FO[illegible]NCISE ENGLISH DICTIONARY

Edited and revised by

H.W. FOWLER

from the original compilation by
H.W. and F.G. Fowler

Wordsworth Editions

This edition published 1989 by Wordsworth Editions Ltd,
8b East Street, Ware, Hertfordshire.

ISBN 1-85326-930-1

Printed and bound in Great Britain by Mackays of Chatham.

FOWLER'S CONCISE ENGLISH DICTIONARY

PREFACE TO THE SECOND EDITION

WHEN we began, more than twenty years ago, the work that took shape as *The Concise Oxford Dictionary*, we were plunging into the sea of lexicography without having been first taught to swim. But lexicography for us was fortunately of the minor or dependent kind ; and, fortunately also, the time was one at which the major or firsthand kind was reaching greater excellence than ever before, and the Oxford English Dictionary, four-fifths completed, already provided popularizers with unlimited material.

The object we set before us, hinted at by the word *current* on our title-page, was to present as vivid a picture as the small dictionary could be made to give of the English that was being spoken and written at the time. The vividness was to be secured by allotting space to words more nearly in proportion to the frequency and variety of their use, and consequently to their practical value, than had been the custom ; and further by an unprecedented abundance of illustrative quotation ; define, and your reader gets a silhouette ; illustrate, and he has it 'in the round'. That at least was our belief ; and we hailed as confirmation of it one or two letters from persons unknown congratulating us on having 'produced a live dictionary', or 'treating English at last as a living language'.

A living language, however, does not remain unchanged through twenty years and a great war ; our picture has needed, and received, a good deal of retouching before being again exhibited in public ; and its owners, the Clarendon Press, have thought it worthy of a slightly larger and more handsome frame, for which I thank them.

The original preface follows, with no change except the interpolation, in square brackets, of some necessary comments, and the insertion in our abbreviation-list of some items that had escaped record.

In the dictionary itself, the object and the methods are what they were, but detailed alterations are numerous, few pages being without them.

H. W. F., 1929.

ACKNOWLEDGEMENTS

A dictionary-maker, unless he is a monster of omniscience, must deal with a great many matters of which he has no firsthand knowledge. That he has been guilty of errors and omissions in some of these he will learn soon after publication, sometimes with gratitude to his enlightener, sometimes otherwise. The first letter we received after C.O.D. appeared was a demand for repayment of the book's cost, on the ground that it failed to give *gal(l)iot*, to settle the spelling of which it had been bought. Even for that announcement of an omission I am now grateful, as affording a good illustration of the less friendly form of correction, and reminding me to assure the public that to one revising for a new edition no correction is (ultimately) unwelcome; all is grist that comes to his mill. At the other end of the scale is the friend, known to me only by correspondence, who for years sent me fortnightly packets of foolscap devoted to perfecting a still contingent second edition—all this for love of the language not as a philological playground, but as the medium of exchange and bond of union among the English-speakers of the world. *Castigavit et emendavit Byron F. Caws* might have stood with justice at the foot of our title-page.

Other helpers have been many, some with systematic lists, others with a few isolated but valuable points; to all those in the list below I would fain offer—what some of them are no longer living to receive—my heartiest thanks:

Leslie J. Berlin Esq.; Major B. F. Caws; Dr R. W. Chapman; Mr S. K. N. Chaudhuri; *Sir Arthur Church K.C.V.O.; Rev. G. P. Ford; H. Gilbert-Carter Esq.; *Prof. Marcus Hartog; the Very Reverend Dr J. H. Hertz; Rev. J. Clare Hudson; Rev. F. E. Hutchinson; Lindsay Johnson M.D., F.R.S.; Rev. D. Evans Jones; Major C. V. N. Lyne; D. C. Macgregor Esq.; F. Morland Esq.; C. O. Ovington Esq.; George Pernet M.D.; Prof. Sir Flinders Petrie F.R.S.; Rev. S. de Saram; Kenneth Sisam Esq.; W. H. Thompson Esq.; B. H. Tower Esq.; F. F. Urquhart Esq.; *Rev. M. N. Walde; E. B. F. Wareing Esq.; *Dr F. H. P. van Wely; J. Beach Whitmore Esq.; Ernest W. Wignall Esq.; C. F. Williams F.G.S.; *Sir Dawson Williams C.B.E.

H. W. F.

* Those whose names are thus marked are known to me to be no longer living; and I fear the same may be true of some others, whom I have failed to reach by postal inquiries.

PREFACE TO THE FIRST EDITION[1]

THE steady advance towards completion of the great *Oxford English Dictionary* has made it possible for the Delegates of the Clarendon Press to authorize the preparation and issue of this book, which in its own province and on its own scale uses the materials and follows the methods by which the Oxford editors have revolutionized lexicography. The book is designed as a dictionary, and not as an encyclopaedia ; that is, the uses of words and phrases as such are its subject matter, and it is concerned with giving information about the things for which those words and phrases stand only so far as correct use of the words depends upon knowledge of the things. The degree of this dependence varies greatly with the kind of word treated, the difference between cyclopaedic and dictionary treatment varies with it, and the line of distinction is accordingly a fluctuating and dubious one. It is to the endeavour to discern and keep to this line that we attribute whatever peculiarities we are conscious of in this dictionary as compared with others of the same size. One of these peculiarities is the large amount of space given to the common words that no one goes through the day without using scores or hundreds of times, often disposed of in a line or two on the ground that they are plain and simple and that every one knows all about them by the light of nature, but in fact entangled with other words in so many alliances and antipathies during their perpetual knocking about the world that the idiomatic use of them is far from easy ; chief among such words are the prepositions, the conjunctions, the pronouns, and such 'simple' nouns and verbs as *hand* and *way*, *go* and *put*. Another peculiarity is the use, copious for so small a dictionary, of illustrative sentences as a necessary supplement to definition when a word has different senses between which the distinction is fine, or when a definition is obscure and unconvincing until exemplified ; these sentences often are, but still more often are not, quotations from standard authors ; they are meant to establish the sense of the definition by appeal not to external authority, but to the reader's own consciousness, and therefore their source, even when authoritative, is not named. A third and a fourth peculiarity are the direct results of the preceding ones ; if common words are to be treated at length, and their uses to be copiously illustrated, space must be saved both by the curtest

[1] The remarks likely to be needed for reference on pronunciation, inflexion, &c., will be found facing the letter A ; on the page before these remarks is a list of the abbreviations used in the Dictionary.

possible treatment of all that are either uncommon or fitter for the encyclopaedia than the dictionary, and by the severest economy of expression—amounting to the adoption of telegraphese—that readers can be expected to put up with.

In attaching this great importance to illustration, by the need of which the relative length of articles, and our manner of expressing ourselves on every page, are governed, we are merely acting, with the exaggeration imposed on us by our limited space, upon the principles of the O.E.D. That may be said to be the first dictionary for which the ideal procedure has been possible, that is, the approaching of each article with an open mind and a collection of examples large enough to be exhaustive, and the extraction from these of classified senses—the first dictionary, to put it another way, in which quotations have served not merely to adorn or convince, but as the indispensable raw material. This procedure—first the collection of sentences from all possible sources as raw material, and then the independent classification—we have often followed even in that part of our book (A–R) in which the O.E.D., with senses already classified and definitions provided, was before us, treating its articles rather as quarries to be drawn upon than as structures to be reproduced in little ; and in the later part (S—Z), where we had no longer the O.E.D. to depend upon, it has been our practice still more often ; for many of the more difficult (i. e. especially the common and 'simple') words, we have collected the quotations given in the best modern dictionaries (the *Imperial*, the *Century*, the *Standard*, Cassell's *Encyclopaedic*, Webster, &c.), added to these what we could get either from other external sources or from our own heads, and then framed our articles, often without reference to the arrangement that we found in any of our authorities. Proceeding in this manner, it was almost inevitable that we should be very much alive to the inadequacy of mere definition and the need of constant illustration. That our examples have some general tendency to the colloquial, and include many usages for which room has not been found in dictionaries many times as large as this, is in harmony with our design of on the one hand restricting ourselves for the most part to current English, and on the other hand omitting nothing to which that description may fairly be applied.

VOCABULARY

The words, or senses of words, given are meant to be such only as are current ; 'current', however, is an elastic term ; we might, but we do not, stretch it to include all words and senses used by Shakspere or in the Bible, on the ground that the whole of Shakspere and the whole of the Bible are still commonly read ; thus the archaic senses of *addition* (title), *buxom* (pliant), *owe* (own), *sad* (serious), *sort* (suit), and the archaic words *shend* (scold), *wood* (mad), familiar as they are to readers of Elizabethan literature, are not given. We do stretch it to include many words and senses that are fossilized, having in themselves no life or capacity for further development, but kept extant by being enshrined in perhaps a single proverb or phrase that is still in use ; of this sort are *coil* (confusion), preserved by ' shuffled off this mortal coil ', and *scotch* (wound), preserved by ' we have scotched the snake, not killed it '.

Again, of the many thousands of old or new scientific and technical terms that have a limited currency some are carried by accident into the main stream of the language and become known temporarily or permanently, vaguely or precisely, to all ordinarily well-informed members of the modern newspaper-reading public. For the purposes of a dictionary that is not to be bulky and yet is to give a fuller treatment than is usual in dictionaries of its size to the undoubtedly current words forming the staple of the language, selection among these intruders is a difficult but very necessary task. The most that can be hoped for is that every one conversant with any special vocabulary may consider us, though sadly deficient on his subject, fairly copious on others ; the meaning of many learned words that have been omitted as having no pretence to general currency may easily be gathered by reference first to the stem, which is often the subject of an article, or to another word of which the stem is clearly the same, and secondly to the suffix.

In another class of words and senses the test of currency has led us to diverge in the opposite direction from the practice usual in dictionaries of this size ; if we give fewer scientific and technical terms, we admit colloquial, facetious, slang, and vulgar expressions with freedom, merely attaching a cautionary label ; when a well-established usage of this kind is omitted, it is not because we consider it beneath the dignity of lexicography to record it, but because, not being recorded in the dictionaries from which our word-list is necessarily compiled, it has escaped our notice ; we have not, however, consulted slang dictionaries nor made any attempt at completeness in this respect.

SPELLING

The spelling adopted is for the most part, but not invariably, that of the O.E.D. For instance, the verbs that contain the suffix *-ize* (which see), and their derivatives in *-ization* &c., are all given without the alternative forms in *-ise* &c., although these are still the commoner in British (as opposed to American) printing ; but such generally established spellings as *judgment*, *rhyme*, *axe*, have not been excluded in favour of the *judgement*, *rime*, *ax*, preferred by the O.E.D., but are retained at least as alternatives having the right to exist. [I have now found salvation, so far as preference for *judgement*, *abridgement*, &c., over the clipped forms is concerned. The simple rule that a mute e is dropped before suffixes beginning with a vowel, but not before suffixes beginning with a consonant, is so nearly universal, and so useful, that it should surely prevail in cases where usage still allows any possibility of choosing the right. The question is discussed in *Modern English Usage*, article Mute E.] In dealing with verbs such as *level*, *rivet*, *bias*, whose parts and derivatives are variously spelt, the final consonant being often doubled with no phonetic or other significance, we have as far as possible fallen in with the present tendency, which is to drop the useless letter, but stopped short of recognizing forms that at present strike every reader as Americanisms; thus we write *riveted*, *riveter*, but not *traveling*, *traveler*. On another point of varying usage—the insertion of a mute e in derivatives in *-able*, *-age*, *-ish*, &c., to indicate the 'long' sound of the stem vowel (*likable* or *likeable*, *milage* or *mileage*, *latish* or *lateish*)—we have thought ourselves justified in taking a bolder line, and have consistently omitted the -e-; it is against all analogy (or why not *smileing*, *Romeish*, *doteage*, *tideal*, *indescribeable*, *desireable*, *exciteable*?), it is used chiefly in words not familiar or important enough to have their form respected as established, it obscures the different and more valuable use by which a soft g or c is indicated as in *manageable* and *serviceable*, and it tempts bad spellers to such monstrosities as *unpalateable*, *loveable*, and *moveable*. In words of the type *ardour*, *colour*, *favour*, where the O.E.D. recognizes both *-our* and *-or*, we have excluded the latter as being (except in particular words like *horror* and *torpor*, in which it is usually the only form) entirely non-British. Words in which -y- has intruded itself without completely dispossessing a more correct -i-, as *sylvan*, *tyro*, *tyre*, we have given with the -i- form either alone or placed first. In stating the plural of words in -o, we have found it impossible to draw any satisfactory line between the words that prefer *-os* and those that prefer *-oes*; it may perhaps be laid down that on the one hand words of which the plural is very commonly used, as *potato*, have almost invariably *-oes*, and on the other hand words still felt to be foreign or of abnormal form, as *soprano*, *chromo* for *chromolithograph*, have almost invariably *-os*; of many other words it may be said with confidence that they use one form only (cf. *punctilios*, *noes*); but the majority fluctuate, and we have not seen our way to doing otherwise. We have also to admit that after trying hard at an early stage to arrive at some principle that should teach us when to separate, when to hyphen, and when to unite the parts of compound words, we had to abandon the attempt as hopeless, and welter in the prevailing chaos. [On this question, too, another simple rule seems capable of converting the chaos referred to in the text into something like order, and thousands of compounds have in this edition been corrected into conformity with it. It is applicable to the countless compounds, far outnumbering all others, in which the second element is a noun, and the first a word, whether an actual adjective or not, whose relation to that noun is adjectival (e.g., *tipsy cake* and *plum cake*, however written, are both compounds, but one has an adjective, the other a noun used adjectivally, preceding the noun). The simple rule is that in such compounds the legitimacy of hyphening depends solely on pronunciation: it must only be done if the two parts are said with a single (or with one clearly predominant) stress, and that falls on the first. This rule, excluding *head-master*, in which the stress is certainly not on *head*, gives the easier choice between *head master* and *headmaster* (either of which will serve); or, excluding *water-ouzel* as having two equal stresses, leaves no doubt that *water ouzel* is the right choice. Ruthless application of this rule results in the disappearance of at least a score of hyphens for every one that for some other reason has been newly inserted; and I have some hope that it will be accepted as both reasonable and useful, though I admit that hyphen-lovers will sometimes feel themselves defrauded. A consequence of this reformed hyphening is that the presence of a hyphen in such a compound assures the reader that the word-stress falls on the first part. Even to an Englishman that assurance is sometimes welcome, and to foreigners it is, as letters from them have convinced me, of great importance.]

PRONUNCIATION

When the pronunciation of a word is not sufficiently determined by the placing of the stress-mark or by vowel quantities, further information follows in round brackets. The phonetic values of the letters employed in these, and the use of the stress-mark, are explained on the page facing the letter A.

Derivatives are to be understood, unless the contrary is indicated, as following the pronunciation of the main word under which they are given or to which they are referred in the etymological note.

The pronunciation of many words is omitted on the assumption that the reader is already familiar with the normal values of some letters and combinations. The hard sounds of th and s, and the sounds of c (s) and g (j) before i, e, and y, are recorded only for special purposes; a vowel that is short before two consonants or a single final consonant, or long before a single consonant followed by e mute, is not usually marked; and the pronunciation of the suffix *-ation* (-āshn) and of the a in *path* &c. (-ah-, -ă-) is not given.

To some suffixes no less familiar than *-ation* pronunciation is added in view of certain ignorant or pedantic tendencies. The pleasant fiction that *cottage* is pronounced kŏtāj, though still prevalent in dictionaries, has perhaps never deceived any one; but we have all heard *furniture* (-tūr), *knowledge* (nō-), and *often* (-t-). Against these and other results of the undue influence of spelling warnings are freely given.

In the choice or rejection of alternative pronunciations the O.E.D. has always been consulted, but is not always followed.

ORDER OF SENSES

From the order in which the senses of a word are here given no inference must be drawn as to their historical or other relations, the arrangement being freely varied according to the requirements or possibilities of the particular word. Sense-development cannot always be convincingly presented without abundant quotation from authorities, and the historical order is further precluded by the uniform omission of obsolete senses. Occasionally, when a rare but still current sense throws light on the commoner senses that follow or forms the connecting link with the etymology, it has been placed at the beginning; but more commonly the order adopted has been that of logical connexion or of comparative familiarity or importance.

ETYMOLOGY

Etymology is given in square brackets at the end of each article.

Words of Teutonic origin are illustrated by all or some of the forms found in cognate languages. With words that have passed through several languages on their way to English, the forms taken in successive languages are recorded in full, with the following exceptions. (1) When OF or the like at the beginning of the etymology is not followed by the old French form written in full, it is because the latter is identical in spelling with the English or differs from it only in some unimportant detail specified in brackets. (2) The Latin form of a Greek word is usually omitted, and is to be inferred according to the rules of transliteration given below. Thus (under *pleonasm*) 'f. L f. Gk *pleonasmos*' is to be read 'f. L *pleonasmus* f. Gk *pleonasmos*'. A similar omission of a word in any other language implies absolute identity of form.

Greek words are written with the corresponding English letters (φ, χ, ψ, ῥ, ῤῥ, = ph, kh, ps, rh, rrh, and ᾳ, ῃ, ῳ, = āi, ēi, ōi), and not according to the Latin transliteration, the rules for which are as follows ; Greek k=Latin c ; ai=ae ; ou=u ; u (exc. in diphthongs) =y; ei=i or e; oi=oe (but in nom. pl.=i); g (before g or k)=n; also, -ŏs (nom. masc.), -ŏn, =-us, -um ; -ēs, -ē, (1st decl. nom.)=-a ; -ōn (nom.)=-o ; -ŏs (genit.)=-is ; -a (accus. sing. masc. or fem.)=-em.

French nouns of Latin origin are with few exceptions derived from the Latin accusative ; but the Latin nominative is here given except when (e. g. in words in *-atio*) a change of stress is involved.

Greek η (ē) and ω (ō), and the e of Latin infinitives of 2nd conj. (-ēre, -ēri), are regularly marked long. The accented letters (á, ǽ, &c.) in forms quoted from Old English or other Teutonic languages are long.

F, G, &c., must not be taken to imply that the word to which they are prefixed is current, or is so spelt, in the modern language ; nor does it follow from a word's being given as OF that it is obsolete.

The etymology often contains references in small capitals to words and suffixes.

Hence introduces one or more of the direct derivatives of the word treated ; *whence* introduces such derivatives under a particular sense to which they are restricted ; *so* introduces words derived from another language ; *hence or cogn.*, *whence or cogn.*, introduce groups of partly English and partly foreign derivation. The suffixes of such derivatives are commonly printed in small capitals, and are thus referred to the suffix article in its alphabetical place. The numbers enclosed in brackets indicate subdivisions of the suffix article, and are often used to distinguish among the possible senses of the derivative word those in which it is chiefly current.

The first element of a Latin or other compound word is often referred to a prefix article, and the remainder treated separately within brackets ; meanings given within the bracket belong to the simple word, those of the compound being added if necessary outside it. Thus *convene* is [f. F *convenir* f. L CON(*venire vent-* come) assemble, agree, fit]. The stem *vent-* and the senses *agree*, *fit*, are here added for the purposes of *convention* and *convenience*, which are referred to *convene*. The first element of a Greek compound similarly treated is sometimes written according to the current (Latin) transliteration, to facilitate reference to the prefix article ; Greek *kakoepeia*, under *cacoepy*, accordingly appears as CACO(*epeia*). Certain similar devices for saving needless repetition will, it is believed, explain themselves.

The etymology of all words from A to R was drawn in the first instance from the O.E.D., but was occasionally modified after reference to Prof. Skeat's *Etymological Dictionary* (Clarendon Press, 4th edition, 1910). From S to Z Prof. Skeat's work has been our main authority, the *Century* and other dictionaries being consulted for the words that he omits. [In the second edition the derivations of all words from S to Z have been examined, and corrected into agreement with the O.E.D. conclusions. This has occasionally required the division of a single article into two or more, or the combining of what we had before treated as separate words into one article.]

REFERENCE BY SMALL CAPITALS

The use of small capitals for etymological purposes is explained above.

In the same way reference is made

(1) from the word treated to another word for the purpose of contrast, distinction, correlation, or the like. Of this kind are the references from *slander* to *libel* and *scandal*, from *creationism* to *evolution* and vice versa, and from *tenon* to *mortise* and vice versa.

(2) from any member of a group to the word under which the group is collected or further explained. *Ruby* (print.) is in this way referred to *type*; *order* (nat. hist.) to *class*[1]; and the *iron*[1], *golden*, and *silver ages* to *brazen*[1].

(3) from one or more words of a proverb or the like to that under which alone the proverb is explained. *Play*[1] and *drake*[2] contain such references to *duck*[1], *flesh* and *herring* to *fish*[1]. [*herring* otherwise treated in second edition.]

(4) from a compound of the word treated to its other component for explanation. The sign (=) prefixed to such a reference indicates that the simple word treated is itself used in the sense of the compound. Thus, under *pie*[1], *sea-pie* is merely referred (SEA-*p.*) to *sea*, but *magpie*, besides being referred to the article *magpie*, is recorded (=MAGPIE) as one of the senses of *pie*.

ABBREVIATIONS

In any article, when the word treated in it is to be quoted or mentioned, its initial letter followed by a period is used instead of the whole word; this stands only for the exact form that heads the article; e.g., in the verb *love*, *l.* means *love* (verb or noun), but not *loving*, *loved*, &c.; the plural of nouns is represented by doubling the letter; e.g., in *extreme*, *nut*, *ee.*, *nn.*, mean *extremes*, *nuts*; in the part of an article obviously restricted to a derivative the letter may stand for that derivative; e.g., *representation*, given in the article *represent*, is followed by a bracket in which *r.* stands not for *represent*, but for *representation* [in the second edition I have corrected all examples of this possibly ambiguous method that I have noticed, substituting a termination, e.g. *-ion* for *r.* in *repre-*

sentation; but the original warning remains as provision for oversights]; in the part of an article restricted to a compound, the hyphened initials of the two parts are used; e.g., when in doing *ground-floor* under the article *ground* the phrase *get in on the ground-floor* is to be explained in a bracket, *g.-f.* is used for *ground-floor.*

Of other abbreviations, a list including all that are not either too obvious to need explanation or generally current (and accordingly to be found in the abbreviation lists given in the first article of each letter of the alphabet) follows on the opposite page. In this list, three points require mention: (1) the appending of *&c.* means that the abbreviation stands for derivatives or inflexions as well as for the simple word given; e.g., *metaphor &c.* means metaphor, metaphorical, or metaphorically; *explain &c.* means explain, explains, explained, explaining, or explanation; this system is used also with abbreviations omitted as obvious; thus *adv.* stands not only for *adverb*, but also for *adverbial* and *adverbially*; (2) abbreviations of nouns, such as *ex.* (example), *prep.* (preposition), are often used with the last letter doubled (*exx.*, *prepp.*) as plurals; it has not been thought necessary to give these plural forms except in one-letter abbreviations (*aa.*, *nn.*); similar plurals occur for forms that have been omitted as obvious (*adjj.* for *adjectives* &c.); (3) abbreviations given in the list with initial capital have always the capital in use; but those given with initial small letter have either form according to circumstances; similarly, though the list is all in Roman type, the abbreviations are sometimes for reasons not affecting their sense printed in italics.

June, 1911

LIST OF ABBREVIATIONS

a., adjective
aa., adjectives
abl., ablative
abs., absolute &c.
acc., according, accusative
aeron., aeronautics &c.
AF, Anglo-French
alch., alchemy &c.
allus., allusive &c.
anal., analogy &c.
ant., antiquities
anthrop., anthropology &c.
arch., architecture &c.
Ass., Assyrian
assim., assimilate &c.
assoc., associated &c.
astr(on)., astronomy &c.
astrol., astrology &c.
attrib., attributive &c.
augment., augmentative &c.
b., born
back form., back formation
bibl., biblical &c.
Boh., Bohemian
Braz., Brazilian
Bret., Breton
Byz., Byzantine
c., century, *c.*, circiter
cc., centuries
cl., classical
cogn., cognate
colloq., colloquial &c.
colon., colonial
com., com(mon)-Teut. &c.
comb., combination &c.
comp., composition, comparative
compd, compound
compl., complement
compp., compounds
conj., conjunction, conjugation
conn., connect &c.
constr., construct &c.
contr., contraction &c.
cop., copulative
Copt., Coptic
Corn., Cornish
correl., correlative &c.
d., died
Da., Danish
dat., dative
dent., dentistry
deriv., derivative &c.
dial., dialectal
diff., different
different., differentiate &c.
dim., diminutive &c.
dissim., dissimilate &c.
Du., Dutch
dub., dubious
E, English
eccl., ecclesiastical &c.
EFris., East Frisian
electr., electricity &c.
ellipt., elliptical &c.
erron., erroneously
eth., ethics &c.
etym., etymology &c.
euphem., euphemism &c.
ex., example
exag., exaggeration &c.
exc., except
excl., exclusive &c., exclamation &c.
expl., explain &c.
expr., expressing &c.
F, French
f., from
facet., facetious &c.
fig., figurative &c.
Fl., Flemish
foll., (the) following (word)
found., founding
Fr., French
Frank., Frankish
freq(uent)., frequentative &c.
Fris., Frisian
G, German
gen., general &c., genitive
Gk, Greek
gr., grammar &c.
Hind., Hindi, Hindustani
hist., history, historical &c.
hort., horticulture &c.
i., intransitive
imit., imitative &c.
incept., inceptive
ind., indicative, indirect
inf., infinitive
infl., influence &c.
instr., instrumental (case)
int., interjection
intr., intransitive
Ir., Irish
joc., jocose &c.
L, Latin
LG, Low German
lit., literal, literally
LL, late Latin
magn., magnetism
ME, middle English (1200–1500)
med., medicine &c.
med. L, medieval Latin
metaph., metaphor &c.
metath., metathesis, metathetic
Mex., Mexican
MHG, middle high German
min., mineralogy
MIt., middle Italian
n., noun
neg., negative &c.
nn., nouns
nom., nominative
N.T., New Testament
num., numeral
O, old (with languages)
obj., object &c.
obs., obsolete
occ(as)., occasional &c.
OHG, old high German
ON, old Norse
ONF, old northern French
opp., (as) opposed (to)
opt., optics &c.
ord., ordinary
orig., origin &c.
OS, Old Saxon
O.T., Old Testament
part., present participle
partic., participial
path., pathology &c.
pharm., pharmacy
phr., phrase
pl., plural
Pol., Polish
pol., politics &c.
pop., popular &c.
poss., possessive
p.p., past or passive participle
Pr., Provençal
pr., pronounced &c.
prec., (the) preceding (word)
pred., predicate &c.
pref., prefix
prep., preposition
pres., present
prob., probable &c.
pron., pronoun &c., pronounce &c.
prop., proper, properly
pros., prosody &c.
Prov., Provençal
prov., proverb &c., provincial &c.
psych., psychology &c.
R.-C., Roman-Catholic
redupl., reduplicated &c.
ref., reference
refash., refashioned &c.
refl., reflexive &c.
rel., relative
repr., represent &c.
Rom., Roman, Romance
s., singular
Sc., Scotch
schol., scholastic
sci., science &c.
sent., sentence
Serb., Serv., Serbian, Servian
Skr., Sanskrit
somet., sometimes
spirit., spiritualism &c.
st., stem
subj., subject &c., subjunctive
suf., suffix
sup., superlative
surv., surveying
Sw., Swedish
t., transitive
term., termination
theosoph., theosophy &c.
thr., through
trans., transitive &c.
transf., in transferred sense
transl., translation &c.
translit., transliteration
typ., typography
ult., ultimately
unexpl., unexplained
U.S., United States
usu., usual, usually
v., vb, verb
var., variant, various
vbl, verbal
voc., vocative
vv., verbs
W, Welsh
w., with
WG, West German

*, sign affixed to all forms not recorded but merely inferred, with the exception of those called Aryan or OTeut. (all of which are inferential)

NOTE ON ACCENT, PRONUNCIATION, INFLEXION, AND FOREIGN WORDS

ACCENT

ACCENT is marked by the turned period (·), which is normally placed after the accented vowel or diphthong (**a·ctor, allow·, a·ccent** noun, **acce·nt** verb, **exaggera·tion, exa·ggerator**); two equal accents in one word are both marked (**ti·tbi·t**); and the · is used for the secondary as well as for the main accent in long words where the former might be doubtful (**cir·cumgyra·te, a·biogene·tically**).

But the place of the turned period in syllables whose vowel sound is modified by r or re is after the whole combination (**por·ter, pure·ly**), any possible confusion being guarded against by the – or ◡ (**mere·ly**, but **herĕ·tical**). Similarly it stands after silent consonants (**migh·ty, deb·tor, black·guard**), consonants that merely modify a vowel sound (**cal·mness**), or e mute following the accented vowel (**blue·bell**).

Some miscellaneous examples are added:—fŏ·rest, fore·noon, for·tnight, forĕ·nsic; bar·ring, ba·rrack; bal·my, ba·lsam; arraig·n; demes·ne; sig·ning, si·gnature; high·er; Cadmē·an; defray·; bye·-law; da·ffadowndi·lly; ca·noniza·tion.

PRONUNCIATION

When necessary, a bracket is placed immediately after a word, with directions for pronouncing it or some part of it. In these brackets,

(1) Vowel sounds have the value shown by the roman-type letters in:—*māte, mēte, mīte, mōte, mūte, mōōt; răck, rĕck, rĭck, rŏck, rŭck, rŏŏk;* caw, cow; bah, boil.

(2) Vowel-combinations with r (the r is not trilled before a consonant or mute e) are as follows:—

mār̃e, mēr̃e, mīr̃e mōr̃e, demūr̃e, moor; *dowry*; par*t*, per*t*, por*t*.

(3) Italicized vowels or vowel-combinations have the indistinct sound shown in *a*gain, mom*e*nt, adm*i*ral, m*o*rose, s*u*pport, cert*ai*n, conn*oi*sseur, comf*or*t, jeal*ou*s, murd*er*.

(4) Each consonant or consonant-combination has only one sound; the value of ambiguous or specially used ones is:—

ch as in *loch* **dh** as in *dhen* (=then); **g** as in *get*; **j** as in *jet*; **ng** as in *singer*; **ngg** as in *finger*; **n-g** as in *un-gardĭd* (=unguarded); **r** as in *rat* (and see vowel-combinations above); **s** as in *sister*; **th** as in *thinketh*; **tsh** as in *tship* (=chip); **w** as in *wit* (and see vowel sounds above); **y** as in *yet*; **zh** as in *fūzhn* (=fusion).

Letters marked – or ◡ in the word itself have the same value as in the brackets, except that ĕ is also used, when there is no danger of confusion, to show that e is not mute or part of a compound sound; so ni·cĕty, ca·ffĕine.

INFLEXION

The rules assumed, exceptions to which are noted in a bracket placed after a word's grammatical description, are as follows:—

1. Verbs add *-s* in 3rd sing. pres., *-ed* in past and p.p., *-ing* in pres. part., *-er* to form agent-noun.
2. Verbs and adjectives drop final mute e before *-ing, -ed, -er, -est.*
3. Before *-ed, -ing, -er, -est, -eth,* monosyllabic verbs and adjectives double a final single consonant (except x) if preceded by a single vowel.
4. (a) nouns, (b) adjectives, (c) verbs, in -y preceded by a consonant have (a) plural *-ies,* (b) comparative *-ier,* superlative *-iest,* adverb *-ily,* noun *-iness,* (c) 3rd sing. pres. *-ies,* past and p.p. *-ied,* agent-noun *-ier.*
5. Nouns in -s, -x, -z, -ch = tsh, and -sh, and some in -o, form plural by adding *-es*; others add *s.*
6. Monosyllabic adjectives and disyllables in -y compare in *-er, -est*; others with *more, most.*

FOREIGN WORDS

Words usually or often printed in italics as either incompletely naturalized or completely foreign are in sloping type. When either the word itself or any of its sounds is distinctly un-English, the reader is warned by a bracket containing, instead of pronunciation, the letter or letters standing for the language it belongs to. Otherwise, pronunciation is given for sloped words to the same extent as for others, but is often to be taken as merely approximate.

ENGLISH DICTIONARY

A, letter (pl. *As*, A's, Aes). (Mus.) note, and the corresponding scale. (In argument) first imaginary person or case. (Alg.) first known quantity. (Naut.) **A1** (ā wŭn), first-class ship in Lloyd's register; excellent, best, (colloq.; **A1** POPULATION). (Naut.) **Æ**, third-class ship at Lloyd's.

Abbreviations (1): ab, **A.U.C.** (urbe condita); able. **A.B.** (-bodied); acting, as **A.A.Q.M.G.** (assistant quartermaster general); adjutant, as **A.G.** (general); admiral, **A.F.** (of the Fleet); aide, **A.D.C.** (-de-camp); Alpine, **A.C.** (Club); amateur, **A.A.A.** (athletic association); Ångström, **A.U.** (unit); anno, **A.D., A.H.** (domini, hegirae); assistant, **A.A.G.** (adjutant general), **A.P.M.** (provost marshal), **A.Q.M.G.** (quartermaster general); associate, **A.R.A.** (of Royal Academy); authorized, **A.V.** (version); automobile, **A.A.** (association); ante, **a.m.** (meridiem).

Abbreviations (2): **ab init.**, ab initio; **Abp,** Archbishop; **a/c,** account; **Adm.,** Admiral; **advt,** advertisement; **aet.,** aetatis; **Ala.,** Alabama; **Alas.,** Alaska; **Alban.,** Bishop of St Albans; **Ariz.,** Arizona; **Ark.,** Arkansas; **arr.,** arrives; **Asaph.,** Bishop of St Asaph.

a[1], **an,** a. (sometimes called indefinite article. Before all consonants except silent *h*, use *a*; *a history, a historian,* though some still write *an* before *h* in unaccented syllable, but *an hour*: before all vowels except *eu, ū,* use *an*; *an ŭlcer,* but *a ūnit, a eulogy*; also *a one.* Placed after *many, such, what,* or any adj. preceded by *how, so, as, too.* Used with apparent plurals of number, *a dozen men* = a dozen of men; also with pl. adjj. *few, good many, great many*). (Unemphatic substitute for) one, some, any; one like (*a Daniel*); (after *all of, many of,* &c.) the same (*all of a size*); (distrib.) each (*£40 a year,* where *a* is orig. = foll.). [weakening of OE *án* ONE]

a[2], prep. On, to, towards, into, in. Mostly now written as pref., or oftener omitted than expressed, or confused w. A[1]. On: *abed, afoot.* To: *ashore.* Towards: *aback, afar, aside.* Into: *apart, asunder.* In: *now-a-days, twice a day*; w. vbl nouns, passively, *a-building,* actively, *was* (*a-*) *fighting,* and esp. w. *go, set,* as *he went a begging, they set the bells a ringing.* [weakening of OE prep. *an,* ON]

a-, pref. f. various sources. (1) OE *ar-* or *a-*, away, on, up, out, and so to express intensity, as *arise*; cf. G *er-*. (2) OE *an, on* prep.; see prec. (3) OE *of* prep., as *akin.* (4) L *ad-* to, either directly, as *aspect,* or through F *a-* as *achieve*; many words derived in the latter way have been later assimilated to L spelling, as *a(d)dress, a(g)grieve.* (5) L *a, ab,* from; directly, as *avert,* or through F *a-*, as *abridge*; again somet. assimilated to L spelling, as *a(b)stain.* (6) L *ex-* out, utterly, through AF *a-* f. OF *e-, es-*, as *amend.* (7) Gk *a-, an-*, not, without; directly, as *amorphous,* through L, as *acatalectic,* or through L and F, as *adamant*; compounded chiefly w. Gk words, but also w. others, as *amoral.*

-a, suf. (1) Nn. f. Gk, L, and Rom. fem. sing., as *idea* (Gk), *arena* (L), *piazza* (It.), *duenna* (Sp.), esp. Nat. Hist. terms, ancient or latinized mod. (*hyena, dahlia*), geogr. names (*Africa*), and names of women, ancient or latinized mod. (*Lydia, Hilda*). (2) Gk and L neut. pl. nouns (*genera, phenomena*), esp. names, often f. mod.L, of classes of animals (*mammalia*).

aard-vark (ard), n. S.-African quadruped between armadilloes and ant-eaters. [f. Du. *aarde* earth + *vark* pig, cf. OE *fearh* and L *porcus* pig]

aard-wolf (ard), n. S.-African carnivore between hyenas and civets. [see prec.]

Aar·on's beard (ār-), n. Kinds of plant, esp. Great St John's wort. [ref. to *Ps.* cxxxiii. 2]

Aar·on's rod (ār-), n. Kinds of plant, esp. Great Mullein and Golden Rod. [ref. to *Num.* xvii. 8]

ab-, pref. Away, from, off, apart. [f. L *ab,* cf. Gk *apo,* E *of, off,* G *ab-*. In L reduced to *a-* before *p, m, v,* changed to *au-* before *f,* and to *abs-* before *c, t*; in F often reduced to *a-*]

aba·ck, adv. Backwards. (Naut.) of square sails pressed against mast by head wind; *take a.,* of ship w. sails in that state; (fig.) surprised. [A[2] + BACK[1]]

ă·bacus, n. (pl. *-ci,* pr. -sī). Calculating-frame w. balls sliding on wires, used before adoption of the nine figures and zero, and still in China &c., and in elementary teaching. (Arch.) upper member, often square flat slab, of capital, supporting architrave. [L *abacus* f. Gk *abax -akos* tablet]

Aba·ddon. Hell; the devil (*Rev.* ix. 11). [Heb. word, destruction (*abad* he perished)]

aba·ft (-ahft), adv. & prep. (naut.). In stern half of ship; nearer the stern than, aft of. [A[2] + *baft* = OE *be* by + OE *æftan* adv. behind]

aba·ndon[1], v.t. Give up to another's control or mercy; yield one*self* completely to a passion or impulse; give up (a possession or habit); forsake (a person, post). [f. OF *abandoner* (*à* to + *bandon* jurisdiction, *mettre à bandon* meaning to put a person under any one's, including his own, control)]

aba·ndon[2] (or as F), n. Careless freedom, letting oneself go. [F; see prec.]

aba·ndoned, a. Profligate. [p.p. of ABANDON[1]]

aba·ndonee·, n. (law). Underwriter to whom salvage of wreck is abandoned. [ABANDON[1] + -EE]

aba·ndonment, n. Giving up or forsaking; being forsaken; self-surrender; careless freedom of manner, impulsiveness. [f. F *abandonnement* (ABANDON[1], -MENT)]

aba·se, v.t. Lower, humiliate, make base. Hence **aba·se**MENT n. [f. OF *abaissier* (now *abaisser*) (*à* to + *baissier* to lower f. LL *bassare* f. *bassus* short)]

aba·sh, v.t. Put out of countenance; (chiefly in pass.) be confounded. Hence **aba·sh**MENT n. [f. OF *esbaïr* astound f. *es-* = A- (6) + *bahir* cry bah!; see -ISH[2] & cf. *punch* = punish]

aba·sk, adv. In warm light. [A[2] + BASK]

aba·te, v.t. & i. Diminish (t. & i.). Do away with (nuisance); blunt (edge); lower (price); deduct (specified or unspecified part of price); mitigate (violence); weaken (energy). Grow less (of flood or epidemic). (In law) quash (writ or action). So **aba·te**MENT n. [f. OF *abatre* (*à* to + *batre* f. LL *batere* f. L *batuere* beat)]

ă·batis, aba·ttis, n. Defence made of felled trees w. boughs pointing outwards. Hence **abă·tis**ED[2] a. [F *abatis*, OF *abateïs* f. LL **abateticius* of throwing down; cf. OF *abatre*, see ABATE]

abattoir (F), n. Public slaughterhouse.

abb, n. Woof. [A- (1) + WEB]

A·bba, n. Father. Used w. *Father* in invoking God (*Mark* xiv. 36). [Aram.]

a·bbacy, n. Office, jurisdiction, or tenure, of an abbot. [earlier *abbatie* (see -CY) f. LL *abbatia* (*abbat-* nom. *-as* ABBOT)]

abba·tial (-āshal), a. Of an abbey, abbot, or abbess. [F, f. LL *abbatialis* (*abbatia* ABBACY, -AL)]

a·bbé (-ā), n. Frenchman (orig. abbot) entitled to wear ecclesiastical dress, esp. without official duties. [F, f. L *abbatem* nom. *-as* ABBOT]

a·bbess, n. Lady superior of a nunnery. [OF *abaësse* (Pr. *abadessa*) f. LL *abbatissa* (*abbat-* ABBOT)]

a·bbey, n. Buildings occupied by monks or nuns under an abbot or abbess; the monks or nuns as a body; a church or house that was once an abbey or part of it (*the A.*, Westminster A.). [f. OF *abaïe*, Pr. *abadia*, f. LL *abbatia* ABBACY]

a·bbot, n. Head of abbey of monks; *Abbot of Misrule* or *of Unreason*, leader in medieval burlesque festivities. Hence **a·bbot**CY, **a·bbot**SHIP, nn. [OE *abbod*, f. L f. Gk *abbas -at-* (ABBA)]

abbrē·viate[1] (-*a*t), a. Relatively short (esp. in nat. hist.). [f. L *abbreviatus* p.p. of *abbreviare* shorten (*ab* off or *ad* to + *brevis* short)]

abbrē·viāte[2], v.t. Make short (chiefly now of writing part of word for whole, but also of visit, story, &c.) Hence **abbrevi**A·TION n. [f. prec.; see -ATE[3]]

A B C, n. The alphabet; rudiments of any subject; alphabetical railway guide.

Abdēr·ite, n. *The A.*, Democritus (see DEMOCRITEAN). [Gk *Abdērītēs* (*Abdēra*, a town, -ITE[1])]

a·bdicate, v.t. Renounce formally or by default (a power, office, right; also abs., esp. of the crown). Hence **abdic**A·TION n., **a·bdicat**ED[1] (2) a. [f. L AB(*dicare* declare), -ATE[3]]

abdō·men, n. (Anat.) belly, including stomach, bowels, and other nutritive organs. (Zool.) hinder part of insects, spiders, &c. [L, etym. dub.]

abdŏ·minal, a. Of the abdomen in either sense; (of fish) having the ventral fins under the belly. [f. *abdomin-* stem of prec. + -AL]

abdŏ·minous, a. Corpulent. [as prec. + -OUS]

abdu·cent, a. (anat.). Drawing away (of muscles that open or pull back the part they are fixed to). [f. L *abducent-* part. st. of AB(*ducere duct-* draw)]

abdu·ct, v.t. Kidnap; take away (esp. a woman) by force or fraud; draw (limb &c.) from its natural position. [f. L *abduct-* see prec.]

abdu·ction, n. Illegal carrying off, esp. of a child, ward; forcible carrying off of any one, as of a voter; withdrawal of limb from natural position; shrinking of sides of a wound, causing it to gape; syllogism of which the minor premiss, and therefore the conclusion, is only probable. [f. L *abductio* (prec., -ION)]

abdu·ctor, n. Person who abducts another; (also *a. muscle*) muscle that abducts a limb. [as ABDUCT + -OR[2]]

abea·m (-ēm), adv. (naut.). On a line at right angles to the ship's length; *a. of us*, opposite our centre, abreast. [A[2] + BEAM]

a·becedār·ian (ābĭsĭ-), a. & n. Arranged alphabetically, as the 119th Psalm; elementary, ignorant. Pupil learning the alphabet (common in U.S.). [f. med. L *abecedarium* alphabet (ABCD + -ARIUM) + -AN]

abe·d, adv. In bed. [A[2] + BED[1]]

abele (abē·l, ā·bl), n. The white poplar. [f. Du. *abeel* f. OF *abel* earlier *aubel* f. LL *albellus* dim. of *albus* white]

aberglaube (G), n. Excessive belief, superstition. [G]

ă·berdevī·ne, n. Birdfancier's name for the siskin. [?]
Aberdō·nian, a. & n. (Inhabitant, native) of Aberdeen. [-IAN]
abĕ·rrant, a. Straying from moral standard; (in nat. hist.) diverging from normal type. Hence **abe·rr**ANCE, **abe·rr**ANCY, nn. [f. L *aberrant-* part. st. of AB(*errare* stray)]
ăberra·tion, n. A straying from the path, lit. and fig.; breaking of rules; moral slip; intellectual deficiency; deviation from type. (Optics) non-convergence of rays to one focus. (Astron.) displacement of heavenly body's true position to observer. [f. L *aberratio*; see prec., -ATION]
abe·t, v.t. (-tt-). Countenance or assist (offence or offender; esp. *aid and a.*). Hence **abe·t**MENT, **abe·tt**ER[1], **abe·tt**OR[2], nn. *Abettor* is the legal and the commoner general form. [f. OF *abeter* (*à* to + *beter* BAIT[1])]
ab e·xtra, adv. From outside. [LL]
abey·ance (-bā-), n. State of suspension, dormant condition liable to revival, (of rights &c.; mostly in phrr. *be in* or *fall into a.*). [f. OF *abeance* (*à* to + *beer* = It. & LL *badare* gape)]
abhor·, v.t. (-rr-). Regard with disgust and hatred. [f. L AB(*horrēre* shudder)]
abhŏ·rrence, n. Detestation; detested thing (*flattery is my a.*). [foll., -ENCE]
abhŏ·rrent, a. Inspiring disgust, hateful, of conduct, &c., often with *to* (person); inconsistent (*from*); (archaic) feeling disgust (*of*), as, *the Greeks were a. of excess.* [f. L *abhorrent-* part. st. see ABHOR].
abhor·rer, n. (hist.). Nickname of those who signed addresses to Charles II in 1680. [ABHOR + -ER[1]]
abī·dance, n. Continuance, dwelling (*in*), abiding (*by* rules, &c.). [ABIDE + -ANCE]
abi·de, v.t. & i. (past & p.p. *abode* sometimes *abided*). Remain over; continue; dwell; stand firm; (with *by*) remain faithful to, act upon (terms). Wait for; encounter, sustain; submit to, suffer; (negatively as *I cannot, who can, a.?*) put up with (noun or infinitive). [OE *abīdan* f. A-(1) + *bīdan* BIDE]
abi·ding, a. Permanent. Hence **abi·ding**LY[2] adv. [part. of ABIDE]
ăbiĕt-, stem of several chemical terms. Of resin, or fir. [L *abiet-* nom. *abies* firtree]
ă·bigail, n. Lady's-maid. [character in Beaumont and Fletcher's *Scornful Lady*, perh. w. ref. to 1 *Sam.* xxv. 24–31]
abi·lity, n. Sufficient power, capacity (*to* do something); legal competency (to act); financial competency to meet a demand; cleverness, mental faculty, (general in sing., special in pl.). [f. OF *ableté* f. L *habilitat-* n. st. f. *habilis* deft; in F and E it was later corrected into *habileté, hability*, whence the mod. form]
ab inī·tio, adv. From the beginning. [L]
ă·biogĕ·nesis, n. Spontaneous generation. (Allied words) **a·biogenĕ·t**IC, connected w. the doctrine; **a·biogene·t**ICALLY adv., by spont. gen. or according to the doctrine; **abiŏ·gen**IST(2) n., one who believes in it; **abiŏ·gen**OUS a., so produced; **abiŏ·geny**[1] n., = abiogenesis. [f. Gk *abios* f. A-(7) + *bios* life + GENESIS]
a·bject, a. & n. Brought low, miserable; craven, degraded, despicable. (Bibl. and archaic) a person of the meanest condition. Hence **a·bject**LY[2] adv., **a·bject**NESS n. [f. L *abjectus* p.p. of AB(*jicĕre* = *jacĕre* throw)]
abje·ction, n. Abasement, low estate. [F, f. L *abjectionem* (ABJECT, -ION)]
abjura·tion, n. Action or form of renunciation on oath, in all senses of ABJURE (in hist. esp. of the Stuart claim). [f. L *abjuratio* (ABJURE, -ATION)]
abjure·, v.t. Renounce on oath (an opinion, heresy, cause, claim, or claimant); swear perpetual absence from (one's country &c.) [f. F *abjurer* f. L AB(*jurare* swear)]
ablacta·tion, n. Weaning from the mother. [f. L AB(*lactatio* f. *lactare* suckle f. *lact-* nom. *lac* milk)]
abla·tion, n. Removal (esp. in surgery, of any part of body); (Geol.) waste of a glacier or rock by melting or water action. [f. L *ablatio* f. AB(*lat-* p.p. st. of *ferre* carry)]
a·blative, a. & n. The case in Latin nouns that expresses source, agent, cause, instrument, of action = *from* or *by* with the noun (usu. noun; adj. with *case, sense,* &c.). *A. absolute,* a construction of noun and participle in L Gram. giving time or circumstances. [F *ablatif* f. L *ablativus* brought from (*ablat-* see prec.)]
a·blaut (or as G), n. Systematic vowel change in derivation, as in *sing, sang, sung.* [G]
abla·ze, adv. & pred. a. On fire; glittering; excited. [A[2] + BLAZE]
a·ble, a. Talented, clever; competent, having the means or power (*to*), esp. w. parts of *be* to supply the deficiencies of *can*; legally qualified; *a.-bodied seaman* (abbr. A.B.), of special class. Hence **a·bly**[2] adv. [f. OF *hable, able,* (now *habile*) f. L *habilis* handy (*habēre* to hold)]
-able, suf. f. F *-able* f. L *-a-* of first conjug. + *-bili-* see -BLE. In F extended to vbs of all conjugg. In E now appended even to native vbs as *bearable,* nouns as *clubbable,* and phrase vbs as *get-at-able*; prob. f. confusion w. the unrelated adj. *able.* (Meaning) able to (*comfortable*), able to be (*eatable*), fit for (*salable*).
ă·blet, ă·blen, n. Name for the freshwater fish bleak. [F *ablette* f. LL *abula* for *albula* dim. of *alba* white]
ā·blings, ā·blins, ai·blins, adv. (Sc. & north.). Possibly, perhaps. [ABLE + -LINGS]

abloo·m, adv. & pred. a. In or into bloom. [A² + BLOOM]
ablu·sh, adv. & pred. a. Blushing. [A² + BLUSH]
ablu·tion, n. (usu. pl.). Ceremonial washing of person, hands, or sacred vessels; ordinary personal washing; (sing.) water in which things have been washed, esp. in Catholic Ritual. Hence **ablu·tion**ARY¹ a. [f. L AB(*lutio* f. *luere lut-* wash, -ION)]
a·bnegate, v.t. Deny oneself (something), renounce (a right or belief). [f. L AB(*negare* deny), -ATE³]
abnega·tion, n. Denial; rejection (of doctrine); self-sacrifice (now oftener *self-a.*). [f. L *abnegatio* (prec., -ATION)]
abnor·mal, a. Exceptional, irregular, deviating from type. Hence **abnorma·l**ITY n., the quality or an instance of it, **abnor·mal**LY² adv. [earlier & F *anormal* f. med. L *anormalus* corrupted f. Gk *anōmalos* ANOMALOUS; but now regarded as f. L *abnormis* see foll.]
abnor·mity, n. Irregularity; a monstrosity. [f. L *abnormitas* f. AB(*normis* f. *norma* rule) see -TY]
aboar·d, adv. & prep. On or into a ship (*ship* either expressed or omitted); alongside, near, esp. *close* or *hard a. Lay* (another ship) *a.*, place one's own alongside of her to fight; *fall a.*, fall foul of (another ship). [A² + BOARD]
abo·de, n. Dwelling-place, house; stay, habit of dwelling, as in *make* one's *a.* [vbl n. of ABIDE; cf. *ride, rode, road*]
aboi·l, adv. & pred. a. A-boiling, boiling. [A² + BOIL]
abŏ·lish, v.t. Do away with (customs, institutions). Hence **abo·lish**ABLE a., **abo·lish**ER¹, **abo·lish**MENT, nn. [f. F *abolir* (-ISH²) f. L *abolescere* inceptive of *abolēre* become effete, destroy, (AB-, **olēre* grow)]
ăboli·tion, n. Doing, being done, away with. In the 18th and 19th cc. w. ref. to negro slavery and the movement against it, whence also **aboli·tion**ISM(3), **aboli·tion**IST(2), nn. [f. L *abolitio* (prec., -ION)]
abŏ·minable, a. Detestable, odious, morally or physically loathsome; (by conscious exaggeration) unpleasant. Hence **abo·minable**NESS n., **abo·minab**LY² adv. [F (*ab.*, *abh.*), f. L *abominabilis* f. AB(*ominari* f. *omen*) deprecate; the older spelling was regularly *abh.*, due to confusion w. *homo*, and the violence of the meaning (*inhuman* instead of *ill-omened*) results from the mistake]
abo·minate¹, v.t. Loathe; (by exaggeration) dislike. [f. L *abominat-*; see prec.]
abo·minate² (-*a*t), a. (poet.). Abominated. [f. L *abominatus* p.p., see ABOMINABLE]
abomina·tion, n. Loathing; odious or degrading habit or act; an object of disgust (*to*). [F (ABOMINATE¹, -ATION)]
abori·ginal, a. & n. Indigenous, existing in a land at the dawn of history, or before arrival of colonists (of races and natural objects); (noun; pl. *-als*, but *aborigines* commoner) aboriginal inhabitant or (rarely) thing. Hence **aborigina·l**ITY n., **abori·ginal**LY² adv. [f. L *ab* from + *origin-* nom. *origo* origin + -AL]
abori·gines (-ēz), n. pl. (*aboriginal* usual for sing.; also the indefensible form *aborĭ·ginĕ*, and rarely *abŏ·rigin* or *-en*). First inhabitants, or those found in possession by colonists (also of native plants and animals). [L, f. phr. *ab origine* from the beginning]
abor·t, v.i. Miscarry, have premature delivery of a child. (Biol.) become sterile, remain undeveloped, shrink away, (of plants and animals—the race, the individual, or part of the body). [f. L *abort-* p.p. st. of AB(*oriri* be born)]
abor·ted, a. Untimely born, undeveloped; rudimentary (*thorns are aborted branches*). [ABORT + -ED¹ (2)]
abor·tion, n. Miscarriage of birth; the procuring of this, whence **abor·tion**IST(1) n.; arrested development of any organ; a dwarfed or mis-shapen creature; failure of a project or action. [f. L *abortio* (ABORT, -ION)]
abor·tive, a. Premature (birth &c.); fruitless, unsuccessful; rudimentary (organ &c.), arrested in development. Hence **abor·tive**LY² adv., **abor·tive**NESS n. [f. L *abortivus* (ABORT, -IVE)]
abou·nd, v.i. (Orig.) overflow, either of vessel or of liquid. Be plentiful; be rich (*in*); teem or be infested (*with*). [f. OF *abunder, abonder, habonder*, f. L AB(*undare*, f. *unda* wave); the *h-* common in older F and E is due to confusion w. L *habēre* have]
abou·t¹, adv. & prep. All round from outside, as *compass it a., He is a. my path, beat a. the bush*; all round from a centre, as *look* or *lay a. you*; somewhere round, as *lie a., hang a.* (the door), *the fields a. Oxford, people* or *objects a. us, have not a penny a. me*; here and there (in, or abs.), as *smallpox is a., move* or *order a., he put the tale a., I was much put a.* (distracted), *dotted a. the fields, man a. town*; near in number, scale, degree, &c., as *a. half, fifty, right, tired, midnight, my size* (somet. *much a.*); facing round, as *right-a. turn* (now *a. turn!* as mil. word of command), *the wrong way a., put* (the ship) or *go a.*; round a party, as *take turns a., read verse a.*; occupied with, as *a. my father's business, send a. his business, what are you a.?, go a. to do, am a. to do* (so all fut. participles); in connexion with, as *quarrels a. trade, something wrong a. it*; circuitously, as *he went a long way a., I brought it a., it came a.* [OE *on-bútan* f. *on* + *bútan* without (*be* by + locative of *út útan* out); orig. meaning is therefore *on the outside* (*of*)]
abou·t², v.t. Change the course of (ship) to the other tack. [f. ABOUT adv.]

abou·t-sledge, n. Largest hammer used by smiths.

abo·ve (-ŭv), adv. & prep. (Adv.) at a higher point (w. spec. meaning acc. to context); overhead, on high; up stream, upstairs; in heaven; on the upper side; earlier in a book or article (*as was remarked a.*; *the a.-cited passages*; *the a.*); in addition (*over and a.*). (Prep.) over, on the top of, higher than (*a. par*; *a. oneself* slang, in unusual spirits &c.; *can't get a. C*—in music), more than (*a. a hundred*), up stream from, projecting from (*head a. water*; *heard a. the tumult*; *a. ground* = alive), further north than, earlier in hist. than (*not traced a. third century*), out of reach of (*a. criticism, measure, my understanding*), too great or good for (*a. meanness*, one's *station*), more important than (*a. all*), of higher rank than. *Above* is also treated as a noun in *from above*. [f. A² + OE *bufan* (*be* by + *ufan* locative of *uf-* cf. G *auf* up)]

abo·ve-board, adv. & pred. a. Undisguisedly; fair, open. [metaph. f. cards]

ab o·vo, adv. (Relating tediously) from the very beginning. [L; Hor. *A.P.* 147]

ă·bracadă·bra, n. Spell, magic formula; gibberish. Cabbalistic word supposed when written triangularly, and worn, to cure agues &c. [L, etym. dub.]

abra·de, v.t. Scrape off, injure, (skin &c.) by violent rubbing. [f. L AB(*radere ras-* scrape)]

abra·nchial, abra·nchiate, (-kĭ-), a. Without gills. [A-(7) + Gk *bragkhia* gills + -AL and -ATE²]

abra·sion (-āzhn), n. Scraping off (of skin &c.); the wounded place that results. [f. L *abrasio* ABRADE, -ION)]

abrea·st, adv. On a level and facing the same way; keeping up, not behind, (*of* or *with* progress, thought, &c., or as prep., *a. the times*). [A² + BREAST¹]

abri·dge, v.t. Shorten (interview &c.); condense or epitomize (book &c.); curtail (liberty; of limbs &c. only now w. playful archaism); deprive (person *of*). [f. OF *abregier, abreger,* f. L *abbreviare* ABBREVIATE]

abri·dgement, -gment, n. Shortening (of time or labour), curtailment (of rights); epitome, abstract. [f. OF *abregement* f. *abreger* (prec., -MENT)]

abroa·ch (-ōtsh), adv. & pred. a. Pierced, so as to let the liquor run (of casks). [A² + BROACH]

abroa·d (-awd), adv. Broadly, widely, in different directions; in motion (*there is a rumour a.*; *the schoolmaster is a.*, education is now becoming generally accessible); out of doors, in or to foreign lands; in error (*all a.*) Also treated as a noun in *from a.* [A² + BROAD a.; cf. *along, at large*]

a·brogate, v.t. Repeal, cancel, (law or custom). So **abrog**ATION n. [f. obs. adj. *abrogate* f. L *abrogatus* p.p. of AB(*rogare* propose law)]

abru·pt, a. Sudden, hasty, disconnected; steep, precipitous; (Bot.) truncated; suddenly cropping out (of geol. strata). Hence **abru·pt**LY² adv., **abru·pt**NESS n. [f. L *abruptus* p.p. of AB(*rumpere* break)]

abru·ption n. Breaking away of part from a mass. [f. L *abruptio* (ABRUPT, -ION)]

abs-, pref. From, away, off. See AB-.

a·bscess (-sĕs), n. Collection of pus formed in a cavity of the body. [f. L *abscessus* a going away f. ABS(*cedere cess-* go)]

a·bsciss(e) (pl. *-es*), **absci·ssa** (pl. *-ae*), (-sĭ-), n. Portion of given line intercepted between fixed point within it and ordinate drawn to it from given point without it. [L *abscissa* (*linea*) p.p. of AB(*scindere sciss-* cut)]

absci·ssion (-sĭ-), n. (surg.). Cutting off, violent separation. [f. L *abscissio* (see prec., -ION)]

absco·nd, v.i. Go away secretly, fly from the law. Hence **absco·nd**ENCE, **absco·nd**ER¹, nn. [f. L ABS(CON*dere* stow, f. *dare* put); orig. transitive in E also, then refl., then intr.]

a·bsence, n. Being away from a place; time of being away; non-existence or want *of*; abstraction of thought (esp. in phr. *a. of mind*); rollcall. [F, f. L *absentia* (*absent-* ABSENT¹)]

a·bsent¹, a. Not present; not existing. Abstracted in mind, whence **a·bsent**LY² adv., **absent-mi·nd**ED² a., **absent-mi·nded**LY² adv., **absent-mi·nded**NESS, **a·bsent**NESS, nn. [F, f. L *absentem* nom. *-ens* part. of AB(*esse* be)]

abse·nt², v.refl. Keep one*self* away. [f. F *absenter* f. L *absentare* f. *absent-* ABSENT¹]

absentee·, n. A person not present. A person habitually living away from home; esp. a landlord so doing, whence **absentee·**ISM (2) n. [ABSENT² + -EE]

absidal. See APSIDAL.

a·bsinth, n. Wormwood, the plant or its essence; a liqueur made (orig. at least) from wine and wormwood. [f. L f. Gk *apsinthion*]

a·bsit o·men, sent. May no ominous significance attach to the words, may my fears not be verified. [L]

a·bsolute (-ōōt, -ūt), a. Complete, perfect, pure (as *a. alcohol*), mere; unrestricted, independent; ruling arbitrarily; out of grammatical relation (*ablative a.* in L, *genitive a.* in Gk, *a. construction* in E, noun & participle used as advl clause, as *dinner being over we left the table*); real, not merely relative or comparative; unqualified, unconditional; self-existent and conceivable without relation to other things (*the a.*, as noun). Hence **a·bsolute**NESS n. [f. mid. F *absolut* (now *absolu*) f. L *absolutus* p.p. see ABSOLVE]

a·bsolutely, adv. Independently, in and

by itself; arbitrarily, without external control; without qualification; without the usual accompaniments (as *a transitive vb used a.*, i.e. without its obj.); unconditionally; positively, though you would not believe it; conclusively, completely, quite; at all (w. negatives); (colloq.) quite so, yes. [f. prec. + -LY²]

absolu·tion, n. Formal setting free from guilt, sentence, or obligation; ecclesiastical declaration of forgiveness of sins; remission of penance; forgiveness. [F, f. L *absolutionem* (ABSOLVE, -ION)]

a·bsolutism, n. (Theol.) doctrine that God acts absolutely in the affair of salvation. (Polit.) principle of absolute government. [ABSOLUTE + -ISM (3)]

a·bsolutist, n. Partisan of political absolutism (also adj., as *a. principles*). A metaphysician who identifies subject and object. [ABSOLUTE + -IST (2)]

abso·lve (-s-, -z-), v.t. Set, pronounce, free (*from* blame &c., *of* sin, *from* obligation &c., or abs.); acquit, pronounce not guilty. [f. L AB(*solvere, solut-* loosen)]

a·bsonant, a. Discordant, alien (*from*), unreasonable. [f. AB- + *sonant-* part. st. of L *sonare* sound on anal. of *dissonant, consonant,* and L *absonus*]

absor·b, v.t. Swallow up, incorporate (*be absorbed by,* lose one's identity in); engross the attention of; suck in (liquids); take in (heat, light, &c.) by chemical or molecular action. [f. F *absorber* f. L AB-*sorbēre sorpt-* suck in)]

absor·bable, a. Easily sucked in. Hence **absorbabi·lity** n. [prec. + -ABLE]

absor·bed, a. Intensely engaged or interested. Hence **absor·bĕdly²** adv. [p.p. of ABSORB]

absorbĕfā·cient (-shnt), a. & n. Causing the absorption or drying up (e.g. of a tumour); agent that does this. [f. L *absorbēre* ABSORB + -FACIENT]

absor·bent, a. & n. Having a tendency to suck in (abs., or *of*); a substance of this kind; one of the vessels in plants and animals (e.g. the root tips) that absorb nutriment. [f. L *absorbent-* part. st. of *absorbēre* ABSORB]

absor·bing, a. Engrossing, intensely interesting. Hence **absor·bingly²** adv. [part. of ABSORB]

absor·ption, n. Disappearance through incorporation in something else; natural or medical removal of tissues; mental engrossment; sucking in of fluid, light &c., or nutriment. [f. L *absorptio* (ABSORB, -ION)]

absor·ptive, a. Having a tendency to suck in. Hence **absor·ptiveness** n. [f. L *absorpt-* (ABSORB, -IVE)]

ȧbsqua·tulate (-kwŏt-), v.i. Make off, decamp. [American-made jocular vb w. L pref. and suf.]

abstai·n, v.i. Keep oneself away, refrain, (*from*). Refrain from alcohol, whence **abstai·ner¹** n., **abstai·ning²** a. [f. F *abstenir* f. L ABS(*tinēre tent-* = *tenēre* hold)]

abstē·mious, a. Sparing, not self-indulgent, esp. in food and drink. Used of persons, habits, meals. Hence **abste·miously²** adv., **abste·miousness** n. [f. L ABS(*temius* f. *temum* strong drink inferred f. *temulentus, temetum*) + -OUS]

abste·ntion, n. Keeping off (abs., or *from* any pleasure); esp., not using one's vote. [F (ABSTAIN, -ION)]

abster·gent, a. & n. Cleansing; a cleansing substance. [f. L *abstergent-* part. st. of ABS(*tergēre ters-* wipe)]

abster·sion, n. Cleansing, purgation. [F, see prec., -ION]

abster·sive, a. Cleansing. [f. F (*-if, -ive*), as prec., -IVE]

a·bstinence, n. Refraining (*from* any pleasure, or abs. in sense of continence, fasting, or, usu. *total a.*, going without alcohol). Somet. = foll. [F, f. L *abstinentia* (ABSTINENT, -ENCE)]

a·bstinency, n. Habit of refraining from pleasures, esp. food. [f. L *abstinentia* see prec. & -ENCY]

a·bstinent, a. Practising abstinence. Hence **a·bstinently²** adv. [F, f. L *abstinent-* (ABSTAIN, -ENT)]

a·bstract¹, a. Separated from matter, practice, or particular examples, not concrete; ideal, not practical; abstruse; (with *the*, as noun) the ideal or theoretical way of regarding things (*in the a.*). Hence **a·bstractly²** adv., **a·bstractness** n. [f. L *abstractus* p.p. of ABS(*trahere* draw)]

a·bstract², n. Essence, summary; abstraction or abstract term. [see prec.]

abstra·ct³, v.t. Deduct, remove, (an obj. *much* &c. is somet. omitted); (euphemism) steal; disengage (obj. *attention* &c. somet. omitted) *from*; consider apart from the concrete; summarize. [f. ABSTRACT¹]

abstra·cted, a. Withdrawn in thought, not attending. Hence **abstra·ctedness** n. [-ED¹]

abstra·ctedly, adv. In the abstract, ideally; separately (*from*—esp. after *consider*); in an absent-minded way. [-LY²]

abstra·ction, n. Taking away, withdrawal; (euphemism) stealing. Process of stripping an idea of its concrete accompaniments; the idea so stripped, something visionary, whence **abstra·ctionmonger** n. Absence of mind. [F, f. L *abstractionem* (ABSTRACT¹, -ION)]

abstru·se, a. Hard to understand, profound. Hence **abstru·sely²** adv., **abstru·seness** n. [f. L ABS(*trusus* p.p. of *trudere* push)]

absur·d, a. Incongruous, unreasonable, ridiculous, silly. Hence **absur·dly²** adv. [f. F *absurde* f. L *absurdus* (*ab-* utterly + *surdus* deaf, dull)]

absur·dity, n. Folly, unreasonableness; an absurd statement or act. [f. F *absurdité* f. L *absurditatem* (ABSURD, -ITY)]

abu·ndance, n. Quantity more than sufficient, plenty; overflowing emotion (*a. of the heart*); many people (*there are a. who*); affluence, wealth. [OF (*ab-, hab-*, see ABOUND), f. L *abundantia* (as foll., -ANCE)]
abu·ndant, a. More than sufficient, plentiful; rich (*in*). Hence **abu·ndant**LY[2] adv. [OF (*ab-, hab-*, see ABOUND), f. L *abundant-* part. st. (ABOUND, -ANT)]
ab ur·be co·nditā, adv. (abbr. A.U.C.). Counting from the foundation of Rome. [L]
abu·se[1] (-ūz), v.t. Misuse, make bad use of; deceive (archaic, but still used esp. in pass.); maltreat (archaic); revile. [f. F *abuser* f. L **abusare* f. AB(*us-* p.p. st. of *uti* use)]
abu·se[2] (-ūs), n. Misuse, perversion (*of*); an established unjust or corrupt practice. Reviling, whence **abu·**SIVE a., **abu·sive**LY[2] adv., **abu·sive**NESS n. [f. F *abus* f. L *abusus* n. f. *abus-* see prec.
abu·t, v.i. (-tt-). Have a common boundary with, border, (*upon*; or somet. without prep. as trans. vb; of estates or countries); end *on* or *against*, lean *on*, (of parts of a building). [mixed meanings f. OF *abouter* place end to end (*à* to + *bout* end), and OF *abuter* touch with one end (*à* to + *but* end)]
abu·tment, n. A lateral support; (esp. in architecture) that on which an arch or bridge rests; point of junction between such support and thing supported. [ABUT + -MENT]
abu·tter, n. (In law) owner of the adjoining property. [ABUT + -ER[1]]
abȳ·, abye·, v.t. (archaic; past and p.p. *abought*). Redeem, pay the penalty of, (an offence; usu. w. *dearly, sore*). [earlier *abuggen, abeggen,* f. A- (1) away + BUY]
abȳ·sm, n. Earlier form, still used in poetical style, of ABYSS. [OF *abisme* f. LL **abyssimus* superl. of *abyssus* ABYSS]
abȳ·smal, a. Bottomless, esp. fig., as *a. ignorance.* Hence **aby·smal**LY[2] adv. [ABYSM + -AL]
abȳ·ss, n. The primal chaos, bowels of the earth, lower world; a bottomless chasm, deep gorge; depth (*a. of light*). [Earlier *abime, abysme,* f. F see ABYSM, later corrected after L *abyssus* f. Gk *abussos* bottomless]
abȳ·ssal, a. More than 300 fathoms below sea surface (water, zone, mud). [f. LL *abyssalis* f. *abyssus*; see ABYSS and -AL]
ac-, pref. to words in *c-, k-, qu-*. Properly the L assimilated form of AD- to, in addition. In passing through OF it became *a-*; this being rectified later, *ac-* was mistakenly written also for *a-* representing other preff. (see A-), e.g. OE *a-* (on) in *acknowledge.*
-ac, suf. forming adjj., which are often also (if not only) used as nouns. From Gk *-akos*, the modification of adj. suf. *-kos* appended to nouns in *-ia, -ios, -ion,* and imitated in L. E wds in *-ac* may be f. Gk (*-akos*), L (*-acus*), or F (*-aque*).
acā·cia (-sha), n. Genus of trees, of Mimosa tribe, yielding gum arabic; the Locust-tree or False Acacia, grown in England for ornament; gum arabic. [L, f. Gk *akakia*; perh. f. *akē* point (in ref. to its thorns)]
ă·cademe, n. (Prop.) = Academus (see ACADEMY); (used by mistake in poetic style for) the Gk Academy, a college, university. [Gk *Akadēmos* see ACADEMY; mistake perh. caused by Milton's 'grove of Academe', *P. R.* iv. 244]
acadĕ·mic, a. & n. Belonging to or agreeing with the philosophic school of Plato (ACADEMY), (w. ref. to some of his successors' views) sceptical; an ancient Platonist. Scholarly, (and by implication) abstract, unpractical, cold, merely logical; (as sing. noun) member of a university, one too much enslaved to the principles (in painting &c.) of an academy; (as pl. noun) merely theoretic arguments, university robes. Of an academician or academy (*a. rank*). [f. med. L *academicus* see ACADEMY]
acadĕ·mical, a. Belonging to a college or university; (as pl. noun) college costume (commoner than *academics*). [prec. + -AL]
acadĕ·mically, adv. Theoretically, unpractically; rarely also in any of the senses of the two precc. [prec. + -LY[2]]
acă·demi·cian, n. Member of an Academy or art society, esp. of the Royal Academy of Arts. [f. F *académicien* f. med. L *academicus* (foll.); see -IAN]
Acă·demy, n. The garden near Athens in which Plato taught; Plato's followers or philosophical system; a place of study, including universities, but gen. used pretentiously or depreciatingly of something between a school and a university; a place of training in a special art (Royal Military A.); a society for cultivating literature, art, &c., of which membership is an honour, esp. the Royal A. of Arts; the R.A.'s annual exhibition. [f. F *académie* f. L f. Gk *akadēmeia* (*Akadēmos* the man or demigod f. whom Plato's garden was named)]
Acā·dian, a. & n. Nova-Scotian. [f. F *Acadie* Nova Scotia + -AN]
-acal, compd suf. = -AC + -AL. Adjj. in *-ac* being often used as nouns also, *-al* was appended to distinguish the adj. (*demoniac, -acal*), and even when there was no noun (*heliacal*). In adjj. *-acal* often differs f. *-ac* in suggesting looser connexion w. the orig. noun; e.g., *cardiac arteries* (*of* the heart), *cardiacal herbs* (*having influence on* the h.).
ă·caleph(e), n. Jellyfish, medusa, sea-nettle. [Gk *akalēphē* nettle]
acalyc- (ăkal- or akăl-), stem of several bot. terms. Without calyx. [A-(7) + Gk *kalux -ukos* flower-cup]

aca·nthus, n. A genus of plants, esp. Bear's Breech or Brank-Ursine; a conventional representation of its leaf used in Gk architecture. Hence **acanth**(o)- comb. form. [L, f. Gk *akanthos* (*akantha* thorn f. *akē* point)]

aca·psular, a. Not having capsule. [A- (7) + L *capsula* CAPSULE + -AR[1]]

acar·diac, a. (physiol.). Without a heart. [f. Gk *akardios* f. A- (7) + *kardia* heart + -AC]

ăcarpe·llous, a. Without carpels. [A- (7), CARPEL, -OUS]

acar·pous, a. (bot.). Not producing fruit. [A- (7) + Gk *karpos* fruit + -OUS]

acătale·ctic, a. & n. (A verse) not docked of a syllable, complete. [f. LL *acatalecticus* f. Gk *akatalēktos*, see A- (7), CATALECTIC)]

acă·talepsy, n. Incomprehensibility (philos. term), the quality in the object answering to agnosticism in the subject. So **acatale·pt**IC a. [f. med. L f. Gk *akatalēpsia* f. A- (7) + *kata* thoroughly + *lēpsis* grasping (*lab-* st. of *lambanō* take)]

acau·lous, a. (also **-e·scent, -ine, -ose**) (bot.). Apparently stemless, having very short stem. [A- (7) + L *caulis* stem + -OUS]

Accā·dian, a. & n. Of Accad in Shinar (*Gen.* x. 10); a language preserved in cuneiform inscriptions.

acce·de (-ks-), v.i. Enter upon (an office); join (a party); assent to (opinion or policy). Abs., or w. *to* if the office &c. is stated, in all senses. [f. L AC(*cedere cess-* come)]

accĕlera·ndo (-ks-), musical direction. Gradually increase speed. [It.]

accĕ·lerate (-ks-), v.t. & i. Make quicker; cause to happen earlier; become swifter (of a motion or process); put on pace. [f. obs. adj. *accelerate* f. L AC(*celerare* f. *celer* swift); see -ATE[2, 3]]

acce·lerated, a. (physics). Progressively quicker (*a. motion*). Hence **acce·lerated**LY[2] adv. [p.p. of prec.]

acce·lerating, a. Causing progressively quicker motion (*a. force*). [-ING[2]]

accelera·tion (aks-), n. Making quicker; being made quicker. (Physics) rate of increase of velocity per time unit, as with falling bodies. (Astr.) *a. of stars*, time gained daily by them over sun; *a. of planets*, increased velocity from aphelion to perihelion; *a. of moon*, increase in speed of mean motion; *a. of tides*, amount of local advance on calculated time. [f. L *acceleratio* (ACCELERATE, -ION)]

acce·lerative, a. Tending to increase speed, quickening. [f. ACCELERATE + -IVE]

acce·lerator, n. Person or thing that increases anything's speed, esp. an attachment in motor-cars for this purpose; one of a class of nerves and muscles. [ACCELERATE + -OR[2]]

a·ccent[1], n. Prominence given to a syllable, whether by higher musical pitch (ancient Gk and L, Swedish and Norw.), or by stress (most mod. langg., but perh. not F). Three marks called *acute* (ʹ), *grave* (ˋ), and *circumflex* (ˆ or ˆ) *accents* (systematically employed only in Gk, and to a less degree in F) used for various purposes, e.g. to indicate syllabic pitch (Gk), quality of vowel sound (F), etymological hist. (F, E), metrical stress, syllabic stress (dictionaries &c.), the fact of a letter's not being silent, or conventional distinction between homonyms (F). Individual, local, or national mode of pronunciation; modulation to express feeling; in pl., speech (poet.). (In prosody) rhythmical stress. (Mus.) stress recurring at intervals. (Fig.) intensity, sharp distinction. [F, f. L AC(*centus -ūs* = *cantus* singing) lit. transl. of Gk *prosōdia* (*pros* to + *ōdē* song)]

acce·nt[2], v.t. Pronounce with accent, emphasize (word or syllable); put the written accents on; heighten, make conspicuous. [f. obs. F *accenter* see prec.]

acce·ntor, n. Kinds of bird (= WARBLER), esp. the hedge-sparrow, which name is now sometimes avoided as misleading. [mod. L, f. *ad* to + *cantor*, see CANTORIS]

acce·ntual, a. Of accent; *a. prosody* or *verse*, of which the principle is accent or stress, not quantity. Hence **acce·ntual**LY[2] adv. [f. L *accentus* ACCENT[1] + -AL]

acce·ntuate, v.t. = ACCENT[2], but more used than it in the fig. sense. [f. med. L *accentuare* (*accentus* ACCENT[1]), -ATE[3]]

acce·ntua·tion, n. Accenting (all senses from ACCENT). [f. med. L *accentuatio* see ACCENTUATE, -ION]

acce·pt, v.t. Consent to receive (gift), answer affirmatively (offer, invitation, suitor); regard with favour (esp. unfair favour, as *a. the person of, a. persons*); receive as adequate (*a. service of writ*), allow the truth of, believe; undertake (office); take responsibility for, agree to meet, (bill of exchange). *Of* may be added (exc. w. *service of writ, bill*) with a slight suggestion of formality or condescension. Hence **acce·pt**ER[1] n. [f. F *accepter* f. L *acceptare* frequent. of AC(*cipere* = *capere* take)]

acce·ptable (*also* ă·-), a. Worth accepting, pleasing, welcome. Hence or cogn. **acce·ptab**LY[2] adv., **acceptab**I·LITY, **acce·ptable**NESS, nn. [F, f. L *acceptabilis* (ACCEPT, -ABLE)]

acce·ptance, n. Consent to receive (gift, payment, pleasure, duty); favourable reception (act. & pass.), approval, belief; *a. of persons*, partiality; engagement to meet a bill; a bill so accepted. [OF; see ACCEPT and -ANCE]

ăccepta·tion, n. A particular sense given to a word or phrase; its generally recognized meaning. [F, f. LL *acceptationem* (ACCEPT, -ATION)]

acce·pted, a. Generally recognized or believed in (*Free & A. Masons*, see FREE[1]-*mason*). Hence **acce·pted**LY[2] adv. [-ED[1]]

acce·ptor, n. One who accepts a bill (preferred to *accepter* in this sense). [AF *acceptour* f. L *acceptorem* (ACCEPT, -OR[2])]

a·ccess (*also* -ě·s, *see etym.*), n. Approach; addition; right or means of approaching (*to*); being approached (*easy of a.*;) advance (*a. and recess*); passage, channel, doorway; adhesion, growth, (usu. now *accession*); attack or outburst (*of* illness, anger, emotion). [The doubtful accent is due to double derivation. 1. (sense *attack*, pron. ă·-) f. F *accès* f. L *accessus* n. f. AC(*cedere cess-* come); 2. (other senses, pron. ăksě·s) direct f. L *accessus*. The two pronunciations, however, have now ceased to be significant]

a·ccessary (*also* aksě·s-), n. & pred. a. (see also ACCESSORY). Helper in any act, one privy *to* it (as pred. a., *be a.*, *were made accessary*); accompaniment, adjunct. [f. ACCESS + -ARY[1] formed as f. L *access-* like *emissary, adversary*; the adj. (first spelt *-ary*) being corrected later to *-ory* on L *accessorius* drew the noun after it, and the two spellings are often confused]

acce·ssible, a. Able to be reached or entered (abs., or *to*); open to influence, to the influence of, (*to*). Hence **accessi**BI·LITY n., **acce·ssib**LY[2] adv. [F, f. L *accessibilis* (ACCEDE, -BLE)]

acce·ssion, n. Coming into presence or contact; coming into an office (esp. the throne) or condition (as manhood); being added; assent; thing added, addition; (in law) improvement or natural growth of property. [F, f. L *accessionem* (ACCEDE, -ION)]

a·ccessory (*also* aksě·s-), a. & n. (see also ACCESSARY). Additional, subordinately contributive (of things), adventitious; a thing of that character, esp. in pl. *the accessories*. [f. LL *accessorius* adj. (ACCEDE, -ORY)]

a·ccidence, n. The part of grammar, or a book, dealing with inflexions (i.e. the accidents or non-essentials of words); the elements of any subject. [corruption of *accidents* = F pl. n. *accidens* transl. of L neut. pl. *accidentia* the things that befall (a word), see ACCIDENT; or perh. direct f. *accidentia* treated as fem. sing. noun]

a·ccident, n. Event without apparent cause, unexpected (so *chapter of aa.*, unforeseen course of events); unintentional act, chance, fortune, (*by a.*); mishap; irregularity in structure; a property not essential to our conception of a substance (so of material qualities of bread and wine after transubstantiation); a mere accessory. [F, f. L *accidens -entis* part. and n. f. AC(*cidere* = *cadere* fall)]

accide·ntal, a. & n. Happening by chance, undesignedly, or unexpectedly; occasional; not essential to a conception (so also *an a.* as n.); subsidiary. (Mus.) *a. sharps, flats, naturals*, and *a.* as noun, signs attached to single notes, not in signature. (Optics) *a. colours*, those presented by subjective sensation, not external. (In painting) *a. lights*, and *accidentals* as n., effects of other than ordinary daylight. [F (now *-el*), prob. f. LL *accidentalis* f. *accidens* see prec.]

accide·ntally, adv. By chance, unintentionally. [-LY[2]]

acci·pitral (aksĭp-), a. Hawklike; rapacious; keensighted. [f. L *accipitr-* nom. *-ter* hawk + -AL]

acclai·m[1], v.t. Applaud loudly or enthusiastically; (w. obj. and compl.) hail as (king, winner, saviour; *acclaimed him king*). [f. L AC(*clamare* shout), spelling assimilated to CLAIM]

acclai·m[2], n. Shout of applause. [f. prec.]

acclama·tion, n. Loud and eager assent to a proposal (*voted, carried, by a.*); shouting in a person's honour (usu. pl.). [f. L *acclamatio* (prec., -ATION)]

acclīma·tion, n. = acclimatization (see foll.), or distinguished from it as a natural process, not imposed on animals by man. [syncopated for *acclimatation* (*acclimate* f. F *acclimater* ACCLIMATIZE)]

acclī·matize (also **a·cclimate**), v.t. & i. Habituate (animals, plants, one*self*) to new climate; (rarely) become so habituated. Hence **accli·matiz**A·TION (also **acclimata·tion**) n. [f. F *acclimater* (*à* to + *climat* CLIMATE) + -IZE]

acclī·vity, n. Upward slope of a hill (cf. DECLIVITY). [f. L *acclivitas* f. AC(*clivis* f. *clivus* slope)]

accola·de (-ād *or* -ahd), n. Sign at bestowal of knighthood, whether embrace, kiss, or stroke on shoulder with flat of sword. (Mus.) vertical line or brace coupling staves. [F, f. It. *accollata* n. from p.p. st. of *accollare* (AC- + L *collum* neck)]

acco·mmodate, v.t. Adapt (thing or person *to* another); prove such adaptation in, harmonize, (somet. w. implication of sophistry); reconcile, settle differences between; compose (quarrel); equip, supply, (person *with*); oblige, confer favour on; find lodging for. [f. obs. adj. *accommodate* f. p.p. of L AC(*commodare -at-* f. *commodus* fitting = COM- + *modus* measure)]

acco·mmodating, a. Obliging, easy to deal with, pliable, lax. Hence **acco·mmodating**LY[2] adv. [-ING[2]]

accommoda·tion, n. Adjustment (e.g. of eyes for various distances); adaptation of anything to a purpose or meaning different from the original; self-adaptation; settlement, compromise; serviceable thing, convenience (so in comp. as *a.-road*; *a.-ladder*, up ship's side); lodgings, entertainment; money loan (so in *a.*-BILL[4]). [F, f. L *accommodationem* (ACCOMMODATE, -ION)]

acco·mpaniment (-ŭm-), n. Appendage, thing that attends another. (Mus.) subsidiary part vocal or instrumental, usu. the latter as used to support the voice. [f. F *accompagnement* (foll., -MENT)]

acco·mpany (-ŭm-), v.t. Supplement (a thing *with*, as word w. blow); go with, escort, attend; coexist with (of things), characterize. (Mus.) support (singer, player, piece) by performing additional part, whence **acco·mpan**IST (also **-nyist**) n. After pass., *by* has almost ousted older *with*, now only used when *accompanied* = *combined*. [f. F *accompagner* (*à* to + *compagne* COMPANION)]

accŏ·mplice, n. Partner, usu. subordinate, in crime. [f. earlier & F *complice* (whether by mistake from *a complice*, cf. NEWT, or by assim. to foll.) f. L *complicem* nom. *-plex* closely connected (COM- + *plic-* fold)]

accŏ·mplish, v.t. Fulfil, perform, complete, finish. Perfect (a person) in graceful acquirements, whence **acco·mplish**ED[1] a. [f. OF *acomplir* f. LL AC(*complēre* COMPLETE); see -ISH[2]]

acco·mplishment, n. Fulfilment, completion; thing done or attained, achievement; faculty that perfects a person for society, (disparagingly) merely superficial acquirement. [f. F *accomplissement*; see prec., -MENT]

accompt, -ant, archaic for ACCOUNT, -ANT.

accor·d[1], v.t. & i. Be in harmony or consistent (abs., or *with*; chiefly of things); grant (indulgence, request, welcome, &c.). [f. OF *acorder* f. LL AC(*cordare* f. *cor cordis* heart)]

accor·d[2], n. Consent (*with one a.*), mutual agreement; treaty of peace; harmonious correspondence in colour, pitch, tone; assent (*of* one's *own a.*). [f. OF *acord* agreement (*acorder* ACCORD[1])]

accor·dance, n. Conformity, agreement, esp. in phr. *in a. with.* [OF *acordance* (as prec., -ANCE)]

accor·dant, a. In tune, agreeing, (abs., or *with*). Hence **accor·dant**LY[2] adv. [OF *acordant* as prec., -ANT]

accor·ding, adv. (only now in the compd conj. *a. as*, and the compd prep. *a. to*). *A. as*: in proportion as (of a process varying w. another); in a manner depending on which of certain alternatives is true. *A. to*: in a manner consistent with or degree proportioned to; on the authority of. [-ING[2]]

accor·dingly, adv. As the (stated) circumstances suggest; therefore; *a. as* = *according as.* [-LY[2]]

accor·dion, n. Portable musical instrument made of bellows, keys, and metal reeds. Hence **accor·dion**IST (3) n. [f. It. and LL *accordare* attune see ACCORD[1]; termination imitated f. CLARION]

accŏ·st[1], v.t. Make up to and address, open conversation with; (of prostitute) solicit. [f. F *accoster* f. LL AC(*costare* f. *costa* rib)]

accŏ·st[2], n. Greeting, opening remark. [f. prec.]

accou·chement (-ōōshmŏng, or as F), n. Lying-in, delivery in child-bed. [F]

accoucheur· (-ōōsher), n. (fem. *-euse* pr. -erz). Man-midwife, midwife. [F]

accou·nt[1], v.t. & i. Consider, regard as, (followed by obj. & complement or infin.; *a. him a hero, wise, to be guilty*). *Be accounted of*, be esteemed (alw. w. *little, much*, &c.). *Account for*: give reckoning of (money held in trust); answer for (conduct, performance of duty); explain the cause of; serve as explanation of (*that accounts for it*); (sport) be responsible for the death of, kill. [f. OF. *aconter* f. LL *accomptare* for *AC(*computare* L = COMPUTE); the form *accompt* is due to 14th-c. correction in F passing into E, the oldest E being *acunte* (see AC-)]

accou·nt[2], n. (1) Counting, calculation, in phrr. *cast accounts* (reckon up), *money of a.* (names not of coins, but of sums, as guinea). (2) Reckoning of debit and credit, in money or service. Statement of money received and expended, with balance; so *open* or *close an a. with, render* or *send in, pay* or *settle, an a.*; *a. current* (whence a/c = account), one kept going w. occasional entries; *a. rendered*, used when a bill previously sent in, but left unpaid, is sent again; *joint a.*, in which two persons not otherwise partners count as one; *keep aa.*, enter all expenditure for comparison w. income; *balance* or *square aa. with some one*, receive or pay the balance due; *cash, profit-and-loss*, &c., *a.*, headings of subdivision in ledger; *sale for the a.*, on the Stock Exch., not for cash, but payable at next periodic settlement; *A in a. with B*, having credit relations with; *for a. of*, to be sold for (person); *on a.*, as interim payment; *on* one's *a.*, for his service; *on* one's *own a.*, for and at one's own purposes and risk, whence generally *on a. of*, because of, and *on no a.*, by no means, certainly not. A favourable result of the reckoning, profit; *find one's a. in*, profit by, *turn to a.*, make useful. Statement of administration as required by creditor; *ask, demand, yield, render, an a., call* or *bring to a.*; extended from money to conduct generally, so *the great a.*, Day of Judgement, *gone to his a.*, dead; *give a. of*, find cause of, explain, (in sport) *give a good a. of*, dispose of (opponents, game) successfully. (3) Estimation. Person or thing *of*, or *held in, some* or *no a.*; *make little a. of*; *take into, leave out of, a.*; *take a. of*; *lay one's a. with*, include in one's calculations, expect. (4) Narration, report, description, of event, person, &c. [f. OF *acont* (*à* to + *cont* f. LL *comptum* for *computum* f. L *computare* COMPUTE)]

accou·ntable, a. Bound to give account,

responsible, (*for* things, *to* persons, or abs.); explicable (somet. followed by *for*). Hence **accountabi·lity, accou·ntableness**, nn., [f. ACCOUNT[1] + -ABLE]

accou·ntant, n. (Law) one liable to render account; defendant in an action of account. Professional keeper and inspector of accounts; *a.-general*, chief a. in public offices; whence **accou·ntantship** n. [F (15th c.) *accomptant* part. of *accompter* OF *aconter* ACCOUNT[1]]

accou·tre (-ōōter), v.t. (-tring, -tred). Attire, equip, esp. w. special costume (chiefly used in p.p.). [f. med. F *accoustrer* (now *accoutrer*) etym. dub. perh. AC- + *coustre* vestry-keeper and so rober which is perh. f. LL **custor* f. *custos* guardian]

accou·trement (-ōōtrem-), n. (usu. in pl.). Equipment, trappings. (Mil.) soldier's outfit other than arms and garments, e.g. belt, straps, valise. [MF *accoustrement* (prec., -MENT)]

accrĕ·dit, v.t. Gain belief or influence for (adviser, advice); send out (ambassador &c.) with credentials *to* person, *to* or *at* a court; *a.* thing (saying, policy) *to* person, or *a.* him *with* it, put it down to him. [f. F AC(*créditer* f. *crédit* CREDIT)]

accrĕ·dited, a. Officially recognized (persons); generally accepted, orthodox, (beliefs). [p.p. of prec.]

accre·te[1], v.t. & i. Grow together or into one; form round or on *to*, as round a nucleus; attract (such additions). [f. L *accret-* p.p. st. of AC(*crescere* grow)]

accre·te[2], a. (bot.). Grown into one with something else. [f. L *accretus* p.p. see prec].

accrē·tion, n. Growth by organic enlargement; the growing of separate things (as particles) into one; the whole resulting from this; adhesion of extraneous matter to anything; the matter so added; (Law) = ACCESSION, also increase of legacy &c. by share of failing co-legatee. [f. L *accretio* (ACCRETE[1], -ION)]

accrue· (-ōō), v.i. Fall (*to* one, *from* a thing) as a natural growth, advantage, result; esp. of interest on invested money. Hence **accrue·d**[1] (2) a. [f. obs. *accrue* n. = F *accrue* p.p. of *accroître* OF *acreistre* f. L *accrescere* ACCRETE[1]]

accū·mūlate, v.t. & i. Heap up, gain by degrees, (usu. fig., a fortune, ill will, &c., or abs.), amass, make money; take (University degrees) by accumulation (obj. expressed, or abs.), i.e. more than one step at a time; grow numerous, form an increasing mass or heap (lit. and fig., as *dirt, disasters, had accumulated*). [f. obs. *accumulate* a. f. L AC(*cumulare* f. *cumulus* heap), -ATE[2, 3]]

accumula·tion, n. Collection (act. or pass.), amassing; money-making; growth of capital by continued interest; combination of distinct acts into one (degrees, see prec., or church services &c.); a mass (as snow, papers, property). [f. L *accumulatio* (prec., -ION)]

accu·mulative, a. Arising from accumulation (*a. proof, evidence*, now being ousted by *cumulative*); so arranged as to accumulate (sinking fund); acquisitive, given to hoarding. Hence **accu·mulatively**[2] adv. [as prec. + -IVE]

accu·mulator, n. One who collects; money-maker; taker of degrees by accumulation; apparatus for storing electricity. [L (as prec., -OR[2])]

a·ccūrate, a. Careful, precise, in exact conformity with a standard or with truth. Hence **a·ccuracy** n., **a·ccurately**[2] adv. [f. L AC(*curare* f. *cura* care), -ATE[2]]

accur·sed (-ĭd), **accur·st**, a. Lying under a curse, ill-fated; involving misery, execrable, detestable. [p.p. f.obs. *accurse* earlier *acurse* (*a*-imitated as intensive f. OE *ar-* see A- (1) + OE *cursian* CURSE v.)]

accu·sal, n. Sometimes used for foll. [f. ACCUSE + -AL (2)]

accusa·tion, n. Accusing; being accused; a charge of offence or crime; indictment. [F, f. L *accusationem* (ACCUSE, -ION)]

accu·sative, a. & n. *A. case* (or *a.* as noun), the grammatical case used in Gk & L for the goal of motion or obj. of action; in uninflected langg., applied to the wd that stands as obj., though with no mark of case. Hence **accusatī·val** adj., **accu·satively**[2] adv. [F (*-if, -ive*), f. L *accusativus* lit. transl. of Gk *aitiatikē* causal (also accusing), the goal or obj. being the final cause of motion or action]

accusator·ial, a. *A. procedure* &c., in which prosecutor and judge are not the same, opposed to *inquisitorial*. [as foll. + -AL]

accu·satory, a. *A. language, manner*, &c, conveying or implying accusation. [f. L *accusatorius* (foll., -ORY)]

accu·se (-z), v.t. Charge with a fault, indict, (person), whence p.p. as noun, *the accused*; blame, lay the fault on, (person or thing, as *the times*). *A. as* offender, *of* offence. Point to (subj. *evidence* &c., obj. a person). Hence **accu·ser**[1] n., **accu·singly**[2] adv. [earlier *acuse* f. OF *acuser* f. L AC(*cusare* = *causare* f. *causa* cause)]

accu·stom, v.t. Habituate (one*self*, person, or thing, *to* do or *to*; commoner in pass.). [earlier *acustom* (see AC-) f. OF *acostumer* (now *accoutumer*) (*à* to, CUSTOM)]

accu·stomed, a. In vbl senses; also, usual. [p.p. of prec. in obs. sense *make usual*]

āce, n. The one on dice; *ambs-ace*, throw of two ones, *deuce ace*, of two and one (formerly two ones); the one on dominoes, cards; one point at rackets &c.; French airman who has brought down ten enemy aeroplanes; (Tennis) service that beats opponent; the smallest possible amount, hair's-breadth, as *within* *an ace of*; *ace-point*, first or starting point on backgammon table. [F *as* f. L *as* unity]

-ācea, L suf. freely used to form names (neut. pl. agreeing w. *animalia*) for orders of animals; the names are L and pl., the sing. being supplied by E adjj. in -ACEAN used as noun; so *the crustacea, a crustacean.* [f. L *-aceus* (*-ac-* + *-e-us*) compd adj. formative]

-āceae, L suf. freely used to form names (fem. pl. agreeing w. *plantae*) for orders of plants. [f. *-aceus* see prec.]

-ācean, a. & n. suf. As adj., = -ACEOUS; as n., see -ACEA. [f. L *-aceus* see -ACEA + -AN]

Ace·ldama (-k-), n. Field of bloodshed, scene of slaughter. [*Acts* i. 19]

-āceous, suf. freely used to form adjj. to the Nat.-Hist. nouns in -ACEA, -ACEÆ, as *crustaceous, rosaceous.* [f. L *-aceus* see -ACEA + -OUS]

acephal-, stem of several bot., zool., & eccl. terms. Headless. [f. LL f. Gk *akephalos* f. A- (7) + *kephalē* head]

acĕ·phalous, a. Headless; recognizing no chief; (Zool.) having no part of body specially organized as head; (Bot.) with head aborted or cut off; (in prosody), (verse) wanting the regular first syllable. [as prec. + -OUS]

ă·cerbate, v.t. Sometimes used for EXACERBATE.

acer·bity, n. Astringent sourness, harsh taste; bitterness of speech, manner, or temper. [f. F. *acerbité* f. L *acerbitatem* (*acerbus* sour-tasting, -TY)]

ă·cervate, a. Growing in compact clusters (of spines &c.). [f. L *acervare* (*acervus* a heap), -ATE[2]]

acĕ·scent, a. Turning sour, rather sour, lit. and fig. [f. L *acescere* inceptive of *acēre* be sour (*ac-* sharp), -ENT]

acet-, stem of many chem. terms. Vinegar. [L *acetum* vinegar (*acēre* be sour)]

ăcētă·bulum, n. (pl. *-la*). (Rom. antiq.) cup to hold vinegar. (Zool.) cup-shaped sucker of cuttle-fish &c.; socket of thigh-bone, or of joints in insects. [f. L *acetum* vinegar + *-abulum* dim. of *-abrum* receptacle]

ăcētar̄·ious, a. (Of plants) used in salads. [f. L *acetaria* salad plants, neut. pl. of *acetaris* (as ACETIC, see -AR[1]) + -OUS]

ă·cetated, a. Treated with acetic acid. [p.p. of *acetate* v. (ACETIC + -ATE[3]) not otherwise used]

acĕ·tic, a. Pertaining to vinegar. [f. L *acetum* vinegar + -IC]

acĕ·tify, v.t. & i. Convert into vinegar; become sour. Hence **aceti**FICA·TION, **ace·tifi**ER[1] (2), nn. [as prec. + -FY]

ă·cetous, a. Having the qualities of vinegar; sour. [as prec. + -OUS]

acĕ·tylene, n. A colourless gas, burning with a bright flame. [as prec., see -YL and -ENE]

acharnement (F), n. Ferocity; gusto.

Achā·tēs (-k-). Faithful friend of Aeneas (Virg. *Aen.*); any faithful friend.

ache[1] (āk), v.i. Suffer continuous or prolonged pain. [OE *acan*; earlier and correct spelling of the verb was *ake*]

ache[2] (āk), n. Continuous pain. [OE *æce* f. *acan* v.; earlier pronunciation of the noun was ātsh (cp. *bake batch, wake watch*)]

ache[3] (ātsh), n. Name of letter H.

achie·ve, v.t. Accomplish, carry out; acquire; reach (an end). Hence **achie·v**ABLE a. [f. F *achever* (*à chef venir* f. LL *ad caput venire* come to a head with)]

achie·vement, n. Completion, accomplishment; thing accomplished; escutcheon or ensign armorial in memory of a distinguished feat; = HATCHMENT. [f. F *achèvement* (*achever* ACHIEVE)]

achi·lous (-k-), a. (bot.). Without lips. [f. Gk *a-* not + *kheilos* lip + -OUS]

ăchlamȳ·deous, a. (bot.). Without calyx or corolla. [f. Gk *a-* not + *khlamus -udos* cloak + -EOUS]

ăchromă·tic, a. (opt.). Free from colour; transmitting light without decomposing it. Hence **achroma·t**ICALLY adv., **achromati·**CITY, **achrō·mat**ISM(2), nn., **achrō·mat**IZE(3) v.t. [f. Gk *akhrōmatos* (*a-* not + *khrōma -matos* colour) + -IC]

ă·cid[1], a. Sour (*a. drops*, kind of sweeties); (Chem.) with the essential properties of an ACID[2]. So **aci·d**ITY n. [f. L *acidus* (*acēre* be sour)]

a·cid[2], n. A sour substance; (Chem.) one of a class of substances that neutralize and are neutralized by alkalis, and are compounded of hydrogen and another element or elements, and of which the principal types are sour and turn vegetable blues to reds; *a. test* (in which a. is applied to test composition &c.; often fig. in morals &c.). [f. prec.]

aci·dify, v.t. & i. Make, become, sour; (Chem.) convert into an acid. Hence **aci·difi**ABLE a., **acidi**FICA·TION, **aci·difi**ER[1](2), nn. [as ACID, see -FY]

acidi·meter, n. Instrument for measuring strength of acids. [as prec., see -METER]

aci·dulated, a. Made somewhat acid. [p.p. of *acidulate* v. (foll. + -ATE[3]), not otherwise used]

aci·dulous, a. Somewhat acid. [f. *acidulus* (dim. of *acidus* sour) + -OUS]

ă·cinus, n. (pl. *acini*). One of the small berries that make up a compound fruit such as the blackberry; the compound fruit itself; seed of a grape or berry; (Anat.) racemose gland. Hence **aci·ni**FORM a. [L, = berry, seed]

-ācious, suf. forming adjj. meaning 'inclined to', 'abounding in'. [f. L *-ax -acis*, added to vb stems to form adjj., + -OUS]

-ăcity, suf. forming nouns of quality corresponding to adjj. in -ACIOUS directly f. L *-acitat-* or thr. F *-acité*.

ack e·mma, adv. & n. (slang). *Ante*

meridiem; air-mechanic. [=A, M, in signallers' alphabet]

acknow·ledge (aknŏl-), v.t. Admit the truth of; own (person &c. *to be* something); recognize the authority or claims of; recognize in legal form; express appreciation of; announce receipt of; reward (a service). [A- (2) + KNOWLEDGE; or from the obs. noun *acknowledge*]

acknow·ledgement, -gment, n. Act of acknowledging; thing given or done in return for a service, message, &c. [prec. + -MENT]

acli·nic, a. *A. line,* magnetic equator, on which magnetic needle has no dip. [f. Gk *aklinēs* (*a-* not + *klinō* bend) + -IC]

ă·cmē, n. Highest point, point of perfection. [Gk, = point]

ă·cnē, n. Pimple; disease marked by pimples. [perh. corrupt. of ACME]

aco·ck, adv. (Of the hat) in cocked fashion. [A prep. + COCK v.]

ă·colyte, n. Inferior officer in the church; attendant, assistant; novice. [f. Gk *akolouthos* follower]

ă·conīte, n. Monk's-hood or wolf's-bane, a poisonous plant; extract from this. Hence **aconi·tic** a., **acŏ·nitine**[5] n. [f. F *aconit* f. Gk *akoniton* (etym. dub.)]

ā·corn, n. Fruit of the oak; *a.-shell,* multi-valve cirriped, allied to barnacles. [OE *æcern,* perh. w. orig. meaning 'fruit of the open country' (OE *æcer*); confus. w. *corn*]

acotylē·don, n. Plant with no distinct seed-lobes. Hence **acotyle·donous** a. [f. mod. L *acotyledonēs* f. Gk *a-* not + *kotulēdōn* cup-shaped hollow (*kotulē* cup)]

acou·chy (-ōōshĭ), n. Small rodent allied to guinea-pig. [f. F *acouchi,* perh. f. native name in Guiana]

acou·stic (-ow-), a. Pertaining to the sense of hearing. Hence **acou·stical** a., **acou·sticaly**[2] adv., **acousti·cian, acou·stics,** nn. [f. F *acoustique* f. Gk *akoustikos* (*akouō* hear)]

acquai·nt, v.t. Make (person, one*self*) aware (*of* or *with* facts, *that, how,* &c.); make one*self* familiar (*with* circumstances &c.); (pass.) have personal knowledge (*with* person or thing). [f. OF *acointer* f. LL ACcognitare f. *cognit-* p.p. st. of CO(*gnoscere* come to know)]

acquai·ntance, n. Knowledge of (*with*) person &c. more than mere recognition and less than intimacy; person(s) with whom one is acquainted (pl. now usu. *-ances* in this sense). Hence **acquai·ntanceship** n. [f. OF *acointance* (*acointer* ACQUAINT)]

acque·st, n. Thing acquired; (Law) property gained otherwise than by inheritance. [f. OF *acquest* f. LL *acquistum* f. L *acquisitum* (see ACQUIRE)]

acquie·sce (-ĭĕs), v.i. Agree tacitly; *a. in,* accept (arrangements, conclusions). So **acquie·scence** n., **acquie·scent** a. [f. MF *acquiescer* f. L AC(*quiescere* rest)]

acquire·, v.t. Gain by oneself and for oneself; (of qualities &c.) win (person a good name &c.); come into possession of; *an acquired taste* (not natural). Hence **acquire·ment** n., acquired mental faculty. [f. OF *acquerre* f. L AC(*quirere quisit-* = *quaerere* seek)]

acquisi·tion, n. Act of acquiring; thing acquired. So **acqui·sitive** a., **acqui·sitiveness** n. [f. L *acquisitio* (as prec., see -ION)]

acqui·t, v.t. (-tt-). Pay (a debt); declare (person) not guilty (*of* offence); discharge one*self of* (duty, responsibility); *a.* one*self* (perform one's part) *well, ill,* &c. [f. OF *aquiter* f. LL *AC(*quitare* = L *quietare* settle f. *quies -etis* rest)]

acqui·ttal, n. Discharge from debt; deliverance from a charge by verdict &c.; performance (of duty). [prec + -AL (2)]

acqui·ttance, n. Payment of debt; release from debt; receipt in full. [f. OF *aquitance* (*aquiter* ACQUIT, see -ANCE)]

acre (ā·ker), n. Measure of land, 4,840 sq. yds; piece of tilled or enclosed land, field (only in special uses, as *broad aa., God's A., Long A.*). Hence (-)**a·cred**[2] a. [f. OE *æcer, acer* (cf. OHG *achar* L *ager* Gk *agros* Skr. *ajras*) tilled or enclosed land (orig. open country); adopted in med. L as *acra,* in OF as *acre,* hence mod. spelling for the regular *aker*]

acreage (ā·kerĭj), n. Amount of acres; acres collectively or in the abstract. [ACRE + -AGE]

ă·crid, a. Bitterly pungent, irritating, corrosive; of bitter temper or manner. Hence **acri·dity** n. [irreg. f. L *acer -cris* pungent + -ID, perh. assimilated to *acid*]

ă·crimony, n. Bitterness of temper or manner. So **acrimō·nious** a., **acrimo·niously**[2] adv. [f. L *acrimonia* pungency (*acer -cris* sharp; see -MONY) perh. thr. F *acrimonie*]

Ă·crita, n. pl. (zool.). Animals with no distinct nervous system. [mod. L f. Gk *akritos* undistinguishable (*a-* not + *krinō* distinguish)]

ăcro- in comb. Highest, topmost, terminal; tipped with; at the point or extremity of. [f. Gk *akros* topmost, outermost]

ă·crobat, n. Rope-dancer, tumbler; politician, reasoner, &c., who changes position nimbly. Hence **acrobă·tic** a., **acroba·tically** adv., **a·crobatism** n. [f. F *acrobate* f. Gk *akrobatos* walking on tiptoe, climbing aloft (ACRO + *batos* vbl adj. f. *bainō* go)]

ă·crogen, n. (bot.). Cryptogamous plant having perennial stem with growing point at extremity, as ferns and mosses. Hence **acrŏ·genous** a. [ACRO- + Gk *-genēs* born]

ă·crolith, n. Statue with head and extremities of stone. [ACRO- + Gk *lithos* stone]

acrŏ·nychal, a. Happening at nightfall (esp. of rising or setting of stars). Hence **acro·nychal**LY[2] adv. [f. Gk *akronukhos* (ACRO- + *nux nuktos* night) + -AL]

acrŏ·petal, a. Developing from below upwards. Hence **acro·petal**LY[2] adv. [ACRO- + L *petere* seek + -AL]

acrŏ·polis, n. Citadel or elevated part of a Greek city, esp. of Athens. [Gk *akropolis* (ACRO- + *polis* city)]

acro·ss, adv. & prep. In the form of a cross, as *with arms a.*; forming a cross with, making angles with, (object expressed or understood), as *a line drawn a.* (*the road*); into contact with, as *came a. a tiger, an instance*; from side to side (of), as *run a.* (*the road*); on the other side (of), as *by this time he is a.* (*the Channel*). [A prep. + CROSS[1]; Caxton has *in cross* f. F *encroix*]

acrŏ·stic, n. Poem or other composition in which the initial (*single a.*), the initial and final (*double a.*,) or the initial, middle, and final (*triple a.*) letters of the lines make words; word-puzzle so made; Hebrew poem of which the lines begin with the successive letters of the alphabet. Hence **acro·stic** a., **acro·st**ICALLY adv. [ACRO- + Gk *stikhos* row, line of verse]

act[1], n. Thing done, deed, this as outward sign of a condition &c. (*a. of faith, contrition*); process of doing, operation, as *in the very a. of, A. of God* (operation of uncontrollable natural forces); decree passed by a legislative body &c.; *a. and deed,* binding legal instrument (esp. *I deliver this as my a. and d.* said at time of signing); main division of a play; (in Universities) thesis maintained by a candidate for a degree &c. [f. F *acte* f. L *actus -ūs* doing and f. L *actum* thing done; see foll.]

act[2], v.t. & i. Carry out (an incident or story) in mimicry, represent, perform a play or part; personate (character in a play or in life), as *a. Othello, a. the fool*; perform actions, behave, as *a.* (behave) *generously, a.* (serve) *as interpreter, a. upon* (execute) *a suggestion, a. up to* put into practice) *a principle*; perform special functions, as *the policeman declined to a., the brake refused to a., alcohol acts on the brain.* [f. L *agere act-* do]

a·cting, a. & n. In vbl senses, esp.: doing duty temporarily, as *A. Captain*; doing alone duties nominally shared with others, as *A. Manager, Trustee*; *acting copy* (for players' use, with stage-directions & cuts). [ACT[2] + -ING[2,1]]

Acti·nia, n. (pl. *-ae, -as*). Genus of Zoophytes belonging to the family Actiniadae; (pop.) sea-anemone. [mod. L f. Gk *aktis -inos* ray]

a·ctinism, n. That property of the sun's rays by which chemical changes are produced, as in photography. So **acti·n**IC a. [as prec. + -ISM]

acti·nium, n. Radio-active substance found in pitchblende; an element that turns dark in sunlight. [as prec. + -IUM]

a·ction, n., & v.t. Process of acting, exertion of energy or influence, as *men of a., put in a., a. of an acid*; thing done, act; (in drama) series of events represented; mode of acting, management of body, &c., as *a. of a player, horse*; mechanism of piano or other instrument; legal process; engagement between troops (*A. Front!*, Artillery word of command); (v.t.) bring a legal a. against. [F, f. L *actionem* (as ACT[2], see -ION)]

a·ctionable, a. Affording ground for an action at law. Hence **a·ctionab**LY[2] adv. [ACTION + -ABLE]

a·ctive, a. Given to outward action; working, effective; energetic, diligent; acting of one's own accord, acting upon others; (Gram.) the *active voice* comprises all forms of intransitive verbs, and those forms of transitive verbs that attribute the verbal action to the person or thing whence it proceeds (the logical subject), as *We punished him*; not, like the forms of the passive voice, to the person or thing to whom it is directed (the logical object), as *He was punished by us.* Less correctly, verbs are themselves called *active.* Hence **active**LY[2] adv. [F (*-if, -ive*), f. L *activus* (as ACT[2], see -IVE); or direct f. L in theol. phr. *vita activa*]

acti·vity, n. Exertion of energy; quality of being active, diligence, nimbleness; (pl.) active forces, spheres of action. [f. F *activité* f. med. L *activitatem* (as prec., see -TY)]

a·cton, n. Jacket of quilted cotton worn under mail; mail-plated jacket of leather &c. [f. OF *auqueton* (mod. *hoqueton*) padding, padded jacket, f. Sp. *alcoton* (mod. *algodon*) cotton f. Arab. *al-qutun* the cotton]

a·ctor, n. Dramatic performer, whence **a·ctr**ESS[1] n.; (rarely) doer. [L, = doer, actor (as ACT[2], see -OR[2])]

a·ctual, a. Existing in fact, real; present, current. [f. F *actuel* f. LL *actualis* (*actus* vbl n. f. *agere* ACT[2]; see -AL)]

actua·lity, n. Reality; realism; (pl.) existing conditions. [f. med. L *actualitas* (as prec., see -TY)]

a·ctualize, v.t. Realize in action; describe realistically. Hence **actualiz**A·TION n. [ACTUAL + -IZE]

a·ctually, adv. In actual fact, really; for the time being even (strange as it may seem). [-LY[2]]

a·ctuary, n. Expert authority on rates of mortality and other details of life, fire, or accident insurance; (formerly) registrar, notary. Hence **actuār·i**AL a. [f. L *actuarius* amanuensis, book-keeper (*actus*; see ACTUAL and -ARY[1])]

a·ctuate, v.t. Communicate motion to (a machine &c.); serve as motive to (person). Hence **actua·tion** n. [f. med. L *actuare* (*actus*, as prec., see -ATE[3])]

acū·ity, n. Sharpness, acuteness (as of needle, acid, disease, wit). [f. F *acuité* f. med. L *acuitatem* (*acus -ūs* needle; see -ITY)]

acū·lĕate (-*at*), **acū·leāted**, aa. (Zool.) having a sting; (Bot.) prickly; pointed, incisive. [f. L *aculeatus* (ACULEUS, see -ATE[2])]

acū·leus, n. (pl. -*ī*). (Zool.) sting; (Bot.) prickle. [L *aculeus* sting, dim. of *acus* needle]

acū·men, n. Keen discernment, penetration. [L *acumen -minis* anything sharp (*acuere* sharpen)]

acū·minate[1] (-*at*), a. (nat. hist.). Tapering to a point. [f. L *acuminare* (prec.), see -ATE[2]]

acu·mināte[2], v.t. Sharpen, point; give poignancy to. Hence **acumina·tion**, n. [as prec., see -ATE[3]]

acū·te, a. Sharp, pointed; (of angles) less than a right angle; (of diseases) coming sharply to a crisis, opp. to *chronic*; (of sensations, senses, intellect) keen; (of sounds) high, shrill; (of letters) bearing the acute ACCENT. Hence **acu·tely**[2] adv., **acu·teness** n. [f. L *acuere -ut-* sharpen]

acuti- in comb. Sharp, as *-foliate* sharp-leaved, *-lobate* sharp-lobed. [L comb. form of *acutus* ACUTE]

-acy, suf. forming nouns of state or quality from or modelled on L *-acia* or *-atia* or Gk *-ateia*. (1) n. of quality f. L *-aci-a* f. adjj. in *-aci-*: *fall-* deceive *fall-aci-* deceitful *fall-aci-a* fallacy. (2) n. of state or quality f. L *-ati-a* f. nouns in *-at-* (nom. *-as*, *-i-* being part of stem or connecting link): med. L *primat- primati-a* primacy; and by analogy *supremacy*. (3) n. of state f. med. L *-ati-a* f. nouns in *-atus*: *advocat-us advocat-ia* advocacy; and by analogy *curacy*. This formation was extended to adjj. f. L *-atus* to form *accuracy*, *obstinacy*, from *accurate*, *obstinate*, where L has nouns in *-atio*; hence other L words in *-atio* appear in E with *-acy* where E has no corresponding adj. in *-ate*, as *conspiracy*; similarly, E *-acy* for L *-atus* (n. of 4th decl.), as *magistratus* magistracy, gives rise to *episcopacy* as if f. E *episcopate*; and *lunacy* is formed to match *lunatic* on anal. of *diplomacy diplomatic*. (4) n. of state, through L, f. Gk *-ateia* f. n. in *-atēs* or vb in *-ateuein*: *peiratēs peirateia* piracy.

ad-, pref. (1) f. L *ad* to, with sense of motion or direction to, change into, addition, adherence, increase, or mere intensification. Before c f g l n p q r s t, and prob. before b, *ad* was in later L assimilated; before vowels and d h j m v, it was unchanged. In OF, L *ad*, wherever recognized as such, became *a-*, even before vowels, as *aörner* f. L *adornare*; but later the spelling was Latinized, sometimes with changed pronunciation, both in F and still more in E, where the OF forms had been adopted. (The use of *ad-*, *ab-*, in pairs like *adoral*, *aboral*, situated *at* and *away from* mouth, is unknown to L.) (2) The pedantic spelling *ad-* for *a-* was sometimes extended to *a-* coming not from L *ad-* but f. L *ab-* (*advance* F *avancer* L *ab-anteare*), f. OF *en-* (*addebted* OF *endetté*), f. OF *es-* f. L *ex-* (*affray* OF *esfrayer*), f. OE *a-* (*accurse* ME *a-curse*), &c.; so *admiral* f. Arab. *amiral*. New native compounds with E *a-* were falsely spelt in the same way.

-ad, suf. of nouns. (1) f. Gk *-ad-* (nom. *-as*), in collective numerals (*monad*, *dyad*, *triad*, *chiliad*, *myriad*); in fem. patronymics (*Dryad*, *Naiad*); in names of poems (*Iliad*, and by anal. *Dunciad*, *Rosciad*); and in family names of plants (*liliad*, *asclepiad*). (2) f. F *-ade*; see the more usual -ADE.

ă·dage (-ĭj), n. Traditional maxim, proverb. [F, f. L *adagium* (*ad* to + *agi-*, root of *aio* I say)]

ada·gio (adahj-), adv. a., n., (mus.). Leisurely; (n.) adagio movement. [It.]

Ă·dam, n. The first man (*not know* one *from A.*, have no knowledge of his looks); *old A.* (unregenerate condition), *A.'s ale* or *wine* (water), *A.'s apple* (projection of the thyroid cartilage of the larynx). [Heb. *a-dam* man]

ă·damant, n. A thing impenetrably hard (*be a.*, stubbornly refuse compliance with requests); (formerly) loadstone; diamond. Hence **adama·ntine**[2] a. [f. OF *adamaunt* f. L *adamantem* (nom. *-mas*) f. Gk *adamas -mantos* untamable (*a-* not + *damaō* I tame); used in Gk of the hardest metal, prob. steel; in med. L of the loadstone, from confusion with *ad-amantem* having an attraction for; from 17th cent., often a synonym for DIAMOND]

A·damite, n. Child of Adam, human being; unclothed man; (Eccles.) name of sects who imitated Adam in this respect; (pl.) a section of humanity supposed by some to be alone derived from Adam. [ADAM + -ITE]

ada·pt, v.t. Fit (a thing *to* another); make suitable (*to* or *for* a purpose); modify, alter, (*plays adapted from the French*). Hence or cogn. **adaptabi·lity**, **adapta·tion**, nn., **ada·ptable**, **ada·ptive**, aa. [f. F *adapter* f. L AD(*aptare* f. *aptus* fit)]

ad capta·ndum (vu·lgus), adv. & a. (Calculated) to take the fancy (of the rabble). [L]

add, v.t. & i. Join (one thing *to* another), as *a. your entreaties to mine*, *a. insult to injury*, *this adds to* (increases) *our difficulties*, *he added* (stated further) *that—*, *a. up* or *together* (find the sum of), *a.* (perform the process of summation) *correctly*, *a. in* (include). [f. L AD(*dere dit* = *dare* put)]

adde·ndum, n. (pl. *-da*). Thing to be

added; appendix, addition. [L gerundive of *addere* ADD]

a·dder, n. Small venomous snake, esp. Common Viper; *Puff, Death, Horned, A.*, species of Viperidae; *Flying A.*, dragonfly; *A.'s tongue,* genus of ferns. [f. OE *nædre* (cf. OLG *nadra,* OHG *natra*) serpent; *n-* lost in ME by wrong division of *a naddre* into *an addre*; *nedder* survives in dial.]

addi·ct, v.t. Devote, apply habitually, (*to* a practice), as *his tastes a. him, he addicts himself* or *his mind, he is addicted, to*; (Rom. Law) deliver over by sentence of a judge. So **addi·ct** n., person addicted to specified drug &c. (*opium a.*), **addi·ct**ION n. [f. L AD(*dicere dict-* say) assign]

addi·tion, n. Process of adding (*in a. to,* as well as); thing added (*a useful a.*). [F, f. L *additionem* (as ADD, see -ION)]

addi·tional, a. Added, supplementary. Hence **addi·tional**LY[2] adv. [prec. + -AL]

a·ddle[1], a. *A. egg,* rotten one, one that produces no chicken; empty, vain; muddled, unsound, as *a.-brained, -head, -pated.* [f. OE *adela* mud (cf. MLG *adele* G *adel*); now used only as adj.]

a·ddle[2], v.t. & i. Muddle, confuse; (of eggs) grow addle. [f. prec.]

a·ddled, a. Made addle. [ADDLE a. assim. to p.p. form, apparently before ADDLE v. existed]

addre·ss[1], v.t. Communicate with (by word or letter), as *a. myself* or *my remarks* or *a letter to a person, a. an audience, a. a letter* (write on cover directions for delivery) *to a person*; apply one*self to* (a task); *a. the ball* (golf), take aim. [f. F *adresser* f. LL *AD(*drictiare* f. *drictum* for *directum* DIRECT)]

addre·ss[2], n. Readiness, skill, dexterity, adroitness; superscription of letter, name of place to which person's letters are directed; act of dispatching a ship; manner, bearing, in conversation; discourse delivered to audience; (pl.) courteous approach, courtship (*pay* one's *aa. to*). [f. prec. and f. F *adresse* n. f. *adresser*]

ăddressee·, n. Person to whom a letter is addressed. [ADDRESS[1] + -EE]

addu·ce, v.t. Cite as proof or instance. Hence **addu·ce**ABLE, **addu·ci**BLE, aa. [f. L AD(*ducere duct-* lead)]

addu·cent, a. (physiol.) (Of muscles) drawing to a common centre. [as prec., see -ENT]

addu·ct, v.t. (physiol.). Draw to a common centre. [as ADDUCE]

addu·ction, n. Act of adducing; act of adducting. [F, f. L *adductionem* (as prec., see -ION)]

-ade, suf. of nouns. (1) f. F *-ade,* the form in which Pr., Sp., or Port. wds in *-ada* f. L *-ata* (fem. sing. p.p. of verbs in *-are*) were adopted in F, often supplanting native F *-ée* direct f. L, as in *accolade* OF *acolée.* Now a living suf. both in F wds, many of which are borrowed by E (*tirade, gasconnade*), and in E (*blockade, orangeade*); E drops F *e* in *ballad, salad.* Meanings: action done (*tirade, fusillade*), body concerned in action or process (*ambuscade, cavalcade*), thing produced by action or from material (*masquerade, lemonade*). (2) f. F *-ade* f. Gk *-ada* (nom. *-as*), as *decade*; but in E usu. -AD. (3) f. Sp. or Port. *-ado,* masc. form corr. to (1) above, with similar meaning (*brocade*), or that of the person concerned (*renegade*).

ă·dĕnoids, n. pl. Mass of spongy tissue between back of nose and throat, often hindering inflation of lungs. [f. Gk *adēn -enos* acorn, gland]

ade·pt, n. & a. (One who is) thoroughly proficient (*in* anything); skilled alchemist. [f. L *adeptus* p.p. of AD(*ipisci* = *apisci* f. root *ap-*) attain, used in med. L as title by alchemists who 'had attained' the great secret]

ă·dequate, a. Proportionate (*to* the requirements); sufficient. Hence **a·dequ**ACY n., **adequate**LY[2] adv. [f. L AD*aequare* make equal (*aequus*), see -ATE[3]]

ad ĕŭ·ndem, adv. *Admitted ad e.,* to the same (degree at another university). [L]

à deux (F), adv. & a. For two; between two.

adhere·, v.i. Stick fast, cleave, *to* (a substance, person, party, opinion). [f. L AD(*haerēre haes-* stick)]

adhē·r·ent, a. & n. Sticking (*to* substance); due *to*; connected with (*to*); (n.) supporter (*of* party &c.). So **adhē·r**ENCE n. [f. F *adhérent* (as prec., see -ENT)]

adhē·sion, n. Adhering (lit. and fig.); *give in one's a.,* announce one's concurrence. [f. F *adhésion* f. L *adhaesionem* (as ADHERE, see -ION)]

adhe·sive, a. Having the property of adhering; sticky. Hence **adhe·sive**LY[2] adv. [f. F *adhésif, -ive* (as ADHERE, see -IVE)]

adhi·bit, v.t. Put on, affix; apply, administer, (remedies). So **adhibi·t**ION n. [f. L AD(*hibēre hibit-* = *habēre* hold) employ]

ad hoc, a. Arranged for this purpose, special. [L]

ădia·ntum, n. Genus of ferns including the True Maidenhair; (pop.) Black Maidenhair. [L, f. Gk *adianton* maidenhair, lit. unwetted (*a-* not + *diainō* wet)]

ădiă·phorism, n. Latitudinarianism. So **adia·phor**IST n. [f. Gk *adiaphoros* (*a-* not + *diaphoros* different f. *dia* apart + *pherō* bear) + -ISM]

adieu (adū·), int. & n. Good-bye; *make, take,* one's *a.,* say good-bye. [F (*à* to + *Dieu* God)]

ad infīni·tum, adv. Without limit, for ever. [L]

ad i·nterim, adv. & a. For the meantime. [L]

ă·dipocere, n. Greyish fatty substance generated in dead bodies subjected to moisture. [f. F *adipocire* (L *adeps -ipis* fat + -O- + *cire* wax f. L *cera*)]

ă·dipose, a. & n. Pertaining to fat, fatty; (n.) animal fat. Hence **adipŏ·SITY n.** [f. L *adeps -ipis* fat + -OSE]

ă·dit, n. Approach; (of mines) horizontal entrance; act of approaching. [f. L AD*itus -ūs* (*ire it-* go)]

adjā·cent, a. Lying near, contiguous. So **adja·CENCY** n. [f. L AD(*jacēre* lie), see -ENT]

a·djective, a. & n. Additional, not standing by itself, dependent: *a. colours* (not permanent without a basis); *Law A.* (subsidiary part of law, procedure); (Gram.) *a., noun a.*, the name of an attribute, added to the name of a thing to describe the thing more fully. Hence **adjectī·VAL** a., **adjecti·valLY**², **a·djectiveLY**² advv. [F (*-if, -ive*), f. L *adjectivus* f. AD(*jicĕre ject-* =*jacĕre* throw), see -IVE]

adjoi·n, v.t. Join, unite, (one thing *to* another); be contiguous with. [f. OF *ajoindre* f. L AD(*jungere junct-* join)]

adjour·n (-ern), v.t. & i. Put off, postpone; break off for later resumption; (intr., of persons met together) suspend joint proceedings and separate; change the place of meeting. Hence **adjou·rnMENT** n. [f. OF *ajorner* f. LL AD*jurnare* appoint a day (*jurnus* day, cf. It. *giorno*, F *jour*, f. L *diurnus* daily f. *dies* day)]

adju·dge, v.t. Adjudicate upon (a matter); pronounce judicially (*that a thing is* or *a thing to be*); condemn (person *to* penalty or *to* do); award judicially (thing *to* person). Hence **adju·dgeMENT** n. [f. OF *ajuger* (as foll.)]

adju·dicate, v.t. & i. (Of a judge or court) decide upon (claim &c.); pronounce (person *to be* something); (intr.) sit in judgement and pronounce sentence. Hence **adjudicA·TION**, **adju·dicatOR**², nn., **adju·dicatIVE** a. [f. L AD(*judicare* f. *judex -icis* judge), see -ATE³]

a·djunct, n. Subordinate or incidental thing, accompaniment (*to, of*); (Gram.) amplification of the predicate, subject, &c.; (Logic) non-essential attribute. Hence **adju·nctIVE** a., **adju·nctiveLY**² adv. [f. L as ADJOIN]

adjure· (-joor), v.t. Charge (a person) under oath or penalty of curse (*to* do); request earnestly. Hence **adjurA·TION** n. [f. L AD(*jurare* swear) in LL sense 'put person to an oath']

adju·st, v.t. Arrange, put in order; harmonize (discrepancies); adapt (*to* standard or purpose). Hence **adju·stABLE** a., **adju·stMENT** n. [f. 16th-c. F *adjuster* (mod. F *ajuster*) f. med. L *adjustare* (not, as was thought, *ad* + *justus* just, but) f. OF *ajuster, ajouster* (mod. F *ajouter*) f. LL AD(*juxtare* bring together f. *juxta* near); those meanings of OF *ajuster* that seemed connected with L *justus* being given to the new *adjuster*, formed when the conn. of OF *ajuster* with *adjustare* came to be concealed by the new spelling *ajouter*]

adju·tage, aj-, n. Mouthpiece of an artificial fountain. [f. F *ajoutage* (*ajouter* add, join; see prec. and -AGE)]

a·djutant, a. & n. Assistant; (Mil.) officer in the army who assists superior officers by communicating orders, conducting correspondence, &c., whence **a·djutanCY** n.; gigantic Indian stork. [f. L *adjutare* frequent. as foll., see -ANT]

a·djuvant, a. & n. Helpful, auxiliary; person, thing, that helps. [F, f. L AD-(*juvare jut-* help), see -ANT]

ad lĭ·bitum, adv. (abbr. *ad lib.*). At pleasure, to any extent. [L]

admea·sure (-zher), v.t. Apportion, assign in due shares. [f. OF *amesurer* f. LL AD(*mensurare* MEASURE)]

admea·surement, n. Process of admeasuring; comparison; dimensions. [f. OF *amesurement* (as prec., see -MENT)]

admĭ·nicle, n. A help; (Law) corroboratory evidence. Hence **admini·culAR**¹ a. [f. L AD*miniculum* prop (*manus* hand)]

admi·nister, v.t. & i. Manage (affairs); dispense (justice, sacraments, *to*); tender (oath *to*); furnish, give, (thing *to*); apply (remedies *to*); (intr.) act as administrator; contribute *to* (one's comfort &c.). Hence **admi·nistrABLE** a. [f. OF *aministrer* f. L AD(*ministrare* MINISTER)]

administra·tion, n. Management (*of* business); management of public affairs, government; the ministry, the Government; (Law) management of deceased person's estate; *Letters of A.*, authority to administer estate of an intestate, opp. to *probate*; dispensation (*of* justice &c.); tendering (*of* oath); application (*of* remedies). [(perh. thr. F) f. L *administratio* (as prec., see -ATION)]

admi·nistrative, a. Pertaining to management of affairs; executive. Hence **admi·nistrativeLY**² adv. [f. L *administrativus* (as prec., see -IVE)]

admi·nistrator, n. Manager; one capable of organizing; one who performs official duties (of religion, justice, &c.); applier or giver (*of*); one authorized to manage estates for legal owner during minority, &c., or estates of one who dies without appointing competent executors. Hence **admi·nistratorSHIP**, **admi·nistraTRIX**, nn. [L, as ADMINISTER, see -OR²]

a·dmirable (-mer-), a. Surprisingly good, excellent. Hence **a·dmirabLY**² adv. [F, f. L *admirabilis* (as ADMIRE, see -ABLE)]

a·dmiral (-mer-), n. Commander-in-chief of a country's navy (in England, formerly *Lord High A.*); naval officer of highest rank, commander of fleet or squadron; *A. of the Fleet, A., Vice-A., Rear-A.*, the four grades of A. in England; privileged commander of fishing or merchant fleet; ship that carries the a., Flagship; *Red A., White A.*, two European species of butterfly. Hence **a·dmiral**SHIP n. [f. OF *amiral* f. Arab. *amir* commander *al* of the (Faithful, Sea, &c.), Latinized as *amiralis*, but refashioned (see AD-) as *admiralis*, and confused with L *admirari* wonder at, whence med. L *admirabilis mundi* ruler of the world]

a·dmiralty, n. Office of admiral; branch of the executive that superintends the navy (in England, *Lords Commissioners of A.*); (Rhet.) command of the seas (esp. *the price of a.*); *Court of A.*, tribunal for trial and decision of maritime questions and offences. [f. OF *admiralté*; see ADMIRAL and -TY]

admira·tion (-mer-), n. Pleased contemplation; (formerly) wonder; *the a. of*, admired by; *note of a.* (!). [F, f. L *admirationem* (as foll., see -ATION)]

admire·, v.t. Regard with pleased surprise or approval; (also, colloq.) express admiration of (*forgot to a. her cat*); (formerly) wonder at, wonder. [f. F *admirer* f. L AD(*mirari* wonder at)]

admir·er, n. One that admires; lover. [ADMIRE + -ER[1]]

admi·ssible, a. (Of idea or plan) worthy to be entertained; (Law) allowable as judicial proof; capable of being admitted (*to* office or position). Hence **admissi**BI·LITY n. [F, f. LL *admissibilis* (as ADMIT, see -BLE)]

admi·ssion, n. Admitting, being admitted, (*to* society of persons or class of things); acknowledgement (*of* thing as true, *that* it is true). [f. L *admissio* (as foll., see -ION)]

admi·ssive, a. Tending to admit. [f. L *admissivus* (as foll., see -IVE)]

admi·t, v.t. & i. (-tt-). Allow (person &c.) entrance or access (*to* place, class, privileges, &c.); accept as valid or true, whence **admi·tted**LY[2] adv.; acknowledge (thing *to be, that* it is); (abs.) *this, I admit, was wrong*; (of enclosed spaces) have room for; *a. of*, leave room for (doubt, improvement). [f. F *admettre* f. L AD(*mittere miss-* let go)]

admi·ttable, a. Capable of being admitted (usu. to a place). [prec. + -ABLE]

admi·ttance, n. Admitting, being admitted, (usu. to a place). [ADMIT + -ANCE]

admi·x, v.t. & i. Add as an ingredient; mingle (*with* something). So **admi·**XTURE n. [AD- + MIX; perh. due to *admixt*, really f. L *admixt-* p.p. of AD(*miscēre mixt-* MIX), but taken for an E p.p.]

admŏ·nish, v.t. Exhort (person *to* do, *that* he should do); give advice; warn (*of* a thing); inform, remind, (*of* a thing, *that*). Hence **admo·nish**MENT n. [OE *amonest* f. OF *amonester* f. LL *admonestare* irreg. f. AD(*monēre monit-* warn); *amonest* having dropped final *-t* (supposed to be p.p. ending) became *admonish* on anal. of *aboliss abolish* &c.]

admoni·tion, n. Admonishing; warning, reproof. So **admo·nit**ORY a. [f. OF *amonition* f. L *admonitionem* (as prec., see -ION)]

ad nau·seăm, adv. To a disgusting extent. [L]

adnŏ·minal, a. Belonging to an adnoun; attached to a noun. [f. L *adnomen* variant of *agnomen* in the sense (not L) 'attached to a noun' (*ad* to + *nomen* noun)]

a·dnoun, n. Adjective, word added to a noun substantive; adjective used substantively. [f. L *ad* to + NOUN on anal. of *adverb*]

adc· (-ōō), n. Action, business, fuss; difficulty. [f. Norse *at* (= *to* with infinitive) + *do*; *much ado* prop. = *much to do*; but *much* being taken as adj., *ado* is treated as n.]

-ado, suf. of nouns. (1) f. Sp. or Port. *-ado* f. L *-atus* p.p. of vbs in *-are*, as *desperado* L *desperatus* (*desperare*); sometimes changed in E to *-ade*, as *renegado*, now *renegade*. (2) Ignorant refashioning of nouns in *-ade* f. F *-ade* = Sp. *-ada* It. *-ata*, as *crusado* Sp. *cruzada*, *scalado* Sp. *escalada*.

ado·be (-ōbĭ, -ōb), n. Unburnt sun-dried brick. [Sp.]

adole·scent (-ĕsnt), n. & a. (Person) growing up, between childhood and manhood (14 to 25) or womanhood (12 to 21). So **adole·s**CENCE, -ENCY, nn. [F, f. L AD(*olescere ult-* incept. of *olēre* grow), see -ENT]

Adō·nis, n. Beautiful youth loved by Venus; beau, dandy; (Bot.) genus including Pheasant's Eye; (Entom.) the butterfly Clifton Blue. [Gk, f. Phoen. *adōn* lord, title of a divinity]

ă·donize, v. refl. & i. Adorn, dandify, (one*self*); play the Adonis. [ADONIS + -IZE]

ado·pt, v.t. Take (person) into a relationship he did not previously occupy; take (idea, &c.) from some one else; choose. Hence **adopta**BI·LITY, **ado·pt**ION, nn., **ado·pt**ABLE a. [f. F *adopter* f. L AD(*optare* choose, frequent. of obs. *opere opt-* wish) adopt esp. child]

ado·ptive, a. Due to adoption, as *a. son, father*; apt to adopt. Hence **ado·ptive**LY[2] adv. [F (*-if, -ive*), f. L *adoptivus*; see prec. and -IVE]

adore·, v.t. Regard with the utmost respect and affection; (poet.) worship as a deity; (in R. C. Church) reverence with representative honours (the Host &c.). So **ador·**ABLE a., **ador·ab**LY[2] adv., **ador**A·TION n. [f. F *adorer* f. L AD(*orare* speak f. *os oris* mouth) salute, worship]

ador·er, n. Worshipper; ardent admirer, lover. [prec. + -ER[1]]

ador·n, v.t. Add beauty or lustre to; furnish with ornaments. So **ador·n**MENT n. [f. F *adorner* f. L AD(*ornare* furnish) deck out]

adow·n, adv. & prep. (archaic, poet.). =DOWN[3]. [f. OE *of dúne* off the mount (see DOWN[1] n.)]

ad rem, adv. & pred. a. To the point; to the purpose. [L]

adrē·nalin, n. A hormone secreted by the adrenal ductless glands and affecting circulation and muscular action; this extracted from animals for medicinal use. [*adrenal* at the kidney (f. L *ad* at + *rēn* kidney) + -IN]

adri·ft, adv. In a drifting condition, at the mercy of wind and tide or of circumstances. [A prep. + DRIFT[1]]

adroi·t, a. Having address, dexterous. Hence **adroi·t**LY[2] adv., **adroi·t**NESS n. [F, orig. =rightly (*à* to + *droit* right f. OF *dreit* f. LL *drictum* f. L *directum* right; see DIRECT[2])]

adry·, adv. & pred. a. Dry; thirsty. [*a-* + DRY[1] on anal. of *acold, athirst,* the prep. A[2] in these being misunderstood]

adsciti·tious, a. Adopted from without; supplemental. [f. L AD(*sciscere scit-* inceptive of *scire* know) + -ITIOUS]

adscri·ptus gle·bae, a. & n. (Serf) attached to the soil. [L]

a·dsum, v.i. I am here. [L]

ă·dūlate, v.t. Flatter basely. So **adu**LA·TION, **a·dulat**OR[2], nn., **a·dulat**ORY a. [f. L *adulari* fawn on, see -ATE[3]]

Adu·llamite, n. M.P. seceding from Liberal Party in 1866. [*Adullam* (1 *Sam.* xxii. 1, 2) + -ITE]

adu·lt, a. & n. (One who is) grown up; mature. [as ADOLESCENT]

adu·lterant, a. & n. (Thing) employed in adulterating. [as foll., see -ANT]

adu·lterate[1] (-*at*), a. Stained (in conduct or in birth) by adultery; (of things) spurious, counterfeit. [as foll., see -ATE[2]]

adu·lterāte[2], v.t. Falsify by admixture of baser ingredients. So **adulter**A·TION, **adu·lterat**OR[2], nn. [f. L *adulterare* corrupt (*adulter* adulterer, perh. f. *ad* to + *alter* other); replaces obs. vb *adulter* f. OF]

adu·lterer, n. One guilty of adultery. So **adu·lter**ESS[1] n. [f. *adulter* v. (see prec. and -ER[1]); obs. *adulter, avouter,* are f. OF *avoutre* f. L *adulter*]

adu·lterīne, a. Of, born of, adultery; adulterated, counterfeit; illegal, unlicensed. [f. L *adulterinus* born of adultery, spurious (*adulter* adulterer, see -INE[1])]

adu·ltery, n. Voluntary sexual intercourse of married person with one of opposite sex, married (*double a.*) or not (*single a.*). So **adu·lter**OUS a., **adu·lterous**LY[2] adv. [f. OF *avoutrie, aülterie* (L *adulter* adulterer, see -Y[1]), re-formed on F *adultère* f. L *adulterium*]

adu·mbral, a. Overshadowing, shady. [f. AD- + L *umbra* shade + -AL]

ă·dumbrate, v.t. Represent in outline; faintly indicate; typify, foreshadow; overshadow. Hence or cogn. **adumbr**A·TION n., **adu·mbra**TIVE a. [f. L AD(*umbrare* f. *umbra* shade), see -ATE[3]]

ad un·guem (fa·ctus), a. Highly finished. [L]

adu·st, a. Scorched, dried up, parched; sunburnt; atrabilious, gloomy. [f. L AD(*urere ust-* burn)]

ad valor·em, adv. & a. (Of taxes) in proportion to estimated value of goods. [L]

adva·nce,[1] v.t. & i. Move or put forward; promote (plans, persons); bring forward (claims, suggestions); accelerate (events); pay (money) before it is due; lend; raise (price); (intr.) move forward; make progress; rise (in price); (p.p.) far on in progress, as *advanced studies, ideas.* So **adva·nce**MENT n. (esp. of promotion of plan or person). [f. OF *avancer* f. LL *abanteare* (*abante* = *ab* away + *ante* before, whence F *avant*; see AD-)]

adva·nce[2], n. Going forward; progress; personal approach, overture; rise in price; payment beforehand, loan; *a. copy* of book &c., supplied before publication; *in a.*, before (of place or time). [f. prec. and f. F *avance* n. (as prec.)]

adva·ntage[1] (-ĭj), n. Better position, precedence, superiority; favourable circumstance, whence **advantā·ge**OUS a., **advanta·geous**LY[2] adv.; (in Tennis) next point or game won after deuce points or games; *have the a. of, gain an a. over,* have, acquire, a better position than (*you have the a. of me,* esp., you know me and I do not know you); *take a.* (avail oneself) *of a circumstance*; *take a. of* (overreach) *a person*; *take a person at a.* (by surprise); *to a.*, in a way to exhibit the merits (*was seen, heard, to a.*); *a.-ground* (usu. *vantage-*), position that gives superiority. [f. F *avantage* (*avant*; see ADVANCE v. and -AGE)]

adva·ntage[2] (-ĭj),v.t. Be beneficial to; be an advantage to; further, promote. [f. F *avantager* (*avantage*; see prec.)]

a·dvent, n. Season before the Nativity; coming of Christ, Incarnation; second coming of Christ; any (important) arrival. [f. OF *advent, auvent* f. L *adventus -ūs* arrival f. AD(*venire vent-* come)]

adventi·tious, a. Coming from without; accidental, casual; (Law, of property) coming from a stranger or by collateral, not direct, succession. Hence **adventi·tious**LY[2] adv. [f. L *adventicius* (med. L *-itius*) coming to us from abroad (as prec., see -ITIOUS)]

adve·nture[1] (-tsh*er*), n. Risk, danger; daring enterprise; unexpected incident; commercial speculation; hazardous activity. [f. OF *aventure* f. L *adventura* (*res* thing) about to happen (as ADVENT)]

adve·nture[2] (-tsh*er*), v.t. & i. Hazard, imperil, (one*self*, thing); incur risk; dare to go or come (*into, in, upon,* a place); dare to enter *on, upon,* (undertaking). [f. OF *aventurer* (as prec.)]

adve·nturer, n. One who seeks adventures; soldier of fortune; speculator; one who lives by his wits. [f. F *aventurier* (as ADVENTURE[1], see -ER[1])]

adve·nturesome, a. Given to adventures. [ADVENTURE[1] + -SOME]

adve·nturess, n. Female adventurer; woman on the look-out for a position. [f. ADVENTURER, see -ESS]

adve·nturous, a. Rash, venturesome; enterprising. Hence **adventurous**LY[2] adv. [f. OF *aventuros* (as ADVENTURE[1], see -OUS)]

a·dverb, n. Word that modifies or qualifies an adjective, verb, or other adverb, expressing a relation of place, time, circumstance, manner, &c. (e.g. *gently, so, now, where, why*). [f. F *adverbe* f. L AD-*verbium* (*verbum* word, verb) transl. of Gk *epirrhēma* addition to a predication]

adver·bial, a. Pertaining to an adverb; of the nature of an adverb. Hence **adver·bial**LY[2] adv. [f. L *adverbialis* (*adverbium*; see prec. and -AL)]

ad ver·bum, adv. & a. Word for word. [L]

a·dversary, n. Opponent, antagonist, enemy; *the A.*, the Devil. [f. OF *aversier* f. L *adversarius* opposed (as ADVERSE, see -ARY[1])]

adver·sative, a. (Of words &c.) expressing opposition or antithesis. Hence **adve·rsative**LY[2] adv. [f. L *adversativus* (*adversari* oppose, see foll. and -IVE)]

a·dverse, a. Contrary, hostile, (*to*); hurtful, injurious, (*to*); placed opposite. Hence **a·dverse**LY[2] adv. [f. OF *avers* f. L AD(*vertere vers-* turn)]

adver·sity, n. Condition of adverse fortune; misfortune. [f. OF *aversité* f. L *adversitatem* (as prec., see -TY)]

adver·t, v.i. Refer *to* (in speaking or writing). [f. 14th-c. E *averte* f. F *avertir* f. LL AD(*vertĕre* = L *vertĕre* turn) draw attention to; F *avertir* (see AD-) was written *adv-* to dist. it from obs. *avertir* f. LL *avertĕre* turn away (*ab*), and E adopted this in *advert* and *advertise*]

a·dvertīse (-z), v.t. & i. Notify, warn, inform, (person *of* thing, *that*); make generally known (thing *by* circular, *in* journal, also abs.); *a. for,* ask for by public notice. [f. F *avertir* (st. *-iss-*); see ADVERT]

adver·tīsement, n. Public announcement (usu. by placards or in journals). [f. F *avertissement* (as prec., see -MENT)]

advī·ce, n. Opinion given or offered as to action, counsel; information given, news; (pl.) communications from a distance; (commerc.) formal notice of transactions. [f. OF *avis* f. LL **advisum* (*ad* to + *visum* p.p. of *vidēre* see)]

advi·sable, a. To be recommended; expedient. Hence **advisa**BI·LITY, **advi·sable**NESS, nn., **advi·sab**LY[2] adv. [f. foll. + -ABLE]

advi·se (-z), v.t. & i. Offer counsel to; (commerc.) announce; take counsel *with*. Hence **advi·**SER[1] n., esp. person habitually consulted. [f. F *aviser* f. LL *advisare* (*advisum*, see ADVICE)]

advi·sed, a. Deliberate, considered, whence **advi·sĕd**LY[2] adv.; judicious; *ill-a.*, injudicious. [p.p. of prec.]

advī·sory (-z-), a. Giving advice; consisting in giving advice. [ADVISE + -ORY]

ad vi·tam aut cu·lpam. adv. During good behaviour. [L]

a·dvocacy, n. Function of an advocate; pleading in support *of*. [f. F *advocacie, -tie*, f. med. L *advocatia* (as foll., see -ACY)]

a·dvocate[1] (-*at*), n. One who pleads for another; one who speaks in behalf *of* (proposal &c.); professional pleader in courts of justice; *Faculty of Aa.*, Scotch bar; *Lord A.*, principal law-officer of crown in Scotland. Hence **a·dvocate**SHIP n., **a·dvocat**ORY a. [f. F *avocat* f. L *advocatus* p.p. (as n.) of AD(*vocare* call)]

a·dvocāte[2], v.t. Plead for, defend, recommend publicly. [f. prec.]

advow·son (-zn), n. Right of presentation to a benefice. [f. OF *avoëson* f. med.L *advocationem* function of patron (as prec., see -ION)]

ădynā·mia, n. Want of vital force; physical prostration. Hence **ădynă·mi**C a. [Gk *adunamia* (*a-* not + *dunamis* power)]

ă·dytum, n. (pl. *-ta*). Innermost part of a temple; private chamber, sanctum. [L f. Gk *aduton* not to be entered (*a-* not + *duton* vbl adj. of *duō* enter)]

adze, n. & v.t. Tool for cutting away surface of wood, like axe with arched blade at right angles to handle; (vb) cut with a. [OE *adesa*, etym. dub.]

æ, ae, symbol repr. a vowel sound betw. *a* and *e*. (1) In OE short *æ* repr. orig. Teut. short *a*, the sound of *a* in *man*; replaced after 1100 usu. by *a* sometimes by *e*. Long *æ* repr. same sound prolonged, and was replaced in 13th c. by *e* or *ee*. (2) In 16th c. *æ* was reintroduced to repr. L *ae* and Gk *ai*; as, *ædify* (L *aedificare*), *æther* (Gk *aithēr*). In familiar wds *æ* gave place to *e*, (*edify, ether*), being kept (pron. *ē*) in some Gk and L proper names (*Æneas, Cæsar*, but *Judea, Etna*), in names of Gk and Roman antiquities (*ædile, ægis*), and in some scientific terms (*ætiology, phænogamous*, but *phenomenon, museum*).

-æ, -ae, pl. suf. of L nouns of 1st decl. in *-a*, and L form of Gk *-ai* pl. of nouns of 1st decl. in *-ē, -a, -ēs, -as*; kept in non-naturalized words (*laminae, larvae*), esp. in proper names (*Heraclidae*) and names of animal and plant orders (*Felidae, Rosidae*); varying with *-as* in some wds acc. to degree of familiarity (*actiniae, -as*) or of technicality (mathematical *formulae*, theological *formulas*); familiar wds take *-as* (*areas, hyenas, Julias*).

ae·dīle, n. Roman magistrate who superintended public buildings, shows, police, &c. Hence **ae·dile**SHIP n. [f. L *aedilis* (*aedes* house, see -ILE)]

ae·ger (ējer), n. (In Eng. univv.) note certifying that student is ill. [L, =sick]

aegis (ē·jĭs), n. Protection, impregnable defence; (Myth.) shield of Zeus or Athene. [L, f. Gk *aigis*, etym. dub.]

aegrō·tăt, n. (In Eng. univv.) certificate that student is too ill to attend examination &c. [L, =he is sick (*aeger*)]

Aeō·lian, a. (1) Of Aeolis, district of Asia Minor colonized by ancient Greeks; (Mus.) *A. mode*, ninth of the church modes. (2) Of Aeolus, god of winds; *A. harp*, stringed instrument producing musical sounds on exposure to wind. [f. L *Aeolius* (1. *Aeolis* Gk *Aiolis*; 2. *Aeolus* Gk *Aiolos*) + -AN]

Aeŏ·lic, a. & n. Aeolian (dialect.) [f. L f. Gk *aiolikos* (as prec., see -IC)]

ae·olipyle, -pile, n. Instrument for showing force of steam escaping through narrow aperture. [f. F *æolipyle* f. L *Aeoli pylae* f. Gk *Aiolou pulai* gates of Aeolus, god of winds]

aeolŏ·tropy, n. Change of physical qualities consequent on change of position. [f. Gk *aiolos* changeful + *-tropia* turning]

ae·on, ē·on, n. An age of the universe, immeasurable period; eternity; (Platonic philosophy) a power existing from eternity, emanation or phase of the supreme deity. [L *aeon* f. Gk *aiōn* age]

ā·erate, v.t. Expose to mechanical or chemical action of air; charge with carbonic acid gas (formerly called *fixed air*). Hence **aer**A·TION n. [f. L *aer* air + -ATE[2]]

āĕr·ial, a. & n. Of air, gaseous; thin as air, ethereal; immaterial, imaginary; of, in the atmosphere, atmospheric; existing, moving, in the air. (N.) antenna-like collecting-wire in wireless telegraphy. Hence **aeria·l**ITY n., **aer·ial**LY[2] adv. [f. L f. Gk *aerios* (*aēr* air) + -AL]

aerie, aery, eyrie, eyry, (ā·erĭ, ĭr·ĭ), n. Nest of bird of prey, esp. eagle, or of raven or other bird that builds high up; human residence perched high on mountain; brood of bird of prey. [f. med. L *aeria, aerea*, f. F *aire*, perh. f. L *area* level ground or L *atrium* hall]

a·eriform, a. Of the form of air, gaseous; unsubstantial, unreal. [f. L *aer* air + -FORM]

a·ero, n. colloq. (pl. *-os*). Aeroplane or airship or aviation; (attrib.) of or for these. [irreg. use of foll.]

a·ero- in comb. Air-, of aircraft, as: *aeroba·tics*, feats of expert aviation; *a·erobus* slang, aeroplane; *aerodrome*, aviation ground; *aerodyna·mics*, the physics of gases in motion; *a·erofoil*, aeroplane wing or plane; *a·erogram*, wireless message; *a·erolite, -lith*, meteorite; *a·eronaut*, air-navigator, whence *-nau·tic*(*al*) aa., *-nau·tics* n.; *a·eroplane*, flying-machine heavier than air; *a·erostat*, balloon (hist.), aviator (rare); *aerosta·tics*, physics of gases in equilibrium, science of air-navigation. [Gk comb.-form of *aēr* air]

aeru·ginous (ērōō-), a. Of the nature or colour of verdigris, or copper-rust. [f. F *érugineux* f. L *aeruginosus* (*aerugo -inis* verdigris f. *aes aeris* brass, see -OUS)]

Aesculā·pius, n. Roman god of medicine; physician. Hence **Aescula·pi**AN a. [L]

ae·sthete (ēs-), n. Professed appreciator of the beautiful. [f. Gk *aisthētēs* one who perceives (as foll.)]

aesthĕ·tic, a. Belonging to the appreciation of the beautiful; having such appreciation; in accordance with principles of good taste. Hence **aesthe·tic**AL a., **aesthe·tical**LY[2] adv., **aesthe·tic**ISM, **aesthe·t**ICS, nn. [f. Gk *aisthētikos* (*aisthanomai* perceive, see -IC)]

aestho-physio·logy, n. Scientific study of the organs of sensation. [irreg. f. Gk *aisth-* perceive + PHYSIOLOGY]

aestival, estival, (ĕ·stĭval, ēstī·val), a. Belonging to, appearing in, summer. [F (*es-*), f. L *aestivalis* f. *aestivus* (*aestus* heat), see -IVE, -AL]

ae·stivate (ĕst-, ēst-), v.i. Spend the summer, esp. (Zool.) in state of torpor. [f. L *aestivare*, see -ATE[3]]

aestiva·tion (ĕst-, ēst-), n. (Zool.) aestivating; (Bot.) arrangement of petals in flower-bud before expansion. [f. prec., see -ATION]

aeta·tis, aet., aetat. Of or at the age of (*aet. 17*); *anno a. suae* —, in the —th year of his age. [L]

aetio·logy, n. Assignment of a cause; philosophy of causation; (Med.) science of the causes of disease. So **aetiolo·gi**CAL a., **aetiolo·gical**LY[2] adv. [f. L f. Gk *aitiologia* (*aitia* cause, see -LOGY)]

af-, pref. = AD- before *f*.

afar·, adv. *From* a distance; at, to, a distance (in prose, usu. *a. off*). [f. OE *feor* FAR adv., with prepp. OF, ON]

a·ffable, a. Easy of address, courteous, complaisant. Hence or cogn. **affa**BI·LITY n., **a·ffab**LY[2] adv. [F, f. L *affabilis* f. AF(*fari* speak), see -BLE]

affair·, n. Thing to be done; concern, business, matter, as *that is my a.*; (pl.) ordinary pursuits of life; *a. of honour*, duel; (colloq., of material things) *a gorgeous* &c. *a.* [f. OF *afaire* (*à faire* to do), cf. ADO]

affaire de cœur (F), n. Love affair.

affe·ct[1], v.t. Practise, use, as *a. a costume*; (of things) tend to assume (form, shape, &c.); assume (character), as *a. the free-thinker*; pretend to have or feel (indifference &c.); pretend (*to* do). [f. F *affecter* f. L *affectare* aim at, pretend to have, frequent. of AF(*ficere fect-* = *facere* do)]

affe·ct², v.t. Attack (as disease); move, touch, (in mind), whence **affe·cting**LY² adv.; produce (material) effect on; (pass., archaic) be assigned, allotted, (*to* particular service &c.). [(perh. thr. F) f. L *afficere* attach to (see prec.)]

affecta·tion, n. Studied display *of*; artificiality of manner; pretence; (rare) declared occupation or employment (*all* ships, whatever their a.). [f. L *affectatio* pursuit after (as AFFECT¹, see -ATION)]

affe·cted, a. Artificially assumed or displayed; pretended; (of persons) full of affectation, artificial, whence **affe·cted**LY² adv., **affe·cted**NESS n.; (with adv.) disposed, inclined, (*towards* or abs.); attacked (as by disease); moved in the feelings; acted upon physically. [AFFECT¹, ² + -ED¹]

affe·ction, n. Affecting; mental state, emotion, whence **affe·ction**AL a.; disposition (*towards*); goodwill, love, (*towards*); bodily state due to any influence; malady, disease; mode of being; property, quality, attribute. [F, f. L *affectionem* (as AFFECT², see -ION)]

affe·ctionate (-*at*), a. Loving; fond; (of things) showing love or tenderness. Hence **affe·ctionate**LY² adv., **affe·ctionate**NESS n. [Latinized f. F *affectionné*]

affe·ctive, a. Pertaining to the affections, emotional. [F (-*if*, -*ive*), f. med. L *affectivus* (as AFFECT², see -IVE)]

a·fferent, a. Conducting inwards or towards, as *a. nerves, a. vessels*. [f. L AF(*ferre* bring), see -ENT]

affettuo·so, adv. (mus.). Feelingly. [It.]

affi·ance¹, n. Faith, trust (*in*); pledging of faith, esp. plighting of troth in marriage. [f. OF *afiance* f. *afier* trust f. LL AF*fidare* (*fides* faith), see -ANCE]

affi·ance², v.t. Promise solemnly in marriage (usu. pass.). [f. OF *afiancer* f. *afiance*, see prec.]

affidā·vit, n. Written statement, confirmed by oath, to be used as judicial proof. (Strictly, deponent *swears* an a., judge *takes* it; but in pop. use deponent *makes* or *takes* it.) [L, = has stated on faith or oath, f. AF*fidare*, see AFFIANCE¹]

affi·liate, v.t. (Of an institution) adopt (persons as members, societies as branches); attach (persons, societies) *to*, connect (them) *with*, (a society); (Law) fix paternity of (illegitimate child *on* putative father) for purpose of maintenance; ascribe (child) *to* its parent; father (a thing) *upon*, trace (it) *to*. So **affili**A·TION n. [f. L AF*filiare* adopt (*filius* son), see -ATE³]

affi·ned, a. Related, connected. [f. F *affiné* (*affin* f. L *affinis*, see foll.) + -ED¹; no vb in F or E]

affi·nity, n. Relationship, relations, by marriage; relations, kindred, in general; structural resemblance (between animals, plants, languages); (fig.) similarity of character suggesting relationship, family likeness; liking; attraction; (Chem.) tendency of certain elements to unite with others. [f. F *affinité* f. L *affinitatem* (AF*finis* related, lit. bordering on, f. *finis* end, see -TY)]

affir·m, v.t. & i. Assert strongly, aver; make formal declaration, (Law) make AFFIRMATION; (Logic, Gram.) state in the affirmative; (Law) confirm, ratify, (judgement). Hence **affir·m**ABLE, **affir·ma**TORY, aa. [f. OF *afermer* f. L AF*firmare* (*firmus* strong)]

affirma·tion, n. Affirming, esp. (Law) solemn declaration by person who conscientiously declines taking an oath. [F, f. L *affirmationem* (as prec., see -ATION)]

affir·mative, a. & n. Affirming, answering yes; (Logic) expressing agreement of the two terms of a proposition; *answer in the a.*, answer yes, say that a thing is so. Hence **affir·mative**LY² adv. [F (-*if*, -*ive*), f. L *affirmativus* (as prec., see -IVE)]

affi·x¹, v.t. Fix, fasten, (thing *to, on*); impress (seal, stamp); add in writing (signature, postscript); attach (censure, salary). [(perh. thr. MF *affixer*, occas. refash. of OF *aficher* F *afficher*) f. med. L *affixare* frequent. of L AF(*figere fix-* fix)]

a·ffix², n. Appendage, addition; (Gram.) addition placed at the beginning or end of root, stem, or word, to modify its meaning. [f. F *affixe* f. L *affigere* (see prec.)]

affi·xture, n. Affixing. [f. AFFIX¹ after FIXTURE; correct form (on L) would be *affixure*]

afflā·tus, n. Communication of supernatural knowledge; divine impulse, poetic or other; inspiration. [L vbl n. f. AF(*flare* blow)]

affli·ct, v.t. Distress with bodily or mental suffering. [f. 14th-c. *afflict* adj., f. OF *aflit* f. L AF(*fligere flict-* dash)]

affli·ctiŏn, n. Misery, distress; pain, calamity. So **affli·c**TIVE a. [F, f. L *afflictionem* (as prec., see -ION)]

a·ffluent¹, a. Flowing freely, copious; abounding (esp. in riches), wealthy. Hence or cogn. **a·fflu**ENCE n., **a·ffluent**LY² adv. [F, f. L AF(*fluere flux-* flow), see -ENT]

a·ffluent², n. Tributary stream. [f. prec., prob. after F]

a·fflux, n. Flow towards a point, esp. of humours; accession. [f. med. L *affluxus -ūs*, vbl n. as AFFLUENT]

affor·d, v.t. (With *can*) have the means, be rich enough, (*to* do), manage to spare; furnish, bestow; (of things) yield supply of. [OE *geforthian* (*ge-* pref. implying completeness + *forthian* advance f. *forth* forward); *ge-* was reduced to *a-*, which was corrupted to *af-* after L (see AD-)]

affŏ·rest, v.t. Convert into forest or hunting-ground. So **afforest**A·TION n. [f. med. L AF*forestare* (*foresta* FOREST)]

affra·nchise, v.t. Free from servitude or

obligation. [f. F *affranchiss-* lengthened st. of *affranchir* (*à* to + *franchir* free f. *franc*, see FRANK)]

affray·, n. Breach of the peace, caused by fighting or riot in a public place. [f. OF *effrei* f. *esfreer*, vb f. LL EX*fridare* (LL *fridus* f. Teut. *fridhu*, OE *fridh*, peace); cf. AFRAID]

affrigh·t[1], v.t. (archaic). Frighten. [late formation on FRIGHT v., partly due to obs. *affright* p.p. of OE **afyrhtan* (*a-* intensive)]

affrigh·t[2], n. (archaic). Alarm, terror. [f. prec.]

affro·nt[1] (-ŭnt), v.t. Insult openly; put to the blush, offend the modesty or self-respect of; face, confront. [f. OF *afronter* slap in the face, insult, f. LL AF*frontare* (*frons -tis* face)]

affro·nt[2] (-ŭnt), n. Open insult, as *put a. upon, offer an a. to, feel it an a.* [f. prec.]

affu·sion, n. Pouring on, esp. of water on the body in one kind of baptism; (Med.) pouring of water, usually 50° to 70° Fahr., upon fever patients. [f. L AF(*fundere fus-* pour), see -ION]

afie·ld, adv. On or in the field (esp. of labour or battle); to the field; away from home, at a distance, as *far a.* [A prep.]

afire·, adv. & pred. a. On fire (lit. & fig.). [A prep.]

afla·me, adv. & pred. a. In flame, in a glow of light, (lit. & fig.). [A prep.]

afloa·t, adv. & pred. a. In a floating condition; at sea, on board ship, in naval service; full of water; floating in the air; out of debt, paying one's way; in full swing; in general circulation, current; (Commerc.) in currency as negotiable document; unsettled, adrift. [OE *on flote* (ON prep. + FLOAT n.)]

à fond (F), adv. Thoroughly, fully.

afoo·t, adv. & pred. On one's own feet; astir, on the move; in operation or employment. [A prep.]

afore·, adv. & prep. (Naut.) in front, in front of, as *a. the mast*; (archaic) previously. [f. OE *on foran* (*on* prep. + *foran*, adv., in front, dat. of *for*, which was used as noun or adj.]

afore- in comb. Before, previously, as *-cited, -going, -named, -said*; *-thought*, premeditated, as *malice a.*; *-time*, previously. [prec.]

ā fortior·ī, adv. With stronger reason, more conclusively. [L]

afrai·d, pred. a. Alarmed, frightened, (abs. or *of*); *a.* (of the consequences, and therefore unwilling) *to do a thing, a. of a thing's happening, a. lest it should happen, a. (that) it will happen.* [p.p. of obs. vb *affray* f. OF *esfreer*, see AFFRAY]

ă·freet, -rit, -rite, n. Evil demon in Mohammedan mythology. [Arab. *'ifrīt*]

afre·sh, adv. Anew, with fresh beginning. [A- (3) + FRESH]

Afrika·nder, n. & a. Native of S. Africa born of European (esp. Dutch) settlers; *A. Bond*, organization for furtherance of A. interests and ultimate formation of United States of S. Africa. [(perh. f. S.-African Du. *Afrikaander*) f. Du. *Afrikaner* n. African, altered on *Englander* &c.]

aft, adv. (naut.). In or near stern of ship; towards the stern; *fore and a.*, from stem to stern, lengthwise (also as adj. *f.-and-a.*). [OE *æftan* cogn. w. Goth. *aftana* from behind, f. *afta* behind (*af* off + *-ta* superl. suf.); *after, aft*, are orig. compar. and superl.]

a·fter[1], adv., prep., & conj. Behind (prep. & adv.; *Gill came tumbling a.*); in pursuit of, as *run a., inquire a.*; concerning, as *look, see, a.*; for, as *hanker, yearn, a.*; following in point of time, afterwards, (*a. you*, formula in yielding precedence; *a. you with*, colloq. request for next turn at; *was sore for months a.*); *a.* (the lapse of) *three months*; in view of, as *a. such behaviour*; next in importance to; according to, as *a. a* FASHION, *a.* one's *own heart* (such as one loves); in imitation of (person), as *a. Rembrandt*; in allusion to, as *named a.*; *a. all*, in spite of all that has happened or been said &c. (*a. all, what does it matter?*) or of one's exertions, expectations, &c. (*tried for an hour and failed a. a.*; *so it did rain a.a.!*); (conj.) in, at, the time subsequent to that at which, as *a. he went, goes, has gone, had gone.* [OE *æfter* (*af* off + compar. suf. *-ter*) cogn. w. OHG *aftar*, Gk *apōterō*; cf. prec.]

a·fter[2], a. Later, following, as *a. years*; (Naut.) hinder, posterior, as *a. cabin, masts.* [f. prec.]

a·fterbirth, n. Membrane enveloping the foetus in the womb, so called because its extrusion follows that of the infant. [AFTER a.]

a·fterdamp, n. Choke-damp, gas left in mine after explosion of fire-damp. [AFTER a.]

a·fterglow, n. Glow in the West after sunset. [AFTER a.]

a·fter-grass, n. Grass that grows after first crop has been mown for hay, or among stubble after harvest. [AFTER a.]

a·ftermath, n. After-grass. [AFTER a. + *math* mowing, OE *mæth* f. OTeut. root *mæ* MOW]

a·ftermost, a. (naut.). Nearest the stern, most aft. [OE *æftemest*, a treble superl. of *af* off with compar. suf. inserted, *af* + *te* (*r*) + *me* + *st*]

afternoo·n, n. The time from noon to evening, as *in, during, the a., on Wednesday a.*, (fig.) *the a. of life.* [AFTER prep.]

a·fterpiece, n. Farce or smaller entertainment after a play. [AFTER a.]

a·fterthought, n. Reflection after the act; later expedient or explanation. [AFTER a. or adv.]

a·fterwards, adv. Later, subsequently. [OE *æftanweard,* a. (*æftan* AFT + WARD, corrupted in OE to *æfterweard,* + adv. genit. suf. -ES]

ag-, pref. = AD- before *g.*

ā·ga (or *agah·*), n. Commander, chief officer in Ottoman empire. [Turk. *agha* master]

agai·n, adv. Another time, once more; *a. and a., time and a.,* repeatedly; *ever and a., now and a.,* occasionally; *as much a.,* twice as much; *half as much a.,* one-and-a-half times as much; further, besides; on the other hand, as *these a. are more expensive*; *back a.* (to the original position or condition); in return, as *answer a.*; in response, as *rocks echoed a., glasses rang a.*; proportionately to specified act or condition, as *the loaded table groaned a.* [OE *ongeán, ongægn* (*on* in + *gagn* opposite), cf. G *entgegen*; 12th-c. *againes* (see -ES) became *against* by confus. w. superlatives]

agai·nst, prep. & conj. In opposition to, as *fight a., I am a. reform*; in contrast to, as *a. a dark background*; in anticipation of, as *a. his coming, a. a rainy day*; in preparation for, as *warned a. pickpockets*; into collision with, as *ran a. a rock,* (colloq.) *ran a.* (chanced to meet) *a friend*; opposite to, as *a. the horsepond* (usu. *over a.*). (Conj.) by the time that (*be ready a. he comes*). [see prec.]

ă·gamĭ, n. Tropical American bird, the Trumpeter. [native name in Guiana]

agă·mic, a. (zool.). Characterized by absence of sexual action. [as foll. + -IC]

a·gamoge·nesis, n. Asexual reproduction. So **agamogenĕ·tic** a., **agamogene·tically** adv. [as foll. + *genesis* birth]

ă·gamous, a. (biol.). Without (distinguishable) sexual organs. [f. L f. Gk *agamos* (*a-* not + *gamos* marriage) + -OUS]

aga·pe[1], adv. & pred. a. On the gape; open-mouthed with wonder or expectation. [A prep.]

ă·gapē[2], n. Love-feast held by early Christians in connexion with Lord's Supper. [Gk, = brotherly love]

ă·garic (or *agă·rĭk*), n. Mushroom; name of various fungi. [f. L f. Gk *agarikon* perh. f. a place *Agaria*]

aga·stric, a. (zool.). Without distinct alimentary canal. [f. Gk *a-* not + *gastēr -tros* belly]

ă·gate (-*at*), n. Name of several varieties of precious stone (semipellucid variegated chalcedonies); burnishing instrument of gold-wiredrawers; (in U.S.) the printing-type called in England *ruby.* [f. F *agathe* (16th-c.) f. It. *agata* f. L f. Gk *akhatēs* agate]

Agā·ve (-ĭ), n. (bot.). Genus of plants including American Aloe. [f. L f. Gk *Agauē,* prop. name in myth.]

aga·ze, adv. On the gaze. [A prep.]

age[1], n. Length of life or of existence; *Moon's a.,* time elapsed since new moon; duration of life required for a purpose, as *come of a., full a.* (in Eng. Law, 21 years), *a. of discretion* (14), *over a.*; latter part of life, as *peevishness of a., a. before honesty,* children must give precedence to their elders; a generation; BRAZEN[1] &c. *a.*; (Hist., Geol.) great period, as *Patriarchal A., Ice A.*; (colloq.) long time, as *waiting for aa.* [f. OF *aage, edage,* f. LL **aetaticum* f. *aetas -atis* contraction of *aevitas* (*aevum* an age); see -AGE]

age[2], v.t. & i. (part. *aging*). (Cause to) grow old. [f. prec.]

-age, suf. OF f. LL *-aticum* 'belongings' neut. of adj. suf. *-aticus* -ATIC (med. L *-agium* is readopted f. F, e.g. *homagium* f. *hommage* instead of *hominaticum*); afterwards added as living suf. in F and in E. Meaning: (1) collective belongings or aggregate of (*cellarage*); (2) function, condition, (*baronage, bondage*); (3) action (*breakage*); (4) fees payable for, cost of using, (*cartage, demurrage*).

aged, a. (ā·jĭd) having lived long, old; (ājd) of the age of, as *a. thirteen,* (of horses) over six years old. Hence **a·gĕd**NESS n. [f. AGE v. + -ED[1]]

a·geless, a. Never growing old. [AGE n. + -LESS]

ā·gency, n. Active operation, action, as *moral, free, a.*; instrumentality, as *by the a. of*; action personified, as *an invisible a.*; (Commerc.) office of agent; establishment for business purposes, as *Reuter's A.* [f. med. L *agentia* (L *agere* do, see -ENCE)]

age·nda, n. Things to be done, items of business to be considered at a meeting; memorandum book. [L, neut. pl. of gerundive of *agere* do]

ā·gent, n. One who exerts power or produces an effect; (of things) efficient cause; a natural force acting on matter, as *chemical a.*; one who does the actual work, esp. one who represents a person or firm in business (*Who is your a. in Paris?*). So **age·ntial** (-shl) a. [as ACT[2], -ENT]

agent provocateur (F), n. Person employed to detect suspected offenders by tempting them to overt action.

agglŏ·merāte[1], v.t. & i. Collect into a mass. Hence **agglomera·tion** n., **agglo·merative** a. [f. L AG*glomerare* (*glomus -meris* ball), see -ATE[3]]

agglo·merate[2] (-*at*), a. & n. (Collected into) a mass; (Geol.) mass of volcanic fragments united under heat, opp. to *conglomerate.* [as prec., see -ATE[2]]

agglu·tinate[1] (-*at*), a. Glued together; consisting of simple words combined into compounds without change of form or loss of meaning. [f. L AG*glutinare* (*gluten -tinis* glue) see -ATE[2]]

agglu·tināte[2], v.t. & i. Unite as with

glue; combine simple words to express compound ideas; (t. & i.) turn into glue. Hence **agglu·tinA·TION** n., **agglu·tina-tIVE** a. [as prec., see -ATE[3]]

a·ggrandize, v.t. Increase the power, rank, wealth, of (person, State); exaggerate, embellish. Hence **aggra·n-dizeMENT,** n. [f. F *agrandir* (st. *-iss-*) prob. f. It. AG(*grandire* f. L *grandis* large)]

a·ggravate, v.t. Increase the gravity of (burden, offence, &c.); (colloq.) exasperate (person). So **aggravA·TION** n. [f. L AG*gravare* make heavy (*gravis*), see -ATE[2]; replacing obs. *aggrege* f. OF *agreger* f. *LL *aggreviare*)]

a·ggregate[1] (-*at*), a. & n. Collected into one body; collective, total; (Law) composed of associated individuals, as *corporation a.*; sum total; assemblage; (Physics) mass of homogeneous particles; *in the a.*, as a whole. [f. L AG*gregare* unite in a flock (*grex gregis*)]

a·ggregāte[2], v.t. & i. Collect together; (trans.) unite (individual to company); amount to (specified total). Hence **ag-gregA·TION** n., **a·ggregatIVE** a. [f. prec.]

aggre·ss, v.i. (rare). Begin a (or the) quarrel. So **aggre·ssION, aggre·ssOR**[2], nn. [f. F *aggresser* f. LL *aggressare* frequent. of AG(*gredi gress-* =*gradi* step)]

aggre·ssive, a. & n. Of attack; offensive; disposed to attack; *assume the a.*, begin the quarrel. Hence **aggre·ssiveLY**[2] adv., **aggre·ssiveNESS** n. [as prec., see -IVE]

aggrie·ve, v.t. Grieve, distress, oppress, (usu. pass.) [f. OF *agrever* as AGGRAVATE]

agha·st (*a*gah-, *a*gă-), a. Terrified; struck with amazement. [p.p. of obs. vb *agast* (A- (1) +*gasten*, OE *gǽstan*, alarm)]

a·gīle (ăj-), a. Quick-moving, nimble, active. Hence or cogn. **agi·lITY** n., **a·gileLY**[2] adv. [F, f. L *agilis* (*agere* do)]

a·gio (ăj-, āj-), n. Percentage charged on exchange of paper-money into cash, or of one currency into another more valuable; excess value of one currency over another; exchange business. [It., =ease]

ă·giotage (-ĭj), n. Exchange business; speculation in stocks; stock-jobbing. [F f. *agioter* (prec. +connecting *-t-*); see -AGE]

agi·st (-j-), v.t. Take in live stock to feed; charge (land or its owner) with a public burden. Hence **agi·stMENT** n. [f. OF *agister* (*à* to +*gister* f. L *jacitare* frequent. of *jacēre* lie)]

ă·gitate, v.t. Move, shake; disturb, excite, (feelings, persons); revolve mentally, discuss, debate, (plans &c.); (abs.) keep up an agitation (*for*). [f. L *agitare* move to and fro, frequent. of *agere* drive, see -ATE[3]]

agita·tion, n. Moving, shaking; commotion, disturbance, (mental or physical); debate, discussion; keeping of a matter constantly before the public; public excitement. [F, f. L *agitationem* (as prec., see -ATION)]

agita·to (-tah-), adv. (mus.). In an agitated manner. [It.]

a·gitator, n. One who agitates, esp. politically; apparatus for shaking or mixing. [L (see AGITATE and -OR[2])]

a·glet, ai·glet, n. Metal tag of a lace; spangle or other metallic ornament of dress; tagged point hanging from shoulder upon breast of some uniforms (usu. *aiguillette*); catkin of hazel, birch, &c. [f. F *aiguillette* dim. of *aiguille* needle f. L *acucula* =*acicula* dim. of *acus* needle]

aglow·, adv. & pred. a. In a glow. [A prep.]

a·gnail, n. Torn skin at root of finger-nail; (formerly) corn on toe or foot. [OE *angnægl* f. *ang-* (Goth. *aggwus*) tight, painful, +*nægl* (Goth. *nagls*) nail (of iron &c.), hard excrescence fixed in the flesh; mod. sense, and forms *hang-nail*, (Sc.) *anger-nail*, result from false etym., *nail* being taken as finger-nail]

a·gnāte, n. & a. (One who is) descended by male links (also, by male or female links) from same male ancestor; sprung from same forefather, of same clan or nation; (fig.) akin, of same nature. So **agnă·tIC** a., **agna·tION** n. [f. F *agnat* f. L *agnatus* related by father's side (*ad* to + *gnatus* born p.p. of (*g*)*nasci* f. stem *gen-* beget)]

agnō·men, n. A fourth name sometimes assumed by Romans; (loosely) nickname. [L (*ad* to +(*g*)*nomen* name)]

agnŏ·stic, n. & a. One who holds that nothing is known, or likely to be known, of the existence of a God or of anything beyond material phenomena; pertaining to this theory. Hence **agno·sticISM** n. [f. Gk *agnōstos* unknown (*a-* not +*gnō-* know); see -IC]

A·gnus Ca·stus, n. Tree once held a preservative of chastity. [L, f. Gk *agnos* (name of tree), confused w. *hagnos* chaste, whence L *castus* is added]

A·gnus Dē·ī, n. Part of Mass beginning *A. D.*; figure of lamb bearing cross or flag; cake of wax stamped with such figure and blessed by Pope. [L, =lamb of God]

ago·, a. & adv. (Adj., always following noun) past, gone by, as *ten years a.*; (adv.) *long a.*, long since. [orig. *agone* p.p. of obs. vb *ago* (A- forth +GO)]

ago·g, adv. & pred. a. On the move, eager, expectant. [perh. f. OF *en gogues* (*gogue* fun, etym. dub.)]

agŏ·nic, a. Making no angle; *a. line*, line of no magnetic variation. [f. Gk *agōnios* without angle (*a-* not +*gōnia* angle) + -IC]

agoni·stic, a. Pertaining to athletic contests (esp. of Ancient Greece); (Rhet.) polemic, combative; strained, aiming at effect. Hence **agoni·sticAL** a., **agoni·s-**

ticalLY² adv. [f. Gk *agōnistikos* pertaining to a combatant, *agōnistēs*, in the games (*agōnes* f. *agō* lead, bring)]
ă·gonize, v.t. & i. Torture; suffer agony, writhe in anguish; contend in arena, wrestle (lit. & fig.); make desperate efforts for effect. Hence **a·gonizing**LY² adv. [f. med. L *agonizare* f. Gk *agōnizomai* contend (*agōn*, see prec.)]
ă·gony, n. Mental anguish; *a. column* (in newspaper), column of advertisements for missing friends &c.; paroxysm of pleasure; pangs of death; extreme bodily suffering; struggle. [prob. formed by Wyclif on Vulgate L *agonia* f. Gk *agōnia* contest, anguish; see AGONISTIC]
ăgoraphō·bia, n. Morbid dread of public places. [Gk *agora* assembly, -PHOBIA]
agou·ti, agou·ty (-gōō-), n. Genus of rodents of Cavy or Guinea-pig family, esp. a hare-like animal of W. Indies. [(thr. F) f. native Ind. *aguti*]
agrār·ian, a. & n. Relating to landed property; *a. outrage* (arising from discord between landlords and tenants); relating to cultivated land; (n.) advocate of redistribution of landed property, whence **agrār·ian**ISM n., **agrār·ian**IZE v.t. & i. [f. L *agrarius* (*ager agri* land, see -ARY¹) + -AN]
agree·, v.i. & t. Consent (*to* proposal, statement, *to* do); concur (*with* person *that*); become, be, in harmony (*with* person); (pl.) *a. together, cannot a.*, get on with one another; suit the constitution of, as *work, lobster, does not a. with him*; (Gram.) take same number, gender, case, person; (trans.) bring (balance, items of accounts) into harmony. [f. OF *agréer* f. LL *AG*gratare* make agreeable (*gratus*)]
agree·able (-rĭabl), a. Pleasing (*to* or abs.); (colloq., of persons) well-disposed (*to* a thing, *to* do, or abs.); conformable *to*, as *a. to all experience.* Hence **agree·able**NESS n., **agree·ab**LY² adv. [f. F *agréable* (*agréer* AGREE, see -ABLE)]
agree·ment, n. Mutual understanding, covenant, treaty; (Law) contract legally binding on parties; accordance in opinion; (Gram.) concord in gender, number, case, person. [OF (*agreer* AGREE, see -MENT)]
agréments (F), n. pl. Agreeable qualities or surroundings.
agre·stic, a. Rural, rustic; uncouth. [f. L *agrestis* (*ager* field) + -IC]
ă·griculture, n. Cultivation of the soil. Hence **agricu·ltur**AL a., **agricu·ltur(al)**IST, nn. [(prob. thr. 17th-c. F) f. L *agricultura* (*ager agri* field + *cultura* CULTURE)]
ă·grimony, n. Genus of plants, esp. species *A. Eupatoria,* common in Britain. [f. L *agrimonia* perh. f. Gk *argemōnē*, etym. dub.]
agrŏ·nomy, n. Rural economy, husbandry. So **agronŏ·mic**(AL) aa., **agronŏ·mic**S, **agro·nom**IST, nn. [f. Gk *agronomos* overseer of land (*agros* land + *-nomos* f. *nemō* dispense), see -Y¹]
agrou·nd, adv. & pred. a. Upon the bottom of shallow water, as *be, run, a.* (of ships). [A prep.]
ā·gue (-ū), n. Malarial fever, with cold, hot, and sweating stages; shivering fit; quaking (lit. & fig.); *a.-cake*, enlargement of spleen or liver caused by a. Hence **a·gu**ED² a. [OF, f. L *acuta* sharp]
ā·gūish, a. Of the nature of ague; tending to produce ague; subject to ague; ague-like, quaking; coming by fits and starts. Hence **a·guish**LY² adv. [f. prec. + -ISH¹]
ah, int. expr. sorrow, regret, surprise, admiration, entreaty, remonstrance, dislike, contempt, mockery. [not in OE; ME has *a*, perh. f. OF *a, ah*]
aha¹ (ahhah·), int. expr. surprise, triumph, mockery, irony. [f. AH + HA; formerly written *a ha*]
aha², n. See HA-HA n.
ahea·d, adv. & pred. a. In advance; in the direct line of one's forward motion, as *breakers a.*; straight forwards; forward at a rapid pace, as *go a.*; in advance *of* (lit. & fig.). [A prep.]
ahea·p, adv. In a heap, all of a heap. [A prep.]
ahe·m, int. used to attract attention or gain time. [lengthened form of *hem*]
ahoy·, int. Nautical call used in hailing. [obs. *a* int. + HOY]
à huis clos (ah wē klō), adv. With closed doors, in private. [F]
ahu·ll, adv. (naut.). With sails taken in and helm lashed on lee side. [A prep. + HULL]
ai (ah·ĭ), n. Three-toed Sloth of S. America. [f. Braz. *aï*, repr. its cry]
aid¹, v.t. Help (person *to* do, or abs.); promote (recovery &c.). [f. OF *aider* f. L *adjutare* frequent. of AD(*juvare jut-*)]
aid², n. Help; (Law) help claimed by defendant from one who has joint-interest; (Hist.) grant of subsidy or tax to king, (later) exchequer loan; helper; material source of help (usu. pl.) as *aa. and appliances.* [f. OF *aide, aiude* (Prov. *ajuda*) f. LL *adjuta*, fem. p.p. of *adjuvare* AID¹ used as n.]
aide-de-camp (ā·dekŏng), n. (pl. *aides-de-camp* pron. ā·dekŏngz). Officer assisting general by carrying orders, &c. [F]
aigrette (ā·grĭt), n. Lesser White Heron (usu. EGRET); tuft of feathers or hair; spray of gems &c. [F, dim. f. OHG *heigir* heron]
aiguille (ā·gwĭl), n. Sharp peak of rock, esp. in Alps. Hence **aiguill**E·SQUE a. [F, see AGLET]
aiguillette (āgwĭlĕ·t), n. See AGLET.
ail, v.t. & i. Trouble, afflict, as *what ails him?*; be ill. Hence **ai·l**MENT n. [f. OE *eglan* (cogn. w. Goth. *agljan*) f. *egle* troublesome (Goth. *aglus*)]

ai·leron, n. (usu. pl.). Lateral-control flap(s) at rear of aeroplane's wingtip(s). [F]

aim¹, v.t. & i. Direct (blow, missile, *at*); point (gun &c.) towards (*at*); direct an act or proceeding against (*at*); (intr.) deliver blow, discharge missile, (*at*); take aim (abs.); form designs (abs.). [prob. f. two vbs (1) Picard. *amer*, OF and Prov. *esmer*, f. L *aestimare* reckon, (2) OF *aësmer* f. LL *adaestimare*; ME sense was *estimate*]

aim², n. Direction of a missile at an object, as *take a.*; design, purpose, object, whence **ai·m**LESS a., **ai·mless**LY² adv., **ai·mless**NESS n. [f. prec.]

ainé (ā·nā), n. Elder son (cf. CADET). [F]

air¹, n. (1) Gaseous substance enveloping earth, mixture of oxygen and nitrogen, breathed by all land animals; atmosphere; free space overhead, as *birds of the a.*; unconfined space, as *open a.*; *fresh a.*, also simply *a.*, a. not exhausted of its oxygen; breeze, light wind; *take a.*, become known; (of projects &c.) *quite in the a.* (uncertain); (of opinions, feelings) *in the a.*, spreading about; *castles in the a.*, visionary projects. (2) Appearance, as *an a. of absurdity*; mien, gesture, as *with a triumphant a.*; affected manner (esp. in pl.), as *gave himself aa.*, *aa. and graces*; (Mus.) melody, tune, esp., in harmonized composition, predominant (usu. soprano) part. (3) Combb.: *a.-ball(oon)*, inflated toy; *a.-bed*, inflated mattress; *a.-bladder*, one filled with a., in animals or plants; *a.-brake* (worked by a.-pressure); *a.-chamber* (in hydraulic machines, for equalizing pressure); *A. Chief Marshal, A. Commodore*, see *A. Force*; *aircraft*, aeroplane(s), airship(s), or balloon(s), *a.-c. carrier*, ship that carries and serves as base for aeroplanes; *Aircraftsman*, see *A. Force*; *a.-cushion* (inflated with a.); *a.-engine* (actuated by heated a.); *A. Force* (*the Royal A.F.*, abbr. R.A.F.), the aircraft service co-ordinate with Navy and Army, with officers as follows: *Marshal of the Air, A. Chief Marshal, A. Marshal, A. Vice-Marshal, A. Commodore, Group-Captain, Wing-Commander, Squadron-Leader, Flight-Lieutenant, Flying-Officer, Pilot-Officer*, and (non-commissioned) *aircraftsman, a.-mechanic*; *a.-gun* (using compressed air as propelling force); *a.-jacket* (inflated, to support wearer in water); *a. liner*, large passenger aircraft; *airman*, aviator; *A. Marshal, a.-mechanic*, see *A. Force*; *airplane*, aeroplane (chiefly U.S.); *a.-pocket*, apparent vacuum in a. causing aircraft to drop some distance; *a.-pump* (for exhausting a vessel of its a.); *a.-raid*, attack by aircraft; *airship*, flying-machine lighter than air; *a. thermometer* (with a. instead of mercury); *a.-threads*, gossamer; *a.-tight*, impermeable to a.; *a.-truck*, aeroplane with truck body for freight; *A. Vice-Marshal*, see *A. Force*; *airway*, ventilating passage in mine, route regularly followed by aircraft; *airworthy*, (of aircraft) fit to fly, *airworthiness*. [(1) OF f. L *aerem*, nom. *aer* f. Gk *aēr* (*aō* breathe). (2) perh. developed f. (1) in F; taken by E f. F about 1600]

air², v.t. Expose to open air, ventilate; dry at fire; (refl.) go out into fresh air; parade (qualities, grievances, theories, fine clothes). [f. prec.]

Aire·dale, n. Large rough-coated terrier. [f. *A.* in Yorks.]

air·less, a. Stuffy; breezeless, still. [AIR + -LESS]

air·y, a. Aerial, lofty; breezy; immaterial; of thin texture; light in movement; sprightly; graceful, delicate; unsubstantial; superficial, flippant. Hence **air·**ILY² adv., **air·**INESS n. [AIR¹ + -Y²]

aisle (īl), n. Division of church, esp. one parallel to and divided by pillars from the nave, choir, or transept; passage between rows of pews. Hence **aisl**ED² a. [f. OF *ele* f. L *ala*, contr. of *axilla* wing; confused in E with *ile* island, refash. with this as *isle*, and again modified to *aisle* after F refash. *aile* (on L *axilla*); the F spelling *aisle* (after med. L *ascella* = L *axilla*) is mere coincidence; sense *passage* from confus. of L *ala* w. OF *allée* ALLEY]

ait (āt), n. Small isle, esp. in a river. [perh. f. OE *iggath, iggeoth*; *eyet, eyot*, are artificial spellings on *islet* and F *îlot*]

aitch, n. = ACHE³.

ai·tch-bone, n. (Cut of beef lying over) buttock or rump bone. [ME *nage* f. OF *nache, nage*, f. LL *natica*, adj. (L *natis* buttock) + BONE; for loss of *n* (*a nage-* becoming *an age-*), cf. ADDER; pop. etym. gives *H-, ice-, edge-*, bone]

ajar·¹, adv. (Of doors) slightly open. [A prep. + *char* (OE *cyrr* a turn)]

ajar·², adv. In a jarring state. [A prep. + JAR n.]

a-ki·mbo, adv. (Of the arms) with hands on hips and elbows turned outwards. [etym. dub.]

aki·n, pred. a. Related by blood; (fig.) of similar or kindred character. [A prep.]

-al, suf. (1) Adj. f. L *-alis* (adj. suf. varying w. *-aris* -AR¹ by dissim. f. prec. syllable, as *regularis* but *generalis*) direct or through F *-el* (since corrected to *-al* in E); now appended freely to L nouns (*cordial*), Gk nouns (*colossal*), L adjj. (*individual*), and Gk adjj. in *-kos, -oidēs*, (*comical, rhomboidal*); *-ical* indicates vaguer connexion w. the orig. n. than *-ic* (*comic* paper, *comical* story), cf. -ACAL; other suff. are sometimes appended, as *generality, centralize*. (2) Nouns f. L *-alis, -al, -ales, -alia*, parts of above used as nouns (*rival, animal, annals, Saturnalia*), with new imitations (*cardinal, regimentals*). *-alia* became in F *-aille*, in E *-aille*, *-ail*, *-al* (L *sponsalia*, OF *espousaille*, E *spousaille* now *espousal*), the last now freely imitated to form vbl nn. (*reprisal, recital, bestowal*), partly on false anal. of BRIDAL, BURIAL.

à la (ah lah), prep. After the manner of, as *à la Russe, à la Reform.* [F, for *à la mode*]

alaba·ster (*or* ă·l-), n. & a. Name of several varieties of carbonate or sulphate of lime; (Mineral.) massive fine-grained sulphate of lime (*Modern, Gypseous, A.*), as distinct from the carbonates used by the ancients for holding unguents (*Oriental, Calcareous, A.*); box made of a.; (adj.) of a., like a. in whiteness or smoothness. So **alaba·strINE**[1] a. [f. OF *alabastre* f. L *alabaster* f. Gk *alabast(r)os*, etym. dub.]

à la carte, adv. By the bill of fare. [F]

ala·ck, int. (archaic) expressing regret or surprise, esp. in phr. *alack-a-day.* [perh. f. *a* int. + *lak* LACK]

ala·crity, n. Briskness, cheerful readiness. [f. L *alacritas* (*alacer* brisk, see -TY)]

Ala·ddin's lamp, n. Talisman enabling holder to gratify any wish. [*Arabian Nights*]

ă·lamode, *à la mode*, adv. & a. In the fashion, fashionable; *a. beef*, scraps of beef boiled down into stew; *a. silk* (also as n., *alamode*), a thin glossy black silk. [F (*à la m.*), = in the fashion]

ā·lar, a. Pertaining to wings; winglike, wing-shaped; (Bot. & Physiol.) axillary. [f. L *alaris* (*ala* wing, see -AR[1])]

alar·m[1], n. Call to arms; warning sound giving notice of danger; warning, as *give, take, the a.*; excited anticipation of danger; (Fencing) stamp on ground made with advancing foot; *a.-post*, place for troops to assemble at in case of alarm; mechanism that sounds the alarm (usu. *ală·rum*); *alarum-clock*, one with apparatus that rings at appointed hour; *alar(u)ms and excursions* (facet.), noise and bustle. [f. OF *alarme* f. It. *allarme* (*all'arme!* to arms); form *alarum* now only of alarm-signal]

alar·m[2], v.t. Arouse to sense of danger; disturb; agitate, excite with fear. Hence **alar·mingly** adv. [f. prec.]

alar·mist, n. One who raises alarms on slight grounds (often attrib., as *these a. reports*); panic-monger. So **alar·mISM** n. [ALARM n. + -IST]

alarum, n. See ALARM n.

ā·lary, a. Pertaining to wings or wing-like parts. [f. L *alarius* (*ala* wing, see -ARY[1])]

ala·s, int. expressing grief, pity, concern. [f. OF *ha las* (mod. F *hélas*) f. *ha* ah + *las lasse* wretched f. L *lassus* weary]

Ala·stor, n. Avenging deity, nemesis. [Gk (*a-* not + *last-* f. *lath-* forget)]

ā·late(d), a. Having wings or winglike appendages. [f. L *alatus* (*ala* wing, see -ATE[2])]

alb, n. White vestment reaching to feet, worn by priests, and by some consecrated kings. [f. LL *alba* (*tunica*) white (tunic)]

a·lbacore, n. Large species of Tunny; other fish of same genus. [f. Port. *albacor* (F *albicore*, also used in E) f. Arab. *al* the + *bukr* young camel, heifer]

albā·ta, n. White metal, German silver. [f. L *albata* whitened (*albus* white)]

a·lbatross, n. Family of birds allied to Petrels, inhabiting Pacific and Southern Oceans; esp. *great A.*, largest of sea-fowls. [17th-c. *algatross*, perh. f. obs. *alcatras* Frigate-bird (f. Sp. and Port. *alcatruz* f. Arab. *alqadus* the bucket, Arab. name of Pelican, from its supposed water-carrying habit); *-b-* under influence of L *albus* white]

albē·it (awl-), conj. Though, as *a. that he failed, a. he failed, he tried a. without success.* [= all though it be that]

a·lbert, n. (Also *A. chain*) kind of watch-chain. [f. Prince *Albert* consort of Queen Victoria]

Albert Hall, in Kensington, used for concerts, demonstrations, &c. [as prec.]

albe·scent, a. Growing white, shading into white. [f. L *albescere* (*albus* white), see -ENT]

Ălbigĕ·nsēs, n.pl. Heretics of 12th–14th cc. in S. France persecuted for criticism of clerical corruptions. [L *Albiga* Albi in S. France, -ESE]

albi·no (-bē-), n. Human being marked by congenital absence of colouring pigment in skin and hair, which are white, and eyes, which are pink and unable to bear ordinary light; any animal so distinguished; plant lacking the normal colouring. Hence **albi·nESS**[1], **a·lbĭnISM,** nn. [Port., orig. of white negroes, f. L *albus* white]

a·lbite, n. White or soda feldspar. [f. L *albus* white + -ITE[1]]

a·lbum, n. Blank book for insertion of autographs, photographs, &c. [L, neut. sing. of *albus* white]

albū·men, n. White of egg; a constituent of animal solids and fluids, of seeds, and of tuberous or fleshy roots, found nearly pure in white of egg; (Bot.) substance found between skin and embryo of many seeds, usu. the eatable part. Hence **albu·minOSE, albu·minOUS,** aa. [L *albumen -minis* white of egg (*albus* white, see -MEN]

albu·menize, v.t. (phot.). Coat (paper) with an albuminous solution. [prec. + -IZE]

albu·minoid, a. & n. Like albumen; (n. pl.) proteids, class of organic compounds forming chief part of organs and tissues of animals and plants. Hence **albuminoi·dAL** a. [f. ALBUMEN + -OID]

albur·num, a·lburn, n. Recently formed wood in exogenous trees, sap-wood. Hence **albur·nous** a. [L *alburnum* (*albus* white)]

alcahest. See ALKAHEST.

Alcā·ic, a. & n. Pertaining to Alcaeus (Gk lyric poet, 600 B.C.), or to the metre he invented; (n. pl.) Alcaic strophes. [f. L f. Gk *Alkaikos* (*Alkaios*)]

alchĕ·mic, a. Pertaining to alchemy. Hence **alche·mical** a., **alche·mically**[2] adv. [f. med. L. *alchimicus* or F *alchimique*: see ALCHEMY and -IC]

a·lchemist, n. One who studies or practises alchemy. Hence **alchemi·stic(al)** aa. [f. OF *alquemiste*; see ALCHEMY and -IST]

a·lchemize, v.t. Change as by alchemy; transmute. [back-formation on prec.]

a·lchemy (-k-), n. Chemistry of the middle ages; esp., pursuit of the transmutation of baser metals into gold (also fig.). [f. OF *alquimie* f. med. L *alchimia* f. Arab. *al-kimia, al* the + *kimia*, apparently = *khemia* (Gk form of native name of Egypt, but confused with Gk *khumeia* pouring f. *khu-* perf. st. of *kheō* pour, whence the spelling *alchymy*)]

a·lcohŏl, n. Pure spirit of wine; any liquor containing this; (Chem.) large class of compounds of same type as spirits of wine. Hence **a·lcoholate**[1](3) n., **alcoho·lic** a. [med. L, f. Arab. *al* the + *koh'l* powder for staining eyelids (*kahala* v. stain)]

a·lcoholism, n. Action of alcohol on human system. [prec. + -ISM]

a·lcoholize, v.t. Saturate with alcohol; subject to alcoholic influence. Hence **alcoholiza·tion** n. [ALCOHOL + -IZE]

alcoholo·meter, n. Instrument for measuring alcoholic strength of spirits. Hence **alcoholo·metry** n. [f. ALCOHOL + -O- + METER]

Alcoran (ă·lkorahn, ălkorah·n), n. Koran, sacred Mohammedan book. Hence **Alcorā·nic** a. [(thr. F) f. Arab. *al-qoran* the reading (*qara'a* v. read)]

a·lcōve, n. Vaulted recess in room-wall, esp. (in Spain) recess for bed; recess in garden wall or hedge; summer-house. [F, f. Sp. *alcova, -ba*, f. Arab. *al-qobbah* the vault (*qubba* v. vault)]

a·ldehyde, n. Colourless volatile fluid of suffocating smell, obtained by oxidation of alcohol; class of compounds of this type. Hence **aldehy̆·dic** a. [abbr. of L *alcohol dehydrogenatum* (deprived of hydrogen)]

a·lder (awl-), n. Tree related to Birch; other trees not related, as *Black, White, Red, A.* [OE *alor, aler* (cf. ON *ölr, elrir*, OHG *elira*, mod. G *erle, eller*) w. phonetic *d*]

a·lderman (awl-), n. Magistrate in English and Irish cities and boroughs, next in dignity to Mayor. Hence **aldermă·nic** a., **a·ldermanship** n. [f. OE *aldor* patriarch (*ald* old + *-or* noun suf.) + -MAN]

a·ldermanry, n. Ward, district of a borough having its own alderman; rank of alderman. [prec. + -RY]

A·ldershot (awl-), n. (Used for) the permanent military camp at A. in Hampshire.

A·ldine (awl-), a. Printed by Aldus Manutius, Venetian printer of 16th cent.; name of certain style of type. [f. *Aldus* + -INE[1]]

ale, n. Liquor made from an infusion of malt by fermentation, flavoured with hops &c.; merry-making at which ale was drunk; *alecost*, costmary; *a.-house*, one at which ale is retailed; *a.-wife*, woman who keeps an alehouse, American fish allied to herring. [OE *alu*]

ā·lĕatory, a. Depending on the throw of a die or on chance. [f. L *aleatorius* (*aleator* dice-player f. *alea* die)]

alee·, adv. & pred. a. On the lee or sheltered side of ship; to leeward. [f. ON *á* on + *hlé* shelter; see LEE]

ā·lĕgar, n. Sour ale; malt vinegar. [f. ALE + *egre* = F *aigre* sour, on anal. of *vinegar*]

ale·mbic, n. Apparatus formerly used in distilling; also fig., as *a. of fancy.* [f. F *alambic* f. Arab. *al* the + *ambig* still f. Gk *ambix -ikos* cup; *lembick, limbeck*, were usu. in 15–17th cc.]

aler·t, a. & n. Watchful, vigilant; lively, nimble; (n.) warning call, alarm; *on the a.*, on the look-out. Hence **aler·tly**[2] adv., **aler·tness** n. [f. F *alerte*, earlier *allerte, à l'airte*, f. It. *all'erta* (*alla* to the + *erta* look-out, watch-tower, fem. p.p. of *ergere* f. L *erigere* ERECT)]

aleur·on, aleur·one, n. Albuminoid substance found in seeds of plants &c. [Gk *aleuron* flour]

Alexa·ndrine, a. & n. *A. (verse)*, iambic line of six feet or twelve syllables. [f. F *alexandrin*, of doubtful orig.]

alexiphar·mic, a. & n. (Having the quality of) an antidote. [earlier *-ac* f. F *alexipharmaque* f. Gk *alexipharmakon* remedy for poison (*alexō* keep off + *pharmakon* poison)]

alfre·sco, adv. & a. In the open air; open-air, as *a. lunch.* [f. It. *al fresco* in the fresh (air)]

a·lga, n. (pl. *-ae*). Sea-weed. Hence **a·lgal, a·lgoid, algolo·gical,** aa., **a·lgist** (3) (-j-), **algo·logist, algo·logy,** nn. [L]

a·lgebra, n. Investigation of the properties of numbers by means of general symbols; *quadruple a.*, quaternions. Hence **algebrā·ic(al)** aa., **algebra·ically**[2] adv., **a·lgebrāist, a·lgebrist,** nn. [It., f. Arab. *aljebr* reunion of broken parts (*jabara* reunite)]

a·lgid (-j-), a. Cold, esp. of cold stage of ague. Hence **algi·dity** n. [f. F *algide* f. L *algidus* (*algēre* be cold, see -ID[1])]

a·lgorism, n. Arabic (decimal) notation; *cipher in a.*, 0, mere dummy. [f. OF *augorisme* f. med. L *algorismus* f. Arab. *al-Khowarazmi* the man of Khiva, surname of a mathematician; mod. misspelling *-ithm* by confus. w. Gk *arithmos* number]

alguazi·l (-gw*a*-), n. Spanish warrant-officer or sergeant. [Sp. (now *-cil*) f. Arab. *al-wazir* the vizier, minister (*wazara* carry on)]

a·lgum, n. Tree mentioned in Bible (2 *Chron.* ii. 8; in 1 *Kings* x. 11 wrongly given as *almug*), prob. a kind of sandal-wood. [Heb.; a foreign word perh. = Skr. *valguka* sandal-wood tree]

Alha·mbra, n. Palace of Moorish kings at Granada. Hence **alhambr**ESQUE a. [f. Arab. *al-hamra'* the red house]

ā·lias, adv. & n. (pl. *-ases*). (Name by which one is called) on other occasions. [L, adv.]

ă·lĭbi, adv. & n. (The plea that when an alleged act took place one was) elsewhere. [L, adv.; old locative of *alius* another]

ă·lidăd, -ade, n. Index of astrolabe, quadrant, &c., showing the degrees cut off on the arc. [F (*-ade*), f. med. L *alhidada* f. Arab. *al-'idadah* the revolving radius ('*add* upper arm)]

ā·lien[1], a. & n. Not one's own; foreign, under foreign allegiance; differing in nature (*from*); repugnant (*to*); stranger; non-naturalized foreigner; one excluded *from*; (Law) *a.-friend, -enemy,* alien owing allegiance to friendly, hostile, country. Hence **a·lien**ISM(2) n., study and treatment of mental diseases, **a·lien**IST n., mad-doctor. [OF, f. L *alienus* belonging to another (*alius*)]

ā·lien[2], v.t. (Poet.) estrange; (Law) transfer ownership of. Hence **a·lien**ABLE a., **aliena**BI·LITY n. [f. OF *aliéner* f. L *alienare* (as prec.)]

ā·lienate, v.t. Estrange; transfer ownership of; turn away, divert (*from*). Hence **a·lienator**[2] n. [f. L as prec., see -ATE[2]]

aliena·tion, n. Estrangement; transference of ownership; diversion to different purpose; (*mental*) *a.*, insanity. [f. MF *aliénacion* f. L *alienationem* (as prec., see -ATION)]

alienee·, n. One to whom transfer to property is made. [ALIEN[2] + -EE]

ā·liform, a. Wing-shaped. [f. L *ala* wing + -FORM]

alīgh·t[1], v.i. Dismount (*from* horse), descend (*from* carriage); settle, come to earth, from the air. [OE *alihtan* (A- (1) + *lihtan* light)]

alīgh·t[2], a. Kindled; on fire; lighted up. [p.p. of obs. *alight* kindle; now only used predicatively, on anal. of *a-blaze* and other adv. compds]

alīg·n, alī·ne, v.t. & i. Place, lay, in a line; bring into line; esp. bring three or more points into a straight line, as *a. the sights* (of rifle) *and bull's-eye*; (intr.) form in line (as troops). Hence **alig·n**MENT n. [f. F *aligner* (*à* to + *ligner* f. L *lineare* (*linea* line)]

alī·ke, pred. a. & adv. Similar, like; (adv.) in like manner. [OE *gelic* a. *gelice* adv. (OHG *gelîh*, mod. G *gleich*) f. *ge-* together + *lic* LIKE; also f. ON *alikr* a. *alika* adv. (cogn. w. OE *anlic* a. *anlice* adv.) f. *a* prep. on, to, + *lik* like]

ă·liment, n. Food; (fig.) support, mental sustenance. Hence **alime·nt**AL a., **alime·ntal**LY[2] adv. [f. L *alimentum* (*alere* nourish, see -MENT)]

alime·ntary, a. Nourishing; performing functions of nutrition, as *a. canal*; providing maintenance. [f. L *alimentarius* (as prec., see -ARY[1])]

alimenta·tion, n. Nourishment; maintenance. [f. med. L *alimentatio* (*alimentare*, as ALIMENT, see -ATION)]

ă·limony, n. Nourishment; maintenance; allowance due to wife from husband's estate, on separation from certain causes. [f. L *alimonia* nutriment (*alere* nourish, see -MONY)]

ă·liquot, a. & n. *A.* (*part*), part contained by the whole an integral number of times, integral factor. [f. F *aliquote* f. L *aliquot* some, so many]

-ality, compd noun-suf. = -AL + -TY. Quality, or instance of it, (*generality, a g.*)

alī·ve, adv. & pred. a. In life, living; fully susceptible *to* (an idea &c.); active, brisk, as (colloq.) *look a.*, be brisk; swarming *with*, as *river a. with boats*; *any man a.* (whatever); *man a.!* (colloq. expletive). [f. A prep. + ME *live*, OE *life* dat. of *lif* LIFE; = on life]

ali·zarin, n. Red colouring matter of madder. [f. F *alizari* madder prob. f. Arab. *al* the + *'açarah* extract (*'açara* v. press); see -IN]

a·lkahest, n. Alchemist's supposed universal solvent (also fig.). [sham Arab., prob. invented by Paracelsus]

alkale·scent, a. & n. Incipiently or slightly alkaline (substance). Hence **alkale·sc**ENCE, **alkale·sc**ENCY, nn. [f. foll., see -ESCENT]

a·lkalī, n. (pl. *-lis, -lies*). (Chem.) series of compounds called bases, including soda, potash, and ammonia, highly soluble in water, producing caustic or corrosive solutions that neutralize strong acids, and turn vegetable yellows to brown, reds to blue, purples to green; (Commerc.) caustic soda, caustic potash, other alkaline products. Hence **a·lkalifi·**ABLE a., **a·lkali**FY v.t. [f. F *alcali* f. Arab. *al-qaliy* calcined ashes (*qalay* fry)]

alkali·metry, n. Measurement of strength of alkalis. Hence **alkalime·tr**ICAL a. [ALKALI + -METRY]

a·lkalīne, a. Of alkalis; of the nature of an alkali; *a. metals*, those whose hydroxides are alkalis. [f. ALKALI + -INE[1]]

a·lkaloid, n. Nitrogenous basic substance; esp. *vegeto-alkaloids,* vegetable alkalis. Hence **alkaloi·dAL** a. [f. ALKALI + -OID]

a·lkanet, n. (Plant whose root yields) a red dye. [f. Sp. *alcana* (f. Arab. *al-henna* the henna shrub) + dim. suf. to dist. this shrub from henna]

all (awl), a., n., adv. (1) (adj. w. noun &c. expressed or understood). The entire, as *a. day, a. England, a. his life, a. this, take it a., a. whom I saw*; the greatest possible, as *a. speed*; (w. pl.) the entire number of, as *a. men, a. the others*; *a. kind of,* every kind of; any whatever, as *renounce a. connexion*; *a. the* TIME¹. (2) (n.). All men, as *a. are agreed*; (w. *of*) the whole, every one, as *a. of it, a. of you*; everything, as *that is a., a. is lost*; one's whole property, as *he lost his a.*; *a. but,* everything short of (used adv.), as *a. but impossible, he was a. but drowned*; *a. in a.,* of paramount or exclusive importance; *at a.,* in any way, as *not at a., did you speak at a.?* (not in affirmative sent.); *in a.,* in total number; *one and a., a. and some* (archaic), *a. and sundry,* a. individually and collectively; *a. along of* (vulg.), owing to; *a. very fine* or *well* (colloq. form of dissatisfaction, as *a. v. f., but I shall stand it no longer*); *a. one,* just the same (*it is a. o. to me*). (3) (adv.). Wholly, quite, as *dressed a.* (orig. an adj.) *in white, a. covered with mud, a. the better, a. at once, a. too soon*; *a. red,* (of cable, line, &c.) British throughout; *all right,* (adv.) satisfactorily, as desired, (pred. a.) safe and sound, in good state, satisfactory, (sent.) I consent, all is well, (also iron. in threats, as *A. r.! you shall repent this*); *a. there,* sane, in one's senses, (*is he a. t.? not quite a. t.*); *a. the same,* just the same, without any difference or any that matters, (*it 's a. t. s. to me whether he goes or not*; *if it 's a. t. s. to you,* if you don't mind), in spite of this, notwithstanding, however, (was *punished a. t. s.,* in spite of extenuating circumstances &c.; *a. t. s., I wish you hadn't done it*). (4) Combb.: *A.-father,* Odin, God; *A. Fools' Day,* first of April; *All Hallows* (archaic), *A. Saints' Day,* general celebration of saints, November 1st; *A. Souls' Day,* day of supplication for souls of faithful deceased, Nov. 2nd. *All* is prefixed to many adjj., as *a.-bountiful, a.-righteous, a.-sufficient,* and esp. to partt., as *a.-sufficing, a.-seeing, a.-knowing.* [com.-Teut.: OHG *al,* ON *allr*]

A·llah, n. Name of God among Mohammedans. [Arab. *allah* contr. of *al-ilah* (*al* the + *ilah* god = Heb. *eloah*]

allay·, v.t. Put down, repress; alleviate (pain &c.); diminish (pleasure &c.). [f. A- (1) + LAY v.; confused with obs. *allege* alleviate and obs. *allay* alloy]

allega·tion, n. Alleging; assertion (esp. one not proved). [f. F *allégation* f. L *allegationem* (*allegare* allege, see -ATION)]

alle·ge (-ĕj), v.t. Affirm; advance as argument or excuse. [f. *adlegiare* E Latiniz. of OF *esligier,* Norm. *alegier,* f. LL *exlitigare* clear at law; but treated as repr. L *allegare* cite, adduce, which would give *alleague* (cf. F *alléguer*)]

allē·giance (-jans), n. Duty of subject to sovereign or government; loyalty (lit. and fig.). [ME *ligeaunce* f. OF *ligeance* (LIEGE); *a-* added in E perh. thr. confusion with obs. *allegeance,* n. f. prec.]

allegŏ·ric, a. Pertaining to, of the nature of, allegory. Hence **allego·ricAL** a., **allego·ricalLY²** adv. [f. F f. L f. Gk *allēgorikos* (as foll., see -IC)]

a·llegorize, v.t. & i. Treat as an allegory; make allegories. Hence **a·llegorIST** n. [f. F *allégoriser* f. L *allegorizare* (as foll., see -IZE)]

ă·llegory, n. Narrative description of a subject under guise of another suggestively similar; emblem. [f. L f. Gk *allēgoria* (*allos* other + *-agoria* speaking f. *agora* assembly)]

allegre·tto (mus.). Somewhat briskly. [It.]

alle·gro (-lā-), a., adv., n. (mus.). Lively, gay; (movement) in brisk time. [It.]

allelu·ia (-lōōya), n. Song of praise to God. [f. L f. (Septuagint) Gk *allēlouia* f. Heb. *halleluyah* praise ye Jehovah]

allē·viate, v. t. Relieve, mitigate. Hence **alleviA·TION, alle·viatOR²,** nn.; **alle·viaTIVE, alle·viatORY,** aa. [f. L AL*leviare* lighten (*levis* light), see -ATE³]

a·lley, n. (pl. *-eys*). Walk, passage, esp. in park or garden; narrow street; *blind a.,* one closed at end; enclosure for skittles &c. [f. OF *alee,* F *allée,* walking, passage, f. *aller* go, etym. dub.]

Alley·nian (alēn-) n. Member of Dulwich College. [E *Alleyn,* founder]

All-ha·llow(s), n. All saints (in heaven), as *All hallows' day, Allhallowmass.* [ALL + *hallow* f. OE *hálga* saint]

alliā·ceous, a. Of the genus *Allium,* including garlic, onions, and leeks; smelling, tasting, of garlic &c. [f. L *allium* garlic + -ACEOUS]

alli·ance, n. Union by marriage; relationship; confederation (esp. between States); community in nature or qualities; (Bot.) group of allied Natural Orders. [f. OF *aliance* (as ALLY¹, see -ANCE)]

a·lligator, n. Genus of saurian reptiles of crocodile family, found in America; other large American saurians; *a. apple, pear,* fruit of W. Indian trees; *a. tortoise,* snapping turtle. [corrupt. of Sp. *el lagarto* the lizard f. L *lacerta*]

alli·terate, v.i. (Use words that) begin with the same letter. Hence **alli·teraTIVE** a., **alli·terativeLY²** adv. [f. L *ad* to + *litera* letter + -ATE³, on anal. of *obliterate*]

allitera·tion, n. Commencement of words in close connexion (esp. in early

Teut. poetry, of accented syllables) with the same letter. [f. prec. + -ATION]

a·llocate, v.t. Assign, devote, (*to* person or object); locate. Hence **alloca·tion** n. [f. med. L ALlocare (*locus* place), see -ATE³]

al(l)ō·dium, n. Estate held in absolute ownership, without acknowledgement to a superior (opp. to *feudum*). Hence **allo·dial** a., **allo·dially²** adv., **allo·dialism, allo·-dialist,** nn. [f. med. L f. G **alôd* entire property (ALL + OLG *ôd* estate); sometimes written *allod, allody*]

allo·gamy, n. (bot.). Cross-fertilization. [f. Gk *allos* other + -GAMY]

allo·nge (F), n. Slip of paper gummed to end of bill of exchange to give room for further endorsements.

allŏ·pathy, n. Curing of a diseased action by inducing another action of a different kind (opp. to *homoeopathy*). Hence **allopa·thic** a., **allopa·thically** adv., **allo·pathist** n. [f. Gk *allos* other + -PATHY]

allophȳ·lian, a. & n. (One whose native tongue is) neither Aryan nor Semitic. [f. L f. Gk *allophulos* (*allos* other + *phulē* tribe) + -IAN]

allo·t, v.t. (-tt-). Distribute by lot or with authority; assign (*to*). [f. OF *aloter* (*à* to + *loter* divide by lot f. *lot,* Teut. wd, OE *hlot*)]

a·llotheism, n. Worship of strange gods. [f. Gk *allos* other + *theos* god + -ISM]

allo·tment, n. Apportioning; lot in life; share allotted to one; small portion of land let out for cultivation. [f. F *allotement* (*aloter,* see prec. and -MENT)]

allo·tropy, n. Variation of physical properties without change of substance. Hence **allotro·pic(al)** aa., **allotro·pically²** adv., **allo·tropism** n. [f. Gk *allotropia* f. *allotropos* (*allos* other + *tropos* manner f. *trepō* turn)]

allottee·, n. One to whom allotment is made. [f. ALLOT + -EE]

allow·, v.t. Admit (thing *to* be, *that*); (U.S.) form the opinion (*that*); permit (practice, person *to* do); (refl.) indulge one*self in* (conduct); (intr.) admit *of*; give (limited periodical sum), as *a. him £200 a year*; add, deduct, in consideration of something; *a. for,* take into consideration, make addition or deduction corresponding to; *a. me* (formula in offering services). Hence **allow·able** a., **allow·ably²** adv.; **allow·edly²** adv., admittedly. [f. OF *alouer* f. (1) L ALlaudare praise, (2) L ALlocare place]

allow·ance¹, n. Permission; tolerance (*of*); limited portion, esp. yearly income; deduction, discount; *make a. for,* allow for. [f. OF *alouance* (as prec., see -ANCE)]

allow·ance², v.t. Make allowance to (person); supply (thing) in limited quantities. [f. prec.]

alloy·¹, n. Standard, quality, (of gold or silver); inferior metal mixed esp. with gold or silver (also fig.); mixture of metals. [orig. *allay* f. OF *aley* (F *aloi*) f. *aleier* combine f. L ALligare bind; meaning influenced by confusion with F *à loi* to law]

alloy·², v.t. Mix with baser metal; mix (metals); debase; moderate. [f. F *aloyer* f. OF *aleier,* see prec.]

a·llseed (awl-), n. Name of various plants producing much seed.

a·llspice (awl-), n. Jamaica pepper. Pimenta, supposed to combine flavour of cinnamon, nutmeg, and cloves; other aromatic shrubs, as *Carolina A., Japan A., Wild A.*

allu·de (-ōō-, -ū-), v.i. Refer covertly, indirectly, *to*; (improp.) *a. to,* mean. [f. L AL(*ludere lus-* play)]

allūre·, v.t. Tempt, entice, win over, (*to, from,* person, place, conduct); fascinate, charm. Hence **allure·ment** n. [f. OF *aleurrer* attract (*à* to + *leurrer* LURE)]

allu·sion, n. Covert, implied, indirect, reference (*to*). [f. L *allusio* (as ALLUDE, see -ION)]

allu·sive, a. Containing an allusion (*to*); abounding in allusions; (Her.) *a.* (canting) *arms.* Hence **allu·sively²** adv., **allu·siveness** n. [as prec., see -IVE]

allu·vion (-ōō-, -ū-), n. Wash of sea, river, against shore, banks; flood; matter deposited by flood; (Law) formation of new land by water's action. [F, f. L ALluvionem (nom. *-vio*) f. *luere* wash]

allu·vium, n. Deposit of earth, sand, &c., left by flood. Hence **allu·vial** a. [L, neut. of adj. ALluvius (*luĕre* wash)]

allȳ·¹, v.t. Combine, unite, for special object *to, with,* (esp. of marriage and alliance with foreign states); (of things) *allied to,* connected with. [f. OF *alier* f. L ALligare bind]

allȳ·², n. Person, state, &c., allied with another. [f. prec.]

a·llȳ³, n. Choice playing-marble of marble or alabaster. [perh. dim. of *alabaster*]

a·lma(h), n. Egyptian dancing-girl. [Arab. *'almah* knowing (*'alama* know)]

a·lmagest (-j-), n. Great astronomical treatise of Ptolemy; other books on astrology and alchemy. [f. F f. Arab. *al* the + *majisti* = Gk *megistē* greatest]

A·lma Mā·ter, n. Name used of Universities and schools. [L, = bounteous mother]

a·lmanac (awl-), n. Annual calendar of months and days, with astronomical and other data. [med. L, etym. dub.]

a·lmandine, n. A garnet of violet tint. [corrupt. of obs. *alabandine* f. L *alabandina* (*Alabanda,* city in Caria)]

almigh·ty (awl-), a. All-powerful, esp. *A. God, the A.*; (slang) great, (adv.) exceedingly. Hence **almigh·tiness** n. [OE *ælmeahtig* (ALL adv. + MIGHTY)]

a·lmond (ahm-), n. Kernel of a stone-fruit borne by two trees (*sweet, bitter, a.*) allied to plum and peach; anything a.-shaped; *A.* (*Tumbler*), kind of pigeon. [f. OF *almande* f. L f. Gk *amugdalē*; *al-* perh. by confus. w. Arab. *al* the]

ă·lmoner (*or* ahmn-), n. Official distributor of alms; *Hereditary Grand A., Lord High A.*, (officers in royal household of Great Britain). [f. OF *aumoner* f. LL *almosinarius* = *eleemosynarius* (as ALMS, see -ARY[1])]

a·lmost (awl-), adv. Very nearly (qualifying v., adv., adj.; also noun, as *his a. impudence*). [f. ALL + MOST adv.]

alms (ahmz), n. (usu. as sing.). Charitable relief of the poor; donation; *a.-folk, almsman*, (supported by charity); *a.-giving*; *a.-house*, one founded by charity for reception of poor. [OE *ælmysse* f. L f. Gk *eleēmosunē* compassionateness (*eleēmōn* adj. f. *eleos* compassion)]

a·lmug. See ALGUM.

ă·loe (-ō), n. Genus of plants with erect spikes of flowers and bitter juice; (pl.) purgative drug procured from juice of aloes; other plants, as *American A.*, Agave. [OE *aluwe* f. L f. Gk *aloē*]

aloĕ·tic, a. & n. (Medicine) containing aloes. [f. Gk *aloē* aloe on false anal. of *diuretic* &c.]

alŏ·ft (*or* -aw-), adv. & pred. a. High up (lit. and fig.); upward. [f. ON *á* on, to, + *lopt* sky, loft]

alo·ne, pred. a. & adv. Solitary; standing by oneself (*in* opinion &c); LET, *leave, a.*, abstain from interfering with; (adv.) only, exclusively. [f. ALL adv. + ONE]

alo·ng, adv. & prep. From end to end of; through any part of the length of; onward, as *get a.*; *a. with*, in company with, in conjunction with; *all a.*, all the time; (*all*) *a. of* (vulg.), owing to; *a.-ships*, directed fore and aft; *a.-shore*, a. by the shore, a. and on the shore; *alongside*, close to side of ship; *alongside of*, side by side with (lit. and fig.). [OE *and-lang* (*and-* against, facing, + *lang* long), orig. adj.]

alōō·f, adv. & pred. a. Away, apart, (lit. and fig.), as *stand, keep, hold, a.*; (Naut.) away to windward, as *spring a.* (cf. LUFF). Hence **aloo·f**NESS n. [f. A prep. + LUFF]

alou·d, adv. Loudly; not in a whisper; (colloq.) palpably, as *reeks a.* [f. A prep. + LOUD; cf. foll.]

alow· (-ō), adv. (naut.). In, into, lower part of vessel. [f. A prep. + LOW a.]

alp, n. Mountain-peak; (in Switzerland) green pasture-land on mountain-side; *Alps*, mountain range separating France and Italy. [(pl.) f. L *Alpes* prop. n., etym. dub.]

alpă·ca, n. Kind of llama with long woolly hair; its wool; fabric thence made. [f. Sp. (Arab. *al* the + *paco*, native Peruv. name)]

a·lpenstock, n. Long iron-shod staff used in climbing Alps &c. [G, = stick of the Alps]

a·lpha, n. Greek letter A (Α, α); *A. and Omega*, beginning and end; (Astr.) chief star of constellation. [Gk, f. Heb. *aleph* ox, leader]

a·lphabet, n. Set of letters used in a language; first rudiments. Hence **alphabe·**TIC a. [f. L *alphabetum* (Gk *alpha, bēta*, first two letters of alphabet)]

alphabĕ·tical, a. Of the alphabet, as *a. order*. Hence **alphabe·tical**LY[2] adv. [as prec. + -ICAL]

A·lpine, a. Of the Alps or any lofty mountains. [f. L *Alpinus* (*Alpes*, see ALP and -INE[1])]

A·lpinist, n. Alpine climber. [f. F *alpiniste* (as prec., see -IST)]

alrea·dy (awl-), adv. Beforehand; by this time, thus early. [f. ALL adv. + READY]

Alsa·tia, n. Province west of Rhine, receded by Germany to France 1919; White Friars in London, once sanctuary for lawbreakers. Hence **Alsa·ti**AN a.; *Alsatian* (*wolf-hound*), a breed of dog.

a·lsike, n. Kind of clover. [*Alsike* in Sweden]

a·lso (awl-), adv. In addition, besides; *a. ran* (slang), person(s) &c. that failed to win distinction. [f. ALL + SO; orig. in antecedent and relat. as well as demonstr. functions, now superseded in relat. by its shortened form AS, and in antec. by AS and SO]

alt, n. (Mus.) high tone, esp. *in a.*, in octave above treble stave beginning with G; (fig.) *in a.*, in an exalted frame of mind. [Pr., f. L *altum* high]

a·ltar (awl-), n. Flat-topped block for offerings to deity; Communion Table; *lead to the a.*, marry; *a.-cloth*, (prop.) linen cloth used at Communion or Mass, (loosely) silk frontal and super-frontal; *a.-piece*, reredos, esp. a painting. [f. L *altare* (*altus* high)]

a·ltarwise, adv. In the manner of an altar.

altă·zimuth, n. Instrument for determining altitude and azimuth of heavenly bodies. [*alt-* for *altitude* + AZIMUTH]

a·lter (awl-), v.t. & i. Change in character, position, &c. Hence or cogn. **altera·**BI·LITY, **alter**A·TION, nn., **a·lter**ABLE a. [f. 14th-c. F *altérer* f. med. L *alterare* (L *alter* other)]

a·lterative, a. & n. Tending to alter; (n.) medicine, treatment, that alters processes of nutrition. [prec. + -ATIVE]

a·ltercate (ălt-, awlt-), v.i. Dispute hotly, wrangle, (*with*). So **alterca·**TION n. [f. L *altercari*, see -ATE[3]]

ă·lter ĕ·go, n. One's other self, intimate friend. [L, = second I]

alter·nant, a. & n. Alternating; (Mineral.) of alternating layers; (n.) a. quantity.

[F, part. of *alterner* f. L *alternare* ALTERNATE]

alter·nate[1] (awl-, -*at*), a. (Of things of two kinds) coming each after one of the other kind; (Biol.) *a. generation* (by a. processes, as first by budding, next by sexual reproduction); *a. leaves, angles* (placed alternately on the two sides of stem, line). Hence **alter·nate**LY[2] adv. [f. L *alternare* do one thing after the other (*alternus* every other f. *alter* other), see -ATE[2]]

a·lternāte[2], v.t. & i. Arrange, perform, (two sets of things) alternately; interchange (one thing) alternately *with, by,* another; (of two things) succeed each other by turns; (of a whole) consist of alternate things; (of one class of things) appear alternately with another. So **altern**A·TION n. [f. prec.]

alter·native, a. & n. (Of two things) mutually exclusive; (strictly) permission to choose between two things; (loosely) either of two possible courses, as *I had no* (*other*) *a.*; one of more than two possibilities. Hence **alter·native**LY[2] adv. [f. med. L *alternativus* (as prec., see -ATIVE)]

although· (awl-), conj. Though. [f. ALL adv. + THOUGH]

ălti·meter, n. Aeronautical aneroid for showing height above sea level. [L *altus* high, -METER]

a·ltitude, n. Height; depth; (Geom.) length of perpendicular from vertex to base; height above sea level; (usu. in pl.) high place; (fig.) eminence. [f. L *altitudo* (*altus* high), see -TUDE]

a·lto, n. (mus.). Highest male voice, counter-tenor; its musical part; female voice of similar range, contralto; its part; singer with alto voice; *a.-clarinet, -viola,* instruments similar to the clarinet, viola, but of higher pitch. [It. *alto* (*canto*) high (singing)]

altoge·ther (awl-), adv. & n. Totally; on the whole; (n.) *an a.,* a whole. [ALL a.]

a·lto-relie·vo (-rĭlē·vō), n. (sculp.). High relief. [It. *alto-rilievo*]

a·ltruism, n. Regard for others as a principle of action. Hence **a·ltru**IST n., **altrui·st**IC a., **altrui·st**ICALLY adv. [f. F *altruisme* (It. *altrui* others' f. L *alteri huic* to this other, see -ISM)]

ă·lum, n. A double sulphate of aluminium and potassium; series of salts including this; family of compounds including these; (Mineral.) various native minerals, alums proper and pseudo-alums. [OF, f. L *alumen*]

alu·mina, n. One of the earths, the only oxide of aluminium. [f. L *alumen* alum, on type of *soda* &c.]

ălūmi·nium, n. White light sonorous ductile malleable metal, not oxidized in air, used for instruments and as an alloy; *a. bronze,* alloy of a. and copper. [f ALUMINA; formerly *alumium, aluminum*]

alu·minous, a. Of the nature of alum or alumina. [f. F *alumineux* f. L *aluminosus* (*alumen* ALUM, see -OUS)]

alu·mnus, n. (pl. -*nī*). Pupil of a school or university. [L, = foster-child]

a·lveolate (-*at*), a. Honeycombed, pitted with small cavities. [f. L *alveolatus* f. foll., see -ATE[2]]

alve·olus, n. Small cavity; socket of tooth, whence **alvē·ol**AR[1] a.; cell of honeycomb; conical chamber of a belemnite. [L, dim. of *alveus* cavity]

a·lways (awl-), adv. At all times; on all occasions (*a. excepting, provided,* &c., legal formulae). [f. ALL a. + WAY; *alway* (now archaic or poet. for *always*) orig. meant 'all the way, continually', *always* (gen. case) having prob. the sense 'on every occasion']

am. See BE.

ă·madou (-ōō), n. German tinder, prepared from fungi, used as a match and styptic. [F f. Pr. (OPr. *amador*), f. L *amatorem* lover (*amare,* see -OR[2])]

amai·n, adv. (archaic, poet.). Vehemently; in all haste. [A prep. + *main,* OE *mægn,* force]

ama·lgam, n. Mixture of a metal with mercury, as *gold a.*; plastic mixture of any substances (also fig.). [f. F *amalgame,* med. L *amalgama,* perh. f. L f. Gk *malagma* an emollient (*malassō,* st. *malak-,* soften)]

ama·lgamate[1] (-*at*), a. Combined, esp. of languages. [f. med. L *amalgamare* (as prec., see -ATE[2])]

ama·lgamāte[2], v.t. & i. Mix; unite (classes, societies, ideas); (of metals) combine with mercury. Hence **amalgam**A·TION, **ama·lgamat**OR[2], nn., **ama·lgamāt**IVE a. [f. prec., see -ATE[3]]

amănūe·nsis, n. (pl. -nsēs). One who writes from dictation. [L, adj. used as n., f. (*servus*) *a manu* secretary + -*ensis* belonging to]

ă·marant(h), n. Imaginary unfading flower; genus, including Prince's Feather and Love-lies-bleeding; purple colour. Hence **amara·nt(h)**INE[1] a. [f. F *amarante* f. L f. Gk *amarantos* everlasting, name of a flower (*a-* not + *maran-* st. of *marainō* fade); *h* by confusion with Gk *anthos* flower]

ămary·llis, n. Genus of autumn-flowering bulbous plants. [L, f. Gk *Amarullis,* name of a country girl]

ama·ss, v.t. Heap together; accumulate (esp. riches). [f. 12th-c. F *amasser* (*à* to + *masser* f. *masse* MASS[2])]

ă·mateur (-tūr), n. One who is fond *of*; one who cultivates a thing as a pastime. Hence **amateur·ish** a., **amateur·ish**LY[2] adv., **amateur·ish**NESS, **amateur·**ISM, nn. [F, f. L *amatorem* (*amare* love, see -OR[2])]

ă·mative, a. Disposed to loving. Hence **a·mative**NESS n. [f. L *amare* love, see -ATIVE]

ă·matol, n. A high explosive. [f. am(monia) + (trinitro)tol(uol); see TOLU]
a·matory, a. Pertaining to a lover or to sexual love. Hence **amator·**IAL a. [f. L *amatorius* (*amare* love, see -ORY)]
amaurō·sis, n. Partial or total loss of sight from disease of optic nerve. Hence **amaurŏ·**TIC a. [Gk, f. *amauroō* darken (*amauros* dark), see -OSIS]
ama·ze[1], v.t. Overwhelm with wonder. Hence **ama·zĕd**LY[2], **ama·zing**LY[2], advv., **ama·ze**MENT n. [A- (1) + *maze* v., etym. dub.]
ama·ze[2], n. (poet.). = AMAZEMENT. [f. prec.]
A·mazon (ă-), n. Fabulous race of female warriors in Scythia; female warrior (lit. and fig.); masculine woman. Hence **Amazō·n**IAN a. [f. L f. Gk (prob. foreign word, but explained by Greeks as *a-* not + *mazos* breast, from destruction of right breast to facilitate use of bow)]
ambā·ges (-jēz), n. pl. Roundabout ways. [L (*amb-* about + *ag-* f. *agere* drive; 16th-c. E had *a·mbage*, pl. *a·mbages*]
amba·ssador, n. Minister sent by one sovereign or State on mission to another (usu. *A. extraordinary*); minister permanently representing sovereign or State at foreign court (*Ordinary, Resident, A.*; formerly *A. Leger*); *A. Plenipotentiary* (with full power to sign treaties &c.); official messenger. Hence **ambassador·ial** a. [f. F *ambassadeur* f. OSp. *ambaxador* f. med. L **ambactiator* agent-noun of *ambactiare* f. *ambactia* office f. Celt. *ambactus* servant (*ambi* about + *ag-* drive, cogn. w. L *agere*)]
amba·ssadress, n. Female ambassador; ambassador's wife. [f. prec. + -ESS[1]]
a·mber, n. Yellow translucent fossil resin, found chiefly on S. shore of Baltic; *a. Fauna, Flora,* animals, plants, of which remains are found in a. [f. F *ambre* f. Arab. *'anbar* ambergris, to which the name orig. belonged]
a·mbergris (-ēs), n. Wax-like substance found floating in tropical seas, and in intestines of sperm-whale, odoriferous and used in perfumery, formerly in cookery. [f. F *ambre gris* grey amber]
ambide·xter, a. & n. (Person) able to use left hand as well as right; double-dealing. Hence **ambidextĕ·**RITY n. [med. L (*amb-* on both sides + *dexter* right-handed]
ambide·xt(e)rous, a. = prec. Hence **ambide·xtrous**LY[2] adv., **ambide·xtrous**NESS n. [as prec. + -OUS]
a·mbient, a. Surrounding, circumfused. [f. L *ambiens -entis* part. of *ambire* go about (*amb-* on both sides + *ire* go)]
ambigū·ity, n. Double meaning; expression capable of more than one meaning. [f. med. L *ambiguitas* (as foll., see -TY)]
ambi·guous, a. Obscure; of double meaning; of doubtful classification; of uncertain issue. Hence **ambi·guous**LY[2] adv., **ambi·guous**NESS n. [f. L *ambiguus* doubtful f. *ambigere* (*amb-* both ways + *agere* drive) + -OUS]
a·mbit, n. Precincts; bounds; compass, extent. [f. L *ambitus* a going round (*ambire,* see AMBIENT)]
ambi·tion, n. Ardent desire for distinction; aspiration (*to* be, *to* do); object of such desire. [F, f. L *ambitionem* (*ambire -it-*, canvass for votes, see AMBIENT and -ION)]
ambi·tious, a. Full of ambition; strongly desirous (*of* a thing, *to* do); showing ambition, as *an a. attempt.* Hence **ambi·tious**LY[2] adv., **ambi·tious**NESS n. [f. L *ambitiosus* (as prec., see -OUS)]
a·mble[1], v.i. (Of horses &c.) move by lifting two feet on one side together; ride an ambling horse, ride at an easy pace; move in a way suggesting an ambling horse. [f. F *ambler* f. L *ambulare* walk]
a·mble[2], n. Pace of an ambling horse; easy pace. [f. F *amble* f. *ambler,* see prec.]
amblyō·pia, n. Impaired vision. Hence **amblyŏ·**PIC a. [Gk, f. *ambluōpos* a. (*amblus* dull + *ōps ōpos* eye)]
a·mbo, n. (pl. *-bos, -bo·nēs*). Pulpit in early Christian churches. [LL, f. Gk *ambōn*]
amboy·na(wood), n. Finely marked wood of an Asiatic tree. [*Amboyna* Island]
ambrō·sia (-zĭa, -zhya), n. (Myth.) food of the gods; anything delightful to taste or smell; bee-bread. [f. L f. Gk, fem. of *ambrosios* of the immortals f. *ambrotos* (*a-* not + (*m*)*brotos* mortal)]
ambro·sial (-zĭal, -zhyal), a. Divinely fragrant; divine. Hence **ambro·sial**LY[2] adv. [f. L f. Gk *ambrosios,* see prec. and -AL]
a·mbry, n. (archaic). Pantry; wall-press; dresser; closed recess in wall of church. [f. L *armarium* tool-chest (*arma* tools, see -ARY[1]), with *l* for *r* by dissim., and phonetic *-b-*]
ambs-a·ce (ămz-), n. Both aces, lowest throw at dice; bad luck; worthlessness. [f. OF *ambes as* f. L *ambas as,* see ACE; also written *ames-*]
a·mbulance, n. Moving hospital following army; conveyance for sick or wounded persons. [F (L *ambulare* walk, see -ANCE)]
a·mbulatory, a. & n. Pertaining to walking; adapted for walking; movable; not permanent. (N.) place for walking; arcade, cloister. [f. L *ambulatorius* (as prec., see -ORY)]
ambusca·de[1], n. Ambush. [f. F *embuscade* f. It. *imboscata* or Sp. *emboscada* (*imboscare,* see AMBUSH v. and -ADE]
ambusca·de[2], v.t. & i. Lie, conceal, in ambush. [f. prec.]
a·mbush[1] (-ŏŏ-), n. Concealment of troops, troops concealed, in a wood &c.;

(generally) lying in wait; *make, lay, an a., lie in a.* [f. OF *embusche* (as foll.); *am-* perh. due to *ambages*]
a·mbush², v.t. & i. Conceal (troops, only in p.p.); lie in wait for; (intr.) lie in wait. [f. OF *embuscher* (Sp. *emboscar*, It. *imboscare*) f. LL *IMBOSCARE (*boscus* BUSH); see prec.]
âme damnée (ahm dahnā·), n. Tool, devoted adherent. [F]
ameer·, amir· (-ēr), n. Title of various Mohammedan rulers in Scinde and Afghanistan. [Arab. *amir* commander (*amara* command)]
amē·liorate, v.t. & i. (Cause to) become better. Hence **amelioraA·TION, ame·lioratoR²**, nn., **ame·liorativE** a. [f. F *améliorer* f. OF *ameillorer* (*à* to + *meillorer* f. L *meliorare* f. *melior* better)]
ame·n (ā-, ah-), int. So be it. [f. L f. Gk f. Heb. *amen* certainty, certainly (*aman* strength)]
amē·nable, a. (Of persons) responsible (*to* law &c. or abs.); (of things) liable *to*; capable of being tested by (*to*); responsive, tractable. Hence **amenaBI·LITY, ame·nableNESS**, nn., **ame·nabLY²** adv. [AF, f. *amener* bring to (*à* to + *mener* bring f. L *minare* threaten), see -ABLE]
ame·nd, v.i. & t. Abandon evil ways; (archaic) improve in health; correct an error in (legal document), make professed improvements in (measure before Parliament); make better. Hence **ame·ndABLE** a., **ame·ndMENT** n. [f. OF *amender* f. L EMENDARE free from faults (*menda* fault)]
amende honorable (F), n. Public apology and reparation.
ame·nds, n. Reparation, restitution, compensation, as *make a.* [f. OF *amendes* penalties, fine, pl. of *amende* reparation f. *amender* AMEND; pl. now treated in E as sing.]
amē·nity, n. Pleasantness (of places, persons, &c.); (pl.) pleasant ways. [f. L *amoenitas* (*amoenus* conn. w. *amare* love, see -TY)]
ā me·nsa et tŏ·ro, adv. From board and bed. [L]
ame·ntum, ame·nt, n. Catkin. Hence **ămentA·CEOUS, amenti·FEROUS, ame·ntiFORM**, aa. [L, = thong]
amer·ce, v.t. Fine; (loosely) punish. Hence **amer·ciABLE** a., **amer·ceMENT, amer·ciaMENT**, nn. [orig. *amercy* f. AF *amercier* (*à* at + *merci* MERCY)]
Ame·rican, a. & n. Belonging to continent of America or to United States. (N.) native of America of European descent; citizen of United States; *A. cloth, leather,* glazed cloth used for covering tables &c. [-AN]
Ame·ricanism, n. Word or phrase peculiar to or extending from United States; attachment to, sympathy with, United States. [prec. + -ISM]
Ame·ricanize, v.t. & i. Naturalize as an American; make American in character; become American in character; use Americanisms. [as prec. + -IZE]
ames-ace. See AMBS-ACE.
ă·methyst, n. Precious stone, kind of quartz, purple or violet; *Oriental A.*, rare violet variety of sapphire. Hence **amethy·sTINE¹** a. [f. OF *ametiste* f. L f. Gk *amethustos* not drunken (*a-* not + vbl adj. f. *methuskō* intoxicate f. *methu* wine), the stone being supposed to prevent intoxication]
ā·miable, a. Feeling and inspiring friendliness; lovable. Hence **amiaBI·LITY, a·miableNESS**, nn., **a·miabLY²** adv. [OF, f. L *amicabilis* AMICABLE; confused with OF *amable* (mod. F *aimable*) f. L *amabilis* lovable (*amare* love, see -BLE)]
amia·nt(h)us, n. Mineral, variety of asbestos, splitting into flexible fibres; green fibrous chrysolite. [L, f. Gk *amiantos* undefiled (*a-* not + vbl adj. f. *miainō*), i.e. purified by fire, being incombustible; for *-h-* cf. AMARANTH]
ă·mic, a. (chem.). Pertaining to ammonia. [f. AMMONIA + -IC]
ă·micable, a. Friendly; done in a friendly spirit. Hence **amicaBI·LITY, a·micableNESS**, nn., **a·micabLY²** adv. [f. L *amicabilis* (*amicare* make friendly f. *amicus,* see -BLE)]
ă·mice¹, n. Square of white linen worn by celebrant priests, formerly on head, now on shoulders. [earlier *amyt* f. OF *amit* f. L *amictus* garment; *-ce,* or *-s,* perh. due to confus. w. foll.]
ă·mice², n. Cap, hood, cape, of religious orders; badge worn by French canons on left arm. [f. OF *aumusse,* perh. f. Arab. *al* the + G *mütze* cap; early confused w. prec.]
amī·cus cūr·iae, n. Friend of the court, disinterested adviser. [L]
ami·d, ami·dst, prep. In the middle of (lit. and fig.); in the course of. [OE *on middan* (dat. of *mid*) in the middle, followed by genitive; see also -ES]
ă·midin, n. Soluble matter of starch; starch in state of solution. [f. *amid-* com.-Rom. form of L *amylum* starch + -IN]
ami·dships, adv. In middle of ship. [f. AMID + SHIP + -ES]
amir, n. See AMEER.
ami·ss, adv. & pred. a. Not up to the mark; out of order; wrongly; untowardly, as *come a.*; *take a.*, take offence at; *not a.*, appropriate. [A prep. + MISS n.]
ă·mity, n. Friendship, friendly relations. [f. F *amitié,* earlier *amisté,* f. pop. L *amicitatem* (*amicus* friend, see -TY)]
a·mmeter, n. Instrument for measuring force of electric currents. [f. AM(PERE) + -METER]
ammō·nia, n. A colourless gas with pungent smell and strong alkaline reaction, spirit of hartshorn; (Chem.)

large series of compounds, analogous to ammonia; *Liquid A.*, solution of a. in water. [f. foll.]

ammo·niac, a. & n. Of the nature of ammonia; *Sal A.*, hard white crystalline salt, said to have been prepared from camels' dung near temple of Jupiter Ammon; *Gum A.* (also *A.*), a gum resin used in medicine and as cement. Hence **ammonī·ac**AL a. [F, f. L f. Gk *ammōniakon* belonging to Ammon]

ammo·niated, a. Combined with ammonia. [f. prec. + -ATE[1] (3) + -ED[1]]

a·mmonite, n. Fossil genus of Cephalopods. [after med. L *cornu Ammonis* horn of (Jupiter) Ammon, see -ITE[1] (2)]

ammūni·tion, n. Military stores (formerly of all kinds, now of powder, shot, shell, &c.): *a. boots, bread, hat* (supplied to soldiers). [f. F *amunition*, vulg. *amonition*, by confus. of *la munition* (see MUNITION) with *l'amonition*]

amnē·sia, n. Loss of memory. [Gk, = forgetfulness]

a·mnesty, n., & v.t. Intentional overlooking; act of oblivion, general pardon; (v.t.) give a. to. [f. L f. Gk *amnēstia* oblivion f. *amnēstos* a. (*a-* not + *mnē-* remember)]

a·mnion, n. (pl. *-ia*). Innermost membrane enclosing foetus before birth. [Gk, = caul (dim. of *amnos* lamb)]

amoe·ba (*amē-*), n. Microscopic animalcule perpetually changing shape. Hence **amoe·bi**FORM, **amoe·b**OID, aa. [f. Gk *amoibē* change]

amoebae·an, a. Alternately answering. [f. L f. Gk *amoibaios* interchanging (*amoibē* change), see -AN]

amo·ng, amo·ngst (*amŭ-*), prep. In the assemblage of, surrounded by; in the number of; within the limits of (collectively or distributively), as *five shillings a. us, divided a. us*; in comparison with, as *one a. many*; by joint action of, as *kill him a. you*; reciprocally, as *quarrelled a. themselves.* [OE *on gemang* (*on* in + *gemang* assemblage f. *gemengan* mingle) foll. by gen. case; see -ES]

ā-mŏ·ral, a. Unconcerned with, out of the sphere of, morals, non-moral. [A- (7)]

a·morous, a. Inclined to love; in love; of, pertaining to, love. Hence **a·morous**LY[2] adv., **a·morous**NESS n. [OF, f. L *amorosus* (*amor* love, see -OUS)]

amor·phous, a. Shapeless; anomalous; (Min., Chem.) uncrystallized; unorganized. Hence **amor·ph**ISM, **amor·phous**NESS, nn. [f. Gk *amorphos* shapeless (*a-* not + *morphē* form) + -OUS]

amor·tise, v.t. Alienate in mortmain; extinguish (debt, usu. by means of sinking fund), whence **amortis**A·TION n. [f. F *amortir* (st. *-iss-*) bring to death f. LL* *admortire* (*ad mortem* to death)]

amou·nt[1], v.i. Come *to* (so much); be equivalent (in significance) *to.* [f. OF *amonter* f. *amont* upward (*à mont* hillward f. L *ad montem*)]

amou·nt[2], n. Total to which a thing amounts; full value, significance, &c.; quantity, as *a considerable a.* (*of*). [f. prec.]

amour· (-moor), n. Love-affair; intrigue. [F, = love f. L *amorem*, nom. *-or*, f. *amare*]

amoure·tte (-moor-), n. Petty love-affair. [F, dim. of *amour*]

amour-pro·pre (ă·moor-prŏ·pr), n. Self-esteem. [F]

ampelo·psis, n. Kinds of vine-creeper. [Gk *ampelos* vine, *opsis* appearance]

a·mpere (-ār), n. (electr.). Current that one volt can send through one ohm, unit of current. [name (*Ampère*) of electrician]

ampersa·nd, n. The sign & (*and*, L *et*). (also *ampus-*, *ampassy-*, *ampussy-*, corrupt. of 'and *per se* (= by itself) *and*']

amphi- in comb. Both, of both kinds, on both sides, around. [Gk, prep.]

Amphĭ·bia, n. pl. Division of Vertebrata, intermediate between reptiles and fishes, as frogs, newts, &c. [f. L f. Gk *amphibia* (*zōa*) (animals) living in both elements (AMPHI- + *bios* life)]

amphi·bian, a. & n. (Animal) living both on land and in water; an airplane designed to rise from and alight on either land or water. [as prec. + -AN]

amphibio·logy, n. Branch of zoology treating of Amphibia. [prec. + -LOGY]

amphĭ·bious, a. Living both on land and in water; connected with both land and water; having two lives, connected with two classes, &c. Hence **amphi·bious**LY[2] adv. [f. AMPHIBIA + -OUS]

amphibo·logy, n. Quibble; ambiguous wording. Hence **amphibolo·g**ICAL a. [f. F *amphibologie* f. L f. Gk AMPHI(*bolia* f. *ballō* throw); assim. to words in -LOGY]

Amphi·ctyons, n. pl. Deputies from ancient Greek states forming council. So **Amphictyŏ·n**IC a. [f. Gk *amphiktuones* neighbours]

a·mphigam, n. (bot.). Plant with no distinct sexual organs. Hence **amphi·gam**OUS a. [f. F *amphigame* (AMPHI- + Gk *gamos* marriage)]

amphigour·i (-oorĭ), **a·mphigory,** n. Nonsensical composition. [?]

amphio·xus, n. The fish Lancelet. [f. AMPHI- + Gk *oxus* sharp]

amphi·poda, n. pl. Order of Crustacea, with feet of two kinds. Hence **a·mphipod** n., **amphi·pod**AN, **amphi·pod**OUS, aa. [AMPHI- + Gk *pous podos* foot]

amphi·prostyle, a. With portico at both ends. [F, f. L f. Gk *amphiprostulos* (AMPHI + *prostulos* PROSTYLE)]

amphisbae·na, n. Fabulous serpent with head at each end; (Zool.) genus of worm-like lizards. [L, f. Gk *amphisbaina* (*amphis* both ways + *bainō* go]

a·mphithēatre, n. Oval or circular building, with seats rising behind and above each other round a central open space; part of a theatre; (fig.) scene of a contest. Hence **amphitheă·trICAL** a. [f. L f. Gk *amphitheatron* (see AMPHI- and THEATRE)]

Amphi·tryon, n. Host, entertainer. [Molière, *Amphitryon*, iii. 5]

a·mphora, n. Greek or Roman two-handled vessel. [L, f. Gk *amphoreus* for AMPHI(*phoreus* f. *pherō* bear)]

amphŏ·ric, a. (med.). Like the sound produced by blowing into large vessel with small mouth. [f. prec. + -IC]

a·mple, a. (-er, -est). Spacious; extensive; abundant; copious; quite enough. Hence **a·mpLY**[2] adv., **a·mpleNESS** n. [F, f. L *amplus*]

a·mpliative, a. (logic). Extending a simple conception. [f. L *ampliare* widen (*amplus*), see -ATIVE]

amplifica·tion, n. Extension, enlargement; making the most of a thing. [f. L *amplificatio* (as foll., see -ATION)]

a·mplifȳ, v.t. & i. Enhance; enlarge (story, statement); expatiate. Hence **a·mplifiER**[1] n., (esp.) appliance increasing force of electric signals for wireless receiving. [f. F *amplifier* f. L *amplificare* (as AMPLE, see -FY)]

a·mplitude, n. Breadth; abundance; wide range; dignity; (Astr.) space by which celestial body rises, sets, wide of due east, west. [F, f. L *amplitudo* (as AMPLE, see -TUDE)]

ampŭ·lla, n. Roman two-handled flask; vessel for sacred uses; (Biol.) dilated end of vessel, canal, duct, in an animal. Hence **ampullA·CEOUS** a. [L, etym. dub.]

a·mputate, v.t. Cut off (part of animal body &c. or abs.). Hence **amputA·TION, a·mputatOR**[2], nn. [f. L *amputare* (*amb-* about + *putare* prune), see -ATE[3]]

amu·ck, adv. *Run a.*, run about in frenzied thirst for blood (also fig.). [f. Malay *amoq* rushing in frenzy]

ă·mulet, n. Thing worn as charm against evil (lit. and fig.). [f. L *amuletum*, etym. dub.]

amu·se (-z), v.t. Divert from serious business (*with* trifles, *by* trifling); tickle the fancy of; *be amused with, by, at.* So **amu·SABLE, amu·SIVE,** aa. [f. OF *amuser* cause to MUSE (causal *à* to + *muser* stare)]

amu·sement, n. Pleasant diversion; excitement of risible faculty; pastime. [f. F *amusement* (*amuser*, see prec. and -MENT)]

ămygdă·lic, a. Of almonds, as *a. acid.* [f. L *amygdala* ALMOND + -IC]

amy·gdaloid, a. & n. (Igneous rock containing mineral nodules) of almond shape. [f. Gk *amugdalē* ALMOND + -OID]

ă·myl, n. (Chem.). The radical of various alcohols some of which are constituents of fusel oil. Hence **amy·lic** a. [f. L *am(ylum)* starch + -YL; named as discovered in distilling fusel oil from starch]

ămylā·ceous, a. Of starch, starchy. [f. L *amylum* starch + -ACEOUS]

ă·myloid, a. & n. Starchy (food). [as prec. + -OID]

an[1], a. See A, adj.

an[2], conj. (archaic). If. [weakening of *and*]

an-, pref. (1) f. *an* = on, as in *anon, anent.* (2) f. L *ad* before *n*, see AD-. (3) f. L *an-* = *ambi-*, as in *anfractuosity.* (4) f. Gk ANA-. (5) f. Gk *an-* = *a-* not (before vowel), as in *anarchy.*

-an, suf. of adjj. (often used as nn.), f. L *-anus* direct or through F *-ain* (the early E form, retained in *certain, captain, chaplain*) or *-en*, or It., Sp., Port., *-ano*, and freely used in new words; added esp. to names of place, system, zool. order, or founder (*Chilian, Anglican, reptilian, Lutheran*); often as E termination to L adjj. in *-ius*, giving -IAN as a mere phonetic variant (cf. *Christ-ian, Mohammed-an*). See also -ANE.

ā·na, n. (With pl. *anas*) collection of person's memorable sayings; (collect. pl.) anecdotes, literary gossip, about a person. [= -ANA]

ăna-, pref. = Gk *ana* up, back, again, anew; before a vowel *an-*.

-ana, suf. Neut. pl. of L adjj. in *-anus* (see -AN) appended in 16th-c. F to names = the sayings of; in E from 18th c., now including anecdotes about, publications bearing on, places or persons, as *Tunbrigiana, Shaksperiana.*

anaba·ptism, n. Re-baptism; doctrine of anabaptists. [f. L f. Gk *anabaptismos* (ANA- + *baptismos* BAPTISM)]

anaba·ptist, n. One who baptizes over again; (opprobriously) = BAPTIST. Hence **anabapti·stICAL** a. [as prec., see -IST]

ă·nabas, n. Genus of fishes that leave water and ascend trees. [Gk part. of *anabainō* walk up]

ană·basis, n. Military advance, esp. that of Cyrus the younger into Asia, narrated by Xenophon. [Gk, = ascent f. ANA(*bainō* go)]

anachrŏ·nic, a. Involving anachronism; out of date. [f. ANA- + Gk *khronos* time + -IC]

ana·chronism, n. Error in computing time; thing out of harmony with the present. So **ana·chroni·stIC** a. [f. F *anachronisme* f. L f. Gk *anakhronismos* f. *anakhronizō* (as prec.)]

anacla·stic, a. Pertaining to refraction; springing back with crackling sound, as *a. glasses.* [f. Gk *anaklastos* refracted f. ANA-(*klaō* bend)]

ănacolū·thon, n. (pl. *-tha*). Sentence, words, lacking grammatical sequence. [f. Gk *anakolouthon* (AN- (5) + *akolouthos* following f. *a-* copul. + *keleuthos* road)]

ănaco·nda, n. Large snake of Ceylon; large S.-American Boa; any large snake that crushes its prey. [?]

anăcreo·ntic, a. & n. (Poem) in the manner or metre of Anacreon's lyrics; convivial and amatory. [f. L *Anacreonticus* (Gk *Anakreōn*, name of poet)]
anacru·sis, n. (prosody). Unstressed syllable at beginning of verse. [f. Gk *anakrousis* (ANA*krouō* strike up)]
ana·dromous, a. (Of fishes) ascending rivers to spawn. [f. Gk ANA(*dromos* running) + -OUS]
anae·mia, n. (med.). Lack of blood, unhealthy paleness. Hence **anae·mic** a. [f. Gk *anaimia* (AN- (5) + *haima* blood)]
anaesthē·sia, n. Insensibility (lit.). [f. Gk *anaisthēsia* (AN- (5) + *aisthēsis* sensation f. st. *aisthe-* perceive)]
anaesthĕ·tic, a. & n. (Agent) that produces insensibility. Hence **anaesthe·tically** adv. [f. Gk *anaisthētos* insensible (as prec.) + -IC]
anae·sthetize, v.t. Render insensible (lit. and fig.). Hence **anae·sthetist** (1), **anaesthetiza·tion**, nn. [as prec. + -IZE]
a·naglyph, n. Embossed ornament in low relief. Hence **anaglў·phic** a. [f. Gk ANA*gluphē* (*gluphō* carve)]
anagnor·isis, n. Dénouement in a drama. [L f. Gk, f. *anagnōrizō* recognize]
anagō·ge (-jē), n. Spiritual or allegorical interpretation. So **anagŏ·gic(al)** aa., **anago·gically**[2] adv. [L, f. Gk *anagōgē* f. *anagō* lead up (AN- 4)]
a·nagram, n. Transposition of letters of word or phrase, to form new word or phrase. Hence **anagramma·tic(al)** aa., **anagramma·tically**[2] adv. [f. F *anagramme* f. Gk ANA(*graphō* write), see -M]
anagra·mmatize, v.t. Form into an anagram. Hence **anagra·mmatism**, **anagra·mmatist**, nn. [f. Gk *anagrammatizō* (as prec., see -IZE)]
ā·nal, a. Pertaining to, situated near, the anus. [f. ANUS + -AL]
a·nalects, anale·cta, n. pl. Literary gleanings. [f. L f. Gk *analekta* things gathered (ANA*legō* pick up)]
analĕ·ptic, a. & n. Restorative (medicine). [f. Gk *analēptikos* f. ANA(*lambanō* take) restore, see -IC]
ănalgē·sia, n. Absence of pain. So **analgĕ·tic,** (irreg.) **analgē·sic,** aa., giving a., & nn., such drug. [Gk (-gēs-), f. *an-* (5), *algeō* feel pain]
analŏ·gic, a. Of analogy. [f. L f. Gk *analogikos* (as ANALOGY, see -IC)]
analŏ·gical, a. According to analogy; expressing an analogy. Hence **analo·gically**[2] adv. [prec. + -AL]
ana·logist, n. One occupied with analogies; philosopher who saw in words images of the things they expressed. [as foll., see -IST]
ana·logize, v.t. & i. Represent by analogy; show to be analogous; employ analogy; be in harmony (*with*). [f. ANALOGY + -IZE]
ana·logous, a. Similar, parallel, (*to*). Hence **ana·logously**[2] adv., **ana·logousness** n. [f. L f. Gk *analogos* (*ana* up to + *logos* proportion) + -OUS]
a·nalogue (-ŏg), n. Analogous, parallel, word or thing. [F, f. Gk *analogon* neut. adj., see prec.]
ană·logy, n. (Math.) proportion; agreement, similarity, (*to, with, between*); analogue; (Logic) process of reasoning from parallel cases; (Lang.) imitation of inflexion or construction of existing words in forming inflexions or constructions of others, without intervention of the formative steps through which these at first arose; (Nat. Hist.) resemblance of form or function between organs essentially different. [f. L f. Gk *analogia* proportion (as ANALOGOUS)]
ă·nalyse, v.t. Examine minutely the constitution of; (Chem., Physics) ascertain the elements of (a compound); find, show, the essence of (treatise &c.); (Gram.) resolve (sentence) into its grammatical elements. Hence **a·nalysable** a. [f. F *analyser* (*analyse*, as foll.); also *-yze* in E by assim. to vbs in -IZE]
ană·lysis, n. (pl. *-ysēs*). Resolution into simple elements (in all senses of the vb); *bowling a.*, register of the result of each ball. [f. L f. Gk *analusis* f. ANA(*luō* loose)]
a·nalyst, n. One skilled in (usu. chemical) analysis. [f. F *analyste* f. *analyser* ANALYSE, on anal. of nouns in *-iste* -IST f. vbs in *-iser* -IZE]
analў·tic, a. Pertaining to analysis. Hence **analy·tics** n. [f. med. L f. Gk *analutikos* (as ANALYSIS, see -IC)]
analy·tical, a. Employing the analytic method; (Lang.) using separate words instead of inflexions. Hence **analy·tically**[2] adv. [prec. + -AL]
anamnē·sis, n. Recollection (esp. of a previous existence). [Gk (ANA*mimnēskō* remind)]
anamor·phosis, n. Distorted drawing appearing regular from one point; (Bot.) abnormal transformation. [Gk *anamorphōsis* (ANA*morphoō* transform f. *morphē* form, see -OSIS)]
ana·nas (anā-, anah-), n. Pine-apple. [prob. f. Peruv. *Nanas*; also *anana*, *-s* being taken for plural]
ana·ndrous, a. (bot.). Without stamens. [f. Gk *anandros* husbandless (AN- (5) + *anēr andros* male) + -OUS]
a·napaest, n. (Prosody) foot consisting of two short syllables followed by one long. Hence **anapae·stic** a. [f. L f. Gk *anapaistos* reversed (ANA- + *paiō* strike)]
ană·phora, n. Repetition of word or phrase in successive clauses. [L, f. Gk *anaphora* = carrying back f. ANA(*pherō* bear)]
ă·narch (-k), n. (poet.). Leader of revolt. [f. Gk *anarkhos* without ruler (AN- (5) + *arkhos*)]

anar·chic, -ical, aa. Lawless. Hence **anar·chical**LY[2] adv. [as prec. + -IC, -ICAL]

a·narchist, n. Advocate of anarchy. So **a·narchi**SM n. [as prec. + -IST]

a·narchy, n. Absence of government; disorder; confusion. [f. Gk *anarkhia* (as prec.)]

anar·throus, a. (Greek Gram.) used without the article; (Physiol.) jointless. [f. AN- (5) + Gk *arthron* joint, article, + -OUS]

anasar·ca, n. A dropsical affection. Hence **anasar·co**US a. [f. Gk *ana* up + *sarka* (nom. *sarx*) flesh]

anastă·tic, a. In relief; *a. printing* (from reliefs on zinc plates). [f. Gk *anastatos* set up (ANA*sta-* stand up) + -IC]

ana·stomose, (-z), v.i. Communicate by anastomosis. [f. F *anastomoser* (*anastomose* = foll.)]

anăstomō·sis, n. Cross connexion of arteries, branches, rivers, &c. [Gk, f. *anastomoō* furnish with mouth (*stoma*), see -OSIS]

ană·thema, n. Accursed thing; curse of God; curse of the church, excommunicating a person or denouncing a doctrine; imprecation. [L, = excommunicated person, excommunication, f. Gk *anathema* thing devoted, (later) accursed thing (ANA*tithēmi* set up)]

ana·thematize, v.t. & i. Curse. [f. F *anathématiser* f. L f. Gk *anathematizō* (as prec., see -IZE)]

anatŏ·mical, a. Belonging to anatomy; structural. Hence **anato·mical**LY[2] adv. [f. L f. Gk *anatomikos* (as ANATOMY, see -IC)]

ana·tomist, n. Dissecter of bodies; (fig.) analyser. [f. F *anatomiste*, see foll. and -IST]

ana·tomize, v.t. & i. Dissect; (fig.) analyse. [f. med. L *anatomizare* f. *anatomia* ANATOMY, as if f. a Gk *anatomizō*]

ană·tomy, n. Dissection; science of bodily structure; anatomical structure; analysis; (pop.) skeleton, mummy, emaciated creature. [f. F *anatomie* f. L f. Gk *anatomia* abstr. n. = ANA(*tomē* f. *temnō* cut)]

ana·tta, n. Orange-red dye, used for colouring cheese. [?]

a·nbury, amb-, n. Soft tumour on horses and oxen; disease of turnips and allied plants. [perh. = *ang-berry* (OE *ang-* painful, cf. AGNAIL)]

-ance, suf. forming nn. of quality or action, chiefly thr. F *-ance* f. L *-antia* and *-entia* f. L pres. part. in *-ant-*, *-ent-* (nom. *-ans*, *-ens*). OF gave *-ance* both for existing L *-antia*, *-entia*, and for wds formed in F on same model; thus, *assistance*, *nuisance*, where L would have *-entia*. Later F followed L vowel; *élégance*, *tempérance* (L *-antia*), but *diligence*, *prudence* (L *-entia*). E adopted F forms of both kinds, and usu. retains F form; but after 1500 *-ence* was in some wds restored where L would have *-entia*, and mod. formations follow L vowel. F *-ance* also became living suf. in E on native vbs as *furtherance*, *forbearance*, *riddance*.

a·ncestor, n. Any of those from whom one's father or mother is descended, forefather. Hence **a·ncestr**ESS[1] n. [f. OF *ancestre*, *ancessor*, f. L *antecessor*, *-orem*, f. ANTE(*cedere cess-* go), see -OR[2]]

ance·stral, a. Belonging to, inherited from, ancestors. [f. OF *ancestrel* (*ancestre*, see prec. and -AL)]

a·ncestry, n. Ancestral lineage; ancient descent; ancestors. [f. OF *ancesserie* (as ANCESTOR, see -Y[1])]

a·nchithere (-kĭthēr), n. Fossil animal, size of small pony, regarded as ancestor of the horse. [f. Gk *agkhi* near + *thērion* wild beast]

a·nchor[1] (-k-), n. Heavy iron, composed of long shank, with ring at one end to which cable is fastened, and at other end two barbed arms, used for mooring ship to bottom of sea &c.; *sheet*, *bower*, *kedge*, *-a.*, (largest, middle, smallest size); (fig.) source of confidence; *cast*, *weigh*, *a.*, let down, take up, a; *at a.*, anchored; *come to (an) a.*, anchor; *a.-plate*, heavy piece of timber or metal serving as point of support for cables of suspension-bridge &c.; *a.-stroke* (Bill.), a kind of cannon; *a.-watch*, watch set while ship lies at anchor. [OE *ancor* f. L *ancora* (not *anch-*) perh. cogn. w. or adoption of Gk *agkura* (st. *agk-* hook)]

a·nchor[2], v.t. & i. Secure (ship) with anchor; (fig.) fix firmly; (intr.) cast anchor, come to anchor. [perh. f. F *ancrer* f. *ancre* anchor]

a·nchorage, n. Anchoring; lying at anchor; anchorage-ground; (fig.) thing to depend upon; anchorage-dues. [prec. + -AGE]

a·nchoress, a·ncress, n. Female anchoret. [f. obs. *anchor* (OE *ancra*, short form of L *anachoreta*, see foll.) + -ESS[1]]

a·nchoret, -ite, n. Hermit; person of secluded habits. Hence **anchorĕ·t**IC a. [f. F *anachorète* f. L *anachoreta* (med. L *-ita*) f. Gk *anakhōrētēs* (ANA*khōreō* retire, see -ETE), influenced by OE *ancra*, see prec.]

anchō·vy (*also* ă·ntsho-), n. Small fish of herring family; *a.-paste* and *a.-sauce*, *a.-toast*, (made, spread, with anchovies); *a.-pear*, W.-Indian fruit eaten like mango. [f. Sp. *anchova* perh. f. Basque *anchua* (perh. = *antzua* dry)]

a·nchўlose (-z), v.t. & i. (Of joints, bones) stiffen, unite. [f. foll.]

anchylo·sis (-k-), n. Formation of stiff joint by consolidation of articulating surfaces. [f. Gk *agkulōsis* (*agkuloō* crook f. *agkulos*, see -OSIS); *-ch-* for *-c-* to preserve hard sound]

ancien régime (F), n. Time before French Revolution.
ā·ncient[1], a. & n. Belonging to times long past (esp. before fall of Western Roman Empire); having existed, lived, long (*a. lights*, window that neighbour may not deprive of light by building); *the A. of Days*, God; *the ancients*, civilized nations of antiquity. Hence **a·ncient**LY[2] adv., **a·ncient**NESS n. [f. F *ancien* f. LL *antianus* (*ante* before, see -AN); *-t* by confus. w. -ENT]
ā·ncient[2], n. (archaic) = ENSIGN. [corrupt.]
a·ncientry, n. Ancientness; old-fashioned style. [ANCIENT + -RY]
a·ncillary, a. Subservient, subordinate, (*to*). [f. L *ancillarius* (*ancilla* handmaid, see -ARY[1])]
ancle. See ANKLE.
a·ncon, n. (Physiol.) elbow; (Arch.) quoin of wall or rafter, console, pretended support to cornice; *A. sheep*, race with long bodies and short legs, the fore-legs crooked. [L, f. Gk *agkōn* bend, elbow]
-ancy, suf. Mod. E different. f. -ANCE (see -Y[1]), usu. denoting only quality or state, as opposed to *-ance*, which has besides this meaning that of action or process.
and, conj. connecting words, clauses, and sentences, as *cakes a. buns, black a. brown bread, buy a. sell.* Special uses: *four a. twenty* (but *twenty-four*); *two hundred a. forty, two thousand a. forty* (but *two thousand four hundred*); *two a. ten pence, two pounds a. ten pence* (but *two pound ten*); *miles a.* (= innumerable) *miles*; *nice a.* (= nicely) *thin*; *try a.* (to) *come, mind a.* (to) *bring*; *there are books a.* (different kinds of, good and bad) *books*; *two a. two*, by twos; *stir, a.* (= if you stir) *you are a dead man*; *and/or*, formula allowing reader to take either or both of two expressions (*contributions in money and/or garments*). [OE *and* prep. = against, *end* conj, f. OTeut. **anda*, **andi*]
anda·ntĕ, adv. & n. (mus.). (Movement) in moderately slow time. [It.]
andantī·no (-tē-), adv. & n. (Movement) rather quicker (orig. slower) than *andante*. [It., dim. of prec.]
a·ndiron (-īrn), n. Firedog, for supporting burning wood on hearth. [f. OF *andier* (mod. F *landier*), etym. dub.]
androe·cium (-rē-), n. (bot.). The stamens taken collectively. [f. Gk *andro-* male + *oikion* house]
andrŏ·gynous (-j-), a. Hermaphrodite, whence **andro·gyn**Y[1] n. (Bot). with stamens and pistils in same flower or on same plant. [f. L f. Gk *androgunos* (*anēr andros* male + *gunē* woman) + -OUS]
-ane, suf. (1) Variant of -AN, usu. w. differentiation (*germane, urbane, humane*), but sometimes alone (*mundane*). (2) (Chem.) formed to give a series with Gk -ENE, -INE, -ONE, for naming hydrocarbon types.
ă·necdōtage, n. Anecdotes; (facet.) garrulous old age. [-AGE]
ă·necdote, n. Narrative of detached incident; (pl.) unpublished details of history. Hence **a·necdōt**IST n., **a·necdōt**AL, **anecdŏ·t**IC(AL), aa. [f. med. L f. Gk *anekdota* things unpublished (AN- (5) + *ekdotos* f. *ekdidōmi* give out)]
anē·le, v.t. (archaic). Anoint; give extreme unction to. [orig. *anelien* (AN- (1) + *elien* oil f. OE *ele*, n. f. L *oleum*]
anĕ·mograph, n. Instrument for recording on paper the direction and force of wind. Hence **anemogra·ph**IC a. [f. Gk *anemos* wind + -GRAPH]
ănemo·meter, n. Instrument for measuring force of wind, whence **anemome·tr**IC a., **anemo·**METRY n.; apparatus for showing wind-pressure in organ. [as prec. + -METER]
anĕ·mone (-nĭ), n. Genus of plants, esp. *A. nemorosa* (also called *Wind-flower*); *Sea A.*, popular name of various actinoid zoophytes. [f. L f. Gk *anemōnē* daughter of the wind (as prec. + *-ōnē* patronymic suf.)]
anemŏ·philous, a. Wind-fertilized. [f. Gk *anemos* wind, see -PHIL]
ane·nt, prep. (archaic, Sc.). Concerning. [OE has *on efen* on a level with]
-aneous, suf. f. L adjj. in *-aneus* (*-an-* + *-eo-*) + -OUS.
ă·neroid, a. & n. *A.* (*barometer*), one that measures air-pressure by its action on elastic lid of box exhausted of air, not by height of fluid column. [f. F *anéroïde* (Gk *a-* not + *nēros* wet, see -OID)]
ă·neurysm, -ism, n. Morbid dilatation of an artery; abnormal enlargement. Hence **aneury·sm**AL, **-i·sm**AL a. [f. Gk *aneurusma* (*aneurunō* widen out f. *eurus* wide)]
anew·, adv. Again; in a different way. [A- (3) + NEW]
anfractuo·sity, n. Circuitousness, intricacy, (lit. and fig.); (usu. pl.) winding passage. [f. F *anfractuosité* f. L *anfractuosus* f. *anfractus* a bending (*amb-* about + *frangere fract-* break), see -OSE and -TY]
a·ngary, n. (Law). Belligerent's right (subject to compensation) of seizing or destroying neutral property under stress of military necessity. [f. med. L *angaria* f. Gk *aggareia* (*aggaros* Persian courier)]
a·ngel, n. Divine messenger; *visits, like those of aa., short and far between*; *entertain an a. unawares*, do service to one who proves to be an important person &c. (*Heb.* xiii. 2); lovely or innocent being; minister of loving offices; old English gold coin (in full *a.-noble*), from 6*s.* 8*d.* to 10*s.*, showing Michael piercing dragon; *good, evil, a.*, attendant spirits; *a.* (messenger) *of death*; *a.-fish*, kind of shark; *aa., devils, -on-horseback*, savoury of oysters wrapped in slices of bacon. [f. L *angelus* f. Gk *aggelos* messenger, used

to transl. Heb. *mal'āk* messenger (of Jehovah)]

ăngĕ·lic, a. Pertaining to angels; like an angel, of superhuman qualities; *A. Doctor*, Thomas Aquinas. Hence **an-ge·lic**AL a., **ange·lical**LY[2] adv. [f. F *angélique* f. L f. Gk *aggelikos* (as prec., see -IC)]

angĕ·lica, n. Aromatic plant, used in cooking and medicine; candied angelica root. [f. med. L (*herba*) *angelica* angelic herb]

āngelo·latry, n. Angel-worship. [f. Gk *aggelos*, see ANGEL and -LATRY]

āngelo·logy, n. Doctrine as to angels. [as prec. + -LOGY]

ă·ngelus, n. Devotional exercise commemorating Incarnation, said by Roman Catholics at morning, noon, and sunset, at sound of bell (*a.-bell* or *a.*). [f. opening words *Angelus domini*]

a·nger[1] (-ngg-), n. Rage, hot displeasure. [f. ON *angr* trouble (root *ang* strait)]

a·nger[2], v.t. Make angry, enrage. [f. ON *angra* vex (as prec.)]

A·ngevin (-jĭ-), a. & n. Of Anjou, of the Plantagenets, including English kings from Henry II to Richard II; (n.) a Plantagenet. [F]

angī·na (-j-), n. Quinsy; *a. pectoris*, spasm of chest resulting from over-exertion when heart is diseased. [L *angĭna* quinsy (formerly thought to be *angīna*, whence usu. E pronunc.), cf. *angĕre* choke and Gk *agkhonē* strangling]

angio- in comb. = Gk *aggeion* vessel dim. of *aggos* chest, chiefly in terms relating to seed- or blood-vessels.

a·ngle[1], n. Space between two meeting lines or planes; inclination of two lines to each other; ACUTE, OBTUSE, RIGHT, *a.*; corner; sharp projection; *a.-iron*, L-shaped piece of iron to strengthen framework; *a.-wise*, angularly. Hence (-)**a·ngl**ED[2] a. [F, f. L *angulus* dim. of **angus*, cf. Gk *agkos* bend]

a·ngle[2], n., & v.i. Fish-hook (obs. exc. in *brother of the a.*, angler); (vb) fish with hook and bait (*for* or abs.), lit. and fig. [OE *angul* cogn. w. OHG *angul* mod. G *angel*, cf. L *uncus* and *angulus*, see prec.]

A·ngle[3], n. (Pl.) Low-German tribe settled in Northumbria, Mercia, and E. Anglia. [f. L *Anglus* f. OTeut. *angli-* (OE *engel*) f. *Angul* a district of Holstein (as prec.)]

a·ngler, n. One who angles; (Zool.) a British fish that preys upon small fish, attracting them by filaments attached to head and mouth. [f. ANGLE[2] + -ER[1]]

A·nglican, a. & n. (Adherent) of the reformed church of England, esp. of High Church principles. Hence **A·nglican**ISM n. [f. med. L *Anglicanus* (*Anglicus* f. *Angli* English)]

A·nglicè (-sē), adv. In English. [L]

A·nglicism, n. English idiom; English political principles. [f. foll., see -ISM]

A·nglicize, v.t. Make English in form or character. [f. L *Anglicus* English + -IZE]

Anglo- in comb. English, as *A.-Catholic*; of English origin, as *A.-American*; half English and half —, as *A.-French* (*entente* &c.); *A.-Indian* a. & n., of British birth but living or having lived long in India, (in Eurasian use) Eurasian. [comb. form of L *Anglus* English]

Anglo-Ca·tholic, a. & n. (Member) of the party that insists on the catholicity of the Church of England and repudiates the epithet *protestant*. [prec.]

Angloma·nia, n. Excessive admiration of English customs. So **A·nglo**PHOBE, **Anglo**PHO·BIA, nn. [prec. + -MANIA]

Anglo-Sa·xon, n. & a. English Saxon (as distinct from Old Saxons of the continent); Old English (people, language) before Norman Conquest (in this dictionary called OE); of English descent (wherever found), whence **Anglo-Sa·xon**DOM n. [f. L *Anglo-Saxones* (pl.)]

Anglo-Sa·xonism, n. Belief in claims of the Anglo-Saxon race. [prec. + -ISM]

angō·la, angor·a, n. Fabric made from wool of angora goat; *A. cat* (long-haired variety). [f. *Angora* (L *Ancyra*, Gk *Agkura*), town in Asia Minor, corrupted to *angola*]

angostūr·a, angus-, a. & n. Bark used as febrifuge and tonic, as *A. bitters*. [f. *Angustura*, town on the Orinoco, now Ciudad Bolivar]

a·ngry, a. Enraged, wrathful, resentful, (*at*, *about*, thing, *at*, *with*, person); irritable, passionate; (of wound, sore, &c.) inflamed, painful. Hence **a·ngri**LY[2] adv. [f. ANGER n. + -Y[2]]

Å·ngström u·nit, n. A hundred-millionth of a centimetre, used in expressing short wave-lengths (abbr. A.U.). [A. J. *Ångström*, Swedish physicist]

a·nguine (-gw-), a. Snake-like. [f. L *anguis* snake, see -INE[1]]

a·nguish (-gw-), n. Severe bodily or mental pain. [f. OF *anguisse*, *angoisse* choking (It. *angoscia*) f. L *angustia* tightness (*angustus*, cf. ANGINA)]

a·ngular, a. Having angles; sharp-cornered; placed in, at, an angle; measured by angle, as *a. divergence*; wanting plumpness; wanting suavity. Hence **angula·**RITY n., **a·ngular**LY[2] adv. [f. L *angularis* (*angulus* ANGLE, see -AR[1]]

a·ngulate (-*at*), a. Formed with corners. Hence **a·ngul**ATE[3] v.t., **angul**A·TION n. [f. L *angulare*, see -ATE[2]]

angusti- in comb. With narrow —, as *-foliate*, *-rostrate*, (leaves, beak). [L *angustus* narrow]

anhȳ·drous, a. (chem.). Without water of crystallization. [f. Gk *anudros* (AN- (5) + *hudōr* water) + -OUS]

anigh·, adv. & prep. Near. [mod. sham archaism, after *afar*]

ă·nil, n. Indigo (shrub and dye). [F, = Sp.

añil f. Arab. *an-nil* (*al* the + *nil* f. Skr. *nili* indigo]

ă·nile, a. Old-womanish; imbecile. [f. L *anilis* (*anus* old woman, see -ILE)]

ă·niline, n. A chemical base, the source of many dyes, obtained originally from indigo, now chiefly from coal-tar. [ANIL + -INE[5]]

ani·lity, n. Dotage. [f. L *anilitas* (ANILE, see -TY)]

ănimadver·sion, n. Criticism; censure. [f. L *animadversio* (*animadvertere -vers-*, see foll. and -ION)]

ănimadver·t, v.i. Pass criticism or censure *on* (conduct, fault, &c.). [f. L *animadvertere* f. *animus* mind + AD(*vertere vers-* turn)]

ă·nimal, n. & a. Organized being endowed (more or less perceptibly) with life, sensation, and voluntary motion; other a. than man; quadruped; man no better than a brute; pertaining to the functions of animals, as *a. spirits* (natural buoyancy), *a. magnetism* (mesmerism); pertaining to animals as opp. to vegetables; carnal. Hence **a·nimal**LY[2] adv. [L, for *animale* neut. of *animalis* having breath (*anima* breath, see -AL); the adj. orig. f. L adj.]

anima·lcule, n. Microscopic animal. [f. L *animalculum* (*animal*, see prec. and -CULE)]

anima·lculism, n. Reference of physiological phenomena to agency of animalcules. So **anima·lcul**IST n. [f. prec. + -ISM]

a·nimalism, n. Animal activity; sensuality; doctrine that men are mere animals. [ANIMAL + -ISM]

anima·lity, n. Animal nature or system; merely animal nature; the animal world. [f. F *animalité* (*animal* a., see -TY)]

a·nimalize, v.t. Convert into animal substance, sensualize. Hence **animaliz**A·TION n. [ANIMAL + -IZE]

a·nimate[1] (-*at*), a. Living; lively. [f. L *animare* quicken, see -ATE[2]]

a·nimāte[2], v.t. Breathe life into; enliven; inspirit (esp. in p.p.); *an animated* (lively) *discussion*; inspire, actuate. Hence **a·nimated**LY[2] adv., **anim**A·TION, **a·nimat**OR[2], nn. [f. prec., see -ATE[3]]

ă·nimé (-mā), n. A W. Indian resin used in making varnish; other resins. [F, = animated (by the many insects contained)]

ă·nimism, n. Doctrine of the *anima mundi* (that phenomena of animal life are produced by an immaterial soul); attribution of living soul to inanimate objects and natural phenomena; spiritualism (as opposed to materialism). Hence **a·nim**IST n., **animi·st**IC a. [f. L *anima* life, soul + -ISM]

animo·sity, n. Active enmity (*against, between*). [f. F *animosité* f. L *animositatem* (*animosus* spirited f. foll., see -OSE and -TY)]

ă·nimus, n. Animating spirit; animosity. [L, = soul, mind, mental impulse]

ă·nise (-ĭs), n. Umbelliferous plant with aromatic seeds. [f. F *anis* f. L f. Gk *anison, anēthon*, anise, dill]

a·niseed, n. Seed of anise, used as a carminative.

anise·tte (-z-), n. Liqueur flavoured with aniseed. [F, dim. of *anis* anise]

aniso- in comb. Unequal, as *-merous*, unsymmetrical, *-sthĕ·nic*, of unequal strength. [f. Gk *anisos* (AN- (5) + *isos* equal)]

a·nker, n. Measure of wine and spirits in Holland, N. Germany, Denmark, Sweden, Russia, and formerly in England (8⅓ imp. gals); cask holding the quantity. [Du., etym. dub.]

a·nkle, a·ncle, n. Joint connecting foot with leg; slender part between this and calf. [earlier *ankel* (Du. *enkel*, G. *enkel*) f. root *ank-* bend (cf. L *angulus*); OE has *ancléow* perh. f. Du. *anklaauw* (ending assim. to *klaauw* claw)]

a·nklet, n. Ornament or support for ankle. [prec. + -LET]

a·nna, n. Sixteenth part of a rupee; *half a., quarter a.*, E. Indian coins. [Hind. *ana*]

a·nnalist, n. Writer of annals. Hence **annali·st**IC a. [f. foll. + -IST]

a·nnals, n. pl. Narrative of events year by year; historical records. [f. L *annales* (*libri*) yearly (books) f. *annus* year, see -AL]

a·nnates, n. pl. (Rom. Cath.) first year's revenue of see or benefice, paid to Pope. [f. F *annate* f. med. L *annata* year's proceeds (*annus*, see -ADE)]

annea·l, v.t. Toughen by gradually diminishing heat, temper (lit. and fig.). [f. AN- (1) + OE *ǽlan* burn, bake; partly also f. OF *neeler* enamel f. LL *nigellare* blacken (*nigellus*, dim. of *niger*)]

anne·ctent, a. Connecting, as *a. link*. [f. L as ANNEX, see -ENT]

Annĕ·lida, n. pl. (zool.) The class of red-blooded worms. Hence **a·nnel**ID[3] n., **anne·lid**AN a. [mod. L, f. F *annelés* ringed (OF *annel* ring f. L *a(n)nellus* dim. of *anulus* ring) + *ida*, cf. -ID[3]]

anne·x, v.t. Add as subordinate part; append (*to* book &c.); take possession of (territory &c.); attach as an attribute, addition, or consequence. Hence or cogn. **anne·x**ABLE a., **annex**A·TION n. [f. F *annexer* f. *annexe* thing joined f. L AN-(*nectere nex-* bind)]

anne·x(e), n. Addition to a document; supplementary building. [F (*-xe*), see prec.]

anni·hilate, v.t. Blot out of existence. Hence **anni·hilat**OR[2] n. [f. L AN*nihilare* (*nihil* nothing), see -ATE[2]]

annīhila·tion, n. Utter destruction; (Theol.) destruction of soul as well as body, whence **annihila·tion**ISM, **annihi-**

la·tionIST, nn. [F (*annihiler* f. L as prec., see -ATION)]

anniver·sary, n. Yearly return of a date; celebration of this. [f. L *anniversarius* (*annus* year + *versus* turned, see -ARY[1])]

a·nno aeta·tis su·ae, phr. In the — year of his or her age. [L]

A·nno Dŏ·mĭnī, phr. In the year of our Lord, of the Christian era, (usu. *A.D.*); (colloq., as n.) advancing age (*A.D. is the trouble*). [L]

a·nnotate, v.t. & i. Furnish with notes (book, author); (intr.) make notes (*on*). So **annot**A·TION, **a·nnotat**OR[2], nn. [f. L AN*notare* (*nota* mark), see -ATE[3]]

annou·nce, v.t. Proclaim; intimate the approach of; make known (without words) to senses or mind. Hence **annou·nce**MENT, **-cer** (esp., of items to be broadcast), nn. [f. OF *anoncer* f. L AD*nuntiare* (*nuntius* messenger)]

annoy·[1], n. (archaic, poet.). Annoyance. [f. OF *anoi, enoi* (OSp. *enoyo*, OVenet. *inodio*) f. L phr. *in odio* in hatred, hateful; *-n-* doubled by assim. to *ennoble* &c.]

annoy·[2], v.t. Irritate; molest, harass. [f. OF *anuier, anoier*, f. com.-Rom. *inodiare* (as prec.)]

annoy·ance, n. Molestation; vexation; disgust. [f. OF *anuiance, anoiance* (*anuier*, see prec. and -ANCE)]

a·nnual, a. & n. Reckoned by the year; recurring yearly; lasting for one year; (plant) that lives only for a year; (book &c.) published in yearly numbers. Hence **a·nnual**LY[2] adv. [f. OF *annuel* f. L *annualis* = class. L *annalis* (*annus* year, see -AL)]

annū·itant, n. One who holds an annuity. [f. foll. + -ANT, by assim. to *accountant* &c.]

annū·ity, n. Sum payable in respect of a particular year; yearly grant; investment of money entitling investor to series of equal annual sums; *life, terminable, perpetual, a.* (ceasing at death of investor, after specified term, on repayment of principal); *immediate, deferred* or *reversionary, a.* (commencing at end of first interval of payment after investment, after specified interval or event). [f. F *annuité* f. med. L *annuitatem* (*annuus* yearly, see -TY)]

annu·l, v.t. (-ll-). Annihilate; abolish, cancel; declare invalid. Hence **annu·l**MENT n. [f. OF *anuller* (mod. F *annuler*) f. LL AN*nullare* (*nullus* none)]

a·nnular, a. Ring-like; *a. space* (between inner and outer surface of cylinder); *a. ligament* (girding wrist and ankle); *a. eclipse* of sun (when moon, projected on sun's disk, leaves ring of light visible). Hence **a·nnular**LY[2] adv. [f. L *an(n)ularis* (*an(n)ulus* ring, see -AR[1])]

a·nnulate(d), a. Furnished, marked, with rings; formed of rings. Hence **annul**A·TION n. [f. L *annulatus* (as foll., see -ATE[2])]

a·nnulet, n. Small ring; (Arch.) small fillet encircling column. [f. L *annulus* ring + -ET[1]]

a·nnuloid, a. Ring-like. So **annulo**·SE[1] a. [as prec. + -OID]

annu·nciate (-shĭ-), v.t. Proclaim; intimate as coming or ready. [f. L *annuntiare* ANNOUNCE, see -ATE[3]]

annuncia·tion (-sĭ-), n. Announcement; (*A-*) that of the incarnation, made by the angel Gabriel to the Virgin Mary, festival commemorating this, Lady-day, March 25th. [f. F *annonciation* f. L *annuntiationem* (as prec., see -ATION)]

annu·nciator, n. Announcer; indicator showing in which direction attendance summoned by bell or telephone is needed. [f. L *annuntiator* (as prec., see -OR[2])]

ă·node, n. (Electr.) positive pole (cf. CATHODE). [f. Gk *anodos* way up (*ana* up + *hodos* way)]

ă·nodȳne, a. & n. (Medicine, drug) able to assuage pain; (anything) mentally soothing. [f. L f. Gk *anōdunos* painless (AN- (5) + *odunē* pain)]

anoi·nt, v.t. Apply ointment, oil, to (esp. as religious ceremony at baptism or on consecration as priest or king); moisten, rub; *the Lord's Anointed*, Christ, (also) king by divine right. [f. obs. adj. *anoint* f. OF *enoint* p.p. of *enoindre* f. L IN(*ungere unct-*)]

anŏmali·stic, a. (astr.). *A. year*, time earth takes to pass from perihelion to perihelion; *a. month*, time moon takes to pass from perigee to perigee. [f. Gk *anōmalos* ANOMALOUS + -IST + -IC]

anŏ·malous, a. Irregular; abnormal. Hence **ano·malous**LY[2] adv., **ano·malous**NESS n. [f. L f. Gk *anōmalos* (AN- (5) + *homalos* even)]

anŏ·maly, n. Unevenness of motion &c.; irregularity; (Astr.) angular distance of planet or satellite from its last perihelion or perigee. [f. L f. Gk *anōmalia* (*anōmalos* see prec.)]

anomo- in comb. Irregular, as ***-carpous***, bearing unusual fruit, ***-phyllous***, with leaves irregularly placed. [f. Gk *anomos* without law (*a-* not + *nomos*)]

ano·n, adv. Soon, presently; (of contrast) now again; *ever and a.*, every now and then. [OE *on an* into one, *on ane* in one (body, mind, state, way, movement, moment)]

ănona·ceous, a. Pertaining to the pineapple. [f. mod. L *anona* pine-apple (cf. ANANAS) + -ACEOUS]

ă·nonym, n. Person who remains nameless; pseudonym. [f. F *anonyme* (as foll.)]

ănonȳ·mity, n. State of being anonymous. [as foll., see -TY]

anŏ·nymous, a. Of unknown name; of unknown authorship. Hence **ano·nymous**LY[2] adv., **ano·nymous**NESS n. [f. Gk *anōnumos* nameless (AN- (5) + *onoma* name)]

anō·phelēs, n. Kinds of (esp. malarial) mosquito. [Gk, =hurtful (*a-* not, *ōpheleō* benefit)]

ano·smia, n. Loss of sense of smell. [mod. L f. AN- (5) + Gk *osmē* smell]

ano·ther (-ŭ-), pron. & a. (pl. *other* a., *others* pron.). An additional (one), as *try a. pear, try a.*; unnamed additional party to legal action (*X versus Y and a.*); (in list of cricket eleven &c., written *A. N. Other*) anonymous player or one still to be selected; a counterpart to, as *a. Solomon*; *such a.*, a. of the same sort; a different (one), as *take this towel away and bring me a.*; (contrasted or coupled with *one*) *one man's meat is a. man's poison, taken one with a.*; ONE *a.* [AN + OTHER; in OE *other* was used by itself, *an* not yet being weakened to indef. article]

anour·ous (-owr-), a. Tailless. [f. AN- (5) + Gk *oura* tail + -OUS]

ă·nserine, a. Of the nature of a goose; silly. (f. L *anserinus* (*anser* goose, see -INE[1])]

a·nswer[1] (-*ser*), n. Reply; defence; solution; thing done in return. [orig. = solemn affirmation to rebut a charge, OE *andswaru* f. OTeut. *andswarâ-* (*and-* against + **swarâ-* affirmation f. *swarjan*, OE *swerian* swear)]

a·nswer[2], v.t. & i. Reply, as *a. me, my question, to me, to my question*; *a. to* (acknowledge, have) *the name of X*; *a.* (summons to) *the door*; reply to (charge); be responsible (*for* person or thing); *a.* (correspond to, also *a. to*) *my hopes, your description*; *a.* (fulfil) *my purpose*; *will not a.* (do, succeed); *a. back* (vulg.), a. rebuke saucily. [OE *andswarian* (as prec.)]

a·nswerable, a. Responsible (*to* person, *for* act); (archaic) corresponding (*to*). [prec. + -ABLE]

ant, n. A small social hymenopterous insect celebrated for industry, emmet, pismire; *a.-eggs*, larvae of aa.; *a.-catcher*, *a.-thrush*, bird of thrush family living on aa.; *a.-eater*, name of various animals that live on aa.; *a.-fly*, winged a., used as bait in angling; *a.-hill*, mound over ant's nest, conical nest of termites; *White A.*, termite, destructive social insect of neuropterous order. [OE *ǽmete*, *ǽmete*, cogn. w. WG **âmaitjô* (*á* off + *maitan* cut); *ǽmete* became *ant*, *émete* EMMET]

ant- = ANTI- before vowel.

-ant, suf. forming adjj. (& nn.) f. F *-ant* (or direct) f. L *-antem*, *-ēntem*, *-ĕntem*, accus. of pres. part, (nom. *-ans*, *-ens*). OF levelled all L partt. under ending *-ant*, though later F preserved L *-ent-*. E adopted F *-ant* as *-aunt*, which on loss of accent reappeared as *-ant* (*defiant* L *diffidentem*, *pliant* L *plicantem*, *serjeant* L *servientem*, *tenant* L *tenentem*). Most old wds retain *-ant*, but since 1500 some have been refash., universally (*apparent*) or partly (*dependent*, *-ant*); *belligerant* (L *belligerare*) is wrongly changed to *-ent* on L *gerĕre*. Mod. wds in *-ant* are f. L *-ant-*, direct or thr. F, or on L anal. (rarely where no vb exists, as *benignant* on anal. of *malignant*). Noun meanings: (1) personal agent, (2) thing, esp. drug, producing effect.

antă·cid, a. & n. Preventive of acidity (esp. in stomach). [ANT- + ACID]

anta·gonism, n. Active opposition (*to*, *against*, thing; *between* two; *come into a. with*); opposing principle. [f. Gk *antagōnisma* (as foll., see -ISM)]

anta·gonist, n. Opponent, adversary; (Phys.) counteracting muscle. Hence **antagoni·stic** a., **antagoni·stically** adv. [f. Gk *antagōnistēs* (as foll., see -IST)]

antă·gonize, v.t. (Of a force &c.) counteract, tend to neutralize, (another); evoke hostility in, provoke to opposition, make into an enemy; (U.S.) oppose, resist. [f. Gk ANT*agōnizomai* (*agōn* contest, see -IZE)]

anta·lkali, n. Substance that counteracts an alkali. Hence **anta·lkaline**[1] a. [ANT- + ALKALI]

antaphrodi·siac (-diz-), a. & n. Preventive of venereal desire. [f. ANT- + APHRODISIAC]

antar·ctic, a. Southern, of south polar regions; *A. Pole*, S. pole of earth or heavens; *A. Circle*, parallel of 66° 32′ S. [refash. f. OF *antartique* f. L f. Gk ANT(*arktikos* ARCTIC)]

ante-, pref. = L *ante* before, prep. and adv., used esp. in E to form adjj. with or without adj. ending, as *ante-reformation(al)*.

antecē·dence, n. Precedence, priority, (in time or causal relation); (Astr.) retrograde motion. [f. L *antecedentia* (as foll., see -ENCE)]

antecē·dent, a. & n. Previous (*to*); presumptive, a priori; preceding thing or circumstance; (Logic) the part of a conditional proposition on which the other depends; (Gram.) noun, clause, sentence, to which a following (esp. relative) pronoun or adverb refers; (Math.) first term of a ratio; (pl.) past history (esp. of persons). Hence **antece·dently**[2] adv. [f. F *antécédent* f. L ANTE(*cedere* go), see -ENT]

a·ntechamber, n. Room leading to chief apartment. [f. F *antichambre* (*anti-* for ANTE- + *chambre* CHAMBER)]

a·ntechapel, n. Outer part at west end of chapel. [ANTE- + CHAPEL]

a·ntedate[1], n. Date before the true time (esp. of writing). [ANTE- + DATE n.]

For other compounds of *ante-* see ANTE-.

anteda·te[2], v.t. Affix, assign, an earlier than the true date to (document, event); precede; anticipate. [f. prec.]
antedilū·vian, a. & n. Belonging, referring, appropriate, to the time before the flood; (n.) old-fashioned person, (also) very old person. [f. ANTE- + L *diluvium* DELUGE + -AN]
a·ntelope, n. Deer-like ruminant genus of animals. [f. OF *antelop* f. L *anthalopus* f. Gk *antholops*, etym. dub.]
ă·ntĕ mĕrī·dīĕm, phr. (abbr. *a.m.*). Between midnight and noon, as *7.30 a.m.* [L]
antemu·ndane, a. Existing, occurring, before creation of world. [f. ANTE- + L *mundus* world + -ANE]
antenā·tal, a. Previous to birth. [ANTE- + NATAL]
ante·nna, n. (pl. *-ae*). Sensory organ found in pairs on heads of insects and crustacea, feeler; (Bot.) irritable processes in male flower of some orchids; (Wireless) = AERIAL n. Hence **ante·nn**AL, **ante·nn**ARY[1], **antenni·**FEROUS, **ante·nni**-FORM, aa. [L, = sail-yard, perh. f. Gk *anateinō* stretch out]
antenu·ptial, a. Born, occurring, &c., before marriage. [f. ANTE- + L *nuptiae* nuptials + AL]
antepe·ndium, n. Veil for front of altar. [L ANTE*pendium* (*pendēre* hang)]
antepenu·lt, a. & n. Last but two (orig. and usu. of syllables). [abbrev. of L (*syllaba*) *antepaenultima*, see foll.]
antepenu·ltimate, a. & n. = prec. [f. L ANTE*paenultimus* (*paene* almost + *ultimus* last) + -ATE[2]]
antepra·ndial, a. Before-dinner. [f. ANTE- + L *prandium* + -AL]
antēr·ior, a. More to the front; prior (*to*). Hence **anterio·**RITY n., **anter·ior**LY[2] adv. [L, = fore, former, f. *ante* before]
a·nte-room, n. Room leading to another. [ANTE- + ROOM]
anth-, pref. = ANTI- before aspirate.
anthē·lion, n. Luminous ring projected on cloud or fog bank opposite to sun. [late Gk, neut. of *anthēlios* opposite to sun (ANTH- + *hēlios* sun)]
anthelmi·ntic, a. & n. (Medicine) of use against intestinal worms. [f. ANTH- + Gk *helmins -minthos* worm + -IC]
a·nthem, n. Composition sung antiphonally; prose composition (usu. from Scriptures or Liturgy) set to sacred music; song of praise or gladness. [OE *antefne* f. Rom. **antefena* f. LL *antifona* f. Gk *antiphōna*, see ANTIPHON, E development being *ante·fne, ante·mne, a·ntem, a·nthem*]
a·nther, n. (bot.). Part of stamen containing pollen; *a.-dust*, pollen; *a.-valve*, opening by which pollen is shed. Hence **a·nther**AL, **antheri·**FEROUS, **a·nther**OID aa. [f. F *anthère* f. L *anthera* medicine extracted from flowers f. Gk *anthēra* flowery, fem. adj. f. *anthos*]
antho·logy, n. Collection of small choice poems, esp. epigrams, (orig. Greek); literary collection. Hence **antho·log**IST n. [f. L f. Gk *anthologia* (*anthos* flower + *-logia* collection f. *legō* gather)]
A·nthony (-*to*-), n. *St A.*, patron of swineherds; *A.*, smallest pig of litter; (*St*) *A.'s fire*, erysipelas.
a·nthracite, n. Non-bituminous variety of coal. Hence **anthraci·t**IC, **a·nthra-cīt**OUS, aa. [f. L f. Gk *anthrakitēs* coal-like (*anthrax -akos* coal)]
a·nthrax, n. Malignant boil; splenic fever of sheep and cattle; malignant pustule caused in man by infection from animals so affected. [L f. Gk, = carbuncle]
anthropo- in comb. = Gk *anthrōpos* man, as: *-ce·ntric*, centring in man; *-geny*, study of origin of man; *-graphy*, science of geographical distribution of mankind; *-lite, -lith*, fossil man; *-metry*, measurement of human body; *-phagous, -phagy*, man-eating.
a·nthropoid, a. & n. Man-like; (n). being that is human in form only, esp. a. ape. [f. Gk *anthrōpoeidēs* (ANTHROPO-, see -OID)]
anthropo·logy, n. Whole science of man; physiological and psychological science of man; study of man as an animal. Hence **anthropolo·g**ICAL a., **anthropo-lo·gical**LY[2] adv., **anthropo·**LOGIST n. [as prec. + -LOGY]
anthropomor·phic, a. Of the nature of anthropomorphism. [as foll. + -IC]
anthropomor·phize, v.t. Attribute human form or personality to (God &c. or abs.). Hence **anthropomor·ph**ISM, **anthropomor·ph**IST, nn. [as foll. + -IZE]
anthropomor·phous, a. Of human form. [f. Gk ANTHROPO*morphos* (*morphē* form) + -OUS]
anti-, pref. = Gk *anti* (before unaspir. vowel *ant-*, before aspirate *anth-*) opposite, against, in exchange, instead, rivalling: in words f. Gk, and as living pref. in E (1) combining with nouns to form nouns, *anti-* having adj. force = rival (*-pope, -king*), opposing, counter, (*-chorus, -league*), reverse of (*-climax*); (2) forming adjj. on nouns governed by *anti-* (*-slavery* society, *-vaccination* league) or on adjj. implying a noun so governed (*-national, -ritualistic*), with sense 'opposed to'; many of these are also nouns, esp. names of medicines (*-dysenteric*); (3) forming derivative nouns and adjj. by addition of a suf., esp. *-ist*, (*-alcoholist, -tobacconist, -sabbatarian*) with sense 'one opposed to', also corresponding abstract nn. in *-ism* (*-Darwinism*)
anti-air·craft, a. *A. gun* &c. (for shooting down hostile aircraft). [prec.]

For other compounds of *ante-* see ANTE-. For other compounds of *anti-* see ANTI-.

a·ntiar, n. Upas tree of Java; poison thence obtained. [Jav. *antjar*]

antibi·lious, a. Of use against biliousness. [ANTI- (2)]

a·nti-body, n. (Physiol.). Kinds of substance in the blood tending to neutralize others that are harmful. [ANTI- (1)]

a·ntic, a. & n. (Archaic) grotesque, bizarre; grotesque posture (usu. pl.); (archaic) mountebank, clown. [f. It. *antico* f. L *antiquus* ancient, apparently from ascription of GROTESQUE work to the ancients]

a·ntichrist, n. Enemy of Christ; great personal opponent of Christ expected by early church to appear before end of world. [f. OF *ante-crist* f. L *antechristus* f. Gk *antichristos* (ANTI- (1)+*khristos* CHRIST)]

antichri·stian, a. Pertaining to Antichrist; opposed to Christianity. Hence **antichri·stian**ISM n. [f. prec., with extended meaning]

anti·cipate, v.t. Use in advance; forestall (person or thing); accelerate, as *a.* one's *ruin*; discuss, consider, realize, beforehand; look forward to, expect, (event, *that* it will happen). Hence **anti·cip**ANT a. & n., **anti·cipat**IVE a., **anti·cipative**LY[2] adv. [f. L *anticipare* (*anti-* for ANTE-+ *-cipare* f. *capere* take) see -ATE[2]]

anticipa·tion, n. Action of anticipating (in senses of the vb); *thanking you in a.*, closing formula in letter of inquiry or request; (Med.) occurrence of phenomena before usual time; (Mus.) introduction beforehand of part of a chord about to follow. [f. L *anticipatio* (as prec., see -ATION)]

anti·cipator, n. One who anticipates. Hence **anti·cipat**ORY a. [L (as prec., see -OR[2])]

anticli·max, n. Opposite of climax, addition of a particular that weakens the effect; descent contrasting with previous rise. [ANTI- (1)]

anticli·nal, a. (Geol.) forming ridge on which strata lean against each other, and from which they slope down in opposite directions; (Anat.) with upright spine towards which spines on both sides incline. [f. ANTI-+Gk *klinō* lean+-AL]

anticy̆·clone, n. Rotary outward flow of air from atmospheric area of high pressure; whole system of pressure and outward flow. [ANTI- (1)]

a·ntidote, n. Medicine given to counteract poison or disease (*against, for, to*). Hence **a·ntidōt**AL a. [f. L f. Gk *antidoton* neut. of ANTI*dotos* given against]

a·ntigen, n. Substance introduced into the blood to stimulate production of anti-bodies. [ANTI(-BODY)+-GEN (1)]

antigrŏ·pelōs, n. pl. Waterproof leggings. [perh. for *anthygropelos* (ANTI- (2)+Gk *hugros* wet+*pēlos* mud)]

anti-Jă·cobin, a. & n. (One) opposed to the Jacobins (revolutionary party in France, 1789) or the French revolution. [ANTI- (2)]

antilo·garithm, n. Number to which a logarithm belongs, as *100 is the a. of 2.* [ANTI- (1)]

anti·logy, n. Contradiction in terms. [f. Gk *antilogia* (ANTI-+*-logia* speaking)]

antimaca·ssar, n. Covering thrown over chairs &c., as protection from grease or as an ornament. [ANTI- (2)]

a·ntimasque, -mask, n. Grotesque interlude between acts of masque. [ANTI- (1)]

antimonar·chical, a. Opposed to monarchy. [ANTI- (2)]

a·ntimony, n. Brittle metallic substance, bluish-white, of flaky crystalline texture. [f. med. L *antimonium*, prob. of Arab. orig.]

antinō·mian, a. & n. Opposed to the obligatoriness of moral law; pertaining to Antinomians; one who maintains that the moral law is not binding on Christians. [f. L *Antinomi*, name of sect in Germany (1535) alleged to hold above opinion (ANTI-+Gk *nomos* law)+-AN]

anti·nomy, n. Contradiction in a law, or between two laws; conflict of authority; paradox. [f. L f. Gk ANTI*nomia* (*nomos* law)]

antipathĕ·tic, a. Opposed in nature or disposition (*to*). Hence **antipathe·tic**AL a., **antipathe·tical**LY[2] adv. [f. Gk ANTI*patheō* (as ANTIPATHY), see -ETIC]

antipă·thic, a. Of contrary character (*to*); (Med.) having, producing, contrary symptoms. [f. F *antipathique* f. *antipathie* (as foll.)]

anti·pathy, n. Constitutional or settled aversion (*against, to, between* persons). [f. L f. Gk *antipatheia* f. ANTI*pathēs* opposed in feeling (*pathos -eos*)]

antiphlogi·stic, a. & n. (Medicine, paste, &c.) reducing inflammation. So **antiphlogi·st**INE[4] n. [ANTI- (2)]

a·ntiphon, n. Versicle, sentence, sung by one choir in response to another; prose or verse composition consisting of such passages; anthem. [f. F *antiphone* f. med. L *antiphona*, fem. sing., f. Gk ANTI*phōna* (neut. pl. of *antiphōnos*) things sounding in response (*phōnē* vocal sound)]

anti·phonal, a. & n. Sung alternately; responsive; collection of antiphons. Hence **anti·phonal**LY[2] adv. [OF (*antiphone*, see prec. and -AL)]

anti·phonary, n. Book of antiphons. [f. med. L *antiphonarium* (as ANTIPHONE, see -ARY[1])]

anti·phony, n. Antiphon; antiphonal singing; response, echo. [f. Gk *antiphōnos*, see ANTIPHON and -Y[1]]

anti·podēs, n. pl. Place(s) diametrically opposite (to each other), esp. region opposite to our own; (sing. *antipode*, pron. -ōd) exact opposite (*of, to*). Hence **anti·pod**AL, **antipodē·**AN, aa. [f. L f.

Gk *antipodes* having the feet opposite, pl. of ANTI*pous* adj. (*pous podos* foot)]

a·ntipole, n. Opposite pole; direct opposite. [ANTI- (1)]

a·ntipope, n. Pope elected in opposition to one (held to be) canonically chosen. [f. F *antipape* f. med. L *antipapa*; assim. to *pope*]

antipyre·tic, a. & n. (Drug) allaying or preventing fever. So **antipyr·in** n., a particular a. [ANTI- (2); see PYRETIC]

antiquār·ian, a. & n. Connected with study of antiquities; large size of drawing paper; antiquary, whence **antiquar·ian**ISM n., **antiquar·ian**IZE v.i. [as foll. + -AN]

a·ntiquary, n. Student, collector, of antiquities. [f. L *antiquarius* (*antiquus* ancient, see -ARY[1])]

a·ntiquate, v.t. Make obsolete (esp. in p.p.), abolish as out of date; make antique. [f. obs. adj. *antiquate* (L *antiquare* f. *antiquus* ancient, see -ATE[2])]

anti·que (-ēk), a. & n. Of old times; existing since old times; old-fashioned; after the manner of the ancients; archaic; relic of ancient art or of old times; *the a.*, antique style. Hence **anti·que**NESS n. [f. L *antiquus, anticus,* former, ancient (*ante* before; cf. *posticus*), whence also ANTIC]

anti·quity, n. Ancientness; old times, esp. time before middle ages; the ancients; (pl.) customs, events, precedents, of ancient times; (usu. pl.) ancient relics. [f. F *antiquité* f. L *antiquitatem* (*antiquus,* see prec. and -TY)]

antirrhī·num, n. Genus of plants, Snapdragon. [L, f. Gk *antirrhinon* (*anti* counterfeiting + *rhis rhinos* nose)]

antisabbatār·ian, a. & n. (Person) opposed to observance of Sabbath. [ANTI- (3)]

antiscorbū·tic, a. & n. (Medicine) against scurvy. [ANTI- (2)]

antiscri·ptural, a. Opposed to Scripture. [ANTI- (2)]

anti-Sē·mite, a. & n. (Person) hostile to Jews. So **anti-Semi·t**IC a., **anti-Se·mīt**ISM n. [ANTI-]

antise·ptic, a. & n. (Agent) counteracting putrefaction (lit. and fig.). Hence **antise·pt**ICALLY adv. [f. ANTI- (3) + Gk *sēptikos* putrefying (*sēptos* adj. f. *sēpō* rot, see -IC)]

antiso·cial, a. Opposed to principles on which society is based. [ANTI- (2)]

anti·strophē, n. (Lines recited during) returning movement from left to right in Greek choruses; inverse relation. [L f. Gk, = turning about (ANTI*strephō* turn against)]

antistrŏ·phic, a. Pertaining to antistrophes. [f. Gk *antistrophikos* (as prec., see -IC)]

antithē·ist, n. One opposed to belief in existence of a God. Hence **antithei·st**IC a., **antithē·**ISM n. [ANTI- (3)]

anti·thesis, n. (pl. *-thesēs*). Contrast of ideas expressed by parallelism of strongly contrasted words; opposition, contrast, (*of, between,* two things); direct opposite (*of, to*). [L f. Gk (vbl n. f. ANTI*tithēmi* set against)]

antithĕ·tic, a. Of the nature of antithesis; contrasted; consisting of two opposites. Hence **antithe·tic**AL a., **antithe·tical**LY[2] adv. [f. Gk *antithetikos* (as prec., see -IC)]

antito·xin, n. A serum serving to neutralize a toxin. So **antito·x**IC a. [ANTI-]

a·nti-trade, a. & n. *A.* (*wind*), one that blows in opposite direction to trade wind. [ANTI- (2)]

antitrinitār·ian, a. & n. (One) opposed to doctrine of the Trinity. Hence **antitrinitar·ian**ISM n. [ANTI- (3)]

a·ntitype, n. That which a type or symbol represents. Hence **antitў·p**ICAL a. [f. Gk ANTI*tupos* responding as an impression to the die (*tupos* stamp f. st. *tup-* strike)]

a·ntler, n. Branched horn, branch of a horn, of stag or other deer. Hence **a·ntler**ED[2] a. [f. OF *antoillier* f. LL *antocularem* (*ramum*) (branch) in front of the eyes (ANTE- + *oculus* eye); orig. = lowest branch]

antonomā·sia, n. Substitution of epithet &c. for proper name (e.g. *the Iron Duke*); use of proper name to express general idea (e.g. *a Solomon*). [L f. Gk, f. ANT*onomazō* name instead (*onoma* name)]

a·ntonym, n. A word of contrary meaning to another, as *bad* to *good* (opp. *synonym*). [ANTI- + (SYN)ONYM]

a·nus, n. Posterior opening of alimentary canal in animals. [L]

a·nvil, n. Block (usu. iron) on which smith works metal; (Physiol.) a bone of the ear. [OE *onfilti*, etym. dub.]

anxi·ety (ăngz-), n. Uneasiness, concern; solicitous desire (*for* a thing, *to* do). [f. L *anxietas -atis* (as foll., see -TY)]

a·nxious (-kshus), a. Troubled, uneasy (*about*); earnestly desirous (*for* a thing, *to* do); causing anxiety, as *an a. business.* Hence **a·nxious**LY[2] adv. [f. L *anxius* (*angere* choke) + -OUS]

a·ny (ĕ-), a., pron., & adv. (With interrog.) one, some, (no matter which), as *have you a. wool? have you a. of them? were a. Frenchmen there?*; (after negative expr. or implied) *cannot see a. difference, to prevent a. loss, cannot find a. of them*; (in affirmative sent.) whichever (of all) is chosen, every, as *a. chemist will tell you, at a. rate*; *a. one* (adj.), whatever individual is chosen; *a. one* (pron.), any person, anybody; (adv., w. compar. in neg. or interrog. context) at all, in a. degree, (*is that a. better?*; *without being a. the wiser*). [OE *ǣnig* (cogn. w. OHG *einîc*, mod. G. *einig*, Du. *eenig*) f. *ān* one + *-ig* adj. ending (see -Y²), here perh. dim.]

a·nybody, n. or pron. Any person; *if you wish to be a.* (of any importance); *two or three anybodies* (ordinary people).

a·nyhow, adv. & conj. In any way whatever; in any case, at any rate; at haphazard, as *does his work a.*, *things are all a.*

a·nything, pron. & n. Whatever thing; a thing, no matter which; a thing of any kind.

a·nyway, adv. & conj. = ANYHOW.

a·nywhere, adv. In any place.

a·nywise, adv. In any wise.

A·nzac, n. & a. (Pl.) *the* Australian and New Zealand Army Corps in the Great War; (sing.) member of the Aa.; (adj.) of the Aa. [= A. & N.-Z. A. C.]

a·orist, a. & n. (Gram.) indefinite, implying no limitation; (Gk Gram.) *a.* (*tense*), one denoting simply occurrence (in indicative, past occurrence), without limitations as to continuance &c. So **aori·stic** a. [f. Gk *aoristos* unlimited (*a-* not + *horizō* limit f. *horos*)]

āor·ta, n. Great artery or trunk of the arterial system, issuing from left ventricle of heart. Hence **aor·tic** a. [f. med. L f. Gk *aortē* that which is hung (*aeirō* lift)]

à outrance (F), phr. To the death.

ap- = AD- before *p*.

apa·ce, adv. Swiftly, quickly. [A prep. + PACE]

Apa·che (-ahsh), n. Violent street ruffian in Paris; (*A-*, pron. *apă·tshĭ*) member of N.-Amer. tribe. [native, lit. = enemy]

a·panage, app-, n. Provision for maintenance of younger children of kings, &c., (orig. province or lucrative office); perquisite; (of territory) dependency; natural accompaniment or attribute. [F, f. *apaner* endow with means of subsistence f. med. L APpanare (*panis* bread), see -AGE]

apar·t, adv. Aside, separately, independently, (*from*); *set a.*, devote, reserve, (*for*); *jesting a.* (laid aside). [f. F *à part* (*à* to, *part* side)]

apar·tment, n. Single room of a house; (pl.) set of rooms. [f. F *appartement* f. med. L *appartimentum* (APpartire apportion, see -MENT)]

ăpathĕ·tic, a. Insensible to emotion; indifferent. Hence **apathe·tically** adv. [f. foll., after PATHETIC]

ă·pathy, n. Insensibility to suffering; passionless existence; indolence of mind. [f. F *apathie* f. L f. Gk *apatheia* f. *apathēs* without feeling (*a-* not + *pathos -eos* suffering]

ape¹, n. Tailless monkey (gorilla, chimpanzee, orang-outan, gibbons); imitator, mimic; *play the a.*, mimic; *Sea A.*, fish (Sea Fox). [OE *apa* masc. *ape* fem. (Du. *aap*, OHG *affo*, MHG *affe*)]

ape², v.t. Imitate, mimic. [f. prec.]

apea·k, adv. & pred. a. (naut.). Vertical, as *oars a.* [f. F *à pic* (*à* to, at, *pic*, summit, see PEAK)]

ape·psy, n. Lack of digestive power. [f. Gk *apepsia* (*a-* not + *peptō* digest)]

aperçu (F), n. Summary exposition, conspectus. [F, p.p. of *apercevoir* perceive]

apĕ·rient, a. & n. Laxative (medicine). [f. L *aperire* open, see -ENT]

apĕ·ritive, a. & n. = prec. [f. F *apéritif* f. med. L *aperitivus* variant of *apertivus* (as prec., see -IVE)]

ă·perture (-tsher), n. Opening, gap; space through which light passes in optical instruments. [f. L *apertura* (as prec., see -URE)]

ā·pery, n. Mimicry; apish performance; ape-house. [APE n. + -RY]

apĕ·talous, a. Without petals. [f. Gk *apetalos* leafless (*a-* not + *petalon* leaf) + -OUS]

ā·pex, n. (pl. *-icēs*, *-exes*). Tip, top, peak; vertex (of triangle, cone). [L, = small rod at top of flamen's cap, peak, tip, perh. as APT; cf. *vertex* f. *vertere*]

aphā·sia, n. Loss of speech, as result of cerebral affection. Hence **aphă·sic** (-z-), a. & n. [Gk, f. *aphatos* speechless (*a-* not + *pha-* speak]

aphē·lion, n. Point farthest from sun (of planet's or comet's orbit). [Graecized f. mod. L *aphelium* f. Gk *aph' hēliou* from the sun]

aphēliotrŏ·pic, a. (bot.). Turning from the sun. Hence **apheliotro·pically** adv., **aphelio·tropism** n. [f. Gk as prec. + *tropikos* turning (*trepō*)]

ă·phesis, n. Gradual loss of unaccented vowel at beginning of word, as in (*e*)*squire*. [Gk, = letting go, f. *aphiēmi* (*apo* away + *hiēmi* send)]

aphĕ·tic, a. Pertaining to aphesis. Hence **a·phetize** v.t. [f. Gk *aphetos* vbl adj. (as prec.) + -IC]

ă·phis, n. (pl. *ă·phidēs*). Plant-lice, minute insects, the food of ladybirds, and tended by ants for the honey-dew they yield. Hence **aphi·dian** a. [?]

aphōnia, n. Total loss of voice. [Gk, f. *aphōnos* voiceless (*a-* not + *phōnē* voice)]

ă·phorism, n. Short pithy maxim; definition. Hence or cogn. **aphori·smic, aphori·stic** [-IST], aa., **aphori·stically** adv. [f. Gk *aphorizō* (APO- + *horizō* f. *horos* boundary), see -ISM]

ăphrodi·siac (-dĭz-), a. & n. Venereal; (drug) producing venereal desire. [f. Gk *aphrodisiakos* f. *aphrodisios* (*Aphroditē* Venus), see -AC]

aphy·llous, a. (bot.). Naturally leafless. [f. Gk *aphullos* (*a-* not + *phullon* leaf) + -OUS]

āpiār·ian, a. Pertaining to bee-keeping. [as foll. + -AN]

ā·piary, n. Place where bees are kept. Hence **a·piar**IST n. [f. L *apiarium* (*apis* bee, see -ARY¹)]

ă·pical, a. Belonging to an apex; placed at the tip. Hence **a·pical**LY² adv. [f. L *apex -icis* + -AL]

ā·piculture, n. Bee-keeping. [f. L *apis* bee + CULTURE]

apie·ce, adv. Severally, each, as *five pounds a.* [orig. *a piece*]

ā·pish, a. Of the nature, appearance, of an ape; ape-like in manner, silly. Hence **a·pish**LY² adv., **a·pish**NESS n. [f. APE n. + -ISH]

aplomb (F), n. Perpendicularity; self-possession. [F, = *à plomb* according to plummet]

apnoe·a (-nē*a*), n. Suspension of breathing. [mod. L, f. Gk *apnoia* f. *apnoos* breathless (*a-* not + *pnoē* breath)]

ăpo-, pref. (before unaspirated vowel *ap-*, before aspirate *aph-*), = Gk *apo* prep. off, from, away, un-, quite; in compds f. Gk, and in mod. scientific wds (not on Gk anal.) with sense 'detached, separate'.

apŏ·calypse, n. Revelation, esp. that made to St John in island of Patmos; book recording this. So **apo·caly·pt**IC(AL) aa., **apo·caly·ptical**LY² adv. [f. L f. Gk *apokalupsis* (APO*kaluptō* uncover)]

apŏ·copē, n. Cutting off of last letter or syllable of word. [Gk (APO*koptō* cut off)]

apŏ·crypha, n. Books of Old Testament included in Septuagint and Vulgate, but not originally written in Hebrew, nor counted genuine by Jews, and excluded from Canon at Reformation. [LL *apocrypha* (*scripta*) hidden writings f. Gk *apokruphos* (APO*kruptō* hide away); treated in E as sing., with pl. *-as*]

apŏ·cryphal, a. Of the apocrypha; of doubtful authenticity; sham, false. [as prec. + -AL]

ă·pod, n. Bird, reptile, fish, without (or with undeveloped) feet or ventral fins. Hence **a·pod**AL a. [f. Gk *apous* footless (*a-* not + *pous podos* foot)]

apodĭ·ctic, -dei·ctic (-dī-), a. Of clear demonstration; clearly established. Hence **apodi·ct**ICALLY adv. [f. L f. Gk *apodeiktikos* (APO*deiknumi* show, see -IC)]

apŏ·dosis, n. Concluding clause of sentence (cf. PROTASIS); consequent clause of conditional sentence, wherever placed. [L f. Gk (APO*didōmi* give back)]

ă·pogee (-j-), n. Point (in orbit of moon or any planet) farthest from earth; greatest distance of sun from earth when latter is in aphelion; (fig.) most distant spot, highest point. Hence **apogē·**AN a. [f. F *apogée* f. L f. Gk APO*gaion* (neut. adj.) away from earth (*gaia, gē,* earth)]

apolau·stic, a. Self-indulgent. [f. Gk *apolaustikos* (APO*lauō* enjoy, see -IC)]

Apollinār·is, n. Mineral water exported from the A. spring in Rhenish Prussia.

Apo·llo, n. Greek sun-god; (poet.) the sun; man of great beauty. [L f. Gk *Apollōn*]

Apo·llyon, n. The Devil. [f. Gk *apolluōn* part. of *apolluō* (APO- + *olluō* destroy)]

apologĕ·tic, a. & n. Regretfully acknowledging, excusing, fault or failure; vindicatory; (n., usu. pl.) argumentative defence, esp. of Christianity. Hence **apologe·tic**AL a., **apologe·tical**LY² adv. [f. F *apologétique* f. L f. Gk *apologētikos* (*apologeomai* speak in defence, see APOLOGY and -IC)]

apo·logist, n. One who defends (esp. Christianity) by argument. [f. F *apologiste* f. Gk *apologia*, see APOLOGY and -IST]

apo·logize, v.i. Make an apology (*for*). [f. APOLOGY + -IZE]

a·pologue (-ŏg), n. Moral fable. [F, f. L f. Gk *apologos* fable (*apo* off + *logos* speech)]

apo·logy, n. Regretful acknowledgement of offence; assurance that no offence was intended; explanation, vindication; *a. for,* bad specimen of (*this a. for a letter*). [f. L f. Gk *apologia* defence (*apo* away + *-logia* speaking)]

a·pophthegm (-ĕm), n. Terse saying; pithy maxim. Hence **apophthegma·t**IC (-ĕg-) a., **apophthegma·t**ICALLY adv. [f. Gk *apophthegma -matos* (APO*phtheggomai* speak out)]

apople·ctic, a. Pertaining to, causing, apoplexy; suffering from, tending to, apoplexy. Hence **apople·ct**ICALLY, adv. [f. L f. Gk *apoplēktikos* (APO*plēssō* strike completely, see -IC)]

a·poplexy, n. Malady arresting powers of sense and motion, usu. caused by effusion of blood or serum in brain. [f. F *apoplexie* f. L f. Gk *apoplēxia* (as prec.)]

aposīopē·sis, n. (rhet.). Sudden breaking-off in speech. [L, f. Gk f. APO(*siōpaō* keep silent)]

apo·stasy, n. Abandonment of religious faith, vows, principles, or party. [f. L f. Gk *apostasia* (APO*sta-* withdraw)]

apo·state (-*a*t), n. & a. (One) guilty of apostasy. So **apostă·t**ICAL a. [F, f. L (*-ta*) f. Gk *apostatēs* (APO*sta-* withdraw)]

apo·statize, v.i. Become an apostate (*from* one *to* another). [f. LL *apostatizare* (as APOSTATE, see -IZE)]

ā pŏstĕriōr·ī, adv. & adj. phr. (Reasoning) from effects to causes; inductive. [L, = from what comes after]

apŏ·stil, n. Marginal note. [f. F *apostille*, etym. dub.]

apo·stle (-sl), n. Messenger, esp. any of the twelve whom Christ sent forth to preach Gospel; first successful Christian missionary in a country, as *a. of Germany*; leader of reform, as *a. of temperance*; *a. spoons* (with figures of aa. on handles). Hence **apo·stle**SHIP n. [f. OF *apostle, apostre* (mod. *apôtre*) f. L f. Gk *apostolos* (APO*stellō* send away); OE had *apostol*]

apo·stolate, n. Apostleship; leadership in a propaganda. [f. L *apostolatus* (as prec., see -ATE[1])]

apostŏ·lic, a. Pertaining to the Apostles; of the character of an apostle; of the Pope, papal, as *A. See, succession.* Hence **aposto·lic**AL a., **aposto·lical**LY[2] adv. [f. F *apostolique* f. L f. Gk *apostolikos* (as APOSTLE, see -IC)]

apo·strophe[1] (-fĭ), n. (rhet.). Exclamatory address, in course of public speech or in poem, to particular person (often dead or absent). Hence **apostrŏ·phi**C a., **apo·stroph**IZE v.t. & i. [L f. Gk, lit. turning away (as foll.)]

apo·strophe[2] (-fĭ), n. Sign of omission of letter, or of possessive case, (e.g. *can't, boy's.*) Hence **apostrŏ·phi**C a. [confused w. prec., but prop. three syllables (-strŏf); F, f. L f. Gk (*hē*) *apostrophos* (*prosōdia*) (the accent) of elision (APO*strephō* turn away)]

apŏ·thecary, n. (archaic). Druggist, pharmaceutical chemist, as *Apothecaries' Company.* [f. OF *apotecaire* f. LL *apothecarius* f. *apotheca* f. Gk *apothēkē* storehouse (APO*tithēmi* lay away), see -ARY[1]]

apotheō·sis, n. Deification (lit. & fig.); canonization; deified ideal; (loosely) release from earthly life. Hence **apo·theos**IZE v.t. [L f. Gk (APO*theoō* make a god of, f. *theos* god, see -OSIS)]

appa·l (-awl), v.t. (-ll-). Dismay, terrify. Hence **appa·lling**LY[2] adv. [perh. f. OF *apalir* make pale; but cf. PALL v.]

appanage. See APANAGE.

apparā·tus, n. (pl. *-uses*). Mechanical requisites, *an* appliance, for doing something; organs by which natural processes are carried on; *a. criticus,* materials for critical study of document. [L (AP*parare* make ready for, see -ATE[1])]

appă·rel[1], v.t. (-ll-). Attire, dress. [f. OF *apareiller* f. Rom. *AD*pariculare* make fit (*pariculus* dim. of *par* equal)]

appă·rel[2], n. Ornamental embroidery on ecclesiastical vestments; (archaic) clothing, dress. [f. OF *aparail* f. *apareiller,* see prec.]

appă·rent (*or* -ār-), a. Manifest, palpable; seeming; *heir a.* (whose right cannot be superseded by birth of nearer heir, cf. PRESUMPTIVE). Hence **appă·rent**LY[2] adv. [f. OF *aparant* f. L as APPEAR, see -ENT]

appari·tion, n. Appearance, esp. of a supernatural being; ghost. [F, f. L *apparitionem* (as APPEAR, see -ION)]

appă·ritor, n. Public servant of Roman magistrate; officer of civil or ecclesiastical court; herald, usher. [L (as prec., see -OR[2])]

appea·l[1], v.i. Call *to* (higher tribunal) for deliverance from decision of lower (also abs.); *a. to the country* (i.e. from parliament), dissolve parliament; call *to* (witness) for corroboration; call attention *to* (evidence); make earnest request (*to* person, *for* thing or *to* do); *pictures a.* (address themselves) *to the eye, do not a.* (prove attractive) *to me.* [f. OF *apeler* f. L AP*pellare* address]

appea·l[2], n. Act of appealing; right of appealing; *Court of A.* (hearing cases previously tried in inferior courts). [f. OF *apel* (as prec.)]

appea·lable, a. That can be appealed against; that can be appealed *to.* [APPEAL v. + -ABLE]

appear·, v.i. Become, be, visible; present oneself formally, publicly; be published; be manifest; seem. [f. *aper*- st. of OF *apareir* f. L AP*parēre -rit-* come in sight]

appear·ance, n. Act of appearing (in vbl senses; *put in an a.,* show oneself); look, aspect; semblance; *to all a.* (so far as can be seen); *save, keep up, aa.* (outward show &c.); apparition, phantom. [f. OF *aparance* f. L *apparentia* (as prec., see -ENCE)]

appea·se (-z), v.t. Pacify, quiet, (strife, anger, person); soothe; satisfy (appetite, prejudice). So **appea·s**ABLE a., **appea·se**MENT n. [f. OF *apeser, apaisier* (*à* to + *pais* peace f. L *pacem,* nom. *pax*)]

appe·llant, a. & n. Appealing; (Law) concerned with appeals; (n). one who appeals to higher court. [F (as APPEAL[1], see -ANT)]

appe·llate (-at), a. Taking cognizance of appeals, as *a. jurisdiction.* [f. L as foll., see -ATE[2]]

appella·tion, n. Name, title; nomenclature. [F, f. L as APPEAL[1], see -ATION]

appe·llative, a. & n. (Of words) designating a class, common (as opp. to *proper*); common noun, applicable to any member of a class; appellation. Hence **appe·llative**LY[2] adv. [f. L as APPEAL[1], see -ATIVE]

appe·nd, v.t. Hang on, annex; add in writing. [f. L AP*pendere*]

appe·ndage, n. Thing attached; addition; accompaniment. [prec. + -AGE]

appe·ndant, a. & n. (Possession, thing, person) attached in subordinate capacity (*to* another). [F, part. of *appendre* f. L *appendĕre* (for *-ēre*) hang to (intr.)]

appe·ndix, n. (pl. *-icēs, -ixes*). Subsidiary addition (*to* book or document); small process developed from surface of any organ, esp. *vermiform a.* (of the intestine), whence **appendici·**TIS n. [L *appendix -icis* (AP*pendĕre* hang to, trans.)]

apperce·ption, n. Mind's perception of itself; mental perception. [f. F *aperception* (LL AP*percipere -cept-* PERCEIVE, see -ION)]

appertai·n, v.i. Belong as possession or right *to*; be appropriate *to*; relate *to.* [f. OF *apartenir* f. LL AP(*pertinēre* PERTAIN)]

a·ppetence, -cy, n. Longing after, desire, (*of, for, after*); affinity (*for*). [f. F *appé-*

tence f. L *appetentia* (APpetere seek after, see -ENCE, -ENCY]

a·ppetent, a. Eagerly desirous (*after, of*). [f. L *appetere*, see prec. and -ENT]

a·ppetite, n. Desire, inclination, (*for*); desire to satisfy natural necessities, esp. hunger; relish. So **appĕ·titIVE** a. [f. OF *apetit* f. L *appetitus* (as prec., see -ITE[2])]

a·ppetize, v.t. (Of things) give appetite (only in part. *-izing*). Hence **a·ppetizer**[1] (2) n. [f. F *appétissant* part. as if f. L *appetitiare* (as prec.), assim. to vbs in -IZE]

applau·d, v.t. & i. (Intr.) express approval loudly, as by clapping hands; (trans.) express approval of, praise. [f. L AP-*plaudere -plaus-* clap hands]

applau·se (-z), n. Approbation loudly expressed; marked approval. Hence **applau·SIVE** (-s-) a., **applau·siveLY**[2] adv. [f. L *applausus, -ūs* (as prec.)]

a·pple, n. Round firm fleshy fruit of a rosaceous tree; (Bot.) any inferior fleshy many-celled fruit; *A. of discord*, golden a. contended for by Juno, Minerva, and Venus; *A. of Sodom, Dead sea a.*, fruit dissolving into ashes; *a. of the eye*, the pupil, any cherished object; *a. brandy*, spirit distilled from cider; *a. butter*, sauce of apples stewed in cider; *a.-cart* (*upset* person's *a.-c.*, spoil his plans); *a. cheese*, compressed a.-pomace; *a. dumpling*, a. cooked in paste; *a. green*, a colour; *a. pomace*, pulp remaining after juice is expressed; *a.-jack*, Amer. name for a. brandy; *a.-john*, kind of a. said to keep two years and to be best when withered; *a.-pie bed*, one with sheets so folded that one's legs cannot get down; *a.-pie order*, perfect order. [com.-Teut.; OE *æppel*, OHG *aphul*, mod. G *apfel*]

appli·ance, n. Applying; thing applied as means to an end. [f. APPLY + -ANCE]

a·pplicable, a. Capable of being applied; having reference, appropriate, (*to*). Hence **applicaBI·LITY** n. [f. L as APPLY, see -ABLE]

a·pplicant, n. One who applies (*for*). [as prec., see -ANT]

applica·tion, n. Putting of one thing *to* another; employment of means; (application of) plaster, liniment, &c.; bringing (*of* a general rule &c.) to bear upon particular case; relevancy; diligence; making of a request; request made. [F, f. L *applicationem* (as foll., see -ATION)]

apply·, v.t. & i. Put close (*to*); administer (remedy &c. *to*; lit. and fig.); devote (*to*); make use of; use as relative or suitable (*to*); set one*self* closely (*to* task, *to* do); have reference (*to*); attend closely (*to*); address oneself (*for* help &c. *to*). [f. OF *aplier* f. L APplicare fold, fasten to]

appoggiatu·ra (-ŏjatōō-), n. (mus.). Grace-note prefixed to an essential note. [It.]

appoi·nt, v.t. Fix (time, place, *for* purpose); prescribe (thing, *that*); (Law) declare the destination of (property, also abs.); nominate, as *a. him governor, to govern, to be governor, a. him*; (p.p.) *well, badly, -appointed*, so equipped. Hence **appointEE·** n. [f. OF *apointer* (*à point* to the point)]

appoi·ntment, n. Appointing; engagement, assignation; decree, ordinance; office assigned; (usu. pl.) outfit; *keep, break, an a.*, appear, fail to appear, at fixed place and time. [f. OF *apointement* (as prec., see -MENT)]

appor·t, n. Material thing produced by occult means at spiritualist seance. [AP- + (*ex*)*port*, (*im*)*port*]

appor·tion, v.t. Assign as due share (*to*); portion out. Hence **appor·tionMENT** n. [f. OF *apportionner* (*à* to + *portionner* f. PORTION)]

a·pposite (-z-), a. Well put; appropriate (*to*). Hence **a·ppositeLY**[2] adv., **a·ppositeNESS** n. [f. L AP(*ponere posit-* put)]

apposi·tion, n. Application (of seal); placing side by side; (Gram.) placing of word in syntactic parallelism with another, esp. addition of one noun to another. Hence **apposi·tionAL** a. [f. L *appositio* (as prec., see -ION)]

apprai·se (-z), v.t. (Esp. of official valuer) fix price for; estimate. Hence **apprai·SAL, apprai·seMENT,** nn., **apprai·SABLE** a. [f. PRAISE v. (formerly used in the same sense), perh. on anal. of APPRIZE]

appre·ciable (-sha-), a. Capable of being estimated; perceptible, sensible. Hence **appre·ciabLY**[2] adv. [as foll., see -BLE]

apprē·ciate (-shĭ-), v.t. & i. Estimate worth, quality, amount, of; estimate aright; be sensitive to; esteem highly; raise in value; rise in value. Hence **appre·ciatIVE, appre·ciatORY** (-sha-), aa., **appre·ciativeLY**[2] adv. [f. L APpre-*tiare* appraise (*pretium* price), see -ATE[3]]

apprecia·tion (-sĭ-), n. Estimation, judgement; perception; adequate recognition; rise in value; critique. [f. F *appréciation* f. *apprécier* (as prec., see -ATION)]

apprehe·nd, v.t. Seize, arrest; perceive (by senses or intellect); understand; fear (thing, *that*). [f. F *appréhender* f. L AP-(*prehendere -hens-* lay hold of), whence also F *apprendre* learn]

apprehe·nsible, a. Capable of being grasped (by senses or intellect). Hence **apprehensiBI·LITY** n. [f. L *apprehensibilis* (as prec., see -BLE)]

apprehe·nsion, n. Seizure, arrest; grasping (of ideas), conception; understanding; dread. [f. L *apprehensio* (as prec., see -ION)]

apprehe·nsive, a. Pertaining to sensuous or mental perception; perceptive (*of*); intelligent; uneasy, fearful, (*of* thing, *that* it may happen, *for* person, *for* his safety). Hence **apprehe·nsiveLY**[2] adv., **apprehe·nsiveNESS** n. [f. med. L *apprehensivus* (as prec., see -IVE)]

appre·ntice[1], n. Learner of a craft, bound to serve, and entitled to instruction from, his employer for specified term; tiro. Hence **appre·ntice**SHIP n. [f. OF *apprentis* f. *apprendre* (see APPREHEND), suggested by words in *-tis, -tif,* f. L *-tivus* (see -IVE)]

appre·ntice[2], v.t. Bind as apprentice. [f. prec.]

appri·se (-z), v.t. Inform; (pass.) be aware *of.* [f. F *appris -ise* p.p. of *apprendre* learn, teach, (see APPREHEND)]

appri·ze, v.t. (archaic). Appraise; appreciate. [f. OF *aprisier* (*à* to +*prisier* PRAISE)]

a·ppro. *On appro.,* (of goods supplied) to be returned if not satisfactory. [=*approval* or *approbation*]

approa·ch[1], v.t. & i. Come near(er); approximate in character &c. *to*; come near to; approximate to; (commerc.) make overtures or proposals to; (Mil.) make approaches to. Hence **approach**ABI·LITY n., **approa·ch**ABLE a. [f. OF *aprochier* f. LL AD*propiare* draw near (*propius* compar. of *prope* near)]

approa·ch[2], n. Act of approaching; approximation; access, passage, (lit. and fig.); (Mil.) entrenchments enabling besiegers to approach. [f. prec.]

a·pprobate, v.t. (U.S.). Approve formally, sanction. [f. L AP(*probare* test f. *probus* good) see -ATE[3]]

approba·tion, n. Sanction; approval. So **a·pprobat**ORY a. [F, f. L *approbationem* (as prec., see -ATION)]

apprō·priate[1] (-*at*), a. Belonging, peculiar, (*to*); suitable, proper, (*to, for*). Hence **appro·priate**LY[2] adv., **appro·priate**NESS n. [f. L AP*propriare* (*proprius* own), see -ATE[2]]

apprō·priāte[2], v.t. Take possession of; take to oneself; devote to special purposes. Hence or cogn. **appropri**A·TION, **appro·priat**OR[2], nn., **appro·priat**IVE a. [f. prec., see -ATE[3]]

appro·val (-ōō-), n. Approbation; sanction. [f. foll. + -AL (2); rare before 1800, *-ance* being used instead]

appro·ve (-ōōv), v.t. & i. Give evidence of (quality); (refl.) show one*self* to be; confirm, sanction; commend; *a. of,* pronounce, consider, good; (p.p.) pronounced satisfactory, accepted, (of persons, reasons, &c.; *approved society,* under Nat. Insurance Act). [f. OF *aprover* f. L as APPROBATE]

appro·ver, n. One who approves; one who turns King's evidence. [f. prec. + -ER[1]]

appro·ximate[1] (-*at*), a. Very near; closely resembling; fairly correct. Hence **appro·ximate**LY[2] adv. [f. L AP*proximare* (*proximus* very near), see -ATE[2]]

appro·ximāte[2], v.t. & i. Bring, come, near (*to* thing, esp. in quality, number, &c.). Hence **approxima**·TION n., **appro·xima**TIVE a., **appro·ximative**LY[2] adv. [f. prec., see -ATE[3]]

appui· (-wē), n. (Mil.) defensive support; *point of a.* (F *point d'a.*), fixed object on which troops commence formation into line. [F, f. *appuyer* f. LL AP*podiare* (*podium* support f. Gk *podion* base f. *pous podos* foot)]

appūr·tenance, n. Belonging; appendage; accessory. [f. AF *apurtenance* (OF *aper-, apar-*) f. LL *appertinentia* (as APPERTAIN, see -ANCE)]

appur·tenant, a. & n. (Thing) belonging, appertaining, pertinent, (*to*). [f. OF *apartenant* part. as APPERTAIN]

ā·pricot, n. Orange-coloured stone-fruit allied to plum. [(also earlier *apricock*) f. Sp. *albar(i)coque* f. Arab. *al* the +*burquq* f. Gk *praikokion* prob. f. L *praecoquum* variant of *praecox* early-ripe; *-cot* by assim. to F *abricot*]

A·pril (ā-), n. Fourth month of year; *A.-fool,* one sportively imposed upon on *A.-fool-day* (April 1). [f. OF *avrill* f. L *aprilis*]

***ā prĭor·ī*,** adv. & a. (Reasoning) from cause to effect; deductively; (loosely) presumptively, as far as one knows. Hence **ā-priŏ·**RITY n. [L, =from what is before]

ā·pron, n. Garment worn in front of body to protect clothes; official dress, as *bishop's, dean's, freemason's, a.*; leather covering for legs in open carriage; skin covering stuffing of roast goose or duck; *tied to a.-strings of* (wife, mother, &c.), unduly controlled by; (Theatr.) advanced strip of stage for playing scenes before curtain. Hence **a·pron**ED[2] a., **a·pron**FUL n. [f. OF *naperon* dim. of *nape* tablecloth f. L *mappa* napkin; for loss of *n-* (an apron =a napron) cf. *adder*]

ăpropos· (-pō), adv., a., n. To the purpose; in respect *of*; appropriate(ness). [F, *à* to +*propos* PURPOSE]

apse, n. Semi-circular or polygonal recess, arched or dome-roofed, esp. in church. [f. APSIS]

a·psidal, a. Of the form of an apse; of the apsides. [f. foll. + -AL]

a·psis, n. (pl. *a·psĭdēs, apsī·dēs*). Aphelion, perihelion, of planet; apogee, perigee, of moon; *line of aa.,* straight line joining these. [L, f. Gk (*h*)*apsis -idos* fastening, felloe of wheel, vault, (*haptō* join)]

apt, a. Suitable, appropriate; having a tendency *to* (do); quick-witted (*at*). Hence **a·pt**LY[2] adv., **a·pt**NESS n. [f. L *aptus* fitted p.p. of **apere* fasten]

a·pterous, a. Wingless; (Bot.) having no membranous expansions. [f. Gk *apteros* (*a-* not +*pteron* wing) + -OUS]

a·pteryx, n. New-Zealand bird with rudimentary wings and no tail. [f. Gk *a-* not +*pterux* wing]

a·ptitude, n. Fitness; natural propensity

(*for*); ability. [F, f. L *aptitudinem* (as APT, see -TUDE)]

ă·qua, n. (chem.). Liquid, solution, as *a. fortis*, nitric acid, *a. rēgia*, mixture of nitric and hydrochloric acids, able to dissolve gold and platinum. [L, = water]

āquamari·ne (-ēn), n. Bluish-green beryl; bluish green (also as adj). [f. L *aqua marina* sea-water]

ăquare·lle (-rĕl), n. Kind of painting with Chinese ink and thin water-colours. [F, f. It. *acquerella* water-colour dim. of *acqua* f. L *aqua* water]

aquār·ium, n. (pl. *-iums, -ia*). Artificial pond or tank for the keeping of live aquatic plants and animals; place of public entertainment containing such tanks. [L (*aqua* water, see -ARIUM)]

Aquār·ius, n. Zodiacal constellation; eleventh sign of Zodiac, which sun enters on Jan. 21. [L, = water-carrier (as prec., see -ARY[1])]

aquă·tic, a. & n. (Plant, animal) growing, living, in or near water; (of sports) conducted in or upon water. [f. F *aquatique* f. L *aquaticus* (*aqua* water, see -ATIC)]

ă·quatint, n. Method of engraving on copper by use of a resinous solution and nitric acid. [f. F *aqua-tinte*, It. *acqua tinta*, f. L *aqua tincta* dyed water (*tingere* dye)]

āqua-vī·tae, n. Ardent spirits, esp. of the first distillation. [L, = water of life]

ă·queduct, n. Artificial channel, esp. elevated structure of masonry, for conveyance of water; conduit; (Physiol.) small canal, esp. in head of mammals. [f. L *aquae ductus* conveyance of water (*ducere duct-* lead)]

ā·queous, a. Of water, watery; (Geol.) produced by water, as *a. rocks*. [as f. a L *aqueus* (*aqua* water) + -OUS]

ă·quiline, a. Of an eagle; eagle-like, as *a. nose* (hooked). [f. L *aquilinus* (*aquila* eagle, see -INE[1])]

aquŏ·sity, n. Wateriness. [f. med. L *aquositas* f. *aquosus* (*aqua* water), see -OSE and -TY]

ar-, pref. = AD- before *r*.

-ar[1], suf. (1) f. L *-aris* (varying with *-alis* -AL), adj. suf. taken direct or thr. F, or imitated with L nouns. OF had *-er*, new F wds have *-aire*; E corrects *-er* (*scholar*), but sometimes uses -ARY[2] instead of *-ar* for *-aire* (*military*). (2) noun suf., f. L *-are, -ar*, neut. of above (*altar, exemplar*).

-ar[2], suf. Occas. (for regular -ER[2], -ARY[1]) f. L *-arius, -arium*, in nouns thr. OF *-ier* (*bursar*) or F *-aire* (*vicar*).

-ar[3], suf. Variant for regular -ER[1], -OR[2], in nouns (*beggar, liar*), perh. on anal. of *scholar* (-AR[1]).

Ă·rab, n. & a. Native of Arabia; Arab horse; *street a.*, homeless child; (adj.) Arabian. [f. F *Arabe* f. L *Arabem* (nom. *-bs*) f. Gk *Araps -abos*]

ărabe·sque, a. & n. Arabian; fantastic; decoration in colour or low relief, with fanciful intertwining of leaves, scroll-work, &c. [F, = Arabian, see -ESQUE]

Arā·bian, a. & n. Of Arabia; *A. nights*, collection of fabulous stories; *A. bird*, phoenix. (N.) = Arab. [f. *Arabia* + -AN]

A·rabic, a. & n. Arabian; *gum A.* (exuded by some kinds of acacia); *A. numerals*, 1, 2, 3, &c.; (n.) language of the Arabs. [f. OF *Arabic* f. L *Arabicus* (*Arabs* ARAB, see -IC)]

A·rabist, n. Student of Arabic. [ARAB + -IST]

ă·rable, a. & n. (Land) fit for tillage. [f. L *arabilis* (*arare* plough, see -BLE)]

ara·chnid (-k-), n. (zool.). Member of the *Arachnida*, class comprising spiders, scorpions, and mites. [f. Gk *arakhnē* spider + -ID[3]]

ara·chnoid, a. & n. (Bot.) covered with long cobweb-like hairs; (n.) serous membrane lining the dura mater, and enveloping brain and spinal cord. [f. Gk *arakhnoeidēs* (*arakhnē* cobweb, see -OID)]

Aramā·ic (ă-), a. & n. (Language) of Aram or Syria; northern branch of Semitic family of languages, including Syriac and Chaldee. [f. L f. Gk *Aramaios* of Aram + -IC]

Aranē·idan, a. & n. (Member) of the *Araneida* or spiders. [f. L *aranea* spider, see -ID[3]]

Araucār·ia, n. Genus of trees including monkey-puzzle. [*Arauco*, name of province]

ar·balest, ar·blast, n. Crossbow. [f. OF *arbaleste* f. L *arcuballista* (*arcus* bow + *ballista* military engine)]

ar·biter, n. Judge; one appointed by two parties to settle dispute, umpire; one who has entire control (*of*). [L, perh. f. *ar-* = *ad* to + *bitere* go, one who goes to see]

ar·bitrage (-ĭj), n. Traffic in bills of exchange or stocks to take advantage of different prices in other markets. [F, f. *arbitrer* as ARBITRATE, see -AGE]

ar·bitral, a. Pertaining to arbitration. [F, f. LL *arbitralis*, see ARBITER and -AL]

arbi·trament, -ement, n. Deciding of dispute by arbiter; authoritative decision. [f. OF *arbitrement* (*arbitrer*, see ARBITRAGE and -MENT)]

ar·bitrary, a. Derived from mere opinion; capricious; unrestrained; despotic; (Law) discretionary. Hence **ar·bitrari**LY[2] adv., **ar·bitrari**NESS n. [f. L *arbitrarius*, see ARBITER and -ARY[1]]

ar·bitrate, v.t. & i. Decide by arbitration. [f. L *arbitrari* judge, see ARBITER and -ATE[3]]

arbitra·tion, n. Settlement of a dispute by an arbiter; *a. of exchange*, determination of rate of indirect exchange between two currencies. [OF, f. L *arbitrationem* (as prec., see -ATION)]

ar·bitrator, n. (Now the legal term for) arbiter. Hence **ar·bitrator**SHIP n. [f. OF

arbitratour by-form of *arbitrour* f. L *arbitratorem* (as ARBITRATE, see -OR²)]
ar·bitress, n. Female arbiter, mediatress; absolute mistress. [f. OF *arbitresse* fem. of *arbitre* f. L ARBITER, see -ESS¹]
ar·bor, n. Main support of machine; axle or spindle on which wheel revolves. [f. F *arbre* tree, axis, f. L *arbor*; refash. on L]
arbora·ceous, a. Tree-like; wooded. [f. L *arbor* tree, see -ACEOUS]
arbor·eal, a. Of, living in, connected with, trees. [f. L *arboreus* (as prec., see -AL)]
arbor·eous, a. Wooded; arboreal; arborescent. [as prec., see -OUS]
arbore·scent, a. Tree-like in growth or general appearance; (Arch.) branching out. Hence **arbore·sc**ENCE n., **arbore·scent**LY² adv. [f. L *arborescere* grow into a tree (*arbor*), see -ENT]
arborē·tum, n. (pl. *-ta*). A botanical tree-garden. [L, f. *arbor* tree]
ar·boriculture, n. Cultivation of trees and shrubs. Hence **arboricu·ltur**AL a., **arboricu·ltur**IST n. [f. L *arbor -oris* tree + CULTURE]
arboriza·tion, n. Tree-like appearance (Min., Chem.) in aggregation of crystals, (Anat.) from distension or injection of capillary vessels. [as prec. + -IZE + -ATION]
ar·bor vi·tae, n. Popular name of several evergreens. [L, = tree of life]
ar·bour, n. Bower, shady retreat with sides and roof formed by trees or latticework covered with climbing plants. Hence **ar·bour**ED² a. [orig. (*h*)*erber* f. OF (*h*)*erbier* grass lawn f. L *herbarium* (*herba* grass, herb, see -ARIUM), phonetic change to *ar-* being assisted by assoc. with L *arbor* tree]
ar·būtus, n. Genus of evergreens including strawberry-tree. [L]
arc, n. Part of circumference of circle or other curve; *diurnal, nocturnal, a.*, part of circle that a heavenly body appears to pass through above, below, horizon; belt contained between parallel curves; (Electr.) luminous bridge formed between two separate carbon poles; *a.-lamp, -light*, using this. [OF, f. L *arcus* bow, curve]
arca·de, n. Passage arched over; any covered walk, esp. with shops along one or both sides; (Arch.) series of arches on same plane. Hence **arca·d**ED² a. [F, f. It. *arcata* arch f. med. L *arcata* (L *arcus* bow), see -ADE]
Ar·cadĕs ă·mbō, sent. Blackguards both (cf. Byron *D. Juan*, iv. 93). [facet. application of Virg. *Ecl.* vii. 4]
Arcā·dian, a. & n. Ideal(ly) rustic. [f. L *Arcadius* (Gk *Arkadia* mountain district in Peloponnese) + -AN]
Ar·cady, -ā·dia, n. (poet.). Ideal rustic paradise. [f. Gk *Arkadia*, see prec.]
arcā·num, n. (Usu. in pl. *-na*) mystery, secret. [L, neut. of *arcanus* (*arca* chest, see -AN)]
arch¹, n. Curved structure, bearing weight or ornamental; curve; vault; *archway*, vaulted passage, arched entrance. Hence **ar·ch**WISE adv. [f. OF *arche* (f. L *arca* chest, but confused with *arc* f. L *arcus* bow)]
arch², v.t. & i. Furnish with an arch; form into an arch; overarch, span; (intr.) form an arch. [f. OF *archer* (as prec.)]
arch³, a. (sup. *-est*). Chief, pre-eminent, as *a. rogue, knave, impostor*, (but now usu. *a.-*); cunning, clever, innocently roguish, whence **ar·ch**LY² adv., **ar·ch**NESS n. [= foll.]
arch- (-tsh, exc. in *archangel*), pref. = Gk *arkhi-*, *arkh-*, *arkhe-*, comb. form of *arkhos* chief cogn. w. *arkhō* begin (OE *erce-*, *arce-*, OF *arce-*, later *arche*; whence G *erz-*, Du. *aarts*); in mod. literary wds f. Gk *archi-* is used, as *archdeacon* but *archidiaconal*. Meaning: (1) in titles of office &c. 'chief, superior', as *archbishop*, *-duke*, esp. in titles of Holy Roman or German empire, as *-butler*, *-chamberlain*; (2) 'pre-eminent, leading', as *-antiquary*, *-builder*, *-prophet*, *-wag*; esp. 'extreme, worst', as *-buffoon*, *-knave*, *-liar*; (3) rarely = 'first, original', as *-founder*, *-messenger*; (4) of things, 'chief', as *-diocese*.
archae·an (-k-), a. Of the earliest geological period. [f. Gk *arkhaios* ancient (*arkhē* beginning) + -AN]
archaeo·logy, n. Study of antiquities, esp. of the prehistoric period. So **archaeolo·g**IC(AL) aa., **archaeolo·gical**LY² adv., **archaeo·log**IST n. [f. Gk *arkhaiologia* (as prec., see -LOGY)]
archā·ic (-k-), a. Primitive, antiquated; (of language) no longer in common use, though retained for special purposes. Hence **archa·**ICALLY adv. [f. Gk *arkhaïkos* (as prec., see -IC)]
ar·chāism, n. Retention, imitation, of what is old or obsolete (esp. in language and art); archaic word or expression. Hence **ar·cha**IST n., **archai·st**IC a. [f. Gk *arkhaïsmos* (*arkhaïzō*, see foll. and -ISM)]
ar·chāize, v.t. & i. Imitate, affect, the archaic; (trans.) render archaistic. [f. Gk *arkhaïzō* copy the ancients (*arkhaios* ancient, see -IZE)]
ar·changel (-k-), n. Angel of highest rank; kind of dead-nettle; kind of pigeon. Hence **archange·l**IC a. [OF, f. L f. Gk *arkhaggelos* (see ARCH- and ANGEL)]
ar·chbi·shop, n. Chief bishop; metropolitan. Hence **arch**BI·SHOPRIC. [f. L *archiepiscopus* (see ARCH- and BISHOP)]
ar·chdea·con, n. Ecclesiastical dignitary next below bishop, superintending rural deans and holding lowest ecclesiastical court, with power of spiritual censure. Hence **archdea·con**SHIP n. [OE *arcediacon* f. L f. Gk *arkhidiakonos* (see ARCH- and DEACON)]

archdea·conry, n. Jurisdiction, rank, residence, of archdeacon. [prec. + -RY]
archdi·ocese, n. See of an archbishop. [ARCH- (4)]
ar·chduchess, n. Wife of an archduke; daughter of Emperor of Austria. [f. F *archiduchesse* (see ARCH- and DUCHESS)]
ar·chduke, n. Son of Emperor of Austria. So **ar·ch**DU·CAL a., **ar·ch**DUCHY n. [f. OF *archeduc* (see ARCH- and DUKE)]
ar·ch-e·nemy, n. Chief enemy; Satan. [ARCH- (2)]
ar·cher, n. One that shoots with bow and arrows; Sagittarius, ninth zodiacal constellation. So **ar·ch**ERY (2) n. [AF, f. OF *archier* f. L *arcarius* (*arcus* bow, see -ARY[1])]
ar·chĕtype (-k-), n. Original model, prototype. Hence **ar·chetyp**AL a., **ar·chetypal**LY[2] adv. [f. L f. Gk *arkhetupon* (*arkhe-* ARCH- +*tupos* stamp)]
arch-fie·nd, n. Satan. [ARCH- (2)]
archibald. See ARCHIE.
archidiă·conal (-k-), a. Pertaining to an archdeacon. [f. L as ARCHDEACON + -AL]
ar·chie, -ibald, nn. (slang). Anti-aircraft gun. [f. name in pop. song]
archiĕpi·scopal (-k-), a. Pertaining to an archbishop. [f. L as ARCHBISHOP + -AL]
ar·chil (-tsh-, -k-), n. (Violet dye from) various kinds of lichen. [corrupt. of *orchil* f. OF *orchel* f. It. *orcello,* etym. dub.]
archima·ndrite (-k-), n. Superior of monastery or convent in Greek church. [f. med. L *archimandrita* f. late Gk *arkhimandritēs* (*arkhi-* ARCH- +*mandra* monastery)]
Archimē·dĕan (-k-), a. Of Archimedes (Greek mathematician); *A. screw,* instrument raising water by tube in form of screw wound round cylinder. [f. L *Archimedeus* + -AN]
archipĕ·lago (-k-), n. Aegean sea; sea with many islands; group of islands. [f. It. *arcipelago* (*arci-* ARCH- (4) +*pélago* gulf, pool, f. L f. Gk *pelagos* sea)]
ar·chitect (-k-), n. Professor of building, who prepares plans and superintends work; designer of complex structure, esp. the Creator; (fig.) achiever, as *a. of his own fortunes.* Hence **ar·chitect**IVE a. [f. L *architectus* f. Gk *arkhitektōn* (*arkhi-* ARCH- +*tektōn* builder); some derivatives formed as if L *-tectus* were p.p. of *tegere* cover]
architectŏ·nic, a. Of architecture or architects; constructive; controlling; pertaining to systematization of knowledge, whence **architecto·**NICS n., **architecto·nic**AL a. [f. L f. Gk *arkhitektonikos* (as prec., see -IC)]
ar·chitecture (-tsh*er*), n. Science of building; thing built, structure; style of building; construction. Hence **archite·ctur**AL a., **archite·ctural**LY[2] adv. [F, f. L *architectura* (*architectus* ARCHITECT, see -URE)]
ar·chitrave (-k-), n. Epistyle, main beam resting immediately on the abacus on capital of column; the various parts surrounding doorway or window; moulding round exterior of arch. [f. *archi-* ARCH- +L *trabs -abis* beam]
ar·chive (-kīv), n. (usu. pl.). Place in which public records are kept; records so kept. [F (*-if, -ive*), f. LL *archi(v)um* f. Gk *arkheion* public office (*arkhē* government)]
ar·chivist (-kĭ-), n. Keeper of archives. [f. prec. + -IST]
ar·chivolt (-k-), n. Under curve of arch from impost to impost; mouldings decorating this. [f. It. *archivolto, arcovolta* (*arco* f. L *arcus* arch + *volta* VAULT, *volto* arched)]
ar·chon (-k-), n. One of nine chief magistrates at Athens; ruler, president. Hence **ar·chon**SHIP n. [Gk, = ruler (part. of *arkhō*)]
ar·ctic, a. Of the north pole, northern; *A. circle* (of earth), parallel of 66° 32′ N. [f. OF *artique* f. L f. Gk *arktikos* (*arktos* bear, Ursa Major, see -IC)]
Arctūr·us, n. Brightest star in constellation Boötes. [L, f. Gk *arktouros* (*arktos* bear + *ouros* guardian)]
ar·cuate(d), a. Bent like a bow; arched. [f. L *arcuatus* (*arcuare* f. *arcus* bow; see -ATE[2])]
-ard, suf. forming nouns, usu. of censure (*sluggard, drunkard*), but cf. *standard* (orig. *stander*), *placard*; also spelt *-art* (*braggart*). [ME & OF, f. G *-hart, -hard,* hardy, in proper names]
ar·dent, n. Burning, red-hot; parching; *a. spirits* (prop. = inflammable, but now understood of their taste), alcoholic spirits; eager, zealous; fervent (of persons and feelings). Hence **ar·d**ENCY n., **ar·dent**LY[2] adv. [f. OF *ardant* f. L *ardentem* (*ardēre* burn), see -ANT]
ar·dour (-*er*), n. Fierce heat; warm emotion; fervour, zeal, (*for*). [OF, f. L *ardorem* (*ardēre* burn, see -OR[1])]
ar·duous, a. Steep, hard to climb; hard to achieve, laborious; strenuous, energetic. Hence **ar·duous**LY[2] adv., **ar·duous**NESS n. [f. L *arduus* steep, difficult + -OUS]
are[1] (ar), n. French metric unit of square measure, square whose side is 10 metres (119·6 sq. yds). [F, f. L *area*]
are[2]**.** See BE.
ār·ea, n. Vacant ground; level space; sunk court railed off from pavement and giving access to basement of house, as *a. bell*; superficial extent; region, tract; scope, range. [L, = vacant piece of ground in town]
ă·rēca, n. Genus of palms; *a.-nut,* astringent seed of a species of a. [Port., f. Tamil *aḍaikay* (*aḍai* close-clustering + *kay* nut)]
arē·na, n. (pl. *-as*). Central part of amphitheatre, in which combats take place; (fig.) scene of conflict, sphere of action.

[L (*h*)*arena* sand, sand-strewn place of combat]

arena·ceous, a. Sand-like; sandy. So **arēno·**SE[1] a. [f. L *arenaceus* (as prec., see -ACEOUS)]

arē·ola, n. (pl. *-ae*). Very small area, as that between veins of a leaf; interstice in tissue; circular spot, as that surrounding the human nipple; (Biol.) cell-nucleus of plant. Hence **arē·ol**AR[1], **arē·ol**ATE[2], aa., **areol**A·TION n. [L, dim. of AREA]

Areŏ·pagite (-g-), n. Member of the court of Areopagus. [f. L f. Gk *areiopagitēs* (see foll. and -ITE)]

Areŏ·pagus, n. Hill at Athens where highest judicial court sat. [L, f. Gk *Areios pagos* Mars' hill]

arê·te (-āt), n. Sharp ascending ridge of mountain. [F, f. L *arista* ear of corn]

ar·gala, n. Adjutant-bird, gigantic Indian stork. [Hind. *hargila*]

ar·gali, n. Asiatic wild sheep. [Mongol]

ar·gand, n. Lamp with cylindrical wick; gas-burner on same principle. [inventor]

ar·gent, n. & a. Silver (colour, esp. in armorial bearings). [F, f. L *argentum*]

argenti·ferous, a. Yielding silver. [f. L *argentum* + -FEROUS]

ar·gentīne, a. & n. Of silver; silvery; imitation silver; silvery lamellae on scales of fish; (Zool.) genus of small fishes; (Min.) slate-spar. [f. F *argentin* f. L *argentinus* of silver (*argentum,* see -INE[1])]

ar·gil (-j-), n. Clay (esp. potter's). So **argill**A·CEOUS a. [f. F *argille* f. L *argilla* f. Gk *argillos* (*argēs* white)]

ar·gle-bargle, v.i., & n., (facet.). Debate. [corrupt. & redupl. of *argue*]

ar·gol, n. Tartar deposited from fermented wines, which when purified becomes cream of tartar. [?]

ar·gon, n. (chem.). A gas, an inert constituent of the atmosphere. [neut. of Gk *argos* idle (A- 7, *ergon* work)]

Ar·gonaut, n. (Pl.) legendary heroes who sailed with Jason in the Argo for the golden fleece; genus of cephalopod molluscs including paper nautilus. Hence **Argonau·t**IC a. [f. L (*-ta*) f. Gk *Argonautēs* sailor in the *Argō*]

ar·gosy, n. (hist., poet.). Large merchant-vessel, esp. of Ragusa and Venice; (poet.) ship, venture. [earlier *ragusye,* prob. f. It. *Ragusea* (*nave*) Ragusan (vessel)]

ar·got (-gō), n. Jargon, slang, of a class, esp. of thieves. [F, etym. dub.]

ar·gue (-ū), v.t. & i. Prove, indicate, as *it argues him* (*to be*) *a rogue, that he is a rogue, roguery in him*; maintain by reasons (*that*), whence **ar·gū**ABLE a.; treat (matter) by reasoning; *a. it away,* get rid of it by argument; *a.* (persuade) *a person into, out of*; reason (*with, against,* person, *for, against, about,* thing). [f. OF *arguer* f. L *argutare* frequent. of *arguere* make clear, prove, accuse]

ar·gument, n. Reason advanced (*for, against,* proposition or course); (Logic) middle term in syllogism; reasoning process; debate; summary of subject-matter of book; *a.* (usu. *argumentum*) *ad hominem,* one that takes advantage of character or situation of particular opponent, *ad crumenam,* of his avarice, *ad ignorantiam,* of his ignorance of the facts. [F, f. L *argumentum* (*arguere,* see prec. and -MENT)]

argumenta·tion, n. Methodical reasoning; debate. [F, f. L *argumentationem* f. *argumentari* (as prec.), see -ATION]

argume·ntative, a. Logical; fond of arguing. Hence **argume·ntative**LY[2] adv., **argume·ntative**NESS n. [F (*-if, -ive*), as prec., see -ATIVE]

Ar·gus, n. Fabulous person with a hundred eyes; watchful guardian; *a.-eyed,* vigilant; *a.-shell,* oculated porcelain-shell. [L, f. Gk *Argos*]

argū·te, a. Sharp, shrewd; (of sounds) shrill. [f. L *argutus* p.p. of *arguere,* see ARGUE]

argyr-, argyro-, (-jĭ-), in comb. = Gk *arguros* silver, as *argy·ria* silver-poisoning, *argyra·nthous,* with silvery flowers, *argyrophy·llous,* silvery-leaved.

ar·ia (ar-), n. (mus.). Air. [It.]

Ar·ian (ār-), a. & n. (Holder) of the doctrine of Arius of Alexandria (4th c.), who denied consubstantiality of Christ. Hence **Ar·ian**ISM n., **Ar·ian**IZE v.t. & i. [f. L *Arianus* (*Arius* f. Gk *Arios, Areios,* see -AN)]

-arian, suf. forming adjj. and nn. chiefly denoting (member) of a sect &c. (*veget-, trinit-, humanit-*), or (person) of an age given by L numerals (*octogen-*). [L *-arius* + -AN; first sense perh. w. ref. to ARIAN]

ă·rid, a. Dry, parched, (lit. & fig.); (of ground) barren, bare. Hence **ari·d**ITY, **a·rid**NESS, nn. [f. L *aridus* (*arēre* be dry)]

ār·iel, n. Species of gazelle in Western Asia and Africa. [f. Arab. *aryil* var. of *ayyil* stag]

Ar·iēs (ār-), n. The Ram, first zodiacal constellation. [L, = *ram*]

arigh·t, adv. Rightly. [A prep. + RIGHT n.]

-arious, compd adj. suf. = L *-arius* (-ARY[1]) + -OUS.

ari·se (-z), v.i. (arose, arisen). (Archaic) rise, get up; (poet.) rise from the dead; (archaic) be heard (of sounds); originate; be born; come into notice; result (*from*); present itself. [A- (1) + RISE v.]

ari·sta, n. Awn, beard, of grain and grasses. [L]

ari·state, a. Awned, bearded. [f. L *aristatus* (ARISTA, see -ATE[2])]

aristo·cracy, n. Government by the best citizens; supremacy of privileged order, oligarchy; state so governed; ruling body of nobles; class from which ruling body is drawn, nobles; the best representatives *of* (intellect &c.). [f. L f. Gk *aristokratia* (*aristos* best + *-kratia* rule)]

a·ristocrat, n. One of a ruling oligarchy; one of the class of nobles. Hence **aris·to·crat**ISM n. [f. F *aristocrate* (as foll.)]

aristocră·tic, a. Pertaining to, attached to, aristocracy; grand, stylish. Hence **aristocra·tic**AL a., **aristocra·tical**LY² adv. [f. F *aristocratique* f. Gk *aristokratikos* (as ARISTOCRACY, see -IC)]

Aristotē·lian, -telē·an, aa. & nn. (Disciple or student) of the Greek philosopher Aristotle. [*-lian* f. L f. Gk *Aristotelēs* Aristotle + -IAN; *-lean* f. L *-lēus* f. Gk *-leios* aa. + -AN]

ari·thmetic, n. Science of numbers; arithmetical knowledge, computation; treatise on computation. Hence **arithmeti·**CIAN n. [f. OF *arismetique* f. LL *arismetica* for L *arithmetica* f. Gk *arithmētikē* (*tekhnē*) (art) of counting f. *arithmeō* count (*arithmos* number), see -IC; corrupted in ME to *arsmetrike*, as if f. L *ars metrica* art of measure]

arithmĕ·tical, a. Of arithmetic; *a. progression,* (series of numbers showing) increase, decrease, by a constant quantity (e.g. 1, 2, 3, 4, &c., 9, 7, 5, 3, &c.). Hence **arithme·tical**LY² adv. [prec. + -AL]

arithmŏ·meter, n. Calculating-machine. [f. F *arithmomètre* (Gk *arithmos* number + -METER]

-arium, noun suf. f. L neut. of adjj. in *-arius* (-ARY¹), chiefly in antiquarian words as *sacrarium,* occas. popularized, as *aquarium.*

ark, n. Chest, box; *A. of the Covenant, A. of Testimony,* wooden coffer containing tables of Jewish law; covered floating vessel in which Noah was saved at the Deluge; *Noah's a.,* toy ark with animals. [com.-Teut.: OE *arc* f. OTeut. *arka* prob. f. L *arca* chest]

arm¹, n. Upper limb of human body from shoulder to hand; *fore-a.* (from elbow to hand); fore limb of an animal; large branch of tree; sleeve; thing resembling a., as *a. of the sea, a.-chair* (with side supports), *a. of lever, balance* (part from fulcrum to point of application of power or weight); *a.-hole* in garment, hole through which a. is put; *a.-pit,* hollow under a. at shoulder; *a.-in-a.* (of two persons with aa. interlinked); *infant in aa.* (too young to walk); *with open aa.,* cordially; *keep at a.'s length,* avoid familiarity with; *secular a.,* authority of secular tribunal. Hence **ar·m**FUL n., **ar·mless¹** [-LESS] a. [com.-Teut. (OE, Du., G) cogn. w. L *armus* shoulder; cf. Gk *harmos* joint f. Aryan root *ar-* join]

arm², n. (usu. pl.). Weapon(s); *fire-aa.* (requiring explosive); *small-aa.* (not requiring carriages); *stand of aa.,* set for one soldier; (sing.) particular kind of weapon; *take up aa.,* arm oneself (often fig.); *bear aa.,* serve as soldier; *lay down aa.,* cease hostilities; *in aa.,* armed; *up in aa.,* actively engaged in rebellion &c. (also fig.); *under aa.,* in battle array; military profession; (sing. & pl.) each kind of troops, infantry, cavalry, &c.; heraldic devices, as *coat of aa.*; *King-of-Aa.,* Chief Herald. Hence **ar·mless²** [-LESS] a. [f. F *armes* f. L *arma* arms, fittings, f. root *ar-* join]

arm³, v.t. & i. Furnish with arms; *armed neutrality* (of nations prepared for war); furnish with tools or other requisites; plate (*with* anything); furnish (magnet) with an armature; (intr.) arm oneself, take up arms. [f. F *armer* f. L *armare* (*arma*)]

armā·da, n. Fleet of ships of war, esp. *the* (*Invincible*) *A.* sent by Philip II of Spain against England in 1588. [Sp., f. L *armata* (*armare* ARM v., see -ADE)]

armadi·llo, n. Burrowing animal of S. America, with body encased in bony armour, and habit of rolling itself into ball when captured; genus of small terrestrial Crustacea with same habit, allied to wood-louse. [Sp., dim. of *armado* one armed f. L as ARM³, see -ADO]

Armage·ddon (-g-) n. (Scene of) supreme conflict between the nations. [*Rev.* xvi. 16]

ar·mament, n. Force (usu. naval) equipped for war; military equipments, esp. great guns on man-of-war; process of equipping for war. [f. L *armamentum* (as prec., see -MENT)]

ar·mature, n. Arms, armour; defensive covering of animals or plants; piece of soft iron placed in contact with poles of magnet, increasing its power; essential part of a dynamo. [f. L *armatura* (as prec., see -URE)]

arme blanche (F), n. Cavalry sword or lance.

Armē·nian, a. & n. Of Armenia; *A. bole,* red Armenian earth, used medicinally; *A. stone,* blue carbonate of copper; native of Armenia; adherent of Armenian church. [-AN]

ar·miger (-j-), n. Esquire, one entitled to bear heraldic arms. [L, = bearing arms (*arma* arms + *gerere* bear)]

armi·llary, a. Pertaining to bracelets; *a. sphere,* skeleton celestial globe of metal rings representing equator, tropics, &c. [f. L *armilla* bracelet, see -ARY¹]

Armĭ·nian, a. & n. (Adherent) of the doctrine of Arminius, Dutch protestant theologian, who opposed the views of Calvin, esp. on predestination. Hence **Armi·nian**ISM n. [f. *Arminius,* Latiniz. of *Harmensen* + -AN]

ar·mistice (-ĭs), n. Cessation from arms (lit. & fig.); short truce; *A. Day,* 11th Nov., kept as anniversary of the a. (1918) that ended hostilities in the Great War. [f. L *arma* arms + *-stitium* (*sistere -stit-* stop)]

ar·mlet, n. Band worn round arm; small inlet of sea or branch of river. [ARM¹ + -LET]

armor·ial, a. & n. (Book) pertaining to heraldic arms. [ARMORY + -AL¹]

ar·mory, n. Heraldry. Hence **ar·mor**IST n. [f. OF *armoirie* f. *armoier* blazoner f. *armoier* v. = It. *armeggiare* f. L *arma* arms]

ar·mour¹ (*-er*), n. Defensive covering worn in fighting; *a.-bearer,* one who carries another's a.; metal sheathing of ship of war, composed of *a.-plates*; *a.-clad,* furnished with this; diver's suit; protective covering of animals or plants; heraldic insignia. [f. OF *armeüre* f. L *armatura* ARMATURE]

ar·mour², v.t. Furnish with protective covering; *armoured* CRUISER. [f. prec.]

ar·mourer, n. Manufacturer of arms; official in charge of ship's, regiment's, arms. [f. AF *armurer,* OF *-urier,* f. *armeüre,* see prec. and -ER²]

ar·moury, n. Place where arms are kept, arsenal; (U.S.) armourer's workshop. [perh. as ARMORY, but treated as f. ARMOUR + -Y¹]

ar·my, n. Organized body of men armed for war; *standing a.,* one of professional soldiers permanently on foot; *the a.,* the military service; vast host; organized body of men, as *Salvation A., Church A., Blue Ribbon A.*; *a.-broker, -contractor* (carrying on business in connexion with the a.); *a.-corps,* main division of a. in the field; *a.-list,* official list of officers; *a.-worm,* larva of cotton-moth. [f. F *armée* (cf. -ADE) f. L *armata* fem. p.p. of *armare* arm]

ar·nica, n. Genus of plants including mountain tobacco; medicine, esp. tincture, prepared from this. [?]

aroi·nt, -oy·nt, v. or int. (archaic). *A. thee,* begone. [?]

arō·ma, n. (pl. *-as*). Fragrance, sweet smell; subtle pervasive quality. [earlier (and OF) *aromat* f. L *aromata* (pl.) f. Gk *arōma -matos*]

aromă·tic, a. Fragrant; spicy. [f. F *aromatique* f. L f. Gk *arōmatikos* (AROMA, see -IC)]

arose. See ARISE.

arou·nd, adv. & prep. On every side, in every direction; (U.S.) about, here and there, at random, as *fool a.*; on, along, the circuit of; about, enveloping. [f. A- (2) + ROUND]

arou·se (-z), v.t. Awaken; stir up into activity. [A- + ROUSE, on anal. of *rise, arise*]

arpe·ggio (-ĕjō), n. (mus.). Striking of notes of chord in rapid (usu. upward) succession; chord so struck. [It.]

arquebus. See HARQUEBUS.

a·rrack, n. Eastern name for any native spirituous liquor, esp. that distilled from the coco-palm, or from rice and sugar. [f. Arab. *'araq* juice]

a·rrah, int., an Anglo-Irish expletive.

arraig·n, v.t. Indict before a tribunal; accuse; find fault with, call in question, (action, statement). So **arraig·n**MENT n. [f. AF *arainer* f. OF *araisnier* f. L AD-*rationare* reason, talk reasonably (*ratio -onis* reason, discourse)]

arrā·nge, v.t. & i. Put into order, adjust; draw up (army); (Mus.) adapt (composition) for new circumstances; settle (dispute &c.); settle beforehand the order, manner, of; (intr.) take steps, form plans, give instructions, (*a. to be there, for the cab to be there*; *a. about it*); come to agreement (*with* person, *about* thing, *to* do, *that,* or abs.). So **arra·nge**MENT n. [f. OF *arangier* (*à* to + *rangier* f. *rang* RANK)]

a·rrant, a. Notorious, downright, thorough-paced, as *a. knave, dunce, hypocrite, nonsense.* Hence **a·rrant**LY² adv. [variant of ERRANT, orig. in phrr. like *a.* (= outlawed, roving) *thief*]

a·rras, n. Rich tapestry; hanging screen of this formerly hung round walls of rooms (often not too closely to admit person). Hence **a·rras**ED² a. [*Arras,* town in Artois famous for the fabric]

array·¹, v.t. Marshal, dispose, (forces); (Law) impanel (a jury); dress, esp. with display; (refl.) dress one*self* up; adorn; (fig.) clothe (in qualities &c.). [f. AF *arayer* = OF *areyer* (Prov. *aredar,* early Rom. *arredare*) f. *ad* to + **redo* (OF *rei, rai*) order, preparation, f. LG *rêde,* Goth. *garaids* ready]

array·², n. Order, as *battle a.*; (Hist.) arming of militia, as *Commission of A.*; military force; imposing series *of* persons or things; order of impanelling jury; (poet.) outfit, dress. [f. AF *arai* = OF *arei* f. *areyer,* see prec.]

arrear·, n. (Archaic) hinder part, esp. of procession; (pl.) outstanding debts; *in aa.* or *a.,* behindhand, esp. in payment; *in a. of,* behind. [orig. adv. f. OF *arere* (mod.F *arrière*) f. LL *ad retro* (*ad* to + *retro* backwards); first used in phr. *in arrear*]

arrear·age, n. Backwardness; unpaid balance; thing in reserve; (pl.) debts. [f. OF *arerage* f. *arere,* see prec. and -AGE]

arre·ct, a. (Of the ears) pricked up; (fig.) on the alert. [f. L *arrectus* p.p. of AR*rigere* raise up (*regere* straighten)]

arre·st¹, v.t. Stop (person, cannon-ball, decay); (Law) *a. judgement,* stay proceedings after verdict, on ground of error; seize (person), esp. by legal authority; catch (attention); catch attention of. Hence **arre·st**IVE a., **arre·st**MENT n. [f. OF *arester* (Prov. *arestar*) f. LL AD*restare* remain, stop (intr.)]

arre·st², n. Stoppage, check; *a. of judgement* (see prec.); seizure; legal apprehension; imprisonment; *under a.* (legal restraint). [f. OF *arest* f. *arester,* see prec.]

arri·de, v.t. (archaic). Please, gratify. [f. L ARridēre smile upon, be pleasing to]

arrière-ban (ă·rĭer-), n. Summoning of vassals to military service by Frankish king; body thus summoned or liable to be summoned; noblesse; (improp.) summoning of inferior (*arrière-*) vassals. [F, f. OF *ariere-ban* for (*h*)*ari-ban* f. OHG *hari* army + *ban* edict, altered in form and sense by pop. etym., whence *ban et arrière-ban* summoning of superior and inferior vassals]

arrière-pensée (F), n. Ulterior motive; mental reservation.

a·rris, n. Sharp edge formed by angular contact of two plane or curved surfaces, as *a.-gutter* (V-shaped), *a.-wise*, ridgewise. [f. F *areste* (mod. *arête*) f. L *arista* ear of corn]

arrī·val, n. Act of coming to end of journey or destination (lit. & fig.); appearance upon scene; person, thing, that has arrived; (colloq.) new-born child; cargo to be delivered when ship arrives. [f. AF *arrivaille* (*arriver*, see foll. and -AL (2))]

arri·ve, v.i. Come to destination (lit. & fig.) or end of journey (*at* Bath, *in* Paris, *upon* scene, *at* conclusion), (as Gallicism) establish one's repute or position; (of things) be brought; (of time) come; (of events) come about. [f. OF *ariver* f. LL *arribare* f. L ADripare come to shore (*ripa*)]

a·rrogant, a. Overbearing; presumptuous; haughty. Hence or cogn. **a·rro**gANCE, -ANCY, nn., **a·rrogant**LY[2] adv. [F (as foll., see -ANT)]

a·rrogate, v.t. Claim unduly (thing, *to* one*self* a thing); claim unduly that one possesses (a quality); claim unduly for (*to*) some one else. [f. L AR(*rogare* ask), see -ATE[3]]

arroga·tion, n. Unjust claim (*of* or abs.); unwarrantable assumption. [f. L *arrogatio* (as prec., see -ATION)]

arrondissement (F), n. Administrative subdivision of French department.

a·rrow, n. Pointed missile shot from bow; index, pin, ornament, of similar shape; *a.* or *broad a.-head*, mark distinguishing British Government stores; *a.-stitch*, triangular set of stitches securing whalebone in stays; *a.-headed characters*, cuneiform; *arrowroot*, plant from which a nutritious starch is prepared. Hence **a·rrow**Y[2] a. [OE *earh*, *arwe*, f. OTeut., Goth. *arhwazna* thing belonging to the bow (*arhw* cogn. w. L *arcus* bow)]

arse, n. Buttocks, rump. [com.-Teut., cogn. w. Gk *orrhos*]

ar·senal, n. Public establishment for storage or manufacture of weapons and ammunition (also fig.). [f. It. *arsenale*, earlier *arzenà* f. Arab. *dar accina'ah* (*dar* house + *al* the + *çina'ah* art f. *çana'a* fabricate; *d-* dropped perh. by confus. w. *de* prep.; *-ale* added in It.]

ar·senic[1], n. (Chem.) brittle steel-green semi-metallic substance, crystallizing in rhombohedrons, and volatilizing without fusion with odour of garlic; (pop.) trioxide of a., white mineral substance, a violent poison; *flowers of a.*, same sublimed. Hence **arsĕ·nic**AL a. [OF, f. L f. Gk *arsenikon* yellow orpiment (identified with *arsenikos* male, from belief that metals were of different sexes, but in fact) f. Arab. *az-zernikh* the orpiment f. Pers. *zerni* (*zar* gold)]

arsĕ·nic[2], a. Of, belonging to, arsenic; esp. (Chem.) applied to compounds in which arsenic combines as a pentad. [f. prec., *-ic* being identified with -IC (1)]

arsē·nious, a. Containing arsenic; esp. applied to compounds in which arsenic combines as a triad. [f. ARSENIC n. + -IOUS; see also -OUS]

ar·sis, n. Accented syllable in English scansion (cf. *thesis*). [L f. Gk, = lifting f. *airō* lift; in what sense, and whether orig. of voice or foot (in beating time), is disputed]

ar·son, n. Wilful setting on fire of another's house or similar property or one's own when insured. [OF, f. LL *arsionem* (*ardēre ars-* burn, intr., see -ION)]

art[1], v. See BE.

art[2], n. Skill, esp. human skill as opposed to nature; skilful execution as an object in itself; skill applied to imitation and design, as in painting &c.; (attrib.) of artistic design &c. (chiefly shop use: *a. needlework, carpet, curtain*); thing in which skill may be exercised; esp. (pl.) certain branches of learning serving as intellectual instruments for more advanced studies, as *Bachelor, Master, of Aa.*, one who has obtained standard of proficiency in these; *black a.*, magic; practical application of any science; industrial pursuit, craft; guild, company of craftsmen; *fine aa.*, those in which mind and imagination are chiefly concerned; knack; cunning; stratagem; *a. and* (*or*) *part*, design and (or) execution, as *be a. and part in* (accessary in both respects). [OF, f. L *artem*, nom. *ars*, prob. f. *ar-* fit]

artē·ial, a. Belonging to, of the nature of, an artery; *a. drainage* (ramifying like artery). [F (*artère* ARTERY, see -AL)]

artē·ialize, v.t. Convert venous into arterial (blood) by exposure to oxygen in lungs; furnish with arterial system. Hence **arter·ializ**ATION n. [prec. + -IZE]

artēriosclē·ro·sis, n. Hardening of the arteries, esp. as concomitant of old age. [see ARTERY, SCLER(O)-, -OSIS]

artēriо·tomy, n. Opening of artery for blood-letting; dissection of arteries. [f. Gk *artēriotomia* (as foll., see -TOMY)]

ar·tery, n. Tube forming part of system by which blood is conveyed from heart (cf. VEIN) to all parts of body (also fig.). Hence **arteri·**TIS n. [f. L f. Gk *artēria* prob. f. *airō* raise]

Artē·sian (-zhn), a. *A. well*, perpendicular boring into strata, producing constant supply of water rising spontaneously to surface. [f. F *artésien* (*Artois*, old French province)]

ar·tful, a. Cunning, crafty, deceitful, (of persons and actions). Hence **ar·tful**LY² adv., **ar·tful**NESS n. [ART + -FUL]

arthrī·tis, n. Inflammation of joint; gout. So **arthri·**TIC a. [L f. Gk (*arthron* joint, see -ITIS)]

arthro-, comb. form of Gk *arthron* joint, as in *arthropathy*, painful affection of joints, *arthrosis*, articulation.

ar·tichoke, n. Plant (of which bottom of flower and bases of its scales are edible) allied to thistles, native of Barbary; *Jerusalem* (corrupt. of *girasole*, sunflower) *A.*, species of sunflower with edible tuberous roots. [f. It. *articiocco* corrupt. of **alcarcioffo* (mod. It. *carciofo*, OSp. *alcarchofa*) f. Arab. *alkharshuf*]

ar·ticle¹, n. Separate portion of anything written; separate clause (of agreement &c.) as *Thirty-nine Aa.*, *Aa. of war, Apprenticeship, Association*; literary composition forming part of magazine &c. but independent; *leading a.* in newspaper, large-type a. expressing editorial opinion; particular; particular thing, as *the next a.*; (Gram.) *definite a.*, 'the', *indefinite a.*, 'a, an'; *in the a.* (moment) *of death* (usu. *in articulo mortis*). [F, f. L *articulus*, dim. of *artus* limb]

ar·ticle², v.t. Set forth in articles; indict; bind by articles of apprenticeship. [f. prec.]

arti·cular, a. Pertaining to the joints. [f. L *articularis* (as ARTICLE¹, see -AR¹)]

arti·culate¹ (-*a*t), a. & n. Jointed; distinctly jointed, distinguishable, as *a. speech*; (n.) articulate animal. Hence **arti·culate**LY² adv., **arti·culate**NESS n. [f. L *articulatus* (as prec., see -ATE²)]

arti·culāte², v.t. & i. Connect by joints, mark with apparent joints (usu. pass.); divide into words, pronounce distinctly; (intr.) speak distinctly. Hence **arti·cula**TORY a. [f. prec., see -ATE³]

articula·tion, n. Act, mode, of jointing; joint; articulate utterance, speech; consonant. [F, f. L *articulationem* (*articulare* joint as ARTICLE¹, see -ATION)]

ar·tifice, n. Device, contrivance; address, skill. [F, f. L *artificium* (*ars artis* art + *-ficium* making f. *facere* make)]

arti·ficer, n. Craftsman; inventor (*of*). [f. prec. + -ER¹]

artifi·cial (-shl), a. Made by art; not natural; not real, as *a. flowers*; real, but produced by art, as *a. ice*. Hence **artificia·**LITY (-shĭ-), **artifi·cial**NESS, nn., **artifi·cial**IZE v.t., **artifi·cial**LY² adv. [F, f. L *artificialis* (as ARTIFICE, see -AL)]

arti·llery, n. Engines for discharging missiles, esp. cannon, ordnance; branch of army that manages cannon; *a.-train*, ordnance mounted on carriages and ready for marching. Hence **arti·ller**IST, **arti·lleryman,** nn. [f. F *artillerie* f. *artiller* maker of artillery f. LL **articularius* (*articula* dim. as art, see -ARY¹)]

artisā·n (-z-), n. Mechanic, handicraftsman. [F, perh. f. It. *artigiano* f. LL **artitianus* (*artitus* p.p. of *artire* instruct in arts, see -AN)]

ar·tist, n. One who practises one of the fine arts, esp. painting; *a.'s proof*, copy of engraving taken for a.'s approval or correction & valued as fresher than ordinary copies; one who makes his craft a fine art (*a. in words* &c.). Hence **arti·s**TIC(AL) aa., **arti·stical**LY² adv., **ar·tist**RY n. [f. F *artiste* f. It. f. LL *artista* (*ars artis* art, see -IST)]

arti·ste (-ēst), n. Professional singer, dancer, &c. [F, see prec.]

ar·tless, a. Unskilful, uncultured; clumsy; natural; guileless, ingenuous. Hence **ar·tless**LY² adv., **ar·tless**NESS n. [ART + -LESS]

ār·um, n. Genus of endogenous plants, including Wake-Robin; *a. lily*, cultivated white lily. [L, f. Gk *aron*]

-ary¹, suf. forming adjj. & nn. f. L *-arius* taken directly or thr. mod. F *-aire*, or imitated w. L nn. (rarely in E words as *bloomary*); adjj. as *arbitrary*; nouns = *-arius*, as *actuary*, = *-arium*, as *dictionary*, = *-aria*, as *fritillary*; words taken thr. OF have sometimes -ER² instead, as *primer*.

-ary², suf. Sometimes in adjj. f. L *-aris* instead of regular -AR¹, owing to passage thr. F *-aire*, as *exemplary*.

Ar·yan (ār-), a. & n. Applied by some to family of languages (also called *Indo-European, Indo-Germanic*) that includes Sanskrit, Zend, Persian, Greek, Latin, Celtic, Teutonic, Slavonic, with their modern representatives, by others only to the Asiatic portion of these; member of A. family. [f. Sk. *arya* noble (in earlier use a national name comprising worshippers of the gods of the Brahmans); earlier *Arian* is f. L *Arianus* of Aria (f. Gk *Areia* eastern Persia, prob. f. OPers. *ariya*, a national name)]

as¹ (ăz, *a*z), adv., conj., rel. pron. 1. adv. (in main sentence, foll. by *as* in subord. clause expressed or understood) in the same degree, as *I came as soon as I could, I know that as well as you, you might as well help me, as* FAR¹ *as*. 2. rel. adv. or conj. in subord. clause, with or without antecedent *as, so*, expressing manner, degree, &c., of the principal sentence; (degree) *you are as good as he, it is not so* (or *as*) *easy as you think, quick as thought he jumped out, fair as* (= though) *she is*; (manner) *do as you like, according as we* *decide, he looks as if he had seen a ghost, treat him as a stranger, you are, as it were* (= as if it were actually so), *compromised, they rose as one man, late as usual, he smiled, as who should say* (= as a man would smile who); (time) *it struck me as I was speaking*; (reason) *as you are not ready, we must go on*; (result) *he so arranged matters as to suit everyone, be so good as to come*; (illustration) *cathedral cities, as Norwich.* 3. rel. pron. That, who, which, as *I had the same trouble as you, such countries as Spain*; (with antecedent inferred from main sentence) *he was a foreigner, as* (which fact) *they perceived from his accent.* 4. Special phrases: *as from* (in formal dating, as *coal will be decontrolled a. f. 31st March*); *as regards,* so far as it concerns; *as to,* with respect to (*said nothing a. t. hours, a. t. when he would come*; *a. t. you, I despise you*); *as yet,* up to this time; *I thought as much,* I thought so; *as well* (*as*), in addition (to); *as good as dead,* practically dead. 5. Phrases in (*as*) . . . *as* expressing by reference to a proverbial type the highest or a high degree of some quality, and in alliterative or punning phrr. modelled on these: *bald as a coot, black as pitch, black as your* or *my hat, blind as a bat, bold as brass, brave as a lion, bright as a button, bright as a new pin, brown as a berry, busy as a bee, cold as charity, common as dirt, cool as a cucumber, cross as two sticks, dead as a doornail, dead as mutton, deaf as a post, drunk as a fiddler, drunk as a lord, dry as a bone, dull as ditch-water, easy as ABC, easy as lying, fat as a porpoise, fit as a fiddle, flat as a pancake, good as gold* (of children's conduct), *good as a play* (amusing), *hard as nails, heavy as lead, hungry as a hunter, jolly as a sandboy, keen as mustard, large as life, light as air, long as your* or *my arm, mad as a hatter, mad as a March hare, meek as Moses, merry as a grig, old as the hills, pale as a ghost, plain as a pikestaff, pleased as Punch, plentiful as blackberries, plump as a partridge, proud as a peacock, proud as Lucifer, quick as thought, quiet as a mouse, rich as a Jew, right as a trivet, right as rain, safe as a house, sharp as a needle, silent as the grave, snug as a bug in a rug, soft as butter, soft as velvet, sound as a bell, stiff as a poker, straight as a die, strong as a horse, stubborn as a mule, sure as fate, sweet as a nut, thick as thieves, thin as a lath, tight as a drum, tight as wax, true as steel, ugly as sin, warm as a toast, weak as a cat, weak as water, white as a sheet.* [OE *allswá* (later *alsa, als*) adv. = wholly so, quite so]

as², n. Roman copper coin, orig. weighing 12 oz., but finally reduced to ½ oz. [L]

as-, pref. = AD- before *s*.

ăsafoe·tida (-fē-), n. Concreted resinous gum with strong smell of garlic used in medicine and cookery. [med. L (*asa* f. Pers. *aza* mastic + *foetida* stinking)]

asbe·stine, a. Of, like, asbestos, incombustible (lit. & fig.) [f. L f. Gk *asbestinos* f. foll., see -INE²]

asbe·stos, n. Fibrous mineral that can be woven into an incombustible fabric (also fig.). Hence **asbe·st**IC, **asbe·st**OID, aa. [L f. Gk, = unquenchable (*a-* not + *sbestos* f. *sbennumi* quench)]

asce·nd, v.t. & i. Go, come, up; (of things) rise, be raised; slope upwards, lie along ascending slope; rise in thought, rank, degree of quality; (of sounds) rise in pitch; go back in point of time; (trans.) go up, climb; *a. a river,* go along it towards its source; mount upon, as *a. the throne.* [f. L *ascendere,* AD(*scendere scens-* = *scandere* climb)]

asce·ndancy, -ency, n. Dominant control, sway, (*over*). [f. foll., see -ANCY]

asce·ndant, -ent, a. & n. Rising; (Astr.) rising towards zenith; (Astrol.) just above eastern horizon; predominant; horoscope; point of ecliptic or degree of zodiac that (esp. at birth of child) is just rising above eastern horizon; *house of the a.* (from 5 degrees of zodiac above this point to 25 below it); *lord of the a.,* any planet within this; *in the a.,* supreme, dominating, (improp.) rising; supremacy; ancestor. [f. OF (*-ant*) f. L as prec., see -ENT]

asce·nsion, n. Act of ascending; ascent of Christ on fortieth day after resurrection; *A.-day,* Holy Thursday, on which this is commemorated; rising of a celestial body, as *right a.* (celestial longitude). Hence **asce·nsion**AL a. [f. L *ascensio* (as ASCEND, see -ION)]

asce·nsive, a. Rising, progressive; (Gram.) intensive. [as prec., see -IVE]

asce·nt, n. Act of ascending; upward movement, rise, (lit. & fig.); way by which one may ascend, slope, flight of steps. [f. ASCEND on anal. of *descent*]

ascertai·n, v.t. Find out. Hence **ascertai·n**ABLE a., **ascertai·n**MENT n. [f. OF *acertener,* st. *acertaine-* (*à* to + CERTAIN)]

ascĕ·tic, a. & n. Severely abstinent, austere; (n.) one who practises severe self-discipline, esp. (Eccl. Hist.) one who retired into solitude for this purpose. Hence **asce·tic**AL a., **asce·tical**LY² adv., **asce·tic**ISM n. [f. Gk *askētikos* f. *askētēs* monk (*askeō* exercise), see -ETE and -IC]

asci·dium, n. Genus of molluscs with leathery enveloping tunic, regarded as link in development of Vertebrata. [f. Gk *askidion* dim. of *askos* wine-skin]

Asclē·piad, n. (Gk and Lat. Prosody) verse consisting of a spondee, two or three choriambi, and an iambus. Hence **Asclepiade·**AN a. [f. L f. Gk *Asklēpiadeios* (*Asklēpiadēs,* Greek poet, the inventor)]

A·scot, n. Race-course on A. Heath, Berks.; race-meeting at A.

ascri·be, v.t. Attribute, impute, (*to*); consider as belonging (*to* person or thing). Hence or cogn. **ascri·b**ABLE a., **ascri·p**TION n., (esp.) preacher's words ascribing praise to God at end of sermon. [earlier *ascrive* f. OF *ascriv-* st. of *ascrire* f. L AD(*scribere script-* write)]

āsē·ity, n. (metaphys.). Underived existence, the being uncreate. [f. L *a se* from oneself + -ITY]

ase·psis, n. Absence of putrefactive matter or harmful bacteria; the aseptic method in surgery. [A- (7) + Gk *sēpsis* decay (*sēpō*, see foll.)]

ase·ptic, a. & n. Free from putrefaction or blood-poisoning; surgically sterile, sterilized, (of wounds, instruments, dressings); (of method &c.) seeking the absence (rather than counteraction, cf. *antiseptic*) of septic matter; (n.) non-putrescent substance. [f. Gk *a-* not + *sēptikos* putrefying (*sēpō* rot, see -IC)]

ase·xual, a. (Biol.) without sex. Hence **asexua·l**ITY n. [f. Gk *a-* not + SEXUAL]

ash[1], n. Forest-tree with silver-grey bark, pinnate foliage, and close-grained wood; wood of this; *a.-fly, a.-grub,* (found on a. and used by anglers); *a.-key,* winged seed of the a.; *a.-leaf,* an early potato; *mountain a.,* rowan-tree. [com.-Teut.; OE *æsc,* G *esche*]

ash[2], n. (usu. pl.). Powdery residue left after combustion of any substance; (pl.) remains of human body after cremation (lit. & fig.); *lay in aa.,* burn to the ground; *sackcloth and aa.* (symbol of repentance); *bring back the aa.* (crick.), wipe out defeat; *a.-fire,* low fire used in chemical operations; *a.-furnace* (used in glass-making); *A.-Wednesday,* first day of Lent (from Rom. Cath. custom of sprinkling aa. on penitents' heads). [com.-Teut.; OE *asce, axe,* Da. *aske*]

asha·med (-md), pred. a. Abashed, disconcerted, by consciousness of guilt; *a. of* (conduct); *a. for* (on account of) *you*; *a. to do* (implying reluctance, but not always abstention). [p.p. of obs. vb *ashame* (A- (1) + OE *scamian* SHAME)]

a·shen[1], a. Pertaining to an ash-tree; made of ash. [ASH[1] + -EN[5]]

a·shen[2], a. Of ashes; ash-coloured, pale. [ASH[2] + -EN[5]]

a·shlar, n. Square hewn stone(s); masonry constructed of this; similar masonry as facing to rubble or brick wall. [f. OF *aiseler* f. L *axillaris* (*axilla* dim. of *axis, assis,* axle, board, see -AR[1])]

a·shlaring, n. Short upright boarding in garrets, cutting off acute angle formed by rafters with floor; ashlar masonry. [prec. + -ING[1]]

ashore·, adv. To, on to, on, shore. [A prep.]

a·shy, a. Of ashes; covered with ashes; ash-coloured, pale. [ASH[2] + -Y[2]]

Asiă·tic (āshĭ-), a. & n. (Native) of Asia. [f. L f. Gk *Asiatikos* (*Asiatēs* f. *Asia,* see -IC)]

asi·de, adv. & n. To, on, one side, away; *set a.,* quash (verdict); *speak a.* (apart, in privacy); (n.) words spoken aside, esp. spoken by an actor & supposed not to be heard by other performers; indirect effort. [orig. *on side,* see A prep.]

ă·sinīne, a. Pertaining to asses; stupid. Hence **asinĭ·n**ITY n. [f. L *asininus* (*asinus* ass, see -INE[1])]

-asis, suf. forming names of diseases. [L *-ăsis* f. Gk *-ăsis* in nouns of state f. vbs in *-aō*]

ask, v.t. & i. Call for an answer to, as *a.* (*him*) *a question, a.* (*him*) *this, a.* (*him*) *who it is, a. him the time, a. a question of a person, a. him about a thing*; make a request (for), as *a. a favour of him, a.* (*him*) *a favour, a.* (*him*) *for it, ask* (abs.), *a. him to do it, a. that it may be done, a. to have time given one*; invite (person *to* dinner &c., or *out*); (of things) demand, require, as *it asks* (*for*) *attention*; *a.* (publish) *the banns*; (pop.) *be asked in church,* have one's banns called. [com.-Teut.; OE *ásciam,* ME *ox ax ex ask esk ash ass,* &c.; *ax* was usu. literary form to 1600]

aska·nce, -ant, adv. Sideways, asquint; with indirect meaning; *look a. at,* view suspiciously. [?]

askew·, adv. & pred. a. Obliquely; *look a.* (not straight in the face); (adj.) oblique. [etym. dub., cf. SKEW]

asla·nt, adv. & prep. Obliquely; (prep.) slantingly across, athwart. [A prep. + SLANT]

aslee·p, adv. & pred. a. In, into, a state of sleep (lit. & fig.); (of limbs) benumbed; (of top) spinning without apparent motion. [A prep. + SLEEP]

aslo·pe, adv. & pred. a. Sloping, crosswise. [prob. f. OE *aslopen* p.p of *aslupan* slip away]

asp[1], n. (also *aspen*). Kind of poplar with specially tremulous leaves. [com.-Teut.; OE *æspæ, æps,* G *espe*]

asp[2], n. Small venomous hooded serpent of Egypt and Libya; (poet.) any venomous serpent. [f. L f. Gk *aspis*]

aspă·ragus, n. Plant, whose vernal shoots are a table delicacy. [L, f. Gk *asparagos,* etym. dub.; earlier *sperage, sparagus, sparrow-grass*]

ă·spect, n. Way of looking; a looking, fronting, in a given direction; side so fronting; phase; look, expression; appearance (esp. to the mind). [f. L *aspectus -ūs* (AD*spicere -spect-* look at)]

a·spen, a. & n. Of, like, the asp (tree); quivering; (n.) = ASP[1]. [ASP[1] + -EN; wrongly taken as noun used attrib. in *aspen leaf* &c.]

ăspergi·llum, n. Brush for sprinkling holy water. [L, f. *aspergere* (*ad* to + *spargere* sprinkle) + *-illum* dim. suf.]

ăspĕ·rity, n. Roughness; rough excrescence; severity (of weather); harshness, sharpness, (of temper). [f. OF *asprete* f. L *asperitatem* (*asper* rough, see -TY)]

asper·se, v.t. Besprinkle (*with*); bespatter (person, character, *with* damaging reports); calumniate. So **asper·SION** n. [f. L *aspergere -ers-*, see ASPERGILLUM]

aspersor·ium, n. Vessel for holy water. [med. L (as prec., see -ORY)]

ă·sphălt[1], n. A smooth hard bituminous substance; mixture of bitumen, pitch, and sand, for pavements &c.; similar mixture of coal-tar with sand &c. Hence **aspha·ltIC** a. [f. Gk *asphaltos*, of foreign orig.]

a·sphălt[2], v.t. Lay (road) with asphalt. [f. prec.]

ă·sphodel, n. Genus of liliaceous plants; (poet.) immortal flower in Elysium. [f. L f. Gk *asphodelos*, etym. dub.; earlier *affodil*, whence DAFFODIL]

asphy·xia, -xy, n. Suspended animation due to lack of oxygen in blood, suffocation. Hence **asphy·xiAL** a., **asphy·xiATE**[3] v.t. [f. Gk *asphuxia* (*a-* not + *sphuxis* pulse)]

ă·spic[1], n. (poet.). = ASP[2]. [F, f. L *aspidem*, nom. *-is*, w. unexpl. *-ic*]

ă·spic[2], n. Savoury meat jelly with cold game, eggs, &c., in it. [F, etym. dub.]

aspidi·stra, n. Foliage plant with broad taper leaves. [mod. L f. Gk *aspis* shield]

a·spirant (or *aspīr·-*), a. & n. (One) who aspires (*to, after, for*). [F, as foll., see -ANT]

ă·spirate[1] (*-at*), a. & n. (Consonant) pronounced with a breathing, blended with sound of *h*; the sound of *h*. [f. L *aspirare*, see ASPIRE and -ATE[2]]

a·spirāte[2], v.t. Pronounce with a breathing; draw out (gas) from vessel. [as prec., see -ATE[3]]

aspira·tion, n. Drawing of breath; desire (*for, after*); action of aspirating. [f. L *aspiratio* (as prec., see -ATION)]

a·spirātor, n. Apparatus for drawing air, gas, through tube; instrument for drawing pus from abscesses; winnowing-machine. [f. L *aspirare*, see foll. and -OR[2]]

aspire·, v.i. Desire earnestly (*to, after, at, to* do, or abs.); mount up (usu. fig.). [f. L AD(*spirare* breathe)]

a·spirin, n. An analgetic & febrifuge. [trade name]

asqui·nt, adv. & pred. a. (With *look* or sim. vb) obliquely, out at the corner of the eyes (esp. through defect in the eyes). [prob. f. or corr. to Du. *schuinte* slant + A prep.]

ass, n. Quadruped of horse family with long ears and tuft at end of tail (used esp. as type of ignorance, stupidity, &c.); *make an a. of*, stultify (oneself, or another); *Asses' bridge* (*Pons Asinorum*), Euclid I, 5. [OE has isolated form *assa*, as well as *esol* for com.-Teut. *esil* f. L *asinus*]

ă·ssagai, -segai (-gī), n. Slender spear of hard wood, esp. a missile of S. African tribes. [f. F *azagaye* f. Arab. *azzaghayah* (*al* the + Berber word *zaghayah*)]

assa·i (-ah-ē), adv. (mus.). Very. [It.]

assai·l, v.t. Make hostile attack upon (lit. & fig.); approach resolutely (task); overwhelm (*with* questions &c.). Hence **assai·lABLE** a., **assai·lANT** n. [f. OF *asalir, asaillir*, f. LL AD*salire -salt-* leap at]

assă·ssin, n. One who undertakes to kill treacherously; (Hist.) Moslem fanatic in time of Crusades, sent by the Old Man of the Mountains to murder Christians. [F, f. med.L *assassinus* f. Arab. *ḥashshash, ḥashishiyy* hashish-eater]

assa·ssinate, v.t. Kill by treacherous violence. Hence **assassinA·TION, assa·ssinatOR**[2], nn. [f. med. L *assassinare* (*assassinus*), see prec. and -ATE[3]]

assau·lt[1], n. Hostile attack (lit. & fig.); *a. of, at, arms*, attack in fencing, display of military exercises; rush against walls of fortress &c., as *carry by a.*; (Law) unlawful personal attack (including menacing words), as *a. and battery*. [f. OF *asaut* f. LL *adsaltus* (as ASSAIL)]

assau·lt[2], v.t. Make violent attack upon (lit. & fig.); assail; attack (fortress) by sudden rush. Hence **assau·ltABLE** a. [f. OF *asauter* f. Rom. *assaltare* spring at, for L AD(*sultare* = *saltare* frequent. of *salire salt-* leap)]

assay·[1], n. Trial of metals, esp. of fineness of coin or bullion; metal to be so tried; (archaic) attempt. [OF, f. L *exagium* weighing (*exigere, -agere*, weigh, try)]

assay·[2], v.t. & i. Try the purity of (precious metals, also fig.); attempt (anything difficult, *to* do). Hence **assay·ABLE** a. [f. OF *asayer, essayer*, f. LL **exagiare* (*exagium*, see prec.)]

asse·mblage, n. Bringing, coming, together; concourse of persons; collection. [F (*assembler*, see foll. and -AGE)]

asse·mble, v.t. & i. Gather together, collect; (Mech.) fit together the parts of (machine, structure). [f. OF *asembler* f. L AS*simulare* in the (late) sense of bring together (*simul*)]

asse·mbly, n. Gathering together, concourse, esp. deliberative body, legislative council; military call by drum or bugle; *a.-room*, room in which balls &c. are given. [f. OF *asemblée* fem. p.p. of *asembler*, see prec.]

asse·nt[1], v.i. Agree (*to* proposal), defer (*to* a desire); express agreement (*to* statement or opinion, or abs.). Hence **asse·ntOR**[2] n. [f. OF *asenter* f. L *assentare, -ari*, irreg. frequent. of AS*sentiri* agree to (*sentire* think)]

asse·nt[2], n. (Official) concurrence, sanction, as *royal a.* (of sovereign to bill passed by Parliament); mental acceptance. [f. OF *asente* (*asenter*, see prec.)]

assenta·tion, n. Obsequious concurrence. [F, f. L *assentationem* (as ASSENT, see -ATION)]
asse·ntient (-shĭ-), a. & n. (Person) that assents. [f. L as ASSENT, see -ENT]
asser·t, v.t. Vindicate a claim to (rights); *a.* one*self*, insist upon one's rights; declare. Hence **asser·t**ABLE, **asser·t**IVE, aa., **asser·tive**LY[2] adv., **asser·tive**NESS n. [f. L AS(*serere sert-* join) put one's hand on slave's head to free him (whence obs. sense 'free' in E) or claim him, claim, affirm]
asser·tion, n. Insistence upon a right; *self-a.*, insistence on recognition of one's claims; affirmation, positive statement. [f. L *assertio* (as prec., see -ION)]
asser·tor, n. One who asserts; champion, advocate, (*of*). [L (as prec., see -OR[2])]
asse·ss, v.t. Fix amount of (taxes, fine); fix amount of and impose (*upon* person or community); fine, tax, (person, community, property, *in, at,* so much); estimate value of (property) for taxation. Hence **asse·ss**ABLE a., **asse·ssab**LY[2] adv., **asse·ss**MENT n. [f. OF *assesser* f. LL *assessare* frequent. of AS(*sidēre sess-* = *sedēre* sit)]
asse·ssor, n. One who sits as assistant, adviser, to judge or magistrate; one who assesses taxes or estimates value of property for taxation. [f. OF *assessour* f. L *assessorem* assistant-judge (as prec., see -OR[2])]
a·ssets, n. pl. (sing. *-et*). (Law) enough goods to enable heir to discharge debts and legacies of testator; property liable to be so applied; effects of insolvent debtor; property of person or company that may be made liable for debts; (sing.) item of this in balance-sheet, (loosely) any possession, (improp.) any useful quality. [f. AF *asetz* f. OF *asez* enough f. LL *ad satis* to sufficiency]
assĕ·verate, v.t. Solemnly declare. So **assever**A·TION n. [f. L AS*severare* (*severus* serious), see -ATE[3]]
assi·bilate, v.t. Give a hissing sound to. Hence **assibil**A·TION n. [f. L AS*sibilare* hiss, see -ATE[3]]
assidu·ity, n. Close attention; (pl.) constant attentions. [f. L *assiduitas* (*assiduus,* see foll. and -TY)]
assi·duous, a. Persevering, diligent. Hence **assi·duous**LY[2] adv., **assiduous**NESS n. [f. L *assiduus* (as ASSESS) + -OUS]
assī·gn[1], v.t. Allot as a share (*to*); make over (esp. personal property, *to*); appoint (place &c. *to*); fix, specify; ascribe, refer, (event *to* date); ascribe (reason *to, for,* thing). Hence **assi·gn**ABLE a., **assign**OR·[2] (-īn-), n. [f. OF *assigner* f. L AS*signare* mark out to (*signum* sign)]
assī·gn[2], n. One to whom property, right, is legally transferred. [ME *assigne* (three syllables) f. F *assigné* p.p. of *assigner* (see prec.) gives both *assign* and *assignee*]

a·ssignăt (-ĭg-), n. Paper money issued by revolutionary government of France. [F, f. L *assignatum*, neut. p.p. of *assignare* assign]
assigna·tion (-ĭg-), n. Apportionment; formal transference; appointment (of time and place); attribution of origin. [f. OF *assignacion* f. L *assignationem* (as ASSIGN[1], see -ATION)]
assignee· (-īnē), n. One appointed to act for another; assign; *aa. in bankruptcy,* persons charged with management of bankrupt's estate. [f. OF *a(s)signé*, see ASSIGN n.]
assig·nment, n. Allotment; legal transference; document effecting this; attribution; statement (of reasons). [f. OF *assignement* f. med. L *assignamentum* (as ASSIGN[1], see -MENT)]
assi·milate, v.t. & i. Make like (*to, with*); compare (*to, with*); absorb into the system (lit. & fig.); (intr.) be so absorbed. Hence or cogn. **assimila**BI·LITY, **assimil**A·TION, **assi·milat**OR[2], nn., **assi·mil**ABLE, **assi·milat**IVE, **assi·milat**ORY, aa. [f. L AS*similare* (*similis* like), see -ATE[3]]
assi·st, v.t. & i. Help (person, process, person *in doing*), whence **assi·st**ANT a. & n., **assi·st**ANCE n.; (intr.) take part (*in*); be present (*at*). [f. F *assister* f. L AS*sistere* take one's stand by]
assi·ze, n. Statutory price (of bread and ale); trial in which sworn assessors decide questions of fact, esp. periodical sessions in each county of England for administration of civil and criminal justice; *great a.*, last judgement. [f. OF *asise,* fem. sing. p.p. (as n.) of *asseoir* sit at f. L *assidēre,* cf. ASSESS]
asso·ciable (-sha-), a. That can be connected in thought (*with*). Hence **associ**ABI·LITY n. [F, f. *associer* (as foll., see -ABLE)]
assō·ciate[1] (-shĭat), a. & n. Joined in companionship, function, or dignity; allied; partner; companion; colleague; subordinate member of an association; thing connected with another. Hence **asso·ciate**SHIP n. [f. L AS*sociare* (*socius* sharing, allied), see -ATE[2]]
asso·ciāte[2] (-shĭ-), v.t. & i. Join (persons, things, or one *with* another); connect in idea; make one*self* a partner *in* (a matter); (intr.) combine for common purpose; have intercourse (*with*). Hence **asso·ciat**IVE, **asso·ciat**ORY, aa., **asso·ciat**OR[2] n. [as prec., see -ATE[3]]
associa·tion (-sĭ-), n. Act of associating (in all senses); organized body of persons; *deed of a.*, document giving particulars of limited liability company; fellowship, intimacy; *a. of ideas,* mental connexion between an object and ideas related to it; *a. football* (abbr. *socker*), kind played with round ball, which must not be handled (cf. RUGBY). [f. L *associatio* (as prec., see -ATION)]

assoi·l, v.t. (archaic). Absolve from sin, pardon; acquit; release; atone for. [f. OF *assoil, assoille*, pres. ind. and subj. of *assoudre* f. L AB(*solvere* loose); Sc. has *assoilzie* (pron. -yĭ) still used in sense 'acquit']

ă·ssonance, n. Resemblance of sound between two syllables; rhyming of one word with another in the accented vowel and those that follow, but not in the consonants (e.g. *sonnet, porridge*); partial correspondence. So **a·ssonANT** a. [F, f. L ASsonare respond to (*sonus* sound), see -ANCE]

assor·t, v.t. & i. Classify, arrange in sorts; group *with* others; furnish (store, shop) with an assortment; (intr.) associate *with*; fall into a class; suit *well* or *ill with*. [f. OF *assorter* (*à* to + *sorte* SORT)]

assor·tment, n. Assorting; assorted set of goods of one or several classes. [-MENT]

assuā·ge (-sw-), v.t. Calm, soothe, (person, feelings, pain); appease (appetite, desire). Hence **assua·geMENT** n. [f. OF *asouager* f. L *ASsuaviare (*suavis* sweet)]

assū·me, v.t. Take upon oneself (aspect, air); *assuming*, taking much upon oneself, arrogant; undertake (office, duty); usurp; simulate; take for granted (thing, thing *to* be, *that*). Hence **assu·mABLE** a., **assu·mabLY²** adv. [f. L AS(*sumere sumpt-* take)]

assu·mption, n. Act of assuming (in all senses); (*A*-) reception of Virgin Mary into heaven, feast in honour of this; thing assumed; arrogance. [f. L *assumptio* (as ASSUME, see -ION)]

assu·mptive, a. Taken for granted; arrogant. [f. L *assumptivus* (as prec., see -IVE)]

assur·ance (ashoor-), n. Formal guarantee; positive declaration; (Law) securing of a title; compact securing value of property in the event of its being lost, or payment of specified sum on person's death (usu. life-*a.*, fire-, marine-, *insurance*); certainty (*make a. double sure*, remove all possible doubt, Shaksp., *Macb.* IV. i. 183); self-confidence; impudence. [f. OF *aseürance* (*aseürer*, see foll. & -ANCE)]

assure (ashoor·), v.t. Make safe; *a. life* (see prec.); make certain, ensure the happening &c. of; make (person) sure (*of* fact); tell (person) confidently (*of* a thing, *of* its being so, *that* it is so). Hence **assur·ĕdLY²** adv., **assure·dNESS** n. [f. OF *aseürer* f. LL ADsecurare (*securus* safe)]

assur·gent, a. Rising; (Bot.) rising obliquely; aggressive. [f. L ASsurgere rise, see -ENT]

Assy̆rio·logy, n. Study of language, history, antiquities, of Assyria. Hence **Assyrio·LOGIST** n. [f. L f. Gk *Assuria* + -LOGY]

astă·tic, a. Not tending to keep one position; *a. needle* (unaffected by earth's magnetism). [f. Gk *astatos* unstable (*a-* not + *sta-* stand) + -IC]

a·ster, n. Genus of plants with showy radiated flowers; *China a.*, flower allied to this. [L f. Gk *astēr* star]

-ăster, suf. expressing contempt, added to L and Rom. nn., as *oleaster, poetaster*, meaning 'petty, sham, would-be'. [L, as in *philosophaster*]

ă·sterisk, n. & v.t. Star (*) used to mark words for reference or distinction; (v.t.) mark with a. [f. L f. Gk *asteriskos* dim. as ASTER]

ă·sterism, n. Cluster of stars; three asterisks (⁂), calling attention. [f. Gk *asterismos* (ASTER, see -ISM)]

aster·n, adv. (naut.). In, at, the stern; away behind; *a. of*, behind (a ship, boat); backwards. [A prep. + STERN]

ă·steroid, a. & n. Star-shaped; (n.) name of small planets revolving round sun between orbits of Mars and Jupiter; kind of firework. Hence **asteroi·dAL** a. [f. Gk *asteroeidēs* (ASTER, see -OID)]

ă·sthma, n. A disease of respiration, characterized by difficult breathing, cough, &c. [Gk *asthma -matos* (*azō* breathe hard, see -M)]

asthmă·tic, a. & n. Pertaining to, suffering from, good against, asthma; (n.) person suffering from asthma. Hence **asthma·ticAL** a., **asthma·ticalLY²** adv. [f. Gk *asthmatikos* (as prec., see -IC-)]

asti·gmatism, n. Structural defect in the eye or a lens, preventing rays of light from being brought to common focus. So **ăstigmă·tIC** a. [f. Gk *a-* not + *stigma -matos* point + -IC]

astir·, adv. & pred. a. In motion; out of bed; in excitement. [A prep. + STIR n.]

astŏ·nish, v.t. Amaze, surprise; *astonied* (archaic p.p. of *astony*, see etym.), dazed, dismayed. Hence **asto·nishMENT** n. [altered f. obs. *astony* unexpl. form of obs. *astone* apparently f. OF *estoner, estuner* (mod. *étonner*), stupefy, shock, f. L *EXtonare (cf. L *attonare* strike with thunderbolt, stun); relation to STUN and G *staunen* is uncertain]

astou·nd (-ow-), v.t. Shock with alarm or surprise; amaze. [f. obs. *astound a.* = *astoned* p.p. of obs. *astone*, see prec.]

astra·ddle, adv. & pred. a. In a straddling position. [A prep. + STRADDLE v.]

ă·stragal, n. (Arch.) small moulding round top or bottom of columns; (Gunn.) ring round cannon near mouth. [f. foll.]

astră·galus, n. Ball of ankle-joint; genus of leguminous plants including milk-vetch. [L, f. Gk *astragalos* huckle-bone, moulding, plant]

astrakha·n (-kăn), n. Skin of young lambs from Astrakhan in Russia, with wool like fur.

ă·stral, a. Connected with, consisting of, stars; *a. spirits* (supposed to live in stars); *a. body,* spiritual appearance of the human form; *a. lamp* (throwing no shadow on table below). [f. L *astralis* (*astrum* star, see -AL)]

astray·, adv. or pred. a. Out of the right way (lit. & fig.). [perh. orig. f. OF *estraié* p.p. of *estraier* f. L **extravagare* wander out of bounds; but confused w. forms like *a-float, a-sleep*; no early noun *stray*]

astri·ct, v.t. (rare). Bind tightly; make costive; bind morally, legally; restrict (*to*). So **astri·ct**ION n. [f. L *astringere -ict-* (*ad* to + *stringere* bind)]

astri·ctive, a. Tending to contract organic tissue; astringent, styptic. [as prec., see -IVE]

astri·de, adv., pred. a., & prep. In striding position; with legs on each side (*of*); *a. of the road* &c., mil., posted across it; (prep.) astride of. [A prep. + STRIDE n.]

astri·nge, v.t. Bind together; compress; constipate. [as ASTRICT]

astri·ngent (-j-), a. & n. Binding, styptic; severe; austere; (n.) astringent medicine. Hence **astri·ngent**LY[2] adv., **astri·ngen**CY n. [as prec., see -ENT]

ăstro-, in comb. = Greek *astron* star; in wds f. Gk, as *astronomy,* and mod. formations as *-gony,* stellar cosmogony, *-lithology,* study of meteoric stones.

ă·stroïte, n. Gem known to the ancients; kind of madrepore. [f. L *astroïtes* (see prec. and -ITE)]

a·strolabe, n. Instrument formerly used for taking altitudes &c. [f. OF *astrelabe* f. med. L *astrolabium* f. Gk ASTRO- (*lab-* take)]

astro·logy, n. (Formerly) practical astronomy (also called *natural a.*); art of judging of reputed occult influence of stars upon human affairs (*judicial a.*). So **astro·**LOGER n., **astrolo·gic**(AL) aa., **astrolo·gical**LY[2] adv. [f. F *astrologie* f. L f. Gk ASTRO(*logia* -LOGY)]

astro·nomy, n. Science of the heavenly bodies. So **astro·nom**ER[1] (3) n., **astrono·mic**(AL) aa., **astrono·mical**LY[2] adv. [f. OF *astronomie* f. L f. Gk *astronomia* f. ASTRO*nomos* a. star-arranging (*nemō* arrange)]

astu·te, a. Shrewd, sagacious; crafty. Hence **astu·te**LY[2] adv., **astu·te**NESS n. [f. L *astutus* length. form of *astus* crafty]

asu·nder, adv. (Of two or more things) apart (in motion or position); *tear a., tear* to pieces. [OE *on sundran,* see A prep. and SUNDER]

asy·lum, n. Sanctuary, place of refuge, esp. for criminals or debtors; shelter, refuge; institution for shelter and support of afflicted or destitute persons, esp. lunatics. [L, f. Gk *asulon* neut. of adj. *asulos* inviolable (*a-* not + *sulē* right of seizure)]

asy·mmetry, n. Want of symmetry. [A-(7) + SYMMETRY]

ă·symptote (-ōt), n. Line that approaches nearer and nearer to given curve but does not meet it within a finite distance. [f. Gk *asumptōtos* not falling together (*a-* not + *sum-* together + *ptōtos* falling f. *piptō*)]

asy·ndeton, n. A rhetorical figure that omits the conjunction. [f. Gk *asundeton* unconnected (*a-* not + *sundetos* f. *sundeō* bind together)]

at, prep. expressing exact, approximate, or vague position, lit. & fig., as *meet a. a point, wait a. the corner, a. the top, a. Bath* (or any town except London and that in which the speaker is), *a. school, a. sea, a. a distance, a. arm's length, out a. elbows, a. work, a. dinner, play a. fighting, good a. repartee, a. daggers drawn, a. a disadvantage, a. his mercy, a. a low price, a. midday, a. first, a. least, a. all events, annoyed a. finding, impatient a. delay*; expr. motion towards, lit. & fig., as *arrive a. a place, get, rush, shoot, laugh, grumble, hint, snatch, aim, a.*; *a. all,* in any degree (in neg. context); *a. best, worst,* assuming best, worst, result &c.; *a. one,* in harmony or agreement (*with*); *a. that,* at that estimate (*will take it a. t.,* accept that account of the matter), moreover, into the bargain (*lost an arm, and the right arm a. t.*). [com.-Teut., but lost in G and Du.; OE *æt,* governing dat., rarely acc.]

at-, pref. = AD- before *t.*

ă·taraxy, -a·xia, n. Stoical indifference. [Gk *ataraxia* (*a-* not + *tarassō* disturb)]

ă·tavism, n. Resemblance to remote ancestors, reversion to earlier type; recurrence of disease after intermission of some generations. Hence **atavi·stic** [-IST, -IC] a. [f. F *atavisme* f. L *atavus* great-grandfather's grandfather, see -ISM]

ata·xic, a. Characterized by ataxy; *a. fever,* malignant typhus fever. [f. foll. + -IC]

ata·xy, n. Irregularity of animal functions; *locomotor a.,* constitutional unsteadiness in use of legs, arms, &c. [f. Gk *ataxia* (*a-* not + *taxis* order f. *tassō* arrange)]

ate. See EAT.

-ate[1], suf. forming nn. orig. f. L *-atus* (gen. *-ūs*) in nouns of state from p.p. stems or nouns, or f. L *-atus, -ata, -atum* (see -ATE[2]), which in OF became *-é* (*-ée*), but in learned words, and later in many reformed words, *-at,* as *prélat, primat, magistrat.* E having adopted *-at* afterwards added *-e* to mark quantity of *a,* and later words took *-ate* at once. E also formed wds either directly on L as *curate* or by anal. as *aldermanate.* Most nn. in *-ate* are (1) nn. of office, as *marquisate, syndicate,* (2) participial nn. as *legate* one deputed, *precipitate* what is thrown down, (3) chem. terms denoting salts formed by action of an acid on a base, as *nitrate, sulphate.*

-ate[2], suf. forming adjj. (1) chiefly (thr. F) f. L p.p. in *-atus* (1st conjug.), which (cf. prec.) became successively *-at, -ate,* as *desolate.* Many such adjj. formed causative vbs (see foll.) and served as p.p. to them, till later the native *-ed* was added; *-ated* also appears without intervention of vb, as *annulated,* and as alternative form to *-ate*; (2) L participial adjj. were also formed on nn., as *caudatus* tailed, and on adjj. as *candidatus* white-robed; these were largely adopted in E, and others formed on anal. Many nouns in -ATE[1] were orig. adjj. In *cordate, ovate,* &c., the sense is 'shaped like'.

-ate[3], suf. forming vbs to correspond to adjj. in -ATE[2], and subsequently to repr. the corr. L vb in *-are* (p.p. *-atus*), as *separate, aggravate.* As these vbs usu. have F equivalents in *-er, -ate* was further used to form vbs on model of F vbs in *-er,* as *isolate* (F *isoler*). *-ate* was also used to form vbs that L might have formed, but did not, on nouns, as *felicitate* (L *felicitas -atis*), and even vbs on nouns not of L orig., as *camphorate.*

atelier (ătl-yā·), n. Workshop, studio. [F]

atelo- in comb. = Gk *atelēs* imperfect (*a-* not + *telos* end), as *-glossia, -gnathia, -stomia,* imperfect development of tongue, jaws, mouth.

Athanā·sian, n. Of Athanasius (archbishop of Alexandria in reign of Constantine), as *A. creed* (that beginning *Whosoever will*). [f. *Athanasius* + -AN]

ā·theism, n. Disbelief in the existence of a God; godlessness. So **a·the**IST n., **athei·st**IC a., **athei·st**ICALLY adv. [f. F *athéisme* f. Gk *atheos* without God (*a-* not + *theos* God), see -ISM]

ăthĕnae·um, n. Literary or scientific club (esp. *the A.,* in London); reading-room, library. [L, f. Gk *Athēnaion* temple of *Athēnē,* goddess of wisdom]

athir·st, pred. a. Thirsty; eager (*for*). [OE *ofthyrst* for *ofthyrsted* p.p. of *ofthyrstan* be thirsty]

ă·thlete, n. Competitor in physical exercises; robust, vigorous, man. [f. L *athleta* f. Gk *athlētēs* f. *athleō* contend for prize (*athlon*), see -ET[2]]

athlĕ·tic, a. & n. Pertaining to athletes; physically powerful; (n. pl.) practice of physical exercises. Hence **athle·t**ICALLY adv., **athle·tic**ISM n. [f. L f. Gk *athlētikos* (as prec.)]

at-ho·me, n. Reception of visitors within certain hours during which host or hostess or both have announced that they will be at home.

athwar·t (-ort), adv. & prep. Across from side to side (usu. obliquely); crosswise, perversely; in opposition to; (of ship) *athwart-hawse,* across stem of another ship at anchor. [A prep. + THWART]

-atic, adj. suf. (= F *-atique*) f. L *-aticus* (orig. *-at-* of p.p. stems + -IC, but extended to nouns as *fanaticus* f. *fanum*), which gives also -AGE; in many modern formations, as *lunatic, lymphatic*; but in many apparent exx. (*dramatic, piratic*) the suf. is *-ic,* and *-at-* part of the stem.

-atile, adj. suf. like -ATIC in orig. and use = *-at-* + -ILE, as *volatile, fluviatile.*

a-ti·lt, adv. Tilted; *run, ride, a.* (in encounter on horseback with thrust of lance, usu. fig.). [A prep. + TILT]

-ation, suf. (= *-at-* of L 1st conj. p.p. stems + -ION) forming abstract nouns on L 1st conj. vbs as *agitation,* Gk vbs in *-izō* (L *-izare* -IZE) as *organization,* F vbs in *-er* as *filtration,* and rarely E vbs as *starvation,* the last on false anal. f. *vexation* &c., formed on L *vexare,* not on E *vex.* The great preponderance of *-ation* over *-ition* &c. is due to F adoption of the *-er* vb (= L 1st conj.) as the type for all new vbs. Wds taken f. OF have often *-ison,* -SON, (*orison, reason*) instead of *-ation.* Most wds have vb in *-ate* corr. (*creation*), many a shortened vb f. L 1st conj. (*plantation, plant,* not *plantate*; *modify,* not *modificate*), a few no vb (*duration*). Meanings: (1) vbl action; (2) instance of this; (3) resulting state; (4) concrete result (*plantation*).

-ative, adj. suf. = *-at-* + -IVE (cf. -ATIC); most exx. are f. vbs in *-ate* as *demonstrative,* or L 1st conj. as *affirmative,* some f. nouns in -TY (L st. *-tat-*) as *authoritative,* and some on E vbs as *talkative.*

Atla·ntic, a. & n. Pertaining to mount Atlas in Libya; hence applied to sea near western shore of Africa, and later to whole ocean between Europe and Africa on east and America on west; (n.) Atlantic ocean. [f. L f. Gk *Atlantikos* f. foll.]

a·tlas, n. Volume of maps; large size of drawing paper; (Physiol.) uppermost cervical vertebra, supporting skull. [*Atlas -antos* (1) Greek god of the older family, who held up pillars of universe; (2) the mountain in Libya, regarded as supporting the heavens]

atmo- in comp. = Gk *atmos* vapour, as *-logy,* science of aqueous vapour, *-lysis,* separation of vapours, *-meter* (for measuring evaporation).

a·tmosphere, n. Spheroidal gaseous envelope surrounding heavenly body; that surrounding earth; one surrounding any substance; mental or moral environment; air (in any place); (w. pl.) pressure of 15 lb. on square inch (that exerted by atmosphere on earth's surface). Hence **atmosphĕ·r**IC(AL) aa., **atmosphe·rical**LY[2] adv.; **atmosphe·rics** n. pl., interfering sounds in wireless or other telephones due to electric disturbance in a. [f. ATMO- + Gk *sphaira* ball]

ato·ll (*or* ă·t-), n. Ring-shaped coral reef

enclosing lagoon. [Maldive *atollon, atoll,* prob. = Malayalam *adal* closing]

ă·tom, n. Body too small to be divided; *physical a.,* supposed ultimate particle of matter; *chemical aa.,* smallest particles in which elements combine with themselves or each other; minute portion; small thing. [f. F *atome* f. L f. Gk *atomos* indivisible (*a-* not + *-tomos* cut f. *temnō*)]

atŏ·mic, a. Of, pertaining to, atoms; *a. philosophy,* doctrine of formation of all things from indivisible particles endued with gravity and motion; (Chem.) *a. theory* (that elemental bodies consist of indivisible atoms of definite relative weight, and that atoms of different elements unite with each other in fixed proportions, which determine the proportions in which elements and compounds enter into chemical combination); *unit of a. weight,* weight of an atom of hydrogen. Hence **ato·mic**AL a., **ato·mical**LY[2] adv. [prec. + -IC]

atomĭ·city, n. The number of atoms in the molecule of an element; (formerly) = VALENCY. [f. prec., see -TY]

a·tomism, n. Atomic philosophy; doctrine of action of individual atoms. [ATOM + -ISM]

a·tomist, n. Holder of atomic theory or philosophy. Hence **atomi·st**IC a. [ATOM + -IST]

a·tomize, v.t. Reduce to atoms. Hence **atomiz**A·TION n. [ATOM + -IZE]

a·tomizer, n. (med.). Instrument for reducing liquids to fine spray. [prec. + -ER[1]]

ă·tomy[1], n. Skeleton; emaciated body. [f. ANATOMY, *an-* being taken as article]

ă·tomy[2], n. Atom, tiny being. [f. *atomi* pl. of L *atomus* ATOM]

atō·ne, v.t. & i. (As v.t., archaic) reconcile (enemies), compose (quarrel); (v.i., in mod. use) make amends (esp. *a. for,* expiate). Hence **atō·ne**MENT n. [AT + ONE, = set at one, unite]

atŏ·nic, a. & n. Unaccented, unstressed; (Path.) wanting tone; (n.) unaccented word (esp. in Gk Gram.). [f. med. L *atonicus* f. Gk *atonos* toneless (*a-* not + *tonos* TONE), see -IC]

ato·p, adv. On the top (*of*). [A prep.]

ătrabĭ·lious, a. Affected by black bile; melancholy; acrimonious. Hence **atrabi·lious**NESS n. [f. L *atra bilis* black bile + -OUS, after L *biliosus* bilious]

atri·p, adv. (Of anchor) just lifted from ground in weighing. [A prep. + TRIP]

ā·trium, n. (pl. *-a, -ums*). Central court of Roman house; covered portico, esp. before church door. [L]

atrō·cious (-shus), a. Heinously wicked; very bad, as *a. pun.* Hence **atro·cious**LY[2] adv., **atro·cious**NESS n. [f. L *atrox -ocis* (*ater* black) + -OUS]

atrŏ·city, n. Heinous wickedness; atrocious deed; bad blunder. [f. L *atrocitas* (as prec., see -TY)]

ă·trophy, n. Wasting away through imperfect nourishment; emaciation (lit. & fig.). Hence **a·trophy** v.t. & i. [f. F *atrophie* f. L f. Gk *atrophia* f. *atrophos* ill-fed (*a-* not + *trophē* food)]

ă·tropine, n. Poisonous alkaloid found in deadly nightshade. [f. *atropa* deadly nightshade f. Gk *Atropos* inflexible, name of one of the Fates, see -INE[5]]

atta·ch, v.t. & i. Fasten (thing *to* another); join one*self* (*to* person, company, expedition); bind in friendship, make devoted, (*has the gift of attaching people to him; is deeply attached to her*); affix (immaterial things, name, liability, &c., *to*); attribute (importance &c. *to*); (Law) seize (person, property) by legal authority; adhere, be incident, as *no blame attaches to.* Hence **atta·ch**ABLE a. [f. OF *atachier* (mod. *attacher,* It. *attaccare*) f. *à* to + root found in Genevese *tache,* Sp. and Port. *tacha,* nail, TACK]

attă·ché (-shā), n. One attached to ambassador's suite; *a. case,* small rectangular valise ostensibly for carrying documents. [F, p.p. of *attacher* (as prec.)]

atta·chment, n. Act of attaching; thing attached; means of attaching; affection; legal seizure, esp. *foreign a.* (of foreigner's goods, to satisfy his creditors). [f. F *attachement* (*attacher* ATTACH, see -MENT)]

atta·ck[1], v.t. Fall upon, assault, (lit. & fig.); (of physical agents or diseases) act destructively upon. Hence **atta·ck**ABLE a. [f. F *attaquer* f. It. *attaccare,* see ATTACH]

atta·ck[2], n. Act of attacking (lit. & fig.); offensive operation. [f. prec.]

attai·n, v.t. & i. Arrive at, reach; gain, accomplish; (intr.) *a. to,* arrive at. Hence **attaina**BI·LITY, **attai·nable**NESS, nn., **attai·n**ABLE a. [f. OF *ataign-* st. of *ataindre* f. L AT*tingere* (*tangere* touch)]

attai·nder, n. Consequences of sentence of death or outlawry (forfeiture of estate, corruption of blood, extinction of civil rights). [OF *ataindre* ATTAIN used as n.; meaning influenced by confus. w. OF *taindre* TAINT]

attai·nment, n. Act of attaining; thing attained, esp. personal accomplishment. [ATTAIN + -MENT]

attai·nt, v.t. Subject to attainder; (of diseases &c.) strike, affect; infect; sully. [f. obs. *attaint* a. f. OF *ataint* p.p. as ATTAIN; confused in meaning with TAINT]

a·ttar, n. Fragrant essential oil from rose-petals. [f. Pers. *'aṭar(-gal)* essence (of roses) f. Arab. *'uṭur* aroma f. *'aṭara* breathe perfume]

atte·mper, v.t. Qualify by admixture; modify temperature of; soothe, mollify; accommodate *to*; attune *to*; temper (metal). Hence **atte·mper**MENT n. [f. OF *atemprer* f. L AT*temperare*]

atte·mpt[1], v.t. Try (thing, action, *to* do); try to master (enemy, fortress); *a. the* *life of*, try to kill. Hence **atte·mpt**ABLE a. [f. OF *attempter*, f. L AT*temptare* strive after]

atte·mpt², n. Attempting; endeavour. [f. prec.]

atte·nd, v.t. & i. Turn the mind *to*; apply oneself (*to* or abs.); be present (*at*); wait *upon*; (trans.) wait upon; escort, accompany; be present at (lecture &c.). [f. OF *atendre* f. L AT*tendere -tent-* stretch]

atte·ndance, n. Act of attending (*upon* person, *at* lecture); *dance a. on*, attend the convenience of; body of persons present. [f. OF *atendance* (as prec., see -ANCE)]

atte·ndant, a. & n. Waiting (*upon*); accompanying, as *a. circumstances*; present, as *a. crowd*; (n.) servant, satellite. [OF, part. as ATTEND]

atte·ntion, n. & int. Act of attending, as *pay, give, a.*; faculty of attending, as *attract, call, a.*; consideration, care; (pl.) ceremonious politeness; *come to, stand at, a.* (military attitude; *A.!*, order to assume it). [f. L *attentio* (as ATTEND, see -ION)]

atte·ntive, a. Heedful, observant; polite, assiduous. Hence **atte·ntive**LY² adv., **atte·ntive**NESS n. [F (*-if, -ive*), f. L as ATTEND, see -IVE)]

attĕ·nuāte¹, v.t. Make slender; make thin in consistence; reduce in force or value. So **attenu**A·TION n. [f. L AT*tenuare* (*tenuis* thin), see -ATE³]

attĕ·nuate² (-*a*t), a. Slender; rarefied. [as prec., see -ATE²]

atte·st, v.t. & i. Testify, certify; put (person) on oath or solemn declaration; (intr.) bear witness *to*. Hence **atte·st**OR² n. [f. F *attester* f. L AT*testari* (*testis* witness)]

attesta·tion, n. Act of testifying; testimony; evidence; formal confirmation by signature, oath, &c.; administration of an oath. [F, f. L *attestationem* (as prec., see -ATION)]

A·ttic¹, a. & n. Of Athens or Attica; *A.* (*dialect*), Greek spoken by the Athenians; *A. salt, wit*, refined wit; *A. order*, square column of any of the five ORDERS. [f. L f. Gk *Attikos*]

a·ttic², n. Structure consisting of small order placed above another of greater height (usu. *Attic*); highest storey of house; room in this. [f. F *attique*, as prec.]

a·tticism, n. Style, idiom, of Athens; refined amenity of speech; attachment to Athens. So **a·ttic**IZE (2) v.i. [f. Gk *attikismos*]

attire·, v.t., & n. Dress, array. [(n. f. vb) f. OF *atirer* (*à* to + *tire*, see TIER)]

a·ttitude, n. Disposition of figure (in painting &c.); posture of body, as *strike an a.* (assume it theatrically); settled behaviour, as indicating opinion; *a. of mind*, settled mode of thinking. [F, f. It. *attitudine* fitness, posture, f. med. L *aptitudinem* (*aptus* fit, see -TUDE)]

attitu·dinize, v.i. Practise attitudes; speak, write, behave, affectedly. [f. prec. + -IZE]

attor·n (-ern), v.t. & i. (law). Transfer; make legal acknowledgement of new landlord. Hence **attor·n**MENT n. [f. OF *atorner* (*à* to + *tourner* TURN)]

attor·ney¹ (-er-), n. One appointed to act for another in business or legal matters; *A. General*, legal officer empowered to act in all cases in which the state is a party; *abuse plaintiff's a.* (iron. advice to lawyer with a weak case). Hence **attor·ney**SHIP n. [f. OF *atorné* p.p. as ATTORN]

attor·ney² (-er-), n. *Letter, warrant, of A.* (by which person appoints another to act for him); *Power of A.*, authority thus conferred. [f. OF *atornée* fem. p.p., see prec.]

attra·ct, v.t. Draw to oneself (esp. of physical forces); excite the pleasurable emotions of (person); draw forth and fix upon oneself (attention &c.). Hence **attract**ABI·LITY n., **attra·ct**ABLE a. [f. L AT(*trahere tract-* draw)]

attra·ction, n. Act, faculty, of drawing to oneself (lit. & fig.); drawing force; thing that attracts (fig.); *a. of gravity* (existing between all bodies, and varying directly as their masses, inversely as the square of their distance apart); *magnetic a.*, action of magnet in drawing iron; *molecular a.* (between molecules of bodies, acting only at infinitesimal distances); *capillary a.* (by which liquid is drawn up through hairlike tube). [F, f. L *attractionem* (as prec., see -ION)]

attra·ctive, a. Attracting, capable of attracting (esp. fig.). Hence **attra·ctive**LY² adv., **attra·ctive**NESS n. [F (*-if, -ive*), as prec., see -IVE]

a·ttribute¹, n. Quality ascribed to anything; material object recognized as appropriate to person or office; characteristic quality; (Gram.) attributive word. [f. L AT(*tribuere -ut-* assign)]

attri·bute², v.t. Ascribe as belonging or appropriate *to*; refer (effect *to* its cause); assign (*to* time or place). Hence **attri·but**ABLE a. [as prec.]

attribu·tion, n. Act of attributing; authority granted (*to* a ruler &c.). [F, f. L *attributionem* (as prec., see -ION)]

attri·butive, a. & n. (Logic) assigning an attribute to a subject; (Gram.) expressing an attribute (e.g. *old* in *the old dog* but not in *the dog is old*); (n.) word denoting an attribute (usu. an adjective or its equivalent). Hence **attri·butive**LY² adv. [F (*-if, -ive*), as ATTRIBUTE¹, see -IVE]

attrī·ted, a. Worn by friction. [f. L AT(*terere trit-* rub)]

attrī·tion, n. Friction; wearing out (*war of a.*, turning on which side can last longest); abrasion; (Theol.) sorrow for sin (short of *contrition*). [f. L *attritio* (as prec., see -ION)]

attu·ne, v.t. Bring into musical accord (*to*, lit. & fig.); tune (instrument). [AT- + TUNE v.]

aubade (ōbah·d), n. Musical announcement of dawn. [F]

auberge (ōbar̄·zh), n. Inn. [F]

au·burn, a. Golden-brown (usu. of hair). [f. OF *auborne* f. L *alburnus* whitish]

au·ction, n. Public sale in which articles are sold to the highest of successive bidders; *Dutch a.*, sale in which price is reduced by auctioneer till a purchaser is found; *a. bridge*, form of bridge in which declaration may be made by any player. [f. L *auctio* increase, auction (*augēre auct-*, see -ION)]

auctioneer·, n., & v.i. (One whose business is to) conduct auctions. [-EER]

audā·cious, a. Daring, bold; impudent. Hence **auda·cious**LY[2] adv., **auda·cious**NESS, **audă·**CITY, nn. [f. L *audax* (*audēre* dare, see -ACIOUS)]

au·dible, a. Perceptible to the ear. Hence **au·dib**LY[2] adv., **audi**BI·LITY, **au·dible**NESS, nn. [f. med. L *audibilis* (*audire* hear, see -BLE)]

au·dience, n. Hearing; *give a.*, listen; formal interview; persons within hearing; assembly of listeners; (of a book) readers. [F (refash. on L), f. OF *oiance* f. L *audientia* (*audire* hear, see -ENCE)]

audio·meter, n. Kind of telephone for testing hearing-power. [f. L *audire* hear + -O- + -METER]

au·diphone, n. Instrument that, pressed against upper teeth, assists hearing. [improp. f. L *audire* hear + Gk *phōnē* sound, on *telephone*]

au·dit[1], n. Official examination of accounts; searching examination, esp. Day of Judgement; periodical settlement of accounts between landlord and tenants; *a. ale* (of special quality, brewed in English Universities, orig. for use on day of a.); *a.-house, -room* (attached to Cathedral for transaction of business). [f. L *auditus -ūs* hearing (*audire -it-*)]

au·dit[2], v.t. Examine (accounts) officially. [f. prec.]

audi·tion, n. Power of hearing; listening; trial hearing of applicant for employment as singer &c. [f. L *auditio* (*audire -it-*, see -ION)]

au·ditive, a. Concerned with hearing. [F (*-if, -ive*), as prec., see -IVE]

au·ditor, n. Listener; one who audits accounts. Hence **au·ditor**SHIP, **au·di-tr**ESS[1], nn. [f. AF *auditour* f. L *auditor* (as prec., see -OR[2])]

auditor·ial, a. Connected with an audit. [f. L *auditorius* (as prec., see -ORY) + -AL]

au·ditory, a. & n. Connected with hearing; received by the ear; assembly of hearers, audience; (also *-orium*) part of building occupied by audience. [f. L *auditorius, -um* (as prec., see -ORY)]

au fait (ō fā·), pred. a. Conversant, instructed; *put a person* au fait *of*, instruct him in. [F]

au fond [F], adv. At bottom (cf. *à fond*).

Auge·an, a. Filthy, like the stables of Augeas, which Hercules cleansed by turning river Alpheus through them. [f. L *Augeas* f. Gk *Augeias* + -AN]

au·ger (-g-), n. Tool for boring holes in wood, having long shank with cutting edge and screw point, and handle at right angles; instrument for boring in soil or strata, with stem that can be lengthened. [OE *nafugár* (*nafu* NAVE + *gár* piercer), cf. G. *näber*, Du. *avegaar*; for loss of *n-* cf. ADDER]

aught (awt), n. & adv. Anything; (adv., archaic) in any degree or respect. [OE *áwiht* (*á* ever + *wiht* wight, whit); later OE *áht*, gives mod. *ought*, now less usu. form]

au·gment[1], n. Vowel (in Sanskrit *a*, in Greek *ĕ*) prefixed to past tenses in the older Aryan languages. [F, f. L *augmentum* increase (*augēre*, see -MENT)]

augme·nt[2], v.t. & i. Make greater, increase; prefix the augment to; (intr.) increase. [f. F *augmenter* f. L *augmentare* increase (*augmentum*, see prec.)]

augmenta·tion, n. Enlargement; growth, increase; addition; (Mus.) repetition of a subject in notes double or quadruple those of the original. [OF, f. LL *augmentationem* (*augmentare*, see prec. and -ATION)]

augme·ntative, a. & n. Having the property of increasing; (Gram., of affixes or derived words) increasing in force the idea of the original word; (n.) augmentative word. [F (*-if, -ive*), f. L as AUGMENT, see -ATIVE]

au grand sérieux (F), adv. Quite seriously (*take* it, him, &c., *a.*)

au·gur[1], n. Roman religious official who foretold future events by omens derived from the actions of birds, appearance of victims' entrails, celestial phenomena, &c.; soothsayer. Hence **au·gur**SHIP n. [L, perh. f. *avis* bird + *-gar*, conn. w. *garrire* talk, Skr. *gar* shout, make known]

au·gur[2], v.t. & i. Forebode, anticipate; *a. well, ill*, have good or bad expectations *of, for*; *it augurs* (promises) *ill*. [f. prec.]

au·gūral, a. Pertaining to augurs; significant of the future. [f. L *auguralis* (AUGUR[1], see -AL)]

au·gūry, n. Divination by flight of birds &c.; augural ceremony; omen; presentiment; promise. [f. OF *augurie* f. L *augurium* (AUGUR[1])]

augu·st[1], a. Majestic, venerable. Hence **augu·st**LY[2] adv., **augu·st**NESS n. [f. L *augustus* consecrated, venerable, prob. f. AUGUR]

Au·gust[2], n. Eighth month of year, named after Augustus Caesar. [earlier *Aust* f. OF *aoust* f. L *augustus* (see prec.), refash. on L]

Augu·stan, a. & n. Connected with reign of Augustus Caesar, best period of Latin literature; (of any national literature) classical; *A. confession* (drawn up by Luther and Melanchthon at Augusta Vindelicorum or Augsburg); (n.) writer of the Augustan age of any literature. [f. L *Augustanus,* see -AN]

auk, n. Northern sea-bird, with short wings used only as paddles. [cogn. with Swed. *alka,* Da. *alke,* f. ON *álka*]

au·lic, a. Pertaining to a court; *A. Council,* (in old German empire) personal council of emperor, (later) council managing Austrian war-department. [f. F *aulique* f. L f. Gk *aulikos* (*aulē* court, see -IC)]

au·mbry, var. of AMBRY.

au nature·l (F), adv. or pred. a. (Cooked) in the simplest way.

aunt (ahnt), n. Father's, mother's, sister; uncle's wife; *A. Sally,* game at fairs, in which players throw sticks at pipe in mouth of wooden woman's head. [f. OF *aunte* (Prov. *amda*) f. L *amita*; E up to 17th c. had also *naunt* (my naunt = mine aunt), still used in dial.; F *tante* perh. = *ta ante*]

au pied de la lettre (ō pyā de lah lĕtr), adv. Literally. [F]

au·ra, n. Subtle emanation (from flowers &c.); atmosphere diffused by or attending a person &c. (esp. in mystical use as a definite envelope of body or spirit); (Electr.) current of air caused by discharge of electricity from a sharp point; (Path.) sensation as of current of cold air rising from some part of body to head, premonitory symptom in epilepsy and hysterics. Hence **au·ral**[1] [-AL] a. [L f. Gk, = breeze, breath]

au·ral[2], a. Pertaining to organ of hearing; received by the ear. Hence **au·ral**LY[2] adv. [f. L *auris* ear + -AL]

aurē·lia, n. (Formerly) chrysalis, esp. of butterfly; (Zool.) genus of phosphorescent marine animals. [It., = silkworm, fem. of *aurelio* golden f. L *aurum* gold]

aure·lian, a. & n. Of an aurelia; golden; (n.) collector, breeder, of insects. [prec. + -AN]

aurē·ola, n. Celestial crown won by martyr, virgin, doctor, by victory over world, flesh, or devil; = foll. [L (*a. corona*) golden (crown) fem. of *aureolus* f. *aureus* (*aurum* gold)]

au·reole, n. Aureola; (prop.) gold disk surrounding head in early pictures; circle of light depicted round head; oblong glory surrounding divine figures; actual halo, esp. that seen in eclipses. [f. prec.]

au revoir (ō revwar·), adv. (Good-bye) till we meet again. [F]

au·ric, a. Pertaining to gold; (Chem.) in which gold combines as a triad. [f. L *aurum* gold, see -IC]

au·ricle, n. External ear of animals; process shaped like lower lobe of ear; either of the two upper cavities of the heart. Hence **au·ricl**ED[2] a. [f. foll.]

auri·cula, n. Species of primula, bear's-ear; genus of molluscs. [L, = external ear, dim. of *auris* ear]

auri·cular, a. Pertaining to the ear; told privately in the ear, as *a. confession*; *a. witness,* one who tells what he has heard; pertaining to auricle of heart; shaped like an auricle. Hence **auri·cular**LY[2] adv. [f. L *auricularis* (AURICULA, see -AR[1])]

auri·culate, a. With ear-shaped projections. [as prec., see -ATE[2]]

auri·ferous, a. Yielding gold. [f. L *aurifer* (*aurum* gold + *-fer* producing) + -OUS]

au·riform, a. Ear-shaped. [f. L *auris* ear + -FORM]

Aurī·ga, n. Northern constellation, the Waggoner. [L, = charioteer]

au·rilave, n. Instrument for cleaning ears. [f. L *auris* ear + *lavare* wash]

au·rist, n. Ear specialist. [as prec. + -IST]

au·rochs (ow-, aw-; -ks), n. Extinct wild ox; (improp.) European bison. [G; OTeut. **urus,* etym. dub., + *ochs* ox]

auror·a, n. Luminous atmospheric (prob. electrical) phenomenon radiating from earth's northern (*a. borealis*) or southern (*australis*) magnetic pole; dawn; colour of sky at sunrise; *A.,* Roman goddess of dawn. Hence **auror·**AL a. [L, = dawn, goddess of dawn]

au·rous, a. (chem.). In which gold combines as a monad. [f. L *aurum* + -OUS]

au·rum, n. Gold; *a. fulminans,* fulminate of gold; *a. mosaicum,* bisulphide of tin, bronze-powder; *a. potabile,* drinkable gold (once in repute as a cordial). [L]

auscultā·tion, n. Act of listening, esp. (Med.) to movement of heart, lungs, &c. So **au·scultat**OR[2] n., **auscu·ltat**ORY a. [f. L *auscultare* listen to (etym. dub.), see -ATION]

Ausgleich (ow·sglĭch), n. (hist.). Political agreement between Austria and Hungary, renewable every tenth year. [G]

au·spicate, v.t. & i. Inaugurate, initiate; (intr.) augur. [f. L *auspicari* (*auspex -icis* observer of birds for *avispex* f. *avis* bird + *-spec-* observe), see -ATE[3]]

au·spice (-ĭs), n. Observation of birds for purposes of taking omens; prognostic; prosperous lead, patronage, as *under the aa. of.* [f. L *auspicium* (*auspex,* see prec.)]

auspi·cious, a. Of good omen, favourable; prosperous. Hence **auspi·cious**LY[2] adv., **auspi·cious**NESS n. [as prec. + -OUS]

Au·ssie, n. (slang). Australian. [abbr.]

austere·, a. Harsh, stern; stringently moral, strict; severely simple; harsh in flavour. Hence **austere·**LY[2] adv., **austere·**NESS, **austĕ·**RITY, nn. [OF, f. L f. Gk *austēros* drying, harsh (*auō* v. dry)]

au·stral, a. Southern. [f. L *australis* (*Auster* south wind, see -AL)]

Australā·sian, a. & n. (Native) of Australasia (Australia and adjoining islands). [f. *Australasia* f. F *Australasie* (L *australis*, see prec. +*Asia*) + -AN]

Austrā·lian, n. & a. Native of, colonist or resident in, Australia; (adj.) of Australia. [f. F *Australien* f. L as AUSTRAL]

aut Cae·sar aut nĭ·llus or ***nī·hil,*** sent. (I will have) the highest place or nothing. [L]

authe·ntic, a. Reliable, trustworthy; of undisputed origin, genuine; (Mus., of ecclesiastical modes) having their sounds comprised within an octave from the final. Hence **authe·nticALLY** adv., **authenti·CITY** n. [f. OF *autentique* f. L f. Gk *authentikos* f. *authentēs* one who does a thing himself (AUTO- + *-hentēs*, cf. *sunentēs* fellow-worker), see -IC]

authe·nticate, v.t. Establish the truth of; establish the authorship of; make valid. Hence **authenticA·TION, authe·nticatOR**², nn. [f. med. L *authenticare* (*authenticus*), see prec. and -ATE³]

au·thor, n. Originator (*of* a condition of things, event, &c.); writer of book, treatise, &c.; (loosely) author's writings. Hence **au·thorESS**¹ n., **author·IAL** a. [f. AF *autour* f. OF *autor* f. L *auctor* (*augēre auct-* increase, originate, promote, see -OR²); *auth-* at first a scribal var. of *aut-*]

authŏ·ritative, a. Commanding, imperative; possessing authority; proceeding from competent authority. Hence **autho·ritativeLY**² adv., **autho·ritativeNESS** n. [f. foll. + -ATIVE]

autho·rity, n. Power, right, to enforce obedience; delegated power (*to* do, *for* an act, or abs.); person having authority; personal influence, esp. over opinion; weight of testimony; book, quotation, considered to settle a question; evidence, declaration, that may be cited in support of a statement (*on the a. of Plato*); person whose opinion is accepted, esp. expert in (*on*) a subject. [f. F *autorité* f. L *auctoritatem* (*auctor*, see AUTHOR and -TY)]

au·thorize, v.t. Sanction; give ground for, justify, (thing); give authority to, commission, (person *to* do). *Authorized Version* (abbr. A.V.), the Bible of 1611. Hence **au·thorizABLE** a., **authorizA·TION** n. [f. F *autoriser* f. med. L *auctorizare* (*auctor*, see AUTHOR and -IZE)]

au·thorship, n. Occupation, career, as a writer; origin (of book). [-SHIP]

auto- in comp. = Gk *auto-* (*autos* self), in sense 'self, one's own, by oneself, independent(ly)', in wds f. Gk and new formations, as *-car·pous*, consisting of pericarp alone, *-gamy*, self-fertilization, *-genous*, self-producing, *-geny*, *-gony*, spontaneous generation, *-mor·phic*, *-mor·phism*, ascribing (of) one's own characteristics to another, *-phagous*, *-phagy*, feeding on oneself (by absorption of tissues, during starvation), *-plasty*, repair of wounds with tissue from same body; *-sugge·stion*, hypnotic suggestion proceeding from the subject himself.

autobio·grapher, n. One who writes his own history. [AUTO-]

autobiogrā·phic, a. Pertaining to, engaged in, autobiography. Hence **autobiogra·phicAL** a., **autobiogra·phicalLY**² adv. [AUTO-]

autobio·graphy, a. Writing the story of one's own life; story so written. [AUTO-]

au·tocar, n. Road vehicle driven by mechanical power. [AUTO-]

autocĕ·phalous, a. Having its own head; (of bishop, church) independent. [f. Gk *autokephalos* (AUTO- + *kephalē* head) + -OUS]

auto·chthon (-k-), n. (usu. pl.; *-onēs*, *-ons*). Original, earliest known, inhabitants; aborigines. Hence **auto·chthonAL, autochthŏ·NIC, auto·chthonOUS,** aa., **auto·chthonISM, auto·chthonY**¹, nn. [Gk, = sprung from that land itself (AUTO- + *khthōn -onos* land)]

auto·cracy, n. Absolute government; controlling influence. [f. Gk *autokrateia* (as AUTOCRAT)]

au·tocrat, n. Absolute ruler; *A. of all the Russias* (title of the Czar). So **autocrā·TIC(AL)** aa., **autocra·ticalLY**² adv. [f. F *autocrate* f. Gk *autokratēs* (AUTO- + *kratos* might)]

auto·cratrix, n. Female autocrat, title of empresses of Russia ruling in their own right. [Latinized fem. of Gk *autokratōr* (AUTO- + *kratos* might)]

auto-da-fé· (-dahfā), n. (pl. *autos-da-fé*). Sentence of the Inquisition; execution of this, esp. burning of heretic. [Port., = act of the faith; also Sp. *-de-fé*]

au·tograph¹, n. Author's own manuscript; person's own handwriting, esp. signature; copy produced by autography. Hence **autogra·phIC(AL)** aa., **autogra·phicalLY**² adv. [f. L f. Gk *autographon* neut. of *autographos* (AUTO- + *-graphos* written)]

au·tograph², v.t. Write with one's own hand; copy by autography; sign. [f. prec.]

auto·graphy, n. Writing with one's own hand; author's own handwriting; lithographic reproduction of writing or drawing. [as prec., see -Y¹]

autogyr·o, n. Form of aeroplane that can descend vertically by means of a windmill revolving freely on its own shaft. [name patented by inventor, Señor de la Cierva; see AUTO-, GYRO-]

automă·tic, a. & n. Self-acting; working

For other words in *auto-* see AUTO-.

of itself, (n.) a. pistol; mechanical, unconscious; unintelligent, merely mechanical. Hence **automa·tic**AL a., **automa·tical**LY[2] adv., **automati·**CITY n. [f. AUTOMATON + -IC]

auto·matism, n. Involuntary action; doctrine attributing this to animals; unthinking routine; faculty of originating action or motion. [f. foll. + -ISM]

autŏ·maton, n. (pl. *-a, -ons*). Thing endued with spontaneous motion; living being viewed materially; piece of mechanism with concealed motive power; living being whose actions are involuntary or without active intelligence. Hence **auto·mat**OUS a. [f. Gk AUTOmaton, neut. adj., acting of itself]

automobi·le (-ēl), n. Autocar. [F]

autŏ·nomous, a. Of, possessed of, autonomy. [f. Gk AUTO(*nomos* law) + -OUS]

auto·nomy, n. Right of self-government; personal freedom; freedom of the will (in Kantian doctrine); a self-governing community. So **autono·**MIC a. **auto·nom**IST n. [f. Gk *autonomia,* as prec.]

auto·psy (*or* aw·t-), n. Personal inspection; post-mortem examination; (fig.) critical dissection. So **auto·pt**IC(AL) aa. [f. Gk *autopsia* f. *autoptos* (AUTO-) + *op*- see]

au·totype, n. Facsimile; permanent photographic printing process for reproducing in monochrome. Hence **au·totype** v.t. [AUTO-]

au·tumn (-m), n. Third season of the year, August, September, October (Astr., Sep. 21 to Dec. 21); (fig.) season of incipient decay. [f. OF *autompne* f. L *autumnus,* etym. dub.]

autu·mnal, a. Of autumn; *a. equinox,* time when sun crosses equator as it proceeds southward (Sep. 23); maturing, blooming, in autumn; past prime of life. [f. L *autumnalis* (as prec., see -AL)]

auxi·liary, a. & n. (One who is) helpful *to*; (Mil.) *a. troops, aa.,* foreign or allied troops in a nation's service; (Gram.) *a.* (*verb*), one used to form tenses, moods, voices, of other verbs. [f. L *auxiliarius* (*auxilium* help, see -ARY[1])]

avai·l[1], v.t. & i. Afford help; be of value or profit; (trans.) help, benefit; *a.* one*self of,* profit by, take advantage of. [prob. f. *vail* f. F *valoir* be worth f. L *valēre*]

avai·l[2], n. Use, profit, only in phrr. *of a., of no a., without a., to little a.* [f. prec.]

avai·lable, a. Capable of being used, at one's disposal, within one's reach. Hence **availa**BI·LITY, **avai·lable**NESS, nn., **avai·lab**LY[2] adv. [AVAIL v. + -ABLE]

ă·valanche (-sh), n. Mass of snow, earth, and ice, descending swiftly from mountain (also fig.). [F, dialect. form of *avalance* f. *avaler* descend (*à val* to the valley), see -ANCE]

avani·a (-nēa), n. (Extortionate) tax levied by Turks. [etym. dub.; common in Levant]

avant-courier (avŏ·ng-kŏŏ·rĭer), n. One who runs, rides, before; esp. (pl.) scouts, advance-guard. [f. F *avant-coureur* (*avant* before + *coureur* runner f. *courir*)]

ă·varice, n. Greed of gain, cupidity; (fig.) eager desire to get or keep. Hence **avari·ci**OUS a., **avari·cious**LY[2] adv. [OF, f. L *avaritia* (*avarus* greedy, see -ICE)]

ava·st, int. (naut.). Stop; cease. [prob. f. Du. *houd vast* hold fast]

ăvatar·, n. (Hind. Myth.) descent of deity to earth in incarnate form; incarnation; manifestation, display; phase. [f. Skr. *avatara* descent (*ava* down + *tar*- pass over)]

avau·nt, int. Begone. [f. F *avant* forward f. LL *ab-ante* before (L *ab* from + *ante* before)]

ā·ve (-ĭ), int. & n. Welcome; farewell; shout of welcome or farewell; *A. Maria* (Hail, Mary), devotional recitation (*Luke* i. 28, 42) and prayer to the Virgin; *a.-bell,* rung when this is to be said. [L, 2nd sing. imper. of *avēre* fare well]

ave·nge, v.t. Inflict retribution, exact satisfaction, on behalf of (person, violated right, &c.); *be avenged,* a. oneself; take vengeance for (injury). [f. OF *avengier* (*à* to + *vengier* f. L *vindicare*)]

ă·vens, n. *Wood a.,* herb bennet; *water a.,* plant of same genus. [f. OF *avence* etym. dub.]

ave·nturĭne, -in, n. Brownish glass with copper crystals, manufactured first at Murano near Venice; variety of quartz resembling this. [F, f. It. *avventurino* (*avventura* chance, from its accidental discovery)]

ă·venue, n. Way of approach (usu. fig.); approach to country house bordered by trees; roadway marked by trees or other objects at regular intervals; (esp. in U.S.) wide street. [F, fem. p.p. (used as n.) of *avenir* f. L ADvenire come to]

aver·, v.t. (-rr-). Assert, affirm; (Law) prove (a plea). Hence **aver·r**ABLE a. [f. F *avérer* f. LL *ADverare verify (*verus* true)]

ă·verage[1] (-ĭj), n. Generally prevailing rate, degree, or amount; ordinary standard; medial estimate, as *on the* or *an a.*; apportionment of loss of ship, cargo, or freight, through unavoidable accident (*particular a.*) or through intentional damage to ship or sacrifice of cargo (*general a.*), among the owners or insurers. [etym. dub.; F *avarie,* Sp. *averia,* Du. *avarij, haverij,* G *havarie*; perh. conn. w. OF *aveir* goods, see AVOIRDUPOIS]

a·verage[2], a. Estimated by average; of the usual standard. Hence **a·verage**LY[2] adv. [f. prec.]

a·verage[3], v.t. Estimate the average of (by dividing the aggregate of several quantities by the number of quantities); estimate the general standard of; amount on an average to; *a.* (work on an average) *six hours a day.* [as prec.]

aver·ment, n. Positive statement, affirmation; (Law) offer to prove, proof of, a plea. [f. F *averement* (as AVER)]
ăverrunca·tor, n. Instrument for cutting off branches of trees high above head. [f. obs. vb *averruncate,* f. L *averruncare* (*a* off + *verruncare* turn), but wrongly explained as f. *eruncare* weed out]
aver·se, a. Opposed, disinclined, (*to, from*); unwilling (*to* do). Hence **aver·se**NESS n. [f. L as AVERT]
aver·sion, n. Dislike, antipathy, (*to, from, for*); unwillingness (*to* do); object of dislike, as *pet a.* [f. L *aversio* (as AVERT, see -ION)]
aver·t, v.t. Turn away (eyes, thoughts, *from*); ward off. Hence **aver·t**IBLE, -ABLE, aa. [f. F *avertir* f. LL *avertēre,* L *-ĕre* (*a* away + *vertere vers-* turn); cf. ADVERT]
ā·vian, a. Pertaining to birds. [f. L *avis* bird + -AN]
ā·viary, n. Place for keeping birds. [f. L *aviarium* (as prec., see -ARIUM)]
ā·viate, v.i. Manage or travel in dirigible balloon, airship, flying-machine, &c. So **avi**A·TION, **a·viat**OR[2], nn. [f. L *avis* bird, -ATE[3]]
aviati·k (ah-), n. Type of German military aeroplane. [G]
ă·vid, a. Eager, greedy (*of, for*). Hence **ă·vid**LY[2] adv. [f. L *avidus* (*avēre* crave)]
avi·dity, n. Ardent desire, greed. [f. F *avidité* f. L *aviditatem* (as prec., see -TY)]
āvie·tte, n. Engineless man-worked aeroplane. [F, f. *avion* aeroplane, see -ETTE]
ā·vifauna, n. Birds (of district, country) collectively. [f. L *avis* bird + FAUNA]
avion (F), n. War aeroplane.
avi·so (-ēzō), n. Advice-boat. [Sp., f. L *advisum,* see ADVICE]
aviza·ndum, n. (Sc. Law). Private consideration. [med. L, gerund of *avizare* consider]
ă·vocate v.t. (legal). Call (case) to higher tribunal. [f. L as foll.]
ăvoca·tion, n. Distraction; minor occupation; vocation, calling. [f. L *avocatio* (*avocare* call away, see -ATION)]
ă·vocet, -set, n. Wading bird allied to snipe. [f. F *avocette* f. It. *avosetta*]
avoi·d, v.t. Shun, refrain from (thing, do*ing*); escape, evade; (Law) defeat (pleading), quash (sentence). Hence **avoi·d**ABLE a. [f. AF *avoider* f. OF *evuider* clear out, get quit of (*es* out + *vuidier* f. *vuit, vuide,* VOID)]
avoi·dance, n. Act of avoiding; vacancy (of office, benefice). [prec. + -ANCE]
avoirdupois (ă·verdūpoi·z), a. & n. *A. (weight),* system of weights used in Great Britain for all goods except precious metals & stones, & medicines; *A. pound* contains 7,000 grains; (U.S.) weight, heaviness. [recent corrupt. of *avoir-de-pois* f. AF, OF, *aveir de peis* (*aveir, avoir,* goods, property, f. L *habēre* have + *de* of + *pois, peis,* weight f. L *pensum*)]
avou·ch (-ow-), v.t. & i. Guarantee; affirm; confess. Hence **avou·ch**MENT n. [f. OF *avochier* f. L ADvocare (in legal use) call upon as defender]
avow·, v.t. Admit, confess; (refl. & pass.) admit oneself to be, as *a. himself the author, the avowed author.* Hence **avow·**ABLE a., **avow·**AL n., **avow·ed**LY[2] adv. [f. F *avouer* (*à* to + *vouer* f. LL *votare* frequent. of *vovēre* vow)]
avu·lsion, n. Tearing away; (Law) sudden removal of land by flood &c. to another person's estate. [f. L *avulsio* (*avellere -vuls-* pluck away)]
avu·ncular, a. Of, resembling, an uncle. [f. L *avunculus* maternal uncle (dim. of *avus* grandfather) + -AR[1]]
awai·t, v.t. Wait for; (of things) be in store for. [f. ONF *awaitier* (*à* to + *waitier,* OF *guaitier,* see WAIT v.)]
awa·ke[1], v.t. & i. (past *awoke,* p.p. *awoke, awaked*). Cease to sleep; (fig.) become active; *a. to,* become conscious of; rouse from sleep (lit. & fig.). [(1) OE *awæcnan, awóc, awacen,* (*a-* prob. = on); of which present tense was early treated as weak vb, with past *awæcnede,* whence AWAKEN *awakened*; (2) OE *awacian, awacode,* in form a compd of *wacian* watch, but in sense = *awæcnan*; (3) in OE these were intr., the trans. sense being given by *awecc(e)an,* ME *awecche,* G *erwecken,* ousted by *awake,* trans., before 1300]
awa·ke[2], pred. a. Roused from sleep; not asleep; vigilant; *a. to,* aware of. [short for *awaken,* orig. p.p. of prec.]
awa·ken, v.t. & i. = AWAKE[1] (lit. & fig.) esp. (fig.) arouse (*to* a sense of). [see AWAKE[1]]
awar·d[1] (-ord), v.t. Adjudge; grant, assign. [f. AF *awarder* f. OF *esguarder* f. Rom. *EX(*wardare, -guardare,* f. OLG **wardên,* OHG *wartên,* watch; cf. WARD)]
awar·d[2], n. Judicial decision; payment, penalty, assigned by this. [AF, f. OF *eswart, esguart,* f. *esguarder,* see prec.]
aware·, pred. a. Conscious, knowing, (*of, that*). [OE *gewær* (OHG *gawar,* MHG *gewar,* G *gewahr*) f. *ge-* quite + *wær* wary]
awa·sh (-wŏ-), pred. a. Flush with or washed by the waves. [A- (2)]
away·, adv. To, at, a distance from the place, person, thing, in question (lit. & fig.), as *go a., throw a., give a., he is a., waste a., fool a., explain a.*; *out & a.,* beyond comparison; constantly, continuously, as *work a., peg a.*; without delay, as *fire a.*; = go away (imper.); *a. with* (imper.), go a. with, take a.; (*cannot*) *a. with,* get on with, tolerate; *make a. with,* destroy. [OE *onweg* (phr. *on weg* on one's way, onward, along), in early E used as separable vbl prefix]
awe[1], n. Reverential fear or wonder, as *stand in a. of, hold, keep, in a.*; *awe-struck,* struck with a. Hence **awe·**LESS, **awe·**SOME, aa. [f. ON *agi*; OE has *ege*; both f. *agan* v. fear]

awe[2], v.t. Inspire with awe. [f. prec.]
awe[3], n. One of the float-boards of an undershot water wheel. [?]
aw·ful, a. Inspiring awe; worthy of profound respect; solemnly impressive; (archaic) reverential; (slang) notable in its kind, as *a. scrawl, bore, relief, something a.* Hence **aw·ful**LY[2] adv., **aw·ful**NESS n. [AWE[1] + -FUL]
awhi·le, adv. For a short time. [OE *áne hwíle* a while]
aw·kward, a. Ill-adapted for use; clumsy (person, thing); bungling; embarrassing; difficult, dangerous, to deal with. Hence **aw·kward**ISH[1](2) a., **aw·kward**LY[2] adv., **aw·kward**NESS n. [f. obs. adj. *awk* backhanded, untoward (prob. f. ON *afug* turned the wrong way) + -WARD]
awl, n. Small tool for pricking, pricker, esp. that used by shoemakers. [OE *æl*, cf. OHG *ala*, G *ahle*]
awn, n. Spinous process, beard, terminating grain-sheath of barley, oats, &c. Hence **awned**[1] [-ED[2]], **aw·n**LESS, aa. [prob. f. ON *ögn* pl. *agnar*; cf. OHG *agana*, G *ahne*]
aw·ning, n. Canvas roof, esp. above deck of vessel; (Naut.) poop-deck beyond bulkhead of cabin; shelter. Hence **awned**[2] (-ED[2]] a. [perh. f. F *auvent*, etym. dub.]
awry (*a*rī·), adv. & a. Crookedly, askew; *look a.*, look askance (lit. & fig.); amiss, improperly; *go, run, tread, a.*, do wrong; (adj., usu. pred.) crooked (lit. & fig.). [A prep. + WRY]
ax(e), n., & v.t. Chopping-tool, usually iron with steel edge & wooden handle; *put the a. in the helve*, solve a puzzle; (U.S. politics) *an a. to grind*, private ends to serve; *the Geddes a.*, (vast reductions of public expenditure advised by) the Geddes Committee appointed 1921; (vb) cut down (costs, services). [com.-Teut.; OE *æx*, OHG *acchus*, G *ax, axt*; akin to Gk *axinē* & perh. L *ascia*]
a·xial, a. Forming, belonging to, an axis; round an axis. Hence **axia·l**ITY n., **a·xial**LY[2] adv. [f. AXIS + -AL]
a·xil, n. Upper angle between leaf & stem it springs from, or between branch & trunk. [f. L *axilla* armpit]
a·xile, a. (bot., physiol.). Belonging to the axis. [f. AXIS, see -IL]
a·xillary, a. Pertaining to the armpit; (Bot.) in, growing from, the axil. [f. F *axillaire* f. L **axillaris* (as AXIL)]
a·xiom, n. Established principle; maxim; self-evident truth. [f. F. *axiome* f. L f. Gk *axiōma* (*axioō* hold worthy f. *axios*, see -M)]
axioma·tic, -ical, aa. Self-evident; characterized by axioms; full of maxims, aphoristic. Hence **axioma·tical**LY[2] adv. [f. Gk *axiōmatikos* (*axiōma -matos*), see prec. & -IC, -AL]
a·xis, n. (pl. *axēs*). Imaginary line about which a body rotates, or by revolution about which a plane is conceived as generating a solid (sphere, cone, cylinder); line dividing regular figure symmetrically; (Optics) ray passing through centre of eye or lens, or falling perpendicularly on it; (Physiol.) central core of organ or organism; (Bot.) central column of inflorescence or other whorl of growth; straight line from end to end of a body, as *a. of equator* (polar diameter of earth). [L, =axle, pivot]
a·xle, n. Spindle upon or with which wheel revolves; (in carriages, prop.) slender end of *a.-tree* (whole bar connecting wheels), (loosely) a.-tree; *wheel & a.*, a MECHANICAL power; *a.-box* (in which ends of aa. revolve); *a.-journal*, polished end of a. revolving under bearing in a.-box. Hence **a·xl**ED[2] a. [first found in *axle-tree*, ON *öxul-tre* (ON *öxull* = Goth. *ahsuls* f. OTeut. *ahsâ*, cogn. w. Skr. *aksha*, Gk *axōn*, L *axis*)]
A·xminster, a. *A. carpet*, kind formerly hand-woven at A., now made at Wilton.
a·xolotl, n. Salamander-like reptile found in Mexican lakes. [Aztec, =servant (*xolotl*) of water (*atl*)]
ay (ī), int. & n. (pl. *ayes*). Yes; (n.) affirmative answer; *the ayes have it*, affirmative voters are in majority. [?]
ayah (ī·*a*), n. Native Hindoo nurse or lady's maid. [Ind. vernacular *āya* f. Port. *aia* nurse, fem. of *aio* tutor]
aye (ā), adv. Ever, always; on all occasions; *for a.*, for ever. [ME *agg, ai, ei*, f. ON *ei, ey*, cogn. w. Goth. *aiw* f. OTeut. *aiwōz*, cogn. w. L *aevum* age; cf. Gk *aei* always]
aye-aye (ī·ī), n. Squirrel-like animal of the size of a cat, found only in Madagascar. [F, f. Malagasy *aiay*]
Azā·lĕa, n. Genus of flowering shrubby plants, natives of northern hemisphere. [f. Gk *azalea* fem. of *azaleos* dry (from its dry wood or the dry soil in which it flourishes)]
ă·zarole, n. Fruit of the Neapolitan medlar. [f. F *azerole* (Sp. *azarolla*) f. Arab. *az-zu'rūr* (*al* the + name of the fruit)]
ă·zimuth, n. Arc of the heavens extending from the zenith to the horizon, which it cuts at right angles; *a.-circle*, one of which this is a quadrant, passing through zenith & nadir; *true a.* of a heavenly body, arc of horizon intercepted between north (in Southern hemisphere, south) point of horizon & the point where the great circle passing through the body cuts the horizon; *magnetic a.*, arc intercepted between this circle & magnetic meridian. Hence **azimū·th**AL a., **azimu·thal**LY[2] adv. [f. F *azimut* f. Arab. *assumut* (*al* the + *sumut* pl. of *samt* way, direction)]
azo·ic, a. Having no trace of life; (Geol.) containing no organic remains. [f. Gk *azōos* (*a-* not + *zōē* life) + -IC]

azo·te, n. Former name of nitrogen. Hence **azŏ·tic** a., **ă·zotize**(3) v.t. [F, f. Gk *a-* not+*zōō* for *zaō*) live, from its inability to support life]

A·ztec, a. & n. (One) of the Aztecs, the Mexican tribe dominant till the conquest of Cortes (1519).

azure (ă·zher, ă·zhyer), n. & a., & v.t. Sky blue; (Herald.) blue; unclouded vault of heaven; bright blue pigment; lapis lazuli; (adj.) sky-blue, (fig.) cloudless, serene; (v.t.) make a. [f. OF *azur* f. med. L *azura* f. Arab. *al* the+*lazward* f. Pers. *lazhward* lapis lazuli]

ă·zygous, a. & n. (physiol.). (An organic part) not existing in pairs. [f. Gk *azugos* unyoked (*a-* not+*zugon* yoke)+ -OUS.]

B

B (bē), letter (pl. *Bs*, B's, Bees). (Mus.) seventh note in scale of C major (*B flat*, jocular euphem, for bug). (In argument) second hypothetical person or thing. (Alg.) second known quantity.

Abbreviations (1): bachelor, as **B.A.** (of Arts), **B.D.** (of Divinity), **B.Sc.** (of Science); beata, **B.V.M.** (virgo Maria); before, **B.C.** (Christ); black, **B, BB, BBB** (black, double black, treble black, in pencils); brandy, **B & S** (& soda); brazen, **B.N.C.** (Brazenose College); British, **B.A.** (Academy), **B.B.C.** (broadcasting corporation), **B.C.** (Columbia), **B.E.** (Empire, Order of the), **B.E.F.** (expeditionary force), **B.S.A.** (South Africa), **B.W.T.A.** (women's temperance association), **B.P.** (public); born, **b.**; bowled, **b.**

Abbreviations (2): **Bart**, baronet; **Bath. & Well.**, Bishop of Bath & Wells; **Beds.**, Bedfordshire; **Berks.**, Berkshire; **Bp**, bishop; **Bros**, Brothers; **Bt**, baronet; **Bucks.**, Buckinghamshire.

baa (bah), n., & v.i. (*baaing, baaed* or *baa'd*). =BLEAT. *Baa-lamb*, nursery name for lamb. [imit.]

Bā·al, n. (pl. *Ba·alim*). Phoenician god; (transf.) a false god. Hence **Ba·alism**(3), **Ba·alist**(2), **Ba·alite**(1), nn. [Heb. *ba'al* lord]

ba·bacoote (bah-), n. Species of lemur (Madagascar). [Malagasy *babakoto*]

Ba·bbit-metal, n. Soft alloy of tin, antimony, & copper. [inventor's name]

ba·bble[1], v.i. & t. Talk half articulately, incoherently, or excessively; murmur (of streams, &c.); repeat foolishly; let out (secrets). Hence **ba·bblement** n. [imit. of infant's *ba, ba*, + -LE(3); cf. F *babiller*, LG *babbelen*, G *pappelen*]

ba·bble[2], n. Imperfect speech; idle talk; murmur of water &c. [prec.]

ba·bbler, n. Chatterer; teller of secrets; Long-legged Thrush. [-ER[1]]

babe, n. (poet.). Young child, baby; inexperienced or guileless person (in pl. often *bb. & sucklings*). [imit. of child's speech, cf. BABBLE]

bā·bel, n. The tower in Shinar (*Gen.* xi); a high structure; visionary plan; scene of confusion, noisy assembly, meaningless noise. [perh. f. Ass. *bab-ilu* gate of God]

babirou·ssa, -ru·ssa (rōō-), n. E.-Asiatic wild hog with upturned horn-like tusks. [Malay *babi* hog+*rusa* deer]

ba·boo (bah-), n. (As Hindoo title) Mr; Hindoo gentleman; Indian English-writing clerk; (contemptuous) half anglicized Hindoo. [Hind. *babu*]

baboo·n, n. Large African & S.-Asiatic monkey. [f. 13th-c. F *babuin* etym. dub.]

babou·che (-ōōsh), n. Oriental slipper. [F, f. Arab. *babush* f. Pers. *paposh* (*pa* foot+*posh* covering); for *p*=*b* cf. *pasha* & *bashaw*]

bā·by, n. Very young child; childish person, whence **ba·byish**[1] a., **ba·byishness**, **ba·byism**(2), nn.; thing small of its kind; *b.-farmer*, one who contracts to keep bb.; *b. grand*, small grand piano; *b.-jumper*, hanging frame in which child is fastened to exercise limbs. Hence **ba·byhood** n. [BABE, -Y[3]]

Bă·bylon, n. Capital of Chaldean empire; any great empire or vicious city; Rome, the papacy (ref. to *Rev.* xvii &c.), London, &c. Hence **Babylō·nian** a. & n. [L, f. Gk *Babulōn* f. Heb. *Babel* BABEL]

baccalau·reate (-rĭat), n. University degree of bachelor. [f. med. L *baccalaureatus* (*baccalaureus* corrupted after *bacca lauri* laurelberry) f. *baccalarius* BACHELOR; see ATE[1]]

ba·ccara, -at (-rah), n. Gambling card game. [F]

ba·ccāte, a. (bot.) Bearing berries, berry-shaped. Hence **bacca·to-** comb. form. [f. L *baccatus* berried (*bacca* berry, -ATE[2])]

Ba·cchanal (-k-), a. & n. Of, like, Bacchus or his rites; riotous, roystering. Priest, priestess, votary, of Bacchus; drunken reveller; dance or song in honour of Bacchus. [f. L *bacchanalis* (L f. Gk *Bakkhos* god of wine, -AL)]

Bacchanā·lia, n. pl. Festival of Bacchus; drunken revelry. [L neut. pl. of *bacchanalis* =prec.]

Bacchanā·lian, a. & n. Of Bacchanals; riotous, drunken. A Bacchanal, tippler. [f. L *bacchanalis* BACCHANAL+-AN]

Ba·cchant, n. masc. or fem., & a.; **Bacchante** (bakă·nt, bă·kant, bakă·ntĭ), n. fem. Priest, priestess, votary of Bacchus; Bacchus-worshipping, wine-loving. Hence **Baccha·ntic** a. [(*-nte* F) f. L *bacchari* (-ANT) f. Gk *bakkheuō* celebrate Bacchic rites]

Ba·cchic, a. =BACCHANAL (adj. meanings). [f. L f. Gk *bakkhikos* of Bacchus]

Ba·cchus, n. Greek god of wine. [L, f. Gk *Bakkhos*]

bacci·ferous, ba·cciform, bacci·vor-

ous, (băks-), aa. Berry-bearing, -shaped, -eating. [L *baccifer* (-FEROUS); L *bacca* berry + -FORM, -VOROUS]

ba·ccy (-kĭ), n. (colloq.) Tobacco. [abbr.]

Ba·charach (bah·charahch). A Rhine wine. [town]

ba·chelor, n. Young knight serving under another's banner (hist.); hence now, *knight b.*, simple knight not belonging to a special order; man or woman who has taken the university degree below Master; unmarried man. *B.'s buttons*, various button-shaped flowers esp. double buttercup, also small ratafia biscuits, also buttons attachable without sewing. Hence **ba·chelor**HOOD, **ba·chelor**SHIP, **ba·chelor**ISM(4), nn. [f. OF *bacheler* f. L **baccalaris*; cf. *baccalaria* piece of land, *baccalarius* farm-labourer, perh. f. *bacca* LL for L *vacca* cow]

baci·llary, a. Of little rods (tissue, membrane); connected with bacilli (disease, research). [BACILLUS + -ARY[1]]

baci·lliform, a. Rod-shaped. [foll. + -FORM]

baci·llus, n. (pl. *-illī*). Genus of schizomycetae, microscopic rodlike vegetable organisms some of which are found in diseased tissues in anthrax, phthisis, &c. [LL dim. of L *baculus* stick]

back[1], n. & a. Hinder surface of human body (*at the b. of*, behind in support, pursuit, or concealment; BEHIND one's *b.*; *give, make, a b.*, bend down at leapfrog; *turn* one's *b. upon*, run away from, abandon; *on* one's *b.*, laid up; *with* one's *b. to wall*, hard pressed); body as needing clothes (*b. & belly*, clothing & food) or as weight-carrier (*b. equal to burden*; *have on* one's *b.*, be burdened with; *put, get, set*, person's *b. up*, make him angry; *break* one's *b.*, overburden him, & see BREAK[1] *b. of*); surface of things corresponding to human b. (less visible, active, or important; *b. of hand, leg, door, book, knife*), side away from spectator; upper surface of animal's body, surface corresponding to this (ridge-shaped, &c.; *b. of hill, ship* esp. in *broke her b.*; *on the b. of*, in addition to); football player stationed behind (*full, three-quarter, half, b.*); *the Bb.*, grounds on the Cam at the b. of certain Colleges at Cambridge, of noted beauty; *backband*, over cart-saddle to keep shafts up; *backboard*, at b. of cart, also strapped across child's b. to straighten it; *backbone*, spine (whence **ba·ckbone**D[2] a.; *to the backbone*, thoroughly), main support, axis, watershed, chief strength, firmness of character (whence **ba·ckbone**LESS a.); *backfall*, throw on b. in wrestling; *backsword*, with only one edge, also singlestick. (Adj.; no comp., superl. *backmost*); situated behind, remote, inferior, (*take b. seat*, humble oneself); overdue (*b. rent*); reversed, counter, (*b. current*); *b.-chat* (slang,) retort(s), recrimination; *backdoor*, lit., & fig. secret means or approach, (adj.) clandestine, underhand; *b.-end*, late autumn; *b. formation*, making from a supposed derivative (as *lazy, banting*) of the non-existent word (*laze, bant*) from which it might have come; *background*, part of scene, picture, or description, that serves as setting to chief figures or objects and foreground, obscurity, retirement; *backhand(ed)*, delivered with b. of hand or in direction counter to the usual, indirect, unexpected, (*backhander*, such blow, indirect attack, extra glass got by bottle's travelling wrong way); *b. number* (of magazine &c.), (slang) out of date method or person; *backset*, counter current, check, reverse; *backside*, posterior, rump; *b.-sight*, that nearer stock of rifle &c., (Surv.) sight taken backwards; *backstairs* n. & a., *backstair* a., as *backdoor* above; *backstays*, ropes slanting abaft from masthead to a lower point; *backstroke*, return or backhand stroke; *backwash*, motion of receding wave (lit. & fig.); *backwater*, water dammed back, currentless water beside stream & fed by its backflow, stagnant condition of things, creek communicating with sea by barred outlets, water cast from ship's paddles, loss of power caused by this; *backway*, bypath (lit. & fig.); *backwoods* n. & a., *backwood a.*, (connected with) remote uncleared forest land (so *backwoodsman*). [a. f. n., OE *bæc*; Teut., now almost confined to E]

back[2], v.t. & i. Put, or be, a back, lining, support, or background, to; assist with countenance, money, or argument, bet upon, whence **ba·ck**ER[1] n.; (of sporting dogs) follow suit to one that points; *b. up*, help by subordinate action, esp. in cricket; ride upon, break in to the saddle; countersign, endorse; cause to move back (horse, boat, engine, &c.; *b. a sail, yard*, lay it aback, i.e. to face wind; *b. water*, reverse boat's motion with oars); go backwards; (of wind) change countersunwise (cf. VEER); *b. out (of)*, withdraw (from undertaking &c.); *b. down*, abandon claim. [f. prec.]

back[3], adv. To the rear (often with omission of vb, esp. in imperative), away from what is considered the front (*push the bolt b.*); away from a promise (*go b. from* or *upon* one's *word*); into the past, into or in an earlier position or condition, home; in return (*answer b.* = retort; *pay b.*); at a distance (*b. from the road*); in a checked condition (*keep b.*); = ago; reckoning backwards (*for years b.*); behindhand; *b. & forth* = to & fro; *b. of* (U.S.) = behind; *backbite*, slander, speak ill of, whence **ba·ckbit**ER[1] n.; *ba·cklash(ing)*, irregular recoil of wheels in machinery due to defects or sudden pressure; *back-pedal*, work pedal backwards; *backslide* v.i., relapse into sin, whence **back-sli·der**[1], **backsli·ding**[1], nn.; *backstitch* n. & v.t. & i., sew(ing) with overlapping stitches. [for ABACK]

back4, n. Shallow vat used in brewing, dyeing, &c. [f. Du. *bak* tub f. F *bac* punt cf. med. L *baccus* ferryboat]

ba·ckfisch (-sh), n. (slang). Girl, flapper. [G]

backga·mmon, n. Game played on special double board with draughts & dice; most complete form of win in this. [BACK[3] (because pieces go back or re-enter), GAME[1]]

ba·cking, n. In vbl senses; esp.: body of supporters; material used to form thing's back or support. [BACK[2],-ING[1]]

backsheesh. See BAKSHEESH.

ba·ckward(s), adv., **ba·ckward,** a. Away from one's front (*look, lean,* &c.); back foremost (*walk* &c.); back to starting-point (*flow, roll,* &c.; not of living things exc. in *b. & forwards*); into a worse state (*go* &c.); into the past (*reckon* &c.); the reverse way (*spell* &c.; *ring the bells b.,* from bass upwards). (Adj.) directed to rear or starting-point; reversed; reluctant, shy, behindhand, dull, whence **ba·ckward**NESS n. [orig. for *abackward,* later referred to BACK[1]; see -WARD, -WARDS]

backwarda·tion, n. (St. Exch.). Percentage paid by seller of stock for right of delaying delivery (cf. CONTANGO). [f. prec. used as vb + -ATION on anal. of *retardation*]

bā·con, n. Cured back & sides of pig (*save* one's *b.,* escape death or injury). [OF, f. OHG *bacho* MHG *backe* buttock cf. BACK[1]]

Bacō·nian, a. & n. Of Francis Bacon or his philosophy, experimental, inductive; a follower of Bacon; believer in B. authorship of Shakspere's plays. [*Bacon* + -IAN]

bā·cony, a. Like bacon (esp. *b. liver,* a disease, fatty degeneration). [BACON + -Y[1]]

bactēr·ium, n. (pl. *-ria*). Genus of schizomycetae, microscopic rod-shaped unicellular organisms in decomposing liquids. Hence **bacter**·IAL a., **bacteriŏ**·LOGY, **-ŏ**·LOGIST, nn. [mod. L, f. Gk *baktērion* dim. of *baktron* stick]

bă·culine, a. Of the stick or flogging (esp. *b. argument*). [f. L *baculum* stick + -INE[1]]

bad, a. (worse, worst), & n. (Negatively) worthless, inferior, deficient, of poor quality, incorrect, not valid, (*b. air,* corrupt; *b. coin,* debased; *b. debt,* not recoverable; *b. food,* not nourishing; *go b.,* decay; *with b. grace,* reluctantly; *b. shot,* wrong guess; *b. law,* not sustainable; *b. form,* want of breeding; *b. pre-eminence,* disrepute; *in a b. sense,* unfavourable; *b. success*); *b. egg, b. hat,* (slang) person of b. character. (Positively) noxious, depraved, vicious, offensive, painful, (*b. blood,* ill feeling; *b. for,* injurious to); in ill health, injured, in pain, (*she is b., worse, to-day*; *a b. leg*); (colloq. of things in no case good) notable, decided, pronounced, (*b. blunder, headache, falling-off*). (N.) ill fortune (*take the b. with the good*), wrong side of account (*£500 to the b.*), ruin (*go to the b.*). Hence **ba·dd**ISH[1] (2) a. [ME *badde,* perh. f. OE *bæddel* hermaphrodite, womanish man; for loss of *l* cf. *mycel* MUCH]

bade. See BID[1].

badge, n. Distinctive mark, formerly of knight, now worn as sign of office or licensed employment or membership of a society; symbol, something that betrays a quality or condition. [ME; etym. dub.]

ba·dger[1], n. (dial.) Hawker, esp. of provisions. [?]

ba·dger[2], n. Grey-coated strong-jawed nocturnal hibernating plantigrade quadruped between weasles & bears; fishing-fly, & painting-brush, made of its hair; *b.-baiting, -drawing,* setting dogs to draw it from its burrow or a cask; *b.-legged,* with legs of unequal length (popular error). [mod. E (older *brock* or *bauson*) perh. f. BADGE + -ARD (*earlier bageard, badgerd*) with ref. to its white forehead mark]

ba·dger[3], v.t. Bait like a badger, worry, tease. [f. prec.]

bă·dinage (-ahzh), n. Light raillery. [F (*badiner* banter f. *badin* silly f. LL *badare* gape)]

ba·dly, adv. (worse, worst). Defectively, unsuccessfully, faultily, wickedly, cruelly, dangerously, by much (*beaten*), very much (*want a thing b.*). [-LY[2]]

ba·dminton, n. A summer drink (claret, soda, sugar); game with net, rackets, & shuttlecocks. [Duke of Beaufort's seat]

ba·dness, n. Poor quality or condition; faultiness, invalidity; wickedness, noxiousness, adverseness. [-NESS]

ba·ffle, v.t., & n. Foil, reduce to perplexity, bar progress of, (person, curiosity, faculties, efforts, ship); *baffling winds,* variable, preventing a straight course; (n.) *b.* or *b.-plate,* plate hindering or regulating passage of fluid through outlet or inlet (e.g. a damper). Hence **ba·ffler** n., = b.-plate. [perh. f. F *beffler* mock & *bafouer* hoodwink, both perh. f. Pr. *bafar* mock perh. f. *baf* interj. of contempt]

bă·ffy, bă·ffing-spoon, nn. Wooden golf club for lofting. [cf. Sc. *baff* a blow]

baft, n. Coarse cheap cotton fabric exported to Africa. [Pers., = woven]

bag[1], n. Receptacle of flexible material with opening at top (*green* or *blue b.,* barrister's for briefs; hyphened with nouns showing contents or purpose, as *mail-b., travelling-b.*; also alone for such compp., e.g. for money-b., so *bags* =

wealth, or for game-b., also for g.-b.'s contents or all a sportsman has shot or caught; *b. of bones*, lean creature; *whole b. of tricks*, every device, everything, all the lot; *in bottom of b.*, as last resource; *let cat out of b.*, reveal secret, esp. involuntarily; *b. & baggage*, with all belongings, esp. of utter expulsion), whence **ba·gg**ING[1] (3) n.; cow's udder; sac in body containing honey, poison, &c.; baggy place under eyes &c.; (slang) *bb.*, trousers; *b. fox*, one brought, not found; *bagman*, commercial traveller, also = b. fox; *bagpipe(s)*, musical instrument (air-b., three drones, & chanter) now used chiefly in Scotland; *b.-sleeve*, loose except at wrist; *b.-wig*, 18th-c. wig with back hair enclosed in b. Hence **ba·g**FUL(2) n. [perh. f. ON *baggi* etym. dub.; no evidence for connexion with BELLY, BELLOWS (OHG *balg*)]

bag[2], v.i. & t. Swell, bulge; (Naut.) drop away from course; hang loosely; put in a bag, secure (game, whether lit. bagged or not), take possession of, (euphem.) steal; (school slang) claim on the ground of being first to claim (*I b.*, but usu. *bags I* or *bags, first innings!*). [prec.]

bag[3], v.t. Cut (wheat &c.) with a hook. [also *badge*; etym. dub.]

baga·sse (-ăs), n. Refuse products in sugar-making. [F; perh. = *bagage* lumber]

băgate·lle, n. Trifle, negligible amount; light piece of music; minor game of billiard kind. [F, f. It. *bagatella* dim. perh. f. *baga* BAGGAGE]

ba·ggage (-ĭj), n. Belongings with which one travels (now ousted exc. in U.S. by *luggage*); portable equipment of army; good-for-nothing woman (now only used playfully), saucy girl. [f. OF *bagage* f. *baguer* tie up or *bagues* bundles pl. of *bague* = It. & LL *baga* chest]

ba·ggy, a. Puffed out, hanging in loose folds. Hence **ba·ggi**NESS n. [BAG[1] + -Y[2]]

bagnio (bă·nyō), n. Bathing-house (not now in England); oriental prison; brothel. [f. It. *bagno* f. L *balneum* bath]

bah, int. of contempt. [F]

Baha·dur (-ahd-), n. Title of respect appended in India to a person's name (& other titles); (Anglo-Ind. slang) consequential official. [Hind., = gallant]

baignoire (bānwah·r). Box at theatre on level of stalls. [F]

bail[1], n. Security for prisoner's appearance, on giving which he is released pending trial (*forfeit one's b.*, fail to appear; *save one's b.*, appear); (joc.) *give leg b.*, run away; person(s) who become(s) surety for prisoner's appearance (*be, become, go, b.*; *go b. for*, guarantee truth of anything; magistrate *accepts, admits to, allows, holds to, takes, b.*; prisoner *gives, offers, surrenders to his, b.*; his *b. surrender, render, bring in, produce*, him). [OF *bail* custody f. *baillier* take charge of f. L *bajulare* bear a burden (*bajulus* porter)]

bail[2], v.t. 1. Deliver (goods) in trust. 2. Admit to bail, release on security given for appearance, (of magistrate; archaic); secure liberation of, by becoming bail or security for (*b. out* if already in prison). [sense 1 f. F *bailler* deliver; sense 2 f. BAIL[1]]

bail[3], n. (Hist.) outer line of fortification formed of stakes; wall of castle court, or court itself. (Mod.) bar separating horses in open stable; *swinging b.*, slung from manger to ceiling; (cricket) one of the cross pieces (orig. one, not two) over stumps. [OF *bail* perh. f. *baillier* enclose, or f. L *baculum* stick]

bail[4], n. Half-hoop for supporting wagon-tilt &c.; hoop-handle of kettle &c.; (Australia) frame holding cow's head at milking. [ME *beyl* f. ON *beygla* sword-guard &c. (*beygya* = OE *bégan* to bend)]

bail[5], v.t. Confine (archaic); (Australia) *b. up*, secure (cow; see prec.); (of bush-rangers) make hold up the arms to rob, (intr. of victim) throw up the arms. [f. OF *baillier* enclose perh. same as in prec. & BAIL[2]]

bail[6], **bale**, v.t. Throw water out of boat with pails &c. (*b. water out, b. out boat*, or abs.). Hence **bai·ler**[1] [-ER[1] (2)] n. [f. obs. n. *bail* bucket f. F *baille* f. LL *bacula* dim. of *baca, bacca*, water-vessel]

bai·lable, a. Admitting of bail (offence). [BAIL[1], [2] + -ABLE]

bailee·, n. One to whom goods are entrusted for a purpose. [BAIL[2] + -EE]

bai·ler[2], n. Ball that hits bails at cricket. [BAIL[3] + -ER[1]]

bai·ley, n. Outer wall of castle; also any of its inner defensive circuits, or any of the courts enclosed between these; *Old B.*, London Central Criminal Court, standing in ancient b. of city wall. [ME variant of BAIL[3] perh. f. med. L form *ballium*]

bai·lie, n. Scotch municipal magistrate = Eng. alderman. [ME *bailli* f. OF *baillis* BAILIFF]

bai·liff, n. (Orig.) King's representative in a district (including mayor, sheriff, &c.,) esp. chief officer of a hundred (still in *High-B. of Westminster, B. of Dover Castle*, &c.; used as Eng. equivalent of F *bailli*, G *landvogt*, Channel-I. *bailly* or first civil officer); officer under sheriff for writs, processes, arrests; agent of lord of manor; landholder's steward. [ME & OF *baillif* obj. case of *baillis* f. LL *bajulivus* (L *bajulus* porter)]

bai·liwick, n. District, jurisdiction, of bailie or bailiff. [BAILIE + WICK[2]]

bai·lment, n. Delivery of goods in trust; bailing of prisoner. [OF *baillement* see BAIL[2] & -MENT]

bai·lor, n. One who delivers goods to another for a stated purpose. [BAIL[2] + -OR[2]]

bai·lsman, n. One who gives bail for another. [f. *bail's* (BAIL[1]) + MAN]

bain-marie (F), n. Vessel of hot water in which stewpans are stood to warm. [F, f. L *balneum Mariae* bath of the Virgin perh. from gentleness of process]

Bairam (bīrah·m), n. Mohammedan festival (twice a year, Lesser & Greater). [Turk. & Pers.]

bairn, n. Child (Sc. form now borrowed in literary Eng., the E *berne* having perished, & *barne* become dialectal). [OE *bearn*, com.-Teut. f. *beran* BEAR[3]]

bait[1], v.t. & i. (Orig.) cause to bite. (1) Worry (chained animal) by setting dogs at it (*with* dogs, or abs.; also of the dogs), whence (*bear, bull,* &c.) **-bait**ING[1] n.; torment (helpless person) with jeers &c. (2) Give food to, take food, (of horses on journey); stop at inn (orig. to feed horses, then also for rest or refreshment). (3) Put food (real or sham) on or in (hook, trap, fishing-place). [sense 3 prob. f. foll.; ME *beyten* f. ON *beita* cause to bite (*bīta* BITE v.) cf. OF *beter*]

bait[2], n. Food to entice prey (*live b.*, small fish so used); (fig.) an allurement, temptation; halt in journey for refreshment or rest. [partly f. ON *beita* food, partly f. prec.]

baize, n. Coarse woollen stuff with long nap used for coverings. [f. F *baies* pl. fem. of *bai* f. L *badius* chestnut-coloured, BAY[6], treated by mistake as sing. cf. BODICE]

bake, v.t. & i. Cook by dry heat in closed place or on hot surface (not by direct exposure to fire), whence **ba·k**ING[1] (5) n.; harden by heat; *half-baked,* immature, half-witted; (of sun) ripen (fruit), tan (skin); (intr.) undergo the process, be cooked, hardened, tanned, by heat; *bakehouse,* house or room for baking bread, or for making loaf-sugar; *bakestone,* flat stone, slate, or iron plate, on which cakes are baked in oven; *baking-powder,* substitute for yeast. [OE *bacan*; com.-Teut., & cf. Gk *phōgō* roast]

ba·ker, n. Professional breadmaker (*pull devil, pull b.*, encouragement to both sides; *b.'s dozen,* thirteen, 13th loaf being huckster's profit; *b.-legged,* knock-kneed); (Fishing) kind of artificial fly. Hence **ba·ker**ESS[1], **ba·k**ERY (3), nn. [OE *bæcere* (*bacan* BAKE + -ER[1])]

ba·ksheesh, ba·khshish (-ē-), n. Gratuity, tip, (article not used). [Pers., f. *bakhshidan* give]

Bā·laam(-lăm) n. Disappointing prophet or ally; (Journalism) matter kept in stock to fill up gaps in newspaper (*Numb.* xxii. 28 or 38; *b.-box* receptacle for this).

bă·lance[1], n. Weighing-apparatus with central pivot, beam, & two scales; spring or lever substitute for this; regulating gear of clock or watch; zodiac constellation (usu. *Libra* or *The Scales*), & (not now corresponding) seventh sign of zodiac. The weighing of actions or opinions, the wavering of fortune or chance, power to decide (*hold the b.*); counterpoise, set-off; equilibrium (*b. of power,* no State greatly preponderant); (Art) harmony of design & proportion; steady position (*lose one's b.*, fall physically or be upset mentally; *b.- wheel,* in watch, regulating the beat); preponderating weight or amount (*the b. of advantage lies with him*). (Accounts) difference between Cr & Dr, statement of this (*strike a b.*, determine it; *b.-sheet,* written statement of it with details); *b. of trade,* difference between exports & imports; *b. in hand,* amount over after realizing assets & meeting liabilities; *b. due,* deficiency; (slang) *the* remainder of anything. [F, = It. *bilancia* f. L (*libra*) BI(*lanx- lancis* plate) two-scaled (balance)]

ba·lance[2], v.t. & i. Weigh (a question, two arguments &c. against each other); match (thing) *with, by, against,* another; bring (thing, one*self*) into, or keep in, equilibrium; equal or neutralize weight of, make up for; oscillate, waver; (dancing) move conversely with one's partner. (Accounts) compare Dr & Cr, make the entry necessary to equalize them; *account balances,* two sides are equal; settle (account) by paying deficit. [f. F *balancer* (*balance* = prec.)]

bă·las, n. Red spinel resembling ruby. [f. OF *balais* ult. f. Pers. *Badakhshan* district of origin]

bă·lcony, n. Outside balustraded platform with access from upper-floor window; (Theatre) tier of seats generally between dress-circle & gallery. Hence **ba·lconi**ED[2] a. [f. It. *balcone* (*balco* f. OHG *balcho* = BALK[1] + *-one* -OON)]

bald (bawld), a. With scalp wholly or partly hairless (*go b.-headed* slang, stake everything, disregard consequences); (of animals &c.) hairless, featherless, treeless, leafless, napless; (of horses) marked with white, esp. on face; (of style) meagre, dull, jejune, monotonous, (of bad qualities) undisguised, whence **ba·ld**LY[2] adv.; *baldhead, baldpate,* (person) with bald head, kinds of duck (*pate* only) & pigeon. Hence **ba·ld**NESS n. [earlier *balled* perh. f. obs. *ball* white spot cf. W (*ceffyl*) *bàl* (horse) with white forehead, Ir. & Gael. *bal* spot, + -ED[2])]

bă·ldachin (-k-), **-quin,** n. (Orig.) rich brocade; (now) canopy projecting, suspended, or on pillars, over altar, throne, &c. [F & Sp. *baldaquin* f. It. *baldacchino* (*Baldacco* It. form of *Bagdad,* place of origin)]

ba·ld-coot, ba·ldicoot, n. The coot, from its bare white forehead; bald person.

ba·lderdash (bawl-), n. (Formerly) frothy liquid, mixture of liquors. (Now) jumble of words, nonsense; foul language. [?]

ba·ldmoney (bawl-), n. Yellow-flowered umbelliferous plant. [?]

ba·ldric (bawl-), n. Belt for sword, bugle, &c., hung from shoulder to opposite hip. Hence **ba·ldric**-WISE adv. [earlier *baudry* f. OF *baudrei* cf. MHG *balderich* perh. f. L *balteus* BELT]

bale[1], n. Evil, destruction, woe, pain, misery, (poet. & archaic). Hence **ba·le**-FUL a., **ba·leful**LY[2] adv. [OE, OSax., & OFris. *balu* f. OTeut. **balwom* neut. adj. evil]

bale[2], n. Package of merchandise usu. done up in canvas & corded or metal-hooped. [ME (perh. through Flem.) f. OF *bale, balle,* f. It. *balla, palla,* either from OHG *balla, palla,* BALL[1], or f. Gk *palla* ball]

bale[3]. See BAIL[6].

balee·n, n. & a. Whalebone. [ME *baleyne* f. OF *baleine* f. L *balaena* whale]

ba·lefire, n. Great fire in the open; funeral pyre; beaconfire (*fire* added only in 19th c.); bonfire. [f. OE *bǣl* & ON *bál* great fire f. OTeut. *balom* (cf. Skr. *bhalas* lustre, Gk *phalos* shining) + FIRE]

balk[1], **baulk**, (bawk), n. Ridge left unploughed; stumbling-block, hindrance; sanctuary area on billiard table (*make a b.,* utilize this); roughly squared timber beam; tie-beam of a house; headline of fishing-net. [OE *balca* ridge & perh. ON *bálkr* beam]

balk[2], **baulk**, (bawk), v.t. & i. Shirk, miss, (topic, turn, duty, chance); jib, shy, pull up; hinder, thwart, disappoint, discourage, startle. [f. prec.]

ball[1] (bawl), n. Solid or hollow sphere; (with distinctive adj.) any of the heavenly bodies; hard or soft, inflated or solid, large or small, sphere used in games; (Cricket) single delivery of it by bowler (*no b.,* delivery breaking rules); solid missile (not always spherical) for cannon, rifle, pistol, &c. (*load with b.,* opposed to blank cartridge); = BALLOT n., & see BLACK[1]; *b. of eye,* eye within lids; material gathered or wound in round mass, as snow, medicine (veterinary), wool, or string; *b. of foot,* rounded part at base of great toe, so *b. of thumb.* (Phrr.) *have the b. at one's feet,* see one's way to success; *keep up the b., keep the b. rolling,* do one's part in talk &c.; *the b. is with you,* it is your turn; *b. & socket,* joint with greatest possible freedom; *three bb.,* pawnbroker's sign; *b.-firing,* with b. cartridge; *b.*-PROOF; *b.-bearings,* axle fittings avoiding friction by use of small bb.; *b.-cock, -tap,* automatic cistern-tap with floating b.; *b.-flower,* archit. ornament. [ME *bal* f. ON *böllr* f. OTeut. *balluz*]

ball[2] (bawl), n. Social assembly for dancing (so *b.-room*; *give a b.,* of the entertainer; *open the b.,* lead first dance, fig. commence operations). [f. F *bal* f. *baler, baller,* = Pr. *balar,* It. & LL *ballare* to dance perh. f. Gk *ballizō* dance]

ball[3], v.t. & i. Squeeze or wind into a ball; grow into a lump or lumps. [BALL[1]]

bă·llad, n. Simple song, esp. sentimental composition of several verses, each sung to same melody, with accompaniment merely subordinate; poem in short stanzas narrating popular story. Hence **ba·llad**-MONGER, **ba·llad**RY (5), nn. [ME & OF *balade* (F *ball-*) f. Pr. *balada* dancing-song f. *balar* (BALL[2]), -ADE (1)]

balla·de (balahd), n. Poem of one or more triplets of seven-lined or eight-lined stanzas, each ending with same refrain line, & envoy; poem of equal (usu. seven or eight line) stanzas; *b. royal,* stanzas of seven or eight ten-syllable lines (also *rhyme royal*). [earlier spelling & pron. of prec., now used technically]

bă·llast[1], n. Heavy material placed in ship's hold to secure stability; *in b.,* in the hold, (of ship) laden with b. only or unladen, (of material) as b.; experience, principles, &c., that give stability to character; slag &c. used to form bed of railroad or substratum of road. [so in most Eur. langg.; perh. OSw. & ODa. *barlast* (now *bal-*) show origin, *bar* bare, mere, + *last* load]

bă·llast[2], v.t. Furnish with, render steady by means of, b. (lit. & fig.); fill in (railroad bed) with b. Hence **ba·llast**ING[1] (3) n. [f. prec.]

bălleri·na (-ēnah), n. Dancing-woman, ballet-girl. [It.]

bă·llet (-lā), n. Combined performance of professional dancers on the stage. [F, dim. of *bal* BALL[2]]

balli·sta (ba-), n. Ancient military engine for hurling great stones &c. [L, f. Gk *ballō* throw]

balli·stic, a. Of projectiles, of hurling-power. Hence **balli·stics** n. [prec. + -IC]

ballon d'essai (F), n. Experiment to see whether the public, or foreign States, will tolerate a new departure in policy &c.

bă·llonet, n. One of the interior gas-bags of an airship. [F (*-nnet*) as foll.]

balloo·n[1], n. (Archit.) large ball crowning pillar, spire, &c.; (Chem.) large hollow glass globe used in distillations; round or pear-shaped airtight envelope inflated with gas lighter than air & rising skywards, whence **balloo·n**IST (3) n., anything hollow & inflated; shape into which, or frame on which, trees & plants are trained. [f. It. *ballone* large ball (*balla* see BALE[2] + *-one* see -OON)]

balloo·n[2], v.i. Ascend in balloon, whence **balloo·n**ER[1] n.; swell out like b. (gowns &c.). [f. prec.]

bă·llot[1], n. (Small ball, ticket, or paper—also *b.-paper*—used in) secret voting; votes so recorded; lot-drawing (whether by balls or not); *b.-box,* used in voting or lot-drawing. [f. It. *ballotta* dim. of *balla* ball see BALE[2]]

ba·llot[2], v.i. Give secret vote; *b. for*, select (officials &c.) by secret vote; draw lots (*for* precedence, esp. in H. of Commons for right of moving resolutions &c.). [f. It. *ballottare* (*ballotta* BALLOT[1])]

bă·llot[3], n. Small bale of 70 to 120 lb. [F dim. of *balle* BALE[2]]

ba·llotage (-ĭj), n. French second ballot, between two highest candidates with less than legal majority. [F, f. *ballotter* = BALLOT[2]; see -AGE]

Ball-platz (bah·lplahts), n. Foreign Office of late Austro-Hungarian Empire. [*B.* in Vienna]

bă·lly, a. & adv. (slang) expr. speaker's disgust or satisfaction (*stung by a b. wasp*; *too b. tired*; *whose b. fault is that?*; *won the b. lot*). [pronunciation of *bl—y* = *bloody*]

bă·llyrag, v.t. & i. (slang) (-gg-). Maltreat by hustling, jeering, or playing practical jokes on; indulge in horseplay. Hence **ba·llyragg**ING[1] n. [etym. dub.; also *bullyrag*, prob. by pop. etym.]

balm (bahm), n. Fragrant & medicinal exudation from certain trees; ointment for anointing, soothing pain, or healing; perfume, fragrance; healing or soothing influence, consolation; tree yielding b. (Asia & N. Africa); *B. Gentle* or *B.-mint*, *Bastard B.*, *Field B.*, fragrant herbs; *B. of Gilead* or *of Mecca*, golden oleo-resin once much used as antiseptic, artificial imitation of this. [ME & OF *basme* f. L *balsamum* BALSAM; the ME has been variously corrected on the L (e.g. *balsme*), whence the mod. *-l-*]

bal·m-cricket (bahm-), n. Cicada. [earlier *baum-*; mistransl. of G *baumgrille* tree-cricket]

bălmŏ·ral, n. Kinds of laced boot, petticoat, Scotch cap. [Queen Victoria's Scotch residence]

bal·my, a. Yielding balm; fragrant, soft, mild, soothing, healing. Hence **bal·mi**LY[2] adv., **bal·mi**NESS n. [BALM + -Y[1]]

ba·lsam (bawl-), n. Resinous product = BALM; *True B.* or *B. of Mecca* = BALM *of Gilead*; other medicinal oleo-resins; *Canada B.*, used in mounting for microscope; artificial oily or resinous ointment, esp. various substances dissolved in oil or turpentine, e.g. *B. of Aniseed*; (fig.) healing or soothing agency; (Chem.) compounds of resins & volatile oils, insoluble in water; tree yielding b.; flowering plant of genus *Impatiens*; *B. Apple*, gourdlike plant with highly coloured fruit. Hence **balsă·mi**C (bawl- *or* băl-) a., **balsă·mi**CALLY adv., **balsami·**FEROUS a., **ba·lsam**Y[2] (bawl-) a. [f. L *balsamum*; from c. 1000 to 1600 either variants of *basme* were used, or the full L; *balsam* before & after those dates]

ba·ltimore (bawl-), n. N.-Amer. orange & black starling. [colours of Lord Baltimore's (proprietor of Maryland) coat of arms]

bă·luster, n. Short pillar, slender above, pear-shaped below; post helping to support rail; (pl.) set of these supporting handrail of staircase (now usu. *banisters*). [f. F *balustre* f. It. *balausta* f. L f. Gk *balaustion* wild-pomegranate flower (from shape of its calyx-tube)]

balustrā·de, n. Row of balusters with rail or coping as ornamental parapet to terrace, balcony, &c. Hence **balustra·d**ED[2] a. [prec., -ADE]

bam, v.t. & n. (slang, archaic). Hoax. [from 18th c.; etym. dub.]

bambi·no (-ē-), n. Image of infant Jesus in swaddling-clothes shown in Italian churches at Christmas. [It., = baby]

bamboo·, n. Genus of tropical giant grasses; the stem, used as stick or material. [*bambu* now in Java & Sumatra, but perh. not native]

bamboo·zle, v.t. (slang). Hoax, mystify, cheat *into* doing something or *out of* property &c. Hence **bamboo·zle**MENT n. [from c. 1700; etym. dub.; cf. BAM, also F *bambocher* play the fool, *bamboche* puppet f. It. *bamboccio* simpleton (*bambo* fool + *-occio*)]

ban[1], v.t. & i. Curse (t. & i., archaic); prohibit, interdict. [OE *bannan* summon & ON *banna* curse f. OTeut. *bannan* proclaim f. root *ba-* (cf. L *fa-*, Gk *pha-*) speak]

ban[2], n. Ecclesiastical anathema, interdict; curse supposed to have supernatural power; angry execration (archaic); formal prohibition; sentence of outlawry, esp. *B. of the* (Holy Roman) *Empire*; tacit prohibition by public opinion (*under a b.*). [OF, f. LL *bannum* f. Teut. *bann* proclamation with penalties (*bannan* BAN[1])]

ban[3], n. Viceroy of districts in Hungary, Croatia, &c., commanding in war. [Pers., = lord]

bā·nal, a. Commonplace, trite. [F (BAN[2], -AL); orig. a feudal word; the use of the lord's mill was compulsory for all tenants (*bannal mill*), whence the sense *common to all*]

bană·lity, n. Triteness; a commonplace. [f. F *banalité* f. prec., see -ALITY]

bana·na (-nah-), n. Tropical & subtropical fruit-tree; its fruit, finger-shaped with yellow rind, in clusters (*hand of bb.*, bunch). [Port. or Sp. f. the native name in Guinea]

banau·sic, a. Suitable for a mere mechanic, illiberal. [f. Gk *banausikos* (*banausos* working by fire f. *baunos* forge, -IC)]

Banbury cake, n. Spiced cake made at Banbury.

banc, *ba·nco*, n. Used in phrases *in banc*, *in banco*, = on the bench, applied to sittings of a Superior Court of Common Law as a full court (not Nisi Prius or circuit). [*banco* L abl. of *bancus* bench; see BANK[5]]

band[1], n. (1) Thing that restrains, binds together, connects, or unites (chiefly archaic, now ousted by the orig. identical BOND); (bookbinding) straps at back holding sheets together; *b.-stone*, one passing through dry-stone wall & binding it. (2) Flat strip of thin material; hoop round anything (of iron, elastic, &c.); strap forming part of a garment (shirt, dress, hat, &c.), (pl.) development of neckband or collar into two pendent strips (clerical, legal); *reef-band*, strip sewn on sail at eyelet holes for strength; (Mech.) belt connecting wheels; stripe of colour or distinguishable material on object; *bandbox*, of paper-covered chip or cardboard for millinery (orig. for clerical bb.; *look as if one came out of bandbox*, of extreme neatness); *b.-saw*, endless saw running over wheels; *b.-wheel*, worked by strap from another. (3) Organized company of armed men, robbers, persons with common object (*B. of Hope*, total-abstinence association), musicians (esp. *regimental b.*; *German b.*, any itinerant open-air musicians; *bandmaster*, conductor; *bandstand*, platform; *bandsman*, member of b.). [all meanings ult. f. OTeut. *bindan* BIND[1], but 1, 2, 3, with different hist. (1) (tie), ME *band* f. ON *band* f. OTeut. (hence also BOND); (2) (strip), late ME *bande* f. F *bande, bende*, =Pr. & It. *benda* f. OHG *bindâ* f. OTeut.; (3) (company), 15th-c. *bande* f. F *bande* = Pr., Sp., It., *banda* ribbon or LL *bandum* banner both f. Teut.]

band[2], v.t. Put a band on; mark with stripes; form into a league (usu. refl. or pass.). [f. F *bander* f. *bande*, see prec.]

ba·ndage (-ĭj), n., & v.t. Strip of material for binding up limb, wound, &c., or anything used for blindfolding; (vb) tie up with b., whence **ba·ndag**ING[1] (3) n. [F, f. *bande* BAND[1]; see -AGE]

banda·nna, -ă·na, n. Richly coloured yellow or white spotted (orig. always silk) handkerchief. [Hind. *bandhnu* method of spot-dyeing]

bandeau· (-dō), n. Fillet for binding woman's hair; fitting-band inside woman's hat. [F]

ba·nderōl(e), n. Long narrow flag with cleft end flown at masthead; ornamental streamer on knight's lance; ribbon-like scroll (*Arch.*, stone band) with inscription; sometimes =BANNEROL. [F *banderole* dim. of *bandière* BANNER]

ba·ndicoot, n. (India) rat as large as cat; (Australia) insectivorous marsupial. [f. Telugu *pandi-kokku* pig rat]

ba·ndit, n. (pl. *-i·ttī, -its*). Outlaw; lawless robber, brigand, (usu. in organized gangs); *a banditti*, set of brigands. [f. It. *bandito* pl. *-iti* p.p. of *bandire* = med. L *bannire* proclaim see BAN[1,2]]

ba·ndog, n. Chained dog; mastiff, bloodhound. [earlier *band-dog* f. BAND[1]]

bandoleer·, -ier·, n. Shoulder-belt with cartridge-loops. [f. 17th-c. F *bandouillere* f. It. *bandoliera* (*bandola* dim. of *banda* BAND[1]]

ba·ndoline, n. Gummy preparation for fixing the hair or moustache. [perh. f. BANDEAU]

ba·ndy[1], v.t. Throw, strike, pass, to & fro (ball, or *fig.* stories, epithets, &c.); often *b. about*; discuss (names &c.); give & take (blows &c.), exchange (something *with* some one). [cf. F *bander* 'bandie at Tennis' perh. f. *bande* side; *-y* unexplained]

ba·ndy[2], n. (Orig.) special form of tennis; (now also *b.-ball*) hockey; the stick, curved at end, used in the game. [perh. f. prec.]

ba·ndy[3], n. Indian cart or buggy. [f. Telugu *baṇḍi*]

ba·ndy[4], a. Wide apart at the knees (of legs); *b.-legged*, (of persons or animals) having b. legs. [perh. f. BANDY[2] curved stick]

bane, n. Poison (lit. now only in comb., as *rat's-b.*); cause of ruin, esp. *the b. of*; ruin, woe, (poet.). Hence **ba·ne**FUL a., **ba·neful**LY[2] adv., **ba·neful**NESS n. [OE *bana* death, murder, cf. OHG *bano*; also Gk *phonos* slaughter]

bang[1], v.t. & i. Strike (t. & i.) noisily; shut (t. & i. of door) with noise; make sound of blow or explosion; thrash; (slang) surpass. [from 16th c.; cf. ON *banga* to hammer, LG *bangen* strike]

bang[2], n. Sounding blow, sound of a blow, report of gun. [f. prec.]

bang[3], adv. & int. With sudden impact, abruptly, completely, explosively; *go b.*, explode; conventional imitation of gunfire. [f. BANG[1]]

bang[4], v.t. & n. Cut (front hair) straight across forehead; fringe resulting; *b.-tail*, horse with tail cut straight across. [f. prec.]

ba·ngle, n. Ring bracelet or anklet. Hence **ba·ngl**ED[2] a. [f. Hind. *bangri*, glass wrist-ring]

bă·nian, bă·nyan, n. Hindoo trader; (Bengal) native broker to European house; Indian flannel jacket; (Naut.) *b.-day*, on which no meat is served out; *b.-hospital*, for animals; *b.-tree* (or *b.*), Indian Fig, branches of which root themselves over great extent. [Port. *banian* f. Arab. *banyan* f. Gujarati *vaṇiyo* man of trading caste. *B. day, hospital*, from caste reverence for animal life; *b. tree*, E name used first of a specimen under which Banians had built pagoda]

bă·nish, v.t. Condemn to exile (person *from* place, or double obj. as *banished him the court*, or obj. of person only); dismiss from one's presence or mind. Hence **ba·nish**MENT n. [f. OF *banir* (-ISH[2]) f. LL *bannire* BAN[1]]

bă·nister, n. (usu. pl.). Upright(s) supporting stair handrail (also in pl. for uprights & rail together). [corruption of BALUSTER]

ba·njo, n. (pl. *-os, -oes*). Stringed musical instrument with guitar neck & head, tambourine body, played with fingers. Hence **ba·njō**IST (3) n. [negro corruption of earlier *bandore* ult. f. Gk *pandoura*]

bank[1], n. Raised shelf of ground, slope, elevation in sea or river bed; artificial slope enabling car &c. to maintain speed round a curve; flat-topped mass of cloud, snow, &c. Sloping margin of river, ground near river (*right, left, b.*, to one looking down stream); edge of hollow place (e.g. top of shaft in mining). [ME *banke* cf. OIcel. *bakki* in same senses f. OTeut. *bankon* cf. BANK[5]]

bank[2], v.t. & i. Contain as a b., confine with bank(s); (of car or aeroplane or its occupant) travel with one side higher; confine watch-escapement (of banking-pins), strike against the banking-pins (or abs.; of escapement); *b. up*, heap or rise into bb. (of snow, clouds), pack tightly (fire, for slow burning). [f. prec.]

bank[3], n. Establishment for custody of money, which it pays out on customer's order; *The B.*, B. of England, managing the public debt, receiving the revenue, issuing legal-tender notes, & having the Government for chief customer; (Gaming) amount of money before keeper of table; *b.-bill*, drawn by one b. on another; *b.-book*, containing customer's private copy of his account with b.; *b.-credit*, arrangement by which customer may overdraw on security given; *b. holiday*, day on which bb. are legally closed, usu. kept as general holiday also; *b.-note*, banker's promissory note payable to bearer on demand & serving as money; *b.-rate*, announced percentage at which B. of England is prepared to discount bills. [f. F *banque* f. It. *banca* f. Teut. *bank* BENCH, see BANK[5]]

bank[4], v.t. & i. Keep b., trade in money (*banking-house*, commercial firm that does some banking); keep money at b.; deposit (money &c.) at b.; convert into money; (Gaming) hold table fund; *b. (up)on*, base one's hopes on, count upon, reckon reliable. [f. prec.]

bank[5], n. Galley-rower's bench; tier *of oars* in galley; row of organ keys; working-table in some trades. [ME *baunck* f. OF *banc* f. Teut. *bank* f. OTeut. *bankiz* BENCH f. *bankon*]

ba·nkable, a. That will be received at a bank (securities &c.). [BANK[3] + -ABLE]

ba·nker[1], n. Proprietor or partner of private bank, governor, director, &c., of joint-stock bank, (*let me be your b.*, lend or give the money you need); (Gaming) keeper of the bank; dealer in some games of chance. [BANK[3] + -ER[1]]

ba·nker[2], n. Labourer (Eastern counties); (Hunting) horse that jumps on & off banks too large to clear. [BANK[1] + -ER[1]]

ba·nker[3], n. Wooden or stone bench for trimming bricks or stone on. [perh. = It. *banco* statuary's bench]

ba·nket, n. Auriferous conglomerate like pudding-stone found in S. Africa. [Du., = kind of hardbake (BANQUET)]

ba·nking, n. In vbl senses of BANK [2,4]; also, fishing on a sea bank (esp. Newfoundland). [BANK[1]]

ba·nkrupt[1], n. (Law) insolvent person whose effects, on creditors' or his own petition to Bankruptcy Court, are administered & distributed for benefit of all creditors; (pop.) insolvent debtor. [earlier *bankrout* &c. f. It. *banca rotta* broken bank (BANK[3], L *rupt-* p.p. of *rumpere* break) corrected to *-rupt* on L]

ba·nkrupt[2], v.t. Reduce to bankruptcy. [f. prec.]

ba·nkrupt[3], a. Under legal process because of insolvency; insolvent; bereft (*of* some quality &c.). [perh. the short p.p. of prec.]

ba·nkruptcy, n. Being declared bankrupt, being insolvent; utter loss (of something, e.g. reputation). [prec. + -CY, irreg. for *-rupcy*]

ba·nksia, n. Australian flowering shrub now grown in Europe. [Sir J. *Banks*, -IA[1]]

ba·nksman, n. Coal-mine overlooker above ground. [BANK[1]]

ba·nner, n. Cloth flag on pole used as standard of emperor, king, lord, knight, for war; flag of a country &c. (*join, follow, the b. of*; now chiefly fig.); ensign (esp. in frame, or with two poles) borne in religious or political demonstrations; anything used as symbol of principles; *b.-screen*, fire screen hung from standing pole or mantelpiece. Hence **ba·nner**ED[2] a. [f. OF *baniere* f. LL **bandaria* f. LL *bandum* f. Goth. *bandwa* perh. f. root of *band, bind*]

ba·nneret, n. Knight having vassals under his banner; one knighted on the field for valour. [ME & OF *baneret* (*baniere* see prec. + *-et* = -ATE[2]) lit. bannered]

ba·nnerol, n. Banner borne at great men's funerals & placed over tomb; = BANDEROLE. [var. of BANDEROLE]

ba·nnock, n. Scotch & N.-Eng. home-made loaf, usu. unleavened, flat, & round or oval. [f. Gael. *bannach* perh. f. L *panicium* (*panis* bread)]

banns, n. pl. Notice in church of intended marriage, thrice read to give opportunity of objection (*ask, publish, put up, forbid, the b.*). [var. of BAN[2]]

ba·nquet[1], n. Sumptuous feast; dinner with speeches in celebration of something or to further a cause. [F, dim. of *banc* bench BANK[5]]

ba·nquet[2], v.t. & i. Regale (person);

feast, carouse, whence **ba·nqueter**[1] n. [f. F *banqueter* (*banquet* = prec.)]

banque·tte (-kĕt), n. Raised way behind rampart &c. for firing from; bench behind driver in French diligence. [F, f. It. *banchetta* dim. of *banca* bench see BANK[3]]

ba·nshee, n. Spirit whose wail portends death in a house (Irish & Scotch). [Ir. *bean sidhe* f. OIr. *ben side* woman of the fairies]

ba·ntam, n. Small kind of domestic fowl, of which the cock is very pugnacious; small but spirited person (*b. battalion,* of men below normal standard enrolled for the great war); *b.-weight,* lightest class in boxing-competitions. [f. Bantam in Java whence they were perh. brought, though perh. orig. Japanese]

ba·nter, n., & v.t. & i. Humorous ridicule, good-humoured personalities. (Vb) make fun of, rally; talk jestingly. [f. 17th c.; etym. dub.]

ba·nting, n. Treatment of obesity by abstinence from sugar, starch, & fat; *bant,* adopt this. [for *Banting's method*]

ba·ntling, n. Young child, brat. [perh. corrupted f. G *bänkling* bastard f. *bank* (bench-begotten, cf. BASTARD); or f. BAND[2] swathe + -LING[1] (2)]

bantu (bahntōō·), n. & a. Used to include many related S.-Afr. languages & races. [native, = people]

ba·nxring, n. Javanese squirrel-like insectivorous animal. [Javanese *bangsring*]

ba·nyan. See BANIAN (used esp. for the tree).

bā·obăb, n. African tree called also Monkey-Bread with enormously thick stem. [mentioned 1592]

ba·ptism, n. Religious rite of immersing (person) in, or sprinkling with, water in sign of purification & (with Christians) of admission to the Church, generally accompanied by name-giving; (fig.) *b. of blood,* martyrdom, *b. of fire,* soldier's first battle; naming of church bells & ships. Hence **bapti·smal** a., **bapti·smally**[2] adv. [ME *bapteme* f. OF *baptesme* f. L f. Gk *baptismos* (*baptizō* BAPTIZE)]

ba·ptist, n. One who baptizes, esp. John the B.; one of a sect (formerly called ANABAPTISTS by opponents) objecting to infant baptism, & practising immersion. [f. OF *baptiste,* f. L *baptista* f. Gk *baptistēs* (*baptizō* BAPTIZE)]

ba·ptist(e)ry, n. Part of church (or formerly separate building) used for baptism; (in Baptist chapel) immersion receptacle. [f. OF *baptisterie* f. L f. Gk *baptistērion* bathing-place (*baptizō* BAPTIZE)]

bapti·ze, v.t. Immerse in or sprinkle with water, as sign of purification or initiation, esp. into the Christian Church; christen; (abs.) administer baptism; (fig.) purify, elevate; name or nickname. [f. F *baptiser* f. L *baptizare* f. Gk *baptizō* bathe (*baptō* dip)]

bar[1], n. Long-shaped piece of rigid material (metal, wood, soap, &c.; *b.-bell,* iron b. with ball at each end used in gymnastics, cf. *dumb-bell*; *barwood,* red wood from Gaboon imported in bb. for dyeing &c.;) (medals) slip of silver below clasp as additional distinction; band of colour &c. on surface, (Herald.) two horizontal parallel lines across shield (*b. sinister,* by mistake for BEND or BATON, supposed sign of illegitimacy); rod or pole used to confine or obstruct (*window, door, grate, gate, -b.*); barrier of any shape (*Temple-b., tollb.*; *harbour-b.,* of sand across mouth); (Mus.) vertical line across stave dividing piece into equal time-parts; immaterial barrier; (Law) plea arresting action or claim; moral obstacle. Barrier with some technical significance, as, in lawcourt, place at which prisoner stands; hence *b. of conscience, opinion,* &c.; *trial at b.,* in King's-Bench division; a particular court (*practise at parliamentary, Chancery,* &c., *b.*); *be called to the b.* (i.e. that in Inns of Court separating benchers), be admitted a barrister; *be called within the b.* (i.e. that in courts within which K.C.s plead), be appointed King's Counsel; *the b.,* barristers, profession of barrister; (Parl.) rail dividing off space to which non-members may be admitted on business; (inn &c.) counter across which refreshments are handed, space behind or room containing it; *barman, barmaid,* attendants at such counter. [ME & OF *barre* f. LL *barra* etym. dub.]

bar[2], v.t. Fasten (door &c.) with bar(s); keep (person) *in* or *out* (*barring-out,* schoolboy rebellion); obstruct (path &c.); stay (process or party) by legal objection; exclude from consideration (esp. in imperative used as prep., e.g. *bar one* in betting); (slang) object to, dislike, (person, habit, &c.); mark with stripe(s). [ME *barren* f. OF *barrer* (*barre* BAR[1])]

bar[3], n. Large European sea-fish. [F]

bărali·pton. See BARBARA.

bă·rathrum, n. Pit at Athens into which criminals were thrown; abyss. [L, f. Gk *barathron*]

barb[1], n., & v.t. Beardlike feelers of barbel &c.; chin-piece of nun's head-dress; lateral filament branching from shaft of feather; subordinate recurved point of arrow, fishhook, &c., (fig.) sting. (Vb) furnish (arrow &c.) with b.; *barbed wire,* for fences & esp. as obstruction in war, with wire prickles at intervals. [f. F *barbe* f. L *barba* beard]

barb[2], n. Breeds of horse & pigeon imported from Barbary. [f. F *barbe* (*Barbarie*)]

bar·bara, first word of the scholastic mnemonic lines for figures & moods of the syllogism (some of these, esp. *barbara, barbara celarent, baralipton,* are used allusively for logic or logical training).

barbăr·ian, n. & a. (Foreigner) differing from speaker in language & customs, esp. in hist., (a) non-Greek, (one) outside the Roman Empire, (a) non-Christian; rude, wild, or uncultured (person). [f. F *barbarien* (BARBAROUS, -IAN)]

barbă·ric, a. Rude, rough, like or of barbarians & their art or taste. Hence **barba·rICALLY** adv. [f. OF *barbarique* f. L f. Gk *barbarikos* (*barbaros* BARBAROUS, & see -IC)]

bar·barism, n. Mixing of foreign or vulgar expressions in talk or writing; such an expression; absence of culture, ignorance & rudeness; instance of this. [f. F *barbarisme* f. L f. Gk *barbarismos* (*barbarizō* speak like a foreigner f. *barbaros* BARBAROUS, -IZE)]

barbă·rity, n. Savage cruelty, instance of it; barbaric style or taste, instance of it, (usu. *barbarism*). [f. L *barbarus* BARBAROUS + -TY]

bar·barize, v.t. & i. Make or become **barbarous**; corrupt (language). Hence **bar·barizA·TION** n. [f. L *barbarus* BARBAROUS + -IZE]

bar·barous, a. (Lang.) not Greek, not Greek or Latin, not pure, illiterate; (people) non-Greek, beyond Roman Empire, non-Christian, outlandish; uncivilized; cruel; coarse. Hence **bar·barousLY**[2] adv., **bar·barousNESS** n. [f. L f. Gk *barbaros* foreign (perh. imit. of gibberish) + -OUS]

bar·bāte, a. (bot., zool.). Having hairy tufts. [f. L *barbatus* bearded (*barba* beard, -ATE[2])]

bar·becue, n. Large wooden or iron framework for smoking or broiling; hog, ox, &c., roasted whole, whence **bar·becue** v.t.; (U.S.) large entertainment with whole-roasting; floor for drying coffee-beans. [f. Sp. *barbacoa* f. Haitian *barbacòa* crate on posts]

bar·bel (-bl), n. Large European freshwater fish with fleshy filaments hanging from mouth; such filament in any fish, whence **bar·bel(l)ED**[2] a. [f. OF *barbel* f. LL *barbellus* dim. of *barbus* barbel (*barba* beard)]

bar·ber, n. One who shaves & trims customers' beards & hair (now usu. *hairdresser*); *b.'s block*, for making & displaying wigs; *b.'s itch*, skin disease said to be communicated in shaving; *b.'s pole*, spirally painted & used as sign. [ME & AF *barbour* f. OF *barbeor* f. L **barbatorem* (*barba* beard), see -OR[2]]

bar·ber(r)y, ber·ber(r)y, n. Shrub with spiny shoots, yellow flowers, & oblong red berries; its berry. [f. med. L *barbaris, berberis*, etym. dub.]

bar·bet, n. Bird with bristle-tufts at base of bill. [perh. OF *barbet* adj. = *barbu* bearded]

barbe·tte (-ĕt), n. Platform within fort or in ship from which guns fire over parapet &c. without embrasure. [F dim. of *barbe* beard (F *barbette* = also linen up to throat showing above dress)]

bar·bican, n. Outer defence to city or castle, esp. double tower over gate or bridge. [f. F *barbacane* etym. dub.; Arab.-Pers. *bab-khanah* gate-house is suggested]

bar·bule, n. Filament branching from barb (of feather) as barb from shaft. [f. L *barbula* dim. of *barba* beard]

bar·carōle, -olle, n. Song of gondolier; imitation of it. [f. F *barcarolle* f. It. *barcaruola* boat-song (*barca* boat)]

bard[1], n. Celtic minstrel, (Wales) poet recognized at Eisteddfod, whence **bar·dIC** a.; early poet; lyric poet; poet, whence **bar·dLING**[1] n. [f. Gael. & Ir. *bàrd*]

bard[2], n. Armour for breast & flanks of warhorse. Hence **bar·dED**[2] a. [f. F *barde* horse-armour perh. = Sp. & Port. *albarda* (f. Arab.?) packsaddle]

bare[1], a. Unclothed, undisguised, uncovered, bald, unfurnished, unprotected, threadbare, unsheathed, ill-provided, empty, unadorned, scanty, mere; *bareback* a. & adv., *-ed* a., with b. back, on unsaddled horse; *barefaced*, without beard &c., without mask, also undisguised, shameless, or impudent, whence **barefa·cĕdLY**[2] adv., **barefa·cĕdNESS** n.; *barefoot* a. & adv., *barefooted* a., without shoes or stockings; *b.-headed*, without hat or cap. Hence **bār·ISH**[1](2) a. [OE *bær*; com.-Teut., cf. G & Du. *baar*]

bare[2], v.t. Uncover, unsheathe, reveal, strip. [f. prec.]

baré·ge (-āzh), n. & a. (Of) silky gauze. [orig. made at Baréges]

bare·ly, adv. Openly, explicitly; merely; only just; scarcely. [BARE[1] + -LY[2]]

bare·ness, n. Lack of covering, unadorned state. [BARE[1] + -NESS]

bare·sark, n. & adv. Wild Norse warrior; without armour. [lit. bare shirt (SARK); mod. form embodying supposed etym. of BERSERKER]

bar·gain[1] (-gĭn), n. Agreement on terms of give and take, compact, thing acquired by bargaining (*good, bad, b.*, result cheaply or dearly bought; *a b.*, thing acquired or offered cheap; *Dutch, wet, b.*, closed with drink; *into the b.*, beyond the strict terms, moreover; *strike a b.*, come to terms; *make best of bad b.*, take misfortune &c. cheerfully). [f. OF *bargaine, -caigne*, f. LL **barcaneum* (*barca* see foll.)]

bar·gain[2], v.i. & t. Haggle (*with* some one, or abs.) over terms of give & take; stipulate *with* person *for* thing or *to* receive, give, &c.; *b. for*, be prepared for, expect, (usu. with neg. or *more than*); (trans.) *b. away*, part with for a consideration. Hence **bar·gainER**[1] n. [f. OF *bargaigner* f. LL *barcaniare* perh. f. *barca* 'barge which carries goods to & fro', giving sense either of 'off & on' or of trading]

barge, n., & v.i. Flat-bottomed freight-boat for canals & rivers, with or without sails; second boat of man-of-war, for use of chief officers; large ornamental oared vessel for state occasions, house-boat (e.g. *College b.*); *b.-pole* (for fending; *would not touch with a b.-p.*, regard with loathing); (vb, slang) lurch or rush heavily *into, against, about.* [OF, prob. = BARK[3]]

barge-, comb. form in architecture = gable. *B.-couple,* two gable beams; *b.-course,* roof projecting beyond them; *b.-board,* ornamental screen to them; *b.-stones,* forming sloping or stepped line of gable. [f. med. L *bargus* gallows]

bargee·, n. Man in charge of barge; *swear like a b.,* fluently, forcibly; *lucky b.* (colloq.), lucky fellow. [-EE]

bā̆r·ic, a. Of or containing barium. [BARIUM + -IC]

bari·lla, n. Plant (*Salsola Soda*) in Spain, Sicily, Canaries; impure alkali made by burning either this or kelp. [Sp.]

baritone, var. of BARYTONE in mus. sense.

bā̆r·ium, n. (chem.). White metallic element, basis of alkaline earth baryta. [BARYTA + -IUM]

bark[1], n. Outer sheath of tree trunks & branches; tan; quinine (also *Peruvian* or *Jesuits' b.*); (slang) skin; *b.-bed,* hot-bed of tan; *b.-bound,* hindered in growth by tight b.; *b.-pit,* of b. & water for tanning; *b.-tree,* E name of cinchona. [f. Scand. *bark-* f. OTeut. *barkuz*]

bark[2], v.t. Strip bark from (tree), kill (tree) by ring-cutting bark (also *ring-b.*); abrade (one's knuckles &c.); encrust. [f. prec.]

bark[3], barque (-ark), n. Three-masted vessel with fore & main masts square-rigged, mizen fore-&-aft rigged (usu. *barque*), whence **bar·k-rigg**ED[2] a. (Poet.) any ship or boat (usu. *bark*). [f. F 15th-c. *barque* f. Pr., Sp., or It., *barca* f. L *barca* ship's boat perh. f. Celt.]

bark[4], n. Usual cry of dogs, foxes, squirrels; (fig.) sound of gunfire, or of cough; *b. worse than bite,* of testy harmless person. [f. foll.]

bark[5], v.i. & t. Utter sharp explosive cry (of dogs & some other animals); speak (& *b. out,* say) petulantly, imperiously; *b. at,* abuse; *b. up the wrong tree,* denounce wrong person &c.; (slang) cough. [OE *beorcan* cf. ON *berkja*; perh. variant of BREAK]

bar·ker, n. Noisy assailant; shop or auction tout; (slang) pistol, cannon. [f. prec.]

bar·ley, n. Hardy awned cereal used as food & in making malt liquors & spirits; its grain; *pearl b.,* the grain ground small; *b.-broth,* strong ale; *barleycorn,* grain of b. (*John Barleycorn,* malt liquor personified), its length as measure, ⅓ inch, top of fore-sight on rifle; *b.-mow,* stack; *b. sugar,* twisted sweetmeat; *b.-water,* soothing decoction of pearl b. for invalids. [OE *bærlic*; for *bær-* cf. obs. *bear* barley f. OTeut. *bariz*; *-lic* = -LY[1] (as if orig. an adj.)]

barm, n. Froth on fermenting malt liquor, yeast, leaven. [OE *beorma*; prob. com.-Teut., cf. G *bärme*]

Bar·mecīde, n. & a. (Giver of benefits that are) illusory, imaginary, disappointing. [name of Arabian-Nights prince whose feast to beggar was rich dish-covers with nothing below]

bar·my, a. Full of barm; frothy; (slang, also *b. on the crumpet*) wrong in the head, cracked. [-Y[2]]

barn, n. Covered building for storing grain &c.; (contempt.) unadorned building; *b.-door,* lit., & fig. target too large to be missed, also adj. of fowls = reared at the b.-d.; *B.-owl,* = White, Church, Screech, Owl; *b.-stormer,* strolling player; *b.-yard,* farmyard. [OE *bere-ern* (*bere* barley + *-ærn* place)]

bar·nacle[1], n. (Usu. pl.) pincers placed on horse's nose to coerce him into quiet for shoeing &c.; (slang; pl.) spectacles. [ME *bernak* f. OF *bernac* muzzle, w. dim. ending see -LE]

bar·nacle[2], n. (1) Arctic goose visiting Britain in winter (also *bernacle* for distinction from 2). (2) Stalked cirriped clinging by fleshy foot-stalk to ship's bottom; follower who cannot be shaken off. [ME *bernekke, bernake,* = OF *bernaque* etym. dub.; *(Hi)bernicula* (Irish goose), *perna* (a shellfish), *bare + neck,* are suggested; pop. mythol. represented the goose as developed out of the shellfish]

bă·rograph, n. Self-recording aneroid. [f. Gk *baros* weight + -GRAPH(2)]

barŏ·logy, n. Science of weight. [as prec. + -LOGY]

barŏ·meter, n. Instrument measuring atmospheric pressure used for forecasting weather & ascertaining height above sea-level; *common, siphon, wheel, aneroid, b.,* various systems; (fig.) *b. of opinion* &c. Hence **baromĕ·tr**IC(AL) aa., **baromĕ·trical**LY[2] adv., **baro·**METRY n. [as prec. + -METER]

bă·ron, n. (Hist.) one who held by military or other honourable service from the king or other superior (restricted later to king's bb., & again to those, *Great Bb.,* attending Great Council or summoned to Parliament; hence, peer). (Mod.) one of the lowest order of nobility; holder of foreign title (called *Baron* ——, not, like English b., *Lord* ——); *b. of beef,* double sirloin undivided. [ME & OF *barun* f. LL *baronem* nom. *baro* man (as in *king's man*), freeman, husband, male, perh. f. L *baro -onis* dunce]

bă·ronage (-ĭj), n. Barons or great vassals of Crown collectively; the nobility; book with list of peers & comments. [ME

& OF *barnage* f. LL **baronaticum* f. *baro* (prec., -AGE)]

ba·roness, n. Baron's wife; lady holding baronial title in her own right. [f. OF *barnesse* see BARON, -ESS¹]

ba·ronet¹, n. Member of lowest hereditary titled order, commoner with precedence of all knights exc. K.G.s; abbr. *bart*, added to name, as *Sir John Jones, Bart.* [dim. of BARON; see -ET]

ba·ronet², v.t. Raise to rank of baronet. [f. prec. on anal. of *knight*]

bă·ronetage (-ĭj), n. Baronets collectively; book with list of them & comments. [-AGE; cf. BARONAGE].

ba·ronetcy, n. Baronet's patent or rank. [-CY]

barō·nial, a. Of, belonging to, befitting, baron(s). [foll. + -AL]

bă·rony, n. Baron's domain, rank, tenure; (Ireland) division of county; (Scotland) large manor. [f. OF *baronie* f. LL *baronia*; see BARON & -Y¹]

baro·que (-ōk), a. & n. Irregularly shaped, grotesque; whimsical style or ornamentation. [F, f. Port. *barroco*, Sp. *barrueco* rough pearl, etym. dub.]

barou·che (-o͞osh), n. Four-wheeled carriage with collapsible half-head, for four occupants & driver. [f. G (dial.) *barutsche* f. It. *baroccio* f. L *birotus* (BI- 1 a + *rota* wheel) perh. after *carroccio* chariot]

barque, n. See BARK³.

barquentine, bark-, (bar·kentēn), n. Vessel with foremast square-rigged, main & mizen fore-&-aft rigged. [f. BARK³ after BRIGANTINE]

ba·rrack, n., & v.t. Permanent building(s) in which soldiers are lodged (usu. pl.); (transf.) building in which others (e.g. children) are similarly herded together; building of severely dull or plain appearance; (vb) place in bb.; hoot, jeer at, (players in cricket-match &c.). [f. F *baraque* f. It. *baracca* or Sp. *barraca* 'souldier's tent' (1617) etym. dub.]

barracoo·n, n. Set of sheds or enclosure for slaves, convicts, &c. [f. Sp. *barracon* (as prec.; see -OON)]

barracu·da, -coo·ta, -cou·ta, (-o͞o-), n. Large W.-Ind. sea-fish. [? Sp.]

bar·rage (-ĭj), n. Damming; dam (esp. of those in Nile); (Mil.) gunfire so directed as to make a given line impassable. [F, f. *barre* BAR¹; see -AGE]

ba·rrator, -er, n. (legal). Vexatious litigant; malicious raiser of discord. [f. OF *barateor* trickster (*barat* fraud perh. f. Celtic, cf. OIr. *mrath*, W *brad*; meaning influenced by ON *barátta*, strife]

ba·rratry, n. (Marine law) fraud or gross negligence of master or crew to prejudice of ship's owners; (Law) vexatious litigation or incitement to it. Hence **ba·rra**TROUS a. [f. OF *baraterie* (*barat* see prec., -ERY)]

barred, a. In vbl senses; also [BAR¹] marked with bars, (of harbour) obstructed with sandbar.

ba·rrel¹, n. Flat-ended cylindrical wooden vessel of hooped staves, cask; varying measure of capacity (*b.-bulk*, 5 cub. ft); revolving cylinder in capstan, watch, & other machines; cylindrical body or trunk of an object, belly & loins of horse, &c.; metal tube of gun; *barrel-*, cylindrical or semi-cylindrical, as *b.-drain, -vault*; *b.-organ*, with pin-studded revolving cylinder acting mechanically on keys. [f. F *baril* perh. f. LL *barra* BAR¹]

ba·rrel², v.t. Put in barrel(s); *barrelled*, also, = *b.-shaped*. [f. prec.]

ba·rren, a. (-est), & n. Not bearing, or incapable of bearing, children, young, fruit, vegetation, or produce; meagre, unprofitable, dull; (noun) barren tract of land; *barrenwort*, purple-&-yellow-flowered wood plant. Hence **ba·rren**LY² adv., **ba·rren**NESS n. [f. OF *baraine* (fem.), *brahain, brehaing*, &c., etym. dub.]

ba·rret, n. Flat cap, esp. the biretta. [f. F *barrette* BIRETTA]

barricā·de¹, (now rarely) **-ā·do,** n. Hastily erected rampart across street &c. of barrels, carts, stones, furniture; any barrier, lit. or fig. [f. F *barricade* or Sp. *barricada* (-ADO) f. F *barrique* or Sp. *barrica* cask]

barricā·de², (now rarely) **-ā·do,** v.t. Block (street &c.) with b.; defend (place or person) with b. [f. prec.]

ba·rrier¹, n. Fence barring advance or preventing access; (ancient chariot-races) barred starting-cells; (foreign towns) gate at which customs are collected; (tilting) the lists or enclosing palisade, also railing parallel to which, but on opposite sides, tilters charged reaching their lances across; any obstacle, boundary, or agency that keeps apart. [ME & AF *barrere* f. OF *barrière* f. LL *barraria* (*barra* BAR¹) later assim. to F spelling]

ba·rrier², v.t. Close or shut in with b. (usu. with *off, in*). [f. prec.]

bar·ring, prep. Except, not including. [part. of BAR²]

ba·rrister, n. Law student called to bar & having right of practising as advocate in superior courts (in full, *b.-at-law*); *revising-b.*, one appointed to revise lists of voters at parliamentary elections. [f. BAR¹ (orig. the bar in Inn of Court, later connected with that in lawcourts); *-ister* (formerly *-ester, -aster*) unexplained; perh. f. form *barre* + -STER]

ba·rrow¹, n. (In local names) hill; (Archaeol.) grave-mound, tumulus. [OE *beorg*; com.Teut., cf. G *berg* mountain f. OTeut. *bergoz* f. Aryan *bhergh* height]

ba·rrŏw², n. (Also *hand-b.*) rectangular frame with short shafts used by two or more men for carrying loads on, stretcher, bier; (also *wheel-b.*) shallow box with shafts & one wheel for similar use by one man; (also *coster's b.*) two-wheeled hand-cart; a barrowful. [ME *barewe* f. OTeut. *barwâ* f. *beran* BEAR[3]]

ba·rrow[3], n. Infant's long sleeveless flannel coat. [cf. OE *beorgan* protect]

bar·ter,[1] v.t. & i. Exchange (goods or immaterial things) *for* other goods (sometimes *away*); part with for a (usu. unworthy) consideration (usu. *away*), whence **bar·ter**ER[1] n.; trade by exchange. [prob. f. obs. *barat* defraud see BARRATOR + -ER[5]]

bar·ter[2], n. Traffic by exchange, truck, (also fig., e.g. of talk); (Arith.) reckoning of quantity of one commodity to be given for another, values being known. [f. prec.]

bartiza·n, n. Battlemented parapet, or overhanging battlemented corner turret, at top of church tower or castle. [mod. form (Scott) prob. f. *bertisene* illit. spelling of *bratticing* see BRATTICE]

bar·ton, n. Farmyard; farm not let with rest of manor, but retained by owner. [OE *bere-tún* (*bere* barley + *tún* enclosure see TOWN)]

Bart's, n. St. Bartholomew's Hospital in London. [abbr.]

bary·ta, n. Protoxide of barium, alkaline earth of great weight. Hence **barȳ·t**IC a., **barȳto-** comb. form. [f. foll.]

barȳ·tēs, n. Native sulphate of barium, called also *heavy spar*, used as white paint. [f. Gk *barus* heavy, or perh. mere translit. of *barutēs* weight, with pronunc. assim. to mineral names in -ITES]

bă·rytone (-tn), n. & a. (Voice, singer with voice, music suited to voice) between tenor & bass; smaller bass saxhorn in B flat or C; (Gk gr.) (word) without acute accent on last syllable. [f. F *baryton* or It. *baritono* f. (gram. meaning direct f.) Gk *barutonos* (*barus* heavy + *tonos* TONE)]

bā·sal, a. Of, at, or forming, the base; fundamental. [f. BASE[1] + -AL]

basalt (bă·sawlt, basaw·lt), n. Dark green or brown igneous rock often in columnar strata, whence **basa·lt**IC, **basa·lti**FORM, aa.; black porcelain invented by Wedgwood. [f. L *basaltes* f. an African word]

bă·san, bă·zan, n. Sheepskin tanned in oak or larch bark (also *basil*). [f. F *basane* f. Pr. *bazana* f. Sp. *badana* f. Arab. *biṭanah* lining]

bas bleu (F), n. Bluestocking.

bă·scule, n. Lever apparatus used in *b.-bridge*, kind of drawbridge raised & lowered with counterpoise. [F, formerly *bacule* see-saw (*battre* bump or *bas* down + *cul* buttocks)]

base[1], n. That on which anything stands or depends, support, bottom, foundation, principle, groundwork, starting-point (*b.-ball*, U.S. national game, more elaborate rounders, also ball used in it); (Arch.) part of column between shaft & pedestal or pavement; (Bot. & Zool.) end at which an organ is attached to trunk; (Geom.) line or surface on which plane or solid figure is held to stand; (Chem.) correlative of ACID, electro-positive compound body that combines with acid to form salt (including, but wider than, ALKALI); (Mil.) town or other area in rear of an army where drafts, stores, hospitals, &c., are concentrated (also *b. of operations*); (Surv.) known line used as geometrical b. for trigonometry; (Math.) starting-number for system of numeration or logarithms (as 10 in decimal counting). [F, f. L f. Gk *basis* (*bainō* step, stand)]

base[2], v.t. Found (something) *on*; establish (with adv., as *firmly*); *b.* oneself *on*, rely upon (in argument &c.). [f. prec.]

base[3], a. (Orig.) of small height (now only in plant names as *b.-rocket*). Morally low, cowardly, selfish, mean, despicable, whence **ba·se**LY[2] adv.; menial; (Law) *b. tenure, estate, fee*, not absolute, but determinable on fulfilment of contingent qualification; (Lang.) not classical (*b. Latinity*); *b.-born*, of low birth, illegitimate; *b.-court*, outer court of castle or court behind farmhouse; *b. metals*, opposed to precious; *b. coin*, spurious, alloyed. Hence **ba·se**NESS n. [f. F *bas* f. LL *bassus* short (in L as cognomen) etym. dub.]

ba·seless, a. Groundless, unfounded. Hence **ba·seless**NESS n. [BASE[1], -LESS]

ba·sement, n. Lowest or fundamental part of structure; inhabited storey sunk below ground level. [BASE n. or v. + -MENT]

bash, v.t. Strike heavily so as to smash in (often *in*). [perh. imit. cf. *bang, smash*; or = Sw. *basa* flog, Da. *baske* cudgel]

bashaw·, n. Earlier form of PASHA.

ba·shful, a. Shy; shamefaced, sheepish. Hence **ba·shful**LY[2] adv., **ba·shful**NESS n. [f. obs. *bash* vb for ABASH + -FUL]

băshi-bazou·k, (-ōōk), n. Mercenary of Turkish irregulars, notorious for pillage & brutality. Hence **bashibazou·k**ERY (4, 5) n. [mod.Turk., lit. brain-turned]

bāsi-, stem of many adjj. in Physiol. Of, at, forming, the base of. [BASE[1], BASIS]

bā·sic, a. Of, at, forming, base; fundamental; (Chem.) having base atomically more than acid (salts); (Min.) slightly silicated (igneous rock); prepared by non-siliceous process (steel). [BASE[1] + -IC]

basi·city, n. An acid's relative power of combining with bases. [prec. + -TY]

bă·sil[1] (-z-), n. Kinds of aromatic herb, esp. *Common* or *Sweet B.* & *Bush* or *Lesser B.*, both culinary. [f. OF *basile* f. L *basilisca* (*basiliscus* BASILISK), the Gk name *basilicon* (= royal) being misinterpreted as antidote for basilisk's venom]

ba·sil[2], n. Corruption of BASAN.
basi·lic, a. (Of vein) starting from elbow & discharging into axillary vein. [f. F *basilique* f. L f. Gk *basilikos* royal (as formerly thought of special importance)]
basi·lica, n. (Orig.) royal palace; hence, oblong hall with double colonnade & apse used for lawcourt & assemblies; such a building used as Christian church; (in Rome) one of the seven churches founded by Constantine. [L, f. Gk *basilikē* (*oikia, stoa*) royal (house, portico) f. *basileus* king, -IC]
basi·licon, -um, n. Kinds of ointment. [*-on* Gk, *-um* L, f. Gk *basilikos* as in prec.; so called as a 'sovereign' remedy]
bă·silisk (-z-), n. Fabulous reptile (also *cockatrice*) hatched by serpent from cock's egg, blasting by its breath or look; (fig.) *b.-glance* &c., evil eye, person or thing that blasts (reputation &c.); (Zool.) small American lizard with hollow crest inflated at will. [f. L f. Gk *basiliskos* kinglet, serpent, golden-crested wren]
basin (bā·sn), n. Hollow round metal or pottery vessel, less deep than wide, & contracting downwards, for holding water &c., bowl; hollow depression; dock with flood-gates; land-locked harbour; tract of country drained by river & tributaries; circular or oval valley; (Geol.) formation with strata dipping towards centre, the deposit (e.g. coal) contained in this. Hence **ba·sin**FUL(2) n. [ME & OF *bacin* (F *bassin*) f. LL *bachinus* perh. for *baccinus* (*bacca* water-vessel)]
bă·sinet, ba·snet, n. Light steel headpiece. [f. OF *bacinet* dim. of *bacin* BASIN]
bā·sis, n. (pl. *bāsēs*). =BASE[1] (chiefly in fig. senses); main ingredient, foundation, beginning, determining principle; common ground for negotiation &c.; military base. [L =BASE[1]]
bask, v.i. Revel in warmth & light (usu. *in* the sun, firelight, &c.); *basking-shark*, largest species of shark (also *Sunfish* & *Sailfish*). [prob. f. ON *bathask* (cf. *or* = *other*) refl. of *batha* BATHE[1]]
ba·sket[1], n. Wicker vessel of osiers, cane, rushes, &c.; the quantity contained in it (also *basketful*); wicker singlestick handguard; *pick of the b.*, best of the lot; *basket-*, of b. shape as *b.-hilt*, of b. material or fashion as *b.-carriage, -work*. Hence **ba·sket**RY(5) n. [etym. dub.; *bascauda* is mentioned by Martial as a British utensil]
ba·sket[2], v.t. Put in a b., waste-paper or other. [f. prec.]
ba·son[1], n. =BASIN.
ba·son[2], n., & v.t. Bench for felting hat material; (vb) felt. [perh. =BASIN]
basque (-sk), n. & a. (1) Biscayan, (native or language) of Western Pyrenees (*B-*). (2) Short continuation of bodice below waist; bodice having this. [F, f. LL *Vasco -onis*; whether 2 is from 1 is not known]
băs-relief, bass-, n. (Piece of) shallow carving or sculpture on background (less than half the true depth). [f. F *bas-relief* f. It. *basso-rilievo* low RELIEF; see BASE[3]]
băss[1], n. Common Perch; *Black B.*, Perch of Lake Huron; European sea-fish (also *Sea-wolf* and *Sea-dace*). [earlier *barse* f. OE *bærs*; com.-Teut. f. root *bars-* bristle]
băss[2], n. Inner bark of lime, used for mats, hassocks, & baskets, & for tying plants, flowers, &c.; *b.-wood*, Amer. lime, its wood. [corruption of BAST]
bāss[3], a. & n. Deep-sounding; (of, suited to) lowest part in harmonized music; (man with) b. voice; *thorough-b., figured b.*, b. part with shorthand indications below of the proper harmony, hence theory of harmony; *b.-viol.*, violoncello. [ME *bas base* see BASE[3]; now *bass* after It. *basso*]
Băss[4], n. B.'s beer, bottle of this (*a small B.*). [*B.*, brewer]
ba·sset[1], n. Short-legged badger-dog. [F, dim. of *bas basse* low; see BASE[3]]
ba·sset[2], n. Obsolete card-game. [f. It. *bassetta* f. *bassetto* dim. of *basso* BASE[3]]
ba·sset[3], n., & v.i., (geol.). Edge of stratum cropping out; (vb) crop out. [?]
ba·sset-horn, n. Tenor clarinet. [transl. of F *cor de bassette* f. It. *bassetto* see BASSET[2]]
bassinĕ·t, n. Hooded wicker cradle or perambulator. [F, dim. of *bassin* BASIN]
bassoo·n, n. Wooden double-reed instrument used as bass to oboe; organ stop & harmonium reeds of similar quality. Hence **bassoo·n**IST(3) n. [f. F *basson* (*bas* BASE[3] + *-on* see -OON, or *bas son* deep sound)]
bąsso-rilievo (It.), n. (pl. *-os*). = BAS-RELIEF.
băst, n. Inner bark of lime (see BASS[2]); other flexible fibrous barks. [OE *bæst*; com.-Teut., etym. dub.]
bă·stard, n. & a. (Child) born out of wedlock or of adultery, illegitimate; (of things) unauthorized, hybrid, counterfeit; *b. slip*, sucker of tree (also fig., = *bastard* n.); (Bot.) nearly resembling another species (*b.* BALM); (Zool.) *b. wing*, rudimentary extra digit with quill-feathers. [OF, f. *bast* (BAT-) packsaddle (used as bed by muleteer) + -ARD; cf. BANTLING]
bă·stardize, v.t. Declare illegitimate. Hence **bă·stardiza**·TION n. [prec. + -IZE]
bă·stardy, n. Illegitimacy; *b. order*, for support of illegitimate child by putative father. [f. AF & OF *bastardie*; see BASTARD, -Y[1]]
bāste[1], v.t. Stitch together, tack, (as prelim. to regular sewing). [f. OF *bastir* (now *bâtir*) perh. f. LL *bastire* construct, build; but cf. also BAST]

bāste², v.t. Moisten (roasting meat) with fat to prevent burning; pour melted wax &c. on (wicks in candlemaking). [?]

bāste³, v.t. Thrash, cudgel. [perh. =Sw. *basa* flog (*basit, baste, baist*, as past or p.p. in early exx.; cf. HOIST¹, ²); or fig. use of prec. (cf. ' dry basting ' Shaksp.)]

băsti·lle (-ēl), n. Fortress; Paris prison-fortress destroyed 1789; prison. [F, f. LL *bastilia* pl. of *bastile* f. *bastire* build]

băstinā·do, n., & v.t. (Punish with) caning on soles of feet. [f. Sp. *bastonada* (*baston* stick) see -ADO(2)]

bă·stion, n. Projecting part of fortification, irregular pentagon with its base in the line (or at an angle) of the main works. Hence **ba·stion**ED² a. [F, f. It. *bastione* f. LL *bastire* build perh. f. same root as *baston* BATON]

bā·sӯl(e), n. (chem.). Body that unites with oxygen to form a base. [f. Gk *basis* BASE¹ + -YL]

bat¹, n. Nocturnal mouse-like quadruped with fingers extended as frame of membranous wings; *bat-*, often = purblind. [f. 1575, displacing ME *bakke* f. Scand.]

bat², n., & v.i. Cricket implement (*off* one's *own b.* cricket or fig., unaided; *carry* one's *b.*, be not out at end of innings); (also *batsman*) performer with it; (vb) use b., have innings. [f. OF *batte* club (*battre* strike see ABATE)]

bat³, n. (slang). Pace of stroke or step (*went off at a rare b.*). [?]

băt-, bät- (bah, baht), comb. form. For officers' baggage on campaign; *b.-horse, b.-pay* or *-allowance, b.-man* (in charge of horse). [f. F *bât* packsaddle f. OF *bast* f. LL *bastum* perh. f. Gk *bastazō* lift]

bata·ta (-ahta), n. W.-Indian plant, Sweet or Spanish potato. [Sp. & Port. f. native American]

Batā·vian, a. & n. (Inhabitant) of ancient Batavia (between Rhine & Waal) or of modern Holland, Dutch(man); of, inhabitant of, Batavia in Java. [f. L *Batavia* (*Batavi* pl.)]

batch, n. Loaves produced at one baking; quantity or number of anything coming at once or treated as a set. [ME *bache* (*bacan* BAKE) cf. *wake watch*]

bate¹, v.t. & i. Let down (*b. hope* &c.), restrain (*bated breath*); deduct (part of; usu. with neg., esp. *not b. a jot of*); fall off in force. [for ABATE]

bate², n., & v.t. Alkaline lye for suppling hides; (vb) steep in this. [=Sw. *beta* to tan, G *beisse* maceration f. *beissen* cause to bite BAIT¹]

bate³, **bait**³, n. (slang). Rage (*was in an awful b.*) [perh. = obs. *bate* var. of *debate*; or f. BAIT¹, = state of baited person]

bath¹ (-th, *pl.* -dhz), **Bath,** n. (1) Washing; immersion in liquid, air, &c. (*air-b., sun-b.*, exposure of naked body to air, sun; *mud-b.*, of mud for rheumatism; *b. of blood*, carnage); water &c. for bathing, wash, lotion, surrounding medium; vessel (*sitz-b.*, like HIP-*b.* but with broad flat bottom [G *sitzbad* sitting bath]; *sponge-b.*, esp. of broad flat saucer shape to facilitate sponging), room (also *b.-room*), or building, for bathing in (see TURKISH); town resorted to for medical bathing. (2) Order of knighthood (*B.*; for C.B., K.C.B., G.C.B., see C, K, G) named from the b. preceding installation. (3) Town in Somerset named from hot springs (*B. bun*; *B. Oliver*, biscuit invented by Dr. W. Oliver of B., d. 1764; *B. brick*, preparation for cleaning metal; *B. chair*, wheeled for invalid; *B.* CHAP²; *B. stone*, oolite building-stone). [OE *bæth*; com.-Teut., cf. G *bad* f. OTeut. *bathom* perh. f. *bajo-* foment cf. L *fovēre* keep warm]

bath² (-ah- or -ă- in all parts), v.t. Subject to washing in b. (child or invalid, of nurse &c.). [f. prec.]

bāthe¹ (-dh), v.t. & i. Immerse (in liquid, air, light, &c.); (of person or river, liquid, &c.) moisten all over; (of sunlight, &c.) envelop; take a bath or bathe, so *bathing-costume, -drawers*; *bathing-machine*, wheeled dressing-box drawn into sea for bathing from. [OE *bathian* (-dh-); com.-Teut., cf. G *baden*; for *bathe* (-dh), *bath*, cf. *graze, grass*]

bāthe², **bā·ther,** nn. Taking, taker, of a bath, esp. in sea, river, swimming-bath. [f. prec. in intr. sense]

bathĕ·tic, a. Marked by bathos. [irreg. f. Gk BATHOS on false anal. of *pathetic* (f. *pathētos*, not *pathos*)]

bathŏ·meter, n. Spring balance used in ascertaining depth of water. [f. Gk *bathos* depth + -METER]

Batho·nian, a. & n. (Inhabitant) of Bath. [mod. L *Bathonia* Bath, -AN]

bā·thos, n. Fall from sublime to ridiculous; anticlimax; performance absurdly below occasion. [Gk, = depth]

bathymĕtr-, stem of scientific words. Of depth-measurement. [f. Gk *bathus* (translit. *-ys*) deep + -METER]

bā·ting, prep. Except. [part. of BATE¹]

bati·ste (-ēst), n. & a. (Of) fine light fabric like cambric in texture. [F, f. *Baptiste* of Cambrai, first maker]

bă·ton (bătn), n., & v.t. Staff of office, esp. *Marshal's b.*; constable's truncheon (vb, strike with this); (Herald.) truncheon in shield (*b. sinister*, badge of bastardy); (Mus.) conductor's wand for beating time. [f. F *bâton* f. OF *baston* etym. dub.]

batrā·chian (-k-), a. & n. Of frogs; (one) of the *Batrachia*, or animals that discard gills & tail. [f. Gk *batrakheios* (*batrakhos* frog) + -AN]

battă·lion, n. Large body of men in battle array (*God is for the big bb.*, force prevails); body of infantry composed of several companies & forming part of regiment, body of engineers. [f. F *bat-*

taillon (now *bata-*) f. It. *battaglione* f. *battaglia* BATTLE[1]]

ba·ttels, n. pl. College account at Oxford for board & provisions supplied, or for all college expenses. [perh. f. obs. vb *battle* fatten f. obs. adj. *battle* nutritious cf. BATTEN[4]]

ba·tten[1], n. Board (6 ft or more long, 7in. ×2½ or less broad & thick) used for flooring; bar of wood used for clamping boards of door &c.; (Naut.) strip of wood nailed on spar to save rubbing, or securing hatchway tarpaulin. Hence **ba·tten**ING[1](6) n. [var. of BATON]

ba·tten[2], v.t. Strengthen with bb.; (Naut.) *b. down,* close the hatches (see BATTEN[1]). [f. prec.]

ba·tten[3], n. Bar in silk-loom striking in the weft. [f. F *battant* (*battre* strike, -ANT)]

ba·tten[4], v.i. Feed gluttonously *on,* revel *in,* (often implying morbid taste); grow fat. [perh. f. ON *batna* get better (*bati* advantage cf. BOOT[2])]

ba·tter[1], v.t. & i. Strike repeatedly so as to bruise or break (person, thing, or abs.; also with advv. *about, down, in*; & intr., *b. at the door*); operate against (walls &c.) with artillery; (fig.) handle severely (theories, persons); beat out of shape, indent; (Printing) deface (type) by use; *battering-charge,* full charge of powder for cannon; *battering-ram,* swinging beam anciently used for breaching walls, sometimes with ram's-head end; *battering-train,* set of siege guns. [f. obs. vb *batt,* cf. OF *batre,* + -ER (5)]

ba·tter[2], n. Mixture of ingredients beaten up with liquid for cooking; defect in printing-type or stereotype plate. [f. prec.]

ba·tter[3], v.i., & n. (Have) receding slope from ground upwards (of walls narrower at top). [perh. F *abattre* depress]

ba·ttery, n. (Law) infliction of blows, or of the least menacing touch to clothes or person (esp. in phr. *assault & b.*); (Mil.) set of guns for combined action with their men & horses, platform or fortification made to contain guns, (fig.) *turn a man's b. against himself* (in argument); (in various sciences & arts) set of similar or connected cells, instruments, or utensils (electric, galvanic, optical, cooking); hammered brass or copper vessels. [f. F *batterie* (*battre* strike, & see -ERY)]

ba·tting, n. In vbl senses; also, cotton fibre prepared in sheets for quilts &c. [BAT[2] + -ING[1]]

ba·ttle[1], n. Combat, esp. between large organized forces (*general's b.,* decided by strategy or tactics, *soldier's b.,* by courage; *pitched b.,* one fought by common consent; *b. royal,* in which several combatants or all available forces engage, free fight); victory (*the b. is to the strong, youth is half the b.*); *join, give, refuse, accept, offer, do, b.*; *b.-axe,* medieval weapon; *b. bowler* (slang), soldier's steel hat; *b.-cruiser,* heavy-gunned ship of higher speed & lighter armour than b.-ship; *b.-piece,* picture or literary description of a battle-scene; *b.-plane,* large fighting aeroplane; *line of b.,* troops or ships drawn up to fight; *l.-of-b. ship,* (obs.) of 74 or more guns; *b.-ship* (mod.), adapted by armour for regular engagement (opp. *cruiser* as l.-of-b. ship to frigate). [ME *batayle* f. OF *bataille* f. LL *battualia* neut. pl. of adj. *battualis* f. *battuere* beat]

ba·ttle[2], v.i. Struggle *with* or *against* (difficulties, the waves, &c.). [f. F *batailler* (*bataille* = prec.)]

ba·ttledore, n. Wooden instrument like canoe paddle used in washing, baking, &c.; wooden, stringed, or parchmented bat used with shuttlecock in the game *b. & shuttle-cock.* [from 1440; perh. f. Pr. *batedor* beater (*batre* beat + *-dor* = -TOR)]

ba·ttlement, n. (usu. in pl.). Indented parapet (raised parts, *cops* or *merlons*; gaps, *embrasures* or *crenelles*); parapet & enclosed roof. Hence **ba·ttlement**ED[2] a. [f. OF *batailles* temporary wooden turrets, *batailler* provide with these; etym. dub.; the F vb was later identified with *bastillier* cf. BASTILLE]

battue (batōō·, or as F), n. Driving of game by beaters to the sportsmen's station; shooting-party on this plan; wholesale slaughter. [F]

bau·ble, n. Showy trinket; court fool's emblem, a stick with ass-eared head carved on it; trifle, toy, thing of no worth. [f. OF *babel* child's toy, & perh. also partly f. ME *babyll* & vb *bablyn* flicker perh. f. BOB[3]]

baulk. See BALK.

baw·bee, n. (Sc.) Halfpenny. [?]

bawd, n. Procuress; obscene talk. [?]

baw·dy, a. & n. Obscene (talk); *b.-house,* brothel. Hence **baw·di**NESS n. [f. prec.]

bawl, v.t. & i. Say, speak, in a noisy way (often with *out,* also with *at, against,* &c.). [f. med. L *baulare* bark]

bawn, n. Court of a castle; cattlefold. [f. Ir. *bábhun* etym. dub.]

bay[1], n. Kind of tree or shrub; (pl.) wreath of its leaves worn by conquerors or poets, heroic or poetic fame; *bayberry,* a West Indian tree (*Pimenta acris*); *b. rum,* a perfume distilled from bayberry leaves. [f. OF *baie* f. L *baca* berry]

bay[2], n. Part of sea filling wide-mouthed opening of land; recess in mountain range; *Bay-state,* Massachusetts. [f. F *baie* f. LL *baia* perh. associated with, but not from, *badata* in foll.]

bay[3], n. Division of wall between columns or buttresses; recess (*horse-b.,* stall; *sick-b.,* part of main deck used as hospital); space added to room by advancing window from wall line (*b. window,* filling such space). [f. F *baie* OF *baée* (=L *badata*) f. *bayer* OF *baer*, *béer*, gape]

bay[4], n. Bark of large dog, of hounds in pursuit, esp. the chorus raised as they draw close; (in phrr. lit. of hounds & quarry, fig. of persecutors & victim, applied to the hunted animal) *stand* or *be at*, *turn to*, *hold hounds* &c. *at*, *b.*, show fight; (applied to hounds) *hold* or *have at*, *bring* or *drive to*, *b.*, come to close quarters with (quarry). [mixture of (1) OF *tenir a bay* = It. *tenere a bada* hold agape or in suspense (see *badata* in prec.) & (2) F *être aux abois* be at (close quarters with) the barking (OF *abai*)]

bay[5], v.i. & t. (Of large dogs) bark; bark at, esp. *b. the moon.* [OF *bayer* (mod. *aboyer*) bark perh. f. LL *badare* gape]

bay[6], a. & n. Reddish-brown (horse). [f. F *bai* f. L *badius*]

Bay·ard, n. Chivalrous person. [French hero, 'chevalier sans peur et sans reproche', 1475–1524]

bay·onet[1], n. Stabbing blade attachable to rifle-muzzle; *the b.*, or *bb.*, military force; (with prefixed number) so many infantry (cf. SABRE); *b.-catch*, securing of cylindrical part in place by a turn as with the triangular b.; *Spanish b.*, a plant, species of Yucca. [perh. f. *Bayonne* as made or first used there]

bay·onet[2], v.t. Stab with b.; *b. into*, coerce by military force (or fig. by pressure) into. [f. prec.]

bayou (bī·ū), n. Marshy offshoot of river in southern N. America. [f. F *boyau* gut f. L *botulus* sausage]

bay-sa·lt, n. Salt in large crystals obtained by evaporation. [perh. = sea salt f. BAY[2]]

bazaar· (-zar), n. Oriental market; fancy fair in imitation of this, esp. sale of goods for charities. [f. Pers. *bazar* prob. through Turk. & It.]

bde·llium, n. Balsam-bearing tree; its resin. [L, f. Gk *bdellion* transl. of Heb. *b'dolakh* of uncertain meaning (carbuncle or crystal or pearl)]

be, v. substantive, copulative, & auxiliary (pres. ind., *am*, *art*, *is*, pl. *are*; past ind., *was* pr. wŏz, *wast* or *wert*, *was*, pl. *were* pr. wār & wer; pres. subj., *be*; past subj., *were*, exc. 2 sing. *wert*; imperat., *be*; part. *being*; p.p., *been* pr. bēn; *'m*, am; *'s*, is; *'re*, are. *Isn't*, *wasn't*, *aren't* pl., *weren't*, are legitimate in actual or printed talk; *ain't*, *an't*, for *am not* is sometimes held vulgar; *ain't* for *is not*, *are not*, is wrong). (1) *Vb subst.*: Exist, occur, live, (often with *there*; *God is*, *there is a God*; *for the time being*, temporarily; *to be or not to be*, see *Haml.* III. i. 56—often facet. in trivial applications); remain, continue, (*let it be*, *do not be long*); (with advv. or adv. phrr.) occupy such a position, experience such a condition, have gone to such a place, busy oneself so, hold such a view, be bound for such a place, (*is in the garden*, *has been to Rome*, *be off*, *how is he?*, *what are you at?*, *I am for tariff reform*, *for London*); *been* colloq., called here, paid a visit, (*has anyone been?*, *has not been for orders*); *been and*, colloq. expletive of protest or surprise (*you have b. a. moved my papers!*); (with dat.) befall (*woe is me*). (2) *Vb cop.*: (with nouns, adjj., or adj. phrr.) belong under such a description (*I am a man*, *sick*, *of good courage*); coincide in identity with, amount to, cost, signify, (*thou art the man*, *twice two is four*, *it is nothing to me*, *what are these pears?*). (3) *Vb aux.*: With p.p. of trans. vbs forming passives (*this was done*); with p.p. of some intr. vbs, as *fall*, *come*, *grow*, forming perfects (*the sun is set*, *Babylon is fallen*); with pres. part. act. forming continuous tenses act. & pass. (*he is building a house*, *the house was building*); with pres. part. pass. forming continuous tenses pass. (*the house was being built*); with infin. expressing duty, intention, possibility, (*I am to inform you*, *he is to be there*, *the house is to let*, *he is to be hanged*, *it was not to be found*); *were* with infin. in hypotheses (*if I were*, or *were I*, *to tell you*). (4) Parts used as adjj., advv., nouns: *may-be*, perhaps, a possibility; *the to-be*, the future; *might-have-beens*, past possibilities; *would-be*, that yearns, or fancies himself, to be; *be-all*, whole being, essence. [f. three vbs (1) Aryan *es-*, Gk, L, & OTeut. *es-*, Skr. *as-*, to be; (2) OTeut. *wes-*, Skr. *vas-*, remain; (3) Skr. *bhu-*, Gk *phu-*, L *fu-*, OTeut. *beo-*, become. From (1) come *am* (cf. Gk *esmi*), *art* (cf. ON *est*, later *ert*), *is*, *are* (cf. ON *erum*, L *sumus*, Gk *esmes*); from (2) come *was*, *wast*, *wert*, *were*; from (3) come *be*, *being*, *been*]

be-, pref. f. OE *be-*, weak form of prep. & adv. *bi* BY, accented form of which appears in *by-law*, *by-word*, *bygone*, &c. The orig. meaning is *about*, which is variously developed as in *before* (about the front), *bespatter* (spatter all about), *bespeak* (speak about, making vbs trans.), *bedevil* (say *devil* about), *benight* (bring night about), *behead* (take the head from about) *bejewel* (put jewels about). As new vbs are constantly formed, & only the well-established or peculiar ones can be given, the chief varieties are here numbered for reference: (1) Adding notion of all over, all round, to trans. vb, as *beset*, *besmear*; (2) adding notion of thoroughness, excess, to trans. vb, as *bedrug*, *bescorch*; (3) making intr. vbs trans, as *bemoan*, *bestraddle*; (4) forming trans. vbs = *to make* from adjj. & nouns as *befoul*, *bedim*, *bebishop*; (5) making trans. vbs = *to call so & so* from nouns, as *bedevil*, *bemadam*;

For compounds of *be-* not given consult BE-.

(6) making trans. vbs = *to surround with, to affect with, to treat in the manner of,* from nouns as *becloud, beguile, befriend*; (7) making adjj. in -ED², from nouns, as *bewigged, beflagged,* (usu. with some contempt).

beach¹, n. Water-worn pebbles; seashore covered with these; shore between high & low water mark; *b.-comber,* white man in Pacific Islands &c. who lives by collecting jetsam; *b.-master,* officer superintending disembarkation of troops; *b.-rest,* chair-back for sitting against on b. [?]

beach², v.t. Run (ship, boat) ashore, haul up. [f. prec.]

bea·con¹ (-ē-), n. Signal, signal-fire on pole or hill; signal station; conspicuous hill (in names); lighthouse; guide or warning. [OE *béacn* f. OTeut. *bauknom* cf. BECKON]

bea·con², v.t. Give light to, guide; supply (district) with beacons. [f. prec.]

bead¹, n. (Orig.) prayer. Small perforated ball for threading with others on string, used in counting one's prayers (*tell* one's *bb.*); the same used for ornament; drop of liquid, bubble; small knob in fore-sight of gun (*draw a b. on,* take aim at); (Arch.) moulding like a bead series, or small one of semicircular section; *b.-roll,* list of names, long series, (orig. of persons to be prayed for); *beadsman,* pensioner bound to pray for benefactor, almsman. [ME *bede* f. OE *gebed* (or **bedu*) prayer, see BID¹]

bead², v.t. & i. Furnish with bb.; string together; form or grow into bb. [f. prec.]

bea·ding, n. In vbl senses; also, a bead moulding. [BEAD¹; see -ING¹]

bea·dle, n. Apparitor of trades guild or company; parish officer appointed by vestry. Hence **bea·dle**SHIP n. [OE *bydel* f. OTeut. *budiloz* f. *biudan* announce]

bea·dledom, n. Stupid officiousness. [-DOM]

bea·dy, a. (Of eyes) small & bright; covered with beads or drops. [BEAD¹]

bea·gle, n. Small dog tracking by scent formerly used in hare-hunting (pl. still in names of harrier packs); spy &c. [perh. f. F *bé-gueule* open throat (*béer* gape)]

beak¹, n. Bird's bill (esp. in birds of prey, & when strong & hooked); similar mandible-end of other animals, as turtle; hooked nose; projection at prow of ancient warship; spout. Hence **beak**ED² a. [f. F *bec* f. LL *beccus* of Gaulish origin]

beak², n. (slang). Magistrate. [?]

bea·ker, n. Large drinking-cup; lipped glass vessel for scientific experiments. [ME *biker* cf. G *becher* perh. f. med. L *bicarium* perh. f. Gk *bikos*]

beam¹, n. Long piece of squared timber supported at both ends; cylinder in loom on which warp, cloth, is wound; chief timber of plough; bar of balance (*kick the b.,* prove the lighter, be defeated; shank of anchor; lever in engine connecting piston-rod & crank; (pl.) horizontal cross-timbers of ship supporting deck & joining sides (*starboard, larboard, b.,* right & left sides, as *land on l. b.* &c.); = ship's breadth (*on her b.-ends,* on her side, almost capsizing, *fig.* in danger, at a loss); ray or pencil of light, or of electric radiation (*b. system,* wireless telegraphy in which a short-wave b. is projected undispersed, by reflection from a parabolic mirror); radiance, bright look, smile. [OE *béam* tree; com.-Teut., cf. G *baum,* Du. *boom,* tree, & perh. Gk *phu-,* Skr. *bhu-,* grow]

beam², v.t.&i. Emit (light, affection, &c.); shine; smile radiantly. Hence **bea·m**ING² a. [f. prec.]

bea·my, a. Radiant (rare); (poet., of spears &c.) huge; broad (of ships). [BEAM¹, -Y²]

bean, n. (Kinds of leguminous plants bearing) smooth kidney-shaped seed in long pods; similar seed of other plants, as coffee; *full of bb., b.-fed,* in high spirits; OLD *b.*; *give* one *bb.* (slang), punish or scold him. [OE *béan*; com.-Teut., cf. G *bohne,* & perh. L *faba*]

bea·n-feast, bea·no (slang, pl. *-os*), n. Employer's annual dinner to workpeople, fête, merry time. [?]

bear¹ (bār), n. Heavy partly carnivorous thick-furred plantigrade quadruped; rough unmannerly person, whence **bear·**ISH¹ a., **bear·ish**NESS n.; *Great, Little, B.,* northern constellations; (St. Exch.) speculator for a fall, one who sells stock for future delivery hoping to buy it cheap meanwhile, & therefore tries to bring prices down (cf. BULL, & see foll.). *B.'s-breech,* acanthus; *B.'s-foot,* kinds of hellebore; *b.-garden,* scene of tumult; *b.'s-grease,* pomade; *bearskin,* (wrap &c.) of b.'s skin, Guards' tall furry cap; *b.-leader,* travelling tutor. [OE *bera*; com.-Teut., cf. G *bär,* & perh. L *ferus* wild]

bear², v.i. & t., & n. (St. Exch.). Speculate for a fall; produce fall in price of (stocks &c.); (n.) this operation. [f. prec., perh. w. ref. to selling the b.'s skin before killing the b.]

bear³ (bār), v.t. & i. (*bore, borne* or *born,* see below*). (1) Carry (poet. or formal, exc. in the senses or contexts following): *b.* or *b. away,* win (the palm, bell, prize); carry visibly, show, be known by, (banner, device, arms, the marks *of,* name, relation or ratio *to*; *b.* one*self well* &c., behave); bring at need (*b. witness, company*; *b. a hand,* help); wield (office, rule); carry internally (*b. a grudge*; *b. in mind,* remember); wear (*b. arms, the sword*); *b. out,* confirm; *be borne away* (by external force or influence, or internal impulse); *is borne in upon* one, becomes one's conviction. (2) Sustain (weight, responsibility, cost; *b. a part in,* share); stand (test &c.), endure (*grin & b. it*), tolerate, put up with (*cannot b. him*), whence **bear·**ABLE a.; be capable of upholding weight (*ice bears*); be fit for (*his language won't b. repeating*); *b. with*, treat forbearingly; *b. up*, (trans.) uphold, (intr.) not despair; *borne on the books of*, paid by. (3) Thrust, strive, apply weight, tend, (*b. down*, overthrow; *b. hard on*, oppress; *b. upon*, be relevant to; *bring to b.*, apply; *b. to the right, away, off*, incline; *b. down*, swoop; *b. up*, bring ship into direction of wind; *b. up for*, change ship's course so as to sail towards. (4) Produce, yield, give birth to. *The p.p. is *borne*, exc. that *born* is used in pass. parts referring to human & other mammal birth; even then *borne* is used before *by* with the mother (*has borne a child*; *born* 1901; *born of, borne by, Eve*). [Aryan; OE, OHG, *beran*, cf. Gk *pher-*, L *fer-*]

beard[1], n. Hair of lower face (excluding usu. the moustache, & sometimes the whiskers); chin tuft of animals; gills of oyster; attachment threads of some shellfish; beak-bristles of birds; awn of grasses; *Old-Man's B.*, =Traveller's Joy. Hence **bear·d**ED[2], **bear·d**LESS, aa., **bear·dless**NESS n. [com.-Teut., cf. G *bart*]

beard[2], v.t. Oppose openly, defy, (*b. the lion in his den*). [f. prec.]

bear·er, n. Person or thing that carries; part-carrier of coffin; (India) palanquin-carrier, domestic servant; bringer of letters or message, presenter of cheque; (with adj. *good* &c.) plant &c. that produces well &c. [BEAR[3] + -ER[1]]

bear·ing, n. In vbl senses; also or esp.: behaviour; heraldic charge or device; relation, aspect, (*consider it in all its bb.*; *what is the b. of this on the argument?*); (pl.) parts of machine that bear the friction; direction in which a place &c. lies, (pl.) relative position (*have lost my bb.*, do not know where I am); *b.-rein*, fixed rein from bit to saddle, forcing horse to arch its neck. [BEAR[3], -ING[1]]

beast, n. Animal; quadruped; (Farming) bovine animal, esp. fatting-cattle (collect. pl. *beast*); animal for riding or driving; brutal man; person that one dislikes; *The B.*, Antichrist; *the b.*, the animal nature in man. [f. OF *beste* f. L *bestia*]

bea·stliness, n. Gluttony, drunkenness, obscenity; disgusting food or drink. [f. foll.]

bea·stly[1], a. Like a beast or its ways; unfit for human use, dirty; (colloq.) undesirable. [-LY[1]]

bea·stly[2], adv. (slang). (Intensifying adjj. & advv. used in bad sense; cf. JOLLY) very, regrettably, (*b. drunk, wet*; *raining b. hard*). [-LY[2]]

beat[1], v.t. & i. (past *beat*; p.p. *beaten*, but *beat* in *dead-beat*, often in sense *surpassed*, & sometimes in other senses). Strike repeatedly (t. & i.; *b. the breast*, in mourning; *b. black & blue*, bruise; *b. the air*, strive in vain; *b. at door*, knock loudly; *b. path*, make it by trampling), inflict blows on, (of sun, rain, wind) strike (*upon* something, or abs.); overcome, surpass (*b. hollow*, easily; *beats cockfighting*, is extremely exhilarating), be too hard for, perplex; move up & down (t. & i. of wings); move rhythmically (*heart* &c. *beats*, *b. time, seconds*, &c.); shift, drive, alter, deform, by blows (*b. down, back, away, off*; *b. in*, crush; *b. down price* or *seller*, cheapen or bargain with; *b. up eggs* &c., reduce to froth, powder, paste; *b.* or *b. out* metal, forge); (Naut.) *b. up, about*, strive, tack, against wind; strike (bushes, water) to rouse game (*b. about the bush*, approach subject slowly, shilly-shally; *b. up recruits* &c., collect; *b. up the quarters of*, visit; *b.* one's *brains*, search for ideas; *b. the bounds*, mark parish boundaries by striking certain points with rods); play on drum (*b. a parley, a retreat*, propose terms, retire). [OE *béatan*; com.-Teut., cf. ON *bauta* f. OTeut *bautan*]

beat[2], n. Stroke on drum, signal so given; movement of conductor's baton; measured sequence of strokes or sounds; throbbing; sentinel's or constable's appointed course; one's habitual round; sportsman's range. [f. prec.]

bea·ten, a. In vbl senses; also or esp.: worn hard, trite; shaped by the hammer; exhausted, dejected. [p.p. of BEAT[1]]

bea·ter, n. In vbl senses; esp.: man employed to rouse game; implement for beating flat. [BEAT[1] + -ER[1]]

bēati·fic, a. Making blessed. [f. L *beatificus* (*beatus* p.p. of *beare* bless, & see -FIC)]

bēă·tifica·tion, n. Making or being blessed; (R.-C. Ch.) first step to canonization, announcement that dead person is in bliss. [F, f. L *beatificare* (prec.), -ATION]

beă·tifȳ, v.t. Make happy; (R.-C. Ch.) announce as in prec. [f. L (prec., -FY)]

bea·ting, n. In vbl senses; esp.: a chastisement; a defeat. [f. BEAT[1]]

bēă·titude, n. Blessedness; (pl.) the blessings in *Matt.* v. 3–11. [F, f. L *beatitudo* (*beatus* see BEATIFIC, -TUDE)]

beau (bō), n. (pl. *beaux*, pr. bōz). Fop; lady's-man, lover. [OF, f. L *bellus* pretty perh. = **benlus* dim. cf. *bene, bonus* good]

beau geste (bōzhĕ·st), n. A display of magnanimity. [F]

beau idē·al (bō), n. One's highest type of excellence or beauty. [F (*-éal*), =the ideal Beautiful (often misconceived in E as a beautiful ideal); see prec. & IDEAL a.]

beau monde (bō mawnd), n. Fashionable society. [F]

Beaune (bōn), n. A red Burgundy wine.

beau·teous (bū-), a. Beautiful (poet.). [ME *beute* BEAUTY + -OUS]

beau·tiful, a. Delighting the eye or ear, gratifying any taste, (*b. face, voice, soup, batting*); morally or intellectually impressive, charming, or satisfactory (*b. patience, organization, specimen*). Hence **beau·tiful**LY[2] adv. [BEAUTY + -FUL]

beau·tifȳ (bū-), v.t. Make beautiful; adorn. Hence **beau·tifi**ER[1] (1, 2) n. [BEAUTY + -FY]

beau·ty (bū-), n. Combination of qualities, as shape, proportion, colour, in human face or form, or in other objects, that delights the sight (*b. is but skin deep*, one cannot judge by appearances); combined qualities delighting the other senses, the moral sense, or the intellect; *a b.*, beautiful person or thing (often ironical), exceptionally good specimen (*here is a b.*); beautiful women; a beautiful trait or feature, ornament, (*that's the b. of it*, the particular point that gives satisfaction); *b.-sleep*, before midnight; *b.-spot*, small patch placed on lady's face as foil to complexion, beautiful scene. [ME *bealte, beute*, f. OF *bealte, beaute*, f. L *bellus* pretty; see BEAU, -TY]

beaux yeux (F), n. Beauty; charms.

bea·ver[1], n. Amphibious broad-tailed soft-furred rodent, building huts and dams; its fur; hat of this. [OE *beofor* = LG *bever*, G *biber*, L *fiber*; reduplicated f. Aryan *bhru-* brown]

bea·ver[2], n. Lower face-guard of helmet. [ME & OF *bavière* bib (*bave* saliva)]

bea·verteen, n. Cotton twilled cloth with pile of loops. [f. BEAVER[1] after *velveteen*]

beca·ll, v.t. (archaic or vulg.). Call (person) names. [BE-(2)]

becal·m (-ahm), v.t. (1) Make calm (sea &c.). (2) Deprive (ship) of wind. [(1) BE-(2) + CALM v., (2) BE-(6) + CALM n.]

became. See BECOME.

becau·se (-ŏz, -awz), adv. and conj. For the reason (*that* & clause, archaic); by reason, on account, (*of* & noun); for the reason that, inasmuch as, since. [BY prep. + *cause* n.; the conj. use arises by omission of *that*]

beccafi·co (-fē-), n. Small migrant bird eaten in Italy. [It. (*beccare* peck + *fico* fig)]

bĕ·chamel (bĕsh-), n. Kind of white sauce. [inventor's name]

bêche-de-mer (F), n. Sea-slug, a Chinese dainty.

beck[1], n. Brook, mountain stream, (northern word). [f. ON *bekkr* cf. G *bach*]

beck[2], n. Significant gesture, nod, &c.; the order implied (*have at* one's *b., be at* person's *b. & call*, of entire dominion & obedience). [f. foll.]

beck[3], v.t. & i. Make mute signal, signal mutely to, (poet.). [shortened f. BECKON]

be·cket, n. (naut.). Contrivance for securing loose ropes, tackle, or spars, (rope-loop, hook, bracket, &c.). [?]

be·ckon, v.t. & i. Summon, call attention of, by gesture; make mute signal (*to* person). [OE *biecnan* f. OTeut. *baukno-* BEACON]

beclou·d, v.t. Cover with clouds; obscure. [BE-(6) + CLOUD n.]

beco·me (-ŭm), v.i. & t. (-came, -come). Come into being; *what has b. of* (happened to) *him?* (copulative) begin to be (followed by n., adj., or adj. phr.); suit, befit, adorn, look well on, whence **beco·ming**[2] a., **beco·ming**LY[2] adv., **beco·ming**NESS n. [OE *becuman* (BE- + *cuman* COME) arrive, attain; com.-Teut., cf. G *bekommen*]

bed[1], n. 1. Thing to sleep on, mattress (*feather b.* &c.), frame-work with mattress & coverings; animal's resting place, litter; (elliptical for) use of b., being in b.; *b. & board*, entertainment, connubial relations; *narrow b.*, the grave; *b. of down, flowers, roses*, easy position; *b. of sickness*, invalid state; *brought to b.*, in child-birth, *of* child or abs.; *die in* one's *b.*, of natural causes; *go to b.*, retire for the night (imperat., slang, cease talking &c.); *take to, keep*, one's *b.*, become, be, ill; *make the b.*, arrange the coverings; *lie in the b.*, one *has made*, take consequences of one's acts; *got out of b. on wrong side*, is bad-tempered for the day; *bedchamber* (archaic exc. of royal, as *Groom, Lady*, &c., *of the b.-c.*), bedroom; *b.-clothes*, sheets, pillows, &c., of b.; *bedfellow*, sharer of b., associate; *bedgown*, woman's night-dress, northern woman's short jacket; *b.-key*, wrench for (un)fastening bedstead; *b.-lift*, appliance for raising invalid to sitting position; *bedmaker*, (wo)man tending college rooms at Oxf. & Camb.; *b.-pan*, invalid's chamber utensil for use in b.; *bedpost*, upright support of b. (*in twinkling of bedpost*, prob. transf. f. *bedstaff*, loose cross-piece of old bedsteads often used as handy weapon; *between you & me & the bedpost*, in confidence); *be·d-rid(den)*, confined to b. by infirmity, decrepit, [OE *bedreda* (*rida* rider), *-en* by confusion w. p.p.]; *bedroom*, for sleeping in; *b.-side*, side of esp. invalid's b. (*good b.-s. manner*, of tactful doctors); *bedsore*, developed in invalid by lying in b.; *b.-spread*, coverlet; *bedstead*, framework of b.; *bedstraw*, kinds of plant, esp. (*Our*) *Lady's b.-s.*; *bedtick*, quadrangular bag holding feathers &c. for b.; *bedtime*, hour for going to b. 2. Flat base on which anything rests; *b.-plate*, metal plate forming base of machine; garden plot filled with plants, swamp with osiers; bottom of sea, river, &c. (*b.-rock*, solid rock underlying alluvial deposits &c., fig. ultimate facts or principles of a theory, character, &c.); foundation of road or railway; slates &c. of billiard table;

central part of gun-carriage; stratum; layer of oysters &c. [com.-Teut., cf. G *bett* perh. f. Aryan *bhodh-* whence L *fodere* dig]

bed[2], v.t. & i. Put or go to bed (poet. or archaic exc. of horses &c.); plant (esp. *b. out*); cover up or fix firmly in something; arrange as, be or form, a layer. [f. prec.]

beda·bble, v.t. Stain, splash, with dirty liquid, blood, &c. [BE-(1) + DABBLE]

beda·d, int. (Irish &c. for) by GAD[1].

bedau·b, v.t. Smear with paint &c.; bedizen. [BE-(1) + DAUB v.]

be·dder, n. In vbl senses; also, plant suited for flower-bed. [-ER[1]]

be·dding, n. In vbl senses; also: mattress, bedclothes, &c.; litter for cattle; bottom layer; (Geol.) stratification. [-ING[1]]

bede·ck, v.t. Adorn. [BE-(1) + DECK v.]

bĕ·deguar (-gar), n. Mosslike excrescence on rose-bush produced by insect's puncture. [f. F *bédeguar* f. Pers. *badawar* wind-brought]

bē·del(l), n. Official at Oxf. & Camb. with duties chiefly processional. [= BEADLE]

bedĕ·vil, v.t. (-ll-, -l-). Treat with diabolical violence or abuse; possess, bewitch; spoil, confound; call devil. [BE-(5, 6) + DEVIL n.]

bede·vilment, n. Possession by devil; maddening trouble, confusion. [prec. + -MENT]

bedew·, v.t. Cover with drops, sprinkle. [BE-(6) + DEW]

Be·dfordshire, n. (nursery). Bed (*go to B.*).

bedīgh·t, v.t. (past & p.p. *bedight*). Array, adorn, (archaic; usu. in p.p.). [BE-(1) + DIGHT]

bedi·m, v.t. (-mm-). Make (eyes, mind) dim. [BE-(4) + DIM a.]

bedī·zen, v.t. Dress out gaudily. [BE-(2) + DIZEN]

be·dlam, n. Hospital of St Mary of Bethlehem used as lunatic asylum; any madhouse; scene of uproar. [f. *Bethlehem*; hospital founded as priory 1247, converted to asylum 1547]

be·dlamite, n. & a. Lunatic. [-ITE[1] (1)]

bedouin (bĕdōō·ēn), n. (pl. same) & a. (Arab) of the desert, wandering; gipsy. [F, f. Arab. *badawin* pl. of *badawiy* dweller in the desert (*badw* desert); *-n* is prop. the pl. sign]

bedra·bbled, a. Dirty with rain and mud. [BE-(1), & see DRABBLE]

bedra·ggle, v.t. Wet (dress &c.) by trailing it, or so that it trails or hangs limp. [BE-(1) + DRAGGLE]

bee, n. Four-winged stinging social insect (queen, drones, & workers) producing wax & honey; allied insects (*Humble, Mason, Carpenter,* &c., *B.*); poet; busy worker; meeting for combined work or amusement (chiefly U.S., exc. *spelling-b.*); *have a b. in* one's *bonnet,* be mad on some point; *b.-bread,* (honey &) pollen used as food by bb.; *b.-eater,* kinds of foreign bird; *bee*HIVE; *b.-line,* straight between two places; *b.-master, -mistress,* keepers of bb.; *B. orchis,* with b.-shaped flowers; *b.-skep,* straw hive; *bees-wax,* secreted by bb. as comb material, (v.t.) polish with this. [OE *béo*; com.-Teut., cf. G *biene* perh. f. Aryan *bhi-* fear, quiver]

beech, n. Smooth-barked glossy-leaved mast-bearing forest tree; its wood; *b.-fern,* kind of polypody; *beechmast,* fruit of b. Hence **bee·chEN**[5] a. [OE *bóece, béce,* cf. G *buche*; com.-Teut. & cf. Gk *phagos, phēgos,* L *fagus*]

beef, n. (pl. *-ves*). Flesh of ox, bull, or cow; (in men) size, muscle; (usu. pl.) ox(en), esp. fattened, or their carcases; *beefeater,* yeoman of guard, warder of Tower of London, (f. obs. sense dependant); *b. tea,* stewed b. juice for invalids; *beef*STEAK; *b.-wood,* red timber of various trees. [f. OF *boef* f. L *bovem* nom. *bos* ox = Gk *bous,* Skr. *go-,* & E COW]

bee·fy, a. Like beef; solid, muscular; stolid. Hence **bee·fiNESS** n. [-Y[2]]

Bee·lzebub (biĕlzĭ-), n. The Devil; a devil. [L, f. Gk *beelzeboub* f. Heb. *ba'alz'būb* fly-lord]

been. See BE.

beer[1], n. Alcoholic liquor from fermented malt &c. flavoured with hops &c., including ale (pale) and porter (dark); other fermented drinks, as *nettle-b.*; GINGER-*b.*; *small b.,* (lit.) weak b., (fig.) trifling matters (*think no small b. of,* have high opinion of); *b.-engine,* for drawing b. at a distance; *beerhouse,* licensed for b., not spirits; *b.-money,* servant's allowance in lieu of b.; *b.-pull,* handle of b.-engine. [OE *béor*; com.-WG, cf. G *bier*; etym. dub.]

beer[2], n. One of the ends (so many threads) into which a warp is divided. [= BIER, cf. *porter* in same sense in Scotland]

beer·y, a. Of, like, beer; esp., betraying influence of beer. [-Y[2]]

bee·stings, n. pl. First milk after parturition. [f. obs. *beest* OE *béost,* com.-WG, cf. G *biest*; etym. dub.]

bee·swing (-z-), n. Second crust in long-kept port; old wine. [BEE + WING, from its filmy look]

beet, n. Two plants with succulent root, *Red B.* used for salad, *White B.* for sugar-making; *beetroot,* root of b. [OE *béte* f. L *beta*]

bee·tle[1], n., & v.t. Tool with heavy head & handle for ramming, crushing, smoothing, &c. (vb, beat with this); *three-man b.,* requiring three to lift it; *b.-brain* &c.,

For compounds of *be-* not given consult BE-.

blockhead. [OE *bietel* f. OTeut. *bautiloz* f. *bautan* BEAT[1]; see -LE(1)]

bee·tle[2], n. Insect having upper wings converted to hard wing-cases (pop. only of the black and large varieties, also wrongly of insects like them, as the *black-b.* or cockroach); short-sighted person (cf. *b.-eyed, blind as a b.*); *b.-crusher*, large boot or foot. [OE *bitula* biter f. *bitan* BITE[1]]

bee·tle[3], a. Projecting, shaggy, scowling, (*b. brows, b.-browed*). [prob. f. prec. w. ref. to tufted antennae of some beetles]

bee·tle[4], v.i. Overhang (of brows, cliffs), hang threateningly (of fate &c.). [f. prec.

beeves. See BEEF.

befa·ll (-awl), v.t. & i. (-fell, -fallen). Happen; happen to (person &c.). [OE *befallan* f. BE-(2) + *fallan* FALL; cf. G *befallen*]

be·fit, v.t. (-tt-). Suit, be fitted for; be incumbent on; be right. Hence **befi·tt**ING[2] a., **befi·tting**LY[2] adv. [BE-(2) + FIT v.]

befo·g, v.t. (-gg-). Envelop in fog; obscure. [BE-(6) + FOG n.]

befoo·l, v.t. Dupe. [BE-(5) + FOOL n.]

before·, adv., prep., & conj. (1) Adv.: ahead (*go b.*); on the front (*b. & behind*); previous to time in question, already, in the past, (*long b.*). (2) Prep.: in front of (*b. the mast*, of common sailors berthed forward), ahead of; under the impulse of (*b. the wind, recoil b., carry all b. you*); in presence of (*appear b. judge, bow b. authority*; *b. God* = as God sees me; *the question b. us*); awaiting (*world all b. them*); earlier than (*b. Christ*, usu. abbr. B.C., appended to dates reckoned backwards from birth of Christ); this side the coming of (future event); farther on than; rather than (*would die b. lying*). (3) Conj.: previous to the time when; rather than (*would die b. I lied*). [OE *beforan* (BE- + *foran* adv. f. OTeut. *fora* FOR)]

before·hand, adv. In anticipation, in readiness; *be b. with*, anticipate, forestall; *b. with the world*, having money in hand. [orig. two wds; sense-development doubtful]

befou·l, v.t. Make foul (lit. or fig.); *b.* one's *own* NEST[1]. [BE-(4) + FOUL]

befrie·nd, v.t. Help, favour. [BE-(6) + FRIEND n.]

beg, v.t. & i. Ask for (food, money, &c.); (abs.) ask alms; ask (*for* alms &c.); live by alms; (of dog) sit up with forepaws raised expectantly; ask earnestly or humbly (thing, *for* thing, *of* person, person *to* do, *of* person *to* do, *that* something may be done); (in formal and courteous phrr.) *b. pardon, leave*; *b. off*, get (person) excused penalty &c.; *b. to* do, take leave to do, take the liberty of doing, (*I b. to differ, enclose, announce*, &c.); *b. the question*, assume the truth of matter in dispute; *go (a-)begging* (of situations, opportunities, &c.), find no accepter. [perh. shortened f. F *béguiner* be a *beghard* or *béguin*, lay brother of mendicant order named f. Lambert Bègue]

bega·d, int. = by God (in fam. speech).

began. See BEGIN.

bege·t, v.t. (-tt-, -got, -gotten). Procreate (usu. of father, sometimes of father and mother, cf. BEAR[3]); give rise to, occasion. Hence **bege·tt**ER[1] n. [OE & Goth. *begitan*; see BE-(2) & GET]

be·ggar[1], n. One who begs; one who lives by begging; poor man or woman (*bb. must not be choosers*, must take what is offered); (depreciatingly) fellow; (playfully) *little b.*, youngster &c.; *a good b.* (= *begger*), good at collecting for charities &c. [perh. = *beghard* see BEG & -ARD]

be·ggar[2], v.t. Reduce to poverty; outshine, reduce to silence (*b. description*); *b.-my-neighbour*, card game. [f. prec.]

be·ggarly, a. Indigent; intellectually poor; mean, sordid. Hence **be·ggarli**NESS n. [BEGGAR[1] + -LY[1]]

be·ggary, n. Extreme poverty. [-Y[1]]

begi·n, v.t. & i. (-nn-, began, begun). Commence (*to* do, do*ing*, *work* &c., or abs.; in pass. sense either *it has begun to be done*, or *it has been begun*); be the first to do something; take the first step (*b. to* colloq., appear likely ever to, make any attempt to); start speaking; *b. at*, start from; *b. with*, take first; *to b. with*, in the first place; *b. upon*, set to work at; come into being, arise; have its commencement, nearest boundary, &c. (at some point in space or time); *b. the world*, start in life. [com.-WG; OE *beginnan* cf. G & Du. *beginnen* (BE- + *ginnan* perh. = OE *ginan* gape f. Aryan *ghi-* open cf. L *hiare*)]

begi·nner, n. In vbl senses; also, tiro. [-ER[1]]

begi·nning, n. In vbl senses; also or esp.: time at which anything begins; source, origin; first part; *the b. of the end*, first clear sign of final result. [-ING[1] (1)]

begir·d, v.t. (-irt). Gird round or encircle. [BE-(1) + GIRD]

bego·ne (-awn, -ŏn), vb imperat. = be gone (more peremptory than *go*).

begō·nia, n. Kinds of plant with coloured perianths but no petals. [Michel *Begon* c. 1680]

begot(ten). See BEGET.

begri·me, v.t. Soil deeply. [BE-(6) + GRIME]

begru·dge, v.t. Feel or show dissatisfaction at (thing), envy (one) the possession of. [BE-(2) + GRUDGE v.]

begui·le (-gīl), v.t. Delude; cheat (person *of, out of*, or *into* doing); charm, amuse; divert attention from (toil, passage of time). Hence **begui·l**ER[1], **begui·le**MENT, nn. [BE-(2) + obs. vb *guile*, see GUILE]

beguinage (bĕ·gĭnahzh), n. House of beguines. [foll. + -AGE]

bĕ·guine (-gēn), n. Member of Netherlands lay sisterhood not bound by vows. [Lambert *Bègue*, founder 1180]

bē·gum, n. Queen or lady of high rank in Hindustan. [Hind. *begam* f. East Turk. *bigim* fem. of *big* prince (Osmanli BEY)]

begun. See BEGIN.

behal·f (-ahf), n. (Only in phrr. ' on *or* in my &c. b.', ' on *or* in——'s b.', ' on *or* in b. of —— ') *on* the part *of, on* account *of,* (a person); *in* the interest *of* (person or principle &c.). [mixture of earlier phrr. *on his halve* & *bihalve him,* either = on his side; see HALF]

behā·ve, v.i. & refl. (Intr., usu. with adv.) conduct oneself, act, (rarely abs., esp. to or of children) conduct oneself with propriety, *b. towards,* treat (*well* &c.); (refl., usu. of or to children, & usu. without adv.) show good manners; (of machines &c., intr. or refl.) work (*well, badly,* &c.); *behaved* p.p. (with *well-, ill-,*) having good, bad, manners or conduct. [BE-(2) + HAVE]

behā·viour, n. Deportment, manners; moral conduct, treatment shown to or towards others; *be on* one's *good b.,* do one's best under probation; way in which ship, machine, substance, &c., acts or works. [f. prec., the ending due to confusion w. obs. *aver, havour, havyoure,* possession, = F *avoir*]

beha·viourism, n. (psychol.). Doctrine that, given adequate knowledge, all human actions admit of analysis into stimulus & response, & that ability to predict them depends on exhaustive study of behaviour in that light. [f. prec. + -ISM]

behea·d, v.t. Cut the head from; kill in that way. [OE *behéafdian* f. *be-* (from) about + *héafod* HEAD n.]

beheld. See BEHOLD.

behemoth (bĭhē·- *or* bē·ĭ-), n. Enormous creature. [perh. Egyptian *p-ehe-mau* water-ox (hippopotamus) assimilated to Heb. pl. (of dignity) of *b'hemah* beast, see *Job* xl. 15]

behe·st, n. Command (poet.). [OE *behæs* cf. *behatan* later *behight* to command, & G *heissen*]

behī·nd, adv., prep., & n. In or to the rear (of), on the further side (of), hidden (by), at one's back, towards what was one's rear, further back in place or time (than), past in relation to, too late, in concealment, in reserve, in support of, in an inferior position (to), under the defence of, in the tracks of, outdone (by), in arrear (with); (n.) the posterior. Phrr.: *stay, leave, b.,* after others', one's own, departure or death; *fall b.,* not keep up; *b. the scenes,* in private; *put b.* one, refuse to consider; *go b.* one's *words* &c., look for secret motives on his part; *b.* one's *back,* without his knowledge; *b. time,* unpunctual; *b. the times,* antiquated. [OE *behindan* (BE- + *hindan* = G *hinten* f. *hind-* HIND[3] + *-ana* from)]

behi·ndhand, adv. & pred. a. In arrear (*with* payments &c.); out of date, behind time; ill-provided (*with*). [prec. + HAND, cf. BEFOREHAND]

beho·ld, v.t. (beheld). See, become aware of by sight; (abs. in imperat.) take notice, attend. Hence **beho·ld**ER[1] n. [OE *bihaldan* f. BE-(2) + *haldan* HOLD v. keep (in view)]

beho·lden, pred. a. Under obligation (*to*). [p.p. (obs. exc. in this use) of prec. = bound]

behoo·f, n. (In phrr. *to, for, on b.,* or *the b., of*) use, advantage. [OE *bihóf* in *bihóf-lic* useful cf. G *behuf* f. OTeut. *bihafjan* (BE- + *hafjan* HEAVE cf. L *capère* take)]

beho·ve, -hoo·ve, v.t. impers. Be incumbent on (person) *to* (do something). [OE *bihófian* f. *bihóf* see prec.]

beige (bāzh), n. Kinds of dress-material made of undyed and unbleached wool; colour of this. [F, = natural-coloured, grey or brown, cf. It. *bigio*]

be·ing, n. In vbl senses; also or esp.: existence (*in b.,* existing); constitution, nature, essence; anything that exists (*the Supreme B.,* God); a person. [BE-, -ING[1], [2]]

bela·bour, v.t. Thrash (lit. & fig.). [BE-(3) + LABOUR v. (exert one's strength upon)]

bela·ted, a. Overtaken by darkness; coming too late. [p.p. of obs. *belate* f. BE-(4) + LATE]

belau·d, v.t. Load with praise. [BE-(2) + LAUD v.]

belay·, v.t. Coil (running rope) round cleat &c. to secure it; (sailor's slang in imperat.) stop!, enough!; *belaying-pin,* fixed wooden or iron pin for belaying on. [OE *belecgan* cf. G *belegen* f. BE-(1) + *lecgan* LAY[3] = lay round]

belch[1] (-tsh), v.i. & t. Emit wind noisily from throat; utter noisily or drunkenly (abusive, blasphemous, or foul talk); (of gun or volcano) send out or up. [OE *bealcian* cf. Du. *balken* bray]

belch[2], n. Eructation; sound of gun, volcano; burst of flame. [f. prec.]

be·lcher (-tsh-), n. Parti-coloured neckerchief. [Jim *B.,* pugilist]

be·ldam, -dame, n. Old woman, hag; virago. [earlier = grandmother f. *bel-* (cf. obs. *belsire,* & see BEAU) expressing relationship + DAM mother]

belea·guer (-ēger), v.t. Besiege (lit. & fig.). [f. Du. *belegeren* camp round f. BE-(6) + *leger* a camp]

bĕ·lemnīte, n. Tapering sharp-pointed fossil bone of extinct cuttlefish. [f. Gk *belemnon* dart + -ITE[1] (2)]

bel esprit (-rē), n. (pl. *beaux esprits* pr. bōz ĕsprē). A wit. [F]

be·lfry, n. Bell tower, attached or separate; bell space in church tower. Hence **be·lfri**ED² a. [by dissim. f. OF *berfrei* f. LL **berefridus* f. Teut. (MHG *bercvrit* prob. f. *bergen* shelter & OHG *fridu* peace); orig. sense, shed or tower for cover in besieging]

Be·lgian, a. & n. (Native) of Belgium. [-AN]

Be·lgic, a. Of the Netherlands; of the ancient Belgae. [f. L *Belgicus* (*Belgae*, -IC)]

Belgrā·via, n. Fashionable residential part of London south of Knightsbridge containing Belgrave Square.

Belgrā·vian, a. Of, suited to, Belgravia, fashionable London district. [f. Belgrave Square f. ground-landlord's Belgrave, Leics.]

Bē·lial, n. The devil; the spirit of evil; *man of B.*, reprobate. [f. Heb. *b'li-yaal* (*b'li* not + *yaal* use) worthlessness]

belie·, v.t. (-lying). Give false notion of; fail to act up to (promise &c.); fail to justify (hope &c.) [OE *belēogan* f. BE-(3) + *lēogan* LIE]

belie·f, n. Trust or confidence (*in*); acceptance of the Christian theology; acceptance as true or existing (of any fact, statement, &c.; *in*, or *of*, with nn., *that* with clause; *to the best of my b.*, in my genuine opinion); thing believed, religion, opinion, intuition; *The B.*, Apostles' Creed. [ME *bileafe* (BE- + OE *lēafa* shortened f. *ge-lēafa* cf. G *glaube* f. OTeut. *galaub-* dear)]

belie·ve, v.t. & i. Have faith *in*, trust word of, (person); put trust *in* truth of a statement, efficacy of a principle, system, machine, &c., existence of anything; give credence to (person, statement, &c., or *that*-clause); be of opinion *that*; *make b.*, pretend. Hence **belie·v**ABLE a., **belie·v**ER¹ n., **belie·v**ING² a. [ME *bileven* f. BE- + OE *gelēfan* cf. G *glauben* f. OTeut. as prec.]

beli·ke, adv. (archaic). Probably, perhaps, (often iron.). [*be-* = BY prep. + LIKE a. (by what is likely)]

beli·ttle, v.t. Make small, dwarf; depreciate. [BE-(4) + LITTLE]

bell¹, n. Hollow body of cast metal in deep cup shape widening at lip made to emit musical sound when struck; (Naut.) *one* to *eight bb.*, half hours of watch; b.-shaped object, as flower corolla (BLUE¹, CANTERBURY, *B.*). *Bear, carry away, the b.*, be first, win; *b., book, & candle*, in allusion to eccles. cursing formula; *sound, clear, as a b.*, quite sound or clear (in other senses besides the acoustic); *b.-bird*, Brazilian and Austral. kinds with b.-like note; *b.-buoy*, with warning b. rung by waves' motion; *b.-flower*, any plant of genus *Campanula*; *b.-founder, -founding, -foundry*, caster, casting, & manufactory, of bb.; *b.-glass*, b.-shaped as cover for plants; *b.-hanger*, artisan who puts up bb. & wires; *b.-hop* (U.S. slang), hotel page; *b.-metal*, alloy of copper & tin (more tin than in bronze) for bb.; *b.-pull*, cord or handle attached to b.-wire; *b.-ringer, -ringing* (of church bb. with changes &c.); *b.-wether*, leading sheep of flock with b. on neck, ringleader. [OE *belle*, com.-LG cf. Du. *bel*]

bell², v.t. Furnish with bell(s); *b. the cat*, take the danger of a common enterprise on oneself (fable of mice & cats). [f. prec.]

bell³, n., & v.i. (Make the) cry of stag or buck at rutting-time. [OE *bellan* cf. G *bellen* bark]

bellado·nna, n. (Bot.) Deadly Nightshade; (Med.) drug prepared from this. [mod. L f. It., = fair lady, perh. because a cosmetic is made from it]

belle, n. Handsome woman; reigning beauty (*the b. of* any place). [F, f. L *bella* fem. of *bellus* pretty see BEAU]

belles-lettres (bĕl-lĕ·tr), n. Studies, writings, of the purely literary kind. Hence **bellĕ·tr**IST (3) n., **belletri·st**IC a. [F]

be·llicōse, a. Inclined to fighting. Hence **bellicŏ·sity** n. [f. L *bellicosus* (*bellum* war, -IC, -OSE¹)]

bellĭ·gerency, n. Status of a belligerent. [f. foll., see -ENCY]

bellĭ·gerent, a. & n. (Nation, party, or person) waging regular war as recognized by the law of nations; of such nation &c.; (loosely) any opponent engaged in conflict. [wrong correction of earlier *belligerant* f. F *belligérant* f. L *belligerare* wage war (*bellum* + *gerere*), -ANT]

Bello·na, n. War personified; woman of commanding presence. [L, = goddess of war f. *bellum* war]

be·llow (-ō), v.i. & t., & n. Roar as a bull; shout, roar with pain; utter loudly and angrily (often *out, forth*); (of thunder, cannon, &c.) reverberate, roar; (n.) bellowing sound. [etym. dub.; cf. BELL³]

be·llows (-ōz), n. pl. Portable or fixed contrivance for driving air into a fire or through apertures of wind instrument; *pair of b.*, two-handled for fire; means used to fan passion &c.; the lungs (*b. to mend*, of broken-winded horse). [earlier *belg* bag = BELLY; the present wd f. northern form *belu, belw*]

be·lly¹, n. Cavity of human body below diaphragm with stomach & bowels & other contents, abdomen; (externally) lower front of body; corresponding parts of animals; stomach; the body as food consumer (cf. BACK¹), appetite, gluttony; the womb; cavity of anything; bulging part (concave or convex); front, inner, or lower surface; *b.-band* (below horse's b., checking play of shafts); *b.-worship*, gluttony; *b.-timber*, food; *b.-pinched*, starving; *b.-ache*, colic. Hence **-bellied**[2] a. [ME *bali*, *bely*, f. OE *bælg* f. OTeut. *balgiz* bag f. *belgan* swell; same wd as BELLOWS]

be·lly[2], v.t. & i. Swell out (usu. of sails, & with *out*). [f. prec.]

be·llyful, n. As much as one wants of anything, esp. of fighting. [-FUL(2)]

belo·ng, v.i. Pertain, be proper, *to* (as duty, right, possession, natural or right accompaniment, example in classification, characteristic, part, member, inhabitant, appendage); *b. under* or *in*, be rightly classified among; *b. here* &c., live here, be rightly placed under this heading &c. [BE-(2) + obs. vb *long* pertain f. OE *gelang* adj. dependent on (cf. the now dialectal 'along of') = OHG *gilang* akin (perh. f. notion *corresponding in length*)]

belo·ngings, n. pl. A person's property, relatives, or luggage; everything connected with a subject. [f. prec.]

belo·ved (*as adj. or n. usu.* -ŭvĭd; *as vb* -ŭvd), p.p., a., & n. (Forming pass. parts of vb obs. in act.) dearly loved (followed by *of* or *by*, or abs.); (n.) darling (common in voc., & with *my, his*, &c.). [BE-(2) + LOVE v.]

below· (-ō), adv. & prep. Adv.: at or to lower level; on earth; in hell; downstairs (esp. Naut. *go b.*, from deck); down stream; in lower rank (*the court b.*); at foot of page, or further on in book. Prep.: lower than (*b.-stairs* now rare, downstairs); too low to be affected by (*b. flattery*); down stream from; on inferior side of dividing line (*b. par*, *b. the gangway*); at or to greater depth than; covered by; lower in amount, degree, &c., than (*b.* one's *breath*, less audibly than); of lower rank &c. than; unworthy of. Cf. BENEATH, UNDER. [*be-* = BY + LOW a.]

belt[1], n. Encircling strip of leather &c. worn round waist or baldric-wise to confine or support clothes or weapons &c. (*hit below the b.*, fight unfairly); cincture of earl or knight; strip of colour, special surface, trees, &c., round or on anything; endless strap connecting wheels; row of armour plates under water-line; *Great* & *Little B.*, channels into Baltic. [com.-Teut., cf. OHG *balz* perh. f. L *balteus*]

belt[2], v.t. Put b. round (*belted cruiser*, with b. & metal-covered deck); fasten on with b.; mark with b. of colour &c.; thrash with b. [f. prec.]

be·lvedere (-ēr), n. Raised turret to view scenery from. [It. (*bel* beautiful, see BEAU, + *vedere* see)]

bely·ing. See BELIE.

bē·ma, n. Platform in ancient Athenian public assembly. [Gk]

bemire·, v.t. Cover or stain with mud; (pass.) be stuck in the mud. [BE-(6) + MIRE n.]

bemoa·n, v.t. Weep or express sorrow for or over. [OE *bemǣnan* f. BE-(3) + *mǣnan* MOAN]

bemu·se (-z), v.t. Stupefy. [BE-(2) + MUSE v.]

bench (-tsh), n., & v.t. Long seat of wood or stone; boat-thwart; judge's seat, office of judge, law-court (*King's, Queen's, B.*); (collect.) judges, magistrates; (Parl.) seats appropriated to certain groups &c. (*Treasury*, FRONT[1], CROSS[3], *bishops'*, bb.); *be raised to, be on, the b.*, be (made) a judge or bishop; working-table of carpenter &c.; ledge in masonry or earthwork; *b.-table*, stone seat in cloister &c.; *b.-mark*, cut by surveyors to mark point in line of levels. (Vb) exhibit (dog) at show. [com.-Teut.; OE *benc*, cf. Sw. *bänk*, G *bank*, f. OTeut. *bankiz*; same wd as BANK[1,5], which came through Rom.]

be·ncher, n. Senior member, sharing management, of Inn of Court. [-ER[1]]

bend[1], n. (Naut.) knot of various kinds (*fisherman's, weaver's*, &c.); (Herald.) parallel lines from dexter chief to sinister base (*b. sinister* in opposite direction, sign of bastardy); shape (half BUTT) in which hides are tanned (*b.-leather*, the thickest, used for soles). [earlier meaning *band, bond*, which wds have taken its place in most senses; OE *bend* f. OTeut. *band-* st. of *bindan* BIND[1]; identified with OF *bende, bande*, BAND[1] (2)]

bend[2], n. Bending, curve; bent part of anything. [f. foll.]

bend[3], v.t. & i. (past *bent*, p.p. *bent* exc. in *bended knees*). Force out of straightness, impart to (rigid object) or receive a curved or angular shape; arch (brows); tighten up, bring to bear, (energies &c.); (pass.) be determined (*on* with gerund or noun); attach with b. or knot (cable, sail); turn (t. & i.) in new direction (steps, eyes); incline (t. & i.) from the perpendicular (head), bow, stoop, submit, (*to* or *before*), force to submit (will &c.). Hence **be·nder**[1] n., esp. (slang) sixpenny bit. [OE *bendan* prob. = ON *benda* join, strain, f. OTeut. *bandjâ-* string, band; the orig. sense is stringing the bow]

benea·ped, a. Left aground by neap-tide. [p.p. f. unused *beneap* see BE-(6) & NEAP]

benea·th, adv. & prep. Below, under, underneath, (poetic, archaic, & literary, but usual in) *b. contempt* &c., not worth despising &c., *b.* one, unworthy of him. [OE *beneothan* = BE- + *neothan* cf. G *nieden* f. OTeut. *nithar* NETHER + *-ana* from]

bĕnĕdī·cĭte (-tĭ), n. Blessing invoked; grace at table; *the B.*, one of the canticles. [L, = *bless ye*, imperat. of *benedicere -dict-* bless (*bene* well + *dicere* speak)]

bĕ·nedick, n. Newly married man,

esp. confirmed bachelor who marries. [Shaksp., *Much Ado*]

bĕnĕdi·ctine, a. & n. (Monk) of the order founded 529 by St Benedict, black monk; a liqueur. [f. F *bénédictin* f. L *benedictus* p.p. see BENEDICITE]

benedi·ction, n. Utterance of a blessing, generally at table, at end of church service, or as special R.-C. service; a blessing, blessedness. [f. L *benedictio* (BENEDICITE, -ION)]

benedi·ctory, a. Of, expressing, benediction. [f. med. L *benedictorius* see prec. and -ORY(1)]

Benedi·ctus, n. One of the canticles. [first word in L version; see BENEDICTINE]

benefa·ction, n. Doing good; gift for charitable purpose. [f. L *benefactio* (BENEFIT[1], -ION)]

bĕ·nefactor, n. Person who has given one friendly aid; patron of or donor to a cause or charitable institution. Hence **be·nefactr**ESS[1] n. [f. L *benefactor* (BENEFIT[1], -OR[2])]

bĕ·nefice (-ĭs), n. Church living. Hence **be·nefic**ED[2] a. [f. L *beneficium* (*bene* well + *-ficium* a doing)]

benĕ·ficence, n., **benĕ·ficent,** a. Doing good, (showing) active kindness. Hence **benĕ·ficent**LY[2] adv. [f. L *beneficentia* n. and *beneficus* a., comparat. *beneficentior,* (*bene* well, and see -FIC, -ENCE)]

benefi·cial (-shl), a. Advantageous; (Law) of, having, the usufruct of property. Hence **benefi·cial**LY[2] adv. [F *bénéficial* f. L *beneficialis* (BENEFICE, -AL)]

benefĭ·ciary (-sha-), a. & n. (Law) holder, holding or held, by feudal tenure; holder of a living; receiver of benefits. [f. L *beneficiarius,* see BENEFICE, -ARY[1]]

bĕ·nefit[1], n. Advantage (*for the b. of,* on behalf of; *the b. of the doubt,* assuming innocence rather than guilt); allowance, pension, attendance, to which person is entitled under Nat. Insurance Act or as member of benefit society &c. (*maternity, medical, b.*); exemption from ordinary courts by the privilege of one's order (*b. of* CLERGY, *peerage*); performance at theatre, game &c., of which proceeds go to particular players (*—'s b., b.-night, b.-match*); *b.-club, -society,* for mutual insurance against illness or age; (slang, iron.) fine time, job, (*had no end of a b. getting things straight*). [ME & AF *benfet* f. L *benefactum* neut. p.p. of *benefacere* do well]

be·nefit[2], v.t. & i. Do good to; receive b. (*by* thing). [f. prec.]

benĕ·volence, n. Desire to do good, charitable feeling; (Eng. Hist.) forced loan. [f. OF *benivolence* f. L *benevolentia* f. *benevolens -entis* = foll.]

benĕ·volent, a. Desirous of doing good, charitable. Hence **benĕ·volent**LY[2] adv. [f. OF *benivolent* f. L *bene volentem* nom. *-ens* well wishing (*velle* wish)]

Benga·l (-awl), a. *B. light,* firework used for signals; *B. stripes,* striped gingham, orig. from B.; *B. tiger,* the tiger proper. [Indian province]

Benga·lĭ, -a·lee, (-aw-), n. & a. (Native, language) of Bengal. [f. native *Bangali*]

benĭgh·ted, p.p. & a. (Forming pass. of vb obs. in act.) overtaken by night; involved in intellectual or moral darkness, ignorant. [BE-(6) + NIGHT]

benĭg·n, a. Gracious, gentle; fortunate, salutary; (of diseases) mild, not malignant. Hence **benig·n**LY[2] adv. [f. OF *benigne* f. L *benignus* prob. = *benigenus* (*bene* well + *-genus* born)]

benĭ·gnant, a. Kind, kindly, to inferiors; gracious; salutary. Hence **benĭ·gn**ANCY n., **beni·gnant**LY[2] adv. [recent formation f. prec. on anal. of MALIGNANT]

beni·gnity, n. Kindliness, kindness, (usu. in the old). [f. OF *benignité* f. L *benignitatem* (BENIGN, -TY)]

bĕ·nison, n. A blessing (archaic). [= BENEDICTION, see -SON]

Be·njamin[1], n. Youngest child, darling, *B.'s mess,* large share. [*Gen.* xlii. 4]

be·njamin[2], n. = BENZOIN; *B. tree,* (a) that yielding benzoin, (b) a N.-Amer. shrub with aromatic bark. [corruption of BENZOIN]

be·nnet, n. See HERB *b.,* and foll.

bent[1], n. Reedy rushlike stiff-stemmed grass of various kinds (with pl., or collect.); (also *bennet*) stiff flower-stalk, old stalk, of grasses; couch-grass; *Way B., Stool B.,* &c., kinds of plant; heath, unenclosed pasture. [OE *beonet* perh. = G *binse* rush]

bent[2], n. Twist, inclination, bias, tendency: *to the top of* one's *b.,* to heart's content. [f. BEND[3] on F anal. of *descent, extent*]

bent[3]. See BEND[3].

Be·nthamism, n. Greatest happiness of the greatest number as guiding principle of ethics. So **Be·nthami**TE[1] (1) n. [Jeremy *Bentham,* 1748-1832; see -ISM (3)]

ben trova·to (-ah-), a. Well invented, characteristic if not true. [It.]

benu·mb (-ŭm), v.t. Make torpid, insensible, powerless, (usu. of cold); paralyse (mind, action). [earlier *benum* (cf. *dumb, limb*) f. OE *benumen* p.p. of *beniman* deprive (BE- + *niman* cf. G *nehmen* take)]

be·nzene, n. An aromatic hydro-carbon got from coal-tar & represented by derivatives in all coal-tar products (formerly, & still in trade use, called *benzol, -ole*). [BENZ(O)- + -ENE]

be·nzine, n. Mixture of liquid hydrocarbons got from mineral oils & used for removing grease-stains (in trade use often called *benzoline* or *benzene*). [foll. + -INE[5]]

benz(o)-, forming derivatives of foll.

be·nzoin (-ōĭn *or* -oin), n. (Also *gum b., benjamin*) fragrant aromatic resin of

Javanese tree. Hence **benzō·ic** a. [earlier *benjoin* through F, Sp., It., f. Arab. *luban jawi* frankincense of Java (*lo-* being dropped in Rom. as if the article)]

be·nzol, -ole, n. = BENZENE. [BENZ(O)- + -OL]

be·nzoline (-ēn, -ĭn), n. = BENZINE. [prec. + -INE⁵]

bequea·th (-dh), v.t. Leave (*to* person) by will (personalty; cf. DEVISE); transmit to posterity (example &c.). [OE *becwethan* f. BE-(3) + *cwethan* say, see QUOTH]

beque·st, n. Bequeathing; thing bequeathed. [ME *biquyste* prob. for *bicwis* (BE- + *cwis* saying cf. prec.; for *-t* cf. BEHEST)]

bera·te, v.t. (now chiefly U.S.). Scold. [BE- + RATE³]

Ber·ber, n. & a. (Member) of the N.-African stock including the aboriginal races of Barbary, speaking allied languages. [f. Arab. *barbar* (*barbara* talk confusedly) or perh. f. Gk *barbaros* BARBAROUS]

ber·berry, n. See BARBERRY.

bere, n. Barley, esp. of six-rowed or four-rowed kinds. [OE]

berea·ve, v.t. (*bereaved* or *bereft*). Rob, dispossess, *of* (usu. of immaterial things, as life, hope); leave desolate (esp. in p.p., usu. *bereaved* in this sense); (of death &c.) deprive of a relation, wife, &c., whence **berea·ve**MENT n. [com.-Teut.; OE *beréafian* cf. G *berauben*; see BE-(2), REAVE v.]

berg, n. = ICEBERG.

ber·gamot¹, n. Tree of orange & lemon kind; perfume extracted from its fruit. [f. *Bergamo* town in Italy]

ber·gamot², n. Kind of pear. [f. F *bergamotte* f. It. *bergamotta* f. Turk. *begarmudi* prince's pear]

ber·gschrund (bărgshrōō-), n. (mountaineering). Crevasse or gap at junction of steep upper slope with glacier or nevé. [G]

berhy·me, v.t. Write verses about, lampoon; put (matter) into rhymed form. [BE- (6) + RHYME n.]

bĕ·ribĕri, n. Disease like dropsy prevalent in India. [Cingalese, f. *beri* weakness]

Berkeleian (barklē·*an*), n. & a. (Follower) of Berkeley or his philosophy, which denied the objective existence of the material world. [Bishop *Berkeley*, d. 1753; see -EAN]

Berli·n, n. & a. Four-wheeled covered carriage with hooded seat behind (also *berline*); *B. black*, iron-varnish; *B. iron*, for casts; *B. warehouse*, shop for *B. wool*, fine dyed knitting wool; *B. gloves*, knitted. [*B.* in Germany]

berm, n. Ledge in fortification between ditch & base of parapet. [f. F *berme* cf. ON *barmr* brim]

Ber·nardine, a. & n. = CISTERCIAN.

be·rry¹, n. (Pop.) any small roundish juicy fruit without stone; (Bot.) fruit with seeds enclosed in pulp; egg in fish-roe (*in b.*, of hen-lobster carrying eggs). Hence (-)**be·rri**ED² a. [com.-Teut., cf. G *beere*, Goth. *basi*]

be·rry², v.i. Come into b., fill out; go gathering bb. [f. prec.]

bersaglieri (It.), n. pl. Italian sharpshooters.

ber·serk(er), n. Wild Norse warrior fighting with mad frenzy. [f. Icel. *berserkr* prob. = bear-sark, bear-coat]

berth¹, n. Convenient sea-room (*give wide b. to*, avoid); room for ship to swing at anchor; ship's place at wharf; proper place for anything; sleeping-place; situation, appointment. [prob. f. BEAR v. (make room by bearing off) + -TH¹; of same formation, but prob. later & independent, as BIRTH (early spellings coincide)]

berth², v.t. Moor (ship) in suitable place; provide sleeping place for. [f. prec.]

ber·tha, berthe (-th), n. Deep falling (usu. lace) collar to low-necked dress. *Big Bertha*, German gun of vast range used in bombarding Paris in the great war. [F (*-e*), the woman's name]

Bertillon system, n. Method of identifying criminals by measurements. [French anthropologist b. 1853]

bĕ·ryl, n. Precious stone, pale-green passing into light blue, yellow, & white; mineral species including also the emerald. [OF, f. L f. Gk *bērullos*]

bery·llium, n. A metal, = GLUCINUM. [prec. + -IUM]

besee·ch (-tsh), v.t. (*-sought* pr. -sawt). Ask earnestly for (esp. *leave* &c.); entreat (person, person *that* or *to* do or *for* thing). [BE-(2) + ME *secen, sechen, seken,* SEEK]

besee·ching, a. Suppliant (of look, tone, &c.). Hence **besee·ching**LY² adv. [-ING²]

besee·m, v.t. Suit, be fitting or creditable to, (abs., or with *well, ill,* &c.). Hence **besee·ming**LY² adv. [BE-(2) + SEEM]

bese·t, v.t. (*-tting*, past & p.p. *-set*). Hem in, set upon, (person); occupy & make impassable (road &c.); (of difficulties, temptations, &c.) assail, encompass, (*besetting sin*, that most frequently tempts one.) [OE *besettan* (BE-(1), & see SET v.)]

bese·tment, n. Besetting sin; being hemmed in. [prec. + -MENT]

beshrew·, v.t. (Now only as mock-heroic imprecation) plague take (*me*, person, or thing). [BE-(2) + ME *schrewen* to curse f. SHREW]

besi·de, prep. (formerly also adv. = foll.). Close to, by, near; on a level with, compared with; wide of (*mark, question,* &c.); *b. oneself*, out of one's wits. [OE *be sīdan* BY, SIDE n.)]

besi·des, adv. & prep. In addition (to),

moreover; otherwise, else, (than); (neg. & interrog.) except. [prec. + -ES]

besie·ge, v.t. Invest, lay siege to; crowd round; assail with requests. Hence **besie·ger**[1] n. [ME *besegen* f. BE-(1) + *segen* f. OF *asegier* f. LL *assediare* (AD- + *sedium* f. L *sedēre* SIT)]

beslă·ver, v.t. Cover with slaver; flatter fulsomely. [BE-(1) + SLAVER v.]

beslo·bber, v.t. = prec.; also, kiss effusively. [BE-(1) + SLOBBER v.]

beslu·bber, v.t. Besmear. [BE-(1) + SLUBBER v.]

besmear·, v.t. Smear with greasy or sticky stuff (also of the stuff as subj.). [OE *bismierwan* see BE-(1) & SMEAR v.]

besmir·ch (-tsh), v.t. Soil, discolour; dim brightness of. [BE-(1) + SMIRCH v.]

bē·som (*or* -z-), n., & v.t. (Sweep with) bundle of twigs tied round stick for sweeping, kind of broom. [OE *besema*, com.-WG cf. G *besen* Du. *bezem*]

beso·t, v.t. (-tt-). Stupefy mentally or morally. [BE-(4) + SOT]

besough·t. See BESEECH.

bespa·ngle, v.t. Set about with spangles. [BE-(6) + SPANGLE]

bespa·tter, v.t. Spatter (object) all over; spatter (liquid &c.) about; cover with abuse or flattery. [BE-(1) + SPATTER]

bespea·k, v.t. (past *-spoke*, p.p. *-spoke*, *spoken*). Engage beforehand; order (goods); stipulate for; speak to (poet.); suggest, be evidence of; *bespoke bootmaker* &c. (prop. *bespoke-boot maker*), opposed to ready-made dealer. [OE *besprecan*; com.-WG cf. G *besprechen*; see BE-(3) & SPEAK]

bespre·nt, p.p. (poet.). Sprinkled (*with*); scattered about. [f. OE *besprengan* f. BE-(1) + OTeut. *sprangjan* causal of *springan* SPRING v.]

bespri·nkle, v.t. Sprinkle or strew over (*with*; lit. & fig.; also with the liquid &c. as subj. or obj.). [ME *besprengil* frequent. of OE *besprengan*, see prec. & -LE]

Be·ssemer, a. & n. *B. process*, for decarbonizing & desiliconizing pig-iron by passing currents of air through it when molten & so making *B. iron*, *B. steel*, or *B.* [Sir H. *B.*, inventor 1856]

best[1], a. & adv. (superl. of *good*, *well*). Of, in, the most excellent kind, way (often, like *good*, *well*, used for specific adjj. & advv. as *kindest*, *most skilfully*). Phrr.: *the b. part*, most; *had b.*, would find it wisest to; one's *b. girl* (slang), sweetheart; *b. man*, bridegroom's supporter; *b. seller* (slang), popular novel &c.; *put b. leg* or *foot foremost*, go at full pace; *bad is the b.*, no good event possible; *with the b.*, as well as anyone; *do* one's *b.*, all one can; *be at* one's *b.*, in the b. state; one's *b.* or *Sunday b.*, b. clothes; *have the b. of it*, win in argument &c.; *make the b. of things*, be contented; *b. abused* (colloq.) most violently or generally abused (*the b. abused book of the year*); *make the b. of* one's *way*, go as fast as possible; *at b.*, on the most hopeful view; *did it for the b.*, with good intentions; *to the b. of* one's *power* &c., as far as one's power &c. allows; *the b. is the enemy of the good*, too high standard bars progress. [OE *betst*; com.-Teut. f. OTeut. *batist* cf. BETTER]

best[2], v.t. (colloq.). Get the better of, circumvent, worst. [f. prec.]

bestea·d (-ĕd), v.t. & i. Avail, help. [BE-(2) + STEAD]

beste·d, p.p. (With *ill*, *hard*, *sore*, &c.) situated, circumstanced, pressed. [ME *bistad* f. BE-(2) + *stad* f. ON *staddr* p.p. of *stethja* stop]

bĕ·stial, a. Of, like, a beast or beasts esp. quadrupeds; brutish, barbarous; depraved, lustful, obscene. Hence or cogn. **bestiă·lity** n., **be·stialize**(3) v.t., **be·stially**[2] adv. [OF, f. L *bestialis* (*bestia* BEAST + -AL)]

be·stiary, n. Medieval moralizing treatise on beasts. [f. med. L *bestiarium* menagerie f. L *bestia* beast]

bestir·, v. refl. (-rr-). Exert, rouse, (one*self*). [OE *bestyrian* f. BE-(2) + *styrian* STIR v.]

bestow· (-ō), v.t. Deposit; provide with lodging; confer (thing) *upon* (person) as gift. Hence **bestow·al**(2) n. [ME *bistowen*, see BE-(2), STOW v.]

bestrew·, v.t. (p.p. *-ewed* or *-ewn*). Strew (surface) *with*; scatter (things) about; lie scattered over. [OE *bestréowian* see BE-(1) & STREW; p.p. *-ewn* is recent, but now common]

bestri·de, v.t. (past *-ode*; p.p. *-idden*, *-id*, *-ode*). Get or sit upon (horse, chair) with legs astride; stand astride over (place or fallen friend or enemy; also fig. of rainbow &c.). [OE *bestrīdan*, see BE-(3), STRIDE v.]

bet, n., & v.i. & t. (bet). (Engagement to) risk one's money &c., risk (an amount &c.) against another's on the result of a doubtful event (*on* or *against* result or competitor, *that* so-&-so will happen); (slang) *you b.*, you may take it as certain; *betting-book*, for entering bb. in. [perh. f. ABET v. (or obs. n.); whether vb or n. is prior is doubtful]

bē·ta, n. Second letter (B, β) of Gk. alphabet, used as name of second star in a constellation, & in other numberings. [Gk]

beta·ke, v. refl. (-took, -taken). Commit one*self to* (i. e. try) some course or means; convey one*self to* (i. e. go to) a place or person. [ME; BE-, TAKE]

bē·tel, n. Leaf of *Piper betle*, which Indians chew with areca-nut parings; (hence by mistake) *b.-nut*, the areca nut. [Port. f. Malayalam *veṭṭila*]

bête noire (bāt nwahr), n. (One's) abomination. [F]

bĕ·thel, n. Hallowed spot (*Gen.* xxviii. 19); nonconformist chapel. [Heb. *beth-el* house of God]

bethe·sda (-z-), n. Nonconformist chapel. [*John* v. 2; Heb., = house of mercy]

bethi·nk, v. refl. (-thought) (alw. with *self* or archaic refl. *me, him,* &c.). Reflect, stop to think; remind one*self of, how,* or *that*; take into one's head *to*. [OE *bethencan,* com.-Teut. cf. G *bedenken*; see BE-(3), THINK]

beti·de, v.i. & t. (only in 3 sing. pres. subj.). Happen (*whate'er b.*); happen to (*woe b. him* &c.). [ME *bitiden* see BE-(2), TIDE v.]

beti·mes, adv. Early in day, year, life, &c.; in good time. [*by time* (ME) + -ES]

bêtise (bātē·z), n. Foolish, ill-timed, remark or action. [F]

beto·ken, v.t. Augur, indicate, suggest. [ME *bitacnien* cf. G *bezeichnen,* see BE-, TOKEN]

bĕ·tony, n. Purple-flowered plant. [f. F *bétoine* f. LL *betonia* f. L *vettonica* f. name of Gaulish tribe]

betook. See BETAKE.

betray·, v.t. Give up treacherously (person or thing *to* enemy); be disloyal to; lead astray; reveal treacherously; reveal involuntarily; be evidence or symptom of. Hence **betray·**AL(2), **betray·**ER[1], nn. [ME *betraien* f. BE-(2) + obs. *tray* f. OF *traïr* f. L *tradere* (*trans* over + *dare* give)]

betro·th (-ōdh), v.t. Bind with a promise to marry (usu. in p.p.). Hence **betro·th**AL(2) n., **betro·th**ED[1] a. & n. [ME *bitreuthien* f. BE-(6) + *treuthe* TRUTH, later assimilated to TROTH]

be·tter[1], a., adv., & n. (comp. of *good, well*). Of, in, a more excellent kind, way (often, like *good, well,* for specific wd as *more virtuous, more plentifully*). Phrr.: *no b. than,* practically; *no b. than* one *should be,* improper; one's *b. feelings,* higher self; *b. part,* most; one's *b. half,* wife; *for b. for worse,* on terms of accepting all results (see Prayer Book, Marriage Service); *b. than* (with number &c.), above; *had b.,* would find it wiser to; *be, get, b.,* less unwell; *b. than* one's *word,* more liberal than one promised to be; one's *b.,* more skilful person; one's *bb.,* people of higher rank; *get the b. of,* defeat, outwit; *know b.,* refuse to accept statement, not be so foolish (as to do something); *think b. of it,* change one's mind; *change for the b.*; *b. off,* richer, more comfortable; *the b. the day the b. the deed* (retort to charge of Sabbath-breaking). [OE *betera*; com.-Teut. cf. G *besser* f. OTeut. *batizon-* f. *bat-* see BOOT[3] + -ER[3]]

be·tter[2], v.t. & i. Amend, improve; surpass (a feat &c.); *b. oneself,* get b. situation, wages, &c. Hence **be·tter**MENT n. [ME *beteren* cf. G *bessern* & see prec.]

be·tter[3]**,-or,** n. One who bets. [BET + -ER[1]]

betwee·n, prep. & adv. (the orig. restriction to relations involving only *two* limits &c. still tends to be observed wherever AMONG is adequate for higher numbers). In, into, along, or across, a space, line, or route, bounded by (two or more points, lines, &c.); in, into, along, or across, an interval; separating; connecting; intermediately in place, time, or order (to); owing partly to, partaking of, shared by, (each); to & fro (*go-b.*); to & from (*plies b. London & Brighton*); reciprocally on the part of; confined to (*b. ourselves, b. you & me*); by combination of; taking one & rejecting the other of (*choose b.*). *Far b.,* at wide intervals; *b. cup & lip,* of dashed hopes; *b.-maid* (now usu. *tweeny*), servant assisting two others, e.g. cook & housemaid; *b. wind & water,* at a vulnerable point; *b. devil & deep sea,* with no escape; *betwixt & b.,* half-&-half; *stand b.,* mediate, be protector; *b. whiles,* in the intervals. [OE *betwéonum, betwéon,* (BE- + dat. & acc. pl. of distrib. num., = L *bini,* of TWO); orig. constr., *bi* (*sæm* &c.) *tweonum* = by (seas &c.) twain]

betwi·xt, prep. & adv. (Poet., archaic, or dial., for) BETWEEN. [earlier *betwixen* (BE- + OSax. *twisc* f. OTeut. *twiskjo-* twofold cf. G *zwischen* between)]

Beu·lah, n. Nonconformist chapel. [*Is.* lxii. 4]

bĕ·vel[1] (-vl), n. Joiner's & mason's tool for setting off angles; a slope from the horizontal or vertical, surface so sloping; *b. edge,* as in a chisel; *b.-gear,* working one shaft from another at angle to it by *b.-wheels,* cogged wheels with working face oblique to axis. [f. OF **bevel* (now *beveau*) etym. dub.]

bĕ·vel[2], v.t. & i. (-ll-). Reduce (square edge) to, take, a slope. [f. prec.]

bĕ·verage (-ĭj), n. Drinking-liquor. [f. OF *bevrage* (*beivre,* now *boire,* f. L *bibere* drink + -AGE)]

bĕ·vy, n. Company (prop. of ladies, roes, quails, larks). [etym. dub.; perh. = drinking company (cf. prec.)]

bewai·l, v.t. & i. Wail (over), mourn (for). [BE-(3) + WAIL v.]

beware·, v.i. & t. (not inflected, and used only where *be* is the vbl part required, as *I will b.,* but not *I b.*). Be cautious, take heed; take heed *of, lest, how, that not.* [as now used, f. BE v. + OE *wær* cautious, but with traces of OE vbs *warian, bewarian,* take care of, defend, (surviving in 'Ware holes!')]

bewi·lder, v.t. Lead astray, perplex, confuse. Hence **bewi·ldering**LY[2] adv., **bewi·lder**MENT n. [BE-(6) + obs. *wilder(n)* WILDERNESS]

bewi·tch, v.t. Affect by magic, put a spell on; delight exceedingly, whence **bewi·tch**ING[2] a., **bewi·tching**LY[2] adv., **bewi·tch**MENT n. [ME *biwicchen* f. BE-(2) + OE *wiccian* enchant f. *wicca* WITCH n.]

bewray (bĭrā·), v.t. Reveal, esp. involuntarily. [BE-(2) + OE *wrégan* accuse cf. G *rügen*)]

bey, bey·lic, (bā-), nn. (*Bey*) Turkish governor; (*beylic*) his district. [formerly *beg* f. Osmanli *bey*]

beyo·nd, adv., prep., & n. At, to, the farther side (of), past, outside, besides; later than; out of reach, comprehension, or range, of (*b. measure*, exceedingly); surpassing; more than (with objective case, as *you have prospered b. me*); (neg. & interrog.) except. (N.) *the b.*, the future life, the unknown; *the back of b.*, the remotest corner of the world. [OE *begeondan* (BE- about + *geond* across + *-ana* from); cf. YON & G *jen-* that]

bĕ·zant (*also* bĭză·nt), n. Gold coin (10/- to 20/-) current in Europe from 9th c.; also silver (1/- to 2/-). [f. OF *besan* f. L *Byzantius* (*nummus* coin) of Byzantium]

bĕ·zel, n. Sloped edge of chisel &c.; oblique faces of cut gem; groove holding watch-glass or gem. [f. OF **bezel* (now *bizeau*) etym. dub.]

bezi·que, (-ēk), n. Card-game for two or four. [f. F *besigue* etym. dub.]

bhang (bă-), n. Indian hemp used as narcotic & intoxicant (smoked, chewed, eaten, & drunk). [earlier *bangue, bang*; f. Hind. &c. *bhang*]

bi-, pref. f. L *bi-* (earlier *dui-*, cf. Gk *di-*, Skr. *dvi*) twice, doubly, having two ——, freely used in English, esp. with wds f. L, but also with E wds (*bi-weekly*). (1) Adjj., (a) having two ——, as *bicentral, bicristate*; (b) doubly, in two ways, as *biconcave*; (c) in Bot. & Zool., twice over, i.e. divided into similarly divided parts, as *bipinnate*; (d) lasting for two ——, appearing every two ——, as *biennial*; (e) appearing twice in a ——, as *biannual, bi-monthly*; many wds are ambiguous between this & the last, & *semi-, half-*, would be better here; (f) joining two —— as *bi-parietal.* (2) Nouns, double, as *bi-millionaire.* (3) Chem. nouns & adjj., having twice the amount of acid, base, &c., indicated by the simple wd, as *bicarbonate.*

bī·as[1], n. (In bowls) lopsided form of a bowl, its oblique course, the weight or influence deflecting it; (metaph. from bowls) inclination, predisposition (*towards*), prejudice, influence; (Dressmaking &c.; as a., n., & adv.) *cut on the b., cut b.*, cut obliquely across the texture, *b. band* &c., band so cut. [f. F *biais* oblique, obliquity, etym. dub.; L *bifacem* nom. *-fax* two-faced is suggested]

bī·as[2], v.t. (-s- *or* -ss-). Give a bias to, influence (usu. unfairly), inspire with prejudice. [f. prec.]

bia·xial, a. With two (optic) axes. [BI-(1 a) + AXIAL]

bib[1], v.i. Drink much or often. [perh. f. L *bibere* drink]

bib[2], n. Child's chin-cloth to keep dress-front clean; adult's apron-top (*best b. & tucker*, best clothes). [perh. f. prec.]

bib[3], n. A fish, the whiting-pout. [from an inflatable membrane on head resembling prec.]

bībā·sic, a. Having two (chem.) bases. [BI-(1 a) + BASE[1] + -IC]

bi·bber, n., **bi·bbing,** n. & a. Tippler, tippling, (usu. in comb., as *wine* &c. *-b.*). [BIB v., -ER[1], -ING[1, 2]]

Bī·ble, n. The Scriptures of the Old & New Testament, a copy of them, a particular edition of them (BREECHes, PRINTERs', VINEGAR, WICKED, *B.*); authoritative text-book; *B.-oath*, taken on the B.; *B.-reader*, one employed to read the B. from house to house; *B.-Christian*, a member of sect so called; *B.-clerk*, student at some Oxford colleges who reads lessons in chapel. [F, f. LL f. Gk *biblia* books pl. of *biblion* dim. of *biblos* papyrus bark]

bi·blical, a. Of, concerning, contained in, the Bible. [f. med. L *biblicus* (see -IC, -AL]

bi·blico-, comb. of BIBLICAL, as *biblico-poetical.* [-O-]

bĭblio-, comb. form of *biblion* see BIBLE. Of books or the Bible.

bibliograph-, See foll., & -GRAPH, -GRAPHER, -GRAPHIC, -GRAPHY.

biblio·graphy, n. History of books, their authorship, editions, &c.; book containing such details; list of books of any author, printer, country, subject. [f. Gk *bibliographia*; see BIBLIO-, -GRAPHY]

bibliŏ·later, n., **bibliŏ·latrous,** a., **bibliŏ·latry,** n. Worshipper of, worshipping, worship of, books, a book, or the Bible. [BIBLIO-, -LATRY]

bibliomā·nia, bibliomā·niac, nn. Rage for collecting, enthusiastic collector of, books. [see BIBLIO-, -MANIA]

bi·bliophil(e), n. Book-fancier, -lover. Hence **bibliŏ·phil**ISM(3), **bibliŏ·phil**IST (3), nn. [F *bibliophile* (BIBLIO-, -PHIL)]

bi·bliopole, bĭbliŏ·poly, nn. Seller, selling, of (esp. rare) books. [f. L (*-la*) f. Gk *bibliopōlēs* (BIBLIO-, *-pōlēs* -seller)]

bi·būlous, a. Absorbent; addicted to drink. Hence **bi·bulous**LY[2] adv. [f. L *bibulus* freely drinking (*bibere* drink) + -OUS]

bică·meral, a. With two (legislative) chambers. [BI-(1 a) + L *camera* CHAMBER + -AL]

bīcar·bonate. See BI-(3).

bīce, n. *B.* or *blue b., green b.*, pigments made from blue, green, hydrocarbonate of copper; similar pigment made from smalt &c.; dull shades of blue and green given by these. [f. F *bis* dark-coloured f. It. *bigio* etym. dub.]

For words in *bi-*, *bin-*, not given consult BI-, BIN-.

bīce·ntenary (*also* -ĕntē·n-), a. & n. (Festival) of the two-hundredth anniversary. [BI- (1 a) + L *centenarius* CENTENARY; used of years by confusion with *centennial*]

bīcente·nnial, a. & n. Lasting, occurring every, two hundred years; (n.) = prec. [BI-(1 d) + CENTENNIAL]

bīcĕ·phalous, a. Two-headed. [BI-(1 a) + -CEPHALOUS]

bī·ceps, n. Muscle with double head or attachment, esp. the upper-arm flexor; muscularity. [L, = two-headed f. BI-(1 a) + *caput* head]

bīchlor·ide, n. Compound in which double amount of chlorine combines with metal &c. [BI-(3)]

bīchrō·mate, n. Salt with double amount of chromic acid. [BI-(3)]

bi·cker, v.i. Quarrel; (of stream, rain, &c.) brawl, patter; (of flame, light, &c.) flash, glitter. [ME *bikeren* perh. frequent. of obs. *bike* to thrust, pierce]

bīcu·spid, a. & n. (Tooth) with two cusps. [BI-(1 a) + L *cuspis -idis* point]

bī·cycle, n., & v.i. (Ride on) two-wheeled velocipede. Hence **bi·cycl**IST(1) n. [F, f. BI- (1 a) + Gk *kuklos* wheel]

bid[1], v.t. & i. (past *bad, bade, bid,* p.p. *bidden, bid*): Command to (usu. without *to*; now literary, archaic, or poet., for *tell* with *to*; also abs., as *do as you are b.*); invite (esp. in *bidden guest*); salute (person) with *welcome, farewell,* &c.; offer price, offer (a certain price) *for* (past & p.p. *bid*), whence **bi·dd**ER[1] n.; proclaim (*defiance, the banns*); *b. fair to do,* show promise of doing; *bidding-prayer,* inviting congregation to join. [mixture of (1) OE *béodan* offer, proclaim, cf. G *bieten* f. OTeut. *beudan* cf. Skr. *budh-* present & perh. Gk *puth-* ascertain, (2) OE *biddan* press, beg, cf. G *bitten* f. OTeut. *bidjan* cf. Skr. *bâdhate* press; the variety of forms is due to this confusion]

bid[2], n. Offer of price, esp. at auction; *make a b. for,* (fig.) make an attempt to secure (favour, the prize, &c.). [f. prec.]

bi·ddable, a. Obedient. [-ABLE]

bi·dding, n. In vbl senses; esp., the offers at auction; a command. [-ING[1] (1)]

bide, v.t. & i. (Archaic and poet. for ABIDE, but the regular wd in) *b.* one's *time,* await best opportunity. [com.-Teut.; OE *bídan* cf. OSax. *bîdan,* OHG *bîtan*]

bidet (bē·dā), n. Raised narrow bath that can be bestridden. [F, = pony, etym. dub.]

bīe·nnial, a. & n. Lasting, recurring every, two years; (n., bot.) plant that springs one year, & flowers, fructifies, & perishes, the next. Hence **bīe·nnial**LY[2] adv. [f. L *biennis* f. BI-(1 d) + *annus* year + -AL]

bienséance (F), n. Decorum.

bier (bēr), n. Movable stand on which coffin (or corpse) is taken to grave. [com. -Teut.; OE *bær* cf. G *bahre* & see BARROW; mod. spelling affected by F *bière*]

biff, n., & v.t. (U.S. slang). A smart blow; (vb) strike (person). [?]

bi·ffin, n. Deep-red cooking-apple. [= *beefing* f. BEEF + -ING(3) with ref. to the colour]

bī·fid, a. Divided by a deep cleft into two parts. [f. L BI(*fidus* f. st. of *findere* cut)]

bīfō·liate (-*at*), a. Of two leaves. [BI-(1 a) + L *folium* leaf + -ATE[2] (2)]

bī·furcāte[1], v.t. & i. Divide into two branches, fork. [f. foll., first in p.p. *-ated*]

bī·furcate[2] (-*at*), a. Forked (esp. in Bot.). [f. med. L BI(*furcatus* f. *furca* fork, -ATE[2])]

bīfurca·tion, n. Division into two branches; the point of division; the branches or one of them. [f. BIFURCATE[1]]

big, a. & adv. Large; grown up; pregnant (*b. with young,* also *b.-bellied,* & esp. fig. as *b. with fate, news*); important (*a b. man*; *the B.* 3, 4, 5, &c., slang, the predominant few in any affair, esp. the SUPREME Council; *get, grow, too b. for* one's *boots,* slang, become conceited, put on airs; *b. bug,* slang, = *bigwig*); boastful(ly) (*b. words, looks*; *look or talk b.*); (as distinctive epithet) *b. drum, toe, game*; *b.-horn,* Rocky-Mountain sheep; *bigwig,* person of importance. Hence **bi·g**NESS n. [?]

bi·gamist, n. Man (woman) with two wives (husbands). [see BIGAMY, -IST]

bi·gamous, a. Guilty of, involving, bigamy, [f. med. L *bigamus* see foll. + -OUS]

bi·gamy, n. Having two wives or husbands at once. [f. F *bigamie* (-Y[1]) f. OF *bigame* bigamous f. med. L BI(*gamus* f. Gk *-gamos* -married)]

bigaroo·, -oo·n, n. Large white heart-cherry. [f. F *bigarreau* f. *bigarre* variegated]

bīgĕ·minal, a. Arranged in two pairs. [BI-(1 c) + L *geminus* twin + -AL]

bigg, big, n. Four-rowed barley. [f. ON *bygg* = OE *béow* grain, cf. Gk *phu-*, Skr. *bhu-*, grow]

bight (bīt), n. Loop of a rope; curve, recess, of coast, river, &c., bay. [OE *byht* cf. G *bucht* f. OTeut. *bugan* to BOW]

bi·got, n. One who holds irrespective of reason, & attaches disproportionate weight to, some creed or view. Hence **bi·got**ED[2] a. [F, etym. dub.; *Visigoth,* & Sp. *bigote* moustache, have been suggested]

bi·gotry, n. Conduct, mental state, act, of a bigot. [f. F *bigoterie*; see BIGOT, -RY]

bi·jou (bē·zhōō), n. (pl. *-oux,* pr. -ōō) & a. Jewel, trinket; small & elegant. [F, prob. f. Breton *bizou* ring with stone f. *biz* = Corn. *bis,* W *bys,* finger]

For words in *bi-*, *bin-*, not given consult BI-, BIN-.

bijou·terie (-zhōō-, or as F), n. Jewelry, trinkets, &c. [F, see prec. & -RY]

bike, n., & v.i. (Abbrev. for) BICYCLE.

bilă·teral, a. Of, on, with, two sides; affecting, between, two parties. Hence **bila·teral**LY[2] adv. [BI-(1 a) + L *latus -eris* side + -AL]

bi·lberry, n. Fruit of dwarf hardy N.-European shrub growing on heaths & in mountain woods (also *blaeberry, whortleberry*). [cf. Da. *böllebær*]

bi·lbo, n. Sword. [f. *Bilbao* in Spain]

bi·lboes, n. pl. Iron bar with sliding shackles for prisoner. [?]

bile, n. Brownish-yellow bitter fluid secreted by the liver to aid digestion; derangement of the b.; peevishness; *b.-stone,* calculus in gall-bladder. [F, f. L *bilis*]

bilge[1], n. Nearly horizontal part of ship's bottom, inside or out; the foulness that collects inside the b.; belly of barrel; *b.-keel,* timber fastened under b. to prevent rolling; *b.-water,* stinking water collected in b. [corruption of BULGE f. OF *boulge* now *bouge*]

bilge[2], v.t. & i. Stave in the b. of, spring a leak in the b.; bulge, swell out. [f. prec.]

bi·liary, a. Of the bile. [f. F *biliaire,* see BILE, -ARY[2]]

bili·ngual (-ĭnggwal), a. Having, speaking, spoken or written in, two languages. [f. L *bilinguis* f. BI-(1 a) + *lingua* tongue + -AL]

bi·lious, a. Liable to, affected by, arising from, derangement of the bile; peevish. Hence **bi·lious**LY[2] adv., **bi·lious**NESS n. [f. F *bilieux* f. L *biliosus*; see BILE, -OSE[1], -OUS]

-bility, suf. See -BLE.

bilk, v.t. Evade payment of (creditor, bill); cheat, give the slip to. [etym. dub.; perh. = BALK; earliest use in cribbage, = spoil opponent's score]

bill[1], n. Obsolete weapon, halberd; (also *billhook*) concave-edged lopping implement for pruning &c. [com.-WG cf. G *bille*]

bill[2], n. Bird's beak (esp. when slender, flattened, or weak, & in pigeons & web-footed birds); muzzle of platypus; narrow promontory (*Portland B.* &c.); point of anchor-fluke. Hence **-bill**ED[2] a. [OE *bile* etym. dub.]

bill[3], v.i. Stroke b. with b. (of doves); exchange caresses (esp. *b. & coo*). [f. prec.]

bill[4], n. Draft of proposed Act of Parliament; (Law) written statement of (esp. plaintiff's) case (*find a true b., ignore the b.,* forms by which Grand Jury sends, does not send, case for trial); note of charges for goods delivered or services rendered; poster, placard, programme of entertainment; (also *b. of exchange*) written order by drawer to drawee to pay sum on given date to drawer or to named payee (if drawn not against value received, but to raise money on credit, the b. is known as an *accommodation b.*); *b. of fare,* list of dishes to be served, menu, (fig.) programme; *b. of health,* certificate regarding infectious disease on ship or in port at time of sailing (*clean b. of h.,* no disease); *b. of lading,* ship-master's detailed receipt to consignor; *b. of sale,* transferring personal property, or authorizing its seizure by lender of money if payment is delayed; *bb. of mortality* (hist.), weekly return of deaths in London and district (*within the bb. o. m.,* in or near London); *b.-poster, -sticker,* man who pastes up placards; *b.-broker, -discounter,* dealer in, discounter of, bb. of exchange. [ME *bille* f. L *bulla* amulet in medieval sense of *seal, papal bull, document*]

bill[5], v.t. Announce, put in the programme; *billed to appear* &c., announced as going to; plaster with placards. [f. prec.]

bi·llet[1], n. Order requiring person to board & lodge the soldier bearing it (*every bullet has its b.,* hits only by providential order), place where troops are lodged; destination; appointment, situation. [ME *billette* dim. of *bille* BILL[4]]

bi·llet[2], v.t. Quarter (soldiers) *on* (town, householder, &c.), *in, at.* [f. prec.]

bi·llet[3], n. Thick piece of firewood; small bar of metal; short roll inserted at intervals in hollow moulding (Norman archit.). [f. F *billette* & *billot* dim. of *bille* tree-trunk etym. dub.]

billet-doux (bĭ·lidōō·), n. Love-letter (jocular). [F]

bi·lliards, n. pl. Game played with cues & ivory balls on cloth-covered table; *billiard-marker,* attendant keeping the score. [f. F *billard* cue dim. of *bille* see BILLET[3]]

bi·llingsgate, n. Abuse, violent invective. [from the scolding of fishwomen in *Billingsgate* market]

bi·llion, n. A million millions; (in U.S.) a thousand millions. [F, coined in 16th c. out of BI- & *million* to denote the second power of a million; meaning afterwards changed in France (so U.S.) but not in England]

bi·llow[1], n. Great wave; (poet.) *the* sea; (fig.) anything that sweeps along, as sound, troops. Hence **bi·llow**Y[2] a. [f. ON *bylgja* f. com.-Teut. *belgan* swell]

bi·llow[2], v.i. Rise, move, in bb. [f. prec.]

bi·lly, n. (Austral.). Tin can used as kettle &c. in camping out. [prob. the male name].

bi·llyboy, n. One-masted trading barge. [?]

bi·llycock, n. Round-crowned hard felt hat, bowler. [*bully-cocked hat* 1721 = cocked after the fashion of the bullies]

bi·lly-goat, n. Male goat. [*Billy* male name]
bīlō·bate (-*at*), a. With two lobes. [BI-(1 a), & see LOBE, -ATE²(2)]
bi·ltong, n. Strips of sun-dried meat. [S.-Afr. Du. f. *bil* buttock (from which it is cut) + *tong* tongue (which it looks like)]
bī·manal, bī·manous, aa., **bī·mane,** n. (Individual) of the *Bimana* or two-handed order of mammalia, two-handed. [*bimane* F f. BI-(1 a) + L *manus* hand, & see -AL, -OUS]
bi·mbo, n. Kind of punch (drink). [= BUMBO]
bīmeta·llic, a., **bīmĕ·tallism,** n., **bime·tallist,** n. & a. Of, system of, advocate of, using both gold & silver as legal tender to any amount at fixed ratio to each other. (f. F *bimétallique* 1869; see BI-(1 a), METALLIC, -ISM(3), -IST(2)]
bin, n. Receptacle (orig. of wicker, now usu. fixed, of wood) for corn, coal, dust, bottled wine, &c.; wine from a special b.; canvas receptacle used in hop-picking. [OE *binn* perh. f. LL *benna* hamper cf. It. *benna* wicker sleigh]
bin-, sometimes used for BI- before vowels, perh. on anal. of F *binocle* (f. L *bini,* not *bi-, oculi*) and of *a an, co- con-*; for meanings see BI-.
bī·nary, a. Dual, of or involving pairs; (Mus.) *b. measure,* of two beats to bar; *b. form,* of movement with two themes; (Astron.) *b. system,* two stars revolving round common centre or each other; (Chem.) *b. compound,* of two elements, *b. theory,* making all acids compounds of hydrogen, all salts similar compounds with metal; (Math.) *b. scale,* with 2 (not 10) as base of notation. [f. L *binarius* f. *bini* two together]
bī·nate, a. In pairs. [f. L *bini* two together + -ATE²(2)]
bīnd¹, v.t. & i. (*bound,* pr. bow-; also archaic p.p. in *bounden duty*). Tie; fasten, attach, *to, on*; put in bonds, restrain; fasten or hold together; be obligatory, exercise authority, impose constraint or duty, upon, (pass.) be required by duty *to* (do something); subject to legal obligation (esp. *b. over to appear, to good behaviour, to keep the peace*; fig., *I'll be bound,* go bail for statement), indenture as apprentice; ratify (*b. the bargain*); make costive; bandage (usu. *b. up*); wreathe (head &c.) *with,* (material) *round, about, on*; edge with braid, iron, &c.; cohere (of snow, &c.); (Bookbind.) fasten (sheets) into stiff, esp. leather, cover (*half-bound,* with leather at back & corners only), *b. up,* together in one vol. [com.-Teut.; OE *bindan* cf. G *binden* f. Aryan *bhendh*]
bīnd², n. Indurated clay between coal strata; (Mus.) curved line between two notes to be sounded continuously; = BINE. [f. prec.]
bī·nder, n. In vbl senses; also or esp.: book-b.; obstetric apparatus; long fencing-withe; tie-beam; through-stone in wall; wisp of straw, part of reaping-machine, for sheaf-binding; loose cover for unbound newspapers &c. [-ER¹]
bī·nding¹, a. Obligatory (*on*). [-ING²]
bī·nding², n. In vbl senses; also, book-cover; braid &c. for protecting raw edges. [-ING¹]
bī·ndweed, n. Kinds of convolvulus & other climbing plants. [BIND¹ + WEED]
bine, n. Flexible shoot; stem of climbing plant, esp. the hop. [orig. dial. form of BIND², now adopted in its place]
bi·nnacle, n. Box on deck holding compass. [earlier *bittacle* f. Sp. *bitácula* f. L *habitaculum* lodge (*habitare* dwell f. *habēre* hold); confusion with BIN]
bīnŏ·cular, a. & n. (Field or opera glass) adapted for two eyes. [f. L *bini* two together + *oculus* eye + -AR¹]
bīnō·mial, a. & n. Consisting of two terms; *B. theorem,* formula for finding any power of a b. without multiplying at length; (n.) algebraic expression of two terms joined by + or —. [f. LL *binomius* (= L *binominis*) having two names, f. BI-(1 a) + *nomen* name]
bīnŏ·minal, a. Of two names (esp. *b. system,* of scientific nomenclature by genus & species). [f. L *binominis* see prec. + -AL]
bio-, comb. form of Gk *bios* (course of) life, which meaning it has in actual borrowings f. Gk, as *biography*; in mod. formations it is extended to include organic life (Gk *zōē*).
bīogĕ·nesis, n. Hypothesis that living matter arises always from living matter. [prec. + Gk GENESIS]
bī·ograph, n. Photographic reproduction of continuous action. [BIO- + -GRAPH]
bīŏ·graphee·, n. Person whose life is written. [formed as correl. to *biographer*; see foll. & -EE]
bīo·graphy, n. Written life of a person; branch of literature dealing with persons' lives; life-course of a living being. So **bio·**GRAPHER n., **bio**GRA·PHIC(AL) aa., **biogra·phical**LY² adv. [f. late Gk *biographia* see BIO-, -GRAPHY]
bīŏ·logy, n. Science of physical life, dealing with the morphology, physiology, origin, & distribution, of animals & plants. So **biolŏ·gic**(AL) aa., **biolŏ·gical**LY² adv., **bīŏ·log**IST n. [BIO-, -LOGY, -LOGIST]
bī·oplasm, bī·oplast, nn. The germinal matter, a small separate portion of it, from which all living things spring. [BIO-

For words in *bi-, bin-,* not given consult BI-, BIN-.

+Gk *plasma*, thing moulded, *plastos* moulded (*plassō* to mould)]

bi·oscope, n. = BIOGRAPH. [BIO-, -SCOPE]

bī·ped, a. & n., **bi·pedal,** a. Two-footed (animal). [f. L *bipes -edis* f. BI-(1 a) + *pes pedis* foot]

bīpi·nnate, a. Having lobes that themselves have lobes. [BI-(1 c) + PINNATE]

bī·plane, n. Two-planed aeroplane. [BI-]

bīpo·lar, a. With two poles or extremities. [BI-(1 a)]

Bīpo·ntine, a. Printed at Zweibrücken (editions of classics). [BI- two + L *pons pontis* bridge (transl. of the name) + -INE[1]]

bīquadră·tic, a. & n. (Number) of the fourth power, square of a square; *b.* (*equation*), in which the unknown quantity is b. [BI-(1 b)]

birch[1] (-tsh), n. Kinds of smooth-barked slender-branched northern forest tree; (also *b.-rod*) bundle of its twigs used for flogging schoolboys &c. Hence **bir·chEN**[5] a. [OE *berc* = ON *bjork* (whence northern *birk*), & OE *bierce* = OHG *biricha*, both f. Aryan *bhergo-* cf. Skr. *bhurja*]

birch[2], v.t. Flog with a b. [f. prec.]

bird, n. Feathered vertebrate; game b., esp. the partridge; (slang) girl; *little b.*, unnamed informant; *old b.*, wary person; *bb. of a feather*, people of like character; *b. in hand, in bush*, certainty, contingency; *b. is flown*, prisoner &c. escaped; *kill two bb. with one stone*, gain two ends at once; *give* one, *get, the b.* slang, hiss him, be hissed; *b. of Jove*, eagle, *of Juno*, peacock, *of paradise*, New Guinea family with beautiful plumage, *of passage*, migratory (also fig. of sojourner), *of prey*, member of orders *Raptores* & *Accipitres*, as hawk, eagle, owl; *b.-cage*, for b. or bb.; *b.-fancier*, one who knows about, collects, breeds, or deals in, bb.; *b.-lime*, sticky stuff spread on twigs to catch bb.; *b.-seed*, special seeds given to caged birds; *b.'s-eye*, kinds of plant with small bright round flowers as Mealy Primrose or Germander Speedwell, (tobacco) in which ribs are cut as well as fibre, *b.'s-eye view*, conspectus of town, district, &c., as seen from above, or résumé of subject, (of pattern &c.) marked with spots; *b.'s-foot*, kinds of vetch, fern, trefoil, & starfish; *b.'s mouth*, re-entrant angle cut in wood or stone; *b.'s nest, b.-nest*, nest of b., kinds of plant as Wild Carrot, b.-n. orchid, (v.i., esp. in gerund) hunt for nests, (of horse) turn head from side to side. [OE *brid*; excl. E, etym. dub.]

bī·reme, n. Ancient galley with two banks of oars. [f. L *biremis* f. BI-(1 a) + *remus* oar]

bĭre·tta, n. Square cap worn by R.-C. and some Anglican clerics. [f. It. *berretta* f. LL *birretum* (*birrus* silk or wool cape prob. f. Gk *purrhos* flame-coloured)]

birth, n. Bringing forth of offspring (so many *at a b.*); coming into the world (*give b. to*); origin, beginning; parentage, descent, inherited position; noble lineage, high-born people; *new b.*, regeneration; *b.-control*, methods of preventing undesired sexual conception, practice of these, policy of popularizing this; *birthday*, (anniversary of) day of one's b. (*b.-d. present*, given on this; *b.-d. book*, for entering friends' b.-dd.; *b.-d. suit* facet., one's skin; *b.-d. honours*, knighthoods &c. given on King's b.-d.); *b.-mark*, on one's body at or from b. (so *b.-blindness* &c.); *b.-place*, at which one was born; *b.-rate*, births per mille of population; *bir·thright*, rights belonging to one as eldest son, as born in a certain station or country, or as a human being. [ME *byrthe* prob. f. ON *byrthr* f. OTeut. (*ga*)*burthiz* f. *beran* BEAR[3] + -TH[1]]

bis, adv. (Mus.) over again, repeat. Twice (calling attention to a double occurrence in references &c.). [F & It. f. L, = twice]

bi·scuit (-kĭt), n. & a. Piece of unleavened bread of various materials, usu. crisp, dry, hard, & in small flat thin cakes; porcelain &c. after baking but before glazing & painting; half-piece of soldier's mattress; (of) light-brown colour; *b.-throw* (naut.), short distance. [earlier *bisket* (now assim. to mod. F.) f. OF *bescoit* (L BIS, *coctus* p.p. of *coquere* cook)]

bis dat quī cĭ·tō dat, sent. He gives twice who gives quickly. (formula in charity appeals.) [L]

bise (bēz), n. Keen dry N. wind in Switzerland, S. France, &c. [F]

bīse·ct, v.t. Cut or divide into two (usu. equal) parts. Hence **bīse·CTION** n. [BI-, L *secare sect-* cut]

bīse·ctor, n. Bisecting line. [-OR[2]]

bīse·xual, a. Of two sexes; having both sexes in one individual. [BI-(1 a) + SEXUAL]

bi·shop, n. Clergyman consecrated as eccl. governor of a diocese; *b. in partibus* (*infidelium*), having the title, & competent to confirm &c., but with no diocese (the nominal one being in heathen possession); mitre-shaped piece in chess; mulled & spiced wine; *Bishops' Bible*, version of 1568; *b.'s-cap, -hat, -leaves, -weed*, various plants. [OE *biscop* f. L f. Gk *episkopos* overseer (*epi* on + *-skopos* -looking]

bi·shopric, n. Office of bishop. [OE *bisceoprīce* (prec. + *rīce* realm cf. G *reich*)]

bisk, n. Rich soup made by boiling down birds &c. [f. F. *bisque* crayfish soup]

Bi·sley (-zlĭ), n. (Used for) the ranges or the shooting competitions of the Nat. Rifle Association at B. in Surrey.

bi·smuth (-z-), n. A reddish-white metal. [G (now *wismut*), etym. dub.]

bi·son, n. Wild ox of two species, (also *aurochs*) formerly over Europe, and still in Lithuania, (also *buffalo*) about Rocky Mountains. [f. L *bison -ontis* f. OTeut. *wisand* cf. OE *wesend*, OHG *wisunt*]

bisque[1] (-k), n. (Tennis) right of scoring one point without winning it at any time in the set; (croquet) right of playing extra turn. [F, etym. dub.]

bisque[2] (-k), n. Unglazed white porcelain used in statuettes. [f. BISCUIT]

bisse·xtile, a. & n. Leap(-year). [f. L *bi(s)sextilis (annus)*, (year) containing the *bis sextus dies* or doubled 24th Feb. (vi Kal. Mart.)].

bi·stort, n. Herb with cylindrical spike of flesh-coloured flowers. [f. L *bistorta* (*bis* twice + *torta* fem. p.p. of *torquēre* twist) w. ref. to twisted form of root]

bi·stoury (-torĭ), n. Surgeon's scalpel. [f. F *bistouri* etym. dub.]

bi·stre (-*ter*), n. & a. Brown pigment prepared from soot; colour(ed) like this. [F, perh. f. OF *behistre* = *besistre* = BISSEXTILE, the meaning *gloomy* from notion of unlucky day]

bit[1], n. Something to eat (*a b. & a sup*); boring-piece of drill, cutting-iron of plane, nipping-part of pincers &c., part of key that grips lock-lever; mouthpiece of bridle, (fig.) control, (*draw b.*, slacken pace; *take b. between teeth*, reject control). [OE *bite*, com.-Teut. f. OTeut. *bitiz* (cf. G *biss*) f. *bītan* to BITE]

bit[2], n. Morsel of food (*dainty, tit-, b.*); small piece of anything (*b. by b.*, gradually; *give a b. of* one's *mind*, speak candidly; *do* one's *b.*, contribute service or money to a cause; piece of scenery actual or painted; short passage in book &c.; *bb. of*, poor little (*children, furniture*); *a b. of a*, rather a (*coward* &c.); *a b.*, rather, *not a b.* (*of it*), not at all, *every b. as*, quite as; a short time (*wait a b.*); small coin (U.S., of fractions of Spanish dollar; in Engl., *three-penny b.*, &c.). [OE *bita* com.-Teut. f. OTeut. *biton-* (cf. G *bisse*) f. *bītan* to BITE]

bit[3], v.t. Put b. into mouth of (horse); accustom to the b.; restrain. [f. BIT[1]]

bitch, n. Female of dog, fox, wolf, (usu. *b. fox*, & *b. wolf*); harlot. [OE *bicce* etym. dub.]

bite[1], v.t. & i. (past *bit*; p.p. *bitten* sometimes *bit*). Cut into or nip with the teeth; (with *off* &c.) detach with the teeth; snap *at*; (of serpents, fleas, &c.) sting, suck; accept bait (lit. & fig.); (of sword &c.) penetrate; cause glowing, smarting, &c., pain to (*frost-bitten*); corrode; (of wheels, anchor, &c.) grip; (now only in pass.) take in, swindle, (*were you bitten?*); *b. the dust* or *ground*, fall & die; *b.* one's *lips*, to control anger &c.; *b. off more than* one *can chew*, attempt too great a task; *bitten with*, infected with (a mania, enthusiasm, &c.) [OE *bītan*; com.-Teut., cf. G *beissen* f. OTeut. *bītan* cf. Skr. *bhid-*, L *fid-* (*findere* cut)]

bite[2], n. Act of, wound made by, piece detached by, biting; food to eat (*b. & sup*); taking of bait by fish; grip, hold, (lit. & fig.). [f. prec.]

bi·ter, n. In vbl senses; also, swindler (only now in *the b. bit*). [-ER[1]]

bi·ting, a. In vbl senses; esp., pungent, stinging, sarcastic. Hence **bi·ting**LY[2] adv. [part. of BITE[1]]

bi·tter, a., adv., & n. Tasting like wormwood or quinine, opposite to sweet (*b.-cup*, cup of quassia wood giving b. tonic property to liquid drunk from it); unpalatable to the mind, full of affliction; virulent, relentless; biting, harsh; piercingly cold (also as adv., *it was b. cold*); *to the b. end*, last extremity; hence **bi·tter**ISH[1] (2) a., **bi·tter**LY[2] adv., **bi·tter**NESS n. (N.) bitterness (*the b. with the sweet, the bb. of life*); (pl.) liquors impregnated with wormwood &c. taken as stomachics; = bitter beer; *b.-sweet*, sweet(ness) with bitter after-taste or element (lit. & fig.), Woody Nightshade. [OE *biter*; com.-Teut. prob. f. *bītan* to BITE; *the b. end* may be f. Naut., where the wds mean the last part of a cable left round the BITTS when the rest is overboard, *bitter* being the turn at any moment on the bitts]

bi·ttern, n. Kinds of marsh bird allied to herons, esp. one known for its booming note. [ME *botor* f. OF *butor* etym. dub.]

bi·ttock, n. Little bit. [BIT[2] + -OCK]

bitts, n. pl. Pair of posts on deck for fastening cables &c. [etym. dub.; in most European langg.; perh. f. *bītan* BITE]

bītu·men, n. Mineral pitch, asphalt; (Sci.) kinds of native oxygenated hydrocarbon, as naphtha, petroleum. Hence **bitu·mini·**FEROUS, **bitu·min**OUS, aa. [L, genit. *-minis*, cf. Skr. *gatu* gum]

bītu·minize, v.t. Convert into, impregnate or varnish with, bitumen. Hence **bītu·minīz**A·TION n. [prec. + -IZE (3, 5)]

bī·valent, a. = DIVALENT.

bī·valve, a. & n., **bi·valved, biva·lvular**, aa. With two valves; (mollusc) with hinged double shell; oyster. [BI-(1 a) + VALVE, *valv*ED[2], & see -ULE, -AR[1]]

bi·vouac (-ŏŏ-), v.i., & n. (-acking, -acked). (Remain, esp. for the night, in) temporary encampment without tents; *bivouacked*, in b., see -ED[1] (2). [F, prob. f. G *beiwacht* (BY, WATCH) additional guard at night (in Argau & Zürich)]

bizarre· (-ar), a. Eccentric, fantastic, grotesque, mixed in style, half barbaric. So ***bizarrerie·*** (-rē) [-ERY] n. [F; cf. Sp. *bizarro* handsome, brave, It. *bizzarro* choleric perh. f. Basque *bizarra* beard]

For words in *bi-*, *bin-*, not given consult BI-, BIN-.

blab, v.t. & i., & n. Talk or tell foolishly or indiscreetly, reveal, let out, (secrets &c., or abs.); hence **bla·bb**ER[1] n. (N.) person who blabs. [etym., & relation of vb to n. & to older obs. vb *blabber,* doubtful]

black[1], a. Opposite to white, colourless from the absence or complete absorption of all light; so near this as to have no distinguishable colour; very dark-coloured (*b. in the face,* purple with strangulation or passion); dark-skinned; dark-clothed; (of sky, deep water, &c.) dusky, gloomy; (of hands, linen) dirty; (as specific epithet) *b. bear, currant, snake, heart-cherry;* deadly, sinister, wicked, hateful, (*b.-hearted; b. ingratitude; crimes of blackest dye*); dismal (*b. despair*); angry, sulky, threatening, (*b.-browed; b. looks; look b.*); implying disgrace or condemnation (*b. mark,* of discredit against one's name; *b. book, list,* of persons suspect, tabooed, &c.; *deep in* one's *b. books,* quite out of his favour). *B. & blue,* discoloured with bruise; *b. & tan,* (dog) so coloured, *B. & Tans,* ex-service recruits of the R.I.C. against Sinn-Feiners 1921 named from mixture of military and constabulary uniforms; *b. & white,* ink drawing (*down in b. & w.,* recorded in writing or print); *b. art,* magic [*b.* partly in sense *wicked,* partly by assoc. w. med. L *nigromantia* corrupt. of NECROMANCY]; *b. ball,* used to reject candidate in club ballot, whence **black-ball** v.t.; *b.-beetle,* cockroach; *blackberry,* bramble or its fruit (*plentiful as blackberries,* as can be; *blackberrying,* gathering them); *blackbird,* European song-bird, kidnapped negro on slave-ship (*blackbirding,* trade in these); *b.-board,* in lecture-room for demonstrations in chalk; *b. bottom,* an American dance; *b. cap,* put on by judge in sentencing to death; *blackcap,* kinds of bird, esp. the B. Warbler; *b.* CATTLE; *b.-cock,* male (opp. *grey-hen*) of B. Grouse; *B. Country,* smoky district in Staffs. &c.; *b. dog,* sulks; *b. draught,* an aperient; *b. eye,* discoloured with bruise, also with dark iris whence **black-ey**ED[2] a.; *b.-face,* dark-faced sheep; *b. fellow,* Australian native; *b.-fish,* a species, also salmon just after spawning; *b. flag,* used by pirates, also signal of execution completed; *b. friar,* Dominican; *b. game,* B. Grouse (& see *b.-cock*); *black·guard,* scoundrel(ly), foul-mouthed (person), whence **black·-guard**LY[1] a., **black·guard**ISM (2) n., (v.t.) call blackguard, abuse scurrilously [orig. collect. n., applied at various times to menials of royal household, camp-followers, bodyguard, criminal class, & vagrants]; *b.-head,* kinds of bird, esp. kind of gull, (also) kind of pimple on the skin; *b. hole,* military lock-up (so *B. H. of Calcutta*); *b. jack,* tarred-leather wine-bottle, also pirates' b. flag, also flexible loaded life-preserver; *b.-lead,* (polish with) PLUMBAGO [named from marking like lead]; *blackleg,* swindler esp. on turf, workman who works for master whose men are on strike (v.i. & t., act as b.-l., betray or injure thus) [orig. of senses unknown]; *b. letter,* old type like the German; *blackmail,* (Hist.) tribute exacted by freebooters for protection & immunity, (mod., v.t. & n.) (force to make) payment for not revealing discreditable secrets &c., whence **black-mai·l**ER[1] n. [obs. *mail* rent, OE *mál* f. ON *mál* agreement perh. = OHG *mahal* assembly]; *b. Maria,* vehicle for taking prisoners from & to gaol, (also, army slang) large shell exploding with much smoke; *b. monk,* Benedictine; *b. pudding,* sausage-shaped of blood, suet, &c.; *B. Rod,* gentleman usher of Lord Chamberlain's department, House of Lords, & Garter; *b. sheep,* scoundrel; *b.-shirts,* fascists; *blacksmith,* smith working in iron (cf. WHITE*smith*); *blackthorn,* thorny shrub bearing white flowers before leaves & small plums or sloes (*blackthorn winter,* time of its flowering, cold with NE winds), cudgel or walkingstick of this; *B. Watch,* 42nd Highlanders [f. orig. uniform]; *b.-water fever,* W.-Afr. disease with bloody urine &c. Hence **bla·ck**ISH[1] (2) a., **bla·ck**NESS n. [OE *blæc, blac,* =OHG *blah-, blach-,* perh. cogn. w. Gk *phlegō* burn]

black[2], n. B. colour; b. paint, dye, varnish; b. speck; fungus, smut, in wheat &c.; particle of soot; b. cloth(es); negro or negrito, whence **bla·ck**Y[3] n. [f. prec.]

black[3], v.t. Make b.; polish with BLACKING; *b. out,* obliterate. [f. BLACK[1]]

bla·ckamoor, n. Negro; dark-skinned person. [BLACK[1] + MOOR]

bla·ckavized (-īzd) a. (archaic). Dark-complexioned. [BLACK + F *vis* face]

bla·cken, v.t. & i. Make, grow, black or dark; speak evil of (person's character). [ME *blaknen* (BLACK[1], -EN[6])]

bla·cking, n. In vbl senses; also, paste or liquid for blacking boots. [-ING[1]]

bla·dder, n. Membranous bag in human & other animal bodies (esp. the urinary b., also gall, air, swimming, -b.); the same or part of it prepared for various uses, inflated &c.; (fig.) anything inflated & hollow, wordy man, windbag; inflated pericarp or vesicle in plants & seaweeds (*b.-wrack,* common sea-weed with these in its fronds). Hence **bla·ddery**[2] a. [OE *blǣdre,* com.-Teut. cf. G *blatter* f. OTeut. *blǣdrôn-* f. vb st. *blǣ-* BLOW[1] + *-drôn* instr. suf. cf. Gk *-tron*]

blade, n. (Vague & poet.) leaf; flat lanceolate leaf esp. of grass & cereals; whole of such plants before ear comes (*in the b.*); (Bot.) expanded part of leaf apart from foot-stalk; flattened part of instrument, as oar, bat, spade, paddle-wheel; cutting-piece of edged tool, as sword, chisel, knife; sword; (also *b.-bone*) flat bone, esp. shoulder-b. as joint of meat or otherwise; jovial, hectoring, gay, &c., fellow (usu. with epithet). Hence (-)**blad**ED[2] a. [OE *blæd*; com.-Teut., cf. G *blatt*, perh. partic. form with *-do-*, Aryan *-to-*, f. OTeut, vb st. *blo-* BLOW[3] cf. L *flos*; OE not using *blæd*, but *léaf*, in the vegetable sense, it is likely that the mod. use is a retransfer f. *sword-b.*, helped by med. L *bladum*, OF *bled* (now *blé*), corn]

blae·berry (-ā-), n. =BILBERRY. [*blae* livid, dark-blue, the direct descendant of the OTeut. *blǣwoz* cf. G *blau* f. which *blue* comes indirectly through F *bleu*]

blague (-ahg), n. Pretentiousness. [F]

blain, n. Inflamed sore on skin, pustule. [OE *blegen* cf. Du. *blein*]

blame[1], v.t. Find fault with (*for* offence &c.); fix the responsibility on; *be to b.*, deserve censure. Hence **bla·m**ABLE a., **bla·mab**LY[2] adv. [f. OF *blâmer*, *blasmer*, f. L as BLASPHEME]

blame[2], n. Censure; responsibility for bad result (*lay the b. on*, *bear the b.*). [f. OF *blâme* cf. prec.]

bla·meful, a. (Rare) conveying, (usu.) deserving, censure. (-FUL]

bla·meless, a. Innocent. Hence **bl·ameless**LY[2] adv., **bla·meless**NESS n. [-LESS]

bla·meworthy, a. Deserving blame. Hence **bla·meworthi**NESS n.

blanch, v.t. & i. Make white by withdrawing colour, peeling (almonds). or depriving of light (plants); make or grow pale with fear, cold, &c.; *b. over*, palliate by misrepresentation. [f. F *blanchir* (*blanc* BLANK)]

blancmange (blamah·nzh), n. Opaque white jelly of isinglass, gelatine, or cornflour, and milk. [f. OF *blancmanger* white food (*blanc* BLANK +*manger* eat f. L *manducare* MANDUCATE)]

bland, a. Gentle, polite, in manner; ironical; balmy, mild. Hence **bla·nd**LY[2] adv., **bla·nd**NESS n. [f. L *blandus*]

bla·ndish, v.t. Flatter, coax. Hence **bla·ndish**MENT n. (usu. in pl.). [f. F *blandir* (-ISH[2]) f. L *blandiri* (*blandus*)]

blank[1], a. Not written or printed on (of paper); (of document) with spaces left for signature or details (*in b.*, *drawn in b.*, so prepared; *b. cheque*, with amount left for payee to fill in, hence =CARTE BLANCHE); empty, not filled, (*b. space* &c.; *b. cartridge*, without ball); void of interest, incident, result, or expression; *look b.*, nonplussed; unrelieved, sheer; unrhymed (*b. verse*, esp. the five-foot iambic). Hence **bla·nk**NESS n. [f. F *blanc* white, com.-Rom. cf. It. *bianco* f. OHG *blanch* f. OTeut. *blankoz* shining cf. BLINK]

blank[2], n. Lottery ticket that gains no prize; space left to be filled up in document, empty surface (one's *mind*, *memory* &c., *is a b.*, has no sensations &c.); words printed in italics in Parl. bills; time without incident, thing without meaning; coin-disk before stamping; =*b. cartridge* (*20 rounds of b.*); dash written instead of word or letter, whence *blank*, *blanky*, *blanked*, as substitutes for abusive nouns and adjj. [uses of prec.]

bla·nket[1], n. Large woollen sheet used for bed covering, for horse-cloth, & by savages for clothes; *wet b.*, person who extinguishes conversation; *born on wrong side of b.*, illegitimate. [f. OF *blanquette* (*blanc* BLANK + -ETTE)]

bla·nket[2], v.t. Cover with a b.; stifle, keep quiet, (scandal, question, &c.); toss in a b. as punishment; take wind from sails of (another craft) by passing to windward. [f. prec.]

bla·nkly, adv. Without expression, vacuously, (*look b.* &c.); flatly (*deny b.* &c.). [BLANK[1] + -LY[2]]

blare, v.i. & t., & n. (Make) sound of trumpet; utter loudly. [perh. imit.; cf. MDu. *blaren*, G *plärren*]

blar·ney, n., & v.t. & i. (Use, assail with) cajoling talk. [*Blarney*, Irish castle with stone conferring a cajoling tongue on whoever kisses it]

bla·sé (-ahzā), a. Cloyed, tired of pleasure. [F]

blasphe·me, v.i. & t. Talk impiously; utter profanity about, revile. So **blasphe·m**ER[2](4), **bla·sphem**Y[1], nn., **bla·sphemous** a., **bla·sphemous**LY[2] adv. [ME *blasfemen* f. OF *blasfemer* f. L *blasphemare* f. Gk *blasphēmeō* f. *blasphēmos* (*blas-* etym. dub., perh. *blab-* hurt + *-phēmos* -speaking)]

blast[1], n. Strong gust of wind; sound of wind-instrument; current of air in smelting &c. (*in*, *out of*, *b.*, of furnace working or not); quantity of explosive used in blasting operation; *b.-furnace*, smelting furnace into which compressed hot air is driven by engine. [OE *blǣst*; com.-Teut. f. OTeut. *blǣstuz*, f. *blǣsan* blow see BLAZE[5]]

blast[2], v.t. Blow up (rocks &c.) with explosives; wither, shrivel, blight, (plant, animal, limb, prosperity, character; esp., with subj. *God* understood, in curses, whence *blasted*, damnable]. [f. prec.]

blasto-, first element in many biological terms, meaning germ, bud. [f. Gk *blastos* sprout]

bla·stoderm, n. Germinal membrane round yolk in impregnated ovum, dividing later into three layers (*epiblast*, *mesoblast*, *hypoblast*) from which all parts of the animal are developed. [prec. + Gk *derma* skin (*derō* flay, -M)]

blā·tant, a. Noisy, vulgarly clamorous. Hence **bla·tant**LY[2] adv., **bla·t**ANCY n. (prob. invented by Spenser, (*F.Q.*, V. xii. 37, *b. beast*) perh. in sense *bleating*]

blather(skite). See BLETHER.

blaze[1], n. Bright flame or fire (*in a b.*, on fire); (slang) *bb.* = hell (*go to bb.*, *what the bb.!*; *like bb.*, impetuously); violent outburst (*b. of passion* &c.); glow of colour, bright display; full light (*b. of publicity*). [OE *blase*, *blæse*, torch, cf. G *blass* pale, & BLAZE[3]]

blaze[2], v.i. Burn with flame (*b. up*, burst into b.); be brilliantly lighted; burn with excitement &c. (*b. up*, burst out in anger); show bright colours; emit light; *b. away*, fire continuously with rifles &c., work enthusiastically at anything; *blazing indiscretion*, rash & conspicuous piece of candour; (Hunting) *blazing scent*, very strong (opp. to *cold scent*). [f. prec.]

blaze[3], n. White mark on horse's or ox's face, or made on tree by chipping bark to mark route. [from 17th c.; = ON *blesi* star on horse's forehead, cf. G *blässe* in same sense & G *blass* pale]

blaze[4], v.t. Mark (tree, and so path) by chipping bark. [f. prec.]

blaze[5], v.t. Proclaim as with trumpet, esp. *b. abroad*, spread (news) about. [prob. f. ON *blása* blow f. OTeut. *blæsan* f. root *blæ-* cf. L *flare* BLOW[1]]

bla·zer, n. Coloured jacket for boating, golf, &c.; (slang) outrageous lie. [BLAZE[2] + -ER[1]]

blā·zon[1], n. Heraldic shield, coat of arms, bearings, or banner; correct description of these; record, description, esp. of virtues &c. [f. F *blason* etym. dub.; orig. meaning *shield* in lit. sense]

blā·zon[2], v.t. Describe or paint (arms) heraldically; inscribe (object) with arms, names, &c., in colours or ornamentally; give lustre to; set forth in fitting words; proclaim. Hence **blā·zon**MENT n. [f. prec. partly confused in sense with BLAZE[5]]

blā·zonry, n. (Art of describing or painting) heraldic devices, armorial bearings; brightly coloured display. [prec. + -RY]

-ble, suf. OF f. L *-bilis* forming vbl adjj. active or passive (*penetrabilis* penetrating or penetrable) f. vb or p.p. stems. L has *-ab.*, *-eb.*, *-ĭb.*, or *-īb.*, acc. to conjug. (*-ĭb.* also f. p.p. stems as *flexĭbilis*). F in making new wds uses only *-able*; E vacillates between this & using *-ible* w. L 3rd-conj. or p.p. stems, *-able* elsewhere; to this confusion, incurable at present, is added that between *-able* & *-eable*; *-eable* is necessary after soft *-c*, *-g*, (cf. *navigable*, *manageable*); it is also used arbitrarily in some wds to affect the vowel of the previous syllable (*tameable*). See also -ABLE, -IBLE. The E meaning in new wds is always passive, in old ones (*capable*) often active. From adjj. in *-ble* are formed nouns in *-bility* (L *-bilitas*, see -TY) as well as in *-bleness*.

bleach (-tsh), v.t. & i. Whiten by exposure to sunlight or by chemical process; *bleaching-powder*, (so-called) chloride of lime. [OE *blǽcan*; com.-Teut. f. OTeut, *blaikjan* cf. OE *blác* pale]

bleak[1], n. Small river fish, & allied sea-fish, of various species. [prob. f. ON *bleikja* f. OTeut. *blaikjôn* white cf. prec.]

bleak[2], a. Wanting colour; bare, exposed, windswept; chilly; dreary. [perh. northern form of obs. *bleach*, *bleche*, OE *blǽc* variant of *blác* see BLEACH]

blear (-ēr), a., & v.t. (Make) dim-sighted, dull, filmy, (eyes or mind); (make) indistinct in outline; *b.-eyed*, having blear eyes, without foresight or penetration. [ME *blere* adj., etym. dub.]

bleat, v.i. & t., & n. (Make) sheep's, goat's, or calf's, cry; speak (& *b. out*, say) feebly or foolishly. [OE *blǽtan*, com.-WG cf. Du. *blaten*, G *blöken*]

bleb, n. Small blister or bubble on skin, in water or glass. [imit. of making bubble with lips, cf. *blab*, *blubber*]

bleed, v.i. & t. (bled). Emit blood (*heart bleeds*, is in acute distress); suffer wounds or violent death (often *for* cause &c.); (of plants) emit sap; part with money, pay lavishly, suffer extortion; draw blood surgically from; extort money from; (part., vulg. euphem., cf. *blinking*, *blooming*, for) bloody; *bleeding heart*, pop. name of various plants, as Wallflower. [OE *blédan* f. OTeut. *blôdjan* (cf. G *bluten*) f. *blôdom* BLOOD]

blĕ·mish[1], v.t. Mar, spoil the beauty or perfection of, sully. [f. OF *blemir* (-ISH[2]) f. *blaisme*, *blesme*, *blême*, pale, etym. dub.]

ble·mish[2], n. Physical or moral defect, stain, flaw. [f. prec.]

blench (-tsh), v.i. & t. Start aside, flinch, quail; close the eyes to, disguise from oneself. [there is OE *blencan* cheat, & prob. connexion & confusion with BLINK]

blend[1], v.t. & i. (*blended* or *blent*). Mix (things) together (esp. sorts of tea, spirit, to get certain quality); mingle (t. & i. of element) intimately *with*; mix (components) so as to be inseparable & indistinguishable; become one, form harmonious compound; pass imperceptibly into each other (esp. of colours). [there is OE *blandan* mix; but ME *blenden* is prob. f. ON *blanda*]

blend[2], n. Mixture made of various sorts of tea, spirits, &c. (f. prec.]

blende, n. Native sulphide of zinc. [G *blendendes Erz* deceiving ore 'because while often resembling galena it yielded no lead']

Ble·nheim (-ĕnĭm), n. & a. Kind of spaniel; *B. Orange*, golden-coloured apple. [Duke of Marlborough's seat at Woodstock]

blenno-, blenn-, stem of many wds in pathology. Of mucus. [Gk *blennos* mucus]

ble·nny, n. Small spiny-finned sea-fish. [as prec. (through L *blennius*) from mucous coating of its scales]

blent. See BLEND[1].

blĕ·pharo-, stem of pathological words. Of the eyelids. [f. Gk *blepharon* eyelid]

bless, v.t. (past & p.p. *blessed,* sometimes *blest,* & see under BLESSED). Consecrate (esp. food; *not a penny to b. oneself with,* w. ref. to cross on silver penny); call holy, adore, (God); attribute good fortune to (esp. one's stars); pronounce words that bring supernatural favour upon (of father, priest, &c.); invoke God's favour on; make happy or successful (abs. or *with* something); *God b. me, b. me, God b. you, b. you, b. the boy, b. my soul, I'm blest,* exclamations of surprise or indignation; (euphem.) = damn, curse, &c. [OE *blóedsian, blédsian, blétsian*; excl. E, but formed on OTeut. *blôdisôjan* f. *blôdom* BLOOD (consecrate by sacrifice); meaning influenced (1) by the word's being used at the Eng. conversion to translate L *benedicere,* (2) by confusion with the independent BLISS]

ble·ssed, blest, (for pronunc. see under etym.), a. Consecrated; revered; fortunate; *b. with,* fortunate in the possession of (esp. iron.); in paradise (esp. as n., *the b.*); blissful, bringing happiness (*b. ignorance* &c.); (euphem.) cursed. [p.p. of prec.; as p.p. & past tense *blessed* is usu. monosyl., as adj. disyl.; of the adj. forms *blessed* is the ordinary, *blest* the poet., also used in some phrr. as *Isles of the Blest*]

ble·ssĕdness, n. Happiness; enjoyment of divine favour; *single b.,* jocular phr. for being unmarried (perversion of Shaksp. *M. N. D.,* I. i. 78). [prec. + -NESS]

ble·ssing, n. Declaration, invocation, or bestowal, of divine favour; grace before or after food (*ask a b.*); gift of God, nature, &c., thing one is glad of; *b. in disguise,* unwelcome but salutary experience &c. [BLESS + -ING[1]]

blĕ·ther, blă·ther, v.i., & n. (Talk) loquacious nonsense. Hence **bla·therskite, ble·therskate,** nn. (dial.), blethering person. [ME *blather* f. ON *blathra* talk nonsense (*blathr* nonsense); *blether* is the Scotch form adopted from Burns &c.]

blew, past of BLOW[1, 3].

blew·it, n. A late edible mushroom with lilac stem. [prob. f. *blue,* cf. dial. name *blue-legs*]

blight[1] (-īt), n. Disease of unknown or atmospheric origin affecting plants; plant disease caused by fungoid parasites, mildew, rust, smut; species of aphis; hazy close state of atmosphere; any obscure malignant influence. [from 17th c., etym. dub.]

blight[2], v.t. Exert baleful influence on, nip in the bud, wither, mar. Hence **bligh·tER**[1] n., esp. (slang) annoying person. [f. prec.]

Bligh·ty, n. (army slang). England, home, after foreign service (*a B. one,* wound that ensures return to B.). [Anglo-Ind. corruption of Hind. *wilāyatī, bilātī,* European, English (*wilāyat* country, cf. Turk. VILAYET]

blī·mey, int. (vulg.) of surprise &c. [= God blind me!]

blimp, n. Small airship used in hunting submarines. [?]

blind[1], a. Without sight (*b. of an eye,* having one eye b.; *turn a* or one's *b. eye to,* affect not to see; without foresight, discernment, or moral or intellectual light (*b. to,* incapable of appreciating; one's *b. side,* direction in which one is unguarded); reckless; mechanical, not ruled by purpose, (*b. forces*); hard to trace (*b. track*); (Post Office) *b. letter, man, reader,* of ill-addressed letters and the officials dealing with them; concealed (*b. ditch*; *b.-stitch,* sewing visible only on one side, also as v.t. & i. sew thus); *b. door* &c., walled up; closed at one end (*b. alley*; *b.-a. occupations,* such as fail to fit one for anything further); (slang) drunk (also *b. drunk, b. to the world*); *b. hazard, hookey,* card-games; *b.-man's-buff,* game in which blindfold player tries to catch others, who push him about [f. obs. *buff* = *buffet*]; *b. stamping, tooling* (in bookbinding without use of ink or goldleaf); *b.-story,* triforium below clerestory admitting no light; *b. man's holiday,* time before candles are lighted; *b. coal,* burning without flame, anthracite; *b.-worm,* = SLOW-*worm* (f. small size of eyes). [com.-Teut.]

blind[2], v.t. Deprive of sight permanently or temporarily; rob of judgement, deceive. [f. prec.]

blind[3], n. Obstruction to sight or light; screen for windows, esp. on roller (*Venetian b.,* of laths running on webbing); (Fortif.) = foll.; pretext, stalking-horse. [f. prec.]

blī·ndage (-ĭj), n. Screen for troops in fortification, sieges, &c. [-AGE]

blī·ndfold[1], v.t. Deprive (eyes, person) of sight with bandage (also fig.). [corruption (through notion of folding) of ME *blindfellen* (FELL v.) strike blind, chiefly used in p.p., whence the *-d,* which helped the confusion]

blī·ndfold[2], a. & adv. With eyes bandaged; without circumspection. [p.p., earlier *blindfelled* see prec.]

blī·ndly, adv. Without seeing, gropingly; recklessly. [-LY[2]]

blī·ndness, n. Want of sight; want of intellectual or normal sense, folly, recklessness. [-NESS]

blink[1], v.i. & t. Move the eyelids; look

with eyes opening and shutting; shut the eyes for a moment; shine with unsteady light, cast momentary gleam; ignore, shirk consideration of, (esp. *the fact*); (part., vulg. euphem., cf. *bleeding, blooming*, for) bloody. [ME *blinken*, more usu. *blenken*; cf. Du. & G *blinken* perh. f. stem *blik-* shine]

blink², n. Momentary gleam or glimpse; (also *ice-b.*) whiteness about horizon, reflection of distant ice-fields. [f. prec.]

bli·nker, n. In vbl senses; also, (usu. pl.) screen(s) preventing horse from seeing sideways. [-ER¹]

bliss, n. Gladness, enjoyment; perfect joy, blessedness; being in heaven. Hence **bli·ss**FUL a., **bli·ssful**LY² adv., **bli·ssful**NESS n. [OE *blīths* (*blīthe* BLITHE + OTeut. suf. *-sjâ-*); the sense has shifted from earthly to heavenly joy by confusion with BLESS]

bli·ster, n., & v.t. & i. Vesicle on skin filled with serum, caused by friction, burning, &c.; similar swelling on surface of plant, metal, painted wood; (Med.) anything applied to raise a b. (Vb) raise b. on; become covered with bb.; (slang) bore, waste time of. [ME *blester* perh. f. OF *blestre* f. ON *blástr* swelling (*blása* to blow)]

blithe (-dh), a. Gay, joyous, (chiefly poet.). Hence **bli·the**LY² adv., **bli·the**SOME adj. [OE *blīthe*, com.-Teut., cf. OHG *blîdi* perh. f. vb st. *blî-* shine]

bli·zzard, n. Blinding snow-storm. [first common in U.S. newspapers in severe winter 1880–1; imit., cf. *blow, blast, blind*, & see -ARD]

bloat¹, v.t., **bloa·ter,** n. Cure (herring) by salting & smoking slightly into *bloated herring* or *bloater*. [f. obs. adj. *bloat* ME *blote* perh. = ON *blautr* soaked]

bloat², v.t. & i., **bloa·ted,** a. Inflate, swell (t. & i.); (chiefly in p.p. as adj.) puffed up, esp. with gluttony, overgrown, too big, pampered (esp. *bloated aristocrat, armaments*). [f. obs. adj. *bloat* ME *blowt, blout*, perh. variant of ME *blote* see prec.]

blob, n. Drop of liquid; small roundish mass; spot of colour; (Cricket) = duck's egg. [imit., cf. BLEB]

blo·bber-lipped, a. With thick protruding lips. [imit., cf. BLEB; *blabber, blubber*, are found in same sense]

block¹, n. Log of wood, tree-stump, (*chip of old b.*, child like his father esp. in character; *cut bb. with razor*, waste ingenuity &c.); large piece of wood for chopping or hammering on (*the b.*, death by beheading) or mounting horse from; mould for shaping hats on, shape; *barber's b.*, wooden head for wigs; pulley, system of pulleys mounted in case; piece of wood engraved for printing; bulky piece of anything; unhewn lump of rock; prepared piece of building-stone; collection of buildings bounded by (usu. four) streets; stolid or hard-hearted person, whence **blo·ck**ISH¹ a.; obstruction, (Parl.) notice that a bill will be opposed, which prevents its being taken at certain times & so often kills it; (traffic) jammed vehicles unable to proceed; *B. system* on railways, by which no train may enter a section till it is clear; (Cricket) spot on which batsman blocks ball & rests bat before playing; *b.-chain*, kind of endless chain used in bicycle &c.; *blockhead*, dolt; *blockhouse*, detached fort (orig. one blocking passage), sometimes one of connected chain of posts, also one-storeyed timber building with loopholes, also house of squared logs; *b. letters, writing* (with each letter separate as in print, & usu. in capitals). [prob. f. F *bloc*, which is perh. f. OHG *bloh* (G *block*)]

block², v.t. Obstruct (passage &c.); put obstacles in way of (progress &c.); *b. up, in*, confine; (Parl.) announce opposition to (bill; see prec.); (Cricket) stop (ball) with bat; shape (hats); emboss (book cover); *b. out, in*, sketch roughly, plan, (work). [f. F *bloquer* f. *bloc* see prec.]

blocka·de¹, n. Shutting-up, total or on land or sea side, of a place by hostile forces in order to starve it into surrender or prevent egress & ingress (*paper b.*, one declared but not made effective; *raise b.*, cease blockading, compel blockaders to cease; *run b.*, evade blockading force; *b.-runner*, ship, captain, &c., doing this); imprisonment by snow &c. [f. prec. on anal. of F wds in -ADE]

blocka·de², v.t. Subject to b. (see prec.); obstruct (door, view, &c.) Hence **blocka·d**ER¹ n. [f. prec.]

bloke, n. (colloq.). Man, fellow, chap; dull or rustic person; *the b.* (Nav. slang), ship's commander. [?]

blond, blonde (see etym.), a. & n. (Of hair) light-auburn-coloured; (of complexion) fair (n., person with such hair & skin); (also *b. lace*) silk lace of two threads in hexagonal meshes (orig. of raw-silk colour, now white or black). [f. F *blond* fem. *blonde* cf. It. *biondo*; OE *blanden-feax* grizzled (*blandan* blend), and the ancient-German custom of dyeing hair yellow, suggest a deriv.; *blonde* is used of the lace, & of the adj. & n. as applied to a woman, *blond* elsewhere]

blood¹ (-ŭd), n. Red liquid circulating in veins of higher animals, corresponding liquid in lower animals, (*flesh & b.*, the animal nature; *let b.*, surgically); (fig.) sap, grape-juice, &c.; taking of life, murder, sacrifice, guilt of bloodshed; passion, temperament, mettle, (*bad b.*, ill feeling; *his b. is up*, he is in fighting mood; *b. out of a stone*, pity from the pitiless; *in cold b.*, deliberately); race (*blue b.*, high birth; *fresh b.*, new members admitted to family, society, &c.; *b. royal*, royal family; *Prince* &c. *of the* *b. royal* or *of the b.*, of royal race; *runs in the b.*, is a family trait); relationship, relations, (*own flesh & b.*; *b. is thicker than water*, the tie of kindred is real); descent, good parentage, (of men, horses, &c.; *bit of b.*, *b.-horse*, thoroughbred); dandy, man of fashion, (*young b.*, either in this sense, or as personal form of *fresh b.* above, =younger member of party); *b. and iron*, relentless use of force (esp. as motto of Bismarckian policy); *b. ally*, red-veined ALLY[3]; *b. feud*, between families of which one has spilt the other's b.; *b.-guilty*, responsible for murder or death, whence **bloo·dguilti**NESS n.; *b.-heat*, ordinary heat of b. in health, 98·4° F.; *bloodhound*, large keen-scented dog with which cattle, slaves, &c., used to be tracked, detective, spy; *b.-letting*, surgical removal of some of patient's b., (facet.) bloodshed; *b.-money*, reward to witness for securing capital sentence, fine paid to next of kin for slaughter of relative; *b. orange*, with red juice; *b.-poisoning*, state resulting from introduction of septic matter into b. esp. through wound; *b.-red*, red as b.; *b.-relation*, one related by b., not marriage; *bloodshed*, spilling of b., slaughter [f. phr. *to shed b.*]; *bloo·dshot*, (of eye) suffused, tinged, with b. (*see things bloodshot*, find incitements to slaughter or traces of b. in them); *b.-stained*, stained with b., disgraced by bloodshed; *bloodstone*, kinds of precious stone spotted or streaked with red, esp. Heliotrope; *b.-sucker*, leech, extortioner; *b.-thirsty*, eager for bloodshed, whence **bloo·dthirsti**NESS n.; *b.-vessel*, flexible tube (vein or artery) conveying b.; *bloodworm*, bright-red kind used in fishing; *b.-wort*, kinds of plant with red roots or leaves, esp. Bloody Dock. [OE *blód*, com.-Teut., cf. G *blut* f. OTeut. *blôdom*]

blood[2], v.t. (Surg.) remove a little of the b. of (usu. *bleed*); allow first taste of b. to (hound; also fig. of inciting persons). [f. prec.]

bloo·dless, a. Without blood; unfeeling; pale; without bloodshed, whence **bloo·dless**LY[2] adv. [-LESS]

bloo·dy[1], a & adv. Of, like, running or smeared with, blood (*b. nose*, bleeding; *b. flux*, dysentery); red (*b. hand*, armorial device of baronet); involving, loving, resulting from, bloodshed; (also *b.-minded*) sanguinary, cruel; (in foul language)=*damned* &c., or as mere intensive (*not a b. one*); (similarly as adv.) =confoundedly, very; (in pop. plant names) *B. Finger*, Foxglove. Hence **bloo·di**LY[2] adv., **bloo·di**NESS n. [OE *blódig*, com.-Teut. cf. G *blutig*; see BLOOD, -Y[2]]

bloo·dy[2], v.t. Make b., stain with blood. [f. prec.]

bloom[1], n. Flower, esp. of plants grown or admired chiefly for the flower, florescence (*in b.*); prime, perfection; flush, glow; powdery deposit on grapes, plums, &c., freshness, (*take the b. off*, stale); kind of raisin. [ME *blom* f. ON *blóm* cf. G *blume* f. OTeut. *blômon-* f. vb st. *blo-* BLOW[3]+suf. *-mon-*]

bloom[2], v.i. Bear flowers, be in flower; come into, be in, full beauty; culminate, flourish. [f. prec.]

bloom[3], n. Mass of puddled iron hammered or squeezed into thick bar. [OE *blóma* in same sense]

bloom[4], v.t. Make (puddled iron) into a BLOOM[3]. Hence **bloo·m**ERY (3) (also *-ary*) n. [f. prec.]

bloo·mer[1], n. & a. (Female costume) of short skirt & trousers (as n., usu. pl.). Mrs *B.*, American inventor]

bloo·mer[2], n. (slang). Blunder. [=*blooming* (see foll.) *error*; -ER[1]]

bloo·ming, a. In vbl senses (BLOOM[2]); also slang, euphemistic substitute for vulgar BLOODY. [-ING[2]]

Bloo͞·msbury (-zberĭ), n. Part of London containing British Museum, formerly a fashionable residential (and now a literary) quarter.

blo·ssom[1], n. Flower, esp. as promising fruit; mass of flowers on fruit-tree &c. (*in b.*); early stage of growth, promise; *b.-faced*, *-nosed*, bloated. Hence **blo·ssom**Y[2], **blo·ssom**LESS, aa. [OE *blóstm* prob. f. same root as BLOOM[1] (*blo-* extended to st. *blos-*, cf. L *flos*, or with double suf. *-st*+*-m*)]

blo·ssom[2], v.i. Open into flower (lit., & fig., as *b. out into a statesman*). [OE *blóstmian* cf. prec.]

blot[1], n. Spot of ink &c., dark patch; disfigurement, blemish, defect; disgraceful act or quality in good character. [f. 14th c., etym. dub.; cf. ON *blettr*, Da. *plet*; there was 16th-c. F *blotte* clod, *blotter* to stain]

blot[2], v.t. & i. Spot with ink; smudge; (of pen, ink) make bb.; cover with worthless writing; sully, detract from, (fair fame); *b. out*, obliterate (writing), exterminate, destroy; dry with *blotting-paper*, absorbent paper for drying wet ink-marks (*blotting-book*, *-case*, *-pad*, arrangements of this), whence **blo·tt**ER[1] (2) n. [f. prec.]

blot[3], n. Exposed piece in backgammon; weak point in strategy &c. [etym. dub.; cf. Da. *blot* naked, G *bloss*]

blotch, n. Inflamed patch, boil, &c., on skin; dab of ink or colour; (school slang) blotting-paper. Hence **blotch**ED[2], **blo·tch**Y[2], aa. [f. 1600; excl. E, perh. compounded f. *blot* & *botch* or *patch*]

blotte·sque, a. & n. (Piece of painting or description) done with heavy blotted touches. [-ESQUE]

blou·se (-owz), n. Workman's loose linen or cotton upper garment usu. belted at waist (chiefly French); woman's loose light bodice visible only to waist, and there belted. [F, etym. dub.]

blow[1] (-ō), v.i. & t. (*blew*; *blown* &, in sense 'cursed', *blowed*). (Of wind, air, 'it') move along, act as air-current, (*b. great guns*, violent gale); send strong air-current from mouth (*b. hot & cold*, vacillate), puff, pant; make or shape (bubble, glass) by blowing; (of whales) eject air & water; cause air-current by means of (*b. bellows*); work bellows of (organ); exhaust of breath (esp. in pass.); send out by breathing (*b. air into*; *b. off steam*, get rid of superfluous energy); (with advv. & prepp.) drive, be driven, by blowing (*b. over*, pass off; *b. in* slang, come in breezily, drop in); sound (wind instrument, note or signal *on* or *with* it, or with it as subject to *blow* t. or i.; *b. one's own trumpet*, praise oneself); direct air-current at (*b. fingers*, *fire*; *b. out*, extinguish); clear by air-current (nose, egg); break *in* or send flying *off* or *out* or *up* by explosion (*b. out* one's *brains*, shoot him, or usu. oneself); *b. up*, inflate, shatter or be shattered by explosion, reprove; (slang) betray; (of flies) deposit eggs in; (slang) curse, confound, (*I'll be blowed if* &c.; *b. the expense*, spend recklessly); (slang) squander, spend (sum) recklessly; *b. upon*, stale, discredit, tell tales of; *blowball*, seed-head of dandelion &c.; *blowfly*, the Meat fly; *blowhole*, nostril of whale &c., vent for air, smoke, &c., in tunnel &c.; *blowpipe*, tube for heating flame by blowing air or other gas into it, tube used in glass-blowing, Amer.-Ind. dart tube. [OE *bláwan* cf. OHG *blâhan* f. OTeut. *blǣjan* cf. L *flare*]

blow[2], n. Blowing, taste of fresh air; blowing of flute, one's nose, &c.; =FLY[1]-*blow*; *b.-out* slang, abundant meal or feed. [f. prec.]

blow[3] (-ō), v.i. (blew, blown). Burst into, be in, flower. [OE *blówan* cf. OHG *bluojan*, G. *blühen*, f. OTeut. *blôjan* cf. L *flos*)

blow[4], n. Blossoming (*in full b.* &c.) [f. prec.]

blow[5] (-ō), n. Hard stroke with fist, instrument, &c.; disaster, shock; *come to, exchange, bb.*, fight; *strike a b. for, against*, help, oppose; *at one b.*, in one operation. [f. 15th c., etym. dub.]

blow·er, n. In vbl senses of BLOW[1,3]; also: apparatus for increasing a fire's draught, esp. sheet of iron before grate-front; escape of gas, or fissure allowing it, in coal mine. [BLOW[1], -ER[1]]

blow·y, a. Windy, wind-swept. [BLOW[1], -Y[2]]

blowzed, blow·zy, (-ow-), aa. Red-faced, coarse-looking, dishevelled. [f. obs. n. *blowze* beggar's wench, etym. dub., but suggesting *blush* & *blow*]

blub, v.i. (schoolboy slang). Shed tears. [short for BLUBBER[3]]

blu·bber[1], n. Whale fat; jelly-fish (sailor's name); weeping. [ME *blober*; prob. imit. (obs. meanings *foaming, bubble*), cf. BLEB, BUBBLE]

blu·bber[2], a. Swollen, protruding, (of lips). [as prec.]

blu·bber[3], v.t. & i. Utter with sobs, weep noisily; wet, disfigure, swell, (face) with weeping. [as prec.]

blu·chers (-k-), n. pl. Old-fashioned low boots or high shoes. [named after the Prussian Field Marshal *Blücher*]

blu·dgeon (-ŭjn), n., & v.t. (Strike repeatedly with) heavy-headed stick. [etym. dub.; from 18th c. only]

blue[1], a. Coloured like the sky or deep sea (also of things much paler, darker, &c., as smoke, distant hills, moonlight, bruise; & qualified by or qualifying other colours &c., as *b.-black*, *deep b.*, NAVY *b.*, *Prussian b.*); *look b.*, nervous, depressed (*things looked b.*, depressing); *b. funk*, uncontrollable; *true b.*, faithful; dressed in b. (*Foot-Guards B.*); *the B.* (*Squadron*), one of three divisions (Red, White, B.) of Navy; belonging to a particular political party, usu. Tory; (of women) learned (see BLUESTOCKING); (of talk &c.) indecent; *drink till all's b.*, to drunkenness. *Bluebell*, (Scotland & N. Eng.) light-blue-flowered *Campanula* growing in dry places & flowering in summer & autumn, harebell, (S. Eng.) wild hyacinth with blue or white flower growing in moist places & flowering in spring; *b. blood*, high birth; *b.-book*, Parliamentary or Privy-Council report; *bluebottle*, B. Cornflower, Meat fly or Blowfly; *b.-coat boy*, scholar in charity school, esp. Christ's Hospital; *b. devils*, depression; *b. gum*, kind of eucalyptus tree; *bluejacket*, seaman in Navy; *b. light*, firework used for signals; *B. Mantle*, one of four pursuivants of College of Arms; *once in a b. moon*, very rarely; *b. mould*, in certain cheeses when mature; *B. Peter*, b. flag with white square, hoisted before sailing; *b. pill*, mercurial & antibilious; *b. ribbon*, ribbon of the Garter, greatest honour in any sphere, sign of teetotalism; *b. rock*, kind of pigeon; *b. ruin*, bad gin; *bluestocking*, woman having or affecting literary tastes & learning [Blue Stocking Society (in sense 'not in full evening dress') name given to meetings about 1750 at houses of Mrs. Montague &c. to talk on literature &c. instead of playing cards; blue-worsted, i.e. ordinary, stockings were worn by some of the men attending instead of black silk]; *b. water*, open sea; *b.-water school*, strategists regarding the fleet as sufficient defence for Gt Britain. Hence **blu·**ISH[1] (2) a., **blue·**NESS n. [ME *blew* f. OF *bleu* f. OHG *blâw-* f. OTeut. *blǣwoz*, cf. L *flavus*]

blue[2], n. B. colour (*Oxford b.*, dark; *Cambridge b.*, light; *the light, dark, bb.*, representatives or supporters of Cambridge, Oxford, in sporting contests); b. pigment; b. powder used by laundresses; b. cloth &c.; *the* sky (BOLT[1] *from the b.*); *the* sea; (pl.) *the* Royal Horseguards; *the Bb.* or *Bb. trot*, dance of fox-trot kind; colour, member, of a political party; (badge given to) one who has represented his university in athletics &c.; =BLUE[1] *stocking*; (pl.) *the* dumps. [f. prec.]

blue[3], v.t. Make b.; treat with laundress's b.; (slang) squander (money). [f. BLUE[1]]

Blue·beard, n. Husband of many wives. [hero of popular story, who hung up in locked chamber the bodies of his murdered wives]

bluff[1], a. With perpendicular broad front (of ship's bows, cliffs); (of person, manner) abrupt, blunt, frank, hearty. Hence **blu·ff**LY[2] adv., **blu·ff**NESS n. [naut. wd, etym. dub., but cf. MDu. *blaf*, flat, broad]

bluff[2], n. Headland with perpendicular broad face. [f. prec., & see foll.]

bluff[3], v.t. & i. (Game of poker) impose upon (opponent) as to value of one's hand & induce him to throw up his cards; treat (political opponents or rival States) so; practise this policy. [earlier meaning, *hoodwink* (lit.); the prec. n. also meant earlier *horse's blinker*; etym. dub.]

bluff[4], n. Overbearing demeanour, threats designed to operate without action. [f. prec.]

blu·nder[1], v.i. & t. Move blindly, stumble, (often *on, along*); *b. upon*, find by fluke; make gross mistake; mismanage (a business &c.); *b. out*, utter thoughtlessly; *b. away*, waste by mismanagement. Hence **blu·nder**ER[1] n., **blu·ndering**LY[2] adv. [ME *blondren*, perh. f. obs. *blond, bland*, mix, cf. BLEND, + -ER[5]]

blu·nder[2], n. Stupid or careless mistake. [prob. f. prec., but found earlier]

blu·nderbuss, n. Ancient short gun with large bore firing many balls. [perverted f. Du. *donderbus* thunder gun (orig. box cf. G. *büchse*)]

blu·nderhead, n. =DUNDERHEAD (cf. prec.).

blunge (-j), v.t. (Pottery) mix (clay, flint-powder, &c.) up with water by revolving machinery. [after *plunge, blend*]

blunt[1], a. & n. Dull, not sensitive; without edge or point; plain-spoken; hence **blu·nt**ISH[1] (2) a. (N.) short thick needle; (slang) ready money. [?]

blunt[2], v.t. Make less sharp or sensitive. [f. prec.]

blu·ntly, adv. Obtusely (shaped &c.); rudely, curtly. [-LY[2]]

blu·ntness, n. Dullness of point or edge; outspokenness. [-NESS]

blur[1], n. Smear of ink &c.; dimness, confused effect. [etym. dub., perh. formed on *blear* & *blot*]

blur[2], v.t. & i. Smear (clear writing &c.) with ink &c.; sully, disfigure; make indistinct; efface; dim (perception &c.) [as prec.]

blurb, n. Publisher's eulogy of book printed on jacket or in advertisements elsewhere. [U.S. slang]

blurt, v.t. Burst *out* with, utter abruptly. [imit. after *blow, spurt*, &c.]

blush[1], v.i. Become red (in the face; also with *face* &c. as subj.) with shame or other emotion (*at* sight or word, *with* or *for* joy or shame, *for* another); be ashamed (*b. to own* &c.]; be red, pink. Hence **blu·shing**LY[2] adv. [ME *blusche, blosche, blysche*, OE *ablisian*; cf. wds in ON & LG pointing to a st. *blusi-* f. vb root *blus-* glow (Du. *blozen* blush)]

blush[2], n. Glance, glimpse, (*at the first b.*, prima facie); reddening of face in shame &c. (*put to the b.*); rosy glow, flush of light; *blush-*, pink, rosy, (*b.-rose, b.-tint*, &c.). [f. prec.]

blu·ster[1], v.i. & t. Storm boisterously (of wind, waves, persons); (trans. with *out, forth*) utter overbearingly; (refl.) storm (one*self*) *into* (anger &c.). Hence **blu·ster**ER[1] n., **blu·stering**LY[2] adv. [perh. imit. on *blow, blast*, &c.; ME *blostre* stray is prob. separate]

blu·ster[2], n. Boisterous blowing, noisy self-asserting talk, threats. Hence **blu·ster**OUS, **blu·ster**Y[2], aa. [f. prec.]

bo, boh, int. used to startle (*can't say bo to a goose*, of shy or timid person).

bo·a, n. S.-Amer. genus of large non-poisonous snakes killing by compression (pop. extended to Old-World pythons; so also *b. constrictor*, prop. a Brazilian species of b.); lady's long fur or feather throat-wrap. [?]

Bo·aner·gēs, n. Loud-voiced preacher or orator. [Gk, f. Heb. *b'ney regesh* sons of thunder (*Mark* iii. 17)]

boar, n. Male uncastrated pig; its flesh; *b's head*, esp. as dish at Christmas or on festive occasion. [OE *bár* cf. G *bär* etym dub.]

board[1], n. 1. Long thin usu. narrow piece of sawn timber (strictly, over 4in. broad, under 2½ thick); wooden slab (of one or more breadths of b. bare or covered with leather &c.) used for various purposes, as in games, for posting notices, &c.; (pl.) the stage (*on the bb.*, employed as actor); thick stiff paper used in bookbinding (covered with paper, 'in bb.', or cloth, 'cloth bb.'), & for other purposes. 2. Table (only in spec. senses or contexts); *above b.*, open(ly); *sweep the b.*, take all the cards or stakes; table spread for meals (*bed & b.*, conjugal relations; *groaning b.*, plentiful meal); food served, daily meals provided at contract price or in return for services (*b.-money, -wages*, servant's pay in lieu of food; esp. *b. & lodging*); council-table, councillors, committee; *B. of Agriculture, B. of Trade, B. of Education, Local Government B.*, government departments; *Road B.*, for construction and improvement of roads; *b.-school* (before 1902), managed by b. according to Elementary Education Act of 1870. 3. Ship's side (only in spec. phrases, cf. *overboard*), *go by the b.*, (of masts &c.) fall overb., *on b.* = ABOARD (in various senses), usu. now on or into ship (orig. meaning within the sides, not on the deck), train, coach, &c. 4. Tack (naut.). [OE *bord* mixture of two com.-Teut. words meaning (1) board (2) border, respectively f. OTeut. *bordom* & *bordoz*; the second was further adopted in F & returned with spec. developments]

board[2], v.t. & i. 1. (f. prec. = wood) cover with boards (*b. up*, close with bb.). 2. (f. prec. = table) provide (lodger or daily guest) with, receive, stated meals at fixed rate; *b. with*, be entertained for pay in the house of. 3. (f. prec. = ship's side) come alongside (usu. to attack); force one's way on b. (ship or abs.); embark on. 4. (Of ship) tack. [f. prec., with influence of F *aborder*]

boar·der, n. One who boards with someone (prec. 2), esp. schoolboy at boarding-school. [prec. + -ER[1]]

boar·ding, n. In vbl senses; also or esp.; erection of boards; *b.-house, -school*, in which persons, boys, board (BOARD[2], 2); *b.-out*, (intr.) feeding elsewhere than at home, (trans.) placing (destitute children) in families; *b.-ship* (examining neutrals for contraband). [BOARD[1,2] + -ING[1]]

boast[1], n. Vain-glorious statement; self-exaltation in words; fact one is proud of; *make b. of*, announce proudly. Hence **boa·stFUL** a., **boa·stfulLY**[2] adv., **boa·stfulNESS** n. [ME *bost* etym. dub.]

boast[2], v.i. & t. Extol oneself (also refl.), brag *of* or *about*; vaunt, brag of, brag *that*; possess as thing to be proud of. Hence **boa·stER**[1] n. [ME *bosten* as prec.]

boat[1], n. Small open oared or sailing vessel, fishing-vessel, mail packet, or small steamer (*take b.*, embark; *have oar in everyone's b.*, of busybodies; *in the same b.*, with like risks &c.); b.-shaped utensil for sauce &c.; *boat-hook*, long pole with hook & spike; *b.-house*, shed at water's edge for keeping b.; *ship's b.*, carried on board ship; *b. train*, timed to catch or meet steam packet; *b.-fly*, water-bug swimming on water on its back; *boatman*, hirer-out or rower or sailer of b. for hire; *b.-bill*, S.-Amer. heron; *boatrace*, between rowing boats; *boatswain* (bō·sn), ship's officer in charge of sails, rigging, &c., & summoning men to duty with whistle [late OE *bátswegen*, cf. Icel. *sveinn* & see SWAIN]. Hence **boa·tAGE**(4), **boa·tFUL** (2), nn. [OE *bát* cf. ON *beit* and (f. the OE) *bátr*; borrowed in other Teut. langg. f. these, & possibly in Rom. also (F *bateau* &c.)]

boat[2], v.i. & t. Go in a b., amuse oneself so (*boating man*); place, carry, in a b. Hence **boa·tER**[1] n., hard straw hat (as worn in boating). [f. prec.]

bob[1], n., & v.t. Weight on pendulum, plumb-line, or kite-tail; knot of hair, tassel-shaped curl (*b.-wig*, also *b.*, with short curls, opp. to full-bottomed; cf. CHERRY-*bob*); horse's docked tail; (Metre) short line at end of stanza; (vb) cut (woman's hair) to hang short of shoulders (*wear it bobbed*), (n.) bobbed hair. [etym. dub.; f. 14th c.]

bob[2], v.i. Fish (*for* eels) with bunch (cf. prec.) of lobworms.

bob[3], v.i. Move up & down, dance, rebound; *b. up like a cork*, become active or conspicuous again after defeat; catch with the mouth (*for* cherries &c. floating or hanging); curtsy. [etym. dub.; cf. BOB[1,7]]

bob[4], n. Jerk, bounding movement; curtsy; (Bellringing) kinds of change in long peals (*treble b.* in which treble bell has a dodging course, *b. minor* on 6 bells, *triple* on 7, *major* on 8, *royal* on 10, *maximus* on 12). [f. prec.]

bob[5], n. *Dry, wet, -b.*, cricketing, boating, Etonian; *light.-b.*, soldier of light infantry. [prob. = *Robert*]

bob[6], n. (slang; pl. same). Shilling. [etym. dub.; quoted f. 1812]

bob[7], v.t. Rap, jerk. [ME *boben* etym. dub.]

Bŏ·badil, n. Braggart. [Jonson, *Every Man in his Humour*]

bo·bbery, n. Disturbance, row, fuss. [Hind. *bap re* O father ! int. of dismay]

bo·bbin, n. Cylinder for holding thread, yarn, wire &c., & giving it off as wanted, reel, spool; small bar & string for raising door-latch. [f. F *bobine*]

bo·bbinet, n. Machine-made cotton net imitating lace made with bobbins on pillow. [prec., *net*]

bo·bbish, a. (slang). Brisk, well, (esp. *pretty b.*). [BOB[3] + -ISH[1] (2) irregularly appended to vb]

bo·bby, n. (slang). Policeman. [as BOB[5] + -Y[3] (Sir *Robert* Peel, Home Sec. 1828)]

bŏ·bolink, n. N.-Amer. songbird. [imit., cf. *cuckoo*]

bo·b-sled, -sleigh, n. Two short sleighs coupled, used for drawing logs, & in tobogganing. [U.S. & Canadian wd, now also Anglo-Swiss]

bo·bstay, n. Rope holding bowsprit down. [?]

bo·btail, n. & a. Docked tail; with this; horse or dog with this; *tag-rag & b.*, the rabble. [BOB[1]]

bocar·do, n. Logical formula, see BARBARA.

Bŏche (-sh), n. & a. (slang). (Contempt.

for) German. [F, perh. abbr. of *Alboche* (*Allemand* German & *-boche* substituted in contempt for other endings)]

bode, v.t. & i. Foresee, foretell, (evil); portend, foreshow; promise *well* or *ill*. Hence **bo·ding**LY[2] adv., **bo·de**MENT n. [OE *bodian* f. *boda* messenger, cf. ON *botha*]

bo·deful, a. Ominous. [mod. formation f. prec. or obs. n. *bode* omen + -FUL(1)]

bodē·ga, n. Cellar or shop selling wine only. [Sp., f. L f. Gk *apothēkē* see APOTHECARY]

bŏ·dice, n. Close-fitting upper part of woman's dress, down to waist; also, inner vest over stays. [orig. *pair of bodies* (cf. pair of stays), being a whalebone corset; now spelt & understood as sing.; cf. BAIZE & (perh.) ACCIDENCE]

bo·died, a. Possessed of body or a body, embodied; esp. in comb., as *full-b., able-b.* [BODY[1] + -ED[2]]

bo·diless, a. Incorporeal; separated from the body. [-LESS]

bo·dily[1], a. Of, affecting, the human body or physical nature; *b. fear*, of physical harm. [BODY[1] + -LY[1]]

bo·dily[2], adv. In the body, in person; with the whole bulk, as a whole. [BODY[1], -LY[2]]

bo·dkin, n. Pointless thick needle with large eye for drawing tape &c. through hem; long pin for fastening hair; person squeezed between two others (*ride, sit, b.*). [etym. dub.; earlier *boydekin*]

bŏ·dy[1], n. Man or animal as material organism (*keep b. & soul together*, remain alive); corpse (*b.-snatcher*, exhumer of corpses for dissection); *b. of Christ*, sacramental bread; *b.-servant*, valet; *b.-guard*, (rarely, member of) dignitary's retinue, escort, personal guard. Trunk, main portion (stem, hull, nave, &c., acc. to context); upper garment (minus sleeves & collar, or = bodice); document minus preamble &c.; majority. Human being, person, (*heir of* one's *b., good sort of b., anyb.*, &c.). Aggregate of persons or things (*in a b.*, all together; *b. politic*, State); society, league, military force; collection *of* precepts, information, &c. Piece of matter (*heavenly b.*, sun, star, &c.), quantity; comparative solidity or substantial character (*b.-colour*, opaque; *wine of good b.*), thing perceptible to senses. [OE *bodig*; now excl. E, unless = G *bottich* cask, referred to med. L *butica* f. Gk *apothēkē* see APOTHECARY]

bo·dy[2], v.t. Provide with b. (rare). (Usu. with *forth*) give mental shape to; exhibit in outward shape; typify. [f. prec.]

Boeotian (bēō·shn), a. & n. Crass, dull, (person). [of Gk nation derided by Athenians]

Bō·er, n. & a. (Of) Dutch or Dutch-descended S.-African(s). [Du., = peasant, farmer, cf. G *bauer* & see BOOR]

bog[1], n. (Piece of) wet spongy ground, morass (in many plant names as *b. violet*, BUTTERwort, *b.-berry*, cranberry); *b. butter*, fatty hydrocarbon found in Irish peat-b.; *b. oak*, ancient preserved in black state in peat; *b.-trotter*, Irishman. Hence **bo·ggy**[2] a., **bo·ggi**NESS n. [f. Ir. or Gael. *bogach* (*bog* soft)]

bog[2], v.t. Submerge in b. (usu. in pass.).

bog[3], n. A privy (vulgar).

bō·gey, Colonel Bogey, (-g-), n. Score that good golf-player should do hole or course in. [f. BOGY as imaginary person?]

bo·ggle, v.i. Start with fright, shy; hesitate, demur, *at* or *about*; equivocate; fumble. [var. of BOGLE used as vb]

bō·gie (-gĭ), n. Under-carriage with two or more wheel-pairs, pivoted below end of locomotive or railway-car; *b.-car* &c., fitted on these. [northern dial. wd, etym. dub.]

bō·gle, n. Phantom, goblin; bugbear; scarecrow. [introduced f. Scotch writers; etym. dub.; earlier *bog* in same sense, & *bug* (now only in BUGBEAR), may be f. W *bwg* ghost]

bō·gus, a. Sham, fictitious. [U.S. wd, etym. dub.]

bo·gy, -gey, (-g-), n. (pl. *-ies, -eys*). The devil; goblin (nursery, *the b. man*); bugbear. [quoted f. 1840 only; etym. dub. see BOGLE]

bohea· (-hē), n. Black tea of lowest quality (last crop of season). [f. Chin. *Wu-i* name of district]

Bohē·mian, a. & n. Socially unconventional (person); of free-&-easy habits, manners, & sometimes morals (esp. of artists &c.). Hence **bohe·mian**ISM(2) n., **bohe·mian**IZE(4) v.i. [f. F *bohémien* gipsy]

boil[1], n. Hard inflamed suppurating tumour. [OE *býl*, ME *bile*; com.-Teut., cf. G *beule* f. root *bul-* blow]

boil[2], v.t. & i. Bubble up, undulate, (of liquid at the heat that converts it to gas; also of containing vessel); *b. over* (of liquid or vessel), overflow or be overflowed thus; seethe, be agitated, like boiling water or its vessel (of sea &c., feelings, feeling person); bring (liquid, vessel) to heat at which it boils; subject to heat of boiling water, cook thus; undergo cookery by boiling; *b. down, away*, reduce, convert to vapour, by boiling; *keep the pot boiling*, get a living; *boiling hot*, boiling, (colloq.) very hot; *blood boils*, with indignation; *boiled shirt* (U.S. slang), cotton or linen shirt with starched front. [f. OF *boillir* (now *bouillir*) f. L *bullire* (*bulla* bubble)]

boil[3], n. = boiling, boiling-point, (esp. *on, at, to, the b.*).

boi·ler, n. One who boils; vessel for boiling, esp. large vessel of riveted wrought-iron plates for making steam in engine; tank attacked to kitchen range; laundry vessel; vegetable &c. suited to boiling; *b.-iron, -plate,* rolled iron ¼ to ½ in. thick; *b.-tube,* internal air-pipe carrying heat through b. [-ER[1]]

boi·ling, n. In vbl senses; esp.: *the whole b.* (slang), all the lot; *b.-point,* temperature at which anything boils (water at sea-level, 212° F., 100° C.), high excitement. [-ING[1]]

bois de rose (bwah-), n. Shades of brown. [F, = rose-wood]

boi·sterous, a. Violent, rough, (wind, sea, behaviour, speech, persons); noisily cheerful. Hence **boi·sterous**LY[2] adv. [earlier *boistous* (also *-eous, -uous*) etym. dub.; AF *boistous* (OF *boisteus* now *boiteux* lame) does not suit sense]

bo·ko, n. (slang). Nose. [?]

bōld, a. Courageous, enterprising, confident; *make (so) b. (as),* presume, venture; forward, immodest; vigorous, free, well-marked, clear, (imagination, drawing, description, features, headland, &c.). Hence **bo·ld**LY[2] adv., **bo·ld**NESS n. [OE *bald*; com.-Teut. cf. G *bald* quickly]

bole, n. Stem, trunk. [f. ON *bolr* cf. G *bohle* plank]

bole·ction, a. & n. (Moulding) raised above panel &c. [?]

boler·o (-ārō), n. Spanish dance; woman's short jacket with or without sleeves resembling zouave jacket. [Sp.]

bō·lide, n. Large meteor, fire-ball. [F, f. L f. Gk *bolis -idos* (*ballō* throw)]

bōll, n. Rounded seedvessel, as in flax or cotton. Hence **bōll**ED[2] a. [=BOWL[1]]

bŏ·llard, n. Post on ship or quay for securing ropes to. [perh. f. BOLE + -ARD]

bolŏ·meter, n. Radiation-measurer. [Gk *bolē* ray + -O- + -METER]

Bo·lshevik, n. Advocate of proletarian dictatorship in Russia by soviets, Russian communist; (pop.) any revolutionary. Hence **bo·lshev**ISM n., **-**VIST n. & a., **Bo·lshy** (slang) n. & a. [f. Russ. *bolsheviki* n. pl. majority party]

bō·lster[1], n. Long stuffed (esp. under-) pillow of bed or couch; pad or support in many machines and instruments. [OE; com.-Teut. cf. G. *polster* f. root *bul-* swell]

bo·lster[2], v.t. & i. (Usu. with *up*) support with b., prop, aid and abet, countenance, preserve from (merited) destruction; pad; (with schoolboys) belabour with b., (intr.) have b.-fight. [f. prec.]

bōlt[1], n. Short heavy arrow of crossbow, quarrel, (*fool's b. soon shot,* soon speaks and is soon silenced); discharge of lightning (*b. from the blue,* complete surprise); door-fastening of sliding bar & staple, sliding piece of lock; headed metal pin for holding things together, usu. riveted or with nut; (as measure) roll of canvas &c., bundle of osiers; *b.-rope* (round sail-edge to prevent tearing). [cf. G *bolz,* Du. *bout*; etym. dub.]

bolt[2], v.i. & t. Dart off or away, (horse) break from control; gulp down unchewed; fasten (door &c.) with b., *b. in* or *out,* shut in, exclude, by bolting door; fasten together with bolts. [f. prec.]

bolt[3], n. Sudden start; running away. [f. prec.]

bolt[4], adv. (With *upright*) = as a bolt, quite.

bolt[5], **boult** (bōlt), v.t. Sift; investigate. [f. OF *bulter* = It. *burattare* (*buratto* sieve perh. f. *bura* kind of cloth see BUREAU)]

bō·lter, n. In vbl senses of BOLT[2, 5]; esp.: horse given to bolting; (also *boulter*) sieve, sifting machine. [-ER[1]]

bō·lus, n. Large pill. [mod. L, f. Gk *bōlos* clod]

bomb (-ŏm), n., & v.t. & i. Hollow iron sphere filled with explosive fired from gun or (now usu.) thrown by hand & exploded by fuse or by striking an object, shell; *b.-proof,* (shelter) strong enough to resist shells; *b.-shell,* artillery b. (now usu. *shell* except in similes, *fell like a b.-s.* &c.). (Vb) assail with bb., throw bb. Hence **bo·mb**ER[1] (-mer) n., soldier, aeroplane, using bb. [f. F *bombe* f. Sp. *bomba* f. L f. Gk *bombos* hum]

bŏmbar·d, v.t. Batter with shot & shell (esp. of warships attacking town); (fig.) assail persistently with abuse, argument, &c. Hence **bombar·d**MENT n. [f. F *bombarder* discharge *bombarde* f. med. L *bombarda* stone-throwing engine prob. f. L *bombus* hum]

bombardier (bŭmbarder·), n. Artillery non-commissioned officer. [F, see prec. & -IER]

bŏ·mbardon, -ō·nĕ, n. Low-toned brass instrument; bass reed-stop on organ. [It. (*-one*), f. *bombardo* + *-one,* see BOMBARD, -OON]

bo·mbasine (-ŏm- or -ŭm-, -zēn), n. Twilled dress-material of worsted with silk, with cotton, or alone, much used for mourning. [f. F *bombasin* f. L *bombycinus* silken (*bombyx -ycis* silk or silk-worm f. Gk *bombux*)]

bŏ·mbast, n. Turgid language, tall talk. Hence **bomba·sti**C a., **bomba·sti**CALLY adv. [earlier & OF *bombace* (*-t* phonetic, cf. *behest*) f. LL *bombacem* nom. *-ax* cotton (& so padding) corruption of *bombyx* see prec.]

bon, bonne, (F), a. French for *good,* common in some senses & phrases. [f. L *bonus*]

bō·na fi·dĕ, a. & adv. Genuine(ly), sincere(ly). [L abl. s. of foll.; as adj. it may be hyphened, not as adv.]

bō·na fi·dēs, n. (legal). Honest intention, sincerity. [L, = good faith; not hyphened]

bona·nza, n. & a. (Prop.) prosperity, good luck; (pop.) greatly prospering, a large output (esp. of mines), worked with all best appliances (*a b. farm*), a run of luck (*in b.*). [U.S. f. Sp., = fair weather f. L *bonus* good]

bon-bon (F), n. Sweetmeat. [BON]
bonce, n. Large playing-marble. [?]
bond[1], n. Thing restraining bodily freedom, imprisonment, (rare, only in pl., esp. *in bb.*); fagot-withe; restraining or uniting force; binding engagement, agreement; deed by which A binds himself & his heirs &c. to pay a sum to B & his; government's or public company's documentary promise to pay borrowed money, debenture, (*bondholder*, person holding such document); (Customs, of goods) *in b.*, stored under charge of Customs in 'bonded warehouse' till importer pays duty (*take out of b.*); (Bricklaying)various methods (*English b., Flemish b.*, &c.) of holding wall together by making bricks overlap; *b.-stone*, stone or brick running through wall. [ME var. of BAND[1]]
bond[2], v.t. Bind together (bricks &c., see prec.), put customable goods into b. (see prec.), whence **bo·nd**ER[1] n., person who puts goods into bond, binding stone or brick; encumber with bonded debt (see BONDED). [f. prec.]
bond[3], n. League, confederation, (see AFRICANDER). [Du., cf. G *bund* f. *binden* BIND]
bond[4], a. In slavery, not free, (archaic). Hence **bo·ndman, bo·ndmaid, bo·ndservant, bo·ndservice, bo·ndslave,** nn. [influenced in sense by, but orig. separate f., BOND[1]; f. OE n. *bonda, bunda*, husbandman f. ON *bónde* = *bóande* part. n. f. *bua, boa*, dwell; after the conquest, the *bonde* sank into a serf, & the wd changed in sense]
bo·ndage (-ĭj), n. Serfdom, slavery; confinement; subjection to constraint, influence, obligation, &c. [ME f. AF; see prec. & -AGE]
bo·nded, a. (Of goods) placed in bond, (of warehouse) for such goods, (BOND[1]); (of debt) secured by bonds (BOND[1]). [BOND[1], -ED[2]]
bo·ndsman, n. Villein, serf; slave (lit. & fig.) [var. of *bondman* (BOND[4]) as though f. *bond's* genit. of BOND[1]]
Bond Street, n. A London street, esp. as resort of fashionable loungers (*a B.-S. exquisite*).
bone[1], n. One of the parts making up vertebrate animal's skeleton; (pl.) the body (*my old bb.* &c.), its remains (*his bb. were laid*); the body's hard, solid, or essential part (*flesh & b.*; *skin & b.*, thin person; *horse with plenty of b.*, well developed frame; *bred in the b.*, ineradicable; *to the b.*, penetrating, of cold, wound, &c.); material of which bb. consist; similar substance, as ivory, dentine, whalebone; thing made of bone, as (pl.) **dice,** castanets, stay-ribs; a small or nearly finished joint of meat (*knuckle-b., broiled bb.*); subject of dispute (*b. of contention, b. to pick with someone*); *make no bb. of, about*, or *to*, not hesitate; *will never make old bb.*, live long; *feel in* one's *bb.*, be quite sure; *b.-dry*, quite dry, (of country &c.) teetotal; *b.-setter*, one who sets broken or dislocated bones, esp. without being qualified surgeon; *b.-shaker*, bicycle without rubber tires; *b.-spavin*, callous growth in horse's leg becoming as hard as b. [OE *bán*; com.-Teut., cf. G *bein*; in most langg. the meaning is *leg* as well as *bone*]
bone[2], v.t. 1. Take out the bones from (meat, fish). 2. (slang) steal. [1 f. prec., & perh. 2 (as dog makes off with b.)]
bo·nfire, n. Large open-air fire in celebration of some event; fire for consuming rubbish (*make a b. of*, destroy). [earlier *bonefire* f. BONE n., bones being the chief material formerly used]
bo·ngo, n. Large striped African antelope. [native]
bonhomie (bŏ·nomē·), n. Geniality. [F (BON, *homme* f. L *homo* man, -Y[1])]
Bŏ·niface, n. Innkeeper. [Farquhar, *Beaux' Stratagem*]
bon mot (F), n. (pl. *bons mots*). Witty saying. [F (BON + *mot* saying f. L *muttum* a grunt)]
bonne, n. (French) nursemaid, maid. [BON]
bonne bouche (-ōōsh), n. Tit-bit, esp. to end up with. [F (BON, *bouche* mouth f. L *bucca* cheek perh. = POUCH); phr. not used in this sense in F]
bonnes fortunes (F), n. Ladies' favours, as a thing to boast of or pride oneself on.
bo·nnet[1], n. (Man's) Scotch cap; woman's out-door head-dress without brim, with strings, & covering no part of forehead; *b. rouge* (F, pr. bŏnā rōōzh), red cap as revolutionary symbol; (Naut.) additional canvas laced to sail-foot; cowl of chimney &c., protective cap in various machines, hinged cover over motor of car; (Gaming, Auctions, &c.) accomplice, decoy; BEE *in b.*, an eccentricity. Hence **bo·nnet**ED[2] a. [ME *bonet* f. OF *bonet* short for *chapel de b.* cap of (med. L) *bon(n)etus* an unknown material]
bo·nnet[2], v.t. Put b. on (person); crush down hat over the eyes of (person). [f. prec.]
bo·nny, a. (chiefly Sc.). Comely, healthy-looking; satisfactory. Hence **bo·nni**LY[2] adv. [etym. dub., perh. f. BON]
bon ton (F), n. Good breeding, the fashionable world, (archaic).
bō·nus, n. Something to the good, into the bargain; esp., extra dividend to shareholders of company, distribution of profits to insurance-policy-holders, gratuity to workmen beyond their wages. [jocular or ignorant use of L *bonus* good (man)]
bon vivant (F), n. Gourmand.
bo·ny, a. Of, like, bone(s); big-boned; with little flesh. [BONE[1] + -Y[2]]
bonze, n. Japanese or Chinese Buddhist

priest. [F, f. Port. *bonzo* perh. f. Jap. *bonzô* f. Chin. *fan seng* religious person]

boo, int., n., & v.t. & i. (Make) sound of disapproval or contempt; hoot (speaker, announcement, &c.). [imit. of cow's lowing]

boo·by, n. Silly dull-witted fool, lout; *b.-trap,* things placed on top of door ajar to fall on first opener; kinds of Gannet. Hence **boo·by**ISH[1] a. [prob. f. Sp. *bobo* (both fool & bird) perh. f. L *balbus* stammering]

boo·dle, n. Crowd, pack, lot, (*the whole b.* or *caboodle*); money for political bribery &c.; a card-game. [now U.S., cf. obs. *buddle*]

boohoo·, n., & v.i. (Make) sound of noisy weeping. [imit.]

bo͝ok[1], n. Portable written or printed treatise filling a number of sheets fastened together (forming roll, or usu. with sheets sewn or pasted hingewise & enclosed in cover); literary composition that would fill such a set of sheets (or several) if printed; (fig.) anything from which one may learn, also imaginary record, list, &c., (*b. of fate*; *b. of life,* list of those who shall be saved); the Bible (esp. *swear on the b.*); main division of treatise or poem (*Bk I* &c.), or of Bible (*B. of Genesis*); = LIBRETTO; back-hinged set of blank sheets for writing accounts, notes, exercises, &c., in (pl., merchant's accounts); (Turf) one's bets on a race or at a meeting (*won't suit my b.,* transf., is inconvenient); set of tickets, stamps, cheques, tricks at whist, &c., bound up or collected. *B. of reference,* not read continuously but used intermittently for information; *speak by the, like a, b.,* in formal phrases, or with correct information; *take a leaf out of ——'s b.,* imitate him; *without b.,* without authority, from memory; *on the bb.,* entered in list of members &c. (so *take* one's *name off the bb.*); *in ——'s bad* or *black, good, bb.,* in disfavour or favour with him; *bring to b.,* call to account. *Bookbinder, -ding,* binder, binding, of bb.; *bookcase* (-k-k-), case containing bookshelves; *b.-keeper, -ping,* one who keeps, art of keeping, the accounts of a merchant, public office, &c.; *b.-learning* or *-lore, -learnĕd,* mere theory, knowing bb. but not life, so **boo·k**ISH[1] a., **boo·kish**LY[2] adv., **boo·kish**NESS n.; *b.-maker, -king,* compiler, compiling, of bb. (esp. for mercenary motives), also professional betting man or **boo·kie** [-Y[3]] n., his profession; *bookman,* literary man; *b.-mark(er),* thing to keep place in b.; *b.-muslin,* fine kind folded in booklike way when sold; *b.-plate,* label with owner's name, crest, &c., for pasting into bb.; *b.-rest,* adjustable support for b. on table; *bookseller*; *b.-slide,* expanding stand for a few bb.; *bookstall* (of bb. exposed for sale out of doors); *b.-work,* study of rules or text-bb. (opp. to working sums, chemical analysis, &c.); *bookworm,* maggot eating its way through bb., person devoted to reading. Hence **boo·k**LET n. [OE *bóc*; com.-Teut. cf. G *buch*; the supposed connexion with BEECH (as providing bark or tablets) is doubtful]

bo͝ok[2], v.t. Enter in book or list; engage (seat &c.) by previous payment, (guest, supporter, &c.) for some occasion; enter name of (person engaging seat &c.), issue railway ticket to; take railway ticket; give, take down, address of (goods to be transmitted); *I'm booked,* caught, cannot escape; *booking-clerk, -office,* person, place, for buying tickets from. [OE *bócian* f. prec.]

boom[1], n. Long spar with one end attached stretching sail-foot; floating barrier of timber across river or harbour mouth. [Du., = BEAM]

boom[2], v.i., & n. (Make) deep resonant sound; hum, buzz; (make) bittern's cry. [imit.]

boom[3], v.t. & i., & n. (Show) sudden activity, development, (esp. of commercial ventures, prices, &c., cf. SLUMP); (win) sudden popularity for (an invention, cause, &c.) by advertising &c., launch with éclat. [U.S. wd perh. f. prec. (cf. *make things hum*)]

boo·merang, n. Australian curved hardwood missile with convex edge returning to its thrower; (fig.) argument or proposal that recoils on its author. [native name, perh. modified]

boon[1], n. Request, thing asked for; favour, gift; blessing, advantage. [f. ON *bón* = OE *bén* prayer; the change f. prayer to gift prob. helped by confusion with foll.]

boon[2], a. Bounteous, benign, (poet.; of nature, air, life, &c.); congenial, jolly, (*b. companion*). [f. BON; from 14th c.]

boor, n. Peasant; clumsy or ill-bred fellow. Hence **boor·**ISH[1] a., **boor·ish**LY[2] adv., **boor·ish**NESS n. [either f. OE *gebúr* dweller f. *búr* BOWER[1] & cf. NEIGHBOUR, or f. the cognate LG *bûr,* Du. BOER]

boost, v.t. (Slang) shove, hoist; (Mech.) raise the electromotive force in (electric circuit, battery), whence **boo·st**ER[1](2) n. [U.S.]

boot[1], n. Outer foot-covering, usu. all or partly of leather, coming above ankle; (Hist.) instrument of torture, luggage-receptacle in coach under guard's & coachman's seat; *b. is on the other leg,* truth or responsibility just the other way round; *like old bb.* (slang), tremendously; *over shoes over bb.,* as well risk much as little; *heart in* one's *bb.,* in terror; *die in* one's *bb.,* not in bed; *b. & saddle* [perversion of F *boute-selle,* place saddle], cavalry signal to mount; *bootjack,* for pulling bb. off; *bootlace,* string or leather strip for lacing bb.; *bootlegger,* liquor-smuggler in U.S.; *bootmaker*; *b.-trees*, moulds for keeping bb. in shape; (slang) *get, give, the b.*, be dismissed, dismiss, from employment. Hence **boo·t**ED[2] a. [ME *bote* f. OF *bote* (now *botte*), etym. dub.]

boot[2], n. Good, advantage, (now only in *to boot*, as well, to the good, additionally). [OE *bót*; com.-Teut. cf. G *busse* making good, expiation; prob. f. root *bat-*, Aryan *bhad-*, whence BETTER]

boot[3], v.t. (archaic; usu. impers. & abs.). Do good (*to*), avail, as, *what boots (it) to, (it) little boots, (it) boots (me) not.* [ME *boten* f. *bot* BOOT[2]]

bootee·, n. Kind of lady's boot; infant's wool boot. [cf. *coatee*, see -EE]

booth (-dh), n. Temporary shelter of canvas &c.; covered stall in market, tent at fair, &c.; *polling-b.*, for voting at elections. [ME *bothe* cf. Da., Sw., *bod*, f. East Norse *bóa* dwell]

boo·tless, a. Unavailing. [OE *botléas*, see BOOT[2], -LESS]

boots, n. Hotel-servant who cleans boots, conveys luggage, &c.

boo·ty, n. Plunder or profit acquired in common & to be divided; gain, a prize; *play b.*, act as decoy for confederates, practise collusion. [perh. f. F *butin* f. ON *býti* barter, influenced in form by *bót* BOOT[2]]

booze, v.i., & n. Drink deeply, go on drinking; (n.) drink, a drinking-bout. [earlier *bouse, bowse*, ME *bousen* perh. f. MDu. *bûsen* (*buise* drinking-cup)]

boo·zy, a. Addicted to drink; fuddled. [prec. + -Y[2]]

bō-pee·p, n. Game of hiding & suddenly appearing to child; *play b.*, of elusive politicians, arguers, &c. [BO + PEEP v.]

borā·cic, a. Of borax (*b. acid*, = BORIC acid). [-IC]

borage (bŭ·rĭj), n. Blue-flowered hairy-leaved plant used to flavour claret-cup &c. [f. med. L *borrago* or F *bourrache*; cf. perh. LL *burra* shaggy garment]

bō̆r·ax, n. A native salt, in white powder or crystal when pure. [ME & OF *boras* f. med. L *borax* f. Arab. *bauraq* prob. f. Pers. *burah*]

Bordeaux· (-dō), n. Southern French wine, claret.

bor·der[1], n. & a. Side, edge, boundary or part near it; frontier of country, (pl. after *within, out of*, &c.) territory; *the B.*, boundary & adjoining districts between England & Scotland, (U.S.) frontier of civilization, (also *Border* adj. in these senses); continuous bed round garden or part of it, distinct edging for strength or ornament or definition round anything. [ME & OF *bordure* = LL *bordatura* f. **bordare* f. *bordus* f. Teut. *bord* BOARD[1]]

bor·der[2], v.t. & i. Put or be a b. to, whence **bor·der**ING[1] (3) n.; adjoin (trans., or intr. with *on, upon*); *b. upon*, resemble. [f. prec.]

bor·derer, n. Dweller on or near frontier, esp. that of England & Scotland. [BORDER n. + -ER[1] (4)]

bore[1], v.t. & i. Make hole in usu. with revolving tool, hollow out evenly (tube &c.), whence **bor·**ING[1] (2) n.; make (a hole, one's way) by boring, persistent pushing, or excavation; (of horse) thrust the head out; (Racing) push (another) out of the course. [OE *borian*; com.-Teut. cf. OE & ON *bor* augur, & L *forare* bore, Gk *pharos* plough]

bore[2], n. Hollow of gun-barrel; diameter of this, calibre; small deep hole made in earth to find water &c. [f. prec.]

bore[3], n. Nuisance (usu. as pred.); tiresome person, twaddler. [f. 1750, etym. dub.; early quotations imply F deriv.; *bourrer* stuff, satiate?]

bore[4], v.t. Weary by tedious talk or dullness. [etym., & relation to prec. & to BORE[1], doubtful; of same date as BORE[3]; *bore* (BORE[1]) one's *ears* = gain a hearing by emphasis or repetition occurs over a hundred years earlier]

bore[5], n. Great tide-wave with precipitous front moving up some estuaries. [perh. f. ON *bára* wave]

bore[6]. See BEAR[3].

bor·ĕal, a. Of the North or north wind. [f. L *borealis* (foll., -AL)]

Bor·ĕăs, n. (God of) the north wind. [L f. Gk]

bore·cole, n. = KAIL. [f. Du. *boerenkool* peasant's cabbage]

bore·dom, n. Being bored, ennui. [BORE[4] + -DOM]

bō̆r·er, n. Person, tool, or machine, that bores holes; horse that bores; kinds of boring insect. [BORE[1] + -ER[1]]

bor·ic, a. Of boron (*b. acid*, a preservative). [-IC]

born, p.p. & a. *Be b.*, come into the world by birth; *b. of*, owing origin to; *b. again*, regenerate; (with compl.) destined to be (*b. rich, tired, to be hanged, a poet*; cf. also *b. orator, an orator b.*, &c.); *b. with silver spoon in mouth, under lucky star*, destined to wealth, good luck; *in all my b. days*, my life; *b. fool, idiot* (utter, hopeless); often in comb. with adjj. & advv., as *base, first, -b.* [p.p. of BEAR[3]]

borne. See BEAR[3].

borné (F), a. Having limitations, of limited ideas, narrow-minded.

boro-, comb. form of foll.

bor·on, n. Non-metallic solid element (a dark-brown powder). [f. BORAX with ending of *carbon*, which it resembles in some respects]

borough (bŭ·ru), n. (Munic.) town with corporation & privileges conferred by royal charter; (Parl.) town sending member(s) to parliament; *the B.*, of Southwark; (Hist.) *own, buy, b.*, power of controlling election of member, *close, pocket, b.*, so controlled, *rotten b.*, no longer (before

1832) having real constituency. [OE *burg, burh*; com.-Teut., cf. G *burg* castle, prob. f. OTeut. *bergan* to shelter; Sc. form, *burgh*]

borough-English (bŭru), n. Tenure in some parts of England, by which all lands & tenements fall to youngest son. [f. AF *tenure en Burgh Engleys* (i.e. not French, but existing in some English boroughs)]

bo·rrow, v.t. Get temporary use of (money &c. to be returned; *of* or *from* person); adopt, use without being the true or original owner or inventor, derive from another, import from an alien source; (Golf) play ball up-hill to roll back, (also) allow for wind or slope; *borrowed light*, internal window; *borrowed* PLUMES. Hence **bo·rrow**ER[1], **bo·rrow**ING[1](2), nn. [OE *borgian* f. *borg, borh*, pledge, f. OTeut. *bergan* protect, cf. G *borgen* borrow; orig. meaning, take on pledge]

Bor·stal, n. *B. system*, of imprisonment for young criminals, based on the INDETERMINATE sentence; *B. Association*, for help of B. prisoners on discharge; *B. Institution*, formerly *B. Prison*, at B. in Kent.

bort, n. Diamond fragments made in cutting. [perh. f. OF *bort* bastard]

bor·zoi, n. Russian wolf-hound. [f. Russ. *borzoy* a. = swift, & n.]

bŏs, n., & v.t. & i., (slang). (Also *b.-shot*) bad shot or guess, miss; bungle, mess; (vb) miss, bungle. [?]

bo·scage, -kage, (-ij), n. Masses of trees or shrubs. [ME *boskage* f. OF *boscage* (LL *boscum* wood & see -AGE)]

bosh[1], n. & int. (slang). Nonsense, foolish talk, folly. [Turk., = empty; introduced by Morier's novel *Ayesha*]

bosh[2], v.t. (school slang). Make a fool of, tease. [f. prec.]

bosk, bo·sket, -quet (-k-), nn. Thicket, plantation. [*bosk* prob. mod. back-formation f. BOSKY (but cf. ME *bosk* var. of *busk* BUSH[1]); *bosket* f. F *bosquet* f. It. *boschetto* dim. of *bosco* wood; cf. BOUQUET]

bo·sky a. Wooded, bushy. [f. BOSK not recorded betw. 14th & 19th cc. + -Y[2]]

bosom (bŏŏ·zm), n. Person's breast; enclosure formed by breast & arms (*wife of* one's *b.*); breast of dress, space between dress & breast, old equivalent of pocket (*put in* one's *b.*); surface of lake, ground, &c.; the midst (*b. of* one's *family, of the church*); the heart, thoughts, desires, &c. (*comes home to* one's *b., b.-friend*). [OE *bósm* cf. G *busen*, etym. dub.]

boss[1], n. Protuberance; round metal knob or stud on centre of shield or ornamental work; (Arch.) projection at intersecting-point of vault-ribs; (Mech.) enlarged part of shaft. Hence **boss**ED[2], **bo·ss**Y[2], aa. [ME & OF *boce* (now *bosse*) = It. *bozza* ulcer]

boss[2], n. (slang). Master, person in authority; (U.S.) manager of political organization; person or thing that is best at any thing, champion. [U.S. wd f. Du. *baas* uncle, master, cf. G *base* female cousin]

boss[3], v.t. (slang). Be master or manager of (*b. the show*, make all arrangements). [f. prec.]

Bo·swell (-z-), n. Biographer like James B., writer of Johnson's life. Hence **Boswe·ll**IAN a., **Bo·swell**ISM(3) n., **Bo·swell**IZE(4) v.i.

bot, bott, n. Parasitic worm; *the botts*, horse disease caused by it.

bŏ·tanist, n. Student of botany. [f. F *botaniste*, see BOTANY, -IST(3)]

bŏ·tanize, v.i. Study plants, esp. by seeking them as they grow. [f. Gk *botanizō* gather plants, see BOTANY, -IZE]

bŏ·tany, n. Science of plants. Hence **bota·n**ICAL a. (also **bota·n**IC in names of old societies), **bota·n**ICALLY adv. [historically *botanic* is the parent word, f. med. L f. Gk *botanikos* (*botanē* plant f. *boskō* feed); *botany* on anal. of *astronomy* -*ic* &c.; see -Y[1]]

botar·go, n. Relish of mullet or tunny roe. [It., f. Arab. *buṭarkhah* f. Copt. *outarakhon* (Copt. *ou-* indef. art. + Gk *tarikhion* pickle)]

botch, n., & v.t. & i. (Make a) clumsy patch; bungle(d) work; repair badly. Hence **bo·tch**ER[1] n. [etym. dub.; cf. PATCH & G *batzen*]

bōth, a., pron., & adv. (Adj.) the two ——s & not only one, as *b.* (*the*) *brothers are dead* (*have it b. ways*, choose now one now the other of alternatives or contradictories to suit one's argument &c.). (Pron.) the two & not only one (a) with no. n., as *b. are dead*; (b) with *of* & n. or pron., as *b. of them* (or *of the brothers*) *are dead*; (c) with n. or pron. as subj., & *b.* in the pred. in apposition, as *they* (or *the brothers*) *are b. dead, they were gentlemen b.* (Adv.) with equal truth in two cases (a) where *b.* might still be held pronominal, as *b. brother & sister are dead*; (b) clearly adv., as *she is b. dead & buried*; (c) of more than two nouns &c., as *b. God & man & beast.* [earlier *bo*, OE *bá*; ME *bathe* f. ON *báthar* cf. G *beide*; *báthar* perh. resulted f. the addition of the def. art. (both the)]

bŏ·ther[1] (-dh-), v.t. & i. Pester, worry; be troublesome; worry oneself, take trouble; (subjunct. as mild imprecation) confound. [etym. dub.; first in Irish writers, Swift, Sterne, &c.]

bo·ther[2], n. Worry, fuss. [f. prec.]

bothera·tion, n. & int. = prec.; (int.) confound it! [BOTHER v. + -ATION]

bo·thersome, a. Annoying, troublesome. [-SOME]

bŏ·thy, -ie, n. (Sc.). Hut, cottage; one-roomed building in which workmen are lodged. [etym. dub.; cf. BOOTH]

bo·ttle[1], n. Narrow-necked vessel, usu. of glass, for storing liquid; the amount of liquid in it; *the b.*, drinking, *over a b.*, while drinking; *bring up on the b.*, of child not fed from the breast; *b.-brush*, cylindrical brush for cleaning bb., kinds of plant as Horsetail; *b.-glass*, coarse dark-green glass; *b.-green*, dark green; *b.-holder*, pugilist's attendant at prizefight, second, supporter, understrapper; *b.-neck*, (of roads) narrow outlet for traffic; *b.-nose*, swollen nose, B.-nosed whale; *b.-washer*, factotum, underling. [f. OF *bouteille* f. LL *buticula* dim. of *butis* BUTT[1]]

bo·ttle[2], v.t. Store in bb.; (slang) nab, catch, (offender, person for duty &c.); *b. up*, conceal ,restrain for a time, (resentment &c.). [f. prec.]

bo·ttle[3], n. Bundle of hay or straw (*look for needle in b. of hay*, of hopeless search). [f. OF *botel* dim. of **bot* (*botte* bundle)]

bo·ttle[4], n. *Blue, White, Yellow, B., B. of all sorts*, kinds of plant. [partly corruption of *buddle, bothel*, etym. dub., partly from shape of ovary or calyx]

bo·ttom[1], n. & a. Lowest part, part on which thing rests (*stand on own b.*, be independent; *b. up*, upside-down); the posterior; seat (of chair); ground under water of lake &c. (*go, send, to the b.*, sink; *touch b.*, be at the lowest point or on firm facts; *to, from, b. of heart*, genuinely, profoundly); river-basin &c., low-lying land; less honourable end of table, class, &c., person occupying this; farthest or inmost point (*b. of bay*); keel, horizontal part near keel, hull, ship esp. as cargo-carrier (*in British bb.*); foundation, basis, origin, (*be at the b. of*, cause); essential character, reality, (*search to the b., get to the b. of; at b.*); stamina. (Adj.) lowest, last (*bet your b. dollar*, stake all); *bottom* GEAR; fundamental; hence **bo·ttom**MOST a. [OE *botm* f. WG **bothm* (G *boden*), cf. Gk *puthmēn*, Skr. *budhná*, L *fundus* (for *fudnus*)]

bo·ttom[2], v.t. & i. Put b. to (saucepan, chair); base (argument &c.) *upon*; touch b. of sea &c.; touch b. of, sound, find the extent or real nature of. [f. prec.]

bo·ttomless, a. Without bottom (chair &c.); unfathomable. [-LESS]

bo·ttomry[1], n. System of lending money to shipowner for purposes of voyage on security of ship, lender losing the money if ship is lost. [BOTTOM n. = ship + -RY after Du. *bodmerij*]

bo·ttomry[2], v.t. Pledge (ship; see prec.).

bŏ·tūlism, n. (med.). Sausage-poisoning. [f. L *botulus* sausage, -ISM]

boudoir (bōō·dwahr), n. Lady's small private room. [F, = sulking-place f. *bouder* sulk, etym. dub.; termin. as in PARLOUR (F *-oir*)]

Bou·gainvillae·a, -vi·lia, (bōō-), n. Tropical plant with large bright-coloured bracts. [*Bougainville*, French navigator, c. 1750]

bough (-ow), n. Tree-branch (if on tree, one of the chief branches). [OE *bóg, bóh*; com.-Teut. (in etym., but not in sense) cf. G *bug*, Du. *boeg*, shoulder, bow of ship; also Skr. *bahus*, Gk *pēkhus* arm; BOW[5] of ship is same wd adopted separately f. Scand. or LG]

bought. See BUY.

bougie (bōō·zhē), n. Wax candle; thin flexible surgical instrument for exploring, dilating, &c., the passages of the body. [F, f. Arab. *Bijiyah* Algerian town with wax trade]

bouillabaisse (bōōlyabā·s), n. French (esp. Marseilles) dish, rich fish-stew. [F]

bouilli (bōōlyē·), n. Stewed or boiled meat. [F]

bouillon (F), n. Broth, soup; (Dress) puffed fold. [F, f. *bouillir* BOIL]

bou·lder (bōl-), n. Water-worn rounded stone, cobble; large erratic block of weather-worn stone (in mining, of detached ore); *b.-clay, -drift, -formation, -period*, geol. terms w. ref. to the Ice Age. [short for *boulderstone*, ME *bulderston*, cf. Sw. dial. *bullersten* large stone in stream (*buller* noise)]

boulevard (bōō·lvahr), n. Broad street with rows of trees. [F, f. G *bollwerk* BULWARK orig. promenade on demolished fortification]

boulever·sement (F), n. Turning upside-down.

bou·lter (bōl-), n. Long fishing-line with many hooks. [?]

bounce[1] (bow-), v.i. & t. Rebound; throw oneself about; burst noisily, angrily, &c., *into* or *out of* (room), *in* or *out*; talk big; hustle (person) by bluff or assumptions *into doing* or *out of* (something); *bouncing girl* &c., big, hearty, bustling, noisy. [ME *bunsen* thump (a now archaic sense of *bounce*); perh. imit. of sound cf. G dial. *bums* for gunfire &c.]

bounce[2], n. Rebound; boast, exaggeration, swagger. [f. prec.]

bounce[3], adv. Suddenly, noisily, (*come b. against* &c. cf. BANG). [as prec.]

bou·ncer, n. In vbl senses; also: unblushing lie; thing big of its kind. [-ER[1]]

bound[1] (bow-), n. Limit of territory or estate; (usu. pl.) limitation, restriction, (*out of bb.*, beyond limits set by school rules; *go beyond the bb. of reason, put bb. to*). [f. OF *bodne* = med. L *bodena* earlier *butina*]

bound[2], v.t. Set bounds to, limit, (esp. in pass. with *by*); be the boundary of. [f. prec.]

bound[3] (bow-), v.i. (Of ball &c.) recoil from wall or ground, bounce; (of living thing, wave, &c.) spring, leap advance lightly. [f. F *bondir* (only of sound till 15th c.) perh. f. L *bombitare* (*bombus* hum)]

bound[4], n. Springy movement upward or forward; (*advance by leaps & bb.*, with startling speed); (of ball &c.) recoil (*on* *the first b.*, between first two touchings of ground). [f. prec.]

bound[5] (bow-), a. Ready to start, having started, *for* (or with preceding adv. as *homeward b.*). [ME *boun*, f. ON *búinn*, Norw. *buen*, p.p. of *búa* get ready; *-d* is due to the ME form's not looking like a p.p.]

bound[6], p.p. of BIND. In vbl senses; esp. *b. up with*, having the same interests as, closely connected with; *b. to win* &c., certain.

bou·ndary, n. Limit-line; thing that limits. [BOUND[1] + -ARY[1]]

bou·nden. See BIND[1].

bou·nder, n. In vbl senses of BOUND[2, 3]; esp., (slang) cheerfully or noisily ill-bred person. [-ER[1]]

bou·ndless, a. Unlimited. Hence **bou·ndless**LY[2] adv., **bou·ndless**NESS n. [BOUND[1] + -LESS]

bou·nteous (bow-), a. Beneficent, liberal; freely bestowed. Hence **bou·nteous**LY[2] adv., **bou·nteous**NESS n. [ME *bontyvous* f. OF *bontif* (*bonté* BOUNTY) + -OUS, altered later as though f. *bounté* BOUNTY + -OUS]

bou·ntiful, a. = prec. (*lady b.*, beneficent lady of a neighbourhood); also, ample. Hence **bou·ntiful**LY[2] adv. [foll. + -FUL]

bou·nty (bow-), n. Munificence, liberality in giving; gift (*King's, Queen's, B.*, grant made to mother of triplets; *Queen Anne's B.*, fund for augmenting poor benefices); gratuity to soldiers & sailors on joining &c.; sum paid to merchants &c. to encourage trade enterprise (*b.-fed products*). [f. OF *bontet* f. L *bonitatem* f. *bonus* good (BON, -TY)]

bou·quet (bo͝o·kā), n. Bunch of flowers; perfume of wine. [F, = It. *boschetto* BOSKET]

bouquetin (bo͝o·ketĭn), n. The Alpine ibex. [F]

bour·don (boor-), n. Bass (usu. 16 ft) stop in organ; similar stop in harmonium. [F, = bagpipe-drone, perh. imit.]

bourgeois[1] (boor·zhwah), n. & a. (Member) of shop-keeping middle class, (person) of humdrum middle-class ideas. [F, f. LL *burgensis* (*burgus* town f. WG *burg* BOROUGH]

bourgeois[2] (berjoi·s), n. & a. (Printing type) between long primer & brevier. [perh. a French printer's name]

bourgeoisie (boorzhwahzē·), n. The middle class. [F]

bourgeon. See BURGEON.

bourn[1] (boorn), n. Small stream. [southern var. of BURN[1]]

bourn(e)[2] (boorn), n. Limit, goal. [f. F *borne* f. OF *bodne* BOUND[1]]

bourse (boors), n. Foreign money-market, esp. that of Paris. [F]

boustrophē·don (bow-), a. & adv. (Written) from right to left & from left to right in alternate lines. [Gk, adv. = as ox turns in ploughing (f. *bous* ox, *-strophos* turning, *-don* adv. suf.)]

bout (bowt), n. Spell of or turn at work or exercise; fit of drinking or illness; trial of strength; *this b.*, on this occasion. [perh. = obs. *bought*, which was perh. (being only from 15th c.) assim. of BIGHT to BOW[3]]

bouts rimés (bo͝o rēmā·), n. pl. Rhymed ends; versifying to set rhymes. [F]

bō·vine a. Of, like, an ox; inert, dull. [f. L *bovinus* (*bos bovis* ox, see COW)]

bŏ·vril, n. A meat extract used like beef tea. [trade name]

bow[1] (bō), n. Curve; rainbow; weapon for shooting arrows (*bend, draw, the b.*; *two strings to* one's *b.*, more resources than one; *draw the long b.*, exaggerate); = SADDLE-*b.*; rod with stretched horse-hair for playing violin &c., single passage of this across strings; = BAIL[4]; = BOW-WINDOW; slipknot with single or double loop, ribbon &c. so tied; *bb., b.-compass(es)*, compass with jointed legs; *b.-head*, Greenland whale; *b.-legged*, bandy; *b.-saw*, narrow saw stretched like bowstring on wooden frame; *bowshot*, distance to which b. can send arrow; *b.-string*, (strangle with) string of b. (Turkish method of execution). [OE *boga*; com.-Teut. cf. G *bogen* f. *bug-* st. of OTeut. *beugan* bend]

bow[2], v.t. Use the bow on (violin &c.; also abs.). [f. prec.]

bow[3] (-ow), v.i. & t. Submit (*to the inevitable* &c.), bend or kneel in sign of submission or reverence *to* or *before* (often with *down*); incline head in salutation, assent, &c. (*bowing acquaintance*, that stops at this, slight); express (thanks &c.) usher *in* or *out*, by bowing; cause to bend (lit. & fig., *knee, back* &c. for burden, *will*); *b. down*, crush, make stoop, (esp. *bowed down by* care &c.) [OE *búgan* f. OTeut. *beugan* f. st. *bug-* cf. Skr. *bhuj-* bend, L *fugere*, Gk *pheugō* flee; *bow* has also taken the senses of obs. *bey* its causal form f. OTeut. *baugjan*]

bow[4], n. Bending of head or body in salutation, respect, consent, &c.; *make* one's *b.*, retire. [f. prec.]

bow[5] (-ow), n. Fore-end of boat or ship from where it begins to arch inwards (often pl.); *on the b.*, of objects within 45° of the point right ahead; rower nearest the b. (*b.-oar*, his oar or himself); *b.-chaser*, see CHASE[1]. [only from 1600; = LG *bug*, Du. *boeg*, Da. *boug*, shoulder, ship's bow; OE had *bóg, bóh*, shoulder, bough, but without the naut. sense; see BOUGH]

Bow bells (bō), n. *Within the sound of B.*, in City of London. [f. *St Mary le Bow*]

bow·dlerize (bow-), v.t. Expurgate (book, author). Hence **bow·dler**ISM(3), **bowdleriz**A·TION, nn. [T. *Bowdler* 1818, expurgator of Shakspere, + -IZE (4)]

bow·el, n. Division of alimentary canal

below stomach, intestine, gut, (sing. only in med. use); (pl.) entrails, inside of body; pity, tender feelings, (*bb. of mercy* &c.); interior of anything. [ME *buel* f. OF *boel* = It. *budello* f. LL *botellus* dim. of *botulus* sausage]

bow·er[1] (bow-), n. Dwelling, abode, (poet.); inner room, boudoir, (poet.); place closed in with foliage, arbour, summerhouse, whence **bow·ery**[2] a.; *b.-bird*, Australian bird of the bird-of-paradise family constructing elaborate runs adorned with feathers, shells, &c. [OE *búr* dwelling (cf. G *bauer* birdcage) f. OTeut. *bûrom* f. Aryan *bhurom* f. *bhu* (Teut. *bu-*) dwell]

bow·er[2] (bow-), n. (Also *b.-anchor, -cable*) either of two anchors (*best* & *small*) carried at ship's bow or of their cables. [BOW[5] + -ER[1]]

bow·er[3] (bow-), n. One of two cards (*right b.*, knave of trumps, *left b.*, knave of same colour) at euchre. [f. G *bauer* peasant, knave at cards, see BOER]

bow·ie-knife (bō-), n. Long knife with 10–15in. blade double-edged at point used as weapon in wild parts of U.S. [Col. J. *Bowie*]

bowl[1] (bōl), n. Basin (hist., deep-shaped basin; now differing only as more dignified or poetic wd); drinking-vessel (*the b.*, conviviality); contents of a b.; b.-shaped part of tobacco-pipe, spoon, balance, &c. Hence **bow·lful**(2) n. [var. of BOLL OE *bolla*; com.-Teut. f. *bul-* swell]

bowl[2] (bōl), n. 1. Wooden ball made slightly out of spherical shape and weighted on one side to make it run curved course (BIAS). 2. Flattened or spherical wooden ball at skittles. 3. (Pl.) game played with bb. (sense 1) on grass, or with round balls in room. 4. (Dial.; pl.) skittles. [ME & F *boule* f. L *bulla* bubble; *bowl*[2] has taken its pronunc. f. *bowl*[1], & *bowl*[1] its spelling f. *bowl*[2]]

bowl[3] (bōl), v.t. & i. Play bb.; trundle (ball, hoop, &c.) along ground; go along by revolving or by means of wheels, esp. *b. along*, go fast & smoothly; (Cricket) deliver (*ball, over*, or abs.), knock *off* (bails) or *down* (wicket), dismiss (batsman; *out* or abs.), whence **bow·ler**[1] [-ER[1]] n.; *b. over*, knock down, (fig.) disconcert, render helpless. [f. prec.]

bow·ler[2] (bō-), n. = BILLYCOCK. [f. BOWL[1] + -ER[1]]

bowline (bō·lĭn), n. Rope from weather side of square sail to bow; (also *b.-knot*) a simple but very secure knot. [in all Teut. langg. connected with BOW[5], but found in E centuries before that, & now with different pronunc.]

bow·ling, n. In vbl senses; esp.: *b.-crease*, line from behind which bowler delivers ball; *b.-alley*, long enclosure for playing skittles; *b.-green*, lawn for playing bowls. [-ING[1]]

bow·man[1] (bō-), n. (pl. *-men*). Archer. [BOW[1]]

bow·man[2] (bow-) n. (pl. *-men*). Oarsman nearest the bow. [BOW[5]]

bow·sprit (bō-) n. Spar running out from ship's stem, to which forestays are fastened. [earlier recorded than BOW[5], & with its first part very various (*bore, boar, bolt-, bole-, bow-*); therefore prob. not an E compd, but borrowed entire; cf. Du. *boegspriet* see BOW[5], SPRIT]

Bow-street (bō-), n. & a. Street near Covent Garden with chief metropolitan police-court; *B.-runner, -officer*, old names for police officer.

bow wi·ndow (bō-), n. Curved (not angular) bay window; (slang) large belly. Hence **bow-wi·ndowed**[2] a. [BOW[1]]

bow-wow, int. & n. Dog's bark; imitation of it; (nursery talk &c.) dog; *the (big) b. style*, dogmatic manner in talk or writing.

bow·yer (bō-), n. Maker, seller, of bows. [BOW[1] + -YER]

box[1], n. Kinds of small evergreen shrub, esp. one with small dark leathery leaves, much used in garden borders; (also *boxwood*) its wood, used by turners & engravers; (with qualification) similar plant (*Bastard B.* &c.). [f. L *buxus*, cf. Gk *puxos*]

box[2], n. Receptacle (usu. lidded, rectangular or cylindrical, & for solids) of wood, cardboard, metal, &c. (*in the same b.*, i.e. predicament); driver's seat (from the box under it); = *boxful* as quantity; money-box (*put in the b.*); separate compartment at theatre, in tavern, &c., in stable or railway truck for horse (*loose b.*, in which it can move about); = JURY-*b.*, WITNESS-*b.*; hut for sentry or signalman; *fishing, shooting*, &c., *-b.*, small country house for such temporary uses; protective case in various machines; *in the wrong b.*, awkward position. *B. bed*, with wooden roof & sides opening with sliding panels, also bed made to fold up & look like b.; *b.-cloth*, close-woven cloth like buff; *b.-coat*, heavy overcoat (for driving); *b.-keeper*, attendant on theatre bb.; *b.-office*, in theatre for booking seats; *b.-pleat*, double fold in cloth; *b.-drain*, of quadrangular section; *b.-iron*, for ironing, hollow for reception of heater; *b. spanner* (with socket head). Hence **bo·xful**(2) n. [either = prec., or f. L *buxum* boxwood, or f. L f. Gk *puxis* PYX]

box[3], v.t. Provide with, put into, a b.; *b. up*, confine uncomfortably, squeeze together; lodge (document) in Law Court; divide off from other compartments; (old slang) *b. the watch*, overturn watchman in his b.; *b. the compass*, (Naut.) rehearse the points in correct order, (fig.) make complete revolution & end where one began (in politics, argument, &c.). [f. prec.]

box[4], n. Slap with hand *on the ear(s)*. [?]

box[5], v.t. & i. Slap person's *ears*; fight (someone, or intr.) with fists (usu. in padded gloves & merely for exercise); *boxing-gloves*; boxing-weights, *Heavy, Middle, Light, Feather*, and *Bantam, -weight*, the divisions being at 11st. 4, 10st., 9st., & 8st. 4 (*Welter-weight*, U.S., 145 lb. & below). [f. prec.]

Box and Cox, n. Two persons who take turns in sustaining a part. [name of play]

bo·xer, n. Pugilist; (slang) top hat; (*B*-) member of Chinese anti-foreign secret society. [prec., -ER[1]]

box-haul, v.i. Veer ship round on her keel (for want of room). [BOX[3]]

Bo·xing-day, n. First week-day after Christmas. [on which Christmas-boxes are given, f. obs. sense of BOX[3] f. (money)-BOX[2]]

boy, n. Male child (strictly till puberty, loosely till 19 or 20, 'the bb.' also of grown-up sons of a family); person who retains tastes or simplicity of boyhood; servant, slave, native labourer, male native, in various countries with subject races (cf. POST[2]-*boy* &c.); (familiar voc.) *old, my, b.*; *the b.* slang, champagne; *boy-*, often = male (*b.-child*), young (*b.-husband*); *b.* SCOUT[1]; *boy's-love*, Southern-wood. [cf. EFris. *boi* young gentleman perh. = Du. *boef* knave f. MHG *buobe* (G *bube*)]

boy·cott, v.t., & n. Punish, coerce, (person, class, nation) by systematic refusal of social or commercial relations; combine in abstaining from (goods &c.) with this aim; (n.) such treatment. [Capt. *B.*, Irish landlord so treated; f. 1880]

boy·hŏŏd, n. Boyish age; boys. [-HOOD]

boy·ish, a. Proper to boys; as of a boy, spirited, puerile. Hence **boy·ish**LY[2] adv., **boy·ish**NESS n. [-ISH[1] (1)]

bra·bble, v.i., & n., (archaic). (Engage in) paltry noisy quarrel. [etym. dub., but cf. Du. *brabbelen* jabber, stammer]

brace[1], n. Thing that clasps, tightens, unites, secures; (pl.) suspenders for trousers; thong for tuning drum; strap suspending carriage-body from springs; connecting mark in printing ({); pair, couple, (dogs, game, contempt. persons; pl. *3, 20*, &c., *brace*); strengthening piece of iron or timber in building; *b. & bit*, revolving tool for boring, screw-driving, &c.; (Naut.) rope attached to yard for trimming sail (*splice the main b.*, drink). [f. OF *brace, brase*, the two arms, f. L *brachia* (pl.) arms; the naut. meaning is perh. f. F *bras* arm]

brace[2], v.t. Fasten tightly, stretch, string up, give firmness to, (*b. oneself up, b.* one's *energies*, &c.; *bracing air*); support; couple together; (Naut.) move (sail) by bb. Hence **bra·cer**[1] n. (U.S. slang), pick-me-up. [partly f. OF *bracier* embrace, partly f. prec.; the naut. perh. f. F *brasser*]

bra·celet, n. Ornamental band, chain, &c., for wrist or arm; wrist-fetter. Hence **bra·celet**ED[2] a. [OF, dim. of *bracel* f. L *brachiale* (*brachium* arm) see -AL (2)]

bra·cer[2], n. Wrist-guard in archery & fencing. [f. OF *brasseüre* as f. L **brachiatura* (*brachium* arm), see -URE & cf. BORDER[1]]

brach (-ătsh), n. Bitch hound. [f. OF *brachet* dim. of *brac* f. OHG *bracco* hound hunting by scent]

bra·chial (-āk-), a. Of the, like an, arm. [f. L *brachialis* (*brachium* arm) see -AL]

bra·chiate (-āk-, -*at*), a. (bot.). With branches in pairs at right angles to stem, each pair at right angles to the last. [f. L *brachiatus* armed see prec. & -ATE[2] (1)]

brăchy- (-k-), comb. form of Gk *brakhus* short, in many scientific terms.

brăchycephă·lic (-kĭsĭ-), a. Short-headed (of skulls with breadth at least four-fifths of length; or of person or race with such skull). [prec. + -CEPHALIC]

brachy·logy (-kĭ-), n. Conciseness of speech, condensed expression, incorrectness of speech due to excessive condensation. [f. Gk *brakhulogia*, see BRACHY-, -LOGY]

bra·cken, n. A fern abundant on heaths &c.; any large fern; (collect.) mass of ferns. [ME (northern) *braken* cf. Sw. *bräken*]

bra·cket[1] n. Flat-topped projection from wall serving as support to statue, arch, &c.; shelf with slanting under-prop for hanging against wall; wooden or metal angular support; side-piece of gun-carriage supporting trunnion; support projecting from wall of gas or other lamp; pairs of marks, ( ), [ ], { } (cf. BRACE), used for enclosing words, figures, &c. (*b.-turn* in skating, like one of the third pair). [earlier *bragget* f. Sp. *bragueta* dim. of *braga* f. L *braccae* breeches, meaning affected by confusion with L *brachium* arm]

bra·cket[2], v.t. Enclose in bb. as parenthetic, spurious, (Math.) having spec. relations to what precedes or follows, &c.; couple (names &c.) with a brace, imply connexion or equality between (*bracketed*, equal); (Mil.) drop two shots one short of & one beyond (target) in range-finding. [f. prec.]

bra·ckish, a. Between salt & fresh (of water). [f. obs. adj. *brack* f. Du. *brak*, -ISH[1]]

bract, n. Small leaf or scale below calyx. So **bra·ctĕ**AL, **bra·ctĕ**ATE[2](2), aa. [f. L *bractea* thin plate, gold leaf]

brad, n. Thin flat slightly-headed nail. [earlier *brod* prob. f. ON *broddr* = OE *brord* spike]

bră·dawl, n. Small non-spiral boring-tool. [perh. f. prec. + AWL]

bra·dbury, n. (slang). Currency note, esp. for £1. [f. signature of Permanent Sec. to Treasury]

brădy-, comb. form of Gk *bradus* slow, as *-pepsy* slow digestion.

brae (-ā), n. Steep bank, hill-side. [Sc. wd used by E writers, f. ON *brá* = OE *brǽw* brow]

brag, n., & v.i. & t. (Indulge in) boastful talk; boast of or *of*, boast *that*; card-game like poker. [etym. dub.; F *braguer* &c. later]

braggadō·cio (-shĭō), n. Empty vaunting. [formed by Spenser (meaning *boaster*) on prec. & It. augmentative *-occhio*]

bra·ggart, n. & a. (Person) given to bragging. [f. F *bragard* f. *braguer* BRAG + -ARD]

brahmapoo·tra, brah·ma, n. Kind of domestic fowl. [river *Brahmaputra*, whence brought]

brah·min, -man, n. Member of Hindu priestly caste. Hence **brahmi·nic**(AL), **-mă·nic**(AL), aa., **brah·minism**(3), **-manism**(3), n. [f. Skr. *brahmaṇa* f. *brahman* worship]

brahminee·[1], n. Female brahmin. [f. Skr. *brahmaṇi* fem. see prec.]

brah·minee[2], a. Belonging to brahmin caste &c. [f. BRAHMIN on anal. of *Bengalee* &c.]

braid[1], n. Entwined hair, plait; band &c. entwined with the hair; silk, thread, &c., woven into a band. Hence **brai·ding**[1] (3, 6) n. [see foll.]

braid[2], v.t. Plait, interweave, (hair, flowers, thread); arrange (hair) in bb.; confine (hair &c.) with ribbon &c.; trim, edge, with b. [OE *bregdan* com.-Teut. move to & fro, move suddenly sideways]

Brai·dism, n. = HYPNOTISM. [first scientifically applied & explained by Dr J. *Braid*, 1842; -ISM (3)]

brail, n., & v.t. (Haul *up* with) small rope(s) on sail-edges for trussing sails before furling. [OF, f. L *bracale* waist-belt (*bracae* breeches) see -AL(2)]

braille (-āl), n. System of writing & printing for the blind. [M. *Braille*, French inventor, 1834]

brain, n., & v.t. Convoluted nervous substance in skull of vertebrates (sing. of the whole as an organ, pl. of the substance; *blow out* one's *bb.*, shoot him in the head); centre of sensation, thought, &c. (usu. pl., sing. with dignified or exalted effect; *cudgel* &c. one's *bb.*, think hard; *have something on the b.*, be crazy about it; *turn* one's *b.*, make him vain & silly); intellectual power (*suck, pick*, one's *b.*, extract & use his ideas); *b.-fag*, nervous exhaustion; *b. fever*, inflammation of the b.; *b.-pan*, skull; *b. sauce*, intelligence; *b.-sick*, mad; hence **brai·nless** a. (Vb) dash out bb. of. [OE *brægen* = Du. *brein*, cf. perh. Gk *brekhmos* forehead]

brai·ny, a. Clever (chiefly U.S.). [-Y[2]]

braird, n., & v.i. (Come up in) fresh shoots. [f. OE *brerd* brim cf. *brord* see BRAD]

braise (-z), v.t. Stew (prop. with fire above & below) tender with bacon, herbs, &c. [f. F *braiser* (*braise* hot charcoal)]

brake[1], n. = BRACKEN. [perh. borrowed f. northern *bracken* with loss of *-en* as though pl. ending]

brake[2], n. Thicket, brushwood. [cf. MLG *brake* tree-stumps (*breken* BREAK v.)]

brake[3], n. Toothed instrument for braking flax & hemp; (also *b.-harrow*) heavy harrow; instrument for peeling off willow-bark. [= MLG *brake* or ODu. *braeke* flax-brake f. Du. *breken* BREAK[1]]

brake[4], v.t. Crush (flax, hemp) by beating. [f. prec.]

brake[5], n. Apparatus for checking wheel's motion; (also *b.-van*) railway-carriage containing this, guard's compartment. Hence **bra·keless** a. [etym. dub.; perh. f. obs. or techn. *brake* = lever f. OF *brac* oblique of *bras* arm]

brake[6], v.t. Apply b. to (wheel, car, train). [f. prec.]

brake[7]. See BREAK[3].

brā·kesman, n. Man in charge of BRAKE[5].

Brā·mah-. (Lock, press, pen, &c.) invented by J. *B.* c. 1790.

bra·mble, n. Rough prickly shrub; blackberry-bush; (Sc.) blackberry. Hence **bra·mbly**[2] a. [OE *brembel* earlier *brémel* (for *-b-* cf. *humble, number*) dim. of OTeut. wd = OE *brom* BROOM cf. G *brom-beere* blackberry]

bra·mbling, n. The Mountain Finch. [prec. + -LING[1] (1)]

bran, n. Husks of grain separated from flour after grinding; *b. pie*, form of LUCKY[1]-*bag*. [f. OF *bren* etym. dub.]

bra·ncard, n. A horse-litter. [F, = litter (foll., -ARD)]

branch[1] (-tsh), n. Limb springing from tree or bough (*bough, b., twig*, is the order, but *b.* sometimes for either of the others); lateral extension or subdivision of mountain-range, river, road, family, genus, subject of knowledge, argument, legislature, bank or other business, &c.; *root-&-b.* adj., *root & b.* adv., thorough(ly), radical(ly). Hence (-)**branched**[2], **bra·nchless**, aa., **bra·nchlet** n. [f. F *branche* branch f. LL *branca* paw]

branch[2], v.i. Put branches *out, forth*; spring *out*, spread *forth*, tend *away* or *off*, diverge *into*. [f. prec.]

***bra·nchia*(*e*)** (-kĭa, -kĭē), n.pl. Gills. Hence **bra·nchial**, **bra·nchiate**[2](2), **branchi·ferous**, **bra·nchiform** aa., **bra·nchio**-comb. form. [L *branchia*, pl. *-ae*, f. Gk *bragkhia* pl.]

bra·nchy a. With many branches. [-Y[2]]

brand[1], n. Burning or charred log or stick (*b. from the burning*, rescued person, convert), torch (poet.); mark made by hot iron; stigma (*the b. of Cain*, blood-guiltiness); trade-mark, particular kind of goods; iron stamp for burning a mark in; kind of blight (leaves &c. with burnt look); sword (poet.; perh. as flashing). [com.-Teut., f. OTeut. *brandoz* (*bran-* pret. st. of *brinnan* BURN[2] + suf. *-do* as in WORD)]

brand[2], v.t. Burn with hot iron (surgically, penally, or showing ownership or quality); impress on memory; stigmatize. [f. prec.]

bra·ndish, v.t. Wave about, flourish, (weapon, threat) as preliminary to action or in display. [f. F *brandir* (-ISH[2]) f. Teut. BRAND[1] sword]

bra·ndling, n. Red worm with brighter rings used as bait. [BRAND[1] + -LING[1](1)]

bra·nd-new, bran-, a. Conspicuously new. [f. BRAND[1], as if freshly stamped]

bra·ndreth, n. Wooden stand for cask, hay-rick, &c. [f. ON *brandreith* grate (*brandr* BRAND[1] + *reith* carriage)]

bra·ndy, n. Strong spirit distilled from wine; *b.-ball,* kind of sweet; *b. pawnee* [Hind. *pani* water], b. & water; *b.-snap,* gingerbread wafer. [earlier *brandwine, brandewine,* f. Du. *brandewijn* = burnt (distilled) wine]

bra·nk-ur·sine, n. Bear's breech, Acanthus. [f. med. L *branca ursina* bear's claw cf. BRANCH]

bran-new. See BRAND-NEW.

brant(-goose). See BRENT.

brash, n. Loose broken rock or ice; hedge refuse, clippings, &c. [perh. f. F *brèche* breach]

brass, n. & a. (Hist.) alloy of copper with tin, zinc, or other base metal; (mod.) yellow alloy of $\frac{2}{3}$ copper with $\frac{1}{3}$ zinc (cf. BRONZE); inscribed sepulchral table of b.; *the b.,* the b. instruments of a band; (slang) money; effrontery, shamelessness; (adj.) made of b.; *b. band,* set of musicians with b. instruments; *b. farthing,* least possible amount, esp. *don't care a b. f.*; *b. hat,* (army slang) officer of high rank; *b. plate,* on door, gate, or window-ledge, with name, trade, &c.; *b. rags,* sailors' cleaning cloths, as *part b. rags* (Naut. slang), dissolve intimacy *with*; *b. tacks,* (slang) actual details, real business, esp. *get down to b. t.* [OE *bræs* etym. dub.]

bră·ssage (-ĭj), n. Mint-charge for coining money. [F, f. *brasser* stir melted metals together; see -AGE]

brassar·d, n. Badge worn on arm. [F (*bras* arm & see -ARD)]

bra·ssy, a. & n. Like brass in colour, sound, taste; impudent; pretentious; hence **bra·ssi**LY[2] adv., **bra·ssi**NESS n. (N.) b.-soled golf-club. [-Y[2]]

brat, n. Child (usu. contempt.). [etym. dub., but cf. obs. or dial. *brat* cloth, applied in OW (*brith* pl.) to swaddling-clothes]

bra·ttice, bra·tticing, nn. (Coal-mining) wooden partition or shaft-lining. [formerly wooden parapet on fortress; ME *brutaske* f. ONF *breteske* perh. f. G *brett* board + Rom. suf. *-esca* -ESQUE]

brava·do (-vah-, -vā-), n. (pl. *-oes, -os*). Show of courage, bold front. [f. Sp. *bravada,* F *bravade*; see foll., -ADO (2), -ADE (1)]

brave[1], a. & n. Courageous (*the b.,* b. men); (archaic-literary) finely dressed, showy, worthy, honest, admirable; hence **bra·ve**LY[2] adv. (N.) Red-Indian warrior. [F, f. It. *bravo* etym. dub.; L *rabidus,* mad, & *barbarus,* have been suggested]

brave[2], v.t. Defy, encounter with courage; *b. it out,* carry oneself defiantly under suspicion or blame. [f. F *braver* see prec.]

bra·very, n. Daring; splendour, ostentation, finery. [prob. f. F *braverie* f. *braver* see prec. (orig. E sense *bravado*); -ERY]

bra·vo[1] (-ah-), n. (pl. *-oes, -os*). Hired assassin, desperado. [It., see BRAVE[1]]

bra·vo[2] (-ah-), n. & int. Cry of approval, esp. to actors &c. (sometimes *brava, bravi,* to actress, company; also *bravissimo* superl.). [It. = BRAVE[1]]

bravur·a (-oora), n. Brilliant or ambitious execution, forced display; passage of music requiring exceptional powers. [It.]

brawl, v.i., & n. Squabble, (engage in) noisy quarrel; (of streams) murmur. Hence **braw·l**ER[1] n. [quoted from 1375, etym. dub.; cf. mod. Du. & G *brallen* brag, shout]

brawn, n. Muscle; pickled or potted boar's flesh. [f. OF *braon* flesh f. WG *brâdo* (*brâdan* roast cf. OE *brǣdan* & G *braten* f. Aryan *bhre-* burn); sense *boar's flesh* is excl. E]

braw·ny, a. Strong, muscular. Hence **braw·ni**NESS n. [-Y[2]]

bra·xy, n. & a. (Sc.). Splenic apoplexy in sheep; (adj.) suffering from b., (of meat) of a b. sheep (also abs. as n., = b. meat). [etym. dub.; cf. OE *bræc* catarrh]

bray[1], n., & v.i. & t. (Make) the cry, or a sound like the cry, of ass or trumpet; *b. out,* utter harshly. [f. F *braire* cf. L *fragor* crackling noise]

bray[2], v.t. Pound, beat small, esp. with pestle & mortar. [f. OF *breier* (now *broyer*) etym. dub.]

braze[1], v.t. Colour like brass. [perh. = OE *brasian* (*bræs* BRASS) make of brass (not found betw. 1000 and 1550), but prob. mod. form on *glass, glaze*]

braze[2], v.t. Solder with alloy of brass & zinc. [perh. f. F *braser* solder f. ON *brasa* expose to fire]

brā·zen[1], a. Made of brass; strong, yellow, or harsh-sounding, as brass; (also *b.-faced*) shameless, whence **bra·zen**LY[2] adv.; *b. age,* third stage in human deterioration (golden, silver, b., iron). [OE *bræsen* (*bræs* BRASS + -EN[5])]

bra·zen[2], v.t. *B. out,* carry off impudently ('it', matter, deed); make shameless. [f. prec.]

brā·zier[1] (-zher), n. Worker in brass. Hence **bra·zi**ERY(1) n. [BRAZE[1] + -IER, cf. GLAZIER, GRAZIER]

brā·zier[2], (-zher), n. Pan for holding lighted charcoal. [f. F *brasier* (*braise* hot coal)]

Brazi·l, n. & a. (Also *B.-wood*) kinds of hard red S.-Amer. wood yielding dyes; *B.-nut*, large three-cornered nut. [etym. dub.; orig. Sp., Port., & F name of E.-Ind. wood, transferred to S.-Amer. similar species & thence to the country]

breach[1] (-ē-), n. (Naut.) breaking of waves (*clear b.*, rolling over without breaking; *clean b.*, carrying away of masts & everything on deck); breaking or neglect (*of* rule, duty, contract, someone's privileged rights, or promise, esp. to marry); *b. of close*, trespass, *of the peace*, riot or affray; breaking of relations, separation, alienation, quarrel; broken state; gap, esp. in fortifications made by artillery (*stand in the b.*, bear brunt of attack, lit. or fig.); whale's leap clear out of water. [OE *bryce* (f. OTeut. st. *brek-* see BREAK) gave ME *bruche*; ME *breche* (f. F *brèche* f. same Teut.) combined with and has displaced *bruche*, helped by such analogies as *speak speech*]

breach[2], v.t. & i. Break through, make gap in; (of whale) leap clear out of water. [f. prec.]

bread (-ĕd), n. Flour moistened, kneaded, & baked, usu. with leaven (*white*, BROWN, *black*, *b.*; *standard b.*, wheaten of mixed flours; *break b.*, take food, join in Lord's supper; *b. & butter*, b. slices spread with butter, necessary food, a livelihood; *b.-&-butter miss*, school-girl; *b. & scrape*, stingily buttered bread; *ship's b.* naut., hard biscuit; *b. & cheese*, simple food, a livelihood; *b. & milk*, broken b. in boiling m.; *b. & wine*, Lord's supper; *b. of life* (see *John* vi. 35); *know which side* one's *b. is buttered*, where one's interest lies; *b. buttered on both sides*, easy prosperity; *take the b. out of* one's *mouth*, take away his living by competition &c.; *eat the b. of idleness, affliction*, be idle, afflicted; *daily b.*, livelihood; *make* one's *b.*, earn a living); *b.-basket*, (slang) stomach; *b.-crumb*, inner part of loaf, b. crumbled for use in cooking; *b.-fruit*, *-tree*, South-Sea tree with farinaceous fruit; *b.-stuffs*, grain, flour; *b.-ticket* (entitling to ration); *b.-winner*, person (also art, trade, tool) that supports a family. Hence **brea·d**LESS a. [OE *bréad* (cf. G *brod*, *brot*) f. OTeut. *braudoz*; orig. sense prob. *fragment* or *piece*, *loaf* being the Teut. wd for bread]

breadth (-ĕ-), n. Broadness, measure from side to side, (*to a hair's b.*, exactly); piece (of cloth &c.) of full b.; extent, distance, room; largeness (*of* mind, view, &c.), liberality, catholicity, toleration; bold effect. Hence **brea·dth**WAYS, -WISE, advv. [formed on obs. *brede*, OE *brǣdu*, in same sense, + -TH[1] on anal. of *length* &c.]

break[1] (-āk), v.t. & i. (*broke & in Bible brake*; *broken* sometimes *broke* see BROKE[2]). 1. (Of a whole) make or become discontinuous otherwise than by cutting, divide into two or more parts, (*b.* BULK[1]; *b. a set*, sell parts separately; *b. up*, dismiss, depart, b. small, (of person) become feeble, show signs of decay; *b. out* a flag, release it when run up from its trussed state; *b. a lance with*, argue against; *b. bread with*, be entertained by; *b. Priscian's head*, use bad grammar; *b. person on wheel*, of medieval execution; *b. butterfly on wheel*, waste power; *b. ground*, plough, begin siege, or fig. any, operations; *b. the ice*, get over initial shyness or reserve; *b. the ranks*, disorder by leaving them; *troops b.*, disperse in confusion; *clouds b.*, show gap; crack, graze, (*b. a head*); shatter; dislocate (neck; *b. the neck* or *back of*, kill, dispose of); make by separating obstacles (*a way* &c.); penetrate by breaking (*b. open*); interrupt, change, (*gloom, spell, journey, silence*, one's *fast*; *voice breaks*, with emotion or at manhood; *b. off*, bring to an end, cease); disrupt (*broken bonds* &c.). 2. (Of a part) disconnect or depart from something otherwise than by cutting (*b.* bough *from* tree, person *of* habit; *b. with*, quarrel or part with; *b. an officer*, dismiss; *b. piece off*; *ball breaks*, changes from its course, *back* from off, *in* from leg, side). 3. Make a way, come, produce, with effort, suddenness, violence, &c. (*b. into* house, *out of* prison, *through* obstacles; *b. in*, intrude, interpose; disease, war, *b. out*; *b. out*, exclaim; *b. news, a jest*, reveal it; *b.* WIND[1]; *day breaks*; *abscess breaks*); escape, emerge from, (prison, bounds, covert; *b. free* or *loose*; *b. away from*). 4. Make or become weak, disable, discourage, ruin, destroy, cease, exhaust, (*b. the heart, heart breaks*; *frost, weather, breaks*; *b. bank*, exhaust its resources; *merchant breaks*, is bankrupt; *b. blow, fall*, weaken its effect; *b. down*, demolish, collapse, fail); tame, discipline, overpower, (with *in, to*, or abs.; *b. a horse*, *b. a horse to the rein*; *b. in child*; *b.* one's *will, spirit*; *b. resistance, a rebellion*); make of no effect, transgress, violate, neglect, (*law, Sabbath, contract, promise*, one's *word*). Hence **brea·k**ABLE a., **brea·k**AGE(3) n. [OE *brecan* cf. G *brechen* f. OTeut. st. *brek-* = L *frag-*]

break[2], n. Breaking; *b. of day*, dawn; (Cricket) deviation of ball on pitching (*b.-back*, f. off side); (Billiards) points scored continuously; gap, broken place, interruption of continuity; (Mus.) point of separation between different registers of voice; irregularity. [f. prec.]

break[3], n. Carriage-frame with no body for breaking in young horses; large wagonette. [f. BREAK[1] (=' b.-horse '), or f. obs. n. *brake* = curb, bridle, which may be special use of BRAKE[3]]

break-down, n. Collapse, stoppage; failure of health or power; negro dance (brā·kdown).

brea·ker[1], n. In vbl senses (esp. in comb. as *horse-b.*); also, heavy ocean-wave breaking on coast or over reefs. [-ER[1]]

brea·ker[2] (-ā-), n. (naut.). Small keg. [f. Sp. *barrica* cask]

brea·kfast (brĕk-), n., & v.i. & t. (Take, entertain at) first meal of day. Hence **brea·kfast**LESS a. [BREAK[1] interrupt + FAST n.]

brea·kneck, a. Dangerous (*b. pace, road, climb*).

break-up, n. Disintegration, decay, collapse, dispersal. [f. phr. *to break up*]

brea·kwater, n. Object breaking, mole &c. built to break, force of waves.

bream[1], n. Yellowish arch-backed freshwater fish; (also *sea-b.*) a salt-water variety of this. [ME *breme* f. F *brême* OF *bresme* f. Teut. (WG *brahsm-, brehsm-*, perh. f. st. of *brehwan* glitter)]

bream[2], v.t. Clear (ship's bottom) by singeing with burning furze &c. [perh. f. Du. *brem* BROOM, furze]

breast[1] (-ĕ-), n. Either milk-secreting organ in woman, corresponding rudiment in man, (sometimes of beast's dug); (fig.) source of nourishment; upper front of human body or of coat, dress, &c.; corresponding part of animals; heart, emotions, thoughts, (*make clean b. of*, confess); *breastbone*, thin flat vertical bone in chest connecting ribs; *b.-drill, -hoe*, &c., pushed with b.; *b.-harness*, with b.-band instead of collar; *b.-high*, high as the b., (submerged) to the b., (of scent) so strong that hounds race with heads up; *b.-pin*, jewelled &c., worn in tie; *breastplate*, piece of armour covering b., lower shell of turtle, tortoise, &c., inscription-plate on coffin; *b.-wall*, confining a bank of earth; *b.-wheel*, waterwheel with water admitted near axle; *breastwork*, temporary defence or parapet a few feet high. Hence **-brea·st**ED[2] a. [OE *brēost* f. OTeut. *breustom* cf. G *brust*; perh. related to OSax. *brustian* to bud]

breast[2], v.t. Oppose the b. to, face, contend with, (waves, hill). [f. prec.]

brea·stsummer, bre·ssummer, n. Beam across broad opening, sustaining superstructure. [BREAST[1] + *summer* beam f. F *sommier* f. L *sagmarius* (*sagma* pack-saddle)]

breath (-ĕth), n. Exhalation as perceptible to sight or smell; slight movement of air; whiff of perfume &c.; air taken into and expelled from lungs (*draw b.*, breathe, live; *a b. of fresh air*; *spend, waste, b.*, talk vainly; *keep b. to cool porridge*, abstain from talk; *b. of life, nostrils*, a necessity; *take away* person's *b.*, render him breathless with astonishment); respiration (*catch, hold*, one's *b.*, in fear or absorbing emotion); one respiration (*say inconsistent things in one or the same b.*); power of breathing (*out of b.*, not able to breathe quick enough; *take b.*, pause, rest); whisper, murmur, (*not a b. heard*; also *below* one's *b.*, in a whisper). [OE *brǣth* smell of burning f. OTeut. *brǣthoz* f. Aryan *bhrēto-* (*bhre-* burn)]

breathe (-ēdh), v.i. & t. Use the lungs; live; seem alive; take breath, pause, (*b. again, freely*, recover from fear &c., be at ease); sound, speak, (of wind) blow, softly (*b. upon*, tarnish, taint): send out (*new life into*; *fragrance*; *b.* one's *last breath* or *last*, die); take in (*b. foul, wholesome, air*); utter softly, also passionately (*b. strife*), exhibit (*b. simplicity*); allow to b., give rest to; force to b., exercise, tire. [ME *brethen* f. prec.]

brea·ther (-ēdh-), n. In vbl senses; esp., short spell of exercise. [-ER[1]]

brea·thing[1] (-ēdh-), n. In vbl senses; esp.: (Gk Gram.) *rough, smooth, b.*, signs (ʽ), (ʼ), indicating that initial vowel is or is not aspirated; *b.-space*, time to breathe, pause. [-ING[1]]

brea·thing[2] (-ēdh-), a. In vbl senses; esp., lifelike (statue &c.) [-ING[2]]

brea·thless (ĕth-), a. Lifeless; panting; holding the breath; unstirred by wind. [-LESS]

brea·thlessly (-ĕth-), adv. Pantingly; in suspense. [-LY[2]]

brea·thy (-ĕth-), a. (Of singing-voice) not clear-cut at beginning of sound, using breath before vocal chords are tense. Hence **brea·thi**NESS n. [-Y[2]]

brĕ·ccia (-tsha), n. Rock of angular stones &c. cemented by lime &c. [It., = gravel or rubbish of broken walls cf. F *brèche* f. Teut. = BREAK]

bred. See BREED v.

breech, n., & v.t. (Pl.) *breeches* (-ĭtshĭz) or *pair of bb.*, short trousers fastened below knee (*Bb. Bible*, Geneva Bible of 1560 with *bb.* for *aprons* in *Gen.* iii. 7) and (now) used only for riding or in court costume &c. (cf. KNICKERBOCKERS); (loosely) trousers or knickerbockers; *wear the bb.*, of wife ruling her husband; (sing., archaic) posterior. (Gunnery) part of cannon behind bore, back part of rifle or gun barrel; *b.-block*, closing b. aperture in guns; *breech-loader, -loading*, (gun) loaded at breech, not through muzzle; *breeches-buoy*, lifebuoy with canvas bb. for user's legs. (Vb, archaic) put (boy) into bb. instead of petticoats. Hence **breech**ED[2] a., (-ĭtsht) wearing breeches, (-ētsht) having a breech. [OE *brēc* pl., f. OTeut. *brōks* loin and thigh garment; *breeches* a double pl., *breech* being a pl. like *feet*]

bree·ching (-ĭtsh-), n. Leather strap round shaft-horse's hind-quarters for pushing back; (Naut.) rope securing gun to ship's side. [f. prec. + -ING[1]]

bree·chless (-ĭtsh-), a. Without breeches. [-LESS]

breed[1], v.t. & i. (bred). Bear, generate, (offspring); cherish in womb or egg; propagate; be pregnant; yield, produce, result in; make propagate, raise, (cattle); train up; fit for being, adapt *to*, (*b. him a lawyer, to the law*), bring up; arise, spread; *b. in & in*, always marry near relations; *what is bred in the bone*, hereditary traits. Hence **bree·dER**[1] n. [OE *brēdan* cf. G *brüten* f. OTeut. *brôdjan* (*brôdâ-* warmth see BROOD)]

breed[2], n. Race, stock, strain; family with hereditary qualities. [f. prec.]

bree·ding, n. In vbl senses; esp., result of training, behaviour, good manners. [-ING[1]]

breeze[1], n. Gad-fly. [OE *briosa* etym. dub.]

breeze[2], n. Gentle wind; wind off land, or sea, at certain hours; (slang) quarrel, display of temper. Hence **bree·zeLESS** a. [earlier *brize* f. OSp. *briza* NE wind perh. = F *bize, bise*, N wind; F *brise* is later]

breeze[3], n. Small cinders, coke, coke-dust, &c., used by brickmakers. [perh. f. F BRAISE, cf. BRAZIER[2]]

bree·zy, a. Wind-swept; pleasantly windy; fresh, lively, jovial. Hence **bree·ziLY**[2] adv., **bree·ziNESS** n. [-Y[2]]

Brē·hon, n. & a. Ancient Irish judge; *B. law*, Irish code abolished under James I. [f. OIr. *brithem* judge]

brent(-goose), brant-, n. Smallest species of wild goose, visiting Britain in winter. [etym. dub.; cf. G *brandgans*]

brer, n. (U.S. negro dial. contraction for) brother (esp. in beast-fable personifications, as *B. Fox, Rabbit*).

bre·ssummer. See BREASTSUMMER.

bre·thren. See BROTHER.

Brĕ·ton, a. & n. (Native) of Brittany in France. [F, = BRITON]

Bretwa·lda (-ŏl-), n. Lord of the Britons, title given to Egbert & Old Eng. Kings of various States who held nominal or real supremacy over the rest.

breve, n. (Hist.) authoritative letter from sovereign or pope; (Mus.) note = two semibreves now rarely used; short prosody mark (˘) in printing. [var. of BRIEF[1]]

brĕ·vet, n., & v.t. Document conferring a privilege from sovereign or government, esp. rank without corresponding pay in army (*b. rank, b. officer*); honorary, nominal, position; (vb) confer b. rank on. [F, = note, dim. of *bref* BRIEF[1]]

brĕvi-, comb. form in scientific terms of L *brevis* short, as *brevirostrate* short-beaked.

brē·viary, n. (R.-C. Ch.) book containing the Divine Office for each day, to be recited by those in orders. [f. L *breviarium* summary (*brevis* short, -ARY[1])]

brevier· (-vēr), n. Printing-type size between bourgeois & minion. [used in *breviaries*]

brĕ·vity, n. Shortness of expression, conciseness; short span (*of* life). [f. AF *brevete* f. L *brevitatem* (*brevis* short, -TY)]

brew[1], v.t. & i. Make (beer &c.) by infusion, boiling, & fermentation (*drink as you have brewed*, take consequences); make (tea, punch) by infusion or mixture; undergo these processes; concoct, bring about, set in train, grow to ripeness, fester, gather force, (usu. of evil results; *mischief is brewing, b. rebellion*); *brewhouse*, = brewery (but now less used). Hence **brew·ER**[1], **brew·ERY** (3), nn. [OE *brēowan*; com.-Teut., cf. G *brauen*; perh. also L *defrutum* new wine boiled down]

brew[2], n. Process of brewing; amount brewed at once; quality of stuff brewed. [f. prec.]

brew·age (-ĭj), n. Concocted drink; process or result of concoction (lit. & fig.). [-AGE]

brew·is, n. Broth (archaic & dial.). [ME *browes* f. OF *brouetz* nom. of *brouet* dim. of *bro* f. OHG *brod* BROTH]

Brew·ster Se·ssions, n. Sessions for issue of licences to trade in alcoholic liquors. [f. obs. *brewster* (orig. female) brewer, see -STER]

bri·ar. See BRIER.

Brī·areus (-rōōs), n. Many-handed person. [Gk mythol.]

bribe[1], n. Money &c. offered to procure (often illegal or dishonest) action in favour of the giver. [perh. f. OF *bribe* piece of bread given to beggar, etym. dub.]

bribe[2], v.t. Pervert by gifts or other inducements the action or judgement of; (abs.) practise bribery. Hence **bri·bER**[1], **brībEE·, bribABI·LITY, bri·bERY**(4), nn., **bri·bABLE** a. [f. prec.]

bric-à-brac (brĭ·kabrăk), n. Curiosities, old furniture, china, fans, &c. [F, perh. = *de bric et de broc* by hook or by crook]

brick[1], n. & a. Clay kneaded, moulded, & baked by fire or sun; block (usu. rectangular & about 9 in. ×4⅜ ×2⅝) of this (*like a hundred of bb.* colloq., with crushing weight or force); b.-shaped loaf, block of tea, &c.; child's wooden toy building-block; (slang) generous or kind person; *b.-bat*, piece of b., esp. as missile [BAT[2]]; *b.-dust*, powdered b., colour like it; *b.-field, -kiln*, in which bb. are made, baked; *bricklayer*, workman building in b.; *brickwork*, building in b.; hence (rare) **bri·ckEN**[5] a. (Adj.) built of b. [prob. f. F *brique* broken piece f. Teut. *brek-* BREAK]

brick[2], v.t. *B. up*, block (window &c.) with b.-work (& used with other advv.). [f. prec.]

bri·cky, a. Littered with coloured or looking like, bricks. [-Y[2]]

bri·cole (-ĭkl), n. Indirect stroke in tennis & billiards. [F, etym. dub.]

bri·dal, n. & a. Wedding-feast, wedding, (Adj.) of bride or wedding (*b. cheer, veil*); hence **bri·dal**LY[2] adv. [= *bride* ALE or festivity; OE *brýd-ealo*; the prevailing adj. use results f. confusion with -AL]

bride[1], n. Woman on her wedding-day & for some days or weeks before & after it; *bri·decake*, rich cake eaten at wedding, sent round to friends, &c. [OE *brýd*; com.-Teut. cf. G *braut*, f. OTeut. *brûdiz* bride, daughter-in-law, perh. f. *bru-* to cook]

bride[2], n. Delicate network connecting the patterns in lace; bonnet-string. [F, = BRIDLE[1], f. Teut.]

bri·degroom, n. Man at or soon before or after his marriage. [OE had *brýd-guma* (*guma* man cf. L *homo*) com.-Teut.; *guma* becoming obs. in ME, perh. *groom* was substituted by mistake; but as there is more than a century's gap between instances of the old & new form, the latter may be independent = *bride lad* (*bride* in 15th & 16th cc. being of either sex)]

bri·desmaid, n. Unmarried woman (usu. one of several) attending bride at wedding. [earlier *bridemaid*, altered when the attrib. sense of *bride* was missed]

bri·desman, n. Bridegroom's attendant, best man. [earlier *brideman*, cf. prec.]

bri·dewell, n. House of correction, gaol. [St Bride's Well, near the London b.]

bridge[1], n. (northern form, in writers for local colour, *brig*). Structure carrying road or path across stream, ravine, road, &c. (*b. of boats*, over boats moored abreast; *b. of gold, golden b.*, easy retreat provided for beaten enemy); (Naut.) platform amidships for officer in command; upper bony part of nose; movable piece over which violin strings are stretched; (Billiards) support for cue formed with left hand; *b.-head*, post held on far side of frontier river giving one access to enemy's territory; *b.-train*, Mil. Engineers with material for building floating bridges. Hence **bri·dge**LESS a. [OE *brycg*; com.-Teut. cf. G *brücke*]

bridge[2], v.t. Span as, with, or as with, a b. [OE *brycgian* see prec.]

bridge[3], n. Card-game of Russian origin resembling whist, in which each player in turn looks on while his exposed hand is played by his partner. [?]

bri·dle[1], n. Head-gear of harness, including head-stall, bit, & rein (*give horse the b., lay b. on his neck*, abandon control; *horse going well up to b.*, willing goer); restraint, curb; (Naut.) mooring-cable; (Physiol.) ligament checking motion of a part; *b.-bridge, -path, -road*, &c., fit for riders but not for vehicles. [OE *bridel* f. *bregdan* twitch see BRAID[2] + -LE (1)]

bri·dle[2], v.t. & i. Put bridle on (horse &c.); curb, hold *in*, bring under control; express offence, vanity, &c., by throwing up head & drawing in chin (often *b. up*). [OE *bridlian* see prec.]

bridoo·n, n. Snaffle & rein of military bridle. [f. F *bridon* (BRIDE[2], -OON)]

Brie (brē), n. A cream cheese. [*B.*, in France]

brief[1], n. Pope's letter on matter of discipline to person or community (less formal than bull); (Law) summary of facts & law-points of a case drawn up for counsel (*hold b. for*, be retained as counsel for, argue in favour of); *watching-b.*, of barrister who watches case for client indirectly concerned; *b.-bag*, small leather hand-bag; *a b.*, piece of employment for barrister, whence **brie·f**LESS a. [ME & OF *bref* f. L *breve* dispatch, note, neut. of *brevis* short]

brief[2], v.t. (Law) reduce (facts &c.) to a b.; instruct (barrister) by b., employ. [f. prec.]

brief[3], a. & n. Of short duration; concise; *be b.*, speak shortly; *in b.*, in short. Hence **brie·f**LY[2] adv., **brie·f**NESS n. [ME & OF *bref* f. L *brevis* short]

bri·er[1], **bri·ar,** n. (also *brere* archaic). Prickly bush, esp. of wild rose; *Sweet B.*, wild rose with fragrant leaves & flowers; *B.-rose*, Dog-rose. Hence **bri·er**Y[2], **-ar**Y[2], a. [OE *brǽr, brér*, etym. dub.; cf. *frere*, FRIAR]

bri·er[2], **bri·ar,** n. The White Heath, of which the root is used for tobacco pipes. [at first (the material was introduced only c. 1859) *bruyer* f. F *bruyère* heath]

brig[1], n. Two-masted square-rigged vessel, but with additional lower fore-&-aft sail on gaff & boom to mainmast. [abbr. of BRIGANTINE, f. which the type of ship was developed]

brig[2]. See BRIDGE[1].

briga·de[1], n. Subdivision of army, varying in different countries & times; organized or uniformed band of workers (*Boys', Church*, &c., *B.*, organizations on military model for disciplining & occupying boys &c.). [F, f. It. *brigata* company (*brigare* brawl f. LL *briga* strife); see -ADE]

briga·de[2], v.t. Form into b. or bb.; join (regiment &c.) *with* others into a b. [f. prec.]

brigadier·, n. (fully *B.-General*). Officer commanding brigade (title now replaced by *Colonel Commandant* or *Colonel-on-the-Staff*, exc. as retired rank). [-IER]

bri·gand, n. Bandit, robber. Hence or cogn. **bri·gand**AGE(3), **bri·gand**ISM(2), nn., **bri·gand**ISH[1] a. [ME f. OF, prob. f. It. *brigante* (*brigare* see BRIGADE[1])]

bri·gantine (-ēn), n. Two-masted vessel with square-sailed fore-mast & fore-&-aft mainmast. [f. F *brigandin* (now *-tin*) f. It. *brigantino* perh. = skirmisher cf. prec.]

bright[1] (-īt), a. Emitting or reflecting much light, shining; lit up with joy, hope, &c.; vivid (*b. red* &c.); illustrious; vivacious, quick-witted, (often iron.). Hence **brigh·tEN**[6] v.t. & i., **brigh·tISH**[1] (2) a., **brigh·tLY**[2] adv., **brigh·tNESS** n. [OE *beorht*; com.-Teut., but now lost exc. in E, f. OTeut. *berhtoz* f. Aryan *bhrag-* cf. L *flagrare*]

bright[2], adv. = brightly (*shine b., b.-beaming,* &c.). [OE *beorhte* with adv. *-e* now lost; see prec.]

Bright's disease, n. Granular degeneration of the kidneys. [Dr R. *Bright*, 1827]

brill, n. Flat-fish resembling turbot. [?]

bri·lliant[1], a. Bright, sparkling; illustrious, striking; talented, showy. Hence **bri·lliANCE, bri·lliANCY,** nn., **bri·lliantLY**[2] adv., [f. F *brillant* part. of *briller* shine referred to LL **berillare* (BERYL)]

bri·lliant[2], n. Diamond of finest cut and brilliance (b. shape has two horizontal tables, joined by facets); a size of TYPE. [f. F as prec. used as n.]

bri·lliantine (-ēn), n. Cosmetic for hair. [f. F *brillantine* see BRILLIANT[1] + -INE[4]]

brim[1], n. Edge or lip of cup, bowl, or hollow; projecting edge of hat; *b.-full,* to the b. Hence **bri·mLESS, brimmED**[2], aa. [ME *brimme* etym. dub.; cf. G *bräme*]

brim[2], v.t. & i. Fill, be full, to the b. (lit. & fig.); *b. over,* overflow. [f. prec.]

bri·mmer, n. Full cup. [BRIM[2] + -ER[1]]

bri·mstone (-on), n. (Old name for) sulphur (*b. & treacle,* nursery medicine); fuel of hell-fire; *b. butterfly, moth,* sulphur-coloured species. Hence **bri·mstonY**[2] a. [ME (*bernen, brinnen,* BURN[2] + STONE)]

bri·ndled, bri·ndle, a. Brownish or tawny with streaks of other colour. [earlier *brinded* (perh. p.p. of a possible vb *brenden* f. BRAND[1] burning) has been ousted by *brindled* (perh. with dim. sense); f. which *brindle* is perh. a mistaken back-formation]

brine[1], n. Salt water; the sea; tears (poet.); *b.-pan,* iron vessel or shallow pit for getting salt by evaporation. Hence **bri·nY**[2] a. (*the briny,* slang, the sea). [OE *brȳne* etym. dub.; cf. Du. *brijn*]

brine[2], v.t. Steep or pickle in, or wet with, b. [f. prec.]

bring, v.t. & i. (brought, *pr.* -awt). Cause to come, come with or conveying whether by carrying, leading, impelling, or attracting, (*take* expresses the corresponding notions with *go* for *come*); cause, result in; prefer (charge), adduce (argument); *b. home to,* convict or convince of; *b. into play,* cause to operate; *b. into world,* give birth to; cause to become (*b. low*); *b. to bear,* apply (influence &c.); *b. to book,* exact account from (offender); *b. to mind,* recall; *b. to pass,* cause to happen; persuade (*cannot b. myself to believe*). *B. about,* cause to happen, reverse (ship); *b. back,* call to mind; *b. down,* kill or wound, cause penalty to alight *on,* abase, lower (price), continue (record) *to* a point, (Theatr.) *b. d. the house,* elicit tumultuous applause; *b. forth,* give birth to, cause; *b. forward,* carry sum of page's figures to next page; *b. in,* introduce (custom), produce as profit, adduce, pronounce (*guilty, not g.*); *b. off,* rescue from wreck &c., conduct (enterprise) to success; *b. on,* lead to, cause discussion of; *b. out,* express, exhibit clearly, introduce (girl) to society, publish; *b. over,* convert; *b. round,* restore to consciousness; *b. through,* save (sick person); *b. to,* check motion of, come to a stop. restore to consciousness; *b. under,* subdue; *b. up,* educate, rear, sue in court, anchor (ship), come to a stop, call attention again to, cause (M.P.) to rise and speak, continue (accounts &c.) to a further point; *b. up the rear,* come last. [com.-Teut. cf. G *bringen*]

brink, n. Edge of steep place or abyss (*on b. of grave,* soon to die); border of water, esp. when steep (*shiver on the b.,* hesitate to plunge); verge (*of* discovery, ruin, eternity, &c.). [ME, prob. f. Scand., cf. Da. *brink* precipice]

bri·o (-ēō), n. Vivacity. [It.]

briquette, brĭ·quet, (-k-), n. Block of compressed coal-dust. [F (*-ette*), dim. of *brique* BRICK]

brise-bise (brēz bēz), n. Curtain stretched across lower part of window. [F]

brisk[1], a. Active, lively, (usu. of movement; *b. pace, trade, wind,* &c.); enlivening, keen, (champagne, air, &c.). Hence **bri·skLY**[2] adv., **bri·skNESS** n. [f. 16th c., perh. f. W. *brisg* quick-footed cf. OIr. *brisc* brittle, or perh. = F BRUSQUE]

brisk[2], v.t. & i. Make or become b. (usu. with *up*). [f. prec.]

bri·sket, n. Breast of animals (esp. as joint of meat). [etym. dub.; there is F *brechet* in same sense]

bri·stle[1] (-ĭsl), n. One of stiff hairs on hog's back & sides; short stiff hair of other animals, man's short-cropped beard, or plants; *set up* one's, another's, *bb.,* show or rouse temper. Hence **bri·stlY**[2] (-islĭ), **bri·stlED**[2], aa. [ME *brustel* f. OE *byrst* & see -LE(1); f. OTeut. *bors-*]

bri·stle[2], v.i. & t. (Cause to) stand upright (hair &c.), raise or rise like bb. or into roughness, (often with *up*); show temper, prepare for fight; be thickly set *with* hair, difficulties, &c. [f. prec.]

bri·s(t)ling, n. A small sardine-like fish. [?]

Bri·stol, n. (attrib.) *B. board,* kind of cardboard for drawing on; (*shipshape &*) *B. fashion* (Naut., & transf.), with all in good order.

Bri·tain (-ĭtn), n. (Also *Great B.*) England, Wales, & Scotland, the British Empire; *North B.*, Scotland; *Greater B.* (descriptive, not official), Gt B. & the dominions & colonies. [ME *Bretayne* f. OF *Bretaigne* f. L *Brittannia* or *Brittania* (L *Britannia* would have produced F *bribreaigne*)]

Brita·nnia, n. Personification of Britain; *B. metal*, alloy of tin & regulus of antimony resembling silver. [L *Britannia, Brittannia, Brittania,* = Gk *Brettania* f. *Brittanni* or *Brittani,* = Gk *Brettanoi*]

Brita·nnic, a. Of Britain (chiefly in phr. *His B. Majesty*). [prob. f. F *britannique* f. L *Britannicus*]

bri·ticism, n. =BRITISHISM. [U.S. wd, non-existent *Britic* + -ISM(4)]

Bri·tish, a. Of the ancient Britons; of Great Britain or its inhabitants (esp. in political or imperial connexion, & in botany &c.); *the B.*, B. soldiers, people, &c.; *B. Academy*, chartered body of 100 for promotion of moral and political sciences; *B. Association* (for advancement of science); *B. Expeditionary Force* (abbr. B.E.F.), any of the armies sent abroad in the great war, esp. Sir J. French's original force in France; *B. Museum*, national museum of antiquities, books, &c., in London; *B. warm*, kind of short military overcoat. [OE *Brettisc* f. *Bret* Briton; see -ISH[1]]

Bri·tisher, n. (U.S. term for) British subject of British descent. [prob. a U.S. wd; cf. *foreigner*, -ER[1]]

bri·tishism, n. Idiom used in Gt Britain & not in U.S. &c. [-ISM (4)]

Bri·ton, n. One of the race found by Romans in S. England; native of Great Britain or the British Empire (poet., melodramatic, &c.); *North B.*, Scotsman. [ME & F *breton* f. L *Brittonem* nom. *Britto*, f. the native name, which displaced *Brittanni* after the Roman conquest]

bri·ttle, a. Apt to break, fragile. Hence **bri·ttle**NESS n. [ME *britul* cf. OE *bréotan* break]

bri·tzka, -tzska, (-ĭtska), n. Open carriage with calash top & space for reclining. [f. Pol. *bryczka* dim. of *bryka* wagon]

brize (-ēz). = BREEZE[1].

broach[1] (-ōtsh), n. Roasting-spit; church spire rising from tower without parapet; boring-bit. [ME & F *broche* = It. *brocca* cf. L *brocci dentes* projecting teeth; var. of BROOCH]

broach[2], v.t. Pierce (cask) to draw liquor, begin drawing (liquor); open and start using (bale, box, &c.); begin discussion of, moot, (subject). [f. prec.]

broach[3], v.t. & i. (Usu. *b. to*) veer or cause (ship) to veer & present side to wind & waves. [perh. f. obs. use of prec. = turn on the spit]

broad (-awd), a., n., & adv. Large across, wide, not narrow; = in breadth (*6 ft b.*); extensive (*b. lands*); full, clear, main, explicit, (*b. daylight, facts, distinction, hint*); coarse (*b. story*); downright in sound, not mincing, (*b. Yorkshire, Scotch*); generalized (*b. rule*); tolerant (*B. Church*, churchmen favouring comprehension & not pressing doctrines); bold in effect or style; *as b. as it is long*, indifferent; *b.* ARROW; *broadcloth*, fine plain-wove double-width dressed black cloth [phr. in Act of Parl. 1482 kept as name for quality rather than width]; *b.* GAUGE; *b.-glass*, window-glass; *broadsheet*, large sheet of paper printed on one side only; *broadside*, ship's side above water between bow & quarter (*broadside on, to*, with this presented), (discharge of) all guns on one side of ship, also = broadsheet; *b.-silk, -weaver*, (of) silk in piece not in ribbons; *broadsword*, b.-bladed cutting-sword. (Noun) the b. part (*b. of the back*); (E. Anglia) large piece of fresh water formed by widening of river. (Adv.) = broadly (*speak b., b. awake*); *b.-blown*, in full bloom. Hence **broa·d**EN[6] v.t. & i., **broa·d**LY[2], **broa·d**WAYS, **broa·d**WISE, advv. [OE *brád*, com.-Teut. cf. G *breit*]

broa·dcast, a., adv., v.t. & i. (past *-casted*, p.p. *-cast*), & n. (Of seed) scattered freely, not in drills or rows, (adv.) in this manner, (v.i. & t.) sow thus, (all also fig. of information, propaganda, &c.); (Wireless, v.t.) issue (news, music, any audible matter) by wireless telephony to owners of receiving-sets, (v.i.) speak, sing, &c., for such transmission, (n., esp. attrib.) the practice &c. of broadcasting (*to-day's b. programme*). [f. prec. + *cast* p.p.]

Broa·dmoor (braw-), n. Asylum in Berkshire for criminal lunatics.

broa·dness, n. (Superseded by *breadth*, exc. in sense) indelicacy (of speech). [-NESS]

Bro·bdingnag, n. Land of giants. Hence **brobdingna·g**IAN (-ăg-) a. [Swift, *Gulliver's Travels*]

brocā·de[1], n. Fabric woven with raised patterns; Indian cloth of gold & silver. [f. Sp. & Port. *brocado* = It. *broccato* cf. BROACH[1] & see -ADE]

brocā·de[2], v.t. Work with raised pattern. [f. prec.]

brŏ·c(c)oli, n. Cultivated cabbage with edible flower head, hardy variety of cauliflower. [It., pl. of *broccolo* cabbage-top dim. of *brocco* see BROACH[1]]

brochure (-ŏ·shoor, or as F), n. Stitched booklet, pamphlet. [F]

brock, n. Badger; stinking fellow. [OE *broc* f. Celt. cf. Gk *phorkos* grey]

bro·cket, n. Second-year stag with straight horns. [f. F *brocart* (*broche* BROACH[1] + -ARD)]

brogue[1] (-ōg), n. Rude Irish & Scotch-Highland shoe of untanned leather;

fishing-bb., waterproof leggings with feet; nailed & goloshed shoe for golf &c. [f. Gael. & Ir. *brog* f. OIr. *broce* shoe perh. f. OCelt. *bracca* whence L *braccae* see BREECH]

brogue[2] (-ōg), n. Dialectal, esp. Irish, accent. [etym. dub.; perh. = speech of those who wear the BROGUE[1]]

broi·der, v.t., broi·dery, n. (Poet. & archaic for) EMBROIDER(Y).

broil[1], n. Quarrel, tumult. [f. obs. vb *broil* mix, quarrel, f. F *brouiller* cf. It. *broglio* n. hurly-burly, & *brogliare* v., etym. dub.]

broil[2], v.t. & i. Cook (meat) or be cooked on fire or gridiron; make, be, very hot (of person in sun &c.). [etym. dub.; the form *brule*, common before 1500, may be assim. to F *brûler* burn]

broil[3], n. Broiled meat. [f. prec.]

broke[1], n. Short-stapled wool on certain parts of fleece. [OE *broc* f. *brecan* BREAK]

broke[2], p.p. of BREAK, still often used in some spec. senses, as = *ruined* (esp., slang, *stony-b.*), & *dismissed the service.*

bro·ken, a. In vbl senses of BREAK[1]; also or esp., *b. meat* &c., remains; *b. tea*, siftings; *b. water*, choppy; *b. ground*, uneven; *b. sleep*, intermittent; *b. weather*, uncertain; *b. English*, imperfect; *b. numbers*, fractions; *b. money*, small change; *b.-hearted*, crushed by grief; *b. man*, reduced to despair; *b.-winded*, (of horse) incapacitated for hard work by ruptured air-cells. [p.p. of BREAK]

bro·kenly, adv. Spasmodically, by jerks, with breaks. [prec. + -LY[2]]

bro·ker, n. Dealer in second-hand furniture &c.; middleman in bargains; agent, commissioner; person licensed to sell or appraise distrained goods. Hence **bro·ker**AGE(4) n. [ME & AF *brocour* f. L **broccatorem* nom. *-or* (see -OR[2]) broacher (BROACH[1]) of cask, retailer of wine]

bro·king, n. Broker's trade, acting as broker. [f. obs. vb *broke* cf. prec.]

bro·lly, n. (slang). Umbrella. [abbr.]

brō·mal, n. Compound produced by action of bromide on alcohol. [BROM(INE) + *al-* of ALCOHOL]

brō·mic, a. Containing bromine in chem. combination. Hence **bro·m**ATE[1](3) n. [BROMINE, -IC]

brō·mide, n. Compound (see -IDE) of bromine, esp. b. of potassium. [foll. + -IDE]

brō·mine, n. Non-metallic element resembling chlorine (poisonous dark liquid with rank smell) used in various preparations as sedative. Hence **bro·m**IZE(5) v.t., **bro·m**ISM(5) n. [f. F *brome* f. Gk *brōmos* stink + -INE[5]]

brōmo-, brōm-, comb. forms of *bromine* as in *bromobenzoic, bromacetic.* [-o-]

bro·nchī, bro·nchia, (-k-), nn. pl. (Form -*i*, with sing. -*us*) two main divisions of windpipe; (-*ia*) ramifications of these in lungs. Hence **bro·nchi**AL a., **bro·nchi**o-, **bro·ncho**-, comb. forms, **broncho·**TOMIST, -TOMY, nn. [L, f. Gk *brogkhos, brogkhia*]

bronchī·tis (-k-), n. Inflammation of bronchial mucous membrane. Hence **bronchi·t**IC a. [prec. + -ITIS]

bro·nchocele (-sēl), n. Swelling of thyroid gland, goitre. [f. Gk *brogkhokēlē* (BRONCHO-, -CELE)]

bro·nco, n. Wild or half-tamed horse of California &c. [Sp., = rough]

bronze[1], n. & a. Brown alloy chiefly of copper and tin (about 8:1; *the b. age*, in which weapons and tools were made of b.); work of art made of this; colour of b.; hence **bro·nz**Y[2] a. (Adj.) made of, coloured like, b. [F, f. It. *bronzo, bronzino*, f. L (*aes*) *Brundusinum* (brass) of Brundusium]

bronze[2], v.t. & i. Give b.-like surface to; make or become brown, tan. [f. prec.]

brooch (-ōtsh), n. Ornamental, jewelled, &c., safety-pin for fastening some part of female dress, esp. the neck. [ME *broche* = BROACH[1]]

brōōd[1], n. Hatch of young birds or other egg-produced animals; (usu. contempt.) human family, children; swarm, crew, of men, animals, or things; *brood-*, for breeding (*b.-mare, -hen*). [OE *bród* cf. G *brut* f. Teut. vb root *bro-* warm]

brood[2], v.i. Sit as hen on eggs; hang close *over* or *on* (of night &c.); meditate *on* or *over* (esp. insults, ill designs, &c.); meditate (often sullenly). [f. prec.]

broo·dy, a. Wishing to sit or incubate (of hen). Hence **broo·di**NESS n. (BROOD[1] + -Y[2])

brōōk[1], n. Small stream; *broo·klime*, kind of Speedwell common in ditches [OE *hleomoc* name of the plant]. Hence **broo·k**LET n. [OE *bróc* cf. G *bruch* moor, marsh; etym. dub.]

brōōk[2], v.t. Put up with, tolerate, (in neg. context). [OE *brúcan*; com.-Teut., cf. G *brauchen* use, f. OTeut. *bruk-* use cf. L *frui fruct-*]

brōōm, n., & v.t. Yellow-flowered shrub growing on sandy banks &c.; genus to which it belongs; sweeping-implement usu. on long handle (vb, sweep with this); *new b.*, newly appointed official eager to sweep away abuses; *broo·mrape*, genus of parasitic herbs on roots of broom &c. (brown, leafless, fleshy-stemmed, bracteate) [med. L *rapum* root-knob]; *b.-stick*, handle of b. (ridden on through the air by witches, and jumped over by parties to sham marriage). [OE *bróm* f. OTeut. *brǣmoz* thorny shrub whence BRAMBLE]

brose (-ōz), n. Dish of oatcake with boiling water or milk poured on it. [= BREWIS]

broth (-aw-, -ŏ-), n. Water in which something, esp. meat, has been boiled, thin soup; (Irish) *b. of a boy*, good fellow. [com.-Teut. f. vb root *bru-* boil, BREW, + -TH[1]]

brŏ·thel, n. House of ill fame, bawdy-house. [orig. = ruined man f. OE *brothen* p.p. of *bréothan* go to ruin, but confused with *bordel* cabin, hut, f. OF f. It. *bordello* (med. L *borda* f. Teut. *bord* BOARD)]

bro·ther (-ŭ-), n. (pl. *brothers* & in some senses *brĕ·thren*, see below). Son of same parents or (strictly *half-b.*) parent as another person (the latter usu. specified by *my* &c. or a possessive case; pl. abbr. *Bros*, in title of firm, as *Smith Bros & Co.*); close friend; fellow citizen, countryman, or man, equal, (*a man & a b.*, esp. of negro slaves); fellow member of religious society (pl. *brethren*); fellow member of guild, order, profession, &c. (pl. *brethren*); official of certain companies &c. (*Elder B., Brethren*, of Trinity House); companion, associate, (pl. *brothers*) often with specification as *b. in arms, of the angle*; member of religious order (as title; either pl.); vocative of sovereigns to each other; *b. german*, on both sides, *b. uterine*, of same mother only; *b.-in-law*, b. of one's husband or wife, husband of one's sister. Hence **bro·ther**LESS a., **bro·ther**LIKE a. & adv., **bro·ther**LY[1, 2] a. & adv., **bro·therli**NESS n. [Aryan; OE *bróthor* cf. G *bruder*, Skr. *bhratr*, Gk *phratēr*, L *frater*, W *brawd*]

bro·therhood, n. Fraternal tie; companionship; (members of) association for mutual help &c.; community of feeling. [OE *brotherred* ME *brotherhede -hode*; see -HEAD]

brougham (-ōōm, -ōō·am), n. One-horse (or electric) closed carriage. [Lord *B.*]

brought. See BRING.

brow[1], n. Arch of hair over eye (usu. in pl.; *knit, bend*, one's *bb.*, frown); forehead (*b.-ague*, megrim); edge, projection, of cliff &c., top of hill in road. Hence **-brow**ED[2] a. [OE *brú* f. OTeut. *brûs* cf. Skr. *bhrus*, Gk *ophrus*]

brow[2], n. (naut.). Gangway, inclined plane of planks. [perh. f. Da. *bru* bridge]

brow·beat, v.t. Bully, bear down, with looks & words. [BROW[1]]

brown[1], a. Of the colour given by mixing orange & black or by toasting bread; as distinctive epithet of species &c. (*b. bear, willow*; *b. coal*, lignite; *b. bread*, of unbolted flour; *b. paper*, coarse unbleached kind used for parcels &c.; *b. sugar*, half refined; *b. ware*, common sort of pottery); dark-skinned, tanned; (slang) *do b.*, take in, cheat; *B. Bess*, old army flintlock musket; *b. study*, reverie. Hence **brow·n**ISH[1](2) a., **brow·n**NESS n., **browny-** comb. form. [OE *brún*; com.-Teut. cf. G *braun* f. OTeut. *brûnoz*, Aryan *bhrûnos*, root *bhru-* cf. BEAVER; Rom. wds, as F *brun*, It. *bruno*, adopted f. the Teut.]

brown[2], n. B. colour; b. pigment; (ellipt. for) b. butterfly, fishing-fly, clothes; (slang) copper coin. [f. prec.]

brown[3], v.t. & i. Make or become b. by roasting, sunburn, or (gun-barrel &c.) chemical process. [f. BROWN[1]]

brow·nie, n. Benevolent shaggy goblin haunting house and doing household work secretly; junior member (ages 8–11) of GIRL *guides*; (Photog.) kind of camera. [BROWN[1] + -Y[3]]

Brow·ning, n. Modern type of automatic pistol. [*B.*, surname]

browse[1] (-z), n. Twigs, young shoots, &c., as fodder for cattle; act of browsing. [foll.]

browse[2] (-z), v.i. & t. Feed *on*, crop, (leaves, twigs, scanty vegetation); (abs.) feed thus, (fig.) read for enjoyment. [f. 16th c. F *brouster* vb, *broust* n. (now *brout*), f. Teut., cf. OSax. *brustian* see BREAST]

Bru·in, n. (Personifying name for) bear. [MDu., = BROWN[1], name in *Reynard the Fox*]

bruise (-ōōz), n. Injury by blow to body (also to fruit &c.) discolouring skin. [f. foll.]

bruise[1] (-ōōz), v.t. & i. Injure by blow that discolours skin without breaking it or any bone, contuse, (human or animal body, also fruit, plant, &c.); dint, batter, (wood, metal); (fig.) disable; pound, bray, grind small; (Hunting) ride recklessly; (with *easily* &c.) show effects of blow. [OE *brysan* crush combined w. AF *bruser* (now *briser*) break perh. f. Teut.]

brui·ser, n. In vbl senses; esp., prize-fighter. [-ER[1]]

bruit[1] (-ōōt), n. (archaic). Report, rumour. [F, = noise (*bruire* roar perh. f. L *rugire*)]

bruit[2] (-ōōt), v.t. (archaic). Spread (report) *abroad, about*, make famous, celebrate. [f. prec.]

Bru·mmagem, n. & a. (Dial. & contempt. form of) Birmingham; (article) made at B., counterfeit, cheap & showy. [allusion to counterfeit groats made there in 17th c., & to its plated goods]

bru·mous (-ōō-), a. Wintry, foggy. [f. L *bruma* (= *brevima* shortest day f. *brevis*) + -OUS]

brunch, n. (slang). Single meal in lieu of breakfast & lunch. [portmanteau wd]

brune·tte (-ōō-), n. & a. Dark-skinned & brown-haired (woman). [F, fem. of *brunet* dim. of *brun* BROWN[1] see -ETTE]

Bru·nswick, a. From B. in Germany; esp., *B. line*, of Eng. sovereigns from George I.; *B. black*, a varnish. [f. G *Braunschweig*]

brunt, n. Chief stress (usu. *of* the attack

&c., & in phr. *bear the b. of*). [etym. dub.; there is ON *bruna* to advance like fire]

brush[1], n. (Archaic & U.S., Austral., &c.) brushwood or underwood, thicket, small trees & shrubs growing or (in U.S.) cut in fagots; implement of bristles, hair, wire, &c., set in wood &c. for scrubbing or sweeping; bunch of hairs &c. in straight handle, quill, &c., for painting &c.; *the b.*, art of painting, *b.*, painter's style, painter (*from the same b.*); tail, esp. of fox; b.-like tuft; (Electr.) b.-like discharge of sparks, piece of metal ending in wires or strips securing good metallic connexion, (also) movable strip of conductible material for making & breaking connexion; (Optics) bright or dark figure with vague edge; application of b., brushing, esp. *b. up* [f. foll.]; short smart encounter, skirmish, graze, abrasion, [f. foll.]; *b.-pencil*, artist's colour-b.; *brushwood*, undergrowth, thicket; *b.-work*, painter's (style of) manipulation. Hence **bru·sh**Y[2] n. [(sense *b.-wood*) ME *brusche* f. OF *brosse*, *broce*, (other senses) ME *brusshe* f. OF *brosse*, *broisse*; whether *broce* & *broisse* are identical in etym., and f. Teut. (cf. G *borste* bristle, *bürste* brush), is uncertain]

brush[2], v.t. & i. Move briskly, esp. *by*, *through*, *against*; sweep or scrub clean, put in order, with b.; *b. up*, furbish, (fig.) renew one's memory of; *b. over*, paint lightly; graze or touch in passing; remove (dust &c.) with b.; *b. aside*, *away* (fig.), ignore, pass over; injure by grazing. [partly f. prec., perh. partly f. F *brosser* dash through underwood (*brosse* brushwood)]

brusque (-ŏŏsk, -ŭsk), a. Blunt, off-hand, (of or in manner, speech). Hence **bru·sque**LY[2] adv., **bru·sque**NESS, **brusquerie·** (-ŏŏskerē) [-ERY], nn. [F, f. It. *brusco* sour, etym. dub.]

Bru·ssels, a. Made or grown at, or adopted from, B., as *B. carpet*, *lace*, *sprouts* (edible buds of kind of cabbage).

bru·tal, a. Sensual, rude, coarse, savagely cruel. Hence **bru·tal**ISM(2), **bruta·l**ITY, nn., **bru·tal**LY[2] adv. [f. L *brutus* BRUTE + -AL]

bru·talize, v.t. & i. Make (*rarely* grow) brutal. Hence **bru·taliz**A·TION n. [prec. + -IZE(3)]

brute, a. & n. (Beast) not gifted with reason; stupid, sensual, unspirited, beastlike, cruel, or passionate (person; & in same adj. senses of acts, motives, &c.); unconscious, merely material, (*b. force*, *matter*); lower animal; lower nature in man. Hence **bru·te**HOOD n., **brut·**ISH[1](1) a., **bru·tish**LY[2] adv., **bru·tish**NESS n., **bru·ti**FY v.t., **bru·ti**FICATION n. [f. F *brut* f. L *brutus* dull]

bru·tum fŭ·lmĕn, n. Empty threat, blank cartridge (fig.). [L]

Bru·tus, n. Style of wig (19th cent.). [F name in honour of Roman hero]

brȳŏ·logist, -logy, nn. Person learned in, the lore of, mosses. [Gk *bruon* kind of seaweed + -LOGIST, -LOGY]

brȳ·ony, n. Genus of climbing plants; *Red* or *White B.*, common species; *Black B.*, *Bastard B.*, plants resembling but not belonging to the genus. [f. L f. Gk *bruōnia* (*bruō* swell)]

bu·bble[1], n. Spherical or hemispherical envelope of liquid enclosing air &c.; air-filled cavity in solidified liquid, as glass, amber; unsubstantial or visionary project, enterprise, &c. (also adj. in this sense; *prick the b.*, unmask futility, pretension, &c.); sound or appearance of boiling; *b.-&-squeak*, cold meat fried with chopped vegetables. Hence **bu·bbl**Y[2] a. [f. foll.]

bu·bble[2], v.i. & t. Send up, rise in, make the sound of, bb. (lit., & fig. as *b. over*, or *b.*, *with* laughter, wrath); delude (archaic). [prob. imit. of sound of bursting bubbles, or of the action of lips in making one; cf. BLEB, BLUBBER]

bu·bbly-jock, n. Turkey-cock. [*bubbly* (BUBBLE[1]) + *Jock* = *Jack*]

bū·bo, n. (pl. *-oes*). Inflamed swelling in glandular part, esp. groin or armpit. Hence **būbŏ·n**IC a. [LL, f. Gk *boubōn* groin].

būbō·nocele, n. Hernia of groin. [prec., -CELE]

buccaneer·, n., & v.i. (Be a) sea-rover, pirate, esp. of the Spanish-American coasts; adventurer. Hence **buccaneer·**ISH[1] a. [f. F *boucanier* hunter of oxen (*boucan* BARBECUE-frame Brazilian wd)]

bu·ccinator (bŭks-), n. Flat thin cheek-muscle. [L (*buccinare* blow the trumpet f. *buccina*, -TOR)]

Būcē·phalus, n. Riding-horse (facet.). [charger of Alexander of Macedon]

buck[1], n. Male of fallow-deer, reindeer, chamois, antelope, hare, rabbit; dandy (also *old b.*, vocative = old fellow), whence **bu·ck**ISH[1] a., **bu·ckish**LY[2] adv.; (attrib., slang) male, of or for males, (*b. nigger*, *lunch*, &c.); *b.-horn*, as material for knife handles &c. (also *buck-*, as *buck-handled*); *b.-hound*, small variety of staghound (not now used for hunting); *b.-shot*, coarse shot (*b.-shot rule*, in Ireland, by armed constabulary); *buckskin*, (leather made of) b.'s skin, (pl.) breeches of it; *b.-tooth*, one that projects. [OE *buc* & *bucca*. cf. G *bock* he-goat; F *bouc*, W *bwch*, are f. the Teut.]

buck[2], v.i. & t. (Of horse) jump vertically with back arched & feet drawn together (also *b.-jump*, whence **bu·ckjump**ER[1] n.); *b. off*, throw (rider) thus. Hence **bu·ck**ER[1] n. [f. prec.]

buck[3], v.i. & t. (slang). (With *up*) make haste, become or make vigorous or cheerful, (esp. intr. in imperat.). [perh. f. BUCK[1] in sense *dandy*]

buck[4], n. Basket for trapping eels. [?]

buck[5], n. Body of cart (chiefly in comb. as *b.-board, b.-cart,* in various local senses). [perh. f. obs. *bouk* belly cf. BULK n.]

bu·ck-bean, n. Water plant with pinkish racemes. [transl. (1578) of Flem. *bocks boonen* goats' beans]

bu·cket[1], n. Wooden or other vessel for drawing or carrying water; piston of pump; compartment of water-wheel, scoop of dredging-machine or grain-elevator; socket for whip, carbine, wooden leg, &c.; *kick the b.*, die (but perh. f. obs. *bucket* beam, yoke); *b.-shop,* (chiefly U.S.) office for gambling in stocks, speculating on markets, &c. [accidental; story connected with elevator of office first so called]. Hence **bu·cket**FUL(2) n. [perh. f. OE *búc* pitcher, or f. OF *buket* tub]

bu·cket[2], v.i. & t. Ride hard (horse, or abs.); (Rowing) hurry the forward swing, row hurried stroke. [f. prec., cf. *pump* = exhaust]

Bu·ckingham Pa·lace, n. London residence of the King.

bu·ckle[1], n. Metal rim with hinged spiked tongue for securing strap, ribbon, &c. [f. F *boucle* f. L *buccula* cheek-strap (*bucca* cheek, see -ULE)]

bu·ckle[2], v.t. & i. Fasten with b. (often *up, on,* &c.); *b. to* (with *to* prep.) prepare for, set about, (with *to* adv.) get to work, start vigorously; (cause to) give way, crumple up, under longitudinal pressure (t. & i. of wheel, saw, &c.). [f. prec.; the last sense perh. f. F *boucler* bulge]

bu·ckler, n., & v.t. Small round shield usu. held by handle; protection, protector, (vb, protect); also technically in various naut., zool, & anat. senses. [f. OF *boucler* (now *bouclier*) f. L **buccularius* f. *buccula* BUCKLE[1], -ER[2](2)]

bu·ckram, n. & a. Coarse linen or cloth stiffened with gum or paste; stiffness, stiff, (of manner); strong, strength, in appearance only; *men in b., b. men,* non-existent (1 *Hen. IV*, II. iv. 210–50). [f. OF *boquerant* or It. *bucherame* etym. dub.]

bu·ckwheat, n. A cereal plant with seed used for horse and poultry food, & in U.S. for breakfast cakes. [= *beech wheat,* from its three-cornered seeds like beechmast; either transl. of Du. *boekweit* or made on obs. *buckmast* = beechmast]

būcŏ·lic, a. & n. Of shepherds, pastoral, rustic; (usu. pl.) pastoral poems (*the Bb.*, those of Virgil). Hence **buco·li**CALLY adv. [f. L f. Gk *boukolikos* f. *boukolos* herdsman (*bous* cow, *kol-* cf. L *colere* tend)]

bud[1], n. Rudiment of branch, leaf-cluster, or flower; flower not fully open; (Zool.) animal forming by GEMMATION, anything still undeveloped; *in b.*, putting forth buds; *nip in the b.*, destroy at early stage (fig.). Hence **bu·d**LESS a., **bu·d**LET n. [ME *budde, bodde,* etym. dub.]

bud[2], v.i. & t. Put forth bb., spring forth; begin to grow or develop (*budding horns, lawyer, cricketer*); (Zool.) produce, be produced, by GEMMATION; (Gardening) ingraft (trans. or abs.) into alien stock. [f. prec.]

bu·dded, p.p. In vbl senses; esp., that has budded, is in bud. [-ED[1](2)]

Buddha (bŏŏ·da), n. The Enlightened, title of successive teachers past & future of the Asiatic religion **bu·ddh**ISM(3) (bŏŏ·dĭ-) n., but applied esp. to Sakyamuni, Gautama, or Siddartha (5th c. B.C., in N. India). Hence **bu·ddh**IST(2) n. & a., **buddhi·st**IC(AL) aa. [Skr., p.p. of *budh* awake]

buddle·ia (-lēa), n. Kinds of shrub with lilac or yellow flowers of various forms. [A. *Buddle,* botanist, -IA[1]]

budge, v.i. & t. Make the slightest movement, force to do this, (in neg. sentences). [f. F *bouger* stir perh. (cf. Pr. *bolegar*) = It. *bulicare* f. LL *bullicare* frequent. of *bullire* boil]

bu·dget, n., & v.i. Contents of a bag or bundle (mostly fig., esp. of news, & as title of newspapers); annual estimate of revenue & expenditure by Chancellor of Exchequer in House of Commons; private person's similar estimate; (v.i.) *b. for,* allow or arrange for in b. Hence **bu·dget**ARY[1] a. [f. F *bougette* dim. of *bouge* leather bag f. L *bulga* (f. Gallic) knapsack]

buff[1], n. & a. (Of) stout velvety dull-yellow leather of buffalo or ox-hide; the human skin (*in b.*, naked); (of) dull-yellow colour (*the Buffs,* East Kent Regt, f. former colour of facings); (Path.) coagulated coating on blood drawn from fever patients, whence **bu·ff**Y[2] a.; *b.-coat, -jerkin,* formerly worn by soldiers as proof against sword-cut; *b.-stick, -wheel,* polishing tools covered with b.; *b.-tip,* kind of moth. [f. F *buffle* BUFFALO]

buff[2], v.t. Polish (metal) with b.; make (leather) velvety like b. [f. prec.]

bu·ffalo, n. Kinds of ox (*Bos bubalus,* India, Asia, Europe, N. Africa; *Bos caffer,* S. Africa; incorrectly, American BISON). [prob. f. Port. *bufalo,* f. L f. Gk *boubalos* antelope]

bu·ffer[1], n. Apparatus for deadening by springs or padding, or sustaining by strength of beams &c., a concussion, esp. of railway vans; *b. State,* small State between two large ones diminishing chance of hostilities. [f. obs. vb *buff* (prob. imit. of sound made by soft body struck, cf. PUFF & F *bouffer*) + -ER[1]]

bu·ffer[2], n. (slang). (Usu. *old b.*) old-fashioned or incompetent fellow. [etym. dub.; Wyclif's Bible has it = stammerer —'*the tunge of bufferes swiftli shal speke*']

bu·ffet[1], n., & v.t. & i. (Strike with) blow of the hand; (of fate &c.) knock, hurt, plague; contend with (waves); contend *with.* [OF, dim. of *buffe* blow (also in obs. E *buff* cf. BLIND[1]-*man's-b.*)]

bŭ·ffet[2], n. 1. Sideboard, recessed cupboard, for china, plate, &c. 2. (pr. bŏŏ·fā, or as F) refreshment bar. [F, etym. dub.; sense 2 of later introduction than 1; there is also *buffet* stool, hassock, (obs. exc. in dial. & in *Little Miss Muffet sat on a b.*)]

buffo (bŏŏ·fō), n. & a. Burlesque, comic, (actor). [It.]

buffoo·n, n., & v.i. (Play the) wag, jester, mocker. Hence **buffoo·n**ERY(4) n. [f. F *buffon* f. It. *buffone* (*buffa* jest, *buffare* to puff), -OON]

bug, n. Flat ill-smelling blood-sucking insect infesting beds; (loosely) small insect (often with defining word as *harvest, May, -b.*; *b.-hunter* &c., entomologist); *big b.* (slang), person of importance. Hence **bu·gg**Y[2] a. [?]

bŭ·gaboo, bu·gbear, nn. Fancied object of fear; false belief used to intimidate or dissuade. [etym. & mutual relation doubtful; cf. BOGY, BOGLE, & obs. *bug* in same sense]

bu·gger, n. (Law) sodomite, man having unnatural intercourse with beast or man, whence **bu·gg**ERY(4) n.; (in foul or low talk, abusively or humorously) fellow, beggar, chap, beast. [f. F *bougre* f. L *Bulgarus* 11th-c. heretic from Bulgaria, supposed capable of any crime]

bu·ggy, n. Light vehicle for one or two persons (esp. in U.S., India, colonies). [?]

bū·gle[1], n., & v.i. & t. Brass instrument like small trumpet used for military signals; (vb) sound b., sound (call) on b. Hence **bu·gl**ER[1] n. [orig. hunting-horn, short for *b.-horn* f. obs. & dial. & OF *bugle* young bull f. L *buculus* dim. of *bos bovis* ox see COW]

bū·gle[2], n. Kinds of plant. [F, f. LL *bugula*]

bū·gle[3], n. Tube-shaped glass bead sewn on dress &c. for ornament. [etym. dub.; there is Du. *beugel* ring]

bū·glet, n. Small (bicyclist's) bugle. [-ET[1]]

bū·gloss, n. Kinds of plant allied with borage. [f. F *buglosse* f. L *buglossa* f. Gk *bouglōssos* ox-tongued (*bous, glōssa*), from shape & roughness of leaves]

buhl (bōōl), n. & a. (Inlaid with) brass, tortoise-shell, &c., cut in ornamental patterns for inlaying. [Germanized f. *Boule* name of carver temp. Louis XIV]

build[1] (bĭ-), v.t. & i. (built). Construct by putting parts or material rightly together (house, ship, carriage, organ, engine, nest, or other structure large relatively to the builder); (abs.) be busy making one's house or nest; *b. up, round, in,* surround (person, place, &c.) with houses &c., block up; (with material as obj.) lay *in(to* wall &c.) in building; establish, make gradually, (often with *up*; system, empire, reputation); base (hopes &c.) *upon,* rely *upon*; *built* (with preceding adv.), of such & such a BUILD[2]. [ME *bulden* f. OE *bold* dwelling f. OTeut. *bu-* dwell, cf. BOOTH]

build[2], n. Style of construction, make; proportions of human body (*sturdy b.* &c.). [prec.]

bui·lder, n. In vbl senses; esp., master-builder, contractor for building houses. [-ER[1]]

bui·lding, n. In vbl senses; esp.: house, edifice; *b.-lease,* permitting lessee to build on the land; *b.-society,* of contributors to fund for loan to members when needing house. [-ING[1]]

bulb[1], n. Nearly spherical underground stem of lily, onion, &c., sending roots downwards & leaves &c. upwards; leaf-bud detaching itself from stem & becoming separate plant; (Anat.) roundish swelling of any cylindrical organ, as of hair-root or spinal cord; dilated part of glass tube (*b.-tube,* ending in a b.); electric-light container. Hence **bulb**ED[2], **bulbi·**FEROUS, **bu·lbi**FORM, aa., **bulbo**-comb. form. [f. L *bulbus* f. Gk *bolbos* onion]

bulb[2], v.i. Swell into bulb(s). [f. prec.]

bu·lbous, a. Of, having, like, springing from, a bulb. [BULB.[1] + -OUS]

bulbul (bŏŏ·lbŏŏl), n. Eastern song-thrush; singer, poet. [Pers. f. Arab.]

bulge[1], n. Convex part, irregular swelling, tendency to swell out, on flat or flatter surface; =BILGE. Hence **bulg**Y[2] a., **bu·lgi**NESS n. [ME, f. OF *boulge, bouge,* (or direct) f. L *bulga* see BUDGET]

bulge[2], v.i. & t. Swell outwards irregularly & usu. faultily; extend (bag &c.) by stuffing it. [f. prec.]

bu·lger, n. (golf). Convex-faced brassy or driver. [prec., -ER[1]]

bū·limy, būlĭ·mia, n. (Med.) morbid hunger; (fig.) voracity (for books &c.). [f. Gk *boulimia* ox- (i.e. vast) hunger (*bous* ox + *limos* hunger); latinized *bulimia* now preferred in medical use]

bŭlk[1], n. Cargo (*break b.,* begin unloading; *b. not equal to sample*; *in b.,* loose, not in package; *load in b.,* put grain &c. in loose; *sell in b.,* in large quantities, as it is in the hold); large shape, person, body; size, magnitude; great size; mass, large mass; *the* greater part or number of. [perh. f. ON **bulki* cargo, but with the meanings also of obs. *bouk* OE *búc* belly cf. G *bauch*]

bulk[2], v.i. & t. Seem in respect of size or importance (*b. large, larger*); *b. up,* form considerable sum &c., amount *to*; pile in heaps (fish); (Customs) ascertain weight of (tea &c.) by emptying out of chest. [f. prec.]

bŭ·lkhead, n. Upright partition dividing ship's cabins or water-tight compartments; compartment, stall. [f. obs. *bulk* framework before shop, stall, perh. f. ON *balkr* BALK[1]]

bu·lky, a. Large; too large. Hence **bu·lkiness** n. [BULK[1] + -Y[2]]

bull[1] (bŏŏl), n. & a. Uncastrated male of ox or any bovine animal (*b. in china shop*, reckless or clumsy destroyer; *take b. by horns*, meet not evade difficulty); male of whale, elephant, & other large animals (usu. *b. whale* or *whale-b.* &c.); constellation & sign Taurus; (St. Exch.) person trying to raise prices (see BEAR[1]); = BULL'*s-eye* (of target); (adj.) like that of a b. (*b. head, neck, voice*; also *b. operations* on St. Exch.); *bull-calf*, male calf, simpleton; *b.-corner* (local), barred refuge, usu. at junction of fields, from b.'s attack; *bulldog*, powerful & courageous large-headed smooth-haired breed of dog, tenacious & courageous (person), University proctor's attendant, gun or pistol (esp. of a certain pattern), [f. use in b.-baiting, or f. its b. head]; *bulldoze*, v.t. (U.S. slang), cow, coerce; *bullfight*, Spanish sport of baiting b. with horsemen &c.; *bullfinch*, strong-beaked handsome-plumaged songbird, also [perh. = *b. fence*, cf. *minch* dial. for *mince*] quickset hedge with ditch; *bullfrog*, large Amer. species; *bullhead*, small big-headed fish = Miller's thumb; *b.-headed*, obstinate, impetuous, blundering; *b.-of-the-bog*, bittern; *b.-puncher* (Austral.) bullock-driver; *b.-pup, -bitch*, young, female, bulldog; *bullring*, arena for bullfight; *bullroarer*, kind of noisy toy; *b.'s-eye*, boss of glass formed at centre of blown glass sheet, hemispherical piece or thick disk of glass as light in ship's side, hemispherical lens, (lantern) with such lens, small circular window, centre of target, kind of sweetmeat; *b.-terrier*, cross between bulldog & terrier; *bulltrout*, fish of salmon tribe. [OE *bule-* (in comb. only), cf. MLG *bulle*, prob. connected with BELLOW]

bull[2], v.i. & t. (St. Exch.) speculate for the rise; try to raise price of (stocks). [f. prec.; BULL[1],[2] perh. merely correl. to the more explicable BEAR[1],[2]]

bull[3] (bŏŏl), n. Papal edict. [f. L *bulla* BILL[4]]

bull[4] (bŏŏl), n. (Often *Irish b.*) expression containing contradiction in terms or implying ludicrous inconsistency (often an intelligible statement made absurd by compression). [etym. dub.; f. 1630 (connexion with *Irish* is more recent; there is OF *boul, bole*, trickery]

bull[5] (bŏŏl), n. Drink made of water flavoured in empty spirit cask. [?]

Bull[6]. = JOHN *Bull*.

bullace (bŏŏ·lĭs), n. Wild (or semi-cultivated) plum tree or fruit. [f. OF *beloce* f. LL *pilota* PELLET]

bŭ·llāte, a. (bot., physiol.). Puffy, blistered-looking. [f. L *bullatus* (*bulla* bubble, -ATE[2])]

bu·llet (bŏŏ-), n. Missile of lead &c., spherical or conical, used in muskets & rifles (*Dumdum, expanding, soft-nosed, explosive, b.*, varieties so shaped &c. as to inflict complicated wound); *b.-drawer*, instrument for extracting b. from wound; *b.-head, -headed*, (with) round & presumably thick head; *b.*-PROOF. [f. F *boulette* dim. of *boule* ball f. L *bulla* knob]

bu·lletin (bŏŏ-), n. Short official statement of public event or of invalid's condition. [F, f. It. *bullettino* dim. of *bulletta* lottery ticket dim. of *bulla* seal, BULL[3]]

bu·llion[1] (bŏŏ-), n. & a. Gold or silver before (or as valued apart from) coining or manufacture; (made of) solid or real gold or silver. [AF, prob. = F *bouillon* soup f. med. L *bullionem* nom. *-io* (L *bullire* BOIL + -ION); but the meanings are E only]

bu·llion[2] (bŏŏ-), n. Fringe of gold & silver thread twists. [f. F *bouillon*, see prec., in sense *bubble* (independent adoption)]

bu·llionist, n. Advocate of metallic currency. [BULLION[1] + -IST(2)]

bu·llock (bŏŏ-), n. Castrated bull, ox. [OE *bulluc* (-OCK)]

bu·lly[1] (bŏŏ-), n. Blusterer, tyrant (esp. among boys), coward & tyrant; hired ruffian. [obs. senses *lover, sweetheart, gallant, fine fellow*, perh. f. Du. *boel* lover cf. G *buhle*]

bu·lly[2], v.t. Persecute, oppress, tease, physically or morally; frighten *into* or *out of*; (abs.) play the b.; *b. off*, perform preliminary crossing of clubs in hockey. [f. prec.]

bu·lly[4], a. & int. (esp. U.S. & colonial). Capital, first-rate; *b. for you, him*, &c., = bravo. [f. BULLY[1]]

bu·lly[5] (bŏŏ-), n. Scrummage in (prop. Eton) football.

bu·lly[1] (bŏŏ-), n. (Also *b. beef*) tinned beef. [perh. = BOUILLI, or f. BULL[1]]

bullyrag. See BALLYRAG.

bu·lrush (bŏŏ-), n. Kinds of tall rush (pop. the Cat's Tail; in Bible, papyrus). [BOLE (strong-stemmed)?, or BULL[1] (big cf. *bullfrog, bulltrout*, & Gk use of *bou-* see BULIMY)?]

bu·lwark (bŏŏ-), n. Rampart, earthwork, &c.; mole, breakwater; person, principle, &c., that acts as a defence; ship's side above deck. [cf. Du. *bolwerk*, G *bollwerk*; perh. = BOLE + WORK (log-rampart)]

bum, n. Backside, buttocks; *b.-bailiff* (also *b.*), employed for arrests (from touching debtor on the back); *b.-boat*, plying with fresh provisions for ships (orig. scavenger boat). [cf. BUMP; earlier than, not contracted f., *bottom* in this sense]

bu·mble, n. Beadle; consequential jack-in-office. Hence **bu·mble**DOM n. [name of beadle in *Oliver Twist*]

bu·mble-bee, n. Large kind of bee. [f. obs. vb *bumble* (BOOM + -LE)]

bu·mble-puppy, n. Whist, tennis, &c., played unscientifically; game with tennis-ball slung to post. [prop. an obs. out-of-door bagatelle; etym. dub.; there is obs. vb *bumble* bungle]

bu·mbo, n. Cold rum-punch. [cf. It. *bombo* child's wd for drink]

bumf, n. (slang). Toilet paper; paper-chase; paper(s), documents. [= *bum-f(odder)*]

bu·mmalo, n. Small fish of S.-Asiatic coasts. [f. Mahratti *bombil*]

bummaree·, n. Middleman at Billingsgate fish-market. [?]

bu·mmer, n. (U.S.). Idler, loafer. [cf. G *bummler*]

bump[1], v.t. & i., & adv. Push, throw down, (box &c.) *against* or *on* (wall, person, floor, &c.); hurt (one's head &c.) by striking it (*against, on,* or abs.); seize by arms & legs & strike the posterior of (person) against floor, wall, &c.; come with a b. *against*; go along with repeated bumps; (Boat-racing, see foll.) overtake; (of cricket-ball) rise abruptly on pitching; (adv.) with a b., suddenly, violently, (*come, go,* &c., *b.,* cf. BANG, BOUNCE). [expressing the sound, or shape of swelling]

bump[2], n. Dull-sounding blow, knock, collision; swelling caused by it; (Phrenol.) prominence on skull, faculty indicated by it; (Boat-racing) touching of boat by next, a win for latter (*b.-supper,* in celebration of this). [f. prec.]

bump[3], n., & v.i. (Make) bittern's cry. [imit.]

bu·mper, n. In vbl senses; also, brim-full glass of wine; (slang) anything unusu. large or abundant (harvest, full theatre); (Whist) score of two games against nil; (Motoring) spring fender for mitigating collisions. [-ER[1]]

bum·pkin, n. Country or awkward or bashful fellow. [perh. f. Du. *boomken* little tree or MDu. *bommekijn* little barrel]

bu·mptious (-sh*u*s), a. Self-assertive. Hence **bu·mptious**LY[2] adv., **bu·mptious**NESS n. [jocular form, on BUMP[2] & e.g. *fractious*]

bu·mpy, a. Full of bumps, causing jolts, (esp. of road or cricket pitch). Hence **bu·mpi**NESS n. [-Y[2]]

bun[1], n. Small soft round sweet cake with a few currants (the usu. Eng. sense, but with local variations); *hot cross b.,* marked with cross & eaten on Good Friday; hair dressed in b. shape. [perh. f. OF *bugne* bump, swelling, (at Lyons = fritter, whence mod. F *beignet*)]

bun[2], n. (Personifying name of) squirrel, rabbit. [etym. dub.; there is Sc. *bun,* hare's tail]

bunch[1], n. Cluster of things growing or fastened together (flowers, grapes, keys), lot (*best of the b.*); *b. of fives* (slang), fist, hand. Hence **bu·nchy**[2] a. [?]

bunch[2], v.t. & i. Make into bunch(es), gather (dress) into folds; come or cling together, (Mil., of skirmishers) fail to keep intervals. [f. prec.]

bu·ncombe. See BUNKUM.

bund, n. (Anglo-Ind.). Embankment, causeway, quay. [Hind. *band,* of Persian orig.]

bundesrat(h) (bo͞o·ndesraht), n. Federal council of German Empire (58 members from 26 states). [G]

bu·ndle[1], n. Collection of things fastened together (esp. clothes & odds & ends in handkerchief); set of sticks, iron rods, &c., bound up; set of parallel fibres, nerves, &c.; 20 hanks of linen yarn. [perh. f. MDu. *bondel* cf. G *bündel* (OTeut. *bindan* BIND); see -LE(1)]

bu·ndle[2], v.t. & i. Tie in, make *up* into, a b.; throw confusedly *in* to any receptacle; go, put or send (esp. a person), in a hurry or unceremoniously *out, off, away,* &c. [f. prec.]

bung[1], n. Stopper, esp. large cork stopping hole in cask; (slang) lie; *b.-hole,* for filling cask. [cf. MDu. *bonghe* = **bonde* f. L *puncta* orifice (*pungere punct-* prick)]

bung[2], v.t. Stop (cask) with b.; *eyes bunged up,* closed with swelling from blow, or sealed with rheum; (slang) throw (stones). [f. prec.]

bungalow (bŭ·nggalō), n. Lightly built one-storeyed or temporary house. [f. Hind. *bangla* belonging to Bengal]

bu·ngle, v.i. & t., & n. (Make) clumsy work, confusion; blunder over, fail to accomplish, (task). Hence **bu·ngl**ER[1] n. [imit., cf. BUMBLE, BOGGLE]

bŭ·nion, n. Inflamed swelling on foot. [perh. f. It. *bugnone* (*bugno* boil, lump, cf. F *bugne* BUN[1], + *-one* -OON)]

bunk[1], n. Sleeping-berth. [?]

bunk[2], v.i., & n., (slang). *B., do a b.,* make off, vanish. [?]

bu·nker, n., & v.t. Ship's coal-bin; (Golf) sandpit or other obstruction to free dealing with balls; (v.t., usu. in p.p.) entangle in b., (fig.) bring into difficulties. [?]

bŭ·nkum, -combe (-km), n. Humbug, claptrap, sophistry. [anecdotic; member for Buncombe in N. Carolina speaking needlessly in Congress to impress his constituents]

bu·nny, n. Pet name for rabbit; *b.-hug,* an American dance. [BUN[2] + -Y[3]]

Bu·nsen('s) (bo͝on-, bŭn-), a. Invented by

Prof. B. of Heidelberg (*B. burner, lamp,* burning air with gas for heating & blowpipe work; *B. battery, cell,* voltaic of spec. kind).

bunt[1], n. Cavity, baggy part, of fishing-net, sail, &c.; *b.-line* (confining b. in furling sail). [?]

bunt[2], n. (Also *Smut-ball*) disease of wheat. [?]

bu·nting[1], n. Sub-family of birds including *Common* or *Corn B., Yellow B.* (or *Yellow-hammer*), *Black-headed, Reed, Snow,* &c., *B.*; grey shrimp. [?]

bu·nting[2], n. (Open-made worsted stuff used for) flags. [perh. = bolting-cloth (BOLT[5]) f. obs. *bunt* sift, or perh. = G *bunt* parti-coloured + -ING[1]]

buoy[1] (boi), n. Anchored float showing navigable course or reefs &c.; (also *life-b.*) something to keep person afloat; also fig. in both senses. [f. OF *boie* or MDu. *boei* f. L *boia* chain]

buoy[2] (boi), v.t. (Usu. with *up*) keep afloat; bring to surface of water; sustain (person, courage, &c.), uplift. (Without *up*, sometimes with *out*) mark with buoy(s). [see prec., but the vb is perh. directly f. a foreign source]

buoy·age (-ĭj), n. Providing of buoys. [-AGE]

buoy·ancy, n. Floating power (of solid to stay, of liquid to keep object, afloat); (Hydrost.) loss of weight by immersion in liquid; elasticity, recuperative power, (of spirits, also of prices, &c.). [f. foll.; see -ANCY]

buoy·ant (boi-), a. Apt to float, rise, keep up, or recover, springy; able to keep things up; light-hearted. Hence **buoy·ant**LY[2] adv. [=, & perh. f., Sp. *boyante*; earlier than BUOY[2]; see BUOY[1]]

bur, burr, n. (Any plant with) clinging seed-vessel or flower; female hop-catkin; person hard to shake off. [= Da. *borre*]

Bur·berry, n. A kind of waterproof cloth, coat &c. of this, made by a company of that name.

burble, v.i. Simmer (*with* rage, mirth). [on *burst, bubble*; but cf. obs. *burble* bubble]

bur·bot, n. Eel-like flat-headed bearded fresh-water fish. [f. F *bourbotte* cf. *bourboter* wallow f. LL *borba* f. Gk *borboros* mud]

bur·den[1], **bur·then** (-dh-), n. (usu. *-den* exc. = *tonnage*). Load (lit., or of labour, duty, sorrow, &c.; *b. of proof,* obligation to prove falling on maker of statement); obligatory expense; ship's carrying-capacity, tonnage; bearing of loads (*ship, beast, of b.*); (bibl.) oracle, heavy fate; (= obs. senses of BOURDON) refrain, chorus, of song, chief theme or gist of poem, book, speech, &c. [OE *byrthen* = OSax. *burthinnia* (st. of BEAR[3] + suf. *-innja*); for *-d-* cf. *murther, murder*]

bur·den[2], **bur·then**, v.t. Load (lit. & fig.), encumber, oppress, tax. [f. prec.]

bur·densome, a. Oppressive, wearying. Hence **bur·densome**NESS n. [-SOME]

bur·dock, n. Coarse plant with prickly flower-heads (BUR) & dock-like leaves. [BUR + DOCK[1]]

bureau (būrō·), n. (pl. *-eaux,* pr. -ōz). Writing-desk with drawers, escritoire; office, government department. [F, = office, desk, orig. baize f. OF *burel* dim. of *bure* coarse cloth cf. *buire* brown f. L *burrus* red perh. f. Gk *purrhos* red]

bureau·cracy (-ŏkra-), n. Government by bureaux, centralization; officialism; officials. Allied wds: **bureau·**CRAT n., **bureaucra·t**IC a., **bureaucra·t**ICALLY adv., **bureau·crat**ISM(2), **bureau·crat**IST(2), nn. [f. prec. + -CRACY]

būre·tte, n. Graduated glass tube for measuring small quantities of liquid. [F, dim. of *buire* vase]

bur·gage, n. An ancient tenure (*hold in b.*). [f. med. L *burgagium* (*burgus* see BOROUGH)]

burgee·, n. Small swallow-tailed pennant used by yachts &c. [?]

bur·geon, bour·geon, (ber·jn), n., & v.i. (Put forth, spring forth as) young shoot(s), bud, begin to grow, (poet., & also in Zool. of GEMMATION). [ME *borioun* f. OF *burjon* etym. dub.]

bur·gess, n. Inhabitant of borough with full municipal rights, citizen; (Hist.) member of parliament for borough, corporate town, or university. [ME & OF *burgeis* = BOURGEOIS[1]]

burgh (bŭ·ru), n. (Sc.). Scotch chartered town (used in E in writing of Scotch borough). [see BOROUGH]

burgher (ber·ger), n. (archaic). Citizen (chiefly of foreign towns). [f. G or Du. *burger* (*burg* fortified town), later assim. to E *burgh*]

bur·glar, n. One who breaks into house by night with intent to commit felony. Hence **bur·glar**Y[1] n., **burglār·**IOUS a., **burglar·ious**LY[2] adv. [f. Anglo-L *burglator, burgator,* perh. made on *burgh-breche* the native term for burglary]

bur·gle, v.i. & t. Commit burglary; enter or rob (house) burglariously. [recent back-formation f. prec., but cf. *burgulare* 1354]

bur·gomaster, n. Mayor of Dutch or Flemish town. [f. Du. *burgemeester* (BOROUGH)]

bur·gonet, n. (hist.). Visored helmet; steel cap. [f. OF *bourguignotte* f. *Bourgogne* Burgundy]

burgoo·, n. (naut. slang). Porridge. [?]

bur·gundy, n. Kinds of (usu. red) wine of Burgundy.

bu·rial (bĕ-), n. Depositing under earth, burying, esp. of dead body, funeral; *b.-ground,* cemetery; *b.-service,* religious form (esp. that in Ch.-of-Engl. prayer-book) at funeral. [f. OE *byrgels* cf. OSax. *burgisli* (*burg-* st. of *bergan* cover), *-s* dropped as though pl., cf. PEA]

bū̆r·in, n. Tool for engraving on copper. Hence **bur·in**IST(1) n. [F, perh. f. OHG *bora* boring-tool (BORE[1])]

burke, v.t. Avoid, smother, (publicity, inquiry); hush up, suppress, (rumour, book). [*Burke* executed 1829 for smothering people to sell bodies for dissection]

burl, n., & v.t. Knot in wool or cloth; (vb) clear of bb. [f. OF *bourle*]

bur·lap, n. Coarse canvas. [cf. Du. *boenlap* etym. dub.]

burle·sque (-ĕsk), a. & n., & v.t. Imitative, imitation, imitate, for purpose of deriding or amusing; bombast(ic), mock-serious(ness); caricature, parody, esp. (of) literary & dramatic work. [F, f. It. *burlesco* (*burla* mockery, -ESQUE)]

Bur·lington House, n. Building in London used as head-quarters of the Royal Academy, British Academy, & British Association.

bur·ly, a. Sturdy, corpulent. Hence **bur·li**NESS n. [ME *borlich* prob. f. an OE *búrlic* handsome, fit for the BOWER[1], see -LY[1]]

Burme·se, a. & n. Of Burma; (n.) B. native (pl. same) or language. **Bur·man** a. & n., = *B.* [*Burma* + -ESE, -AN]

burn[1], n. (Sc., north., poet.). Small stream. [com.-Teut. cf. Du. *born*, & S.-Engl. BOURN[1]]

burn[2], v.t. & i. (*burnt* sometimes *burned*). Consume, waste, by fire (t. & i., the heat, heating person, or heated thing, being subject; *b. away, out,* to nothing, to extinction; *b. up,* get rid of by fire; *b. out,* consume contents of; *b.* one's *boats,* commit oneself irrevocably to a course); blaze, glow, with fire (*b. up,* flash into blaze; *b. down, low,* less vigorously as fuel fails); give, make to give, light (lamp, candles, gas, oil, &c.; *b. blue* &c., give blue &c. light; *b. candle at both ends,* not husband energy; *b. daylight,* use artificial light by day; *b. the midnight oil,* work late); put, be put, to death by fire; harden, produce, (bricks, lime, charcoal) by heat; make (hole &c.) by heat (*money burns hole in pocket,* clamours to be spent); injure, be injured, by fire or great heat (*b.* one's *fingers,* suffer for meddling or rashness); char, scorch, in cooking (t. & i.), adhere to saucepan &c.; cauterize, brand, (*b. in, into,* impress indelibly); eat, make acid &c. eat, its way (*into* material, material, or abs.); parch, freckle, tan, colour, (t. & i.; abs. or with *brown, dry,* &c.); give, feel, sensation or pain (as) of heat (*burnt child dreads fire*; *ears b.,* when one is talked of; *b.,* get near discovery or truth, as in child's game); make, be, hot or passionate, glow, blaze, rage, yearn; *b.* person *out,* expel him by fire; *b. the water,* spear salmon by torchlight; *burning-glass,* convex lens or concave mirror concentrating sun's rays enough to ignite object at focus; *burnt almond* (enclosed in burnt sugar); *burnt ochre, sienna* (calcined); *burnt offering,* sacrifice made by burning. [OE *brinnan* intr., *bærnan* trans.; com.-Teut. cf. G *brennen*]

burn[3], n. Sore, mark, on body made by burning. [f. prec.]

bur·ner, n. In vbl senses, esp. in comb. as *brick-b.*; also, part of lamp &c. that shapes the flame. [-ER[1]]

bur·net, n. Kinds of brown-flowered plant. [f. obs. adj. *burnet* f. OF *burnete* see BRUNETTE]

bur·ning, a. In vbl senses; also: flagrant (*b. shame, disgrace*); hotly discussed, exciting, (*b. question*); *b. scent* (in hunting), strong. [-ING[2]]

bur·nish, v.t. & i. Polish by friction; (with *well* &c.) take a polish. Hence **bur·nish**ER[1](2) n. [f OF *burnir* = *brunir* (*brun* BROWN), see -ISH[2]]

burnou·s(e) (-ōōs, -ōōz), n. Arab, Moorish, & lady's, hooded cloak. [F (*-s*), f. Arab. *burnus*]

burr[1], n. Nebulous disk round moon or star; rough ridge left on cut or punched metal or paper (*b.-drill,* dentist's); siliceous rock used for mill-stones; whetstone; kinds of limestone; rough sounding of letter *r* as in Northumberland; whirring sound; = BUR. [etym. dub.; perh. four different wds; & cf. BUR]

burr[2], v.t. & i. Pronounce with sound of Northumbrian *r*, also of French *r*; speak without clear articulation. [cf. prec.]

bu·rrow, n., & v.i. & t. (Make, live in) hole excavated in earth, as of foxes, rabbits, &c.; make by excavating (hole, one's way); retire out of sight; (fig.) investigate mysteries &c. Hence **bu·rrow**ER[1] n. [perh. = BOROUGH]

bur·sar, n. Treasurer, esp. of a college; exhibitioner in Scotch University or school, whence **bur·sar**Y[1] n. [f. med. L *bursarius* (*bursa* bag f. Gk = hide)]

bursā̆r·ial, a. Of bursar(y). [-AL]

burst[1], v.t. & i. (past & p.p. *burst*). Fly by expansion of contents, send (containing case), violently asunder, split, (powder, shell, &c.; exaggeratively, *b. with food* or *emotion, heart bursts*); get away from or through, make way *out* or *in*, express one's feelings, by force or suddenly (*river bursts banks*; *b. in,* come into room, interrupt; *b. out,* exclaim; *b. into tears, out laughing,* break into tears, laughter; *b. upon enemy's country,* overrun it); open, come open, be opened, forcibly (*boil, bud, cloud, b.*; *b. door, door bursts, in* or *open*); fill, be full, to overflowing (*grain bursts granary, granary bursting*; *b. with joy, envy, pride, a secret*); appear suddenly (*b. into flame, upon the view*; *sun, war, disease, b. out*);

suffer bursting of (some part; *b. a blood-vessel*, one's *heart, sides with laughing, buttons with food*; *b. up*, explode, bring or come to utter collapse, (colloq., & often spelt *bust up*). [OE *berstan* f. OTeut. *brestan* perh. f. *brek-* BREAK; there has been double metathesis, OTeut. *brest-*, OE *berst-*, ME *brest-*, mod. *burst*]

burst[2], n. Bursting, split; *b.-up* (often *bust-* colloq.), collapse; sudden issuing forth (*b. of flame*), explosion, outbreak, (lit. & fig.); spurt; continuous gallop; bout of drunkenness &c. (often vulg. *bust*; *on the bust*). [f. prec.]

bur·then. See BURDEN.

bury (bĕ·rĭ), v.t. Deposit in, commit to, earth, tomb, or sea (corpse); (of relatives) *to have buried*, lost; perform burial rites over; put under ground (*b. alive*; *b. the hatchet*, renounce quarrel); put away, forget; (chiefly refl. & pass.) consign to obscurity; hide in earth (treasure &c.), cover up, submerge; withdraw from view (face in hands, hands in pockets); (p.p.) immersed (*buried in sloth*); *burying-ground, -place*, graveyard, cemetery. [OE *byrgan* cf. BURIAL]

bus, 'b-, n. (pl. *-es*), & v.i. (Go by) OMNIBUS; (slang) aeroplane.

bu·sby (-z-), n. Tall fur cap of Hussars & R.H.A. [?]

bush[1] (bo͝osh), n. Shrub, clump of shrubs; bunch of ivy as ancient vintner's sign (*good wine needs no b.*); luxuriant growth of hair, whisker, &c.; woodland, untilled district, (esp. in colonies; *take to the b.*, become bushranger); BEAT[1] *about b.*; *bush-* in many bird, beast, & plant names; *b.-fighter, -ing*, (person used to) fighting in the b., guerilla warfare; *b.-harrow*, heavy frame with bars between which branches are inserted for harrowing grass land or covering seed, (vb) harrow with this; *bushman*, aboriginal of a S.-Afr. tribe, dweller, farmer, or traveller in the Australian b., whence **bu·shman**SHIP(3) n. [After Du. *boschjesman* (*bosch* bush)]; *b.-ranger*, Australian brigand (at first escaped convict) living in the bush; *b.-rope*, tropical wild vine netting trees together. [ME *busk* f. ON *buskr*, cf. G *busch*, Du. *bosch* (whence prob. the sense *woodland* above), f. Rom. *bosco* see BOSK]

bush[2], v.t. Set (ground) with bb. to frustrate net-poaching; b.-harrow (ground) [prec.]

bush[3] (bo͝osh), n., & v.t. Metal lining of axle-hole or other circular orifice, perforated plug; (vb) furnish with b. [prob. f. MDu. *busse* BOX[2] cf. BLUNDERBUSS]

bu·shel (bo͝oshl), n. Measure of capacity (8 gal.) for corn, fruit, &c. (*not hide light* or *candle under b.*, set example; *measure others' corn by* one's *own b.*, judge others by oneself). Hence **bu·shel**FUL(2) n. [ME *boyschel* f. OF *boissiel* f. LL *buscellus* f. *buxis* BOX[2]]

Bushido (bo͝oshē·dō), n. The code of honour & morals evolved by the samurai. [Jap., = military knight way]

bu·shy, a. Abounding in bushes; growing thickly. Hence **bu·shi**NESS n. [-Y[2]]

business (bĭ·znĭs), n. Being busy (orig. sense, now obs., see BUSYNESS); task, duty, province, (*make it* one's *b. to*, undertake); cause of coming (*what is your b.?*); habitual occupation, profession, trade; serious work (*means b.*, is in earnest; *on b.*, with definite purpose; *b. as usual*, things will proceed in spite of disturbing circumstances; *b. end of tin tack*, point; *b. hours, hours of b.*, of regular work, open shop or office, &c.); thing needing attention, agenda, (*the b. of the day, meeting*, &c.); dealings with men & matters (*b. man*, one used to these, & see below; *man of b.*, agent, attorney); difficult matter (*what a b. it is!, make a great b. of it*); thing that concerns one, that one may meddle with, (*mind your own, go about your, send about his, b.*, reproof or dismissal; *has no b. to*, no right); (contempt.) device, machine, process, concern, course of events, (*sick of the whole b.*; *a lath-&-plaster b.*); (Theatr.) action, dumb-show; buying & selling, bargaining, (*doing a great b.*; *good stroke of b.*; *b. man*, engaged in commerce, also see above); commercial house, firm; *do* one's *b.*, kill him; *good b.!* well done! [OE *bisignis* (BUSY[1] + -NESS)]

business-like, a. Systematic, practical, prompt, well-ordered. [-LIKE]

busk, n. Rigid strip stiffening corset-front. [f. F *busc* etym. dub.]

bŭ·skin, n. Boot reaching to calf or knee; thick-soled boot lending height to Athenian tragic actor; the tragic vein, tragedy, (see SOCK; *put on the b.*, write or act tragedy). Hence **bu·skin**ED[2] a. [in many Europ. langg.; the E perh. f. OSp. *boszegui*, F *brousequin*, Du. *brozeken*, &c., having *br-*; etym. dub.; MIt. *borzachino* suggests *borza* PURSE]

buss, n., & v.t., (archaic). Kiss. [earlier *bass* n. & v.; cf. F *baiser*, L *basiare*, *basium*]

bust[1], n. Sculpture of person's head, shoulders, & chest; upper front of body, bosom, esp. of woman. [f. F *buste* f. It. *busto* etym. dub.]

bust[2]. See BURST[1], [2].

bu·stard, n. Genus of large swift-running birds. [perh. mixture of OF *bistarde*, *oustarde*, both f. L *avis tarda* slow bird (the inappropriate adj. unexplained)]

bu·stle[1] (bŭsl), v.i. & t. Bestir oneself; make show of activity, hurry *about*; make (others) hurry or work hard. [perh. var. of obs. *buskle* f. obs. *busk* prepare (ON *buask* refl. of *búa* prepare cf. BOUND[5])]

bu·stle[2], n. Excited activity, fuss. [f. prec.]

bustle[3] (bŭ·sl), n. Pad or frame puffing out top of woman's skirt behind. [perh. =prec.]

busy[1] (bĭ·zĭ), a. Occupied, working, engaged, with attention concentrated, (*b. in, with, at*; also, prep. being dropped, with vbl n. now looking like part., as *he was b. packing*); unresting, ever employed, stirring, (*b. as a bee*); fussy, meddlesome, prying, mischievous; *b. idle(ness)*, spending energy on trifles; *b.-body*, meddlesome person, mischief-maker. Hence **bu·si**LY[2] adv. [OE *bisig*; only E & LG cf. Du. *bezig*; the *-u-* unexplained]

bu·sy[2], v.t. Occupy (esp. one*self*, one's hands, eyes, &c.), keep b., (*with, in, at, about*, or with *-ing*, or abs.). [OE *bisgian* see prec.]

bu·syness, n. State or quality of being busy. [mod. form differentiated in spelling & pronunc. f. BUSINESS]

but[1] (orig. adv. & prep. = outside, without; developed into conj., under which most mod. uses belong; but it is now adv., prep., negative rel. pron., subord. & coord. conj.; clear distinction of these is not here possible). Only (*she is b. a child, I can b. do it*); except, if not, short of, except that, if it were not that, short of the condition that, (*they are all wrong b. he, him*; *no one b. me, I*; *never b. once*; *he all b. did it*; *what can he do b. die*; *nothing would content him b. I must come*); otherwise than (*cannot choose b., cannot b., do it*); who *or* that not (*no one b. knows that*); without the result &c. that (*never rains b. it pours*; *justice was never done b, some one complained*); rather than so-&-so shall prove untrue (*it shall go hard b. I will get there*; *ten to one b. it was you*); that not (*not such a fool b.*—also *b. that, b. what—he can see that*; *it is impossible b. that offences will come*); to say (that) not (*not b. that*—also *what—he believed it himself*); *b. for this* &c., were it not so, without this; *b. then*, b. on the other hand (*it is hot, no doubt, b. t. the heat is dry*); (after neg.) that (*I don't deny, doubt, b. that*); on the contrary, nevertheless, however, on the other hand, moreover, yet. [OE *be-útan, bútan, búta*, (BE-, OUT) outside, without]

but[2], n., & v.t. An objection; (vb) utter, use, (bb.; *but me no buts*). [uses of prec.]

bu·tcher[1] (bŏŏ-), n. Slaughterer of animals for food; dealer in meat (*the b., the baker, the candlestick-maker*, people of all trades); judge, general, &c., who has men killed needlessly or brutally; a salmon-fly; *b.'s bill*, list of killed in war; *b.-bird*, kind of shrike; *b.'s-broom*, low spiny-leaved evergreen = *Knee Holly*; *b.'s meat*, excluding poultry, game, & bacon &c. [f. OF *bochier* (*boc* BUCK[1]) lit. dealer in goat's flesh]

bu·tcher[2], v.t. Slaughter (people) wantonly or cruelly; ruin by bad reading or editing, damage by harsh criticism. [f. prec.]

bu·tcherly, a. Fit for, like, a butcher, coarse, brutal, bloody. [-LY[1]]

bu·tchery, n. Shambles (in barracks, camp, ship, &c.); (attrib.) butcher's trade (*b. trade, business*, &c.); needless or cruel slaughter of people. [f. F *boucherie* (BUTCHER, -Y[1])]

bŭ·tler, n. Servant in charge of wine-cellar & plate &c., head servant. [f. AF *butuiller* f. OF *bouteillier*, see BOTTLE[1], -ER[2](2)]

butt[1], n. Wine or ale cask (108–140 gals); any barrel. [f. Rom. (F & It. *botte*) f. LL *buttis*]

butt[2], n. Thicker end, esp. of tool or weapon (*give fish the b.*, turn b. of rod towards him for firmer hold); trunk of tree just above ground; *b.* or *b.-end*, remnant (*b.-end* also = thicker end); base of leaf-stalk; kinds of flat-fish, as sole, plaice, turbot; hide of back & flanks trimmed to rectangle, thickest leather (cf. BEND[1]); square end of plank meeting a similar end (also *b.-end*). [cf. Da. *but*, Du. *bot*, stumpy, Sw. *but* stump; whether senses belong together, & relation to other wds *butt*, doubtful]

butt[3], n. Mound behind target; (pl.) shooting-range; target; end, aim, object; object *of* (ridicule &c.); object of teasing & ridicule. [f. F *but* goal cf. foll.]

butt[4], v.i. & t., & n. Push (v. & n.) with the head (*come b.* or *full b. against*, run into; *b. in*, fig., intervene, meddle); meet end to end (*b. against, upon*); come, place (timber &c.), with end flat *against* wall &c. [f. OF *boter, buter*, (now *bouter*) thrust, project, influenced by ABUT]

bu·tter[1], n. Fatty substance made from cream by churning (*look as if b. would not melt in mouth*, demure; *melted b.*, sauce of b., flour, &c.); kinds of substance of similar consistence or look, as *b. of almonds*; fulsome flattery; *b.-&-eggs*, kinds of plant with two yellows in flower, as toad-flax; *b.-bean*, yellow-pod kind usu. cooked in the pod unsliced, wax-pod, (also) large flat kind of haricot; *b.-boat*, sauce-boat; *b.-knife*, blunt, of silver &c., for cutting b.; *b.-scotch*, kind of toffee; *butterbur*, plant with large soft leaves; *buttercup*, kinds of yellow-flowered Ranunculus; *b.-fingers, -fingered*, (person) unable to hold things, esp. a catch at cricket; *buttermilk*, liquid left after churning b.; *b.-nut*, N.-Amer. oily nut (-tree); *b.-print*, wooden stamp for marking b.; *butterwort*, fleshy-leaved violet-flowered bog-plant. Hence **bu·tter**Y[2] a., **bu·tteri**NESS n. [OE *butere*, f. L f. Gk *bouturon* (*bous* cow, *turon* cheese, or perh. barbarian wd so accounted for)]

bu·tter[2], v.t. Spread, cook, sauce, with b. (*fine wds b. no parsnips*, mere professions are valueless); for other phrr. see BREAD); (also *b. up*) flatter. [f. prec.]

bu·tterbump, n. =BITTERN. [see BUMP[3]]

bu·tterfly, n. & a. Diurnal erect-winged insect with knobbed antennae; showy or fickle (person), trifler; *b.-nut, -screw* (Mech.), with wings to be turned by thumb & finger; BREAK[1] *b. on wheel.* [OE *buttor-fléoge* cf. Du. *botervlieg,* connexion with *butter* unexplained]

bu·tterine (-ēn), n. Imitation butter of oleo-margarine & milk. [-INE[1]]

bu·tteris, n. Farrier's tool for paring hoof. [cf. F *boutoir* & obs. E *butter*]

bu·ttery, n. Place in colleges &c. where bread & ale, butter, &c., are kept; *b.-hatch,* half-door over which provisions are issued. [f. OF *boterie* =*bouteillerie* (BOTTLE[1], -ERY)]

bu·ttock[1], n. Half of rump (usu. in pl.); manœuvre in wrestling (usu. *cross-b., running-b.,* &c.); *b.-steak,* = rumpsteak. [BUTT[2] + -OCK]

bu·ttock[2], v.t. Throw by using b. [f. prec.]

bu·tton[1], n. Knob or disk sewn to garment to fasten it by passing through buttonhole, or for ornament (*boy in bb.,* page; *take by the b.,* detain, see *buttonhole* below); bud; unopened mushroom; in plant names, as BACHELOR'*s b.*; knob, handle, catch, as in electric bell (*touch the b.,* produce complicated result by simple action); small bar revolving on pivot as door-fastening; small rounded body; terminal knob (on foil, making it harmless; also as ornament); *b.-boot,* fastened with bb.; *buttonhole,* slit made to receive fastening b., (fig.) small mouth, flower(s) worn in buttonhole, (vb) make buttonholes (in), hold by a coat or waistcoat b., detain, (reluctant listener), whence **bu·ttonhol**ER[1] n. [last sense by confusion with earlier *b.-hold*]; *buttonhook,* for pulling b. into place; *b.-stick,* soldier's appliance for b.-polishing. Hence (-) **button**ED[2], **bu·tton**LESS, aa., **bu·ttonless**NESS n. [f. OF *boton* bud f. LL **bottonem* nom. *-to* f. *bottare* push, cf. BUTT[4]]

bu·tton[2], v.t. & i. Furnish with button(s); fasten (t. & i.) with bb. (often *up*); enclose within buttoned garment (person, or object carried with one; usu. *up*). [f. prec.]

bu·ttons, n. Liveried page. [pl. of BUTTON[1]]

bu·ttony, a. With many buttons. [-Y[2]]

bu·ttress, n., & v.t. Support built against wall &c. (FLYING *b.*); prop (lit. & fig.); b.-like projection of hill; (vb) support (lit. & fig., often with *up*) with b., by argument, &c. [perh. f. OF *bouterez,-et,* flying buttress (*bouter* push cf. ABUT)]

būtyr-, būtyro-, st. & comb. form of technical wds as *butyr*A·CEOUS, *butў·r*IC, *butyroacĕ·tic*; of BUTTER, esp. in its chem. aspect.

bu·xom, a. Plump, comely. Hence **bu·xom**NESS n. [earlier sense *pliant*; ME *buhsum* f. st. of *búgan* BOW[3] + -SOME]

buy (bī), v.t. (*bought,* pr. bawt). Obtain by paying a (usu. money) price; serve to procure (*money cannot b.*); get by some sacrifice (*dearly bought*); gain over (person) by bribery &c.; *b. in,* b. a stock of, withdraw at auction by naming higher price than highest offered; *b. into,* b. stock or shares in (the Funds or a company); *b. off,* get rid by payment of (claim, claimant, blackmailer), get (soldier) discharged so; *b. out,* pay person to give up post, property, &c.; *b. over,* bribe; *b. up,* b. as much as possible of, absorb (other firm &c.) by purchase; *b. pig in poke,* commit oneself inconsiderately. Hence **buy·**ABLE a., **buy·**ER[1] n. [OE *bycgan* cf. Goth. *bugjan* etym. dub.]

buz(z)[1], int. =Stale news !

buzz[2], v.i. & t. Make humming sound; move, hover, *about* (person or abs.) annoyingly like bluebottle; (of a company or place) sound confusedly; circulate (t. & i. of rumour &c.); utter by speaking together (*b. applause*); throw hard (*b. stones*). [imit.]

buzz[3], n. Hum of bee &c.; sound of people talking, stir, general movement. [f. prec.]

buzz[4], n. Downy beetle, fishing-fly like it. [perh. as expressive, cf. FUZZY & obs. *buzz* (large bushy) *wig*]

buzz[5], v.t. Finish (bottle of wine). [?]

bu·zzard, n. Kinds of falcon (*B., Bald B.* or osprey, *Honey B., Moor B.,* &c.). [f. OF *busart* f. L *buteo* falcon + -ARD]

bu·zzer, n. In vbl senses; esp. steam-whistle, (also) electric buzzing-machine for sending signals, (army slang) signaller. [BUZZ[2], -ER[1]]

by[1], prep. & adv. Prep. (bī, *sometimes* bĭ); Near, at *or* to side of, in postal district of, about person *or* in possession of, in company of, in region of, slightly inclining to, (*Bromley-by-Bow, Coniston-by-Ambleside*; *come here by me*; *stand by,* be faithful to, help; *abide by,* accept, observe; *have not got it by me*; *come by,* obtain; *by oneself,* alone; *North by East,* between N & NNE; *by the head, stern,* deeper in water there; *by land & sea, adventures by flood & field*); along, in passing along, through, via, avoiding, passing, out-stripping, (*by nearest road*; *by the way,* as one goes, parenthetically; so *by the by,* esp. as formula introducing digression; *travel by Bâle, Paris*; *pass him by, go by him*); during, in the circumstances of, (*by day, night, daylight*; *by the space of,* biblical for *during*); through the agency, means, instrumentality, or causation, of, owing to, in such a manner, with, (*by oneself,* without help or prompting; *know, say, by* HEART; *multiply, divide, by*; *3 ft by 2 ft*; *lead by the hand*; *set by the ears,* egg on to quarrel; *go, be known, by the name of*——; *what do you mean by that?*; *travel by rail*; *by all, no, means*; *live by bread*; *do it by* one's *deputy*; *have children by such a father, mother*; *authorized, hanged, made, by*; *no gas to read by*; *case goes by default*; *begin, end, by ——ing*; *by way of a joke*, *be by way of knowing everybody*, profess or be supposed to; *cautious by nature*; *by cheque, £6. 5. 4*, in Cr entries; *by chance*; *by dint of*; *by reason of*); as soon as, not later than, (*by now, next week, tomorrow, the time*—with or oftener without—*that*); according to, after, from, (*by rote*; *by right*; *by rights*, if right were done; *take warning, example, by*; *by your leave*; *judge by appearances*; *sell, buy, by retail, measure, the yard, packet*); with succession of, succeeding, (*by degrees, by hundreds, man by man, little by little*); to the extent of (*missed by a foot, too moral by half, better by far, much*); concerning, in respect of, (*do* one's *duty by*; *French by blood, Jones by name*; *pull up by the roots*); as surely as I believe in (*by God*; *swear by all* one *holds sacred*; *swear by vegetarianism*, declare complete belief in it). Adv. (bī): Near (*stand by*, be inactive, also be ready for action, esp. Naut.); aside, in reserve, (*put, lay, set, by*, abandon or store up); past (*they marched by*; *all that is gone by*). [OE *bī, bi, be*; cf. OHG *bî, bi*, (G *bei, be-*); in OE the prep. was sometimes *be*; in mod. E the adv. is always *bȳ*, the prep. usu. *bȳ* sometimes *bў*, & the pref. either *bȳ-* or BE-]

by[2], **bye**, a. Subordinate, incidental, secondary, side, out-of-the-way, secret, as *by(e) road, the by(e) effects, a by(e) consideration*; *b.* ELECTION. [*by* adv. used attrib.; often hyphened with noun; usu. *by* when this is done, & *bye* as sep. wd]

by[3], n. =BYE (*-e* usu. exc. in *by the by*).

by-, pref. (1) usu. with one of the meanings of BY a.; it may be written as separate wd (*by path* or *bye path*), hyphened (*by-path*), or, if the combination is often used, as one wd with the other (*bypath*); (2) sometimes with meanings of BY adv. as in *bystander, bygone*.

by· and by·, adv. & n. Before long, presently; (n.) the future. [perh. f. BY prep. denoting succession (*one by one* &c.)]

by·-blow, n. Side blow at someone else than the main opponent; bastard child. [BY a.]

bye, n. Something subordinate (*by the by* or *bye*, incidentally, parenthetically); (Cricket) run scored for ball that passes batsman and wicket-keep, *leg-b.*, for one that touches batsman; (Golf) hole(s) remaining after decision of match and played as a new game; (in games where competitors are paired off) odd man, being odd man. [BY[1] as n.]

bye·-bye[1], n. (Nursery word for) sleep, bed. [sound used in lullabyes cf. *hushaby, lullaby, bye baby bunting*]

bye-bye·[2], int. =Good-bye. [colloq. & childish clipping of *good-bye*]

by·-end, n. Side or secret purpose. [BY a.]

by·gone, a. & n. Past, departed; antiquated; (pl. n.) the past, past offences (*let bb. be bb.*, forgive & forget). [BY adv.]

by·-lane, n. See BY-.

by·-law, bye·-law, n. Regulation made by local authority or corporation, as town or railway company. [prob. f. obs. *byrlaw* local custom (ON *býjar* genit. pl. of *byr* OE *bý* town, cf. *Derby* &c.), but associated with BY a.]

by·-name, n. Secondary name, sobriquet; nickname. [BY a.]

by·-pass, n. Secondary gas-jet always alight from which main jet is lit when wanted; piece of new road relieving traffic by connecting two points of the old. [BY a.]

by·past, a. Gone by, elapsed. [BY adv.]

by·path, n. Retired path (lit., & fig. as *bb. of history*). [BY a.]

by·play, n. Action apart from the main course of events; esp., dumb-show of minor characters on stage. [BY a.]

by·-product, n. Thing produced incidentally in manufacturing something else. [BY a.]

byre (-īr), n. Cow-house. [OE *býre* perh. cogn. w. *búr* BOWER]

by·-road, n. Little-frequented road. [BY a.]

bў·ssus, n. Fine ancient textile fibre & fabric of flax; tuft of silky filaments by which some molluscs adhere to rock. Hence **byss**A·CEOUS, **by·ss**AL, **byssi·**FEROUS, **by·ss**INE[2], **by·ss**OID, aa. [L, f. Gk *bussos*]

by·stander, n. Spectator. [BY adv.]

by·street, n. Out-of-the-way street. [BY a.]

by·-way, n. Secluded road or track (often *highway and b.*); short cut; less known department of any subject. [BY a.]

by·word, n. Proverb; person, place, &c. taken as type of some (usu. bad) quality (esp. *a b. for iniquity* &c.) [BY a.]

by·-work, n. Work done by the way, at leisure moments. [BY a.]

byza·ntine (ȳ *or* ў), a. & n. (Inhabitant) of Byzantium or Constantinople (*B. historians*, of Eastern Empire from 6th to 15th c.); of the style in architecture &c. developed in the Eastern Empire (round arch, cross, dome, circle, mosaic). Hence **Byzantin**E·SQUE a., **Byza·ntin**ISM n., **Byza·ntin**IZE(4) v.t. [f. L *Byzantinus* f. L f. Gk *Buzantion*]

C

C (sē), letter (pl. *C*s, C's, Cees). *C springs*, see CEE. *C3* POPULATION. (Mus.) first note of natural major scale (In argument) third hypothetical person or thing. (Alg.) third known quantity.

Abbreviations (1): **C**, centum, 100, as CI 101, CV 105, CCL 250, CM 900, DC 600, XC 90. **C.**, cash, **C.O.D.** (on delivery);

centigrade, as 15° **C.**; centimetre, **C.G.S.** (gramme, second); Ceylon, **C.C.S.** (civil service); Channel, **C.I.** (Islands); chaplain, **C.F.** (of the Forces); charity, **C.O.S.** (organization society); chartered, **C.A.** (accountant); chief, **C.I.G.S.** (of imperial general staff), **C.J.** (Justice); church, **C.E.** (of England), **C.E.T.S.** (temperance society); city, **C.I.V.** (imperial volunteers); civil, **C.E.** (engineer); commander, **C.B.E.** (of British Empire), **C. in C.** (chief), **C.V.O.** (of Victorian Order); commanding, **C.O.** (officer); companion, **C.B.**, **C.B.E.**, **C.H.**, **C.I.E.**, **C.M.G.**, **C.S.I.**, (of the Bath, British Empire, Honour, Indian Empire, St Michael & St George, Star of India); company, **C.S.M.** (sergeant major); confined, **C.B.** (to barracks); conspicuous, **C.G.M.** (gallantry medal); contagious, **C.D.** (diseases); co-operative, **C.W.S.** (wholesale society); Corpus, **C.C.C.** (Christi College); county, **C.C.** (council, -lor); cricket, **C.C.** (club); criminal, **C.I.D.** (investigation department); crown, **C.I.** (of India, Order of the); cyclists', **C.T.C.** (touring club). **c.**, candle, **c.-p.** (power); caught, **c. & b.** (bowled); circa; circiter; cost, **c.i.f.** (insurance & freight). **c**, care, **c/o** (of).

Abbreviations (2): **Cal.**(ifornia); **Cambs.**, Cambridgeshire; **Can.**(ada); **Cant.**(icles); **Cantab.**(rigian); **Cantuar.**, Abp of Canterbury; **cap.**, chapter, capital letter; **caps**, capital letters; **Capt.**(ain); **Carliol.**, Bp of Carlisle; **cd**, command paper; **Cels.**(ius); **Cestr.**, Bp of Chester; **cf.**, confer (L = compare); **cg.**, centigram; **ch.**(apter); **Ch.Ch.**, Christ Church; **Ches.**(hire); **Chron.**(icles); **Cicestr.**, Bp of Chichester; **circ.**(iter); **cl.**, centilitre; **cm.**, centimetre; **cmd**, command paper; **Co.**(mpany); **Co.**(unty in Ireland); **Col.**(onel); **Col.**(ossians); **Colo.**(rado); **Conn.**(ecticut); **Copec**, Conference on politics, economics, & citizenship; **Cor.**(inthians); **Corn.**(wall); **Corp.**(oral); **cp.**, compare; **Cr**, Creditor; **crim. con.**, criminal conversation; **Cumb.**(erland); **cwt**, hundredweight.

Caaba (kah·*aba*), n. Sacred building at Mecca, Mohammedan Holy of Holies containing the black stone. [Arab. *ka'bah*]

cab[1], n., & v.i. (Go in a) hackney carriage esp. of brougham or hansom shape or taxi; driver's shelter on locomotive; *cabman*, driver of c.; *c.-rank*, row of cc. on *cabstand*, where cc. are authorized to wait; *c.-runner*, *-tout*, men earning pay by fetching, or unloading luggage from, cc. Hence **ca·b**LESS a. [short for CABRIOLET]

cab[2], n., & v.i. (slang). (Use secretly in preparing lessons) a translation, crib. [short for archaic *cabbage* v. & n. pilfer(ing) perh. f. F *cabas* basket f. L *capacem* nom. *-ax* CAPACIOUS]

cabă·l, n., & v.i. (-ll-). (Join in a) secret intrigue; clique, faction; (Hist.) *the C.*, 'Committee for Foreign Affairs' under Charles II, esp. Clifford, Arlington, Buckingham, Ashley, & Lauderdale (1672), precursor of modern Cabinet. Hence **caba·ll**ER[1] n. [f. F *cabale(r)* f. med. L *cabala* CABBALA; not f. initials of Clifford &c., being quoted from 1646]

caba·na (-bah-), n. Brand of cigar. [maker]

că·baret (-ā), n. French tavern; (in England, U.S., &c.) entertainment provided in restaurant &c. while guests are at table. [F]

ca·bbage (-ĭj), n. Kinds of cultivated vegetable with round heart or head; *Sea C.*, sea KALE; *c. butterfly*, Large White or Small White; *c.-net*, for boiling **c. in**; *c.-rose*, double red rose with large compact round flower; *c.-tree*, various trees, esp. certain palms with terminal bud eaten like c. [earlier *cabbage-cole* head-vegetable f. ME & F *caboche* head = It. *capocchia* f. *capo* f. L *caput*]

ca·b(b)ala, n. Jewish oral tradition; mystic interpretation, esoteric doctrine, occult lore. Hence **ca·b(b)al**ISM(3), **ca·b(b)al**IST(2), nn., **cab(b)ali·st**IC a., **cab(b)ali·st**ICALLY adv. [med. L, f. Heb. *qabbalah* tradition]

ca·bby, n. (colloq.). Cab-driver. [-Y[3]]

cā·ber, n. Roughly trimmed pine-trunk used in Sc. Highland sport of *tossing the c.* [f. Gael. *cabar* pole]

că·bin, n., & v.t. Small rude dwelling; room or compartment in ship for sleeping or eating in, officer's or passenger's room; *c.-boy*, waiting on officers or passengers; (vb, chiefly in p.p.) confine in small space, cramp. [ME & F *cabane* f. LL *capanna*]

ca·binet, n. & a. Small private room, closet; case with drawers &c. for keeping valuables or displaying curiosities. (Pol.) council-room of about twelve or twenty chief ministers of state; those ministers collectively; *c. council*, one of their meetings; *C. Minister*, one of them; *c. crisis*, difficulties involving change of government or resignation of some member(s) of c. *C. edition*, between library & popular in cost &c.; *c. photograph*, size larger than carte-de-visite; *c. pudding*, made of sponge-cakes, eggs, milk, &c.; *c.-maker*, *-king*, skilled joiner, joinery, (also facet. of prime minister forming new government). [CABIN + -ET[1], influenced also by F *cabinet*]

cā·ble[1], n. Strong thick rope (Naut., 10 in. or more in circumf., cf. CABLET, HAWSER) of hemp or wire strands; (Naut.) rope or chain of anchor, (as measure) 100 fathoms; (Teleg.) submarine or underground line containing insulated wires, also = CABLEGRAM; (Arch. & goldsmith's work) rope-shaped ornament; *c.-laid rope*, of three triple strands. [cf. Du. *kable* f. Rom. cf. F *câble*, It. *cappio*, f. LL *capu-*

lum halter cf. L *capulus* hilt (*capere* take); but the F may be f. L **catabola* kind of BALLISTA]

ca·ble², v.t. & i. Furnish, fasten, with c.; (Arch.) fill lower part of flutings of (column) with convex mouldings; transmit (message), communicate, inform (person), by c. [f. prec.]

ca·blegram, n. Message by submarine cable. [CABLE¹ + -GRAM (hybrid on TELEGRAM)]

cā·blet, n. Cable-laid rope under 10 in. in circumference. [-ET¹]

cabo·bs, n. pl. Meat cooked in small pieces with ginger, garlic, &c. [Arab. *kabab*]

caboo·dle, n. (slang). *The whole c.*, all the lot (persons or things). [U.S. wd etym. dub.]

caboo·se, n. Cooking-room on ship's deck, [cf. Du. *kabuis* perh. = **kaban-huys* cabin-house]

că·botage (-ĭj), n. Coasting-trade. [F, f. *caboter* to coast, etym. dub.]

cabriolet· (-ā), n. Light two-wheeled hooded one-horse chaise. [F, f. *cabriole* goat's leap f. It. *capriola* (*caprio* f. L *caprum* nom. *-per* goat)]

cacā·o, n. & a. Seed of tropical Amer. tree, giving cocoa & chocolate; the tree (also *c.-tree*). [Sp., f. Mex. *caca(-uatl* -tree)]

că·chalot (-shalŏt, -shalō), n. Kinds of whale with teeth in lower jaw, esp. *Common C.*, Sperm whale. [F, =toothed f. Gascon *cachau* large tooth]

cache (kăsh), n., & v.t. Hiding-place for treasure, provisions, ammunition, &c., esp. as used by explorers; the hiding (*make a c.*) or stores hidden; (vb) place in c. [F, f. *cacher* to hide f. L co(*actare* collect frequent. of *agere* bring)]

cachĕ·ctic (-k-), a. Of, suffering from, CACHEXY. [f. Gk *kakhektikos* of CACHEXY]

că·chet (-shā), n. Stamp (fig.), distinguishing mark, internal evidence of authenticity. [obs. sense *seal*, cf. F *lettre de c.* letter under king's private seal (*cacher* see CACHE)]

cache·xy (-k-), n. Ill-conditioned state of body or mind. [f. Gk *kakhexia* (CACO- + *hexis* habit f. *ekhō* hold, be)]

că·chinnate (-k-), v.i. Laugh loudly. So **cachin**NA·TION n., **ca·chinnat**ORY a. [f. L *cachinnare*, -ATE³]

că·cholong (-tsh-), n. Kind of opal. [f. Kalmuck *kaschtschilon* beautiful stone]

că·chou (-shōō), n. =CATECHU; pill used by smokers to sweeten breath. [F, = CASHEW]

cachu·cha (-tshōōtsha), n. A dance. [Sp.]

caci·que (-sēk), n. W.-Indian & Amer.-Indian native chief. [Sp., f. Haytian]

ca·ckle, v.i. & t., & n. (Make) clucking of hen after laying; (indulge in) glib noisy inconsequent talk; boast; chuckle; *c. out* &c., say cacklingly. Hence **ca·ckl**ER¹ n. [ME *cakelen*; imit., cf. Du. *kakelen*, G *gackeln*]

căco-, pref. =Gk *kako-* (*kakos* bad), found in some wds taken direct or through L (& F) f. Gk; & prefixed in med. terms (=*disease of*, as *cacophthalmia* eye-disease, or *mal-*, as *cacomorphia* malformation) usu. to Gk components, rarely to L as *cacodorous* ill-smelling.

cacodē·mon, -ae·mon, n. Evil spirit; malignant person. [f. Gk *kakodaimōn* (prec. + *daimōn* spirit)]

ca·codyl, n. Stinking poisonous compound of arsenic & methyl. Hence **caco-dy̆·l**IC a. [Gk *kakōdēs* stinking (CACO- + *od-* root of *ozō* to smell) + -YL]

caco·epy, n. Bad pronunciation (cf. ORTHOEPY). [f. Gk CACO(*epeia* f. *epos* word, see -Y¹)]

cacoē·thes (-ēz), n. Ill habit, itch for doing something unadvisable, usu. in *scribendi c.*, scribbling-mania. [f. Gk *kakoēthes* neut. adj. (CACO- + *ēthos* disposition]

caco·graphy, n. Bad handwriting or spelling. Hence **caco·**GRAPHER n., **caco-**GRA·PHIC(AL) aa. [CACO-, -GRAPHY]

caco·logy, n. Bad choice of words or pronunciation. [f. Gk *kakologia* vituperation (CACO-, *-logos* -speaking f. *legō* speak)]

cacoo·n, n. Large flat polished bean of tropical shrub with 6–8ft pods. [African ?]

caco·phonous, a. Ill-sounding. [Gk CACO- (*phōnos* -sounding f. *phōnē* sound) + -OUS]

caco·phony, n. Ill sound (cf. EUPHONY); discord (lit. & fig.). [f. F *cacophonie* f. Gk *kakophōnia* as prec. & see -Y¹]

ca·ctus, n. Kinds of succulent plant with thick fleshy stem, usu. no leaves, & clusters of spines. Hence **cact**A·CEOUS, **ca·ct**AL, **ca·ct**OID, aa. [L, f. Gk *kaktos* cardoon]

cad, n. Omnibus conductor; hanger-on employed about (esp. school & college) games; member of lower classes; person of low manners; person guilty or capable of ungentlemanly conduct, blackguard, whence **ca·dd**ISH¹ a. [quoted f. 1831; prob. short for CADET (cf. CADDIE) & started at Eton & Oxford as name for townsmen]

cada·stral, a. Of, showing, the extent, value, & ownership, of land for taxation (esp. *c. survey*). (F, f. *cadastre* f. L *capitastrum* register of *capita* (*caput* head) units made for Roman *capitatio terrena* land-tax]

cadavĕ·ric, a. (med. & physiol.). Characteristic of a corpse. [L *cadaver* corpse (perh. f. *cadere* fall) + -IC]

cadă·verous, a. Corpse-like; deadly pale. [f. F *cadavéreux* f. L *cadaverosus* (prec., -OSE¹)]

ca·ddie, n. Golf-player's attendant. [Sc. (also *cadie*) f. F CADET²]

ca·ddis, -ice, n. Larva of May-fly &c.,

living in water & making cylindrical case of hollow stems &c., used as bait; also *c.-bait, -worm.* [also *cad, cod,* etym. dub.]

ca·ddy, n. Small box for holding tea. [f. Malay *kati* weight = $1\frac{1}{3}$ lb.]

cā·dence, n. Rhythm; measured movement, esp. of sound; fall of voice, esp. at end of period; intonation; close of musical phrase. Hence (-)**ca·dence**D[2] a. [F, f. It. *cadenza* (L *cadere* fall, -ENCE)]

cā·dency, n. Descent of younger branch, cadetship. [as prec., -ENCY]

cade·nza (-tsa), n. (mus.). Flourish of voice or instrument at close of movement. [It.]

cade·t[1], n. Younger son; student in naval or military college, whence **cade·t**SHIP n.; member of Russian Constitutional-Democratic party. [f. foll. f. 15th-c. *capdet* f. Rom. **capitetto* dim. of L *caput* head = little chief]

cadet[2] (F), n. (Appended to surname of younger brother for distinction, cf. AÎNÉ) the younger (as *Coquelin c.*).

cadge, v.i. & t. Go about peddling or begging; get by begging. [perh. var. of *catch*]

ca·dger, n. Carrier; itinerant dealer in eggs, butter, &c., between remote farms and towns; street hawker; beggar, loafer. [-ER[1]]

ca·di (kah-, kā-), n. Civil judge, usu. of town &c., among Turks, Arabs, Persians. [Arab.]

Cadmean. See VICTORY.

ca·dmium, n. Bluish-white metal resembling tin; *c.-yellow,* intense yellow pigment. Hence **cadmi·**FEROUS, **ca·dm**IC, aa. [f. obs. *cadmia* CALAMINE f. L f. Gk *kadmia (gē)* Cadmean (earth), -IUM]

cadre (kah·dr), n. Framework, scheme; (Mil.) permanent establishment of regiment forming nucleus for expansion at need. [F, f. It. *quadro* f. L *quadrum* SQUARE]

cadu·cēŭs, n. (pl. *-ēī*). Ancient herald's wand, esp. as carried by messenger-god Hermes. [L, f. Gk *karukion* (*kērux* herald)]

cadu·city, n., **cadu·cous,** a. Fleeting (nature); perishable(ness); (Zool. & Bot., of organs and parts) falling off (n. & a.) when work is done. [n. thr. F *caducité* (-TY), a. f. L *caducus* falling (*cadere* fall) + -OUS]

cae·cum (sē-), n. (pl. *-a*). The blind gut, first part of large intestine in mammals &c.; any tube with closed end. Hence **cae·**CAL, **cae·ci**FORM, aa., **cae·cal**LY[2] adv., **caeci·**TIS n. [L, for *intestinum caecum* f. *caecus* blind]

Cae·sar, n. Roman Emperor from Augustus to Hadrian; heir presumptive of later Roman Emperor; (loosely) any Roman Emperor; an autocrat; the civil power (*Matt.* xxii. 21); *C.'s wife,* person required to be above suspicion. [L, family name of C. Julius]

Caesā·rean, -ian, a. & n. Of Caesar or the Caesars, imperial; *C. birth, operation,* delivery of child by cutting walls of abdomen (as with Julius); (n.) adherent of Caesar or an autocratic system. [f. L *Caesarianus* see -EAN]

Cae·sarism, -ist, nn. (Believer in) autocracy. [-ISM(3), -IST(2)]

cae·sious (sē-), a. (bot.). Bluish or greyish green. [f. L *caesius* + -OUS]

cae·sium (sē-), n. (chem.). An alkali-metal. [as prec. f. its spectrum lines]

caesūr·a (-z-), n. (Clas. prosody) break between words within a metrical foot; (Eng. prosody) pause about middle of line. Hence **caesur·**AL a. [L (*caedere caes-* cut, -URE)]

că·fé[1] (-ā), n. Coffee-house, restaurant (esp. foreign; *c. chantant,* with music and entertainments, often in open air). [F, = coffee(-house)]

café[2] (kafā·), n. Coffee; *c. au lait* (ō lā), with milk; *c. noir* (nwahr), without milk. [F]

caffē·ic, a. (chem.). Of coffee (esp. *c. acid*). [f. F *caféique,* see prec., -IC]

ca·ffēine, n. Vegetable alkaloid found in coffee & tea plants. [f. F *caféine* (CAFÉ[1],[2], -INE[5])]

Caffre. See KAFIR.

că·ftan (*also* kăftah·n), n. Eastern long under-tunic with waist girdle. Hence **ca·ftan**ED[2] a. [f. Turk. *qaftan*]

cage, n., & v.t. Fixed or portable prison, of wire or barred, esp. for birds or beasts; prison (lit. or fig.); (Mining) frame for hoisting & lowering cars; open framework of various kinds; (vb) place or keep in c. [F, f. L *cavea* (*cavus* hollow) cf. *rage* f. *rabies*]

caiman. See CAYMAN.

Cain, n. Fratricide, murderer. [*Gen.* iv]

cainozo·ic (kī-), a. (geol.). Of the third geological period (= *tertiary,* cf. *palaeozoic, mesozoic*). [f. Gk *kainos* new + *zōon* animal + -IC]

caique (ka-ē·k), n. Light Bosporan rowboat; Levantine sailing-ship. [F, f. Turk. *kaik*]

cairn, n. Pyramid of rough stones as memorial, sepulchre, landmark, &c. [f. Gael. *carn*]

cairngor·m, n. (Also *c. stone*) yellow or wine-coloured precious stone. [found on *C.,* Scotch mountain (Gael. *carn gorm* blue cairn)]

cai·sson (also kasōō·n), n. Ammunition chest or wagon; large water-tight case used in laying foundations under water; boat-shaped vessel used as dock gate. [F (*caisse* f. L *capsa* CASE[2], -OON)]

cai·tiff, n. & a. (poet. & archaic). Base, despicable, (person); coward(ly). [f. ONF *caitif* f. L *captivus* CAPTIVE]

cajo·le, v.t. Persuade or soothe by flattery, deceit, &c. (also *c.* person *into doing, out of,* something; or *c.* something *out of* person). Hence **cajo·le**MENT,

cajo·ler[1], **cajo·lery**(4), nn., **cajo·lingly**[2] adv. [f. F *cajoler* etym. dub.; Cotgrave has also *cageoler* 'jangle like a jay', whence it has been referred to *cage*]

cake, n., & v.i. & t. Small flattish loaf of bread (archaic, as in *King Alfred & the cc.*); thin oaten bread (Sc. & north.; also *oatc.*; *land of cc.*, Scotland); (usu. Eng. sense) bread with other ingredients besides flour, as currants, spice, eggs, sugar —the substance (*c.*) or (*a c.*) a portion of it baked in a thick disk or ornamental shape—; flattish compact mass of other food (*fish-c.*, PAN[1]-*c.*) or of any compressed substance (*c. of soap, wax, tobacco*); *cc. and ale*, merry-making; *c.-walk*, kinds of dance developed from negro contest in graceful walking with c. for prize; *take the c.*, carry off the honours; *cannot eat your c. and have it*, do mutually exclusive things; hence **ca·ky**[2] a. (Vb) form into compact flattish mass. [prob. f. ON *kaka* cf. G *kuche* etym. dub. (not cogn. with L *coquere* cook)]

că·labash, n. Kinds of gourd whose shell serves for holding liquid; fruit of American C.-tree, so used; pipe &c. made from these or of like shape. [f. F *calebasse* f. Sp. *calabaça*, Sicil. *caravazza*, perh. f. Pers. *kharbuz* melon]

că·laber, -ar, n. Fur of grey squirrel. [prob. f. F *Calabre* Calabria]

călama·nco, n. Glossy Flemish woollen stuff much used in 18th-c. [etym. dub.; cf. Du. *kalamink*, F *calmande*]

călama·nder, n. Hard cabinet wood of Ceylon & India. [etym. dub.; perh. f. *Coromandel*]

că·lamary, n. Kinds of cuttlefish with pen-shaped internal shell. [f. L *calamarius* (*calamus* pen, -ARY[1])]

că·lamine, n. A zinc ore found in England. [F, f. med. L *calamina* (L *cadmia* CADMIUM)]

că·lamint, n. Kinds of aromatic herb. [ult. f. Gk *kalaminthē*]

că·lamite, n. Fossil plant allied to Mare's Tail. [f. L *calamus* reed + -ITE(2)]

cală·mitous, a. Marked by, causing, calamity. Hence **cala·mitously**[2] adv. [f. F *calamiteux* f. L *calamitosus* see foll., & -ITOUS]

cală·mity, n. Adversity, deep distress; grievous disaster. [f. F *calamité* f. L *calamitatem* (-TY) cf. *incolumis* safe]

cala·ndo, mus. direction. Diminish tone & pace gradually. [It.]

cala·sh, n. Light low hooded carriage; carriage hood; (Canada) two-wheeled one-seated vehicle with driver's seat on splash-board; woman's hooped silk hood. [f. F *calèche* f. Slav. (Boh. *kolésa* &c.)]

calc- comb. form = lime; *c.-sinter*, crystalline deposit from lime-springs; *c.-spar*, crystallized carbonate of lime; *c.-tuff*, porous calcareous deposit. [f. G *kalk* f. L *calx -cis* corrected to L spelling]

calcār·eous, -ious, a. Of, containing, carbonate of lime or limestone. Hence **calcar·eo-**, comb. form. [f. L *calcarius* (CALC-, -ARY[1]) + -OUS; first spelling wrong but usu.]

calcĕolār·ia, n. Kinds of plant with flower like ancient slipper. [f. L *calceolus* dim. of *calceus* shoe + fem. of *-arius* -ARY[1]]

ca·lceolate, a. (bot.). Slipper-shaped. [as prec., -ATE[2]]

ca·lcic, a. Of calcium. [-IC]

calci·ferous, a. Yielding carbonate of lime. [CALC-, -I-, -FEROUS]

ca·lcify, v.t. & i. Convert, be converted, into lime; replace by lime; harden by deposit of salts of lime; petrify. Hence **calci·fic** a., **calcifica·tion** n. [CALC-, -I-, -FY]

ca·lcine, v.t. & i. Reduce to quick-lime or friable substance by roasting or burning; desiccate; refine by consuming grosser part; burn to ashes; (intr.) suffer these processes. Hence **calcina·tion**, **ca·lciner**[1](2), nn. [f. med. L *calcinare* reduce to CALX]

ca·lcite, n. Native carbonate of lime. [f. L *calx -cis* lime + -ITE[1]]

ca·lcium, n. Chem. element, yellow metal, the basis of lime (in many compd terms, as *c. chloride*). Hence **calcio-** comb. form. [as prec. + -IUM]

ca·lculable, a. That may be reckoned, measured, computed, or relied upon. Hence **ca·lculabi·lity** n. [f. L *calculare* (foll.), -ABLE]

ca·lculate, v.t. & i. Compute (w. noun or clause, or abs.) by figures (*calculating-machine*, that does sums automatically), ascertain beforehand (event, date, &c.) by exact reckoning; plan deliberately (t. & i., esp. in intr. part. & p.p. = cold-blooded, selfish); (usu. pass.) arrange, adapt, (conduct, apparatus, &c.) *for* (purpose), *to* (do); (in p.p.) fit, suitable, *to* do; rely *upon*; (U.S.) suppose, believe. Hence **ca·lculative** a. [f. L *calculare* (CALCULUS), -ATE[3]]

calcula·tion, n. (Result got by) reckoning; forecast. [F, f. L *calculationem* (prec., -ATION)]

ca·lculator, n. In vbl senses; also: set of tables for use in calculation; calculating-machine. [L (CALCULATE, -OR[2])]

ca·lculous, a. Of, suffering from, stone or calculus. [f. L *calculosus* (foll., -OSE[1])]

ca·lculus, n. (pl. -ī). (Med.) stone, concretion in some part of body (*renal* &c. *c.* f. the particular part; *uric acid* &c. *c.* f. its composition); (Math.) particular method of calculation, as *differential, integral, c.* [L, = small stone (*calx -cis* stone, -ULE) used in reckoning on abacus]

căldār·ium, n. (archaeol.). Roman hot bath room. [f. L *calidus* hot, see -ARY[1]]

caldron. See CAULDRON.

Caledō·nian, a. & n. (Native) of ancient Scotland (also used in mod. titles of clubs

&c., & facetiously = Scotch or Scot). [f. L *Caledonia* northern Britain, -AN]
cālĕfā·cient, a. & n. (Medical agent) producing warmth. So **calefa·**CTION n., **că·lefact**IVE a. [f. L *calefacere* (*calēre* be warm, *facere* make), -ENT, -ANT]
calefa·ctory, a. & n. Producing warmth; (Archaeol.) warm room in monastery. [f. L *calefactorius* see prec., -TORY]
calembour (F), n. Pun.
că·lendar[1], n. System by which beginning, length, & subdivision, of civil year is fixed, esp. the Gregorian c., used in Engl. from 1752; table(s) with months, weeks, & festivals &c., of a given year, or with dates important for certain classes, as *Gardener's c.*; register, list, esp. of canonized saints, prisoners for trial, or documents chronologically arranged with summaries; *c.* MONTH. [f. OF *calendier* f. L *calendarium* account-book (CALENDS, -ARY[1])]
ca·lendar[2], v.t. Register, enter in list; arrange, analyse, & index (documents), whence **ca·lendar**ER[1] n. [f. prec.]
că·lender[1], v.t., & n. Press (cloth, paper, &c.) in a c. or roller-machine to smooth it; steam mangle; (archaic) person who calenders. Hence **ca·lend**RY n. [f. F *calandre(r)* f. med. L *calendra* f. L f. Gk *kulindros* roller]
că·lender[2], n. Mendicant dervish in Turkey or Persia. [f. Pers. *qalander*]
că·lends, k-, n. pl. First of month in Roman calendar; *on the Greek C.*, never. [f. L *kalendae* (*cal-* cf. *calare*, Gk *kaleō*, proclaim)]
că·lenture, n. Tropical fever or delirium in which sailors &c. leap into sea. [F, f. Sp. *calentura* fever f. part. st. of L *calēre* be hot, -URE]
calf[1] (kahf), n. (pl. *-ves*). Young of bovine animal, esp. domestic cow, for first year (*cow in, with, c.*, pregnant; *slip her c.*, suffer abortion); *golden c.*, wealth as object of worship (*Ex.* xxxii); stupid fellow; MOON-*c.*; child (so *c.-love*, childish love affair); (also *calfskin*) = c.-leather, esp. in bookbinding (*c.-bound*) & shoemaking; young of elephant, whale, deer, &c.; *sea-c.*, seal; (Naut.) floating piece of ice; *c.-knee*, knock-knee; *calf's teeth*, milk teeth; *calves-foot jelly*. Hence **cal·f**HOOD n., **cal·f**ISH[1](1) a. [com.-Teut., cf. G *kalb*]
calf[2] (kahf), n. (pl. *-ves*). Fleshy hinder part of leg-shank; c. part of stocking. Hence **cal·f**LESS, **-calv**ED[2], aa. [f. ON *kálfi* etym. dub.]
Că·liban, n. Man of degraded bestial nature. [Shaksp., *Tempest*, & see CANNIBAL]
că·librate, v.t. Find calibre of; calculate irregularities of (tube, gauge) before graduating. Hence **calibr**A·TION n. [foll. + -ATE[3]]
că·libre (*-er*), **ca·liber,** n. Internal diameter of gun or any tube; weight of character, standing, importance. Hence **-ca·libr**ED[2] a. [F (*-bre*), f. It. *calibro* perh. f. Arab. *qalib* mould]
că·licle, n. (biol.). Small cup-like body. So **cali·cul**AR[1] a. [f. L *caliculus* dim. of *calix* cup]
că·lico, n. & a. (Of) cotton cloth, esp. plain white unprinted, bleached or unbleached (*c.-ball*, dance at which only cotton dresses are worn); *c.-printer, -ting*, producer, production, of coloured patterns on c. [orig. *Calicut-cloth* f. town on Malabar coast]
că·lipash, ca·lipee, nn. Gelatinous substances in turtle regarded as dainties (*-ash*, dull green next upper shell; *-ee*, light yellow next lower shell). [perh. W.-Ind.; perh. *-ash* = CARAPACE, & *-ee* formed for distinction f. it]
că·liph, -if, n. Successor of Mohammed, Mohammedan chief civil & religious ruler. Hence **ca·liph**ATE[1] n. [f. F *caliphe* f. med. L *calipha* f. Arab. *khalifah* successor]
că·lix, n. (anat.; pl. *-icēs*). Cup-like cavity or organ. [L, = cup, often confused w. L CALYX]
calk[1] (kawk), v.t., & n. (Provide with) sharp iron to prevent horse-shoe or boot from slipping. [f. L *calx calcis* heel, cf. CALKIN]
calk[2] (kawk), v.t. Trace by colouring back of design & pressing along outlines. [f. F *calquer* f. It. & L *calcare* tread]
cal·kin (kaw-, *also* kăl-), n. Turned-down heels of horse-shoe, also turned edge in front, esp. when sharpened in frost; iron guards on boots or shoes. [perh. f. OF *calcain* heel f. L *calcaneum* (*calx calcis* heel)]
call[1] (kawl), v.t. & i. 1. Cry, shout, speak loudly, (lit. & fig. &c., as): (bird, trumpet, &c.) utter characteristic note; cry *out*; cry *to* (person); signal (*for* trumps); pay brief visit (*at* house, *on* person); read *over* (names to ascertain presence); *c. for*, order, demand, need, go & fetch; *c. on*, invoke, appeal to. 2. Summon (lit. & fig. &c., as): demand presence of (cab, witness, actor after curtain); *c. into being*, create; *c. to* ACCOUNT[2]; *c. into play*, give scope for; *c. in question*, dispute; *c. to mind* &c., also *c. up*, recollect; *c. away, off*, divert, distract; *c. in* money lent, doctor &c. for advice; *c. forth*, elicit; *c. out*, elicit, challenge to duel, summon (troops) esp. to aid the civil authorities; *c. over the* COALS; *c. up*, imagine, summon to talk by telephone, summon to serve in army &c.; rouse from sleep; fix the moment for (*c. case* in law-court; *c. a halt*; *c. a meeting*); urge, invite, nominate, (*duty, pleasure, calls*; *many are called*; *c. to the* BAR[1], *ministry*; *c. attention to*; *c. to witness*). 3. (with n. or adj. as compl.) name, describe as, (*c. a* SPADE *a spade*; *c. him John, c. him by the name of John*; c. person

names, abuse him; *c.* COUSINS *with*); consider, regard as, (*c. that mean*); *c.* (thing) one's *own*, possess. [f. ON *kalla*, com.-Teut. cf. Du. *kallen*]

call[2], n. Shout, cry; (also *c.-over*) = ROLL-*c.*; special cry of bird &c., imitation of this, instrument imitating it; signal on bugle &c., signalling-whistle; looking-in on business (so *house of c.*); short formal visit (*pay c.*, make one); invitation, summons, (to actor for applause; to the BAR[1]; from God, conscience, or congregation, to be pastor); duty, need, occasion, (*no c. to blush*); demand for money, esp. for unpaid capital from company shareholders; (St. Exch.) option of claiming stock at given date; *c.-loan*, *-money*, lent subject to recall without notice; *at*, *within*, *c.*, ready for orders; *c.-boy*, prompter's attendant summoning actors; *c.-day*, *-night*, at Inns of Court, for calling students to bar. [f. prec.]

cal·ler[1], n. In vbl senses; esp., person who pays call or visit. [-ER[1]]

că·ller[2], a. (Sc.). Fresh, not decaying, (of herring &c.); cool (of air). [?]

calli·graphy (ka-), n. Beautiful handwriting; handwriting. So **că·lli**GRAPH(1, 2, 3) n. & v.t., **calli·**GRAPHER, **calli·graph**IST(1), nn., **călli**GRA·PHIC a. [ult. f. Gk *kalligraphia* (*kallos* beauty, -GRAPH)]

cal·ling, n. In vbl senses; also or esp.: divine summons to salvation or self-devotion; impulse to do something as right; occupation, profession, trade; persons following a particular business. [-ING[1]]

că·l(l)iper, n. & a., & v.t. *C. compasses* or *cc.*, compasses with bowed legs for measuring diameter of convex bodies, or with out-turned points for measuring calibre; *c.-square*, rule with movable cross-heads for taking internal or external diameters; (vb) measure with cc. [prob. = CALIBRE]

callisthĕ·nic, a. Suitable for producing strength with beauty (esp. of girls' gymnastics). Hence **callisthe·n**ICS n. [f. Gk *kallos* beauty + *sthenos* strength + -IC]

callŏ·sity, n. Abnormal hardness & thickness of skin; hardened insensible part, lump, (from friction, or natural as on horses' legs). [f. F *callosité* f. L *callositatem* (see foll. -TY)]

că·llous, a. (Physiol., Zool.) hardened, hard, (of parts of skin); (of person, heart, &c.) unfeeling, insensible, whence **ca·llous**NESS n. [f. L *callosus* (*callum* or CALLUS, -OSE[1])]

că·llow, a. Unfledged; downy like young birds; raw, inexperienced; (Irish, a. & n.) low-lying, often flooded, (meadow). [OE *calu* f. WG *kalwo-* (cf. G *kahl*) perh. f. L *calvus* bald]

ca·llus, n. (physiol.,path.,bot.). Thickened part of skin or soft tissue; bony material formed while bone-fracture heals. [L]

calm[1] (kahm), n. Stillness, serenity, (of weather, air, sea, the mind, social or political conditions); (colloq.) impudent (*pretty c. of him*); *a c.*, windless period. [f. F *calme* f. It., Sp., or Port., *calma* perh. (with infl. of L *calor* heat) f. Gk *kauma* heat (*kaiō* burn)]

calm[2], a., & v.t. & i. Tranquil, quiet, windless, (lit. & fig.); hence **cal·m**LY[2] adv., **cal·m**NESS n. (Vb) make c., pacify; (intr.; alw. w. *down*) become c. [f. F *calme* n. & a., see prec.]

că·lmative (*also* kahm-), a. & n. (med.). Calming (agent), sedative. [prec. + -ATIVE]

că·lomel, n. (med.). Mercurous chloride used as purgative. [F, f. Gk *kalos* fair, *melas* black (explained anecdotically in various ways)]

calore·scence, n. (physics). Change of heat-rays to light-rays. [for *calescence* (L *calescere* grow hot) by confusion w. foll.]

calori-, comb. form of L *calor* heat in Physics & Physiol. Hence **calŏ·ri**FA·CIENT, **calori·**FIC, **calo·ri**ME·TRIC(AL), aa., **calori·f**ICALLY adv., **calo·ri**FICA·TION, **calori·**METER, -METRY, nn., **calo·ri**FY v.t.

calŏ·ric, n. Heat; *c.-engine*, driven by hot air. [f. F *calorique* (L *calor* heat, -IC)]

că·lorie, n. (physics). Unit of heat. [F, f. L *calor* heat + *-ie* (-Y[1]) irregularly used]

calŏ·rimōtor, n. Voltaic battery with large plates generating heat. [CALORI- + MOTOR]

calo·tte, n. Skull-cap of priests &c. [F, dim. of *cale* CAUL]

călp, n. Irish dark-grey limestone. [?]

că·ltrop, n. Four-spiked iron ball thrown on ground to maim cavalry horses; kinds of plant, as Star-thistle. [found earliest as plant name; but prob. transf. f. the iron; f. L *calx -cis* heel + LL *trappa* f. OHG *trapo* TRAP]

că·lūmet, n. Amer.-Ind. clay-bowled reed-stemmed tobacco-pipe; symbol of peace; *smoke the c. together*, make peace. [F, esp. Fr.-Canadian form of *chalumet* tube f. L *calamellus* dim. of *calamus* reed]

calu·mniate, v.t. Slander. Hence or cogn. **calumnia**·TION, **calu·mniat**OR[2], nn., **calu·mniā**TORY a. [f. L *calumniari*, see -ATE[3]]

calu·mnious, a. Given to, marked by, calumny. Hence **calu·mnious**LY[2] adv. [f. L *calumniosus* (see foll., -OUS)]

că·lumny, n. Malicious misrepresentation; false charge; slanderous report. [f. L *calumnia* (& F *calomnie*) f. *calvi* deceive]

Că·lvary, n. Place, (R.-C. Ch.) representation, of Crucifixion. [f. L *calvaria* skull (*calvus* bald) transl. of *Golgotha*, *Matt.* xxvii. 33]

calve (kahv), v.i. & t. Give birth to a calf; (esp. in pass. of calf) give birth to; (of iceberg &c.) throw off mass of ice. [OE *cealfian* (CALF[1])]

-calved. See CALF[2].

Că·lvinism, n. Calvin's theology (esp. the doctrines of Particular election & redemption, Moral inability in a fallen state, Irresistible grace, Final perseverance); adherence to this. So **Ca·lvin**IST(2) n. & a., **Calvini·stic**(AL) aa., **Calvini·stical**LY[2] adv., **ca·lvin**IZE(4) v.i. & t. [John *Calvin*, 1509–1564]

căl x, n. (pl. *calcēs*). Powder or friable substance left when a metal or mineral has been burnt, residuum. [L, genit. *calcis*, lime]

calyc-, calyci-, st. of CALYX. **calyciflor·**AL, **-flor·**ATE[2], **-flor·**OUS, aa., with stamens & petals inserted in calyx; **ca·lyci**FORM a.; **calў·cin**AL, **ca·lyc**INE[2], aa., having a, on the, calyx; **calў·cin**AR[1] a., = **-al**, also (of flower) double by increase of calyx-lobes; **ca·lyc**OID, **calycoi·d**EOUS, aa.

că·lycle, n. (bot.). Row of bracts surrounding calyx-base; adherent crown of seed. Hence or cogn. **ca·lycl**ED[2], **caly·cul**AR[1], **caly·cul**ATE[2], aa. [f. L *calyculus* dim. of CALYX (-ULE)]

calyptr-, st. of bot. terms = having, like, a hood. [f. Gk *kaluptra* veil (*kaluptō* to cover)]

cā̆·lyx, n. (pl. *-ycēs*, *-yxes*). (Bot.) whorl of leaves (SEPAL) forming outer case of bud (for derivatives see CALYC-); (Physiol. & Biol.) = CALIX. [L, f. Gk *kalux* (cf. *kaluptō* to cover) case of bud, husk]

cam, n. Projecting part of wheel &c. in machinery, grooved, toothed, or otherwise adapted to convert circular into reciprocal or variable motion. [var. of COMB, cf. Du., Da., Sw., *kam*, G *kamm*]

cămara·derie· (-ahderē), n. The intimacy, mutual trust, & sociability, of comrades. [F]

cămari·lla, n. Cabal, clique, junto. [Sp.]

că·mber, n., & v.i. & t. Slight convexity above, arched form, (of beam, deck, road, &c.); (also *c.-beam*) slightly arched beam; small dock or tidal basin; (vb) have, impart to (beam &c.), such convexity. [f. F *cambre(r)* f. L *camerare* to vault (CAMERA)]

Cămberwell Beauty, n. A butterfly.

că·mbist, n. Expert in, manual of, exchanges; dealer in bills of exchange. [f. F *cambiste* f. L *cambium* exchange, -IST]

că·mbium, n. Cellular tissue, below bark of exogens, in which annual growth of wood & bark occurs. [L, = exchange]

că·mbrel, n. Butcher's bent wood or iron for slinging carcases by ankles. [perh. f. W *cambren* (*cam* crooked + *pren* wood)]

Că·mbrian, a. & n. Welsh(man); (Geol.) (of) palaeozoic rocks lying below the Silurian in Wales & Cumberland. [f. L *Cambria* var. of *Cumbria* f. Celt. *Cymry* Welshman or *Cymru* Wales (OCelt. *Combroges* compatriots)]

cā·mbric, a. & n. (Of) fine white linen; handkerchiefs. [*Cambray* orig. place of making]

Cā·mbridge, n. *C. blue*, light blue.

came[1], n. Grooved slip of lead as used in lattice windows. [cf. Sc. *calm* casting-mould]

came[2]. See COME.

că·mel, n. Large hornless ruminant long-necked cushion-footed quadruped with (Arabian) one hump or (Bactrian) two humps; thing hard to believe or put up with (*Matt.* xxiii. 24); machine for floating ship over shoals &c.; type of aeroplane; *c.-brown*, fishing-fly; *c.'s-hair*, made of c.'s hair or (paint-brushes) of squirrel's tail hairs. [OE, f. L f. Gk *kamēlos* f. Semit. (cf. Heb. *gāmāl* camel, Arab. *jamala* carry)]

cameleer·, n. Camel-driver. [-EER]

camĕ̄·llia, n. Flowering evergreen from China & Japan. [*Kamel*, Jesuit & botanist, -IA[1]]

camĕ·lopard (*or* kă·-), n. = the now usu. GIRAFFE. [f. L *camelopardus* f. Gk *camēlopardalis* (CAMEL, PARD)]

ca·melry, n. Troops on camels. [-RY]

Că·membert (-ār, or as F), n. Small soft rich Norman cheese. [name of village]

că·meo, n. Piece of relief-carving in stone (sardonyx, agate, &c.) with colour-layers utilized to give background (cf. INTAGLIO). [f. It. *caméo* cf. med. L *cammaeus* etym. dub.]

că·mera, n. *In camerâ* (Lat.), in the judge's private room, not in open court; (for *c. obscura*) photographing-apparatus; *c. obscura*, *lucida* (L, = dark, light, chamber), two kinds of apparatus projecting on paper, for tracing, image of distant object. [L, = vault, cf. Gk *kamara* anything with arched cover]

Camerō·nian, a. & n. (Follower) of Richard Cameron or his doctrines; Scottish reformed presbyterian; (pl.) first battalion of Scottish Rifles (formed orig. of Cc.). [-IAN]

cămi-kni·ckers, n.pl. Woman's undergarment of camisole & knickers combined. [*cami(sole)* + *knicker(bocker)s*]

că·mion, n. Low flat four-wheeled horse or motor truck. [F]

că·misole, n. Under bodice, usu. embroidered &c. [F, f. Sp. *camisola* (*camisa* CHEMISE)]

ca·mlet, n. Light cloth of various materials for cloaks &c. [orig. a costly Eastern stuff of silk & camel's hair; f. F *camelot* perh. f. CAMEL, perh. f. Arab. *khaml* nap]

ca·mmock, n. Rest-harrow; kinds of yellow-flowered plant. [OE *cammoc* etym. dub.]

că·momile, ch-, n. Aromatic creeping composite plant with daisy-like flowers used as tonic; allied kinds of plant, *Dog's*, *Stinking*, *Purple*, *C.*; *c. tea*, infusion of the flowers. [f. F *camomille* f. L *chamomilla* f. Gk *khamaimēlon* earth-apple]

Camo·rra, n. Secret society in Naples &c.

că·mouflage (-ŏŏflahzh), n., & v.t. Disguise of guns, ships, &c., effected by obscuring outline with splashes of various colours; use of smoke-screens, boughs, &c., for same purpose; (transf.) means of throwing people off the scent; (vb) hide by c. [F, f. *camouflet* smoke-puff]

camp[1], n. Place where troops are lodged in tents &c.; army on campaign; military life (*courts & cc.*); temporary quarters of nomads, gypsies, travellers; camping-out; persons camping out; adherents of a doctrine; *c.-bed, -chair, -stool,* folding and portable; *c.-colour,* flag used in marking out c.; *c.-fever,* esp. typhus; *c.-follower,* non-military hanger-on of camp, male or female; *c.-meeting,* American religious open-air or tent meeting lasting several days. [F, f. It. or Sp. *campo* (cf. F *champ* direct) f. L *campus* level ground, esp. the Campus Martius, exercising-ground]

camp[2], v.i. & t. Encamp, lodge in c.; (also *c. out*) lodge in tent or the open, take up quarters; station (troops) in c. [f. F *camper* (prec.)]

Campagna (-ah·nya), n. *The C.,* Italian plain S.E. of Tiber. [f. L *Campania* (CAMP[1])]

campaig·n, n., & v.i. Series of military operations in a definite theatre or with one objective or from taking the field to a temporary or final cessation of hostilities (*the Gallipoli, Moscow, 1704, c.*); organized course of action, esp. (Pol.) attempt to rouse public opinion for or against a policy; *Plan of C.,* in Ireland 1886–7 for forcing landlords to reduce rents. (Vb) serve on a c.; hence **campaig·n**ER[1] n. (*old campaigner,* person practised in adapting himself to circumstances). [f. F *campagne* open country, campaign, f. It. CAMPAGNA (cf. F *champagne* CHAMPAIGN)]

campani·le (-ēlĭ), n. Bell-tower, usu. detached. [It., f. *campana* bell]

campano·logy, n. The subject of bells (founding, ringing, &c.). Hence **campano·**LOGER, **campano·**LOGIST, nn., **ca·mpanolo·gic**AL a. [f. LL *campana* bell + -LOGY]

campă·nula, n. Kinds of plant with bell-shaped flowers, usu. blue or white, as Canterbury Bell. Hence **campa·nul**A·CEOUS a. [mod. L, dim. of *campana* bell]

campă·nulate, a. (zool. & bot.). Bell-shaped. [as prec. + -ATE[2]]

ca·mphor, n. Whitish translucent crystalline volatile substance with aromatic smell and bitter taste. Hence **camphŏ·**RIC a. [f. F *camfre,* med. L *camphora,* f. Arab. *kafur* f. Malay *kapur* chalk]

ca·mphorate, v.t. Impregnate or treat with camphor. [-ATE[3]]

ca·mpion, n. Kinds of flowering plant, esp. the Red and the White C. [?]

ca·mpo sa·nto, n. Cemetery in Italy. [It., = sacred field]

ca·mpshed, v.t. Face with campshot.

ca·mpshot, ca·mpshedding, ca·mpsheeting, nn. Facing of piles & boarding to resist water-action on, or out-thrust of, a bank. [etym. dub.; cf. WAINSCOT]

ca·mpylo-, comb. form. in bot. terms = bent-. [f. Gk *kampulos*]

ca·mwood, n. Hard red W.-African wood yielding dye. [native name *kambi*?]

can[1], n., & v.t. Vessel for liquids, usu. of metal, esp. tin, and with handle over top, whence **ca·n**FUL(2) n.; *c.-buoy,* large conical buoy over sands &c.; *c.-dock,* water lily; (U.S.) (put in a) tin-plate box for hermetic sealing (meat, fish, fruit, &c.), whence (-)**ca·nn**ER[1] n. [com.-Teut.; OE *canne* f. WG *kanna* cf. G *kanne*]

can[2], v.aux. (2 s., *canst*; 3 s., *can*; neg., *cannot, can't*; past & condit., *could, couldst* or *couldest*; infin., part., & p.p., wanting; defective parts supplied f. *be able to*). Be able to; have the right to; be permitted to (*you can go*; also as mild imperat.); *could,* feel inclined to (*could laugh for joy*; *really couldn't think of it*); *cannot* AWAY *with*; (with ellipse) *will do what I can.* [OE *cunnan,* com.-Teut., cf. G *können,* OTeut. sense *know,* cogn. w. KEN, KNOW, & w. L (*g*)*nosco,* Gk *gignōskō,* learn; as in DARE, MAY, MUST, the tense used as pres. is an old past, *could* being a later development; *could* (earlier *cúthe, couthe, coud*) has *-l-* merely on anal. of *would, should*; infin. *can* is now obs. or a conscious archaism or jocular exc. in Sc.; part. *cunning* now only as adj., preserving orig. sense *know*]

Cā·naan (-nyan, -nan), n. Land of promise, paradise. [O.-T. name of Palestine]

Că·nada, a. Of, from, C. (in names of plants, animals, products, as *C.* BALSAM).

Canā·dian, a. & n. (Native) of Canada. [-IAN]

canaille (F), n. The rabble.

cană·l, n., & v.t. (-ll-). Duct in plant or animal body for food, liquid, air, &c.; artificial watercourse for inland navigation (*cc. of Mars,* markings of doubtful nature on planet Mars); (Zool.) groove in shell for protrusion of breathing-tube. (Vb) make c. through; provide with cc. [F, f. L *canalis*]

cănalĭ·culate(d), a. (nat. hist.). With longitudinal groove(s); striated. [f. L *canaliculus* dim. of CANAL*is* + -ATE[2, 3]]

că·nalize, v.t. = CANAL vb; convert (river) into canal by embanking, straightening course, locks, &c. Hence **canaliz**A·TION n. [prob. f. F *canaliser* (CANAL + -IZE)]

că·napé (-ā), n. Piece of fried bread with anchovies &c. [F]

canard (kă·nar, kanar·d, or as F), n. False report, hoax. [F, = duck, false report]

canār·y, a. & n. From the C. Islands; (also *c.-bird*) yellow-feathered song-bird (green in wild state); (also *C.-wine*) a favourite wine in 16th-18th cc.; yellow fishing-fly; *c.-coloured*, bright yellow; *C. creeper*, yellow-flowered used esp. in window-boxes; *c.-seed*, used as food for the bird. [f. F *Canarie* f. Sp. & L *Canaria* (*canis* dog), one of the islands being noted in Roman times for large dogs]

cană·ster, n. Tobacco prepared by coarsely breaking the dried leaves. [orig. the rush basket used for packing it; f. Sp. *canastra* f. *L f. Gk *kanastron* basket see CANISTER]

cancan (F), n. High-kicking dance.

ca·ncel[1], v.t. & i. (-ll-). Obliterate, cross out, annul, make void, abolish, countermand, neutralize, balance, make up for, (intr., *c. out* or *c.*, of items) neutralize each other; (Arith.) strike out (same factor) from numerator & denominator, from two sides of equation, &c. Hence **cancell**A·TION n. [f. F *canceller* f. L *cancellare* (*cancelli* cross-bars, lattice)]

ca·ncel[2], n. Countermand; suppression & reprinting of sheet set up, the suppressed or the substituted sheet; (*pair of*) *cc.*, pincers for punching tickets [f. prec.]

ca·ncellate(d), a. (bot. & zool.). Marked with crossing lines, reticulated; (of bone) formed of interlacing fibres & plates with cavities, porous. [f. L *cancellatus* (CANCEL[1], -ATE[2], [3])]

ca·ncellous, a. (Of bone) = prec. [-OUS]

ca·ncer, C-, n. Zodiacal constellation the Crab (*C-*); fourth sign of zodiac (*C-*); TROPIC *of C.*; malignant tumour eating the part it is in, spreading indefinitely, & recurring when removed, (fig.) evil (sloth, bribery, &c.) acting similarly, whence **ca·ncer**ED[2], **ca·ncer**OUS, aa. [OE (later CANKER, corrected to *-cer* for disease c. 1600) f. L *cancer -cri* crab, cancer; tumour named from swollen veins, like crab's limbs]

ca·ncroid, a. & n. Crab-like; like cancer. (N.) crustacean of crab family; disease like cancer. [as prec. + -OID]

candelā·brum, n. (pl. *-bra*; also sing. *-bra*, pl. *-bras*). Large, usu. branched, candlestick or lampstand. [L (*-um*), f. *candela* CANDLE]

cande·scent, a. Glowing (as) with white heat. Hence **cande·sc**ENCE n. [f. L *candescere* (*candēre* be white, -ESCENT)]

ca·ndid, a. Unbiased; not censorious; frank; *c. friend*, nominal friend glad to tell home-truths. Hence **ca·ndid**LY[2] adv., **ca·ndid**NESS n. [f. L *candidus* white, see prec.]

ca·ndidate, n. One who puts himself or is put forward for appointment to an office or honour; person thought likely to gain any position. [f. L *candidatus*, as prec., -ATE[2] (2), orig. white-robed (Roman cc. wearing white)]

ca·ndidāture (-tsher), n. Standing for election, being candidate. [F, as prec. + -URE]

8469

ca·ndied. See CANDY.

ca·ndle, n. Cylinder of wax, tallow, spermaceti, &c., enclosing wick, for giving light; (also *c.-power*) unit of light-measurement; *Roman c.*, firework, tube discharging coloured balls; *can't, is not fit to, hold a c. to*, is not to be compared with; *sell by inch of c.*, by auction, last bid before small candle expires winning; BELL *book & c.*; *game not worth the c.*, result not justifying the cost or trouble; BURN[2] *c. at both ends*; *hide c. under* BUSHEL; *candleberry-myrtle* (N.-Amer.), *candleberry-tree* (Moluccas), yielding wax & nut-kernels used for cc.; *c.-ends*, remnants of c., odds-&-ends hoarded by the stingy; *candlelight*, light of cc., any artificial light, evening; *candlestick*, support for (usu. single) c.; *c.-tree*, Amer., with c.-like fruit some feet long. [OE *candel* f. L *candela* (*candēre* shine)]

Ca·ndlemas (-*a*s), n. Feast of purification of Virgin Mary; (as date) 2nd Feb. [OE *Candelmæsse* (CANDLE, MASS[1])]

ca·ndour, n. Open-mindedness, impartiality; freedom from malice; frankness. [f. L *candor* whiteness (*candēre* shine, -OR[1])]

ca·ndy, n., & v.t. & i. Crystallized sugar made by repeated boiling and slow evaporation (also *sugar-c.*); (U.S., w. pl.) sweety. (Vb) preserve by coating with c.; form (t. & i.) into crystals; (p.p.) glistening, (archaic) honeyed, flattering. [f. F (*sucre*) *candi* f. Arab.-Pers. *qand* crystallized sugarcane juice cf. Skr. *khaṇḍa* piece]

ca·ndytuft, n. Plant with white, pink, or purple flowers in flat tufts. [f. obs. *Candy* (*Candia* Crete) + TUFT]

cane[1], n. Hollow jointed stem of giant reeds & grasses (bamboo, sugar c.) or solid stem of slender palms (rattan, Malacca, &c.) collectively & as material (*c.*), or with pl. (*a c., cc.*) of the stem or a length of it used for walking-stick or instrument of punishment; any slender walking-stick; stick of sealing-wax, sulphur, glass; *c.-apple*, Strawberry-tree; *c.-brake*, genus of grasses; *c. chair*, with seat of woven c. strips. Hence **ca·n**Y[2] a. [OF (now *canne*), f. L f. Gk *kanna* reed perh. f. Semit. cf. Heb. *qaneh*]

cane[2], v.t. Beat with c., whence **ca·n**ING[1] (1) n.; drive (lesson) *into* (person) with c.; insert c. into (chair-frame &c.). [f. prec.]

canē·phorus, n. (pl. *-ī*). Sculptured Greek youth or maid bearing basket on head at feast of Demeter. [L, f. Gk *kanēphoros* (*kaneon* basket, *pherō* carry)]

cangue (kăngg), **cang,** n. Heavy wooden board worn round neck by Chinese criminals. [F (*-gue*), f. Port. *cango* cf. *canga* yoke]

căn·icide, n. Dog-killing, -killer (esp. of reckless motorists & riders). [L *canis* dog, -CIDE]

cā·nine (*also* kanī·n), a. & n. Of, as of, a dog or dogs; *c. tooth* or *c.*, one of the four strong pointed teeth between incisors & molars. [f. L *caninus* (*canis* dog, -INE¹)]

că·nister, n. Small box usu. of metal for tea, shot, &c.; (R.-C. Ch.) vessel holding wafers before consecration; *c.-shot* or *c.*, = CASE²*-shot.* [f. L *canistrum* f. Gk *kanastron* wicker basket (*kanna* CANE¹)]

ca·nker, n., & v.t. Ulcerous disease of human mouth; disease of horse's foot; disease of fruit-trees; (fig.) corrupting influence, rotten tendency; *c.-worm* or *c.*, caterpillar or larva destroying leaves or buds; *c.-rash,* variety of scarlet fever with ulcerated throat; hence **ca·nker**OUS a. (Vb) consume with c.; infect, corrupt; (p.p.) soured, malignant, crabbed. [f. ONF *cancre* f. L *cancrum* nom. CANCER]

ca·nna, n. Plant with bright yellow, red, or orange flowers & ornamental leaves. [L (CANE¹)]

ca·nnel, n. (Also *c.-coal*) bituminous coal burning with bright flame & used in making coal oils & gas. [perh. f. CANDLE]

ca·nnibal, n. & a. Man who eats human flesh; animal feeding on its own species; hence **ca·nnibal**ISM(2) n., **cannibali·st**IC a. (Adj.) of, having, these habits. [16th-c. E & Sp. *Canibales* pl., var. of Carib name of W.-Ind. nation; *Caliban* is prob. another variant]

ca·nnikin, n. Small can. [-KIN]

ca·nnon¹, n. 1. (Now being ousted by *gun*) piece of ordnance, gun of the kind that needs mounting, (collect. sing. usu. instead of pl.); *c.-ball,* projectile; *c.-bone,* tube-shaped bone between hough & fetlock; *c.-clock,* fired at noon by burning-glass. 2. (Mech.) hollow cylinder moving independently on shaft; watchkey barrel. 3. (Also *c.-bit*) smooth round bit for horse. 4. (Billiards) hitting of two balls successively by player's ball. 5. (Also *c.-curl*) sausage-shaped, prop. horizontal, curl. [in 16th c. also *canon* f. F *canon* cf. It. *cannone* great tube (*canna* CANE¹, -OON); sense 4 is corruption of obs. *carom* short for *carambole* (F, f. Sp. *carambola* etym. dub.); sense 5 = obs. *canion* f. Sp. *cañon* ornamental roll on breeches-legs (*canna* as above)]

ca·nnon², v.i. Make a c. at billiards (of player or ball); come into collision, strike obliquely, *against, into, with.* [f. prec.]

cannonā·de, n., & v.t. & i. Continuous gunfire. (Vb) fire continuously; bombard, fire fast at. [CANNON¹ + -ADE]

cannot. See CAN².

ca·nny, a. Shrewd, worldly-wise; natural, safe to meddle with, (esp. w. neg.); thrifty; gentle, quiet, circumspect, (*ca' c.*, Sc. for *drive* or *go gently,* as name for trade-union policy of limiting output); sly, pawky. Hence **ca·nni**LY² adv., **ca·nni**NESS n. [Sc. wd (w. senses differing f. above) f. CAN² know + -Y²]

canoe· (-ōō), n., & v.i. (Go in, paddle) boat propelled with paddle(s). Hence **canoe·**IST(3) n. [f. Sp. & Haytian *canoa*]

că·non, n. Church decree; *c. law,* eccl. law; general law governing treatment of a subject; criterion; list of Bible books accepted by Church; part of Mass containing words of consecration; (Mus.) piece with different parts taking up same subject successively in strict imitation; (Typ.) largest size of type with specific name; metal loop on bell for hanging it; member of cathedral CHAPTER, whence **ca·non**RY(2) n.; MINOR *c.* [OE, f. L f. Gk *kanōn* rule (*kanna* CANE); in last sense short for CANONIC, meaning (person) living (with others) according to rule]

cañon. See CANYON

canŏ·nical, a. & n., **cano·nic,** a. (archaic). Appointed by canon law (*c. hours,* for prayer, or for celebration of marriage, 8 a.m. to 3 p.m.; *c. dress,* of clergy, also *cc.* as n. pl.); included in canon of Scripture; *C. Epistles,* the seven of Peter, James, John, Jude; authoritative, standard, accepted; (Mus.) in canon form; of a cathedral chapter or a member of it. Hence **cano·nical**LY² adv. [f. med. L *canonicalis* f. *canonicus* (CANON, -IC) + -AL]

canŏ·nicate, n. = CANON*ry.* [f. med. L *canonicatus* (as prec., -ATE¹)]

canonĭ·city, n. Status as canonical book. [f. *canonicus* CANONICAL, -TY]

ca·nonist, n. Canon-lawyer. Hence **canoni·st**IC(AL) aa. [f. F *canoniste* (CANON, -IST)]

ca·nonize, v.t. Admit formally to calendar of saints; regard as a saint; recognize (book) as canonical; sanction by church authority. So **ca·noniz**A·TION n. [f. med. L *canonizare* (CANON, -IZE)]

canoo·dle, v.i. & t. (U.S. slang). Cuddle, fondle. [?]

că·nopy, n., & v.t. Covering suspended or held over throne, bed, person, &c. (also fig. of any overhanging shelter, sky, &c.); (Arch.) roof-like projection over niche &c.; (vb) supply, be, such a covering to. [f. F *canapé* (now) couch f. med. L *canopeum* f. Gk *kōnōpeion* mosquito-net (*kōnōps* gnat)]

canor·ous, a. Melodious, resonant. [f. L *canorus* (*canor* song f. *canere* sing) + -OUS]

cănt¹, n. Bevel, oblique face, of crystal, bank, &c.; push, toss, movement, that partly or quite upsets; tilted or sideways position; *c.-board,* sloping board. [cf. Du. *kant,* OF *cant,* It. *canto,* corner, edge, &c., perh. f. L f. Gk *kanthos* corner of eye]

cănt², v.t. & i. (Trans.) bevel off; tilt; turn *over,* turn upside down; push, pitch, sideways. (Intr.) take inclined position; lie aslant; (Naut.) swing round. [f. prec.]

cănt³, n. & a., & v.i. Peculiar language of class, profession, sect, &c., jargon; temporary catchwords (esp. as adj., *c. phrase* &c.); words used for fashion without being meant, unreal use of words implying piety; hypocrisy. (Vb) use talk of these kinds; (Herald.) *canting arms, heraldry, coat,* containing allusion to name of bearer; hence **ca·ntER**[1] n. [earlier of musical sound, of intonation, & of beggars' whining, perh. f. singing of religious mendicants; prob. f. L *cantus* song, *cantare* frequent. of *canere* sing]

can't. See CAN[2].

Că·ntăb, n., **Cantabri·gian,** n. & a. (Member) of Cambridge University. [f. L *Cantabrigia* Cambridge + -AN]

că·ntaloup (-ōōp), n. Kind of melon. [F, f. It. *Cantalupo* in Italy]

cănta·nkerous, a. Cross-grained, quarrelsome. Hence **canta·nkerousLY**[2] adv., **canta·nkerousNESS** n. [perh. f. ME *contak* contention on anal. of *traitorous, rancorous*]

cănta·ta (-tah-), n. (mus.). Choral work, kind of short oratorio, or lyric drama set to music but not acted. [It. (*cantare* sing, -*ata* -ADE)]

Canta·te (-ahtě), n. Psalm xcviii (O sing—) as a canticle. [L, =sing ye]

cantatri·ce (-ētshā, -ēs), n. Professional woman singer. [It. & F]

căntee·n, n. Provision & liquor shop in camp or barracks (*dry, wet, c.,* without, chiefly for, liquor); box of cooking-utensils for use in camp, soldier's mess-tin; soldier's water-vessel of tin, wood, &c. [f. F *cantine* f. It. *cantina* cellar etym. dub.]

că·nter, n., & v.i. & t. Easy gallop (*win in a c.,* easily). (Vb) go at this pace (of horse or rider); make (horse) go thus. [short for *Canterbury pace, gallop, trot,* &c., f. easy pace of Canterbury pilgrims]

că·nterbury, n. Stand with partitions for music &c.

Canterbury Bell, n. Kind of Campanula. [f. bells of Canterbury pilgrims' horses]

cănthă·ridēs, n. pl. (med.). Dried Spanish Fly. [L, pl. of L f. Gk *kantharis* blister-fly]

că·nticle, n. Little song, hymn; one of the Prayer-Book hymns, as the *Benedicite, Nunc Dimittis, Te Deum*; *Canticles,* Song of Solomon. [f. L *canticulum* dim. of *canticum* song (*cantus* song f. *canere* sing)]

că·ntilēver, n. Bracket (of length many times breadth & more than twice depth) projecting from wall to support balcony &c.; *c. bridge,* with piers each of which has two cc., with long girders connecting cc. of adjacent piers. [prob. f. CANT[1] & LEVER]

că·ntle, n. Piece, slice, cut off; hind-bow of saddle. [f. ONF *cantel* dim. of CANT[1]]

că·nto, n. (pl. -*os*). Division of long poem. [It., = song, as CANT[3]]

canto·n[1] (*also* kă·-), n. Subdivision of country; State of Swiss confederation; (Herald.) square division less than a quarter in upper corner of shield. Hence **ca·ntonAL** a. [OF, =corner (CANT[1], -OON)]

cantŏ·n[2] (*also* -tōō·n), v.t. Divide into cc. (-tŏn); (-tōōn) quarter (soldiers). [f. prec.]

canto·nment (-ōōn-), n. Lodging assigned to troops (in India also permanent military station). [prec. + -MENT]

cantor·ial, a. Of the precentor, of N. side of choir (cf. DECANAL). [f. L as foll. + -AL]

cantor·is, mus. direction. To be sung by cantorial side in antiphonal singing. [L, genit. of *cantor* precentor (*canere cant-* sing, -OR[2])]

Canu·ck, n. & a. (slang). French Canadian; (U.S.) Canadian. [U.S. word]

ca·nvas, n. Strong unbleached cloth of hemp or flax, for sails, tents, painting on; open kind used as basis for tapestry & embroidery; *under c.,* in tent(s), with sails spread; racing-boat's covered end; picture; *C.-back,* N.-Amer. duck (f. colour of back feathers). [ME & ONF *canevas* f. LL **cannabaceus* (L f. Gk *kannabis* hemp, -ACEOUS)]

ca·nvass, v.t. & i., & n. Discuss thoroughly; solicit votes, solicit votes from (constituency), ascertain sentiments of, ask custom of, whence **ca·nvassER**[1] n.; (n.) canvassing for votes. [f. prec., orig. sense being toss in a sheet, & so shake up, agitate, &c.]

ca·nyon, n. Deep gorge with stream. [f. Sp. *cañon* tube (*caña* f. L *canna* CANE[1])]

canzone·t, n. Short light song. [f. It. *canzonetta* (*canzone* f. L *cantionem* f. *canere* sing)]

caoutchouc (kow·tshōōk), n. & a. (Of) India-rubber. [F, f. Carib. *cahuchu*]

cap[1], n. Head-dress (woman's, esp. of muslin &c. worn indoors, but also now, like man's or boy's, for out-door use, brimless & of cloth or soft material; *c. in hand,* humbly; *c. fits,* person feels that general remark is true of him; *set* one's *c. at,* try to attract as suitor); special head-dress (*college* or *square c.*; *steel c.,* helmet; *Scotch c.,* part of Highland costume; *football c.,* of velvet &c., sign of inclusion in team; *c. of* MAINTENANCE; *c. of liberty,* conical, given to Roman slave on emancipation, now Republican symbol; *c. & bells,* jester's insignia; FOOL'S *c.*); caplike covering, natural (mushroom top, knee-c., &c.), or added for various purposes (windmill top, toe-c., inner watch-case; *percussion c.,* for igniting explosive in cartridges &c.); (Naut.) doubly pierced block for lengthening mast by extra spar; conical paper bag, cornet; *c.-paper,* whity-brown for packing, also a size of writing-paper; *c.-stone,* top stone, coping. [OE *cæppe* f. LL *cappa,* the Rom. forms of which meant *cloak, cape, cope*; *cape, cope,* are separate E adoptions of the same wd through Rom. or in its med. L form *capa*]

cap[2], v.t. & i. Put c. upon; (Sc. Univv.)

confer degree on; put percussion c. on nipple of (gun); protect (end of beam &c.) with metal &c., whence **ca·pp**ING[1] (3) n.; lie on top of, crown; outdo (*c. anecdote, quotation,* &c., produce a better or another apposite one; *c. verses,* reply with one beginning with the last's last letter); touch or take off one's hat to (also intr. with *to*); injure at point (*horse caps its hocks*). [f. prec.]

cāpabi·lity, n. Power *of* (action &c., act*ing* &c.), *for* (be*ing* done something to), *to* (do something); undeveloped faculty (*has cc.*). [foll., -BILITY]

cā·pable, a. Susceptible (*of*, or abs.); having the power or fitness for (*of*); wicked enough for (*of*); gifted, able. Hence **ca·pab**LY[2] adv. [F, f. LL *capabilis* irreg. for *capibilis* (L *capere* hold, -BLE); earlier sense *having room* (*for*)]

capa·cious, a. Roomy. Hence **capa·-cious**NESS n. [L *capax* (*capere* hold), -ACIOUS]

capă·citate, v.t. Render capable (*for, to* do); make legally competent. [foll., -ATE[3]]

capă·city, n. Holding-power, receiving-power, (*for* happiness, heat, moisture; *filled to c.*, quite full; *c. house,* packed theatre &c.); cubic content (*measure of c.*, for vessels & liquids, grain, &c.); mental power, faculty; capability, opportunity, *to* do, *of* do*ing*, &c. (rare); position, relative character, (*in a civil c.*; *in my c. as critic*); legal competency. [f. F *capacité* f. L *capacitatem* (CAPACIOUS, -TY)]

cap-à-pie (kă·papē·), adv. From head to foot, (armed, ready, &c.). [f. OF *cap a pie*]

capă·rison (-zn), n. (often pl.), & v.t. Horse's trappings; equipment, outfit; (vb) put c. upon. [f. F *caparasson* (now *-açon*) f. Sp. *caparazon* f. med. L *caparo* (*capa* CAPE[1])]

cape[1], n. Short sleeveless cloak, either as separate garment or as fixed or detachable part of longer cloak or coat. Hence **cap**ED[2] a. [F, f. Sp. *capa* or It. *cappa*; see CAP[1]]

cape[2], C-, n. & a. Headland, promontory; *the C.*, of Good Hope, also = C. Colony (*C. boy,* S.-African of mixed black & white descent), & as adj. of its products (*C. wine* &c.). [f. F *cap* f. Rom. *capo* f. L *caput* head]

cā·per[1], n. Bramble-like S.-European shrub; (pl.) its flower-buds pickled (esp. *c. sauce*); *English cc.*, seed vessels of Nasturtium pickled. [ME *caperis, caperes,* (sing.) f. L f. Gk *kapparis*; *-s* lost as though pl. sign cf. PEA, MACE]

cā·per[2], n., & v.i. (Give a) frisky movement, leap; fantastic proceeding; *cut a c.*, *cc.*, = *c.* vb. [short for CAPRIOLE]

căpercai·lyĕ, -cai·lzie, n. Wood-grouse, largest European gallinaceous bird (Scotland &c.). [f. Gael. *capull coille* horse of the wood]

ca·perer, n. In vbl senses; esp., caddis-fly (from its flight). [CAPER[2], -ER[1]]

ca·pful, n. Enough to fill a cap; esp., *c. of wind,* passing gust. [-FUL (2)]

că·pias, n. Writ of arrest. [L, = take thou]

capillă·rity, n. (Power of exerting) capillary attraction or repulsion. [f. F *capillarité* see foll., -TY]

capi·llary (*also* kă·-), a. & n. Of hair; hair-like, thin as a hair; (tube, blood-vessel) of minute or hair-like diameter (e.g. one of ramified blood-vessels intervening between arteries & veins); so *c.* ATTRACTION, REPULSION. [f. L *capillaris* (-ARY[2]) f. *capillus* hair]

că·pital[1], n. Head or cornice of pillar. [= L *capitellum* (cf. F *chapiteau*) dim. of *capitulum* dim. of *caput* head]

că·pital[2], a. & n. Involving loss of life, punishable by death, (*c. sentence, offence*); vitally injurious, fatal, (*c. error*); standing at the head (*c. letter,* also *c.* as noun); chief (*c. manor,* held in capite or direct from king; *c. messuage,* occupied by owner of estate with several messuages; *c. town* or *city,* or *c.* as noun, head town of country, county, &c.); important, leading, first-class, (*c. ship,* battleship or battle cruiser); excellent, first-rate, (often as interj. of approval); original, principal, (*c. fund* or *c.*, stock with which company or person enters into business, accumulated wealth used in producing more, holders of this as a class, as *C. & Labour*; *fixed c.*, machinery &c., *circulating* or *floating c.*, goods, money, &c.; so fig., *make c. out of,* turn to account). Hence **ca·pital**LY[2] adv. [F, f. L *capitalis* (*caput -itis* head, -AL)]

ca·pitalism, ca·pitalist, nn. Possession or influence or system, possessor, of capital or fund used in production, (mod., Pol.) dominance of private capitalists (opp. *socialism*). Hence **ca·pitali·st**IC a. [prec., -ISM(3), -IST(3)]

ca·pitalize, v.t. Convert into, use as, capital; compute or realize present value of (income). Hence **ca·pitaliz**A·TION n. [-IZE(3)]

ca·pitate(d), a. (nat. hist.). Having distinct head; with clustered flowers &c. [f. L *capitatus* headed (*caput -itis,* -ATE[2])]

capita·tion, n. (Levying of) tax or fee of so much a head; *c. grant,* of so much for every person fulfilling conditions. [f. L *capitatio* poll-tax (*caput -itis* head, -ATION)]

Că·pitol (-tl), n. Roman temple of Jupiter on Tarpeian hill (later *Capitoline hill* or *Capitoline*); (U.S.) Congress house. [f. L *capitolium* (*caput* head)]

capĭ·tular, a. Of a cathedral chapter; (Physiol.) of a terminal protuberance of bone. [f. med. L *capitularis* (L *capitulum* CHAPTER, -AR[1])]

capi·tulary, n. Collection of ordinances, esp. of Frankish kings. [f. med. L *capitularius* (as prec., -ARY[1])]

capi·tulate, v.i. Surrender on terms. [f. med. L *capitulare* draw up under heads (see CAPITULAR), -ATE[3]]

capi·tula·tion, n. Stating heads of subject; agreement, conditions, (esp. *the Cc.*, by which foreign residents in Turkey had exterritoriality); surrender on terms, instrument containing these. [F, f. med. L *capitulationem* (prec., -ATION)]

cā·pon, n. Castrated cock. Hence **ca·pon-**IZE(3) v.t. [OE *capun* f. L *caponem*, nom. *capo*]

căponier·, n. Covered passage across ditch of fort. [f. F *caponnière* f. Sp. *caponera* orig. a capon-cote (see prec.)]

că·poral (-ahl), n. A French tobacco. [F]

capo·t, n., & v.t. (-tt-). (In piquet) winning of all tricks by one player; (vb) do this against (opponent). [F]

capo·te, n. Soldier's, traveller's, &c., long cloak with hood. [F, dim. of *cape* CAPE[1]]

că·pric, a. (chem.). *C. acid*, obtained from butter, coco-nut oil, &c. [f. L *caper -pri* goat + -IC (from its goatlike smell)]

capri·ce (-ēs), n. Unaccountable change of mind or conduct, fancy, freak; inclination to these; work of sportive fancy in art &c. [F, f. It. *capriccio* sudden start (*capro* goat f. L *caper -pri*)]

capri·cious (-sh*us*), a. Guided by whim, inconstant, irregular, incalculable. Hence **capri·cious**LY[2] adv., **capri·cious**NESS n. [f. F *capricieux* f. It. *capriccioso* (prec., -OUS)]

Că·pricorn, n. Zodiacal constellation Goat; tenth sign of zodiac; TROPIC *of C.* [f. L *capricornus* (*caper -pri* goat, *cornu* horn)]

căprifica·tion, n. Hastening of ripeness in figs by subjecting them to puncture by wild-fig gall-insects. [f. L *caprificatio* f. *caprificus* wild fig (*caper* goat, *ficus* fig), -ATION]

că·prine, a. Of, like, a goat. [f. L *caprinus* (*caper -pri*, -INE[1])]

că·priole, n., & v.i. (Give a) leap, caper, esp. (in manège) horse's high leap & kick without advancing. [F (now *cab-*), or f. It. *capriola* dim. of L *capra* she-goat]

capro·ic, a. (chem.). *C. acid*, found with capric & butyric acids in butter &c. [var. of CAPRIC for differentiation]

caps, abbr. of *capitals* (capital letters) in direction to printers &c.

ca·psicum, n. Kinds of plant with hot capsules & seeds, Guinea Pepper &c.; the prepared fruit. [irreg. prob. f. L *capsa* CASE[2]]

capsi·ze, n., & v.t. & i. Upset, overturn, (of ship, boat). Hence **capsi·**ZAL(2) n. [perh. f. Sp. *cabezar* pitch or *capuzar* sink by the head (*cabo* f. L *caput* head)]

ca·pstan, n. Revolving barrel, worked by men walking round & pushing horizontal levers, or by steam &c., for winding cable in, hoisting heavy sails, &c. [f. F or Pr. *cabestan* f. L *capistrare* (*capistrum* halter f. *capere* hold), -ANT]

ca·psule, n. (Physiol.) membranous envelope; (Bot.) dry seed-case opening when ripe by parting of valves; (Chem.) shallow saucer for evaporating &c.; (Med.) gelatine envelope enclosing pill; metallic top for bottle. Hence **ca·psul**AR[1], **ca·psuli**FORM, aa., **capsuli-** comb. form. [F, f. L *capsula* (CASE[2], -ULE)]

ca·ptain[1] (-ĭn), n. Chief, leader; great soldier, strategist, experienced commander; (Army) chief company or troop officer. (Navy) officer commanding man-of-war (also used, by courtesy, of commander); *C. of the Fleet*, adjutant-general of a force, with rear-admiral's uniform; chief sailor of special gang (*c. of forecastle* &c.). Master of merchant ship; manager of Cornish mine; foreman; head boy; leader of side in games; = Grey Gurnard. Hence **ca·ptain**CY, **ca·ptain**SHIP, nn., **ca·ptain**LESS a. [ME & OF *capitain* f. LL *capitaneus* (a. & n.) chief (L *caput* head)]

ca·ptain[2], v.t. Be c. of, lead. [f. prec.]

capta·tion, n. Use of *ad captandum* arguments or appeals. [f. L *captatio* (*captare* catch at, frequent. of *capere* take, -ATION)]

ca·ption, n. Legal arrest; (Law) certificate attached to or written on document; (U.S.) heading of chapter, article, &c. (e.g. on cinema screen). [f. L *captio* (*capere* take, -TION); last meaning f. second]

ca·ptious, a. Fallacious, sophistical; fond of taking exception, trying to catch people in their words. Hence **ca·ptious**LY[2] adv., **ca·ptious**NESS n. [f. L *captiosus* (prec., -OSE[1])]

ca·ptivate, v.t. Fascinate, charm. Hence **captiva·tion** n. [f. L *captivare* take CAPTIVE, -ATE[3]]

ca·ptive, a. & n. (Person, animal) taken prisoner, kept in confinement, under restraint, unable to escape; of, like, prisoner (*c. state*); *lead, take, hold, c.*; *c. balloon*, held by rope from ground. So **capti·**VITY n. [f. F *captif* f. L *captivus* (*capere capt-* take, -IVE)]

ca·ptor, n., **ca·ptress,** n. fem. One who takes a captive or prize. [*-or* L (as prec., -OR[2]); & see -ESS[1]]

ca·pture (-tsh*er*), n., & v.t. Seizing, taking possession of; thing or person seized. (Vb) take prisoner, seize as prize; hence **ca·ptur**ER[1] n. [F, f. L *captura* as prec., -URE]

Că·puchin (-tsh-), n. & a. Franciscan (friar) of new rule of 1528; woman's cloak and hood; *C. monkey, pigeon*, kinds with head hair or feathers like cowl. [F (now *-cin*), f. It. *capuccino* (*capuccio* cowl f. *cappa* CAP[1])]

că·put mor·tūŭm, n. Worthless residue. [L, = dead head; alch. term for residuum of any substance after distillation or sublimation]

căpȳbar·a, n. Large S.-Amer. rodent allied to guinea-pig. [Brazilian]

car, n. Wheeled vehicle (chiefly poet. = chariot; *c. of the sun, triumphal c., c. of Juggernaut,* &c.; or with specification as JAUNT[1]*ing-c.,* MOTOR-*c., tramway-c., dining-c.*; in U.S. of any railway carriage or van; in Engl. also of motor-car, of low two-wheeled truck for hogsheads &c., & of other low heavy carts); pendant of airship or balloon holding passengers; *carman,* driver of van or jaunting-c., carter, carrier. Hence **car·**FUL(2) n. [ME & ONF *carre* f. LL *carra* cf. L *carrus* four-wheeled vehicle f. Bret. *karr* cf. OW. *carr*]

cărabineer·, carb-, n. Soldier with carbine; *The Carabineers,* 6th Dragoon Guards. [f. F *carabinier* (CARBINE, -IER)]

că·racăl, n. Kind of lynx. [F, f. Turk. *qarah-qulaq* black-ear]

că·racol(e), n., & v.i. (Execute) half-turn(s) to right or left (of horse or rider). [f. F *caracole(r)* f. It. *caracollo* f. Sp. *caracol* snail, spiral shell]

cara·fe (-ahf), n. Glass water-bottle for table. [F, cf. It. *caraffa,* Sp. *garrafa* perh. f. Arab. *gharafa* draw water]

că·ramel, n. Burnt sugar used for colouring spirits &c.; a sweetmeat. [F, f. Sp. *caramelo*]

că·rapace, n. Upper shell of tortoise & crustaceans. [F, f. Sp. *carapacho* etym. dub.]

că·rat, n. Measure of weight for precious stones, about $3\frac{1}{6}$ grains; measure of purity of gold, pure gold being 24 c. [F, f. It. *carato* f. Arab. *qirat* perh. f. Gk *keration* fruit of carob tree (dim. of *keras* horn)]

carava·n, n. Eastern or N.-African company of merchants, pilgrims, &c., travelling together for safety, esp. through desert; covered cart or carriage, house on wheels (esp. of menagerie &c.). [16th-c. *carouan* f. Pers. *karwan,* perh. assim. to F *caravane*]

carava·nserai, -sera, -sary, n. Eastern quadrangular inn with great inner court where caravans put up. [f. Pers. *karwan-sarai* (prec., *sara* mansion)]

că·ravel, car·vel, n. (hist.). Small light fast ship, chiefly Spanish & Portuguese of 15th-17th cc. [f. F *caravelle* f. It. *caravella*; cf. LL f. Gk *karabos*]

că·raway, n. Umbelliferous plant with fruit (*c.-seeds*) used in cakes. [f. med. L *carui* cf. Arab. *al-karawiya* & Gk *karon* cummin]

carb-, carbo-, comb. forms of CARBON. Hence **car·b**IDE n. (often for *calcium carbide* used in making acetylene gas).

car·bīne, că·ra-, n. Short fire-arm for cavalry use. [F (*cara-*) weapon of *carabin* soldier perh. f. *Calabria* perh. f. med. L *chadabula* kind of ballista (Gk *katabolē* overthrow)]

car·bo-hȳ·drate, n. (chem.). Organic compound of carbon with oxygen & hydrogen in the proportion to form water (starch, sugar, glucose).

carbŏ·lic, a. (chem.). *C. acid,* powerful antiseptic & disinfectant. Hence **car·bol**IZE(5) v.t. [CARB-, -OL, -IC]

car·bon, n. (chem.). Non-metallic element occurring as diamond, graphite, & charcoal, in carbonic acid gas, the carbonates, & most organic compounds; (Electr.) charcoal pencil used in one form of electric lighting; *c. printing, process,* producing permanent prints in black and white; *c.-paper,* for taking copies of letters &c. Hence **car·bon**ATE[1](3) n. [f. F *carbone* f. L *carbonem* nom. *-o* charcoal]

carbona·ceous, a. Of, like, coal or charcoal; consisting of or containing carbon. [as prec., -ACEOUS]

carbonar·i (-ē), n. Neapolitan secret society of republican revolutionists. [perh. f. disguising themselves as charcoal-burners]

car·bonāte, v.t. (chem.). Form into a c.; impregnate with carbonic acid gas, aerate. [f. *carbonate* n. see CARBON, -ATE[3]]

carbŏ·nic, a. (chem.). Of carbon; *c. acid (gas),* the gas formed in combustion of carbon, given out in breathing, & constituting choke-damp. [-IC]

carboni·ferous, a. Producing coal; (Geol.) *c. strata, system, formation,* palaeozoic next above Old Red Sandstone; *c. age, era, period,* in which these strata were deposited. [CARBON, -I-, -FEROUS]

car·bonize, v.t. Convert into carbon; reduce to charcoal or coke; cover (paper) with carbon for taking copies. Hence **carboniza·**TION n. [-IZE(3, 5)]

carboru·ndum, n. Compound of carbon and silicon used for polishing by abrasion. [CARBON + CORUNDUM]

car·boy, n. Large coloured-glass bottle protected with basket-work. [f. Pers. *qarabah*]

car·buncle, n. Red precious stone (formerly of many kinds, e.g. ruby; now garnet cut in boss shape); malignant tumour, anthrax, pimple on nose or face, whence **car·buncl**ED[2], **carbu·ncul**AR[1], aa. [ME & OF *charbucle* f. L *carbunculus* small coal (CARBON, -UNCLE)]

carbure·t, v.t. (-tt-). Combine (any element) chemically with carbon; charge with carbon. Hence **carbure·tt**OR[2] (2) or **carbure·tt**ER[1] (2) n., carburetting apparatus used in motor engines &c. [CARBON, -URET]

car·cass, -ase, n. Dead body (of human body now only with contempt); (with butchers) beast's trunk without head, limbs, or offal; mere body, dead or alive (*to save* one's *c.*), worthless remains (*of*); skeleton, framework, (of house, ship, &c.); (Mil.) kind of fire-ball from gun for igniting buildings. [partly f. OF *charcois* f. med. L *carcosium,* partly f. 16th-c. F *carcasse* f. It. *carcassa*; etym. and mutual relations of *carcosium, carcassa*, doubtful]

card[1], n., & v.t. (Cleanse, comb, get into order, also scratch or torture, with) toothed instrument, wire-brush, or wire-set rubber or vulcanite strip, for raising nap on cloth or preparing wool, hemp, &c.; *c.-thistle*, teasel; *carding-machine*, with card-strips fixed on rollers. [f. F *carde* teasel-head ult. f. L *carduus* thistle]

card[2], n. (Also *playing-c.*) one of pack of 52 oblong pieces of pasteboard used in games (COURT[1]-*c.*; *make a c.*, take trick with it; *house of cc.*, insecure scheme &c.; *cc.*, card-playing; *sure, safe, doubtful*, &c., *c.*, such a plan, expedient; *knowing, queer, c.*, such a person; *throw up, show*, one's *cc.*, give up, let out, one's plan; *c. up* one's *sleeve*, plan in reserve; *on the cc.*, likely, possible); flat piece of thick paper or pasteboard for various purposes (*speak by the c.*, with precision, f. obs. use = mariner's compass; POST-*c.*; *correspondence-c.*, for short notes; = ticket of admission; = invitation; *c.* or *visiting-c.*, with name &c., sent or left in lieu of formal visit, so *leave a c. on*; *wedding, Christmas*, &c., *c.*, sent in notification or compliment to friends; *collecting-c.*, for entering subscribers to charities; programme of events at race-meetings &c., or of cricket scores, esp. *correct c.*; *the c.*, the correct thing, what is expected; printed or written notice, rules, &c., for hanging in window or on wall); *c.-case*, for carrying visiting-cc.; *c.-basket, -rack*, for keeping visitors' cc.; *cardboard*, pasteboard for cutting cc. from or making boxes &c.; *c.-sharper*, swindler at c.-games; *c. vote* (of delegates each counting for the number of his constituents). [f. F *carte* f. It. *carta* (cf. *charte* direct) f. L *charta* f. Gk *khartēs* papyrus-leaf; *-d* for *-te* unexplained]

car·damom, n. Spice from seed-capsules of E.-Ind. plants. [f. L f. Gk *kardamōmon* (*kardamon* cress, *amōmon* a spice plant)]

car·diac, a. & n. Of the heart (esp. path., as *c. symptoms*, of heart-disease); of upper orifice of stomach; (n.) heart-stimulant, cordial. [f. F (*-aque*) f. L f. Gk *kardiakos* (*kardia* heart, -AC)]

car·digan, n. Knitted woollen over-waistcoat with or without sleeves. [named after Earl of *C.* c. 1855]

car·dinal, C-, a. & n. On which something hinges, fundamental, important, (*c. virtues*, the four natural & three theological, see VIRTUE; *c. numbers*, the simple ones, as one, six, cf. ORDINAL; *c. points, winds*, North, S., E., W.; *c. church* hist., one of principal churches in Rome, to which others were subordinate, whence *Cardinal*, noun, orig. person in charge of one of these, now one of seventy princes of R.-C. Ch., members of Pope's council of 6 c. bishops, 50 c. priests, & 14 c. deacons, & electors of new Pope, whence **car·dinal**ATE[1], **car·dinal**SHIP, nn.; also prefixed to other titles, as *C.-Legate*), whence **car·dinal**LY[2] adv.; of deep scarlet; woman's short hooded (orig. scarlet) cloak; small scarlet bird; (Zool.) of the hinge of a bivalve; *c.-flower*, Scarlet Lobelia. [F, f. L *cardinalis* (*cardo -inis* hinge, -AL); sense *scarlet* f. Cardinal's robes]

cardio-, comb. form of Gk *kardia* heart.

cardoo·n, n. Composite kitchen-garden plant allied to artichoke. [f. F *cardon* f. It. *cardone* (*cardo* f. L *cardus, carduus* thistle, -OON)]

care[1], n. Solicitude, anxiety: occasion for these; serious attention, heed, caution, pains, (*take, have a, c.*, be cautious); charge, protection, (*A, c/o* or *c. of B*, in addresses; *have the, take, c. of*; *in, under*, one's *c.*); thing to be done or seen to (*cc. of State* &c.; *that shall be my c.*); *c.-laden, -worn*, with anxieties; *c.-taker*, person hired to take charge, esp. of house in owner's absence. [OE *caru*, com.-Teut. f. OTeut. *karâ-*; not related to L *cura*]

care[2], v.i. Feel concern or interest *for* or *about*; provide food, attendance, &c., *for* (children, invalids, &c.); (w. neg. expressed or implied) feel regard, deference, affection, *for*, be concerned *whether* &c., (often with expletive *a pin, a damn, a farthing*; *I don't c. if I do*, am willing); be willing or wishful *to* (*should not c. to be seen with him*; *do you c. to try them?*). [OE *carian* f. prec.]

caree·n, v.t. & i. Turn (ship) on one side for cleaning, caulking, &c.; (cause to) heel over. [ult. f. L *carina* keel]

caree·nage, n. Careening a ship; expense of it; place for it. [-AGE]

career·, n., & v.i. Swift course, impetus, (*in full, mid*, &c., *c.*); course or progress through life; development & success of party, principle, nation, &c.; way of making a livelihood; (vb) go swiftly or wildly (often *about*). [f. F *carrière* race-course f. LL *carraria* (*via*) carriage-(road) f. L *carrus* CAR[1]]

care·ful, a. Concerned *for*, taking care *of*; painstaking, watchful, cautious, (*to* do, *that, what, whether*, &c.); done with or showing care. Hence **care·ful**LY[2] adv., **care·ful**NESS n. [-FUL]

care·less, a. Unconcerned, light-hearted; inattentive, negligent (*of*), thoughtless; inaccurate. Hence **care·less**LY[2] adv., **care·less**NESS n. [-LESS]

carĕ·ss, n., & v.t. Fondling touch, kiss; blandishment. (Vb) bestow these on; pet, make much of; hence **care·ssing**LY[2] adv. [f. F *caresse*(*r*) f. It. *carezza*(*re*) f. LL **caritia* (L *carus* dear)]

că·ret, n. Mark (^) placed below line to show place of omission. [L, = it needs (*carēre*)]

car·go, n. Freight of ship. [Sp., =loading

f. med. L *carricum* f. LL *carricare* to load (L *carrus* CAR[1])]

Că·rib, n. & a. (One) of aboriginal inhabitants of Southern W.-Ind. islands. So **Caribbē·an** a. [f. Sp. *Caribe* cf. CANNIBAL]

caribou· (-ōō), **-boo·**, n. N.-Amer. reindeer. [-*ou* Canad. F, prob. f. native wd]

căricature·, n., & v.t. Grotesque representation of person or thing by over-emphasis on characteristic traits (pictorial, literary, or mimetic); hence **caricatūr·**IST(1) n. (Vb) make, give, a c. of; hence **caricatūr·**ABLE a. [F, f. It. *caricatura* (*caricare* to load see CARGO, -URE)]

cār·ĭēs, n. Decay (of bones or teeth). [L]

că·rillon (-lyon, or as F), n. Set of bells that can be rung either by hand or mechanically; air played on bells; instrument (or part of organ) imitating peal of bells. [F, f. med. L *quadrilionem* nom. *-o* quaternary (formerly four bells)]

carī·na, n. (zool. & bot.). Ridge-shaped structure. Hence **carī·**NAL, **că·rin**ATE[2], aa., **carīno-** comb. form. [L, = keel]

cār·ious, a. Decayed (esp. of bones, teeth). [f. L *cariosus* (CARIES, -OSE[1])]

car·king, a. Burdensome (alw. with *care*). [f. obs. vb *cark* f. ONF *carkier* f. LL *carricare* (CARGO)]

carl(e), n. (Sc.). Man, fellow. [OE in comb. as *hús-carl* f. ON *karl* cogn. w. CHURL]

car·line[1], n. (Sc.). Old woman. [ME & ON *kerling* fem. of prec.]

car·line[2], n. Genus of composite plants allied to thistle. [F, f. med. L *carlina* for *Carolina* named f. *Carolus* Charlemagne]

Car·lism, Car·list, nn. Spanish legitimism, legitimist, support(er) of Don Carlos second son of Charles IV. [-ISM(3), -IST(2)]

Carlovi·ngian, Caroli·ngian, (-j-), a. & n. (One) of second French dynasty founded by Charlemagne. [f. F *carlovingien* after *merovingien* MEROVINGIAN]

Car·lowitz (-w-, -v-), n. A red wine of C. on the Danube.

Car·lton Club, n. The chief Conservative club in England.

Carlȳ·lism, n. Principles, literary manner, a mannerism, of Carlyle. So **Car·lyl**E·AN, **Carly·l**IAN, aa., **Carlyl**E·SE a. & n. [Thomas *Carlyle* 1795–1881; -ISM(3, 4)]

Carmagno·le (-anyōl), n. Song & dance among French revolutionists of 1793. [F]

Car·melite, n. & a. (Member) of mendicant order of friars (also *White Friars* f. their white cloak); fine woollen stuff, usu. grey. [Mt *Carmel*, place of foundation (12th c.), -ITE[1](2)]

car·minative, a. & n. (Drug) curing flatulence. [f. L *carminare* card, -IVE, gross humours being combed out like tangled wool]

car·mine, n. & a. (Coloured like, colour of) crimson pigment made from cochineal. [f. F or Sp. *carmin* f. med. L *carminus* for *carmesinus* CRIMSON]

car·nage (-ĭj), n. Great slaughter, esp. of men. [F, f. It. *carnaggio* f. LL *carnaticum* (L *caro carnis* flesh, -AGE)]

car·nal, a. Sensual, fleshly; sexual; unsanctified, worldly. Hence **car·nal**ISM(2), **carnă·l**ITY, nn., **car·nal**IZE(3) v.t., **car·nal**LY[2] adv. [f. L *carnalis* (*caro* see prec., -AL)]

carna·tion[1], n. & a. (Of) rosy pink colour. [orig. flesh-colour f. L *carnatio* (*caro* see CARNAGE) fleshiness]

carna·tion[2], n. Cultivated kinds of Clove-pink. [formerly also *incarnacyon, coronation, cornation*; perh. orig. *coronation* as indented like coronet, later confused w. the colour; for *corn-*, *carn-*, cf. foll.]

carnē·lian. = CORNELIAN. [*ca-* by confusion w. L (CARNATION[1]) as flesh-coloured]

car·nifȳ, v.t. & i. (path.). Change (t. & i. of bone, lungs, &c.) to structure of flesh or muscle. Hence **car·ni**FICA·TION n. [L *caro carnis* flesh, -FY]

car·nival, n. Half-week or week before Lent; festivities usual during this in R.-C. countries; riotous revelry; reckless indulgence in something (*of*; *c. of bloodshed* &c.). [f. It. *carnevale* orig. name for Shrove Tuesday only, f. L phr. *carnem levare* put away meat]

carnĭ·vora, n. Large order of flesh-eating mammalia, including cats, dogs, bears, &c. [L neut. pl. see CARNIVOROUS]

car·nivore, n. Carnivorous animal or plant. [F, as foll.]

carnĭ·vorous, a. Feeding on flesh (esp. of the CARNIVORA, & of plants digesting animal substance). [f. L *carnivorus* (*caro carnis* flesh, -VOROUS)]

car·ny, -ey, v.t. (colloq.). Coax, wheedle. [?]

că·rob, n. Horn-like pod of Levantine c.-tree. [f. F *carobe* f. Arab. *kharrubah* bean-pod]

că·rol, n., & v.t. & i. (-ll-). Joyous song, human or of birds, esp. Christmas hymn. (Vb) utter, celebrate with, these; hence **ca·roll**ER[1] n. [obs. senses *dance, ring*; f. OF *carole(r)* perh. f. L *choraula* f. Gk *khoraulēs* flute-player for chorus-dancing (*khoros* chorus, *aulos* flute), or f. L COROLLA ring]

Că·rolīne, a. Of Charlemagne; of the time of Charles I & II of England. [f. L *Carolus* Charles + -INE[1]]

Carolingian. See CARLOVINGIAN.

că·rom, n. (U.S.). Cannon at billiards. [see CANNON[1]]

carō·tid, a. & n. Of, near, the two great arteries carrying blood to head; (n.) one of these. [f. Gk *karōtides* pl. (*karoō* stupefy, compression of these arteries being thought to do this)]

carou·se (-owz), v.i., & n. (Have, engage in) a drinking-bout; drink deep. Hence

carou·sAL(2) n. [orig. as adv. = right out, in phr. *drink c.* f. G *gar aus trinken*]

carp[1], n. A fresh-water fish usu. bred in ponds. [f. OF *carpe* f. LL *carpa* cf. OHG *charpho*, G *karpfen*]

carp[2], v.i. Talk querulously, find fault, (usu. *at*); esp. *carping tongue, criticism*, captious. [obs. senses *talk, say, sing*, prob f. ON *karpa* to brag, but mod. sense influenced by L *carpere* pluck at, slander]

car·pal, a. Of the CARPUS. [CARPUS, -AL]

car·pel, n. (bot.). Pistil-cell, whether pistil is one cell or several. Hence **car·pell**ARY[1] a. [mod. dim. f. Gk *karpos* fruit, see -LE (2)]

car·penter, n., & v.i. & t. Artificer in wood-work (esp. of rough solid kinds as in ship or house building, cf. JOINER, CABINET-*maker*; *the c.'s son*, Jesus); *c.-ant, -bee*, kinds boring into trees; *c.-scene*, played before a painted scene (also *c.-scene*) to give c. time for preparing elaborate scene behind; so **car·pent**RY (2, 5) n. (Vb) do, make by, c.'s work. [f. ONF *carpentier* (now *ch-*) f. LL *carpentarius* (*carpentum* wagon f. Celt.)]

car·pet[1], n., & v.t. Thick fabric, usu. woollen & patterned, for covering floor & stairs (at first of table-covering, whence *on the c.*, under discussion; & as floor-covering long a boudoir luxury, whence *c.-knight*, stay-at-home soldier, ladies' man); smooth, soft, or bright expanse of grass, flowers, &c.; *c.-bed*, garden bed with dwarf plants arranged in pattern; *c.-dance*, informal; *c.-rods*, keeping stair-c. in place; *c.-snake*, variegated Australian kind; *c.-bag*, travelling-bag, orig. made of c.; *c.-bagger*, candidate for election or political agitator unconnected with district; hence **car·pet**LESS a. (Vb) cover (as) with a c., whence **car·pet**ING[1] (3) n.; summon (servant &c.) into the room for reprimand, reprove. [f. OF *carpite* or It. *carpita* p.p. of *carpire* f. L *carpere* pluck, the fabric being perh. a patchwork; cf. F *charpie* lint]

carpho·logy, n. Delirious fumbling with bed-clothes &c. [f. Gk *karphologia* (*karphos* twig, *legō* pick, -Y[1])]

carpo-[1], comb. form of CARPUS.

carpo-[2], comb. form of Gk *karpos* fruit. Hence **carpo·**LOGY n.

car·pus, n. (anat.). Part of skeleton that unites hand &c. to fore-arm, eight small bones in higher vertebrates (in man, wrist; in horse, knee). [f. Gk *karpos* wrist]

ca·rriage (-rĭj), n. Conveying, transport; cost of conveying (*c.*-FREE; *c.-forward*, not prepaid); management (*of* enterprise &c.); passing (*of* Parl. motion &c.); manner of carrying (*c. of head, body*, &c.), bearing, deportment; wheeled vehicle for persons (*hackney, railway, -c.*), esp. four-wheeled private vehicle with two (*c. & pair*) or more horses (*c.-company, -folk*, who keep these), whence **ca·rriage**FUL (2) n.; wheeled support of gun (usu. *gun-c.*); wheeled framework of vehicle apart from body; (Mech.) sliding &c. part of machinery for shifting position of other parts; *c. candle* (hard kind worked by spring in tube); *c. clock* (going in any position); *c.-dog*, spotted Dalmatian; *c.-drive*, road in parks &c. Hence **ca·rriage**LESS a. [f. ONF *cariage* f. *carier* (CARRY, -AGE)]

ca·rriageable, a. Available for carriages (of road). [-ABLE]

ca·rrick bend, n. (naut.). Kind of knot or splice. [BEND[1]; *carrick* perh. f. obs. *carrack* armed merchant ship]

ca·rrier, n. In vbl senses; esp.: person plying for hire with cart for conveyance of parcels (*common c.*, legal term including also railway and steamship companies &c.); part of bicycle &c. for carrying luggage; person or animal that without catching a disease conveys its germs; *c.*-PIGEON; *c.-nation* &c., conducting oversea trade for others. [CARRY + -ER[1]]

ca·rriole, n. Small open carriage for one; covered light cart; Canadian sledge. [f. F *carriole*, med. L *carriola* dim. of *carra* CAR[1]]

ca·rrion, n. & a. Dead putrefying flesh; anything vile, garbage, filth; *c.-crow*, between raven & rook, feeding on c., small animals, &c.; (adj.) rotten, loathsome. [ME & ONF *caroine* perh. f. Rom. **caronia* f. L *caro carnis* flesh]

carronā·de, n. Short large-calibred ship's gun. [*Carron* orig. place of making + -ADE]

ca·rrot, n. (Plant with) tapering orange-coloured edible root; (pl.) red hair, red-haired person, whence **ca·rrot**Y[2] a. [f. F *carotte* f. L *carota* f. Gk *karōton* perh. f. *kara* head]

ca·rry[1], v.t. & i. Convey in vehicle, ship, hand, or head (as *news*), or on person (also of vehicle &c., or water, wind, &c., as subject; *c. corn*, from field to stack; *fetch & c.*, be underling; *c. all before* one, succeed; *c. weight*, be handicapped in horse-racing or fig.); conduct (*pipes c. water, wires c. sound*; *c. into effect*; *c. one back*, in fancy to earlier times; *c. off to prison*); transfer (figures to column of higher notation; *c. conviction*, implant one's own in other minds; *c. over, forward*, entries to new page or account); propel to specified distance (of gun &c., with obj. usu. omitted; also intr. = *go* of missile); cause or enable to go *to* (of motive, journey-money, &c.); bring *to* (of day's journey &c.); prolong, continue, *to* (*c. tower to 500 ft, modesty to excess*); win (prize; *c. it, the day*, succeed; *c. fortress* &c., capture; *c. hearers with* one, persuade); win victory for (candidate; *c.* one's *point, a motion, bill*); wear, have with one, possess, involve, (arms, a watch, &c.; *c.* one's BAT²; *c. weight, authority,* be influential; *c. with* one, remember; *loans c. interest, principles c. consequences*); hold in a certain way (*c.* one's *head, body,* one*self*; *c. sword* &c., in saluting-position); endure weight of, support, (*ships c. sail, piers c. dome*); *c. away,* inspire, transport, deprive of self-control, (Naut.) lose (mast &c.) by breakage; *c. off,* remove from life, win, render passable, *c. it off well,* make brave show; *c. on,* advance (process) a stage, continue, manage (business), (v.i.) go on with what one is doing, (colloq.) behave strangely, flirt or have amorous intrigue (*with*); *c. out,* put (principles, instructions, &c.) in practice; *c. over* (St. Exch.), keep over to next settling-day; *c. through,* bring safely out of difficulties, complete. [f. ONF *carier* f. LL *carricare* (L *carrus* CAR¹)]

ca·rry², n. (Mil.) *the* position of carrying sword; (Golf) ball's flight before pitching; portage between rivers &c.; range of gun &c.; *c.-over* (St. Exch.), process of carrying or amount carried over. [prec.]

cart, n., & v.t. & i. Strong two-wheeled vehicle (cf. WAGON) used in farming & for heavy goods, (also *spring, mail, dog,-c.*) light two-wheeled one-horse vehicle for driving in, (*put c. before horse,* reverse order, take effect for cause); *c.-horse,* thickset & fit for heavy work; *c.-ladder,* rack at sides or ends for increasing capacity; *c.-load,* = cartful, also large quantity of anything; *c.-road, -way,* too rough for carriages; *c.-wheel,* wheel of c., large coin as crown &c., lateral summersault of street urchins (*turn c.-w.*); *c.-whip,* long & heavy; *c.-wright,* maker of cc.; hence **car·t**AGE(4), **car·t**ER¹, **car·t**FUL(2), nn. (Vb) carry in a c.; work with a c.; (slang) defeat easily (in match, game, &c.). [prob. f. ON *kartr* cart cf. OE *cræt* of doubtful meaning]

carte, quarte (kart), n. Fencing position (*c. & tierce,* sword-play). [F (*q*-), f. It. *quarta* fourth]

carte blanche (F), n. Blank paper given to person to write his own terms on; full discretionary power. [F (CARD², BLANK)]

carte-de-visi·te (de, -zēt), n. Photograph 3½in. × 2¼. [F, = visiting card, its orig. purpose]

car·tel, n. Written challenge to duel; (agreement for) exchange of prisoners; (also *kartell*) manufacturers' union to keep up prices. [F, f. It. *cartello* dim. of *carta* CARD²]

Cartē·sian (-zhn), a. & n. (Follower) of Descartes or his philosophy or mathematical methods. Hence **Carte·sian**ISM (3) n. [*Cartesius* mod. L name of René Descartes, 1596–1650, -AN]

Carthu·sian (-z-), a. & n. (Member) of order of monks founded by St Bruno 1086; (member) of Charterhouse school founded on site of C. monastery. [f. L *Cartusianus* f. *Chatrousse,* place of their first monastery]

car·tilage (-ij), n. (Structure, part, in vertebrates, of) firm elastic tissue, gristle, (*temporary c.,* in the young, changing later to bone). So **cartilā·gin**OID a. [F, f. L *cartilago -inis*]

cartilā·ginous, a. Of, like, cartilage (*c. fish,* with c. skeleton). [f. L (*-osus,* see prec., -OUS)]

carto·graphy, n. Map-drawing. So **carto·**GRAPHER n., **carto**GRA·PHIC(AL) aa. [f. F *carte* chart (CARD²) + -GRAPHY; the correct form f. Gk would have *ch-*]

car·tomancy, n. Fortune-telling by playing-cards. [f. It. *carta* CARD², -MANCY]

car·ton, n. White disk within bull's-eye of target; cardboard box for holding goods or the cardboard used for these. [f. F as foll.]

cartoo·n, n., & v.i. & t. Drawing on stout paper as design for painting, tapestry, mosaic, &c.; full-page (or large) illustration, esp. on politics in comic paper; hence **cartoo·n**IST(3) n. (Vb) draw c., represent (person &c.) in a c. [f. F *carton* or It. *cartone* (*carta* CARD², -OON)]

cartou·che (-ōōsh), n. (Arch.) scroll ornament, e. g. volute of Ionic capital; tablet imitating, or drawing of, scroll with rolled-up ends, used ornamentally or bearing inscription; (Archaeol.) oval ring containing hieroglyphic names & titles of Egyptian kings &c. [F, f. It. *cartoccio* augmentative of *carta* CARD²]

car·tridge, n. Charge of explosive for firearms or blasting made up in case of paper, flannel, metal, &c. (small-arm *ball c.,* or *c.,* contains bullet also, *blank c.* the explosive only); *c.-belt,* with sockets for cc.; *c.-paper,* thick & rough, used also for drawing & for strong envelopes. [corrupt of prec.]

car·tulary, n. Collection of records; register. [f. med. L *c(h)artularium* f. L *cartula* dim. of *c(h)arta* CARD², -ARY¹]

că·runcle (*also* karŭ·-), n. Fleshy excrescence, as turkeycock's wattles. [f. 16th-c. F *caruncule* f. L *caruncula* (*caro carnis* flesh, -UNCLE)]

carve, v.t. & i. (p.p. *-ed,* sometimes *-en*). Cut (in gen. sense now only fig., as *c.* one's *way*); produce by cutting (statue, portrait, representation in relief or intaglio, inscription, design, *out of, in,* or *on,* material), change by cutting (material *into* something), cover or adorn (material) *with* figures cut in it, cut designs &c., whence **car·**VING¹(2) n.; cut up meat, cut up (meat &c.), at or for table (*carving-knife,* long for this purpose); subdivide (usu. *up*); *c. out,* take from larger whole, acquire esp. by the sword. [OE *ceorfan,* com.-Teut. cf. Du. *kerven,* prob. cogn. w. Gk *graphō* write]

car·vel, = CARAVEL; *c.-built,* with planks flush (cf. CLINKER-BUILT).

car·ver, n. In vbl senses; also, carving-knife, (pl.) carving knife & fork. [-ER[1]]

căryă·tid, n. Female figure used as pillar. [f. L f. Gk *karuatis -idos* priestess at Caryae]

cascā·de, n., & v.i. (Fall like a) waterfall, or one section of large broken waterfall; wavy fall of lace &c. [F, f. It. *cascata* (*cascare* to fall for *casicare* f. L *cas-* see CASE[1])]

cascar·a sagra·da (-ahda), n. Laxative drug from the bark of a tree. [Sp., = sacred bark]

case[1], n. Instance of thing's occurring; actual state of affairs (*is, is not, the c.,* is true, false); position, circumstances, in which one is, plight, (*in good, evil, c.,* well, badly, off); (Med.) person's diseased condition; instance of any disease. (Law) cause, suit, for trial; statement of facts in cause *sub judice,* drawn up for higher court's consideration (*judge states a c.*); cause that has been decided & may be cited (*leading c.,* one often cited & governing subsequent decisions); sum of arguments on one side (*that is our c.*; *make out* one's *c.,* prove it); (fig.) *c. of conscience,* matter in which conscience has to decide between conflicting principles. (Gram.) form of noun, adj., or pronoun, in inflected languages expressing relation to some other word in sentence (in uninflected languages, this relation itself apart from form). *In c.,* if, in the event that, lest; *in c. of,* in the event of; *in the c. of,* as regards (*i. t. c. o. Jones an exception was made*); *put* (*the*) *c. that,* suppose; *in any c.,* whatever the fact is, whatever may happen; *in that c.,* if that is true, should happen; *c.-law,* law as settled by precedent. [ME & OF *cas* f. L *casus -ūs* fall (*cadere cas-* fall)]

case[2], n., & v.t. Enclosure of something, box, bag, sheath, &c.; frame for plant-growing; glass box for showing specimens, curiosities, &c.; outer protective covering (of watch, sausage, seed-vessel, book, &c.); box with proper contents (*dressing-c.*); (Print.) receptacle with compartments (*upper c.,* capitals, *lower c.,* small letters); *c.-bottle,* square for fitting into c. with others; *ca·se-harden* v.t., harden surface of, esp. give steel surface to (iron) by carbonizing, (fig.) render callous; *c.-knife,* worn in sheath; *c.-shot,* or c., bullets in tin box fired from cannon without fuse, also = SHRAPNEL; *c.-worm,* = CADDIS. (Vb) enclose in c., surround *with,* (also with *up, over*); hence **ca·s**ING[1](3) n. [f. ONF *casse* (now *châsse*) f. L *capsa* (*capere* hold)]

cā·sĕin, n. A proteid or albuminoid, the basis of cheese. [L *caseus* cheese + -IN]

ca·semate, n. Vaulted chamber in thickness of wall of fortress, with embrasures. Hence **ca·semat**ED[2] a. [F, f. It. *casamatta* (*casa* house, perh. *matto* mad, also pseudo-)]

ca·sement (-s- *or* -z-), n. Metal or wooden hinged frame with glass forming (part of) window (often *c.-window*); (poet. &c.) window. [f. med. L *casamentum,* or f. CASE[2] + -MENT]

cā·sĕous, a. Of, like, cheese. [f. L *caseus* cheese + -OUS]

caser·n(e) (-z-), n. (Usu. pl.) small building(s) for troops between ramparts & houses of fortress. [F (*-e*), f. Sp. *caserna* (*casa* house)]

cash[1], n. (no pl.), & v.t. Ready money (*in, out of, c.,* having, not having, money; *c. down,* paid on the spot); *c. on delivery* (abbr. C.O.D.), forwarding of goods against c. to be paid to postman; (Banking &c.) specie, or specie and bank-notes; (Book-keeping) *c.-account,* to which only c. is carried, & from which all payments are made, *c.-book,* for record of c. received and paid; *c. payment,* in ready money; *c. price,* lowest, for ready money; hence **ca·sh**LESS a. (Vb) give or obtain c. for (note, cheque, &c.). [f. F *casse* (now *caisse*) box f. L *capsa* CASE[2]]

cash[2], n. (pl. *cash*). Kinds of E.-Ind. and Chinese small coin, esp. a Chinese coin perforated for stringing = $\frac{1}{1000}$ of tael. [ult. f. Tamil *kasu* a small coin by confusion with CASH[1]]

că·shew, n. W.-Ind. &c. tree with kidney-shaped fruit (*c.-nut*). [f. F *acajou* f. Braz. *acajoba*]

cashier·[1], n. Person in charge of bank's or merchant's cash. [f. F *caissier* (CASH[1], -IER)]

cashier·[2], v.t. Dismiss from service, depose; discard. [f. Flem. or Du. *casseren* cf. F *casser* f. L *quassare* (*quatere quass-* shake), with senses also of L *cassare* annul (*cassus* vain)]

ca·shmere, n. (Also *c. shawl*) shawl of fine soft wool of Cashmere goat; the material; imitation of it. Hence **cashmēr**E·TTE(2) n.

casi·no (-sē-), n. Public music or dancing room. [It., dim. of *casa* house f. L *casa* cottage]

cask, n. Wooden vessel (= BARREL[1]); this and its contents; varying measure of capacity. [perh. f. F *casque* helmet]

ca·sket, n. Small box, often of precious material & workmanship, for jewels, letters, cremated ashes, &c. [perh. dim. of prec. (-ET[1]), but quoted from a century earlier]

casque (kăsk), n. (hist., poet.). Helmet. [F, f. Sp. *casco*]

Cassa·ndra, n. Prophet of ill; unregarded prophet. [Trojan prophetess fated to prophesy truly & be unbelieved]

cassa·tion, n. Annulment; *Court of C.,* court of appeal (esp. of foreign countries). [f. LL *cassatio* (L *cassare* CASHIER[2], -ATION)]

cassa·va (-sah-), n. W.-Ind. &c. plant with tuberous roots; its starch or flour, bread made from these. [f. Haytian *casávi* &c.]

ca·sserole, n. A heat-proof earthenware vessel in which meat &c. is cooked & served (*en c.*, so served). [F]

ca·ssia (*also* -sha), n. Inferior kind of cinnamon; genus of plants yielding senna-leaves. [f. L f. Gk *kasia* f. Heb. *q'tsi'ah* (*qatsa'* cut off bark)]

ca·ssock, n. Long close tunic worn by some Anglican clergymen under gown or short surplice, or as ordinary attire. Hence **ca·ssock**ED[2] n. [f. F *casaque* etym. dub., perh. f. It. *casacca* habitation, also long coat, (*casa* see CASINO); cf. CHASUBLE]

cassole·tte, n. Vessel for burning perfumes; perfume-box with perforated top. [F, dim. of *cassole* dim. of *casse* pan]

ca·ssowary, n. Kinds of large running bird related to ostrich. [f. Malay *casuari*]

cast[1], v.t. & i. (*cast*). Throw (poet. or archaic exc. in spec. uses, as: *c. dice*; *c. a vote*, give or deposit it; *c.* LOTS; *c. ashore*; *c. net, hook, fly*; *casting-net*, one thrown & at once drawn in; *c. the* LEAD[1], in sounding; *c. anchor*; *c. in* one's *teeth*, reproach him with, *that*; *c. an eye, glance, look*; *c. a spell on*, bewitch; *c. light, a shadow, on*; *c. blame*, one's *cares, upon*; *c. into prison*); overthrow in a lawsuit; throw off, get rid of, lose, (*c. not a* CLOUT *till May be out*; *c. aside*, give up using, abandon; horse casts shoe; snake, deer, c. slough, horns; *cow, tree, c. calf, fruit*, drop prematurely; *c. soldier, policeman, horse*, dismiss, reject; *c. loose*, detach, detach oneself); reckon, calculate, (*c. accounts*, do sums; *c. a column of figures* &c., add up; *c. a* HOROSCOPE or *nativity*); arrange (c. facts into such a shape; c. actors *for* parts, parts *to* actors); form, found, (molten metal) *into* some shape, (figure &c.) *of* metal, whence **ca·st**ING[1](2) n.; *c. about*, go this way & that in search, devise means, (*for, to* do, *how*); *c. away*, reject, (pass., of ship) be wrecked; *c. back*, revert; *c. down*, depress; *c. in* one's *lot with*, share fortunes of; *c. off*, abandon, (Knitting) close loops & make selvedge; *c. up*, calculate. [f. ON *kasta* perh. cogn. w. L *gerere gest-*; it displaced OE *weorpan*, & has been displaced in ordinary literal use by *throw*]

cast[2], n. Throw of missile &c., distance so attained, (archaic); throw, number thrown, at dice, whence chance or try; throw of net, sounding-lead, or fishing-line (also in fishing the fly with hook & gut; & *good, bad*, &c. place for casting); casual lift in cart &c.; undigested food thrown up by hawk, owl, &c.; calculation, adding of columns in account; set of actors taking the parts in play, or the distribution among them; form into which any work is thrown; model made by running molten metal or pressing soft material into mould (also the negative mould itself); twist, inclination, (*c. in eye*, slight squint); tinge, shade, of colour; type, quality, (esp. *c. of features, c. of mind*). [f. prec.]

Că·staly, n. Fount of poesy. So **Castā·li**AN a. [f .L f. Gk *Kastalia* fountain of the Muses + -AN]

că·stanet (*or* -ĕ·t), n. (Usu. pl.) hard-wood or ivory instrument(s) used in pairs to rattle in time with dancing. [f. Sp. *castañeta* dim. of *castaña* f. L *castanea* chestnut]

ca·staway, n. & a. Reprobate; ship-wrecked (person). [p.p. of CAST[1], AWAY]

caste, n. Indian hereditary class, with members socially equal, united in religion, & usu. following same trade, having no social intercourse with persons of other cc.; hereditary more or less exclusive class elsewhere; this system, the position it confers (*lose, renounce, c.*, descend in social scale). Hence **ca·ste**LESS a. [f. Sp. & Port. *casta* lineage perh. orig. fem. of *casto* CHASTE]

că·stellan, n. Governor of castle. [ME & ONF *castelain* f. L *castellanus* (CASTLE, -AN)]

că·stellated, a. Castle-like; battlemented; (of district &c.) having castles. [f. med. L *castellatus* (CASTLE, -ATE[2])]

că·stigāte, v.t. Chastise, punish with blows or words; correct & emend (book &c.). Hence **castig**A·TION, **ca·stigat**OR[2], nn., **ca·stiga**TORY a. [f. L *castigare* (see -ATE[3]) perh. =*castum agere* make CHASTE]

ca·sting-vote, n. Vote that decides between two equal parties. [part. of CAST[1] in obs. sense, cf. CASTOR[2]]

cast iron, n., **cast-iron**, a. Iron shaped by being run into mould. (Adj.) made of c.i.; hard, untiring, rigid, unadaptable.

castle[1] (kah·sl, kă·sl), n. Large fortified building or set of buildings, stronghold; mansion that was once such; (Ireland) *The C.*, government system (f. Dublin C., seat of vice-regal court & government); *Englishman's house his c.*, none may force entrance; (Chess) piece made with battlemented top, also *Rook*; *c. in the air*, or as Gallicism *c. in Spain*, visionary project, day-dream, (so *c.-builder*). Hence **ca·stl**ED[2] a., **ca·stle**WISE adv. [f. ONF *castel* f. L *castellum* dim. of *castrum* fort]

ca·stle[2], v.t. & i. (chess). Move c. next king & king round c. (*c. the king*, or abs.). [f. prec.]

ca·stor[1], n. Substance obtained from beaver used in medicine & perfumery; (slang) hat. [obs. wd for beaver, F, f. L f. Gk *kastōr*]

ca·stor[2], **-er**, n. 1. Condiment-bottle for table, (pl.) cruet-stand; *c. sugar*, white, powdered. 2. Small swivelled wheel on leg of chair, table, &c. [CAST[1] + -OR[2], -ER[1];

sense 1 orig. of perforated-top bottle for casting pepper &c.; sense 2 f. obs. sense of CAST[1] = veer, turn]

ca·stor[3], n. Horny external knob inside horse's leg (also *chestnut*). [perh. = obs. *castane* chestnut (ONF *castanie* f. L *castanea*)]

ca·stor oil, n. Nauseous vegetable oil used as purgative (*cold-drawn c.o.*, expressed from seeds without heat) & lubricant. [etym. dub.; perh. so called as having succeeded CASTOR[1] in med. use]

castrameta·tion, n. (archaeol.). Laying out of camps. [f. F *castramétation* f. L *castra* camp, *metari* measure, -ATION]

castra·te, v.t. Remove testicles of, geld; deprive of vigour; expurgate (book). Hence **castra**TION n. [f. L *castrare*, -ATE[3]]

că·sual (-zhōō-, -zū-), a. & n. Accidental; irregular; undesigned; unmethodical, careless; *c. labourer*, who works when the chance comes; *c. poor*, who sometimes need poor-relief (also *c.* as noun); *c.-ward*, for their relief in work-house. Hence **ca·sual**LY[2] adv., **ca·sual**NESS n. [f. F *casuel* f. L *casualis* (*casus* CASE[1], -AL)]

ca·sualty, n. Accident, mishap, disaster, esp. (pl.) list or number of killed, wounded, & invalided, in a battle, march, war, &c., (sing.) wounded &c. person. [f. L *casualitas* (prec., -TY) on anal. of *royalty* &c.]

ca·suist (-zhōō-, -zū-), n. Person, esp. theologian, who lays down application of ethical rules to special cases, weighs conflicting obligations, classifies exceptions, & draws distinctions; sophist, quibbler. Hence **casui·st**IC(AL) aa., **casui·stical**LY[2] adv., **ca·suist**RY n. [f. F *casuiste* f. L *casus* CASE[1], -IST(3)]

cā·sus, L n. *c. belli*, act justifying war; *c. foederis*, circumstances contemplated in treaty as requiring the action of the parties when they arise.

cat[1], n. Small domesticated carnivorous quadruped (male, *Tom-c.*); *Wild C.*, larger native British kind; spiteful woman, scratching child; (Zool.) any member of genus *Felis*, as lion, tiger, panther, leopard (esp. *the Cc., the great Cc.*); c.-like animal of other species (*civet, musk, -c.*); (Hist.) pent-house in sieges; (also *cathead*) horizontal beam from each side of ship's bow for raising & carrying anchor; (also *c.-o'-nine-tails*) rope whip with nine knotted lashes formerly used for flogging sailors & soldiers, & still ordered by magistrates sentencing for certain criminal offences; six-legged tripod always standing on three of its legs; tapered short stick in game tip-c.; *turn c. in pan*, change sides, be turncoat; *c. may look at king*, rebuke to the exclusive; *care killed the c.* (for all its nine lives; therefore be cheerful); *wait for the c. to jump, see which way the c. jumps, cult of the jumping c.*, &c., of politician refusing to advise until public opinion has declared itself; *fight like Kilkenny cc.*, to mutual destruction; BELL[2] *the c.*; *not room to swing a c.*, confined space; *c.-&-dog life* &c., full of quarrels, esp. that of husband & wife; *c.- & -mouse Act* (slang), that enabling hunger-strikers to be released temporarily; *rain cc. & dogs*, very hard; *catbird*, Amer. thrush; *c. burglar* (who enters by climbing); *catcall*, shrill whistle (sound or instrument) expressing disapproval at theatre &c. (also as v.i. & t., use, reprove with, this); *c.-eyed*, able to see in dark; *catfish*, of various kinds, esp. large Amer. river-fish; *c.-ice*, milky-looking, bubbly, not solid, irregular by receding of water; *c.-lap*, slops, tea, &c.; *c.-mint*, blue-flowered aromatic plant; *c.-nap, -sleep*, brief, in chair &c.; *c.'s-cradle*, child's game with transfers of string between fingers of two players; *c.'s-eye*, precious stone of Ceylon & Malabar; *c.'s-foot*, ground-ivy; *c.'s-meat*, horse-flesh prepared & hawked as food for cc.; *c.'s-paw*, person used as tool by another, slight breeze rippling water in places; *c.'s-tail*, various plants, as Reed-mace; *c.-whisker*, fine adjustable wire in crystal wireless receiver. Hence **ca·t**HOOD n., **ca·t**LIKE a. [com.-Europ. f. L *catta*]

cat[2], v.i. & t. (colloq.). Vomit. [f. prec.]

cata-, cat-, cath-, pref. in wds taken from Greek, and in others formed with Gk materials or on Gk analogy; meanings: down, away, wrongly, mis-, entirely, down upon, according to, alongside of, thoroughly. [f. Gk *kata* prep.]

cătachrē·sis, n. Perversion, improper use, of words. So **catachrĕ·st**IC(AL) aa., **catachre·stical**LY[2] adv. [L, f. Gk CATA-(*khrēsis* f. *khraomai* use)]

că·taclasm, n. Violent break, disruption. [f. Gk CATA(*klasma* f. *klaō* to break)]

că·taclÿsm, n. Deluge (esp. in Geol. as required by theory of school that believed in repeated destructions of all life followed by new creations); political or social upheaval. Hence **catacly·sm**AL, **catacly·sm**IC, aa., **catacly·sm**IST(3) n. [f. F *cataclysme* f. Gk CATA(*klusmos* flood f. *kluzō* wash)]

că·tacomb (-kōm), n. Subterranean cemetery (orig. that under basilica of St Sebastian near Rome, supposed burying-place of Peter & Paul); (usu. pl.) the many Roman subterranean galleries with recesses excavated in sides for tombs; similar works elsewhere (in Paris, worked-out stone-quarries with bones from emptied churchyards); wine-cellar. [etym. dub.; the cc. generally, while in use, were not so called; that of St Sebastian was, *catacumbas* (Gk CATA- *kumbas* at the boats?) being possibly name of district or an inn]

cată·dromous, a. (zool.). Descending to

lower river or sea to spawn. [f. Gk CATA-(*dromos* -running) + -OUS]

că·tafălque (-k), n. Decorated stage for coffin or effigy of distinguished person during funeral service; open hearse. [F, f. It. *catafalco* etym. dub.; but cf. F *échafaud* SCAFFOLD]

Că·talan, a. & n. (Native, language) of Catalonia.

cătale·ctic, a. Wanting a syllable in last foot (of verse). [f. LL f. Gk CATA(*lēktikos* ceasing f. *lēgō* cease)]

că·talepsy, n. Disease in which trances occur; (Philos.) apprehension, grasping by mind. [f. med. L *catalepsia* f. Gk CATA(*lēpsis* seizure) see foll.]

catale·ptic, a. & n. Of, subject to, the disease catalepsy (n., c. person); (Philos.) of mental apprehension. [f. LL *catalepticus* f. Gk CATA(*lēptikos* seizing f. *lambanō* seize)]

că·talogue (-ŏg), n., & v.t. (Enumerate, enter, in a) complete list, usu. alphabetical or under headings, & often with particulars added to items; *c. raisonné* (-zonā), descriptive c. arranged according to subjects or branches of subject. Hence **ca·taloguer**[1] n. [F, f. LL f. Gk *katalogos* f. CATA(*lĕgō* choose) enroll]

cata·lpa, n. Kinds of tree with heart-shaped leaves & trumpet-shaped flowers. [W.-Ind.]

cată·lysis, n. (chem.). Effect produced by a substance that without undergoing change itself aids a chemical change in other bodies. So **catalȳ·tic** a. [f. Gk CATA(*lusis* loosing f. *luō* to loose) dissolution]

cătamară·n, n. Raft or float of logs tied side by side, longest in middle, used for communication with shore or short voyage; raft of two boats fastened side by side; quarrelsome woman. [f. Tamil *kaṭṭa-maram* tied tree]

că·tamīte, n. Sodomite's minion. [f. L *catamitus* f. Gk *Ganumēdēs* cup-bearer of Zeus]

catamou·ntain, cat-o'-m-, n. Leopard; wild quarrelsome person.

că·tapŭlt, n., & v.t. & i. Ancient engine worked by lever & ropes for discharging darts, stones, &c.; boy's shooting contrivance of forked stick & elastic; (vb) shoot or pepper (bird &c., or abs.) with this. [f. L *catapulta* f. Gk *katapeltēs* perh. f. CATA- + *pallō* hurl]

că·taract, n. Waterfall (prop. large & sheer, cf. CASCADE); downpour of rain, rush of water; (Path.) eye-complaint producing partial blindness; (Mech.) steam-engine governor acting by flow of water. [f. F *cataracte* f. L *cataracta* f. Gk *katarrhaktēs* f. CAT(*arassō* dash) or CATA-(*rrhēgnumi* break); the path. sense prob. f. obs. sense *portcullis*]

catarrh·, n. Inflammation of mucous membrane, a cold. Hence **catar·rhal** a. [f. F *catarrhe* f. L *catarrhus* f. Gk *katarrhous* f. *katarrheō* (CATA-, *rheō* to flow)]

că·ta(r)rhine, a. & n. (zool.). (Monkey) having nostrils close together, oblique, & directed downwards, & opposable thumbs on all limbs. [f. Gk CATA-, *rhis rhinos* nostril]

cata·strophĕ, n. Dénouement of drama; disastrous end, ruin; event subverting system of things, esp. in Geol. (cf. CATACLYSM, UNIFORMITARIAN), whence **catastro·phic(al)** aa., **cata·strophism**(3), **cata·strophist**(2), nn.; sudden, widespread, or signal disaster. [f. Gk CATA(*strophē* turning f. *strephō* to turn)]

Cataw·ba, n. U.S. grape & wine. [river *C.*]

catch[1], v.t. & i. (*caught pr.* kawt). Capture, ensnare (*c.* CRAB[1]), overtake (also *c. up*; *caught in storm*), lay hold of (also *c. hold of*; *c. a* TARTAR; *c. up habit* &c., adopt), be in time for (train &c.); surprise, detect, (*at* or *in*, or *doing*; *c. me!, him!*, you may be sure we shall not); hit (usu. with part specified; *caught him on the nose*; also *caught him a blow* or *one*); (of fire or combustible) ignite, be ignited, (*c. fire* or *c.*); be entangled, take hold, (usu. *c. in* a thing; *bolt catches*; *c. on*, become popular); snatch (esp. *c. up, away*; *c. at*, often fig. = be glad to get); intercept motion of (nail catches dress; at cricket, *c. ball*, prevent its touching ground off bat, also *c.* or *c. out* batsman, dismiss by doing this); *c. out*, (fig.) c. in a mistake &c., c. napping; check suddenly (*c.* one's *breath*; *c. up* speaker, interrupt); receive, incur, be infected with, (cold, a cold, a fever; a scolding, thrashing, or 'it'; enthusiasm, a habit, an accent; *c.* one's DEATH; *pond* &c. *catches*, is coated with ice); grasp with senses or mind (meaning, sound, tune; *c. a likeness*, see & reproduce it; *c. glimpse of*, see for a moment; *don't c. on*, fail to see meaning); arrest, captivate, (attention, eye, fancy; *c. Speaker's eye*, succeed in being called on to speak in H. of Commons); *c.-as-c.-can*, Lancashire wrestling style; *c.-drain*, along hillside to prevent water's running off; *c.-'em-alive-o*, sticky flypaper; *c.-fly*, a sticky-stemmed plant; *catch-penny* (adj.), claptrap, intended merely to sell; *catchweed*, Goosegrass; *catchword*, word so placed as to draw attention, e.g. first of dictionary article, rhyming word in verse, last word (cue) of actor's speech, first word of page anticipated at foot of previous one, also influential temporary phrase in politics, religion, &c. Hence **ca·tchable** a., (-)**catcher**[1](1, 2) n. [*catch* & CHASE are respectively f. ONF *cachier* & OF *chacier* (now *chasser*) both f. LL **captiare* (L *captus* captive f. *capere* take); the gen. sense of *catch* (*take*, not *pursue*) is excl. E, the orig. meanings (still in Rom.) having been taken by the later adoption CHASE[2]]

catch[2], n. Act of catching; amount of fish caught; chance of, success in, catching at cricket (also *a good, safe, c.*, one skilful at it); cunning question, deception, surprise; *c.-out*, act of catching out, circumstance that upsets calculations; contrivance for checking motion of door &c.; thing or person caught or worth catching (*no c.*, bad bargain, unwelcome acquisition); (Mus.) composition for several voices, second &c. beginning same melody when first &c. is a line further on, usu. with arrangement for ludicrous verbal combinations. [f. prec.]

ca·tching, a. In vbl senses; esp.: infectious; attractive. [-ING[2]]

ca·tchment, n. *C.-basin,-area*, from which rainfall flows into river &c. [CATCH[1], -MENT]

ca·tchpole, -pōll, n. Sheriff's officer, bum-bailiff. [f. med. L *cacepollus* cf. OF *chacepol* chase-fowl (CHASE, L *pullus* fowl)]

ca·tchup, mis-spelling of KETCHUP.

ca·tchy, a. Attractive; easily caught up (of tune &c.) [CATCH[1] + -Y[2]]

cate, n. (Usu. pl.) choice food. [for obs. *acate* f. OF *acat* purchase f. *acater* now *acheter* buy f. LL AC(*captare* frequent. of L *capere* take) catch at]

cateche·tic(al) (-kĕ-), aa. Of, by, oral teaching; according to a, or the Church, catechism; consisting of, proceeding by, question & answer. Hence **cateche·tical**LY[2] adv. [f. L f. Gk *katēkhētikos* f. *katēkhētēs* oral teacher (*katēkheō* CATECHIZE), -IC]

că·techism (-k-), n. Instruction by question & answer; published example of this, esp. on religious doctrine (*Church C.*, the Anglican; *Longer & Shorter C.*, of Presbyterians); series of questions put to any one. Hence **catechi·sm**AL a. [f. L *catechismus* (foll., -ISM)]

că·techize (-k-), v.t. Instruct by question & answer, or by use of Church Catechism; put questions to, examine. Hence or cogn. **ca·techi**ST(1), **ca·techiz**ER[1], nn. [f. L *catechizare* f. Gk *katēkhizō* f. CAT(*ēkheō* sound) make hear]

că·techu (-tshōō), n. Astringent substances with much tannin from bark, wood, or fruits, of Eastern plants. [f. Malay *kachu*]

cătechu·men (-kū-), n. A convert under instruction before baptism. [f. F *catéchumène* f. pass. part. of Gk *katēkheō* CATECHIZE]

cătego·rical, a. (Logic: of proposition) unconditional, absolute; explicit, direct, plain-speaking; (Ethics) *c. imperative*, bidding of conscience as ultimate moral law. Hence **catego·rical**LY[2] adv. [f. L f. Gk *katēgorikos* f. CAT(*ēgoros* -speaking) + -AL]

că·tegory, n. (Orig. Gk meaning, *statement*) one of a possibly exhaustive set of classes among which all things might be distributed (the cc. of Aristotle are: substance, quantity, quality, relation, place, time, posture, possession, action, passion); one of the *a priori* conceptions applied by the mind as frames to material supplied by sense; class, division. [f. L f. Gk *katēgoria* statement as prec.]

catē·na, n. Connected series. [L, = chain]

catē·nary, catenār·ian, aa. & nn. (Like) curve formed by uniform chain hanging freely from two points not in one vertical line (*c. bridge*, suspension, hung from such chains). [f. L *catenarius* (prec., -ARY[1], -AN)]

că·tenate, v.t. Connect like links. So **caten**ATION n. [f. L *catenare* as prec., -ATE[3]]

cā·ter[1], n. The four of cards or dice. [f. F *quatre* f. L *quatuor* four]

cā·ter[2], v.i. Purvey food (usu. *for*); provide amusement &c. *for*. Hence **ca·ter**ER[1] n. [f. obs. noun *cater* (now *caterer*) = obs. *acater* f. OF *acateor* buyer (CATE, -OR[2])]

că·teran, n. (Sc.). Highland fighting-man, marauder, cattle-lifter. [f. Gael. *ceathairne* peasantry]

cā·ter-cousin, n. Intimate; *be cc.*, on good or familiar terms. [perh. f. CATER[2] as feeding together]

că·terpillar, n. Larva of butterfly or moth; rapacious person; (Mech.) endless articulated steel band passing round & worked by two wheels of a tank, tractor, or vehicle required to cope with rough ground. [perh. f. OF *chatepelose* lit. hairy-cat, with *-s* dropped as pl. sign, & spelling influenced by vb *pill* rob, strip]

că·terwaul, v.i., & n. (Make) cat's screaming; quarrel like cats. [CAT, WAUL]

ca·tgut, n. Material used for strings of fiddle &c. made of twisted intestines of sheep, horse, or ass (not cat); stringed instruments. [expl. of *cat* doubtful]

cath-. See CATA-.

cathar·sis, n. (Med.) purgation; outlet to emotion afforded by drama (ref. to Arist., *Poet.* 6). [f. Gk *katharsis* (*kathairō* cleanse f. *katharos* clean)]

cathar·tic, a. & n. (med.). Purgative (medicine). [f. L f. Gk *kathartikos* as prec.]

Cathay·, n. (Archaic & poet. for) China. [*Kitah*, race name]

cathē·dral, a. & n. (Also *C. church*) principal church of diocese, with bishop's throne; *c. utterance* &c., delivered EX CATHEDRA. [f. med. L *cathedralis* f. L f. Gk CAT(*hedra* chair f. *hed-* sit), -AL]

Ca·therine-wheel, n. Circular spoked window or window-compartment; rotating firework; lateral summersault (*turn cc.*). [spiked wheel in St Catherine's martyrdom]

că·theter, n. (med.). Tubular instrument for passing into bladder. [L, f. Gk *kathetēr* f. CAT(*hiēmi* send)]

că·thode, n. (electr.). Negative pole of current. [f. Gk CAT(*hodos* way) descent]

că·tholic, a. & n. 1. Universal; of interest or use to all men; all-embracing, of wide sympathies, broad-minded, tolerant; *C. Epistles*, encyclical (those of James, Peter, Jude, & John—2 & 3 *John* being irregularly included—; cf. CANONICAL). 2. (Eccl.) *C. Church*, whole body of Christians; *c.*, belonging (a) to this, (b) to the church before separation into Greek or Eastern & Latin or Western, (c) to the Latin church after that separation (cf. ORTHODOX), (d) to the part of the Latin church that remained under the Roman obedience after the reformation, (e) to any church (as the Anglican) claiming continuity with (b); orthodox, in accord with the church in any of above senses, esp. = ROMAN CATHOLIC as (d) in contrast with Protestant, Reformed, Lutheran, &c.; *C. King, his C. Majesty*, of Spain; hence **catho·li**CALLY, **ca·tholic**LY[2], advv., **catho·lic**ISM(2, 3) n., **catho·lic**IZE(3), v.t., **catho·lico-** comb. form. (N.) member of the church in above senses; a Roman Catholic (cf. *C. emancipation* &c., i.e. of Roman Cc.); *Old C.*, member of party that seceded from Rome 1870–1 in Germany. [f. F *catholique* f. L f. Gk *katholikos* f. CATH- *holou* on the whole, universally]

catholi·city, n. Comprehensiveness, freedom from prejudice; wide prevalence; agreement with Catholic or R.-C. Church doctrine, catholicism. [prec., -ITY]

cathŏ·licŏn, n. Panacea. [F, f. Gk *katholikon* neut. CATHOLIC]

Că·tiline, n. Profligate conspirator. [*Catilina* Roman noble d. 63 B.C.]

ca·tkin, n. Downy hanging inflorescence of willow, birch, &c. [f. Du. *katteken* (CAT[1], -KIN)]

ca·tling, n. Small cat; fine cat-gut; amputating knife. [-LING[1](2); surg. sense unexpl.]

cato·ptric, a. Of mirror, reflector, or reflexion. Hence **cato·ptr**ICS n. [f. Gk *katoptrikos* f. CAT(*optron* f. *op-* see, *-tron* instr. suf.)]

ca·tsup. Var. of KETCHUP.

ca·ttle, n. Live stock; oxen (as *c. & sheep*); (slang) horses; *black c.*, oxen of Scotch & Welsh highland breeds, orig. black; contemptible persons; *c.-feeder*, machine regulating amount of food for c.; *c.-leader*, nose-ring; *c.-lifter*, c.-stealer; *c.-*PEN[1]; *c.-piece*, picture with c.; *c.-plague*, contagious disease of c., rinderpest. [ME & ONF *catel* f. LL *captale* f. L *capitale* neut. CAPITAL in sense *chief property*; cf. CHATTEL, to which the orig. meaning of c. now belongs]

Caucā·sian (-shn), a. & n. (Member) of the white race, Indo-European. [the *Caucasus*, supposed starting-place, + -IAN]

cau·cus, n., & v.t. & i. Local political usu. elective party committee for fighting elections, defining policy, &c. (gen. used only of opponents' organization); *the c.*, c. system as a political power; hence **cau·cus**DOM n. (Vb) use the c. system; organize, dictate to, by its means; hence **cau·cus**ER[1] n. [U.S. wd (in sense *meeting*) perh. f. Algonkin = elder]

cau·dal, a. Of, at, like, tail. Hence or cogn. **cau·dal**LY[2] adv., **cau·d**ATE[2] a. [f. L *cauda* tail + -AL]

cau·dle, n. Warm gruel with spice, sugar, & wine, for invalids, esp. women in childbed. [f. ONF *caudel* f. med. L *caldellum* dim. of L *cal(i)dum* hot drink (*calidus* warm)]

caught. See CATCH[1].

caul, n. Plain part at back of woman's cap; membrane enclosing foetus; portion of this sometimes found on child's head (good omen, & charm against drowning); = OMENTUM. [f. F *cale* small cap etym. dub.]

cau·ldron, cal-, n. Large boiling-vessel (usu. of deep basin shape with hoop handle & removable lid). [f. ONF *caudron* f. L *caldarium* hot bath (L *calidus* warm, -ARY[1]), -OON]

caule·scent, a. (bot.). With visible stem. [f. L *caulis* stalk after *arborescent* &c.]

cau·liflower (kŏ-), n. Cabbage with large fleshy flower-head. [f. F *chouflori* (now *-fleur*) f. L *caulis* stem + F p.p. of L *florēre* to flower, w. assim. in E to L *caulis* & E *flower*]

cau·līne, a. (bot.). Of, on, stem. [f. L *caulis* stem, -INE[1]]

caulk (kawk), v.t. Stop up seams of (ship), stop up (seams), with oakum & melted pitch (or, in iron ship, by striking plate-junctions with blunt chisel). Hence **caul·k**ER[1] n. (in vbl senses, &, slang, = final dram). [f. OF *cauquer* squeeze f. L *calcare* tread (*calx* heel)]

caulo-, comb. form of Gk *kaulos* or L *caulis* stem. [-O-]

cau·sal (-z-), a. Of, acting as, expressing, due to, a cause or causes; of the nature of cause and effect. Hence **cau·sal**LY[2] adv. [f. L *causalis* (*causa*, -AL)]

causă·lity, n. The being, having, or acting as, a cause; relation of cause and effect, doctrine that everything has cause(s). [prec., -ITY]

causa·tion (-z-), n. Causing, producing an effect; relation of cause and effect; doctrine that all things have causes, whence **causa·tion**ISM(3), **causa·tion**IST (2), nn. [f. L *causatio* pretext, but w. sense f. med. L *causare* to cause (L *causa*), -ATION]

cau·sative (-z-), a. Acting as cause, productive *of*; (Gram.) expressing cause. Hence **cau·sative**LY[2] adv. [f. F *causatif* f. L *causativus* (*causari* give as pretext, -IVE)]

cause[1] (-z), n. What produces an effect; antecedent(s) invariably and unconditionally followed by a certain phenomenon; person who, agent that, occasions something; ground, reason, motive, for action; adequate motive or justification (esp. *show c.*); *efficient c.*, producing force, *material c.*, the requisite matter, *formal c.*, the idea or definition, *final c.*, purpose; *First C.*, the Creator. (Law, and from law) matter about which person goes to law; his case (*plead a c.*); law-suit; side of any dispute espoused by person or party, militant movement, propaganda, (*make common c. with*); *c.-list*, of cases awaiting trial. [F, f. L *causa*]

cause[2] (-z), v.t. Effect, bring about, produce; induce, make, (person or thing *to* do, *to be* done something to). Hence **cau·**SER[1] n. [f. med. L *causare* (cf. L *causari* plead causes, give as pretext)]

cause célèbre (kōz sĕlĕ·br), n. (pl. *causes célèbres*, pr. as sing.). Law-suit that excites much attention. [F]

cau·seless, a. Fortuitous; without natural cause; unjustifiable, groundless, whence **cau·seless**LY[2] adv. [-LESS]

causerie (kōzerē·), n. (pl. *-s*, pr. as sing.). Newspaper article (or spoken address) of an informal or conversational kind, esp. on literary subjects. [F]

causeuse (kōzer·z), n. (pl. *-s*, pr. as sing.). Small sofa for two. [F]

cau·seway, cau·sey, (-z-), n., & v.t. Raised road across low or wet place or piece of water; raised footway by road; (vb) provide with c. [*causeway* = *causey* (ONF *caucie* f. LL *calciata* trodden f. L *calcare* f. *calx -cis* heel) + WAY]

cau·stic, a. & n. (Substance) that burns or corrodes organic tissue (*Common* or *Lunar c.*, nitrate of silver for surg. use); sarcastic, biting, whence **cau·sti**CALLY adv.; (Math.) (surface, curve) formed by intersection of rays reflected or refracted from curved surface. Hence **causti·**CITY n. [f. L f. Gk *kaustikos* (*kaustos* burnt f. *kaiō* burn, -IC)]

cau·terize, v.t. Sear with hot iron or caustic; (fig.) make callous. Hence **cauteriz**A·TION n. [f. F *cautériser* f. LL *cauterizare* f. Gk *kautērion* branding-iron (*kaiō* burn)]

cau·tery, n. Metal instrument for searing tissue; cauterizing. [f. L f. Gk *kautērion* see prec.; second sense on anal. of nouns in -ERY]

cau·tion (-shn), n., & v.t. Prudence, taking care, avoidance of rashness, attention to safety, (*c. money*, deposited as security for good conduct, esp. at Universities & Inns of Court), whence **cau·ti**OUS a., **cau·tious**LY[2] adv.; warning (in drill, preliminary word of command), fact that acts as warning, warning with reprimand (*dismissed with a c.*), whence **cau·tion**ARY[1] a.; (slang) extraordinary thing, hideous or strange person. (Vb) warn (person, often *against*, *to* or *not to* do); warn & reprove. [F, f. L *cautionem* (*cavēre caut-* take heed, -ION)]

cavalcā·de, n. Company of riders. [F, f. Pr. *cavalcada* f. *cavalcar* ride f. LL *caballicare* f. L *caballus* horse; see -ADE]

căvalier·, n. & a. Horseman; courtly gentleman, gallant, esp. as escorting a lady, whence **cavalier·** v.t.; 17th-c. royalist; (adj.) off-hand, curt, supercilious, whence **cavalier·**LY[2] adv. [earlier *-llero*, *-liero*, f. Sp.; present form F, f. It. *cavaliere* (*cavallo* see CAVALRY, -IER)]

cava·lly, n. Kinds of tropical fish, horse-mackerel. [f. Sp. *cavalla* mackerel]

că·valry, n. Horse-soldiers (usu. w. pl. vb). [f. F *cavallerie* f. It. *cavalleria* (*cavallo* f. L *caballus* horse, -ERY)]

cavati·na (-tē-), n. Short simple song; smooth melodious air. [It.]

cave[1], n. Underground hollow usu. with horizontal opening, den; IDOLS *of the c.*; (Pol.) secession of part of party on some question (ADULLAMITE), the seceders; *c.-dweller*, esp. of prehistoric men living in cc.; *c.-fish*, *-man*, *-rat*, *-spider*, *-swallow*, kinds living in caves (also *c.-bear* &c. of extinct kinds whose remains are found in cc.). Hence **ca·ve**LET n. [F, f. L *cava* neut. pl. of *cavus* adj. hollow]

cave[2], v.t. & i. Hollow out, make into a c.; form political CAVE[1]. *C. in*: subside, recede, (of earth &c. over hollow; of wall yielding inwards cf. BULGE); yield to pressure, submit, withdraw opposition; smash in (esp. person's hat or head), spoil shape of. [f. prec.; but *c. in* may be f. obs. *calve* fall in cf. Flem. *inkalven* Du. *af-kalven*, in similar sense]

cā·vē[3], int. (schoolboy slang). Look out! (warning of master's approach). [L, = beware]

cā·vĕăt, n. (Law) process to suspend proceedings (*enter, put in, a c.*). Warning; proviso. [L, = let him beware]

cā·vĕăt e·mptor, L sent. (= let the buyer see to it) disclaiming responsibility for buyer's disappointment.

că·vendish, n. Tobacco softened, sweetened, & pressed into cake, negro-head. [?]

că·vern, n. Underground hollow (rhet.). [f. F *caverne* f. L *caverna* (*cavus* hollow)]

ca·verned, a. Like, in, with, cavern(s). [-ED[2]]

ca·vernous, a. Full of caverns; as of, huge or deep as, a cavern (*c. darkness, mouth, eyes*); porous. [f. L *cavernosus* (CAVERN, -OSE[1])]

căviar·, caviare· (-ar), n. Sturgeon-roe pickled, eaten as relish; *c. to the general*, good thing unappreciated by the ignorant. [16th-c. It. has *caviale*, etym. dub.]

că·vil, v.i. (-ll-), & n. (Raise) captious objection (*at, about*). Hence **ca·vill**ER[1] n.

[f. OF *caviller* f. L *cavillari* (*cavilla* mockery)]
că·vity, n. Empty space within solid body. [f. F *cavité* (L *cavus* hollow, -TY)]
cavor·t, v.i. (U.S. slang). Prance. [?]
că·vy, n. Amer. rodent. [f. *cabiai* native name in French Guiana]
caw, n. & int., & v.i. & t. (Make) rook's, crow's, raven's, cry; *c. out,* utter in cawing tone. [imit.]
Ca·xton, n. Book printed by W. C. (first Engl. printer, d. 1492); printing-type in imitation of C.'s.
cay, n. Insular bank or reef of coral, sand, &c. [=QUAY]
caye·nne, n. (Also *C. pepper*) pungent red pepper of capsicum. [f. Braz. *kyynha* assim. to *Cayenne* capital of French Guiana]
cay·man, cai·man, n. Kinds of large saurian of crocodile family (prop. an American genus with round short muzzle). [prob. f. Carib *acdyouman*]
cd, cmd, = COMMAND² *paper.*
ce, = CEE.
cēanō·thus, n. A flowering shrub. [Gk]
cease¹, v.i. & t. Desist *from*; stop do*ing*, be*ing*, &c.; (of feelings, actions) come to an end; bring to an end (strife, endeavours, &c.); (Mil.) *c. fire,* discontinue firing. [ME *cessen* f. F *cesser* f. L *cessare* frequent, of *cedere cess-* yield]
cease², n. Ceasing (obs. exc. in *without c.*, incessantly). Hence **cea·se**LESS a., **cea·seless**LY² adv., **cea·seless**NESS n. [f. OF *ces* (*cesser* see prec.)]
cĕ·cils, n. pl. Kind of fried forcemeat balls. [?]
cē·city, n. Blindness (usu. fig.). [f. L *caecitas* (*caecus* blind, -TY)]
cē·dar, n. Kinds of cone-bearing tree including C. of Lebanon, Atlas C., & Deodar; various trees resembling c.; = c.-wood. Hence (poet.) **ce·darn** (-EN⁵) a. [ME & OF *cedre* f. L f. Gk *kedros*]
cede, v.t. Give up, grant, admit, surrender (territory). [f. L *cedere* retreat]
cedi·lla, n. Mark (¸) written under c to show that it is sibilant. [Sp., f. It. *zediglia*, dim. of *zēta* Gk name of Z]
cee, n. The letter C; *cee spring, C-spring,* spring so shaped supporting carriage body.
ceil (sēl), v.t. Line roof of (room), whence **cei·l**ING¹(2) n. [prob. f. F *ciel* heaven, ceiling, f. L *caelum* heaven, w. infl. of L *caelare* emboss]
cĕ·ladon, n. & a. Willow green. [F, perh. f. name of character in D'Urfé's *Astrée*]
cĕ·landīne, n. Two yellow-flowered plants, Greater C., & Lesser C. (Pilewort, Fig-wort). [f. OF *celidoine* f. L *chelidonia* f. Gk *khelidonion* (*khelidōn* swallow); for *-n-* cf. *passenger*]
cĕlane·se, n. Kind of artificial silk. [proprietary name]
-cele (sēl), in medical compound words, = tumour of the —. [f. Gk *kēlē* tumour]
cĕ·lebrant, n. Officiating priest, esp. at Eucharist. [f. L *celebrare* (foll.), -ANT]
cĕ·lebrate, v.t. & i. Perform publicly & duly (religious ceremony &c.); officiate at Eucharist; observe, honour, with rites, festivities, &c. (festival, event); publish abroad, praise, extol, (p.p.) famous. Hence **celebr**A·TION n. [f. obs. *celebrate* adj. f. L *celebrare* (*celeber -bris* frequented), -ATE²,³]
celĕ·brity, n. Being famous; well-known person. [f. L *celebritas* (*celeber* see prec., -TY)]
celĕ·riăc, n. Turnip-rooted celery. [f. CELERY, *-ac* unexplained]
celĕ·rity, n. Swiftness, dispatch (of living movement or agency). [f. F *célérité* f. L *celeritatem* (*celer* swift, -TY)]
cĕ·lĕry, n. Plant of which blanched stem is used as salad & vegetable. [f. F *céleri* ult. f. Gk *selinon* parsley]
cele·ste, n. & a. Sky blue; (also *voix c.*) organ & harmonium stop; (adj.) sky-blue. [f. F *céleste* f. L *caelestis* (*caelum* heaven)]
cele·stial, a. & n. Of the sky (*c. globe, map*); heavenly, divine, divinely good, beautiful, &c., whence **cele·stial**LY² adv.; *C. Empire,* China (transl. of native title; so *C.* =Chinese, a. & n.). [OF (L *caelestis* see prec., -AL)]
cĕ·libate (-*at*), a. & n. (Person) not married, bound or resolved not to marry; unmarried (of life, habits). So **ce·lib**ACY n., **celibat**AR·IAN a. & n. [f. L *caelebs -ibis* unmarried + -ATE²(2)]
cell, n. 1. Dependent nunnery or monastery (hist.); anchoret's one-roomed dwelling; cottage (poet.); grave (poet.); single person's small room in monastery or prison (*condemned c.*, for one condemned to death); compartment in bees' comb; (Electr.) voltaic apparatus with only one pair of metallic elements, unit of battery. 2. Enclosed cavity in organism or mineral (*cc. of brain,* imaginary compartments assigned to various faculties); (Biol.) portion of protoplasm usu. enclosed in membrane, ultimate element of organic structures; (Zoophytes) cup-like cavity of individual polype in compound polypidom. Hence (-)**cell**ED², **ce·lli**FORM, aa. [f. OF *celle* f. L *cella* small room]
ce·llar, n., & v.t. (Put, store, in an) underground room; (also *wine-c.*) place in which wine is kept, one's stock of wine (*keeps a good c.*); *c.-flap,* trapdoor into c.; *c.-plate,* in pavement over hole into coal-c. Hence **ce·llar**AGE n. [f. OF *celier* f. L *cellarium* (prec., -AR², -ARY¹)]
ce·llarer, n. Monastic keeper of wine & provisions. [f. OF *celerier* (*celier* see prec., -IER)]
cellare·t, n. Case or sideboard for keeping winebottles in dining-room. [-ET¹]
'ce·llo (tsh-), n. (Short for) VIOLONCELLO.

ce·llular, a. Of, having, small single rooms or compartments or cavities; *c. shirt* &c. (of open texture); (Physiol.) consisting of cells (as *c. tissue*); *c. plant*, without distinct stem, leaves, &c. Hence **cellulă·rITY** n. [as foll., -AR[1]]

ce·llule, n. (anat.). Cell or cavity (see CELL, 2; the derivatives are formed from *cellule*, not *cell*). Hence or cogn. **ce·llulATE**[2], **-ated, celluli·FEROUS, ce·llulOUS.** aa., **cellulA·TION** n., **ce·llulo-** comb. form. [f. L *cellula* (*cella* CELL, -ULE)]

ce·lluloid, a. & n. Like cells: (n.) substance like ivory, made chiefly of cellulose. [irreg. f. CELLULOSE[2] + -OID]

ce·llulose[1], a. Consisting of cells. Hence **cellulŏ·sITY** n. [CELLULE, -OSE[1]]

ce·llulose[2], n. (chem.). Substance forming solid framework of plants. [F, f. L *cellula* CELLULE + -OSE[2]]

Ce·lsius. See CENTIGRADE.

Celt[1], Kelt, n. Member of one of the peoples akin to the ancient Galli (Bretons, Cornish, Welsh, Irish, Manx, Gaels). [f. F *Celte* f. L *Celta*; cf. Gk *Keltoi, Keltai*, pl.]

celt[2], n. (archaeol.). Bronze or stone (or iron) chisel-edged prehistoric implement. [wd founded on a perh. false reading in Vulgate of *Job* xix. 24—*stylo ferreo, et plumbi lamina, vel celte* (v.l. *certe*) *sculpantur*; cf. FYLFOT]

Ce·ltic, K-, a. & n. (Language) of the Celts; *the C. fringe*, the Scots, Irish, Welsh, & Cornish, in relation to the U.K. Hence **ce·ltICALLY** adv., **ce·lticISM**(2,4) n., **ce·lticIZE**(2, 3) v. i. & t. [f. L *celticus* (CELT[1], -IC)]

ce·lto-, comb. form of CELT[1]. Hence **celto·LOGIST, celtoMA·NIAC, ce·ltoPHIL,** nn. [-O-]

ceme·nt, n., & v.t. Substance applied as paste & hardening into stony consistence for binding together stones or bricks & for forming floors, walls, &c., strong mortar of calcinated lime & clay (*hydraulic c.*, hardening under water); any substance applied soft for sticking things together; (fig.) principle of union; substance for stopping teeth; bony crust of tooth-fang. (Vb) unite (as) with c.; apply c. to, line or cover with c. [ME *cyment* f. OF *ciment* f. L *caementum* for *caedimentum* (*caedere* cut, -MENT) chippings of stone]

cĕ·metery, n. Place for burials, not being a churchyard. [f. L f. Gk *koimētērion* dormitory (*koimaō* put to sleep)]

cē·nobite. See COENOBITE.

cĕ·notaph, n. Sepulchral monument to person whose body is elsewhere; *the C.*, that in Whitehall commemorating the dead of the great war; tomb from which one has risen. [f. F *cénotaphe* f. L f. Gk *kenotaphion* (*kenos* empty, *taphos* tomb)]

cense, v.t. Perfume, worship, with burning incense. [f. obs. *cense* noun short for INCENSE[2]]

ce·nser, n. Vessel in which incense is burnt. [f. OF (*en*)*censier* f. L *incensum* INCENSE[1], -ER[2](2)]

ce·nsor, n., & v.t. Ancient-Roman magistrate drawing up register or census of citizens & supervising public morals; person expressing opinions on others' morals & conduct; official licensing, or suppressing as immoral, seditious, or inopportune, books, plays, news, or military intelligence (vb, exercise such control over, make excisions or changes in); various University officials; (Psycho-anal.) *censor*(*ship*), a power by which elements of the Unconscious are inhibited from emerging into the consciousness. Hence or cogn. **censor·IAL** a., **ce·nsorSHIP** n. [L, f. *censēre* tax, -OR[2]]

censor·ious, a. Fault-finding, over-critical. Hence **censor·iousLY**[2] adv., **censor·iousNESS** n. [f. L *censorius* (CENSOR, -ORY) + -OUS]

ce·nsure (-sh*er*), n., & v.t. Adverse judgement, expression of disapproval, reprimand. (Vb) blame, criticize unfavourably, reprove; hence **ce·nsurABLE** a. [f. F *censure(r)* f. L *censura* (*censēre* tax, -URE)]

ce·nsus, n. Official numbering of population with various statistics (in Gt Britain taken every ten years); *c.-paper*, form left at every house to be filled up with names, ages, &c., of inmates. [L, f. *censēre* to rate]

cent, n. *Per c.*, for, to, in, every hundred (in stating proportion, esp. of interest); *three* &c. *per cents*, public securities at 3 % &c.; *c. per c.*, interest equal to principal; (U.S. &c.) hundredth of a dollar; typical small coin (*don't care a c.*). [f. F *cent* or L *centum* hundred]

ce·ntal, n. Weight of 100 lb. used for corn. [f. L *centum* hundred, perh. after QUINTAL]

ce·ntaur, n. Horse with human body, arms, and head, taking the place of its neck and head; hybrid creation, person or thing of double nature; name of a constellation; perfect horseman. Hence **ce·ntaurESS**[1] n. [f. L f. Gk *kentauros* etym. dub.]

ce·ntaury, n. Name of various plants. [ult. f. Gk *kentaurion* (*kentauros* see prec.) said to have been used medicinally by centaur Chiron]

centenā·rian, a. & n. (Person) a hundred years old. [as foll. + -AN]

centē·nary (*also* sĕ·-), a. & n. Of a hundred years. (N.) space of a hundred years reckoned from any point in a century; centennial anniversary, celebration of it. [f. L *centenarius* (*centeni* a hundred each, -ARY[1])]

cente·nnial, a. & n. Of, having lived or lasted, completing, a hundred years; (of) the hundredth anniversary. [f. L *centum* hundred, & as BIENNIAL]

centĕ·simal, a. Reckoning, reckoned, by hundredths. Hence **cente·simal**LY[2] adv. [f. L *centesimus* hundredth (*centum* hundred) + -AL]

centi-, comb. form of L *centum* hundred, =1/100 of the denomination in the metric system. Hence **ce·nti**GRAMME, **ce·nti**LITRE (-lēter), **ce·nti**METRE, nn.

ce·ntigrade, a. Having a hundred degrees (of Celsius's thermometer, with freezing-point 0° & boiling-point 100°). [F, f. L *centum* a hundred + *gradus* step]

centi·llion, n. Hundredth power of a million (1 with 600 ciphers). [*centum* (prec.), BILLION]

centime (sahntē·m, or as F), n. French coin = 1/100 of a franc. [F]

ce·ntipede, n. Many-footed wingless crawling animal. [f. L *centipeda* (*centum* hundred, *pes pedis* foot)]

ce·ntner, n. German weight, about 1 cwt. [G, f. L *centenarius* CENTENARY]

ce·nto, n. Composition made up of scraps from other authors. [L, = patchwork garment]

ce·ntral, a. Of, in, at, from, containing, the centre; leading, principal, dominant; *C. Empires, Powers,* Germany & Austria-Hungary. Hence **centra·li**TY n., **ce·ntral**LY[2] adv., **ce·ntral**NESS n. [f. L *centralis* (*centrum* CENTRE, -AL)]

ce·ntralism, ce·ntralist, nn. (Upholder of) a centralizing system. [prec. + -ISM(3), -IST(2)]

ce·ntralize, v.i. & t. Come, bring, to a centre; concentrate (administration) at single centre; subject (State &c.) to this system. Hence **ce·ntraliza·**TION n. [CENTRAL, -IZE(3)]

ce·ntre[1], ce·nter, n. & a. Middle point (strictly, equidistant from ends of line measuring along it, or from extremities of regular surface or body, or from all points in circumference of circle or sphere, & at mean distance from all points in periphery of irregular surface or body); point, pivot, axis, of revolution (in lathe, conical adjustable bearing to hold revolving object); point of concentration or dispersion, nucleus, source; (Fenians &c.) organizer, leader, (esp. *head-c.*); (hit on) part of target between bull's-eye and outer; (Arch.) wooden mould for arch or dome while building; (Mil.) main body of troops between wings; (Pol.; orig. f. French) *the C.*, men of moderate opinions (*left-c., left,* radical grades; *right-c., right,* reactionary); (Footb.) *c. forward* or c. (player in Assoc. game); *c. of attraction,* (Physics) to which bodies tend by gravity, (fig.) drawing general attention; *c. of gravity,* that point in body which being supported body remains at rest in any position; *c. of mass,* point (in relation to body) any plane passing through which divides body into two parts of equal weight; DEAD *c.*; *c.-piece,* ornament for middle of table; *c.-rail,* third rail on mountain railways for cogged wheel &c.; *c.-second(s),* seconds hand mounted on centre arbor of clock or watch; *c.-bit,* boring-tool with c. point & side cutters; *c.-board,* (flat-bottomed boat with) board for lowering through keel to prevent lee-way; hence **ce·ntre**LESS, **ce·ntr**IC(AL), aa., **ce·ntrical**LY[2] adv., **centri·ci**TY n. (Adj.) at, of, the c.; hence **ce·ntre**MOST a. [F (-*re*), f. L f. Gk *kentron* spike (*kenteō* to prick)]

ce·ntre[2], ce·nter, v.i. & t. Be concentrated *in, on, at, round, about*; place in c.; mark with a c.; concentrate *in* &c.; find c. of. [f. prec.]

centri·fugal, a. Flying, tending to fly, from centre; *c. force,* with which body revolving round centre tends to fly off, inertia; *c. machine* &c., in which c. force is utilized; (Bot.) *c. inflorescence,* in which end flower opens first & side ones in downward order. Hence **centri·fugal**LY[2] adv. [f. L *centrum* CENTRE[1] + *-fugus* -flying (*fugere* flee) + -AL]

centri·petal, a. Tending towards centre; *c. force, machine* &c., *inflorescence,* opposite of CENTRIFUGAL. Hence **centri·petal**LY[2] adv. [f. L *-petus* -seeking (*petere* seek) and as prec.]

ce·ntro-, comb. form of L *centrum* CENTRE[1], =centre-, central, centrally.

ce·ntūple, a., n., & v.t. Hundredfold; (vb) multiply by a hundred. [f. LL *centuplus* for L *centuplex* (*centum* hundred, *-plic-* fold)]

centū·plicate, a. & n. (-*at*), & v.t. (-āt). =prec., esp. *in c.*, of things of which a hundred copies are produced. [f. L *centuplicare* as prec., -ATE[2,3]]

centūr·ion, n. Commander of century in Roman army. [f. L *centurio -onis* (foll.)]

ce·ntury, n. (Rom. hist.) company in army, orig. of 100 men; political division for voting. A hundred of something (esp., 100 runs at cricket); one of the hundred-year periods counting from a received epoch, esp. from birth of Christ (*first c.*, 1–100, *nineteenth c.*, 1801–1900, &c.); any hundred successive years, centenary. [f. L *centuria* (*centum* hundred)]

cephă·lic, a. Of, in, the head. [f. F *céphalique* f. L f. Gk *kephalikos* (*kephalē* head, -IC)]

-cepha·lic. = -CEPHALOUS.

cĕ·phalo-, comb. form = head-, head-&—. [see CEPHALIC, -O-]

ce·phalopod, n. Mollusc with distinct tentacled head. [prec. + Gk *pous podos* foot]

cephalothor·ax, n. Coalesced head & thorax of spider, crab, &c. [CEPHALO-, THORAX]

-cĕ·phalous, last element esp. of anthropological terms = -headed, as *brachyc.*, with short head. [f. Gk *kephalē* head + -OUS]

cerā·mic, k-, a. Of the art of pottery. Hence **cera·mics, cĕ·ramist**(2), nn. [f. Gk *keramikos* (*keramos* pottery, -IC)]

cera·stium, n. Kinds of hoary-leaved herb. [mod. L, f. Gk *kerastēs* horned (*keras* horn)]

ce·rato-, comb. form of Gk *keras -atos* horn, = horn-&-—, horny-, & esp. of the cornea.

Cer·berus, n. Three-headed dog guarding entrance to Hades (*sop to C.*, something to propitiate an official, guard, &c.). [L, f. Gk *Kerberos*]

cere, n. Naked wax-like membrane at base of some birds' beaks. [f. F *cire* f. L *cera* wax]

cēr·ēal, a. & n. Of corn or edible grain; (n., usu. pl.) kind(s) of grain used for human food. [f. L *Cerealis* (*Ceres* goddess of corn, -AL)]

cĕrebe·llum, n. Little or hinder brain. [L, dim. of CEREBRUM]

cĕ·rebral, a. Of the brain; *c. letter*, consonant sounded by turning tongue-tip to top of palate. [f. F *cérébral* (CEREBRUM, -AL)]

cerebra·tion, n. Working of the brain, esp. *unconscious c.*, of results reached without conscious thought. [CEREBRUM + -ATION]

cĕ·rĕbrum, n. The brain proper, in front of and above the cerebellum. Hence **ce·rebro-** comb. form; *cerebro-spī·nal*, of brain & spine (*c.-s. meningitis*, spotted fever). [L]

cere·ment (sēr-), n. (usu. pl.). Grave-clothes. [f. F *cirement* (*cirer* to wax, wrap in waxed cloth, see CERE)]

cĕremō·nial, a. & n. With or of ritual or ceremony, formal; hence **ceremo·nialism**(3), **ceremo·nialist**(2), nn., **ceremo·nially**[2] adv. (N.) system of rites; formalities proper to any occasion; observance of conventions; (R.-C. Ch.) book of ritual. [f. L *caerimonialis* (CEREMONY, -AL)]

cĕremō·nious, a. Addicted or showing addiction to ceremony, punctilious. Hence **ceremo·niously**[2] adv., **ceremo·niousness** n. [f. L *caerimoniosus* (foll., -OUS)]

cĕ·remony, n. Outward religious rite or polite observance; empty form; stately usage; formalities; punctilious behaviour (*without c.*, off-hand; *stand upon c.*, insist on conventions, keep one's distance); *Master of the Cc.*, superintending forms observed on state or public occasions. [prob. f. OF *cerymonie* f. L *caerimonia* cf. Skr. *karman* work, rite, (*kri* do)]

ce·riph, (now rare for) SERIF.

ceri·se (-ēz), a. & n. (Of) a light clear red. [F, = CHERRY]

cēr·ium, n. A metal. Hence **cer·ic**(1), **cer·ous,** aa. [f. planet *Ceres*, discovered (1801) just before, + -IUM]

cēro-, comb. form of L *cera* or Gk *kēros* wax.

cēropla·stic, a. Modelled, of modelling, in wax. Hence **ceropla·stics** n. [f. Gk *kēro-* = CERO(*plastikos* adj. f. *plassō* to mould)]

cert, n. (slang). Event or result certain to happen. [abbr. *certain*]

cer·tain (-tn, -tĭn), a. Settled, unfailing; unerring, reliable; sure to happen; indisputable; convinced (*of, that*); destined, undoubtedly going, *to* do; that might but need not or should not be specified (*a c. person, lady of a c. age*), some though perhaps not much (*felt a c. reluctance*), existing but probably unknown to hearer (*a c. John Smith*); *for c.*, assuredly. [OF (L *certus* orig. p.p. of *cernere* decide, -AN)]

cer·tainly (-tn-), adv. Indubitably; infallibly; confidently; admittedly; (in answers) I admit it, no doubt, yes. [prec. + -LY[2]]

certainty (-tn-), n. Undoubted fact (*bet on a c.*, usu. dishonestly with secret knowledge of result), indubitable prospect; thing in actual possession; absolute conviction (*of, that*); *to, for, a c.*, beyond possibility of doubt. [f. OF *certaineté* (CERTAIN, -TY)]

cer·tēs (-z), adv. (archaic). Assuredly, I assure you. [OF, also *a certes* perh. f. L *a certis* from sure (grounds)]

certi·ficate (-at), n., & v.t. Document formally attesting a fact, esp. the bearer's status, acquirements, fulfilment of conditions, right to company shares, &c.; *bankrupt's c.*, stating that he has satisfied legal requirements & may recommence business. (Vb) furnish with, license by, c.; hence **certi·fica·tion** n. [f. med. L *certificatum* neut. p.p. (foll.)]

cer·tify̆, v.t. Attest formally, declare by certificate; (of doctor) officially declare (person) insane, whence **cer·tifiable** a.; inform certainly, assure. Hence **cer·tifīer**[1] n. [f. F *certifier* f. med. L *certificare* (CERTAIN, -FY)]

certiorār·ī, n. Writ from higher court for records of case tried in lower. [L wd in writ]

cer·titude, n. Feeling certain, conviction. [F, f. LL *certitudinem* (CERTAIN, -TUDE)]

ceru·lĕan (-ōō-), a. Deep-blue. [f. L *caeruleus* prob. for *caelul-* (*caelum* sky) + -AN]

ceru·men (-ōō-), n. Ear-wax. So **ceru·minous** a. [f. L *cera* wax on anal. of *albumen*]

cēr·use (-ōōs), n. (Also *white lead*) a white paint from carbonate & hydrate of lead, esp. as cosmetic. [f. L *cerussa* prob. f. a Gk *kēroussa* fem. of *kēroeis* waxy (CERO-)]

cervī·cal (*also* ser·vī-), a. (physiol.). Of the neck. So **cervi·co-** comb. form. [f. L *cervix -īcis* neck + -AL]

cer·vīne, a. Of, like, deer. [f. L *cervinus* (*cervus* deer + -INE[1])]

Cesare·vitch, -witch, (-rā-), n. Tsar's eldest son. [Russ.]

cess, n. Tax, rate, (now displaced by *rate* in Engl., but used in various senses in Ireland, Scotland, and India). [prop. *sess* for obs. *assess* n. see ASSESS]

cessa·tion, n. Ceasing; pause. [f. L *cessatio* (*cessare* CEASE[1], -ATION)]

ce·sser, n. (legal). Coming to an end, cessation, (*of* term, liability, &c.). [F (CEASE[1], -ER[4])]

ce·ssion (-shn), n. Ceding, giving up, (of rights, property, or esp. of territory by State). [F, f. L *cessionem* (*cedere cess-* go away, -ION)]

ce·ssionary, n. = ASSIGN[2]. [f. med. L *cessionarius* as prec. + -ARY[1]]

ce·sspit, n. Midden. [see foll.]

ce·sspool, n. Well sunk for soil from water-closet &c., retaining solids & letting liquid escape (also fig., as *c. of iniquity*). [prob. f. It. *cesso* privy f. L *secessus* SECESSION]

ce·stoid, a. & n. (zool.). Ribbon-like (intestinal worm, as tape-worm). [f. L f. Gk *kestos* girdle + -OID]

cēt-, comb. form = of spermaceti, in chem. names. [f. L *cetus -i* f. Gk *kētos -eos* whale]

cēta·cean, a. & n. (Member) of the mammalian order containing whales. So **ceta·ceous** a. [as prec., -ACEAN]

cē·teosaur, -saur·us, n. Fossil saurian. [f. Gk *kētos -eos* whale & *sauros* lizard]

cĕ·terach (-k), n. Kinds of fern with frond-backs covered with scales. [med. L, etym. dub.]

cē·teris pă·ribus, adv. Other things being equal. [L]

Chablis (shă·blē), n. A French white wine. [place name]

Cha·dband, n. Unctuous hypocrite. [person in Dickens's *Bleak House*]

chafe (tsh-), v.t. & i., & n. Rub (skin, to restore warmth); make, become, sore by rubbing; (of beast, river) rub itself *against* (bars, rocks); irritate; show irritation, fume, fret. (N.): (sore made by) friction; state of irritation, pet, (*in a c.*). [f. OF *chaufer* f. L *calefacere* (*calēre* be hot, *facere* make)]

chā·fer (tsh-), n. Kinds of beetle, usu. the COCKCHAFER. [OE *cefer* cf. G *käfer* perh. f. *kaf-* gnaw cf. JOWL]

chaff (tsh-), n., & v.t. 1. Separated grain-husks; chopped hay and straw; bracts of grass-flower; spurious substitute (*caught with c.*, easily deceived or trapped); worthless stuff; *c.-cutter*, machine chopping fodder; hence **cha·ffy**[2] a.; (vb) chop (straw &c.). 2. Banter (n. & v.t.). [OE *ceaf* cf. OHG *cheva* perh. f. *kef-* gnaw cf. JOWL; sense 2 may be fig. use of 1 (starting with noun), or (starting with vb) be = CHAFE (anger playfully)]

chă·ffer (tsh-), v.i. & t., & n. Haggle, bargain (*c. away*, = BARGAIN *away*); hence **cha·fferer**[1] n. (N.) = chaffering. [ME *ch(e)apfare* f. OE *céap* see CHAPMAN + *faru* FARE]

chă·ffinch (tsh-), n. Common British small bird. [CHAFF (f. haunting barndoor) + FINCH]

chā·fing-dish, n. Vessel with burning charcoal &c. inside for keeping warm things placed on it. [f. obs. sense of CHAFE = warm]

chagrin (sha*grē·n*), n., & v.t. (Affect with) acute disappointment or mortification. [f. F *chagrin(er)* f. Turk. *saghri* rump of horse, prepared hide, SHAGREEN; sense by metaphor f. use of shagreen for friction]

chain (tsh-), n., & v.t. Connected series of metal or other links (ENDLESS *c.*); fetters, confinement, restraining force; necklace, watchguard, &c.; sequence, series, set, (*of* proof, events, posts, mountains; *ladies' c.*, movement in quadrille); jointed metal-rod measuring-line, its length (66 ft); (also *c.-shot*) two balls or half balls joined by c. for cutting masts &c.; (Naut.) fastening for shrouds below CHANNEL[2] (also *c.-plate*), *the cc.* (also the *fore, mizen, main, -cc.*), whole contrivance (channel, c.-plate, & DEAD-eyes) for widening basis of shrouds; *c. armour, mail*, made of interlaced rings; *c. bridge*, = suspension; *c. coupling*, extra coupling of railway vans in case of accident to screw coupling; *c. moulding*, archit. ornament with link carving; *c.-stitch*, ornamental sewing like chain, (sewing machine) simple sewing (cf. LOCK[3]-*stitch*); *c.-wale*, = CHANNEL[2]; *c.-wheel*, transferring power by c. fitted to its edge; hence **chai·nless** a., **chai·nlet** n. (Vb) secure, confine, with c. (lit. & fig.). [f. OF *chaeine* f. L *catena*]

chair (tsh-), n., & v.t. Separate seat for one, of various forms (ARM[1] or *elbow*, BATH[1], CURULE, DECK[1], EASY[1]; *take a c.*, sit down); seat of authority; professorship; mayoralty (*past* or *above the C.*, *below the C.*, of alderman who has, has not, been mayor); seat, office, of person presiding at meeting, public dinner, &c. (*take, leave, the c.*, begin, end, the proceedings); chairman (*address, appeal to, the c.*; '*chair! chair!*', protest against disorder); (Railway) iron or steel socket holding rail in place; (Hist.) = SEDAN; *c. bed*, that can be unfolded into c. (Vb) install in c. of authority; place in c. and carry aloft (winner of contest, election, &c.). [f. OF *chaëre* f. L f. Gk *kathedra* (CATHEDRAL)]

chair·man, n. (pl. *-men*; fem. *chair-*

woman). Person chosen to preside over meeting, permanent president of committee, board, &c. (*C. of Committees*, in Houses of Parl., presiding instead of Lord Chancellor & Speaker when House is in Committee), whence **chair·man**SHIP n.; keeper of Bath chair; (Hist.) one of two sedan-bearers.

chaise (shāz), n. Pleasure or travelling carriage of various shapes, usu. now low, four-wheeled, & open, with one or two ponies; POST-c. [F, var. of *chaire* f. OF *chaëre* CHAIR]

chalcĕ·dony (k-), **cal-**, n. Precious stone of quartz kind with many varieties as agate, cornelian, chrysoprase. [f. L *c(h)alcedonius* f. Gk *khalkēdōn* etym. dub.]

chalco- (k-), comb. form esp. in mineralogical terms =copper-, brass-. [f. Gk *khalkos*]

chalco·graphy, n. Art of engraving on copper. [prec., -GRAPHY]

chalcopyr·īte (-īr-), n. A copper ore, yellow or copper pyrites. [CHALCO-, PYRITE]

Chaldē·an, Chăldee·, (k-), a. & n. (Native) of Chaldea or Babylon; soothsayer, astrologer. [f. L f. Gk *khaldaios* + -AN]

cha·ldron (tshawl-), n. Coal measure, 36 bushels. [f. OF *chauldron* as CAULDRON]

chalet (shă·lā), n. Swiss mountain dairy-hut; Swiss peasant's wooden cottage; villa in this style; street lavatory. [F-Swiss wd perh. dim. of *casella* dim. of It. *casa* house]

chă·lice (tsh-), n. Goblet; eucharistic wine-cup (*mixed c.*, with water ceremonially added); (poet.) flower-cup, whence **cha·lic**ED[2] a. [OF (now *calice*), f. L CALIX]

chalk[1] (tshawk), n. White soft earthy limestone used for burning into lime & for writing & drawing; coloured preparation of like texture used in crayons for drawing; *as like as c. & cheese*, unlike in essentials; *by (a) long chalk(s)*, by far (f. use of c. to score points in games); *c.-bed*, stratum of c.; *c.-pit*, quarry; *c.-stone*, gouty concretion like c. in tissues & joints esp. of hands & feet. [OE *cealc*, com.-WG, cf. G *kalk*, f. L *calx -cis* lime]

chalk[2], v.t. Rub, mark, draw, write, write *up*, with c.; *c. out*, sketch, plan as thing to be accomplished (often *for* oneself). [f. prec.]

chal·ky, a. Abounding in, white as, chalk; like or containing chalk-stones. Hence **chal·ki**NESS n. [-Y[2]]

chă·llenge[1] (tsh-), n. Calling to account (*sentry's c.*, 'Who goes there?'); exception taken (e.g. to juryman); summons to trial or contest, esp. to duel, defiance. [f. OF *chalenge* f. L *calumnia* CALUMNY]

cha·llenge[2], v.t. Call to account (of sentry, & fig.); take exception to (evidence, juryman), dispute, deny; claim (attention, admiration, &c.); invite to contest, game, or duel, defy. Hence **cha·llenge**ABLE a., **cha·lleng**ER[1] n. [f. OF *chalenger* f. LL *calumniare* (CALUMNY)]

chă·llis (tsh-), n. Lady's-dress fabric. [?]

chalў·bēate (k-), a. Impregnated with iron (of mineral water or spring). [irreg. for *chalybate* f. L f. Gk *khalups -ubos* steel + -ATE[2]]

cham (k-), n. *Great c.*, autocrat (of dominant critic &c., esp. Dr Johnson). [obs. form of KHAN]

chamade (shamah·d), n. Signal for retreat on drum or trumpet. [F, f. Port. *chamada* (*chamar* f. L *clamare* call, -ADE)]

cha·mber (tshā-), n. Room, esp. bedroom (poet. or archaic; but *c. music*, for performance in room, not at theatre, church, &c.; *c. concert*, of c.-music); (pl.) set of rooms in larger building, esp. in Inns of Court, let separately, judge's room for hearing cases not needing to be taken in court; (hall used by) deliberative or judicial body, one of the houses of a parliament; *C. of Commerce, Agriculture*, board organized to forward these in a district; (also *c.-pot*) vessel for urine; *c. counsel*, lawyer giving opinions in private, not practising in court; *chambermaid*, housemaid at inn; enclosed space in body of animal or plant, or in machinery &c. (esp. part of gun-bore, of larger diameter in some cannon, separate in revolver, that contains charge). Hence (-)**chamber**ED[2] a. [f. F *chambre* f. L *camera* f. Aryan *kam-* cover over cf. Gk *kamara* vault]

chamberlain (tshā·mberlĭn), n. Officer managing household of sovereign or great noble; *Lord Great C. of England*, hereditary holder of ceremonial office; *Lord C. of the Household*, with part management of Royal Household, & licenser of plays. Hence **cha·mberlain**SHIP n. [OF, f. Teut. **kamarling* (OHG *chamarling*) f. *kamara* f. L *camera* see prec.]

chamē·leon (k-), n. Small prehensile-tailed long-tongued lizard with power of changing colour & of living long without food; inconstant person. Hence **chameleŏ·nic** a., **chame·leon-**LIKE, a. & adv. [f. L f. Gk *khamaileōn* (*khamai* on ground, *leōn* lion)]

chă·mfer (tsh-), v.t., & n. Bevel symmetrically (right-angled edge or corner); (n.) surface so given (*hollow* or *concave c.*, made as with gouge instead of chisel); channel, flute, (v.t. & n.). [f. OF *chanfraindre* (CANT[1], L *frangere*) lit. break-corner]

chamois (shă·mwah, *in sense 2* shă·mĭ), **n.** 1. Wild mountain antelope of goat size. 2. (Also *c.-leather, shammy, shammy-leather*) soft pliable leather from sheep, goats, deer, &c. [F, prob. f. Swiss Rom.;

cf. It. *camozza*, also G *gemse* (OHG *gamz*)]

cha·momile, = CAMOMILE.

champ (tsh-), v.t. & i., & n. Munch (fodder) noisily; work (bit) noisily in teeth; (make) chewing action or noise. [prob. imit.]

champāg·ne (sh-), n. Kinds of wine from E. France (usu. white & sparkling). [name of province, = foll.]

champaign (tshă·mpān), n. (Expanse of) open country. [f. OF *champaigne* = CAMPAGNA]

cha·mperty, n. (law). The offence of assisting a party in a suit in which one is not naturally interested with a view to receiving a share of the disputed property. **cha·mpert**ous a. [f. F *champart* feudal lord's part of produce, f. L *campus* field, *pars* part]

cha·mpion (tsh-), n. & a., & v.t. Person who fights, argues, &c., for another or for a cause (*King's, Queen's, C.*, or *C. of England*, hereditary official at coronations); athlete &c., animal, plant, &c., that has defeated all competitors (often as adj., *c. boxer, c. turnip, c. idiot, c. blunder*). Hence **cha·mpion**LESS a., **cha·mpion**SHIP n. (Vb) maintain the cause of. [OF, f. LL *campionem* nom. *-io* fighter (L *campus* CAMP[1])]

champlevé (shă·mplevā), a. & n. *C. enamel* or *c.*, enamel in which the colours are filled into hollows made in the surface (cf. CLOISONNÉ) [F, =raised field]

chance[1] (tsh-), n. & a. Way things fall out, fortune; undesigned occurrence; opportunity; possibility; probability (esp. in pl., as *the cc. are against it*); absence of design or discoverable cause; course of events regarded as a power, fate; *by c.*, as it falls or fell out, without design; *on the c.*, in view of the possibility (*of, that*); *take* one's *c.*, let things go as they may, consent to take what comes; *the main c.*, that of getting rich; *stand a* (*good, fair*) *c.*, have a prospect; *chance-*, = by c., as *c.-sown tree*; (adj.) fortuitous (*a c. companion, meeting*). [f. OF *cheance* f. LL *cadentia* n. (L *cadere* fall, -ENCE)]

chance[2], v.i. & t. Happen (archaic in abs. use, getting rare in constrr. *it chanced that, he chanced to* do); *c. upon*, happen to find, meet, or come upon; (colloq.) risk (esp. *c. it*). [f. prec.]

cha·ncel (tsh-), n. Eastern part of church reserved for clergy, choir, &c., & usu. railed off. [OF, f. LL *cancellus* f. L *cancelli* lattice-bars]

cha·ncellery (tsh-), **-ory,** n. Position, staff, department, official residence, of a chancellor; office attached to embassy or consulate. [f. OF *chancelerie* (*chancelier* see foll., -RY)]

cha·ncellor (tsh-), n. State or law official of various kinds; *Lord C.* (also *C. of England, Lord High C.*), highest judge, presiding in H. of Lords & in Chancery Div. of Supreme Court; *C. of* EXCHEQUER; *C. of Duchy of Lancaster*, member of government (legally representative of King as Duke of Lancaster), often Cabinet minister who does not desire departmental work; *C. of bishop* or *diocese*, bishop's law officer; *C. of Garter* or other order, who seals commissions &c.; titular head of university (Vice-C. performing duties); (Germany, Austro-Hungary) chief minister of State. Hence **cha·ncellor**SHIP n. [ME *c(h)anceler* f. OF *c(h)ancelier* (-OR[2]) f. L *cancellarius* law-court usher (*cancelli* grating)]

chance-me·dley, n. (Law) action, esp. homicide, mainly but not entirely unintentional; inadvertency. [AF *chance medlée* (see MEDDLE) mixed chance]

cha·ncery (tsh-), n. Lord Chancellor's court, a division of High Court of Justice (formerly a separate court of equity for cases with no remedy in common-law Courts, whence the meaning, still in U.S. & in literature, of court of equity); office for public records; (Boxing) *in c.*, with head held under opponent's arm being pommelled (from difficulty of getting clear of old Court of C.). [shortened f. CHANCELLERY]

chancre (shă·nk*er*), n. Venereal ulcer. [F, =CANCER]

cha·ncy, a. Uncertain, risky. [CHANCE[1], -Y[2]]

chăndelier· (sh-), n. Branched hanging support for several lights. [F, see foll.]

cha·ndler (tsh-), n. Dealer in candles, oil, soap, paint, & groceries (*corn-c.*, in corn; *ship-c.*, in cordage, canvas, &c.). Hence **cha·ndl**ERY(1) n. [f. OF *chandelier* (L *candela* CANDLE, -ARY[1])]

change[1] (tshānj), n. Alteration; substitution of one for another, variety (*for a c.*); whence **cha·nge**FUL(1), **cha·nge**LESS, aa.; *Change* (now usu. but wrongly *'Change*), place where merchants meet (*on C.*, engaged there); arrival of moon at fresh phase (prop. at new moon only); *c. of clothes*, second outfit in reserve; lower coins given for higher one or for foreign money; money returned as balance of that tendered for article (*take* one's, *the, c. out of*, avenge oneself on); (bell-ringing, usu. pl.) different orders in which peal can be rung (*ring the cc.* fig., exhaust ways of putting or doing thing). [OF, f. LL *cambium* (*cambire* CHANGE[2])]

change[2], v.t. & i. Take another instead of (*c.* one's *coat*); resign, get rid of, *for*; give or get smaller or foreign coin for (money); put on different clothes; go from one to another of (*thing changes hands*, passes to different owner; *c. houses, carriages*; also abs. = c. trains, boats, &c.); give & receive, exchange, (*c. places with, we changed places*); make or become different (often *to, into, from*), (moon) arrive at fresh phase, esp. become new moon; *c. colour*, turn pale or blush; *c.* one's *feet* (colloq.), put on other shoes &c.; *c. front*, take new position in argument &c.; *c.* one's *condition*, marry; *c.* one's *mind*, adopt new plan or opinion; *c.* one's *note* or *tune*, become more humble, sad, &c.; *c. step, foot, feet*, time other foot to drum in marching. [f. OF *changer* f. LL *cambiare* (*cambium* f. L *cambire* barter cf. Gk *kamp-* turn back)]

cha·ngeable, a. Irregular, inconstant; alterable. Hence or cogn. **cha·nge**ABI·LITY, **cha·ngeable**NESS, nn. [F, see prec., -ABLE]

cha·ngeling, n. Thing or child substituted for another by stealth, esp. elf-child thus left by fairies. [CHANGE² + -LING¹]

cha·nnel¹ (tsh-), n., & v.t. (-ll-). Natural or artificial bed of running water; (Geog.) piece of water, wider than strait, joining two larger pieces, usu. seas (*The C.*, English C.); tubular passage for liquid; course in which anything moves, direction, line; medium, agency; groove, flute. (Vb) form cc. in, groove; cut out (*way* &c.). [f. OF *chanel* var. of CANAL]

cha·nnel² (tsh)-, n. Broad thick plank projecting horizontally from ship's side abreast of mast to broaden base for shrouds; (mod., sing. or pl.) level of deck (*rolling cc. under*). [for *chainwale* (WALE) cf. *gunnel* for *gunwale*]

chant (tsh)-, n., & v.i. & t. Song; (Mus.) short melody with long reciting-note for psalms & canticles (*single, double, quadruple*, as one, two, four, verses are sung to it); measured monotonous song; singsong intonation in talk. (Vb) sing; utter musically; intone, sing to a c.; *c. the praises of*, constantly praise; *c. horses*, sell fraudulently. [f. F *chant(er)* song, sing, f. L *cantus -ūs, cantare*, (*canere cant-* sing)]

chantage (F) n. Blackmailing.

cha·nter, n. In vbl senses; also: melody-pipe, with finger-holes, of bagpipe; (also *horse-c.*) swindling horse-dealer. [-ER¹]

chantere·lle (tsh-), n. Yellow edible fungus. [F, dim. f. L f. Gk *kantharos* drinking-cup]

cha·nticleer (tsh-), n. (Personal name for) domestic cock. [f. OF *chantecler* (CHANT, CLEAR), name in *Reynard the Fox*]

cha·ntress (tsh-), n. Female singer (archaic or poet.). [f. OF *chanteresse*, see CHANTER, -ESS¹]

cha·ntry (tsh-), n. Endowment for priest(s) to sing masses for founder's soul; priests, chapel, altar, so endowed. [f. OF *chanterie* (*chanter* CHANT, -ERY)]

chă·nty (sh-), n. Sailors' song in heaving. [prob. f. F *chantez*, imperat. pl. of *chanter* see prec.]

chā·ŏs (k-), n. Formless void or great deep of primordial matter (*C.*, this personified as eldest of the gods); utter confusion. Hence (irreg.) **chaŏ·tic** a., **chao·tic**ALLY adv. [L, f. Gk *khaos*; *-otic* on false anal. of *erotic* &c.]

chap¹ (tsh-), v.t. & i., & n. Crack (t. & i.) in fissures (usu. of skin, by wind &c., also of dried-up earth &c.). (N., usu. pl.) crack(s), open seam(s), esp. in skin; hence **cha·ppy**² a. [ME *chappen*, cf. MDu. *cappen*, & CHIP, CHOP]

chap², chop, n. (Pl.) jaws, esp. of beasts (*lick* one's *cc.*, w. relish or anticipation), cheeks (*fat-chops*, fat-faced person); (sing.) lower jaw or half of cheek, esp. of pig as food (*Bath chap*; *c.-fallen*, with jaw hanging down, dispirited, dejected); *chops of the Channel*, entrance from Atlantic to Channel. [f. prec.]

chap³ (tsh-), n. (colloq.). Man, boy, fellow. [short for CHAPMAN cf. *customer*]

cha·p-book (tsh-), n. (bibliog.). Specimen of popular literature (usu. small pamphlet of tales, ballads, tracts) formerly hawked by chapmen. [mod. wd, see CHAPMAN]

chape (tsh-), n. Metal cap of scabbard-point; back-piece of buckle attaching it to strap &c.; sliding loop on belt or strap. [F, f. LL *capa* CAP¹]

chapeau-bras (shapō-brah·), n. (hist.). Three-cornered flat silk hat of 18th c. carried under arm. [F, = arm-hat]

chă·pel (tsh-), n. Place of Christian worship other than parish church or cathedral, esp. one attached to private house or institution (*c. royal*, of royal palace); oratory in larger building, with altar, esp. compartment of cathedral &c. separately dedicated (*Lady-c.*, dedicated to Virgin, usu. E. of high altar); subordinate Anglican church, esp. *c. of ease*, for convenience of remote parishioners; R.-C. or dissenters' place of worship in England; c. service or attendance at c. (*keep a c.*, be present, in colleges); (Print.) printing-office, journeyman printers' association or meeting. [f. OF *chapele* f. LL *cappella* dim. of *cappa* cloak (CAP¹); first c. was sanctuary in which St Martin's sacred cloak was kept by *cappellani*]

chă·pelry, n. District served by chapel. [-RY]

chă·peron (sh-), n., & v.t. Married or elderly woman in charge of girl on social occasions; hence **cha·peron**AGE n. (Vb) act as c. to. [F, = hood, chaperon, dim. of *chape* cope (CAP¹)]

chă·piter (tsh-), n. (bibl.). Capital of column. [earlier form of CHAPTER]

cha·plain (-ĭn), n. Clergyman officiating in private chapel of great person or institution, on board ship, or for regiment &c.; nun reciting inferior services in nunnery. Hence **cha·plain**CY n. [f. OF *chapelain* f. LL *cappellanus* (CHAPEL, -AN)]

cha·plet (tsh-), n. Wreath of flowers, leaves, gold, gems, &c., for head; string of beads for counting prayers (one-third of rosary number), or as necklace; string of eggs in toad &c.; bead-moulding. Hence **cha·plet**ED² a. [f. OF *chapelet* dim. of CHAPE, see -LET]

cha·pman (tsh-), n. Pedlar. [OE *céapmann* (*céap* n. barter, *mann* man) cf. G *kaufmann* merchant, Du. *koopman*, & see CHEAP]

cha·ppie, -y, (tsh-), n. (colloq.). Exquisite, man about town. [CHAP³ + -Y³]

cha·pter, n. Main division of a book (abbr. *cap., ch., c.*), (fig.) limited subject, piece of narrative, &c.; Act of Parl. numbered as part of session's statutes for reference (5 & 6 Will. IV. cap. 62 = Statutory Declarations Act 1835); general meeting, whole number, of canons of collegiate or cathedral church or members of monastic or knightly order (*c.-house*, used for such meetings); *c. & verse*, exact reference to passage, exact authority *for* statement; *to end of c.*, for ever; *c. of* ACCIDENTS. [for CHAPITER f. OF *chapitre* f. L *capitulum* dim. of *caput -itis* head]

char¹ (tsh-), n. Hill trout of Wales &c. [?]

char². See CHARE.

char³ (tsh-), v.t. & i. Burn (t. & i.) to charcoal, scorch, blacken with fire. [prob. back-formation f. CHARCOAL]

char-à-banc(s) (shă·rabăng, or as F), n. Long vehicle, with many seats looking forward, for holiday excursions. [F *char à bancs* = benched carriage]

chă·racter (k-), n., & v.t. Distinctive mark; (pl.) inscribed letters or figures; national writing-symbols (*in the German c.*); person's handwriting; characteristic (esp. of species &c. in Nat. Hist.); collective peculiarities, sort, style; person's or race's idiosyncrasy, mental or moral nature; moral strength, backbone; reputation, good reputation; description of person's qualities; testimonial; status; known person (usu. *public c.*); imaginary person created by novelist or dramatist; actor's or hypocrite's part (*in, out of, c.*, appropriate to these or not, also more widely of actions that are in accord or not with person's c.); eccentric person (*c. actor*, who devotes himself to eccentricities). (Vb, poet. & archaic) inscribe; describe. [f. F *caractère* f. L f. Gk *kharaktēr* stamp (*kharattō* engrave)]

characteri·stic, a. & n. Typical, distinctive, (trait, mark, quality), whence **characteri·sti**CALLY adv.; (Math.) index of logarithm. [f. Gk *kharaktēristikos* (prec., -IST, -IC)]

cha·racterize, v.t. Describe character of; describe *as*; be characteristic of, impart character to. Hence **cha·racteriza**·TION n. [f. med. L f. Gk *kharaktērizō* (CHARACTER, -IZE)]

cha·racterless, a. Ordinary, undistinguished; without testimonial. [-LESS]

charade (sharah·d), n. Game of guessing word from written or acted clue given for each syllable & for the whole. [F, f. Pr. *charrada* (*charrà* chatter)]

char·coal (tsh-), n. Black porous residue of partly burnt wood, bones, &c., form of carbon (somet. w. allus. to use of the fumes as method of suicide); *c.-burner*, maker of this. [perh. f. CHARE + COAL in sense (*wood*) *turned coal*]

chare (tshār), **char,** n., (usu. pl.), & v.i. (-r-, -rr-). (Do) odd job(s); work by the day at housecleaning. [OE *cerr, cerran*, turn; U.S. *chore*]

charge¹ (tsh-), n. Material load; right quantity to put into thing, esp. of explosive for gun; figurative load; (Herald.) device, bearing; expense (*at his own c.*); price demanded for service or goods; task, duty, commission; care, custody, (*of*; *nurse in c. of child, child in c. of nurse*; CURATE *in c.*; *give* person *in c.*, hand over to police); thing or person entrusted, minister's flock; exhortation, directions, (*parting c., bishop's c., judge's c. to jury*); accusation (*lay to* one's *c.*, accuse him of; *c.-sheet*, record of cases at police station); impetuous attack, rush, (*return to the c.*, begin again, esp. in argument); (Mil.) signal sounded for attack. [F, f. Rom. *carga* f. LL *carrica* (L *carricare* see foll.)]

charge², v.t. & i. Load, fill to the full or proper extent, (vessel, gun with explosive); saturate (air with vapour, water with chemicals, accumulator with electricity, memory with facts); entrust *with* (*c. oneself with*, undertake); command *to* do, exhort (esp. of bishop, judge); accuse, impute, (person *with* action, fault *upon* person); saddle *with* (liability), place (liability) *on*; demand (price) *for* (also *c. person price for*); attack (t. & i.) impetuously, esp. on horseback; place (weapon) in position for use (*c. bayonets*, bring down to receive cavalry c.). [f. OF *charger*, cf. prec., f. L *carricare* (*carrus* CAR¹)]

char·geable, a. 1. Expensive (archaic). 2. Liable to be charged *with* (accused of); subject to a money demand; liable to be made an expense (*c. to the parish*); imputable to (*on*); proper to be added *to* an account. Hence **char·gea**BI·LITY n. [1 f. CHARGE¹, 2 f. CHARGE², + -ABLE]

chargé (d'affaires) (shar·rzhā dafār·), n. (pl. *-és d'-*). Deputy ambassador; ambassador at minor court. [F, = one charged with affairs]

char·ger¹, n. (archaic). Large flat dish. [ME *chargeour* perh. f. CHARGE² + -OR² (loader), or f. OF **chargeoir* (CHARGE² & as PARLOUR)]

char·ger², n. In vbl senses; esp., (Mil.) officer's horse. [-ER¹]

chă·riot (tsh-), n., & v.t. Stately vehicle, triumphal car, (poet. & esp. fig. of sun's c. &c.); 18th-c. four-wheeled carriage with back seats only; (Hist.) car used in ancient fighting & racing, whence **chariot**EER· n.; (vb) convey as or in c. [OF, augment. of *char* CAR]

chă·ritable (tsh-), a. Liberal in giving to the poor; connected with such giving; wont to judge favourably of persons, acts, & motives. Hence **cha·ritable**NESS n., **cha·ritab**LY[2] adv. [OF (*charité* = foll., -ABLE)]

chă·rity (tsh-), n. Christian love of fellow men (*in, out of, c. with*); kindness, natural affection, (*c. begins at home*, is due first to kith and kin); candour, freedom from censoriousness, imputing of good motives when possible, leniency; beneficence, liberality to the poor, almsgiving (*cc.*, acts of this), alms; institution for helping the helpless, help so given, (*cold as c.*, in allusion to mechanical administration; *c.-boy, -girl*, brought up in such place); *Brother, Sister, of C.*, member of religious society devoted to relieving poor; *C. Commission(ers)*, board created 1853 to control charitable trusts. [f. OF *charité* f. L *caritatem* (*carus* dear, -TY)]

char·ivar·i (sh-), n. Medley of sounds, hubbub. [F, etym. dub.; prop. a serenade of pans, trays, &c., to unpopular person]

char·lady, slang var. of CHARWOMAN.

char·latan (sh-), n. & a. Impostor in medicine, quack; of, as of, empty pretender to knowledge or skill. Hence **char·latan**ISH[1](1) a., **char·latan**ISM(2), **char·latan**RY, nn. [F, f. It. *ciarlatano* (*ciarlare* patter)]

Charles's Wain, n. (Also *Plough, Great Bear*) constellation *Ursa Major* or its seven bright stars. [OE *Carles wægn*; wain of Arcturus, neighbouring constellation, became wain of Arthur, who was confused with the other great hero Charlemagne]

Char·leston, n., & v.i. An American dance with side-kicks from the knee; (vb) dance this, kick thus. [f. *C.* in S. Carolina]

char·lock (tsh-), n. Field mustard. [OE *cerlic*]

char·lotte (sh-), n. Kinds of pudding made of stewed fruit with casing or layers or covering of bread, biscuits, sponge-cake, or bread-crumbs; *c. russe*, custard enclosed in sponge cake. [F]

charm[1] (tsh-), n. Verse, sentence, word, act, or object having occult power (*against*), spell; thing worn to avert evil &c., amulet; trinket on watch-chain &c.; quality, feature, exciting love or admiration (*cc.*, beauty); attractiveness, indefinable power of delighting, (esp. as literary critics' word). [f. F *charme* f. L *carmen* song]

charm[2], v.t. Bewitch, influence (as) by magic, (abs. or with pred. as *c. asleep, away*); *c.* (secret, consent, &c.) *out of*; endow with magic power (*bear a charmed life*); captivate, delight, (*charmed with*); give pleasure to (*I shall be charmed* as polite formula); (part.) delightful, whence **char·ming**LY[2] adv. [f. F *charmer* (CHARM[1])]

charmante, charmeuse, (F) nn. Ladies' dress-fabrics.

char·mer, n. In vbl senses; esp., beautiful woman (now joc. or archaic). [-ER[1]]

char·nel-house (tsh-), n. House or vault in which dead bodies or bones are piled. [OF *charnel* burying-place f. LL *carnale* (CARNAL)]

Chār·on (k-), n. Ferryman conveying souls across Styx to Hades in Gk mythol. (*C.'s boat, ferry*, &c., phrr. for hour of death). [f. Gk *Kharōn*]

char·poy (tsh-), n. (Anglo-Ind.). Light Indian bedstead. [f. Hind. *charpai*]

chart (tsh-), n., & v.t. Navigator's sea map, with coast outlines, rocks, shoals, &c.; outline map with conspectus of special conditions, as *magnetic c.*; record by curves &c. of fluctuations in temperature, prices, &c.; sheet of tabulated information; hence **char·t**LESS a. (Vb) make c. of, map. [OF, f. L *carta* CARD[2]]

char·ter[1] (tsh-), n. Written grant of rights by sovereign or legislature, esp. creation of borough, company, &c. (*Great C.*, MAGNA CHARTA); deed conveying land; = CHARTER-PARTY; privilege, admitted right. [f. OF *chartre* f. L *cartula* dim. of *carta* CARD[2]]

char·ter[2], v.t. Grant c., give privilege, to (*chartered accountant*, member of Institute of Accountants with royal c.; *chartered libertine*, one allowed to take liberties); hire (ship) by c.-party, (loosely) hire (vehicle &c.). Hence **char·ter**ER[1] n. [f. prec.]

Char·terhouse, n. Alms-house in London for aged pensioners on site of Carthusian monastery, (also *C. School*) public school of same foundation at Godalming. [corrupt. of CHARTREUSE]

char·ter-party (tsh-), n. Deed between ship-owner & merchant for hire of ship & delivery of cargo. [f. F *charte partie* divided document, INDENTURE]

char·tism, -ist, (tsh-), nn. (hist.). Principles, adherent, of reform movement of 1837–48. [f. L *charta* + -ISM(3), -IST(2), name taken from the democratic manifesto 'People's Charter']

charto·graphy (k-), &c. See **car-**.

chartreuse (shartrer·z), n. Carthusian monastery; kinds (*green, yellow, c.*) of liqueur; pale apple-green colour. [made by CARTHUSIAN monks]

char·tulary (k-). See **car-**.

char·woman (tsh-), n. Woman hired by the day for house-work. [CHARE]

chār·y (tsh-), a. Cautious; shy *of*, sparing

in, do*ing*; stingy *of* (*c. of praise*). Hence **char·i**LY[2] adv., **char·i**NESS n. [OE *cearig* =OSax. *karag* f. OTeut. *karâ* CARE]
Charў·bdis (k-), n. See SCYLLA.
chase[1] (tsh-), n. Pursuit (*in c. of*, pursuing; *give c.*, go in pursuit), hunting (*the c.*, hunting as sport); (also *chace*) unenclosed park-land; hunted animal or pursued ship; (Hist.) *c.*, *c.-port*, *c.-gun*, *chaser*, *bow-c.*, *stern-c.*, *bow*, *stern*, *-chaser*, gun, port, in bow or stern for use while chasing or being chased; (Tennis) a certain stroke. [ME & OF *chace* (LL **captiare* CATCH[1])]
chase[2] (tsh-), v.t. Pursue; drive *from*, *out of*, *to*, &c. [see CATCH[1]]
chase[3] (tsh-), v.t. Emboss, engrave, (metal). [for poet. & archaic *enchase* = set (jewels), inlay, engrave, enshrine, f. F *enchâsser* (*en* in, CASE[2])]
chase[4], n. Part of gun enclosing bore; groove cut to receive pipe &c. [f. F *chas* f. LL *capsum* hollow of the chest (L *capere* hold)]
chase[5], n. Iron frame holding composed type for page or sheet. [f. F *châsse* CASE[2]]
chasm (kă·zm), n. Deep fissure; break of continuity, hiatus; wide difference of feeling, interests, &c., between persons or parties; void, blank. Hence (poet.) **cha·sm**Y[2] a. [f. L f. Gk *khasma* (*khaskō* gape, -M)]
chasse (shahs), n. Liqueur after coffee &c. [F]
chassé (shă·sā), n., & v.i. (Make) gliding step in dancing; *c. croisé* (F, pl. *-s -s*), double c., (fig.) idle manœuvring. [F]
chassepot (shă·spō), n. French army breech-loading rifle. [inventor's name]
chassis (shă·sē), n. (pl. the same). Base-frame of gun-carriage, motor-car, &c.; company's stock of motor-cars, motor-buses, &c. [f. F *châssis* (LL *capsus* wagon-body f. L *capere* take)]
chaste (tshā-), a. Abstaining from unlawful or immoral (also from all) sexual intercourse, pure, virgin; decent (of speech); restrained, severe, pure in taste or style, unadorned, simple. Hence **cha·ste**LY[2] adv. [OF, f. L *castus*]
chasten (tshā·sn), v.t. Discipline, correct by suffering, (usu. of God, Providence, &c., or of trouble &c.); make chaste in style &c., refine; temper, subdue, (esp. in p.p.). Hence **chasten**ER[1] (-sen*er*) n. [prec. + -EN[6]]
chăsti·se (tsh-, -z), v.t. Punish; beat. Hence **cha·stise**MENT, **chasti·se**R[1], nn. [form unexplained; ME has *chastien*, *chasten*, (later *chasty*, *chaste*) f. OF *chastier* f. L *castigare*]
chă·stity, n. Continence; virginity, celibacy; simplicity of style or taste. [f. OF *chastete* f. L *castitatem* (*castus* CHASTE, -TY)]
cha·suble (tshăzū-), n. Sleeveless vestment of celebrant at Mass or Eucharist. [F, f. med. L *casubula* dim. of *casa* cottage]
chat[1] (tsh-), v.i., & n. (Indulge in) easy familiar talk. Hence **cha·tt**Y[2] a., **cha·tti**NESS n. [short for CHATTER]
chat[2], n. Kinds of bird, chiefly Warblers (usu. in comb. as *Stone*, *Whin*, *-c.*). [f. prec.]
château (shă·tō), n. (pl. *-x*, pr. -z). Foreign country house. [F]
chă·telaine (sh-), n. Set of short chains attached to woman's belt for carrying keys, watch, pencil, &c. [F (*châ-*), = mistress of prec.]
cha·ttel (tsh-), n. Movable possession (usu. pl., esp. *goods & cc.*). [f. OF *chatel* see CATTLE]
cha·tter (tsh-), v.i., & n. (Of birds) utter quick series of short notes; (of persons) talk quickly, incessantly, foolishly, or inopportunely; (of teeth) rattle together (also of ill-adjusted parts of machine). (N.) any of these sounds; *chatterbox*, child &c. given to c. [imit., see -ER[5]]
chau·ffer (tsh-), n. Metal basket holding fire; portable furnace with air-holes. [f. F *chauffoir* f. L *calefactorius* CALEFACTORY]
chauffeur (shōfer·), n. Motor-car driver. [F]
chaumonte·l (shō-), n. Large kind of pear. [name of French village]
chaussure (F), n. Boots or shoes.
chau·vinism (shō-), n. Bellicose patriotism, foreign jingoism. So **chau·vin**IST(2) n. & a., **chauvini·st**IC a. [*Chauvin*, Napoleonic veteran, person in Cogniard's *Cocarde Tricolore* 1831]
chaw (tsh-), v.t., & n. (now vulg.). Chew; (U.S.) *c. up*, utterly defeat; *c.-bacon*, bumpkin; (n.) quid of tobacco. [var. of CHEW]
cheap (tsh-), a. Inexpensive (of thing, price, shop, dealer; *c. & nasty*, of low cost and bad quality); worth more than its cost; easily got; worthless, of little account, staled, (*hold c.*, despise); (as pred.) = cheaply (*got it c.* &c.); *dirt c.*, very c.; *feel c.* (slang), be out of sorts; *on the c.*, in c. manner; *C. Jack*, travelling hawker; *c. trip(per)*, excursion(ist) by rail &c. at reduced fares. Hence **chea·p**LY[2] adv., **chea·p**ISH[1](2) a., **chea·p**NESS n. [f. phr. *good cheap* f. obs. *cheap* n., OE *céap* barter, price, com.-Teut. cf. G *kauf* purchase]
chea·pen, v.t. & i. Haggle for (archaic); make or become cheap, depreciate. [-EN[6]]
cheat (tsh-), n., & v.t. & i. Trick, fraud; swindler, deceiver; card-game in which undetected cheating is licensed. (Vb) deceive, trick (person *out of* thing); deal fraudulently; while away (time, fatigue). [ME *chete* short for ESCHEAT]
check[1] (tsh-), int. & n. (Announcement of) exposure of chess king to attack;

sudden arrest given to motion, rebuff, repulse; slight military reverse; (Hunt.) loss of the scent; stoppage, pause; restraint on action (*keep in c.*, under control); person or thing that restrains; control to secure accuracy; token of identification for left luggage, seat-holder, &c.; (U.S.) counter at cards (hence colloq., *hand in* one's *cc.*, die); *c.-action* in piano, restraining hammer from striking string twice; *c.-nut*, screwed on over nut to prevent its working loose; *c.-rein*, attaching one horse's rein to other's bit, also rein preventing horse from lowering head; *c.-string*, in carriage for signalling to driver to stop; *c.-taker*, collector of pass tokens in theatre &c.; *c.-till*, in shop, recording receipts. [f. OF *eschec* f. Arab. f. Pers. *shah* king]

check², v.t. & i. Threaten opponent's king at chess; suddenly arrest motion of; (of hounds) stop on losing scent, or to make sure of it; restrain, curb, (Mil., of superior) find fault with, rebuke; test (statement, account, figures, employés) by comparison &c., examine accuracy of. [f. OF *eschequier* play chess, check, as prec.]

check³ (tsh-), n. Cross-lined pattern; fabric woven or printed with this. So **check**ED² a. [perh. short for CHEQUER]

check⁴, n. = CHEQUE.

che·cker. See CHEQUER.

checkma·te, int. & n., & v.t. (also *mate*, now more usu. in chess but not in fig. sense). (Announcement to opponent of) inextricable check of king at chess, final defeat at chess or in any enterprise; (vb) defeat, frustrate. [f. OF *eschec mat* (see CHECK¹) f. Arab. *shah mata* king is dead]

Che·ddar (tsh-), n. Kind of cheese. [place]

cheek (tsh-), n., & v.t. Side-wall of mouth, side of face below eye, (*c.-tooth*, molar; *c.-bone*, that below eye; *c. by jowl*, close together, intimate; *to* one's *own c.*, not shared with others); saucy speech (vb, address saucily), whence **chee·ky**² a., **chee·ki**LY² adv., **chee·ki**NESS n.; cool confidence, effrontery, (*have the c. to*); side post of door &c.; (pl.) jaws of vice, side-pieces of various parts of machines arranged in lateral pairs. [OE *céce* cf. Du. *kaak*]

cheep (tsh-), v.i., & n. (Utter) shrill feeble note as of young bird. Hence (of young partridge or grouse) **chee·p**ER¹ n. [imit.]

cheer¹ (tsh-), n. Frame of mind (*what c.?*, how do you feel?; *be of good c.*, stout-hearted, hopeful); food, fare, (*make good c.*, feast; *the fewer the better c.*, more to eat); shout of encouragement or applause (*three cc.*, successive united hurrahs, often *for* person or thing honoured). [obs. sense *face*, ME & OF *chere* f. LL *cara* face perh. f. Gk *kara* head]

cheer², v.t. & i. Comfort, gladden; incite, urge *on*, esp. by shouts; applaud (t. & i.), shout for joy; *c. up*, comfort, take comfort. [f. prec.]

cheer·ful, a. Contented, in good spirits, hopeful; animating, pleasant; willing, not reluctant. Hence **cheer·ful**LY² adv., **cheer·ful**NESS n. [CHEER¹ + -FUL]

cheer·less, a. Dull, gloomy, dreary, miserable. Hence **cheer·less**LY² adv., **cheer·less**NESS n. [CHEER¹ + -LESS]

cheer·ly, adv. (naut.). Heartily, with a will. [formerly adj. & adv. (see -LY²) f. CHEER¹]

cheer·y, a. Lively, in spirits, genial. Hence **cheer·i**LY² adv., **cheer·i**NESS n., **cheer·io** (slang), int. of encouragement. [-Y²]

cheese¹ (tshēz), n. Food made of pressed curds; *a c.*, complete cake or ball of this within rind; *green c.*, immature, not yet dried; BREAD *& c.*; CHALK *& c.*; *make cc.* (of schoolgirls), spin round and sink suddenly, inflating petticoats; fruit of mallow; *c.-cutter*, with broad curved blade; *c.-cake*, tartlet filled with sweet yellow compound of curds &c.; *c.-hopper*, maggot of c.-fly; *cheesemonger*, dealer in c., butter, &c.; *c.-paring*, stingy, stinginess, (pl.) worthless odds and ends; *c.-plate*, 5 or 6 in. in diameter, also large coat-button; *c.-rennet*, name for Lady's bedstraw; *c.-scoop*, *-taster*, instrument for extracting small piece as sample; *c.-straws*, savoury of grated cheese &c. made up into thin strips. [OE *cése*, cf. G *käse* f. L *caseus*]

cheese², n. *The c.*, the correct thing. [prob. Anglo-Ind. f. Pers. & Hind. *chiz* thing]

cheese³ (tshēz), v.t. (slang). *C. it*, stop, cease, give over, (only as imperat.). [?]

chee·sy, a. Like, tasting of, cheese; (slang) stylish. Hence **chee·si**NESS n. [CHEESE¹,², -Y²]

chee·tah (tsh-), n. Kind of leopard, tamed in India & trained to hunt deer. [f. Hind. *chita* f. Skr. *chitraka* speckled]

chef (sh-), n. Head cook (male). [F]

chef-d'œuvre (shĕder·vr), n. (pl. *chefs-*, same pronunc.). A, one's, master-piece. [F]

cheil(o)- (kī-). = CHIL(O)-.

cheir(o)- (kīr-). = CHIR(O)-.

cheiro·pteran, n., **cheiro·pterous,** a., (kīr-). (Member) of mammal order with membraned hands serving as wings, the Bats. [prec. + Gk *pteron* wing + -AN, -OUS]

che·la (tshā-), n. Novice qualifying for initiation in esoteric Buddhism. [Hind., = pupil]

Chellē·an (sh-), a. (archaeol.). Of the palaeolithic epoch represented by remains found at Chelles in France. [-AN]

Che·lsea Royal Hospital, n. An institution for old or disabled soldiers.

Cheltō·nian, a. & n. (Member) of Cheltenham College. [-IAN]

che·mical (kĕ-), a. & n. Of, made by, relating to, chemistry; *c.* COMBINATION; (usu. pl.) substance obtained by or used in c. process. Hence or cogn. **che·mical**LY[2] adv., **che·mico**- comb. form. [obs. *chemic* (F *chimique* or mod. L *chymicus*, assim. of *alchimicus* ALCHEMIC to supposed Gk etym.) + -AL]

chemise (shĭmē·z), n. Woman's body under-garment. [OF, f. LL *camisia* shirt]

chemise·tte (shĕ-), n. Bodice with upper part like chemise; lace, muslin, &c., filling up opening of dress below throat. [F, dim. of prec.]

che·mist (kĕ-), n. Person skilled in chemistry; dealer in medical drugs, apothecary. [f. F *chimiste* f. mod. L *chymista* see ALCHEMIST]

che·mistry, n. Science of the elements & their laws of combination & behaviour under various conditions; *applied* or *practical c.*, art of utilizing this knowledge; (fig.) mysterious change or process. [prec., -RY]

che·mitype, n. [Process for getting) relief cast of engraving. [CHEMICAL &c. + TYPE]

chenille (shĭnē·l), n. Velvety cord used in trimming dresses and furniture. [F, = caterpillar f. L *canicula* small dog]

cheque (tshĕk), **check,** n. Written order to banker to pay named sum on drawer's account to bearer or named person; BLANK[1] *c.*; CROSS[2]*ed c.*; *c.-book*, number of stamped & engraved forms for drawing cc. bound & issued to customer. [var. of CHECK[1] formerly used of counterfoils for checking forgery]

chequer[1] (tshĕ·ker), **che·cker,** n. (Pl.) chess-board as inn-sign; (often pl.) pattern made of squares or with alternating colours, whence **che·quer**-WISE adv.; *Chequers*, Prime Minister's official country house. [f. OF *eschekier* f. LL *scaccarium* chess-board, EXCHEQUER]

che·quer[2], **che·cker,** v.t. Mark with squares, esp. of alternate colours; variegate, break uniformity of, (often fig., esp. in p.p. as *chequered lot, fortunes*). [prob. f. prec.]

chĕ·rish (tsh-), v.t. Foster, nurse, keep warm; value, hold in one's heart, cling to, (esp. hopes, feelings, &c.). [f. F *chérir* (see -ISH[2]) f. *cher* f. L *carus* dear]

cheroo·t (sh-), n. Cigar with both ends open. [f. Tamil *shuruṭṭu* roll]

che·rry (tsh-), n. & a. Small stone-fruit; tree bearing this (also *c.-tree*), its wood (also *c.-wood*); *make two bites at a c.*, boggle, be unenterprising or formal; *c.-bob*, two cc. with joined stems (BOB[1]); *c. brandy*, dark-red liqueur of brandy in which cc. have been steeped; *c.-pie*, garden heliotrope; *c. ripe*, fruit hawker's cry; (adj.) red (*c. lips, ribbon*; *c.-breeches*, 11th Hussars). [ME *chery* f. ONF *cherise* (*s* lost as if pl. cf. PEA) f. L f. Gk *kerasos* perh. f. town name; OE *ciris* (cf. G *kirsche*) was prob. not source of ME]

cher·sonese (k-, -ēs), n. Peninsula. [f. L f. Gk *khersonēsos* (*khersos* dry, *nēsos* island)]

chert (tsh-), n. A flint-like quartz. [?]

chĕ·rub (tsh-), n. (pl. *-s, -im*). Angelic being; one of the second order of ninefold celestial hierarchy, gifted with knowledge as the first (seraphim) with love; (Art) winged (head of) child; beautiful or innocent child. Hence **cheru·b**IC (-ōō-) a. [earlier *cherubin* sing., *-ins* pl., *cherubim* sing., *-ims* pl.; f. F *cherubin* through L, Gk, f. Heb. *k'rub* pl. *k'rubim*]

cher·vil (tsh-), n. Garden herb used in soup, salad, &c. [OE *cærfille* f. L f. Gk *khairephullon* perh. f. *khairō* rejoice + *phullon* leaf]

Chĕ·shire (tsh-), a. *C. cheese*, made in C.; *C. cat*, person with fixed grin. [prov. *grin like a C. cat* unexpl.]

chess (tsh-), n. Game for two players with thirty-two pieces or *c.-men* on *c.-board* chequered with sixty-four squares. [ME *ches* f. OF *eschès* pl. of *eschec* CHECK[1] (lit. sense *kings*)]

che·ssel (tsh-), n. Cheese-making mould. [prob. f. CHEESE[1] + WELL[1]]

chest (tsh-), n. Large strong box; box for sailor's belongings; *carpenter's, medicine*, &c., c., holding special requisites; treasury, coffer, of institution (usu. fig. for the sums in it); case of some commodity, esp. tea (& so as variable measure); *c. of drawers*, frame with drawers for keeping clothes in bedroom; part of human or lower animal's body enclosed in ribs (*get* thing *off* one's *c.* slang, say & be quit of it), whence **-chest**ED[2] a.; *c.-note, -voice*, of lowest speaking or singing register; *c.-protector*, flannel &c. worn on c.; *c.-trouble*, lung disease esp. chronic. [OE *cest* f. L f. Gk *kistē*]

che·sterfield (tsh-), n. Kind of overcoat, also of couch. [19th-c. Earl of C.]

che·stnut (tsh-), n. & a. Tree (also *c.-tree*, *Spanish c.*, or *Sweet c.*) or its edible fruit; =c.-wood; =HORSE[1]-*c.*; =CASTOR[3]; stale anecdote; (of) c.-colour, deep reddish-brown; horse of this colour. [f. obs. *chesten* (f. OF *chastaigne* f. L f. Gk *kastanea* prob. f. place-name) + NUT]

chevă·l-glass (she-), n. Tall mirror swung on uprights. [f. F *cheval* horse, frame]

chĕvalier· (sh-), n. Member of certain orders of knighthood, & of French Legion of Honour &c.; (Hist.) *The C.* or *C. de St George*, Old Pretender, *The Young C.*, Young Pretender; soldier cadet of old French noblesse; *c. of industry* (oftener in F form *c. d'industrie*), adventurer, swindler. [OF (L *caballus* horse, -ARY[1], orig. sense *horseman*), cf. CAVALIER]

chevaux de frise (shevō·defrē·z), n. pl. Iron spikes set in timber &c. to repel cavalry &c. in war, or to guard palings in peace; natural protective line of hair in plants, eyelashes, &c. [F, lit. horses of Friesland, invented by 17th-c. Frisians who had no cavalry]

chevelure· (F), n. (Arrangement of) the hair.

chě·viot (tsh-), n. & a. (Wool, cloth) got, made, from sheep of Cheviot hills.

chě·vron (sh-), n. Bent bar of inverted V shape, in escutcheons, as archit. ornament (*c.-moulding*, consisting of series of these), & on sleeve of army N.C.O. indicating rank (3 bars for sergeant, 2 for corporal, &c.). [F, = rafter, chevron, circumflex, f. L **caprionem* nom. *-io* (L *caper* goat); L *capreolus* chamois was used in pl. as pair of rafters]

chě·vrotain, -tin (sh-), n. Small Musk Deer. [F, dim. of OF *chevrot* (*chèvre* goat)]

chě·vy, chi·vy, (tsh-; usu. spelt -e- & pron. -ĭ-), n., & v.t. & i. Chase (n. & v.), scamper (n. & v.); game of prisoners' base. [prob. f. ballad *Chevy Chase* (place-name)]

chew (tshōō), v.t. & i., & n. Work about between teeth, grind to pulp or indent with repeated biting; (abs.) c. tobacco, whence **chew·**ER[1] n.; turn over in mind; meditate *upon* or *over*; *c. the cud*, bring back half-digested food into mouth for further chewing, (fig., usu. with *of* reflection, fancy, &c.) meditate. (N.) act of chewing; quid of tobacco. [OE *céowan* cf. G *kauen*]

Chia·nti (kĭah-), n. Dry red Ital. wine. [It.]

chiaroscuro (kyar·oskoor·ō), n. & a. Treatment of light & shade in painting; light & shade effects in nature; variation, relief, handling of transitions, use of contrast, in literature &c. (Adj.) of c.; half-revealed. [It., = bright-dark (L *clarus, obscurus*)]

chīa·smus (k-), n. Inversion in second phrase of order followed in first (*I cannot dig, to beg I am ashamed*). [mod. L, f. Gk *khiasmos* cross arrangement f. *khiazō* make letter *khi* (shaped as Eng. X)]

chibouk, -que, (tshĭbōō·k), n. Long Turkish tobacco pipe. [f. Turk, *chibuk* tube]

chic (sh-), n. & a. Skill, effectiveness, style, stamp of superiority; (adj.) stylish, in the fashion. [F, etym. dub. (adj. use Engl.)]

chicā·ne (sh-), v.t. & i., & n. Use chicanery; cheat (person) *into, out of*, &c.; (n.) chicanery; (holding of) no-trump hand in bridge. [f. F *chicane(r)* perh. f. med. Gk *tzoukanizō* play polo f. Pers. *tchaugan* polo-stick]

chicā·nery, n. Legal trickery, pettifogging; sophistry. [f. F *chicanerie* (prec., -ERY)]

chick, n. Young bird before or after hatching; *the cc.*, children of a family (so *chickabiddy*, term of endearment of or to child); *c.-weed*, small plant. [short for foll.]

chi·cken (tsh-), n. (pl. *-ens, -en*). Young bird, esp. of domestic fowl, flesh of this; youthful person (esp. in *no c.*); *Mother Cary's c.*, Stormy Petrel; *count* one's *cc. before they are hatched*, be over-sanguine, precipitate; *c.-breast(ed)*, (having) malformed projection of breast-bone; *c. hazard*, game at dice; *c.-heart(ed)*, (with) no courage; *c.-pox*, children's mild eruptive disease. [OE *cicen* cf. Du. *kieken* prob. cogn. w. COCK[1]]

chi·ckling (tsh-), n. Common cultivated Vetch. [earlier *chicheling* dim. of ME & OF *chiche* ult. f. L *cicer*]

chi·ck-pea, n. Dwarf pea. [earlier *chich-pease* as prec. + PEASE]

chĭ·cory (tsh-), n. Blue-flowered plant cultivated for its root; its root ground for use with or instead of coffee. [f. F *cichorée* (now *chico-*) f. L *cichorium* f. Gk *kikhora* succory]

chide (tsh-), v.t. & i. (*chid, chidden* or *chid*). Make complaints, speak scoldingly, (esp. fig. of hounds, wind, &c.); scold, rebuke. [OE *cīdan*]

chief[1] (tsh-), n. (Herald.) upper third of shield; leader, ruler; head man of tribe, clan, &c., whence **chie·f**ESS[1] n.; head of a department, highest official; *in c.*, most of all, especially, (for *many reasons, & this one in c.*); *-in-c.*, supreme, as *Commander, Colonel, -in-c.* Hence **chie·f**DOM, **chie·f**SHIP, nn., **chie·f**LESS a. [f. OF *chef* f. L *caput* head]

chief[2], a. & adv. (*-er, -est*, now rare). First by title (*C. Justice* &c.); first in importance, influence, &c.; prominent, leading; (adv.) chiefly, especially, (*but c.* or *chiefest of all, forget not*). [orig. CHIEF[1] used in apposition]

chie·fly[1], a. Proper for a chief. [CHIEF[1] + -LY[1]]

chie·fly[2], adv. Above all; mainly but not exclusively. [CHIEF[2] + -LY[2]]

chie·ftain (tsh-, -tĭn), n. Military leader (poet.); captain of robbers; chief of Highland clan or uncivilized tribe. Hence **chie·ftain**CY, **chie·ftain**ESS[1], **chie·ftain**RY, **chie·ftain**SHIP, nn. [f. OF *chevetaine* CAPTAIN]

chi·ff-chaff (tsh-, -tsh-), n. Bird of Warbler family. [imit.]

chiffon (F), n. (Usu. pl.) adornments of female dress; (sing.) thin gauze. [F, f. *chiffe* rag]

chiffonier· (sh-), n. Movable low cupboard with sideboard top. [F (prec. -IER)]

chignon (F), n. Mass of hair on pad at

back of head. [F, f. 13th-c. *chaaignon* nape of neck = *chaînon* link (*chaîne* CHAIN)]

chi·goe (tsh-), n. W.-Ind. flea, burrowing into skin. [W.-Ind.]

chi·lblain, n. Itching sore on hand, foot, &c., from exposure to cold. [Hence **chi·lblain**ED², **chi·lblain**Y², aa. [CHILL + BLAIN]

child (tsh-), n. (pl. *children*). Unborn or newborn human being (pronoun *it*, or *he, she*); boy or girl (*from a c.*, from childhood on); childish person; (slang) *this c.*, I, me; son or daughter (at any age) *of* (or with *my* &c.), offspring; descendant lit. or fig. or follower or adherent *of* (*c. of God, of the devil*; *cc. of Izaak Walton*, anglers; *fancy's c.*; *c. of nature*); result *of*; *with c.*, pregnant; *c.'s-play*, easy task; BURNT *c. dreads fire*; *childbed, -birth*, parturition; *c. wife*, very young wife. Hence **chi·ld**LESS a., **chi·ldless**NESS n. [OE *cild* cf. Goth. *kilthei* womb]

Chi·ldermas, n. Festival of Holy Innocents, 28th Dec. [OE *cildra* (prec.) of infants + *mæsse* MASS¹]

chi·ldhood, n. Child's state; time from birth to puberty; *second c.*, dotage. [-HOOD]

chi·ldish, a. Of, proper to, a child; puerile, improper for a grown person. Hence **chi·ldish**LY² adv., **chi·ldish**NESS n. [-ISH¹]

chi·ldlike, a. Having good qualities of child, as innocence, frankness, &c. [-LIKE]

chi·ldly, a. & adv. (poet.). Like a child. [mod. revival of obs. wd; -LY¹,²]

chi·liad (k-), n. A thousand; a thousand years. [f. L f. Gk *khilias -ados* f. *khilioi* adj. a thousand, -AD(2)]

chi·liasm, chi·liast, (k-), nn. Doctrine of or belief in, believer in, the millennium. Hence **chilia·st**IC a. [f. Gk *khiliasmos, -astēs* (prec. + endings used w. vbs in *-azō* cf. -ISM, -IST)]

chill¹ (tsh-), n. Cold sensation, lowered temperature of body, feverish shivering, (*catch a c.*; also of special part as *liver-c.*); unpleasant coldness of air, water, &c. (*take c. off water* or *claret*, warm slightly); depressing influence (*cast a c. over*); coldness of manner. [OE *cele* cogn. w. COLD; but the noun, after giving CHILL²,³, was dormant 1400–1600, & revived as deriv. of CHILL³]

chill², a. Unpleasantly cold to feel; feeling cold; unfeeling, unemotional, abstract. Hence **chi·ll**NESS n. [prob. f. prec.]

chill³, v.t. & i. Make, become, cold; deaden, blast, with cold; depress, dispirit; harden (molten iron) by contact of cold iron; (colloq.) take the c. off (liquid). [prob. f. CHILL¹]

chi·lli, -y, (tsh-), n. Dried pod of Capsicum (as relish, or made into cayenne). [Mex.]

chi·lly¹, a. Rather cold to feel; feeling rather cold; sensitive to cold; not genial, cold-mannered. Hence **chi·lli**NESS n. [CHILL¹ + -Y²]

chi·lly² (-l-lĭ), adv. (rare). In cold manner (lit. & fig.). [CHILL² + -LY²]

chīl(o)-, cheil(o)-, (k-), comb. form of Gk *kheilos* lip, in zool. terms as *chilopod* (having feet serving as jaws).

Chi·ltern Hu·ndreds (tsh-), n. pl. *Apply for, accept, the C.H.*, resign seat in House of Commons. [a Crown manor, administration of which, being titular office under Crown, requires the otherwise illegal vacation of seat]

chime¹ (tsh-), n. Set of attuned bells; series of sounds given by this; harmony, melody, rhythm, sing-song; agreement, correspondence. [ME *chymbe* f. L f. Gk *kumbalon* CYMBAL]

chime², v.i. & t. Make (bell) sound; ring cc. (of person or bells); ring cc. on (bells); show (hour) by chiming (also of hour, = sound); summon by bells *to*; repeat mechanically; be in rhyme, make to rhyme; be in agreement (*together, with*, or abs.); join *in*, express eager agreement. [as prec.]

chime³, chimb, (tshīm), n. Projecting rim at ends of cask. [ME *chimbe* cf. Du. *kim* edge]

chimēr·a, -aer·a, (k-), n. Monster with lion's head, goat's body, and serpent's tail. Bogy; thing of hybrid character; fanciful conception; whence **chimĕ·r**ICAL a., **chime·rical**LY² adv. [f. F *chimère* f. L f. Gk *khimaira* she-goat, chimera, (*khimaros* goat)]

chimere· (tsh-), n. Bishop's robe. [= OF *chamarre* etym. dub.]

chi·mney (tsh-), n. Flue carrying off smoke or steam of fire, furnace, engine, &c.; (also *c.-stalk, -top*) part of flue above roof; glass tube providing draught for lamp-flame; natural vent, e.g. of volcano; (Mountaineering) narrow cleft by which cliff may be climbed; *c.-corner*, warm seat within old-fashioned fire-place; *c.-jack*, rotating cowl; *c.-piece*, = MANTEL; *c.-pot*, earthenware or metal pipe added to c.-top (*c.-pot hat*, tall silk hat); *c.-stack*, united group of c.-stalks; *c.-stalk*, see above, also = tall factory c.; *c.-swallow*, common swallow; *c.-sweep*, man who sweeps cc.; *c.-sweeper*, = *c.-sweep*, also = jointed c.-cleaning brush. [f. OF *cheminée* f. LL *caminata* (perh. *camera*) fireplaced (chamber) f. L *caminus* oven, -ATE²]

chi·mpănzee· (tsh-), n. African ape resembling man. [native name in Angola]

chin (tsh-), n. Front of lower jaw; *up to the c., c.-deep*, deeply immersed. Hence **-chinn**ED² a. [OE *cin* cf. G. *kinn*, & Gk *geneion* chin, *genus* check]

Chī·na, a., **chī·na,** n. & a., (tsh-). From China (*C. crape, C.* ASTER, &c.; *C.* (or *c.*)

orange, common orange, orig. from C.; *Chinaman*, native of C.). (Made of) a fine semi-transparent earthenware, porcelain; things made of this; whence **chi·na**MA·NIA(C) nn.; *c.-closet*, for keeping or displaying one's c.; *c.-clay*, KAOLIN. [not native name; found in Skr. about 1st c.]

chinchi·lla (tsh-, -tsh-), n. Small S.-Amer. rodent; its soft grey fur. [Sp., dim. of *chinche* bug f. L *cimex -icis* (from supposed smell)]

chi·n-chi·n, int. of greeting & farewell (Anglo-Chin.; also as n. & vb). [Chin. *ts'ing ts'ing*]

chine[1] (tsh-), n. Deep narrow ravine (now only in Isle of Wight & Hampshire). [OE *cinu* cf. Du. *keen* chap in skin]

chine[2] (tsh-), n. Backbone; animal's backbone or part of it as joint; ridge, arête. [f. OF *eschine* perh. f. OHG *scina* splinter]

Chīnee· (tsh-), n. (slang). Chinaman, Chinese; *the heathen C.*, (facet., w. ref. to Bret. Harte's *Truthful James*, for) the typical Chinaman. [due to taking *Chinese* for pl.]

Chīne·se, a. & n. (pl. the same). (Native, language) of China; *C. lantern*, collapsible of paper used esp. in illuminating; *C. white*, a pigment, white oxide of zinc. [*China* + -ESE]

chink[1] (tsh-), n. Crevice; long narrow opening, slit, peep-hole. [f. 16th c.; excl. E.; etym. dub., perh. f. CHINE[1], which it has replaced]

chink[2] (tsh-), n., & v.i. & t. Sound as of glasses or coins striking together; (slang) ready money. (Vb) make this sound; cause (coin &c.) to make it. [imit.]

Chink[3], n. (slang.) Chinaman. [abbr.]

Chi·no-, comb. form of *China*. [-o-]

chintz (tsh-), n. & a. (Of) cotton cloth fast-printed with particoloured pattern & usu. glazed. [earlier *chints* pl. f. Hind. *chint* f. Skr. *chitra*; for sing. use cf. BAIZE]

chip[1], n. Thin piece cut from wood or broken from stone &c.; thin slice of potato, fruit, &c.; (pl., colloq.) potato-cc. fried (*fish & cc.*); wood split into strips for making hats &c. (*c. bonnet, basket*); *dry as a c.*, flavourless, uninteresting; *c.* (scion) *of*, esp. *c. of old block*, son resembling father; place in china &c. from which a c. has been knocked off. [f. foll.]

chip[2] (tsh-), v.t. & i. Cut (wood), break (stone, crockery), at surface or edge; shape thus; cut or break (piece &c.) *off, from*; be susceptible to breakage at edge; carve (inscription); crack (egg-shell; esp. of chickens); (slang) *c. in*, interrupt. [dim. of CHOP[1], cf. *drip drop, tip top*; cf. also EFris. *kippen* cut]

chip[3] (tsh-), n., & v.t. Wrestling-trick; (vb) trip up. [cf. Du. *kippen* ensnare]

chi·pmuck, -unk, (tsh-), n. North-American squirrel. [prob. Amer.-Ind.]

Chi·ppendale. n. A light style of drawing-room furniture. [*C.*, 18th-c. cabinet-maker]

chi·ppy, a. (slang). Dry, uninteresting; parched & queasy after drunkenness &c.; irritable. Hence **chi·ppi**NESS n. [CHIP[1] + -Y[2]]

Chips, n. (Naut). Ship's carpenter. [pl. of *chip*[1], cf. BUTTONS]

chir(o)-, cheir(o)-, (kīr-), comb. form of Gk *kheir* hand, as *chiro·*GRAPHY handwriting, *chir·*OMANCY palmistry.

chir·ograph, n. Document of various kinds formally written or signed. [f. F *chirographe* f. L f. Gk *kheirographon* (prec., -GRAPH)]

chiro·podist, chiro·pody, nn. Treater, treatment, of hands, feet, nails, corns, bunions, &c. [prob. f. CHIRO-, Gk *pous podos* foot, -IST(3); but there is Gk *kheiropodēs* with chapped feet (*kheiras* chap f. *kheir* hand)]

chirp (tsh-), v.i. & t., & n. (Make) short sharp note (as) of small bird; utter (song), express (joy &c.), thus; talk merrily; speak feebly. [imit.; from 15th c., displacing earlier *chark* (OE *cearcian* creak), *chirk, chirt*]

chir·py, a. Lively, cheerful. Hence **chir·pi**NESS n. [prec., -Y[2]]

chirr (tsh-), v.i., & n. (Make) prolonged trilling sound (as) of grasshopper. [imit.]

chi·rrup, v.i., & n. (Make) series of chirps, twittering; (make) imitative chirping to baby &c.; (slang) act as paid applauder at theatre &c., whence **chi·rrup**ER[1] n. [form of CHIRP]

chisel (tshĭ·zl), n., & v.t. (-ll-). (Cut, shape, with) steel-edged tool with square bevelled end for shaping wood, stone, or metal (*cold c.*, all of steel or iron for trimming cold iron; *chiselled features* &c., clear-cut); *the c.*, sculptor's c., (art of) sculpture; (slang) defraud, unfair treatment. [ONF, dim. of L *-cisum* neut. p.p. of *-cidere* (*caedere* cut)]

chit[1] (tsh-), n. Young child; young, small, or slender woman (depreciatingly, esp. *c. of a girl*). [earlier = whelp; var. of *kit*, KITTEN]

chit[2] (tsh-), **chi·tty,** n. (Anglo-Ind.). Note or written paper, esp. character given to servant. [f. Hind. *chiṭṭhi* f. Skr. *chitra* mark]

chit-chat (tsh-, -tsh-), n. Light conversation; subjects of it, gossip. [redupl. of CHAT[1]]

chī·tin (k-), n. Substance forming horny cover of beetles & crustaceans. Hence **chi·tin**OUS a. [should be *chitonin*; f. F *chitine* f. Gk *khitōn -ōnos* tunic + -IN]

chi·tterling (tsh-), n. (usu. pl.). Smaller intestines of beasts, esp. as cooked for food. [etym. dub.; cf. G *kutteln*]

chi·tty. See CHIT[2].

chi·valrous, (poet. &c.) **-ric,** (see foll.), a. Of, as of, the Age of Chivalry; of, as of, the ideal knight, gallant, honourable, courteous, disinterested; quixotic. Hence **chi·valrous**LY[2] adv. [f. OF *chevalerous* (CHEVALIER, -OUS); *chivalric* f. foll. + -IC]

chi·valry (formerly tsh-; now usu. sh-, as though a recent F importation), n. Horsemen, cavalry, (archaic); gallant gentlemen; knightly skill (archaic); medieval knightly system with its religious, moral, & social code; ideal knight's characteristics; devotion to service of women; inclination to defend weaker party; *flower of c.*, pattern knight, élite of nation's soldiers. [f. OF *chevalerie* f. L *caballarius* CAVALIER, -ERY]

chive (tsh-), **cive** (s-), n. Small herb allied to onion & leek. [F (*cive*) f. L *cepa* onion]

chĭ·vy. See CHEVY.

chlor-[1, 2]. =CHLORO-[1, 2], used before vowel.

chlor·al, n. *C. hydrate* or *c.*, a hypnotic & anaesthetic. Hence **chlor·al**ISM(5) n., **chlor·al**IZE(5) v.t. [pop. misuse of *chloral*, strictly a chem. substance first got by action of *chlorine* on *al(cohol)*, whence the name]

chlor·ide, n. (Chem.) compound of chlorine (-IDE); (pop.) kinds of bleaching agent not true cc., as *c. of lime, soda, potash*. [CHLOR-[2], -IDE]

chlor·ine, n. (chem.). Non-metallic element, a yellowish-green heavy ill-smelling gas. [f. Gk *khlōros* green + -INE[5]]

chloro-[1], **chlor-**, comb. form in bot. & mineral. terms of Gk *khlōros* green.

chloro-[2], **chlor-**, comb. form in chem. terms of CHLORINE. Hence **chlor·**ATE[1](3) n., **chlor·**IC(2), **chlor·**OUS (chem.), aa.

chlor·odyne, n. Patent medicine, narcotic & anodyne. [foll. + Gk *odunē* pain]

chlor·oform, n., & v.t. Anaesthetic, thin colourless liquid whose inhaled vapour produces insensibility. (Vb) treat (person) with, render insensible by, c., whence **chlor·oform**IST (1) n.; soak (thing) in c. [f. F *chloroforme* f. CHLORO-[2] + *form(yl)* see FORMIC]

chlor·ophy̆ll, n. Colouring-matter of green parts of plants. [F CHLORO[1](*phylle* f. Gk *phullon* leaf)]

chloro·sis, n. Green sickness, anaemic disease of young women, with greenish complexion; (Bot.) blanching of green parts, or turning green of petals &c. Hence **chloro·**TIC a. [CHLOR-[1], -OSIS]

chock[1] (tsh-), n. Block of wood, esp. wedge for stopping motion of cask or wheel, also in various senses on ship esp. of wedges supporting boat on deck; (Turning; earlier form of) CHUCK[4]. [perh. f. ONF *choque* log]

chock[2], v.t., & adv. Make fast with cc.; place (boat) on cc.; *c. up*, wedge in tightly, encumber (room &c.) with furniture &c.; (adv.) closely, tightly, close up; *c.-full*, stuffed. [f. prec.; the var. *choke-full* for *c.-full* is prob. an etym. guess & misrepresents pronunc.]

chŏ·colate (tsh-), n. & a. (Cake) of cacao-seed paste; drink of this in hot milk or water; dark brown (n. & a.); *c. cream*, sweetmeat of c. enclosing sweet paste. [f. F *chocolat* f. Mex. *chocolatl* etym. dub. (not f. *cacao* or *cocoa*)]

cho·ctaw (tsh-), n. (skating). Step from either edge to edge on other foot in opposite direction. [fancy name, cf. MOHAWK]

choice[1] (tsh-), n. Choosing, selection, (*make c. of*, select; *take* one's *c.*, decide between possibilities; *the girl of* one's *c.*; *for c.*, by preference, if one must select); power, right, faculty, of choosing (*at c.*, at pleasure; *have* one's *c.*; *have no c.*, not care which; *Hobson's c.*, to take or leave the one offer); élite, flower, *of*; variety to choose from; thing or person chosen; alternative (*have no c. but*). [f. OF *chois* f. *choisir* choose f. Rom. *causire* f. Teut. (Goth. *kausjan* test)]

choice[2], a. Of picked quality, exquisite; carefully chosen, appropriate. Hence **choi·ce**LY[2] adv., **choi·ce**NESS n. [perh. mixture of prec. w. obs. *chis* (OE *cis* etym. dub.) fastidious]

choir (kwīr), **quire,** n., & v.t. & i. Band of singers performing or leading in musical parts of church service; chancel of cathedral, minster, or large church; choral society, company of singers (also of birds, angels, &c.); band of dancers; *c.-organ* (corruption of *chair-*) softest of three parts (*great, swell, c., organ*) making up large compound organ, with lowest of three key-boards; (vb) sing in chorus (intr., or with *strain, hymn*, &c., as obj.). [ME *quere* f. OF *cuer* f. L f. Gk *khoros* song and dance]

choke[1] (tsh-), v.t. & i., & n. Stop breath of, suffocate, temporarily or finally, by squeezing throat from without, blocking it up within, or (of water, smoke, &c.) being unbreathable; (fig., of emotion) paralyse (*c.-pear*, fact, reproof, &c., hard to swallow); suffer temporary stoppage of breath, become speechless from anger &c., (n., this condition); smother, stifle, kill, (plant, fire, &c.) by deprivation of light, air, &c.; suppress (feelings); block up wholly or partly (tube by narrowing part of it; as n., the narrowed part, whence *c.-bore*, of gun with bore narrowing towards muzzle; also of channel with sand, stones, &c., *stones c.* or *c. up channel, channel chokes*), fill chock-full; *c. down*, swallow (food), conceal (emotion), with difficulty; *c. off*, make (person) relinquish an attempt; *c.-damp*, carbonic acid gas in mines, wells, &c. [OE *acéocian* etym. dub.]

choke[2], n. Centre part of artichoke. [prob. confusion of ending w. prec.]

cho·ker, n. In vbl senses; esp. clerical or

stand-up collar; *white c.*, white tie (slang). [-ER¹]

chŏl(ĕ)- (k-), comb. form in med. & chem. wds of Gk *kholē* gall, bile.

chŏ·ler (k-), n. (Hist.) one of the four HUMOURS, bile; (poet., archaic) anger, irascibility. [ME & OF *colre* f. L f. Gk *kholera* cholera perh. f. *kholē* bile]

chŏ·lera (k-) n. (Also *English, bilious, summer, c.*, or in L *c. nostras* = of our country) bilious summer & autumn disorder with diarrhoea and vomiting; (also *Asiatic, epidemic, malignant, c.*) non-bilious often fatal disease endemic in India & epidemic in Europe; *chicken c.*, infectious disease of fowls; *c.-belt*, flannel or silk waistband worn as preventive. Hence **cholerā·**IC a. [L, in orig. Gk sense (prec.) of summer c.]

cho·leric, a. Irascible; angry. [f. F *cholérique* f. L f. Gk *kholerikos* (CHOLER, -IC)]

cho·lerīne (*also* -ēn), n. Summer cholera; diarrhoea often prevalent at same time as Asiatic cholera. [F (-*é*-), f. *choléra* CHOLERA]

chō·liamb (k-), n. =SCAZON. Hence **cholia·mb**IC a. [f. L f. Gk *khōliambos* (*khōlos* lame, *iambos* IAMBUS)]

chondri-, -o-, (k-), comb. form of Gk *khondros*, in Med. & Physiol. =cartilage-.

choose (tshōōz), v.t. & i. (chose, chosen). Select out of greater number; (Theol., esp. in p.p.) destine to be saved; decide (*to* do one thing rather than another); think fit, be determined, *to* do; make choice *between*; *cannot c. but*, must, have to, (archaic); (with compl.) select as (*was chosen king*); *pick & c.*, select carefully, be fastidious; *nothing* &c. *to c. between them*, of things nearly equal. Hence **choo·**SER¹ n. [OE *céosan* cf. G *kiesen*]

chop¹ (tsh-), v.t. & i. Cut by a blow, usu. with axe (*c. up, c.* into small pieces, mince; often *c. off, away, down*); deliver such blow *at*; make one's way by such blows *through*; mince (esp. in p.p.); (fig.) cut (words &c.) short or into distinct parts; *c. in*, intervene in talk; *c. back*, reverse one's direction suddenly, double; *chopping sea*, with jerky motion; (of strata) *c. up, out*, come to surface. [var. of CHAP¹ cf. Du. & G *kappen*]

chop², n. Cutting stroke with axe &c.; thick slice of meat, esp. mutton or pork, usu. including rib (*c.-house*, cheap restaurant); broken motion of sea. [f. prec.]

chop³. See CHAP².

chop⁴, v.t. & i., & n. *C. & change* (emphatic for *change*, usu. intr.), vacillate, be inconstant, (n., *cc. & changes*, variations); *c. round, about*, (esp. of wind) change direction suddenly; *c. logic*, bandy arguments. Hence **cho·ppy**² a. [etym. dub., but cf. CHOP¹ in some senses]

chop⁵, n. (India, China) seal, licence, passport, permit; (China) trade-mark, a brand of goods; (Anglo-Ind. & colloq.) *first, second, -c.*, first, second, -class. [f. Hind. *chhāp* stamp]

cho·pper, n. One who chops; large-bladed short axe; butcher's cleaver. [CHOP¹ + -ER¹]

cho·pstick, n. Small slip of ivory &c. of which two held in one hand are used by Chinese as fork. [transl. of Chin. *k'wai-tsze* nimble ones f. Chin. *chop* quick + STICK]

chor·al¹ (k-), a. Of, sung by, choir (*c. service*, with canticles, anthems, &c., so sung; *full c. service*, with versicles & responses also sung); of, with, chorus. Hence **cho·ral**LY² adv. [f. med. L *choralis* (CHORUS, -AL)]

choral(e)² (korah·l), n. (Metrical hymn to) simple tune usu. sung in unison, orig. in German reformed church. [G (-*l*), *e* added merely to suggest foreign accent as in *morale, locale*]

chor·alist, n. Chorus singer. [CHORAL¹, -IST]

chord¹ (k-), n. String of harp &c. (poet.; also fig., as *touch the right c.*, appeal skilfully to emotion); (Physiol.) structure resembling string, as *vocal c., spinal c.*, (also *cord*); (Math.) straight line joining ends of arc. [16th-c. correction of CORD¹ after L f. Gk *khordē*]

chord² (k-), n. (Mus.) combination of three or more (rarely two) simultaneous notes according to rules of harmony (*common c.*, also *c.*, any note with its major or minor third, perfect fifth, & octave; *break* or *spread c.*, play its notes successively); harmonious combination of colours. [earlier *cord* for ACCORD² later confused w. prec.]

chor·dal (k-), a. Of, like, &c., CHORD¹,². [-AL]

chore (tsh-), n., & v.i., (U.S.). =CHARE.

chorē·a (k-), n. St. Vitus's dance. [L]

choree· (k-), n. =TROCHEE. [f. L f. Gk *khoreios* of dance]

chorē·ic, a. Of, having, chorea; of, marked by, chorees. [-IC]

chŏ·reograph (k-), n. Designer of ballet. So **choreo·**GRAPHER, **choreo·**GRAPHY, nn., **choreo**GRA·PHIC a. [f. Gk *khoreia* dancing (*khoros* dancing-company) + -GRAPH]

chori(s)- (k-), pref. f. Gk *khōri(s)* apart, used in bot. terms, as *choripetalous* with separate petals.

chŏ·riamb, choria·mbus, n. Metrical foot (–⏑⏑–). Hence **choria·mb**IC a. [f. L f. Gk *khoriambos* (CHOREE, IAMB)]

chor·ic, a. Of, like, chorus in Greek play. [f. Gk *khorikos* (CHORUS, -IC)]

chor·ion (k-), n. Outer membrane of foetus. [f. Gk *khŏrion*]

chŏ·rister (k-), n. Member of choir, esp. choir-boy (also fig. of angels, birds). [f. med. L *chorista* (CHOIR, -IST, & cf. BARRISTER)]

choro·graphy (k-), n. Describing, description, of districts (more limited than *geography*, less than *topography*). Hence or cogn. **choro·**GRAPHER n., **choro-**GRA·PHIC(AL) aa., **chorogra·phical**LY² adv. [f. F *chorographie* f. Gk *khōrographia* (*khōra* land, -GRAPHY)]

chor·oid, a. & n. Like chorion in shape or vascularity, esp. *c. coat* (or *c.* as noun), membrane lining eye-ball. [f. Gk *khoroeidēs* wrong reading in Gk MSS. for *khorioeidēs* (CHORION, -OID)]

choro·logy (k-), n. Local distribution of species &c. Hence **chorolo·gi**CAL a. [f. Gk *khōra* land + -LOGY]

chor·tle (tsh-), v.i. Chuckle loudly. [invented by Lewis Carroll, perh. f. *chuckle, snort*]

chor·us (k-), n., & v.t. & i. (Gk Ant.) band of dancers & singers in religious ceremonies & dramatic performances (also representing interested spectators in play; so in some Eng. plays); (one of) their utterances; personage speaking prologue & commenting on action in Elizabethan plays; band of singers, choir; thing sung by many at once; any simultaneous utterance of many (*in c.*, all speaking &c. together); (Mus.) composition in several (oftenest four) parts each sung by several voices; refrain of song in which audience joins; (vb) sing, speak, say, in c. [L, f. Gk *khoros*]

chose jugée (F), n. Thing it is idle to discuss, as already settled.

chose(n). See CHOOSE.

chou (shōō), n. Rosette or ornamental knot of ribbon, chiffon, &c., on woman's hat or dress. [F, f. L *caulis* cabbage]

chough (tshŭf), n. Red-legged crow. [cf. Du. *kauw*, OF *choue*]

chouse (tshows), v.t., & n. Swindle, trick. [f 1610; f. Turk. *chiaus* official messenger, in allusion to one of these who defrauded Turkish merchants in England 1609]

Chow (tsh-), a. & n. (Slang, Austral.) Chinese (a. & n.); dog of a Chinese breed.

chow-chow (tsh-), n. Chinese preserve of orange-peel, ginger, &c. [Chin.]

chow·der (tsh-), n. Newfoundland & New England dish, stew of fresh fish or clams with bacon, onions, biscuit, &c. [f. F *chaudière* pot f. L *caldaria* (*calidus* hot, -ARY¹)]

chrēmati·stic, a. Of money-making, economic. Hence **chremati·sti**CS n.. [f. Gk *khrēmatistikos* (*khrēmatizō* traffic f. *khrēmata* pl. money f. *khraomai* use), see -IST, -IC]

chrestŏ·mathy, n. Collection of choice passages. [f. Gk *khrēstomatheia* (*khrēstos* good, *math-* st. of *manthanō* learn)]

chrism, n. Consecrated oil, unguent, anointing, esp. in sacred rites. [OE *crisma* f. L f. Gk *khrisma* (*khriō* anoint, -M); cf. CREAM]

chrĭ·som, n. (hist.). Child's white robe at baptism, used as shroud if it died within a month; *c.-child*, in its first month. [var. of prec., perh. orig. a headcloth to keep chrism from being rubbed off]

Chrīst, n. Messiah or Lord's anointed of Jewish prophecy; (title, now treated as name, given to) Jesus as fulfilling this; divine ruler, saviour, inspirer, (esp. *the* or *a C.*); *the C.-child*, C. as a child. Hence **Chri·st**HOOD n., **Chri·st**LESS, **Chri·st-**LIKE, **Chri·st**LY¹, aa., **Chri·stless**NESS, **Chri·stlike**NESS, nn., **Chri·st**WARD(S) adv. [OE *crist* f. L f. Gk *khristos* anointed one (*khriō* anoint) transl. of Heb. see MESSIAH]

Chrīst-cross-row, criss-, n. (archaic). The alphabet. [*Christ's cross*, a cross before alphabet in horn-books, + ROW (of letters)]

chri·sten (-ĭsn), v.t. & i. Admit as Christian by baptism; administer baptism; give name to (person at baptism, or as nickname; *c. him, c. him John*; also ships, bells, &c., with analogous ceremony). [OE *cristnian* make Christian (*cristen* f. WG *cristin* f. L CHRISTIAN*us*)]

Chri·stendom (-ĭsn-), n. Christians; Christian countries. [f. *cristen* adj., see prec., + -DOM]

Chri·stian (-ĭstshn), a. & n. (Person) believing in, professing, or belonging to, the religion of Christ (also as adj. of communities); of Christ or his religion; (person) showing character consistent with Christ's teaching, of genuine piety, Christ-like, (also as adj. of conduct, feelings, communities, &c.); human (person) as opposed to *brute, brutal*; (slang) civilized, decent, (person); *C. burial* (with the ceremonies of the church); *C. name*, given at baptism; *C. era*, reckoned from supposed birth of Christ; *C. science, scientist*, (adherent of) a system of combating disease &c. without medical treatment by mental effect of patient's C. faith. Hence or cogn. **chri·stian**IZE(2, 3) v.i. & t., **chri·stianīz**A·TION n., **chri·stian**LIKE a., **chri·stian**LY¹,² a. & adv., **christiă·no-** comb. form. [f. L *Christianus* (CHRIST, -I-, -AN)]

Christiă·nity (*or* -tshĭ-), n. The Christian faith, doctrines of Christ & his apostles; a Christian religious system; being a Christian, Christian quality or character. [f. L *Christianitas* (as prec., -TY)]

Chrĭ·stie's, n. A sale-room in London esp. for art sales.

Christmas (-ĭ·smas), n. (abbr. *Xmas*). (Also *C.-day*) festival of Christ's birth, 25th Dec., devoted esp. to family reunion & merrymaking, & a quarter-day (*Father C.*, personification of family festivity); (also *C.-tide*) week or more beginning 24th Dec. (*C. eve*); (attrib.) appropriate to C., as *C. book, card* (of greeting by post), *number* (of magazine), *present, pudding*;

C.-box (cf. BOXING-DAY), money given at C. to postman &c. in general acknowledgement of indefinite or continuous services; *C.-tree*, small tree set up in room & hung with candles, presents, &c.; *C. rose*, white-flowered hellebore blooming Dec.-Feb. Hence **Chri·stmas**Y² a. [OE *Cristes mæsse* (MASS¹)]

Chri·sto-, comb. form of L *Christus* or Gk *Khristos* CHRIST, as *-phany*, manifestation of Christ. Hence **Christŏ**·LATRY, **Christo**MA·NIAC (-mā-), **Christŏ**·LOGY, **Christŏ**·LOGIST, nn., **Christo**LO·GICAL a.

Christy minstrels, n. pl. Negro-song troupe with blacked faces. [inventor's name]

chromă·tic, a. Of, produced by, full of bright, colour (*c. printing*, from blocks inked with various colours; *chromatics*, science of colour). (Mus.) of, having, notes not included in diatonic scale, admitting notes marked with accidentals; *c. scale*, proceeding by semitones; *c. semitone*, interval between note & its flat or sharp. Hence **chroma·t**ICALLY adv. [f. Gk *khrōmatikos* (*chrōma -atos* colour, -IC)]

chrō·mato-, chrō·mo-, comb. forms of Gk *khrōma -atos* colour, as in *chromatopsy* abnormally coloured vision, *chromophotograph(y)*, photograph(y) in the natural colours, *chromosphere*, red gaseous envelope of sun.

chrō·matrope, n. Lantern slide of two circular disks, one rotating in front of other, giving kaleidoscopic movement of colours. [irreg. f. prec. + Gk *-tropos* -turning (*trepō*)]

chrome, n. (Also *c.-yellow*) yellow pigment & colour got from chromate of lead; *c. green, orange, red*, pigments from other compounds of chromium. [F, orig. name of *chromium*, f. Gk *khrōma* colour]

chrō·mic, a. Of chromium. [prec. + -IC]

chrō·mium, n. (chem.). Metallic element. Hence **chro·m**ATE¹(3) n. [CHROME + -IUM]

chromo-¹, comb. form of prec.

chromo-². See CHROMATO-.

chrō·mograph, n., & v.t. (Reproduce with) gelatine copying-apparatus in which aniline dye is used for ink. [CHROMO-², -GRAPH]

chrōmoli·thograph, chrō·mo (pl. *-os*), n. Picture printed in colours from stone. So **chromolitho**·GRAPHER, **chromolitho**·GRAPHY, nn., **chro·molitho**GRA·PHIC a. [CHROMO-² + LITHOGRAPH]

chrŏ·nic, a. Lingering, lasting, inveterate, (of disease, cf. ACUTE; *c. invalid*, with c. complaint; also of other states as *c. doubt, rebellion*); (vulg.) bad, intense, severe. Hence **chro·ni**CALLY adv., **chroni·ci**TY n. [f. F *chronique* f. L f. Gk *khronikos* (*khronos* time, -IC)]

chrŏ·nicle, n., & v.t. (Enter, relate, in a) continuous register of events in order of time; *Chronicles*, two books of O.T.; narrative, account; *C.*, newspaper name. Hence **chro·nicl**ER¹ n. [f. OF *cronique* f. med. L *cronica -ae* f. L f. Gk *khronika* neut. pl. see prec.]

chronique scandaleuse (F), n. Body of scandalous gossip current at any time & place.

chrŏ·nogram, n. Phrase &c. of which the Roman-numeral letters added give a date, as LorD haVe MerCIe Vpon Vs =50+500+5+1000+100+1+5+5=1666. Hence **chronogramma·t**IC a. [f. Gk *khronos* time + -GRAM; *-matic* after Gk *grammatikos* adj. f. *gramma*]

chrŏ·nograph, n. Instrument recording time with extreme accuracy; stop-watch. Hence **chrono**GRA·PHIC a. [as prec. + -GRAPH]

chrono·logy, n. Science of computing dates; arrangement of events with dates, table or treatise displaying this. Hence or cogn. **chrono·**LOGER, **chrono·**LOGIST, nn., **chrono**LO·GICAL a., **chronolo·gical**LY² adv., **chrono·log**IZE(3) v.t. [as prec. + -LOGY]

chrono·meter, n. Time-measuring instrument, esp. one with complete provision against disturbance by temperature, used for fixing longitude at sea &c. [as prec. + -METER]

chrono·metry, n. Scientific time-measurement. So **chrono**ME·TRIC(AL) aa., **chronome·trical**LY² adv. [as prec. + -METRY]

chrŏ·nopher, n. Apparatus for distributing electric time-signals. [as prec., Gk *-phoros* -bearing (*pherō* bear)]

chrŏ·noscope, n. Apparatus measuring velocity of projectiles. [as prec. + -SCOPE]

chrȳs-, comb. form of Gk *khrusos* gold, = yellow in chem. & mineral. wds, of gold, golden, yellow, &c., in general wds.

chry·salis, -id, n. (pl. *-ises, -ids, chrysă·lidēs*). Form taken by insect in the torpid stage of passive development between larva (caterpillar &c.) & imago (butterfly &c.); case then enclosing it; (fig.) preparatory or transition state. [f. L f. Gk *khrusallis -idos* lit. golden thing, see prec.]

chrysa·nthemum, n. (Bot.) genus including Corn Marigold; (Gardening) cultivated varieties of this brought from Japan & blooming in Nov. & Dec.; *land of the c.*, Japan. [f. L f. Gk *khrusanthemon* (CHRYS-, *anthemon* flower)]

chrysĕlepha·ntine, a. Overlaid with gold & ivory as by ancient Greek sculptors. [f. Gk *khruselephantinos* (CHRYS-, ELEPHANT, -INE²)]

chrȳso-. = CHRYS-.

chrysobĕ·ryl, n. Yellowish-green gem. [f. L f. Gk *khrusobērullos* (CHRYSO-BERYL)]

chry·solite, n. (Formerly) green gem of various kinds; (now) olivine. [f. OF *crisolite* f. L f. Gk *khrusolithos* (CHRYSO-, *lithos* stone)]

chry·soprase (-āz), n. (N.T.) prob. a golden-green variety of beryl; (now) apple-green variety of chalcedony. [f. OF *crisopace* f. L f. Gk *khrusoprasos* (CHRYSO-, *prason* leek)]

chub (tsh-), n. Thick coarse-fleshed river fish, dusky green above. [?]

chubb (tsh-), n. Kind of lock. [inventor]

chu·bby, a. Round-faced, plump. Hence **chu·bbi**NESS n. [CHUB + -Y[2]]

chuck[1] (tsh-), int., n., & v.i. (Make) call of fowl or person calling fowls or urging horse. [imit.]

chuck[2] (tsh-), n. Term of endearment. Hence **chu·ck**Y[3] n. [prob. var. of CHICK]

chuck[3] (tsh-), v.t., & n. Jerk *under the chin* (n. & v.); fling, throw, (n. & v.) with contempt, carelessness, ease, (*the c.*, slang, dismissal, as *give* one *the c.*); *c. away*, waste, lose (*chance* &c.); *c. up the sponge*, give up contest or attempt; *c. up*, abandon in disgust; *c. out*, expel (troublesome person) from meeting, music-hall, &c., whence **chuck**ER[1]**-out** n.; (slang) *c. it*, cease; *c.-farthing*, kind of quoit game with coins, also pitch and toss. [in 16th c. *chock*, perh. f. F *choc*, *choquer*]

chuck[4] (tsh-), n., & v.t. Contrivance in lathe & the like for holding work to be operated on; (vb) fix (wood &c.) to this. [var. of CHOCK[1]]

chŭ·cker, n. (polo). Each of the periods into which the game is divided. [Hind. *chakar*]

chu·ckle (tsh-), v.i., & n. (Indulge in) suppressed laughter, laugh with closed mouth, (show) signs of glee; exult *over*; (make) hen's call. [imit. & cf. CHUCK[1], -LE(3)]

chu·ckle-head, n., **chu·ckle-headed**, a., (tsh-). Dolt(ish); stupid (fellow). [f. obs. *chuckle* adj. hulking cf. CHUCK[4], CHOCK[1]]

chum (tsh-), v.i., & n. Occupy rooms together, whence **chu·mm**ERY(3) n.; be intimate; *c. up* (colloq.), form intimacy (*with*). (N.) familiar friend (esp. now among boys); (Australia) *new c.*, recent immigrant, greenhorn. [from 1684; etym. dub.]

chump (tsh-), n. Short thick lump of wood; thick end, esp. of loin of mutton (so *c. chop*); (colloq.) head, esp. *off* one's *c.*, mad with excitement &c.; (slang) fool, blockhead. [mod. wd perh. on *chop* & *lump*]

chunk (tsh-), n. Thick lump cut off (wood, bread, cheese, &c.). [prob. var. of CHUCK[4]]

church[1] (tsh-), n. Building for public Christian worship, esp. according to established religion of country; all Christians (*C. militant*, Christians on earth warring against evil); an organized Christian society of any time (*primitive C.*), place (*C. of Scotland*), or distinguishing principle (*reformed C.*); *C. of England*, *English* or *Anglican C.*, English branch of Western or Latin Church rejecting Pope's supremacy since reformation; *Established C.*, recognized by State, as *E.C. of England, Scotland*; organization, clergy & other officers, of a religious society or corporation; clerical profession (*go into the C.*, take holy orders); HIGH, LOW[1], BROAD, *c.*, parties with different views of doctrine & discipline, whence **-chur·chman, -chur·ch**ISM(3), nn.; public worship (*go to, after, c.*; *c.-time*; *c.-goer, -going*); *churchman, churchwoman, churchmanship*, member, membership, of c.; *poor as a c. mouse*, of poor person; *c.-rate*, levied by vestry for maintenance of parish c. & its services; *c. service*, public worship, book with Common Prayer, proper lessons, &c.; *c.-text*, black letter in monumental inscriptions; *churchwarden*, elected lay representative of parish (usu. one of two, elected one by incumbent, one by parishioners), also long clay pipe; *churchyard*, enclosed ground in which c. stands, sometimes used for burial (*churchyard cough*, heralding death; *fat churchyard*, many deaths). Hence **chur·ch**LESS a., **chur·ch**WARD(S) adv. [OE *circe* f. WG *kirika* f. Gk *kuriakon* (perh. *dōma*) Lord's (house) f. *kurios* lord, -AC]

church[2], v.t. Bring (woman) to c. to have thanks offered for delivery of child. [f. prec.]

chur·chy, a. Obtrusively or intolerantly devoted to church or opposed to dissent. Hence **chur·chi**FY v.t., **chur·chi**NESS n. [-Y[2]]

churl (tsh-), n. Person of low birth (*gentleman or c.*); peasant, boor; ill-bred fellow; cross-grained or niggardly person, whence **chur·l**ISH[1] a., **chur·lish**LY[2] adv., **chur·lish**NESS n. [OE *ceorl* f. WG *kerl* man]

churn (tsh-), n., & v.t. & i. (Agitate *milk* or *cream*, produce *butter*, in) butter-making machine; work this machine; stir (liquid) about, make it froth; (of sea &c.) wash to and fro, foam, seethe; large milk-can of c. shape; *c.-dash(er), -staff*, appliance for agitating milk in c.; *a churning*, amount of butter made at once. [OE *cyrin* com.-Teut. cf. Du. *karn*]

churr (tsh-), v.i., & n. (Make) deep trill as of night-jar. [imit., cf. CHIRR]

chŭt (tsh-), int. of impatience.

chute (shōōt), n. Smooth rapid descent of water over slope; sloping channel, slide, with or without water, for conveying things to lower level (also *shoot*); slope for shooting rubbish down; toboggan-slide. [mixture of F *chute* = It. *caduta* (L *cadere* fall) & SHOOT]

chu·tney, -nee, (tsh-), n. Hot Indian condiment of fruits, chillies, &c. [f. Hind. *chatni*]

chyle (k-), n. White milky fluid formed by action of pancreatic juice & bile on chyme. [F, f. L f. Gk *khulos* juice (*khu-* pour)]

chylo- (k-), comb. form of Gk *khulos* CHYLE.

chyme (k-), n. Food converted by gastric secretion into acid pulp. [f. L f. Gk *khumos* juice (*khu-* pour); *khumos* & *khulos*, synonyms, were differentiated by Galen]

chў·mist. See CHEMIST.

chymo- (k-), comb. form of Gk *khumos* CHYME.

cibor·ium, n. (Arch.) canopy, canopied shrine; receptacle for reservation of Eucharist, shaped like shrine, or cup with arched cover. [f. med. L f. Gk *kibōrion*, seed-vessel of water-lily, cup so shaped]

cicā·da, cica·la (-kah-), **ciga·la** (-gah-), n. Transparent-winged shrill-chirping insect. [(*-cala* It.; *-gala* f. F *-gale*) f. L (*-da*)]

ci·catrice, cicā·trix, n. (*-ix*, pl. *-īcēs*, L form in scientific use). Scar of healed wound; scar on tree bark; (Bot.) mark left by fall of leaf &c., hilum of seed. Hence **cicatri·ci**AL, **cică·trico**SE[1], aa. [F (*-ice*), f. L *cicatricem* nom. *-ix*]

cică·tric(u)le, n. (Biol.) germ of chick, round white spot on yolk, tread; (Bot.) =prec. [f. L *cicatricula* (prec., -ULE)]

cĭ·catrize, v.t. & i. Heal, skin over, (t. & i.); mark with scars. Hence **cicatrī-za·tion** n. [f. F *cicatriser* f. L *cicatricare* (CICATRICE) w. assim. to -IZE (prop. *cicatricize*)]

ci·cely, n. Kinds of umbelliferous plant (Sweet, Wild, Rough, C.). [f. L f. Gk *seselis* SESELI w. assim. to the woman's name (=*Cecilia*)]

cicerone (tshĭtsherō·nĭ), n. (pl. *-oni* pr. -ōnē), & v.t. (Conduct *traveller* &c. as) guide who understands & explains antiquities &c. [It., f. L *Ciceronem* nom. *-o* the Roman orator]

Cicerō·nian, a. & n. Eloquent, classical, or rhythmical, as Cicero's style; person learned in or admiring Cicero. Hence **Cicero·nian**ISM(3, 4) n. [f. L *Ciceronianus* (prec., -IAN)]

cicisbeo (tshĭtshĭzbā·o), n. (pl. *-bei* pr. -bāē). Recognized gallant of married woman. So **cicisbe·**ISM(3) n. [It.]

Cid, n. *The C.*, title (lord) of Ruy Diaz, 11th-c. Christian champion against Moors, & of epic relating his deeds. [Sp., f. Arab. *sayyid*]

-cīde, suf. forming nouns meaning (1) slayer of (F, f. L *-cida*) or (2) slaughter of (F, f. L *-cidium*) both f. L *caedere* kill; taken f. L as *parricide*, or formed on L nn. as *regicide* or facetiously on E nn. as *birdicide*.

cĭ·der, n. Fermented drink from apple-juice; *c.*-CUP; *c.-press*, for squeezing juice from apples. [f. OF *sidre* f. LL f. Gk *sikera* f. Heb. *shekar* strong drink (*shakar* drink deeply)]

ci-devant (F), a. or adv. Former(ly), that has been (with the earlier name or state).

cigar·, n. Roll of tobacco-leaf for smoking; *c.-shaped*, cylindrical with pointed end(s); *c.-holder*, mouthpiece holding c. [f. Sp. *cigarro* perh. f. *cigarra* cicada (of similar shape)]

cigare·tte, n. Small cylinder of cut tobacco or of narcotic or medicated substance rolled in paper for smoking. [dim. of prec.]

cĭ·lia, n. pl. Eyelashes; similar fringe on leaf, insect's wing, &c.; (Physiol.) hair-like vibrating organs on animal & vegetable tissue, serving many lower water animals for locomotion. Hence **ci·li**ARY[1], **ci·li**ATE[2], **ci·liated,** aa., **cilia·**TION n. [pl. of L *cilium* eyelash]

cĭ·lice, n. (Garment of) hair-cloth. [F, also OE *cilic*, f. Gk *kilikion* (*Kilikia* Cilicia)]

Cimmĕ·rian, a. Thick, gloomy, (of darkness, night, &c.). [f. L f. Gk *kimmerios* (of Cimmerii, people in perpetual night)+ -AN]

cinch (sĭntsh), n. (U.S.). Saddle-girth used in Mexico &c.; (slang) sure thing, a certainty. [Sp. *cincha*]

cincho·na (-kō-), n. Kinds of evergreen tree yielding c. bark or Peruvian bark & quinine; the bark, drug made from it & highly esteemed as tonic & febrifuge. Hence **cinchon**A·CEOUS a., **ci·nchon**INE[5], **ci·nchon**ISM(5), nn., **ci·nchon**IZE(5) v.t. [Countess of *Chinchon*, introducer of drug in Spain 1640]

Cincinna·tus, n. Great man in retirement who can be called upon in a crisis. [Roman hero called from plough to dictatorship]

ci·ncture, n., & v.t. (Surround with or as with a) girdle, belt, fillet, border. [f. L *cinctura* (*cingere cinct-* gird, -URE)]

ci·nder, n. Slag; residue of coal, wood, &c., that has ceased to flame (whether cold or not) but has still combustible matter in it; (loosely in pl.) ashes; *c.-path*, running-track laid with fine cc.; *c.-sifter*, for separating cc. from ashes. Hence **ci·ndery**[2] a. [OE *sinder* cf. G *sinter*, Sw. *sinder*, w. assim. to the unconnected F *cendre* & L *cinis -eris*]

Cindere·lla, n. Person of unrecognized merit or beauty; *C. dance* or *C.*, dance closing at twelve o'clock. [allusions to fairy-tale]

cĭ·nema, n. Cinematograph theatre; *the c.*, cinematography, moving pictures. [abbr. of foll.]

cĭnema·tograph, n., & v.t. & i. Apparatus producing pictures of motion by the rapid projection on a screen of a great number of photographs taken successively on a long film; =prec.; (v.t.) make c. film of scene, film; (v.i.) use c. Hence **cinematogra·phic** a., **-ical**LY[2] adv., **cinemato·graphy**[1] n. [f. F *cinématographe* f. Gk *kinēma -atos* movement (*kineō* move), see -GRAPH]

cinerār·ia, n. Bright-flowered composite plant, grown chiefly under glass. [f. L *cinerarius* of ashes f. *cinis -eris* ashes (ash-coloured down on leaves)]

ci·nerary, a. Of ashes (esp. *c. urn*, holding ashes of dead after cremation). [as prec.]

cinēr·eous, a. Ashen-grey (esp. of birds or plumage). [f. L *cinereus* (*cinis -eris* ashes) + -OUS]

Ci·ngale·se, a. & n. (Native, language) of Ceylon. [f. Skr. *siṅhalas*]

ci·ngūlum, n. Belt (used technically in Surg., Anat., Zool., &c.). [L]

ci·nnabar, n. & a. Red mercuric sulphide, vermilion (n. & a.). [f. L *cinnabaris* f. Gk *kinnabari* f. Oriental source]

ci·nnamon, n. & a. (E.-Ind. tree yielding) aromatic inner bark used as spice; c.-colour(ed), (of) yellowish-brown; *c.-stone*, brown or yellow garnet. Hence or cogn. **ci·nnam**ATE[1](3) n., **cinnamō·**MIC, **cinnamŏ·**NIC, aa. [f. F *cinnamome* f. L f. Gk *kinnamōmon* f. Semit. (Heb. *qinnāmōn*)]

cinque, cinq, (sĭnk), n. The five at dice & cards. [f. OF *cink* f. L *quinque* five]

cinquece·nto, **cinquece·ntist,** (tshĭnkwĭtshĕ-), nn. Italian style of art, artist, of the 16th c. (15-) with reversion to classical forms. [It. (*-o, -ista*) with omission (in It.) of *mil*]

ci·nq(ue)foil (sĭnkf-), n. Kinds of plant with compound leaf of five leaflets; (Arch.) five-cusped ornament in circle or arch. [thr. OF f. L *quinquefolium* five-leaf]

Cinque Ports (sĭnk), n. pl. Certain ports (orig. five only) on SE coast with ancient privileges. [f. OF *cink porz* five ports]

ci·pher[1]**, cy-,** n. Arithmetical symbol (0) of no value in itself but multiplying number it is placed after, and dividing decimal number it is placed before, by ten; person or thing of no importance; any Arabic figure; secret writing, thing so written, key to it; interlaced initials of person, company, &c., monogram; continued sounding of organ-note owing to defective valve. [f. OF *cyfre* f. Arab. *çifr* zero (orig. adj. = empty)]

ci·pher[2]**, cy-,** v.i. & t. Do arithmetic; work (usu. *out*) by arithmetic, calculate; put into secret writing (cf. DECIPHER); (of organ-note) go on sounding when not pressed. [f. prec.]

ci·polin, n. Italian white-&-green marble. [F, f. It. *cipollino* (*cipolla* onion) from resemblance of structure to coats of onion]

cir·ca, cir·citer, prepp. (abbr. *c.* or *circ.*). About (with dates). (L)

Cir·cē, n. Enchantress, temptress. Hence **Circē·**AN a. [proper name in Gk mythol.]

cir·cinate, a. (bot.). (With leaves) rolled up from apex to base, as in most ferns. [f. L *circinare* make round (*circinus* compasses, -ATE[2])]

cir·cle[1], n. (Line enclosing) perfectly round plane figure (*square the c.*, find square of same area as given c., attempt impossibilities; *great, small, c.*, c. on surface of sphere whose plane passes, does not pass, through sphere's centre; POLAR, ARCTIC, ANTARCTIC, *c.*); (loosely) roundish enclosure; orbit of planet; ring; curved tier of seats at theatre &c. (*dress c., upper c.*, more & less expensive); (Archaeol.) ring of stones as at Stonehenge; period, cycle, round, (*come full c.*, end at starting-point); circling-feat in gymnastics; complete series; (Logic, often *vicious c.*) fallacy of proving proposition from another that rests on it for proof; action & reaction that intensify each other (often *vicious c.*); persons grouped round centre of interest; set, coterie, class, (*first, upper, cc.*; *cc. in which* one *moves*); area of influence, action, &c., sphere. Hence **cir·cle**WISE adv. [OE *circul* (ME *cercle* f. F) f. L *circulus* dim. of *circus* ring]

cir·cle[2], v.t. & i. Encompass (poet.); encompass *round, about*; move in a c. *round, about*; (Gym.) revolve round bar in various ways; be passed round (of wine &c.); (Mil.) sweep round on moving flank (of cavalry, cf. WHEEL[2]); (p.p.) rounded, marked with cc. [f. prec.]

cir·clet, n. Small circle; circular band, esp. of gold, jewelled, &c., worn on head or elsewhere. [f. F *cerclet* (CIRCLE[1], -ET)]

cir·cuit (-kĭt), n. Line enclosing an area, distance round; area enclosed; roundabout journey; sequence of changes, acts, &c.; journey of judge in particular district to hold courts, this district (eight in Eng. & Wales), the barristers (*member of a c.*) making the c.; Methodist-Church district with series of itinerant preachers; (Electr.) path of current (*short c.*, faulty shortening of a c. by defective insulation). [F, f. L *circuitus* f. CIRCUM(*ire it-* go)]

circū·itous, a. Roundabout, indirect. Hence **circu·itous**LY[2] adv., **circu·itous**NESS n. [f. LL *circuitosus* (CIRCUIT, -OSE[1])]

cir·cular, a. & n. Round in superficies; moving in a circle (*c. tour*, ending where it began by different route, *c. ticket*, for this); (Logic) of, using, the *vicious* CIRCLE[1]; addressed to a circle of persons, customers, &c. (*c. note*, banker's letter of credit in traveller's favour to several foreign bankers; *c. letter* or *c.*, notice, advertisement, &c., reproduced for sending round); of, like, the geometrical circle; *c. saw*, toothed disk revolving by machinery for sawing. Hence **circulă·**RITY n., **cir·cular**LY[2] adv. [f. OF *circulier* f. L *circularis* (CIRCLE, -AR[1])]

cir·cularize, v.t. Send circulars to. [-IZE(1)]

cir·culate, v.i. & t. Go round (blood circulates through veins, water in pipes, wine on table, newspaper to circle of readers); (of decimals) = RECUR; send round, give currency to, (book, report, scandal, &c.); *circulating library*, with books taken by subscribers in succession; *circulating medium*, notes, gold, &c., used in exchange. [f. L *circulare* (CIRCLE[1]), -ATE[3]]

circula·tion, n. Movement of blood from and to heart, similar movement of sap &c.; movement to and fro (*c. of water, atmosphere*, &c.); transmission, distribution, (of news, books, &c.); number of copies sold, esp. of newspapers; currency, coin, &c. [F, f. L *circulationem* (*circulare* see prec., -ATION)]

cir·culative, a. Inclined to, promoting, circulation. [as prec., -IVE]

cir·culator, n. One who circulates news, coin, &c. [as prec., -OR[2]]

cir·culatory, a. Of circulation of blood or sap. [f. L *circulatorius* (as prec., -ORY)]

circum-, pref. =L adv. & prep. *circum* round, about, used (1) adverbially, as *circumvagant* wandering round or about; (2) prepositionally, as *circumocular* surrounding the eye. E wds are some f. L (direct, as *circumscribe*, or thr. F as *circumcise*), some formed in E on L elements as *circumambient*, & some facetious hybrids as *circumbendibus*.

circuma·mbient, a. Surrounding (esp. of air or other fluid). Hence **circuma·mbi**ENCY n. [CIRCUM-(1) + AMBIENT]

circuma·mbulate, v.t. & i. Walk round (place &c.); walk about; beat about the bush. Hence **circumambul**A·TION n., **circuma·mbulat**ORY a. [f. L CIRCUM-(*ambulare* walk), -ATE[3]]

circumbe·ndibus, n. (facet.). Roundabout method; circumlocution. [CIRCUM-(1), BEND, ending of L abl. case]

cir·cumcise (-z), v.t. Cut off foreskin of (as Jewish or Mohammedan rite, or surgically); purify (*c. the heart, passions*, &c.). [f. OF *circonciser* f. L CIRCUM(*cīdere -cīs-* =*caedere* cut)]

circumci·sion (-ĭzhn), n. Act or rite of, spiritual purification by, circumcising; (Bibl.) *the c.*, the Jews; (Eccl.) festival of C. of Christ, 1st Jan. [f. OF *circumcisiun* f. L *circumcisionem* (as prec., -ION)]

circu·mference, n. Encompassing boundary, esp. of figure enclosed by curve, as circle; distance round. So **circumfere·nti**AL a. [f. L CIRCUM(*ferentia* f. *ferent-* part. st. of *ferre* bear, & see -ENCE)]

cir·cumflex, a. & n., & v.t. *C. accent* or *c.*, mark (⌒ in Gk, ^ elsewhere) placed over vowel to indicate contraction, length, or special quality (vb, mark thus); (Anat.) curved, bending round something else, (*c. artery, muscle*, &c.). [f. L CIRCUM(*flexus* p.p. of *flectere* bend) transl. of Gk *perispōmenos*]

circu·mfluent, a. Flowing round, ambient. Hence **circu·mflu**ENCE n. [f. L CIRCUM(*fluens* f. *fluere* flow, -ENT)]

circu·mfluous, a. =prec.; surrounded by water. [f. L CIRCUM*fluus* flowing or flowed round (*fluere* flow) + -OUS]

circumfu·se (-z), v.t. Pour (fluid) *about* or *round* (object); surround, bathe, (object *with*, or of fluid as subj.). So **circumfu·s**ION (-zhn) n. [f. L CIRCUM-(*fundere fus-* pour)]

cir·cumgȳra·te, v.i. Turn, wheel, travel, round. Hence **circumgȳr**A·TION n., **circumgȳra·t**ORY a. [CIRCUM-(1) + GYRATE]

circumjā·cent, a. Situated around. [f. L CIRCUM(*jacent-* part. st. of *jacēre* lie)]

circumli·ttoral, a. Bordering the shore. [CIRCUM-(2) + L *littus -oris* shore + -AL]

circumlocu·tion, n. Use of many words where few would do; evasive talk; a roundabout expression; *C. Office*, dilatory Government office. Hence **circumlocu·tion**AL, **circumlocu·tion**ARY[1], **circumlŏ·cut**ORY, aa., **circumlocu·tion**IST(1) n. [f. L CIRCUM(*locutio* LOCUTION)]

circum-merĭ·dian, a. [astr.). Near the meridian (of observations taken of star &c. when so placed). [CIRCUM-(2)]

circumnă·vigate, v.t. Sail round (esp. *the globe* or *world*). Hence **circumna·vigat**OR[2] n. [f. L CIRCUM(*navigare* NAVIGATE)]

circumnū·tate, v.i. (bot.). Bend towards all points of compass successively (of growing parts of plant). Hence **circumnut**A·TION n. [CIRCUM-(1), NUTATE]

circumor·al, a. (physiol.). Placed round mouth. [CIRCUM-(2), L *os oris* mouth, -AL]

circumpo·lar, a. (Astr.) *c. star, motion*, &c., above horizon throughout diurnal course; (Geog.) about, near, one of the earth's poles. [CIRCUM-(2), L *polus* POLE[2], -AR[1]]

cir·cumscribe, v.t. Draw line round; (Geom.) describe (figure) round another touching it at points, but not cutting it; lay down limits of, confine, restrict; define logically; sign (round robin), whence **circumscri·b**ER[1] n. [f. L CIRCUM(*scribere script-* write)]

circumscri·ption, n. Having, marking out, or imposing, of limits; boundary; limited district; definition; (Geom.) circumscribing (see prec.); inscription round coin &c. [f. L *circumscriptio* (prec., -ION]

circumsō·lar, a. Revolving round, being near, the sun. [CIRCUM-(2), SOL[1], -AR[1]]

cir·cumspect, a. Cautious, wary, taking everything into account. Hence or cogn. **circumspe·ct**ION, **cir·cumspect**NESS, nn., **cir·cumspect**IVE a., **cir·cumspect**LY[2] adv. [f. L CIRCUM(*spectus* p.p. of *-spicere* look at) considered, of act, & transf. of persons]

cir·cumstance, n. (Pl.) time, place, manner, cause, occasion, &c., surroundings, of an act; external conditions affecting or that might affect an agent (*in, under, the cc.*, owing to or making allowance for them; *under no cc.*, not whatever happens, never); material welfare (*in good, bad, easy, reduced, straitened, cc.*). (Sing.) full detail in narrative; ceremony, fuss, (*without c.*, unceremoniously; *pomp & c.*); incident, occurrence, fact (esp. *the c. that*). Hence **cir·cumstanc**ED[2] a. [OF f. L CIRCUM-(*stantia* f. part. of *stare* stand) surrounding state]

circumsta·ntial (-shl), a., Depending on subordinate details (*c. evidence*, establishing the doubtful main fact by inference from known facts otherwise hard to explain); adventitious, incidental; with many details (*c. story*). Hence **circumstantia·l**ITY (-shĭ-) n., **circumsta·ntial**LY[2] adv. [as prec. + -AL]

cir·cumvallāte, v.t., **circumvalla·tion,** n. (Surround with) rampart or entrenchment; process of doing this. [f. L CIRCUM(*vallare* f. *vallum* rampart), see -ATE[3], -ATION]

circumve·nt, v.t. Entrap; overreach, outwit. So **circumve·nt**ION n. [f. L CIRCUM(*venire vent-* come)]

circumvolu·tion, n. Rolling round; coil; period; sinuous movement. [f. L CIRCUM-(*volvere volut-* roll), -ION]

cir·cus, n. Rounded or oval arena lined with tiers of seats for equestrian & other exhibitions; amphitheatre of hills; open circle with streets converging on it; travelling show of horses, riders, &c. [L, =ring]

cirque (-k), n. Arena, natural amphitheatre, (chiefly poet. & rhet.). [F, f. L as prec.]

cirrho·sis, n. Disease of liver, chiefly alcoholic. [Gk *kirrhos* tawny, -OSIS]

cirri-, cirro-, comb. form of CIRRUS. Hence **cirri·**FEROUS, **ci·rri**FORM, aa., & names of cloud-forms as *cirro-cumulus*. [-I-, -O-]

ci·rriped(e), n. Marine animal in valved shell attached to other bodies, with legs like curl of hair. [f. F CIRRI(*pède* f. L *pes pedis* foot)]

ci·rrus, n. (pl. *-rī*). (Bot.) tendril; (Zool.) slender appendage, as beard of fishes, feet of cirripeds; (Meteor.) form of cloud with diverging filaments like lock of hair or wool. Hence **cirro·**SE[1], **ci·rr**OUS, aa. [L, =curl]

cis-, pref. =on this side of, opp. to *trans-* or *ultra-*, retaining in some orig. L wds the Roman sense (*cispadane, cisalpine*, S. or Rome-wards of Po, Alps), but usu. w. ref. to speaker's or majority's position (*cismontane*, N. of Alps or non-Italian; *cis-Leithan*, W. of Leitha, Austrian, non-Hungarian; *cis-pontine*, in London, on northern or better known side of bridges or Thames); prefixed to the adj. form of the second element; often used in wds made for the nonce in opposition to wds in *trans-* or *ultra-* (*transatlantic & cisatlantic*); also of time as *cis-Elizabethan*. [L prep.]

cist, n. (archaeol.). Prehistoric stone or hollowed-tree coffin; box for sacred utensils in Gk mysteries. [f. L f. Gk *kistē* box]

Cister·cian (-shn), n. & a. (Monk) of order founded 1098 at Cistercium or Cîteaux, stricter offshoot of Benedictines, also called *Bernardine* as patronized by St Bernard of Clairvaux. [-AN]

ci·stern, n. Reservoir for storing water, usu. on upper storey with pipes supplying taps on lower levels (also fig., of pond). [f. OF *cisterne* f. L *cisterna* (*cista* see CIST) cf. *caverna*]

ci·stus, n. Kinds of shrub with large white or red short-lived flowers. [f. Gk *kistos*]

ci·tadel, n. Fortress, esp. one guarding or dominating city; last retreat of hard-pressed party, belief, &c. [f. F *citadelle* f. It. *cittadella* dim. of *cittade* f. L *civitatem* CITY]

cite, v.t. Summon to appear in law-court; quote (passage, book, author) in support of a position; mention as example. Hence or cogn. **ci·t**ABLE a., **cīt**A·TION n. [f. F *citer* f. L *citare* frequent. of *ciēre* set moving]

ci·ther(n), ci·ttern, n. (archaic or poet.). Lute, guitar. [f. L f. Gk *kithara* harp with seven to eleven strings]

ci·tizen, n. Burgess, freeman, of city; townsman; civilian; member, native or naturalized, of a State (usu. *of*; *c. of the world*, cosmopolitan); inhabitant *of*. Hence **ci·tizen**HOOD, **ci·tizen**SHIP, nn. [ME *citesein* (*-s-* perh. on anal. of DENIZEN) f. OF *citeain* (CITY, -AN)]

citr-, comb. form of foll. Hence **ci·tr**ATE[1] (3) n.

ci·tric, a. (chem.). Of citron (esp. *c. acid*). [f. L *citrus* CITRON + -IC]

ci·trine, a. Lemon-coloured. [f. F *citrin* f. L *citrus*, -INE[1]]

citro-. =CITR-.

ci·tron, n. (Tree bearing) lemon-like but larger, less acid, & thicker-skinned fruit; lemon colour. [F. f. It. *citrone* (L *citrus*, -OON)]

ci·ty, n. (Loosely) important town; (strictly) town created c. by charter, esp. as containing cathedral (but all cathedral towns are not cc., nor vice versa); *c. of* REFUGE; *Holy C.*, Jerusalem, Heaven; *Eternal C., C. of the Seven Hills*, Rome; *Celestial C., Heavenly C., C. of God*, Paradise; *the C.*, part of London governed by Lord Mayor & Corporation, business part of this, commercial circles, (*C. man*, in commerce or finance; *C. article*, in newspaper on these; *C. Company*, corporation representing ancient trade-guild). Hence (-)**citi**ED[2], **ci·ty**LESS, aa., **ci·ty**WARD(S) adv. [f. OF *cité* f. L *civitatem* (*civis* citizen, -TY) citizenship, community]

ci·vet, n. (Also *c.-cat*) carnivorous quadruped between fox & weasel in size & look; strong musky perfume got from anal glands of this. [f. F *civette* f. Arab. *zabad*]

ci·vic, a. Of, proper to, citizens (*c. crown*, oak-garland, Roman honour to one who saved fellow-citizen's life in war); of city, municipal; of citizenship, civil, (*c. virtues, activity*), whence **ci·vics** n. Hence **ci·vically** adv. [f. L *civicus* (*civis* citizen, -IC)]

ci·vies, n. pl. (army slang). Civilian clothes. [abbr.]

ci·vil, a. Of gregarious men (*c. society, life*); of a citizen community (*c. institutions*; *c. war*, confined to this, between fellow-citizens, *The C. W.*, in Engl., between Charles I & Parliament, in U.S., War of Secession); of, becoming, a citizen (*c. rights, liberty*; *c. spirit*); polite, obliging, not rude, whence (with pl. = favours) **civi·lity** n.; not naval or military (*c. engineer*; *C. Service*, all non-warlike branches of State administration, *C. Servant*, member of one of them); not ecclesiastical (*c. magistrates*, & formerly *c. law*; *c. marriage*, solemnized as c. contract without religious ceremony); not criminal (*c. law*, concerning questions of private rights merely); not natural or astronomical (*c. day, year*, as recognized for dating &c.); *C. Law*, Roman law (so D.C.L.; & see above); *c. list*, Parliamentary allowance for King's household & royal pensions. Hence **ci·villy**[2] adv. [F, f. L *civilis* (*civis* citizen, -IL)]

civi̇·lian (-yan), n. & a. (Person) not of navy or army; (also *Indian C.*) member of Indian Civil Service. [archaic sense, one learned in Civil Law, f. OF *civilien* as prec., -IAN]

ci·viliza·tion, n. Making or becoming civilized; stage, esp. advanced stage, in social development; civilized States. [f. foll. + -ATION]

ci·vilize, v.t. Bring out of barbarism, enlighten, refine; *c. away*, get rid of (barbarous habits &c.). Hence **ci·vilizable** a., **ci·vilizer**[1] n. [f. F *civiliser*, see CIVIL, -IZE(3)]

clack, n., & v.i. Sharp sound as of boards struck together; flap-valve in pumps &c.; clatter of tongues. (Vb) chatter loudly; make sound as of clogs on stone. [prob. imit.; cf. F *claque(r)*, Du. *klakken*]

clad. See CLOTHE.

clăd(o)-, comb. form of Gk *klados* young shoot, in bot. terms as *cladocarpous* with fruit on lateral branchlets.

claim[1], v.t. Demand as one's due (recognition &c., *to* be, *that* one should be, recognized &c.); represent oneself as having (*c. the victory, accuracy*); profess *to* (*be* the owner, *have told* the truth); demand recognition of the fact that; (U.S.) contend, assert; (of things) deserve (esp. *attention*). Hence **clai·mable** a., **clai·mant**(1) n. [f. OF *cla(i)mer* f. L *clamare* call out]

claim[2], n. Demand for something as due (*lay c. to*); right, title, *to* thing, right to make demand *on* person; (Mining &c.) piece of land allotted. [f. OF *claime* see prec.]

clairau·dience, n., **-ent** a. & n. = foll. with 'hearing' for 'sight' 'seeing'. [L *audio* hear]

clairvoy·ance, n. Faculty of seeing mentally what is happening or exists out of sight; exceptional insight. [F (L *clarus* clear, *vidēre* see, -ANCE); first sense given in E]

clairvoy·ant, n. (sometimes fem. *-te*), & a. (Person) having clairvoyance. [F, as prec., -ANT]

clam[1]. See CLAMP[1].

clam[2]. n. Various bivalve shell-fish, esp. the N.-Amer. Hard or Round, & Soft or Long, C., used for food. [orig. *c.-shell* f. *clam* = CLAMP[1]]

clā·mant, a. Noisy, insistent; urgent. [f. L *clamare* cry out, -ANT]

cla·mber, v.i., & n. Climb with hands & feet; climb with difficulty or labour. [prob. f. CLIMB + -ER[5], but cf. CLAMP[1] & G *sich klammern* hook oneself on]

cla·mmy, a. Moist, usu. cold, & sticky or slimy (of the hand, ill-baked bread, any surface). Hence **cla·mmily**[2] adv., **cla·mminess** n. [perh. f. OE *clām* clay]

clă·mour, n., & v.i. & t. Shout(ing); (make) loud appeal, complaint, or demand (abs., or *for, against, to* do; also as v.t., *c. down*, silence, *c. out of, into*, force by c.); (make) confused noise. So **cla·morous** a., **cla·morously**[2] adv. [f. OF f. L *clamor* (*clamare* call out)]

clamp[1], n., & v.t. (also *clam* in some technical uses of n.). Brace, clasp, or band, usu. of iron, for strengthening other materials or holding things together; various appliances or tools with opposite sides connected by screw for holding or compressing; (vb) strengthen, fasten together, with c. or cc. [f. 15th c.; there was OE *clam* in same sense]

clamp[2], n., & v.t. Pile (of bricks for burning, potatoes &c. under straw & earth, turf, peat, garden rubbish, &c.); (vb) pile (bricks &c.) *up*. [perh. = prec.; cf. Du. *klamp* a heap]

clan, n. Scotch highlanders with common ancestor, esp. while under patriarchal control (*clansman*, member, fellow member, of c.); tribe; family holding together, whence **cla·nnish**[1] a., **cla·nnishly**[2] adv., **cla·nnishness** n.; party, coterie; genus, species, class. [f. Gael. *clann* f. L PLANT*a*]

clande·stine, a. Surreptitious, secret. Hence **clande·stinely**[2] adv. [f. L *clandestinus* (*clam* secretly, cf. *intestine, matutine*)]

clang, n., & v.i. & t. Loud resonant metallic sound (esp. of trumpet, arms, large bell, some birds); (vb) make, cause (thing) to make, this. [f. L *clangere* cf. Gk *klag-*]

cla·ngour (-ngg-), n. Succession, prevalence, of clanging noises. Hence **cla·ngor**OUS a., **cla·ngorous**LY[2] adv. [f. L *clangor* (prec., -OR[1])]

clank, n., & v.i. & t. Sound as of heavy chain rattling; (vb) make, cause (bucket, chain, &c.) to make, this. [f. 17th c., perh. on *clang, clink*; but cf. Du. *klank*]

cla·nship, n. The clan system; division into mutually jealous parties; devotion to a leader. [-SHIP]

clap[1], n. Explosive noise (*of* thunder, of hand-palms struck together); slap, pat, (archaic). [perh. f. foll.]

clap[2], v.i. & t. *C.* one's *hands, c.* (t. & i.), applaud by striking palms together loudly (also, usu. w. *hands*, strike them for warmth, as signal, &c.); flap (wings) audibly; *c. on the back*, slap so in encouragement or congratulation; put, place, quickly or energetically (spurs *to* horse, person *in* prison, duty *on* goods; *c. on all sail*; *c. up peace, bargain*, make hastily or carelessly; *c. eyes on*, catch sight of, esp. w. neg.); *c.-net*, fowler's or entomologist's, shut by pulling string. [cf. G *klappen*, ON *klappa*]

clap[3], n. (not in decent use). Venereal disease, gonorrhoea, [?]

cla·pboard, n. (U.S.) = WEATHER-*board*. [anglicized f. LG *klappholt* cask-stave]

cla·pper, n. Tongue or striker of bell; hand or wind rattle for scaring birds. [CLAP[2] + -ER[1]]

cla·pperclaw, v.t. Scratch & hit; abuse, criticize spitefully. [prec., CLAW]

cla·ptrap, n. & a. Language, sentiment, meant to catch applause; showy. [CLAP[1], TRAP]

claque (-ahk), ***claqueur·*** (-ker), nn. Hired body of applauders, hired applauder. [F]

clar·abella, n. Powerful fluty organ-stop. [f. L *clarus* clear, *bellus* pretty]

clă·rence, n. Four-wheeled close carriage with seats for four inside & two on box, four-wheeler cab. [Duke of *C.* (William IV)]

Clă·renc(i)eux (-sū), n. Second KING[1]-of-Arms. [AF (*-ceux*), f. *Clarence* (*Clare* in Suffolk), dukedom of Lionel son of Edw. III]

clă·rendon, a. & n. (typog.). Thick-faced (type), **thus,** of various sizes.

clă·ret, n. & a. Kinds of red French wine imported from Bordeaux (usu. blends of light wine with Benicarlo); (slang) blood (*tap* one's *c.*, make his nose bleed with blow of fist); c.-colour(ed), reddish-violet; artificial salmon-fly so coloured; *c.*-CUP[1]. [OF (*vin c.*), =*clairet* dim. of *clair* f. L *clarus* clear (orig. of light red wines between white & red)]

clă·rifȳ, v.t. & i. Make clear (obscure subject, mind, sight); free from impurities, make transparent, (liquid, butter, air, &c.); become transparent (lit., & fig. of literary style &c.). [f. OF *clarifier* f. L *clarificare* (*clarus* clear, -FY)]

clă·rinet (*also* -ĕ·t), n. Wooden single-reed instrument played by holes & keys; organ-stop of like quality. So **clarine·t**-TIST(3) n. [f. F *clarinette* dim. of *clarine* = foll.]

clă·rion, n. & a. Shrill narrow-tubed trumpet formerly used in war; rousing sound; organ-stop of c. quality; (adj.) clear & loud. [f. OF *claron* f. med. L *clarionem* nom. *-io* (CLEAR)]

clărione·t, n. = CLARINET. [prec., -ET[1]]

clă·rity, n. Clearness. [ME & OF *clarté* f. L *claritatem* (*clarus* clear, -TY)]

clar·kia, n. Kinds of annual with showy flowers. [W. *Clarke*, U.S. explorer]

clār·y, n. Kind of pot-herb. [OE *slarie* f. med. L *sclarea* etym. dub.]

clash, v.i. & t., & n. (Make) loud broken sound as of collision, striking weapons, cymbals, bells rung together; encounter, conflict, (v.i., & n.); disagree(ment); be at variance *with*; *colours c.*, are discordant; rush or charge (vb) *into, against, upon*; ring (bells) all together. [prob. imit., perh. on *clang, crash*]

clasp[1], n. Contrivance of interlocking parts for fastening, buckle, brooch; metal fastening of book-cover; embrace, reach; grasp, handshake; bar of silver on medal-ribbon with name of occasion (in campaign commemorated by medal) at which wearer was present; *c.-knife*, folding, with catch fixing blade when open. [f. 14th c.; excl. E; etym. dub.; var., *clapse*, cf. *hasp hapse, ask ax*]

clasp[2], v.t. & i. Fasten (c.); fasten (t. & i.) with or as c.; encircle, hold closely, embrace; grasp (another's hand; *c. hands*, shake hands emotionally, make common cause; *c.* one's *hands*, interlace fingers). [f. prec.]

cla·sper, n. In vbl senses; esp., (pl.) appendages of some male fish & insects for holding the female. [-ER[1]]

class, n., & v.t. Rank, order, of society (*higher, upper, middle, lower, working, cc.*; *the cc.*, the rich or educated, opp. *the masses*); *c.-conscious*(*ness*), esp. realizing & taking part in the conflict between the labouring & other cc.; caste system; set of students taught together, their time of meeting, their course of instruction, (U.S.) all college students of same standing, (*c.-fellow, -mate*, present or past member of same c. with one; *c.-book*, used by c.); (in foreign armies) all the recruits of a year (*the* 1917 c.); division of candidates after examination (*take a c.*, gain honours; so *classman* opp. to *passman*; *c.-list*, issued by examiners); division according to quality (so *high, low, first, second*, &c., -c., as adjj. of praise or depreciation, & *first, second, third, c.*, of railway carriages &c.; *no c.* slang, quite inferior); number of individuals having common name as like in any respect; (Nat. Hist.) highest division (*c., order, family, genus, species*) of animal, vegetable, or mineral kingdom. (Vb) place in a c.; hence **cla·ss**ABLE a. [f. F *classe* f. L *classis* assembly (*calare* convoke)]

clă·ssic, a. & n. Of the first class, of allowed excellence; of the standard ancient Latin & Greek authors, art, or culture; of Latin & Greek antiquity; in the c. style, simple, harmonious, proportioned, & finished (cf. ROMANTIC); having literary associations (*c. ground*); *the c. races*, Two & One Thousand, Derby, Oaks, St Leger. (N.) writer or artist of admitted excellence; ancient Greek or Latin writer; Latin and Greek scholar; follower of c. models (cf. ROMANTIC); (pl.) classical studies. [f. L *classicus* (prec., -IC) of the first class]

clă·ssical, a. Standard, first-class, esp. in literature; of ancient Greek or Latin standard authors or art; learned in these; based on these (*c. education*); in, following, the restrained style of c. antiquity (as prec., cf. ROMANTIC). Hence **cla·ssical**ISM(3), **classica·l**ITY, nn., **cla·ssical**LY[2] adv. [as prec. + -AL]

cla·ssicism, -ist, nn. Following, follower, of classic style; classical scholar(ship); advocacy, advocate, of classical education; (*-ism*) a Latin or Greek idiom. [-ISM(3, 4), -IST(2, 3)]

cla·ssicize, v.t. & i. Make classic; imitate the classical style. [-IZE(2, 3)]

classico-, comb. form of L *classicus* w. senses of CLASSIC. Hence **classicŏ·**LATRY n.

cla·ssifȳ, v.t. Arrange in classes; assign to a class. So **cla·ssifi**ABLE, **cla·ssifica**TORY, aa., **classifica·**TION, **cla·ssifi**ER[1], nn. [f. L CLASS*is* + -FY]

cla·ssy, a. (slang). Superior. [-Y[2]]

cla·tter, v.i. & t., & n. (Make) dry confused sound as of many plates struck together; (resound with) noisy talk; *c. along, down*, &c., move, fall, with a c.; (v.t.) cause (plates &c.) to c. [OE *clatrian* cf. Du. *klateren*]

clause, n. Short sentence; (Gram.) subordinate words including subject & predicate but syntactically equivalent to noun, adj., or adv.; single proviso in treaty, law, or contract. [OF, f. LL *clausa* = L *clausula* conclusion (*claudere claus-* shut, -ULE)]

clau·stral, a. Of the cloister, monastic, narrow. [f. LL *claustralis* (CLOISTER, -AL)]

claustropho·bia, n. Morbid dread of closed places. [f. L *claustrum* (see CLOISTER) + -PHOBIA]

clā·vate, a. (bot.). Club-shaped. [f. L *clava* club + -ATE[2]]

clă·vichord, n. Predecessor of piano, first string-instrument with key-board. [f. 15th-c. L *clavichordium* (L *clavis* key, CHORD[1])]

clă·vicle, n. Collar-bone. So **clavi·cul**AR[1] a. [f. L *clavicula* dim. of *clavis* key]

clă·viform, a. Club-shaped. [L *clava*, -FORM]

claw[1], n. Pointed horny nail of beast's or bird's foot (*pare, cut, the cc. of*, disarm); foot so armed, pincers of shellfish; (contempt.) hand; contrivance for grappling, holding, &c. (*c.-hammer*, with bent split end for extracting nails; *c.-h. coat*, dress coat). Hence (-)**claw**ED[2] a. [OE *clawu* f. obl. cases of *cléa* cf. *clee* still dial.; cf. Du. *klaauw*, G *klaue*]

claw[2], v.t. & i. Scratch, tear, seize or pull towards one. with cc. or hands (*c. me & I'll c. thee*, of mutual flattery f. obs. sense, still Sc., *scratch gently*); (Naut.) beat to windward, esp. *c. off*, away from shore. [f. prec.]

clay, n. Stiff tenacious earth, material of bricks, pottery, &c.; (material of) human body (*wet, moisten*, one's *c.*, drink); (also *c. pipe*) tobacco-pipe made of c. (*yard of c.*, long one); *c.-cold*, cold as c. (usu. of the dead). Hence (with *-e-* to separate *yy*, & comp. *more, most*) **clay·e**Y[2] a. [OE *clǽg*, com.-Teut. cf. Du. & G *klei*, f. *kli-* to stick cf. Gk *gloios*, L *gluten*]

clay·more, n. Ancient Scottish two-edged broadsword; (incorrectly) basket-hilted often single-edged broadsword introduced in 16th c. [f. Gael. *claidheamh mòr* great sword]

clean[1], a. Free from dirt, unsoiled, clear, (land of weeds, ship of barnacles, paper of writing, printing-proof of corrections; *c.* BILL[4]; *c. hands, c.-handed, c.-handedness*, innocence, innocent; *c.-fingered*, unbribed; *c. slate*, fig., freedom from all commitments; *c. tongue*, abstinence from foul talk; *c.* BREAST[1]; *show c. pair of heels*, escape by speed; *c.-bred*, thoroughbred); (bibl.) free of ceremonial defilement or of disease; (of beasts &c.) fit for food (esp. *c. fish*, not at or soon after spawning); hostile to dirt (*c. servant*), cleanly; well-formed, shapely, (joints, figure, so *c.-limbed*; *c. ship*, with tapering lines); smart, adroit, not bungling, (*c. fielding*); even, unobstructed, clear-cut, complete, (*c. sweep*, complete riddance; *c. timber*, without knots). Hence **clea·n**NESS n. [OE *clǽne*; com.-Teut. cf. G *klein* small]

clean[2], adv. Completely, right, outright, altogether, simply, absolutely, (*c. gone, c. bowled, cut c. through, c. mad, c. wrong*); *c.-cut*, sharply outlined. [OE *clæne* adv. f. prec.]

clean[3], v.t., & n. Make clean (*of* dirt &c.); empty (one's plate); make one*self*, make oneself, become, c. (also *c. up*); *c. up*, put things tidy, put (things) tidy, clear (mess) away; *c. out*, empty, strip, (esp. slang, person of his money); *c. down*, c. by brushing or wiping; hence **clea·n**ABLE a., (-)**clea·n**ER[1](1, 2), n. (N.) cleaning (*give it a c.*). [f. CLEAN[1]]

clea·nly[1] (-ēn-), adv. In clean way. [OE *clǣnlīc* (CLEAN[1] + -LY[2])]

clea·nly[2] (-ĕn-), a. Habitually clean, attentive to cleanness. Hence **clea·nli**LY[2] adv., **clea·nli**NESS n. [OE *clǣnlīc* (CLEAN[1] + -LY[1])]

cleanse (-ĕnz), v.t. Make clean (now formal or archaic for *clean* in lit. sense); purify (*of* sin &c., or with *sin* &c. as obj.); (bibl.) cure (leper &c.). [OE *clǣnsian* (*clǣne* CLEAN[1])]

clear[1], a. & adv. Unclouded, transparent, not turbid, lustrous, unspotted, (so *clear-starch* v.t., = starch well; *c. conscience*, feeling that one is innocent); distinct, unambiguous, intelligible, not confused, manifest, (*in c.*, not in cipher or code); discerning, penetrating, (so *clear-sighted, -sightedness*, usu. fig.); confident, decided, certain, (*on* point, *of* fact, *that*); easily audible; without deduction, net; rid *of*; complete (*three c. days*); open, unobstructed, (*coast is c.*, no one about to see or interfere); unengaged, free, unencumbered by debt. (Adv.) clearly (*speak loud & c.*; *c.-cut*, well defined; *show, shine, c.*); quite (*c. away, off, out, through*; *three feet c.*); apart, without contact, (*stand, hang, steer, get, c.*). [ME & OF *cler* (now *clair*) f. L *clarus*]

clear[2], v.t. & i. Make, become, c. (*of*; *c. the air*, lit. of sultriness, fig. of suspicion, constraint, sulks, &c.; *c.* one's *throat*, by slight coughing); show or declare innocent (*of*); free from or *of* obstruction (*c. the decks for action*, make ready to fight; *c. land*, cut down trees &c. before cultivating); remove (obstruction, esp. *c. out of the way*); melt away (also slang of persons, go away); empty, become empty; pass over or by without touching (esp. in jumping, *c. 6 ft, 22 ft, a gate*); (Naut.) free (ship) by paying all dues, (intr. of ship) sail; defray (prospective charges) by single payment; make (sum) as net gain; *c. away*, remove, remove meal from table, (of mist &c.) disappear; *c. off*, get rid of, melt away, (of intruders) go away; *c. out*, empty, make off; *c. up*, solve (mystery), make tidy, (of weather &c.) grow c. [f. prec.]

clear·ance, n. Making clear; removal of obstructions; passing of cheques through Clearing-House; (certificate of) clearing of ship at Custom-House; permit to leave government employ; (Mech.) space allowed for the passing of two parts. [prec. + -ANCE]

clear·cole, n., & v.t. (Paint with) size and whiting or white-lead as first coat in house-painting. [f. F *claire colle* clear glue]

clear·ing, n. In vbl senses; esp.; piece of land in primeval forest cleared for cultivation; *C.-House*, banker's institution in London at which cheques & bills are exchanged, the balances only being paid in cash. [CLEAR[2], -ING[1]]

clear·ly, adv. Distinctly to, with, senses or mind; manifestly; undoubtedly, (in answers) yes, no doubt. [CLEAR[1], -LY[2]]

clear·ness, n. Transparence; distinctness to, of, senses or mind; freedom from obstruction. [CLEAR[1], -NESS]

cleat, n. Wedge; projecting piece bolted on spar, gangway, &c., to give footing or prevent rope from slipping; piece of wood or iron bolted on for fastening ropes to. [cf. Du. *kloot* ball; cogn. w. CLOT]

clea·vage, n. Way in which thing (mineral, party, opinion, State) tends to split (esp. *lines, planes, of c.*). [foll. + -AGE]

cleave[1], v.t. & i. (*clove* or *cleft*; *cloven* or *cleft*). Split (often *asunder, in two*); chop, break, or come, apart, esp. along the grain or line of cleavage (*cleft palate*, malformation in mouth; *in a cleft stick*, in tight place allowing neither retreat nor advance; *cloven hoof*, of ruminant quadrupeds, of god Pan, & so of devil, whence *show the c. h.*, reveal an evil nature); make way through (water, air); hold (ground, persons) apart (of chasm lit. & fig.). Hence **clea·v**ABLE a. [OE *clēofan*, com.-Teut. cf. G *klieben*, also Gk *gluph-* carve]

cleave[2], v.i. (*cleaved* or *clave*; *cleaved*). Stick fast, adhere, *to* (archaic exc. in fig. sense of *be faithful*). [OE *clifan* & *clifian*, com.-Teut., cf. G *kleben* f. *kli-* stick]

clea·ver, n. In vbl. senses; esp. butcher's chopping-tool for carcases. [CLEAVE[1] + -ER[1]]

clea·vers, cli·v-, n. (used as sing. or pl.). Goose-grass, creeper sticking to clothes. [earlier *-er*; perh. f. CLEAVE[2] + -ER[1]]

cleek, n. Iron-headed golf-club. [Sc., cogn. w. ME *cleche* to clutch]

clef, n. One of the three symbols (*C*, *tenor*, or *alto*; *G* or *treble*; *F* or *bass*) indicating pitch of stave in music. [F, f. *clavis* key]

cleft[1], n. Fissure, split. [earlier *clyft, clift*, cf Du. & G *kluft*, cogn. w. CLEAVE[1]]

cleft[2], see CLEAVE[1].

cleg, n. Large grey fly, horse-fly. [f. ON *kleggi*]

cleistogă·mic (klī-), a. (bot.). Permanently closed & self-fertilizing (of certain flowers). [Gk *kleistos* closed (*kleiō*) + *-gamos* -married]

clem, v.t. & i. (northern). Starve. [cf. Du. & G *klemmen* pinch, & CLAM[1]]

clĕ·matis, n. Kinds of climbing shrub (British wild species, Traveller's Joy or Old Man's Beard.) [L, f. Gk *klēmatis*]

clĕ·mency, n., **clĕ·ment**, a. Mild(ness) of

temper or weather; (showing) mercy. [f. L *clementia, clemens -entis*]

clench, clinch, v.t., & i., & n. (choice between *e* & *i* as indicated). Secure (nail, rivet) by driving point sideways when through (e, i); close (t. & i. of teeth or fingers) tightly (e); grasp firmly (e); (of boxers) come to quarters too close for full-arm blow (i); (Naut.) fasten (rope) with special bend (e, i); confirm, settle (argument, bargain) conclusively (i, e); (n.) any of above actions or the resulting state. [OE *clenc(e)an*, cf. OHG *klenkan*, cogn. w. CLING, w. causal sense]

clencher. See CLINCHER.

Cleopa·tra's nee·dle, n. Egyptian obelisk on Thames embankment.

cle·psȳdra, n. Ancient clock worked by flow of water. [L, f. Gk *klepsudra* (*kleptō* steal, *hudōr* water)]

clere·stōry (-ērs-), n. Part of wall of cathedral or large church, with series of windows, above aisle roofs. [perh. f. CLEAR[1] + STOR(E)Y]

cler·gy, n. The clerical order, all persons ordained for religious service (*the c.* usu. has pl. vb; *a c.*, i.e. the c. of a country or church, has usu. sing. vb); clergymen (*30 c. were present*); (Hist.) membership of, learning proper to, c. (*benefit of c.*, exemption from trial by secular court, & later from sentence for first conviction, enjoyed by all who could read); *clergyman*, ordained minister, esp. of Established Church; *c.-m.'s week, fortnight*, holiday including 2, 3, Sundays; *clergywoman*, wife, daughter, &c., of clergyman, esp. if dominating parish. [f. OF *clergie* (*clerc* f. LL CLERIC*us*, -Y[1])]

clĕ·ric, a. (archaic), & n. Clergyman; of clergy. Hence **clerico-** comb. form. [f. LL f. Gk *klērikos* (*klēros* lot, *Acts* i. 17, *Deut.* xviii. 2)]

cle·rical, a. & n. Of clergy, clergyman, or clergymen; of, made by, clerk(s) (*c. error*, in writing out; *c. duties, staff*); (n.) member of c. party in a parliament &c. Hence **cle·rical**ISM(3), **cle·rical**IST(2), nn., **cle·rical**IZE(3) v.t., **clerica·l**ITY n., **cle·rical**LY[2] adv. [f. LL *clericalis* (prec., -AL)]

clerk (-ark), n. (Also *c. in holy orders*) clergyman (archaic, legal, & sometimes appended to signature to show status of writer); lay officer of parish church with various duties; (*no*) *great c.*, (no) scholar (archaic); officer in charge of records &c., secretary, man of business, of town (*Town c.*), corporation, &c. (usu. a lawyer); person employed in bank, office, shop, &c., to make entries, copy letters, keep accounts, &c.; *C. of the Weather*, personification of meteorology; *c. of the works*, overseer of materials &c. in buildings done by contract. Hence **cler·k**DOM, **cler·k**ESS[1], **cler·k**SHIP(1, 3), nn., **cler·k**LY[1] a. [OE *cleric, clerc*, as CLERIC]

clĕ·ver, a. Adroit, dexterous, neat in movement (*c. horse*, good fencer); skilful, talented; ingenious (of doer or thing done). Hence **cle·ver**ISH[1](2) a., **cle·ver**LY[2] adv., **cle·ver**NESS n. [etym. dub.; *cliver* occurs 1220 = quick at seizing; cf. EFris. *clüfer*, & ME *clivers* claws]

clĕ·vis, n. U-shaped iron at end of beam for attaching tackle. [perh. cogn. w. CLEAVE[1]]

clew (-ōō), n., & v.t. Ball of thread or yarn; this as used in mythol. story to guide through labyrinth; = CLUE. (Naut.) small cords suspending hammock; lower or aft corner of sail by which it is extended; (vb) *c. up*, draw lower ends of (sails) to upper yard or mast ready for furling. [OE *cliwen* n. prob. dim. of OHG *kliu*; CLUE is a var. spelling merely, but the two are now usu. differentiated]

cli·ché (-ēshā), n. Metal cast esp. stereo or electro duplicate; hackneyed literary phrase. [F]

click[1], n., & v.i. (Make) slight sharp sound as of cocking gun; catch in machinery acting with this sound; (of horse) touch shoes of fore & hind feet (n., this fault); (S.-Afr. langg.) (make) sharp non-vocal sucking sound as articulation. [imit., cf. Du. *klikken*, F *cliquer*]

click[2], v.i. (slang). Have luck, secure one's object. [perh. f. dial. vb = snatch, as CLEEK]

cli·ent, n. (Rom. Ant.) plebeian under protection of noble; (archaic) dependant, hanger-on; employer of lawyer; employer of any professional man, customer. Hence **cli·ent**AGE, **cli·ent**SHIP, nn., **cli·ent**LESS a. [f. L *cliens -entis* (*cluere* hear, obey, -ENT)]

clī·entēle, n. 1. Person's dependants, following. 2. Customers, supporters, (of physician, shop, theatre, &c.). [f. L *clientela* as prec. in sense 1, but dropped & later readopted f. F in sense 2, & often pronounced & written (*-tèle*) as F]

cliff, n. Steep rock-face, usu. overhanging sea; *cliffsman*, skilled climber. [OE, cf. Du., *clif*]

clīmactē·ric, a. & n. Constituting a crisis, critical; (Physiol. & Med.) occurring at period of life (45-60) at which vital force begins to decline; (n.) critical period in life (multiples of 7, odd multiples of 7, &c.; *grand c.*, 63rd year). [f. L f. Gk *klimaktērikos* f. *klimaktēr* rung of ladder (*klimax*), -IC]

cli·mate (-*at*), n. (Region with certain) conditions of temperature, dryness, wind, light, &c. Hence **climă·t**IC a., **clima·t**ICALLY adv., **climato·**LOGY n., **cli·mato-lo·g**ICAL a. [f. F *climat* f. LL f. Gk *klima -at-* (*klinō* slope, -M)]

cli·max, n., & v.i. & t. Ascending scale; series of ideas or expressions so arranged; last term in these; culmination, apex; hence (irreg.) **clima·ct**IC a. (Vb) come, bring, to a c. [L, f. Gk *klimax -akos* ladder, climax]

climb (-īm), v.t. & i. (past *climbed* & archaic *clomb* pr. -ōm), & n. Ascend, mount, go *up*, (t. & i.) esp. with help of hands; *c. down* (t. & i.), descend (cliff &c., or abs.) similarly, (intr.) retreat from position taken up, give in; (of sun, aeroplane, &c.) go slowly up; (of plants) get support by tendrils or twining from tree, trellis, &c.; slope upwards; rise by effort in social rank, intellectual or moral strength, &c.; *climbing-iron*, spikes attachable to boot for climbing trees or ice slopes; hence **cli·mb**ABLE (-*ma*-) a. (N.) piece of climbing (*c. down*, abandonment of declared intention), place (to be) climbed. [cf. G *klimmen*; prob. cogn. w. CLEAVE[2]]

cli·mber (-īm*er*), n. In vbl senses; esp.: climbing plant; kinds of bird, usu. with two forward & two backward toes; person climbing socially. [-ER[1]]

clime, n. (poet.). Tract, country, (with or without ref. to climate). [f. LL as CLIMATE]

clinch. See CLENCH.

cli·ncher, cle·ncher, n. In vbl senses; esp.: remark, argument, that triumphantly settles a question; *clincher-built* = CLINKER-BUILT. [prec. + -ER[1]]

cling, v.i. (clung). *C. together*, remain in one body or in contact, resist separation; stick, adhere *to*, (whether by stickiness, suction, grasping, or embracing; *clinging garments*, showing form of body or limbs); remain faithful *to* (friend, habit, idea); *clingstone*, kind of peach or nectarine in which flesh adheres to stone. [OE *clingan* cf. EFris. *klingen* shrink, Sw. *klänge* climb, tendril]

cli·nic, n. Teaching of medicine or surgery at the hospital bed-side; class, institution, so taught, conducted. [f. F *clinique* f. Gk *klinikē* (*tekhnē*) CLINICAL (art)]

cli·nical, a. (med.). Of, at, the sick-bed (esp. of lectures, teaching, so given; *c. thermometer*, for taking patient's temperature). Hence **cli·nical**LY[2] adv. [f. L f. Gk *klinikos* (*klinē* bed + -AL]

clink[1], n., & v.i. & t. (Make, cause *glasses* &c. to make) sharp ringing sound; *clinking* (slang as a. & adv.), exceedingly (good, fine), as *a clinking*, or *clinking good, race*; *clinkstone*, kinds of felspar (f. ringing like iron when struck). Hence **cli·nker**[1] (-ER[1]) n. (slang), clinking specimen. [imit.; cf. Du. *klinken*]

clink[2], n. Prison, lock-up, (esp. *in c.*). [name of a Southwark prison; prob. = CLINCH]

cli·nker[2], n. Very hard yellow Dutch brick; brick with surface vitrified by great heat; mass of bricks fused together or of slag or lava. [f. Du. *klinckaerd* (now *klinker*) f. *klinken* CLINK[1]]

cli·nker-built, a. (Of boats) made with external planks overlapping downwards & fastened with clinched copper nails. [f. obs. *clink* vb = CLINCH]

clino·meter, n. Instrument for measuring slopes. [f. Gk *klinō* to slope, -o-, -METER]

Cli·o, n. (The Muse of) history. [f. Gk *Kleiō* (*kleiō* celebrate)]

clip[1], v.t., & n. Surround closely, grip tightly; (n.) appliance for holding things together or for attachment to object as mark; set of attached cartridges for magazine rifle. [OE *clyppan* embrace cf. ON *klypa* pinch]

clip[2], v.t., & n. Cut with shears or scissors, trim thus, take away part of (hair, wool) thus, remove hair or wool of (sheep, person) thus, (*c.* one's *wings*, disable him from pursuing his ambition); pare edge of (coin); omit letters or syllables of (words); omit (letter &c.; *clips his gs*). (N.) operation of shearing or haircutting; quantity of wool clipped from sheep, flock, &c. [prob. f. ON *clippa*]

cli·pper, n. In vbl senses; also or esp.: instrument for clipping hair; swift mover (esp. of horse or ship); ship with forward-raking bows & aft-raking masts; (slang) thing excellent of its kind. [CLIP[2], -ER[1]]

cli·pping[1], n. In vbl senses; esp., piece clipped off. [CLIP[2], -ING[1]]

cli·pping[2], a. In vbl senses; esp., (slang) first-rate. [CLIP[2], -ING[2]]

clique (-ēk), n. Small exclusive party, set, coterie. Hence **cli·quish**[1], **cli·qu**(e)Y[2], aa., **cli·quish**NESS, **cli·qu**ISM(2), nn. [F, f. *cliquer* CLICK[1] cf. CLAQUE]

cli·toris, n. Rudimentary internal part of female genitals analogous to penis. [Gk *kleitoris*]

clivers. See CLEAVERS.

cloā·ca, n. (pl. *-ae*). Sewer; excrementory cavity in birds, reptiles, &c.; gathering-place of moral evil. Hence **cloā·c**AL a. [L]

cloak, (archaic) **cloke**, n., & v.i. & t. Loose usu. sleeveless outdoor upper garment; covering (*c. of snow*); pretence, pretext, (*under the c. of*); *c.-room*, for leaving cc., hats, &c., or any luggage. (Vb) put on one's c.; put c. on (one*self* or another); conceal, disguise. [f. ONF *cloke* f. med. L *cloca* horseman's cape named from its bell shape (CLOCK[1])]

cloche (F), n. *C.(hat)*, woman's bell-shaped hat. [F, = bell]

clock[1], n. Time-measuring instrument periodically wound up, kept in motion by springs or weights acting on wheels, & recording hours, minutes, &c., by hands on a dial (*o'clock* now usu. only appended to the actual hour, as *six o'clock*, but *quarter to six, six fifteen, 7.25*; *what o'clock is it?*, what is the time?; *of the clock* still in formal or facetious use); downy head of dandelion &c.; *clockwise, counter-clockwise*, moving in curve from left to right, right to left, as seen by spectator at centre; *c.-work*, mechanism on c. principle (*like c.-w.*, regularly, automatically), (attrib.) regular, mechanical. [f. MDu. *clocke* (cf. G *glocke* bell), or ONF *cloke* f. LL *cloca* cf. prec.; orig. meaning *bell*, prob. in imit. of the sound]

clock[2], n. (shop pl., *clox*). Pattern worked in silk on side of stocking. Hence (-)**clock**ED[2] a. [?]

clo·cking, a. *C. hen*, one sitting on eggs. [part. of dial. vb *clock* = CLUCK]

clod, n., & v.t. Lump *of* earth &c.; lump of earth (vb, pelt with cc.); *the c.*, soil, land, mere matter; (also *c.-hopper*, *c.-pole*) bumpkin, lout, (so *c.-hopping*, loutish), whence **clo·dd**ISH[1] a., **clo·ddish**NESS n.; coarse part of neck of ox as meat. [var. of CLOT now differentiated]

clog[1], n. Block of wood fastened to leg to impede motion; impediment, encumbrance; woman's wooden-soled overshoe for wet ground; wooden-soled shoe with metal rim; *c.-dance*, performed in cc. [?]

clog[2], v.t. & i. Confine (animal) with c.; be an encumbrance to, burden; impede, hamper; choke up, obstruct by stickiness; fill up with choking matter; stop or act badly from being choked up. [f. prec., & cf. dial. vb *clag* stick]

clo·ggy, a. Lumpy, knotty; sticky. [-Y[2]]

cloisonné (klwahzŏnā·), a. & n. *C. enamel* or *c.*, enamel in which colours of pattern are kept apart by thin outline plates. [F]

cloi·ster, n., & v.t. (Enclose, shut *up*, in) convent, monastic house, (*the c.*, monastic seclusion); covered walk, often round quadrangle with wall on outer & colonnade or windows on inner side, esp. of convent, college, cathedral buildings, whence **cloi·ster**ED[2] a. Hence **cloi·str**AL a. [ME & OF *cloistre* f. L *claustrum* (*claudere* shut, *-trum* instr. suf.)]

cloke. See CLOAK.

clō·nus, n. (path.). Spasm with violent successive muscular contractions & relaxations. Hence **clŏ·n**IC a. [f. Gk *klonos*]

cloop, n., & v.i. (Make) sound (as) of cork being drawn. [imit.]

close[1] (-ōs), a. & adv. 1. Shut: (of vowels) pronounced with lips or mouth cavity contracted (e.g. *o* in *not* is open, in *note* c.); narrow, confined, contracted, stifling, (*c. siege, prisoner, air*); covered, concealed, secret, given to secrecy, (*keep, lie, c.*, be in hiding; *c.-stool*, chamber-pot mounted in stool with cover); niggardly (so **close-fist**ED[2] a., **close-fi·sted**NESS n.); restricted, limited, (*c. corporation* &c.; *c. scholarship*, not open to all; *c.* BOROUGH); under prohibition (*c. season, time*, in which something is forbidden, esp. killing of game &c.). 2. Near: dense, compact, with no or slight intervals, (*c. texture, thicket, writing*; *c. order, combat*; *c. quarters*, immediate contact; *c. reasoner, argument, analysis*, leaving no gaps or weak spots, coherent; also adv., as *shut c.*, *c. ranked*, *c.-grained*, without visible interstices, *stand, sit, c.*); in or nearly in contact (*c. proximity*; *a c. shave*, near the skin, also fig., narrow missing of collision &c.; *c.-hauled*, with sail-tacks hauled c. to side to windward; SAIL *c. to the wind*; esp. in adv. or prep. phrr. *c. by*, *c. to*, *c. upon*, as *he was c. by*, *c. to the road*, *c. upon two hundred*); fitting exactly (*c. cap*, *c. resemblance*); near & dear; nearly equal (*c. contest*); concentrated (*c. examination, attention*); *c.-up* n., part of cinema film taken at short range and showing person(s) &c. on large scale. Hence **clo·se**LY[2] adv., **clo·se**NESS n. (f. F *clos* f. L *claudere claus-* shut]

close[2] (-ōs), n. Enclosed place (*break* one's *c.* legal, trespass on his land); precinct of cathedral; school playground; (Sc.) entry from street to court at back. [f. F *clos* f. L *clausum* neut. p.p. as prec.]

close[3] (-ōz), v.t. & i., & n. Shut (t. & i. of lid or box, door or room or house; lit., or = declare or be declared not open, of place of business &c.; *closing-time*, at which shops stop business; *c. upon*, of hand, box, &c., grasp or imprison, also of eyes, lose sight of by shutting); be the boundary of, conclude, bring or come to an end, complete, settle, (*c.* one's *days*, die; *c. bargain*; abs. stop speaking, often *with* the remark &c.); bring or come into contact (*c. the ranks* or, intr., *c. up*; c. electric *current* or *circuit*, give it continuity), come within striking distance, grapple *with*, (Naut., as v.t. approach or come alongside of (other ship &c.); (Mil., as v.i., to men in rank) *right c.*, *left c.*, move sideways to right, left; express (often eager) agreement *with* (offer, terms, or person offering them); *c. in*, enclose, come nearer, (of days) get successively shorter; *c. up*, block, fill, coalesce. (N.) conclusion, end; grappling of combatants. [f. OF *clos-* st. of *clore* f. L *claudere* shut]

clo·set (-ŏz-), n., & v.t. Private or small room, esp. for private interviews (so vb, *be closeted with, together*, hold consultation) or for study (*c. play*, to be read not acted; *c. strategist* &c., theoretical); cupboard, as *china-c.*; = WATER-*c.* [OF (CLOSE[3], -ET[1])]

clo·sure (-zher), n., & v.t. Closing, closed condition. (Parl.) decision by vote of House of Commons, under certain restrictions, to put the question without further debate; (vb) apply c. to (motion, speakers, &c.). [OF, f. L *clausura* (*claudere claus-*, -URE)]

clot, n., & v.i. & t. Mass of material stuck together; semi-solid lump of coagulated liquid, esp. of blood (*c. of blood*, pop.

name for THROMBOSIS). (Vb) form (t. & i.) into cc. (*clotted hair*, stuck together in locks; *clotted cream*, got by scalding milk; *clotted nonsense*, utter absurdity). [cf. G *klotz* & CLEAT, CLOD]

cloth (-awth, -ŏth, *pl.* -awdhz, -ŏths), n. (pl. *cloths*, & in differentiated sense CLOTHES). (Piece, used for any purpose, of) woven or felted stuff; (also *table-c.*) covering for table, esp. of linen at meals (*lay the c.*, prepare table for meal); woollen woven fabric as used for clothes; *c. of gold, silver*, tissue of gold or silver threads interwoven with silk or wool; *American c.*, enamelled c. like leather; *cut coat according to c.*, adapt expenditure to resources; profession as shown by clothes, esp. clerical (*respect due to his c.*; also *the c.*, clergy); *c.-binding*, cover of book in linen or cotton c.; (Hist.) *c.-yard shaft*, arrow a yard long. [OE *cláth* (earliest sense *a c.*) cf. G *kleid*, prob. f. *cli-* stick cf. CLAY]

clothe (-ōdh), v.t. (*clothed* or *clad*). Provide with clothes, put clothes upon; cover like or as with clothes or a cloth (*leaves c. trees*; *clothed with righteousness, with plantations*; *body clothes soul*; also *c. face in smiles, ideas in words*). Hence **clo'th**ING[1](4) n. [OE *clathian*, whence *clothe*, & *clǽthan*, whence *clad*, f. *cláth* CLOTH; cf. G *kleiden*]

clothes (-ōz, -ōdhz), n. pl. Wearing-apparel; BED[1]-c.; linen &c. to be washed (*c.-bag, -basket*, for conveying this; *c.-horse*, for airing it on; *c.-line, -post, -prop, -peg*, rope, supports of rope, wooden clips on rope, for drying it after washing); *c.-brush*; *c.-moth*, destructive to c.; *c.-press*, cupboard with shelves for c.; (*old-*)*c.-man*, dealer in usu. old c. [the orig. pl. of CLOTH, *cloths* being modern]

clo'thier (-ōdh-), n. Maker of cloth; dealer in cloth or clothes. [orig. *clother*, see -ER[1]]

cloud (-owd), n., & v.t. & i. (Mass of) visible condensed watery vapour (see CIRRUS, CUMULUS, NIMBUS, STRATUS) floating high above general level of ground (*c.-drift*, c. in motion; *c.-rack*, pile of broken cc.; *c.-burst*, violent rainstorm; *c.-capped*, of hill with top veiled in c.; *c.-scape*, picture, picturesque grouping, of cc.; *c.-kissing*, of high hill or building); unsubstantial or fleeting thing; mass of smoke or dust (*c.-compeller*, smoker, facet. use of Greek epithet of Zeus); local dimness or vague patch of colour in or on liquid or transparent body; great number *of* birds, insects, horsemen, arrows, moving together; light woollen scarf; obscurity (*under c. of night*; *a c. of words*); *in the cc.*, mystical, unreal, imaginary, (so *c.-castle*, daydream; *c.-land, c.-world*, utopia, fairyland), (of person) abstracted, inattentive; state of gloom, trouble, suspicion, louring or depressed look, (*c. on brow*; *under a c.*, out of favour, discredited); *cloudberry*, mountain shrub with white flower & orange-coloured fruit; hence **clou'd**LESS a., **clou'dless**LY[2] adv., **clou'dless**NESS, **clou'd**LET, nn., **clou'd**Y[3] a., **clou'di**LY[2] adv., **clou'di**NESS n., **clou'd**WARD(S) adv. (Vb) overspread, darken, with cc., gloom, or trouble; variegate with vague patches of colour; become overcast or gloomy (*c. up, over*). [prob. f. OE *clúd*, meaning, & cogn. w., CLOD]

clough (-ŭf.) n. Ravine, steep valley usu. with torrent bed. [cf. G *klinge*]

clout (-owt), n., & v.t. (archaic & dial.). Patch (n. & v.); a cloth (esp. *dish -c.*); piece of clothing; rap, knock, (n. & v., esp. on head with knuckles); iron plate on boot &c. to save wear, (also *c.-nail*) broad-headed nail for attaching c.; (Hist.) canvas on frame as mark at archery (*in the c.*, a hit!) [OE *clút* cogn. w. CLOT]

clove[1], **cloven.** See CLEAVE[1].

clove[2], n. One of small bulbs making up compound bulb of garlic, shallot, &c. (usu. *of*). [OE *clufu* cogn. w. CLEAVE[1]]

clove[3], n. (Pungent aromatic dried bud of) tropical tree (*oil of cc.*, extracted from cc. & used in medicine); (also *c.-gillyflower*) c.-scented Pink, original of carnation & other double pinks. [ME *clow(e)* f. F *clou* (*de girofle*); *girofle* (see GILLYFLOWER) was orig. name of the spice; *clou* (f. L *clavus* nail) *de girofle* was used of it w. ref. to its shape, transferred to the similarly shaped bud of Pink, & later divided into *clove* for the spice, & *gillyflower* for the Pink]

clove hitch, n. Hitch by which rope is secured at any intermediate part round spar or rope that it crosses at right angles. [old p.p. of CLEAVE[1], as showing parallel separate lines]

clō'ver, n. Kinds of trefoil used for fodder (*be, live, in c.*, in ease & luxury]. [OE *cláfre* cf. Du. *klaver*, G *klee*]

clown, n. Rustic; ignorant or ill-bred man, whence **clow'n**ISH[1] a., **clow'nish**LY[2] adv., **clow'nish**NESS n.; jester, esp. in pantomime or circus, whence **clow'n**ERY(4) n. [prob. cogn. w. CLOT, & = lump; cf. Icel. *clunni*]

clox. See CLOCK[2].

cloy, v.t. Satiate, weary, by richness, sweetness, sameness, excess, of food or pleasure (usu. *with*). [f. obs. *accloy* choke (put nail into) f. OF *encloyer* (AC-) f. LL IN(*clavare* f. L *clavus* nail)]

club[1], n. 1. Stick with one thick end as weapon (*Indian cc.*, pair swung to develop muscles; *c.-law*, rule by physical force); kinds of stick used in games, esp. golf; structure or organ in Bot. &c. with knob at end; *c.-foot(ed)*, (with) congenitally distorted foot; *c.-moss*, kind with upright spikes of spore-cases; *c.-root*, disease of turnips &c.; playing-card of suit bearing black trefoil (*cc.*, the suit). 2. Association of persons united by some common interest, meeting periodically for co-operation (*Alpine, golf, yacht,* BENEFIT, *c.*) or conviviality; body of persons with cooptation by ballot combined for social purposes & having premises (*c.-house*) for resort, meals, temporary residence, &c. (*c.-land,* St. James's in London, where cc. cluster), whence **clu·b**DOM n., **clu·b**LESS a. [ME *clubbe* perh. f. ON *clubba* by assim. f. *clumba* = CLUMP; sense 2 prob. = knot of persons]

club², v.t. & i. Beat with c.; use butt of (gun) as c.; bring, come, into a mass; contribute (money, ideas) to common stock; (intr.) combine *together, with,* for joint action, making up a sum, &c.; (Mil.) get (one's men) into a confused mass. [f. prec.]

clu·bbable, a. Fit for membership of a club. [CLUB¹, -ABLE]

club-haul, v.t. Tack (*ship,* or abs.) by anchoring & cutting cable, as device for getting off lee-shore when there is not room to wear. [?]

cluck, n., & v.i. (Make) guttural cry of hen. Hence **clucky**² a., = CLOCKING. [cf. obs. & dial. *clock* (OE *cloccian*); imit.]

clue (-ōō), n. Fact or principle that serves as guide, or suggests a line of inquiry, in any problem, investigation, or study; thread of story, train of thought; (also rarely in other senses of) CLEW. Hence **clue·**LESS a. [= CLEW]

clu·mber, n. Kind of spaniel. [*C.* in Notts.]

clump, n., & v.i. & t. Cluster of trees or shrubs (usu. *of*); (also *c.-sole*) extra thickness of leather added to sole, usu. nailed on. (Vb) tread heavily; heap or plant together; provide (boot) with c. [cf. G *klumpen,* Du. *klomp,* ON *clumba* & *clubba* CLUB]

clu·msy (-zĭ), a. Awkward in movement or shape, ungainly; ill-contrived; without tact. Hence **clu·msi**LY² adv., **clu·msi**NESS n. [f. obs. *clumse* be stiff with cold; cf. Norw. *klumsa* paralyse, & CLEM, CLAMMY]

clunch (-tsh), n. Soft white limestone used for internal carving-work. [perh. var. of CLUMP, cf. *bump bunch, hump hunch*]

clung. See CLING.

clu·ster, n., & v.t. & i. Group of similar things, esp. such as grow together, bunch; swarm, group, of persons, animals, &c.; (vb) bring or come into, be in, a c. or cc. (*clustered columns, pillars, shafts,* several close together, or disposed round or half detached from pier). [OE *clyster* prob. cogn. w. CLOT]

clutch¹, v.t. & i. Seize eagerly, grasp tightly; snatch *at.* [OE *clyccean* f. OTeut. (foll.)]

clutch², n. Tight grasp; (pl.) grasping hands, cruel grasp; a grasping *at*; (Mech.) arrangement for throwing working parts into or out of action, gripping-piece of crane. [ME *cloke* claw n. f. OTeut. *kluk-*]

clutch³, n. Set of eggs; brood of chickens. [earlier *cletch* f. *cleck* to hatch f. ON *clekja*]

clu·tter, n., & v.i. & t. (Bustle, run, with) confused noise or movement, loss of self-possession; confused mass, untidy state, litter n. & (esp. in *cluttered up with*) v.t. [var. of obs. *clotter* (CLOT, -ER⁵)]

clȳ·pĕŭs, n. Shield-like part of insect's head. Hence **cly·pe**AL, **cly·pe**ATE², **cly·pĕi**FORM, aa., **clypeo-** comb. form. [L, = shield]

cly·ster, n., & v.t., (med., now rare). = ENEMA; (vb) treat with c. [L, f. Gk *klustēr* syringe (*kluzō* wash)]

cmd, = CD.

co-, pref. L short form of *com-* (*cum* prep. with), used in L only before vowels, h, gn, & (in the correct clas. form) n, but in E as living pref. before any letter. (1) Prefixed to vbs, = with other subjects (*cooperate*) or objects (*co-adjust*); to adjj. & advv., = jointly, together, mutually, (*coeternally, coadjacent*); & to nouns, = joint, mutual, (*coheir, coequality*). (2) In some math. words, short for *complement,* = 'of the complement', 'complement of' as *cosine, co-declination.* In unfamiliar words, a hyphen or diaeresis is used to indicate pronunciation, and the three methods (cooperate, co-operate, coöperate) are employed arbitrarily.

cōăcerva·tion, n. Heaping together, pile. [f. L CO(*acervatio* f. *acervare* f. *acervus* heap, see -ATION)]

coach (-tsh), n., & v.i. & t. State carriage; (also *stage-c.*) large four-wheeled & usu. four-horsed close carriage with seats inside and on the roof carrying passengers at fixed rates & times with stoppages for meals & relays of horses; HACKNEY-c.; MOURNING-c.; SLOW-c.; (official name for) railway carriage; (Naut.) room near stern of man-of-war; private tutor; trainer of athletic team &c,; *drive c. & six through Act of Parliament,* stultify it; *c.-box,* driver's seat; *c.-dog,* = CARRIAGE-*dog*; *c.-house,* outhouse for carriages; *coachman,* driver of any carriage, whence **coa·chman**SHIP(3) n.; hence **coa·ch**FUL(2) n. (Vb) travel in, go by, stage-c. (*in the old coaching days*); tutor, train, (pupil for examination, crew for race); give hints to, prime with facts; (intr.) read with tutor. [f. F *coche* f. Magyar *kocsi* adj. f. *Kocs* place-name]

cōă·djutor, n. Assistant (esp., with prospective succession, to infirm bishop). (f. OF *coadjuteur* f. L CO(*adjutorem* f. AD*juvare -jut-* help, -OR²)]

cōă·dūnate (-*at*), a. (physiol. & bot.).

For compounds of *co-* not given consult CO-.

Congenitally united. [f. L co(*adunatus* p.p. of ADunare make one f. *unus* one)]

cōă·gulate, v.t. & i. Change (t. & i.) from fluid to more or less solid state, clot, curdle, set, solidify. Hence or cogn. **coagul**A·TION, **coa·gulat**OR[2](2), **coa·gu-l**ANT(2), nn. [f. obs. *coagulate* adj. f. L *coagulare* f. *coagulum* n. f. co(*agere* bring) usu. *cogere* collect; -ATE[2,3]]

coai·ta (kōī-), n. Small S.-Amer. monkey (Red-faced Spider-monkey). [f. Braz. *coatá*]

coal, n., & v.t. & i. Hard opaque black or blackish mineral of carbonized vegetable matter found in seams or strata below earth's surface & used as fuel & in manufacture of gas, tar, &c. (*cc.*, pieces of it ready for supplying fire; chief kinds, ANTHRACITE, BITUMINOUS, LIGNITE; *heap cc. of fire*, return good for evil, cf. *Rom.* xii. 20; *blow the cc.*, fan flame of passion &c.; *haul, call, over the cc.*, reprimand; *cc. to Newcastle*, superfluous action); *c.-bed, -seam*, stratum of c.; *c.-black*, quite; *c.-box, -scuttle*, (vulg.) *-vase*, receptacle for c. to supply room fire (*c.-scuttle bonnet*, with front projection as of inverted c.-box); *c.-box* (army slang), German shell emitting black smoke; *c.*-BUNKER; *c.-dust*, small cc.; *c.-factor*, middleman between c.-owners & customers; *c.-field*, district with series of c. strata; *c.-fish*, black cod; *c.-flap, -plate*, cover of c.-cellar opening in pavement; *c.-gas*, mixed gases extracted from c. & used for lighting & heating; *c.-heaver*, man employed in moving c., whence **coa·lie** [-Y[3]] n.; *c.-hole*, small c.-cellar; *c.-master, -owner*, owner or lessee of *c.-mine* or *c.-pit* = COLLIERY; *c.-measures* (geol.), series of rocks formed by seams of c. & intervening strata; *c.-screen*, frame for parting large from small cc.; *c.-tar*, TAR extracted from bituminous c., & yielding paraffin, naphtha, benzene, creosote, & aniline dyes; *c.-tit*, = COALMOUSE; *c.-whipper*, man, machine, raising c. from ship's hold; hence **coa·l**LESS, **coa·l**Y[2], aa. (Vb) put c. into (ship &c.); take in supply of c. [OE *col*, cf. G *kohle*]

coalesce (kōalĕ·s), v.i. Come together & form one (of material or immaterial things); combine in a coalition (of statesmen, parties). So **coale·sc**ENCE n., **coale·sc**ENT a. [f. L co(*alescere alit-* grow f. *alere* nourish)]

coali·tion, n. Union, fusion; (Pol.) temporary combination for special ends between parties that retain distinctive principles. Hence **coali·tion**IST(1) n. [f. L *coalitio* (prec., -ION)]

coa·lmouse, cole-, n. Small dark-coloured bird (also COAL*tit*). [ME *colmose* f. OE *colmáse* (*col* coal + *máse* f. WG *maisa* kinds of small bird)]

coa·ming (kō-), n. Raised border round hatches &c. of ship to keep out water. [?]

coarse (kōrs), a. Common, inferior, (*c. fish, fare*); rough, loose, or large, in texture, grain, or features; not delicate in perception, manner, or taste, unrefined; rude, uncivil, vulgar; obscene (of language); *c.-fibred, -grained*, lit. of things, also fig. of persons = without delicacy. Hence **coar·se**LY[2] adv., **coar·se**N[6] v.t. & i., **coar·se**NESS n., **coar·s**ISH[1](2) a. [f. phr. *in* or *of course* = ordinary, cf. sense of *mean* (average, low) & *plain* (ordinary, ugly)]

coast[1], n. (Also *sea-c.*) border of land near sea, sea-shore; CLEAR[1] *c.*; (U.S. & Canada) toboggan slide; (hence through COAST[2]) downhill run on bicycle with feet up or still; *c.-guard(sman)*, Admiralty c. police(man). Hence **coa·st**WARD(S) adv., **coa·st**WISE a. & adv. [ME & OF *coste* (now *côte*) f. L *costa* rib, side]

coast[2], v.i. Sail along c., trade between ports on same c.; slide down-hill on toboggan, bicycle down-hill without pedalling. [f. OF *costeier* (now *côtoyer*) f. Rom. **costicare* as prec.]

coat, n., & v.t. Man's sleeved usu. cloth body garment (*dress-c.*, with swallow tails for the evening; *c. of* MAIL; FROCK-*c.*; *greatc., top-c.*, out-door, worn over another; *red c.*, traditional uniform of British soldier; so *redcoat*, soldier; *c. of arms*, herald's tabard, gentleman's heraldic bearings or shield; *c. armour*, blazonry, heraldic arms; *c.-card*, now usu. *court-*, playing-card with coated figure, king, queen, or knave; *trail* one's *c.-tails*, for some one to tread on, = seek to pick quarrel; *dust* one's *c.*, beat him; *turn* one's *c.*, change sides, desert; *wear the king's c.*, serve as soldier); woman's stout buttoned overcoat, (also, esp. in *c. & skirt*) shorter tailor-made garment falling over skirt; petticoat (archaic & dial.; in literature esp. in KILT one's *cc.*); covering compared to garment; beast's hair, fur, &c.; (Physiol.) investing membrane &c. of organ; skin, rind, husk, layer of bulb &c.; covering of paint &c. laid on at once; hence (-)**coat**ED[2], **coa·t**LESS, aa. (Vb) put or (with *paint* &c. as subj.) be c. of paint, tin, &c., upon, (p.p.) covered over *with* dust &c. [f. OF *cote* (now *cotte* petticoat) f. med. L *cotta* cf. OHG *chozza* (garment of) shaggy woollen stuff]

coatee·, n. Short-tailed (esp. mil.) coat. [-EE]

cōa·ti (-ah-), n. American carnivorous mammal like civet & racoon with long flexible snout. [Braz. (*cua* cincture, *tim* nose)]

coa·ting, n. Layer of paint &c.; material for coats. [-ING[1]]

coax, v.t. & i. Persuade by blandishments (*to* do, *into* doing or good temper &c.; *c.* thing *out of* person; *c. fire to light, key into lock,* &c.); *c. away, out,* &c., entice; practise wheedling. Hence **coa·x**ER[1] n. [=fool vb f. obs. *cokes* fool n. perh. cogn. w. COCKNEY]

cōă·xal, -ial, a. (math.). Having common axis. [CO-, AXIS, -AL]

cob[1], n. Male swan; stout short-legged riding-horse, whence **co·bb**Y[2] a.; (also *c.-nut*) large kind of hazel-nut; roundish lump of coal &c.; round-headed loaf; CORN-*c.* [?]

cob[2], n. Composition of clay, gravel, & straw, used for building walls. [?]

cō·balt (-awlt), n. Reddish-grey metal similar in many respects to nickel; deep-blue pigment made from it. Hence **coba·lt**IC, **co·balti·**FEROUS, **coba·lt**OUS (chem.), aa., **cobalt**O- comb. form. [G, prob. =*kobold* goblin of mines]

co·bble[1], n., & v.t. (Also *c.-stone*) water-worn rounded stone of size used for paving (vb, pave with these); (pl.) coals of this size. [cf. COB[1]]

co·bble[2], v.t. Put together roughly; mend, patch *up,* (esp. shoes). [etym. dub.; foll. is quoted a century earlier]

co·bbler, n. Mender of shoes; clumsy workman; (often *sherry c.*) iced drink of wine, sugar, lemon, sucked through straw (origin unknown; from U.S.); *c.'s wax,* resinous substance used for waxing thread. [?]

Co·bdenism, n. Policy based on Free Trade, international cooperation, & retrenchment, peace, non-intervention, and opposition to Empire. Hence **Co·bden**ITE[1](1) a. & n. [R. *Cobden,* b. 1804, -ISM]

cō·ble, n. Kinds of fishing-boat in Scotland & N.E. England. [cf. W *ceubal,* Bret. *caubal*]

cō·bra (de cape·llo) (dĭ), n. The venomous Hooded Snake of India, with neck dilated like hood under irritation. [Port.; *cobra* f. L *colubra* snake, *capello* hood, = F *chapeau*]

co·bweb, n. & a. Spider's network, material of it, thread of this; thing of flimsy texture (so adj., thin, flimsy), subtle fanciful reasoning; musty rubbish (esp. fig. as *cc. of the law, of antiquity*; *blow away the cc.,* take an airing); entanglement, mesh. Hence **co·bwebb**ED[2], **co·bwebb**Y[2], aa., **co·bwebb**ERY(5) n. [obs. *cob* spider is prob. f. *cobweb*; but cf. Flem. *cobbe, coppe,* spider]

co·ca, n. (Leaves of) Bolivian shrub (chewed as stimulant). [Sp., f. Peruv. *cuca*]

cocai·ne, n. Drug from coca producing local insensibility. Hence **cocai·n**IZE(5) v.t., **cocainiz**A·TION, **cocai·n**ISM(5), nn. [-INE[1]]

co·ccagee, n. A cider apple, cider from it. [f. Ir. *cac a ghéidh* goose dung (so coloured)]

co·ccyx (kŏks-), n. Small triangular bone ending spinal column in man; analogous part in birds &c. Hence or cogn. **coccȳ·gĕ**AL a., **coccy·geo-, co·ccyg**(O)-, comb. forms. [L, f. Gk *kokkux -ugos* cuckoo (like its bill)]

co·chin-chi·na (kŏtsh-), n. & a. (Fowl) of Cochin China breed.

cochineal (kŏ·tshĭnēl), n. Dried bodies of insect reared on cactus in Mexico &c., used for making scarlet dye & carmine. [f. F *cochenille* f. It. *cocciniglia* (*coccino* f. L *coccinum* scarlet robe f. *coccum* scarlet, orig. berry)]

co·chlea (-k-), n. (pl. *-leae*). Spiral cavity of internal ear. [L, =snail]

cock[1], n. 1. Male bird (alone of domestic fowl, as below, also of BLACK-*c.*; of other birds only when aided by context; in comb. in bird-names, as PEACOCK, WOOD-*cock,* & prefixed= male as *c. robin*; *c. sparrow,* male sparrow, small lively pugnacious person; *c. of the wood,* capercailye; *c. of the north,* brambling; *c.-nest,* built by some cc., as wren, to roost in); (short for) woodcock (w. collect. sing. for pl.); male of domestic fowl (*cock-a-doodle-doo,* its crow, child's name for c.); GAME[1]-*c.*; *c.-&-bull story,* idle invention, incredible tale; *c.-crow, -crowing,* dawn; *c.-fighting,* setting cc. to fight as sport; *this beats c.-fighting,* is inexpressibly delightful; *live like fighting cc.,* on best of fare; *that c. won't fight,* that plea, plan, will not do; *c. lobster,* male; *c.-shot, -shy,* object set up to be thrown at with sticks, stones, &c., as formerly cc. at Shrovetide, a throw at this; *cockscomb,* crest of c., Yellow Rattle & other plants, & see COXCOMB; *cocksfoot,* a pasture grass; *cockshead,* kinds of trefoil; *cockspur,* cock's spur, gas-burner of same shape; *c. of the walk,* dominant person (so *c. of the school* among boys); *old c.,* familiar vocative. 2. Tapped spout, tap, (*c.-metal,* two parts copper to one of lead); (not decent) penis; lever in gun raised ready to be released by trigger (*at half, full, -c.,* of gun half-ready or ready to be let off); indicating-tongue of balance. [OE *cocc,* cf. F *coq.* LL *coccus*; prob. imit. from its cluck; sense 2 perh. f. resemblance of tap to c.'s head & comb]

cock[2], v.t. & i. Erect, stick or stand *up,* jauntily or defiantly (*c. the ears,* in attention; *c.* one's *nose,* in contempt; *c. a* SNOOK; *c.* one's *eye,* glance knowingly, wink); *c.* one's *hat,* set it on aslant, also turn up the brim (*cocked hat,* formerly, with brim fixed so, now, brimless triangular hat pointed before, behind, & above, of various uniform costumes; *knock into a cocked hat,* out of shape or recognition); raise c. of (gun) in readiness for firing. [f. prec. w. ref. to cock's comb, crowing-attitude, &c.]

cock[3], n. Upward bend (of nose &c.); significant turn (of eye); way of cocking hat; cocked state of gun (see COCK[1]). [f. prec.]

cock[4], n., & v.t. (Heap *hay*, rarely *corn*, into) small conical heap(s) in the field. (cf. Norw. *kok* a heap, ON *kökkr* lump]

cockabo·ndy, n. Kind of fishing-fly. [f. W *coch a bon ddu* red with black trunk]

cockā·de, n. Rosette &c. worn in hat as badge of office or party or part of livery, esp. black leather rosette (badge of House of Hanover) worn by servants of persons serving Crown. Hence **cocka·d**ED[2] a. [f. F *cocarde* fem. of 16th-c. *coquard* pert (*coq* COCK[1], -ARD)]

co·ck-a-hoo·p, a. & adv. Exultant(ly), with boastful crowing. [orig. doubtful; there were inn-signs *Hart, Swan, Cock*, &c., *on the Hoop*; early quotations do not suggest the bird; an explanation (1670) is that the spigot (*cock*) being taken out and laid on hoop of barrel, the running of the ale produced jollity]

Cockaig·ne, -ayne, n. Imaginary land of idleness and luxury; (punningly w. ref. to COCKNEY) London. [f. OF *coquaigne* perh. = cake-land (L *coquere* cook)]

cock-a-lee·kie. = COCKY-LEEKY.

cockatoo·, n. Kinds of parrot with movable crest. [f. Malay *kakatúa* w. assim. to COCK[1]]

co·ckatrice (-ĭ- *or* -ī-), n. = BASILISK. [f. OF *cocatris* f. L **calcatricem* nom. *-ix* treader, transl. of Gk *ikhneumōn* ichneumon (*ikhneuō* trace)]

co·ckboat, n. Small ship's boat. [f. obs. *cock* cf. OF *coque*, Du. *kog*, etym. dub.]

co·ckchafer (-tshā-), n. Greyish-chestnut beetle flying with loud whirring sound. [COCK[1] perh. expressing size or vigour + CHAFER]

cocker[1], v.t. Indulge, pamper, coddle, (child, invalid, &c.; usu. *up*). [perh. f. obs. *cock* vb in same sense, & cf. etym. of COCKNEY]

Co·cker[2], n. *According to C.*, exact, correct. [E. *C.*, famous teacher of arithmetic d. 1675]

co·cker[3], n. Breed of spaniel. [COCK[1] (as starting woodcock &c.) + -ER[1]]

co·ckerel, n. Young cock; pugnacious youth. [dim. of COCK[1], cf. *pickerel, mongrel*]

co·ck-eyed, a. (slang). Squinting; crooked, set aslant, not level. [COCK[2]]

co·ck-horse, adv. (Also *a-cock-horse*, see A[2]) astride, mounted. [in 16th c. = toy horse]

co·ckle[1], n. (Also *Corn-c.*) purple-flowered plant growing among corn, esp. wheat; disease of wheat turning grains black. [OE *coccul*; excl. E.; perh. f. a L dim. of *coccum* berry]

co·ckle[2], n. An edible bivalve; its shell; small shallow boat (also *c.-shell, c.-boat*); *cc. of the heart*, one's feelings (*delight, warm, the cc.* &c.) [f. F *coquille* shell f. L *conchylia* pl. of L f. Gk *kogkhulion* dim. of *kogkhē* mussel]

co·ckle[3], v.i. & t., & n. (Make to) bulge, curl up, pucker; (n.) bulge or wrinkle in paper, glass, &c. [cf. F *coquiller* blister (of bread)]

co·ckle[4], n. Radiating-stove for heating room. [perh. f. Du. *kakel* f. G *kachel* stove-tile]

co·ck-loft, n. Small upper loft. [?]

co·ckney, n. & a. (Characteristic of a) native of London (usu. contemptuous, esp. *c. accent*). Hence **co·ckney**DOM, **cockney**E·SE, nn., **co·ckney**FY v.t., **co·ckney**ISH[1] a., **co·ckney**ISM(2, 4) n., **co·ckney**IZE(3) v.t. & i. [ME *coken-ey* cock's egg (*coken* gen. pl., *ey* f. OE *æg*); orig. sense prob. small or ill-shaped egg (still *cock's egg* in dial., cf. G *hahneneier*); obs. senses are 'child that sucketh long', 'one made a wanton or nestle-cock of', townsman, the limitation to London being later]

co·ckpit, n. Place made for cockfights; arena of any struggle; after part of man-of-war's orlop deck, quarters of junior officers, used in action as hospital; (Aeronaut.) space for pilot &c. in fuselage of aeroplane.

co·ckroach, n. Nocturnal voracious dark-brown beetle-like insect (also *black-beetle*) infesting kitchens. [f. Sp. *cucaracha* etym. dub.]

cock-sure, a. Certain to happen, undoubtedly about *to* do; quite convinced *of, about*; self-confident, dogmatic, presumptuous, whence **cocksure·**NESS n. [COCK[1] used intensively, SURE]

cocksy, coxy, coxiness. = COCKY &c.

co·cktail, n. & a., **co·cktailed**, a. (Horse) with docked tail, of racing stamp but not thorough-bred; (person) placed above his birth or breeding; kind of beetle; drink of spirit with bitters, sugar, &c. (origin doubtful; from U.S.). [tail like that of cock, or that cocks up; sense *half-bred* f. docking of hunters & stage-coach horses]

co·ck-up, n. (typog.). Initial letter much taller than the rest. [COCK[2]]

co·cky, co·cksy, co·xy, a. Conceited, pert. Hence **co·cki**LY[2], **co·xi-**, adv., **co·cki**NESS, **co·xi-**, n. [COCK[1], -Y[2]]

cocky-lee·ky, n. Scotch soup of cock boiled with leeks.

cockyŏ·lly bird, n. (Nursery phr. for) bird.

co·co, co·coa[1] (-kō), **co·ker**, n. (Also *c.-nut, c.-tree, c.-nut-tree*) tropical palm-

For compounds of *co-* not given consult CO-.

tree; *c.-nut,* its large ovate brown hard-shelled seed with edible white lining enclosing whitish liquid (*c.-nut milk*), (slang) human head; *that accounts for the milk in the c.-nut,* (facet.) now all is explained; *c.-nut matting,* made from fibre of nut's outer husk; *double c.-nut,* much larger two-lobed seed of Seychelles palm. [-*a* added f. confusion w. foll.; f. Port. & Sp. *coco* grimace; *coker* chiefly in commerc. use to avoid ambiguity]

co·coa² (-kō), n. Powder made from crushed cacao seeds often with other ingredients; drink made from this or from the seeds; *c. bean,* cacao seed; *c. nib,* cotyledon of this; *c. powder,* kind of gunpowder; *C. Press,* nickname of certain free-trade anti-imperialist newspapers as owned by c.-makers. [corruption of CACAO]

cocoo·n, n., & v.t. & i. Silky case spun by larva to protect it as chrysalis, esp. that of silkworm, whence **cocoo·nERY**(3) n.; similar structure made by other animals; (vb) form, wrap (one*self,* thing &c.) in, c. [f. F. *cocon* dim. of *coque* shell]

cod¹, n. Large sea fish (also *c.-fish*); *c.-bank,* submarine bank frequented by it; *c.-liver oil,* used as medicine. [excl. E, etym. dub.]

cod², v.t. & i. (slang). Hoax, fool. [?]

co·ddle, v.t., & n. Treat as invalid, keep from cold & exertion, feed *up*; (n.) person who coddles himself or others. [perh. = CAUDLE]

code, n., & v.t. Systematic collection of statutes, body of laws so arranged as to avoid inconsistency & overlapping, whence **cŏ·diFY** v.t., **co·difiER**¹, **codi-FICA·TION,** nn.; set of rules on any subject; prevalent morality of a society or class (esp. *c. of honour*); system of mil. or nav. signals; (Telegr.) set of letter or figure or word groups with arbitrary meanings for brevity or secrecy; (vb; also *codify*) put (message) into c. words. [F, f. L CODEX]

co-declina·tion, n. (astr.). Complement of the declination, North-Polar distance. [CO-(2)]

cō·dĕine, n. Alkaloid in opium used as hypnotic. [f. Gk *kōdeia* poppy-head + -INE⁵]

cō·dex, n. (pl. *-dicēs*). Manuscript volume, esp. of ancient Bible or classical texts. [L, earlier *caudex* tree-trunk, tablet, book]

co·dger, n. (colloq.). Fellow, buffer, queer old person. [perh. var. of CADGER]

cŏ·dicil, n. Supplementary addition, esp. modifying or revoking will. So **codici·lLARY**¹ a. [f. L *codicillus* (usu. pl.) dim. of CODEX]

co·dling¹, n. Small cod-fish. [-LING¹(2)]

co·dlin(g)², n. Kinds of apple of long tapering shape; *cc.-&-cream,* willow-herb. [earlier *querdling* perh. f. Ir. *cueirt* apple + -LING¹]

co-educa·tion, n. Education of boys & girls together. Hence **co-educa·tionAL** a. [CO-]

cōĕffi·cient, n. Joint agent or factor; (Alg.) number placed before and multiplying another quantity known or unknown; (Physics) multiplier that measures some property (*c. of friction, expansion,* &c.); *differential c.,* quantity measuring rate of change of a function of any variable with respect to that variable. [CO-]

coe·liac (sē-), a. (physiol.). Of the belly. [f. L f. Gk *koiliakos* (*koilia* belly f. *koilos* hollow)]

coe·l(o)- (sē-), in scientific wds, f. Gk *koilos* hollow.

coe·n(o)- (sē-) in comb. = Gk *koinos* common.

coe·nobīte (sē-), **ce·n-,** n. Member of monastic community. Hence **coeno-bĭ·TIC(AL)** aa., **coe·nobītISM**(3) n. [f. LL *coenobita* f. LL f. Gk *koinobion* convent (COENO-, *bios* life)]

cōē·qual, a. & n. (Archaic, theolog., or emphatic, for) equal. Hence **coequa·lITY** (-kwŏl-) n., **coe·qualLY**² adv. [CO-]

cōer·ce, v.t. & i. Forcibly constrain or impel (person) into quiet, obedience, or any course (*into,* rarely *to* do, or abs.); use force, secure by force (*a coerced obedience*). Hence **coer·CIBLE** a. [f. L CO(*ercēre ercit-* = *arcēre* shut up)]

coer·cion (-shn), n. Controlling of voluntary agent or action by force; government by force, esp. of Ireland by suspension of ordinary liberties (*C. Act, Bill,* with such exceptional provisions). Hence **coer·cionARY**¹ a., **coer·cionIST**(2) n. & a. [f. OF *cohercion* f. L *coerc(i)tionem* (COERCE, -ION)]

coer·cive, a. Of, acting by, exercising, coercion. Hence **coer·civeLY**² adv., **coer·civeNESS** n. [irreg. f. COERCE + -IVE]

cōĕsse·ntial, a. Of the same substance or essence. [CO-]

cōētā·neous, a. = COEVAL a. [f. LL CO(*aetaneus* f. L *aetas* age) + -OUS]

cōēter·nal, a. Alike eternal. So **coeter·-nalLY**² adv. [CO-]

cōē·val, a. & n. (Person) of same date of origin, of same age, existing at same epoch, of same duration. Hence **coevă·lITY** n., **coe·valLY**² adv. [f. L CO(*aevus* f. *aevum* age)]

co-exĕ·cutor, co-exĕ·cutrix, nn. Joint executor, executrix. [CO-]

cōexi·st, v.i. Exist together or *with.* So **coexi·stENT** a., **coexi·stENCE** n. [CO-]

cōextensive, a. Extending over same space or time. [CO-]

cŏ·ffee, n. Drink made from seeds of a shrub roasted & ground; light meal with c., c. as final course at dinner; the shrub, its seeds raw, roasted, or ground; ***c.-bean,*** the seed; *c.-cup,* of special shape or size; ***c.-grounds,*** sediment after infusion; *c.-*

house, -palace, refreshment house; *c.-mill,* for grinding seeds; *c.-pot,* for making or serving c. in; *c.-room,* public dining-room of hotel; *c.-tavern,* temperance refreshment house. [f. Turk. f. Arab. *qahweh* the drink]

cŏ·ffer, n. Box, esp. for valuables; (pl.) treasury, funds; sunk panel in ceiling &c.; *c.-dam,* water-tight case in bridge-building, caisson. [f. OF *cofre* f. L f. Gk *kophinos* basket; cf. *order,* F. *ordre,* L *ordinem*]

cŏ·ffin, n., & v.t. Chest in which corpse is buried; *drive nail into* one's *c.,* hasten his, one's, death by annoyance, intemperance, &c.; unseaworthy ship; horse's hoof below coronet (*c.-bone,* last phalangeal bone of foot; *c.-joint* at top of hoof); *c.-plate,* of metal in lid with deceased's name &c.; hence **co·ffin**LESS a. (Vb) put in c., store away (e.g. books) inaccessibly. [f. OF *cofin* f. L as prec.]

co·ffle, n. Train of beasts, slaves, &c., fastened together. [f. Arab. *qāfilah* caravan]

cog[1], n. One of series of projections on edge of wheel or side of bar transferring motion by engaging with another series; *hunting c.,* extra c. on one wheel &c. securing constant variation in the cc. engaged; *c.-wheel,* with cc. Hence **co·gg**ED[2] a. [cf. Sw. *kugge,* Norw. *kug*]

cog[2], v.t. *C. dice,* fraudulently control the way they fall (*cogged dice* for loaded dice is a mistake of modern archaists). [?]

cō·gent, a. Forcible, convincing, (of argument, &, usu. now playfully as though by transf. from this, of motive, compulsion, &c.). Hence **co·g**ENCY n., **co·gent**LY[2] adv. [F, f. L *cogere* = CO(*agere* drive), -ENT]

cŏ·gitable, a. Able to be grasped by reason, conceivable. [f. L *cogitabilis* (foll., -ABLE)]

cŏ·gitate, v.i. & t. Ponder, meditate; devise; (Philos.) form conception of. Hence or cogn. **cogit**A·TION n., **co·gi·t**ATIVE a., **co·gitative**LY[2] adv., **co·gi·tative**NESS n. [f. L *cogitare* = CO(*agitare* AGITATE) think, -ATE[3]]

cognac (kŏ·nyăk), n. French brandy, prop. that distilled from C. wine. [place-name]

co·gnāte, a. & n. Descended from common ancestor (cf. AGNATE), akin in origin, nature, or quality; a relative. (Philol.) of same linguistic family; representing same original word; of parallel development in different allied languages (*father* is c. with L *pater, paternal* is derived from it); a c. word; (Gram.) *c. object* or *accusative,* one of kindred meaning to vb, used adverbially, not as true object (in *die the death, death* is c., in *he slew death* it is object). Hence **co·gnate**NESS n. [f. L CO(*gnatus* born usu. *natus* f. *gn-, gen-, gon-,* beget)]

cogna·tion, n. Cognate relationship, now esp. in philology. [f. L *cognatio* (prec., -ION)]

cogni·tion, n. (philos.). Action or faculty of knowing, perceiving, conceiving, as opposed to emotion & volition; a perception, sensation, notion, or intuition. So **cogni·tion**AL, **co·gnit**IVE, aa. [f. L *cognitio* f. CO(*gnoscere -gnit-* apprehend f. *gno-* KNOW, usu. *noscere*)]

cŏg·nizable (*also* kŏ·g-), a. Perceptible; recognizable; within the jurisdiction of a court &c. Hence **cog·nizab**LY[2] adv. [f. foll. + -ABLE]

cŏg·nizance (*also* kŏ·g-), n. Being aware, notice, sphere of observation, (*have c. of,* know, esp. in a legitimate or official way; *take c. of,* attend to, not allow to go unobserved; *fall within, be beyond,* one's *c.,* of things that fairly concern, do not concern, one); (right of) dealing with a matter legally or judicially (with phrr. as above in legal sense); distinctive mark, as crest, coat of arms, badge. [f. OF *conis(s)ance* var. of *conoissance* f. L *cognoscent-* part. st. of *cognoscere* see COGNITION, -ANCE; *-z-* (cf. the later COGNIZE) due to confusion w. -IZE]

cŏg·nizant (*also* kŏ·g-), a. Having knowledge, being aware, *of*; (Philos.) having cognition. [f. prec., see -ANT]

cogni·ze (kŏg-), v.t. (philos.). Have cognition of. [on anal. of COGNIZANCE & RECOGNIZE & of vbs rightly ending in -IZE]

cogno·men, n. Nickname; surname; name; (Rom. Ant.) third or family name, as *Cicero, Caesar,* or fourth name or personal epithet, as *Africanus.* [L, CO-, (*g*)*nomen* name f. st. of (*g*)*noscere* KNOW]

cogno·scible, a. Capable of being known (esp. philos.). [f. L *cognoscere* see COGNITION + -IBLE]

cogno·vit, n. (legal). Defendant's acknowledgement, to save expense, that plaintiff's cause is just. [L, = he has acknowledged]

cohă·bit, v.i. Live together, esp. as husband & wife (usu. of persons not married). So **cohabit**A·TION n. [f. F *cohabiter* f. L CO(*habitare* dwell frequent. of *habēre* hold)]

coheir·, coheir·ess (kōār-), nn. Male, female, joint heir. [CO-]

cohere·, v.i. Stick together, remain united, (of parts or whole); be consistent, well knit, (of arguments, style, &c.). [f. L CO(*haerēre -haes-* stick)]

cohēr·ent, a. Cohering; consistent, easily followed, not rambling or inconsequent, (of argument, narration, &c.). So **coher·**ENCE, **coher·**ENCY, nn., **coher·ent**LY[2] adv. [f. F *cohérent* f. L (prec., -ENT)]

cohĕ·ritor, n. = COHEIR. [CO-]

cohē·sion (-zhn), n. Sticking together, force with which molecules cohere; tendency to remain united. So **cohe·sive** a., **cohe·sively**² adv., **cohe·siveness** n. [f. F *cohésion* (L *cohaes-* see COHERE, -ION)]
co·hort, n. Division of Roman army; band of warriors; persons banded together. [f. F *cohorte* f. L *cohortem* nom. *-ors* (CO-, *hort-* enclose, cf. L *hortus* garden, E GARTH, GARDEN)]
coif, n. (hist.). Close cap covering top, back, and sides, of head; serjeant-at-law's white cap. [f. OF *coife* perh. f. MHG *kupfe*]
coiffeur (kwahfer·), n. Hair-dresser. [F]
coiffure (kwahfoor·, or as F), n. Way one's hair is dressed.
coign (koin), n. *C. of vantage,* place affording good view of something. [old form of COIN, QUOIN, preserved by *Macb.* I. vi. 7]
coil¹, v.t. & i. Dispose (rope &c.) in concentric rings; twist (t. & i., often *up*) into circular or spiral shape; move sinuously. [perh. =F *cueillir* f. L COL-(*ligere* =*legere* gather)]
coil², n. Length of coiled rope, spring, &c.; arrangement, thing arranged, in concentric circles; single turn of coiled thing, e.g. snake; lock of hair twisted & coiled; wire, piping, &c., in circles or symmetric curves; (Electr.) spiral wire for passage of current. [f. prec.]
coil³, n. (archaic & poet.). Disturbance, much ado, noise, (*this mortal c.,* turmoil of life). [?]
coin¹, n. Piece of metal made into money by official stamp; metal money; money; *false c.,* imitation in base metal &c., (fig.) anything spurious; *pay* one *in* his *own c.,* give tit for tat. Hence **coi·nless** a. [F, =wedge, corner (cf. COIGN, QUOIN), stamping-die, f. L *cuneus*]
coin², v.t. Make (money) by stamping metal (*c. money,* get money fast); make (metal) into money; make money by means of (one's *brains* &c.); invent, fabricate, (esp. new word). [f. OF *coignier* f. *coin* see prec.]
coi·nage, n. Coining; coins; system of coins in use (*decimal c.,* in which each value is ten times the next below); fabrication (*the c. of* one's *brain*), invention, coined word. [f. OF *coignaige* see prec., -AGE]
cōinci·de, v.i. Occupy same portion of space; occur at and occupy same time; agree together or *with*; concur in opinion &c. [f. F *coïncider* f. med. L CO-IN(*cĭdere* =*cadere* fall)]
cōĭ·ncidence, n. (Instance of) being coincident; notable concurrence of events or circumstances without apparent causal connexion. [F, see foll., -ENCE]
cōĭ·ncident, a. Coinciding. Hence **coi·ncidently**² adv. [F, see COINCIDE, -ENT]
cōĭncide·ntal, a. Of the nature of (a) coincidence. [f. prec. + -AL]
coi·ner, n. In vbl senses; esp., maker of counterfeit coin. [COIN² + -ER¹]
cōinstanta·neous, a. Exactly at the same moment. [CO-]
coir, n. Coco-nut fibre, used for ropes, matting, &c. [f. Malayalam *kayar* cord]
cōĭ·tion, n. Sexual copulation. [f. L *coitio* f. CO(*ire it-* go)]
coke, n., & v.t. (Convert *coal* into) solid substance left when volatile parts have been distilled from coal. [prob. f. obs. *colk* core cf. OFris. & LG *kolk* hole]
coker(nut). See COCO.
cŏl, n. Depression in mountain-chain. [F, =neck, col, f. L *collum* neck]
col-, form taken by COM- before *l.*
cō·la, k-, n. W.-Afr. tree; (also *c.-nut, -seed*), its seed, used as condiment, tonic, and antidote to alcohol. [W.-Afr.]
co·lander (kŭ-), **cu·llender,** n., & v.t. (Pass through a) perforated vessel used as strainer in cookery; similar appliance for casting shot. [corruption of med. L *colatorium* (*colare* strain, -ORY)]
co-lă·titude, n. (astr.). Complement of latitude, difference between it & 90°. [CO-(2)]
colca·nnon, n. Irish dish of cabbage and potatoes pounded and stewed. [?]
co·lchicum (-kĭ-), n. Meadow-saffron; drug extracted from it used for gout. [L, f. Gk *kolkhikon* neut. adj. (*Kolkhis* on Black Sea, -IC)]
co·lcothar, n. Red peroxide of iron used in polishing glass &c. [f. Arab. *qolqoṭar*]
cōld¹, a. Of low temperature, esp. when compared with human body or with that usual in things like the one in question (*ice, key, stone, -c.,* c. as these; *c.-blooded,* of fish & reptiles, also fig. of sluggish persons, & see below; *c.-livered,* unemotional; *c. steel,* sword, bayonet, &c., opposed to fire-arms, *inch* or *few* &c. *inches of c. s.,* thrust); not heated or having cooled after heat (*c. water*; *throw c. water on plan,* discourage it; *c. in death* or *c.,* dead; *c. pig,* water thrown on sleeper to wake him, also *c.-p.* as v.t.; *c.-hammer,* work metal in c. state; *c.-*CHISEL; *c. without,* c. sugarless spirit & water; *c. meat,* that has cooled after cooking, *the c.-m. train* slang, conveying corpses to necropolis; *c. shoulder,* of roast mutton, *give the c. s. to,* entertain poorly, show distaste for company of, also *c.-s.* as v.t.; *in c. blood,* without the excuse of heat or excitement, of cruelty &c., whence **coldblooded**² a., **cold-bloo·dedness** n.); feeling c.; slow to absorb heat (of clayey soil); without ardour, friendliness, or affection, undemonstrative, apathetic, (so **cold-hearted**² a., **cold-hear·tedness** n., **cold-hear·tedly**² adv.; *idea leaves* one *c.,* unmoved, not impressed); chilling,

depressing, uninteresting, (*c. comfort, counsel, news*); faint (of scent in hunting); *c. colours*, blue, grey, &c., opp. red, yellow, &c.; *c.-drawn* CASTOR OIL; *c. coil*, tube coiled round inflamed part with c. water running in it; *c. blast*, of c. air forced into furnace; *c.* CREAM; *c. feet*, (army slang) disinclination to fight or go to or remain at the front. Hence **co·ld**ISH[1](2) a., **co·ld**LY[2] adv., **co·ld**NESS n. [OE *cald*, com.-Teut. cf. G *kalt*, cogn. w. L *gel-*]

cold[2], n. Prevalence in atmosphere, or rarely in any object, of low temperature (*left out in the c.*, not looked after); inflamed state of mucous membrane, with hoarseness, running at nose, sore throat, &c. (CATCH[1] *c.*; often *c. in the head*). Hence **co·ld**PROOF a. [OE *cald* neut. adj. see prec.]

co·ld-short, a. Brittle in its cold state (of iron). [f. Scand. (Da. *kold-skjör*) *skjör* brittle w. assim. to *short* as in *shortbread*]

cole, n. (Old name, now rare exc. in comb., for) kinds of cabbage &c., as Rape, Sea-Kale; *c.-seed*, plant from which colza oil is got. [f. L *caulis* stem, cabbage]

cŏleo·pterous, a. Of the order of *Coleoptera* or beetles, with front wings converted into sheaths for hinder. [f. Gk *koleopteros* (*koleon* sheath, *pteron* wing) + -OUS]

cŏ·lic, n. Severe griping pains in belly. Hence **co·lick**Y[2] a. [f. F *colique* f. L f. Gk *kolikos* (COLON[1], -IC)]

collă·borate, v.i. Work in combination (*with*, or abs.) esp. at literary or artistic production. So **collabor**A·TION, **col·la·borat**OR[2], nn. [f. L COL(*laborare* LABOUR[2]), -ATE[3]]

colla·pse, n., & v.i. (Undergo, experience, a) falling in, sudden shrinking together, giving way, prostration by loss of nervous or muscular power, breakdown of mental energy, loss of courage. Hence **colla·ps**ED[1](2) a. [(n. f. L *collapsus -ūs*) f. COL(*labi laps-* slip)]

colla·psible, -able, a. So made as to collapse when required for packing &c. [-BLE]

co·llar[1], n. Neckband, upright or turned over, of coat, dress, shirt, &c.; band of linen, lace, &c., completing upper part of costume; neck-chain of order of knighthood; *c. of SS* or *esses*, formerly badge of House of Lancaster, still in some officials' costume; leather or metal band round dog's or prisoner's neck; roll round horse's neck bearing weight of draught (*c.-harness*, opp. BREAST[1]*-harness*; *c.-work*, hard pulling esp. up hill, & fig. of severe effort, so also *against the c.*); restraining or connecting band, ring, pipe, in machines &c.; arrangement connecting several fishing-flies; coloured stripe round animal's neck; piece of meat, brawn, fish, tied in roll; *c.-bone*, joining breast-bone & shoulder-blade, clavicle. Hence (-)**co·llar**ED[2], **co·llar**LESS, aa. [f. OF *colier* f. L *collare* (*collum* neck, -AR[1])]

co·llar[2], v.t. Seize (person) by the c., capture; (Footb.) lay hold of and stop (opponent holding ball); (slang) appropriate; press (meat &c.) into roll. [f. prec.]

cŏllare·t(te), n. Woman's collar of lace, fur, &c. [f. F *collerette* (*collier* COLLAR[1], -ETTE)]

colla·te, v.t. Compare in detail (copies of text or document, one copy *with* another); (Bookbinding) verify order of (sheets) by signatures; appoint (clergyman) to benefice (only of the Ordinary). So **colla·t**OR[2] n. [f. L COL(*lat-* p.p. st. of *ferre* bring)]

collă·teral, a. & n. Side by side, parallel; subordinate but from same source, contributory, connected but aside from main subject, course, &c.; of common descent but by different line (so as noun = c. kinsman); *c. security* or *c.*, property pledged as guarantee for repayment of money (opp. *personal* giving right of action for recovery). Hence **colla·teral**LY[2] adv. [f. med. L COL(*lateralis* f. *latus -eris* side)]

colla·tion, n. In vbl senses of COLLATE; also: (R.-C. Ch.) light repast in evening of fast-day; light meal (usu. *cold c.*) often at exceptional time. [OF, f. L *collationem* (COLLATE, -ION); sense *repast* from Benedictine monastery readings of Lives of the Fathers (*collationes patrum*; *collatio* also of the reading & debate on it) followed by light repast]

co·lleague (-ēg), n. One of two or more holders of joint office (usu. with *my* &c.). [f. F *collègue* f. L COL(*lega* f. *legere* choose)]

co·llect[1], n. Short prayer of Common Prayer Book, esp. one of those appropriated to days or seasons & read before Epistle & in morning & evening prayer. [f. F *collecte* f. L *collecta* fem. p.p. of *colligere* COLLECT[2]; orig. sense perh. *summing up* (of thought appropriate to occasion); for noun use of p.p. cf. e.g. *army*]

colle·ct[2], v.t. & i. Assemble, accumulate, bring or come together; get (taxes, contributions) from a number of people; secure (specimens, books, &c.) for addition to a set; regain control of, concentrate, recover, (*oneself*, one's thoughts, energies, courage; *collected*, not distracted, cool, whence **colle·cted**LY[2] adv.; *c. a horse*, keep him in hand, not let him sprawl); infer, gather, conclude. Hence **colle·ct**ABLE, -IBLE, a. [f. obs. *collect* adj. f. L *collectus* p.p. of COL(*ligere* = *legere* pick)]

cŏllectā·nea, n. pl. Collected passages, miscellany. [L, neut. pl. adj.]
colle·ction, n. Collecting; collecting of money, money collected, at meeting or Church service for charitable or religious purpose; accumulation *of* water, dust, &c.; group of things collected & belonging together (literary materials, specimens, works of art, &c.); (pl.) college terminal examination at Oxford &c. [OF, f. L *collectionem* (COLLECT², -ION)]
colle·ctive, a. & n. Formed by, constituting a, collection, taken as a whole, aggregate, (*c. fruit*, resulting from many flowers, as mulberry); of, from, many individuals, common, (*c. note*, signed by several States; *c. ownership*, of land, means of production, &c., by all for benefit of all, whence **colle·ctiv**ISM, **colle·ctiv**IST, nn.); (Gram. & Log.) *c. noun, c. idea*, or *c.*, used in sing. to express many individuals, as *cattle, troop, duck*. Hence **colle·ctive**LY² adv., **cŏllecti·**VITY n. [f. L *collectivus* (as prec., -IVE)]
colle·ctor, n. One who collects (specimens, curiosities, railway tickets at station, money due, esp. taxes, rent, & subscriptions); collecting-apparatus in various machines; (I.C.S.) chief official of district collecting revenue & holding magisterial powers, whence (office & district) **colle·ctor**ATE¹ n. Hence **colle·ctor**SHIP n. [med. L, as prec. + -OR²]
collee·n, n. (Anglo-Ir.). Girl. [Ir. *cailin*, dim. of *caile* country-woman]
co·llege (-ĭj), n. Body of colleagues with common functions & privileges (*Sacred C., c. of cardinals*, the Pope's council of 70; *Herald's C.* or *C. of Arms*; *C. of Physicians, Preceptors*, &c.); independent corporation of scholars in university, usu. with master, fellows, scholars, & students not on foundation; similar foundation outside university (as Eton. Dulwich); small degree-giving university; institution for higher education affiliated to university; place of professional study (army, naval, of agriculture, &c.); large public secondary school (Marlborough); (pretentious name for) private school; buildings of any of these; *c. living*, benefice in gift of a c.; *c. pudding*, small plum pudding for one person. Hence **collē·gi**AL a. [f. OF *collége* f. L *collegium* (*collega* COLLEAGUE)]
co·lleger, n. One of seventy foundation scholars at Eton. [-ER¹]
collē·gian, n. Member of a college. [-AN]
collē·giate¹ (-*at*), a. Constituted as, belonging to, a college or body of colleagues, corporate; *c. church*, endowed for chapter but with no see, (Sc. & U.S.) under joint pastorate; *c. school*, of high pretensions. Hence **colle·giate**LY² adv. [f. L *collegiatus* (COLLEGE, -ATE²)]
colle·giāte², v.t. Make c. [as prec., -ATE³]
co·llet, n. Encompassing band, ferrule, socket, flange holding gem, bezel. [F, dim. of COL]
colli·de, v.i. Come into collision; be in conflict. [f. L COL(*lidere lis-* = *laedere* hurt)]
co·llie, -y, n. Scotch sheep-dog. [cf. obs. adj. *colly* = *coaly*; perh. as orig. black]
cŏ·llier, n. Coal-miner, whence **co·lli**ERY (3) n.; coal-ship; sailor on this. [COAL, -IER]
co·lligāte, v.t. Bring into connexion (esp. isolated facts by a generalization). So **collig**A·TION n. [f. L COL(*ligare* bind), see -ATE³]
co·llimāte, v.t. Adjust line of sight of (telescope &c.), make parallel (telescopes, rays). Hence **collim**A·TION n. [*collimare* false reading in Cicero for COL(*lineare* f. *linea* line)]
co·llimātor, n. Small attached telescope for collimating an instrument; tube in spectroscope throwing parallel rays on prism. [-OR²]
colli·nĕar, a. In same straight line. [COL-]
Co·llins, n. (colloq.). = ROOFER. [Jane Austen, *P. & P.*, ch. xxii]
colli·sion (-ĭzhn), n. Dashing together, violent encounter of moving body, esp. ship or railway train, with another; (fig.) harsh combination (of consonants); clashing of opposed interests &c. (esp. *in c., come into c. with*); (Naut.) *c.-mat*, ready for putting over hole made by c. [f. L *collisio* (COLLIDE, -ION)]
co·llocate, v.t. Place together; arrange; station, set in particular place. So **colloc**A·TION n. [f. L COL(*locare* f. *locus* place) station]
co·llocutor, n. Partaker in talk, as *my c. said*. [LL, f. COL(*loqui locut-* talk), -OR²]
collō·dion, n. Solution of gun-cotton in ether filming when exposed, used in photography & surgery. Hence **collo·dion**ED² a., **collo·dion**IZE(5) v.t., **collodio-** comb. form. [f. Gk *kollōdēs* (*kolla* glue, -ODE)]
collo·gue (-ōg), v.i. Talk confidentially (with suggestion of plotting, an obs. sense). [cf. F *colloque* conference, & obs. *colleague* vb plot]
colloid, a. & n. Gluey (substance); (Path.) *c. tissue* &c., degenerated into homogeneous gelatinous consistency (also *c.*, such substance); (Chem.) (substance) of non-crystalline semi-solid kind suspended or dispersed in some medium, e.g., gelatine & starch. Hence **colloi·d**AL a. [Gk *kolla* glue, -OID]
co·llop, n. Slice of meat; (bibl.) fold of skin in fat person or animal. [f. 14th c., orig. sense *fried ham and eggs*, etym. dub.]
collō·quial, a. In or of talk, oral; belonging to familiar speech, not used in formal or elevated language. Hence **collo·quial**ISM(3, 4), **collo·quial**IST(1), nn., **collo·quial**LY² adv. [COLLOQUY, -AL]

co·lloquist, n. =COLLOCUTOR. [foll., -IST(1)]
co·lloquy, n. Converse; a conversation; judicial and legislative court in Presbyterian Church. [f. L COL(*loquium* f. *loqui* speak)]
co·llotype, n. Thin plate of gelatine etched by actinic rays & then printed from (*c. plate, process,* &c.). [f. Gk *kolla* glue + TYPE]
collu·de (-ōō-, -ū-), v.i. (archaic). Practise collusion. [f. L COL(*ludere lus-* play)]
collu·sion (-ōō-, -ū-), n. Fraudulent secret understanding, esp. between ostensible opponents as in law-suit. Hence **collu·**SIVE a. **collu·sive**LY² adv. [F, f. L *collusionem* (prec., -ION)]
collȳ·rium, n. (pl. *-ia*). Eyesalve; suppository. [f. L f. Gk *kollurion* poultice]
co·llywobbles, n. pl. (colloq.). Rumbling in the intestines. [imit.]
Cō·lney Hatch, n. (Used for) C. H. Lunatic Asylum for County of London.
cŏ·locȳnth, n. Bitter-apple, gourd plant with bitter-pulped fruit used as purgative drug; the drug. [f. L f. Gk *kolokunthis*]
cō·lon¹, n. (anat.). Greater part of larger intestine, from caecum to rectum. Hence **coloni·**TIS n. [L, f. Gk *kŏlon*]
cō·lon², n. Punctuation-mark (:) ranking between period and semicolon, & used esp. to mark antithesis, illustration, or (often with dash :—) quotation. [L, f. Gk *kōlon* limb, clause]
colō·nate, n. Serf system in later Roman Empire. [f. LL *colonatus* (L *colonus,* see COLONY, -ATE¹)]
colonel (ker·nl), n. Highest regimental officer; *C. Commandant,* rank replacing Brigadier General. Hence **colonel**CY n. [corrected f. *coronel* f. F *coronnel* f. It. *colonnello* (*colonna* column)]
colonelship, n. Being a colonel (cf. *colonelcy,* ordinary word for the office). [-SHIP]
colō·nial, a. & n. (Inhabitant) of a colony, esp. of a British self-governing or Crown Colony; *C. Office,* State department in charge of the Colonies. Hence **colo·nial**ISM(2, 4) n., **colo·nial**LY² adv. [f. L *colonia* COLONY + -AL]
cŏ·lonist, n. Settler in, part-founder or inhabitant of, a colony. [COLONIZE, -IST]
cŏ·lonize, v.t. & i. Establish colony in; establish in a colony; establish or join a colony. Hence **co·loniz**A·TION, **co·loniz**ER¹, nn. [f. L *colonus* farmer (*colere* till) + -IZE]
cŏlonnā·de, n. Series of columns with entablature; row of trees. Hence **colonna·d**ED² a., [F (*colonne* COLUMN, -ADE)]
cŏ·lony, n. (Gk hist.) independent city founded by emigrants; (Rom. hist.) settlement usu. of veterans in conquered territory acting as garrison; settlement, settlers, in new country forming community fully or partly subject to mother State; their territory; people of one nationality or occupation in a city, esp. if living in a special quarter (so of animals, *c. of sparrows* &c.); (Biol.) aggregate of animals as in coral. [f. L *colonia* (*colonus* farmer f. *colere* till)]
cŏ·lophon, n. Tail-piece in old books, often ornamental, giving information now placed on title-page (*from title-page to c.,* from cover to cover). [LL, f. Gk *kolophōn* summit]
colŏ·phony, n. Dark resin distilled from turpentine & water. Hence **colo·phon**ATE¹(3) n., **coloph-, colophon-,** comb. forms. [f. L *colophonia* (*resina* resin) of *Colophon* in Lydia]
cŏloqui·ntida, n. =COLOCYNTH.
Cŏlora·do (-ah-) **bee·tle,** n. Yellow black-striped b. destructive to potatoes. [*C.* in U.S.]
colo(u)ra·tion (kŭ-, kŏ-), n. Colouring, method of putting on or arranging colour: natural, esp. variegated, colour of living or other things. [F, f. L *colorare* COLOUR², -ATION]
cŏlori·fic, a. Producing colour; highly coloured. [f. F *colorifique* (COLOUR¹, -I-, -FIC)]
cŏlorĭ·meter, n. Instrument measuring intensity of colour. [L *color,* -I-, -METER]
colo·ssal, a. Of, like, a colossus; gigantic, huge; (colloq., f. G) remarkable, splendid, delightful. Hence **colo·ssal**LY² adv. [foll. + -AL]
colo·ssus, n. (pl. *-ī, -uses*). Statue of much more than life size; gigantic person or personified empire &c., esp. conceived (like C. of Rhodes) as standing astride over dominions. [L, f. Gk *kolossos*]
colŏ·tomy, n. (surg.). Incision in COLON¹ to provide artificial anus in stricture &c. [COLON¹, -TOMY]
co·lour¹ (kŭ-), n. Sensation produced on eye by rays of decomposed light (cf. *black,* effect produced by no light or by surface reflecting no rays, & *white,* effect produced by rays of undecomposed light); a particular hue, one, or any mixture, of the constituents into which light decomposes as in spectrum, including loosely black, white (ACCIDENTAL *c.*; *complementary c.,* that combined with given c. makes white; *fundamental, primary, simple, cc.,* red, green, & violet, or with painters red, blue, & yellow, giving all others by mixture; *secondary c.,* mixture of two primary; *c.-blind,* unable to distinguish certain colours, see DALTONISM, also fig. in U.S., impartial between whites & blacks, whence

co·lour-blindNESS n.; *see the c. of* one's *money*, receive some payment from him); *man, woman, &c., of c.*, of non-white race, esp. negro (*c. bar*, legal or social distinction between whites & people of c.); ruddiness of face (*lose, gain, c.*; *change c.*, turn pale or red); appearance, light, (*paint in bright, dark, cc.*; *see in its true cc.*; *put false cc. upon*); (Art) colouring, c.-system, -perception, effects as of c. got by light and shade in engraving, whence **co·lour**IST(3) n., **colour-i·stic** a.; pigment, paint, (*c.-box*, of assorted artists' paints; WATER-*cc.*; *c.-man*, dealer in paints). (Pl.) coloured ribbon, dress, &c., worn as symbol of party, membership of club, &c. (*get* one's, *give* one *his, cc.*, of inclusion in athletic team; *show* one's *cc.*, one's party or character); flag of ship, pair of silken flags (*King's* or *Queen's c., regimental c.*) carried by regiment (TROOP*ing of the c.* or *cc.*; *with the cc.*, serving in army; *sail under false cc.*, fig. of hypocrite or impostor; *come off with flying cc.*, win credit; *nail cc. to mast*, persist, refuse to climb down; *c.-sergeant*, senior sergeant of infantry company, now *Company Sergeant-Major* or *Quartermaster Sergt*, with duty of guarding cc.); coloured dresses. Show of reason, pretext, false plea, (*give no c. for saying*; *under c. of*); (Mus.) timbre, quality, also variety of expression; (Gen.) character, tone, quality, mood, shade of meaning, (*take* one's *c. from*); (Literature) picturesqueness, ornate style, (*local c.*, use of details giving verisimilitude, background, or atmosphere). [f. OF *color* f. L *colorem* nom. *-or*]

co·lour² (kŭ-), v.t. & i. Give c. to; paint, stain, dye; disguise; misrepresent (*highly coloured details*); imbue with its own c. (*motive colours act*); take on c.; blush; *coloured person* (not wholly of white descent). [f. OF *colorer* f. L *colorare* (*color* COLOUR¹)]

co·lourable (kŭ-), a. Specious, plausible; counterfeit. Hence **co·lourab**LY² adv. [f. OF *colorable* (as prec., -ABLE)]

co·louring (kŭ-), n. In vbl senses; esp., style in which thing is coloured, or in which artist employs colour. [-ING¹]

co·lourless, a. Without colour; pale; dull-hued; wanting in character or vividness; neutral, impartial, indifferent. Hence **co·lourless**LY² adv., **co·lourless**NESS n. (-LESS]

co·loury (kŭ-), a. (commerc.). Having the colour that goes with good quality (of hops, coffee, &c.). [-Y²]

colporteur· (-ter; *also* kŏ·-), n. Book-hawker, esp. one employed by Society to distribute Bibles. [F (*colporter* vb f. L *collum* neck, *portare* carry, -OR²)]

cōlt¹, n., & v.t. Young of horse from when it is taken from dam to age of 4 (with thoroughbreds 5); inexperienced person, esp. cricket professional in first season; (Naut.) rope used for chastisement (vb, thrash with c.); *coltsfoot*, common large-leaved yellow-flowered weed; *c.'s tail*, ragged-edged cloud. Hence **co·lt**HOOD n., **co·lt**ISH¹ a. [?]

Cōlt², n. (Used for) C. revolver, automatic gun, or pistol. [S. *C.*, inventor]

cŏ·lūbrīne, a. Snake-like; esp., of, like, the *coluber* (genus of harmless snakes). [f. L *colubrinus* (*coluber* snake)]

cŏ·lumbīne¹, n. Garden plant with flower like five clustered pigeons. [f. F *columbine* f. med. L *columbina* f. L *columba* dove, -INE¹]

Cŏ·lumbīne², n. Mistress of Harlequin in pantomine. [f. It. *Columbina* character in comedy, proper name f. L as prec.]

co·lumn (-*um*), n. (Arch.) long vertical often slightly tapering cylinder usu. supporting entablature or arch, or alone as monument, (fig.) support; c.-shaped object, organ in Anat. or Bot., part of machine, &c. (*c. of water, mercury*, confined vertical cylindrical mass; *c. of smoke*, rising straight); vertical division of page for figures &c., or to reduce length of lines esp. in newspapers (also part of newspaper, sometimes more or less than c., devoted to special subject, as AGONY *c., advertisement cc.*; *our cc., the cc. of The Times*, contents of newspaper); narrow-fronted deep arrangement of troops in successive lines (*in c. of sections, platoons, companies*, with one section &c. forming each line & one section's &c. length between lines; *quarter c.*, with 6 paces between lines); body of ships, esp. following one another. Hence or cogn. **colu·mn**AR¹, **c·olumn**ED² (-*umd*), **colu·mni**FORM, aa. [f. OF *colompne* f. L *columna* (*cel-* whence *celsus* high)]

colūre·, n. One of two great circles intersecting rectangularly at poles & dividing equinoctial & ecliptic into four equal parts, one passing through equinoctial, & one through solstitial, points of ecliptic. [f. L f. Gk *kolouros* truncated]

cŏ·lza, n. =COLE-*seed*; *c.-oil*, made from it & used in lamps. [F, f. LG *côlsât* COLE-seed]

com-, pref. =L *cum* in comb., retained as *com-* before b, p, m, & rarely before vowels, changed to *cor-* before r, *col-* before l, *co-* before vowels, h, & gn, & *con-* before other consonants; *com-* occurs in E also before f (*comfort*). Meaning, *with, together, altogether, completely.*

cō·ma¹, n. Unnatural heavy sleep, stupor, lethargy. Hence **co·mat**OSE a. [f. Gk *kōma -atos* cf. *koimaō* put to sleep]

cō·ma², n. (pl. *-ae*). (Bot.) tuft of silky hairs at end of seed; (Astr.) nebulous envelope round nucleus of comet. [L, f. Gk *komē* hair of head]

comb¹ (kōm), n. Toothed strip of horn,

metal, ivory, &c., for arranging, cleaning, or confining the hair; =CURRY[3]-*comb*; thing of same shape, look, or purpose, in many machines, esp. for dressing wool, or collecting electricity, or in animal structure; red fleshy crest of fowl esp. cock, analogous growth in other birds, (*cut the c. of*, humiliate); crest of hill or wave; = HONEYCOMB[1]; *c.-out*, process or instance of COMB[2]ing out. Hence (-)**comb**ED[2] a. [com-.Teut., cf. Du. *kam*, G *kamm*; also Gk *gomphos* pin, Skr. *gambhas* tooth]

comb[2], v.t. & i. Draw c. through (hair), curry (horse), dress (wool, flax) with c.; (of wave) curl over; *c.out*, secure or get rid of (as) by combing (esp. of getting recruits from among those previously exempted from service). [earlier *kemb*; present vb f. prec.]

combat (kŭ·mbat *or* kŏ·mbăt), n., & v.t. & i. (Do) battle; *single c.*, duel; (engage in) contest, struggle; oppose, strive against. [f. F *combat* & *combattre* f. LL (COM-, *battere, batuere*, fight)]

co·mbatant (kŭ-), a. & n. Fighting, fighter. [OF part. as prec.]

co·mbative (kŭ-), a. Pugnacious. Hence **co·mbative**LY[2] adv., **co·mbative**NESS n. [COMBAT v. + -IVE]

combe. See COOMB.

cō·mber (-mer), n. In vbl senses; esp., machine for combing cotton or wool very fine; long curling wave, breaker. [-ER[1]]

combina·tion, n. Combining; combined state (*in c. with*); combined set of things or persons; (Math., pl.) different collections possible of given number of individuals in groups of given smaller number; (Chem.) union of substances in compound with properties differing from theirs; united action; (pl.) single under-garment for body & legs; *c.-room*, at Cambridge = COMMON[1]-*room*. [OF, f. LL *combinationem* (COMBINE, -ATION)]

combi·ne, v.t. & i., & n. Join together (persons, or things material or other); possess (esp. qualities usu. separate) together; (cause to) coalesce in one substance, form chemical compound; co-operate; (n.) combination of persons, esp. to raise prices or obstruct course of trade. So **co·mbinātive** a. [f. LL COM-(*binare* f. *bini* two together)]

co·mbing (-mĭ-), n. In vbl senses; esp., (pl.) hairs combed off. (-ING[1)]

combu·stible, a. & n. (Matter, thing) capable of or used for burning; excitable. Hence **combusti**BI·LITY, n. [F. f. LL *combustibilis* f. L *comburere -ust-* perh. =COM- + *urere* burn (-*b*- unexplained)]

combu·stion (-ŭstshn), n. Destruction by fire (SPONTANEOUS *c.*). (Chem. &c.) development of light & heat going with chemical combination; oxidation of organic tissue. [OF, f. LL *combustionem* (prec., -ION)]

come[1] (kŭm), v.i. (came, come). Start, move, arrive, towards or at a point, time, or result (often not specified because obvious, while point of departure, if it matters, is always specified; cf. GO; *c. into world*, be born; *c. to an end*, cease; *c. to hand*, of letter &c., be delivered; *c.* SHORT; *c. to a point*, taper; *c. to blows*, fight; *c. home to*, be realized by; *c. & go*, pass to & fro, pay brief visit, be transitory; *let 'em all c. !*, slang announcement of readiness; *light c. light go*, what is easily won is soon lost; *coming nineteen*, in nineteenth year; *two years c. Christmas*, including time from now to Christmas); be brought (*the dinner came; c. under notice, before judge*); fall, land, *on* (*came on my head*); move relatively by motion of beholder &c. towards one (*c. into sight, to* one's *knowledge, in* one's *way; c. to light*, be revealed); reach point with hand, instrument, or missile; occur, fall *to* lot of, (*comes on such a page; one comes before, after, another; c. into* one's *head; the work, ill luck, comes to me*); happen (*how comes it that—?; to c.* pred. adj., future; *for a year to c.; the to-c.*, the future; *c. what may*, whatever happens); become present from future (*c. to pass; the time will c. when*); spring *of*, be the result *of*, (*that's what comes of grumbling; c. of noble parents*); enter, be brought, *into* (collision, play, prominence; *c. to harm*, be injured); amount *to* (*comes to 2/6; it comes to this, that—*, is as much as to say that); take form (*the butter will not c.*); find oneself under compulsion or in a position *to* (*have c. to believe, has c. to be used*); (with cogn. obj.) traverse, accomplish, (*have c. 3 miles, a long way*); play a part (slang; *c. the bully over; c. it strong*, show vigour; *c. it too strong*, overdo something, exaggerate); become, get to be, prove, (*string comes untied, things c. right, he came alive; comes expensive, easy, true, natural*); (imperat. as exclamation) now then (encouraging), think again, don't be hasty. *C. about*, happen; *c. across*, meet with; *c. along*, (colloq.) make haste; *c. at*, reach, discover, get access to; *c. away*, get detached; *c. back*, recur to memory; *c. by* (prep.) obtain, (adv.) pass; *c. down*, extend downwards *to*, be handed down by tradition, fall, be humbled (esp. *in the world*, lose caste); *c. down upon*, rebuke, punish, exact reparation from; *c. down with*, pay (money); *c. forward*, present oneself, answer appeal; *c. in*, enter house or room, begin innings, take such a place in race &c. (*c. in third*), be elected, come to power, be received as income, become seasonable or fashionable, serve a purpose (esp. *c. in useful*), find a place (*where does the joke c. in?*; *where do I c. in?* how are my interests advanced?); *c. in for*, get *share of*, get; *c. into*, receive possession of; *c. near doing*, narrowly escape or fail; *c. off*, be detached, extricate oneself from contest &c. in such state (*with flying* COLOURS, *badly*), be accomplished, fulfilled; *c. on*, (prep.) =*c. upon*, (adv.) continue coming, advance esp. to attack, progress, thrive, supervene (of wind, storm, disease), arise to be discussed, appear on stage, begin to bowl, (imperat.) follow me, I defy you; *c. out*, go on strike, emerge from examination &c. with such success, emerge from clouds, be found out, be solved, show itself (of photograph, smallpox, arrogance), be published (*comes out on Saturdays*), make début on stage or in society; *c. out of that*, slang order to clear out or desist; *c. out with*, utter; *c. over*, (prep.) master as an influence, (adv.) c. from some distance or across obstacle (*came over with the Conqueror, over from London to see us*), change sides or opinion; *c. round*, look in for casual visit, recover from ill temper, swoon, &c.; *c. to*, (prep.) inherit, return to (one*self*, one's *senses* from fainting-fit or from folly), (adv.) cease moving, revive; *c. under*, be classed as or among, be subjected to (influence); *c. up*, join university, approach person for talk, get abreast *with*, spring out of ground, become fashionable, be mooted, be equal *to* standard &c., (imperat., to horse) go faster; *c. upon*, attack by surprise, strike or lay hold of (mind), make demand on, be a burden to, meet by chance with. [OE *cuman*, com.-Teut. cf. Du. *komen*, G. *kommen*; cogn. also w. Skr. *gam*, Gk *bainō*, L *venire*]

come², n. *C.-&-go*, passing to & fro; *c.-down*, downfall, degradation. [f. prec.]

come-ă·t-able, a. Accessible. [-ABLE]

comē·dian, n. Actor, writer, of comedies. [f. F *comédien* f. L *comoedia* COMEDY + -AN]

cŏmedie·nne (-mĭ-), n. Comedy actress. [F]

comēdie·tta, n. Short or slight comedy. [It., dim. of *comedia* COMEDY]

cŏ·mēdist, n. Writer of comedies. [foll., -IST(3); to avoid ambiguity of COMEDIAN]

cŏ·medy, n. Stage-play of light, amusing, & often satirical character, chiefly representing everyday life, & with happy ending (cf. TRAGEDY); branch of drama concerned with ordinary persons & employing familiar language; life, or an incident in it, regarded as a spectacle; *Old, Middle, New, C.*, classification of ancient Greek c., the first farcical & largely political, the last corresponding to modern c., & the second transitional. [f. F *comédie* f. L f. Gk *kōmō(i)dia* f. *kōmō(i)dos* f. *kōmos* revel, *aoidos* singer]

comely (kŭ·mlĭ), a. Pleasant to look at (usu. of personal appearance, sometimes of behaviour or conduct). Hence **co·meli**NESS n. [OE *cýmlic* (*cýme* fine f. WG *kūmi-*, -LY¹)]

co·mer (kŭ-), n. One who comes (usu. qualified, as *first c.*); *all cc.*, any one who applies, takes up a challenge, &c. [-ER¹]

comĕ·stible, n. (usu. pl.). Thing to eat. [F, f. LL *comestibilis* (*comest-* var. of *comes-* p.p. st. of L COM*ĕdere* eat up)]

co·met, n. Body with star-like nucleus & train or tail of light moving round sun in elliptical or towards & from it in parabolic course; *c.-year*, in which conspicuous comet comes; *c.-wine*, made in c.-year, supposed of superior quality. Hence **co·met**ARY¹, **comĕ·t**IC, aa. [f. L f. Gk *komētēs* long-haired (star) f. *komaō* wear hair long (*komē* hair)]

co·mfit (kŭ-), n. Sweetmeat, sugar-plum. [f. OF *confit* f. L CON(*fectum* =*factum* neut. p.p. of *facere* make)]

co·mfort (kŭ-), n., & v.t. Relief in affliction, consolation, being consoled; person who consoles one or saves one trouble; cause of satisfaction; conscious well-being, being comfortable; possession of *cc.*, things that make life easy; *creature cc.*, good food, clothes, &c. (Vb) soothe in grief, console; make comfortable; *c. the king's enemies* (archaic), give them aid. [f. OF *confort(er)* f. L CON-(*fortare* f. *fortis* strong)]

co·mfortable (kŭ-), a. Such as to obviate hardship, save trouble, & promote content, ministering to comfort; at ease, free from hardship, pain, & trouble; tranquil, with easy conscience. Hence **co·mfortab**LY² adv. [f. AF *confortable* (prec., -ABLE)]

co·mforter (kŭ-), n. One who comforts (*the C.*, Holy Ghost; *Job's c.*, professed consoler who depresses); woollen scarf. [-ER¹]

co·mfortless, a. Dreary, without provision for comfort. [-LESS]

co·mfrey (kŭ-), n. Tall rough-leaved ditch plant with clusters of whitish or purplish bells. [f. OF *confirie* etym. dub.]

co·mfy (kŭ-), a. (colloq.). Comfortable. [abbr.]

cŏ·mic, a. Of comedy (*c. opera*, with c. treatment & much spoken dialogue, also mere burlesque set to music); mirth-provoking, laughable or meant to be so, facetious, burlesque, funny, (*c. song, paper*; *c. history of Rome* &c.; *has its c. side*). Hence **comico-** comb. form. [f. L f. Gk *kōmikos* prob. f. *kōmos* revel]

cŏ·mical, a. Mirth-provoking, laughable; odd, queer. Hence **comica·l**ITY n., **co·mical**LY² adv. [as prec. + -AL]

cŏminter·n. See INTERNATIONAL.

cŏmita·dji, n. Band of irregular soldiery in the Balkans. [Serb., ult. f. L as COUNTY]

cŏ·mity, n. Courtesy; *c. of nations,* friendly recognition as far as practicable of each other's laws & usages. [f. L *cōmitas* (*cōmis* courteous)]

co·mma, n. Punctuation-mark (,) of the least separation indicated between parts of sentence, also used to separate figures &c.; (Mus.) definite minute interval or difference of pitch; *inverted cc.,* raised or superior cc. used to begin & end a quotation, the first (or first pair) inverted (he said 'no' or "no"); *c. bacillus,* c.-shaped found in cholera. [f. L f. Gk *komma* clause (*koptō* cut, -M)]

comm·and[1], v.t. & i. Order, bid, (*what God commands, commands us, commands us to do, commands that we should do, commands to be done*; also ellipt., *let us do as God commands*; & abs., *God commands & man obeys*); have authority over, control of; be supreme; be in c.; be in c. of (ship, forces, &c.); *c. in chief,* be commander-in-chief of, or abs.); restrain, master, (passions, one*self*); have at disposal or within reach (sum, skill, person; so *yours to c.,* obediently); deserve & get (sympathy &c.); dominate (strategic position) from superior height, look down over. [f. OF *comander* f. LL COM-(*mandare* entrust)]

comma·nd[2], n. Order, bidding, (*word of c.,* customary order for movement in drill; *at* or *by* one's *c.,* in pursuance of his bidding); *c. paper* (usu. abbr. Cd or Cmd with register number as *Cd 5723*), paper laid by c. of the Crown before Parliament &c.; exercise or tenure of authority, esp. naval or military (*in c. of,* commanding; *under c. of,* commanded by); control, mastery, possession, (*great c. of language,* skill in speech; *at c.,* ready to be used at will; *c. of the passes* &c.); body of troops, district, under commander; *c.-in-chief,* supreme c.; *c.-night,* with theatre &c. performance given by royal c. [f. or as prec.]

cŏmmandă·nt, n. Commanding officer, esp. governor of fortress. Hence **comma·nt**SHIP n. [F (COMMAND[1], -ANT)]

cŏmmandeer·, v.t. Impress (men), seize (stores), for military service. [f. S.-Afr.-Du. *kommanderen* (-ăr-) f. F as prec.]

comma·nder, n. In vbl senses; also or esp.: *C. of the Faithful,* title of Caliph; *C., Lieut. C.,* naval OFFICERS; *Wing-C.,* AIR[1]-*force* officer; member of higher class in some Orders of Knighthood; large wooden mallet; *C.-in-Chief,* (Army) of all military land-forces of State, of portion of them quartered in colony, or of expedition in foreign country, (Navy) of all ships on a station. Hence **comma·nder**SHIP(1) n. [f. OF *comandere* (COMMAND[1], -ER[1])]

comma·nding, a. In vbl senses; esp.: exalted, impressive, (of persons, looks, ability, &c.); with wide view (of hill, position). [-ING[2]]

comma·ndment, n. Divine command (*the ten cc.,* Mosaic decalogue; *eleventh c.,* any precept jestingly classed with these). [f. OF *comandement* (COMMAND[1], -MENT)]

comma·ndo, n. Party called out for military service, body of troops. [Port., f. *commandar* COMMAND[1], wd used by S.-Afr. Dutch, & familiarized in Boer war]

comme il faut (kŏm ēl fō), pred. a. Well-bred. [F]

commĕ·morate, v.t. Celebrate in speech or writing; preserve in memory by some celebration; (of things) be a memorial of. Hence **comme·morat**IVE a. [f. L COM*memorare* bring to remembrance, see -ATE[3]]

commemora·tion, n. Act of commemorating; service, part of service, in memory of saint or sacred event; (Oxford Univ.) annual celebration in memory of founders. [f. L *commemoratio* (as prec. see -ATION)]

comme·nce, v.t. & i. Begin (work, do*ing*, *to* do); (archaic) start, set up, as (lawyer &c.); take the full degree of (M.A. &c.). [f. OF *cumencer* f. LL *COM*initiare* (see INITIATE)]

comme·ncement, n. In vbl senses; also, ceremony when degrees of Master & Doctor are conferred at Cambridge, Dublin, & U.S. univv. [OF (*cumencer,* see prec. & -MENT])

comme·nd, v.t. Entrust for safe keeping (archaic exc. in *c.* one's *soul to God, c.* thing *to* person's *care*); praise; (archaic) *c. me to,* remember me kindly to (person); *c. me to,* give me by choice (often iron.). [f. L COM(*mendare* = *mandare* entrust, see MANDATE)]

comme·ndable, a. Praiseworthy. Hence **comme·ndable**NESS n., **comme·ndab**LY[2] adv. [OF, f. L *commendabilis* (prec., -BLE)]

comme·ndăm, n. Tenure of benefice in absence of regular incumbent. [med. L (*in*) *commendam* (*depositum*) given in trust]

commenda·tion, n. Praise; act of commending person to another's favour. (OF, f. L *commendationem* (as COMMEND, see -ATION)]

comme·ndatory, a. Commending, holding, held, in commendam. [f. LL *commendatorius* (as prec., see -ORY)]

comme·nsal, a. & n. (One) who eats at the same table; (animal, plant) living as another's tenant & sharing its food (cf. PARASITE). Hence **comme·nsal**ISM, **commensa·l**ITY, nn. [F, f. med. L COM(*mensalis* f. *mensa* table, see -AL)]

comme·nsurable (-sher-), a. Measurable by the same standard (*with, to*); (of numbers) divisible without remainder by the same quantity; proportionate *to*. Hence **commensura**BI·LITY, **comme·nsurable**NESS, nn., **comme·nsurab**LY[2] adv. [f. L COM(*mensurabilis*, as MEASURE, see -BLE)]

comme·nsurate (-*at*), a. Coextensive (*with*); proportionate (*to, with*). Hence **comme·nsurate**LY[2] adv., **comme·nsurate**NESS n. [f. L COM(*mensuratus*, prec., -ATE[2])]

co·mment[1], n. Explanatory note or remark; criticism; (fig., of events &c.) illustration. [OF, =commentary f. L *commentum* device, comment, neut. p.p. of COM(*minisci* f. root *men*- cf. *mens* mind)]

co·mment[2], v.i. Write explanatory notes (*upon* a text); make (esp. unfavourable) remarks (*upon*). [f. prec.]

co·mmentary, n. Expository treatise; set of running comments on a book or remarks on a speech or performance; comment. [f. L *commentarius* a. (COMMENT[1], -ARY[1])]

commenta·tion, n. Making of comments. [f. L *commentatio* (*commentari* discuss, frequent. of *comminisci*, see COMMENT & -ATION)]

co·mmentator, n. Writer of commentary. [L (as prec., see -OR[2])]

co·mmerce, n. Exchange of merchandise, esp. on a large scale; CHAMBER *of c.*; intercourse (esp. sexual); card game; *c.-destroyer*, warship harrying enemy's merchant-ships. [F, f. L COM(*mercium* f. *merx mercis* merchandise)]

commer·cial (-shl), a. & n. Of, engaged in, bearing on, commerce; *c.* (*traveller*), trader's agent, showing samples & soliciting orders; *c. room* (in hotel for c. travellers). Hence **commer·cial**ISM, **commer·cial**IST, **commerciă·**LITY(-shĭ-), nn., **commer·cial**IZE v.t., **commer·cial**LY[2] adv. [f. L *commercium* COMMERCE + -AL]

commina·tion, n. Threatening of divine vengeance; recital of divine threats against sinners in Anglican Liturgy. [F, f. L *comminationem* f. COM(*minari* threaten), see -ATION)]

co·mminatory, a. Threatening, denunciatory. [f. L *comminatorius* (as prec., see -ORY)]

commi·ngle, v.t. & i. Mingle together. [COM-]

co·mminūte, v.t. Reduce to small fragments; divide (property) into small portions. So **comminu·**TION n. [f. L COM(*minuere* -*ut*- f. *minor* less)]

commi·serate (-z-), v.t. Feel, show, express, pity for. Hence or cogn. **commisera·**TION n., **commi·serat**IVE a., **commi·serative**LY[2] adv. [f. L COM(*miserari* f. MISER), -ATE[3]]

commissar·, n. Head of a government department of the U.S.S.R. (see U). [Russ. *kommissar* f. F *commissaire* (as COMMISSARY)]

commissār·ial, a. Of a commissary. [-AL]

commissār·iat, n. Department (esp. Mil.) for supply of food &c. [as foll., see -ATE[1]]

co·mmissary, n. Deputy, delegate; representative of a bishop in part of his diocese, or of absent bishop; officer charged with supply of food &c. for body of soldiers; *C. general*, chief c., esp. (Mil.) chief of a commissariat service. Hence **co·mmissary**SHIP n. [f. med. L *commissarius* person in charge (COMMIT, -ARY[1])]

commi·ssion[1], n. Command, instruction; authority, body of persons having authority, to act; *c. of the peace*, (authority given to) Justices of the Peace; *on the c.*, having this; warrant conferring authority, esp. that of officers in the army and navy from lieutenant upwards; *in c.*, (of persons) having delegated authority, (of an office) placed by warrant in charge of a body of persons instead of the constitutional administrator, (of ship of war) manned, armed, & ready for sea; entrusting of authority &c. to a person; charge, matter, entrusted to person to perform; authority to act as agent for another in trade, as *have goods on c.*; pay of a c.-agent, percentage on amount involved; committing (*of* crime &c.); *c.-day*, opening day of assizes, when judge's commission is read. [F, f. L *commissionem* (as prec., -ION)]

commi·ssion[2], v.t. Empower by commission; give (officer) command of ship; order (ship) for active service; (of officer) assume command of (ship); give (artist &c.) a commission for piece of work. [f. prec.]

commissionaire· (-shonār), n. Member of the *corps of Cc.* organized in London for employment as messengers &c. [as COMMISSIONER]

commi·ssioned, a. Authorized; (of officers) holding rank by commission; (of ships) put in commission. [-ED[1]]

commi·ssioner, n. One appointed by commission; member of a commission, esp. of government boards &c., as *Charity, Civil Service, C.*; representative of supreme authority in a district, department, &c. Hence **commi·ssioner**SHIP n. [f. F *commissionnaire* f. med. L *commissionarius* (COMMISSION, -ARY[1])]

co·mmissūre, n. Juncture, seam; joint between two bones; line where lips, eyelids, meet; bands of nerve substance connecting hemispheres of brain, two sides of spinal cord, &c. So **commissūr·**AL a. [f. L *commissura* junction [as foll., see -URE]

commi·t, v.t. (-tt-). Entrust, consign, for treatment or safe keeping (*to* person, his care, his judgement, *to* writing, memory, earth, the flames); *c.* (*to* prison), consign officially to custody; refer (bill) to committee; perpetrate (crime, blunder), whence **commi·tt**ABLE a.; compromise, involve, (character, honour, one*self*); bind one*self to* (a course). Hence **commi·tt**AL n. (committing to prison, reference to committee, committing of oneself), **commi·t**MENT n. (esp., engagement that restricts freedom of action). [f. L COM(*mittere miss-* send) join, entrust]

commi·ttee (-tĭ), n. Body of persons appointed for special function by (& usu. out of) a (usu. larger) body, as (Parl.) *C. of Supply, Ways & Means, House resolves itself into a C., goes into C., is in C., C. of the whole House*; *Standing C.* (permanent during existence of appointing body); *Joint C.* (of members nominated by different bodies); *c.-man*, member of a c.; (Law, pron. kŏmitē·) person entrusted with charge, as *cc. for lunatics.* [late AF, for F *commis* p.p. of *commettre*, as prec.]

commi·x, v.t. & i. (archaic, poet.). Mix. So **commi·xt**URE n. [back-formation on *commixt*, see MIX v.]

commo·de, n. Chest of drawers; chiffonier; (esp. *night-c.*) close-stool. [F, f. L COM(*modus* measure) convenient]

commō·dious, a. Roomy; (archaic) handy. Hence **commo·dious**LY[2] adv., **commo·dious**NESS n. [f. F *commodieux, -euse*, f. med. L *commodiosus* irreg. f. L *commodum* (neut. adj. as n.), see prec.]

commŏ·dity, n. Useful thing; article of trade (*staple c.*); (archaic) convenience. [f. F *commodité* f. L *commoditatem* (COMMODE, -TY)]

co·mmodore, n. Naval officer above captain and below rear-admiral (in Brit. navy a temporary rank); *Air C.*, officer of AIR[1] *Force*; (courtesy title) senior captain when three or more ships cruise together, captain of pilots, president of yacht-club; c.'s ship. [17th c. (*-mand-*) f. L *commandator* COMMANDER]

co·mmon[1], a. (-er, -est). Belonging equally to, coming from, or done by, more than one, as *our c. humanity, c. cause, c. consent*; belonging to, open to, affecting, the public, as *c. crier, goal, alehouse, nuisance, scold*; of ordinary occurrence, as *a c. experience* (*c. or garden*, slang, of the familiar kind); ordinary, of ordinary qualities, as *c. honesty, no c. mind*; without rank or position, as *c. soldier, the c. people*; of the most familiar type, as *C. Nightshade, Snake*; of inferior quality; vulgar; (Math.) belonging to two or more quantities, as *c. factor, multiple*; (Gram.) *c. noun*, name applicable to any one of a class, *c. gender*, masculine or feminine; (Pros.) of variable quantity; (Mus.) *c. time, measure*, (two or four beats in bar), *c.* CHORD; *c. ground*, basis for argument &c. accepted by both sides; *c. law*, unwritten law of England, administered by the King's courts, purporting to be derived from ancient usage; *Court of C. Pleas* (for trial of civil causes, abolished 1875); *C. Prayer*, liturgy set forth in Book of C. P. of Edward VI; *c.-room* (at Oxford), room to which fellows retire after dinner; *c. sense*, normal understanding, good practical sense in everyday affairs, general feeling (of mankind or community), *philosophy of c. sense* (accepting primary beliefs of mankind as ultimate criterion of truth); *c. weal, commonweal*, archaic, public welfare, (also) = COMMONWEALTH. Hence **co·mmon**NESS n. [f. OF *comun* f. L *communis* (COM- + *-munis* bound, obliged, or + *unus* one)]

co·mmon[2], n. Land belonging to a community, esp. unenclosed waste land; (*right of*) *c.*, a man's right over another's land, as *c. of pasturage*; *out of the c.*, unusual; *in c.*, in joint use, shared; *in c. with*, in the same way as (*i. c. w. all sensible people I hold that . . .*). [prec. as n.]

co·mmonable, a. (Of animals) that may be pastured on common land; (of land) that may be held in common. [f. obs. vb *common* f. OF *comuner* (as COMMON[1]) + -ABLE]

co·mmonage (-ĭj), n. Right of common; land, condition of land, held in common; commonalty. [-AGE]

co·mmonalty, n. The common people; general body (of mankind &c.); body corporate. [f. OF *comunalté* f. *comunal* f. L *communalis* (*commune* neut. adj. as n., see COMMON[1] & -AL), see -TY]

co·mmoner, n. One of the common people (below rank of peer); (rarely) member of House of Commons, esp. *the great C.*, elder Wm Pitt, *First C.*, the Speaker; (in some Eng. colleges) student not on foundation; one who has right of common. [COMMON[2] & obs. vb *common* (see COMMONABLE) + -ER[1]]

co·mmoney, n. Inferior playing-marble. [COMMON[1] + -Y[3]]

co·mmonly, adv. Usually; to an ordinary degree, as *c. honest*; meanly, cheaply. [-LY[2]]

co·mmonplāce[1], n. & a. Notable passage, entered for use in a *c.-book*; ordinary topic; everyday saying; platitude; anything common or trite; (adj.) lacking originality, trite. Hence **co·mmonplace**NESS n. [= L *locus communis* = Gk *koinos topos* general theme]

co·mmonplāce[2], v.t. & i. Extract commonplaces from; enter in commonplace-book; utter commonplaces. [f. prec.]

For compounds of *co-* not given consult CO-.

co·mmons, n. pl. The common people; third estate in English or other similar constitution, represented by Lower House of Parliament (*House of C.*); provisions shared in common; common table, as DOCTORS' COMMONS; (Oxf., Camb.) definite portion of food supplied at fixed charge; daily fare, as *short c.* [pl. of COMMON[2]]

co·mmonwealth, n. Body politic, independent community; republic (also fig., as *c. of learning*); republican government in England, 1649–60; title of federated Australian States; company of actors sharing receipts; (formerly) public welfare. [COMMON[1] + WEALTH, cf. F *bien public*, L *res publica*]

commo·tion, n. Physical disturbance; bustle, confusion; tumult, insurrection. [f. OF *comocion* f. L *commotionem* (as foll., see -ION)]

commo·ve (-ōōv), v.t. Move violently (lit. & fig.); excite. [f. F *commouvoir* f. L COM(*movēre mot-* move)]

commū·nal (*or* kŏ·mū-), a. Of a commune; of the Paris Commune; of the commonalty, of or for the community, for the common use (esp. *c. kitchens* in the great war). [F, f. med. L *communalis* (as COMMUNE, see -AL)]

communalism (as prec.), n. Theory of government by local autonomy. So **communal**IST n., **communali·st**IC a. [prec. + -ISM]

commu·nalize, v.t. Make (thing) the property of a local community. Hence **communaliz**A·TION n. [-IZE]

co·mmune[1], n. French territorial division, smallest for administrative purposes; similar division elsewhere; *The C. (of Paris)*, (1) usurping body during the Reign of Terror, (2) communalistic government in 1871. [F, f. med. L *communa* f. LL *communia* (neut. pl. adj. as noun), see COMMON[1]]

commu·ne[2] (*or* kŏ·m-), v.i. Hold intimate intercourse (*with* person, one's own heart, *together*); (U.S.) receive Holy Communion. [f. OF *comuner* (as COMMON[1])]

commu·nicable, a. That can be imparted; communicative. Hence **communica**BI·LITY, **commu·nicable**NESS, nn., **commu·nicab**LY[2] adv. [prob. F (as foll., see -BLE)]

commu·nicant, n. One who (esp. regularly) receives Holy Communion; one who imparts information. [as foll., see -ANT]

commū·nicate, v.t. & i. Impart, transmit, (heat, motion, feeling, news, a discovery, *to*); share (a thing) *with*; receive, administer, Holy Communion; hold intercourse *with*; (of rooms &c.) have common door (*with*). [f. L *communicare* (as COMMON[1] + *-ic-* factitive suf.), see -ATE[3]]

communica·tion, n. Act of imparting (esp. news); information given; intercourse; common door or passage or road or rail or telegraph or other connexion between places, (Mil., pl.) connexion between base & front. [f. OF *comunicacion* f. L *communicationem* (prec., -ATION)]

commu·nicative, a. Ready to impart; open, talkative. Hence **commu·nicative**LY[2] adv., **commu·nicative**NESS n. [F (*-if, -ive*), as COMMUNICATE, see -IVE]

commu·nicator, n. Person, thing, that communicates; part of telegraph instrument used in sending message; contrivance for communicating with guard or driver of train. [L (as prec., see -OR[2])]

commū·nion, n. Sharing, participation; fellowship (esp. between branches of Catholic Church); body professing one faith; intercourse; participation in Lord's Supper (also *Holy C.*); *close, open, c.*, exclusion from, admission to, c. of persons not baptized according to Baptist principles; *c.-cloth, -cup* (used at Holy C.); *c.-rail* (in front of c.-table in some churches); *c.-table* (used for Holy C.). [F, f. L *communionem* (as COMMON[1], see -ION)]

commu·nionist, n. *Close, open, c.*, adherent of close, open, communion; *fellow-c.*, member of same communion. [-IST]

communiqué (F), n. Official intimation.

co·mmūnism, n. Vesting of property in the community, each member working according to his capacity and receiving according to his wants. Hence **co·mmun**IST n., **communi·st**IC a. [f. L as COMMON[1] + -ISM]

communitā·rian, n. Member of community practising communism. [-ARIAN]

commū·nity, n. Joint ownership, as *c. of goods*; identity of character; fellowship (*c. of interest* &c.; also attrib., as *c. singing*, in which all present join); organized political, municipal, or social body; body of men living in same locality; body of men having religion, profession, &c., in common, as *the mercantile c., the Jewish c.*; *the c.*, the public; monastic, socialistic, or other, body practising c. of goods. [f. OF *communeté* f. L *communitatem* (as COMMON[1], see -TY)]

co·mmunize, v.t. Make (land &c.) common property. Hence **communiz**A·TION n. [f. L as COMMON[1] + -IZE]

commu·table, a. Exchangeable; that can be compounded for. Hence **commuta**BI·LITY n. [f. L *commutabilis* (as foll., see -BLE)]

commuta·tion, n. Commuting; money paid by way of c.; *C. Act* (for c. of tithes in England, 1836). [F, f. L *commutationem* (as foll., see -ATION)]

commu·tative (*also* kŏ·m-), a. Relating

to or involving substitution. [f. med. L *commutativus* (as foll., see -ATIVE)]

co·mmutator, n. Person, thing, that commutes; contrivance for altering course of electric current. [as foll., see -OR[2]]

commu·te, v.t. Interchange (two things); buy off one obligation by (*for, into*) another; change (punishment *into* another less severe); change (one kind of payment *into, for,* another). [f. L COM*mutare* exchange]

cōmo·se, a. Having a COMA[2]; hairy, downy. [f. L *comosus* (COMA[2], see -OSE[1])]

co·mpact[1], n. Agreement between parties; *general c.,* common consent; FAMILY, SOCIAL, *c.* [f. L COM(*pacisci pact-* covenant)]

compa·ct[2], a. Closely or neatly packed together; (of style) condensed, terse. Hence **compa·ct**LY[2] adv., **compa·ct**NESS n. [f. L COM(*pingere pact-* =*pangere* fasten)]

compa·ct[3], v.t. Join firmly together; condense; make up, compose, (*of*). [f. prec.]

compā·gēs, n. Framework, complex structure (lit. & fig.). [L COM(*pages* f. *pangere* fix)]

compă·ginate, v.t. Join firmly together. So **compagin**A·TION n. [f. LL *compaginare* (*compago -ginis* =prec.), see -ATE[3]]

compă·nion[1], n., & v.t. & i. One who accompanies another; associate *in,* sharer *of,* as *c.-in-arms,* fellow-soldier, *c. of his retreat*; title of handbooks, as *Gardener's C.*; member of lowest grade of order of knighthood, as *C. of the Bath*; *C. of Honour* (of the order of Cc. of H.); person (usu. woman) paid to live with another; thing that matches another (also adj., as *c. volume*); (v.t.) accompany; (v.i.) consort *with.* [f. OF *compaignon* f. LL COM(*panionem* f. *panis* bread); vb f. n.]

compă·nion[2], n. (naut.). Raised frame on quarter-deck for lighting cabins &c. below; *c. hatch,* wooden covering over c.-way; *c. hatchway,* opening in deck leading to cabin; *c.-ladder* (from deck to cabin); *c.-way,* staircase to cabin (cf. Du. *kompanje,* It. (*camera della*) *compagna* storeroom = LL *companaticum* (*panis* bread)]

compa·nionable, a. Sociable. Hence **compa·nionab**LY[2] adv., **compa·nionable**NESS n. [COMPANION[1] + -ABLE]

compa·nionship, n. State of being companion(s); (Printing) company of compositors working together. [-SHIP]

co·mpany (kŭm-), n., & v.t. & i. Companionship; *in c.,* not alone; *bear, keep, a person c.,* accompany him; *part c.* (*with*), part (from); *weep for c.* (because one's companion weeps); *keep c.,* associate as lovers; number of persons assembled; one's usual associates, as *addicted to low c.*; *he is good, bad, c.* (a pleasant, dull, companion); social party; guests; *I sin in good c.,* better men have done the same; *c. manners,* the artificial behaviour put on before strangers; body of persons combined for common (esp. commercial) object, as JOINT[2] *Stock C., Limited Liability C.* (liability of each member limited usu. to amount subscribed by him), *John C.* (*East India C.*); partner(s) not named in title of firm, as *Smith & Co.*; party of players; subdivision of infantry regiment commanded by captain (cf. TROOP, BATTERY; *get* one's *c.,* be promoted captain; *c. officer,* captain or lower commissioned officer; *c. sergeant-major,* senior warrant officer of c.); *ship's c.,* entire crew; (v.t., archaic) accompany; (v.i.) consort *with.* [(vb f. OF *compaignier*) f. OF *compaignie* formed on *compaignon* COMPANION[1]]

cŏ·mparable, a. That can be compared (*with*); fit to be compared (*to*). Hence **compara**BI·LITY n. [F, f. L *comparabilis* (as COMPARE[1], see -BLE)]

compă·rative, a. & n. Of or involving comparison, as *the c. method,* esp. of sciences, as *c. anatomy*; (Gram.) *c. adjective, adverb,* one in the comparative degree, expressing a higher degree of the quality denoted by the simple word; estimated by comparison, as *the c. merits of*; perceptible by comparison, as *in c. comfort*; (n.) c. degree. Hence **compa·rative**LY[2] adv. [f. L *comparativus* (foll., -ATIVE)]

compare·[1], v.t. & i. Liken, pronounce similar, (*to*), esp. with negative, as *not to be compared to*; estimate the similarity of (one thing *with, to,* another; two things together); observe the similarity or relation between (passages of book &c.; abbr. *cp.*); *c. notes,* exchange views; (Gram.) form comparative & superlative degrees of (adjective, adverb); (intr.) bear comparison, as *no lady can c. with Sally.* [f. L COM*parare* (*par* equal)]

compare·[2], n. Comparison, as *beyond, without, past, c.* [f. prec.; prob. arising f. obs. *compare* = COMPEER, misunderstood in *without c.*]

compă·rison, n. Act of comparing; simile, illustration; *in c. with,* compared to; *degrees of c.,* positive, comparative, superlative, (of adjectives & adverbs). [f. OF *comparaison* f. L *comparationem* (as COMPARE[1], see -SON)]

compar·t, v.t. Divide into compartments. [f. L COM*partiri* (*pars partis* part)]

compar·tment, n. Division separated by partitions esp. of railway carriage; water-tight division of ship. [f. F *compartiment* f. LL *compartimentum* (as prec., see -MENT)]

co·mpass[1] (kŭm-), n. *(Pair of) cc.*, instrument for describing circles, with two legs connected at one end by movable joint; *beam-cc.* (with sliding sockets, for large circles); *bow-cc.* (with legs jointed to bend inwards); circumference, boundary; area, extent, (also fig., as *beyond my c.*); range of a voice; roundabout way, as *fetch, go, a c.*; instrument showing magnetic meridian or one's direction with respect to it (*Mariner's C.*); BOX[3] *the c.*; *c.-plane* (convex, for planing concave surfaces); *c.-saw* (with narrow blade, for curves); *c. window*, semicircular bay window. [f. F *compas* f. med. L COM*passus* pair of compasses (perh. *passus* step); sense-history of *compassus* and vb *compassare* is obscure]

co·mpass[2] (kŭm-), v.t. Go round; hem in; grasp mentally; contrive; accomplish. Hence **co·mpass**ABLE a. [f. F *compasser* measure, contrive, f. L **compassare*, see prec.]

compa·ssion, n. Pity inclining one to spare or help, as *have c. on us.* [F, f. LL *compassionem* f. COM(*pati pass-* suffer), see -ION]

compa·ssionate[1] (-at), a. Sympathetic, pitying. Hence **compa·ssionate**LY[2] adv., **compa·ssionate**NESS n. [f. F *compassionné* p.p. of *compassionner* (as prec.), -ATE[2]]

compa·ssionāte[2], v.t. Regard, treat, with compassion. [f. prec.]

compă·tible, a. Consistent, able to coexist, (*with*). Hence or cogn. **compati**BI·LITY n., **compa·tib**LY[2] adv. [F, f. med. L *compatibilis* (COM*pati* suffer with, -BLE)]

compă·triot, n. Fellow-countryman. Hence **compatriŏ·t**IC a. [f. F *compatriote* f. L COM(*patriota* PATRIOT)]

compeer·, n. Equal, peer; comrade. [f. OF COM(*per* PEER[1])]

compe·l, v.t. (-ll-). Constrain, force, (*to* do, *to* a course); bring about (an action) by force, as *c. submission*; (poet.) drive forcibly. Hence **compe·ll**ABLE a. [f. OF *compeller* f. L COM(*pellere puls-* drive)]

co·mpend, n. =COMPENDIUM.

compe·ndious, a. Brief but comprehensive (of works & authors). Hence **compe·ndious**LY[2] adv., **compe·ndious**NESS n. [f. OF *compendieux* f. L *compendiosus* (foll., see -OUS)]

compe·ndium, n. (pl. *-ums, -a*). Abridgement; summary; abstract. [L, lit. what is weighed together f. COM(*pendĕre* weigh)]

co·mpensate, v.t. & i. Counterbalance; make amends (*for* thing, *to* person, *with, by,* another thing, or abs.); recompense (person *for* thing); (Mech.) provide (pendulum &c.) with mechanical compensation. Hence **compe·nsat**IVE a. & n., **co·mpensat**OR[2] n., **compe·nsat**ORY a. [f. L COM(*pensare* frequent. of *pendĕre pens-* weigh)]

compensa·tion, n. Compensating; thing given as recompense; *c.-balance, c.-pendulum,* of chronometer (neutralizing effect of temperature). Hence **compensa·tion**AL a. [f. L *compensatio* (as prec., see -ATION)]

compē·te, v.i. Strive (*with* another *for* thing, *in* doing, or abs.); vie (*with* another *in* a quality). [f. L COM(*petere -tit-* seek), in class. L = coincide, be fitting]

co·mpetence, -cy, nn. Sufficiency of means for living, easy circumstances; ability (*to* do, *for* a task); (of court, magistrate, &c.) legal capacity, right to take cognizance. [f. F *compétence* f. L *competentia* (as prec., see -ENCE, -ENCY)]

co·mpetent, a. Properly qualified (*to* do, *for* a task); legally qualified (judge, court, witness); (of things) belonging, permissible, *to,* as *it was c. to him to refuse.* Hence **co·mpetent**LY[2] adv. [f. F *compétent* (as COMPETE, see -ENT)]

competi·tion, n. Act of competing (*for*), by examination, in market, &c.; (Anglo-Ind.) *c.-wallah,* member of I.C.S. chosen by c. [f. L *competitio* (as foll., see -ION)]

compĕ·titive, a. Of, by, offered for, competition. Hence **compe·titive**LY[2] adv. [f. L (as COMPETE, see -IVE)]

compĕ·titor, n. One who competes, rival. Hence **compe·tit**ORY a., **compe·titr**ESS[1] n. [L (as prec., see -OR[2])]

compila·tion, n. Compiling; thing compiled. [F, f. L *compilationem* (foll., -ATION)]

compi·le, v.t. Collect (materials) into a volume; make up (volume) of such materials; (Cricket slang) score (so many runs). [f. F *compiler* (perh.) f. L COM*pilare* plunder (*pīlare* thrust home or *pĭlare* plunder)]

complā·cence, -cy, nn. Tranquil pleasure; self-satisfaction. [f. med. L *complacentia,* whence F *complaisance,* f. L COM(*placēre* please), see -ENCE, -ENCY]

compla·cent, a. Self-satisfied. Hence **compla·cent**LY[2] adv. [f. L as prec., see -ENT]

complai·n, v.i. Express dissatisfaction with (*of*); announce that one is suffering from (*of* a headache &c.); state a grievance (*to* an authority *of* offender or offence), whence **complai·n**ANT (1) n., plaintiff in certain suits; (poet.) emit mournful sound. [f. F *complaindre* (st. *-aign-*) f. LL COM(*plangere planct-* beat the breast) bewail]

complai·nt, n. Utterance of grievance; formal accusation; (U.S.) plaintiff's case in civil action; subject, ground, of c.; bodily ailment. [f. F *complainte* f. LL fem. p.p. as prec.]

complaisă·nce (*or* kŏ·m-), n. Obligingness, politeness; deference. So **complais**A·NT a. [F (see COMPLACENCE)]

co·mplement[1] (-ment), n. That which

completes; (Gram.) *c. of* (words completing) *the predicate*; full number required (to man ship, fill conveyance, &c.); (Math.) *c. of an angle,* its deficiency from 90° (cf. SUPPLEMENT). Hence **compleme·ntAL** a., **compleme·ntalLY**[2] adv. [f. L *complementum* (COMPLETE[1], -MENT)]

co·mplemĕnt[2], v.t. Complete, form complement to. [f. prec.]

compleme·ntary, a. Serving to complete; *c. angles* (making up 90°); *c.* COLOURS. [-ARY[1]]

comple·te[1], a. Having all its parts, entire; finished; unqualified, as *c. surprise*; (archaic, of persons) accomplished, as *c. horseman.* Hence **comple·teLY**[2] adv., **comple·teNESS** n. [f. L *completus* p.p. of com*plēre* fill up]

comple·te[2], v.t. Finish; make whole or perfect; make up the amount of. So **comple·TION** n., **comple·TIVE** a. [f. prec.]

co·mplex[1], n. Complex whole; (Psychol.) kinds of mental abnormality set up by some body of suppressed tendencies or experience. [f. L *complexus -ūs* (as foll.)]

co·mplex[2], a. Consisting of parts, composite; complicated; *c. sentence,* one containing subordinate clause(s). Hence **comple·XITY** n., **co·mplexLY**[2] adv. [f. L COM(*plectere plex-* plait) embrace]

comple·xion, n. Natural colour, texture, & appearance, of the skin (esp. of face); (fig.) character, aspect, as *his conduct wears another c.* Hence **-complexionED**[2], **comple·xionLESS,** aa. [F, f. L *complexionem* (as prec., see -ION); orig. = combination of supposed qualities determining nature of a body]

compli·ance, n. Action in accordance with request, command, &c.; *in c. with,* according to (wish &c.); base submission. [COMPLY, -ANCE]

compli·ant, a. Disposed to comply, yielding. Hence **compli·antLY**[2] adv. [-ANT]

co·mplicacy, n. Complexity; complicated structure. [f. L as foll., see -ACY]

co·mplicate, v.t. Mix up (*with* other things); make intricate (esp. in p.p.). [f. L COM(*plicare* fold), see -ATE[3]]

complica·tion, n. Involved condition; entangled state of affairs; complicating circumstance, as *here is a further c.* [f. L *complicatio* (as prec., see -ATION)]

complĭ·city, n. Partnership in an evil action. [f. L COM(*plex -plicis* f. *plic-* fold), see -TY]

co·mpliment[1], n. Polite expression of praise, as *pay, make, a c.*; act implying praise; (pl.) formal greetings, as *make, pay, send,* one's *cc.,* (as accompaniment to message, note, present, &c.) *with Mr —'s cc.*; *cc. of* (greetings appropriate to) *the season*; (archaic) gift, gratuity. Hence **complime·ntARY**[1] a. [F, f. It. *complimento* f. Sp. *cumplimiento* fulfilment of the duties of courtesy f. L as COMPLEMENT[1]; cf. COMPLY]

co·mplimĕnt[2], v.t. Pay a compliment to (person *on* thing); present (person *with* thing) as mark of courtesy. [f. F *complimenter* (prec.)]

co·mplĭn(e), n. (Eccl.) last service of the day. [ME *cumplie* f. OF *conplie* f. L *completa* (*hora*) see COMPLETE; *-in* unexplained; mod. E often uses pl., after F *complies*; *-e* is mod.]

comply·, v.i. Act in accordance (*with* wish, command, &c., or abs.). [f. It. *complire* f. Sp. *cumplir* COMPLETE, cf. COMPLIMENT]

co·mpo, n. (pl. *-os*). Abbr. of COMPOSITION, esp. = stucco, plaster.

compo·nent, a. & n. Contributing to the composition of a whole; (n.) c. part. [f. L COM(*ponere* put), -ENT]

compor·t, v.t. & i. Conduct, behave, one*self*; *c. with,* suit, befit. [f. L COM-(*portare* carry)]

compo·se (-z), v.t. (Of elements) make up, constitute, (esp. pass., *be composed of*); construct in words, produce in literary form, (poem &c., or abs.); (Mus.) invent & put into proper form; set (words) to music; (Print.) set up (type) to form words & blocks of words, set up (article &c.) in type; put together, arrange, artistically; adjust (dispute &c.); arrange in specified or understood manner, or for specified purpose, as *c. yourself to write, c. your countenance, c. your thoughts for action*; tranquillize (one*self*, passions, &c.), esp. in p.p., whence **compo·sĕdLY**[2] adv., **compo·sĕdNESS** n. [f. F COM(*poser* f. LL *pausare* cease, lie or lay down, see POSE; confused with & replacing in compounds *pondre* f. L *ponere posit-* place)]

compo·ser, n. One who composes (usu. music). [prec. + -ER[1]]

compo·sing, n. In vbl senses; *c.-machine* (for setting up type); *c.-stick,* metal instrument of adjustable width in which type is set. [-ING[1]]

co·mposite (-zī- *or* -zĭ-), a. & n. (Thing) made up of various parts; (Arch.) fifth classical ORDER, Ionic & Corinthian mixed; (plant) of the Natural Order *Compositae,* in which the so-called flower is a head of many flowers (as daisy, dandelion, &c.); (of ships) built of both wood & iron; *c.* (railway) *carriage,* one with compartments of different classes; *c. candle* (of stearic acid & stearin of coco-nut oil). Hence **co·mpositeLY**[2] adv., **co·mpositeNESS** n. [f. L COM(*ponere posit-* put)]

composi·tion, n. Act of putting together; formation, construction; formation of words into a compound word; con-

For compounds of *co-* not given consult CO-.

struction of sentences, art of literary production; act, art, of composing music; setting up of type; mental constitution, as *a touch of madness in his c.*; arrangement (of the parts of a picture &c.); thing composed, mixture; piece of music or writing; agreement for cessation of hostilities; compromise; compound artificial substance, esp. one serving the purpose of a natural one (often attrib., as *c. billiard-balls*); agreement for payment of sum in lieu of larger sum or other obligation, as *made a c. with his creditors.* [F, f. L *compositionem* (as prec., see -ION)]

compŏ·sitive, a. Combining. [f. L *compositivus* (as prec., see -IVE)]

compŏ·sitor, n. Type-setter. [f. AF *compositour* f. L *compositorem* (as prec., see -OR²)]

co·mpŏs (me·ntis), a. In one's right mind; *non c.*, not in one's right mind. [L]

compo·ssible, a. Able to coexist (*with*). [F, f. med. L COM(*possibilis* POSSIBLE)]

co·mpŏst¹, n. Compound manure; combination. [OF, f. L as COMPOSITE]

co·mpost², v.t. Treat with, make into, compost. [f. OF *composter* (prec.)]

compo·sure (-zher), n. Tranquil demeanour, calmness. [f. COMPOSE + -URE]

compota·tion, n. Tippling together. So **co·mpotat**OR² n. [f. L *compotatio* f. *COM(*potare* drink) see -ATION]

co·mpote, n. Fruit preserved in syrup. [F, f. OF *composte* f. L fem. p.p. as COMPOSITE]

compou·nd¹, v.t. & i. Mix (ingredients, lit. & fig.); combine (verbal elements) into a word; make up (a composite whole); settle (matter by mutual concession, debt by partial payment, subscription by lump sum, or abs.); condone (liability, offence) for money &c.; *c. a felony*, forbear prosecution on private motive; (intr.) come to terms (*with* person *for* forgoing claim &c. *for* offence). Hence **compou·nd**ABLE a. [ME *compounen* f. OF *compondre* f. L COM(*ponere* put), whence obs. *compone*]

co·mpound², a. & n. Made up of several ingredients; consisting of several parts; combined, collective; *c. fracture* (complicated with skin wound); *c. addition, subtraction*, &c. (dealing with various denominations); *c.* INTEREST¹; (Zool., Bot.) consisting of a combination of organisms, or simple parts, as *c. animal, c. flower*; *c. householder* (whose rates are paid by landlord & included in rent); (n.) mixture of elements, c. thing, esp. c. word. [orig. p.p. of *compoun*, see prec.]

co·mpound³, n. (In India, China, &c.) enclosure in which house or factory stands. [perh. f. Malay *kampong*]

comprador·, n. (In China) chief native servant in European house of business. [Port., = buyer, f. LL *comparatorem* f. COM(*parare* furnish), see -OR²]

comprehe·nd, v.t. Grasp mentally, understand, (person, thing); include, take in. [f. L COM(*prehendere -hens-* grasp)]

comprehe·nsible, a. That may be understood; that may be comprised. Hence **comprehensi**BI·LITY n., **comprehe·nsib**LY² adv. [f. L *comprehensibilis* (as prec., see -BLE)]

comprehe·nsion, n. Act, faculty, of understanding; inclusive power, as *a term of wide c.*; toleration of divergent opinions (esp. Eccl.). [f. L *comprehensio* (as prec., see -ION)]

comprehe·nsive, a. Of understanding, as *c. faculty*; including much, as *c. term, c. grasp* (fig. & lit.). Hence **comprehe·nsive**LY² adv., **comprehe·nsive**NESS n. [f. L *comprehensivus* (as prec., see -IVE)]

compre·ss¹, v.t. Squeeze together; condense (air, language, thoughts). Hence **compre·ss**IVE a. [f. OF *compresser* f. L *compressare* f. COM(*primere press-* = *premere* press)]

co·mpress², n. Soft pad of lint &c. for compressing artery &c.; piece of wet cloth covered with waterproof bandage, for relief of inflammation. [f. F *compresse* f. L fem. p.p. as prec.]

compre·ssible, a. That may be compressed. Hence **compressi**BI·LITY n. [COMPRESS¹ + -IBLE, as if on L *comprimere*, not *compressare*]

compre·ssion, n. Squeezing together, condensation, (lit. & fig.). So **compre·ss**OR² n. [F, f. L *compressionem* (as COMPRESS¹, see -ION)]

compri·se (-z), v.t. Include, comprehend; consist of, as *the house comprises 9 bedrooms &c.*; condense (*within* limits &c.). Hence **compri·s**ABLE a. [f. F *comprendre* (p.p. *compris*) f. L as COMPREHEND, prob. after ENTERPRISE]

co·mpromise¹ (-z), n. Settlement of dispute by mutual concession; adjustment of (*between*) conflicting opinions, courses, &c., by modification of each. [f. F *compromis* f. L COM(*promittere* PROMISE)]

co·mpromise², v.t. & i. Settle (dispute) by mutual concession; (intr.) make a compromise; bring (person, one*self*) under suspicion by indiscreet action. [f. prec.]

comprovi·ncial, a. & n. (Person, esp. bishop) of the same (esp. archiepiscopal) province. [f. med. L *comprovincialis* (COM-, PROVINCE, -AL)]

comptro·ller (kon-), n. Mis-spelling of CONTROLLER in some titles, as *C. of accounts.*

compu·lsion, n. Constraint, obligation; *under, upon, c.*, because one is compelled. [F, f. L *compulsionem* (as COMPEL, see -ION)]

compu·lsive, a. Tending to compel. Hence **compu·lsive**LY² adv. [f. L as COMPEL, -IVE]

compu·lsory, a. (Of action, agent) enforced; compelling (*c. legislation* &c., opp. *permissive*). Hence **compu·lsori**LY[2] adv., **compu·lsori**NESS n. [as prec., -ORY]

compu·nction, n. Pricking of conscience; slight regret, scruple, as *without c.* Hence **compu·nct**IOUS a., **compu·nctious**LY[2] adv. [OF, f. L *compunctionem* f. COM-(*pungere punct-* prick), see -ION]

compurga·tion, n. Clearing from a charge, vindication, esp. (Eng. Hist.) trial & purgation by oath. So **co·mpurgat**OR[2] n., **compur·gat**ORY a. [f. L *compurgatio* f. COM(*purgare* purify) see -ATION]

compu·te, v.t. Reckon (number or amount often *at* figure, *that*, or abs.). So **compu·t**ABLE (*or* kŏ·m-), **compu·t**ATIVE (*or* kŏ·m-), aa., **comput**A·TION n. [f. F *computer* f. L COM(*putare* reckon)]

cŏ·mrade, n. Mate or fellow in work or play or fighting, equal with whom one is on familiar terms, (usu. of males, cf. *companion*); (as prefix) fellow member of trade union, benefit society, &c. (*C. Smith*). Hence **co·mrade**SHIP n. [f. F *camarade* f. Sp. *camarada* chamber-mate, lit. chamberful (*camara* room f. L *camera*, see -ADE); *-o-* prob. to repr. sound of Sp. *a*].

Cŏ·mtism, n. =POSITIVISM. So **Cŏ·mt**IST n. [Auguste *Comte*, founder, +-ISM]

con[1], v.t. *C.* (*over*): study; learn by heart. [earlier spelling and pron. *cun*, a differentiation of CAN (pres. st. *cun-*)]

con[2], v.t. Direct steering of (ship, or abs.); *conning-tower*, shot-proof pilot-house of ironclad. [perh. weakened form of *cond, condue*, f. F *conduire* f. L *conducere* CONDUCT v.]

con[3], prep. (It.). With (esp. Mus.), as *c. brio* (spirit), *espressione* (expression), *fuoco* (fire), *moto* (spirited movement).

con[4]. See CONTRA.

con-, pref. =L *cum* (see COM-) before *c d f g j l m n p q s t v*.

cŏ·nācre (-ker), n. (In Ireland) letting by tenant of small portions of land prepared for crop. [CORN+ACRE]

con amor·ĕ, adv. Zealously. [It.]

cona·tion, n. (Philos.). The exertion of willing that desire or aversion shall issue in action. Hence **cŏ·native** a. [f. L *conationem* (*conari* to try)]

concă·tenate, v.t. Link together (fig.). So **concaten**A·TION n. [f. L CON(*catenare* f. *catena* chain), see -ATE[3]]

co·ncāve, a. & n. With outline or surface curved like interior of circle or sphere (cf. CONVEX); (n.) c. surface, esp. vault of heaven. Hence or cogn. **co·ncave**LY[2] adv., **concă·**VITY n. [F. f. L CON(*cavus* hollow)]

conca·vo-, in comb. Concavely, concave & —, as *c.-concave*, concave on both sides, *c.-convex*, concave one side, convex the other. [-O-]

concea·l, v.t. Keep secret (*from*); hide. Hence **concea·l**MENT n. [f. OF *conceler* f. L CON*celare*]

conce·de, v.t. Admit, allow, (statement, *that*); grant (right, privilege, points or start in game &c.; *to* person); (Sport. slang) lose (game &c.). [f. F *concéder* f. L CON(*cedere, -cess-* yield)]

concei·t[1] (-ēt), n. Personal vanity; fanciful notion, far-fetched comparison or other euphuism; *in my own c.* (judgement); *out of c.*, no longer pleased *with*. [f. CONCEIVE on *deceit*]

concei·t[2] (-ēt), v.t. (archaic). Imagine; persuade one*self* (*that*). [f. prec.]

concei·ted, a. Vain (orig. *self-c.*). Hence **concei·ted**LY[2] adv. [CONCEIT[1]+-ED[2]]

concei·vable, a. That can be (mentally) conceived. Hence **conceivab**I·LITY, **concei·vable**NESS, nn., **concei·vab**LY[2] adv. [f. foll.+-ABLE]

concei·ve (-ēv), v.t. & i. Become pregnant with; become pregnant; form in the mind, imagine, (also *c. of*); fancy, think, (*that*); formulate, express, (usu. pass., as *conceived in plain terms*). [f. OF *conceveir* (st. *conceiv-*) f. L CON(*cipere cept-* =*capere* take)]

concĕ·lebrate, v.i. (R.-C. Ch., of newly ordained priest) celebrate mass with ordaining bishop. Hence **concelebr**A·TION n. [f. L CON(*celebrare* CELEBRATE)]

co·ncentrate, v.t. & i. Bring together to one point (troops, power, attention); (Chem.) increase strength of (liquid &c.) by contracting its volume, (fig. in p.p. of hate &c.) intense; (intr.) employ all one's power or attention (*upon*). Hence **concentr**A·TION n. (*-ation camp*, at which a population is collected to facilitate feeding &c.); **co·ncentrative**NESS, **co·ncentrat**OR[2], nn., **co·ncentrat**IVE a. [as f. a L CON(*centrare* f. *centrum* CENTRE), -ATE[3]]

conce·ntre, v.t. & i. Bring, come, to a common centre. [f. F *concentrer* (as prec.)]

conce·ntric, a. Having a common centre (*with* or abs.); (Mil.) *c. fire*, firing concentrated on a point. Hence **conce·ntr**ICALLY adv., **concentri·**CITY n. [f. med. L CON(*centricus*, as CENTRE)]

co·ncept, n. Idea of a class of objects, general notion. [f. L as CONCEIVE]

conce·ption, n. Conceiving (in all senses); thing conceived, idea. Hence **conce·ption**AL a. [F, f. L *conceptionem* (as prec., -ION)]

conce·ptive, a. Conceiving (mentally), of conception. [f. L *conceptivus* (as prec., see -IVE)]

conce·ptual, a. Of mental conceptions.

[f. med. L *conceptualis* (*conceptus -ūs* as prec., -AL]
conce·ptualism, n. Doctrine that universals exist as mental concepts (only); doctrine that the mind can form ideas corresponding to abstract terms. So **conce·ptualIST** n. [-ISM]
concer·n[1], v.t. Relate to, affect; interest oneself (*with, in, about,* matter, *to* do); *be concerned* (take part) *in*; *I am not concerned,* it is not my business (*to*); (in p.p.) troubled, as *a concerned air, am concerned to hear, at, for* person, *about*; *concerning* (prep.), about. [f. F *concerner* f. L CON(*cernere* sift, regard), in med. L = have regard to]
concer·n[2], n. Relation, reference, (*with*); *have no c.* (nothing to do) *with*; *have a c.* (interest, share) *in*; anxiety, solicitous regard, as *asked with deep c.*; matter that affects one, as *no c. of mine*; (pl.) affairs, as *meddling in my cc.*; business, firm, as a *flourishing c.*; (colloq.) thing, as *smashed the whole c.* [f. prec.]
concer·nment, n. Affair, business; importance, as *of vital c.*; being concerned (*with*); anxiety. [-MENT]
co·ncert[1], n. Agreement, union, as *work in c.* (*with*); *the C. of Europe,* chief Powers acting together occasionally from 1815; combination of voices or sounds, as *voices raised in c.*; musical entertainment; *c. grand,* grand piano of brilliant tone for cc.; *c. pitch* (slightly higher than the ordinary; transf., state of unusual efficiency or readiness). [F, f. It. *concerto,* as foll.]
concer·t[2], v.t. Arrange (by mutual agreement, also of one person). [f. F *concerter* f. It. *concertare* accord together; connexion with L *concertare* contend, doubtful]
concer·ted, a. In vbl senses; also (Mus.) arranged in parts for voices or instruments. [-ED[1]]
concerti·na (-tē-), n. Portable musical wind instrument, with set of keys at each end. [CONCERT[1] + -INA[1]]
concer·to (-tshār-), n. Composition (usu. in three movements) for solo instrument(s) accompanied by orchestra. [It., see CONCERT[1]]
conce·ssion, n. Act of conceding; thing conceded, esp. (diplom.) grant to CONCESSIONAIRE, piece of territory of which the occupation & use is granted to a State, company, or person. Hence **conce·ssionARY**[1] a. [F, f. L *concessionem* (as CONCEDE, see -ION)]
concession(n)aire·, n. Holder of concession, grant, &c., esp. of monopoly given by government to foreigner. [F (*-nn-*), prec., -ARY[1]]
conce·ssive, a. Of, tending to, concession; (Gram.) expressing concession. [f. L *concessivus* (as CONCEDE, see -IVE)]
conce·ttism (-tshĕt-), n. Use of fanciful turns (It. *concetti*) in literature. [-ISM]
conch (-k), n. Shell-fish; shell of a mollusc, esp. (Rom. Myth.) as trumpet of a Triton; (Arch.) domed roof of semicircular apse; (also *concha*) external ear, its central concavity; (Naut. slang, *C-*) native of Bahamas. [f. L *concha* shell f. Gk *kogkhē* mussel &c.]
conchi·ferous (-k-), a. (zool., geol.). Shell-bearing. [as prec., see -FEROUS]
concho·logy (-k-), n. Study of shells & shell-fish. So **concholo·gICAL** a., **concho·logIST** n. [as CONCH, see -LOGY]
co·nchy (-tsh-), n. (slang.). Conscientious objector to conscription in the great war. [abbr.]
concierge (F), n. (In France &c.) doorkeeper, porter, (esp. of flats &c.).
conci·liar, a. Of ecclesiastical councils. [f. L *concilium* COUNCIL + -AR[1]]
conci·liate, v.t. Gain (esteem, goodwill); pacify; win over (*to* one's side &c.); reconcile (discrepant theories). Hence or cogn. **conci·liatIVE, conci·liatORY,** aa., **conci·liatOR**[2], **conci·liatoriNESS,** nn. [f. L *conciliare* (as prec.,) see -ATE[3]]
concilia·tion, n. Reconcilement; use of conciliating measures; *Court of c.* (offering parties a voluntary settlement). [f. L *conciliatio* (as prec., see -ATION)]
conci·nnity, n. Elegance, neatness, of literary style. [f. L *concinnitas* (*concinnus* well-adjusted, etym. dub., see -TY)]
conci·se (-s), a. Brief in expression (of speech, style, person). Hence **conci·seLY**[2] adv., **conci·seNESS** n. [f. L CON(*cidere cis-* = *caedere* cut)]
conci·sion (-zhn), n. Mutilation (in *Phil.* iii. 2, = circumcision, contemptuously); conciseness. [F, f. L *concisionem* (as prec., see -ION)]
co·nclāve, n. Meeting-place, assembly, of cardinals for election of Pope; private assembly, as *in c.* [F, f. L CON(*clave* lock-up place f. *clavis* key)]
conclu·de, v.t. & i. Bring to an end, make an end, (*c.* one's *speech* &c., or *c., with* remark &c., *by* saying &c.); (of things) come to an end; infer (*from* premises &c.); settle, arrange, (treaty &c.); resolve (*to* do). [f. L CON(*cludere clus-* = *claudere* shut)]
conclu·sion, n. Termination; final result; *in c.,* lastly, to conclude; inference; decision; (Logic) proposition deduced from previous ones, esp. last of three forming a syllogism; *try cc. with,* engage in a trial of skill &c. with; settling, arrangement, (*of* peace &c.). [F, f. *conclusionem* (as prec., see -ION)]
conclu·sive, a., Decisive, convincing. Hence **conclu·siveLY**[2] adv., **conclu·siveNESS** n. [f. LL *conclusivus* (as prec., see -IVE)]
conco·ct, v.t. Make up of mixed ingredients (soup, drink, story, plot). Hence or cogn. **conco·ctION, conco·ctOR**[2], nn., **conco·ctIVE** a. [f. L CON(*coquere coct-* cook)]

conco·lorous (-cŭl-), a (nat. hist.). Of uniform colour. [f. L CON(*color* colour) + -OUS]
concŏ·mitance, -cy, n. Coexistence, esp. (*-ance*) of body & blood of Christ in each of the eucharistic elements. [f. L *concomitantia* (as foll., see -ANCE, -ANCY)]
concŏ·mitant, a. & n. Going together, as *c. circumstances*; (n.) accompanying thing. Hence **conco·mitantLY**[2] adv. [f. L CON(*comitari* f. *comes -mitis* companion), see -ANT]
co·ncord, n. Agreement, harmony, between persons or things; treaty; (Mus.) chord satisfactory in itself without others to follow; (Gram.) agreement between words in gender, number, &c. [f. F *concorde* f. L *concordia* f. CON(*cors* f. *cor cordis* heart) of one mind]
concor·dance, n. Agreement; alphabetical arrangement of chief words (*verbal c.*) or subjects (*real c.*) occurring in a book (esp. the Bible) or author, with citations of the passages concerned. [F, f. LL *concordantia* (foll., -ANCE)]
concor·dant, a. Agreeing, harmonious, (*with* or abs.); in musical concord. Hence **concor·dantLY**[2] adv. [F, f. L *concordare* (*concors*), see CONCORD and -ANT]
concor·dăt, n. Agreement between Pope and a secular government. [F, f. L *concordatum* neut. p.p. as prec.]
co·ncourse, n. Crowd; confluence of things, as *fortuitous c. of atoms*. [f. OF *concours* f. L *concursus -ūs* (as CONCUR)]
concre·scence, n. (biol.). Coalescence, growing together. [f. L *concrescentia* (as foll., see -ENCE)]
co·ncrete[1], a. & n. (Gram., of noun) denoting a thing as opposed to a quality, state, or action, not ABSTRACT; existing in material form, real; *in the c.*, in sphere of reality. (N.) c. thing; composition of gravel, cement, &c., for building, (attrib.) made of this. Hence **co·ncreteLY**[2] adv. [f. L CON(*crescere cret-* grow)]
concrete[2], v.t. & i. (-krē·t) form into a mass, solidify; (kŏ·n-) treat with concrete [f. prec.]
concrē·tion, n. Coalescence; concrete mass, esp. (Path.) morbid formation in the body, stone, (Geol.) mass formed of solid particles, whence **concre·tionARY**[1] a.; embodiment in concrete form. [f. L *concretio* (as CONCRETE[1], see -ION)]
concu·binage, n. Cohabiting of man and woman not legally married; having, being, a concubine. [F, as CONCUBINE, see -AGE)]
concu·binary, a. & n. (Person) living in concubinage; of, sprung from, concubinage. [f. L *concubinarius* (as foll., see -ARY[1])]
co·ncŭbīne, n. Woman who cohabits with a man, not being his wife; (among polygamous peoples) secondary wife. [F, f. L CON(*cubina* f. *cubare* lie)]
concū·piscence, n. Sexual appetite; (N.T.) desire for worldly things. [f. L *concupiscentia* (as foll., see -ENCE)]
concū·piscent, a. Lustful, eagerly desirous. [f. L *concupiscere* inceptive of CON(*cupere* desire), see -ENT]
concur·, v.i. (-rr-). Happen together, coincide; (of circumstances &c.) cooperate (*with* or abs.); agree in opinion (*with*). So **concŭ·rrENCE** n. [f. L CON(*currere curs-* run)]
concŭ·rrent, a. & n. Running together, as parallel lines; existing together; cooperating; agreeing; *c. lease* (made before the former expires); *c. fire insurance* (of which the risk is definitely proportioned among several companies); (n.) c. circumstance. Hence **concu·rrentLY**[2] adv. [as CONCUR, see -ENT]
concu·ss, v.t. Shake violently, agitate, (usu. fig.); intimidate. [f. L CON(*cutere cuss-* = *quatere* shake)]
concu·ssion, n. Violent shaking; shock; (Surg.) injury to brain &c. caused by heavy blow &c.; *c.-bellows*, self-acting reservoir regulating wind in organ; *c.-fuse* (in shell, ignited by c.) [f. L *concussio* (as prec., see -ION)]
conde·mn (-ĕm), v.t. Censure, blame; give judgement against; bring about conviction of, as *his looks c. him*; doom (*to* death, *to* be beheaded; also fig. *to* toil &c.; *condemned cell, pew, sermon* (for condemned persons); pronounce forfeited (smuggled goods &c.), unfit for use, incurable. Hence **conde·mnABLE** (-mn-) a. [f. OF *condemner* f. L CON(*demnare* = *damnare* damage, condemn)]
condemna·tion (-mn-), n. Censure; judicial conviction; ground for condemning, as *his own conduct is his c.* [f. L *condemnatio* (as prec., see -ATION)]
conde·mnatory (-mn-), a. Expressing condemnation. [f. L as CONDEMN, see -ORY]
condensa·tion, n. Act of condensing (t. & i.); condensed mass. [f. L *condensatio* (as foll., see -ATION)]
conde·nse, v.t. & i. Compress; *condensed milk* (reduced by evaporation); concentrate (rays of light); increase intensity of (electricity); reduce, be reduced, from gas or vapour to liquid; compress into few words. Hence or cogn. **condensaBI·LITY, condensA·TION,** nn., **conde·nsABLE** a. [(prob. thr. F *condenser*) f. L CON(*densare* f. *densus* thick)]
conde·nser, n. In vbl senses; esp.: chamber in steam-engine in which steam is condensed on leaving cylinder; apparatus for accumulating electricity; lens, system of lenses, concentrating light. [-ER[1]]
condesce·nd, v.i. Deign, stoop, (*to* an act, *to* do); waive one's superiority (*to* a

person); (Sc.) *c. upon,* specify (particulars). [f. F *condescendre* f. L CON(*descendere* DESCEND)]
condesce·nding, a. Showing condescension, esp. patronizing. Hence **condesce·nding**LY² adv. [prec. + -ING²]
condesce·nsion, n. Affability to inferiors; patronizing manner. [f. L *condescensio* (as CONDESCEND, see -ION)]
condi̅g·n, a. Adequate (*c. punishment, vengeance*). Hence **condig·n**LY² adv. [f. F *condigne* f. L CON(*dignus* worthy)]
co·ndiment, n. Thing used to give relish to food. Hence **condime·nt**AL a. [F, f. L *condimentum* (*condire* pickle, see -MENT)]
condi·tion¹, n. Stipulation, thing upon the fulfilment of which depends that of another, (*c. precedent,* that must be fulfilled before a bequest &c. becomes valid); *on c. that,* if, provided that; (Gram.) clause expressing a c.; (pl.) circumstances, esp. those essential to a thing's existence, as *the cc. of equilibrium, favourable cc., under existing cc.*; state of being, as *eggs arrived in good c., persons of humble c.*; *in, out of, c.,* in good, bad, c.; *change* one's *c.,* marry. [f. OF *condicion* f. L *condĭcionem* f. CON(*dīcere,* weak st. *dĭc-,* say) agree upon, see -ION]
condi·tion², v.t. Stipulate (*that*); agree by stipulation (*to* do); *the size is conditioned by* (depends on) *the requirements*; *the two things c.* (are essential to) *each other*; *they c. the universe* (impose conditions on it) *anew*; (Commerc.) test the condition of (material). [f. OF *condicionner* f. med. L *conditionare* (as prec.)]
condi·tional, a. & n. Not absolute, dependent (*on* or abs.); (Gram.) *c. clause,* one expressing a condition, PROTASIS, *c. mood* in French and Italian verbs, that used in the apodosis; (n.) c. word, conjunction, mood, clause. Hence **conditiona·l**ITY n., **condi·tional**LY² adv. [f. OF *condicionel* f. L *condicionalis* (as CONDITION¹, see -AL)]
condi·tioned, a. 1. Having a (specified) disposition, as *ill, well, -c.*; in a (specified) condition, as *well-c. ground, cattle*; circumstanced. 2. Subject to conditions. [CONDITION¹, ² + -ED², ¹]
condō·latory, a. Expresssing condolence. [f. foll. on anal. of *consolatory* &c.]
condo·le, v.i. Express sympathy (*with* or abs., *upon* loss &c.). Hence **condo·l**ENCE n. [f. L CON(*dolēre* suffer)]
cŏndomĭ·nium, n. (diplom.). Joint control of a State's affairs vested in two or more other States. [CON-, L *dominium* DOMINION]
condo·ne, v.t. Forgive, overlook, (offence, esp. matrimonial infidelity); (of actions) atone for (offence). So **condon**A·TION n. [f. L CON(*donare* give)]
co·ndor, n. Large S.-Amer. kind of vulture; *California C.,* great vulture of California. [Sp., f. Peruvian *cuntur*]
condottier·e (-tyārĭ), n. (pl. *-ri,* pron. -rē). Leader of troop of mercenaries. [It. (*condotto* hired, as CONDUCT², + *-iere* for *-iero* -ARY¹)]
condu·ce, v.i. (Usu. of events, rarely of persons) lead, contribute, *to* (result). Hence **condu·c**IVE a., **condu·cive**NESS n. [f. L CON(*ducere* lead)]
co·nduct¹, n. Leading, guidance, (cf. SAFE-*conduct*); *c.-money* (paid to a witness for travelling expenses); manner of conducting (business &c.); (Art) mode of treatment; behaviour (esp. in its moral aspect, as *good, bad, c.*). [partly f. F *conduite* f. LL **conducta* (fem. p.p. as noun), partly f. F *conduit* (whence also CONDUIT) f. L *conductus -ūs*; both as foll.]
condu·ct², v.t. & i. Lead, guide, *to*; (of road) lead *to*; command (army); direct (orchestra, concert, or abs.); direct, manage, (business &c.); *c. oneself,* behave (*well, with* judgement, &c.); (Physics) transmit (heat &c.). [f. F *conduit* p.p. of *conduire* f. L CON(*ducere duct-* lead); refash. on L in 16th c.]
co·nduct³, n. An Eton chaplain. [f. L *conductus* hired (p.p. of *conducere* see prec.)]
condu·ctible, a. Capable of conducting (heat &c.) or (rarely) being conducted. Hence **conducti**BI·LITY n. [f. prec., see -BLE]
condu·ction, n. Transmission (of heat by contact &c.); conducting (of liquid through pipe &c., esp. of natural processes). So **condu·ct**IVE a., **conducti·v**ITY n. [f. L *conductio* (as CONDUCT², see -ION)]
condu·ctor, n. Leader, guide; manager; director of orchestra; official in charge of passengers on omnibus, tram, or (U.S.) train; thing that conducts or transmits (esp. heat &c., as *good, bad, non-, c.*); *lightning-c.,* rod at top of building, conducting electricity away into earth. Hence **condu·ctor**SHIP, **condu·ctr**ESS¹, nn. [f. F *conducteur* f. L *conductorem* (as CONDUCT², see -OR²)]
conduit (kŭ·ndĭt, kŏ·n-), n. Channel or pipe for conveying liquids (or fig.). [see CONDUCT¹]
condū·plicate, a. (bot.). Folded lengthwise along middle. [f. L CON(*duplicare* DUPLICATE)]
co·ndyle (-ĭl), n. (anat.). Rounded process at end of bone, forming articulation with another bone. Hence **co·ndyl**OID a. [F, f. L f. Gk *kondulos* knuckle]
Co·ndy('s fluid). A solution of sodium permanganate as disinfectant. [maker]
cone, n., & v.t. & i. Solid figure with circular (or other curved) base, tapering to a point (generated by straight line that always passes through a fixed point, and describes any fixed curve); fruit of pine or fir; marine shell of genus *Conus*; c.-shaped thing, esp. (Meteorol.) foul-

weather signal; *cones*, fine flour used by bakers for dusting troughs; (v.t.) shape like c.; (v.i.) bear cc. [(vb f. n.) f. L f. Gk *kōnos*]

cō·ney. See CONY.

confa·b, n., & v.i. Colloq. abbr. of CONFABULATION or foll.

confă·bulate, v.i. Converse, chat, (*with* or abs.). Hence or cogn. **confabul**A·TION n., **confa·bulat**ORY a. [f. L CON(*fabulari* f. *fabula* tale), see -ATE[3]]

confe·ction, n., & v.t. Mixing, compounding; thing compounded, esp. preserve, sweetmeat, whence **confe·ction**ARY[1] a.; ready-made article of (usu. female) dress, mantle, wrap, &c.; (v.t.) prepare, make, (a c.). [(vb f. n.) F, f. L *confectionem* f. CON(*ficere fect-* =*facere* make), see -ION]

confe·ctioner, n. Maker of sweetmeats, pastry, &c. (usu. for sale). Hence **confe·ction**ERY(1, 2) n. [-ER[1]]

confĕ·deracy, n. League, alliance; conspiracy; collusion; body of confederate persons or States, as *Southern C.*, Confederate States of America. [as foll., see -ACY (3)]

confe·derate[1] (-*at*), a. & n. Allied (lit. & fig.); *C. States* of America (seceding from the Union, 1860–5); (n.) ally, esp. in bad sense, accomplice. [f. L CON(*foederare* f. *foedus -eris* league), see -ATE[2]]

confe·derāte[2], v.t. & i. Bring (person, State, one*self*), come, into alliance (*with*). So **confeder**A·TION n. [as prec., see -ATE[3]]

co·nfer[1], v. (imperat.). Compare (abbr. *cf.*). [L]

confer·[2], v.t. & i. (-rr-). Grant, bestow, (title, degree, favour, &c., *on*); (intr.) converse, take counsel, (*with* or abs.). Hence **confer·**MENT n., **confer·r**ABLE a. [f. L CON(*ferre* bring)]

co·nference, n. Consultation; annual assembly of Wesleyan Methodist Connexion. So **confere·nti**AL a. [f. med. L *conferentia* (as prec., see -ENCE)]

confe·ss, v.t. & i. Acknowledge, as *I c. my fault, that I did it, to doing it, to having done it, to a dread of spiders*; formally declare one's sins, esp. to a priest, whence **confe·ss**ANT n.; (of priest) hear (penitent) c. Hence **confe·ssĕd**LY[2] adv. [f. OF *confesser* f. LL *confessare* frequent. of L CON(*fitēri fess-* =*fatēri*)]

confe·ssion, n. Acknowledgement (of offence, fact, &c.); *auricular c.* (of sins to priest), whence **confe·ssion**ARY[1] a.; thing confessed; *c. of faith*, declaration of religious doctrine, creed, statement of one's principles in any matter; (formerly) tomb of CONFESSOR. [F, f. L *confessionem* (as prec., see -ION)]

confe·ssional, a. & n. Of confession; (n.) stall in which priest hears confession, as *secrets of the c.* [(adj.) prec. + -AL; (n.) F, f. med. L *confessionale* (neut. adj. as n.)]

confe·ssionist, n. Adherent of a creed, esp. of the Augsburg Confession (Lutheran). [f. F *confessioniste* (-IST)]

confe·ssor, n. One who confesses; one who avows his religion in face of danger, but does not suffer martyrdom; *The C.*, King Edward the C.; priest who hears confession. [L (as CONFESS, see -OR[2])]

confe·tto, n. (usu. in pl., *-tī*). Plaster bonbons, bits of coloured paper, used as missiles in the carnival, at weddings, &c. [It., =sweetmeat]

confida·nt, n. (fem. *-ante*, pron. -ănt). Person trusted with private (usu. love) affairs. [18th c.; perh. meant to repr. sound of F *confident, -ente* (as foll., see -ANT)]

confi·de, v.t. & i. Repose confidence *in*, (part.) unsuspicious; impart (secret *to*); entrust (object of care, task, *to*). [f. L CON(*fidere* trust)]

co·nfidence, n. Firm trust; assured expectation; boldness; impudence; imparting of private matters (*in* one's *c.*, allowed to know his private affairs); thing so imparted; *told in c.* (as a secret); *c. trick*, persuading victim to entrust valuables to one as sign of c. [f. L *confidentia* (as prec., see -ENCE)]

co·nfident, a. & n. Trusting, fully assured (*that, of*, or abs.), bold; impudent; (n.) confidant, sharer *of* (secret).] Hence **co·nfident**LY[2] adv. [as CONFIDE, see -ENT]

confide·ntial (-shl), a. Spoken, written, in confidence; entrusted with secrets; charged with secret service. Hence **confidentia·l**ITY (-shĭ-), **confide·ntial**NESS, nn., **confide·ntial**LY[2] adv. [as CONFIDENCE + -AL]

configūra·tion, n. Mode of arrangement, conformation, outline, (Astr.) relative position of planets &c. [f. L *configuratio* (foll., -ATION)]

confi·gure (-*ger*), v.t. Give shape to (usu. fig.). [f. L CON(*figurare* FIGURE)]

co·nfīne[1], n. (usu. pl.). Border-land, esp. (fig.) between two classes of ideas &c. [f. F *confins* pl. f. med. L CON(*fines* pl. adj. f. *finis* end, limit)]

confi·ne[2], v.t. & i. Keep (person, thing, one*self*, *within, to*, limits); imprison; (pass.) be in childbed, be brought to bed; (rarely) *c. with*, be adjacent to. [f. F *confiner* f. It. *confinare* (*confino* f. L as prec.)]

confi·nement, n. Imprisonment; being confined, esp. in childbed; limitation. [F (-MENT)]

confir·m, v.t. Establish more firmly (power, possession, person *in* possession); ratify (treaty; possession, title, *to* person); corroborate (statement, evidence), whence **confir·m**ATIVE, **confir·mat**ORY, aa., **confir·mative**LY[2] adv.; establish, encourage, (person *in* habit, opinion, &c.); administer religious rite of confirmation to, whence **cŏnfirma·**ND[1] (candidate for confirmation), **cŏnfirm**EE·, nn.; *a confirmed* (inveterate) *drunkard, disease.* [f. OF *confermer* f. L CON(*firmare* f. *firmus* firm)]

confirma·tion, n. Act of confirming; corroboration; rite administered to baptized persons in various Christian Churches. [OF, f. L *confirmationem* (as prec., see -ATION)]

co·nfiscate, v.t. Appropriate to the public treasury (by way of penalty); seize as by authority. So **confi·s**CABLE, **confi·scat**ORY, aa., **co·nfiscat**OR[2] n. [f. L CON(*fiscare* f. *fiscus* treasury), see -ATE[3]]

confisca·tion, n. Act of confiscating; (colloq.) legal robbery with sanction of ruling power. [f. L *confiscatio* (prec., -ATION)]

conflagra·tion, n. Great & destructive fire (lit. & fig.). [f. L *conflagratio* (CON-*flagare* burn up, see FLAGRANT)]

confla·tion, n. Fusing together esp. fig. of two variant readings into one. [f. L *conflatio* f. CON(*flare* blow), see -ATION)]

co·nflict[1], n. Fight, struggle, (lit. & fig.); collision; clashing (*of* opposed principles &c.); *in c.,* discrepant (often *with*). [f. L *conflictus -ūs* (as foll.)]

confli·ct[2], v.i. Struggle (*with* or abs., usu. fig.); clash, be incompatible, whence **confli·ct**ION n. [f. L CON(*fligere flict-* strike)]

co·nfluent, a. & n. Flowing together, uniting, (of streams, roads, &c., & fig.), so **co·nflu**ENCE n.; *c. smallpox* (when vesicles run together); (n.) stream flowing with another (prop. of same size). [f. L CON(*fluere flux-* flow), -ENT]

co·nflux, n. Confluence. [as f. a L *confluxus -ūs* (as prec.)]

confor·m, v.t. & i. Form according to a pattern, make similar (*to*); adapt one*self to*; (intr.) comply with (*to*), be conformable (*to* or abs.). Hence **confor·m**ANCE n. [f. F *conformer* f. L CON(*formare* f. *forma* shape)]

confor·mable, a. Similar (*to*); consistent, adapted, (*to*); tractable. Hence **conforma**BI·LITY n., **confor·mab**LY[2] adv. [-ABLE]

conforma·tion, n. Manner in which a thing is formed, structure; adaptation (*to*). [f. L *conformatio* (as CONFORM, see -ATION)]

confor·mist, n. One who conforms to usages of Church of England. [-IST]

confor·mity, n. Likeness (*to, with*); compliance (*with, to*). [f. F *conformité* f. L CON(*formis* f. *forma* shape), see -TY]

confou·nd (-ow-), v.t. Defeat (plan, hope); (mild oath) *c. it, you,* (=God c.), esp. in p.p., whence **confou·nded**LY[2] adv.; (bibl.) put to shame; throw into perplexity; throw (things) into disorder; mix up; confuse (in idea). [f. OF *confondre* f. L CON(*fundere fus-* pour) mix up]

confrater·nity, n. Brotherhood (esp. religious or charitable); body, gang. [F (*-té*), f. L CON(*fraternitatem* FRATERNITY)]

confrère (F), n. Fellow member of profession, scientific body, &c.

confro·nt (-ŭnt), v.t. Meet face to face, stand facing; be opposite to; face in hostility or defiance; (of difficulties &c.) oppose; bring (person) face to face *with* (accusers &c.); compare. Hence **confront**A·TION n. [f. F *confronter* f. med. L CON(*frontari* f. *frons -ntis* face)]

Confū·cian, a. & n. (Follower) of Confucius, the Chinese Philosopher. Hence **Confu·cian**ISM n. [f. *Confucius,* latiniz. of *K'ung Fû tsze* K'ung the master, + -AN]

confu·se (-z), v.t. Throw into disorder; mix up in the mind; abash, perplex, (usu. pass.). Hence **confu·sĕd**LY[2] adv., **confu·sĕd**NESS n. [f. L as CONFOUND]

confu·sion, n. Act of confusing; confused state; tumult; (as imprecation) *c. !, drink c. to*; *c. worse confounded,* made worse than it was. [OF, f. L *confusionem* (as prec., see -ION)]

confu·te, v.t. Convict (person) of error by proof; prove (argument) false. So **cŏnfut**A·TION n. [f. L CON(*futare* perh. f. same root as *fundere* pour)]

congé (kŏ·nzhā, or as F), **cŏ·ngee** (-jĭ), n. Dismissal without ceremony; (archaic) bow, esp. at parting; (F) *congé d'élire,* royal permission to elect bishop. Hence **co·ngé, -gee,** v.t. & i. [ME *congye* f. OF *congiez* f. L *commeatus -ūs* leave of absence f. COM(*meare* go) go & come; now usu. treated as mod. F]

congea·l, v.t. & i. Freeze, solidify by cooling; coagulate (t. & i. of blood &c. or fig.). Hence **congea·l**ABLE a., **congea·l**MENT n. [f. OF *congeler* f. L CON(*gelare* f. *gelu* frost)]

congela·tion, n. Congealing; congealed state; congealed substance. [f. L *congelatio* (as prec., see -ATION)]

co·ngener, n. & a. One of the same kind as (*of*) another; (adj.) akin, allied, (*to*). [(n. thr. F *congénère*) f. L CON(*genus -eris* kind)]

congenĕ·ric, a. Of same genus, kind, race; allied in nature or origin. [-IC]

congĕ·nerous, a. Of same genus or (loosely) family; of same kind; *c. muscles* (concurring in same action). [-OUS]

congē·nial, a. (Of persons, characters, &c.) kindred, sympathetic, (*with, to*); suited, agreeable, (*to*). Hence **congenia·**LITY n., **conge·nial**LY[2] adv. [CON-+GENIAL]

congĕ·nital, a. Belonging to (*with*) one from birth (esp. of diseases, defects, &c.). Hence **conge·nital**LY[2] adv. [f. L CON-(*genitus* p.p. of *gigno* beget)+-AL]

co·nger (-ngg-), n. Large sea eel (also *c. eel*). [f. OF *congre* f. L *conger -gri* f. Gk *goggros*]

congĕrĭēs (-j-), n. Collection, mass, heap. [L (as foll.)]
conge·st (-j-), v.i. & t. (Intr.) accumulate to excess (esp. in p.p.); affect with congestion; (Med.) *congested organ* (overcharged with blood). Hence **conge·st**IVE a. [f. L CON(*gerere gest-* bring)]
conge·stion, n. Abnormal accumulation of blood in a part of the body (fig. of population, traffic, &c.). [F, f. L *congestionem* (as prec., see -ION)]
co·nglobāte, v.t. & i., & a. Form into a ball; (adj.) so formed. So **conglob**A·TION n. [f. L CON(*globare* f. *globus*), see -ATE[2, 3]]
conglo·be, v.t. & i. =prec. [as prec.]
conglŏ·merate[1] (-*at*), a. & n. Gathered into a round mass; (Geol.) (pudding-stone, water-worn fragments of rock) cemented into a mass (cf. AGGLOMERATE). [f. L CON(*glomerare* f. *glomus -eris* ball), see -ATE[2]]
conglo·merāte[2], v.t. & i. Collect into a coherent mass (lit. & fig.). So **conglomer**A·TION n. [as prec., see -ATE[3]]
conglu·tinate (-ōō-), v.t. & i. Stick together (as) with glue. So **conglutin**A·TION n. [f. L CON*glutinare* (*gluten -inis* glue), see -ATE[3]]
co·ngou (-nggōō, -ō), n. Kind of black Chinese tea. [f. Chin. *kung-fu(-ch'a)* labour (tea)]
congrăˑtulate, v.t. Address (person) with expressions of sympathetic joy (*on* an event); *c. oneself*, think oneself happy (*on*). Hence **congra·tul**ANT a. & n., **congra·tulat**IVE, **congra·tulat**ORY, aa., **congra·tulat**OR[2] n. [f. L CON(*gratulari* f. *gratus* pleasing), see -ATE[3]]
congratula·tion, n. Congratulating; (pl.) congratulatory expressions. [f. L *congratulatio* (as prec., see -ATION)]
co·ngregate, v.t. & i. Collect, gather, into a crowd (of persons) or mass (of things). [f. L CON(*gregare* f. *grex gregis* flock), see -ATE[3]]
congrega·tion, n. Collection into a body or mass; assemblage; general assembly of (qualified) members of university; (bibl.) collective body of Israelites in wilderness, also, public solemn assembly of the nation; (bibl.) *C. of Saints, the wicked,* &c., (whole body); body assembled for religious worship; permanent committee of Roman College of Cardinals, as *the C. de propaganda fide.* [f. F *congrégation* f. L *congregationem* (as prec., see -ATION)]
congrega·tional, a. Of a congregation; (with cap. *C*) of, adhering to, Congregationalism. [-AL]
Congrega·tionalism, n. System of ecclesiastical polity that leaves legislative, disciplinary, and judicial functions to the individual church. So **Congrega·tional**IST n., **Congrega·tional**IZE v.t. [prec. + -ISM]
co·ngress, n. Coming together, meeting; formal meeting of delegates for discussion, esp. of envoys or persons engaged in special studies, as *Church C.*, annual meeting of Church of England, *Social Science C.*, &c.; national legislative body of U.S. or S. & Central Amer. republics; its session; *C.-man*, member of C. [f. L *congressus -ūs* f. CON(*gredi gress-* = *gradi* walk)]
congre·ssional, a. Of a congress. [f. L *congressio* (as prec., see -ION) + -AL]
Co·ngreve, a. & n. *C. (match)*, kind of friction match; *C. (rocket)*, kind formerly used in war. [Sir W. *C.*, inventor]
co·ngruence, -cy, n. Agreement, consistency, (*of* one *with* another, *between* two). [f. L *congruentia* (as foll., see -ENCE, -ENCY)]
co·ngruent, a. Suitable, accordant, (*with*). [f. L CON(*gruere* not otherwise found), see -ENT]
co·ngruous, a. Accordant, conformable, (*with*); fitting. Hence or cogn. **congru·**ITY n., **co·ngruous**LY[2] adv. [f. L *congruus* (as prec.) + -OUS]
cŏnic, a. & n. Cone-shaped; of a cone, as *c. section*; (n. pl.) study of plane c. sections. Hence **co·nic**AL a., **co·nical**LY[2] adv., **co·nical**NESS n. [f. Gk *kōnikos* (CONE, -IC)]
conico-, in comb. With a conical tendency, as *c.-cylindrical.* [as prec.]
cōnifer, n. Cone-bearing plant. Hence **conĭ·**FEROUS a. [L (as CONE, see -FEROUS)]
cōniform, a. Cone-shaped. [CONE, -FORM]
cōnine, cōniine, n. An alkaloid, the poisonous principle of hemlock. [f. L *conium* f. Gk *kōneion* hemlock + -INE[5]]
conje·ctural, a. Involving, given to, conjecture. Hence **conje·ctural**LY[2] adv. [f. L *conjecturalis* (as foll., see -AL)]
conje·cture[1], n. Formation of opinion without sufficient grounds, guessing, esp. in textual criticism, of a reading not in the text; *a c.*, a guess, proposed reading. [F, f. L *conjectura* f. CON(*jicere ject-* = *jacĕre* throw), see -URE]
conje·cture[2], v.t. & i. Guess; propose (a conjectural reading); (intr.) make a guess. Hence **conje·ctur**ABLE a., **conje·cturab**LY[2] adv. [f. F *conjecturer* (prec.)]
conjoi·n, v.t. & i. Join (t. & i.); combine. [f. F *conjoindre* f. L CON(*jungere junct-*)]
conjoi·nt, a. United; associated. Hence **conjoi·nt**LY[2] adv. [F, p.p. as prec.]
co·njugal, a. Of marriage, as *c. rights*; of husband and/or wife, as *c. affection.* Hence **conjuga·**LITY n., **co·njugal**LY[2] adv. [f. L *conjugalis* f. CON(*jux -jugis* f. root of *jungere* join) consort, see -AL]
co·njugāte[1], v.t. & i. (Gram.) inflect (verb) in voice, mood, tense, number, person; (intr.) unite sexually; (Biol.) become fused. [f. L CON(*jugare* f. *jugum* yoke) yoke together, see -ATE[3]]

For compounds of *co-* not given consult CO-.

co·njugate[2] (-*at*), a. & n. Joined together, esp. coupled; (Gram.) derived from same root; (Math.) joined in a reciprocal relation; (Biol.) fused; (n.) c. word or thing. [as prec., see -ATE[2]]

conjuga·tion, n. Joining together; (Gram.) scheme of verbal inflexion; (Biol.) fusion of two (apparently) similar cells for reproduction. Hence **conjuga·tion**AL a. [f. L *conjugatio* (as prec., see -ATION)]

conju·nct, a. & n. Joined together; combined; associated, joint; (n.) c. person or thing. Hence **conju·nct**LY[2] adv. [f. L as CONJOIN]

conju·nction, n. Union, connexion; *in c.*, together (*with*); (Astr.) apparent proximity of two heavenly bodies; combination of events or circumstances; number of associated persons or things; (Gram.) uninflected word used to connect clauses or sentences, or to co-ordinate words in same clause. Hence **conju·nction**AL a., **conju·nctional**LY[2] adv. [OF, f. L *conjunctionem* (as prec., see -ION)]

conjunctī·va, n. Mucous membrane connecting inner eyelid & eye-ball. Hence **conjunctivi·**TIS n. [mod. L (for *membrana c.*) as foll.]

conju·nctive, a. & n. Serving to join, as *c. tissue*; (Gram.) (1) of the nature of a conjunction, (2) uniting sense as well as construction, cf. DISJUNCTIVE, (3) *c. mood* of verb, one used only in conjunction with another verb, cf. SUBJUNCTIVE; (n.) c. word or mood. Hence **conju·nctive**LY[2] adv. [f. L *conjunctivus* (as CONJOIN, see -IVE)]

conju·ncture (-tsh*er*), n. Combination of events, posture of affairs. [f. F *conjoncture* f. L as CONJOIN, see -URE]

cŏnjura·tion, n. Solemn appeal; incantation. [OF, f. L *conjurationem* (foll., -ATION)]

conjure, v.t. & i. 1 (konjoor·). Appeal solemnly to (person *to* do). 2 (kŭ·nj*er*). Constrain (spirit) to appear by invocation (also *c. up, down, out of* person); effect, bring *out*, convey *away*, by juggling; juggle, produce magical effects by natural means, perform marvels (*a name to c. with*, of vast influence); *c. up*, cause to appear to the fancy. [f. OF *conjurer* f. L CON-(*jurare* swear) band together by oath]

co·njurer, -or, n. One who practises legerdemain, juggler; unusually clever person, as *he is no c.* [(-*er*) f. prec. + -ER[1]; (-*or*) f. OF *conjureor* f. L *conjuratorem* (as prec., see -OR[2])]

conk, n. (slang). Nose. Hence **co·nk**Y[2] a. & n., big-nosed (person). [perh. = CONCH]

co·nnāte, a. Born with a person, innate; (of two or more qualities &c.) born together, coeval in origin; (Bot., Zool.) congenitally united (of leaves united at base &c.). [f. L CON(*nasci nat-* be born)]

conna·tural, a. Innate, belonging naturally, (*to*); of like nature. Hence **conna·tural**LY[2] adv. [f. med. L CON(*naturalis* NATURAL)]

conne·ct, v.t. & i. Join (two things, one *with, to*, another); make coherent (arguments &c.); (pass.) have practical relations *with*; associate mentally; unite *with* others in relationship &c. (usu. pass. or refl.); (intr.) join on (*with*). Hence **conne·ct**ER[1](2), -OR[2], nn., **conne·ct**IBLE a. [f. L CON(*nectere nex-* bind)]

conne·cted, a. In vbl senses, esp.: joined in sequence, coherent, whence **conne·cted**LY[2] adv., **conne·cted**NESS n.; related, as *well c.* (with persons of good position). [-ED[1]]

conne·ctive, a. Serving, tending, to connect; *c. tissue* of the body, fibrous tissue connecting & supporting the organs. [-IVE]

conne·xion, -nection, n. Act of connecting; state of being connected (*cut the c.*, separate things, have no more to do with something); relation of thought, as *in this c.*; connecting part, as *hot water cc.*; personal intercourse; sexual relation, as *criminal c.* (abbr. *crim. con.*); family relationship; relative; religious body, as *Wesleyan c.*, whence **conne·xion**AL a.; body of customers &c., as *business with a good c.*; *in c. with*, connected with, esp. of trains, boats, &c., taking on passengers from others. [f. L *connexio* (as CONNECT, see -ION)]

conni·vance, n. Conniving (*at, in*); tacit permission, as *done with his c.* [earlier -*ence*, f. L *conniventia* (as foll., see -ENCE, -ANCE)]

connī·ve, v.i. Wink *at* (what one ought to oppose). [f. L CON(*nivēre*, cf. *nicere* make a sign, *nictare* wink)]

connī·vent, a. (nat. hist.). Gradually convergent. [as CONNIVE, see -ENT]

connoisseur (kŏnas*er*·), n. Critical judge (*of, in*, matters of taste). Hence **connoisseur·**SHIP n. [F, f. L *cognoscitorem* f. CO(*gnoscere* become acquainted with), see -OR[2]]

conno·te, v.t. (Of words) imply in addition to the primary meaning; (of facts &c.) imply as a consequence or condition; (Logic) imply the attributes while denoting the subject; (loosely) mean. Hence or cogn. **connota·**TION n., **connō·tat**IVE a., **conno·tative**LY[2] adv. [f. L CON(*notare* f. *nota* mark) mark together]

connū·bial, a. Of marriage; of husband and/or wife. Hence **connubia·l**ITY n., **connu·bial**LY[2] adv. [f. L *connubialis* f. CON(*nubium* f. *nubere* marry), see -AL]

cō·noid, a. & n. Cone-shaped; (n.) solid generated by revolution of a conic section about its axis, also, any more or less cone-shaped body. Hence **conoi·d**AL a. [f. Gk *kōnoeidēs* (as CONE, see -OID)]

co·nquer (-k*er*), v.t. & i. Overcome by force; get the better of (habit, passion,

&c.); *stoop to c.*, use indirect means for gaining one's end; acquire, subjugate, (land). Hence **co·nquer**ABLE a. [f. OF *conquerre* f. L CON(*quaerere* seek, get)]

co·nqueror (-ke-), n. One who conquers; *the C.*, William I; (colloq.) *play the c.* (decisive game); horse-chestnut that has broken others in boys' game of *cc.* [f. OF *conquereor* f. L **conquaeretorem* (*conquaerēre* for *-ĕre*, see prec. & -OR²)]

co·nquest (-kw-), n. Subjugation (of country &c.); *the (Norman) C.*, acquisition of English crown by William of Normandy, 1066; conquered territory; person whose affections have been won; *make a c. (of)*, win (person's) affections. [f. OF (1) *conquest* thing acquired by c.; (2) *conqueste* action of c., f. L *conquisita*, fem. p.p. of *conquirere* (*-quaerere*) CONQUER]

consa·nguine, a. =foll. [F (*-in, -ine*), as foll.]

consangui·neous, a. Of the same blood, akin. [f. L CON(*sanguineus* f. *sanguis -inis* blood) + -OUS]

consangui·nity, n. Blood-relationship (also fig.). [f. F *consanguinité* f. L *consanguinitatem* (as prec., see -TY)]

co·nscience (-shens), n. Moral sense of right & wrong; *good* or *clear*, *bad* or *guilty*, *c.*, consciousness that one's actions are right, wrong; *have on* one's *c.*, feel guilty about; *in all c.*, *upon* one's *c.*, (forms of asseveration); *have the c. to*, have the impudence to; *for c.* (or *c.'*) *sake*, to satisfy one's c.; *c. clause* in act, one ensuring respect for the cc. of those affected; *c. money* (sent to relieve the c., esp. in payment of evaded income-tax). Hence **co·nscience**LESS a. [F, f. L *conscientia* f. CON(*scire* know) be privy to, see -ENCE]

conscie·ntious (-shĕnsh-), a. Obedient to conscience, scrupulous, (of persons or conduct); *c. objector*, person who avails himself of CONSCIENCE *clause*, man (often abbr. *c.o.*) who pleaded conscience & refused to serve in the great war. Hence **conscie·ntious**LY² adv., **conscie·ntious**NESS n. [f. F *conscientieux, -euse*, f. med. L *conscientiosus* (as prec., see -OUS)]

co·nscious, a. Aware, knowing, (*of* fact, *of* external circumstances, *that*, or abs.); with mental faculties awake; (of actions, emotions, &c.) realized by the actor &c. (*with c. superiority*; *a hardly c. movement*); =SELF-CONSCIOUS. Hence **co·nscious**LY² adv. [f. L *conscius* f. CON(*scire* know) be privy to + -OUS]

co·nsciousness, n. State of being conscious; totality of a person's thoughts & feelings, or of a class of these, as *moral c.*; perception (*of, that*). [-NESS]

conscri·be, v.t. Enlist by conscription. [f. L CON(*scribere script-* write) enrol]

co·nscript, a. & n. (Recruit) enrolled by conscription; *c. fathers* (collective title of Roman senators). [as prec.]

conscri·ption, n. Compulsory enlistment for military or naval service (esp. enrolment by lot); *c. of wealth*, taxation or confiscation of property for war purposes to impose equality of sacrifice on non-conscripts. [f. L *conscriptio* (as prec., see -ION)]

co·nsecrāte¹, a. Consecrated. [f. L CON(*secrare*=*sacrare* f. *sacer -cri* sacred), see -ATE²]

co·nsecrāte², v.t. Set apart as sacred (*to*); devote *to* (purpose); sanctify. So **co·nsecrat**OR² n., **co·nsecrat**ORY a. [prec., -ATE³]

consecra·tion, n. Act of consecrating, dedication, esp. of church, churchyard, &c., by bishop; ordination to sacred office, esp. of bishop; devotion *to* (a purpose). [f. L *consecratio* (as prec., see -ATION)]

conse·ctary, n. Deduction, corollary. [f. L *consectarium* (neut. adj. as n.) f. *consectari* frequent. as foll.]

consecu·tion, n. Logical sequence; sequence of events; (Gram.) sequence of words, tenses, &c. [f. L *consecutio* f. CON(*sequi secut-* pursue) overtake, see -ION]

consĕ·cutive, a. Following continuously; (Gram.) expressing consequence, as *c. clause*; (Mus.) *c. intervals* (of the same kind, esp. fifths or octaves). Hence **conse·cutive**LY² adv., **conse·cutive**NESS n. [f. F *consécutif, -ive* (as prec., see -IVE)]

consene·scence, n. General decay by age. [f. L CON(*senescere* grow old f. *senex*), -ENCE]

conse·nsual, a. (physiol.). Caused by sympathetic action. [f. foll. + -AL]

conse·nsus, n. Agreement (*of* opinion, testimony, &c.); (Physiol.) agreement of different organs in effecting purpose. [L (as foll.)]

conse·nt¹, v.i. Acquiesce, agree, (*to* a thing, *to* do, *that*, or abs.). [f. OF *consentir* f. L CON(*sentire sens-* feel) agree]

conse·nt², n. Voluntary agreement, compliance; permission; *age of c.* (at which c., esp. of girl to seduction, is valid in law); (prov.) *silence gives c.*; *with one c.*, unanimously. [f. OF *consente* (as prec.)]

consentā·neous, a. Accordant, suited, (*to, with*); unanimous, concurrent. Hence **consentanē·i**TY, **consenta·neous**NESS, nn., **consenta·neous**LY² adv. [f. L *consentaneus* (as CONSENT¹) + -OUS]

conse·ntient (-shnt), a. Agreeing; concurrent; consenting (*to*). [f. L as CONSENT¹, see -ENT]

co·nsequence, n. Result (of something preceding; *take the cc.*, accept whatever results from one's choice or act); logical inference; *in c.*, as a result (*of*); importance; *of (no) c.*, (un)important; social distinction, rank, as *persons of c.* [f. F *conséquence* f. L *consequentia* (as foll., -ENCE]

co·nsequent[1], n. Event that follows another; second part of conditional proposition, dependent on the antecedent; (Math.) second of two numbers in a ratio, second & fourth of four proportionals. [as foll.]

co·nsequent[2], a. Following as a result (*on*); following logically; logically consistent. [f. F *conséquent* f. L CON(*sequi* follow), see -ENT]

conseque·ntial, a. Following as a result or inference; following or resulting indirectly, as *c. damages*; self-important. Hence **consequentia·lity** (-shĭ-), n., **conseque·ntially**[2] adv. [f. L as CONSEQUENCE + -AL]

co·nsequently, adv. & conj. As a result; therefore. [-LY[2]]

conser·vancy, n. Commission, court, controlling a port, river, &c., as *Thames C.*; official preservation (of forests &c.). [f. L as CONSERVE[2], see -ANCY]

conserva·tion, n. Preservation; *c. of energy*, invariability in quantity of total energy of any system of bodies (including the universe). [f. L *conservatio* (as prec., -ATION)]

conser·vative, a. & n. Preservative (a. & n.); (*C. party*, English political party) disposed to maintain existing institutions; (improp., of estimate) moderate, cautious, purposely low; (n.) one so disposed, member of the C. party. So **conser·vatism** n. [F (*-if, -ive*), f. med. L *conservativus* (as foll., see -IVE)]

***conservatoire*·** (-twar·r), n. Public school of music & declamation (on Continent). [F, f. L *conservatorium* (as foll., see -ORY)]

co·nservator, n. Preserver; official custodian (of museum &c.); *cc. of the peace*, the King, Lord Chancellor, &c.; *cc. of a river* (see CONSERVANCY). [f. F *conservateur* f. L *conservatorem* (as foll., see -OR[2])]

conser·vatory, n. Greenhouse for tender plants; =CONSERVATOIRE. [f. L *conservatorius* a. (as foll., see -ORY)]

conser·ve[1], n. (usu. pl.). Confection, preserve. [F, f. med. L *conserva* (as foll.)]

conser·ve[2], v.t. Keep from harm, decay, or loss. [f. F *conserver* f. L CON(*servare* keep)]

consi·der, v.t. & i. Contemplate mentally; weigh the merits of (course, claim, &c.); reflect (*that, whether*, &c., or abs.), reckon with, make allowance for; be of opinion (*that*); regard as, as *I c. him* (*to be*) *a knave*, *c. yourself under arrest*; (archaic) *c. of*, think over. [f. F *considérer* f. L CON(*siderare* perh. f. *sidus -eris* star) examine]

consi·derable, a. Worth considering; (of persons) notable, important; (of immaterial things) much, no small, (trouble, annoyance, pleasure), whence **consi·derably**[2] adv. [f. med. L *considerabilis* (as prec., see -ABLE)]

consi·derate (-*at*), a. Thoughtful for others; (archaic) careful. Hence **consi·derately**[2] adv., **consi·derateness** n. [as prec., -ATE[2]]

considera·tion, n. Act of considering; meditation; *take into c.*, consider; *under c.*, being considered; *in c. of*, in return for, on account of; fact, thing, regarded as a reason, as *that is a c.*, *on no c.*; compensation, reward, as *for a c.*; (Law) thing given, done, as equivalent by person to whom a promise is made; thoughtfulness for others; importance (now rare). [f. F *considération* f. L *considerationem* (as prec., see -ATION)]

consi·dering, prep. In view of, as *it is excusable c. his age, how young he is*, (*that*) *he has no experience*; (ellipt.) *that is not so bad, c.* (the circumstances). [-ING[2]]

consi̅·gn, v.t. Hand over, deliver, *to* (misery, watery grave, person, person's care); transmit, send by rail &c., *to* (person), whence **consi̅gnee·**, **consi̅gnor·**[2], nn.; deposit (money *in* bank). Hence **consi̅·gnable** a. [f. L CON*signare* mark with a seal (*signum*)]

consigna·tion (-ĭg-), n. Formal payment of money to person legally appointed; act of consigning goods; *to the c. of*, addressed to. [f. L *consignatio* (as prec., see -ATION)]

consi̅·gnment, n. Consigning; goods consigned. [-MENT]

consi·lient, a. (Of inductions from different phenomena) accordant. Hence **consi·lience** n. [f. L *CON(*silire* = *salire* jump), see -ENT]

consi·st, v.i. Be composed *of* (esp. material things); be comprised *in*, as *virtue consists in being uncomfortable*; harmonize *with*; (bibl., *Col.* i. 17) exist. [f. L CON(*sistere* stop) exist]

consi·stence, -cy, n. Degree of density, esp. of thick liquids; firmness, solidity, (lit. & fig.); (*-cy*) state of being consistent, esp. of persons. [as prec., see -ENCE, -ENCY]

consi·stent, a. Compatible, not contradictory, (*with*); (of person) constant to same principles. Hence **consi·stently**[2] adv. [as prec., -ENT]

co·nsistory (*also* konsĭ·s-), n. Senate composed of Pope & Cardinals; (also *C. Court*) bishop's court for ecclesiastical causes & offences; Lutheran clerical board; court of presbyters. So **consistor·ial** a. [f. F *consistoire* f. L *consistorium* (as CONSIST, see -ORY)]

conso̅·ciate[1] (-shĭat), a. & n. Associate(d). [f. L CON(*sociare* f. *socius* fellow), see -ATE[2]]

conso·ciāte[2], v.t. & i. Associate. So **consocia·tion** (-sĭ-), n. [as prec., see -ATE[3]]

consola·tion, n. Act of consoling; consoling circumstance; *c. race, prize, stakes* (open to competitors unsuccessful in former events). [F, f. L *consolationem* (as foll., see -ATION)]

conso·latory, a. Tending, meant, to console. Hence **conso·latori**LY² adv. [f. L *consolatorius* (as foll., see -ORY)]

conso·le¹, v.t. Comfort. Hence **conso·l**ABLE a. [f. F *consoler* f. L CON*solare, -ri*]

co·nsole², n. (Arch.) kind of bracket or corbel; frame enclosing manuals, draw-knobs, &c., of organ; *c.-table, -mirror* (supported by bracket against wall). [F, etym. dub.]

conso·lidate, v.t. & i. Solidify (t. & i); strengthen (usu. fig., power &c.); combine (territories, estates, companies, statutes, debts) into one whole; *consolidated annuities, consols,* Government securities of Great Britain, consolidated in 1751 into a single stock at 3% (now 2½), *Consolidated Fund,* united product of various taxes &c., whence interest of national debt &c. is paid. Hence **consolid**A·TION, **conso·lida**TOR², nn., **conso·lidat**ORY a. [f. L CON(*solidare* f. *solidus*), see -ATE³]

conso·ls, n. pl. See prec. [abbr.]

consommé (F), n. Strong meat soup.

co·nsonance, n. Recurrence of same or similar sounds in words, assonance; sounding of two notes in harmony; (Mus.) consonant interval, concord; (fig.) agreement, harmony. [F, f. L *consonantia* (as foll., see -ANCE)]

co·nsonant¹, a. Agreeable *to,* consistent *with*; harmonious; agreeing in sound; (Mus.) making concord. Hence **co·nsonant**LY² adv. [F, f. L CON(*sonare* sound f. *sonus*), see -ANT]

co·nsonant², n. Alphabetical element other than vowel; sound that in forming a syllable is combined with vowel. Hence **consona·nt**AL a. [F, f. L *consonantem* (*litteram* letter) sounding with another (as prec.)]

co·nsort¹, n. Husband or wife; *queen c.,* king's wife; *king, prince, c.,* queen's husband; ship sailing with another. [F, f. L CON(*sors -rtis* lot) sharer, comrade]

consor·t², v.t. & i. Class or bring together, keep company, (*with*); agree, harmonize, (*with*). [f. prec., and f. vb *sort*]

conspeci·fic, a. Of the same species. [CON-]

conspe·ctus, n. General view of subject, scene, &c.; tabulation of details, synopsis. [L, vbl n. f. CON(*spicere* look at)]

conspi·cuous, a. Clearly visible, striking to the eye; attracting notice, remarkable, as *c. by its absence, for his loyalty.* Hence **conspicu·**ITY, **conspi·cuous**NESS, nn., **conspi·cuous**LY² adv. [f. L *conspicuus* (as prec.) + -OUS]

conspi·racy, n. Act of conspiring (in good or bad sense); combination for unlawful purpose; plot. [f. L *conspiratio* (as foll., see -ATION), with -ACY(3) substituted]

conspi·rator, n. One engaged in a conspiracy. Hence **conspi·ratr**ESS¹ n. [f. F *conspirateur* f. L *conspiratorem* (as foll., see -OR²)]

conspire·, v.i. & t. Combine privily for unlawful purpose, esp. treason, murder, sedition; combine, concur, (*to* do); plot, devise, as *c. his ruin, c. an attack.* [f. F *conspirer* f. L CON(*spirare* breathe) agree, plot]

conspue·, v.t. Express detestation, clamour for the abandonment or abolition, of (person, policy, &c.). [f. F *conspuer* f. L CON(*spuere* spit) spit upon]

co·nstable (kŭn-), n. (Also *police c.*) policeman; *Chief C.,* head of police force of county &c.; *special c.,* person sworn in to act as c. on special occasion; *outrun the c.,* run into debt; *C. of France,* principal officer of household of early French kings, commander-in-chief in king's absence; *C. of England, Lord High C.,* similar officer in English Royal household (now temporary officer on special occasions). [f. OF *conestable* f. LL *comes stabuli* count of the stable]

consta·bulary, a. & n. (Organized body) of constables. [f. med. L *constabularius* (n. *-aria*) f. *constabulus* CONSTABLE, see -ARY¹]

co·nstancy, n. Firmness, endurance; faithfulness; unchangingness. [f. L *constantia* (as foll., see -ANCY)]

co·nstant, a. & n. Unmoved, resolute; faithful (*to*); unchanging; unremittent, as *c. attention, chatter*; (Math., n.) quantity that does not vary; (Physics) number expressing a relation, property, &c., that remains the same for same substance in same conditions, as *c. of friction.* [F, f. L CON(*stare* stand), see -ANT]

Consta·ntia, n. Wine from the C. farm near Cape Town.

co·nstantly, adv. Always; often. [-LY²]

co·nstellate, v.t. & i. Form into a constellation. [f. L *CON(*stellare* f. *stella* star), see -ATE³]

constella·tion, n. Number of fixed stars grouped within an imaginary outline (also fig.). [f. L *constellatio* (as prec., see -ATION)]

co·nsternate, v.t. Dismay (usu. pass.). [f. L CON(*sternare, -sternere,* throw down), see -ATE³]

consterna·tion, n. Dismay. [f. L *consternatio* (as prec., see -ATION)]

co·nstipate, v.t. Confine (bowels); render costive. [f. L CON(*stipare* press), see -ATE³]

constipa·tion, n. Costiveness. [f. L *constipatio* (as prec., see -ATION)]

consti·tuency, n. Body of voters who elect a representative member; place, body of residents in place, so represented;

body of customers, subscribers, &c. [f. foll., see -ENCY]

consti·tuent, a. & n. Composing, making up, a whole; appointing, electing; able to frame or alter a (political) constitution, as *c. assembly, power*; one who appoints another his agent; component part; member of a constituency. [as foll., see -ENT]

co·nstitute, v.t. Appoint, as *c. him president, c. oneself a judge*; establish, found; give legal form to (assembly &c.); frame, form, (esp. pass. of bodily or mental constitution); make up, be the components of. [f. L CON(*stituere -ut-* = *statuere* set up)]

constitu·tion, n. Act, mode, of constituting; character of the body as regards health, strength, &c.; mental character; mode in which State is organized; body of fundamental principles according to which a State is governed; *written c.*, document embodying these; (Hist.) decree, ordinance, as *Cc. of Clarendon* (1164). [F, f. L *constitutionem* (as prec., see -ION)]

constitu·tional, a. & n. Of, inherent in, affecting, the bodily or mental constitution; essential; of, in harmony with, authorized by, the political constitution, as *c. sovereign, government* (limited by c. forms), whence **constitutiona·lITY** n.; adhering to the political constitution; (n.) c. walk, for health's sake. Hence **constitu·tionalLY**^{2} adv. [-AL]

constitu·tionalism, n. Constitutional government; adherence to constitutional principles. [-ISM]

constitu·tionalist, n. Writer on the political constitution; adherent of constitutional principles. [-IST]

constitu·tionalize, v.t. & i. Make constitutional; (intr.) take a constitutional. [-IZE]

co·nstitutive, a. Constructive, formative; essential; component. Hence **co·nstitutiveLY**^{2} adv. [f. CONSTITUTE + -IVE]

co·nstitutor, n. Person that constitutes. [L (as CONSTITUTE, see -OR^2)]

constrai·n, v.t. Compel (person *to* do, *to* course or state, or abs.); bring about by compulsion; confine forcibly, imprison (lit. & fig.); (p.p.) forced, embarrassed, as *constrained voice, manner*, whence **constrai·nĕdLY**^{2} adv. [f. OF *constreindre* f. L CON(*stringere strict-* tie)]

constrai·nt, n. Compulsion (*under c.*); confinement; restraint of natural feelings, constrained manner. [f. OF *constreinte*, fem. p.p. as n., see prec.]

constri·ct, v.t. Contract, compress; cause (organic tissue) to contract. So **constri·ctION** n., **constri·ctIVE** a. [f. L as CONSTRAIN]

constri·ctor, n. Muscle that draws together or narrows a part; compressor (surgical instrument); BOA-*c.* [L (as prec., see -OR^2)]

constri·nge (-j), v.t. Compress; cause (organic tissue) to contract. Hence **constri·ngENCY** n., **constri·ngENT** a. [as prec.]

constru·ct, v.t. Fit together, frame, build, (also fig.); (Gram.) combine (words) syntactically; draw, delineate, as *c. a triangle.* [f. L CON(*struere struct-* pile, build)]

constru·ction, n. Act, mode, of constructing; thing constructed; syntactical connexion between words; construing, explanation, (of words); interpretation (of conduct &c.), as *put a good, bad, c. upon his refusal.* [f. L *constructio* (as prec., see -ION)]

constru·ctional, a. Of construction; structural, belonging to the original structure. [-AL]

constru·ctive, a. Of construction; tending to construct, esp. opposed to *destructive* as *positive* to *negative*, as *c. criticism*; belonging to the structure of a building; inferred, not directly expressed, virtual, as *a c. denial, permission, blasphemy, treason.* Hence **constru·ctiveLY**^{2} adv. [f. med. L *constructivus* (as CONSTRUCT, see -IVE)]

constru·ctor, n. One who constructs, esp. supervisor of naval construction. Hence **constru·ctorSHIP** n. [-OR^2]

co·nstrue (*or* -strōō·), v.t. & i. Combine (words *with* others) grammatically, as *'rely' is construed with 'on'*; analyse (sentence), translate word for word; admit of grammatical analysis, as *this passage does not c.*; expound, interpret, (words, actions). [as CONSTRUCT]

consubsta·ntial, a. Of the same substance, esp. of the three Persons in the Godhead. Hence **consubstantia·lITY** n. [f. L CON(*substantialis* as SUBSTANCE, see -AL)]

consubsta·ntiate, v.t. & i. Unite in one substance. [f. L CON(*substantiare* as prec.), -ATE^3]

consubstantia·tion, n. (Doctrine of) real substantial presence of body & blood of Christ together with bread & wine in Eucharist (cf. TRANSUBSTANTIATION). [f. 16th-c. L *consubstantiatio* (as prec., see -ATION)]

co·nsuetude (-swĭ-), n. Custom, esp. as having legal force; social intercourse. [OF, f. L *consuetudo -inis* (cf. CUSTOM) f. *consuetus* accustomed p.p. of CON*suescere*, see -TUDE]

consuetū·dinary, a. & n. Customary, as *c. law*; (n.) manual of customs, esp. of monastic house, cathedral, &c. [f. L *consuetudinarius* (as prec., see -ARY^1)]

co·nsul, n. Title of two annual magistrates exercising supreme authority in Roman republic; title of three chief magistrates of French Republic 1799–1804 (*First C.*, Napoleon); State agent residing in foreign town and protecting subjects there; local representative of Cyclists'

Touring Club. Hence **co·nsul**SHIP n. [L (CON- + *sal-* root of *salire* leap)]
co·nsular, a. & n. Of a consul; (Roman) of c. rank. [f. L *consularis* (as prec., see -AR[1])]
co·nsulate (-*at*), n. Office, establishment, of a (modern) consul; (period of) consular government in France; office of (Roman) consul. [f. L *consulatus* (as prec., see -ATE[1])]
consu·lt, v.t. & i. Take counsel (*with* person or book, or abs.); seek information or advice from (person, book); *c. one's pillow*, take a night for reflection; take into consideration (feelings, interests); *consulting physician*, (who is called in by colleagues or applied to by patients for advice in special cases). Hence **consu·lt**ABLE, **consu·lt**ATIVE, aa., **consult**EE· n. [f. L *consultare* frequent. of *consulere -sult-* (as CONSUL)]
consu·ltant, n. One who consults; consulting physician. [as prec., see -ANT]
consulta·tion, n. Act of consulting; deliberation; conference. [f. L *consultatio* (as prec., see -ATION)]
consu·me, v.t. & i. Make away with; use up; eat, drink, up; spend, waste, (time, trouble, &c.); (p.p.) eaten up (*with envy*); (intr.) waste away. [f. L CON(*sumere sumpt-* take up)]
consu·mĕdly, adv. Excessively. [prec., -LY[2]]
consu·mer, n. In vbl senses, esp. (Pol. Econ.) user of an article, opp. to *producer*. [-ER[1]]
consu·mmate[1] (-*at*), a. Complete, perfect, as *c. general, skill, ass.* Hence **consu·mmate**LY[2] adv. [f. L CON(*summare* complete f. *summus* utmost), see -ATE[2]]
co·nsummāte[2], v.t. Accomplish, complete, esp. marriage (by sexual intercourse). Hence **co·nsummat**IVE a., **co·nsummat**OR[2] n. [as prec., see -ATE[3]]
consumma·tion, n. Completion (esp. of marriage, see prec.); desired end, goal; perfection; perfected thing. [f. OF *consommation* f. L *consummationem* (as prec., see -ATION)]
consu·mption, n. Using up; destruction; waste; amount consumed; wasting disease, esp. *pulmonary c.*, phthisis. [f. L *consumptio* (as CONSUME, see -ION)]
consu·mptive, a. & n. Tending to consume; tending to, affected with, consumption, whence **consu·mptive**LY[2] adv. **consu·mptive**NESS n.; (n.) c. patient. [as CONSUME, see -IVE]
contabe·scence, n. (bot.). Suppression of pollen formation in anthers of flowers. So **contabe·s**CENT a. [f. L CON(*tabescere* waste away f. *tabes* consumption), see -ENCE]
co·ntact, n. State, condition, of touching, as *be in c. with*; (fig.) *come into c. with*, come across, meet; *make, break, c.*, complete, interrupt, electric circuit (so *c.-maker, -breaker*); (Math.) touching of straight line & curve, two curves, or two surfaces. [f. L *contactus -ūs* vbl n. f. CON-(*tingere tact-* = *tangere* touch)]
contadi·no (-dē-), n. (fem. *-na*; pl. *-ni* pr. -nē, fem. *-ne* pr. -nā). Italian peasant. [It.]
contā·gion, n. Communication of disease from body to body; contagious disease; moral corruption; contagious influence (fig.). [F, f. L CON(*tagionem* f. *tangere* touch, -ION)]
conta·gionist, n. One who thinks a disease (plague, cholera, &c.) contagious. [-IST]
conta·gious (-*jus*), a. Communicating disease by contact (lit. & fig.); (of diseases) so communicable; (fig.) catching, infectious. Hence **conta·gious**LY[2] adv., **conta·gious**NESS n. [f. OF *contagieus* f. LL *contagiosus* (as CONTAGION, see -OUS)]
contai·n, v.t. Have, hold, as contents; comprise, include; (of a measure) be equal to, as *a pound contains 16 ounces*; (pass.) be included (*within* a space, *between* limits); (Geom.) enclose, form boundary of; (of numbers) be divisible by (number) without remainder; restrain, as *could not c. himself for joy, c. your anger*; (Mil.) keep (enemy force) from moving, esp. with a view to operations elsewhere. Hence **contai·n**ABLE a. [f. OF *contenir* f. L CON(*tinēre tent-* = *tenēre* hold)]
contă·minate, v.t. Pollute, infect. So **contamin**A·TION n. (also, in literary criticism, the blending of two plays, tales, &c., into one). [f. L *contaminare* f. CON(*tamen* f. *tag-* root of *tangere* touch), see -ATE[3]]
conta·ngo, n. (pl. *-oes*). Percentage paid by buyer of stock for postponement of transfer (cf. BACKWARDATION); *c.* (also *continuation*)*-day*, second day before settling-day. [perh. = Sp. *contengo* I check, stop, f. *contener* f. L as CONTAIN]
conte·mn (-ĕm), v.t. Despise, treat with disregard. Hence **conte·mn**ER[1] (-mn-) n. [f. OF *contemner* f. L CON(*temnere tempt-*)]
co·ntemplate, v.t. & i. Gaze upon; view mentally; expect; intend, purpose; (intr.) meditate. So **contempla·**TION n. (*in contemplation*, intended), **co·ntemplat**OR[2] n. [f. L CON(*templari* f. *templum* TEMPLE, open space for observation), see -ATE[3]]
co·ntemplative, a. Meditative, thoughtful; (of life in middle ages) given up to religious contemplation, opp. to *active*. Hence **co·ntemplative**LY[2] adv., **co·ntemplative**NESS n. [OF (*-if, -ive*), f. L *contemplativus* (prec., -IVE)]
contemporā·neous, a. Existing, occurring, at the same time (*with*); covering

For compounds of *co-* not given consult CO-.

the same time; of the same period. Hence **contemporanē·i**TY, **contempora·neous**NESS, nn., **contempora·neous**LY² adv. [f. L CON(*temporaneus* f. *tempus -oris* time, see -ANEOUS)]

conte·mporary, a. & n. (Person) belonging to the same time; (person) equal in age; (newspaper) published during same period. [CON- + TEMPORARY; in 18th c. *cotemporary* was preferred]

conte·mporize, v.t. Make contemporary, cause to agree in time. [f. st. of prec. + -IZE]

conte·mpt, n. Act, mental attitude, of despising; condition of being despised; *have, hold, in c., bring, fall, into c.*; (Law) disobedience to sovereign's lawful commands or to authority of Houses of Parliament or other legislative body, esp. *c. of court*, disobedience to, interference with administration of justice by, courts of law. [f. L *contemptus -ūs* (as CONTEMN)]

conte·mptible, a. Deserving contempt, despicable; *Old Contemptibles*, Sir J. French's army of 1914 (w. ref. to Kaiser's alleged 'French's c. little army'). Hence **contemptibi·li**TY, **conte·mptible**NESS, nn., **conte·mptib**LY² adv. [f. L *contemptibilis* (as CONTEMN, see -BLE)]

conte·mptuous, a. Showing contempt (*of*); scornful; insolent. Hence **conte·mptuous**LY² adv., **conte·mptuous**NESS n. [as CONTEMPT + -OUS]

conte·nd, v.i. & t. Strive, fight, (*with* person *for* thing); struggle *with* (feelings, natural forces); compete, be in rivalry, as *contending passions*; argue (*with*); (trans.) maintain (*that*). [f. L CON(*tendere tent-* stretch, strive)]

conte·nt,¹ n. (Pl.) *cc. of*, what is contained in (vessel &c., book, document); (*table of*) *cc.*, summary of subject-matter of book; (*also* kŏ·ntĕnt) capacity (of vessel), volume (of solid). [f. L as CONTAIN]

conte·nt², n. Contented state, satisfaction, esp. *to* one's *heart's c.* [f. CONTENT v. or a.]

conte·nt³, a. & n. Satisfied; willing (*to* do); *well c.*, well pleased; (House of Lords) *c.*, *not c.*, (= *ay, no*, in House of Commons); (n. pl.) those who vote 'c.' [F (as CONTENT¹); orig. = bounded (in desires by what one has)]

conte·nt⁴, v.t. Satisfy; *c. oneself*, be satisfied (*with* thing, *with* doing). Hence **conte·nted**LY² adv., **conte·nted**NESS, **conte·nt**MENT, nn. [f. F *contenter* (as prec.)]

conte·ntion, n. Strife, dispute, controversy; emulation; point contended for in argument. [F, f. L *contentionem* (as CONTEND, see -ION)]

conte·ntious, a. Quarrelsome; involving contention. Hence **conte·ntious**LY² adv., **conte·ntious**NESS n. [f. F *contentieux* f. L *contentiosus* (as prec., see -IOUS)]

conter·minal, a. Having a common boundary. [f. med. L *conterminalis* (as foll., see -AL)]

conter·minous, a. Having a common boundary (*with, to*); (of two things) meeting at their ends; coextensive (in space, time, meaning). Hence **conter·minous**LY² adv. [f. L CON(*terminus* boundary) + -OUS]

co·ntest¹, n. Debate, controversy; strife; (friendly) competition. [f. foll.]

conte·st², v.t. & i. Debate, dispute (point, statement, &c.); strive in argument (*with, against*); strive *for*; dispute with arms (field, victory, issue, battle); contend or compete for (seat in Parliament &c.). Hence **conte·st**ABLE a. [f. F *contester* call to witness, argue, gainsay, f. L CON*testari* (*litem*) bring witnesses to an action, bring an action (*testis* witness)]

conte·stant, n. One who contests. [F (-ANT)]

contesta·tion, n. Disputation; assertion contended for; *in c.*, in dispute. [f. L *contestatio* (as CONTEST², see -ATION)]

co·ntext, n. Parts that precede or follow a passage & fix its meaning; *in this c.* (connexion). So **conte·xtu**AL a., **conte·xtual**LY² adv. [f. L *contextus -ūs* f. CON(*texere text-* weave)]

conte·xture, n. Act, mode, of weaving together; structure; fabric; mode of literary composition. [F (as prec., see -URE)]

contigū·ity, n. Contact; proximity; (Psychol.) proximity of ideas or impressions in place or time, as principle of association. [f. L *contiguitas* (as foll., see -TY)]

conti·gūous, a. Touching, adjoining, (*to*); next in order (*to*); neighbouring. Hence **conti·guous**LY² adv. [f. L *contiguus* f. CON(*tingere* = *tangere* touch) + -OUS]

co·ntinent¹, a. Temperate; chaste. Hence or cogn. **co·ntin**ENCE n., **co·ntinent**LY² adv. [OF, f. L as CONTAIN, see -ENT]

co·ntinent², n. Continuous land, mainland; *the C.*, mainland of Europe; one of the main continuous bodies of land (Europe, Asia, Africa, N. & S. America, Australia). [as prec.]

contine·ntal, a. & n. Of a continent; belonging to, characteristic of, the Continent, whence **contine·ntal**ISM, **contine·ntal**IST, nn., **contine·ntal**IZE v.t., **contine·ntal**LY² adv.; (n.) inhabitant of the Continent. [-AL]

conti·ngency, n. Uncertainty of occurrence; chance occurrence; thing that may happen hereafter; thing dependent on an uncertain event; thing incident to another, incidental expense &c. [f. L as foll., see -ENCY]

conti·ngent, a. & n. Of uncertain occurrence; accidental; incidental *to*; true only under existing conditions; non-essential; conditional; (n.) force contributed to form part of army or navy (or fig.). Hence **conti·ngent**LY[2] adv. [F, f. L CON(*tingere* = *tangere* touch), see -ENT]

conti·nual, a. Always going on; very frequent. Hence **conti·nual**LY[2] adv. [f. OF *continuel* f. L as CONTINUOUS, see -AL]

conti·nuance, n. Going on, duration; *of long c.,* lasting long; remaining, stay, (*in* place, condition, &c.). [OF (CONTINUE, -ANCE)]

conti·nuant, a. & n. (Consonant) of which the sound can be prolonged (as *f v s r*), opp. of stop or check. [f. L as CONTINUE, see -ANT]

continua·tion, n. Carrying on, resumption, (of an action, course, story, book, &c.); (Stock Exch.) carrying over an account to next *c.* (or CONTANGO) *-day*; that by which a thing is continued, additional parts; gaiters continuous with knee-breeches; (slang) trousers; *c. school* (for additional teaching in leisure time of those who have left primary and other schools). [F, f. L *continuatio* (as prec., see -ATION)]

conti·nuative, a. Tending, serving, to continue. [f. L *continuativus* (as prec., see -IVE)]

conti·nuator, n. One who writes continuation to another's work. [f. L as foll., -OR[2]]

conti·nue, v.t. & i. Maintain, keep up, (action &c.); retain (person *in* office &c.); take up, resume, (narrative &c. or abs.); (Law) adjourn; remain in existence; stay (*in, at,* place, *in* a state); *if you c.* (are still) *obstinate*; not cease (do*ing, to* do). Hence **conti·nu**ABLE a. [f. F *continuer* f. L *continuare* as CONTINUOUS]

continu·ity, n. State of being continuous; *law of c.* (that all changes in nature are continuous, not abrupt). [f. F *continuité* f. L *continuitatem* (as foll., see -TY)]

conti·nuous, a. (Of material things) connected, unbroken; uninterrupted in time or sequence; *c. brake* of train, c. series of carriage brakes controlled from one point; (Arch.) *c. style* (with mullions of window continued in tracery); *c. voyage* (name of the doctrine that consignment to a neutral on the way to a belligerent amounts to consignment to the latter & does not relieve contraband of its character). Hence **conti·nuous**LY[2] adv., **conti·nuous**NESS n. [f. L *continuus* f. CON(*tinēre* = *tenere* hold) + -OUS]

conti·nuum, n. (Philos.). An unbroken mass or tissue or course of or *of* matter, sensation, events, &c. (SPACE-*time c.*). [L, neut. of *continuus,* see prec.]

co·nt-line, n. Spiral interval between strands of rope; space between casks stowed side by side. [?]

contor·niate, a. & n. (Medal) with deep furrow round disk within edge. [f. It. *contorno* contour f. *contornare* compass about f. CON- + L *tornare* turn in lathe (*tornus*)]

contor·t, v.t. Twist, distort. [f. L CON-(*torquēre tort-*)]

contor·tion, n. Twisting; twisted state (esp. of face or body). [f. L *contortio* (prec. -ION)]

contor·tionist, n. Artist whose work, gymnast whose body, exhibits contortions. [-IST]

co·ntour (-oor), n., & v.t. Outline; line separating differently coloured parts of design; artistic quality of outline; outline of coast, mountain mass, &c.; *c. line,* one representing horizontal c. of earth's surface at given elevation, as in a *c. map* (v.t.) mark with c. lines, carry (road) round c. of hill. [(vb f. n.) F, f. CON-(*tourner* TURN)]

co·ntra (-*a*), prep. & n. *Pro & contra* (usu. *con*) for & against; *pros & cons,* arguments for & against; (Bookkeeping) opposite side of account, esp. credit side. [L, as foll.]

contra-, pref. Against; in Ital. mus. terms, of parts marked on the stave alongside of, opposite to, bass, alto, &c. (*contrabasso* &c.). [L]

co·ntrabănd, n. & a. Prohibited traffic, smuggling; smuggled goods; *c. of war,* anything forbidden to be supplied by neutrals to belligerents (*absolute, conditional, c.,* things that may under no, some, circumstances be supplied, as, *a. c.,* weapons, *c. c.,* cotton); (adj.) forbidden to be imported or exported, as *c. goods,* concerned with these, as *c. trade(r).* [f. Sp. *contrabanda* f. It. CONTRA(*bando* proclamation f. LL *bandum* BAN)]

co·ntrabandist, n. Smuggler. [f. Sp. *contrabandista* (as prec., see -IST)]

co·ntrabāss, n. = DOUBLE[1]-*bass.* [f. It. CONTRA(*basso* BASS)]

contrace·ptive, a. & n. Preventive of uterine conception. So **contrace·ption** n., use of cc. [CONTRA- + (CON)CEPTION]

co·ntract[1], n. Agreement between parties, States, &c.; business agreement for supply of goods or performance of work at fixed price; agreement enforceable by law (NUDE *c.*); accepted promise to do or forbear; formal agreement for marriage; conveyance of property; *c. bridge,* a form of auction bridge. [OF, f. L *contractus* *-ūs* (as foll.)]

contra·ct[2], v.t. & i. Enter into business or legal engagement (*to* do, *for* do*ing, for* piece of work, or abs.); *c.* one*self out of, c. out of,* or abs. *c. out,* c. for exemption or exclusion from provisions of (law &c.); *c.* (enter into) *marriage*; form (friendship, habit); incur (debt); draw together (muscles, brow, &c.); make smaller, whence **contracti**BI·LITY n., **contra·ct-**

IBLE a.; restrict, confine, (lit. & fig.); (Gram.) shorten (word) by combination or elision; shrink, become smaller; (p.p.) narrow, mean, (of ideas &c.). [f. L CON-(*trahere tract-* draw)]

contra·ctile (-īl, -ĭl), a. Capable of or producing contraction, as *c. muscles, metal, force.* So **contracti·lITY** n. [F (as prec., see -ILE)]

contra·ction, n. Shrinking, contracting; restriction, confinement; shortening of word by combination or elision; contracted word; contracting (*of* debt, disease, habit). [F, f. L *contractio* (as prec., see -ION)]

contra·ctive, a. Serving to contract. [-IVE]

contra·ctor, n. Undertaker of contract; contracting muscle. [L (as CONTRACT², -OR²)]

contra·ctual, a. Of (the nature of) a contract. [as CONTRACT¹ + -AL]

contrad·ict, v.t. Deny (statement); deny the words of (person); be contrary to, as *these rumours c. each other.* Hence or cogn. **contradi·ctABLE** a., **contradi·ctOR²** n. [f. L CONTRA(*dicere dict-* say)]

contradi·ction, n. Denial; opposition; statement contradicting another; inconsistency; *c. in terms,* plainly self-contradictory statement or words, as '*almost quite ready*' *is a c. in terms.* [F, f. L *contradictionem* (as prec., -ION)]

contradi·ctious, a. Inclined to contradict; disputatious. Hence **contradi·ctiousLY²** adv., **contradi·ctiousNESS** n. [-IOUS]

contradi·ctory, a. & n. Making denial; mutually opposed or inconsistent; contradictious; (n.) contradictory assertion. Hence **contradi·ctoriLY²** adv., **contradi·ctoriNESS** n. [f. L *contradictorius* (as prec., see -ORY)]

contradisti·nction, n. Distinction by contrast. [CONTRA-]

contradisti·nguish, v.t. Distinguish (things, one *from* another) by contrast. [CONTRA-]

contrā·lto, n. & a. (Part, singer, voice) next above alto. [It. (CONTRA- + ALTO)]

contraposi·tion, n. Opposition, contrast; (Logic) a mode of conversion (*if all A is B, then by c. all not-B is not-A, or no not-B is A*). So **contrapo·sitIVE** a. [f. L *contrapositio* (as foll., see -ION)]

contra·ption, n. (slang). Queer machine, makeshift contrivance. [perh. f. *contrive,* cf. *conceive, -ception*]

contrapu·ntal, a. Of, according to rules of, counterpoint. [f. It. *contra(p)punto* COUNTERPOINT + -AL]

contrapu·ntist, n. One skilled in counterpoint. [f. It. *contra(p)puntista* (as prec., -IST)]

contrār·iant, a. Opposed (*to*). [F, f. med. L *contrariare* (as CONTRARY), see -ANT]

contrari·ety (-tra-), n. Opposition in nature, quality, or action; disagreement, inconsistency. [f. OF *contrarieté* f. LL *contrarietatem* (as CONTRARY, see -TY)]

contrār·ious, a. (archaic). Opposed; perverse; (of things) adverse. [f. OF *contrarios* f. med. L *contrariosus* (as prec., see -OUS)]

co·ntrariwise (*also* kontrār·-), adv. On the other hand; in the opposite way; perversely. [foll. + -WISE]

co·ntrary (see below), a., n., adv. Opposed in nature or tendency (*to*); (of wind) impeding, unfavourable; *the* opposite (of two things); (pop., pron. kontrār·ĭ) perverse, self-willed, whence **contrār·iNESS** n.; opposite in position or direction; (n.) *the* opposite; *on the c.* (corroborating a denial expressed or understood, as *Have you nearly done?—On the c., I have only just begun*); *interpret by cc.,* understand Yes for No &c.; *to the c.,* to the opposite effect, as *there is no evidence to the c.*; (adv.) in opposition *to,* as *act c. to nature.* Hence **co·ntrariLY²** adv. [f. OF *contrarie* f. L *contrarius* (CONTRA, see -ARY¹)]

contra·st¹, v.t. & i. Set (two things, one *with* another) in opposition, so as to show their differences; (intr.) show striking difference on comparison (*with*). [f. OF *contraster* (=It. *contrastare*) f. L CONTRA-(*stare* stand)]

co·ntrast², n. Juxtaposition (esp. of forms, colours, &c.) showing striking differences (*between*; *in c. with*); thing showing such a difference (*to*). [f. F *contraste* f. It. *contrasto* (see prec.)]

co·ntrate, a. *C. wheel,* one with teeth at right angles to its plane. [CONTRA- + -ATE²]

contravalla·tion, n. Chain of redoubts and breastworks placed by besiegers between their camp and the town. [f. F *contrevallation* (CONTRA-, see CIRCUMVALLATION)]

contrave·ne, v.t. Infringe (law); dispute (statement); (of things) conflict with. [f. F *contrevenir* f. L CONTRA(*venire vent-* come)]

contrave·ntion, n. Infringement (*in c. of,* violating). [F (as prec., see -ION)]

contretemps (kŏ·ntretŏng, or as F), n. Unlucky accident; hitch.

contri·bute, v.t. & i. Pay, furnish, (*to* common fund &c.); (intr.) *c. to,* help to bring about. [f. L CON(*tribuere, -ut-* bestow)]

contribu·tion, n. Act of contributing; thing, help, literary article, contributed; imposition levied for support of army in the field; *lay under c.,* exact cc. from. [F, f. L *contributionem* (as prec., see -ION)]

contri·butor, n. One who contributes (esp. literary articles). [f. AF *contributour* (as CONTRIBUTE, see -OR²)]

contri·butory, a. & n. That contributes

(*c. negligence*, of injured person who has failed to take proper precautions against accident); (n.) person liable, when a company fails, to share in paying off its debts. [CONTRIBUTE, -ORY]

co·ntrīte, a. Broken in spirit by sense of sin, completely penitent; (of actions) showing a c. spirit. Hence **co·ntrite**LY[2] adv. [f. F *contrit* f. L CON(*terere trit-* rub) bruise]

contri·tion, n. Being contrite, penitence. [f. OF *contriciun* f. L *contritionem* (prec., -ION)]

contri·vance, n. Act of contriving; deceitful practice; invention; mechanical device; inventive capacity. [-ANCE]

contrī·ve, v.t. Invent, devise; bring to pass, manage, (thing, *to* do; also of undesired event, as *c. to make matters worse*); (abs.) manage household affairs (*well* &c.), whence **contri·**VER[1] n. Hence **contri·v**ABLE a. [f. OF CON(*trover* find f. L *turbare* disturb, stir up)]

contrō·l, n. Power of directing, command; restraint; means of restraint, check; standard of comparison for checking inferences deduced from experiment; (Spirit.) personality actuating a medium; station at which aeroplanes, motors, &c., in races are allowed time to stop for overhauling &c.; (pl.) various devices in aeroplanes used to assist stability in turning &c. [perh. f. F *contrôle* for *contrerolle* copy of a roll f. med. L CONTRA(*rotulus* see ROLL); but prob. f. foll.]

contrō·l[2], v.t. (-ll-). Dominate, command; hold in check (*oneself*, one's anger); check, verify. Hence **contrō·ll**ABLE a., **contro·l**MENT n. [f. F *contrôler* OF *contreroller* keep copy of roll of accounts (as prec.)]

contrō·ller, n. In vbl senses; also one who checks expenditure, steward, esp. of royal household, Mint, Navy, &c. (often spelt *compt-*). Hence **contro·ller**SHIP n. [f. OF *contre-rolleor* (as prec., see -OR[2]); spelling *compt-* by confus. w. obs. *compte* count]

controver·sial, a. Of, open to, given to, controversy. Hence **controver·sial**ISM, **controver·sial**IST, nn., **controver·sial**LY[2] adv. [f. L *controversialis* (as foll., -AL)]

co·ntroversy, n. Disputation; *without, beyond, c.*, unquestionably. [f. L *controversia* (as foll., see -Y[1])]

co·ntrovert (*also* -ver·t), v.t. Dispute about, discuss; dispute, deny. Hence **co·ntrovert**IST n. [f. L *controversus* turned against, opposed (*contro-* against +p.p. of *vertere* turn) whence **controvertere* was assumed]

contūmā·cious, a. Insubordinate, disobedient, esp. to order of court. Hence or cogn. **contuma·cious**LY[2] adv., **contuma·cious**NESS, **co·ntum**ACY, nn. [f. L CON(*tumax -acis* perh. f. *tumēre* swell or *temnere* despise), see -ACIOUS]

contumē·lious, a. Opprobrious; insolent. Hence **contume·lious**LY[2] adv. [f. OF *contumélieus* f. L *contumeliosus* (as foll., see -OUS)]

co·ntūmely (-mĭ-), n. Insolent, reproachful, language or treatment; disgrace. [f. OF *contumelie* f. L *contumelia* (cf. CONTUMACIOUS)]

contu·se (-z), v.t. Injure by blow without breaking skin, bruise. So **contu·**SION n. [f. L CON(*tundere tus-* thump)]

conu·ndrum, n. Riddle; hard question. [?]

convale·sce (-ĕs), v.i. Regain health. [f. L CON(*valescere* incept. of *valēre* be well)]

convale·scent, a. & n. (Person) recovering from sickness; *c. hospital* (for cc.). So **convale·**SCENCE n. [as prec., see -ENT]

conve·ction, n. Transportation of heat or electricity, by movement of heated or electrified substance. [f. L *convectio* f. CON(*vehere vect-* carry), see -ION]

convenance (F), n. (usu. pl.). Conventional propriety.

conve·ne, v.t. & i. Assemble (t. & i.); convoke (assembly); summon (person *before* tribunal). Hence **convē·n**ABLE a. [f. F *convenir* f. L CON(*venire vent-* come) assemble, agree, fit]

convē·nience, n. Suitableness, commodiousness; material advantage, as *marriage of c.*; personal comfort, as *at your c.*, in a way, at a time, convenient to you; advantage, as *a great c.*; *make a c. of* one, utilize him unconscionably, abuse his good nature; useful appliance; water-closet; (archaic) vehicle; (pl.) material comforts. [f. L *convenientia* (as prec., see -ENCE)]

conve·nient, a. Suitable, commodious; not troublesome, as *if it is c. to you.* Hence **conve·nient**LY[2] adv. [as CONVENE, see -ENT]

co·nvent, n. Religious community (usu. women, cf. MONASTERY) living together; building occupied by this. [f. AF *covent* (cf. *Covent Garden*) f. OF *convent* f. L *conventus -ūs* (as prec.)]

conve·nticle, n. (hist.). Clandestine religious meeting, esp. of Nonconformists or Dissenters; building used for this. [f. L *conventiculum* (place of) assembly, dim. as prec.]

conve·ntion, n. Act of convening; formal assembly, esp. (Eng. Hist.) of Parliament without summons of King, 1660 & 1688; agreement between parties; general (often tacit) consent; practice based on this. [F, f. L *conventionem* (as CONVENE, see -ION)]

conve·ntional, a. Depending on convention, not natural, not spontaneous; (Art) following traditions. Hence **conve·ntional**ISM, **conve·ntional**IST, **con-**

ventiona·lITY, nn., **conve·ntional**IZE v.t., **conve·ntionally**[2] adv. [f. L *conventionalis* (as prec., -AL)]
conve·ntionary, a. & n. (Tenant, tenure) on terms orig. fixed by convention, not by custom. [f. med. L *conventionarius* (as prec., -ARY[1])]
conve·ntual, a. & n. (Member, inmate) of a convent; (member) of the less strict branch of Franciscans, living in large convents. [f. med. L *conventualis* (as CONVENT, see -AL)]
conver·ge, v.i. & t. (Of lines) tend to meet in a point (also fig.); (Math., of series) approximate in some of its terms towards a definite limit; (trans.) cause to c. So **conver·g**ENCE, -ENCY, nn., **conver·g**ENT a. [f. LL CON(*vergere* VERGE)]
conver·sable, a. Easy, pleasant, in conversation; fit for social intercourse. Hence **conver·sable**NESS n., **conver·sably**[2] adv. [F, f. med. L *conversabilis* (as foll., see -BLE)]
co·nversance, -cy, n. Familiarity, acquaintance, (*with*). [as foll., see -ANCE]
co·nversant, a. Having frequent intercourse, well acquainted, (*with* person, subject, &c.); (of things) concerned (*in, about, with*). [f. L *conversari* CONVERSE[1], see -ANT]
conversa·tion, n. Talk, whence **conversa·tion**IST n.; *c.* (*piece*), kind of genre painting of group of figures; sexual intercourse, as *criminal c.* (*crim. con.*, cf. CONNEXION). [OF, f. L *conversationem* (as prec., see -ATION)]
conversa·tional, a. Fond of, good at, pertaining to, conversation. Hence **conversa·tional**IST n., **conversa·tionally**[2] adv. [-AL]
conversaziō·nĕ (-āts-), n. (pl. *-nes, -ni* pron. -nē). Soirée given by learned or art society. [It., f. L as CONVERSATION]
conver·se[1], v.i. Talk (*with* person, *on, about,* subject). [f. F *converser* f. L *conversari* keep company (with), frequent. as CONVERT[1]]
co·nverse[2], n. (archaic). Discourse; intercourse. [f. prec.]
co·nverse[3], a. & n. Opposite, contrary; (Logic) converted proposition; form of words produced by transposition of some terms of another (*he had learning without wealth* is the c. of *he had wealth without learning*); (Math.) *this proposition is the c. of the former* (assumes its conclusion & proves its datum). Hence **conver·sely**[2] adv. [as CONVERT[1]]
conver·sion, n. Transposition, inversion, esp. (Logic) of subject & predicate (*if no A is B, then by c. no B is A*); bringing over (*to* an opinion, party, faith, &c.); turning of sinners to God; changing (*to, into*); change (of debentures, stocks, &c.) into others of different character. [F, f. L *conversionem* (as foll., see -ION)]
conver·t[1], v.t. Change (*into*); cause to turn (*to* opinion, faith, &c.), cf. PERVERT; turn to godliness; (Stocks &c.) see prec.; (Logic) see prec. [f. L CON(*vertere vers-* turn) turn about]
co·nvert[2], n. Person converted, esp. to religious faith or life. [f. prec.]
conver·tible, a. That may be converted; *c. terms,* synonymous; (of paper-money) exchangeable for specie; *c. husbandry,* rotation of crops. Hence **converti**BI·LITY n., **conver·tibly**[2] adv. [F, f. LL *convertibilis* (as prec., see -BLE)]
co·nvex, a. Curved like the outside of circle or sphere (cf. CONCAVE). Hence or cogn. **conve·x**ITY n., **co·nvexly**[2] adv. [f. L *convexus* prob. =*convectus* p.p. of CON(*vehere* bring)]
convexo- in comb. Convex and —, as *c.-concave.* [as prec., see -O-]
convey· (-ā), v.t. Transport, carry; transmit (sound, smell, &c.); impart, communicate, (idea, meaning); (Law) make over (property *to*, or abs.). Hence **convey·**ABLE a. [f. OF CON*veier,* mod. *convoyer* (*veie, voie,* f. L *via* way)]
convey·ance, n. Carrying; transmission; communication (of ideas &c.); (document effecting) transference of property; carriage, vehicle. [-ANCE]
convey·ancer, n. Lawyer who prepares documents for conveyance of property. [-ER[1]]
convey·ancing, n. Work of prec. [-ING[1]]
co·nvict[1], n. Condemned criminal undergoing penal servitude. Hence **co·nvict**ISM(3) n. [f. obs. adj. *convict* (as foll.)]
convi·ct[2], v.t. Prove guilty (*of* offence); declare guilty by verdict of jury or decision of judge; impress (person) with sense of error. Hence **convi·ct**IVE a. [f. L CON(*vincere vict-* conquer)]
convi·ction, n. Proving or finding guilty; *summary c.* (by judge or magistrates without jury); act of convincing; settled belief; (Theol.) awakened consciousness of sin. [f. L *convictio* (as prec., see -ION)]
convi·nce, v.t. Firmly persuade (*of, that*; esp. pass.); produce in (person) a moral conviction (*of* sin &c.). Hence **convi·nce**MENT, **convi·ncing**NESS, nn., **convi·ncingly**[2] adv. [as CONVICT[2]]
convi·ncible, a. Open to conviction. [as prec., see -IBLE]
convi·vial, a. Of, befitting, a feast; festive, jovial. Hence **convi·vial**IST, **convivia·l**ITY, nn., **convi·vially**[2] adv. [f. L *convivialis* f. *convivium* feast f. *conviva* fellow feaster f. CON(*vivere* live)]
convoca·tion, n. Calling together; assembly; (Ch. of Eng.) synod of clergy of province of Canterbury or York; legislative assembly of Oxford or Durham Univ. Hence **convoca·tional** a. [f. L *convocatio* (as foll., -ATION)]
convo·ke, v.t. Call together, summon to assemble. [f. L *convoquer* f. F CON(*vocare* call)]

co·nvolute, a. & n. (bot., conch.). Rolled together, coiled; (n.) coil. [as CONVOLVE]
convolu·ted, a. (zool.). Coiled, twisted. [f. vb *convolute* (as prec.) otherwise rare]
convolu·tion, n. Coiling, twisting; fold, twist. [as foll., see -ION]
convo·lve, v.t. & i. Roll together, roll up, (esp. in p.p.). [f. L CON(*volvere volut-* roll)]
convo·lvŭlus, n. (pl. *-luses*). Genus of plants including bindweed. [L, as prec. with dim. suf.]
convoy·[1], v.t. (Of ship of war) escort (merchant or passenger vessel); escort with armed force; (archaic) conduct (guests, lady, &c.). [f. F as CONVEY]
co·nvoy[2], n. Act of convoying; protection; escort (for honour or protection); company, supply of provisions, &c., under escort; number of merchant ships under escort or able to defend themselves. [f. F *convoi* (as prec.)]
convu·lse, v.t. Shake violently (lit. & fig.); throw into convulsions (usu. pass.); cause to be violently seized with laughter (usu. pass.). [f. L CON(*vellere vuls-* pull)]
convu·lsion, n. Violent irregular motion of limb or body due to involuntary contraction of muscles (usu. pl., & esp. as a disorder of infants); (pl.) violent fit of laughter; violent social or political agitation; violent physical disturbance. Hence **convu·lsion**ARY[1] a. [f. L *convulsio* (as prec., see -ION)]
convu·lsive, a. Attended or affected with, producing, convulsions (lit. & fig.). Hence **convu·lsive**LY[2] adv. [CONVULSE, -IVE]
co·ny, -ney, n. Rabbit (now used only in statutes &c., & as shop name for the fur); (bibl.) small pachyderm of Palestine living in clefts of rocks, hyrax; (archaic) *c.-catcher,* sharper. [sing. f. pl. *conies* f. OF *coniz* pl. of *conil* f. L *cuniculus* rabbit, etym. dub.; formerly pron. kŭ-]
coo, v.i. & t., & n. (Make) soft murmuring sound of or as of doves & pigeons; *bill & c.,* converse amorously; say cooingly. [imit.]
coo·ee, coo·ey, n. Sound adopted as signal by Australian colonists from the aborigines.
cŏŏk[1], n. One whose business is to cook food; *too many cc. spoil the broth,* one director is enough; *c.-house,* camp kitchen, outdoor kitchen in warm countries, (on ship, also *c.-room*) galley; *c.-shop,* eating-house. [OE *coc* f. L *coquus*]
cŏŏk[2], v.t. & i. Prepare (food or abs.) by heat; (intr.) undergo cooking; (also *c. up*) concoct (fig.); (colloq.) tamper with (accounts &c.); (slang, of exertion &c.) exhaust (runner &c., esp. in p.p.); *c. his goose,* do for him, settle his hash. [prec.]
coo·ker, n. Cooking-apparatus, -stove; vessel food is cooked in; fruit &c. that cooks well; one who cooks (accounts &c.) or concocts. [-ER[1]]
coo·kery, n. Art, practice, of cooking; *c.-book* (dealing with c.). [-ERY]
cŏŏ·kie, n. (Sc.) plain bun; (U.S.) small flat cake. [prob. f. Du. *koekje* dim. of *koek* cake]
coo·ky, n. (colloq.). (Usu. female) cook. [-Y[3]]
cōōl[1], a. & n. Moderately cold; (Hunt.) *c. scent* (faint, weak); unexcited, calm; lacking zeal, lukewarm; wanting cordiality; calmly audacious, as *a c. hand* (person); (complacently or emphat. of large sums of money) *it cost me a c. thousand*; (n.) c. air, c. place, coolness; *c.-headed,* not easily excited; *c. tankard,* cooling drink of wine, water, lemon-juice, &c. Hence **coo·l**ISH[1] a., **coo·l**LY[2] (-l-lĭ) adv., **coo·l**NESS n. [OE *cól* f. OTeut. *kôluz* (*kal-* =L *gel-* cold)]
cool[2], v.i. & t. Become cool (lit. & fig.; also *c. down*); make cool (lit. & fig.); *c.* one's COPPERS; *c.* one's *heels,* be kept waiting. [OE *cólian* f. OTeut. *kôlôjan* (as prec.)]
coo·ler, n. Vessel in which a thing is cooled, as *wine, butter, -c.* [-ER[1]]
cōō·lie, -ly, n. Indian or Chinese hired labourer. Hence **coo·lie**ISM(3) n. [f. Hind. *quli*]
coomb, combe, (kōōm), n. Valley on flank of hill; short valley running up from coast. [OE *cumb,* etym. dub.]
cōōn, n. (U.S.). =RACOON; sly fellow; *gone c.,* one whose case is hopeless. [abbr.]
cōōp[1], n. Basket placed over sitting or fattening fowls; fowl-run; basket used in catching fish. [=ME *cupe* basket; cf. G *kufe* cask]
coop[2], v.t. Put in coop; confine (persons; also *c. up, in*). [f. prec.]
coo·per[1], n., & v.t. Maker of casks for dry goods (*dry c.*) or liquids (*wet c.*); *white c.,* maker of pails, tubs, &c.; (on ship) repairer of casks &c.; (also *wine-c.*) one who samples, bottles, or retails wine; equal mixture of stout & porter; (v.t.) repair (cask), stow in casks, furbish *up.* [vb f. n. f. med. L *cuparius* (as prec., -ARY[1])]
cooper[2], see COPER[2].
coo·perage, n. Cooper's work or workshop. So **coo·per**Y(3) n. [-AGE]
co(-)ŏ·perate, v.i. Work together (*with* person *in* a work, *to* an end); (of things) concur in producing an effect. So **co-o·per**ANT a. & n., **co-o·perat**OR[2] n. [f. L CO(*operari* f. *opus operis* work), see -ATE[3]]
co-opera·tion, n. Working together to same end; (Pol. Econ.) co-operative combination. [f. L *cooperatio* (as prec., see -ION)]
co-o·perative, a. Of, tending to, co-operation; (Pol. Econ.) *c. society* (for production or distribution of goods, profits

being shared by members), *c. store* (belonging to c. society). Hence **co-o·perative**LY[2] adv. [as CO-OPERATE, see -IVE]

co-o·pt, v.t. Elect into body by votes of existing members. So **co-opt**A·TION n. [f. L co(*optare* choose)]

co(-)or·dinate[1] (*-at*), a. & n. Equal in rank, esp. (Gram.) of clauses of compound sentence (cf. SUBORDINATE); consisting of c. things; (n.) c. thing, esp. (Math.) each of a system of magnitudes used to fix position of point, line, or plane. Hence **co-or·dinate**LY[2] adv. [f. CO- + L *ordinare* (*ordo -inis* order), see -ATE[2]]

co-or·dināte[2], v.t. Make co-ordinate; bring (parts) into proper relation. Hence **co-ordin**A·TION n., **co-or·dinat**IVE a. [prec., -ATE[3]]

cōōt, n. Name of several swimming & diving birds, esp. the *Bald C.*, web-footed bird with base of bill extended to form white plate on forehead, whence *bald as a c.* [ME *cote* = Du. *koet*, etym. dub.]

cop[1], n. (spinning). Conical ball of thread wound upon spindle. [OE *cop* top]

cop[2], n. (slang). Policeman. [cf. foll., COPPER[2]]

cop[3], v.t. (slang). Catch. [etym. dub.]

copai·ba, -va, (-pī-, -pā-), n. Aromatic balsam used in medicine & the arts. [(*-ba*) Sp., f. Braz. *cupauba*]

cō·pal, n. Kinds of resin used for varnish. [Sp., f. Mex. *copalli* incense]

copar·cenary, -ery, copar·cener, nn. = PARCENARY, PARCENER. [CO-]

copar·tner, n. Partner, sharer, associate. Hence **copar·tner**SHIP n. (*labour c.-ship*, system designed to interest workmen in their business by means of profit-sharing). [CO-]

copar·tnery, n. Copartnership. [f. prec., see -ERY(2)]

cope[1], n. (Eccl.) long cloak worn by ecclesiastics in processions; (fig.) *c.* (cloak) *of night*, *c.* (canopy) *of heaven*; (Founding) outer portion of mould; = COPING; *c.-stone*, head stone of building, finishing touch. [f. med. L *capa* CAP]

cope[2], v.t. & i. Furnish with a cope; cover (wall &c.) with COPING; cover as with a vault; (intr.) *c. over*, project like a coping. [f. prec.]

cope[3], v.i. Contend evenly, grapple successfully, *with* (person, task). [f. F *couper* strike (COUP)]

cō·peck, n. Russian copper coin (about a farthing). [f. Russ. *kopeika* dim. of *kopyé* lance]

cō·per[1], n. (Also *horse-c.*), horse-dealer. [f. obs. *cope* buy, barter (as foll.)]

cō·per[2], **coo·per**[2] (kō-), n. Floating grog-shop for North Sea fishers. [f. Flem. & Du. *kooper* f. *koopen* buy (cf. CHEAP)]

Coper·nican, a. *C. system, theory*, (that the planets, including earth, move round sun). [f. *Copernicus* latinized f. *Koppernik*, astronomer (d. 1543) + -AN]

co·ping, n. Top (usu. sloping) course of masonry in wall; overhanging ledge protecting wall-fruit; *c.-stone* (used for c.). [COPE[2] + -ING[1]]

cō·pious, a. Plentiful; abounding in information; profuse in speech; (of languages) having large vocabulary. Hence **co·pious**LY[2] adv., **co·pious**NESS n. [f. L *copiosus* (*copia* plenty, see -OUS)]

co·pper[1], n. & a. Reddish malleable ductile metal; bronze (formerly c.) coin, penny, halfpenny, farthing; cooking or laundry boiler of iron or c.; *hot cc.*, mouth & throat parched by drinking, *cool* one's *cc.* (by drinking); *c.-bit*, soldering tool pointed with c.; *c.-bottom* v.t., sheathe bottom of (ship) with c. (esp. in p.p.); *c. captain*, sham captain; *c. Indian*, red Indian of N. America; *copperhead*, venomous American snake; *copperplate*, polished c. plate for engraving or etching, print from this, (adj., of writing) neat; *c.-smith*, one who works in c.; (v.t.) cover (ship's bottom &c.) with c. Hence **co·pper**Y[2] a. (esp., c.-coloured). [(vb f. n.) OE *coper* f. pop. L *cuprum*, L *Cyprium* (*aes*), Cyprian metal]

co·pper[2], n. (slang). Policeman. [cf. COP[2]]

co·pperas (*-as*), n. Proto-sulphate of iron, green vitriol. [f. med. L *cup(e)rosa* perh. = *aqua cuprosa* copper water]

co·ppice, n. Small wood of underwood & small trees, grown for periodical cutting; *c.-wood*, underwood. [f. OF *copeïz* f. LL **colpaticium* f. *colpare* cut (*colpus* f. L f. Gk *kolaphos* blow, cuff)]

cŏ·pra, n. Dried kernels of coco-nut. [Port., prob. f. Malayalam *koppara* coconut]

cŏ·pro- in comb. = Gk *kopros* dung, as: *-lite*, fossil dung, so *-li·tic* a.; *-logy*, treatment of filthy subjects in literature &c.; *-phagous*, (of beetles) dung-eating.

copse, n., & v.t. = COPPICE; *copsewood*, underwood; (v.t.) treat as copsewood, cover with cc. Hence **co·psy**[2] a. [syncop. form of COPPICE]

Copt, n. Native Egyptian Christian of Jacobite sect of Monophysites. [f. Copt. *gyptios, kyptaios*, f. Gk *Aiguptios* Egyptian]

Co·ptic, a. & n. (Language) of the Copts. [-IC]

cŏ·pula, n. (Logic, Gram.) verb *be* (as mere sign of predication); (Anat.) connecting part (bone, cartilage, ligament); (Mus.) short connecting passage. Hence **co·pul**AR[1] a. [L (CO- + *ap-* fasten + dim. suf.)]

cŏ·pulate, v.i. Unite sexually. Hence **co·pulat**ORY a. [f. L *copulare* fasten together (prec.), see -ATE[3]]

copula·tion, n. Sexual union; grammatical or logical connexion. [F, f. L *copulationem* (as prec., see -ION)]

co·pulative, a. & n. Serving to connect;

(Gram.) connecting words or clauses that are connected in sense (cf. DISJUNCTIVE), also, connecting subject & predicate; (Zool., Anat.) relating to sexual union; (n.) c. conjunction or particle. Hence **co·pulative**LY² adv. [F (*-if*, *-ive*), f. L *copulativus* (as prec., see -IVE)]

cŏ·py¹, n. Reproduction (of writing, picture, &c.); imitation; page written after model (of penmanship); (Law) transcript of manorial court-roll, containing entries of admissions of tenants to land hence called COPYHOLD; written or printed specimen (of book &c.); *rough, foul, c.*, original draft; *fair, clean, c.* (transcribed from rough c.); *c. of verses*, short set as school exercise; *fair c.*, model version of this; model to be copied; manuscript or matter to be printed (*incident* &c. *will make good c.*, lends itself to interesting narration in newspapers &c.); *c.-book*, one containing cc. for learners to imitate; *c.-book maxims, morality* (commonplace). [f. F *copie* f. L *copia* abundance, in phr. *dare copiam legendi* give the power of reading, i.e., give a copy]

co·py², v.t. & i. Transcribe (*from* original), whence **co·py**IST n.; make copy of; imitate; crib from neighbour in examination. [f. F *copier* f. med. L *copiare* (as prec.)]

co·pyhold, n. & a. Tenure by COPY¹; (land) so held. Hence **co·pyhold**ER¹ n.

co·pyright, n. & a., & v.t. Exclusive right given by law for term of years to author, designer, &c., or his assignee to print, publish, or sell, copies of his original work; (adj.) protected by c. (of books &c.); (v.t.) secure c. for (book &c.).

coque·t¹ (-k-), a. Coquettish. [F (orig. noun, dim. of *coq* cock)]

coquĕ·t², **coque·tte,** (-k-), v.i. (-tt-). Play the coquette; flirt (*with*); dally, trifle, *with* (matter, proposal, &c.). [f. F *coqueter* f. prec.]

cō·quetry, n. Coquettish behaviour or act; (fig.) trifling; attractive prettiness as result of art. [f. F *coquetterie* (*coqueter*, as prec.; see -ERY)]

coque·tte, n. Woman who trifles with man's affections; crested humming-bird. Hence **coque·tt**ISH¹ a., **coque·ttish**LY² adv. [F, fem. of COQUET]

coqui·to (-kē-), n. Chilian palm-tree yielding palm-honey. [Sp., dim. of *coco* coco-nut]

cor-, pref. = COM- before *r*.

cŏ·racle, n. Wicker boat covered with watertight material used on Welsh & Irish lakes & rivers. [f. W *cwrwgl* f. *cwrwg* = Ir. *curach* boat]

cŏ·raco- in comb. (anat.). Of the *coracoid process* (beak-shaped process extending from shoulder-blade towards breastbone). [f. Gk *korax -akos* crow]

cŏ·ral, n. & a. Hard calcareous substance (red, pink, white, &c.) secreted by many tribes of marine polyps for support & habitation; *c.-reef*, accumulation of this; toy of polished c. for children cutting teeth; unimpregnated roe of lobster; (adj.) like coral, esp. red; *c.-island* (formed by growth of coral); *c.-rag*, limestone containing beds of petrified cc. [OF, f. L *corallum* f. Gk *korallion*]

coralli- in comb. Coral, as *-ferous, -form*, bearing, shaped like, coral. [as prec., see -I-]

co·ralline¹, n. Genus of seaweeds with calcareous jointed stem; (pop.) name of various plant-like compound animals; *c. zone* of sea-depths, that in which these abound. [f. It. *corallina* dim. of *corallo* CORAL]

co·ralline² (-ī-, -ĭ-), a. Coral-red; *c. ware*, Italian red-paste pottery (17th–18th c.); like, composed of, coral. [f. L *corallinus* (CORAL, -INE¹)]

co·rallite, n. Fossil coral; coral skeleton of polyp; coralline marble. [-ITE¹]

co·ralloid, a. & n. (Organism) like, akin to, coral. [-OID]

cor·ăm, prep. In the presence of (*judice*, a judge, *populo*, the public, &c.). [L]

cor·bel, n., & v.t. & i. (-ll-). (Arch.) projection of stone, timber, &c., jutting out from wall to support weight, whence **cor·bell**ED² a.; (also *c.-block*) short timber laid on wall or pier longitudinally under beam; *c.-table*, projecting course resting on cc.; (v.t. & i.) *c. out, off*, (cause to) project on cc. [(vb f. n.) OF, f. LL *corvellus* dim. of *corvus* raven]

cor·bie, n. (Sc.). Raven; carrion crow; *c.-steps*, step-like projections on sloping sides of gable. [f. OF *corb* CORBEL + -Y³]

cord, n., & v.t. Thin rope, thick string; (Anat.) cord-like structure in animal body, as SPINAL, UMBILICAL, *c.*, VOCAL *cc.*; cord-like rib on cloth; ribbed cloth, esp. corduroy; *cc.*, corduroy breeches or trousers; measure of cut wood (usu. 128 cub. ft); (fig.) *cc. of discipline, fourfold c. of evidence*, &c.; (v.t.) bind with c. [(vb f. n.) f. F *corde* f. L f. Gk *khordē* gut, string of musical instrument]

cor·dage (-ĭj), n. Cords, ropes, esp. in rigging of ship. [F (as prec. + -AGE)]

cor·date, a. Heart-shaped. [f. L *cor cordis* heart, see -ATE²]

cor·ded, a. Bound with cords; furnished with cords; (of cloth &c.) ribbed. [-ED²,¹]

cordelier· (-lēr), n. Franciscan friar of strict rule (wearing knotted cord round waist). [F (*cordelle* dim. as CORD, see -IER)]

cor·dial, a. & n. (Medicine, food, drink) that stimulates the heart, esp. (Commerc.) aromatized & sweetened spirit; hearty, sincere; warm, friendly, whence

cordia·lity[1] n., **cor·dially**[2] adv. [f. med. L *cordialis* (*cor cordis* heart, -AL)]
cordiller·a (-lyāra), n. Mountain ridge (one of parallel series), esp. of the Andes & same system in Central America & Mexico. [Sp.]
cor·dite, n. A smokeless explosive. [f. CORD (from its appearance) + -ITE[1](2)]
cor·don, n. Projecting course of stone in wall; chain of military posts; line or circle of police &c.; (also *sanitary c.*) guarded line between infected & uninfected districts; ornamental cord or braid; (pron. as F) ribbon of knightly order (*c. bleu* facet., first-class cook); fruit-tree pruned to grow as single stem. [F (as CORD, see -OON)]
cor·dovan, a. & n. (Leather) of Cordova. [f. Sp. *cordovan(o)*]
corduroy·, n. & a. Coarse thick ribbed cotton stuff, worn chiefly by labourers; (pl.) c. trousers; (U.S.) *c. road,* of tree-trunks laid across swamp. [perh. f. F **corde du roi* king's cord]
cor·dwain, n. (archaic). Spanish leather formerly used for shoes. [f. OF *cordoan* CORDOVAN]
cor·dwainer, n. Shoemaker (now only as guild-name &c.). [f. OF *cordoanier*, as prec.]
core, n., & v.t. Horny capsule containing seeds of apple, pear, &c.; central part cut out (esp. of rock in boring); bar of soft iron forming centre of electro-magnet or induction coil; central strand of rope; innermost part, as (fig.) *rotten at the c., English to the c.*; heart; a disease, tumour, in sheep; (v.t.) remove c. from, whence **cor·ER**[1](2) n. Hence **core·LESS** a. [?]
co-rela·tion. See CORRELATION.
co-reli·gionist, n. Adherent of same religion. [-IST]
cŏrĕo·psis, n. Plant with rayed usu. yellow flowers. [mod. L, f. Gk *koris* bug, *opsis* appearance, w. ref. to shape of seed]
co-respo·ndent, n. Person proceeded against together with the RESPONDENT in divorce suit.
corf, n. Large basket formerly used in mining; basket in which fish are kept alive in water. [cf. Du. *korf*, G *korb*, perh. f. L *corbis*]
cŏriā·ceous, a. Like leather, leathery. [f. L *coriaceus* (*corium* leather, see -ACEOUS)]
cŏria·nder, n. Annual plant with aromatic fruit (pop. called *c. seed*) used for flavouring. [F, f. L *coriandrum* f. Gk *koriannon*]
Cori·nthian, a. & n. (Native) of Corinth; (archaic) man of fashion & pleasure; *Epistles to the Cc.*, books in N.T.; (Arch.) *C. order,* one of the three Grecian ORDERS, having bell-shaped capital with rows of acanthus leaves, whence **Corinthian-E·SQUE** a. [f. L f. Gk *Korinthios* (*Korinthos*) + -AN]
cork, n. & a., & v.t. Bark of cork-oak (*c.-tree*); piece of c. used as float for fishing line &c. (*like a c.*, buoyant, recovering quickly from depression &c.); bottle-stopper of c.; (Bot.) inner division of the bark in higher plants; (adj.) made of c., as *c. jacket* (for supporting person in water); *cork-screw,* steel screw for drawing c. from bottle, *c.-s. curl* (spirally twisted), (v.t. & i.) move spirally; *cork-wood,* name of various light porous woods; (v.t.) stop, stop *up*, (as) with c., blacken with burnt c. [(vb f. n.) f. Sp. *corche* f. L *cortex -icis* bark; or f. Sp. *alcorque*, etym. dub.]
cor·kage (-ĭj), n. Corking, uncorking, of bottles; hotel-keeper's charge for serving wine &c. not supplied by himself. [-AGE]
corked, a. Stopped with, blackened with burnt, cork; (of wine) tasting of cork. [-ED[1]]
cor·ker, n. (slang). Circumstance that precludes further discussion, esp., notable lie. [-ER[1]]
cor·ky, a. Cork-like; (colloq.) frivolous, lively, skittish, restive. [-Y[2]]
corm, n. (bot.) Bulb-like subterraneous stem, solid bulb. [f. Gk *kormos* trunk with boughs lopped off (*keirō* cut)]
cormo- in comb. Trunk, stem, (in terms referring to evolution of races &c.). [as prec.]
cor·morant, n. A voracious sea-bird, 3 ft in length; rapacious person. [f. F *cormoran* f. L *corvus marinus* sea-raven]
corn[1], n. A grain, seed, esp. of cereals (also of pepper &c.); (collect. sing.) grain, also cereal plants while growing; (U.S.) maize, Indian c.; *c.-chandler*, retail dealer in c.; *c.-cob*, part to which grains are attached in ear of maize; *c.-cob pipe* (made of this); *c.-crake*, the bird Landrail; *c.-exchange* (for trade in c.; *c.-factor*, dealer in c.; *c.-flag*, plant of genus Gladiolus; *c.-flour*, fine-ground Indian c., also, flour of rice or other grain; *c.-flower*, name of various plants growing among corn; *c.-laws* (regulating c.-trade, esp. the English laws restricting importation, and repealed in 1846); *c.-rent* (paid in c. or varying with price of c.); *c.-stalk* (colloq.), tall person (applied as nickname to Europeans born in Australia, esp. in N.S.W.). [com.-Teut. f. Aryan **grnóm* (*ger-* wear down), cf. L *granum* grain]
corn[2], v.t. Sprinkle, preserve, with salt (esp. in p.p.). [f. prec.]
corn[3], n. Horny place esp. on feet; *tread on my cc.*, hurt my feelings; *c.-plaster* (for application to cc.). [OF, f. L *cornu* horn]
cor·nbrash, n. (geol.). Coarse calcareous sandstone. [CORN[1] + *brash* rubble, etym. dub.]
cor·nea (-ĭa), n. Transparent horny part of anterior covering of eyeball. [L *cornea* (*tela*) horny (web)]
cor·nel, n. Genus including Cornelian

Cherry & *Common C.* or Dogwood. [ult. f. L *cornus*]

cornē·lian, car-, n. Dull red or reddish-white chalcedony. [f. F *corneline,* etym. dub.]

cor·neous, a. Horn-like, horny. [f. L *corneus* (*cornu* horn) + -OUS]

cor·ner, n., & v.t. & i. Place where converging sides or edges meet; projecting angle, esp. where two streets meet; *turn the c.,* pass round it into another street, (fig.) pass critical point (in illness &c.); *cut off a c.,* avoid it by a short cut; (slang) *the C.,* Tattersall's betting-rooms (orig. near Hyde Park C.); hollow angle enclosed by meeting walls &c.; *put* (child) *in the c.* (as punishment); (fig.) *drive into a c.* (difficult position from which there is no escape); secret or remote place, as *done in a c., hole-&-c. transactions* (underhand); region, quarter, as *all the cc. of the earth*; (Commerc.) buying up the whole of any stock in the market, so as to compel speculative sellers to buy from one to fulfil their engagements, (loosely) any combination to raise price by securing monopoly; *c.-chisel, -punch,* &c. (angular, for cutting, cleaning, &c., cc.); *c.-boy, -man*[1], street rough, loafer; *c.-man*[2] (at either end of row of nigger minstrels, playing bones or tambourine & contributing comic effects); *c.-stone,* one in projecting angle of wall, (fig.) indispensable part, basis; (v.t.) furnish with cc., set in c., drive into c. (esp. fig.), force (dealers) or control (commodity) by means of c.; (v.i.) form c. (*in* commodity). [(vb f. n.) f. OF *cornier* ult. f. L *cornu* horn, see -ARY[1]]

cor·net[1], n. (Also *cornet-à-piston(s), cornopean*) brass musical instrument of trumpet class, with valves or pistons; c.-player, also **cor·net**IST n.; conically-rolled piece of paper for groceries &c.; *solo c., echo c.,* organ-stops. [OF, dim. of *corn, cor,* f. L *cornu* horn]

cor·net[2], n. White head-dress of Sister of Charity; (formerly) fifth commissioned officer in cavalry troop, who carried the colours (from obs. sense *pennon, standard*), whence **cor·net**CY n. [f. F *cornette* dim. of *corne* f. Rom. *corna* f. L *cornua* horns]

cor·nice, n. (Arch.) horizontal moulded projection crowning a building &c., esp. uppermost member of entablature of an order, surmounting frieze; ornamental moulding round wall of room just below ceiling; (Mountaineering) overhanging mass of hardened snow at edge of precipice. Hence **cor·nic**ED[2] a. [F f. It., etym. dub.; L has *corona* cornice, *cornix -icis* crow]

corni·ferous, a. (geol.). Producing or containing hornstone. [f. L *cornifer* horn-bearing (*cornu* horn, see -FEROUS)]

Cor·nish, a. & n. Of Cornwall. (N.) the C. language. [-ISH[1]]

cornō·pean. See CORNET[1].

cor·nstone, n. Mottled red and green limestone, subordinate bed in Old Red Sandstone formation. [CORN[1]]

cornūcō·pia, n. (pl. *-as*). Horn of plenty; goat's horn represented in art as overflowing with flowers, fruit, and corn; ornamental vessel shaped like this; overflowing store, whence **cornuco·pi**AN a. [LL, f. L *cornu copiae* horn of plenty (that of the goat Amalthea by which Zeus was suckled)]

cornu·ted, a. Having horns or horn-like projections. [f. obs. *cornute* f. L *cornutus* (*cornu* horn) + -ED[1]]

cor·ny[1], a. Of, abounding in, corn. [-Y[2]]

cor·ny[2], a. Of, having, corns. [CORN[2] + -Y[2]]

coro·lla, n. (bot.). Whorl of leaves (petals), separate or combined, forming inner envelope of flower. Hence **coroll**A·CEOUS a. [L, dim. of *corona* crown]

coro·llary, n. Proposition appended to one already demonstrated, as self-evident inference from it; immediate deduction; natural consequence, result. [f. L *corollarium* money paid for chaplet, gratuity, neut. adj. f. prec., -ARY[1]]

corō·na, n. (pl. *-ae*). Small disk of light round sun or moon; similar disk opposite sun, ANTHELION; halo of white light seen around disk of moon in total eclipse of sun (now known to belong to sun); circular chandelier hung from roof of a church; (Arch.) member of cornice, with broad vertical face, usu. of considerable projection; (Anat.) various crown-like parts of body; (Bot.) appendage on top of seed or inner side of corolla. [L, = crown]

cŏ·ronach (-ch), n. Funeral-song, dirge, in Scotch Highlands and Ireland. [Ir., = Gael. *corranach* (*comh-* together + *ranach* outcry)]

cŏ·ronal[1], n. Circlet (esp. of gold or gems) for the head; wreath, garland. [prob. f. AF **corounal* (*coroune* f. CORONA)]

corō·nal[2] (*also* kŏ·-), a. (Anat.) *c. suture,* transverse suture of skull separating frontal bone (*c. bone*) from parietal bones; of the crown of the head; (Bot.) of a corona. [F, f. L *coronalis* (CORONA, see -AL)]

cŏ·ronate(d), a. (bot. & zool.). Furnished with a corona or crown-shaped part. [f. L *coronare* (CORONA, see -ATE[2])]

corona·tion, n. Ceremony of crowning sovereign or sovereign's consort; *c.-oath,* taken by sovereign at c. [OF (as prec., -ATION)]

cŏ·roner, n. Officer of county, district, or municipality, holding inquest on bodies of persons supposed to have died by violence or accident; *c.'s inquest,* inquiry held by c.'s court as to cause of death; (orig.) officer charged with maintaining rights of private property of crown. Hence **co·roner**SHIP n. [f. AF *corouner* f. *coroune* CROWN, see -ER[2](2)]

cŏ·ronet, n. Small crown (implying dignity inferior to that of sovereign); fillet of precious materials, esp. as decorative part of woman's head-dress; garland; (Anat.) lowest part of horse's pastern. [f. OF *coronette* dim. of *corone* CROWN]

co·roneted, a. Wearing a coronet (esp. as belonging to peerage). [-ED[2]]

corō·noid, a. (anat.). Curved like crow's beak (of processes of bones). [f. Gk *korōnē* crow + -OID]

corō·zo, n. S.-American tree, allied to palms; *c.-nut*, its seed, from which vegetable ivory is made. [native]

cor·poral[1], a. Of the human body, as *c. punishment*; personal; (archaic) *c. oath*, one ratified by touching a sacred object. Hence **cor·poral**LY[2] adv. [OF, f. L *corporalis* (*corpus -oris* body, see -AL)]

cor·poral[2], **-as,** n. Cloth on which consecrated elements are placed during celebration of mass. [f. med. L *corporalis* (*palla*) body cloth (as prec.); *-as* f. OF *corporaus, -als*, nom. sing.]

cor·poral[3], n. Non-commissioned officer ranking below sergeant (*the little C.*, Napoleon I); *ship's c.*, officer attending to police matters under master-at-arms. [F, var. of *caporal* f. It. *caporale* prob. f. L *corporalis* (as prec.) confused w. *capo* head]

corpora·lity, n. Material existence; body; (pl.) bodily matters, wants, &c. [f. LL *corporalitas* (as CORPORAL[1], see -TY)]

cor·porate (-*a*t), a. Forming a body politic or corporation, as *c. body, body c.*; *c. town* (having municipal rights); forming one body of many individuals; of, belonging to, a body politic. Hence **cor·porate**LY[2] adv. [f. L *corporare* form into a body (*corpus -oris*), see -ATE[2]]

corpora·tion, n. United body of persons, esp. one authorized to act as an individual; artificial person created by charter, prescription, or act of the legislature, comprising many persons (*c. aggregate*) or one (*c. sole*); *municipal c.*, civic authorities of borough, town, or city; (colloq.) abdomen, esp. when prominent. [f. L *corporatio* (as prec., see -ATION)]

cor·porative, a. Of a corporation. [f. L *corporativus* (as prec., see -ATIVE)]

cor·porator, n. Member of a corporation. [as CORPORATE, see -OR[2]]

corpor·ĕal, a. Bodily; material; (Law) tangible, as *c. hereditament* (of material objects). Hence **corporea·**LITY n., **corpor·eal**LY[2] adv. [f. L *corporeus* (*corpus -oris* body) + -AL]

corporē·ity, n. Quality of being or having a material body; bodily substance. [f. med. L *corporeitas* (as prec., see -TY)]

cor·posant (-znt), n. Ball of light sometimes seen on ship during storm, St Elmo's fire. [Port. *corpo santo* = L *corpus sanctum* holy body]

corps (kor), n. (pl. same, pron. korz). Division of an army; body of troops for special service; *c. d'armée* (pron. -mā·), Army-c.; *C. Diplomatique* (F), all the ambassadors & attachés of foreign states at a Court or capital; *c.-de-ballet* (pron. -lā·), dancers in ballet. [F (as foll.)]

corpse, n. Dead (usu. human) body; *c.-candle*, lambent flame seen in churchyard or over grave, regarded as omen of death. [f. OF *cors* (mod. *corps*) f. L *corpus* body]

cor·pulent, a. Bulky (of body); fat. So **cor·pul**ENCE, -ENCY, nn. [F, f. L *corpulentus* (*corpus* body, see -ULENT)]

cor·pus, n. Body, collection, of writings; *c. juris*, body of law; *c. delicti*, all that goes to make a breach of law; (Physiol.) structure of special character in the animal body; *C. Christi*, Feast of the body of Christ (Thursday after Trinity Sunday). [L, = body]

cor·puscle (-sl), **corpu·scule** (-kūl), n. Minute body forming distinct part of the organism, esp. (pl.) those constituting large part of the blood in vertebrates; atom (esp. of electricity). [f. L *corpusculum* (as prec., see -CULE)]

corpu·scular, a. Of corpuscles or atoms; *c.* (EMISSION) *theory of light*. [as prec. + -AR[1]]

corră·l, n., & v.t. (-ll-). Pen for horses, cattle, &c. (in U.S. & Span. Amer.); defensive enclosure of wagons in encampment; enclosure for capturing wild animals; (v.t.) form (wagons) into c., confine in c. [(vb f. n.) Sp. (*corro* ring of spectators f. *correr toros* give bull-fight f. L *currere* run)]

corre·ct[1], v.t. Set right, amend; substitute right for (wrong); mark errors in (proof-sheet &c.) for amendment; admonish (person); cure (person) of fault; punish (person, fault); counteract (hurtful quality); bring into accordance with standard (reading of barometer &c.). [f. L COR(*rigere rect-* = *regere* guide)]

corre·ct[2], a. True, accurate; right, proper, (of conduct, manners, &c.); in accordance with a good standard (of taste &c.); *the c. card* (slang), programme of events at a sports-meeting &c., etiquette or one of its requirements. Hence **cor·re·ct**LY[2] adv., **corre·ct**NESS n. [as prec.]

corre·ction, n. Correcting; *I speak under c.*, I may be wrong; thing substituted for what is wrong; punishment, as *house of c.* (bridewell). Hence **corre·ction**AL a. [F, f. L *correctionem* (as prec., see -ION)]

corre·ctitude, n. Correctness esp. of conduct. [mod., = *correct* + *rectitude*]

corre·ctive, a. & n. (Thing) serving, tending, to correct or counteract what is harmful. Hence **corre·ctive**LY[2] adv. [F (*-if, -ive*), as CORRECT[1], see -IVE]

corre·ctor, n. One who corrects; censor, critic; *c. of the press,* proof-reader; one who punishes. [f. AF *corectour* f. L *correctorem* (as CORRECT[1], see -OR[2])]

cŏ·rrelāte[1], n. Each of two related things (esp. so related that one implies the other). [COR- + L *relatum* p.p. of *referre* REFER]

cŏ·rrelāte[2], v.i. & t. Have a mutual relation (*with, to*); bring (thing) into such relation (*with* another). [as prec.]

cŏrrĕ·lative, a. & n. Having a mutual relation (*with, to*); analogous; (Gram., of words) corresponding to each other & regularly used together, e.g. *either* & *or*; (n.) c. word or thing. Hence or cogn. **correla·**TION n., **corre·lative**LY[2] adv., **correlati·**VITY n. [COR-]

cŏrrespo·nd, v.i. Be in harmony (*with, to*); be similar, analogous, (*to*); agree in amount, position, &c. (*to*); communicate by interchange of letters (*with*). Hence **correspo·nding**LY[2] adv. [f. med. L COR(*respondēre* RESPOND)]

correspo·ndence, n. Agreement, harmony, (*with, to*; *between* two); communication by letters; letters. [as prec., see -ENCE]

correspo·ndent, n. & a. One who writes letters (to person or newspaper, esp. one employed for that purpose, as *our New York c., war-c.*); person, firm, having regular business relations with another esp. in another country; (adj.) corresponding (*to, with,* or abs.), whence **correspo·ndent**LY[2] adv. [as prec., -ENT]

co·rridor, n. Main passage in large building, on which many rooms open; outside passage connecting parts of building; (Pol.) strip of a State's territory that runs through that of another & secures access to the sea &c. (*Polish c.,* through Prussia to Danzig); *c. train* (with narrow passage from end to end. [F, f. It. *corridore* corridor for *corridoio* (*correre* run + *-orio* -ORY) by confus. w. *corridore* runner]

co·rrie, n. (Sc.). Circular hollow on mountain side. [f. Gael. *coire* cauldron]

cŏrrige·ndum (-j-), n. (pl. *-da*). Thing to be corrected (esp. fault in printed book). [L (as CORRECT[1], -ND[1])]

co·rrigible, a. Capable of being corrected; (of persons) submissive, open, to correction. [F (as CORRECT[1], see -BLE)]

corri·val, n. = RIVAL. [COM-]

corrŏ·borant, a. & n. Strengthening (medicine); corroborating (fact). [F (as foll., see -ANT)]

corrŏ·borate, v.t. Confirm formally (law &c.); confirm (person, statement) by evidence &c. Hence or cogn. **corro·bora**TIVE, **corro·borat**ORY, aa., **corro·bora**TOR[2] n. [f. L COR(*roborare* f. *robur -oris* hard wood), -ATE[3]]

corrobora·tion, n. Confirmation by further evidence. [F (as prec., see -ATION)]

corrŏ·boree, n. Native dance of Australian aborigines. [native]

corro·de, v.t. & i. Wear away, destroy gradually, (of rust, chemical agents, diseases, & fig.); (intr.) decay. So **corro·**SION n. [f. L COR(*rodere ros-* gnaw)]

corro·sive, a. & n. (Thing) tending to corrode (lit. & fig.); *c. sublimate,* mercuric (bi-)chloride of mercury, a strong acrid poison. Hence **corro·sive**LY[2] adv., **corro·sive**NESS n. [F (*-if, -ive*), as CORRODE, see -IVE]

co·rrugate, v.t. & i. Contract into wrinkles or folds (t. & i.); mark with, bend into, ridges, as *corrugated iron.* Hence **corrug**A·TION n. [f. L COR(*rugare* f. *ruga* wrinkle), -ATE[3]]

co·rrugator, n. Muscle that contracts the brow in frowning. [as prec., see -OR[2]]

corru·pt[1], a. Rotten; depraved, wicked; influenced by bribery; (of language, texts, &c.) vitiated by errors or alterations; *c. practices,* forms of bribery esp. at elections. Hence **corru·pt**LY[2] adv., **corru·pt**NESS n. [f. L COR(*rumpere rupt-* break)]

corru·pt[2], v.t & i. Infect, taint, (lit. & fig.); bribe; destroy purity of (language); (intr.) become corrupt. So **corru·pt**IVE a. [f. prec., displacing earlier *corrump*]

corru·ptible, a. Liable to corruption, perishable; capable of moral corruption. Hence or cogn. **corrupti**BI·LITY n., **corru·ptib**LY[2] adv. [F, f. L *corruptibilis* (CORRUPT[1], -BLE)]

corru·ption, n. Decomposition; moral deterioration; use of corrupt practices (bribery &c.); perversion (of language &c.) from its original state; (Law) *c. of blood,* effect of attainder upon person attainted. [F, f. L *corruptionem* (as prec., see -ION)]

cor·sac, -ak, n. (zool.). Tartar fox. [Turki]

corsage (korsah·zh, kor·sĭj), n. What a woman is wearing about the bust. [OF (*cors* body, see CORPSE & -AGE)]

cor·sair, n. Privateer, privateering vessel, esp. of Barbary. [f. F *corsaire* f. med. L *cursarius* (*cursus -ūs* inroad, f. *currere* run, -ARY[1])]

corse, n. (archaic, poet.). = CORPSE.

cor·set, n. Woman's closely fitting inner bodice stiffened with whalebone & fastened by lacing, stays. Hence **cor·set**ED[2] a. [F, dim. of OF *cors* body, see CORPSE]

cor·slet, corse-, n. Piece of armour covering body; garment (usu. tight-fitting) covering body as distinct from limbs; (Zool.) insect's thorax, part between head & abdomen. [F (*corse-*), double dim. as prec.]

cortè·ge (-āzh), n. Train of attendants; procession. [F]

Cor·tēs, n. pl. Two chambers making legislative assembly of Spain or Portugal. [Sp., Port.]

cor·tex, n. (pl. *-tĭcēs*). Bark; outer grey matter of brain, outer part of kidney. [L, =bark]

cor·tical, a. (Bot.) of the bark or rind; (Anat., Zool.) forming the outer part of animal body or organ. [f. prec. + -AL]

cor·ticate(d), a. Having bark; bark-like. [f. L *corticatus* (as prec., see -ATE²)]

coru·ndum, n. Crystallized mineral of same species as sapphire & ruby, blue, grey, brown, black; mineral species of crystallized alumina. [f. Tamil *kurundam*]

co·ruscate, v.i. Sparkle, flash, (lit., & fig. of wit &c.). So **coru·sc**ANT a., **corusca·**TION n. [f. L *coruscare*, see -ATE³]

corvée· (-vā), n. (feudal). Day's work of unpaid labour due by vassal; statute labour, e.g. that exacted of French peasants before 1776. [F, f. Rom. *coruada* f. LL COR*rogata* (*opera*) requisitioned (work) f. *rogare* ask]

corve·tte, n. (naut.). Flush-decked war-vessel with one tier of guns. [F, f. Sp. *corbeta*; cf. L *corbita* (*navis*) ship of burden (*corbis* basket)]

cor·vīne, a. Of, akin to, the raven or crow. [f. L *corvinus* (*corvus* raven, see -INE¹)]

Cŏ·rybant, n. (pl. *-s*, *-ēs*). Priest of Phrygian worship of Cybele, performed with extravagant dances. Hence **Coryba·n**TIAN, **Coryba·nt**IC, **Coryba·nt**INE, aa. [f. F *Corybante* f. L *Corybantem* (nom. *-as*) f. Gk *Korubas*]

Cŏ·rydon, n. Typical rustic in pastoral poetry. [L, f. Gk *Korudōn*]

cŏ·rymb, n. (bot.). Species of inflorescence; raceme in which lower flower-stalks are proportionally longer. Hence **corymbo·**SE¹ a. [f. F *corymbe* f. L f. Gk *korumbos* cluster]

coryphae·us (-fē-), n. Leader of a chorus (also fig.). [L, f. Gk *koruphaios* (*koruphē* head)]

corȳ·za, n. Catarrh. [L, f. Gk *koruza* running at nose]

cos¹, n. (Also *C. lettuce*) kind of lettuce introduced from Cos (now Stanchio). [f. Gk *Kōs*]

cos², n. Abbr. of COSINE.

cosa·que (-ahk), n. Cracker bon-bon. [F]

cose (-z), v.i. Make oneself cosy. [back-formation on COSY, cf. LAZE f. *lazy*, & COZE]

cosĕ·cant, n. (trig.). Secant of complement of given angle (abbr. *cosec*). [CO-]

cosei·smal (-sīz-), a. & n. (Line or curve connecting points) of simultaneous shock from earthquake wave. [CO-]

cŏ·sher, v.t. Pamper, cocker up. [?]

co-si·gnatory, a. & n. (Person) signing jointly with others. [CO-]

co·sine, n. (trig.). Sine of complement of given angle (abbr. *cŏs*). [CO-]

cosmĕ·tic (-z-), a. & n. (Preparation) designed to beautify hair, skin, or complexion. [f. Gk *kosmētikos* (*kosmeō* adorn f. *kosmos* order, adornment, see -ETIC)]

co·smic, a. Of the universe or COSMOS (esp. as distinguished from the earth); *c. philosophy*, =foll. Hence **co·smic**AL a., **co·smical**LY² adv. [f. Gk *kosmikos* (*kosmos* world, see -IC)]

co·smism, n. Conception of the cosmos as a self-acting whole. So **co·sm**IST n. [COSMOS + -ISM]

cosmo- in comb. = Gk *kosmos* universe, as *-geny*, evolution of the universe, *-logy*, *-logist*, *-lo·gical*, science of, student of, concerned with, the universe, *-pla·stic*, moulding the universe.

cosmo·gony, n. (Theory of) the creation of the universe. So **cosmogŏ·n**IC(AL) aa., **cosmo·gon**IST(3) n. [f. Gk *kosmogonia* (COSMO- + *-gonia* f. *-gonos* -begetting)]

cosmo·graphy, n. Description, mapping, of general features of universe or earth. So **cosmo·**GRAPHER n., **cosmo**GRA·PHIC(AL) aa. [f. Gk *kosmographia*, see COSMO-, GRAPHY]

cosmopŏ·litan, a. & n. Belonging to all parts of the world; (person) free from national limitations. Hence **cosmopo·litan**ISM n., **cosmopo·litan**IZE v.t. & i. [f. foll. + -AN]

cosmŏ·polite, n. & a. Citizen of the world; (adj.) free from national prejudices. Hence **cosmo·polit**ISM n. [f. Gk *kosmopolitēs* (COSMO- + *politēs* citizen)]

cosmopoli·tical, a. Belonging to universal polity. [f. prec. + -ICAL]

cosmora·ma (-rah-), n. Peep-show illustrating all parts of the world. Hence **cosmoră·m**IC a. [f. COSMO- + Gk *horama* spectacle (*horaō* see)]

co·smos (-z-), n. The universe as an ordered whole; ordered system of ideas, &c., sum-total of experience. [f. Gk *kosmos*]

Co·ssack, n. Name of a Turkish people subject to Russia, esp. as light horse in Russian army; *cc.*, (shop name for) trousers. [f. Turki *quzzaq* adventurer]

co·sset, n., & v.t. Pet lamb; (v.t.) pet, pamper. [(vb f. n.) perh. = OE *cotsæta* cot-sitter (i.e. animal brought up in house)]

cost¹ (kaw-, kŏ-), n. Price (to be) paid for thing; *prime c.* (also *c. price*), that at which merchant buys; (pl.) law expenses, esp. those allowed in favour of winning party; expenditure of time, labour, &c.; *at the c. of*, at the expense of losing; *to a person's c.*, to his loss; *c.-book* (showing expenses, profit, &c., of mine). Hence **co·st**LESS a. [OF (as foll.)]

cost[2] (kaw-, kŏ-), v.i. (*cost*). Be acquirable at, involve expenditure of, as *c. him five shillings, c. the writer infinite labour*; result in the loss of, as *c. him his crown*; *c. him dear(ly)*, involved a heavy penalty; (Commerc.) fix prices. No pass.; the person is indirect object, the price is expressed adverbially, *in* being understood. [f. OF *coster, couster*, f. L CON(*stare* stand) with dative of person, locative of price]

cŏ·stal, a. Of the ribs. [F, f. med. L *costalis* (*costa* rib, see -AL)]

cŏ·stard, n. Large kind of apple; (archaic) head. [perh. f. OF *coste* rib (as prec.,) + -ARD]

cŏ·state, a. Ribbed, having ribs. [f. L *costatus* (as COSTAL, see -ATE[2])]

cŏstea·n, -een, v.i. (mining). Sink pits down to rock to find direction of lode. [f. Corn. *cothas stean* dropped tin]

cŏ·ster(monger), n. Man who sells fruit, fish, &c., from barrow in street. [COSTARD]

cŏ·stive, a. With confined bowels, constipated; (fig.) niggardly. Hence **co·stive**NESS n. [f. OF *costivé* f. L *constipatus* CONSTIPATED]

co·stly, a. Of great value; expensive. Hence **co·stli**NESS n. [-LY[1]]

cŏ·stmāry, n. Aromatic perennial plant, formerly used in medicine & for flavouring ale. [OE *cost* f. L f. Gk *kostos* + (St) *Mary*]

cŏ·stume (*also* -tū·m), n., & v.t. Style, fashion of dress or attire (including way of wearing hair); complete set of outer garments; *c. piece*, play in which actors wear historical costume; (v.t.) provide with c. [(vb f. n.) F, f. It. *costume* f. L *consuetudinem* CUSTOM]

costū·mier, -mer, n. Maker of, dealer in, costumes. [F (*-ier*), f. *costumer* (COSTUME)]

cō·sy (-zĭ), **-zy**, a. & n. Comfortable, snug, (of person or place); (n.) canopied corner seat for two (cf. F *causeuse*), *tea, egg, -c.*, quilted covering to retain heat in teapot, egg. Hence **co·si**LY[2] adv., **co·si**NESS n. [?]

cot[1], n., & v.t. Small erection for shelter, as *bell-, sheep-, c.*; (poet.) cottage; (v.t.) put (sheep) in c. [(vb f. n.) OE, f. OTeut. **kutom*]

cot[2], n. (Anglo-Ind.) light bedstead; (Naut.) swinging bed for officers, sick persons, &c.; small (usu. swinging) bed for child; bed in children's hospital. [Anglo-Ind., f. Hind. *khaṭ* bedstead, bier]

cot[3], n. Abbr. of foll.

cōta·ngent, n. (trig.). Tangent of complement of given angle (abbr. *cŏt*). [CO-]

cote, n. Shed, stall, shelter, esp. for animals as *dove-, hen-, sheep-, c.* [OE, parallel to COT[1]]

co-temporary &c. See CONTEMPORARY &c.

co-te·nant, n. Joint tenant. [CO-]

cō·terie (-rĭ), n. Circle, set, of persons associated by exclusive interests; select circle in society. [F, orig. = association of country people, f. *cotier* COTTAR, see -ERY]

cothur·nus, n. Buskin, thick-soled boot of Athenian tragic actor (also fig., of elevated style &c.). [L, f. Gk *kothornos*]

co-ti·dal, a. *C. line* on map (connecting places at which high water occurs at same time.) [CO-]

coti·llion, *cotillon* (F), n. Name of several dances; music for these. [F (*-llon*), = petticoat]

co·ttage (-ĭj), n. Labourer's or villager's small dwelling; small country residence; *c. hospital* (in c., without resident medical staff); *c. loaf* of bread (of two round masses, smaller on top of larger); *c. piano* (small upright). [prob. f. AF **cotage* (COTE + -AGE)]

co·ttager, n. Inhabitant of a cottage. [-ER[1]]

co·ttar, -er[1], n. Scotch peasant occupying cottage on farm, and labouring on farm at fixed rate when required; = COTTIER. [f. med. L *cotarius* (*cota* COTE, see -ARY[1])]

co·tter[2], n. Key, wedge, bolt, for securing parts of machinery &c.; esp., split pin that opens after passing through hole; *c.-pin*, pin to keep c. in place. [?]

co·ttier, n. Cottager; Irish peasant holding under *c. tenure* (letting of land in small portions at rent fixed by competition). [OF (as COTTAR)]

co·tton[1], n. White downy fibrous substance clothing seeds of *c.-plant*, used for making cloth, thread, &c.; c.-plant; thread spun from c. yarn (also *sewing-c.*); cloth made of cotton; GUN-*c.*; *c.-cake*, compressed c. seed as food for cattle; *c.-grass*, kinds of plant with white silky hairs; *c.-lord*, magnate of c. trade; *c.-spinner*, workman who spins cotton, owner of c. mill; *c. waste*, refuse yarn used for cleaning machinery &c.; *c. wool*, raw c., esp. as prepared for wadding; *c. yarn*, c. prepared for weaving into fabrics. Hence **co·tton**Y[2] a. [f. F f. OSp. *coton* f. Arab. *qutun*]

co·tton[2], v.i. Agree, harmonize, (*together, with* each other); *c. up*, make friendly advances (*to* or abs.); become attached *to*. [f. prec.]

cottono·cracy, n. The magnates of the cotton trade. So **Cottono·polis** n. (joc.), Manchester. [COTTON[1] + -O- + -CRACY, Gk *polis* city]

cŏtylē·don, n. Primary leaf in embryo of higher plants, seed-leaf; genus of plants including navelwort or pennywort. [L, f. Gk *kotulēdōn* cup-shaped cavity (*kotulē* cup)]

cotylē·donous, a. Having cotyledons. [-OUS]

cŏ·tyloid, a. (anat.). Cup-shaped. [f. Gk *kotuloeidēs* (*kotulē* cup, see -OID)]

couch[1] (kowtsh), n. Bed; thing one sleeps on; lounge like sofa, but with half-back and head-end only; (Malting) bed in which grain germinates after steeping. [f. F *couche* (as foll.)]

couch[2] (kowtsh), v.t. & i. Lay one*self* down (now only in p.p.); (Malting) lay (grain) on floor to germinate; lower (spear &c.) to position of attack; remove (cataract; also *c. person, person's eye,* for cataract); express (thought &c. *in* words); veil (meaning *under* words); (of animals) lie (esp. in lair); crouch, cower; lie in ambush. [f. F *coucher* f. L COL(*locare* place)]

couch[3] (kow-, kōō-), n. (More usu. *c.-grass*) kind of grass with long creeping roots, a common weed. [var. of QUITCH]

cou·chant (kow-), a. (herald.). (Of animals) lying with body resting on legs and head raised. [F, part. as COUCH[2]]

Couéism (kōō·āĭsm), n. Systematic auto-suggestion of a sanguine kind. [Emile *Coué*, French psychologist, + -ISM]

cou·gar (kōō-), n. Large American feline quadruped, puma. [f. F *couguar* repr. Guarani *guazu ara*]

cough[1] (kawf, kŏf), n. Act of coughing; tendency to cough, diseased condition of respiratory organs. [f. foll.]

cough[2] (as prec.), v.i.& t. Expel air from lungs with violent effort and noise produced by abrupt opening of glottis; (trans.) *c. out, up,* eject by, say with, cough; *c. down,* silence (speaker) by coughing. [ME *coghen*; OE has *cohhetan*; cf. MDu. *cuchen,* Du. *kuchen,* cough, G *keuchen* pant; all imit.]

could. See CAN[2].

couleur de rose (F), a. & n. =ROSE-*colour*(*ed*).

coulisse (kōōlē·s), n. Side-scene in theatre; space between two of these; groove in which sluice-gate moves. [F, f. OF *couleïs* f. L **colaticius* (*colare* flow)]

couloir (kōōlwar·r), n. Steep gully on mountain side. [F]

coulomb (kōōlŏ·m), n. Quantity of electricity conveyed in one second by current of one ampere. [*de C.,* French physicist]

cou·lter (kō-), **cō·l-,** n. Iron blade fixed in front of share in plough. [OE *culter* f. L *culter*]

cou·marin (kōō-), n. Aromatic crystalline substance found in seeds of Tonka bean &c. [f. F *coumarine* (*coumarou,* name in Guiana of Tonka bean, see -IN)]

cou·ncil (kow-), n. Ecclesiastical assembly, as *oecumenical, diocesan, c.*; (N.T.) Jewish Sanhedrin; advisory or deliberative assembly, as (Hist.) *Great C.,* c. of tenants-in-chief & great ecclesiastics (last summoned in 1640), CABINET *c.*; body of councillors, as PRIVY *c.* (*the King, Queen, Crown, in C.,* Privy C. as issuing Orders in C. or receiving appeal petitions from colonies &c.), *C. of State* (of foreign countries); body assisting governor of British crown colony or dependency; local administrative body of town, city, or administrative county, as *County C.*; *C. of War,* assembly of officers called in special emergency, (in some foreign countries) permanent military board; *c.-board,* table at which c. sits, c. in session; *c.-chamber, -house* (in which c. meets). [(1) in eccles. sense f. OF *cuncile* f. L CON*cilium* assembly, meeting (*calare* call); (2) f. OF *conseil* f. L CON*silium* advisory body, COUNSEL; E confused the two words; acc. to mod. different. (begun in 16th c.) *council* =any deliberative body, *counsel* =act of counselling, advice, &c.]

cou·ncillor, n. Member of a council. Hence **cou·ncillor**SHIP n. [16th-c. different. f. COUNSELLOR]

cou·nsel[1] (kow-), n. Consultation; *take c.,* consult (*with* or abs.); advice; (Theol.) *c. of perfection,* injunction (orig. of Christ or Apostles) not regarded as universally binding (*Matt.* xix. 21); plan; *keep one's* (*own*) or *another's c.* (secret); body of legal advisers in cause; barrister; *King's, Queen's, C.* (abbr. *K.C., Q.C.*), c. to the crown, taking precedence of ordinary barristers. [f. OF *conseil* f. L CON(*silium* f. *sal-* jump =Skr. *sar-* go) deliberative body, plan, cf. COUNCIL]

cou·nsel[2], v.t. (-ll-). Advise (person *to* do); recommend (thing, *that*). [f. F *conseiller* f. LL *consiliare* (L *-ari*), as prec.]

cou·nsellor, n. Adviser; (also *c.-at-law*) advising barrister (now only in Ireland). [f. OF *conseillere, -eor,* f. L *consiliator*(*em*); as prec., -OR[2]]

count[1] (kow-), n. Counting; one's reckoning (*keep, lose, c.,* be aware, fail to know, how many there have been); sum total; (Law) each charge in an indictment; (H. of Commons) *c.-out, c.,* adjournment when fewer than 40 members are present; *c. out* (boxing), counting of 10 sec. to give fallen man time to rise, failing which he loses the match. [f. OF *conte* f. LL *computum* (as foll.)]

count[2], v.t. & i. Enumerate, reckon up; repeat numerals in order; *c. up,* find the sum of; *c. out,* count while taking from a stock; (of boxer) *be counted out,* fail to rise in time (see prec.); *c. out the House,* procure adjournment (as prec.); include in reckoning; consider (a thing) to be (so & so); *c. on, upon,* expect confidently; be included in reckoning, as *that does not c.*; *c. for,* be worth (much &c.); (Sc.) *c. kin* (*with*), be demonstrably related (to). [f. OF *conter* COMPUTE]

count[3] (kow-), n. Foreign noble corresp. to earl; *c.* PALATINE. Hence **cou·nt**SHIP n. [f. OF *conte* f. L *comitem* (nom. *-mes*) companion]

cou·ntenance[1] (kow-), n. Expression of face, as *change* (one's) *c.* (from emotion), *keep* one's *c.*, maintain composure, esp. refrain from laughing; face; composure, as *put out of c.*, disconcert, *keep* (person) *in c.* (usu. by show of support). [f. OF *contenance* bearing, aspect, f. L *continentia* (as CONTAIN, see -ENCE)]

cou·ntenance[2], v.t. Sanction (act); encourage (person, practice, person *in* practice). [f. OF *contenancer* (as prec.)]

cou·nter[1], n. Small (usu. round) piece of metal, ivory, &c., used for keeping account in games, esp. cards; imitation coin; banker's table; table in shop on which money is counted out & across which goods are delivered; *c.-jumper*, shop assistant. [f. OF *conteoir* f. L *computatorium* (as COMPUTE, see -ORY(2)]

cou·nter[2], n. Part of horse's breast between shoulders and under neck; curved part of stern of ship. [perh. f. COUNTER[5]]

cou·nter[3], n. (fencing). Circular parry in which hand retains same position while point describes a circle. [f. F *contre* COUNTER-]

cou·nter[4], n. (shoemaking). Back part of shoe or boot round heel. [abbr. of COUNTERFORT]

cou·nter[5], a. Opposed; opposite; duplicate; *c.* (*rocking turn* or *rocker*), skating figure (see ROCK[3]). [arising f. combb. w. COUNTER-]

cou·nter[6], v.t. & i. Oppose, contradict; (Chess) meet with counter move; (Boxing) give (opponent, or abs.) return blow while parrying. [partly f. ENCOUNTER, partly f. COUNTER-]

cou·nter[7], adv. In the opposite direction, as *hunt, run, go, c.* (i.e. to direction taken by game); contrary, as *act, go, c.* (*to* instructions &c.). [f. F *contre* COUNTER-]

cou·nter[8], n. (Abbr. for) counter rocking turn (see ROCK[3]).

cou·nter- (kow-), pref. f. F *contre* (It. *contra*) f. L *contra* against, in return, orig. in words f. OF, F, or It., but now a living prefix of vbs, nouns, adjj., and advv., with sense (1) reciprocation, opposition, frustration, rivalry, (2) opposite position or direction, (3) correspondence, match, (of things having naturally two opposite parts), (4) duplicate, substitute.

countera·ct, v.t. Hinder, defeat, by contrary action; neutralize. Hence **countera·ction** n., **countera·ctive** a. [COUNTER-(1)]

counter-a·gent, n. Counteracting agent or force. [COUNTER-(1)]

cou·nter-approach, n. (mil.). Work constructed by besieged outside permanent fortifications to check besiegers. [COUNTER-(1)]

cou·nter-attraction, n. Attraction of contrary tendency; rival attraction. [COUNTER-(1)]

cou·nterba·lance, n., & v.t. Weight balancing another; (v.t.) act as c. to. [COUNTER-(1)]

cou·nterblast, n. Energetic declaration against something. [COUNTER-(1)]

cou·nter-ceiling, n. Layer of dry material between joists of floor. [COUNTER-(4)]

countercha·nge, v.t. & i. Interchange; chequer; (intr.) change places or parts. [f. F *contrechanger* (see COUNTER-(1) and CHANGE v.)]

cou·ntercharge, n. Charge in opposition to another, charge against accuser. [COUNTER-(1)]

cou·ntercheck, n. Check that opposes a thing; check that operates against another; (archaic) retort (*the c. quarrelsome*, see *As You Like It*, v. iv. 85). [COUNTER-(1)]

cou·nter-claim, n. Claim set up against another; claim set up by defendant in suit. [COUNTER-(1)]

counter-clo·ckwise. See CLOCK[1].

cou·nterfeit[1] (-ĭt, -ēt), a. & n. (Thing) made in imitation, not genuine, (of coins, writings, persons, &c.). [f. OF *contrefet, -fait*, p.p. of *contrefaire* f. med. L CONTRA-(*facere* make)]

cou·nterfeit[2] (-ĭt, -ēt), v.t. Imitate; forge (coin, bank-notes, hand-writing); simulate (feelings); (fig.) resemble closely. [f. prec.]

cou·nterfoil, n. Complementary part of bank cheque, official receipt, &c., with note of particulars, retained by drawer. [COUNTER-(3)]

cou·nterfort, n. Buttress supporting wall or terrace. [f. F *contrefort* (COUNTER-, FORT)]

counter-i·rritant, n. Thing used to produce surface irritation and thus counteract disease (also fig.). So **counter-irrita·tion** n. [COUNTER-(1)]

counterma·nd, v.t., & n. Revoke (command); recall (person, forces, &c.) by contrary order; cancel order for (goods &c.); (n.) order revoking previous one. [f. OF *contremand(er)* n. & vb f. med. L CONTRA(*mandare* order)]

cou·ntermarch, v.i. & t., & n. (Cause to) march in the contrary direction. [COUNTER-(2)]

cou·ntermark, n. Additional mark, for greater security &c.; additional mark on bale of goods belonging to several merchants; hallmark added to that of the maker. [f. F *contremarque*, see COUNTER-(3) & MARK]

cou·ntermine, n., & v.t. & i. (Mil.) mine made to intercept that of besiegers; submarine mine sunk to explode enemy's mines by its explosion; (fig.) counterplot; (v.t.) oppose by c.; (v.i.) make a c. [COUNTER-(1)]

cou·ntermure, n. Wall raised within or

behind another as reserve defence. [f. F *contremur* (COUNTER-(2), *mur* f. L *murus* wall)]

cou·nterpane (-ĭn, -ān), n. Outer covering of bed, coverlet, quilt. [f. obs. *counterpoint* f. OF *contrepointe* corrupt. of *cuiltepointe* f. L *culcita puncta* stitched QUILT; assim. to PANE in obs. sense *cloth*]

cou·nterpart, n. Duplicate; person, thing, forming natural complement to another; opposite part of INDENTURE. [COUNTER-(3)]

cou·nterplot, n., & v.t. Plot contrived to defeat another; (v.t.) frustrate by c., devise c. against. [COUNTER-(1)]

cou·nterpoint, n. (mus.). Melody added as accompaniment to given melody; art, mode, of adding melodies as accompaniment according to fixed rules; *double c.* (in which the melodies can be placed in any order above or below one another). [f. OF *contrepoint* f. med. L CONTRA-*punctum* pricked opposite, i.e. to the original melody (*pungere punct-* prick)]

cou·nterpoise[1] (-z), n. Counterbalancing weight; thing of equivalent force &c. on opposite side; equilibrium. [f. OF *contrepois* (*contre* COUNTER-(1) +*pois* f. L *pensum* weight)]

cou·nterpoise[2] (z-), v.t. Counterbalance; compensate; bring into, keep in, equilibrium (lit. & fig.). [f. OF *contrepeser* (*contre* COUNTER- +*peser* f. L *pensare* assim. to prec.)]

cou·nter-reforma·tion, n. Reformation running counter to another, esp. that in Church of Rome following on Protestant Reformation. [COUNTER-(1)]

cou·nterscarp, n. (fortif.). Outer wall or slope of ditch, supporting covered way. [f. F *contrescarpe* f. It. CONTRA(*scarpa* SCARP)]

cou·ntersign[1], n. Watchword, pass-word, given to all men on guard (cf. PAROLE); mark used for identification &c. [f. OF *contresigne* (see COUNTER-(3) & SIGN)]

cou·ntersign[2], v.t. Add signature to (document already signed); ratify. [f. OF *contresigner* (as prec.)]

countersi·nk, v.t. Bevel off (top of hole) to receive head of screw or bolt; sink (screw-head) in such hole. [COUNTER-(3)]

counter-tĕ·nor, n. (mus.). (Part for, singer with) male voice higher than tenor, alto. [f. obs. F *contre-teneur* (see CONTRA- & TENOR)]

countervai·l, v.t. & i. Counterbalance (esp. in *-ing duty,* one put on imports that are bounty-fed to give home goods an equal chance); avail against. [f. OF *contrevaloir* f. L CONTRA *valēre*]

cou·nterwork, n., & v.t & i. (Mil.) work raised in opposition to those of enemy; (gen.) opposing work; (v.t.) counteract. frustrate; (v.i.) work in opposition. [COUNTER-(1)]

cou·ntess, n. Wife, widow, of count or earl; lady ranking with count or earl in her own right. [f. OF *contesse* f. LL *comitissa* fem. of *comes -itis* COUNT]

cou·nting-house, n. Building, room, devoted to keeping accounts; office.

cou·ntless, a. Too many to count. [-LESS]

cou·ntrified, -ryfied, a. Rural, rustic, in appearance, manners,&c. [p.p. of *countrify,* else little used (COUNTRY + -FY)]

cou·ntry (kŭ-), n. Region; territory of a nation; land of a person's birth, citizenship, &c., fatherland; rural districts as opp. to towns, esp. the rest of a land as opp. to the capital; (Cricket slang) *in the c.,* far from the wickets; APPEAL[1] *to the c.* (body of electors); *c. cousin,* relation of countrified manners or appearance; *c.-house, -seat,* residence of c. gentleman; *c. note,* bank-note issued by local bank; *c. party,* political party supporting agricultural against manufacturing interests; *c.-side,* particular rural district, its inhabitants. [f. OF *cuntrée* f. LL *contrata* land lying opposite (CONTRA)]

cou·ntry dance, n. Any rural or native English dance, esp. those in which couples stand face to face in two long lines. [COUNTRY + DANCE; perverted to *contredance* &c.]

cou·ntryman, n. (fem. *cou·ntrywoman*). Man of one's own (or a specified) country; person living in rural parts.

cou·nty (kow-), n. Territorial division in Great Britain and Ireland, chief unit for administrative, judicial, and political purposes; administrative division in most British colonies; (U.S.) political and administrative division next below State; people of a c.; *c.* PALATINE; *c. corporate,* city, town, ranking as administrative c.; *c. borough,* one of over 50,000 inhabitants ranking (since 1888) as administrative c.; *c. council,* representative governing body of administrative c.; *c. court,* local court esp. for recovery of small debts, whence *c.-court* (v.t. colloq.), sue in this; *c. family* (with ancestral seat in a c.); *c. society* (of c. families & their associates); *c. town,* chief town in county. [f. OF *cunté* f. L *comitatus* (as COUNT[3], see -ATE[1])]

coup (kōō), n. Notable or successful stroke or move; (Billiards) direct holing of ball; *c. d'état* (dĕtah·), violent or illegal change in government; *c. de grâce* (de grahs), finishing stroke; *c. de main* (F), sudden vigorous attack; *c. d'œil* (F), comprehensive glance, general view; *c. de théâtre* (tāah·tr), dramatically sudden or sensational act. [F, f. LL *colpus* f. L f. Gk *kolaphos* blow]

coupé (kōō·pā), n. Four-wheeled close carriage for two inside & driver; half-compartment at end of railway carriage. [F, p.p. of *couper* cut, as noun]

cou·ple[1] (kŭ-), n. Leash for holding two hounds together, whence (fig.) *go, hunt, run, in cc.*; pair, brace, esp. of hunting dogs (collect. sing. for pl., as *15 couple*); wedded or engaged pair; pair of partners in dance; *a c. of*, two; pair of rafters; (Dynam.) pair of equal and parallel forces acting in opposite directions. [f. OF *cople* f. L COPULA]

cou·ple², v.t. & i. Fasten, link, together (esp. dogs in pairs); connect (railway carriages) by a coupling; unite, bring together, (persons); marry (t. & i.); associate in thought or speech (two things *together*, one *with* another); (intr.) unite sexually. [f. OF *copler* (as prec.)]

cou·pler, n. In vbl senses; esp. contrivance for connecting two manuals, or manual with pedals, or two keys, of organ. [prec. + -ER¹]

cou·plet, n. Pair of successive lines of verse. [F, dim. of COUPLE]

cou·pling, n. In vbl senses; esp.: link connecting railway carriages; contrivance for connecting parts of machinery. [-ING¹]

coupon (kōō·pŏn, or as F), n. Detachable ticket entitling holder to periodical payments of interest, services of excursion agency, ration under food-control, &c.; (Pol. slang) party leader's recognition of parliamentary candidate as deserving election. [F, = piece cut off (*couper*, see COUPÉ, -OON)]

cou·rage (kŭ·rĭj), n. Bravery, boldness, as *take, pluck up, lose, c.*; (Gallicism) *take* one's *c. in both hands*, nerve oneself to a venture; *Dutch c.* (induced by drinking); *c. of* one's *opinions*, c. to act up to them. [OF (*cœur* f. L *cor* heart, see -AGE)]

courageous (kerā·jus), a. Brave, fearless. Hence **coura·geous**LY² adv., **coura·geous**NESS n. [f. OF *corageus* f. prec., see -OUS]

cou·rier (kōō-), n. Servant employed to make travelling arrangements on continent; title of newspapers, as *Liverpool C.*; running messenger. [(1) ME *corour* f. OF *coreor* f. LL *curritorem* (*currere curs-* run, see -OR²); (2) 16th-c. F, f. It. *corriere* (*corre* run f. L *currere*)]

course¹ (kōrs), n. Onward movement; pursuit of game esp. of hares with (grey)hounds; direction taken, as *hold, take, change*, one's *c., ship's c., a dangerous c.* (line of conduct), *c. of events, c. of nature* (ordinary procedure); (pl.) *evil cc.* (behaviour); ground on which race is run (also *race-c.*); channel in which water flows, watercourse; *c. of* EXCHANGE; career; series (of lectures &c.); rota for duty among members of cathedral body; each of successive divisions of meal (esp. soup, fish, joint, &c.); continuous layer of stone &c. in building; (Naut.) *fore, main, -c.*, fore, main, -sail; *in the c. of*, during; *by c. of*, according to ordinary procedure of (law &c.); *in due c.*, in the natural order; *of c.*, naturally; *matter of c.*, natural thing. [(1) f. F *cours* f. L *cursus -ūs* (as prec.); (2) f. F *course* fem. noun f. L p.p. of *currere* run, cf. -ADE]

course², v.t. & i. Pursue (game, as prec.); run about, run, (esp. of liquids); give (horse) a run; use (hounds) in coursing. [f. prec.]

cour·ser, n. (poet.). Swift horse. [f. OF *corsier* f. L **cursarius* (*cursus* COURSE, see -ARY¹); orig. = warhorse, charger]

court¹ (kōrt), n. (Also *courtyard*) space enclosed by walls or buildings; (Camb. Univ.) college quadrangle; subdivision of an Exhibition building, museum, &c., open to the general roof; confined yard opening off street; enclosed quadrangular area, open or covered, for games, as *tennis, fives, -c*; plot of ground marked out for lawn-tennis; sovereign's residence; his establishment and retinue; the body of courtiers; sovereign and his councillors as ruling power, as *C. of St James's* (British sovereign's c.); assembly held by sovereign, state reception; *High C.* (assembly) *of Parliament*; assembly of judges or other persons acting as tribunal, as *c. of law, law-c., c. of justice, c. of judicature*, COUNTY, *criminal*, POLICE, *c., C. of* ADMIRALTY, COMMON¹ *pleas*, EQUITY, &c.; place, hall, in which justice is administered; *out of c.*, (of plaintiff, and fig. of arguments) not entitled to be heard; (meeting of) qualified members of company or corporation; (in some friendly societies) = LODGE¹; attention paid to one whose favour, affection, interest, is sought, as *pay c. to*; *c.-card* (orig. *coat-card*), king, queen, knave; *c. circular*, daily report of c. doings published in newspapers; *c. guide*, directory containing (theoretically) names of those who have been presented at c.; *c. martial*, judicial c. of military or naval officers, (v.t., *c.-m.*) try by this; *drumhead c. m.* (held round upturned drum in time of war); *c. plaster*, sticking-plaster for cuts &c. (formerly used by ladies at c. for face-patches). [f. OF *cort* f. L *c(oh)ortem* (nom. *-ors*), yard, COHORT; the senses of assembly, judicial court, by confus. in F with L *curia*]

court², v.t. Pay court to; make love to (also abs.); entice (person, *into, to, from*, &c.); seek to win (applause &c.); invite (inquiry &c.; *you are courting disaster*). [prec.]

courteous (kōr·tyus, ker-). Polite, kind, considerate, in manner or address. Hence **cour·teous**LY² adv., **cour·teous**NESS n. [f. OF *corteis* = It. *cortese* (*corte* COURT¹, see -ESE), assim. to wds in -OUS]

courtesă·n (-z-), **-ză·n**, (kōr-), n. Prostitute. [f. F *courtisane* f. It. *cortigiana*, fem. adj. as n. (as prec. + *-ano* -AN)]

cour·tesy, n. Courteous behaviour or disposition; *by c.*, by favour, not of right; *c. title*, one held by c., having no legal validity; (Law) *c. of England, Scotland*, husband's tenure after wife's death of certain kinds of property inherited by her; =CURTSY. [f. OF *cortesie* = It. *cortesia* (*cortese* COURTEOUS)]

cour·tier (kōr-), n. Attendant at, frequenter of, sovereign's court. [prob. f. OF *cortoyeur* f. *cortoyer* vb (*corte* COURT[1])]

cour·tly (kōr-), a. Polished, refined, in manners; obsequious, flattering. Hence **cour·tli**NESS n. [-LY[1]]

cour·tship, n. Courting, wooing, with view to marriage. [-SHIP]

couscous(sou) (kōō·skōōsōō), n. African dish of granulated flour steamed over broth. [F, f. Arab. *kuskus* (*kaskasa* bruise)]

cousin (kŭ·zn), n. (Also *first c., c. german*) child of one's uncle or aunt; *my second c.*, my parent's first c.'s child; *my first* (*second* &c.) *c. once* (*twice* &c.) *removed*, my first (second &c.) c.'s child (grandchild &c.), also, my parent's (grandparent's &c.) first (second &c.) c.; *call cc.*, claim kinship (*with*); title used by sovereign in addressing another sovereign or a nobleman of same country; *c. Jacky*, (nickname for) Cornishman. Hence **cou·sin**HOOD, **cou·sin**SHIP, nn., **cou·sin**LY[1] a. [F, f. L CON(*sobrinus, -na*, f. *soror* sister) c. by mother's side]

coûte que coûte (kōōtkekōō·t), adv. At all costs. [F]

cove[1], n. Small bay or creek; sheltered recess; (Arch.) concave arch, curved junction of wall with ceiling or floor. [com.-Teut.; OE *cofa*]

cove[2], v.t. Arch (esp. ceiling at junction with wall); slope (fireplace sides) inwards. [prec.]

cove[3], n. (slang). Fellow, chap. [thieves' cant, etym. dub.]

co·venant (kŭ-), n., & v.t. & i. Compact, bargain; (Law) contract under seal, clause of this; (bibl.) compact between God and the Israelites, as ARK *of the c., land of the c.* (Canaan); *Solemn League and C.* (establishing Presbyterianism in England and Scotland, 1643); *C. of the League of Nations*, document constituting the League, incorporated in the Treaty of Versailles & other treaties concluding the great war (1919); (v.t. & i.) agree (*with* person *for* thing, *to* do, *that*). [(vb f. n.) OF, part. of *convenir*, see CONVENE]

co·venanted, a. Bound by a covenant, esp. of Indian Civil servants (*the c. service*). [-ED[1]]

co·venanter, n. One who covenants, esp. (Sc. Hist.) adherent of the National Covenant (1638) or Solemn League & COVENANT. [-ER[1]]

Cŏ·vent Garden, n. (Used for) the C. G. fruit and vegetable market in London.

Cŏ·ventry (also kŭ-), n. Town in Warwickshire; *send person to C.*, refuse to associate with him.

co·ver[1] (kŭ-), v.t. Overspread, overlay, (*with* cloth, lid, &c., also fig. *with* disgrace &c.); strew thoroughly (*with*); lie over, be a covering to; extend over, occupy the surface of; protect; *covering letter*, explanatory one with enclosure; (of fortress, guns, &c.) command (territory); conceal (feelings &c.); *c. with gun*, present gun at; (Mil., Cricket) stand behind (front-rank man, another player to stop balls he misses; *c.-point*, fielder behind point, his place); include, comprise; suffice to defray (expenses); protect by insurance; (of stallion) copulate with; *c. in*, complete the covering of, fill in (grave &c.) with earth; *c. up*, conceal, esp. by wrapping up. Hence **co·ver**ING[1] (3) n. [f. OF *cuvrir* f. L CO(*operire opert-*)]

co·ver[2], n. Thing that covers; lid; binding of book; either board of this, as *from c. to c.*; wrapper, envelope, of letter, as *address* person *under c. to another*; case of bicycle tire; hiding-place, shelter, (*take c.*, mil., utilize lie of ground for protection); screen, pretence, as *under* (*the*) *c. of humility*; woods or undergrowth sheltering game, COVERT[2]; (Commerc.) funds to meet liability or secure against contingent loss; plate, napkin, &c., laid for each person at table. [f. prec.]

co·verlet, -lid, n. Counterpane, quilt; covering. [earlier *coverlite* perh. f. OF **covre-lit* (as COVER[1] + *lit* bed)]

co·vert[1] (kŭ-), a. (Of threat, glance, &c.) secret, disguised. Hence **co·vert**LY[2] adv. [OF (as COVER[1])]

co·vert[2] (kŭ·vert, *-er*), n. Shelter, esp. thicket hiding game; *c. coat*, short light overcoat. [f. F *couvert* p.p. as n. (COVER[1])]

coverture (kŭ·vertsher), n. Covering, cover; shelter; condition of married woman under husband's protection. [OF (as COVER[1], see -URE)]

co·vet (kŭ-), v.t. Desire eagerly (usu. what belongs to another). Hence **co·vet**ABLE a. [f. OF *cuveitier* f. L **cupiditare* (as CUPIDITY)]

co·vetous, a. Eagerly desirous (*of* another's property &c.); grasping, avaricious. Hence **co·vetous**LY[2] adv., **co·vetous**NESS n. [f. OF *coveitus* (as prec., see -OUS)]

co·vey (kŭ-), n. Brood of partridges; family, party, set. [f. OF *covée* f. *couver* hatch f. L *cubare*, see -ADE]

co·vin (kŭ-), n. (legal, archaic). Conspiracy, collusion. [OF, f. LL *convenium* f. *convena* one who meets others (as CONVENE)]

cō·ving, n. Arched piece of building; (pl.) curved sides of fire-place. [COVE[2] + -ING[1]]

cow[1], n. (pl. *cows*, archaic *kine*). Female of any bovine animal, esp. of the domestic species (*the c. with the iron tail*, pump as used in adulterating milk); female of elephant, rhinoceros, whale, seal, &c.; *c.-bane*, water hemlock; *c.-boy*, boy in charge of cc., (U.S.) man in charge of grazing cattle on ranch; *c.-catcher* (U.S.), apparatus fixed in front of locomotive engine to remove cattle & other obstructions; *c.-fish*, (1) sea-cow, (2) Indian & American fish with horn-like spines over eyes; *c.-grass*, wild species of Trefoil; *c.-heel*, foot of cow or ox stewed to jelly; *cowherd*, one who tends cc. at pasture; *c.-hide*, (leather, whip, made of) c.'s hide; *cowitch*, =COWAGE; *c.-puncher* (U.S.), =*c.-boy*; *cowshot* (cricket slang), violent pull made in crouching position; *c.-tree*, S.-American tree with milk-like juice. Hence **cow·**ISH[1] a. [com.-Teut.; OE *cú* f. OTeut. *kouz* f. Aryan *gwous* (Skr. *gaus*, Gk *bous*, L *bos*)]

cow[2], v.t. Intimidate. [perh. f. ON *kuga*]

cow·age, cowh-, (-ĭj), n. Tropical plant with stinging hairs on pod. [f. Hind. *kawanch*]

cow·ard, n. & a. Faint-hearted, pusillanimous, (person). Hence **cow·ardli**NESS n., **cow·ard**LY[1] a., **cow·ard**LY[2] adv. [f. OF *coart* = It. *codardo* (*coda* tail f. L *cauda*, -ARD)]

cow·ardice, n. Faint-heartedness; *moral c.*, fear of disapprobation. [f. OF *couardise* (as prec., see -ICE)]

cow·er, v.i. Stand, squat, in bent position; crouch, esp. from fear. [etym. dub.; cf. Icel. *kúra* sleep, Da. *kure* squat; also G *kauern*]

cowl[1], n. Monk's hooded garment; hood of this; hood-shaped covering of chimney or ventilating shaft. Hence **cowl**ED[2] a. [(1) OE *cugele* f. LL *cucullа* f. L *cucullus* hood of cloak; (2) OE *cufle* cogn. w. Du. *keuvel*, conn. w. Icel. *kofl* cowl]

cowl[2], **coul**, n. Tub for water, esp. one with two ears, carried by two men on *c.-staff*. [prob. f. OF *cuvelle* f. L *cupella* dim. of *cupa*]

cow·-pox, n. Disease on teats of cows, communicated to human beings by vaccination.

cowr·ie, -y, n. Shell of small gastropod found in Indian Ocean, used as money in Africa & S. Asia; the animal; kinds of gastropod including *common c.* of British coast. [f. Hind. *kauri*]

cow·slip, n. Wild plant growing in pastures, with fragrant yellow flowers; *c. tea, wine* (made from these). [OE *cú-slyppe* prob. = cow-dung (*cú-* cow- + *slyppe* slimy substance)]

co·xa, n. Hip. Hence **co·x**AL a. [L]

co·xcomb (-ōm), n. Conceited showy person. Hence **coxco·mb**ICAL (-mĭ-) a. [= *cock's comb*; orig. (cap worn by) professional fool]

co·xcombry (-komrĭ), n. Foppery, behaviour of a coxcomb. [-RY]

coxswain (kŏ·kswān, kŏ·ksn), n. (abbr. *cox*). Helmsman of boat; person on board ship permanently in charge of, & (unless superior officer is present) commanding, boat & crew. Hence **co·xswain**LESS a., **co·xswain**SHIP n. [earlier *cockswain* (*cock* = COCKBOAT + SWAIN), cf. BOATSWAIN]

coxy. See COCKY.

coy, a. Modest, shy, (usu. of girl); (of place) secluded; *c. of*, backward, reserved, in (speech &c.). Hence **coy·**LY[2] adv., **coy·**NESS n. [f. F *coi* (fem. *coite*) f. L *as* QUIET]

coyote (kŏyō·tĭ, -yō·t), n. N.-American prairie-wolf. [Mex. Sp., f. Mex. *coyotl*]

coz (kŭz), n. (archaic). Abbr. of COUSIN.

coze, v.i., & n. (Have a) chat. [(vb) prob. f. F *causer*; n. perh. influenced by COSY]

cozen (kŭ·zn), v.t. Cheat, defraud, (*of*, *out of*); beguile (*into* do*ing*). Hence **co·zen**AGE(3) n. [?]

co·zy, a. See COSY.

crab[1], n. Kinds of ten-footed crustacean, esp. edible species found near most seacoasts; zodiacal constellation, CANCER; machine (orig. with claws) for hoisting heavy weights; (pl.) lowest throw at hazard, two aces, whence *turn out cc.*, end in failure; *catch a c.* in rowing, get oar jammed under water by faulty stroke; *c.'s eyes*, round concretion of carbonate of lime, found in stomach of crayfish; *c.(-louse)*, parasitical insect infesting human body; *c.-pot*, wicker trap for cc. Hence **cra·b**LET n., **cra·b**LIKE a. & adv. [OE *crabba* = ON *krabbi*, Du. *krabbe*, cogn. w. LG *krabben* scratch, claw]

crab[2], v.t. & i. (Of hawks) scratch, claw, fight with, (each other or abs.); (colloq.) cry down, pull to pieces. [prob. = LG as prec.]

crab[3], n. (Also *c.-apple*) wild apple (fruit & tree); sour person. [?]

cra·bbed, a. Cross-grained, perverse; churlish, irritable; (of writings or authors) ruggedly intricate, difficult to make out; (of handwriting) ill-formed & hard to decipher; sour, harsh. Hence **cra·bbĕd**LY[2] adv., **cra·bbĕd**NESS n. Also (in first two senses only) **cra·bby** a. [CRAB[1] + -ED[2], influenced in sense by CRAB[3]]

crack[1], n. & a. Sudden sharp noise (of whip, rifle, thunder); *c. of doom*, thunder-peal of Day of Judgement; sharp blow, as *a c. on the head*; *in a c.*, in a moment; (archaic, slang) boast, lie; (Sc. & North.) brisk talk, (pl.) news; fissure formed by breakage; partial fracture (the parts still cohering); good player, horse, &c.; burglar; house-breaking; (adj., colloq.) first-rate; *c.-brained*, crazy. [f. foll.; not in OE]

crack[2], v.t. & i. (Cause to) make sharp noise, as *c. a whip*, *whips c.*; *c.* (utter) *a joke*; chat; *c. up*, praise; break (nut, skull, &c.) with sudden sharp report; *c. a bottle*, empty, drink it; (slang) *c. a crib*, break into a house; break (t. & i.) without complete separation of parts; *voice cracks, is cracked* (becomes dissonant, esp. at age of puberty); damage, ruin, (credit &c.); (p.p., colloq.) crazy, insane; *c.-jaw* (colloq.), (word) difficult to pronounce. Hence **crac·k**ABLE a. [com.-Teut.; OE *cracian*, Du. *kraken*, G *krachen*]

cra·cker, n. In vbl senses; also or esp.: firework exploding with sharp report; explosive bon-bon; instrument for cracking, as *nut-cc.*; thin hard biscuit; (U.S.) biscuit; smash, breakdown; (school slang) lie. [-ER[1]]

cra·ckle, v.i., & n. Emit slight cracking sound; (n.) such sound, (also *c.-china, -glass, -ware*) china, glass, with appearance of minute cracks. [(n. f. vb) CRACK[2] + -LE(3)]

cra·ckling, n. In vbl senses; also, crisp skin of roast pork. [prec. + -ING[1]]

cra·cknel, n. Light crisp kind of biscuit. [prob. f. F *craquelin*]

cra·cksman, n. Burglar. [CRACK[1], MAN]

cra·cky, a. Full of cracks; apt to crack; (colloq.) crazy. [-Y[2]]

-cracy, noun suf. added to Gk stems (and as *-ocracy* to E wds), meaning 'rule of, ruling body of, class influential by'; thus *democracy* = popular government, *the d.* = the lower classes as political power; *plutocracy* = government by the rich, *the p.*, those whose wealth gives them power; so *cottonocracy* &c. [f. F *-cratie* f. Gk *-kratia* (*kratos* power)]

crā·dle, n., & v.t. Bed, cot, for infant, mounted on rockers; *from the c.*, from infancy; (fig.) place in which thing is nurtured in earliest stage, as *c. of an art, of a nation*; framework resembling c., esp. (Naut.) that on which ship rests during construction or repairs; frame attached to scythe to lay corn evenly; (Engraving) kind of serrated chisel, rocking-tool; (Mining) trough on rockers in which auriferous earth is shaken in water; CAT's-*c.*; (v.t.) place in (child's, ship's) c., contain or shelter as c., mow (corn) with c.-scythe. [OE *cradol*, etym. dub.]

cra·dling, n. In vbl senses; also (Arch.) wood or iron framework. [prec. + -ING[1]]

craft, n. Skill; cunning, deceit; art, trade, (esp. in combb., as *handic., priestc., statec.*); *the gentle c.*, angling; members of a c.; *the c.*, brotherhood of Freemasons; boat, vessel, (pl. *craft*); *c.-brother, -guild*, workman, guild of workmen, of same trade; *craftsman*, one who practises a c., whence **cra·ftsman**SHIP(3) n. [com.-Teut.; OE *cræft*, G *kraft* strength]

cra·fty, a. Cunning, artful, wily. Hence **cra·fti**LY[2] adv., **cra·fti**NESS n. [com.-Teut.; OE *cræftig* (CRAFT, see -Y[2])]

crag[1], n. Steep or rugged rock; *cragsman*, skilled climber of cc. Hence **cra·gg**ED[2], **cra·gg**Y[2], aa., **cra·ggĕd**NESS, **cra·ggi**NESS, nn. [prob. Celt.; cf. Ir. *creag*]

crag[2], n. (geol.). Deposits of shelly sand found in Norfolk, Suffolk, Essex. [perh. = prec.]

crake, n., & v.i. Kinds of bird including CORN-*c.*; cry of the corn-c.; (v.i.) utter this. [imit., cf. CROAK]

cram, v.t. & i., & n. Fill overfull; force (thing *into, down*; *c. down* one's *throat*, tell him repeatedly); stuff (poultry &c. *with* food); eat greedily; (fig.) prepare t. & i.) for examination; learn, get up, (subject) for special purpose; *c.-full*, as full as cramming can make it; (n.) crowd, cramming for examination, (slang) lie. [(n. f. vb) OE *crammian* f. *crimman* insert, cf. OHG *krimman*, pinch]

cra·mbo, n. Game in which one player gives word to which each of the others must find rhyme; *dumb c.*, game in which one side must guess word agreed upon by other side, who represent rhymes to it in dumb show. [prob. f. L *crambe repetita* cabbage served up again]

cra·mmer, n. In vbl senses, esp.: one who crams (esp. pupils); lie. [-ER[1]]

crā·moisy, -mesy, a. & n. (archaic). Crimson (cloth). [f. It. *cremesi, chermesi*, f. Arab. *qirmazi* of the KERMES]

cramp[1], n. Contraction of muscles from sudden chill, strain, &c.; *c.-fish*, electric ray, torpedo. [f. OF *crampe* f. same root as CRAM]

cramp[2], n. (Also *c.-iron*) metal bar with bent ends for holding masonry &c. together; portable tool for pressing two planks &c. together; restraint. [as prec., but thr. Du.]

cramp[3], a. Hard to make out, as *c. word, handwriting*; contracted, cramped. Hence **cra·mp**NESS n. [f. CRAMP[1] or OF *crampe* a.]

cramp[4], v.t. Affect with CRAMP[1]; confine narrowly (also *c. up*); (fig.) restrict (energies &c.); fasten with CRAMP[2]. Hence **cra·mped**NESS n.

cra·mpon, n. Metal hook, grappling-iron; iron plate with spikes for walking on ice &c. [F, f. LL *cramponem*, nom. *-o*, f. root of CRAM[1]]

cran, n. (Sc.). Measure for fresh herrings (37½ gal.). [?]

crā·nage, n. Use of crane; dues paid for this. [CRANE[1] + -AGE]

cra·nberry, n. Small dark-red acid berry, fruit of dwarf shrub native of Britain, N. Europe, N. America, &c. [recent in E, thr. N. Amer. colonists f. LG *krônbere*]

crane[1], n. Large wading bird with long legs, neck, and bill; machine for moving heavy weights; siphon; (also *water-c.*) tube for supplying water to locomotive; *c.-fly*, daddy-long-legs; *c.'s-bill*, various species of geranium. [OE *cran*, cf. Du. *kraan*, G *kranich*]

crane[2], v.t. & i. Move with crane; stretch (neck), stretch neck, like crane; *c. at*, pull up at, shrink from, (hedge, difficulty). [f. prec.]

cranio- in comb. =foll., as *cranio*LOGICAL, -LOGIST, -LOGY, -METRY.

crā·nium, n. (pl. *-ia*). Bones enclosing the brain; bones of the whole head, skull. Hence **crā·ni**AL a. [med. L f. Gk *kranion* skull]

crank[1], n., & v.t. Part of axis bent at right angles for converting reciprocal into circular motion, or vice versa; elbow-shaped connexion in bell-hanging; revolving disk turned by criminals as punishment; (v.t.) bend into c. shape, furnish or fasten with c. [(vb f. n.) OE *cranc* prob. f. *crincan* (past *cranc*) rare by-form of *cringan* contract, curl up]

crank[2], n. Fanciful turn of speech; eccentric idea or act; eccentric person. [different. f. prec.]

crank[3], a. Weak, shaky, (usu. of machinery). [f. CRANK[1]]

crank[4], a. (naut.). Liable to capsize. [?]

cra·nkle, v.i., & n. Bend in and out, twist; (n.) bend, twist. [(n. f. vb) CRANK[1] vb + -LE]

cra·nky, a. Sickly; shaky, crazy; capricious; crotchety, eccentric; full of twists; (Naut.) =CRANK[4]. Hence **cra·nki**LY[2] adv., **cra·nki**NESS n. [CRANK[1,2,3,4] + -Y[2]]

cra·nnog, n. Ancient lake-dwelling in Scotland or Ireland. [Ir. (*crann* tree, beam)]

cra·nny, n. Chink, crevice, crack. Hence **cra·nni**ED[2] a. [prob. f. F *cran*, etym. dub.]

crape, n., & v.t. Gauze-like fabric with wrinkled surface, usu. of black silk or imitation silk (of other colour or material now usu. CRÊPE), used for mourning dress; band of this round hat &c. as sign of mourning; *c.-cloth*, c.-like woollen material; (v.t.) cover, clothe, drape, with c. Hence **cra·p**Y[2] a. [f. CRÊPE]

craped, a. In vbl senses; also, crisped, crimped. [CRAPE + -ED[2,1]]

crā·pulent, a. Given to, suffering from effects of, resulting from, intemperance. Hence or cogn. **cra·pul**ENCE n., **cra·pu-lo**US a. [f. L *crapulentus* (*crapula* debauch f. Gk *kraipalē* drunken headache, see -LENT)]

crash[1], v.i. & t., & n. Make a c. (see n.); move, go, with a c., (of aircraft) fall to earth; (trans.) dash in pieces, throw, force, drive, with a c.; *go, fall, c.* (with a c.); (n.) noise as of broken crockery, thunder, loud music, &c., violent percussion or breakage, (fig.) ruin, collapse of mercantile credit. [imit.]

crash[2], n. Coarse linen for towels &c. [?]

crā·sis, n. (Gk gram.). Combination of the vowels of two syllables (as *kǎgō* for *kai egō*). [Gk, =mixture (*kerannumi* mix)]

crăss, a. Thick, gross; (fig.) gross, as *c. stupidity*; grossly stupid. Hence **cra·ss**LY[2] adv., **cra·ss**NESS n. [f. L *crassus* solid, thick]

cra·ssitude, n. Grossness; gross stupidity. [f. L *crassitudo* (as prec., see -TUDE)]

-crat, noun suf. =supporter, member, of a -CRACY, & used & appended similarly (*-crat, -ocrat*). Hence **-cra·tic**(AL) adj. suff. [f. F *-crate* formed f. adjj. in *-cratique* (on anal. of Gk *autokratēs* or independently) f. Gk *-kratia* -CRACY]

cratch, n. Rack for feeding beasts out of doors. [f. OF *creche*; cf. OHG *chrippa* CRIB]

crate, n. Large open-work case or basket for carrying glass, crockery, fruit, &c. Hence **cra·te**FUL n. [prob. f. L *cratis* hurdle]

crā·ter, n. Mouth of volcano; bowl-shaped cavity, esp. that made by a shell-explosion. Hence **cra·teri**FORM a. [L, f. Gk *kratēr* mixing-bowl for wine (*kerannumi* mix)]

cravă·t, n. Neckcloth, tie, (now archaic or shop). Hence **crava·tt**ED[2] a. [f. F *cravate* f. G *Krabate* Croatian]

crave, v.t. & i. Beg for; long for; beg, long, *for*. [OE *crafian*]

crā·ven, a. & n. Cowardly, abject, (person); *cry c.*, surrender. Hence **cra·ven**LY[2] adv. [?]

craw, n. Crop of birds or insects. [ME *crawe* cogn. w. Du. *kraag* neck]

crawfish. See CRAYFISH.

crawl[1], n. Pen in shallow water for fish, turtles, &c.; =KRAAL. [f. Du. KRAAL]

crawl[2], v.i., & n. Move slowly, dragging body along close to ground, or on hands & knees; walk, move, slowly; creep abjectly; (of ground &c.) be alive *with* crawling things; feel creepy sensation, whence **craw·l**Y[2] a.; (n.) crawling; *the c.*, a modern high-speed swimming stroke. [(n. f. vb) prob. f. Norse; cf. Da. *kravle* crawl, Sw. *krafla* grope]

craw·ler, n. In vbl senses; esp.: baby's overall; louse; cab moving slowly in search of fare.

cray·fish, craw·-, n. Small lobster-like fresh-water crustacean; spiny lobster. [ME & OF *crevice* f. OHG *crebig* f. same st. as CRAB[1]]

cray·on (or as F), n., & v.t. Stick, pencil, of coloured chalk or other material for drawing; carbon point in electric arc lamp; (v.t.) draw with cc., (fig.) sketch. [(n.) F (*craie* f. L *creta* chalk, see -OON); (vb) f. F *crayonner*]

craze, v.t., & n. Render insane (usu. in p.p.); produce small cracks on (pottery); (intr.) have such cracks; (n.) insane fancy, mania, crazy condition, (*be the c.*, be generally sought or affected). [(n. f. vb) orig. =break, shatter, perh. (direct or thr. OF *acraser* =*écraser*) f. Sw. *krasa*]

cra·zing, n. In vbl senses; *c.-mill* (for crushing tin ore). [-ING[1]]

cra·zy, a. (Of ship, building, &c.) unsound, shaky; sickly; insane, mad; (of paving, quilts, &c.) made of irregular pieces fitted together. Hence **cra·zi**LY[2] adv., **cra·zi**NESS n. [CRAZE + -Y[2]]

creak, n., & v.i. Harsh strident noise, as of unoiled hinge, new boots, &c.; (v.i.) make this. Hence **crea·k**Y[2] a. [prob. imit.]

cream[1], n. Oily part of milk, which gathers on the top, & by churning is made into butter; CLOT*ted* (also *Devonshire*) *c.*; fancy dish, sweet, like or made of c.; best part of anything, esp. the point of an anecdote; part of a liquid that gathers at the top; *c. of tartar*, purified & crystallized bitartrate of potassium, used in medicine &c.; *c. of lime* (pure slaked); c.-like preparation, as *cold c.* (cooling unguent); c.-coloured horse; *c. cheese*, soft rich kind made of unskimmed milk & cream; *c.-fruit*, a c.-like fruit of Sierra Leone; *c.-coloured*, yellowish white; *c.-laid, -wove, paper*, laid, wove, paper of c. colour; *c. separator*, machine for separating c. from milk. Hence **crea·m**Y[2] a., **crea·mi**NESS n. [f. F *crème* f. L as CHRISM]

cream[2], v.i. & t. (Of milk & liquids) form cream or scum; cause (milk) to c.; take cream from (milk); take the best part of (anything); add cream to (tea &c.). [f. prec.]

crea·mer, n. Flat dish for skimming cream off milk; machine for separating cream. [-ER[1]]

crea·mery, n. Butter-factory; shop where milk, cream, &c., are sold. [f. F *crémerie* (as CREAM[1], see -ERY)]

crease, n., & v.t. & i. Line caused by folding, fold, wrinkle; (Cricket) line defining position of bowler & batsman, as *bowling c.* (from behind which bowler delivers ball); (v.t.) make cc. in (material); (v.i.) fall into cc. Hence **crea·s**Y[2] a. [?]

crēa·te, v.t. Bring into existence, give rise to; originate, as (of actor) *c. a part*; invest (person) with rank, as *c. a man a peer, c. a peer*; (slang as v.i.) make a fuss (*you needn't c. about it*). Hence **crea·t**IVE a., **crea·tive**LY[2] adv., **crea·tive**NESS n. [f. L *creare*, see -ATE[3]]

crē·atine, n. An organic base found in the juice of flesh. [f. Gk *kreas -atos* meat + -INE[5]]

crea·tion, n. Act of creating (esp. the world); investing with title, rank, &c. (*c. of peers*, ultimate means of overcoming resistance of House of Lords to will of Commons); all created things; a production of the human (esp. dressmaker's, actor's) intelligence, esp. of the imagination. [f. F *création* f. L *creationem* (as prec., see -ATION)]

creā·tionism, n. Theory that God creates a soul for every human being at birth; theory that attributes origin of matter & species to special creation (not EVOLUTION). So **crea·tion**IST n. [-ISM]

creā·tor, n. *The C.*, the Supreme Being; one who creates, whence **crea·tr**ESS[1] n. [OF, f. L *creatorem* (as CREATE, see -OR[2])]

creature (krē·tsh*er*), n. Created thing; animate being; animal (often as distinct from man); human being, person, (often expr. admiration, contempt, patronage, &c.); one who owes his fortune to another; mere instrument; *the c.* (often spelt as Ir., *cratur* &c.) whisky or other intoxicant; *c.* COMFORTS. [f. F *créature* f. L *creatura* (as prec., see -URE)]

crea·turely, a. Of creatures. [-LY[1]]

crèche (krāsh), n. Public nursery for infants. [F (as CRATCH)]

crē·dat Judae·us (Ape·lla), sent. expressing incredulity. [L, = let the Jew Apella believe it, see Hor. *Sat.* I. v. 100]

crē·dence, n. Belief; *give c. to*, believe; *letter of c.* (introduction); small side table for eucharistic elements before consecration. [f. med. L *credentia* (*credere* believe, see -ENCE)]

crede·ntial, n. (usu. pl.). Letter(s) of introduction (also fig.). [as CREDENCE + -AL]

crē·dible, a. (Of persons or statements) believable, worthy of belief. Hence or cogn. **credibi·li**TY n., **cre·dib**LY[2] adv. [f. L *credibilis* (as CREDENCE, see -BLE)]

crē·dit[1], n. Belief, trust; *give c. to*, believe (story); good reputation; power derived from this; acknowledgement of merit, as *have the c. of, get c. for*; source of honour, as *a c. to the school, it does him c.*; trust in person's ability & intention to pay, as *give c., deal on c., long c.*; reputation of solvency & honesty; sum placed at person's disposal in books of a bank &c.; *letter of c.* (authorizing person to draw money from writer's correspondent in another place); (Bookkeeping) acknowledgement of payment by entry in account, sum entered on c. side of account (cf. DEBIT), this side, *give* person *c. for*, enter (sum) to his c., (fig.) ascribe (quality) to him. [f. F *crédit* f. L *credere -it-* believe, trust]

cre·dit[2], v.t. Believe; carry to credit side of account (c. amount *to* person, person *with* amount); (fig.) c. person *with*, think he has (a quality). [f. prec.]

crē·ditable, a. That brings credit or honour (*to*). Hence **cre·ditab**LY[2] adv. [-ABLE]

crē·ditor, n. One to whom a debt is owing; (Bookkeeping) *c.* (abbr. *Cr*) *side* of account, right-hand side. [f. OF *crediteur* f. L *creditorem* (as CREDIT[1], see -OR[2])]

crē·do, n. Creed (esp. Apostles' & Nicene, beginning in Latin with c.); musical setting of Nicene Creed. [L, = I believe]

crĕ·dūlous, a. Too ready to believe; (of things) showing such readiness. Hence or cogn. **credū·li**TY, **crĕ·dulous**NESS, nn.,

cre·dulousLY[2] adv. [f. L *credulus* (*credere* believe)]

creed, n. Brief formal summary of Christian doctrine, esp. *Apostles'* (also *the C.*), *Nicene, Athanasian, C.*; system of religious belief; set of opinions on any subject. Hence **cree·d**LESS a. [OE *créda,* f. L CREDO]

creek, n. Inlet on sea-coast; small harbour; short arm of river; (U.S. & Colon.) tributary river; narrow plain between mountains. [etym. dub., prob. G; ME *crike* (cf. F *crique*), later *creke* (cf. Du. *kreke*), *crick* (cf. Sw. *krik*)]

creel, n. Large wicker basket for fish; angler's fishing-basket. [orig. Sc., etym. dub.]

creep, v.i. (crept), & n. Move with body prone & close to ground; move timidly, slowly, or stealthily; insinuate oneself *into,* come *in, up,* unobserved; proceed, exist, abjectly; (of plants) grow along ground, wall, &c.; *flesh creeps,* feels as if things were creeping over it (result of fear, repugnance, &c.); (Naut.) drag with creeper at bottom of water; *c.-mouse* (adj.), timid, shy. (N.) creeping; shrinking horror, as (colloq. pl.) *gave me the cc.*; low arch under railway embankment; opening in hedge &c. [(n. f. vb) com.-Teut.; OE *créopan,* Du. *kruipen*]

cree·per, n. In vbl senses, esp.: plant that creeps along ground or up wall; grapnel for dragging bottom of water. [-ER[1]]

cree·py, a. Having a creeping of the flesh; productive of this; given to creeping. So **cree·py-craw·ly** a. [-Y[2]]

creese, crease, kris (-ēs, -ĭs), n. Malay dagger with wavy blade. [Malay (*k*(*i*)*ris, kres*]

crema·te, v.t. Consume (esp. corpse) by fire. So **crem**A·TION, **crema·tion**IST(2), nn. [f. L *cremare,* see -ATE[3]]

crema·tor, n. Person, furnace, cremating corpses or rubbish. Hence **crĕmator·ium, crĕ·mat**ORY(2), nn. [L (as prec., see -OR[2])]

crème (-ām), n. *C. de menthe,* peppermint liqueur; *c. de la c.,* the very pick, élite. [F]

cremō·na, n. Violin made at C.; cromorne.

crena·te(d), a. (bot., zool.). With notched or toothed edge. Hence **cren**A·TION n. [f. It. *crena* notch, etym. dub., see -ATE[2]]

cre·nature (-ē- *or* -ĕ-), n. Rounded tooth on edge of leaf &c. [as prec. see -URE]

crĕ·nel, crene·lle (-ĕl), n. Open space in embattled parapet, for shooting through &c. [OF (*-el*), dim. of *cren* = It. *crena* (see CRENATE)]

crĕ·nel(l)ate, v.t. Furnish with battlements or loopholes. Hence **crenell**A·TION n. [on F *créneler* (as prec.), see -ATE[2]]

crē·ōle, n. & a. (Descendant of) European (also *c. white*) or negro (*c. negro*) settler in W. Indies, Mauritius, &c.; (adj.) of such descent, (of animals &c.) naturalized in W. Indies &c. [f. F *créole* f. Sp. *criollo* perh. f. **criadillo* dim. of *criado* bred, domestic, p.p. of *criar* CREATE]

crē·osōte, n. Colourless oily fluid distilled from wood-tar, a strong antiseptic; (Commerc). carbolic acid. [f. Gk *kreas* meat + *sōzō* save]

crêpe (-ā-), n. Crapy fabric other than black mourning crape; *c. de Chine* (made of raw silk); *c. rubber,* very durable rubber used for boot soles &c. [F, f. L *crispa* curled, fem. adj.]

crĕ·pitate, v.i. Make crackling sound; (of beetles) eject pungent fluid with sharp report. Hence **cre·pit**ANT a., **crepit**A·TION n. [f. L *crepitare* frequent. of *crepare* creak, see -ATE[3]]

crépon (krĕ·pon, or as F), n. Stuff like crape, but of firmer substance. [F (as CRÊPE, see -OON)]

crept. See CREEP.

crepu·scular, a. Of twilight; (Zool.) appearing, active, in twilight; dim, not yet fully enlightened. [f. L *crepusculum* twilight + -AR[1]]

cresce·ndo (krĕsh-), adv., n., & a. (mus.) (Passage of music to be played) with gradually increasing volume (abbr. *cres., cresc.*); (fig.) progress towards a climax. [It., part. of *crescere* grow (as foll.)]

cre·scent (-sent), n. & a. Increasing moon; figure of moon in first or last quarter; this as badge of Turkish Sultans; the Turkish power; the Mohammedan religion; any figure of c. shape, esp. row of houses; (adj.) increasing, c.-shaped. [f. L *crescere* grow, see -ENT]

cress, n. Name of various plants usu. with pungent edible leaves, as *Garden C.,* WATER[1]-*c.* [OE *cresse,* f. root of OHG *chresan* creep]

cre·sset, n. Metal vessel for holding grease or oil for light, usu. mounted on pole; (mod.) fire-basket for lighting wharf &c. [OF (also *craisset*), f. *graisse* GREASE]

crest, n., & v.t. & i. Comb or tuft on animal's head; *c.-fallen,* with drooping c., dejected, abashed; plume, tuft, of feathers; (apex of) helmet; head, top, esp. of mountain; surface line of neck in animals; mane; (Anat.) ridge along surface of bone, as *frontal, occipital, c. of skull*; (Herald.) device above shield & helmet on coat of arms, or separately, as on seal, notepaper, &c.; (v.t.) furnish with c., serve as c. to, reach c. of (hill, wave); (v.i., of waves) form into a c. [(vb f. n.) f. OF *creste* f. L *crista* tuft]

crētā·ceous, a. Of (the nature of) chalk. [f. L *cretaceus* (*creta* chalk, see -ACEOUS)]

crē·tic, n. Metrical foot (–⏑–). [f. L *creticus* (*Creta* Crete, see -IC)]

crē·tifȳ, v.t. Impregnate with salts of lime. Hence **creti**FICA·TION n. [f. L *creta* chalk + -FY]

crē·tin, n. Deformed idiot of a kind found esp. in Alpine valleys. Hence **cre·tin**ISM (2) n., **cre·tin**IZE v.t., **cre·tin**OUS a. [f. F *crétin* f. L *Christianus* CHRISTIAN in mod. Rom. sense ' (barely) human creature ']

cretŏ·nne (*also* krĕ·t-), n. Stout unglazed cotton cloth with pattern printed on one or both sides. [F]

crevă·sse, n. Deep fissure in ice of glacier. [F, readopted as different. f. foll.]

crĕ·vice, n. Chink, fissure. [ME & OF *crevace* f. LL *crepatia* (*crepare* creak, crack)]

crew[1], n. Whole body of men manning ship or boat; associated body, company, of persons; set, gang, mob. [f. OF *creue* increase fem. p.p. (as n.) of *croistre* grow f. L *crescere*]

crew[2]. See CROW[3].

crew·el, n. Thin worsted yarn for tapestry & embroidery; *c.-work*, design in worsted on linen or cloth ground. [?]

crib[1], n. Barred receptacle for fodder; hovel, hut; small bed for child, with barred sides; wicker salmon-trap; framework lining shaft of mine; (also *c.-work*) heavy crossed timbers used in foundations in loose soil &c.; (U.S.) bin for maize, salt, &c.; set of cards given to dealer at cribbage, taken from other players' hands; (colloq.) plagiarism; translation for (esp. illegitimate) use of students; CRACK[2] *a c.*; *c.-biting* (of horses), habit of seizing manger in teeth & at same time noisily drawing in breath. [com.-WG; Du. *krib*]

crib[2], v.t. Confine in small space; furnish (cowshed &c.) with cribs; pilfer; copy unfairly or without acknowledgement. [f. prec.]

cri·bbage, n. Card game for two, three, or four persons. [f. CRIB[1] + -AGE]

crĭ·briform, a (anat., bot.). Having small holes, like a sieve. [f. L *cribrum* sieve + -FORM]

crick, n., & v.t. Spasmodic affection of muscles of neck, back, &c., sudden stiffness; (v.t.) produce c. in (neck &c.). [prob. imit.]

cri·cket[1], n. (Also *house-c*) a jumping chirping insect. [f. OF *criquet* conn. w. *criquer* creak; imit.]

cri·cket[2], n., & v.i. Open-air game played with ball, bats, & wickets, between two sides of 11 players each (*not c.* colloq., infringing the code of fair play between honourable opponents in any sphere); (v.i.) play c. Hence **cri·cket**ER[1] n. [etym. dub.; OF has *criquet*, a game, (also) a stick to aim at]

cri·coid, a. & n. Ring-shaped (cartilage of larynx). [f. Gk *krikoeidēs* (*krikos* ring, -OID)]

cri·er, n. One who cries; officer who makes public announcements in court of justice or (*town c.*) in a town. [ME & OF *criere*, nom. of *crieur* (*crier* CRY, see -OR[2])]

crĭ·key, int. (slang), expr. astonishment. [perh. substituted for L *Christe* O Christ]

crime, n., & v.t. Act (usu. grave offence) punishable by law; evil act, sin; *c.-sheet*, record of soldier's offences against regulations. Hence **cri·me**LESS a. (Vb, mil.) charge with or convict of military offence. [F, f. L *crimen -minis* judgement, offence (*cernere cret-* decide)]

crĭ·minal, a. & n. Of (the nature of) crime; *c.* CONVERSATION, CONNEXION; (person) guilty of crime. Hence or cogn. **crimina·**LITY n., **crĭ·minal**LY[2] adv. [f. F *criminel* f. L *criminalis* (as prec., see -AL)]

crĭ·minate, v.t. Charge with crime; prove (one*self* &c.) guilty of crime; censure. Hence or cogn. **crimin**A·TION n., **crĭ·minat**IVE, **crĭ·minat**ORY, aa. [f. L *criminari* (*crimen* CRIME), see -ATE[3]]

crĭ·minĕ, -nȳ, int. expr. astonishment. [perh. = It. *crimine* CRIME, or suggested by *jiminy* for *Gemini*]

crimino·logy, n. Science of crime. [f. L *crimen -minis* CRIME + -O- + -LOGY]

crĭ·minous, a. Guilty of crime, only in phr. *c. clerk* (clergyman). [f. OF *crimineux* f. L *criminosus* (as prec., see -OUS)]

crimp[1], n., & v.t. Agent who entraps men for seamen or soldiers (also fig.); (v.t.) entrap thus, impress, (seamen, soldiers). [?]

crimp[2], v.t. Compress into plaits or folds, frill; make flutings in, corrugate; contract (flesh of freshly-caught fish) by gashing; mould, bend, into shape. [f. same root as CRAMP[1], cf. Du. *krimpen* contract (intr.)]

cri·mson, a. & n., & v.t. & i. Deep-red (colour); (v.t. & i.) turn c. [(vb f. n.) f. Sp. *cremesin, car-*, (*carmesi* CRAMOISY, -INE[1])]

cringe (-j), v.i., & n. Cower; bow servilely; behave obsequiously (*to*); (n.) fawning obeisance, cringing. [(n. f. vb) earlier *crenge* f. *cringan*, see CRANK[1]]

cri·ngle, n. (naut.). Eye of rope containing thimble for another rope to pass through. [cf. G *kringel* dim. of *kring* ring f. root of CRANK[1]]

cri·nite, a. (bot., zool.). Hairy. [f. L *crinitus* (*crinis* hair, cf. -ATE[2](2)]

cri·nkle, v.t. & i., & n. Twist, wrinkle. Hence **cri·nkl**Y[2] a. [(n. prob. f. vb) frequent. of OE *crincan*, see CRANK[1] & -LE (3)]

cri·nkum-cra·nkum, n. & a. (Thing) full of twists & turns (lit. & fig.). [playful f. CRANK[1]]

cri·noid, a. & n. (zool.). Lily-shaped (echinoderm). Hence **crinoi·d**AL a. [f. Gk *krinoeidēs* (*krinon* lily, see -OID)]

crinole·tte, n. Contrivance for distending back of woman's skirt. [dim. f. foll.]

cri·noline (*also* -ēn), n. Stiff fabric of horsehair &c. formerly used for skirts;

hooped petticoat; netting round warship as defence against torpedoes. [F (L *crinis* hair + *linum* thread)]

crio- in comb. = Gk *krios* ram, as *-sphinx* (ram-headed), *-ceratite*, ram's-horn ammonite.

cri·pple, n., & v.t. & i. Lame person; staging for cleaning windows &c.; (v.t.) lame, (fig.) disable, impair; (v.i.) hobble, walk lamely, (*along* &c.). Hence **cri·pple**DOM, **cri·pple**HOOD, nn. [(vb f. n.) OE *crypel* f. OTeut. *krupilo-* (*kriupan* creep)]

cris. = CREESE.

crī·sis, n. (pl. *crisēs*). Turning-point, esp. of disease; moment of danger or suspense in politics, commerce, &c., as *cabinet, financial, c.* [L, f. Gk *krisis* decision (*krinō* decide)]

crisp, a., n., & v.t. & i. Hard but fragile, brittle; bracing, as *c. air*; brisk, decisive, as *c. manner, style*, &c.; (of hair &c.) curly; (n. collect., slang) banknotes; (v.t. & i.) curl in short stiff folds, make or become c. Hence **cri·sp**LY[2] adv., **cri·sp**NESS n. [(vb f. adj.) f. L *crispus* curled]

cri·spate, a. Crisped, (Bot., Zool.) with wavy margin. [f. L *crispare*, -ATE[2]]

crispa·tion, n. Curling; undulation; contraction (esp. = GOOSE-*skin*). [as prec., -ATION]

cri·spy, a. Curly; brittle; brisk. [-Y[2]]

cri·ss-cross, n., a., adv., & v.i. & t. Crossing lines, currents, &c. (for *c. row* see CHRIST-CROSS-ROW); (adj.) in cross lines (*c. pattern, traffic*), (of persons or temper) peevish; (adv.) crosswise, at cross purposes (*everything went c.*); (vb) move crosswise, work with c. pattern. [partly f. *Christ's Cross*, partly redupl. of *cross*]

cri·state, a. (nat. hist.). Having a crest. [f. L *cristatus* (as CREST, see -ATE[2])]

critēr·ion, n. (pl. *-ia*). Principle, standard, a thing is judged by. [f. Gk *kritērion* as foll.]

cri·tic, n. One who pronounces judgement; censurer; judge of literary or artistic works; one skilled in textual criticism. Hence **critic**A·STER n. [f. L f. Gk *kritikos* (*kritēs* judge f. *krinō*, see -IC)]

cri·tical, a. Censorious, fault-finding; skilful, engaged, in criticism; belonging to criticism; involving risk or suspense, as *c. condition, operation*; (Math., Physics) marking transition from one state &c. to another, as *c. angle, temperature.* Hence **cri·tical**LY[2] adv. [-AL]

cri·ticism, n. Work of a critic; critical essay or remark; *textual c.* (dealing with text, character, &c., of literary documents, esp. the Bible); *the higher c.* (other than verbal). [-ISM]

cri·ticize, v.t. Discuss critically (often abs.); censure. Hence **crit·iciz**ABLE a. [-IZE]

cri·tico- in comb. = critically, critical & —, as *-historical.* [CRITIC + -O-]

criti·que (-ēk), n. Critical essay or notice; art of criticism. [F (as CRITIC)]

croak, n., & v.i. & t. Deep hoarse sound of frog or raven; (v.i.) utter c., forebode evil, (slang) die; (v.t.) utter dismally. Hence **croa·k**Y[2] a. [prob. imit.]

croa·ker, n. In vbl senses; esp., prophet of evil. [-ER[1]]

Crō·at, n. Member of the race from which Croatia is named. [Slav.]

crō·ceāte (-sĭ-), a. Saffron, saffron-coloured. [f. L *croceus* (CROCUS), see -ATE[2]]

crō·chet (-shĭ), n., & v.t. (*-cheted* pron. -shĭd). Knitting (material or work) done with hooked needle; (v.t.) make (shawl &c. or abs.) in c. [(vb f. n.) F, dim. of *croche, croc*, hook]

crŏ·cidolite, n. A fibrous silicate of iron & sodium, blue asbestos; yellow mineral produced from this, used for ornament. [f. Gk *krokis -idos* nap of cloth + -LITE]

crock[1], n. Earthen pot or jar; (dial.) metal pot; broken piece of earthenware used for covering hole in flowerpot. [OE *croc, crocca*, cf. Icel. *krukka*]

crock[2], n., & v.i. & t. (Slang) inefficient person; broken-down horse; (Sc.) old ewe; (v.i., slang) *c. up*, break down; (v.t.) disable (usu. in p.p.). [prob. cogn. w. CRACK v.; cf. Norw. *krake* sickly beast, MDu. *kraecke* broken-down horse or house]

cro·ckery, n. Earthenware vessels. [f. obs. *crocker* potter (CROCK[1]), see -ERY]

cro·cket, n. Small ornament (usu. bud or curled leaf) on inclined sides of pinnacles &c. [f. AF *croket* = F CROCHET]

crŏ·codile, n. Large amphibious reptile (esp. the Nile species); *c. tears* (hypocritical, from belief that the crocodile wept while devouring, or to allure, its victim); (colloq.) girl's school walking two & two. Hence **crocodĭ·l**IAN a. [f. L f. Gk *krokodeilos*]

crō·cus, n. (pl. *-uses*). Genus of dwarf bulbous plants with brilliant (usu. yellow or purple) flowers; *c. sativus*, species of this yielding saffron; a peroxide of iron used for polishing. [L, f. Gk *krokos* crocus, saffron]

Croe·sus (krē-), n. Wealthy person. [*C.*, king of Lydia]

croft (-aw-, -ŏ-), n. Enclosed piece of (usu. arable) land; small holding of CROFTER. [etym. dub., cf. Du. *kroft* high & dry land]

cro·fter, n. One who rents a small holding, esp. joint tenant of Scotch divided farm. [-ER[1]]

cro·mlech (-k), n. Prehistoric structure consisting of large flat stone laid horizontally on upright ones. [W (*crom* bent, *llech* flat stone)]

cromor·ne, cremō·na, n. An organ reed-stop. [F, f. G *krummhorn* crooked horn]

crone, n. Withered old woman; old ewe. [ult. f. ONF *caroine*, see CARRION]

crō·ny, n. Intimate friend. [?]

crōōk, n. & a., & v.t. & i. Shepherd's, bishop's, hooked staff; anything hooked; hook; bend, curve; act of bending; (slang) rogue, swindler; *by* HOOK *or by c.*; (slang) *on the c.*, dishonestly; *c.-back(ed)*, hunch-back(ed); (adj.) = CROOKED; (v.t. & i.) bend, curve. [(vb f. n.) ME *crok* prob. f. ON *krókr*]

crōō·ked, a. Not straight, bent, twisted; deformed; bent with age; (fig.) not straightforward, dishonest; (of stick, pron. -ōōkt) having a cross handle, crutched. Hence **croo·ked**LY[2] adv., **croo·kĕd**NESS n. [-ED[1]]

crōōn, v.t. & i., & n. (Hum, sing, mutter, in) low undertone. [chiefly Sc. till 19th c.; cf. Du. *kreunen* groan]

crop[1], n. Pouch-like enlargement of gullet in birds, where food is prepared for digestion; stock, handle, of whip; (also *hunting-c.*) short whipstock with loop instead of lash; produce of cultivated plants, esp. cereals; *in, under, out of, c.* (cultivation); season's total yield (of cereal &c.); entire hide of animal tanned; cropping of hair; style of wearing hair cut short; piece cut off end; name of some cuts of meat; NECK *& c.*; *c.-eared*, with ears (also, hair) cut short. [OE, = bird's crop, rounded top of plant, cf. LG & Du. *krop*, OHG *chropf*, bird's c.; other senses developed in E]

crop[2], v.t. & i. Cut off; (of animals) bite off (tops of plants); gather, reap; cut short (ears, tail, hair, nap of cloth, edges of book); sow, plant, (land *with* barley &c.); (intr.) bear a crop; turn *up* unexpectedly; *c. out, forth*, appear; (Geol.) *c. up, out*, come to surface. [f. prec.]

cro·pper, n. Person, thing, that crops; pigeon with large crop, pouter; *good, heavy, light, c.*, plant yielding good &c. crop; (slang) heavy fall, as *came a c.* [CROP[1,2] + -ER[1]]

cro·ppy, n. Person with short cropped hair, esp. (Hist.) Irish rebel, sympathizer with French revolution, in 1798. [CROP[1] + -Y[2]]

crō·quet[1] (-kĭ), n. Game, played on lawn, in which wooden balls are driven with mallets through hoops; act of croqueting a ball. [perh. North. F, dial. form of CROCHET]

cro·quet[2] (-kĭ), v.t. (*croqueting*, pron. krō·kĭing; *croqueted*, pron. krō·kĭd). (In game of croquet) drive away (opponent's ball or abs.) by placing the two together & striking one's own (cf. ROQUET). [f. prec.]

croque·tte (-kĕt), n. Seasoned & fried ball of rice, potato, meat, &c. [F (*croquer* crunch)]

crore, n. (Anglo-Ind.). Ten millions, one hundred lakhs (usu. of rupees). [f. Hind. *kror*]

crō·sier, -zier, (-zhyer), n. Bishop's, abbot's, pastoral staff; (improp.) archbishop's cross. [orig. = bearer of a crook, f. OF *crocier* f. med. L *crociarius* (*crocia* crook) confused w. F *croisier* f. L **cruciarius* cross-bearer (*crux* cross); mod. *crosier* = *c.'s staff* (16th c.)]

cross[1] (-aw-, -ŏ-), n. Stake (usu. with transverse bar) used by the ancients for crucifixion, esp. that on which Christ was crucified; model of this as religious emblem; sign of c. made with right hand as religious act; staff surmounted with c. & borne before archbishop or in processions, *c.-bearer*, person who carries this; monument in form of c., esp. (also *market-c.*) one in centre of town; Christian religion; trial, affliction; annoyance; c.-shaped thing; (*Southern*) *C.*, a constellation; *Greek c.* (upright with limbs of equal length); *Latin c.* (with long lower limb); *St Andrew's c.* (like X); *Tau c., c. of St Anthony*, (like T); *Maltese c.* (with equal limbs, narrow where they join & widening out towards outer extremities, which are indented); *fiery c.*, Scotch signal (orig. two bloody sticks) sent through district to rouse inhabitants; decoration in orders of knighthood (*Grand C.*, highest degree of this; *Victoria C.*, decoration for personal valour); intermixture of breeds; animal resulting from this; mixture, compromise, *between* two things; (slang) fraud, swindle; *on the c.*, diagonally. Hence **cro·ss**LET n., **cro·ss**WISE adv. [ult. f. L *crux crucis*; late OE has *cruc*, ME *cruche, crouche*, & (thr. OF) *crois*]

cross[2], v.t. & i. Place crosswise, as *c. swords* (in fighting, also fig.); make sign of cross on or over (esp. one*self*, as sign of awe, to invoke divine protection, &c.); *c. fortune-teller's hand with*, give her (coin); draw line across, as *c. out, off*, cancel, *c. cheque* (with two lines usu. filled up with *& Co.* or name of bank through whom alone it may be paid); write across (what is already written, a letter); go across (road, river, sea, or abs.); bestride (saddle, horse); carry, move, across; meet and pass (*each other* or abs.); *two persons' letters c.* (each being dispatched before receipt of the other); *c.* one's *mind*, occur to one; *c. the path of*, meet with, thwart; thwart (person, will, plans); (cause to) inter-breed; cross-fertilize (plants.) [f. prec.]

cross[3], a. Passing from side to side, transverse, (*c. bench*, in Parliament, for members who are of neither party; so *c.-b.*, adj., impartial, as *the c.-b. mind*; *c. voting*, when in Parliamentary divisions &c. some of either or each side vote against their own party, as *there was no c. voting*); intersecting; contrary, opposed, (*to* a purpose &c., or abs.); (colloq.) peevish, out of humour, as *as c. as two sticks*, whence **cro·ss**LY[2] adv., **cro·ss**NESS n.; *c.-patch*, ill-natured person; *c. reference* (from one part of book to another for further information); (Bookkeeping) *c. entry* (transferring amount to different account or neutralizing previous entry); *cross-bred*, hybrid; (slang) dishonest, dishonestly got. [CROSS¹]

cross- in comb. 1. f. CROSS n., objectively, as *c.-bearer*, or attrib. = having a transverse part, as CROSS-BOW, marked with a c., as *c.*-BUN. 2. f. CROSS a. = crossing, transverse, as *c.-bar, -beam, -keys, -piece, -section*, CROSS-BONES. 3. adv., in vbs as *c.-breed, -fertilize* (animals, plants, from individuals of different species), CROSS-EXAMINE, CROSS-QUESTION; in vbl nouns as *c.-fire*, firing in two crossing directions. 4. prep. = across, as *c.-country*, adj., across fields, not following roads.

cro·ssbelt, n. Belt for cartridges &c. from shoulder to opposite hip. [CROSS-(2)]

cro·ssbill, n. Bird the mandibles of whose bill cross when bill is closed. [CROSS-(2)]

cro·ss-bones, n. pl. Figure of two thigh-bones laid across each other, usu. under skull as emblem of death. [CROSS-(2)]

cro·ss-bow, n. Bow fixed across wooden stock, with groove for the missile (stone, arrow, &c.) and mechanism for holding and releasing string. [CROSS-(1)]

cross-bu·ttock, n., & v.t. Throw over the hip, in wrestling. [CROSS-(4)]

cro·ss-cut, n. Diagonal cut, path, &c.,; figure in skating. [CROSS-(2)]

crosse, n. Long racquet-like implement used in LACROSSE. [F, f. OF *croce, croc*, hook]

cross-exa·mine, v.t. Examine (esp. witness in legal action) minutely, with a view to checking previous examination or eliciting suppressed facts. Hence **cross-examin**A·TION n. [CROSS-(3)]

cro·ss-grain, n. Grain running across the regular grain. [CROSS-(2)]

cro·ss-grained, a. (Of wood) with grain running irregularly or in crossing directions; (fig.) perverse, intractable. [-ED²]

cro·ss-hatch, v.t. Engrave with intersecting series of parallel lines. [CROSS-(3)]

cross head(ing), n. (In newspaper &c.) indication of the contents of the following passage inserted here & there across the column for the reader's guidance in an article or report. [CROSS-(2)]

cro·ssing, n. In vbl senses; also or esp.: intersection of two roads, railways, &c., as *level c.* (of road and railway, or two railways, on same level); place where street is crossed; *c.-sweeper*, one who sweeps this. [-ING¹]

cro·ss-legged, a. (Of person squatting) with legs crossed; (of person sitting on chair) with one leg laid across the other. [CROSS-(3)]

cro·ss-light, n. Light that crosses another; (fig.) illustration of subject from another point of view. [CROSS-(2)]

cross purposes, n. pl. Contrary or conflicting purposes; name of a game; *be at c.*, misunderstand one another, (also) have conflicting plans with same object. [CROSS-(2)]

cross question, n. Question asked in CROSS-QUESTIONing; *c.qq. & crooked answers*, game in which each question gets answer written for another.

cross-que·stion, v.t. Question in order to elicit details or test accuracy. [CROSS-(3)]

cro·ss-road, n. Road that crosses another or joins two main roads; (also *cross roads*) intersection of two roads. [CROSS- (2)]

cro·ss-stitch, n. Stitch formed of two crossing each other; kind of needlework characterized by these. [CROSS-(2)]

cro·ss-trees, n. pl. Two horizontal cross-timbers bolted to head of lower mast to support mast above. [CROSS-(2)]

cro·ss-word, n. Puzzle in which words written horizontally & others written vertically on chequered paper have to fit each other. [CROSS²]

cro·tchet, n. (Mus.) black-headed note with stem, half of minim; whimsical fancy, whence **crotchet**EER·, **cro·tche-ti**NESS, nn., **cro·tchet**Y² a.; hook. [f. F *crochet* dim. of *croc* hook]

crō·ton, n. Genus of plants, from one species of which *c. oil*, a drastic purgative, is obtained. [f. Gk *krotōn* tick, croton]

crouch (-ow-), v.i., & n. Stoop, bend, esp. timidly or servilely; (n.) crouching. [?]

croup(e)¹ (-ōō-), n. Rump, hind-quarters, (esp. of horse). [F (*-pe*), f. Teut. cf. CROP¹]

croup² (-ōō-), n. Inflammatory disease in larynx & trachea of children, marked by sharp cough. [f. obs. vb *croup* croak (imit.)]

crou·pier (-ōō-), n. Raker in of money at gaming table; assistant chairman at public dinner. [F, orig. = rider on the CROUPE¹]

crow¹ (-ō), n. Genus of birds, esp. *Carrion C.*, large black bird; *white c.*, a rarity; *have a c. to pluck* (fault to find) *with him*; *as the c. flies, in a c. line*, straight; *c.(-bar)*, bar of iron (usu. with beak-like end) used as lever; *crowberry*, fruit of a small heath-like shrub; *c.-bill*, forceps for extracting bullets &c.; *crowfoot*, name of various plants, esp. species of buttercup, (Naut.) arrangement of small ropes for suspending awning, (Mil., also *c.'s-foot*) caltrop; *c.'s-footed*, marked with c.'s-feet; *c.-quill*, c.'s quill or steel pen for fine writing; *c.'s-foot*, wrinkle at outer corner of eye; *c.'s-nest*, barrel fixed at mast-head of whaler &c. as shelter for look-out man; *c.-toe*, bluebell (& other flowers, as buttercup). [OE *crāwe* f. *crāwan* CROW³]

crow², n. Crowing of cock; joyful cry of infant. [f. foll.]

crow³ (-ō), v.i. (past *crew* or *crowed*, p.p. *crowed*). Utter loud cry of cock; (of child) utter joyful cry; exult loudly; *c. over*, triumph over. [OE *crāwan*, cf. Du. *kraaijen*, G *krähen*; imit.]

crowd[1], n. Throng, dense multitude, (*would pass in a c.*, is not conspicuously defective); *the c.*, the masses; (colloq.) company, set, lot; large number (of things); (Naut.) *c. of sail*, large number of sails hoisted. [f. foll.]

crowd[2], v.i. & t. Collect (t. & i.) in a crowd; fill, occupy, cram, (space &c. *with*); fill (place &c.) as a crowd does; force one's way *into, through*, &c. (confined space &c. or abs.); force (thing, person) *into* &c.; *c. out*, exclude by crowding; (Naut., of ship or crew) hasten on; *c. sail*, hoist unusual number of sails. [OE *crúdan* press, drive, cf. MDu. *cruden*]

crown[1], n. Wreath of flowers &c. worn on head, esp. as emblem of victory, (also fig. as *martyr's c., no cross no c.*); monarch's head-covering of gold &c. & jewels; (fig.) king or queen, regal power, supreme governing power in a monarchy; any c.-shaped ornament; (British coin worth) five shillings; foreign coin, esp. = KRONE; top part, esp. of skull; whole head; upper part of cut gem above girdle; highest or central part of arch or arched structure, as *c. of the causeway*; top of hat; part of tooth projecting from gum; size of paper, 15″×20″; *c.-glass*, made in circular sheets without lead or iron and used chiefly for windows; *c.-land* (belonging to the c.); *C. Colony* (controlled by the C.); *c. Derby*, kind of china made at Derby & often marked with c. surmounting D; *c. law*, criminal law; *c. lawyer* (in service of the C.); *C. office* (transacting common law business of Chancery); *C. prince*, heir-apparent or designate to a sovereign throne (esp. in Germany and N. Europe); *C. princess*, his wife; *c. -wheel*, CONTRATE wheel. [f. ONF *corune* f. L *corona* wreath, crown]

crown[2], v.t. Place crown on (person, head); invest (person) with regal crown or dignity (*c. him, c. him king*; *crowned heads*, kings & queens); (fig.) reward; occupy the head of, form chief ornament to, (lit. & fig.); put finishing touch to, as *to c. all*; bring (efforts) to happy issue; (Draughts) make (piece) a king; (Dent.) *c. a tooth*, protect its remains with a gold &c. cap cemented on. [f. OF *coroner* f. L *coronare* (as prec.)]

crowned, a. In vbl senses; (of hat) *high, low, -c.*, with high, low, crown. [-ED[1,2]]

crow·ner, n. (obs. or dial.). *=CORONER.

croy·don, n. Two-wheeled carriage of gig class. [*C.*, town in Surrey]

cru·cial (-ōōshl), a. Decisive, critical, (case, point, test, &c.); (Anat.) cross-shaped, as *c. incision*. [F, f. L *crux crucis* cross + -AL]

cru·cian, -sian, (-ōōshn), n. Yellow fish allied to carp. [f. LG *karusse* (etym. dub.), -AN]

cru·ciāte (-ōōsh-), a. (zool., bot.). Cross-shaped. [f. med. L *cruciatus* (as CRUCIAL, -ATE[2])]

cru·cible (-ōō-), n. Melting-pot (usu. of earthenware); (fig.) severe trial. [f. med. L *crucibulum*, etym. dub.]

cruci·ferous, a. Wearing, adorned with, a cross; (Bot.) of the order *Cruciferae*, having flowers with four equal petals arranged crosswise. [f. LL *crucifer* (as CRUCIAL, see -FEROUS)]

cru·cifix (-ōō-), n. Image of Christ on the cross; (improp.) cross. [f. OF *crucefix* f. L *cruci fixus* one fixed to the CROSS (see FIX)]

crucifi·xion, n. Crucifying; *the C.* (of Christ); picture of this. [f. mod. L *crucifixio* (L *cruci figere*, as prec., see -ION)]

cru·ciform, a. Cross-shaped. [f. L *crux crucis* cross, see -FORM]

cru·cify, v.t. Put to death by fastening to a cross; (fig.) mortify (passions, sins, flesh); (Mil.) tie up (soldier) with arms out in field punishment. [f. OF *crucifier* f. LL **crucificare* (see -FY) = *cruci figere*, see CRUCIFIX]

crude, a. In the natural or raw state; (of food &c.) not digested; unripe; (of diseases &c.) not matured; (fig.) ill-digested, unpolished, lacking finish; rude, blunt, (action, statement, manners); (Gram., of form of word) uninflected. Hence or cogn. **cru·de**LY[2] adv., **cru·de**NESS, **cru·d**ITY, nn. [f. L *crudus* raw]

cru·el (-ōōĭl), a. Indifferent to, delighting in, another's pain; (of actions) showing such indifference or pleasure; painful, distressing. Hence or cogn. **cru·el**LY[2] adv., **cru·el**TY n. [F, f. L *crudelis* (*crudus* CRUDE)]

cru·et (-ōōĭt), n. Small glass bottle with stopper for vinegar, oil, &c., for table; small vessel for wine or water in celebration of Eucharist; *c.-stand* (for cc. & castors). [f. OF **cruete* dim. of *cruie* f. OLG *crûca* pot]

cruise (-ōōz), v.i., & n. Sail to & fro on look-out for ships for protection of commerce in time of war, for plunder, or for pleasure, making for no particular port (also fig.); (n.) cruising voyage. [(n. f. vb) f. Du. *kruisen* or Sp., Port., *cruzar*, F *croiser*, f. L *cruciare* cross (*crux*)]

crui·ser, n. War-ship adapted for cruising; *armoured c.* (with lighter armour than battleship); *battle*,[1] BELT[2]*ed*, *c.*; (*un*)-*protected c.*, one with(out) protective deck. [-ER[1]]

cruive (-ōōv), n. (Sc.). Wicker salmon-trap. [?]

crumb (-m), n., & v.t. Small fragment, esp. of bread; (fig.) small particle, atom, (*of* comfort &c.); soft inner part of bread; *c.-cloth* (laid over carpet, esp. under table); (v.t.) cover, thicken, with cc., break into cc. Hence **cru·mb**Y[2] (-mĭ) a. [(vb f. n.) OE *cruma*, cf. Du. *kruim*]

cru·mble (-bl), v.t. & i. Break, fall, into

crumbs or fragments (lit. & fig.). [earlier *crimble* f. OE *cruma* CRUMB]
cru·mbly (-blĭ), a. Apt to crumble (intr.). [CRUMB + -LY¹; now treated as f. prec. + -Y²]
cru·mmy, a. (slang). (Of women) plump, comely; rich. [CRUMB + -Y²]
crump, v.t., & n. (colloq.). Hit (esp. cricket-ball) hard; (n.) hard hit, heavy fall, (army slang) bursting shell. [imit.]
cru·mpet, n. Soft cake of flour, egg, milk, &c., baked on iron plate; (slang) head (BARMY *on the* c.). [?]
cru·mple, v.t. & i. Crush together or *up* into creased state; ruffle, wrinkle; become creased. [f. obs. *crump* v. & a. (make, become) curved + -LE(3)]
crunch, v.t. & i., & n. Crush with teeth, esp. noisily; grind under foot (gravel &c.); make one's way (*up, through*, &c.) thus; (n.) crunching (noise). [replaces *cra(u)nch*, imit.]
cru·pper, n. Strap buckled to back of saddle & passing under horse's tail; hindquarters of horse. [f. OF *cropiere* (as CROUP¹)]
crur·al (-oor-), a. (anat.). Of the leg. [f. L *cruralis* (*crus cruris* leg, see -AL)]
crusā·de, n., & v.i. (Hist.) Christian expedition to recover Holy Land from Mohammedans; war instigated by Church for alleged religious ends; (fig.) aggressive movement against public evil &c., as *Temperance c.*; (v.i.) engage in c. Hence **crusa·d**ER¹ n. [(vb f. n.) f. 16th-c. F *croisade* & Sp. *cruzada* f. med. L *cruciata* p.p. of *cruciare* mark with CROSS]
crusā·do, n. Portuguese coin worth about 2*s.* 4*d.* [f. Port. *cruzado* marked with cross]
cruse (-s, -z), n. (archaic). Pot, jar, of earthenware (*widow's c.*, inexhaustible supply, see 1 *Kings* xvii. 12 &c.). [cf. Du. *kroes*, G *krause*, etym. dub.]
crush¹, v.t. & i. Compress with violence, so as to break, bruise, &c.; crumple (dress &c.) by rough handling; (fig.) subdue, overwhelm, as *a crushing defeat, reply*; *c. out*, extinguish, stamp out; *c. a cup of wine*, drink it; (intr.) squeeze one's way (*into* &c.). [prob. f. OF *croissir* crash, prob. of Teut. orig.]
crush², n. Act of crushing; crowded mass (esp. of persons); (colloq.) crowded social gathering; *c.-room* in theatre &c. (for promenade during intervals); *c. hat*, collapsible opera hat with spring. [f. prec.]
crust, n., & v.t. & i. Hard outer part of bread; similar casing of anything, e.g. harder layer over soft snow (*c.-hunt* n. & v.t. & i., of hunting elks &c. over a c. that supports hunters but not quarry); hard dry scrap of bread; pastry covering pie; hard dry formation, scab, on skin; (Geol.) outer portion of earth; coating, deposit, on surface of anything; *c. of wine*, deposit on sides of bottle; hard external covering of animal or plant; (fig.) anything superficial; (v.t.) cover with, form into, c.; (v.i.) become covered with c. [(vb f. n.) f. L *crusta*, partly thr. OF *crouste*]
Crustā·cea (-sha), n. pl. Large class of animals, mostly aquatic, with hard shell, as crabs, lobsters, shrimps. Hence **crust**A·CEAN a. & n.; **crustacĕo·**LOGY n. [neut. pl. of mod. L CRUST(*aceus* -ACEOUS)]
crusta·ceous, a. Crust-like; (of animals) having a hard covering, esp. (Zool.) belonging to the *Crustacea*. [as prec.]
cru·sted, a. Having a crust; (of wine) having deposited a crust; (fig.) antiquated, venerable, as *c. prejudice, theory*. [-ED²]
cru·sty, a. Crust-like, hard; irritable; curt. Hence **cru·sti**LY² adv., **cru·sti**NESS n. [-Y²]
crutch, n. Staff (usu. with crosspiece at top) for lame person (usu. *pair of cc.*); support, prop, (lit. & fig.); (Naut.) various forked contrivances; crosspiece, whence **crutch**ED² a. [com.-Teut.: OE *crycc*, Du. *kruk*, G *krücke*, f. OTeut. *kruk*- bend]
Cru·tchĕd Fri·ars, n. pl. Minor order of friars wearing a cross; site of their convent in London. [f. ME *crouch* CROSS¹ + -ED²]
crux, n. Difficult matter, puzzle. [L, = cross]
cry¹, n. Loud inarticulate utterance of grief, pain, fear, joy, &c.; loud excited utterance of words; appeal, entreaty; proclamation of wares to be sold in streets; rumour; voice of the public; watchword, as *war-c., battle-c.*; fit of weeping; yelping of hounds (also fig.), as *full c.* (pursuit); *within c.*, within calling distance (*of*); *a far c.*, a long way; *c.-baby*, one who cries childishly; *much c. & little wool*, fuss to no purpose, as when pigs are shorn. [f. F *cri*, as foll.]
cry², v.t. & i. Utter loudly, exclaim, (with sentence as object, or *that*); make loud utterance, as *c. out, c. to* (person &c.); announce for sale, as *c. muffins*; *c. stinking fish*, condemn one's own wares; weep (*bitter tears*, one's *heart out*, one*self to sleep*, or abs.; *c. over spilt milk*, waste regrets); (of animals, esp. birds) make loud call; (of hounds) yelp; ask *for* (esp. *c. for the moon*); *cry down*, disparage; *c. off*, withdraw *from* bargain; *c. up*, praise, extol; *c.* CRAVEN; *c. halves*, claim share (*in*); *c.* QUARTER, QUITS; *c. shame upon*, protest against (act, person). [f. F *crier* f. L *quiritare* cry aloud, orig. ask aid of the citizens (*Quirites*)]
cry·ing, a. In vbl senses; esp. (of evils) calling for notice, flagrant. [-ING²]
crȳ·ogen, n. (chem.). Freezing-mixture; thing mixed with ice to make this. [f. Gk *kruos* frost + -GEN(1)]

crypt, n. Underground cell, vault, esp. one beneath church, used as burial-place. [f. L f. Gk *kruptē* (*kruptō* hide)]

cry·ptic, a. Secret, mystical. [f. L f. Gk *kruptikos* (as prec., see -IC)]

cry·pt(o)- in comb. =Gk *kruptos* hidden, secret, as *-branchiate*, with concealed gills, *-Calvinist*, secret sympathizer with Calvinism, *-logy*, enigmatical language.

cry·ptogam, n. Plant having no stamens or pistils, & therefore no proper flowers. Hence **cryptogă·mic, cryptŏ·gamous,** aa., **crypto·gamist**(3), **crypto·gamy**[1], nn. [f. F *cryptogame* (prec. + Gk *-gamos* wedded), after Linnaean class-name *Cryptogamia*]

cry·ptogram, -graph, nn. Thing written in cipher. So **crypto·grapher, crypto·graphy,** nn., **cryptogra·phic** a. [CRYPTO- + -GRAM, -GRAPH]

cry·stal, n. & a. A clear transparent ice-like mineral; *rock-c.*, a form of pure quartz; piece of this; *c. set*, simple form of receiving apparatus in broadcasting; (poet.) any clear transparent thing, esp. water; *c.-gazing*, concentration of one's gaze on ball of rock-c., pool of ink, &c., for the purpose of inducing a hallucinatory picture of future or distant events (*crystal* colloq., view of the future thus obtained, prophetic utterance); (also *c. glass*) glass of very transparent quality; vessel &c. of this; *C. Palace*, building of glass & iron built in Hyde Park for the 1851 Exhibition & re-erected at Sydenham; (Chem., Min.) aggregation of molecules with definite internal structure & external form of solid enclosed by symmetrically arranged plane faces; (adj.) made of, like, clear as, c. [f. OF *cristal* f. L *crystallum* f. Gk *krustallos* ice, crystal, f. *krustainō* freeze (*kruos* frost)]

cry·stalline (-ī- *or* -ĭ-), a. Made of, clear as, like, crystal; *c. heaven* (in Ptolemaic system, between primum mobile & firmament, assumed to explain precession of equinox &c.); *c. lens* of eye, transparent body in membranous capsule behind iris. [f. L f. Gk *krustallinos* (as prec., see -INE[2])]

cry·stallize, v.t. & i. Form into crystals or (fig.) definite or permanent shape. Hence **cry·stallizable** a., **crystalliza·tion** n. [-IZE]

crystallo- in comb. =Gk *krustallos* CRYSTAL, as *-ge·nic*, *-geny*, forming, formation of, crystals, *-grapher*, *-gra·phic*, *-graphy*, student of, pertaining to, science of, crystal structure.

cry·stalloid, a. & n. Crystal-like; (body) of crystalline structure (cf. COLLOID). [-OID]

ctē·noid (t-), a. & n. (Fish with scales or teeth) like a comb. [f. Gk *ktenoeidēs* (*kteis ktenos* comb, see -OID)]

cub, n., & v.t. & i. Young of fox, as *c.-hunting*; young of bear or other wild beast; unpolished youth (usu. *unlicked c.*); (vb) bring forth (cc., or abs.). Hence **cu·bbish**[1] a., **cu·bhood** n. [?]

cū·bage, n. (Finding of) cubic content. [CUBE + -AGE]

cu·bature, n. =prec. [f. mod. L *cubare -at-* (LL *cubus* CUBE), see -URE]

cu·bbing, n. CUB-hunting. [CUB + -ING[1]]

cube, n., & v.t. Solid contained by squares; block of anything so or similarly shaped; product of a number multiplied by its square (*c. of 2* = *8*, *c.-root of 8* = *2*); *c. powder*, gunpowder in cubical grains; (v.t.) find c. of (number), find cubic content of (solid), pave with cc. [(vb f. n.) F, f. LL f. Gk *kubos* cube, die]

cū·bĕb, n. Pungent berry of a Javan shrub, used in medicine & cookery. [f. F *cubèbe* f. Arab. *kababah*]

cū·bic, a. Cube-shaped; of three dimensions; *c. foot, inch*, volume of a cube whose edge is one foot, inch; *c. content* of solid, its volume expressed in c. feet &c.; involving the cubes of numbers, as *c. equation*. Hence **cu·bical** a., **cu·bically**[2] adv. [f. F *cubique* f. L f. Gk *kubikos* (as CUBE, see -IC)]

cū·bicle, n. Small separate sleeping compartment in schools &c. [f. L *cubiculum* (*cubare* lie down)]

cū·biform, a. Cube-shaped. [-I-, -FORM]

cū·bism, n. A recent style in art in which objects are so presented as to give the effect of an assemblage of geometrical figures. So **cu·bist** n. [CUBE, -ISM]

cu·bit, n. Ancient measure of length, 18 to 22 in. [f. L *cubitus* elbow, length of fore-arm]

cū·bital, a. Of the fore-arm or corresponding part in animals. [f. L *cubitalis* (prec., -AL)]

cū·boid, a. & n. Cube-shaped, like a cube, as *c. bone* (of the foot); (n.) rectangular parallelepiped. Hence **cuboi·dal** a. [f. Gk *kuboeidēs* (as CUBE, see -OID)]

cu·cking-stool, n. (hist.). Chair in which disorderly women &c. were ducked as punishment. [prob. f. obs. *cuck* f. ON *kúka* void excrement, *stool*]

cŭ·ckold, n., & v.t. Husband of unfaithful wife; (v.t.) make a c. of. [(vb f. n.) ME *cokewold* f. OF *cucuault* (*cucu* CUCKOO; mod. F *coucou* cuckoo, *cocu* cuckold)]

cu·ckōō (kŏŏ-), n. Migratory bird reaching British Islands in April & depositing its eggs in nests of small birds; simpleton; *c. clock* (striking with sound like c.'s note); *c.-flower*, meadow plant with lilac-white flower, ladysmock; *c.-pint*, common arum, wake-robin; *c.-spit*, froth exuded by the larvae of certain insects as a protection. [f. F *coucou*, imit.]

cū·cullate(d), a. (bot., zool.). Shaped like, covered with, a hood. [f. LL *cucullatus* (*cucullus* hood, see -ATE[2])]

cū·cumber, n. (Creeping plant with) long fleshy fruit eaten in thin slices as salad;

cool as a c., quite cool, self-possessed. [f. F *cocombre* (mod. *conc-*) f. L *cucumerem* (nom. *-mis*)]
cūcur·bit, n. Gourd. Hence **cucurbit**A·CEOUS a. [f. L *cucurbita*]
cud, n. Food that ruminating animal brings back from first stomach into mouth & chews at leisure; (fig.) *chew the c.*, reflect, ruminate. [OE *cwidu*, cf. OHG *chuti, quiti*, glue]
cu·dbear, n. Purple or violet dyeing-powder prepared from various lichens; kind of lichen. [named by *Cuthbert* Gordon, patentee]
cu·ddle, v.t. & i., & n. Hug, embrace, fondle; lie close & snug; nestle together; curl oneself *up*; (n.) hug, embrace. Hence **cu·ddle**SOME, **cu·ddl**Y², aa., given to cuddling or tempting to c. [?]
cu·ddy¹, n. Cabin of half-decked boat, (hist.) saloon of large ship; closet, cupboard. [?]
cu·ddy², n. (Sc.). Donkey; fool, ass; young of the coal-fish; lever on tripod for lifting stones &c. [?]
cu·dgel, n., & v.t. (-ll-). Short thick stick used as weapon; *c.-play*, contest with cc.; (fig.) *take up the cc. for*, defend vigorously; (v.t.) beat with c., esp., fig., *c.* one's *brains for*, try to think of. [(vb f. n.) OE *cycgel*, etym. dub.]
cu·dweed, n. Composite plant with chaffy scales round flower-heads, given to cattle that had lost their cud.
cue¹, n. Last words of a speech in a play, serving as signal to another actor to enter or speak; (Mus.) similar guide to singer or player; hint how to act; proper course to take. [?]
cue², n. Pigtail (also QUEUE); long straight tapering leather-tipped rod for striking ball in billiards &c. [f. F *queue* (OF *cue*) f. L *cauda* tail]
cue·ist, n. Billiard-player. [prec. + -IST (3)]
cuff¹, n. Ornamental bottom part of sleeve; separate band of linen worn round wrist. Hence (-)**cuff**ED² a. [?]
cuff², v.t., & n. Strike with fist or open hand; such blow. [etym. dub.; Sw. has *kuffa* thrust]
Cū·fic, K-, a. & n. (Of) rude form of the Arabic alphabet found chiefly in inscriptions. [f. *Cufa*, city S. of Bagdad, -IC]
cui bō·no? (kī), sentence. Who profited by it? (i.e. who is most likely to have brought it about?); (pop.) to what purpose? [L]
cuira·ss (kwĭ-, kū-), n. Body armour, breastplate & back-plate fastened together; woman's close-fitting sleeveless bodice. [f. F *cuirasse* f. L *coriacea* (fem. adj.) leathern (*corium* leather, see -ACEOUS)]
cuirassier (kwĭrasēr·, kūr-), n. Horse-soldier wearing cuirass. [F (as prec., see -EER)]
cuisine (kwĭzē·n), n. Kitchen arrangements; style of cooking. [F, = kitchen f. L *coquina* (*coquere* cook)]
cuisse (kwĭs), **cuish** (kw-), n. (hist.). Thigh armour (usu. pl.). [earlier *cuissues, -ies, -es*, (pl.) f. OF *cuissel* f. L *coxale* (*coxa* hip)]
cul-de-sac (F), n. Blind alley; (Anat.) tube &c. open at one end only.
-cule, dim. suf. = F *-cule* f. L *-culus, -cula, -culum*; the L suf. appears in E as *-cle*, as *-cule*, or in full: *article, corpuscule, corpuscle, fasciculus, Auricula, vasculum.*
cū·linary, a. Pertaining to a kitchen or cooking; fit for cooking, as *c. plants.* [f. L *culinarius* (*culina* kitchen, see -ARY¹)]
cull, v.t., & n. Pick (flower &c.); select; (n.) animal removed from flock (& usu. fattened) as inferior or too old for breeding. [f. OF *cuillir* (mod. *cueillir*) f. L as COLLECT]
cullender. See COLANDER.
cu·llet, n. Refuse glass with which crucibles are replenished. [later form of COLLET now disused in this sense]
cu·lly, n. (slang). Dupe, simpleton. [?]
culm¹, n. Coal-dust (esp. of anthracite). [?]
culm², n. (bot.). Stem of plant (esp. of grasses). So **culmi**·FEROUS a. [f. L *culmus*]
cu·lminant, a. At, forming, the top; (of heavenly body) on the meridian. [foll., -ANT]
cu·lminate, v.i. Reach its highest point (*in*; lit. & fig.); (Astr.) be on the meridian. Hence **culmin**A·TION n. [f. LL *culminare* (*culmen* top) see -ATE³]
cu·lpable, a. Criminal, blameworthy, as *c. negligence, hold him c.* Hence **culpa**BI·LITY, **cu·lpable**NESS, nn., **cu·lpab**LY² adv. [f. OF *coupable* f. L *culpabilis* (*culpa* fault)]
cu·lprit, n. Offender; prisoner at the bar. [17th c.; orig. in formula *Culprit, how will you be tried?*, said by Clerk of Crown to prisoner pleading Not Guilty; abbr. of *Culpable: prest d'averrer* &c. (You are) guilty: (I am) ready to prove &c.]
cult, n. System of religious worship; devotion, homage, to person or thing (*the c. of*). [f. L *cultus -ūs* worship (*colere cult-* till, worship)]
cu·ltivate, v.t. Till, whence **cu·ltiv**ABLE a.; (fig.) improve, develop, (person, mind, manners; esp. in p.p.); pay attention to, cherish, (faculty, art, person, his acquaintance); prepare (ground) with CULTIVATOR. [f. LL *cultivare* f. *cultiva* (*terra*) tilled (land), as prec., -IVE, -ATE³]
cultiva·tion, n. Cultivating, cultivated state, (lit. & fig.). [F (as CULTIVATE, see -ATION)]
cu·ltivator, n. One who cultivates; implement for breaking up ground & uprooting weeds. [-OR²]
cu·ltrate, a. (nat. hist.). Knife-edged. So

cu·ltriFORM a. [f. L *cultratus* (*culter* *-tri* knife, -ATE²)]

cu·lture (-tsher), n., & v.t. Tillage; rearing, production, (of bees, oysters, fish, silk, bacteria); set of bacteria thus produced; improvement by (mental or physical) training; intellectual development; (v.t.) cultivate (lit. & fig., chiefly in p.p.). Hence **cu·lturAL** a., **cu·lturIST**(2) n. [(vb f. F *culturer*) F, f. L *cultura* as CULT, -URE)]

cu·lver, n. (dial.). Wood-pigeon; *culverkeys*, cowslip, other plants. [OE *culfre*, etym. dub.]

cu·lverin, n. (hist.). Large cannon, small firearm. [f. F *coulevrine* snake (L *colubra*, -INE¹)]

cu·lvert, n. Channel, conduit, carrying water across under road, canal, &c.; channel for electric cable. [?]

cum, prep. With; *c. grano* (*salis*), with caution or reserve (lit. with a grain of salt); *cum dividend* (abbr. *cum div.*), including dividend about to be paid; also in names of combined parishes, as *Stow-cum-Quy*. [L]

cu·mber, v.t., & n. Hamper, hinder; burden; (n.) hindrance, obstruction. [(vb) f. OF *combrer* f. LL *cumbrus* heap, etym. dub., perh. f. L CUMULUS; (n.) f. vb or f. G *kummer* trouble]

cu·mbersome, a. Unwieldy, clumsy. Hence **cu·mbersomeLY²** adv., **cu·mbersomeNESS** n. [-SOME]

Cu·mbrian, a. & n. (Native) of Cumberland; of the ancient British kingdom of Cumbria. [-AN]

cu·mbrous, a.=prec. Hence **cu·mbrousLY²** adv., **cu·mbrousNESS** n. [CUMBER + -OUS]

cŭ·m(m)in, n. Umbelliferous plant like fennel, with aromatic seed. [f. L f. Gk *kuminon*]

cu·mmer, ki·mmer, n. (Sc.). Godmother of one's child or godchild; female companion; woman. [f. F *commère* f. LL COM(*mater* mother)]

cŭ·mmerbŭnd, n. (Anglo-Ind.). Waist sash. [f. Hind. & Pers. *kamar-band* loin band]

cū·mūlate¹ (-*at*), a. Heaped up, massed. [as foll., see -ATE²]

cū·mūlāte², v.t. & i. Accumulate. Hence **cumulA·TION** n. [f. L *cumulare* (*cumulus* heap), see -ATE³]

cu·mulative, a. Tending to accumulate; increasing in force &c. by successive additions, as *c. evidence*; *c. voting*, system in which each voter has as many votes as there are representatives, & may give all to one candidate; *c. preference shares* (entitling holder to arrears of interest before other shares receive any on current year). Hence **cu·mulativeLY²** adv., **cu·mulativeNESS** n. [f. prec. + -IVE]

cū·mūlus, n. (pl. *-lī*). Heap; set of rounded masses of cloud heaped on each other & resting on horizontal base. So **cumulo-**, comb. form, **cu·mulOUS** a. [L]

cū·nēate (-*at*), a. Wedge-shaped. [f. L *cuneare* (*cuneus* wedge), see -ATE²]

cū·nēiform (*also* kūnē·ĭ-), a. & n. Wedge-shaped; (n.) c. writing in ancient inscriptions of Persia, Assyria, &c. [f. L *cuneus* wedge, -FORM]

cu·nning¹, n. Artfulness, craft; ability, dexterity. [vbl n. f. CAN²]

cu·nning², a. Artful, crafty; skilful, ingenious; able. Hence **cu·nningLY²** adv. [part. (orig. **cunnende*) of CAN²]

cup¹, n. Drinking-vessel, with or without handle & stem, as *tea, coffee, -c.*; *challenge c.* (prize for race &c., usu. of gold or silver, esp. one held by winner only until next race &c.); rounded cavity, esp. calyx of flower, socket of some bones, &c.; cupful, as *c. of tea, half a c.*; chalice used, wine taken, at Communion; fate, portion, experience, as *a bitter c.*, *his c. was full* (happiness, misery, was complete); *the cups that cheer but not inebriate*, tea (Cowper *Task* iv. 39); *in* one's *cc.*, while (getting) drunk; wine, cider, &c., with various flavourings, as *claret-c.*; *a. c. too low*, out of spirits; *c. & ball*, c. at end of stem, with attached ball to be thrown & caught in c. or on spiked end of stem; *c.-bearer*, one who serves wine, esp. officer of royal or noble household; *c.-moss*, lichen with c.-shaped processes arising from the thallus. Hence **cu·pFUL** n. [perh. f. LL *cuppa*, whence OF *cope*, It. *coppa*, &c.]

cup², v.t. Bleed (person) by means of a *cupping-glass*; (Golf) strike (ground) with club in driving ball. [f. prec.]

cupboard (kŭ·berd), n. Shelved closet or cabinet for crockery, provisions, &c.; SKELETON *in the c.*; *c. love* (simulated for sake of what one can get by it). [CUP¹ + BOARD]

cŭ·pel, n., & v.t. (-ll-). Small flat circular vessel used in assaying gold or silver with lead; (v.t.) assay in c. Hence **cupellA·TION** n. [(vb f. n.) f. F *coupelle* f. med. L *cupella* f. *cupa* cask]

Cū·pid, n. Roman god of love; beautiful boy. [f. L *Cupido* (*cupere* desire)]

cūpi·dity, n. Greed of gain. [f. F *cupidité* f. L *cupiditatem* (*cupidus* desirous, see -TY)]

cū·pola, n. Rounded dome forming roof; ceiling of dome; (also *c.-furnace*) furnace for melting metals; revolving dome protecting mounted guns on iron-clad; (Anat., Zool.) dome-like organ or process. [It., f. L *cupula* dim. of *cupa* cask]

cū·preous, a. Of or like copper. [f. L *cupreus* (*cuprum* COPPER) + -OUS]

cū·pric, a. Containing copper. So **cupri·FEROUS, cu·prOUS**, aa. [f. L *cuprum*, -IC(1)]

cū·pule, n. (bot., zool.). Cup-shaped organ, receptacle, &c. [f. L as *cupola*]

cur, n. Worthless, low-bred, or snappish dog; surly, ill-bred, or cowardly fellow. [cf. MDu. *korre*, cf. ON, Sw., *kurra* grumble]

cūr·açao, -çoa, (-sō), n. Liqueur of spirits flavoured with peel of bitter oranges. [Du. island in Caribbean sea; *-çoa* is E mis-spelling]

cūr·acy, n. Curate's office; benefice of perpetual curate. [f. CURATE, see -ACY(3)]

cūrar·ĕ, -ĭ, n. Resinous bitter substance from some S. American plants, paralysing the motor nerves, used by Indians to poison arrows. Hence **cur·ar**INE⁵ n., **cur·ar**IZE(5) v.t. [corrupt. of native *wurali*]

cūr·assow (-ō), n. Turkey-like bird of Central & S. America. [=CURAÇAO]

cūr·ate (-*at*), n. Assistant to parish priest; *c.-in-charge*, clergyman appointed to take charge of parish during incapacity or suspension of incumbent; (facet.) small extra poker meant for use. [f. med. L *curatus* one having a charge (*cura*), see -ATE²]

cur·ative, a. & n. (Thing) tending to cure (esp. disease). [F (*-if, -ive*), f. L *curare* CURE², see -ATIVE]

cura·tor, n. Person in charge, manager; keeper, custodian, of museum; member of board managing property or having general superintendence in University; (Sc. law; kūr·*a*-) guardian of minor, lunatic, &c. Hence **curator·**IAL a., **cura·tor**SHIP n. [L (as prec., -OR²)]

curb, n., & v.t. Chain, strap, passing under lower jaw of horse, used as a check; (fig.) check, restraint; hard swelling on horse's leg, whence **cur·b**Y² a.; frame round top of well; timber or iron plate round edge of circular structure; = KERB; *c. roof*, one of which each face has two slopes, the lower one steeper; (v.t.) put c. on (horse), (fig.) restrain. [(vb f. n.) f. F *courbe* (adj.) f. L *curvus* bent]

cur·cūma, n. Turmeric, substance used in curry-powder, as test for alkalis (*c. paper*), &c.; genus of tuberous plants yielding this & other commercial substances. [mod. L, f. Arab. *kurkum* saffron, turmeric, cf. CROCUS]

curd, n. Coagulated substance formed (naturally or artificially) by action of acids on milk, and made into cheese or eaten (often pl.; *cc. & whey*, junket); fatty substance found between flakes of boiled salmon; *c. soap* (white, of tallow & soda). Hence **cur·d**Y² a. [perh. f. OE as CROWD²]

cur·dle, v.t. & i. Congeal, form into curd; (fig.) *c. the blood* (with horror). [*curd* v.t. & i. (now rare) + -LE(3)]

cure¹, n. Remedy; course of medical or other treatment (esp. of specified kind, as *grape, milk, -c.*), success with this; spiritual charge, as *c. of souls*. Hence **cure·**LESS a. [OF, f. L *cura* care]

cure², v.t. & i. Restore to health (also fig.); remedy (an evil); preserve (meat, fruit, tobacco) by salting, drying, &c. (also intr.). Hence **cura**BI·LITY n., **cur·**ABLE a. [f. F *curer* f. L *curare* take care of (*cura*)]

cure³, n. (slang). Odd or eccentric person. [?]

curé (F), n. Parish priest in France &c.

cūre·tte, n., & v.t. & i. Surgeon's small scraping-instrument; (vb) scrape with c. [F (as CURE¹, -ETTE)]

cur·few, n. Medieval regulation for extinction of fires at fixed hour in evening; hour for this; (also *c.-bell*) bell announcing it; ringing of bell at fixed evening hour, still surviving in some towns; (under martial law &c.) signal or time after which inhabitants may not be abroad. [f. AF *coeverfu* f. OF *covrefeu* (*couvrir* cover + *feu* fire)]

cūr·ia, n. One of the ten divisions of any of the three ancient Roman tribes; its place of worship; Roman senate-house; senate of ancient Italian towns; court of justice (esp. under feudal organization); the Papal court. [L]

cūr·ial, a. Of a curia; of the Papal court, whence **cur·ial**ISM n. [F, f. L *curialis* (CURIA, see -AL)]

cūr·io, n. (pl. *-ōs*). Curious object of art. [=foll.]

cūriŏ·sity, n. Desire to know; inquisitiveness; strangeness; *a c.*, strange or rare object. [f. OF *curioseté* f. L *curiositatem* (as foll., see -TY)]

cūr·ious, a. Eager to learn; inquisitive; minutely careful, as *c. inquiry*; strange, surprising, odd. Hence **cur·ious**LY² adv., **cur·ious**NESS n. [f. OF *curius* f. L *curiosus* f. *cura* care, see -IOUS(1)]

curl¹, n. Spiral lock of hair; *c.-paper* (used for twisting hair into cc.); anything spiral or incurved; act of curling, as *c. of the lip* (expressing scorn); state of being curled, as *keep the hair in c.*; disease of potatoes &c. in which shoots or leaves are curled up. [f. foll.]

curl², v.t. & i. Bend, coil, into spiral shape (t. & i.); *c. up*, roll up into a curl, (intr., slang) collapse; move in spiral form (of smoke &c.); play at CURLING. [f. obs. adj. *croll, crull*, curly; cf. Du. *krullen*, G *krollen, kröllen*]

cur·lew, n. Wading bird with long slender curved bill. [f. OF *courlieus* perh. imit. of cry, but assim. to *corliu* courier f. *courir* run]

cur·ling, n. In vbl senses; esp.: Scotch game played on ice with large round stones; *c.-irons, -tongs* (for curling hair). [-ING¹]

cur·ly, a. Having, arranged in, curls; *c.-pate*, c.-headed person. Hence **cur·li**NESS n. [-Y²]

curmu·dgeon, n. Churlish or miserly fellow. Hence **curmu·dgeon**LY¹ a. [?]

cu·rrach (-*ra*, -*rach*), n. Coracle. [f. Ir. *curach*, cf. CORACLE]

cu·rrant, n. Dried fruit of a seedless variety of grape grown in the Levant, much used in cookery; *Red, White, Black, C.*, (fruit of) species of Ribes. [orig. *raisins of Corauntz* (Corinth)]

cu·rrency, n. Time during which a thing is current; (of money) circulation; money current in actual use in a country (*c. note*, inconvertible legal-tender note for £1 or 10s. issued by Treasury during & after the great war); prevalence (of words, ideas, reports). [f. L *currere* run, see -ENCY]

cu·rrent[1], a. In general circulation or use (of money, opinions, rumours, words); *pass, go, run, c.*, be generally accepted as true or genuine; (of time) now passing, as *c. week, month*; belonging to the c. time, as *c. issue* (of journal); *c. handwriting*, cursive. Hence **cu·rrent**LY[2] adv. [f. OF *corant* part. of *courir* f. L *currere* run (refash. on L)]

cu·rrent[2], n. Running stream; water, air, &c., moving in given direction; course, tendency, (of events, opinions, &c.); transmission of electric force through a body. [prec. as n.]

cu·rricle, n. Light two-wheeled carriage (usu. for two horses abreast). [f. foll.]

cŭrri·culum, n. Course (of study). [L, = course, race-chariot, f. *currere* run]

cŭ·rrier, n. One who dresses & colours tanned leather. [f. OF *corier* f. L *coriarius* (*corium* hide, leather, see -ARY[1])]

cur·rish, a. Like a cur; snappish; mean-spirited. Hence **cur·rish**LY[2] adv., **cur·rish**NESS n. [-ISH[1]]

cŭ·rry[1], n., & v.t. Dish of meat &c. cooked with bruised spices & turmeric; *c.-paste, -powder*, preparations of turmeric &c. for making c.; (v.t.) prepare, flavour, with c.-powder. [(vb f. n.) f. Tamil *kari* sauce]

cŭ·rry[2], v.t. Rub down or dress (horse &c.) with *c.-comb*; dress (tanned leather); (fig.) thrash; *c. favour* (orig. *favel* f. OF *faveau, favel*, the chestnut horse), ingratiate oneself (*with* person) by officiousness &c. [f. OF *correier*, earlier CON(*reder* prepare see ARRAY)]

curse[1], n. Utterance of deity or person invoking deity, consigning person or thing to destruction, divine vengeance, &c. (*cc. come home to roost*, injure the curser; *under a c.*, feeling or liable to its effects); sentence of excommunication; profane oath, imprecation; accursed object; evil inflicted in response to a c.; great evil, bane; (Cards) *c. of Scotland*, nine of diamonds. [?]

curse[2], v.t. & i. Utter curse against: excommunicate; blaspheme; afflict *with* (esp. in pass.); (intr.) utter curses. [?]

cur·sed, -st, a. & adv. In vbl senses; also: damnable, abominable; (archaic; usu. *curst*) cantankerous; (adv.) cursedly. Hence **cur·sĕd**LY[2] adv., **cur·sĕd**NESS n. [p.p. of prec.]

cur·sive, a. & n. Running (writing in manuscript), opp. to UNCIAL. [f. med. L *cursivus* (L *currere curs-* run, see -IVE)]

cursor·ial, a. Having limbs adapted for running (*c. birds* &c.). [as CURSORY, -AL]

cur·sory, a. Hasty, hurried, (*c. inspection*). Hence **cur·sori**LY[2] adv., **cur·sori**NESS n. [f. L *cursorius* of a runner (as CURSIVE, see -ORY)]

curt, a. Discourteously brief; terse, concise; (lit.) short. Hence **cur·t**LY[2] adv., **cur·t**NESS n. [f. L *curtus* short]

curtai·l, v.t. Cut short (lit. & fig.); deprive *of*. Hence **curtai·l**MENT n. [f. obs. *curtal* horse with docked tail f. OF *cortald* (*court* short f. L *curtus* + Teut. suf. *-ald*); assim. to *tail*]

cur·tail-step, n. Lowest step of stair, with outer end carried round. [?]

cur·tain (-tn), n., & v.t. Suspended cloth used as screen; *draw the c.* (back or aside to reveal objects, forward to conceal them); screen separating stage of theatre from auditorium (*c. falls, drops, is dropped*, at end of action, *rises, is raised*, at beginning; also fig.; *c.!*, narrator's word drawing attention to dramatic situation just described, = *tableau*); *fire-proof c.* in theatre, metal sheet cutting off stage; plain wall of fortified place, connecting two towers &c.; piece of plain wall not supporting a roof; partition, cover, in various technical senses; *c.-fire*, = BARRAGE (mil.); *c. lecture*, wife's reproof to husband in bed; *c.-raiser* in theatre, short opening piece; (v.t.) furnish, cover, shut *off*, with cc. [(vb f. n.) f. OF *cortine* f. L *cortina*, etym. dub.]

curtā·na (*or* -ah-), n. Pointless sword borne before kings of England at Coronation, as emblem of mercy. [Anglo-L *c.* (*spada*) curtailed (sword) (as CURT, see -AN)]

cur·tilage, n. (law, dial.). Area attached to dwelling-house. [f. OF *courtillage* (*courtil* small COURT + -AGE)]

cur·tsy, -sey, n., & v.i. Feminine salutation made by bending knees & lowering body; *make, drop, a c.*; (v.i.) make c. (*to* person). [var. of COURTESY]

cūr·ule, a. Pertaining to any high civic dignity; (Rom. Antiq.) *c. chair*, one like camp-stool, inlaid with ivory; *c. magistrate*, one entitled to this. [f. L *curulis* perh. f. *currus* chariot]

cur·vature, n. Curving; curved form; (Geom.) deviation (of curve) from straight line. [f. L *curvatura* (as foll., see -URE)]

curve[1], v.t. & i. Bend so as to form a curve. [f. L *curvare* (as foll.)]

curve[2], n. Line of which no part is straight; curved form or thing; (statistics &c.), line presenting diagrammatically a continuous variation of quantity, force, &c., graph. [f. L *curvus* bent]

curve·t (*also* ker·-), n., & v.i. (-tt-, -t-). Horse's leap with fore-legs raised together & hind-legs raised with spring before fore-legs reach ground; (v.i., of horse or rider) make c. [(vb f. It. *corvettare*) f. It. *corvetta* dim. of *corvo* curve (as prec.)]

curvi- in comb. = L *curvus* curved, as *-caudate, -costate, -dentate, -rostrate,* with curved tail, ribs, teeth, beak; *-foliate,* with leaves bent back; *-form,* of curved shape; *-nervate* (of leaves), with veins diverging from mid-rib & converging towards margin.

curvili·nĕar, a. Contained by, consisting of, curved line(s). Hence **curvilineă·r**ITY n., **curvili·near**LY[2] adv. [prec. + LINEAR]

cŭ·scŭs, n. Aromatic root of an Indian grass, used for fans &c. [f. Hind. *khas khas*]

cŭ·shat, n. (Sc., dial.). Wood-pigeon, ring-dove. [?]

cu·shion[1] (kŏŏ-), n. Mass of soft material stuffed into cloth or silk covering, for sitting, kneeling, reclining, on; PIN-*c.*; pad worn by woman under hair; pad beneath skirt of woman's dress; elastic lining of sides of billiard table; steam left in cylinders as buffer to piston; fleshy part of buttock (of pig &c.); frog of horse's hoof; sweety in c. shape; *c.-tire* of bicycle (rubber tubing stuffed with rubber shreds). Hence **cu·shion**Y[2] a. [f. F *coussin,* etym. dub.; the earlier (ME) form *cuisshin* is f. OF *coissin* f. L **coxinum* (*coxa* hip, see INE[1])]

cu·shion[2], v.t. Furnish with cushions; protect with cushions (also fig.); suppress quietly (complaints &c.); (Billiards) place, leave, (ball) against cushion. [f. prec.]

cu·shy (kŏŏ-), a. (slang). (Of a post, task, &c.) easy, pleasant, comfortable. [Anglo-Ind., f. Hind. *khush* pleasant]

cusp, n. Apex, peak; (Geom.) point at which two branches of curve meet & stop; (Arch.) projecting point between small arcs in Gothic tracery; (Bot.) pointed end, esp. of leaf. Hence **cusp**ED[2] a. [f. L *cuspis -idis* point]

cu·spidal, a. Of (the nature of) a cusp. So **cu·spidāte(d)** [-ATE[2](2)] aa. [as prec., -AL]

cu·spidor(e), n. (U.S.). Spittoon. [Port. (*-or*), = spitter (*cuspir* f. L CON*spuere,* see -OR[2])]

cuss, n. (U.S.). Curse; person, creature, (often disparaging). [vulg. pron. of CURSE[1]]

cu·ssĕdness, n. (U.S.). Perversity, esp. *pure c.* [vulg. pron. of *cursedness*]

cu·stard, n. Mixture of eggs & milk, baked or served liquid; *c.-apple,* W. Indian fruit with pulp like c. [orig. a kind of pie; prob. f. obs. *crustade* f. F *croustade* (as CRUST, -ADE)]

custō·dial, a. Relating to custody. [-AL]

custō·dian, n. Guardian, keeper. So **custo·di**ER[1] n. [as foll. + -AN]

cu·stody, n. Guardianship, care, (*parent has c. of child, child is in the c. of father*); imprisonment, esp. *take into c.,* arrest. [f. L *custodia* (*custos -odis* guardian, see -Y[1])]

cu·stom, n. Usual practice; (Law) established usage having the force of law; (pl.) duty levied upon imports from foreign countries; *c.-house,* office (esp. in seaport) at which cc. are collected; business patronage or support. [f. OF *costume* f. L *consuetudinem* f. CON(*suescere suet-* grow accustomed), see -TUDE]

cu·stomary, a. & n. Usual; (Law) subject to, held by, custom (of the manor &c.); (n. also *-tumary*) written collection of the customs of a country. Hence **cu·stomari**LY[2] adv., **cu·stomari**NESS n. [f. med. L *custumarius* = L *consuetudinarius* (as prec., see -ARY[1])]

cu·stomer, n. Buyer; (colloq.) *queer, awkward,* &c., *c.* (person to deal with). [prob. f. CUSTOM + -ER[1]]

cu·stŏs, n. Guardian, keeper; *c. rotulorum,* keeper of the rolls, principal justice of the peace in a county. [L]

cut[1], n. Act of cutting; stroke, blow, with knife, sword, whip; *c. & thrust,* hand-to-hand struggle; excision (of part of a play &c.); act, speech, that wounds the feelings; particular stroke in cricket, lawn tennis, croquet, &c.; refusal to recognize an acquaintance (esp. *give* one *the c. direct*); *short c.,* crossing that shortens the distance; fashion, style, (of clothes, hair, &c.; *the c. of* one's JIB[1]); *a c.* (degree, stage) *above*; wound made by cutting; railway cutting; narrow opening in floor of stage of theatre, by which scenes are moved up & down; = WOOD-*cut*; piece (esp. of meat) cut off; *draw cc.,* draw lots with sticks of unequal length (prob. a different word); *c.-out,* device in motor-car for releasing gas rapidly without passage through silencer. [f. foll.]

cut[2], v.t. & i. (cut). Penetrate, wound, with edged instrument, as *the knife* c. *his finger, he c. his finger with a knife,* (fig.) *argument cuts both ways* (tells for both sides); (fig.) *a cutting wind, cutting retort, it c. him to the heart,* whence **cu·tting**LY[2] adv.; divide with knife &c. *in two, in* or *into* pieces (*c. the knot* fig., solve problem in irregular but efficient way, cf. GORDIAN); (fig.) *c.* (renounce) *a connexion*; detach by cutting; carve (meat); cross, intersect, as *two lines c. each other*; (intr.) pass *through, across,* &c., (slang) run (*c. & run,* run away); reduce by cutting (hair &c.); reduce (wages, prices, time, &c.; *c. it fine,* allow only the minimum; *c. a loss,* abandon losing speculation in good time; *c. the record*, reduce the recorded shortest time for race &c., or surpass record otherwise); shape, fashion, by cutting (coat, gem, &c.); perform, execute, make, as *c. a* CAPER, DASH, *joke*, FIGURE; divide (pack of cards, or abs.) to select dealer, prevent cheating, &c.; hit (ball, or abs.) in certain way, in cricket &c.; renounce acquaintance of (person), decline to recognize him, esp. *c. him dead*; absent oneself from, avoid, renounce, as *c. a lecture, c. the whole concern*; *c. a tooth*, have it appear through gum (*c.* one's *eye* or *wisdom teeth*, fig. develop insight or wisdom); *c. short*, shorten by cutting (lit. & fig.), also interrupt; *c.* one's *stick*, go; *c. coat according to* CLOTH; *c. down*, bring or throw down by cutting, (fig.) reduce (expenses); *c. in* (intr.), enter abruptly, interpose (in conversation), (Cards) join in game by taking place of player who cuts out; *c. no ice* (slang), effect little or nothing; *c. off*, remove by cutting, bring to an end, intercept (supplies, communications), exclude (*from* access &c.); *c. off with a shilling*, disinherit by bequeathing a shilling; *c. out*, remove by cutting, (fig.) out-do or supplant (rival), fashion or shape (lit. & fig.), prepare, as *his work is c. out for him*, (Cards, intr.) be excluded from game as result of cutting, (Nav.) capture (enemy ship) by getting between it & shore; *c. up*, c. in pieces, destroy utterly, (fig.) criticize severely, (usu. pass.) distress greatly, *c. up* (*well*), leave (large) fortune, *c. up rough*, show resentment; *c.-&-come-again*, abundance; *c. & dried* or *dry* (of opinions &c.), ready-made, lacking freshness; *cutpurse*, thief; *cut-throat*, murderer. [?]

cūtā·neous, a. Of the skin. [f. mod. or med. L *cutaneus* (*cutis* skin, see -ANEOUS)]

cu·t-away, a. & n. (Coat) with skirt cut back from the waist.

cutche·rry, cu·tchery, n. (Anglo-Ind.). Public office, court-house; office of planter &c. [f. Hind. *kachahri*]

cute, a. (colloq.). Clever, shrewd; ingenious. Hence **cu·te**LY[2] adv., **cu·te**NESS n. [for ACUTE]

Cu·thbert, n. (slang). Evader of military service esp. on plea of indispensability in Civil Service. [the pers. name]

cu·ticle, n. Epidermis or other superficial skin; (Bot.) superficial film of plants. Hence **cuti·cul**AR[1] a. [f. L *cuticula* dim. of CUTIS]

cū·tis, n. (anat.). True skin, underlying the epidermis. [L, =skin]

cu·tlass, n. Short sword with wide slightly curved blade, esp. that used by sailors. [f. F *coutelas* augment. of *couteau* (*-tel*) knife, dim. f. L as COULTER]

cu·tler, n. One who makes or deals in knives & similar utensils. [f. OF *coutelier* f. *coutel*, see prec. & -ER[2](2)]

cu·tlery, n. Trade of the cutler; things made or sold by cutlers. [f. OF *coutelerie* (as prec., see -ERY)]

cu·tlet, n. Neck-chop of mutton, small piece of veal, broiled or fried in bread-crumbs, imitation of mutton-c. in minced fish &c. [f. F *côtelette* double dim. of *côte* rib f. L *costa*]

cu·tter, n. Person, thing, that cuts; superior kind of brick that can be cut; boat belonging to ship of war, fitted for rowing & sailing; small single-masted vessel rigged like sloop, but with running bowsprit. [-ER[1]]

cu·tting, n. In vbl senses; esp. excavation of high ground for railway, road, &c.; *press c.*, paragraph &c. cut from newspaper. [-ING[1]]

cu·ttle, n. (Usu. *c.-fish*) fish ejecting black fluid when pursued; *c.-bone*, its internal shell, used for polishing. [OE *cudele*, etym. dub.]

cu·tty, a. & n. (Sc. & north.). Cut short, abnormally short; (n.) short pipe; *c.-stool*, seat in Sc. churches where unchaste women sat to receive public rebuke during service. [CUT[2], -Y[2]]

cu·twater, n. Knee of head of ship, dividing water before it reaches bow; forward edge of prow.

cu·tworm, n. Caterpillar that cuts off young plants level with the ground.

-cy, suf., special form of the abstract suf. -Y[1], repr. L *-cia*, *-tia*, & Gk *-kia*, *-keia*, *-tia*, *-teia* (see -ACY, -ANCY, -ENCY). On anal. of wds in *-acy*, *-ncy*, with corresp. nn. in *-ate*, *-nt*, as *advocacy, advocate, infancy infant*, *-cy* was extended to wds in *-n*, as *chaplaincy, captaincy*, after *incumbency, lieutenancy*, &, being thus regarded as independent suf. = *-ship*, to other wds as *colonelcy*; it is even added to wds ending in *-t* (where *-c-* should have been substituted for *-t-*), as *bankruptcy, idiotcy*, normal form being *idiocy* f. Gk *idiōteia*.

cȳā·nic, a. Blue; (Chem.) of, containing, cyanogen. [as foll. + -IC]

cyano- in comb. 1. Dark-blue, as *-meter*, instrument for measuring blueness of sky. 2. of, containing, cyanogen. [f. Gk *kuanos*, a dark-blue mineral]

cyă·nogen, n. (chem.). Compound radical consisting of one atom of nitrogen and one of carbon. Hence **cy·an**IDE n. [f. F *cyanogène* (as prec. + -GEN)]

cyanō·sis, n. Blue jaundice, due to circulation of imperfectly oxygenated blood. [f. Gk *kuanōsis* (as prec., see -OSIS)]

cȳ·cad, n. (bot.). Kinds of palm-like plant.

cȳ·clamen, n. Kinds of plant cultivated for their early-blooming flowers. [med. L, f. Gk *kuklaminos*, etym. dub.]

cȳ·cle, n., & v.i. Recurrent period (of events, phenomena, &c.); *Metonic* or *Lunar c.*, one of 19 years, used for finding date of Easter; period of a thing's completion; complete set or series; series of poems collected round a central event &c.; bicycle, tricycle, or similar machine; *c.-car*, very light motor vehicle of simplified design with 3 (rarely 4) wheels, usu. fitted with chain drive & engine of 1 or 2 cylinders; (v.i.) revolve in cc., ride c. [(vb f. n.) f. L f. Gk *kuklos* circle]

cȳ·clic, -ical, aa. Recurring in cycles; belonging to a chronological cycle; (*-ic*) of a cycle of poems, as *c. poet*; (Gk Ant., *-ic*) *c. chorus.* dithyrambic chorus, danced in ring round altar; (Bot., of flower) with its parts arranged in whorls. [f. L f. Gk *kuklikos* (as CYCLE)]

cȳ·clist, n. Rider of a cycle. [CYCLE + IST)

cyclo- in comb. = Gk *kuklos* circle, as *-graph*, instrument for tracing circular arcs, *-meter*, instrument for measuring (1) circular arcs (2) distance traversed by bicycle &c., *-stomous*, with round mouth, *cyclorama*, circular panorama.

cȳ·cloid, n. Curve traced by a point on a radius of a circle within (*prolate c.*), on (*common c.*), or without (*curtate c.*), its circumference, as the circle rolls along a straight line. Hence **cycloi·d**AL a. [f. Gk *kukloeidēs* (as CYCLE, see -OID)]

cȳ·clone, n. System of winds rotating round a centre of minimum barometric pressure; violent hurricane of limited diameter. Hence **cyclŏ·n**IC a. [irreg. f. Gk *kuklos* circle]

cȳclop(a)e·dia, n. = ENCYCLOPAEDIA. Hence **cyclopae·d**IC a. [abbr. of ENCYCLOPAEDIA]

Cȳclopē·an, -clō·pian, a. Of, like, a cyclops; huge; *C. masonry*, an ancient style made with huge irregular stones. [f. L *Cyclopeus, -pius*, f. Gk *kuklōpeios, -pios*, (as foll.)]

Cȳ·clop(s), n. (pl.- *ops, -opses, -ōpēs*). (Gk Myth.) one-eyed giant; one-eyed person. [L -(*s*), f. Gk *kuklōps* (*kuklos* circle + *ōps* eye)]

cȳ·clostyle, n. Apparatus printing copies of writing from stencil-plate cut by pen with small toothed wheel. [CYCLO-]

cy·gnet, n. Young swan. [f. L *cygnus* swan + -ET[1]]

cȳ·linder. n. (Geom.) solid generated by straight line moving parallel to itself and describing with its ends any fixed curve, esp. circle; roller-shaped body, hollow or solid; barrel-shaped object of baked clay covered with cuneiform writing and buried under Babylonian or Assyrian temple; stone of similar shape used as seal by Assyrians; cylindrical part of various machines, esp. chamber in which steam acts upon piston; metal roller used in printing. [f. L f. Gk *kulindros* (*kulindō* roll)]

cyli·ndrical, a. Cylinder-shaped. [f. Gk *kulindrikos* (as prec., see -IC) + -AL]

cy·lindroid, a. & n. (Figure) like a cylinder. [f. Gk *kulindroeidēs* (as prec., -OID)]

cȳ·ma, n. (pl. *-mas*). Ogee moulding of cornice (*c. recta* with concave, *c. reversa* with convex, curve uppermost); = CYME. [mod. L, f. Gk *kuma* wave, anything swollen]

cȳmar·, n. Woman's loose light garment esp. under-garment. [f. F *simarre* OF *chimarre*, cf. CHIMERE]

cy·mbal, n. One of a pair of concave brass or bronze plates, struck together to make ringing sound. Hence **cy·mbal**IST n. [f. L f. Gk *kumbalon* (*kumbē* cup)]

cy·mbalo, n. Stringed musical instrument, played with hammers. [f. It. *cembalo*, as prec.]

cy·mbiform, a. (anat., bot.). Boat-shaped. [f. L *cymba* boat + -FORM]

cymbocephă·lic, a. With boat-shaped (i.e. long and narrow) skull. [f. Gk *kumbē* boat + *kephalē* head + -IC]

cȳme, n. (bot.). Inflorescence in which primary axis bears single terminal flower that develops first, system being continued by axes of secondary and higher orders (cf. RACEME). Hence **cymo·**SE[1] a. [F, = top (as CYMA)]

Cȳ·mric (k-), a. Welsh. [f. W *Cymru* Wales]

cȳ·nic, a. & n. Of, characteristic of, the Cynic philosophers; = foll.; (n.) philosopher of sect founded by Antisthenes, marked by ostentatious contempt for pleasure; sneering fault-finder. Hence **cy·nic**ISM n. [f. L f. Gk *kunikos* (*kuōn kunos* dog, nickname for Cynic)]

cy·nical, a. Churlish; captious; incredulous of human goodness; sneering. Hence **cy·nical**LY[2] adv. [-AL]

cyno- in comb. repr. Gk *kuōn kunos* dog, as *-phobia*, dread of dogs.

cȳnocē·phalus, n. Fabulous dog-headed man; (Zool.) dog-faced baboon. [L, f. Gk *kunokephalos* (prec. + *kephalē* head)]

cȳ·nosūre (*or*-shoor), n. (Constellation containing) Pole-star, Little Bear; guiding star; centre of attraction or admiration. [F, f. L f. Gk *kunosoura* dog's tail, Little Bear (*kuōn kunos* dog + *oura* tail)]

cypher. See CIPHER.

cy pres (sēprā·), adv., n., & a. (Law) as near as possible (to testator's intentions); (adj.) approximate; (n.) approximation. [AF, = F *si près* so near (as &c.)]

cȳ·press, n. Coniferous tree with hard wood and dark foliage; branch of this as symbol of mourning. [f. OF *ciprès* f. LL *cypressus* f. Gk *kuparissos*]

Cȳ·prian, a. & n. (Inhabitant, native) of Cyprus; licentious (person). [f. L *Cyprius* (*Cyprus*) + -AN]

Cȳ·priot(e), a. & n. = prec. (first sense). [-OT[2]]

Cȳrena·ic, a. & n. (Philosopher) of the hedonistic school of Aristippus of Cyrene. [f. L f. Gk *Kurēnaikos* (*Kurēnē*)]

Cy̆ri·llic, a. *C. alphabet,* that used by Slavonic peoples of the Eastern Church. [St *Cyril,* supposed inventor, + -IC]

cyrto- in comb. = Gk *kurtos* curved, as *-meter,* instrument measuring curves of chest.

cyst, n. (Biol.) hollow organ, bladder, &c., in animal or plant, containing liquid secretion; (Path.) sac containing morbid matter, parasitic larva, &c.; cell containing embryos &c. [f. Gk *kustis* bladder]

cyst-, cysti-, cysto-, in comb. repr. Gk *kustis, kustē,* bladder, as *cystiform,* bladder-shaped, *cysto*CELE, -SCOPE, -TOMY.

cy·stic, a. Of the urinary bladder; of the gall-bladder; of the nature of a cyst. [f. F *cystique* (as CYST, see -IC)]

-cyte, suf. in biol. wds meaning *cell,* as LEUCO*cyte.* [f. Gk *kutos* vessel]

cyto- in comb. = cell, as *-blast,* protoplasmic nucleus of a cell. [as prec.]

czar, tsar, tzar, (z-, ts-), n. Emperor of Russia. [f. Russ. *ts(is)ari* f. L *Caesar*]

czarevitch, -wich, tsar-, (tsar·ĭvĭtsh, z-), n. Son of a czar (not now an official title; cf. CESAREVITCH). [f. Russ. *tsarevitsh*]

czare·vna, tsar-, n. Daughter of a czar. [Russ.]

czari·na, tsar-, (-ē-), n. Wife of a czar, Russian empress. [f. G *czarin* f. CZAR]

czari·tza, tsar-, n. Russian form of prec.

Czech, -kh, (tshĕk), n. & a. Bohemian. [f. Boh. *Cech*]

Czecho-Slovak (tshĕkō-slovah·k), a. & n. (Native) of the new State called *Czecho-Slovakia* including Bohemia, Moravia & the northern Slavs of the former Austrian Empire. [*Czech, Slovak,* native race-names, -O-]

D

D (dē), letter (pl. *Ds,* D's, Dees). *D block, trap, valve,* shaped like the letter; also D = DEE. (Mus.) second note of natural major scale.

Abbreviations (1); D (half of M or CIƆ), 500, as XD 490, MDCLXVI 1666. **D.,** *dal* in **D.S.** (*segno*); Dame in **D.B.E.** (of British Empire); *dat* in **D.D.D.** (*dicat, dedicat,* = he gives, devotes, & dedicates; also **d.d.d.**); De, **D.H.,** De Havilland; defence, **D.O.R.A.,** (of the realm act); *delirium,* **D.T.** (*tremens*); *Deo,* **D.V.** (*volente*), **D.O.M.** (*optimo maximo*); deputy, as **D.A.A.G.** (assistant adjutant-general), **D.A.Q.M.G.** (assistant quarter-master-general), **D.L.** (lieutenant); dictionary, **D.N.B.** (national biography); distinguished, **D.C.M.** (conduct medal), **D.F.C., D.F.M.,** (flying cross, medal), **D.S.C., D.S.M., D.S.O.,** (service cross, medal, order); district, **D.C.** (of Columbia); doctor, as **D.C.L.** (civil law), **D.D.** (divinity), **D.Lit.** (literature); *dono,* **D.D.** (*dedit,* = gave as a gift; also **d.d.**). **d.,** daughter, died (as *d. 1789*); *denarius* (penny, as £1 10s. **6d.**). **d—,** damn (also *d—d,* damned).

Abbreviations (2); **Dak.**(ota); **Dan.**(iel, O.T. book); **Del.**(aware); **del.**(*ineavit* = drew this); **dep.**(arts); **Deut.**(eronomy); **do,** ditto; **Dr,** Debtor, Doctor; **Dunelm.,** bishop of Durham; **Dur.**(ham); **dwt,** pennyweight.

'd. Colloq. clipping of *had* & *would,* chiefly after *I, we, you, he, she, they.*

-d, p.p. suf. (*heard* &c.); see -ED[1], & cf. DEAD.

da. See DAD.

dab[1], v.t. Strike lightly or undecidedly, hit feebly *at,* tap, peck; press but not rub (surface) with sponge &c., whence **da·bb**ER[1](2) **n.**; press (brush, dabber, &c.) against surface. [f. 1300; etym. dub.]

dab[2], n. Slight or undecided but sudden blow, tap, peck; brief application of sponge, handkerchief, &c., to surface without rubbing; moisture, colour, &c., so applied. [f. prec.]

dab[3], n. Kind of flat-fish. [?]

dab[4], n. (colloq.). Adept (*at* games &c., do*ing*). [f. 1690; etym. dub.]

da·bble, v.t. & i. Wet intermittently, slightly, or partly, soil, moisten, splash; move the feet, hands, bill, about in water; engage *in* or *at* pursuit &c. as a hobby, whence **da·bbl**ER[1] **n.** [cf. Du. *dabbelen* & DAB[1], -LE(3)]

da·bchick, n. Water-bird, the Little Grebe. [early forms *dap-, dop-*; perh. cogn. w. DIP]

da·bster, n. = DAB[4]; = DAUB*ster.* [-STER]

da ca·po (dahcah-), mus. direction. Repeat from the beginning. [It.]

dace, n. Small fresh-water fish. [ME *darse* f. OF *darz* DART[1]]

dachshund (dah·ks-hŏŏnt), n. Short-legged breed of dog. [G, = badger-dog]

dacoi·t, n. Member of Indian or Burmese armed robber band. [f. Hind. *ḍakait* f. *ḍaka* gang-robbery]

dacoi·ty, n. (Act of) gang-robbery. [f. Hind. *ḍakaiti* as prec.]

da·ctyl, n. Metrical foot —⏑⏑. [f. L f. Gk *daktulos* finger]

dacty̆·lic, a. & n. Of dactyls; (noun, usu. pl.) d. verse(s). [f. L f. Gk *daktulikos* (prec., -IC)]

dad, da (dah), **dă·da, da·ddy,** nn. (colloq.). Father (esp. as voc.); *daddy-lo·nglegs,* crane-fly. [f. 16th c.; infantile sound]

dā·do, n. Cube of pedestal between base & cornice; lower few feet of room-wall when faced with wood or coloured differently from upper part. Hence **da·do**ED[2] **a.** [It., = DIE[1]]

dae·dal (dē-), a. (poet.). Skilful, inventive; mazy; manifold, complex, mysterious. [f. L f. Gk *daidalos* skilful, variegated]

Daedā·lian, -ēan, a. In the manner of Daedalus the Greek artificer; intricate; labyrinthine. [f. L *Daedaleus* of Daedalus (cf. Gk *daidaleos* cunningly wrought) + -AN]

daemonic. See **dem-.**

daff, v.t. (archaic). Put aside, waive. [var. of DOFF, preserved by *1 Hen. IV,* IV. i. 96]

dă·ffodil (also **daffodi·lly, da·ffadown-di·lly,** in poetry &c.), n. & a. Lent Lily, pale-yellow-flowered Narcissus (alternative to leek as Welsh national emblem); pale yellow (n. & a.). [f. earlier *affodill* (*d*-unexplained) f. L f. Gk *asphodelos*]

daft, a. Foolish, reckless, wild, crazy. [OE *gedæfte* mild, meek, whence also DEFT; orig. sense (cf. Goth. *gadaban* be fit) *fitting, suitable*; for change of meaning cf. *innocent*]

da·gger, n. Stabbing-weapon with short pointed and edged blade (*at dd. drawn,* on the point of fighting, in strained relations, *with* person, or abs.; *look, speak, dd.,* bitterly, so as to wound); (Print.), *d., double d.,* =(*double*) OBELISK. [cf. F *dague,* & ME *dag* to pierce]

dā·go, n. (U.S.). American Spaniard, Portuguese, or Italian. [f. Sp. *Diego* = James]

dague·rreotype (-gĕro-), n. (Portrait taken by) early photographic process. [*Daguerre* 1839 inventor, -o-, TYPE]

dahabee·yah (dah-ha-), **-bi·ah** (-bē-), n. Nile sailing-boat. [Arab., =the golden, orig. sense *gilded barge*]

dah·lia (dāl-), n. Mexican composite plant cultivated in Europe for its many-coloured single & double flowers (*blue d.,* impossibility); shade of red. [*Dahl* 1791 botanist]

Dail Eireann (dhawlyār·*a*n), n. Chamber of Deputies in the Irish Free State legislature. [Ir., =assembly of Ireland]

dai·ly, a., adv., & n. (Recurring, appearing, done) every day or week-day, from day to day, constant, often; *d. bread,* one's necessary food or livelihood; a d. newspaper (pl. *dailies*). [OE *-dæglic* (DAY, -LY[1])]

dai·mio (-yō). n. Japanese feudal vassal, noble, (hist.). [Jap., f. Chin. *dai* great, *myo* name]

dai·nty[1], n. Choice morsel, dish, &c., delicacy, tit-bit, (lit. & fig.). [f. OF *dainté* f. L *dignitatem* (*dignus* worthy, -TY)]

dai·nty[2], a. Delicate, choice; tasteful, pretty, of delicate beauty, scrupulously clean; particular, nice, of delicate tastes & sensibility, fastidious; inclined to luxury. Hence **dai·nti**LY[2] adv., **dai·nti**NESS n. [f. prec.]

dair·y, n. Room or building for keeping milk & cream & making butter &c. (*dairymaid,* in charge of this); the milk department in farming; shop for milk &c. (*dairyman,* dealer in milk &c.), cows of a farm. Hence (f. rare vb) **dair·y**ING[1] n. [f. obs. *dey* OE *dǽge* maid-servant cogn. w. *dáh* DOUGH + -ERY]

dais (dās), n. Raised platform, esp. at end of hall for high table, throne, &c., or terrace. [f. OF *deis* f. L *discus* disk in LL sense *table*]

dai·sy (-zĭ), n. Small European wild & garden flower; other plants resembling it, esp. the larger Ox-eye D.; (slang) first-rate specimen of anything; *d.-chain,* string of dd. fastened together; *d.-cutter,* horse lifting feet very little, ball travelling along ground at cricket. Hence **dai·si**ED[2] a. [OE *dæges éage* day's eye]

dak, dâk. See DAWK.

dale, n. Valley (esp. in north; also in poet. use, as *hill & d.*); *dalesman,* inhabitant of dd. in north. [OE *dæl,* com.-Teut. cf. G *t(h)al*]

dă·lly, v.i. & t. Amuse oneself, make sport; toy amorously (*with* or abs.); coquet *with* temptation &c.; be evasive *with* person or business; idle, loiter, delay; *d. away,* consume (time, opportunity) to no purpose. Hence **da·lli**ANCE n. [f. OF *dalier* chat]

Dălma·tian (-āshn), n. (Also *D. dog*) spotted dog kept to run with carriage. [*Dalmatia,* -AN]

dălmă·tic, n. Wide-sleeved loose long vestment with slit sides worn by deacons & bishops on some occasions, & by kings & emperors esp. at coronation. [f. F *dalmatique* f. L *dalmatica* (*vestis* robe) of Dalmatia]

dal segno (sā·nyō), mus. direction (abbr. *D.S.*). Repeat from point indicated. [It.]

da·ltonism (dawl-), n. Colour-blindness, esp. inability to distinguish green from red. [f. F *daltonisme* f. John *Dalton,* Eng. chemist so affected, d. 1844, -ISM(2)]

dam[1], n., & v.t. Barrier constructed to hold back water & raise its level, to form a reservoir, or to prevent flooding; causeway; water confined by d. (Vb) furnish or confine with d. (usu. *up*); block *up,* obstruct, (lit. & fig.). [com.-Teut., cf. Du. *dam,* G *damm*]

dam[2], n. Mother (usu. of beast); *the devil & his d.,* the powers of evil. [var. DAME]

dă·mage (-ĭj), n., & v.t. Harm (*to* one's *great d.*), injury impairing value or usefulness; (Law; pl.) sum of money claimed or adjudged in compensation for loss or injury; (slang) cost (*what's the d.?*). (Vb) injure (usu. thing) so as to diminish value; detract from reputation of (person &c.; *trying to d. the Government*; *a damaging admission*); hence **da·mage**ABLE a. [f. OF *damage(r)* f. *dam* loss f. L *damnum* + -AGE]

damasce·ne (-*a*sēn), **damaskee·n,** v.t. Ornament (metal) with inlaid gold or silver; ornament (steel) with watered pattern produced in welding. [f. *Damascus, -cene* thr. L f. Gk *damaskēnos, -keen* thr. F & It.]

dă·mask, n. & a., & v.t. *D. rose,* old variety brought from Damascus; its colour; figured woven material (prop. of silk); twilled table-linen with woven designs shown by reflection of light; steel of or as of Damascus, with wavy surface-pattern due to special welding of iron & steel together. (Adj.) coloured like d. rose, blush-red; made of or resembling the silk, linen, or steel. (Vb) Weave with figured designs; =DAMASCENE; ornament with pattern; make (cheek &c.) red. [f. It. *Damasco* f. L *Damascus*]

dame, n. (Archaic, poet., or facetious, for) lady; keeper, male or female, of Eton boarding-house; (Law; prefixed title of) wife of knight or baronet (*Lady* in ordinary use; cf. *D. Fortune, D. Nature*); lady member of Order of British Empire (also as prefix corresp. *Sir*); *D. Commander, D. Grand Cross,* (ranks in O.B.E.); higher female member of Primrose League; *d.-school,* elementary kept by old lady. [OF, f. L *domina* mistress]

damn (dăm), v.t. & i., & n. Condemn, censure, (*d. a person's character*); (Theatr., of audience) receive coldly, secure the withdrawal of, (play); bring condemnation upon, be the ruin of; *d. with faint praise,* commend so frigidly as to suggest disapproval; doom to hell (so in optative, often *d—,* = *may God d.* person or thing, or with object omitted; *damned,* or *I'll be damned, if I know* &c., colloq. negation); cause the damnation of; curse (person or thing, or abs.; esp. *d. your eyes,* or *impudence!*); (N.) an uttered curse; a negligible amount (*don't care, not worth, a d.*). [f. OF *damner* f. L *damnare* (*damnum* loss, harm)]

da·mnable (-mn-), a. Subject to, deserving, damnation; hateful, confounded, annoying. Hence **da·mnab**LY[2] adv. [F, f. L *damnabilis* as prec., -ABLE]

damna·tion (-mn-), n. & int. Damning of play; (condemnation to) eternal punishment in hell; (int.) =may d. take a person or thing. [F, f. L *damnationem* (DAMN, -ATION)]

da·mnatory (-mn-), a. Conveying, causing, censure or damnation. [f. L *damnatorius* (*damnare* DAMN, -ORY)]

damned (-md), a. & adv. In vbl senses; also or esp.: *the d.,* souls in hell; damnable, infernal, unwelcome; confoundedly, extremely, (*d.* or *d—d hot, funny,* &c.). [-ED[1]]

da·mnify̆ (-mn-), v.t. (legal). Cause injury to. Hence **damni**FICA·TION n. [f. OF *damnifier* f. L *damnificare* (*damnum* loss, -FY)]

da·mning[1] (-mĭ-), n. In vbl senses; esp., cursing. [-ING[1]]

da·mning[2] (-mn-, -mĭ-), a. In vbl senses; esp., *d. evidence,* that secures conviction. [-ING[2]]

damno·sa hērē̆·ditas, n. Inheritance that brings more burden than profit. [L]

Dă·moclēs, n. *Sword of D.,* imminent danger in midst of prosperity. [Greek who was feasted with sword hung by a hair over him]

Dā·mon & Pў̆·thiăs, n. & a. (As of) devoted friends (*D.-&-P. friendship*). [Gk tale]

damp, n., a., & v.t. & i. =CHOKE[1]-*d.* (also *black d.*); =FIRE[1]-*d.*; moisture in air, on surface, or diffused through solid; dejection, chill, discouragement, (*cast* or *strike a d. over* or *into*); *d.(-proof) course,* layer of slate &c. in wall to keep d. from rising; hence **da·mp-**PROOF a. (Adj.) slightly wet; hence **da·mp**EN[6] v.t. & i. (chiefly U.S.), **da·mp**ISH[1](2) a., **da·mp**LY[2] adv., **da·mp**NESS n. (Vb) stifle, choke, dull, extinguish, (*d. down a fire,* heap with ashes &c. to check combustion); (Mus.) stop vibration of (string); discourage, depress, (zeal, hopes); moisten; (Gardening) *d. off,* rot & fall off from d. [vb f. adj. f. noun; cf. Du. & Da. *damp,* G *dampf,* vapour]

da·mper, n. Person or thing that depresses; (Piano) pad silencing string except when removed by loud pedal or by note's being struck; metal plate in flue controlling combustion; contrivance for wetting paper, stamps, &c.; (Austral.) unleavened cake baked in wood ashes. [-ER[1]]

da·msel (-zl), n. (archaic & literary). Young unmarried woman. [f. OF *dameisele* f. med. L *domnicella* dim. of L *domina* mistress]

da·mson (-zn), n. & a. Small dark-purple plum (*d. plum,* larger but similar); tree bearing it; *d. cheese,* solid conserve of dd. & sugar; (adj.) d.-coloured. [ME *damascene* f. L *damascenum* (*prunum* plum) of Damascus]

Danaos. See TIMEO.

dance[1], v.i. & t. Move with rhythmical steps, glides, leaps, revolutions, gestures, &c., usu. to music, alone or with a partner or set (*d. to* one's *tune* or *pipe,* follow his lead); jump about, skip, move in lively way (of heart, blood, &c.); bob up and down on water &c. (*d. upon nothing,* be hanged); perform (minuet, waltz, &c.); *d. attendance* (*upon* person), be kept waiting (by), follow about; cause to d. (bears &c.); toss up & down, dandle, (baby); *d. away, off, into,* &c., lose, bring, &c., by dancing (*his head off, his chance away, herself into favour*). [f. OF *dancer, -ser,* perh. f. OHG *dansôn* stretch out]

dance[2], n. Dancing motion (see prec.);

some special form of this; single round or turn of one; tune for dancing to, or in d. rhythm; dancing-party; *lead* (person) *a d.*, entangle him in useless pursuit or toil; *D. of Death* or *of Macabre*, medieval picture-subject of Death leading all ranks to grave; *St Vitus's dance*, disorder chiefly in children with convulsive involuntary movements. [f. prec.]

da·ncer, n. In vbl senses; esp.: one who dances in public for money; *merry dd.*, aurora borealis. [-ER[1]]

dă·ndelī·on, n. Yellow-flowered composite plant with widely toothed leaves. [f. F *dent de lion* lion's tooth]

dă·nder, n. (colloq., esp. U.S.). Temper, anger, indignation, (*get* one's *d. up*, grow, make him, angry). [?]

Da·ndie Di·nmont, n. Breed of terrier. [character in *Guy Mannering*]

dă·ndle, v.t. Dance (child) on knee or in arms; pet. [cf. It. *dandolare* (*dandola* doll)]

dă·ndruff, -iff, n. Dead skin in small scales among the hair, scurf. [also *dander*; ending perh. Yorksh. *hurf* f. Icel. *hrufa* scab]

dă·ndy[1], n. & a. (Person) devoted to smartness esp. of costume, neat, smart, decorated, whence **dandī·**ACAL a., **da·n-di**FY v.t., **dandi**FICA·TION n., **da·ndy**ISH[1] a., **da·ndy**ISM(2) n.; sloop with special rig; (also *d.-cart*) spring-cart used by milkmen; *d.-brush*, of whalebone &c. for cleaning horse. [1780 in Scotland, where *Dandy* also stands for *Andrew*]

dă·ndy[2], n. =DENGUE. [negro corrupt. of *dengue*, perh. w. assim. to prec. w. ref. to stiff attitude caused by pain]

Dane, n. Native of Denmark; (Hist.) Northman invader of England; (also *Great D.*) powerful short-haired breed of dog. [f. Da. *Daner* f. OTeut. *Daniz* pl.]

dā·nger, n. Liability or exposure to harm, risk, peril, (*of* one's life, *of* death or other evil; *in d. of*, likely to incur &c.); position of railway signal directing stoppage or caution (*signal is at d.*); thing that causes peril (*a d. to the peace of Europe, to navigation*). So **da·nger-**OUS a., **da·ngerous**LY[2] adv. [earlier sense *power* (*within his d.* = at his mercy), f. OF *dangier* f. LL **dominiarium* (L *dominium* f. *dominus* lord, -ARY[1])]

da·ngle, v.i. & t. Be suspended & sway to & fro; hold or carry (thing) swaying loosely; hold (hopes &c.) as temptation *before* person, *in* his sight, &c.; hover *after, round, about*, person as a follower, lover, &c., whence **da·ngl**ER[1] n. [etym. dub.; cf. Da. *dangle*]

Dăn·iel, n. Upright judge, person of infallible wisdom. [*Dan.* i–vi, & *Merchant of Venice*, IV. i. 223, 333]

Dā·nish, a. & n. (Language) of Denmark or the Danes. [OE *Denisc* (-ISH[1])]

dank, a. Soaked, oozy; unpleasantly or unwholesomely damp (of air, weather, &c.). [cf. Sw. *dank* marshy spot]

Dantē·an, a. & n. (Student) of Dante; in Dante's style or recalling his descriptions. So **Dant**E·SQUE a., **Da·nt**IST(3) n. [-AN]

dap, v.i. & t., & n. Fish by letting bait bob on water; dip lightly; make (ball) bounce, (of ball) bounce, on ground; (n.) bounce of ball. [cf. DAB[1]]

da·phnē, n. Kinds of flowering shrub. [Gk (-ē), =laurel]

da·pper, a. Neat, smart, in appearance or movement. [cf. Du. *dapper*, G *tapfer*, valiant]

da·pple, v.t. & i., & n. Variegate, become variegated, with rounded spots or patches of colour or shade. (N.) dappled effect; *d.-grey*, (horse) of grey with darker spots. [perh. =Icel. *depill* spot dim. of *dapi* pool; but G *apfelgrau*, F. *gris-pommelé*, & other parallels, suggest some connexion with *apple*]

dar·bies, n. pl. (slang). Handcuffs. [?]

Dar·by & Joan (jōn), n. Devoted old married couple. [perh. f. poem 1735 in *Gentleman's Mag.*]

dare, v.t. (before expressed or implied infin. without *to*, the 3 sing. pres. is usu. *dare*, the past & conditional often *durst*; otherwise *dares, dared*; infin. without *to* is usual only after the sense *venture* in negative or virtually negative sentence). Venture (to), have the courage or impudence (to), (*I d. swear*, feel sure that; *d. he do it?*; *he dares to insult me*; *I would if I durst* or *dared*; *they dared* or *durst not come, did not d. to come*); attempt, take the risks of, (*d. all things, a leap, the event*, person's *anger*); defy (person); challenge (person) *to* do, *to it*, &c.; *I dare say* (rare exc. in 1st person; 3rd sing. in reported speech, *he dares to say*, past *he dared say* or *to say*), am prepared to believe, do not deny, =very likely (often iron.); *d.-devil*, reckless (person). [OE *durran* f. Aryan *dhers-* cf. Gk *tharseō* be bold; the pres. (cf. CAN) is an old past, whence *dare* as 3rd sing.]

dar·i, n. =DURRA.

dār·ing[1], n. In vbl senses; esp., adventurous courage. [-ING[1]]

dār·ing[2], a. In vbl senses; esp., adventurous, bold. Hence **dar·ing**LY[2] adv. [-ING[2]]

dark[1], a. With no or relatively little light, unilluminated (*d. lantern*, that can have its light covered), gloomy, sombre; of colour more or less near black (esp. as pref. to adjj. of colour as *d.-brown*; *d.* BLUE[2]s); brown-complexioned, not fair; evil, atrocious; cheerless (*d. side of things*; sad, sullen (*a d. humour*), frowning; obscure (*d. saying, d. oblivion*); secret (*keep* thing *d.*; *keep d.*, remain in hiding); little known of (*d. horse*, unexpected winner of race, & fig. of persons); unenlightened (*in the darkest ignorance*; *the* *d. ages,* Middle Ages); *the D. Continent* (in last two senses), Africa; *d. room,* with actinic rays excluded for treating photographic plates. Hence **dar·**KISH[1](2) a., **dar·**KLY[2] adv., **dar·**KNESS n. (*Prince of darkness,* the Devil). [OE *deorc*; as adj. exclusively E, but cf. OHG *tarchanjan* to hide]

dark[2], n. Absence of light (esp. *in the d.*); nightfall (*at d.*); d. colour (esp. in art, *the lights and dd. of a picture*); want of knowledge (*am in the d. about it*; *leap in the d.,* rash step or enterprise). Hence **dar·k**SOME a. (poet.). [f. prec.]

dar·ken, v.t. & i. Make or become DARK[1]; *d.* one's *door,* pay him a visit (usu. neg.); *d. counsel,* make perplexity worse. [-EN[6]]

dar·kle, v.i. Lie concealed; grow dark. [mod. back-formation f. foll. misunderstood as part.]

dar·kling, adv. & a. In the dark. [-LING[2]]

dar·k(e)y, n. (colloq.). Negro. [-Y[3]]

dar·ling, n. & a. Loved, best loved, lovable, (person or animal). [OE *déorling* (DEAR, -LING[1])]

darn[1], v.t., & n. Mend (esp. knitting) by interweaving yarn with needle across hole, whence **dar·**NING[1](5) n.; *darning-ball, -last,* for stretching work during operation; (n.) place so mended. [perh. f. obs. vb & adj. *dern* hide, hidden, = OHG *tarnan* hide]

darn[2], v.t. (slang). Damn (as imprecation.) [deformation of DAMN]

dar·nel (-nl), n. Kind of grass growing as weed among corn. [cf. Walloon *darnelle*]

dart, n., & v.t. & i. Pointed missile, esp. light javelin, (pl.) indoor game with toy *dd.* & target; sting of insect &c.; sudden rapid motion; act of throwing missile. (Vb) throw (missile), throw missile; emit suddenly (glance, flash, anger); start rapidly in some direction. [OF accus. of *darz* cf. DACE]

dar·ter, n. In vbl senses; also: web-footed bird of pelican tribe; (pl.) order of birds including kingfishers & bee-eaters; kinds of fish. [-ER[1]]

Dar·tmoor, n. (Used for) D. convict prison near Princetown, Devon.

Dar·tmouth, n. (Used for) Royal Naval College, D., Devon.

dar·tle, v.t. & i. Keep on darting. [-LE(3)]

dar·tre (-*ter*), n. Kinds of skin disease, esp. herpes. So **dar·tr**OUS a. [F, etym. dub.]

Darwi·nian, a. & n. Of, person believing in, Charles Darwin or his doctrines esp. on evolution of species. So **Dar·win**ISM(3) n., **Dar·win**IST(2) n. & a., **Darwini·s**TIC a., **Dar·win**ITE[1](1) n. & a., **Dar·win**IZE(2, 4) v.t. & i.

dash[1], v.t. & i. Shatter *to pieces* (rarely abs., as *flowers dashed by rain*); knock, drive, throw, or thrust, *away, off, out, down,* &c.; fling, drive, splash, (thing or person) *against, upon, into*; bespatter *with* water &c. (*d.-board,* of wood or leather in front of vehicle to keep out mud; *dashed with colour*); dilute, qualify, (water *with* spirit, joy *with* pain); frustrate (*d.* one's *hopes*), daunt, discourage, confound; write *down* or throw *off* rapidly (composition, sketch); underline; (slang) = *damn* as mild imprecation; fall, move, throw oneself, with violence; come into collision *against, upon*; ride, run, or drive *up,* move about, behave, with spirit or display, whence **da·sh**ING[2] a., **da·shing**LY[2] adv. [cf. Sw. *daska* drub; but perh. imit., cf. *clash, crash,* &c.; imprecatory use perh. f. use of dashes in *d—, d—d,* cf. BLANK[2]]

dash[2], n. Sound of water striking or struck; splash of colour; infusion (*d. of brandy, of good blood*); hasty pen-stroke; horizontal stroke in writing or printing to mark a break in sense, a parenthesis (two dd.), omitted letters or words, &c.; rush, onset, sudden advance; (capacity for) vigorous action; showy appearance or behaviour (*cut a d.,* make a brilliant show). [f. prec.]

da·sher, n. In vbl senses; esp., contrivance for agitating cream in churn. [-ER[1]]

da·stard, n. Coward, skulker, esp. one who commits brutal act without endangering himself. Hence **da·stard**LY[1] a., **da·stardli**NESS n. [prob. f. *dazed* p.p. + -ARD]

data. See DATUM.

da·taller, day-taler, (-*tal*-), n. Workman engaged and paid by the day. [DAY, TALE in sense *reckoning,* -ER[1]]

date[1], n. W.-Asiat. & N.-Afr. tree (also *d.-palm*), or its fruit, an oblong single-stoned drupe. [OF, f. L f. Gk *daktulos* finger]

date[2], n. Statement in document, letter, book, or inscription, of the time (& often place) of execution, writing, publication, &c.; time at which thing happens or is to happen; period to which antiquities &c. belong; person's age, duration, term of life, (archaic or poet.); (*go*) *out of d.,* (become) obsolete; *up to d.* (f. book-keeping phr. for accounts completed to current day, now as slang adj. & adv.), meeting, according to, the latest requirements or knowledge; *d.-line,* meridian 180° from Greenwich, east & west of which the d. differs. [F, f. L *data* fem. p.p. of *dare* = (letter) given (at such a time & place)]

date[3], v.t. & i. Mark (letter &c.) with d. (dated *from* London), whence **da·t**ER[1](2) n.; refer (event) to a time; count time, reckon, (*dating from the Creation*); bear d., be dated; have origin *from* (*church dates from the 14th c.*); (of art, style, &c.) become recognizable as of a past or particular period. Hence **dā·t**ABLE a. [f. prec.]

da·teless, a. Undated; endless; immemorial. [f. DATE[2], [3], -LESS]

dā·tive, a. & n. *D. case* or *d.*, the case in nouns, pronouns, & adjj., proper to the remoter object or recipient. So **datī·**VAL a., **da·tive**LY[2] adv. [f. L *dativus* (*dare dat-* give, -IVE)]

dā·tum, n. (pl. *-ta*). Thing known or granted, assumption or premiss from which inferences may be drawn; fixed starting-point of scale &c. (ORDNANCE *d.*). [L, neut. p.p. of *dare* give]

datūr·a, n. Kinds of poisonous plant, including stramonium, yielding strong narcotic. [f. Hind. *dhatura*]

daub, v.t. & i., & n. Coat (wall &c.) *with* plaster, clay, &c. (n., the material); smear (surface; n., a smear), lay *on* (greasy or sticky stuff); soil, stain; paint (t. & i.) inartistically, lay (colours) *on* so, (n., a coarse painting), whence **dau·b**ER[1], **dau·b**STER, nn., **dau·b**Y[2] a. [f. OF *dauber* f. L DE(*albare* f. *albus* white) whitewash]

daugh·ter, n. One's female child; female descendant, female member *of* family, race, &c.; woman who is the spiritual or intellectual product of person or thing; product personified as female (*Carthage d. of Tyre*; *Fortune and its d. Confidence*; *d.-language*, as French of Latin); *d.-in-law*, son's wife, (loosely) step-d. Hence **daugh·ter**HOOD n., **daugh·ter**LY[1] a. [Aryan; OE *dohtor*, Du. *dochter*, G *tochter*, Gk *thugatēr*, cf. Skr. *duh-* to milk]

daunt, v.t. Discourage, intimidate; press (herrings) down in barrel. [f. OF *danter* (now *dompter*) f. L *domitare* frequent. of *domare* tame]

dau·ntless, a. Intrepid, persevering. Hence **dau·ntless**LY[2] adv., **dau·ntless**NESS n. [perh. f. obs. *daunt* a check f. prec. + -LESS]

dau·phin, dau·phiness, nn. (Wife of) King of France's eldest son. [family name (f. L *delphinus* DOLPHIN) of lords of Dauphiné, last of whom ceded it on condition of *dauphin*'s being accepted as French heir-apparent's title]

dă·venport, n. Escritoire with drawers & hinged writing-slab. [prob. maker's name]

Dă·vid & Jŏ·nathan, n. Any pair of devoted friends. [1 *Sam.* xviii &c.]

dă·vit, n. Crane at ship's bow for hoisting anchor clear of side; one of pair of cranes for suspending or lowering ship's boat. [formerly also *david* prob. f. the male name; cf. *jemmy*]

Dā·vy (lamp), n. Miner's wire-gauze safety lamp. [Sir H. *D.*, inventor]

dā·vy, n. (slang). *Take* one's *d.*, swear (*that, to* fact). [short for AFFIDAVIT]

Davy Jones's locker, n. The deep, a watery grave (in the sea). [?]

daw, n. =JACKDAW. [cf. OHG *tâha*, G *dohle*]

daw·dle, v.i. & t., & n. Idle, dally; *d. away* (time &c.) waste; hence **daw·dl**ER[1] n. (N.) dawdling person. [cf. DODDER[2], & dial. *daddle* totter as baby; -LE(3)]

dawk, dâk, n. (Anglo-Ind.). Post or transport by relays of men or horses; relay; *d. bungalow*, house for travellers at d. station. [Hind.]

dawn, v.i., & n. Begin to appear or grow light (of day, day-light, morning, country shone upon, things becoming evident to mind, intelligence, civilization, &c.); *first dawnings* &c., beginning; *dawning*, the East; *d. upon*, begin to be perceptible to; (n.) first light, daybreak, rise or incipient gleam of anything. [back formation f. *dawning* prob. f. ON, which displaced *dawing* vbl n. f. obs. *daw* OE *dagian* become day]

day, n. Time while sun is above horizon, (loosely) including twilights (*d. & night*, adv., throughout these or in both alike; *all d., all the d.*, adv., throughout it; *d.-break, break of d.*, dawn; *d.-dream, -ing, -er*, reverie or castle in air, indulgence, indulger, in them); dawn (*before, at, d.*); daylight (*by d.*; *was broad d.*; *clear as d.*); twenty-four hours (*solar* or *astronomical d.*, from noon; *civil d.*, from midnight; *sidereal d.*, between two meridional transits of first point of Aries, about 4′ shorter than *solar*; *natural d.*, =*sidereal*, also in first sense above); civil d. as point of time, date, &c. (*one d.*, adv., on an unspecified date past or future; *the other d.*, on a d. not long ago; *one of these dd.* or *fine dd.*, before long, in prophecy or promise; *some d.*, adv., in the future; *on* one's *d.*, when he is at his best; *d. of* GRACE); date of specified festival &c. (*first d.*, Sunday; *Christmas d., birthd., pay-d., last D.* or *D. of* JUDGEMENT; *the D.* or *der Tag*, that of victory over Gt Britain expected by Germans); date agreed upon (*keep* one's *d.*, be punctual; one's *d.*, for being at home to guests, esp. once a week); victory (*carry, win, lose, the d.*); period (often pl., *in the dd. of, the dd. of old, in dd. to come, men of other dd.*; *better dd.*, when one was or will be better off; *fallen on evil dd.*, in misfortune; sing., *at, to, this d.*; *present-d.*, adj. =modern; *these dd.*, adv., nowadays; *the d.*, the current d., *sufficient for the d. is the evil thereof*, do not anticipate trouble; *men of the d.*, persons of importance at any time; *creature of a d.*, short-lived); one's *d.*, lifetime, period of prosperity, activity, power, &c., (also pl. *end* one's *dd.*, die; *every dog has his d.*, no one always unlucky); *this d. week, month, year*, reckoning forward or back from today; *d. about*, on alternate dd.; *d. by d., d. after d., from d. to d., every d.*, advv. of daily repetition or progress; *twice* &c. *a d.*, in each d. (see A[3]); *know the time of d.*, be wide awake, knowing; *the d. before, after, the fair*, advv., too early, late, for opportunity. *D.-boarder*, schoolboy feeding but not sleeping at school; *d.-book* in bookkeeping, book in which esp. sale transactions are entered at once for later transfer to ledger; *d.-boy*, schoolboy boarding at home; *d.-fly*, ephemerid; *d.-labourer*, hired by d. at fixed wage; *d.-long* a. & adv., (lasting) for whole d.; *d.-owl*, Hawk-owl hunting by day; *d.-room*, used by d. only, esp. common living-room at schools; *d.-school*, opp. Sunday, evening, or boarding school; *d.-spring*, dawn (poet.); *d.-ticket*, covering return on same d.; *d.-time*, not night, esp. *in the d.-time*. [OE *dæg*, com.-Teut. cf. Du. *dag*, G *tag*; not cogn. w. L *dies*]

day·light, n. Light of day (BURN² *d.*); openness, publicity; *let d. into* (slang), stab or shoot; dawn (*before, at, d.*); visible interval as between boats in race, wine & glass-rim (*no d.*, fill up), or rider & saddle; *d.-saving*, use of fictitious time in summer making lamps &c. needless.

daze, v.t., & n. Stupefy, bewilder; dazzle; hence **da·zĕd**LY² adv. (N.) stupefaction, bewilderment. [ME *dasen* cf. Icel. *dasask* refl. vb become weary]

da·zzle, v.t., & n. Confuse or dim (sight, eye, person) with excess of light, intricate motion, incalculable number, &c.; confound or surprise (mind, person) by brilliant display lit. or fig.; *dazzled with* or *by*; *d. lamps* or *lights* (over-bright, on motor-car); *d. paint* (so patterned on ship as to deceive enemy about her type or course); hence **da·zzle**MENT n., **da·zzling**LY² adv. (N.) glitter. [f. prec. + -LE(3)]

de-, pref. From L *de* (prep. &) pref. = down (*depend*), away (*defend*, orig. fend off, *deduce, deprecate*), completely (*declare, denude*), un- (in L oftener *dis-*, but also *de-*, which is now a living pref. in this sense, as *decentralize*; many such E wds in *de-* are also f. F in *dé-*, which represents L *dis-*, OF & Rom. *des-*, as well as L *de-*), twice over or doubly (in chem. & bot. wds as *decomposite, decompound*; a LL use).

deacon (dē·kn), n. (Primitive Church) appointed minister of charity (*Acts* vi. 1–6); (Episcopal) member of third order of ministry below bishop & priest; (Presbyterian) officer attending to congregation's secular affairs. Hence **dea·con**SHIP n. [f. L f. Gk *diakonos* servant]

dea·coness, n. Woman in primitive & some modern Churches with functions analogous to deacon's. [-ESS¹]

dead (dĕd), a., n., & adv. That has ceased to live (*the d.*, noun, d. person or persons, or all who have ever died; *from the d.*, from among these; *d. men tell no tales*, argument for killing possessor of secret; *d.-house*, mortuary; *d. march*, funeral music; *d.-office*, funeral service; *d. as a doornail*, quite d.; *d. & gone*; *wait for d. men's* SHOES; FLOG *d. horse*; *d. men* or *marines*, empty bottles; *d. man's finger, hand, thumb*, kinds of orchid; *d. man's handle*, the controlling handle in electric trains which must be held and pressed down for current to pass, so that slackening by death or illness cuts the current & stops the train); benumbed, insensible, (of hands &c.; also *d. to*, unconscious or unappreciative of, hardened against); without spiritual life; obsolete, past, not effective, (*d. language*, e.g. ancient Gk; *d. letter*, law no longer observed, unclaimed or undelivered letter at post office); inanimate (*d. fence*, of timber &c., opp. *quickset*; *d. matter*); extinct, dull, lustreless, without force, muffled, (*d. brand, coal*; *d. gold*, unburnished; *d. colour*, first layer in picture, cold & pale; *d.-nettle*, non-stinging weed like nettle; *d.-alive*, spiritless; *d. sound*, not resonant); inactive, motionless, idle, (*D. Sea*; *d. point* or *d. centre*, least & greatest extension of piston or crank, where it exerts no effective power; *d. weight*, inert, of lifeless matter, also fig. of debt &c.; *d. pull, lift*, at thing too heavy for one to move; *d. freight*, sum paid in chartering ship for part not occupied by cargo; *d. arch, window*, &c., sham; *d. end*, terminus of branch line of railway &c.; *d. hand*, = MORTMAIN, usu. implying protest; *d. hours*, still, in night; *d. season*; *d. stock*, unemployed capital, unsalable goods; *d. ball*, out of play; *wind falls d.*; as noun, = d. time, *at d. of night, in the d. of winter*); abrupt, complete, unrelieved, exact, (*come to d. stop*; *a d. faint*; *on a d. level*; *d. heat*, exact equality in race; *d. spit* colloq., very counterpart *of*; *a d. calm*; *d. loss*, without compensation; *be in d. earnest*; *a d. certainty*; *d. on the target*, quite straight, so *d. shot*, unerring; *d.-lock*, utter standstill); *d.-alive*, (of place, occupation, &c.) dull, tedious, monotonous; *d.-eye* (naut.), round flat three-holed block for extending shrouds; *d.-fire*, St. Elmo's fire, as presaging death; *d.-head*, non-paying theatre-goer or passenger; *d.-light* (naut.), shutter protecting cabin-window or porthole in storm; *d. man's* (or *men's*) *fingers*, finger-like divisions of gills in lobster or crab; *d. reckoning* (naut.), of ship's position by log, compass, &c., when observations are impossible; *D.-Sea* APPLE; hence **dea·d**NESS n. (Adv.) profoundly, absolutely, completely, (*d. asleep, level, straight, tired, drunk*; *d.-beat*, tired out; CUT² *d.*; *d. against*, directly opposite to). [OE *déad*, com.-Teut. cf. Du. *dood*, G *tot*, f. OTeut. *daudoz* p.p. of vb st. *dau-* DIE²]

deaden (dĕ·dn), v.t. & i. Deprive of or

For compounds of *de-* not given consult DE-.

lose vitality, force, brightness, feeling, &c.; make insensible *to*. [-EN[6]]

dea·dly[1] (dĕd-), a. Causing fatal injury; of poisonous nature (*D. Nightshade*); entailing damnation (*d. sin*); implacable, internecine; deathlike (*d. paleness, faintness, gloom*); intense (*in d. haste*; *d. dullness*). Hence **dea·dli**NESS n. [OE *déadlic* (DEAD, -LY[1])]

dea·dly[2] (dĕd-), adv. As if dead (*d. white, faint*); extremely (*d. tired, dull*). [OE *déadlīce* (DEAD, -LY[2])]

deaf (dĕf), a. Wholly or partly without hearing (*the d.*, d. people; *d. of an*, or *in one, ear*; *d. as adder* or *post*; *none so d. as those that won't hear*); insensible *to* harmony, rhythm, &c.; not giving ear *to*, uncompliant, (*turn a d. ear to*); *d. nut*, with no kernel; *d.-&-dumb alphabet, language*, &c., signs for communication by the d.; *d.-mute*, d. & dumb person. Hence **dea·f**LY[2] adv., **dea·f**NESS n. [OE *déaf*, com.-Teut. cf. Du. *doof*, G *taub*, also Gk *tuphlos* blind]

deafen (dĕ·fn), v.t. Deprive of hearing by noise; make (sound) inaudible by louder one; make (floor &c.) impervious to sound. [-EN[6]]

deal[1], n. *A great, good, d.*, large, considerable, amount; (slang) *a. d.*, =a great d.; (same phrases used adv.) to a large, considerable, extent, (esp. with comparative or superl.) by much, considerably. [OE *dǣl*, com.-Teut. cf. G *teil* part; also cogn. w. DOLE]

deal[2], v.t. & i. (*dealt* pr. dĕlt), & n. Distribute, give *out*, (gifts &c.) among several; deliver as his share or deserts to person (esp. of Providence &c.; *dealt him happiness, good measure*; of persons, esp. *d. a blow*, abs. or with *at*, lit. & fig.); distribute cards to players for a game or round (n., such distribution, player's turn for it, as *my d.*, or round played after it), give (card, hand, &c.) to player; associate *with* (esp. neg. as *refuse to d. with*); do business *with* person, *in* goods (n., slang, a bargain or transaction; also dishonest job); occupy oneself, grapple by way of discussion or refutation, take measures, *with*; (with adv.) behave (*d. honourably, cruelly*, esp. *with* or *by* person). Hence **dea·l**ING[1](1) n. [OE *dǣlan* as prec.]

deal[3], n. Piece of sawn fir or pine wood over 7 in. broad & 6 ft long, & not over 3 in. thick; a quantity of these; fir or pine wood. [cogn. w. OE *thille* THILL, but f. LG cf. Du. *deel*, G *diele*]

dea·ler, n. In vbl senses; esp.: player dealing at cards; trader, usu. in comb. as *corn-d.* [-ER[1]]

dēămbula·tion, n., **dēă·mbulatory**, a. Walking. [f. L *deambulatio, deambulatorius*, f. DE(*ambulare* walk), -ATION, -ORY]

dean[1], n. Head of cathedral or collegiate-church chapter; (also *rural d.*) clergyman invested with jurisdiction or precedence over division of archdeaconry; (colleges) resident fellow, or one of several, with disciplinary & other functions; (foreign, Scotch, & modern universities) president of a faculty; =DOYEN. [earlier sense *one set over ten monks* f. L (Vulgate &c.) *decanus* prob. f. *decem* ten]

dean[2], **dene**, n. Vale (esp. in names ending in *-dean, -dene, -den*). [OE *denu*, cogn. w. DEN]

dea·nery, n. Office, house, of dean; group of parishes presided over by rural dean. [-ERY]

dear, a., n., adv., & int. Beloved (often as merely polite or even ironical form in talk, esp. *my d. sir, my d. Jones*, & now used at beginning of most letters not intended to be markedly business-like; as noun, *d.* or *dearest*, esp. in voc., =*d. one*; *a d.*, esp. in coaxing formulae); precious *to*; one's cherished (*for d. life*, as though life were at stake); high-priced, costly, (as adv., *sell, buy, pay*, COST[2] one *d.*; *d. year, shop*, in which prices run high); hence **dear·**LY[2] adv., **dear·**NESS n. (Int.) *dear, dear!, dear me!, oh dear!*, expressing surprise, distress, sympathy, &c. [OE *déore*, com.-Teut. cf. Du. *dier* loved, *diuer* costly, G *teuer*]

dearth (der-), n. Scarcity & dearness of food; scanty supply *of*. [ME *derthe* (prec., -TH[1])]

dear·y, -ie, n. (usu. voc.). Dear one. [-Y[3]]

death (dĕth), n. Dying (DIE[2] *the d.*; *d.-bed*, on which one dies, *d.-b. repentance*, fig. change of policy made too late to bear fruit; *d.-rattle*, sound in dying person's throat; *d.-roll*, list of the killed or dead; *d.-watch*, kinds of insect whose ticking portends d.); end of life (*civil d.*, ceasing to count as citizen by outlawry, banishment, &c.; *catch* one's *d.*, i.e. fatal chill &c.; *d.-duties*, tax levied before property passes to heir; *d.-rate*, yearly number of dd. to 1000 of population; *d.-trap*, unwholesome or dangerous place); being killed or killing (*field of d.*, battle-field &c.; *be the d. of*, kill; *do, put, stone*, &c., *to d.*; *war to the d.*, *d.-feud*, till one kills or is killed; *it is, we make it, d. to*, d. is the penalty; *be in at the d.*, see fox killed, or fig. any enterprise ended; *be d. on* slang, skilful at killing game &c., or fig. at doing anything; *sick unto, tired to, d.*, to utmost limit; *d.-adder*, kinds of venomous snake; *d.-blow*, mortal, lit. & fig.; *d.-warrant*, for criminal's execution, abolition of custom &c.); ceasing to be, annihilation, personified power that annihilates, (*at d.'s door*, soon to die; *d.'s-head*, skull as emblem of mortality, also kind of moth with skull marked on back; *sure, pale, as d.*; *hold on like grim d.*; *d. on rats*, good rat-killer, of dogs; *death!*, archaic imprecation); being dead (*d.-mask*, cast taken of dead person's face; *eyes closed in d.*); want of spiritual life (*everlasting d.*, damnation); *Black D.*, (mod. name, transl. f. G for) great pestilence of Oriental Plague in Europe in 14th c. Hence **dea·th**LESS a., **dea·th-less**LY[2] adv., **dea·thless**NESS n., **dea·th-**LIKE a. & adv., **dea·th**LY[1] a. & adv., **dea·th**WARD(S) a. & adv. [OE *déath*, com.-Teut. cf. Du. *dood*, G *tod*, f. vb st. *dau-* DIE[2], *-th* cogn. w. L p.p. *-tus*]

débâcle (F), n. Break-up of ice in river; (Geol.) sudden rush of water carrying along blocks of stone and other debris; confused rush, rout, stampede; collapse, downfall, e.g. of a government.

debar·, v.t. (-rr-). Exclude *from* admission or right (also *d.* person *the crown* &c.); (rare) prevent, bar, (entrance &c.). [f. 1430; F *débarrer*, OF *desbarer*, LL *debarrare*, have almost contrary sense *unbar*; cf. DE- in *defend*]

debar·k, v.t. & i. =DISEMBARK. Hence **debark**A·TION n. [f. F *débarquer* (DE-, BARK[3])]

deba·se, v.t. Lower in quality, value, or character; adulterate (coin). Hence **deba·se**MENT n. [DE- + obs. *base* for ABASE]

debā·table, a. Questionable, subject to dispute, (*d. ground* lit. or fig., for which parties contend, borderland). [OF (foll., -ABLE)]

deba·te, v.t. & i., & n. Contest, fight for, (*long debated the victory*); dispute about, discuss, (a question); hold argument, esp. in Parliament or public meeting (*debating-society*, for practice); consider, ponder, (t. & i.); hence **deba·t**ER[1] n. (esp. of one skilled rather in argument than in oratory). (N.) controversy, discussion, public argument. [f. OF *debatre* & 13th-c. F *debat* (DE-, Rom. *battere* fight)]

debauch (-tsh), v.t., & n. Pervert from virtue or morality; make intemperate or sensual; seduce (woman); vitiate (taste, judgement); hence **debau·ch**ABLE a. (N.) bout or habit of sensual indulgence; hence **debauch**ERY(4) n. [f. F *débaucher* entice from a master (DE-, perh. *bauche* workshop)]

debauchee (dĕbōshē·), n. Viciously sensual person. [f. F *débauché* p.p. see prec., -EE]

debe·nture (-tsher), n. (Archaic or techn.) voucher given to person supplying goods to Royal Household or Government Office, entitling him to payment, Custom-House certificate to exporter of amount due to him as drawback or bounty. (Ord. sense) sealed bond of corporation or company acknowledging sum on which interest is due till principal is repaid, esp. fixed interest constituting prior charge on assets; *d. stock*, dd. consolidated or created as stock whose nominal capital represents debt of which interest only is secured as perpetual annuity. [perh. (w. assim. to -URE) = L *debentur* are due, as initial word of voucher]

debĭ·litate, v.t. Enfeeble (constitution &c.). [f. L *debilitare*, see foll., -ATE[3]]

debĭ·lity, n. Feebleness (of health, purpose, &c.). [f. F *débilité* f. L *debilitatem* (*debilis* weak, -TY)]

dĕ·bit, n., & v.t. Entry in account of sum owing; side of account (left-hand) in which these entries are made (cf. CREDIT). (Vb) charge (person) *with* sum; enter (sum) *against* or *to* person. [f. L *debitum* DEBT]

dĕ·bonair·, a. (archaic). Genial, pleasant, unembarrassed. [f. OF *debonaire* = *de bonne aire* of good disposition]

debo·shed, a. (Archaic for) debauched.

debouch (dĭboo·sh), v.i. Issue from ravine, wood, &c., into open ground (of troops; also of stream). So **debou·ch**MENT n. [f. F *déboucher* (L *dis-* see DE- + F *bouche* mouth)]

Debre·tt, n. (Used for) D.'s Peerage &c. [John *D.*, compiler]

debris, dé-, (dĕ·brē), n. Scattered fragments, wreckage, drifted accumulation. [F (*dé-*), f. obs. *débriser* break down]

debt (dĕt), n. Money, goods, or service, owing (*d. of honour*, not legally recoverable, esp. of sum lost in gambling; *d.-collector*, one whose business it is to collect dd. for creditors; *d. of nature*, death; *National D.*, sum owed by State to persons who have advanced money to it; *funded d.*, the part of this converted into fund of which interest only is to be paid; *floating d.*, part of it repayable on demand, or at stated time; *small d.*, of limited amount recoverable in County Court); being under obligation to pay something (*in, out of, get into, d.* or person's *d.*). [ME & OF *dette* f. L *debitum* neut. p.p. of *debēre* owe]

deb·tor, n. One who owes money or an obligation or duty; (Book-keeping) *Debtor, Dr*, heading of left-hand or debit side of account. [ME & OF *dettour* f. L *debitorem* (prec., -OR[2])]

debu·s, v.t. & i. (Mil.). Unload (men, stores) or alight from motor vehicles. [DE- + BUS, after *detrain*]

début (F), n. First appearance in society, or on stage &c. as performer.

dé·butant (F), n. (fem. *-ante*). Male or female performer making début; (fem.) girl coming out or being presented.

deca-, dec-, pref. f. Gk *deka* ten in many technical terms as *decagynous* [Gk *gunē* female] with ten pistils, *decahedral* [Gk *hedra* base] ten-sided (*-hedron*, such solid), *decandrous* [Gk *andr-* male] with ten stamens, *decastyle* [Gk *-stulos*] ten-columned (portico); esp. in French metric system = ten of the specified unit (cf. DECI-), whence **dĕ·cagram(me),** .353 oz avoird.; **dĕ·calitre** (-ēt*er*), about 2⅕ gal.; **dĕ·cametre,** about 32 ft 9 in.

dĕ·cade (-*a*d), **dĕ·cad,** n. Set, series, of ten; ten years; ten books (1–10, 11–20, &c.) of Livy. So **dĕ·cad**AL, **decă·d**IC, aa. [13th-c. F (-*e*), f. L f. G *dekas -ad-* f. *deka* ten, -AD, -ADE(2)]

dĕ·cadence, n., **dĕ·cadent,** a. & n. Falling away, declining, deteriorating, (used esp. of a period of art or literature after culmination); (literary slang) *decadent,* (writer or artist) affecting certain vices, obscurities, & turgidities of style. [f. F *décadence* f. med. L *decadentia* (DE-, Rom. *cadēre* = L *cadĕre* fall, -ENCE)]

dĕ·cagon, n. Plane figure with ten sides and angles. So **decă·gon**AL a. [f. med. L DECA(*gonum* f. Gk *-gōnos* -angled)]

dēca·lcify̆, v.t. Deprive (bone &c.) of its lime. [DE-]

dĕ·calogue (-ŏg), n. The ten commandments. [f. F *décalogue* f. L f. Gk *dekalogos* (*hoi deka logoi* the ten words)]

decă·meron, n. Collection of tales like the D. of Boccaccio (100 tales told by a company in ten days). [f. It. DEC(*amerone* wrong form f. Gk *-aēmeron* in *hexaēmeron* neut. adj. of six days]

deca·mp, v.i. Break up or leave camp; go away suddenly, take oneself off, abscond. So **deca·mp**MENT n. [f. F *décamper* (DE-, CAMP[1])]

decā·nal, a. Of dean, deanery, or south side, on which dean sits, of choir. [f. L *decanus* DEAN + -AL]

decā·nī, mus. direction. To be sung by decanal side in antiphonal singing (cf. CANTORIS). [L genit. as prec.]

deca·nt, v.t. Pour off (liquid of solution) by gradual inclination of vessel without disturbing sediment; pour (wine) similarly from bottle into decanter. [f. F *décanter* f. med. L DE(*canthare* f. L f. Gk *kanthos* CANT[1] used of lip of beaker)]

deca·nter, n. Stoppered glass bottle in which wine or spirit is brought to table. [-ER[1]]

decă·pitate, v.t. Behead (esp. as legal punishment); cut the head or end from. So **deca·pit**ABLE a., **decapit**A·TION n. [f. F *décapiter* f. LL DE(*capitare* f. *caput -itis* head)]

dĕ·capŏd, n. Ten-footed crustacean. [f. F *décapode* f. Gk DECA(*pous -podos* foot)]

dēcar·bonize, v.t. Deprive of its carbon or carbonic acid. [DE-]

deca·sualize, v.t. Do away with the casual employment of (labour). Hence **decasualiz**A·TION n. [DE-, -IZE]

dĕcasyllă·bic, a. & n., **decasy·llable,** n. & a. (Line) of ten syllables. [DECA-]

dēcathŏ·licize, v.t. Divest of its catholic character. [DE-]

decay·[1], v.i. & t. Deteriorate, lose quality, decline in power, wealth, energy, beauty, &c.; rot (t. & i.); cause to deteriorate. [f. OF *decair* f. Rom. DE(*cadēre* for L *cadĕre* fall)]

decay·[2], n. Decline, falling off; ruinous state, wasting away (*phonetic d.*, wearing down of word-forms); break-up of health, decomposition; rotten tissue (*remove the d.*). [f. prec.]

decea·se (-ēs), n., & v.i. (Esp. in legal and formal use for) death, die, depart(ure) from life. Hence **decea·s**ED[1](2) a. and n. (with or without *the*). [f. F *décès* f. L DE(*cessus* n. f. *cedere cess-* go)]

decei·t, n. Misrepresentation, deceiving; trick, stratagem; the vice of deceitfulness; misleading appearance. Hence **decei·t**FUL a., **decei·tful**LY[2] adv., **decei·tful**NESS n. [f. OF *deceite* n. f. fem. p.p. of *deceveir* f. L DE(*cipere -cept-* = *capere* take) deceive]

decei·ve, v.t. & i. Persuade of what is false, mislead, (*d.* one*self*, juggle with one's own convictions, also be mistaken); use deceit; disappoint (esp. *hopes*). So **decei·v**ABLE a., **decei·v**ER[1] n. [f. OF *deceveir* f. L as prec.]

Dece·mber, n. Twelfth month of year. Hence **Dece·mbr**IST n., member of Russian revolutionary conspiracy in D. 1825. [f. OF *décembre* f. L *December* (*decem* ten) orig. tenth month of Roman year]

dece·mvir, n. (pl. *-rs, -rī*). (Rom. Hist.) member of board of ten acting as council or ruling power, esp. that appointed 451 B.C. to draw up laws of Twelve Tables; member of any ruling body of ten, as at Venice. So **dece·mvir**AL a., **dece·mvir**ATE[1] n. [L, f. *decem viri* ten men]

dē·cency, n. Propriety of behaviour; what is required by good taste or delicacy; avoidance of obscene language & gestures & of undue exposure of person; respectability; *the dd.*, decorous observances, requirements of a decent life; *d. forbids* (appeal to passengers not to defile place). [f. L *decentia* (*decēre* be fitting, -ENCY)]

dece·nnary, a. & n. (Of) period of ten years. [f. L *decennis* (*decem, annus*) ten-year + -ARY[1]]

dece·nniad, dece·nnium (pl. *-a*), n. Ten-year period. [*-ad* irreg. f. L (*-um*) f. *decennis* (prec.); see -AD]

dece·nnial, a. Of ten-year period; recurring in ten years. Hence **dece·nnial**LY[2] adv. [f. L *decennium* see prec. + -AL]

dē·cent, a. Seemly, not immodest or obscene or indelicate; respectable; passable, good enough, tolerable, whence

de·centISH[1](2) a.; (school slang) kind, not severe or censorious, Hence **de·cent**LY[2] adv. [f. L *decēre* beseem, -ENT]

dēce·ntralize, v.t. Undo the centralization of; confer local government on. Hence **decentraliz**A·TION n. [DE-]

dece·ption, n. Deceiving, being deceived; trick, sham. [f. F *déception* f. L *deceptionem* (*decipere* see DECEIT, -ION)]

dece·ptive, a. Apt to deceive, easily mistaken. Hence **dece·ptive**LY[2] adv., **dece·ptive**NESS n. [f. F *déceptif* (prec., -IVE)]

dēchri·stianize (-stsh*a*-), v.t. Divest of its christianity. [DE-]

dĕci-, pref. shortened from L *decimus* tenth, used (as *déci-* in F) in French metric system in sense $\frac{1}{10}$ of specified unit. So **de·cigram(me), de·cilitre** (-ēt*er*), **de·cimetre,** nn.

deci·de, v.t. & i. Settle (question, issue, dispute) by giving victory to one side; give judgement (*between, for, in favour of, against,* or abs.); bring, come, to a resolution (*that decides me*; *d. to* do, *on, for,* or *against* doing). Hence **deci·d**ABLE a. [f. F *décider* f. L DE(*cīdere cis-* = *caedere* cut)]

deci·ded, a. In vbl senses; also: definite, unquestionable, (*a d. difference*); (of persons) of clear opinions or vigorous initiative, not vacillating. Hence **deci·ded**LY[2] adv. [-ED[1]]

deci·der, n. In vbl senses; also, (Racing) heat in which tie is run off. [-ER[1]]

deci·duous, a. Shed periodically or normally (of leaves, teeth, horns, &c.); shedding its leaves annually; shedding its wings after copulation (of ants &c.); fleeting, transitory. [f. L *deciduus* f. DE-(*cīdere*=*cadere* fall) + -OUS]

deci·llion, n. Tenth power of million (1 with 60 ciphers). Hence **deci·llion**TH[2] a. & n. [f. L *decem* ten & *million,* see BILLION]

dĕ·cimal, a. & n. Of tenths or ten, proceeding by tens, (*d. numeration,* ordinary counting-system with ten for basis, reckoned by decades; *d. system,* of weights and measures, with denominations rising by tens; *d. notation,* by the Arabic figures; *d. arithmetic,* using this notation, also in narrower sense that, also called *dd.,* treating of d. fractions; *d. fraction* or *d.,* one whose denominator is a power of ten, esp. when expressed by figures written to right of the *d. point* or dot placed after the unit figure, & denoting tenths, hundredths, &c., according to their place; RECUR*ring d.*; *d.* COINAGE); of d. coinage, whence **de·cimal**IST(2) n. Hence **de·cimal**IZE(3) v.t., **decimaliz**A·TION n., **de·cimal**LY[2] adv. [f. med. L *decimalis* f. L *decima* tithe, but treated as f. L *decimus* tenth, -AL]

dĕ·cimāte, v.t. Put to death one in ten of (mutinous or cowardly soldiers); destroy tenth or large proportion of (esp. of epidemic or other visitation). So **decim**A·TION n. [f. L *decimare* take the tenth man (*decimus*), see -ATE[3]]

dĕcimo-se·xto. = SEXTODECIMO.

dĕ·cimus. See PRIMUS[1].

decī·pher (dĭ-), v.t., & n. Turn into ordinary writing or make out with key (thing written in cipher); make out meaning of (bad writing, hieroglyphics, anything perplexing); (n.) interpretation of cipher document. Hence **deci·pher**ABLE a., **deci·pher**MENT n. [DE-]

deci·sion (-ĭzhn), n. Settlement (*of* question &c.), conclusion, formal judgement; making up one's mind, resolve; resoluteness, decided character. [F (*dé*-), f. L *decisionem* (DECIDE, -ION)]

deci·sive, a. Deciding, conclusive, (esp. *d. battle*); = DECIDED (*d. character, d. superiority*). Hence **deci·sive**LY[2] adv., **deci·sive**NESS n. [f. med. L *decisivus* (DECIDE, -IVE)]

dēcī·vilize, v.t. Divest of civilization. [DE-]

deck[1], n. Platform of planks or wood-covered iron extending from side to side of ship or part of it (in large ships *main, middle, lower, dd.,* also *upper* or *spar d.* above *main,* & ORLOP below *lower*; *poop* & *forecastle dd.,* short ones in stern & bow); CLEAR[2] *the dd.*; *on d.,* not below; *d.-chair,* camp-stool, also long-armed reclining chair, used in passenger steamers; *d.-house,* room erected on d. [perh. as foll. f. MDu., but found in E 160 years earlier than the corresp. Du. in same sense]

deck[2], v.t. Array, adorn; furnish with, cover as, a d. [prob. f. MDu. *deken* cover f. OTeut. *thakjan* whence also OE *thæc* THATCH]

de·ckle, n. Contrivance in papermaking-machine for limiting size of sheet (*d.-edge,* rough uncut edge). [f. G *deckel* dim. of *decke* cover]

declai·m, v.i. & t. Speak rhetorically (often *against,* = inveigh), practise speaking or recitation; deliver impassioned rather than reasoned speech; utter rhetorically. Hence **declai·m**ER[1] n. [earlier *declame* f. L DE(*clamare* cry out) w. assim. to CLAIM]

dĕclama·tion, n. Act or art of declaiming; rhetorical exercise, set speech; impassioned speech, harangue. So **declă·mat**ORY a. [f. L *declamatio* (prec., -ATION)]

declār·ant, n. One who makes legal declaration. [f. L *declarare* DECLARE, -ANT]

dĕclara·tion, n. Stating, announcing; positive, emphatic, solemn, or legal assertion, announcement, or proclamation (*d. of war,* before beginning hostilities, not now usual; *d. of the poll,* of vote-totals of election-candidates);

manifesto, written announcement of intentions, terms of agreement, &c. (*D. of* INDULGENCE; *D. of* RIGHTS; *D. of Independence*, of 4th July 1776 by N.-Amer. British colonies; *D. of Paris* 1856, *of London* 1909 unratified by Gt Britain, international agreements on maritime law); (Law) plaintiff's statement of claim, affirmation in lieu of oath, Custom-House statement (see foll.). [f. L *declaratio* (foll., -ATION)]

declare·, v.t. & i. Make known, proclaim publicly, formally, or explicitly, (*d. war, a dividend*); (abs.) *Well, I d.* (excl. of incredulity, surprise, or vexation); pronounce (person &c.) to be something, as *d. him* (*to be*) *an enemy to humankind*; *d. oneself*, avow intentions, reveal character; *d. for, against*, side with, against; *d. innings closed*, or *d.*, elect to cease batting as though all were out; *d. off*, break off (bargain &c., or abs.); (Customs) name (dutiable goods) as in one's possession. Hence or cogn. **declă·r**ATIVE, **declă·rat**ORY, aa., **declă·rative**LY², **declār·ed**LY², advv. [f. F *déclarer* f. L DE(*clarare* f. *clarus* clear)]

déclassé (dĕklă·sā), a. (fem. *-ée*). That has lost caste or sunk in social scale. [F]

decle·nsion, n. Deviation *from* uprightness &c.; deterioration, decay; (Gram.) case-inflexion, one of the noun-classes distinguished by their different methods of case-inflexion, declining. [irreg. f. L DE(*clinatio* f. *-clinare* cf. Gk *klinō* bend, -ATION); perh. thr. F *déclinaison* & a form *declin'son* corresp. to *venison*]

dĕclina·tion, n. Downward bend; (Astron.) angular distance of star &c. north or south of celestial equator, celestial latitude; (Compass) deviation of needle from true N. & S. variation. Hence **declina·tion**AL a. [f. OF *déclinacion* f. L *declinationem* see prec.]

decli·ne¹, v.i. & t. Slope downwards (usu. intr.); bend, droop, (i., & also t. as *with head declined, declines its blossoms*); (of day, life, &c.) draw to close; sink morally (*d. on*, descend to); fall off, decay, decrease, deteriorate; turn away from, refuse, (discussion, challenge, battle; *d. to* do, *doing, to be* treated in such a way); say one cannot accept (invitation &c., or abs.; *d. with thanks* iron., reject scornfully); (Gram.) inflect, recite the cases of, whence **decli·n**ABLE a. [f. F *décliner* f. L, see DECLENSION; *de-* in the L = *away*, in the E chiefly *down*]

decli·ne², n. Sinking, gradual loss of vigour or excellence, decay, deterioration; phthisis, consumption; fall in price; setting, last part of course, (of sun, life, &c.). [f. F *déclin* f. *décliner* see prec.]

dĕclino·meter, n. Instrument for measuring magnetic declination. [irreg. f. L *declinare* see DECLENSION + -METER]

declĭ·vity, n. Downward slope. [f. L *declivitas* f. DE(*clivis* f. *clivus* slope) + -TY]

declī·vous, a. Sloping down (esp. in Zool. of profile). [f. L *declivus, -is*, see prec., + -OUS]

deco·ction, n. Boiling down so as to extract essence; liquor resulting. [OF, f. L DE(*coctionem* f. *coquere coct-* boil, -ION)]

deco·de, v.t. Decipher (code telegram &c.). [DE-]

deco·llāte, v.t. Behead, truncate (p.p., of spiral shell without apex). So **decoll**A·TION n. [L DE(*collare* f. *collum* neck), -ATE³]

déco·lleté (dĕ-, -tā), a. (fem. *-ée*). Low-necked (of dress); wearing low-necked dress. [F]

dēco·lo(u)rize (-kŭl-), v.t. Deprive of colour. Hence **deco·lo(u)rīz**A·TION, **deco·lo(u)rīz**ER¹(2), nn. [DE-, COLOUR¹, -IZE(3)]

dē·complex (-ko-), a. Doubly complex, having complex parts. [DE-]

dēcompo·se, v.t., & i. Separate into its elements (substance, light, &c.); analyse (thought, motive); rot (t. & i.) Hence **decompo·s**ABLE a., **decompo·s**ER¹(2), **decomposi**·TION, nn. [f. F *décomposer* (DE-, COMPOSE)]

deco·mposite (-ĭ-, -ī-), a. & n. (Substance, word, &c.) made by compounding a compound with another element, further composite. [f. LL *decompositus* transl. of Gk *parasunthetos* used of words derived from compounds; see DE-]

dē·compound (-ko-), a. & n. = DECOMPOSITE (esp. in Bot.). [DE-]

dēco·nsecrate, v.t. Secularize. [DE-]

decontro·l, v.t., & n. Release from (esp. war-time) control by Government. [DE-]

décor (F), n. All that makes up the appearance of a room or the stage.

dĕ·corate, v.t. Furnish with adornments (esp. church with flowers &c.); serve as adornment to; invest with order, medal, &c.; *decorated* as adj. or n., (of) third English STYLE of architecture. Hence **de·corāt**IVE a. [f. L *decorare* (*decus -oris* beauty), -ATE³]

decora·tion, n. In vbl senses; esp.; (pl.) flags, wreaths, &c., put up on occasion of public rejoicing; medal, star, &c., worn as honour. [f. L *decoratio* (prec., -ATION)]

de·corātor, n. In vbl senses; esp., tradesman who papers, paints, &c., houses. [-OR²]

decōr·ous (or dĕko-), a. Not violating good taste or propriety, dignified and decent. Hence **decor·ous**LY² adv. [f. L *decōrus* (*decor* f. *decēre* be fit, -OR¹) + -OUS]

decor·um, n. Seemliness, propriety, etiquette; particular usage required by politeness or decency. [L, neut. adj. as prec.]

decoy·, n., & v.t. (Entice, esp. by help of trained bird &c., into) pond with narrow netted arms into which wild duck may be tempted and caught; allure *into, out of, away*, &c., ensnare; bird &c. trained to entice others; (also *d.-duck*) swindler's confederate, tempter; bait, enticement. [earlier *coy* f. Du. *kooi* f. WG *cawia* f. L *cavea* CAGE[1]; *de-* unexplained (*duck-coy* n. & v. is early, but not earliest, E form)]

decrea·se, v.i. & t., **dē·crease,** n. Lessen, diminish, (i. & t.); hence **decrea·sing**LY[2] adv. (N.) diminution, lessening. [vb f. OF *descreiss-* part. st., n. f. OF *descreis-* vb st., of *descreistre* f. (Rom. *dis-*) L DE(*crescere cret-* grow)]

decree·, n., & v.t. Ordinance or edict set forth by authority; decision (in other courts called *judgement*) in Admiralty cases, (in Divorce cases) order declaring nullity or dissolution or giving judicial separation (*d. nisi*, order for divorce unless cause to the contrary is shown within a period, at least six months); will, as shown by result, of God, Providence, Nature, &c.; (vb) ordain by d. [f. OF *decré* f. L DE(*cretum* neut. p.p. of *cernere* sift) thing decided]

dē·crement, n. Decrease, amount lost by diminution or waste, (esp. as scientific term opp. INCREMENT). [f. L *decrementum* (DECREASE, -MENT)]

decrē·pit, a. Wasted, worn out, enfeebled with age & infirmities, (of persons or institutions). So **decre·pi**TUDE n. [f. F *décrépit* f. L DE(*crepitus* p.p. of *crepare* creak)]

decrē·pitate, v.t. & i. Calcine (mineral or salt) till it ceases to crackle in fire; crackle under heat. Hence **decrepit**A·TION n. [DE-, L *crepitare* frequent. of *crepare* creak]

decresce·ndo (dākrĕsh-). =DIMINUENDO. [It.]

decre·scent, a. Waning, decreasing, (usu. of moon). [f. L *decrescens* (DECREASE, -ENT)]

decrē·tal, n. Papal decree; (pl.) collection of these, forming part of canon law. [f. F *décrétal* f. L *decretalis* (letter) of DECREE, -AL]

decry·, v.t. Disparage, cry down. [f. F *décrier* (DE-, CRY[2])]

dĕ·cūman, a. Especially large or powerful (usu. of wave lit. or fig.). [f. L *decu-, decimanus*, used of main gate of camp where tenth cohort was quartered (*decimus* tenth, -AN)]

decu·mbent, a. (bot. & zool.). Lying along ground or body (of plant, shoot, bristles). [f. L DE(*cumbere* lie), -ENT]

dĕ·cūple, a., n., & v.t. & i. Tenfold (amount); (vb) multiply by ten. [F (*dé-*), f. L *decuplus* (*decem* ten, *-plus* cf. *duplus* DOUBLE)]

decu·ssate, a. (-*at*), & v.t. & i. (-āt). X-shaped, intersecting; (Bot.) with pairs of opposite shoots, each at right angles to pair below; (Rhet.) chiastic. (Vb) arrange in these ways; intersect; hence **dĕcuss**A·TION n. [f. L *decussare* (*decussis* number ten, X,) -ATE[2], [3]]

dĕ·dicate, v.t. Devote with solemn rites (*to* God or *to* sacred use; of church &c. esp. without certain forms necessary for legally consecrating ground or buildings); give up (*to* special purpose); inscribe (book &c.) *to* patron or friend. So **de·dicat**OR[2], **dedicat**EE·, nn., **de·dica**TIVE, **de·dicat**ORY, aa. [f. L DE(*dicare* declare), -ATE[3]]

dedica·tion, n. In vbl senses; also, dedicatory inscription on building &c. or in book. [f. OF *dédication* f. L *dedicationem* (prec., -ION)]

dedu·ce, v.t. Bring down (annals &c.) *from* or *to* a time; trace descent of (person &c.) *from*; infer, draw as conclusion, *from*. So **dedu·**CIBLE a. [f. L DE(*ducere duct-* lead)]

dedu·ct, v.t. Take away, put aside, (amount, portion, &c., *subtract* being now used of numbers) *from* (or abs.). [f. L *deduct-* see prec.]

dedu·ction, n. Deducting; amount deducted; deducing, inference from general to particular, *a priori* reasoning, (cf. INDUCTION); thing deduced. [f. L *deductio* (DEDUCE, -ION)]

dedu·ctive, a. Of, reasoning by, deduction, *a priori*. Hence **dedu·ctive**LY[2] adv. [f. L *deductivus* (DEDUCE, -IVE)]

dee, n. Letter D; D-shaped harness-ring.

deed, n. Thing done intentionally; brave, skilful, or conspicuous act; actual fact, performance, (*in word & d.*; *in d. & not in name*, whence INDEED; *in very d.*); (Law) written or printed instrument effecting legal disposition & sealed & delivered by disposing party (in practice now always signed also but not always delivered); *d.-poll*, deed made & executed by one party only (paper polled or cut even, not indented). Hence **dee·d**LESS a. [OE *dǣd* cf. Du. *daad*, G. *tat*, cogn. w. DO[1]]

deem, v.t. Believe, consider, judge, count, (abs. in parenthesis, as *it was, I deemed, time to go*; *d. highly of*, have high opinion of; *d. it* one's *duty*; *was deemed sufficient, to suffice*; *deemed that this would do*). [OE *dēman* com.-Teut. f. OTeut. *dômjan* f. *dômoz* DOOM]

dee·mster, n. One of two justices of Isle of Man. [prec., -STER]

deep[1], a. Going far down from top (*d. hole, water, draught, drink, drinker, gaming, gamester*; *in d. waters*, plunged in grief &c.); going far in from surface or edge (*d. wound, shelf, border*; *d. mourning*, expressed by wide crape &c.; *d. plunge*; *d. reader, thinker*); hard to fathom, profound, not superficial, penetrating, (*d. dissimulation*; *a d. one* slang, cunning or secretive; *the deeper causes*; *d. learning, study*; *d. influence*; *d. insight*); heartfelt, absorbing, absorbed, (*d. feelings, interest, curses*; *d. in a pursuit*, dead to everything else); intense, vivid, extreme, heinous, (*d. disgrace, sleep, night, sin, colour*; *d.-red* &c.); going or placed (so) far down, back, or in (*water 6 ft d.*; *ankle-d. in mud*; *drawn up six d.*; *ship d. in the water, hands d. in pockets*; *d. in debt*; *d. in the human heart*, fully versed in it); brought from far down (*d. sigh*); not shrill, low-pitched, full-toned, (note, bell, voice; *d.-mouthed*, of dog). Hence **dee·pEN**[6] v.t. & i., **dee·pLY**[2] adv., **dee·pMOST** a., (rare, for *depth*) **dee·pNESS** n. [OE *diop, déop*, com.-Teut. cf. Du. *diep*, G *tief*, cogn. w. DIP]

deep[2], n. *The d.* (poet.), the sea; (usu. pl.) d. part(s) of the sea; abyss, pit, cavity; mysterious region of thought or feeling. [as prec. (neut. adj. in OE)]

deep[3], adv. Deeply, far in, (*read d. into the night*; *still waters run d.*, real feeling or knowledge not showy); esp. in comb. as *d.-drawn* (of sighs), *d.-laid* (of scheme, secret & elaborate), *d.-rooted* (esp. of prejudice), *d.-seated* (of emotion or disease). [OE *diope, déope*, (DEEP[1])]

dee·ping, n. Section, one fathom deep, of fishing-net. [-ING[3]]

deer, n. (collect. sing. usu. for pl.). Kinds of ruminant quadruped with deciduous branching horns (*small d.*, insignificant animals or things collectively, cf. *King Lear* III. iv. 144); *d.-hound*, large rough greyhound; *d.-forest*, wild land reserved for stalking d.; *d.-lick*, spring or damp spot impregnated with salt &c. where d. come to lick; *d.-neck*, horse's thin neck; *d.'s-foot*, a fine grass; *deerskin*, (made of) d.'s skin; *d.-stalker*, sportsman stalking d., cloth cap peaked before and behind. [OE *díor, déor*, beast, quadruped, com.-Teut. cf. Du. *dier*, G *tier*]

defa·ce, v.t. Mar appearance or beauty of, disfigure; discredit; make illegible. Hence **defa·ceABLE** a., **defa·ceMENT** n. [f. obs. F *defacer* (DE-, FACE[1])]

dē fa·cto, a. & adv. In fact, whether by right (DE JURE) or not (*king d. f., the d.-f. king*). [L]

dē·falcate, v.i. Commit defalcations, misappropriate property in one's charge. So **de·falcatOR**[2] n. [f. med. L DE(*falcare* lop f. L *falx -cis* scythe), -ATE[3]]

dēfalca·tion, n. Defection, shortcoming; fraudulent deficiency of money owing to breach of trust, misappropriation, amount misappropriated. [f. med. L *defalcatio* (prec., -ATION)]

defa·me, v.t. Attack the good fame of, speak ill of. So **dēfamA·TION** n., **defă·matORY** a. [f. OF *diffamer* f. L *diffamare* spread abroad (DIS-, *fama* report), see DE-; there are also LL *defamis, -atus*, infamous]

defau·lt[1], n. Want, absence, (*in d. of*, if or since such a thing is wanting); failure to act or appear, neglect, (*make d.*; *judgement by d.*, given for plaintiff on defendant's failure to plead); failure to pay, defaulting. [f. OF *defaute* f. *defaillir* see foll. & cf. FAULT]

defau·lt[2], v.i. & t. Make, be guilty of, d.; fail to appear in court; not meet money calls, break; hence **defau·ltER**[1] n. Declare (party) in d. & give judgement against him. [f. OF *defaillir* (3 sing. *default*) f. DE-, L *fallere* deceive]

defea·sance (-fēz-), n. Rendering null & void. [f. OF *defesance* f. *desfaire* undo (DE-, L *facere* do), -ANCE]

defea·sible (-fēz-), a. Capable of annulment, liable to forfeiture. Hence **defeasiBI·LITY** n. [as prec., -IBLE]

defea·t, v.t., & n. Frustrate, frustration; (Law) annul(ment); (archaic) disappoint *of*; overthrow (v. & n.) in contest esp. in battle. [n. prob. f. vb, which is f. OF *defeit* p.p. of *desfaire* see DEFEASANCE]

defea·tism, n. Conduct tending to bring about acceptance of defeat, esp. by action on civilian opinion. So **defea·tIST** n. & a. [f. F *défaitisme* (as prec., -ISM)]

defea·ture (-tsher), v.t. Make unrecognizable. [f. obs. noun f. OF *desfaiture* (prec., -URE)]

dĕ·fecāte, v.t. Clear of dregs, refine, purify, (lit. & fig.); get rid of (dregs, excrement, sin). Hence **defecA·TION**, **de·fecatOR**[2](2), nn. [f. L DE(*fecare* f. *faex -cis* dregs), -ATE[3]]

defe·ct, n. Lack of something essential to completeness; shortcoming, failing, (*has the dd. of his qualities*, the particular ones that often accompany his particular virtues); blemish; amount by which thing falls short. [f. L *defectus* n. f. DE(*ficere fect-* =*facere* do) desert, fail]

defe·ction, n. Falling away from allegiance to leader, party, religion, or duty, desertion, apostasy. [f. L *defectio* (prec., -ION)]

defe·ctive, n. Having defect(s), incomplete, faulty, wanting or deficient (*in* some respect); (Gram.) not having all the usual inflexions. Hence **defe·ctiveLY**[2] adv., **defe·ctiveNESS** n. [f. F *défectif* f. L *defectivus* as prec., -IVE]

defe·nce, n. Defending from, resistance against, attack (cf. OFFENCE; *best d. is offence*, advantage goes with the initiative; in cricket, guarding of one's wicket, also batting as opposed to bowling; *science* or *art of d.*, boxing or fencing); (Mil., pl.) fortifications (also *line of d.*, series of fortified posts); thing that protects; justification, vindication, speech or writing used to this end; (Law) accused party's denial, pleading, & proceedings, counsel for the d.; *D. of the Realm Act* (abbr. D.O.R.A., joc. *Dora*), Act of August, 1914, providing Government with wide powers during war. Hence **defe·nce**LESS a., **defe·nce-less**LY² adv., **defe·nceless**NESS n. [f. OF *defens* f. L *defensum* neut., thing forbidden, & OF *defense* f. L *defensa* fem. used as noun cf. -ADE(1), both p.p. see foll.]

defe·nd, v.t. & i. Forbid, avert, (archaic; still in *God d.!*); ward off attack from, keep safe, protect (*against, from*); uphold by argument, vindicate, speak or write in favour of; (Law) make defence in court (*d. oneself*, conduct one's own defence), (of counsel) appear for defendant, conduct defence of. [f. OF *defendre* f. L DE(*fendere -fens-* FEND)]

defe·ndant, n. Person sued in law-suit (cf. *plaintiff*); (attrib.) holding this relation (*the d. company*). [f. F *défendant* part. (prec., -ANT)]

defe·nder, n. One who defends; *D. of the Faith*, title of Eng. Sovereigns from Henry VIII, who received it from Pope for writing against Luther; (Sport) holder of championship &c. defending the title (opp. *challenger*). [f. OF *defendeor* f. Rom. **defenditorem* (DEFEND, -OR²)]

defe·nsible, a. Easily defended (in war or argument); justifiable. Hence **defe·nsi-bi·lity** n., **defe·nsib**LY² adv. [f. L *defensibilis* (DEFEND, -IBLE)]

defe·nsive, a. & n. Serving, used, done, for defence, protective, not aggressive; hence **defe·nsive**LY² adv. (N.) state or position of defence (esp. *be, stand, act, on the d.*). [f. F *défensif* f. med. L *defensivus* (DEFEND, -IVE)]

defer·¹, v.t. & i. (-rr-). Put off, postpone, (*deferred* ANNUITY; *deferred pay*, part of esp. soldier's pay held over to be paid at discharge or death; *deferred* SHARE¹*s*); procrastinate, be dilatory. Hence **defer·**MENT n. [ME *differren* f. OF *différer* f. L DIF(*ferre* carry)]

defer·², v.t. (-rr-). Submit or make concessions in opinion or action *to* (person). [f. F *déférer* f. L DE(*ferre* bring)]

dĕ·ference, n. Compliance with advice &c. of one superior in wisdom or position (*pay* &c. *d. to*); respect, manifestation of desire to comply, courteous regard, (*in d. to*, out of respect for authority of). So **defere·nti**AL a., **deferen·tial**LY² adv. [f. F *déférence* (prec., -ENCE)]

dĕ·ferent, a. (Physiol.) conveying to a destination (of ducts &c.); (rare for) deferential. [first sense (f. F or direct) f. L *deferens* part. of DE(*ferre* carry); second f. DEFER², -ENT]

defi·ance, n. Challenge to fight or maintain cause, assertion, &c.; open disobedience, setting at nought, (*bid d. to, set at d., in d. of*). [OF (DEFY, -ANCE)]

defi·ant, a. Openly disobedient; rejecting advances, suspicious and reserved. Hence **defi·ant**LY² adv. [f. F *défiant* (DEFY, -ANT)]

defi·ciency (-ĭshn-), n. Being deficient; want, lack; thing wanting; amount by which thing, esp. revenue, falls short. [f. LL *deficientia* (*deficere* see DEFECT, -ENCY)]

defi·cient (-ĭshnt), a. Incomplete, defective, wanting *in* specified quality; insufficient in quantity, force, &c.; half-witted. Hence **defi·cient**LY² adv. [f. L *deficiens* (*deficere* see DEFECT, -ENT)]

de·ficit (dē-, dĕ-), n. Amount by which esp. sum of money is too small; excess of liabilities over assets. [f. F *déficit* f. L *deficit* 3 sing. pres. of *deficere* see DEFECT]

de fi·dē, pred. a. Required to be held as article of faith. [L]

defi·er, n. One who defies. [DEFY, -ER¹]

dĕfilā·de, v.t. & n. Secure (fortification), against enfilading fire; (n.) this precaution or arrangement (also *defilement*). [n. f. vb, f. F *défiler* unthread, -ADE]

defi·le¹, v.i., **dē·file,** n. March by files, in file; (n.) narrow way through which troops can only march so, gorge. [f. F *défiler* & *défilé* p.p. (DE-, *file* FILE³)]

defi·le², v.t. Make dirty, befoul; pollute, corrupt; desecrate, profane; make ceremonially unclean. Hence **defi·le**MENT n. (see DEFILADE). [earlier *defoul* f. OF *defouler* trample (DE-, L *fullo* fuller, f. treading of cloth in fulling), altered on anal. of E vbs *befoul* & obs. *befile* in same sense f. OE *fȳlan* f. *fūl* FOUL]

defi·ne, v.t. Settle limits of; make clear, esp. in outline (*well-defined image*; *d. one's position*, state it precisely); set forth essence of, declare exact meaning of, (also abs., frame definitions); (of properties) make up total character of. Hence **defi·n**ABLE a. [f. OF *definer* (now displaced by correct *définir*, which would have given E *definish*) f. L DE(*finire* f. *finis* end)]

dĕ·finite, a. With exact limits; determinate, distinct, precise, not vague; (Gram.) *d. inflexions*, those of German and early E adjj. used after d. article & similar wds; *d. article*, the; *past* or *preterite d.*, simple past tense in French, as *il vint* he came. Hence **de·finite**LY² adv., **de·finite**NESS n. [f. L *definitus* p.p. see prec.]

dĕfini·tion, n. Stating the precise nature of a thing or meaning of a word; form of words in which this is done; making or being distinct, degree of distinctness, in outline (esp. of image given by lens or shown in photograph). [OF (-*cion*), f. L DE(*finitio* f. *finire* f. *finis* end, -ION)]

defi·nitive, a. Decisive, unconditional,

final, (of answer, treaty, verdict, &c.). Hence **defi·nitive**LY[2] adv. [f. OF *definitif* f. L *definitivus* (prec., -IVE)]

dē·flagrate, v.t. & i. Burn away with rapid flame. Hence **deflagr**A·TION, **de·flagrat**OR[2](2), nn. [f. L DE(*flagrare* blaze), -ATE[3]]

defla·te, v.t. Let inflating air &c. out of (pneumatic tire &c.); (Finance) reduce the inflation of (State's currency), (abs.) adopt this policy. Hence **defla·t**ION n. [f. L DE*flare* blow away (w. changed sense), -ATE[3]]

defle·ct, v.t. & i. Bend aside or (rarely) down, (make) deviate (*from*). Hence **defle·ct**OR[2](2) n. [f. L DE(*flectere flex-* bend)]

defle·xion, -ction, n. Lateral or downward bend, deviation, (lit. & fig.; in Electr. & Magn., of needle from its zero). [f. L *deflex-* (prec., -ION)]

dēflora·tion, n. Deflowering. [OF (*-cion*) f. L *deflorationem* (foll., -ATION)]

deflower (dĭflowr·), v.t. Deprive of virginity, ravish; ravage, spoil; strip of flowers. [f. OF *desflorer* f. L DE*florare* (*flos floris* flower)]

dē·fluent, a. & n. Down-flowing (part; e.g. lower end of glacier). [f. L DE(*fluere* flow), -ENT]

defŏ·rest, v.t. =DISFOREST. [f. OF *desforester*]

defor·m, v.t. Make ugly, deface; put out of shape, mis-shape, (esp. in p.p. of person with mis-shapen body or limb). [f. OF *deformer* f. L DE(*formare* f. *forma* shape)]

dēforma·tion, n. Disfigurement; change for the worse (esp. as opponent's name for Reformation); perverted form of word (*dang* for *damn* &c.); (Physics) changed shape *of*. [f. L *deformatio* (prec., -ATION)]

defor·mity, n. Being deformed, ugliness, disfigurement, (physical or moral); a malformation esp. of body or limb. [f. OF (*-té*) f. L *deformitatem* f. DE(*formis* f. *forma* shape), -TY]

defrau·d, v.t. Cheat (person, person *of*, or abs.). [f. OF *defrauder* (DE-, L *fraudare* f. *fraus -dis* FRAUD)]

defray·, v.t. Settle, discharge by payment, (cost, expense). Hence **defray·**ABLE a., **defray·**AL(2) n. [f. F *défrayer* (DE-, *frai* sing. of *frais* expenses perh. = LL *fredum* fine f. OHG *fridu*, G *friede*, peace)]

defro·ck, v.t. =UNFROCK.

deft, a. Dextrous, skilful, handling things neatly. Hence **de·ft**LY[2] adv., **de·ft**NESS n. [var. of DAFT]

defu·nct, a. Dead (*the d.*, way of mentioning a particular dead person), no longer existing. [f. L DE(*functus* p.p. of *fungi* perform) dead]

defy·, v.t. Challenge to combat or competition (archaic or facet.); challenge *to* do or prove something; resist openly, set at nought; (of things) present insuperable obstacles to (*defies definition, capture, attack,* &c.). [f. OF *defier* f. Rom. *DIS(*fidare* trust f. *fidus* faithful)]

dégagé (F), a. (fem. *-ée*). Easy, unconstrained.

degĕ·nerate[1] (*-at*), a. & n. Having lost qualities proper to race, sunk from former excellence; (Biol.) having reverted to lower type; hence **dege·ner**ACY n. (N.) d. person or animal. [f. L p.p. see foll., -ATE[2]]

dege·nerāte[2], v.i. Become d. (see prec.). [f. L *degenerare*, f. DE(*gener* f. *genus -eris* race) ignoble, -ATE[3]]

degenera·tion, n. Becoming degenerate; (Path.) morbid disintegration of tissue or change in its structure (esp. *fatty d. of heart*). [f. F *dégéneration* (prec., -ION)]

dēgluti·tion (-glōō-), n. Swallowing. [f. F *déglutition* f. L DE(*glutire* swallow), -ION]

degra·de, v.t. & i. Reduce to lower rank; depose as punishment; lower in estimation, debase morally, whence **degra·d**ING[2] a.; reduce (Biol.) to lower organic type, (Physics) to less convertible form (energy), (Geol.) to disintegration (rocks &c.); degenerate; (Camb. Univ.) put off entering for honours examination for a year beyond regular time. So **dĕgrad**A·TION n. [f. OF *degrader* f. LL DE*gradare* (*gradus* step)]

degree·, n. Step (as) of staircase (archaic; perh. so in 2 *Kings* xx. 9, & in Psalm-title *Song of Dd.*); thing placed like step in series, tier, row; stage in ascending or descending scale or process (*by dd.*, gradually; *fine by dd. & beautifully less*, see Prior, *Henry & Emma*, 431, often misquoted *small by* &c.); step in direct genealogical descent (*prohibited dd.*, number of these too low to allow of marriage, i.e. first, second, & third, reckoning from one party up to common ancestor & down to the other); social or official rank; relative condition (*each good in its d.*); stage in intensity or amount (*to a high* or *the last d.*, also colloq. in latter sense *to a d.*; in law, *principal in the first, second, d.*); academic rank conferred as guarantee of proficiency, or (*honorary d.*) on distinguished person; masonic rank; (Gram.) stage (POSITIVE, COMPARATIVE, SUPERLATIVE) in comparison of adjj. & advv.; (Geom. &c.) unit of angular or circular-arc measurement, 1/90 of right angle or 1/360 of circumference (symbol °, as 45°; *d. of* LATITUDE, about 69 miles); (Therm.) unit of temperature in any scale. Hence **degree·**LESS a. [f. OF *degre* f. LL DE(*gradus* step)]

de haut en bas (F), adv. In a condescending or superior manner.

dehi·sce (-ĭs), v.i. Gape, burst open, (esp. in Bot. of seed-vessels, & in Physiol.). So **dehi·scENCE** n., **dehi·scENT** a. [f. L DE(*hiscere* incept. of *hiare* gape)]

dehor·tative, a. & n. Dissuasive; thing meant to dissuade. [f. L DE(*hortativus* f. *hortari* exhort, -IVE)]

dēhu·manize, v.t. Divest of human characteristics. [DE-]

dēhȳ·drāte, v.t. (chem.). Deprive (substance) of water or its elements. [DE-, Gk *hudōr* in comb. *hudr-* water, -ATE³]

dēhy·pnotize, v.t. Rouse, release, from hypnotic state. [DE-]

de·icīde, n. Killer, killing, of a God. [f. L *deus* god, -I-, -CIDE]

dei·ctic (dī-), a. (philol., gram.). Pointing, demonstrative. [f. Gk *deiktikos* (*deiktos* f. *deiknumi* show, -IC)]

de·iform, a. Godlike in form or nature. [f. med. L *deiformis* (*deus* god, -I-, -FORM)]

de·ifȳ, v.t. Make a god of; make godlike; regard as a god, worship. Hence **dei-FICA·TION** n. [f. F *déifier* f. L *deificare* (*deus* god, -FY)]

deign (dān), v.t. Think fit, condescend, *to* do; condescend to give (answer &c.). [f. OF *degnier* f. L *dignare* (usu. *-i*) deem worthy]

de·ī grā·tiā, adv. By God's grace. [L]

dē i·ntegro, adv. Afresh. [L]

de·ism, de·ist, nn. Belief, believer, in the existence of a god without accepting revelation; (adherent of) natural religion. Hence **de·istIC(AL)** aa. [f. F *déisme, déiste,* f. L *deus* god + -ISM(3), -IST(2)]

de·ity, n. Divine status, quality, or nature; a god; *the D.*, the Creator, God. [f. F *déité* f. L *deitatem* (*deus* god, -TY)]

deje·ct, v.t. Dispirit, depress (usu. in p.p.). Hence **deje·ctedLY²** adv. [f. L DE(*jicĕre -ject-* =*jacĕre* throw)]

deje·cta, n. pl. Person's or animal's excrements. [L, neut. pl. p.p. as prec.]

deje·ction, n. Downcast state, low spirits; (Med.) evacuation of bowels, excrement. [OF, f. L *dejectionem* (prec., -ION)]

déjeuner (dĕ·zhonā, or as F), n. Breakfast; lunch, esp. of ceremonial kind. [F]

dē jure (joor·ī), a. & adv. Rightful, by right, (*king* &c. *d. j.*; *the d.-j. king*; cf. DE FACTO). [L]

delai·ne (dĭ-), n. Light dress-fabric. [f. F (*mousseline*) *de laine* woollen (muslin)]

dela·te, v.t. Inform against, impeach, (person); report (offence). So **dela·tION, dela·tOR²,** nn. [f. L DE(*lat-* p.p. st. of *ferre* carry)]

delay·, v.t. & i., & n. Postpone(ment), defer(ring), put(ting) off, loiter(ing), be(ing) tardy, wait; hinder, hindrance. [(n. f. F *délai*) f. OF *delaier* perh. irreg. f. L *dīlatare* frequent. of DIF(*ferre lat-* carry) defer]

del cre·derĕ (-ād-), a., adv., & n. (commerc.). Under, charge made for, selling agent's guarantee that buyer is solvent. [It.]

dē·lē, printing direction (abbr. *d*). Delete indicated letter, word, or passage (written in margin). [L, imperat. of *delēre* DELETE]

dele·ctable, a. Delightful, pleasant, (archaic exc. in irony). [OF, f. L *delectabilis* f. DE(*lectarĕ* frequent. of *lacere* snare) delight]

dēlecta·tion, n. Enjoyment (usu. *for* one's *d.*). [OF (prec., -ATION)]

dele·ctus, n. School reading-book of selected passages. [L, n. f. DE(*ligere lect-* =*legere* choose)]

dĕ·legacy, n. System of delegating; appointment as delegate; body of delegates. [foll., -ACY]

dĕ·legate¹ (-*at*), n. Deputy, commissioner; elected representative sent to conference. [f. OF *delegat* f. L *delegatus* (foll., -ATE²)]

dĕ·legāte², v.t. Depute (person), send as representative; commit (authority &c.) to or *to* agent. [f. L DE(*legare* depute), -ATE³]

dĕlega·tion, n. Entrusting of authority to deputy; body of delegates (U.S., Congress representatives of a single state; Austro-Hungary, *the Dd.*, two bodies appointed by Austrian & Hungarian Parliaments to deal jointly with imperial questions). [f. L DE(*legatio* LEGATION)]

dele·te, v.t. Strike out, obliterate, (letter, word, passage; also fig.). So **dele·tION** n. [f. L DE(*lēre -let-* cf. *linere* smear)]

dĕletēr·ious, a. Noxious physically or morally, injurious. Hence **deleter·iousLY²** adv. [f. Gk *dēlētērios* f. *dēlētēr* destroyer (*dēleomai* injure) + -OUS]

delf(t), n. Glazed earthenware made at Delft (earlier *Delf*) in Holland.

deli·berate¹ (-*at*), a. Intentional; considered, not impulsive; slow in deciding, cautious; leisurely, not hurried, (of movement &c.). Hence **deli·berateLY²** adv., **deli·berateNESS** n. [f. L *deliberatus* (foll., -ATE²)]

deli·berāte², v.i. & t. Consider, think carefully, (intr., or with indirect question *how it might be done, what to do*); take counsel, consult, hold debate. [f. L DE(*liberare* =*librare* weigh f. *libra* balance), -ATE³]

delibera·tion, n. Weighing in mind, careful consideration; discussion of reasons for & against, debate; care, avoidance of precipitancy; slowness of movement. [f. F *délibération* f. L *deliberationem* (prec., -ATION)]

deli·berative, a. Of, appointed for purpose of, deliberation or debate (usu. *d. assembly* or *functions*). Hence **deli·berativeLY²** adv. [f. L *deliberativus* (DELIBERATE², -IVE)]

dĕ·licacy, n. Fineness of texture, graceful slightness, tender beauty; weakliness, susceptibility to disease or injury, need of care, discretion, or skill; nicety of perception, sensitiveness, (of persons, senses, or instruments); consideration for others' feelings; shrinking from, avoidance of, the immodest or offensive; choice kind of food, dainty; a nicety. [foll., -ACY]

dĕ·licate (-*at*), a. Delightful (poet.); palatable, dainty, (of food); sheltered, luxurious, effeminate, (*d. living, nurture, upbringing*); fine of texture, soft, slender, slight; of exquisite quality or workmanship; subdued (of colour); subtle, hard to appreciate; easily injured, liable to illness; requiring nice handling, critical, ticklish; subtly sensitive (of persons or instruments); deft (*a d. touch*); avoiding the offensive or immodest; considerate (esp. of actions). Hence **de·licate**LY[2] adv. [f. L *delicatus* cogn. or associated w. *deliciae* delight see foll.]

deli·cious, a. Highly delightful, esp. to taste, smell, or the sense of humour. Hence **deli·cious**LY[2] adv., **deli·cious**NESS n. [OF, f. LL *deliciosus* f. L *deliciae* delight f. DE(*licere* =*lacere* allure), -OSE[1]]

deli·ct, n. Violation of law, offence, (*in flagrant d.*, =IN FLAGRANTE DELICTO). [f. L *delictum* neut. p.p. of DE(*linquere* leave) come short]

deligh·t, v.t. & i., & n. Please highly (*shall be delighted to*, in accepting invitation; *was delighted with* or *at the result*); take, find, great pleasure *in* (so in p.p., *the books delighted in by the many*), be inclined and accustomed *to* do. (N.) high pleasure, thing that causes it; hence **deligh·t**FUL a., **deligh·tful**LY[2] adv., **deligh·t**SOME a. (literary). [ME *deliten* f. OF *delitier* f. L *delectare* see DELECTABLE, now mis-spelt after *light*]

Deli·lah, Da-, n. Temptress, false & wily woman. [*Judges* xvi]

deli·mit(āte), vv.t. Determine limits or territorial boundary of. So **delimit**A·TION n. [-*it* thr. F *délimiter*, -*itate* direct, f. L DE(*limitare* f. *limes* -*itis* boundary), -ATE[3]]

deli·nĕate, v.t. Show by drawing or description, portray. So **deline**A·TION, **deli·neat**OR[2], nn. [f. L DE(*lineare* f. *linea* line), -ATE[3]]

delĭnĕā·vit, -vēr·unt, L vb sing. & pl. (usu. abbr. *del.*). So-&-so drew this. [f. L as prec.]

deli·nquency, n. Neglect of duty; guilt; a sin of omission; misdeed. [f. L *delinquentia* f. *delinquens* part. (DELICT, -ENCY)]

deli·nquent, a. & n. Defaulting, guilty; (n.) offender. [f. L *delinquens* (prec., -ENT)]

dēlique·sce (-ĕs), v.i. Become liquid, melt, (fig.) melt away. So **delique·sc**ENT a., **delique·sc**ENCE n. [f. L DE(*liquescere* incept. of *liquēre* be liquid)]

deli·rious, a. Affected with delirium, temporarily or apparently mad, raving; wildly excited, ecstatic; betraying delirium or ecstasy. Hence **deli·rious**LY[2] adv. [as foll. + -OUS]

deli·rium, n. Disordered state of mind with incoherent speech, hallucinations, & frenzied excitement; great excitement, ecstasy; *d. trēmens* (abbr. *d.t.*), special form of d. with terrifying delusions to which heavy drinkers are liable. [L, f. DE*lirare* (*lira* furrow)]

dēlite·scent, a., **delite·scence,** n. Latent (state). [f. L DE(*litescere* incept. of -*litēre* =*latēre* lie hid), -ENT, -ENCE]

deli·ver, v.t. Rescue, save, set free *from*; disburden (woman in parturition) *of* child (usu. pass.; also fig. *was delivered of a sonnet*); unburden oneself (*of* esp. a long-suppressed opinion &c.) in discourse; give *up* or *over*, abandon, resign, hand on *to* another; distribute (letters, parcels, ordered goods) to addressee or purchaser (*d. the goods* fig., carry out one's part of agreement); present, render, (account); (Law) hand over formally (esp. sealed deed to grantee, so *seal & d.*); launch, aim, (blow, ball, attack; *d. battle*, accept opportunity of engaging); recite (*well-delivered sermon*). Hence **deli·ver**ABLE a. [f. F *délivrer* f. LL *deliberare* (DE-, L *liberare* f. *liber* free)]

deli·verance, n. Rescue; emphatically or formally delivered opinion, (in jurors' oath) verdict. [f. OF *delivrance* (prec., -ANCE)]

deli·verer, n. In vbl senses; esp., saviour, rescuer. [f. OF *delivrere* nom. of *delivreor* f. LL *deliberatorem* (DELIVER, -OR[2])]

deli·very, n. Childbirth; surrender *of*; delivering of letters &c., a periodical performance of this (*the first, the two-o'clock, d.*); (Law) formal handing over of property, transfer of deed (formerly essential for validity) to grantee or third party; sending forth of missile, esp. of cricket-ball in bowling, action shown in doing this (*a good, high, d.*); uttering of speech &c. (*its d. took two hours*), manner of doing this (*a telling d.*). [AF *delivrée* fem. part. used as n. of F *délivrer* DELIVER, -Y[4]]

dell, n. Small hollow or valley usu. with tree-clad sides. [cf. Du. *del*, G *telle*, DALE]

De·lla Cru·scan, a. & n. (Member) of the Florentine Academy della Crusca, a society for purifying the Italian language, which issued an authoritative dictionary; following artificial literary methods; member of a late 18th-c. artificial English school of poetry. [f. It. (*Accademia*) *della*

Crusca (Academy) of the bran (i. e. sifting) + -AN]

De·lphian, De·lphic, aa. (As) of the oracle of Delphi; obscure, ambiguous. [-*ic* f. L f. Gk *Delphikos*, -*ian* f. L f. Gk *Delphoi* + -IAN]

De·lphin, a. *The D. classics* or *text*, in an edition prepared for the Dauphin, son of Louis XIV. [L f. Gk, = dolphin; see DAUPHIN]

de·lphinine, n. (chem.). A poisonous alkaloid used medically. [f. bot. L f. Gk *delphinion* (dim. of *delphin* dolphin) larkspur]

de·lta, n. Letter D (Δ, δ) of Greek alphabet (capital an equilateral triangle); triangular alluvial tract at mouth of river enclosed or traversed by its diverging branches, esp. that of Nile, whence **deltā·**IC a. [Gk]

de·ltoid, a. & n. Triangular; *d. muscle* or *d.*, muscle of shoulder lifting upper arm; like a river delta. [f. Gk *deltoeidēs* (prec., -OID)]

delu·de (-ōōd, -ūd), v.t. Impose upon, deceive. [f. L DE(*ludere lus-* play)]

dĕ·luge (-ūj), n., & v.t. Great flood, inundation, (*the D.*, Noah's flood); heavy fall of rain; flood of words &c.; (vb) flood, inundate, (lit. & fig.). [F (*dé-*), f. L *diluvium* (*diluere* DILUTE)]

delu·sion (ōō-, -ū-), n. Imposing or being imposed upon; false impression or opinion, esp. as symptom or form of madness, whence **delu·sion**AL a. [f. L *delusio* (DELUDE, -ION)]

delu·sive (-ōō-, -ū-), a. Deceptive, disappointing, unreal. Hence **delu·sive**LY² adv., **delu·sive**NESS n. [DELUDE, -IVE]

delve, v.t. & i., & n., (archaic, poet., & dial.). Dig; make research in documents &c.; (of road &c.) make sudden dip. (N.) cavity; depression of surface, wrinkle. [OE *delfan*, com.-WG cf. Du. *delven*]

dēma·gnetize, v.t. Deprive of magnetic quality. Hence **dema·gnetiz**A·TION n. [DE-]

dĕ·magogue (-ŏg), n. Popular leader; political agitator appealing to cupidity or prejudice of the masses, factious orator. Hence or cogn. **demagŏ·g**IC (-gĭk) a., **de·magog**ISM(2), **de·magog**Y¹ (-gĭ), nn. [f. Gk *dēmagōgos* (DEMOS, *agōgos* leading)]

dema·nd¹, n. Request made as of right or peremptorily, thing so asked, (*payable on d.*, as soon as the d. is made); call of would-be purchasers *for* commodity (*laws of supply and d.* in Pol. Econ.; *in d.*, sought after); urgent claim (*many dd. on my time*). [f. F *demande* f. *demander* see foll.]

dema·nd², v.t. Ask for (thing) as right or peremptorily or urgently (*of* or *from* person; obj. a noun, infin., or *that*-clause); require, need, (*piety demands it*; *task demands skill*); ask to be, insist on being, told (*d.* one's *business*, what he wants). Hence or cogn. **dema·nd**ABLE a., **dema·nd**ANT(1) n. [f. F *demander* f. L DE(*mandare* order cf. MANDATE)]

dēmarca·tion, n. Marking of boundary, esp. *line of d.* Hence (by back-formation) **de·marcate** v.t. [Sp. (-*cion*), f. *demarcar* mark bounds of (DE-, MARK)]

démarche (F), n. (In E diplomatic journalese) political step or proceeding.

dēmatēr·ialize, v.t. & i. Make, become, non-material, spiritual. [DE-]

deme, n. (Gk hist.) township of ancient Attica; (Biol.) undifferentiated aggregate of cells. [f. Gk *dēmos*]

demea·n¹, v. refl. *D. oneself*, behave, conduct oneself, (always w. adv. or adv. phr.). [f. OF *demener* (DE- + *mener* lead f. L *minare* threaten & in LL drive cattle)]

demea·n², v.t. (usu. refl.). Lower in dignity. [DE-, MEAN³, but prob. generated by misunderstanding of prec.; chiefly used by the uneducated or in imitations of them]

demea·nour, n. Bearing, outward behaviour. [earlier -*ure*, -*er*; see -URE, -ER⁴, DEMEAN¹; assim. to *honour* &c.]

deme·nt, v.t. Drive mad, craze, (usu. in p.p.). Hence **deme·nted**LY² adv. [f. L *dementare* f. DE*mens* out of one's mind (*mens mentis*)]

démenti (F), n. Official denial of rumour &c.

deme·ntia (-tĭa, -sha), n. (med.). Species of insanity consisting in feebleness of mind. [L (*demens* see prec., & cf. -ENCE)]

demerar·a, n. Kind of brown sugar from Demerara.

dēmĕ·rit, n. Ill desert; fault, defect. Hence **deme·ritor·**IOUS [-ORY, -OUS] a. [f. L *demeritum* neut. p.p. of DE*mereri* deserve; orig. sense desert (good or bad, like *merit*); the two have now been fixed to opposite senses]

demēs·ne (*also* -ān), n. (Law) possession (of real property) as one's own (esp. *hold in d.*); an estate held in d., all of an owner's land not held of him by freehold tenants, or all that he actually occupies himself; *Royal d.*, Crown lands; *State d.*, land held by State. Sovereign's or State's territory, domain; landed property, estate; region, sphere, *of*. [f. OF *demeine* f. L *dominicus* (*dominus* lord, -IC)]

dĕ·mi-, pref. usu. written with the hyphen, still used as living pref. to form temporary words, but more or less ousted by SEMI-. Half-size, half, imperfect, partial(ly), semi-. [F, f. L *dimidium* half (DIS-, *medius* middle)]

dĕ·migod, n. Partly divine being, son of god and mortal, or deified man. [prec.]

dĕ·mijohn (-jŏn), n. Bulging narrow-necked bottle of 3–10 gal., usu. cased in wicker & with wicker handles. [corrupt. of F *dame-jeanne* Dame Jane; found in many langg., but earliest in F, prob. as playful personification]

dĕ·milune (-ōōn), n. (fortif.). Outwork protecting bastion or curtain. [F, = half moon]

dĕ·mi-mŏnde (or as F), n. Class of women on outskirts of society, of doubtful reputation & standing. [F, = half world]

dĕ·mi-rep, n. Woman of suspected chastity. [abbr. for *demi-reputable*]

demi·se (-īz), v.t., & n. Convey, grant, (estate) by will or lease (n., this process); transmit (title &c.) by death or abdication (n., this event, esp. *d. of the Crown*; transf., death). Hence **demi·sABLE** a. [vb f. n., prob. f. p.p. of OF *desmettre* DISMISS, in refl. abdicate]

dĕ·misĕmiquā·ver, n. (mus.). Note, with three-hooked symbol, equal to half a semiquaver. [DEMI-]

demi·ssion, n. Resigning, abdication, *of*. [f. F *démission* f. LL *dis-* for L DI(*missionem* f. *mittere miss-* send, -ION)]

demi·t, v.t. & i. (-tt-). Resign (office, or abs.). [f. F *démettre* (DIS- +*mettre* send, put, f. L *mittere* send)]

dē·miurge (-erj), n. Creator of world (in Platonic philosophy; also of Christian God, & of supposed subordinate agents in creation). Hence **demiur·gIC** a. [f. Gk *dēmiourgos* craftsman (*dēmios* f. DEMOS, *-ergos* -working)]

demo·b, v.t. (slang). Demobilize (esp. in p.p. of individuals released by demobilization). [abbr.]

demō·bilize, v.t. Release from mobilized state, disband, (troops, ships). Hence **demo·bilizA·TION** n. [DE-]

demo·cracy, n. (State practising) government by the people, direct or representative; *the* politically unprivileged class. [f. F *démocratie* f. L f. Gk *dēmokratia* (DEMOS, -CRACY)]

dĕ·mocrat, n. Advocate of democracy; (U.S.) member of Democratic party. Hence **demo·cratISM**(3) n. [f. F *démocrate* (prec.)]

dĕmocră·tic, a. Of, like, practising, advocating, democracy; (U.S.) *D. party*, opposed to Republican & supporting State, local, & individual liberty against federal powers. So **democra·tICALLY** adv., **demo·cratIZE**(3) v.t. & i., **demo·cratizA·TION** n. [f. F *démocratique* f. med. L f. Gk *dēmokratikos* (DEMOS, -CRATIC)]

Demŏ·critē·an, a. Of Democritus, his humour, or his theory of atoms. [f. L f. Gk *Dēmokriteios* of Democritus (Gk philosopher of 5th c. B.C. called the laughing philosopher, & an atomistic physicist) + -AN]

Dēmogor·gon, n. A mysterious & terrible infernal deity. [LL; perh. assim. of some Oriental name to Gk DEMOS, *gorgos* grim]

dēmŏ·graphy, n. Statistics of births, diseases, &c., illustrating condition of communities. Hence **demo·GRAPHER** n., **demoGRA·PHIC** a. [DEMOS, -GRAPHY]

demoiselle (dĕ·mwazĕ·l), n. The Numidian crane. [F, = DAMSEL]

demŏ·lish, v.t. Pull or throw down (building), destroy; overthrow (institution, theory); eat up. So **dĕmoli·TION** n. [f. F *démolir* (-ISH[2]) f. L DE(*moliri* construct f. *moles* mass)]

dē·mon, dae-, n. (Gk mythol.; often *dae-*) supernatural being, inferior deity, spirit, ghost, in-dwelling or attendant spirit, genius; evil spirit (as in demoniacs); heathen deity; devil; malignant supernatural being; cruel, malignant, destructive, or fierce person (*d. bowler*, very fast; *is a d. for work*, works strenuously); personified vice or passion. Hence **dēmono-** comb. form, **demonŏ·LATRY, demono·LOGY,** nn. [f. L f. Gk *daimōn* deity, w. sense also of L f. Gk *daimonion* divine (power &c.) neut. adj.]

demŏ·netize (*or* -mŭ-), v.t. Deprive (metal &c.) of its status as money. [f. F *démonétiser* (DE-, L *moneta* MONEY, -IZE)]

demō·niac, a. & n. (Person) possessed by an evil spirit; of such possession; devilish; fiercely energetic, frenzied. [f. LL *daemoniacus* (Gk *daimonion* see DEMON, -AC)]

dēmonī·acal, a. = prec. adj. (esp. in phr. *d. possession*, & in sense *devilish*). [prec. + -AL]

demŏ·nic, dae-, a. = prec.; inspired, of supernatural genius or impulses. [f. L f. Gk *daimonikos* (DEMON, -IC)]

dē·monism, n. Belief in the power of demons. [-ISM(3)]

dē·monize, v.t. Make into or like, represent as, a demon. [f. med. L *daemonizare* (DEMON, -IZE)]

demo·nstrable, a. Capable of being shown or logically proved. Hence **demo·nstrABI·LITY** n., **demo·nstrabLY**[2] adv. [f. L *demonstrabilis* (foll., -ABLE)]

dĕ·monstrate, v.t. & i. Show (feelings &c.); describe & explain by help of specimens or experiments, teach as a demonstrator; logically prove the truth of; be a proof of the existence of; make a military demonstration; take part in a demonstration by public meeting, whence **demo·nstrANT**(1) n. [f. L DE(*monstrare* show, see MONSTER), -ATE[3]]

demonstra·tion, n. Outward exhibition *of* feeling &c.; logical proving, clear proof, (*to d.*, conclusively); thing serving as proof; exhibition & explanation of specimens or experiments as way of teaching; show of military force to intimidate, to mask other operations, or in peace to show readiness for war; exhibition of opinion on political or other question, esp. public meeting or procession, whence **demonstra·tion**IST(1) n. Hence **demonstra·tion**AL a. [f. L *demonstratio* (prec., -ION)]

demo·nstrative, a. & n. Serving to point out or exhibit (esp. in Gram., *d. pronoun* or *adjective,* or *d.* as noun, this &c.); giving proof *of;* logically conclusive; concerned with proof; given to or marked by open expression of feelings (*d. person, behaviour, affection,* &c.). Hence **demo·nstrative**LY[2] adv., **demo·nstrative**NESS n. [f. F *démonstratif* f. L *demonstrativus* (as prec., -IVE)]

dĕ·monstrator, n. One who demonstrates; teacher by demonstration, assistant to professor doing practical work with students; partaker in demonstration by public meeting. [L (DEMONSTRATE, -OR[2])]

demŏ·ralize, v.t. Corrupt morals of, deprave; destroy the discipline, cohesion, courage, or endurance of (esp. troops; see MORALE). Hence **demo·raliz**A·TION n. [f. F *démoraliser* (DE-, MORAL, -IZE)]

dē mor·tŭīs nĭl nĭ·sĭ bŏ·num, sent. Nothing but good should be spoken of the dead. [L]

Dē·mos, n. Personification of the populace or democracy. [Gk, = people]

Dēmosthĕ·nic, a. Like Demosthenes or his oratory; eloquent, patriotic, denunciatory, (of speech). [f. Gk *Dēmosthenikos* of Demosthenes (Attic orator 4th c. B.C.)]

dēmŏ·tic, a. Popular, vulgar; (Archaeol.) in the popular form (opp. *hieratic*) of ancient Egyptian writing. [f. Gk *dēmotikos* (*dēmotēs* one of the DEMOS + -IC)]

demu·lcent, a. & n. Soothing (medicine). [f. L DE(*mulcēre* soothe), -ENT]

demur·, v.i. (-rr-), & n. Make difficulties, raise scruples or objections *to* or *at;* (Law) put in a demurrer, whence **demu·rr**ANT(1) n.; (n.) objecting, objection, (usu. *without, no, d.*). [earlier sense *tarry(ing),* f. F *demeure(r)* f. L DE(*morare* pop. for *-i* delay)]

demure·, a. Sober, grave, composed; ironically reserved; affectedly coy, prudish. Hence **demure·**LY[2] adv., **demure·**NESS n. [DE- + obs. *mure* f. OF *meur* f. L *maturus* ripe]

demŭ·rrable, a. That may be demurred to, open to objection, (esp. legal). [DEMUR, -ABLE]

demŭ·rrage, n. Rate or amount payable to ship-owner by charterer for failure to load or discharge ship within time allowed, similar charge on railway trucks; charge ($1\frac{1}{2}$*d.* per oz.) of Bank of Engl. deducted in giving notes or gold for bullion. [f. OF *demorage* (DEMUR, -AGE)]

demŭ·rrer, n. Legal objection to relevance of opponent's point even if granted, which stays action till relevance is settled; exception taken. [f. OF *demourer* infin. = DEMUR; -ER[4]]

demȳ·, n. (pl. *-ies,* pr. -īz). Size of paper (printing, $17\frac{1}{2} \times 22\frac{1}{2}$; writing, $15\frac{1}{2} \times 20$); scholar of Magd. Coll., Oxford (orig. w. half fellow's allowance), whence **demy·**SHIP n. [var. of DEMI-]

den, n. Wild beast's lair; lurking-place of thieves &c.; small room unfit to live in; room in which person secludes himself to work &c. [OE *denn* cf. G *tenne,* Du. *denne*]

denār·ius, n. (pl. *-ĭī*). Ancient-Roman silver coin (orig. about 8*d.*), whence Engl. *d.* for penny. [f. *deni* ten each, -ARY[1]; *denarius* (*numus*) = (coin) of ten (asses)]

dē·nary, a. Of ten, decimal. [f. L (prec.)]

dēna·tionalize (-năsh-), v.t. Deprive (nation) of its status or characteristics, (person) of membership or characteristics of his nation, (institution) of its position as national property. Hence **dena·tionaliz**A·TION n. [f. F *dénationaliser* (DE-, NATIONAL, -IZE)]

dēna·turalize (-nătshra-), v.t. Change nature of, make unnatural; (usu. refl.) divest of citizenship or membership of State. Hence **dena·turaliz**A·TION n. [DE-, NATURAL, -IZE(3); also DE- + NATURALIZE]

denā·ture (-tsher), v.t. Change nature or essential qualities of (esp. tea or alcohol by adulteration). So **denă·turant** n., substance used in denaturing. [f. F *dénaturer* (DIS-, NATURE)]

de·ndrite, n. (Stone or mineral with) natural tree-like or moss-like marking. Hence **dendrĭ·t**IC a. [f. Gk *dendritēs* adj. (*dendron* tree)]

dendr(o)-, -i-, comb. forms, f. Gk *dendron* tree. Hence **de·ndri**FORM, **de·ndro**ID, aa., **dendro·**LOGY, **dendro·**LOGIST, nn.

dene[1], n. Bare sandy tract, low sandhill, by sea. [cf. G *düne,* Du. *duin,* F *dune*]

dene[2]. See DEAN[2].

dēnega·tion, n. (archaic). Denial. [F (*déne-*), f. L DE(*negationem* f. *negare* deny, -ATION)]

dene-hole, dane-, n. (archaeol.). Artificial cave in chalk entered by vertical shaft often 60 ft deep. [etym. dub.; perh. f. DANE]

de·ngue (-nggā), n. Infectious eruptive fever with acute pains in joints. [prob. f. Zanzibar name, w. assim. to Sp. *dengue* prudery, w. ref. to stiffness of patient's neck & shoulders]

deni·able, a. That one can deny. [-ABLE]

deni·al, n. Refusal of request; = SELF-*d.*; statement that thing is not true (*meet charge with flat d.*) or existent, contradiction; disavowal of person as one's leader &c. [DENY, -AL(2)]

deni·er[1], n. One who denies. [DENY, -ER[1]]

denier·[2] (-nēr), n. (archaic). Very small sum or coin. [OF, 1/12 of sou, f. DENARIUS]

dē·nigrāte, v.t. Blacken; defame, whence or cogn. **de·nigrat**OR[2], **denigr**A·TION, nn. [f. L DE(*nigrare* f. *niger* black)]

deni·m, n. Twilled cotton fabric used for overalls &c. [for *serge de Nim* (*Nîmes* in France)]

dēnī·trate, dēnī·trifȳ, vv.t. Free of nitric or nitrous acid or nitrates. [DE-]

dĕ·nizen, n., & v.t. Inhabitant, occupant, (*of* place); foreigner admitted to residence & certain rights; naturalized foreign word, animal, or plant; hence **de·nizen**SHIP n. (Vb) admit as d. (usu. pass.). [f. AF *deinzein* (*deinz* = F *dans* f. L DE-, *intus* within, *-aneus* see -ANEOUS)]

denŏ·minate, v.t. Give name to, call or describe as so-&-so (w. obj. & compl.). [f. L DE(*nominare* NOMINATE)]

denŏmina·tion, n. Name, designation, esp. characteristic or class name; class of units in numbers, weights, money, &c. (*reduce to the same d.*; *money of small dd.*); class, kind, with specific name; religious sect, whence **deno·mina·tion**AL a. (*denominational education*, according to principles of a Church or sect, whence **denomina·tional**IZE(3) v.t.). [OF (*-cion*), f. L *denominationem* (prec., -ATION)]

denŏ·minative, a. Serving as, giving, a name. [f. L *denominativus* (as prec., -ATIVE)]

denŏ·minator, n. Number below line in vulgar fraction, divisor. [med. L (as prec., -OR[2])]

dēnota·tion, n. Denoting; expression by marks or symbols; sign, indication; designation; meaning of a term; (Log.) aggregate of objects that may be included under a word (cf. CONNOTATION), extension. [f. L *denotatio* (DENOTE, -ATION)]

denō·tative, a. Indicative *of*; (Log.) merely designating, implying no attributes, (cf. CONNOTATIVE). Hence **deno·tative**LY[2] adv. [DENOTE, -ATIVE]

deno·te, v.t. Mark out, distinguish, be the sign of; indicate, give to understand, (esp. *that*-clause); stand as name for; (Log.) be a name for, be predicated of, (*the word* white *denotes all white things, as snow, paper, foam*). Hence **deno·te**MENT n. [f. F *dénoter* f. L DE(*notare* mark f. *nota* NOTE[1])]

dénouement (F) n. Unravelling of plot or complications, catastrophe, final solution, in play, novel, &c. [F (*dénouer* unknot, f. DE-, L *nodare* f. *nodus* knot, -MENT)]

denou·nce (-ow-), v.t. Prophesy (woe, vengeance); inform against; openly inveigh against; give notice of termination of (armistice, treaty). Hence **denou·nce**MENT n. [f. OF *denoncier* f. L DE(*nuntiare* f. *nuntius* messenger perh. for *noventius* f. *novus* new)]

de nouveau (de nōōvō·), adv. Afresh, starting again. [F]

dē nō·vō, adv. = prec. [L]

dense, a. Closely compacted in substance; crowded together; crass, stupid. Hence **de·nse**LY[2] adv., **de·nse**NESS n. [f. L *densus*]

de·nsity, n. Closeness of substance; (Physics) degree of consistence measured by ratio of mass to volume or by quantity of matter in unit of bulk; crowded state; stupidity. [f. F *densité* f. L *densitatem* (prec., -TY)]

dent, n., & v.t. (To mark with a) surface impression (as) from the blow of a blunt-edged instrument. [var. of DINT]

de·ntal, a. & n. Of tooth, teeth, or dentistry; *d. letter* or *d.*, made with tongue-tip against upper front teeth (as *th*) or front of palate (as *d, t*), whence **de·ntal**IZE(3) v.t. [f. L *dens dentis* tooth + -AL]

de·ntate, a. (bot. & zool.). Toothed, with tooth-like notches. So **dent**A·TION n., **denta·to-** comb. form. [f. L *dentatus* (prec., -ATE[2])]

denti-, comb. form of L *dens dentis* tooth, as *dentilingual* formed by teeth & tongue. Hence **de·nti**FORM, **denti·**GEROUS, aa.

de·nticle, n. Small tooth or tooth-like projection; = DENTIL. So **denti·cul**AR[1], **denti·cul**ATE[2] (-*at*) or **-ated,** aa., **denticul**A·TION n. [f. L *denticulus* (prec., -CULE)]

de·ntifrĭce, n. Powder, paste, &c., for tooth-cleaning. [f. L DENTI(*fricium* f. *fricare* rub)]

de·ntil, n. One of series of small rectangular blocks under bed-moulding of cornice in classical architecture (often *d.-cornice, -band, -moulding*). [f. obs. F *dentille* dim. of *dent* tooth f. L *dens dentis*]

de·ntine, n. Hard dense tissue forming main part of teeth. [f. L as prec. + -INE[4]]

de·ntist, n. Tooth-doctor. Hence **de·ntist**RY n. [f. F *dentiste* f. *dent* see DENTIL, -IST(3)]

denti·tion, n. Cutting of teeth, teething; characteristic arrangement of teeth in animal. [f. L *dentitio* (*dentire* to teethe, -ION)]

de·nture, n. Set of (usu. artificial) teeth. [F, f. *dent* tooth (see DENTIL) + -URE]

denū·de, v.t. Make naked; strip *of* clothing, covering, possession, attribute; (Geol.) lay (rock, formation) bare by removal of what lies above. Hence **dēnud**A·TION n., **denu·d**ATIVE a. [f. L DE(*nudare* f. *nudus* naked)]

denuncia·tion (-sĭ-), n. Denouncing; invective. So **denu·nciat**IVE, **denu·n-**

ciatORY, (-shă-) aa., **denu·nciātor**[2] (-shĭ-) n. [f. L *denuntiatio* (DENOUNCE, -ATION)]

deny·, v.t. Declare untrue or non-existent (*d. the charge, the possibility, that it is so, this to be the case*; rarely with *but* after neg., *I don't d. but he may have thought so*); disavow, repudiate, (*d.* one's *word, signature, faith, leader*); refuse (person, thing, person a thing, thing *to* person; *I was denied this, this was denied me* or *to me*); *d.* one*self*, be abstinent; report as not at home, refuse access to, (person visited). [f. F *dénier* f. L DE(*negare* say no)]

dē·odand, n. (hist.). Thing forfeited to Crown to be used in alms &c. as having caused a human death. [f. L *deo dandum* thing to be given to God]

dē·odar, n. Himalayan cedar. [f. Hind. *de'odar* f. Skr. *deva-dara* divine tree]

deŏ·dorize (*or* -ōd-), v.t. Deprive of odour, disinfect. Hence **deodoriz**A·TION, **deo·doriz**ER[1](2), nn. [DE-, L *odor*, smell, -IZE]

dēonto·logy, n. Science of duty, ethics. So **deonto**LO·GICAL a., **deonto·**LOGIST n. [f. Gk *deont-* part. st. of *dei* it is right, -O-, -LOGY]

Dē·o o·ptimo ma·ximo, phr. To God the best & greatest (in dedications). [L]

De·o vole·ntĕ, adv. (abbr. *D.V.*). God willing; if nothing occurs to prevent it. [L]

depar·t, v.i. & t. (Poet., archaic, &c.) go away (*from*), take one's leave; set out, start, leave, (esp. in time-tables, as *dep. 6.30 a.m.*); die, leave by death, (*d. from life, d. this life*); diverge, deviate, (*d. from received account, custom*). [f. OF DE(*partir* f. L *partire* divide)]

depar·ted, a. & n. Bygone (*d. greatness*); deceased (person; esp. *the d.*). [-ED[1](2)]

depar·tment, n. Separate part of complex whole, branch, esp. of municipal or State administration; French administrative district. So **dēpartme·nt**AL a., **departme·ntal**LY[2] adv. [f. F *département* (DEPART, -MENT)]

depar·ture (-tsh*er*), n. Going away; deviation *from* (truth, standard); starting, esp. of train (*the d. platform*); setting out on course of action or thought (esp. *new d.*); (Naut.) amount of ship's change of longitude in sailing. [OF (DEPART, -URE)]

depa·sture, v.t. & i. (Of cattle) graze upon, graze; put (cattle) to graze; (of land) feed (cattle). Hence **depa·stur**AGE n. [DE-]

depau·perate, v.t. Impoverish; reduce in vigour, stunt, make degenerate. So **depauper**A·TION n. [f. med. L DE(*pauperare* f. L *pauper* poor), -ATE[3]]

dēpau·perize, v.t. Raise from, rid of, pauperism. [DE-, PAUPER, -IZE]

depe·nd, v.i. Hang down (poet., archaic, &c.); be contingent (*it depends upon himself*, i.e. upon his efforts, skill, wisdom, &c.; also abs. in *that depends*, i.e. can only be answered conditionally; be grammatically dependent (*up*)*on*; rest for maintenance &c. *upon* (*she depends upon her own efforts, her pen, her mother, my help*); reckon confidently *upon* (esp. in imperat., *d. upon it*, you may be sure); be waiting for settlement (of lawsuit, Bill, &c.). [f. OF DE(*pendre* f. L *pendĕre* suspend but with sense of *pendēre* be suspended)]

depe·ndable, a. That may be depended on. Hence **depe·ndable**NESS n., **depe·ndab**LY[2] adv. [-ABLE]

depe·ndant, -ent[1], n. One who depends on another for support, retainer, servant. [f. F *dépendant* part. (DEPEND, -ANT)]

depe·ndence, n. Depending (*upon*), being conditioned or subordinate or subject; living at another's cost; reliance, confident trust; thing relied on. [f. F *dépendance* (prec., -ANCE)]

depe·ndency, n. Something subordinate or dependent, esp. country or province controlled by another. [as prec., -ANCY, -ENCY]

depe·ndent[2], a. Depending (*on*), contingent, subordinate, subject; maintained at another's cost; (Gram. of clause, phrase, or word) in subordinate relation to a sentence or word. [earlier *-ant* = DEPENDANT]

dēpho·sphorize, v.t. Rid (ore) of phosphorus. Hence **dephosphoriz**A·TION n. [DE-]

depi·ct, v.t. Represent in drawing or colours; portray in words, describe. Hence or cogn. **depi·ct**ER[1], **depi·ct**OR[2], **depi·ct**ION, nn., **depi·ct**IVE a. [f. L DE-(*pingere pict-* paint)]

depi·cture (-tsh*er*), v.t. Picture, depict. [DE- + PICTURE v.]

dē·pilate, v.t. Remove hair from. Hence **depil**A·TION, **de·pilat**OR[2](2), nn., **depi·la**TORY a. & n. [f. L DE(*pilare* f. *pilus* hair), -ATE[3]]

deplĕ·nish, v.t. Empty of its contents, deprive of its stock. [DE-, & as REPLENISH]

deple·te, v.t. Empty out, exhaust; relieve of congestion. So **deple·t**ION n., **deple·t**IVE a. & n., **deple·t**ORY a. [f. L DE(*plēre -plet-* fill)]

deplore·, v.t. Bewail, grieve over, regret; be scandalized by. Hence **deplor·**ABLE a., **deplor·ab**LY[2] adv., **deplor**ABI·LITY, **deplor·able**NESS, nn. [f. L DE(*plorare* bewail)]

deploy·, v.t. & i., & n., (mil.). Spread out (t. & i. of troops) from column into line; so **deploy·**MENT n. (N.) doing this. [f. F *déployer* f. L DIS(*plicare* fold), whence also DISPLAY]

deplu·me, v.t. Pluck, strip of feathers. [f. F *déplumer* (DE-, L *pluma* feather)]

dēpō·larize, v.t. (Opt.) change direction of polarization of (ray); (Electr. &

Magn.) deprive of polarity; (fig.) disturb, shake loose, dissolve, (convictions, prejudices). Hence **depolariza·tion, depo·larizer**[1](2), nn. [DE-]

depo·nent, a. & n. (L & Gk gram.) (verb) passive in form but active in sense (named from notion that they had laid aside the pass. sense); person making deposition under oath or giving written testimony for use in court &c. [f. L DE(*ponere posit-* place), -ENT]

depŏ·pulate, v.t. & i. Reduce population of; decline in population. So **depopula·tion** n. [f. L DE(*populari* lay waste f. *populus* people), -ATE[3]]

depor·t, v.t. 1. Bear or conduct *oneself* in such a manner. 2. Remove, esp. into exile, banish, whence **dēporta·tion** n. [sense 1 f. OF *deporter* (DE-, *porter* carry f. L *portare*); sense 2 f. F *déporter* f. L DE(*portare* carry)]

depor·tment, n. Bearing, demeanour, manners; way a thing (e.g. metal in chem. experiment) behaves. [OF (*-ement*), as prec. 1, -MENT]

depo·se (-z), v.t. & i. Remove from office, esp. dethrone, whence **depo·sable** a.; bear witness *that*, testify *to*, esp. on oath in court. [f. F *déposer* (DE- + *poser* f. LL *pausare* PAUSE, POSE[1])]

depŏ·sit[1] (-z-), n. Thing stored or entrusted for safe keeping; sum placed in bank, usu. at interest & not to be drawn on without notice (*on d.*, so disposed of; *has a current & a d. account*); sum required and paid as pledge or earnest or first instalment; layer of precipitated matter, natural accumulation. [f. L DE(*positum* neut. p.p. of *ponere* place)]

depŏ·sit[2] (-z-), v.t. Lay down in a (usu. specified) place; lay (eggs; usu. with adv. &c.); (of water or natural agency) leave (layer of matter) lying; store or entrust for keeping (esp. sum at interest in bank); pay as pledge for fulfilment of contract or further payment. [f. obs. F *depositer* f. med. L *depositare* frequent. of L *deponere* see prec.]

depo·sitary, n. Person to whom thing is committed, trustee. [f. L *depositarius* (DEPOSIT[1], -ARY[1])]

dĕposi·tion, n. (Picture of) taking down of Christ from the cross; deposing from office, esp. dethronement; (giving of) sworn evidence, allegation, (usu. -dĕ); depositing. [OF, f. L *depositionem* f. *deponere* (DEPOSIT[1], -ION), but w. senses chiefly of unconnected DEPOSE]

depo·sitor, n. Person who deposits money, property, &c.; apparatus for depositing some substance. [L (*deponere* see DEPOSIT[1], -OR[2])]

depo·sitory, n. Storehouse (lit. & fig.); = DEPOSITARY. [f. med. L *depositorium* (DEPOSIT[1], -ORY)]

dĕ·pot (-ō), n. (Mil.) place for stores; head-quarters of regiment; recruit-drilling station; part of regiment not on foreign service. Storehouse, emporium; (U.S.; *pr.* dē·pō) railway station. [f. F *dépôt* f. L as DEPOSIT[1]]

depra·ve, v.t. Make bad, deteriorate, pervert, corrupt, esp. in moral character or habits. So **dēprava·tion** n. [f. L DE(*pravare* f. *pravus* crooked)]

deprā·vity, n. Moral perversion, viciousness; (Theol.) innate corruption of man. [DE- + obs. *pravity* f. L *pravitas* (prec., -TY)]

dĕ·precate, v.t. Plead against (*d.* one's *anger*, beseech him not to be angry); express wish against or disapproval of (*d. war, hasty action, panic*). Hence or cogn. **de·precatingly**[2] adv., **depreca·tion** n., **de·precative, de·precatory,** aa. [f. L DE(*precari* pray), -ATE[3]]

deprē·ciate (-shĭ-), v.t. & i. Diminish (t. & i.) in value; lower market price of; reduce purchasing power of (money); disparage, belittle. Hence **depre·ciatingly**[2] adv., **depre·ciatory** (-sha-) a. [f. L DE(*pretiare* f. *pretium* price), -ATE[3]]

deprecia·tion (-ēsĭ-, -ēshĭ-), n. Depreciating or being depreciated; allowance made in valuations, estimates, and balance sheets, for wear & tear. [prec., -ATION]

dĕpreda·tion, n. (usu. pl.). Spoliation, ravages. [F (*dé-*), f. L DE(*praedationem* f. *praedare* f. *praeda* prey, -ATION)]

dĕ·predātor, n. Spoiler, pillager. [f. L *depraedator* (prec., -OR[2])]

depre·ss, v.t. Push or pull down, lower; bring low, humble; reduce activity of (esp. trade); lower (voice) in pitch; dispirit, deject. So **depre·ssible** a. [f. OF *dépresser* f. L *DE(*pressare* frequent. of *premere* PRESS)]

depre·ssant, a. & n. (med.) Lowering, sedative, (medicine). [prec. + -ANT]

depre·ssion (-shn), n. Lowering, sinking; (Astron.) angular distance of star &c. below horizon; sunk place, hollow, on surface; reduction in vigour (esp. of trade), in pitch (of voice), vitality, or spirits; (Meteorol.) lowering of barometer or atmospheric pressure, esp. centre of minimum pressure or system of winds round it. [f. L DE(*pressio* f. *premere press-* press, -ION)]

depre·ssor, n. (anat.). *D. muscle* or *d.*, one pulling down some organ &c. [L (prec., -OR[2])]

dĕpriva·tion (*or* -ĭ-), n. Loss, being deprived, *of*; deposition from esp. ecclesiastical office; felt loss (*that is a great d.*). (f. med. L *deprivatio* (foll., -ATION)]

depri·ve, v.t. Strip, bereave, debar from enjoyment, *of*; depose (esp. clergyman) from office. Hence **depri·**VABLE a., **depri·**VAL(2) n. [f. OF DE(*priver* f. L *privare* deprive)]

dē profu·ndis, n. & adv. (Cry) from the depths of sorrow &c. [initial L wds of *Ps.* cxxx]

depth, n. Being DEEP; measurement from top down, from surface inwards, or from front to back; abstruseness; sagacity; intensity of colour, darkness, &c.; (pl.) deep water, deep place, abyss, lowest or inmost part; middle (*in the d. of winter*); deep or mysterious region of thought, feeling, &c. (*cry from the dd., d. of inspiration, dd. of degradation*); *out of* one's *d.*, in water too deep to stand in, (fig.) engaged on too hard a task or subject; *d.-charge*, bomb for dropping on submerged submarine, set to explode at desired d. [DEEP, -TH[1]]

dĕ·pūrate, v.t. & i. Make, become, free from impurities. So **depur**A·TION, **de·purat**OR[2](2), nn., **depūr·at**IVE a. & n. [f. med. L DE(*purare* f. L *purus* pure)]

dĕputa·tion, n. Body of persons appointed to represent others. [foll., -ATION]

depu·te, v.t. Commit (task, authority) to substitute; appoint as one's substitute. [f. F *députer* f. L DE(*putare* think) regard as, allot]

dĕ·putize, v.i. Act as deputy or understudy (*for*), esp. in musical engagements. [foll. + -IZE]

dĕ·puty, n. Person appointed to act for another or others (*by d.*, by proxy; *d. lieutenant*, abbr. D. L., d. of Lord Lieutenant of county); member of deputation; parliamentary representative (*Chamber of Dd.*, lower house in French & other Parliaments); *d.-*, deputed, acting-. Hence **de·puty**SHIP(1) n. [f. F *député* p.p. of *députer* DEPUTE, -Y[4]]

dera̋·cinate, v.t. Tear up by the roots. [f. F *déraciner* (DE-, *racine* f. LL *radicina* dim. of *radix* root), -ATE[3]]

derai·l, v.t. & i. Cause (train &c.) to leave the rails (usu. pass.); (rarely) leave the rails. So **derai·l**MENT n. [f. F *dérailler* (DE-, *rail* rail)]

dera·nge (-ānj), v.t. Throw into confusion or out of gear, disorganize; cause to act irregularly; make insane (esp. in p.p.); disturb, interrupt. So **dera·nge**MENT n. [f. F *déranger* (DE-, *rang* rank)]

Der·by (dar-), n. Annual horse-race at Epsom; *D. day*, of the race; *D. dog*, any dog straying on course, (fig.) trivial untimely interruption. [Earl of *D.* founder 1780]

Der·bўite (dar-), n. Soldier attested under Lord Derby's scheme of 1915 (as half-way between voluntary and compulsory recruits).

Der·byshire (dar-), a. *D. neck*, goitre, bronchocele; *D. spar*, fluor-spar.

de règle (F), pred. a. Customary, proper.

dĕ·relict, a. & n. Abandoned, ownerless, (esp. of ship at sea); abandoned property, esp. ship. [f. L DE(*relict-* see RELINQUISH)]

dĕreli·ction, n. Abandoning, being abandoned; retreat of sea exposing new land; neglect *of duty*; failure in duty, short-coming. [f. L *derelictio* (prec., -ION)]

deri·de, v.t. Laugh to scorn. [f. L DE(*ridēre ris-* laugh)]

de rigueur (F), pred. a. Required by etiquette (*evening dress is* d. r.).

deri·sion (-zhn), n. Ridicule, mockery, (*hold, have, in d.*, mock at; *be in d.*, be mocked at; *bring into d.*); laughing-stock. [f. L *derisio* (DERIDE, -ION)]

derī·sive, deri·sory, aa. Scoffing (*d. cheers*, ironical); (*-ory* only; of offer &c.) ridiculously futile, not to be taken seriously. Hence **deri·sive**LY[2] adv. [f. L *deris-* see DERIDE, + -IVE, -ORY]

dĕriva·tion, n. Obtaining from a source; extraction, descent; formation of word from word or root, tracing or statement of this; theory of evolution, whence **deriva·tion**IST(2) n. [F (*dé-*), f. L *derivationem* (DERIVE, -ATION)]

derī·vative, a. & n. (Thing, word, chemical substance) derived from a source, not primitive or original. Hence **deri·vative**LY[2] adv. [f. F *dérivatif* f. L *derivativus* (foll., -IVE)]

der·ive, v.t. & i. Get, obtain, (*from* a source, or with the source present in thought); have one's or its *origin* &c. *from*; gather, deduce, (knowledge, truth, ideas, &c.) *from*; (pass., refl., & intr.) be descended or have one's origin *from*; (pass., of words) be formed *from*; trace, show, or assert, descent, origin, or formation, of (person, thing, word) *from*. Hence **deri·**VABLE a. [f. F *dériver* f. L *derivare* (DE-, *rivus* stream) divert, derive]

derm, n. Skin; true skin or layer of tissue below epidermis. Hence or cogn. **der·m**AL, **der·m**IC, aa., **der·mat**(O)-, **derm**O-, comb. forms, **dermato·**LOGY, **dermato·**LOGIST, nn. [f. Gk *derma* skin (*derō* flay, -M)]

dern. = DARN[2].

dernier ressort (F), n. Last resort, desperate expedient.

dĕ·rogate, v.i. Detract, take away part, *from* (a merit, right, &c.); sink in the scale, do something derogatory. [f. L DE(*rogare* ask), -ATE[3]]

dĕroga·tion, n. Lessening or impairment *of* law, authority, position, dignity, &c.; deterioration, debasement. [F (*dé-*), f. L *derogationem* (prec., -ATION)]

derŏ·gatory, a. Tending to detract *from*, involving impairment, disparagement, or discredit, *to*; lowering, unsuited to one's dignity or position; depreciatory. [f. L *derogatorius* (DEROGATE, -ORY)]

de·rrick, n. Contrivance for moving or hoisting heavy weights, kind of crane with adjustable arm pivoted at foot to central post, deck, or floor. [obs. senses *hangman, gallows*, f. name of hangman c. 1600]

de·rring-do·, n. (pseudo-archaic). Desperate courage. [f. Chaucer's *In dorryng don that longeth to a knyght* (in daring to do that which belongeth &c.) misinterpreted by Spenser]

de·rringer (-j-), n. Small large-bore pistol. [U.S. inventor's name]

der·vish, n. Mohammedan friar vowed to poverty & austerity (*dancing* or *whirling d., howling d.*, according to the practice of his order). [f. Pers. *darvesh* poor]

dĕ·scant[1], n. (poet.). Melody, song; (Mus.) melodic independent treble accompaniment. [f. OF *deschant* f. med. L DIS(*cantus* CHANT)]

descă·nt[2], v.i. Talk at large, dwell freely, *upon* (esp. in praise, *d. upon the beauties of*). [f. OF *deschanter* (prec., L *cantare*)]

desce·nd (-sĕ-), v.i. & t. Come or go down, sink, fall, (*descending letter* in Typog., with tail below line); slope downwards; make sudden attack *upon*; proceed in narrative &c. from earlier to later time, from greater to less (so Math., *descending series* of numbers), from general to particular; stoop *to* do; (rare) be DESCENDED *from*; be transmitted by inheritance *from* (of qualities, property, privileges), pass (*to* heir, or abs.); go down (hill, stairs). [f. F *descendre* f. L DE(*scendere* = *scandere* climb)]

desce·ndant, n. Person or thing DESCENDED (*of*, or with *his* &c.) [F (prec., -ANT)]

desce·nded, p.p. Sprung, having origin, *from* ancestor or stock (*is d.* &c. usual instead of the rare *descends* &c.). [-ED[1](2)]

desce·ndible, -able, a. Transmissible by inheritance. [OF (*-able*); see -BLE]

desce·nt, n. Descending, downward motion; downward slope; way down; sudden attack, esp. from sea; decline, sinking in scale, fall; being descended, lineage; single generation (*lineal succession of four dd.*); transmission of property, title, or quality, by inheritance. [f. F *descente* (*descendre* DESCEND)]

descri·be, v.t. Set forth in words, recite the characteristics of; qualify *as* (*should d. him as a scoundrel*); mark out, draw, (esp. geom. figure); move in (such a line, curve); (abs.) deal in, give a, description. Hence **descri·b**ABLE a. [f. L DE(*scribere script-* write)]

descri·ption, n. Describing, verbal portrait(ure), of person, object, or event (*answers to the d.*, has the qualities specified), more or less complete definition; sort, kind, class, (*no food of any d., tyrant of the worst d.*). [F, f. L *descriptionem* (DESCRIBE, -ION)]

descri·ptive, a. Serving to describe (*d. touches*), fond of describing (*d. writer*). Hence **descri·ptive**LY[2] adv. [f. LL *descriptivus* (DESCRIBE, -IVE)]

descr̄y·, v.t. Catch sight of, succeed in discerning (lit. & fig.). [prob. var. of DESCRIBE, & often confused in early use with DECRY]

dĕ·secrate, v.t. Deprive of sacred character; outrage, profane, (sacred thing); dedicate *to* (evil). Hence **desecr**A·TION, **de·secrat**OR[2], nn. [DE- + (CON)SECRATE]

deser·t[1] (-z-), n. Deserving, worthiness of recompense good or bad; character that deserves good, virtue, whence **deser·t**LESS a.; deserving people; (pl.) acts or qualities deserving good or bad recompense, such recompense, (*reward him according to, give him, he has got, his dd.*). [OF obs. p.p. of *deservir* DESERVE]

dĕ·sert[2] (-z-), a. & n. Uninhabited, desolate; uncultivated, barren; (n.) waterless & treeless region, (fig.) uninteresting or barren subject, period, &c. [OF (a. & n.), f. L p.p. see foll.]

deser·t[3] (-z-), v.t. & i. Abandon, give up, (thing); depart from (place, haunt); forsake (person or thing having claims on one, as *wife, post, the colours, ship*); fail (*his presence of mind deserted him*); run away (esp. from service in army or navy), whence **deser·t**ER[1] n. So **deser·**TION n. [f. F *déserter* f. LL *desertare* frequent. of L DE(*serere sert-* join)]

deser·ve (-z-), v.t. & i. Be entitled by conduct or qualities to (good or bad); have established a claim to be *well* or *ill* treated at the hands *of*. Hence **deser·v-ĕd**LY[2] adv. [f. OF *deservir* f. L DE(*servire* serve)]

deser·ving, a. Meritorious; worthy (*of* praise, censure, &c.). [-ING[2]]

déshabillé (F), n. = DISHABILLE.

dĕ·siccate (*also* dĭsĭ·k-), v.t. Dry, dry up, (esp. milk &c. for preservation). So **desicc**A·TION, **de·siccat**OR[2](2), nn., **de·sicc**ATIVE a. [f. L DE(*siccare* f. *siccus* dry), -ATE[3]]

desĭ·derāte, v.t. Feel to be missing, regret absence of. [f. L DE(*siderare* see CONSIDER), -ATE[3]]

desĭ·derative (-*at*-), a. & n. (gram.). (Verb, conjugation, &c.) formed on another verb &c. & expressing desire of doing the action. [f. L *desiderativus* (prec., -IVE)]

desĭdera·tum, n. (pl. *-ta*). Thing missing, felt want. [L (neut. p.p. see DESIDERATE)]

desig·n[1] (-zīn), n. Mental plan; scheme of attack *upon* (*has dd. upon me*); purpose (*whether by accident or d.*); end in view; adaptation of means to ends (*the argument from d.*, maintaining existence of a

God by pointing to such adaptation); preliminary sketch for picture &c.; delineation, pattern; artistic or literary groundwork, general idea, construction, plot, faculty of evolving these, invention. [f. 15th-c. F *desseing* f. *desseigner* see foll.]

desig·n[2] (-zīn), v.t. & i. Set (thing) apart *for* person; destine (person, thing) *for* a service; contrive, plan; purpose, intend, (*designs an attack, to* do, *doing*, or *that* —, thing or person *to* be or do something), whence **desig·nĕd**LY[2] adv.; make preliminary sketch of (picture); draw plan of (building &c. to be executed by others); be a designer; conceive mental plan for, construct the groundwork or plot of, (book, work of art). [f. F *désigner* appoint f. L *designare* DESIGNATE[2], with senses also of obs. F *desseigner* purpose & mod. F *dessiner* draw]

dĕ·signate[1] (-*at*), a. (placed after its noun). Appointed to office but not yet installed (*bishop d.* &c.). [f. L p.p. (foll., -ATE[2])]

dĕ·signāte[2] (-z-), v.t. Specify, particularize; serve as name or distinctive mark of; style, describe as; appoint to office (*as, to, for*). [f. L DE(*signare* f. *signum* mark), -ATE[3]]

dĕsigna·tion (-z-), n. Appointing to office; name, description, title. [f. L as prec., -ATION]

desig·ner, n. In vbl senses; esp. draughtsman who makes plans for manufacturers. [-ER[1]]

desig·ning, a. In vbl senses; esp. crafty, artful, scheming. [-ING[2]]

dēsi·lverize, v.t. Extract the silver from (esp. lead). [DE-, SILVER, -IZE]

desi·pience, n. Trifling, silliness. [f. L *desipientia* f. DE(*sipere* = *sapere* be wise)]

desīr·able (-z-), a. Worth wishing for. Hence **desira**BI·LITY, **desir·able**NESS, nn., **desir·ab**LY[2] adv. [DESIRE[2], -ABLE]

desire·[1] (-z-), n. Unsatisfied appetite, longing, wish, craving; request; thing desired. [f. OF *desir* cf. foll.]

desire·[2], v.t. Long for, crave, wish, (noun, infin., noun & infin., or *that*-clause); (abs.) feel d.; ask for; pray, entreat, command, (*d. him to wait*; *she desired we would wait*). [f. OF *desirer* f. L *desiderare* DESIDERATE]

desīr·ous, pred. a. Wishful *to* do, ambitious *of* (success &c.), having the desire *of* doing, wishful *that*. [f. OF *desireus* f. LL *desiderosus* (st. of *desiderare* see prec. + -OSE[1])]

desi·st (-zĭ-, -sĭ-), v.i. Cease (*from doing, from* sin). [f. OF *desister* f. L DE(*sistere* stop)]

desk, n. Fixed or movable piece of furniture or box having (often in combination with drawers, seat, &c.) a board usu. sloped serving as rest for writing or reading at; *the d.*, clerical, office, or literary work. Hence **de·sk**FUL(2) n. [f. med. L *desca* f. L *discus* disk]

dĕ·solate[1] (-*at*), a. Left alone, solitary; uninhabited; ruinous, neglected, barren, dreary; forlorn, disconsolate, wretched. Hence **de·solate**LY[2] adv., **de·solate**NESS n. [f. L DE(*solare* f. *solus* alone), -ATE[2]]

de·solāte[2], v.t. Depopulate; devastate; make (person) wretched. Hence **de·solat**OR[2] n. [f. prec., see -ATE[3]]

desola·tion, n. Desolating; neglected, ruined, solitary, or barren state; being forsaken, loneliness; dreary sorrow. [f. L *desolatio* (as prec., -ATION)]

despair·, n., & v.i. Loss, utter want, of hope; thing that causes this, whether by badness or unapproachable excellence. (Vb) lose, be without, hope (*of*, or abs.; *his life is despaired of*); hence **despair·ing**LY[2] adv. [f. OF *despeir*- stressed st. of *desperer* f. L DE(*sperare* hope)]

despatch. See **disp-.**

desperā·do, n. Person ready for or given to reckless, esp. criminal, undertakings. [OSp. (adj. only), f. L *desperatus* see foll.]

de·sperate (-*at*), a. Leaving no or little room for hope, extremely dangerous or serious, utterly impracticable; reckless from despair, violent, lawless, staking all on a small chance, whence **desper**A·TION n.; extremely bad (*a d. night, storm*, &c.); very great (*d. fear, a d. fool*). Hence **de·sperate**LY[2] adv., **de·sperate**NESS n. [f. L DE(*sperare* hope), -ATE[2]]

dĕ·spicable, a. Vile, contemptible. Hence **de·spicab**LY[2] adv. [f. L *despicabilis* f. DE(*spicari* cf. *specere* look at), -BLE]

despi·se (-z), v.t. Look down upon, contemn. [f. *despis*- st. of OF *despire* f. L DE(*spicere* = *specere* look at)]

despi·te, n. & prep. Outrage, injury, contumely, (archaic); malice, spite, offended pride (*died of mere d.*); *in d. of, d. of, d.*, notwithstanding the opposition of, in the teeth of, in spite of, (also *in my* &c. *d.*, in spite of my &c. efforts, archaic). Hence **despi·te**FUL a., **despi·teful**LY[2] adv. [f. OF *despit* f. L *despectus* -*ūs* f. *despicere* see prec.]

despoi·l, v.t. Plunder, spoil, rob, deprive, (person or place; often *of*). Hence or cogn. **despoi·l**ER[1], **despoi·l**MENT, **despō-li**A·TION, nn. [f. OF *despoiller* (now *dépouiller*) f. L DE(*spoliare* spoil)]

despo·nd, v.i., & n. Lose heart, be dejected; so **despo·nd**ENCY n., **despo·n-d**ENT a., **despo·ndent**LY[2], **despo·nd-ing**LY[2], advv. (N., archaic, only in SLOUGH *of D.*) dejection. [f. L DE(*spondēre* promise) give up, resign]

de·spot, n. Absolute ruler, whence **de·s-pot**IST(2) n.; tyrant, oppressor. So **despŏ·t**IC a., **despo·t**ICALLY adv. [OF, f. Gk *despotēs*]

de·spotism, n. Arbitrary rule; State under a despot. [f. F *despotisme* (prec., -ISM)]

dĕ·squamate, v.t. & i. Strip of (in p.p.), come off in, scales. Hence **desquamA·**TION n., **desquă·matIVE, desquă·ma**tORY, aa. [f. L DE(*squamare* f. *squama* scale)]

desser·t (-z-), n. Course of fruit, sweetmeats, &c., at end of dinner; *d.*-SPOON. [F, f. *desservir* (*des-* f. L *dis-*, *servir* SERVE) clear the table]

destina·tion, n. Place to which person or thing is bound. [f. L *destinatio* (foll., -ATION)]

de·stine, v.t. Appoint, fore-ordain, devote, set apart, (person or thing *to* do, *to* or *for* a service, achievement, &c.; of God, Fate, &c., or of persons; but chiefly in pass.); *was destined to*, was, as we now know, to. [f. F *destiner* f. L DE(*stinare* prob. causative of *stare* stand)]

de·stiny, n. Predetermined events; person's, country's, &c., appointed or ultimate lot; power that fore-ordains, invincible necessity. [f. OF *destinée* (prec., -Y[4])]

de·stitute, a. Without resources, in want of necessaries; devoid *of*. So **destitu·**TION n. [f. L DE(*stituere -tut-* =*statuere* place) forsake]

de·strier, n. (hist.). War-horse. [OF, f. LL *dextrarius* hand-led (DEXTER, -ARY[1])]

destroy·, v.t. Pull down, demolish, undo, make useless, kill, annihilate, nullify, neutralize effect of. Hence **destroy·**ABLE a. [f. OF *destruire* ult. f. L DE(*struere struct-* build)]

destroy·er, n. In vbl senses; esp. as abbr. for TORPEDO-*boat d.* [-ER[1]]

destru·ctible, a. Able to be destroyed. Hence **destructi**BI·LITY n. [f. L *destructibilis* (DESTROY, -BLE)]

destru·ction, n. DESTROYing or being destroyed; what destroys, cause of ruin, (*is our d.*). [OF, f. L *destructionem* (DESTROY, -ION)]

destru·ctive, a. & n. Destroying; deadly *to*, causing destruction *of*; (of criticism or policy) merely negative, refuting &c. without amending, not constructive; hence **destru·ctive**LY[2] adv., **destru·ctive**NESS n. (N.) person, thing, that aims at or effects destruction. [OF (*-if, -ive*), f. L *destructivus* (DESTROY, -IVE)]

destru·ctor, n. Refuse-burning furnace. [L, =destroyer (DESTROY, -OR[2])]

dē·suetude (-swĭ-), n. Passing into, state of, disuse. [f. F *désuétude* f. L DE(*suetudo* f. *suescere suet-* be wont, -TUDE)]

dēsu·lphurize (*-fer-*), v.t. Free from sulphur. Hence **desu·lphuriz**A·TION n. [DE-]

dĕ·sultory, a. Skipping from one subject to another, disconnected, unmethodical. Hence **de·sultori**LY[2] adv., **de·sultori**NESS n. [f. L *desultorius* f. *desultor* circus-rider f. DE(*sult-* =*salt-* p.p. st. of *salire* leap)]

dēsȳnŏ·nȳmize, v.t. Differentiate in sense (synonymous words). [DE-, SYNONYM, -IZE]

deta·ch (-tsh), v.t. Unfasten & remove (*from*, or abs.; *detached mind, view*, &c., regarding things impartially, free from prejudice; *detached house*, not joined to another on either side); (Mil. & Nav.) send (ship, regiment, &c.) on separate mission. Hence **deta·ch**ABLE a., **deta·chĕd**LY[2] adv., **deta·ched**NESS -(ătsht-) n. [f. F *détacher* (DE-, Rom. *tacca* nail, tack)]

deta·chment, n. Detaching; portion of army, navy, or large body, separately employed; standing aloof from or unaffected by surroundings, public opinion, &c., independence of judgement, selfish isolation. [f. F *détachement* (prec., -MENT)]

dē·tail[1], n. Dealing with things item by item (*in d.*; *go into d.*, give the items separately; *army beaten in d.*, in small sectional engagements); minute account, number of particulars; item, small or subordinate particular, (*but that is a d.*, often iron. to call special attention), whence **de·tail**ED[2] a., with particulars; minor decoration in building, picture, &c., way of treating this; (Mil.) distribution of orders of the day, small detachment. [f. F *détail* f. *détailler* see foll.]

detai·l[2], v.t. Give the particulars of, relate circumstantially; (Mil.) tell off for special duty. [f. F *détailler* (DE-, *tailler* cut, see TAILOR)]

detai·n, v.t. Keep in confinement; withhold (money due &c.); keep waiting, hinder. [f. OF DE(*tenir* f. L *-tinēre -tent-* =*tenēre* hold)]

detai·ner, n. (legal). Detaining of goods taken from owner for distraint &c.; keeping of person in confinement; writ by which person already arrested may be detained on another suit. [f. AF *detener* f. OF *detenir* see prec., -ER[4]]

dete·ct, v.t. Find out (guilty person, person *in doing*); discover existence or presence of. Hence or cogn. **dete·ct**ABLE a., **dete·ct**ION, **dete·ct**OR[2](1, 2,) nn. [f. L DE(*tegere tect-* cover)]

dete·ctive, a. & n. Serving to detect; policeman employed to investigate special cases (*private d.*, person undertaking special inquiries for pay; *amateur d.*, person who sets up theories on police cases); *d. story* &c. (that tempts readers to solve d. problems). [prec., -IVE]

dete·nt, n. Catch by removal of which machinery is set working, (in clocks &c.) catch that regulates striking. [f. F, *détente* f. *détendre* slacken (DE-, L *tendere* stretch)]

détente (F), n. Cessation of strained relations between States. [as prec.]

dete·ntion, n. Detaining, being detained;

arrest, confinement, (*House of D.*, lock-up); compulsory delay; (at schools) keeping in as punishment. [f. L *detentio* (DETAIN, -ION)]

deter·, v.t. (-rr-). Discourage or hinder (*from*, or abs.) by or as fear, dislike of trouble, &c. Hence **dete·rr**ENT(2) a. & n., **dete·rr**ENCE, **deter·**MENT, nn. [f. L DE(*terrēre* frighten)]

deter·gent, a. & n. Cleansing (agent). [f. L DE(*tergēre ters-* wipe), -ENT]

detĕr·iorate, v.t. & i. Make, grow, worse. Hence or cogn. **deterior**A·TION n., **deter·iorat**IVE a. [f. L *deteriorare* (*deterior* worse f. *de* down), -ATE³]

determinant, a. & n. Determining, decisive, conditioning, defining, (agent, factor, element, word). [DETERMINE, -ANT]

deter·minate (-*at*), a. Limited, definite, distinct, finite, definitive. Hence **deter·minate**LY² adv., **deter·minate**NESS n. [f. L p.p. (DETERMINE, -ATE²)]

determina·tion, n. (Law) cessation of estate or interest; conclusion of debate; judicial sentence; fixing of date &c.; delimitation, definition; exact ascertainment *of* amount &c.; fixed direction, decisive bias, (*d. of blood to* some part, tendency to flow there); settling of purpose, fixed intention; resoluteness. [f. L *determinatio* (DETERMINE, -ATION)]

deter·minative, a. & n. (Thing) that impels in a certain direction; (attribute, mark, symbol) serving to define or qualify. [f. F *déterminatif* (foll., -IVE)]

deter·mine, v.t. & i. Bring, come, to an end (esp. in law); limit in scope, define; fix beforehand (date); settle, decide, (dispute, person's fate, *what* is to be done, *that* —, *whether*, &c.), come to a conclusion, give decision; be the decisive factor in regard to (*demand determines supply*); ascertain precisely, fix; give an aim to, direct, impel *to*; decide (person) *to* do; resolve (*to* do, *that* —, *on doing, on* a course; *be determined*, have resolved). Hence **deter·min**ABLE a. [f. OF *determiner* f. L DE(*terminare* f. *terminus* end)]

deter·mined, a. In verbal senses; also, resolute, unflinching. [-ED¹]

deter·minism, n. Theory that human action is not free but determined by motives regarded as external forces acting on the will. So **deter·min**IST(2) n. & a., **determini·st**IC a. [DETERMINE + -ISM]

deter·sive, a. & n. Cleansing (substance). [f. F *détersif* (DETERGENT, -IVE)]

dete·st, v.t. Abhor, dislike intensely. Hence or cogn. **dete·st**ABLE a., **dete·stable**NESS n., **dete·stab**LY² adv. [f. F *détester* f. L DE*testari* call God to witness against]

dĕtesta·tion, n. Abhorrence (*have, hold, in d.*, abhor); detested person or thing. [F (*dé*-), f. L *detestationem* (prec., -ATION)]

dethro·ne, v.t. Depose (ruler, dominant influence). Hence **dethro·ne**MENT n. [DE-]

dĕ·tinue, n. (legal). *Action of d.*, suit for recovery of thing wrongfully detained. [f. OF *detenue* f. p.p. of *detenir* DETAIN]

dē·tonate (*or* dĕ-), v.i. & t. (Cause to) explode with loud report. Hence or cogn. **deton**A·TION n., **de·tonāt**IVE a. [f. L DE(*tonare* thunder), -ATE³]

de·tonator, n. Detonating contrivance, esp. as part of bomb or shell; railway fog-signal. [-OR²]

detour (dĭtoor·), **détour** (F), n. Deviation, roundabout way, digression, (esp. *make a d.*). [F (*dé*-), f. *détourner* (DE-, TURN)]

detra·ct, v.t. & i. Take away (*much, something*, &c., or abs.) *from* a whole (esp. in sense *reduce the credit due to, depreciate*). Hence or cogn. **detra·ct**ION, **detra·ct**OR², nn., **detra·ct**IVE a. [f. L DE(*trahere tract-* draw)]

detrai·n, v.t. & i. Discharge, alight, from train (troops &c.; cf. ENTRAIN), [DE- + TRAIN n.]

dĕ·triment, n. Harm, damage, (esp. *without d. to*). [F (*dé*-), f. L DE(*trimentum* f. *terere trit-* rub, wear, -MENT)]

detrime·ntal, a. & n. Harmful, causing loss, whence **detrime·ntal**LY² adv.; (n., slang) undesirable suitor, e.g. younger son. [-AL]

detri·ted, a. (geol.). Disintegrated, formed as detritus. [DETRITUS as p.p. + -ED¹]

detrĭ·tion, n. Wearing away by rubbing. [f. L *detrit-* see DETRIMENT, -ION]

detrī·tus, n. Matter produced by detrition, as gravel, sand, silt; debris. Hence **detri·t**AL a. [wrong use of L *detritus -ūs* = wearing down for *detritum* neut. p.p. see DETRIMENT]

de trop (de trō·), pred. a. Not wanted, unwelcome, in the way. [F]

deuce¹, n. The two at dice or cards; (Tennis) state of score (40 all, games all) at which either party must gain two consecutive points or games to win. [f. F *deux* f. L *duos* nom. *-o* two]

deuce², n. Plague, mischief; the devil (*d. take it*; *who, where, what*, &c., *the d.?*; *the d. is in it if I cannot*, I certainly can; *play the d. with*, spoil, ruin; *the d. to pay*, trouble to be expected; *a d. of a* mess; *d. knows*; *d. a bit*, not at all; *the d. he isn't*, it is incredible that he is not). [perh. = prec., the two at dice being the worst throw; cf. G *daus* in same sense]

deu·cĕd (dū-, dōō-), a. & adv. Confounded(ly); great (*in a d. hurry*). Hence **deu·ced**LY² adv. [-ED²]

dē·us ex mā·chĭnā (-k-), n. Power, event, that comes in the nick of time to solve difficulty, providential interposition, esp. in novel or play. [L, = god from the machinery (by which in ancient theatre gods were shown in air)]

Dē·us mĭsereā·tur (-zĕrĭ-), n. The canticle God be merciful. [L]

deuteragō·nist (*also* -ă·go-), n. Person of next importance to PROTAGONIST in drama. [f. Gk *deuteragōnistēs* (foll., *agōnistēs* actor)]

deutero-, comb. form of Gk *deuteros* second, as *d.-Isaiah,* supposed later author of *Is.* xl–lxvi, *d.-canonical* of Bible books, admitted later to Canon, *deuterogamy,* second marriage.

Deuterŏ·nomist, n. Author, joint-authors, or compiler, of *Deuteronomy.* [-IST]

Deutero·nomy (*also* dū·-), n. Fifth book of Pentateuch. Hence **Deuterono·m**IC(AL) aa. [f. L f. Gk DEUTERO(*nomion* f. *nomos* law) second book of law]

deu·tzia (dū-, doi-), n. White-flowered shrub. [J. *Deutz* 1781, -IA[1]]

deux-temps (F), n. Kind of waltz more rapid than the trois-temps. [F, =two-time]

dĕ·vastāte, v.t. Lay waste, ravage. Hence or cogn. **devast**A·TION, **de·vastā**TOR[2], nn. [f. L DE(*vastare* f. *vastus* waste), -ATE[3]]

devĕ·lop, v.t. & i. Unfold (t. & i.), reveal, bring or come from a latent to an active or visible state; (Mil.) open (an attack); make or become fuller, more elaborate or systematic, or bigger; (Photog.) treat (plate, film) so as to make picture visible; make progress; exhibit (*has developed a tendency to*), come or bring to maturity. Hence **deve·lop**ABLE a., **deve·lop**ER[1] (1, 2) n. [f. F *développer* etym. dub.; cf. It. *viluppo* wrapping]

deve·lopment, n. Gradual unfolding, fuller working out; growth; evolution (of animal & plant races); well-grown state; stage of advancement; product; more elaborate form; developing of photograph; *D. Commission,* public body set up in 1909 & provided with funds from which grants may be made in aid of schemes for the improvement of agriculture, stock-breeding, industrial processes, &c. [-MENT]

developme·ntal, a. Incidental to growth, (*d. diseases*); evolutionary. Hence **deve·lopme·ntal**LY[2] adv. [-AL]

dē·viate, v.i. Turn aside, diverge, (*from* course, rule, truth, &c., or abs.), digress. [f. L DE(*viare* f. *via* way), -ATE[3]]

devia·tion, n. In vbl senses; esp.; deflexion of compass-needle by iron in ship &c.; divergence of optic axis from normal position. [-ATION]

devi·ce, n. Make, look, (archaic; *things of rare, strange, d.*); (pl.) fancy, will, (*left to* one's *own dd.*); plan, scheme, trick; contrivance, invention, thing adapted for a purpose; drawing, design, figure; emblematic or heraldic design; motto. [ME & OF *devis, devise,* f. L *divisum, -a,* neut. & fem. p.p. of *dividere* DIVIDE]

dĕ·vil[1] (-vl), n. *The D.,* supreme spirit of evil, tempter of mankind, enemy of God, Satan; heathen god; evil spirit possessing demoniac; superhuman malignant being; wicked or cruel person; mischievously energetic, clever, knavish, or self-willed person, luckless or wretched person (usu. *poor d.*); vicious animal; junior legal counsel working for a leader (*Attorney-General's d.,* junior Counsel to Treasury); literary hack doing what his employer takes the credit and pay for; *printer's d.,* errand-boy in printing-office; personified evil quality (*the d. of greed* &c.); fighting-spirit, energy or dash in attack; (name of) kinds of animal, bird, firework, & implement; highly seasoned dish, esp. devilled bones. Phrases (see also those in DEUCE[2], in all of which *d.* may be substituted): *a d. of a—,* one of an unwelcome or remarkable or amusing kind; *— is the d.,* a great difficulty or nuisance; *like the d.,* with great energy &c.; *go to the d.,* be ruined, (imperat.) be off; *the d.!,* excl. of annoyance or surprise; *d. a one,* not one; *the d. & all,* everything bad; *between the d. & the deep sea,* in a dilemma; *dd.-on-horseback,* see ANGEL; *d. take the hindmost* (motto of selfish competition); *give the d. his* DUE; *the d. to pay,* trouble ahead; *talk of the d.* (*& he will appear*), said when one comes just after being mentioned; *the d. among the tailors,* row, disturbance; *d. on two sticks,* older name for DIABOLO; *d.'s advocate, -acy* (one who puts) the d.'s case against canonization, (transf.) depreciator, depreciation; *d.'s bedpost,* four of clubs; *d.'s bones,* dice; *d.'s books,* cards; *D.'s Own,* 88th Foot, Inns of Court Volunteers; *d.'s* TATTOO; *devil's* in many plant-names, esp. *d.'s-bit,* kind of scabious; *d.'s coach-horse,* large cocktail beetle; *d.'s dust,* shoddy. *D.-dodger,* preacher, parson; *d.-fish,* name of many kinds; *d.-may-care,* reckless, rollicking. Hence **de·vil**DOM, **de·vil**HOOD, nn., **de·vil**WARD(S) adv. [OE *déofol* (perh. f. L) f. Gk *diabolos* slanderer (*diaballō* slander f. *dia* through, *ballō* throw)]

de·vil[2], v.i. & t. (-ll-). Work as lawyer's or author's d. (usu. *for* principal); grill with hot condiments. [f. prec.]

de·vilish, a. (-vĭl-), & adv. (-vl-). Like, worthy of, the devil, damnable; hence **de·vilish**LY[2] adv., **de·vilish**NESS n. (Adv.) very. [-ISH[1]]

de·vilism (-vĭl-), n. Devilish quality or conduct; worship of devils. [-ISM]

de·vilment (-vl-), n. Mischief, wild spirits; devilish or strange phenomenon. [-MENT]

de·vilry (-vl-), **-try,** n. Diabolical art,

magic; the devil and his works; wickedness, cruelty; reckless mischief, daring, or hilarity; demonology; devils. [(-*try* corrupt. of) -RY]

dē·vious, a. Remote, sequestered; winding, circuitous, erratic; erring. Hence **de·vious**LY[2] adv., **de·vious**NESS n. [f. L DE(*vius* f. *via* way) + -OUS]

devi·se (-z), v.t., & n. (Law) assign, give, (realty; cf. BEQUEATH) by will (n., this act, clause effecting it), whence **devi·**SOR[2], **devis**EE·, nn.; plan, contrive, invent, plot, scheme, (thing, *how*, or abs.). Hence or cogn. **devi·**SABLE a., **devi·**SER[2] (4), n. [f. OF *deviser* f. LL frequent. of L *dividere -is-* DIVIDE]

dēvī·talize, v.t. Make lifeless or effete. Hence **devitaliz**A·TION n. [DE-]

dēvĭ·trify, v.t. Deprive of vitreous quality, make (glass or vitreous rock) opaque & crystalline. Hence **devitri**FICA·TION n. [DE-]

devoi·d, a. Destitute, empty, *of*. [short p.p. of obs. *devoid* f. OF DE(*vuidier* f. *vide* VOID)]

dĕ·voir (-vwar), n. Duty, one's best, (*do* one's *d.*); (pl.) courteous attentions (*pay* one's *dd. to*). [ME *dever* f. OF *deveir* f. L *debēre* owe]

dē·volute (-ōōt), v.t. Transfer by devolution, depute, (work). [f. L p.p. st. see DEVOLVE]

dēvolu·tion (-lōō-), n. Descent through a series of changes; descent of property by due succession; lapse of unexercised right to ultimate owner; (Biol.) degradation of species (cf. EVOLUTION); deputing, delegation, of work or power (esp. by House of Parliament to its committees). [f. med. L *devolutio* (foll., -ION)]

devo·lve, v.t. & i. Throw (duty, work), (of duties) be thrown, fall, descend, *upon* (deputy, or one who must act for want of others); descend, fall by succession, (*to*, *upon*, or abs.). [f. L DE(*volvere volut-* roll)]

Devō·nian, a. & n. (Native) of Devonshire; (Geol.) (of) the formation lying above the Silurian & below the Carboniferous. [-IAN]

De·vonshire, n. *D.* (i.e. clotted) *cream*.

devo·te, v.t. Consecrate, dedicate, give up exclusively, (one*self*, another, thing, esp. abilities &c.) *to* (God, person, pursuit, purpose); give over to destruction &c. Hence **devo·te**MENT n. [f. L DE(*vovēre vot-* vow)]

devo·ted, a. In vbl senses; esp.: zealously loyal (*d. friend*), whence **devo·ted**LY[2] adv.; doomed (esp. *d. head*). [-ED[1]]

dĕvotee·, n. Votary *of*, one devoted *to*; zealously or fanatically pious person. [-EE]

devo·tion, n. Devoutness; devoting; divine worship, (pl.) prayers, praying, (*was at his dd.*), whence **devo·tion**AL a., **devo·tional**LY[2] adv., **devo·tional**ISM(3), **devo·tional**IST(2), nn.; enthusiastic addiction or loyalty (*to*, or abs.). [OF (*-cion*) f. L *devotionem* (DEVOTE, -ION)]

devour· (-owr), v.t. Eat (of beasts); eat like a beast or ravenously; (bibl.) consume recklessly, waste, destroy, pillage, (substance, property, or its owners); kill, decimate, (of fire, sword, plague, &c.); engulf; take in greedily with ears or eyes (book, story, beauty or beautiful person); absorb the attention of (*devoured by anxiety*); (poet.) *d. the way* &c., go fast, esp. of horses. Hence **devour·ing**LY[2] adv. [f. OF *devorer* f. L DE(*vorare* swallow)]

devou·t (-owt), a. Reverential, religious, pious, (of person, act, &c.), whence **devou·t**NESS n.; earnest, hearty, genuine. Hence **devou·t**LY[2] adv. [f. OF *devot* f. L p.p. (DEVOTE)]

dew[1], n. Atmospheric vapour condensed in small drops on cool surfaces from evening to morning; freshness, refreshing or gently stealing influence, (usu. *of* sleep, eloquence, youth, music, &c.); any beaded or glistening moisture, esp. tears, sweat; *mountain d.*, illicitly distilled whisky; *dewberry*, kind of blackberry; *d.-claw*, rudimentary inner toe of some dogs; *d.-drop*; *d.-fall*, time when d. begins to form, evening; *d.-point*, temperature at which it forms; *d.-rake*, for surface of grass or stubble; *d.-ret* v.t., RET by exposure to d. instead of steeping in water; *d.-worm*, large garden worm. Hence **dew·**LESS, **dew·**Y[2], aa., **dew·i**LY[2] adv., **dew·i**NESS n. [OE *déaw*, com.-Teut. cf. Du. *dauw*, G *tau*]

dew[2], v.t. & i. (Impers.) form or fall as d. (*it is beginning to d.*); bedew, moisten. [ME *dewen* as prec.]

dew·lap, n. Fold of loose skin hanging from throat of cattle (& transf. of other animals or men). Hence **dew·lapp**ED[2] a. [*dew-* of doubtful etym. & sense, cf. Da. *doglæb*; *-lap* f. OE *læppa* skirt, lobe]

de·xter, a. Of or on the right-hand side (in Heraldry, to the spectator's left). [L, comparative (cf. -THER) f. *dex-* cf. Gk *dexios*, Goth. *taihswa*, Skr. *daksha*]

dextĕ·rity, n. Manual or mental adroitness, skill, neatness of handling; right-handedness, using of right hand. [f. L DEXTER*itas* -ITY)]

de·xtrin, n. (chem.). Soluble gummy substance obtained from starch & used on adhesive stamps &c. [as foll. + -IN]

dextro-, comb. form of L DEXTER, esp. in terms concerned w. chem. property of causing plane of polarized light ray to rotate to right (opp. LAEVO-, which see for compounds).

de·xtrose, n. (chem.). Dextro-rotatory form of glucose. [prec., -OSE[2]]

de·xtrous, -ter-, a. Neat-handed, deft; mentally adroit, clever; using right hand by preference. Hence **de·xt(e)rous**LY[2] adv. [DEXTER + -OUS; *-tr-* correct but less common]

Dey (dā), n. (hist.). Commander of janizaries at Algiers; governor of Algiers or Tripoli. [F, f. Turk. *dāī* maternal uncle]

d(h)ow (dow), n. Single-masted Arabian-Sea ship of about 200 tons; any Arab ship, esp. as used in E.-Afr. slave-trading. [etym. dub.; spelling *dow* more correct but rare]

d(h)u·rrie, n. Indian rectangular fringed cotton carpet used for sofa-covers, curtains, &c. [f. Hind. *dari*; spelling as prec.]

di-[1], pref. Form of L DIS- (which see for meaning) used before *b, d, l, m, n, r, s* + cons., *v*, usu. *g*, & sometimes *j*. In LL & Rom. often replaced by *dis-* (so *dismiss*), in OF & ME often varying with *de-* (so *defer*[1] f. L *differre*). Not a living pref. in E.

di-[2], pref. f. Gk *di-* = *dis* twice, two-, double-. In many E wds, & as living pref. in Chem. with various special uses.

di-[3], pref. = foll. before vowel.

di(a)-, pref. f. Gk prep. or pref. *dia* through, thorough(ly), apart, across. In Gk words taken direct, or through L or F & L; also in many scientific words made with Gk elements or on Gk analogy.

dīabē·tēs, n. Disease with excessive glucose-charged urine, thirst, & emaciation. [L f. Gk, f. DIA(*bainō* go)]

diabē·tic, a. & n. Of diabetes; (person) suffering from diabetes. [f. F *diabétique* f. L *diabeticus* (prec., -IC)]

dia·blerie (-ah-), n. Devil's business; sorcery; wild recklessness; devil-lore. [F (*diable* f. L *diabolus* DEVIL, -RY)]

dīabŏ·lic(al), aa. Of, having to do with, proceeding from, externally like, the devil (usu. *-ic*); fiendish, atrociously cruel or wicked, (usu. *-ical*). Hence **diabo·lical**LY[2] adv. [f. F *diabolique* f. L f. Gk *diabolikos* (DEVIL, -IC) + -AL]

dīă·bolism, n. Sorcery; devilish conduct or nature; belief in or worship of the devil. [f. Gk *diabolos* DEVIL + -ISM]

dīă·bolize, v.t. Make into, represent as, a devil. [as prec. + -IZE]

dīă·bolo (*or* dĭ-), n. Game with two-headed top & sticks. [mod. fancy formation; older DEVIL *on two sticks*]

dīă·chȳlon, -chylum, (-k-), **-cūlum,** n. Sticking-plaster of litharge, olive oil, & water, on linen. [med. L (*-ylum*) f. Gk *dia khulōn* by juices; *-culum* by confus. w. -CULE]

dīă·conal, a. Of a deacon. [f. LL *diaconalis* (DEACON, -AL)]

dīă·conate (-at), n. Office of, one's time as, deacon; deacons. [f. LL (*-tus*), as DEACON, -ATE[1]]

dīacrĭ·tical, a. Distinguishing, distinctive, esp. *d. marks* used in printing to indicate different sounds of a letter, accents, diaeresis, cedilla, &c.; capable of seeing distinctions. [f. Gk DIA(*kritikos* see CRITIC) + -AL]

dīăctĭ·nic, a. Transmitting, transparent to, the actinic rays. [DI-[3], Gk *aktis -inos* ray, -IC]

dīade·lphous, a. (bot.). With stamens united in two bundles (cf. MONADELPHOUS, POLY*adelphous*). [DI-[2], Gk *adelphos* brother]

di·adĕm, n. Crown, or plain or jewelled fillet, as badge of sovereignty; wreath of leaves or flowers worn round head; sovereignty; crowning distinction or glory. Hence **di·adem**ED[2] a. [f. 13th-c. F *dyademe* f. L f. Gk DIA(*dēma* f. *deō* bind, -M)]

diaer·esis (dīēr-), n. (pl. *-esēs*). Mark (as in *aërate*) over second of two vowels indicating that they are not one sound. [L, f. Gk *diairesis* (DI-[3], *haireō* take) separation]

dīagno·se (-z), v.t. Determine from symptoms the nature of (a disease). [f. foll.]

dīagno·sis, n. (pl. *-osēs*). Identification of disease by means of patient's symptoms &c., formal statement of this; classification of person's character, assignment of species &c. [L f. Gk (DIA-, *gignōskō* recognize)]

dīagnŏ·stic, a. & n. Of, assisting, diagnosis; symptom. Hence **diagno·st**ICS n., **diagno·st**ICALLY adv., **diagnost**I·CIAN n. [f. Gk DIA(*gnōstikos* f. *gnōstos* known, prec., -IC)]

dīă·gonal, a. & n. (Straight line) joining two non-adjacent angles of rectilineal figure or solid contained by planes; obliquely placed like the d. of a parallelogram (*d. row* or *d.*, as of the squares of the same colour on chess-board), inclined at other than a right angle, having some part so inclined (*d. cloth* or *d.*, twilled with ridges oblique to the lists). Hence **dia·gonal**LY[2] adv. [f. L *diagonalis* f. Gk DIA(*gōnios* f. *gōnia* angle), -AL]

di·agram, n. (Geom.) figure made of lines used in proving &c.; sketch showing the features of an object needed for exposition; symbolic representation, by lines, of process, force, &c. Hence or cogn. **diagrammă·t**IC a., **diagramma·t**ICALLY adv., **diagra·mmat**IZE(1) v.t. [f. F *diagramme* f. L f. Gk DIA(*gramma -atos* f. *graphō* write, -M)]

di·agraph, n. Instrument for drawing projections, enlarging maps, &c., mechanically. [f. F *diagraphe* (prec., -GRAPH)]

di·al, n., & v.t. (-ll-). (Usu. *sun-d.*) instrument showing hour by sun's shadow on graduated plate; (also *d.-plate*) face of clock or watch; plate in steam-gauge, gas-meter, &c., on which pressure, consumption, &c., are indicated by index-finger; (vb) measure, indicate, (as) with

d. [prob. f. med. L (*rota*) *dialis* daily (wheel) f. L *dies* day, -AL; hardly found outside E]

di·alect, n. Form of speech peculiar to a district, class, or person, subordinate variety of a language with distinguishable vocabulary, pronunciation, or idioms. Hence **diale·ct**AL a., **diale·ct-al**LY[2] adv., **dialecto·**LOGY, **dialecto·**LO-GIST, nn. [f. L f. Gk *dialektos* f. DIA-*legomai* converse]

diale·ctic[1], n. (often in pl.). Art of investigating the truth of opinions, testing of truth by discussion, logical disputation; (Mod. Philos.; not in pl.) criticism dealing with metaphysical contradictions & their solutions. So **dialect-i·**CIAN n. [f. OF *dialectique* f. L f. Gk *dialektikē* (*tekhnē* art) of debate (prec., -IC)]

diale·ctic[2], a. & n. Logical, of disputation; (person) skilled in critical inquiry by discussion; =DIALECT*al*. [f. L f. Gk *dialektikos* (-IC)]

diale·ctical, a. =DIALECTIC[2] (adj.); = DIALECT*al*; belonging to DIALECTIC[1] in mod.-philos. sense. Hence **diale·ct-ical**LY[2] adv. [-AL]

dialŏ·gic (-j-), a. In, of, dialogue. [f. med. L *dialogicus* (DIALOGUE, -IC)]

diă·logist (-j-), n. Speaker in, writer of, dialogue. [f. L f. Gk *dialogistēs* (foll., -IST)]

di·alogue (-ŏg), n. Conversation; piece of written work in conversational form, this kind of composition (*written in d.*); the conversational part in a novel. Hence **di·alogue-**WISE adv. [f. 13th-c. F *dialoge* f. L f. Gk *dialogos* (DIA*legomai* converse)]

diă·lȳsis, n. (pl. *-ysēs*). Parting of colloid from crystalloid parts of mixture by filtration through parchment floating in water. Hence **di·alȳse** (-z), v.t. [f. Gk DIA(*lusis* f. *luō* loose)]

dialȳ·tic, a. (chem.). Of, by, dialysis. [f. Gk DIA(*lutikos* f. *lutos* loosed f. *luō* loose, -IC)]

diamagnĕ·tic, a. & n. Tending to lie E. & W., across the magnetic axis, when suspended freely & acted on by magnetism; of d. bodies or diamagnetism; a d. body or substance. Hence **diamagne·t-**ICALLY adv., **diama·gnet**IZE(3) v.t. [DIA-]

diama·gnetism, n. Diamagnetic tendency; the diamagnetic branch of magnetism. [DIA-]

diamanté (F), a. & n. (Material) scintillating with powdered crystal &c. [F, see DIAMOND]

diamantī·ferous, a. Diamond-yielding. [f. F *diamant* DIAMOND, -I-, -FEROUS]

diă·meter, n. Straight line passing from side to side of any body or geom. figure through centre (with special geom. applications for curves), transverse measurement, width, thickness; unit of linear measurement of magnifying-power (*lens magnifying 2000 dd.*). So **dia·-metr**AL a., **dia·metral**LY[2] adv. [f. OF *diametre* f. L f. Gk DIA*metros* (*grammē* line) measuring across f. *metron* measure]

diame·trical, a. Of, along, a diameter, diametral; (of opposition, difference, &c.) direct, complete, like that between opposite ends of diameter. Hence **dia-me·trical**LY[2] adv. [f. Gk *diametrikos* (prec., -IC) + -AL]

di·amond, n., a., & v.t. Colourless or tinted precious stone of pure carbon crystallized in octahedrons & allied forms, harder than any other known substance (cut into TABLE, ROSE, & BRILLIANT[2]; *Bristol, Cornish,* &c., *d.*, kinds of rock crystal; *black d.*, dark-coloured d., coal; *rough d.*, not yet cut, person of intrinsic worth but rough manners; *d. cut d.*, of persons well matched in wit or cunning); glittering particle or point; (usu. *glazier's* or *cutting d.*) tool with small d. for glass-cutting; figure shaped like section of d., rhomb (*d. panes*, small panes so shaped set in lead), playing-card bearing this (*dd.*, the suit; *a small d.*, one of lower cards); a printing TYPE; *d.-back*, kinds of moth & turtle; *d. cement*, for setting dd.; *d.-drill*, set with dd. for boring hard substance; *d.-field*, tract yielding dd.; *d.-point*, d.-tipped stylus used in engraving, (usu. pl.) place where two lines or rails intersect obliquely; *d.-snake*, Australian & Tasmanian kinds; *d. wedding*, 60th anniversary; hence **diamondi·**FEROUS a., **di·amond-**WISE adv. (Adj.) made of, set with, d. or dd., rhomb-shaped. (Vb) adorn with dd., dewdrops, &c. [ME & OF *diamant* f. LL *diamantem* nom. *-as* f. L f. Gk *adamas* ADAMANT]

Dīā·na, n. Horsewoman, lady who hunts; woman bent on remaining single. [L, goddess of the chase]

dīapā·son (-zn), n. Combination of notes or parts in harmonious whole; melody, strain, esp. grand swelling burst of harmony; compass of voice or intrument; range, scope; fixed standard of musical pitch; *open, closed* or *stopped, d.*, two principal foundation-stops in organ. [L, f. Gk DIA *pasōn* (*khordōn*) through all (strings) f. *pas* all]

di·aper, n., & v.t. Linen fabric with small diamond pattern; baby's napkin of this; sanitary towel; ornamental design of diamond reticulation for panels, walls, &c. (vb, decorate with this). [f. OF *diapre* f. Byzant. Gk *diaspros* adj. f. DIA-, *aspros* white]

diă·phanous, a. Transparent. [f. med. L *diaphanus* f. Gk DIA(*phanēs* -showing f. *phainō* show) + -OUS]

diaphorĕ·tic, a. & n. (Drug, treatment) productive of perspiration. [f. L f. Gk *diaphorētikos* f. DIA(*phoreō* carry f. *pherō*), -ETIC]

di·aphragm (-ăm), n. Muscular & tendinous partition separating thorax from abdomen in mammals; partition in shell-fish, plant tissues, & various instruments, esp., in optics, telephony, & wireless, disk pierced with circular hole. So **diaphragmă·**TIC (-gm-) a. [f. L f. Gk DIA(*phragma -atos* f. *phrassō* hedge in, -M)]

di·archy (-kĭ), **dy-**, n. Government by two independent authorities, esp. the reformed Indian constitution started in 1921. [DI-[2], Gk *archō* rule; *dy-* less correct]

di·arist, n. One who keeps a diary. Hence **diari·st**IC a. [DIARY + -IST]

di·arize, v.i. & t. Keep, enter in, a diary. [DIARY, -IZE]

diarrhoea (dīarē·*a*), n. Excessive looseness of bowels. Hence **diarrhoe·**AL, **diarrhoe·**IC, aa. [L, f. Gk DIA(*rrhoia* f. *rheō* flow)]

di·ary, n. Daily record of events, journal; book prepared for keeping this in; calendar with daily memoranda esp. for persons of a particular profession. Hence **diār·**IAL a. [f. L *diarium* (*dies* day, -ARY[1])]

di·astase, n. (chem.). A ferment converting starch to sugar, important in digestion. So **diasta·tic,** (irreg.) **-a·sic,** aa. [f. Gk *diastasis* separation (DIA-, *histēmi* set)]

dia·stolĕ, n. Dilatation of heart or artery alternating with systole, & with it forming pulse (*systole & d.* often fig. of reaction, fluctuation, &c.). [med. L f. Gk, f. DIA(*stellō* send)]

dīate·ssaron, n. Harmony of the four gospels. [OF, f. L f. Gk *dia tessarōn* by four]

dīather·mancy, n., **diather·manous, diather·mic,** aa. (Having the) quality of transmitting radiant heat. [f. F *diathermansie, diathermane* + -OUS, *diathermique*, f. Gk DIA(*thermansis* f. *thermainō* f. *thermos* warm)]

dīă·thesis, n. (med.; pl. *-esēs*). Constitutional predisposition. [Gk, f. DIA-(*tithēmi* place)]

di·atŏm, n. Member of genus *Diatoma*. microscopic unicellular Algae found esp. at bottom of sea & forming fossil deposits. So **diatom**A·CEOUS a. [f. Gk DIA(*tomos* f. *temnō* cut) alluding to the cells' being connected in easily separable chains]

dīatŏ·mic, a. (chem.). Consisting of two atoms; having two replaceable atoms of hydrogen. [DI-[2], ATOM, -IC]

dīatŏ·nic, a. (mus.). (Of scale) proceeding by notes proper to key without chromatic alteration; (of melodies & harmonies) constructed from such a scale. [f. F *diatonique* f. L f. Gk DIA(*tonikos* TONIC) with intervals of a tone]

di·atribe, n. Piece of bitter criticism, invective, denunciation. [F, f. L f. Gk (*-ē*) = wearing away of time, discourse, f. DIA(*tribō* rub)]

dib, v.i. = DAP. [var. of DAB, whence also *dap*]

dībā·sic, a. (chem.). Having two bases or two atoms of a base. [DI-[2], BASE[1]]

di·bber, n. Instrument for dibbling, dibble. [f. DIB, now used thus only in *dibbing-stick*]

di·bble, n., & v.t. & i. Instrument for making holes in ground for seeds &c. (Vb) prepare (soil) with this; sow or plant thus; use a d. [perh. f. DIB + -LE(1), but found much earlier]

dibs, n. pl. (Child's game with) sheep's knuckle-bones; counters at cards; (slang) money. [prob. f. DIB; cf. earlier *dibstones*]

dĭ·cast, dica·stery, nn. (Gk Antiq.). (Member of) Athenian jury (*-ery*), which gave both verdict & sentence. [f. Gk *dikastēs, dikastērion,* (*dikazō* to judge f. *dikē* right)]

dice[1], n. pl. See DIE[1].

dice[2], v.i. & t. Play DICE[1], whence **di·**CER[1] n.; gamble *away* at dice; chequer, mark with squares. [f. prec.]

di·ce-box, n. Box of hour-glass shape from which dice are thrown; *d. insulator*, piece of porcelain so shaped supporting telegraph wire.

dīchlamў·deous, a. (bot.). Having calyx & corolla. [DI-[2], Gk *khlamus -udos* cloak, -EOUS]

dīchŏ·gamous (-k-), a. (bot.). Having stamens & pistils that mature at different times, so that self-fertilization is impossible. [f. Gk *dikho-* asunder, *-gamos* -married]

dīchŏ·tomy (-k-), n. Division into two; binary classification; (Bot. & Zool.) repeated bifurcation. So **dichotŏ·mic**, **dicho·tom**OUS, aa., **dichŏ·tom**IST(1) n., **dicho·tom**IZE(1, 3) v.t. & i., **dicho·tom**OUSLY[2] adv. [as prec., -TOMY]

dīchro·ic, a. Showing two colours (esp. of doubly refracting crystals). [f. Gk DI[2](*khroos* f. *khrōs* colour) + -IC]

dīchromă·tic, a. Two-coloured (esp. of animal species of which individuals show different colorations). [DI-[2] + Gk *khrōmatikos* (*khrōma -atos* colour, -IC)]

dīchrō·mic, a. With only two colours (esp. of colour-blind vision seeing two of three primary colours). [Gk *dikhrōmos* (prec.) + -IC]

dick, n. (slang). *Take* one's *d. that* or *to it*, swear, affirm. [prob. for *declaration*]

di·ckens, n. (colloq.). Devil, deuce. [from 1598; prob. use of *Dickon* = Richard, or the surname *Dickens*, as alliterative substitute for *devil*]

di·cker[1], n. (commerc.). Half-score, ten, esp. of hides. [ME *dyker* cf. G *decher* f. L *decuria* set of ten (*decem*)]

di·cker[2], v.i. (U.S.). Trade by barter, chaffer, haggle. [prob. f. prec. through the barter in skins with Indians]

di·cky[1], **-ey,** n. (colloq. & slang). Donkey;

(also *d.-bird*) small bird; false shirt-front; pinafore or apron; driver's seat; servant's seat at back of carriage. [etym. dub.; some senses f. the male name]
di·cky², a. (slang). Unsound, shaky. [?]
dīcotylē·don, n. Flowering plant with two cotyledons. Hence **dicotyle·don**OUS a. [DI-²]
di·ctaphone, n. Machine recording, for subsequent reproduction in type, what is spoken into it. [proprietary name, f. foll. + PHONE¹]
di·ctate¹, n. Authoritative direction (usu. *of* reason, conscience, nature, &c.; often pl.). [f. L *dictatum* neut. p.p. see foll.]
dicta·te², v.t. & i. Say or read aloud (matter to be written down, often *to* writer; also abs.); prescribe, lay down authoritatively, (terms, thing to be done; of person, also of motive &c.); lay down the law, give orders, (*will not be dictated to*). So **dict**A·TION n. [f. L *dictare* frequent. of *dicere dict-* say, -ATE³]
dicta·tor, n. Absolute ruler, usu. temporary or irregular, of a State, esp. one who suppresses or succeeds a republican government; person with absolute authority in any sphere; one who dictates to writer. Hence **dicta·tor**SHIP, **dicta·tr**ESS¹, nn. [L (prec., -OR²)]
dictator·ial, a. Of dictator; imperious, overbearing. Hence **dictator·ial**LY² adv. [f. L *dictatorius* f. prec. + -AL]
di·ction, n. Wording & phrasing, verbal style. [f. L *dictio* (*dicere dict-* say, -ION)]
di·ctionary, n. Book dealing, usu. in alphabetical order, with the words of a language or of some special subject, author, &c., wordbook, lexicon, (*French-English* &c. *d.*, of French &c. words with English &c. explanation; *d. of architecture* or *the Bible, Shakspere d.*, &c.); *walking* or *living d.*, well-informed person; *d. English, style*, &c., over-correct, pedantic. [f. med. L *dictionarium* (prec., -ARY¹)]
di·ctum, n. (pl. *-a, -ums*). Formal saying, pronouncement; (Law) judge's expression of opinion not having legal validity; maxim, current saying. [L, neut. p.p. of *dicere* say]
did. See DO.
dida·ctic (*or* dī-), a. Meant to instruct; having the manner of a teacher. Hence **dida·cti**CALLY adv., **dida·ctici**SM n. [f. Gk *didaktikos* (*didaskō* teach)]
dī·dapper, n. Small diving water-fowl. [for *dive-dapper* f. earlier *divedap* f. OE *dufedoppa* (*dúfan* dive + *doppa* cf. *dip*)]
di·ddle, v.t. (slang). Cheat, swindle. [perh. back-formation f. *Jeremy Diddler* in Kenney's *Raising the Wind*, 1803]
didst. 2 sing. past of DO.
dĭdy·mium, n. (chem.). A rare metal. [f. Gk *didumos* twin + -IUM (from its being always found with lanthanum)]
die¹, n. (pl. *dice, dies*). 1. (Pl. *dice*) small cube with faces bearing 1–6 spots used in games of chance; *dice*, game played with these; *the d. is cast*, course irrevocably decided; *upon the d.*, at stake; *as straight, true, as a d.* 2. (Pl. *dies*): (Arch.) plinth, cubic part of pedestal between base & cornice; engraved stamp for coining, striking medal, embossing paper, &c.; *d.-sinker*, engraver of dd. [ME & OF *de* f. L *datum* neut. p.p. of *dare* give, perh. in sense *what is given by fate*; for pl. *dice* (perh. felt as collective) cf. *pence*, the orig. pl. *truce*, also *mice* &c.]
die², v.i. (dying). Cease to live, expire, (*of* illness, hunger, &c., *by* violence, the sword, one's own hand, *from* wound &c., *through* neglect, *on* scaffold, *at* the stake, *in* battle, *for* friend, cause, &c., *in* poverty; *d. a beggar, martyr*; *d. a glorious, dog's, death*; *d. the death*, be put to death, archaic or playful; *d. game*, fighting, not tamely; *d. hard*, not without struggle; *d. in* one's *bed*, of age or illness, *in* one's *shoes*, by violence, *in harness*, while still at work, *in last ditch*, desperately defending something; *never say d.*, not give in, keep up courage); (bibl.) suffer as in death (*I d. daily*), suffer spiritual death, *d. unto*, escape thraldom of (sin); *be dying for, to* do, have great desire; *d. of laughing*, laugh to exhaustion; (of plants &c.) lose vital force, decay; come to an end, cease to exist, go out, disappear, be forgotten, fade away, (of flame, fame, sound, &c.; *secret dies with* one; often *away, down, off, out*); *die-away* adj., languishing; *d.-hard*, person who dies hard or resists compulsion &c. to the last, obstinate politician &c.; *Die-hards*, 57th Regiment of Foot. [ME *deghen* perh. f. ON *deyja* cf. OHG *touwan* f. OTeut. *daw-j-an*]
dīēle·ctric, a. & n. Insulating (medium or substance), non-conductive, non-conductor. [DI-³ + ELECTRIC = through which electricity is transmitted (without conduction)]
dī·ēs īr·ae, n. Day of Judgement; Latin hymn beginning so. [L, = day of wrath]
dī·ēs nŏn, n. (Law) day on which no legal business is done; (transf.) day that does not count or cannot be used. [L, short for *d. n. juridicus* non-judicial day]
di·et¹ (-et), n., & v.t. Way of feeding; prescribed course of food, regimen, whence **diet**AR·IAN (-ār-) n.; one's habitual food; (vb) feed (person, one*self*) on special food as medical regimen or punishment. [f. OF *diete*(*r*) f. L f. Gk *diaita* way of life perh. f. *zaō* live]
di·et², n. Conference, congress, on national or international business; meeting of the estates of the realm or confederation (esp. as Engl. name for foreign parliamentary assemblies). [f. med. L *dieta* assembly, day's work; prob. f. *diaeta* DIET¹ confused with *dies* day]

di·etary, n. & a. (Course) of diet; allowance or character of food in hospital, workhouse, &c. [f. L *diaetarius -um* (DIET[1], -ARY[1])]
dīĕtĕ·tic, a. Of diet. Hence **diete·tic**S n., **diete·tic**ALLY adv. [f. L f. Gk *diaitētikos* (*diaitēt-* f. *diaitaō* vb f. *diaita* DIET[1], -IC)]
dif-, pref. = DIS- before *f* in L wds. Sometimes changed in OF to *de-* (*defy, defer*[1]).
di·ffer, v.i. Be unlike; be distinguishable *from*; be at variance, disagree, (*from, with*, or abs.; *agree to d.*, give up attempt to convince each other). [f. F *différer* (cf. DEFER[1]) f. L DIF(*ferre* bear, tend)]
di·fference, n., & v.t. Being different, dissimilarity, non-identity (DISTINCTION *without d.*); point in which things differ; quantity by which amounts differ, remainder after subtraction, (*split the d.*, come to compromise); change in price of stocks &c. between certain dates (*pay, meet, the d.*); disagreement in opinion, dispute, quarrel; characteristic mark distinguishing individual or species, differentia (vb, serve as distinguishing mark of, differentiate); *make a d. between*, treat differently; *it makes a great d.*, is important. [f. F *différence* f. L *differentia* (foll., -ENCE)]
di·fferent, a. Not the same, unlike, of other nature, form, or quality, (*from, to, than*, all used by good writers past and present, *than* chiefly where a prep. is inconvenient). Hence **di·fferent**LY[2] adv. [f. F *différent* f. L *different-* part. st. (DIFFER, -ENT)]
differe·ntia (-shĭa), n. (pl. *-ae*). Distinguishing mark, esp. of species. [L, see DIFFERENCE]
differe·ntial (-shl), a. & n. Of, exhibiting, depending on, a difference (*d. duties, charges, tariff*, that differ according to circumstances); constituting a specific difference, distinctive, relating to specific differences (*d. diagnosis*); (Physics, Mech.) concerning the difference of two or more motions, pressures, &c. (*d. gear*, or *d.* as n., gear enabling car's hind-wheels to revolve at different speeds in rounding corners); (n., math.) infinitesimal difference between consecutive values of continuously varying quantity (*d. calculus*, method of calculating this). Hence **differe·ntial**LY[2] adv. [f. med. L *differentialis* (DIFFERENCE, -AL)]
differe·ntiate (-shĭ-), v.t. & i. Constitute the difference between, of, or in; develop (t. & i.) into unlikeness, specialize, (species, organs, functions, synonyms); discriminate, discriminate between. Hence **differenti**A·TION n. [f. med. L DIFFERENT*iare*, -ATE[3]]
di·fficile (-ēl), a. Unaccommodating, exigent, hard to deal with, persuade, &c. [F]
di·fficult, a. Hard to do or practise, troublesome, perplexing, (often *d. of access, to answer*, &c.); = prec. [perh. back-formation f. foll.]
di·fficulty (-ĭkl-), n. Being hard to do (*with d.*, often as adv. = not easily) or obscure; something hard or obscure; hindrance; embarrassment of affairs, esp. want of money; reluctance, demur, objection, (*make dd.*, be unaccommodating). [f. L DIF(*ficultas* = *facultas* FACULTY)]
di·ffidence, n. Self-distrust, excessive modesty, shyness. [f. L *diffidentia* (foll., -ENCE)]
di·ffident, a. Wanting in self-confidence, bashful. Hence **di·ffident**LY[2] adv. [f. L DIF(*fidere* trust), -ENT]
di·ffluence, n., **di·ffluent,** a. Flowing apart, becoming fluid; deliquescence, deliquescent. [f. L DIF(*fluere* flow), -ENT, -ENCE]
diffra·ct, v.t. (opt.). (Of edge of opaque body) break up (beam of light) into series of dark and light bands or coloured spectra. So **diffra·ct**ION n., **diffra·ct**IVE a., **diffra·ctive**LY[2] adv. [f. L DIF(*frangere fract-* break)]
diffu·se[1] (-s), a. Spread out, diffused, not concentrated, (of light, inflammation, &c.); not concise, long-winded. Hence **diffu·se**LY[2] adv., **diffu·se**NESS n. [f. L DIF(*fundere fus-* pour)]
diffu·se[2] (-z), v.t. & i. Send forth, shed abroad, (light, particles, heat, geniality, knowledge, rumour); (Physics) intermingle (t. & i. of gases or fluids) by diffusion, whence **diffu·s**IBLE (-z-) a., **diffusi**BI·LITY (-z-) n. Hence or cogn. **diffu·s**ION (-zhn) n., **diffu·s**IVE (-s-) a., **diffu·sive**LY[2] (-s-) adv., **diffu·sive**NESS (-s-) n. [f. L *diffus-* see prec.]
dig, v.t. & i. (*dug*, formerly also *digged*), & n. Use spade or mattock, claws, hands, or snout, in excavating or turning over ground; make research (*for* information, *into* author &c.); make way by digging *into, through, under*; excavate or turn up (ground) with spade &c.; make (hole &c.) by digging (*d. a pit for* fig., try to entrap); get by digging (potatoes); thrust (spurs, one's nails, feet, point of weapon) *into* something or *in*; poke (person *in the ribs*); *d.* (*-self, -selves*, or abs.) *in*, prepare defensive trench or pit; *d. out*, get, find, make, by digging; *d. up*, break up (fallow land). (N.) piece of digging; thrust, poke, (esp. *in the ribs*; also fig. *d. at*, remark directed against). [prob. f. F *diguer* cf. F *digue* dike; from 14th c. only, not in OE, nor directly related to *dike*]
dīga·mma, n. Sixth letter (F, in sound = w) of original Gk alphabet, later disused, but important in philology. [L f. Gk (DI-[2], GAMMA)]
di·gamy, n. Taking, having, a second spouse. Hence or cogn. **di·gam**IST(1) n., **di·gam**OUS a. [f. L f. Gk DI[2](*gamia* f. *-gamos* -married)]

dīga·stric, a. & n. (anat.). With two swelling ends (of muscles); muscle of lower jaw. [DI-², Gk *gastēr -tr-* belly, -IC]
di·gby, Di·gby chi·cken, nn. Smoked herring from Digby, Nova Scotia.
dī·gest¹ (-j-), n. Methodical compendium or summary, esp. of a body of laws (*the D.*, that compiled by order of Justinian). [f. L *digesta* neut. pl. p.p. see foll.]
dige·st², v.t. & i. Reduce into systematic form, classify; summarize; think over, arrange in the mind; prepare (food) in stomach and bowels for assimilation (intr. of food, admit of digestion; *digests well, will not d.*); (of drugs, wine, &c.) promote digestion of; assimilate (conquered territory &c.); brook, endure, be reconciled to, (insult, opinion); get mental nourishment from. Hence **dige·st**IBLE a., **digesti**BI·LITY n., **dige·stib**LY² adv. [f. L DI¹(*gerere gest-* carry) sort]
dige·ster, n. In vbl senses; esp. in cookery, stock-pot (cf. foll.). [-ER¹]
dige·stion (-stshn), n. Digesting (*hard, easy, of d.*) of physical or mental food; power of digesting (*a good, weak, d.*); long steeping in hot fluid to extract essence, stewing. [F, f. L *digestionem* (DIGEST², -ION)]
dige·stive, a. & n. Of, promoting, digestion; substance aiding digestion; ointment to promote suppuration. Hence **dige·stive**LY² adv. [F (*-if, -ive*), f. L *digestivus* (DIGEST², -IVE)]
di·gger, n. In vbl senses; also or esp.: (also *gold-d.*) one who digs or searches for gold in gold-fields; (slang) Australian; *Dd.*, N.-Amer. Indians living on roots; digging-part of various machines; (also *d.-wasp*) division of *Hymenoptera*. [-ER¹]
di·gging, n. In vbl senses; also or esp.: (pl., sometimes *a diggings*) mine or goldfield; (pl., colloq., also abbr. *digs*) lodgings. [-ING¹]
dight (dīt), v.t. (archaic, & chiefly in p.p. *dight*). Clothe, array, adorn; make ready. [common in ME, with many meanings; obs. exc. dial. f. 1670 to 1800; revived by Scott, & now as above; OE *dihtan* f. L *dictare* dictate, whence also G *dichten* write poetry]
di·git (-j-), n. Finger or toe (facet., or in Zool. or Anat.); finger's breadth; any numeral from 0 to 9; (Astron.) twelfth part of sun's or moon's diameter (in measuring eclipse). So **di·git**AL a. [f. L *digitus*]
digitā·lis (-j-), n. Medicine prepared from fox-glove. [mod. L, =fox-glove, transl. of its G name *fingerhut* thimble (DIGIT, -AL)]
di·gitate (-at), **-ated,** a. (zool., bot.). With divided fingers or toes; with deep radiating divisions. Hence **digit**A·TION n., **digita·to-** comb. form. [f. L *digitatus* (DIGIT, -ATE²)]
di·gitigrade, a. (zool.). Walking on toes, not touching ground with heel, (cf. PLANTIGRADE). [F (L *digitus*, -I-, *-gradus* -walking)]
di·gnifȳ, v.t. Make worthy; confer dignity upon, ennoble; make stately (p.p., marked by dignity, self-respecting, stately); speak of by high-flown title (*school dignified with name of college*). [f. OF *dignifier* f. med. L *dignificare* (*dignus* worthy, -FY)]
di·gnitary, n. Person holding high office, esp. ecclesiastical. [f. L as foll. + -ARY¹]
di·gnity, n. True worth, excellence, (*the d. of labour*); high estate or estimation (*beneath* one's *d.*, unfit for one to do); honourable office, rank, or title; elevation of manner, proper stateliness. [f. OF *dignete* f. L *dignitatem* (*dignus* worthy, -TY); cf. DAINTY]
dī·graph, n. Group of two letters expressing one sound, as *ch, ea.* [DI-², Gk *graphē* writing]
dīgre·ss (*or* dĭ-), v.i. Diverge from the track, stray; depart from or *from* the main subject temporarily in speech or writing. Hence or cogn. **digre·ss**ION n., **digre·ss**IVE a. [f. L DI¹(*gredi* = *gradi* walk *gress-*)]
dike, dyke, n., & v.t. Ditch; natural watercourse; low wall esp. of turf; embankment, long ridge, dam, against flooding, esp. those in Holland against sea; causeway; (fig.) barrier, obstacle, defence; (Mining & Geol.) fissure in stratum filled with deposited matter, this matter; *d.-reeve*, officer in charge of drains, sluices, & sea-banks, of fen district; (vb) provide, defend, with dike(s). [OE *dīc*, whence also *ditch*; cf. G *teich* pond]
dilă·pidate, v.t & i. Bring, come, into disrepair or decay (building, furniture, clothing, estate, fortune). [f. L DI¹(*lapidare* f. *lapis* stone) understood in E as *take stone from stone*, in L perh. *throw away like stones*]
dilapida·tion, n. Squandering; bringing or coming into, being in, disrepair; sum charged against incumbent &c. for wear & tear during his tenancy; falling away of cliffs &c., debris resulting. [f. L *dilapidatio* (prec., -ATION)]
dila·te (dī-, dĭ-), v.t. & i. Make or become wider or larger, expand, widen, enlarge, (*with dilated eyes*), whence **dila·t**ABLE a., **dilata**BI·LITY n., **dilat**A·TION (& irreg. **dila·tion**) n.; expatiate, speak or write at large (usu. *upon*). [f. F *dilater* f. L DI¹(*latare* f. *latus* wide); the L p.p. st. being *dilatat-*, *dilation* is irreg.]
dīla·tor, n. (anat.). (Also *d. muscle*) muscle that dilates an organ (cf. CONSTRICTOR). [irreg. for less used *dilatator*; see prec., -OR²]
di·latory, a. Tending to, designed to cause, given to, delay. Hence **di·latori**LY² adv., **di·latori**NESS n. [f. L *dilatorius* (DI¹*lat-* p.p. st. of *differre* DEFER¹, -ORY)]

dĭle·mma (*or* dī-), n. Argument forcing opponent to choose one of two alternatives (*horns of the d.*) both unfavourable to him; position that leaves only a choice between equal evils. So **dilemmă·tic** a. [L, f. Gk DI²(*lēmma -atos* assumption f. *lambanō* take, -M)]

dĭletta·ntĕ, n. (pl. *-ti*, pr. *-tē*) & a. Lover of the fine arts; amateur; smatterer, one who toys with subject or concentrates on nothing; hence **diletta·ntish**¹ a., **diletta·ntism**(1) n. (Adj.) trifling, not thorough, amateur. [It., f. *dilettare* f. L *delectare* DELIGHT, -ANT]

dĭ·ligence¹, n. Persistent effort or work; industrious character. [F, (DILIGENT, -ENCE)]

di·ligence² (often as F), n. Foreign public stage-coach. [F, as prec.]

dĭ·ligent, a. Hard-working, steady in application, industrious, attentive to duties. Hence **di·ligently**² adv. [F, f. L DI¹(*ligere lect-* =*legere* choose) love, take delight in, -ENT]

dill, n. Umbelliferous annual yellow-flowered herb. [OE *dili* cf. G *dill* etym. dub.]

di·lly-dălly, v.i. (colloq.). Vacillate; loiter. [redupl. of DALLY]

dĭ·lūent (*or* -ōō-), a. & n. Diluting (agent); (substance) increasing proportion of water in the blood &c. [f. L *diluere* DILUTE², -ENT]

dī·lūte¹, a. Weakened by addition of water; (of colour) washed-out, faded; (fig.) watery, watered down. [f. L *dilutus* p.p. see foll.]

dilute² (dīlōō·t, dĭ-), v.t. Reduce strength of (fluid) by adding water; diminish brilliance of (colour); water down (doctrine, zeal); *d. labour*, substitute a proportion of women or unskilled men for skilled men. So **dilu·tion** n. [f. L DI(*luere lut-* wash)]

dilu·vial (-ōō-, -ū-), a. Of a flood, esp. of the Flood in Genesis. (Geol.) *d. theory, changes*, &c., depending on general deluge or catastrophic water-action, whence **dilu·vialist**(2) n.; of the drift formation now called Glacial Drift. [f. L *diluvialis* (*diluvium* DELUGE, -AL)]

dim, a., & v.i. & t. Faintly luminous or visible; not bright, clear, or well-defined; obscure; seeing or seen, hearing or heard, apprehending or apprehended, indistinctly; hence **di·mly**² adv., **di·mmish**¹ (2) a., **di·mness** n. (Vb) become or make d., becloud, outshine. [OE, cf. OHG *timbar*]

dīme, n. (U.S.). Silver coin, 1/10 of dollar (*d. novel*, cheap shocker). [obs. sense *tithe*, f. OF *disme* f. L *decima* fem. of *decimus* tenth]

dime·nsion (*or* dī-), n. Measurable extent of any kind, as length, breadth, thickness, area, volume, (usu. pl.; *of great dd.*, very large); *the three dd.*, length, breadth, & thickness (point has no dd., line one, surface two, body three; *fourth d.* in math. speculations, property of matter that should be to solids as solids are to planes); (Alg.) number of unknown quantities contained as factors in a product (x^3, x^2y, xyz, all of three dd.). Hence (-)**dime·nsional**, **dime·nsionless**, aa. [F, f. L DI¹(*mensionem* f. *metiri mensus* measure, -ION)]

dī·merous, a. (bot., entom.). With two parts. [DI-², -MEROUS]

dĭ·meter, n. Verse of two measures (measure in some metres has one foot, in others two). [f. L f. Gk DI²(*metros* f. *metron* measure)]

dīmi·diate (-*at*), a. Halved, split in two. [f. L (*-diare*) f. DI¹(*midium* f. *medius* mid), -ATE²]

dimĭ·nish, v.t. & i. Make or become, actually or in appearance, less (*hide* one's *diminished head*, i.e. reduced power &c.; in Mus., *diminished*, of intervals less by a chromatic semitone than the full, as *diminished fifth* &c.); (Arch.) taper (t. & i.). Hence **dimi·nishable** a., **dimi·nishingly**² adv. [mixture of MINISH with obs. *diminue* f. F *diminuer* f. L DI¹*minuere -minut-* cf. *minor* less]

dĭmĭ·nue·ndo, mus. direction (abbr. *dim.*) & n. Gradually decrease loudness (cf. CRESCENDO); gradual decrease, musical passage marked by it, (also fig.). [It.]

diminu·tion, n. Diminishing, amount of it. [F, f. L *diminutionem* (DIMINISH, -ION)]

dimi·nutive, a. & n. (Gram.) (word) describing small specimen of the thing denoted by corresponding primitive word; remarkably small, tiny. Hence **dimi·nuti·val** a. (gram.), **dimi·nutively**² adv., **dimi·nutiveness** n. [F (*-if, -ive*), f. L *diminutivus* (DIMINISH, -IVE)]

dĭ·mity, n. Stout cotton fabric woven with raised stripes or fancy figures used for bedroom hangings &c. [f. It. *dimito* (pl. *-i*) f. LL *dimitum* f. Gk DI²(*mitos* warp-thread)]

dīmor·phic, dīmor·phous, aa. (bot., zool., chem., mineral.). Exhibiting, occurring in, two distinct forms. So **dimor·phism**(2) n. [f. Gk DI²(*morphos* f. *morphē* form) + -IC, -OUS]

di·mple, n., & v.t. & i. Small hollow esp. in cheek or chin; ripple in water, hollow in ground; hence **di·mply**² a. (Vb) produce dd. in, show dd. [f. 15th c. only; perh. cogn. w. G *tümpel* pool (cf. DAPPLE) f. OHG *dumphilo*]

din, n., & v.t. & i. Continued confused stunning or distracting noise. (Vb) assail with d.; repeat ad nauseam *into* person or person's *ears*; make a d. [vb f. n., OE *dyne* cf. ON *dynr*]

dine, v.i. & t. Take dinner (*d. out*, away from home; *d. off* or *on*, have for dinner; *d. with Duke Humphrey*, go without dinner—perh. w. allusion to those who walked during dinner-time in Duke Humphrey's Walk in St Paul's); entertain (persons) at dinner, (of room &c.) provide dining-accommodation for (some number); *dining-room*, used for meals. [f. F *dîner* perh. f. LL *DIS(*jejunare* f. *jejunus* fasting) breakfast cf. DÉJEUNER]

di·ner, n. One who dines; railway dining-car; *d.-out*, one who often dines from home, esp. one much invited for his social qualities. [-ER[1]]

di·ng-do·ng, adv., n., & a. (With) alternating strokes as of two bells (*hammer away at it d.*; *d. race*, in which each has the better alternately); sound of bell(s); jingle of rhyme. [imit.]

dinghy, dingey, (dĭ·nggĭ), n. Small ship's-boat; small pleasure rowing-boat. [orig. native rowing-boat on Indian rivers, f. Hind. *ḍeṅgi*]

di·ngle, n. Deep dell, usu. shaded with trees. [etym. dub.; perh. = DIMPLE]

di·ngo, n. Wild or half-domesticated Australian dog. [native]

di·ngy (-jĭ), a. Dull-coloured, grimy, dirty-looking. Hence **din·gi**LY[2] adv., **di·ngi**NESS n. [perh. f. DUNG + -Y[2]]

di·nky, a. (colloq.). Pretty, neat, of engaging appearance. [cf. Sc. *dink* trim, f. 1508]

di·nner, n. Chief meal of day, whether at midday or evening (formal meal with distinct courses); public feast in honour of person or event; *d.-bell, -hour, -time, -party*; *d.-claret, -sherry*, &c. (inferior to *dessert-*); *d.-jacket*, tailless dress coat; *d.-set*, of plates, dishes, &c.; *d.-wagon*, movable tray on castored legs; *d. without grace*, ante-nuptial sexual intercourse. Hence **di·nner**LESS a. [f. F *dîner* DINE used as n.; -ER[4]]

dī·nosaur, n. Extinct gigantic reptile. Hence **dinosaur·**IAN a. & n. [f. Gk *deinos* terrible + *sauros* lizard]

dī·nothēre, n. Huge extinct proboscidean quadruped. [as prec., Gk *thērion* wild beast]

dint, n., & v.t. (Archaic) stroke, blow, (whence, mod.) *by d. of*, by force or means of; mark made by blow or pressure, dent; (vb) mark with dd., dent. [OE *dynt* cf. ON *dyntr*]

dīŏ·cĕsan (-zn), a. & n. Of a diocese. (N.) bishop in relation to diocese or clergy; member of diocese in relation to bishop (corresp. to *parishioner*). [f. F *diocesain* (foll., -AN)]

di·ocese (-ĕs, -ēs), n. Bishop's district. [f. OF *diocise* f. med. L *diocesis* f. L f. Gk DI[3](*oikēsis* f. *oikeō* inhabit) administration]

dioe·cious (dīē-), a. (Bot.) Having the male & female flowers on separate plants; (Zool.) with the two sexes in separate individuals. [DI-[2], Gk *-oikos* -housed, -OUS]

dīo·ptric, a. & n. Serving as medium for sight, assisting sight by refraction, (*d. glass, lens, system*); of refraction, refractive; of dioptrics; hence **dio·ptri**CALLY adv. (N.) unit of refractive power, power of lens with focal distance one metre; (pl.) part of optics dealing with refraction (cf. CATOPTRICS). [f. Gk *dioptrikos* f. DI[3](*optra* f. *op-* see + instr. suf. *-tra*) optical instrument, -IC]

dīora·ma (-ah-), n. Spectacular painting in which, by changes in the colour & direction of light thrown on or through it, effects of such natural processes as sunrise are produced. Hence (irreg.) **dioră·mic** a. [DI-[3], Gk *horama -atos* (*horaō* see, -M)]

dio·xide, n. (chem.). Oxide formed by combination of two equivalents of oxygen with one of metal or metalloid (*carbon d.* &c.). [DI-[2]]

dip[1], v.t. & i. Put or let down into liquid, immerse, (*d.* one's *pen in gall*, write bitterly); dye thus; make (candles) by immersing wick in hot tallow; wash (sheep) in vermin-killing liquid; take *up* (liquid, grain, &c.) in scoop, pan, &c.; lower (flag, sail, scale of balance) for a moment; involve in debt (colloq.); go under water & emerge quickly; put hand, ladle, &c., *into* to take something out (*d. into* one's *purse* &c., spend freely); go below any surface or level (*sun dips below horizon*; *bird dips & rises in flight*; *scale dips*); extend downwards; have downward slope (esp. of magnetic needle, & of strata; *dipping-needle*, one so mounted as to measure magnetic dip); make investigations (*d. deep into the future*); look cursorily or skippingly *into* (book). [OE *dyppan*, cogn. w. DEEP; cf. G *taufen* baptize]

dip[2], n. A dipping (see prec.); quantity dipped up; (colloq.) bathe in sea &c.; amount of submergence; (Astron., Surv.) apparent depression of horizon due to observer's elevation; angle made by magnetic needle with horizon; downward slope of stratum; depression of sky-line &c.; tallow candle; washing-preparation for sheep &c.; *d.-needle*, = dipping-needle (see prec.); *d.-net*, small fishing-net with long handle; *d.-pipe, -trap*, arranged to cut off communication of gas &c. by downward bend in which liquid stands. [f. prec.]

diphthē·ria, diphtherī·tis, (-fth-), nn. Acute infectious disease with inflammation of a mucous membrane esp. of throat, & exudation forming a false membrane. Hence **diphthē·r**IAL, **diphthĕ·r**IC, **diphtherĭ·t**IC, **di·phther**OID, aa. [f. F *diphthérie*, *diphthérite* (earlier name), f. Gk *diphthera* hide, -Y[1], -ITIS]

di·phthong (-fth-), n. Union of two vowels pronounced in one syllable (ou, oi); two vowel characters representing sound of single vowel (ea in *feat*), digraph; compound vowel character, ligature, (æ).

Hence **diphtho·ng**AL a., **di·phthong**IZE (3) v.t., (-ngg-), [f. F *diphthongue* f. L f. Gk DI[2](*phthoggos* -sounded f. *phthoggos* voice)]

dipl(o)-, comb. form of Gk *diplous* double, in many scientific words as *diploblastic* with two germinal layers, *diplocardiac* with right & left sides of heart separate.

diplō·ma, n. (pl. *-s*, rarely *-ta*). State paper, official document, charter; document conferring honour or privilege, esp. University or College certificate of degree, whence **diplo·ma'd, -ma**ED[2], **diplo·ma**LESS, aa. [L f. Gk (-ō-), f. *diploō* (*diplous* double), -M; orig. folded paper]

diplō·macy, n. Management of, skill in managing, international relations; adroitness, artful management, tact. [f. F *diplomatie* f. *diplomate* see foll., -Y[1]]

di·plomăt, n. = DIPLOMATIST. [f. F *diplomate* back-formation f. *diplomatique* see foll.]

diplomă·tic, a. Of official or original documents, charters, &c.; of diplomacy (*d. body*, ambassadors & legation-officials at a court; *d. service*, officials concerned with foreign legations); skilled in diplomacy; proceeding by negotiation; (of statements, dealings, persons) uncandid, deceiving. Hence **diploma·ti**CALLY adv. [f. F *diplomatique* f. mod. L *diplomaticus* f. Gk DIPLOMA *-atos*, -IC]

diplō·matist, n. One officially engaged in diplomacy; adroit negotiator. [DIPLOMAT, -IST]

diplō·matize, v.i. Act as diplomatist; use diplomatic arts. [DIPLOMAT, -IZE]

di·pper, n. In vbl senses; also or esp.: Anabaptist or Baptist; kinds of bird, esp. water ouzel; kind of ladle; (Photog.) apparatus for immersing negatives; *the D.* (U.S.), the Great Bear. [DIP[1], -ER[1]]

dipsomā·nia, n. Morbid craving for alcohol. Hence **dipso**MA·NIAC n. [Gk *dipso-* (*dipsa* thirst, -O-), -MANIA]

di·pteral, a. With double peristyle. [f. L f. Gk DI[2](*pteros* -winged f. *pteron* wing), -AL]

di·pterous, a. (Entom.) two-winged, belonging to the order *Diptera* (insects with one pair of membranous wings); (Bot.) with two wing-like appendages. [as prec. + -OUS]

di·ptych (-ĭk), n. Ancient hinged two-leaved writing-tablet with inner sides waxed; painting, esp. altarpiece, of two leaves closing like book. [f. L f. Gk DI[2](*ptukha* neut. pl. of *-ptukhos* -folding f. *ptukhē* fold]

dire, a. Dreadful, calamitous, (*d. sisters*, the Furies). Hence **dire·**LY[2] adv. [f. L *dirus*]

dire·ct[1], v.t. & i. Address (letter, parcel, *to* person or place); utter or write *to* or to be conveyed *to* (*I d. my remarks to you*); control, govern the movements of, (*soul directs body, commander troops*); turn (thing, person, eyes, attention) straight *to* something; tell (person) the way (*to*; *directing-post*, = FINGER-*post*); guide as adviser, principle (*duty directs my actions*), &c.; order (person) *to* do, thing *to be* done; give orders (*that* or abs.). So **direc·ti**VE a. [f. L DI[1](*rigere rect-* = *regere* put straight)]

dire·ct[2], a. & adv. Straight, not crooked(ly) or round about, (*the d. road*; *went d. to heaven*; *d. action*, exertion of pressure on the community by strikes instead of on Parliament by votes to force political measures on the Government; *d. ray*, not reflected or refracted; *d. shot, hit*, without ricochet); (Astron.) proceeding from E. to W., not retrograde; (of descent) lineal(ly), not collateral(ly); (of argument) following uninterrupted chain of cause & effect &c.; diametrical (*d. opposite, contrary, contradiction*); (Mus.) not inverted (of interval, chord), not contrary (of motion); straightforward, frank, going straight to the point, not ambiguous; immediate(ly), personal(ly), not by proxy; (Gram.) *d. speech* or *oration*, the words as actually spoken, not modified (cf. OBLIQUE, INDIRECT) in reporting; *d. tax*, levied originally (income tax &c.) on person who bears the burden ultimately (cf. INDIRECT). Hence **dire·ct**NESS n. [(prob. F) f. L *directus* p.p. see prec.]

dire·ction (dĭ-, dī-), n. Directing, aiming, guiding, managing; = DIRECTORATE; instruction what to do, order, (usu. pl.); address on letter or parcel; course pursued by moving body, point to which one moves or looks, (*in the d. of London*, Londonwards); scope, sphere, subject, (*new dd. of inquiry, improvement in many dd.*). [f. L *directio* (DIRECT[1], -ION)]

dire·ctly, adv. & conj. In a DIRECT[2] manner; at once, without delay; presently, in no long time; (colloq.) as soon as (*went d. I knew*). [-LY[2]]

dire·ctor, n. Superintendent, manager, esp. member of managing-board of commercial company; (Fr. Hist.) member of Directory; (Eccl.) priest acting as spiritual adviser; apparatus controlling direction in instruments &c. Hence **dīrec·tor·**IAL a., **dire·ctor**SHIP, **dire·ctr**ESS[1], nn. [f. F *directeur* (DIRECT[1], -OR[2])]

dire·ctorate, n. Office of director; board of directors. [-ATE[1]]

dire·ctory[1], a. Directive, advisory, (esp. of part of law advising procedure omission of which does not invalidate action). [f. L *directorius* (DIRECT[1], -ORY)]

dire·ctory[2], n. Book of rules, esp. for public or private worship; book with lists of inhabitants of district, members of professions, &c., with various details; (Fr. Hist.) revolutionary executive of five directors in power 1795–9 (*D-*). [f. med. L *directorium* neut. adj. see prec.]

dire·ctrix, n. (pl. *-ices*). = DIRECTRESS;

(Geom.) fixed line used in describing curve or surface. [DIRECTOR, -TRIX]

dire·ful, a. Terrible, dread. Hence **dire·ful**LY² adv. [DIRE, -FUL(1)]

dirge (-j), n. Song sung at burial, or in commemoration of the dead; lament. [f. L *dirige* imperat. of *dirigere* DIRECT¹, first wd in Latin antiphon in Matins part of Office of the Dead]

di·rigible, a. & n. Capable of being guided (esp. of balloons); (n.) d. balloon or airship as opp. *aeroplane.* [as DIRECT¹, -IBLE]

di·riment, a. Nullifying (*d. impediment,* making marriage null & void from the first). [f. L *dirimere* (DIS-, *emere* take), -ENT]

dirk, n., & v.t. Kind of dagger (esp. of Highlanders); (vb) stab with this. [earlier *dork* (1602) perh. f. Du. *dolk* cf. G *dolch*]

dirt, n. Unclean matter that soils, wet mud (*d. pie,* made by children in gutters &c.); anything worthless (*yellow d.,* gold; *d.,* scornful name for land; *d.-cheap,* very cheap); earth, soil; dirtiness; foul talk; *fling d.,* talk abusively or slanderously; *eat d.,* put up with insult &c.; *d.-eating,* disease with morbid craving to eat earth. [ME *drit* prob. f. ON *drit* excrement]

dir·ty, a., & v.t. & i. Soiled, foul, mixed with or like or connected with dirt, (*D. Shirts,* 101st Foot, from fighting in shirt-sleeves at Delhi); unclean, obscene; sordid, mean, despicable; *d. work,* esp. dishonourable proceedings, (also) drudgery (*do person's d. work for him*); ill-gotten; (of weather) rough, squally; (of colour) not pure or clear; *D. Allan,* sea-bird getting food by forcing gulls &c. to disgorge; hence **dir·ti**LY² adv., **dir·ti**NESS n., **dir·ty**ISH¹(2) a. (Vb) make, become, d. [-Y²]

dis-, pref. f. L *dis-* (which was changed to DI-¹ or DIF- before certain letters; see also DE-) related to *bis* (orig. **dvis* = Gk *dis* twice) & *duo* two. In wds taken direct or thr. F f. L; in wds taken f. LL in which *dis-* or Rom. *des-* had displaced *de-*; & used as living pref. to modify sense of E wds. Meanings: asunder, away, apart or between, one by one, utterly (in wds already negative, as *disannul*), un-, not, the reverse of, deprivation of, expulsion from.

disabi·lity, n. Thing, want, that prevents one's doing something, esp. legal disqualification. [f. obs. adj. DIS*able* (= *unable*), -BILITY]

disā·ble, v.t. Incapacitate *from* doing or *for* work &c.; cripple, deprive of power of acting; disqualify legally, pronounce incapable, hinder. Hence **disa·ble**MENT n. [DIS-, -ABLE]

disabu·se, v.t. Undeceive, disillusion. [DIS-]

disaccor·d, n., & v.i. Disagree(ment), (be at) variance. [DIS-]

disadva·ntage, n. Unfavourable condition (*taken at a d.*); loss, injury. [f. F *désavantage* (DIS-, ADVANTAGE)]

disa·dvanta·geous, a. Involving disadvantage or discredit, derogatory. Hence **disa·dvanta·geous**LY² adv. [DIS-]

disaffe·cted, a. Estranged, unfriendly, disloyal, esp. to Government. [p.p. of scarcely used vb DIS*affect*]

disaffe·ction, n. Political discontent, disloyalty. [as prec. after AFFECTION]

disaffir·m, v.t. (legal). Reverse (previous decision); repudiate (settlement). Hence **disăffirm**A·TION n. [DIS-]

disaffŏ·rest, v.t. Reduce from legal state of forest to ordinary land. Hence **disaffŏrest**A·TION n. [f. med.L DIS(AFFOREST*are*)]

disagree·, v.i. Differ, be unlike, not correspond; differ in opinion, dissent, quarrel; (of food, climate, &c.) prove unsuitable, have bad effects, (*with* person, his health, digestion, &c.). Hence **disagree·**MENT n. [DIS-]

disagree·able (-grĭa-), a. & n. Not to one's taste, unpleasant; unamiable, bad-tempered; hence **disagree·able**NESS n., **disagree·ab**LY² adv. (N., usu. pl.) unpleasant experience(s), trouble(s), worries. [f. F *désagréable* (DIS-, AGREEABLE)]

disallow·, v.t. Refuse to sanction or accept as reasonable or admit, prohibit. [f. OF *desalouer* (DIS-, ALLOW)]

disannu·l, v.t. (-ll-). Cancel, annul. [DIS-]

disappear·, v.i. Cease to be visible, vanish, die away from sight or existence, be lost. Hence **disappear·**ANCE n. [DIS-]

disappoi·nt, v.t. Not fulfil desire or expectation of, break appointment with, (person; *disappointed at, in, of, with*; *agreeably* &c. *disappointed,* glad to find one's fears groundless); belie, frustrate, (hope, purpose, &c.). Hence **disappoi·nt**ING² a., **disappoi·nted**LY², **disappoi·nting**LY², advv., **disappoi·nt**MENT n., event &c. that disappoints, distress resulting. [f. F *désappointer* (DIS-, APPOINT)]

disăpproba·tion, n. Disapproval. So **disa·pprobāt**IVE, **disa·pprobāt**ORY, aa. [DIS-]

disappro·ve, v.t. & i. Have, express, unfavourable opinion of or *of.* Hence **disappro·**VAL(2) n., **disappro·ving**LY² adv. [DIS-]

disar·m, v.t. & i. Deprive *of* weapons; deprive of weapons (esp. in fencing, jerk foil &c. out of hand of); dismantle (city, ship), reduce, be reduced, to peace footing (of army or navy), abandon or cut down military establishment, whence **dis**AR·MAMENT n.; deprive of power to

For compounds of *dis-* not given consult DIS-.

injure; pacify hostility or suspicions of. [f. F *désarmer* (DIS-, ARM[3])]

disarra·nge, v.t. Put into disorder, disorganize. Hence **disarra·nge**MENT n. [DIS-]

disarray·, n., & v.t. (Throw into) disorder; (poet.) unclothe. [DIS-]

disarti·culate, v.t. Separate, undo the articulation of, take to pieces. Hence **disarti·cul**A·TION n. [DIS-]

di·sassimila·tion, n. (physiol.). Conversion of assimilated into less complex or waste substances. [DIS-]

disa·ster, n. Sudden or great misfortune, calamity; ill luck (*a record of d.*). So **disa·stro**US a., **disa·strous**LY[2] adv. [f. F *désastre* (DIS-, *astre* f. L f. Gk *astron* star)]

disavow·, v.t. Say one does not know or approve of, repudiate. Hence **disavow·**AL(2) n. [f. F *désavouer* (DIS-, AVOW)]

disba·nd, v.t. & i. Break up, disperse, (t. & i. of troops &c.). Hence **disba·nd**MENT n. [f. 16th-c. F *desbander* see DIS-, BAND[1] (3)]

disbar·, v.t. (-rr-). Expel from membership of the bar, deprive of status of barrister. Hence **disbar·**MENT n. [DIS-, BAR[1]]

disbelie·ve, v.t. & i. Refuse credence to (person or statement &c.); be a sceptic; have no faith *in*. So **dis**BELIE·F n. [DIS-]

disbe·nch, v.t. Deprive of status of bencher. [DIS-, BENCH n.]

disbra·nch, v.t. Strip of branches. [DIS-]

disbu·d, v.t. (-dd-). Remove (esp. the superfluous) buds of. [DIS-]

disbur·den, v.t. Relieve of or *of* a burden; get rid of, discharge, (load, thoughts). [DIS-]

disbur·se, v.t. & i. Expend, defray; pay money. Hence **disbur·se**MENT n. [f. OF *desbourser* (DIS-, BOURSE)]

disc. =DISK.

discă·lcĕate (-*at*), a. & n., **discă·lceāted**, **discă·lced** (-st), aa. Barefooted or only sandalled (friar, nun). [(-*ed* anglicized) f. L DIS(*calceatus* p.p. of *calceare* f. *calceus* shoe)]

discar·d, v.t. & i., & n. Throw out or reject from hand at cards (specified card, or abs. esp. at whist of playing non-trump that does not follow lead); cast aside, give up, (clothes, habit, belief, &c.); dismiss, cashier; (n.) discarding at cards, discarded card. [DIS-, CARD[2]]

discar·nate, a. Parted from the flesh, disembodied. [DIS-, (IN)CARNATE]

discer·n (-s-, -z-), v.t. & i. (Archaic) distinguish, see the difference between, (good *&* bad, good *from* bad, *between* good & bad). Perceive clearly with the mind or senses, make out by thought or by gazing, listening, &c.; so **discer·n**IBLE a., **discer·nib**LY[2], adv. [f. F *discerner* f. L DIS(*cernere cret-* sift)]

discer·ning, a. Having quick or true insight, penetrating. [-ING[2]]

discer·nment, n. Discerning; keenness of perception, penetration, insight. [-MENT]

discer·ptible, a. That can be plucked apart, not indestructibly one. Hence **discerpti**BI·LITY n. [f. L DIS(*cerpere -cerpt-* =*carpere* pluck) + -IBLE]

discer·ption, n. Pulling apart, severance; severed piece. [f. L *discerptio* (prec., -ION)]

dischar·ge[1], v.t. & i. Relieve of load (ship &c.; *d. gun*, fire it off; *d. bankrupt*, relieve him of further liability), withdraw electricity from; dismiss, cashier, (*was discharged from*, or rarely *discharged, the service*); release (prisoner), let go (patient, jury); put forth, get rid of, send out, emit, unload from ship, (cargo, missile, liquid, purulent matter, abuse; also abs., as *ship, abscess, is discharging*); (of river, refl. or intr.) disembogue; (Law) cancel (order of court); acquit oneself of, pay, perform, (duty, debt, vow); (Dyeing) remove (colour), undye (fabric). [f. OF *descharger* (DIS-, CHARGE[2])]

dischar·ge[2], n. Unloading (*of* ship or cargo); firing off of gun &c. (*a d. of arrows*, several arrows shot); emission (of liquid, electricity, purulent matter); release, exoneration, exemption, acquittal, written certificate of these; dismissal; liberation; payment (*of* debt); performance (*of* obligation); (Dyeing) process of, composition used in, discharging. [f. prec.]

dischar·ger, n. In vbl senses; esp., appliance for producing electric discharge. [-ER[1]]

disci·ple, n. One of Christ's personal followers, esp. one of the Twelve; any early believer in Christ; follower, adherent, of any leader of thought, art, &c. Hence **disci·ple**SHIP n., **disci·pul**AR[1] a. [OE *discipul* f. L *discipulus* (*discere* learn)]

disciplinār·ian, n. Maintainer of discipline (*strict, good, poor, no, d.*). [as foll. + -AN]

di·sciplinary (*also* -plĭ·-), a. Of, promoting, discipline; of the nature of mental training. [f. med.L *disciplinarius* (foll., -ARY[1])]

di·scipline[1], n. Branch of instruction (archaic); mental & moral training, adversity as effecting this; military training, drill, (archaic); trained condition; order maintained among schoolboys, soldiers, prisoners, &c.; system of rules for conduct; control exercised over members of church; chastisement; (Eccl.) mortification by penance. So **di·sciplin**AL (or -ī·*nal*) a. [F, f. L *disciplina* (*discipulus* DISCIPLE, -INE[3])]

di·scipline[2], v.t. Bring under control,

train to obedience & order, drill, whence **di·sciplin**ABLE a.; chastise. [f. med.L (*-nare*) as prec.]

disclai·m, v.t. & i. Renounce legal claim to, renounce claim; disown, disavow, (authorship, character). [AF *desclamer* (DIS-, CLAIM[1])]

disclai·mer, n. Act of disclaiming, renunciation, disavowal. [AF (=prec. as n., -ER[4])]

disclo·se (-z), v.t. Remove cover from, expose to view, make known, reveal. [f. OF *desclore* (DIS-, L *claudere claus-* shut)]

disclo·sure (-zh*er*), n. Disclosing; thing disclosed. [-URE]

discŏ·bolus (pl. -ī), n. Ancient quoit-thrower; statue of one in act of throwing. [L, f. Gk *diskobolos* (*diskos* stone or metal quoit, *-bolos* -throwing f. *ballō* throw)]

di·scoid, a. Disk-shaped. [f. L f. Gk *diskoeidēs* (prec., -OID)]

disco·lour (-kŭl-), v.t. & i. Change or spoil the colour of, stain, tarnish; become stained &c. Hence or cogn. **discolo**(**u**)**r**A·TION, **disco·lour**MENT, nn. [f. OF *descolorer* f. med.L DIS*colorare* = L DE(*colorare* COLOUR[2])]

disco·mfit (-kŭ-), v.t. Defeat in battle; thwart, disconcert. So **disco·mfit**URE (-tsh*er*) n. [orig. p.p. = defeated f. OF *desconfit* f. LL DIS(*confectus* p.p. see CONFECTION) undone]

disco·mfort (-kŭ-), n., & v.t. Uneasiness of body or mind; want of comfort; (vb) make uneasy. [f. OF *desconfort*(*er*) (DIS-, COMFORT)]

discommo·de, v.t. Put to inconvenience. [DIS- + obs. *commode* f. L *commodare* (*commodus* see COMMODE)]

disco·mmon, v.t. Debar (tradesman) from serving undergraduates; enclose (common land). [DIS-, COMMON[1, 2]]

disco·mmons, v.t. Deprive (member of college) of commons; discommon (tradesman). [DIS-, COMMONS]

discompo·se, v.t. Disturb composure of, ruffle, agitate. Hence **discompo·sĕd**LY[2], **discompo·sing**LY[2], advv., **discompo·sure** (-zh*er*) n. [DIS-]

disconcer·t, v.t. Derange, spoil, upset, (plan, concerted measures); disturb self-possession of, ruffle, fluster. Hence **disconcer·t**MENT n. [f. obs. F DIS(*concerter* CONCERT[2])]

disconne·ct, v.t. Sever the connexion of (thing *from*, *with*, another) or between. [DIS-]

disconne·cted, a. In vbl senses; esp. (of speech or writing) incoherent, with bad connexion or transitions, whence **disconne·cted**LY[2] adv., **disconne·cted**NESS n. [-ED[1]]

disconne·xion, -ction, n. Disconnecting; want of connexion, disconnectedness. [DIS-]

disco·nsolate (-*at*), a. Forlorn, inconsolable, unhappy, disappointed. Hence **disco·nsolate**LY[2] adv. [f. med.L DIS(*consolatus* p.p. of L *consolari* CONSOLE[1])]

disconte·nt, n., a., & v.t. Dissatisfaction, want of contentment; grievance. (Adj.) not content, dissatisfied, (*with*). (Vb, usu. in p.p.) make dissatisfied; hence **disconte·nted**LY[2] adv., **disconte·nted**NESS, **disconte·nt**MENT, nn. [DIS-, CONTENT[2, 3, 4]]

disconti·gūous, a. (With parts) not in contact. [DIS-]

disconti·nue, v.t. Cause to cease; cease from, give up, (do*ing*, habit &c.); cease taking, paying (newspaper, subscription). So **disconti·nu**ANCE n. [f. F *discontinuer* f. med.L DIS*continuare* CONTINUE])

disconti·nuous, a. Wanting continuity in space or time, having interstices, intermittent. Hence or cogn. **disco·ntinu**·ITY n., **disconti·nuous**LY[2] adv. [f. med.L DIS(*continuus* CONTINUOUS) + -OUS]

di·scord[1], n. Disagreement, variance, strife; harsh noise, clashing sounds; whence or cogn. **discor·d**ANT a., **discor·d**ANCE n., **discor·dant**LY[2] adv. (Mus.) want of harmony between notes sounded together; chord unpleasing or unsatisfactory in itself & requiring to be resolved by another; any interval except unison, octave, perfect fifth & fourth, major & minor third & sixth, & their octaves; single note dissonant with another. [f. OF *descord* (foll.)]

discor·d[2], v.i. Disagree, quarrel, be different or inconsistent, (*with*, *from*); be dissonant, jar, clash. [f. OF *descorder* f. L *discordare* f. DIS(*cors -cord-* -hearted f. *cor -dis* heart)]

di·scount[1] (-ow-), n. Deduction from amount due or price of goods in consideration of its being paid promptly or in advance; deduction from amount of bill of exchange &c. by one who gives value for it before it is due; discounting; allowance for exaggeration in accepting story; *at a d.*, below par, depreciated, not in demand. [f. 16th-c. F *descompte* (foll.)]

discou·nt[2] (-ow-), v.t. Give or get present worth of (bill not yet due); leave out of account; lessen, detract from; part with for immediate but smaller good; allow for exaggeration in; use up effect of (news &c.) beforehand, stale by anticipation. Hence **discou·nt**ABLE a. [f. OF *desconter*, *-compter*, f. med.L DIS(*computare* L = COMPUTE)]

discou·ntenance, v.t. Refuse to countenance, discourage, show disapproval of. [f. obs. F *descontenancer* (DIS-, COUNTENANCE[2])]

discou·rage (-kŭrĭj), v.t. Deprive of courage, confidence, or energy; deter *from*; discountenance. Hence **discou·rage**MENT n., **discou·raging**LY[2] adv. [f. OF *descoragier* (DIS-, COURAGE)]

di·scourse[1] (-ors), n. Talk, conversation,

(archaic); dissertation, treatise, sermon. [f. F *discours* f. L DIS(*cursus* COURSE[1])]
discour·se[2] (-ōrs), v.i. & t. Talk, converse; hold forth in speech or writing on a subject (*of, upon*, or abs.); give forth (some kind of music; ref. to *Hamlet* III. ii. 374). [f. prec.]
discour·teous, a., **discour·tesy,** n.,(-ker-, -kōr-). Rude(ness), uncivil, incivility. Hence **discour·teous**LY[2] adv. [DIS-]
disco·ver (-kŭ-), v.t. Disclose, expose to view, reveal, make known, exhibit, manifest, betray; (Chess) *d. check*, check by removing piece or pawn; find out (fact &c., *that* &c., unknown country), suddenly realize, whence or cogn. **disco·ver**ABLE a., **disco·ver**ER[1] n. [f. OF *descovrir* f. med. L DIS(*cooperire* COVER[1])]
disco·vert (-kŭ-), a. (legal). Unmarried or widowed (of woman). [f. OF *descovert* p.p. (prec.)]
disco·very (-kŭ-), n. Revealing, disclosure, (in Law, compulsory disclosure by party to action of facts or documents on which he relies; in play, poem, &c., revelation unravelling plot); finding out, making known; thing found out. [f. DISCOVER on anal. of RECOVERY (OF *recovrée*, OF for *discovery* being *descoverte*)]
discre·dit[1], n. Loss of repute, thing involving this; doubt, lack of credibility, (*throws d. upon*); loss of commercial credit. [DIS-]
discre·dit[2], v.t. Refuse to believe; bring disbelief or disrepute upon. [DIS-]
discre·ditable, a. Bringing discredit, shameful. Hence **discre·ditab**LY[2] adv. [DIS-]
discree·t, a. Judicious, prudent, circumspect, not speaking out at inopportune times. Hence **discree·t**LY[2] adv. [f. F *discret* f. L DIS(*cretus* p.p. of *cernere* sift) separate, with LL sense f. its derivative *discretio* discernment]
di·screpant (*or* -krĕ·-), a. Different, inconsistent, (of stories &c.). So **discrĕ·p**ANCY n. [f. L DIS(*crepare* sound), -ANT]
di·screte, a. Separate, individually distinct, discontinuous; (Metaphys.) abstract not concrete. Hence **di·screte**NESS n. [f. L *discretus* see DISCREET]
discrĕ·tion, n. Liberty of deciding as one thinks fit, absolutely or within limits (*it is within* one's *d. to*; *at the d. of*, to be settled or disposed of by the wish of; *at d.*, at one's own pleasure; *surrender at d.*, unconditionally), whence **discre·tion**ARY[1] a.; discernment, prudence, judgement, (*years, age, of d.*, time at which one is fit to manage oneself—in Eng. law, 14; *d. is the better part of valour*, used as facet. excuse for cowardice). [f. OF *discrecion* f. L *discretionem* (DISCREET, -ION)]
discri·mināte, v.t. & i. Be, set up, or observe, a difference between (also intr. with *between*), distinguish *from* another; make a distinction (*d. against*, distinguish unfavourably, of taxes &c.), observe distinctions carefully. So **discrimin**A·TION n., **discri·min**ATIVE a. [f. L *discriminare* (*discrimen* distinction f. *discernere* DISCERN), -ATE[3]]
discri·minating, a. In vbl senses; esp.: discerning, acute; *d. duty, rate*, varying in amount according to country sending goods or person rated, differential. [-ING[2]]
discrow·n, v.t. Take crown from, depose, (sovereign lit. or fig.). [DIS-]
discur·sive, a. Rambling, digressive, expatiating; proceeding by argument or reasoning, not intuitive. Hence **discur·sive**LY[2] adv., **discur·sive**NESS n. [f. L DIS(*currere curs-* run), -IVE]
discu·ss, v.t. Examine by argument, debate, whence **discu·ss**IBLE a.; consume with enjoyment (food, wine, meal). [f. L DIS(*cutere -cuss-* = *quatere* shake)]
discu·ssion (-shn), n. Examination by argument; a debate; consumption with enjoyment *of* food. [OF, f. L *discussionem* (prec., -ION)]
disdai·n, n., & v.t. Scorn, (regard with) contempt; think beneath oneself (*to* do, *doing*, or noun) or one's notice. Hence **disdai·n**FUL a., **disdai·nful**LY[2] adv. [f. OF *desdeign(er)* f. L DE(*dignare* f. *dignus* worthy)]
disea·se (-zēz), n. Morbid condition of body, plant, or some part of them, illness, sickness; any particular kind of this with special symptoms & name; deranged or depraved state of mind or morals. [f. OF *desaise* (DIS-, EASE n.)]
diseased (-zēzd), a. Affected with disease; morbid, depraved. [p.p. of obs. *disease* vb f. OF *desaaisier* as prec.]
disembar·k, v.t. & i. Put, go, ashore. Hence **dise·mbark**A·TION n. [f. F *désembarquer* (DIS-, EMBARK)]
disemba·rrass, v.t. Free from embarrassment, rid or relieve (*of*); disentangle (*from*). Hence **disemba·rrass**MENT n. [DIS-]
disembo·dy, v.t. Separate, free, (soul, idea) from body or the concrete; disband (troops). Hence **disembo·di**MENT n. [DIS-]
disembo·gue (-ōg), v.i. & t. (Of river &c.) pour forth at mouth (intr., or *itself*, waters, &c.); (fig.) discharge, pour forth, (t. & i. of speech, crowd, &c.). [f. Sp. *desembocar* (DIS-, *en* in, *boca* mouth)]
disembo·som, v.t. & i. Disclose, reveal; unburden oneself, make confidences. [DIS-]
disembow·el, v.t. (-ll-). Remove entrails of, rip up so as to cause bowels to protrude. Hence **disembow·el**MENT n. [DIS-]
disembroi·l, v.t. Extricate from confusion or entanglement. [DIS-]

disencha·nt, v.t. Free from enchantment or illusion. Hence **disencha·nt**MENT n. [f. F *désenchanter* (DIS-, ENCHANT)]

disencu·mber, v.t. Free from encumbrance. [f. F *désencombrer* (DIS-, ENCUMBER)]

disendow·, v.t. Strip (esp. Church) of endowments. Hence **disendow·**MENT n. [DIS-]

disenga·ge, v.t. & i., & n. Detach, liberate, loosen; (Fencing) pass point of sword to other side of opponent's (n., this movement); come apart, break contact. [DIS-]

disenga·ged, a. In vbl senses; esp.: at leisure to attend to any visitor or business that comes; vacant, not bespoken. [-ED[1]]

disenga·gement, n. Disengaging; liberation (of chem. component); freedom from ties, detachment; easy natural manner; dissolution of engagement to marry; (Fencing) = DISENGAGE n. [-MENT]

disentai·l, v.t. (legal). Free from entail, break the entail of. [DIS-]

disenta·ngle, v.t. & i. Extricate, free from complications; unravel, untwist; come clear of tangle. Hence **disenta·ngle**MENT n. [DIS-]

disenthra·l(l), v.t. (-ll-). Free from bondage. Hence **disenthra·l**MENT n. [DIS-]

disento·mb, v.t. Take out of tomb; unearth, find by research. [DIS-]

disesta·blish, v.t. Undo establishment of; deprive (Church) of State connexion, depose from official position. Hence **disesta·blish**MENT n. [DIS-]

diseur (dēzer·), n. (fem. *-euse*, pron. -er·z). Artiste entertaining with monologue. [F, = talker]

disfa·vour, n., & v.t. Dislike, disapproval; being disliked (*fall into, be in, d.*); (vb) regard, treat, with d. [DIS-]

disfea·ture (-tsh*er*), v.t. Mar features of, disfigure. [DIS-]

disfi·gure, v.t. Mar beauty of, deform, deface, sully. Hence **disfigur**A·TION, **disfi·gure**MENT, nn. [f. OF *desfigurer* (DIS-, L *figurare* f. *figura* FIGURE[1])]

disfo·rest, v.t. = DISAFFOREST; clear of forests. [f. OF *desforester* (DIS-, FOREST)]

disfra·nchise (-tshīz), v.t. Deprive of citizen rights; deprive (place) of right of sending, (person) of right of voting for, parliamentary representative. Hence **disfra·nchise**MENT n. [DIS-, obs. *franchise* vb = ENFRANCHISE]

disfro·ck, v.t. Deprive of clerical (garb &) status. [DIS-]

disgor·ge (-j), v.t. & i. Eject (as) from throat (esp. fig., trans. or abs., of giving up ill-gotten gains, booty, &c.); (of river &c., trans., refl., or intr.) disembogue, discharge (waters). [f. OF *desgorger* (DIS-, GORGE[1])]

disgra·ce[1], n. Loss of favour, downfall from position of honour; ignominy, shame; thing involving dishonour, cause of reproach. Hence **disgra·ce**FUL a., **disgra·ceful**LY[2] adv., **disgra·ceful**NESS n. [f. F *disgrâce* f. It. *disgrazia* f. med.L DIS(*gratia* GRACE)]

disgra·ce[2], v.t. Dismiss from favour, degrade from position; bring shame or discredit upon, be a d. to. [f. F *disgracier* as prec.]

disgru·ntled, a. Discontented, moody. [from 17th c.; DIS-, *gruntle* obs. frequent. of GRUNT]

disgui·se[1] (-gīz), v.t. Conceal identity of (*d.* one*self*, person or thing, *as* someone or something else, *by* do*ing*, *with* false beard &c., *in* costume &c.); misrepresent, show in false colours; conceal, cloak, (*d.* one's *intention, opinion*); *disguised in* or *with drink* or *liquor*, drunk. Hence **disgui·se**MENT n. [f. OF *desguisier* (DIS-, Rom. *guisa* GUISE)]

disgui·se[2], n. Use of changed dress or appearance for concealment's sake, disguised condition (*blessing in d.*, one that seems to be a misfortune); garb used to deceive; artificial manner, deception. [f. prec.]

disgu·st[1], n. Loathing, nausea, repugnance, strong aversion, (*at, for, towards, against*). [f. 16th-c. F *desgoust* (DIS-, L *gustus* taste)]

disgu·st[2], v.t. Excite loathing, aversion, or indignation, in (*disgusted with, at, by*). Hence **disgu·sted**LY[2], **disgu·sting**LY[2], advv. [f. 16th-c. F *desgouster* (DIS-, L *gustare* taste)]

disgu·stful, a. Disgusting, repulsive; (of contempt, curiosity, &c.) inspired by, full of, disgust. [-FUL]

dish[1], n. Shallow flat-bottomed usu. oval or oblong vessel of earthenware, glass, or metal, for holding food at meals; food so held, particular kind of food (SIDE-*d.*; *made d.*, of various ingredients; *standing d.*, that appears daily, also fig.); (archaic) cup, esp. *d. of tea*, tea-drinking, whence *d. of gossip*, a chat; d.-shaped receptacle used for any purpose; *d.-cover*, of metal &c. for keeping food in d. hot; *d.-cloth* & (archaic) *-clout*, for washing dd. & plates; *d.-wash, -water*, in which dd. have been washed; *d.-washer*, water wagtail. [OE *disc* (cf. G *tisch* table) f. L *discus* DISK]

dish[2], v.t. & i. Put (food) into dish ready for serving; *d. up*, serve meal, (fig.) present (facts, argument) attractively; make concave or dish-shaped; (of horse) move fore-feet not straight but with scooping motion; circumvent, outmanœuvre, (esp., pol.) defeat (opponents) by adopting their policy (*dishing the Whigs*, of Reform Bill 1867). [f. prec.]

dishabille (dĭsabē·l), n. Being negligently or partly dressed, undress, (usu. *in d.*); undress garment or costume. [f. F *déshabillé* p.p. of *déshabiller* (DIS-, *habiller* clothe f. *habile* ready, ABLE)]

dishabĭ·tuate (-h-), v.t. Make (person) unaccustomed (*for* &c.). [DIS-]

dishallu·cina·tion (-h-), n. Disillusion. [DIS-]
dishar·monize (-h-), v.t. Put out of harmony, make discordant. [DIS-]
dishar·mony (-h-), n. Discord, dissonance. So **disharmō·nious** a. [DIS-]
dishear·ten, v.t. Make despondent, rob of courage. Hence **dishear·ten**MENT n. [DIS-]
dishĕ·rison (-h-), n. Disinheriting. [f. OF *disheriteisun* (DIS-, L *hereditare* f. *heres* heir, -ATION, -SON)]
dishĕ·velled, a. With disordered hair; (of hair) loose, flung about, unconfined; (of person) untidy, ruffled, unkempt. Hence **dishe·vel**MENT n. [f. OF *deschevelé* (DIS-, OF *chevel* hair f. L *capillus*, p.p. suf. *-é*)]
disho·nest (dĭsŏ-), a. Fraudulent, knavish, insincere, (of person, act, statement). Hence **disho·nest**LY[2] adv. [f. OF *deshoneste* f. L DE(*honestus* HONEST)]
disho·nesty (dĭsŏ-), n. Want of honesty, knavery, deceitfulness, fraud. [f. OF *desonesté* f. L DIS*honestus* after *honestatem* HONESTY]
disho·nour[1] (dĭsŏ-), n. State of shame or disgrace, discredit; thing that involves this; refusal to honour cheque, bill of exchange, &c. [f. OF *deshonor* (DIS-, L *honorem* HONOUR[1])]
disho·nour[2] (dĭsŏ-), v.t. Treat with indignity; violate chastity of; disgrace; refuse to accept or pay (cheque, bill of exchange). [f. OF *deshonnorer* f. LL DIS-(*honorare* L = HONOUR[2])]
disho·nourable (dĭsŏ-), a. Involving disgrace, ignominious; unprincipled, base, against dictates of honour. Hence **disho·nourable**NESS n., **disho·nourab**LY[2] adv. [DIS-]
dishor·n (-h-), v.t. Cut off horns of. [DIS-]
dishou·se (-howz), v.t. Deprive (population &c.) of house(s). [DIS-]
disillu·sion, n., & v.t., **disillu·sionize,** v.t. Disenchant(ment), free(dom) from illusions. Hence **disillu·sion**MENT n. [DIS-, -IZE]
disi·nclina·tion, n. Want of liking or willingness (*for* or *to* course, *to* do). [DIS-]
disincli·ne, v.t. Make indisposed (*to* do, *for* or *to* course). [DIS-]
disincor·porate, v.t. Dissolve (corporate body). [DIS-]
disinfe·ct, v.t. Cleanse (room, clothes, &c.) of infection. Hence or cogn. **disinfe·ct**ANT(2) a. & n., **disinfe·ct**ION n. [DIS-]
disingĕ·nuous, a. Insincere, having secret motives, not candid. Hence **disinge·nuous**LY[2] adv., **disinge·nuous**NESS n. [DIS-]
disinhĕ·rit, v.t. Reject as heir, deprive of inheritance. Hence **disinhe·rit**ANCE n. [DIS-, *inherit* in obs. sense *make heir*]
disi·ntegrate, v.t. & i. Separate into component parts, deprive of or lose cohesion. Hence **disintegr**A·TION, **disi·ntegrat**OR[2](2), nn. [DIS-]
disinter·, v.t. (-rr-). Unbury, exhume; unearth. Hence **disinter·**MENT n. [f. F *désenterrer* (DIS-, INTER[1])]
disi·nterest, v.t. & refl. To divest of interest, (refl.) cease to concern one*self* (esp., in Diplom., renounce intention or right of intervening &c.). [DIS-]
disi·nterested (-re-), a. Not biased by self-seeking, impartial; *d. management* (of public house by manager who does not profit by sale of liquor). Hence **disi·nterested**LY[2] adv., **disi·nterested**NESS n. [DIS-]
disje·cta me·mbra, n. pl. Fragments, scattered remains. [L]
disjoi·n, v.t. Separate, disunite, part. [f. OF *desjoindre* f. L DIS(*jungere junct-* join)]
disjoi·nt, v.t. Dislocate, disturb working or connexion of (p.p., esp. of talk, incoherent, desultory, whence **disjoi·nted**LY[2] adv., **disjoi·nted**NESS n.); take in pieces at the joints. [f. obs. *disjoint* adj. f. p.p. of OF as prec.]
disju·nction, n. Disjoining, separation. [f. L *disjunctio* (DISJOIN, -ION)]
disju·nctive, a. & n. Disjoining, involving separation; (Log., Gram.) alternative (adj.), involving choice between two words &c., (n., d. proposition or conjunction). Hence **disju·nctive**LY[2] adv. [f. L *disjunctivus* (DISJOIN, -IVE)]
disk, disc, n. Thin circular plate (e.g. coin); round flat or apparently flat surface (*sun's d.*) or mark; round flattened part in body, plant, &c. [f. L f. Gk *diskos* quoit]
disli·ke, v.t., & n. Not like, have aversion or objection to; (n.) aversion (*to, of, for*). [DIS-]
di·slocate, v.t. Put out of joint (limb, or fig. machinery, affairs); (Geol.) make (strata) discontinuous; displace. So **disloc**A·TION n. [f. med.L DIS(*locare* L = place), -ATE[3]]
dislo·dge, v.t. Remove, turn out, (esp. fortified enemy) from position. Hence **dislo·dg(e)**MENT n. [f. OF *desloger* (DIS-, LODGE v.)]
disloy·al, a. Unfaithful to or *to* friendship &c.; untrue to allegiance, disaffected to government, whence **disloy·al**IST(2) n. & a. Hence or cogn. **disloy·al**LY[2] adv., **disloy·al**TY n. [f. OF *desloial* (DIS-, LOYAL)]
di·smal (-z-), a., **di·smals,** n. pl. Depressing, miserable, sombre, dreary; hence **di·smal**LY[2] adv., **di·smal**NESS n.; *the d. science*, political economy; *the dd.*, low spirits, dumps. [orig. noun = unlucky days f. OF *dis mal* f. L *dies mali* ill days; these were two special days in each month in medieval calendars]

For compounds of *dis-* not given consult DIS-.

disma·ntle, v.t. Strip *of* covering, protection, &c.; deprive (fortress, ship, &c.) of defences, rigging, equipment. Hence **disma·ntle**MENT n. [f. obs. F *desmanteller* (DIS-, MANTLE n.)]

disma·st, v.t. Deprive (ship) of mast(s). [DIS-]

dismay·, v.t., & n. (Fill with) consternation, discourage(ment). [prob. thr. OF f. DIS- + OHG *magan* be powerful (MAY v.)]

disme·mber, v.t. Tear or cut limb from limb; partition (empire, country), divide up. Hence **disme·mber**MENT n. [f. OF *desmembrer* (DIS-, L *membrum* limb)]

dismi·ss, v.t., & n. Send away, disperse, disband, (assembly, army; Mil., imperat., word of command closing drill, also as n., *the d.*, release at end of drill); allow to go; discharge, cashier, from service or office (*was dismissed the*, or *from the*, *army*); send away from one's presence; put out of one's thoughts, cease to feel; treat (subject) summarily; (Law) send out of court, refuse further hearing to, (case); (Cricket, of batsman) send (ball), send ball of (bowler), usu. *to boundary* or *for four* &c., (of fielding side) put (batsman, side) out (usu. *for* score). Hence **dismi·ss**AL(2), (now rare) **dismi·ss**ION, nn., **dismi·ss**IBLE a. [prob. f. L DI[1](*mittere miss-* send) with *dis-* due to obs. *dismit* f. OF *desmetre* in same sense]

dismou·nt, v.i. & t., & n. Alight, cause to alight, from or *from* horseback &c. (n., alighting); unseat, unhorse, (of horse, enemy, or stumble &c.); remove (thing) from its mount (esp. gun from carriage). [DIS-]

disobe·dience, n., **disobe·dient,** a. Disobeying (*d. to* orders, master, &c.), rebellious(ness), rule-breaking. Hence **disobe·dient**LY[2] adv. [f. OF (*des-*), see DIS-, OBEDIENCE, OBEDIENT]

disobey· (-bā), v.i. & t. Disregard orders, break rules; not obey (person, law). [f. F *désobéir* (DIS-, OBEY)]

disobli·ge, v.t. Refuse to consult convenience or wishes of. Hence **disobli·ging**[2] a., **disobli·ging**LY[2] adv., **disobli·ging**NESS n. [f. F *désobliger* (DIS-, OBLIGE)]

disor·der[1], n. Want of order, confusion; tumult, riot, commotion; ailment, disease. [DIS-]

disor·der[2], v.t. Disarrange, throw into confusion; put out of health, upset. [assim. to ORDER v. of earlier *disordain* f. OF *desordener* (DIS-, ORDAIN)]

disor·derly, a. Untidy, confused; irregular, unruly, riotous; hence **disor·derli**NESS n. Constituting public nuisance (*d. house*, bawdy, gaming, or betting, -house) [DISORDER[1], -LY[2]]

disor·ganize, v.t. Destroy system &c. of, throw into confusion. Hence **disorganiza·tion** n. [f. F *désorganiser* (DIS-, ORGANIZE)]

disŏ·rientāte (-*en*-), v.t. Place (church) with chancel not directly eastwards; confuse (person) as to his bearings (lit. & fig.). Hence **disorienta·tion** n. [DIS-]

disow·n, v.t. Refuse to recognize, repudiate, disclaim; renounce allegiance to. [DIS-]

dispă·rage (-ij), v.t. Bring discredit on, lower; speak slightingly of, depreciate. So **dispa·rage**MENT n., **dispa·raging**LY[2] adv. [f. OF *desparagier* marry unequally (DIS-, *parage* equality f. L *par* equal, -AGE)]

di·sparate (-*at*), a. & n. Essentially different, diverse in kind, incommensurable, without relation; hence **di·sparate**LY[2] adv., **di·sparate**NESS n. (N., usu. pl.) thing(s) so unlike that there is no basis for comparison. [f. L DIS(*paratus* p.p. of *parare* provide) separate, influenced in sense by L *dispar* unequal]

dispă·rity, n. Inequality, difference, incongruity. [f. F DIS(*parité* PARITY)]

dispar·k, v.t. Convert (park-land) to other uses. [DIS-]

dispar·t[1], n. (gunnery). Difference between semidiameters of gun at base-ring and at muzzle, to be allowed for in aiming; sight making the allowance. [?]

dispar·t[2], v.t. & i. Separate, part asunder, (t. & i.); go in different directions; distribute. [f. L DIS(*partire* f. *pars* part) distribute)]

dispa·ssionate, a. Free from emotion, calm, impartial. Hence **dispa·ssionate**LY[2] adv., **dispa·ssionate**NESS n. [DIS-]

dispa·tch[1], **des-,** v.t. & i. Send off to a destination or for a purpose; give the deathblow to, kill; get (task, business) promptly done, settle, finish off; eat (food, meal) quickly; (archaic) make haste. [f. Sp. *despachar* expedite (DIS-, L *pactus* p.p. of *pangere* fasten); not connected w. F *dépêcher*]

dispa·tch[2], **des-,** n. Sending off (*of* messenger, letter, &c.); putting to death (*happy d.*, suicide as practised by Japanese); prompt settlement of business, promptitude, efficiency, rapidity; written message, esp. official communication on State affairs (*d.-box*, for carrying these & other documents); agency for conveying goods &c.; *d.-rider*, esp. motorcyclist or horseman carrying military messages. [f. prec.]

dispe·l, v.t. (-ll-). Dissipate, disperse, (fears, darkness). [f. L DIS(*pellere* drive)]

dispe·nsable, a. That can be relaxed in special cases (canon, law, oath); not necessary, that can be done without. [f. med. L *dispensabilis* (DISPENSE, -ABLE)]

dispe·nsary, n. Place, esp. charitable institution, where medicines are dispensed; apothecary's shop. [DISPENSE, -ARY[1]]

dispensa·tion, n. Distributing, dealing out; ordering, management, esp. of the world by Providence; arrangement made by Nature or Providence; special dealing of Providence with community or person; religious system prevalent at a period (*Mosaic, O.T., Christian, d.*); exemption from penalty or duty laid down in esp. eccl. law (*with, from*); doing without (*with*). [f. L *dispensatio* (foll., -ATION)]

dispe·nse, v.t. & i. Distribute, deal out; administer (sacrament, justice); make up & give out (medicine); grant dispensations; release *from* obligation. *D. with*: relax, give exemption from, (rule); annul binding force of (oath); render needless (usu. *the need of* &c.); do without. Hence **dispe·nser**[1] n., (esp.) professional maker-up of medical prescriptions. [f. OF *dispenser* f. L *dispensare* frequent. of DIS-(*pendĕre pens-* weigh)]

dispeo·ple (-pēp-), v.t. Depopulate. [f. OF *despeupler* f. L DE(*populare* f. *populus* people)]

disper·se, v.t. & i. Scatter (t. & i.), drive, go, throw or send, in different directions, rout, dispel, be dispelled; send to or station at separate points; put in circulation, disseminate; (Opt.) divide (white light) into its coloured rays. Hence **disper·sal**(2) n., **disper·sĕdly**[2] adv., **disper·sive** a., **disper·sively**[2] adv., **disper·siveness** n. [f. F *disperser* f. L DI[1](*spergere -spers-* =*spargere* scatter)]

disper·sion, n. Dispersing (see prec.); *the D.*, the Jews dispersed among Gentiles after Captivity. [f. L *dispersio* (prec., -ION)]

dispi·rit, v.t. Make despondent, depress. Hence **dispi·ritedly**[2] adv. [DIS-]

dispi·teous, a. Pitiless. [19th-c. revival with changed sense as if f. DIS-, PITEOUS, of 16th-c. *despiteous* (DESPITE)]

displa·ce, v.t. Shift from its place; remove from office; oust, take the place of, put something else in the place of, replace. [f. OF *desplacer* (DIS-, PLACE n.)]

displa·cement, n. Displacing, being displaced; amount by which thing is shifted from its place; ousting, replacement by something else; amount or weight of fluid displaced by solid floating or immersed in it (*a ship with a d. of 11,000 tons*). [prec., -MENT]

display·[1], v.t. Exhibit, expose to view, show; show ostentatiously; reveal, betray, allow to appear. [f. OF *despleier* f. L DIS(*plicare* fold) cf. DEPLOY]

display·[2], n. Displaying; exhibition, show; ostentation; (Print.) arrangement of type with a view to calling attention. [f. prec.]

displea·se (-z), v.t. Offend, annoy, make indignant or angry, be disagreeable to; *be displeased* (*at, with*, or abs), disapprove, be indignant or dissatisfied. Hence **displea·sing**[2] a., **displea·singly**[2] adv. [f. OF *desplaisir* (DIS-, L *placēre* please)]

displea·sure (-ĕzher), n., & v.t. Displeased feeling, dissatisfaction, disapproval, anger; (vb) cause d. to, annoy. [f. OF as prec., assim. to PLEASURE]

displu·me, v.t. (poet.). Strip of feathers, lit. & fig. [DIS-]

dispor·t, v. refl. & i., & n. (archaic). Frolic, gambol, enjoy one*self*, display one*self* sportively; (n.) relaxation, pastime. [f. OF *desport(er)* f. DIS-, L *portare* carry]

dispo·sable, a. That can be disposed of, got rid of, made over, or used; at disposal. Hence **disposabi·lity** n. [DISPOSE, -ABLE]

dispo·sal, n. Disposing of, getting rid of, settling, dealing with, bestowal, assignment; sale; control, management, (*at* one's *d.*); placing, disposition, arrangement. [foll., -AL(2)]

dispo·se (-z), v.t. & i. Place suitably, at intervals, or in order; bring (person, mind) into certain state (esp. in p.p. *well-, ill-, disposed*); incline, make willing or desirous, *to* something or *to* do; give (thing) tendency *to*; determine course of events (*man proposes, God disposes*). *D. of*: do what one will with, regulate; get off one's hands, stow away, settle, finish, kill, demolish (claim, argument, opponent), dismiss (cricket XI *for* certain score), consume (food); sell. [f. OF DIS(*poser* see POSE[1]) substituted for L *disponere* thr. such derivatives as foll.]

disposi·tion, n. Setting in order, arrangement, relative position of parts; (usu. pl.) plan, preparations, stationing of troops ready for attack, defence, &c.; ordinance, dispensation, (*a. d. of Providence* &c.); bestowal by deed or will; control, disposal, (*at* one's *d.*); bent, temperament, natural tendency; inclination *to*. [F, f. L DIS(*positionem* f. *ponere posit-* place)]

disposse·ss (-zĕs), v.t. Oust, dislodge, (person); deprive *of*; rid (person) of or *of* evil spirit. Hence **disposse·ssion**, **disposse·ssor**[2], nn. [f. OF *despossesser* (DIS-, POSSESS)]

disprai·se (-z), v.t., & n. Disparage(ment), censure. [n. f. vb, f. OF *despreisier* f. L DE*pretiare* DEPRECIATE]

disproo·f, n. Refutation; thing that disproves. [DIS-]

dispropor·tion, n. Want of proportion; being out of proportion. Hence **dispropor·tioned**[2] a. [DIS-]

dispropor·tionate (-*a*t), a. Wanting proportion; relatively too large or small. Hence **dispropor·tionately**[2] adv. [DIS-]

dispro·ve (-ōōv), v.t. (p.p. *-d*, rarely *-n*). Prove false, show fallacy of, refute. [f. OF *desprover* (DIS-, PROVE)]

di·sputable, a. Open to question, uncertain. Hence **di·sputably**[2] adv. [f. L *disputabilis* (DISPUTE[1], -ABLE)]

disputa·tion, n. Argument, controversy. Hence **disputa·tious** a., **disputa·tious-**

LY[2] adv., **disputa·tious**NESS n. [f. L *disputatio* (foll., -ATION)]
dispu·te[1], v.i. & t. Argue, hold disputation, (*with, against*, person, *on, about*, subject), whence **di·sput**ANT(1) n. & a.; quarrel, have altercation; discuss (*whether, how*, &c.; point, question); controvert, call in question, (statement, fact); resist (landing, advance, &c.); contend for, strive to win, (pre-eminence, victory, every inch of ground). [f. OF *desputer* f. L DIS(*putare* reckon)]
dispu·te[2], n. Controversy, debate, (*in d.*, being argued about; *beyond, past, without, d.*, certainly, indisputably); heated contention, quarrel, difference of opinion. [f. prec.]
disqualifica·tion, n. In vbl senses; esp., thing that disqualifies. [foll., -FICATION]
disqua·lify, v.t. Unfit, disable, (*for* some purpose or office); incapacitate legally, pronounce unqualified. [DIS-]
disqui·et, v.t., a., & n. Deprive of peace, worry; (adj.) uneasy, disturbed, whence **disqui·**ETUDE, **disqui·et**NESS, nn.; (n.) anxiety, unrest. [DIS-]
disquisi·tion (-zĭshn), n. (Archaic) investigation, inquiry; (mod.) long or elaborate treatise or discourse *on* subject. Hence **disquisi·tion**AL a. [f. L DIS(*quisitio* f. *-quirere -quisit-* = *quaerere* seek, -ION)]
disra·te, v.t. (naut.). Reduce to lower rating or rank. [DIS-]
disregar·d, v.t., & n. Pay no attention to, ignore, treat as of no importance; (n.) indifference, neglect (*of, for*). [DIS-]
disrĕ·lish, n., & v.t. Dislike, (regard with) distaste, aversion. [DIS-]
disreme·mber v.t. (dial. &c.). Fail to remember. [DIS-]
disrepair·, n. Bad condition for want of repairs (usu. *is* &c. *in d.*). [DIS-]
disre·putable, a. Discreditable; of bad repute, not respectable in character or appearance. Hence **disre·putable**NESS n., **disre·putab**LY[2] adv. [DIS-]
disrepu·te, n. Ill repute, discredit. [DIS-]
disrespe·ct, n. Rudeness, want of respect. So **disrespe·ct**FUL a., **disrespe·ctful**LY[2] adv., **disrespe·ctful**NESS n. [DIS-]
disro·be, v.t. & i. Divest of robe or garment (also fig.); undress (refl. or intr.). [DIS-]
disroo·t, v.t. Uproot; dislodge. [DIS-]
disru·pt, v.t. Shatter, separate forcibly. [19th-c. vb f. L *disrupt-* see foll.]
disru·ption, n. Bursting asunder, violent dissolution, rent condition; *the D.*, split in Church of Scotland 1843. So **disru·pt**IVE a. [f. L DIS(*ruptio* f. *rumpere rupt-* break, -ION)]
dissa·tisfy, v.t. Fail to satisfy, make discontented (*dissatisfied with, at*). So **dis**SATISFA·CTION n. [DIS-]
dissea·t, v.t. Unseat. [DIS-]
disse·ct, v.t. Cut in pieces; anatomize, cut up, (animal, plant) to show its structure &c.; examine part by part, analyse, criticize in detail. Hence or cogn. **disse·ct**ION, **disse·ct**OR[2], nn. [f. L DIS(*secare sect-* cut)]
dissei·se, -ze, (-sēz), v.t. Oust, dispossess, *of* estates (or fig.). [f. OF *dessaisir* (DIS-, SEIZE)]
dissei·sin, -zin, (-sēz-), n. (legal). Disseising, wrongful dispossession of real property. [f. OF *dessaisine* (DIS-, SEIZIN)]
disse·mble, v.t. & i. Cloak, disguise, conceal, (character, feeling, intention, act); pretend not to see, ignore, (insult &c.; archaic); fail to mention (fact); conceal one's motives &c., be a hypocrite, whence **disse·mbl**ER[1] n. [perh. assim. to *resemble* of obs. *dissimule* f. OF *dissimuler* f. L DIS(*simulare* SIMULATE)]
dissĕ·minate, v.t. Scatter abroad, sow in various places, (lit., seed; usu. fig., doctrines, sedition, &c.). So **dissemin**A·TION, **disse·minat**OR[2], nn. [f. L DIS(*seminare* f. *semen -inis* seed), -ATE[3]]
disse·nsion, n. Discord arising from difference in opinion. [F, f. L DIS(*sensionem* f. *sentire sens-* feel, -ION)]
disse·nt[1], v.i. Refuse to assent; disagree, think differently or express such difference (*from*), esp. in religious doctrine from an established church (*dissenting minister*, nonconformist clergyman). Hence **disse·nting**LY[2] adv. [f. L DIS(*sentire* feel)]
disse·nt[2], n. (Expression of) difference of opinion; refusal to accept doctrines of established church, nonconformity, (collect.) dissenters. [f. prec.]
disse·nter, n. One who dissents, esp. from a national church; member of a sect that has separated itself from the Church of England or Scotland. [-ER[1]]
disse·ntient (-shĭ-, -shnt), a. & n. (One) disagreeing with a majority or official view (*D. Liberals* = Liberal Unionists). [f. L DIS(*sentire* feel), -ENT]
dissĕ·piment, n. (bot. & zool.). Partition, septum. [f. L DIS(*saepimentum* f. *saepire* f. *saepes* hedge, -MENT)]
disser·t, di·ssertate, vv.i. Discourse, give an exposition, disquisition, or **dis**sert**A·TION** n. [f. p.p. stems of L DIS(*serere sert-* join) & its frequent. *dissertare*, -ATE[3]]
disser·ve, v.t. Do an ill turn to. So **dis**SER·VICE n. [DIS-]
dissĕ·ver, v.t. & i. Sever, divide. [DIS-]
di·ssidence, n. Disagreement, dissent. [f. L *dissidentia* (foll., -ENCE)]
di·ssident, a. & n. Disagreeing, at variance; dissentient (a. & n.); dissenter. [f. L DIS(*sidēre* = *sedēre* sit), -ENT]
dissigh·t, n. Unsightly thing, eyesore. [DIS-]
dissi·milar, a. Unlike (*to*, also rarely *from, with*). Hence **dissi·milă·**RITY n., **dissi·milar**LY[2] adv. [DIS-]

dissi·milate, v.t. (philol.). Make unlike (sounds repeating each other, as in cinnamo*n*, orig. cinnamo*m*). Hence **dissimil**ATION n. [f. L DIS(*similis* like), after ASSIMILATE]

dissimi·litude, n. Unlikeness. [f. L *dissimilitudo* (prec., -TUDE)]

dissi·mūlate, v.t. & i. Pretend not to have or feel (cf. SIMULATE); dissemble, be hypocritical. So **dissi·mul**ATION, **dissi·mulat**OR[2], nn. [f. L DIS(*simulare* SIMULATE), -ATE[3]]

di·ssipate, v.t. & i. Disperse, dispel or disappear, (cloud, vapour, care, fear, darkness); dissolve to atoms, bring or come to nothing; squander (money); fritter away (energy, attention); engage in frivolous or dissolute pleasures (*people go there to d.*). Hence **di·ssipāt**IVE a. [f. L DIS(*sipare* throw), -ATE[3]]

di·ssipated, a. In vbl senses; esp., given to dissipation, dissolute. [-ED[1]]

dissipa·tion, n. Scattering, dispersion, disintegration; wasteful expenditure *of*; distraction, want of concentration, *of* faculties &c.; frivolous amusement; intemperate or vicious living. [f. L *dissipatio* (DISSIPATE, -ION)]

disso·cialize (-sha-), v.t. Make unsocial, disincline for society. [DIS-, SOCIAL, -IZE]

disso·ciate (-shĭ-), v.t. Disconnect, separate, in thought or in fact (*from*); (Chem.) decompose, esp. by heat. So **dissoci**A·TION (-sĭ-), n., **disso·ci**ABLE, **disso·cia**tIVE, (-sha-), aa. [f. L DIS(*sociare* f. *socius* comrade), -ATE[3]]

di·ssoluble (-ōōbl), a. That can be disintegrated, untied, or disconnected. Hence **di·ssolu**BI·LITY n. [f. L DIS(*solubilis* SOLUBLE)]

di·ssolute (-ōōt), a. Lax in morals, licentious. Hence **di·ssolute**LY[2] adv., **di·ssolute**NESS n. [f. L *dissolutus* p.p. (DISSOLVE)]

dissolu·tion (-ōō-), n. Disintegration, decomposition; liquefaction (of ice or snow); undoing *of* bond, partnership, marriage, or alliance; dismissal of assembly, esp. ending of a Parliament with a view to fresh election; death; coming to an end, fading away, disappearance. [f. L *dissolutio* (foll., -ION)]

disso·lve (-z-), v.t. & i. Decompose (t. & i.); make or become liquid esp. by immersion in liquid (*dissolved in tears*, weeping copiously), relax, enervate; vanish (*dissolving views*, of magic lantern, one fading while another replaces it); disperse (t. & i.), esp. *d. Parliament* or *d.*, declare DISSOLUTION; put an end to (partnership &c.), annul. Hence **disso·lv**ABLE a. [f. L DIS(*solvere solut-* loosen)]

disso·lvent (-z-), a. & n. (Thing) that dissolves something (usu. *of*). [-ENT]

di·ssonant, a. Discordant, harsh-toned, incongruous. Hence or cogn. **di·sso**NANCE n., **di·ssonant**LY[2] adv. [L DIS(*sonare* sound), -ANT]

dissua·de (-swād), v.t. Advise against, deprecate, (action); give advice to hinder, divert, (person *from*). So **dissua·s**ION n., **dissua·s**IVE a. [f. L DIS(*suadēre suas-* persuade)]

dissyllable &c. See **disy-** &c.

dissymme·trical, a., **dissy·mmetry,** n. Symmetrical, symmetry, in opposite directions, as in the two hands (esp. of crystals with two corresponding forms). [DIS-]

di·staff, n. Cleft stick about 3 ft long on which wool or flax was wound for spinning by hand; corresponding part of spinning-wheel; woman's work; *d. side*, female branch of family (cf. *spear-side* for the male). [OE *distæf* (LG *diesse* bunch of flax + STAFF)]

di·stal, a. (anat., bot.). Away from centre of body or point of attachment, terminal. [irreg. f. DISTANT, -AL]

di·stance, n., & v.t. Being far off, remoteness; extent of space between, interval, (*within striking-d.*, near enough to deliver blow); avoidance of familiarity, reserve, (esp. *keep* one's *d.*); distant point (*at, to, from, a d.*); remoter field of vision (*in the d.*; *middle d.*, in painted or actual landscape, between foreground & far part); space of time (*at this d. of time*); (in adv. phrr.) *a good* &c. *d. off.* (Vb) place or make seem far off; leave far behind in race or competition. [f. OF *destance* f. L *distantia* (DI[1]*stare* stand apart]

di·stant, a. Far, or a specified distance, away or *from* (*three miles d.*); remote, far apart, in position, time, resemblance, &c. (*a d. likeness, connexion*; *d. ages*; *d. signal* on railway, one in advance of home signal to give warning); not intimate, reserved, cool. Hence **di·stant**LY[2] adv. [F, f. L *distant-* part. st. see DISTANCE]

distā·ste, n. Dislike, repugnance, slight aversion, (*for*). [DIS-]

dista·steful, a. Disagreeable, repellent, (*to*). Hence **dista·steful**NESS n. [-FUL]

diste·mper[1], v.t. (archaic, usu. in p.p.). Upset, derange, in health or sanity (*a distempered fancy*). [f. med. L DIS(TEMPERare L)]

diste·mper[2], n. Derangement, an ailment, of body or mind; dog-disease with catarrh, cough, & weakness; political disorder. [f. prec.]

diste·mper[3], n., & v.t. Method of painting on plaster or chalk with colours mixed with yolk of egg, size, &c., instead of oil, used for scene-painting & internal walls (*paint in d.*); (vb) paint (wall &c., or abs.) thus. [n. f. vb, f. OF *destemprer* f. L as DISTEMPER[1]]

diste·nd, v.t. & i. Swell out by pressure

from within (balloon, vein, nostrils, &c.). So **diste·nsIBLE** a., **distensiBI·LITY, diste·nsION,** nn. [f. L DIS(*tendere tens-* stretch)]

di·stich (-k), n. Pair of verse lines, couplet. [f. L f. Gk DI[2](*stikhon* f. *stikhos* line) neut. adj.]

di·stichous (-k-), a. (bot.). (Having fruit &c.) arranged in two vertical lines on opposite sides of stem. [f. L f. Gk as prec., -OUS]

disti·l, v.i. & t. (-ll-). Trickle down; come or give forth in drops, exude; turn to vapour by heat, condense by cold, & recollect (liquid); extract essence of (plant &c., or fig. doctrine &c.); drive (volatile constituent) *off* or *out* by heat; make (whisky, essence) by distillation; undergo distillation. So **distillA·TION** n., **disti·llatORY** a. [f. L DI[1](*stillare* drop)]

di·stillate (-*at*), n. Product of distillation. [as prec., -ATE[2]]

disti·ller, n. One who distils, esp. alcoholic spirit, whence **disti·llERY**(3) n.; apparatus for distilling salt water at sea. [-ER[1]]

disti·nct, a. Not identical, separate, individual, different in quality or kind, unlike, (*from*, or abs.); clearly perceptible, plain, definite; unmistakable, decided, positive. Hence **disti·nctLY**[2] adv., **disti·nctNESS** n. [f. L *distinctus* p.p. see DISTINGUISH]

disti·nction, n. Making of a difference, discrimination, the difference made (*d. without a difference*, a merely nominal or artificial one); being different; thing that differentiates, mark, name, title; showing of special consideration, mark of honour; distinguished character, excellence, eminence; (of literary style) individuality. [F, f. L *distinctionem* (DISTINGUISH, -ION)]

disti·nctive, a. Distinguishing, characteristic. Hence **disti·nctiveLY**[2] adv., **disti·nctiveNESS** n. [DISTINGUISH, -IVE]

distingué (F), a. Of distinguished air, features, manners, &c.

disti·nguish, v.t. & i. Divide *into* classes &c.; be, see, or point out, the difference of (thing, thing *from* another; also intr. with *between*), differentiate, draw distinctions; characterize, be a mark or property of; make out by listening, looking, &c., recognize; make one*self* prominent (often *by* gallantry &c.). Hence **disti·nguishABLE** a., **disti·nguishabLY**[2] adv. [f. L DI[1](*stinguere stinct-* extinguish prob. cogn. w. Gk *stizō* prick), with irreg. use of -ISH[1]]

disti·nguished, a. In vbl senses; esp.: remarkable (*for* or *by* quality &c.), eminent, famous, of high standing; = DISTINGUÉ. [-ED[1]]

distor·t, v.t. Put out of shape, make crooked or unshapely, (actually or, as by curved mirror &c., apparently); misrepresent (motives, facts, statements). Hence or cogn. **distor·tedLY**[2] adv., **distor·tION** n., **distor·tionAL** a. [f. L DIS-(*torquēre tort-* twist)]

distor·tionist, n. Caricaturist; acrobat who distorts his body. [-IST]

distra·ct, v.t. Divert, draw away, (attention, the mind, usu. *from*); draw in different directions, divide or confuse the attention of, (often p.p. with *between*) bewilder, perplex; (chiefly p.p.) drive mad or infuriate (*-ed with, by, at*). Hence **distra·ctedLY**[2], **distra·ctingLY**[2], advv. [f. L DIS(*trahere tract-* draw)]

distra·ction, n. Diversion of, thing that diverts, the mind; interruption; lack of concentration; amusement, relief from over-absorption; confusion, perplexity, internal conflict, dissension; frenzy, madness, (*to d.*, to a mad degree). [f. L *distractio* (prec., -ION)]

distrai·n, v.i. (legal). Levy a distress (*upon* person or his goods, or abs.), seize chattels to compel person to pay money due (esp. rent) or meet an obligation, or to obtain satisfaction by sale of the chattels. Hence **distrai·nER**[1], **distrai·nOR**[2], **distrainEE·**, **distrai·nMENT** & (in same sense) **distrai·nt,** nn. [f. OF *destreindre* f. L DI[1](*stringere strict-* squeeze)]

distrait· (-ā), a. (fem. *-te*, pr. -āt). Absent-minded, not attending. [F]

distraugh·t, a. (archaic). Violently agitated; crazy. [var. of obs. *distract* a. f L *distractus* p.p. see DISTRACT]

distre·ss[1], n. Severe pressure of pain, sorrow, &c., anguish; want of money or necessaries; straits, dangerous position; exhaustion, being tired out, breathlessness; (Law) = DISTRAINT; *d.-gun, -rocket*, signals from ship in danger; *d.-warrant*, authorizing distraint. Hence **distre·ssFUL** a. (*the -ful country*, Ireland). [f. OF *destrece* f. LL **districtia* (DISTRAIN, -Y[1])]

distre·ss[2], v.t. Subject to severe strain, exhaust, afflict; cause anxiety to, vex, make unhappy. Hence **distre·ssingLY**[2] adv. [f. F *destresser* f. LL *districtiare* as prec.]

distri·bute, v.t. Deal out, give share of to each of a number; spread abroad, scatter, put at different points; divide into parts, arrange, classify; (Log.) use (term) in its full extension so that it includes every individual of the class. Hence (orig. *-er*) **distri·butOR**[2](1, 2) n., **distri·butABLE** a. [f. L DIS(*tribuere tribut-* assign)]

distribu·tion, n. Distributing, apportionment; (Pol. Econ.) dispersal among consumers effected by commerce, also extent to which individuals or classes share in aggregate products of community; spreading abroad, dispersing, scattered situation or arrangement; division into parts, arranging, classification; (Log.) application of term to all individuals of the class. Hence **distribu·tionAL** a. [F, f. L *distributionem* (prec., -ION)]

distri·butive, a. & n. Of, concerned with, produced by, distribution; (Log., Gram.) referring to each individual of a class, not to the class collectively; (n., gram.) d. word (as *each, neither, every*). Hence **distri·butive**LY[2] adv. [F (*-if, -ive*), f. L as DISTRIBUTE, -IVE]

di·strict, n., & v.t. Territory marked off for special administrative purpose; division of parish with its own church or chapel & clergyman; urban or rural division of county with D. Council; assigned sphere of operations; tract of country with common characteristics, region; *D. Railway*, serving parts of London & suburbs; *d. visitor*, person working under clergyman's direction in section of parish; (vb) divide into dd. [F, f. med. L *districtus* jurisdiction f. L *district-* see DISTRAIN]

distru·st[1], n. Want of trust, doubt, suspicion. Hence **distru·st**FUL a. (*of*), **distru·stful**LY[2] adv. [DIS-]

distru·st[2], v.t. Have no confidence in, doubt, not rely on. [DIS-]

distur·b, v.t. Agitate, trouble, disquiet, unsettle; perplex. [f. OF *destorber* f. L DIS(*turbare* f. *turba* crowd)]

distur·bance, n. Interruption of tranquillity, agitation; tumult, uproar, outbreak; (Law) molestation, interference with rights or property. [f. OF *destorbance* (prec., -ANCE)]

disu·nion, n. Separation, want of union, dissension. So **dis**UNI·TE v.t. & i. [DIS-]

disu·se[1] (-s), n. Discontinuance, want of use or practice, desuetude. [DIS-]

disu·se[2] (-z), v.t. Cease to use. [DIS-]

disy·llable, diss-, n. Word, metrical foot, of two syllables. So **dis(s)yllă·b**IC a., **dis(s)ylla·b**ICALLY adv. [f. F *dissyllabe* (DI-[2], SYLLABLE); *-ss-* in F as sign of hard sound]

ditch, n., & v.i. & t. Long narrow excavation, esp. to hold or conduct water or serve as boundary; watercourse; DIE[2] *in last d.*; *d.-water*, stagnant in d. (esp. *dull as d.-water*). (Vb) make or repair dd. (esp. *hedging & ditching*), whence **di·tch**ER[1] (1, 2) n.; provide with dd., drain; (pass., of vehicle) stick in a d. [OE *dīc*, whence also DIKE]

dī·thĕism, n. Religious dualism, belief in independent principles of good & evil. [DI-[2]]

di·ther (-dh-), v.i., & n. Tremble, quiver. [prob. imit.]

dĭ·thyramb (-ăm), n. Greek choric hymn of wild character; Bacchanalian song; vehement or inflated poem, speech, or writing. So **dithyra·mb**IC (-mb-) a. & n. [f. L f. Gk *dithurambos* etym. dub.]

di·ttany, n. A herb, formerly of medicinal repute. [f. OF *ditan* f. L f. Gk *diktamnon* perh. f. *Diktē* in Crete]

di·tto, a. & n. (*abbr.* d°, do; pl. *-os*). The aforesaid, the same, (in accounts, inventories, & commerc. or colloq. talk, instead of repeating word); duplicate, similar thing, (*d. suit, suit of dd.*, clothes all of one material); *say d. to*, agree with, endorse opinion of. [It. (now *detto*), f. L *dictus* p.p. of *dicere* say]

dittŏ·graphy, n. Copyist's mistaken repetition of letter, word, or phrase. Hence **dittogra·ph**IC a. [f. Gk *dittos* double, -GRAPHY]

di·tty, n. Short simple song. [ME *dite* f. OF *dité* f. L *dictatum* neut. p.p. of *dictare* DICTATE[2]]

di·tty-bag, -box, nn. Sailor's, fisherman's, receptacle for odds & ends. [?]

dīūrĕ·tic, a. & n. (Substance) exciting discharge of urine. [f. L f. Gk *diourētikos* f. DI[3](*oureō* make water), -IC]

dīur·nal, a. (Astron.) occupying one day; (archaic) daily, of each day; of the day, not nocturnal. Hence **diur·nal**LY[2] adv. [f. L *diurnalis* (*dies* day)]

div (dēv), n. Evil spirit in Persian mythology. [Pers., =Skr. *deva* god]

di·va (dē-), n. Great woman singer, prima donna. [It. f. L, =goddess]

dī·vagate, v.i. Stray, digress. Hence **divag**A·TION n. [f. L DI[1](*vagari* wander), -ATE[3]]

dī·valent, a. Combining with two atoms of hydrogen &c., having two combining equivalents. [DI-[2], L *valēre* be worth, -ENT]

dĭvă·n, n. Oriental council of State, esp. Turkish privy council; oriental council-chamber, court of justice; long seat against room-wall; smoking-room, cigar-shop. [Turk., f. Pers. *devan* brochure, account-book, custom-house (see DOUANE), tribunal, senate, bench]

dīvă·ricāte (*or* dĭ-), v.i. Diverge, branch, (of roads, branches, &c.). Hence or cogn. **diva·ric**A·TION n., **diva·ric**ATE[2] (*-at*) a. (bot., zool.). [f. L DI[1](*varicare* f. *varicus* straddling), -ATE[3]]

dive, v.i., & n. Plunge, esp. head foremost, into water &c.; go down or out of sight suddenly; put one's hand *into* water, vessel, pocket; penetrate or search mentally *into*; *diving-bell*, open-bottomed box or bell in which person can be let down into deep water. (N.) plunge, header, swim under water; sudden dart out of sight; (U.S.) drinking-den. [mixture of sense of OE *dúfan* sink with form of OE *dýfan* immerse]

di·ver, n. In vbl senses; esp.: person who dives for pearls, to examine sunk ships, &c.; kinds of diving bird. [-ER[1]]

dīver·ge (*or* dĭ-), v.i. & t. Proceed in different directions from point or each other; go aside *from* track; differ, deviate; make d., deflect. Hence **diver·g**ENCE,

diver·gENCY, nn., **diver·gENT** a., **diver·gentLY**², **diver·gingLY**², advv. [f. DI-¹, L *vergere* VERGE v.]

di·vers (-z), a. (archaic or facet.). Sundry, several, more than one. [OF, f. L DI¹- (*versus* p.p. of *vertere* turn) = foll.]

diver·se (*or* dī-), a. Unlike in nature or qualities; varied, changeful. Hence or cogn. **diver·seLY**² adv., **diver·siFORM** a. [as prec.]

diver·sify̆ (prec.), v.t. Make diverse, vary, modify, variegate. So **diversiFICA·TION** n. [f. OF *diversifier* f. med. L *diversificare* (prec., -FY)]

diver·sion (prec.), n. Deflecting, deviation; diverting of attention, manœuvre to secure this, feint; recreation, pleasant distraction, pastime. [f. med. L *diversio* (DIVERT, -ION)]

diver·sity (prec.), n. Being diverse, unlikeness; different kind; variety. [f. OF *diversité* f. L *diversitatem* (DIVERS, -ITY)]

diver·t (prec.), v.t. Turn aside, deflect, (stream &c., *from*, *to*, or abs.); turn elsewhere, get rid of, ward off; draw off attention of (*from* one thing *to* another), distract; entertain, amuse, whence **diver·tING**² a., **diver·tingLY**² adv. [f. OF *divertir* f. L DI¹*vertere* & DE*vertere* *-vers-* turn in different directions, turn away]

Di·vēs, n. (Typical name for) rich man; (Law) *d. costs*, costs on higher scale (opp. *pauper costs*). [L, = rich, ref. to *Luke* xvi. 19, where Vulgate has *d.*]

dive·st (*or* dī-), v.t. Unclothe; strip *of* garment &c.; deprive, rid, *of* (*d. oneself of*, abandon). Hence **dive·stMENT**, **dive·stitURE**, nn. [earlier *devest* f. OF *desvestir* (DIS-, L *vestire* f. *vestis* garment)]

divi·de¹, v.t. & i. Separate (t. & i.) into or *in(to)* parts, split or break up; make way through, make (way &c.) *through*; mark out actually or mentally in parts, fall into parts, make classification in, distinguish kinds of; sunder, part, cut off, (things, thing *from*); cause to disagree, set at variance, distract; distribute, deal out, (*among*, *between*); share *with* others; (Math.) see how often number contains another (*d.* 20 *by* 3), do DIVISION, (of number) go into (number) without remainder; part (t. & i. of House of Parliament, meeting, &c.) into two sets in voting. [f. L DI¹(*vidĕre* *-vis-* cf. *vidua* WIDOW)]

divi·de², n. (U.S. &c.). Watershed. [f. prec.]

di·vidend, n. (Math.) number to be divided by DIVISOR; sum payable as interest on loan or as profit of joint-stock company (EX *d.*, CUM *d.*) or to creditors of insolvent estate; individual's share of it (*d.-warrant*, order to pay this). [f. F *dividende* f. L *dividendum* (DIVIDE¹, -ND¹)]

divi·der, n. In vbl senses; esp., (pl.) measuring-compasses, esp. those provided with screw for setting to small intervals. [-ER¹]

divi·dual, a. Separate; separable. Hence **divi·dualLY**² adv. [f. L *dividuus* + -AL]

divina·tion, n. Divining, insight into or discovery of the unknown or future by supernatural means; skilful forecast, good guess. [OF, f. L *divinationem* (DIVINE², -ATION)]

divi·ne¹, a. (-er, -est) & n. Of, from, like, God or a god (*d. right of kings*, independent of their subjects' will); devoted to God, sacred, (*d. service*, public worship); superhumanly excellent, gifted, or beautiful; hence **divi·neLY**² adv. (N.) person (usu. cleric) skilled in theology. [f. OF *devin* f. L *divinus* cf. *divus, deus*, god]

divi·ne², v.t. & i. Make out by inspiration, magic, intuition, or guessing, foresee, predict, conjecture; practise divination; *divining-rod*, see DOWSING. Hence **divi·nER**²(4) n. [f. F *deviner* f. L *divinare* (*divinus* DIVINE¹)]

divĭ·nity, n. Being divine, godhood; a god, godhead; *the D.*, God; adorable person; theology, University theological faculty; (Bookbind.) *d. calf* (dark brown with *blind* TOOLING). [f. OF *devinité* f. L *divinitatem* (DIVINE¹, -TY)]

dĭ·vinize, v.t. Deify. Hence **diviniZA·TION** n. [f. F *diviniser* f. *divin* = *devin* DIVINE¹]

divĭ·sible (-z-), a. Capable of being divided actually or in thought; (Math.) *d. by*, containing (a number) some number of times without remainder. Hence **divisiBI·LITY** n. [f. L *divisibilis* (DIVIDE¹, -IBLE)]

divi·sion (-ĭzhn), n. Dividing or being divided, severance; distribution, sharing, (*d. of labour*, time-saving arrangement giving different parts of manufacturing process &c. to different persons); disagreement, discord; (Math.) process of dividing number by another (*long, short, d.*, methods usual with divisors greater, not greater, than 12); (Log.) classification, enumeration of parts, distinction of meanings; (Parl.) separation of House into two sets for counting votes; dividing line, boundary; part, section; administrative &c. district, definite part, under single command, of army or fleet, esp. (Mil.) unit of two or more brigades usu. of infantry with artillery &c. attached; (Nat. Hist.) section of kingdom, order, genus, &c.; (Civil Service) *second d.*, lower grade of clerks; (Prison) *1st, 2nd, 3rd, d.*, lenient, medium, severe, treatment in prison prescribed by judge. Hence **divi·sionAL** a. (*-al rest*, period for which a d. is relieved from trench fighting & sent behind the line), **divi·sionalLY**² adv. [OF, f. L *divisionem* (DIVIDE¹, -ION)]

divi·sor (-z-), n. (math.). Number by which another (the DIVIDEND) is to be divided; number that divides another without remainder. [L (DIVIDE[1], -OR[2])]

divor·ce[1], n. Legal dissolution of marriage (*d. ā vi·ncŭlō matrimō·nii*, i.e. from the bonds of marriage) opp. to judicial separation of married pair (*d. ā me·nsā et thŏ·ro*, i.e. from board and bed); (loosely) decree of nullity of marriage; (fig.) severance, sundering. [F, f. L *divortium* f. DI[1](*vortere* later *vertere* turn)]

divor·ce[2], v.t. Legally dissolve marriage between; separate (spouse) by d. *from*; put away, repudiate, (spouse); dissolve (union); sever (things, thing *from*). Hence **di-** or **divorcEE·** (also F *divorcé* masc., *-ée* fem.), **divor·ceMENT**, nn. [f. F *divorcer* f. med. L *divortiare* (prec.)]

di·vot, n. (Sc., north.). A turf, sod; (golf) piece of turf cut out by bad stroke. [?]

divu·lge (-j), v.t. Let out, reveal. Hence or cogn. **divulgA·TION**, **divu·lgeMENT**, **divu·lgENCE**, nn. [f. L DI[1](*vulgare* publish f. *vulgus* people)]

Di·xie('s land), n. The U.S.A. south of Mason & Dixon's line, the former slave States. [corrupt. of *Dixon*, surveyor]

di·xy, n. Large iron pot in which stew, tea, &c., are made or carried on campaign. [?]

di·zen (*or* dī-), v.t. Array with finery, deck *out* or *up*, bedizen. [cf. LG *diesse* bunch of flax, & *distaff*; from 1530]

di·zzy, a., & v.t. Giddy, dazed, unsteady, tottering, confused; making giddy; (of mountain, tower, &c.) very high; (of stream, wheel, &c.) whirling rapidly; hence **di·zziLY**[2] adv., **di·zziNESS** n. (Vb) make d., bewilder. [OE *dusig* n., *dysigan* v., cf. LG *dusen* v.]

djibba(h). See JIBBA(H).

do[1] (dōō), v.t. & i. & aux. (sing. pres. 2, *doest* as t. & i., *dost* pr. dŭst as aux.; 3, *does* pr. dŭz & archaic *doth* pr. dŭ-, *doeth*; past *did, didst*; p.p. *done* pr. dŭn; *dōn't, didn't*, are common for *do not, did not*; *doesn't*, & vulg. *dōn't*, for *does not*). 1. Vb trans.: (archaic) put (now only in *do to death*); bestow, impart, grant, render, give, (*does him credit, does credit to his intelligence*; *does me good, harm*; *did a service to his country*; *do justice to*); perform, carry out, effect, bring to pass, (thing, work, good, right, wrong, duty, bidding, penance; *it is not done*, is bad form), whence **do·ING**[1](1) n. (usu. pl.); (p.p. & perf.) complete, bring to an end, (*it is, I have, done*); exert, use, (*do* one's *endeavour*, one's *best*, &, slang, one's *damnedest*); produce, make, (*have done six copies*); operate on, deal with, repair, set in order, (*does the French books for the Athenaeum*; *paper-hanger does a house, housemaid a room*; *do* one's *hair*); cook, roast, &c., to the right degree (*chop done to a turn*; *well, over, under, -done*); solve (sum, problem); translate *into* English &c.; work at (lesson); play the part of (*did Lear, the cicerone*; hence *do the polite* &c.); exhaust, tire out; (slang) cheat (also *do in the eye*); traverse (such a distance); (colloq.) see the sights of (city, museum); (slang) undergo (term of punishment); (with noun of action as compd vb) *do battle* &c., fight &c.; (slang) provide food &c. for (*they do you very well*; *do* one*self well*, make liberal provision for one's own comfort). 2. Vb intr.: (w. adv. or advl phr.) act, proceed, (*do as they do at Rome*; *would do wisely to withdraw*); perform deeds (*do or die*); make an end (*have done!*, cease; *let us have done with it*); fare, get on, (well, badly, &c.; of person or thing; *how do you do?* or *how d'ye do?*); be suitable, answer purpose, serve, suffice. 3. Vb substitute: (a) replacing vb and taking its construction, as *I chose my wife as she did her gown*; (b) replacing vb & obj. &c., as *if you saw the truth as clearly as I do*; (c) as elliptical auxiliary, as '*did you see him?*' '*I did*'; (d) with *so, it, which*, &c., as: *I wanted to see him, & I did so*; *in passing through the market, which he seldom did*; *if you want to tell him, do it now*. 4. Vb aux.: used with infin. for simple pres. & past (a) when special emphasis is to be laid on a fact, as *I do so wish I could*, esp. in contrast with what has preceded, as *But I did see him*; also for imperat. in urgent petitions, as *do tell me, do but think*; or when the pronoun is inserted & emphasized, as *do* you *go rather*; (b) when inversion is desired, as *rarely does it happen that*; (c) the usual form in questions except with *have, be*, & some monosyl. vbs, as *did you recognize her?, do you dare?* or *dare you?*; (d) usual in *not* statements except with *be, have, dare, need*, &c.; also in *not* commands. 5. Phrr. &c.: *a to-do*, bustle, fuss; *well-to-do*, rich enough, thriving; *have to do with*, be concerned or connected or have dealings with; *nothing doing*, going on; *done*, used in accepting offer or bet; *do-nothing*, a. & n., idle(r). 6. With prepp.: *do by*, treat, deal with, in such a way; *do for* (colloq.), act as housekeeper &c. for, ruin, destroy, kill; *do to, unto*, = do by; *do with*, get on with, tolerate (jocularly, *could do with a drink*), find sufficient; *do without*, dispense with. 7. With advv.; *do away* (*with*), abolish; *do in* (slang), kill; *do up*, restore, repair, wrap up (parcel), tire out. Hence **do·ABLE** (dōō-) a., **do·ER**[1] (dōō-) n. [com.-WG, OE *dón* cf. G *tun*, f. Aryan *dhe-, dho-*, put, cf. Gk *tithēmi*, L *-dere* in *condere* &c.]

do[2] (dōō), n. (slang). Swindle, imposture, hoax. [f. prec.]

dō[3], n. (mus.). Key-note of scale (*movable do*); the note C (*fixed do*). [arbitrary]

dō[4], abbr. of DITTO.

doat. See DOTE.

do·bbin, n. Draught or farm horse. [pet-name = Robert]

Docē·tic, a., **Docē·tist, Docē·tism,** nn. (Of, holder of) the heresy that Christ's body was not human but phantasmal or of celestial substance. [med. L f. Gk *dokētai* lit. seemers (*dokeō* seem) + -IC, -IST, -ISM]

do·chmiăc (dŏk-), a. & n. Composed of dochmii (dochmius, ⏑——⏑—); (n., usu. pl.) line(s) so composed. [f. Gk *dokhmiakos* f. *dokhmios* adj. (*dokhmē* hand-breadth f. *dekhomai* receive)]

dŏ·cile (*or* -īl), a. Teachable; submissive; easily managed. So **doci·lity** n. [F, f. L *docilis* (*docēre* teach, -IL)]

dock[1], n. Kinds of coarse weedy herb, popular antidote for nettle stings. [OE *docce*, cf. G *docken-blätter*]

dock[2], n. Solid fleshy part of animal's tail; crupper of saddle or harness. [= Icel. *dockr* stumpy tail, cf. G *docke* bundle, plug]

dock[3], v.t. Cut short (animal in tail, person in hair; or tail &c.); lessen, deprive *of*, put limits on (person, supplies); (Law) *d. the entail*, cut it off; *docktailed*, with tail docked. [f. prec.]

dock[4], n., & v.t. & i. Basin with floodgates in which ships may be loaded, unloaded, or repaired (*dry* or *graving d.*, for repairing or building, water being pumped out; *wet d.*, with water kept at high-tide level; *floating d.*, floating structure usable as dry d.); (usu. pl.) range of d. basins with wharves and offices, dockyard; (Railway) platform-enclosure in which line terminates; *d.-dues*, charge for use of dock, also **do·ckage**(4) n.; *d.-glass* (large, for wine-tasting); *d.-master*, superintendent of *dockyard* or enclosure with dd. & all ship building & repairing appliances, esp. in connexion with Navy. (Vb) bring (ship), (of ship) come, into d.; furnish with dd. [cf. 16th-c. Du. *docke*]

dock[5], n. Enclosure in criminal court for prisoner; *d. brief* (undertaken gratis by barrister in court selected by poor prisoner in d.). [=Fl. *dok* rabbit-hutch]

do·cker, n. Labourer in DOCK[4]. [-ER[1]]

do·cket, n., & v.t. (Law) register of legal judgements (vb, enter in this); endorsement on letter or document showing its contents or subject (vb, endorse thus); Custom-House warrant certifying payment of duty; certificate of cotton clearing-house entitling presenter to delivery. [f. 15th c.; etym. dub.]

do·ckize, v.t. Make (river) into range of docks. Hence **dockiza·tion** n. [-IZE]

do·ctor[1], n. (Archaic) teacher, learned man, (*Dd. of the Church*, certain, esp. four Eastern & four Western, early fathers; *who shall decide when dd. disagree?*); holder of the highest university degree in any faculty (often honorary; used as prefix to surname, usu. abbr. *Dr*), esp. d. of medicine male or female (also pop. of any medical man, M.D. or not, esp. in voc.); kinds of mechanical appliance for regulating &c.; artificial fly; *d.'s stuff*, physic. Hence or cogn. **do·ctoral, doctor·ial, do·ctorless**, aa. **do·ctorate**[1], **do·ctorship**(1, 3), **do·ctorhood, do·ctress**[1] (facet. &c. for usu. *d.* fem.), nn. [OF f. L (*docēre doct-* teach, -OR[2])]

do·ctor[2], v.t. & i. Confer degree of d. on; treat (patient, one*self*) medically; patch up (machinery &c.); adulterate, falsify; practise as physician (esp. in gerund). [f. prec.]

Doctors' Commons, n. pl. Common table, buildings (in which certain courts were held), of former College of Doctors of Civil Law in London (frequent literary allusions to probate, marriage-licence, & divorce business once transacted there). [COMMONS]

doctrinaire·, doctrinār·ian, nn. & aa. Pedantic theorist, person who applies principle without allowance for circumstances; hence **doctrinair·ism**(2), **doctrinar·ianism**(2), nn. (Adj.) theoretic and unpractical. [-*aire* F (L *doctrina* DOCTRINE, -ARY[1]) name of French political party 1815; -ARIAN]

doctrī·nal (*also* dŏ·ktrĭ-), a. Of, inculcating, doctrine(s). Hence **doctrinally**[2] adv. [f. LL *doctrinalis* (foll., -AL)]

do·ctrine, n. What is taught, body of instruction; religious, political, scientific, &c., belief, dogma, or tenet (*Monroe d.*, U.S. policy foreshadowed by President Monroe 1823 discountenancing European State interference in America). Hence **do·ctrinism**(1), **do·ctrinist**(1), nn., **do·ctrinize**(2) v.i. [F, f. L *doctrina* (DOCTOR[1], -INE[3])]

dŏ·cument, n., & v.t. Thing, esp. deed, writing, or inscription, that furnishes evidence (*human d.*, description, incident, &c., illustrating human nature); hence **docume·ntary**[1] a. (Vb) prove by, provide with, dd. or evidence; so **documenta·tion** n. [OF, f. L *documentum* (*docēre* teach, -MENT)]

do·dder[1], n. Kinds of slender leafless threadlike parasitic plant. (ME *doder* cf. G *dotter*]

do·dder[2], v.i. Tremble, nod, with frailty, palsy, &c. (*d.-grass*, Quaking-grass); totter, potter, be feeble. [?]

do·ddered, a. Having lost the top or branches (of oaks & other trees). [prob. f. frequent. of obs. vb *dod* poll, lop]

dōdec(a)-, pref. =twelve-, as *dodĕ·cagon*, plane figure of twelve sides, *dodecahĕ·dron* (*or* -hē-), solid figure of twelve faces, *dodecasy·llable*, verse of twelve syllables. [f. Gk *dōdeka* twelve]

dodge[1], v.i. & t. (Intr.) move to & fro, change position, shuffle; move quickly *round*, *about*, or *behind*, obstacle so as to elude pursuer, blow, &c.; play fast &

loose, quibble, prevaricate; (of bell in chime) sound one place out of the normal order. (Trans.) baffle by finesse, trifle with; elude (pursuer, opponent, blow) by sideward deviation &c.; move (thing) to & fro; ask (person) questions in unexpected order. [?]

dodge², n. Piece of dodging, quick side-movement; trick, artifice; (colloq.) clever expedient, mechanical &c. contrivance; sounding of bell out of normal place in chimes. Hence **do·dg**Y² a. [f. prec.]

do·dger, n. In vbl senses; esp., artful or elusive person. [-ER¹]

dō·do, n. (pl. *-oes, -os*). Large extinct bird of Mauritius. [f. Port. *doudo* simpleton]

doe (dō), n. Female of fallow deer (cf. BUCK¹), hare, or rabbit; *doeskin*, skin of d., leather of this, fine cloth resembling it. [OE *dá* perh. f. L *dama* deer]

does, doest. See DO¹.

doff, v.t. Take off (hat, clothing); (rarely) abandon, discard, (custom, condition). [=*do off*]

dog¹, n. Quadruped of many breeds wild & domesticated; hunting-dog (fig., *dd. of war*, havoc, rapine); male of d., wolf (also *d.-wolf*), (fem. *bitch*), or fox (also *d.-fox*); worthless or surly person; fellow (*sly, lucky, jolly, d.*; SEA-*d.*); (Astron.) *Greater* & *Lesser D.*, constellations, also Sirius or Procyon, chief star in either (also *d.-star*, usu. Sirius; *d.-days*, hottest part of year in July & Aug., variously dated according to heliacal & cosmical rising of Sirius); kinds of mechanical device for gripping &c.; (pl., also *fire-dd.*) pair of metal supports for burning wood, or for grate, or for fire-irons; (also *sea-d.*) light near horizon portending storm; *sun-d.*, parhelion. Phrr.; *go to the dd.*, be ruined; *throw to the dd.*, throw away, sacrifice; *not have* WORD¹ *to throw at d.*; *every d. has his* DAY; *love me, love my d.*, accept my friends as yours; *rain* CATS *& dd.*; *die like a d., a d.'s death*, miserably, shamefully; *not a d.'s chance*, not even the least chance; *take hair of d. that bit you*, drink more to cure effects of drink; *help lame d. over stile*, be friend in need; *lead, lead* one, *a d.'s life*, be worried, worry another; *give d. ill name & hang him*, of power of nickname or slander; *let sleeping dd. lie*, let well alone; *d. in the manger*, one who prevents others' enjoying what is useless to him; *d. in a blanket*, rolled currant dumpling or jam pudding. *Dogberry*, fruit of *dogwood* or wild cornel; *d.-biscuit*, for feeding dd.; *d.-box*, railway van for dd.; *dog-cart*, two-wheeled driving-cart with cross seats back to back; *d.-cheap*, very; *d.-collar*, lit., & fig. of person's straight high collar; *d.-faced*, epithet of kind of baboon; *d.-fall*, in which wrestlers touch ground together; *d.-fennel*, Stinking Camomile; *d.-fish*, kinds of small shark & other fish; *d.('s)-grass*, Couch-grass; *d.-hole, -hutch*, mean room; *d. latin*, incorrect, mongrel; *d.-lead*, string &c. for leading d.; *d.-leg(ged) staircase*, going back & forward without well-hole; *d.-rose*, wild hedge rose; *d.('s)-ear* n. & v.t., corner of page turned down with use, fill (book) with these; *d.-shore*, prop used in launching; *d.-skin*, leather of or imitating d.'s skin used for gloves; *d.-sleep*, light & fitful; *d.'s letter*, r (f. snarling sound); *d.'s-meat*, horseflesh, offal; *d.'s-nose*, beer & gin; *d.('s)-tail*, kind of grass; *d.'s-tongue*, plants of borage kind; *d.'s-tooth*, plant with speckled leaves & flowers; *d.-tired*, tired out; *d.-tooth*, small pyramidal ornament esp. in Norman & Early English architecture; *d.-violet*, scentless kind; *d.-watch* (Naut.), short half watch of two hours (4–6, 6–8, p.m.); *d.-whip*, for keeping dd. in order. Hence **do·gg**ISH¹, **do·g**LESS, **do·g**LIKE, aa., **do·ggy¹** or **do·ggie** (-Y³), **do·g**HOOD, nn. [OE *docga* etym. dub.]

dog², v.t. Follow closely, pursue, track, (person, his *steps*; of person or calamity &c.); (Mech.) grip with d. [f. prec.]

dō·gāte, n. Office of doge. [f. F *dogat* f. It. *dogato* (foll., -ATE¹)]

doge (-j), n. (hist.). Chief magistrate of Venice, Genoa. [F f. It., f. L *ducem* nom. *dux* leader]

do·ggĕd (-g-), a. Obstinate, tenacious, persistent, unyielding, (*it's d. does it*, persistency succeeds). Hence **do·gged**LY² adv., **do·gged**NESS n. [-ED²]

do·gger (-g-), n. Two-masted bluff-bowed Dutch fishing-boat. [f. 14th c., etym. dub.]

do·ggerel (-g-), a. & n. Trivial, mean, halting, or irregular, (verse). [?]

do·ggo, adv. (slang). *Lie d.* (motionless, making no sign). [*dog*]

do·ggy², a. (for *doggy¹* see DOG¹). Of dogs; devoted to dogs. Hence **do·ggi**NESS n. [-Y²]

do·gma, n. (pl. *-s*, rarely *-ta*). Principle, tenet, doctrinal system, esp. as laid down by authority of Church; arrogant declaration of opinion. [L f. Gk (gen. *-atos*), f. *dokeō* seem, -M]

dogmă·tic (rarely **-ical**), a. Of dogma(s), doctrinal; based on *a priori* principles, not on induction; (of person, book, &c.) authoritative, laying down the law, arrogant. Hence **dogma·t**ICS n., **dogma·t**ICALLY adv. [f. L f. Gk *dogmatikos* (prec., -IC)]

do·gmatize, v.i. & t. Deal in positive unsupported assertions, speak authoritatively; express (principle &c.) as a dogma. So **do·gmat**ISM(1), **do·gmat**IST (1), nn. [f. F *dogmatiser* f. L f. Gk *dogmatizō* (DOGMA, -IZE)]

doi·ly, n. Small napkin placed below finger-glass. [fabric named from 17th-c. inventor]

doit, n. Very small sum or coin; merest trifle (esp. *don't care a d.*). [f. Du. *duit* etym. dub.]

doi·ted, a. (Sc.). Crazed, esp. with age. [?]

do·lce far nie·nte (dawltshā), n. Pleasant idleness. [It.]

dŏ·ldrums, n. pl. Dullness, dumps, depression; (of ship, usu. *in the d.*) becalmed state; region of calms & light baffling winds near equator. [prob. formed on *dull*, cf. *tantrums*; the geog. sense prob. due to mistake]

dole[1], n., & v.t. (Archaic) lot, destiny, (*happy man be his d.*, may he be happy); charitable distribution; charitable (esp. sparing, niggardly) gift of food, clothes, or money; *the d.* (colloq.), relief claimable by the unemployed; *dolesman, -woman*, recipient of d.; (vb) deal *out* sparingly, esp. as alms. [OE *dál* cogn. w. *dǽl* DEAL[1]]

dole[2], n. (poet.). Grief, woe; lamentation. [revived obs. wd, f. OF *doel* (now *deuil* mourning) f. LL *dolium* grief cf. L *dolor*]

do·leful, a. Dreary, dismal; sad, discontented, melancholy. Hence **do·lefu**LY[2] adv., **do·leful**NESS n. [prec., -FUL]

dŏ·lichocephă·lic (-ko-), a. Long-headed (of skull with breadth less than 4/5 of length; or of person or race with such skull). [f. Gk *dolikhos* long + -CEPHALIC]

doll, n. Toy baby, puppet; pretty silly woman (so *d.'s face*). Hence **do·ll**ISH[1] a., **do·llish**LY[2] adv., **do·llish**NESS n. [short for *Dorothy*]

do·llar, n. (Orig.) English name for German thaler, also for Spanish piece of eight; unit of U.S. gold & silver coinage =100 cents, about 4*s*. 1½*d*. (symbol or *d. mark*, $; *the almighty d.*, money, mammon); corresponding coin in Canada &c.; (slang) five-shilling piece, crown. [earlier & Du. *daler* = G *taler*, f. *Joachimstaler* gulden from silver mine of the Joachims(*tal* valley)]

do·llop, n. (colloq.). Clumsy or shapeless lump of food &c. [?]

do·lly, n. (Pet-name, esp. in voc., for) doll; kinds of appliance in clothes-washing, ore-washing, pile-driving, iron-punching, polishing, &c.; *d.-shop*, marine store. [-Y[3]]

Do·lly Var·den, n. Kinds of woman's hat & dress. [character in *Barnaby Rudge*]

dŏ·lman, n. Long Turkish robe open in front; hussar's jacket worn with sleeves hanging loose; woman's mantle with flaps for sleeves. [ult. f. Turk. *dolaman*]

dŏ·lmen, n. (F name for) cromlech. [F, perh. f. Cornish (*doll* hole, *men* stone)]

dŏ·lomīte, n. Kind of rock (double carbonate of lime & magnesia); *The Dd.*, mountains of this, esp. those in Tyrol. Hence **dolomi·t**IC a. [*Dolomieu*, French geologist 1794, -ITE[1]]

dŏ·lorous, a. (usu. poet. or facet.). Distressing, painful; dismal, doleful; distressed. Hence **do·lorous**LY[2] adv. [OF f. LL *dolorosus* (DOLOUR, -OUS)]

dolo·se, a. (legal). Having criminal intent; intentionally deceitful. [f. L *dolosus* (*dolus* guile, -OSE[1])]

dŏ·lour, n. (poet.). Sorrow, distress. [OF, f. L *dolorem* nom. *-or*]

do·lphin, n. Cetaceous mammal resembling porpoise, but with beak-like snout; (pop.) the fish dorado, which changes to many colours in dying; curved fish in heraldry, sculpture, &c.; kinds of esp. naut. appliance. [earlier *delphin* f. L *delphinus* f. Gk *delphis -inos*]

dōlt, n. Dull fellow, blockhead. Hence **do·lt**ISH[1] a., **do·ltish**NESS n. [perh. = *dulled*]

Dom, title prefixed to names of R.-C. dignitaries, esp. Benedictine & Carthusian monks, and in Portugal & Brazil to Christian names of persons of the royal family, cardinals, bishops, &c. [abbr. of L *dominus* lord]

-dom, suf. forming nouns expressing rank, condition, domain, f. nn. or adjj. (*earldom, freedom, kingdom*), & (f. nouns) used collectively for the pl. or = the ways of (*officialdom*). [OE *dóm* cf. G *-tum* (st. of DO[1], *-m* as in *seam*).

domai·n, n. Estate, lands, dominions; district under rule, realm, sphere of influence; scope, field, province, of thought or action; (Internat. & U.S. law) *Eminent D.*, lordship of sovereign power over all property in State, with right of expropriation. So **domā·n**IAL a. [f. F *domaine* f. L *dominicum* neut. adj. (*dominus* lord, -IC)]

dome, n., & v.t. Stately building, mansion, (poet.); rounded vault as roof, with circular, elliptical, or polygonal base, cupola; natural vault, canopy, (of sky, trees, &c.); rounded summit of hill &c.; hence **dom**ED[2], **dō·m**IC(AL), **do·me**-LIKE, **do·m**Y[2], aa. (Vb) cover with, shape as, d. [F, f. It. *duomo* cathedral, dome, (& direct) f. L *domus* house]

Do·mesday (Book) (dōōmz-), n. Record of Will. I's Great Inquisition of lands of England made 1086. [ME, = DOOM[1]*sday*, pop. name given to the book as final authority]

dome·stic, a. & n. Of the home, household, or family affairs; of one's own country, not foreign; native, home-made; (of animals) tame, kept by or living with man; home-keeping, fond of home; hence **dome·st**ICALLY adv. (N.) household servant. [f. F *domestique* f. L *domesticus* (*domus* home)]

dome·sticāte, v.t. Naturalize (colonists, animals); make fond of home (esp. in p.p.); bring (animals) under human control, tame; civilize (savages). So **dome·stic**ABLE a., **domestic**A·TION n. [f. med. L *domesticare* (prec., -ATE[3])]

dŏmesti·city (*or* dō-), n. Domestic character; home life or privacy; homeliness; *the dd.*, domestic affairs; domesticated state. [-ITY]
dŏ·mett, n. Fabric of wool & cotton used for shrouds &c. [?]
dŏ·micīle (*or* -ĭl), n., & v.t. & i. Dwelling-place, home; (Law) place of permanent residence, fact of residing; place at which bill of exchange is made payable (v.t., make payable *at* a place). (Vb, also **domici·li**ATE[3]) establish, settle (t. & i.), in a place; so **domicili**A·TION n. [F, f. L *domicilium* f. *domus* home]
domicĭ·liary, a. Of a dwelling-place (*d. visit*, of officials to search or inspect private house). [as prec., -ARY[1]]
dŏ·minant, a. & n. Ruling, prevailing, most influential; (of heights) outstanding, overlooking others; (Mus.) fifth note of scale of any key (adj., of this, as *d. chord, seventh,* &c.). Hence **do·min**ANCE n., **do·minant**LY[2] adv. [F, f. L *dominari* see foll., -ANT]
dŏ·minăte, v.t. & i. Have commanding influence over (also intr. with *over*); be the most influential or conspicuous (of person, power, sound, feature of scene); (of heights) overlook, hold commanding position *over*. [f. L *dominari* (*dominus* lord), -ATE[3]]
domina·tion, n. Ascendancy, sway, control; (pl.) angelic powers of fourth rank (see ORDER[1]1). [F,f. L *dominationem* (prec., -ATION)]
domineer·, v.i. Act imperiously, tyrannize, be overbearing. Hence **domineer·ing**LY[2] adv. [f. Du. (*-neren*) f. F *dominer* DOMINATE]
domi·nical, a. Of the Lord (Christ; *d. year*, date A.D.); of the Lord's day, Sunday-, (*d. letter*, the one of the seven A-G denoting Sundays in any year). [f. med. L *dominicalis* f. L *dominicus* (*dominus* lord, -IC) + -AL]
Domi·nican, a. & n. Of St Dominic or his order of preaching friars; (n.) Black or D. friar. [f. eccl. L *Dominicanus* f. *Dominicus* L name of *Domingo* de Guzman + -AN]
dŏ·minie, n. (Sc.). Schoolmaster. [= *domine* sir voc. of L *dominus* lord]
domi·nion, n. Lordship, sovereignty, control; domains of feudal lord, territory of sovereign or government (*D. of Canada*, name given to Canadian colonies united 1867; *D. of New Zealand*, title given 1907); (Law) right of possession. [OF, f. LL *dominionem* nom. *-o* f. L *dominium* (*dominus* lord)]
dŏ·mino, n. (pl. *-oes*). Loose cloak with half mask worn to conceal identity esp. at masquerade, whence **do·mino**ED[2] a.; person wearing this; one of 28 small brick-shaped pieces marked with pips used in game of *dd.* [F, prob. f. L *dominus* lord, but unexplained]
don[1], n. Spanish title prefixed to Christian name (*D. Juan*, rake, libertine; *D.* QUIXOTE); Spanish gentleman, Spaniard; distinguished person; adept *at* something; head, fellow, or tutor, of college, whence **do·nn**ISH[1] a., **do·nnish**NESS n. [Sp., f. L *dominus* lord]
don[2], v.t. Put on (garment). [= *do on*]
dō·na(h), n. (slang). Woman; sweetheart. [f. Sp. *doña* or Port. *dona* f. L *domina* lady]
dona·tion, n. Bestowal, presenting; thing presented, gift, (esp. of money given to institution), whence **dona·te** v.t. (U.S.), present. [F, f. L *donationem* (*donare* give, -ATION)]
dŏ·native (*or* dō-), a. & n. (Benefice) given directly, not involving presentation to or investment by the Ordinary; gift, present, esp. official largess. [f. L *donativus* adj. (*donare* give, -IVE)]
dō̆·natory, n. Recipient of donation. [f. med. L *donatorius* (*donare* give, -ORY)]
done (dŭn), p.p. of DO[1]. *D. brown*, duped, swindled; *d. up*, tired.
dōnee·, n. Recipient of gift. [as DONOR, -EE]
do·nga (-ngga), n. Gully, ravine. [S.-Afr.]
dŏ·njon (*also* dŭ-), n. Great tower of castle, keep. [archaic spelling of DUNGEON]
do·nkey, n. (pl. *-eys*). (Usual word for) ass; stupid person; *d.-engine*, hauling or hoisting steam-engine on ship's deck. [perh. f. DUN[1] with double dim. ending]
Do·nnybrook Fair, n. Scene of uproar, free fight. [*Donnybrook* in Ireland]
do·nor, n. Giver. [f. OF *doneur* f. L *donatorem* (*donare* give, -OR[2])]
don't[1]. See DO[1].
don't[2], n. (facet.). Prohibition. [use of prec.]
doo·lie, -y, n. Simple form of Indian litter used as army ambulance. [f. Hind. *doli* (Skr. *dul-* to swing)]
doom[1], n. (Hist.) Statute, law, decree; (archaic) decision, sentence, condemnation; fate, destiny, (usu. evil); ruin, death; the Last Judgement (now only in *crack, day, of d.*, & in *doomsday*; *till doomsday*, for ever; cf. DOMESDAY). [com.-Teut.; OE *dóm* f. OTeut. (*dôm* DO[1])]
doom[2], v.t. Pronounce sentence against, condemn *to* some fate, *to* do; consign to misfortune or destruction (esp. in p.p.); (archaic) decree (*doomed his death*). [f. prec.]
door (dōr), n. Hinged or sliding barrier usu. of wood or metal for closing entrance to building, room, safe, &c. (*front d.*, chief d. from house to street &c.; *lives* &c. *next d.*, in next house or room; so *three dd. off* &c.: *next d. to* fig., nearly, almost, near to; so *at death's d.*; entrance, access, exit, (*show* one *the d.*, expel him; *open a d. to, close the d. upon*, make possible, impossible); *out of dd.*, abroad,

in the open air; *within dd.*, in the house; *lay, lie, at the d. of*, impute, be imputable, to; DARKEN *d.*; *d.-bell*, inside bell worked by handle outside d.; *d.-case, -frame*, structure in which d. is fitted: *d.-keeper*, porter; *d.-mat*, for rubbing off mud from boots; *d.-money*, taken at d. of place of entertainment; *d.-nail*, with which dd. used to be studded (*dead, deaf*, &c., *as a d.-n.*); *d.-plate*, usu. of brass bearing occupant's name; *d.-posts*, uprights of d.-case; *d.-step*, leading up to usu. outer d.; *d.-stone*, slab in front of d.; *d.-way*, opening filled by d. Hence (-)**door**ED², **door·**LESS, aa. [OE *duru* cf. G *thüre*, also Gk *thura*, L *fores*]

dope, n., & v.t. Thick liquid used as food or lubricant; kinds of varnish esp. in aeroplane manufacture; (slang) narcotic, stupefying drink; (vb, slang) administer d. to, drug. [f. Du. *doop* sauce (*doopen* to dip)]

doppel-gänger. See DOUBLE¹*-ganger*.

dor, n. Insect flying with loud humming noise; black dung-beetle, cockchafer, rose-beetle, &c. [OE *dora* etym. dub.]

Dor·a, n. See DEFENCE.

dora·do (-ah-), n. Splendidly coloured sea-fish, dolphin. [Sp., f. L DE(*auratus* gilt f. *aurum* gold, -ATE²)]

Dor·cas (-*as*), n. Meeting of ladies to make clothes for the poor. [*Acts* ix. 36]

Dōr·ian, a. & n. (Inhabitant) of Doris, district of ancient Greece; (member) of one of three divisions (*Aeolian, Ionian, D.*) of ancient Greeks (*D.* MODE, of simple & solemn character). [f. L f. Gk *Dōrios* (*Dōris* as above) + -AN]

Dŏ·ric, a. & n. =prec. adj.; *D.* ORDER (also *D.* as n.); (of dialect) broad, rustic; (n.) dialect of ancient Greece (cf. *Attic, Ionic, Aeolic*), rustic English. [f. L f. Gk *Dōrikos* (prec., -IC)]

Dor·king, a. & n. (Fowl) of the D. breed. [*Dorking* in Surrey]

dor·mant, a. Lying inactive as in sleep (of some animals through winter, undeveloped buds, potential faculties); (Herald., of beast) with head on paws; not acting, in abeyance, (often *lie d.*; *d. warrant* &c., drawn in blank; *d. partner*, sleeping). Hence **dor·m**ANCY n. [OF (*dormir* f. L *dormire* sleep, -ANT)]

dor·mer, n. (Also *d.-window*) projecting upright window in sloping roof. [f. OF *dormeor* f. L *dormitorium* (prec., -ORY)]

dormeu·se (-erz), n. Travelling-carriage for sleeping in; kind of couch. [F, fem. of *dormeur* sleeper (DORMANT, -OR²)]

dor·mitory, n. Sleeping-room with several beds & sometimes cubicles; suburban or country district of city people's residences. [f. L (DORMER)]

dor·mouse, n. (pl. *-mice*). Small hibernating rodent between mouse and squirrel. [perh. f. st. of F *dormir* (DORMANT) + MOUSE]

dor·my, a. (golf). As many holes ahead as there are holes to play (*d. one, five*, &c.). [?]

dŏ·rothy bag, n. Lady's open-topped handbag slung by loops from wrist. [fem. name]

dor·sal, a. (Anat., Zool., Bot.) of, on, near, the back; ridge-shaped. Hence **dor·sal**LY² adv. [f. med. L *dorsalis* (foll., -AL)]

dors(o)-, comb. form = back-&-, as in *dorsabdominal* of back & belly, *dorsolateral* of back & sides. [L *dorsum* back, -O-]

dor·tour, -ter, n. (hist.) Bedroom, dormitory, esp. in monastery. [OF (*-our*), as DORMER]

dor·y¹, n. (Also *John D.*) sea-fish used as food. [f. F *dorée* fem. p.p. of *dorer* gild, as DORADO]

dor·y², n. Flat-bottomed skiff, esp. fishing-vessel's boat in U.S. [?]

dō·sage (-sĭj), n. Giving of medicine in doses; size of dose. [-AGE]

dose (-s), n., & v.t. Amount of medicine to be taken at once (also fig. of flattery, punishment, &c.); (vb) give physic to (person), adulterate, blend, (esp. wine with spirit). [vb f. noun, F, f. med. L f. Gk *dosis* (*didōmi* give)]

doss, n., & v.i., (slang). Bed in *d.-house* or common lodging-house. (Vb) sleep in this; hence **do·ss**ER¹ n. [perh. f. F *dos* f. L *dorsum* back]

do·ssal, n. Hanging behind altar or round chancel. [f. med. L *dossale* (L *dorsum* back, -AL)]

do·ssier (*or* -syā), n. Set of documents, esp. record of person's antecedents. [F, = bundle of papers (as DOSS, from bulging shape)]

dŏ·ssy, a. (slang). Smart-looking. [?]

dost. See DO¹.

dot¹, n. Small spot, speck, roundish pen-mark; (Orthogr.) period, point over *i* or *j*, point used as diacritical mark; (Mus. writing) point used with various meanings; small child, tiny object; *d.-&-dash*, using dd. & dashes, as in Morse telegraphy; *d.-wheel*, used for making dotted line. [OE *dott* head of boil cf. OHG *tutto* nipple]

dot², v.t. Mark with dot(s); place d. over (letter i; *d. the is & cross the ts*, fill in details, make meaning quite clear); (Mus.) *dotted crotchet* &c., with time value increased by half; diversify as with dd. (*sea dotted with ships*); scatter (*about, all over*) like dd.; *d. & carry* (*one*), child's formula for remembering to carry in addition sum; *d. & go one*, n., a., & adv., limp, limping(ly). [f. prec.]

dō·tard, n. One in his dotage. [foll., -ARD]

dote, doat, v.i. Be silly, deranged, infatuated, or feeble-minded, esp. from age, whence **do·t**AGE(2) n.; concentrate one's affections, bestow excessive fondness, (*up*)*on*. Hence **do·ting**LY[2] adv. [cf. MDu. *doten*, OF *redoter*]

doth. See DO[1].

do·tt(e)**rel,** n. Kind of plover. [DOTE + -REL, named from the ease with which it is caught]

do·ttle, -tel, n. Plug of tobacco left unsmoked in pipe. [DOT[1], -LE]

do·tty, a. Dotted about, sporadic, marked with dots; (colloq.) shaky of gait (*d. on his legs*), feeble-minded, half idiotic. [DOT[1] + -Y[2]]

douane (dōō·ahn), n. Foreign customhouse. [F, f. Arab. *diwan* DIVAN]

dou·ble[1] (dŭ-), a. & adv. 1. Adj.: consisting of two members, things, layers, &c., forming a pair, twofold (*d. chin*, with roll of fat below chin proper); folded, bent, stooping much; with some part d. (*d. axe*, with two edges, *eagle*, with two heads); (of flowers) with petals multiplied by conversion of stamens &c.; having twofold relation, dual, ambiguous (*d. meaning* = DOUBLE ENTENDRE); twice as much or many (*of*, or, with prep. omitted, seeming to govern following wd;) of twofold or extra size, strength, value, &c. (*d. ale, d. florin*); (Mus.) lower in pitch by an octave (*d. bassoon* &c.); (Mil.) *d. time* (also formerly, & still in general use, *d.-quick time*), regulation running pace; deceitful, hypocritical; *d.* ENTRY; *d.* first, (person who has taken) first-class University honours in two subjects; *d. star*, two stars so close as to seem one, esp. when forming connected pair; *work d.* TIDES; hence **dou·ble**NESS n., **dou·b**LY[2] adv. 2. Adv.; to twice the amount &c. (*d. as bright*; *see d.*, two things when there is only one, esp. of drunken man); two together (*ride d.*, two on horse; *sleep d.*, two in bed). 3. *Double-*, a. or adv., is freely used in new or obvious compounds, as well as in the following: *d.-acting*, in two ways, directions, &c., esp. of engine in which steam acts on both sides of piston; *d.-barrel*, = d.-barrelled, or d.-barrelled gun; *d.-barrelled*, with two barrels (also fig. = ambiguous, of compliment &c.; & of compound surname); *d.-bass*, deepest-toned instrument of violin kind; *d.-bedded*, with two beds or double bed; *d.-bitt* v.t. (naut.), pass (cable) twice round bitts or round two pairs of bitts; *d.-breasted* of coat or waistcoat, made to button on either side; *d.-dealer, -ling* n. & a., deceiver, deceit(ful); *d.-dyed* usu. fig., deeply stained with guilt (*d.-d. scoundrel*); *d.-edged*, with two cutting edges, (of argument, sarcasm, &c.) telling against as well as for one; *d.-faced*, insincere; *d.-gănger* (-ng-), wraith [f. G *doppel-gänger* double-goer]; *d. harness* (fig.), matrimony; *d.-leaded* (-lĕd-), of printed matter with wide spaces between lines to draw attention; *d.-lock* v.t., turn key of (some locks) twice; *d.-quick* (see *d. time* above; also) adv., very quickly; *d.-reef* v.t. (naut.), contract spread of (sail) by two reefs; *d.-refine*, refine twice over. [OF, f. L *duplus* (*duo* two, *-plus* f. *ple-* fill)]

dou·ble[2], n. D. quantity, twice as much or many (*d. or quits*, game, throw, toss, deciding whether person shall pay twice his loss or debt or nothing); counterpart of thing or person; wraith; (Mil.) *at the d.*, running; score (short whist) of five to less than three, (long whist) of ten to nothing, (stake being doubled); (Lawn-tennis &c.) game between two pairs; Guernsey copper coin, ⅛*d.*; sharp turn of hunted animal, or of river. [f. prec. & foll.]

dou·ble[3] (dŭ-), v.t. & i. Make d., increase twofold, multiply by two; amount to twice as much as; (Mus.) add same note in higher or lower octave to; (of actor) *d. part*(*s*), play two in same piece; (Mil.) move in d. time, run; put (passenger &c.) in same quarters with another (also *d. up*); bend, turn, (paper, cloth) over upon itself (often *up*); *d. up*, bend one's body into stooping or curled-up position, cause (another) to do this by blow, (of paper, leaf, &c.) become folded; clench (fist); (Billiards) rebound, make to rebound; (Naut.) get round (headland); turn sharply in flight, pursue tortuous course. [f. OF *doubler* f. L *duplare* (*duplus* DOUBLE[1])]

double entendre (F), n. Ambiguous expression, phrase with two meanings, one usu. indecent; use of such phrases. [from 1673; obs. F (now *d. entente*, which is often needlessly substituted in E for the established *d. entendre*)]

dou·blet (dŭ-), n. (Hist.) close-fitting body-garment worn by men with or without sleeves & short skirts (*d. & hose*, masculine attire, also light attire without cloak); one of a pair, esp. one of two words of same derivation but different sense (*fashion* & *faction*); (pl.) same number on two dice thrown at once; two birds killed with double-barrel; (Microscope &c.) combination of two simple lenses. [F (DOUBLE[1], -ET)]

doubloo·n (du-), n. Spanish gold coin, double pistole (formerly 33–36*s.*, now slightly over £1). [f. F *doublon* or Sp. **doblon* (DOUBLE[1], -OON)]

doublure (F), n. Ornamental usu. leather lining inside book-cover.

doubt[1] (dowt), n. Feeling of uncertainty (*about*), undecided frame of mind, inclination to disbelieve (*of, about*; *have no doubt that . . .*), hesitation; uncertain state of things, want of full proof (*give* one *the benefit of the d.*, assume his innocence rather than guilt) or of clear signs of the future; *make no d.*, feel sure;

no d., certainly, admittedly; *without d.*, certainly. [f. OF *doute* f. *douter* DOUBT[2]]

doubt[2] (dowt), v.i. & t. Feel uncertain (about); waver; be undecided about or *about*, hesitate to believe or trust, call in question, (person, fact expressed by noun or by clause with *whether*, *if*, or, in negative or interrog. sentences, *that*, *but*, *but that*; *I d. whether*, *I don't d. that*, *can you d. that*, *he will win*); have dd. *of* (esp. w. neg., as *never doubted of success*); (archaic & dial.) be afraid, rather think, suspect, that (*I d. we are late*). [f. OF *douter* f. L *dubitare* (*dubius* DUBIOUS); *-b-* inserted f. the L as correction]

doub·tful, a. Of uncertain meaning, character, truth, or issue, undecided, ambiguous, questionable, (*d. syllable*, *letter*, that can be either long or short); unsettled in opinion, uncertain, hesitating. Hence **doub·tful**LY[2] adv., **doub·tful**NESS n. [-FUL]

doub·tless, adv. Certainly, no doubt, I admit, (usu. concess., cf. UNDOUBTEDLY). [-LESS]

douce (dōōs), a. (Sc.). Sober, gentle, sedate. [ME, f. OF *doux* fem. *douce* f. L *dulcis* sweet]

douceur (dōōser·r), n. Gratuity; bribe. [F]

douche (dōōsh), n., & v.t. & i. Jet of water applied to body externally or internally as form of bathing or for medicinal purpose; (vb) administer d. to, take d. [F, f. It. *doccia* pipe ult. f. L *ductus* conduit (*ducere* lead)]

dough (dō), n. Kneaded flour, bread-paste; pasty mass; (slang) money; *d.-boy*, boiled dumpling, (slang) U.-S. infantry-man; *doughnut*, cake of d. sweetened & boiled in fat. Hence **dough·**Y[2] a., **dough·**INESS n. [com.-Teut.; OE *dáh* cf. G *teig*, also Skr. *dih-* besmear, L *fig-* shape, Gk *teikhos* wall]

dough·ty (dow-), a. (archaic or facet.). Valiant, stout, formidable. Hence **dough·ti**LY[2] adv., **dough·ti**NESS n. [OE *dohtig* var. of *dyhtig* (cf. *dugan* be strong, & G *tüchtig*)]

Dou·khobors (dōō-), n. pl. Religious sect, with some likeness in doctrines to Quakers, of which large numbers migrated from Russia to Canada after persecutions for refusing military service. [f. Russ. = spirit-fighters]

doum (dowm, dōōm), n. (Also *d.-palm*) Egyptian palm-tree. [f. Arab. *daum*, *dum*]

dour (-oor), a. (Sc.). Severe, stern, obstinate. Hence **dour·**LY[2] adv., **dour·**NESS n. [prob. f. L *durus* hard]

douse (-ows), **dowse,** v.t. (Naut.) lower (sail), close (port-hole); extinguish (light; *d. the glim* slang, put out the light); throw water over, drench. [?]

dove (dŭv), n. Kinds of pigeon (*cushat*, *ground*, *ring*, *rock*, *stock*, *turtle*, *wood*. *-d.*); the Holy Spirit; type of gentleness or innocence (so *d.-eyed*); messenger of good news or peace (*Gen.* viii); darling (esp. *my d.*); *d.-colour(ed)*, (of) warm grey; *d.'s-foot*, kinds of crane's-bill; *d.-hawk*, hen-harrier (from its colour); *d.-cot(e)*, pigeon-house (*flutter the d.-cc.*, alarm quiet people). Hence **do·ve**LIKE a. [cf. G *taube*; perh. cogn. w. OE *dúfan* DIVE]

do·vetail, n., & v.t. & i. Tenon shaped like dove's spread tail or reversed wedge, fitting into corresponding mortise & forming joint; such a joint. (Vb) put together with dd.; (fig.) fit together (t. & i.) compactly. [from 16th c.]

dow. See D(H)OW.

dow·ager, n. Woman with title or property derived from her late husband (often in comb. as *Queen d.*, *d. duchess*). [f. OF *douagere* f. *douage* dower, -ER[2](2)]

dow·dy, n. & a. (Woman) shabbily, badly, or unfashionably dressed; (of dress &c.) unattractive, unfashionable. Hence **dow·di**LY[2] adv., **dow·di**NESS, **dow·dy**ISM(2), nn., **dow·dy**ISH[1] a. [f. obs. *dowd* slut, etym. dub.]

dow·el, n., & v.t. Headless pin of wood, metal, &c., for keeping two pieces of wood, stone, &c., in their relative position; (vb) fasten with d. [cf. G *döbel* plug, OF *doelle* barrel-stave]

dow·er, n., & v.t. Widow's share for life of husband's estate; property or money brought by wife to husband, dowry; endowment, gift of nature, talent. Hence **dow·er**LESS a. (Vb) give dowry to; endow *with* talent &c. [vb f. n., OF *douaire* f. LL *dotarium* (L *dos dotis*, -ARY[1])]

dow·las, n. Kind of strong calico. [*Doulas* in Brittany]

down[1], n. Open high land, esp. (pl.) treeless undulating chalk uplands of S. England used for pasture; = DUNE; *The Dd.*, part of sea (opposite North Dd.) within Goodwin Sands. [OE *dún* hill cf. ODu. *dúna* whence F *dune*]

down[2], n. First covering of young birds; bird's under plumage, used in cushions &c.; fine short hair, esp. first hair on face, also on fruit &c.; fluffy substance. [f. ON *dún*, cf. G *daune*]

down[3], adv. (superl., a. or adv., *downmost*). 1. (Motion): from above, to lower place, to ground, (*come d.*, from bedroom; *knock*, *fall*, *d.*; *sun*, *ship*, *goes d.*, sets, sinks; *food goes d.*, is swallowed; *get d.*, swallow, alight; *book* &c. *goes d.*, finds acceptance; *get*, *set*, *d.*, from carriage &c.; *brought d. by river*; *money d.*, *pay d.*, at once, as though on counter; *write*, *set*, *put*, *take*, *copy*, *d.*, on paper; so *Bill d. for second reading today*); to place regarded as lower, into helpless position, with current or wind, southwards, from capital or university, (*Lord's amendments sent d. to Commons*; *bear d.*, sail to leeward;

run, ride, hunt, d., bring to bay; *shout, hiss, d.*, silence; *d. to Norfolk* from Scotland, *to Scotland* or *the country* from London; *go d.*, for vacation or at end of university life; *send d.*, university punishment; *up & d.*, to & fro); (ellipt. for imperat. of) lie, get, put, &c., d. (*d., Ponto !*; *d. helm*, put the HELM d.; & with *with, d. with the aristocrats !*). 2. (Station): in lower place (*blinds were d.*; *is not d. yet*, i.e. out of his bedroom); not up in capital or university; in fallen posture, prostrate, at low level, in depression, humiliation, &c., (*hit man who is d.*; *many d. with fever*; *sun, tide, are d.*; *down in the mouth* or *d.* or *d.-hearted*, dispirited; *are we d.-hearted ?*, slang assertion of confidence; *bread is d.*, cheaper). 3. (Order, time, quality): inclusively of lower limit in series (*from King d. to cobbler*); from earlier to later time (*custom handed d.*); to finer consistence (*boil, grind, wear, thin, d.*); into quiescence (*calm d.*). 4. (Phrases): *be d. on*, pounce upon, treat severely; *d. to the ground*, completely; *d. at* HEEL; *d. on* one's LUCK; *d. & out*, unable to resume the fight in boxing, beaten in the struggle of life, done for; *d.-easter* (U.S.), New-Englander, esp. inhabitant of Maine; *d. under*, at the antipodes, in Australia &c. [OE *dúne* for *adúne* ADOWN]

down[4], prep. Downwards along, through, or into; from top to bottom of; at a lower part of (*situated d. the Thames*); *up & d.*, to & fro along; *d. town*, into the town from higher or outlying part; *d. the wind*, with it (*let go d. the w.*, abandon, discard). [f. prec.]

down[5], a. (not compared). Directed downwards (*d. leap, look*; *d. grade*, descending slope in railroad, fig. deterioration); *d.-draught*, downward draught, esp. one driving down chimney into room; *d. train*, going, coming, from London, *d. platform*, for such train's departure or arrival. [f. DOWN[3]]

down[6], v.t. (colloq.). Put, throw, knock, (usu. person or aeroplane) d.; *d. tools*, cease work for the day &c., go on strike. [f. DOWN[3]]

down[7], n. Reverse of fortune (usu. *ups & dd.*); (Dominoes) =POSE[1]; *have a d. on*, dislike, tend to be d. upon, (colloq.). [f. DOWN[3]]

dow·ncast[1], n. (Also *d.-shaft*) shaft for introducing fresh air into mine. [DOWN[3] + CAST[2]]

dow·ncast[2], a. (Of looks) directed downwards; dejected.

dow·nfall, n. Great fall of rain &c.; fall from prosperity, ruin.

downhill, n., adj. & adv. (N., dow·nhĭ·l) downward slope, decline, (*d. of life*, later half); (adj. dow·-) sloping down, declining; (adv., -ĭ·l) in descending direction, on a decline.

Dow·ning street, n. Street in London containing some government offices, (home of) the Government of the day (*does not find favour in D. s.*; *D. s. disapproves*).

dow·npour, n. Heavy fall of rain &c.

dow·nright (downrī·t *if placed late*), a. & adv. (Archaic) vertical; plain, definite, straightforward, blunt, whence **down-righ·t**NESS n.; not short of, out-&-out, (*a d. lie, atheist*; *d. nonsense*); (adv.) thoroughly, positively, quite, (*d. scared, insolent*). [DOWN[3] + RIGHT a. & adv.]

downstair·s, adv., **dow·nstair(s)**, a. Down the stairs; to, on, of, a lower floor.

dow·nthrow, n. (geol.). Depression of strata on one side of fault.

dow·ntrodden, a. Oppressed, kept under.

dow·nward, a. & adv., **dow·nwards**, adv. (Moving, pointing, leading) towards what is lower, inferior, or later. [OE *adúnweard* (DOWN[3], -WARD)]

dow·ny[1], a. Like, of, downs. [DOWN[1], -Y[2]]

dow·ny[2], a. Of, like, covered with, down; (slang) wide awake, knowing. So **dow·n-**ILY[2] adv., **dow·ni**NESS n. [DOWN[2], -Y[2]]

dowr·y, n. Portion woman brings to her husband; talent, natural gift. [f. OF as DOWER]

dow·sing, n. Searching for latent water or minerals with the *d.-* (or *divining-*) *rod*, a forked twig held by the *dowser* & dipping over the right spot. [?]

doxo·logy, n. Liturgical formula of praise to God, as *Glory be to* &c. [f. med. L f. Gk *doxologia* (*doxa* glory, -LOGY)]

do·xy[1], n. Beggar's wench, paramour. [?]

do·xy[2], n. Opinion, esp. on theology. [facet. use of end of *orthodoxy, heterodoxy*]

doy·en (F), n. Senior member *of* a body, esp. senior ambassador at a court. [F, f. L as DEAN[1]]

doyley. See DOILY.

doze, v.i., & n. Sleep drowsily, be half asleep; *d. off*, fall lightly asleep; (n.) short slumber. [cf. Da. *döse* make drowsy]

do·zen (dŭ-), n. (Pl. *dozen*, used adjectivally or as noun, when with numeral or equivalent except *some*) twelve, as *a, three, several, how many, d. figs* or *of the best figs, of these*, but *some dd. of people*, cf. *some* (about a) *d.* (*of*) *people, dd. of* (=many) *times*; (pl. *dozens*) set of twelve, as *pack them in dd.*; *baker's, devil's, long, printer's, d.*, thirteen; *talk nineteen to the d.*, incessantly. [f. OF *dozeine* (L *duodecim* twelve)]

drab[1], n., & v.i. Slut, slattern; prostitute; (vb) whore. [cf. Irish *drabog*, Gael. *drabag*]

drab[2], a. & n. (Of) dull light brown colour; dull, monotonous; monotony. [prob. f. obs. & F *drap* cloth]

dra·bbet, n. Drab twilled linen used for smock-frocks. [prec., -ET[1]]

dra·bble, v.i. & t. Go splashing *through*,

make dirty and wet with, water or mud. [=EFris. *drabbeln* paddle]

drachm (-ăm), n. Ancient Greek silver coin, drachma, (9¾*d.*); (Apoth. wt) 60 grains, ⅛oz; (Avoird.) 27⅓ grains, 1/16 oz; small quantity. [f. F *drachme* f. L as foll.]

dra·chma (-k-), n. (pl. *-mas, -mae*). Ancient Greek coin (see prec.); modern Greek franc. [L, f. Gk *drakhmē* (*drassomai* grasp)]

Dracō·nian, Dracō·nic, a. (Of laws) rigorous, harsh, cruel. [*Drakōn* Athenian legislator 621 B.C. + -IAN, -IC]

draff, n. Dregs, lees; hog's-wash; refuse of malt after brewing. [from 1205; ME, MDu., Icel., Sw., *draf*, cf. G *träber* husks]

draft[1], n. (Selection of) detachment of men from larger body for special duty, contingent, reinforcement; drawing of money by written order (*make a d. on* fund &c., also fig. *on* person's confidence, friendship, &c.), bill or cheque drawn, esp. by one branch of bank on another; sketch of work to be executed; rough copy of document; (Masonry) chisel-dressing along margin of stone's surface. [var. of DRAUGHT[1]]

draft[2], v.t. Draw off (part of larger body, esp. of troops) for special purpose; prepare, make rough copy of, (document, esp. Parliamentary Bill), whence **dra·ft-ER**[1] n.; (Masonry) cut d. on (stone). [f. prec.]

dra·ftsman, n. One who makes drawings or designs; one who drafts documents or Parliamentary Bills. [=DRAUGHTSMAN]

drag[1], v.t. & i. Pull along with force, difficulty, or friction; allow (feet, tail, &c.) to trail; *ship drags her anchor, anchor drags*, anchor fails to hold; *d. in*, introduce (subject) needlessly (also *d. in by the head & shoulders*); (Mus.) go too slowly, be wanting in life; trail, go heavily; *d. on*, continue (t. & i.) tediously; *d. out*, protract; use grapnel or d. (often *for* drowned person or lost object), dredge, search bottom of, (river &c.) with grapnels, nets, &c.; harrow (land); apply d. to (wheel, vehicle); (colloq.) *d. up* (child), rear roughly. [per. var. of DRAW]

drag[2], n. Heavy harrow; rough sledge; four-horsed private vehicle like stage coach; (also *d.-net*) net drawn over bottom of river &c. or surface of field to enclose all fish or game; apparatus for dredging or recovering drowned persons &c.; muckrake; iron shoe for retarding vehicle downhill; obstruction to progress; strong-smelling lure for hounds in lieu of fox (so *d.-hounds*), club for pursuing this sport; slow motion, impeded progress; *d.-anchor*, floating frame on hawser to check lee-way of drifting ship; *d.-chain*, used to retard vehicle by fixing wheel, (fig.) impediment. [f. prec.]

dra·ggle, v.t. & i. Make wet, limp, & dirty, by trailing; hang trailing; lag, straggle in rear; *d.-tail(ed)*, (woman) with draggled or untidily trailing skirts. [prob. f. DRAG[1] + -LE(3)]

drăgoman, n. (pl. *-ans, -en*). Interpreter, esp. in Arabic, Turkish, or Persian. [F, f. OArab. *targuman*, cf. TARGUM]

dră·gon, n. Mythical monster like crocodile or snake with wings & claws & often breathing fire; (with allusion to legends) guardian of treasure &c. or of female chastity, watchful person, duenna; (bibl.) whale or shark, serpent, crocodile, jackal; *the old D.*, Satan; kinds of lizard & pigeon; *d.-fly*, neuropterous insect with long slender body & two pairs of large wings; *d.'s-blood*, bright red gum exuding from kind of palm fruit. [F, f. L *draconem* nom. *-o* f. Gk *drakōn* serpent perh. f. *derkomai* see st. *drak-*]

drăgonnā·de, n., & v.t. (Pl.) persecutions of Protestants under Louis XIV by quartering dragoons on them; persecution carried on by means of troops; (vb) persecute thus. [F (*dragon* DRAGOON, -ADE)]

dragoo·n, n., & v.t. Cavalryman (orig. mounted infantryman armed with carbine called *d.*; now of certain cavalry regiments that were formerly mounted infantry); rough fierce fellow; kind of pigeon (also *dragon*); (vb) set dd. upon, persecute (see prec.), force *into* a course by persecution. [f. F *dragon* carbine, so named as breathing fire (DRAGON)]

drail, n. Fish-hook & line weighted with lead for dragging at depth through water. [perh. a mixture of *draw, trail*]

drain[1], v.t. & i. Draw (liquid) *off* or *away* by conduit, d.-pipes, &c. (also fig., *d. the wealth of England*); drink (liquid), empty (vessel), to the dregs; dry (land &c.) by withdrawing moisture; (of river) carry off superfluous water of (district), deprive (person, thing) *of* property, strength, &c.; trickle *through*, flow *off* or *away*; (of wet cloth, vessel, &c.) get rid of moisture by its flowing away (*set it there to d.*). [OE *dréahnian* cogn. w. DRY]

drain[2], n. Channel carrying off liquid, artificial conduit for water, sewage, &c., (Surg.) tube for drawing off discharge from abscess &c.; constant outlet, withdrawal, demand, or expenditure (*a great d. on my resources*); (slang) small draught, drink. [f. prec.]

drai·nage (-ĭj), n. Draining; system of drains, artificial or natural; *d.-basin*, district drained by river; what is drained off, sewage. [-AGE]

drai·ner, n. In vbl senses; esp., vessel in which things are put to drain. [-ER[1]]

drake[1]. n. Kinds of ephemeral fly used in fishing (*green d.*, common day-fly). [OE *draca* f. L *draco* DRAGON]

drake[2], n. Male duck (*play* DUCKS *& dd.*). [cf. G dial. *draak*, perh. seen in G *enterich* earlier *endtrich*, of which *end-* is perh. = *ente* duck]

dram, n. A weight (see DRACHM); small draught of spirit &c. (*d.-drinker*, *-ing*, tippler, -ing; *d.-shop*, public-house). [for DRACHM]

dra·ma (-ah-), n. Stage-play; *the d.*, the dramatic art, composition & presentation of plays; set of events having the unity & progress of a play & leading to catastrophe or consummation. [LL f. Gk (gen. *-atos*), f. *draō* do, -M]

dramă·tic, a. Of drama; as of a play-actor, theatrical; fit for theatrical representation, sudden, striking, impressive; (of utterances &c.) not to be taken as one's own, representing another person's thoughts. Hence **drama·tic**ALLY adv. [f. LL f. Gk *dramatikos* (prec., -IC)]

dră·matis persō·nae, n. pl. (often with sing. constr.). (List of) characters in a play. [L]

dră·matist, n. Playwright. [DRAMA, -IST]

dră·matize, v.t. & i. Convert (novel &c.) into a play, admit of such conversion. Hence **dramatiz**A·TION n. [DRAMA, -IZE]

dră·maturge, n. Playwright. So **dramatur·g**IC a., **dra·maturg**IST(1), **dra·maturg**Y[1], nn. [F, f. Gk *dramatourgos* (DRAMA, *-ergos* -working)]

drank. See DRINK[1].

drape, v.t. Cover, hang, adorn, with cloth &c.; arrange (clothes, hangings) in graceful folds. [f. F *draper* (*drap* cloth)]

drā·per, n. Dealer in cloth, linen, &c. [f. F *drapier* (prec., -IER)]

drā·pery, n. Cloth & linen & cotton fabrics; draper's trade; arrangement of clothing in sculpture &c.; clothing or hangings disposed in folds, whence **dra·peri**ED[2] a. [f. OF *draperie* (*drap* cloth, -ERY)]

dră·stic, a. Acting strongly, vigorous, violent, esp. (Med.) strongly purgative. Hence **dra·stic**ALLY adv. [f. Gk *drastikos* (*drastos* vbl adj. of *draō* do, -IC)]

drat, v.t. 3 sing. subjunct. (vulg.). Confound, curse, bother, (as woman's imprecation). Hence **dra·tt**ED[1] a. [for *'od* (God) *rot*]

draught[1] (-ahft), n. (also *draft* in some senses, as stated). Drawing, traction, (*beast of d.*, *d.-horse*, &c., for drawing cart, plough, &c.); drawing of net for fish &c., take of fish at one drawing; single act of drinking, amount so drunk, (also fig. of joy, love, pain, &c.); dose of liquid medicine (*black d.*, a purgative); (Naut.) depth of water ship draws or requires to float her; (pl.) game with 24 similar pieces on *d.* (same as *chess*) *-board*; current of air in room, chimney, &c. (*forced d.*, of furnace, made by rarefying air above or compressing it below; *feel the d.*, slang, suffer from adverse conditions), whence **drau·ght**Y[2] a., **drau·ghti**NESS n.; outline, preliminary drawing for work of art; plan of something to be constructed (also *-ft*); rough copy, first conception, of document (usu. *-ft*); (selection of) military detachment, party, reinforcement, (usu. *-ft*); (written order for) withdrawing of money from fund in bank &c., cheque, bill of exchange, (now *-ft*); drawing of liquor from vessel (*beer on d.*, in tapped cask; so *d. beer*, opp. *bottled*). [ME *draht* cf. G *tracht* vbl n. f. com.-Teut. *dragan* DRAW]

draught[2] (-ahft), v.t. Draw off (party for military service &c.) from larger body (now *draft*); make plan or sketch of (also *-aft*). [f. prec.]

drau·ghtsman (-ahft-), n. (pl. *-men*). One who makes drawings, plans, or sketches (*good, bad, no, d.*, one who draws well &c.), whence **drau·ghtsman**SHIP(3) n., **drau·ghtswoman** n. fem.; (usu. *draftsman*) person who drafts document, esp. Parliamentary Bill; piece in game of draughts. [*draught's + man*]

draw[1], v.t. & i. (drew, drawn). 1. Pull (boat up from water, hat over face, belt tighter, pen across paper, friend aside); pull after one (plough, cart, cartload, &c.); drag (criminal) on hurdle &c. to execution; contract, distort, (*with drawn face*); haul in (net); bend (bow; *d. a* BEAD[1] *on*); pull at (*d. bit, bridle, rein*, check horse, & fig. oneself); pull (curtain, veil) open or shut; *d. cloth*, clear table after meal; (Cricket) divert (ball) to on side with bat; (Golf) drive (ball) too much to left. 2. Attract, bring to one, take in, (*drew a deep breath*; & abs., *chimney, pipe, draws well*, promotes, allows, draught; *I felt drawn to him*; *drew my attention*; *d. him into talk, out of temptation*; *draws customers*, & abs., attract attention or custom); induce *to* do; be attracted, assemble, *round* or *about* some centre (*drew round the table*); bring about, entail, (*drew after it great consequences*; *d. ruin upon oneself*). 3. Extract (cork, tooth, gun-charge, nail, cricket-stumps from ground, card from pack; pistol, sword from sheath, also abs. = d. one's sword or pistol; *d.* one's *sword against*, attack; *d.* LOTS, also abs. = d. lots, & trans. = obtain by lot, as *drew the winner*); drag (badger, fox) from hole; haul up (water) from well; bring out (liquid, blood) from vessel, body (*d. it mild*, i.e. orig. beer, now = be moderate, not exaggerate); extract essence of (*d. the tea*, also intr. *the tea draws*); (of poultice) drain (gathering &c.); take, get, from a source (*d. inspiration*, one's *salary*; *tax draws well, draws from the rich only*); (Cards) cause to be played (*d. all the trumps*); bring (person) out, make him reveal information, talent, irritation, &c.; deduce, infer, (conclusion); extract something from, empty, drain (*calf draws cow*), disembowel (*hanged, drawn, & quartered*, of criminal; *d. fowl* before cooking); (Hunt.) search (covert) for game (*d. blank*, find none). 4. Protract, stretch, elongate, (*long-drawn agony*; *d. wire*, make it by pulling piece of metal through successively smaller holes); (Naut., intr. of sail) swell out with wind. 5. Trace (furrow, figure, line; *d. the line at*, refuse to go as far as or beyond); delineate, make (picture), represent (object), by drawing lines, (abs.) use pencil thus; describe in words; practise delineation; frame (document) in due form, compose, (often *up, out*); formulate, institute, (comparisons, distinctions); write out (bill, cheque, draft, *on* banker &c.), (abs.) make call *on* person or his faith, memory, &c., *for* money or service. 6. Make way, move, *towards, near, off, back*, &c. (*d. to an end* or *close*); (Racing) get further *away* to the front, come *level*, gain *on*. 7. (Of doubtful origin); (of ship) require (such a depth of water) to float; *d. game* or *battle*, part without deciding it. 8. (With advv. in special senses); *d. back*, withdraw from undertaking; *d. in*, entice, persuade to join, (of day) close in, (of successive days) become shorter; *d. off*, withdraw (troops; or intr. of troops etc.); *d. on*, lead to, bring about, allure, approach (intr.); *d. out*, lead out, detach, or array (troops), prolong, elicit, induce to talk, write out in proper form, (of days) become longer; *d. up*, (refl.) assume stiff attitude, (intr.) come up *with* or *to* = overtake, come to a stand, (t. & i. of troops) bring or come into regular order, (trans.) compose (document &c.). [com.-Teut., OE *dragan*, cf. G *tragen* carry]

draw[2], n. Act of DRAWing; esp.: strain, pull; attractive effect, thing that draws custom, attention, &c.; drawing of lots, raffle; drawn game; remark &c. meant to elicit information or set person off on pet subject. [f. prec.]

draw·back, n. Amount of excise or import duty paid back or remitted on goods exported; deduction *from*; thing that qualifies satisfaction, disadvantage; *d. lock*, with spring bolt that can be drawn back by inside knob. [DRAW[1]]

draw·bridge, n. Bridge hinged at one end for drawing up to prevent passage or to open channel. [DRAW[1]]

Drawca·nsir, n. & a. (Person) formidable both to friend and foe; fierce swashbuckler. [name of character in Villiers's *Rehearsal*]

drawee·, n. Person on whom draft or bill is drawn. [-EE]

draw·er, n. In vbl senses; also or esp.: (archaic) tapster; receptacle sliding in & out of special frame (*dd.* or *chest of dd.*) or of table &c., for holding clothes, papers, &c., whence **draw·erFUL**(2) n.; (pl.) two-legged (usu. under-) garment suspended from waist. [-ER[1]]

draw·ing, n. In vbl senses; esp.: art of representing by line, delineation without colour or with single colour, (*out of d.*, incorrectly drawn); product of this, black-&-white or monochrome sketch; *d.-block*, of detachable leaves of d.-paper adhering at edges; *d.-board*, for stretching d.-paper on; *d.-compass(es)*, with pen or pencil substituted for one point; *d.-pin*, for fastening d.-paper to d.-board. [-ING[1]]

draw·ing-room, n. Room for reception of company, to which ladies retire after dinner; levee, formal reception esp. at court. [for earlier *withdrawing-*]

drawl, v.i. & t., & n. Speak, utter (often *out*), with indolent or affected slowness; (of words, esp. in part.) be so uttered; hence **draw·lingLY**[2] adv. (N.) slow utterance. [prob. intensive f. DRAW[1]; cf. Du. *dralen*, EFris. *draulen*, loiter]

drawn, p.p. of DRAW[1]; *d.-work*, fancy work in linen &c. done by drawing out threads.

draw·-well, n. Deep well with rope and bucket. [DRAW[1]]

dray, n. Low esp. brewer's cart without sides for heavy loads (*d.-horse*, large & powerful; *drayman*, brewer's driver). [f. OE *dragan* DRAW[1], cf. Sw. *drög*]

dread[1] (-ĕd), v.t., & n. Be in great fear of; shrink from, look forward to with terror; fear greatly (*that, to* learn &c.), be afraid (*to* do). (N.) great fear, awe, apprehension; object of fear or awe. [n. f. vb, ME *dreden, drǣden*, cf. OE *andrǣden*, etym. dub.]

dread[2], a. Dreaded, dreadful; awful, revered. [ME p.p. of DREAD[1]]

dread·ful, a. Terrible, awe-inspiring (*penny d.* ellipt, story-book full of horrors); troublesome, disagreeable, boring, very bad or long, horrid. Hence **drea·dfulLY**[2] adv. [-FUL]

drea·dnought (-ĕdnawt), n. (Cloth used for) thick coat for stormy weather; (*D-*) type of 20th-c. battleship greatly superior in tonnage & power to all predecessors (f. name of first built).

dream[1], n. Vision, series of pictures or events, presented to sleeping person; act, time, of seeing such vision; *waking d.*, similar experience of one awake; conscious indulgence of fancy, reverie, castle in the air, (also *day-d.*); thing (ideal, person, dress, dish, &c.) of dreamlike goodness, beauty, or refinement; *d.-reader*, interpreter of dd.; *d.-world, -land*, region outside the laws of nature. Hence **drea·mLESS, drea·mLIKE**, aa. [cf. G *traum*, perh. cogn. w. G *trügen* deceive]

dream[2], v.i. & t. (*dreamt* pr. -ĕmt, or *-ed*).

Have visions in sleep; see, hear, &c., in sleep (*dreamt a d., did you d. it?, d. that ...*); imagine as in a dream, think possible; (with negative &c.) think *of* even in a d., so much as contemplate possibility *of*, have any conception *of*; fall into reverie; form imaginary visions *of*; be inactive or unpractical (& trans. *d. away* one's *time*). Hence **drea·mER**[1] n. [as prec.]

drea·m-hole, n. Hole left in wall of tower &c. to admit light. [perh. f. OE *dréam* mirth, music (the holes letting sound of bells issue)]

drea·my, a. Full of dreams (rare or poet.); given to reverie, fanciful, unpractical; dreamlike, vague, misty. Hence **drea·mILY**[2] adv., **drea·miNESS** n. [-Y[2]]

drear·y, (poet.) **drear,** a. Dismal, gloomy, dull. Hence **drear·(i)LY**[2] adv., **drear·(i)NESS** n. [OE *dréorig* (*dréor* gore) prob. cogn. w. *dréosan* to drop & G *traurig* sad]

dredge[1], n., & v.t. & i. Apparatus for bringing up oysters, specimens, &c., or clearing out mud &c., from river or sea bottom. (Vb) bring *up*, clear *away* or *out*, with d.; clean out (harbour, river) with d.; use d.; hence **dre·dger**[1] [-ER[1] (1, 2)] n. [earlier *dreg* perh. f. DRAG[1]]

dredge[2], v.t. Sprinkle with flour or other powder; sprinkle (flour &c.) *over*; *dredging-box*, =foll. [f. obs. *dredge* sweetmeat, f. OF *dragee* f. L f. Gk *tragēma* (*trōgō* chew)]

dre·dger[2], n. (for *dredger*[1] see DREDGE[1]). Box with perforated lid for sprinkling flour &c. [prec., -ER[1]]

dree, v.t. (archaic). Endure (still in *d.* one's *weird*, submit to one's lot). [OE *dréogan*]

dreg, n. (usu. pl.). Sediment, grounds, lees, (*drink, drain, to the dd.*, leaving nothing); worthless part, refuse; (sing.) small remnant (esp. *not a d.*). Hence **dre·ggY**[2] a. [cf. Icel. *dreggjar*, Sw. *drägg*]

Dreibund (drī·boŏnd), n. = TRIPLE *Alliance* (3). [G (*drei* three, *bund* league)]

drench[1] (-tsh), n. Draught or dose administered to animal; (archaic) large, medicinal, or poisonous draught; a soaking or downpour. [OE *drenc* cogn. w. DRINK]

drench[2] (-tsh), v.t. Make to drink largely; force (animal) to take draught of medicine; (Sheep-washing, Tanning) steep, soak; wet all over with falling liquid (or of the liquid; *drenched with, by*). [OE *drencan* cf. G *tränken*, causative of DRINK]

dre·ncher, n. In vbl senses; esp.: drenching shower; apparatus for giving drench to beast. [-ER[1]]

Dre·sden (-z-), n. *D. china, porcelain*, kind produced in Saxony esp. in 18th c.

dress[1], v.t. & i. (Mil.) correct the alignment of (companies &c. in relation to each other, or men in line), (intr.) come into correct place in line &c. (*up*, i.e. forward, *back*, or abs.); array, clothe, (*dressed in black, serge*, &c.); provide oneself with clothes (*d. well* &c.); put on one's clothes; put on evening d. (esp. *d. for dinner*); *d. up*, attire oneself, attire (another), elaborately or in masquerade; *d. out*, attire conspicuously; deck, adorn, (ship with flags, shop-window with tempting wares); provide (play) with costumes; treat (wound, wounded man) with remedies, apply dressing to; subject to cleansing, trimming, smoothing, &c.; brush, comb, do up, (hair); curry (horse, leather; & fig., often *d. down*, thrash, scold); finish surface of (textile fabrics, building-stone); prepare, cook, (food); prune (plant); manure. [f. OF *dresser* cf. It. *dirizzare* f. L *directus* DIRECT]

dress[2], n. Clothing, esp. the visible part of it, costume (*full d.*, that worn on great occasions; *evening d.*, or *d.*, that worn at dinners or evening parties; *morning d.*, ordinary; *a d.*, lady's gown, frock); external covering, outward form, (*birds in their winter d., French book appearing in English d.*); *d. circle*, first gallery in theatres, in which evening-d. was once required; *d. coat*, swallow-tailed for evening d.; *d.-guard*, on bicycle &c. to protect d.; *d.-improver*, =BUSTLE[3]; *dressmaker, -king*, (woman) making women's dd.; *d. rehearsal*, final one in costume. [f. prec.]

dre·sser[1], n. Kitchen sideboard with shelves for dishes &c. [f. OF *dresseur* (*dresser* DRESS[1]) cf. med. L *directorium*]

dre·sser[2], n. In vbl senses; esp., surgeon's assistant in hospital operations, whence **dre·sserSHIP**(1) n. [-ER[1]]

dre·ssing, n. In vbl senses; esp.: scolding or thrashing; sauce, stuffing, &c.; manure; bandages, ointments, &c., for wound; stiffening used in finishing fabrics; *d.-bell*, &c. signal to dress for dinner; *d.-case*, of toilet necessaries; *d.-gown*, worn while making toilet or in dishabille; *d.-room*, attached to bedroom for toilet; *d.-table*, for looking-glass &c. [-ING[1]]

dre·ssy, a. Fond of, smart in, dress; (of clothes) stylish. Hence **dre·ssiNESS** n. [-Y[2]]

drew. See DRAW[1].

dri·bble, v.t. & i., & n. Flow, let flow, in drops or trickling stream (n., such flow); (of child, idiot, &c.) run at the mouth; (Football) work (ball) forward with slight touches of alternate or different players' feet (n., piece of dribbling); (Billiards) make (ball) just roll (or intr. of ball) into pocket. Hence **dri·bblER**[1] n. [frequent. of obs. *drib* v. var. of DRIP]

dri·b(b)let, n. Small quantity, petty sum, (esp. *by dd.*). [f. *drib* see prec. + -LET]

dried, drier. See DRY[2,1].

drift[1], n. Being driven by current; slow course or current; ship's deviation due to currents; projectile's deviation due to rotation; (Forest Law) driving of cattle to one place on appointed day to determine ownership &c.; natural or unperceived progress, tendency; waiting on events, inaction, (esp., contempt., *the policy of d.*); purpose, meaning, tenor, or scope, of person or his words; shower, driving mass; snow, sand, &c., accumulated by wind; (also *d.-ice, -wood,* &c.) matter driven by water; (Geol.) superficial deposit made by current of water or air (*D-*, pleistocene ice detritus, boulder clay); (also *d.-net*) large net for herrings &c. allowed to d. with tide; (Mining) horizontal passage following mineral vein; S.-Afr. ford; tool for enlarging or shaping hole in metal; *d.-anchor,* = DRAG²-*anchor.* [f. OE *drifan* DRIVE¹]

drift², v.i. & t. Be carried (as) by current of air or water, (of current) carry; go passively or aimlessly; pile, be piled, by wind into dd.; cover (field, road) with dd.; form or enlarge hole (see prec.). Hence **dri·ft**AGE(1) n., **dri·ft**ER¹ n., (esp.) boat used in d.-net fishing (much also in mine-sweeping during the great war). [f. prec.]

drill¹, n., & v.t. & i. Pointed steel &c. tool, or machine, for boring holes (vb, bore, of person or tool, with *metal* &c., or *hole* &c., as obj.; also intr., *d. through,* perforate); boring shell-fish; instruction or exercise in military evolutions (*d.-sergeant,* instructor in d., also fig.), rigorous discipline, exact routine, (vb, subject to, or undergo, such discipline; *B Company will d. at 10.0 a.m.*; *d. him in what he is to say, in Latin Grammar*). [n. in sense *tool* f. Du. *dril* f. *drillen* v.; vb in sense *bore* f. n.; other n. senses f. vb]

drill², n., & v.t. Small furrow for sowing seed in, ridge with such furrow on top, row of plants so sown; machine for furrowing, sowing, & covering seed; (vb) sow (seed) thus, plant (ground) in dd. [perh. = prec.]

drill³, n. Kind of baboon. [perh. W.-Afr.]

drill⁴, n. Coarse twilled linen or cotton fabric. [earlier *drilling* f. G *drillich* f. L *trilicem* nom. *-ix* (*tri-* three-, *licium* thread)]

drily. See DRY¹.

drink¹, v.t. & i. (*drank*; *drunk* & poet. *drunken*). Swallow (liquid); take (*the waters* at a spa) medicinally; *d. off, up,* d. the whole of at once; (of plants, porous things, &c.) absorb (moisture; often *up* or *in*); (fig.) *d. in,* contemplate, listen to, with delight; empty (vessel, *the cup of* pain or joy); spend (wages &c.) on d.; swallow liquid, take draught, (often *of* a source; *d. deep,* take large draught, or be great drinker as in next sense); take spirituous liquor esp. to excess, tipple, be a drunkard, (*d. hard, heavily, like a fish*; *drinking*-BOUT; *drinking-water* (reserved, pure enough, for drinking); *d.* one*self drunk, to death, out of a situation*; *d. down* or *under the table,* outlast in retaining control of oneself while drinking); *d. to,* pledge, toast; wish good &c. to in drinking (*d.* one's *health, d. success* or *confusion to*). Hence (-)**dri·nk**ER¹ n. [com.-Teut.; OE *drincan* cf. G *trinken*]

drink², n. Liquid swallowed or absorbed; beverage; intoxicating liquor (also *strong d.*), excessive indulgence in it, intemperance (*on the d.*, giving way to this; *in d.*, drunk); glass &c. or portion of liquor (STAND *dd. round*); *d.-offering,* libation. Hence **dri·nk**LESS a. [OE *drinc* & *drinca* f. *drincan* = prec.]

dri·nkable, a. & n. Good to drink; (n., esp. in pl.) thing(s) to drink. [-ABLE]

drip¹, v.i. & t. Fall, let fall, in drops; let drops fall, be so wet (*with* blood &c.) as to shed drops (*dripping wet,* very wet). [OE *dryppan* cf. G *triefen*]

drip², n. Act of dripping; dripping liquid; (Arch.) projection keeping rain from parts below (so *d.-moulding, dripstone*); *d.-drop,* persistent dripping. Hence **dri·ppy**² a. [f. prec.]

dri·pping, n. In vbl senses; also: fat melted from roasting meat, & used for frying or as food; *dd.*, water, grease, &c., dripping from anything. [-ING¹]

drive¹, v.t. & i. (drove, driven). Urge in some direction by blows, threats, violence, &c. (usu. with adv. or prep. as *away, back, in, out, from, to, through*; *d. out,* oust, take place of); chase or frighten (game, wild beasts, enemy esp. in guerilla warfare) from over large area into small in order to kill or capture; scour (district), (Forest Law) hold a DRIFT¹; (urge &) direct course of (animal drawing vehicle or plough, vehicle &c., or locomotive); convey in vehicle; act as driver of vehicle; travel, go, in carriage at one's disposal (cf. *ride* in omnibus, tram, train); impel forcibly, constrain, compel, (*to, into, to* do; *d. mad, out of* one's *senses*); overwork (*was very hard driven*); impel, carry along (of wind, water), throw, propel, send in some direction, (inanimate things); (Cricket) return (ball) from freely swung bat to or past bowler; (Golf) strike (ball, or abs.) with DRIVER; force (stake, nail, &c.) *into* ground &c. with blows; bore (tunnel, horizontal cavity); (also *let d.*) aim blow or missile (*at*); (of steam or other power) set or keep (machinery) going (also of person, *d. a quill, pen,* write); carry on, effect, conclude, (*drove a roaring trade, good bargain*); defer (*d. it to the last minute*); dash, rush, hasten; work hard *at*; float along, drift, tend, (*driving rain*; *d. at,* seek, intend, mean; *what is he driving at?*); *driving-iron, -pütter,* golf-clubs. [com.-Teut., OE *drifan* cf. G *treiben*]

drive[2], n. Excursion in vehicle (see prec.); driving of game or enemy (see prec.); stroke at cricket, golf, &c. (see prec.); energy, push; tendency; carriage-road, esp. private road to house; WHIST[3]-*d.* [f. prec.]

drĭ·vel, v.i. & t. (-ll-), & n. Run at mouth or nose like child; talk childishly or idiotically; fritter *away*; hence **dri·vel-l**ER[1] n. (N.) silly nonsense, twaddle. [ME *drevelen, dravelen,* OE *dreflian,* prob.cogn. w. DRAFF]

dri·ver, n. One who drives (DRIVE[1]), coachman (also *cab-d., engine-d.,* &c.; *slave-d.,* overseer of slave gang); (Golf) supple wooden-headed club for driving long distance; (Mech.) driving-wheel or other part that receives power directly; *front, rear, -d.,* bicycle in which power is applied to front, rear, wheel; QUILL-*d.* Hence **dri·ver**LESS a. [-ER[1]]

dri·ving-wheel, n. Wheel communicating motion to other parts of machine; large wheel of locomotive; cycle wheel that is directly worked.

dri·zzle, v.i., & n. (Fall in, be wet with) fine dense drops of rain (subj., *the day, rain, it*). Hence **dri·zzl**Y[2] a. [cf. OE *drēosan* fall, -LE(3)]

drō·gher (-ger), n. W.-Ind. coasting vessel; slow heavy craft. [thr. F f. 16th-c. Du. *drogher* (*droogen* to dry) named from drying herrings]

drogue (-ōg), n. Buoy at end of harpoon line. [perh. var. of DRAG[2]]

droit (-oit, or as F), n. Right, due, legal perquisite, (esp. *dd. of Admiralty,* proceeds of enemy's ships, wrecks, &c.). [F, f. LL *drictum* f. L *directum* neut. adj. = in LL legal right (DIRECT[2])]

drōll, a., n., & v.i. Facetious, amusing; queer, odd, surprising; hence **dro·l**LY[2] (-ōl-lĭ) adv., **dro·ll**NESS n. (N., now rare) jester, wag. (Vb, now rare) play the buffoon, jest *with, at, on.* [f. F *drôle(r)* etym. dub.]

dro·llery, n. Jesting; a facetious composition; quaint humour. [-ERY]

drŏ·medary (*also* -ŭm-), n. Light fleet usu. Arabian or one-humped camel bred for riding. [f. OF *dromedaire* f. LL *dromedarius* f. L f. Gk *dromas -ados* runner, -ARY[1]]

drŏ·mond, n. (hist.). Large medieval ship for war or commerce. [f. OF *dromon* f. LL f. Byz. Gk *dromōn* (*dromos* race)]

drone, n., & v.i. & t. Male of honey-bee, which does not work; idler; deep humming sound; monotonous speech or speaker; bass-pipe of bagpipe; fixed continuous note emitted by this. (Vb) buzz like bee or bagpipe, talk or utter monotonously, whence **dro·ning**LY[2] adv.; idle; idle *away* (life &c.). [OE *dran, dræn,* (sense *bee*); cf. G *drohne*]

droop, v.i. & t., & n. Hang down, slope, incline, as in weariness; (of eyes) look downwards; (poet., of sun &c.) sink; languish, decline, flag, lose heart; let (head, face, eyes) fall forward or down; hence **droo·ping**LY[2] adv. (N.) drooping attitude, loss of spirit, fall of tone. [f. ON *drúpa* vb cogn. w. foll.]

drop[1], n. 1. Round, pear-shaped, or hemispherical portion of liquid such as hangs or falls separately or adheres to surface (*of* water, tears, sweat, dew, rain, blood, or abs. in these senses); (Med.) smallest separable quantity of a liquid (in pl., liquid medicine to be measured by dd.); minute quantity (*d. in bucket* or *ocean,* infinitesimal factor); glass &c. of intoxicating liquor (*take a d.*; *has taken a d. too much,* is drunk; *have a d. in* one's *eye,* show signs of having drunk); pendant, hanging ornament, (*ear-dd.,* earrings; dd. of glass chandelier); sugar-plum (*acid, pear* &c., *dd.*); hence **dro·p**LET n. 2. Act of dropping, fall, social comedown, descent in prices, temperature, &c.; thing that drops or is dropped, as (Theatr.) painted curtain let down between acts (also *d.-curtain*), (in gallows) platform withdrawn from under feet of condemned (also, distance he is allowed to fall, as *d. of 3 ft*); abrupt fall in level of surface, amount of this; (also *d.-kick*) kick at football made by dropping ball and kicking it as it rises (*d.-off, -out,* such kick to start play after goal, try, or touchdown); *d.-shutter,* appliance for giving instantaneous exposure in photography; *d.-sulphur, -tin,* granulated by being dropped molten into water; *dropwort,* kinds of plant with tuberous root fibres. [sense 1 f. OE *dropa* cf. G *tropfen,* cogn. w. *drip, droop*; sense 2 f. foll.]

drop[2], v.i. & t. Fall in dd.; give off moisture in dd.; fall by force of gravity from not being held &c., (fig.) be uttered casually (*the remark dropped from him*), disappear (*a letter has dropped out*); sink to ground exhausted, wounded, &c. (*d. on* one's *knee,* kneel), (of setter) crouch at sight of game; fall naturally *asleep,* (*back*) *into* habit &c.; die; cease, lapse, (*affair was allowed to d.*; *the correspondence dropped*); fall in direction, condition, amount, degree, pitch, (*prices, voice, d.*); go *down* stream; fall *behind, to the rear,* &c.; come or go casually *in* as visitor, *into* place, *across* person; *d. on* or *across,* reprimand or punish; let fall (liquid, tears) in dd., shed; let go, relinquish, cease to hold, (*d. anchor,* anchor ship); give birth to (esp. lambs); utter casually as if unconsciously (esp. *d. a hint*; so *d. a postcard, line, note*); lose (money, esp. in gaming); fell with axe, blow of fist, or bullet; set down (passenger, parcel); omit (*letter,* one's hs, *syllable*) in speech; let (eyes) droop; lower (voice); *d.* CURTSY; (Football) send (ball), make (goal), by d.-kick (see prec.; also intr. = take d.-kick); cease to associate with, have done with (*d. it!*, stop that); *d. away, in*, depart, enter, one by one; *d. off*, = d. away, also fall asleep. [OE *dropian*, see prec.]

dro·ppings, n. pl. What falls or has fallen in drops, e.g. wax from candles; dung of beasts or birds. [-ING[1]]

dro·p-scene, n. = drop-curtain (DROP[1]); final scene, finale, of drama in real life.

dro·psy, n. Disease in which watery fluid collects in cavities or tissue of body, (fig.) overswollen state. Hence **dro·psi**CAL a., **dro·psical**LY[2] adv. [f. OF *ydropisie* f. L *hydropisis* f. Gk *hudrōps -ōpos* (*hudōr, hudr-*, water)]

dro·s(h)ky, n. Russian low four-wheeled carriage; cab in German towns. [f. Russ. *drozhki* dim. of *drogi* wagon (*droga* perch)]

dross, n. Scum thrown off from metals in melting; foreign matter mixed with anything, impurities; refuse, rubbish. Hence **dro·ss**Y[2] a. [OE *drós* cf. G *drusen* husks, dregs]

drought (-owt), (poet.) **drouth** (-ow-), n. (Archaic) dryness, lack of moisture, also thirst; continuous dry weather, want of rain. Hence **drough·t**Y[2], **drou·th**Y[2], a. [OE *drúgad* (*drýge* DRY[1], -TH[1])]

drove[1], n. Herd, flock, being driven or moving together; crowd, multitude, shoal, large number, esp. as moving together; mason's broad chisel. [OE *dráf* (*drífan* DRIVE[1])]

drove[2]. See DRIVE[1].

dro·ver, n. Driver of droves to market, cattle-dealer. Hence **drove**[3] v.t., **dro·v**ING[1] n. [DROVE[1] + -ER[1]]

drown, v.i. & t. Suffer death by suffocation in liquid (now usu. *be drowned*; but *drowning man* &c.); suffocate (person, animal) by submersion (subj., person &c., or the liquid); submerge, flood, drench, (esp. fig. *drowned in tears, sleep, wine*; *like drowned rat*, in soaked condition; *d. out*, drive out by flood); deaden (grief &c.) with or *in* drink; overpower (esp. of louder sound making voice &c. inaudible). [perh. f. *drunken* p.p. of *drink*, cf. MDa. *drukne* drown f. *drucken* p.p. of *drikke* drink]

drowse (-z), v.i. & t., & n. Be dull & sleepy, half asleep; be sluggish; make drowsy; pass *away* (time) in drowsing; (n.) half-asleep condition. [perh. = OE *drúsian* sink, become slow, cogn. w. *dréosan* fall; but not found in 11th-15th cc.; prob. back-formation from foll.]

drow·sy (-zĭ), a. Sleepy, half asleep, dozing; lulling, soporific; sluggish; *d.-head*, sleepy person. Hence **drow·si**HEAD (archaic), **drow·si**NESS, nn., **drow·si**LY[2] adv. [prob. cogn. w. OE *drúsian* see prec.; found earlier than prec.]

drub, v.t. Cudgel, thump, belabour; beat in fight; beat (notion) *into, out of*, person. Hence **dru·bb**ING[1] n. [earlier sense *bastinado*; perh. f. Arab. *darb* beating]

drudge, n., & v.i. Servile worker, slave, hack; hence **dru·dg**ERY(2, 5) n. (Vb) work slavishly at distasteful work; hence **dru·dging**LY[2] adv. [perh. cogn. w. DREE]

drug, n., & v.t. & i. Original simple medicinal substance, organic or inorganic, used alone or as ingredient (*the d. habit*, of taking opiates &c.); unsalable commodity, thing no longer in demand (usu. *d. in the market*); hence **dru·gg**Y[2] a. (Vb) adulterate with d., esp. with narcotic or poison; administer dd., esp. narcotics, to; indulge in narcotics &c.; nauseate, cloy. [f. F *drogue* cf. Pr. *drogua*, Sp., It., *droga*, etym. dub.]

dru·gget (-g-), n. (Over-carpet or floor-cloth of) coarse woollen stuff used for floor or table coverings. [f. F *droguet* etym. dub.]

dru·ggist, n. Dealer in drugs, pharmaceutical chemist. [-IST]

Dru·id, n. Priest, magician, soothsayer, among Celts of ancient Gaul & Britain; officer of Welsh Gorsedd or national assembly. Hence **Dru·id**ESS[1], **Dru·id**ISM (3), nn., **Drui·d**IC(AL) aa. [f. F *druide* f. L pl. *druidae, -des*, f. OCelt. *druid-* magician]

drum[1], n. Musical instrument sounded by striking & made of hollow cylinder or hemisphere with parchment stretched over opening(s) (*bass, tenor, big*, KETTLE, &c., *d.*); (Zool.) natural organ giving resonance, as howling monkey's hyoid bone; sound (as) of d., esp. bittern's cry; player of d., drummer; cylindrical structure (*d. of ear*, hollow part of middle ear) or object, cylinder or barrel in machinery on which something is wound or for other purposes; solid part of Corinthian or composite capital; stone block forming section of shaft; cylindrical receptacle for packing dried fruit, holding oil, &c.; evening or afternoon-tea party; (also *d.-fish*) kinds of American fish able to make drumming noise; *d.-fire*, heavy continuous rapid artillery fire usu. heralding infantry attack; *d.-head*, skin or membrane of d. (*d.-h.* COURT[1] *martial*), membrane across d. of ear, circular top of capstan; *d.-major*, N.C.O. commanding drummers of regiment; *drumstick*, stick with knob or pad for beating d., lower joint of cooked fowl's leg. [cf. Du. *trom*, & MHG *trumme* orig. trumpet]

drum[2], v.i. & t. Play the d., whence **dru·mm**ER[1] n., player of drum, (U.S.) commercial traveller; beat, tap, or thump, continuously on something (*on* piano, *at* door; *feet d. on floor*; *a drumming in the ears*); (of birds, insects) make loud hollow noise with quivering wings; summon, beat *up*, as by drumming; *d. out*, cashier by beat of d.; drive (person) *into* apathy &c., (lesson) *into* person, by persistence; strike (hands &c.) repeatedly (*up*)*on* something; play (tune &c.) on or as on d. [f. prec.]

drum[3], **dru·mlin,** nn. (geol.). Long narrow hill of drift or diluvial formation. [f. Gael. & Ir. *druim* ridge; *-lin* perh. for -LING[1]]

Dru·mmond light, n. Limelight or oxyhydrogen light. [Capt. T. *D.*, inventor c. 1825]

drunk, pred. a. & n. (also p.p. of DRINK[1]). Intoxicated, overcome with liquor, (*beastly, blind, dead, half,* &c., *d.*; *d. as a fiddler* or *lord*; also fig., *d. with joy, success, rage*); hence **dru·nk**ARD n. (N., slang) drinking-bout, drunken fit; (from police charge-sheets) case of drunkenness, (hence gen.) man charged with drunkenness, drunken man. [p.p. of DRINK[1]]

dru·nken, a. (rarely pred., cf. prec.). Intoxicated; given to drinking, often drunk; caused by or exhibiting drunkenness (*d. frolic, brawl*). Hence **dru·nken**LY[2] adv., **dru·nken**NESS n. [as prec., see -EN[1]]

drupe, n. Stone-fruit, fleshy or pulpy fruit enclosing stone or nut with kernel, as olive, plum, cherry. Hence **drup**A·CEOUS a. [f. L f. Gk *druppa* over-ripe (olive)]

dru·pel, dru·pelet (-plĭt), nn. Small drupe in compound fruit, as blackberry. [-EL, -LET]

druse[1], n. Crust of crystals lining rock-cavity, cavity so lined. [G, f. Boh. *druza*]

Druse[2] (-z), n. Member of political & religious sect of Mohammedan origin about Mt Lebanon. [Ismail al-*Darazi*, founder 1040]

dry[1], a. (drier, -est). Without moisture (*d. eyes*, free from tears; *d. shampoo*, applied as powder); not rainy, with deficient rainfall; parched, dried up, (colloq.) thirsty, (of liquid) having disappeared by evaporation, draining, wiping, &c.; (of country, legislation, &c.) teetotal, prohibiting sale of intoxicants (*go d.*, accept such legislation); not yielding water, milk, &c. (*cow, well, is d.*); without butter (*d. bread, toast*); solid, not liquid, (*d. goods*, see below; *d. measure*, measure of capacity for these); (of wine) free from sweetness & fruity flavour; unconnected with liquid (*die a d. death*, not by drowning or bloodshed; *d. cough*, without phlegm; *d.*-BOB[5]); impassive, unsympathetic, stiff, hard, cold, (*d. jest, sarcasm, humour*, expressed in matter-of-fact tone with show of unconsciousness); meagre, plain, bare, not enlarged upon, (*d. facts, thanks*); uninteresting, dull, unprofitable; untinged by prejudice or interest (*d. light*); *d.-bulb thermometer*, one of pair in hygrometer with wet & d. bulbs; *d. cooper*, maker of casks for d. goods; *d.-cure*, cure (meat &c.) without pickling in liquid; *d.*-DOCK[4]; *d.-fly* a. & v.i., (fish) with fly dangled just over water; *d. goods*, non-liquid goods, as corn, also (esp. U.S.) drapery, mercery, haberdashery; *d. lodging*, without board; *d.-nurse*, tending but not suckling child, (v.t.) bring up by hand; *d. pile*, electric pile or battery in which no liquid is used; *d.-plate*, photographic plate with sensitized film hard & d. for convenience of keeping, developing at leisure, &c.; *d.-point*, needle for engraving without acid on bare copper plate (also v.i., use this process, & n., engraving produced so); *d.-rot*, decayed state of wood not exposed to air caused by fungi, also the fungi, (fig.) unsuspected moral or social decay; *d.-salt* v.t., = *d. cure*; *dry·-salter(y)*, dealer, dealing or shop that deals, in drugs, dyes, gums, oils, pickles, tinned meats, &c.; *d.-shod* a. or adv., without wetting the feet. Hence **dry·**ISH[1](2) a., **dri·**LY[2] (or **dry·ly**) adv. (esp. in fig. senses), **dry·**NESS n. [OE *drȳge* cf. Du. *droog*, G *trocken*]

dry[2], v.t. & i. Make or become d. by wiping, evaporation, draining, &c.; cause (cow) to cease giving milk; *d. up*, make utterly d., (of moisture) disappear utterly, (of well &c.) cease to yield water, (colloq., esp. in imperat.) cease talking or doing something. Hence **dri·**ER[1] (1, 2) (also **dry·er**) n. [OE *drȳgean* (*drȳge* DRY[1])]

drȳ·ad, n. Nymph inhabiting tree, wood-nymph. [f. L f. Gk *druas -ados* (*drus* tree)]

Dry·asdust, n., **d-,** a. Dull laborious antiquary or historian; (adj.) very dry, uninteresting. [Dr *D.*, fictitious person (*dry as dust*) to whom Scott dedicated]

'dst, clipping of *wouldst, hadst.*

du·ad, n. (Incorrect for) DYAD.

du·al, a. & n. Of two, twofold, divided in two, double, (*d. ownership, skirt*); *the D. Monarchy*, former Austro-Hungarian Empire; (Gram.) *d. number* or *d.*, inflected form proper to two persons or things (additional to *singular* & *plural*). So **duă·**LITY n., **du·al**IZE(3) v.t., **du·al**LY[2] adv. [f. L *dualis* (*duo* two, -AL)]

du·alin, n. Powerful explosive of nitre, nitroglycerin, & sawdust. [prec. (dual nitre) + -IN]

du·alism, n. Duality; use of dual number; theory recognizing two independent principles (mind & matter, cf. *idealism* & *materialism*; good & evil in the universe; two personalities in Christ), so **du·al**IST (2) n., **duali·s**TIC a., **duali·s**TICALLY adv. [DUAL + -ISM]

dub[1], n. Deep pool in northern streams. [?]

dub[2], v.t. Make (person) into *a knight* by striking shoulders with sword; invest with (new title), name, nickname, (person or thing, with complement; *dubbed me Doctor, quack, a scribbler*); dress (artificial fishing-fly); smear (leather) with grease. [perh. f. OF *aduber*, com.-Rom. cf. It. *addobare*, etym. dub.]

du·bbing, n. In vbl senses; esp., prepared grease for leather (also *dubbin*). [-ING[1]]

dūbī·ĕty, n. Feeling of doubt; doubtful matter. [f. LL *dubietas* (*dubius* doubtful, -TY)]

dū·bious, a. Indistinct (*d. light*), vague, unreliable (*d. friend*), of questionable value or truth (*a d. compliment*); of doubtful issue (*d. undertaking, struggle*); of suspected character (*d. gains, company*); hesitating, doubting. Hence **du·bious**LY[2] adv., **du·bious**NESS n. [f. L *dubiosus* (*dubius* doubtful, -OSE[1])]

dūbita·tion, n. Doubt, hesitation. [F, f. L *dubitationem* (*dubitare* DOUBT[2], -ATION)]

dū·bitātive, a. Of, expressing, inclined to, doubt or hesitation. Hence **du·bitative**LY[2] adv. [f. L *dubitativus* as prec. + -IVE]

dū·cal, a. Of, like, bearing title of, duke. [F, f. LL *ducalis* (*dux* DUKE, -AL)]

dŭ·cat, n. Gold coin about 9*s*., formerly current in most European countries; coin, (pl.) money. [F, f. It. *ducato* f. LL *ducatus* DUCHY (prob. named from Duke of Apulia 1140)]

Duce (dōō·chā), n. Chief (*Il*, or *the*, *D.*, Signor Mussolini as leader of the Fascisti). [It., f. L *dux ducis*]

dŭ·chess (-tsh-), n. Duke's wife or widow; imposing woman; (slang) costermonger's wife (abbr. *dutch*). [F (-*e*), f. LL *ducissa* (DUKE, -ESS[1])]

dŭ·chy (-tshĭ), n. Territory of reigning duke or duchess; royal dukedom of Cornwall or Lancaster, each with certain courts of its own. [f. OF *duché* f. LL *ducatus* (*dux* DUKE, -ATE[1])]

duck[1], n. (pl. often *duck* collective; also -*s*). Kinds of swimming-bird, esp. the domesticated form of the mallard or wild-d. (*like d. in thunderstorm*, with upturned eyes, looking flabbergasted, faint, &c.; *like water off d.'s back*, producing no effect; *take to* anything *like d. to water*; *fine day for young dd.*, rainy weather; *lame d.*, disabled person, defaulter on Stock Exchange; *in two shakes of d.'s tail*, in an instant); female of this (cf. DRAKE[2]); its flesh; darling (esp. in voc.), whence **du·ck**Y[3] n. (also *ducky diamond*); (Cricket; also *d.'s-egg*) batsman's score of 0; *Bombay d.*, BUMMALO; *d. & drake*, game of making flat stone skip along water (*make dd. & drakes of, play dd.* &c. *with*, squander); *d.-bill*, red wheat, also = d.-billed PLATY*pus* or ORNITHO*rhynchus*; *d.-boards* (army slang), narrow path of wooden slats in trench or over mud; *d.-hawk*, marsh harrier; *d.-shot*, of size for shooting wild d.; *duckweed*, plant that carpets surface of still water. Hence **du·ck**LING[1](2) n. (UGLY *duckling*). [OE *duce* cogn. w. foll.]

duck[2], v.i. & t., & n. Plunge, dive, dip head, under water & emerge; bend quickly, bob, to avoid blow &c. or by way of bow or curtsy; plunge (person &c.) momentarily *in* water, or abs., whence **du·ck**ING[1](1) n.; lower (head) suddenly; (n.) quick dip below water in bathing, or lowering of head. [ME *d(o)uke* f. OE **dúcan* com.-WG cf. G *tauchen*]

duck[3], n. Strong untwilled linen or cotton fabric for small sails & outer clothing esp. of sailors; (pl.) trousers of this. [prob. f. Du. *doeck* = G *tuch* cloth]

du·cker[1], n. Kinds of diving-bird, esp. dabchick & water ouzel. [DUCK[2], -ER[1]]

du·cker[2], n. Breeder of ducks. [DUCK[1], -ER[1]]

duct, n. Conduit, tube, for conveying liquid; tube or canal in body conveying chyle, lymph, or secretions (named from function, as *biliary d.*, or from discoverer, as *Eustachian d., dd. of Bellini*); vessel of plant's vascular tissue holding air, water, &c. Hence **du·ct**LESS a. (-*less glands*, of which the secretion is not carried off by a duct, but acts directly on the blood). [f. L *ductus* leading, aqueduct (*ducere duct-* lead)]

du·ctile, a. (Of metals) malleable, flexible, not brittle, (in technical use) capable of being drawn out into wire, tough; plastic (of clay &c., or of person or character), pliable, tractable, docile. Hence **ducti·li**TY n. [F, f. L *ductilis* (*ducere* see prec., -IL)]

dud, n. (slang). (Pl.) clothes, rags; (sing.) scarecrow (also *dudman*), shell &c. that fails to go off, futile plan or person. [?]

dude, n. (U.S. slang; fem. *dudi·ne* pr. -ēn). Fastidious aesthetic person, often imitating English speech, dress, & manners; dandy, swell. Hence **du·d**ISH[1] a. [?]

dudgeon (dŭ·jn), n. Resentment, feeling of offence, (usu. *in d.*). [etym. dub.; obs. *dudgeon* hilt may be same word or not]

dud(h)ee·n (dŏŏ-), (Ir.). Short clay pipe. [?]

due[1], a. & adv. Owing, payable, as a debt or obligation (*fall, become, d.*, as bill reaching maturity); that ought to be given *to* person (*first place is d. to Milton, it is d. to him to say*), merited, appropriate, (*has his d. reward*), rightful, proper, adequate (*after d. consideration*), to be looked for, calculated or foreseen (*in d. time*); to be ascribed *to* cause, agent, &c. (*the difficulty is d. to our ignorance; the discovery is d. to Newton*; the advl use for *owing*, as *I came late d. to an accident*, is incorrect); under engagement *to* do something (*is d. to speak tonight*) or to arrive at certain time (*train d. at 7.30, already d. & over-d.*); (adv., of points of compass) exactly, directly, (*went d. east, a d. N. wind*). [f. OF *deü* (p.p. of *devoir* owe) f. LL *debutus* for L *debitus* (*debēre* owe)]

due[2], n. Person's right, what is owed him, (*give* one, esp. *the devil, his d.*, not be unjust to him, even though he deserves little or is no friend); what one owes (*pay* one's *dd.*); (usu. pl.) toll, fee, legally demandable (*harbour, light, tonnage, dd.*); (Naut.) *for a full d.*, for good, thoroughly, completely. [f. prec.]

du·el, n., & v.i. (-ll-). Fight with deadly weapons between two persons, in presence of two seconds, to settle quarrel (*the d.*, duelling & its code of rules); any contest between two persons, animals, parties, causes; hence **du·ell**IST(1) n. (Vb) fight d. [F, f. med.L sense of archaic L *duellum* (*duo* two) orig. form of *bellum* war; for *duel- bel-* cf. BIS]

dūĕ·nna, n. Elderly woman acting as governess & companion in charge of girls (orig.&esp.inSpanish family); chaperon. [f. Sp. *dueña* f. L *domina* mistress]

dūĕ·t, -tt, n. Musical composition for two voices or instruments; (fig.) dialogue, scolding-match; pair, couple. Hence **due·tt**IST(1) n. [f. It. *duetto* dim. of *duo* duet f. L *duo* two]

duff[1], n. (Dial. &c. for) DOUGH; PLUM-*d.*

duff[2], v.t. (slang). Fake up (goods), give look of newness &c. to, (*duffing*, counterfeit); (Austral.) steal & alter brands on (cattle). [perh. back formation f. DUFFER]

du·ffel, du·ffle, n. Coarse woollen cloth with thick nap; sportman's, camper-out's, change of clothes. [*Duffel* in Brabant]

du·ffer, n. One who sells trash as valuable, pretending it to be smuggled, stolen, &c.; pedlar, hawker; faker of sham articles; counterfeit coin, picture, &c.; unproductive mine; thing of which no use can be made; inefficient, useless, or stupid person. [etym. dub.; first sense a century older than last, & than DUFF[2]]

dug[1], n. Udder of female mammals, also teat, nipple, (not now used of women exc. contempt.). [cf. Sw. *dægga* suckle]

dug[2]. See DIG[1].

duge·nto (dōō-), n. The 13th century in Italian art &c. [It., = 200 (for 1200)]

du·gong (dōō-), n. (pl. often *dugong*). Large herbivorous mammal of Indian seas. [f. Malay *duyong*]

du·g-out, n. Canoe made by hollowing tree-trunk; underground shelter esp. for troops in trenches; (slang) retired officer &c. recalled to service.

duke, n. (Hist.) provincial military commander under later Roman emperors; (bibl.) chief of tribe; (in some parts of Europe) sovereign prince ruling duchy or small State; (Gt Britain & some other countries) person holding highest hereditary title of nobility outside royal family (also *royal d.*, d. who is also royal prince, with precedence); DINE *with D. Humphrey*; kind of cherry; (slang) hand, fist. [f. F *duc* f. L *dux ducis* leader]

du·kedom, n. Territory ruled by, dignity of, duke. [-DOM]

Du·keries, n. pl. District in Notts. containing several ducal estates. [-ERY]

dŭ·lcet, a. Sweet, soothing, (esp. of sounds). [f. F *doucet* dim. of *doux* f. L *dulcis* sweet]

du·lcifȳ, v.t. Sweeten, make gentle. Hence **dulci**FICA·TION n. [f. L *dulcificare* (*dulcis* sweet, -FY)]

du·lcimer, n. Musical instrument with strings of graduated length over sounding board or box struck with hammers, prototype of piano. [f. OF *doulcimer* perh. f. L *dulce melos* (not found in required sense) sweet tune]

Dŭlcinē·a (*or* -sĭ·nĭa), n. Idolized & idealized mistress. [name of Don Quixote's mistress]

dull, a., & v.t. & i. Slow of understanding, obtuse, stupid, whence **du·ll**ARD n.; (of ears, eyes, &c.) without keen perception; (of inanimate things) insensible; (of pain &c.) indistinctly felt; sluggish, slow-moving, stagnant, (of person, animal, trade); (of goods, stocks) not easily salable, not in demand; listless, depressed; tedious, monotonous; blunt (esp. of edge); (of colour, light, sound, taste) not bright, vivid, or keen; (of weather) overcast, gloomy; hence **du·ll**ISH[1] a., **du·l(l)**NESS n., **du·l**LY[2] (dŭl-lĭ) adv. (Vb) make d. (*d. the edge of*, blunt, make less sensitive, interesting, effective); lose force, intensity, clearness, or keenness. [ME, cf. OE *dol*, also G *toll* mad]

dulse, n. Edible kind of sea-weed. [f. Ir. & Gael. *duileasg*]

du·ly, adv. Rightly, properly, fitly; sufficiently; punctually. [DUE[1] + -LY[2]]

du·ma (dōō-), n. Russian parliament, 1906–17. [previously name of elective municipal councils]

dumb[1] (-m), a. (compar. & superl., pron. -*mer*, -mĭst). Unable to speak, abnormally (of human beings; *the d.*, *the deaf & d.*, as nouns) or normally (*d. animals*, used in pity or contempt); inarticulate, having no voice in government &c., (*the d. millions*); silenced by surprise, shyness, &c. (esp. *strike d.*; *d. in mixed company*); taciturn, reticent, (*Nature is d. on the point*; *English a d. people*); without speech (*d. crambo*; *d. show*, significant gestures, part of play given in early drama without words); unheard, giving no sound; without the voice, sound, or other property, usual in things of the name (*d. piano*, set of keys for exercising fingers; *d.-waiter*, an upright with revolving shelves enabling waiter to be dispensed with in dining-room; *d. barge*, *craft*, without sails or motive power; *d.-bell*, short bar with weight at each end used in pairs for exercising muscles, v.i., use these; *d. well*, sunk merely to carry off surface water). Hence **du·mb**LY[2] (-mlĭ) adv., **du·mb**NESS n. [com.-Teut.; OE *dumb*, cf. Du. *dom*, G *dumm*, stupid]

dumb[2], v.t. Make d. [f. prec.]
dumbfou·nd (-mf-), v.t. Strike dumb, confound, nonplus. [*dumb, confound*]
du·mbledore, n. (dial.). Bumble-bee; cockchafer. [?]
du·mdum (bullet), n. Kind of soft-nosed bullet that expands & inflicts laceration. [*D.* in India, with cantonment & arsenal]
du·mmy, n. & a. (Whist) imaginary fourth player whose hand is turned up & played by partner (*d. whist* or *d.*, game so played; *double d.*, game with two such hands); person taking no real part, or present only for show, figurehead, mere tool, man of straw; dolt, blockhead; counterfeit object, sham package &c., clothes-block, lay figure, man's figure as target; (adj.) sham. [DUMB[1] + -Y[3]]
dump[1], n. Short thick object of various kinds; leaden counter used in games; obs. Australian coin, (slang) small coin (*not worth a d.*); kind of bolt in ship-building; rope quoit for game on board ship; kind of skittle; kind of sweetmeat; short stout person. [prob. back-formation f. DUMPY]
dump[2], v.t. & i., & n. Shoot, deposit, tilt down, (rubbish); let fall with a bump; (Commerc.) send (goods unsalable at high price in home market) to foreign market for sale at low price, to avoid lowering home price & capture new market; drop down (t. & i.) with a thud; land (superfluous immigrants) in foreign country; hence **du·mp**ER[1] n. (N.) dull blow, thud; (U.S.) heap of refuse, place for shooting this; (Mil.) temporary depot of munitions at front. [cf. Da. *dumpe*, Norw. *dumpa*, fall plump]
du·mpling, n. Mass of dough boiled or baked either plain or enclosing apple &c. [cf. LG *dump* damp, heavy, & see -LING[1]]
dumps, n. pl. Depression, melancholy, (usu. *in the d.*). [f. 1523; etym. dub.]
du·mpy, a. & n. Short & stout (*d. level*, kind used in surveying); hence **du·mpi**NESS n. (N.) short-legged Scotch breed of fowls; (pl.) 19th Hussars. [etym. dub.; earlier than DUMP[1]]
dun[1], a. & n. (Of) dull greyish-brown colour as of ass or mouse (*d.-bird*, pochard; *d. diver*, female or young male of goosander); (poet.) dark, dusky; d. horse; kinds of artificial fishing-fly. [OE, cf. Ir. & Gael. *donn*, W *dwn*]
dun[2], n., & v.t. Importunate creditor; debt-collector; demand for payment. (Vb) importune for payment of debt; pester. [perh. var. of DIN]
dunce, n. One slow at learning, dullard, (*d.'s cap*, paper cone put on head of d. at school). [f. John *Duns* Scotus, schoolman, d. 1308, whose followers were ridiculed by 16th-c. humanists and reformers as enemies of learning]
du·nderhead, n., **du·nder-headed,** a. Blockhead, stupid (person). [?]
Dundrear·y, n. *D. whiskers*, long side whiskers worn without beard. [*D.*, character in T. Taylor's comedy *Our American Cousin*]
dūne, n. Mound or ridge of loose sand on coast. [F, f. ODu. *dûna* = OE *dún* DOWN[1]]
dung, n., & v.t. Manure; excrement of animals (rarely of man; *d.-beetle*, whose larvae develop in d.; *d.-fly*, feeding in it; *d.-worm*, found in cow-d. & used as bait; *d.-cart, -fork*, for conveying, loading & spreading, manure); moral filth; (vb) manure (land; of farmer, grazing animals, or the manure). [OE, cf. G *dung, dünger*, manure, & Sw. *dynga* dung]
du·ngaree (-ngg-), n. Coarse Indian calico. [f. Hind. *dungrī*]
dungeon (dŭ·njn), n., & v.t. (Now usu. *donjon*) great tower of castle in innermost court or bailey; strong subterranean cell for prisoners; (vb) shut *up*, imprison in d. [f. F *donjon* f. LL *domnionem* nom. *-o* f. *domnus* for L *dominus* lord; doublet of DOMINION]
du·nghill, n. Heap of dung or refuse in farmyard (*cock on his own d.*, household, parish, &c., tyrant or bully; *d. cock* &c., barn-door not game, whence *d.* as adj., craven).
du·niwă·ssal (dōō-), n. (Sc.). Highland gentleman of secondary rank. [Gael. *duine* man, *vasal* noble]
du·nlin, n. Red-backed sand-piper. [-LING[1]]
du·nnage, n. Mats, brushwood, gratings, &c., stowed under or among cargo to prevent moisture & chafing. [earlier *din-*, etym. dub.]
du·nnock, n. Hedge-sparrow. [DUN[1], -OCK]
duodĕ·cimal, a. & n. Of twelve or twelfths, proceeding by twelves; (n. pl.) cross-multiplication, method used for lengths given in feet, inches, & twelfths of inch, used by painters &c. [f. L *duodecimus* twelfth + -AL]
duodĕ·cimo, n. (usu. 12mo). Book-size in which each leaf is 1/12 of printing-sheet; book of this size; diminutive thing or person. [L (*in*) *duodecimo* abl. see prec.]
duodē·nary, a. Proceeding by twelves, in sets of twelve. [f. L *duodenarius* (*duodeni* twelve at once, -ARY[1])]
duodē·num, n. (anat.). First portion of small intestine immediately below stomach. Hence **duode·n**AL a., **duoden**I·TIS n. [med. L (*duodeni* see prec., from its length of 12 in.)]
du·ologue (-ŏg), n. Conversation between two persons, dramatic piece with two actors. [irreg. f. Gk *duo* two, after *monologue*]
duo·mo (dwō-), n. Italian cathedral. [It.]
dupe, n., & v.t. Victim of deception, gull; hence **du·p**ERY(2) n. (Vb) cheat, make a fool of; hence **du·p**ABLE a., **dup**ABI·LITY, **du·p**ER[1], nn. [F, etym. dub.]

dū·ple, a. Double (now only in: *d. ratio,* that of 2 to 1; *d. time, rhythm,* of two beats to the bar). [f. L *duplus* (*duo* two, *-plus* f. *ple-* fill)]

dū·plex, a. Of two elements, twofold, (*d. gas-burner,* with two jets combining into one flame; *d. lamp,* with two wicks); *d. telegraphy,* by which one wire transmits messages both ways at once. [L, gen. *-plicis* (*duo* two, *plic-* fold)]

dū·plicate[1] (*-at*), a. & n. With two corresponding parts, existing in two examples; doubled, twice as large or many; *d. proportion, ratio,* proportion of squares in relation to that of their radicals; exactly like a thing already existing (of any number of copies or specimens). (N.) one of two things exactly alike, esp. that made after the other; second copy, with equal legal force, of letter or document; second copy of bill drawn in two parts, second of exchange; pawnbroker's ticket; one of two or more specimens of thing exactly or virtually alike; synonym; exact correspondence between two things (*made in d.*). [f. L as foll., -ATE[2]]

dū·plicāte[2], v.t. Double, multiply by two; make in d., make exact copy of, produce copies of, whence **du·plicat**OR[2] (2) n. Hence **duplic**A·TION n. [f. L *duplicare* (DUPLEX, -ATE[3])]

dūpli·city, n. Double-dealing, deceitfulness; doubleness. [f. F *duplicité* f. L *duplicitatem* (DUPLEX, -TY)]

dūr·able, a. Lasting, not transitory; resisting wear, decay, &c. Hence **dura**BI·LITY, **dur·able**NESS, nn., **dur·ab**LY[2] adv. [F, f. L *durabilis* (*durare* f. *durus* hard, -ABLE)]

dūr·a mā·ter, n. (anat.). Tough outer membrane enveloping brain & spinal cord. [med. L, = hard mother, transl. of Arab. phrase]

dūr·ance, n. Imprisonment (usu. *in d. vile*). [earlier sense *endurance*; F (*durer* last f. L *durare* see DURABLE, -ANCE)]

dura·tion, n. Continuance in, length of, time; time for which thing continues (*for the d.,* phr. common in war-time contracts). [obs. F, f. LL *durationem* (prec., -ATION)]

dur·bar, n. Indian ruler's court; public levee of Indian prince or Anglo-Ind. governor or viceroy. [f. Pers. & Hind. *darbar* court]

dūr·ess(e) (*or* dūrĕ·s), n. Forcible restraint, imprisonment; compulsion, esp. imprisonment, threats, or violence, illegally used to force person to do something (*under d.*; *plea of d.,* for voiding contract so made). [obs. F (*-e*), f. L *duritia* (*durus* hard, -ESS[2])]

dūr·ing, prep. Throughout, at some point in, the continuance of. [part. of obs. *dure* last, used in abs. construction after F f. L; L *vita durante,* OF *vie durant,* E *life d.* or *d. life*]

dur·mast, n. Kind of oak. [etym. dub.; cf. *mast* fruit of forest tree]

durn, v.t. = DARN[2].

du·rra, dh-, (dōō-), n. Indian millet. [f. Arab. *durah*]

durst. See DARE.

dusk, n., a., & v.i. & t. Shade, gloom; darker stage of twilight. (Adj., poet.) shadowy, dim, dark-coloured, whence **du·sk**ISH[1] a., & (in ordinary use) **du·sk**Y[2] a., **du·ski**LY[2] adv., **du·ski**NESS n. (Vb, poet.) become, look, make, dim or dark or shadowy. [n. f. much earlier adj. ME *dosc* f. OE *dox,* cf. Norw. *dusk* mist]

dust[1], n. Finely powdered earth or other matter lying on ground or on surfaces or carried about in clouds by wind (*shake off the d. of* one's *feet,* depart indignantly; *throw d. in* one's *eyes,* mislead him by misrepresentation or diverting attention from point; *bite the d.,* fall wounded or slain); household refuse (*dustbin, d.-hole,* receptacles for this; *dustman,* scavenger who empties these); pollen; (with *a*) cloud of d. (*what a d.!, a great d., make* or *raise a d.*); dead person's remains (*honoured d.*; also *in the d.,* dead); the human body, man; humiliation (*humbled in, to, the d.*); confusion, turmoil, excitement, row, contest, (*d. & heat,* the burden of a struggle); (slang) cash; *d.-brand,* disease of corn, smut; *d.-cloak, -coat, -gown, -wrap, -cloth,* worn or put over objects to keep off d.; *d.-colour,* dull light brown; *d.-cover,* book's jacket; *d.-guard,* in machine, or on bicycle to protect dress; *dustman,* = SAND*man*; *dustpan,* into which d. is brushed from floor; *d.-shot,* smallest-sized shot. Hence **du·st**LESS a. [OE *dúst,* cf. MDu. *donst,* & G *dunst* vapour]

dust[2], v.t. & i. Sprinkle with d. or powder (intr., of birds, take d.-bath; *d. the eyes of,* deceive, take in); make dusty; sprinkle (d., powder); clear of d. by brushing, wiping, or beating (*d.* one's *jacket,* beat him); clear away (d. &c.), clear furniture of d. [f. prec.]

du·ster, n. Cloth for dusting furniture &c.; person who does this. [-ER[1]]

du·sting, n. In vbl senses; esp. (slang), thrashing, tossing in storm at sea. [-ING[1]]

du·sty, a. Full of, strewn with, finely powdered like, dust; dry as dust, uninteresting; (slang) *not so d.,* fairly good; *d. miller,* plant auricula, artificial fishing-fly. Hence **du·sti**LY[2] adv., **du·sti**NESS n. [-Y[2]]

Dutch[1], a. & n. (Hist.) of Germany including Netherlands (*High D.,* of Southern Germans. *Low D.,* of Germans of sea-coast, Netherlands, & Flanders); of the language or people of Holland & Netherlands (*D. school,* of painters distinguished by artistic treatment of everyday subjects; *the D.,* people of Holland & Netherlands); coming from Holland, made or invented by the D., (*D. clock, chair,* *cheese*, HOE, OVEN); characteristic of or attributed to the D. (*D.* AUCTION, COURAGE; *talk to* one *like a D. uncle*, lecture him paternally; *D. wife*, frame of cane &c. for resting the limbs in bed, long bolster similarly used). (N.): (Hist.) the German language in any of its forms (*High D.*, German; *Low D.*, Low German including language of Holland & other northern varieties); language of Holland & Netherlands (*double D.*, gibberish). [f. MDu. *dutsch* Hollandish, Netherlandish, German, =G *deutsch* German, f. OHG *diutisc* popular, vulgar, national, (*diota* people cf. OE *théod*); in E the sense has narrowed f. *Teutonic* to *Hollandish*; in G & Du., from *Teutonic* to *German*]

dutch[2], n. See DUCHESS.

Du·tchman, n. (pl. *-men*, fem. *-woman*). Hollander or Netherlander (*or I'm a D.*, *I'm a D. if—*, forms of positive & negative asseveration); Dutch ship (*Flying D.*, spectral ship, also certain express train on G.W.R.).

du·tēous, a. Dutiful, obedient, (of person or conduct). Hence **du·teous**LY[2] adv., **du·teous**NESS n. [DUTY + -OUS, cf. *beauteous*]

du·tiable, a. Liable to customs or other duties. [-ABLE]

du·tiful, a. Regular or willing in obedience & service. Hence **du·tiful**LY[2] adv., **du·tiful**NESS n. [foll. + -FUL]

du·ty, n. Behaviour due to superior, deference, expression of respect; payment to public revenue levied on import, export, manufacture, or sale, of goods (CUSTOMS, EXCISE, *dd.*), transfer of property (DEATH, PROBATE, *succession, stamp, dd.*), licences, legal recognition of documents, &c. (d. is levied on article or transaction, tax usu. on persons); moral or legal obligation, what one is bound or ought to do (*d. call*, visit one would rather not but feels bound to pay); binding force of what is right; business, office, function, performance of or engagement in these (*on, off, d.*, actually so engaged or not), (Eccl.) performance of church services (*took my d. for me*); (Mech.) measure of engine's effectiveness in units of work done per unit of fuel; *do d. for*, serve or pass for (something else); *d.-paid, -free*, of goods on which customs or excise d. has been paid or is not leviable. [AF *dueté* (no corresp. F) see DUE[1], -TY]

dūū·mvir, n. (pl. *-s, -ī*). Member of board of two equal officials. Hence **duu·mvir**ATE[1] n. [L, lit. man of the two]

du·vet (F), n. Eider-down quilt.

dux, n. (no pl.). Top boy in class (chiefly Sc.). [L, =leader]

dwale, n. Deadly Nightshade. [prob. f. Scand. (ON *dvöl* delay, Sw. *dvala* trance)]

dwarf (-orf), n., a., & v.t. Person, animal, or plant, much below ordinary size of species, whence **dwar·**FISH[1] a., **dwar·fish**LY[2] adv., **dwar·fish**NESS n.; small supernatural being in esp. Scandinavian mythology skilled in metal-working. (Adj.) undersized (in many plant names); puny, stunted. (Vb) stunt in growth, or in intellect &c.; make look small by contrast or distance. [com.-Teut.; OE *dweorh*, cf. Du. *dwerg*, G *zwerg*]

dwell, v.i. (dwelt), & n. Keep one's attention fixed, write or speak at length, (*up*)*on* subject (*d. upon note, syllable, &c.*, prolong it); make one's abode, spend one's time, live, *in, at, near, on*, &c. (now usu. *live* in talk); (of horse) be slow in raising feet, pause before taking fence; (n., mech.) slight regular pause for some purpose in motion of machine. [OE *dwellan* lead astray, delay, be delayed, cf. OHG *twellan* retard, MDu. *dwellen* stun; also Skr. *dhur* mislead]

dwe·ller, n. Inhabitant, resident *in, on*, &c.; horse that DWELLS at fence. [-ER[1]]

dwe·lling, n. In vbl senses; also: place of residence, house; *d.-house*, used as residence, not as office, warehouse, &c.; *d.-place*, =d. [-ING[1]]

dwi·ndle, v.i. Become smaller, shrink, waste away; lose importance, decline, degenerate. [obs. *dwine*, OE *dwīnan*, cf. ON *dvína*, Du. *verdwijnen*, vanish, + -LE(3)]

dȳ·ad (-*ad*), n. The number two; group of two, couple; (Chem.) atom, radical, or element, with combining-power of two atoms of hydrogen. Hence **dȳă·d**IC a. [f. L f. Gk *duas -ad-* (*duo* two, -AD)]

dyarchy. See DIARCHY.

dye[1] (dī), n. Colour produced by or as by dyeing, tinge, hue, (also fig., *crime, scoundrel, of blackest, deepest, d.*); matter used for dyeing, colouring-matter in solution; *d.-stuff, -ware, -wood*, yielding d.; *d.-house, -works*, where dyeing is done. [OE *déag*]

dye[2], v.t. & i. (*dyed*; part. *dyeing*). Colour, stain, tinge; impregnate (tissue) with colouring-matter (*d. in the wool, in grain*, while material is in raw state, giving more permanent result); make (thing) such a colour (*d. cloth red, a rose colour*, &c.); (of material) take colour *well, badly*, &c. [OE *déagian* (prec.)]

dy·er, n. One who dyes cloth &c. (*dyer's* in many names of plants yielding dye, as *d.'s bugloss, broom, oak*). [-ER[1]]

dy·ing, n. In vbl senses of DIE[2]; esp. (attrib.) connected with, at time of, death (*d. bed, declaration, wish*; *d. oath*, made at, or with solemnity proper to, death). [-ING[1]]

dyke. See DIKE.

dȳnă·mic, a. & n. Of motive force (cf. *static*); of force in actual operation (cf. *potential*); active, potent, energetic; of dynamics; (Med.) functional (cf. *organic*); (Philos.) accounting for matter or mind as being merely the action of forces, so

dy·namISM(3), **dy·namist**[1] [-IST(2)] (& see DYNAMICS), nn.; (n.) energizing or motive force. [f. F *dynamique* f. Gk *dunamikos* (*dunamis* power, -IC)]

dynă·mical, a. Of dynamics; of force or mechanical power actively operative; (Theol., of inspiration) endowing with divine power, not impelling mechanically; of dynamism (see prec.). Hence **dyna·mical**LY[2] adv. [-AL]

dynă·mics, n. pl. used as sing. Branch of physics treating of the action of force (now including *statics*, which deals with equilibrium under action of force, & *kinetics* formerly called *d.*, which deals with force as producing or affecting motion), whence **dy̆·namist**[2] [-IST(3)] (& see DYNAMIC) n.; branch (*of* any science) in which forces are considered; moving forces, physical or moral, in any sphere. [-ICS]

dy̆·namīte, n., & v.t. High explosive of nitro-glycerine mixed with inert absorbent; (vb) shatter with d. [Gk *dunamis* force, -ITE]

dy·namīter, -ard, nn. User of explosive esp. for revolutionary purposes. So **dy̆namĭ·t**IC a., **dy·namīt**ISM(1), **dy·namīt**IST(1), nn. [prec., -ER[1]; *-ard* after F *communard* (-ARD)]

dy̆namo-, comb. form of Gk *dunamis* power, as in *d.-electric* = of current (formerly *dynamic*) electricity, also = converting mechanical into electric energy.

dy·namo, n. (pl. *-os*). Machine converting mechanical into electric energy by rotating coils of copper wire in magnetic field. [short for *d.-electric machine*, see prec.]

dynamŏ·meter, n. Kinds of instrument measuring energy expended by animal, engine, or mechanical force; gauge for telescope's magnifying-power. [DYNAMO-, -METER]

dy̆·nast, n. Ruler, member of a dynasty. [f. LL f. Gk *dunastēs* (*dunamai* be able)]

dy̆·nasty, n. Line of hereditary rulers. So **dy̆na·st**IC a., **dy̆na·st**ICALLY adv. [f. F *dynastie* f. LL f. Gk *dunasteia* lordship (prec.)]

dyne, n. (physics). Unit of force (the amount that, acting for one second on one-gramme mass, gives it velocity of one centimetre per second). [F, f. st. of Gk *dunamis* force]

dy̆s-, pref. = Gk *dus-* bad-, opp. *eu-* good-, chiefly in medical or other scientific words taken f. Gk or made with Gk elements.

dy̆·sentery, n. Disease with inflamed mucous membrane & intestinal glands, griping pains, & mucous & bloody evacuations. So **dysentĕ·r**IC a. [f. OF *dissenterie* f. L f. Gk *dusenteria* (DYS-, *entera* bowels)]

dy̆slogi·stic (-j-), a. Disapproving, opprobrious, (of sense in which term is used). Hence **dyslogi·st**ICALLY adv. [DYS- + (EU)LOGISTIC)]

dy̆spe·psia, -sy, n. Indigestion. So **dy̆spe·ptic** a. & n., (person) subject to d. or the attendant depression. [L f. Gk DYS(*pepsia* f. st. of *pessō* cook)]

dyspnoe·a (-nēa), n. (path.). Difficult breathing. Hence **dyspnoe·**IC a. [L, f. Gk *duspnoia* (DYS-, *pneō* breathe)]

E

E, e, (ē), letter (pl. *E*s, E's). (Mus.) note, & corresp. scale; second-class ship in Lloyd's register.

Abbreviations (1): early, as **E.E.T.S.** (English text society); east, as **E.N.E., E. by N.,** (north), **E.S.E., E. by S.,** (south), **E., E.C.** (central), London postal districts; **E.R. (et I.),** *Edvardus Rex* (*et Imperator*), Edward King (& Emperor); English, as **E.C.U.** (Church Union), **E.D.D., E.D.S.,** (dialect dictionary, society); excess, **E.P.D.** (profits duty); **E. (& O.) E.,** errors (& omissions) excepted; **e.g.,** *exempli gratia*, for example.

Abbreviations (2): **Ebor.,** Abp of York; **Eccl**(es)**.,** Ecclesiastes; **Ecclus,** Ecclesiasticus; **Eph.**(esians); **Esq.**(uire); **Esth.**(er); **etc.**(etera); **exc.**(ept); **Exod.**(us); **Exon.,** Bp of Exeter; **exor, exrx,** executor, -trix; **Ezek.**(iel).

e-, pref. Shortened form of EX-(1)

each, a. & pron. (Of two or more) every (one) taken separately, as *e. man has two votes, e. of us has two votes, we have two votes e., they cost a penny e., e. is worse than the one before*; *they hate e. other*, e. hates the other; *sides of two triangles are equal e. to e.* (a side of one to the corresponding side of the other). [OE has (1) *ǣlc* (cf. OHG *eogilîh*, G *jeglich*) perh. f. **aiwon galîkô* ever alike, (2) *gehwilc* (cf. OHG *gihwelîh*, & see Y- & WHICH), (3) *ǣghwilc* (cf. OHG *eogihwelîh*, & see AYE)]

ea·ger, a. Full of keen desire; strongly desirous (*to* do, *for, after, about*, &c.); (of passions &c.) keen, impatient; (archaic) *e.* (cold) *air*. Hence **ea·ger**LY[2] adv., **ea·ger**NESS n. [f. OF *aigre* keen, f. L *acrem* (nom. *acer*)]

ea·gle, n. Large bird of prey, with keen vision & powerful flight; figure of this, esp. as ensign of Roman or French army, or as lectern in church; (U.S.) *double e.*, coin worth twenty dollars; *e.-eyed*, keen-sighted; *e.-owl*, largest European owl. [f. OF *aigle* f. L *aquila*]

ea·glet, n. Young eagle. [f. F *aiglette* (as prec., see -ET[1])]

eagre (ā·ger, ē-), n. Large tidal wave, esp. in the Humber, Trent, and Severn. [?]

-ean, suf. of adjj. & nn. (also *-aean, -eian*), with sense 'of, belonging to, like'; = -AN w. end of stem, usu. Gk *-ai(os)*, L *-ae(us)*, or Gk *-ei(os)*, L *-ei(us)*; *-aean* chiefly in unfamiliar wds as *Ascraean, Achaean*; *-eian* (apart from Gk & L as *Pompeian* &c.) is used w. E names in *-ey, -y*, as

Bodleian, Rugbeian; *-ean* is pron. with ē (*Macitēan, empyrēan*), exc. in familiar adjj. as *Pro·tean, Hercu·lean*, (-ĭan), but cf. *pygmēan*; some have *-ean* incorrectly for *-ian* (*antipodean*), & some vary betw. the two (*Aristotelean, -ian*).

ear[1], n. Organ of hearing, esp. external part of this; faculty of discriminating sound, as *an e. for music*; ear-shaped thing, esp. handle of pitcher; *bring* (storm, hornet's nest, &c.) *about* one's *ee.*; *prick up* one's *ee.*, assume expectant attitude; *I would give my ee.*, make any sacrifice (*for* a thing, *to* do); *over head and ee.*, deeply immersed *in* (lit. & fig.); *set* (persons), *be, by the ee.* (at variance); *a word in your e.* (in private); *be all ee.* (deeply attentive); *it goes in at one e. & out at the other*, it leaves no impression; *give e.*, listen *to*; *have a person's e.* (favourable attention); *were your ee. burning last night?* (we were talking about you); *sent him away with a flea in his e.*, told him some home truths &c.; *e.-ache*, pain in drum of e.; *e.-mark*, (n.) mark on e. of sheep &c. as sign of ownership, (fig.) mark of ownership, (v.t.) mark (sheep &c.) with this, (fig.) assign (fund &c.) to definite purpose; *e.-phone*, =HEAD-*phone*; *e.-ring* (worn in lobe of ear for ornament); *e.-shot*, hearing distance, as *within, out of, e.-shot*; *e.-trumpet*, tube used by persons partly deaf; *e.-wax*, viscid secretion in e. Hence (-)**ear**ED[2], **ear**·LESS, aa. [com.-Teut.; OE *éare*, G *ohr*; cogn. w. L *auris*, Gk *ous*]

ear[2], n. Spike, head, of corn, containing its flowers or seeds. [OE *éar* (cf. G *ähre*, Du. *aar*), cogn. w. L *acus -eris* husk]

ear·ing, n. (naut.). Small rope (one of several) fastening upper corner of sail to yard. [EAR[1] + -ING[1]; or =*ear-ring*]

earl (erl), n. (fem. *countess*). Nobleman ranking between marquis & viscount (cf. COUNT[3]); *E. Marshal*, officer presiding over Heralds' College &c. Hence **ear·l**DOM n. [OE *eorl*, cf. ON *earl, jarl*]

Ear·lswood (erlz-), n. (Used for) E. Asylum for feeble-minded persons, Redhill, Surrey.

ear·ly (er-), a. & adv. Absolutely or relatively near to the beginning of a portion of time, as *an e. visit, e. risers, rise e., keep e. hours* (rise & go to bed e.), *e. peaches* (maturing e. in the year), *E. English* STYLE, *fix an e. date* (not long hence), *at your earliest convenience* (as soon as you conveniently can), *the e. part* (beginning) *of the century*; *the e. spring, morning*, &c., the e. part of spring &c.; *e. bird*, (facet.) e. riser (w. ref. to proverb *the e. bird gets the worm*); *e.-Victorian* a. & n., (writer &c.) of Victoria's e. reign, antiquated. Hence **ear·li**NESS n. [(adj. f. adv.) OE *ǽrlíce* (*ar* posit. degree of *ǽr* ERE, -LY[2])]

earn (ern), v.t. (Of person, action, conduct, &c.) obtain as reward of labour or merit. [OE (*ge-*)*earnian* f. OTeut. *aznôjan* (*aznâ* field-labour, cf. G *ernte* harvest)]

ear·nest[1] (ern-), a. & n. Serious, zealous, not trifling; ardent (*desire* &c.); *in e.*, serious(ly), not jesting(ly). Hence **ear·nest**LY[2] adv., **ear·nest**NESS n. [OE *eorneste* a. f. *eornust* n. (cf. G *ernst*) perh. f. root *ers* seen in obs. *erre* anger]

ear·nest[2] (ern-), n. Money paid as instalment, esp. to confirm contract &c.; foretaste, presage, betokening, (*is an, in, e. of what is to come*). [prob. conn. w. *erles, arles*(*-penny*) f. L **arrhula* dim. of *arrha*]

ear·ning, n. In vbl senses, esp. (pl.) money earned. [-ING[1]]

earth[1] (er-), n. (pl. only as below). The ground, as *it fell to e.*; (w. pl.) hole of badger, fox, &c.; the dry land; land & sea opp. the sky; this planet; this world opp. heaven or hell (*why* &c. *on e.?*, why EVER?); (w. pl.) soil, mould; (Chem., w. pl.) any of certain metallic oxides, uninflammable, & having little taste or smell; (Electr., w. pl.) communication with e. as completion of circuit; *e.-born*, of mortal race, (Myth.) emerging from e. at birth; *e.*-(substitute for WATER[1]-) *closet*; *e.-light, -shine*, partial illumination of dark part of moon by light from e.; *e.-nut*, pig-nut & other plants; *earthwork*, bank of e. used in fortification; *earthworm*, worm living in ground, (fig.) grovelling person. Hence **ear·th**WARD(S) adv. [com.-Teut.: OE *eorthe*, Du. *aarde*, G *erde*]

earth[2], v.t. & i. Cover (roots of plants) with heaped-up earth; drive (fox) to earth; (intr., of fox) run to earth; (Electr.) =GROUND[2]. [f. prec.]

ear·then, a. Made of earth; made of baked clay. [-EN[5]]

ear·thenware, n. (often attrib.). Vessels &c. made of baked clay; baked clay. [WARE[1]]

ear·thly, a. Of the earth, terrestrial; (colloq.) *no e. use, reason, chance*, no use &c. at all; *not an e.* (slang), no chance whatever. Hence **ear·thli**NESS n. [-LY[1]]

ear·thquake, n. Volcanic convulsion of earth's surface; (fig.) social or other disturbance.

ear·thy, a. Like, of, earth or soil; (fig.) grossly material. Hence **ear·thi**NESS n. [-Y[2]]

ear·wig, n., & v.t. (-gg-). Insect once held to get into the head through the ear; (v.t.) influence (person) by secret communications. [(vb f. n.) OE *éarwicga* (*éare* EAR[1] + *wicga* earwig)]

ease[1] (ēz), n. Freedom from pain or trouble; freedom from constraint, as *at* one's *e.*; (Mil.) *stand at e.* (in informal attitude, with right foot drawn back & taking most of body's weight); relief from pain; CHAPEL *of e.*; facility, esp. *with e.* Hence **ea·se**LESS a. [f. OF *aise* (cf. It. *agio* etym. dub.]

ease², v.t. & i. Relieve from pain &c.; give mental ease to (person, one*self*, one's *mind*); (facet.) rob (person *of* his purse &c.); relax, adjust, (what is too tight); (Naut.) slacken (rope, sail, *away, down, off*), *e. her*, reduce speed of engine; (intr.) *e. off*, become less burdensome. [f. prec.; F had *aaisier* = It. AD(*agiare*, see prec.)]

ea·seful, a. Comfortable, soothing; at rest; slothful. Hence **ea·seful**LY² adv., **ea·seful**NESS n. [-FUL]

ea·sel (-zl), n. Wooden frame to support picture, blackboard, &c. [f. Du. *ezel* = G *esel* ass]

ea·sement, n. (Law) right of way or similar right over another's ground; supplementary building, shed, &c.; (archaic) relief from pain or burden. [f. OF *aisement* (as EASE², -MENT)]

east, adv., n., & a. (Towards, at, near) the point of the horizon where the sun rises (90° to right of North); *to the e.* (*of*), in an eastward direction (from); *e.* (*wind*), wind blowing from the e.; eastern part of the world, orient; *far E.*, China, Japan, &c.; *near E.*, Turkey; *E.* INDIES; *E. End*, eastern part of London. Hence **ea·st**WARD a. & n., **ea·st**WARD(S) adv. [OE (1) *éastan* (cf. Du. *oost*, G *osten*) f. OTeut. *austonô* from the east (*aus-* seen in L *aurora* dawn), (2) *éast* perh. shortened f. **éaster* eastwards]

Ea·ster, n. Festival of Christ's resurrection, corresponding to Passover, & observed on 1st Sunday (*E. day, Sunday*) after calendar full moon on or after March 21 (also archaic *Eastertide*); (also *E.-week*) week commencing with E. day; *E. eggs* (painted & presented to friends at E.); *E. eve*, day before E. day. [OE *éastre* perh. f. *Eostre*, dawn-goddess (*aus-*, see prec.)]

ea·sterly, a. & adv. In an eastern position or direction; (coming) from the east, as *e. wind*. [f. obs. *easter* (perh. compar. of EAST) + -LY¹]

ea·stern, a. & n. Of, dwelling in, the east part of the world; *E. Church* (Greek); *E. question*, political problem relating to E. Europe, esp. Turkey; lying towards the east; (n.) inhabitant of the East, member of E. Church. Hence **ea·stern**MOST a. [OE *éasterne* (see EAST & -ERN)]

ea·sting, n. (naut.). Course gained to the eastward; easterly direction. [-ING¹]

ea·sy (-zĭ), a., adv., & n. Free from pain, discomfort, annoyance, anxiety, &c.; *e. circumstances*, affluence; free from embarrassment or stiffness, as *e. manners, free & e.* (not stiff, not strict); not difficult (*to* do, or abs.; *e. of access*, easily got at); easily persuaded, compliant; (Commerc., of commodity) not much in demand, (of market) not showing eager demand, (cf. TIGHT); (adv.) in an e. manner, as *take it e.*, proceed comfortably; (as command) *e.!*, move gently, *e. all!*, stop (prop. rowing), whence *an e.*, a short rest, *stand e.!* (mil.), permission to squad standing at ease to relax attitude further; *e. chair*, one designed for comfort, usu. with arms; *e.-going*, (of horse) having an e. gait, (of person) fond of comfort, indolent. Hence **ea·si**LY² adv., **ea·si**NESS n. [f. OF *aisié* p.p. of *aisier* EASE²]

eat, v.t. & i. (past *ate, eat*, pron. ĕt; p.p. *eaten*, pron. ētn). Masticate & swallow (solid food); swallow (soup); *e.* one's *words*, retract them in humiliating manner; *e.* one's *terms* or *dinners*, be studying for the bar; *e.* HUMBLE *pie*; *e.* (person) *out of house & home*, ruin him by eating (lit. & fig.) all he has; *horse* &c. *eats its head off*, costs more to feed than it is worth; *well, don't e. me!*, joc. reply to vehement protest &c.; (intr. as pass.) *the cakes e. crisp*; destroy, consume, as *e.* one's *heart out*, suffer silently; *e. away*, destroy gradually (lit. & fig.); *e. up*, consume completely, waste, (lit. & fig.), absorb, as *eaten up with pride*. Hence **ea·t**ABLE a. & n. (usu. pl.). [com.-Teut.: OE *etan*, Du. *eten*, G *essen*]

ea·ting, n. In vbl senses; *e.-house*, restaurant. [-ING¹]

eau (ō), n. *E.-de-Cologne*, perfume made at Cologne; *e.-de-Luce*, an antidote to snake-bites; *e.-de-vie*, brandy; *e. sucrée*, water and sugar. [F, = water]

eaves, n. (now pl.). Overhanging edge of roof or thatch; *eavesdrop*, stand under this to listen to secrets; *eavesdropper*, one who does this (usu. fig.). [OE *efes* (cf. dial. G *obsen*), prob. f. same root as OVER; *-s* being now taken as pl. *eave* is sometimes used for sing.]

ebb, n., & v.i. Reflux of tide, as *e. & flow*, *e.-tide*; decline, decay, as *at a low e.*; (v.i.) flow back, recede, decline, decay. [OE (*ebbian* vb f.) *ebba* (cf. Du. *eb, ebbe*), etym. dub.]

ĕ·bon, a. (poet.). Made of, black as, ebony. [f. L f. Gk *ebenos*, perh. of oriental orig.]

ĕ·bonite, n. = VULCANITE. [f. foll. + -ITE¹]

ĕ·bony, n. & a. Kinds of hard black wood; (adj.) made of, black as, this. Hence **e·bon**IZE(3) v.t. [ME *hebenyf* f. L *hebeninus* (perh. misread *-ivus*) f. Gk *ebeninos* EBON]

ēbrī·ety, n. (now rare). Drunkenness. [f. F *ébriété* f. L *ebrietatem* (as foll., see -TY)]

ē·brious, a. (now rare). Drunk; given to, of, drunkenness. [f. L *ebrius* + -OUS]

ēbŭ·llient, a. Boiling; exuberant. So **ebu·lli**ENCE, -ENCY, nn. [f. L E(*bullire -it-* boil), -ENT]

ĕbulli·tion, n. Boiling; effervescence; (fig.) sudden outburst (*of* passion, war, &c.). [f. L *ebullitio* (as prec., see -ION)]

écarté (ĕkar·tā), n. Card-game for two persons. [F (*écarter* discard)]

Ecce Hō·mō (ĕ·ksĭ), n. Picture of Christ wearing crown of thorns. [L, = behold the man (*John* xix. 5)]

ecce·ntric (ĭks-), a. & n. Not concentric (*to* another circle); not placed, not having its axis &c. placed, centrally; (of orbit) not circular; (of heavenly body) moving in an e. orbit; irregular; odd, whimsical; (n., Mech.) e. contrivance for changing rotatory into backward-&-forward motion, esp. for slide-valve of steam-engine; *e. strap, rod,* parts of this. Hence **ecce·ntr**ICALLY adv., **eccentri·c**ITY n. [f. LL *eccentricus* f. Gk *ekkentros* (*ek* out of + *kentron* CENTRE), see -IC]

ecclē·sia (-z-), n. (Gk Ant.). Regular assembly (esp. of Athenian citizens). [med.L, f. Gk *ekklēsia* (*ekkaleō* call out); in later Gk = church]

ecclē·siast, n. Member of Athenian ecclesia; 'the Preacher', Solomon, regarded as author of *Eccles.*). [f. Gk *ekklēsiastēs* (as prec.)]

Ecclēsia·stēs, n. An O.T. book. [as ECCLESIAST]

ecclesia·stic, n. & a. Clergyman; (adj., now rare) = foll. [f. Gk *ekklēsiastikos* (as prec.)]

ecclesia·stical, a. Of the church or the clergy; *E. Commission(ers)*, body administering part of Church of England revenues. Hence or cogn. **ecclesia·stical**LY² adv., **ecclesia·stic**ISM n. [-AL]

Ecclesia·sticus, n. A book of the Apocrypha. [as ECCLESIASTIC, = of (i.e. to be read in) church]

ecclēsio·logy, n. Science of churches, esp. of church building & decoration. Hence **ecclesiolo·gic**(AL) aa., **ecclesio·log**IST n. [f. ECCLESIA + -O- + -LOGY]

e·cdȳsis, n. Casting off (esp. of slough in serpents &c.; also fig.); slough. [f. Gk *ekdusis* (*ekduō* put off)]

echelon (ĕ·shelon, or as F), n., & v.t. Formation of troops in parallel divisions, each with its front clear of that in advance; *in e.* (or F *en é.*), so drawn up; (v.t.) draw up thus. [(vb f. n.) f. F *échelon* (*échelle* ladder f. L *scala*, see -OON)]

echi·dna (ĕk-), n. Australian toothless burrowing animal like hedgehog. [f. Gk *ekhidna* viper]

e·chinite (ĕk-), n. Fossil echinoderm or sea-urchin. [f. ECHINUS + -ITE¹]

echinoderm (ĭkī·-, ĕ·kĭ-), n. Class of animals including sea-urchins. [as foll. + DERM]

echī·nus (-k-), n. Sea-urchin, animal inhabiting spheroidal prickly shell. [f. L f. Gk *ekhinos* hedgehog, sea-urchin]

echo¹ (ĕ·kō), n. Repetition of sound by reflexion of sound-waves (*cheer* person &c. *to the e.*, loudly); *E.*, cause of this personified; close imitation; obsequious imitator or adherent; artifice by which last syllables of one verse are taken up by next. Hence **e·cho**LESS a. [f. L f. Gk *ēkhō*, conn. w. *ēkhē* sound]

e·cho², v.i. & t. (Of places) resound with an echo; (of sounds) be repeated, resound; (trans.) repeat (sound) by echo; repeat (another's words), imitate the words or opinions of (person). [f. prec.]

e·choism, n. = ONOMATOPOEIA. So **e·choic** a. [-ISM]

é·clair (ĕ-), n. Small finger-shaped cake filled with cream and iced. [F]

éclaircissement (F), n. Clearing up, explanation, (of conduct &c.).

éclat (ĕklah·), n. Conspicuous success, general applause, as *with great e.*; social distinction. [F]

ecle·ctic, a. & n. (Ancient philosopher) selecting such doctrines as pleased him in every school; (person) borrowing freely from various sources, not exclusive in opinion, taste, &c. Hence **ecle·ct**ICALLY adv., **ecle·ctic**ISM(3) n. [f. Gk *eklektikos* (*eklegō* pick out, see -IC)]

ecli·pse¹, n. Interception of the light of a luminous body (sun, moon, &c.), by intervention of another body between it & the eye or between the luminous body and what illuminates it; ANNULAR, PARTIAL, TOTAL, *e.*; deprivation of light; loss of brilliance or splendour (*in e.*, of birds, having lost the courting plumage); periodical obscuration of light-house light. [OF, f. L f. Gk *ekleipsis* vbl n. f. *ekleipō* fail to appear, be eclipsed (*leipō* leave)]

ecli·pse², v.t. (Of a heavenly body) obscure another by passing between it & spectator or between it and the source of its light; intercept (light, esp. of lighthouse); (fig.) deprive of lustre, outshine, surpass. [f. prec.]

ecli·ptic a. & n. Of eclipse; (n.) sun's apparent orbit. [f. L f. Gk *ekleiptikos* (ECLIPSE¹, -IC)]

ĕ·clogue (-ŏg), n. Short poem, esp. pastoral dialogue, such as Virgil's Bucolics. [f. L f. Gk *eklogē* selection (*eklegō* pick out)]

ecology, var. of OECOLOGY.

ēconŏ·mic, a. & n. Of economics; maintained for profit, on a business footing, paying expenses, (of rent) high enough to compensate builder, owner, &c.; connected with industrial arts; (n. pl.) practical science of the production & distribution of wealth, (also) condition of a country as to material prosperity. [f. L f. Gk *oikonomikos* (see ECONOMY & -IC)]

econo·mical, a. Saving, thrifty, not wasteful (*of*); relating to economics or to political economy. [-AL]

econo·mically, adv. Thriftily; from an economic point of view. [-LY²]

ecŏ·nomist, n. Manager (*of* money &c.); thrifty person; writer on economics or political economy. [as ECONOMY + -IST]

ecŏ·nomize, v.t. & i. Use sparingly; turn to the best account; (intr.) practise economy, cut down expenses. Hence **economiza·**TION n. [as foll. + -IZE]

ecŏ·nomy, n. Administration of concerns & resources of a community; *Political E.*, theory of production & distribution of wealth; frugality; (w. pl.) instance of this; (Theol.) judicious handling of doctrine, whence (with play on sense *frugality*) *e. of truth*; organization; organized body, society, &c. [f. L f. Gk *oikonomia* f. *oikonomos* steward (*oikos* house + *-nomos* f. *nemō* manage)]

ĕcru· (-ōō, or as F *écru*), n. Colour of unbleached linen. [F, = unbleached]

e·cstasize, v.t. & i. Throw, go, into ecstasies, [f. foll. + -IZE]

e·cstasy, n. Exalted state of feeling, rapture, (esp. of delight); (Med.) morbid state of nerves in which mind is occupied solely by one idea; trance; poetic frenzy. [f. OF *extasie* f. med. L f. Gk *ekstasis* vbl n. f. *existēmi* put (person) out of (his senses)]

ecstă·tic, a. Of, subject to, producing, ecstasies (esp. of joy). Hence **ecsta·ti**CALLY adv. [f. Gk *ekstatikos* (as prec., see -IC)]

ecto- in comb. = Gk *ektos* outside, as, *-gene·tic*, (of child &c.) born without gestation; *-plasm*, (Biol.) outer layer of protoplasm, (Spirit.) emanation from medium's body; *-zōon*, external parasite.

ecumenical. See OECUMENICAL.

e·czema, n. Inflammation of the skin, of several kinds. [f. Gk *ekzema* (*ek* out + *zeō* boil, see -M)]

-ed¹, suf. forming p.p. of weak vbs (also *-d*, *-t*, as in *sold*, *bought*); *-ed* (now reduced in sound to *-d* or *-t* except in *-ded*, *-ted*, in some bibl. wds, as *blessed*, & in *learned*) was in OE *-ed*, *-ad*, *-od*, acc. to vb class, *-d* alone being the participial element, f. OTeut. *-do-* f. Aryan *-tó-* (cf. Gk vbl adj. *-tos*, L p.p. *-tus*); *-t* is used in vbs that shorten in p.p. a long vowel of stem, as *crept*, *dreamt* (*dreamed* if pronounced with ē), and in some ending in *-d* after *l*, *n*, *r*, as *gilt*, *sent*, *girt*. (2) p.pp. in *-ed* (and *-en*) are used (rarely f. intr., commonly from trans. vbs) as adjj., meaning when intr. 'that has done so-&-so' (*vanished hand*, *fallen idol*, *escaped convict*); a special use, w. resultant force, is seen in *outspoken*, *well-read*; sometimes it is doubtful whether adjj. in *-ed* are trans. (or intr.) p.p. or belong to foll.: *decayed* may be *that has been decayed*, *that has decayed*, or *that is affected with decay*; reference to -ED¹(2) is made only for the rare intr. p.p. adjj.

-ed² (as prec.), suf., distinct f. prec. in OE (*-ede*), though perh. a form of the p.p. suf. in OTeut. (cf. *caudatus* tailed in L), appended to nn. to form adjj. meaning possessed of, affected with, &c., as *talented*, *wooded*, *diseased*; esp. used to make adj. out of adj. & n., usu. stressed (apart from demands of context) in attrib. use on first component (*a qui·ck-witted lad*, *me·tal-cornered chest*), in pred. use on second (*he seems quick-wi·tted enough*) exc. where this is more or less otiose (*ru·by*, *co·ffee*, &c., *-coloured*, attrib. & pred.); sometimes = 'having the ways of' instead of simply 'having', as *bigoted*, *crabbed*, *dogged*; sometimes indisting. f. prec. (2).

edā·cious, a. Of eating; greedy. So **edă·**CITY n. [f. L *edax -acis* (*edere* eat, see -ACIOUS)]

E·dam (ē-), n. Spherical Dutch cheese. [*E.*, in Holland]

E·dda, n. (*Older*, *Poetic*, *E.*) collection of ancient Icelandic poems; (*Younger*, *Prose*, *E.*) miscellaneous handbook (c. 1230) to Icelandic poetry. [perh. f. a name in an ON poem]

e·ddy, n., & v.t. & i. Small whirlpool; wind, fog, smoke, moving like this; (v.t. & i.) whirl round in ee. [?]

edelweiss (ā·dlvīs), n. Alpine plant with white flower, growing in rocky places. [f. G *edel* noble + *weiss* white]

E·den (ē-), n. Abode of Adam & Eve at their creation; delightful abode; state of supreme happiness. [f. Heb. *'eden* orig. = delight]

ede·ntate, a. & n. (Animal) without incisor & canine teeth; toothless (animal). [f. L E(*dentatus* f. *dens -ntis* tooth, see -ATE²]

edge¹, n. Sharpened side of blade of cutting instrument or weapon; sharpness of this, as *the knife has no e.*; *take the e. off*, blunt, weaken, dull, (appetite, argument, &c.); *set* (person's) *teeth on e.*, jar his nerves, affect him with repulsion; e.-shaped thing, esp. crest of a ridge; (fig.) critical position or moment; meeting-line of two surfaces of a solid; (Skating) *do the inside, outside, e.*, skate on the inner, outer, e. of skates; boundary-line of surface; brink (of precipice); *e.-bone*, see AITCH-BONE; *e.-tool*, cutting-tool (in fig. sense also *edged tool*). Hence **e·dge**LESS a. [OE *ecg* (cf. Du. *egge* edge, corner, G *ecke*, *eck*, corner) f. root *ak-* whence L *acies*, Gk *akis*, point]

edge², v.t. & i. Sharpen (tool &c., also fig.); *e. on*, = EGG² *on*; furnish with border, form border to; insinuate, push, (thing, oneself) *into*, *in*, *out*, *off*, &c.; (intr.) advance obliquely. [f. prec.]

e·dgeways, -wise, adv. With edge uppermost or foremost; (fig.) *get a word in e.* (in talkative person's silent interval); (of two things) edge to edge. [-WAYS, -WISE]

e·dging, n. In vbl senses, esp. border, fringe; *e.-shears* (for trimming edges of lawn). [-ING¹]

e·dgy, a. Sharp-edged; (of painting) of too sharp outline. [-Y²]

ĕ·dible, a. & n. (Thing) fit to be eaten. Hence **edibi·lity** n. [f. LL *edibilis* (*edere* eat, see -BLE)]

ē·dict, n. Order proclaimed by authority; *E. of Nantes,* issued by Henry IV of France to grant toleration to Protestants, and revoked by Louis XIV. Hence **edi·ct**AL a. [f. L *edictum* f. E(*dicere dict-* say) proclaim]

ĕ·difice, n. Building (esp. large one; also fig.). [f. F *édifice* f. L *aedificium* (*aedis* temple + *-ficium* f. *facere* make)]

ĕ·dify, v.t. Benefit spiritually; improve morally (often iron.). So **edi**FICA·TION n. [f. F *édifier* f. L *aedificare* (as prec., see -FY)]

ĕ·dit, v.t. Prepare an edition of (another's work); set in order for publication (material chiefly provided by others); garble, cook, (dispatches &c. in newspaper); act as editor of (paper &c.). [(1) f. L E(*dere dit-* = *dare* give) put out; (2) back-formation f. EDITOR]

edi·tion, n. Form in which a literary work is published (*library, cabinet, popular, e.*); whole number of copies of book, newspaper, &c., issued from same types & at same time (see also IMPRESSION). [f. F *édition* f. L *editionem* (as EDIT, see -ION)]

édition de luxe (F), n. Handsome edition.

edi·tio pri·nceps, n. First printed edition of a book. [L]

e·ditor, n. One who prepares the work of others for publication; one who conducts a newspaper or periodical. Hence **e·ditor**SHIP, **e·ditr**ESS[1], nn. [L (as EDIT, see -OR[2])]

editor·ial, a. & n. Of an editor; (n.) newspaper article written by or under responsibility of the editor. Hence **edi·tor·ial**LY[2] adv. [-IAL]

e·ducate, v.t. Bring up (young persons); give intellectual & moral training to; provide schooling for; train (person, one*self*, a faculty, *to* do); train (animals). Hence **educa**BI·LITY, **e·ducat**OR[2], nn., **e·duc**ABLE, **e·ducat**IVE, aa. [f. L *educare* conn. w. EDUCE, see -ATE[3]]

educa·tion, n. Bringing up (of the young); systematic instruction; course of this, as *classical, commercial, art, e.*; development of character or mental powers; training (of animals). Hence **educa·tion**AL a., **educa·tion(al)**IST(3) nn., **educa·tional**LY[2] adv. [f. L *educatio* (as prec., see -ATION)]

edu·ce, v.t. Bring out, develop, from latent or potential existence; (Chem.) disengage (substance) from a compound; infer (number, principle, *from* data). Hence **edu·c**IBLE a. [f. L E(*ducere duct-* lead)]

ē·duct, n. (Chem.) body disengaged from another in which it previously existed; inference. [as prec.]

edu·ction, n. Educing; (in steam-engine) *e.-pipe, -valve,* &c., EXHAUST[1]-pipe &c. [f. L *eductio* (as prec., see -ION)]

edu·lcorate, v.t. Free from acrid properties or from soluble particles, purify. Hence **edulcor**A·TION n. [f. L E(*dulcorare* f. *dulcor* sweetness f. *dulcis*), see -ATE[3]]

-ee, suf. forming nn. expr. the person affected by the vbl action, corresp. to agent nn. in *-or,* prop. in legal terms (*lessee, vendee*) on anal. of AF (*apelour, apelé,* summoner, summoned), but extended to the indirect obj.; now also in non-techn. wds, & without corresp. *-or,* as *employee, payee*; & without consciousness of its meaning, as *bargee, absentee*; a few wds are adoptions f. mod. F *-é, -ié,* as *debauchee, refugee.* In *committee* (orig. a person), accent has changed with meaning. *Epopee* is not an instance; in *coatee, -ee* perh. = -Y[3]; in *settee, goatee, -ee* is unexplained. [AF *-é* of p.p. f. L *-atus*]

eel, n. A snake-like fish; (fig.) slippery creature; (pop.) minute animal found in vinegar & in sour paste; *e.*-BUCK[4]; *e.-spear* (for transfixing ee.). Hence **ee·l**Y[2] a. [com.-Teut.: OE *ǣl,* Du. & G *aal*]

e'en. See EVEN[1,3].

-eer, suf. expr. person concerned with, f. L *-iarius* or *-arius* -ARY[1]; F *-ier* is retained in the less familiar wds (*muleteer* but *bombardier*); *-eer* is freely used for new nn., as *auctioneer, mountaineer,* often contempt., as *sonneteer.* Vbs are also formed (*electioneer*) by back formation on *auctioneering* &c.

e'er. See EVER.

eer·ie, -y, a. Superstitiously timid; strange, weird. Hence **eer·i**LY[2] adv., **eer·i**NESS n. [ME *eri,* etym. dub.]

ef-, pref. = EX-(1) before *f.*

effa·ce, v.t. Rub out; (fig.) obliterate, wipe out; utterly surpass, eclipse; treat, regard, one*self* as unimportant. Hence **effa·ce**ABLE a., **effa·ce**MENT n. [f. F *effacer* f. L *ex* out + *facies* face]

effe·ct[1], n. Result, consequence (*cause and e.,* causation); efficacy, as *of no e.*; combination of colour or form in picture &c., as *a pretty e.*; (pl.) property, as *personal ee., no ee.* (written by banker on dishonoured cheque); *give e. to, take e.,* make, become, operative; impression produced on spectator, hearer, &c., as *calculated for e.*; *bring to, carry into, e.,* accomplish; *in e.,* for practical purposes. Hence **effe·ct**LESS n. [OF, f. L *effectus -ūs* f. EF(*ficere fect-* = *facere* make)]

effe·ct[2], v.t. Bring about, accomplish; *e.* (take out) *a policy* (of insurance). [f. prec.]

effe·ctive, a. & n. Having an effect; *e. range* (of weapon), range within which it is e.; powerful in effect; striking; (of soldiers or sailors) fit for service; actual, existing; (n.) e. soldier, e. part of army. Hence **effe·ctive**LY[2] adv., **effe·ctive**NESS n. [F (*-if, -ive*), f. L *effectivus* (as EFFECT[1], see -IVE)]

effe·ctual, a. Answering its purpose; valid. Hence **effe·ctual**LY[2] adv.,

effe·ctualNESS n. [f. OF (*-el*) f. LL *effectualis* (EFFECT¹, -AL)]
effe·ctuate, v.t. Bring to pass, accomplish. Hence **effectuA·TION** n. [f. F *effectuer* (as EFFECT¹), on anal. of ACTUATE]
effĕ·minate (*-at*), a. Womanish, unmanly; voluptuous. Hence **effe·minACY** n., **effe·minateLY**² adv. [f. L EF(*feminare* f. *femina* woman), see -ATE²]
effe·ndi, n. Turkish title of respect applied to government officials & members of learned professions. [f. Turk. *efendi* lord, corrupt. of Gk *authentēs* (see AUTHENTIC)]
e·fferent, a. (physiol.). Conveying outwards, discharging. [f. L EF(*ferre* carry), see -ENT]
efferve·sce (-ĕs), v.i. Give off bubbles of gas, bubble, (often fig. of persons); (of gas) issue in bubbles. Hence **efferve·sCENCE, -ENCY,** nn., **efferve·sCENT** a. [f. L EF(*fervescere* incept. of *fervēre* be hot)]
effe·te, a. Exhausted, worn out; feeble, incapable. Hence **effe·teNESS** n. [f. L EF*fetus* worn out by breeding (*fetus*)]
effica·cious, a. (Of thing) producing, sure to produce, desired effect. Hence or cogn. **effica·ciousLY**² adv., **effica·ciousNESS, e·fficACY,** nn. [f. L *efficax* (as foll., -ACIOUS)]
effi·cient, a. Productive of effect; (of persons) competent, capable; *e.* CAUSE¹, that which makes a thing what it is. Hence or cogn. **effi·ciENCY** n., **effi·cientLY**² adv. [F, f. L, as EFFECT¹, see -ENT]
e·ffigy, n. Portrait, image; *hang, burn,* (person) *in e.*, hang, burn, his image. [f. F *effigie* f. L *effigies* (EF*fingere* fashion)]
efflore·sce (-ĕs), v.i. Burst out into flower (lit. & fig.); (Chem., of crystalline substance) turn to fine powder on exposure to air, (of salts) come to the surface & there crystallize, (of ground or wall) become covered with saline particles. So **efflore·sCENCE** n., **efflore·sCENT** a. [f. L EF(*florescere* FLOURISH)]
e·ffluence, n. Flowing out (of light, electricity, &c., or fig.); what flows out. [foll., -ENCE]
e·ffluent, a. & n. Flowing forth; (n.) stream flowing from larger stream, lake, sewage tank, &c. [f. L EF(*fluere flux-* flow), see -ENT]
efflu·vium (-ōō-), n. (pl. *-ia*). Exhalation affecting lungs or sense of smell; (supposed) stream of minute particles emitted by magnet &c. [LL, as prec.]
e·fflux, n. Flowing out (of liquid, air, gas; also fig.); that which flows out. Hence **efflu·xION** n. [f. L *effluxus -ūs* (as prec.)]
e·ffort, n. Strenuous exertion; (of oratory &c.) display of power. [F, f. *efforcer* f. med.L EX(*fortiare* f. *fortis* strong)]
e·ffortless, a. Making no effort, passive; (of skill &c.) without effort, easy. [-LESS]
effro·ntery (-ŭnt-), n. Shameless audacity. [f. F *effronterie* f. *effronté* f. L EX(*frontatus* f. *frons -ntis* forehead) shameless]
effu·lgent, a. Radiant. Hence **effu·lgENCE** n., **effu·lgentLY**² adv. [f. L EF(*fulgēre* shine), see -ENT]
effu·se¹ (-s), a. (Bot., of inflorescence) spreading loosely; (Conch.) with lips separated by groove. [as foll.]
effu·se² (-z), v.t. Pour forth (liquid, air, light, smell; also fig.). [f. L EF(*fundere fus-* pour)]
effu·sion (-zhn), n. Pouring forth (lit. & fig.); unrestrained utterance (often contempt., of literary work). [f. L *effusio* (as prec., see -ION)]
effu·sive (-s-), a. (Of speech or emotions) exuberant, demonstrative. Hence **effu·siveLY**² adv., **effu·siveNESS** n. [as EFFUSE², see -IVE]
eft, n. Newt. [OE *efeta* etym. dub.]
eftsoo·n(s), adv. (archaic). Soon afterwards. [OE *eftsóna* (see AFT & SOON); *-s* = -ES]
ega·d, int. By God. [prob. orig. *a* ah + *God*]
egg¹, n. Spheroidal body produced by female of birds &c. esp. of domestic fowl, containing germ of a new individual; ADDLE, WIND¹, *e.*; (fig.) *in the e.*, in an early stage; *as full as an e.*, chock-full; *bad e.*, person, scheme, that comes to no good; *as sure as ee. is ee.*, undoubtedly; *teach your grandmother to suck ee.*, offer advice to persons more experienced than yourself; *have all your ee. in one basket*, risk all on a single venture; *e. & anchor, dart, tongue,* (Arch.) kinds of moulding; *e.-&-spoon race* (in which runners carry e. in spoon); *e. cleavage* (biol.), process of cleavage in fertilized e.-shell; *e.-cup* (for holding e. boiled in shell); *e.-dance,* dance blindfold among ee., (fig.) intricate task; *e.-flip, -nog,* hot beer, cider, wine, &c., with ee. stirred in; *e.-plant,* white-fruited *Solanum esculentum*; *e.-shell,* shell of e., fragile thing (*e.-s. china,* very thin kind); *e.-slice,* utensil for taking omelette from pan; *e.-spoon,* small spoon for eating boiled ee.; *e.-tooth,* protuberance on bill-sheath of embryo bird for cracking shell; *e.-whisk,* utensil for beating ee. [com.-Teut.; OE *ǣg*, Du. & G *ei*]
egg², v.t. Urge (person) *on* (*to* an act, *to* do). [f. ON *eggja* = EDGE v.]
e·glantine, n. Sweet-briar. [f. F *églantine* f. OF *aiglent* prob. f. L *acus* needle, see -LENT]
ĕ·go, n. (metaphys.). The conscious thinking subject, opp. to the non-ego or object. [L, = I]
ĕ·gōism, n. (Ethics) theory that treats self-interest as foundation of morality; systematic selfishness; self-opinionatedness; = foll. Hence **e·goIST** n., **egoi·st-**

IC(AL) aa., **egoi·sticalLY²** adv. [f. F *égoïsme* (as prec., see -ISM)]

ĕ·gotism, n. Too frequent use of 'I' & 'me'; practice of talking about oneself; self-conceit; selfishness. Hence **e·gotIST** n., **egoti·sTIC(AL)** aa., **egoti·sticalLY²** adv., **e·gotIZE** v.i. [f. EGO + -ISM; *-t-* perh. on F *idiotisme* &c.]

egrē·gious, a. (Archaic) surpassing; (mod.) shocking, as *e. folly, blunder, ass.* Hence **egre·giousLY²** adv., **egre·giousNESS** n. [f. L E(*gregius* f. *grex gregis* flock) lit. towering above the flock]

ē·gress, n. (Right of) going out; (Astr.) end of eclipse or transit; way out (lit. & fig.). [f. L *egressus -ūs* f. L E(*gredi gress-* =*gradi* step)]

egre·ssion, n. Going out or forth. [f. L *egressio* (as prec., see -ION)]

e·gret (ēg- *or* ĕg-), n. Lesser White Heron; feathery down on seeds of dandelion, thistle, &c. [var. of AIGRETTE]

Egy·ptian, a. & n. (Native) of Egypt; *E. pound* (usu. abbr. £E, as £E10), coin worth about 20/6; *E. printing-type* (thick-stemmed); =GIPSY. [-IAN]

Egypto·logy, n. Study of Egyptian antiquities. So **Egypto·LOGIST** n. [-O-, -LOGY]

eh (ā), int. expr. inquiry or surprise, or inviting assent. [ME *ey*]

ei·der (ī-), n. An Arctic species of duck; *e.* (*-down*), small soft feathers from breast of this (*e.-down*, also, quilt stuffed with e.-d.). [ult. f. Icel. *æðar*]

ei·dograph (ī-), n. Instrument for enlarging or reducing drawings. [f. Gk *eidos* form + *graphō* write]

eidō·lon (ī-), n. (pl. *-ons, -a*). Spectre, phantom. [Gk, see IDOL]

eight (āt), a. & n. One more than seven (8, viii); (Skat.) figure of two adjacent circles; crew of e. in rowing-boat; *the Ee.*, boatraces at Oxford & Cambridge between such crews. Hence **eighTH²** (ātth) a. & n., **eigh·thLY²** adv. [com.-Teut. (OE *ahta*, Du. & G *acht*) & Aryan (L & Gk *oc-*, *oktō*, Skr. *ashtau*)]

eightee·n, a. & n. One more than seventeen (18, xviii); *eighteenmo*, = OCTODECIMO. Hence **eightee·NTH²** a. & n. [OE *e(a)htatýne, -téne* (as prec., see -TEEN)]

eighty (ā·tĭ), a. & n. Eight times ten (80, lxxx); *E. Club*, Liberal club founded in 1880. Hence **eigh·tiETH** a. & n. [OE *eahtatig* (as EIGHT + *-tig* decade)]

eirē·nicon (īr-), n. Proposal tending to make peace. [Gk, neut. adj. (*eirēnē* peace, see -IC)]

eisteddfod (āstĕ·dhvōd), n. Congress of Welsh bards. [W, lit. = session f. *eistedd* sit]

ei·ther (īdh-, ē-), adj., pron., & adv. (conj.). Each of two, as *at e. end was a lamp, e. view is tenable, e. is tenable*; one or other of two, as *put the lamp at e. end, there is no lamp at e. end, e. of you can go*; (adv. or conj.) on one or other supposition, which way you will, as *he is e. drunk or mad, e. come in or go out*; (w. neg. or interrog.) any more than the other, as *if you do not go, I shall not e.* [OE *ǣghwædher* f. WG *aiwon always + *gihwatharoz* each of two (see Y- & WHETHER)]

ejă·culate, v.t. Utter suddenly (words or abs.); eject (fluids &c.) from the body. Hence **ejaculA·TION** n., **eja·culatORY** a. [f. L E(*jaculari* f. *jaculum* javelin) dart]

eje·ct¹, v.t. Expel (*from* place, office, property); dart forth, emit. Hence or cogn. **eje·cTION**, **eje·ctMENT**, **eje·ctOR²**, nn. [f. L *ejectare* frequent. of E(*jicĕre ject-* =*jacĕre* throw)]

ē·ject², n. Something inferred, not an actual nor a conceivable object of our own consciousness. [f. L *ejectum* neut. p.p. of *ejicere* (see prec.)]

eje·ctive, a. Tending to eject; pertaining to an eject. Hence **eje·ctiveLY²** adv. [-IVE]

eke¹, v.t. *E. out*: supplement (defective means &c. *with*); (improp.) contrive to make (livelihood) or support (existence). [dial. form of obs. *eche* (OE *écan*) f. OTeut. *aukan* cogn. w. L *augēre* increase; partly also f. obs. n. *eke* (same root)]

eke², adv. (archaic). Also. [com.-Teut.: OE *éac*, Du. *ook*, G *auch*]

-el. See -LE(2).

elă·borate¹ (*-at*), a. Carefully or minutely worked out; highly finished. Hence **ela·borateLY²** adv., **ela·borateNESS** n. [f. L E(*laborare* f. *labor* work), see -ATE²]

elă·borāte², v.t. Produce by labour; work out (invention, theory, &c.) in detail; (of natural agencies) produce (substance &c.) from its elements or sources. Hence or cogn. **elaborA·TION** n., **ela·boratIVE** a. [as prec., -ATE³]

elaeo- in comb. = Gk *elaion* oil, as *-meter*, instrument for determining purity of oils.

élan (F), n. Vivacity; impetuous rush.

ē·land, n. S.-African antelope of heavy build. [Du., = elk]

ela·pse, v.i. (Of time) pass away. [f. L E(*labi laps-* glide)]

ela·stic, a. & n. Spontaneously resuming its normal bulk or shape after contraction, dilatation, or distortion (of solids, liquids, & gases); springy; (of feelings or persons) buoyant; flexible, adaptable, as *e. conscience*; *e.-side boots* or *e.-sides*, 19th-c. boots with e. web at sides instead of buttons or laces; (n.) e. cord or string, usu. woven with india-rubber. Hence **ela·sTICALLY** adv., **ĕlăsti·CITY** n. [f. Gk *elastikos* impulsive (*elaunō* drive, st. *ela-*)]

ela·te, v.t., & a. Inspirit, stimulate, (esp. in p.p.); make proud; (adj.) in high spirits, exultant, proud. So **ela·TION** n. [f. L EFferre Elat- bring out, raise]

e·lbow[1], n. Outer part of joint between fore & upper arm; e.-shaped bend or corner; *at* one's *e.*, close at hand; *up to the ee.*, busily engaged *in*; *out at ee.*, (of coat) worn-out, (of person) poor; *e.-grease*, vigorous polishing, hard work; *e.-room*, plenty of room. [com.-Teut.: OE *elnboga*, Du. *elleboog*, G *ell(en)bogen*, f. OTeut. *alino-bogon* (see ELL & BOW[1])]

e·lbow[2], v.t. & i. Thrust, jostle, (person, one*self*, *into*, *in*, &c.; also intr.). [f. prec.]

e·lchee (-tshĭ), n. Ambassador. [f. Turk. *ilchi* representative of a tribe (*il*)]

eld, n. (archaic, poet, dial.). Old age; the olden time. [OE *eldo* (*ald* OLD)]

e·lder[1], a. & n. (The) senior (of relations, or of two indicated persons), as *his e. brother*, *which is the e.?*; (Cards) *e. hand*, first player; (n. pl.) persons of greater age, as *respect your ee.*; person advanced in life; member of a senate; official in early Christian Church (=Gk *presbuteros*), & in some Protestant (esp. Presbyterian) churches, whence **e·lder**SHIP n.; *E.* STATESMAN. [OE *eldra* (*ald* OLD)]

e·lder[2], n. Low white-flowered tree; *e.(-berry) wine* (made from fruit of this). [OE *ellærn*, cf. MLG *ellern*, *alhorn*]

e·lderly, a. Getting old. [ELDER[1] + -LY[1]]

e·ldest, a. First-born or oldest surviving (member of family, son, daughter, &c.). [OE *eldest(a)* superl. of *ald* OLD]

El Dora·do (-ah-), n. Fictitious country or city abounding in gold. [Sp., = the gilded]

e·ldritch, a. (Sc.). Weird, hideous. [?]

ĕlĕcămpā·ne, n. Plant with bitter aromatic leaves & root; sweetmeat flavoured with this. [corrupt. of med. L *enula* (L *in-*) *campana*; *campana* may = of Campania, or of the fields]

ele·ct[1], a. Chosen; select, choice; (Theol.) chosen by God, as *the e.*; chosen to office &c., as *bride e.* [f. L E(*ligere lect-* = *legere* pick)]

ele·ct[2], v.t. Choose (thing, *to* do); choose (person) by vote, as *e. a magistrate*, *e. him to the magistracy*, *e. him* (*to be*) *magistrate*; (Theol., of God) choose (persons) in preference to others for salvation. [as prec.]

ele·ction, n. Choosing, esp. by vote; *general e.* (of representatives, esp. members of House of Commons, throughout the country), *by-e.* (of M.P. to fill vacancy); (Theol.) see prec. [OF, f. L *electionem* (as prec., see -ION)]

electioneer·, v.i. Busy oneself in political elections. [prec. + -EER]

ele·ctive, a. (Of official, office, authority) appointed by, filled up by, derived from, election; having power to elect; (Chem.) *e. affinity*, tendency to combine with some substances rather than others. Hence **ele·ctive**LY[2] adv. [f. F *électif*, *-ive* (as ELECT[1], -IVE)]

ele·ctor, n. One who has right of election (esp. of M.P.); (Hist.) German Prince entitled to share in election of Emperor. Hence **ele·ctor**AL a., **elec·tor**SHIP n. [L (as ELECT[1], -OR[2])]

ele·ctorate (-*at*), n. Dignity, dominions, of German Elector; body of electors. [-ATE[1]]

ele·ctress, n. Female elector; wife of German Elector. [as prec. + -ESS[1]]

elec·tric, a. & n. Of, charged with, capable of developing, electricity; *e. charge*, accumulation of electricity in Leyden jar &c.; *e. eel*, one able to give e. shock; *e. light* (produced by electricity); *e. shock*, effect of sudden discharge from Leyden jar &c.; *e. blue*, steely blue; (n.) substance in which e. force can be excited by friction. Hence **ele·ctr**ICALLY adv., **ĕlectri·**CIAN n. [f. L f. Gk *ēlektron* amber, see -IC]

ele·ctrical, a. Relating to electricity (rare in other senses of prec.). [-AL]

ĕlectri·city, n. Peculiar condition of the molecules of a body or of the ether surrounding them, developed by friction (*frictional e.*), chemical action (*galvanic e.*), heat (*thermal e.*), or magnetism (*magnetic e.*); *positive* or *vitreous*, *negative* or *resinous*, *e.*, two kinds now held to differ only in POTENTIAL; science of this. [-ITY]

electrifica·tion, n. Electrifying; conversion of steam railway into electric. [as foll., see -FICATION]

ele·ctrify, v.t. Charge (body with electricity; subject (person &c.) to electric shock; convert (railways, transport, manufactures, &c.) to electric working; (fig.) startle, excite. [f. ELECTRIC + -FY]

ele·ctrize, v.t. = prec. Hence **electriza·**TION n. [as prec. + -IZE]

ele·ctro, n. & v.t. (colloq.). = ELECTRO-*plate*, *type*. [abbr.]

electro- in comb. Of, pertaining to, caused by, electricity, as: *-bath*, liquid holding metal in solution for e.-plating; *-biology*, science of the electrical phenomena of living beings; *-chemistry*, electricity as applied to chemistry; *-dynamics*, dynamics of electricity; *-engraving* (done by electricity); *-graph*, instrument for registering electrical conditions; *-kinetics*, science of electricity in motion; *-logy*, electric science; *-lysis*, chemical decomposition by galvanic action, science of this, (Surg.) breaking up of tumours or calculi by electric agency; *-lyte*, body decomposed by this; *-lyse*, decompose thus; *-magnet*, piece of soft iron surrounded by wire coil through which electricity is passed; *-magnetism*, production of magnetism by electric current; *-meter*, instrument measuring electricity; *-motion*, motion of galvanic current, mechanical motion produced by electricity; *-motor*, machine for using electricity as motive power;

-negative, -positive, of negative, positive, electricity; *-pathy,* electrical treatment of disease; *-phore, -phorus,* instrument for generating statical electricity by induction; *-plate,* (v.t.) coat with silver by electrolysis, (n.) ware thus produced; *-scope,* instrument indicating presence or quality of electricity; *-statics,* science of statical electricity; *-tonus,* condition of motor nerve under galvanic current; *-type,* (n.) model, copy, formed by deposition of copper on a mould by galvanic action, (v.t.) copy thus. [f. Gk *ēlektron* amber]

electrocu·tion, n. Killing by electricity (as capital punishment). Hence **ele·ctrocute** v.t. [f. prec., suggested by *execution*]

ele·ctrode, n. Either pole (ANODE, CATHODE) of galvanic battery. [ELECTRO- + Gk *hodos* way]

electrolier· (-lēr), n. Cluster of electric lamps. [f. ELECTRO- on *chandelier*]

ele·ctron, n. (Physics, Chem.). Indivisible unit of the charge of negative electricity of an atom, rotating (in numbers constant for each element) about the positive nucleus of every atom. Hence **electro·nic** a. [f. ELECTRO- or ELECTRIC, with Gk *-on* appended]

ele·ctrum, n. Alloy of silver & gold used by the ancients; (Mineral.) native argentiferous gold. [L, f. Gk *ēlectron* amber, e.]

ele·ctuary, n. Medicinal powder &c. mixed with honey or syrup. [f. LL *electuarium* perh. corrupt. of Gk *ekleikton* (*ekleikhō* lick out)]

eleemŏ·synary (ĕlĭē-), a. Of, dependent on, alms; charitable; gratuitous. [f. med. L *eleemosynarius* (as ALMS, see -ARY¹)]

ĕ·legant, a. & n. (Of movements, style, author, manners) graceful; tasteful; refined; (of modes of life &c.) of refined luxury; (vulg.) excellent; (n.) person with pretensions to taste & fashion. Hence or cogn. **e·leg**ANCE n., **e·legant**LY² adv. [f. F *élégant* f. L *elegantem,* cf. ELECT¹]

ĕlĕgī·ac, a. & n. (Of metre) suited to elegies, esp. *e. couplet,* (usu. Gk or Lat.) dactylic hexameter & pentameter; mournful; (n. pl.) e. verses. [f. L f. Gk *elegeiakos* (as ELEGY, see -AC)]

ĕ·legize, v.i. & t. Write an elegy (*upon*); write in mournful strain; write an elegy upon. [-IZE]

ĕ·legy, n. Song of lamentation, esp. for the dead (often vaguely used of other poems); poem in elegiac metre. [f. F *élégie* f. L f. Gk *elegeia* (*elegos* mournful poem)]

ĕ·lement, n. Component part, as *reduced to its ee.,* analysed, *the ee. of national wealth, there was an e. of cant, cant was a notable e., in his style*; (Chem.) any of the many substances that defy analysis; *the four ee.,* earth, water, air, fire; one of these as a being's abode or sphere, as (usu. fig.) *in, out of, his e.*; atmospheric agencies, as *war of the ee.*; rudiments of learning (i.e. the A B C) or of an art or science; *Euclid's Ee.* (of Geometry); *ee. of trenches* (Mil.), short lengths of them e.g. those between the traverses. [OF, f. L *elementum,* etym. dub.]

eleme·ntal, a. & n. Of the four elements; of the powers of nature, as *e. worship*; comparable to these, as *e. grandeur, tumult*; uncompounded; essential. (N., theosoph.) spirit of earth, air, &c. [prec. + -AL]

eleme·ntary, a. Rudimentary, introductory; (Chem.) not decomposable. Hence **eleme·ntari**LY² adv., **eleme·ntari**NESS n. [f. L *elementarius* (as ELEMENT, see -ARY¹)]

ĕ·lĕmi, n. A stimulant resin used in ointments, varnish, &c. [?]

ele·nchus (-k-), n. Logical refutation; *Socratic e.,* mode of eliciting truth by short question & answer. [L, f. Gk *elegkhos*]

ele·nctic, a. Of, given to, refutation or cross-examination. [f. Gk *elegktikos* (*elegkhō* refute, as prec., see -IC)]

ĕ·lephant, n. Huge four-footed pachyderm with proboscis & long curved ivory tusks; *white e.,* burdensome possession (from cost of maintenance); size of paper (28 × 23 in.; *double e.,* 40 × 26½). Hence **elepha·nt**OID a. [ME *olifaunt* f. OF *olifant* corrupt. f. L *elephantum* (nom. *-tus*), *-ntem* (nom. *-phas*), f. Gk *elephas -antos,* etym. dub.]

elephănti·asis, n. Skin disease causing part affected to resemble elephant's hide. [L f. Gk (as prec., see -ASIS)]

elepha·ntine, a. Of elephants; *e. epoch* (when large pachydermata abounded); clumsy, unwieldy, as *e. movements, humour, task.* [f. L f. Gk *elephantinos* (as prec., -INE²)]

Eleusi·nian, a. *E. mysteries* (of Demeter, celebrated at Eleusis in Attica). [f. L f. Gk *Eleusinios* (*Eleusis -inos*) + -AN)]

eleu·thero- (ilū)- in comb. = Gk *eleutheros* free, as *-mania,* mad zeal for freedom, *-phyllous,* with distinct leaves.

ĕ·levate, v.t. Lift up; hold up (the Host) for adoration; raise (one's eyes, voice, hopes); raise axis of (gun); exalt in rank &c.; raise morally or intellectually (aims, style; esp. in p.p.); (p.p., colloq.) slightly drunk. Hence **e·levat**ORY a. [f. L E(*levare* lift f. *levis* light), see -ATE³]

eleva·tion, n. Elevating, being elevated, (in all senses); angle (esp. of gun) with horizon; height above given (esp. sea) level; drawing made in projection on vertical plane, flat drawing of front, side, or back, of house &c.; grandeur, dignity. [f. L *elevatio* (as prec., see -ATION)]

e·levator, n. Person, thing, that elevates; muscle that raises limb &c.; machine for hoisting corn &c., lift. [L (as prec., see -OR²)]

elē·ven, a. & n. One more than ten (11, xi); *an e.*, e. persons forming side at cricket &c.; *the E.* (disciples, without Judas); *elevens* dial., lunch, snack. So **ele·venTH²** a. & n. (*the eleventh* HOUR). [com.-Teut.: OE *endleofon*, Du. & G *elf*, f. OTeut. *ainlif-* (*ain* ONE + *-lif-* etym. dub.)]

elf, n. (pl. *elves*). (Teut. Myth.) a supernatural being; mischievous creature; dwarf; little creature; *e.-bolt*, flint arrowhead; *e.-lock*, tangled mass of hair; *e.-struck*, bewitched. Hence **e·lfISH¹, e·lv-,** aa. [OE *ǣlf*, cf. G *alp* nightmare]

e·lfin, a. & n. Of elves, elfish; (n.) dwarf, child. [f. prec., *-in* unexpl.]

eli·cit, v.t. Draw forth (what is latent, usu. fig.); educe (truths *from* data), draw out, evoke, (admission, answer *from* person). [f. L E(*licere licit-* for *lacere* entice)]

eli·de, v.t. Omit (vowel, syllable) in pronunciation. [f. L E(*lidere lis-* = *laedere* dash)]

ĕ·ligible, a. Fit to be chosen (*for* office &c.); desirable, suitable. Hence **e·ligiBI·LITY** n., **e·ligibLY²** adv. [f. F *éligible* (ELECT¹, -BLE)]

eli·minate, v.t. Remove, get rid of; (Physiol., Chem.) expel (waste matter *from* tissues, substance *from* a compound); ignore (part of question &c.); (Alg.) get rid of (quantities) from equation; (improp.) extract (desired element from compound, also fig.). So **eli·minABLE** a., **eliminA·TION** n. [f. L E(*liminare* f. *limen -minis* threshold), see -ATE³]

eli·sion, n. Suppression of vowel or syllable in pronouncing, (rarely) of passage in book &c. [f. L *elisio* (as ELIDE, see -ION)]

élite (ĕlē·t), n. The choice part, the best, (*of*). [F, =choice]

eli·xir (*-er*), n. Alchemist's preparation designed to change metals into gold or (also *e. of life*) to prolong life indefinitely; sovereign remedy; PAREGORIC *e.* [med. L, f. Arab. *aliksir* the elixir (*iksir* prob. f. late Gk *xērion* desiccative powder)]

Elizabē·than, a. & n. (Person, writer) of the time of Queen Elizabeth. [-AN]

elk, n. Large animal of the deer kind found in N. Europe and (also *moose*) N. America; species of deer & antelope. [etym. dub.; OE *elch*; also *alke*, influenced by L *alces*, Gk *alkē*]

ell, n. Measure of length (*English e.* = 45 in.; now obs. as measure); *give him an inch* (a little) *& he'll take an e.* (much). [com.-Teut.: OE *eln*, Du. *el*, G *elle*, f. OTeut. *alina* forearm (cogn. w. Gk *ōlenē*, L *ulna*), whence med. L *alena*, F *aune*]

E·lliman, n. (Used for) E.'s embrocation. [*E.*, maker]

elli·pse¹, n. Regular oval; figure produced when a cone is cut by a plane making smaller angle with the base than the side of the cone makes, whence **ellipti·CITY** n.; = foll. Hence or cogn. **elli·ptic(al¹)** aa., **-ically¹** adv. [f. Gk *elleipsis* f. *elleipō* come short (*en* in + *leipō* leave)]

elli·psis, -pse², n. (pl. *-pses*). Omission from sentence of words needed to complete construction or sense. So **elli·ptical²** a., **-ically²** adv. [as prec.]

elli·psoid, n. Solid of which all plane sections through one axis are ellipses & through the other ellipses or circles. [-OID]

elm, n. Tree with rough doubly serrated leaves. Hence **e·lmY²** a. [OE *elm* (cf. Swed. *alm*, Da. *ælm*), = L *ulmus*]

elocū·tion (ē- *or* ĕ-), n. Manner, style, art, of oral delivery. Hence **elocu·tionARY¹** a., **elocu·tionIST(3)** n. [f. L *elocutio* f. E(*loqui locut-* speak), see -ION]

éloge (F), n. Discourse in honour of deceased person (esp. member of French Academy, pronounced by his successor). [F]

Elō·hist, n. Author(s) of the *elohistic* parts of the Hexateuch, marked by use of *Elohim* for *Yahveh* (Jehovah). [f. Heb. *elohim* God + -IST]

ē·longate (-ngg-), v.t. & i., & a. Lengthen, prolong; (Bot.) be of slender or tapering form; (adj., Bot., Zool.) long, slender, tapering. [f. LL E(*longare* f. *longus* long), see -ATE³, ²]

ēlonga·tion, n. Lengthening; the part (of line &c.) produced; (Astr.) angular distance of planet from sun. [f. LL *elongatio* (as prec., see -ATION)]

elo·pe, v.i. (Of woman) run away from husband or home (*with* paramour, lover); abscond. Hence **elo·peMENT** n. [AF *aloper* perh. f. ME **alope* p.p. of **aleapen* (*a-* = *and-* against + LEAP), cf. G *entlaufen* run away]

ĕ·loquence, n. Fluent, forcible, & apt use of language; rhetoric, as *Professor of E.* So **e·loquENT** a., **e·loquentLY²** adv. [F (*é-*), f. L *eloquentia* f. E(*loqui* speak), see -ENCE]

else, adv. (Following indef. or interrog. pron.) besides, in addition, as *any one, anybody, anything, e., who e.? who else's?, whose else?*; (same constr.) instead, as *what e. could I say?*; otherwise, if not, as *run, (or) e. you will be late*; *elsewhere*, in, to, some other place. [OE *elles* f. OTeut. *aljo-* other = L *alius*, -ES]

ēlu·cidate (-ōō-, -ū-), v.t. Throw light on, explain. Hence **elucidA·TION, elu·cidatOR²,** nn., **elu·cidatIVE, elu·cidatORY,** aa. [f. LL E(*lucidare* f. *lucidus* bright f. *lux lucis* light)]

ēlu·de (-ōōd, -ūd), v.t. Escape adroitly from (blow, danger, difficulty, person's grasp, person, inquiry, observation); avoid compliance with (law, request) or fulfilment of (obligation); escape from, baffle, (the understanding). So **elu·sion**, **elu·siveness**, nn., **elu·sive**, **elu·sory**, aa., **elu·sively**² adv. [f. L E(*ludere lus-* play)]

e·lvan, n. Hard rock of igneous origin; broad vein or dyke of this. [perh. f. Corn. *elven* spark]

elvish. See ELF.

Élysée (ĕlēzā·), n. Official residence of French President. [F]

Elȳ·sium (-z-), n. (Gk Myth.) abode of the blessed after death; place, state, of ideal happiness. Hence **Ely·sian** a. [f. L f. Gk *Elusion* (*ē*-) (*pedion* plain)]

ĕ·lytron, n. (pl. *-ra*). Outer hard wing-case of coleopterous insect; the vagina. [f. Gk *elutron* sheath (*eluō* roll round)]

E·lzevir (*-er*), a. & n. (Book) printed by Elzivier family at Amsterdam, the Hague, &c.

em, n. The letter M; (Typog.) unit for measuring amount of printed matter in line.

em-, pref. = EN- before *b*, *p*, and (often) *m*.

emă·ciate (-shĭ-), v.t. Make lean, waste, (esp. in p.p.); impoverish (soil). So **emacia·tion** (-sĭ-) n. [f. L E(*maciare* f. *macies* leanness), see -ATE³]

ĕ·manate, v.i. Issue, originate, (*from* source, person, &c.); (of gases, light, &c.) proceed, issue, (*from*). [f. L E(*manare* flow), see -ATE³]

emana·tion, n. Issuing (*from*); thing proceeding from a source (esp. fig., of virtues, qualities, moral powers); person, thing, proceeding from the Divine Essence. So **e·manative** a. [f. L *emanatio* (as prec., see -ATION)]

ema·ncipate, v.t. (Rom. Law) release (child, wife) from power of *pater familias*; free from legal, social, political, intellectual, or moral restraint. Hence **ema·ncipator**² n., **ema·ncipatory** a. [f. L E(*mancipare* f. *manceps* purchaser f. *manus* hand + *capere* take), -ATE³]

emancipa·tion, n. Setting free, esp. from slavery or from legal disabilities, whence **emancipa·tionist** n.; setting free, freedom, from intellectual or moral fetters. [f. F *émancipation* f. L *emancipationem* (prec., -ATION)]

ema·ncipist, n. (Austral.). Ex-convict who has served his term. [f. EMANCIPATE + -IST]

ema·scŭlate¹ (*-at*), a. Castrated; effeminate. [f. L E(*masculare* f. *masculus* dim. of *mas* male), see -ATE²]

ema·scŭlāte², v.t. Castrate; weaken, make effeminate; impoverish (language); weaken (literary composition) by excisions. Hence **emascula·tion** n., **ema·sculative**, **ema·sculatory**, aa. [as prec., see -ATE³]

embal·m (-ahm), v.t. Preserve (corpse) from decay with spices; preserve from oblivion; endue with balmy fragrance. Hence **embal·mment** (-ahm-m-) n. [f. F EM(*baumer*, as BALM)]

emba·nk, v.t. Shut in, confine, (river &c.) by banks, raised stone structure, &c. Hence **emba·nkment** n. [EM-]

embar·go, n., & v.t. Order forbidding ships of a foreign power to enter, or any ships to leave, the country's ports; suspension of (a branch of) commerce, as *be under*, *lay on*, *an e.*; impediment; (v.t.) lay (ships, trade) under e.; seize (ship, goods) for State service. [Sp., f. *embargar* f. LL *IMbarricare (*barra* BAR)]

embar·k, v.t. & i. Put, go, on board ship (*for* destination), whence **embarka·tion** n.; engage (*in*, *upon*, undertaking, war, &c.). [f. F *embarquer* f. LL IM(*barcare* f. *barca* BARK³)]

embarras de choix, de richesse (F), n. More alternatives, wealth, than one knows how to deal with.

embă·rrass, v.t. Encumber, impede; (p.p.) encumbered with debts; complicate (question &c.); perplex. Hence **emba·rrassingly**² adv., **emba·rrassment** n. [f. F *embarrasser* f. *embarras* n. conn. w. EM(*barrer* BAR²)]

e·mbassy, n. Ambassador's function or office; his residence; deputation to a sovereign &c. [f. OF *ambassée* f. L **ambactiata* (*ambactia*, see AMBASSADOR, & cf. -ADE)]

emba·ttle¹, v.t. Set (army) in battle array. [f. OF EM(*bataillier* f. *bataille* BATTLE)]

emba·ttle², v.t. Furnish (building, wall) with battlements. [EM- + obs. vb *battle* f. OF *bataillier*, see BATTLEMENT]

embay·, v.t. Lay (vessel) within a bay; (of wind) force (vessel) into a bay; enclose as in a bay, shut in. Hence **embay·ment** n. [EM-]

embe·d, im-, v.t. (-dd-). Fix firmly in surrounding mass (esp. in p.p.); (of the mass) surround thus. [EM-]

embe·llish, v.t. Beautify, adorn; heighten (narrative) with fictitious additions. Hence **embe·llishment** n. [f. OF EM(*bellir* f. *bel* f. L *bellus* handsome), see -ISH²]

e·mber¹, n. (usu. pl.). Small piece of live coal or wood in dying fire (& fig.). [OE *ǣmerge*, cf. Da. *emmer*, Sw. *mörja*; *-b-* phonetic]

e·mber², a. *E. days*, days of fasting and prayer, the Wed., Fri., & Sat., after (1) 1st Sun. in Lent, (2) Whitsunday, (3) Holy Cross Day (Sep. 14), and (4) St Lucia's day (Dec. 13). [OE *ymbren* n. perh. f. *ymbryne* period (*ymb* about + *ryne* course)]

e·mber³, n. (Usu. *e.-goose*, *-diver*) an Orkney sea-fowl, the Loon. [f. Norw. *emmer*]

embe·zzle, v.t. Divert (money &c., also abs.) fraudulently to one's own use. Hence **embe·zzlement** n. [f. AF EN-(*besiler* = OF *besillier* maltreat, ravage, perh. f. L *bis-* used in LL as pejorative pref.)]

embi·tter, v.t. Make bitter (fig.); aggravate (evil); exasperate (person, feeling). Hence **embi·tter**MENT n. [EM-]

emblā·zon, v.t. Portray conspicuously, as on heraldic shield; adorn (shield) with heraldic devices (also fig.); celebrate, extol. Hence **embla·zon**MENT n. [EM-]

embla·zonry, n. = BLAZONRY. [EM-]

e·mblem, n., & v.t. Symbol, typical representation; (archaic) pictorial parable; (of person) type (of a quality); heraldic device; (v.t.) symbolize, show forth by e. [(vb f. n.) f. L f. Gk *emblēma -matos* insertion f. EM(*ballō* throw)]

emblema·tic(al), aa. Serving as a type (*of*). Hence **emblema·tical**LY[2] adv. [prec., -IC]

emblĕ·matist, n. Maker of emblems or of allegories. [as prec. + -IST]

emblĕ·matize, v.t. Serve as emblem of; represent by an emblem. [as prec. + -IZE]

e·mblĕment, n. (legal; usu. pl.). Profits of sown land; natural products of soil. [f. OF *emblaement* f. *emblaer* f. med. L IM*bladare* sow with wheat (*bladum*), see -MENT]

embo·dy, v.t. Clothe (spirit) with body; give concrete form to (ideas &c.); express tangibly (principles *in* actions &c.); (of things) be an expression of (ideas &c.); form into a body; include, comprise. Hence **embo·di**MENT n. [EM-]

embo·g, v.t. (-gg-). Plunge into, hamper in, a bog (lit. & fig.). [EM-]

embō·lden, v.t. Make bold, encourage (often *to* do). [EM- + BOLD + -EN[3]]

e·mbolism, n. Obstruction of artery &c. by clot of blood &c., esp. as cause of paralysis. [f. Gk *embolos* peg, stopper (*en* in, *ballō* throw)]

embonpoint (F), n. Plumpness (chiefly of women; usu. euphem.). [F, f. phr. *en bon point* in good condition]

embo·som, v.t. Embrace; (p.p.) enclosed *in*, surrounded *with*, (trees, hills, &c.). [EM-]

embo·ss, v.t. Carve, mould, in relief; cause figures &c. to stand out on (surface); make protuberant. Hence **embo·ss**MENT n. [prob. f. OF *EM*bocer* (see BOSS[1])]

embouchure (F), n. Mouth of river; opening of valley; (Mus.) part of musical instrument applied to mouth, mode of applying this.

embow·el, v.t. (-ll-). Remove the bowels from (body). [f. OF EN*boweler* for *esboueler* (*es-* = EX- + *bouel* BOWEL)]

embow·er, v.t. Enclose as in bower. [EM-]

embra·ce, v.t., & n. Fold (person &c.; in pl. abs. = e. one another) in the arms, usu. as sign of affection; clasp, enclose; accept eagerly (offer, opportunity, &c.); adopt (course of action, doctrine, party, cause); (of things) include, comprise; (of persons) comprise (thing *in* a formula, report, &c.); take in with eye or mind; (n.) folding in the arms, (euphem.) sexual intercourse. Hence **embra·ce**ABLE a., **embra·ce**MENT n. [(n. f. vb) f. OF EM(*bracer* f. L *bracchium* arm)]

embra·nchment, n. Branching out (of arm of river &c.). [EM- + BRANCH n. + -MENT]

embra·ngle, im-, v.t. Entangle, confuse. Hence **embra·ngle**MENT n. [EM- + obs. *brangle* perh. suggested by *brawl, wrangle*]

embrā·sure (-zher; *also* ĕmbrazhoor·), n. Bevelling off of wall at sides of door or window, splaying; opening in parapet for gun, widening from within. [F (EM*braser* splay, mod. F *ébraser*; see -URE)]

e·mbrocate, v.t. Bathe, foment, (limb &c.) to mitigate disease. [f. med. L *embrocare* f. *embrocha* f. Gk *embrokhē* f. EM(*brekhō* wet)]

embroca·tion, n. Liquid used for rubbing diseased part. [f. prec., see -ATION]

embroi·der, v.t. Ornament (cloth &c., or abs.) with needlework; embellish (narrative) with fictitious additions. [EM- + *broider* f. F. *broder*, orig. = work on the edge (*bord*); *-er* perh. f. wrong division of foll.]

embroi·dery, n. Embroidering; embroidered work; adventitious ornament. [-ERY]

embroi·l, v.t. Bring (affairs, narrative, &c.) into state of confusion; involve (person) in hostility (*with* another). Hence **embroi·l**MENT n. [f. F EM(*brouiller*, see BROIL[1])]

embrow·n, v.t. Make brown. [EM-]

e·mbryo, n. & a. (pl. *-os*). Offspring of animal before birth (or emergence from egg); thing in rudimentary stage; *in e.*, undeveloped; (adj.) undeveloped. Hence **embryŏ·n**IC a. [med. L *embryo -onis* corrupt. of Gk EM(*bruŏn* perh. f. *bruō* swell, grow)]

e·mbryo- in comb. = prec., as *-ctony*, destruction of foetus in womb, *-genesis*, formation of e., *-logy*, science of the e., *-tomy*, cutting up of foetus in womb.

embu·s, v.t. & i. (Mil.; -ss-). Put (men, stores) or get into motor vehicles. [EM- + BUS, after *entrain*]

eme·nd, v.t. Remove errors from (text of book &c.). Hence **emend**A·TION, **ē·mendat**OR[2], nn., **eme·ndat**ORY a. [f. L E(*mendare* f. *menda* fault)

ĕ·merald, n. Bright-green precious stone; colour of this; size of TYPE; *E. Isle*, Ireland. Hence **e·merald**INE[1] a. [f. OF *emeraude* f. com.-Rom. **smaralda* f. L f. Gk *smaragdos*]

emer·ge, v.i. Come up out of a liquid; come into view (*from* enclosed space &c.); issue (*from* state of suffering &c.); (of facts &c.) come out as result of inquiry; (of question, difficulty, &c.) crop up. So **emer·g**ENCE n., **emer·g**ENT a. [f. L E(*mergere mers-* dip)]

emer·gency, n. Sudden juncture demanding immediate action; *e. door, exit,* &c., for use in ee. only, e.g., in case of fire; *e. man,* (in Ireland) bailiff's officer recruited for special service, esp. in evictions. [f. LL *emergentia* (as prec., see -ENCY)]

ēmē·ritus, a. Honourably discharged from service, as *e. professor* (retired). (L, p.p. of E(*merēri* earn)]

ĕ·merods, n. pl. (bibl.). = HAEMORRHOIDS.

emer·sion, n. Emerging; reappearance of sun, moon, star, after eclipse or occultation. [as EMERGE, see -ION]

ĕ·mery, n. Coarse corundum used for polishing metal, stones, &c.; *e.-cloth, -paper, -wheel* (covered with e. powder). [f. F *émeri(l)* f. LL *smericulum* f. Gk *smēris* polishing powder]

emĕ·tic, a. & n. (Medicine) that causes vomiting (also fig.). [f. Gk *emetikos* (*emeō* vomit, see -ETIC)]

émeute (F), n. Popular rising.

ĕ·migrate, v.i. & t. Leave one country to settle in another; (colloq.) change one's place of abode; (trans.) assist (person) to emigrate. So **e·migr**ANT a. & n., **emigr**A·TION n., **e·migrat**ORY a. [f. L E(*migrare* MIGRATE)]

émigré (F), n. French emigrant, esp. Royalist who fled at French Revolution.

e·minence, n. Rising ground; distinguished superiority (social, intellectual, &c.); (*E*-) cardinal's title. [f. L *eminentia* (as foll., see -ENCE)]

ĕ·minent, a. Exalted distinguished; *e.* DOMAIN; (of qualities) remarkable in degree, whence **e·minent**LY[2] adv. [f. L E(*minēre* jut, cf. *minae* projecting points, threats), -ENT]

ēmir· (-ēr), n. Saracen or Arab prince or governor; descendant of Mohammed. [= AMEER]

ĕ·missary, n. Person sent on (usu.) an odious or underhand mission. [f. L *emissarius* (as EMIT, see -ARY[1])]

emi·ssion, n. Giving off or out (*of* light, heat, smell, &c.); thing thus given out; *e. theory* (that light is e. of streams of imponderable particles from luminous bodies). So **emi·ss**IVE a. [f. L *emissio* (as foll., see -ION)]

emi·t, v.t. (-tt-). Give out, send forth, (stream, light, heat, sound, opinion, paper currency, &c.). [f. L E(*mittere miss-* send)]

e·mma gee, n. (slang). Machine gun. [= M, G, in signallers' alphabet]

e·mmet, n. Ant. [see ANT]

emŏ·llient, a. & n. (Application) that softens living animal textures (also fig.). [f. L E(*mollire* f. *mollis* soft), see -ENT]

emŏ·lument, n. Profit from office or employment, salary. [f. L *emŏlumentum, emoli-,* f. E(*mōlere* grind or *mōliri* work out), -MENT]

emo·tion, n. Agitation of mind, feeling; excited mental state. Hence **emo·tion**LESS a. [f. L *emotio* f. E(*movēre mot-* move), see -ION]

emo·tional, a. Of the emotions; liable to emotion, whence **emo·tional**ISM(1), **emo·tional**IST(2), **emotiona·l**ITY, nn., **emo·tional**LY[2] adv. [prec. + -AL]

emo·tive, a. Of, tending to excite, emotion. Hence **emo·tive**LY[2] adv. [f. L *emovēre,* see EMOTION & -IVE]

empa·nel, im-, v.t. (-ll-). Enter on panel, enrol, (jury). [f. AF EM(*paneller* PANEL)]

e·mperor, n. (fem. *empress*). Sovereign of Roman, Western, or Eastern Empire; head of Holy Roman Empire; sovereign (title superior in dignity to king); *Purple E.,* kind of butterfly. Hence **e·mperor**SHIP n. [f. OF *emperere, -pereor,* f. L *imperator, -orem,* f. IM(*perare* = *parare* prepare, order) command, see -OR[2]]

e·mphasis, n. Stress laid on word(s) to indicate special significance; vigour, intensity, of expression, feeling, action, &c.; importance assigned to a thing; prominency, sharpness of contour. [L f. Gk, f. EM(*phainō* show)]

e·mphasize, v.t. Lay stress upon (word in speaking); bring (fact &c.) into special prominence. [f. prec. + -IZE]

emphă·tic, a. (Of language, tone, gesture) forcibly expressive; (of words) bearing the stress; (of person) expressing himself with emphasis; (of actions) forcible, significant. Hence **empha·t**ICALLY adv. [f. Gk *emphatikos* (as EMPHASIS, see -IC)]

e·mpire, n. Supreme & wide (political) dominion; absolute control (*over*); government in which sovereign is called emperor; territory of an emperor; (Hist.) *the E.,* (usu.) Holy Roman E.; *E. Day,* May 24th, birthday of Q. Victoria, largely kept as (esp. school) holiday in British E.; (U.S.) *E. City, State* (of New York). [F, f. L *imperium* conn. w. *imperare,* see EMPEROR]

empĭ·ric, a. & n. Based, acting, on observation & experiment, not on theory, whence **empi·ric**IST(2) n.; (person) relying solely on experiment; quack. Hence **empi·ric**AL a., **empi·rical**LY[2] adv., **empi·ric**ISM n. [f. L f. Gk EM(*peirikos* f. *peira* trial, see -IC)]

emplā·cement, n. Situation; placing; platform for guns. [F (EM- + PLACE + -MENT)]

empla·ne, v.i. & t. Go or put on board aeroplane. [EM- + (AERO)*plane*]

employ·, v.t., & n. Use (thing, one's power, &c., *for, in, on, about,* an object); use services of (person); keep (person) in one's service; busy, keep occupied, (*oneself,* others, *doing, in,* &c.); (n.) *in the e. of,* employed by. Hence **employ·**ABLE a., **employ·**ER[1] n. [(n. f. F *emploi*) f. F *employer* f. L IM(*plicare* fold), cf. IMPLY]

employé (ŏmploi·ā, or as F), n. (fem. *-ée*). Person employed for wages. [F p.p. (prec.)]

ĕmployee·, n. =prec. [-EE]

employ·ment, n. In vbl senses; esp., one's regular trade or profession. [-MENT]

empoi·son, v.t. Put poison into, taint; corrupt (fig.); embitter (person's mind *against*). [f. F EM(*poisonner* POISON)]

empor·ium, n. Centre of commerce, mart; (vulg.) shop. [f. L f. Gk *emporion* f. EM*poros* merchant (*por-* journey)]

empow·er, v.t. Authorize, license, (person *to* do); enable. [EM-]

e·mpress, n. Wife of emperor; woman governing an empire or (fig.) having absolute power. [f. OF *emperesse* fem. of *emperere* EMPEROR, see -ESS[1]]

empressement (F), n. Display of cordiality.

emprī·se (-z), n. (archaic). (Chivalrous) enterprise. [OF, fem. p.p. as n. of *emprendre* f. LL *IM(*pre(he)ndere* take)]

e·mpty[1], a. & n. Containing nothing; devoid *of* (qualities); (colloq.) hungry; (of house) devoid of furniture or inmates; (of van, ship, &c.) without load; (of persons, plans, &c.) lacking sense; meaningless; (n.) e. truck, box, &c.; *e.-handed*, bringing no gift, carrying nothing away; *e.-headed, -pated*, witless. Hence **e·mpti**NESS n. [OE *ǣmetig* at leisure (*ǣmetta*, see -Y[2])]

e·mpty[2], v.t. & i. Remove contents of (vessel &c. *upon* &c.); transfer (contents of one thing *into* &c. another); (of river) discharge itself (*into*); (intr.) become empty. [f. prec.]

empur·ple, v.t. Make purple, redden. [EM-]

empȳrē·an, a. & n. (Of) the highest heaven, as the sphere of fire or as the abode of God; (of) the visible heavens. So **empȳ·re**AL a. [f. med. L *empyreus* f. Gk EM(*puros* f. *pur* fire) + -AN]

ē·mu, ē·meu (-ū), n. Large Australian bird allied to the Cassowary. [perh. f. Port. *ema* crane, ostrich]

ĕ·mulate, v.t. Try to equal or excel; rival; imitate zealously. So **emul**A·TION, **e·mulat**OR[2], nn., **e·mulat**IVE a. [f. L *aemulari* (as foll.), see -ATE[3]]

ĕ·mulous, a. Zealously, jealously, imitative (*of*); desirous (*of* renown &c.); actuated by spirit of rivalry. Hence **e·mulous**LY[2] adv. [f. L *aemulus* + -OUS]

emu·lsifȳ, v.t. Convert into an emulsion. [f. L E(*mulgēre muls-* milk) + -FY]

emu·lsion, n. Milky liquid with oily or resinous particles suspended in it. Hence or cogn. **emu·lsion**IZE(3) v.t., **emu·ls**IVE a. [as prec., see -ION]

emu·nctory, a. & n. Of nose-blowing; (organ, duct) conveying waste matter from the body. [f. L E(*mungere munct-*), see -ORY]

en, n. Unit of width in printing, narrower than EM.

en-, pref. (1) *en-, em-*, f. F *en-, em-*, f. L IN-, IM- (*enamour, embarrass, engage*); now used to form E vbs (a) on nouns, with sense ' put (the object) into or on something ' (*embed, engulf, entrust*) or ' put something into or on (the object) ' (*enjewel*); (b) on nn. or adjj., w. sense ' bring into such condition ' (*englad, enslave*); often with suf. -EN[6] (*embolden, enlighten*); (c) on vbs with sense ' in ', ' into ', ' upon ', (*enfold*) or w. intensive force (*encarnalize*). (2) *en-, em-*, f. Gk *en-* (*em-* before *b, m, p, ph*; *el-, er-*, before *l, r*), w. sense ' in ' (*energy, enthusiasm, emphasis*).

-en[1], **-n**, suf. forming p.p. of strong vbs (*spoken, sworn*); often obs. or archaic (*gotten, graven*); in some not recorded (*flung*); also displaced by *-ed* (*shaped* for *shapen*); or surviving only in adj. sense (*drunken, lorn*). For adj. sense see -ED[1](2).

-en[2], suf. forming dimm., as *chicken, maiden*. [f. OTeut. *-înom*]

-en[3], suf. forming femm. (now only in *vixen*), and found in some nouns, as *burden*. [f. WG *-innja* f. OTeut. *-inî*]

-en[4], suf. seen in *oxen*; orig. part of stem in weak-decl. nouns, but retained only in pl., & added to other old plurals, as in *brethren, children, kine*, (earlier *-ther, -der, ky*). [OE *-an*]

-en[5], **-n**, suf. forming adjj. f. nn., usu. expr. material; mostly obs. or archaic (*silvern*) or only in metaph. senses (*golden*), the noun being used as adj.; but *wooden, woollen*, & a few others, remain. [f. OTeut. *-īno-*, cf. Gk & L *-īno-*]

-en[6], suf. forming vv.t. & i. from adjj. (*deepen, moisten*) on anal. of a few in OE (*fasten*), & f. nouns as *listen* (OE), *happen* (14th c.), *heighten, hearten*, &c., (mod.).

ena·ble, v.t. Authorize, empower, (person *to* do); supply (person &c.) with means *to* (do); *Enabling Act*, esp. that of 1920 conferring on the Established Church a certain measure of autonomy subject to parliamentary veto. [EN-]

ena·ct, v.t. Ordain, decree, (thing, *that*), whence **ena·ct**ION, **ena·ct**MENT, nn., **ena·ct**IVE, **ena·ct**ORY, aa.; *enacting clauses* (containing new provisions); play (scene, part, on stage or in life). [EN- + ACT n. & v.]

enă·mel[1], n. Glass-like opaque or semi-transparent coating of metallic surfaces for ornament or as preservative lining (also fig.); any smooth hard coating; kinds of complexion-veneer; coating of teeth; painting done on e.; (poet.) smooth bright surface colouring, verdure, &c. [f. foll.]

enă·mel[2], v.t. (-ll-). Inlay, encrust, (metal &c., the face or skin) with enamel; portray (figures &c.) with enamel; adorn with varied colours. [f. AF EN(*amayller* f. OF *esmal* f. med. L *smaltum* of Teut. orig., cf. OE *smaltan* SMELT)]

enă·mour, v.t. Inspire with love (*of*, esp.

in p.p.); charm, delight. [f. OF EN-(*amourer* f. *amour* love f. L *amorem*, nom. *-or*)]
enarthrō·sis, n. (anat.). Ball-&-socket joint. [Gk, f. EN(*arthros* f. *arthron* joint), -OSIS]
en bloc (F), adv. In a lump, wholesale.
encae·nia (-sē-), n. Dedication festival; (Oxf.) =COMMEMORATION. [L, f. Gk *egkainia* (EN- + *kainos* new)]
enca·ge, in-, v.t. Confine (as) in cage. [EN-]
enca·mp, v.t. & i. (Of troops) settle (t. & i.) in camp; lodge (t. & i.) in the open in tents. [EN-]
enca·mpment, n. In vbl senses; also, place where troops are encamped. [-MENT]
enca·se, in-, v.t. Put into a case; surround as with a case. Hence **enca·se**MENT n. [EN-]
enca·sh, v.t. Convert (bills &c.) into cash; receive in form of cash, realize. Hence **enca·sh**MENT n. [EN-]
encau·stic, a. & n. (Painting, art of painting) by burning in; *e. brick, tile*, (inlaid with coloured clays burnt in). [f. Gk *egkaustikos* f. *egkaiō* (EN- + *kaiō* burn)]
-ence, suf. forming nn. of quality or action f. F *-ence* or direct f. L *-entia* f. L pres. part. in *-enti-* (nom. *-ens*); rarely repr. L *-entia* f. adjj. in *-lentus* (*corpulence*); see -ANCE, -ENCY.
enceinte (F), a. & n. (Of women) pregnant; (n.) enclosure (in fortification).
encĕpha·lic, a. Of the brain. [f. Gk *egkephalon* brain (EN- + *kephalē* head) + -IC]
enchai·n, v.t. Chain up, fetter; hold fast (attention, emotions). Hence **enchai·n**MENT n. [f. OF EN(*chainer* CHAIN)]
encha·nt (-tsh-), v.t. Bewitch (lit. & fig.); charm, delight. Hence or cogn. **encha·nt**ER[1], **encha·nt**MENT, **encha·ntr**ESS[1], nn., **encha·nting**LY[2] adv. [f. F *enchanter* f. L IN(*cantare* sing, frequent. of *canere cant-*)]
enchiri·dion (-kīr-), n. Handbook. [Gk (*egkheir-*), f. *en* in, *kheir* hand]
encir·cle, v.t. Surround, encompass, (*with*); form a circle round. [EN-]
encla·sp, v.t. Hold in clasp or embrace. [EN-]
enclā·ve (or as F), n. Territory surrounded by foreign dominion. [F, f. *enclaver* f. LL IN(*clavare* f. *clavis* key or *clavus* nail)]
encli·tic, a. & n. (gram.). (Word) so unemphatic as to be pronounced as part of preceding word, esp. (Gk) throwing its accent back on preceding word. Hence **encli·tic**ALLY adv. [f. L f. Gk *egklitikos* (EN- + *klinō* lean), see -IC]
enclo·se, in-, v.t. Surround, fence in, (land &c. *with, in*, walls &c.); shut up in receptacle (esp. something besides letter in envelope); bound on all sides, contain, (esp. Math.); hem in on all sides. [EN-]
enclo·sure (-zher), n. Enclosing (esp. of common land, to make it private property, as *E. Act*); enclosing fence &c.; enclosed place; paper &c. enclosed with letter in envelope. [F (OF EN*clore* p.p. *-clos*, see CLOSE[3] and -URE]
enclo·the, v.t. Clothe. [EN-]
enclou·d, v.t. Envelop in cloud. [EN-]
encō·miast, n. Composer of an encomium; flatterer. Hence **encomia·stic** a. [f. Gk *egkōmiastēs* (*egkōmiazō*, as foll., *-ast* = IST(1) w. vbs in *-azō*)]
encō·mium, n. Formal or high-flown praise. [L, f. Gk *egkōmion* (EN- + *kōmos* revelry)]
enco·mpass (-ŭm-), v.t. Surround (esp. with friendly or hostile intention); contain. Hence **enco·mpass**MENT n. [EN- + COMPASS n.]
encore (ŏngkōr·, or as F), int., n., & v.t. (Spectator's or auditor's demand for song &c. to be sung &c.) again, once more; (v.t.) demand repetition of (song &c.), summon (performer) for this. [(vb f. n.) F, = still, again, (cf. It. *ancora*) perh. f. L (*in*) *hanc horam* to this hour]
encou·nter (-ow-), v.t., & n. Meet hostilely; fall in with; (n.) meeting in conflict, falling in, (*with*). [(n. f. OF *encontre*) f. OF *encontrer* f. LL IN(*contrare* f. L *contra* against)]
encou·rage (-kŭ-), v.t. Embolden; incite, advise, (person *to* do); promote, assist, (commerce, opinion, &c.). Hence or cogn. **encou·rage**MENT n., **encou·raging**LY[2] adv. [f. OF EN(*coragier*, as COURAGE)]
E·ncratite, n. Member of early Christian heretical sect abstaining from meat, wine, & marriage. [f. LL f. late Gk *egkratitēs* (*egkratēs* continent, -ITE[1])]
encri·mson, v.t. Make crimson. [EN-]
encroa·ch, v.i. Intrude usurpingly (*on* others' territory, rights, &c., or abs.). Hence **encroa·ch**MENT n. [f. OF EN-(*crochier* f. *croc* hook)]
encru·st, in-, v.t. & i. Cover with a crust; overlay (surface) with ornamental crust of precious material; (intr.) form into a crust. Hence **encru·st**MENT n. [f. F *incruster* f. L IN(*crustare*, as CRUST); also f. EN- + CRUST]
encu·mber, v.t. Hamper (person, movement, action, *with* burden, difficulty, &c.); burden (person, estate, *with* debts); fill, block, (place *with* lumber &c., lit. & fig.). Hence **encu·mber**MENT n. [f. F EN(*combrer* CUMBER[1])]
encu·mbrance, n. Burden; annoyance; impediment; *without e.*, having no children; claim, mortgage, &c., on property. [f. OF *encombrance* (as prec., see -ANCE)]
encu·mbrancer, n. One who has an encumbrance on another's estate. [-ER[1]]
-ency, suf., mod. E different. of -ENCE (-Y[1]), usu. denoting quality or state, not action.

ency̆·clic(al), aa. & nn. (Pope's letter) for extensive circulation. [f. LL *encyclicus*, for *-ius*, f. Gk *egkuklios* (EN- + *kuklos* circle)]

encyclop(a)e·dia, n. Book giving information on all branches of knowledge or of one subject, usu. arranged alphabetically; esp. the French e. of Diderot, D'Alembert, and others; general course of instruction. Hence **encyclopae·dic**(AL) aa., **encyclopae·dism**(3), **encyclopae·dist**(3), nn. [LL, f. false Gk *egkuklopaideia* for *egkuklios paideia* allround education (as prec., *paideia* f. *paideuō* educate f. *pais paidos* boy)]

ency·st, v.t. Enclose in a cyst. Hence **encysta·tion, ency·stment,** nn. [EN-]

end[1], n. Limit, as *there is no e. to it*; extremity (of line &c.); *East, West, E.* (part of London); surface bounding a thing at either extremity, head of cask &c.; remnant, as *candle ee., odds & ee.*; *rope's e.*, short piece bound at ends with thread for flogging; *shoemaker's e.*, length of thread armed with bristle; conclusion (of period, action, state, book, &c.); latter part; destruction; death; result; purpose, as *to gain his ee., to what e?*; object for which a thing exists, final cause; *place on e.* (upright); *turn e. for e.*, reverse; *world without e.*, for ever; *placed e. to e.* (lengthwise, continuously); *e. on*, with its e. fronting one; *no e.*, much, many, *of*; *on e.*, continuously (*for three weeks on e.*); *be at, come to, an e.*, be, become, exhausted or completed; *in the e.*, finally, after all; *at* one's *wits' e.*, quite perplexed; *put an e. to*, stop, abolish; *keep* one's *e. up*, acquit oneself well in conversation, bargain, &c.; *go (in) off the deep e.* (sc. of swimming-bath) fig., take risks; *make an e. of*, put a stop to; *at a loose e.*, unoccupied; *make both ee. meet*, live within one's income; *is at the e. of his tether*, knows, can do, no more; *e.-iron*, movable plate changing size of grate in range. [com.-Teut.: OE *ende*, Du. *einde*, G *ende*]

end[2], v.t. & i. Bring (action, speech, life, &c.) to an end; put an end to, destroy; come to an end; *e. by doing*, eventually do (*will e. by marrying a duke*); result *in*; *e. up*, conclude, finish. [OE *endian* (as prec.)]

enda·mage, v.t. = DAMAGE. [EN-]

enda·nger, v.t. Cause danger to. [EN-]

endear·, v.t. Render (person, thing, one*self*) dear (*to*). Hence **endear·ingly**[2] adv., **endear·ment** n. [EN-]

endea·vour (-dĕ-), v.t. & i., & n. Try (*to* do); strive *after*; (n.) attempt (*to* do, *at doing*). [(n. f. vb) f. EN- + DEVOIR]

endĕ·mic, a. & n. Regularly found among (specified) people, in (specified) country; (n.) e. disease. Hence **ende·mically** adv., **endemi·city** n. [f. Gk EN- + *dēmos* people + -IC]

ender·mic, a. Acting on the skin. Hence **ender·mically** adv. [EN- + DERM + -IC]

e·nding, n. In vbl senses, esp. latter part (of word, story, &c.). [-ING[1]]

e·ndive, n. Species of chicory, with curled leaves, used as salad. [F, f. L *intibus*]

e·ndless, a. Infinite; eternal; incessant; (Mech.) *e. band, cable, chain* (with ends joined for continuous action over wheels &c.). Hence **e·ndlessly**[2] adv., **e·ndlessness** n. [OE *endeléas*, see END[1] and -LESS]

endo- in comb. = Gk *endon* within, as; *-car·dium*, lining membrane of heart; *-carp*, inmost layer of pericarp; *-crane*, inner surface of skull; *-crine*, secreting internally, ductless, of the e. glands, [Gk *krinō* sift]; *-derm*, inner layer of blastoderm; *-gamous, -gamy*, (of) marrying within the tribe; *-gen*, plant that develops wood in interior of stem; *-genous*, growing from within; *-lymph*, fluid in membranous labyrinth of ear; *-metrī·tis, -metrium*, (inflammation of) lining membrane of womb; *-morph*, mineral enclosed in another; *-pa·rasite*, internal parasite; *-plasm, -sarc*, inner soft layer of protoplasm; *-scope*, instrument for viewing internal parts of body; *-ske·leton*, internal framework of vertebrates; *endo·smose, -osmo·sis*, passage of a fluid inwards through a porous septum; *-sperm*, albumen enclosed with embryo in seeds; *-spore*, inner coat of spore, spore formed in a case; *-the·lium*, layer of cells lining blood-vessels &c.

endor·se, in-, v.t. Write on back of (document), esp. sign one's name on back of (bill, cheque, &c.); write (explanation, comment, *on* back of document); *e. over*, make over one's rights in (bill &c. *to* another person, also fig.); confirm (statement, opinion), (vulg. in advertisements) confirm advertiser's praise of (—'s pills &c.); motorist's, publican's, *licence is endorsed*, has record of offence written on the back. Hence **endor·sement** n. [refash. on L; ME *endosse* f. OF *endosser* f. med. L IN(*dorsare* f. *dorsum* back)]

endow·, v.t. Bequeath, give, permanent income to (person, institution); invest (person) *with* (privileges &c.); furnish (person) *with* (ability &c.; esp. in p.p.). Hence **endow·ment** n. [f. EN- + F *douer* f. L *dotare* (as DOWER)]

endue·, in-, v.t. Put on (clothes &c., also fig.); clothe (person) *with*; (usu. pass.) furnish (person *with* qualities &c.). [f. OF *enduire* f. L IN(*ducere* lead, draw), associated in sense w. *induere* put on (clothes)]

endūr·ance, n. Habit, power, of enduring; enduring. [-ANCE]

endure·, v.t. & i. Undergo (pain &c.); submit to; bear (*to* do, esp. w. neg.); last. Hence **endūr·able** a., **endur·ingly**[2] adv., **endur·ing**NESS n. [f. OF *endurer* f. L IN(*durare* make hard f. *durus*)]

e·ndways, -wise, adv. With the end turned towards the spectator or uppermost or foremost; end to end. [-WAYS, -WISE]

-ene, suf. forming names of hydrocarbons, as *benzene, camphene.*

ĕne·ma (*or* ĭnē·-), n. Injection of liquid or gaseous substance into the rectum; the syringe used. [Gk *ĕnĕma* f. EN(*hiēmi* send), see -M]

ĕ·nemy, n. & a. Hostile person; opponent (*of, to,* another); *the E.,* the Devil; member of hostile army or nation; hostile force or ship; (colloq.) *how goes the e.?*, what is the time?; (adj.) of, or belonging to, the e. (*e. ships, goods, alien*). [f. OF *enemi* f. L IN[2](*imicus* = *amicus* friend)]

energĕ·tic, a. & n. Strenuously active; forcible, vigorous; powerfully operative; (n. pl.) science of energy. Hence **energe·t**ICALLY adv. [f. Gk *energētikos* f. EN(*ergeō* f. *ergon* work), see -IC]

ener·gic, a. (rare). = prec. [f. ENERGY + -IC]

e·nergize, v.t. & i. Infuse energy into (person, work); be in active operation. [-IZE]

energū·men, n. Demoniac; enthusiast, fanatic. [f. LL f. Gk *energoumenos* (pass. part., see ENERGETIC)]

ĕ·nergy, n. Force, vigour, (of speech, action, person, &c.); active operation; (pl.) individual powers in exercise, as *devote your ee. to this*; (latent) ability; (Physics) *actual, kinetic, motive, e.,* a body's power of doing work by virtue of its motion (half product of mass into square of velocity), *potential, static, latent, e.,* body's power of doing work by virtue of stresses resulting from its relation to other bodies; CONSERVATION *of e.* [f. LL f. Gk *energeia* f. EN(*ergēs* f. *ergon* work)]

ener·vate[1] (-*a*t), a. Wanting in (physical, moral, literary, artistic) vigour. [f. L E(*nervare* f. *nervus* sinew), see -ATE[2]]

ĕ·nervāte[2], v.t. Weaken (physically &c. as prec.). So **enerva·tion** n. [as prec., -ATE[3]]

enfa·ce, v.t. Write, print, stamp, (form of words) on bill &c.,; do this to (bill &c.). Hence **enfa·ce**MENT n. [EN-]

en famille (F), adv. At home, among one's family.

enfant terrible (F), n. Child who asks awkward questions, repeats what he has heard, &c.

enfee·ble, v.t. Make feeble. Hence **enfee·ble**MENT n. [f. OF EN(*feblir* as FEEBLE)]

enfeo·ff (-ĕf), v.t. Invest (person) with fief; (fig.) hand over. [f. OF EN*feffer* (FIEF)]

enfeoffment (-ĕf-), n. Enfeoffing; document effecting this; fief. [-MENT]

en fête (F), adv. & pred. a. Engaged in, attired &c. for, holiday-making.

enfe·tter, v.t. Bind in fetters (lit. & fig.); enslave (person *to*). [EN-]

enfilā·de, n., & v.t. Fire from guns &c. sweeping line of works or men from end to end; (v.t.) subject (troops, road, &c.) to e. [(vb f. n.) F, f. EN(*filer* f. *fil* thread), see -ADE]

enfo·ld, in-, v.t. Wrap up (person &c. *in, with*); clasp, embrace; shape into folds. [EN-]

enfor·ce, v.t. Urge, press home, (argument, demand); impose (action, conduct, *upon* person &c.); compel observance of (law &c.). Hence or cogn. **enfor·ce**ABLE a., **enfor·cēd**LY[2] adv., **enfor·ce**MENT n. [f. OF *enforcer* f. LL IN(*fortiare* f. *fortis* strong)]

enfra·me, v.t. Set (picture &c.) in frame; serve as frame to. [EN-]

enfra·nchīse (-z), v.t. Set free; invest (town) with municipal rights, esp. that of representation in parliament; admit (person) to electoral franchise. Hence **enfra·nchise**MENT n. [f. OF EN(*franchir* f. *franc* FRANK a.), see -ISH[2]]

enga·ge, v.t. & i. Bind by contract or promise (esp. of marriage, as *engaged couple*); hire (servant); bespeak (seats, cab, &c.); pledge oneself (*to* do, *that*); *e. for,* guarantee, promise; induce; attract, charm, (esp. in part.), whence **enga·ging**LY[2] adv.; (Arch.) fasten (pillar) into wall; interlock (thing *with* another); hold fast (attention); employ (usu. pass.); embark *in* (politics &c.); bring (troops) into conflict; enter into conflict with (also *with*). Hence **enga·ge**MENT n. [f. F EN(*gager* f. GAGE)]

en garçon (F), adv. & pred. a. As a bachelor, unmarried.

engar·land, v.t. Put a garland upon; wreathe (*with* flowers &c.). [EN-]

enge·nder, v.t. Beget (now only fig.); (of situation, condition, &c.) bring about. [f. F *engendrer* f. L IN(*generare* GENERATE)]

e·ngīne, n., & v.t. Mechanical contrivance consisting of several parts; = STEAM-*e.*; FIRE-*e.*; machine, instrument, used in war; instrument, means; *e.-driver* (of steam-e., esp. locomotive); *e.-lathe* (worked by machinery); *e.-sized paper* (sized by machine); *e.-turning,* engraving of symmetrical patterns on metals by machine; (v.t.) fit (ship) with steam-ee. [(vb f. n.) f. OF *engin* f. L *ingenium* (see INGENIOUS)]

engineer·[1], n. One who designs & constructs military works; soldier of branch of army called *Ee.*, trained to engineering; (also *civil e.*) one who designs works of public utility, bridges, canals, gasworks, &c.; maker of engines; one who has charge of steam-engine (only in U.S. of locomotive). Hence **engineer·**SHIP n.

[f. OF *engigneor* f. LL *ingeniatorem* (*ingeniare*, as ENGINE, see -OR[2])]

engineer·[2], v.i. & t. Act as engineer; construct, manage, (bridge, work, &c.) as engineer; (colloq.) arrange, contrive, bring about. [f. prec.]

e·nginery, n. Engines; machinery (often fig.). [-ERY]

engir·d(le), vv.t. Surround with or as with girdle. [EN-]

E·nglander, n. *Little E.*, one opposed to imperial policy. [-ER[1]]

E·nglish[1] (ĭ-), a. & n. Of England; *the E.* (people, soldiers, &c.); *Englishman, -woman*, one who is E. by birth, descent, or naturalization; of, written or spoken in, the E. language; (n.) the E. language (also *the king's, queen's, E.*, as *mishandle the king's E.*); *Old E.* (ending about 1150), *Middle E.* (ending 1500); *in plain E.*, in plain words; size of TYPE; *Early E.* STYLE. [OE *englisc, ænglisc* f. OTeut. *anglisko* (*angli-* ANGLE[3])]

e·nglish[2], v.t. (archaic, affected). Render into English. [f. prec.]

engor·ge, v.t. Devour greedily; (pass.) be crammed, (Path.) be congested with blood. Hence **engor·ge**MENT n. [f. F EN-(*gorger* GORGE)]

engra·ft, in-, v.t. Insert (scion of one tree *into, upon*, another); implant (principles &c. *in* the mind &c.); incorporate (thing *into* another); add (adventitious thing *upon*). [EN-]

engrai·l, v.t. Indent the edge of, give serrated appearance to, (esp. Herald.). [f. OF EN*gresler* perh. f. *gresle* hail]

engrai·n, in-, v.t. Cause (dye &c.) to sink deeply into a thing (usu. fig.); (p.p., cf. INGRAINED) inveterate, as *an engrained rogue*. [EN-]

engra·ve, v.t. Inscribe, ornament, (hard surface *with* incised marks); carve (figures &c. *upon* surface); (fig.) impress deeply (*upon* memory &c.); cut (figures &c.) in lines on metal plates for printing. [EN- + GRAVE[2]]

engra·ving, n. In vbl senses, esp. copy of picture &c. from engraved plate. [-ING[1]]

engrō·ss, v.t. Write (document) in large letters; express in legal form; (Hist.) buy whole stock of (corn &c.) so as to get monopoly; monopolize (conversation &c.); absorb (person, his attention, time, &c.; esp. in p.p. *engrossed in* subject &c.). Hence **engro·ss**MENT n. [1. f. AF EN-*grosser* (*grosse* f. med.L *grossa* large writing); 2. f. phr. *in gross* wholesale]

engu·lf, in-, v.t. Plunge into, swallow up (as) in, a gulf. Hence **engu·lf**MENT n. [EN-]

enha·nce, v.t. Heighten, intensify, (qualities, powers, &c.); exaggerate; raise (price). Hence **enha·nce**MENT n. [f. AF *enhauncer* prob. corrupt. of OF *enhaucer* f. LL *IN(*altiare* f. *altus* high)]

enharmŏ·nic, a. (mus.). Of, having, intervals smaller than semitone (esp. such intervals as that between G sharp & A flat). Hence **enharmo·nic**ALLY adv. [f. L f. Gk EN*armonikos* (*harmonia* HARMONY, see -IC)]

eni·gma, n. Riddle; puzzling person or thing. Hence or cogn. **ēnigma·tic**(AL) aa., **enigma·tical**LY[2] adv., **eni·gma-tize**(3) v.t. [f. L f. Gk *ainigma -matos* f. *ainissomai* speak allusively (*ainos* fable)]

enis·le, in-, v.t. Make into an isle; place on an isle; isolate. [EN-]

enja·mbment (-m-m-), n. (pros.). Continuation of sentence beyond second line of couplet. [f. F *enjambement* f. EN(*jamber* f. *jambe* leg), see -MENT]

enjoi·n, v.t. Prescribe, impose, (action, conduct, *on* person); command (person *to* do); issue instructions (*that*). [f. F *enjoindre* (st. *-joign-*) f. L IN(*jungere* join)]

enjoy·, v.t. *E. oneself*, experience pleasure; take delight in, whence **enjoy·**ABLE a., **enjoy·able**NESS n., **enjoy·ab**LY[2] adv.; have the use of (advantages &c.); experience, as *e. poor health*. Hence **enjoy·**MENT n. [f. OF EN(*joier* f. *joie* JOY) give joy to, (refl.) enjoy; or f. OF EN(*joir* f. L *gaudēre* rejoice)]

enki·ndle, v.t. Cause (flame, passions, war, &c.) to blaze up; inflame with passion. [EN-]

enla·ce, v.t. Encircle tightly; enfold; entwine. Hence **enla·ce**MENT n. [f. F *enlacer* f. LL IN(*laciare* f. *lacius* = *laqueus* noose)]

enlar·ge, v.t. & i. Increase, extend; widen, expand, (mind, heart, ideas); (archaic) release; grow larger; expatiate *upon*. Hence **enlar·ge**MENT n. [f. OF EN*larger* (LARGE)]

enligh·ten, v.t. Instruct, inform, (person *on* subject); (poet.) shed light on (object), give light to (person); free (person) from prejudice or superstition (esp. in p.p.). Hence **enligh·ten**MENT n. [EN- + LIGHT n. + -EN[6]]

enli·nk, v.t. Link together, connect closely, (*with, to*; lit. & fig.). [EN-]

enli·st, v.t. & i. Engage (t. & i.) for military service; secure the co-operation or support of (persons, feelings, natural forces, sciences, &c., *in* enterprise &c.). Hence **enli·st**MENT n. [EN-]

enlī·ven, v.t. Animate, inspirit, (persons, feelings, trade, &c.); brighten (picture, scene). [EN- + LIFE + -EN[6]]

en masse (F), adv. In a mass; all together.

enme·sh, emm-, imm-, v.t. Entangle in or as in a net. Hence **enme·sh**MENT n. [EN-]

e·nmity, n. Hatred; state of hostility. [f. OF *enemistie* f. LL *inimicitatem* (as ENEMY, see -TY)]

e·nnĕăd, n. Set of nine (discourses, books, points). [f. Gk *enneas* nine, see -AD)]

enno·ble, v.t. Make (person) a noble; make noble, elevate. Hence **enno·ble**MENT n. [f. F EN*noblir* (NOBLE)]

ennui (ŏ·nwē, or as F), n. Mental weariness from lack of occupation or interest. Hence **ennui**ED² (ŏnwē·d), ***ennuyé*** (F, fem. *-ée*, pl. *-és*, *-ées*), aa. [F, f. L *in odio*, cf. ANNOY¹]

E·no (ē-), n. (Used for) E.'s Fruit Salt, a patent medicine. [*E.*, maker]

enor·mity, n. Monstrous wickedness; crime. [f. F *énormité* f. L *enormitatem* (as foll., see -TY)]

enor·mous, a. Huge, very large, as *e. beast, difference.* Hence **enor·mously**² adv., **enor·mous**NESS n. [f. L E(*normis* f. *norma* pattern, standard) + -OUS]

enou·gh (-ŭf), (poet.) **enow·**, a., n., & adv. Not less than the required number, quantity, degree, as: (adj.) *we have apples e., e. apples, beer e., e. beer, he made e. noise* (to justify supposition &c.), *e. noise to wake the dead, for his purpose*; (n.) *we have e. of everything except beer, e. of* (stop) *this folly, e.!* (say no more), *e. is as good as a feast, cry 'e.'* (acknowledge defeat), *I have had e.* (am tired) *of him, I had e. to do* (my work cut out) *to catch the tram, you have done more than e., e. and to spare*; (pred.; adj. or n.) *five men are e., five quarts is not e.*; (adv.) *it is boiled* (*just*) *e., he does not advertise e., are you warm e.?, he does not e.* (usu. *sufficiently*) *realize the difficulties, she sings well e.* (tolerably), *you know well e.* (quite well) *what I mean*; *oddly e.* (to justify the term *oddly*), *he had lost his purse*; *sure e.* (to satisfy rational doubt), *there it was.* [OE *genóg* (Du. *genoeg*, G *genug*) f. *geneah* it suffices f. OTeut. *ga-* pref. + *nah* f. Aryan *nak* seen in L *nancisci nact-* obtain]

enou·nce (-ow-), v.t. Enunciate; pronounce (words). Hence **enou·nce**MENT n. [f. F *énoncer* (as ENUNCIATE)]

en passant (F), adv. By the way; (Chess) *take* (pawn that advances two squares at once) *e. p.* (with your own pawn by which it could have been taken if it had advanced only one).

enquire, enquiry. See INQUIRE, INQUIRY.

enra·ge, v.t. Make furious (*enraged at, by, with*). [f. OF EN*rager* (RAGE)]

en rapport. See RAPPORT.

enra·pture, v.t. Delight intensely. [EN-]

enre·giment, v.t. Form (men) into a regiment; discipline. [f. F EN(*régimenter* f. *régiment* REGIMENT)]

en règle (F), adv. In due form.

enri·ch, v.t. Make rich; add to contents of (collection, museum, book); make richer in quality, flavour, &c. Hence **enri·ch**MENT n. [f. F EN(*richir* f. *riche* RICH)]

enro·be, v.t. Put a robe upon. [EN-]

enrō·l, -ll, v.t. (-ll-). Write name of (person on list, esp. of army; incorporate (person) as member (*in* society &c.); enter (deed &c.) among rolls of court of justice; record, celebrate. Hence **enro·l**MENT n. [f. OF EN*roller* f. *rolle* ROLL n.]

en route (F), adv. On the way (*to, for,* place &c. or abs.).

ensa·mple, n. (archaic). = EXAMPLE. [earlier *asaumple* f. OF *essample* EXAMPLE]

ensa·nguined, a. Blood-stained, bloody, (lit. & fig.) [EN- + L *sanguis -inis* blood + -ED¹]

ensco·nce, v.t. Establish (oneself &c. in secret, safe, snug, &c., place). [EN-]

ensemble (F), n. (Also *tout e.*) thing viewed as a whole; general effect.

enshri·ne, v.t. Enclose (relic &c.) in shrine; serve as shrine for (precious thing, lit. & fig.). Hence **enshri·ne**MENT n. [EN-]

enshrou·d, v.t. Cover completely, hide from view. [EN-]

e·nsign (-īn), n. Badge (of office &c.); banner, flag, esp. (Brit. naut.) white, blue, or red, flag with union in corner (*white e.*, of Royal Navy & Royal Yacht Squadron, *blue e.*, of naval reserve &c., *red e.*, of merchant service); standard-bearer (formerly, lowest commissioned officer of foot, cf. ANCIENT²), whence **e·nsign**CY n. [f. OF *enseigne* f. L *insignia* neut. pl. of IN*signis* (*signum* sign) conspicuous]

e·nsilage (-ĭj), n., & v.t. Preservation of green fodder in silo or pit without drying; fodder thus preserved; (v.t.) treat (fodder) by e. [(vb f. n.) F (as foll., see -AGE)]

ensi·le, v.t. Put (fodder) into a silo. [f. F *ensiler* f. Sp. EN*silar* (SILO)]

ensla·ve, v.t. Make (person &c.) a slave (lit., or fig. *to* habit, superstition, &c.). Hence **ensla·ve**MENT n. [EN-]

ensla·ver, n. In vbl senses, esp. woman by whose charms a man is enslaved. [-ER¹]

ensnare·, v.t. Entrap (lit. & fig.). [EN-]

ensou·l, in-, v.t. Infuse a soul into. [EN-]

ensphere·, v.t. Encircle, enclose. [EN-]

ensue·, v.i. & t. Happen afterwards; result (*from, on*); (bibl.) seek after. [f. OF *ensuivre* f. LL IN(*sequere* = L *sequi* follow)]

ensure· (-shoor), v.t. Make (person, thing) safe (*against, from,* risks); make certain (thing, *that* it shall happen); secure (thing *to, for,* person &c.); (formerly) = INSURE. [f. AF EN(*seurer* f. OF *seur* SURE)]

enswā·the, v.t. Bind, wrap, in bandage (lit. & fig.). Hence **enswa·the**MENT n. [EN-]

-ent, suf. forming adjj. & nn., repr. L *-ent-* (nom. *-ens*) of pres. part. in 2nd, 3rd, & 4th conjj. See -ANT. For noun meanings (1, 2) see -ANT.

entă·blature, n. (archit.) The part of an order above the column, including architrave, frieze, & cornice. [f. It. *intavolatura* f. IN(*tavolare* f. *tavola* TABLE), see -URE]

entā·blement, n. Horizontal platform(s) supporting statue, above dado & base. [F, f. EN*tabler* (TABLE), see -MENT]

entai·l¹, n. Settlement of succession of landed estate so that it cannot be bequeathed at pleasure; estate so secured; (fig.) inalienable inheritance (of qualities, beliefs, &c.). [f. foll.]

entai·l[2], v.t. Settle (land &c.) as in prec.; bestow (thing) as inalienable possession (*on* person); impose (expense, labour, *on* person); necessitate. Hence **entai·l**MENT n. [EN- + TAIL[2]]

enta·ngle, v.t. Catch in snare or among obstacles; involve (person &c.) in difficulties; make (thing) tangled or intricate (lit. & fig.). Hence **enta·ngle**MENT n. [EN-]

entĕ·lechy (-kĭ), n. (philos.). Realization, the becoming or being actual of what was potential, developed perfection, (*Aristotle defines the soul, the Form or E. of an organized body*); what gives perfection, informing spirit. [f. Gk *entelekheia* (*en telei ekhein* to be in perfection)]

entente (F), n. (diplom.). Friendly understanding between States; group of States in such relation; *E. cordiale*, of Gt Britain & France 1904; *the* (*Triple*) *E.*, of these with Russia 1908; *the Little E.*, of Czecho-Slovakia, Jugo-Slavia, & Roumania 1921. [F, = understanding]

e·nter, v.i. & t. 1. (intr.). Go, come, in, (*into* place, room, &c., or abs.); (3rd pers. imperat. as stage direction) come upon stage, as *E. Macbeth*; *e. into*, engage in (conversation, relations, agreement, inquiry, &c.), sympathize with (person's feelings &c.), form part of (calculations, plans, &c.), bind oneself by (recognizances, treaty, contract); *e.* (*up*)*on*, assume possession of (property), begin (process &c.), begin to deal with (subject). 2. (trans.). Go, come, into (place &c.); penetrate (flesh &c.); become member of (army, church, &c.); give initial training to (dog), break in (horse); write (name, details, &c., in list, book, &c.); record name of (person) as competitor *for* (contest, race, &c.; also intr., announce oneself as competitor); *e. an appearance*, show oneself at a meeting &c.; (of minority in deliberative body, esp. House of Lords) *e. a protest*, record it in journals or minutes, make it; admit, procure admission for, (pupil, member of a society); *e. up*, complete series of entries in (account-books &c.). Hence **e·nter**ABLE a. [f. F *entrer* f. L *intrare* (*intra* within)]

entĕ·ric, a. & n. Of the intestines; *e.* (*fever*), typhoid. So **enteri·**TIS n. [f. Gk *enterikos* (*enteron* intestine, see -IC)]

entero- in comb. = Gk *enteron* intestine, as *-lite*, stony concretion of stomach &c., *-tomy*, cutting open intestine.

e·nterprise (-z), n. Undertaking, esp. bold or difficult one; courage, readiness, to engage in ee., as *he has no e.* [f. OF *entreprise* f. *entreprendre* (*entre* between + *prendre* take f. L *pre*(*he*)*ndere*)]

e·nterprising, a. Ready to undertake enterprises. Hence **e·nterprising**LY[2] adv. [part. of archaic vb *enterprise* (f. prec.)]

entertai·n, v.t. Maintain (correspondence, discourse); amuse, occupy agreeably, (person &c., often iron.), whence **entertai·n**ING[2] a., **entertai·ning**LY[2] adv.; receive hospitably (*e. angels unawares*, see *Heb.* xiii. 2; also abs., as *they e. a great deal*); harbour, cherish, welcome or consider, (idea, feeling, proposal). [f. F *entretenir* f. LL INTER(*tenēre* hold)]

entertai·nment, n. In vbl senses, esp.: amusement, as *much to my e.*; public performance or show. [-MENT]

enthra·l(l) (-awl), v.t. (-ll-). Enslave (usu. fig.); charm. Hence **enthra·l**MENT n. [EN-]

enthro·ne, v.t. Place (king, bishop, &c.) on throne, esp. as formal induction (also fig.). Hence **enthro·ne**MENT n. [EN-]

enthroniza·tion, n. Enthronement (lit. & fig.). [f. obs. vb *enthronize* f. OF *introniser* f. LL (*in-*) f. Gk EN(*thronizō* as THRONE, -IZE)]

enthū·se (-z), v.i. (colloq.). Show enthusiasm, gush. [back formation on foll.]

enthū·siasm (-zĭ-), n. Ardent zeal (*for, about*, an object, cause, &c.). [f. LL f. Gk *enthousiasmos* f. *enthousiazō* f. *enthousia* f. EN(*theos* god) possessed by a god]

enthū·siast, n. One who is full of enthusiasm (*for* cause &c.), whence **enthusia·s**TIC a., **enthusia·st**ICALLY adv.; visionary, self-deluded person. [f. Gk *enthousiastēs* (as prec.)]

e·nthymēme, n. (logic). Syllogism in which one premiss is suppressed. [f. L f. Gk *enthumēma* f. EN*thumeomai* consider (*thumos* mind)]

enti·ce, v.t. Allure (person &c. *from* place, course of conduct, &c., *into* another; *to* do). So **enti·ce**MENT n. [f. OF EN*ticier* prob. lit. set on fire (L *titio* firebrand)]

entire·, a. & n. Whole, complete; not broken or decayed; not castrated; unqualified, as *e. affection*; mere, as *an e. delusion*; all of one piece, continuous; pure, unmixed; (n., hist., & on inn-signs) blend of former ale, beer, & twopenny. Hence **entire·**NESS n. [f. OF *entier* f. L IN[2](*teger*, f. *tag-*, *tangere* touch)]

entire·ly, adv. Wholly; solely. [-LY[2]]

entire·ty (-īrtĭ), n. Completeness, esp., *in its e.*; sum total (*of*); (Law) *possession by ee.* (undivided). [f. OF *entiereté* f. L *integritatem* (as ENTIRE, see -TY)]

enti·tle, v.t. Give (book &c.) the title of (*Adam Bede* &c.); give (person) the title of (sultan &c.); (of circumstances, qualities, &c.) give (person &c.) a claim (*to* a thing, *to* do). [f. OF *entiteler* f. LL IN-(*titulare*, as TITLE)]

e·ntity, n. A thing's existence, as opp. to its qualities or relations; thing that has real existence. So **e·ntit**ATIVE a. [f. LL *entitas* (*ens* LL part. of *esse* be, suggested by *absens*; see -TY)]

ento- in comb. = Gk *entos* within, as *-pa·rasite*, *-zo·on*, internal parasite, *-phyte*, plant growing inside a plant or animal.

ento·mb (-ōōm), v.t. Place in tomb (lit. & fig.); serve as tomb for. Hence **ento·mb**MENT (-ōōm-m-) n. [f. OF EN-*toumber* (as TOMB)]

entŏ·mic, a. Of insects. [as foll. + -IC]

entomo- in comb. Insect, as: *-lite*, fossil insect, *-phagous*, insect-eating, *-philous* (Bot.), fertilized by means of insects, *-tomy*, insect anatomy. [f. Gk EN(*tomos* f. *temnō* cut) cut up, in neut. pl. = insects]

entomo·logy, n. Study of insects. Hence **entomolo·gic**AL a., **entomo·log**IST n., **entomo·log**IZE v.i. [f. F ENTOMO(*logie* -LOGY)]

entourage (F), n. Surroundings; attendant persons.

en-tout-cas (F), n. Umbrella-sunshade.

entr'acte (F), n. (Performance in) interval between acts of play.

e·ntrails, n. pl. Bowels, intestines; (fig.) (inner parts (*of* the earth &c.). [f. OF *entraille* f. LL *intralia* (neut. pl. taken in F as fem. sing.) f. *inter* among]

entrai·n, v.t. & i. Put (esp. troops), get, into a train. [EN-]

entra·mmel, v.t. Entangle, hamper. [EN-]

e·ntrance[1], n. Coming or going in; coming of actor upon stage; entering *into*, *upon* (office &c.); right of admission; (in full *e. fee*) fee paid on admission to club, school, &c.; door, passage, &c., one enters by. [OF (as ENTER, -ANCE)]

entra·nce[2], v.t. Throw into a trance; overwhelm (*with* joy, fear); carry away as in trance (*from, to*). Hence **entra·nce**MENT n. [EN-]

e·ntrant, n. One who enters room, profession, &c., or *for* (race &c.). [F, part. as ENTER]

entra·p, v.t. (-pp-). Catch in or as in trap; beguile (person *to* destruction &c., *into* doing). [f. OF EN(*traper* TRAP)]

entrea·t, v.t. (Also *e. of*) ask (person) earnestly (*to* do, *that*), whence **entrea·t-ing**LY[2] adv.; (bibl.) *evil e.*, treat ill. [f. OF EN(*traiter* TREAT)]

entrea·ty, n. Earnest request. [prec. + -Y[4]]

entrechat (F), n. Striking together of the heels several times during leap from ground, in dancing.

entrée (ŏ·ntrā, or as F), n. Right, privilege, of admission; made dish served between fish & joint. [F, = ENTRY]

entre·nch, in-, v.t. Surround (post, army, town) with trench (also fig., esp. one*self*); (rarely) encroach, trespass, *upon*. Hence **entre·nch**MENT n. [EN-]

entre nous (F), adv. Between you & me.

entrepôt (F), n. Storehouse for deposit; commercial centre for import & export, collection & distribution.

entrepreneur (F), n. Organizer of (esp. musical) entertainments.

entresol (F), n. Low storey between first & ground floor.

e·ntropy, n. (physics). Measure of the unavailability of a system's thermal energy for conversion into mechanical work. [f. EN- + Gk *tropē* transformation (*trepō* turn), on *energy*]

entru·st, in-, v.t. Charge (person) *with* (duty, object of care); confide (duty, person, thing, its safety, *to* person). [EN-]

e·ntry, n. Coming or going in; ceremonial entrance; (Law) taking possession; place of entrance, door, gate, lobby, mouth of river; registration in records, account-books, &c.; item so entered; *bookkeeping by double, single, e.* (in which each item is entered twice, once, in ledger); list of competitors for race &c. [f. F *entrée* f. LL *intrata* (as ENTER, cf. -ADE)]

entwi·ne, in-, v.t. Interweave (lit. & fig.); wreathe (thing *with, about, round*, another); embrace. [EN-]

entwi·st, in-, v.t. Clasp with, form into, a twist; twist (thing) in *with* (another). [EN-]

ēnū·clēate, v.t. Explain, clear up; (Surg.) extract (tumour &c.) from shell &c. Hence **enucle**A·TION n. [f. L E(*nucleare* f. NUCLEUS)]

enū·merate, v.t. Count; specify (items). Hence or cogn. **enumer**A·TION, **enu·merat**OR[2], nn., **enu·merat**IVE a. [f. L E(*numerare* NUMBER)]

enu·nciate (-shĭ-), v.t. Express definitely (proposition, theory); proclaim; pronounce (words). So **enunci**A·TION (-sĭ-), **enu·nciat**OR[2] (-shĭ-), nn., **enu·nciat**IVE (-sha-) a. [f. L E(*nuntiare* announce f. *nuntius* messenger), -ATE[3]]

enure·, v.i. (& t.). See INURE.

envĕ·lop, v.t. Wrap up (person, thing, subject, &c., *in* garment, flames, clouds, mystery, or w. *flame* &c. as subject); (Mil.) effect the surrounding of (enemy). Hence **enve·lop**MENT n. [f. OF EN*veloper* (as DEVELOP)]

ĕ·nvelōpe (*or* ŏn-), n. Wrapper, covering, (lit. & fig.), esp. folded & gummed cover of letter. [f. F *enveloppe* (as prec.)]

envĕ·nom, v.t. Put poison on or into (weapon, air, &c.); infuse venom into (feelings, words, actions); corrupt (mind &c.). [f. OF EN(*venimer* as VENOM)]

e·nviable, a. Calculated to excite envy (said of desirable thing or its possessor). Hence **e·nviab**LY[2] adv. [f. ENVY v. + -ABLE]

e·nvious, a. Full of envy; feeling envy *of* (person, thing). Hence **e·nvious**LY[2] adv. [f. OF *envieus* f. L *invidiosus* (as ENVY[1], see -OUS)]

envīr·on, v.t. (Of persons or things) form a ring, be stationed, round; surround (person, place, &c.) hostilely, protectively, as attendants, &c.; surround (person, thing, *with* others). [f. F *environner* f. adv. as ENVIRONS]

envīr·onment, n. Surrounding; surrounding objects, region, or circumstances. [-MENT]
envīr·ons (*or* ĕnvī-), n. pl. District surrounding town &c. [f. OF ENviron (n. f. adv.) f. **viron* circuit, cf. *virer* VEER]
envi·sage, v.t. Look in the face of; face (danger, facts); contemplate, esp. under particular aspect. Hence **envi·sage**MENT n. [f. F EN*visager* (VISAGE)]
e·nvoy¹, n. (archaic). (Author's parting words, esp.) short stanza concluding certain archaic forms of poem. [OF, f. *envoiier* send (*en voie* on the way f. L *via*)]
e·nvoy², n. Messenger, representative; esp. minister plenipotentiary, ranking below ambassador & above *chargé d'affaires.* Hence **e·nvoy**SHIP n. [prob. f. F *envoyé*, p.p. as prec.]
e·nvy¹, n. Grudging contemplation (*of* more fortunate persons, *of, at,* their advantages, or abs.; often playfully); object, ground, of this, as *she, her poodle, is the e. of Bath.* [f. F *envie* f. L *invidia* f. *invidus* f. IN(*vidēre* see) envy]
e·nvy², v.t. Feel envy of, as *I e. him, e. his impudence, e. him his impudence.* [f. F *envier* f. med.L *invidiare* (*invidia* ENVY¹)]
enwi·nd, v.t. (Of thing) wind itself round (another). [EN-]
enwo·mb, v.t. Enclose (as) in womb. [EN-]
enwra·p, in-, v.t. (-pp-). Wrap, enfold, (*in*; lit. & fig.). [EN-]
enwrea·the, v.t. Surround as or (as) with wreath; intertwine. [EN-]
enzoō·tic, a. & n. (Disease) regularly affecting cattle &c. in a particular district or at a particular season. [f. EN-(2), Gk *zōion* animal, -IC]
e·nzȳme, n. (Chem.). A chemical or unorganized ferment as distinguished from yeast & other living ferments. [EN-(2) + Gk *zumē*, see ZYMOSIS]
ē·ocēne, a. (geol.). Of the lowest division of Tertiary strata. [f. Gk *ēōs* dawn + *kainos* new]
ēolī·thic, a. Of the period preceding the PALAEOlithic age. [Gk *ēōs* dawn, *lithos* stone]
eon. See AEON.
-eous, suf. = L *-eus* + -OUS, forming adjj. meaning 'of the nature of', as *ligneous* like wood; a few are f. L nn. direct (*aqueous* f. *aqua*); some add -OUS to *-te* (now *-ty*) as *duteous*, or are changed f. *-tivous* (*bounteous* f. F *bontif*); *righteous, courteous*, are by false anal.
ēozō·ic, a. (Geol.). (Of strata) showing the earliest indications of animal life. [Gk *ēōs* dawn, *zōion* animal]
ep- in comb. = EPI- before unaspirated vowels.
ĕ·pact, n. Age of moon on Jan. 1; excess of solar over lunar year. [f. F *epacte* f. L f. Gk *epaktē* f. EP(*agō* bring) intercalate]
ĕ·parch (-k), n. Governor, bishop, of an eparchy. [f. Gk EP(*arkhos* ruler)]
ĕ·parchy, n. Subdivision of modern kingdom of Greece; diocese in Russian (Greek) Church. [f. Gk *eparkhia* (as prec., see -Y¹)]
ĕ·paulet(te), n.. Ornamental shoulder-piece of uniform; (of private soldier) *win his ee.*, earn promotion to rank of officer. [f. F *épaulette* dim. of *épaule* shoulder f. L *spatula*]
epergne (ĭper·n), n. Centre ornament (esp. in branched form) for dinner-table. [?]
epexegē·sis (-j-), n. Additional, addition of, words to make meaning clear (e.g. 'difficult *to do*'). So **epexegē·t**IC(AL) aa., **epexege·tical**LY² adv. [Gk (EP- + EXEGESIS)]
eph-, pref. = EPI- before *h.*
ephē·be, n. (Gk Ant.). Citizen aged 18 to 20. [f. L f. Gk EPH*ēbos* (*hēbē* early manhood)]
ephĕ·mera (pl. *-ras*), **-ron** (pl. *-rons, -ra*), nn. Insect living only a day; genus of insects including May-fly; short-lived thing. [f. Gk EPH*ēmeros* lasting only a day (*hēmera*)]
ephĕ·meral, a. (Of diseases) lasting only a day; (of insects, flowers, &c.) lasting a day or a few days; short-lived, transitory. Hence **ephemera·l**ITY n. [f. Gk as prec. + -AL]
ephĕ·meris, n. (pl. *-idēs*). Astronomical almanac or table. [Gk (*-ēm-*), = calendar (as prec.)]
ĕ·phod, n. Jewish priestly vestment. [Heb., f. *aphad* put on]
ĕ·phor, n. One of five Spartan magistrates controlling the kings; (in mod. Greece) overseer. [f. Gk EPH*oros* (*horaō* see)]
ĕpi-, pref. = Gk *epi* upon, at, on the ground of, in addition.
e·piblăst, n. (biol.). Outermost layer of blastoderm. [f. EPI- + Gk *blastos* sprout, germ]
ĕ·pic, a. & n. (Poem) narrating continuously achievements of one or more heroes, as the *Iliad* & *Odyssey*; fit for recital in an e., of heroic type or scale; *E. dialect*, form of Gk in which the e. poems were written; *national e.*, poem, of any form, embodying nation's conception of its past history. Hence **e·pic**AL a., **e·pical**LY² adv. [f. L f. Gk *epikos* (EPOS, -IC)]
epicē·dium, n. Funeral ode. [f. L f. Gk EPI(*kēdeion* f. *kēdos* care)]
ĕ·picēne, a. & n. (Lat. & Gk Gram.) denoting either sex without change of gender; for, used by, both sexes; (person) with characteristics of both sexes. [f. L f. Gk EPI(*koinos* common)]
epice·ntrum, -tre, nn. Point at which earthquake breaks out. [f. Gk EPI(*kentros* a. as CENTRE)]
ĕ·picure, n. One who is choice & dainty in eating & drinking. Hence **e·picur**ISM (2) n. [f. L f. Gk *Epikouros* Epicurus, or LL *epicurius* a.]

epicurē·an, a. & n. (Follower) of Epicurus, Athenian philosopher (300 B.C.) who taught that highest good was pleasure (i.e. practice of virtue); (person) devoted to pleasure, esp. refined sensuous enjoyment. Hence **epicure·an**ISM(3) n. [f. L (*-eus*) f. Gk *Epikoureios* (prec.)]

e·picȳcle, n. Small circle having its centre on circumference of a greater. Hence **epicȳ·cl**IC a. [f. L f. Gk EPI(*kuklos* circle)]

epicȳ·cloid, n. Curve traced by point in circumference of a circle rolling on exterior of another. Hence **epicycloi·d**AL a. [prec. + -OID]

epidei·ctic (-dī-), a. Meant for display. [f. Gk *epideiktikos* f. EPI(*deiknumi* show), see -IC)]

epidē·mic, a. & n. (Disease, lit. & fig.) prevalent among community at special time, cf. ENDEMIC. Hence **epide·mic**AL a., **epide·mical**LY[2] adv. [f. F *épidémique* f. *épidémie* f. LL f. Gk *epidēmia* f. *epidēmios* a. (*dēmos* people)]

epidēmio·logy, n. Science of epidemics. [f. Gk as prec., -LOGY]

epider·mis, n. Outer layer of skin of animals, cuticle; outer animal integument of shell; true skin of plant below cuticle. Hence **epider·m**AL, **epider·m**IC, **epider·m**OID, **epidermoi·d**AL, aa. [Gk EPI*dermis* (DERM)]

epiga·strium, n. Part of abdomen immediately over stomach. Hence **epiga·str**IC a. [f. Gk EPI*gastrion* (*gastēr* stomach)]

e·pigene (-j-), a. (Geol.) produced on surface of earth; (of crystal) chemically altered since its formation. [f. F *épigène* f. Gk EPI(*genēs* born)]

epige·nesis, n. Formation of organic germ as a new product; *theory of e.* (that the germ is brought into existence, not merely developed, in process of reproduction). [EPI-]

epiglŏ·ttis, n. Erect cartilage at root of tongue, depressed during swallowing to cover glottis. Hence **epiglŏ·tt**IC a. [Gk EPI(*glōttis* f. *glōtta* tongue)]

e·pigram, n. Short poem ending in witty turn of thought; pointed saying or mode of expression. So **epigramma·t**IC a., **epigramma·t**ICALLY adv., **epigra·mmat**IST(3) n., **epigra·mmat**IZE(1, 2) v.t. & i. [f. F *épigramme* f. L f. Gk EPI(*gramma* -GRAM)]

e·pigraph, n. Inscription on stone, statue, coin, &c., whence **epigra·ph**IC a., **epi·graph**IST(2), **epi·graph**Y[1], nn.; motto. [f. Gk EPI(*graphē* f. *graphō* write)]

e·pilepsy, n. Nervous disease in which patient falls to ground unconscious, with spasms & foaming at mouth. [f. OF *epilepsie* f. L f. Gk *epilēpsia* f. EPI(*lambanō* take)]

epile·ptic, a. & n. Of epilepsy; (person) subject to epilepsy. [f. F *épileptique* f. L f. Gk *epilēptikos* (as prec.)]

epi·logist (-j-), n. Writer, speaker, of epilogue. [f. foll. + -IST]

e·pilŏgue (-g), n. Concluding part of literary work; speech, short poem, addressed to spectators by actor at end of play. [F, f. L f. Gk EPI(*logos* speech)]

epi·phany, n. Manifestation of Christ to the Magi; manifestation of a superhuman being. [f. OF *epiphanie* f. LL (neut. pl. used as fem. sing.) f. late Gk *epiphania* (neut. pl. adj.) f. EPI(*phainō* show); partly also f. Gk *epiphaneia* (*epiphanēs* manifest)]

ĕpiphenŏ·menon, n. (med., philos.; pl. *-ena*). Secondary symptom, mere concomitant of something else not regarded as its cause or result. [EPI-, PHENOMENON]

e·piphyte, n. Plant growing on (usu. not fed by) another; vegetable parasite on animal body. Hence **epiphȳ·t**AL, **epiphȳ·t**IC, aa. [f. EPI- + Gk *phuton* plant]

Epīr·ot, n. Inhabitant of Epirus. [f. Gk *ēpeirōtēs* (*ēpeiros*, -OT[2])]

epi·scopacy, n. Government of church by bishops; *the* bishops. [as EPISCOPATE, -ACY]

epi·scopal, a. Of bishop(s); *e. church*, constituted on principle of prec. Hence **epi·scopal**ISM(3) n., **epi·scopal**LY[2] adv. [f. F *épiscopal* f. LL *episcopalis* (as BISHOP, see -AL)]

episcopā·lian, a. & n. (Adherent) of episcopacy; (member) of episcopal church. Hence **episcopa·lian**ISM(3) n. [f. L as prec. + -AN]

epi·scopate (-*at*), n. Office, see, tenure, of bishop; *the e.*, the bishops. [f. L *episcopatus* (*episcopus* BISHOP, see -ATE[1])]

e·pisode, n. Part between two choric songs in Gk tragedy (orig. interpolation); incidental narrative or series of events. Hence **episŏ·d**IC(AL) aa., **episo·dical**LY[2] adv. [f. Gk EP*eisodion* f. *eisodos* entry (*eis* into + *hodos* way)]

epispa·stic, a. & n. (med.). Blistering (plaster, substance). [f. Gk *epispastikos* f. EPI(*spaō* draw), see -IC]

epistēmo·logy, n. Theory of the method or grounds of knowledge. [f. Gk *epistēmē* knowledge + -O- + -LOGY]

epi·stle (-sl), n. Letter (now only facet. of ordinary modern letters), esp. one of an apostle, part of the canon of Scripture; *the E.*, extract from apostolical e. read in Communion service; literary work, usu. verse, in form of letter. [OF, f. L f. Gk *epistolē* f. EPI(*stellō* send)]

epi·stolary, a. Of, carried on by, suited to, letters. [f. F *épistolaire* f. L *epistolaris* (as prec., see -ARY[2])]

epi·stoler, n. (eccl.). Reader (cf. GOSPELLER) of the Epistle. [f. F *epistolier* f. L *epistolaris* as prec., -ER[2](1)]

epi·strophe (-fī), n. (rhet.). Ending of several sentences or clauses with same word. [Gk EPI(*strophē* turning f. *strephō*)]

e·pistyle, n. (archit.). = ARCHITRAVE. [f. L f. Gk EPI(*stulion* f. *stulos* pillar)]

e·pitaph, n. Words (supposed to be) inscribed on tomb. [f. L f. Gk EPI(*taphion* f. *taphos* tomb), neut. adj. as n.]

epithalā·mium, n. (pl. *-iums, -ia*). Nuptial song or poem. Hence **epithalā·mi**AL, **epithală·m**IC, aa. [f. L f. Gk EPI(*thalamion* f. *thalamos* bride-chamber), neut. adj. as n.]

epithē·lium, n. Tissue forming outer layer of mucous membrane; (Bot.) epidermis formed of young cells. Hence **epithē·li**AL a. [mod.L, f. EPI- + Gk *thēlē* teat]

e·pithet, n. Adjective expressing quality or attribute; significant appellation. Hence **epithĕ·t**IC(AL) aa., **epithe·tical**LY[2] adv. [f. L f. Gk *epitheton* f. EPI(*tithēmi* place)]

epi·tome (-mĭ), n. Summary, abstract, of book; condensed account; (fig.) thing that represents another in miniature, as *man, the world's e.* Hence **epi·tom**IST(1) n., **epi·tom**IZE(3) v.t. [Gk *epitomē* f. EPI(*temnō* cut) abridge]

epi·zoō·tic, a. & n. (Disease) temporarily prevalent among animals (cf. ENZOOTIC, EPIDEMIC). [EPI-, Gk *zōion* animal, -IC]

ē·pŏch (-k), n. Beginning of era in history, science, life, &c., as *this made an e., an e.-making event*; date; period in history or life marked by special events. Hence **ĕ·poch**AL a. [f. LL f. Gk *epokhē* stoppage f. EP(*ekhō* hold)]

ĕ·pode, n. Form of lyric poem, used by Horace; third division of lyric ode. [OF, f. L f. Gk *epōdos* f. EP(*adō* sing)]

ĕ·ponym, n. One who gives his name to a people, place, or institution. So **epŏ·nym**OUS a. [f. L f. Gk EP(*ōnumos* f. *onoma* name)]

ĕ·popee, n. Epic poem or poetry. [f. F *épopée* f. Gk *epopoiia* f. *epopoios* (foll. + *poieō* make)]

ĕ·pos, n. Early unwritten epic poetry; epic poem. [L f. Gk *epos* word, song]

ĕpsī·lon, n. Greek letter (Ε, ε) ĕ (cf. ETA). [Gk (*psilos* bare)]

E·psom, n. Town in Surrey; *E. salt,* magnesium sulphate; (used for) racecourse at E., principal race-meeting there held, including Derby and Oaks.

ĕ·quable, a. Uniform, even, not easily disturbed. Hence **equa**BI·LITY n., **e·quab**LY[2] adv. [f. L *aequabilis* (as EQUATE, -BLE)]

ē·qual[1], a. & n. The same in number, size, value, degree, &c. (*to, with,* or abs.), as *twice three is e. to six, the totals are e., talks French & Dutch with e. ease, the two are e. in ability*; having strength, courage, ability, &c., adequate *to* (*the occasion, a cup of tea, doing,* &c.); uniform in operation &c., as *e. laws*; evenly balanced (fight &c.); (n.) person e. to another in rank &c., as *mix with your ee.*, or in power &c., as *he has no e.*; (n. pl.) e. things, as *if ee. be added to ee.* [f. L *aequalis* (*aequus* even, see -AL)]

e·qual[2], v.t. (-ll-). Be equal to (person, thing, *in* quality, number, &c.). [f. prec.]

equa·lity (-ŏl-), n. Condition of being equal (*between* two or more; *with* person &c. *in* quality &c.; usu. abs.); *is on an e. with,* is on equal terms with. [f. OF *équalité* f. L *aequalitatem* (as EQUAL[1], see -TY)]

e·qualize, v.t. & i. Make (thing &c.) equal (*to, with*); (Footb. &c.) bring score to equality with opponent's. Hence **equaliz**A·TION n. [-IZE]

e·qually, adv. In an equal degree; in equal shares; uniformly. [-LY[2]]

ēquani·mity, n. Evenness of mind or temper; composure; resignation. [f. F *équanimité* f. L *aequanimitatem* f. *aequanimis* (*aequus* even + *animus* mind), see -TY]

equa·te, v.t. State equality of (thing *to, with,* another); treat as equivalent. [f. L *aequare* (*aequus* equal), see -ATE[3]]

equa·tion, n. Making equal, balancing, (of demand & supply &c.); (amount or process of) compensation for inaccuracy, as (Astr.) *personal e.*, allowance for individual slowness in noting phenomena (also fig.), *e.* (difference between mean & apparent places) *of the equinoxes*; (Math.) formula affirming equivalence of two expressions connected by the sign =. Hence **equa·tion**AL a., **equa·tional**LY[2] adv. [f. L *aequatio* (as prec., see -ATION)]

equa·tor, n. A great circle of the earth, equidistant from the poles; = EQUINOCTIAL; *magnetic e.*, ACLINIC line. [LL (as prec., -OR[2])]

ēquator·ial, a. Of, near, the equator; *e. telescope* (attached to axle revolving in direction parallel to plane of equator). Hence **equator·ial**LY[2] adv. [-IAL]

ĕ·querry (*or* ĭkwĕ·rĭ), n. Officer of prince or noble charged with care of horses; officer of British royal household. [f. F *écurie* f. med.L *scuria* stable f. OHG *scûr* shed; confused in E with L *equus* horse]

eque·strian, a. & n. Of horse-riding; *e. statue* (of person on horse); (Rom. Ant.) of the order of Equites or Knights; (n.) rider, performer, on horseback. [f. L *equestris* (*eques* horseman f. *equus* horse) + -AN]

equi- in comb. = L *aequus* equal, as *-angular*, having equal angles.

ēquidi·stant, a. Separated by equal distance(s). [f. F *équidistant* f. LL *aequidistantem* (see EQUI- & DISTANT)]

ēquilă·teral, a. Having all the sides equal. [f. LL *aequilateralis* (see EQUI- & LATERAL]

ēquilī·brate, v.t. & i. Cause (two things) to balance; balance (t. & i.); counterpoise. Hence **equilibr**A·TION n. [f. EQUI- + L *libra* balance + -ATE[3]]

equi·librist, n. Rope-walker, acrobat. [f. F *équilibriste* (*équilibre* EQUILIBRIUM)]

ēquili·brium, n. State of balance (lit. & fig.); *a body in stable e.* (tending to recover e. after disturbance); neutrality of judgement &c. [L (EQUI-, *libra* balance)]

ēquimu·ltiple, n. (usu. pl.). Number having a common factor with another. [EQUI-]

ĕ·quine, a. Of, like, a horse. [f. L *equinus* (*equus* horse, see -INE[1])]

ĕquino·ctial, a. & n. Of equal day & night; *e. line,* circle of celestial sphere whose plane is perpendicular to earth's axis; happening at or near time of equinox, as *e. gales*; at, near, the (terrestrial) equator; (n.) e. line, (pl.) e. gales. [f. L *aequinoctialis* (as foll., see -AL)]

ĕ·quinox, n. Time at which sun crosses equator & day & night are equal (*vernal e.*, March 20; *autumnal e.*, Sep. 22 or 23); (pl.) two points at which sun crosses equator; PRECESSION *of ee.* [f. L *aequinoctium* (*nox -ctis* night, EQUI-)]

equi·p, v.t. (-pp-). Furnish (ship, army, person, *with* requisites); provide (one*self* &c.) for journey &c. Hence **equi·p**MENT n. [f. F *équiper, esq-*, prob. f. ON *skipa* man (ship) f. *skip* SHIP]

ĕ·quipage, n. Requisites for an undertaking; outfit for journey &c.; carriage & horses with attendants. [f. F *équipage* (as prec., -AGE)]

ĕ·quipoise, n., & v.t. Equilibrium (often fig.); counterbalancing thing; (v.t.) counterbalance, hold (mind) in suspense. [EQUI-]

ēquipo·llent, a. & n. Equal in power, force, &c.; practically equivalent; (n.) e. thing. So **equipo·ll**ENCE, -ENCY, nn. [f. OF *equipolent* f. L *aequipollentem* (EQUI-, *pollēre* be strong)]

ēquipo·nderate, v.t. Counterbalance. So **equipo·nder**ANT a. & n. [f. med.L *aequi*(*ponderare* weigh f. *pondus -eris* weight), see EQUI- & -ATE[3]]

ēquipote·ntial, a. (physics). In which the potential of a force is the same or constant at all points. [EQUI-]

ĕ·quitable, a. Fair, just, whence **e·quitable**NESS n., **e·quitab**LY[2] adv.; (of claims &c.) valid in equity as opposed to law. [f. F *équitable* (as EQUITY + -ABLE)]

ĕquita·tion, n. (usu. facet.). Riding on horse; horsemanship. [f. L *equitatio* f. *equitare* f. *eques -itis* horseman f. *equus* horse, see -ATION]

ĕ·quity, n. Fairness; recourse to principles of justice to correct or supplement law; system of law coexisting with and superseding common and statute law. [f. OF *equité* f. L *aequitatem* (*aequus* fair, see -TY)]

equi·valent, a. & n. Equal in value (*to*); (of words) meaning the same; (Chem.) equal in combining value (*to*); having the same result; corresponding; (n.) e. thing, amount, word, &c. So **equi·val**ENCE, -ENCY, nn. [f. LL *aequi*(*valēre* be worth), see EQUI- & -ENT]

equi·vocal, a. Of double meaning, ambiguous; of uncertain nature; *e. generation* (spontaneous); undecided; (of persons, character, &c.) questionable, suspicious. Hence **equivoca·l**ITY, **equi·vocal**NESS, nn., **equi·vocal**LY[2] adv. [f. LL *aequivocus* (EQUI-, *vocare* call), see -AL]

equi·vocate, v.i. Use ambiguous words to conceal the truth, prevaricate. Hence **equivoca·**TION, **equi·vocat**OR[2], nn. [f. LL *aequivocare* (as prec., see -ATE[3])]

ĕ·quivōque (-k), **-oke,** n. Pun; ambiguity. [f. LL *aequivocus* EQUIVOCAL]

-er[1], suf. forming esp. agent nn. f. nn. & vbs. Orig. = 'one who has to do with', f. OTeut. *-ārjoz* (cf. L *-arius* -ARY[1]); so E wds as *hatter* & (after *-w*) *bowyer, sawyer, lawyer*, & perh. on their anal. *collier, grazier*, &c.; also colloq. wds of action, as *header, out-&-outer*, and of number, as *fiver, tenner*; add *Londoner, foreigner*, &c. As many wds so formed correspond to vbs, *-er* took agent sense (*clothier* one connected with cloth, one who clothes), & can now be added to any vb not otherwise provided (*correspondent, translator*); *-or* (*-our, -ier*) & *-er* may coexist, with or without differentiation (*saviour, -er; assertor, -er*); some wds seem to double -er (*caterer, fruiterer, poulterer*); *-er* is sometimes used to anglicize L *-us* (*astronomer, geographer*, perh. *philosopher*). Meanings: (1) person, animal, that does something; (2) instrument, machine, occurrence, &c. (*poker, paper-cutter, deodorizer, eye-opener*); (3) person concerned with thing (*hatter, geographer*); (4) person belonging to place &c. (*Londoner, Britisher*; (5) slang distortion of word with other ending (*Rugger, Socker, footer*, Rugby, Association, football).

-er[2], suf. in nn. & adjj. f. OF, of various orig., esp.: (1) OF *-er* f. L *-arem* -AR[1] as *sampler.* (2) AF *-er* f. OF *-ier* f. L *-arius* -ARY[1], as *butler, carpenter, danger.* (3) OF *-eure* f. L *-aturam* = -URE, as *border.* (4) see -OR[2].

-er[3], suf. forming comparatives; now (exc. in poetry and mannered prose) only in adjj. of one syllable, or of two ending in *-y, -ly, -le, -er, -ow*, & a few others (esp. w. accent on last syllable; see -EST), & in advv., chiefly those identical with adjj., as *hard*; the vowel change seen in German &c. now remains only in *elder*, BETTER. [OE: (adj.) *-ra* f. OTeut. *-izon-* & *-ôzon-*; (adv.) *-or* f. OTeut. *-ôz*]

-er[4], suf. esp. in Law terms, as *cesser, disclaimer, misnomer, user*; also *dinner, supper.* Meaning: (single instance of) the vbl action, document effecting this. [F infin.]

-er[5], suf. forming frequent. vbs f. others (*wander, waver*, f. *wend, wave*) or on sound imitations (*twitter*); *batter, flicker, shimmer, slumber.*

ēr·a, n. System of chronology starting from some particular point of time, as *Christian e., e. of the* HEGIRA; historical or other period; date forming commencement of this. [f. LL *aera* number expressed in figures (pl. of *aes aeris* money, treated as fem. sing.)]

erādia·tion, n. Emission of rays. [E-]

erā·dicate, v.t. Tear up by roots; extirpate, get rid of. So **era·dic**ABLE a., **eradic**A·TION n. [f. L E(*radicare* f. *radix -icis* root), -ATE[3]]

era·se (-z), v.t. Rub out; obliterate. Hence **era·**SABLE a., **era·**SER[1](2), **era·s**URE (-zher), nn. [f. L E(*radere ras-* scrape)]

Era·stian, a. & n. (Adherent) of the supposed doctrines of Erastus, subordinating ecclesiastical to secular power. Hence **Era·stian**ISM(3) n., **Era·stian**IZE(3) v.t. & i. [f. *Erastus*, Heidelberg physician of 16th c., + -IAN]

ere (ār), prep. & conj. (poet., archaic). Before (of time); *e. long*, before long; *erewhile*, formerly. [OE *ǣr* (Du. *eer*, G *eher, ehe*) f. OTeut. *airiz* compar. of *air* adv. early]

E·rebus (ĕ-), n. (Gk myth.). Place of darkness between earth & Hades. [L, f. Gk *Erebos*]

ere·ct[1], a. Upright, not stooping, (lit. & fig.); vertical; (of hair &c.) set up, bristling. Hence **ere·ct**LY[2] adv., **ere·ct**NESS n. [f. L E(*rigere rect-* = *regere* direct) set up]

ere·ct[2], v.t. Raise, set upright, (*oneself*, body, &c.); build (lit. & fig.); form (persons, principles, &c.) *into* (class, system, &c.). [as prec.]

ere·ctīle, a. That can be erected; *e. tissue* in animals (capable of being distended & becoming rigid under excitement). [f. F *érectile* (as ERECT[1], see -IL)]

ere·ction, n. Erecting; building, structure, (lit. & fig.). [f. LL *erectio* (as prec., see -ION)]

ere·ctor, n. Person, thing, that erects, as *e.-muscle*. [-OR[2]]

ĕ·rĕmīte, n. Hermit (esp. of Christian solitaries from 3rd c. onwards). Hence **eremi·t**IC(AL) aa. [f. LL as HERMIT]

ĕ·rethism, n. (path.). Abnormal excitement (of organ or tissue, fig. of mind). [f. F *éréthisme* f. Gk *erethismos* (*erethizō* irritate, see -ISM)]

erg, er·gon, n. (physics). Work done by a force that acting for one second on mass of one gramme produces velocity of one centimetre per second. [f. Gk *ergon* work]

ergato·cracy, n. Rule of the workers. [Gk *ergatēs* worker, -O-, -CRACY]

er·go, adv. (usu. facet.). Therefore. [L]

er·got (-ot), n. Disease of rye &c. caused by fungus; diseased rye seed as medicine. [F, f. OF *argot* cock's spur, f. appearance produced]

er·gotism, n. = prec.; disease produced by bread made from flour affected by this. [-ISM]

E·rin (ĕ-), n. (Ancient name of) Ireland.

eri·stic, a. & n. (Art) of disputation; (of argument or arguer) aimed or aiming at victory rather than truth. [f. Gk *eristikos* (*erizō* f. *eris* strife, see -IC)]

er·mīne, n. Animal of weasel tribe, whose fur is brown in summer & white (except black tail-tip) in winter; its fur, used in robes of judges & peers (often poet. as emblem of purity), whence **er·min**ED[2] (-ĭnd) a.; (Herald.) white marked with black spots. [f. OF *(h)ermine* (Prov. *ermini*), etym. dub.]

-ern, suf. in *northern* &c. f. OTeut. *-rônjo-* (*-ro-* + *-ônjo-* = L *-aneus*).

erne, n. Golden Eagle; Sea-Eagle. [OE *earn* (Du. *arend*) f. OTeut. *arnuz*, cf. Gk *ornis* bird]

ēro·de, v.t. (Of acids, currents, &c.) gnaw away, destroy gradually, wear out. So **ero·**SION (-zhn) n., **ero·**SIVE (-s-) a. [f. F *éroder* f. L E(*rodere ros-* gnaw)]

ĕrŏ·tic, a. & n. Of love, amatory; (n.) e. poem. [f. Gk *erōtikos* (*erōs -ōtos* sexual love, see -IC)]

ĕrō·tomā·nia, n. (path.). Melancholy, madness, arising from love. [f. Gk *erōs* (as prec.) + -MANIA]

err (er), v.i. (part. & vbl n. pron. er·ĭng). Make mistakes; (of statements &c.) be incorrect; sin. [f. F *errer* f. L *errare*]

ĕ·rrand, n. Short journey on which an inferior is sent to carry message &c., as *run, go, (on) ee., e.-boy*; object of journey; purpose. [OE *ǣrende*, cf. Da. *ærinde*, etym. dub.]

ĕ·rrant, a. & n. Roaming in quest of adventure, esp. *knight-e.*; itinerant; erring, deviating from correct standard; whence **e·rr**ANCY n.; (n.) knight-e. [F (1) f. OF *errer, esrer, edrer*, f. vulg. L *iterare* (*iter* journey), (2) as ERR; see -ANT]

e·rrantry, n. Condition, conduct, notions, of a knight-errant. [-RY]

ĕrră·tic, a. Uncertain in movement; (of diseases) moving from one part to another; irregular in conduct, habit, opinion; (Geol.) *e. blocks*, stray masses foreign to surrounding strata. Hence **erra·t**ICALLY adv. [f. L *erraticus* (as ERR, see -ATIC]

ĕrrā·tum, n. (pl. *-ta*). Error in printing or writing, esp. (pl.) errors noted in list attached to book. [L, neut. p.p. as prec.]

ĕrrō·neous, a. Mistaken, incorrect. Hence **erro·neous**LY[2] adv., **erro·neous**NESS n. [f. L *erroneus* (*erro -onis* vagabond, as ERR) + -OUS]

ĕ·rror, n. Mistake, as *make, commit, an e.*, CLERICAL *e.*; condition of erring in opinion; wrong opinion; *in e.*, mistaken(ly), by mistake; *e. of a planet*, difference between its observed & calculated positions; (Law) *writ of e.* (to procure reversal of judgement on ground of e.); transgression.

Hence **e·rror**LESS n. [OF, f. L *errorem* (as ERR, -OR[1])]

Erse, a. & n. Highland Gaelic (dialect); (vulg.) Irish. [early Sc. form of *Irish*]

erst, adv. (archaic). (Also *erstwhile*) formerly, of old. [OE *ǣrest* superl. of *ǣr*, see ERE]

ĕrube·scent, a. Reddening, blushing. [f. L E(*rubescere* incept. of *rubēre*), see -ENT]

ēructa·tion, n. Belching (lit. & fig., esp. of volcano). [f. L *eructatio* (E*ructare*, see -ATION)]

ĕ·rudite, a. (Of persons & writings) learned. Hence or cogn. **e·rudite**LY[2] adv., **erudi·tion** n. [f. L E*rudire -it-* train (*rudis* rude)]

eru·pt, v.i. (Of teeth) break through gums; (of volcano) break out. [f. L E(*rumpere rupt-* break)]

eru·ption, n. Outbreak (of volcano, whence **eru·ption**AL a.; also of geyser, disease, war, passion, mirth, wit); (Path.) breaking out (of rash, pimples, &c.); (of teeth) breaking through gums. [f. L *eruptio* (as prec., see -ION)]

eru·ptive, a. Bursting forth; tending to burst forth; of, formed by, forced up by, volcanic eruption. Hence **eru·ptive**LY[2] adv., **eru·ptive**NESS, **erupti·**VITY, nn. [f. F *éruptif, -ive* (as ERUPT, see -IVE)]

-ery, -ry, suf. forming nouns, orig. after F *-erie*: (a) f. com.-Rom. *-aria* = L *-ario-* (F *-ier, -er*) + *-ia* -Y[1]; F wds in *-ier* usu. denote person having some occupation, wds in *-erie* the class of goods he deals in, as *draperie*, his employment, as *archerie*, his place of work, as *boulangerie*; *-erie* was also used without existing wd in *-ier*, as *soierie* (*soie*) silk goods, *niaiserie* (*niais*) foolishness. (b) f. OF *-ere, -eor* (mod. F *-eur*) f. L *-ator* + *-ie*. On anal. of wds thus formed, *-erie* was added to vb stems direct, w. sense class of actions (*tromperie* deceit), occupation (*confiserie* confectioner's business), place of this (*brasserie* brewery). Many E wds are f. F; others are formed on nn. in *-er* (*bakery, fishery, pottery*), or on others (*knavery, slavery, popery*). Meanings: (1) class of goods (*drapery*); (2) employment or condition (*archery, dupery*); (3) place of work or cultivation or breeding (*brewery, vinery, piggery*); (4) conduct (*foolery*); (5) all that has to do with (*popery*), things of the nature of.

ĕrȳsĭ·pelas, n. (Also *St Anthony's fire, the rose*) local febrile disease producing deep red colour on skin. [Gk *erusipelas*, etym. dub.]

ĕrȳthē·ma, n. Superficial inflammation of the skin in patches. [f. Gk *eruthēma* f. *eruthainō* be red (*eruthros*)]

-es, old genit. termination used to give adv. force; appearing as *-s* (*needs*), *-ce* (*once*), & (by confus. w. superl.) *-st* (*against*); also in the emphatic absolute forms *ours, yours, hers*, &c. Often on false anal., as *betimes, besides, nowadays*.

escalā·de, n. Scaling of walls with ladders. [F, f. Sp. *escalada* f. med. L *scalare* (*scala* ladder), see -ADE]

e·scalator, n. Moving staircase for carrying passengers up or down. [as ESCALADE, -OR[2]]

escallō·nia, n. S.-Amer. genus of flowering shrubs. [*Escallon*, discoverer, -IA[1]]

esca·llop. See SCALLOP.

escapa·de, n. Breaking loose from restraint; flighty piece of conduct. [F, f. Sp. *escapada* (as ESCAPE[2], see -ADE)]

esca·pe[1], n. Act of escaping; fact of having escaped (*a narrow, hairbreadth, e.*); leakage (of gas &c.); garden plant growing wild; = FIRE-*e.*; *e.-pipe, -valve* (for e. of steam or water); *e.-shaft* (for e. of miners when other shaft is blocked). [f. foll.]

esca·pe[2], v.i. & t. Get free (*from* prison, person, &c.); (of steam, fluids, &c.) find a way out; get off safely, go unpunished; (trans.) get clear away from (person, his grasp, &c.), avoid (unpleasant thing, do*ing*); elude notice or recollection of, as *his name had escaped me*; (of words) issue unawares from (person, his lips). [f. OF *eschaper*, ONF *escaper* (Sp. *escapar*), f. LL EX(*cappare* f. *cappa* cloak)]

esca·pement, n. Outlet; (of watch or clock) mechanism connecting motive power & regulator. [-MENT]

escar·p, n., & v.t. Steep bank immediately in front of & below rampart; similar natural formation; (v.t.) cut into form of e., so **escar·p**MENT n. [(vb f. F *escarper*) f. F *escarpe* f. It. *scarpa* SCARP]

-escent, suf. forming adjj. f. L part. of inceptive vbs (*-escens -ntis*), as *effervescent*, & thence in wds usu. describing play of colour, as *iridescent, opalescent*, or merely adjectival, as *alkalescent*.

eschalo·t (ĕsh-). See SHALLOT.

eschato·logy (ĕsk-), n. Doctrine of death, judgement, heaven, & hell. Hence **eschatolo·gic**AL a. [f. Gk *eskhatos* last + -LOGY]

eschea·t[1] (ĕstsh-), n. Lapsing of property to crown or lord of manor on owner's dying intestate without heirs; property so lapsing. [f. OF *eschete* f. *escheoir* f. LL EX(*cadere* fall)]

eschea·t[2], v.t. & i. Confiscate; hand over (property) as an escheat (*to* person, *into* his hands); revert by escheat (*to* or abs.). [prec.]

eschew (ĕstshōō·), v.t. Avoid, abstain from, (action, conduct, kind of food, &c.). [f. OF *eschiver* f. com.-Rom. *skivare*, cf. G *scheuen* & SHY[1]]

eschscho·ltzia (ĭshŏl-), n. A plant with usu. yellow flowers, Noah's nightcap. [*Eschscholtz*, explorer, -IA[1]]

esclandre (F), n. Scandal; disturbance.

e·scort[1], n. Body of armed men acting as guard to persons, baggage, &c.; person(s) accompanying another on journey for protection or guidance, or for courtesy's sake. [f. F *escorte* f. It. *scorta* f. *scorgere* conduct f. LL *EX(CORrigere f. *regere* direct)]

escor·t², v.t. Act as escort to. [f. prec.]

ēscri·be, v.t. (math.). Describe (circle) so as to touch one side of triangle exteriorly & the other two produced. [f. E- + L *scribere* write]

escritoire (-twar·r), n. Writing-desk with drawers &c. for stationery. [F (now *éc-*), f. LL *scriptorium* (as prec., see -ORY)]

ĕ·sculent, a. & n. (Thing) fit for food. [f. L *esculentus* (*esca* food, see -LENT)]

escu·tcheon (-tshn), n. Shield with armorial bearings; *a blot on his e.* (stain on reputation); middle of ship's stern where name is placed; pivoted keyhole-cover. [f. ONF *escuchon* f. LL **scutionem* (L *scutum* shield, see -ION)]

-ese, suf. forming adjj. (& nn.), f. OF *-eis* = It. *-ese* f. L *-ensis* local suf. (usu. now *-ian*, as *Atheniensis* Athenian); applied to some foreign countries & towns (*Japanese, Milanese*), either as adj. or meaning 'inhabitant' (pl. *-ese*) or 'language'; also used spec. (adj. or n.) of diction of mannered writers (*Carlylese*), as though a non-English language.

e·skar, n. (geol.). Mound of post-glacial gravel in Irish river valleys. [f. Ir. *eiscir*]

Eskimo·, -quimau· (-kĭmō), n. (pl. *-oes, -aux*, pr. -mōz). Member of a race in N. America.

ĕsotĕ·ric, a. (Of philosophical doctrines &c.) meant only for the initiated; (of disciples) initiated; private, confidential. Hence **esote·ric**AL a., **esote·rical**LY² adv. [f. Gk *esōterikos* (*esōterō* compar. of *esō* within, see -IC)]

espagnole·tte (-ănyolĕt), n. Fastening of French window. [F, dim. of *espagnol* Spanish]

espă·lier, n. Lattice-work on which trees or shrubs are trained; tree so trained. [F, f. It. *spalliera* (*spalla* shoulder)]

espar·to, n. (Also *e. grass*) kinds of grass imported from Spain for paper-making. [Sp., f. L f. Gk *sparton* rope of the plant *spartos*]

espĕ·cial (-shl), a. Pre-eminent, exceptional, as *my e. friend, thing of e. importance*; particular (opp. to *ordinary*, cf. SPECIAL); belonging chiefly to one case (*for your e. benefit*). Hence **espe·cial**LY² adv. [OF, f. L as SPECIAL]

Espera·nto, n. An artificial language designed as a medium for persons of all nations.

espi·al, n. Acting as a spy; watching; espying. [f. OF *espiaille*, as ESPY, see -AL(2)]

espièglerie (F), n. Roguishness.

e·spionage (-ĭj, -ah·zh), n. Practice of spying or using spies. [f. F *espionnage* f. *espion* spy f. It. *spione* (of Teut. orig., cf. ESPY), see -AGE]

esplana·de, n. Level piece of ground, esp. one used for public promenade; level space separating citadel of fortress from town. [F, f. Sp. *esplanada* f. *esplanar* f. L EX*planare* make level (*planus*), see -ADE]

espou·sal (-zl), n. (archaic). (Usu. pl.) marriage or betrothal; (fig.) espousing *of* (a cause &c.). [f. OF *espousailles* f. L *sponsalia* neut. pl. (*sponsus* p.p. as foll., see -AL)]

espou·se (-owz), v.t. (Usu. of man) marry; give (woman) in marriage (*to*); adopt, support, (doctrine, cause, &c.). [f. OF *espouser* f. L *sponsare* (*sponsus* p.p. of *spondēre* betroth)]

espressi·vo (-ēvō), adv. (mus.). With expression. [It.]

esprit (ĕsprē·), n. Sprightliness; wit; *e. de corps* (de kōr), regard for honour & interests of body one belongs to; *e. fort* (*pron.* for), strong-minded person, free-thinker. [F, f. L as SPIRIT]

espy·, v.t. Catch sight of; detect (flaw &c.). [f. OF *espier* ult. f. OHG *spehôn* SPY]

-esque, suf. forming adjj., = F *-esque* f. It. *-esco* f. med. L *-iscus* in Teut. wds; cf. OHG *-isc* (mod. *-isch*) = -ISH¹; meaning 'after the manner of', as *arabesque, Dantesque, burlesque.*

Esquimau. See ESKIMO.

esquire·, n. Title appended to name of one regarded as gentleman by birth, position, or education, esp. in address of letter (abbr. *Esq.*); (archaic) = SQUIRE. [f. OF *esquier* f. L *scutarius* shield-bearer (*scutum* shield, -ARY¹)]

ess, n. S(-shaped thing); COLLAR¹ *of ee.*

-ess¹, suf. forming female nn. f. F (*countess, lioness*) or on E wds (*goddess*); in 15th c. the OE fem. *-ster* (now only in *spinster*) came to be regarded as masculine, & could take fem. *-ess* (*seamstress*); agent nn. in *-ter, -tor*, regularly have *-tress* (*chantress*); other exx. are *authoress* &c. (*author* &c. now preferred), *giantess, quakeress*; *governess* (formed on vb) is irreg., perh. on anal. of *sorceress* (formed on old *sorcer* not on *sorcerer*, which has double agent suf.); euphony leads to same clipping in *adventuress, murderess*; *-tress* is now recognized angliciz. of F *-trice* (L *-trix -tricis*), though of diff. orig. [f. F *-esse* f. LL f. Gk *-issa*]

-ess², suf. in abstr. nn. f. adjj., as *duress, largess*; *riches, laches*, are exx., mistaken for pl. [ME & OF *-ęsse* = It. *-ezza* f. L *-itia* -ICE]

e·ssay¹, n. Attempt (*at*); a literary composition (usu. prose & short) on any subject, whence **e·ssay**IST(3) n. [f. OF *essai* = ASSAY¹]

essay·², v.t. & i. Try, test, (person, thing); attempt (task, *to* do, or abs.). [refash. f. ASSAY² on F *essayer*]

e·ssence, n. An existence or entity (spiritual or immaterial); absolute being, reality underlying phenomena; all that makes a thing what it is; intrinsic nature; indispensable quality or element; extract obtained by distillation &c. (lit. & fig.); perfume, scent, whence **e·ssenc**ED[2] a. [F, f. L *essentia* f. **essens -ntis* fictitious part. of *esse* be, repr. Gk *ousia*]

Esse·ne, n. Member of an ancient Jewish sect, of mystical tenets & coenobitical life. [f. L f. Gk *Essēnos*, etym. dub.]

esse·ntial (-shl), a. & n. Of, constituting, a thing's essence; indispensable (*to*); *e. proposition*, one that predicates of a subject what is implied in its definition; *e. character* (of species, genus, &c.), marks that distinguish it from others included with it in next superior division; *e. harmony* (belonging to one particular key); *e. oil*, volatile oil, marked by characteristic odour &c.; (n.) indispensable element. Hence **essentia·l**ITY n., **esse·ntial**LY[2] adv. [f. LL *essentialis* (as ESSENCE, -AL)]

-est, suf. forming superl. adjj. & advv. (& FIRST, LAST); for limits of use see -ER[3], but many adjj. can bear *-est* though not *-er*, as *awkward, barren, fragile, loyal, legible*, & many in *-id*, as *limpid*; in poetry & mannered prose *-est* is used w. almost any adj., & appended to advv. in *-ly*, as *quickliest*. [OE *-ost, -ust, -ast*, f. OTeut. *-ôsto-*, & OE *-est, -st*, f. OTeut. *-isto-* (compar. *-ôz-, -iz-*, + Aryan *-to-*), cf. Gk *-isto-*; *-iz-* required vowel change, now only in *eldest*, BEST]

estă·blish, v.t. Set up (government, house of business, &c.) on permanent basis; settle (person, one*self, in* office &c.); secure permanent acceptance for (custom, precedent, belief, &c.); place beyond dispute (fact, *that*); make (church) legally national. [f. OF *establir* (st. *-iss-*, see ISH[2]) f. L *stabilire* (as STABLE a.)]

esta·blishment, n. Establishing; *Church E., the E.*, church system established by law; organized body of men maintained for a purpose, as army, navy, civil service; *peace, war, e.*, reduced, increased, army in time of peace, war; staff of servants &c.; public institution, house of business; household, as *separate e.* (of man maintaining paramour). [-MENT]

establishmentăr·ian, a. & n. (Person) adhering to, advocating the principle of, an established church. [-ARIAN]

estaminet (F), n. French café selling wine, beer, & coffee, or cottage with barroom.

esta·te, n. Order, class, forming part of body politic & sharing in government; *the Three Ee.* (in England), Lords Spiritual, Lords Temporal, Commons; *third e.*, (usu.) French bourgeoisie before Revolution; (facet.) *fourth e.*, the press; person's interest in landed property (*real e.*) or movables (*personal e.*), whence **esta·t**ED[2] a.; a landed property (*e. agent*, steward of e., go-between in sales of houses & land); one's collective assets & liabilities; (archaic) condition, as *the holy e. of matrimony*. [f. OF *estat* f. L as STATE]

estee·m, v.t., & n. Think highly of; consider, as *I shall e. it (as) a favour*; (n.) favourable opinion, regard, respect. [(n. f. vb) f. OF *estimer* f. L as ESTIMATE[2]]

e·ster, n. (chem.). Any of a class of compounds formed by the condensation of an alcohol & an acid with elimination of water. [arbitrary]

e·stimable, a. Worthy of esteem. [F, f. L *aestimabilis* (as prec., see -BLE)]

e·stimate[1] (-*at*), n. Approximate judgement (of number, amount, &c.); quantity assigned by this; *the Ee.*, forecasts of national expenditure, presented annually to parliament; contractor's statement of sum for which he will undertake specified work; judgement of character or qualities. [f. L *aestimatus -ūs* (as foll.)]

e·stimāte[2], v.t. Form an estimate of; fix (number &c.) by estimate *at* (so much); form an opinion of. So **e·stimat**IVE a., **e·stimat**OR[2] n. [f. L *aestimare*, see -ATE[3]]

estima·tion, n. Judgement of worth, as *in my e.*; esteem, as *hold in e., be in e.* [f. OF *estimacion* f. L *aestimationem* (as prec., see -ATION)]

estival &c. See **aest-.**

esto·p, v.t. (law) (-pp-). Bar, preclude, (*from* thing, *from* doing). Hence **esto·p**PAGE n. [f. OF *estoper* (*estoupe* f. L *stuppa* tow)]

esto·ppel, n. (legal). The being precluded from a course by previous action of one's own. [f. OF *estoupail* bung]

estra·de (-ahd), n. Raised platform, dais. [F, f. Sp. *estrado* f. L *stratum* neut. p.p. of *sternere* spread (with carpets)]

estrā·nge, v.t. Alienate (person) in feeling (*from* another). Hence **estra·nge**MENT n. [f. OF *estranger* f. L *extraneare* (as STRANGE)]

estrea·t, v.t. (law). Take out record of (fine, bail, &c.) & return it to Court of Exchequer to be prosecuted. [f. *estreat* n. record f. OF *estraite* fem. p.p. of *estraire* extract f. L EX(*trahere tract-* draw)]

e·stuary, n. Tidal mouth of large river. Hence **e·stuar**INE[1] a. [f. L *aestuarium* neut. adj. as n. (*aestus -ūs* tide, see -ARY[1])]

esur·ient, a. (facet.). Hungry; needy and greedy. So **esur·**IENCE, -ENCY, nn. [f. L *esurire*, desiderative f. *edere es-* eat]

-et[1], suf. forming (orig.) dimm., many not now realized as such; mostly in ME adoptions f. F (*bullet, hatchet, sonnet*); double dim. -LET (F *-el* + *-et*) is living suf. [OF *-et* & *-ette* (dist. only in mod. E) = It. *-etto, -etta*, etym. dub.]

-et[2], **-ete,** suf. in agent nn. f. Gk, *-et* in older or familiar wds, as *poet, comet, anchoret*, *-ete* in newer or learned ones, as *athlete, aesthete, exegete*. [f. Gk *-ētēs* (*-tēs* of agent n. as appended esp. to vbs in *-eō, -aō*); *epithet, paraclete,* are not exx.; *diabetes* retains full form]

ē·ta, n. Greek letter (Η, η) = ē (cf. EPSILON). [Gk]

e·tacism (ā-), n. Pronunciation of Gk ē as English ā (cf. ITACISM). [f. Gk *ēta* letter *ē*, -ISM]

état-major (F), n. (mil.). Staff, staff-office.

et cē·tera, etcē·tera, phr. & n. (pl. *-as*). (Abbr. *etc., &c.*) & the rest, & so on, as *I remain yours etc.*; (n. pl.) extras, sundries. [L]

etch, v.t. & i. Reproduce (pictures &c.), portray (subject), by engraving metal-plate &c. by means of acids or corrosives, esp. for purpose of printing copies; (intr.) practise this art. [f. Du. *etsen* f. G *ätzen* etch f. OHG *ezjan* cause to eat or be eaten f. OTeut. *atjan* make EAT]

e·tching, n. In vbl senses, esp. copy from etched plate; *e.-needle,* used in e. [-ING[1]]

eter·nal, a. That always (has existed &) will exist, as *e. life, punishment*; *the E.,* God; *e.* CITY; (colloq.) incessant, too frequent, as *these e. bickerings*; *the e. triangle,* two males & a female or *vice versa.* Hence or cogn. **eter·n(al)**IZE(3) vv.t., **eter·nal**LY[2] adv. [OF, f. LL *aeternalis* (*aeternus* for *aeviternus* f. *aevum* age, see -AL)]

eter·nity, n. Being eternal; immortal fame; (pl.) eternal truths; infinite time, esp. future; the future life. [f. F *éternité* f. L *aeternitatem* (*aeternus,* see prec. & -TY)]

Etē·sian, a. *E. winds* (blowing annually in Mediterranean from N.W. for about 40 days in summer). [f. L f. Gk *etēsios* (*etos* year) + -AN]

-eth, suf. See -TH[2].

ē·ther, n. Clear sky, upper regions beyond clouds; (Physics) subtle elastic fluid permeating space & filling interstices between particles of air & other matter, medium through which light-waves are propagated, whence **e·ther**IC a.; (Chem.) colourless light volatile liquid produced by action of sulphuric acid & other acids on alcohol, an anaesthetic. [f. L f. Gk *aithēr* f. root of *aithō* burn, shine]

ēthēr·eal, -ial, a. Light, airy; heavenly; of unearthly delicacy of substance, character, or appearance, whence **ethe-rea·l**ITY, **etherealiz**A·TION, nn., **ether·-eal**IZE(3) v.t., **ether·eal**LY[2] adv.; (Physics, Chem.) of, like, ETHER, so **e·theri**FICA·TION n., **e·theri**FY v.t.; *e. oil,* essential or volatile oil. [f. L (*-eus, -ius*) f. Gk *aitherios* (as prec.) + -AL]

ē·therize, v.t. Put (patient) under influence of ether. Hence **etheriz**A·TION n. [-IZE]

ĕ·thic, a. & n. (Now usu. *ethical*) relating to morals, treating of moral questions; *e. dative* (of person indirectly interested in fact stated); (n. pl., & rarely sing.) science of morals, treatise on this, moral principles, rules of conduct, whole field of moral science. Hence **e·thic**AL a., **e·thical**LY[2] adv., **e·thic**IZE(3) v.t. [f. L f. Gk *ēthikos* (ETHOS, -IC)]

Ethiō·pian (ē-), a. & n. (Native) of Ethiopia, esp. (Anthropol.) as epithet of one of the races into which human species is divided. [-AN]

e·thnic, -ical, aa. Pertaining to race, ethnological, whence **e·thnical**LY[2] adv.; (*-ic*) gentile, heathen, whence **e·thnic**ISM(2) n. [f. Gk *ethnikos* (*ethnos* nation, see -IC)]

ethno·graphy, n. Scientific description of races of men. So **ethno·**GRAPHER n., **ethnogra·phic**(AL) aa., **ethnogra·phical**LY[2] adv. [f. Gk *ethnos* nation + -GRAPHY]

ethno·logy, n. Science of races & their relations to one another & characteristics. So **ethnolo·gic**(AL) aa. (*-ic frontier,* corresponding to a division of races), **ethnolo·gical**LY[2] adv., **ethno·**LOGIST n. [as prec. + -LOGY]

et hoc gĕ·nus ŏ·mne (-ĭ). And all that kind of thing (often as ornamental substitute for *et cetera*). [L]

etho·logy, n. Science of character-formation. Hence **etholo·gic**AL a. [f. L f. Gk *ēthologia* (ETHOS, see -LOGY)]

ē·thos, n. Characteristic spirit of community, people, or system. [Gk (*ē-*) = character, nature, disposition]

ĕ·thyl, n. (chem.). Base of ordinary alcohol, common ether, & acetic acid. [f. ETHER, -YL]

-etic, suf. of adjj. & nn. = Gk agent suf. *-ĕt-* or *-ēt-* + -IC, in wds f. Gk or on Gk models, as *emetic* (Gk *emĕtikos*), *ascetic* (Gk *askētikos*).

ē·tiolate, v.t. Make (plant) pale by excluding light; give sickly hue to (person). Hence **etiol**A·TION n. [f. F *étioler* f. Norm. *étieuler* make into haulm (*éteule* f. L *stipula* straw)]

ētiology. See AETIOLOGY.

ĕtique·tte (-kĕt), n. Conventional rules of personal behaviour in polite society; ceremonial of court; unwritten code restricting professional men in what concerns interests of their brethren or dignity of their profession, esp. *medical, legal, e.* [f. F *étiquette* TICKET, etiquette]

e·tna, n. Vessel for heating small quantity of liquid by burning spirit. [f. the volcano]

E·ton (ē-), n. *E. collar* (broad, stiff, worn outside coat-collar); *E. crop,* cutting of woman's hair short like boy's; *E. jacket,* boy's short coat reaching only to waist. [f. *Eton* College]

Etru·scan, a. & n. (Native) of ancient Etruria. [f. L *Etruscus* + -AN]

et seqq., sequentes, -tia, (in reference to books &c.). And the words, pages, &c., that follow. [L]

-ette, suf. forming dim. nn. (rarely adjj.), repr. OF *-ette,* the fem. corresp. to -ET. Older adoptions f. F now have *-et, -ette* appearing chiefly in wds introduced since 17th c., as *cigarette, etiquette.* (2) A mod. commerc. use, =' sham ', is seen in *leatherette, Brusselette* (carpet).

ĕtui· (-wē), **etwee·**, n. Small case for needles, tooth-picks, &c. [f. F *étui*, etym. dub.]

etymo·logize, v.t. & i. Give, trace, the etymology of; suggest etymology for; study etymology. [f. LL *etymologizare* (as foll., -IZE)]

etymo·logy, n. Account of, facts relating to, formation & meaning of word; branch of linguistic science concerned with this; part of grammar treating of individual words & their formation & inflexions. Hence or cogn. **etymo·**LOGER, **etymo·lo**GIST, nn., **etymolo·gic**(AL) aa., **etymolo·gical**LY[2] adv. [f. OF *ethimologie* f. L f. Gk *etumologia* (as foll., -LOGY)]

ĕ·tymŏn, n. Primary word that gives rise to a derivative. [L, f. Gk *etumon* (neut. of *etumos* true) literal sense, original form, of a word]

eu- in comb. = Gk *eu* well, cf. DYS-.

eucaly·ptus, n. Genus of plants including Australian Gum tree; *e. oil*, a disinfectant. [f. EU- + Gk *kaluptos* covered (*kaluptō*), flower being protected by cap]

eu·charis (ūk-), n. (Also *e. lily*) S.-Amer. bulbous plant with white bell-shaped flowers. [Gk EU(*kharis* grace) pleasing]

eu·charist (ūk-), n. Lord's Supper; consecrated elements, esp. the bread, as *give, receive, the E.* Hence **euchari·st**IC(AL) aa. [f. OF *eucariste* f. LL f. Gk *eukharistia* f. EU(*kharistos* f. *kharizomai* offer willingly) grateful]

euchlor·ine, n. Bright yellow-green compound gas discovered by Davy. [EU- + Gk *khlōros* on anal. of CHLORINE]

eu·chre (-ker), n., & v.t. American card game for 2, 3, or 4 persons; (v.t.) gain advantage over (opponent) by his failure to take three tricks at euchre (also fig.). [?]

Eu·clid, n. Alexandrian mathematician (c. 300 B.C.); his *Elements* or treatise on geometry, a copy of this; (pop.) geometry as a science or subject; (mod.) the geometry of ordinary experience, accepting E.'s axioms as indisputable (cf. RELATIVITY). Hence **Euclide·**AN a. [f. Gk *Eukleidēs*]

eud(a)e·monism, n. System of ethics basing moral obligation on tendency of actions to produce happiness. So **eude·mon**IST(2) n. [f. Gk EU(*daimōn* guardian genius) happy, -ISM]

eudio·meter, n. Instrument showing quantity of oxygen in air. So **eudiome·tric**(AL) aa., **eudiome·trical**LY[2] adv., **eudio·**METRY n. [f. Gk EU(*dios*, st. of *Zeus*, gen. *Dios*, god of the sky) clear + -METER]

eugĕ·nic (-j-), a. & n. Of the production of fine (esp. human) offspring; (n. pl.) science of this. So **eu·gen**IST(2) n., student of eugenics. [f. EU- + Gk *gen-* produce + -IC]

euhē·merism, n. Reference of myths to historical basis. So **euhē·mer**IST(2) n., **euhēmeri·st**IC a., **euhē·mer**IZE(4) v.t. & i. [f. *Euhemerus*, Sicilian author c. 316 B.C., + -ISM]

eu·logize, v.t. Extol, praise, in speech or writing. So **eu·log**IST(1) n., **eulogi·st**IC a., **eulogi·st**ICALLY adv. [f. foll. + -IZE]

eu·logy, n. Speech, writing, in praise of person &c., as *pronounce his e., pronounce a e. on him*; praise. [prob. f. med. L (also used as E) *eulogium* irreg. f. Gk EU(*logia* -LOGY)]

eu·nuch (-*uk*), n. Castrated male person, esp. one employed in harem, or (in Oriental courts & under Roman empire) employed in state affairs. [f. L f. Gk *eunoukhos* lit. bedchamber attendant (*eunē* bed + *okh-* st. of *ekhō* hold)]

euŏ·nymus, n. Genus of shrubs. [f. L f. Gk EU(*ōnumos* f. *onoma* name) of lucky name]

eupe·ptic, a. Of, having, good digestion. [f. Gk EU(*peptos* f. *pessō, peptō*, digest) + -IC]

eu·phemism (-fĭ-), n. Substitution of mild or vague expression for harsh or blunt one; expression thus substituted, as *' queer ' is a e. for ' mad '*. So **euphemi·st**IC a., **euphemi·st**ICALLY adv., **eu·phem**IZE(1, 2) v.t. & i. [f. Gk *euphēmismos* f. EU(*phēmos* f. *phēmē* speaking, fame), see -ISM]

euphō·nium, n. (mus.). Bass instrument of saxhorn family. [mod. L, f. Gk *euphōnos* see foll.]

eu·phony, n. Pleasing sound; quality of having this (usu. of words, phrases, &c.); tendency to phonetic change for ease of pronunciation. So **euphŏ·n**IC, **euphō·ni**OUS, aa., **euphŏ·n**ICALLY, **euphō·nious**LY[2], advv., **eu·phon**IZE(3) v.t. [f. F *euphonie* f. Gk *euphōnia* f. EU*phōnos* (*phōnē* sound)]

eu·phrasy, n. = EYE*bright*. [f. med. L f. Gk *euphrasia* cheerfulness f. EU*phrainō* gladden (*phrēn* mind)]

eu·phuism, n. Artificial or affected style of writing (prop., in imitation of Lyly's *Euphues*, 1580); high-flown style. So **eu·phu**IST n., **euphui·st**IC a., **euphui·st**ICALLY adv. [-ISM]

Eurā·sian (-shan), a. & n. (Person) of mixed European & Asiatic parentage; of Europe & Asia. [f. *Europe* + *Asia* + -AN]

eurē·ka, int. & n. (The exulting exclamation) ' I have (found) it ! ' (also as trade name). [f. Gk *heurēka* 1st pers. perf. of *heuriskō* find]

eurhy·thmic, a. In or of harmonious proportion (esp. in architecture). Hence **eurhy·thmics** n. pl., harmony of bodily movement, esp. as developed with the aid of music into a system used in education. [f. L f. Gk *eurūthmia* good rhythm (see EU-, RHYTHM) + -IC]

Europē·an, a. & n. (Native) of Europe;

happening in, extending over, Europe, as *a E. reputation.* Hence **Europe·an**ISM(2, 3, 4), **Europeaniz**A·TION, nn., **Europe·an**IZE(3) v.t. [f. F *européen* f. L *Europaeus* (L f. Gk *Eurōpē* Europe) + -AN]

Euter·pē, n. A Muse, goddess of music, whence **Euter·pe**AN a.; genus of palms. [Gk]

euthanā·sia (-z-, -s-), n. Gentle & easy death; bringing about of this, esp. in case of incurable & painful disease. [Gk (EU- + *thanatos* death)]

evă·cuate, v.t. Empty (esp. stomach or bodily organ *of* contents), whence **eva·cu**ANT(2) a. & n.; withdraw from (place; esp. of troops); discharge (excrement &c.; also fig.). So **evacu**A·TION n. [f. L E(*vacuare* f. *vacuus* empty)]

eva·de, v.t. Escape from, avoid, (attack, pursuit, designs, adversary, blow, obstacle, &c.); avoid doing (duty &c.), answering (question), yielding to (argument &c.); defeat intention of (law &c., esp. while complying with its letter); (of things) elude, baffle. Hence **eva·d**ABLE a. [f. F *évader* f. L E(*vadere vas-* go)]

evă·ginate, v.t. (physiol.). Turn (tubular organ) inside out. So **evagin**A·TION n. [f. L E(*vaginare* f. *vagina* sheath), see -ATE[3]]

evă·luate, v.t. Ascertain amount of; find numerical expression for. So **evalu**A·TION n. [f. F *évaluer* (*é-* EX-, VALUE)]

ĕvane·sce (-s), v.i. Fade out of sight; become effaced; disappear. [f. L E(*vanescere* VANISH)]

ĕvane·scent, a. (Of impression, appearance, &c.) quickly fading; (Math.) infinitesimal. Hence **evane·sc**ENCE n., **evane·scent**LY[2] adv. [f. F *évanescent* (as prec., see -ENT)]

eva·ngel (-j-), n. (archaic). The Gospel; any of the Four Gospels; doctrine, principle, (of politics &c.). [f. OF *evangi(l)le* f. eccl. L f. Gk EU(*aggelion* cf. ANGEL) fee for good news]

ĕvange·lic(al), aa. & nn. Of, according to, the teaching of the Gospel or the Christian religion; esp. (usu. *-ical*) of the Protestant school maintaining that the essence of the Gospel consists in doctrine of salvation by faith, good works & sacraments having no saving efficacy, whence **evange·lical**ISM(3) n.; (n.) member of this school. Hence **evange·lical**LY[2] adv. [f. LL f. eccl. Gk *euaggelikos* (as prec., see -IC, -AL)]

eva·ngelism, n. Preaching of the Gospel; = EVANGELICALISM. [-ISM]

eva·ngelist, n. One of the writers of the Four Gospels; preacher of the Gospel; layman doing home missionary work. [f. F *évangéliste* f. L (*-ta*) f. Gk *euaggelistēs* (as EVANGELIZE, -IST)]

evangeli·stic, a. Of the Four Evangelists; of preachers of the Gospel; = EVANGELICAL. [-IC]

eva·ngelize, v.t. Preach the Gospel to (persons, also abs.); win over (person) to Christianity. Hence **evangeliz**A·TION n. [f. eccl. L *evangelizare* f. Gk *euaggelizomai* (as EVANGEL)]

evă·nish, v.i. Vanish; die away. Hence **eva·nish**MENT n. [f. OF *evanir* (-ISH[2]) f. pop. L **exvanire* = L *evanescere* EVANESCE]

evă·porate, v.t. & i. Turn (t. & i.) from solid or liquid into vapour (also fig.; esp. colloq., disappear, die); remove the liquid part of; (intr.) exhale moisture. So **eva·por**ABLE, **eva·porat**IVE, aa., **evapor**A·TION, **eva·porat**OR[2], nn. [f. LL E*vaporare* (as VAPOUR), see -ATE[3]]

eva·sion (-zhn), n. Act, means, of evading; shuffling excuse. So **eva·s**IVE (-s-) a., **eva·sive**LY[2] adv., **eva·sive**NESS n. [f. F *évasion* f. LL *evasionem* (as EVADE, see -ION)]

Eve[1], n. The first woman; *daughter of E.*, woman (often w. allusion to feminine curiosity &c.). [f. Heb. *Havvah* orig. = life, living]

eve[2], n. Evening or day before (*of*) a church festival or any date or event; time just before anything, as *on the e. of an election*; (archaic) evening. [= EVEN[1]; for loss of *-n* cf. *morrow*]

eve·ction, n. Inequality in moon's longitude. [f. L *evectio* f. E(*vehere vect-* carry), -ION]

ē·ven[1], n. (poet.). Evening; *evensong*, evening prayer in Church of England; *eventide*, evening. [OE *ǽfen*, *éfen*; Du. *avond*, G *abend*]

ē·ven[2], a. (-er, -est). Level; smooth; uniform in quality; in same plane or line (*with*); equally balanced, as *e.-handed justice*; equal in number or amount; (Law, Commerc.) *of e.* (same) *date*; (of temper &c.) equable, unruffled; (of numbers) integrally divisible by two, opp. to ODD; ODD *& e.*; *be e. with*, have one's revenge on. Hence **e·ven**LY[2] adv., **e·ven**NESS n. [com.-Teut.: OE *efen*, Du. *even*, *effen*, G *eben*]

ē·ven[3], adv. inviting comparison of the assertion, negation, &c., made with a less strong one that might have been made, as *He disputes e. the facts* (not merely the inferences from them), *I never e. opened* (much less read) *it*, *does he e. suspect* (not to say realize) *the danger?*, *e. if my watch is right we shall be late* (later if it is slow), *this applies e. more* (not merely equally) *to French* (*than to English*); (archaic) neither more nor less than, just, simply, as *e.* (quite) *so*, (emphasizing identity) that is, as *God, e. our own God.* [OE *efne*, as prec.]

ē·ven[4], v.t. Make even; treat as equal or comparable (*to*). [OE *efnan*, as prec.]

e·vening (ēvn-), n. Close of day, esp. sunset to bedtime; this time spent in particular way, as *musical ee.*; (fig.) decline of life, closing period; *e. dress*, that prescribed by fashion to be worn in the e.; *e.-star*, Jupiter, Mercury, or other planet, & esp. (*the e. star*) Venus, when seen in West after sunset. [OE *ǣfnung* vbl n. f. *ǣfnian* (as EVEN[1])]

eve·nt, n. Fact of a thing's happening, as *in the e. of his death, his coming*, if he dies, comes; thing that happens, esp. important thing, as *quite an e.*, whence **eve·nt**FUL, **eve·nt**LESS, aa.; (in doctrine of chances) any of several possible but mutually exclusive occurrences; *double e.*, combined occurrence of two ee., esp. as subject of bets; (Sport.) something on the issue of which money is staked; result, outcome; *in any* or *either e., at all ee.*, in any case. [OF, f. L *eventus -ūs* f. E(*venire* come)]

eve·ntual, a. That will happen under certain circumstances; ultimately resulting, whence **eve·ntual**LY[2] adv. [f. F *éventuel* (prec., -AL)]

eventua·lity, n. Possible event. [-ITY]

eve·ntuate, v.i. Turn out (*well, ill*, &c.); result (*in* or abs.); (chiefly U.S.) happen, come to pass. [f. L as EVENT, -ATE[3]]

ĕ·ver, adv. Always, at all times, (archaic exc. as foll.); *for ever* (*& e., & a day*), for all future time, incessantly; *evermore*, always; *e. after, e. since*; (archaic) *e. & anon*, now & then; (w. negative, question, condition, comparison) at any time, as *nothing e. happens, did you e. hear such stuff?, if I e. catch him, the best thing I e. heard, as good as e., better than e.*; strengthening *as*) *be as quick as e. you can*; (emphasizing question, colloq.) *what e.* (vulg. *whatever*) *does he want?, who e. can it be?, which e. Brown do you mean?, when, where, how, e. did I drop it?, why e. didn't you say so?*; *e. so* (earlier *never so*), very, as *it is e. so much easier*; (appended to superl. as slang ellipsis for that e. was or were (*the back-benchers were the most docile e.*); *did you e.?* (as complete sentence), did you ever see or hear the like?. [OE *ǣfre*, etym. dub., perh. conn. w. AYE]

e·verglade, n. (U.S.). Marshy tract of land, esp. (pl.) swamp in S. Florida. [prec. + GLADE]

e·vergreen, a. & n. Always green or fresh (lit. & fig.); (tree, shrub) having green leaves all the year round (cf. DECIDUOUS).

everla·sting, a. & n. Lasting for ever; lasting long; lasting too long, repeated too often; (of plants) keeping shape and colour when dried; (n.) eternity, as *from e.*, e. flower, strong twilled woollen stuff. Hence **everla·sting**LY[2] adv., **everla·sting**NESS n.

ever·t, v.t. (Physiol.) turn (organ &c.) inside out; (archaic) overthrow (government &c.). So **ever**SION n. [f. L E(*vertere vers-* turn)]

every (ĕ·vrĭ), a. Each, all (w. sing. vb), as *e. word of it is false*, (w. possess. pron.) *it engaged his e. thought*, (of succession or alternation) *he comes e. day, e. other* (i.e. second) *day, e. three days, e. third day*; *e. now & then, e. now & again*, from time to time; *e. bit* (quite) *as much*; *everybody* (*else*), every (other) person; *everyday* (adj.), occurring daily, worn or used on ordinary days, commonplace; *e. one*, each, as *e. one of them is wrong*; *e·veryone* (also *e. one*), everybody, as *everyone likes to have his way*; *everything*, all things, as *everything depends on that*, thing of first importance, as *pace is everything*; *everyway*, in e. way, in e. respect; *everywhere*, in e. place. [OE *ǣfre ǣlc* EVER EACH]

evi·ct, v.t. Expel (person; esp. tenant *from* land &c.); recover (property, title to it, *of, from*, person) by legal process. So **evi·ct**ION, **evi·ct**OR[2], nn. [f. L E(*vincere vict-* conquer)]

ĕ·vidence, n., & v.t. Clearness, obviousness, esp. *in e.*, conspicuous; indication, sign, (*of* quality, treatment, &c.); testimony, facts, making *for* (also *of*) a conclusion, esp. (pl.) *the Ee. of Christianity*; INTERNAL, EXTERNAL, *e.*; (Law) information (given personally or drawn from documents &c.) tending to establish fact, as *call* (person) *in e.* (as a witness), CIRCUMSTANTIAL, PRESUMPTIVE, *verbal e.*; *turn King's, Queen's, e.*, (of accomplice in crime) give e. against one's accomplices; statements, proofs, admissible as testimony in court; (v.t.) serve to indicate, attest. So **evide·nti**AL (-shl), **evide·nti**ARY[1] (-sha-), aa., **evide·ntial**LY[2] adv. [(vb f. n.) f. F *évidence* f. L *evidentia* (as foll., see -ENCE)]

ĕ·vident, a. Obvious (to eyes or mind). Hence **e·vident**LY[2] adv. [f. L E(*vidēre* see), see -ENT]

evil (ē·vl), a., n., & adv. Bad, harmful; *the E. One*, the Devil; *of e.* (bad) *repute, an e.* (slanderous) *tongue*; *e. eye*, malicious look, pop. believed to do material harm; (n.) e. thing, sin, harm, (*of two ee. choose the less*); *e.-doer*; *Aleppo e.*, a disease of boils; = KING'S *e.*; (adv.) in e. manner, as *speak e. of*, (bibl.) *e. entreat, e.-disposed*. Hence **e·vil**LY[2] adv. [ME *uvel*, OE *yfel*, Du. *euvel*, G *übel*; perh. f. root of *up*, w. sense 'excessive']

evi·nce, v.t. Show, indicate, (quality &c., *that* &c.); show that one has (quality). Hence **evi·nc**IVE a. [as EVICT]

ĕ·virate, v.t. Castrate (male); (fig.) deprive of manly qualities. So **evira·**TION n. [f. L E(*virare* f. *vir* man), see -ATE[3]]

evi·scerate, v.t. Disembowel; (fig.) empty (thing) of vital contents. Hence **eviscer**A·TION n. [f. L E*viscerare* (VISCERA), see -ATE[3]]

evo·ke, v.t. Call up (spirit from the dead, feelings, memories, energies); summon (cause) to higher court. So **ĕvoca·**TION n., **evŏ·cat**IVE, **evŏ·catory,** aa. [f. F *évoquer* f. L E(*vocare* call)]

ĕ·volute, a. & n. *E.* (*curve*), locus of centres of curvature of another curve that is its INVOLUTE. [f. L p.p. as EVOLVE]

ĕvolu·tion, n. Opening out (of roll, bud, &c.; usu. fig.); appearance (of events &c.) in due succession; evolving, giving off, (of gas, heat, &c.); unfolding of curve; (Math.) extraction of root from any given power (cf. INVOLUTION); development (of organism, design, argument, &c.); *Theory of E.* (that the embryo is not created by fecundation, but developed from a pre-existing form); origination of species by development from earlier forms, not by special creation (cf. CREATIONISM), whence **evolu·tion**ISM, **evolu·tion**IST, nn., **evolutioni·st**IC a.; formation of heavenly bodies by concentration of cosmic matter; change in disposition of troops or ships; wheeling about, movement, in dancing &c. Hence **evolu·tion**AL, **evolu·tion**ARY[1], aa. [f. L *evolutio* (as EVOLVE, see -ION)]

e·volutive, a. Tending to evolution. [-IVE]

evo·lve, v.t. & i. Unfold, open out, (fig.); set forth in due sequence; give off (heat &c.); develop, deduce, (theory, facts, &c.); develop (t. & i.) by natural process; *e. from* one's *inner consciousness,* create imaginatively (often joc. of romancing &c.). Hence **evo·lve**MENT n. [f. L E(*volvere volut-* roll)]

evu·lsion, n. Forcible extraction. [f. L *evulsio* f. E(*vellere vuls-* pluck), see -ION]

ewe (ū), n. Female sheep; one's *e. lamb,* one's most cherished possession (2 *Sam.* xii). [com.-Aryan; OE *eowu,* Du. *ooi,* L *ovis,* Gk *ois,* Skr. *avi*]

ew·er (ū-), n. Pitcher; (Commerc.) bedroom water-jug. [f. OF *aiguiere* f. L **aquaria,* fem. adj. as n. (*aqua* water, see -ARY[1])]

ex, prep. (commerc.). (Of goods) out of, sold from, (*ship, store,* &c.); (of stocks or shares) *ex dividend* (abbr. *ex div.* or *x.d.*), not including next dividend. [L]

ex-, pref. (1) = L *ex* before *h, c, p, q, s* (which is often dropped), and *t*; becoming *ef-* before *f*, *e-* before other consonants; forming vbs with sense 'out', 'forth', (*exclude, exit*), 'thoroughly' (*excruciate*), 'make so-&-so' (*exasperate*), 'remove, expel, free, from' (*expatriate, -onerate, -coriate*), and adjj. w. sense 'not having', esp. in form *e-* (*ecaudate* tailless). (2) = Gk *ex* (= *ek* before vowels) out, as *exodus.* (3) L *ex* is prefixed to nn. and rarely adjj. (orig. to titles of office &c.) in sense 'formerly', 'quondam', as *ex-chancellor, ex-Prime-Minister.*

exă·cerbate, v.t. Aggravate (pain, disease, anger); irritate (person &c.). So **exacerb**A·TION n. [f. L EX(*acerbare* f. *acerbus* bitter)]

exa·ct[1], a. Precise, rigorous, (rules, order, &c.); (of person, judgement, description, report, answer, &c.) accurate, strictly correct; *e. sciences* (admitting of absolute precision). Hence or cogn. **exa·cti**TUDE, **exa·ct**NESS, nn. [f. L p.p. as foll.]

exa·ct[2], v.t. Demand & enforce payment of (money, fees, &c., *from, of,* person), insist upon (act, conduct, *from, of*), whence **exa·ct**ING[2] a.; (of circumstances) require urgently. Hence or cogn. **exa·ct**ABLE a., **exa·ct**OR[2] n. [f. L EX(*igere act-* = *agere* drive)]

exa·ction, n. Exacting (*of* money &c.); sum, thing, thus exacted; illegal or exorbitant demand, extortion; arbitrary & excessive impost. [F, f. L *exactionem* (as prec., see -ION)]

exa·ctly, adv. In adj. senses, esp. (as answer or confirmation) quite so, just as you say. [-LY[2]]

exa·ggerate (-ăj-), v.t. Magnify (thing described, or abs.) beyond limits of truth; intensify, aggravate; make (physical features &c.) of abnormal size. Hence or cogn. **exa·ggerated**LY[2], **exa·ggerative**LY[2], advv., **exagger**A·TION, **exa·ggerat**OR[2], nn., **exa·ggerat**IVE a. [f. L EX(*aggerare* heap up, f. *agger* heap), see -ATE[3]]

exa·lt (-aw-), v.t. Raise, place high in rank, power, &c.; praise, extol, (often *e. to the skies*); dignify, ennoble, (esp. in p.p.); intensify (colours &c.). [f. L EX(*altare* f. *altus* high)]

exalta·tion, n. Raising, lifting up, (usu. fig.); elation, rapturous emotion; intensification. [F, f. L *exaltationem* (prec., -ATION)]

examina·tion, n. Minute inspection (*of, into*); POST-MORTEM *e.*; (colloq. abbr. *exam*). testing of knowledge or ability (of pupils, candidates) by questions oral or written; *e.-paper,* series of such questions or of examinee's answers to them. Hence **examina·tion**AL a. [F, f. L *examinationem* (as foll., see -ATION)]

exă·mine, v.t. & i. Investigate, scrutinize, (accounts, person *in* or *on* subject, organ, baggage for contraband goods, theory, statement, one's own conscience, *whether*); (intr.) inquire *into.* Hence **exa·min**ANT, **exa·min**EE·, **exa·min**ER[1], nn., **examinator·**IAL a. [f. F *examiner* f. L *examinare* (*examen,* for *exagmen,* tongue of balance, examination, as EXACT[2])]

exa·mple, n., & v.t. Fact, thing, illustrating general rule; problem, exercise, designed to do this; specimen of workmanship, picture &c.; warning to others, as *make an e. of* (punish) *him*; precedent, as *beyond, without, e.*; conduct as object of imitation, as *give, set, a good e.*; *take e. by,* copy; (v.t., rare exc. in p.p.) exemplify. [(vb f. n.) OF f. L *exemplum* (as EXEMPT[1])]

exă·nimate (-*a*t), a. Dead; lacking animation, spiritless. [f. L EX*animare* deprive of life (*anima*), see -ATE[2]]

e·xarch (-k), n. (Under Byzantine

emperors) governor of distant province; (in Eastern Church) patriarch, bishop, patriarch's deputy. So **e·xarch**ATE[1] n. [f. L f. Gk *exarkhos* f. EX(*arkhō* rule)]

exa·sperate, v.t. Make worse (ill feeling, disease, pain); irritate (person; *-ed at, by*); provoke (person *to* ill, *to* do). Hence or cogn. **exa·speratingly**[2] adv., **exaspera·tion** n. [f. L EX(*asperare* f. *asper* rough), see -ATE[3]]

ex cathĕ·drā, adv. & a. Authoritative(ly). [L, =from the (teacher's) chair]

e·xcavate, v.t. Make hollow; make (hole, channel) by digging; dig out (soil) leaving a hole; unearth, get out, by digging. Hence or cogn. **excava·tion, e·xcavator**[2], nn. [f. L EX(*cavare* f. *cavus* hollow), see -ATE[3]]

excee·d, v.t. & i. Do more than is warranted by (one's commission, rights, &c.); be greater than (quantity, thing, *by* so much); surpass (person &c. *in*); be pre-eminent, whence **excee·ding**[2] a. & (archaic) adv., **excee·dingly**[2] adv.; be immoderate in feeding &c.; exaggerate. [f. F *excéder* f. L EX(*cedere cess-* go)]

exce·l, v.t. & i. (-ll-). Surpass (others *in* quality, *in* doing); be pre-eminent (*in, at*, thing, *in* quality, *in* doing). [f. F *exceller* f. L EX(*cellere*, cf. *celsus* lofty)]

e·xcellence, n. Surpassing merit; thing in which person &c. excels. [F, f. L *excellentia* (as prec., see -ENCE)]

e·xcellency, n. Title (*Your, His, Her, E.*) of ambassadors, governors & their wives, & some other officers. [as prec., see -ENCY]

e·xcellent, a. Pre-eminent; very good. Hence **e·xcellently**[2] adv. [F (as prec., see -ENT)]

exce·lsior, int. & n. Higher (as trade mark &c.); (U.S.) soft shavings of wood for stuffing. [L, compar. of EX*celsus* lofty]

exce·pt[1], v.t. & i. Exclude (thing) from enumeration, statement, &c., as *present company excepted, e. him from the general pardon*; make objection *against*. So **exce·ptive** a. [f. F *excepter* f. EX(*cipere cept-* =*capere* take)]

exce·pt[2], **exce·pting,** prep. & conj. (*-ing* is required only after *not, without*, as *we are all fallible, except the pope*, but *not excepting the pope*; *-ing* is also usual after *always*). Not including, but, as *we all failed e. him, he is everywhere e. in the right place, never to be found e. in the wrong place, it is right e. that the accents are omitted, e. for the omission of accents*; (conj., archaic) unless, as *e. he be born again.* [*except* orig. p.p. (f. L as prec.) in abs. constr. (*e. you*=*you being excepted*); *-ing*, abs. use of part. of prec.]

exce·ption, n. Excepting; thing excepted, thing that does not follow the rule; *the e. proves the rule*, (prop.) the excepting of some cases shows that the rule exists, or that it applies to those not excepted, (pop.) the weaker my case, the stronger my conviction; *with the e. of*, except; *take e.*, object *to*; *subject, liable, to e.* (objection), whence **exce·ptionable** a. [f. AF *excepcioun* f. L *exceptionem* [EXCEPT[1], -ION)]

exce·ptional, a. Forming an exception; unusual, as *e. advantages.* Hence **exceptiona·lity** n., **exce·ptionally**[2] adv. [-AL]

e·xcerpt[1] (or ĭkser·-), n. Extract from book &c., article from learned society's Transactions &c. printed off separately for private circulation. [as foll.]

excer·pt[2], v.t. Extract, quote, (passage *from* book &c., or abs.). Hence or cogn. **excer·ptible** a., **excer·ption** n. [f. L EX(*cerpere cerpt-* =*carpere* pluck)]

exce·ss, n. (Usu. pl.) outrage; intemperance in eating or drinking; overstepping of due limits; fact of exceeding, esp. *in e. of*, more than; amount by which one exceeds another; *e. fare* on railway, payment due for travelling further or in higher class than ticket warrants; *e. luggage* (over the weight for free carriage); superabundance, extreme degree, (*of* cruelty &c.); exceeding of the proper amount or degree, esp. *in, to, e.*; *e. profits duty*, tax on profits swollen by war conditions. So **exce·ssive** a., **exce·ssively**[2] adv. [f. F *excès* f. L *excessus -ūs* (as EXCEED)]

excha·nge[1], n. Act, process, of exchanging (*of* goods, prisoners of war, blows, words, &c.; *e. is no robbery*, joc. excuse for unfair e.); exchanging of coin for its equivalent in coin of same or another country; money-changer's trade; *par of e.*, standard value of coinage of one country in terms of that of another; (*rate, course, of*) *e.*, price at which bills drawn in a foreign currency may be bought, also, difference between this & par; system of settling debts between persons (esp. in different countries) without money, by *bills of e.* (*first, second, third, of e.*, separate bills of even tenor & date as security against miscarriage); thing exchanged for another; building where merchants assemble to transact business, as STOCK-*e.* [f. OF *eschange* f. LL *excambium* (as foll.)]

exchānge[2], v.t. & i. Give, receive, (thing) in place of (*for*) another; interchange (blows, words, glances, &c.); (intr., esp. of coin) be received as equivalent *for*; pass (*from* one regiment or ship *into* another) by exchange with another officer. [f. OF *eschangier* f. LL EX(*cambiare* CHANGE)]

excha·ngeable, a. That may be exchanged (*for*); *e. value* (estimated by that of the goods for which a thing may be exchanged). Hence **exchangeabi·lity** n. [-ABLE]

exche·quer (-tshĕker), n. Department of public service charged with receipt & custody of revenue; *Chancellor of the E.*, finance minister of United Kingdom; royal or national treasury; money of private person &c.; (also *Court of E.*) court of law, now merged in King's Bench Division (orig. using table with chequered cloth for accounts); *e. bill* (issued by authority of Parliament, bearing interest at current rate). [f. OF *eschequier* f. med. L *scaccarium* chess-board (*scacchi* chess, see -ARIUM)]

exci·se[1] (-z), n., & v.t. Duty charged on home goods during manufacture or before sale to home consumers; government office collecting e. (now *Department of Inland Revenue*); *exciseman*, officer collecting e. & preventing infringement of e. laws; (v.t.) force (person) to pay e., overcharge (also fig.). Hence **exci·s**ABLE a. [(vb f. n.) prob. f. MDu. *excijs* f. LL **accensus* f. ACcensare tax (CENSUS)]

exci·se[2] (-z), v.t. Cut out (passage of book, limb, organ, &c.); (Bot., Zool.) cut out, notch. So **exci·s**ION (-ĭzhn) n. [f. L EX(*cidere cis- =caedere* cut)]

exci·te, v.t. Set in motion, rouse up, (feelings, faculties, &c.); provoke, bring about, (action, active condition); promote activity of (bodily organs &c.) by stimulus; move (person) to strong emotion; (Electr., Magnet.) induce activity in (substance), set (current) in motion, whence **excit**A·TION n.; (Photog.) sensitize (plate). Hence or cogn. **excītab**I·LITY, **exci·te**MENT, nn., **e·xcīt**ANT a. & n., **excī·t**ABLE (esp., of persons, easily excited, unbalanced), **excī·t**ATIVE, **excī·tat**ORY, aa., **exci·ted**LY[2] adv. [f. F *exciter* f. L *excitare* frequent. of EX(*ciēre* set in motion)]

exclai·m, v.i. & t. Cry out, esp. from pain, anger, &c.; utter (words quoted direct or with *that*) thus; *e. against*, accuse loudly. [f. F *exclamer* f. L EX(*clamare* shout)]

exclama·tion, n. Exclaiming; words exclaimed; *note of e.* (!). So **exclă·m-at**ORY a. [F, f. L (prec., -ATION)]

exclu·de, v.t. Shut out (person, thing, *from* place, society, privilege, &c.); prevent the occurrence of, make impossible, (doubt &c.); expel & shut out. So **exclu·s**ION -(zhn) n. [f. L EX(*cludere clus- =claudere* shut)]

exclu·sive (-s-), a. Shutting out; not admitting *of*; desirous of excluding others, (of social circles &c.) chary of admitting members, select, whence **exclu·siv**ISM(2) n.; (shop, newspaper) not to be had, not published, elsewhere; (of terms &c.) excluding all but what is specified; employed, followed, to the exclusion of all else, as *his e. occupation*; (quasi-adv.) not counting, as *20 men, e. of our own.* Hence **exclu·sive**LY[2] adv., **exclu·sive**NESS n. [f. med. L *exclusivus* (prec., -IVE)]

excŏ·gitate (-j-), v.t. Think out, contrive. So **excogit**A·TION n., **exco·gitat**IVE a. [f. L EX(*cogitare* COGITATE)]

excommū·nicate, v.t. (Eccl.) cut off (person) from participation in sacraments, or from all communication with the Church. So **excommunic**A·TION, **ex-commu·nicat**OR[2], nn., **excommu·ni-cat**IVE, **excommu·nicat**ORY, aa. [f. LL EX(*communicare* f. *communis* COMMON), see -ATE[3]]

excŏ·riate, v.t. Remove part of skin of (person &c.) by abrasion &c.; strip, peel off, (skin). So **excori**A·TION n. [f. L EX*coriare* (*corium* hide), see -ATE[3]]

e·xcrement, n. Waste matter discharged from bowels, dung, (often pl.). Hence or cogn. **excreme·nt**AL, **excrementi·**TIOUS[1] aa. [f. F *excrément* f. L *excrementum* (as EXCRETE, see -MENT)]

excre·scence, n. Abnormal or morbid outgrowth on animal or vegetable body (also fig.). So **excresce·nt**IAL a. [f. L *excrescentia* (as foll., see -ENCE)]

excre·scent, a. Growing abnormally; redundant; (Gram., of sound in word) due merely to euphony. [f. L EX(*crescere cret-* grow), -ENT]

excrē·ta, n. pl. Waste expelled from body, esp. faeces & urine. [L, p.p. as foll.]

excre·te, v.t. (Of animals or plants) separate & expel (waste matters, also abs.) from system. Hence or cogn. **excre·t**ION n., **excre·t**IVE, **excre·t**ORY, aa. [f. L EX(*cernere cret-* sift)]

excru·ciate (-shĭ-), v.t. Torment acutely (person's senses; now esp. in part. as adj.); torture mentally (now rare). Hence or cogn. **excru·ciating**LY[2] adv., **excru-ci**A·TION (-sĭ-) n. [f. L EX(*cruciare* torment f. *crux crucis* cross), see -ATE[3]]

e·xculpate, v.t. Free from blame; clear (person *from* charge &c.). Hence **ex-culp**A·TION n., **excu·lpat**ORY a. [f. EX- + L *culpa* blame + -ATE[3]]

excu·rrent, a. Running out; (of blood) flowing from heart, arterial; affording an exit; (Bot.) projecting. [as foll., see -ENT]

excur·se, v.i. (rare). Wander, digress (usu. fig.); make an excursion. Hence **excur·s**IVE a., **excur·sive**LY[2] adv., **ex-cur·sive**NESS n. [f. L EX(*currere curs-* run)]

excur·sion, n. Journey, ramble, with intention of returning (also fig.); pleasure trip of number of persons, whence **ex-cur·sion**IST n.; *e. train* (for excursionists, usu. at reduced rates); (archaic) sortie (*alarms & ee.*); (Astr.) deviation from regular path. Hence **excur·sion**AL, **excur·sion**ARY[1], aa. [f. L *excursio* (as prec., see -ION)]

excur·sus, n. (pl. *-uses*). Detailed discussion of special point in book, usu. in appendix at end. [L vbl n. as EXCURSE]

excu·se[1] (-z), v.t. Attempt to lessen the blame attaching to (person, act); obtain exemption for (person, one*self*, *from* duty &c.); (of things) serve as exculpation for (person, act); accept the exculpation of (person, act, person *for* act); release (person *from* a duty; also double obj., as *we e. him the fee*); dispense with, as *we will e. your presence*; *e. me* (as apology for lack of ceremony, interruption, &c.; also as form of dissent). So **excu·**SABLE, **excu·sat**ORY, aa., **excu·s-ab**LY[2] adv. [f. OF *excuser* f. L EX*cusare* (*causa* CAUSE)]

excu·se[2] (-s), n. Apology offered, exculpation (usu. *in e. of*); ground of this; plea for release from duty &c. [OF (as prec.)]

e·xĕăt, n. (In schools, colleges, &c.) permission for temporary absence. [L, 3rd sing. subj. of EX(*ire* go)]

e·xecrable, a. Abominable. Hence **e·xe-crab**LY[2] adv. [f. L *execrabilis* (foll., -BLE)]

e·xecrate, v.t. & i. Express, feel, abhorrence for; (intr.) utter curses. Hence or cogn. **execr**A·TION n., **e·xecrat**IVE, **e·xe-crat**ORY, aa. [f. L EX(*s*)*ecrari* (*sacrare* devote f. *sacer* sacred, accursed), see -ATE[3]]

exĕ·cutant, n. One who executes, performer, (*of* music &c.). [f. F *exécutant*, part. as foll.]

e·xecute, v.t. Carry (plan, command, law, judicial sentence, will) into effect; perform (action, operation, &c.); make (legal instrument) valid by signing, sealing, &c.; convey (estate) in property; discharge (office, function); perform (musical composition); inflict capital punishment on. Hence **e·execut**ABLE a. [f. F *exécuter* f. med. L *exsecutare* f. L EX(*sequi secut-* follow)]

execu·tion, n. Carrying out, performance; dexterity in performing music; (of weapons) destructive effect, as *do e.* (also fig. of personal charms &c.); seizure of goods or debtor in default of payment; infliction of capital punishment, whence **execu·tion**ER[1] n. [f. F *exécution* f. L *executionem* (as prec., -ION)]

exĕ·cutive, a. & n. Pertaining to, having the function of, executing; (branch of government) concerned with executing laws, decrees, & sentences (cf. JUDICIAL, *legislative*). [-IVE]

executor, n. (Pron. ĕ·ks-) one who carries out or performs; (ĭkzĕ·k-) person appointed by testator to execute his will, *literary e.*, person charged with writer's unpublished works &c. Hence **exe·cu-tor**·IAL a., **exe·cutor**SHIP, **exe·cu**TRIX (pl. *-cū·trīces*), nn. [f. AF *executour* f. L *executorem* (EXECUTE, -OR[2])]

exegē·sis (-j-), n. Exposition esp. of Scripture. So **exegĕ·tic**(AL) aa., **exege·ti-cal**LY[2] adv. [Gk *exēgēsis* f. EX(*hēgeomai* lead)]

exe·mplar, n. Model, pattern; type (of a class); parallel instance. [f. OF *exemplaire* f. LL *exemplarium* (EXAMPLE, -ARY[1])]

exe·mplary, a. Fit to be imitated; typical; illustrative; serving as a warning (*e. damages* in law, exceeding amount needed for compensation). Hence **exe·mplar**ILY[2] adv., **exe·mplari**NESS n. [f. L *exemplaris* (as EXAMPLE, see -ARY[2])]

exe·mplify̆, v.t. Illustrate by example; be an example of; make attested copy of (document) under official seal. So **exe·mpli**FICA·TION n. [f. med. L *exemplificare* (EXAMPLE, -FY)]

exe·mpt[1], a. & n. Free (*from* taxation, control, failings, &c.); (n.) person exempted, esp. from tax; one of four officers sometimes commanding Yeomen of Guard (now usu. *exon*). [F, f. L EX(*imere empt-* =*emere* take)]

exe·mpt[2], v.t. Free *from* (as prec.). So **exe·mpt**ION n. [f. F *exempter* (prec.)]

exe·nterate, v.t. Disembowel (only fig.). So **exenter**A·TION n. [f. L EX*enterare* (Gk *enteron* intestine), see -ATE[3]]

exequā·tur, n. Recognition of a country's consul by a foreign government; temporal sovereign's authorization of bishop under Papal authority, or of publication of Papal bulls. [L, =he may perform]

e·xequies (-kwĭz), n. pl. Funeral rites. [OF, f. L *exsequiae* f. EX(*sequi* follow)]

e·xercise[1] (-z), n. Employment (of organ, faculty, power, right); practice (of virtues, profession, functions, religious rites); exertion of muscles, limbs, &c., esp. for health's sake; bodily, mental, or spiritual training; task set for this purpose; (pl.) military drill, athletics, &c.; academical declamation &c. required for degree; composition set to pupils; act of worship. [f. OF *exercice* f. L *exercitium* f. EX(*ercēre -cit-* = *arcēre* restrain) keep at work)]

e·xercise[2] (-z), v.t. & i. Employ (faculty, right, &c.); train (person &c.); tax the powers of; perplex, worry; discharge (functions); take, give (horse &c.), exercise. Hence **e·xercis**ABLE a. [f. prec.]

exercita·tion, n. Practice, training; literary or oratorical exercise. [f. L *exercitatio* f. *exercitare* frequent, as EXERCISE[1], -ATION]

exergue (ĕ·kserg, ĕkzer·g), n. Small space usu. on reverse of coin or medal, below principal device; inscription there. Hence **exer·gu**AL (-gl) a. [F, prob. f. Gk EX- +*ergon* work]

exer·t, v.t. Exercise, bring to bear, (quality, force, influence); *e. oneself*, strive (*to* do, *for* object). So **exer·t**ION n. [f. L EX(*serere sert-* bind) put forth]

E·xeter Hall, n. Building in Strand formerly used for May meetings &c. (see MAY).

e·xĕŭnt, v.i. (Stage direction) they (two, or more actors) leave the stage; *e. omnes*, all leave the stage. [L, =they go out]

exfō·liate, v.i. (Of bone, skin, minerals, &c.) come off in scales or layers; (of tree) throw off layers of bark. So **ex-foli**A·TION n. [f. LL EX(*foliare* f. *folium* leaf), see -ATE[3]]

exhala·tion (ĕkz*a*-), n. Evaporation; puff of breath; short burst (*of* anger &c.); mist, vapour; effluvium. [f. L *exhalatio* (foll., -ATION)]

exha·le, v.t. & i. Give off (fumes &c., also fig.) in vapour; be thus given off, evaporate, (*from, out of*); (Path., of animal fluids) pass off in minute quantities through blood-vessel &c.; breathe out (life, soul, words, &c.); get rid of (anger &c.) as if by blowing. [f. F *exhaler* f. L EX(*halare* breathe)]

exhau·st[1] (ĭkzaw-), n. (In steam or motor engine) exit of steam or motive fluid from cylinder when its work is done; *e.-pipe* &c. (for this); process of exhausting vessel of air; (apparatus for) production of outward current of air by creating partial vacuum. [f. foll.]

exhau·st[2] (ĭkzaw-), v.t. Draw off (air, also fig.); consume entirely; use, account for, the whole of; empty (vessel) of contents; say, find out, all that is worth knowing of (subject); drain (person, kingdom, &c.) of strength, resources, &c. (esp. in p.p.); tire out. Hence **ex-hausti**BI·LITY n., **exhau·st**IBLE a. [f. L EX(*haurire haust-* draw)]

exhau·stion (-tshn), n. Exhausting (in all senses); total loss of strength; arrival at a conclusion by eliminating alternatives. [-ION]

exhau·stive, a. Tending to exhaust esp. a subject; comprehensive. Hence **ex-hau·stive**LY[2] adv., **exhau·stive**NESS n., [-IVE]

exhi·bit[1] (ĭkzĭ-), n. Document or thing produced in lawcourt & referred to in written evidence; thing, collection of things, sent by person, firm, &c., to an exhibition; showing, display. [f. L neut. p.p. as foll.]

exhi·bit[2] (ĭkzĭ-), v.t. Show, display; submit for consideration; manifest (quality); show publicly (for amusement, in competition, &c.). So **exhi·bit**OR[2] n., **exhi·bi-tory** a. [f. L EX(*hibēre hibit-* =*habēre* hold)]

exhibi·tion, n. Showing, display, (of thing); *make an e. of oneself*, behave so as to excite contempt; public display of works of art &c.; *the Great E.*, first e. on large scale, London, 1851; fixed sum given to student for term of years from funds of school, college, &c., whence **exhibi·tion**ER[1] n. [f. OF *exhibicion* f. LL *exhibitionem* (as prec., see -ION); last use f. prec. in obs. sense 'provide maintenance']

exhi·larate (ĭkzĭ-), v.t. Enliven, gladden, (person, spirits). So **exhi·lar**ANT(2) a. & n., **exhilar**A·TION n., **exhi·larat**IVE a. [f. L EX(*hilarare* f. *hilaris* cheerful), see -ATE[3]]

exhort (ĭkzor·t), v.t. Admonish earnestly; urge (person *to* do, *to* a course); advocate (reform &c.). So **exhor·tat**IVE, **exhor·ta-tory**, aa. [f. L EX(*hortari* see HORTATORY)]

exhorta·tion, n. Exhorting; formal, liturgical, address. [f. L *exhortatio* (prec., -ATION)]

exhu·me, v.t. Dig out, unearth, (lit. & fig.). So **exhum**A·TION n. [f. F *exhumer* f. L EX(*humare* f. *humus* ground)]

e·xigence, -cy, nn. Urgent need; emergency. [F (*-ce*), f. L *exigentia* (foll., -ENCY)]

e·xigent (-j-), a. Urgent, pressing; requiring much, exacting; *e. of*, demanding. [f. L EX(*igere* =*agere* drive), see -ENT]

e·xigible (-j-), a. That may be demanded or exacted (*against, from*, person). [as prec., -BLE]

exi·gūous, a. Scanty, small. Hence or cogn. **exigū·**ITY, **exi·guous**NESS, nn. [f. L *exiguus* (as prec.) + -OUS]

e·xile[1], n. Penal banishment; long absence from one's country (also fig.). [f. OF *exil* f. L EX*silium* (*salire* leap)]

e·xile[2], n. Banished person (lit. & fig.). [perh. f. prec.; L has *exsul* (as prec.)]

e·xile[3], v.t. Banish (person *from*; lit. & fig.). [f. OF *exilier* f. LL *exsiliare* (as EXILE[1])]

exĭ·lian, a. Of the Jews' exile in Babylon. So **exĭ·l**IC a. [f. L as EXILE[1] + -IAN]

exi·lity, n. Thinness; subtlety. [f. L *exilitas* (*exilis* thin, etym. dub., see -TY)]

exi·st, v.i. Have place in the domain of reality; have being under specified conditions; *e. as* (in the form of); (of circumstances &c.) occur, be found; live; continue in being. [f. F *exister* f. L EX(*sistere* redupl. f. *stare* stand)]

exi·stence, n. Being, existing, esp. *in e.*; life, as *a wretched, precarious, e.*; mode of existing; existing thing; all that exists. So **existe·nt**IAL a. [OF, f. med. L *existentia* (as prec., see -ENCE)]

exi·stent, a. Existing, actual, current. [-ENT]

e·xit[1], n. Departure of player from stage (also fig.); death; going out or forth; liberty to do this; passage to go out by. [f. L *exitus -ūs* going out (as foll.); partly also from foll.]

e·xit[2], v.i. (Stage direction) — goes off stage, as *E. Macbeth* (also fig.). [3rd sing. pres. of L EX(*ire it-* go)]

ex-lī·bris, n. Book-plate, label with arms, crest, &c., & owner's name pasted into book. [L *ex libris* from library (of so-&-so)]

exo- in comb. =Gk *exō* outside as: *-derm*, outer layer of blastoderm; *-gamous, -gamy*, (of, following) custom compelling man to marry outside his own tribe; *-gen* n., *-genous* a., = DICOTYLEDON(*ous*), w. ref. to external growth of stem;

-pa·thic, (of disease) originating outside the body; *-phagous*, *-phagy*, not eating members of one's own tribe; *-plasm*, outermost layer of protoplasm; *-ske·leton*, external integument, bony or leathery; *exosmo·sis*, passage of a fluid outwards through a porous septum.

e·xodus, n. Departure, going forth, (esp. of body of emigrants); departure of Israelites from Egypt; book of O.T. relating this. [L, f. Gk EX*odos* (*hodos* way)]

ex offi·cio (-shĭō), adv. & a. In virtue of one's office, as *e.-o. members of committee.* [L]

e·xon, n. See EXEMPT[1]. [repr. F pron.]

exŏ·nerate, v.t. Exculpate; free (person) *from* (blame &c.); release (person *from* duty &c.). Hence or cogn. **exoner**A·TION n., **exo·nerat**IVE a. [f. L EX(*onerare* f. *onus -eris* burden), see -ATE[3]]

exophtha·lmus, -ŏs, n. Protrusion of eyeball. Hence **exophtha·lm**IC a. [f. Gk EX(*ophthalmos* eye) adj.]

exor·bitant, a. Grossly excessive (of price, demand, ambition, person). Hence **exor·bit**ANCE n., **exor·bitant**LY[2] adv. [f. L EX*orbitare* go out of the wheel-track (ORBIT), -ANT]

e·xorcize, v.t. Expel (evil spirit *from*, *out of*, person or place) by invocation or use of holy name; clear (person, place, *of* evil spirits). So **e·xorc**ISM, **e·xorc**IST, nn. [f. LL *exorcizare* f. Gk EX*orkizō* (*horkos* oath)]

exor·dium, n. (pl. *-iums*, *-ia*). Beginning, introductory part, esp. of discourse or treatise. Hence **exor·di**AL a. [L, f. EX(*ordiri* begin)]

exotĕ·ric, a. & n. (Of doctrines, modes of speech, &c.) intelligible to outsiders (cf. ESOTERIC); (of disciples) not admitted to esoteric teaching; commonplace, ordinary, popular; (n. pl.) e. doctrines or treatises. Hence **exote·ric**AL a., **exote·rical**LY[2] adv. [f. LL f. Gk *exōterikos* (*exōterō* compar., see EXO-, -IC)]

exŏ·tic, a. & n. (Of plants, words, fashions) introduced from abroad; (n.) e. plant (also fig.). [f. L f. Gk *exōtikos* (*exō* outside, see -IC)]

expa·nd, v.t. & i. Spread out flat (t. & i.); expound, write out, in full (what is condensed or abbreviated, algebraical expression, &c.); develop (t. & i.) *into*; swell, dilate, increase in bulk, (t. & i.); become genial, throw off reserve. So **expansi**BI·LITY n., **expa·nsi**BLE a. [f. L EX(*pandere pans-* spread)]

expa·nse, n. Wide area or extent; expansion. [as prec.]

expa·nsile, a. (Capable) of expansion. [-IL]

expa·nsion, n. Expanding; (Commerc.) extension of transactions; *e.* (increase) *of the currency*, whence **expa·nsion**IST(2) n.; increase in bulk of steam in cylinder of engine; *triple-e. engine* (in which steam passes through 3 cylinders). [f. LL *expansio* (prec., -ION)]

expa·nsive, a. Able, tending, to expand (t. & i.); extensive; comprehensive; (of persons, feelings, speech) effusive. Hence **expa·nsive**LY[2] adv., **expa·nsive**NESS, **expansi·**VITY, nn. [as prec., see -IVE]

ex par·tē, adv. & a. (law). On, in the interests of, one side only; (adj., *ex-p.*) made or said thus, as *an ex-p. statement.* [L]

expā·tiate (-shĭ-), v.i. Speak, write, copiously (*on* subject); wander unrestrained (usu. fig.). Hence **expati**A·TION n.; **expa·tiat**ORY a. [f. L EX(*spatiari* walk about, as SPACE), -ATE[3]]

expā̆·triate, v.t. Banish; (refl.) emigrate; (Law of Nations, refl.) renounce citizenship. Hence **expatri**A·TION n. [f. LL EX(*patriare* f. *patria* native land), see -ATE[3]]

expe·ct, v.t. Look forward to, regard as likely, as *I e. a storm*, *e. to see him*, *e. him to come*, *e.* (*that*) *he will come*, *e. him next week*, *don't e. me*, *e. payment today*, *not so bad as I expected* (*it to be*), *just what I expected of him*; *shall not e. you till I* &c. *see you*, leave you to arrive when you please; look for as due, as *I e. you to be punctual*, *that you will be punctual*, *do you e. payment for this?*; (colloq.) think, suppose, (*that*). [f. L EX(*spectare* look, frequent. of *specere* see)]

expe·ctancy, n. State of expectation; prospect, esp. of future possession; prospective chance (*of*). [f. L *expectantia* (prec., -ANCY)]

expe·ctant, a. & n. Expecting (*of* or abs.); having the prospect, in normal course, of possession, office, &c.; characterized by waiting for events, esp. (Med.) *e. method*; (Law) reversionary; (n.) one who expects, candidate for office &c. Hence **expe·ctant**LY[2] adv. [-ANT]

expecta·tion, n. Awaiting; anticipation, as *beyond*, *contrary to*, *e.*; ground for expecting (*of*); (pl.) prospects of inheritance; thing expected; *e. of* LIFE; probability of a thing's happening. [f. L *expectatio* (as prec., see -ATION)]

expe·ctative, a. Of reversion of benefices, reversionary. [f. LL *expectativus* (prec., -ATIVE)]

expe·ctorant, a. & n. (Medicine) that promotes expectoration. [as foll., see -ANT]

expe·ctorate, v.t. (chiefly U.S.). Eject (phlegm &c.) from chest or lungs by coughing or spitting; (abs.) spit. Hence **expector**A·TION n. [f. L EX*pectorare* relieve the mind (*pectus -oris* breast), -ATE[3]]

expē·dient, a. & n. (Usu. predic.) advantageous, suitable, as *do whatever is e.*, *it is e. that he should go*; politic rather than just; (n.) contrivance, device. Hence or cogn. **expe·di**ENCE, -ENCY, nn., **expedi·ential** a., **expe·dient**LY[2] adv. [f. F *expédient* (as foll., see -ENT)]

e·xpedite, v.t. Assist the progress of (measure, process, &c.); dispatch (business). [f. L EX*pedire -dit-* lit. free feet of (*pes pedis* foot)]

expedi·tion, n. Warlike enterprise; journey, voyage, for definite purpose; men, fleet, sent on this; promptness, speed. Hence **expedi·tion**ARY[1] a., **expedi·tion**IST(3) n. [f. L *expeditio* (as prec., see -ION)]

expedi·tious, a. Doing or done speedily; suited for speedy performance. Hence **expedi·tious**LY[2] adv., **expedi·tious**NESS n. [f. prec., see -IOUS(2)]

expe·l, v.t. (-ll-). Eject (person *from* place, bullet *from* gun, &c.) by force; turn out (person *from* a community, school, &c.; also w. *from* omitted *was expelled the school*). Hence **expe·ll**ENT a. [f. L EX(*pellere puls-* drive)]

expe·nd, v.t. Spend (money, care, time, *on* object, *in doing*); use up; (Naut.) wind (spare rope) round spar &c. [f. L EX-(*pendĕre pens-* weigh)]

expe·nditure (-tsher), n. Laying out (*of* money &c.); consuming; amount expended. [as prec. (irreg. p.p. *penditus*), see -URE]

expe·nse, n. Expenditure; cost; (pl.) outlay in execution of commission &c., reimbursement of this, as *he paid my ee.*, *offered me £10 & ee.*; *at the e.* (cost) *of*, esp. (fig.) by bringing discredit &c. on, as *you defend his veracity at the e. of his understanding*, if what he says is true he is a fool; *a laugh at his e.* (at him). [AF, f. LL *expensa* orig. fem. p.p. (as EXPEND)]

expe·nsive, a. Costly. Hence **expe·nsive**LY[2] adv., **expe·nsive**NESS n. [EXPEND, -IVE]

exper̄·ience[1], n. Actual observation of facts or events; knowledge resulting from this, whence **exper·ience**D[2] a.; event that affects one, as *an unpleasant e.*; fact, process, of being so affected, as *I learnt by e.*; (usu. pl.) state, phase, of religious emotion. [f. F *expérience* f. L *experientia* f. EX(*periri pert-* go through), see -ENCE]

exper·ience[2], v.t. Meet with, feel, undergo, (pleasure, treatment, fate, &c.); learn, find, (*that, how*, &c.). [f. prec.]

experie·ntial, a. Of experience; *e. philosophy* (treating all knowledge as based on experience), whence **experie·ntial**ISM, **experie·ntial**IST, nn. Hence **experie·ntial**LY[2] adv. [f. L as EXPERIENCE[1], see -AL]

expĕ·riment[1] (-ment), n. Test, trial, (*of*); procedure adopted on chance of its succeeding or for testing hypothesis &c. [OF, f. L *experimentum* (as prec., see -MENT)]

expe·rimĕnt[2], v.i. Make experiment (*on, with*). Hence **experiment**A·TION n. [prec.]

expĕrime·ntal, a. Based on experience, not authority or conjecture; based on experiment, as *e. philosophy*, whence **experime·ntal**ISM, **experime·ntal**IST, nn.; tentative; used in experiments. Hence **experime·ntal**IZE(2) v.i., **experime·ntal**LY[2] adv. [-AL]

exper·t[1], a. Trained by practice, skilful, (*at, in*). Hence **exper·t**LY[2] adv., **exper·t**NESS n. [OF, f. L as EXPERIENCE[1]]

e·xpert[2], n. Person having special skill or knowledge (*at, in*), as *mining e.*, (attrib.) *e. evidence.* [F (prec. as n.)]

exper·tō crē·de (-ī), sent. You may take my word for it, because I have tried. [L, = believe one who has tried]

e·xpiate, v.t. Pay the penalty of, make amends for, (sin). So **e·xpi**ABLE, **e·xpiatory**, aa., **expi**A·TION, **e·xpiat**OR[2], nn. [f. L EX(*piare* seek to appease f. *pius* devout), -ATE[3]]

expira·tion (-per-), n. Breathing out (*of* air &c.); termination (*of* period, truce, &c.). [f. L *expiratio* (as foll., see -ATION)]

expire·, v.t. & i. Breathe out (air *from* lungs, or abs.), whence **expīr·at**ORY a.; die; (of fire &c.) die out; (of period) come to an end; (of law, patent, truce, &c.) become void, reach its term; (of title &c.) become extinct. [f. F *expirer* f. L EX-(*spirare* breathe)]

expīr·y, n. Termination (of period, truce, &c.) [f. prec. + -Y[4]]

expi·scate, v.t. (Sc.) Find by scrutiny &c. [f. L *expiscari* (EX-, *piscari* to fish)]

explai·n, v.t. Make known in detail (thing, *that, how*, &c.); make intelligible (meaning, difficulty, &c., also abs.); account for (conduct &c.); *e. away*, modify, do away with, (esp. offensive language) by explanation; *e. oneself*, make one's meaning clear, (also) give an account of one's motives or conduct. Hence **explai·n**ABLE a. [f. L EX(*planare* f. *planus* flat)]

explana·tion, n. Explaining, esp. with view to mutual understanding or reconciliation; statement, circumstance, that explains. [f. L *explanatio* (as prec., see -ATION)]

explă·natory, a. Serving, meant, to explain. Hence **expla·natori**LY[2] adv. [as EXPLAIN, see -ORY]

explē·tive (*or* ĕ·ksplĭ-), a. & n. Serving to fill out (esp. sentence, metrical line, &c.); (n.) e. thing, word, &c., esp. oath or meaningless exclamation. [f. L *expletivus* f. EX(*plēre* fill), -IVE]

e·xplicate, v.t. Develop (notion, principle, &c.), whence **explic**A·TION n.; (archaic) explain, whence **e·xplic**ABLE, **e·xplicat**IVE, **e·xplicat**ORY, aa. [f. L EX(*plicare plicat-* or *plicit-* fold) unfold, see -ATE[3]]

e·xplicit[1], v.i. Here ends (formerly written at end of book). [med. L; prob.

abbr. of p.p. as prec., but treated as 3rd sing.]

expli·cit[2], a. Stated in detail, leaving nothing merely implied; definite; (of persons) outspoken; *e. faith*, acceptance of doctrine with clear understanding of all it involves (cf. IMPLICIT). Hence **expli·cit**LY[2] adv., **expli·cit**NESS n. [f. F *explicite* (as EXPLICATE)]

explo·de, v.t. & i. Expose, bring into disrepute, (theory, fallacy, &c.); (of gas, gunpowder, boiler, &c.) go off with loud noise; cause (these) to do this. [f. L EX(*plodere plos-* = *plaudere* clap) hiss off stage]

e·xploit[1], n. Brilliant achievement. [f. OF *esploit(e)* f. L neut. & fem. p.p. as EXPLICATE]

exploi·t[2], v.t. Work, turn to account, (mine &c.); utilize (person &c.) for one's own ends. Hence or cogn. **exploi·t**ABLE a., **exploi·t**AGE, **exploit**A·TION, nn. [f. OF *exploiter* f. L **explicitare* frequent. as prec.]

explore·, v.t. Inquire into; examine (wound) by touch; examine (country &c.) by going through it. Hence or cogn. **explor**A·TION, **explor·**ER[1], nn., **explor·a**TIVE, **explor·at**ORY, aa. [f. F *explorer* f. L EX(*plorare* perh. = make flow f. *pluere* flow) search out, reconnoitre]

explo·sion (-zhn), n. Going off with loud noise; such noise; outbreak (of anger &c.). [f. L *explosio* (as EXPLODE, see -ION)]

explo·sive (-s-), a. & n. Tending to eject something with loud noise; (of consonant sound) produced by explosion of breath, stopped; tending to explode or cause explosion (lit. & fig.); (n.) e. agent or material, e. letter; *high e.*, kinds having very violent shattering effect & used not as propellents but in shells &c. Hence **explo·sive**LY[2] adv., **explo·sive**NESS n. [as EXPLODE, see -IVE]

expo·nent, a. & n. (Person, thing) that sets forth or interprets; executant (of music &c.); type, representative; (Alg.) index, symbol indicating what power of a factor is to be taken, whence **expone·nt**IAL a. [f. L EX(*ponere posit-* put), see -ENT]

expor·t[1], v.t. Send out (goods) to another country. Hence or cogn. **expor·t**ABLE a., **export**A·TION n. [f. L EX(*portare* carry)]

e·xport[2], n. Exported article; (usu. pl.) amount exported; exportation; *e. duty* (paid on e.). [f. prec.]

expo·se (-z), v.t. Leave (person, thing) unprotected (esp. from weather); subject *to* (risk &c.); (Photog.) subject (plate) to light; turn (child) out of doors to perish; (p.p.) open *to* (the East &c.); exhibit, display; put up for sale; disclose (secret, project, &c.); unmask (villain, villany). [f. F EX(*poser*, see COMPOSE)]

expo·sé (-zā), n. Statement of facts; showing up (of discreditable thing). [F, p.p. as prec.]

exposi·tion, n. Setting forth, description; explanation; commentary; = EXPOSURE; exhibition of goods &c. [F, f. L *expositionem* (as EXPONENT, see -ION)]

expŏ·sitive, a. Descriptive; explanatory. So **expo·sit**OR[2] n.; **expo·sit**ORY a. [f. L *expositivus* (as prec., see -IVE)]

ex pōst fa·cto, a. Acting retrospectively, as *e. p. f. law*. [L, = from what is made (i.e. enacted) afterwards]

expŏ·stulate, v.i. Make friendly remonstrance; remonstrate (*with* person *about, for, on*). Hence or cogn. **expostul**A·TION n., **expo·stulat**ORY a. [f. L EX(*postulare* POSTULATE)]

expo·sure (-zh*e*r), n. Exposing, being exposed, (*to* air, cold, danger, &c.); abandoning (of child); display, esp. of goods for sale; unmasking of imposture &c.; aspect, as *southern e.* [-URE]

expou·nd (-ow-), v.t. Set forth in detail (doctrine &c.); explain, interpret, (esp. Scripture). [ME *expounen* f. OF *espondre* (as EXPONENT)]

expre·ss[1], a., adv., & n. (Of likeness) exact; definitely stated, not merely implied; done, made, sent, for special purpose; *e. train* (fast, stopping at few intermediate stations); *e. rifle* (discharging bullet with high initial velocity & low trajectory); *e. bullet* (expanding, for e. rifle); *e. delivery* (by special postal messenger); (adv.) with speed, by e. messenger or train; (n.) e. train, messenger, rifle. Hence **expre·ss**LY[2] adv. [f. F *exprès, -esse* (as foll.)]

expre·ss[2], v.t. Squeeze out (juice, air, *from, out of*); emit, exude; represent by symbols, as (Math.) *e.* (quantity) *in terms of* (another); reveal, betoken, (feelings, qualities); put (thought) into words; *e. oneself*, say what one means (*strongly* &c. *on* subject, *well, aptly*, &c.). Hence **expre·ss**IBLE a. [f. OF EX(*presser* PRESS[2])]

expre·ssion, n. Expressing (in all senses); wording, diction, word, phrase; (Alg.) collection of symbols expressing a quantity; aspect (of face), intonation (of voice), whence **expre·ssion**LESS a.; (Art) mode of expressing character &c., whence **expre·ssion**IST(2) n.; (Mus.) execution that expresses the feeling of a passage, as *e.-mark*, sign, word, indicating e. required, *e.-stop* (in harmonium, producing e. by varied air-pressure). [F, f. L *expressionem* f. EX(*primere* = *premere* PRESS[2], -ION)]

expre·ssional, a. Of verbal, facial, or artistic expression. [-AL]

expre·ssive, a. Serving to express (*e. of* motion &c.); (of word, gesture, &c.) significant. Hence **expre·ssive**LY[2] adv., **expre·ssive**NESS n. [F (*-if, -ive*), as EXPRESSION, see -IVE]

exprobra·tion, n. Reproachful language. [f. L *exprobratio* f. EX(*probrare* f. *probrum* shameful deed), see -ATION]

exprō·priate, v.t. Dispossess (*from* estate &c.); take away (property). So **expropri**A·TION n. [f. LL EX(*propriare* f. *proprium* property), see PROPER & -ATE[3]]

expu·lsion, n. Expelling. So **expu·ls**IVE a. & n. (med.). [f. L *expulsio* (as EXPEL, see -ION)]

expu·nge (-j), v.t. Erase, omit, (name *from* list, passage *from* book, &c.). So **ex-pu·nct**ION n. [f. L EX(*pungere punct-* prick)]

e·xpurgate, v.t. Purify (book &c.) by removing objectionable matter; clear away (such matter). Hence or cogn. **expurg**A·TION, **e·xpurgat**OR[2], nn., **ex-purgator·**IAL, **expur·gat**ORY, aa. [f. L EX(*purgare* cleanse), -ATE[3]]

e·xquisite (-zĭt), a. & n. Of consummate excellence or beauty; acute (*e. pain, pleasure*); keen (*e. sensibility* &c.); (n.) coxcomb, fop. Hence **e·xquisite**LY[2] adv., **e·xquisite**NESS n. [f. L EX(*quirere quisit-* =*quaerere* seek)]

exsa·nguinate, v.t. Drain of blood. [f. L EX(*sanguinare* f. *sanguis -inis* blood), see -ATE[3]]

exsa·nguine, a. Lacking blood. [EX-]

exsci·nd, v.t. Cut out, excise, (lit. & fig.). [f. L EX(*scindere* cut)]

exser·t, v.t. (biol.). Put forth. [=EXERT]

ex-ser·vice, a. That has been (esp. during the great war) but is no longer in one of the fighting services. [EX-(3)]

e·xsiccate, v.t. Dry up; drain dry. [f. L EX(*siccare* f. *siccus* dry)]

e·xtant (*or* -ă·nt), a. Still existing (esp. of documents &c.). [f. L EX(*stare* stand), see -ANT]

extasy. See ECSTASY.

exte·mporĕ, adv. & a. (Spoken, done) without preparation; off-hand; *speak e.* (without notes.) Hence or cogn. **extem-por**A·NEOUS, **exte·mpor**ARY[1], aa., **ex-tempora·neous**LY[2], **exte·mporari**LY[2], advv., **extempora·neous**NESS n. [L *ex tempore* from the time]

exte·mporize, v.t. & i. Compose, produce, extempore; (intr.) speak extempore. Hence **extemporiz**A·TION n. [f. prec. + -IZE]

exte·nd, v.t. & i. Lay out (esp. body, limbs, &c.) at full length; write out (shorthand &c.) at full length; *e. an invoice,* write in the columns the total of items in each line; (intr. & refl.) reach (*to* point, *over, across,* &c., space); cause to do this; prolong (period); enlarge (scope, meaning of word, &c.); (Mil., of line &c.) spread out into open order with regular intervals between men (trans., cause to e.); (Sport. slang) tax powers of (horse, athlete) to the utmost (usu. pass.); stretch forth (hand, arm); accord (kindness, patronage, *to*); (Law) value (land &c.), seize (land &c.) for debt. Hence or cogn. **extensi**BI·LITY n., **ex-te·nd**IBLE, **exte·nsi**BLE, aa. [f. L EX(*tendere tens-* or *tent-* stretch)]

exte·nsile, a. Capable of being stretched out or protruded. [as prec., see -ILE]

exte·nsion, n. Extending (in all senses exc. Law); extent, range; prolongation; enlargement; additional part (of railway, plan, theory, &c.); word(s) amplifying subject or predicate; *University E.*, admission of non-resident students to some forms of Univ. teaching & examination. [f. L *extentio, -sio,* (as prec., see -ION)]

exte·nsive, a. (Of space, purchase, operation, &c.) large; far-reaching, comprehensive; (of agricultural production &c.) depending on extension of area (cf. INTENSIVE). Hence **exte·nsive**LY[2] adv., **exte·nsive**NESS n. [f. LL *extensivus* (as prec., see -IVE)]

exte·nsor, n. *E.* (*-muscle*), one that straightens out part of the body. [LL, as prec., -OR[2]]

exte·nt, n. Space over which a thing extends; width of application, scope, as *to a great e., to the full e. of his power*; large space, as *a vast e. of marsh*; (Law) valuation (of land &c.); seizure, writ for seizure, (of land &c.). [f. AF *estente* p.p. of *estendre* (as EXTEND)]

extĕ·nuate, v.t. Lessen seeming magnitude of (guilt, offence) by partial excuse, as *we must not e., nothing can e., his baseness,* whence **exte·nuat**ORY a.; (improp.) lessen seeming guilt of, as *do not e. yourself, his conduct*; (archaic) make thin or weak. Hence **extenu**A·TION n. [f. L EX(*tenuare* f. *tenuis* thin), -ATE[3]]

extēr·ior, a. & n. Outer; situated or coming from without; *e. angle,* that between side of rectilineal figure & adjacent side produced; (n.) outward aspect or demeanour. Hence **exteriŏ·**RITY n., **exter·ior**LY[2] adv. [L, compar. of *exterus* outside]

exter·iorize, v.t. Realize (conception) in outward form; attribute external existence to. Hence **exterioriz**A·TION n. [-IZE]

exter·minate, v.t. Root out (species, race, sect, opinion). Hence or cogn. **extermin**A·TION, **exter·minat**OR[2], nn., **exter·minat**ORY a. [f. L EX*terminare* (TERMINUS), -ATE[3]]

exter·nal, a. & n. Situated outside; (of remedies &c.) applied to the outside of the body; (Theol.) consisting in outward acts, whence **exter·nal**ISM(2) n.; belonging to the world of phenomena (*e. world*), outside the conscious subject; *e. evidence* (derived from source independent of the thing discussed); (n. pl.) outward features or aspect, e. circumstances, nonessentials. Hence **externa·**LITY n., **ex-ter·nal**LY[2] adv. [f. L *externus* outward + -AL]

exter·nalize, v.t. Give, attribute, external existence to. Hence **externa-liz**A·TION n. [-IZE]

exterritor·ial, a. (Of ambassadors &c.) free from jurisdiction of the territory in which one resides. So **exterritoria·l**ITY n. [EX-]

exti·nct, a. (Of fire &c.) no longer burning; (of volcano) that has ceased eruption; (of life, hope, &c.) quenched; (of family, class, species) that has died out; (of office &c.) obsolete; (of title of nobility) having no qualified claimant. [f. L EX(*stinguere stinct-* quench)]

exti·nction, n. Extinguishing; making, being, becoming, extinct; wiping out (of debt); annihilation. So **exti·nct**IVE a. [f. L *extinctio* (as prec., see -ION)]

exti·nguish, v.t. Put out, quench, (light, hope, life, faculties); eclipse, obscure, (person) by superior brilliancy; reduce (opponent) to silence; destroy; wipe out (debt); annihilate. Hence **exti·nguish**ABLE a., **exti·nguish**MENT n. [as EXTINCT, see -ISH²]

exti·nguisher, n. In vbl senses, esp. hollow conical cap for putting out candle. [-ER¹]

e·xtirpate, v.t. Root out, destroy, (tree, weed, species, nation, tumour, heresy, &c.). So **extirp**A·TION, **e·xtirpat**OR², nn. [f. L EX(*s*)*tirpare* (*stirps* stem), see -ATE³]

extŏ·l, v.t. (-ll-). Praise enthusiastically (*e. him to the skies*). [f. L EX(*tollere* raise)]

extor·t, v.t. Obtain (money, promise, &c.) by violence, intimidation, importunity, &c. (*from*); extract forcibly (meaning, inference, *from* words, data). Hence **extor·t**IVE a. [f. L EX(*torquēre tort-* twist)]

extor·tion, n. Extorting, esp. of money; illegal exaction. Hence **extor·tion**ER¹ n. [f. L *extortio* (as prec., see -ION)]

extor·tionate (-*at*), a. Using, given to, extortion; (of prices &c.) exorbitant. [-ATE²]

e·xtra, a., adv., & n. Additional; larger than its name indicates, as *e. foolscap octavo*; of superior quality, as *e. binding*; (adv.) more than usually, as *e. strong*; additionally; *e.-special* (latest) *edition* (of evening paper); (n.) e. thing, one for which e. charge is made, as *dancing is an e.*, (Crick.) run not scored off bat. [prob. for EXTRAORDINARY, perh. f. F]

extra- in comb. = L *extra* in senses 'situated outside of a thing', 'not coming within its scope'; chiefly in wds f. med. L or mod. L (L has only *extraordinarius*), as: *-atmospheric*, of the space beyond the atmosphere; *-cosmical*, acting outside the universe; *-cranial*, outside the skull; *-essential*, not included in the essence of a thing; *-judicial*, not belonging to the case before the court, not legally authorized, (of confession) not made in court; *-mundane*, outside of our world or of the universe; *-mural*, outside the walls or boundaries (of town or city), (of lecturers &c.) from outside a university; *-official*, not pertaining to an office; *-parochial*, outside, not concerned with, the parish; *-physical*, not subject to physical laws; *-spectral*, lying outside the visible spectrum; *terrestrial*, outside the earth or its atmosphere; *-territorial-(ity)*, = EXTERRITORIAL(ITY).

e·xtract¹, n. The tough or viscid matter got by treating a substance with solvents & then evaporating them; preparation containing the active principle of a substance in concentrated form; passage from book &c. [as foll.]

extra·ct², v.t. Copy out (passage in book &c.); make extracts from (book &c.); take out by force (teeth, anything firmly fixed); draw forth (money, admission, &c.) against person's will; obtain (juices &c.) by suction, pressure, &c.; derive (pleasure &c. *from*); deduce principle &c. *from*); (Math.) find (root of a number). Hence **extra·ct**ABLE a., **extra·ct**OR² n. [f. L EX(*trahere tract-* draw)]

extra·ction, n. Extracting; lineage (*of Indian e.*). [F, f. med. L *extractionem* (prec., -ION)]

extra·ctive, a. & n. (Thing) of the nature of an extract; *e. industries* (concerned with obtaining natural productions). [-IVE]

extradi·table, a. Liable to, (of crime) warranting, extradition. [f. foll. + -ABLE]

e·xtradite, v.t. Give up (fugitive foreign criminal) to the proper authorities; obtain the extradition of. [back formation f. foll.]

extradi·tion, n. Delivery of fugitive criminal to proper authorities; (Psychol.) localizing of sensation at distance from the centre of sensation. [F (EX-, see TRADITION)]

extrā·dŏs, n. Upper or outer curve of arch. [F EXTRA(*dos* back f. L *dorsum*)]

extrā·neous, a. Of external origin; foreign *to* (object to which it is attached &c.); not belonging (*to* matter in hand, class). Hence **extra·neous**LY² adv., **extra·neous**NESS n. [f. L *extraneus* (*extra* outside) + -OUS]

extraor·dinary (-tror-, -traor-), a. & n. Out of the usual course; (of officials &c.) additional, specially employed; *envoy e.*, diplomatic minister of second class, ranking next to ambassador; exceptional, surprising; unusually great; (n. pl.) extra allowances to troops. Hence **extraordi·nari**LY² adv., **extraor·dinari**NESS n. [f. L *extraordinarius* (*extra ordinem* outside the usual order, -ARY¹)]

extrā·vagance, n. Being extravagant; absurd statement or action. [F (foll., -ANCE)]

extrā·vagant, a. Immoderate; exceeding the bounds of reason; profuse, wasteful; (of price &c.) exorbitant. Hence

extra·vagantLY[2] adv. [f. L EXTRA(*vagari* wander), see -ANT]

extrăvaga·nza, n. Fantastic composition (literary, musical, dramatic), language, or behaviour. [f. It. *estravaganza* (prec., -ANCE)]

extră·vagate, v.i. (rare). Wander away (*from* right course, *into* error &c.); exceed due bounds. [as EXTRAVAGANT, see -ATE[3]]

extră·vasate, v.t. & i. Force out (fluid) from its proper vessel; flow out. Hence **extrăvas**A·TION n. [EXTRA-, L *vas* vessel, -ATE[3]]

extre·me, a. & n. Outermost, farthest from centre, situated at either end; *divided in e. & mean ratio* (the whole being to one part as that part to the other); utmost; last, as (R.-C. Ch.) *e. unction,* anointing by priest of dying person; reaching a high degree, as *e. old age, in e. danger*; *an e. case* (having some characteristic in the utmost degree); (of actions, measures) severe, stringent; (of opinions, persons, &c.) going to great lengths, opp. to *moderate,* whence **extre·m**ISM, **extre·m**IST, nn.; *in the e.,* extremely; (n.) thing at either end of anything, esp. (pl.) things as remote or as different as possible, as *ee. meet*; (Logic) subject or predicate in proposition, major or minor term in syllogism; (Math.) first, last, term of ratio or series; *run to an e., go to ee.,* take an e. course. Hence **extre·me**LY[2] adv. **extre·me**NESS n. [OF, f. L *extremus* superl. of *exterus* outward]

extrĕ·mity, n. Extreme point, very end; *the ee.,* hands & feet; extreme adversity, embarrassment, &c., as *driven to e., what can we do in this e?*; (usu. pl.) extreme measure(s). [f. F *extrémité* f. L *extremitatem* (prec., -TY)]

e·xtricate, v.t. Disentangle, release, (person, thing, *from* confinement, difficulty); (Chem.) liberate (gas &c.) from state of combination. Hence **e·xtric**ABLE a., **extric**A·TION n. [f. L EX(*tricare* f. *tricae* perplexities), -ATE[3]]

extri·nsic, a. Lying outside, not belonging, (*to*); operating from without; not inherent or essential. Hence **extri·nsic**ALLY adv. [f. F *extrinsèque* f. LL (adj.) f. L (adv.) *extrinsecus* (*exter* outside + *-in* local suf. + *secus* beside)]

extror·se, a. (bot.). (Of anthers) turned outwards. [F, f. L *extrorsus* outwards (EXTRA- + *versus* towards)]

e·xtrovert, n. (psychol.). Person not given to introspection (chiefly in antithesis with INTROVERT n.). [f. L *extra* outside (w. assim. to INTRO-) + *vertĕre* turn, after *convert* n.]

extru·de, v.t. Thrust out (person, thing, *from*). Hence **extru·s**ION (-zhn) n., **extru·s**IVE (-s-) a. [f. L EX(*trudere trus-* thrust)]

exū·berant, a. Luxuriantly prolific (lit. & fig.); growing luxuriantly; (of health, emotions, &c.) overflowing, abounding; (of persons, actions, &c.) effusive, overflowing with spirits; (of language) copious, lavish in ornament; abundant. Hence or cogn. **exu·ber**ANCE n., **exu·berant**LY[2] adv. [f. L EX(*uberare* be fruitful f. *uber* fertile, cf. *uber* udder), -ANT]

exū·berate, v.i. Abound, overflow; indulge freely *in.* [as prec., see -ATE[3]]

exū·de, v.i. & t. Ooze out, give off (moisture &c.), like sweat. Hence or cogn. **exud**A·TION n., **exu·dat**IVE a. [f. L EX(*sudare* sweat)]

exu·lt, v.i. Rejoice exceedingly (*at, in,* thing, *to* find &c.); triumph (*over* person). Hence or cogn. **exu·lt**ANCY, **exult**A·TION, nn., **exu·lt**ANT a., **exu·ltant**LY[2] adv. [f. F *exulter* f. L EX(*sultare* = *saltare* frequent. of *salire salt-* leap)]

exū·viae, n. pl. Animal's cast skin, shell, or covering, (recent or fossil, also fig.). Hence **exu·vi**AL a. [L, = animal's skin, spoils of enemy, f. EX*uere* divest oneself of]

exū·viate, v.t. & i. Shed (exuviae, also fig.), slough. Hence **exuvi**A·TION n. [prec., -ATE[3]]

ex vō·to, adv. & n. (Offering made) in pursuance of a vow. [L (as adv. phr.)]

eyas (ī·*as*), n. Young hawk taken from nest for training, or not yet completely trained. [orig. *nyas* f. F **niais* f. L **nidiacem* (nom. *-ax*) f. *nidus* nest; for loss of *n-* cf. ADDER]

eye[1] (ī), n. Organ of sight; iris of this, as *blue, brown, ee.*; region of the ee., as BLACK[1] *e.*; *e. of day,* sun; EVIL *e.*; *in the wind's e.* (direction of the wind); (Mil.) *ee. right, left, front,* (turn them thus); *mind your e.,* take care; (contempt.) *pipe, put* one's *finger in,* one's *e.,* weep; *beam, mote, in* one's *e.* (*Matt.* vii. 3); *e. for e.,* retaliation (*Exod.* xxi. 24); *clap, set, ee. on,* behold; *be all ee.,* watch intently; *up to the ee.,* deeply (engaged), as *up to the ee. in work, mortgaged up to the ee.*; *his ee. are bigger than his belly* (said of a person who has helped himself to more than he can eat); *made him open his ee.* (stare with astonishment); *open* one's *ee. to,* make him realize; *wipe the e. of* (shooter), kill game he has missed; *all my e.* (*& Betty Martin*), humbug, nonsense; *my eye(s)!,* int. expr. astonishment; *lose an e.,* (often) lose the sight of it; *if you had half an e.* (were not wholly blind or dull); *saw with half an e.* (at a glance); *the* NAKED *e.*; *have an e. to,* have as one's object; *with an e.* (a view) *to*; *keep an e. on,* keep watch on (lit. & fig.); *have an e. for* (a due sense of) *proportion* &c.; *in the ee.* (judgement) *of*; *in the e.* (from the point of view) *of the law*; *in the mind's e.,* in anticipation or imagination; *see e. to e.,* agree entirely (*with*); *view with a friendly,* *jealous, e.* (with such feelings); *throw* DUST *in the ee. of*; *make ee.* (look amorously) *at*; *cast* SHEEP'*s ee.*; thing like an e., as spot on peacock's tail, *e. of needle* &c. (hole for thread &c.), *hook & e.* (kind of fastening for dress), loop of cord or rope, leafbud of potato; BULL[1]'*s-e.*; *glass e.* (artificial, of glass &c.); APPLE *of the e.*; *eyeball*, pupil of the e., e. within lids & socket; *e.-bath, -cup*, small glass for applying lotion &c. to e.; *e.-bolt*, bolt, bar, with e. at end for hook &c.; *eyebright* (also *euphrasy*), plant formerly used to cure weak eyes; *eyebrow*, fringe of hair over e.; *e.-glass*, lens for assisting defective sight, (pl.) pair of these held in position by hand or by spring on nose (cf. SPECTACLE); *eyehole*, hole containing e., hole to look through; *eyelash*, hair, row of hairs, on edge of eyelid; *eyelid*, upper or lower cover of e., (fig.) *hang on by the eyelids*, have only slight hold; *e.-opener*, enlightening or surprising circumstance; *eyepiece*, lens(es) at *e.-end* of telescope &c.; *e.-servant* (working properly only under employer's e.); *e.-service* (performed only thus); *eyeshot*, seeing-distance, as *beyond, in, out of, eyeshot (of)*; *eyesight*, power, faculty, of seeing; *eyesore*, ugly object, thing that offends the sight; *e.-splice* (made by turning up end of rope & interlacing its strands with those of upper part); *eyestrings*, muscles, nerves, tendons, of e.; *e.-tooth* (canine, just under or next to e., in upper or lower jaw); *eyewater*, tears, lotion for e., aqueous or vitreous humours of e.; *e.-wash*, lotion for e., (slang) bunkum, mere professions; *eyewitness*, one who can bear witness from his own observation. Hence **(-)eye**ED[2], **eye·**LESS, aa. [OE *éage*, Du. *oog*, G *auge*, f. OTeut. *augon*, etym. dub.]

eye[2], v.t. (part. *eying*). Observe, watch, (*jealously, narrowly, with disgust*, ASKANCE, &c.). [f. prec.]

eye·let (ī-), n. Small hole in cloth, sail, &c., for lace, ring, rope, &c.; loophole; *e.-hole*, small hole to look or shoot through; small eye. [ME *oilet* f. F *œillet* dim. of *œil* eye f. L *oculus*]

eyot. See AIT.

eyre (ār), n. (hist.). Circuit, circuit court, as *Justices in E.* [f. OF *eire* f. *errer* (ERRANT 1)]

eyrie. See AERIE.

F

F (ĕf), letter (pl. *F*s F's). (Mus.; also *fa*) fourth note in diatonic scale of C major (*F sharp*, joc. for flea).

Abbreviations (1): (F) fine (in pencils); (F.) Fahrenheit, as 45° F.; federated, **F.M.S.** (Malay States); federation, **F.B.I.** (of British industries); Fellow, as **F.B.A.** (British Academy), **F.G.S.** (Geological Society), **F.R.A.S.** (Royal Astronomical Soc.), **F.R.C.P.** (Royal College of Physicians), **F.R.C.S.** (ditto Surgeons), **F.R.G.S.** (Royal Geographical Soc.), **F.R.I.B.A.** (Royal institute of British architects), **F.R.S.** (Royal Soc.), **F.S.A.** (Soc. of Antiquaries), **F.Z.S.** (zoological soc.); *Fidei*, **F.D.** (*defensor* = Defender of the Faith); Field, **F.M.** (Marshal), **F.P.** (punishment); fire, **F.P.** (plug); football, **F.A.** (association), **F.C.** (club); foreign, **F.O.** (office); four, **F.W.B.** (wheel brake). (f.) *falsa*, **f.l.** (*lectio* = false reading); feet, as *5 f.*; feminine; filly; francs; free, as **f.a.a.** (of all average), **f.a.s.** (alongside ship), **f.o.b.** (on board), **f.o.r.** (on rail). (*f.*), forte.

Abbreviations (2): **Fahr.** (enheit); **fcap, fcp**, foolscap; **fec.**(*it* or *-erunt*); **fi. fa.**, fieri facias; **fig.**(ure, as fig. *e*, or -uratively); **fl.**(orins); **Fla**, Florida; **flor.**(uit); **foll.**(owing, as *pp. 76 foll.*); Father, **Fr**; **fr.**(ancs); **Frl.**, Fräulein; **ft**, feet, as *60 ft long*.

fa (fah), n. Fourth note of octave in solmization. [first syl. of *famuli*, see GAMUT]

Fā·bian, a. Employing cautious & dilatory strategy to wear out an enemy (esp. *F. policy*); *F. Society* (of socialists following such policy). [f. L *Fabianus* (Q. *Fabius* commander against Hannibal, -AN)]

fā·ble[1], n. Story, esp. of supernatural character, not founded on fact; (collect.) myths, legendary tales; idle talk (*old wives' ff.*); false statement, lie; thing only supposed to exist; short story, esp. with animals for characters, conveying a moral, apologue; plot of play &c. [F, f. L *fabula* (*fari* speak)]

fa·ble[2], v.i. & t. (archaic & poet.). Romance, tell fictitious tales, whence **fa·bl**ER[1] n.; state fictitiously; (p.p.) celebrated in f., legendary, fictitious. [f. OF *fabler* f. L *fabulari* see prec.]

fă·bliau (-ĭō), n. (pl. *-x*, pr. -z). Metrical tale of early French poetry. [F]

fă·bric, n. Thing put together; edifice, building; frame, structure, (lit. & fig.); (often *textile f.*) woven material; construction, texture, tissue. [f. F *fabrique* f. L *fabrica* (*faber* artificer)]

fă·bricate, v.t. Construct, manufacture, (rare); invent (facts), forge (document). So **fabric**A·TION, **fa·bricat**OR[2], nn. [f. L *fabricare* as prec., -ATE[3]]

fă·bulist, n. Composer of fables or apologues; liar. [f. F *fabuliste* (FABLE[1], -IST)]

fă·bulous, a. Given to legend (*f. historians*); celebrated in fable; unhistorical, legendary, incredible, absurd, exaggerated. Hence or cogn. **fabulŏ·**SITY, **fa·bulous**NESS, nn., **fa·bulous**LY[2] adv. [f. L *fabulosus* (FABLE[1], -OUS)]

faça·de (-sahd), n. Face of building towards street or open space. [F (foll., -ADE[1])]

face[1], n. Front of head from forehead to chin (*look* one *in the f.*, confront him steadily; *show* one's *f.*, appear; *f. to f.*, confronted; *f. to f. with*, confronting; *set* one's *f. against*, oppose; *with wind, sun, in* one's *f.*, straight against one; *fly in the f. of*, openly disobey; *in f. of*, opposite to; *in the f. of*, or *in f. of*, despite; *to* one's *f.*, openly in his sight or hearing; *in the f. of day*, openly; *her f. is her fortune*, beauty her only dower); expression of countenance (*pull, wear, a long f.*, look serious or dismal); grimace (*make, pull, a f.* or *ff.*); composure, coolness, effrontery, (*have the f.*, be shameless enough; *save* one's *f.*, forbear from or evade shaming him or oneself openly); outward show, aspect, (*on the f. of it*, to judge by appearance; *put a new f. on*, alter aspect of; *put a good, bold, f. on matter*, make it look well, show courage in facing it); surface (*from the f. of the earth*); front, façade, right side, obverse, dial-plate of clock &c., working surface of implement &c.; *f.-ache*, neuralgia; *f. value*, nominal value as stated on coin, note, &c. Hence **-fac**ED[2] a. [F, f. pop. L *facia*=*facies* (*facere* make, or *fa-* shine)]

face[2], v.t. & i. Meet confidently or defiantly (*f.* matter *out*, carry it through; *f.* opponent *down*, browbeat him), not shrink from, stand fronting, (*f. the music*, not quail at moment of trial); present itself to (*the problem that faces us*); turn (card) f. upwards; (of persons &c.) look, (of things) be situated, in a certain direction (*on, to*, or *North, Eastwards*, &c.); front towards, be opposite to, (*to f. page 20*); (Golf) strike (ball) full with middle of club-f. in driving from tee; (Mil.) turn in certain direction on one's ground (*left, about, f.*; also trans., *he faced his men about*); supply (garment) with FACINGS; cover (surface) with layer of other material; dress surface of; coat (tea) with colouring matter. [f. prec.]

fa·cer, n. Blow in the face; great & sudden difficulty. [FACE[1]+-ER[1]]

fă·cet, n. One side of a many-sided body, esp. of a cut gem; one segment of a compound eye. Hence **fa·cet**ED[2] a. [f. F *facette* (FACE[1], -ETTE)]

facē·tiae (-shĭē), n. pl. Pleasantries, witticisms; (book catalogues) books of humorous or obscene character. [L (*facetus* urbane)]

face·tious (-sh*u*s), a. Addicted to or marked by pleasantry, waggish. Hence **face·tious**LY[2] adv., **face·tious**NESS n. [f. F *facétieux* (*facétie* f. L *facetia* sing. of prec.)]

fă·cia (-sh*a*), n. Plate over shop-front with occupier's name &c. [var. of FASCIA]

fā·cial (-shl), a. Of the face (esp. in Anat., as *f. artery*); *f. angle*, that formed by two lines from nostril to (1) ear & (2) forehead. [F, f. med. L *facialis* (FACE[1], -AL)]

-fācient (-shnt), suf. forming adjj. representing L *-facient-* (*facere* make, -ENT) added to infin. in *-ē(re)*, as *calefacere, liquefacere*, w. sense *producing the action of* the vb. E forms, on strict anal. w. L, *absorbefacient* &c.,&,loosely, *abortifacient, calorifacient*, &c., where L would have vbs in *-ficare*, adjj. in *-ficus* -FIC.

fă·cile, a. Easily done or won; working easily, ready, fluent; of easy temper, gentle, flexible, yielding. [F, f. L *facilis* (*facere* do)]

fă·cilĕ pri·nceps, pred. a. Easily first. [L]

faci·litate, v.t. Make easy, promote, help forward, (action or result). Hence **faci·li**TA·TION n. [f. F *faciliter* (FACILE, -ATE[3])]

faci·lity, n. Being easy, absence of difficulty, unimpeded opportunity (*give ff. for, of doing*); ease or readiness of speech &c., aptitude, dexterity, fluency; pliancy. [f. L *facilité* f. L *facilitatem* (FACILE, -TY)]

fa·cing, n. In vbl senses of FACE[2]; esp.: (pl.) cuffs, collar, &c., of soldier's jacket, differently coloured from rest; coating of different material, esp. of stone &c. on wall; turning in some direction (*put* person *through his ff.*, test his qualities, proficiency, &c.; *go through* one's *ff.*, be thus tested). [-ING[1]]

făcsĭ·milĕ, n., & v.t. Exact copy, esp. of writing, printing, picture, &c. (*reproduced in f.*, exactly); (vb) make f. of. [L *fac* imperat. of *facere* make+neut. of *similis* like]

fact, n. Perpetration of act, occurrence of event, (now only in *before, after, the f., confess the f.*); thing certainly known to have occurred or be true, datum of experience, (often with explanatory clause or phrase, as *the f. that fire burns, of my having seen him*); thing assumed as basis for inference (*his ff. are disputable*); (sing. without *a*) the true or existent, reality, (so *matter of f.*, independent of inference; MATTER[1]*-of-f.*; *in f.*; *as a matter of f.*; *in point of f.*; *the f. of the matter is*). [f. L *factum* neut. p.p. of *facere* do]

fa·ction, n. Self-interested, turbulent, or unscrupulous party, esp. in politics; prevalence of party spirit. Hence or cogn. **fa·ction**AL, **fa·ct**IOUS, aa., **fa·ctious**LY[2] adv., **fa·ctious**NESS n. [F, f. L *factionem* (*facere fact-* do, -ION) way of making (FASHION), class, clique]

-faction, suf. repr. L *-factio*, forming nn. of action related to vv. in -FY, prop. only when *-fy* represents L *-facere*, F *-faire*, as in *satisfaction*, but also used when *-fy* represents L *-ficare*, F *-fier*, as in *petrifaction*.

facti·tious, a. Designedly got up, not natural, artificial. Hence **facti·tious**LY[2] adv., **facti·tious**NESS n. [f. L *facticius* (*facere fact-* make)+-OUS]

fa·ctitive, a. (gram.). *F. verb,* one with sense *make, call,* or *think,* that takes obj. & compl. (*he thought her mad*). Hence **fa·ctitive**LY[2] adv. [irreg. f. L *facere fact-* make, -IVE]

fa·ctor, n. Agent, deputy; merchant buying & selling on commission, whence **fa·ctor**AGE(4) n.; (Sc.) land agent, steward; (Math.) one of the components that make up a number or expression by multiplication; circumstance, fact, or influence, contributing to a result. [f. F *facteur* f. L *factor* (prec., -OR[2])]

factor·ial, a. & n. (math.). Product of series of factors in arithmetical progression; product of an integer & all lower integers (adj., *f. 4,* symbol $\underline{4|}$, $=4\times3\times2\times1$). [-IAL]

fa·ctory, n. Merchant company's foreign trading station; manufactory, workshop, (*F. Acts,* regulating management in interest of the hands). [ult. f. med. L *factoria* (FACTOR, -Y[1])]

facto·tum, n. Man of all work; servant managing his master's affairs. [med. L, as FACSIMILE + neut. of L *totus* whole]

fa·ctual, a. Concerned with, of the nature of, fact. Hence **fa·ctual**LY[2] adv. [f. FACT on false anal. of ACTUAL]

fa·ctum, n. Statement of facts or points in controversy, memorial. [L, see FACT]

fă·cula, n. (astron.; pl. *-ae*). Bright spot or streak on sun. Hence **fa·cul**AR[1], **fa·cul**OUS, aa. [L, dim. of *fax fac-* torch]

fă·cultative, a. Permissive; optional; contingent; of a faculty. [F (*-if, -ive*); foll., -IVE]

fă·culty, n. Aptitude for any special kind of action; executive ability (chiefly U.S.); power inherent in the body or an organ; a mental power, e.g. the will, reason; branch of art or science, department of University teaching (*the four ff.,* Theology, Law, Medicine, Arts), Masters & Doctors in any of these (pop., *The F.,* members of medical profession); liberty of doing something given by law or a superior, authorization, licence, (esp. eccl.). [f. F *faculté* f. L *facultatem* (*facilis* easy)]

fad, n. Pet notion or rule of action, craze, piece of fancied enlightenment. Hence **fa·dd**ISH[1], **fa·dd**Y[2], aa., **fa·dd**INESS, **fa·ddish**NESS, **fa·dd**ISM(3), **fa·dd**IST(2), nn. [?]

fade, v.i. & t. Droop, wither, lose freshness & vigour; (of colour &c.) grow dim or pale; cause to lose colour; disappear gradually. Hence **fa·de**LESS a., **fa·deless**LY[2] adv. [f. OF *fader* (*fade* dull, insipid, perh. f. L *vapidus*)]

fae·cēs (fē-), n. pl. Sediment; excrement of the bowels. Hence **fae·**CAL a. [L, pl. of *faex*]

Fā·erie, -y, n. & a. Fairyland, the fairies, esp. as represented by Spenser; (attrib.) visionary, fancied. [var. of FAIRY]

fag, v.i. & t., & n. Toil painfully; (of occupation) tire, make weary; (at schools, of seniors) use the service of (juniors), (of juniors) do service for seniors; (Cricket) *f. out,* field; *f.-end,* inferior or useless remnant. (N.) drudgery, unwelcome task (*what a f.!*), exhaustion (*brain-f.*); (at schools) junior who has to f.; (slang) cigarette. [perh. corrupt. of FLAG v.]

fa·ggot, fă·got, n., & v.t. & i. Bundle of sticks or twigs bound together as fuel; bundle of steel rods; dish of liver chopped, seasoned, & baked; *f.-vote,* manufactured by transferring sufficient property to unqualified person, so *f.-voter*; (vb) bind in ff., make ff. [F (*fagot*), etym. dub.]

Fah·renheit (-īt), a. (*abbr.* F.). *F. thermometer,* with 32° & 212° for freezing & boiling points (used esp. in giving temperatures, as 50° F.). [Prussian inventor d. 1736]

faience (F), n. Earthenware & porcelain of all kinds. [f. F *faïence* f. *Faenza* Italian town]

fail[1], n. *Without f.,* for certain, irrespective of hindrances, (emphasizing injunction or promise). [f. OF *faile* (*faillir* FAIL[2])]

fail[2], v.i. & t. (strictly, intr. with ind. obj.). Be missing (see FAILING[2]) or insufficient, not suffice for needs of (person), run short, (*time would f. me to tell*; *words f. me,* I cannot adequately describe &c.; *his heart failed him*); neglect, not remember or not choose, *to* (*he failed to appear*; *don't f. to let me know*); become extinct, die away; flag, break down; prove misleading, disappoint hopes of, (*the prophecy failed*; *the wind failed us*); be insufficiently equipped *in,* not succeed in the attainment *of*; not succeed (*in doing* or *to* do); miscarry, come to nothing; suspend payment, go bankrupt; be rejected as candidate. [f. OF *faillir* f. pop. L ***fallire** = L *fallere* deceive]

fai·ling[1], n. In vbl senses; also, foible, shortcoming, weakness. [-ING[1]]

fai·ling[2], prep. In default of (*f. this,* if this does not happen; *whom f.* or *f. whom* in proxy appointments). [-ING[2]]

fai·lure (-yer), n. Non-occurrence, nonperformance; running short, breaking down; ill success; unsuccessful person, thing, or attempt; insolvency. [earlier *failer* for F *faillir* FAIL[2], cf. -ER[4], -URE]

fain[1], pred. a., & adv. Willing under the circumstances *to*; left with no alternative but *to*; (adv.) *would f.,* would be glad to. [OE *fægen* cogn. w. OHG (*gi*)*fehan* rejoice]

fain[2], **fains, fen(s),** child's formula (usu. *fains I* as v.t.) stipulating for exemption from unwelcome office &c. (*f. I wicket-keeping!*). [?]

fainéant (F), n. & a. Idle(r), inactive (official). [F, perversion on *faire* do, *néant* nothing, of OF *faignant* sluggard (*faindre* skulk)]

faint[1], a. Sluggish; timid (*f.-heart*, coward; so **faint-heart**ED[2] a., **faint-hear·ted**LY[2] adv., **faint-hear·ted**NESS n.); feeble (*a f. show of resistance*); dim, indistinct, pale (*f.* or *feint lines, ruled f.* or *feint*, of paper with lines to guide writing; *a f. idea*, inadequate); giddy or languid with fear, hunger, &c., inclined to swoon; (of air, scents, &c.) sickly, oppressive. Hence **fai·nt**ISH[1](2) a., **fai·nt**LY[2] adv., **fai·nt**NESS n. [OF, p.p. of *faindre* FEIGN]

faint[2], v.i., & n. Lose courage, give way, (archaic); swoon (v. & n.; *fainted away*; *in a dead f.*, utterly insensible). [f. prec.]

faints, n. pl. Impure spirit coming over at beginning & end of distillation. [f. FAINT[1]]

fair[1], n. Periodical gathering for sale of goods, often with shows & entertainments, at place & time fixed by charter, statute, or custom (*a day after the f.*, too late); FANCY *f.* [f. OF *feire* (now *foire*) f. L *feria* holiday]

fair[2], a. & n. Beautiful (*the f. sex, the f.*, women; also archaic as n., *a f.* =a woman); satisfactory, abundant, (*a f. heritage*); specious (*f. speeches*); blond, not dark, (*a f. man, complexion, hair*, whence **fair-hair**ED[2] a.); clean, clear, unblemished, (*f. water*; *f.* COPY[1]; *f. fame*); just, unbiased, equitable, legitimate, (*f. & square* a. & adv., without finesse, above-board; *f. trade*, principle that reciprocity should be the condition of free trade; *a f.* FIELD[1] *& no favour*; *all's f. in love & war*; *f. play*, equal conditions for all); of moderate quality, not bad, pretty good, whence **fair·**ISH[1](2) a.; favourable, promising, gentle, unobstructed, (*f. or foul weather*; *f.-weather friends*, not good at need; *in a f. way to succeed*; *by f. means*, without violence or fraud; *fairway*, navigable channel, regular course or track of ship or on golf-links); *fairlight*, =TRANSOM *window*; *f.-maid*, =FUMADE; *February Fair-maids*, snowdrops. Hence **fair·**NESS n. [com.-Teut.; OE *fæger* cf. OHG *fagar*]

fair[3], adv. *Speak* one *f.*, address him courteously; *f.-spoken* (of person), courteous, bland; *write out f.*, as FAIR[2] copy; *hit, fight, f.*, according to the rules; BID[1] *f.*; *f. & softly*, gently, not so fast, (esp. as protest against assumptions &c.); (with *strike, fall*, &c.) straight, plump, clean. [OE *fægre* (prec.)]

fair·ing, n. Present bought at a fair. [-ING[1]]

Fair Isle, n. One of the Shetlands; *F.I.* (*sweater, pull-over*, &c.), jersey knitted in designs said to be Moorish & to be traceable to Armada wrecks.

fair·ly, adv. In adj. senses; (also) utterly, completely, (*f. beside himself*; there is sometimes doubt between this sense & that of *rather, tolerably*, as in *f. good*). [-LY[2]]

fair·y, n. & a. Small supernatural being with magical powers; *f. lamps* (of glass, for esp. outdoor decoration); *Fairyland*, home of ff., enchanted region; *f. ring*, circular band of darker grass caused by fungi & attributed to f. dancing; *f.-tale*, about ff., also account of strange incident, coincidence, marvellous progress, &c.; hence **fair·y**DOM, **fair·y**HOOD, **fair·y**ISM, nn. (Adj.) of ff.; imaginary, fictitious; f.-like, beautiful & delicate or small, whence **fair·i**LY[2] adv. [f. OF *faerie* (now *féerie*) f. OF *fae* FAY]

fait accompli (F), n. Thing done & no longer worth arguing against.

faith, n. Reliance, trust, *in*; belief founded on authority (*pin* one's *f. to* or *upon*, believe implicitly); (Theol.) belief in religious doctrines, esp. such as affects character & conduct, spiritual apprehension of divine truth apart from proof; system of religious belief (*the Christian, Jewish, f.*; DEFENDER *of the F.*; *the f.*, the true religion); things (to be) believed; warrant (*on the f. of*); promise, engagement, (*give, pledge, plight, keep, break, violate*, one's *f.*); loyalty, fidelity, (*good f.*, honesty of intention; *bad f.*, intent to deceive; *Punic f.*, treachery); *f.-cure, -curer, -healing, -healer*, acting by prayer, not drugs &c. [f. OF *feid* f. L *fides*]

fai·thful, a. Loyal, constant, (*to* person, one's word), conscientious; trustworthy; true to fact, the original, &c., accurate; *the f.* (pl.), true believers, esp. Mohammedans (*Father of the f.*, Caliph). Hence **fai·thful**NESS n. [-FUL]

fai·thfully, adv. In adj. senses; esp.: *yours f.*, formula of rather distant tone for closing letter; *deal f. with*, speak home truths to or of; *promise f.*, emphatically (colloq.). [-LY[2]]

fai·thless, a. Unbelieving; perfidious, false to promises; unreliable. Hence **fai·thless**LY[2] adv., **fai·thless**NESS n. [-LESS]

fake[1], v.t., & n. (naut.). Coil (rope); (n.) one round of a coil. [?]

fake[2], v.t., & n. (slang). Do *up*, make presentable or specious, contrive out of poor material; (n.) piece of faking, thing faked up, dodge, cooked report. Hence **fa·ke**MENT n., f. [perh. f. G *fegen* sweep]

fakir· (-ēr), n. Mohammedan (or Hindu) religious mendicant, devotee. [f. Arab. *faqir* poor man]

fă·lbala, n. Flounce, trimming. [?]

fă·lcate, a. (anat., bot., zool.). Hooked, sickle-shaped. [f. L *falcatus* f. *falx* sickle, -ATE[2](2)]

fă·lcāted, a. (astron.). =prec. (of moon &c.). [as prec., see -ATE[2]]

falchion (faw·ltshn), n. Broad curved convex-edged sword. [f. OF *fauchon* f. pop. L **falcionem* nom. *-o* (L *falx* sickle)]

fă·lciform, a. (anat.). Sickle-shaped. [f. L *falx -cis* sickle + -FORM]

falcon (faw·kn, faw·lkn), n. Small diurnal bird of prey, esp. as trained to hawk for sport (in falconry the female only, cf. TERCEL). So **fal·con**RY(2, 5) n. [f. OF *faucon* f. LL *falconem* perh. f. L *falx* sickle]

fal·coner (fawk-), n. Keeper and trainer of hawks; one who hunts with hawks. [f. OF *faulconnier*, see prec., -ER²(2)]

fal·conet (fawk-), n. (Hist.) light cannon; species of shrike. [first sense f. It. *falconetto* dim. of *falcone* FALCON; last f. FALCON + -ET¹]

fălderă·l, n. Gewgaw, trifle. [earlier as meaningless refrain in songs]

fa·ldstool (faw-), n. Bishop's armless chair; movable desk for kneeling at; desk for litany to be said from. [f. med. L *faldistolium* f. OHG *faldstuol* (*faldan* to fold, STOOL)]

Faler·nian, n. A famous wine of ancient Campania. [f. L (*vinum*) *Falernum* Falernian (wine) + -IAN]

fall¹ (fawl), v.i. (*fell*; *fallen* often conjugated with *be*, see -ED¹(2), & used as adj.). Descend freely (*falling star*, meteor), drop, (*the remark fell from him*; *lambs f.*, are born), come down, lose high position (*statesmen f.*; *fallen angel*, one of those cast out of heaven), swoop (*vengeance fell*); become detached, hang down; sink to lower level (*barometer, prices, f.*), decline, slope; disembogue *into*; subside, ebb, abate; show dismay (*faces f.*), droop (*eyes f.*); cease to stand (*falling sickness* archaic, epilepsy), become prostrate, come to ground, sin, be overthrown, perish (*f. prostrate, flat*; *plans f. to the ground*, are abandoned, fail; *f. on* one's *sword*, in suicide; *wicket falls*, batsman is out; *fortress falls*, is taken; *woman falls*, loses chastity; *many fell*, were killed in battle; *seven lions fell to his rifle*; *fallen on evil times*, in misfortune; *f. a prey* or *sacrifice to*; *f. into error*; *houses f.*, tumble in fragments; *f. to pieces, in two, asunder*); take such a direction (*his eye fell upon me*), have such a place (*accent falls on first syllable*), alight, come by chance &c., (*the lot fell upon me*; *it fell to my lot to*; *cost falls to you*; *it fell in my way*; *f. amongst thieves, upon a corrupt age*; *subject falls into three divisions*); pass into such a state (*fell into a rage, in love*), become so-&-so (*f. dumb, due*); lapse, revert, (*revenues f. to the Crown*); occur, have date, (*Easter falls early*), find place (*what now falls to be described*). With prepp.: *f. a- —ing*, begin; *f. behind*, be passed by; *f. for* (U.S. slang), be captivated by, admire, yield to the charms or merits of; *f. into*, (*line*) take one's place in the ranks, combine with others, (*conversation with*) begin talking to, (*habit* &c.) adopt it; *f.* (*up*)*on*, assault, come across, (one's *feet* or *legs*) get well out of difficulty; *f. to —ing*, take to, begin, (also *f. to work*); *f. under*, be classed among, be subjected to (*observation* &c.); *f. within*, be included in. With advv.: *f. astern*, (of ship) drop behind; *f. away*, desert, revolt, apostatize, decay, vanish; *f. back*, retreat; *f. back upon*, have recourse to; *f. behind*, lag; *f. foul of*, come into collision with, quarrel with, attack; *f. in*, (Mil.) take or cause to take places in line, (of buildings &c.) give way inwards, (of debt &c.) become due, (of land &c.) become available, (of lease) run out; *f. in with*, happen to meet, accede to (views), agree with (person), coincide with, humour; *f. off*, withdraw, decrease, degenerate (so *falling off*, n.), (of ship) refuse to answer helm, (of subjects) revolt; *f. on*, join battle, begin feeding; *f. out*, quarrel, come to pass, result *well* &c., (Mil.) leave the ranks; *f. out of*, give up (habit) &c.; *f. short*, become insufficient, (of missile) not go far enough; *f. short of*, fail to obtain; *f. through*, miscarry, fail; *f. to*, begin eating or fighting. [com.-Teut.; OE *feallan* cf. G *fallen*; also L *fallere* deceive]

fall², n. Act of falling (see prec.); also or esp.: amount of rain &c. that falls; (now chiefly U.S.; also *f. of the year* or *leaf*) autumn; number of lambs born; cataract, cascade, (often pl.); downward trend, amount of descent; wrestling-bout, throw in this, (*try a f.*, lit. & fig.); rope of hoisting-tackle; amount of timber cut down; succumbing to temptation (*the F. of man*, Adam's sin and its results); kind of woman's veil. [f. prec.]

fă·llacy, n. Misleading argument, sophism, (Log.) flaw that vitiates syllogism, one of the types of such flaws; delusion, error, (PATHETIC *f.*); unsoundness, delusiveness, disappointing character, (of arguments or beliefs). So **fallA·cious** a., **falla·cious**LY² adv., **falla·cious**NESS n. [f. L *fallacia* (*fallax* deceiving f. *fallere* deceive) see -ACY]

făl-lă·l, n. Piece of finery. Hence **falla·l**LERY(5) n. [contemptuous reduplication, cf. *gewgaw*, perh. f. FALBALA]

fă·llible, a. Liable to err or be erroneous. Hence **fallibi·lity** n. [f. LL *fallibilis* (*fallere* deceive, -BLE)]

fă·llow¹, n., a., & v.t. (Ground) ploughed and harrowed but left uncropped for a year; uncultivated (land); (vb) break up (land) for sowing or to destroy weeds. [ME *falwe* ploughed land, cf. OE *fealga* harrows]

fă·llow², a. Of pale brownish or reddish yellow (now only in *f.-deer*, species smaller than red deer). [OE *falu* cf. G *fahl*, prob.. cogn. w. L *pallidus* pale & Gk *polios* grey]

false (fawls), a. & adv. Erroneous, wrong, incorrect, (*f. idea, verdict*; *f. concord*, breach of agreement rules in grammar; *f. quantity*, incorrect length of vowel in verse or pronunciation; *f. note* in music; *f. drawing*; *f. imprisonment*, illegal; *f. weights*

&c.; *f. pride, shame,* based on wrong notions; *f. position,* one that forces person to act against his principles; *f. step,* stumble, transgression; *f. start,* wrong start in racing); lying, deceitful, treacherous, unfaithful *to*; deceptive (*f. mirror, medium*); spurious, sham, artificial, (*f. coin, god, prophet, hair, teeth*; *f. colours,* flag one has no right to, lit. & fig.); improperly so called, pseudo-, (*f. acacia*; *f. bottom,* horizontal partition in vessel; *f.* KEEL); hence or cogn. **fa·lse**LY[2] adv., **fa·lse**NESS, **fa·ls**ITY, nn. (Adv.) *play* person *f.*, cheat, betray. [OE *fals* f. L *falsus* p.p. of *fallere* deceive]

fa·lsehood, n. Falsity; something untrue, contrariety to fact; lying, lie(s). [-HOOD]

false·tto (fawl-), n. Forced shrill voice above one's natural range (*in f., a f. tone,* &c., often of sham indignation). [It., dim. of *falso* FALSE]

fa·lsify̆ (fawl-), v.t. Fraudulently alter (document); misrepresent; make wrong, pervert; disappoint (hope, fear, &c.). So **falsific**A·TION n. [f. F *falsifier* f. LL *falsificare* (FALSE, -FY)]

fa·lter (fawl-), v.i. & t. Stumble, stagger, go unsteadily; stammer, speak hesitatingly, (*f. out,* utter, say, thus); waver, lose courage, flinch. Hence **fa·ltering**LY[2] adv. [?]

fame[1], n. Public report, rumour; reputation (*house of ill f.*, bawdy-house), good reputation; renown, celebrity. [F, f. L *fama* = Gk *phēmē* (*fa-* speak)]

fame[2], v.t. (Pass.) be currently reported *as, for, to* be or do; (p.p.) famous, much spoken of, (*for valour* &c.). [f. OF *famer* (prec.)]

fami·liar (-*yar*), a. & n. Of one's family (archaic for *family* attrib.); intimate (*with*), in close friendship (*f. spirit,* or *f.* as n., demon attending & obeying witch &c.); closely acquainted *with* (some subject); well-known, no longer novel, (*to*); common, current, usual; unceremonious, free, over-free; amorously or sexually intimate (*with*). (N.): (R.-C. Ch.) person rendering certain services in Pope's or bishop's household; intimate friend or associate; f. spirit. Hence **fami·liar**LY[2] adv. [f. OF *familier* f. L *familiaris* (FAMILY, -AR[1])]

fami·lĭă·rity, n. Close intercourse, intimacy *with* person or some subject; amorous intimacy, (pl.) caresses &c.; unceremoniousness, treating of inferiors or superiors as equals, (*f. breeds contempt*). [f. F *familiarité* f. L *familiaritatem* (prec., -TY)]

fami·liarize (-*ya*-), v.t. Make (thing) well known; make (person, person's *mind* &c., one*self*) well acquainted or at home *with*. Hence **fami·liarīz**A·TION n. [-IZE]

fă·mily, n. Members of a household, parents, children, servants, &c. (*happy f.*, animals of different kinds in one cage); set of parents & children, or of relations, living together or not (*Holy F.*, the Virgin, Jesus, St Joseph, & often St John Baptist & St Elizabeth, as grouped in pictures); person's children; all descendants of common ancestor, house, lineage, (*of f.*, nobly born); race, group of peoples from common stock; brotherhood of persons or nations united by political or religious ties; group of objects distinguished by common features; group of allied genera, usu. subdivision of ORDER; *f. butcher* &c., supplying ff. as opp. to the army &c.; *f. hotel,* with special terms for ff.; *in a f. way,* without ceremony; *in the f. way,* with child; *f. Bible,* large Bible with fly-leaves for registering births &c.; *f. coach,* large closed carriage, a game of forfeits; *F. Compact,* in 18th c. between Bourbons of France, Spain, & Two Sicilies, esp. against England & Austria; *f. likeness,* that between relations, vague resemblance; *f. living,* benefice in gift of head of f.; *f. man,* one with f., domestic person; *f. tree,* genealogical chart. [f. L *familia* household (*famulus* servant, -IA[1])]

fă·mine, n. Extreme scarcity of food in a district &c.; dearth of something specified, as *water f.* (*f. prices,* raised by scarcity); hunger, starvation, (*die of f.*). [F, f. LL **famina* f. L *fames* hunger, -INE[1]]

fă·mish, v.t. & i. Reduce, be reduced, to extreme hunger; (colloq.) *be famishing,* feel hungry. [obs. *fame* v. f. L *fames* hunger, -ISH[2]]

fā·mous, a. Celebrated (*for* quality &c.), well known; (colloq.) capital, excellent, whence **fa·mous**LY[2] adv. [f. OF *fameus* f. L *famosus* (FAME, -OSE[1])]

fă·mulus, n. (pl. *-lī*). Attendant on magician. [L, = servant]

fan[1], n. Winnowing-machine; instrument, usu. folding & sector-shaped when spread out, on radiating ribs, for agitating air to cool face; anything so spread out, as bird's tail, wing, leaf, kind of ornamental vaulting (*f. tracery*); rotating apparatus giving current of air for ventilation &c.; (Naut.) (blade of) screw, propeller; (in windmill) small sail for keeping head towards wind; *f.-light,* f.-shaped window over door; *f.-tail,* f.-shaped tail or end, kind of pigeon, coal-heaver's hat or sou'-wester. [OE *fann* f. L *vannus* winnowing-basket]

fan[2], v.t. & i. Winnow (corn), whence **fa·nn**ER[1](2) n.; winnow away (chaff), sweep *away* (as) by wind from f.; move (air) with f.; drive current of air (as) with f. upon, to cool (face &c.) or to kindle (flame; *f. the flame,* increase excitement &c.); (of breeze) blow gently on, cool; spread out (t. & i.) in f. shape. [f. prec.]

fan[3], n. (slang). Devotee of a specified amusement, as ***film ff., football ff.*** [abbr. of foll.]

fană·tic, a. & n. (Person) filled with excessive & mistaken enthusiasm, esp. in religion. Hence **fana·ticAL** a., **fana·ticalLY**[2] adv., **fana·ticISM** n., **fana·ticIZE**(2, 3), v.i. & t. [f. L *fanaticus* (*fanum* temple, -ATIC)]

fa·ncier, n. Connoisseur in some article or animal (of which the name is usu. prefixed, as *dog, rose, -f.*). [FANCY[2]. -ER[1]]

fa·nciful, a. Indulging in fancies, whimsical, capricious; fantastically designed, ornamented, &c., odd-looking; imaginary, unreal. Hence **fa·ncifulLY**[2] adv., **fa·ncifulNESS** n. [-FUL]

fa·ncy[1], n. & a. Delusion, unfounded belief; faculty of calling up things not present, of inventing imagery; mental image; arbitrary supposition; caprice, a whim; individual taste, inclination, (*take a f. to, for*; *catch the f. of,* please); *the f.,* those who have a certain hobby, =*-fanciers,* esp. the patrons of boxing; art of breeding animals with certain points of excellence; *f.-free,* not in love. (Adj.; not pred.) ornamental, not plain, (*f. bread*; *f. dress,* masquerade costume, so *f.-d.* or *f.-ball*; *f.-work,* ornamental sewing &c.; *f. fair,* bazaar for sale of f. goods); (of flowers &c.) particoloured; capricious, whimsical, extravagant, (*at a f. price*; *f. franchise,* based on complicated or arbitrary qualifications; *f. dog, pigeon,* &c., bred for particular points of beauty &c.); based on imagination, not fact (*f. picture*); *f. man,* sweetheart, (slang) man living on earnings of a prostitute. [contraction of FANTASY]

fa·ncy[2], v.t. Picture to oneself, conceive, imagine, (*f. oneself dead*; *f. a blue dahlia*; *f. him to be here, that he is here*; imperat. as excl. of surprise, *fancy !, f. his believing it !*); be inclined to suppose, rather think; (colloq.) have good conceit of (*oneself,* one's *game* &c.); take a f. to, like; breed, grow, (animals, plants) with attention to certain points. [f. prec.]

fanda·ngle, n. Fantastic ornament, tomfoolery. [perh. f. foll.]

fanda·ngo, n. Lively Spanish dance; tune for this. [Sp.]

fane, n. (poet.). Temple. [f. L *fanum*]

fa·nfare (or as F), n. Flourish of trumpets, bugles, &c. [F]

fanfaronā·de (or as F), n. Arrogant talk, brag; =prec. [f. F *fanfaronnade* f. *fanfaron* (prec., -OON), -ADE]

fang[1], n. Canine tooth, esp. of dogs & wolves; serpent's venom-tooth; spike of tool held in the stock; (prong of) root of tooth. Hence (-)**fangED**[2], **fa·ngLESS,** aa. [OE, cf. G *fangen* seize]

fang[2], v.t. Prime (pump) by pouring in water to start it. [f. prec.]

fantasia (*-azē·a,* -ah·zĭa), n. Musical composition in which form is subservient to fancy. [It., =FANTASY]

fa·ntast, ph-, n. Visionary, dreamer. [f. med. L f. Gk *phantastēs* (*phantazomai* make a show f. *phainō* show)]

fanta·stic, a. Fancied (rare); extravagantly fanciful, capricious, eccentric; grotesque or quaint in design &c. Hence (thr. obs. *-ical*) **fantastica·lITY, fanta·sticalNESS, fanta·sticISM,** nn., **fanta·sticalLY**[2] adv. [f. med. L *fantasticus* f. LL f. Gk *phantastikos* (prec., -IC)]

fa·ntasy, ph-, n. Image-making faculty, esp. when extravagant or visionary; mental image; fantastic design; =FANTASIA; whimsical speculation. [f. OF *fantasie* f. L f. Gk *phantasia* (see FANTAST)]

fantocci·ni (-tshēnē), n. pl. Mechanically worked puppets; marionette show. [It.]

faquir. See FAKIR.

far[1], adv.(FARTHER,-thest, FURTHER,-thest), & n. At a great distance, a long way off, (often with *away, off, out*; also fig., as *f., so f., from doing, f. from it*; *f. be it from me to,* I would on no account); to a great distance or advanced point (*driven f. into the ground*; *f. gone,* advanced (see below also); *he will go f.,* do much; *go f. to effect* &c., nearly do so; by a great interval, by much, (*f. different, better, the best*; also *f. & away*); *so f.,* to such a distance, (also) up to now; *how f.,* to what extent; *as f. as,* right to, not short of, (place); *as* or *so f. as, in so f. as,* to whatever extent; *f.-away,* remote, long-past, (of look &c.) absent, dreamy; *f.-between,* infrequent; *f.-famed,* widely known, *f.-fetched,* (of simile, illustration, &c.) studiously sought out, strained; *f.-flung* (rhet.), widely extended; *f.* FORTH; *f. gone,* very ill or mad or drunk or much in debt; *f. off,* remote; *f.-reaching,* widely applicable, carrying many consequences; *f.-seeing, -sighted,* prescient, prudent, (*-sighted*) seeing distant things more clearly than near ones. (N.) a distance (*do you come from f.?*); large amount (*by f.,* with compar. & superl., *prefer, surpass,* &c.). [OE *feor(r)* f. OTeut. *fer-* f. Aryan *per-* cf. Gk *peran* beyond]

far[2], a. (farther, -est, further, -est). Distant, remote, (*a f.* CRY[1]). [OE *feorr* f. prec.]

fă·rad, n. (electr.). Electro-magnetic unit of capacity. [f. *Faraday,* electrician, d. 1867]

farada·ic, a. (electr.). Inductive, induced, (of current). [as prec., -IC]

farce[1], n. Dramatic work merely to excite laughter; this species of drama; absurdly futile proceeding, pretence, mockery. Hence **far·cICAL** a., **far·cicalLY**[2] adv., **farcica·lITY** n. [F, orig. =stuffing, f. L *farcire* to stuff, used metaph. of interludes &c.]

farce[2], v.t. (archaic). Season, spice, stuff, (in cookery, & fig. of literary compositions). [f. OF *farsir* f. L as prec.]

farceur· (-ser), n. Person who habitually indulges in mystifications. [F]

far·cy, n. Disease, esp. of horses, allied to glanders; *f. bud, button*, small tumour in this. [f. F *farcin* f. L *farciminum* (*farcire* stuff)]

far·del (-dl), n. (archaic). Bundle, burden. [OF, dim. of *farde* burden perh. f. Arab. *fardah*]

fare[1], n. 1. Cost of passenger's conveyance, passage-money; passenger in hired vehicle. 2. Food provided (usu. *good, bad, plentiful*, &c., *f.*; BILL[1] of *f.*). [OE *fær* (sense 1), & *faru* (sense 2), f. st. of foll.]

fare[2], v.i. Journey, go, travel, (poet.; so *f. forth*, start); happen, turn out, (*how fares it?*); get on *well, ill*, &c., have such luck; be entertained, be fed or feed oneself, *well* &c. [com.-Teut.; OE & OHG *faran* f. Aryan *por-* pass through cf. Gk *poros* ford, L *portare* carry]

farewe·ll, int. & n. Good-bye!, Adieu!, (*f. to*, no more of); (n.) leave-taking, parting good wishes. [imperat. of prec. +*well*]

fari·na, n. Flour or meal of corn, nuts, or starchy roots; powdery substance; (Bot.) pollen; (Chem.) starch. Hence **farin**A·CEOUS a. [L (*far* corn, -INE[4])]

fă·rinose (-s), a. Mealy, sprinkled with powder. [prec., -OSE[1]]

farl, n. (Sc.). Thin cake, orig. quadrant-shaped, of oatmeal or flour. [for obs. *fardel* quarter (FOURTH, DEAL), cf. FARTHING]

farm[1], n. Tract of land used under one management for cultivation (orig. only of leased land; *home f.*, reserved & worked by owner of estate containing other ff.); (also *f.-house*) dwelling-place attached to f.; place where children are farmed (see foll.); *f.-stead*, f. with buildings on it; *f. yard*, enclosure attached to f.-house. [f. F *ferme* f. med. L *firma* fixed payment (*firmare* fix f. FIRM*us*)]

farm[2], v.t. & i. Take proceeds of (tax, office, &c.) on payment of fixed sum; (also *f. out*) let out proceeds of (tax &c.) to person for fixed sum; let the labour of (persons) for hire; contract to maintain and care for (persons, esp. children) for fixed sum; cultivate, till; till the soil, be a farmer. Hence **far·m**ER[1], **far·m**ING[1], nn. [f. prec.]

fā̆r·o, n. Gambling card-game. [f. *Pharaoh* (significance doubtful)]

farou·che (-ōōsh), a. Sullen, shy. [F]

farra·go (-ah-, -ā-), n. Medley, hotchpotch. Hence **farrā·gin**OUS a. [L (genit. *-inis*), =mixed fodder (*far* corn)]

fa·rrier, n. Shoeing-smith; horse-doctor; N.C.O. in charge of cavalry regiment's horses. Hence **fa·rri**ERY(2) n. [f. OF *ferrier* f. L *ferrarius* f. *ferrum* iron, -ER[2](2)]

fa·rrow, n., & v.t. & i. Giving birth to, litter of, pigs (*20 at one f.*); (vb) produce (pigs), produce pigs. [vb f. n., OE *fearh* f. OTeut. *farhoz* cf. L *porcus*]

fart, n., & v.i. (indecent). Emission of, emit, wind from the anus. [Aryan, cf. Gk *perdomai*]

far·ther (-dh-), adv. & a. (used as comp. of FAR[1, 2], see etym.), & v.t. To or at a more advanced point or greater extent or distance (*I'll see you f.* or FURTHER *first*); in addition, also, besides, moreover, (now usu. *further*). (Adj.) more extended, additional, more; more distant or advanced, whence **far·ther**MOST a. (Vb, rare) = FURTHER. [var. of FURTHER; both used as comp. of *far*, but with tendency to restrict *f.* to lit. & *further* to secondary senses]

far·thest (-dh-), a. & adv. Most distant (*at the, at, f.*, at the greatest distance, at latest, at most); (adv.) to or at the greatest distance. [var., now more usu., of FURTHEST]

far·thing (-dh-), n. Quarter of a penny; least possible amount (*doesn't matter a f.*). [OE *féorthing* (*féortha* FOURTH, -ING[3])]

far·thingale, n. (hist.). Hooped petticoat. [f. OF *verdugale* f. Sp. *-ado* (*verdugo* rod, -ADO)]

fa·scēs, n. pl. (Rom. hist.). Bundle of rods with axe in the middle carried by lictor before high magistrate; ensigns of authority. [L (pl. of *fascis* bundle)]

fascia (fă·shĭa), n. (Arch.) long flat surface of wood or stone under eaves or cornice; (Anat.) thin sheath of fibrous tissue; stripe, band, fillet, belt. [L]

fa·sciated (făshĭ-), a. (Bot.; of contiguous parts) compressed, growing, into one (so **fa·sci**A·TION n.); striped. [f. obs. *fasciate* f. L *fasciare* (prec.), -ATE[2]]

fa·scicle, -icule, -i·cūlus, (făsĭ-), n. (Bot. &c.) bunch, bundle, whence **fa·scicl**ED[2], **fasci·cul**AR[1], **fasci·cul**ATE[2], **-ated**, aa., **fascicul**A·TION n.; one part of book published by instalments. [f. L *fasciculus* (FASCES, -CULE)]

fa·scinate, v.t. Deprive (victim) of power of escape or resistance by one's look or presence (esp. of serpents); attract irresistibly, enchant, charm, whence **fa·scinat**ING[2] a., **fa·scinating**LY[2] adv. Hence or cogn. **fa·scin**A·TION, **fa·scinat**OR[2] (esp., =opera-hood), nn. [f. L *fascinare* (*fascinum* spell), -ATE[3]]

fasci·ne (-sēn), n. Long faggot used for engineering purposes & esp. in war for lining trenches, making batteries, &c.; *f. dwelling*, prehistoric lake dwelling supported by cross layers of sticks sunk below surface. [F, f. L *fascina* (*fascis* bundle, -INE[1])]

fa·scism, *fasci·smo* (-shēzmō), n. Principles & organization of the patriotic & anti-communist movement in Italy started during the great war, culminating in the virtual dictatorship of Signor Mussolini, & imitated by fascist or black-shirt associations in other countries. So **fa·scist, *fasci·sta*** (-shē-; pl. *-ti* pron. *-tē*), n. [It. *fascismo* (*fascio* bundle, group, f. L as FASCES, see -ISM)]

fash, v.t., & n. (Sc.). Bother, trouble, inconvenience. [n. f. vb, f. OF *fascher* (now *fâcher*)]

fă·shion (-shn), n., & v.t. Make, shape, style, pattern, manner, (*after the f. of*, like; so *-f.* = -WISE, as *walk crab-f.*); *after, in, a f.*, not satisfactorily, but somehow or other; prevailing custom, esp. in dress (*f.-plate*, picture showing style of dress); conventional usages of upper-class society (*the f.*, whatever is in accord with these for the time being; *set the f.*, give the example in changing them; *the f.*, also admired & discussed person or thing; *in, out of, f.* or *the f.*, agreeing or not with current usage; *man* &c. *of f.*, of social standing, moving in & conforming with upper-class society); hence **-fashion**ED[2] a. (Vb) give shape to, form, mould, (*into, to*, or abs.). [f. OF *façon*, ONF *fachon*, f. L *factionem* (*facere fact-* make, -ION)]

fa·shionable, a. & n. Following, suited to, the fashion; characteristic of, treating of, or patronized by, persons of fashion. Hence **fa·shionable**NESS n., **fa·shionab**LY[2] adv. (N.) f. person. [prec. n., -ABLE]

fast[1], v.i. 1. Abstain from all or some kinds of food as religious observance or in sign of mourning (*fasting-day*, = FAST[2]-*day*). 2. Go without food. [com.-Teut.; OE *fæstan* cf. Goth. *fastan* = orig. keep, observe, f. OTeut. *fastêja*]

fast[2], n. Act of fasting (prec., 1); season or (also *f.-day, fasting-day*) day appointed for fasting; going without food (*break one's f.* = BREAKFAST v.). [prob. f. ON *fasta* f. OTeut. as prec.]

fast[3], a. Firmly fixed or attached (*stake f. in the ground*; *f. friend* or *friendship*, steady, close; *ship f. aground*; *f. asleep*; *a f. prisoner*; *f. colour*, unfading, not washing out; *make f.*, fasten; *play f. & loose*, ignore obligations, be unreliable; *door is f.*, locked &c.; *take f. hold of*, tight; *f. with gout*, confined); rapid, quick-moving, producing quick motion, (*f. train*; *f. cricket-ground, racquet-court, billiard-table*, on which ball bounds smartly; *watch is f.*, shows too advanced time; *f. person*, dissipated, see foll.). Hence **fa·st**ISH[1](2) a. [com.-Teut.; OE *fæst* cf. G *fest* cogn. w. Goth. *fastan* FAST[1]]

fast[4], adv. (-er, -est). Firmly, fixedly, tightly, securely, (*stand, sit, stick, f.*; *f. bind, f. find*, lock up what you would not lose; *eyes f. shut*; *sleep f.*, soundly); (poet. & archaic) close *beside, by, upon*, &c.; quickly, in quick succession; *live f.*, live in a dissipated way, expend much energy in short time. [OE *fæste* (prec.)]

fa·sten (-sn), v.t. & i. Make fast, attach, fix, secure by some tie or bond, (*to, upon, on* adv. or prep., *together, up, in* adv. or prep.; or abs.; *f. parcel, garment, door*, &c., or *string, bolt*, &c.; *f. off thread* &c., secure with knot or otherwise), whence **fa·sten**ING[1](4) (-sn)- n.; direct (look, thoughts, &c.) keenly (*up*)*on*; fix (nickname, imputation, &c.) (*up*)*on*; *f. quarrel upon*, pick quarrel with; become fast (*door will not f.*); *f.* (*up*)*on*, lay hold of, single out for attack, seize upon (pretext). Hence **fa·sten**ER[1](2) n. [OE *fæstnian* cf. G *festnen* (FAST[3], -EN[6])]

fă·sti, n. pl. Chronological register of events, annals. [L, = calendar]

făsti·dious, a. Easily disgusted, squeamish, hard to please. Hence **fasti·dious**LY[2] adv., **fasti·dious**NESS n. [f. L *fastidiosus* (*fastidium* loathing, -OSE[1])]

fastĭ·giate, a. (bot.). With conical or tapering outline. [f. L. *fastigium* gable + -ATE[2]]

fa·stness, n. In adj. senses (FAST[3]); also, stronghold, fortress. [-NESS]

fat, a., n., & v.t. & i. Fed up for slaughter, fatted; well-fed, plump, (*cut up f.*, leave much money), corpulent; thick, substantial, (esp. of printing-type); greasy, oily, unctuous, (*cut it f.*, make a display); (of coal) bituminous; (of clay &c.) sticky; fertile, rich, yielding abundantly, (*f. lands, benefice, job*; *a f. lot* slang, a great deal usu. iron. = very little); slow-witted, indolent, (*f.-head*, dolt; *f.-witted*, stupid); *f.-guts*, corpulent person; *f.-hen*, kinds of GOOSE-*foot*; hence **fa·tt**ISH[1](2) a., **fa·t**NESS n. (N.) the f. part of anything (*live on the f. of the land*, have the best of everything); oily substance composing f. parts of animal bodies (*the f. is in the fire*, there will be an explosion); (Theatr.) part of role that enables actor to show off; (Chem.) organic compound of glycerin with acid; hence **fa·t**LESS a. (Vb) = FATTEN; *kill the fatted calf for*, receive (returned prodigal) with joy. [OE *fætt*(*ian*) cf. Du. *vet* f. OTeut. *faitjan* fatten (*faito-* adj. fat)]

fā·tal, a. Like fate, inevitable, necessary; of, appointed by, destiny (*f. sisters*, the Fates; *f. thread*, allotted length of life; *f. shears*, death); fateful, important, decisive; destructive, ruinous, ending in death, (*to*); deadly, sure to kill; (by exagg.) mischievous, ill-advised. Hence **fa·tal**LY[2] adv. [f. L *fatalis* (FATE, -AL)]

fa·talism, n. Belief that all events are predetermined by arbitrary decree; submission to all that happens as inevitable. So **fa·tal**IST(2) n. & a., **fatali·st**IC a., **fatali·st**ICALLY adv. [-ISM]

fată·lity, n. Subjection to, supremacy of, fate, predestined liability to disaster; fatal influence; misfortune, calamity; death by accident, in war, &c. [f. F *fatalité* f. LL *fatalitas*, see FATAL, -ITY]

fa·talize, v.i. & t. Incline to fatalism; subject to government by fate. [-IZE]

fa·ta morga·na (fah-, -gah-), n. Kind of mirage seen esp. in strait of Messina. [It. (*fata* FAY, *Morgana* female name)]

fate, n., & v.t. Power predetermining events unalterably from eternity; (Mythol.) goddess, one of the three Greek goddesses, of destiny; what is destined to happen; appointed lot of person &c.; person's ultimate condition (*decide, fix, seal,* one's *f.*); death, destruction. (Vb, usu. pass.) preordain (*he was fated to* do or be; *it was fated that*); (p.p.) doomed to destruction. [f. L *fatum* neut. p.p. of *fari* speak]

fa·teful, a. Prophetic; fraught with destiny, important, decisive; controlled by, showing power of, fate. Hence **fa·teful**LY[2] adv. [-FUL]

fa·ther[1] (fahdh-), n. Male parent (also fig.; *the wish is f. to the thought,* one believes because one wishes to; *the child is f. to the man,* lays down the lines of his development); =f.-in-law; =step-f.; (also *adoptive f.*), one who has adopted a child; progenitor, forefather; originator, designer, early leader, (*f. of English poetry*; *F. of lies,* the devil; *F. of the* FAITHFUL; *Ff. of the Church* or *Ff.*, Christian writers of first five centuries); one who deserves filial reverence (*f. of his country*); religious teacher; God; First Person of the Trinity; confessor; priest belonging to religious order, superior of monastic house; *Right, Most, Reverend F. in God,* titles of bishop, archbishop; *The Holy F.*, the Pope; *=priest* as prefixed title; venerable person, god, (*F. Christmas, Thames, Time,* personifications); oldest member, doyen, (*F. of House of Commons,* member with longest continuous service); (pl.) leading men, elders, (*Ff. of the City*; *Conscript Ff.*, Roman senators); *f.-in-law,* father of one's wife or husband; *fatherland,* native country (*the F.-l.*, Germany). Hence **fa·ther**HOOD, **fa·ther**SHIP, nn., **fa·ther**LESS a., **fa·ther**LIKE, **fa·ther**LY [1,2], aa. & advv., **fa·therli**NESS n. [Aryan; OE *fæder* cf. G *vater,* L *pater,* Gk *patēr*]

fa·ther[2], v.t. Beget; be the f. of; originate (statement &c.); pass as, confess oneself, the f., author, of (child, book); govern paternally; fix paternity of (child, book) *upon.* [f. prec.]

fă·thom[1] (-dh-), n. (pl., with numbers, often *fathom*). Measure of six feet, chiefly used in soundings; quantity of wood 6 ft square in section, whatever the length. [OE *fæthm* the outstretched arms, cf. G *faden* 6 ft cogn. w. Gk *petannumi* spread]

fa·thom[2], v.t. Encircle with the arms (archaic); measure with f.-line, sound, (depth of water); (fig.) get to the bottom of, comprehend, whence **fa·thom**LESS a., **fa·thomless**LY[2] adv. [OE *fæthmian* (prec.)]

fati·dical, a. Gifted with prophetic power. [f. L *fatidicus* (FATE, *-dicus* -saying) + -AL]

fati·gue (-ēg), n., & v.t. Weariness after exertion; weakness in metals after repeated blows or long strain; task &c. that wearies; soldier's non-military duty (*f.-party* or *f.*, party told off for this; so *f.-dress*). (Vb) tire, exhaust, whence **fati·gue**LESS, **fati·gu**ING[2], aa.; weaken (metal; see above). [f. F *fatigue(r)* f. L *fatigare* prob. cogn. w. *fatiscere* gape]

fa·tling, n. Young fatted animal. [-LING[1]]

fa·tten, v.t. & i. Make fat (esp. animals for slaughter); grow fat; enrich (soil). [-EN[6]]

fa·tty[1], a. Like fat, unctuous, greasy; consisting of fat, adipose; with morbid deposition of fat (*f. degeneration* of heart or kidney). [-Y[2]]

fa·tty[2], n. Fat child &c. (usu. voc.). [-Y[3]]

fă·tuous, a. Vacantly silly, purposeless, idiotic. Hence or cogn. **fatu·**ITY n., **fa·tuous**LY[2] adv., **fa·tuous**NESS n. [f. L *fatuus* + -OUS]

faubourg (fō·boorg, or as F), n. Suburb, esp. of Paris. [F]

fau·cal, a. & n. (phonol.). Of the throat, deeply guttural (sound). [f. L *fauces* throat + -AL]

fau·cet, n. (dial. & U.S.). Tap for barrel. [f. F *fausset* vent-peg etym. dub.]

faugh (faw), int. of disgust.

fault, n., & v. (geol.) i. & t. Defect, imperfection, blemish, of character or of structure, appearance, &c. (*generous* &c. *to a f.*, excessively; *with all ff.*, at buyer's risk); transgression, offence, thing wrongly done, (Racquets &c.) ball wrongly served; *find f.* (*with*), complain (of), whence **fau·ltfind**ER[1] n., **fau·ltfind**ING [1,2] n. & a.; responsibility for something wrong (*the f. was mine*; *it will be our own f.*), defect that causes something (*the f. is in the patient*); *in f.*, guilty, to blame, (*who is in fault?*); (Hunt.) loss of the scent, check so caused, (*be at f.*, also fig. = be puzzled, not know what to do); (Geol.) break in continuity of strata or vein (vb, break continuity of, show such break); (Telegr.) imperfect insulation, leakage. Hence **fau·lt**LESS a., **fau·ltless**LY[2] adv., **fau·ltless**NESS n., **fau·lt**Y[2] a., **fau·lti**LY[2] adv., **fau·lti**NESS n. [ME & OF *faut(e)* f. pop. L **fallita* fem. p.p. of *fallere* FAIL[2]]

faun, n. One of a class of Latin rural deities with horns & tail. [f. L *Faunus* Latin god identified w. Gk Pan]

fau·na, n. (pl. *-ae*). The animals of a region or epoch; treatise upon these. Hence **fau·n**AL a., **fau·n**IST(3) n., **fauni·s**TIC(AL) aa. [mod. L, f. name of goddess sister of Faunus see prec.]

fauteuil (F), n. Arm-chair; theatre stall.

faux pas (fō pah), n. Act that compromises one's, esp. a woman's, reputation. [F]

fā·vour[1], n. Friendly regard, goodwill, (*find f. in the eyes of,* be liked by; CURRY[2] *f.*), approval (*look with f. on*), good graces (*be, stand high* &c., *in* person's *f.*); kindness beyond what is due (*should esteem it a f.*; *by f. of* —, written on letter conveyed by friend; *do me the f. of —ing*; *have received your f. of yesterday*, letter; *woman bestows her ff. on lover*, yields); leave, pardon, (archaic; *by your f.*; *under f.*, if one may venture to say so); partiality, too lenient or generous treatment (FEAR[1] *or f.*); aid, furtherance, (*under f. of night*); *in f. of*, on behalf or in support of, on the side of, to the advantage or account of, (*am in f. of woman's suffrage*; *cheques to be drawn in f. of the treasurer*); thing given or worn as mark of f., knot of ribbons, rosette, cockade, badge; (archaic) looks, countenance, whence *well, ill, hard*, &c., **-favour**ED[2] a. [OF, f. L *favorem* (*favēre* show kindness to, -OR[1])]

fa·vour[2], v.t. Look kindly upon, approve; treat kindly, countenance; oblige *with*; treat with partiality, be unjust on behalf of; aid, support; serve as confirmation of (theory &c.); prove advantageous to (person), facilitate (process &c.), whence **fa·vour**ING[2] a.; resemble in features (*f. one's father*); (p.p.) having unusual advantages (*most —ed nation*, to which a State accords lowest scale of import duties); *favoured by* (of letter), by f. of. [f. OF *favorer* f. med. L *favorare* as prec.]

fa·vourable, a. Well disposed, propitious; commendatory, approving; giving consent (*f. answer*); promising, auspicious, (*f. aspect*); helpful, suitable, (*to*). Hence **fa·vourable**NESS n., **fa·vourab**LY[2] adv. [f. F *favorable* f. L *favorabilis* (FAVOUR[1], -ABLE)]

fa·vourite, n. & a. (Person) preferred above others (*the f. of, a f. with* or *of*); (Racing) *the f.*, competitor generally expected to win; person chosen as intimate by king or superior & unduly favoured, whence **fa·vourit**ISM(3) n. [f. OF *favorit, -ri*, p.p. of *favorir* favour]

fawn[1], n., a., & v.i. & t. Young fallow deer, buck or doe of first year (*in f.*, pregnant); *f.* or *f.-colour(ed)*, (of) light yellowish brown; (vb; of deer) bring forth (young, or abs.). [f. OF *faon* f. med. L *fetonem* nom. *-o* (FOETUS)]

fawn[2], v.i. (Of animals, esp. dog) show affection by tail-wagging, grovelling, &c. (*f. on, upon*, lavish caresses on); (of persons) behave servilely, cringe (*upon* patron, or abs.), whence **faw·n**ING[2] a., **faw·ning**LY[2] adv. [OE *fahnian* cogn. w. FAIN[1]]

fay, n. Fairy. [f. OF *fae* f. Rom. *fata* sing. f. L *fata* pl. the fates]

fē·alty, n. Feudal tenant's or vassal's (acknowledgement of obligation of) fidelity to his lord (*do, make, receive, swear, f.*). [f. OF *feaulte* f. L *fidelitatem* (*fidelis* f. *fides* faith, -TY)]

fear[1], n. Painful emotion caused by impending danger or evil, state of alarm (*was in f.*), dread *of, that*, or *lest*; *for f. of*, (*that*), *lest*, in order that so-&-so may not occur; *without f. or favour*, impartially; dread & reverence (*the f. of God*); anxiety for the safety *of* (*in f. of his life*); *no f.*, it is not likely. Hence **fear·**LESS a. (*of* danger &c.), **fear·less**LY[2] adv., **fear·less**NESS n. [OE *fǣr* cf. G *gefahr* danger]

fear[2], v.i. & t. Be afraid (also as archaic refl. in parenthesis, *I f. me*; *never f.*, there is no danger of that); be afraid of; hesitate *to* do, shrink from do*ing*; revere (God); apprehend, have uneasy anticipation of; be afraid *that* (or with *that* omitted; also *need not* &c. *f. but* or *but that*). [OE *fǣran* f. prec.]

fear·ful, a. Terrible, awful; (by exagg.) annoying &c. (*in a f. mess*); frightened, timid; apprehensive *of, lest*, (*that*); wanting resolution *to*; reverential. Hence **fear·ful**LY[2] adv., **fear·ful**NESS n. [-FUL]

fear·nought (-awt), n. Stout woollen cloth used at sea for clothing & for protecting portholes &c. [FEAR[2], NOUGHT]

fear·some, a. Appalling, esp. in appearance (usu. joc.). Hence **fear·some**LY[2] adv., **fear·some**NESS n. [-SOME]

fea·sible (-z-), a. Practicable, possible; (loosely) manageable, convenient, serviceable, plausible. Hence **feasi**BI·LITY n. [OF (*fais-* imperf. st. of *faire* f. L *facere* do + -IBLE)]

feast, n., & v.i. & t. Joyful religious anniversary (*movable, immovable, f.*, recurring on different, same, date); annual village festival; sumptuous meal, esp. one given to number of guests and of public nature, (fig.) gratification to the senses or mind (*f. of reason*, intellectual talk). (Vb) partake of f., fare sumptuously, whence **fea·st**ER[1] n.; pass (night &c.) *away* in feasting; regale (guests, one's *eyes on* beauty &c.). [f. OF *feste(r)* f. L *festa* neut. pl. of *festus* festal]

feat[1], n. Noteworthy act, esp. deed of valour (often *f. of arms*); action showing dexterity or strength, surprising trick. [f. OF *fait* FACT]

feat[2], a. (archaic). Adroit, smart, dextrous, neat. Hence **fea·t**LY[2] adv. [f. OF *fait* made f. L *factus* p.p. of *facere* make]

fea·ther[1] (fĕdh-), n. One of the appendages growing from bird's skin, consisting of quill, shaft, & two vanes of barbs (*show the white f.*, betray cowardice—white f. in game-bird's tail being mark of bad breeding—; *crop* one's *ff.*, humiliate him); (collect.) plumage (*in high* or *full f.*, in good spirits &c.; *birds of a f.*, people of one sort); feathered game (*fur & f.*, game beasts & birds); piece(s) of f. attached to arrow; plume worn in hat &c. (*a f. in* one's *cap*, something one may be proud of); very light object (*could have knocked me down with a f.*); ridge of upright hair; f.-like flaw in gem; (Rowing) action of feathering (see foll.); *f. bed*, mattress stuffed with ff.; *f.-edge*, (n.) fine edge of wedge-shaped board, (v.t.) bring (board) to this; *f.-head(ed), -brain(ed), -pate(d)*, silly (person); *f.-stitch*, ornamental zigzag sewing; *f.-weight*, very light thing or person, esp. jockey not over 4 st. 7 lb., boxer 9 st. Hence **(-)featherED**[2], **fea·therLESS, fea·therY**[2], aa., **fea·therINESS, fea·therLET**, nn. [com.-Teut.; OE *fether* cf. G *feder*, also Gk *pteron* wing, *petomai* fly]

fea·ther[2], v.t. & i. Furnish, adorn, line, coat, with ff. (*f. an arrow*; *f.* one's *nest*, enrich oneself; TAR *& f.*); form f.-like covering or adornment for; float, move, or wave, like ff.; turn (oar), turn oar, so as to pass through the air edgeways; (Shoot.) knock ff. from (bird) without killing; (Hunt.; of hound) make quivering motion of body & tail while seeking scent. [OE *gefithrian* f. prec.]

fea·thering, n. In vbl senses; esp.: plumage; feathers of arrow; feathery structure in animal's coat; (Arch.) cusps in tracery; featherlike marking in flower. [-ING[1]]

feature (fē·tsh*er*), n., & v.t. (Usu. pl.) part(s) of the face, esp. with regard to shape & visible effect; distinctive or characteristic part of a thing, part that arrests attention; *f. film, f. picture*, cinema drama of some length in several reels. (Vb) stand as distinctive mark upon; portray, sketch the prominent points of; (U.S.) show on cinema screen, have as chief f., give special prominence to. Hence **-featurED**[2], **fea·tureLESS**, aa. [f. OF *faiture* f. L *factura* (*facere fact-* make, -URE)]

fē·brifuge, n. Medicine to reduce fever, cooling drink. Hence **febri·fugAL** a. [f. F *fébrifuge* (L *febris* fever, *fugare* drive away)]

fē·brile, a. Of fever, feverish. [F, f. L *febrilis* (prec., -IL)]

Fĕ·bruary, n. Second month of year (*F. fill-dike*, name referring to its rain & snow). [f. L *Februarius* (*februa* purification)]

fē·cit, fēcēr·ŭnt, (abbr. *fec.*), v. sing. & pl. 3rd pers. (So-&-so) made this picture &c. (used with artist's signature). [L, perf. of *facere* make]

fe·ckless, a. Feeble, futile, inefficient. Hence **fe·cklessLY**[2] adv., **fe·cklessNESS** n. [Sc. *feck* perh. for EFFECT + -LESS]

fĕ·culent, a. Turbid, fetid. So **fe·culENCE** n. [F (*fé-*) f. L *faeculentus* (FAECES, -ULENT)]

fĕ·cund, a. Prolific, fertile; fertilizing. So **fecu·ndITY** n. [f. F *fécond* f. L *fecundus*]

fĕ·cundate, v.t. Make fruitful; impregnate. Hence **fecundA·TION** n. [L FECUNDare, -ATE[3]]

fed. See FEED[1].

fĕ·deral, a. (Theol.) based on doctrine of Covenants; (Pol.) of the polity in which several States form a unity but remain independent in internal affairs, concerning this whole & not the separate parts; (U.S. Hist.) favouring central government, of Northern party in Civil War., Hence **fe·deralISM**(3), **fe·deralIST**(2), nn., **fe·deralIZE**(3) v.t., **federalizA·TION** n., **fed·eralLY**[2] adv. [f. F *fédéral* (L *foedus -eris* covenant, cogn. w. *fides* FAITH, + -AL)]

fĕ·derāte, v.t. & i. Band together (t. & i.) in league for some common object; organize (t. & i. of States) on a FEDERAL basis. So **fe·derATE**[2] (-*at*), **fe·derATIVE**, aa., **fe·derativeLY**[2] adv. [L *foederare* (prec.), -ATE[3]]

federa·tion, n. Federating, whence **federa·tionIST**(2) n.; federated society, esp. federal empire or group of States; IMPERIAL *f.* [f. F *fédération* f. L *foederationem* (prec., -ATION)]

fee, n., & v.t. (feed). Fief, feudal benefice, (hist.); inherited estate (*f. simple*, without limitation to particular class of heirs; *f.-tail*, with such limitation; *hold in f. simple* or *f.*, have as absolute property); sum payable to public officer for performing his function; remuneration of lawyer, physician, or any professional man (RETAIN*ing-f.*); entrance money for examination, society, &c.; terminal school-money; gratuity; (vb) pay f. to, engage for a f. [f. OF *fé, fief, fiu*, med. L *feodum, feudum*, etym. dub.]

fee·ble, a. & n. Weak, infirm; deficient in character or intelligence; wanting in energy, force, or effect; dim, indistinct; hence **fee·bleNESS** n., **fee·blISH**[1](2) a., **fee·bLY**[2] adv. (N., Fenc.) = FOIBLE. [f. OF *feble, foible*, (now *faible*) f. L *flebilis* lamentable (*flēre* weep)]

feed[1], v.t. & i. (fed). Supply with food (*f. a cold*, eat plentifully when you have a cold); put food into mouth of (*cannot f. himself*); graze (cattle); gratify (*vanity* &c., also *eyes* &c.), comfort (person) *with* hope &c.; take food, eat, (*at the high table*; *well, high*, &c.; often *f. on*, consume); serve as food for; nourish, make grow, (*f. up*, fatten, also satiate; *fed up* slang, having had too much of something, bored *with*); keep (reservoir, fire, &c.) supplied; supply (machine) with material (*f.-pipe*, doing this); use (land) as pasture often *f. down, close*); deal out (fodder) *to* animals; supply (material) (*in*)*to* machine; (of cattle) eat, eat *down*, (pasture); *feeding-bottle*, for hand-fed infants. [OE *fēdan* cf. OHG *fuotan*, & see FOOD]

feed[2], n. Act of feeding, giving of food, (*two biscuits at one f.*; *out at f.*, turned out to graze; *off* one's *f.*, with no appetite; *on the f.* of fish, feeding or looking out for food); pasturage, green crops; horse's allowance of oats &c.; fodder; (colloq.) meal, feast; feeding of machine, material supplied, charge of gun; *f.-tank, -trough*, holding water for locomotive. [f. prec.]

feed[3]. See FEE.

fee·der, n. In vbl senses; esp.: *large, quick, gross*, &c., *f.*, one who eats much

&c.; child's feeding-bottle; child's bib; tributary stream (also fig.); (Rounders &c.) player who tosses ball to striker; hopper or feeding apparatus in machine. [-ER[1]]

fee·ding, a. In vbl senses; also, *f. storm*, one that constantly increases. [-ING[2]]

fee-faw-fum, int. & n. Ogreish exclamation; (n.) nonsense fit only to terrify child. [in *Jack the Giant-Killer*]

feel, v.t. & i. (felt), & n. Explore by touch (*f. the pulse of*, lit., & fig. = cautiously ascertain sentiments of; *f.* one's *way*, grope it out, proceed carefully); search (*about*) with hand *after, for*; try to ascertain by touch *whether, if, how*; (Mil.) reconnoitre (ground, enemy); perceive by touch (*f. a hard substance, heat, pain, a blow*; *I felt him move, moving, that he was cold*; *f.* one's *legs* or *feet*, find firm standing, also fig., be at ease); have sensation of touch; be conscious of (sensation, emotion, conviction; *a felt want*, desideratum); be consciously (*f. well, warm, angry,* CHEAP; *f. quite* one*self*, be fit, self-possessed, &c.; *f.* UP *to work* &c.; *f. like doing*, have inclination to do); experience, undergo, (*he shall f. my vengeance*; *felt the storm severely*), be affected by, behave as if conscious of, (*ship feels her helm*); be emotionally affected by, have sympathy *with* or compassion *for*, (*f. the censure keenly*); have vague or emotional conviction (*that*; esp. *f. in* one's *bones*); (quasi-pass.) be realized as, seem, produce impression of being, (*air feels chilly*; *feels like velvet*). (N.) sense of touch (*firm to the f.*); testing by touch; sensation characterizing something. [com.-WG; OE *félan*, cf. G *fühlen*, f. Aryan *pal-* whence Gk *palamē*, L *palma*, palm of hand]

fee·ler, n. In vbl senses; esp.: organ in certain animals for testing things by touch or searching for food; (Mil.) scout; tentative proposal or hint, *ballon d'essai*. [-ER[1]]

fee·ling[1], n. In vbl senses; esp.: sense of touch; physical sensation; emotion (often *of* hope, fear, &c.); (pl.) susceptibilities, sympathies, (*hurts my ff.*, offends me); readiness to feel, tenderness for others' sufferings, (*good f.*, avoidance of unkindness &c.); consciousness *of* (*had a f. of safety*), conviction not based solely on reason; sentiment (*the general f. was against it*); (Psychol.; differently used by various writers) state of consciousness, sensation or desire or emotion (not perception or thought), element of pleasure or pain in any mental state, intuitive belief; (Art) general emotional effect produced. [-ING[1]]

feeling[2], a. In vbl senses; esp.: sensitive; sympathetic; showing emotion; heartfelt (*a f. pleasure*). Hence **fee·ling**LY[2] adv. [-ING[2]]

feet. See FOOT.

feign (fān), v.t. & i. Invent (excuse, story, accusation), forge (document), represent in fiction, imagine, (archaic); simulate, pretend, (*f. that* one *is mad*, one*self mad, madness*); practise simulation. [f. OF *feindre* f. L *fingere*]

feint[1] (fā-), n., & v.i. Sham attack (blow, cut, thrust, or military assault) to divert attention or deceive opponent; pretence (*make a f. of doing*); (vb) make f. (*at, upon, against*). [f. F *feinte* n. (*feindre* FEIGN)]

feint[2], a. & adv. *F. lines, ruled f.*, = FAINT[1]. [old spelling often kept in this use]

fe·l(d)spar, n. Kinds of crystalline white or flesh-red mineral. So **fel(d)spă·thic** a. [f. G *feldspat(h)* f. *feld* field, *spat(h)* spar; spelling *fels-*, commoner but incorrect, due to false deriv. f. G *fels* rock]

fē·librist, n. Member of the *Félibrige*, a society of modern Provençal poets & writers (Mistral &c.). [f. F *Félibrige*, -IST]

fē·licide, n. Cat-killing. [f. L *feles* cat + -CIDE]

fēlici·fic, a. (eth.). Tending to happiness. [f. L *felicificus* (*felix* happy, -FIC)]

feli·citate, v.t. Make happy (rare); congratulate (usu. *on*), whence (usu. pl.) **felicit**A·TION n. [f. L *felicitare* (*felix* happy), -ATE[3]]

feli·citous, a. Blissful (rare); (of expression, quotation, civilities, or person in these connexions) strikingly apt, pleasantly ingenious. Hence **feli·citous**LY[2] adv. [foll., -OUS]

feli·city, n. Being happy, intense happiness; a blessing; fortunate trait; happy faculty in expression, appropriateness; well chosen phrase. [f. OF *felicité* f. L *felicitatem* (*felix* happy, -TY)]

fē·lid, n. One of the *Felidae* or cat-tribe [f. L *feles* cat, -ID[3]]

fē·līne, a. & n. Of cats; catlike (*f. amenities*, veiled spite, women's innocent-seeming thrusts), whence **feli·**NITY n.; (n.) = prec. [f. L *felinus* (prec., -INE[1])]

fell[1], n. Animal's hide or skin with the hair (also transf. of human skin); thick or matted hair or wool, fleece, (*f. of hair*, unkempt hair of head); *f.*-MONGER. [com.-Teut., cf. G *fell*, cogn. w. Gk *pella*, L *pellis*; also w. FILM]

fell[2], n. Mountain (in names, as *Sca F.*); stretch of N.-English moorland. [f. ON *fiall* perh. cogn. w. G *fels* rock]

fell[3], a. (poet.). Fierce, ruthless, terrible, destructive. [f. OF *fel* f. pop. L *fello* FELON]

fell[4], v.t., & n. Strike (person, animal) down by blow or cut; cut down (tree; n., amount of timber cut); stitch down (projection of seam). [causative of FALL[1], cf. G *fällen*]

fell[5]. See FALL[1].

fe·llah, n. (pl. *fellaheen, fellahs*). Egyptian peasant. [Arab.]

fe·lloe, fe·lly, (usu. spelt *-oe* & pronounced -ĭ), n. Outer circle (or one piece of it) of wheel, attached by spokes. [OE *felg*, cf. G *felge*]

fe·llow, n. One associated with another, comrade, (usu. in pl., as *separated from his ff.*; *good f.*, boon companion; HAIL[3]-*f.-well-met*; *f.-feeling*, sympathy); counterpart, match, other of pair, equal, one of same class, contemporary, (*stone dead hath no f.*, no keeper of secrets like a dead man; *shall never find his f.*; *passed all his ff.*); co-opted graduate incorporated member of college (*f. commoner*, undergraduate privileged to dine at fellows' table); elected graduate holding stipend for certain years on condition of research; member of governing body in some Universities; member of various learned Societies; man, boy, (*poor f.!*, *my dear* or *good f.*, *old f.*; *a f.*, sometimes = *one*, *I*, as *a f. can't work all day long*; *the f.*, contemptuously); (in comb. with nn.; *f.* or *f.-*) belonging to same class (*f. creature*, person or animal also created by God), associated in joint action (*f. soldier*), in same relation to same object (*f. citizen*, whence **fellow-ci·tizen**SHIP n.; *f.-countryman*). [OE *féolaga* (FEE, LAY) one who lays down money in partnership]

fe·llowship, n. Participation, sharing, community of interest; companionship, intercourse, friendliness, (often *good f.*); body of associates, company, (*right hand of f.*, sign of admission); guild, corporation; brotherhood, fraternity; dignity or income of college fellow. [-SHIP]

felly. See FELLOE.

fĕ·lo de sē· (dĭ), n. (pl. *felonēs*, *felos*). Self-murderer, (no. pl.) self-murder. [Anglo-L, = FELON about himself]

fĕ·lon[1], a. (poet.), & n. Cruel, wicked, murderous; (n.) one who has committed felony. [OF, f. LL *fellonem* nom. *-o* perh. f. L *fel* gall]

fe·lon[2], n. Small abscess esp. under or near nail, whitlow. [perh. as prec.]

felō·nious, a. Criminal; (Law) of, involving, felony; who has committed felony. Hence **felo·nious**LY[2] adv. [FELONY + -OUS]

fe·lonry, n. The class or body of felons. [-RY]

fe·lony, n. Crime of kind legally graver than misdemeanour. [f. F *félonie* (FELON, -Y[1])]

felspar. See FELDSPAR.

fe·lstone (-on), n. Compact felspar occurring in amorphous rock masses. [f. G *felsstein* (*fels* rock, *stein* stone)]

felt[1], n., & v.t. & i. Kind of cloth made by rolling & pressing wool with lees or size; (attrib.) made of this (esp. *f. hat*); hence **fe·lt**Y[2] a. (Vb) make into f., mat together; become matted; cover with f. [OE; cf. Du. *vilt*, G *filz*]

felt[2]. See FEEL.

fe·lteric, n. A horse-disease. [?]

felu·cca, n. Small Mediterranean coasting vessel with oars or lateen sails or both. [It., perh. f. Arab.]

fē·male, a. & n. Of the offspring-bearing sex (*f. child*, *slave*, *dog*); (of plants or their parts) fruit-bearing, having pistil & no stamens, (also used of some plants by mere metaphor suggested by their colour &c., as *f. fern*, *bamboo*, *myrtle*); of women (*f. sex*, *education*, *suffrage*, *weakness*); of inferior vigour &c. (*f. sapphire*, pale variety); (in instruments &c.) fitted to receive corresponding male part (*f. screw*, as in nuts). (N.) f. person (*the law is harsh to all ff.*) or animal; (vulg.) woman, girl, (*a young f. has called*). [ME & OF *femelle* n. f. L *femella* dim. of *femina* woman, w. assim. to *male*]

feme co·vert (fĕm kŭ-), **feme sole,** nn. (legal). (*Covert*) married woman; (*sole*) spinster, widow, or married woman entirely independent of her husband as regards property. [AF (*soul*)]

fĕmină·lity, n. Female nature; female peculiarity; woman's knick-knack &c. [obs. *feminal* f. OF (L *femina* woman, -AL) + -ITY]

fĕminē·ity, n. Womanliness; womanishness. [f. L *femineus* (*femina* woman) + -ITY]

fĕ·minĭne, a. Of female sex (rare); of women; womanly; (Gram.) having the gender proper to women's names; (Pros.) *f. rhyme*, of two syllables, the second being unstressed (orig. in F verse, of words ending in mute *-e*), *f. ending*, of line with last accent on penult, *f. caesura*, not immediately following stress. Hence **fe·minine**LY[2] adv., **fe·minine**NESS, **femini·**NITY, nn. [f. OF *feminin* f. L *femininus* (*femina* woman, -INE[1])]

fe·minism, n. Advocacy, extended recognition, of the claims of women. So **fe·min**IST n. [f. L *femina* woman + -ISM]

femi·nity, n. = FEMININITY (prec.). [f. OF *feminité* (L *femina* woman, -ITY)]

fĕ·minize, v.t. & i. Make or become feminine. Hence **feminiz**A·TION n. [f. L as prec. + -IZE]

femme de chambre (F), n. Lady's maid; chambermaid.

fē·mur, n. (pl. *-s*, *femora*). Thigh-bone; corresponding part of insect. So **fĕ·mor**AL. [L]

fen[1], n. Low marshy or flooded tract of land (*the ff.*, low-lying districts in Cambs. &c.; *f.-berry*, cranberry; *f.-fire*, will-o'-the-wisp; *f.-man*, inhabitant of ff.; *f.-pole*, for use in jumping ditches; *f.-reeve*, officer in charge of f.-lands; *f.-runners*, kind of skates. Hence **fe·nn**Y[2] a. [OE; cf. Du. *ven*, G *fenne*]

fen[2], **fens.** See FAIN[2].

fence[1], n. Art of fencing, use of the sword, (*master of f.*, skilled swordsman, often fig. = good debater); (archaic) bulwark;

hedge, wall, railing, &c., keeping out intruders from field &c. (*sunk f.*, placed along bottom of ditch; *sit on the f.*, remain neutral in contest, not take sides; *come* &c. *down on right side of f.*, join winner; PUT *horse at f.*); guard, guide, gauge, in various machines; receiver, receiving-house, of stolen goods; *f.-month, -season, -time*, close time for game or fish. [for DEFENCE]

fence[2], v.i. & t. Practise sword-play, use the sword scientifically, (*f. with question* or *questioner*, parry, evade answering); screen, shield, protect, (*from, against*); repel, keep *off* or *out*; surround (as) with f., enclose, fortify, (*fenced cities* in O.T.; often *about, in, round, up*); (of horse) leap ff.; deal in stolen goods. Hence **fe·nc**ER[1] n. (esp. of swordsman, also of horse). [f. prec.]

fe·nceless, a. Unenclosed; (poet.) unfortified, defenceless. [FENCE[1] + -LESS]

fe·ncible, n. (hist.). Soldier liable only for defensive service. [for DEFENSIBLE]

fe·ncing, n. In vbl senses; also: railing; fences; material for fences; *f.-cully, -ken*, storer, store, of stolen goods. [-ING[1]]

fend, v.t. & i. Ward *off*, keep *away*, repel *from*; provide *for* (usu. one*self*). [for DEFEND]

fe·nder, n. Thing used to keep something off, prevent collision, &c., guard, esp. metal frame for fire to keep coals from rolling into room; *f.-stool*, long footstool before f. Hence **fe·nder**LESS a. [-ER[1]]

fĕneste·lla, n. (archit.). Niche in wall S. of altar holding piscina & often credence. [L, dim. of *fenestra* window]

fene·strate, a. (bot., zool.). With small window-like perforations. [f. L *fenestrare* (prec.), -ATE[2]]

fenestra·tion, n. (Arch.) arrangement of windows in a building; (Bot. & Zool.) being fenestrate. [prec., -ATION]

Fē·nian, n. & a. One of a league among the Irish in U.S. for promoting revolution & overthrowing English government in Ireland; hence **Fe·nian**ISM(3) n. (Adj.) of Ff. or Fenianism. [f. OIr. *féne* name of ancient Irish people confused w. *fiann* guard of legendary kings]

fenks, n. pl. Fibrous parts of whale's blubber, refuse of blubber when melted. [?]

fe·nnel, n. Yellow-flowered fragrant umbelliferous herb used in sauces. [OE *finugl* f. L *faeniculum* (*faenum* hay, -CULE)]

fĕ·nugreek, n. Leguminous plant with seeds used in farriery. [f. L *faenugraecum* (*faenum* hay, *Graecus* Greek)]

feoff. See FIEF.

feoffee· (fĕf-), n. Person to whom freehold estate in land is conveyed by a feoffment; *f. in* or *of trust*, trustee invested with such estate. [f. AF *feoffé* p.p. f. OF *fieffer* (FEE), see -EE]

feo·ffment (fĕf-), n. Particular mode of conveying freehold estate. [as prec., -MENT]

feo·ffor, -er, (fĕf-), n. One who makes feoffment to another. [as FEOFFEE, -OR[2]]

fĕr·ae natūr·ae, a. (pred. or placed after noun). Not domesticated, living in a wild state, (*hares are, the hare is*, f. n.; *animals* f. n.). [L, = of a wild nature]

fēr·al, a. Wild, untamed, uncultivated; brutal. [f. L *fera* wild beast + -AL]

fĕ·retory, n. Shrine for saint's relics, tomb; bier; chapel in which shrines were deposited. [ME *fertre* f. L *feretrum* f. Gk *pheretron* (*pherō* bear), w. assim. to -ORY]

fēr·ial, a. (eccl.). (Of day) ordinary, not appointed for festival or fast (*f. service* &c., for use on f. day). [f. F *férial* f. L *ferialis* (*feria* holiday + -AL)]

fēr·ine, a. = FERAL. [f. L *ferinus* (*fera* wild beast, -INE[1])]

Feri·nghee (-ĭnggĭ), n. (Indian term for) European, esp. Indian-born Portuguese. [corrupt. of FRANK[1]]

fer·ment[1], n. Leaven, fermenting-agent; fermenting, fermentation; agitation, excitement, tumult. [F, f. L *fermentum* (*fervēre* boil, -MENT)]

ferme·nt[2], v.i. & t. Suffer, subject to, fermentation; (make) effervesce; excite, stir up, foment. Hence **ferme·nt**ABLE a. [f. F *fermenter* f. L *fermentare* (prec.)]

fermenta·tion, n. Process like that induced by leaven in dough, with effervescence, heat, & change of properties; agitation, excitement. Hence **ferme·nt**ATIVE a. [f. L *fermentatio* (prec., -ATION)]

fern, n. One of a large group of vascular cryptogams with feathery fronds (also collect., *go through heath & f.*); *f.-owl*, Nightjar. Hence **fer·n**LESS, **fer·n**Y[2], aa., **fer·n**ERY(3) n. [OE *fearn* cf. G *farn* cogn. w. Skr. *parṇa* wing, feather, leaf]

ferō·cious, a. Fierce, savage, cruel. Hence **fero·cious**LY[2] adv. [f. L *ferox -ocis* + -OUS]

ferŏ·city, n. Ferocious character or act. [f. F *férocité* f. L *ferocitatem* (prec., -TY)]

-ferous, suf. (in actual use *-iferous*, see -I-) forming adjj., f. L *-fer* -producing (*fĕrre* bear) + -OUS; in adjj. taken direct or thr. F *-fère* f. L as *auriferous*, & now a living suf., esp. in Nat. Hist., = -bearing, -having.

fĕ·rox, n. Great lake trout. [L name *Salmo ferox* fierce salmon]

fe·rrate, n. A salt of ferric acid. [f. L *ferrum* iron + -ATE[1](3)]

fe·rreous, a. Of, containing, iron. [f. L *ferreus* (prec.) + -OUS]

fe·rret[1], n. Half-tamed variety of polecat kept for driving rabbits from burrows, killing rats, &c.; searcher, detective. Hence **fe·rret**Y[2] a. [f. OF *furet* dim. of *furon* f. LL *furonem* nom. *-o* robber (L *fur*)]

fe·rret[2], v.i. & t. Hunt with ff. (*go ferret-*

ing); clear out (holes, ground), take or drive away (rabbits &c.), with ff. (*about, away, out,* &c.); rummage, search *about,* (*for*); search *out* (secrets, criminals, &c.). [f. prec.]

fe·rret[3], n. Stout cotton or silk tape. [f. It. *fioretti* floss-silk pl. of *fioretto* dim. of *fiore* f. L *flos -oris* flower]

ferri-, comb. form used to indicate presence of iron in the ferric state (cf. FERRO-). [f. L *ferrum* iron]

fe·rriage (-ĕj), n. Conveyance by, charge for using, ferry. [-AGE]

fe·rric, a. Of iron; (Chem.) containing iron in its highest combining-power (cf. FERROUS). [as FERRI- + -IC]

ferri·ferous, a. Iron-yielding. [as prec. + -FEROUS]

ferro-, comb. form of L *ferrum* iron, as *ferro-calcite*; *f.-concrete,* = REINFORCED *concrete*; (Chem.) containing iron in the ferrous state (cf. FERRI-).

ferro-magne·tic, a. Magnetic as opp. to diamagnetic. [prec.]

fe·rrotype, n. Positive photograph taken on thin iron plate; this process. [FERRO-, TYPE]

fe·rrous, a. (chem.) Containing iron as a divalent (cf. FERRIC). [as FERRO- + -OUS]

ferru·ginous (-ōō-), a. Of, containing, iron-rust or iron as a chemical constituent; rust-coloured, reddish-brown. [f. L *ferrugo -ginis* rust (*ferrum* iron) + -OUS)]

fe·rrule, -rel, n. Metal ring or cap strengthening end of stick or tube; band strengthening or forming joint. Hence **fe·rrul**ED[2] a. [earlier *verrel* f. OF *virelle* f. med. L *virola* f. L *viriola* dim. of *viriae* bracelets, altered as though dim. of *ferrum* iron]

fe·rry, v.t. & i., & n. Convey or pass in boat, work (boat), (of boat) pass to & fro, over river, canal, or strait. (N.) Place, provision, for ferrying; (Law) right of ferrying & levying toll for it; *f.-boat*; *ferryman*; *f.-bridge,* large f.-boat transporting railway train entire. [n. f. vb, OE *ferian* cogn. w. FARE]

fer·tile (-īl, -ĭl), a. Bearing abundantly, fruitful, (lit. & fig.; *f. of, in*). So **fer·ti·li**TY n. [f. OF *fertil* f. L *fertilis* (*ferre* bear)]

fer·tilize, v.t. Make fertile or productive (esp. soil); (Bot. &c.) fecundate (individual, organ). Hence **fer·tiliz**ABLE a., **fertiliz**A·TION, **fer·tiliz**ER[1](1, 2), nn. [-IZE]

fĕ·rula, fe·rule, nn. (Bot.) giant fennel (*-ula*); flat ruler with widened pierced end for punishing boys, whence **fe·rule** v.t. [L (*-a*)]

fer·vent a. Hot, glowing; ardent, intense, (*f. soul, lover, hatred*), so **fer·**VENCY n. Hence **fer·vent**LY[2] adv. [F, f. L *fervēre* boil, -ENT]

fer·vid, a. =prec. (poet. in first sense). Hence **fer·vid**LY[2] adv. [f. L *fervidus* (prec.)]

fer·vour, n. Glowing condition, intense heat; vehemence, passion, zeal. [f. OF *fervor* f. L *fervorem* nom. *-or* (FERVENT, -OR[1])]

Fe·scennine, a. *F. verses,* scurrilous lampoons. [f. L *Fescenninus* (*Fescennia* town in Etruria, -INE[1])]

fe·scue, n. Small stick, teacher's pointer: kinds of grass. [f. OF *festu* f. L *festuca*]

fesse (fĕs), n. (herald.). Two horizontal lines as bar across middle of field. [OF, f. FASCIA]

fe·stal, a. Of a feast; keeping holiday; gay. Hence **fe·stal**LY[2] adv. [OF (FEAST, -AL)]

fe·ster, v.i. & t., & n. (Of wound or sore) generate matter, ulcerate; (of poison, disease, grief) cause suppuration, rankle; putrefy, rot; cause festering in; (n.) festering condition. [f. obs. n. *fester* f. OF *festre* f. L FISTULA]

fe·stival, a. (not pred.), & n., Festal day, celebration, merry-making; periodic musical performance(s); (adj.) of a feast (-day). [adj. use earlier; OF, f. med. L *festivalis* (foll., -AL)]

fe·stive, a. Of a feast; joyous; fond of feasting, jovial. Hence **fe·stive**LY[2] adv. [f. L *festivus* (*festum* FEAST, -IVE)]

festi·vity, n. Gaiety, rejoicing; festive celebration, (pl.) festive proceedings. [f. OF *festivité* f. L *festivitatem* (prec., -TY)]

festoo·n, n., & v.t. Chain of flowers or leaves, or ribbons &c., hung in curve between two points; (vb) adorn (as) with, form into, ff. Hence **festoo·n**ERY(5) n. [f. F *feston* f. It. *festone* perh. f. *festa* feast + -OON]

fetch[1], v.t. & i., & n. (Go for &) bring back (person or thing; *f.,* or *go & f., a doctor*; FAR[1]*-fetched*; *f. & carry,* run backwards & forwards with things, be a servant); cause to come, draw forth, (blood, tears; *f. up,* vomit); bring in, realize, sell for, (a price); move the feelings of, delight (whence **fe·tch**ING[2] a.) or irritate; heave (sigh), draw (breath); deal (blow; usu. with ind. obj., *f. him a box on the ears*); *f. a* COMPASS[1]; *f. up,* come to a stand. (N.) far-reaching effort (archaic); dodge, trick; *f. of the sea,* distance of a coast &c., from nearest weather shore (esp. as affecting height of waves). [OE *fecc(e)an* perh. var. of *fetian* etym. dub. whence obs. *fet* in same sense]

fetch[2], n. Person's wraith or double. [?]

fête (fāt), n., & v.t. Festival, great entertainment, (*f.-day,* appointed for f.); day of saint after whom child is named, observed in R.-C. countries like birthday; (vb) entertain, make much of, (person). [f. F *fête(r)* FEAST]

fête-champêtre (F), n. Outdoor fête.

fē·tial (-shl), a. & n. (Rom. ant.). *F. law,* of declarations of war & treaties of peace; (n.) one of Roman college of priests who

served as heralds. [f. L *fetialis* etym. dub.]
fē·tid, foe-, a. Stinking. Hence **fe·tid**LY² adv., **fe·tid**NESS n. [f. L *fetidus* (*fetēre* stink)]
fē·tish, -ch(e), (-sh), n. Inanimate object worshipped by savages for its magical powers or as being inhabited by a spirit; principle &c. irrationally reverenced. Hence or cogn. **fetish**EER·, **fe·tish**ER¹, **fe·tish**ISM(3), **fe·tish**IST(2), nn., **fetishi·stic** a. [f. F *fétiche* f. Port. *feitiço* charm, orig. adj. =FACTITIOUS]
fe·tlock, n. Part of horse's leg where tuft of hair grows behind pastern-joint (*f.-deep*, so as to cover ff.). [ME *fytlok* cf. G *fiszloch* etym. dub.]
fē·tor, n. Stench. [L, see FETID, -OR¹]
fe·tter, n., & v.t. Shackle for the feet; bond, (pl.) captivity; check, restraint; *fetterlock*, (heraldic representation of) D-shaped fetter for tethering horse by leg; (vb) bind (as) with ff., impede, restrain. Hence **fe·tter**LESS a. [OE *feter* cf. G *fesser* f. OTeut. *fet-* cogn. w. *fôt* FOOT; also w. L *pedica*, Gk *pedē*, fetter]
fe·ttle, n. Condition, trim, (*in good f.* &c.). [f. dial. vb *fettle* put right cf. OE *fetel* bond]
fetus. See FOETUS.
fe·twa, n. Decision given by Moslem judicial authority. [Arab.]
feu, n. (Sc.). Perpetual lease at fixed rent; piece of land so held. [var. of FEE]
feud¹, n. Lasting mutual hostility (*be at f. with*), esp. (often *deadly f.*) between two tribes, families, &c., with murderous assaults in revenge for previous injury. [ME & OF *fede* f. OHG *fêhida*=OE *fǣhthu* enmity; cogn. w. FOE]
feud², n. Fief, feudal benefice; territory held in fee. [f. med. L as FEE]
feu·dal, a. Of a feud or fief; *f. system*, medieval European polity based on relation of vassal & superior arising from holding of lands in feud; of, resembling, according to, this system. Hence **feu·dal**LY² adv., **feu·dal**ISM(3), **feu·dal**IST(2), nn., **feudali·stic** a., **feu·dal**IZE(3) v.t., **feudaliza**·TION n. [f. med. L *feudalis* (prec., -AL)]
feudă·lity, n. Feudal system or principles; feudal holding, fief. [f. F *feudalité* (prec., -TY)]
feu·datory, a. & n. Feudally subject *to*, under overlordship; (n.) feudal vassal. [f. med. L *feudare* enfeoff (FEUD²), -ORY]
feu de joie (F), n. Gun-firing on occasion of public rejoicing.
feuilleton (F), n. Ruled-off portion at foot of (esp. French) newspapers, devoted to fiction, criticism, light literature, &c. [F, =leaflet].
fē·ver, n., & v.t. Morbid condition with high temperature & excessive change & destruction of tissues; any of a group of diseases so characterized, each with distinctive name, as *scarlet*, *typhoid*, *f.*; nervous excitement, agitation; *f. heat*, high temperature of body in f.; *f.-trap*, place that collects f.-germs; (vb) throw into f. [OE *féfor* f. L *febris*]
fē·verfew, n. A herb formerly used in medicine. [OE *féferfuge* f. L *febrifugia* (prec., *fugare* drive away)]
fe·verish, a. Having symptoms of fever; excited, fitful, restless; (of places) infested by fever, feverous. Hence **fe·verish**LY² adv., **fe·verish**NESS n. [-ISH¹]
fe·verous, a. Infested with or apt to cause fever; feverish. [-OUS]
few, a. & n. Not many (*f.* is opp. to *many*, *a f.* to *none*, *only a f.*=*f.*; *a man of f. words*; *he spoke a f. words*; *f. have such a chance*; *f.*, *a f.*, *of his friends were there*; *a f. know the truth*; *a faithful f. remained*; *visitors are f.*); *in f.* (archaic), in f. words, briefly; *some f.*, no great number; *the f.*, the minority, the elect, &c.; *not a f.*, many; (colloq). *a good f.*, a fair number (*of*); *every f. days* &c., once in every group of a f. days; (slang) *a f.*, very much, beyond a doubt. Hence **few·**NESS n. [com.-Teut.; OE *féawe* cf. OHG *fao*; cogn. w. L *paucus* & *paullus*, Gk *pauros*. In the use with *a* (cf. *hundred* &c.) *f.* forms with the n. a collective, which however is followed by pl. vb]
fey (fā), a. (Sc.). Fated to die, at point of death; disordered in mind (often with over-confidence &c.) like person about to die. [com.-Teut.; OE *fǣge* cf. G *feige* cowardly]
fĕz, n. Turkish cap, a tasselled dull-red truncated cone. [f. Turk. *fes* perh. f. *Fez*, town]
fiancé, -ée (F), n. One's betrothed, (*-é*) male, or (*-ée*) female.
fiă·sco, n. Failure or break-down (orig. in dramatic &c. performance), ignominious result. [It., = bottle (significance doubtful)]
fī·at (-*at*, -ăt), n., & v.t. Authorization; decree, order, (n., & rarely vb =authorize). [L, =be it done]
fib¹, n., & v.i. (Tell) trivial or venial lie. Hence **fi·bb**ER¹, **fi·b**STER, nn. [perh. f. obs. *fible-fable* nonsense, redupl. of FABLE]
fib², n., & v.t. A blow (vb, strike, hit about) in pugilism &c. [?]
fī·bre (-ber), n. Thread-like filament forming with others animal & vegetable tissue or textile substance; substance consisting of ff.; fibrous structure; structure, grain, character, (*man of coarse f.*); substance that can be spun, woven, or felted; small root or twig. Hence (-)**fi·bred**², **fi·bre**LESS, **fi·bri**FORM, **fi·b**ROUS, aa., **fi·brous**LY² adv., **fi·brous**NESS n., **fibro-** comb. form. [F, f. L *fibra* etym. dub.]
fi·bril, n. Small fibre; subdivision of fibre; ultimate subdivision of root. Hence **fibri·ll**AR(Y), **fibri·ll**ATE², **-ated, fibri·l-**

li*form*, **fi·brill***ose*[1], aa., **fibrill***a·tion* n. [also *fibrilla* mod. L dim. of prec.]

fi·brin, n. Coagulable lymph found in animal & vegetable matter. Hence **fi·brino-** comb. form, **fi·brin***ous* a. [FIBRE + -IN]

fi·broid, a. & n. Of fibrous structure or appearance; (n.) f. uterine tumour. [-OID]

fi·broin, n. Chemical substance of which silk & cobweb mainly consist. [FIBRO- + -IN]

fibro·ma, n. (pl. *-ta*). Fibrous tumour. [mod. L (FIBRE, & cf. SARCOMA)]

fi·bula, n. (pl. *-ae, -as*). Splint bone on outer side of leg. Hence **fi·bul***ar*[1] a. [L, =brooch (*figere* fix)]

-fic, suf. (in actual use, *-ific*, see -I-) repr. L *-ficus* f. weakened root of *facere* make, do, forming adjj. f. nn. as *pacificus* peace-making, f. adjj. as *magnificus*, f. vv. as *horrificus*, & f. the advv. *male, bene*. E adopted many L adjj. of this type thr. F; & later formations, arising in various langg., are usu. of international currency, as *acidific, morbific*.

-fication, suf. (in actual use *-ification*, see -I-) repr. L*-fication-* (nom. *-tio*), which formed nn. of action f. vv. in *-ficare* -FY. E adopted many pairs of words, n. & vb, f. L thr. F or of F formation, as *purify, purification*; hence *-fication* has become the recognized means of forming nn. corresp. to vv. in *-fy* exc. when these repr. L vv. in *-facere* (see -FACTION); as a rule the formation is based only on possible L types; exceptions are *beautif., Frenchif., transmogrif.*

fice·lle, a. String-coloured. [F, =string]

fi·chu (-shōō), n. Woman's small triangular shawl of lace &c. for shoulders & neck. [F]

fi·ckle, a. Inconstant, changeable. Hence **fi·ckle***ness* n. [OE *ficol* cf. *befician* deceive]

fi·ctīle, a. Made of earth or clay by potter; of pottery. [f. L *fictilis* (*fingere fict-* fashion, -IL)]

fi·ction, n. Feigning, invention; thing feigned or imagined, invented statement or narrative; literature consisting of such narrative, esp. novels, whence **fi·ction***ist*(3) n.; conventionally accepted falsehood (esp. *legal, polite, f.*). Hence **fi·ction***al* a. [F, f. L *fictionem* (prec., -ION)]

ficti·tious (-sh*u*s), a. Counterfeit, not genuine; (of name or character) assumed; imaginary, unreal; of, in, novels; regarded as what it is called by legal or conventional fiction. Hence **ficti·tious***ly*[2] adv., **ficti·tious***ness* n. [f. L *ficticius* (prec.) + -OUS]

fi·ctive, a. Creating, created, by imagination. [F (*-if, -ive*), see FICTION, -IVE]

fid, n. (Naut.) conical wooden pin used in splicing; square wooden or iron bar for supporting topmast. Small thick piece or wedge of anything. [?]

fi·ddle, n., int., & v.i. & t. (Fam. or contempt. for) violin (*fit as a f.*, in good condition & spirits; *hang up* one's *f. when* one *comes home*, be witty abroad & dull at home; *play first, second, f.*, take leading, subordinate, position; *face as long as a f.*, dismal); (Naut.) contrivance for stopping things from rolling off table; *f.*-BOW[1]; *f.-case*, for holding f.; *fiddlededee*, int. & n., nonsense; *f.-faddle*, (n.) trivial matters, idler, (adj.) petty, fussy, (int.) nonsense, (v.i.) fuss, trifle; *f.-head*, carving at ship's bows; *f. pattern*, of spoons & forks with f.-shaped heads; *fiddlestick*, (n.) = f.-bow, (also *fiddlestick end*) mere nothing, nonsense (also as int.). (Int.) = fiddlestick. (Vb) play the f., play (tune &c.) on f.; be idle or frivolous, make aimless movements, (*about, at, with*, &c.); fritter *away*. [ME *fithele*, cf. MDu. *vedel*, G *fiedel*, etym. dub.; there is med. L *vitula*, whence VIOL]

fi·ddler, n. Player on fiddle, esp. for hire (*F's Green*, sailor's Elysium); kind of small crab. [OE *fithelere* (prec., -ER[1])]

fiddley (fi·dl-ĭ), n. (naut.). Iron framework round opening of stokehole. [?]

fi·ddling, a. In vbl senses; esp., petty, futile, contemptible, inconsiderable. [-ING[2]]

fidě·lity, n. Faithfulness, loyalty, (*to*); strict conformity to truth or fact, exact correspondence to the original. [f. F *fidélité* f. L *fidelitatem* (*fidelis* faithful f. *fides* faith, -TY)]

fi·dget[1] (-j-), n. 1. Bodily uneasiness seeking relief in spasmodic movements (often *the ff.*); restless mood. 2. One who fidgets or causes others to; act of bustling &c., rustle of dress &c. Hence **fi·dget***y*[2] a., **fi·dgeti***ness* n. [sense 1 f. obs. *fidge* to twitch, cf. G *ficken*; sense 2 f. foll.]

fi·dget[2], v.i. & t. Move restlessly (often *about*); be uneasy, worry; make uncomfortable, worry, (person). [f. prec.]

fi·dibus, n. Paper spill for lighting candles, pipes, &c. [?]

fīdu·cial, a. (surv., astron., &c.). *F. line, point*, &c., one assumed as fixed basis of comparison. [f. L *fiducialis* (*fiducia* trust, -AL)]

fīdu·ciary (-sh*a*-), a. & n. Of trust or trustee(ship); held or given in trust; (of paper currency) depending for its value on public confidence or securities; (n.) trustee. [f. L *fiduciarius* (prec., -ARY[1])]

fī·dus Achā·tes (-k-), n. Devoted follower, henchman. [L, =faithful A., follower of Aeneas in *Aeneid*]

fie (fī), int. expr. sense of outraged propriety, usu. iron. or to children (often *f. upon you!*) [f. OF f. L *fi* excl. of disgust at stench]

fief (fēf), **feoff** (fĕf), n. = FEUD[2].

fie·-fie, a. Improper, scandalous. [FIE]

field, n., & v.i. & t. (Piece of) ground, esp. one used for pasture or tillage, & usu.

bounded by hedges &c., tract abounding in some natural product (*diamond, coal,* &c., *-f.*); ground on which battle is fought (often *battle-f.*; also fig., *left his rival in possession of the f.*; *fair f. & no favour,* equal conditions in contest; *hold the f.,* not be superseded); scene of campaign (*in the f.,* campaigning; *take, keep, the f.,* begin, continue, campaign); battle (*hard-fought, stricken, f.*); *F. of Cloth of Gold,* scene of meeting between Henry VIII & Francis I, 1520; ground for playing cricket, football, &c.; players, partakers, in outdoor contest or sport; all competitors or all except the favourite (*a good f.,* many & good competitors); (Cricket) side not batting, one of this side (see also LONG[1] *f.*); large stretch, expanse, of sea, sky, ice, snow, &c., also fig. (*the whole f. of history*); (Herald.) surface of escutcheon or of one of its divisions; groundwork of picture, coin, flag, &c.; area or sphere of operation, observation, &c. (*each supreme in his own f.*; *filled the f. of the telescope*; *wide f. of vision*; *outside the magnetic f.,* not near enough to be attracted); (attrib. in names of animals &c.) found in the open country (*f.-mouse, f.-ash*); *f.-allowance,* to officer on campaign to meet increased expenditure; *f.-artillery, -battery, -gun* or *-piece,* light & mobile for use on campaign & in battle; *f.-cornet,* magistrate of township in Cape Colony &c.; *f.-day,* (Mil.) manœuvring-exercise or review, (fig.) great occasion, important debate; *f. dressing,* appliances for wound in battle; *f.-glass,* binocular telescope for outdoor use, one of the lenses of astronomical telescope or compound microscope; *f. greys,* German soldiers in service uniform; *f. hospital,* ambulance, temporary hospital near battlefield; *F. Marshal,* general officer of highest rank; *f.-night,* = *f.-day* (fig. sense); *f.-officer,* above captain & below general; *f.-preacher, -ing,* in open air; *f. punishment* (mil.), kinds of penal servitude for offences on campaign; *fieldsman,* fielder at cricket; *f.-sports,* outdoor, esp. hunting, shooting, fishing; *f. telegraph,* movable for use on campaign; *f.-work,* temporary fortification; hence **fie·ld**WARD(S) adv. (Vb) act as fieldsman in cricket, base-ball, or rounders; stop (& return) ball; hence **fie·ld**ER[1] n. [com.-WG; OE & G *feld*]

fie·ldfare, n. Species of thrush visiting Britain in autumn. [ME *feldefare* perh. = fieldgoer (FARE[2])]

fiend (fēnd), n. The devil; evil spirit, demon; person of superhuman wickedness, esp. cruelty (often jocular, as *the interviewer-f.*). Hence **fie·nd**ISH[1] a., **fie·ndish**LY[2] adv., **fie·ndish**NESS n., **fie·nd**LIKE a. [com.-Teut.; OE *fēond* cf. G *feind* enemy, f. OTeut. vb = hate, -ND[2]]

fierce (fērs), a. Violent in hostility, angrily combative; raging, vehement; ardent, eager. Hence **fier·ce**LY[2] adv., **fier·ce**NESS n. [f. OF *fiers* nom. of *fier* (F = proud) f. L *ferus* savage]

fi·eri fā·ciās, n. (legal; abbr. *fi. fa.*). Writ to sheriff for executing judgement. [L, = see that (the sum) is made]

fiery (fīr·ĭ), a. Consisting of, flaming with, fire; (of arrows &c.) fire-bearing; looking like fire, blazing-red; (of eyes) flashing, ardent; hot as fire; acting like fire, inflaming, (*f. taste* &c.); eager, pugnacious, spirited, irritable; (of horse) mettlesome; (of gas, mine, &c.) inflammable, liable to explosions; (of cricket-pitch) making ball rise dangerously; *f.* CROSS[1]. Hence **fier·i**LY[2] adv., **fier·i**NESS n. [FIRE[1] + -Y[1]]

fife, n., & v.i. & t. Kind of small shrill flute used with drum in military music; = fifer. (Vb) play the f.; play (air &c.) on the f.; hence **fi·f**ER[1] n. [f. G *pfeife* PIPE, or f. F *fifre* fife(r) f. OHG *pfīfâri* piper (*pfīfan* to pipe)]

fi·fe-rail, n. (naut.). Rail round mainmast with belaying-pins. [perh. f. prec. because fifer sat on it while anchor was weighing]

fiftee·n (*also* fĭ·-), a. & n. One more than fourteen, 15, XV; (Rugby football) side of 15 players; *the F.,* Jacobite rising of 1715. Hence **fiftee·n**TH[2] a. & n. [OE *fiftēne, -tȳne,* (FIVE, -TEEN)]

fifth, a. & n. Next after fourth (*smite under the f. rib,* kill; *f. wheel* of coach &c., something superfluous, also as name of two horizontal half-circles sliding one over the other when a carriage-front turns); *f. part,* one of five equal parts into which thing is or might be divided. (N.) = f. part; (Mus.) interval of three tones & a semitone, concord of two tones so separated; (pl.) f.-rate material; *F. Monarchy,* last of the five great empires (*Dan.* ii. 44; *f.-m.-man,* 17th-c. zealot expecting immediate second coming of Christ & repudiating all other government). [OE *fifta* (still *fift* in diall.) cogn. w. G *fünfte,* Gk *pemptos,* L *quin(c)tus, -th* on anal. of FOURTH see -TH[2]]

fi·fthly, adv. In the fifth place (in enumerations). [-LY[2]]

fi·fty, a. & n. Five times ten, 50, L, (*f.-one, -seven,* &c.; *f.-first, -third,* &c.); *f.-f.* (U.S.), half & half, equal shares (*go f.-f.*; *on a f.-f. basis*); large indefinite number (*have f. things to tell you*); hence **fi·fty**FOLD a. & adv., **fi·fti**ETH a. & n. (N.) set of f. persons or things (*hid them by ff. in a cave*; *the ff.,* years between 49 & 60 in life or century). [OE *fiftig* cf. G *fünfzig* (FIVE, -TY[2])]

fig[1], n. (Broad-leaved tree, usu. *f.-tree,* bearing) soft pear-shaped many-seeded fruit eaten fresh (*green ff.*) or dried (esp. *Turkey* or *Smyrna ff.*; *pulled ff.,* superior hand-picked Turkey ff.); *under* one's *vine & f.-tree*, safe at home; anything valueless (*don't care a f. for*; also *a f. for—!*, as excl.); *f.-leaf*, device for concealing what is indecorous (*Gen.* iii. 7); *f.-wort*, brown-flowered herb. [f. F *figue* f. pop. L **fica* f. L *ficus*]

fig[2], n. Dress, equipment, (*in full f.*); condition, form, (*in good f.*). [prob. f. foll.]

fig[3], v.t. *F. out* or *up* (horse), make lively; *f. out* (person), dress up, bedizen. [=obs. *feague* perh. f. G *fegen* furbish]

fight[1] (fīt), v.i. & t. (*fought*, pr. fawt). Contend in battle or single combat (*against, with*; *for*, on behalf of person or to secure thing); maintain (cause, suit at law, quarrel) against opponent, contend over (question), win one's *way* by fighting; contend with in battle or duel, or with the fists; set on (cocks, dogs) to f. (*fighting*-COCK[1]); manœuvre (troops, ship) in battle; *f. off*, repel with effort; *f.* (dispute &c., or *it*) *out*, settle by fighting; *f. shy of*, keep aloof from (person, undertaking, &c.). Hence **figh·t**ER[1] n. [com.-WG; OE *feohtan*, cf. G *fechten*)

fight[2], n. Act of fighting (*give, make a, f.*; *valiant in f.*); battle; combat, esp. pugilistic or unpremeditated, between two or more persons, animals, or parties (*running f.*, kept up while one party flies & one pursues; *sham f.*, between troops for practice or display; *stand-up f.*, open & formal); (fig.) strife, conflict; appetite or ability for fighting (*has f. in him yet*; *show f.*, not yield tamely). [f. prec.]

fi·gment, n. Invented statement; thing that has no existence except in imagination. [f. L *figmentum* (*fig-* see FIGURE[1], -MENT)]

fi·gūrant masc., **-*ante*** fem., (or as F), ***figūra·ntĕ*** (pl. *-ti*, pr. *-tē*), nn. Ballet-dancer. [F (first two forms) & It. (third)]

figūra·tion (*also* -ger-), n. Determination to a certain form; the resulting form; shape, outline; allegorical representation; ornamentation by designs; (Mus.) use of florid counterpoint. [F, f. L *figurationem* (FIGURE[2], -ATION)]

fi·gurative (-ger-, -gūr-), a. Emblematic, typical; pictorial or plastic; metaphorical, not literal; metaphorically so called; abounding in, addicted to, figures of speech. Hence **fi·gurative**LY[2] adv., **fi·gurative**NESS n. [F (*-if, -ive*), f. LL *figurativus* (as prec., -ATIVE)]

fi·gure[1] (-ger), n. External form, shape; (Geom.) superficial space enclosed by line(s), or three-dimensional space enclosed by surface(s), any of the classes of these, as triangle, sphere; bodily shape (*has a well-developed f.*; *keep* one's *f.*, not grow stout); a person as seen (*saw a f. leaning against the door*; *f. of fun*, grotesque person); a person as contemplated mentally (*the most terrible f. in our history*); conspicuous appearance (*make* or *cut a brilliant, poor, f.*, produce such impression; *person of f.*, distinguished); image, likeness; representation of human form, statue, person in picture; emblem, type, simile; diagram, illustrative drawing, (abbr. for ref., *fig.*); horoscope; decorative pattern; evolution in dancing, division of set dance; (Skating) movement, series of movements, beginning & ending at centre; numerical symbol, esp. one of the ten in Arabic notation (*double ff.*, number between 9 & 100; *income of five ff.*, between £10,000 & £100,000; *reach three ff.*, in cricket, get century; *got it at a low, high, f.*, cheap, dear); (Rhet.; also *f. of speech*) recognized form of abnormal expression giving variety, force, &c., e.g. aposiopesis, hyperbole, metaphor, (*f.o.s.* only) piece of exaggeration; (Gram.) permitted deviation from rules of construction. e.g. ellipse; (Log.) particular form of syllogism according to position of middle term; (Mus.) short succession of notes producing single impression; *f.-dance*, dance or dancing exhibition with distinct divisions, *f.-dancer*, performer in this; *f.-head*, carving, usu. bust or full-length f., over ship's cutwater, nominal leader or president without real authority, (joc.) person's face. Hence **fi·gure**LESS a. [F, f. L *figura* (*fig-* st. of *fingere* fashion, -URE)]

fi·gure[2], v.t. & i. Represent in diagram or picture; picture mentally, imagine, (often *to* one*self*); be symbol of, represent typically; embellish with pattern (*figured satin*); mark with numbers or prices, do arithmetic, cipher (*f. up*, reckon amount of); *f. out*, give result in ff. (*figures out at £45*); make appearance, appear, (*f. as*, pass for, assume character of), be conspicuous. [f. prec.]

figuri·ne (-gūrē·n, -gerē·n), n. Statuette. [F, f. It. *figurina* dim. of *figura* FIGURE[1]]

fi·lament, n. Slender thread-like body, fibre, (esp. in animal or vegetable structure); non-fusible conductor in incandescent electric lamp, raised to incandescence by current; (of air, light, &c.) imaginary portion of stream, row of particles following each other; (Bot.) part of stamen that supports anther. Hence **filame·nt**ARY[1], **fi·lament**ED[2], **filame·nt**OUS, aa. [f. LL *filare* spin f. L *filum* thread, -MENT]

fi·lature (-tsher), n. (Establishment for) reeling silk from cocoons. [F, as prec., -URE]

fi·lbert, n. (Nut of) cultivated hazel. [short for *f.-nut*=dial. F *noix de filbert*, ripe about St *Philibert's* day (Aug. 22)]

filch (-tsh), v.t. Steal, pilfer. [?]

file[1], n., & v.t. Instrument usu. of steel with roughened surface(s) for reducing or smoothing objects (*bite, gnaw, f.*, attempt vain task); (slang) artful person, dodger, (usu. *old, deep,* &c., *f.*), person. (Vb) smooth, reduce surface of, with f.; elaborate to perfection (esp. literary work); *f. away* (roughnesses &c.), remove with f. [OE *féol* cf. Du. *vijl*, G *feile*]

file[2], n., & v.t. Stiff pointed wire on which documents &c. are run for keeping; kinds of appliance for holding papers arranged for reference; set of papers so kept, esp. in court of law referring to a cause; series of issues of a newspaper in order; (vb) place (papers) on f. or among public records. [f. F *fil* f. L *filum* thread]

file[3], n., & v.i. & t. (Mil.) a front-rank man & the man or men straight behind him (*in f.*, marching with the men of a double line faced towards one of its ends; *single, Indian, f.*, similar formation of single line; RANK[1] *& f.*; *a f. of men*, two told off for some purpose); row of persons or things one behind another; (Chess) line of squares from player to player (cf. RANK[1]). (Vb) march in f.; *f. off, away, go off* by ff.; (trans.) order (soldiers) to move *off* by ff. [F (L *filare* vb f. *filum* thread)]

fi·lĕmot, a. & n. Dead-leaf colour(ed), brownish yellow. [f. F *feuille morte* dead leaf]

fi·lial, a. Of, due from, son or daughter. Hence **fi·lial**LY[2] adv. [f. LL *filialis* (L *filius, -a*, son, daughter, -AL)]

fi·liate, v.t. (Rare for) AFFILIATE.

filia·tion, n. Being some one's child; descent (*from*); formation of offshoots, branch of a society or language; genealogical relation or arrangement. [F, f. med. L *filiationem* (*filiare* give birth to f. L *filius* son, -ATION)]

fi·libeg, n. (Sc.). Kilt. [f. Gael. *feileadh-beag* little fold]

fi·libuster, n., & v.i. One who engages in unauthorized warfare against foreign State; (U.S. pol.) obstructionist; (vb) act as f. [ult. f. Du. *vrijbuiter* FREEBOOTER affected by F *flibustier*, Sp. *filibustero*, f. same]

fi·ligree, fila-, n. Ornamental work of fine gold or silver or copper wire formed into delicate tracery, fine metal openwork; anything delicate, light, showy, & frail. Hence **fi·ligree**ED[2] a. [f. F *filigrane* f. It. *filigrana* (L *filum* thread, *granum* grain)]

fi·ling, n. In vbl senses of FILE[1]; also, (usu. pl.) particle(s) rubbed off by file. [-ING[1]]

fill, v.t. & i., & n. Make or become full (*with*; *sails f.*, are distended with wind); stock abundantly; occupy whole capacity or extent of, spread over, pervade, (*f. the bill*, be the only conspicuous item, also in U.S., do all that is required, suffice); (of dentist) block up (hollow tooth, cavity) with gold &c., whence **fi·ll**ING[1](4) n.; satisfy, satiate, (esp. in part., of kinds of food); hold (position), discharge duties of (office); occupy (vacant time); appoint holder of (vacant post); adulterate (esp. cotton fabrics; usu. in p.p.); *f. in*, complete (outline), add what is wanted to complete (unfinished document, blank cheque, &c.); *f. out*, enlarge, become enlarged, to the proper limit; *f. up*, f. completely, supply vacant parts or places or deficiencies in, do away with (pond &c.) by filling, grow full; FEBRUARY *f.-dike*; hence **fi·ll**ER[1](1, 2) n. (N.) full supply of drink or food (*drink, have*, &c., one's *f.*; also with intr. vbs as *fret her f.*); enough to f. something (*a f. of tobacco*). [OE *fyllan* cf. G *füllen*, cogn. w. FULL[1]]

fille (F), n. *F. de chambre*, chambermaid; *f. de joie*, prostitute. [F, = daughter]

fi·llet, n., & v.t. Head-band, ribbon, string, or narrow band, for binding the hair or worn round head; band, bandage; thin narrow strip of anything; (pl.) animal's loins; fleshy detachable piece of meat near loins or ribs, undercut of sirloin; one of the thick slices into which a fish may be divided; middle part of leg of veal boned, rolled, & tied up; piece of beef, fish, &c., similarly prepared; (Arch.) narrow flat band separating two mouldings, small band between flutes of column; (Herald.) horizontal division of shield, quarter of CHIEF[1] in depth; raised rim or ridge on any surface; (Book-bind.) plain line impressed on cover. (Vb) bind (hair, person as to hair) with f.; encircle with ornamental band; divide (fish) into ff. [f. F *filet* f. L *filum* thread + -ET[1]]

fi·llip, n., & v.t. & i. Sudden release of finger or thumb when it has been bent & checked by thumb or finger; slight smart stroke thus given; stimulus, incentive; mere trifle (*not worth a f.*). (Vb) propel (coin, marble, &c.) with a f.; stimulate (*f.* one's *memory* or *wits*); strike slightly & smartly; make a f. [prob. imit., cf. FLIP]

fi·llister, n. Rabbeting-plane for window-sashes &c. [?]

fi·lly, n. Female foal (cf. COLT); young lively girl. [perh. f. ON *fylja* cogn. w. FOAL]

film, n., & v.t. & i. Thin skin, plate, coating, or layer; (Photog.) coating of collodion, gelatin, &c., spread on photographic paper or plate, or used instead of plate, celluloid roll used in cinematography, its contents as shown (*f.*-FAN[3]; *f. star*, eminent cinema actor); dimness over eyes; slight veil of haze &c.; fine thread or filament; hence **fi·lm**Y[2] a., **fi·lm**ILY[2] adv., **fi·lm**INESS n. (Vb) cover, become covered, (as) with f.; reproduce (scene &c.) for the cinema. [OE *filmen* membrane cf. OFris. *filmene* skin, & FELL[1]]

fi·loselle, n. Floss silk. [F, f. It. *filosello* perh. f. pop. L **follicellus* cocoon, dim.

of L *follis* bag, influenced by It. *filo* thread]

fils (fēs), n. The son, junior, (appended to name to distinguish between father & son of same names, cf. PÈRE). [F]

fi·lter, n., & v.t. & i. Contrivance for freeing liquids from suspended impurities, esp. by passing them through stratum of sand, charcoal, &c.; *f.-bed,* tank or pond with false bottom covered with sand &c. for filtering large quantities. (Vb) pass (liquid), flow, through f.; (of f.) purify (liquid); make way *through, into,* &c., percolate, (of news &c.) leak *out* or come *through*; obtain by filtering. [vb f. n., f. OF *filtre* f. med. L *filtrum* f. Teut. st. whence FELT[1] (earliest filter being of felt)]

filth, n. Loathsome dirt; uninviting food, garbage; vileness, pollution, obscenity; foul language. Hence **fi·lthy**[2] a. (*filthy lucre,* dishonourable gain, also facet., money), **fi·lthi**LY[2] adv., **fi·lthi**NESS n. [OE *fýlth* (FOUL[1], -TH[1])]

fi·ltrate[1], n. Filtered liquor. [FILTER v., -ATE[1](2)]

fi·ltrate[2], v.t. & i. =FILTER v. So **filtra·tion** n. [f. mod. L *filtrare* (as prec., -ATE[3])]

fi·mbriate(d), aa. (bot., zool.). Fringed, bordered with hairs &c. [f. L *fimbria* fringe + -ATE[2]]

fin, n. Organ for propelling & steering attached to fish & cetaceans at various parts of body (*anal, caudal, dorsal, pectoral, ventral,* &c.); (slang) hand (*tip us your f.,* shake hands). Hence (-)**finn**ED[2], **fi·n**LESS, aa. [OE *finn,* cf. MDu. *vinne,* & L *pinna*]

fī·nal, a. & n. At the end, coming last, ultimate; putting an end to doubt, conclusive, definitive, unalterable; concerned with the purpose or end aimed at (*f.* CAUSE[1]; *f. clause* in Gram., introduced by *in order that, lest,* &c.); hence **fi·nal**LY[2] adv. (N.) last or deciding heat or game in athletics; (sing. or pl.) last of a series of examinations. [F, f. L *finalis* (*finis* end, -AL)]

fĭna·le (-ahlĭ), n. (Mus.) last movement of instrumental composition, piece of music closing act in opera; close of drama &c.; conclusion, final catastrophe. [It., as prec.]

fīnă·lity, n. Principle of final cause viewed as operative in the universe; being final; belief that something is final; final act, state, or utterance. [F (*-té*) f. LL *finalitatem* (FINAL, -TY)]

fĭna·nce, n., & v.t. & i. (Pl.) pecuniary resources of sovereign, state, company, or person; management of (esp. public) money, science of revenue. (Vb) furnish with ff., find capital for; engage in financial operations. [OF (*finer* settle debt f. *fin* end; -ANCE)]

fĭna·ncial (-shl), a. Of revenue or money matters (*f. year,* annual period for which public accounts are made up). Hence **fina·ncial**LY[2] adv. [prec. + -IAL]

fĭna·ncier[1] (-sĭ-), n. One skilled in levying & managing public money; capitalist. [F (FINANCE, -IER)]

fĭnancier·[2] (-sēr), v.i. & t. Conduct financial operations (usu. contempt.); (U.S.) cheat, swindle, (*f.* money *away*; *f.* one *out of*). [f. prec.]

finch, n. Kinds of small bird (usu. with distinctive epithet or prefix, as *mountain f.,* BULL[1]*-f.*). [OE *finc* cf. G *fink*]

fīnd, v.t. (found), & n. Come across, fall in with, light upon, (*was found dead*; *we f. St John saying*; *administer the law as you f. it*; *found a treasure*); obtain, receive, (*f. favour, mercy,* one's ACCOUNT[2] *in*; *f.* one's *feet,* get the use of them, develop one's powers); recognize as present, acknowledge or discover to be so-&-so, (*I f. no sense in it, f. the terms reasonable*; *how do you f. yourself?*; *must take us as you find us,* put up with us as we are); discover by trial to be or do or (*that*) or *to* (*has been found wanting*; *finds rest agreeable*; *is found to pay*; *I find it pays, pay,* or *to pay,* or *that it pays*; *f. it impossible, necessary, to* —); discover by search; discover (game), discover game, in hunting; *f.* one*self,* discover one's vocation, & see below; succeed in obtaining (money, bail, sureties; *can't f. time to read*; *found courage to* —; *could f. it in my heart to* —, am inclined; *f. expression, place, vent*); come home to, reach the conscience of; ascertain by study or calculation or inquiry (*f.* one's *way to,* contrive to reach, arrive at); (Law) determine & declare (*it,* i.e. the offence, *murder*; person *guilty* &c.; *that* —; *find true* BILL[4]), whence **fi·nd**ING[1](2) n.; supply, provide, furnish, (*they found him in clothes*; *hotel does not f. tea*; *all found,* with all necessaries provided, of servants' wages; *f.* one*self,* provide for one's own needs, & see above); *f. out,* discover, devise, solve, detect in offence; hence **fi·nd**ABLE a. (N.) finding of fox; discovery of treasure, minerals, &c.; *sure f.,* place where something (esp. fox) is sure to be found. [com.-Teut.; OE *findan* cf. Du. *vinden,* G *finden*; perh. cogn. w. L *petere* seek]

fī·nder, n. In vbl senses; esp.: small telescope attached to large one to find object; contrivance for same purpose in microscope & in photographic camera. [-ER[1]]

fin de siècle (F), a. Characteristic of end of nineteenth century, advanced, modern; decadent.

fine[1], n., & v.i. & t. End (now only in *in f.,* to sum up, finally, in short); sum of money paid by in-coming tenant in consideration of small rent; sum of money fixed as penalty for offence. (Vb) pay consideration *for* privilege or appointment; punish by a f., whence **fi·**NABLE a. [ME & OF *fin* settlement of dispute f. L *finis* end]

fine[2], a., n., adv., & v.t. & i. Of high quality; clear, pure, refined, (of gold or silver) containing specified proportion of pure metal, as *gold 22 carats f.*, *silver 11 oz f.*; delicate, subtle, exquisitely fashioned, (of feelings) elevated; of slender thread, in small particles, thin (*f. pencil*, of hard lead for making f. lines); sharp (*f. pen*, narrow-pointed); (Athlet.) reduced to perfect condition; capable of delicate perception or discrimination, perceptible only with difficulty (*a f. distinction*); excellent, of striking merit, good, satisfactory, fortunate, of good effect, (*had f. sport*; *has been a f. thing for him*; often iron., as *a f. friend you have been!*); well conceived or expressed; of handsome appearance or size, dignified, (*f. potatoes*; *a man of f. presence*); bright, cloudless, free from rain, (*f. weather*; *one f. day*, once upon a time; *one of these f. days*, some day, in prophecies); ornate, showy, smart, (*f. feathers*, gaudy plumage, lit. & fig., as *f. feathers make f. birds*); fastidious, dainty, affecting refinement, (of speech or writing) affectedly ornate; complimentary, euphemistic, (*say f. things about person*, *call things by f. names*); *f. arts*, those appealing to sense of beauty, as poetry, music, & esp. painting, sculpture, architecture; *f.-draw*, sew together (two pieces of cloth, rent, garment) so that the join is imperceptible; *f.-drawn*, subtle, extremely thin, (Athlet.) trained down in weight; *f. gentleman*, *lady*, person of fashion, person who thinks himself above working; *f.-spun*, delicate, flimsy, (of theories &c.) excessively subtle, unpractical; hence **fi·**NISH[1](2) a., **fi·ne**LY[2] adv., **fi·ne**NESS n. (N.) f. weather (*in rain or f.*). (Adv.) finely (*talk f.*). (Vb) make (beer) clear (often *down*); (of liquid) become clear; *f. away*, *down*, *off*, make or become finer, thinner, less coarse, (make) dwindle, taper. [f. F *fin* f. Rom. *fino* prob. back formation f. *finito* FINISHed]

fine champagne (F), n. Liqueur brandy.

fi·nery[1], n. Smartness, stylishness, (rare); showy dress or decoration. [FINE[2] adj., -ERY]

fi·nery[2], n. Hearth where cast iron is made malleable or steel made from pig-iron. [F (*-ie*) f. *finer* refine f. Rom. *finare* (L *finis* end), -ERY]

fine·sse, n., & v.i. & t. Delicate manipulation, subtle discrimination; artfulness, cunning strategy; (Whist) attempt to take trick by inferior card, with higher one in reserve. (Vb) use f.; wheedle *into*, trick *away*, manage by f.; (Whist) make a f., play (card) by way of f. [F (Rom. *fino* FINE[2], -ESS[2])]

fi·nger (-ngg-), n., & v.t. One of five terminal members of hand (*thumb*, & *index, middle, ring*, & *little*, *ff.*), or four excluding thumb (usu. now numbered thus, but cf. *fourth f.*, i.e. ring f., in marriage service), (*done by the f.*, i.e. agency, *of God*; *more wit in his little f. than in your whole body*; *lay, put, a f. upon*, touch however slightly; *lay, put*, one's *f. on* ailing part or cause of evil, point with precision to; *look through* one's *ff. at*, pretend not to see; *stir a f.*, make the least effort; *turn* or *twist* person *round* one's (*little*) *f.*, cajole him; *my ff. itch*, I long, am impatient, *to* do; *his ff. are all thumbs*, he is clumsy; *with a wet f.*, with ease; BURN[2] one's *ff.*; *have a f. in the pie*, take part in a matter; *let slip through* one's *ff.*, lose hold of; *have at* one's *f.-tips* or *f.-ends*, be versed in, know familiarly; *to the f.-nails*, completely); part of glove that holds f.; f.-like object, esp. such part of a fruit &c., & in various machines; *f.-alphabet*, *-language*, conventional signs for talking with the deaf; *f.-bowl*, *-glass*, for rinsing ff. after dessert; *f.-fern*, kind of spleenwort; *f.-fish*, starfish; *f.-plate*, fastened on door to prevent f.-marks; *f.-post*, giving directions at parting of roads; *f.-print*, impressions of person's ff., used for identifying criminals &c.; *f.-stall*, cover of leather or rubber to protect f. in dissections &c. or when wounded; hence **fi·nger**LESS, (-)**fi·nger**ED[2], aa. (Vb) touch with, turn about in, the ff.; take (bribes &c.); play upon (instrument) with the ff., play (passage) with ff. used in particular way, mark (music) with signs showing which ff. are to be used, whence **fi·ngering**[1] [-ING[1]] n. [com.-Teut.; OE, OFris., Sw., Da., *finger*; perh. cogn. w. FIVE]

fi·ngering[2], n. (for *fingering*[1] see prec.). Wool for stockings. [earlier *fingram*, *-im*, &c., perh. f. F *fin grain* fine grain, cf. GROGRAM]

fi·nial, n. (archit.). Ornament finishing off apex of roof, pediment, gable, tower-corner, canopy, &c. [var. of FINAL]

fi·nical, a. Over-nice, precise, fastidious; too much finished in details. Hence **fi·nical**LY[2] adv., **fi·nical**NESS, **finică·**LITY, nn. [perh. f. FINE[2], or var. of foll.]

fi·nicking, fi·nikin, a. = prec. [etym. dub.; cf. MDu. *fijnkens* accurately, neatly]

fi·nis, n. (no pl.). (At end of book) the end; end of anything, esp. of life. [L]

fi·nish, v.t. & i., & n. Bring to an end, come to the end of (often *f. doing*; f. *off*, provide with an ending), complete; consume, get through, the whole or remainder of (food, book); kill, dispatch, overcome completely; perfect, put final or finishing touches to, (*finished manners, gentleman*; also with *off*, *up*); complete education of; (intr.) reach the end, cease, leave *off*; end *in* something or *by* doing. (N.) last stage, termination, esp. of a fox-hunt (*be in at the f.*, often fig.); *fight to a f.*, till one party is completely worsted; what serves to give completeness; accomplished or completed state. [f. OF *fenir f.* L *finire* (*finis* end), -ISH[2]]

fi·nisher, n. In vbl senses; esp. workman or machine doing last operation in manufacture; discomfiting thing, crushing blow, &c. [-ER[1]]

fī·nīte, a. Bounded, limited, not infinite; (Gram.) limited by number and person, not infinitive. Hence **fi·nite**NESS n. [f. L *finitus* p.p. of *finire* FINISH]

Fin(n), n. One of N.-Eastern European people who call themselves *Suomi*. [OE *Finnas* pl., etym. dub.]

fi·nnan, n. (Also *f. haddock*) haddock cured with smoke of green wood, turf, or peat. [perh. f. river *Findhorn*]

fi·nner, n. Kinds of whale, esp. rorqual, having dorsal fin. [-ER[1]]

Fi·nnic, a. Of the group of peoples allied to the Finns; Finnish. [-IC]

Fi·nnish, a. & n. (Language) of the Finns; Finnic. [-ISH[1]]

fi·nny, a. Having fins; like a fin; of, teeming with, fish. [FIN + -Y[2]]

fiord, fjord, (fyord), n. Long narrow arm of sea between high cliffs as in Norway. [Norw.]

fī·orin, n. Kind of grass. [f. Ir. *fiorthán*]

fir, n. (Also *f.-tree*) kinds of coniferous tree with needles placed singly on the shoots (*Scotch, Silver, Spruce, F.*); their wood; *f.-apple, -ball, -cone,* fruit of f.; *f.-needle,* its leaf. Hence **fir·**RY[2] a. [cf. Da. *fyr*, G. *föhre*, prob. cogn. w. L *quercus* oak]

fire[1], n. Active principle operative in combustion, flame, incandescence, (*set f. to*, kindle; *strike f.*, elicit sparks by friction or blow; *no smoke without f.*, always some ground for rumour); state of combustion (*on f.*, burning, fig. excited; *set on f.*, ignite, excite; *set Thames on f.*, do something remarkable; *catch, take, f.*, be ignited); burning fuel in grate, furnace, &c. (*heap* COALS *of f.*; *burnt child dreads the f.*; *out of* FRY*ing-pan into f.*; FAT *is in the f.*), whence **fīr·**ING[1](3) n.; conflagration, destructive burning, (*fire!*, call for aid at a f.; *pour oil on f.*, add to excitement while deprecating it; *go through f. & water*, face all perils; *f. & sword*, burning & slaughter); *Greek f.*, combustible composition for igniting enemy's ships &c.; luminosity, glow, (*St. Elmo's f.*, corposant); burning heat, fever, (*St Anthony's f.*, erysipelas); vehement emotion, fervour, spirit, lively imagination, vivacity, poetic inspiration; firing of guns (*open, cease, f.*; *running f.*, successive shots from line of troops &c., esp. fig. of criticism, objections, &c.; *between two ff.*, shot at from two directions; *line of f.*, path of bullet about to be shot; *under f.*, being shot at; HANG, MISS[2], *f.*); *f.-alarm*, automatic arrangement for giving notice of f.; *f.-arm* (usu. pl.), rifle, gun, pistol, &c.; *fireback*, Sumatran pheasant; *f.-ball*, large meteor, globular lightning, (Mil.) ball filled with combustibles; *f.-balloon*, made buoyant by heat of combustible burning at its mouth; *f.-bird*, kind of bee-eater; *f.-blast*, disease of plants; *f.-blight*, disease of hops; *f.-box*, fuel-chamber of steam-boiler; *f.-brand*, piece of burning wood, person or thing kindling strife; *f.-brick* (proof against f., used in grates &c.); *f.-brigade*, organized body of firemen; *f.-clay* (kind used for f.-bricks); *f.-control*, system of regulating f. of ship's or fort's guns; *f.-cross*, = *fiery* CROSS[1]; *f.-damp*, miner's name for carburetted hydrogen, explosive when mixed in certain proportion with air; *f.-dog*, andiron; *f.-eater*, juggler who eats fire, great fighter, duellist; *f.-engine*, machine for throwing water to extinguish ff.; *f.-escape*, apparatus for saving people in burning house; *f.-eyed* (poet.), with glowing eyes; *f.-flair*, a fish, the sting-ray; *f.-fly*, winged insect emitting phosphorescent light; *f.-guard*, wire frame or grating to keep children, coals, from falling into f., room; *f.-hose*, hose-pipe for extinguishing ff.; *f.-insurance*, against losses by f.; *f.-irons*, tongs, poker, & shovel; *f.-light*, light from f.-place; *f.-lighter*, prepared kindling-fuel; *firelock*, antiquated musket in which priming was ignited by sparks; *fireman*, tender of furnace or steam-engine f., man employed to extinguish ff.; *f.-new* (archaic), = brand-new; *f.-office*, insuring against f.; *f.-pan*, brazier; *f.-place*, grate or hearth for room-f.; *f.-plug* (abbr. F.P.), connexion in water-main for f.-hose; *f.-policy*, f.-insurance office's certificate guaranteeing compensation in case of f.; *f.-raising*, arson; *f.-screen*, to keep off heat of f.; *f.-ship*, freighted with combustibles and sent adrift to ignite enemy's ships &c.; *fireside*, space round f.-place, home life; *f.-step*, = firing-step (FIRE[2]); *f.-stone*, kind that resists f., used for furnaces &c.; *f.-teazer*, stoker; *f.-trap*, building without proper exits in case of f.; *f.-water*, ardent spirits; *firewood*, wood prepared for fuel; *firework*, kinds of apparatus giving spectacular effects by use of combustibles &c., squib, rocket, &c., (fig., pl.) display of wit, passion, &c.; *f.-worship*, treatment of f. as a deity. Hence **fire·**PROOF, **fire·**LESS, aa. [com.-WG; OE *fýr* cf. G *feuer*; also Gk *pur*]

fire[2], v.t. & i. Set f. to with intention of destroying; kindle (explosives); (of explosives, mines) catch f.; become heated or excited (*f. up*, show sudden anger); redden (t. & i.); bake (pottery, bricks), cure (tea, tobacco) by artificial heat; (Farriery) cauterize; supply (furnace, engine) with fuel; cause (explosive, gun) to explode (often *off*; *f. salute*, discharge number of guns as salute; *f. broadside*, discharge all guns on one side of ship), (abs.) shoot, discharge gun &c. (*at, into, on, upon*), (fig.) *f. away*, begin, go ahead; (of gun &c.) go off; propel (missile) from gun &c. (fig. *f. off a postcard, a remark*); (U.S.) *f. out* or *f.*, expel, dismiss, reject, (person); *firing-step* (on which soldier in trench stands to f.). [f. prec.]

fir·er, n. In vbl senses; esp. *single* &c. *-f.*, gun that fires once &c. without reloading. [-ER[1]]

fir·kin, n. Small cask for liquids, butter, fish, &c.; (as measure) half of kilderkin. [earlier *ferdekyn* prob. f. MDu (*vierde* fourth, -KIN)]

firm[1], n. Partners carrying on business (*long f.*, set of swindlers who obtain goods & do not pay). [earlier senses *signature, style*, f. Rom. *firma* (L *firmare* confirm); doublet of FARM[1]]

firm[2], a., adv., & v.t. & i. Of solid or compact structure; fixed, stable; steady, not shaking; established, immutable, (of offer &c.) not liable to cancellation after acceptance; steadfast, unflinching, resolute; constant *to*; (Commerc., of prices, goods) maintaining their level or value; hence **fir·mLY**[2] adv., **fir·mNESS** n. (Adv.) firmly (*stand f., hold f. to*). (Vb) solidify (t. & i.), compact, (soil after planting &c., cheese); fix firmly (plants in soil). [f. OF *ferme* f. L *firmus*]

fir·mament, n. Vault of heaven with its clouds & stars. Hence **firmame·ntAL** a. [f. L *firmamentum* (*firmare* as prec., -MENT)]

fir·man, n. Oriental sovereign's edict, grant, licence, passport. [f. Pers. *ferman*]

first, a., n., & adv. Earliest in time or order (*at f. sight, view*, or *blush*, prima facie; *F.* CAUSE[1]; *come in f.*, win race; *shall do it f. thing* colloq., before anything else; *in the f. place*, to begin with; *the f. two* &c., lit., or = the f. & second &c.; often further defined, as *the f. man you meet, was the f. to do it*); foremost in position, rank, or importance (*head* &c., *f.*, with the head in front; *the f. men in the country*; *F. Lord of the* TREASURY; *F. Lord of the Admiralty*, parliamentary chief of Navy; *F. Sea Lord*, professional chief of Navy); coming next after a specified or implied time (*shall take the f. train*; *the f. cuckoo*); unsupported by others, sufficient by itself, (*obeyed at her f. word*); *f. aid*, help given to wounded man before doctor comes; *f.-born*, eldest (child); *f.*-CHOP[5]; *f. class*, set of persons or things grouped together as better than others, best accommodation in railway train &c., highest division in examination list, place in this; *f.-class*, (adj.) belonging to the f. class, of best quality, very good, (adv.) by the f. class (*travels f.-c.*); *f. coat*, f. layer of paint; *f. cost*, cost not including profit; *f.-day*, Sunday; *f. floor*, above ground-floor; *f. form*, lowest class in schools; *f.-fruit* (usu. pl.), f. products of agriculture for the season esp. as offered to God, f. results of work &c., (Hist.) payment to some superior by new holder of office; *f.-hand*, direct, without intermediate agency (*at f. hand*, directly); *f.-night(er)*, (habitual frequenter of) f. performance of play; *f.-offender* (against whom no previous conviction is recorded); *f.-rate*, of the highest class (*the f.-r. Powers*, great states of f.-rate importance), excellent, very well, (*a f.-r. machine, feeling f.-r.*), (as n., Naut.) line-of-battle-ship of the old type, three-decker. (N.) *the f.*, person or thing f. mentioned; *from the f.*, from the beginning; *from f. to last*, throughout; *at f.*, at the beginning; = f. day *of* June &c.; *the F.* (of September, when partridge-shooting begins); (Commerc.) *f. of exchange*, f. of set of bills of even tenor & date; place in f. class in examination, person who takes this; f. place in race, winner of it; (pl.) best quality of flour, butter, &c. (Adv.) before anyone or anything else (often *f. of all, f. & foremost*; *f. come f. served*; *f. & last*, taking one thing with another, on the whole; *f. or last*, sooner or later); before some specified or implied event, time, &c. (*must get this done f.*); in preference, rather, (*will see him damned f.*); for the f. time (*when did you see him f.?*). [com.-Teut.; OE *fyrst* cf. G *fürst* prince, superl. f. st. of FOR, cf. (with different superl. suf.) FORMER]

fir·stling, n. (usu. pl.). First result of anything, first-fruits; first offspring, first born of season. [-LING[1]]

fir·stly, adv. In the first place, first, (only in enumerating topics; & many writers still prefer *first*). [-LY[2]]

firth, frith, n. Arm of sea; estuary. [Sc. wd prob. f. ON = *fiord*]

fisc, fisk, n. Treasury of ancient Rome, Roman emperor's privy-purse; (rare) State treasury, exchequer. [f. L *fiscus*]

fi·scal, a. & n. Of public revenue; (n.) legal official in some foreign countries. Hence **fi·scalLY**[2] adv. [F, f. LL *fiscalis* (prec., -AL)]

fish[1], n. (pl. often *fish*). (Pop.) animal living in the water, (strictly) vertebrate cold-blooded animal having gills throughout life & limbs (if any) modified into fins, (*pretty kettle of f.*, confusion, muddle; *f. out of water*, person out of his element; *drunk, dull, mute, as a f.*; *drink like a f.*, excessively; *feed the ff.*, be drowned, be sea-sick; *all 's f. that comes to his net*, he takes all he can get; *there's as good f. in the sea as ever came out of it*, no fear of scarcity; FLAT, FLYING, GOLD, JELLY, SHELL[1], SUN, SWORD, &c.,-*f.*); person who is angled for; (colloq.) person of specified kind (*cool, loose, queer*, &c., *f.*); the flesh of f. (*f., flesh, & fowl*; *neither f., flesh, nor good red herring*, thing of indefinite character; *other f. to fry*, more important business to attend to); *the F.* or *Ff.*, zodiac constellation; *f.-carver*, knife for serving f.; *f.-globe*, for keeping gold-f. &c. in; *f.-glue*, isinglass; *f.-hook*, used for catching f., (Naut.) part of anchor-raising tackle; *f.-kettle*, oval pan for boiling f.; *f.-knife*, of silver &c. for eating f.; *f.-pond*, in which f. are kept, (joc.) the sea; *f.-pot*, wicker trap for eels, lobsters, &c.; *f.-slice*, carving-knife for f., cook's implement for turning or taking out f.; *f.-sound*, f.'s swimming-bladder; *f.-tail*, shaped like f.'s tail (of jet of gas, whence *f.-t. burner*), *f.-tail wind* in rifle shooting, one blowing down range & varying in direction; *f.-torpedo*, torpedo shaped like f. & with automatic propulsion; *fishwife*, woman selling f. Hence **fi·sh**LET, **fi·sh**MONGER, nn. [com.-Teut.; OE *fisc* cf. G *fisch*, cogn. w. L *piscis*]

fish[2], v.i. & t. Try to catch f. (*f. in troubled waters*, make one's profit out of disturbances), whence **fi·sh**ERY(2, 3) n.; search *for* something in or under water; seek by indirect means *for* (secrets, compliments, &c.), whence **fi·sh**ING[2] a.; (rare) try to catch (f.) or get (coral &c.) from below water; draw *out of* water, pocket, &c., draw *out*; (Naut.) *f. the anchor*, draw flukes up to gunwale; try to catch f. in (pool &c.; *f. out*, exhaust the f. in), whence **fi·sh**ABLE a.; get (fact, opinion, secret) *out*; *fishing-rod*, long tapering usu. jointed rod to which fishing-line is attached. [OE *fiscian* cf. G *fischen* & see prec.]

fish[3], n., & v.t. (Naut.) piece of wood, convex & concave, used to strengthen mast &c.; flat plate of iron, wood, &c., strengthening beam or joint (so *f.-plate*, one of two holding rails together); (vb) mend or strengthen (spar &c.), join (rails) with f. [perh. = FISH[1] or foll.]

fish[4], n. Piece of ivory &c. used as counter in games. [f. F *fiche* in same sense, also = peg (*ficher* fix perh. ult. f. L *figere*)]

fi·sher[1], n. Fisherman (archaic; *f. of men*, evangelist, see *Matt.* iv. 19); fishing animal; *fisherman*, man who lives by fishing, (rare) angler, fishing-boat. [OE *fiscere* (FISH[1], -ER[1])]

fi·sher[2], n. (slang). Currency note, esp. for £1. [f. signature of Permanent Sec. to Treasury]

fi·shy, a. Abounding in fish; like fish's (*f. eye*, dull, vacant-looking); smelling or tasting like fish; consisting of fish (*a f. repast*); (slang) of dubious character, questionable. Hence **fi·shi**LY[2] adv. **fi·shi**NESS n. [-Y[2]]

fisk. See FISC.

fissi-, fisso-, comb. forms of L *fissus* see FISSURE, as *fissida·ctyl* with digits divided, *fissi·parous* reproducing by fission.

fi·ssile, a. Cleavable, tending to split. Hence **fissi·li**TY n. [f. L *fissilis* (FISSURE, -IL)]

fi·ssion (-shn), n. (biol.). Division of cell &c. into new cells &c. as mode of reproduction. [f. L *fissio* (foll., -ION)]

fi·ssure (-sher), n., & v.t. & i. Cleft made by splitting or separation of parts; (Bot., Anat.) narrow opening in organ &c., esp. depression between convolutions of brain; cleavage; (vb) split (t. & i.). [F, f. L *fissura* (*findere fiss-* cleave, -URE)]

fist, n., & v.t. Clenched hand, esp. as used in boxing (*f. law*, the right of the strongest); (joc.) hand (*give us your f.*, shake hands), hand-writing (*writes a good f.*; *I know his f.*). (Vb) strike with f.; (Naut.) handle (sail, oar, &c.). Hence **-fist**ED[2] a. [OE *fýst* cf. G *faust*]

fi·stic(al), aa. (jocular). Pugilistic. [-ICAL]

fi·sticuffs, n. pl. Fighting with the fists. [FIST + CUFF; cf. *handiwork*]

fi·stŭla, n. Long pipe-like ulcer with narrow mouth; natural pipe or spout in whales, insects, &c. Hence **fi·stul**AR[1], **fi·stul**OUS, aa. [earlier *fystel, fistle*, &c., f. L *fistula* pipe, flute]

fit[1], **fȳtte**, n. (archaic). Section of a poem. [OE *fitt* cf. OHG *fiza* list of cloth]

fit[2], n. Paroxysm of periodic ailment, sudden transitory attack of some illness; sudden seizure, with loss of consciousness or convulsions, of hysteria, apoplexy, fainting, paralysis, or epilepsy (*give* one *a f.*, surprise or outrage him; *beat* one *into, give* one, *ff.*, defeat him easily); sudden transitory state (*a f. of energy, idleness, devotion, indifference*, &c., whence **fi·t**FUL a., **fi·tful**LY[2] adv., **fi·tful**NESS n.; *by ff.* (*& starts*), spasmodically); caprice, mood, (*when the f. was on him*). [OE *fitt*, perh. = prec.]

fit[3], a. Well adapted or suited (*for* some purpose or status or *to* do or be; SURVIVAL *of the fittest*); good enough *for* (*a dinner f. for a king*); becoming, proper, right, (*it is f., that*; *see or think f. to*, decide to); qualified, competent, worthy, *to* do (*not f. to hold a* CANDLE *to*); in suitable condition, ready, *to* do or *for* (also vulg. as adv., *crying f. to burst himself*); angry, troubled, or exhausted enough *to* (do something violent, sink to the ground, &c.); in good athletic condition or health (*f. as a* FIDDLE). Hence **fi·t**LY[2] adv. [from 1440; etym. dub.]

fit[4], v.t. & i., & n. Be in harmony with, become, befit; be of right measure, shape, & size for (esp. of dress; often abs., as *the* CAP[1] *fits*); fill up, exactly correspond to, (receptacle, fellow, &c., or abs.; often *in, into, in with*), make to do this; make suitable, adapt, *for, to* with n.

or inf.; make competent *for* or *to*; *f. on*, try on (garment); supply, furnish, (ship &c., rarely person) *with*; *f. out, up*, equip; hence (-)**fitTER**[1] n. (N.) adaptation, adjustment, style in which garment fits (*a tight, bad, excellent, f.*); *f.-out*, equipment. [from 16th c., prob. f. prec.]

fitch, n. (Brush made of) polecat's hair. [f. MDu. *fisse* polecat]

fi·tchew, n. Foumart, polecat. [f. OF *fissel* dim. of MDu. *fisse* (prec.)]

fi·tment, n. Piece of furniture. [FIT[4], -MENT]

fi·tness, n. Being fit; moral worthiness; propriety (*the f. of things*, what is right or appropriate). [-NESS]

fi·tting[1], n. In vbl senses; esp.: (usu. pl.) fixture(s), apparatus, furniture; (Engin.) *f.-shop*, place where parts are put together. [-ING[1]]

fi·tting[2], a. In vbl senses; esp. becoming, proper, right, whence **fi·ttingly**[2] adv. [-ING[2]]

five, a. & n. One more than four, 5, V, (*twenty-f., f.-&-twenty; f. o'clock; How old are you?—F.*); the number f. (*twice f. is ten*); set of f. things; card, die, or domino with f. pips; (also **fi·VER**[1] n.) hit at cricket for f. runs, £5 note; *bunch of ff.*, hand; (pl.) gloves, shoes, &c., of fifth size; (pl.) the f.-per-cents; *f.-finger exercise*, on piano for practising all fingers; *f.-finger*, kinds of plant, also star-fish; *f.-line(d) whip*, urgent summons to attend in House of Parliament (now disused); *f.-o'clock tea*, light afternoon meal; *fivepenny* (*also pr.* fĭp-), costing, rated at, 5*d.*, (Guernsey &c.) half-franc; *f.-per-cents*, stock or shares paying 5%. Hence **fi·veFOLD** a. & adv. [Aryan; OE *fif* cf. G *fünf*, Gk *pente*, L *quinque*]

fives, n. Ball-game played with hands or bat in court with two, three, or four walls. [pl. of *five* used as sing.; significance unknown]

fix[1], v.t. & i. Make firm or stable, fasten, secure, implant (principles, memory, &c.) (*in, on, to*, &c.); direct steadily, set, (eyes, gaze, affection, attention) *on* or *upon*; (of object) attract & hold (attention, eyes, &c.); make (eyes, features), or become, rigid; deprive of, lose, volatility or fluidity, congeal (t. & i.); make (colour, photographic image) fast, whence **fi·xER**[1](2) n.; single out (person) *with* one's eyes &c.; place definitely or permanently, station, establish; take up one's position; settle one's choice, decide, (*up*)*on*; assign precise position of; refer (thing, person) to definite place or time; determine incidence of (liability &c.); settle, determine, specify, (price, date, place); arrest changes or development in (language, literature); (U.S.; often *up*) arrange, organize, prepare. [ult. f. L *fixus* p.p. of *figere* fix; perh. thr. obs. *fix* a., or F *fixer* or med. L *fixare*]

fix[2], n. Dilemma, position hard to escape from. [f. prec.]

fixa·tion, n. Fixing, being fixed; process of rendering solid, coagulation; process of combining a gas with a solid. [f. med. L *fixatio* (*fixare* see FIX[1], -ATION)]

fi·xative, a. & n. Tending to fix; (n.) substance used to fix colours or drawings; [-ATIVE]

fi·xature (-tsher), n. Gummy preparation for fixing the hair. [as prec., -URE]

fixed, a. In vbl senses; esp.: *f. idea*, one tending to become a monomania; *f. acid* or *oil*, one not evaporable without decomposition; *f. point*, where policeman is permanently stationed; *f. star*, one seeming to keep same relative position to others (opp. *planet*); *f.* CAPITAL[2]; *f. property*, land & houses. [-ED[1]]

fi·xĕdly, adv. In fixed manner; esp. (of looking) intently. [-LY[2]]

fi·xĕdness, n. Fixed state, immobility, permanence, steadfastness. [-NESS]

fi·xings, n. pl. (U.S.). Apparatus, equipment; trimming of dress or dish, adjuncts. [-ING[1]]

fi·xity, n. Fixed state; (Physics) property of enduring heat without being volatilized or losing weight; stability, permanence. [f. L *fixus* see FIX[1] + -ITY]

fi·xture (-tsher), n. Thing fixed or fastened in position; (Law; pl.) articles of a personal nature affixed to the freehold; person or thing confined to or established in one place (chiefly in pred., as *seems to be a f.*); (Athlet. &c.) (date appointed for) meet, race, &c. [changed f. obs. *fixure* f. LL *fixura* (*figere fix-*, -URE)]

fizz, v.i., & n. (Make) hissing or spluttering sound, whence **fi·zzY**[2] a.; champagne. [imit.]

fi·zzle, v.i., & n. Hiss or splutter feebly (n., this sound); *f. out*, come to lame conclusion; (n.) fiasco. [f. obs. *fise* break wind + -LE(3)]

fla·bbergast, v.t. Dumbfound, so astonish as to incapacitate. [from 1722; etym. dub.]

fla·bby, a. Hanging down, flaccid, limp, (usu. of flesh); nerveless, feeble, (of language or character). Hence **fla·bbiNESS** n. [earlier *flappy* (FLAP, -Y[2])]

flabe·llate, flabe·lliform, aa. (bot. & zool.). Fan-shaped. [f. L *flabellum* fan (*flare* blow) + -ATE[2], -FORM]

fla·ccid (-ks-), a. Hanging loose or wrinkled, limp, flabby, (usu. of flesh); relaxed, drooping; wanting vigour, feeble. Hence **flacci·dITY** n. [f. F *flaccide* f. L *flaccidus* (*flaccus* flabby)]

flag[1], n. Kinds of plant with bladed leaf growing on moist ground, esp. various species of iris; *ff.* or *f.* collect., kind of coarse grass; long slender blade of a plant. Hence **fla·ggY**[2] a. [cf. Du. *flag*]

flag[2], n. & v.t., (Also *flagstone*) flat slab of rock for paving, (pl.) pavement made of these, also **fla·gg**ING^1(6) **n.**; (vb) pave with ff. [earlier sense *sod*, cf. Icel. *flag* spot whence sod has been cut, & FLAKE^2]

flag^3, n. (Also *f.-feather*) quill-feather of bird's wing. [perh. f. obs. *flag* drooping f. OF *flac* f. L *flaccus* flabby]

flag^4, n., & v.t. Piece of bunting or other stuff, usu. oblong or square, attached by one edge to staff or halyard & used as standard, ensign, or signal (*black f.*, pirate's ensign, also f. hoisted outside prison to announce execution of criminal; *Black Ff.*, irregular Chinese soldiers, orig. rebels, in Tonquin; *white f.*, f. of truce, f. disclaiming hostile intention; *yellow f.*, displayed by ship with infectious disease on board, hospital ship, or ship in quarantine; *f. of truce*, white, indicating desire to parley; DIP^1 *f.*; *lower* or *strike* one's *f.*, take it down as salute or sign of surrender); (Naut.) f. carried by flagship as emblem of admiral's rank afloat (*hoist, strike*, one's *f.*, assume, relinquish, command); tail of setter or Newfoundland dog; *f.-boat*, serving as mark in aquatic matches; *f.-captain*, captain of flagship; *f.-day* (on which money is raised for a cause by sale to passengers of ff. to be worn as evidence of having given); *f.-lieutenant*, admiral's A.D.C.; *f.-list*, roll of *f.-officers*, i.e. admirals, vice-admirals, or rear-admirals; *flagman*, signaller at races &c.; *f.-rank* (of f.-officers); *flagship*, having admiral on board; *flagstaff*, pole on which f. is hung; *f.-station*, where trains stop only if signalled; *f.-wagging* (mil. slang), signalling; *f.-waver*, agitator. (Vb) place f. on or over; mark out with ff.; inform (person), communicate (information, *that*), by f.-signals. [perh. imit. of flapping sound; in all mod. Teut. langg., earliest in E (15th c.)]

flag^5, **v.i.** Hang down, flap loosely; droop, fade, become limp; lag, lose vigour, grow languid; fall off in interest. [perh. as FLAG^3]

flage·llant (-j-; *also* flă·j-), n. & a. (One) who scourges himself; given to flogging. [f. L *flagellare* (FLAGELLUM), -ANT]

flă·gellate^1, v.t. Scourge. Hence or cogn. **flagell**A·TION, **fla·gellat**OR^2, nn., **fla·gellat**ORY a. [as prec., -ATE^3]

flage·llum (-j-), n. (pl. *-lla*). (Bot.) runner, creeping shoot; (Zool., Biol.) lashlike appendage. Hence **flă·gellate^2** (-*at*; see -ATE^2), **flage·lli**FORM, aa. [L, =whip]

flăgeole·t^1 (-jo-; *also* flă·-), n. Small wind instrument with mouth-piece at end, six holes, & sometimes keys. [F, dim. of OF *flajol* etym. dub.]

flăgeole·t^2 (-jo-; *also* -lā), n. Kind of kidney-bean. [F, =*fageolet* dim. of *fageol* f. L *faseolus*]

flagi·tious (-jĭshus), a. Deeply criminal, atrocious, heinous, villanous. Hence **flagi·tious**LY^2 adv., **flagi·tious**NESS n. [f. L *flagitiosus* (*flagitium* crime, -OSE^1)]

flă·gon, n. Large vessel usu. with handle, spout, & lid, to hold liquor for table; similar vessel for Eucharist; (Wine-trade) flattened globular glass bottle holding nearly two bottles. [ME *flakon* f. OF *flacon* (FLASK, -OON)]

flā·grant, a. Glaring, notorious, scandalous, (of offence or offender). Hence or cogn. **fla·gr**ANCY n., **fla·grant**LY^2 adv. [f. L *flagrare* blaze (Aryan *bhleg-*), -ANT]

flail, n. Hand threshing-implement, wooden staff at end of which a short heavy stick hangs swinging. [OE *fligel* cf. Du *vlegel*, G *flegel*, prob. f. L FLAGELLUM]

flair, n. Selective instinct for what is excellent, paying, &c. [F (*flairer* to smell f. pop. L *flagrare* =*fragrare* see FRAGRANT)]

flake^1, n. Rack for storing oatcake &c.; stage for drying fish &c. [perh. f. ON *flake* hurdle cf. L *plectere*, Gk *plekō*, weave]

flake^2, n., & v.i. & t. Light fleecy tuft, esp. of snow; portion of ignited matter thrown off; thin broad piece peeled off; natural division of fish's flesh; layer; carnation with striped petals; *f.-white*, pigment made from white-lead in ff.; hence **fla·k**Y^2 a. (Vb) fall like, sprinkle as with, snow; take, come, *away* or *off* in ff. [perh. ult. f. Aryan *plag-* cf. Gk *plēgnumi* beat]

flam, n. Sham story, trick, deception. [?]

flă·mbeau (-bō), n. (pl. *-s* or *-x*, pr. -z). Torch, esp. of several thick waxed wicks. [F, f. *flambe*FLAME^1(=med. L *flambellum*)]

flămboy·ant, a. & n. Marked by wavy flamelike lines (of French 15th & 16th c. archit.); floridly decorated; gorgeously coloured; (n.) kinds of flame-coloured flower. [F, part. of *flamboyer* (*flambe* FLAME^1)]

flame^1, n. (Portion of) ignited gas (*the ff.*, fire, esp. as consuming); visible combustion (*in ff.*; *burst into f.* or *ff.*); bright light, brilliant colouring; passion, esp. of love (*fan the f.*, make it more intense); (joc.) sweetheart (*an old f. of mine*); kinds of moth; *f.-projector* or *-thrower*, =FLAMMENWERFER. Hence **fla·me**LESS (poet.), **fla·m**Y^2, aa. [f. OF *flambe* f. L *flamma* (*flagrare* blaze or *flare* blow)]

flame^2, v.i. & t. Emit ff., blaze, (often *away, forth, out, up*); (of passion) burst out; (of persons) break *out*, blaze *up*, into anger; shine, gleam, (*f. up*, blush violently); move like f.; send (signal) by fire; subject to action of f. (*sterilized by flaming*). [f. OF *flamber* as prec.]

flā·men, n. (Rom. ant.). A god's priest. [L]

fla·ming, a. In vbl senses; esp.: very hot (*a f. sun*); bright-coloured; exaggerated, over-laudatory, (*a f. description*). [-ING^2]

flami·ngo, n. Large long-legged long-necked heavy-billed scarlet-feathered bird. [Port. (*-engo*) perh. f. Rom. *flama* flame + *-enc* = -ING[3]]

fla·mmable, a. (Rare, & chiefly in *non-f.*, for) INFLAMMABLE.

fla·mmenwerfer (-vārfer), n. Machine spouting liquid fire in war. [G, = flame-thrower]

flânerie, flâneur, (F), nn. Idling, idler.

flānge (-j), n., & v.t. Projecting flat rim, collar, or rib; (vb) provide with f. [perh. f. OF *flanche* FLANK]

flank, n., & v.t. Fleshy part of side between ribs & hip; side of building, mountain, &c.; right or left side of army or body of troops (*in f.*, at the side; TURN[1] *f. of*). (Vb) guard or strengthen on the f., menace f. of, take in f., enfilade, rake; be posted or situated at f. of; march past f. of. [f. F *flanc* etym. dub.]

fla·nker, n. Fortification guarding or menacing flank; (Mil., usu. pl.) flank skirmisher(s); thing that flanks anything. [-ER[1]]

fla·nnel (-nl), n. & a. Open woollen stuff, usu. without nap (pl., kinds of this, f. goods); (pl.) underclothing of f., f. bandages, garments esp. trousers of f. for games, whence **fla·nnell**ED[2] a.; piece of f. used in washing person or scrubbing floor, whence **fla·nnel** (-ll-) v.t.; hence **flannel**E·TTE (2) n., **fla·nnell**Y[2] a. (Adj.) made of f. [perh. f. W *gwlanen* (*gwlân* wool)]

flap, v.t. & i., & n. Strike with something broad, drive (flies &c.) *away* or *off*; (of birds) strike (something) with flat of wing; swing or sway about, flutter, oscillate; move (t. & i. of wings) up & down; beat the wings. (N.) light blow with something broad; motion of wing &c.; broad hanging piece hinged or attached by one side only, e.g. trapdoor, pocket-cover, hat-brim, table-leaf, valve, fish's gill-cover, piece of skin left in amputations; open mushroom-top (cf. *button*). [imit.]

flapdoo·dle, n. Nonsense, bunkum. [?]

fla·pjack, n. Small cake of flour fried in grease. [FLAP + JACK[1]]

fla·pper n. Flat fly-killing instrument; bird-scaring clapper; young wild-duck or partridge, (slang) girl not yet out; hinged or hanging piece, flap; broad fin; crustacean's tail; (slang) hand; (w. ref. to Laputans) person, thing, that jogs one's memory or wits. [-ER[1]]

flare, v.t. & i., & n. (Cause to) bulge gradually upwards (of ship's sides); blaze with bright unsteady flame, glow as with flame, (often *about, away, out*; part., gaudy, over-conspicuous); *f. up*, burst into sudden blaze or anger. (N.) dazzling irregular light, unshaded flame in open air; sudden outburst of flame; signal light used at sea; ostentation; upward bulge in ship's sides; *f.-up*, sudden breaking into flame, short brilliant popularity or display, burst of anger, uproarious merrymaking. [?]

flash[1], v.i. & t. Break suddenly into flame, give out flame or sparks, (*f. in the pan*, fail after showy start, like priming of old guns); emit or reflect light, gleam; send, reflect, (something) like a f. or in ff. (*eyes f. fire, f. back defiance*); burst suddenly into view or perception (*flashed upon me that* —); move swiftly; *f. up* or *out*, show sudden passion; cause to gleam (*flashed his sword*; *had a lantern flashed in my face*); send by telegraph (*news was flashed over England*); (Glass-making) spread out (t. & i.) into a sheet, cover (plain glass) with coloured film; (of water) rush along, rise & flow, fill or flood (stream &c.) with water; *f.-board*, for sending more water from mill-dam into mill-race; *f.-pipe*, extra pipe with line of holes for lighting high gas-lamp; *flashing-point*, temperature at which vapour from oil &c. may be ignited. [prob. imit. in sense *flood* &c. (the earliest)]

flash[2], n. Sudden transitory blaze (*f. in pan*, abortive effort; see prec.), time occupied by it, instant, (*in a f.*); ostentation; sudden short access of feeling (*a f. of hope*); preparation for colouring spirits; rush of water let down weir to take boat over shallows, contrivance for producing this; *f.-light*, used for signals & in lighthouses, also for photographing by night &c., (also) electric torch; *f.-point*, (now more usu. for) FLASH[1]ing-point. [f. prec.]

flash[3], a. Gaudy, showy, counterfeit (*f. notes, money*); cant, slang; connected with thieves, tramps, &c. [f. prec.]

fla·shing, n. Strip of metal to obviate flooding or soaking at joint of roofing &c. [?]

fla·shy, a. Brilliant but shallow or transitory, cheaply attractive; showy, gaudy; given to display. Hence **fla·shi**LY[2] adv., **fla·shi**NESS n. [-Y[2]]

flask, n. (Usu. *powder-f.*) leather or metal case for carrying sportsman's supply of gunpowder; Italian narrow-necked wickered wine or oil bottle; traveller's pocket bottle of metal or (usu. leather-covered) glass for wine, spirit, &c. [cf. It. *fiasco*, G *flasche*; perh. ult. f. L *vasculum* dim. of *vas* vessel]

fla·sket, n. Long shallow basket (archaic); clothes-basket; small flask. [f. OF *flasquet* (*flasque* FLASK, -ET[1])]

flat[1], n. Storey; suite of rooms on one floor as residence. [OE *flet* floor cogn. w. foll.]

flat[2], a. & adv., n., & v.t. Horizontal, level; spread out, lying at full length, (*fell f.*; *f. against the wall*; *with the f. hand*); even, smooth, unbroken, without projection, (*f. tint*, uniform); with broad level surface & little depth; unqualified, plain, downright, (*f. denial, refusal*; *f. nonsense, blasphemy*; *that's f.*, let there be no doubt about it); dull, lifeless, monotonous, (*fall f.*, prove a failure, not win applause; *market is, prices are, f.*, inactive, sluggish); slow-witted; dejected, without energy, (*f. beer*, that has lost its effervescence); (Mus.) below the true pitch (*B, D*, &c., *f.*, a semitone lower than B, D, &c.; *sings f.*); *f. aback* (emphat. for ABACK naut. & fig.); *f.-boat*, with f. bottom for transport in shallow water; *f. candlestick*, with broad base & short stem for carrying about; *f.-fish*, family including sole, turbot, plaice, &c.; *f.-foot(ed)*, (having) foot not normally arched; *f.-iron*, for ironing linen &c.; *f. race*, over level ground (opp. hurdle-race or steeplechase); *f. rate* (the same in all cases, not proportional &c.); hence **fla·t**LY[2] adv., **fla·t**NESS n., **fla·tt**EN[6] v.t. & i., **fla·tt**ISH[1](2) a., **fla·t**WAYS, **fla·t**WISE, advv. (N.) what is f. (*on, from, the f.*, of drawings &c. as opposed to sculpture), f. part of anything (*the f. of the hand, with the f. of his sword*); level ground, plain, low land, swamp; f.-bottomed boat; shallow basket; (Theatr.) section of scenery mounted on frame (*join the ff.*, transf., make a thing into a coherent whole, preserve appearance of a consistent attitude); (slang) duffer, dupe; (Mus.) note lowered a semitone below natural pitch, sign indicating this lowering, *sharps & ff.*, black notes on piano. (Vb) make f. (chiefly in manufacturing processes; elsewhere *flatten*). [f. ON *flatr* etym. dub.]

fla·tter, v.t. Court, fawn upon; compliment unduly, overpraise; gratify vanity of, make feel honoured; inspire with (esp. unfounded) hope; please one*self* with the belief (*that*); gratify (eye, ear, &c.); *flattering unction*, salve one administers to one's own conscience or self-esteem (*Haml.* III. iv. 145); (of portrait, painter, &c.) exaggerate good looks of. Hence **fla·tter**ER[1], **fla·tt**ERY(4, 5), nn., **fla·tter-ing**LY[2] adv. [perh. irreg. f. OF *flater* (to smooth)]

flă·tulent, a. Generating gas in the alimentary canal; caused by, attended with, troubled with, accumulation of such gas; inflated, puffed up, windy, pretentious. Hence or cogn. **fla·tul**ENCE, **fla·tul**ENCY, nn., **fla·tulent**LY[2] adv. [F (foll., -ULENT)]

flā·tus, n. Wind in stomach or bowels. [L, vbl n. (*flare* blow)]

flaunt, v.i. & t., & n. Wave (t. & i.) proudly; display oneself or one's finery; show off, parade, (one*self*, finery, &c.); hence **flau·nting**LY[2] adv., **flau·nt**Y[2] a. (N.) flaunting motion. [?]

flau·tist (-aw-), n. Flute-player. [f. It. *flautista* (*flauto* FLUTE)]

flave·scent, a. Turning yellow, yellowish. [f. L *flavescere* (*flavus* yellow, -ESCENT)]

flā·vin, n. Surgical antiseptic, & yellow dye, got from dyer's oak. [L *flavus* yellow, -IN]

flā·vour, n., & v.t. Aroma, mingled sensation of smell & taste, distinctive taste; undefinable characteristic quality; hence **fla·vor**OUS, **fla·vour**LESS, **fla·vour**SOME, aa. (Vb) give f. to, season; hence **flavour-**ING[1](3) n. [prob. f. OF *flaur, fraor*, smell, perh. f. L *fragrare* be FRAGRANT]

flaw[1], n., & v.t. & i. Crack, breach, rent; imperfection, blemish; (Law) invalidating defect in document, procedure, evidence, &c.; hence **flaw·**LESS a., **flaw·less**LY[2] adv., **flaw·less**NESS n. (Vb) crack (t. & i.), damage, mar. [perh. f. ON *flaga* slab cf. FLAKE[2]]

flaw[2], n. Squall of wind; short storm. [cf. Du. *vlaag*, Sw. *flaga*; perh. cogn. w. FLAY]

flawn, n. (archaic.) Kind of custard. [f. OF *flaon* (now *flan*) f. med. L *fladonem* nom. *-o* f. OHG *flado* flat cake]

flax, n. Blue-flowered plant cultivated for its textile fibre & its seeds called linseed; (with qualifying word prefixed or suffixed) kinds of similar plant, as *dwarf, toad, -f., f.-lily, -dodder*; fibres of f., dressed or undressed; cloth of f., linen; *f.-seed*, linseed. [com.-WG; OE *fleax* cf. G *flachs*, perh. cogn. w. G *flechten*, L *plectere*, Gk *plekō*, weave]

fla·xen, a. Of flax; (of hair) coloured like dressed flax, pale yellowish-brown. [-EN[5]]

flay, v.t. Strip off skin or hide of; (fig.) criticize severely; pillage, plunder, (person); peel off (skin, bark, peel); pare off (turf); *f.-flint*, extortioner, miser. [com.-Teut.; OE *flēan* cf. MDu. *vlaen*, Gk *plēssō* strike, FLAKE[2], FLAW]

flea (-ē), n. Small wingless jumping insect feeding on human & other blood (*send one away with a f. in his ear*, discomfited by a reproof or repulse); *sand-f., water-f.*, small jumping crustaceans; = f.-beetle; small or contemptible creature; *f.-bane, f.-wort*, kinds of plant; *f.-beetle*, jumping beetle infesting hops; *f.-bite*, lit., & fig. slight inconvenience or expense, mere trifle, also small reddish spot in animal's colouration (*f.-bitten*, sprinkled with these on lighter ground; also lit.); *f.-dock*, butter-bur; *f.-louse*, jumping plant-louse. [com.-Teut.; OE *flēah* cf. G *floh*, prob. cogn. w. FLEE]

fleam, n. Lancet for bleeding horses. [f. OF *flieme* f. med. L *fledomum* f. LL *flebotomum* f. Gk *phlebotomon* see PHLEBOTOMY]

flèche (-āsh), n. Slender spire, esp. at intersection of nave & transept. [F, orig. = arrow]

fleck, n., & v.t. Spot in the skin, freckle; patch of colour or light; small particle, speck; hence **fle·ck**LESS a. (Vb) mark with ff., dapple, variegate. [f. or cogn. w.

ON *flekkr* blow, spot, cf. G *fleck* spot & *flicken* to patch]

fle·cker, v.t. Dapple, variegate; scatter in patches. [prec. + -ER[5]]

fled. See FLEE.

fledge, v.t. Provide with feathers or plumage, wing for flight, deck with feathers or down. Hence **fle·dge**LESS a. [f. obs. adj. *fledge* feathered cf. OE *unfligge* unfledged, & G *flügge*, cogn. w. FLY[2]]

fle·dg(e)ling, n. Young bird; inexperienced person. [as prec. + -LING[1]]

flee, v.i. & t. (fled; *fly, flying*, are now usu. substituted for *flee, fleeing*; *is fled*, see -ED[1](2), or *has fled*). Run away, seek safety in flight, (*from, before*); vanish, cease, pass away; run away from, leave abruptly; eschew, shun. [com.-Teut.; OE *flēon* cf. G *fliehen*, Goth. *thliuhan*]

fleece, n., & v.t. Woolly covering of sheep or similar animal (*Golden F.*, Austrian & Spanish order of Knighthood); quantity of wool shorn from a sheep at once; rough, abundant, or woolly head of hair; thing like a f., white cloud, falling snow, &c.; (Carding) thin sheet of cotton or wool fibre; hence (-)**fleece**D[2], **flee·c**Y[2], aa. (Vb) shear (sheep; rare); strip of money, property, &c. (also *of*), whence **flee·ce**ABLE a.; overspread as with f. (*sky fleeced with clouds*). [com.-WG; OE *flēos* cf. Du. *vlies*, G *fliess*, perh. cogn. w. L *pluma* feather]

fleer, v.i., & n. Laugh impudently or mockingly, gibe, jeer, sneer; (n.) mocking look or speech. [cf. Norw. & Sw. dial. *flira* to grin]

fleet[1], n. Naval armament, number of warships under one command-in-chief (*the f.*, the navy); number of ships or boats sailing in company; *f. of cabs, taxis*, &c., those owned by one proprietor. [OE *flēot* ship, shipping (*flēotan* FLEET[5])]

fleet[2], n. Creek, inlet; *The F.*, stream, now covered sewer, running into Thames E. of F. Street, also the prison that stood near it (*F. marriage*, performed by a *F. parson* or disreputable clergyman in & about the F. ready to marry clandestinely; *F. Street*, (used for) the press. [OE *flēot* cf. Du. *vliet*, G *fliess*, cogn. w. FLEET[5]]

fleet[3], a. (poet. or literary). Swift, nimble. Hence **flee·t**LY[2] adv., **flee·t**NESS n. [cf. ON *fliótr*, cogn. w. FLEET[5]]

fleet[4], a. & adv. Shallow (of water); at or to no great depth (*plough* or *sow f.*). [cf. Du. *vloot*, cogn. w. foll.]

fleet[5], v.i. Glide away, vanish, be transitory; pass rapidly, slip *away*; move swiftly, fly. Hence **flee·t**ING[2] a., **flee·ting**LY[2] adv. [earlier senses, *float, swim, flow*; com.-Teut.; OE *flēotan* cf. G *fliessen*, cogn. w. Gk *pleō* sail, L *pluere* rain]

Flĕ·ming, n. Inhabitant of Flanders. [f. MDu. *Vlâming* (*Flâm-*, whence *Flanders*, + -ING[3])]

Flĕ·mish[1], a. & n. (Language) of Flanders; *F.* BOND[1]. [f. MDu. *Vlaemisch* (prec., -ISH[1])]

flĕ·mish[2], v.i. (Of hound) make quivering movement of tail & body while searching for trail, feather. [?]

flench, flinch[1], **flense,** v.t. Cut up (whale); flay (seal). [f. Da. *flense*, cf. Norw. *flinsa* flay]

flesh[1], n. Soft substance between the skin & the bones, esp. the muscular part of animal bodies (*f. & blood*, the body or its material, mankind, human nature with its emotions & infirmities; as adj., actually living, not supernatural or imaginary; one's *own f. & b.*, near relations, descendants: *f. & fell*, the whole body; as adv., entirely: *one f.*, united as one personality, see *Gen.* ii. 24: *proud f.*, overgrowth of granulations springing on wound: *make his f. creep*, frighten or horrify him esp. with dread of the supernatural); pulpy substance of fruit or plant; plumpness, fat, (*lose, put on, f.*, grow thin, fat); *in f.*, fat; tissue of animal bodies (excluding fish & sometimes fowls) as food, meat, (*f.-feeding, f.-eater*, &c.; *neither* FISH[1], *f., nor* &c.); visible surface of human body (*f.-colour, -ed*, yellowish pink); =*f. & blood* above (*all f.*, whatever has bodily life; *in the f.*, in bodily form, in life; *after the f.*, corporeally); the sensual appetites (*sins of the f.*, unchastity); *f.-brush, -glove*, for stimulating circulation by rubbing; *f.-fly*, depositing eggs or larvae in dead f.; *f.-pots* (w. ref. to *Exod.* xvi. 3), high living; *f. side* or *f.*, side of a hide that adjoined the f.; *f. tints*, esp. painter's rendering of f.-colour; *f. tights*, fleshings; *f.-wound*, one not reaching bone or vital organ. Hence **fle·sh**LESS a. [com.-WG & Scand.; OE *flǣsc* cf. G *fleisch*, Da. *flesk* pork]

flesh[2], v.t. Incite (hound &c.) by taste of blood; initiate in bloodshed; inflame by foretaste of success; use *sword* &c. for first time on f. (or fig. *pen, wit*, &c.). [f. prec.]

fle·sher, n. (Sc.). Butcher. [f. FLESH + -ER[1]]

fle·shings, n. pl. Close flesh-coloured garment usu. of silk worn on stage &c. to represent natural skin. [FLESH[1], -ING[1]]

fle·shly, a. Carnal, lascivious, sensual, (esp. of appetites &c., rarely of persons); mortal, material, not divine or spiritual; worldly. Hence **fle·shli**NESS n. [OE *flǣsclic* (FLESH[1], -LIKE)]

fle·shy, a. Plump, fat; of flesh, without bone; (of plant or fruit tissue) pulpy; like flesh. Hence **fle·shi**NESS n. [-Y[2]]

fleur-de-lis (flerdelē·; pl. *fleurs-* pr. as sing.), **flower-de-lu·ce** (archaic & U.S.), n. Iris flower; heraldic lily; (sing. or pl.) royal arms of France, French royal family, France. [F (first form), =lily flower (*lis* lily); the archaic E form is corrupt. of F]

fleur·et (-oor-), n. Ornament like small flower. [f. F *fleurette* (*fleur* FLOWER, -ETTE)]

fleuron (F), n. Flower-shaped ornament in architecture, on coins, &c.

fleur·y (-oorĭ), **flor·y**, a. (herald.). Decorated with fleurs-de-lis. [f. F *fleuré*, OF *floré* (*fleur* FLOWER, -Y⁴)]

flew. See FLY².

flews, n. pl. Hanging lips of bloodhound &c. [?]

flex¹, v.t. Bend (in scientific use of bending limb &c. by flexor, or in Geol. of distorted strata). [f. L *flectere flex-*]

flex², n. Flexible insulated wire used in electric lighting. [abbr. of foll.]

fle·xible, a. That will bend without breaking, pliable, pliant; easily led, manageable; adaptable, versatile; supple, complaisant. Hence or cogn. **flexi**BI·LITY n., **fle·xib**LY² adv. [F, f. L *flexibilis* (FLEX¹, -IBLE)]

fle·xile, a. Supple, mobile; tractable; versatile. Hence **flexi·l**ITY n. [f. L *flexilis* (FLEX¹, -IL)]

fle·xion, n. Bending, curvature, bent state, (esp. of limb or joint); bent part, curve; (Gram.) = inflexion, whence **fle·xion**AL, **fle·xion**LESS, aa.; (Math.) = flexure. [f. L *flexio* (FLEX, -ION)]

fle·xor, n. (Also *f. muscle, tendon*) muscle that bends a part (opp. EXTENSOR). [FLEX¹, -OR²]

fle·xuose, a. (bot.). Serpentine, undulating. Hence **flexuo·so-** comb. form. [f. L *flexuosus* (*flexus -ūs* a bend see FLEX¹, -OSE¹)]

fle·xuous, a. Full of bends, winding. Hence or cogn. **flexuŏ·**SITY n., **fle·xuous**LY² adv. [as prec., -OUS]

fle·xure (-ksher), n. Bending, curvature, bent state; bend, curve, turn; (Math.) curving of line or surface or, in theory of elasticity, of surface or solid (*f. of a curve*, its bending to or from a straight line); (Geol.) bending of strata under pressure. [f. L *flexura* (FLEX, -URE)]

fli·bbertigi·bbet (-j-), n. Gossiping, flighty, frivolous, or restless person. [imit. of chatter]

flick, n., & v.t. Light sharp blow with whiplash &c. shot out and withdrawn, or with finger-nail; sudden movement, jerk; slight sharp cracking sound. (Vb) strike with a f.; dash or jerk (dust &c.) *away, off*; give a f. with (whip, towel, &c.). [imit.]

fli·cker, v.i., & n. Quiver, vibrate, wave to and fro, blow lightly & unsteadily, (of flags, leaves, serpents' tongues, wind, &c.); (of flame &c., & fig. of hope &c.) flash and die away by turns; hence **fli·ckering**LY² adv. (N.) flickering movement or light. [OE *flicorian* imit.]

flier. See FLYER.

flight¹ (-īt), n., & v.t. Act or manner of flying through air (*take* one's or *a, wing* one's, *f.*, fly), pursuit of game by hawk; migration, migrating body, flock, of birds or insects; swift movement of projectiles &c.; (of time) swift passage; soaring, excursion, sally, (*of* wit, fancy, ambition, &c.); distance that bird, aircraft, or missile, can fly; series (*of* stairs &c. mounting without change of direction, or *of* hurdles or rails for racing over); volley (*of* arrows &c.); *in the first f.*, taking a leading place; oat-chaff; *f.-feather, -muscle*, used in flying; *f.-lieutenant*, see AIR¹*-force*. (Vb) shoot (wildfowl; also abs.) in f. [OE *flyht* (OTeut. *fleugan* FLY²)]

flight² (-īt), n. Running away, hasty retreat, absconding, (*take, take to, betake* one*self to, f.*, run away; *put to f.*, rout). [ME *fluht* (OTeut. *thleuhan* FLEE)]

flīgh·ty, a. Guided by whim or fancy, fickle; half-witted, crazy. Hence **fligh·ti**LY² adv., **fligh·ti**NESS n. [FLIGHT¹ + -Y²]

fli·m-flam, n. Trifle, nonsense, idle talk; piece of humbug, deception. [?]

fli·msy (-zĭ), a. & n. Easily destroyed, frail, slightly put together; paltry, trivial; frivolous, superficial; hence **fli·msi**LY² adv., **fli·msi**NESS n. (N.) banknote(s) (slang); thin paper, reporter's copy. [from 18th c.; prob. imit.]

flinch² (for *f.*¹ see FLENCH), v.i. Give way, draw back, (*from* duty, course, &c.); wince. [f. OF *flenchir* etym. dub.]

fli·nders, n. pl. Fragments, splinters, (*break, fly, in f.*). [cf. Norw. *flindra*, Du. *flenter*]

fling, v.i. & t. (flung), & n. Rush, go angrily or violently (*f. out of the room; flung away in a rage*); (of horse &c.) kick and plunge (often *out*), (of person; usu. *out*) break into invective; throw, hurl, (often *about, aside, away, by, out, up, at*; rejected thing, missile, flotsam, dice); throw one*self into* person's arms, a boat, &c., *on* person's compassion &c., or *into* an enterprise (i.e. take it up with all one's might); suddenly spread *out* (arms), kick *up* (heels); cast (one's eyes) carelessly (*up*)*on*; send, emit, (sound, smell, light); put person suddenly or violently *into* prison; launch (troops &c.) *on* enemy or *against* fortress or enemy; (of wrestler or ridden horse) throw to the ground; *f.* (fact &c.) *in* one's *teeth*, reproach him with it; *f.* (door &c.) *open* or *to*, open or shut violently. (N.) throw, cast, (*have a f. at*, make an attempt at, jeer at); impetuous dance (esp. *Highland f.*); violent movement, plunge; spell of indulgence in impulse (*have* one's *f.*). [cf. ON *flengja*]

flint, n. Hard stone of nearly pure silica found in pebbly lumps steel-grey within & encrusted with white; anything hard and unyielding; piece of f. used with steel to produce fire (*f. & steel*) esp. in f.-lock gun; pebble of f. (*wring water from a f.*, work miracles; *skin a f.*, be miserly or avaricious; *set* one's *face like a f.*, be determined); *f.-glass*, pure lustrous kind orig. made with f.; *f.-lock*, (lock of) gun discharged by spark from f. Hence **fli·nty**[2] a., **fli·ntiness** n. [OE, cf. Da. *flint*, perh. cogn. w. Gk *plinthos* brick]

flip[1], v.t. & i., & n. Put (pellet, coin) in motion with a fillip; fillip (person's ear, cheek, &c.), strike lightly; make a fillip with fingers; move (fan, whip, fishing-fly) about with sudden jerk(s); strike smartly *at* with whip &c.; (n.) smart light blow, fillip, flick. [imit.]

flip[2], n. Beer and spirit mixed, sweetened, & heated with hot iron; EGG[1]-*f.* [perh. f. prec. in sense *whip up*]

fli·p-flap, n. Kind of somersault; kind of firework, cracker; (in places of amusement) machine with passenger cars hung at ends of long moving arms. [imit.]

fli·ppant, a. Lacking in gravity, treating serious things lightly, disrespectful. Hence **fli·ppancy** n., **fli·ppantly**[2] adv. [from 1605, orig. = nimble, voluble, perh. f. FLIP[1], -ANT]

fli·pper, n. Limb used to swim with, as in turtle & penguin; (slang) hand. [FLIP[1] + -ER[1]]

fli·pperty-flo·pperty, a. Loose, dangling.

flirt, v.t. & i., & n. Fillip, send with a jerk; wave or move briskly (fan, bird's tail); play at courtship (*with*), pretend to make love, whence **flirta·tion** n., **flirta·tious** a. (N.) sudden jerk, quick motion quickly checked; man who pays, or usu. woman who invites or accepts, attentions merely for amusement, whence **flir·tish**[1], **flir·ty**[2], aa. [imit.]

flit, v.i., & n. Migrate, be gone, depart; change one's abode, move, (n., change of abode); pass lightly, softly, or rapidly (often *about, by, to & fro*); fly lightly, make short flights, (of birds & esp. bats). [f. ON *flytja* cogn. w. FLEET[5]]

flitch, n., & v.t. Side of hog salted and cured (*f. of Dunmow*, there given yearly to any couple proving conjugal harmony for year and day); square of blubber; steak of halibut; slice (usu. outside one) of timber from tree-trunk; *f.-beam* (compound, esp. of iron plate between two slices of wood); (vb) cut (log or halibut) into ff. [OE *flicce* cf. MLG *vlike*]

fli·tter, v.i. Flit about, flutter; *f.-mouse*, bat. [FLIT + -ER[5]]

fli·vver, n. (U.S. slang). Cheap motor-car. [?]

flix, n. Kinds of fur; beaver's down. [?]

float[1], n. Floating (rare; *on the f.*, afloat); mass of floating weeds, ice, &c.; raft; cork or quill used on fishing-line as indicator; cork supporting edge of fishing-net; inflated part supporting fish &c.; hollow ball regulating cistern tap; French night-light; (Theatr.; sing. or pl.) footlights; (also *f.-board*) one of the boards of water-wheel or paddle-wheel; kind of low-bodied cart; platform on wheels with show used in processions; tool for smoothing plaster (*f.-stone*, for smoothing curved bricks, & cf. foll.); single-cut file; passing of weft-threads over part of warp without being interwoven, thread so passed; *f.-bridge*, of rafts; *f.-grass*, kinds of sedge. [mixture of OE *flot* floating state, OE *flota* ship, fleet, FLOAT[2], & F *flotte*]

float[2], v.i. & t. Rest on surface of liquid; (of stranded ship) get afloat; move with moving liquid, drift; be suspended freely *in* liquid; move or be suspended in air as if buoyed up; hover *before* eye or mind; (Commerc., of acceptance) be in circulation, awaiting maturity; (Commerc.) bring (company, scheme) into favour, launch, (of scheme &c.) be launched; cover with liquid, inundate; (of water &c.) support, bear along, (buoyant object); set afloat; circulate (rumour); waft through air; *f.-stone*, kinds of light stone that f. (& see prec.). [OE *flotian* cf. ON *flota*, cogn. w. FLEET[5]]

floa·table, a. Capable of floating; (of stream) in which rafts &c. can float. [-ABLE]

floa·tage (-ĭj), n. Floating; (right of appropriating) flotsam; ships &c. afloat on river; floating masses; buoyancy; part of ship above water-line. [-AGE]

floata·tion, flot-, n. Floating (*centre of f.*, of gravity in floating body); starting of company or enterprise. [*flot-* is attempt to disguise hybrid formation; FLOAT[2], -ATION]

floa·ter, n. In vbl senses; esp. (St. Exch.) government stock certificate, railway bond, &c., recognized as security. [-ER[1]]

floa·ting, a. In vbl senses; esp. (Commerc.; of cargo) at sea (*f. trade, rates*, &c., concerned with cargoes at sea); *f.* CAPITAL[2], DEBT, RIB; fluctuating, variable, (*the f. population*); *f. anchor* = DRAG[2]-*anchor*; *f.* DOCK[4]; *f. bridge*, kinds of bridge & ferry, also part of bridge that can be swung away on pontoon; *f. kidney*, abnormal condition in which the kidneys are movable; *f. light*, light-ship, life-buoy with lantern. [-ING[2]]

flocci-nauci-nīhĭli-pīlĭ-fica·tion (-ŏks-), n. Estimating as worthless (*the f. of wealth*). [four L wds = at little or nothing + -FICATION]

flocco·se, a. (bot.). Tufted. [f. LL *floccosus* (L *floccus* FLOCK[1], -OSE[1])]

flo·ccule, n. Small portion of matter like flock of wool. [f. FLOCCULUS]

flo·cculent, -lose, -lous, aa. Like tufts of wool; in, showing, tufts. Hence **flo·cculence** n. [foll., -ULENT, -OSE[1], -OUS]

flo·ccŭlus, n. (pl. *-lī*). = FLOCCULE; (Anat.) small lobe in under surface of cerebellum. [mod. L, dim. of foll.]

flo·ccus, n. (pl. *-ci*, pr. -ŏksī). Tuft of woolly hairs or filaments. [L, = foll.]

flock[1], n. Lock, tuft, of wool, cotton, &c.; (pl.) material for quilting & stuffing made of wool-refuse or torn-up cloth; (pl. or collect. sing.) powdered wool or cloth for making f.-paper; (Chem.; pl.) light loose masses precipitated; *f.-bed*, stuffed with ff. *f.-paper*, wall-paper sized & then powdered with f. either all over or in patterns. Hence **flo·cky**[2] a. [prob. f. OF *floc* f. L *floccus*]

flock[2], n., & v.i. Large number of people (chiefly in such phrr. as *come in ff.*); number of animals of one kind, esp. birds, feeding or travelling together; number of domestic animals, usu. sheep, goats, or geese, kept together (*ff. & herds*, sheep & cattle); the Christian body; a congregation esp. in relation to its pastor; family of children, number of pupils, &c.; *f.-master*, sheep-farmer; (vb) congregate, go in great numbers, troop, (often *about, after, into, to, in, out, together*). [OE *flocc* cf. ON *flokkr* perh. cogn. w. FOLK]

floe (-ō), n. Sheet of floating ice. [perh. f. Norse *flo* layer]

flog, v.t. Beat with birch, whip, cat, &c., whence **flo·gging**[1](1) n.; drive (learning, laziness, &c.) *into* or *out of* person; urge (horse &c.) on with whip (*f. dead horse*, waste energy); (slang) defeat, excel; cast fishing-line repeatedly over (stream). [perh. imit., or school slang f. L *flagellare* to whip]

flong, n. Prepared paper for stereotyping. [f. F *flan* FLAWN]

flood (-ŭd), n., & v.t. & i. (Also *f.-tide*) inflow of tide (opp. EBB); (poet.) river, stream, sea, (*f. & field*, sea & land); irruption of water over land, inundation, (*the F., Noah's F.*, that in Genesis), whence **floodŏ·meter** n.; outpouring of water, torrent, downpour, (*ff. of rain, a f. of tears* or *words*); *f.-gate*, opened & closed to admit or exclude water, esp. lower gate of lock, also sluice. (Vb) inundate, cover with a f. (also fig., *was flooded with letters*); irrigate; deluge (burning house, mine) with water; (of rain) fill (river) to overflowing; come in great quantities (usu. *in*); have uterine haemorrhage. [com.-Teut.; OE *flōd* cf. G *flut*, Du. *vloed*, cogn. w. FLOW[1]]

floor (-ōr), n., & v.t. Lower surface of room, (also *flooring*) boards &c. of which it is made; bottom of sea, cave, &c.; part of House of Parliament where members sit and speak (*take the f.*, esp. U.S., speak in debate); set of rooms &c. on same level in house (*ground f.*, on ground level, *first f.*, above this), storey; level area; *f.-lamp*, mounted on metal &c. pillar standing on f.; *f.-cloth*, substitute for carpet; hence **floor·less** a. (Vb) furnish with f., pave; serve as f. of; bring to the f. or ground, knock down; confound, nonplus; (at school) tell (boy) to sit down as not knowing lesson; overcome, get the better of, (*f. the paper*, answer every question in it). [OE *flōr* cf. Du. *vloer*, G *flur*]

floor·er (-ōr-), n. Knock-down blow; disconcerting news or argument; paper or question hard to answer. [-ER[1]]

flop, v.i. & t., n., int., & adv. Sway (intr.) about heavily; walk &c. in ungainly way; sit, kneel, lie, *down* awkwardly; throw *down* negligently or noisily; make dull sound of soft body falling or of flat thing slapping water; hence **flo·ppy**[2] a. (N.) flopping motion, sound made by it. (Int. & adv.) with a f. [=FLAP]

flōr·a, n. (List of) plants of particular region or epoch (cf. FAUNA). [L goddess of flowers (*flos -oris* flower), used in L titles of bot. bks]

flōr·al, a. Of flora(s) (*f. zone*, tract of earth with special vegetable characteristics); of flower(s). [f. L *floralis* of Flora (prec.)]

Flŏ·rentīne, a. & n. (Inhabitant) of Florence in Tuscany (*F. iris*, white or pale blue one); kind of twilled silk. [f. L *Florentinus* (*Florentia* Florence, -INE[1])]

flore·scence, n. Flowering time or state. [f. L *florescere* (*florēre* bloom, -ESCENT, -ENCE)]

flor·et, n. (Bot.) one of small flowers making up a composite flower (*f. of the disk, the ray*, of the flower's centre or circumference); small flower, floweret. [f. OF *florete* (FLOWER, -ETTE)]

flor·iate, v.t. Decorate with flower-designs &c. [as foll., -ATE[3]]

flor·iculture, n. Cultivation of flowers. Hence **floricu·ltural** a., **floricu·lturist** (3) n. [f. L *flos -oris* flower + CULTURE]

flŏ·rid, a. Profusely adorned as with flowers, elaborately ornate, (of literary, artistic, or musical style); ostentatious, showy; ruddy, flushed, high-coloured. Hence **flori·dity**, **flo·ridness**, nn., **flo·ridly**[2] adv. [f. L *floridus* (*flos* FLOWER)]

Flŏ·rida, n. State in U.S. (*F. water*, a perfume; *F. wood*, kind used for inlaying).

flori·ferous, a. (Of seeds or plants) producing many flowers. [f. L *florifer* (*flos* FLOWER, -FEROUS)]

florilē·gium, n. (pl. *-ia*). Anthology. [transl. into mod. L (L *flos* FLOWER, *legere* gather) of Gk *anthologion* ANTHOLOGY]

flŏ·rin, n. Foreign coin of gold or silver current at different times; (Hist.) English gold coin (6/8) of Edw. III; current English coin (2/-). [F, f. It. *fiorino* dim. of *fiore* f. L *florem* nom. *flos* FLOWER (stamped with lily)]

flōr·ist (*also* flŏ·-), n. One who deals in, raises, or studies flowers. [L *flos -oris* flower, -IST]

flōr·uit (-ŏŏit), n. Period (failing exact birth and death dates) at which a person was alive. [L, = he flourished]

flory. See FLEURY.

flo·scular, -lous, aa. Having florets, composite-flowered. [f. L *flosculus* (FLOWER, -CULE)]

floss, n. Rough silk enveloping silkworm's cocoon (*f. silk*, this used in cheap silk goods). Hence **flo·ss**Y[2] a. [perh. f. OF *flosche* down]

flotation. See FLOATATION.

floti·lla, n. Small fleet; fleet of boats or small ships. [Sp., dim. of *flota* fleet]

flo·tsam, n. Wreckage found floating (cf. JETSAM); oyster-spawn. [AF *floteson* (OF *floter* =FLOAT[2], -SON)]

flounce[1] (-ow-), v.i., & n. Go with agitated or violent motion, flop, plunge, throw the body about, (*away, out, about, down, up*); (n.) fling, jerk, of body or limb. [cf. Norw. *flunsa* hurry (found later)]

flounce[2] (-ow-), n., & v.t. Strip gathered & sewn by upper edge round woman's skirt, & with lower edge hanging, as ornament; (vb) trim with f. or ff. [earlier *frounce* f. OF *fronce, froncir,* wrinkle, perh. f. L *frons -tis* brow]

flou·nder[1] (-ow-), n. A small flat-fish. [prob. f. OF *flondre* cf. Norw. *flundra,* Da. *flynder*]

flou·nder[2] (-ow-), v.i., & n. Struggle & plunge (as) in mud or wading; make mistakes, manage business badly or with difficulty; (n.) piece of floundering, staggering attempts to get on. [cf. Du. *flodderen*]

flour (-owr), n., & v.t. Finer part of meal obtained by bolting; wheat meal; fine soft powder; *f.-box*, tin box for dredging f.; hence **flour·**Y[2] a. (Vb) sprinkle with f.; (U.S.) grind into f. [form of FLOWER; orig. sense *finest part*]

flou·rish[1] (flŭ-), v.i. & t. Grow vigorously; thrive, prosper, be successful; be in one's prime; spend one's life, be active, *in, at, about,* &c., a certain time (cf. FLORUIT); use ff. in handwriting or literary work or speech; show ostentatiously; wave (weapon) about; throw (limbs) about; prelude fancifully in music &c. [f. OF *florir* (-ISH[2]) f. L *florēre* (*flos* FLOWER)]

flou·rish[2], n. Prosperity, vigour, (rare; *in full f.*). Ornament of flowing curves about letter or word in handwriting; rhetorical embellishment, florid expression; ostentatious waving of weapon, hand, &c.; (Mus.) fanfare of horns &c. for person's arrival, florid passage, extemporized addition or prelude; hence **flou·rish**Y[2] a. [f. prec.]

flout (-owt), v.t. & i., & n. Mock, insult, express contempt for by word or act; scoff *at*; (n.) mocking speech or action. [from 16th c.; perh. var. of FLUTE v.]

flow (-ō), v.i., & n. Glide along as a stream; (of blood) circulate; (of persons or things) come, go, in numbers; (of talk, literary style, &c.) move easily; (of garment, hair, &c.) hang easily, undulate; (Math.; of numbers) increase or diminish continuously by infinitesimal quantities; gush out, spring; (of blood) be spilt; result *from*; run full, be in flood (*ebb & f.*; *flowing tide*, progressive tendency); (of wine) be poured out without stint; be plentifully supplied *with* (archaic; *land flowing with milk & honey*). (N.) flowing movement in stream; amount that flows; flowing liquid; (of dress, figure, &c.) undulation; outpouring, stream, copious supply; rise of tide (*ebb & f.*); overflowing of Nile &c.; *f. of spirits,* habitual cheerfulness; *f. of soul,* genial conversation (as complement to FEAST *of reason*). [OE *flōwan,* cf. ON *flóa*; cogn. w. FLOOD; unconnected with L *fluere*]

flow·er (-ow-; *also* flowr), n., & v.i. & t. (Bot.) reproductive organ in plant containing one or more pistils or stamens or both, & usu. a corolla & calyx, (pop.) coloured (i.e. not green) part of plant from which fruit or seed is later developed, whence **flow·er**AGE(1) n.; (Old Chem.; pl.) powder left after sublimation (*ff. of sulphur* &c.); scum formed by fermentation (*ff. of tan*); a blossom apart from the plant (*No ff.*, intimation that wreaths &c. are not desired at funeral); flowering plant; (pl.) ornamental phrases (usu. *ff. of speech* often iron.); *the* pick or choice *of*; *the* best part, essence; *the* choicest embodiment *of*; state of blooming (*in f.*), prime (*in the f. of his age*); *f.-de-luce,* see FLEUR-DE-LIS; *f.-girl,* who sells ff.; *f.-piece,* picture of ff.; *flower-pot,* usu. of red earthenware holding soil in which plant may be set; *flower-show,* competitive or other exhibition of ff.; hence **(-)flower**ED[2], **flower·**LESS, aa., **flower·**ET[1] n. (Vb) produce ff., bloom or blossom, whence **flower·**ING[2] a.; (Gardening) cause or allow (plant) to f.; embellish with worked ff. or floral design. [ME & OF *flour* f. L *florem* nom. *flos,* cogn. w. BLOW[3]]

flower·er, n. Plant that flowers at specified time &c. (*late, abundant, f.*). [-ER[1]]

flow·ery, a. Abounding in flowers; full of fine words, compliments, figures of speech, &c., whence **flower·**INESS (-owr-) n. [-Y[2]]

flow·ing, a. In vbl senses; also or esp.: (of style) fluent, easy; (of lines, curves, contour) smoothly continuous, not abrupt; (Naut.) *with f. sheet* or *sail,* sailing with lee clews eased off when wind is nearly across course. Hence **flow·ing**LY[2] adv. [-ING[2]]

flown[1] (-ōn), a. (archaic). Swollen, puffed up, (*f. with insolence and wine*). [obs. p.p. of FLOW]

flown[2]. See FLY[2].

flu·ctuate, v.i. Move up & down like waves (rare); vary irregularly, rise & fall, be unstable; vacillate, waver. So **fluctua·**TION n. [f. L *fluctuare* (*fluctus -ūs* wave f. *fluere* flow), -ATE[3]]

flue[1], n. Kind of fishing-net. [from 14th c.; cf. MDu. *vluwe*]

flue[2], n. Substance formed by loose particles of cotton &c., fluff. Hence **flue·**Y[2] a. [cf. Flem. *vluwe* perh. f. F *velu* hairy]

flue[3], n. Smoke-duct in chimney; channel for conveying heat, esp. hot-air passage in wall, tube for heating water in some kinds of boiler; fissure in organ mouth-pipes (also called *f.-pipes*). [perh. cogn. w. FLUE[5]]

flu(e)[4], n. (colloq.). (Short for) INFLUENZA.

flue[5], v.i. & t. Splay, make (opening) widen inwards or outwards. [f. obs. adj. *flue* shallow perh. cogn. w. FLOW]

flu·ency, n. Smooth easy flow, esp. in speech; ready utterance. [f. L *fluentia* (foll., -ENCE)]

flu·ent, a. & n. Flowing (rare in lit. sense); ready to flow, liquid, (rare); fluid, not settled, liable to change, (rare); (of motion, curves, &c.) graceful, easy; (of speech or style) copious, coming easily, ready; expressing oneself quickly & easily; (Math., in fluxions) that FLOWS (n., the variable quantity that flows). Hence **flu·ent**LY[2] adv. [f. L *fluere* flow, see -ENT]

fluff, n., & v.t. Light feathery stuff given off by blankets &c.; soft fur; soft downy mass or bunch; soft short hair on lip or cheek; (slang) theatrical part imperfectly known; hence **flu·ff**Y[2] a., **flu·ffi**NESS n. (Vb) put soft surface on (flesh side of leather); make into f.; shake (one*self*, one's feathers &c.) *up* or *out* into fluffy mass; (slang) blunder in theatrical part. [perh. modification of FLUE[2]]

flu·id, a. & n. (Substance) consisting of particles that move freely among themselves & yield to the slightest pressure (including gases, liquids, & the assumed pervasive imponderable media of electricity &c.); moving readily, not solid or rigid, not stable; liquid constituent or secretion. Hence **flui·di**FY v.t., **flui·di**TY n. [f. F *fluide* f. L *fluidus* (*fluere* flow, -ID[4])]

fluke[1], n. Kinds of flat-fish, the flounder, (now rare); kinds of parasitic worm found in sheep's liver; kind of kidney potato. [OE *flóc* cf. ON *flóke*, cogn. w. G *flach* flat]

fluke[2], n. Broad triangular plate on arm of anchor; barbed head of lance, harpoon, &c.; (pl.) whale's tail. [perh. f. prec.]

fluke[3], n., & v.i. & t. (Make) lucky accidental stroke; get, hit, &c., by f. Hence **flu·k**Y[2] a., **flu·ki**LY[2] adv., **flu·ki**NESS n. [etym. dub.; first in billiards]

flume, n., & v.i. & t., (chiefly U.S.). Artificial channel conveying water for industrial use; ravine with stream; (vb) build ff., convey down a f. [in early use = stream; f. OF *flum* f. L *flumen* river (*fluere* flow)]

flu·mmery, n. Food made by boiling oatmeal down to a jelly (archaic or dial.); kinds of sweet dish made with milk, flour, eggs, &c.; empty compliments, trifles, nonsense. [f. W *llymru* etym. dub.]

flu·mmox, v.t. (slang). Confound, bewilder, disconcert. [prob. imit.]

flump, v.i. & t., & n. Fall or move heavily, set or throw *down*, with a dull noise (n., the action or sound). [imit.]

flung. See FLING v.

flu·nkey, n. (pl. *-eys*). Liveried servant, footman, (usu. contempt.); toady, snob. Hence **flu·nkey**DOM, **flu·nkey**ISM, nn. [orig. Sc.; perh. f. FLANK, with sense *sidesman*]

fluo(r)-, fluoro-, comb. forms of FLUORINE, as *fluoboric*, *fluorhydric*; *fluoro*SCOPE, instrument with fluorescent screen used instead of dark room to show Röntgen-ray effects. [foll.]

flu·or, n. Kinds of gemlike readily fusible mineral containing fluorine; *f.-spar*, calcium fluoride. [L, = flow (*fluere* flow, -OR[1])]

fluore·scence, n. Coloured luminosity produced in some transparent bodies by direct action of light, esp. of violet & ultra-violet rays; property of rendering ultra-violet rays visible. Hence **fluore·sce** v.i., **fluor**E·SCENT a. [prec., -ESCENT, -ENCE]

flu·orine, n. Non-metallic element grouped with bromine, chlorine, & iodine. Hence **flu·or**IDE n. [FLUOR, -INE[5]]

flu·rry, n., & v.t. Gust, squall; commotion, excitement, nervous hurry, agitation; whale's death-throes; (vb) confuse by haste or noise, agitate. [imit.; cf. *flaw*, *hurry*]

flush[1], v.i. & t., & n. Take wing & fly away; cause to do this, put up, (birds); (n.) number of birds put up at once. [perh. imit.; cf. *fly*, *rush*]

flush[2], v.i. & t. Spurt, rush out; cleanse (drain &c.) by flow of water; flood (meadow); (of plant) throw out fresh shoots (also causative, *rain flushes the plants*); glow with warm colour; (of blood) rush into & redden face; (of face) become red or hot, blush; cause to glow or blush, suffuse with warm colour; inflame with pride or passion, encourage, (*flushed with exercise, joy, victory, insolence*, &c.). [perh. = prec. influenced by *flash* & *blush*]

flush[3], n. Rush of water; sudden abundance; stream from mill-wheel; rush of emotion, elation produced by it or by victory &c.; fresh growth of grass &c.; cleansing of drain by flushing; glow of light or colour; rush of blood to face, reddening caused by it; hot fit in fever; freshness, vigour. [f. prec.]

flush[4], a., & v.t. Full to overflowing, in flood; (usu. pred.) having plentiful supply of or *of* money &c., (of money) abundant; even, in same plane, level *with*, without projections or raised edges. (Vb) level; fill in (joint) level with surface. [prob. f. FLUSH[2]]

flush[5], n. Set of cards all of one suit. [cf. F & Sp. *flux* prob. f. L FLUX*us*]
flu·ster, v.t. & i., & n. Confuse with drink, half-intoxicate; flurry, make nervous; be agitated, bustle; (n.) flurry, flutter, agitation. [cf. Icel. *flaustr* n., *flaustra* v.]
flu·stra, n. (pl. *-ae, -as*). Sea-mat, polyzoic species resembling sea-weed. [arbitrary mod. L coinage by Linnaeus]
flute, n., & v.i. & t. Musical wind-instrument, long wooden pipe with holes along it stopped by fingers or keys, & blow-hole in side near upper end, whence **flu·**TIST(3) n.; f.-player; organ stop with f.-like tone; semicylindrical vertical groove in pillar, similar groove elsewhere, e.g. in frills, whence **flu·**TING[1](6) n. (Vb) play f.; whistle, sing, or speak, in f.-like tones; play (air &c.) on f.; make ff. or grooves in. [f. OF *fleüte, flaüte, flahute,* etym. dub.]
flu·tter, v.i. & t., & n. Flap wings, flap (wings), without flying or in short flights; come or go with quivering motion (usu. to the ground); go about restlessly, flit, hover; quiver, vibrate, (of pulse) beat feebly & irregularly; tremble with excitement, be agitated; move (flag &c.) irregularly, agitate, ruffle; throw (person) into confusion or agitation. (N.) fluttering; tremulous excitement (*be, put, in a f.*); stir, sensation, (*make a f.*); (slang) gambling venture, speculation. [OE *floterian* frequent. cf. *fléotan* FLEET[5]]
flu·ty, a. Like flute in tone, soft & clear. [-Y[2]]
flu·vial, a. Of, found in, river(s). [F, f. L *fluvialis* (*fluvius* river, -AL)]
flu·viatile, a. Of, found in, produced by, river(s). [F, f. L *fluviatilis* (prec., -ATILE)]
flu·vio-, comb. form of L *fluvius* river, as *fluvio-marine, fluviometer.*
flux, n., & v.i. & t. Morbid or excessive discharge of blood, excrement, &c., (formerly) dysentery; flowing out, issue; flowing; inflow of tide (usu. *f. & reflux,* often fig.); flood *of* talk &c.; continuous succession of changes (*in a state of f.*); (Math.) continued motion (*line is the f. of a point*); (Physics) rate of flow of any fluid across given area, amount crossing area in given time; substance mixed with metal &c. to promote fusion. (Vb) issue in a f., flow copiously; make fluid, fuse, treat with a fusing f. [F, f. L *fluxus* (*fluere flux-* flow)]
flu·xion, n. Flowing (rare); continuous change (rare); (Math.) rate or proportion at which a flowing or varying quantity increases its magnitude (*method of ff.,* the Newtonian calculus). Hence **flu·xion**AL, **flu·xion**ARY[1], aa. [F, f. L *fluxionem* (*fluere flux-* flow, -ION)]
fly[1], n. Two-winged insect (*f. in amber,* curious relic; *f. on wheel,* person who over-estimates his own influence; *break f. on wheel,* expend disproportionate energy; *a f. in the ointment,* trifling circumstance that mars enjoyment; *no ff. on him* &c., slang praise of person's or thing's efficiency; HESSIAN, SPANISH, TSETSE, *f.*); kinds of plant-disease caused by various ff. (*a good deal of f. exists*); natural or artificial f. used as fishing-bait; *f.-bane,* kinds of plant, esp. CATCH[1]-f. & Ploughman's spikenard; *f.-blow,* (n.) f.'s egg in meat &c., (v.t.) deposit eggs in, taint, (*f.-blown,* tainted, lit. & fig.); *f.-book,* case for keeping fishing-ff. in; *f.-catcher,* trap for ff., kinds of bird; *f.-fish* (v.i.), fish with f.; *f.-flap,* for driving away ff.; *f.-net,* net or fringe protecting horse from ff.; *f.-paper,* for catching or poisoning ff.; *f.-trap,* for catching ff., also kinds of plant esp. *Venus's f.-t.,* Dionaea; *f.-whisk,* for driving away ff. [OE *fléoge, flýge,* cf. Du. *vlieg,* G *fliege,* cogn. w. foll.]
fly[2], v.i. & t. (*flew, flown* pr. -ōn; *is, has flown,* see -ED[1](2); *fly* is preferred in talk & ordinary prose for *flee,* but not *flew* or *flown* for *fled*). Move through air with wings (*f. high,* be ambitious; *high-flown,* exalted, turgid, bombastic; *as the* CROW[1] *flies*; *the bird is flown,* person wanted has escaped; often *about, away, forth, off, out*) or in aircraft; make (pigeon, hawk) f.; (Hawk.) soar by way of attack *at* (fig., *f. at higher game,* have nobler ambitions); pass or rise quickly through air; jump clear over or *over* fence &c.; make (kite) rise & stay aloft (*f. a kite,* raise money by accommodation bill, also try how the wind blows, feel one's way by ballon d'essai); (of flag, hair, garment, &c.) flutter, wave; set or keep (flag) flying; travel swiftly, rush along, pass rapidly; spring, start, hasten, (*f. to arms,* take up arms eagerly; *f. in the* FACE[1] *of*; *f. at, upon,* attack violently; *f. into* a passion, raptures, &c.; *f. out,* burst into violent language or action); be driven or forced off suddenly (*made sparks f.*; *send flying*; *make the money f.,* spend quickly; *door flew open*; *glass* &c. *flies,* breaks in pieces); *let f.,* discharge (missile), (abs.) shoot, hit, or use strong language, *at*; run away, flee, flee from (*must f. the country*); *f.-away,* (of garments) streaming, loose, negligé, (of persons) flighty; *f.-by-night,* one who makes night excursions or decamps by night; *f.-the-garter,* kind of leap-frog. [com.-Teut.; OE *fléogan,* cf. G *fliegen*; unconnected with *flee*]
fly[3], n. Flying, distance flown, (*on the f.,* on the wing, in motion); one-horse hackney-carriage; lap on garment to contain or cover buttonholes, flap at entrance of tent; part of flag furthest from staff, also its breadth from staff to end; (Theat.; pl.) space over proscenium; speed-regulating device in clockwork & machinery; *f.-leaf,* blank leaf at beginning or end of book, blank leaf of circular &c.; *flyman,* driver of f. = carriage, man

stationed in ff. of theatre to work ropes &c.; *f.-sheet*, 2 or 4 page circular &c.; *f.-wheel*, heavy-rimmed on revolving shaft to regulate machinery or accumulate power. [f. prec.]

fly[4], a. (slang). Knowing, wide awake. [?]

fly·er, fli·er, n. Bird &c. that flies (usu. *high, poor*, &c., *f.*); animal, vehicle, &c., going with exceptional speed; airman; flying jump. [-ER[1]]

fly·ing, a. In vbl senses; also or esp.: making movements like flight (*f. boat*, form of SEA-*plane* in which a boat serves as both fuselage & float; *f.-dog*, kind of vampire-bat; *f.* DUTCHMAN; *f. fish*, kinds rising into air by wing-like pectoral fins, also nickname for native of Barbadoes; *f. fox*, kinds of fruit-eating bat; *f. man*, airman; *f. officer*, rank in AIR[1] Force; *f. pig*, slang, trench-mortar projectile; *f. squad*, police detachment with motor-cars &c. for rapid pursuit; *f. squirrel*, kinds floating in air by skin connecting fore & hind legs); hanging loose, fluttering, (*f. jib*, light sail set before jib on f. jib-boom; *with f.* COLOUR[1]*s*); done or taken in passing (*f. jump*, with running start; *f. handicap, mile, start*, in which starting-post is passed at full speed); passing, hasty, (*f. visit*); temporary (*f. bridge*); designed for rapid movement (*f. squadron, column*); *f. buttress*, slanting from pier &c. to wall & usu. carried on arch. [-ING[2]]

foal, n., & v.t. & i. Young of horse, ass, &c., colt or filly, (*in, with, f.*, pregnant); give birth to (f.), give birth to f. [com.-Teut.; OE *fola*, cf. G *fohlen*, cogn. w. Gk *pōlos*, L *pullus*]

foam, n., & v.i. Collection of small bubbles formed in liquid by agitation, fermentation, &c.; froth of saliva or perspiration; (poet.) the sea. (Vb) emit f., froth at the mouth; (of water &c.) froth, gather f., run foaming *along, down, over*, &c., pass *off* or *away* in f.; (of cup &c.) be filled with foaming liquor. Hence **foa·m**LESS, **foa·m**Y[2], aa. [vb f. n., OE *fám* cf. G *feim*]

fob[1], n., & v.t. Small pocket for watch &c. formerly made in waistband of breeches; (vb) put in one's f., pocket. [?]

fob[2], v.t. Cheat, take in; palm (something inferior) *off upon* (person); put (person) *off with* (something inferior). [from 16th c.; cf. G *foppen* befool]

fō·cal, a. Of, situated or collected at, a focus; (Opt.) *f. distance* or *length*, distance between centre of mirror or lens & its focus. [FOCUS, -AL]

fō·calize, v.t. =FOCUS v.t. Hence **focaliz**A·TION n. [prec., -IZE]

fo'c's'le. See FORECASTLE.

fo·cus, n. (pl. *-ci* pr. -sī, *-uses*), & v.t. & i. (-s-, -ss-). (Plane geom.) one of points from which distances to any point of given curve are connected by linear relation; (Opt., Heat, &c.) point at which rays meet after reflection or refraction, point from which rays appear to proceed, point at which object must be situated for image given by lens to be well defined (*in, out of, bring into, f.*), focal length of lens, adjustment of eye or eyeglass necessary to produce clear image; point to which sound-waves converge; principal seat (of disease, activity, &c.). (Vb) converge, make converge, to a f.; adjust f. of (lens, eye); bring into f. [L, =hearth]

fo·dder, n., & v.t. Dried food, hay, straw, &c., for stall-feeding cattle; hence **fo·dder**LESS a. (Vb) give f. to. [OE *fódor*, cf. Du. *voeder*, G *futter*, f. Aryan *pat-* feed]

foe (fō), n. (poet. &c.). Enemy, adversary, opponent, ill-wisher; *foeman* (archaic), enemy in war. [OE *fáh* adj. & *gefá* noun f. OTeut. *faiho-, gafaiho-*, cogn. w. Gk *pikros* bitter]

foe·tus (fē-), **fē·tus,** n. Fully developed embryo in womb or egg. Hence **f(o)e·t**AL a., **f(o)e·ti**CIDE(2) n. [L *fetus -ūs* offspring]

fog[1], n., & v.t. Aftermath; long grass left standing in water. (Vb) leave (land) under f.; feed (cattle) on f. [from 14th c.; etym. dub.]

fog[2], n., & v.t. & i. Vapour suspended in atmosphere at or near earth's surface, obscurity caused by this (*in a f.*, puzzled, at a loss); abnormal darkened state of atmosphere; (Photog.) cloud on developed plate; *f.-bow*, like rainbow produced by light on f.; *f.-horn*, sounding instrument for warning ships in f.; *f.-signal*, detonator placed on railway line in f. to guide driver. (Vb) envelop (as) with f.; bewilder, perplex; (Gardening) die *off* from damp; (Photog.) make (negative) obscure or cloudy; (Railway) place f.-signals on line, whence **fo·gg**ER[1] n. [prob. back formation f. FOGGY; from 16th c.]

fo·ggy, a. Thick, murky; of, like, infested with, FOG[2]; obscure, dull, confused, (*has only a f. idea of it*); beclouded, indistinct. Hence **fo·ggi**LY[2] adv., **fo·ggi**NESS n. [earlier senses, *covered with coarse grass, boggy, flabby*; prob. f. FOG[1], FOG[2] being formed f. *foggy*]

fō·gle, n. (thieves' slang). Silk handkerchief. [?]

fo·gy, -gey (-g-), n. (Usu. *old f.*) old-fashioned fellow, old man behind the times. Hence **fo·g(e)y**DOM, **fo·gy**ISM, nn., **fo·gy**ISH[1] a. [perh. var. of FOGGY in obs. sense *moss-grown*]

Föhn (G), n. Hot southerly wind in the Alps. [G, perh. f. L *Favonius*]

foi·ble, n. Weak point, weakness of character, quality on which one mistakenly prides oneself; (Fenc.) part of sword-blade from middle to point (cf. FORTE). [F, obs. form of *faible* FEEBLE]

foil[1], n., & v.t. (Arch.) arc or space between cusps of window (vb, ornament with ff., as *foiled arch*); metal hammered or rolled into thin sheet (usu. *gold, tin,* &c., *f.*); sheet of this, or now amalgam of tin & quicksilver, placed behind mirror-glass, backing; leaf of it placed under precious stone &c. to brighten or colour it or enhance its brightness by contrast (vb, supply with this); anything that sets something off by contrast (vb, set off thus). [OF, f. L *folium* leaf cogn. w. Gk *phullon*]

foil[2], v.t. & i., & n. (Hunt.) run over or cross (scent, ground) so as to baffle hounds (also abs. of deer &c., spoil the scent thus); beat off, repulse, frustrate, parry, baffle. (N.) Track of hunted animal (*run, run upon, the f.*, over same track a second time); (archaic) repulse, defeat, check. [f. OF *fouler* full cloth, trample, (L *fullo* fuller)]

foil[3], n. Blunt-edged sword with button on point used in fencing. [etym. dub.; perh. f. prec. in sense *parry*; or f. obs. *foin* thrust (& =foil in 17th c.) f. OF *foine* f. L *fuscina* fish-spear]

foi·son (-zn), n. (archaic). Plenty. [OF, f. L *fusionem* (*fundere fus-* pour, -ION, -SON)]

foist, v.t. Introduce surreptitiously or unwarrantably *into* or *in* (adv.); palm (*off*) *on* or *upon*, father (composition) *upon*. [orig. of palming false die; prob. f. Du. dial. *vuisten* take in the hand (*vuist* fist)]

Fo·kker, n. Type of fighting aeroplane used by Germans. [A. H. G. *F.*, Dutch inventor]

fōld[1], n., & v.t. (Usu. *sheep-f.*) enclosure for sheep; (fig.) church, body of believers. (Vb) shut up (sheep &c.) in f.; place sheep in f. or ff. on (land) to manure it. [OE *fald*, cf. Du. *vaalt*; unconnected w. foll.]

fōld[2], v.t. & i., & n. Double (flexible thing) over upon itself (also *in, over, together*; *f. up*, make more compact by folding); bend portion of (thing) *back, down*; become, be able to be, folded (*-ing door*(*s*), in 2 parts, often themselves folding, hung on 2 jambs); wind, clasp, (arms &c.) *about, round*; lay together & interlace (arms), clasp (one's hands); swathe, envelop, (*f. it in paper*; *hills folded in mist*); embrace *in* arms or *to* breast. (N.) doubling of folded object; hollow between two thicknesses (*carried it in a f. of her dress*), hollow or nook in mountain &c.; coil of serpent, string, &c.; folding (*another f. gives 32mo*); line made by folding. [com.-Teut.; n. f. vb, OE *fealdan*, cf. G *falten*, also Gk (*di*)*plasios* double, & Gk *plekō*, L *plicare*, plait]

-fold, suf. (OE *feald*; cf. Du. *-voud*, G *-falt*) cogn. w. FOLD[2], Gk *-paltos, -plasios,* & *-plo-* in *haplos* single, & prob. L *-plex* (*simplex* &c.); added to cardinals to form adjj. w. sense *multiplied by* (orig. sense *folded in* —, *plaited in* — *strands*). Now largely superseded by wds f. L in *-ble, -ple,* (*treble, quadruple*), but retained in the advl use (*repaid tenfold*), & in adjj. when there is a plurality of things more or less different (*a twofold charm*).

fō·lder, n. In vbl senses; esp.: paper-folding instrument; folded circular &c.; (pl.) folding eyeglasses. [-ER[1]]

fōlia·ceous (-shus), a. Leaf-like; with organs like leaves; of leaves; laminated. [f. L *foliaceus* (*folium* leaf, -ACEOUS)]

fō·liage (-ĕj), n. Leaves, leafage, (lit., or as represented in art; *f. leaf*, excluding petals &c.; *f. plant*, cultivated for f., not for flowers). Hence (-)**foliag**ED[2] a. [f. F *feuillage* (*feuille* leaf f. L *folia* leaves, -AGE) corrected on L]

fō·liar, a. Of leaves. [f. L *folium* leaf, -AR[1]]

fō·liate[1] (-*a*t), a. Leaf-like; having leaves; having specified number of leaflets (*1, 5,* &c., *-f.*). [f. L *foliatus* (*folium* leaf, -ATE[2])]

fō·liāte[2], v.i. & t. Split (intr.) into laminae; decorate (arch, door-head) with foils; number leaves (not pages) of (volume) consecutively. So **foli**A·TION n. [f. L *folium* leaf, -ATE[3]]

fō·lio, n. (pl. *-os*). Leaf of paper, parchment, &c., numbered only on front; (Bookkeep.) two opposite pages of ledger &c. used concurrently, page of ledger &c. used for both sides of account; page-number of printed book; number of words (72 or 90) taken as unit in reckoning length of document; sheet of paper folded once (*in f.*, of books on such paper, volume made of such sheets, largest-sized volume, (also attrib., *a f. book, in six volumes f.*). [L, abl. of *folium* leaf (abl. f. use in reff., =*on leaf 50* &c.)]

fō·liole, n. Division of compound leaf, leaflet. [F, f. L *foliolum* dim. of *folium* leaf]

folk (fōk), n. (Archaic) a people, nation, race; (pl., the sing. being archaic or dial.) people in general, people of specified class, (now being ousted by *people*); *folk-*, of the people (chiefly in compounds imitated f. German, as *f.-custom, -song*; *f.-etymology*, perversion of word's form to make it significant; *f.-lore*, traditional beliefs &c., study of these). [OE *folc*, cf. G *volk*]

fo·llicle, n. Small sac or vesicle; cocoon. So **folli·cul**AR[1], **folliculated** [-ATE[2]], aa. [f. L *folliculus* (*follis* bellows, -CULE)]

fo·llow, v.t. & i., & n. Go or come after (moving thing or person; *f. the hounds*, hunt; *f. my leader*, game in which each player must do as leader does; *f.* one's *nose*, leave one's route to chance; *f. the plough*, be ploughman); go along (path); come after in order or time; accompany, serve; go after as admirer; result from, be the necessary consequence of, be involved in, (*trade follows the flag*); strive after, aim at; treat or take as guide or master, obey, espouse opinions or cause of; conform to (*f.* SUIT), act upon, take as rule; practise (profession &c.; *f. the sea*, be sailor); keep up with mentally, grasp the meaning of, (argument, speaker); go or come after person or thing (*f. in his steps*; *f. in the wake of*); come next in order, as *his arguments are as follows* (not *follow*); happen after something else, ensue; result, be deducible, (*it follows that he was not there*); *f. after* (prep. & adv.), =*f.* (in most senses, but with slightly formal effect); (Cricket, of side) *f. on*, go in again out of turn after getting less than opponents by certain number (n., *f.-o.*, doing this); *f. out*, pursue to the end; *f. through* (Golf), carry stroke through to fullest possible extent after striking ball (*f.-through* n., this action); *f. up*, pursue steadily, add another blow &c. to (previous blow &c.), (Footb. &c.) keep near (player with) ball to support; (n., Billiards) stroke causing player's ball to roll on after object-ball, motion so given; (n., at restaurants) supplementary portion of half the quantity. [OE *folgian*, cf. G *folgen* perh. cogn. w. FULL[1]]

fo·llower, n. In vbl senses; esp.: adherent, disciple; man courting maid-servant. [-ER[1]]

fo·llowing[1], n. In vbl senses; also, body of adherents, followers. [-ING[1]]

fo·llowing[2], a. In vbl senses; esp., now to be mentioned (also as pron. sing. or pl., *the f. are noteworthy*). [-ING[2]]

fo·lly, n. Being foolish, want of good sense, unwise conduct; foolish act, idea, or practice, ridiculous thing; costly structure (considered) useless (usu. with originator's name, —*'s F.*). [f. OF *folie* (*fol* mad, see FOOL[1]); last sense perh. starts f. F use of *folie* =favourite abode]

fome·nt, v.t. Bathe with warm or medicated lotions, apply warmth to; foster, stimulate, or instigate (sentiment, conduct, sedition, &c.), whence **fome·nt**ER[1] n. [f. F *fomenter* f. LL *fomentare* f. L *fomentum* (*fovēre* cherish, -MENT)]

fōmenta·tion, n. In vbl senses; esp., (application of) warm flannels &c. for fomenting purposes. [f. LL *fomentatio* (prec., -ATION)]

fond, a. Foolishly credulous or sanguine; over-affectionate, doting; tender, loving; *f. of*, full of love for, much inclined to. Hence **fo·nd**LY[2] adv., **fo·nd**NESS n. [p.p. of obs. *fon* become insipid]

fo·ndant, n. Kind of sweetmeat. [F (*fondre* melt f. L *fundere* pour, -ANT)]

fo·ndle, v.t. & i. Caress; toy amorously (*with, together*). [f. obs. *fond* vb (FOND), -LE(3)]

font, n. Receptacle for baptismal water; receptacle for holy water; oil-reservoir of lamp. [f. L *fons -tis* fountain in eccl. L sense]

fo·ntal, a. Primary, original, of the fountain-head; baptismal. [f. med. L *fontalis* (prec., -AL)]

fontane·l(le), n. Membranous space in infant's head at adjacent angles of parietal bones. [F (*-lle*), dim. of *fontaine* FOUNTAIN]

fōōd, n. Victuals, nourishment, provisions, (*be f. for worms*, dead; *be f. for fishes*, drowned; *f. for powder*, soldiers); edibles (*f. & drink*); particular kind of f.; nutriment of plants; material for the mind (*mental, intellectual, f.*; *f. for thought* or *meditation*); *f.-card* (entitling to rations under f.-control); *f.-controller*, minister regulating f. supplies in war-time; *f.-stuff*, thing used as f. Hence **foo·d**LESS a. [OE *fóda* f. Teut. *fad-, fôd-*, f. Aryan *pat-* whence Gk *pateomai* FEED]

fōōl[1], n., & v.i. & t. Silly person, simpleton, person whose conduct one disapproves of, (*be a f. to*, be nothing in comparison with; *play the f.*, blunder, trifle; *no f. like an old f.*, esp. of aged lover; *f.'s bolt is soon shot*, his stock of argument is soon exhausted; *man is f. or physician at thirty*, sensible man needs no doctor); jester, clown, in medieval great house (*play the f.*, indulge in buffoonery); dupe (*make a f. of*; *be a f. for one's pains*, take trouble to no end; *All Fools' day*, 1st April; *April f.*, person taken in or sent on f.'s errand on that day; *send, go, on f.'s errand*, fruitless one; *f.'s* MATE[1]; *f.'s paradise*, illusory happiness); *f.'s-cap, foolscap*, cap with bells worn by medieval jester, dunce's conical paper cap, watermark of some 17th-c. paper, long folio writing or printing paper 15–17 ×12–13½ in.; hence **foo·l**ERY(4, 5), **foolo·**CRACY, nn., **foo·l**ISH[1] a., **foo·lish**LY[2] adv., **foo·lish**NESS n., **foo·l**PROOF[2] a. (of rules &c. so plain as to defy misinterpretation). (Vb) play the f., idle, trifle, (also *about* &, U.S., *around*); cheat (person) *out of* money &c. or *into doing*, get (money &c.) by cajolery *out* of person; throw (time, money) *away* foolishly; make a f. of, dupe, play tricks on. [f. OF *fol* f. L *follis* bellows in pop. LL sense *windbag, empty-headed person*]

fōōl[2], n. Creamy liquid of fruit stewed, crushed, & mixed with milk, cream, &c. (esp. *gooseberry f.*). [prob. f. prec.]

foo·lhardy, a. Foolishly venturesome, delighting in needless risks. Hence **foo·lhardi**NESS n. [f. OF *fol hardi* (FOOL[1], HARDY)]

fōōt, n. (pl. *feet*). Termination of leg beginning at ankle (FIND[1] one's *feet*; *have ff. of clay*, be liable to overthrow, see *Dan.* ii. 33); step, pace, tread, (*swift of f.*; *has a light f.*); infantry (*the 4th f.* or *regiment of f.*; *f.-soldier*; *a captain of f.*; *f. & horse*); lower end of bed, grave, couch, &c. (opp. *head*), part of stocking &c. covering f.; metrical unit with varying number of syllables one of which is accented; lineal measure of 12 in. (*10 feet long*; *a ten-f. pole*; *six f.* or *feet three*; see also SQUARE a., CUBIC); lower usu. projecting part, base; (Zool.) kinds of locomotive or adhesive organ in invertebrates; (Bot.) part by which petal is attached, root of hair; lowest part, bottom, of hill, ladder, wall, list, page, class, &c.; dregs, oil refuse, coarse sugar, (pl. *foots*). Phrr.: *have one f. in grave*, be near death; (*with* one's) *feet foremost*, being carried to burial; *find, know, length of* one's *f.*, learn his weaknesses, be able to manage him; *measure* another's *f. by* one's *own last*, judge others by oneself; *set, put, have*, one's *f. on the neck of*, utterly subdue, hold in subjection; *on* one's *feet*, standing, in health, with a livelihood; *carry* one *off his feet*, make him enthusiastic, greatly excite; FALL[1] *on* one's *feet*; *keep* one's *feet*, not fall; *put* one's *f. down*, take up firm position (fig.); *put* one's *f. in it*, blunder; BEST[1] *f.*; *f.'s pace*, walk; CHANGE[1] *f.* or *feet*; *at* one's *feet*, as his disciple, subject, or suppliant; *have* BALL[1] *at* one's *feet*; *with foal at f.*, of mare that has foaled; *on f.*, walking, not riding &c., also in motion (*set agitation, movement*, &c., *on f.*, start it), busy, projected, proceeding; *tread under f.*, oppress; *wet* &c. *under f.*, on the ground. *F.-&-mouth* (*disease*), kind of fever esp. in horned cartle; *football*, large round or elliptical inflated ball, game played with it, *footballer*, player at this; *f-.bath*, washing of feet, small bath used for this; *footboard*, footman's platform at carriage-back, board for getting in or out of carriage by, sloped board for driver's feet; *footboy*, page, boy servant in livery; *f.-bridge, -path, -road, -way*, &c., for f.-passengers only; *f.-drill, -pump*, &c., worked by or with help of f.; *footfall*, sound of footstep; *f.-gear*, boots, socks, &c.; *footguards*, Grenadier, Coldstream, Scots, Irish, Welch, Guards; *f.-hill*, lying at base of mountain; *foothold*, support for feet, surface for standing on; *footlights*, screened lights in front of stage (GET[1] *across the f.-l.*); *footman*, infantryman, liveried servant for carriage, door, & table, trivet to hang on grate bars; *f.-mark*, footprint; *f.-muff*, for keeping feet warm; *f.-note*, inserted at f. of page; *f.-pace*, walking pace, dais; *footpad*, unmounted highwayman; *f.-page*, boy servant; *f.-pan*, for washing feet; *f.-passenger*, one who walks, not rides or drives; *f.-path* (for f.-passengers); *f.-plate*, driver's and fireman's platform in locomotive; *f.-pound*, quantity of energy that will raise 1 lb. to height of 1 ft; *footprint*, impression left by f.; *f.-race*, running-match between persons; *f.-rot*, disease of f. in sheep & cattle; *f.-rule*, rigid measure 1 ft long; *f.-slogger* (slang), walker, infantryman, & so *f.-slogging* n. & a.; *footsore*, having sore feet, esp. with walking; *footstalk*, (Bot.) stalk of leaf or peduncle of flower, (Zool.) attachment of barnacle &c.; *footstep*, tread, footprint, (*follow in* one's *footsteps*, do as he did); *f.-stone*, foundation stone, stone at foot of grave; *footstool*, for resting feet on; *footwarmer*, thing to warm feet, esp. flat hot-water tin used in railway carriages; *f.-wear*, = *f.-gear*. Hence (-)**foot**ED[2], **foo·t**LESS, aa. [Aryan; OE *fōt*, cf. G *fuss*, Skr. *pad*, Gk *pous podos*, L *pes pedis*],

foot[2], v.i. & t. *F. it*, dance, (rare) pace, go; set f. on, traverse on f., (rare); put new f. to (stocking); add up or *up* (account); pay (bill); (of bill, items, &c.) mount *up to*. [f. prec.]

foo·ter, n. (slang). The game football. [-ER[1]]

foo·ting, n. Placing of feet, foothold; surface for standing on, secure position, (lit. & fig.); conditions, relations, position, status, in which person is towards others, degree of intimacy &c.; entrance on new position, admittance to trade, society, &c., (only in *pay for* or *pay* one's *f.*, i.e. a customary fee for it); projecting course at foot of wall &c.; (reckoning of) sum total of column of figures &c. [FOOT[2] + -ING[1]]

foo·tle, v.i., & n. (slang). Trifle, play the fool; hence **foo·tl**ING[2] a. (N.) twaddle, folly. [?]

foo·zle, v.t., & n. (slang, esp. golf). Do clumsily, bungle, make a mess of; (n.) clumsy failure. [cf. G dial. *fuseln* work badly or slowly]

fop, n. Dandy, exquisite, vain man. Hence **fo·p**LING[1](2), **fo·pp**ERY(4, 5), nn., **fo·pp**ISH[1] a., **fo·ppish**LY[2] adv., **fo·ppish**NESS n. [?]

for (for, fŏr, fer, *according to position or emphasis required*), prep. & conj. 1. Prep.: Representing, in place of, in exchange against, as price or penalty of, in requital of, (*sits f., member f., Liverpool*; *once f. all*, instead of many repetitions, finally; *substituted f.*; *agent f.*; *got it f. 2d.*; *thrashed f. his pains*; *do you take me f. a fool?*); in defence or support or favour of, on side of, (*take my word f. it*, be assured; *hurrah f. person* or *thing*; *am f. tariff-reform*); with a view to, in order to be, conducive(ly) to, (*go f. a walk*; *went f. a soldier*; *is, did it, f. her good*; *f. sale*, to be sold); to get, win, or save (*send, go, f. a cab*; *would not do it f. the world*; *not paid f.*; *play f. penny points*; *he has forgotten it, f. a guinea!*; *was tried f. his life*; *cannot do it f. the life of me*; *run f.* IT); to reach, arrive at, be received by, or belong to (*left, sailed, f. India*; *made f. shelter*; *go f.* slang, attack; *getting on f. two o'clock*; *bought gowns f. the maids*; *won a name f. himself*); (after vbs, adjj., nn., & interjections, of emotion, faculty, or fitness; after adjj. & advv. with *too, enough*; after expressions implying fitness &c.) as regards, in the direction of, (*don't care f. games*; *a longing f. praise*; *fit f. nothing*; *ready f. dinner*; *oh f. wings!*; *now f. it!*; *too beautiful f. words*; *good enough f. me*; *time f.*

school; *is not long f. this world*, will soon die; *nothing f. it but to submit*, submission the only course open; *is the man f. the job*; *it is f. you to make the move*; *the motive f. retreating*); with the result, at the cost, to the amount, of (*all out f. 44*; *150 f. 6 wickets*; *drew on him f. £100*); to affect, as affecting, beneficially or the reverse (*they live f. each other*; *can shift f. myself*; *things look bad f. you*; *it is bad f. him to smoke*; & hence *f.* with noun or pron. & infin. as neutral noun-phrase = Latin acc. & inf., *it is wicked f. him to smoke*, *it is usual f. hats to be worn* = that hats should be worn); in the character of, as, as being, (*hold it f. certain*; *mistaken f. him*; *be hanged f. a pirate*; *take f. granted*; *I f. one do not believe it*; *did it f. the second time*; *f.* GOOD); by reason, under influence, because, on account, of (*did it f. pure wantonness*; *avoid it f. fear of accidents*; *I tremble f. him*; *notorious f. parsimony*; *do it f. my sake*; *fie f. shame!*; *alas f. him!*); in spite of (*f. all that*, *f. all you say*, *f. all he seems to dislike me, I still like him*); on account of the hindrance of (*were it not, but, except, f. one thing I might be happy*); corresponding to, in contrast with, (*f. one enemy he has a hundred friends*; *bulk f. bulk*, taking equal bulk of each; *word f. word*, literally, verbatim); so far as concerns, regarding, (*f. the rest*; *f. my part*; *f. all, aught, I know*; *hard up f. money*; *wants f. nothing*); considering, making the allowance required by, the usual nature of (*a humane man f. an executioner*; *very bright f. a winter day*); during, over, to the extent of, (*has been so f. months*; *walk f. two miles*; *made comfortable f. life*, *f. the present*; *left him alone f. once*); *f. all the world*, exactly (*looked f. a t. w. like a porpoise*); *be for it* (army slang), be destined for punishment. 2. Conj. (introducing new sentence or series of sentences containing proof of or reason for believing what has been previously stated) seeing that, since, in order to be convinced of this observe or remember that . . . [prob. shortened f. FORE[2]]

for-, pref. formerly very common, but remaining only in some dozen common words. Meanings: (1) away, off, apart, (*forby, forget, forgive*); (2) prohibition (*forbid, forfend*); (3) abstention, neglect, (*forbear, forgo, forsake, forswear*); (4) bad effect (*fordo*); (5) excess, intensity, (*forlorn, forpine, forworn*). [OE *for-*, *fær-*, cf. G *ver-*, cogn. w. Gk *peri, pro, para*, & L *per, pro*]

fŏ·rage (-ĭj), n., & v.t. & i. Food for horses & cattle, esp. for horses in army; foraging (*on the f.* &c.); *f.-cap*, infantry undress cap. (Vb) collect f. from, ravage; search for f. or (fig.) *for* anything, rummage; supply with f.; get by foraging; so **fo·rager** [-IER] n. [f. OF *fourrage(r)* (*feurre* f. Rom. **fodro* f. Teut. see FODDER]

forā·men, n. (pl. *-mĭna*). Orifice, hole, passage, (esp. in Anat., Zool., Bot.). Hence **forā·min**ATE[2], **-ated**, aa. [L (*forare* bore, -MEN)]

forasmu·ch as, conj. Seeing that, since. [= *for as much as*]

fŏ·ray, n., & v.i. (Go on, make) incursion, raid, inroad. [f. Rom. **fodro* (FORAGE)]

for·bear[1] (-bār; *also* -bār·), n. (usu. pl.). Ancestor(s). [FORE[2] + obs. *beer* (BE, -ER[1])]

forbear·[2] (-bār), v.t. & i. (-bore, -borne). Abstain or refrain from or *from*; not use or mention; be patient. Hence **forbear·**ANCE n., **forbear·ing**LY[2] adv. [FOR-(3), BEAR[2]]

forbi·d, v.t. (*-bad* or *-băde*; *-bidden*). Command (person &c.) not *to* do, (person &c.) not to go to (place), not allow (person &c. something; person or thing to exist or happen), (*f. him to go, him the court, him wine*; *f. gladiators, bullfights*; *was forbidden wine*); (of circumstances, hindrance, &c.) exclude, prevent, make undesirable, (*God f.!*, may it not happen!); *forbidden* or *prohibited* DEGREES; *forbidden fruit*, thing desired because not allowed. [OE *forbéodan* see FOR-(2), BID]

forbi·dding, a. Repellent, of uninviting appearance. Hence **forbi·dding**LY[2] adv., **forbi·dding**NESS n. [-ING[2]]

forbȳ(e)·, prep. & adv. (Sc. & archaic). Besides; not to mention; in addition. [FOR-(1) + BY; cf. G *vorbei*]

force[1], n. Strength, power, impetus, violence, intense effort; military strength; body of armed men, army, (pl.) troops; body of police (*the f.*, the police); strength exerted on an object, coercion, (*by f.*, by compulsion); mental or moral strength; influence, controlling power, efficacy, power to convince, vividness of effect, (*the f. of circumstances brought it about*; *there is f. in what you say*; *described with much f.*); (loose use) desirability, good sense, (*can't see the f. of doing what one dislikes*); binding power, validity, (*law remains in, comes into f.*; *put in f.*, enforce); real import, precise meaning; (Physics) measurable and determinable influence inclining body to motion, intensity of this, (formerly) kinetic energy (CONSERVATION *of f.* or *energy*), (formerly) cause of any class of physical phenomena, e.g. of heat or motion, conceived as inherent in matter, (fig.) agency likened to these (*considers himself a f. in the world*); *by f. of*, by means of; (Mil.) *in f.*, in large numbers; *in great f.*, vigorous, fit, lively; *f.-pump*, that forces water beyond range of atmospheric pressure. Hence **for·ce**LESS a. [F, f. pop. L **fortia* (L *fortis* strong)]

force[2], v.t. Use violence to, ravish; constrain, compel, (*f. one's hand*, compel him to act prematurely or adopt policy unwillingly), put strained sense upon (words), (Whist) compel (player) to trump or reveal his strength, compel player to play (certain card); compel (person) *to* do, *into* doing, or *into* specified action; strain to the utmost, urge, (*f. the pace* or *running,* adopt high speed in race to tire adversary out quickly; so *f. the bidding* at auction; *f.* one's *voice,* strain to get notes beyond usual compass; *forced march,* requiring special effort; *forced* DRAUGHT[1]; *f. the game,* run risks to score quickly; *f. an analogy, simile,* &c., apply it too closely, run it to death); overpower, capture, make way through, break open, (stronghold, defences, pass, lock, door) by f.; drive, propel; impose, press, (thing) *upon* person (*f. a card,* in conjuring, make one choose a particular card unconsciously); effect, produce, by effort (*f. a smile,* make oneself smile; *f.* one's *way, a passage*); take by f., extort, wring, (*f. it out of his hands*; *forced loan*; *f. tears from his eyes, the facts out of him*); artificially hasten the maturity of (plant, scholar). Hence **for·cĕd**LY[2] adv. [f. F *forcer* (prec.)]

force[3], n. (northern). Waterfall. [f. ON *fors*]

for·ceful, a. (Archaic or literary or affected for) forcible. Hence **for·cefu**lLY[2] adv., **for·ceful**NESS n. [-FUL]

force majeure (mahzher·), n. Irresistible compulsion, coercion diplomatically recognized as irresistible; war, strike, act of God, &c., excusing fulfilment of contract. [F]

for·ce-meat, n. Meat chopped, spiced, & seasoned for stuffing. [f. obs. *force* corruption of FARCE[2]]

for·ceps, n. sing. & pl. Surgical pincers; (Anat., Entom., Zool.) organ resembling f., whence **for·cip**ATE[2] a. [L (genit. *-ipis*)]

for·cible, a. Done by, involving, force; telling, vivid, convincing, (of acts, words, style, artist, &c.); *f.-feeble,* disguising feebleness under show of force. Hence **for·cible**NESS n., **for·cib**LY[2] adv. [OF (FORCE[1], -IBLE)]

for·cite, n. An explosive. [FORCE[1], -ITE[1] (2)]

ford[1], n., & v.t. & i. Shallow place where river &c. may be crossed by wading; (vb) cross (water), cross water, by wading. Hence **for·d**ABLE, **for·d**LESS, aa. [cf. G *furt*; cogn. w. FARE, also w. L *portus* PORT[1]]

Ford[2], n. (Used for) motor-car made by Henry F.

fordo· (-ōō), v.t. (archaic; *-did, -done* pr. dŭn). Kill, destroy, spoil; (p.p.) exhausted, tired out. [OE *fordón* see FOR-(4), DO[1]]

fore[1], a. & n. Situated in front (opp. HIND, BACK, AFT). (N.) f. part, bow of ship; (Naut.) *at the f.,* on the f.-royal mast-head; *to the f.,* on the spot, ready to hand, available, alive, (recently) conspicuous (*come to the f.,* take leading part). [developed f. compounds w. FORE-]

fore[2], adv. & prep. (Adv.) in front (still in *f. & aft,* at bow & stern, all over ship, backwards & forwards or lengthwise in ship; *f.-&-aft rigged,* having f.-&-aft sails, i.e. sails set lengthwise, not to yards, as chief sails; *f.-&-aft cap,* with peak at each end); (prep.) in presence of (in adjurations) as *f. George* = by George. [com.-Teut.; OE *fore,* cf. G *vor,* cogn. w. L *pro, prae, per,* Gk *pro, para, peri*; prep. often mistakenly *'fore* as if short for *before*]

fore[3], int. (golf), warning people in front of stroke. [prob. for BEFORE]

fore-, pref. freely used with vbs, their participial adjectives, vbl nouns, & nouns of action; also with other nouns. Meanings with vbs &c.: (1) in front (*forerunner*); (2) beforehand, in advance, (*foreordain*). Meanings with nouns other than verbal or of action: (3) in front, front-, (*forequarter*); (4) front part of (*forearm*); (5) of, near, or towards stem of ship or connected w. foremast (*forecastle*); (6) anticipatory, precedent, (*foreknowledge*). [see FORE[2]]

fore·arm[1], n. Arm from elbow to wrist or finger-tips; corresponding part in foreleg or wing. [FORE-(4)]

forear·m[2], v.t. Arm beforehand. [FORE-(2)]

forebo·de (fer-), v.t. Predict (rare); betoken, portend; have presentiment of (usu. evil) or *that.* Hence **forebo·ding**LY[2] adv. [FORE-(2)]

forebo·ding, n. Prediction (rare), presage or omen, presentiment, (esp. of evil). [-ING[1]]

fore·-ca·bin, n. Cabin in fore part of ship, usu. for second-class passengers. [FORE-(5)]

foreca·st[1], v.t. (*forecast* or *-ed,* see in etym.). Estimate, conjecture, beforehand. [FORE-(2) + CAST[1]; *forecasted* depends on mistaken assumption that the vb is derived f. foll.]

fore·cast[2], n. Foresight, prudence, (rare); conjectural estimate of something future, esp. of coming weather. [f. prec.]

forecastle (fō·ksl), **fō·c's'le,** n. (Hist.) short raised deck at bow, (in war-ship, later but now obs.) part of upper deck forward of aftermost fore-shroud; (in merchant-ship) forward part under deck where sailors live. [FORE-(5)]

foreclo·se (-z), v.t. & i. Bar, preclude, prevent, shut out from enjoyment *of*; (Mortgage Law) bar (person entitled to redeem) upon nonpayment of money due, bar (right of redemption), take away power of redeeming (mortgage), whence **foreclo·**SURE n.; settle (arguable point

For words in *fore-* not given see FORE-.

&c.) by anticipation. [f. F *forclore* (OF *for* out f. L *foris*, CLOSE[3])]
fore·court, n. Enclosed space before building, outer court. [FORE-(3)]
fore·father, n. (Pl.) the persons, esp. in earlier generations, from whom one's father or mother is descended, (loosely) the past generations of a family or race; (sing., rare) man from whom one is descended. [FORE-(6)]
fore·finger, n. Finger next thumb (also called *first* or *index finger*). [FORE-(3)]
fore·foot, n. One of beast's front feet; (Naut.) foremost piece of keel, course in front of this (*crossing our f.*). [FORE-(3, 5)]
fore·front, n. Very front, foremost part, van, (*in the f. of the battle*). [FORE-(3)]
foregather. See FORGATHER.
fore·gift, n. (law). Premium for lease. [FORE-(6)]
forego·[1], v.t. & i. (*-went, -gone* pr. -gawn). Precede in place or time (*foregoing*, previously mentioned); *foregone conclusion*, decision or opinion come to in advance of the evidence or necessary facts, prejudice, result that can be or could have been foreseen. [FORE-(2)]
forego[2]. See FORGO.
forego·er, n. Predecessor. [FORE-(1)]
fore·ground, n. Part of view, esp. in picture, nearest observer; most conspicuous position. [FORE-(3)]
fore·hand, n. & a. Part of horse before rider; (adj., of stroke at tennis &c.) not backhanded. [FORE-(3)]
forehead (fŏ·rĕd), n. Part of face above eyebrows & between temples. [OE *forhéafod* see FORE-(4), HEAD[1]]
fŏ·reign (-rĭn), a. Belonging to, proceeding from, other persons or things; alien *from* or *to*, irrelevant, dissimilar, or inappropriate, *to*; introduced from outside (esp. *f. body* or *substance* in the tissues &c.); situated outside, coming from another district, parish, society, &c.; outside the country, not in one's own land; of, in, characteristic of, coming from, dealing with, some country not in the United Kingdom or English-speaking colonies (*f., colonial, & home trade*; *f. parts*, countries; *F. Office*, department for f. affairs or its building; *f. letter-paper*, thin to reduce postage). Hence **fo·reign**ISM(2, 4) n., **fo·reign**IZE(3) v.t. & i. [f. OF *forain* (L *foris* outside, -AN)]
fo·reigner, n. Person born in foreign country or speaking foreign language; foreign ship, imported animal or article. [-ER[1]]
foreju·dge, v.t. Judge or determine before hearing the evidence. [FORE-(2)]
foreknow (fŏrnō·), v.t. (-knew, -known). Know beforehand, have prescience of. So **fore**KNOW·LEDGE n. [FORE-(2)]
fŏ·rel, fo·rrel, n. Vellum-like parchment for covering account-books. [OF *forrel* dim. of *forre* sheath]
fore·land (-*a*nd), n. Cape, promontory; strip of land in front of something. [FORE-(3)]
fore·leg, n. Beast's front leg. [FORE-(3)]
fore·lock[1], n. Lock of hair growing just above forehead (*take time, occasion*, &c., *by the f.*, not let chance slip). [FORE-(3)]
fore·lock[2], n., & v.t. Wedge put through hole in bolt to keep it in place; (vb) secure thus. [FORE-(3), LOCK[2]]
fore·man, n. President & spokesman of jury; principal workman superintending others (*working f.*, one who both works & supervises). [FORE-(3)]
fore·mast (-m*a*-), n. Forward lower mast of ship (*f. man, seaman, hand*, sailor below rank of petty officer). [FORE-(5)]
fore·most (-ōst, -*o*st), a. & adv. superl. Most advanced in position, front, (*head, end*, &c., *f.*, with head &c. in front); most notable, best, chief; (adv.) before anything else in position, in the first place, (usu. *first & f.*). [OE *formest* double superl. with *-m-* (cf. L *primus*) & -EST f. st. of FORE[2], assimilated to *most*]
fore·noon, n. The day till noon, morning. [FORE[2] + NOON]
forĕ·nsic, a. Of, used in, courts of law (*f. medicine*, medical jurisprudence). Hence **fore·ns**ICALLY adv. [f. L *forensis* (FORUM) + -IC]
foreordai·n, v.t. Predestinate, appoint beforehand. So **fore**ORDINA·TION n. [FORE-(2)]
fore·peak, n. (naut.). End of forehold in angle of bows. [FORE-(5)]
fore·plane, n. First plane used after saw or axe. [FORE-(6)]
fore-rea·ch, v.i. & t. Shoot ahead; gain upon, pass. [FORE-(1)]
fore-ru·n, v.t. (-nn-; -ran, -run). Be precursor of, foreshadow. Hence **foreru·n**NER[1] (1, 2) n. [FORE-(1)]
fore·sail (-sl, -sāl), n. Principal sail on foremast (lowest square sail, or fore-&-aft bent on mast, or triangular before mast). [FORE-(5)]
foresee·, v.t. (-saw, -seen). See beforehand, have prescience of, (noun, or *that*); exercise foresight (obs. exc. in **foresee·**ING[2] a., **foresee·ing**LY[2] adv.). [FORE-(2)]
foreshă·dow, v.t. Prefigure, serve as type or presage of. [FORE-(2)]
fore·-sheets, n. pl. Inner part of bows of boat with gratings for bowman. [FORE-(5)]
fore·shore, n. Part of shore between high & low water marks, or between water & land cultivated or built on. [FORE-(4)]
foreshor·ten, v.t. Show, portray, (object) with the apparent shortening due to visual perspective. [FORE-(1)]
foreshow·, v.t. (p.p. *-shown*). Foretell;

foreshadow, portend, prefigure. [OE *foresceāwian* see FORE-(1), SHOW]
fore·sight, n. Foreseeing, prevision; care for the future; front sight of gun. [FORE-(2, 3)]
fore·skin, n. Prepuce. [FORE-(3)]
fŏ·rest, n., & v.t. Large tract covered with trees & undergrowth sometimes mixed with pasture, trees growing in it (lit., & fig. as *a f. of masts*); (with proper name prefixed) district formerly f. but now cultivated, as *Sherwood F.*; (Law) unenclosed woodland district kept for hunting usu. owned by sovereign; *f.-tree*, of large growth fitted for f.; (vb) plant with trees, convert into f. [OF, f. med. L *forestis* (*silva* wood) outside (walls of park) f. L *foris* outside]
foresta·ll (-awl), v.t. (Hist.) buy up (goods) in order to profit by enhanced price; be beforehand with in action, anticipate and so baffle; deal with before the regular time, anticipate. [f. OE *foresteall* n. ambush, see FORE-(6), STALL]
fore·stay, n. Stay from foremast-head to ship's stem; sail hoisted on this. [FORE-(5)]
fŏ·rester, n. Officer in charge of forest, or of growing timber; dweller in forest; bird or beast of forest, e.g. New-Forest pony; kinds of moth. [f. OF *forestier* (FOREST, -IER)]
fŏ·restry, n. Wooded country, forests; science & art of managing forests. [f. OF *foresterie* (FOREST, -ERY)]
fore·tāste[1], n. Partial enjoyment or suffering (*of*) in advance, anticipation. [FORE-(2)]
foretā·ste[2], v.t. Taste beforehand, anticipate enjoyment &c. of. [FORE-(2)]
forete·ll, v.t. (-tōld). Predict, prophesy; presage, be precursor of. [FORE-(2)]
fore·thought, n. Previous contriving, deliberate intention; provident care. [FORE-(6)]
fore·time, n. The past, early days, old times. [FORE-(6)]
fore·token[1], n. Sign of something to come, prognostic. [FORE-(6)]
foreto·ken[2], v.t. Portend, point to. [FORE-(2)]
fore·top, n. TOP of foremast; *fore-top-gallant mast*, mast above *fore-topmast*, i.e. mast above foremast; *fore-topgallant-sail*, sail above *fore-topsail*, i.e. sail above fore-sail. [FORE-(5)]
fore·type, n. Type of coming thing. [FORE-(2)]
forewar·n (-orn), v.t. Warn beforehand (esp. in *forewarned is forearmed*). [FORE-(2)]
fore·woman, n. President & spokeswoman of jury of matrons; chief work-woman supervising others. [FORE-(3)]
fore·word (-erd), n. Preface; introductory remarks, esp. by another than the author of the book &c. [from 1842; mod. formation of the anti-Latinists, cf. G *vorwort*; FORE-(3)]
fore·yard, n. Lowest yard on FOREMAST.
for·fars, n. Coarse linen cloth of unbleached flax. [*Forfar* in Scotland]
for·feit (-fĭt), n. & a., & v.t. (Thing) lost owing to crime or fault (*his life was the f.* or *was f., his f. life*); penalty for breach of contract or neglect, fine; trivial fine for breach of rules in clubs &c. or in games (*play ff.*), article surrendered by player in game of ff. to be redeemed by performing ludicrous task; forfeiture. (Vb) lose right to, be deprived of, have to pay, as penalty of crime, neglect, &c., or as necessary consequence of something; hence **for·feit**ABLE a., **for·feit**URE n. [f. OF *forfait* p.p. of *forfaire* f. med. L *foris facere* transgress (L *foris* outside, *facere* do)]
forfe·nd, v.t. Avert, keep off, (usu. in *God f.!*). [FOR-(2)]
for·ficate, a. (zool.). Scissor-shaped. [f. L *forfex -icis* scissors + -ATE[2]]
forgā·ther, v.i. Assemble, meet together, associate, converse. [FOR-(5)]
forgave. See FORGIVE.
forge[1], n. Smithy; blacksmith's hearth or fireplace with bellows; furnace or hearth for melting or refining metal, workshop containing it. [OF, f. L *fabrica* FABRIC]
forge[2], v.t. & i. Shape by heating in fire and hammering; fabricate, invent, (tale, lie), make in fraudulent imitation, esp. write (document, signature) in order to pass off as written by another, whence **for·g**ER[1] n. Hence **for·ge**ABLE a. [f. OF *forgier* f. L *fabricare* FABRICATE]
forge[3], v.i. Make way, advance, gradually or with difficulty, esp. *f. ahead*, take lead in race, get start. [?]
for·gery, n. Forging, counterfeiting, or falsifying, of document; spurious thing esp. document or signature. [FORGE[2], -ERY]
forge·t (-g-), v.t. & i. (*-got, -gotten* & poet. *-got*; -tt-). Lose remembrance of or *about* (noun, *that, how to*, or abs.); neglect (usu. *to* do), inadvertently omit to bring or mention or attend to; put out of mind, cease to think of, (esp. *forgive & f.*); disregard, slight; *f. oneself*, neglect one's own interests, act unbecomingly or unworthily, lose consciousness; *f.-me-not*, kinds of myosotis, esp. one with small yellow-eyed blue flowers (*f.-m.-n. blue* as name of colour). Hence **forge·tful** a. (*of*), **forge·tful**LY[2] adv., **forge·tful**NESS n., **forge·tt**ABLE a. [OE *forgietan* cf. G *vergessen* see FOR-(1), GET]
forgi·ve, v.t. (-gave, -given). Remit, let off, (debt, person debt); pardon (offence, offender, offender offence, or abs.). Hence **forgi·**VABLE a., **forgi·veness** [*forgiven* + -NESS] n., **forgi·**VING[2] a., **forgi·ving**LY[2] adv., **forgi·ving**NESS n. [OE *forgiefan* see FOR-(1), GIVE]

forgo·, v.t. (-went, -gone). Abstain from, go without, let go, omit to take or use, relinquish. [OE *forgán* see FOR-(3), GO]

fork, n., & v.i. & t. Pronged agricultural implement for digging, lifting, carrying, or throwing; two, three, or four, -pronged instrument used in eating at table or cooking; (also *tuning-f.*) steel instrument giving when struck a fixed musical note; stake with forked end used as prop for vines &c.; forking, bifurcation, e.g. that of human legs, of diverging roads, or of branches; flash of forked lightning; hence **for·kY**[2] a. (poet.). (Vb) Form f., have or develop branches; lift, carry, dig, or throw with f.; (slang) *f. out* or *over*, hand over, pay. [OE *forca* f. L *furca*]

forked, a. With fork or fork-like end, branching, divergent, cleft, (*three-f.* &c., with three &c. prongs); two-legged. [-ED[2]]

forlor·n, a. Desperate, hopeless, (cf. foll.); abandoned, forsaken, (poet.) deprived *of*, in pitiful condition, of wretched appearance. [p.p. of obs. *forlese*, OE *forléosan* see FOR-(1), LOSE]

forlor·n hope, n. Storming-party; desperate enterprise. [f. Du. *verloren hoop* lost troop (*hoop* = HEAP)]

form[1], n. Shape, arrangement of parts, visible aspect (esp. apart from colour), shape of body (*face & f.*); person or animal as visible or tangible (*saw a f.*, *the f. of —, before me*); (Philos.) that which makes anything (*matter*) a determinate species (Scholastic), conditions of thing's existence by knowing which we can produce it (Baconian), formative principle holding together the elements of thing (Kantian); mode in which thing exists or manifests itself (*in, under, take, the f. of*), species, kind, variety; (Gram.) one of the shapes taken by a word in spelling, pronunciation, or inflexion, external characteristics of words apart from meaning; class in some (esp. the Public) schools (usu. numbered from *sixth* down to *first*); arrangement & style in literary or musical composition; customary method (*in due f.*; *that is common f.*, is of no special significance), set order of words, formula, regularly drawn document, document with blanks to be filled up; formality, mere piece of ceremony; behaviour according to rule or custom (*good, bad, f.*, satisfying or offending current ideals); condition of health & training (*in, out of, f.*, fit or not for racing &c., of horses or athletes; *lose* one's *f.*), good spirits (*was in great f.*); long seat without back, bench; (Print.; also *forme*) body of type secured in chase for printing at one impression; hare's lair. [f. OF *forme* f. L *forma*]

form[2], v.t. & i. Fashion, mould, (*into* certain shape; *after, by, from, upon*, pattern; or abs.); assume shape, become solid; mould by discipline, train, instruct, (person, or faculty &c.); embody, organize, *into* a company &c.; frame, make, produce; articulate (word); conceive (idea, judgement); develop (habit); contract (alliance); be material of, make up, make *one* or *part of*; (Gram.) construct (new word) by derivation, inflexion, &c.; (Mil. &c.) draw up (t. & i.; often *up*) in order, assume specified formation (*f.* FOURS, *line, column*). [f. OF *fourmer* f. L *formare* (prec.)]

form-, comb. form of FORMIC or FORMYL, as *form*ALDEHYDE, a disinfectant & antiseptic, *formal*IN a solution of this.

-form, suf. (in actual use *-iform*, see -I-) f. F *-forme* f. L *-formis* (FORM[1]) giving adjj. (1) w. sense *having the form of* (*cruciform, cuneiform*), (2) referring to number of forms (*uniform, multiform, diversiform*). *Chloroform* does not contain this suf.

for·mal, a. (Metaphys.) of the essence of a thing (*f.* CAUSE[1]), essential not material; of the outward form, shape, appearance, arrangement, or external qualities, (Log.) concerned with the form, not the matter, of reasoning; valid in virtue of its form, explicit and definite, not merely tacit; ceremonial, required by convention (*a f. call*), perfunctory, having the form without the spirit; observant of forms, precise, prim, excessively regular or symmetrical, stiff, methodical, whence **for·mal**ISM(2), **for·mal**IST(2), nn., **formali·st**IC a. Hence **for·mal**LY[2] adv. [f. L *formalis* (FORM[1], -AL)]

formă·lity, n. Conformity to rules, propriety; ceremony, elaborate procedure; formal or ceremonial act, requirement of etiquette or custom; being formal, precision of manners, stiffness of design. [f. L *formalitas* (prec., -TY)]

for·malize, v.t. Give definite shape or legal formality to; make ceremonious, precise, or rigid, imbue with formalism. Hence **formaliz**A·TION n. [-IZE]

for·mat (-ah), n. Shape & size of book. [F]

forma·tion, n. Forming, being formed; thing formed; arrangement of parts, structure, (Mil.) disposition of troops; (Geol.) assemblage of rocks or series of strata having some common characteristic. [f. L *formatio* (FORM[2], -ATION)]

for·mative (-*a*-), a. & n. Serving to fashion, of formation; (Gram., of flexional & derivative suffixes and prefixes) used in forming words, (n.) f. element. [OF (*-if, -ive*) see FORM[2], -ATIVE]

forme, n. (print.). See FORM[1].

for·mer, a. & pron. Of the past or an earlier period (*in f. times*; *more like her f. self*; *our f. haunts*), whence **for·mer**LY[2] adv.; *the f.* (with noun, or oftener as pron. with possessive *the f.'s*), the first or first mentioned of two (opp. LATTER). [back-formation f. *formest* FOREMOST; from 12th c.]

for·mic, a. (chem.). *F. acid*, colourless irritant volatile acid contained in fluid emitted by ants. Hence **for·m**ATE[1](3), **for·m**ENE, **for·m**YL, nn. [for *formicic* f. L *formica* ant + -IC]

for·midable, a. To be dreaded; likely to be hard to overcome, resist, or deal with. Hence **for·midable**NESS n., **for·midab**LY[2] adv. [F, f. L *formidabilis* (*formidare* fear, -ABLE)]

for·mless, a. Shapeless, without determinate or regular form. Hence **for·mless**LY[2] adv., **for·mless**NESS n. [-LESS]

for·mūla, n. (pl. *-ae, -as*). Set form of words, definition, enunciation of principle, statement prescribed for use on some occasion; rule unintelligently followed, conventional usage or belief, whence **for·mul**ISM(3), **for·mul**IST(2), nn., **formuli·st**IC a.; recipe; principle serving to accommodate differences of aim or opinion (*diplomatists seeking a f.*); (Math.) rule or principle in algebraic symbols; (Chem.) expression by symbols of substance's constituents; tabulation of certain facts by symbols & figures. Hence **for·mular**IZE(3) [through obs *formular* a.], **for·mul**IZE(3), vv.t. = FORMULATE, **formulariz**A·TION, **formuliz**A·TION, nn. [L, dim. of *forma* FORM[1]]

for·mūlary, n. & a. Collection of formulas; document or book of set forms esp. for belief or ritual; (adj.) in or of formulas. [f. F *formulaire* f. neut. of L *formularius* (prec., -ARY[1])]

for·mulate, v.t. Reduce to, express in, a formula; set forth systematically. Hence **formul**A·TION n. [FORMULA + -ATE[3]]

for·nicate, v.i. Commit fornication. So **for·nicat**OR[2] n. [f. L *fornicari* (*fornix -icis* brothel), -ATE[3]]

fornica·tion, n. Voluntary sexual intercourse between man (sometimes restricted to unmarried man) & unmarried woman (cf. *adultery*). [OF, f. LL *fornicationem* (prec., -ION)]

forpi·ned, a. (archaic). Wasted by hunger, torture, &c. [p.p. of obs. *forpine* see FOR-(5)]

forrader. See FORWARD[2].

forrel. See FOREL.

forsa·ke, v.t. (-so͝ok, -saken). Give up, break off from, renounce; withdraw one's help, friendship, or companionship from, desert, abandon. [earlier senses *deny, repudiate, refuse*; OE *forsacan* f. FOR-(3) + *sacan* contend]

forsoo·th (-th), adv. Truly, in truth, no doubt, (used parenthet. always in irony). [OE *forsóth* (FOR, SOOTH n.)]

forspe·nt, a. Tired out. [p.p. of obs. *forspend* see FOR-(5), SPEND]

forswear· (-wār), v.t. (-swore, -sworn). Abjure, renounce on oath; *f.* one*self*, swear falsely, perjure oneself; (p.p.) perjured. [OE *forswerian*, see FOR-(3, 1), SWEAR]

fort, n. Fortified place (usu. single building or set of connected military buildings, cf. FORTRESS); trading-station, orig. fortified, in N. America. [F, abs. use of *fort* strong f. L *fortis*]

for·talice, n. (Archaic & poet.) fortress; (mod.) small outwork of fortification, small fort. [f. med. L *fortalitia* (L *fortis* strong)]

forte[1], n. Person's strong point; (Fenc.) sword-blade from hilt to middle (cf. FOIBLE). [f. F *fort* abs. use of adj. = strong; fem. form ignorantly adopted for masc., cf. *morale, locale*]

for·tĕ[2], mus. direction (abbr. *f.*). Loud; *forte forte* (abbr. *ff.*), very loud; *forte piano* (abbr. *fp.*), loud & then immediately soft. [It.]

forth, adv. & prep. Forwards (now only in *back & f.*, to & fro); onwards in time (now only in *from this time f.*, & in comb. as *hencef.*); forward, into view, (*bring, come, show*, &c., *f.*); out from home &c. (*sail, issue, f.*); out of doors (*cast f.*); *& so f.*, & so on, & the like; *so far f.*, to that extent; *so far f. as*, to whatever extent; (prep.; archaic) from out of. [cf. G *fort* (root of FORE[2] + suf. *-to-*)]

forthco·ming (-kŭ-), a. About or likely to come forth; approaching; ready to be produced when wanted. [prec., COME, -ING[2]]

forthrīgh·t, adv., **for·thright,** a. & n., (archaic). (Adv.) straight forward; straightway. (Adj.) going straight; outspoken, unswerving; decisive, dextrous. (N.) straight course (*ff. & meanders*). [FORTH + RIGHT a. & adv.]

forthwi·th (-th, -dh), adv. Immediately, without delay. [for *forth with* used abs.]

fortifica·tion, n. Fortifying; strengthening of wine with alcohol; (Mil.) providing, art or science of providing, with defensive works, (usu. pl.) defensive work(s), wall(s), earthwork(s), tower(s), &c. [F, f. L *fortificationem* act of strengthening (foll., -ATION)]

for·tify̆, v.t. & i. Strengthen structure of; impart vigour or physical strength or endurance to, strengthen mentally or morally, encourage; strengthen (liquors) with alcohol; corroborate, confirm, (statement); provide (town, army, one*self*) with defensive works; erect fortifications. Hence **for·tifi**ABLE a. [f. F *fortifier* f. L *fortificare* (*fortis* strong, -FY)]

forti·ssimo, mus. direction (abbr. *ff., ffor., fortiss.*). Very loud. [It.]

fortiter. See SUAVITER.

for·titude, n. Courage in pain or adversity. [F, f. L *fortitudo* (*fortis* strong, -TUDE)]

for·tnight (-īt), n. Period of two weeks (*today, this day, Monday*, &c., *f.*, a f. from today &c.; *would rather keep him* &c. *a week than a f.*, he &c. is a large eater). [OE *féorwertýne niht* fourteen nights]

for·tnightly, a. & adv. (Happening, appearing) once every fortnight. [-LY[1,2]]
for·tress, n., & v.t. Military stronghold, esp. strongly fortified town fit for large garrison; (vb, poet.) serve as f. to, protect. [f. OF *forteresse* strength, strong place, f. *fort* see FORT]
fortu·itism, fortu·itist, nn. Belief, believer, in chance & natural causes, not design, as causing adaptations in nature (cf. *teleology*, *-ist*). [foll., -ISM, -IST]
fortu·itous, a. Due to or characterized by chance, accidental, casual. Hence **fortu·itous**LY[2] adv., **fortu·itous**NESS n. [f. L *fortuitus* (*fors -tis* chance) + -OUS]
fortu·ity, n. Fortuitousness; a chance occurrence; accident; unstudied or unintended character. [f. L as prec. (for *fortuitity*)]
for·tunate (-tshŏŏ-), a. Favoured by fortune, lucky, prosperous; auspicious, favourable. [f. L *fortunatus* (FORTUNE[2], -ATE[2])]
for·tunately, adv. Luckily, successfully, (esp. as parenthesis qualifying whole sentence = it is a fortunate thing that). [-LY[2]]
for·tune[1] (-tshŏŏn, -tūn), n. Chance, hap, luck, as a power in men's affairs (*F.*, this power personified as goddess; *try the f. of war*, see what it will bring, risk it; SOLDIER *of f.*); luck good or bad that falls to any one or to an enterprise &c. (in sing. or pl.; *try* one's *f.*, take some risky step), coming lot (*tell* person his *f.*, *tell ff.*, of gipsies &c., whence **for·tune-tell**ER[1] n.); good luck; prosperity, prosperous condition, wealth, (*make* one's *f.*, prosper; *make a f.*, become rich; *spent a small f. on it*, large sum; *marry a f.*, heiress), whence **for·tune**LESS a.; *f.-hunter*, man seeking rich wife. [F, f. L *fortuna* cogn. w. *fors -tis* chance & *ferre* bring]
for·tune[2], v.i. (archaic & poet.). Chance, occur, (esp. impers., *it fortuned that*); come by chance *upon*. [f. OF *fortuner* f. L *fortunare* make fortunate (prec.)]
for·ty, a. & n. Four times ten, 40, XL, (*f.-one*, *f.-first*, &c., *f. winks*, short nap esp. after dinner); hence **for·ti**ETH a. & n. (N.) age of f. years (*after f.*, *over f.*; *the ff.*, years of life or century between 39 & 50); *roaring ff.*, stormy ocean tracts between lat. 39° & 50° N. & S.; *f.*-PENNY *nail*; *the F.-five*, Jacobite rebellion of 1745. [OE *féowertig* cf. G *vierzig* (FOUR, -TY[2])]
fōr·um, n. (Rom. Ant.) public place, market-place, place of assembly for judicial & other business, esp. at Rome; place of public discussion; court, the law courts, (fig. *the f. of conscience* &c.). [L]
for·ward[1] (-*ard*), a. & n. (Naut.) belonging to fore part of ship; lying in one's line of motion (*the f. horizon*), onward or towards the front (*the f. path*; *f. play* in cricket, see foll.; *f. movement*, special effort at political &c. progress; *f. school*, *party*, *opinions*, advanced or extreme); (Commerc.) relating to future produce (*f. contract*). Advanced, progressing to maturity or completion, (of plant, crop, season) well advanced or early; ready, prompt, eager, (often *to* do); precocious; presumptuous, pert, whence **for·ward**LY[2] adv.; hence **for·ward**NESS n. (N.) one of the first-line players in football. [OE *foreweard* (FORE[2], -WARD), a.]
for·ward[2]**(s),** adv. (-d is added below to senses in which the -s form is rare or not used). Towards the future, continuously onwards, (-d; *from this time f.*; *look f.*, ahead; CARRIAGE *f.*; *date f.*, of commercial orders, post-date); towards the front in the direction one is facing, (Cricket; -d) *play f.*, reach f. to play short-pitched ball; with continuous f. motion (*rushing f.*), (Mil., as word of command, -d, = go f., advance); in advance, ahead, (-d; *send him f.*); *backward(s) & f.*, to & fro; to the front, into prominence, (-d; *bring f.*, draw attention to; *come f.*, offer oneself for task, post, &c.; *put* or *set f.*, allege, make one*self* too conspicuous); (Naut.; -d) to, at, in, fore part of ship; onward so as to make progress (-d; *go f.*, be going on, progress; *can't get any forwarder*, or usu. colloq. *forrader*, make no progress). [OE *foreweard*, prob. neut. acc. of prec.]
for·ward[3], v.t. Help f., promote; accelerate growth of; send (letter &c.) on to further destination, (loosely) dispatch (goods &c.). [f. prec.]
forwear·ied, forwor·n, aa. (archaic). Tired out. [FOR-(5), WEARY, WEAR, vv.]
fosse, n. Long narrow excavation, canal, ditch, trench, esp. in fortification; (Anat.) groove, depression, also **foss**E·TTE n. [F, f. L *fossa* orig. fem. p.p. of *fodere* dig]
fo·ssick, v.i. (slang). Rummage, search about. [dial. wd current in Austral. gold-mining = search in crevices or abandoned workings]
fossil (fŏ·sl), a. & n. Found buried, dug up, (*f. fuel* &c.; now rare); (thing) preserved in strata of earth with more or less chemical or other change of texture & recognizable as remains of plant or animal of past (usu. prehistoric) ages (*f. bones*, *shells*, *ivory*; *hunting for ff.*; also fig., as *words are f. thoughts*); (person or thing) belonging to the past, antiquated, incapable of further development. Hence **fo·ssil**ATE[3] v.t., **fossil**A·TION n., **fossili·**FEROUS a., **fo·ssil**IZE(3) v.t. & i., **fossilīz**A·TION n. [f. F *fossile* f. L *fossilis* (*fodere foss-* dig, -IL)]
fossor·ial, a. (zool.). Burrowing; used in burrowing. [f. L *fossorius* (*fossor* digger f. *fodere* see prec., -OR[2]) + -AL]
fo·ster[1], n. Food (obs. exc. in comb., as *f.-child*, *-father*, *-mother*, *-parent*, *-son*, *-daughter*, *-brother*, *-sister*, = having the specified relationship not by blood, but in virtue of nursing or bringing up); acting

or treated as —; *f.-mother,* (also)=INCUBATOR. [OE *fóstor* (FOOD, suf. *-tro-*)]

fo·ster[2], v.t. (Archaic) tend affectionately, cherish, keep warm (in bosom), promote growth of; encourage or harbour (feeling); (of circumstances) be favourable to. Hence **fo·ster**ER[1], **fo·str**ESS[1], nn. [f. prec.]

fo·sterage (-ĭj), n. Fostering; custom of employing foster-mothers. [-AGE]

fo·sterling, n. Foster-child, nursling, protégé. [OE *fóstorling* (FOSTER[1], -LING[1])]

fought. See FIGHT[1].

foul (fowl), a., n., adv., & v.i. & t. Offensive to the senses, loathsome, stinking, (*foul brood,* a disease of larval bees); dirty, soiled (*f. linen*), filthy; defaced with corrections (*f. copy*); charged with noxious matter (*f. air, water*); clogged, choked, (*f. gun-barrel*); (of ship's bottom) overgrown with weed, barnacles, &c.; morally polluted, obscene, disgustingly abusive, (*the f. fiend,* the devil; *f. deed, motive, talk*; *f.-mouthed, -tongued*); (of fish at or after spawning) in bad condition; ugly (now dial. exc. in *fair or f.*); unfair, against rules of game &c., (*f. blow, stroke, riding*; *f. play,* in games, & fig. treachery); (of weather) wet, rough, stormy; (of wind) contrary; in collision (FALL[1] *f. of*); entangled (*rope is f.*). (N.) something f. (*through f. & fair,* through everything); collision, entanglement, esp. in riding, rowing, or running, irregular stroke or piece of play. (Adv.) in irregular way (*hit him f.*; *play* one *f.,* deal treacherously with him). (Vb) become f., get clogged; make f. or dirty; pollute with guilt, dishonour; cause (anchor, cable) to become entangled, jam or block (crossing, railway line, traffic); become entangled; run f. of, collide with. [OE *fúl* cf. G *faul* f. Aryan *pu-* stink, rot, cf. Gk *puon,* L PUS; the v.i. f. OE *fúlian*]

fou·lard (fōō·lahr), n. Thin flexible material of silk or silk & cotton; handkerchief of it. [F]

foully (fow·l-lĭ), adv. Abominably, cruelly, wickedly, (*was f. murdered*); with unmerited insult (*f. slandered*). [-LY[2]]

fou·lness, n. Foul condition; foul matter; disgusting wickedness. [-NESS]

fou·mart (fōō-), n. Polecat. [ME *fulmard* (FOUL, *mearth* marten)]

found[1] (fow-), v.t. & i. Lay base of (building &c.); be original builder, begin building, of (town, edifice); set up, establish (esp. with endowment), originate, initiate, (institution); construct, base, (tale, one's fortunes, classification, rule, &c.) (*up*)*on* some ground, support principle, &c. (also *is founded in justice* &c.; *well, ill,* &c., *founded,* reasonable, justified, baseless, &c.); rely, base oneself, (of argument &c.) be based, (*up*)*on.* [f. F *fonder* f. L *fundare* (*fundus* bottom)]

found[2] (fow-), v.t. Melt & mould (metal), fuse (materials for glass); make (thing of molten metal, glass) by melting. So **fou·ndr**Y(3) n. [f. F *fondre* f. L *fundere fus-* pour]

found[3]. See FIND.

founda·tion (fow-), n. Establishing, constituting on permanent basis, esp. of an endowed institution; such institution, e.g. monastery, college, or hospital (*on the f.,* entitled to benefit by its funds, whence **founda·tion**ER[1] n.), or its revenues; solid ground or base, natural or artificial, on which building rests, lowest part of building usu. below ground-level; basis, ground-work, underlying principle, (*report has no f.*; *base religion on a moral f.*); body or ground on which other parts are overlaid, e.g. under-skirt, first set of stitches in crochet or knitting; *f.-muslin, -net,* gummed fabrics for stiffening dresses & bonnets; *f.-school,* endowed; *f.-stone,* esp. one laid with ceremony to celebrate founding of edifice. [f. L *fundatio* (FOUND[1] -ATION)]

fou·nder[1], n. In vbl senses of FOUND[1]; esp., one who founds institutions (*f.'s kin,* relatives of f. entitled to election or preference); *f.'s shares,* shares issued to ff. of public company as part-consideration for business taken over, & separate from ordinary capital. Hence **fou·nder**SHIP, **fou·ndr**ESS[1], nn. [-ER[1]]

fou·nder[2], n. In vbl senses of FOUND[2]. [-ER[1]]

fou·nder[3] (fow-), v.i. & t., & n. (Of earth, building, &c.) fall down or in, give way; (of horse; or with rider substituted as subject) fall from overwork, collapse, fall lame, stick fast in bog &c.; cause (horse) to break down by overwork; (of ship) fill with water & sink, cause (ship) to do this; (Golf) hit (ball) into ground. (N.) inflammation of horse's foot from overwork; (also *chest, body, -f.*) rheumatism of chest-muscles in horses. [f. OF *fondrer* submerge, collapse, (L *fundus* bottom)]

fou·ndling (fow-), n. Deserted infant of unknown parents. [p.p. of FIND + -LING[1]]

fount[1] (fow-), n. (poet. or rhet.). Spring, source, fountain; (shop) reservoir of oil in lamp or of ink in pen. [f. L *fons -tis* on anal. of *mount*; from late 16th c.]

fount[2] (fow-), n. (print.). Set of type of same face & size. [f. F *fonte* (*fondre* FOUND[2])]

fountain (fow·ntĭn), n. Water-spring; source *of* river &c. (also fig., *Crown is the f. of honour*; *poison the ff. of trust*); jet of water made to spout, structure provided for it, (also *drinking-f.*) public erection with constant supply of drinking-water; reservoir in lamp, printing-press, &c., for oil, ink, &c. (*f.-pen,* having this); *f.-head,* original source. Hence (-)**fountain**ED[2] a. [f. OF *fontaine* orig. fem. of LL *fontana* orig. fem. of L *fontanus* adj. (FOUNT[1], -AN)]

four (fōr), a. & n. One more than three, 4, IV, (*f. corners of earth* &c., remotest parts;

f. corners of document &c., its scope; *within the f. seas,* in Gt Britain; *f. figures,* some number from 1000 to 9999; *twenty* &c. *-f.* or *f.-&-twenty* &c.; *f.-&-twentieth* &c.); (ellipt.) f. hours (*f. o'clock*), f. horses (*carriage* &c. *& f.*); *f.-ale,* sold at 4*d.* a quart; *f. by two,* rifle pull-through cloth; *f.-coupled,* with f. coupled wheels; *f.-course,* with fourfold rotation (of crops); *f.*-DIMENSIONAL; *f.-footed,* quadruped (adj.); *f.-foot way,* space (4 ft 8½ in.) between pair of rails; *f.-handed,* (of monkeys) quadrumanous, (of games) for f. persons, (of piece of music) for two players; *f.-horse(d),* drawn by f. horses; *f.-in-hand,* vehicle with f. horses & no outrider (also adv., *drive* &c. *f.-i.-h.*); *f.-oar,* (boat) with f. oars; *f. o'clock,* the plant Marvel of Peru; *f.-part,* arranged for f. voices to sing; *fourpence,* sum or coin = 4*d.*; *fourpenny,* costing 4*d.*, silver coin = 4*d.*; *f.-post* (of bed), having f. posts to support canopy, *f.-poster,* such bed, (also) 4-masted ship; *f.-pounder,* gun throwing 4 lb. shot; *f.-rowed barley,* with f. rows of awns; *fourscore,* eighty, age of 80 years; *f.-square,* square-shaped, solidly based or steady; *f.-wheel,* f.-wheeled carriage; *f.-wheeler,* f.-wheeled hackney carriage; hence **four·**FOLD a. & adv., **four**TEE·N a., **fourtee·nTH**[2] a. & n. (N.) the number f.; set of f. persons or things, esp. f.-pipped card, domino, or side of die, f.-oared boat & crew (*ff.*, races for these), hit &c. at cricket for f. runs; *on all fours* (earlier *four* = f. limbs), crawling on hands & knees, (also, fig.) completely analogous or corresponding (*the cases are not o. a. f.*; *is the simile o. a. f. with the thing illustrated?*); (Mil.; pl.) formation f. deep usu. faced flankwards (*ff. right* or *left*) for marching (FORM[2] *ff.*); f.-pennyworth *of* spirits; (pl.) f.-per-cent. stock. [Aryan; OE *féower*, cf. Du. & G *vier*, Gk *tessares*, L *quatuor*]

fourgon (F), n. Luggage-van.

Fou·rierism (fōō-), n. Fourier's system for reorganization of society (PHALANSTERY). [Charles *Fourier*, French socialist, 1772–1837]

four·some (fōr-), n. Game of golf between two pairs. [FOUR, -SOME; orig. adj.]

fourth (fōr-), a. & n. Next after third (*the, a, f.*, ellipt. as n., esp. = 4th day of month; *f. part,* quarter). (N.) quarter, f. part; (Mus.) tone four diatonic degrees above or below tone given, this interval, harmonic combination of tone & its f.; *F. of June,* principal annual celebration at Eton College, speech-day and procession of boats; *F. of July,* U.S. anniversary of declaration of Independence; *f. party* (hist.), Lord R. Churchill, Sir H. D. Wolff, Sir J. Gorst, Mr. Balfour, and a few other Conservatives who (1880–5) attacked impartially the Liberal Government & the Conservative front bench; (pl.) articles of f. quality. [OE *féortha* cf. G *vierte*, Gk *tetartos*, L *quartus*]

four·thly, adv. In the fourth place (in enumerations). [-LY[2]]

fowl, n., & v.i. Bird (rare), birds (rare exc. in *wild-f.*), their flesh as food (only in *fish, flesh, & f.*); domestic cock or hen (often qualified, as *barndoor f., game, guinea, -f.*; *f.-run,* place where ff. may run, breeding establishment for ff.), its flesh as food. (Vb) catch, hunt, shoot, or snare, wild-f., whence **fow·**LER[1], **fow·**LING[1], nn.; *fowling-piece,* light gun used in fowling. [com.-Teut.; OE *fugel* cf. G *vogel* perh. by dissim. f. **fluglo-* (*flug-* FLY[2])]

fox[1], n. (fem. VIXEN, also *bitch-f.*). Red-furred sharp-snouted bushy-tailed quadruped preserved in England as beast of chase & proverbial for cunning; crafty person; northern constellation; FLYING *f.*; *f. & geese,* game played on board; *f.-brush,* tail of f.; *f.*-EARTH[1]; *foxglove,* tall purple or white flowered plant; *foxhound,* kind bred & trained to hunt ff.; *f.-hunt* n. & v.i., chasing of, chase, f. with hounds, whence **fo·xhunt**ER[1] n.; *fox-hunting* a. & n., (given to) this sport; *foxtail,* f.'s tail, kinds of grass; *f.-terrier,* short-haired for unearthing ff., but kept chiefly as pet; *foxtrot,* an American dance. [com.-Teut.; cf. G *fuchs*]

fox[2], v.i. & t. Act craftily, dissemble; discolour (leaves of book, engraving, &c.) with brownish spots (esp. in p.p.). [f. prec.]

fo·xy, a. Fox-like, crafty(-looking); reddish-brown, (Paint.) over-hot in colour; damaged with mildew &c. Hence **fo·xi**NESS n. [-Y[2]]

foyer (fwah·yā), n. Large room in theatre &c. for audience's use during interval. [F]

fra (-ah), n. = FRATE as prefixed title. [It.]

fră·cas (-ah), n. (pl. same). Noisy quarrel, row. [F, f. It. *fracasso* uproar]

fra·ction (-shn), n. Dividing of Eucharistic bread; (Arith.) numerical quantity that is not an integer, one or more aliquot parts, (*vulgar f.*, expressed by numerator above & denominator below a line; DECIMAL *f.*; *proper, improper, f.*, with numerator less, greater, than denominator); small piece or amount, scrap, (esp. *not a f.*). Hence **fra·ction**AL, **fra·ction**ARY[1], aa. [f. OF *fraccion* f. eccl. L *fractionem* (L *frangere fract-* break, -ION)]

fra·ctionate, v.t. Separate (mixture) into portions of different properties by distillation &c. [prec. + -ATE[3]]

fra·ctionize, v.t. Break up into fractions (Math.), or portions. [-IZE]

fra·ctious (-shus), a. Unruly, cross, peevish. Hence **fra·ctious**LY[2] adv., **fra·ctious**NESS n. [f. FRACTION in obs. sense brawling + -OUS, after *captious* &c.]

fra·cture (-tsher), n., & v.t. & i. Breaking, breakage, esp. of bone or cartilage (COMPOUND[2] *f.*); surface shown by mineral when broken with hammer; substitution of diphthong, diphthong substituted, for simple vowel owing to influence of following consonant; (vb) cause f. in, break continuity of, crack (t. & i.). [F, f. L *fractura* (FRACTION, -URE)]

frae·num, fre-, n. (pl. *-na*). Small ligament checking motion of organ. [L, = bridle]

fră·gile (-j-), a. Easily snapped or shattered, weak, perishable, of delicate frame or constitution. So **fragi·l**ITY n. [F, f. L *fragilis* (*frag-* root of *frangere* break)]

fra·gment, n. Part broken off, detached piece; isolated or incomplete part, remainder of lost or destroyed whole, esp. extant remains or unfinished portion of a writing or work of art. Hence **fra·gment**ARY[1] a. [f. L *fragmentum* (as prec., -MENT)]

frā·grant, a. Sweet-smelling. So **fra·gr**ANCE n. [f. L *fragrare* smell sweet (-ANT

frail[1], n. Rush basket for packing figs, raisins, &c. [f. OF *frayel* etym. dub.]

frail[2], a. Fragile; transient (*f. life, bliss,* &c.); in weak health; morally weak, unable to resist temptation, (euphem., of women) unchaste. [f. OF *fraile* FRAGILE]

frai·lty, n. Liability to err or yield to temptation; fault, weakness, foible. [f. OF *fraileté* f. L *fragilitatem* (FRAGILE, -TY)]

fraise[1] (-z), n. (fortif.). Horizontal or down-sloping palisade round berm. [F, orig. = mesentery of calf]

fraise[2] (-z), n. Tool for enlarging circular hole or cutting teeth in watch wheels. [F (*fraiser* enlarge hole f. *fraise* as prec.)]

framboe·sia (-bēz-)-, n. Chronic contagious negro disease with raspberry-like swellings, the yaws. [mod. L, f. F *framboise* raspberry perh. f. Du. *braambezie* (BRAMBLE, BERRY)]

frame[1], v.t. & i. Shape, direct, dispose, (thoughts, acts, another person) to a purpose (*for, to, to do,* or with adv.); give promise of being skilful &c. (usu. *well*); adapt, fit, *to* or *into*; construct by combination of parts or adaptation to design, contrive, devise, invent, compose, express, (complex article, plot, rule, story, theory); articulate (words); conceive, imagine; [f. foll.] set in a f., serve as f. for (*landscape framed in an archway*), whence **fra·m**ING[1](3) n. Hence **frā·m**ABLE a., **fra·m**ER[1] n. [OE *framian* be helpful (*fram* forward cf. FROM)]

frame[2], n. Construction, constitution, build; established order, plan, system, (*the f. of society* or *government*); temporary state (*of* mind); framed work or structure (*the f. of heaven* or *earth*), human or animal body (*sobs shook her f., man of gigantic f.*); skeleton of building, underlying support or essential substructure of anything; case or border enclosing picture, pane of glass, &c., whence **fra·me**LESS a.; (Gardening) glazed structure protecting plants from cold; (Mining) inclined board for washing ore; *f.-house,* of wooden skeleton covered with boards; *f.-saw,* stretched in f. to make it rigid; *f.-up* (U.S.), conspiracy; *framework,* f., substructure, upon or into which casing or contents can be put (lit., fig.). [f. prec.]

franc, n. French monetary unit, before the great war a silver coin of about 9½*d.*, but after depreciation stabilized 1928 at 125 to £1, or about 2*d.* [F, perh. f. *Francorum Rex* king of the FRANK[1]s, legend on earliest coin so called (gold = 10/6)]

frā·nchīse (-z), n. (Chiefly hist.) legal immunity or exemption from some burden or jurisdiction, privilege or exceptional right, granted to person, corporation, &c.; full membership of corporation or State, citizenship; right of voting at public elections esp. for member of Parliament, principle of qualification for this (FANCY[1] *f.*). [OF) *franc* FRANK[2], -ISE)]

Franci·scan, a. & n. (Friar) of the order founded 1209 by St Francis of Assisi; of the Ff. [f. med. L *Franciscus* Francis + -AN]

Fra·nco-, comb. form of med. L *Franci* the Franks, now used = French-&-, as *F.-German.* Hence **Fra·nco**PHIL(E), **Fra·nco**PHOBE, nn. & aa. [FRANK[1], -O-]

fra·ncolin, n. Kind of partridge resembling pheasant. [F, f. It. *francolino*]

franc-tireur (F), n. (pl. *-cs -rs*). Man of irregular light-infantry corps.

fra·ngipane (-nj-), n. (Perfume of) red jasmine; kind of almond cream or paste. [F, prob. f. *Frangipani,* maker]

Frank[1], n. One of the Germanic nation or coalition that conquered France in 6th c.; (in Levantine use) person of Western nationality. Hence **Fra·nk**ISH[1] a. [f. L *Francus* f. OHG *Franko* perh. f. weapon (OE *franca* javelin)]

frank[2], a. Ingenuous, open, candid, outspoken; undisguised, avowed. Hence **fra·nk**LY[2] adv., **fra·nk**NESS n. [f. OF *franc* f. med. L *francus* free f. prec. (full freedom being confined to the Franks)]

frank[3], v.t., & n. (Hist.) superscribe (letter &c.) with signature ensuring gratis conveyance; facilitate coming & going of (person), give social passport to; convey (person) gratuitously; exempt from future payment &c. (*a franking duty, imposition*); (n.; hist.) franking signature, franked cover. [f. prec. in obs. sense *free of charge*]

Fra·nkenstein (-tīn), n. *F.'s monster,* thing that becomes formidable to the person who has created it. [M. W. Shelley, *Frankenstein*]

Frankfort black, n. Fine black pigment used in copperplate engraving. [German town]

fra·nkincense, n. Aromatic gum resin (prop. from trees of genus *Boswellia*) used for burning as incense. [f. OF *franc* *encens* (FRANK[2] in obs. sense *luxuriant*, INCENSE[1])]

fra·nklin, n. (hist.). Land-owner of free but not noble birth in 14th & 15th cc. [FRANK[2], perh. -LING[1]]

fra·nk-pledge, n. (hist.). System by which each member of tithing was responsible for every other (also rarely fig., e.g. of relation between members of a Government). [AF *franc plege* (FRANK[2], PLEDGE), perh. mistransl. of ON *frithborh* peace-pledge (not free-pledge)]

fră·ntic, a. Wildly excited, beside oneself with rage, pain, grief, &c.; showing frenzy, uncontrolled. Hence **fra·nt**ICALLY, **fra·ntic**LY[2], advv. [f. OF *frenetique* f. LL *phreneticus* f. Gk *phrenitikos* (*phren*-ITIS f. *phrēn -ĕnos* brain)]

frap, v.t. (naut.). Bind tightly. [f. OF *fraper* bind, strike]

frăss, n. Excrement of larvae; refuse left by boring insects. [f. G *frass* (*fressen* devour)]

fra·te (-ahtā), n. (pl. *-ti* pr. -tē). Friar. [It.]

frā·ter, n. (hist.). = REFECTORY. [f. OF *fraitur* as REFECTORY]

frater·nal, a. (As) of brother(s), brotherly. [f. L *fraternus* (*frater* brother) + -AL]

frater·nity, n. Being fraternal, brotherliness; religious body; guild, company with common interests, set of men of same class &c. [f. OF *fraternité* f. L *fraternitatem* (prec., -TY)]

fră·ternize, v.i. Associate, make friends, behave as intimates, (*with, together*, or abs.). So **fra·terni**ZA·TION n. [f. F *fraterniser* (L *fraternus* FRATERNAL, -IZE)]

fră·tricīde, n. Killing of one's, one who kills his, brother or sister. Hence **fra·tricid**AL a. [F, f. L *fratricidium, -cida*, (*frater -tris* brother, -CIDE)]

frau (-ow), n. (Of German wife or widow) Mrs; German woman. [G]

fraud, n. Deceitfulness (rare); criminal deception, use of false representations, (in Law, *in f., to the f., of*, so as to defraud); dishonest artifice or trick (*pious f.*, deception intended to benefit deceived, & esp. to strengthen religious belief); person or thing not fulfilling expectation or description. [f. OF *fraude* f. L *fraudem* nom. *fraus*]

frau·dūlent, a. Guilty of, of the nature of, characterized or effected by, fraud. Hence or cogn. **frau·dul**ENCE n., **frau·dulent**LY[2] adv. [OF, f. L *fraudulentus* (prec., -ULENT)]

fraught (-awt), a. Stored, equipped, *with* (poet.); (fig.) *f. with*, involving, attended with, full of, threatening or promising, destined to produce, woe, danger, meaning, &c. [p.p. of obs. *fraught* v. load with cargo (obs. *fraught* cargo prob. f. MDu. *vracht* FREIGHT)]

fräu·lein (-oilīn), n. (Of German spinster) Miss (with surname; also alone as voc.); German spinster; German governess. [G]

fraxine·lla, n. Kinds of garden dittany. [mod. L, dim. of L *fraxinus* ash]

fray[1], n. Noisy quarrel, brawl; fight, conflict, (lit. or fig.; *eager for the f.*). [for AFFRAY]

fray[2], v.t. & i. (Of deer) *f. head*, or *f.*, rub velvet off new horns; wear through by rubbing, ravel *out* edge or end of, (usu. woven material); become ragged at edge. [f. F *frayer* f. L *fricare* rub]

frāzi·l, n. (Canad. & U.S.). Anchor-ice, ice at bottom of stream. [perh. f. F *fraisil* cinders]

frazzle, n. (U.S.). Worn or exhausted state (esp. *worn, beaten, to a f.*). [perh. as FRAY[2]]

freak (-ēk), n. Caprice, vagary; capriciousness (*out of mere f.*); product of sportive fancy; (also *f. of nature*) monstrosity, abnormally developed specimen. Hence **frea·k**ISH[1] a., **frea·kish**LY[2] adv., **frea·kish**NESS n. [from 16th c.; etym. dub.; cf. OE *frician* to dance]

freaked, a. Oddly flecked or streaked. [-ED[2]]

fre·ckle, n., & v.t. & i. Light brown spot on skin, (pl.) sporadic sunburn; (vb) spot, be spotted, with ff. [earlier *frecken* f. ON *freknur* pl.]

free[1], a. (*freer, freest*, pr. -ēer, -ēĭst). 1. Not in bondage to another, having personal rights & social & political liberty, (*f. labour*, of f. men not slaves, & see 2); (of State, its citizens or institutions) subject neither to foreign dominion nor to despotic government, having national & civil liberty; *f.-born*, inheriting citizen rights & liberty; *freehold*, (estate held by) tenure in fee simple or fee-tail or for term of life (also of corresponding tenure of office), (adj.) held by freehold; *freeholder*, possessor of freehold estate; *freeman*, person not slave or serf, citizen of f. State (& see 4); *freemason*, member of fraternity for mutual help & brotherly feeling called *F. & Accepted Masons* having elaborate ritual & system of secret signs (the orig. f. masons were prob. skilled masons emancipated & allowed to move from place to place in & after 14th c., & the *accepted* may have been honorary members of the f. masons' societies); *freemasonry*, system & institutions of the freemasons, secret understanding between like characters, instinctive sympathy. 2. Loose (*f. wheel* in bicycle, driving-wheel able to revolve while pedals are at rest), unrestricted (*f. love*, sexual relations irrespective of marriage), at liberty, not confined, released from ties or duties, unimpeded (*f. trade*, left to its natural course without customs duties to restrict imports or protect home industries, this principle; *f.- trader*, believer in it), unfettered in action (*have* or *give a f. hand*, right of acting at discretion), permitted *to* do, independent (*F. Church*, unconnected with State; *the F. Cc.*, nonconformists; *F. C. of Scotland*, seceders of 1843 from Presbyterian establishment; *f. lance*, medieval mercenary, modern politician or controversialist with no party allegiance, unattached journalist; *f. labour*, of workmen not belonging to trade unions, & see 1; *f.-thinker, -thinking* n. & a., *-thought*, rejector &c. of authority in religious belief, rationalist &c.), unconstrained (*f. step, gestures*); (of literary style) not observing strict laws of form (*f. verse*, =VERS LIBRE), (of translation) not literal; allowable (*it is f. for* or *to him to do so*); open to all comers (*f. fight*, in which any one present joins); clear of obstructions, clear *of* or *from* something undesirable, (of wind) not adverse; not fixed, not in contact, (Chem.) not combined, (of power or energy) disengaged or available; *f.-board*, part of ship's side between line of flotation & deck-level; *f.-hand* (of drawing), done without artificial aid to the hand; *f.-stone*, kind of peach of which when ripe the stone is loose (& see 3); *f. will*, power of directing our own actions without constraint by necessity or fate (& see 3). 3. Spontaneous, unforced, unearned, gratuitous, willing, (*f. grace*, unmerited favour of God; *f. gift*, not in requital; *did it of my own f. will*, & so *f.-will* adj., voluntary; *f. quarters*, gratuitous entertainment; *am f. to confess*, not unwilling); lavish, profuse, unstinted, copious, (*f. of his money*, open-handed; so *f.-handed*, liberal; *f. flow of water*; *f. liver, living*, indulger, indulgence, in pleasures esp. of the table); frank, unreserved, (*f.-spoken*, not concealing one's opinions, blunt; *f. & easy*, unceremonious, also as n., smoking-concert &c.), forward, familiar, impudent, (*make* or *be f.*, take liberties *with*); (of talk, stories, &c.) broad, not quite decent; *freestone*, fine-grained easily sawn sandstone or limestone (& see 2). 4. Released or exempt *from* (*f. from the ordinary rules, disease, difficulty*, &c.); having burgess rights (*made f. of the city*), having the entrée & use *of* (*f. of the house*); not subject to tax, toll, duty, trade-restrictions, or fees (*f. port*, open to all traders alike; *f.-list*, of persons to be admitted f., duty-f. articles, &c.; *f. school*, with no fees charged; *f. pass*, not paid for; also adv., as *the gallery is open f.*, & in comb. as *carriage-f.*, without charge for conveyance); *freeman*, one who has the freedom of a city, company, &c. (& see 1). Hence **free·**LY[2] adv. [com.-Teut.; OE *frēo* cf. G *frei* f. Aryan *pri* to love]

free[2], v.t. (freed). Make f., set at liberty, (*freedman*, emancipated slave, esp. in Rom. Hist.); relieve *from*, rid or ease *of*; clear, disengage, disentangle. [OE *frēon* (prec.)]

free·booter, n. Pirate, piratical adventurer. Hence by back formation **free·boot** v.i., **free·boot**ING[1,2] n. & a. [f. Du. *vrijbuiter* (FREE[1], BOOTY, -ER[1])]

free·dom, n. Personal liberty, non-slavery; civil liberty, independence; liberty of action, right *to* do; power of self-determination, independence of fate or necessity; frankness, outspokenness, undue familiarity (*take ff. with*); facility, ease, in action; boldness of conception; (Physics) capability of motion; exemption *from* defect, disadvantage, burden, duty, &c.; privilege possessed by city or corporation; participation in privileges of membership *of* company &c. or citizenship *of* city (often given *honoris causa* to distinguished persons); unrestricted use *of* (*has the f. of the library*). [OE *frēodōm* (FREE[1], -DOM)]

free·martin, n. Hermaphrodite or imperfect female of ox kind. [?]

free·sia (-z-), n. Kinds of iridaceous bulbous plant from Cape of Good Hope. [?]

freeze, v.i. & t. (froze, frozen), & n. (Impers.) *it freezes* &c., there is &c. frost; be converted into or covered with ice; become rigid as result of cold; become fastened *to* or *together* by frost, (slang) *f. on to*, take or keep tight hold of; feel very cold (*f. to death*, die by frost); be chilled by fear; cause to congeal, form ice upon, (fluid or moist thing; often *in, over, up*), preserve (meat &c.) by refrigeration; (by exagg.) *f.* one's *blood*, terrify him; chill (feelings), paralyse (powers); stiffen, harden, injure, kill, by chilling (*frozen to death*); (slang) *f. out*, exclude from business, society, &c., by competition or boycotting &c.; *freezing-mixture*, salt & snow or other mixture used to f. liquids; *freezing-point*, temperature at which liquid, esp. water, freezes; (n.) state, coming, period, of frost. [com.-Teut.; OE *frēosan* cf. G *frieren*, also L *pruina* hoarfrost]

free·zing, a. In vbl senses; esp.: (by exagg.) very cold; (of manners) chilling, distant. Hence **free·zing**LY[2] adv. [-ING[2]]

freight (-āt), n., & v.t. Hire of ship for transporting goods; transport of goods by water (in U.S. by land also), charge for this; cargo, shipload; load, burden. (Vb) load (ship) with cargo; hire or let out (ship) for carriage of goods & passengers. [prob. f. MDu. *vrecht* var. of *vracht* see FRAUGHT]

freigh·tage (-ĭj), n. Hire of ship for, cost of, conveyance of goods; freighting or hiring of ship; cargo. [-AGE]

freigh·ter (-āt-), n. One who (charters &) loads ship; one who consigns goods for carriage inland; one whose business is to receive & forward freight; cargo ship. [-ER[1]]

French, a. & n. Of France or its people; having the qualities attributed to F. people; *F. bean,* kidney or haricot bean used as vegetable both in unripe sliced pods & in ripe seeds; *F. bread,* kind of fancy bread; *F. chalk,* kind of steatite used for marking cloth & removing grease & as dry lubricant; *F. drain* (of rubble, letting water soak away); *F. grey,* tint composed of white with ivory black, Indian red, & Chinese blue; *F.* HORN[1]; *take F. leave,* depart, act, without asking leave or giving notice; *F. letter,* a mechanical contraceptive; *Frenchman,* man of F. birth or nationality, (*good* &c.) F.-speaker, F. ship; *F. polish,* kind of polish for wood; *F.-polish* v.t., polish with this, whence **French-po·lish**ER[1] n.; *F. roof,* mansard: *F. toast,* fried bread; *F. window,* glazed folding-door serving as window & door; *Frenchwoman,* woman of France. (N.) the F. language (*F. lesson, master,* &c., concerned with this); *the F.* (pl.), the F. people. Hence **Fre·nch**NESS n., **Fre·nch**Y[2, 3] a. & n. [OE *frencisc* (FRANK[1], -ISH[1])]

Fre·nchifȳ, f-, v.t. Make French in form, character, or manners (usu. in p.p.). Hence **Frenchi**FICA·TION n. [-FY]

Fre·nchless, a. Knowing no French. [-LESS]

frenum. See FRAENUM.

fre·nzy, n., & v.t. Mental derangement, temporary insanity, paroxysm of mania, (rare); delirious fury or agitation, wild folly; (vb, usu. in p.p.) drive to f., infuriate, (*frenzied rage,* that of a frenzied person). [f. OF *frenesie* f. LL *phrenesis* (Gk *phrenitikos* FRANTIC)]

frē·quency n. Frequent occurrence, being repeated at short intervals, (of pulse) rapidity; (Physics) rate of recurrence (of vibration &c.), number of repetitions in given time (*high, low, f.,* abbr. H.F., L.F., w. ref. to sound-waves, electric currents, &c.). [f. L *frequentia* (foll., -ENCY)]

frē·quent[1], a. Found near together, numerous, abundant; often occurring, common, happening in close succession, (of pulse) rapid, (*it is a f. practice to*), whence **fre·quent**LY[2] adv.; (with agent-noun) habitual, constant, (*a. f. caller*). [f. L *frequens -entis* crowded cogn. w. *farcire* FARCE[2]]

freque·nt[2], v.t. Go often or habitually to (place, meetings, company, house). Hence or cogn. **frĕquent**A·TION, **freque·nt**ER[1], nn. [f. L *frequentare* (prec.)]

freque·ntative, a. & n. (gram.). (Verb or verbal form or conjugation) expressing frequent repetition or intensity of action. [f. L *frequentativus* (prec., -ATIVE)]

fre·sco, n. (pl. *-ōs, -oes*), & v.t. Method of painting (esp. *in f.*), picture, in water-colour laid on wall or ceiling before plaster is dry; (vb) paint (wall &c., picture or subject) thus. [It., orig. adj. = foll.]

fresh, a., adv., & n. New, novel, not previously known, used, met with, or introduced, (*break f. ground,* try something unhackneyed); additional, other, different, further, (*begin a f. chapter*); recent, lately made or arrived , just come *from*; raw, inexperienced, (*freshman,* first-year man at University); not preserved by salting, pickling, smoking, tinning, &c. (*f. herrings, meat, fruit,* & see below; *f. butter,* & see next sense); not salt (*f. water*; *freshwater* a., of f. water, not of the sea, as *freshwater fish, fishing, sailor*; *f. butter,* not flavoured with salt, & see prec. sense), not salt or bitter, drinkable, (*f. water*); pure, untainted, invigorating, refreshing, cool, (of air, wind, water); not stale, musty, or vapid (*f. fish, meat, fruit,* & see above; *f. egg*); not faded (*f. flowers, memories*); unsullied, bright & pure in colour (*a f. complexion*), looking healthy or young; not weary, brisk, vigorous, fit, (*never felt fresher*; *as f. as paint,* quite brisk, prob. a pun on the warning 'f. paint'; *a f. wind,* of some strength); excited with drink; (U.S.) presumptuous, forward. (Adv.) freshly, newly, esp. in comb. as *f.-caught, -coined*; *f.-run* (of salmon), lately come up from the sea. (N.) f. part of day, year, &c. (*in the f. of the morning*); rush of water in river, flood. Hence **fre·sh**EN[1] v.t. & i., **fre·sh**NESS n. [OE *fersc* cf. G *frisch* affected by OF *freis* fem. *fresche* from same Teut. origin]

frĕ·sher, n. (slang). =FRESH*man.* [-ER[1]]

frĕ·shet, n. Rush of fresh water flowing into sea; flood of river from heavy rain or melted snow. [FRESH n. + -ET[1]]

fre·shly, adv. Recently (only with participles, =*fresh* adv.); afresh (rare); with unabated vigour; with fresh appearance, odour, &c. [-LY[2]]

fret[1], n., & v.t. Ornamental pattern made of continuous combinations of straight lines joined usu. at right angles (also *Greek f.*). (Vb) variegate, chequer; adorn (esp. ceiling) with carved or embossed work. *F.-saw,* very narrow saw stretched on frame for cutting thin wood in ornamental patterns; *fretwork,* carved work in decorative patterns esp. of straight lines, also wood cut with f.-saw. [prob. f. OF *frete* trellis-work & *freter* vb]

fret[2], v.t. & i., & n. Gnaw, wear or consume or torment by gnawing, (of moths &c., horses champing bit, action of frost, rust, corrosives, friction, &c., or the passions); make (passage &c.) by wearing away; chafe, irritate, annoy, worry, distress; distress oneself with regret or discontent (*at*; *f. away* or *out* one's *life* &c.); *f. & fume,* show angry impatience; (of stream &c.) flow or rise in little waves, chafe; ruffle (water). (N.) irritation, vexation, querulousness, (*in a f.*; *f. & fume*; *on the f.*); hence **fre·t**FUL a., **fre·tful**LY[2] adv., **fre·tful**NESS n., **fre·tt**Y[2] a. [OE *fretan* cf. G *fressen* (*fra-* cogn. w. FOR-, EAT)]

fret[3], n. Bar or ridge on fingerboard of stringed instrument to regulate fingering. Hence **fre·tt**ED[2] a. [perh. f. OF *frete* ferrule])

Freu·dian (froid-), a. & n. (Disciple) of Freud or his doctrines of PSYCHO-*analysis*. [Sigmund *Freud*, psychologist, + -IAN]

fri·able, a. Easily crumbled. Hence or cogn. **fria**BI·LITY, **fri·able**NESS, nn. [F, f. L *friabilis* (*friare* crumble)]

fri·ar, n. Member of certain religious orders esp. the four mendicant orders of Franciscans (*Grey Ff.*), Augustines (*Austin Ff.*), Dominicans (*Black Ff.*), & Carmelites (*White Ff.*); *f.'s balsam*, tincture of benzoin. Hence **fri·ar**LY[1] a. [ME & OF *frere* f. L *fratrem* nom. *-ter* brother]

fri·ary, n. Convent of friars. [f. obs. *frary* f. OF *frairie, frerie* (*frere* see prec.) w. assim. to prec.; or f. prec. w. *-y* for -RY(3) by mistake of *-ar* for -ER[1]]

fri·bble, v.i., & n. Trifle, be frivolous; (n.) trifler. [imit.; earlier senses *stammer, totter*]

fri·candeau (-dō), n. (pl. *-x* pr. -z), & v.t. (Slice of) fried or stewed meat, esp. veal, served with sauce; (vb) make into ff. [F]

fricassee·, n., & v.t. Meat cut up, fried or stewed, & served with sauce, esp., ragout of birds or small animals cut up; (vb) make f. of. [f. F *fricassée* (*fricasser* vb etym. dub.])

fri·cative (*-a-*), a. & n. (Consonant) made by friction of breath in narrow opening, as *f, th*, Scotch *ch*. [f. L *fricare* rub + -ATIVE]

fri·ction, n. Medical chafing; rubbing of two bodies, attrition; (Physics, Mech.) resistance body meets with in moving over another (*angle of f.*, maximum angle at which one will remain on another without sliding); *f.-ball*, used in bearings to lessen f.; *f.-clutch, -cone, -coupling, -disk, -gear(ing)*, contrivances for transmitting motion by f. Hence **fri·ction**AL, **fri·ction**LESS, aa. [F, f. L *frictionem* (*fricare* rub, -ION)]

Fri·day, n. Sixth day of week (*Good F.*, F. before Easter-day, commemorating Crucifixion; *Black F.*, used as name for various disasters that fell on F.). [OE *frigedæg*; com.-WG transl. of LL *dies Veneris* day of planet Venus, cf. G *Freitag* = day of *Frig* wife of Odin]

friend (frĕnd), n., & v.t. One joined to another in intimacy & mutual benevolence independently of sexual or family love; person who acts for one, e.g. as second in duel; (loosely) acquaintance, stranger that one comes across or has occasion to mention anew, (*my f. in the brown hat now left me*; used in voc. as polite form or in irony, & by Quakers as ordinary address; preceding a name, as *f. Jones, Dick*; *my honourable f.*, of another M.P. in House of Commons; *my learned f.*, of another lawyer in court); (pl.) one's near relations, those responsible for one; sympathizer, helper, patron, (*no f. of* or *to order, virtue*, &c.; *a f. at court*, one whose influence may be made use of); helpful thing (*my shyness was here my best f.*); one who is not an enemy, who is on the same side; *be, keep, make, ff.*, be or get on good terms; (*F-*) Quaker (*Society of Ff.*, the Quakers as a communion); hence **frie·nd**LESS a., **frie·ndless**NESS n. (Vb, poet.) befriend, help. [com.-Teut.; OE *fréond*, cf. G *freund*; p.p. of OTeut. *frijôjan* love (OE *fréon* see FREE[1, 2]), -ND[2]]

frie·ndly, a., n., & adv. Acting, disposed to act, as friend; characteristic of friends, expressing, showing, or prompted by, kindness (*f. lead* among London poor, entertainment to raise funds for distressed person); not hostile, on amicable terms, (*a f. nation*; *f. action* at law, brought merely to get a point decided; *f. match*, played for honour merely, not in competition for cup &c.); favourably disposed, ready to approve or help, (of things) serviceable, convenient, opportune; *F. Society*, for mutual insurance against distress in sickness or old age; hence **frie·ndli**LY[2] (rare) adv., **frie·ndli**NESS n. (N., w. pl.) native of f. tribe. (Adv., rare) in f. manner (*used, received, us f.*). [OE *fréondlic* a., *fréondlice* adv., see -LY[2]]

frie·ndship, n. Being friends, relation between friends; friendly disposition felt or shown. [-SHIP]

frieze[1], n. Coarse woollen cloth with nap usu. on one side only. [f. F *frise* (*friser* curl)]

frieze[2], n. Member of entablature coming between architrave & cornice; horizontal broad band of sculpture filling this; band of decoration elsewhere. [f. F *frise* prob. connected w. It. *fregio* fringe f. L *Phrygium* (*opus* work) of Phrygia]

fri·gate (-at), n. (Hist.) warship next in size & equipment to ships of the line, with 28–60 guns on main deck & raised quarter-deck & forecastle; (mod., loosely for) cruiser; (also *f.-bird*) large swift tropical bird of prey. [f. F *frégate* f. It. *fregata* etym. dub.]

fright (-īt), n., & v.t. Sudden fear, violent terror, alarm; grotesque-looking person; (vb, poet.) frighten. [OE *fryhto* metathetic form of *fyrhto* cf. OE *forht* cf. OE *forht*, G *furcht*]

frigh·ten, v.t. Throw into a fright, terrify, (often *out of, into, doing*); drive *away, out of* (place &c.), *into* (submission &c.), by fright; *frightened at* or *of* (*at* w.

ref. to an occasion, *of* to habitual fear). [prec. (n.) + -EN[1]]

frigh·tful, a. Frightening (archaic); dreadful, shocking, revolting; ugly, hideous, whence **frigh·tful**NESS n. (esp., as mistransl. f. G, terrorizing of civilian population as military resource); (slang) very great, awful. Hence **frigh·tful**LY[2] adv. [-FUL]

frĭ·gid (-j-), a. Cold (esp. of climate or air; *f. zone*, region enclosed by either polar circle); without ardour, apathetic, formal, forced; chilling, depressing; dull, flat, insipid. Hence or cogn. **frigi·d**ITY, **fri·gid**NESS, nn., **fri·gid**LY[2] adv. [f. L *frigidus* (*frigēre* be cold f. *frigus* n. cold)]

frill, n. Ornamental edging of woven material, one side of strip being gathered & the other left loose with fluted appearance; similar paper ornament on ham-knuckle &c.; natural fringe of feathers, hair, &c., on bird, animal, or plant; (pl.) airs, affectation, (*puts on ff.*); mesentery of animal; (Photog.) puckered gelatine film at edge of plate. Hence **frill**ED[2] a., **fri·ll**ERY(5), **fri·ll**ING[1](3, 6), nn. [?]

frĭ·llies, n. pl. (colloq.). Frilled petticoats &c. [-Y[2] or -Y[3]]

fringe (-j-), n., & v.t. Ornamental bordering of threads left loose or formed into tassels or twists; such bordering made separately; border, edging, (*Newgate f.*, beard allowed to grow below shaven chin); front hair cut short & allowed to hang over forehead; natural border of hair &c. in animal or plant; hence **frin·ge**LESS, **fri·ng**Y[2], aa. (Vb) adorn or encircle with f., serve as f. to; hence **fri·ng**ING[1](3) n. [ME & OF *frenge* f. L *fimbria*]

fri·ppery, n. Finery, needless or tawdry adornment esp. in dress; empty display esp. in literary style; knick-knacks, trifles. [f. OF *freperie* (*frepe* rag, -ERY)]

Frisco, n. (U.S. slang). San Francisco. [abbr.]

frise·tte (-z-), n. Band of small artificial curls on forehead. [F (*friser* FRIZZ)]

friseur (frēzer·), n. Hair-dresser. [as prec.]

Fri·sian (-z-), a. & n. (Native, language) of Friesland. [f. L *Frisii* pl. f. OFris. *Frise* + -AN]

frisk, v.i., & n. Move sportively, gambol (v. & n.). Hence **fri·sk**Y[2] a., **fri·ski**LY[2] adv., **fri·ski**NESS n. [f. obs. *frisk* a. f. OF *frisque* lively perh. cogn. w. FRESH]

fri·sket, n. (print.). Thin iron frame with tapes across it keeping sheet in position while printing. [f. F *frisquette* etym. dub.]

frit, n., & v.t. Calcined mixture of sand & fluxes as material for glass-making; vitreous composition from which soft porcelain is made; (vb) make into f., partially fuse, calcine. [f. It. *fritta* fem. p.p. of *friggere* FRY[2]]

fri·t-fly, n. Small fly destructive to wheat. [?]

frith. See FIRTH.

fri·tillary (*or* -tĭ-·), n. Kinds of liliaceous plant, esp. Snakeshead; kinds of butterfly. [f. L *fritillus* dice-box + -ARY[1]]

fri·tter[1], n. Piece of fried batter often containing slices of fruit &c. (*apple, oyster*, &c., *f.*); (pl.) = FENKS. [f. F *friture* (L *frigere frict-* FRY[2], -URE), see -ER[2](3)]

fri·tter[2], v.t. Subdivide minutely; throw (time, money, energy, &c.) *away* on divided aims. [f. obs. n. *fritter*(*s*) = obs. *fitters* n. pl. f. obs. *fitter* v. perh. cogn. w. G *fetzen* rag, scrap; or f. OF *freture* f. L *fractura* FRACTURE]

Fritz, nickname for the Germans or a German. [G, abbr. of *Friedrich* Frederick]

fri·vol (-vl), v.i. & t. Be a trifler, trifle; throw (money, time) *away* foolishly. [back formation f. foll.]

frĭ·volous, a. Paltry, trumpery, trifling, futile; given to trifling, not serious, silly. Hence or cogn. **frivŏ·l**ITY, **fri·volous**NESS, nn., **fri·volous**LY[2] adv. [f. L *frivolus* (perh. f. *fricare* rub) + -OUS]

friz(z)[1], v.t., & n. Curl, crisp, form into mass of small curls, (hair, or person &c. in regard to it); dress (wash-leather &c.) with pumice or scraping-knife. (N.) frizzed state, frizzed hair, row of curls; hence **fri·zz**Y[2] a. [f. F *friser*]

fri·zz[2], v.i. Make sputtering noise in frying. [f. FRY[2] w. imit. termin.]

fri·zzle[1], v.t. & i., & n. Curl (t., & i. esp. with *up*, of hair &c.) in small crisp curls. (N.) frizzled hair; hence **fri·zzl**Y[2] a. [etym. dub.; older than FRIZZ[1]; cf. OFris. *frisle* head of hair]

fri·zzle[2], v.i. & t. Fry, toast, or grill, with sputtering noise. [FRIZZ[2] + -LE(3)]

fro, adv. Away (only in *to & f.*, backwards & forwards, or of repeated journeys between two places). [f. ON *frá* prep. = OE FROM]

frock, n., & v.t. Monk's long gown with loose sleeves, (fig.) priestly character (v.t., invest with priestly office, cf. UNFROCK); = SMOCK-*f.*; sailor's woollen jersey; child's skirt & bodice as outer dress for indoor use, (in recent fashionable use) woman's dress; (also *f.-coat*) man's long-skirted coat not cut away in front; military coat of like shape. [f. F *froc* cf. med. L *froccus, floccus*; perh. = FLOCK[1] as woollen, or f. OHG *hroch* (G *rock*) coat]

frog[1], n. Tailless amphibious animal developed from tadpole; (contempt. for) Frenchman (as eating ff.), whence **Fro·gg**Y[2] n.; *f.-eater*, Frenchman; *f.-fish*, kinds of fish esp. the Angler; *f.-in-the-throat*, hoarseness; *f.'s, f., -march*, carrying of prisoner face downwards by four men holding a limb each; *f.-spawn*, lit., & as name for kinds of freshwater algae. Hence **fro·gg**Y[2] a. (esp. = cold as a f.). [OE *frogga*, also *frox* cf. G *frosch*]

frog[2], n. Elastic horny substance in middle of sole of horse's foot. [?]

frog[3], n. Attachment to waistbelt to support sword, bayonet, &c.; military coat-fastening of spindle-shaped button & loop, whence **frogg**ED[2] a. [perh. f. Port. *froco* f. L *floccus* FLOCK[1]]

frog[4], n. Grooved piece of iron at place in railway where tracks cross. [?]

frŏ·lic, a. (archaic), v.i. (-ck-), & n. Joyous, mirthful, sportive, full of pranks; (vb) play pranks, gambol; (n.) outburst of gaiety, prank, merriment, merry-making, gay party. Hence **fro·lic**SOME a., **fro·licsome**LY[2] adv., **fro·licsome**NESS n. [f. Du. *vrolijk* adj. cf. G *fröhlich* (MDu. *vrô* glad, -LIKE)]

from, prep. expressing separation & introducing:—person, place, &c., whence motion takes place (*comes f. the clouds*; *repeated f. mouth to mouth*); starting-point (*f. title to colophon,* throughout book; *f. 2nd July*; *f. day to day,* daily; *f. time to time,* occasionally; *f. a child,* since childhood); inferior limit (*saw f. 10 to 20 boats*); object &c. whence distance or remoteness is reckoned or stated (*ten miles f. Rome*; *am far f. saying*; *f. home,* out, away; *absent, away, f. home*; *apart f. its moral aspect*); thing or person got rid of, escaped, avoided, of which one is deprived &c., person or thing deprived, (*took his sword f. him*; *released him f. prison*; *cannot refrain f. laughing*; *appeal f. lower court, dissuade f. folly*); state changed for another (*f. being attacked became the aggressor*; *raise penalty f. banishment to death*); thing distinguished (*doesn't know black f. white*); source (*dig gravel f. pit*; *draw conclusion f. premisses*; *quotations f. the fathers*); place of vantage &c. (*saw it f. the poop*; *f. his point of view,* as he sees things); giver, sender, &c. (*gifts f. Providence*; *frocks f. Worth's*; *things not required f. me*); model (*painted f. nature*); reason, cause, motive, (*died f. fatigue*; *suffering f. dementia*; *f. his looks you might suppose*); advbs or advl phrr. of place or time (*f. long ago, of old, above,* &c), or prepositions (*f. under her spectacles*; *f. out the bed*). [OE *fram, from,* forward cf. FRO]

frond, n. (Bot.) leaf-like organ formed by union of stem & foliage in certain flowerless plants, esp. ferns, & differing from leaf in usu. bearing fructification; (Zool.) leaf-like expansion in some animal organisms. Hence **fro·nd**AGE(1) n., **frondo·**SE[1] a. [f. L *frons -dis* leaf]

Fronde (-awnd), n. Party that rebelled against Mazarin & Court during minority of Louis XIV; malcontent party; violent political opposition. [F, orig. = sling]

front (-ŭ-), n. & a., & v.i. & t. Forehead (poet.; *head & f.,* chief part or item); face (*f. to f.*; *have the f.,* be impudent enough usu. *to* do; *present, show, a bold f.*); (Mil.) foremost line or part of army &c., line of battle, part of ground towards real or imaginary enemy, scene of actual fighting (*go to the f.,* join troops on campaign), direction in which formed line faces (*change f.*); (Arch.) any face of building, esp. that of main entrance; fore part of anything (opp. BACK); band of false hair, set of false curls, worn over woman's forehead; breast of man's shirt, also dicky; (with prep.) forward position (*in f. of,* before, in advance of, confronting; *in f.*; *come to the f.,* become conspicuous); (ellipt.) = in f. as adv. or adj. (*were beset f. & rear*; *two-pair f.,* second-floor room in f.); *frontsman,* salesman stationed on pavement in f. of shop; hence **fro·nt**WARD a. & adv., **fro·nt**WARDS adv. (Adj.) of the, situated in, f. (*f. bench,* reserved for ministers or ex-ministers in Parliament houses; *f. door,* chief entrance of house). (Vb) face, look, *to, towards,* (*up*)*on*; face, stand opposite to; have f. on side of (street &c.); confront, meet, oppose; furnish with f. (*fronted with stone*); (Mil.) turn (i. & t.) to the f. (often as word of command). [n. OF, f. L *frons frontis*; vb f. OF *fronter*]

fro·ntage (-ŭ-, -ĭj), n. Land abutting on street or water, land between front of building & road, whence **fro·ntag**ER[1](4) n.; extent of front; front of building; ground occupied by troops in camp or on parade; facing a certain way, exposure, outlook. [-AGE]

fro·ntal[1] (-ŭ-), n. Covering for front of altar; façade. [f. OF *frontel* f. LL *frontale* (FRONT, -AL)]

fro·ntal[2] (-ŭ-), a. Of forehead (*f. bone, artery*); of, on, front (*f. attack,* delivered direct, not on flank or rear). [-AL]

fro·ntier (-ŭ-, -ŏ-), n. Part of a country that borders on another; (attrib.) of, on, the f. [OF (FRONT, *-aria* -ARY[1])]

Frŏ·ntignac (-ĭnyăk), n. A muscat wine. [erron. for *-nan,* name of French town]

fro·ntispiece (-ŭ-), n., & v.t. (Arch.) principal face of building, decorated entrance, pediment over door &c.; illustration facing title-page of book or one of its divisions (vb, supply *with* as f.); face (esp. in boxing slang). [f. F *frontispice* f. med. L *frontispicium* countenance (FRONT, *specere* look) w. assim. to *piece*]

fro·ntless (-ŭ-), a. Unblushing (rare); without front. [-LESS]

fro·ntlet (-ŭ-), n. Band worn on forehead; = PHYLACTERY; animal's forehead; cloth hanging over upper part of altar frontal. [f. OF *frontelet* (FRONTAL[1], -LET)]

frŏnto-, comb. form of L *frons -tis* = of the forehead & —, as *f.-nasal.* [for *fronti-* (-I-, -O-)]

fro·nton (frŭ-), n. Pediment. [F, f. It. *frontone* (FRONT, -OON)]

frore, a. (poet.). Frozen, frosty. [archaic p.p. of FREEZE]

frost (-aw-, -ŏ-), n., & v.t. Freezing, prevalence of temperature below freezing-point of water (*ten* &c. *degrees of f.*; *hard, sharp, f.*; *white* or *hoar, black, f.*, with, without, rime; *Jack F.*, f. personified), frozen state or consistence (*there is still f. in the ground*), frozen dew or vapour (*windows covered with f.*); influence that chills, makes grey, &c.; (slang) failure; *f.-bite*, inflammation or gangrene of & below skin from severe cold, *f.-bitten*, affected with this; *f.-work*, tracery made by f. on glass &c.; hence **fro·st**LESS a. (Vb) nip, injure, (plants &c.) with f.; cover (as) with rime, powder with coating of sugar &c., whence **fro·st**ING[1](3) n.; give roughened or finely granulated surface to (glass, metal); turn (hair) white; arm (horse's shoes) against slipping by nails &c. [com.-Teut.; cf. G *frost*; cogn. w. FREEZE]

fro·sty, a. Cold with frost; cold, chilling, frigid, lacking in warmth of feeling; covered, seeming to be covered, with hoar-frost. Hence **fro·sti**LY[2] adv., **fro·sti**NESS n. [-Y[2]]

froth (-aw-, -ŏ-), n., & v.i. & t. Collection of small bubbles, foam; impure matter on liquid, scum; worthless matter, idle talk, &c.; hence **fro·th**Y[2] a., **fro·thi**LY[2] adv., **fro·thi**NESS n. (Vb) emit, gather, f.; cause (beer &c.) to foam. [perh. f. ON *frotha* cf. OE *á-fréothan* to f.]

frou·-frou (-ōō-, -ōō), n. Rustling, esp. of dresses. [F, imit.]

frow (-ow), n. Dutchwoman. [f. Du. *vrouw* = G *frau* woman]

froward (frō·*ard*), a. (archaic). Perverse, refractory. Hence **frow·ard**LY[2] adv., **frow·ard**NESS n. [FRO-, WARD]

frown, v.i. & t., & n. Knit brows esp. to express displeasure or concentrate attention; (of things) present gloomy aspect; express disapprobation (*at, on, upon*); put (interrupter, interruption, &c.) *down* with f.; express (defiance &c.) with f.; hence **frow·ning**LY[2] adv. (N.) vertically furrowed state of brow; look expressing severity, disapproval, or deep thought. [f. OF *froignier* perh. f. Teut. cf. Sw. dial. *fryna*, Norw. *fröyna*, make wry face]

frowst, n., & v.i. Fusty heat in room (vb, stay in, enjoy, this,). Hence **frow·st**Y[2] a. [?]

frow·zy, a. Ill-smelling, fusty, musty, close; slatternly, unkempt, dingy. Hence **frow·zi**NESS n. [?]

froze(n). See FREEZE.

fructi·ferous, a. Bearing fruit. [f. L *fructifer* (FRUIT, -FEROUS)]

fructifica·tion, n. (bot.). Fructifying; reproductive parts of plant, esp. of ferns & mosses. [f. L *fructificatio* (foll., -FICATION)]

fru·ctifȳ, v.i & t. Bear fruit (lit. & fig.); make fruitful, impregnate. [f. F *fructifier* f. L *fructificare* (FRUIT, -FY)]

fru·ctose, n. Fruit sugar. [f. L *fructus* FRUIT + -OSE[2]]

fru·ctuous, a. Full of, producing, fruit (lit. & fig.). OF, f. L *fructuosus* (FRUIT, -OUS)]

fru·gal (-ōō-), a. Careful, sparing (*of*), economical, esp. as regards food; sparingly used or supplied, costing little. Hence or cogn. **frugă·li**TY n., **fru·gal**LY[2] adv. [f. L *frugalis* (*frugi* indecl. adj. orig. dat. of *frux* profit + -AL]

frugi·vorous, a. Feeding on fruit. [f. L *frux frugi-* fruit + -VOROUS]

fruit (-ōōt), n., & v.i. & t. (Usu. pl.) vegetable products fit for food (usu. *ff. of the earth*), so **frui·t**AGE(1) n.; plant's or tree's edible product of seed with its envelope (also collect. in sing., as *feeds on f.*); vegetable seed with envelope as means of reproduction; (bibl.) offspring (usu. *f. of the body, loins, womb*); produce of action, (pl.) revenues produced (*the ff. of industry*); (sing. or pl.) result, issue, consequence; *f.-cake*, containing currants &c.; *f. clipper*, fast ship carrying f.; *f.-knife*, with silver &c. blade against acid; *f.-piece*, picture of f.; *f. salad*, of various ff. cut up & mixed in bowl often with cream &c.; *f.-sugar*, glucose, levulose, or fructose; *f.-tree*, grown for its f.; hence, (-)**fruit**ED[2] a. (Vb.) bear, make bear, f. [OF, f. L *fructus -ūs* (*frui* enjoy)]

fruitār·ian, n. Feeder on fruit. [-ARIAN]

frui·ter, n. Fruit-ship; tree producing fruit (*a sure f.*); fruit-grower. [FRUIT n. & v., -ER[1]]

frui·terer, n. Dealer in fruit. [-ER[1] doubled]

frui·tful, a. Productive, fertile, causing fertility; productive of offspring, prolific, (lit. & fig.; *a session f. in great measures*); beneficial, remunerative, whence **frui·tful**LY[2] adv. Hence **frui·tful**NESS n. [-FUL]

fruition (frōōĭ·shn), n. Enjoyment, attainment of thing desired, realization of hopes &c. [OF, f. L *fruitionem* (*frui fruit-*, enjoy, -ION)]

frui·tless, a. Not bearing fruit; yielding no profit, ineffectual, useless, empty, vain. Hence **frui·tless**LY[2] adv., **frui·tless**NESS n. [-LESS]

frui·tlet, n. (bot.). = DRUPEL. [-LET]

frui·ty, a. Of fruit; (of wine) tasting of the grape, whence **frui·ti**NESS n. [-Y[2]]

fru·menty (ōō-), **fur·mety,** n. Hulled wheat boiled in milk & seasoned with cinnamon, sugar, &c. [f. OF *frumentée* (*frument* f. L *frumentum* corn), -Y[1]]

frump, n. Old-fashioned dowdily-dressed woman. Hence **fru·mp**ISH[1], **fru·mp**Y[2], aa. [?]

fru·strāte, a. (archaic). Frustrated. [f. L *frustratus* (foll., -ATE[2])]

frustra·te (*also* frŭ·-), v.t. Balk, baffle, neutralize, counteract, disappoint. So **frustra·**TION n. [f. L *frustrari* (*frustra* in vain), -ATE[3]]

fru·stule, n. Two-valved shell of diatom. [F, f. LL *frustulum* (foll., -ULE)]

fru·stum, n. (pl. *-ta, -tums*). Remainder of regular solid whose upper part has been cut off by plane parallel to base, or part intercepted between two planes. [L, = piece broken off]

frute·scent, a. (bot.). Of the nature of a frutex. [for *fruticescent* (foll., -ESCENT)]

fru·tex, n. (bot.). Woody-stemmed plant smaller than tree, shrub. [L (genit. *-icis*)]

fru·ticose, a. (Bot.) shrubby; (of minerals, zoophytes, &c.) looking like shrub. [prec., -OSE¹]

fry¹, n. Young fishes fresh from the spawn; young of salmon in second year; young of other creatures produced in large numbers, e.g. bees or frogs; *small f.*, young or insignificant beings, children &c. [f. ON *frió* seed]

fry², v.t. & i., & n. Cook (t. & i.) in boiling fat (*other* FISH¹ *to f.*; *frying-pan*, shallow pan used; *out of frying-pan into fire*, from bad to worse). (N.) fried meat; various internal parts of animals usu. fried, esp. LAMB'*s f.* [f. F *frire* f. L *frigere* cf. Gk *phrugō*]

fry·er, fri·er, n. Vessel for frying fish. [-ER¹]

fu·bsy (-zĭ), a. Fat or squat. [f. obs. *fubs* small fat person]

fuchsia (fū·sha), n. Drooping-flowered shrub. [mod. L (*Fuchs* 16th-c. German botanist, -IA¹)]

fu·chsine (fo͝ok-), n. Salt of rosaniline forming deep red dye. [prec. (f. resemblance of colour to flower) + -INE⁴]

fū·cus, n. (pl. *-ci* pr.-sī). Kinds of seaweed with flat leathery fronds. Hence **fu·**COID a. [L, = rock-lichen, cf. Gk *phōkos*]

fu·ddle, v.i. & t., & n. Tipple, booze; intoxicate; stupefy, confuse; (n.) spell of drinking (*on the f.*), intoxication, confusion. [cf. Du. *vod* slack, G dial. *fuddeln* swindle]

fudge¹, int. & n. Nonsense!; nonsense. [?]

fudge², v.t. & i., & n. Fit together, patch, make up, in a makeshift or dishonest way, cook, fake; practise such methods; (n.) piece of fudging. [perh. f. obs. *fadge* v.i., fit]

fū·el, n., & v.t. & i. (-ll-). Material for fires, firing, coal, wood, &c.; something that feeds or inflames passion &c. (Vb) supply (fire) with f.; get f. [f. OF *fowaille* f. pop. L *focalia* neut. pl. of *focalis* (*focus* hearth, -AL)]

fug, n. Fustiness of air in room; fluff & dust collected in corners &c. Hence **fu·gg**Y² a. [?]

fūga·cious, a. Fleeting, evanescent, hard to capture or keep. So **fugă·**CITY n. [f. L *fugax* (*fugere* flee, -ACIOUS)]

fū·gal, a. Of the nature of a fugue. Hence **fu·gal**LY² adv. [-AL]

-fuge, suf. in adjj. & nn. f. mod. L in *-fugus*. Acc. to L anal. the sense should be *fleeing from* (*fugere*) as in L *lucifugus, erifuga*; but in the mod. formations it is *putting to flight* (*fugare*) as in *febrifuge, vermifuge.*

fū·gitive, a. & n. Flying, running away, that has taken flight; flitting, shifting; evanescent, of short duration, quickly fading; (of literature) of passing interest, ephemeral, occasional. (N.) one who flees esp. from danger, enemy, justice, or owner; exile, refugee. [F (*-if, -ive*), f. L *fugitivus* (*fugere fugit-* flee, -IVE)]

fū·gleman, n. (pl. *-men*). Soldier placed in front of regiment &c. while drilling to show the motions & time; leader, organizer, spokesman, whence by back formation **fu·gle** v.i. [f. G *flügelmann* (*flügel* wing, *mann* man)]

fugue (fūg), n., & v.i. & t. Polyphonic composition on one or more short themes contrapuntally harmonized & re-introduced from time to time; hence **fu·**GUIST(1) n. (Vb) compose or perform f. (*fuguing* or *fugued*, in the form of a f.). (F, f. It. & L *fuga* flight]

-ful, suf. orig. = FULL a. (1) forming adjj. f. nn., w. sense *full of* (*beautiful*), & sometimes *having qualities of* (*masterful*); also adjj. f. adjj. or f. L adj. stems (*direful, grateful, tristful*), perh. on anal. of older synonyms in *-ful*; also f. vv. (*forgetful*), arising perh. f. cases in which first component might in form be either n. or v. (*helpful*, & esp. *thankful* where the sing. n. being disused *thank* would naturally be taken for verb); a pass. sense is seen in *bashful* = abashable. (2) forming nn., w. sense *amount required to fill* (*handful*). *Handful* is a differentiation f. *hand full*, which in the Teut. langg. had orig. besides its literal sense that of *quantity that fills a hand.* The differentiation is not carried out equally in all langg., G *handvoll* &c. taking their gender f. first component, though written as single wds. In mod. E *-ful* is a living suf. freely added to nn. (*boxful, houseful, churchful*); a reminiscence of its orig. is seen in *spoonsful, cupsful*, which are ambiguous & contrary to good mod. usage.

fū·lcrum, n. (pl. *-ra*). (Mech.) point against which lever is placed to get purchase or on which it turns or is supported; means by which influence &c. is brought to bear; (Bot.; usu. pl.) accessory organs, appendages, e.g. bracts, tendrils. [L, = post of couch (*fulcire* to prop)]

fulfi·l (fo͝o-), v.t. (-ll-). Bring to consummation, carry out, (prophecy, promise), satisfy (desire, prayer); perform, execute, do, (command, law); answer (purpose), comply with (conditions); bring to an end, finish, complete, (period, work). Hence **fulfi·l**MENT n. [OE *fullfyllan* (FULL¹, FILL)]

fū·lgent, a. (poet. & rhet.). Shining, brilliant. [f. L *fulgēre* shine, -ENT]

fŭ·lgŭrite, n. (Geol.) rocky substance fused or vitrified by lightning, tube made by passage of lightning into sand; an explosive. [f. L *fulgur* lightning + -ITE[1](2)]

fu·lham, n. (hist.). Loaded DIE[1]. [?]

Fulham Palace (fŏŏ·lam), n. Official residence of the Bishop of London.

fūlĭ·ginous, a. Sooty, dusky. [f. L *fuliginosus* (*fuligo -inis* soot, -OUS)]

full[1] (fŏŏl), a., v.t., & adv. Filled to utmost capacity, holding all (*of*, or abs.) its limits will allow, replete, (*f. to the brim, to overflowing,* & colloq. *up*), (of heart &c.) overcharged with emotion (*f.-hearted,* stirred with deep feeling, also zealous, confident, courageous); holding or having abundance *of,* crowded (*in a f. house,* with a good proportion of members present), showing marked signs *of* (*f. of vitality*); engrossed with the thought *of* (*f. of himself, of his subject; f. of the news* &c., unable to keep from talking of it); replete with food (archaic of persons; *a f. stomach*); (chiefly bibl.) having had one's fill *of* (*f. of years & honours*); abundant, sufficient, copious, satisfactory, (*a f. meal; turned it to f. account; give f. details; he is very f. on this point*); complete, entire, perfect, answering completely to its name, reaching the specified or usual limit, entirely visible, (*f. point* or *stop,* period in punctuation; *f. daylight, membership; f. brother, sister,* born of same father and mother; *of the f. blood,* of pure descent, not hybrid, so *f.-blooded,* & see below; *f. pay,* that allowed on active service; *f. age,* after minority; *f.* DRESS[2], & so *f.-dress rehearsal; f.-dress debate* in Parliament, prearranged on important question, not arising casually; *f.* SWING n.; *at f. length,* lying stretched out, also = *in f.* below; *f.-length portrait* &c., of whole figure; *f. moon,* with whole disk illuminated, also the time when this comes; *f. face,* turned straight to spectator; *waited a f. hour; it was f. summer*); (of light) intense, (of colour) deep, (of motion &c.) vigorous (*a f. pulse; f. gallop, speed,* &c., used adv. with *come* &c.; *f. speed ahead!,* order to pursue course with energy); swelling, plump, protuberant, (of dress) containing superfluous material arranged in folds &c. (vb, make f., gather, pleat); *f.-back,* football player stationed behind; *f.-blooded,* vigorous, hearty, sensual, & see above; *f.-bodied,* esp. of wine with much BODY; *f.-bottomed* of wig, long behind, opp. BOB[1]; *f.-mouthed,* (of cattle) with f. complement of teeth, (of dogs) baying loudly, (of oratory, style, &c.) sonorous, vigorous; *f.-timer,* child who attends during all school-hours (opp. *half-timer*); (used abs. as n.) whole (*cannot tell you the f. of it; in f.,* without abridgement; *to the f.,* to the utmost extent, quite); height, acme, (*season, moon, is past the f.*); hence **fu·llISH**[1](2) a. (Adv.) very (chiefly poet.; *f. fain; f. many a; know it f. well*); quite, fully, (*f. six miles; f. as useful as*; often in comb., as *f.-blown,* of flowers, quite open, also fig. as *f.-b. dignity; f.-grown,* having reached maturity); exactly (*hit him f. on the nose*); more than sufficiently (*this chair is f. high*). [Aryan; cf. G *voll,* Skr. *purṇa,* L *plenus,* Gk *plērēs*]

full[2] (fŏŏl), v.t. Cleanse & thicken (cloth). [f. OF *fouler* see FOIL[2]]

fu·ller[1] (fŏŏ-), n. One who fulls cloth; *f.'s earth,* hydrous silicate of alumina. [-ER[1]]

fu·ller[2] (fŏŏ-), n., & v.t. Grooved tool on which iron is shaped; groove made by this esp. in horse-shoes; (vb) stamp with f. [?]

ful(l)ness, n. Being FULL[1]; esp.: (bibl.) *the f. of the heart,* emotion, genuine feelings, *the f. of time,* the destined time, *the f. of the world* &c., all that fills it; (of sound, colour, &c.) richness, volume, body. [-NESS]

fully (fŏŏ·lĭ), adv. Completely, without deficiency; quite (esp. with numbers). [-LY[2]]

fu·lmar (fŏŏ-) n. Sea-bird of petrel kind & gull's size. [perh. f. ON *fúll* FOUL[1] + *már* MEW[1]]

fŭ·lminant, a. Fulminating; (Path., of diseases) developing suddenly. [f. L as foll., -ANT]

fŭ·lminate, v.i. & t. Flash like lightning, explode, detonate, (*fulminating gold, mercury,* &c., various fulminates, see FULMINIC); thunder forth, utter or publish, (censure); issue (usu. official) censures *against* (esp. of Pope). Hence or cogn. **fulminA·TION** n., **fu·lminātORY** a. [f. L *fulminare* (*fulmen* lightning, -ATE[3])]

fŭ·lmĭne, v.t. & i. (poet.). Send forth (lightning, thunder); thunder (lit. & fig.). [as prec.]

fŭlmĭ·nic, a. (chem.). *F. acid,* nitro-acetonitril, an acid forming explosive salts with some metals. Hence **fu·lminATE**[1](3) n. [f. L *fulmen -inis* lightning + -IC]

fu·lness. See FULLNESS.

fu·lsome (fŭ-, fŏŏ-), a. Cloying, excessive, disgusting by excess, (of flattery, servility, exaggerated affection). Hence **fu·lsomeLY**[2] adv., **fu·lsomeNESS** n. (FULL[1], -SOME]

fŭ·lvous, a. (nat. hist.). Reddish-yellow, tawny. So **fulvE·SCENT** a. [f. L *fulvus* + -OUS]

fūmā·de, n. Smoked pilchard. [f. Sp. *fumado* smoked, f. L *fumare* FUME, -ADO[1]]

fū·marole, n. Crevice in cone of volcano through which vapour issues. [f. F *fumerolle* f. L *fumariolum* dim. of *fumarium* smoke-chamber (*fumus* smoke, -ARY[1])]

fu·mble, v.i. & t., & n. Use the hands

awkwardly, grope about, (*at*, *with*, fastening &c.; *for*, *after*, thing sought); handle or deal with awkwardly or nervously (*f. the ball*, not stop it cleanly); hence **fu·mbl**ER[1] n. (N.) bungling attempt. [perh. f. OE *folm* palm of hand; cf. Du. *fommelen*]

fume, n., & v.t. & i. Odorous smoke, vapour, or exhalation; watery vapour; noxious vapour supposed to rise from stomach to brain (*the ff. of wine* &c.; also fig. of excitement, enthusiasm, &c.); fit of anger (*in a f.*); hence **fu·m**Y[2] a. (Vb) perfume with incense; subject to chemical fumes esp. those of ammonia (photographic film, oak, to darken tints); emit ff.; (of vapour &c.) rise, be emitted; be pettish, chafe (*at*). [n. f. OF *fum*, vb f. F *fumer*, f. L *fumus, fumare*, smoke]

fū·migate, v.t. Apply fumes to; disinfect or purify with fumes; perfume. Hence **fumig**A·TION, **fu·migat**OR[2](1, 2), nn. [f. L *fumigare* (*fumus* smoke), -ATE[3]]

fū·mitory, n. Herb formerly used in medicine. [f. OF *fumeterre* f. med. L *fumus terrae* earth-smoke, w. assim. to -ORY]

fun, n., & v.i. Sport, amusement, jocularity, drollery, (*make f. of*, *poke f. at*, ridicule; *for* or *in f.*, as a joke, not seriously; *is good, great, f.*, very amusing; *like f.*, vigorously, quickly, much; *what f.!*, how amusing!); (vb; rare) indulge in f., joke. [perh. f. obs. *fon* befool, etym. dub.]

fūna·mbūlist, n. Rope-walker. [f. L *funambulus* (*funis* rope, *ambulare* walk), -IST]

fu·nction, n., & v.i. Activity proper to anything, mode of action by which it fulfils its purpose; office-holder's duty, employment, profession, calling; religious or other public ceremony or occasion, social meeting of formal or important kind; (Math.) variable quantity in relation to other(s) in terms of which it may be expressed or on which its value depends; hence **fu·nction**LESS a. (Vb) fulfil a f., operate, act. [OF, f. L *functionem* (*fungi funct-* perform, -ION)]

fu·nctional, a. Official, merely formal, (rare); (Physiol.) of, affecting, the functions of an organ &c. only, not structural or organic (esp. of diseases), (of organ) having a function, not functionless or rudimentary; (Math.)of a FUNCTION. Hence **fu·nctional**LY[2] adv. [-AL]

fu·nctionary, n. & a. (N.) official; (adj.) =prec. (not in math. sense). [-ARY[1]]

fu·nctionate, v.i. =FUNCTION v. [-ATE[3]]

fund, n., & v.t. Permanent stock of something ready to be drawn upon (*a f. of common sense, tenderness, labour, knowledge*); stock of money, esp. one set apart for a purpose (SINK[1]*ing f.*); (pl.) pecuniary resources (*in ff.*, having money, flush); *the ff.*, stock of national debt as mode of investment (*has £10,000 in the ff.*; *f.-holder*, such investor). (Vb) convert (floating debt) into more or less permanent debt at fixed interest; put into a f., collect, store, (rare); invest (money) in the ff. [f. L *fundus* bottom]

fu·ndament, n. The buttocks. [f. L *fundamentum* (FOUND[1], -MENT) foundation)]

fundame·ntal, a. & n. Of the groundwork, going to the root of the matter, serving as base or foundation, essential, primary, original, from which others are derived, (*a f. change*; *the f. rules*; *the f. form*); (Mus.) *f. note*, lowest note of chord, *f. tone*, produced by vibration of whole sonorous body (opp. *harmonics* produced by that of its parts); hence **fundamenta·**LITY n., **fundame·ntal**LY[2] adv. (N.) principle, rule, article, serving as groundwork of system (usu. pl.); (Mus.) f. note or tone. [-AL]

fundame·ntalism, n. (U.S.). Maintenance, in opposition to modernism, of traditional orthodox beliefs such as the inerrancy of Scripture & literal acceptance of the creeds as fundamentals of protestant Christianity. So **fundame·ntal**IST n. & a. [prec. + -ISM]

fūne·brial, a. (rare). Of funeral (*custom is f. in origin*). [f. L *funebris* (*funus* see foll.) + -AL]

fū·neral, a. & n. Of, used &c. at, burial or cremation of the dead (*f. pile, pyre*, pile of wood &c. on which corpse is burnt; *f. urn*, holding ashes of cremated dead; *f. oration*). (N.) burial of the dead with its observances, obsequies; burial procession. [adj. OF, f. med. L *funeralis* (L *funus -eris* funeral + -AL); n. f. OF *funeraille* f. med. L *funeralia* neut. pl. of *funeralis*, -AL(2)]

fū·nerary, a. =FUNEBRIAL. [f. LL *funerarius* (prec., -ARY[1])]

funer·ĕal, a. Appropriate to funeral, gloomy, dismal, dark. Hence **funer·eal**LY[2] adv. [f. L *funereus* (FUNERAL) + -AL]

fu·ngible (-j-), a. (legal). That can serve for, or be replaced by, another answering to the same definition (of goods &c. contracted for, when an individual specimen is not meant). [f. med.L *fungibilis* f. *fungi* (*vice*) serve (turn), -IBLE]

fu·ngicide (-j-), n. Fungus-destroying substance. [FUNGUS, -I-, -CIDE]

fu·ngin (-j-), n. Substance forming cell-walls of fungus. [-IN]

fu·ngous, a. Of fungi, having nature of a fungus; springing up like a mushroom, transitory. [f. L *fungosus* (foll., -OSE[1])]

fu·ngus, n. (pl. *-gi* pr. -jī, *-uses*). Mushroom, toadstool, or allied plant including moulds; (Bot.) cryptogamous plant without chlorophyll feeding on organic matter; thing of sudden growth; (Path.) spongy morbid growth or excrescence; skin-disease of fish. Hence **fu·ngAL**, **fu·ngiFORM** (-j-), **fungi·VOROUS** (-j-), **fu·ngOID**, **fu·ngusY**[2], aa. [L, perh. cogn. w. Gk *sphoggos* SPONGE]

fūni·cular, a. Of a rope or its tension (*f. railway*, worked by cable & stationary engine). [f. L *funiculus* (*funis* cord, -CULE) + -AR[1]]

funk, n., & v.i. & t., (slang). Fear, panic, (*blue f.*, terror); coward; hence **fu·nkY**[2] a.; *f.-hole*, trench dug-out, employment used as pretext for evading military service. (Vb) flinch, shrink, show cowardice; (try to) evade (undertaking), shirk; be afraid of; inspire fear in. [called Oxford slang in 1743; etym dub.]

fu·nnel, n. Diminishing tube, or truncated cone & tube, for conducting liquid, powder, &c., into small opening; ventilating or lighting shaft; metal chimney of steam engine or ship; f.- shaped lower part of chimney. Hence **(-)funnelLED**[2] a. [ME *fonel* perh. thr. OF (cf. Breton *founil*) f. L *infundibulum* f. IN(*fundere* pour)]

fu·nniment, n. Joke, drollery. [foll., -MENT]

fu·nny[1], a. Affording fun, comical; curious, queer, perplexing, hard to account for; *f.-bone*, part of elbow over which ulnar nerve passes; *f.-man*, professional jester. Hence **fu·nniLY**[2] adv., **fu·nniNESS** n. [-Y[2]]

fu·nny[2], n. Narrow clinker-built boat for one sculler. [perh. f. prec.]

fur, n., & v.t. & i. Trimming or lining made of dressed coat of certain animals, e.g. ermine, beaver; coat of such animals, as material for trimming &c.; (usu. pl.) garment(s) of or having f.; short fine soft hair of certain animals distinguished from the longer hair, (pl.) skins of such animals with the f.; (collect.) furred animals (esp. *f. & feather*; *hunt f.*, hares); crust adhering to surface, e.g. deposit of wine; coating formed on tongue in sickness; crust of carbonate of lime in kettle &c.; hence **fur·rY**[2] a. (Vb; esp. in p.p.) provide (garment, animal), clothe (person), coat (tongue, inside of kettle; also intr., become coated), with f., clean f. from (boiler); (Carpent.) level (floor-timbers) by inserting strips of wood. [n. f. vb, OF *forrer* (now *fourrer*) f. Rom. *foderare* sheathe, line, f. Teut. (OE *fóddor* cf. G *futter* lining)]

fur·below, n., & v.t. Flounce, pleated border of skirt or petticoat; (pl., contempt.) showy ornaments; kind of wrinkled seaweed; (vb) adorn with ff. [corrupt. of FALBALA]

fur·bish, v.t. Remove rust from, polish *up*, burnish; give new look to, renovate, revive, (something antiquated; usu. *up*). [f. OF *forbir* (-ISH[2]) f. OHG *forban*]

fur·cate[1] (-āt, -*at*), a. Forked, branched. Hence **furca·to-** comb. form. [f. med. L *furcatus* (L *furca* fork, -ATE[2])]

furca·te[2], v.i. Form a fork, divide. So **furcA·TION** n. [f. L *furca* fork + -ATE[3]]

fū̆r·ious, a. Full of fury, raging, frantic, violent; *fast & f.*, (of mirth &c.) eager, uproarious. Hence **fur·iousLY**[2] adv. [f. OF *furieus* f. L *furiosus* (FURY, -OUS)]

furl, v.t. & i. Roll up & bind (sail) on yard or boom; close, fold up, draw away, relinquish, (fan, umbrella, wings, curtain, hopes); become furled, roll away like clouds. [prob. f. obs. *furdle* furl var. of obs. *fardel* vb (FARDEL)]

fur·long, n. Eighth of mile. [OE *furlang* (*furh* furrow, LONG adj.); orig. =length of furrow in common field, regarded as square containing ten acres]

fur·lough (-lō), n., & v.t. Leave of absence, esp. to soldier; (vb) grant f. to. [f. Du. *verlof* cf. G *verlaub* (FOR-, LEAVE[1])]

fur·mety. See FRUMENTY.

fur·nace (-ĭs), n., & v.t. Apparatus including chamber for combustibles in which minerals, metals, &c., may be subjected to continuous intense heat; hot place; severe test (esp. *tried in the f.*); closed fireplace for heating building by hot pipes; (vb) heat in f. [f. OF *fornais* f. L *fornacem* nom. *-ax* (*fornus* oven)]

fur·nish, v.t. Provide *with* (*furnished with*, having); fit up (house, room) with all necessary appliances, esp. movable furniture (*furnished house, rooms*, &c., esp. let with furniture); provide, afford, yield. [f. OF *furnir* (-ISH[2]) f. Rom. *fornire* f. Teut. (OHG *frummen* promote f. root of FROM)]

fur·niture (-tsh*er*), n. Contents of receptacle (*f. of his pocket*, money; *f. of my shelves*, books; *f. of* one's *mind*, knowledge & intelligence); harness &c. of horse &c. (archaic); movable contents of house or room, tables, chairs, &c. [f. F *fourniture* (*fournir* FURNISH)]

fūror·ĕ, n. Enthusiastic admiration, rage, craze. [It., f. L *furorem* (*furere* be mad, -OR[1])]

fŭ·rrier, n. Dealer in, dresser of, furs. [-IER]

fur·ring, n. In vbl senses; also (Shipbuild.), doubling of planks on ship's side. [-ING[1]]

fu·rrow (-ō), n., & v.t. Narrow trench made by plough; ship's track; rut, track, groove, long indentation, deep wrinkle, hollow between ridges; *f.-slice*, slice of earth turned up by mould-board of plough; hence **fu·rrowLESS**, **fu·rrowY**[2], aa. (Vb) plough; make ff., grooves &c., in; mark with wrinkles. [com.-Teut.; OE *furh* cf. Du. *voor*, G *furche*]

fur·ther (-dh-), adv. & a. (for usage of *fur-*, *far-*, see FARTHER etym.), & v.t. To or at more advanced point in space or time (*unsafe to proceed f.*; *& then to lapse unless f. continued*); to greater extent, more, (*inquire f.*); (also *furthermore*) in addition, moreover, also (esp. introducing fresh consideration in argument); at greater distance (*I'll see you f. first*, euphem. for *in hell*, as strong refusal of request). (Adj.) going beyond what exists or has been dealt with, additional, (*threats of f. punishment*; *till f. notice*, in announcing arrangement to continue during pleasure); more distant (*on the f. side*), whence **fur·ther**MOST a. (Vb) help on, promote, favour, (undertaking, movement, cause); hence **fur·ther**ANCE n., **fur·ther**SOME a. [OE *furthor* adv., *furthra* adj., (FORE[2], -THER), *fyrthrian* vb]

fur·thest (-dh-), a. & adv. =FARTHEST. [superl. formed f. prec.]

fur·tive, a. Done by stealth, clandestine, meant to escape notice; sly, stealthy; stolen, taken secretly; thievish, pilfering. Hence **fur·tive**LY[2] adv., **fur·tive**NESS n. [F (*-if*, *-ive*), f. L *furtivus* (*furtum* theft, -IVE)]

fū̆r·uncle, n. Boil, tumour. Hence **fū̆r·uncul**AR, **fū̆ru·ncul**OUS, aa. [f. L *furunculus* (*fur* thief, -UNCLE)]

fū̆r·y, n. Fierce passion, wild anger, rage, (*in a f.*, fit of rage); impetuosity in battle &c. (*the Spanish F.*, massacre by Spaniards at Antwerp 1576); violence of weather, disease, &c. (*like f.*, furiously, hard); (usu. pl.) snake-haired goddess(es) of Gk myth sent from Tartarus to punish crime, (fig.) avenging spirits, remorseful pangs, (*haunted by the ff. of her father's blood*); virago, angry or malignant woman. [f. F *furie* f. L *furia* (*furere* be mad)]

furze, n. Spiny yellow-flowered evergreen shrub growing on European waste lands, gorse, whin. Hence **fur·z**Y[2] a. [OE *fyrs* etym. dub.]

fu·scous, a. (nat. hist.). Sombre, dark, in colour. So **fu·sco**- comb. form [L *fuscus*, -OUS]

fuse[1] (-z), v.t. & i. Melt (t. & i.) with intense heat; blend, amalgamate, (t. & i.) into one whole (as) by melting (of metals, living bones, institutions, motives, &c.). Hence **fu·s**IBLE a., **fusi**BI·LITY n. [f. L *fundere fus-* pour]

fuse[2] (-z), n., & v.t. Tube, casing, cord, &c., filled or saturated with combustible matter for igniting bomb, blasting-charge, &c.; (vb) fit f. to. [f. It. *fuso* f. L *fusus* spindle]

fusee· (-z-), n. Conical pulley or wheel esp. in watch or clock; exostosis or bony tumour on horse's cannon-bone; large-headed match for lighting cigar or pipe in wind. [f. F *fusée* f. med. L *fusata* spindleful (L *fusus* spindle)]

fū·selage (-zelij), n. Framework of aeroplane. [F, f. *fuseler* cut in spindle form (*fuseau* spindle f. LL *fusellus* dim. of *fusus*), -AGE]

fu·sel oil (-z-), n. Mixture of several alcohols, chiefly amylic, formed in making some spirits. [f. G *fusel* bad spirit, cf. *fuseln* FOOZLE]

fu·siform (-s-), a. (nat. hist.). Shaped like spindle or cigar, tapering at both ends. [f. L *fusus* spindle, -I-, -FORM]

fu·sil (-z-), n. Obsolete light musket. [F, =It. *focile* (L *focus* hearth, fire, -IL)]

fusilier· (-z-), n. (usu. pl.). (Man of) certain (now ten) British regiments formerly armed with fusils. [F (prec., -IER)]

fusillā·de, n., & v.t. (Wholesale execution by) continuous discharge of firearms; (vb) assault (place), shoot down (persons), by f. [F (*fusiller* shoot f. FUSIL, -ADE)]

fu·sion (-zhn), n. Fusing; fused mass; blending of different things into one; coalition, whence **fu·sion**IST(2) n. [f. L *fusio* (FUSE[1], -ION); cf. FOISON]

fuss, n., & v.i. & t. Bustle, excessive commotion, ostentatious or nervous activity; treatment of trifles as important; abundance of petty detail; hence **fu·ss**Y[2] a., **fu·ss**ILY[2] adv., **fu·ss**INESS n. (Vb) make f.; busy oneself restlessly with trifles; move fussily *about*, *up & down*, &c.; agitate, worry, (person). [perh. imit. of sputtering or bubbling]

fūstane·lla, n. Man's white petticoat in modern Greece. [It., dim. of mod. Gk *phoustani* perh. f. It. *fustagno* FUSTIAN]

fu·stian (-t-), n. Thick twilled short-napped cotton cloth usu. dyed dark; turgid speech or writing, bombast; (attrib.) made of f., (fig.) bombastic, worthless, sorry, pretentions. [f. OF, *fustaigne* (med. L *fustaneus* adj. perh. = from *Fostat* suburb of Cairo)]

fu·stic, n. Two kinds of wood yielding yellow dye (*young f.*, Venetian sumach; *f.* or *old f.*, Amer. & W. Ind.); dye from these. [f. F f. Sp. *fustoc* f. Arab. *fustuq* f. Gk as PISTACHIO]

fu·stigate, v.t. (joc.). Cudgel. So **fustigā**·TION n. [L *fustigare* (*fustis* cudgel), -ATE[3]]

fu·sty, a. Stale-smelling, musty, mouldy; close, stuffy; antiquated, old-fashioned. Hence **fu·sti**NESS n. [f. obs. *fust* (smell of) wine-cask f. OF *fust* cask f. L *fustis* cudgel]

fū̆tchel(l), n. One of timbers supporting shafts, pole, or axle-bar, of carriage. [?]

fu·thorc (fōō-), n. Runic alphabet. [its first six letters (*th* being one)]

fū·tile (-ī-, -ĭ-), a. Useless, ineffectual, vain, frivolous. Hence or cogn. **futi·l**ITY n., (rare) **fu·tile**LY[2] adv. [f. L *futilis* leaky, futile, perh. f. *fud-* st. of *fundere* pour]

fŭttock, n. One of ship's middle timbers between floor & top timbers. [perh. = *foot-hook*]

fū·ture (-tsh*er*), a. & n. About to happen, that will be hereafter (*f. life, state,* existence after death), that will be something specified (*my f. wife*); of time to come, (Gram., of tense) describing event yet to happen. (N.) time to come (*for the f., in f.,* from now onwards; *past, present, & f.*); what will happen in the f.; person's, country's, &c., prospective condition; (Gram.) f. tense; one's betrothed; (Commerc.; pl.) goods & stocks sold for f. delivery, contracts for these; hence **fu·ture**LESS a. [OF (*-ur, -ure*), f. L *futurus* fut. part. of *esse* be f. st. *fu-* BE]

fu·turist, n. & a. (Theol.) (one) believing that the prophecies of the Apocalypse &c. are still to be fulfilled; (Art) adherent of **fu·tur**ISM n., a recent movement in (esp. Italian) art, literature, &c., marked by violent departure from traditional methods and by the use of arbitrary symbols in the expression of emotion. [-IST]

futūr·ity, n. Future time; (sing. or pl.) future events; future condition, existence after death. [-ITY]

fuzz, n. Loose volatile matter, fluff; fluffy or frizzed hair; *f.-ball,* a fungus, the puff-ball. [perh. imit. of blowing]

fu·zzy, a. Frayed, fluffy; blurred, indistinct; frizzed; *F.-wuzzy,* Soudanese warrior. Hence **fu·zzi**LY[2] adv., **fu·zzi**NESS n. [-Y[2]]

fy, fye. =FIE.

-fy, suf. forming vv. In the older E vv. *-fy* represented F *-fier,* L *-ficare.* L formed vv. in *-ficare* (with or without intervention of adjj. in *-ficus*) f. nn., w. sense *make, produce,* (*pacificare,* orig. intr., make peace) or *make into* (*deificare* deify); f. adjj. w. sense *bring into a state* (*sanctificare*); & f. vb stems w. causative sense (*horrificare* horrify). In med L *-ficare* was often substituted for *-facere*; hence F & E vv. in *-fier, -fy,* sometimes repr. L vv. in *-facere* (F *stupéfier,* but p.p. *stupéfait* as well as *stupéfié,* stupefy; OF *satisfier,* but mod. F *satisfaire*; F *liquéfier* liquefy, *rubéfier* rubefy). Apart f. these in *-efy* E has always *-ify* (-I-), which is freely added to E adjj. & nn. to form vv. chiefly jocular or colloq. (*speechify, Frenchify*; also, on vb, the irreg. *argufy*). Vbs formed on adjj. have often intr. as well as trans. sense (*solidify* make or become solid). Vv. in *-ify* have nn. in *-ification,* those representing L vv. in *-facere* have nn. in -FACTION; but E has *petrifaction* where F has the correct *pétrification.*

fȳ·lfot, n. Equal-armed cross of which each arm is continued rectangularly, all clockwise or all counterclockwise. [name based on ancient direction for design of painted window, in which *f.* may mean either the particular pattern or something to *fill the foot* of the window; cf. CELT[2]]

fytte. See FIT[1].

G

G (jē), letter (pl. *G*s, G's). (Mus.) fifth note of diatonic scale of C major; corresponding scale or key; *G* CLEF.

Abbreviations (1): General, **G.H.Q.** (headquarters), **G.O.C.** (officer commanding), **G.P.** (practitioner), **G.P.O.** (post office); Georgius, **G.R.** (Rex); Grand, as **G.B.E., G.C.B., G.C.M.G., G.C.V.O.,** (cross of British Empire, Bath, St Michael & St George, Victorian Order), **G.C.I.E.** (Commander of Indian Empire), **G.C.S.I.** (Commander of Star of India), **G.O.M.** (old man); great, **G.W.R.** (western railway); greatest, **G.C.F.** or **M.** (common factor or measure); Greenwich, **G.M.T.** (mean time).

Abbreviations (2): **Ga,** Georgia; **Gal.** (atians); **gal.,** gallon(s); **Gen.**(eral; mil. title); **Gen.**(esis); **Geo.**(rge); **geog.**-(raphy); **geol.**(ogy); **geom.**(etry); **Glam.**(organshire); **Glos.,** Gloucestershire; **gr.,** grain(s); **grm.,** gramme(s); **gs.** guineas; **gym.**(nasium, -nastics).

gab, n. (fam.). Talk, prattle, twaddle, (*stop your g.,* hold your tongue; *gift of the g.,* talent for speaking, also loquacity). [?]

ga·bble, v.i. & t., & n. Talk volubly or inarticulately, read aloud (t., often *over,* & i.) too fast; utter too fast; (n.) voluble confused unintelligible talk. [imit.]

gabe·lle, n. Tax (usu. foreign tax), esp. the French pre-Revolution salt-tax. [F, f. med. L *gabella* (*gabulum*=OE *gafol* see GAVELKIND)]

gă·berdine (-ēn), n. Loose long upper garment esp. of Jews & almsmen; a fine hard-laid cloth. [f. OF *gauvardine* perh. f. MHG *wallevart* pilgrimage]

gā·bion, n. Cylinder of wicker or woven metal bands to be filled with earth for use in fortification or engineering. [F, f. It. *gabbione* (*gabbia* CAGE, -OON)]

gabionā·de, n. Line of gabions. [-ADE(1)]

gā·ble, n. Triangular upper part of wall at end of ridged roof; (also *g.-end*) g.-topped wall; g.-shaped canopy over window or door, whence **gā·bl**ET[1]n. Hence (-)**ga·bl**ED[2] a. [OF, f. ON *gafl*; cf. G *gabel* fork; prob. cogn. w. OHG *gebal,* Gk *kephalē,* head]

gā·by, n. Simpleton. [?]

gad[1], int. of surprise, asseveration, &c. (also *by g., begad*). [=GOD]

gad[2], v.i., & n. Go about idly, rove, wander, (usu. *about, abroad, out*); (of plants, esp. in part.) straggle; (*up*)*on the g.,* going about, on the move; *gadabout,* (person) given to gadding. [perh. back formation f. obs. *gadling* companion, OE *gædling* (*gæd* fellowship, -LING[1])]

ga·d-fly, n. Breeze, cattle-biting fly; irritating or worrying person; violent impulse, oestrum. [f. obs. *gad* spike f. ON *gaddr* cogn. w. YARD & L *hasta* spear]
ga·dget, n. (colloq.). Small fitting or contrivance in machinery &c.; (transf.) dodge, device. [first in naut. use; perh. dim. of GAUGE]
Gadhe·lic (-dĕ-), a. & n. = GAELIC in its wider sense. [literary f. Ir. *Gaedheal* Gael + -IC]
gā·doid, a. & n. (Fish) of the cod family. [f. Gk *gados* cod + -OID]
gadroo·n, n. (usu. pl. or attrib.). Convex curve(s) in series forming ornamental edge like inverted fluting. [f. F *godron* etym. dub.]
Gael (gāl), n. Scottish Celt; (rarely) Irish Celt. [f. Sc.-Gael. *Gaidheal*]
Gae·lic (gā-), a. & n. (Language) of Scottish Celts, of Scottish & Irish & Manx Celts. [-IC]
găff[1], n., & v.t. Barbed fishing-spear; stick with iron hook for landing large fish; spar extending top of fore-&-aft sail not set on stays; (vb) seize (fish) with g. [f. F *gaffe* boat-hook]
găff[2], n. (slang). *Blow the g.*, let out plot. [?]
găff[3], n. (slang). Public place of amusement, esp. (usu. *penny g.*) low theatre or music-hall. [?]
ga·ffer, n. Elderly rustic, old fellow, (also as prefix to name); foreman of gang. [contr. of *godfather* or *grandfather*; cf. GAMMER]
gag, n., & v.t. & i. Thing thrust into mouth to prevent speech or outcry or (Surg.) hold it open for operation, (Parl.) closure or GUILLOTINE, (vb, apply g. to, silence, deprive of free speech); actor's interpolations in dramatic dialogue (vb, make these); *g.-bit*, specially powerful for horse-breaking, *g.-rein*, arranged to make bit more powerful, (*gag*, v.t.) apply g.-bit to (horse); (slang) imposture, lie, (v.t., deceive; v.i. practise deceit). [n. f. vb, perh. imit. of choking sound; slang sense perh. unrelated]
gage[1], n., & v.t. Pledge, thing deposited as security; (glove thrown down as, any symbol of) challenge to fight; (vb) stake, pledge, offer as guarantee. [n. f OF *guage* f. Teut. (WED); vb f. F *gager* of same orig., or for ENGAGE]
gage[2]. See GAUGE.
gage[3] n. (shop). Greengage. [abbr.]
ga·ggle, v.i. (Of geese) cackle. [imit.]
gai·ety, n. Being gay, mirth; (usu. pl.) merrymaking, festive occasion(s), amusements; bright appearance. [f. F *gaieté* (GAY, -TY)]
Gai·kwar, Gaek-, (gīk-), n. Ruler of Baroda. [Marathi, = cowherd]
gaily. See GAY.
gain[1], n. Increase of possessions &c., profit, advance, improvement; acquisition of wealth, lucre, pelf; (pl.) sums acquired by trade &c., emoluments, winnings; increase in amount. [OF (*gaaignier* GAIN[2])]
gain[2], v.t. & i. Obtain, secure, (desired or desirable thing; *g. time*, obtain delay by pretexts or slow methods; *g. the ear of*, get favourable hearing from); win (sum) as profits or as result of changed conditions, earn, whence **gai·nings** [-ING[1] (2)] n. pl.; make a profit, be benefited, improve or advance *in* some respect, be enhanced *by* comparison or contrast; win (land from sea, battle, victory; *g. the upper hand*, be victorious); bring over to one's interest or views, win *over*, persuade, prevail upon; reach, arrive at, (desired place); *g. ground*, progress, advance, encroach (*up*)*on*; *g.* (*ground*) (*up*)*on*, get closer to (person or thing pursued); (of sea) encroach (*up*)*on* land; *g.* (*up*)*on*, win the favour of. Hence **gai·nable** a., **gai·ner**[1] n. [f. F *gagner* f. OF *gaaignier* cf. It. *guadagnare* f. OHG (*weidenen* v. pasture, forage, cf. G *weide* pasturage, OE *wáth* hunting)]
gai·nful, a. Lucrative, remunerative; bent on gain. [-FUL]
gainsay·, v.t. (*-said*, pr. -ād or -ĕd). Deny, contradict. Hence **gainsay·er**[1] n. [f. obs. *gain* prep. against f. ON *gegn* cf. G *gegen* + SAY]
gainst, 'gainst. (Poet. for) AGAINST.
gait, n. Manner of walking, bearing or carriage as one walks. [var. of GATE[2]]
gai·ter, n. Covering of cloth, leather, &c., for leg below knee or for ankle; *ready to the last g. button* (completely; said of French army before Franco-German war). Hence **gai·tered**[2] a. [f. F *guêtre* etym. dub.]
gā·la, n. Festive occasion, fête, (often attrib., as *g. day, dress*, &c.). [F f. It.]
gala·ctic, a. (astron.). Of the Galaxy. [f. Gk *galaktikos* (foll., -IC)]
gala·cto-, comb. form of Gk *gala -aktos* milk used in scientific terms as *galactogogue*, (substance) inducing a flow of milk.
gă·lantine (-ēn), n. White meat boned, spiced, tied, boiled, & served cold. [F, altered f. *galatine* a fish sauce]
gală·nty show, n. Pantomime on screen made by shadows of puppets. [perh. f. It. *galanti* pl. of *galante* GALLANT]
gă·laxy (-la-), n. Irregular luminous band of stars indistinguishable to naked eye encircling the heavens, Milky Way; brilliant company (*of* beauties, talent, &c.). [f. F *galaxie* f. L f. Gk *galaxias* (*gala -aktos* milk)]
gă·lbanum, n. Gum resin from some Persian species of ferula. [L, f. Gk *khalbanē* prob. f. Oriental wd]
gale[1], n. (Also *Sweet-g.*) bog-myrtle. [OE (also Du. & G) *gagel*]
gale[2], n. Rather strong wind, (Naut.)

storm, (poet.) gentle breeze. [perh. cogn. w. Da. *gal*, Norw. *galen*, mad, furious]

gale[3], n. Periodical payment of rent (*hanging g.*, arrears of rent). [perh. = obs. *gavel* see GAVELKIND]

gā·lĕa, n. (bot., zool.). Structure like helmet in shape, function, or position. So **ga·le**ATE[2], **-ated,** aa. [L, = helmet]

galee·ny, n. Guinea-fowl. [f. Sp. *gallina* (*morisca* Moorish) hen]

Gā·len, n. (facet.). Physician. [f. L f. Gk *Galēnos*, Pergamene 2nd-c. physician]

galĕ·nic, n., **gale·nical,** a. & n. Of, according to, Galen; esp. (remedy) made of vegetable, not chemical, components. [prec. + -IC(AL)]

Gă·lilee, g-, n. Porch or chapel at entrance of church. [perh. as less sacred than church w. ref. to Galilee as opp. Judea, or esp. to *Matt.* iv. 15 (*G. of the Gentiles*)]

gălima·tias (-ăsĭah, or as F), n. Confused or meaningless talk, rigmarole. [F (formerly half naturalized, now only as foreign word)]

gă·lingale (-ngg-), n. Aromatic root of E.-Ind. plants used in cookery & medicine; (also *English g.*) kind of sedge. [f. OF *galingal* f. Arab. *khalanjan* perh. f. Chin. *ko-liang-kiang* mild ginger from Ko]

galiot. = GALLIOT.

gă·lipot, n. Kind of hardened turpentine. [F, etym. dub.]

gall[1] (gawl), n. Secretion of liver, bile, (now only of lower animals); typical bitter substance, bitterness, (*g. & wormwood*); g.-bladder & its contents; asperity, rancour, (*dip* one's *pen in g.*, write violently), whence **ga·ll**-LESS a.; *g.-bladder*, vessel containing the g.; *g.-stone*, calculous formation in g.-bladder. [OE *gealla* cf. G *galle*, also Gk *kholē*, L *fel*; perh. also cogn. w. YELLOW]

gall[2] (gawl), n. Painful swelling, pustule, blister, esp. in horse; sore produced by chafing; mental soreness or its cause; place rubbed bare, flaw; bare spot in field or coppice. [OE *gealla* sore on horse, perh. = prec.]

gall[3] (gawl), v.t. & i. Rub sore, injure by rubbing; vex, annoy, harass, humiliate, whence **ga·ll**ING[2] a. [f. prec., perh. orig. as back formation f. *gall*ED[2]]

gall[4] (gawl), n. Excrescence produced by insect on trees, esp. on oak (also *oak-g.*, used in making ink & tannin, & in dyeing & medicine); *g.-fly*, insect producing gg.; *g.-nut*, = g. So (in *gallic acid*) **gă·llic**[1] a. [f. F *galle* f. L *galla*]

gă·llant (also, *in senses indicated below, sometimes* -ă·nt), a., n., & v.t. & i. Showy, finely dressed, (archaic); grand, fine, stately, (of ship, horse, &c.); brave, chivalrous, (also Parl., as conventional epithet of military or naval member, as *the honourable & g. member*); markedly attentive to women (-a·nt); concerned with love, amatory, (-a·nt); hence **ga·llant**LY[2] (or as above *galla·ntly*) adv. (N.) man of fashion, fine gentleman; ladies' man, lover, paramour, (-a·nt). (Vb; -a·nt) play the g., flirt *with*, flirt with; escort, act as cavalier to, (lady). [f. F *galant* part. of OF *galer* make merry cf. GALA perh. f. OHG *wallôn* wander]

ga·llantry, n. Bravery, dashing courage; courtliness, devotion to women; a polite or amorous act or speech; conduct of a gallant, amorous intercourse or intrigue, sexual immorality. [f. F *galanterie* (prec., -ERY)]

gă·lleon, n. (hist.). Vessel shorter & higher than galley; ship of war (usu. Spanish); large Spanish ship used in American trade. [f. Sp. *galeon*, f. med. L *galeonem* nom. *-o*. (GALLEY)]

gă·llery, n., & v.t. Covered space for walking in partly open at side, porticó, colonnade; balcony; long narrow passage in thickness of wall or supported on corbels, open towards interior of building; platform projecting from inner wall of church, hall, &c., providing extra room for audience or reserved for musicians, reporters, strangers, &c.; (Theatr.) highest such balcony, persons there seated, least refined part of audience (*play to the g.*, appeal to lower taste, use claptrap); long narrow room (e.g. *shooting-g.*, for indoor target practice or matches), passage, corridor; room or building used for showing works of art; chimney-holder of lamp; (Mil., Mining) horizontal underground passage; *g. hit* (Cricket, & fig., from theatre) piece of showy play, so *g. shot, stroke*; hence **ga·llery**FUL(2) n. (Vb) provide, pierce, &c., with g. or gg. [f. F *galerie* etym. dub.]

gă·lley, n. (Chiefly hist.) low flat single-decked vessel using sails & oars, & usu. rowed by slaves or criminals; ancient Greek or Roman war-ship with one or more banks of oars; large open row-boat, e.g. that used by captain of man-of-war; ship's kitchen; (Print.) oblong tray to which type is transferred from composing stick (*g. proof*, in slip form, not in sheets or pages); *g.-slave*, person condemned to row in g., (fig.) drudge; *galleyworm*, kind of many-footed insect (from likeness of its legs to oars). [f. OF *galie*, med. L *galea*, etym. dub.]

găllia·mbic, a. & n. In the metre of Catullus's *Attis* (imitated in Tennyson's *Boadicea*); (n., usu. pl.) such verse(s). [f. L *galli*AMBUS song of Galli or priests of Cybele + -IC]

Gă·llic[2] (for *g.*[1] see GALL[4]), a. Of the Gauls, Gaulish; (usu. facet.) French, whence **ga·llic**ISM(4) n., **ga·llic**IZE(2, 3) v.t. & i. [f. L *Gallicus* (*Gallus* Gaul, -IC)]

Ga·llican, a. & n. Of the ancient church of Gaul or France; (adherent) of the school of French Roman Catholics following Bossuet & claiming partial autonomy (opp. ULTRAMONTANE), whence **ga·llicanism**(3), **ga·llicanist**(2), nn. [f. L *Gallicanus* (prec., -AN)]

gă·llicē, adv. In French (used in giving F for English phrase &c.). [L, = in Gaulish]

găligă·skins, n. pl. (facet.). Breeches, trousers. [orig. wide hose of 16th & 17th cc., f. F *garguesque* for *greguesque* f. It. *grechesca* fem. of *grechesco* Greek (-ESQUE)]

găllimau·fry, n. Heterogeneous mixture, jumble, medley. [f. F *galimafrée* etym. dub.]

găllina·ceous, a. Of the order *Gallinae* including domestic poultry, pheasants, partridges, &c. So **gallina·cean** a. & n. [f. L *gallinaceus* (*gallina* hen, -ACEOUS)]

găllinā·zo, n. An American vulture, the Turkey buzzard. [f. Sp. *gallinaza* (L *gallina* hen, *-aza* augment.)]

Gă·llio, n. Person, esp. official, refusing to meddle outside his province. [*Acts* xviii]

ga·lliot, n. Dutch cargo-boat or fishing-vessel; small (usu. Mediterranean) galley. [f. F *galiote* dim. of OF *galie* GALLEY]

gă·llipot, n. Small earthen glazed pot used for ointments &c. [prob. f. GALLEY, as brought in galleys from the Mediterranean]

gă·llium, n. Soft bluish-white metal. [f. L *gallus* cock, transl. of *Lecoq* de Boisbaudran the discoverer 1875, + -IUM]

gă·lliva·nt, v.i. Gad about (usu. in part. or vbl n.). [perh. perversion of *gallant* v.]

Găllo-, comb. form = *French-*, as *-Briton*, *-German*. Hence **Galloma·nia** n., **Galloma·niac** a. & n. **Ga·llophil**, **Ga·llophobe**, nn. & aa., **Gallopho·bia** n. [*Gallus* GAUL, -O-]

gă·llon, n. A measure of capacity (*imperial g.*, 277¼ cubic inches; *wine g.*, 231) for liquids or corn &c. [f. ONF *galon* cf. F *jale* bowl]

galloo·n, n. Narrow close-woven braid for binding dresses &c., of gold, silver, silk, or cotton. [f. F *galon* f. 12th-c. *galonner* tie the hair with bands, perh. cogn. w. *gallant*]

gă·llop, n., & v.i. & t. Horse's or other quadruped's fastest pace, with all feet off ground together in each stride (*full g.*, *at a g.*, going thus), a ride at this pace. (Vb) go at a g. (of horse, or with its rider as subj., or of other quadruped); make (horse &c.) g.; read, recite, or talk, fast (often *through*, *over*); move or progress rapidly (*in a galloping consumption*). [f. F *galop(er)* prob. earlier *walop(er)* etym. dub.]

gallopā·de, n. Lively, orig. Hungarian, dance. [F, see GALOP, -ADE(1)]

ga·lloper, n. In vbl senses; esp., (Mil.) aide-de-camp, light field gun. [-ER[1]]

Găllovi·dian, a. & n. (Native) of Galloway. [f. med. L *Gallovidia* + -AN]

gă·lloway, n. Horse of small strong breed from Galloway; small-sized horse.

ga·llows, n. pl. (usu. treated as sing.). Structure, usu. of two uprights & cross-piece, on which criminals are hanged; punishment of hanging (*a g. look*, *have the g. in* one's *face*, of sinister appearance), similar structure used for cookery, gymnastics, &c.; *g.-bird*, person fit to be hanged; *g.-ripe*, fit to be hanged; *g.-tree*, = g. [OE *galga* cf. G *galgen*]

gă·lop, n., & v.i. Lively dance in 2–4 time; (vb) dance a g. [vb f. n., F, see GALLOP]

galore·, adv. & n. (In) abundance (*with beef & ale g.*; *g. of alcohol*; also *in g.*). [f. Ir. *go leór* to sufficiency]

galo·sh, gol-, n. Over-shoe usu. of rubber to keep shoes clean or dry; piece of leather &c. round lower part of boot or shoe uppers, whence **galo·shed**[2], **gol-**, a. [f. F *galoche* perh. ult. f. Gk *kalopous* boot-last (*kālа* pl. logs, *pous* foot)]

galu·mph, v.i. Go prancing in triumph. [made by L. Carroll perh. on *gallop*, *triumph*]

gălvă·nic, a. Of, produced by, as of, galvanism (*g. battery*, *pile*, producing g. electricity; *g. belt*, for applying it to the body; *g. electricity*, = foll.); (fig., of smile &c.) sudden & forced. Hence **galva·nically** adv. [foll., -IC]

ga·lvanism, n. Electricity produced by chemical action; use of this for medical purposes. Hence **ga·lvanist**(3) n. [f. F *galvanisme* (L. *Galvani* discoverer 1792, -ISM)]

ga·lvanize, v.t. Apply galvanism to, stimulate thus (also fig., *g. into life*, rouse by shock or excitement); coat with metal by galvanism (incorrectly of *galvanized iron*, which is covered with zinc usu. without galvanism). Hence **galvanīza·tion**, **ga·lvanizer**[1], nn. [f. F *galvaniser* (prec., -IZE)]

ga·lvano-, comb. form of GALVANIC, GALVANISM, as *-graphy*, method of producing copperplate engravings by *-plasty*, metal-coating by galvanism, -METER, -SCOPE.

Gălwē·gian, a. & n. = GALLOVIDIAN. [f. *Galloway* on anal. of *Norwegian*]

ga·mba, n. (Also *g. stop*) organ stop with violin or 'cello tone. [earlier =, & short for, VIOLA[1] *da gamba*]

gambā·de, gambā·do (pl. *-oes*), n. Horse's leap or bound; fantastic movement, freak, escapade. [*-ade* F, readopted (cf. GAMBOL) by Scott; *-ado* f. Sp. *gambada* of same orig.]

ga·mbier, n. Astringent extract of oriental plant used in tanning &c. [f. Malay *gambir* the plant]

ga·mbit, n. Kinds of opening in chess in which player sacrifices pawn or piece to secure certain ends, many gg. having special names as *King's*, *Queen's*, *Cunningham's*, *g.* [ult. f. It. *gambetto* tripping up (*gamba* leg)]

ga·mble, v.i. & t., & n. Play games of chance for money, esp. for high stakes (*g. away*, lose thus); take great risks to secure great results in war, finance, &c.; hence **ga·mbl**ER[1] n., **ga·mble**SOME a. (N.) gambling (esp. *on the g.*); risky undertaking or attempt. [prob. f. OE *gamenian* to sport (*gamen* GAME[1])]

gambo·ge (-ōōzh), n. Gum resin from Cambodian & Siamese trees used as yellow pigment. [f. mod. L *gambogium* f. *Cambodia*]

ga·mbol (-bl), n., & v.i. (-ll-). Caper, frisk. [f. F *gambade* leap f. It. *gambata* (*gamba* leg)]

game[1], n. Jest (*make g. of*, ridicule); diversion, spell of play (*a g. of ball*); amusing incident (*what a g.!*); contest played according to rules & decided by skill, strength, or luck (ROUND, SQUARE, *g.*; *have the g. in* one's *hands*, be sure to win or able to direct it; *play the g.* lit. & fig., observe the rules, behave honourably; *play a good, poor, g.*, be skilful or not); (Gk & Rom. Ant.; pl.) athletic, dramatic, & musical contests, gladiatorial &c. shows; scheme, undertaking, &c., followed up like a g. (*was playing a deep, double, winning, losing,* &c., *g.*; *the g. is up*, success now impossible; *so that's your little g.*; *spoilt my g.*; *play* one's *g.*, advance his schemes unintentionally; *g. not worth* CANDLE); (pl.) dodges, tricks, (*none of your gg.!*); single round in some contests, e.g. whist or tennis (*g. & g.*, one g. scored to each side); (Commerc.) apparatus for a g.; winning score in g. (*g. and*, short for *g. & set* in tennis); state of g. (*the g. is four all, love three,* &c.); hunted animal, quarry, object of pursuit, (*fair g.*, legitimately to be pursued or attacked; so *forbidden g.*); (collect.) wild animals, birds, &c., hunted for sport or food, flesh of these; kept flock *of swans*; *g.-act, -law* (usu. pl.), regulating the killing & preservation of g.; *g.-bag*, for holding g. killed by sportsman; *g. ball*, state of g. in tennis &c. at which one point may win; *g.-chicken, -cock, -egg, -fowl*, of kind bred for cock-fighting; *gamekeeper*, man employed to breed g., prevent poaching, &c.; *g.-licence*, to kill or deal in g.; *g.-preserver*, landowner &c. who breeds g. & applies g.-laws strictly; *g.-tenant*, lessee of shooting or fishing. [com.-Teut.; OE *gamen* cf. OHG *gaman* joy]

game[2], a. Like a game-cock, spirited, (DIE[2] *g.*); having the spirit *to* do, *for*. Hence **ga·me**LY[2] adv., **ga·me**NESS n. [f. GAME[1]*-cock*]

game[3], v.i. & t. Play at gg. of chance for money, gamble; throw *away* in gambling; *gaming-house, -table*, frequented for gambling. Hence **ga·me**STER n. [f. GAME[1]]

game[4], a. (Of leg, arm, &c.) lame, crippled. [?]

ga·mesome, a. Sportive. Hence **ga·mesome**LY[2] adv., **ga·mesome**NESS n. [-SOME]

gamē·te, n. (biol.). Sexual protoplasmic body, which unites with another for reproduction. [f. Gk *gametē* wife, *gametēs* husband, (*gameō* marry)]

gamin (F), n. Street Arab, neglected boy.

ga·mma, n. Third letter (Γ, γ, = G) of Greek alphabet, used sometimes in enumerations to supplement 3 & c; kind of moth. [Gk]

gammā·dion, n. = FYLFOT. [late Gk, dim. of prec., fylfot consisting of four gammas (Γ)]

ga·mmer, n. (Rustic name for) old woman. [f. *godmother* or *grandmother*, cf. GAFFER]

ga·mmon[1], n., & v.t. Bottom piece of flitch of bacon including hind leg (usu. *g. of bacon*); smoked or cured ham; *g. & spinach* (as dish, &, with pun on *g.*[3], = humbug); (vb) cure (bacon). [f. ONF *gambon* (*gambe* leg, -OON)]

ga·mmon[2], n., & v.t. Complete victory scoring two games at backgammon; (vb) defeat (adversary) thus. [perh. = ME *gamen* GAME[1]]

ga·mmon[3], n., int., & v.i. & t. Humbug, deception; (int.) nonsense!. (Vb) talk plausibly; feign (intr.); hoax, deceive. [perh. as prec.]

ga·mmon[4], v.t., & n., (naut.). Lash (bowsprit) to stem; (n., also *-ing*) the lashing. [?]

gămo-, comb. form of Gk *gamos* marriage, used esp. in Bot. describing plants with specified parts united as *gamope·talous* with petals united; also *gamoge·nesis* sexual reproduction.

gamp, n. (facet.). Umbrella, esp. large untidy one. [f. Mrs. *G.* in *Martin Chuzzlewit*]

gă·mut, n. (Hist.) lowest note in medieval scale = modern G on lowest line of bass stave; the Great Scale consisting of all notes used in medieval music (G as above to E in highest space of treble). (Mod.) whole series of recognized notes; major diatonic scale; people's or period's recognized scale; voice's or instrument's compass; whole range or scope of anything (*the whole g. of crime*; *run up & down the g.*). [f. med. L *gamma ut* (GAMMA taken as name for note one tone lower than A of classical scale + *ut* first of six arbitrary names of notes forming hexachord, being the italicized syllables of a Sapphic stanza, *Ut* queant laxis *re*sonare fibris *Mi*ra gestorum *fa*muli tuorum, *Sol*ve polluti *la*bii reatum, Sancte Johannes]

gā·my, a. Abounding in game; = GAME[2] (rare); having flavour or scent of game kept till it is high. [-Y[2]]

ga·nder, n. Male goose (*sauce for the goose is sauce for the g.*, used in retorting an argument &c. on its first user); fool, simpleton. [OE *gan(d)ra*, *-d-* being prob. euphonic as in THUNDER, cf. Du. *gander*; perh. f. same st. as GOOSE, perh. orig. the name of another bird]

gang, n., & (Sc.) v.i. Company of workmen, or of slaves or prisoners; band of persons acting or going about together esp. for criminal purpose or one disapproved by speaker; set *of* tools &c. arranged to work simultaneously; *g.-board*, plank usu. with cleats nailed on it for walking into or out of boat. (Vb, Sc.) go (*g.agley*, go awry; *g.* one's *ain gait*, take one's own course). [earlier senses *mode of going, way*, cf. G & Du. *gang*, & obs. & Sc. vb *gang* walk, go, f. OE *gangan*, also OHG]

gānge (-j), v.t. Protect (fish-hook, part of fishing-line) with fine wire. Hence **ga·ng**ING[1] (-j-) n. [?]

ga·nger (-ng-), n. Foreman of gang. [-ER[1]]

Gangĕ·tic (-j-), a. Of the Ganges. [f. L *Gangeticus* (L f. Gk *Gaggēs*, -IC)]

ga·nglion (-ngg-), n. (pl. *-lia*). Enlargement or knot on nerve, from which nerve-fibres radiate; mass of grey matter in central nervous system forming a nerve-nucleus (*g.-cell*, *-corpuscule*, *-globule*, nerve-cell in this); (fig.) centre of force, activity, or interest. Hence **ga·ngliated, ga·nglionated,** [-ATE[3], -ED[1]], **ga·ngli**FORM, **gangliŏ·n**IC, aa. [f. Gk *gagglion*]

ga·ngrene (-ngg-), n., & v.i. & t. Necrosis, usu. with decomposition, of part of the body (often fig.); hence **ga·ngren**OUS a. (Vb) become affected, affect, with mortification. [f. L f. Gk *gaggraina*]

gangue (-ng), n. Earth &c., matrix, in which ore is found. [F, f. G *gang* lode = GANG]

ga·ngway (-ng-), n. Passage esp. between rows of seats (in House of Commons, cross-passage half-way down giving access to back benches; members *above, below, g.* are more, less, closely associated with official policy of their party); passage &c. on ship, esp. platform connecting quarterdeck & forecastle; opening in bulwarks by which ship is entered or left, bridge laid across from this to shore &c. [OE *gangweg* (GANG, WAY)]

ga·nnet, n. A sea-bird, the Solan goose. [OE *ganot* cogn. w. Du. *gent* GANDER]

gă·noid, a. & n. (Of fish-scale) enamelled, smooth & bright; (fish) having g. scales. [f. F *ganoïde* f. Gk *ganos* brightness + -OID]

ga·ntry, gau·n-, n. Four-footed wooden stand for barrels; structure supporting travelling crane, railway signals, &c. [perh. f. obs. *gawn* contr. of GALLON + *tree*, or f. OF *gantier* var. of *chantier*]

Gă·nymede, n. (Facet.) waiter, potboy; (Astron.) largest satellite of Jupiter. [f. L f. Gk *Ganumēdēs* cupbearer of Zeus]

gaol (jāl), **jail,** n., & v.t. (*g-* in official, *g-* & *j-* indifferently in literary use). Public prison for detention of persons committed by process of law, (without article) confinement in this; *g., j., -bird*, prisoner, habitual criminal, rogue; *g., j., -delivery*, clearing of g. esp. at assizes by trying all prisoners awaiting trial; *g., j., fever*, virulent typhus formerly endemic in gg.; (vb) put in g. [f. ONF *gaiole*, OF *jaiole*, (now *geôle*) f. Rom. dim. of L *cavea* CAGE]

gao·ler (-jāl-), **jai·ler, jai·lor,** n. (see prec.). Man in charge of gaol or prisoners in it. Hence **gao·ler**ESS[1], also **jai·leress, jai·loress,** n. [as prec. + -ER[2](2)]

gap, n. Breach in hedge or wall; gorge, pass; unfilled space or interval, blank, break in continuity, (*stop, fill, supply, a g.*, make up deficiency); wide divergence in views, sympathies, &c. Hence **gapp**ED[2], **ga·pp**Y[2], aa. [ON, = chasm, cogn. w. foll.]

gape, v.i., & n. Open mouth wide, (of mouth, oysters, wounds, chasm, &c.) open or be open wide, split, part asunder; stare, gaze curiously, *at*; yawn. (N.) yawn; open-mouthed stare; *the gg.*, poultry disease with gaping as symptom, (facet.) fit of yawning; expanse of open mouth or beak, part of beak that opens; rent, opening; *g.-seed* (facet.), staring, occasion for staring, thing stared at. [f. ON *gapa* vb cf. G *gaffen*]

ga·per, n. In vbl senses; esp. kinds of bird, kind of mollusc. [-ER[1]]

gă·rage (-ij, or as F), n. Building or shed for storing or repair of horseless vehicles, esp. motor-cars. [F (*garer* shunt f. Teut., cf. OE *werian* defend, -AGE)]

garb, n., & v.t. Dress, costume, esp. of distinctive kind, way one is dressed; (vb) attire, put (esp. distinctive) clothes upon (person; usu. pass. or refl.). [f. It. *garbo* elegance, f. Teut. cf. OHG *garawî* preparation cogn. w. GEAR]

gar·bage (-ij), n. Offal used for food, refuse, filth; foul or worthless reading. [perh. f. OF *garbe* sheaf, bundle, + -AGE]

gar·ble, v.t. Select best in, take pick of, (rare); make (usu. unfair or malicious) selections from (facts, statements, &c.), mutilate in order to misrepresent. [f. It. *garbellare* f. Arab. *gharbala* sift cf. *kirbal* sieve]

gar·board (strake), n. First range of planks laid on ship's bottom next keel; corresponding plates in iron ship. [f. Du. *gaarboord* (GATHER, BOARD)]

garçon (F), n. Waiter in French hotel &c.

gar·den (-dn), n., & v.i. Piece of ground devoted to growing flowers, fruit, or vegetables (KITCHEN, MARKET, *g.*); (pl.) ornamental grounds for public resort (usu. *botanical, zoological*, &c., *gg.*);

specially fertile region (*the g. of England*, Kent, Worcestershire, &c.); (pl. with name prefixed as *Onslow, Spring, Gg.*) set of houses in street, square, &c.; *the G.*, philosophy or school of Epicurus (cf. PORCH, ACADEMY); (attrib.; with or without hyphen) cultivated, not wild, (*g. plants, g.-cress; common or g.* slang, ordinary), living in gg. (*g.-spider; g.-white*, kind of butterfly; *g.-warbler*, kind of bird); *g. city*, industrial or other town laid out systematically with a view to spacious and attractive surroundings; so *g. suburb*; *g.-engine*, portable force-pump for watering; *g.-frame*, forcing-frame for plants; *g.-glass*, bell-glass for covering plant; *g.-party*, social meeting on lawn or in g.; *g.-plot*, piece of ground used as g.; *g. seat*, bench &c. for use in g., similar seat for one or two on top of omnibus; *g.-stuff*, vegetables & fruit; hence **gar·den**ED², **garden**E·SQUE, aa., **gar·den**ING¹(1) n. (Vb) cultivate a g. [f. ONF *gardin* ult. f. Teut., cf. G *garten*, also GARTH, YARD]

gar·dener (-dn-), n. Person who gardens, esp. servant employed to tend a garden. [as prec. + -ER²(2), cf. F *jardinier*]

gardē·nia, n. Genus of trees & shrubs with large white or yellow flowers & usu. fragrant scent. [mod. L (Dr. A. *Garden* d. 1791, -IA¹)]

gare·fowl, n. The great auk. [f. ON *geirfugl* (*geir* of doubtful meaning)]

gar·fish, n. Fish with long spearlike snout & green bones. [perh. f. OE *gár* spear cogn. w. Gk *gaison*]

garga·ntuan, a. Enormous, gigantic. [*Gargantua* giant in Rabelais + -AN]

gar·get (-g-), n. Inflamed state of head or throat in cattle, pigs, or poultry; inflammation of cow's or ewe's udder. [perh. f. obs. *garget* throat f. OF *gargate* etym. dub.]

gar·gle, v.t. & i., & n. Wash (throat), wash throat, with liquid kept in motion by breath; (n.) liquid used thus. [f. F *gargouiller* (foll.)]

gar·goyle, gur-, n. Grotesque spout usu. with human or animal mouth, head, or body, projecting from gutter of (esp. Gothic) building to carry water clear of wall. [f. OF *gargouille* throat, gargoyle]

găribă·ldĭ, n. Kind of woman's or child's blouse, orig. of bright red. [f. red shirts of *G.* (Italian patriot 1807–82) & his followers]

gār·ish, a. Obtrusively bright, showy, gawdy, over-decorated. Hence **gar·ish**LY² adv., **gar·ish**NESS n. [perh. f. obs. *gaure* to stare, etym. dub.]

gar·land, n., & v.t. Wreath of flowers, leaves, &c., worn on head or hung on something as decoration; distinction, palm, prize, for victory &c.; (archaic) anthology, miscellany; metal &c. imitation of g.; (vb) crown with g., deck with gg., serve as g. to. [OF (-*e*), etym. dub.]

gar·lic, n. Plant with bulbous strong-smelling pungent-tasting root used as flavouring in cookery. Hence (esp. of smell) **gar·lick**Y² a. [OE *gárléac* (*gár* spear, LEEK)]

gar·ment, n., & v.t. Article of dress, esp. gown or cloak, (pl.) clothes; outward and visible covering of anything; (vb; poet., usu. in p.p.) attire. [f. OF *garniment* GARNISH, -MENT)]

gar·ner, n., & v.t. (poet. & rhet.). Storehouse for corn, granary, (also fig.); (vb) store, deposit, collect. [f. OF *gerner* f. L *granarium* GRANARY]

gar·net, n. Vitreous mineral, of which a deep transparent red kind is used as gem. [f. OF *grenat* f. med. L *granatum* POMEGRANATE (from resemblance to its seeds)]

gar·nish, v.t., & n. Decorate, embellish, (esp. dish for table); (Law) serve notice on (person, called **garnish**EE· n.) for purpose of attaching money belonging to debtor, summon (person) as party to litigation started between others; hence **gar·nish**ER¹, **gar·nish**MENT, nn. (N.; also **gar·nish**ING¹ n.) things used to decorate dish for table (also fig. of literary embellishments). [f. OF *garnir* (-ISH²) fortify, prob. f. Teut. cogn. w. WARN]

gar·niture (-tsh*er*), n. Appurtenances, accessories; adornment, trimming esp. of dish; costume. [F (GARNISH, -URE)]

garotte. See GARROTTE.

ga·rret¹, n. Room on top floor, room partly or entirely in roof, attic; (slang) head (*be wrong in the g., have* one's *g. unfurnished*, &c.). [f. OF *garite* watch-tower (*garir* defend, f. Teut. cf. OE *werian* defend)]

ga·rret², v.t. (archit.). Insert small pieces of stone in joints of (coarse masonry). [?]

gărreteer·, n. Dweller in garret, esp. poor literary hack. [-EER]

ga·rrison, n., & v.t. Troops stationed in fortress, town, &c., to defend it (*g. town*, having g.). (Vb) furnish with, occupy as, g.; place (troops, soldier) on g. duty. [f. OF *garison* (*garir* see GARRET¹, -SON) defence, w. sense of F & obs. E *garnison* (GARNISH)]

ga·rron, n. Small inferior horse bred in Scotland & Ireland. [f. Gael. *gearran*]

ga·rrot, n. Kind of sea duck. [F]

gar(r)o·tte, n., & v.t. Spanish method of capital punishment by strangulation, apparatus used in it; highway robbery performed by throttling victim. (Vb) execute by strangulation; throttle in order to rob, whence **gar(r)o·tt**ER¹ n. [f. Sp. *garrote*(*ar*), the n. (etym. dub.) meaning stick (used in twisting cord tight)]

ga·rrulous (-rōō-), a. Given to talk, loquacious, wordy; (of bird, stream, &c.) chattering, babbling. Hence or cogn. **garru·l**ITY (-rōō-), **ga·rrulous**NESS, nn., **ga·rrulous**LY² adv. [f. L *garrulus* (*garrire* chatter) + -OUS]

gar·ter, n., & v.t. Band worn above or below knee to keep stocking up; *the G.*, (badge of) highest order of English knighthood, membership of this; (*G*-) = G. King of Arms; (vb) fasten (stocking), encircle (leg), with g. [f. OF *gartier* (*garet*, now *jarret*, bend of knee, perh. f. Celt., cf. Breton *gar*, W *gâr*, leg-bone)]

garth, n. (archaic & dial.) Close, yard, garden, paddock, open space within cloisters. [f. ON *garthr* = OE *geard* YARD²]

găs, n. (pl. *găses*), & v.t. & i. Any aeriform or completely elastic fluid (used chiefly of those that do not become liquid or solid at ordinary temperatures, other gg. being usu. called *vapours*); such fluid, esp. COAL-*g.* or various mixtures with carburetted hydrogen, used for lighting or heating; (Mining) explosive mixture of firedamp with air; hydrogen &c. used to fill balloon; nitrous oxide g. as anaesthetic (often *laughing-g.*); (also *poison-g.*) kinds used to asphyxiate enemy in war; jet of g. used for lighting; empty talk, boasting, humbug, windbag eloquence; *g.-bag*, bag for holding gas, empty talker, airship's g.-container, (contempt.) airship or balloon (opp. aeroplane); *g.-bracket*, pipe with burner(s) projecting from wall; *g.-coal*, bituminous from which g. can be made; *g.-coke*, residuum of coal when g. has been made from it; *g.-engine*, *-motor*, with power obtained by production or rhythmical combustion & explosion of g. in closed cylinder; *g.-fitter*, tradesman or workman providing house with *g.-fittings*, apparatus for heating or lighting with g.; *g.-helmet*, *g.-mask*, kinds of appliance including respirator worn as defence against poison-g.; *g.-light*, light given by esp. coal g., jet of burning g.; *g.-main*, main pipe supplying g.; *g.-man*, manufacturer of g., collector of sums due for g.-supply; *g.-mask* (as *g.-helmet*); *g.-meter*, apparatus registering amount of g. consumed (*he lies like a g.-m.*, prodigiously); *g.-oven* (heated by gas; recently notorious as means of suicide); *g.-ring*, perforated with small holes & fed with g. for cooking &c.; *g.-shell* (charged with poison-g. instead of explosive); *g.-tar*, COAL-tar produced in making g.; *g.-works*, manufactory of g.; hence **gă·s**EOUS a., **gasē·**ITY n., **gă·si**FORM, **ga·s**LESS, aa., **gă·si**FY v.t., **ga·sifi**ABLE a., **gasifi**CA·TION n. (Vb) supply (room, railway-carriage, &c.) with g.; project poison-g. upon (enemy, place), (pass.) be poisoned with g.; pass (thread, lace) through g.-flame to remove loose fibres; talk emptily or boastfully. whence **ga·ss**ER¹ n. [wd invented by Van Helmont on Gk *khaos* CHAOS]

Gă·scon, n. Native of Gascony; braggart. [F]

gasconā·de, n., & v.i. Boast(ing). [f. F *gasconnade* (prec., -ADE)]

găselier·, n. Gas-lamp, usu. suspended from ceiling, with several burners often on branches. [f. GAS after CHANDELIER]

gash, n., & v.t. Long & deep slash, cut, or wound; cleft such as might be made by slashing cut; act of making such cut; (vb) make g. in, cut. [earlier *garse* v. & n. f. OF *garser* perh. f. LL *caraxare* f. Gk *kharassō* incise]

gă·sket, n. Small cord for securing furled sail to yard; strip of tow &c. for packing piston or caulking joint. [?]

gasogene. See GAZOGENE.

gă·solene, -ine (-ēn), n. Volatile inflammable liquid got in distilling petroleum & used for heating & lighting. [GAS, -OL, -ENE, -INE¹]

gasŏ·meter, n. (Chem.) vessel for holding gas; large reservoir in which gas is stored for distribution by pipes. [f. F *gazomètre* (*gaz* GAS, *mètre* f. Gk *metron* measure)]

gasp, v.i. & t., & n. Catch breath, strain *for* air or breath, with open mouth as in exhaustion or astonishment; *g. life* &c. *away* or *out*, expire; *g. out*, utter with gg.; hence **ga·sping**LY² adv., **ga·sp**ER¹ n., (esp., slang) cheap cigarette. (N.) convulsive catching of breath (*at one's last g.*, at point of death). [f. ON *geispa* to yawn cf. *geip* idle talk]

gă·ssy, a. Of, full of, like, gas; (of talk &c.) empty, verbose. Hence **ga·ssi**NESS n. [-Y²]

gă·st(e)ropod, n. Mollusc (e.g. snail) with locomotive organ placed ventrally. So **gasterŏ·pod**OUS a. [GASTRO-, Gk *pous podos* foot]

găstrae·a, n. (Assumed) primitive sac-like animal consisting of two layers (ectoderm & endoderm) of cells. [mod. L (GASTRO-)]

gă·stric, a. Of the stomach (*g. fever*, enteric; *g. juice*, thin clear acid nearly colourless fluid secreted by stomach glands & effecting digestion). [f. Gk as foll. + -IC]

găstr(o)-, comb. form of Gk *gastēr* -(*e*)*ros* stomach, as *gastro-enteric*, of stomach & intestines, -CELE, -TOMY, *gastri·*TIS.

gastro·logy, n. Science of cookery. So **gastro·**LOGER, **gastro·**LOGIST, nn. [f. Gk *gastrologia* (prec., -LOGY)]

ga·stronome, n. Judge of cookery. [F, back formation f. *gastronomie* see foll.]

gastro·nomy, n. Art & science of good eating. So **gastro·nom**ER¹ n., **gastronŏ·mic**(AL) aa., **gastrono·mical**LY² adv., **gastro·nom**IST(3) n. [f. F *gastronomie* f. Gk GASTRO*nomia* on anal. of *astronomia* ASTRONOMY]

gate[1], n., & v.t. Opening in wall of city or enclosure made for entrance & exit & capable of being closed with barrier; (bibl.) place of judicial assembly in city; mountain pass; means of entrance or exit (*g. of ivory, horn*, by which false, true, dreams come; *Bosphorus & Hellespont are the two gg. of Constantinople*); barrier closing the opening of a wall, wooden or iron framework, solid or of bars or gratings, hung on hinges, turning on pivots, or sliding, single or double; contrivance regulating passage of water; number entering by payment at gg. to see football match &c., amount of money thus taken (also *g.-money*); *g.-bill* (Oxf. & Camb.), record of undergraduate's returns to college after hours. fines imposed for these; *g.-crasher* slang (also *crasher*), uninvited intruder at ball &c.; *gatehouse*, lodge of park &c., room over city gate often used as prison; *g.-keeper*, attendant at g., kind of butterfly; *g.-meeting*, at which money is taken for admission; *g.-post*, on which g. is hung or against which it shuts (*between you & me & the g.-p.*, or *bedpost*, in close confidence); *gateway*, =g. (first sense), frame of or structure built over g., means of entrance or exit; hence **ga·te**LESS a. (Vb; Oxf. & Camb.) confine to college entirely or after certain hours. [OE *geat* = OFris. *gat, jet*, hole]

gate[2], n. (With prefixed name in North &c.) street. [f. ON *gata* cf. G *gasse* lane]

ga·ther (gădh-), v.t. & i. Bring together, cause to assemble, (*be gathered to* one's *fathers*, die); acquire by collecting, amass; cull, pluck; collect (grain &c.) as harvest; receive addition of (*rolling stone gathers no moss*, change of calling does not pay; *complexion gathers colour*; *invalid gathers strength*; *g. head*, acquire strength, swell as a festering sore; *g. way*, begin to move, of ship); summon up (energies), gain or recover (breath); infer, deduce, (*that*); draw (garment, brow) together in folds or wrinkles, esp. pucker (part of dress) by running thread through; pick *up* from ground; draw *up* (limbs, person) into smaller compass; sum *up* (scattered facts); summon *up* (thoughts, strength, &c.) for an effort; come together, congregate, form a mass; receive additions (*the tale gathered like a snowball*); come to a head, develop purulent swelling. [OE *gaderian*, cf. Du. *gaderen* gather & OE *geador* together]

ga·thering, n. In vbl senses; esp.: purulent swelling; assembly, meeting; *g.-coal*, large piece to keep fire in. [-ING[1]]

ga·thers, n. pl. Part of dress that is gathered or drawn in. [f. GATHER]

Ga·tling, n. (Also *G. gun*) machine gun with clustered barrels. [inventor's name]

gauche (gōsh), a. Tactless, without ease or grace, socially awkward. [F]

gaucherie (gōsherē·), n. Gauche manners, a gauche action. [F]

gaucho (gow·tshō, gaw-), n. One of a mixed European & Amer.-Ind. race of mounted herdsmen. [Sp., prob. f. native S.-Amer. lang.]

gaud, n. Something gaudy, showy ornament, gewgaw; (pl.) showy ceremonies, gaieties. [f. OF *gaudir* make merry f. L *gaudēre* rejoice]

gau·dy[1], n. Grand entertainment, esp. annual college dinner to old members &c.; *g.-day*, day of rejoicing, day on which college g. is held. [f. L *gaudium* joy]

gau·dy[2], a. Tastelessly or inappropriately fine, showy, or brilliant (of dress, decoration, literary style, &c.). Hence **gau·d**ILY[2] adv., **gau·di**NESS n. [earliest sense *luxurious*, of food &c.; perh. orig. attrib. use of prec., later taken as GAUD + -Y[2]]

gauffer. See GOFFER.

gauge[1] (gāj), **gage**[2] (in naut. sense), n. Standard measure to which things must conform, esp. measure of capacity or contents of barrel, diameter of bullet, or thickness of sheet iron; capacity, extent, scope, (*take the g. of*, estimate); distance between pair of rails (*broad, narrow, g.*, of more, less, than 4ft 8½in., *standard g.*); (Naut.; *gage*) relative position in respect to wind (*have the weather g. of*, be to windward of, fig. have advantage of; also rarely *lee, southerly*, &c., *g.*); graduated instrument measuring force or quantity of rainfall, stream, tide, wind, &c.; contrivance attached to vessel to show height of its contents; instrument for testing and verifying dimensions of tools, wire, &c.; adjustable carpenter's tool for marking parallel lines; (Print.) strip regulating depth of margin &c.; means of estimating, criterion, test. [ONF, etym. dub.]

gauge[2] (gāj), v.t. Measure exactly (esp. objects of standard size, as wire, bolts; fluctuating quantities or forces, as rainfall, wind; depth of liquid content); find capacity or content of (cask &c.) by measurement & calculation (*gauging-rod*, exciseman's instrument for this); estimate, take measure of, (person, character); make uniform, bring to standard size or shape. Hence **gau·ge**ABLE a., **gau·g**ER[1] (1,2) n., (gāj-). [f. ONF *gauger* etym. dub.]

Gaul, n. Inhabitant of ancient Gaul; (facet.) Frenchman. [f. *Gaul* the country f. F *Gaule* f. L *Gallia* (*Gallus* a Gaul)]

Gau·lish, a. & n. (Language) of ancient Gauls; (facet.) French (adj.). [prec. + -ISH[1]]

gault, n. (geol.). Series of clay and marl beds between upper & lower greensand. [?]

gaunt, a. Lean, haggard; grim or desolate looking. Hence **gau·nt**NESS n. [etym. dub.; from 1440; cf. Norw. *gand* thin stick or man]

gau·ntlet[1], n. (Hist.) armoured glove (*fling, throw, down the g.*, issue challenge; *pick, take, up the g.*, accept challenge); stout glove with long wrist for driving, fencing, wicket-keeping, &c. Hence **gau·ntlet**ED[2] a. [f. F *gantelet* (*gant* glove f. OSw. *wante*, -LET)]

gau·ntlet[2], n. *Run the g.*, pass between rows of men who strike one with sticks, cords, &c., as military, naval, or school punishment (also fig. of being subjected to criticism). [earlier *gantlope* f. Sw. *gatlopp* (GATE[2], *lopp* course, cf. G *gassenlaufen*) w. assim. to prec.]

gauntry, -tree. See GANTRY.

gauze, n. Thin transparent fabric of silk, cotton, wire, &c.; slight haze. Hence **gau·zy**[2] a., **gau·zi**NESS n. [f. F *gaze* etym. dub.]

gă·vel, n. (U.S.). Auctioneer's or chairman's hammer. [?]

gă·velkind, n. (legal). Land-tenure, especiallyin Kent, involving equal division of intestate's property among all his sons. [f. obs. *gavel*, OE *gafol*, tribute, cf. med. L *gabulum*, cogn. w. GIVE, +KIND]

gavo·tte, n. Minuet-like but more lively dance; music for it; piece of music in common time, moderately quick, with two parts each repeated. [F, f. Pr. *gavoto* (*Gavot* native of Alps)]

gawk, n. Awkward or bashful person. [?]

gaw·ky, a. & n. Awkward, ungainly, bashful, (person). Hence **gaw·ki**NESS n. [perh. f. prec., but found earlier]

gay, a. (gayer, -est). Full of or disposed to or indicating mirth, light-hearted, sportive; airy, off-hand; (euphem.) dissolute, immoral, living by prostitution; showy, brilliant, bright-coloured, finely dressed, (*with*). Hence **gai·**LY[2] adv. [f. F *gai* perh. f. OHG *wâhi* pretty]

gaze, v.i., & n. Look fixedly (*at, on, upon*); hence **ga·z**ER[1] n. (N.) intent look (*stand at g.*, looking thus). [?]

gazē·bo, n. Structure whence a view may be had, belvedere, lantern, turret, balcony, &c. [perh. facet. formation f. prec. on L future (cf. LAVABO), or f. some Oriental word]

gaze·lle, n. Small graceful soft-eyed kinds of antelope. [F, f. Arab. *ghazal*]

gaze·tte, n., & v.t. (Hist.) news-sheet, periodical publication giving current events; one of three official journals (*London, Edinburgh, Dublin, G.*) issued by authority twice a week with lists of government appointments & bankrupts & other public notices; (in newspaper titles as *Westminster, Pall Mall, G.*) newspaper; (vb) publish in official g. (esp. in pass. of officials so announced). [F, f. It. *gazzetta* perh. f. Venetian small coin so called]

găzetteer·, n. Geographical dictionary. [so called as first provided for gazette-writers, earlier sense of g.]

gă·zogene, gas-, n. Apparatus making aerated waters. [f. F *gazogène* (GAS, -GEN)]

gear (g-), n., & v.t. & i. Equipment, apparel, &c. (archaic); harness of draught animals; apparatus, appliances, tackle, tools; combination of wheels, levers, &c.; wheels working on one another by teeth &c.; arrangements connecting motor with its work (*in, out of, g.*, connected or working, with connexion interrupted or not working; *high, low, g.*, by which driven part of bicycle, motor-car, &c., revolves faster, slower, relatively to driving part (similarly *top, bottom, g.* of the available extremes), whence **gear·**ING[1](6) n.; rigging; goods, household utensils; *g.-box, -case*, enclosing gearing of bicycle &c.; *g.-wheel*, cogwheel, esp. that in bicycle which transmits motion of pedals to axle; hence **gear·**LESS a. (Vb) harness (draught animal; often *up*); put (machinery) in g., provide with g. (*g. up, down*, provide with high, low, g.); (of cog-wheel) fit exactly *into*, be in g. *with*. [prob. f. ON *gervi* = OHG *garawî* f. OTeut. *garwu* ready]

ge·cko (g-), n. House lizard found in warm climates. [f. Malay *gekoq*, imit. of its cry]

gee[1], **gee·-gee,** (jē), n. (colloq.). Horse. [orig. child's wd, f. foll.]

gee[2], **gee·-ho·, gee·-(h)u·p, gee·-wo·,** (jē), int. (Words of command to horse &c.) go on, go faster, (sometimes) turn to right.

gee[3], int. (U.S.) of asseveration, discovery, &c. [abbr. *Jesus*]

geese. See GOOSE.

gee·zer (g-), n. (slang). Old person, old creature. [var. of north. *guizer* mummer (as GUISE + -ER[1])]

Gehe·nna (g-), n. Hell; place of burning, torment, or misery. [eccl. L, f. Hellenistic Gk *geenna* f. Heb. *gehinnom* hell, orig. valley of Hinnom where children were sacrificed]

gei·sha (gā-), n. Japanese dancing-girl. [Jap.]

geist (gī-), n. Intellectuality & sensibility, capacity for or tendency to mental fervour. [G, as GHOST]

gĕ·latin(e) (j-; *also* -ēn), n. Amorphous brittle transparent tasteless slightly yellow substance, basis of the jellies resulting from stewing skin, tendons, ligaments, bone-matrix, &c. (*vegetable g.*, constituent of gluten identical with animal g.; *blasting-g.*, an explosive nitroglycerine compound; *g. paper*, coated with sensitized g. for photography). Hence **gelatĭ·ni**FORM a., **gelă·tino-** comb. form. [f. F *gélatine* f. It. *gelatina* (*gelata* JELLY, -IN)]

gelă·tinous, a. Jelly-like in consistence &c.; of gelatin. So **gela·tini**ZE(3) v.t. & i., **gela·tino**ID a. & n. [f. F *gélatineux* (prec., -OUS)]

gela·tion (j-), n. Solidification by freezing. [f. L *gelatio* (*gelare* freeze, -ATION)]
geld (g-), v.t. Deprive (usu. male animal) of generative power, castrate, excise testicles or ovaries of. Hence (-)**ge·ld**ER[1] n. [f. ON *gelda*]
ge·lding, n. Gelded horse or other animal. [f. ON *geldingr* (prec., -ING[3])]
gĕ·lid (j-), a. Icy, ice-cold; chilly, cool. [f. L *gelidus* (*gelu* frost) cogn. w. COLD]
ge·lignite, n. A nitro-glycerine explosive. [f. GELATINE, L *ignis* fire, -ITE[1](2)]
gem (j-), n., & v.t. Precious stone, esp. when cut and polished; object of great beauty or worth, choicest part *of*, prized thing; precious or semi-precious stone with engraved design; hence **ge·mm**Y[2] a. (Vb) adorn (as) with gg. [f. L *gemma* bud, jewel]
Gemar·a (g-), n. Later part of Talmud, commentary on MISHNA. [Aram., = completion]
gĕ·minate[1] (j-, -*at*), a. (nat. hist.). Combined in pairs. [f. L *geminare* (*geminus* twin), -ATE[2]]
ge·minăte[2], v.t. Double, repeat, arrange in pairs. So **gemin**A·TION **n.** [as prec., -ATE[3]]
Gĕ·minī (j-), n. & (-ī) int. Constellation Castor and Pollux or the Twins, third sign of Zodiac, (also as archaic or vulg. int. of surprise, pr. jĭmĭnĭ). [L, = twins]
ge·mma (j-), n. (bot., zool.; pl. -*ae*). Leafbud; (in mosses &c.) small cellular body that separates from mother-plant & starts fresh one; (Zool.) bud-like growth on animal of low organization becoming detached & developing into individual. [L, see GEM]
ge·mmate[1], a. Having buds, reproducing by gemmation. [f. L *gemmatus* (prec., -ATE[2])]
gemma·te[2], v.i. Put forth buds, propagate by gemmation. [f. L *gemmare* (GEMMA), -ATE[3]]
gemma·tion, n. Act, manner, of budding, arrangement of buds; reproduction by gemmae, formation of new individual by protrusion & separation of part of the parent. So **ge·mm**ATIVE a. [F, f. L as prec., -ATION]
gemmĭ·ferous, a. Producing precious stones; bearing buds; = foll. [f. L *gemmifer* (GEMMA, -I-, -FEROUS)]
gemmĭ·parous, a. Of, propagating by, gemmation. Hence **gemmi·parous**LY[2] adv. [GEMMA, L -*parus* (*parere* bring forth)]
ge·mmūle, n. Growing point of plant embryo; reproductive cell of cryptogam; (Zool.) small gemma. [F, f. L *gemmula* (GEMMA, -ULE)]
-gen (j-), suf. forming nn. in scientific use f. F -*gène* f. Gk -*genēs* -born, of such a kind, (*gen-*, *gn-*, seen in *gi-gn-omai* be born, become). (1) in *oxygen* & later chem. formations -*gen* has the sense (not Gk) *that which produces* (*hydrogen, nitrogen, cyanogen*); (2) in *endogen, exogen*, &c. (bot.) -*gen* = growth (*acrogen, thallogen*).
gena·ppe (j-), n. Smooth kind of worsted. [f. *Genappe* in Belgium]
gendar·me (F), n. (pl. -*s*). Soldier, mounted or on foot, employed in police duties esp. in France; (Mountaineering) rock-tower occupying & blocking arête.
gendarmerie (F), n. Force of gendarmes.
ge·nder[1] (j-), n. Grammatical classification (or one of the two, or three, classes) of objects roughly corresponding to the two sexes & sexlessness (MASCULINE, FEMININE, & NEUTER; see also COMMON[1], EPICENE), (of nouns & pronouns) property of belonging to such class, (of adjj.) appropriate form for accompanying a noun of any such class; (joc.) sex. Hence **ge·nder**LESS a. [f. OF *gen(d)re* f. L GENUS]
ge·nder[2] (j-), v.t. (poet.). = ENGENDER. [f. OF *gen(d)rer* f. L *generare* (prec.)]
gene, n. (biol.). One of the factors or elements of which a germ-cell contains a pair transmitted each from one parent. [mod. formation, cf. -GEN]
gĕnealŏ·gical, a. Of genealogy; tracing family descent; *g. tree*, table showing descent of family or of animal species in shape of tree with branches. Hence **genealo·gical**LY[2] adv. [f. F *généalogique* f. med. L f. Gk *genealogikos* (GENEALOGY, -IC) + -AL]
gĕneă·logize (-j-), v.t. & i. Trace genealogy of; draw up genealogies. Hence **genea·log**IST(1) n. [foll., -IZE]
gĕneă·logy, n. Account of descent from ancestor by enumeration of intermediate persons, pedigree; investigation of pedigrees; plant's or animal's line of development from earlier forms. [OF (-*gie*) f. LL f. Gk *genealogia* (*genea* race, -LOGY)]
genera. See GENUS.
ge·neral (j-), a. & n. Completely or approximately universal, including or affecting all or nearly all parts, not partial, particular, local, or sectional, (*g. confession*, to be made by whole congregation; *G. Council*, summoned by invitation to the Church at large; *g.* ELECTION; *G. Post Office*, head office in London; *G. Post*, first morning delivery, also name of indoor game); prevalent, widespread, usual, (*in a g. way*, ordinarily); not limited in application, relating to whole class of objects, occasions, &c., true of all or (opp. *universal*) nearly all cases (*as a g. rule*, in most cases), including points common to individuals of a class & neglecting differences (*g. word, term, notion*); not restricted to one department, not specialized, (*g. dealer*, trader in many articles; *g. practitioner*, doctor treating cases of all kinds; *g. servant*, maid-of-all-work; *g. reader*, of miscellaneous literature);

roughly corresponding or adequate, sufficient for practical purposes, (*g. resemblance, idea*); vague, indefinite, (*spoke only in g. terms*); (Mil., of officer) above rank of colonel; (appended to titles, as ADJUTANT *g.*, ATTORNEY *g.*, POST[2]-*master g.*) chief, head, with unrestricted authority or sphere, (also joc. with other nn., as *lover g.*, one who makes love to all women); *in g.*, generally, in all ordinary cases, barring special exceptions, for the most part. (N.) *the g.* (archaic), the public; (pl.; now rare) g. principles, notions, or rules; chief of religious order, e.g. of Jesuits, Dominicans; (Mil.) officer next below Field Marshal (also by courtesy of *lieutenant g.* & *major g.*); commander of army; tactician, strategist, of specified merit (*a good, bad, great, g.*; *no g.*); =g. servant above (colloq.). [OF, f. L *generalis* (GENUS, -AL)]

generali·ssimo, n. Commander of combined military & naval force, or of several armies. [It., superl. of *generale* GENERAL]

generă·lity, n. Being general, applicability to whole class of instances; vagueness; general point, principle, law, or statement; main body, bulk, majority, *of*. [f. F *généralité* f. L *generalitatem* (GENERAL, -TY)]

generalīza·tion, n. (Forming of) general notion or proposition obtained by induction (often used disparagingly, esp. *hasty g.*, one based on too few instances). [foll., -ATION]

ge·neralize, v.t. & i. Reduce to general laws, form into a general notion, give a general character to, call by a general name; infer (law, conclusion) by induction; base general statement upon (facts &c.); (Math., Philos.) throw into general form, extend application of; form general notions by abstraction; (Paint.) render only the typical characteristics of; make vague, use generalities, speak vaguely; bring into general use. Hence **ge·neraliz**ER[1] n. [-IZE]

ge·nerally, adv. For the most part, extensively; in a general sense, without regard to particulars, not specially, (*g. speaking*, in general); as a general rule, commonly. [-LY[2]]

ge·neralship, n. Office of a general; strategy, military skill; skilful management, tact, diplomacy. [-SHIP]

gĕ·nerate, v.t. Bring into existence, produce, evolve, (plants, animals, &c., usu. in pass.; heat, force, light, friction, electricity, &c.; result, state of things, state of mind, &c.); (Math.; of point, line, surface, conceived as moving) make (line, surface, solid). [f. L *generare* beget (GENUS), -ATE[3]]

genera·tion, n. Procreation, propagation of species, begetting or being begotten, (*equivocal* or SPONTANEOUS *g.*); production by natural or artificial process; single step in descent or pedigree (*have known them for three gg.*; *his descendant in the tenth g.*); whole body of persons born about same time, average time in which children are ready to replace parents (reckoned at ⅓ of a century or at 30 years as a time-measure). [f. L *generatio* (prec., -ATION)]

ge·nerative (-āt-, -*at*-), a. Of procreation; able to produce, productive. [prec., -ATIVE]

ge·nerātor, n. Begetter; apparatus for producing gases, steam, electricity, &c. [L (GENERATE, -OR[2])]

genĕ·ric, a. Characteristic of a genus or class; applied to (any individual of) a large group or class; general, not specific or special. Hence **gene·r**ICALLY adv. [f. L GENUS + -IC]

ge·nerous, a. Magnanimous, noble-minded, not mean or prejudiced, free in giving, munificent, so **genero·**SITY n.; (of soil) fertile; ample, abundant, copious; (of diet, colour, wine) rich & full. Hence **ge·nerous**LY[2] adv. [f. F *généreux* f. L *generosus* (GENUS, -OUS) well-born, generous]

gĕ·nesis, n. First book of O.T., with account of the Creation (G-); origin, mode of formation or generation, (also in comb. as *abiog.*, *parthenog.*). [L f. Gk (root of *gignomai* become)]

ge·net (jĕ-), n. (Fur of) kind of civet-cat. [f. OF *genete* f. Arab. *jarnait*]

genĕ·tic (jĭ-), a. Of, in, concerning, origin; of genetics. Hence **gene·t**ICALLY adv., **gene·t**ICS n. pl., the study of heredity & variation, including loosely the physiology of reproduction & the art of breeding. [f. GENESIS on anal. of *antithesis -etic*]

genē·va[1], n. Spirit distilled from grain & flavoured with juniper berries, Hollands. [f. Du. *genever* f. OF *genevre* f. L *juniperus* JUNIPER w. assim. to foll.]

Genē·va[2], a. (attrib.), & n. Of, from, Geneva (*G. bands*, clerical BAND[1]'s like those of Swiss Calvinists; *G. Conventions*, of 1864–5 neutralizing ambulances &c. in war; *G. cross*, red Greek cross on white ground distinguishing ambulances &c. in war; *G. gown*, black, worn by Calvinists & low-churchmen in pulpit); (as n., used for) the G. Conventions, the League of Nations or its proceedings. Hence **Gene·**VAN, **Gĕneve·**SE, aa. & nn.

gē·nial[1], a. Nuptial, generative, (*g. bed, instinct*; rare); conducive to growth, mild, warm. (of air, climate, &c.); cheering, enlivening; jovial, kindly, sociable, whence **geniă·l**ITY n., **ge·nial**IZE(3) v.t.; of genius (rare). Hence **ge·nial**LY[2] adv. [f. L *genialis* (GENIUS, -AL)]

genī·al[2], a. (anat.). Of the chin. [f. Gk *geneion* chin (*genus* jaw cf. L *gena*) + -AL]

genĭ·culate (-*at*), **geni·culāted,** aa. (nat. hist.). Having knee-like joints. [f. L *geniculatus* (*geniculum* f. *genu* knee, -CULE, -ATE[2])]

gē·nie (-ĭ), n. (pl. usu. *genĭī* see GENIUS). Jinnee, sprite or goblin of Arabian tales. [f. F *génie* f. L GENIUS]

genī·o-, comb. form of Gk *geneion* chin, as *-hy·oid* of chin & hyoid bone.

geni·sta (j-), n. Genus of yellow-flowered shrubs (including in some classifications the common broom). [L]

gĕ·nital (j-), a., & n. (pl.). Of animal generation; (n. pl.) external organs of generation. [f. L *genitalis* (*gignere genit-* beget, -AL)]

gĕ·nitive, a. & n. *G. case* or *g.*, grammatical form of nouns, pronouns, adjectives, & participles, corresponding in inflected langg. to *of, from,* & other prepositions with the noun representing the source, possessor, &c. (*g. absolute*, Gk construction corresponding to Latin ablative absolute). Hence **genitī·**VAL a. [f. L *genitivus* (*casus* case) of generation, mistransl. of Gk *genikē* (*ptōsis* case) of class; *genitivus* as prec. + -IVE]

gĕ·nito-, comb. form of GENITAL, as *-urinary* of the genital & urinary organs.

gē·nius, n. (pl. *-iuses, -iī*). Tutelary spirit of person, place, or institution (*good, evil, g.*, two opposed spirits or angels working for person's salvation or damnation, also person who powerfully influences one for good or ill); (usu. pl., *genii*, w. sing. GENIE) demon(s), supernatural being(s); nation's, age's, &c., prevalent feeling, opinions, or taste; character, spirit, drift, method, of a language, law, &c.; associations or inspirations *of* a place; natural ability, special mental endowments; (no pl.) exalted intellectual power, instinctive & extraordinary imaginative, creative, or inventive capacity, (pl. *-iuses*) person having this; *g. loci* (L), presiding deity, associations &c., of the place. [L, in first sense, f. root of *gignere* beget]

Gĕ·nōa (j-), n. Italian city (*G. cake*, rich with almonds on top). Hence **Geno**E·SE a. & n.

genre (F), n. Kind, style; (also *g.-painting*) portrayal of scenes &c. from ordinary life.

Ge·nro, n. pl. =Elder Statesmen (see STATESMAN). [Jap., =old men]

gens (j-), n. (Rom. ant.; pl. *gentēs*). Clan, sept, among Greeks or Romans. [L, genit. *gentis* (*gignere* beget)]

gent, n. Gentleman (vulg.); person pretending to status of gentleman (joc.). [short for GENTLEMAN]

gentee·l, a. (usu. iron.; vulg. in serious use). Appropriate to, characteristic of, belonging to, the upper classes, stylish, fashionable, well-dressed, elegant. Hence **gentee·**LY[2] (-l-lĭ) adv. [16th-c. adoption of *gentil* (cf. 13th-c. GENTLE) see GENTILE]

ge·ntian (-shn, -tĭan), n. Kinds of usu. blue-flowered plant found esp. in mountain regions; *g.-bitter*, tonic extracted from its root. [f. L *gentiana* (*Gentius* king of Illyria, -AN)]

ge·ntile, a. & n. (Person) not of Jewish race, (in Mormon use) non-Mormon, whence **ge·ntile**DOM n.; of a nation or tribe, (a. & n. in Gram.) (word) indicating nationality; heathen, pagan. [f. F *gentil* f. L *gentilis* (GENS, -IL)]

gentili·tial (-shl), a. Of a nation, gens, or family (*g. noun, name, insignia*). [f. L *gentilitius* (*gentilis* GENTILE) + -AL]

gentĭ·lity, n. Gentle birth, status of gentleman or lady, (now rare); (usu. iron.) being genteel, social superiority, good manners, upper-class habits, (*shabby g.*, endeavour to keep up genteel appearances). [f. OF *gentilité* f. L *gentilitatem* (GENTILE, -TY)]

ge·ntle, a. (-er, -est), & n. Well-born, (Herald.) having right to bear arms, (now only in *g. & simple*, & in comb. as *gentlefolks*, GENTLEMAN); (of birth, blood, family, pursuits, &c.) honourable, belonging to or fit for the class of gentlemen; (archaic) generous, noble, courteous (still playfully in *g. reader*, author's apostrophe); tame, quiet, (*the g. craft*, angling), easily managed; not stormy, rough, or violent; (of medicine) mild, not drastic; (of rule &c.) not severe; moderate (*a g. heat*), gradual (*a g. slope*); kind, mild, tender, (*the g. sex*, women); *gentlefolk(s)*, people of good position & family. (N.): (pl.; vulg.) gentlefolks; maggot, larva of flesh-fly or bluebottle, used as fishing-bait (f. obs. sense *soft* of adj.). [f. OF *gentil* see GENTILE]

ge·ntlehood, n. Position or character attaching to gentle birth. [from 1860; -HOOD]

ge·ntleman, n. Man entitled to bear arms but not included in the nobility (chiefly hist.); member of certain professions &c. (archaic); man of gentle birth attached to household of sovereign or great person (*g. in waiting* &c.; *g.-at-arms*, one of sovereign's bodyguard); man of chivalrous instincts, fine feelings, & good breeding (*the g.'s psalm*, Ps. XV); man of good social position, man of wealth & leisure (*g. at* LARGE); (courteous synonym for) man, (pl., in voc.) male members of audience, also in letters= Sirs; (pl. as sing. n.) men's public urinal; (Law) man who has no occupation; (facet.) *old g.*, the devil, *my g.*, the fellow I was speaking of, *g.'s g.*, valet; *g.-commoner* (hist.), privileged undergraduate at Oxf. & Camb.; *g. farmer*, country g. who farms; *g.* RANKER; *g. usher*, g. acting as usher to great person. Hence **ge·ntleman**HOOD, **ge·ntleman**SHIP(1), nn. [GENTLE + MAN after OF *gentilz hom*]

ge·ntlemanlike, a. Appropriate to, resembling, a gentleman. [-LIKE]

ge·ntlemanly, a. Feeling, behaving, or looking, like a gentleman; befitting a gentleman. Hence **ge·ntlemanli**NESS n. [-LY[1]]

ge·ntleness, n. Kindliness, mildness; freedom from severity, suddenness, violence, steepness, &c. [-NESS]

ge·ntlewoman, n. Woman of good birth or breeding, lady. Hence **ge·ntlewoman-**HOOD n., **ge·ntlewoman**LIKE, **ge·ntlewoman**LY[1], aa., **ge·ntlewomanli**NESS n. [GENTLE + WOMAN after OF *gentilfemme*]

ge·ntly, adv. As gentleman or gentlewoman (only in *g. born,* of gentle birth); quietly, moderately, softly, slowly, (as remonstrance) not so fast &c.; mildly, tenderly, kindly. [-LY[2]]

ge·ntry, n. People next below the nobility in position & birth; (contempt., esp. *these g.*) people. [prob. f. obs. *gentrice* f. OF *genterise* var. of *gentelise* (*gentil* GENTILE)]

gĕ·nūal (j-), a. Of the knee. [L *genu* knee, -AL]

gĕ·nūflect, v.i. Bend the knee, esp. in worship. Hence or cogn. **ge·nuflect**OR[2], **genufle·**XION, nn., **ge·nuflect**ORY a. [f. med. L *genuflectere -flex-* (prec., *flectere* bend)]

gĕ·nuine, a. Of the original stock, purebred; really proceeding from its reputed source or author; having the supposed character, not counterfeit, properly so called. Hence **ge·nuine**LY[2] adv., **ge·nuine**NESS n. [f. L *genuinus* (cf. *ingenuus* INGENUOUS) f. Aryan *gen-* beget]

gē·nus, n. (pl. *gĕ·nera*). (Logic) kind of things including subordinate kinds or SPECIES (*highest g.*, not itself subordinated as species to higher g.; *subaltern g.*, so subordinated); (Zool., Bot.) group of animals or plants having common structural characteristics distinct from those of all other groups, & usu. containing several species (see CLASS; the generic & specific names, the former with capital initial, form the proper name; *the genus* Homo, mankind); (loosely) kind, class, order, tribe. [L, genit. *-eris* race f. Aryan as prec.]

-geny (j-), suf. forming nn. indicating mode of production f. F *-génie* (-GEN), as *anthropogeny* history of human evolution, often with corresp. nn. in *-genesis* & adjj. in *-genetic.*

gēō- (j-), comb. form of Gk *gē* earth (Gk *geō-*), as *-dyna·mic* of the latent forces of the earth, *-selē·nic* of earth & moon.

geoce·ntric, a. Considered as viewed from the earth's centre (*g. latitude of planet,* in which it would appear to observer at earth's centre); having or representing the earth as centre, not HELIO*centric.* [prec., *centric* (CENTRE[1], -IC)]

gē·ode (j-), n. (Concretionary stone containing) cavity lined with crystals or other mineral matter. Hence **geŏ·di**C a. [f. F *géode* f. L f. Gk *geōdēs* earthy (*gē* earth, -ODE)]

geŏ·desy, n. Branch of mathematics dealing with figure & area of the earth or large portions of it. So **geodĕ·**SIC, **geodĕ·**TIC, aa. (*-sic, -tic, line,* shortest possible on surface between two points), **geode·**TICAL a., **geode·tical**LY[2] adv., **geo·desi**ST(3) n. [f. F *géodésie* f. mod. L f. Gk GEO(*daisia* f. *daiō* divide)]

geo·gnosy, n. = GEOLOGY; geology of a district; knowledge of the mineral character, grouping, & distribution, of particular rocks. So **geogno·sti**C(AL) aa. [f. F *géognosie* (GEO-, Gk *gnōsis* knowledge, *gnōstos* known]

geogra·phic(al), aa. Of geography (*-ic latitude,* angle made with plane of equator by perpendicular to earth's surface at any point; *-al mile,* = 1′ of longitude on equator or about 2000 yds). Hence **geogra·phical**LY[2] adv. [f. Gk GEO(*graphikos* GRAPHIC) + -AL]

geo·graphy, n. Science of the earth's surface, form, physical features, natural & political divisions, climate, productions, population, &c. (*mathematical, physical, & political, g.*, the science in these aspects); subject-matter of g.; features, arrangement, *of* place; treatise or manual of g. So **geo·**GRAPHER n. [f. F *géographie* f. L f. Gk GEO(*graphia* -GRAPHY)]

geo·logize, v.i. & t. Devote time to examining places geologically, collecting specimens, &c.; examine (place) thus. [foll. + -IZE]

geo·logy, n. Science of the earth's crust, its strata, & their relations & changes; geological features *of* district. Hence **geolo·gi**C(AL) aa. (*-ic* now only of things forming part of subject-matter of g.), **geo·lo·gical**LY[2] adv., **geo·**LOGIST n. [f. med. L f. Gk GEO(*logia* -LOGY)]

ge·omancy, n. Divination from figure given by handful of earth thrown down, & hence from figures given by dots made at random. Hence or cogn. **ge·omanc**ER[1] n., **geoma·nti**C a. [f. F *géomancie* f. L f. Gk GEO(*manteia* -MANCY)]

geo·meter, n. Person skilled in geometry; kinds of caterpillar & corresp. moth (from caterpillar's seeming to measure ground by its mode of walking). [f. L f. Gk GEO(*metrēs* measurer)]

geome·tric(al), aa. Of, according to, geometry (*-al tracery,* with openings of g. form, as circles, trefoils, &c.; *-al proportion,* involving equal ratios in its two parts, as 1 : 3 :: 4 : 12; *-al progression,* with constant ratio between successive quantities, as 1 : 3 : 9 : 27 : 81; *g. spider,* constructing web of g. pattern). Hence **geome·trical**LY[2] adv. [f. L f. Gk *geōmetrikos* (prec., -IC) + -AL]

geo·metrize, v.i. & t. Work, form, by geometrical methods. [foll. + -IZE]

geŏ·metry, n. Science of properties &

relations of magnitudes (as lines, surfaces, solids) in space. So **geometri·**CIAN n. [f. F *géométrie* f. L f. Gk GEO(*metria* measuring)]

geŏ·phagy (-jĭ), n. = DIRT-*eating*. So **geo·phag**IST(1) n. [GEO-, Gk -*phagia* -eating]

geopŏ·nic, a. (pedantic or facet.). Agricultural. [f. Gk GEO(*ponikos* f. *ponos* toil + -IC)]

Geor·die (jor-), n. (Sc. & north.). = COLLIER (all senses). [*George*, -Y[3]]

George (jorj), n. *St G.*, patron saint of England from time of Edw. III who chose him as patron of Order of the Garter (*St G.'s day*, 23rd April; *St G.'s cross*, vertical & horizontal red bars crossing in centre); (*G-*) jewel forming part of Garter insignia; *brown G.*, vessel of brown earthenware; *by G.*, oath or exclamation. [f. L f. Gk *Geōrgios* supposed prince of Cappadocia martyred under Diocletian]

george·tte, (jor-), n. A thin silk dress-material. [f. dressmaker's name]

Geor·gian[1] (jorjĭ-), a. Of the time of the first four Georges Kings of England; of the time of George V. [-IAN]

Geor·gian[2] (jorjĭ-), a. & n. (Inhabitant, language) of Georgia in the Caucasus; (inhabitant) of Georgia in U.S. [-AN]

Geor·gic (jor-), n. One book (*first, fourth, G.*) of *the Gg.*, Virgil's poem on husbandry. [f. L f. Gk *geōrgika* pl. neut. adj. (*geōrgos* husbandman f. GEO-, *erg-* work, -IC)]

geŏ·tropism, n. Plant-growth in relation to gravity (*positive g.*, tendency of roots to grow towards, *negative g.*, of stems to grow away from, centre of earth). So **geotrŏ·pic** a., **geotro·pic**ALLY adv. [GEO-, Gk *tropikos* (*tropē* a turning f. *trepō* turn + -IC, -ISM)]

gerā·nium, n. Kinds of wild herbaceous plant bearing fruit like crane's bill, Crane's-bill; kinds of cultivated pelargonium; colour of the scarlet g. [L, f. Gk *geranion* (*geranos* crane)]

ger·falcon (j-), n. Any large northern falcon, esp. the Icelandic. [f. OF *gerfaucon* prob. f. OHG *gîr* vulture cf. G *geier*, FALCON]

germ, n., & v.i. Portion of organism capable of developing into a new one (*germ-*, usu. of female reproductive element, opp. *sperm-*), rudiment of animal or plant; micro-organism or microbe, esp. one of those supposed to cause disease (*g.*-CARRIER); (fig.) that from which something may spring, elementary principle (*in g.*, not yet developed); (vb) germinate, sprout, (fig. only). [f. F *germe* f. L *germen* etym. dub.]

ger·man[1], a. (Now only as appended to BROTHER, SISTER, COUSIN) in the fullest sense of relationship; = GERMANE. [f. OF *germain* f. L *germanus* of same parents cogn. w. prec.]

Ger·man[2], a. & n. Of, characterizing, Germany or its inhabitants or language (*G. measles*, contagious disease like mild measles; *G. Ocean*, North Sea; *G. sausage*, large kind stuffed with spiced partly cooked meat; *G. text*, black letter; *G. silver*, white alloy of nickel, zinc, & copper). (N.) native, language, of Germany (*High G.*, form of G orig. spoken in South, but now in literary use throughout Germany; *Low G.*, dialects of Germany that are not High G., also, all forms of WG, including English & Dutch, except High G. Hence **Ger·man**ISH[1] a., **Ger·man**ISM(2, 3, 4), **Ger·man**IST(1, 3), nn., **Ger·man**IZE(2, 3, 4) v.t. & i., **Germanīz**A·TION, **Ger·maniz**ER[1], nn., **Germā·no-** comb. form., **Germa·no**MA·NIA n., **Germa·no**PHIL, **Germa·no**PHOBE, aa. & nn., **Germanŏ·phil**IST, **Germa·no-**PHO·BIA, nn. [f. L *Germanus* a. & n. of related peoples of central & N. Europe, name perh. given by Celts to their neighbours (cf. OIr. *gair* neighbour)]

germa·nder (j-), n. Kinds of plant esp. the blue-flowered *G. speedwell.* [f. med. L *germandra* f. late Gk *khamandrua* (*khamaidrus* f. *khamai* on the ground, *drus* oak)]

germa·ne, a. Relevant, pertinent, *to* the matter or subject. [var. of GERMAN[1]]

Germă·nic, a. & n. Of the Germans (chiefly hist. in *G. Confederation, G. Empire*); of the Teutonic race or any Teutonic people (of language, = primitive Teutonic; also with limiting word: *East G.*, Gothic & some almost lost languages as Burgundian & Vandal; *North G.*, Scandinavian; *West G.*, High & Low German, English, Frisian, Dutch, &c.; see also INDO-*G.*). [f. L *Germanicus* (GERMAN[2], -IC)]

Germă·nity, n. Characteristic German qualities. [-ITY]

ger·mĕn, n. (bot.). Rudiment of seed-vessel, ovary. [L, genit. -*inis*, = GERM]

ger·micide, n. & a. (Substance) having power to destroy (esp. disease-)germs. Hence **germici·d**AL a. [-I-, CIDE]

ger·minal, a. Of germs, of the nature of a germ; in the earliest stage of development. Hence **ger·minal**LY[2] adv. [GERMEN, -AL]

ger·minate, v.i. & t. Sprout, bud, put forth shoots, (lit. & fig.); cause to shoot, develop (trans.), produce. Hence or cogn. **ger·min**ANT a. (intr. usu. fig.), **germin**A·TION, **ger·minat**OR[2](2), nn., **ger·min**ATIVE a. [f. L *germinare* (GERMEN), -ATE[3]]

ger·mon (j-), n. Long-finned tunny. [F]

gĕrŏnto·cracy (g-, j-), n. Government by, governing body of, old men. [f. Gk *gerōn-ontos* old man, -CRACY]

-gerous, suf. (in use *-igerous*, see -I-) f. L *-ger* bearing (*gerere* bear) + -OUS; in some words taken f. L, & freely added to L stems, as in *frondigerous* leaf-bearing.

gerrymă·nder (g-), v.t. & n. Manipulate

(constituency &c.) unfairly so as to secure disproportionate influence at election for some party or class; hence **gerryma·nder**ER[1] n. (N.) such manipulation. [vb f. n., orig. U.S.; anecdotic; substitution of name of governor Gerry of Massachusetts for *sala-* in *salamander*]

gĕ·rund, n. Forms of Latin verb (*-ndum, -ndi, -ndo*) serving as cases of the infinitive in its noun use, constructed as nouns but able to govern like their verb; English verbal noun in -ING[1] when used distinctly as part of verb (*his doing this is doubtful*); *g.-grinder*, teacher of Latin. So **geru·nd**IAL a. [f. L *gerundium* prob. f. *gerundum* neut. gerundive & gerund of *gerere* do = thing to be done, doing]

geru·ndive, a. & n. Of, like, the gerund; (n.; in L Gram.) verbal adjective from gerund stem having sense *that should be done* &c. Hence **gerundī·**VAL a., **geru·nd-ive**LY[2] adv. [f. LL *gerundivus* (prec., -IVE)]

ge·sso (j-), n. Plaster of Paris, gypsum, prepared for use in painting & in sculpture. [It., f. L GYPSUM]

gesta·tion, n. Carrying or being carried in the womb between conception & birth, this period. [f. L *gestatio* (*gestare* frequent. of *gerere* carry, -ATION)]

gestator·ial, a. *G. chair*, for carrying the Pope on certain occasions. [f. L *gestatorius* (*gestator* carrier as prec. + -OR[2], -ORY)]

gestĭ·culate, v.i. & t. Use expressive motion of limbs or body with or instead of speech; express thus. So **gesti·cul**A·TION, **gesti·culat**OR[2], nn., **gesti·cul**ATIVE, **gesti·culat**ORY, aa. [f. L *gesticulari* (*gesticulus* dim. of *gestus* GESTURE, -ATE[3])]

ge·sture (-tsher), n., & v.i. & t. Significant movement of limb or body; use of such movements as expression of feeling or rhetorical device; (transf.) step or move calculated to evoke response from another or to convey (esp. friendly) intention; (vb) = GESTICULATE. [f. med. L *gestura* (L *gerere gest-* wield, -URE)]

get[1] (g-), v.t. & i. (*got*; also p.p. *-gotten* in comb., as *ill-gotten*). Obtain, procure, by effort or contrivance (*g. coal*, extract it from mine), earn (*cannot g. a living*), gain (*got little by it*), win (*g. the upper hand, start, advantage, sun, wind, better, of* a person; *g. the best of it*, be victorious; *g. fame, credit, glory,* &c.; *g. knowledge* or *wind of*, learn, hear rumours of); learn *by heart* or *rote*; obtain as result of calculation (*we g. 9·5 as the average*); receive as gift, wages, &c.; extract by prayer, demand, inquiry, &c. (*from, out of*; *could not g. leave, any supper*); come to have (desired thing, as *rest*, one's *way*, *speech of* some one, *a sight of, possession of*; *g. religion*, be converted); contract (idea &c.; also *g. it into* one's *head*, be convinced *that*; *g. measles*; *g.* person or thing *on the brain*, think of him exclusively, *on* one's *nerves*, be irritably affected by him); (of story &c.) *g. wind*, become known; have inflicted on one, suffer, receive as one's lot or penalty, (*fall, blow, the worst of it, six months*; *g. it*, be punished, scolded, &c.; *g. the* BOOT[1], SACK[1], MITTEN); (with *for* or ind. obj.) procure, provide, (*got him a place*; *we can g. it for you*); catch (fish &c.); bring in, carry home, (crop); *what has got him?*, become of him; (colloq.) corner, puzzle, catch in argument, (esp. in perf. & past); (colloq.) take, eat, (dinner &c.); (colloq., in perf.) have (*have not got a penny*; *it has got to be done*, must); (of animals) beget; (with compl.) succeed in bringing, placing, &c. (*got it over* or *across* see below, *through door, into room*, &c.), bring into some state (*g. with child*, make pregnant; *g. them ready*; *g.* person *upon* a subject, make him talk of it; *g. ship under way*, start her; esp. with p.p. as *g. it done, got the laws obeyed*), suffer injury &c. to some part of one (*got my wrist dislocated*; *shall g. my feet wet*); induce, prevail upon, (person) *to* do. (Intr.): succeed in coming or going *to, from, into, out of, through, over, here, there, as far as*, &c. (*where has it got to?*, what has become of it; *g. across* or *over* (sc. the footlights) slang, reach audience, be effective; *g. there* slang, succeed); (slang) be off, clear out; (with infin.) acquire habit (one *soon gets to like it*); come to be doing (*they got talking*); become (*g. tired, hot, excited, drunk*; *g. well, better*, recover from illness; *g. clear, rid*, or *quit, of*; *g. under way*, begin to sail; *g. done with*, bring to an end; *g. married, used to it, shelved*). (With prepp.): *g. at*, reach (whence **get-a·t-**ABLE a.), get hold of, ascertain, (slang) tamper with, bribe, &c., (slang) attack, banter, (*who are you getting at?*, often = trying to impose upon—expressing incredulity); *g. into*, (colloq.) put on (boots, clothes), (of liquor) affect, confuse, (one's *head*); *g. off*, dismount from, obtain release from (engagement &c.), not remain on (the grass &c.); *g. on*, mount (horse &c.), rise on one's *feet* or *legs* to speak in public; *g. over*, surmount (difficulty), show (evidence, argument) to be unconvincing, recover from (illness) or from surprise at, accomplish (distance, task, &c.), (slang) circumvent; *g. round*, cajole, evade; *g. through*, bring to an end, (of Bill &c.) be passed by (Lords, Commons, &c.), while away (time &c.); *g. to*, begin (business &c.); *g. upon*, = g. on. (With advv.): *g. about*, go from place to place, begin walking after illness &c., (of rumours) be circulated; *g. abroad*, (of rumours) = g. about; *g. along*, advance, meet with success, fare *ill* or *well* &c., manage *without* something, live harmoniously *together* or *with*, (colloq.) *g. along with you!*, be off, nonsense; *g. away*, escape, start, (imperat.) be off!; *g. back*, come home &c., recover (lost thing; *g. b.* one's or *some of* one's *own*, slang, have revenge); *g. down*, dismount; *g. in*, be elected as M.P., enter carriage, bring home (crop), collect (debts &c.), fit (work &c.) into given time, succeed in placing (blow), *g.* one's *hand in*, become at home with some operation, *can't g. in a word* EDGEWAYS; *g. off*, escape (t. & i.), start, go to sleep, be acquitted or pardoned, be let off *with* or *for* specified penalty, procure acquittal or slight penalty for (person); *g. on*, don, display (pace; *g. a move on*, slang, make a start), advance, make progress (*g. on or g. out*, work or go), prosper, fare, manage *without* something, agree or live sociably *with*, *be getting on for*, approaching (an age &c.); *g. out*, (imperat.) be off!, nonsense!, transpire, elicit, succeed in uttering, publishing, &c.: *g. out of*, issue or escape from (*got out of bed on wrong side*, is in bad temper; *g. out of sight*, one's *depth*, disappear, be in too deep water to stand; *g. out of hand*, break from control, also finish *work* &c.), abandon (habit) gradually, evade *doing*, elicit (information) or obtain (money) from (person); *g. over*, bring (troublesome task) to an end; *g. through*, bring to or reach destination, (of Bill) be passed in Parliament, succeed in an examination; *g. through with*, succeed in doing or enduring; *g. together*, collect (t. & i.); *g. under*, subdue (fire); *g. up*, rise esp. from bed, mount esp. on horseback, (of fire, wind, sea) begin to be violent, (of game) rise from cover, (of cricket-ball) rise sharply from pitch, organize, set on foot, (of laundress) dress (linen), make presentable, arrange the appearance of, (hair, the person, mounting of play, binding & print of book), make rise (*I got my, his, back up*, became, made him, angry or stubborn), produce (*g. up steam*, enough to work engine, also fig. of working oneself into anger or energy; *g. the wind up*, slang, feel afraid), work up (factitious emotion; subject for examination &c.). Hence **ge·tt**ABLE a. [f. ON *geta* = OE *-gietan* cf. G (*ver*)*gessen*, f. Aryan *ghed-* seize, whence L *praeda* = *prae-heda* & Gk *khandanō* hold (root *khad*)

get², n. Begetting, offspring, (of animals, esp. in sporting talk). [f. prec.]

get-up, n. Style of equipment or costume, style of production of book &c. [GET¹]

gē·um (j-), n. Kinds of rosaceous plant, Avens, as HERB-bennet. [L, prob. = herb-bennet]

gew·gaw (g-), n. Gaudy plaything or ornament, bauble; paltry showy trifle. [from 13th c.; ME *giuegoue* etym. dub.]

gey (gā), adv. (Sc.). Very, considerably, (also adj. *g. & —*, in same sense). [var. of GAY]

gey·ser¹ (gāz-, gīz-), n. Intermittent hot spring throwing up column of water; apparatus for heating water. [f. Icel. *Geysir* name of a particular specimen in Iceland (*geysa* to gush)]

gey·ser², = GEEZER.

gha·stly (gah-, gă-), a. & adv. Horrible, frightful, shocking; (exagg.) objectionable; deathlike, pale, wan, lurid; (of smile &c.) painfully forced; (adv., chiefly with adj. as *g. pale*) ghastlily. Hence **gha·stli**LY² adv., **gha·stli**NESS n. [f. obs. *gast*, OE *gǣstan* terrify cogn. w. GHOST]

gha(u)t (gawt), n. (Anglo-Ind.). *Eastern, Western, Gg.*, two mountain chains along E. & W. sides of Southern Hindostan; mountain pass, defile; flight of steps leading to river landing-place. [Hind. *ghaṭ*]

Ghazi (gah-), n. Mohammedan anti-infidel fanatic. [Arab. p.p. of *ghaza* fight]

ghee (gē), n. Indian buffalo-milk butter clarified to resemble oil. [f. Hind. *ghi*]

gher·kin (ger-), n. Young green, or small kind of, cucumber used for pickling. [f. Du. **gurkkijn* (now *gurkje*) f. Slavonic cf. late Gk *aggourion* etym. dub.]

ghe·tto (gĕ-), n. Jews' quarter in city. [It., perh. abbr. of *borghetto* (*borgo* BOROUGH)]

Ghi·belline (gĭ-), n. & a. One of emperor's faction (opp. GUELPH) in medieval Italian States; hence **Ghi·bellin**ISM(3) n. (Adj.) adhering to Gg. [f. It. *Ghibellino* perh. f. G *Waiblingen* estate belonging to Hohenstaufen emperors]

ghost (gō-), n. Principle of life (now only in *give up the g.*, die); Spirit of God (now only in *Holy G.*, Third Person of Trinity); soul of dead person in Hades &c.; dead person appearing to the living (*raise, lay, g.*, cause it to appear or cease appearing), apparition, spectre; emaciated person; shadowy outline or semblance (*not the g. of a chance*, none at all); (Opt.) bright spot or secondary image in field of telescope due to defect of lens; artistic or literary hack doing the work for which his employer takes credit; *g.-word*, one of which the existence is imaginary or based on a delusion, as CELT², FYLFOT. Hence **gho·st**HOOD n., **gho·st**LIKE a. [com.-WG; OE *gást* cf. G *geist*; prob. cogn. w. ON *geisa* rage & Goth. *usgaisjan* terrify]

gho·stly, a. (Archaic) spiritual, incorporeal, concerned with sacred or ecclesiastical matters, (*our g. enemy*, the Devil; *g. father, adviser, director*, &c., confessor; *g. comfort, counsel*, &c., administered by priest; *g. weapons*, religious arguments, ecclesiastical penalties, &c.); (as) of a ghost, spectral. Hence **gho·stli**NESS n. [OE *gástlic* (prec., -LY¹)]

ghoul (gōōl), n. Spirit preying on corpses in Eastern tales. Hence **ghou·l**ISH[1] a., **ghou·lish**LY[2] adv. [f. Arab. *ghul* f. vb =seize]

ghyll, var. of GILL[2].

gia·llo anti·co (jah-, -tē-), n. Rich yellow marble found in Italian ruins. [It.]

gi·ant, n. & a. Being of human form but superhuman stature, (Gk mythol.) one of the sons of Gaea (Earth) & Uranus (Heaven) or Tartarus (Hell) who warred against the Gods; agency of enormous power; abnormally tall person, animal, or plant; person of extraordinary ability, courage, strength, &c. (*there were gg. in those days,* our fathers were superior to us); *g. cement,* specially tenacious kind; *g.-powder,* kind of dynamite; *g.('s)-stride,* gymnastic apparatus of pole with revolving head & hanging ropes enabling user to take huge strides round pole; hence **gi·ant**ESS[1] n., **gi·ant**LIKE a. (Adj.) of extraordinary size or force, gigantic, monstrous, (often in plant-names). [ME *geant* (afterwards affected by L) f. OF *géant* f. L f. Gk *gigant-* nom. *-gas* etym. dub.]

giaour (jowr), n. (Turkish contemptuous name for) infidel, esp. Christian. [f. Pers. *gaur*]

gi·bber (j-, g-), v.i., & n. Speak fast & inarticulately, chatter like an ape; (n.) such speed or sound. [imit.]

gi·bberish (g-), n. Unintelligible speech, meaningless sounds, jargon, blundering or ungrammatical talk. [perh. f. prec. (but found earlier) + -ISH[1] as used in names of langg.]

gi·bbet (j-), n., & v.t. (Orig.) gallows; (later) upright post with arm on which bodies of executed criminals were hung up; death by hanging. (Vb) put to death by hanging; expose on g.; hang up as on g.; hold up to infamy or contempt. [f. OF *gibet* gallows dim. of *gibe* club]

gi·bbon (g-), n. Kinds of long-armed ape esp. of Indian archipelago. [F, etym. dub.]

gi·bbous (g-), a. Convex, protuberant; (of moon or planet) having bright part greater than semicircle & less than circle; humped, hunchbacked. Hence or cogn. **gibbŏ·**SITY n., **gibbo·**so- comb. form, **gi·bbous**LY[2] adv. [f. L *gibbus* hump + -OUS, cf. L *gibbosus*]

gibe (j-), **jibe,** v.i. & t., & n. Flout, jeer, mock, (as vb, with *at,* or trans., or abs.). Hence **gi·**BER[1] n., **gi·bing**LY[2] adv. [perh. f. OF *giber* handle roughly, use horse-play, or cogn. w. ON *geip* idle talk]

gi·blets (j-), n. pl. Parts of goose taken out or cut off before cooking, as liver, gizzard, pinions, feet; *giblet soup,* made with these. [f. OF *gibelet* ragout etym. dub.]

gi·bus (j-), n. Opera or crush hat. [*G.,* maker]

gi·ddy (g-), a., & v.t. & i. Dizzy, disposed to fall, stagger, or spin round (*with* sickness, success, &c.); making dizzy (*a g. precipice, maze, success*); circling with bewildering speed; mentally intoxicated, incapable of attention, excitable, frivolous (*play the g. goat,* fool), inconstant, flighty; *g.-go-round,* MERRY[2]-go-round; hence **gi·ddi**LY[2] adv., **gi·ddi**NESS n. (Vb) make or become g. [OE *gydig* insane perh. cogn. w. GOD cf. Gk *entheos*]

gift (g-), n., & v.t. Giving (*would not have it at a g.,* even gratis; *the living is in the g. of* —, is his to bestow; *came to me by free g.*); (Law) voluntary transference of property without consideration; thing given, present, donation; faculty miraculously bestowed, virtue looked upon as emanation from heaven &c., (*g. of* TONGUES); natural endowment (*g. of the* GAB), talent, whence **gi·ft**ED[2] a.; *g.-book,* one given or suitable for giving as present; *g.*-HORSE, one given; hence **gi·ftie** (-Y[3]) n. (Sc.; *the giftie gie us to see oursels as others see us*). (Vb) endow with gg., present *with* as g.; bestow as g. (*to* person; *away*). [prob. f. ON *gift;* com.-Teut., cf. OE *gift* payment for bride, Du. & G *gift* gift, f. OTeut. *giftiz* (GIVE)]

gig[1] (g-), n. Light two-wheeled one-horsed carriage (*g.-lamps* slang, spectacles; *gigman,* person who keeps g., member of GIGMANITY); light narrow clinker-built ship's-boat for oars or sails; rowing-boat chiefly used for racing. [f. obs. *gig* whipping-top, etym. dub.]

gig[2] (g-), n. Kind of fish-spear. [short for *fizgig* f. Sp. *fisga* harpoon (corrupted to *fishgig* & mistaken for compd]

giga·ntic (j-), a. Giant-like in size, stature, &c.; abnormally large, huge Hence or cogn. **gigant**E·SQUE a., **giga·nt**ICALLY adv. [f. L *gigas -antis* GIANT, -IC]

gi·ggle (g-), v.i., & n. Laugh like an affected, ill-bred, or undisciplined girl, titter, have small bursts of half suppressed laughter; (n.) such laugh. [imit.; cf. Du. *giggelen,* G *gichelen*]

gi·glet, -ot, (g-), n. Giggling girl. [orig. = lewd woman, from 14th c., etym. dub.; now associated with prec.]

gigmă·nity (g-), n. The respectable unimaginative middle classes, Philistines. [*gigman* (GIG[1]) + -ITY (Carlylese wds)]

gig-mill (g-), n. Machine for raising nap on cloth; building in which these stand. [f. obs. *gig* whipping-top]

Gilber·tian (g-), a. Of the humorously topsy-turvy kind characteristic of Gilbert & Sullivan opera (*a G. situation*). [W. S. *Gilbert,* librettist, d. 1911, -IAN]

gild[1] (g-), v.t. (p.p. usu. *gilded* in the fully verbal use & in fig. use as adj., *gilt* as adj. in lit. sense). Cover with thin layer of gold laid on as gold leaf or otherwise (*g. pill,* soften down unpleasant necessity), whence **gi·ld**ER[1],

gi·lding[1] (2, 4), nn.; make (condition &c.) tolerable or reputable by money (or with *money* &c. as subj.); tinge, adorn, with golden colour or light; give specious brilliance to by fair words; *Gilded Chamber*, House of Lords; *gilded* or *gilt spurs*, emblem of knighthood; *gilded youth*, the young men of fashion & wealth; *gilt-cup*, buttercup. [f. OE (*be*)*gyldan* (GOLD)]

gild[2]. See GUILD.

gill[1] (g-), n. (usu. pl.), & v.t. Respiration organ(s) in fishes & other water-breathing animals; wattles or dewlap of fowls; vertical radiating plates on under side of mushrooms &c.; flesh below person's jaws & ears (*rosy about the gg.*, healthy-looking); *g.-cover*, bony case protecting fish's gg.; *g.-net*, for entangling fishes by the gg.; hence (-)**gilled**[2] a. (Vb) gut (fish); cut off gg. of (mushroom); take in g.-net. [etym. dub.; cf. Sw. *gäl*, also Gk *kheilos* lip]

gill[2] (g-), n. Deep usu. wooded ravine; narrow mountain torrent. [f. ON *gil* glen]

gill[3] (j-), n. Quarter-pint liquid measure (in some parts half-pint). [f. OF *gille*, med.L *gillo*]

Gill[4] (j-), n. *Jack & G.*, lad & lass. [abbr. of *Gillian* f. F *Juliane* f. L *Juliana* (*Julius*)]

gillaroo· (g-), n. Irish trout. [f. Ir. *giolla* fellow, *ruadh* red]

gi·llie (g-), n. (Hist.) Highland chief's attendant; man or boy attending sportsman in Scotland. [f. Gael. *gille* lad, servant]

gi·llyflower (j-), n. (now rare). Clove-scented pink; other similarly scented flowers, as wallflower, white stock. [f. OF *girofle* f. LL f. Gk *karuophullon* (*karuon* nut, *phullon* leaf) w. assim. to *flower*)]

gilt[1]. See GILD[1] (*cloth g.*, book-binding of cloth with g. letters or tooling).

gilt[2], n. Gilding (*take the g. off the gingerbread*, strip thing of adventitious attractions); *g.-edged paper, securities, stocks*, &c., such investments as trustees prefer or are restricted to. [f. prec.]

gi·mbal (j-), n. (pl. exc. in comb. as *g.-ring* &c.). Contrivance (usu. of rings & pivots) for keeping articles (esp. compass & chronometer) horizontal at sea. [f. obs. & OF *gemel* finger-ring &c. f. *gemellus* dim. of *geminus* twin]

gi·mcrack (j-), n. & a. Trumpery article, knick-knack, useless ornament; hence **gi·mcrackery**(5) n., **gi·mcracky**[2] a. (Adj.) showy & flimsy, worthless, trumpery. [earlier *gibecrake* perh. connected w. OF *giber* shake & CRACK]

gi·mlet (g-), n. Kind of boring-tool (usu. semi-cylindrical with wooden crosspiece as handle & worm at pointed end). [f. OF *guimbelet* dim. of the unrecorded Rom. equivalent of obs. *wimble* boring-tool, cf. LG *wemel* boring-tool, Du. *wemelen* move about]

gimp, gymp, (g-), n. Silk, worsted, or cotton twist with cord or wire running through it; fishing-line of silk &c. bound with wire; (Lacemaking) coarser thread outlining design. [etym. dub.; cf. Du. *gimp*, F *guipure*]

gin[1] (j-), n., & v.t. Snare, net, trap, (n. & v.t.); hoisting apparatus, kinds of crane & windlass; machine for separating cotton from its seeds (vb, remove seeds of with this). [shortened f. OF *engin* ENGINE]

gin[2] (j-), n. Spirit distilled from grain or malt, GENEVA[1]; *g.-palace*, gaudily decorated public-house; *g.-shop*, dramshop esp. for g.; *g. sling*, American cold drink of g. flavoured & sweetened. [short for GENEVA[1]]

gi·ngall (j-), **j-**, n. Musket fired from a rest, or light swivel gun, in China & India. [f. Hind. *janjal*]

gi·nger (jĭnj-), n., a., & v.t. (Plant with) hot spicy root used in cooking & medicine & preserved in syrup or candy as sweetmeat (*black g.*, unscraped, from E. Indies; *white g.*, scraped, from Jamaica; *g. shall be hot in the mouth*, the love of pleasure is immortal); mettle, spirit; stimulation (see vb; *g. group* in Parliament, that urges Government to more decided action); (of) light reddish-yellow colour (n. & a.); *g. ale, beer, pop*, kinds of aerated g.-flavoured drink; *g. brandy*, a cordial; *gingerbread*, a cake made with treacle & flavoured with g. (*g.-b. nut*, small button-like cake of it; *take the* GILT[2] *off the g.-b.*), also (as adj., with allusion to fancy and often gilded shapes in which it was made) gaudy, showy, tawdry, (esp. *g.-b. Gothic*); *g.-nut*, gingerbread nut; *g.-race*, a root of g.; *g. wine*, a British wine of fermented sugar, water, & bruised g.; hence **gi·ngery**[2] a. (Vb) flavour with g.; put g. up fundament of (horse) to produce liveliness, (fig.) rouse up (person). [OE & LL *gingiber* f. L *zingiber* f. Gk *ziggiberis* f. Skr. *çrngavera* (*çrnga* horn, *vera* body)]

gingerā·de, n. =GINGER *beer*. [f. prec. after LEMONADE]

gi·ngerly (jĭnj-), adv. & a. With, showing, extreme caution so as to avoid making a noise or injuring oneself or what is touched or trodden on. [perh. f. OF *gensor* compar. of *gent* graceful f. L *genitus* (well-) born]

gingham (gĭ·ngam), n. Kind of cotton or linen cloth of dyed yarn often in stripes or checks; (colloq.) umbrella. [f. F *guingan* ult. f. Malay *ginggang* (orig. adj. =striped)]

gi·ngili (jĭnj-), n. (E.-Ind. plant yielding) a sweet oil. [f. Hind. *jinjali* f. Arab. *juljulan*]

gingi·val (jĭnj-), a. Of the gums. [L *gingiva* gum + -AL]

gi·ngko (g-), n. Japanese tree with fan-shaped leaves. [Jap., f. Chin. *yinhing* silver apricot]

gi·nglymus (j-), n. (anat.). Hinge-like joint in body with motion only in two directions (e.g. elbow). [f. Gk *gigglumos* hinge]

gi·nseng (j-), n. (Root of) medicinal plant found in China, Nepaul, Canada, & Eastern U.S. [f. Chin. *jên shên* (*jên* man) perh. = image of man, w. allusion to forked root]

gi·ppo, n. (army slang). Soup, gravy, stew. [?]

Gi·ppy, n. (army slang). Egyptian soldier. [abbr.]

gi·psy, gy-, (j-), n. Member of a wandering race (called by themselves *Romany*) of Hindu origin with dark skin and hair, living by basket-making, horse-dealing, fortune-telling, &c., & speaking a much corrupted Hindi; (playful) mischievous or dark-complexioned woman; *g. bonnet,* with large side flaps; *g. rose,* scabious; *g. table,* light round one on tripod. Hence **gi·psy**DOM, **gi·psy**HOOD, **gi·psy**ISM(2), nn., **gi·psy**ISH[1] a., **gi·psy**FY (usu. in p.p. *-fied*) v.t. [earlier *gipcyan* for *Egyptian,* the race being supposed to come from Egypt when it appeared in England in early 16th c.]

giraffe (jĭrah·f, -ăf), n. African ruminant quadruped with spotted skin & long neck & legs, camelopard. [ult. f. Arab. *zarifah*]

gi·randole (j-), n. Revolving firework, discharge of rockets from revolving wheel; revolving jet of water; branched candle bracket or candlestick; ear-ring or pendant with large central stone surrounded by small ones. [F, f. It *girandola* (*girare* f. L *gyrare* revolve f. L f. Gk *guros* circle)]

gi·rasŏl(e) (j-), n. Kind of opal reflecting reddish glow, fire-opal. [It. (*-e*), f. *girare* see prec. + *sole* sun, orig. = sunflower]

gird[1] (g-), v.t. (poet. or rhet.; *girded* or *girt*). Encircle (waist, person as to waist) with belt &c. esp. to confine clothes (*g. oneself,* one's *loins,* prepare for action, often with *up*); invest *with* strength, power, &c.; equip *with* sword in belt; fasten (sword &c.) on with belt (*on* adv. or prep., *upon, to*); secure (clothes) on body with girdle or belt; put (cord &c.) *round*; encircle (town &c.) *with* besiegers or siege-works; (of belt, fence, &c.) encircle. [OE *gyrdan* cf. G *gürten* cogn. w. GIRTH & perh. w. GARTH, YARD[2], GARDEN]

gird[2] (g-), v.i., & n. Jest, gibe, *at.* [?]

gi·rder, n. Beam supporting joists of floor; iron or steel beam for like use; latticed or other compound structure of steel &c. forming span of bridge, roof, &c. [GIRD[1] + -ER[1]]

gir·dle[1], n., & v.t. Belt or (now usu.) cord used to gird waist; something that surrounds like a g.; part of cut gem dividing crown from base & embraced by the setting; (Anat.) bony supports for upper & lower limbs (*shoulder* or *pectoral, pelvic* or *hip, g.*); ring round tree made by removal of bark; (vb) surround with g. (often *about, in, round*); kill (tree) or make it more fruitful by girdling. [OE *gyrdel* see GIRD[1], -LE(1), cf. G *gürtel*]

gir·dle[2], n. (Sc. & north.). Circular iron plate hung over fire for toasting cakes; *g.-cake,* so made [var. of GRIDDLE]

girl (gerl), n. Female child, unmarried woman, (*old g.*, affectionate or disrespectful address or description for woman, mare, &c.; *the gg.*, daughters of family, married or not); maidservant; man's sweetheart (often *best g.*); *g. guides,* organization parallel to *boy* SCOUTS; *g. of the period* (19th-c. nickname for one lacking demureness). Hence **gir·l**HOOD, **gir·lie** [-Y[3]], nn., **gir·l**ISH[1] a., **gir·lish**LY[2] adv., **gir·lish**NESS n. [cf. LG *gör* child]

Giro·ndist (j-), n. & a. (Member) of moderate republican party in French assembly 1791–3; (person) of such views. [f. F *Girondiste* (*Gironde* French department from which leaders of party came)]

girt[1] (g-), n., & v.t. Measurement across or round surface that is not flat, with account taken of elevations & depressions. (Vb) measure g. of; (of trees &c.) measure (so much) in g. [var. of GIRTH]

girt[2]. See GIRD[1].

girth (g-), n., & v.t. Leather or cloth band tightened round body of horse &c. to secure saddle &c.; measurement round any more or less cylindrical thing; *g.-web,* woven material for gg. (Vb) surround; encircle (horse &c.), secure (saddle &c.), with g.; measure (so much) in g. [f. ON *georth* cogn. w. GIRD[1]]

gist (j-), n. Real ground or point, substance or pith of a matter. [OF, 3rd sing. pres. of *gésir* lie f. L *jacēre*]

gi·ttern (g-), n. = CITHERN. [f. OF *guiterne* perh. as CITHERN]

give[1] (g-), v.t. & i. (gave, given). (General sense) make another the recipient of something in subject's possession or at subject's disposal (with obj. of thing given, & ind. obj. usu. preceding obj. if without *to* & following it if with *to*; in pass., either obj. may become subj., the other being retained without *to* if direct, with or without *to* if indirect. Thus; *I gave him a book*; *I gave £50 to the S.P.C.A.*, *I gave it him*; *he was given a book*; *a book was given him*; *the S.P.C.A. was given £50*; *£50 was given to,* or *given, the S.P.C.A.* Corresponding constructions are to be assumed with the various senses unless they are inapplicable or exceptions are mentioned). 1. Bestow gratuitously, hand over as present, confer ownership of with or without actual delivery, render (benefit &c.) without payment, (abs.) bestow alms or donations (*to*); confer, grant, (favour, honour, &c.); accord (one's heart, affection, confidence); (of God &c.) grant (faculty &c., or *to* be or do; *g. me*, in imperat., I prefer or admire, as *g. me the good old times*); bequeath; sanction marriage of (daughter &c.; usu. *in marriage*). 2. Deliver, hand over, without reference to ownership, put (food &c.) before one, (*g.* MITTEN, SACK[1], BOOT[1], cf. GET), administer (medicine); deliver (message, love, compliments, &c.); commit, consign, entrust, (*g. into custody* or *in* CHARGE[1]); pledge, assign as guarantee, (one's *word, honour*, &c.). 3. Make over in exchange or payment, pay, sell *for* price, (*g. as good as* one *gets*, retort adequately in words or blows; so *g. a* ROLAND *for an Oliver*; *g.* one *his due*, admit any merits he may have; *would g. the world*, one's *ears*, make any sacrifice *to* secure or *for* something, or *if*). 4. Devote, dedicate, addict, (*gave his life to it*; *much given to these pursuits*). 5. Put forth (some action or effort) to affect another or simply (*g. him a kick*; *g. a jump, cry*, &c.; *g. orders*; *g.* person one's *blessing*; *g. you joy*, prob. orig. with ellipse of *God*, now taken as = *wish* with *I* expressed or omitted; *g. the time of day*, say good morning, evening, &c.); deliver (judgement &c.) authoritatively (*g. the case*, or *it*, *for* or *against* person; in cricket, *g. batsman out* or *not out*); (p.p., of document) dated; provide (ball, party, dinner) as host. 6. Present, offer, expose, hold out, show, (*g.* person one's *hand*; *g. a back*, stand to be leapfrogged over; *g. good example*; *the Times gives the facts*; *gives no sign of life*; *thermometer gives 80° in the shade*); read, recite, sing, act, perform, (piece &c.). 7. Make partaker of, impart, be source of, (*gave me his sore throat*; *gave its name to the battle*; *g. a piece of* one's *mind*, scold, reproach; *g. to the world*, publish; *g.* person *to understand, know*, &c., inform, assure). 8. Allot, assign, ascribe, grant, assume, (*he was given the contract, the name of John, quarters*; *under the given conditions*; *given health, the thing can be done*). 9. Yield as product or result (*lamps g. a bad light*; *analysis gives the following figures*). 10. Cause or allow to have (*solitude gives it its only charm*; *gave me much pain*; *this gives him a right to complain*; *g. oneself trouble*, take pains; *g. oneself airs*, be pretentious; *gave myself an hour to get there*; *was given a rest*). 11. Collapse, lose firmness, yield to pressure, become relaxed, make room, shrink. 12. (Of window, passage, &c.) look, lead, (*up*)*on*, *into*. 13. (In phrr. with obj.): *g. birth to*, bring forth (lit. & fig.); *g. chase*, start in pursuit; *g. ear* listen; *g.* TONGUE; *g. ground*, retreat; *g. it him* &c., administer punishment (often *hot*); *g. child* &c. *something to cry for*, chastise for causeless crying; *g.* one *what for*, slang, punish or scold; *g. place*, make room, yield precedence, be superseded or succeeded (by); *g. rise to*, occasion; *g. way*, retire, fail to resist, be superseded by (*to*), be dislodged, break down, make concessions, abandon oneself *to* grief &c., fall in price, begin to row or row harder. 14. (With advv.); *g. away*, alienate by gift, hand over (bride) to bridegroom, betray or expose to ridicule or detection (esp. slang *g. a. the* SHOW[2]), distribute (prizes); *g. back*, restore; *g. forth*, emit, publish, report; *g. in*, yield, cease fighting or arguing, hand in (document) to proper official, (p.p.) added as supplement; *g. off*, emit (vapour &c.); *g. out*, announce, emit, distribute, cease or break down from exhaustion &c., run short; *g. over*, cease from do*ing*, abandon (habit &c.), desist, hand over (*given over*, abandoned *to* evil courses &c.); *g. up*, resign, surrender, part with (*g. up the* GHOST). deliver (fugitive &c.) into hands of pursuers &c., abandon one*self to* a feeling &c., cease to have to do with, cease from effort, (refl. & p.p.) devote or addict *to*, divulge (names of accomplices &c.), pronounce incurable or insoluble, renounce hope of. Hence **gi·**VER[1] n. [com.-Teut.; OE *giefan* cf. Du. *geven*, G *geben*]

give[2], n. Yielding to pressure, elasticity, (*there is no g. in a stone floor*); *g. & take*, mutual concession, compromise, exchange of talk. [f. prec.]

gi·zzard (g-), n. Bird's second stomach for grinding the food mixed in the first with gastric juice; specially muscular stomach of some fish, insects, & molluscs; *fret* one's *g.*, worry; *sticks in* one's *g.*, is unpalatable (fig.). [f. OF *g(u)iser* perh. f. L *gigeria* pl. cooked entrails of fowl]

glā·brous, a. (anat. &c.). Free from hair or down, smooth-skinned. [f. L *glaber* + -OUS]

gla·cé (-ah-sā), a. (Of cloth, leather, &c.) smooth, polished; (of fruits) iced, sugared. [F]

gla·cial (-āsĭal, -āshĭal, -āshl), a. Of ice, icy; (Chem.) crystallized; (Geol.) characterized, produced, by the presence or agency of ice (*g. epoch, era, period*, when northern hemisphere was mostly covered with ice-sheet). Hence **gla·cial**LY[2] adv. [F, f. L *glacialis* (*glacies* ice, -AL)]

glă·ciated (-s-, -sh-), a. Marked or polished by ice-action; covered with glaciers or ice-sheet. So **glaci**A·TION n. [p.p. of unused *glaciate* f. L *glaciare* freeze, -ATE[3]]

glă·cier, n. Slowly moving river or mass of ice formed by accumulation of snow on high ground. Hence **gla·cier**ED[2] **a.** [F (*glace* ice)]

glă·cis (or as F), n. Bank sloping down from fort, on which attackers are exposed to fire. [F, orig. =slippery place (OF *glacier* to slip)]

glad, a., & v.t. Pleased (pred. only; *I am g., g. of it, g. to hear it, g. that it is so, g. it is so, shall be g. to come* &c.; iron., *should be g. to know*); (of looks, feelings, &c.) marked by, filled with, expressing, joy; (of news or events) giving joy; (of nature &c.) bright, beautiful; *the g. eye* (slang), amorous or festive glance; *g. rags* (U.S. slang), Sunday or dress clothes; hence **gla·dd**EN[6] v.t., **gla·d**LY[2] adv., **gla·d**NESS n., (poet.) **gla·d**SOME a., **gla·dsome**LY[2] adv., **gla·dsome**NESS n. (Vb; archaic) make g. [OE *glæd* cf. Da. & Sw. *glad,* & G *glatt* smooth (the orig. sense cf. L *glaber*)]

glade, n. Clear open space or passage between forest trees. [perh. cogn. w. prec.]

glă·diātor, n. Man trained to fight with sword or other weapon at ancient Roman shows; political &c. champion in argument, controversialist. So **gladiator**·IAL a. [L (*gladius* sword)]

glă·diolus (*or* gladī·-), n. (pl. *-luses, -li*). Iridaceous plant with sword-shaped leaves & bright flower-spikes. [L, dim. of *gladius* sword]

Gla·dstone, n. & a. *G.* (*bag*), kind of light portmanteau; *G. claret,* of cheap kinds that became common by Gladstone's reduction of duty 1860. [W.E. *G.*, statesman d. 1898]

glair, n., & v.t. White of egg; kinds of adhesive preparation made from it; any similar viscid substance; hence **glair·**EOUS, **glair·**Y[2], aa.; (vb) smear with g. [f. 13th-c. F *glaire* perh. f. L *clara* fem. of *clarus* clear]

glaive, n. (archaic & poet.). Broadsword, sword. [OF, perh. f. L *gladius* sword]

glă·mour, n., & v.t. Magic, enchantment, (*cast a g. over,* enchant); delusive or alluring beauty or charm; hence **gla·mor**OUS a. (Vb) affect with g., bewitch, enchant. [corruption of GRAMMAR, cf. for sense GRAMARYE]

glance, v.i. & t., & n. (Of weapon) glide off object instead of striking it full (often *aside, off*); (of talk or talker) pass quickly *over,* glide *off* or *from,* subject; *g. at,* make passing & usu. sarcastic allusion to; (of bright object or light) flash, dart, gleam; (of eye) cast momentary look, flash, (*g. at,* give brief look at; *g. over,* read cursorily; *g. down, up,* &c.; *g.* one's *eye,* direct it *at, over,* &c.; hence **gla·ncing**LY[2] adv. (N.) swift oblique movement or impact, (Cricket) stroke with bat's face turned slantwise to ball; (sudden movement producing) flash or gleam; brief look (*at, into, over,* &c.). [perh. nasalized form of OF *glaichier* to slip]

glănd, n. (Physiol.) simple or complex organ composed of nucleated cells secreting constituents of the blood for use or ejection; (Bot.) secreting cell or group of cells on surface of plant-structure. So (see -UL-) **gla·nd**ULE n., **gla·ndul**AR[1], **glandulī·**FEROUS, **gla·ndul**OSE[1] (bot.), **gla·ndul**OUS, **gla·nd**LESS, aa. [f. F *glande* f. OF *glandre* f. L **glandula* (*glans -dis* acorn, -ULE)]

glă·nders, n. pl. Contagious horse-disease with swellings below jaw & mucous discharge from nostrils; the same communicated to man. Hence **gla·nder**ED[2], **gla·nder**OUS, aa. [f. OF *glandre* see prec.]

glandi·ferous, a. Bearing acorns. [f. L *glandifer* (GLAND, -FEROUS)]

gla·ndiform, a. Acorn-shaped; like gland. [GLAND, -FORM]

glare, v.i. & t., & n. Shine dazzlingly or disagreeably; be over-conspicuous or obtrusive, whence **glār·ing**LY[2] adv., **glār·ing**NESS n.; look fixedly or fiercely (*at, upon*); express (hate, defiance) by look. (N.) strong fierce light, oppressive unrelieved sunshine; tawdry brilliance; fierce or fixed look; hence **glār·**Y[2] a. [ME, also MDu. & MLG, *glaren* perh. cogn. w. GLASS]

glass[1], n. Substance, usu. transparent, lustrous, hard, & brittle, made by fusing sand with soda or potash or both & other ingredients (CROWN[1], FLINT, PLATE, WATER[1], *-g.*); substances of similar properties or composition, as *g. of antimony,* vitreous oxy-sulphide fused; g. utensils, ornaments, windows, greenhouses; g. vessel esp. for drinking, amount of liquid contained in this, drink (*a friendly g., fond of his g.*; *has had a g. too much,* is rather drunk); sand-g., hour-g.; carriage window; plate of g. covering picture; glazed frame for plants; looking-g.; eye-g., (pl.) pair of spectacles; lens; g. disk covering watch-face; telescope, spy-g., field-g., opera-g., microscope; barometer, weather-g.; *g.-blower,* one who blows & shapes g.; *g. case,* chiefly of g. for exhibiting or protecting objects; *g.-cloth,* linen cloth for drying gg., cloth covered with powdered g. like g.-paper; *g. cloth,* woven fabric of fine-spun g.; *g.-cutter,* workman, tool, cutting g.; *g.-culture,* of plants under g.; *g.-dust,* powdered g. for polishing; *g. eye,* false eye of g., kind of blindness in horses; *g.-house,* building where g. is made, greenhouse, g.-roofed photographing-room; *g.-paper,* covered with g.-dust; *g.-ware,* articles made of g.; *glasswort,* kinds of plant formerly used in g.-making. Hence **gla·ss**FUL(2) n., **gla·ss**LESS a. [OE *glæs* cf. G *glas* perh. f. OTeut. *gla-, glǣ-,* shine]

glass[2], v.t. Fit with g., glaze, (rare); enclose in g. (rare); make (the eye) glassy (rare); mirror, occasion reflection of (often refl., as *trees g. themselves in the lake*); *glassing-jack*, machine used in dressing leather. [f. prec., cf. earlier GLAZE]

gla·ssy, a. Having properties of, resembling, glass; (of eye &c.) lacking fire, dull, fixed; (of water) lustrous & transparent, or smooth, as glass (so *g. calm, surface*, &c.). Hence **gla·ssi**LY[2] adv., **gla·ssi**NESS n. [-Y[2]]

Glaswē·gian, a. & n. (Inhabitant) of Glasgow. [perh. on GALWEGIAN]

Glau·ber's salt(s) (-aw-, -ow-), n. Sulphate of sodium. [J. R. *Glauber*, German chemist.]

glauco·ma, n. An eye-disease with tension of the globe & gradual loss of sight. Hence **glaucō·mat**OUS a. [f. Gk *glaukōma -atos* (*glaukoō* as foll., -M)]

glau·cous, a. (esp. nat hist.). Of dull greyish green or blue; (Bot.) covered with bloom as of grapes. [f. L f. Gk *glaukos* + -OUS]

glaze, v.t. & i., & n. Fit (window, picture) with glass, furnish (building) with glass windows (*g. in*, enclose thus); cover (pottery &c.) with vitreous substance fixed by fusion (n., this substance, smooth surface resulting); fix (paint) *on* pottery thus; overlay (cloth, leather, pastry, &c.) with smooth lustrous coating (n., this coating, surface produced); cover (eye) with a film (n., filmy look); cover (painted surface) with thin coat of different transparent colour to modify tone (n., this coat); give glassy surface to, e.g. by rubbing (n., polished look) become glassy (esp. of eyes). Hence **gla·z**ER[1](1, 2) n., **gla·z**Y[2] a. [ME *glasen* (GLASS[1])]

glā·zier (-zher, -zier), n. One whose trade is to glaze windows &c.; *is your father a g.?* (facet. question, = you are opaque, to person obstructing one's view). Hence **gla·zi**ERY(2) n. [GLASS[1] + -ER[1] w. assim. to Rom. wds in -IER]

gla·zing, n. In vbl senses; also: windows; material used to produce glaze. [-ING[1]]

gleam, n., & v.i. Subdued or transient light; faint, temporary, or intermittent show *of* some quality &c. (*an occasional g. of humour*; *not a g. of hope*); hence **glea·m**Y[2] a. (Vb) emit gg., shine with subdued or interrupted brightness. [OE *glǣm* cf. OHG *glīmo* glow-worm; cogn. w. GLIMMER, GLIMPSE]

glean, v.i. & t. Gather ears of corn left by reapers, gather (such remains); strip (field &c.) thus; collect in small quantities, scrape together, (news, facts, &c.). Hence **glea·n**ER[1], **glea·n**ING[1](1, 2), nn. [f. OF *glener* etym. dub.]

glebe, n. (Poet.) earth, land, a field; portion of land going with clergyman's benefice. [f. L *gleba* clod, soil]

glee, n. Musical composition for three or more voices, one to each part, set to words grave or gay, often with contrasted movements & prop. without accompaniment; mirth, lively & manifest delight, whence **glee·**FUL, **glee·**SOME, aa., **glee·ful**LY[2] adv. [OE *glīw, glēo*]

gleet, n. Thin morbid discharge from wound, ulcer, &c. (rare), or from the urethra. Hence **glee·t**Y[2] a. [f. OF *glette* slime]

glen, n. Narrow valley. [f. Gael. *gleann*]

gle·ndoveer, n. Beautiful sprite of kind represented by Southey as occurring in Hindu myths. [altered f. *grandouver* in F travel-book perh. f. Skr. *gandharva* semi-divine spirit]

glenga·rry, n. Kind of Highland cap. [place]

Glenli·vet, n. Kind of Scotch whisky. [place]

glē·noid, a. (anat.). *G. cavity, fossa, surface*, shallow cavity on bone (esp. scapula & temporal bone) receiving projection of other bone to form joint. [f. Gk *glēnoeidēs* (*glēnē* socket, -OID)]

glib, a. & adv. (Of surface &c.) smooth, offering no resistance, (of movement) unimpeded, easy, (rare); (of speaker, speech, &c.) fluent, ready, more voluble than sincere or thoughtful; hence **gli·b**LY[2] adv., **gli·b**NESS n. (Adv.) volubly (now rare). [perh. imit.; cf. GLIDE]

glide, v.i. & t., & n. Pass, change place, by smooth continuous movement (of liquid, ship, bird, carriage, snake, person skating, &c.); = VOLPLANE, whence **gli·d**ER[1](2) n., engineless aeroplane; go quietly or stealthily; (of time &c.) pass gently & imperceptibly; pass gradually, shade off insensibly, *into*; cause to g. (*light airs glided her on her course*); hence **gli·ding**LY[2] adv. (N.) act of gliding; (Mus.) succession of sounds made in passing from one tone to another without silencing voice or instrument; (Phon.) gradually changing sound made in passing from one position of speech organs to another. [com.-WG; OE *glīdan* cf. G *gleiten*]

glim, n. (slang). Light, candle, lantern, (DOUSE *the g.*). [prob. cogn. w. GLEAM, GLIMPSE]

gli·mmer, v.i., & n. Shine faintly or intermittently; (n.; also **gli·mmer**ING[1] n.) feeble or wavering light, faint gleam *of* hope &c., glimpse, half view. [as prec.; cf. G *glimmern*]

glimpse, n., & v.t. & i. Faint & transient appearance, momentary or imperfect view *of*, (*the gg. of the moon*, the earth by night, sublunary affairs). (Vb) catch g. of, see faintly or partly; (poet.) appear faintly, dawn. [n. f. vb, ME *glymsen* cf. MHG *glimsen* & see prec.]

glint, v.i. & t., & n. Flash, glitter, sparkle, (v. & n.); make flash, reflect, (light). [n. f. vb, earlier *glent* cogn. w. G *glänzen*]

glissa·de (-ahd), n., & v.i. (mountaineering). Slide (n. & v.) down steep slope esp. of ice or snow usu. on the feet with support of ice-axe &c. [vb f. n., F (*glisser* slip, -ADE)]

gli·sten (-ĭsn), v.i., & n. Shine fitfully; glitter, sparkle, (v. & n.). [n. f. vb, OE *glisnian* (*glisian* shine, -EN[6])]

gli·ster, v.i., & n., (archaic). Sparkle, glitter. [f. OE *glisian* see prec. + -*t*- + -ER[5]]

gli·tter, v.i., & n. (Shine with) brilliant tremulous light, gleam, sparkle; be showy or splendid (*with* jewels &c.). [prob. f. ON *glitra* cf. G *glitzern* f. Teut. *glit-* shine + -ER[5]]

gloa·ming, n. Evening twilight. [OE *glómung* (*glóm* twilight cogn. w. GLOW, -ING[1])]

gloat, v.i. Feast eyes or mind lustfully, avariciously, malignantly, &c., (*up*)*on* or *over*. Hence **gloa·ting**LY[2] adv. [cf. G *glotzen* stare]

globe, n., & v.t. & i. Spherical body; *the* earth; planet, star, sun; spherical chart of (*terrestrial g.*) the earth or (*celestial g.*) the constellations (*use of the gg.* archaic, teaching of geography & astronomy by these); golden orb as emblem of sovereignty; (Anat.) eyeball; approximately spherical glass vessel, esp. lampshade or fishbowl; *g.-fish,* able to inflate itself into globular form; *g.-flower,* ranunculaceous plant with round yellow flowers; *g. lightning,* =FIRE[1]-*ball*; *g.-trotter, -ting,* hurried traveller, -ling, through foreign countries for sight-seeing; so **glō·b**OID a. & n., **globo**·SE[1] a., **globŏ**·SITY n. (Vb) make (usu. in pass.), or become, globular. [F, f. L *globus*]

glŏ·bular, a. Globe-shaped, spherical; composed of globules. Hence **globulă**·RITY n., **glo·bular**LY[2] adv. [foll., -AR[1], & see -UL-]

glŏ·bule, n. Small globe, e.g. blood corpuscle, drop, pill. [F, f. L *globulus* (GLOBE, -ULE)]

glo·bulin, n. Proteid found in blood, constituent of haemoglobin. [prec., -IN]

glochĭ·diate (-k-), a. (bot.). Barbed at tip. [f. Gk *glōkhidion* (*glōkhis* arrowhead), -ATE[2]]

glŏ·merate, a. (bot., anat.). Compactly clustered. [L *glomerare* (*glomus -eris* ball), -ATE[2]]

glŏ·merule, n. Clustered flower-head; cluster of small organisms, tissues, blood-vessels, &c. [f. F *glomérule* (L *glomus* see prec., -ULE)]

gloom[1], n. Darkness, obscurity; melancholy, despondency. [perh. back formation f. GLOOMY]

gloom[2], v.i. & t. Look sullen, frown, be melancholy; (of sky &c.) lour, be dull or threatening; appear darkly or obscurely; cover with g., make dark or dismal. [ME *gloume* cf. MG *glûmen* be savage; cogn. w. GLUM]

gloo·my, a. Dark, unlighted; depressed, sullen; dismal, depressing. Hence **gloo·mi**LY[2] adv., **gloo·mi**NESS n. [perh. f. prec. + -Y[2]]

glor·ia, n. (Short for) *G. Patri,* doxology *Glory be to the Father* &c., *G. tibi,* response *Glory be to thee* &c., or *G. in excelsis,* hymn *Glory be to God on high*; aureole. [L, =glory]

glor·ifȳ, v.t. Make glorious, exalt to the glory of heaven; invest with radiance; transform into something more splendid, invest (common or inferior thing) with charm or beauty (*nothing more than a glorified,* or *glorification of a, cottage*); extol, laud. Hence **glori**FICA·TION n. [f. F *glorifier* f. LL *glorificare* (*glorificus* f. L *gloria* glory, -FIC)]

glor·iole, n. Aureole, halo. [F, f. L *gloriola* dim. of *gloria* glory]

glor·ious, a. Possessing glory, illustrious; conferring glory, honourable; splendid, magnificent, intensely delightful, (*a g. view, day*; also joc., as *g. fun*; & iron., as *the g. uncertainty of cricket, a g. muddle*); ecstatically happy with drink. Hence **glor·ious**LY[2] adv. [AF, f. L *gloriosus* (foll., -OSE[1])]

glor·y[1], n. Exalted renown, honourable fame; subject for boasting, special distinction, ornament, pride; adoring praise & thanksgiving (*g. be!* or *g.!,* vulgar excl. of surprise or delight); resplendent majesty, beauty, or magnificence, effulgence of heavenly light, imagined unearthly beauty; bliss & splendour of heaven (*go to g.,* die; *send to g.* facet., kill); state of exaltation, prosperity, &c. (*is in his g.*); circle of light round head or figure of deity or saint, aureole, halo; *g.-hole* (slang), untidy room, drawer, or receptacle. [f. OF *glorie* f. L *gloria*]

glor·y[2], v.i. Exult, pride oneself, *in* thing or do*ing, to* do. Hence **glor·ying**LY[2] adv. [f. L *gloriari* boast (*gloria* glory)]

gloss[1], n., & v.t. & i. Word inserted between lines or in margin to explain word in text; comment, explanation, interpretation, paraphrase; misrepresentation of another's words; glossary, interlinear translation, or set of notes. (Vb) insert gg. in (text &c.); write gg.; make comments esp. of unfavourable sort; read different sense into, explain away. [vb f. n., earlier *gloze* f. OF *glose* f. med. L *glosa* f. L f. Gk *glōssa* (foreign) tongue, obscure or foreign word]

gloss[2], n., & v.t. Superficial lustre; deceptive appearance, fair outside; hence **glo·ss**Y[2] a., **glo·ssi**LY[2] adv., **glo·ssi**NESS n. (Vb) make glossy; give specious appearance to (often *over*). [vb f. n.; from 16th c., cf. obs. Du. *gloos,* Icel. *glossi,* nn., glow, blaze]

glo·ssal, a. (anat.). Of the tongue, lingual. [f. Gk *glōssa* tongue + -AL]

glo·ssary, n. Collection of glosses; list & explanations of abstruse, obsolete, dialectal, or technical terms, partial dictionary. Hence **glossār·**IAL a., **glo·ssar**IST(1) n. [f. L *glossarium* (*glossa* GLOSS[1], -ARY[1])]

glossā·tor, n. Commentator, esp. medieval commentator on Civil & Canon Law. [med. L (*glossare* f. *glossa* GLOSS[1], -OR[2]]

glŏ·ss(o)-, comb. form of Gk *glōssa* tongue, as *gloss(o)-epiglottic* of tongue & epiglottis, *glossi·tis*; also of GLOSS[1], as *glosso·grapher* commentator, *glosso·logy* terminology.

glo·ttis, n. Opening at upper part of windpipe & between vocal chords, affecting modulation of voice by contracting or dilating. Hence **glo·tt**AL, **glo·tt**IC, aa. [Gk *glōttis* (*glōtta* var. of *glōssa* tongue)]

Gloucester (glŏ·ster), n. Kind of cheese (usu. *single, double, G.*, the latter of richer milk) made in Gloucestershire.

glove (-ŭv), n., & v.t. Covering of leather, cotton, silk, wool, or formerly steel, for the hand, usu. with separated fingers (*throw down, take up, the g.*, make, accept, challenge; *fit like a g.*, exactly; HAND[1] *&* or *in g.*); (also *boxing-g.*) padded g. for boxing (*take off, without*, &c., *the gg.*, of arguing or contending in earnest, mercilessly, &c.); *g.-fight*, fight with boxing-gloves (opp. *prize-fight* with bare fists); *g.-sponge*, in shape of g.; *g.-stretcher*, instrument for enlarging g.-fingers; hence **glo·ve**LESS a., **glo·v**ER[1](3) n. (Vb) provide with gg. [OE *glóf* perh. f. OTeut. *galôfâ* (*ga-* = Y-, *lôf-* cogn. w. Sc. *loof* hand]

glow (-ō), v.i., & n. Be heated to incandescence, throw out light & heat without flame; shine like thing intensely heated; show warm colour; burn with bodily heat or emotional fervour (*with*); *g.-worm*, coleopterous insect with winged male & wingless female, the latter emitting green light at tail; hence **glow·ing**LY[2] adv. (N.) glowing state (*in a g., all of a g.*, hot or flushed); brightness & warmth of colour, e.g. red of cheeks; ardour, passion; *g.-lamp*, with carbon &c. incandescent under electric current. [OE *glówan* cf. G. *glühen*; cogn. w. GLOAMING & obs. or dial. *gleed* ember]

glower (-owr), v.i. Stare, scowl, (usu. *at*). Hence **glower·ing**LY[2] adv. [?]

gloxi·nia, n. American tropical plant with large bell flowers of various colours. [B. P. *Gloxin* botanist c. 1785 + -IA[1]]

gloze, v.i. & t. Comment (*up*)*on* (archaic); palliate, explain away, extenuate, (usu. *over*); talk speciously, use fair words, fawn. Hence **glo·zing**LY[2] adv. [f. F *gloser* (*glose* GLOSS[1])]

gluci·num (-ōōs-), n. White metal obtained from beryl, beryllium. [f. Gk *glukus* sweet (some compds of it being sweet)]

gluco·se (-ōō-), n. (chem.). Grape-sugar or dextrose; any member of group of sugars including dextrose, laevulose, mannitose, &c. Hence **glucŏ·s**IC a., **glu·cos**IDE n. [f. Gk *gleukos*, see -OSE[2]]

glue (-ōō), n., & v.t. Hard brittle brownish gelatin made by boiling hides & hoofs & used warm as cement; g.-like cement or sticky substance; *g.-pot*, with outer coat holding water to heat g.; hence **glue·**Y[2] a. (Vb; part. *gluing*) fasten or join (as) with g.; attach tightly or closely (*eye, ear, glued to the keyhole*). [f. OF *glu* f. LL *glus glutis*]

glum, a. Sullen, looking dejected or displeased. Hence **glu·m**LY[2] adv., **glu·m**NESS n. [cogn. w. GLOOM[2]; cf. LG *glum* turbid]

glume, n. (bot.). Chafflike bract in calyx of grasses &c.; husk of grain. Hence **glum**A·CEOUS, **glumo·s**E[1], aa. [f. L *gluma*]

glut, v.t., & n. Feed (person, stomach) or indulge (appetite, desire) to the full, overload with food (lit. or fig.), satiate, cloy; choke up, fill to excess; overstock (market) with goods. (N.) full indulgence, one's fill, surfeit; supply exceeding demand (*a g. in the market*). [n. f. vb, prob. f. obs. & OF *glut* GLUTTON]

glu·tĕn (-ōō-), n. Sticky substance, whence **glu·tin**IZE(3) v.i., **glu·tin**OUS a., **glu·tinous**LY[2] adv., **glutinŏ·s**ITY n.; viscid animal secretion; nitrogenous part of flour remaining as viscid substance when starch is washed out. [L, genit. *-inis*, glue]

glu·tton (-tn), n. Excessive eater, gormandizer; greedy reader *of books*, person with great appetite *for work*; voracious animal of weasel kind but larger, wolverene. Hence or cogn. **glu·tton**IZE(2) v.i.; **glu·tton**OUS a., **glu·ttonous**LY[2] adv., **glu·tton**Y[1] n. [f. OF *glutun* f. LL *glutonem* nom. *-o* (*glutire* swallow)]

glȳ·cerinate, v.t. Treat with glycerine (esp. vaccine lymph). [-ATE[3]]

glȳ·cerine, -in, n. Colourless sweet syrupy liquid got from animal & vegetable oils by saponification, used as ointment, as vehicle for drugs, in explosives, &c. Hence **glycĕ·r**IC a. (chem.), **gly·cer**ATE[1] (3), **gly·cer**IDE, **gly·cer**YL, nn., **gly·cero-** comb. form. [Gk *glukeros* sweet, -IN]

glȳ·cerol, n. (chem.). (Name preferred in scientific use for) glycerine. [prec., -OL(1)]

glȳco-, comb. form, irreg. for *glycy-*, of Gk *glukus* sweet, also used in names of chem. compounds containing glycerol or other substance in *glyc-*.

glȳ·cogen, n., **glycogĕ·nic,** a., (-j-), (chem). (Substance) producing sugar in animal tissues. So **glyco**GE·NESIS n. [prec., -GEN(1)]

glȳ·col, n. Any of the fatty diatomic alcohols. Hence **glyco·l(l)**IC a. [GLYCO-, -OL(1)]

glȳcŏ·nic, a. & n. (Gk & L pros.). (Line, metre) consisting of three trochees & dactyl, the dactyl variously placed, esp.

of the catalectic form (-⏒- ⏑⏑ -⏑⏒) used by Horace & Catullus. [*Glukōn* Gk poet, -IC]

glўcosūr·ia, n. (path.). Diseased condition with sugar in the urine. Hence **glycosur·**IC a. [F *glycose* GLUCOSE, Gk *ouron* urine, -IA[1]]

glў·phograph, glypho·graphy, nn. (Plate or copy, *-ph,* made by) electrotype process giving raised copy of engraved plate for use in letter-press printing (*-y*). So **gly·phograph** v.t. & i., **glypho·**GRAPHER n., **glypho**GRA·PHIC a. [f. Gk *gluphē* carving (*gluphō* carve), -GRAPHY]

glў·ptic, a. Of carving esp. on precious stones. [f. Gk *gluptikos* (*gluphō* carve, -IC)]

gly·ptodon, n. Extinct S.-Amer. quadruped allied to armadillos with fluted teeth. [f. Gk *gluptos* carved as prec. + *odous -ontos* tooth]

glypto·graphy, n. Art & science of gem-engraving. [as prec., -GRAPHY]

gnarled, gnar·ly, (n-), aa. (Of tree; & fig.) covered with protuberances, twisted, rugged. [var. of obs. *knurled* (*knurl* knob); -ED[2], -Y[2]]

gnăsh (n-), v.i. & t. (Of teeth) strike together; grind the teeth, grind (the teeth). [earlier *gnast* cf. ON *gnastan* prob. imit.]

gnăt (n-), n. Small two-winged fly of which female has blood-sucking proboscis; (as type) insignificant annoyance, tiny thing, (*strain at g.,* be scrupulous about trifles). [OE *gnæt*]

gnā·thic, a. Of jaws. [Gk *gnathos* jaw, -IC]

gnaw (n-), v.t. & i. (p.p. *gnawed, gnawn*). Bite persistently, wear away thus (often *away, off, in two,* &c.; also intr. with *at, into*); (of destructive agents, pain, &c.) corrode, waste away, consume, torture. Hence **gnaw·ing**LY[2] adv. [OE *gnagan* cf. G *nagen*]

gneiss (gnīs, nīs), n. (geol.). Laminated rock of quartz, feldspar, & mica. Hence **gnei·**SSIC, **gnei·**SSOID, **gnei·**SSOSE[1], **gnei·**SSY[2], aa. [G (OHG *gneistan* sparkle)]

gnō·mē[1] (n-; *also* nōm), n. Maxim, aphorism. [f. Gk *gnōmē* (*gignōskō* know)]

gnome[2] (n-), n. Diminutive spirit of subterranean race guarding treasures of earth (cf. SYLPH, SALAMANDER, NYMPH), goblin, dwarf. Hence **gno·**MISH[1] a. [used by Paracelsus; perh. for *genomos* (Gk *gē* earth, *-nomos* -dwelling, or spec. use of prec.]

gnō·mic, a. Of, consisting of, using, GNOME[1]s, sententious; (Gram.) *g. aorist,* used without past sense to express a general truth. [f. Gk *gnōmikos* (GNOME[1], -IC)]

gnō·mon (n-), n. Pillar, rod, pin or plate of sundial, showing time by its shadow on marked surface; column &c. used in observing sun's meridian altitude; (Geom.) part of parallelogram left when similar one has been taken from its corner. Hence **gnomŏ·nic** a. [Gk (*gnōmōn*), = inspector, g. of dial, (*gignōskō* know)]

gnō·sis (n-), n. Knowledge of spiritual mysteries; Gnosticism. [Gk (*-ō-*), = knowledge, as prec.]

gnŏ·stic (n-), a. & n. Relating to knowledge, cognitive; having esoteric spiritual knowledge; of the Gnostics, occult, mystic; (n., usu. pl.; *G-*) early Christian heretic(s) claiming GNOSIS, whence **gno·sti**CISM(3) n., **gno·sti**CIZE(2, 3, 4) v.i. & t. [f. Gk *gnōstikos* (as prec., -IC)]

gnu (nū), n. Oxlike antelope. [Hottentot]

go[1], v.i. (*went, gone,* pr. gawn, gŏn; 2nd sing. *gōest,* 3rd *goes* pr. gōz & archaic *gōeth*). Start, depart, move, continue moving, with self-originated or imparted motion, from some place, position, time, &c. (often not specified because obvious, whereas the goal &c. is always specified if it matters; cf. COME); journey, travel, proceed, progress, (*going strong,* with vigour; *he will go far,* reach distinction; *go easy, straight*; *go west,* army slang, be killed or die; *go the* PACE; *went miles round*; *go a walk, journey, voyage*; *go the same, the shortest, way*); (of line &c.) lie, point, in certain direction; be guided *by,* act in harmony *with,* judge or act *upon,* (*a good rule to go by*; *have nothing to go upon*; *always goes with his party*; *promotion goes by favour*; *go with tide* or *times,* do as others do); be habitually in specified state (*go hungry, armed, in rags, in fear of* one's *life*; *six months* &c. *gone with child,* having spent that time in gestation); be moving, acting, working, &c. (*Who goes there?* sentry's challenge; *a going concern,* business in working order; *clock does not go, goes well*; *tongue goes nineteen to the* DOZEN); make specified motion (*go like this with your left foot*); (of bell, striking clock or hour, gun, &c.; also with interjections of sound as *go bang, crack*) sound (*go phut* slang, collapse); (of time) pass, elapse; be current (*the sovereign goes anywhere*; *the story goes,* it is said), be known *by,* or *under, the name of,* be on the average (*is a good actor as actors go nowadays*); (of document &c.) run, have specified tenor; (of verse, song) be rhythmical, be adaptable *to* a tune; (of events) turn out *well, ill,* HARD, &c., (of election &c.) issue *for* or *against,* (of constituency, politician, voter) take certain course or views (*Liverpool went Tory*; *America goes dry,* adopts prohibition of intoxicants; *case goes by default,* takes its course against absent party; *dinner, play, went well,* succeeded; *goes without* SAY*ing*); begin motion (*Go!,* starter's word in race; HERE *goes!*); get away *free, unpunished,* &c.; be sold (*go cheap, for 2/6,* &c.;

going!, *gone!*, auctioneer's announcement that bidding is almost, quite, closed; (of money) be spent (often *in* books &c.); be relinquished, abolished, or lost (*Greek, the carriage, must go*; *my sight, our trade, is going*; *next wicket went for nothing*); die (esp. in p.p.; & in many phrr., as *go the way of all the earth* or pop. *of all flesh, to a better world, to* one's *account* or *own place, aloft, off the hooks*, &c.); fail, give way, succumb, break down, crack; make way *to, towards, into*, &c. (*go to Jericho, Bath, blazes, hell*, &c., be off out of speaker's presence; *go to Canossa*, humble oneself after recalcitrance, w. ref. to Emperor Henry IV in 1077; *go to the* DEVIL[1]; *which way goes to Bristol*; *go to a ball, to church, market*, &c., attend it; *go to school*, get instruction; *go to the bar, to sea*, become barrister, sailor; *go on the stage, the streets*, become actor, prostitute; *go to* STOOL); proceed *to* do (*went to find him*), *and* do (esp. colloq. = be so foolish as to do; also vulg. *have been & gone & done it*, made a blunder &c.), (*a*-)*doing, on* pilgrimage, an errand, the spree, &c.; act as *bail* (*for* person; also abs. in parenthesis *I'll go bail*, I assure you); have recourse, refer, appeal, *to* (*go to the* COUNTRY, test opinion by general election; *go to war, work*, &c.; vulg., *would not go to* or *for to do it*, be so inconsiderate &c. as to); carry action to certain point (*went all lengths*; *will go so far as to say*; *will go as high as £100*, in bidding or offering price; *go halves* or *shares*, share equally *with*, or abs.; *went to great expense, trouble*, &c.; *go the whole* HOG; *go better* or *one better*, outbid or outdo adversary); penetrate, sink, (*ship went to the bottom*; *goes to* one's *heart*, grieves him), find room, (of number) be capable of being contained in another either without remainder or simply, (*will not go into* or *in the basket*; *6 into 12 goes twice, into 5 will not go, into 13 goes twice and one over*; *thread too thick to go through needle*); belong *in* receptacle, *on* shelf &c.; pass, be allotted, &c., *to* person (of prize, victory, inheritance, office, &c.), be applied *to* purpose, contribute *to* or *towards* result, amount together *to* (*12 inches go to the foot*), tend *to show* &c.; reach, extend, (*the difference goes deep*; *as, so, far as it goes*, caution against taking statement too widely; *goes a long* &c. *way*, has great &c. effect *towards*, also of food, money, &c., lasts long &c., buys much &c,); pass into certain condition (*go brown, blind, mad, to seed*; *go hot & cold*, have accesses of fever or shame; *go to pieces*, break up); *go sick* (Mil.), enter oneself on the sick list; (slang) *go it*, act vigorously, furiously, &c., indulge in dissipation; *going fifteen* &c., in one's fifteenth &c. year; *going to*, about to, intending to (used as fut. part.); *be gone*, take oneself off; *gone*, dead (often *dead & gone*); *gone on* (slang), infatuated with; *far gone*, very ill, deeply entangled; *go fetch!* (order to dog). With prepp.: *go about*, set to work at; *go at*, attack, take in hand energetically; *go behind* (decision &c.), re-examine grounds of; *go for*, go to fetch, pass or be accounted as *nothing, little*, &c., strive to attain, (slang) attack; *go into*, enter (profession, Parliament), frequent (society), take part in, allow oneself to pass into (hysterics &c.), dress oneself in (mourning &c.), investigate; *go off* one's HEAD[1]; *go on*, become chargeable to (parish, relief fund, &c.); *go over*, inspect details of, rehearse, retouch; *go over the top* or *bags* (mil.), issue from trench to attack enemy; *go through*, discuss in detail, scrutinize, perform, (ceremony, recitation, &c.), undergo, (of book) be sold out in (so many editions); *go up the line* (mil.), leave the base for the front; *go with*, be concomitant of, take same view as, match, follow the drift of; *go without*, not have, put up with want of. With advv.: *go about*, move from place to place, endeavour *to* do; *go ahead*, proceed without hesitation; *go along with*, = go with; *go back from* or *upon* one's word &c., fail to keep it; *go by*, pass; *go down*, sink (of ship), be continued *to* specified point, fall *before* conqueror, be recorded in writing, be swallowed, find acceptance *with*; *go in*, enter as competitor (*go in & win!*, form of encouragement), (Cricket) take or begin innings, (of sun &c.) be obscured; *go in for*, take as one's object, pursuit, style, principle, &c.; *go off*, leave the stage, begin, explode, die, gradually cease to be felt, deteriorate, become unconscious in sleep, faint, &c., be got rid of by sale, succeed *well, badly*, &c.; *go on*, continue, persevere, (*doing, with, in*, or abs.), proceed as next step *to* do, conduct oneself *shamefully* &c., rail *at* (colloq.), appear on stage, begin bowling, take one's turn to do something, (colloq. in imperat.) don't talk nonsense, *going on for*, approaching (a time, age, &c.); *go out*, leave room or house, fight duel, be extinguished, leave office (of Government), cease to be fashionable, depart *to* colony &c., (esp. of girls) leave home for employment usu. *as* governess &c., mix in society, (of workmen) strike, (of heart &c.) expand with love &c. *to* person; *go over*, change one's party or religion; *go round*, pay informal visit *to*, be long enough to encompass, (of food &c.) suffice for whole party; *go through with*, complete, not leave unfinished; *go to* (imperat.; archaic) interjection of remonstrance, incredulity, impatience, &c.; *go together*, be concomitant, match; *go under*, sink, fail, succumb. *Go-ahead*, enterprising; *go-as-you-please*, unfettered by regulations; *go-between*, intermediary, negotiator; *go-by*, passing (usu. in *give the go-by to*, outstrip, leave behind, elude, disregard, cut, slight); *go·-cart*, wheeled frame for teaching child to walk, kind of perambulator, litter, palankeen, hand-cart; *go-o·ff*, start (usu. *at the first go-off*); *go-to-meeting*, (of hat, clothes, &c.) fit or kept for going to church in. [com.-Teut.; OE *gán* cf. G *gehen*; past supplied f. WEND]

go[2], n. (pl. *goes*). Act of going (*come-&-go*, traffic, movement to & fro); mettle, spirit, dash, animation; (colloq.) embarrassing turn of affairs (*here's, what, a go!*; *a rum go*); turn at doing something (*have a go at*); portion of liquor or food served; (Cribbage) player's inability to play, counting one to opponent; (colloq.) *it's no go*, nothing can be done; (colloq.) *all* or *quite the go*, in fashion; (colloq.) *near go*, close shave; (colloq.) *on the go*, in motion, also in a state of decline; LITTLE-*go*. [f. prec.]

goad, n., & v.t. Spiked stick used for urging cattle; thing that torments, incites, or stimulates. (Vb) urge with g.; irritate; instigate, drive, by annoyance (often *on*; also *to* do, *into* doing, *to* or *into* fury &c.). [OE *gád* cf. Lombard *gaida* arrowhead; not related to obs. *gad* in same sense]

goal, n. Point marking end of race; object of effort or ambition; destination; posts between which ball is to be driven in football &c., points so won (DROP[2], *make*, PLACE[2], *score, a g.*); (Rom. Ant.) pillar at turning-point in chariot race; *g.-keeper*, player stationed to protect g.; *g.-line*, line between each pair of g.-posts produced as end-boundary of field of play (cf. TOUCH-*line*). [etym. dub.; once in 1315 =limit, then not till 1531; prob. not f. F *gaule* rod]

goat, n. Hardy lively wanton strong-smelling usu. horned & bearded ruminant quadruped (*sheep & gg.*, the good & the wicked, see *Matt.* xxv. 32, 33); (pl.) subfamily to which g. belongs; zodiacal sign Capricorn (*G-*); licentious person; *play the* GIDDY *g.*; *g.-god*, Pan; *goatherd*, one who tends gg.; *goat's-beard*, meadowsweet, also salsify; *goatskin*, (garment, bottle, made of) skin of g.; *goatsucker*, nightjar; *goat's wool*, non-existent thing. Hence **goa·tish**[1], **goa·ty**[2], aa., **goa·tishly**[2] adv., **goa·tishness** n. [com.-Teut.; OE *gát* cf. G *geiss*, cogn. w. L *haedus* kid]

goatee·, n. Chin-tuft like goat's beard. [-EE]

goa·tling, n. Goat 1–2 years old. [-LING[1]]

gob, n., & v.i. (vulg.). Clot of slimy substance, e.g. spittle; (vb) spit. [f. OF *gobe* mouthful]

gōba·ng, n. Game played on chequer-board. [f. Jap. *goban* f. Chin. *k'i pan* chessboard, w. assim. to *go, bang*]

go·bbet, n. (archaic). Piece, lump, esp. of raw flesh or food. [f. OF *gobet* (GOB, -ET[1])]

go·bble[1], v.t. & i. Eat hurriedly & noisily; *g.-stitch*, one made too long from hurry. Hence **go·bbler**[1] (-ER[1]) n. [perh. f. GOB + -LE(3)]

go·bble[2], n. (golf). Rapid straight putt into the hole. [perh. f. prec.]

go·bble[3], v.i. (Of turkeycock) make characteristic sound in throat; make such sound when speaking, from rage &c. Hence **go·bbler**[2] n., turkeycock. [imit.]

gŏ·belin, a. *G. tapestry*, made, or imitated from that made, at the state-factory in Paris called *Gobelins* after its founders.

gobemouche (gŏ·bmōōsh), n. (pl. *-es* pr. like sing.). Credulous newsmonger. [f. F *gobemouches* lit. fly-catcher (*gober* swallow, *mouches* flies) mistaken by E writers for pl.]

gŏ·blet, n. (Archaic) metal or glass drinking-cup, bowl-shaped & without handles, sometimes with foot & cover; (Poet.) drinking-cup; (Commerc.) glass with foot & stem. [f. OF *gobelet* (*gobel* cup etym. dub. + -ET[1])]

gŏ·blin, n. Mischievous ugly demon. [f. F *gobelin* perh. f. med. L f. Gk *kobalos* rogue, *kobaloi* sprites invoked by rogues]

gō·bȳ, n. Small fish with ventral fins joined into a disk or sucker. [f. L *gobius, co-*, f. Gk *kōbios* GUDGEON]

gŏd[1], n. Superhuman being worshipped as having power over nature & human fortunes, deity, (usu. *g-*; *g. of heaven*, Jupiter; *g. of hell*, Pluto; *g. of the sea*, Neptune; *g. of day*, sun, Phoebus; *g. of fire*, Vulcan; *g. of war*, Mars; *g. of love, blind g.*, Cupid; *g. of wine*, Bacchus; *g. of this world*, the Devil; *Ye gg.!*, *Ye gg. & little fishes!*, mock-heroic exclamations; *feast, sight, for the gg.*, something exquisite &c.); image, animal, or other object, worshipped as symbolizing, being the visible habitation of, or itself possessing, divine power, an idol, (*g-*); adored, admired, or influential person (*g-*); (Theat., pl.) occupants of gallery. Supreme being, Creator & Ruler of universe, (*G-*; often *the Lord G., Almighty G., G. Almighty*; *G. the Father, Son, Holy Ghost*, Persons of Trinity; ACT[1] *of G.*, *with G.*, dead & in heaven; *God's truth*, the absolute truth; *God's earth*, the whole earth; *oh, my, good*, &c., *G.!*, exclamations of pain, grief, or anger; *G. bless, damn, help, you!, him!*, &c., *G. forbid!, grant —!*, prayers or imprecations; *G. bless me!*, *my life!, my soul!, you!*, &c., exclamations of surprise; *G. willing*, if circumstances allow; *under G.*, used to qualify attribution of full agency to man; *thank G.!*, parenthetic expression of pleasure at turn of events &c.; *G. knows*, it is beyond mortal or my knowledge, I do not know, (also) I call G. to witness that; *for God's sake*, with urgent petitions; *by G.*, confirmatory oath; *so* HELP[1] *me G.!*). *Godfather, godmother, g.-parent, g.-papa, g.-mamma*, sponsor at baptism, & so of the converse relation *g.-child, godson, g.-daughter*; *godfather* (fig.), person after whom person or thing is named, (vb) be responsible for, give one's name to; *g.-fearing*, sincerely religious; *g.-forsaken*, devoid of all merit, dismal, (*what a g.-f. hole!*); *go·dma·n*, Christ; *God's-acre* (imit. of German), churchyard; *God's book*, bible; *go·dsend* (-s-), unexpected welcome event or acquisition; *God's image*, human body; *g.-speed*, utterance of words *G. speed you!*, usu. in *bid* person *g.-s.*, wish him success in undertaking, journey, &c. Hence **go·d**HOOD, **go·d**SHIP, nn., **go·d**WARD adv. & a., **go·d**WARDS adv. [com.-Teut.; cf. Du. *god*, G *gott*; perh. f. Aryan *gheu* invoke or *gheu* sacrifice]

god[2], v.t. Deify; *g. it*, play the g. [f. prec.]

go·ddess, n. Female deity in polytheism (esp., in Latin mythol.: *g. of heaven, hell, love, wisdom, moon, corn, war*, Juno, Proserpine, Venus, Minerva, Diana, Ceres, Bellona); woman one adores. [-ESS[1]]

godē·tia (-sha), n. Free-flowering hardy annual plant. [*Godet* Swiss botanist, -IA[1]]

go·dhead (-ĕd), n. Being God or a god, divine nature, deity; *the G.*, God. [-HEAD]

go·dless, a. Without a god; not recognizing God; impious, wicked. Hence **go·dless**NESS n. [-LESS]

go·dlike, a. Resembling God or a god in some quality; fit for, like that of, a god. [-LIKE]

go·dly, a. Religious, pious, devout. Hence **go·dli**NESS n. [-LY[1]]

godow·n, n. (Anglo-Ind.). Warehouse in parts of Asia, esp. India. [f. Malay *godong* w. assim. to *go down*]

go·dwit, n. Marsh bird like curlew but with upward-curved bill. [?]

go·er, n. Person, thing, that goes (*good, slow*, &c., *g.*; *comers & gg.*). [-ER[1]]

Goethian (ger·tĭan), a. & n. (Follower) of Goethe, like Goethe, his writings, views, &c. [J. W. von *Goethe*, German poet 1749–1832, -IAN]

gō·fer, n. Thin batter-cake stamped with honeycomb pattern by the irons it is baked in. [f. F *gaufre* honeycomb, gofer, see WAFER]

gŏ·f(f)er, go·pher, gau·ffer (gō-), v.t., & n. Make wavy, flute, crimp, (lace edge, trimming, &c.) with heated irons; *goffered edges* of book, embossed. (N.) iron used for goffering; ornamental plaiting used for frills &c. [f. F *gaufre* see prec., *gaufrer* stamp with patterned tool)]

go·ggle, v.i. & t., a., & n. Squint, roll eyes about (or with *eyes* as subj.), (of eyes) project; turn (eyes) sideways or from side to side. (Adj.; of eyes) protuberant, full & rolling; so **go·ggle-eye**ED[2] a. (N.; pl.) kind of spectacles for protecting eyes from glare, dust, &c., often with coloured glasses, wire gauze, &c.; (slang) round-lensed spectacles; sheep disease, staggers. [a. & n. f. vb; f. 14th c.; etym. dub., cf. W *gogi* shake, Gael. *gog* nodding of head]

go·glet, gu·gglet, n. (Anglo-Ind.). Long-necked vessel usu. of porous ware for keeping water cool. [f. Port. *gorgoleta*]

Goi·del, n. Member of GADHELIC races. Hence (=GADHELIC) **Goidĕ·l**IC a. & n. [f. OIr. *Góidel*]

go·ing, n. In vbl senses; esp.: condition of ground for walking, riding, &c.; (for *a-going*, & now regarded as part.) in action (*set the clock g.*), existing, to be had, (*one of the best fellows g.*; *there is cold beef g.*); *goings-on*, (usu. *strange, such*, &c.) behaviour. [-ING[1]]

goi·tre (-ter), n. Morbid enlargement of thyroid gland, often showing as large pendulous swelling in neck, bronchocele, dewlap. Hence **goi·tr**ED[2] (-terd) a. [F, back formation f. *goitreux* (L *guttur* throat, -OUS)]

goi·trous, a. Affected with, like, of, (of places) characterized by prevalence of, goitre. [f. F *goitreux* see prec.]

Golco·nda, n. Mine of wealth (lit. or fig.). [old name of Hyderabad]

gōld, n. & a. Precious yellow non-rusting malleable ductile metal of high specific gravity (*as* GOOD *as g.*); coins made of this, money in large sums, wealth; (fig.) brilliant, beautiful, or precious things, stuff, &c. (*a heart, voice, of g.*; *age of g.*, =GOLDEN *age*; *she is pure g.*; *all that glisters* or *glitters is not g.*); the metal used for coating surface or as pigment, gilding; the colour of the metal (*old g.* n., dull brownish-golden yellow; *old-g.* adj., thus coloured); *g. amalgam*, g. combined with mercury in plastic state; *g.-beater*, one who beats g. out into g.-leaf, *g.-beater's skin*, membrane used to separate leaves of g. during beating, also as covering for slight wounds; *g.*-DIGGER; *g.-dust*, g. in fine particles as often found; *g.-fever*, rage for going in search of g.; *g.-field*, district in which g. is found; *goldfinch*, bright-coloured song-bird with patch of yellow on wings, (slang) gold coin, sovereign; *g.-fish*, small red Chinese carp kept for ornament; *g.-foil, g.-leaf*, g. beaten into thin sheet, *-foil* being the thicker; *g.-mine*, lit. & fig. source of wealth; *g. plate*, vessels made of g.; *g.-rush*, a rush to some new g.-field; *goldsmith*, worker in g. (*g.-s. beetle*, with g.-coloured wing-covers); *G. stick*, (bearer of) gilt rod borne on State occasions by colonel of Lifeguards or captain of Gentlemen-at-arms. (Adj.) wholly or chiefly of, coloured like, g.; (of sums in depreciated currencies) reckoned at par (*g. francs* &c., the stated amount at the nominal undepreciated value of the franc &c.). [com.-Teut.; cf. G *gold*; cogn. w. YELLOW]

gō·lden, a. Made, consisting, of gold (*G.* FLEECE; *g. key*, money used to remove obstacle); abounding in, yielding, gold; coloured, shining, like gold; precious, excellent, important, (*g. opinions*, high respect; *g.-mouthed*, eloquent; *a g. remedy, opportunity, saying*; *the g. rule*, that in *Matt.* vii. 12; *g. mean*, neither too much nor too little, principle of moderation; *g. number* named as important in fixing Easter, year's number in Metonic lunar cycle of 19 years; *g. age*, first of four ages, see BRAZEN[1], when men were happy & innocent, also most prosperous period of nation's condition or literature); *g. balls*, =*three* BALL[1]*s*; *g.-eye*, kind of sea-duck; *G. Horn*, curved inlet of Bosporus, the harbour of Constantinople; *g.-knop*, ladybird; *g. rain*, kind of firework; *g.-rod*, plant with rod-like stem & spike of bright yellow flowers; *g.* SYRUP; *g. wedding*, fiftieth anniversary. [-EN[5]; earlier *gilden*]

gō·ldilocks, n. Kinds of plant, esp. a species of buttercup. [f. obs. *gold*Y[2], LOCK[1]]

gŏlf (*also* gŏf), n., & v.i. Game for two persons or couples played with small hard ball & clubs on links or moorland provided with smooth greens each having small cylindrical hole; *g.-club*, society for playing g., also one of the implements used; (vb) play g., whence **go·lf**ER[1] n. [perh. f. Du. *kolf* cf. G *kolbe* club]

Goli·ath, n. Giant. [1 *Sam.* xvii]

go·lliwog, n. Grotesque doll; bugbear. [?]

go·lly, int. (Used, esp. by negroes, for) God, *by* God. [deformation of GOD]

golosh. See GALOSH.

golu·ptious, golop-, a. (joc.). Luscious, delightful. [perh. facet. for *voluptuous*]

gombee·n, n. (Anglo-Ir.). Usury (*g.-man*, money-lender). [f. Ir. *gaimbín* perh. f. same OCelt. as med. L *cambium* CHANGE]

gom(b)roo·n, n. Persian pottery, imitated in Chelsea ware. [town on Persian gulf]

Gomo·rrah, n. (Type of) wicked town. [*Gen.* xviii, xix]

-gon, suf. f. Gk *-gōnos* -angled, forming nn. as *hexagon, polygon, n-gon*, figure with six, several, *n*, angles.

go·ndola (do-), n. Light flat-bottomed boat with cabin amidships & high point at each end worked by one oar at stern, used on Venetian canals; car suspended from airship. [It., etym. dub.]

gondolier·, n. Rower of gondola. [F, f. It. *gondoliere* (prec., -IER)]

gone (gawn, gŏn), a. In vbl senses; esp.: lost, hopeless, (*a g. man*, also **go·n**ER[1] n.; *a g. case*, COON); past bygone, (usu. *past & g.*). [p.p. of GO]

go·nfalon, n. Banner, often with streamers, hung from cross-bar, esp. as standard of some Italian republics. [f. It. *gonfalone* f. OHG *gundfano* f. OTeut. *gunthjâ* war, *fano* banner]

gonfalonier·, n. Standard-bearer; chief magistrate in some Italian republics. [f. It. *gonfaloniere* (prec., -IER)]

gong, n. Metal disk with turned rim giving resonant note when hung & struck with soft mallet, used esp. as signal for meals; saucer-shaped bell. [imit. of its sound]

go·ngorism, n. A Spanish literary style marked by inversion, antithesis, & classical allusion, corresponding to EUPHUISM in England. [*Gongora* y Argote, Sp. poet, 1561–1627, + -ISM]

gōniŏ·meter, n. Instrument for measuring angles. So **gonio·**METRY n., **goniome·tric**(AL) aa. [F (*-mètre*), f. Gk *gōnia* angle, -METER]

gŏnorrhoe·a (orōa), n. Inflammatory discharge of mucus from urethra or vagina. Hence **gonorrhoe·**AL a. [med. L, f. Gk *gonorrhoia* (*gonos* seed, *rhoia* flux)]

gŏŏd, a. (BETTER, BEST), & n. Having the right qualities, satisfactory, adequate, (*a g. fire*, not too small or dull; *meat keeps g.*, untainted; *g. soil*, fertile; *not g. enough* colloq., not worth doing, accepting, &c.; *g. money*, genuine; as conventional epithet in *the g. ship* —, *the g. town of* —; *g. law*, valid, sound; *is g. eating* &c., attractive to eat &c.); commendable (esp. in *g. men & true*; *g. old— !*, colloq. form of approval; *that's a good un !* slang, a lie worth telling; also in courteous, patronizing, ironically polite, or indignant address, as *my g. friend, man, sir*, or in polite or indulgently contemptuous description, as *your g. lady, the g. man*; *the g. people*, fairies; *of g. family*, well-born; *in g. spirits*, not depressed; *a g. leg*, well shaped); right, proper, expedient, (*it is g. to be here*; *I thought, it seemed, g. to* do something; also abs. as excl. of approval or consent); morally excellent, virtuous; kind, benevolent, (so of God &c., esp. in prayers & exclamations, as *g. God !, g. heavens !, g. gracious !*; *be so g. as, g. enough, to*, = please to; *how g. of you !*; *did me a g. turn* or *office*; *has always been g. to me*; *say a g. word for*, commend, defend); (esp. of child) well behaved, not giving trouble, (often *as g. as gold*); gratifying, agreeable, favourable, advantageous, beneficial, wholesome, (*g. news*; *things are in g. train*, going well; so in forms of greeting or parting, as *g. morning, g. day, good night*; *have a g. time*, enjoy oneself;

have a g. night, sleep well; *a g. saying* or *story* or *thing, as g. as a play*, amusing; *oil is g. for burns*; *beer is not g. for him* or *his health*; *are acorns g. to eat?*; *take in g. part*, not be annoyed at); adapted to an end, efficient, suitable, competent, (esp. with agent-nouns, as *a g. driver*; *g. at* describ*ing* &c.; *has been a g. wife to him*); reliable, safe, sure, (*a g. man*, financially sound, able to meet liabilities; *g. debts*, sure to be paid; *a g. life*, likely to last long, such as insurance office will accept; *g. for* an amount, safely to be trusted to pay it, also of draft &c., drawn for so much; *g. for*, inclined for, up to, as *g. for a ten-mile walk*); valid, sound, thorough, ample, considerable, (*gave her a g. beating*; *did it for g. reasons*; *rule holds g.*; *a g. excuse*; *a g.* DEAL[1], FEW, MANY; *have a g. mind*, be much inclined *to* do; often as intensive before adj., as *went a g. round pace*, *will take a g. long time*); not less than (*played for a g. hour*; *it is three miles g. from the station*); *as g. as*, practically (*he as g. as told me so*; *as g. as dead*; *it is as g. as done*); *make g.*, compensate for, pay (expense), fulfil (promise), effect (purpose), demonstrate (statement), substantiate (charge), gain & hold (position), replace or restore (thing lost or damaged), (without obj.) accomplish what one has attempted; *g. breeding* correct or courteous manners; *g. fellow*, sociable person, agreeable companion, *g.-fellowship*, conviviality, sociability; *g.-for-nothing*, *g.-for-nought*, aa. & nn., worthless (person); *G.* FRIDAY; *g. humour*, cheerful mood or disposition, amiability, whence **good-hu·mour**ED[2] a., **good-hu·moured**LY[2] (-merdlĭ) adv.; *g.-loo·king*, handsome; *goo·d-looking*, of virtuous appearance; *g. looks*, personal beauty; *g. luck*, being fortunate, happy chance, (often *g. l. to you!*, as wish); *goodman* (archaic), head of household, husband, father, &c.; *g. money* (vulg.), high wages; *g. morrow* (archaic), =g. morning; *g. nature*, kindly disposition, willingness to postpone one's own interests, whence **good-na·tur**ED[2] a., **good-na·tured**LY[2] adv.; *g.-neighbourhood*, *-neighbourliness*, *-neighbourship*, friendly conduct; *g. sense*, soundness of judgement, practical wisdom; *g. temper*, freedom from irritability, whence **good-te·mper**ED[2] a., **good-te·mpered**LY[2] adv.; *g. thing*, advantageous bargain or speculation, witty saying, (pl.) dainties; *goodwife*, mistress of house (esp. Sc.). (N.): (adj. used as pl. n.) virtuous persons (*the g.*; *g. & bad alike respect him*); what is g. or beneficial, well-being, profit, benefit, advantage, (*is a power for g.*; *deceive him for his g.*; *what g. will it do?*; *much g. may it do you!*, often iron.: *do g.*, show kindness *to*, act philanthropically, be beneficial *to* or benefit; *to the g.*, as balance on right side, net profit, something extra, &c.; *come to g.*, yield g. result; *for g.*, *for g. & all*, permanently, finally, definitively; *be any, some, no, much, g.*, be of any &c. use; *what is the g. of it?*; *what g. is it*); desirable end or object, thing worth attaining; *no g.*, some mischief (*is up to, after, no g.*); (pl.) movable property; (pl.) merchandise, wares, (*piece of gg.* facet., person); (pl.) things for transmission by rail &c. (opp. *passengers*; so *gg. agent, station, train*, &c.). Hence **goo·d**ISH[1](2) a. [com.-Teut.; OE *gód* cf. G *gut*; perh. f. same root as GATHER]

go͝od-bye·, int. & n. (Saying of) farewell. [contr. of *God be with you!*, with *good* substituted on anal. of *good-night* &c.]

goo·dly, a. Comely, handsome; of considerable size &c.; (Iron.) fine, grand. Hence **goo·dli**NESS n. [OE *gódlic* (GOOD, -LY[1])]

goo·dness, n. Virtue; positive or comparative excellence; benevolence, kindness, generosity, (*have the g.*, be kind enough *to*); what is good in thing, its essence or strength; (in exclamations, substituted for) God (*g. gracious!*, excl. of surprise or indignation; *g. knows*, I do not know, I appeal to Heaven to witness; *I wish to g.*; *thank g.!*; *for goodness' sake*). [OE *gódnes* (GOOD, -NESS)]

goodwi·ll, n. Kindly feeling to person, favour; cheerful acquiescence, heartiness, zeal; privilege granted by seller of business, of trading as recognized successor.

Go͝o·dwins, n. pl. *The G.*, the Goodwin sands.

Goo·dwood, n. (Used for) race-meeting on course near G. Park, Sussex (*G. cup*, chief prize at this).

goo·dy[1], n. (archaic). Elderly woman of lower class (often as prefix to surname). [for GOOD*wife*, cf. HUSSY]

go͝o·dy[2], n. A sweetmeat, bonbon. [-Y[3]]

goo·dy[3], **goo·dy-goody**, a. Primly, pretentiously, inopportunely, obtrusively, weakly, or sentimentally virtuous (*talk g.*, in g. manner). Hence **goo·di**NESS n. [-Y[3]]

goo·gly, n. (cricket). Off-break ball bowled with leg-break action. [?]

goosa·nder, n. Bird allied to duck but with sharp serrated bill. [?]

goose, n. (pl. *geese* pr. g-). Kinds of web-footed bird between duck & swan in size, female of this (opp. GANDER), its flesh, (*all his geese are swans*, he over-estimates; *kill the g. that lays the golden eggs*, sacrifice future profit to present necessities; COOK[2] person's *g.*; *say* BO *to g.*; *sauce for g. is sauce for* GANDER); simpleton, whence **goo·sey**[3] n.; tailor's smoothing iron (with handle like g.'s neck; pl. *gooses*); FOX[1] *& geese*; *g.-club*, for providing poor people with Christmas goose paid for by small instalments; *g.-flesh*, rough bristling state of skin produced by cold or fright; *g.-foot*, kinds of plant named from shape of leaves; *g.-grass*, silverweed, cleavers; *gooseherd*, one who tends geese; *g.-quill*, quill-feather of g. esp. used as pen; *g.-skin*, =g.-flesh; *g.-step*, balancing-drill taught to army recruits & much used in German army. [Aryan; OE *gós*, cf. G *gans*, L *anser*, Gk *khēn*; *gander* perh. unrelated]

goo·seberry (-z-), n. (Edible berry of) any thorny species of *Ribes*; wine made of gg.; *play g.*, act as chaperon, play propriety, for pair of lovers; *g.*-FOOL². [perh. f. prec.]

goo·segog (-zg-), n. (colloq.). Gooseberry, [facet. corruption]

gopher. See GOFFER.

Gor·dian, a. *G. knot*, intricate knot, difficult problem or task, (*cut the G. k.*, solve problem by force or by evading the conditions). [f. *Gordius*, tier of knot cut by Alexander the Great, + -AN]

gore¹, n. Blood shed & thickened or clotted. Hence **gor·y**² a., **gor·ILY**² adv. [OE *gor* dung, dirt, cf. Du. *goor* mud]

gore², n., & v.t. Wedge-shaped piece of cloth adjusting width of a garment; triangular or lune-shaped piece in umbrella, balloon, dome, globe, &c.; (vb) shape, narrow, with g. [OE *gára* triangular piece of land cogn. w. *gár* spear, w. ref. to shape of spear-head]

gore³, v.t. Pierce with the horn or (rarely) tusk (also transf. of rocks piercing ship). [perh. f. OE *gár* a spear]

gorge¹, n. (Rhet.) internal throat; what has been swallowed, contents of stomach, (*cast the g. at*, reject with loathing; one's *g. rises at*, one is sickened or disgusted by); (Fortif.) neck of bastion or other outwork, rear entrance to a work; narrow opening, usu. with stream, between hills; solid object meant to be swallowed as bait for fish. [OF, etym. dub.]

gorge², v.i. & t., & n. Feed greedily; satiate, glut; swallow, devour greedily; fill full, distend, choke up; (n.) act of gorging, surfeit. [f. OF *gorger* (prec.)]

gor·geous (-jus), a. Richly coloured, sumptuous, magnificent; (of diction) ornate, dazzling. Hence **gor·geousLY**² adv., **gor·geousNESS** n. [f. OF *gorgias* finely dressed, etym. dub.]

gor·get¹, n. (Hist.) piece of armour for throat, woman's wimple; necklace; patch of colour on throat of bird &c. [f. OF *gorgete* (GORGE¹, -ET¹)]

gor·get², n. (surg.). Channel-shaped steel instrument used in operations for stone &c. [f. F *gorgeret* (GORGE¹, as tubular)]

Gor·gio, n. (pl. *-os*). (Gipsy for) non-gipsy. [Romany]

gor·gon, n. (Gk mythol.) one of three snake-haired women whose looks turned any beholder to stone; terrible or ugly person, repellent woman. Hence **gorgō·NIAN** a. [f. L *Gorgo -onis* f. Gk *Gorgō -ous* (*gorgos* terrible)]

gor·gō·nia, n. (pl. *-iae*, *-ias*). Sea-fan, kind of polyp. [prec., as hardening in air, + -IA¹]

gor·gonize, v.t. Stare at like gorgon. [-IZE]

Gorgonzo·la, n. A rich cheese. [*G.* in Italy]

gori·lla, n. Large powerful ferocious arboreal anthropoid ape. [Afr. for wild man in Gk account of Hanno's voyage 5th or 6th c. B.C.]

gor·mandize, n., & v.i. & t., ***gourmandise*** (F), n. Habits of a GOURMAND, indulgence in good eating, gluttony; (vb) eat, devour, voraciously, whence **gor·mandizER**¹ n. [vb f. n., f. F *gourmandise* (GOURMAND, -ISE)]

gorse, n. Prickly yellow-flowered shrub, whin, furze. Hence **gor·SY**² a. [OE *gorst* cogn. w. G *gerst*, L *hordeum*, barley]

gosh, int. (Also *by g.*) by God. [for *God*]

gō·shawk (-s-h-), n. Kinds of large short-winged hawk. [OE *gós-hafoc* (GOOSE, HAWK)]

Gō·shen, n. Place of light or plenty. [*Gen.* xlv. 10 &c., *Exod.* viii. 22, ix. 26]

gō·sling (-z-), n. Young goose. [-LING¹]

go·spel, n. Glad tidings preached by Christ; religious doctrine of Christ & his apostles, Christian revelation; protestant or evangelical doctrine (opp. *mass*); record of Christ's life in books of four evangelists; any of those books; portion from one of them read at Communion service; thing that may safely be believed (*takes his dreams for g.*); principle that one acts upon, believes in, or preaches (*the g. of efficiency, laissez faire, soap & water*); *g.-book*, containing gg. read at Communion; *g. oath*, sworn on the gg.; *g.-shop*, Methodist chapel; *g. side*, N. side of altar, at which g. is read; *g. truth*, truths contained in g., something as true as g. [OE *godspel* corrupted by confusion w. *God* f. *gód spel* good tidings (GOOD, SPELL)]

go·speller, n. Reader of gospel in Communion service; *hot g.*, zealous puritan, rabid propagandist. [-ER¹]

go·ssamer, n. & a. Light filmy substance, the webs of small spiders, floating in calm air or spread over grass; *a* thread of this; something flimsy; delicate gauze; hence **go·ssamerED**², **go·ssamerY**², aa. (Adj.) light & flimsy as g. [ME *gossomer* perh. = goose-summer or St Martin's summer, i.e. early November when geese were eaten, g. being most seen then]

go·ssip, n., & v.i. (Archaic) familiar acquaintance, friend, (esp. of women); idle talker, newsmonger, tattler, (esp. of women); idle talk, groundless rumours, tittle-tattle; easy unconstrained talk or writing esp. about persons or social incidents; hence **go·ssipRY**(4, 5) n., **go·ssipY**² a. (Vb) Talk idly or lightly, tattle; write in gossipy style; hence **go·ssip-**

ER[1] n. [earlier senses, *sponsor, fellow-sponsor, one's child's sponsor, at baptism*; OE *godsibb* person related to one in God (*sibb, sib,* akin)]

gossoo·n, n. (Anglo-Ir.). Lad. [f. F *garçon*]

got, past & p.p. of GET. *G.-up*, factitious, artificially produced, adorned, &c., with a view to effect or deception.

Goth, n. One of a German tribe who invaded Eastern & Western Empires in 3rd–5th cc. & founded kingdoms in Italy, France, & Spain; rude, uncivilized, or ignorant person, esp. one who destroys works of art (cf. VANDAL), whence **Go·th**ISH[1] a. [OE *Gotan* pl. f. LL f. Gk *Gothoi*]

Gō·tha (-tȧ), n. Type of large German aeroplane. [G]

Gŏ·tham (-t-h-), n. Typical foolish town (*wise man of G.*, fool). Hence **Go·tham**ITE[1](1) n. [perh. f. the village in Notts.]

Gŏ·thic, a. & n. Of the Goths or their language; (Arch.) in the pointed-arch style prevalent in Western Europe in 12–16th cc., including in England the Early English, Decorated, & Perpendicular (orig. sense *not classical*); barbarous, rude, uncouth; (Print., a. & n.) German, also black-letter, (type); hence **Go·thic**ALLY adv., **Go·thic**ISM(2, 3, 4) n., **Go·thic**IZE(2, 3) v.i. & t. (N.) G. language; G. architecture. [f. L *Gothicus* (GOTH, -IC)]

gotten, p.p. (archaic, & U.S.) of GET[1].

gouache (gōō·ahsh), n. Way of painting in opaque colours ground in water & thickened with gum & honey. [F, f. It. *guazzo*]

gouge (gowj, gōōj), n., & v.t. Concave-bladed chisel used in carpentry & surgery. (Vb) cut with g.; cut *out* (a cork, a channel) (as) with g.; force (*out*, esp. person's eye with thumb) (as) with g.; force out eye of. [F, f. LL *gubia*]

Goular·d (gōō-), n. Lotion of sub-acetate of lead in solution. [T. *G.*, French surgeon]

gourd (gōrd, goord), n. (Large fleshy fruit of) kinds of trailing or climbing plant; rind of the fruit emptied, dried, & used as bottle &c., whence **gour·d**FUL(2) n. [f. F *gourde* f. L *cucurbita*]

gourmand (goor·mȧnd, or as F), a. & n. Gluttonous, fond of eating; (n.; usu. as F) lover of delicate fare, judge of good eating. Hence **gour·mand**ISM(2) n. [F, etym. dub.]

gourmandise. See GORMANDIZE.

gourmet (F), n. Connoisseur of table delicacies, esp. of wine. [F]

gout (gowt), n. Paroxysmal disease with inflammation of smaller joints, esp. that of great toe, & chalk-stones (*rich, poor, man's g.*, ascribed to over, under, -feeding); wheat-disease caused by *g.-fly*; drop, splash, or spot. Hence **gou·ty**[2] a. (*-ties* as n. pl., over-shoes), **gou·ti**LY[2] adv., **gou·ti**NESS n. [f. OF *goute* f. L *gutta* drop w. ref. to medieval theory of defluxion of humours]

go·vern (gŭ-), v.t. & i. Rule with authority, conduct the policy, actions, & affairs, of (State, subject) despotically or constitutionally, regulate proceedings of (corporation &c.; *governing body*, managers of hospital, school, &c.); be in military command of (fort, town); exercise function of government in person (*king reigns but does not g.*, merely selects those who are to g.); sway, rule, influence, regulate, determine, (person, his acts, course or issue of events); be the predominating influence; conduct one*self* in some way; curb, bridle, (one's passions, one*self*); constitute a law, rule, standard, or principle, for, serve to decide (case); (Gram., esp. of vb or prep.) have (noun, case) depending on it, require (a certain case). Hence **go·vern**ABLE a., **governa**BI·LITY n. [f. OF *governer* f. L *gubernare* steer, govern, f. Gk *kubernaō* steer]

go·vernance, n. Act, manner, fact, or function, of governing, sway, control. [f. OF *gouvernance* (prec., -ANCE)]

go·verness, n. Female teacher, instructress, esp. of children in private household; *g.-car*(*t*), light two-wheeled vehicle with side seats face to face. [earlier *governeress* f. OF *gouverneresse* (*gouverneur* GOVERNOR, -ESS[1])]

go·vernment, n. (More modern word for) GOVERNANCE; portion of country ruled by a governor, province; system of governing, form of polity; body or successive bodies of persons governing a State, the State as an agent, an administration or ministry (*form a g.*, of Prime Minister selecting colleagues); (Gram.) relation between GOVERNing & other word; *g. house*, official residence of governor; *g. paper, securities,* bonds, exchequer bills, &c., issued by g. Hence **governme·nt**AL a., **governme·ntal**LY[2] adv. [OF (*-ement*), see GOVERN, -MENT]

go·vernor, n. One who governs, ruler; official appointed to govern province, town, &c., representative of Crown in dominion (*G. General*) or colony, executive head of each of U.S.; officer commanding fortress or garrison; head, or one of governing body, of institution; (slang) one's employer, one's father, sir; (Mech.) automatic regulator of supply of gas, steam, water, &c., to machine, ensuring even motion; kind of fishing-fly; *g. general*, g. with deputy gg. under him, whence **go·vernor-ge·neral**SHIP n. Hence **go·vernor**SHIP(1, 2) n. [f. OF *governeür* f. L *gubernatorem* (GOVERN, -OR[2])]

gow·an, n. (Sc.). Daisy. [prob. var. of obs. *golland* & connected w. obs. *gold*, OE *golde*, marigold, perh. f. GOLD]

gowk, n. (Dial.) cuckoo; awkward or

half-witted person, fool. [f. ON *gaukr* cf. G *gauch*]

gown, n., & v.t. Loose flowing upper garment, esp. woman's dress (usu. of dress with pretensions to elegance, or in comb. as *tea, dinner, -g.*), frock; ancient Roman toga (*arms, gown,* war & peace); official or uniform robe of various shapes worn by alderman, judge, lawyer, clergyman, member of university, college, or school, &c. (*town & g.*, non-members & members of university at Oxf. & Camb.); *gownsman,* civilian, member of university; (vb, chiefly in p.p.) attire in g. [f. OF *goune* f. med. L *gunna* fur garment (in LL = fur)]

Graa·fian (-rahf-), a. *G. follicle, vesicle,* one of small sacs in mammal ovary in which ova are matured. [R. de *Graaf,* Dutch anatomist d. 1673, -IAN]

grab, v.t. & i., & n. Seize suddenly; appropriate rapaciously; capture, arrest; make snatch *at*; hence (-)**gra·bb**ER[1] n. (N.) sudden clutch, grasp, seizure, or attempt to seize; practice of grabbing, rapacious proceedings esp. in politics or commerce; *have the g. on* (slang), have great advantage of; (Mech.) device or implement for clutching; children's card game. [n. f. vb; cf. MDu. & MLG *grabben,* perh. modification of GRIP]

gra·bble, v.i. Grope about, feel for something; sprawl on all fours (often *for* something). [prec. + -LE(2)]

gra·bby, n. (Naut. slang). Soldier. [?]

grace, n., & v.t. Pleasing quality, attractiveness, charm, esp. that belonging to elegant proportions or ease & refinement of movement, action, expression, or manner, whence **gra·ce**FUL a., **gra·ceful**LY[2] adv., **gra·ceful**NESS n.; becomingness, air with which something is done, (*cannot with any g. ask him*; *have the g. to* do something that decency requires; *with a good g.*, as if willing; *with a bad g.*, reluctantly, ungraciously); attractive feature, accomplishment, ornament, (*airs & gg.*, behaviour put on with a view to effect or attraction); (Mus.; also *g.-note, -notes*) embellishment of extra note(s) not essential to harmony or melody; (Gk Myth.) *the Gg.*, three beautiful goddess sisters, the bestowers of beauty & charm; favour, benignant regard or its manifestation, on part of superior (*be in* one's *good gg.*, enjoy his favour or liking); unconstrained goodwill as ground of concession (*act of g.*, privilege, concession, that cannot be claimed as right, & see below; *by the g. of God,* appended to royal titles); boon; (Univv.) permission of Congregation, also of College or Hall, to take degree, dispensation from statutes; (Theol.) unmerited favour of God, divine regenerating, inspiring, & strengthening influence, condition (also *state of g.*) of being so influenced, divinely given talent &c., (*the —th year of g.*, with date = A.D.; *in this y. of g.* usu. iron., when Christianity has been so long established); favour shown by granting delay (*give a day's, year's,* &c., *g.*; *days of g.*, time allowed by law for payment of bill of exchange or insurance premium after it falls due, in England three days); mercy, clemency, (*Act of g.*, formal, esp. general, pardon by Act of Parliament; & see above); short thanksgiving before or after meal (*g.-cup,* cup of wine &c. passed round after g., parting draught); *his, her, your, g.*, forms of address or description for duke, duchess, or archbishop. (Vb) add g. to, adorn, set off *with*; confer honour or dignity on, honour *with* title &c.; do credit to. [f. F *grâce* f. L *gratia* (*gratus* pleasing, GRATEFUL)]

gra·celess, a. Unregenerate, depraved, (archaic or facet.); wanting sense of decency, unabashed; without charm or elegance (rare). Hence **gra·celess**LY[2] adv., **gra·celess**NESS n. [-LESS]

gra·cious (-sh*u*s), a. & int. Agreeable, pleasing, (archaic); kindly, benevolent, courteous, (chiefly poet.); condescending, indulgent & beneficent to inferiors, (of exalted persons, or sarcastic or facet.; esp. as polite epithet of royal or ducal persons or their acts); (of God) dispensing grace, merciful, benignant; hence **gra·cious**LY[2] adv., **gra·cious**NESS n. (Int.; ellipt. for *g. God,* as) *good g.!, my g.!*, excll. of surprise (also in *g. me!, g. goodness!*). [OF, f. L *gratiosus* (GRACE, -OSE[1])]

gra·ckle, n. Kinds of bird allied to jackdaw. [ult. f. L *graculus* jackdaw]

grada·te, v.i. & t. (Cause to) pass by imperceptible degrees from one shade of colour to another; arrange in steps or grades. [back formation f. foll.]

grada·tion, n. (Usu. pl.) stage(s) of transition or advance; series of degrees in rank, merit, intensity, divergence, &c., (pl.) such degrees; arrangement in such degrees; (Fine arts) insensible passing from one shade, tone, &c., to another; (Philol.) ablaut. Hence **grada·tion**AL a., **grada·tional**LY[2] adv. [f. L *gradatio* (*gradus* step, -ATION)]

grade, n., & v.t. (Math.) hundredth part of right angle; degree in rank, proficiency, quality, value, &c., class of persons or things alike in these; (Cattle-breeding) variety produced by crossing native stock with superior breed; (Zool.) group supposed to have branched from parent stock at same stage of development; (Philol.) relative position in ablaut-series; (esp. U.S.) gradient, slope, rate of ascent or descent, (*on the up, down, g.*, rising or falling, lit. & fig.). (Vb) arrange in gg., class, sort; blend so as to affect g. of; colour with tints passing into each other; reduce (road, canal, &c.)

to easy gradients; (Cattle-breeding) cross with better breed (*g. up*, improve thus); (Philol., in pass.) be changed by ablaut. [vb f. n., F, f. L *gradus* step]

grā·dely (-dlĭ), a. (dial.). Excellent, thorough; handsome, comely; real, true, proper. [ME *greidhlic* f. ON *greidhlig-r* (*greidh-r* = OE *gerǣde* READY, -LY[1])]

grā·dient, n. Amount of slope, inclination to the horizontal, in road, railway, &c.; proportional rise or fall of thermometer or barometer in passing from one region to another. [perh. formed on GRADE after *quotient*]

grā·dĭn(e) (*also* -adē·n), n. One of series of low steps or tier of seats; ledge at back of altar. [f. F *gradin* f. It. *gradino* (*grado* GRADE)]

grā·dual[1], n. Antiphon sung between Epistle & Gospel. [so called as sung at steps of altar or while deacon mounted ambo; f. med. L *graduale* neut. adj. as n., see foll.]

gra·dual[2], a. Taking place by degrees, slowly progressive, not rapid, steep, or abrupt; *g. psalm*, = *song of* DEGREES. Hence **gra·dual**LY[2] adv., **gra·dual**NESS n. [f. med. L *gradualis* (L *gradus -ūs* step, -AL)]

grā·duate[1] (-*a*t), n. One who holds academic degree; chemist's graduated measuring-glass. [f. med. L *graduatus* (foll., -ATE[2])]

gra·duāte[2], v.i. & t. Take, admit to (chiefly U.S.), academic degree, (transf.) qualify or perfect oneself *as*; mark out in degrees or portions; arrange in gradations, apportion incidence of (tax) according to a scale; pass *away* by degrees, change (intr.) gradually *into*; concentrate (solution) by evaporation. Hence **gradu**A·TION, **gra·duat**OR[2](1, 2), nn. [f. med. L *graduare* (*gradus -ūs* step), -ATE[3]]

grā·dus, n. Dictionary of Latin prosody used in schools to help in writing Latin verse. [for *g. ad Parnassum* step to Parnassus]

Gr(a)e·cism, n. A Greek idiom, esp. as imitated in another language; Greek spirit, style, mode of expression, &c., imitation of these. [f. F *grécisme* f. med. L *graecismus* (*Graecus* GREEK, -ISM)]

Gr(a)e·cize, v.t. & i. Give a Greek cast, character, or form, to; favour, imitate, the Greeks. [f. L *graecizare* (prec., -IZE)]

Gr(a)e·co-, comb. form of L *Graecus* GREEK, as *-Roman*. Hence **Gr(a)eco**MA·NIA(C) nn., **Gr(a)e·co**PHIL a. & n.

graffi·to (-fē-), n. (pl. *-ti* pr. -tē). Drawing or writing scratched on wall &c., esp. on ancient wall as at Pompeii; decoration by scratches through plaster showing different-coloured under-surface. [It.]

graft[1], n., & v.t. Shoot or scion inserted in slit of another stock, from which it receives sap; (Surg.) piece of transplanted living tissue; process of grafting; place where g. is inserted. (Vb) insert (scion) as g. (*in, into, on, upon, together*), (fig.) insert or fix *in* or *upon* so as to produce vital or indissoluble union; insert graft(s); insert graft(s) upon (stock); (Surg.) transplant (living tissue); (Naut.) cover (ring-bolt &c.) with weaving of small cord; *grafting-clay, -wax*, composition for covering united parts of g. & stock. [for earlier *graff* n. & v. f. OF *grafe* f. LL f. Gk *graphion* stylus (*graphō* write), named f. similarity of shape; *-t* perh. due to use of *g.* as p.p. of *graff*, cf. HOIST, BASTE[3]]

graft[2], n. Depth of earth that may be thrown up at once with spade; crescent-bladed spade. [cogn. w. GRAVE[2]]

graft[3], n., & v.i., (U.S. colloq.). Illicit spoils in connexion with politics or municipal business, practices intended to secure these; (vb) seek, make, g., whence **gra·ft**ER[1] n. [?]

grail[1], n. = GRADUAL[1]. [f. OF *grael* f. eccl. L *gradale* var. of *graduale*]

grail[2], n. (Also *holy* or *saint g.*, or *sangreal*) platter used by Christ at Last Supper, & in which Joseph of Arimathea received his blood at the Cross. [f. OF *graal* f. med. L *gradalis* cup or platter, etym. dub.; *sangreal* as = *blood real* or *royal* (F *sang*) is erron. division]

grail[3], n. Comb-maker's file. [f. F *grêle* (*grêler* make thin f. *grêle* adj. f. L *gracilis*)]

grain, n., & v.t. & i. A fruit or corn of a cereal; (collect. sing.) wheat or the allied food-grasses or their fruit, corn, a particular species of corn; (pl.; also *gg. of Paradise* or *Guinea gg.*) capsules of W.-Afr. plant used as spice & drug; (pl.) refuse malt after brewing or distilling; small hard particle of sand, gold, SALT, gunpowder (*large, small, -g. powder*), incense, &c.; smallest unit of weight, 1/5760 of lb. Troy, 1/7000 of lb. av., smallest possible quantity (*without a g. of vanity, love*, &c.); (Hist.) kermes, cochineal, or dye made from either of these (*dye in g.*, dye in kermes, dye in any fast colour, dye in the fibre or thoroughly; *in g.*, thorough, genuine, by nature, downright, indelible); (Poet.) dye, colour; granular texture, roughness of surface, mottling; texture, arrangement & size of constituent particles, in flesh, skin, wood, stone, &c.; lines of fibre in wood giving a pattern, lamination or planes of cleavage in coal, stone, &c., (fig.) nature, temper, tendency, (*against the g.*, contrary to inclination); *g.-leather*, dressed with the *g.-side* (on which the hair was) out; *g.-sick* n., cattle-disease, distension of rumen; hence **grai·n**LESS, **grai·n**Y[2], **(-)grain**ED[2], aa. (Vb) form (t. & i.) into gg.; dye in g.; give granular surface to; remove hair from (hides); paint in imitation of g. of wood or marble;

hence **grai·n**ER[1](1, 2) n. [OF, f. L *granum*, & f. OF *graine* f. pop. L *grana* collect. fem., orig. neut. pl. of L *granum*]

grains, n. Forked fish-spear or harpoon. [orig. pl. of obs. *grain* fork, prong, f. ON *grein* division; now used as sing.]

grăllator·ial, a. (zool.). Of the *grallatores* or long-legged wading birds. [f. L *grallator* stilt-walker (*grallae* stilts)]

gră·lloch (-ch), n., & v.t. Dead deer's viscera; (vb) disembowel (deer &c.). [f. Gael. *grealach* intestines]

gram[1], n. Chick-pea; any pulse used as horse-fodder. [f. Port. *grão* f. L *granum* grain]

gram[2]. See GRAMME.

-gram, suf. (chiefly) f. Gk *gramma -atos* (*graphō* write, -M) thing written, letter of alphabet, forming nn. (1) prepositional compds f. Gk (*anagram, diagram, epigram*), (2) n. compds (*chronogram, logogram*), (3) compds of numeral with *gramma* or with *grammē* line, where Gk would have *-grammon* neut. adj., (4) the improper compd *telegram* f. adv. *tēle*, suggested by which are (5) the hybrids *cablegram, pistolgram,* & the correctly formed *phonogram.*

gră·ma, gra·mma, n. (Also *g. grass*) kinds of low pasture grass in W. & S.W. parts of U.S. [f. Sp. *grama*]

gră·marye, n. (archaic). Magic, necromancy. [f. OF *gramaire* learning, GRAMMAR]

gramer·cy, int. (archaic). Thank you. [f. OF *grant merci* (God give you) great reward (GRAND, MERCY)]

grāminā·ceous, grami·neous, aa. Of, like, grass, grassy. So **grāmini·**VOROUS a. [f. L *gramen -inis* grass, -ACEOUS, & L *gramineus* (-EOUS)]

gra·mmalogue (-ŏg), n. (shorthand). Word represented by single sign; letter or character standing for word, logogram. [irreg. f. Gk *gramma* (-GRAM), *logos* word]

gra·mmar, n. Art & science dealing with a language's inflexions or other means of showing relation between words as used in speech or writing, & its phonetic system (usu. divided into phonology, accidence, & syntax; *general, philosophical,* or *universal g.*, science of the distinctions of thought recognized & variously expressed in the grammatical systems of actual languages; *historical g.*, study of the development of a language's inflexions & syntax; *comparative g.*, study of the relation between two or more gg.); treatise or book on g.; person's manner of using grammatical forms, speech or writing regarded as good or bad by the rules of g., what is correct according to those rules; body of forms & usages in a language; elements, rudiments, of an art or science; *g.-school*, school founded about 16th c. for teaching Latin, of which many are now of the public-school type. Hence **gra·mmar**LESS a. [f. OF *gramaire* irreg. f. L f. Gk *grammatikē* (*tekhnē* art) of letters (*gramma* see -GRAM)]

grammār·ian, n. One versed in grammar, philologist. [f. OF *gramarien* (prec., -IAN)]

grammă·tical, a. Of grammar (*g. gender*, not determined by sex; *g. sense*, literal, irrespective of other considerations than the rules of grammar); conforming to the rules of grammar, or to the formal principles of an art, so (f. earlier *grammatic*) **gramma·tic**IZE(3) v.t. Hence **gramma·tical**LY[2] adv. [f. L f. Gk *grammatikos*, see GRAMMAR, + -AL]

gramme, gram, n. Unit of weight in metric system, weight of cubic centimetre of distilled water at maximum density weighed in vacuo, 15·432 Troy grains; *g.-centimetre*, unit = work done in raising one g. vertically one centimetre; similarly *gramme·tre.* [F, f. LL f. Gk *gramma* small weight, see -GRAM]

gră·mophone, n. Phonograph, esp. of the kind reproducing music, speech, &c., from hard rubber records. [irreg. form perh. made by inverting PHONOGRAM]

gra·mpus, n. Kinds of blowing spouting blunt-headed delphinoid cetacean; person who breathes loud. [f. 16th-c. *graundepose* prob. f. earlier *grapeys* f. OF *grapois* f. L *crassus piscis* fat fish]

grănadi·lla, grĕ-, n. Kinds of passion-flower. [Sp., dim. of *granada* pomegranate]

gră·nary, n. Storehouse for threshed grain; region producing, & esp. exporting, much corn. [f. L *granarium* (*granum* grain, -ARY[1])]

grand, a. & n. (In official titles) chief over others, of highest rank, (*G. Almoner, Falconer,* &c., holders of old offices still existing; *G.* CROSS[1]; *G. Duke, Duchess,* ruler of some European States called *G. Duchy*, also child of Tsar, whence **Grand-du·**CAL a.; *g. duke*, also, Great Horned Owl; *G. Master*, head of military order of knighthood, head of Freemasons or of one of their provinces, & of Odd Fellows &c.; *G. Signior*, pr. sēn-, *G. Turk*, Sultan of Turkey; *G. Vizier*, chief minister of Turkey); (Law) great, principal, (opp. *petty, common*; *g. assize, inquest, jury*); of most or great importance (*that is the g. question*; *made a g. mistake*); final, summing up minor constituents, (*g. total*; *g. finale*; *the g. sum* or *result of his achievements*); (distinguishing parts of large building) main (*the g. staircase, entrance,* &c.); (in F phrases or imitations) great (*g. army, G. Canal, G. Hotel*; *G. Fleet*, main British fleet in the great war); (Mus.) full, of full dimensions, for full orchestra, in full classical form, (*g. sonata, chorus, concerto*); conducted with solemnity, splendour, &c.; fine, splendid, gorgeous; belonging to high society, distinguished, (*do the g.* put on airs); imposing, impressive, great & handsome; dignified, lofty, in conception, treatment, or expression (*g. style*, fitted for great subjects); morally imposing, noble, admirable, (*the Grand Old Man* or *G.O.M.*, W. E. Gladstone); (colloq.) very satisfactory (*had a g. run*; *ground was in g. condition*); (in names of relationships) in the second degree of ascent or descent (*grandson*, one's child's son; *g.-nephew*, one's nephew's or niece's son; *grandmother*, *g.-aunt*, one's parent's mother or aunt; so *grandchild*; *g.-daughter*; *grandfather*, *grandfather's clock*, worked by weights in tall wooden case; *grandmamma*; *grandmother*, whence **gra·ndmother**LY[1] a., esp. of legislation &c. = excessively PATERNAL; *teach your grandmother to suck* EGGS; *grandmother* v.t., coddle &c., *g.-m. the cups*, prevent their slipping by wetting the saucers; *g.-niece*; *grandpapa*; *grandparent*; *grandsire*, esp. of animal's sire, also = ancestor, old man, & a method of ringing changes on bells; *g.-uncle*); *g. air*, distinguished appearance; *g. committee*, one of two standing committees of House of Commons sessionally appointed to consider Law & Trade Bills; *g.* LODGE; *G. Monarch*, Louis XIV of France; *G. National*, annual steeplechase at Liverpool; *g. piano-(forte)*, large harp-shaped horizontal piano with special mechanism; *g. stand*, principal stand for spectators at races &c.; *g. tour* (archaic), tour of chief towns &c. of Europe completing education. (N.) g. piano (*upright g.*, kind with mechanism of the g. accommodated to an upright shape). Hence **gra·nd**LY[2] adv., **gra·nd**NESS n. [OF, f. L *grandis* full-grown]

gra·ndăm(e), n. (archaic). Grandmother; (*-m* only) animal's dam's dam; ancestress; old woman. [f. AF *graund dame* (prec., DAM[2])]

gra·n(d-)dad, n. (Childish or affectionate for) grandfather. [GRAND, DAD]

grande (F), fem. of GRAND (*g. toilette*, ceremonial costume; *g. passion*, engrossing love affair).

grāndee·, n. Spanish or Portuguese nobleman of highest rank; person of high rank or eminence. [f. Sp. & Port. *grande* GRAND]

gra·ndeur (-jer, -dyer), n. Great power, rank, or eminence; great nobility of character; sublimity, majesty, of appearance or effect; conscious dignity; splendour of living, surroundings, &c. [F (GRAND)]

Grand Guignol (F), n. Dramatic entertainment in which short pieces often of strongly sensational type are played successively. [name (= Great Punch) of theatre in Paris; F *Guignol* perh. f. *Chignolo Po* in Italy, native place of Italian who introduced puppets at Lyons]

grandi·loquent, a. Pompous in language; given to tall talk. Hence **grandi·lo·qu**ENCE n., **grandi·loquent**LY[2] adv. [after *eloquent* f. L *grandiloquus* (GRAND, *-loquus* -speaking f. *loqui* speak)]

gra·ndio·se, a. Producing, intended or trying to produce, an impression of greatness, planned on a magnificent scale, pompous. Hence **grandiŏ·**SITY n., **grandio·se**LY[2] adv. [F, f. It. *grandioso* (GRAND, -OSE[1])]

Grandisō·nian, a. Marked by stately courtesy & chivalric magnanimity. [Sir C. *Grandison* in Richardson's novel, -IAN]

grānge, n. Barn (archaic); country house with farm-buildings attached. [f. AF *graunge* f. med. L *granea* (*granum* grain)]

grā·ngerize, v.t. Extra-illustrate (book) by inserting prints &c. often cut from other books. Hence **grangerīz**A·TION, **gra·ngeriz**ER[1], **gra·nger**ISM(1), **gra·nger**ITE(1), nn. [J. *Granger* published 1769 a Hist. of England with blank leaves for illustrations]

grani·ferous, a. Producing grain or grain-like seed. So **grā·ni**FORM, **grani·**VOROUS, aa. [f. L *granifer* (GRAIN, -FEROUS)]

gră·nite, n. Granular crystalline rock of quartz, orthoclase feldspar, & mica, used for building (*bite on g.*, waste pains, persist in vain); *g.-ware*, speckled pottery imitating g., kind of enamelled ironware. Hence **granĭ·t**IC a., **gra·nit**OID a. & n., **granĭ·ti**FORM a. [f. It. *granito* orig. grained (*grano* f. L *granum*)]

gra·nnom, gră·nam, n. Kind of water-fly; imitation of it for fly-fishing. [?]

gra·nny, n. (Fam., affectionate, or contempt. for) grandmother; (also *g.'s bend* or *knot*) reef-knot crossed the wrong way. [prob. f. obs. *grannam* for GRANDAM + -Y[3]]

grănoli·thic, a. Of a kind of concrete. [L *granum* grain, Gk *lithos* stone, -IC]

grant, v.t., & n. Consent to fulfil (request &c.; in p.p. formerly common, now rare, as answer to *I beg your pardon*); concede as indulgence, allow (person) to have (thing; noun, *that*, or *to* do); bestow (possession, right) formally, transfer (property) legally, whence **grant**EE·, **grant**OR·[2], nn.; concede (proposition) as basis for argument (noun, *this* &c., *that*-clause, or something *to be* something; *I g. you*, I admit; *take for granted*, assume); hence **gra·nt**ABLE a. (N.) granting (*the g. or refusal of*); formal conferment, legal assignment; thing, esp. sum, granted (often *capitation g.*, *g.-in-aid*); conveyance by written instrument. [f. OF *greanter* f. pop. L **credentare* f. part. of *credere* entrust]

gră·nular, a. Of, like, grains, with granulated surface or structure. Hence

granulă·RITY n., **gra·nularLY**[2] adv., **gra·nulo-** comb. form, **gra·nulOUS** a. [f. LL *granulum* small grain (*granum*, -ULE), -UL-, -AR]

gra·nulāte, v.t. & i. Form (t. & i.) into grains; roughen surface of; (of wound &c.) form small prominences as beginning of healing or junction, heal, join. Hence or cogn. **gra·nulATE**[2] (-*at*) a., **granuLA·TION**, **gra·nulatOR**[2](2), nn. [as prec., -ATE[3]]

gra·nule, n. Small grain. [as prec.]

grape, n. Green or purple berry growing in clusters on vine, eaten as fruit or used in making wine (*the g., the juice of the g.*, wine; *the gg. are sour, sour gg.*, said when person disparages what he vainly desires); g.-shot; diseased growth like bunch of gg. on pastern of horse &c., or on pleura; *g.-brandy*, distilled from gg., or wine, alone; *g.*-CURE[1]; *g.-fruit*, kind of small shaddock; *g.-house*, vinery; *g.-scissors*, for thinning g.-bunches at early stage of growth, also for dividing bunches at table; *g.-shot*, small balls put several together in bag &c. to make scattering charge for cannon; *g.-stone*, one of seeds inside g.; *g.-sugar*, dextrose or glucose; *g.-vine*, vine, also skating figure in which both feet are on ice together & form interlacing lines. Hence **grā·PERY**(3) **n., gra·PY**[2] a. [OF, bunch of gg., prob. f. *graper* gather with vine-hook (*grape* hook ult. f. Teut. cf. OHG *krapfo*)]

graph[1], n. Symbolic diagram expressing system of mathematical or chemical connexion. [abbr. of *graphic formula*]

graph[2], n., & v.t. Gelatine copying apparatus; copy, multiply, with this. [colloq. abbr. of *chromograph, hectograph*, &c.]

-graph, suf. f. Gk *-graphos*, -written, -writing, -writer, denoting (1) thing written in such a way (f. Gk, as *autograph, chirograph*; *holograph*; on Gk st., as *lithograph, photograph*; & in hybrids, as *pictograph*); (2) instrument that records something or by some means (*heliograph, seismograph, telegraph*); (3) write in such a way (*calligraph, hectograph*).

-grapher, suf. repr. Gk *-graphos* & forming nn. denoting one versed in -GRAPHY. [-ER]

grā·phic(al rare), aa. Of drawing, painting, engraving, etching, &c.; vividly descriptive, lifelike; of writing; (of minerals) showing marks like writing on surface or in fracture; of diagrams or symbolic curves. [f. L f. Gk *graphikos* (*graphē* writing, -IC)]

-graphic(al), suff. = of or by -GRAPHY.

gra·phically, adv. As in a picture, vividly; by writing; by diagrams or GRAPH[1]S. [-LY[2]]

grā·phite, n. PLUMBAGO. Hence **graphi·tIC, gra·phitOID,** aa. [f. G *graphit* (Gk *graphō* write, -ITE[1])]

grā·phiure, n. S.-Afr. rodent with tail ending in pencil of hairs. [f. Gk *grapheion* pencil, *oura* tail]

grapho·logy, n. Study of, art of inferring character from, handwriting; system of graphic formulae, notation for GRAPH[1]S. [f. Gk *graphē* writing, -LOGY]

grā·photype, n. (Process for making) relief block for surface-printing. [as prec. + TYPE]

-graphy, suf. f. Gk *-graphia* forming nn. denoting (1) styles of writing, drawing, &c. (*litho-, brachy-, steno-, calli-*), (2) descriptive science (*geo-, biblio-, seleno-*).

gra·pnel, n. Iron-clawed instrument thrown with rope to seize object, esp. enemy's ship; small anchor with several flukes used for boats & balloons. [dim. of OF *grapin* (GRAPE)]

gra·pple, n., & v.t. & i. Clutching-instrument, grapnel; hold or grip (as) of wrestlers, close contest. (Vb) seize, fasten, (as) with grapnel; take hold of, grip, with the hands, come to close quarters with; contend *with, together*, or abs., in close fight, battle *with*; *g. with*, try to overcome, accomplish, or deal with. [vb f. n. in first sense; second sense of n. f. vb; n. f. OF dim. of *grape* hook]

gra·ppling, n. In vbl senses; also, g.-iron, grapnel. [-ING[1]]

grasp, v.t. & i., & n. *G. at*, try to seize, accept with avidity; clutch at, seize greedily, (part.) avaricious, whence **gra·spingLY**[2] adv., **gra·spingNESS** n.; hold firmly (*g. nettle*, tackle difficulty or danger boldly), grip; get mental hold of, comprehend; hence **gra·spABLE** a. (N.) fast hold, grip, (*within, beyond*, one's *g.*, close, not close, enough to be grasped); control, mastery; mental hold, comprehensiveness of mind. [by metath. for *grapsen* cogn. w. GROPE, cf. *clean cleanse*, & HASP]

grass, n., & v.t. Herbage of which blades or leaves & stalks are eaten by cattle, horses, sheep, &c. (*not let g. grow, g. does not grow, under* one's *feet*, of person who wastes no time in doing something; *hear the g. grow*, be of preternatural acuteness); any species of this (including in bot. use, excluding in pop. use, the cereals, reeds, & bamboos; usu. with defining words, as *bunch, spear, -g., g. of Parnassus*); grazing, pasture, (*be at, go, put, send, turn out, to, g.*; *at g.* fig., out of work, making holiday, &c.; so perh. *g. widow*, wife whose husband is absent); pasture land; grass-covered ground (*keep off the g.*); (Mining) earth's surface, pit-head; *send, go, to g.*, knock (person), be knocked or fall, down; *gra·sshopper*, kinds of jumping & chirping insect (*grasshopper-beam*, working-beam in engine pivoted at end instead of in middle); *g.-snake*, common ringed snake;

g.-tree, kinds of Australasian tree; hence **gra·ssLESS, gra·ssY²**, aa. (Vb) cover with turf; lay (flax &c.) on g. to bleach; knock down, fell, (opponent); bring (fish) to bank, (bird by shot) to ground; (p.p., of golf-club) with face slightly sloped backward. [com.-Teut.; OE *græs* cf. G *gras*, cogn. w. GREEN, GROW, & w. L *gramen* grass]

grate¹, n. = GRATING (rare), whence **gra·tED²** a.; (frame of metal bars for confining fuel in) fireplace or furnace. Hence **gra·teLESS** a. [f. med. L f. It. *grata* f. L *cratis* hurdle]

grate², v.t. & i. Reduce to small particles by rubbing on rough surface, whence (-)**gra·tER¹**(2) n.; have irritating effect (*up*)*on*; grind (teeth); rub (i. & t.) with harsh scraping noise *against* or (*up*)*on* something else; sound harshly or discordantly (*a grating laugh, voice*); (of hinge &c.) creak. Hence **gra·tingLY²** adv. [f. OF *grater* f. Teut., cf. G *kratzen* scratch]

gra·teful, a. Acceptable, comforting, refreshing; thankful, feeling or showing gratitude (*to* person, *for* thing). Hence **gra·tefulLY²** adv., **gra·tefulNESS** n. [f. obs. *grate* adj. f. L *gratus* + -FUL]

gră·tifȳ, v.t. Remunerate, fee, make present usu. of money to; bribe; please, satisfy, oblige, delight, whence **gra·tifyING²** a. (*to*), **gra·tifyingLY²** adv.; please by compliance, assent to wish of, give free course to or indulge (desire, feeling, impulse). So **gratiFICA·TION** n. [f. L *gratificari* (*gratus* pleasing ,-FY)]

gratin (F), n. Way of cooking, dish cooked, by bread-crumbing & cooking between two fires to produce light crust; *au g.*, so prepared.

gra·ting, n. Framework of parallel or crossed wooden or metal bars; (Opt.) set of parallel wires, or surface of glass &c. ruled with parallel lines, for producing spectra by diffraction. [GRATE¹ + -ING¹]

gra·tis, adv. & a. Gratuitous(ly), (given, done) for nothing, without charge, free. [L, contracted abl. pl. of *gratia* favour]

gră·titude, n. Being thankful, appreciation of & inclination to return kindness. [f. LL *gratitudo* (*gratus* thankful, -TUDE)]

gratu·itous, a. Got or given free, not earned or paid for; uncalled for, unwarranted, motiveless, done or acting without good or assignable reason (*a g. lie* or *liar*). Hence **gratu·itousLY²** adv., **gratu·itousNESS** n. [f. L *gratuitus* spontaneous, cogn. w. *gratia* favour, + -OUS]

gratu·ity, n. Money present of amount fixed by giver in recognition of an inferior's good offices, tip; bounty to soldiers on retirement or some other occasions. [f. med. L *gratuitas* gift (*gratus* grateful, -TY)]

gră·tulate, -a·tion. (Archaic for) **congr-.**

gră·tulatory, a. Expressing joy at another's success &c., complimentary, congratulatory. [f. L *gratulari* congratulate + -ORY]

gravā·men, n. (pl. *-mina*, rare). Grievance; memorial from Lower House of Convocation to Upper on disorders or grievances of Church; essence, worst part, *of* accusation. [LL, inconvenience (*gravare* to load f. *gravis* heavy, -MEN)]

grave¹, n. Excavation to receive corpse, mound or monument over it, (*secret as the g.*, quite; *make* one *turn in his g.*, of act &c. that he would have been pained by while alive; *some one walking on my g.*, said when one shivers unaccountably; *one* FOOT¹ *in g.*), whence **gra·veLESS** a.; being dead, death, Hades, whence **gra·veWARD** adv. & a.; receptacle of or for what is dead (*g. of reputations*, place where many reputations have been lost); trench for earthing up potatoes &c.; *g.-clothes*, wrappings in which corpse is buried; *g.-digger*, lit., also kinds of insect that bury bodies of insects &c. as food for their larvae; *gravestone*, stone over g., inscribed stone at head or foot of g.; *graveyard*, burial ground. [OE *græf*, (*grafan* GRAVE²)]

grave², v.t. (p.p. *-en, -ed*, as stated). (Archaic) bury (*-ed*); (archaic) carve, sculpture, engrave, (material, representation; *-en, -ed*; *graven image*, idol); (fig.) fix indelibly (*on, in*, mind &c.; *-en, -ed*). [com.-Teut.; OE *grafan*, cf. Du. *graven*, G *graben*, dig; cogn. w. GROOVE]

grave³, a. & n. Important, weighty, needing serious thought; (of faults, difficulties, responsibilities, symptoms) formidable, threatening, serious; dignified, solemn, slow-moving, not gay; sombre, plain, not showy; hence **gra·veLY²** adv. (Of accent) low-pitched, not acute, (*g.* ACCENT¹; n., g. accent). [F, f. L *gravis* heavy]

grave⁴, v.t. Clean (ship's bottom) by burning off accretions & tarring while aground or in graving-dock. [perh. f. OF *grave* = *grève* shore]

gră·vel (-vl), n., & v.t. Coarse sand & small water-worn or pounded stones, much used for laying paths & roads; (Geol., Mining) stratum of this, esp. one containing gold (*pay g.*, containing enough gold to yield profit); (Path.) (disease with) aggregations of visible urinary crystals; *g.-blind*, more than SAND-BLIND (Shksp., *M. of V.*, II. ii. 38); hence **gra·vellY²** a. (Vb) lay, strew, with g.; perplex, puzzle, non-plus, (f. obs. sense *run aground*). [f. OF (& F in path. sense) *gravelle* dim. of OF *grave* gravel, shore, f. Celt. cf. W *gro*]

gra·ver, n. In vbl senses; esp., burin. [-ER¹]

gră·vid, a. Pregnant. [f. L *gravidus* (GRAVE³)]

gră·vitate, v.i. & t. Move or tend by

force of gravity *towards* a body; sink (as) by gravity, tend to low level, settle down; (Diamond-digging) manipulate (gravel) so that heavy stones sink to bottom; (transf.) be strongly attracted *to*(*wards*) some centre of influence. Hence **gravitA·TION** n., **gravita·tionAL**, **gra·vi-tATIVE**, aa. [f. mod.L *gravitare* (GRAVE[3]), -ATE[3]]

grā·vity, n. Being grave, solemnity; importance, seriousness; staidness, sobriety, serious demeanour; weight (CENTRE[1] *of g.*; *specific g.*, relative weight of any kind of matter, expressed by ratio of given volume to same volume of a standard—usu. water for liquid or solid, & air for gas); attractive force by which bodies tend to centre of earth, degree of intensity of this measured by acceleration, degree of intensity with which any body is similarly attracted by any other. [f. L *gravitas* (GRAVE[3], -TY)]

gravure·, n. (Short for) PHOTOGRAVURE.

grā·vy, n. Juices that exude from flesh during & after cooking; dressing for food made from these with other materials; *g.-boat*, boat-shaped vessel for g.; *g. beef*, part of leg of beef cooked for its g. [etym. dub.; perh. a misreading as *gravé* of *grané* in OF cookery books, cf. OF *grain* anything used in cookery]

gray. See GREY.

gray·ling, n. Silver-grey freshwater fish with long high dorsal fin; butterfly with grey under-side to wings. [GREY + -LING[1]]

graze[1], v.i. & t. Feed (esp. cattle, or intr. of cattle) on growing grass &c. or **gra·z-ING**[1](3) n.; feed on (grass &c., often *down*); tend grazing cattle; pasture cattle. [OE *grasian* (GRASS n.)]

graze[2], v.t. & i., & n. Touch lightly in passing; abrade (skin &c.) in rubbing past; suffer slight abrasion of (part of body); go with passing contact *against, along, through, by, past*, &c.; (n.) grazing abrasion. [etym. dub.; perh. by transf. f. prec. cf. *shave*]

gra·zier (-zher), n. One who feeds cattle for market. Hence **gra·ziERY**(2) n. [GRASS + -IER]

grease[1] (-s), n. Fat of deer or other game (*in g.*, *in pride* or *prime of g.*, fit for killing, fat); melted fat of dead animals, esp. when soft; oily or fatty matter, esp. as lubricant; oily matter in wool, uncleansed wool, (*wool in the g.*, in fleeces); disease in horses' heels; *g.-box*, attached to train-wheel for lubrication; *g.-paint*, composition for painting actors' faces; *g.-trap*, appliance for catching g. in drains. [f. OF *graisse* (L *crassus* a. fat)]

grease[2] (-z), v.t. Anoint, soil, or lubricate, with g. (*g. the wheels*, make affairs go smoothly, esp. by money; *g. palm of*, bribe; *like greased lightning* slang, very fast); affect (horse) with g. [f. prec.]

grea·ser (-z-), n. In vbl senses, esp.: head fireman on steamer; (U.S. slang) native Mexican or Spanish-American. [-ER[1]]

grea·sy (-zĭ), a. Smeared or covered with, containing, made of, like, with too much, grease; (of wool) uncleansed; (of horse) affected with the grease; slimy with mud or moisture; (of manners or expression) disagreeably unctuous; *g. fritillary*, kind of butterfly; *g. pole*, greased for climbing or walking on in sports. Hence **grea·siLY**[2] adv., **grea·siNESS** n. [-Y[2]]

great (grāt), a. & n. Large, big, (usu. with implied surprise, contempt, indignation, &c., as *made a g. blot, look at that g. wasp*; often colloq. preceding other adj., *a g. big loaf* or *thick stick*; as distinctive epithet of the larger species or individual, as *g. A*, Z, the capital letters, *G. St John's wort*, also *Greater Celandine* &c., *G. Titmouse*, *G.* BEAR[1], *G. Malvern* &c., *G. Portland Street*; also in a few phrases, as *a g.* DEAL[1], MANY, *the g. majority*, much the larger part, *greatest common* MEASURE, *lived to a g. age*, *a g. while ago*; *g. with child* archaic, pregnant); beyond the ordinary (*take g. care*; *of g. popularity*; *shows g. ignorance*); important, elevated, distinguished, critical, *the* chief, pre-eminent, (*it is a g. thing to have* —; *a g. occasion*; *the g. attraction*; *the G. Powers of Europe*, chief States; *the g. world*, high society; in excll., as *G. God!*, *Caesar!*, *Scott!*; *the G.*, appended in sense *the best known of the name*, as *Alexander the G.*, or prefixed in titles, as *the G. King*, of ancient Persia, *the G. Mogul*, &c., & burlesqued in *the G.* UNPAID, UNWASHED); of remarkable ability, genius, intellectual or practical qualities, loftiness or integrity of character, (*a g. judge, painter*, &c.; *the truly g. man*; *g. thoughts*), whence **great-heartED**[2] a.; (pred.) having much skill *at* or information *on*; highly satisfactory (*wouldn't it be g. if* —?); fully deserving the name of, (with agent-nouns) doing the act much or on a large scale, (*a g. scoundrel, fiasco*; *g. friends*; *is a g. dancer, landowner*); (prefixed once or more to *uncle, aunt, nephew, niece*, & kinship words compounded with GRAND) one degree further removed upwards or downwards; *G. Assize, Day*, or *Inquest*, Day of Judgement; *G. Bible*, Coverdale's Version 1539; *G.* BRITAIN, CHARTER, CIRCLE[1]; *great-*COAT[1], whence **greatcoatED**[2], **great-coa·tLESS**, aa.; *the g.* COMMONER; *greater* BRITAIN; *greatest happiness of the greatest number*, test principle of Benthamism; *g. go*, final examination for B.A. at Cambridge, cf. *greats* below; *g. house*, chief house in village &c.; *g.* ORGAN, SEAL; *g.* PRIMER; *g. toe*, now usu. BIG *toe*. Hence **grea·tEN**[6] v.t. & i. (archaic), **grea·tNESS** n. (N.): (abs. use of adj.) *the g.*, (pl.) g. persons (also without *the* in *g. & small*), (sing.) what is g.; *greats*, Oxford B.A. final examination, esp. that for honours in Lit. Hum. [com.-WG; OE *gréat* cf. G *gross*, Du. *groot*]

grea·tly, adv. Much, by much, (usu. with vbs, participles, or comparatives; *g. esteemed, superior; should g. prefer*); nobly, loftily. [-LY[2]]

greave, n. (usu. pl.). Piece(s) of armour for shin(s). [f. OF *greve* shin, greave, etym. dub.]

greaves, n. pl. Fibrous tallow refuse, used as food of dog &c. or fish-bait. [f. LG *greven* pl.]

grebe, n. Kinds of short-bodied lobe-footed almost tailless diving bird; its plumage as trimming. [f. F *grèbe* etym. dub.]

Grē·cian (-shn), a. & n. Greek (rare except of architecture & facial outline; also in *G. bend,* affected attitude in walking prevalent c. 1870, *G. gift,* = GREEK *gift, G. knot,* way of dressing woman's hair at back of head, *G. nose,* straight & continuing forehead line without dip, *G. profile,* with G. nose, *G. slippers,* trade name for oriental shape). (N.) Greek scholar; boy of highest class at Christ's Hospital. [f. L *Graecia* Greece + -AN]

Grecism, Grecize, Greco-. See **grae-.**

greed, n. Insatiate longing esp. for wealth. [back formation f. foll.]

gree·dy, a. Ravenous, voracious, gluttonous, avaricious, covetous, rapacious, (often *of*); eager, keen, intensely desirous (*to* do). Hence **gree·di**LY[2] adv., **gree·di**NESS n. [OE *grǣdig* cf. OHG *grâtag,* cogn. w. Skr. *grdh* be greedy]

Greek, n. & a. Native of Greece, member of Greek race, (*when G. meets G., then comes the tug of war,* orig. *Gg. joined Gg., then was,* said of equal encounter); member of G. Church; cunning person, sharper; the G. language (*G. to me,* beyond my comprehension), whence **Gree·k**LESS a. (Adj.) of Greece or its people, Hellenic; of, according to, written or spoken in, G. (*G. Fathers,* FATHER[1]*s of the Church* who wrote in G.); *G. Church,* also *Orthodox* or *Eastern,* Church acknowledging Patriarch of Constantinople, divided from Rome in 9th c., & including esp. Christians of Greece, Russia, & Turkish Empire; *G.* CALENDS, FIRE[1], FRET[1] or *key*; *G.* CROSS[1]; *G. gift,* one given with intent to harm (Virg. *Aen.* ii. 49). [adj. f. n.; OE *Crécas* pl. f. L *Graecus* f. Gk *Graikoi* prehistoric name of Hellenes]

green[1], a. & n. Of the colour between blue & yellow in the spectrum, coloured like grass, sea-water, emerald, olive, &c.; covered with herbage, verdant, in leaf, (*a. g. Christmas, season, Yule,* mild, without snow); (of complexion) pale, sickly-hued, (*g. eye,* jealousy, whence **green-eye**ED[2] a.; *g. jaundice,* kind in which patient's skin is g.); (fig.) jealous, envious; vegetable (*g. food,* MEAT); (of fruit &c.) unripe, young & tender, flourishing, not dried; full of vitality, not withered or worn out, (*in the g., dry, tree,* under good, bad, conditions; *a g. old age*); immature, undeveloped, inexperienced, gullible; not dried, seasoned, or tanned; fresh, not healed, (*a g. wound*); *greenback,* U.S. legal-tender note, note issued by any U.S. national bank; *g.-blind,* having retina insensitive to g. rays; *g.-book,* official publication of Indian Government; *g. cheese,* unripened cheese, whey cheese, cheese coloured g. with sage; (*Board of*) *G. Cloth,* Lord Steward's department of Royal Household; *g. crop,* used for food in g. state (opp. *hay* &c.); *g. drake,* mayfly; *g. earth,* hydrous silicate of potassium, iron, & other bases; *g. fat,* of turtle, esteemed by epicures; *greenfinch* or *g. linnet,* bird with gold & g. plumage; *g. goose,* killed under four months old and eaten without stuffing; *g. fly,* kind of aphis; *greengage,* roundish g. fine-flavoured plum (Sir W. Gage c. 1725); *gree·ngrocer(y),* (business of, things sold by) retail dealer in fruit & vegetables; *greenheart,* a British Guiana timber tree; *greenhorn,* ignoramus, raw hand, simpleton; *greenhouse,* of glass for rearing delicate plants; *g.-man,* golf-course keeper; *g. manure,* growing plants ploughed into soil; *g.-peak,* G. Woodpecker (transl. of It. *picchio verde*); *g.-room,* accommodating actors & actresses when off stage; *greensand,* = g. earth, kind of sandstone largely of this earth, stratum largely of this sandstone; *greenshank,* large kind of sandpiper; *greensick(ness),* (affected with) CHLOROSIS; *g.-stick,* bone-fracture, esp. in children, in which one side of bone is broken & one only bent; *greenstone,* kinds of g. eruptive rock containing feldspar & hornblende, also kind of jade; *g.-stuff,* vegetation, g. vegetables; *greensward,* turf; *g. table,* gaming table; *greentail,* grannom; *g. tea,* made from steam-dried leaves; *greenweed,* kind of genista used for dyeing; *greenwood,* woodlands in summer, esp. as scene of outlaw life; *greenyard,* enclosure for stray beasts, pound; hence **gree·n**ISH[1](2), & (in comb. as *greeny-yellow*) **gree·n**Y[2], aa., **gree·n**LY[2] adv., **gree·n**NESS n. (N.) what is g., g. part of anything, g. colour, (*do you see any g.,* i. e. sign of gullibility, *in my eye?*); g. dye (usu. with epithet, as *mineral, Paris, g.*); vigour, youth, virility, (usu. *in the g.*); verdure, vegetation, also **gree·n**ERY n.; (pl.) g. vegetables before or after cooking; piece of public or common grassy land, grass-plot used for special purpose (esp. in comb. as *bleaching, bowling, putting, -g.*). [OE *gréne* cf. Du. *groen,* G *grün,* cogn. w. GROW]

green[2], v.i. & t. Become g., esp. with verdure; dye g., soil &c. with g.; (slang) hoax, take in. [OE *grénian* (prec.)]

gree·ner, n. (slang). Raw hand, esp.

newly arrived foreigner seeking work. [-ER[1]]

gree·ning, n. Kind of apple, green when ripe. [-ING[3]]

greenth, n. (rare). Verdure. [-TH[1]]

Greenwich (grĭ·nĭj), n. Town in Kent with State observatory (*G. time*, mean time for meridian of G., standard time in England & some other countries); *G. Hospital*, formerly used to accommodate old and disabled navy seamen (who are now out-pensioners), now occupied by the Royal Naval College for officer students.

greet[1], v.t. Accost with salutation; salute *with* words or gestures, receive on meeting or arrival *with* speech or action (friendly or not); (of cheers &c.) hail; (of sight &c.) meet (eye, ear). Hence **gree·t**ING[1] n. [com.-WG; OE *grœ́tan*, cf. Du. *groeten*, G *grüssen*, etym. dub.]

greet[2], v.i. (Sc.). Weep. [OE *grḗtan* & *grḗotan*]

gre·ffier, n. Registrar, notary, (esp. in foreign countries & Channel Islands). [F (*greffe* = OF *grafe* GRAFT[1], -IER)]

gregār·ious, a. Living in flocks or communities; fond of company; (Bot.) growing in clusters; of flocks, of crowds. Hence **gregar·ious**LY[2] adv., **gregar·ious**NESS n. [f. L *gregarius* (*grex -egis* flock, -ARY[1]) + -OUS]

grege (-āzh), a. & n. (Of) colour between grey & beige. [portmanteau wd]

Gregor·ian, a. & n. Of, according to, the plain-chant or plain-song ritual music named after Pope Gregory I (n., a G. chant); established by Pope Gregory XIII (*G.* CALENDAR, correction 1582 of the Julian; *G. style* = *new* STYLE; *G. epoch*, from 1582). [f. LL f. Gk *Grēgorios* Gregory + -AN]

grĕ·gory-powder, n. Compound powder of rhubarb, used as aperient. [J. *Gregory*, Scottish physician d. 1822]

grē·mial, n. Silk apron placed on bishop's lap at some ceremonies. [f. LL *gremialis* (L *gremium* lap, -AL)]

grena·de, n. Small explosive shell thrown by hand or (*rifle-g.*) shot from rifle-barrel; glass receptacle thrown to disperse chemicals for testing drains, extinguishing fires, &c. [F, f. Sp. *granada* POMEGRANATE]

grĕ·nadier·, n. (Orig.) soldier who threw grenades; (now) *Gg.* or *G. Guards*, first regiment of household infantry; S.-Afr. weaver-bird with red & black plumage. [F (prec., -IER)]

grĕ·nadīne[1], n. Dish of veal or poultry fillets, trimmed, larded, & glazed. [f. F *grenadin* perh. f. *grain* see GRAVY]

grĕ·nadīne[2], n. Dress-fabric of open silk or silk & wool. [F, perh. f. *Granada* Spanish city]

grĕ·nadine[3] (-ēn), n. French cordial syrup of pomegranate. [see POMEGRANATE]

gressor·ial, a. (zool.). Walking, adapted for walking. [f. L *gradi gress-* walk, -OR[2] -IAL]

grew. See GROW.

grey (-ā), **gray**, a. & n., & v.i. & t. Intermediate between black & white, coloured like ashes or lead, (*g. monk*, Cistercian; *g. friar*, Franciscan; *g. sister*, of third order of St Francis; *g. eye*, with g. iris; *g. mare is better horse*, wife rules husband); between light & dark, dull, clouded, depressing, dismal; (of person or his hair) turning white with age &c.; ancient, immemorial; belonging to old age, experienced, mature; *g. crow* or *g.-back*, hooded crow; *greybeard*, old man, large stoneware jug for spirit, kind of lichen; *g.-coat*, Cumberland yeoman; *g.-drake*, kind of ephemera; *g. goose*, GREYLAG; *g.-headed*, old, of long service *in*, ancient, time-worn; *g.-hen*, female of black grouse (cf. BLACK[1]*-cock*); *g. matter*, material of active part of brain; *greystone*, g. volcanic rock; hence **grey·**ISH[1](2) a., **grey·**LY[2] adv., **grey·**NESS n. (N.) g. clothes; cold sunless light; g. colour; g. pigment; g. horse (*the Gg.* or *Scots Gg.*, 2nd Dragoons). (Vb) become, make, g.; (Photog.) dull surface of (glass), give mezzotint effect to (photograph) by covering negative with such glass. [OE *grǣg*, cf. Du. *grauw*, G *grau*]

grey·hound, n. Slender long-legged keen-sighted swift dog used in coursing hares &c. (*ocean g.*, swift ship); *g.-racing*, modern sport in which mechanical hare is coursed by gg. as opportunity for betting. [OE *grighund* (*grig-* etym. dub., not connected w. GREY)]

grey·lag (goose), n. Common European wild goose. [*lag* said to refer to its staying long in England for a migrant]

grid, n. Frame of spaced parallel bars, grating, (Electr.) part of amplifying valve; network of lines, railways, electric-power connexions, &c.; gridiron (for cooking, & docking). [back formation f. GRIDIRON]

gri·ddle, n., & v.t. Circular iron plate for baking cakes on; miner's wire-bottomed screen (vb, screen with g.). [prob. f. OF *gredil* (cf. 16th-c. Norman *grédil* gridiron) perh. f. L *craticula* (*cratis* hurdle, -CULE)]

gride, v.i., & n. Cut, scrape, *along, through*, &c., with strident or grating sound (also *grides its way*); (n.) grating sound. [orig. sense *pierce*, prob. by metath. f. GIRD[2]]

grĭ·diron (-īrn), n. Barred metal cooking utensil for broiling; (Naut.) frame of parallel beams for supporting ship in dock; (Theatr.) plank structure over stage supporting mechanism for drop-scenes &c.; a naval evolution; (also *g.-pendulum*) compensation pendulum with parallel rods of different metals. [earlier *gredire* prob. = GRIDDLE, later confused w. *iron*, cf. ANDIRON]

grief, n. Deep or violent sorrow, keen regret, (*come to g.*, meet with disaster, fail, fall). [OF (*grever* GRIEVE)]

grie·vance, n. Real or fancied ground of complaint. [f. OF *grevance* (prec., -ANCE)]

grieve, v.t. & i. Give deep sorrow to; feel grief (*at, for, about, over*). [f. F *grever* f. L *gravare* (*gravis* heavy)]

grie·vous, a. Bringing serious trouble, injurious; (of pain &c.) severe; flagrant, heinous; exciting grief. Hence **grie·vous**LY[2] adv. [f. OF *grevos* (prec., -OUS)]

gri·ff(in[1]**),** n. (Anglo-Ind.). Newly arrived European, novice, greenhorn. Hence **gri·ffin**AGE(2), **gri·ffin**HOOD, **gri·ffin**SHIP, nn., **gri·ffin**ISH[1] a. [?]

gri·ffin[2]**, gri·ffon**[1]**, grȳ·phon,** n. Fabulous creature with eagle's head & wings & lion's body; *the Griffin*, monument on site of Temple Bar, London; (*-fon*) kind of vulture (also *g.-vulture*). [f. OF *grifoun* (L *gryphus* f. Gk *grups*, -OON)]

gri·ffon[2]**,** n. Kind of foreign coarse-haired terrier-like dog. [F, perh. = prec.]

grig, n. Small eel; grasshopper or cricket (*merry, lively, as a g.*; sense *cricket* doubtful, perh. invented to account for phrase). [?]

grill[1]**,** v.t. & i., & n. Broil (t. & i.) on gridiron (also fig. of torture or great heat), whence **gri·ll**ER[1](1, 2) n.; scallop (oysters &c.). (N.) grilled food; (also *g.-room*) room where steaks &c. are grilled & served. [f. F *griller* (foll.)]

grill[2]**,** n. Gridiron. [f. F *gril* (OF *grail* perh. as GRIDDLE)]

gri·llage, n. Heavy framework of cross-timbering as foundation for building in treacherous soil. [F (foll., -AGE)]

grille, grill[3]**,** n. Grating, latticed screen, esp. in door for observing callers, in convent separating nuns from visitors, formerly in front of ladies' gallery in House of Commons, &c.; (Tennis) square opening in wall; spawn-hatching frame. Hence **grill**ED[2] a. [F (*-e*), as GRIDDLE]

grilse, n. Young salmon that has been only once to the sea. [from 15th c.; etym. dub.]

grim, a. Stern, unrelenting, merciless, severe; of forbidding or harsh aspect (often of death; *hold on like g. death*, tight); sinister, ghastly, unmirthful, (*has a g. truth in it*; *a g. smile*; *g. laughter, pastime*, &c.). Hence **gri·m**LY[2] adv., **gri·m**NESS n. [cf. G *grimm*, also obs. *grame* angry]

grima·ce, n., & v.i. Wry face expressing annoyance &c. or meant to raise a laugh; affected look; use of such looks, affectation; (vb) make wry face. Hence or cogn. **grima·c**ER[1], **grima·c**IER, nn. [F, etym. dub.]

grima·lkin (-awl-, -ăl-,) n. Old she-cat; spiteful old woman. [prob. f. *grey* + *Malkin* (*Matilda*, -KIN)]

grime, n., & v.t. Soot, dirt, ingrained in some surface, esp. the skin; hence **gri·m**Y[2] a., **gri·mi**NESS n. (Vb) blacken, befoul. [cf. Flem. *grijm(en)*]

Grimm's law. See LAW.

grin, v.i. & t., & n. Show teeth in sign of pain or in forced or unrestrained or stupid smile (often *at*; *g. & bear it*, take pain &c. stoically; *g. like Cheshire cat*, constantly & meaninglessly; *g. through horse-collar*, in grimacing-match at rustic sports); express (contempt, satisfaction) by grinning; (n.) act of grinning (often *on the g.* or *broad g.*). [OE *grennian* cf. OHG *grennan* mutter]

grīnd, v.t. & i. (*ground*, pr. -ow-), & n. Reduce to small particles or powder by crushing between mill-stones, teeth, &c. (often *down, small, to pieces, into dust*, &c.); (quasi-pass.) admit of being ground (*will not g. fine*); oppress, harass with exactions, (often *down*; *a grinding tyranny*; also *g. the faces of* the poor &c.); produce (flour) by grinding; sharpen or smooth by friction (*has an* AXE *to g.*; *g. lenses, diamonds*, &c.); work (hand-mill); turn handle of (hurdy-gurdy; also abs.); produce, bring *out*, (music) from hurdy-gurdy; toil monotonously, study hard; teach (subject, pupil *in* it) laboriously; rub (t. & i.) gratingly *on, into*, or *against* (*ground his heel into it*; *ship was grinding on rocks*), rub (teeth) hard together (*g. out an oath*, utter while grinding teeth); *grindstone*, thick revolving stone disk for grinding, sharpening, & polishing (*hold, keep*, one's *nose to the grindstone*, make him work incessantly), kind of stone used for these. (N.) grinding; hard monotonous work or task; walk for exercise; steeplechase; (at Cambridge) a ferry. [only in E & in Du. *grenden*; perh. cogn. w. L *frendere* gnash teeth]

gri·nder, n. Molar tooth; grinding-machine; upper mill-stone; person who grinds (esp. in comb. as *organ, knife, -g.*); crammer. [-ER[1]]

grī·ndery, n. Cobblers' material of all kinds. [GRIND, -ERY; perh. extended f. the cobbler's whetstone]

grip[1]**,** n. Firm hold, tight grasp or clasp (*at, come to, gg.*, close combat), grasping power; way of clasping hands; control, mastery, intellectual hold; power of arresting attention; part in machinery &c. that clips, part of weapon &c. that is held; (U.S.) = GRIP[2]*sack*; *g.-brake*, worked by gripping with hand. [f. OE *gripe* grasp & *gripa* handful, both f. root of GRIPE]

grip[2]**,** v.t. & i. Seize, grasp, or hold, tightly; take firm hold; compel attention of; *gripsack* (U.S.), handbag. Hence **gri·pp**ER[1](2) n. [cf. MHG *gripfen*; cogn. w. GRIPE]

grip[3]**,** n. Small open ditch. [OE *grype* cogn. w. *grēop* burrow]

gripe, v.t. & i., & n. Clutch, grip; oppress, pinch; affect with colic pains; (Naut.) secure with gg., (of ship) come up into wind in spite of helm. (N.) act of griping, clutch; hold, control, (*in the g. of*); (pl.)

colic pains; handle of implement or weapon; (Naut., pl.) lashings securing boat in its place; *g.-water*, horse-medicine for colic. [com.-Teut.; OE *gripan*, cf. Du. *grijpen*, G *greifen*]

grippe, n. Influenza. [F]

grisai·lle (-zāl, or as F), n. Method of decorative painting, stained-glass window &c., in grey monochrome representing objects in relief. [F (*gris* grey f. OHG *grîs*)]

gri·seous (-zĭ-), a. (bot., zool.). Bluish or pearl grey. [f. med.L *griseus* (prec.), -OUS]

grise·tte (-z-), n. French working-class girl (formerly dressed in grey). [F (*gris* see GRISAILLE, -ETTE)]

gri·skin, n. Lean part of loin of bacon pig. [perh. f. obs. *grice* f. ON *griss* young pig + -KIN]

gri·sly (-z-), a. Causing horror, terror, or superstitious dread. [OE *grislic*; cf. obs. *grise* to shudder]

grist[1], n. Corn for grinding (*brings g. to the mill*, is profitable; *all is g. that comes to his mill*, he utilizes everything); malt crushed for brewing. [OE *grist* (GRIND, cf. BLAST f. BLOW)]

grist[2], n. Size or thickness of yarn or rope. [perh. cogn. w. GIRD[1]]

gri·stle (-sl), n. Whitish tough flexible tissue in vertebrates, cartilage, (*in the g.*, immature—infants having g. for bone). Hence **gri·stl**Y[2] a. [OE, cf. OFris. & MLG *gristel*, etym. dub.]

grit[1], n. Small particles of stone or sand, esp. as causing discomfort or clogging machinery &c., whence **gri·tt**Y[2] a., **gri·tt**INESS n.; (also *gritstone*) coarse sandstone; grain or texture of stone; (colloq.) strength of character, pluck, endurance. [OE *gréot*, cf. G *griess*]

grit[2], v.i. & t. Produce, move with, grating sound; grind (teeth). [f. prec.]

grits, n. pl. Husked but unground oats; coarse oatmeal. [OE *grytt*(*e*), cf. G *grütze*, cogn. w. GROATS]

gri·zzled, a. Grey(-haired). [f. obs. *grizzle* grey, grey hair, + -ED[2]]

gri·zzly, a. & n. Grey, greyish, grey-haired, (*g. bear*, large fierce N.-Amer. kind); *g. king, queen*, fishing-flies; (n.) g. bear. [prec., -Y[2]]

groan, v.i. & t., & n. (Make) deep inarticulate sound expressing pain, grief, or disapproval (*g. inwardly*, be distressed); utter with gg. (often *out*); be oppressed or loaded *under, beneath, with*, (*g. under injustice*; *shelf groans with books*; *groaning board*, well-loaded table); long *for*; *g. down*, silence (speaker) with gg. Hence **groa·ning**LY[2] adv. [OE *grânian* cogn. w. GRIN]

groat, n. (hist.). Silver coin = 4*d.* issued 1351–1662 (occasionally used of the fourpenny piece 1836–56); small sum (*don't care a g.*). [f. MDu. *groot* orig. great, in sense *thick* (*penny*), cf. GROSCHEN]

groats, n. pl. Hulled (sometimes also crushed) grain, esp. oats. [cogn. w. obs. OE *grot* fragment & GRITS]

Grō·bian, n. Clownish slovenly person. [G, f. med.L *Grobianus* used as typical name]

gro·cer, n. Dealer in spices, dried fruits, sugar, & miscellaneous domestic stores (*g.'s itch*, eczema caused by handling sugar). Hence **gro·**CERY(2, &, usu. pl., 1) n. [orig. one who sells in the gross, f. OF *grossier* f. med.L *grossarius* (GROSS, -ARY[1])]

grog, n., & v.i. & t. Drink of spirit & water; social meeting with g.; *g.-blossom*, pimple or redness on nose from intemperance. (Vb) drink g.; extract spirit from (empty cask) by pouring in hot water. [perh. short for GROGRAM, nickname (from his cloak) of Adm. Vernon, who first had g. served out instead of neat rum]

gro·ggy, a. Drunk(en); bibulous; (of horse) weak in forelegs, tottering; unsteady, shaky. Hence **gro·gg**INESS n. [-Y[2]]

grŏ·gram, n. Coarse fabric of silk, mohair & wool, or these mixed, often stiffened with gum. [f. F *gros grain* large grain]

groin, n., & v.t. Depression between belly & thigh; (Arch.) edge formed by intersecting vaults, fillet covering this, (vb, build with gg.), whence **groi·**NING[1](6) n. [earlier *grynde* etym. dub.; cf. OE *grynde* abyss cogn. w. GROUND]

gro·mwell, n. Kinds of plant with stony seeds formerly used in medicine. [f. OF *gromil* etym. dub.]

groom, n., & v.t. One of certain officers of Royal Household (*G. of the stole, in waiting*, &c.); servant having care of horses (vb, curry, feed, tend, &c.; also in p.p. of persons, as *well groomed*, neatly got up, esp. with well-trimmed hair, beard, &c.); bridegroom (rare); *groomsman*, unmarried friend officially attending bridegroom at wedding. [perh. shortened f. OF *gromet* (also GOURMET) servant, etym. dub.]

groove, n., & v.t. Channel or hollow, esp. one made to direct motion or receive corresponding ridge (vb, make g. or gg. in); piece of routine, undeviating course, rut, whence **groo·v**Y[2] a., **groovi·**NESS n. [f. Du. *groeve* furrow, cf. G *grube* pit, cogn. w. GRAVE[1]]

grope, v.i. Feel about as in dark (*for, after*, or abs.), search blindly (lit. & fig.); *g. one's way*, find it by feeling, proceed tentatively. Hence **gro·ping**LY[2] adv. [OE *grápian* (*gráp* a grasp) cogn. w. GRIP]

grō·sbeak, n. Kinds of small bird with large strong beak, esp. the hawfinch. [f. F *grosbec* (GROSS[2], BEAK)]

gro·schen (-ōshn), n. Small obsolete silver German coin. [G]

gros de Naples (grō·denah·pl), n. Heavy silk fabric. [F (*gros* GROSS[2], *Naples*)]

grōss[1], n. (pl. *gross*). Twelve dozen. [f. F *grosse* orig. fem. of *gros* GROSS[2]]

grōss[2], a. Luxuriant, rank; overfed, bloated, repulsively fat; flagrant, glaring; total, without deductions, not net; dense, thick, solid, not ethereal, transparent, or impalpable; (of food) coarse, greasy, uncleanly, repulsive, (*g. feeder*, one who likes such food); (of senses &c.) not delicate, dull; coarse in manners or morals, unrefined, indecent; (abs.) *in* (*the*) *g.*, in a general way, apart from detail, on the whole. Hence **gro·ss**LY[2] adv., **gro·ss**NESS n. [f. F *gros grosse* big f. LL *grossus* etym. dub.]

grot, n. (poet.). Grotto. [f. F *grotte* GROTTO]

grote·sque (-k), n. & a. Decorative painting or sculpture with fantastic interweaving of human & animal forms with foliage; (pop.) comically distorted figure or design. (Adj.): (Arch.) in the above style; distorted, bizarre; ludicrous from incongruity, absurd; hence **grote·sque**LY[2] adv., **grote·sque**NESS, **grote·squerie** [-ERY(5)], nn. [f. F *crotesque* f. It. *grottesca* antique work (GROTTO, -ESQUE) perh. because *grotta* was used of excavated chambers with mural paintings]

gro·tto, n. (pl. *-oes, -os*). Picturesque cave; artificial ornamental cave, room &c. adorned with shells &c. in imitation of cave, as cool retreat (*the G.*, London streetboys' celebration on 5th Aug. of end of close time for oysters). Hence **gro·tto**ED[2] a. [f. It. *grotta* f. L f. Gk *kruptē* vault (*kruptō* hide) cf. CRYPT]

ground[1] (-ow-), n. Bottom of sea (now chiefly fig., as *touch g.*, come to something solid after vague talk &c.; of ship, *take g.*, strand), (pl.) dregs, esp. of coffee, whence **grou·nd**Y[2] a.; (Electr.) = EARTH[1]; base, foundation, motive, valid reason, (*on the g. of*, by reason or under pretext of; *on public* &c. *gg.*), whence **grou·nd**LESS a., **grou·ndless**LY[2] adv., **grou·ndless**NESS n.; substratum, underlying part, surface worked upon in embroidery, painting, &c., undecorated part, prevailing colour or tone, (Etching) composition spread on metal & cut through with needle where acid is to act; surface of earth (*fall, be dashed, to the g.*, be abandoned, fail, of scheme, hope; BREAK[1] *g.*; *down to the g.*, colloq., in all respects, thoroughly; *above g.*, alive; *cut the g. from under* one's *feet*, anticipate & stultify his arguments or plans); (pl.) enclosed land for ornament or recreation attached to house; position, area, or distance, on earth's surface (*cover much g.*, of inquiry, report, &c., be far-reaching; *stand, shift*, one's *g.*, maintain, change, one's argument or intention; *gain g.*, advance; *lose, give, g.*, retreat, decline); area of special kind or use (*fishing-gg.*; *forbidden g.*, subject that must be avoided; *classic g.*, historic place; *cricket* &c. *-g.*); person's property in land; (Cricket) *his* &c. *g.*, behind popping-crease (*in, out of*, his *g.*), paid staff of players attached to club; (in names of birds) terrestrial, (of beasts) burrowing or lying on g., (of plants) dwarfish or trailing; *g.-ash*, ash sapling, walking-stick of this; *g.-bait* n. & v.t., (prepare with) bait thrown to bottom of intended fishing-g. to attract fish; *g.-box*, small BOX[1] used to edge garden beds; *g.-colour*, first coat of paint, prevailing colour on which design is done; *g.-fish*, living at bottom; *g.-fishing*, with bait near bottom; *g. floor*, rooms &c. on level of outside g. (*get in on the g.-f.*, be admitted to company &c. on same terms as promoters); *g. game*, hares, rabbits, &c.; *g.-gudgeon*, loach; *g.-hog*, Amer. marmot; *g.-ice*, formed at bottom of water, anchor-ice; *g. ivy*, ale-hoof, creeping herb with bluish-purple flower & kidney-shaped leaf; *g. landlord*, owner of g. leased for building; *g.-man* (in charge of cricket &c. g.); *g.-note*, on which a common chord is built, fundamental bass; *g.-nut*, (edible tuber of) N.-Amer. wild bean, also W.-Ind. & W.-Afr. pea with pod ripening under g.; *g.-pine*, herb with resinous smell, also clubmoss; *g.-plan*, plane drawing of divisions of building at g. level, also outline or general design of anything; *g.-rent*, that paid to g.-landlord; *g. sea*, heavy sea without apparent cause; *groundsman* = *g.-man*; *g. swell*, heavy sea caused by distant or past storm or earthquake; *g. torpedo*, fixed to bottom of sea; *groundwork*, foundation or basis (usu. fig.), chief ingredient, general surface of thing showing where not overlaid with embroidery or other ornament. [com.-Teut.; OE & G *grund*, cf. Du. *grond*]

ground[2], v.t. & i. Base, establish, (institution, principle, belief) *on* some fact or authority (in pass. also *in*; p.p., *well, ill*, &c., founded, also abs. = well founded, whence **grou·nded**LY[2] adv.); instruct thoroughly (*in* elements), whence **grou·nd**ING[1] n.; prepare g. of (embroidery &c.); lay (esp. arms) on g., (Electr.) connect with earth as conductor; alight on g.; run (t. & i.) ashore, strand. [f. prec.]

ground[3], p.p. of GRIND. *G. glass*, made non-transparent by grinding.

grou·ndage (-ĭj), n. Duty on ship lying on beach or entering port. [-AGE]

grou·ndling, n. Kinds of GROUND[1]*-fish*; creeping or dwarf plant; spectator or reader of inferior taste (ref. to *Hamlet* III. ii. 12). [-LING[1]]

grou·ndsel[1] (-ow-), n. Kinds of weed, of which the commonest is used as food for cage-birds. [OE *gundæswelgiæ* perh. f. *gund* pus, SWALLOW[1], = pus-absorber, as being used for poultices, later assimilated to *ground*]

grou·ndsel[2], n. (archaic). Timber serving as foundation, lowest part of wooden framework; threshold. [SILL]

group (-ōōp), n., & v.t. & i. (Fine arts) two or more figures or objects forming complete design or distinct part of one; number of persons or things standing near together, knot, cluster; number of persons or things belonging or classed together (in Pol., used of smaller unit than the party, & esp. in assemblies where the two-party system does not prevail; in scientific classification, used vaguely of cross-divisions outside the regular hierarchy of class-terms); *g.-captain*, officer of AIR[1] *Force*. (Vb) form (t. & rarely i.) into a g., place in a g. *with*; form (t. & i. of colours, figures, &c.) into well-arranged & harmonious whole; classify. Hence **grou·p**AGE(3) n. [f. F *groupe* f. It. *gruppo* prob. f. Teut. (CROP[1])]

grou·per (-ōō-), n. Kinds of W.-Ind. & Austral. fish. [f. Port. *garupa* (prob. S.-Amer.)]

grouse[1] (-ows), n. (pl. *grouse*). (Prop.) any gallinaceous bird with feathered feet; (pop.) Moor Fowl or Game or Red G., reddish game-bird of British Isles (*Black G.*, BLACK[1] *game*; *Wood* or *Great G.*, capercailye; *White G.*, ptarmigan), its flesh. [?]

grouse[2] (-ows), v.i., & n., (slang). Grumble. [?]

grout[1] (-owt), n., & v.t. Thin fluid mortar for filling interstices; (vb) finish with this. [cf. 16th-c. F *grouter*]

grout[2] (-owt), v.i. & t. (Of pigs) turn up earth, turn up (earth &c.), with snout. [perh. f. obs. *groot* mud cogn. w. OE *grēot* GRIT]

grove, n. Small wood, group of trees, (in Bible, mistransl. of Hebrew word = pillar used as idol, or name of goddess). Hence **grove**D[2], **gro·ve**LESS, **gro·v**Y[2], aa. [excl. E, OE *grāf*]

grŏ·vel, v.i. (-ll-), Lie prone, humble oneself, (often *in the dirt* or *dust*); (part.) abject, low, base, whence **gro·velling**LY[2] adv. Hence **gro·vell**ER[1] n. [back formation f. obs. *grovelling* adv. (obs. *on grufe* f. ON *á grúfu* on one's face, -LING[2]) taken as part. in *lay grovelling* &c.]

grow (-ō), v.i. & t. (*grew*, *grown* p.p. often as act. intr. with *is*, cf. -ED[1](2), & as adj.). Develop or exist as living plant (also joc. of lifeless things &c., be found in some place; *g. into one*, *together*, &c., coalesce), germinate, sprout, spring up, be produced, come naturally into existence, arise; increase in size, height (*grow*ING[1] *pains*, neuralgic pains in limbs of the young), quantity, degree, power, &c. (*g. downwards*, diminish; *habit*, *person*, *picture*, &c., *grows on* one, becomes more influential with or admired by him), whence **grow·ing**LY[2] adv.; become gradually (*g. rich*); *g. up*, advance to maturity (*grown-up* a. & n., adult), emerge from soil, reach full size, (of custom) arise, become common; produce by cultivation, bring forth, let (beard &c.) g., whence **grow·**ABLE a.; (pass.) be covered (often *up* or *over*) with some growth. [OE *grōwan* cf. Du. *groeien* f. OTeut. *grô-* cogn. w. GRASS]

grow·er, n. Plant that grows in specified way (*fast*, *free*, &c., *g.*); person growing produce (often in comb., as *fruit-g.*). [-ER[1]]

growl (-owl), v.i. & t., & n. (Make) guttural sound of anger (*at*); rumble; murmur angrily, angry murmur, complain(t); utter with a g. (*out*). Hence **grow·ling**LY[2] adv. [prob. imit.]

grow·ler, n. In vbl senses; also: four-wheeled cab; kinds of fish. [-ER[1]]

grow·lery, n. Growling; place to growl in, private room, den. [-ERY; cf. BOUDOIR]

grown, p.p. of GROW. *G. man* &c., mature.

growth, n. Growing, development, increase, (*of foreign* &c. *g.*, grown abroad &c.; *full g.*, size ultimately attained); cultivation *of* produce; what has grown or is growing, (Path.) morbid formation. [-TH[1]]

groyne, n., & v.t. Timber framework or low broad wall run out to check drifting of beach & so stop encroachment of sea; (vb) supply (beach) with gg. [perh. f. obs. *groin* snout f. OF *groign* (L *grunnire* grunt)]

grub[1], n. Larva of insect, caterpillar, maggot; dull drudge, literary hack, sloven, smug; ball bowled along ground at cricket; (slang) food, a feed. [perh. f. foll.]

grub[2], v.i. & t. Dig (t. & i.) superficially; clear (ground) of roots & stumps, clear away (roots &c.), (often *up*); fetch *up* or *out* by digging (fig., discover in books &c.); search, rummage, (intr.); plod, toil, *on*, *along*, *away*; (slang) feed, provide (boarder &c.) with food, [prob. f. prec.]; *g.-axe*, *-hoe*, *-hook*, for grubbing up stumps. Hence (-)**gru·bb**ER[1](1, 2) n. [prob. cogn. w. GRAVE[2]; cf. ON *gryfja* pit]

gru·bby, a. Of, infested with, grubs; dirty, grimy, slovenly, whence **gru·bbi**NESS n. [-Y[2]]

Gru·b-street, n. & a. (Region inhabited by) the tribe of needy authors & literary hacks; (adj.) of these. [a London street (now Milton St) so inhabited in 17th c.]

grudge, v.t., & n. Be unwilling to give, grant, or allow (thing, person thing, thing *to* person), or *to* do; (part.) reluctant, whence **gru·dging**LY[2] adv.; (n.) feeling of resentment or ill will (*have a g. against*; *bear*, *owe*, one *a g.*). [earlier *grutch* f. OF *groucier* etym. dub.]

gru·el, n., & v.t. (-ll-). Liquid food chiefly for invalids of oatmeal &c. boiled in milk or water (*have*, *get*, one's *g.*, be punished, severely defeated, or killed; so *give* one his *g.*, & *g.* vb slang in same sense, whence **gru·ell**ING[1] n.). [OF, f. med.L **grutellum* dim. of *grutum* f. Teut. cf. OE *grút* coarse meal, & GROATS]

grue·some, a. Grisly, disgusting. Hence **grue·some**LY[2] adv., **grue·some**NESS n. [f. obs. *grue* to shudder cf. G *grauen* + -SOME]

gruff, a. Surly, laconic, rough-mannered, rough-voiced. Hence **gru·ff**LY[2] adv., **gru·ff**NESS n., **gru·ff**ISH[1](2) a. [cf. G. *grob*]

gru·mble, v.i. & t., & n. (Utter) dull inarticulate sound, murmur, growl faintly; rumble; complain(t) (*at*, *about*, *over*); utter complainingly (often *out*). Hence **gru·mbl**ER[1] n., **gru·mbling**LY[2] adv. [cf. F *grommeler*, Du. *grommelen*, G *grummeln*]

grume, n. (med.). Clot of blood, viscous fluid. So **gru·m**OUS a. [f. LL *grumus* small heap]

gru·mmet, n. (naut.). Ring usu. of twisted rope as fastening, rowlock, wad, &c. [f. 15th-c. F *gromette* curb (*gourmer* to curb, etym. dub.)]

gru·mpy, gru·mpish, a. Ill-tempered, surly. Hence **gru·mpi**LY[2] adv., **gru·mpi**NESS n. [f. obs. *grump* offence, snub, etym. dub.]

Gru·ndyism, n. Conventional propriety, prudery. [f. 'What will Mrs Grundy (a neighbour) say?' in Morton's *Speed the Plough* 1798]

grunt, v.i. & t., & n. (Utter) low gruff sound characteristic of hogs; express discontent, dissent, fatigue, &c., by this; utter with g. (often *out*). Hence **gru·nting**LY[2] adv. [OE *grunettan* (cf. G *grunzen*) frequent. of *grunian* imit.]

gru·nter, n. In vbl senses; esp.: pig; kinds of fish. [-ER[1]]

gru·yère (-yār), n. Swiss pale cows'-milk cheese with many cavities. [*G.*, Swiss town]

grȳ·sbok, n. Small grey S.-Afr. antelope. [f. Du. *grijsbok* (*grijs* grey, BUCK[1])]

guacho, incorrect for GAUCHO.

guai·ac(um) (gwī-), n. Genus of W.-Ind. trees & shrubs (*-um* only); brownish-green wood of two kinds of these used in medicine, lignum vitae; resin from these, drug made from it. [*-um* mod.L f. Sp. *guayaco* of Haytian orig.]

guan (gwahn), n. Kinds of S.-Amer. gallinaceous bird allied to curassow. [prob. native]

guana (gwah·na), n. Iguana; any large lizard. [var. of IGUANA]

guana·co (gwanah-), n. Wild llama with reddish-brown wool. [native S.-Amer. *huanaco*]

gua·no (gwah-), n., & v.t. Excrement of sea-fowl found esp. in islands about Peru used as manure; artificial manure esp. that made from fish; (vb) fertilize with g. [Sp., f. native *huanu*]

guarantee· (gă-), n., & v.t. Person making guaranty or giving security; guaranty; thing given or existing as security for fulfilment of conditions or permanence &c. of something; person to whom guaranty is given [correl. to *guarantor*; prop. a separate formation with -EE]; *g. fund*, sum pledged as contingent indemnity for loss. (Vb) be g. for, answer for due fulfilment of (contract &c.) or genuineness &c. of (article), assure permanence &c. of; engage *that* something has happened or will happen; secure possession of *to* person; secure *against* or *from* (risk &c.), or *in* (possession &c.); hence **gua·rant**OR[2] n. [in first sense, orig. *garanté*, prob. f. Sp. *garante* = F *garant* WARRANT[1]; other senses of n. by confusion w. foll. or misuse of -EE]

gua·ranty (gă-), n., & v.t. Undertaking written or other to answer for payment of debt or performance of obligation by another person liable in first instance; ground or basis of security; (vb) guarantee (now rare). [f. AF *guarantie* (*guarant* WARRANT)]

guard[1] (gard), n. Defensive posture or motion in fencing, boxing, &c. (in cricket, position of bat to defend wicket; *take*, *give*, *g.*, of batsman, umpire, ascertaining correct spot on ground for this); watch, vigilant state, (*keep g.*, *be on g.*, act as sentry &c.; *on*, *off*, one's *g.*, prepared, unprepared, against attack, surprise, or one's own impulses &c.); protector, defender, sentry, official in charge of stage-coach or train, (pl.) household troops (including *Foot-gg.*, *Horse-gg.*, *Life-gg.*, & by extension seven regiments of *Dragoon Gg.*); body of soldiers &c. serving as protectors of place or person, escort, separate portion of army, &c. (*advance*, *rear*, *-g.*; *g. of honour*; *mount*, *relieve*, *g.*, earlier *the g.*, take up, take others' place in, sentry duty); contrivance to prevent injury or accident (often in comb., as *fire*, *trigger*, *-g.*); *g.-boat*, boat going rounds of fleet in harbour to see that good watch is kept, also official harbour boat enforcing quarantine or customs regulations; *g.-chain*, securing watch, brooch, &c.; *g.-house*, accommodating military g. or securing prisoners; *g.-rail*, hand or other rail to prevent falling &c.; *g.-ring*, preventing other ring from slipping off finger, keeper; *g.-room*, as *g.-house* above; *g.-ship*, warship protecting harbour & receiving seamen till they can join their ships; *guardsman*, soldier, esp. officer, of Gg.; *g.-tent*, as *g.-house* above. Hence **guar·d**LESS a. [f. F *garde* f. Teut. see WARD]

guard[2], v.t. & i. Keep safe, stand g. over, keep (door &c.) so as to control passage, protect, defend (*from*, *against*); secure by explanations or stipulations &c. from misunderstanding or abuse, (Med.) administer correctives with (drug); keep (thoughts, speech) in check (*guarded language* &c., cautious, measured), whence **guar·ded**LY[2] adv., **guar·ded**NESS n.; use a fencing g.; take precautions *against*; (Curling, Bowling) protect (stone, bowl) by placing one's own between it & later player, (Chess) protect (piece, pawn) with another. [f. prec.]

guar·dian (gar-), n. Keeper, defender, protector, (*G. of the poor*, or *G.*, member of Board elected to administer poor-laws in parish or district); (Law) one having custody of person or property or both of infant, idiot, &c. (cf. WARD); superior of Franciscan convent; *g. angel*, spirit watching over person or place. [f. OF *g(u)arden* (*garde* GUARD[1])]

guar·dianship, n. Office of guardian, legal tutelage; keeping, guard, (*under the g. of the laws*). [-SHIP]

gua·va (gwah-), n. (Tropical myrtaceous tree yielding) acid fruit used for making jelly. [f. Sp. *guayaba* prob. f. S.-Amer. or W.-Ind. name]

gūbernator·ial, a. Of a governor. [f. L *gubernator* GOVERNOR + -IAL]

gudgeon[1] (gŭ·jn), n. Small freshwater fish used as bait; credulous person. [f. F *goujon* f. L *gobionem* nom. *-o* GOBY]

gudgeon[2] (gŭ·jn), n. Pivot at end of beam, axle, &c., on which bell, wheel, &c., works; ring of gate fitting on hook of post; socket in which rudder works; pin holding two blocks of stone &c. together; *g.-pin*, (esp.) that holding piston & connecting-rod together. [f. OF *gojon* perh. = prec.]

Guebre (gē·b*er*, gā·-), n. Zoroastrian, fire-worshipper, Parsee. [f. F *guèbre* f. Pers. *gabr*]

gue·lder rose (gĕ-), n. Plant with round bunches of white flowers, snowball tree. [*Guelders* in Prussia]

Guelph, -lf, (gw-), n. Member of medieval Italian party supporting Pope against Emperor (cf. GHIBELLINE). Hence **Gue·lph**IC a. [f. It. *Guelfo* f. MHG *Welf* name (of founder of princely family of Guelphs, ancestors of British Royal Family) used as war-cry at battle of Weinsberg 1140 against Conrad III]

guerdon (ger·dn), n., & v.t., (poet.). Reward, recompense. Hence **guer·don**LESS a. [OF, f. med. L *widerdonum* f. OHG *widarlôn* (*wider* again, LOAN) w. assim. to L *donum* gift]

Guer·nsey (-z-), n. One of Channel Islands; (also *G. shirt, coat, frock*) thick knitted woollen usu. blue outer tunic or jersey worn by sailors, workmen, & children; G. cow; *G. lily*, kind of amaryllis orig. from Japan.

guer(r)i·lla (ge-), n. (Usu. now *g. war*) irregular war waged by small bodies acting independently; man engaged in this. [Sp. (*-rr-*) dim. of *guerra* WAR]

guess (gĕs), v.t. & i., & n. Estimate without measurement or detailed calculation; think likely, think one divines nature of, form hypothesis as to, conjecture, hazard opinion about, (noun, *that, how, when, whether*, &c., thing *to be*; also intr. with *at*; often abs. in parenthesis; *I g.*, chiefly U.S., I feel sure or know well); conjecture (answer to riddle, solution of problem) rightly, divine. (N.) rough estimate, conjecture, hypothesis, (*by g.*, at haphazard); *g.-work*, (procedure based on) guessing; OTHER-*g*. [n. f. vb, ME *gessen* cf. Du. *gissen*; f. root of GET]

guest (gĕ-), n. Person entertained at another's house or table (*paying g.*, boarder); person lodging at hotel, boarding-house, &c.; animal or vegetable parasite (cf. HOST[2]); *g.-chamber*, kept for gg.; *g.-night*, on which gg. are entertained at club, college, &c. Hence **gue·st**SHIP n. [W Aryan; OE *giest* cf. ON *gestr*, G *gast*, & L *hostis* enemy, orig. stranger]

gue·st-rope, gue·ss-, n. Second rope fastened to boat in tow to steady it; rope slung outside ship to give hold for boats coming alongside. [?]

guffaw·, n., & v.i. & t. Coarse or boisterous laugh; (vb) make, say with, g. [orig. Sc.; imit.]

guggle. = GURGLE.

guide[1] (gīd), n. One who shows the way; hired conductor of traveller or tourist; (Mil.) one of company formed for reconnoitring &c.; (Mil.) *right* & *left g.*, subalterns of company superintending & acting as pivots &c. in evolutions; (Naut.) ship on which rest of fleet regulate their movements; adviser; directing principle or standard (*the feelings are a bad g.*; *Scripture is our g.*); book of rudiments, manual, (also *g.-book*) book of information on a city, cathedral, museum, &c., (*to*); (Mech.) bar, rod, &c., directing motion of something, gauge &c. controlling tool; thing marking a position or guiding the eye; *g.-post*, FINGER-*post*; *g.-rope*, GUY[1], also small rope attached to load of crane to guide it; *guideway*, groove, track. Hence **gui·de**LESS a. [F, orig. fem., f. OF *guie* (by assim. to Pr. or It. *guida*) f. *guier* to guide prob. f. Teut. cogn. w. OE *witan* know]

guide[2], v.t. Act as g. to, go before, lead, direct course of; arrange course of (events); be the principle, motive, or ground, of (action, judgement, &c.); conduct affairs of (State &c.); *guiding-stick*, mahlstick. Hence **gui·d**ABLE a., **gui·d**ANCE n. [f. F *guider* f. OF *guier* as prec.]

guidon (gī·dn), n. Pennant narrowing to point at free end (used as standard of dragoons). [F, f. It. *guidone* perh. f. *guida* GUIDE[1]]

g(u)ild (gi-), n. Society for mutual aid or prosecution of common object; *G.-hall*, in which a medieval g. met, (often, from being used as meeting-place of Corporation) town-hall; *the G.-hall*, hall of the Corporation of the City of London, used for state banquets, municipal meetings, &c.; *g. socialism*, system by which the resources, methods, & profits, of each industry should be controlled by a council of its members. [OE *gild* guild, payment, sacrifice, cf. Du. & G *geld* money]

gui·lder (gĭ-), n. Obsolete coin gold of Netherlands &c.; Dutch silver coin = 1/8. [corruption of Du. *gulden*]

guile (gīl), n. Treachery, deceit, cunning devices. Hence **gui·le**FUL a., **gui·leful**LY[2] adv., **gui·leful**NESS n., **gui·le**LESS a., **gui·leless**LY[2] adv., **gui·leless**NESS n. [OF, prob. f. Teut.; cf. WILE]

gui·llĕmot (gĭ-), n. Kinds of sea-bird. [F, prob. f. *Guillaume* William]

guilloche (gĭlō·sh, or as F), n. Architectural ornament imitating braided ribbons [f. F *guillochis*, or f. F *guilloche* the tool used]

guillotine (gĭ·lotēn, *or* tē·n), n., & v.t. Machine with knife-blade sliding in grooves for beheading; surgical instrument for excising uvula &c., kinds of machine for cutting paper &c.; (Parl.) method of preventing obstruction by fixing times at which parts of Bill must be voted on; (vb) use the g. upon. [F (*Guillotin* inventor 1789)]

guilt (gĭ-), n. The having committed a specified or implied offence; criminality, culpability. [excl. E; OE *gylt*]

gui·ltless, a. Innocent (often *of* offence); not having knowledge or possession *of* (*g. of Greek, soap, moustache*, &c.). Hence **gui·ltless**LY[2] adv., **gui·ltless**NESS n. [-LESS]

gui·lty, a. Criminal, culpable; conscious of, prompted by, guilt (*g. conscience, behaviour, look*); having committed a particular offence (*of*; *g., not g.*, verdicts in criminal trials). Hence **gui·lti**LY[2] adv., **gui·lti**NESS n. [-Y[2]]

guimp. = GIMP.

Guinea, g-, (gĭ·nĭ), n. Part of W. coast of Africa; (*g-*) former gold coin named as first coined for the African trade (1663–1717 nominally 20/- but of fluctuating value; from 1717 fixed at 21/-; last coined 1813), & now money of account 21/- used in stating professional fees, amount of subscriptions, & prices of pictures, horses, estates, &c.; *g.-fowl, -hen*, gallinaceous bird with slate-coloured white-spotted plumage domesticated in Europe; *G.* GRAINS; *g.-pig*, S.-Amer. rodent now half-domesticated in Europe &c. as pet (origin of name doubtful), person receiving g. fees, esp. company director or deputy clergyman, whence **gui·nea-pigg**ING[1] n.; *G. worm*, tropical parasite in human skin. [f. Port. *Guiné*]

guipure (gē·poor, or as F), n. Kind of lace; kind of gimp. [F]

guise (gīz), n. Style of attire, garb, (archaic); external appearance; semblance, assumed appearance, pretence, (*under, in, the g. of*). [F, f. Teut. (WISE[1])]

guitar (gĭ-), n., & v.i. (-rr-). Six-stringed lute played with hand with fretted fingerboard; hence **guitar**·IST(3) n. (Vb) play g. [f. Sp. *guitarra* f. Gk *kithara*; cf. CITHER, GITTERN]

gŭlch (-tsh), n. (U.S.). Ravine, esp. one with gold deposit. [perh. f. obs. *gulch* to swallow]

gu·lden (gōō-), n. Dutch & Austro-Hung. silver coin 1/8. [Du. & G, = golden (orig. name of various gold coins)]

gules, n., & a. (usu. after noun), (herald.). Red. [f. OF *goules* pl. ermine dyed red]

gulf, n., & v.t. (Geog.) portion of sea, proportionally narrower at mouth than bay, partly surrounded by coast; deep hollow, chasm, abyss, (poet.) profound depth or the sea; whirlpool, what swallows up anything; impassable dividing line (*Luke* xvi. 26); (Univ. slang) degree allowed to honour-candidate who fails but deserves pass; *G.-stream*, oceanic warm current issuing from G. of Mexico. (Vb) engulf, swallow up; (Univ.) give g. to. [f. F *golfe* f. Pr. *golfo* f. late Gk *kolphos* (Gk *kolpos*)]

gull[1], n. Kinds of long-winged web-footed mostly marine bird, usu. white with mantle varying from pearl-grey to black, & bright bill. Hence **gu·ll**ERY(3) n. [perh. f. W *gŵylan*]

gull[2], n., & v.t. Dupe, fool. So **gu·ll**IBLE a., **gull**IBI·LITY n., **gu·ll**ISH[1] a. [perh. vb f. n. in fig. sense of prec.; perh. n. f. vb in fig. sense of obs. *gull* to gorge, cf. *cram* & *stuff* = take in]

gu·llet, n. Food-passage from mouth to stomach, oesophagus; throat; water-channel, strait, defile, (archaic & dial.). [f. OF dim. of *gole* (now *gueule*) f. L *gula*]

gu·lly[1], n., & v.t. Water-worn ravine; deep artificial channel, gutter, drain, sink; *g.-drain*, to sewer from *g.-hole*, opening in street for drainage; *g.-trap*, anti-gas TRAP[1] in g.-drains; (vb) make gg. in, form (channels) by water action. [prob. f. prec.]

gu·lly[2], n. Large knife. [perh. orig. butcher's for cutting *gullet*]

gūlŏ·sity, n. (rare). Gluttony. [f. LL *gulositas* (L *gulosus* gluttonous f. *gula* GULLET)]

gulp, v.t. & i., & n. Swallow (usu. *down*) hastily, greedily, or with effort (*g. down sobs, tears*, suppress them); perform act of swallowing with difficulty, gasp, choke; hence **gu·lping**LY[2] adv. (N.) act of gulping (*drained it at one g.*); effort to swallow; large mouthful; hence **gu·lp**Y[2] a. [imit., cf. Du. *gulpen*]

gum[1], n. (usu. pl.). Firm flesh in which the teeth stand; *gumboil*, small abscess on gg. [OE *góma* cf. G *gaumen*]

gum², n., & v.t. & i. Viscid secretion of some trees & shrubs that hardens in drying but is soluble in water (cf. RESIN), used to stick paper &c. together & stiffen linen &c.; secretion collecting in inner corner of eye; (also *g.-tree*) any tree exuding g., esp. kinds of eucalyptus (*up a g.-t.*, in a fix, at end of one's resources); morbid secretion of g. as disease of fruit-trees; (pl., slang) rubber boots; *g.* ARABIC; *g. dragon*, tragacanth; *g. juniper*, sandarac; *g. resin*, vegetable secretion of resin mixed with g., as gamboge; *g. senegal*, kind of g. arabic from Senegal. (Vb) stiffen, smear, with g.; fasten *down*, *together*, *up*, *in*, &c., with g.; exude g. [f. OF *gomme* f. L *gummi* f. Gk *kommi*]

gum³, n. (vulg.). God (in oaths, as *my*, *by*, *g.!*). [deformation of *God*]

gu·mma, n. (path.; pl. *-s*, *-ta*). Syphilitic tumour. Hence **gu·mmat**OUS a. [mod. L, f. L *gummi* GUM², from nature of contents]

gu·mmy, a. Viscid, sticky; abounding in, exuding, gum; (of ankles & legs) puffy, swollen. Hence **gu·mmi**NESS n. [-Y²]

gu·mption (-shn), n. (colloq.). Resource, enterprising spirit, go, ready practical sense; (Painting) vehicle for colour. [Sc., etym. dub.]

gun, n. Metal tube for throwing missiles with gunpowder or some explosive force, piece of ordnance, cannon, musket, fowling-piece, rifle, carbine, (*sure as a g.*, certainly, beyond question; *stand*, *stick*, *to* one's *gg.*, maintain position; *son of a g.*, contemptible fellow; *great g.*, eminent person; *blow great gg.*, violently, a gale); (U.-S. slang) revolver; member of shooting-party; *g.*-BARREL¹; *gunboat*, small warship carrying heavy gun(s); *g.-bus* (slang), aeroplane carrying g.; *g.*-CARRIAGE; *g.-case*, case for sporting g., also judge's tippet; *g.-cotton*, explosive made by steeping cotton in nitric & sulphuric acids used for blasting; *g.-fire*, firing of g., esp. (Mil., Naut.) of morning or evening g. to show time; *g.-harpoon*, propelled from g., not by hand; *g.-house*, shelter for g. & gunner in action; *g.-lock*, mechanism by which charge of g. is exploded; *gunman*, (esp., U.-S. slang) armed robber; *g.-metal*, alloy of copper & tin or zinc (formerly used for gg.); *g.-pit*, to protect gg. from enemy's fire; *gunpowder*, explosive of saltpetre, sulphur, & charcoal, for use in guns & blasting (*gunpowder plot*, 5th Nov. 1605 to blow up Parliament), fine green tea of granular appearance, *white gunpowder*, kinds of modern explosive; *g.-room*, compartment in warship fitted up for junior officers or as lieutenants' mess-room (orig. for gunner & his mates); *g.-runner*, *-ning*, (person engaged in) illegal introduction of fire-arms into dependent country; *gu·nshot*, range of g. (*out of*, *within*, *gunshot*); *g.-shy*, frightened at report of g. (esp. of sporting dog); *gunsmith*, maker and repairer of small fire-arms; *g.-stock*, wooden mounting of g.-barrel. Hence (*heavily* &c.) **gunn**ED², **gu·n**LESS, aa. [perh. f. *Gunna* pet-form of ON *Gunnhildr* woman's name used as personal name (as with ships, & cf. *Mons Meg* cannon kept at Edinburgh) for ballistae & cannon (*una magna balista de cornu quae vocatur Domina Gunilda*, 1330)]

gu·nnel¹, n. A small eel-shaped sea-fish, the butter-fish. [?]

gunnel². See GUNWALE.

gu·nner, n. Officer or man of artillery (as official term, private); (Naut.) warrant officer in charge of battery, magazine, &c. (*g.'s daughter*, gun to which sailors were lashed for flogging; *kiss*, *marry*, *the g.'s d.*, be flogged); game-shooter. [-ER² (2)]

gu·nnera, n. The prickly rhubarb, an ornamental foliage plant with gigantic leaves. [f. J. E. *Gunnerus*, naturalist; see -A(1)]

gu·nnery, n. Construction & management of large guns (*g.-lieutenant*, with warrant of competence to supervise g. from *g.-ship*, for training in g.); firing of guns. [-ERY]

gu·nning, n. Shooting, esp. of game (usu. *go g.*). [-ING¹]

gu·nny, n. Coarse sacking, sack, usu. of jute fibre. [f. Hind. *goni* f. Skr. *goṇi* sack]

gu·nter, n. (Also *G.'s scale*) flat 2-ft rule with scales, logarithmic lines, &c., used for solving mechanically problems in surveying & navigation; topmast, or its sail, sliding up & down lower mast on rings (from resemblance to sliding G.'s scale). [E. *G.*, mathematician d. 1626]

gunwale (gŭ·nl), **gu·nnel**, n. Upper edge of ship's or boat's side (*g. to*, *under*, level with, below, water). [GUN + WALE (formerly used to support guns); cf. CHANNEL²]

gŭ·nyah, n. Native Australian hut. [native]

gŭp, n. (Anglo-Ind.). Gossip. [Hind.]

gurgita·tion (-jĭ-), n. Surging, bubbling motion or sound. [f. L *gurgitare* to surge (*gurges -itis* whirlpool) + -ATION]

gur·gle, v.i. & t., & n. (Make) bubbling sound as of water from bottle or among stones; utter with such sounds. [imit.; or f. Du. *gorgelen*, G *gurgeln*, or It. *gorgogliare*, f. L (*gurgulio* gullet); cf. GARGLE, GUGGLE]

gur·jun, n. E.-Ind. tree yielding g. balsam or oil, used medicinally. [native]

Gurkha (goor·ka), n. Member of ruling Hindu race in Nepal (*G. regiments*, of Gg. in British army). [native]

gur·nard, **gur·net**, n. Kinds of sea-fish with large head, mailed cheeks, & three free pectoral rays. [prob. f. F *grognard* grumbler (*grogner* grunt, -ARD)]

gŭ·rry, n. Small Indian fort. [Hind. *gaṛhī*]

guru (gōō·rōō), n. Hindoo spiritual teacher. [Skr., =grave, dignified]

gush, v.i. & t., & n. (Issue in, send forth) sudden or copious stream (often fig. of speech, tenderness, &c.); emit (water) copiously; (speak, behave, with) effusiveness, sentimental affectation, whence **gu·sh**ER[1] n., **gu·shing**LY[2] adv., **gu·sh**Y[2] a. [ME *gosshe* perh. imit.]

gu·sset, n. Triangular piece let into garment to strengthen or enlarge some part; iron bracket strengthening angle of structure. Hence **gu·sset**ED[2] a. [f. OF *gousset* (*gousse* nut-shell) flexible piece filling up joint in mail-coat]

gust[1], n. Sudden violent rush of wind; burst of rain, fire, smoke, sound, or passion. Hence **gu·st**Y[2] a., **gu·sti**LY[2] adv. [prob. f. ON *gustr*, cf. *gióṡa* gush]

gust[2], n. (archaic & poet.). Sense of taste; keen relish (*have a g. of*, appreciate); flavour. [f. L *gustus* taste]

gusta·tion, n. Tasting. So **gu·st**ATIVE, **gu·stat**ORY, aa. [f. L *gustatio* (*gustare* f. *gustus* taste, -ATION)]

gu·sto, n. Special flavour (archaic; *enjoy the full g. of*); zest, enjoyment with which something is done. [It., as GUST[2]]

gut, n., & v.t. & i. (Pl.) bowels or entrails (esp. of animals), contents of anything (*has no gg. in it*, is of no real value or force); particular part of lower alimentary canal, intestine, (*blind g.*, caecum); (usu. pl.) belly as seat of appetite (vulg.); material for violin strings made from intestines of animals; material for fishing-lines made from intestines of silkworm; narrow water-passage, sound, straits, (Oxf., & Camb.) bend of rivers in racing-course; defile, narrow lane or part of street. (Vb) take out gg. of, clean, (fish); remove or destroy internal fittings of (house &c.); extract essence of (book &c.); eat greedily (vulg.). [OE *guttas* pl., prob. cogn. w. *géotan* pour]

gu·ttae, n. pl. Drops in a row as ornament esp. in Doric architecture. [pl. of L *gutta* drop]

gutta-per·cha (-tsha), n. Greyish horny substance flexible when thin, of inspissated juice of various Malayan trees. [f. Malay *getah* gum, *percha* name of tree]

gu·ttate, a. (nat. hist.) Speckled. [f. L *guttatus* (*gutta* drop, -ATE[2])]

gu·tter, n., & v.t. & i. Track made by running water (rare); shallow trough below eaves, or channel at side of street, carrying off rain-water (*g.-child*, street arab; *take child* &c. *out of g.*, remove from poor surroundings); open conduit for outflow of fluid; groove; *g.-man*, cheap street-vendor of trifles; *g. press*, *journalism* (catering for depraved or vulgar tastes); *g.-snipe*, street arab. (Vb) furrow, channel; flow in streams; (of candle) melt away by becoming channelled so that wax &c. runs down. [f. OF *gutiere* (*goutte* drop f. L *gutta*)]

gu·ttle, v.i. & t. Eat gluttonously. Hence **gu·ttl**ER[1] n. [prob. f. GUT after GUZZLE]

gu·ttural (-er-), a. & n. Of the throat; (of sounds) produced in throat or by back of tongue & palate (n., g. sound or letter, as k, g). Hence **gu·ttural**IZE(3) v.t., **gu·ttural**ISM(1) n., **gu·ttural**LY[2] adv. [f. L *guttur* throat + -AL]

gu·tturo-, comb. form of L *guttur* throat (see -O-), as *-maxillary* of throat & jaws.

gu·tty, n. (golf). Gutta-percha ball. [-Y[3]]

guy[1] (gī), n., & v.t. Rope, chain, &c., to steady load of crane &c. or hold tent &c. in place; (vb) secure with guy(s). [f. OF *guis* cf. GUIDE]

guy[2] (gī), n. (pl. -*s*), & v.t. & i. Effigy of Guy Fawkes burnt on 5th Nov.; grotesquely dressed person, fright; (U.-S. slang) man, fellow; (slang) act of decamping (*give the g. to*, escape from; *do a g.*, disappear). (Vb) exhibit in effigy; ridicule; (slang) run away.

Guy's (gīz), n. (Used for) Guy's Hospital in London.

gu·zzle, v.i. & t. Drink, eat, greedily (i. & t.); consume (money &c.) in guzzling (often *away*). Hence **gu·zzl**ER[1] n. [perh. f. OF *gosiller* vomit (*gosier* throat)]

gwȳ·niad, n. White-fleshed lake fish of salmon kind. [W (*gwyn* white)]

gybe (j-), v.i. & t., & n. (Of fore-&-aft sail or boom) swing across, make (sail) do this, in wearing or running before wind; (of ship, crew, &c.) change course so that this happens. [prob. f. Du. *gijben*]

gyle (g-), n. Quantity of beer brewed at once; fermenting wort; fermenting-tun. [f. Du. *gijl* (*gijlen* to ferment)]

gym, n. (slang). Gymnasium, gymnastics. [abbr.]

gymkha·na (jĭmkah-), n. (Anglo-Ind.). Public place with facilities for athletics; athletic-sports display. [mixture of *gym-(nastics)* & Hind. (*gend-*)*khana* ball-house, racquet court]

gymnā·sium (j-), n. (pl. -*ums*, -*a*). Place, room, or building, with appliances for practice in gymnastics; Continental, esp. German, school of highest grade preparing for universities (*often pr.* gĭmnah·-; pl. sometimes -*ien*), whence **gymna·si**AL a. [L, f. Gk *gumnasion* (*gumnazō* exercise f. *gumnos* naked)]

gy·mnast, n. Expert in gymnastics. [f. Gk *gumnastēs* (*gumnazō* see prec.)]

gymna·stic, a. & n. Of gymnastics, involving bodily or (rarely) mental exercise, discipline, effort, or activity; hence **gymna·sti**CALLY adv. (N.) course of instruction regarded as discipline (*grammar is a good g.*); (pl.) exercises developing the muscles, esp. such as are performed in gymnasium (also in same sense as sing.). [f. L f. Gk *gumnastikos* (prec., -IC)]

gymno- (jĭ-), comb. form of Gk *gumnos* naked, bare, used in many bot., zool., & biol. terms, as *-spermous* having seeds unprotected by seed-vessels.

gymno·sophist, n. One of ancient Hindu philosophic sect going nearly naked & given up to contemplation; mystic, ascetic. So **gymno·sophy**[1] n. [f. L f. Gk *gumnosophistai* pl. (prec., SOPHIST)]

gy̌naecē·um (g-, j-), n. (Gk & Rom. Ant.) women's apartments in house; (Bot.; often incorrectly *-oe·cium*) female organs of flower. [L, f. Gk *gunaikeion* (*gunē -aikos* woman); *-oecium* from confusion with Gk *oikion* house]

gy̌nae·co- (g-, j-), comb. form of Gk *gunē -aikos* woman, as *-logy*, science of diseases of women. Hence **gynaeco·**CRACY n.

gy̌na·ndrous (g-, j-), a. (bot.). With stamens & pistil united in one column as in orchids. [f. Gk *gunandros* (*gunē* woman, *anēr andros* man) of doubtful sex + -OUS]

gy̌n(o)- (g-, j-), shortened form of GYNAECO-, esp. in Bot. = pistil-, ovary-, as *gy·nobase*, enlargement of receptacle supporting gynaeceum, *gy·nophore*, pedicel supporting ovary, also (Zool.) bud-bearing branch in hydrozoa; also = woman-, whence **gyno·**CRACY n.

-gy̌nous (g-, j-), suf. f. Gk *-gunos* (*gunē* woman) + -OUS, forming adjj. = having specified female organs or pistils, as *mono·g.*, *tetra·g.*, *andro·g.*

gy̌p[1] (j-), n. College servant at Cambridge & Durham (cf. SCOUT); *g.-room*, g.'s pantry. [perh. for obs. *gippo* scullion, orig. man's short tunic, f. obs. F *jupeau*]

gy̌p[2], n. (slang). *Give* one *g.*, scold or punish or defeat him unmercifully. [?]

gypsŏ·phila, n. Kinds of garden plant with thread-like stalks & airy lightness of appearance. [foll., -phil]

gy̌·ps(um) (j-), n. Hydrous calcium sulphate, mineral from which plaster of Paris is made, whence **gypso·**GRAPHY n.; this used as manure, whence **gy·psum** v.t. Hence **gy·ps**EOUS, **gypsi·**FEROUS, **gy·ps**OUS, aa. [L, f. Gk *gupsos*]

gypsy. See GIPSY.

gyr·ate[1] (jīr-), a. (bot.). Arranged in rings or convolutions. [f. L *gyratus* (GYRE, -ATE[2])]

gyra·te[2] (jīr-), v.i. Go in circle or spiral, revolve, whirl. Hence **gyra·**TION n., **gyr·at**ORY a. [f. L *gyrare* (foll.), -ATE[3]]

gyre, v.i., & n., (poet.). = prec.; (n.) gyration. [vb as prec.; n. f. L f. Gk *guros* ring]

gy̌r·o, n. Gyroscope (see foll.); *gyro-compass*, gyroscope arranged to serve as compass when magnetic compass cannot be used. [abbr. of foll.]

gyro-, comb. form of Gk *guros* ring, as *-graph*, instrument recording revolutions; *gyroidal*, spirally arranged; *-scope*, *-stat*, instruments illustrating dynamics of rotating bodies, also (*-scope*) rapidly spinning wheel fixed in something, e.g. car on single rail, to keep it in equilibrium, & having, by the independent stability of its axis, great value in mechanics.

gyro·se, a. (bot.). Folded & waved, marked with wavy lines. [GYRE, -OSE[1]]

gyve (j-), n. (usu. pl.), & v.t., (poet.). Shackle, fetter. [ME *give* (*pr.* g-), etym. dub.]

H

H, h, (ātsh), letter (pl. *Hs*, H's). DROP[2] o'nes *hs*; *H-iron*, girder of H-shaped section.

Abbreviations (1): (H) hard (in pencils), **HB**(lack), **H, HH, HHH,** (hard, double, treble, hard). (H.) head, **H.Q.** (quarters); Her or His, as **H.B.M.** (Britannic Majesty), **H.E.** (Excellency), **H.I.H., H.R.H., H.S.H.,** (Imperial, Royal, Serene, Highness), **H.I.M.** (Imperial Majesty), **H.M., H.M.A., H.M.S.,** (Majesty, Majesty's Airship, Ship); high, **H.E.** (explosive), **H.G.** (German); highest, **H.C.F.** (common factor); Home, **H.O.** (Office); Honourable, **H.A.C.** (Artillery Company), House, **H.C., H.L.,** (of Commons, Lords). (h.) **h.,** hour(s).

Abbreviations (2): **Hab.**(akkuk); **Hag.**-(gai); **Hants.,** Hampshire; **Heb.**(rews); **Herts.,** Hertfordshire; **hg.,** hectogram; **hhd,** hogshead; **hl.,** hectolitre; **hm.,** hectometre; **Hon.**(ourable); **Hon.**(orary) **Sec.**(retary); **Hos.**(ea); **h.**(orse) **p.**(ower); **Hunts.,** Huntingdonshire.

ha[1] (hah), int. expr. surprise, joy, suspicion, triumph, &c. [com.-Teut., Gk, L]

ha[2]. See HUM v.

haaf (hahf), n. (In Shetland & Orkney) deep-sea fishing ground. [f. ON *haf* high sea]

hā·bēăs cor·pus, n. Writ requiring body of person to be brought before judge or into court, esp. to investigate lawfulness of his restraint; *H.C. Act* (of Charles II, 1679, facilitating use of this). [L, = you must have the body]

hă·berdasher, n. Dealer in small articles of dress &c. Hence **ha·berdash**ERY(1) n. [conn. w. obs. *haberdash* small wares, prob. f. AF *hapertas*, etym. dub.]

hă·bergeon (-jn), n. (hist.). Sleeveless coat of mail. [f. F *haubergeon* (HAUBERK, -OON)]

hă·bile, a. Skilful, dextrous. [var. of ABLE]

habi·liment, n. (Pl.) dress suited to any office or occasion (facet. of ordinary clothes); (sing.) equipment, attire. [f. OF *habillement* (*habiller* fit out f. *habile* ABLE, see -MENT)]

habi·litate, v.t. & i. Furnish (mine) with working capital; (intr.) qualify for office (esp. in German Univ.). So **habilita·**TION n. [f. L *habilitare* (as ABILITY), see -ATE[3]]

hă·bit[1], n. Settled tendency or practice, as *he is in*, *has* (*fallen into*), *the* or *a h. of* *contradiction*; mental constitution, esp. *h. of mind*; bodily constitution, as *a man of corpulent h.*; (Bot., Zool.) mode of growth; (archaic) dress, esp. of religious order; (also *riding-h.*) lady's riding-dress. [OF, f. L *habitus -ūs* f. *habēre habit-* have, (refl.) be]

ha·bit², v.t. Clothe; (archaic) inhabit. [f. F *habiter* f. L *habitare* inhabit, as prec.]

ha·bitable, a. That can be inhabited. Hence **habita**BI·LITY, **ha·bitable**NESS, nn., **ha·bitab**LY² adv. [F, f. L *habitabilis* (as prec., see -ABLE)]

ha·bitant, n. Inhabitant; (pron. as F) Canadian of French descent. [F (HABIT², -ANT)]

ha·bităt, n. Natural home of plant or animal; habitation. [L, 3rd sing. pres. as HABIT²]

habita·tion, n. Inhabiting, as *fit for human h.*; place of abode; branch of Primrose League. [F, f. L *habitationem* (as HABIT², -ATION)]

habi·tual, a. Customary; constant, continual; given to (specified) habit, as *a h. drunkard*. Hence **habi·tual**LY² adv., **habi·tual**NESS n. [f. med. L *habitualis* (as HABIT¹, -AL)]

habi·tuate, v.t. Accustom (*to* thing, *to doing*). So **habitu**A·TION n. [f. L *habituare* (as HABIT¹), see -ATE³]

ha·bitude, n. Mental or bodily constitution; custom, tendency. [F, f. L *habitudo* (*habēre* have, see -TUDE)]

habĭ·tūé (-ā, or as F), n. Habitual visitor or resident. [F, p.p. of *habituer* (as HABITUATE)]

hachures (F), n. pl. Lines used in hill-shading to indicate slope.

hacĭĕ·nda (ă-, ah-), n. Estate, plantation, with dwelling-house (in Spain or Sp. colonies). [Sp., f. L *facienda* neut. pl. gerund. of *facere* do]

hack¹, n. Mattock; miner's pick; gash, wound, esp. from kick with toe of boot. [prob. cogn. w. G *hacke*, Da. *hakke*, mattock]

hack², v.t. & i. Cut, notch, mangle; kick shin of (opponent at football); deal cutting blows (*at*); emit short dry coughs; *a hacking* (short dry frequent) *cough*; *h.-saw* (for metal-cutting). [ME *hacken* f. com.-WG *hakkôn*, cf. G *hacken*, Du. *hakken*; conn. w. prec.]

hack³, n. Board on which hawk's meat is laid; (of eyas hawk) *be at h.* (not allowed to prey for itself); frame for drying bricks. [var. of HATCH¹]

hack⁴, n. Horse let out for hire; jade; horse for ordinary riding; common drudge (also attrib., as *h. writer*). [abbr. of HACKNEY]

hack⁵, v.t. & i. Make common, hackney; ride (horse), ride on horseback, on road at ordinary pace; use hired horses. [f. prec.]

ha·ckery, n. Indian bullock-cart. [?]

ha·ckle¹, n., & v.t. Steel flax-comb; long feathers on neck of domestic cock & other birds; *with his hh. up*, (of cock, dog, man) angry, ready to fight; artificial fly dressed with h.; (v.t.) dress (flax, fly) with h. [vb f. n.; MHG has *hachele*, perh. f. *hak-* root of OHG **hakjan* prick]

ha·ckle², v.t. Hack, mangle. [HACK² + -LE(3)]

ha·ckly, a. Rough, jagged. [f. prec. + -Y²]

ha·ckmatack, n. Amer. Larch. [native]

ha·ckney, n., & v.t. Horse of middle size & quality for ordinary riding; drudge, hireling; *h.-carriage, -coach* (kept for hire); (v.t., esp. in p.p. *-eyed*) make common or trite. [(vb f. n.) f. OF *haquenée* ambling horse, etym. dub.]

had. See HAVE.

ha·ddock, n. Fish allied to cod. [?]

hade, v.i. (Geol., Mining). Incline from the vertical. [?]

Hā·dēs, n. (Gk Myth.). Lower world, abode of departed spirits. [Gk, orig. a name of Pluto]

Ha·dji, Ha·jji, n. (Title of) Mohammedan pilgrim who has been to Mecca. [f. Arab. *haji*]

haeccē·ity (hěks-), n. (philos.). Thisness; individuality. [f. med. L *haecceitas* (*haec* fem. of *hic* this, see -TY)]

hae·mal, a. (anat.). Of the blood; situated on same side of body as the heart & great blood-vessels. [f. Gk *haima* blood + -AL]

haemă·tic, a. & n. Of or containing blood; (n.) medicine acting on the blood. [f. Gk *haimatikos* (as foll., see -IC)]

hae·matin, n. (chem.). Bluish-black amorphous substance, constituent of haemoglobin. [f. Gk *haima -matos* blood + -IN]

hae·matite, hě·m-, n. A red, brown, or blackish, iron ore. [f. L f. Gk *haimatitēs* (*lithos*) blood-like stone (as prec., see -ITE)]

haemato-, hemato-, in comb. = Gk *haima -matos* blood, as *-cele*, tumour containing extravasated blood.

haemoglō·bin, n. Colouring matter of the red corpuscles of the blood. [f. HAEMATIN + GLOBULIN]

hae·morrhage, he·m-, (hě-), n. Escape of blood from blood-vessels, bleeding. [f. F *emorogie* f. L f. Gk *haimorrhagia* (*haima* blood + st. of *rhēgnumi* break)]

hae·morrhoids, he·m-, (hěm-), n. pl. Piles. [f. OF *emoroyde* (cf. EMERODS) f. L f. Gk *haimorrhoïdes* (*phlebes*) bleeding (veins) (*haima* blood + *-rhoos* -flowing)]

ha·fiz (hah-), n. Mohammedan who knows Koran by heart (used as title). [Arab.]

ha·fnium, n. (chem.). Metal discovered 1923. [Da. (*Kjöben*)*havn* Copenhagen + -IUM]

haft, n., & v.t. Handle (of dagger, knife, &c.); (v.t.) furnish (knife &c.) with h. [(vb f. n.) OE *hæft*(*e*) f. OTeut. *haftjom* f. root *haf-* HEAVE]

hag[1], n. Ugly old woman; witch; (formerly) evil spirit in female form; (also *h.-fish*) a parasite fish allied to lamprey; *h.-ridden*, afflicted by nightmare. Hence **ha·gg**ISH[1] a. [?]

hag[2], n. Soft place in moor; firm place in bog. [cf. ON *hogg* ravine]

hagga·dah (-gah-), n. Legendary part of the Talmud. [Heb., = tale, f. *higgid* tell]

ha·ggard, a. & n. Wild-looking (esp. as a result of fatigue, privation, worry, &c.); (of hawk) caught in her adult plumage, untamed; (n.) such a hawk. Hence **ha·ggard**NESS n. [cf. F *hagard*, etym. dub.]

ha·ggis, n. Heart, lungs, & liver, of sheep &c., boiled in maw with suet, oatmeal, &c. [?]

ha·ggle, v.i., & n. Dispute, wrangle, (*about, over*). [f. dial. *hag* chop f. ON *hoggva* + -LE(3)]

hă·giarchy (-g-), n. Rule, order, of saints. [f. foll. + Gk *arkhē* rule]

hagio- (-g-) in comb. = Gk *hagios* saint(ly), as: *-cracy*, government of holy persons; *-grapha*, books of the Hebrew Scriptures not included under Law & Prophets; *-grapher*, *-gra·phic*, (writer) of any of these, or of saints' lives; *-graphy*, writing of saints' lives; *-latry*, worship of saints; *-logy*, literature treating of lives & legends of saints; *-scope*, (modern term for) squint (eccl.).

hah, int. & v.i. = HA[1,2].

ha ha (hah hah), int. repr. laughter.

ha-ha (hah·hah), n. Sunk fence bounding park or garden. [F, etym. dub.]

hai(c)k (hah·ik, hāk), n. Arabian outer wrapper for head & body. [Arab. *ḥayk* f. *ḥak* weave]

hail[1], n. Pellets of frozen vapour falling in shower, as *h.-storm*; shower *of* missiles, curses, questions, &c.; *h.-stone*, pellet of h. Hence **hai·l**Y[2] a. [com.-Teut.: OE *hagol*, Du. & G *hagel*]

hail[2], v.i. & t. *It hails*, hail falls; (fig.) pour down (blows, words, &c.), come down, violently. [OE *hagalian* f. OTeut. *hagalojan* (cf. prec.)]

hail[3], int. of greeting; *h.-fellow*, *h. fellow well met*, intimate, too intimate, *with*. [ellipt. use of obs. adj. *hail* f. ON *heill* sound, HALE]

hail[4], v.t. & i., & n. Salute; greet (person &c. *as* king &c., also *h. him king*); call to (ship, person) to attract attention; (of ship, person) be come *from* (place); (n.) salutation, esp. *within h.*, near enough to be hailed. [f. prec.]

hair, n. One or (collect. sing.) all of the fine filaments growing from skin of animals, esp. from human head (pl. *hairs* in collect. sense is archaic); (of plants) elongated cell growing from epidermis; h.-like thing; jot, tittle; *against the h.*, against the grain; *to a h.*, exactly; *a h. of the* DOG *that bit you*; (slang) *keep your h. on*, keep cool; (of girl) *put up, turn up, her h.*, dress it in woman's fashion; *do* or *put up, let down, her h.* (in the toilet); *not turn a h.*, show no sign of exhaustion or discomposure; *h. stands on end* (with fright or horror); *hairbreadth* or *hair's breadth*, minute distance (*hairb. escape*, very narrow); *hairbrush*, toilet brush for h.; *haircloth* (made of h., for various purposes); *hairdresser*, one whose business is to dress and cut h.; *h.-line*, line, rope, made of h., (also) up-stroke in writing; *h.-net*, *-oil* (used for the h.); *hairpin* (for fastening the h.; *h.-p. bend*, doubling back of road); *h.-powder*, scented powder for hair, now used by men-servants; *h. shirt* (of haircloth, for ascetics); *h.-splitting* a. & n., over-subtle(ty); *h.-spring*, fine spring in watch, regulating balance-wheel; *h.-stroke*, fine up-stroke in writing; *h. trigger*, secondary trigger releasing main one by slight pressure. Hence **hair·**INESS n., (-)**hair**ED[2], **hair·**LESS, **hair·**LIKE, **hair·**Y[2], aa. [com.-Teut.: OE *hǽr*, *hér*, Du. & G *haar*]

hake[1], n. Fish like cod. [?]

hake[2], **haik,** n. Wooden framework for drying bricks & other purposes. [prob. = HACK[3]]

hakee·m, -ki·m[1] (-ēm), n. (In India & Mohammedan countries) physician. [Arab. *ḥakīm* wise, physician]

ha·kim[2] (hah-), n. (As prec.) judge, ruler, governor. [Arab. *ḥākim*]

hal·berd, -rt, n. (hist.). Combined spear & battle-axe. [f. OF *halebarde* f. MHG *helmbarde* (*helm* helmet or *helm* handle + *barta* broad-axe f. OTeut. *bardoz* beard)]

halberdier· (-ēr), n. Man armed with halberd. [f. OF *hallebardier* (as prec., see -IER)]

ha·lcyon, n. & a. Bird fabled by the ancients to breed in floating nest on sea at winter solstice, and to charm wind & waves into calm for the purpose; (Zool.) Australasian kingfisher; (adj.) calm, esp. *h. days* (orig. 14 days about winter solstice). [f. L *halcyon* f. Gk *alkuōn* kingfisher]

hale[1], a. Robust, vigorous, (esp. of old persons). Hence **ha·le**NESS n. [north. repr. of OE *hál* WHOLE]

hale[2], v.t. (archaic). Drag, draw, forcibly (lit. & fig.). [f. OF *haler* f. OHG *halôn* (G *holen* fetch)]

half (hahf), n. (pl. *halves*), a., & adv. One of two equal or corresponding parts into which a thing is divided, as *the h. of 10 is 5*, *cut it in h.* (into hh.), *your h. is bigger than mine*, *two pounds & a half* (pound) or *two & a half pounds*, *h. of it is* (but *of them are*) *rotten*; (colloq.) = h.-pint, -mile, -back, -holiday; school term (the school year being formerly divided into two portions); *better h.*, wife; *do a thing by hh.* (imperfectly); *too clever by h.* (far); *go hh.*, share equally (*with* person *in* thing); *cry hh.*, claim equal share; (adj.) forming a h., as *a h. length, a h. share*; (adj. now viewed as = *the h. of*) *h. the men, h. your time, h. a crown* (2/6), *h. a pound* (*is h. the battle*, goes a long way towards success); (adv.) to the extent of h., (loosely) to a considerable extent, as *it is h. cooked, a h.-cooked potato, h. dead, I h. wish, not h.* (nearly) *long enough*, (colloq.) *not h.* (not at all) *bad, not h. a bad fellow*; *not h.* (slang), to the greatest possible extent, as *he didn't h. swear* (swore violently); (adv., prob. orig. adj.) *h.* (an hour) *past two* (o'clock); (Naut.) *h. three*, 3½ (fathoms), *east h.-south* (5⅝° south of east); *h.-&-h.*, (what is) h. one thing & h. another, esp. mixture of ale & porter; *h. as much* or *many again*, 1½ times the amount; *h.-back*, (Footb.) position, player, immediately behind forwards; *h.-baked*, (fig.) not thorough, not earnest, half-witted; *h.-ball* (Billiards &c.), with moving ball directed at edge of object ball; *h. binding* of book, leather back & corners, cloth or paper sides (similarly *h.-bound, h.-calf, h.-morocco*, &c.); *h.-blood*, person having one parent in common with another, this relationship, (also) person of mixed nationality; *h.-blooded*, born of different races; *h.-boot* (reaching up to the calf); *h.-bred*, of mixed breed, mongrel; *h.-breed*, h.-blooded person; *h.-brother, -sister* (by one parent only); *h. butt*, cue of length between ordinary cue & long butt; *h.-caste* a. & n., h.-bre(e)d, esp. (child) of European father & Indian mother; *h.* COCK¹(2); *halfcrown*, (n.) silver coin of 2/6, (usu. *h. a crown*, see above) amount of 2/6, (adj.) priced at or worth 2/6; *h.-hearted*, lacking courage or zeal, so *h.-heartedly, -ness*; *h.* HITCH; *h. holiday*, day of which (the latter) h. is taken as holiday; *h.-length*, portrait of upper h. of person; *h.-mast high*, (of flag) lowered to h. height of mast as mark of respect for the dead; *h. measures*, compromise, h.-&-h. policy &c.; *h. moon*, moon of which only h. is illuminated, crescent, crescent-shaped thing; *h. mourning*, black relieved by grey &c.; *h. pay*, reduced allowance to army or navy officer when neither retired nor in actual service; *h.-seas-over*, h. drunk; *h.-timer*, child who attends school for h. usual time, earning money in other h.; *h.-truth*, statement that conveys only part of the truth; *h.* VOLLEY; *h.-way house*, inn midway between two towns &c., (fig.) compromise; *h.-witted*, imbecile; *h.-yearly* a. & adv., (occurring) every h. year. [com.-Teut.: OE *h(e)alf*, G *halb*]

hālf·penny, n. (pl. as PENNY). Bronze coin worth half a penny (*turn up again like a bad h.*, persistently, unfailingly; *h. lick*, slang, ice-cream as sold in the street); *three halfpence*, (usu. for) a penny h., 1½*d.*; *halfpennyworth* (usu. pron. hāpath), *ha'p'orth*, as much as a h. will buy.

hă·libut, hŏ·l-, n. Large flat fish used for food. [prob. f. *haly* HOLY + *butt* flat fish, because eaten on holy-days]

hă·lidom, n. (archaic). Holy thing, esp. (as oath) *by my h.* [OE *hāligdōm* (HOLY, -DOM)]

hălieu·tic, a. & n. Of fishing; (n. pl.) art of fishing. [f. L f. Gk *halieutikos* (*halieuō* fish f. *hals* sea, see -IC)]

hall (hawl), n. Large public room in palace &c.; *servants' h.*, room in which servants dine; residence of landed proprietor; (Univv.) institution governed by a head without fellows, (also) building for students having or not having Univ. privileges; (in Eng. colleges &c.) common dining-room, dinner in this; building of guild, as *Saddlers' H.*; large room for public business; entrance-passage of house; *Liberty H.*, place where one may do as one likes; *h.-mark*, mark used at Goldsmiths' H. (& by Government assay offices) for marking standard of gold & silver, (v.t.) stamp with this (often fig.). [com.-Teut.: OE *heall*, Du. & Da. *hal*]

hallelujah, -luiah. See ALLELUIA.

halliard. See HALYARD.

hallo·, -loa· (-lō), int., n., & v.i. Int. calling attention or expr. surprise; (n., & v.i.) (the) cry *h.* [perh. var. of HOLLO]

halloo·¹, int. inciting dogs to the chase, calling attention, or expressing surprise (also as n., the cry *h.*). [perh. var. of HOLLO]

halloo·², v.i. & t. Cry 'halloo!', esp. to dogs; urge on (dogs &c.) with shouts; shout (t. & i.) to attract attention; (prov.) *do not h. until you are out of the* WOOD. [f. prec.; or = HALLOW³]

ha·llow¹ (-ō), n. Holy person, saint, (now only in *all hallows, hallowmas*, feast of All-hallows, = ALL *Saints' Day*; *hallowe'en* Sc., eve of this). [OE *hālga*, form of *hālig* holy]

ha·llow², v.t. Make holy; honour as holy. [com.-Teut.: OE *hālgian*, G *heiligen*, f. *hailag-* HOLY]

ha·llow³, v.t. & i. Chase with shouts; incite with shouts; shout to incite dogs &c. [ME *halowen* prob. f. OF *halloer*]

hallu·cinate, v.t. Produce false impressions in the mind of (person). [f. L (*h*)*allucinari* wander in mind, see -ATE³]

hallucina·tion, n. Illusion; apparent perception of external object not actually present. So **hallu·cinat**ORY a. [f. LL (*h*)*allucinatio* (as prec., see -ATION)]

halm. See HAULM.

ha·lma, n. Game played on board of 256 squares. [Gk, = leap, f. *hallomai* leap, see -M]

hā·lo, n., & v.t. Circle of light round luminous body, esp. sun or moon; circle, ring; disk of light surrounding head of saint, nimbus; (fig.) ideal glory investing person &c.; (v.t.) surround with h. [(vb f. n.) F, f. L f. Gk *halōs* threshing-floor, disk of sun or moon]

hă·loid, a. & n. (chem.). (Salt) having a composition like that of common salt. [f. Gk *hals* salt + -OID]

halt[1] (hawlt), n., & v.i. & t. Temporary stoppage on march or journey; (v.i.) make a h.; (v.t., Mil.) bring to a stand. [vb f. n.) orig. in phr. *make halt* f. G *halt machen* (*halt* hold)]

halt[2] (hawlt), a. (archaic). Lame; crippled. [com.-Teut.: OE & Da. *halt*]

halt[3], v.i., & n. Walk hesitatingly; hesitate, as *h. between two opinions*; (of argument, verse, &c.) be defective; (archaic) be lame; (n., archaic) halting, limp. Hence **ha·lting**LY[2] adv. [(n. f. vb) OE *haltian*, f. prec.]

ha·lter (hawl-), n., & v.t. Rope, strap, with noose or headstall for horses or cattle; rope with noose for hanging person; death by hanging; *h.-break* v.t., accustom (horse) to h.; (v.t.) fasten (often *up*) with h., hang (person) with h. [(vb f. n.) OE *hælftre* f. root *halb*, whence HELVE]

halve (hahv), v.t. Divide into halves; share equally; reduce to half; (Golf) *h. a hole with*, reach it in same number of strokes as (other player); fit (crossing timbers) together by cutting out half thickness of each. [ME HALF*en*]

ha·lyard, ha·lliard, hau·lyard (haw-), n. (naut.). Rope, tackle, for raising or lowering sail, yard, &c. [orig. *hallyer* (HALE v., -YER)]

ham[1], n. Back of thigh, thigh & buttock; (formerly) bend of the knee; thigh of hog salted & dried in smoke or otherwise for food. [OE, prob. f. OTeut. *ham-* be crooked]

ham[2], n. (hist.). Town, village. [OE *hám* HOME; seen in *Oakham* &c.]

hă·madrȳ·ad, n. (Gk Myth.) nymph living & dying with the tree she inhabited; venomous Indian serpent; Abyssinian baboon. [f. L f. Gk *hamadruas* (*hama* with + *drus* tree)]

Ha·mburgh (-berg, -b*uru*), n. Black variety of grape; small variety of domestic fowl. [*Hamburg* in Germany]

hames, n. pl. Two curved pieces of wood or metal forming (part of) collar of draught horse. [cf. Du. *haam*]

Hă·mite[1], n. (Supposed) descendant of Ham, member of Egyptian or other African race. Hence **Hamĭ·t**IC a. [-ITE]

hā·mite[2], n. Fossil cephalopod with hook-shaped shell. [f. L *hamus* hook, see -ITE]

ha·mlet, n. Small village, esp. one without church. [f. OF *hamelet* dim. of *hamel* dim. f. Teut. (OE *hám* HOME)]

ha·mmer[1], n. Instrument for beating, breaking, driving nails, &c., with solid (usu. metal) head at right angles to handle; machine with metal block serving same purpose; similar contrivance, as for exploding charge in gun (whence **ha·mmer**LESS a.), striking string of piano, &c.; auctioneer's mallet indicating by rap that article is sold; *come under the h.*, be sold by auction; *knight of the h.*, blacksmith; *throwing the h.*, athletic contest with heavy h.; *h. & tongs*, with might & main; *h.-beam* (projecting from wall at foot of principal rafter); *h.-cloth* (covering driver's seat in coach; hist. unexpl.); *h.-head*, head of h., kind of shark, African bird; *hammerman, hammersmith*, smith who works with h. [com.-Teut.: OE & Du. *hamer*, G *hammer*]

ha·mmer[2], v.t. & i. Strike, beat, drive, (as) with hammer; (colloq.) inflict heavy defeat(s) on in war or games; *h. out*, devise; *h.* (force) *idea into* person's *head*; work hard *at*; (St. Exch.) declare (person) a defaulter with three taps of h. [f. prec.]

ha·mmock, n. Hanging bed of canvas or netting suspended by cords at ends, used esp. on board ship; *h. chair* (made of canvas suspended on adjustable framework). [f. Sp. *hamaca* of Carib. orig.]

ha·mper[1], n. Basketwork packing-case. [f. obs. *hanaper* f. OF *hanapier* case for goblet (*hanap* f. OFrank. **knapp*)]

ha·mper[2], v.t., & n. Obstruct movement of (person &c.) with material obstacles; (fig.) impede, hinder; (n., Naut.) necessary but cumbrous part of equipment of vessel. [?]

Ha·mpton Court, n. (Used for) H. C. Palace, now partly occupied by persons of rank in reduced circumstances, partly open to the public.

ha·mshackle, v.t. Shackle (horse &c.) with rope connecting head and foreleg. [?]

ha·mster, n. Rodent like large rat, with cheek-pouches for carrying grain to its winter store. [G]

ha·mstring, n., & v.t. (*-inged* or *-ung*). (In man) one of five tendons at back of knee; (in quadrupeds) great tendon at back of knee in hind leg; (v.t.) cripple (person, animal) by cutting the hh. [HAM[1]]

hă·mulus, n., (anat., zool., bot.) (pl. *-lī*). Hook-like process. [L, dim. of *hamus* hook]

hand[1], n. Terminal part of human arm beyond wrist; similar member of all four limbs of monkey; forefoot of quadruped; authority, disposal, as *in the hh. of*; agency, as *by the hh. of, pass through many hh.*; share in action, as *have a h. in it*; pledge of marriage, as *give* one's *h. to*; (usu. pl.) manual worker(s) of factory &c; person who does something, as *a picture by the same h., all hh.*, the whole crew, *a good h.* (skilful) *at singlestick* or *acrostics, an old parliamentary h., an old h. at test matches*; person, source, from which thing comes, as *first*, SECOND, *h.* (*at 1st* &c. *h.*, directly, more or less indirectly; *first* &c. *-h.*, of hearsay); COOL *h.*; skill, as *a h. for pastry*; style of workmanship; turn, innings, at cricket, billiards, &c.;

style of writing, as *a legible h.*; signature, as *witness the h. of A.B.*; h.-like thing, esp. pointer of clock or watch (*h. of* BANANAS); fixed quantity of various commodities, e.g., bundle of tobacco leaves; a lineal measure of horse's height, =4 in.; (Cards) cards dealt to a player, player holding these, as *first, third, h.*; *at h.*, close by, about to happen soon; *by h.*, by manual labour (*brought up by h.*, of child fed from bottle); *for* one's *own h.*, on one's own account; (*live*) *from h. to mouth*, improvidently; *in h.*, held in the hand, at one's disposal, under control, receiving attention; *off h.*, without preparation, then & there; *on h.*, in one's possession; *on* one's *hh.*, resting on one as a responsibility; *on all hh.*, to, from, all quarters; *on the one h., on the other h.*, (of contrasted points of view &c.); *out of h.*, at once, extempore, (also) out of control; *to h.*, within reach; *to* one's *h.*, ready for one without exertion on one's own part; *bear a h.*, take part *in*; *come to h.*, turn up, be received; *do a h.'s turn*, make the slightest effort; *lay hh. on*, touch, seize; *take in h.*, undertake; *change hh.*, (of property) pass from one person to another; *clean hh.*, (fig.) innocence; *with a heavy h.*, oppressively; *with a high h.*, boldly, arrogantly; *have, keep*, one's *h. in*, be in practice; *his h. is out*, he is out of practice; (*win*) *hh. down*, easily; *hh. off !*, do not touch; *hh. up !* (direction to persons to hold up their hands as a sign of assent &c., or to preclude resistance); *h. in h.*, with hh. mutually clasped; *go h. in h. with*, keep step with, lit & fig.; *h. over h.* or *fist*, with each h. successively passing over the other, as in climbing rope, (fig.) with steady or rapid progress (in overtaking &c.); *h. to h.*, (of conflict &c.) at close quarters; *bind* one *h. & foot* (completely), *serve* (person) *h. & foot* (assiduously); *be h. in* (or *&*) *glove* (intimate) *with*; *hand-* (opp. *machine-*, as *h.-knitted, -sewn, -painted*); *h.-bag* (small, for carrying about); *h.-ball*, ball for throwing with h., game played with this between two goals; *h.-barrow* (carried by h.); *handbell*, bell rung by h., esp. one of a set for musical performance; *handbill*, printed notice circulated by h.; *handbook*, short treatise, manual, guide-book; *h.-canter*, gentle canter; *h.-cart* (pushed or drawn by h.); *handcuff* v.t., secure with *handcuffs* (pair of metal rings joined by short chain, for securing prisoner's hh.); *h.-gallop*, easy gallop; *h.-glass*, magnifying glass held in h., small mirror with handle; *handgrip*, grasp, seizure with the h. (friendly or hostile); *handhold*, something for the hh. to grip on (in climbing &c.); *h.-line*, fishing-line worked without rod; *h.-made*, made by h. (esp. opp. to *machine-made*); *handmaid(en)*, female servant (archaic, exc. fig.); *h.-organ*, portable barrel-organ with crank turned by h.; *h.-rail*, railing along edge of stairs &c.; *handshake*, shake of person's h. with one's own, as greeting; *handspike*, wooden lever shod with iron, used on shipboard & by artillery; *handwriting*, writing with the h., esp. of particular person. Hence (-)**hand**ED[2], **ha·nd**LESS, aa. [com.-Teut.: OE *hand, ho-*, OHG *hant*]

hand[2], v.t. Help (person) with the hand (*into, out of*, carriage &c.); (Naut.) take in (sail); deliver, transfer, by hand or otherwise (*over to* person, *down to* succeeding generations, *in* at office, *on, up*, &c.). [f. prec.]

ha·ndful, n. (pl. *-fuls*). Quantity that fills the hand; small number (of men &c.); (colloq.) troublesome person or task. [OE *handfull* (HAND[1], see -FUL)]

ha·ndicap, n., & v.t. (-pp-). Race, competition, in which chances of competitors are equalized by start, difference in weight to be carried (in horse-races), &c.; extra weight or other condition imposed on competitor, (fig.) hindrance; (v.t.) impose h. on (competitor), (fig., of circumstances) place (person) at disadvantage. Hence **ha·ndicapp**ER[1] n. [?]

ha·ndicraft, n. Manual skill; manual art or trade; *handicraftsman*, man who exercises a h. [earlier *handcraft*]

ha·ndiwork, n. Work done, thing made, by the hands or by any one's personal agency. [OE *handgeworc* (HAND[1]+collect. form of *weorc* WORK)]

handkerchief (hă·ngkertshĭf), n. Square of linen, silk, &c., carried in pocket (*pocket-h.*) for wiping nose &c. or worn about neck (also *neck h., neckerchief*); *throw the h. to* (person, in certain games, to invite him to pursue), also, express condescending preference for (person). [HAND[1]+KERCHIEF]

ha·ndle[1], n. That part of a thing which is made to hold it by; *h.-bar* of bicycle &c., steering-bar with h. at each end; *h. of the face*, (facet.) nose; *h. to* one's *name*, title; fact that may be taken advantage of. [OE (HAND[1]+-LE)]

ha·ndle[2], v.t. Touch, feel, with the hands; manipulate; manage (thing, person); treat (person *roughly, kindly*, &c.); treat of (subject); deal in (goods). [OE *handlian* (HAND[1]), cf. G *handeln*]

Ha·ndley-Page, n. Type of large aeroplane. [maker].

ha·n(d)sel, n., & v.t. (-ll-). Gift at beginning of New Year, or on entering on new circumstances; earnest-money; foretaste; (v.t.) give h. to, inaugurate, be the first to try. [(vb f. n.) OE has *handselen* giving into a person's hands; Da. has *handsel* earnest-money]

ha·ndsome, a. Of fine form or figure; (of conduct &c.) generous, as *a h. present*, *h. treatment*; (prov.) *h. is that h. does*; (of price, fortune, &c.) considerable. Hence **ha·ndsome**LY[2] adv., **ha·ndsome**NESS n. [HAND[1], -SOME]

ha·ndy, a. Ready to hand; convenient to handle; clever with the hands; *h.-dandy*, child's game in which one player guesses which of other player's hands conceals some object; *h.-man* (useful for odd jobs, often of sailors). Hence **ha·ndi**LY[2] adv., **ha·ndi**NESS n. [-Y[2]]

hang[1], v.t. & i. (*hung*, exc. as below). Suspend, attach loosely, (*from, to*, hook or other object above); suspend (meat, game) to dry (*hung beef*, so cured) or become tender or high; place (pictures) on wall (*hung on the line*, at best height for seeing; HANGING *committee* of Royal Academy &c.); attach (wall-paper); fit up (bells in house); suspend floating in space; rest (door on hinges, coach on springs) in free swinging position; (past & p.p. *hanged*) suspend on gibbet as capital punishment, (as imprecation) *hang!, h. it, h. you, I'll be hanged if* —; let droop, as *h. the head* (from shame &c.); remain, be, suspended, lit. & fig., as *sword, punishment, hangs over his head, rogue shall h. for it, hangs in the balance*, is undecided, *curtain hangs loose, in folds*, &c.; decorate *with* (things suspended); *h.* (loiter) *about*; *h. fire*, (of firearm) be slow in going off (also fig.); *h. heavy*, (of time) pass slowly; *h. on*, depend, rely, on, attend carefully to (& see below); *h. back*, show reluctance to act or move; *h.* (lag) *behind*; *h. off*, h. back; *h. on*, stick closely (*to*; & see above) *h. out*, suspend from window &c., (intr.) protrude downwards, (slang) reside; *h. together*, be coherent, be associated; *h. up*, suspend, (fig.) put aside, postpone indefinitely; *h.-dog* n. & a., base & sneaking (fellow); *hangman*, executioner; *h.-nail*, = ĀGNAIL. [(1) OE *hōn* trans., cf. OHG *hāhan*, MDu. *haen*; (2) OE *hangian* intr., cf. OFris. *hangia*; (3) ON *hengjan* causal, cf. MDu *hengen*]

hang[2], n. Downward droop or bend; the way a thing hangs; *get the h. of*, get the knack of, understand; (colloq.) *not a h.*, not at all. [f. prec.]

hă·ngar (-ngg-), n. Shed for housing aeroplane &c. [F, = shed for carriages &c., etym. dub.]

ha·nger[1], n. Wood on side of steep hill. [OE *hangra* f. HANG[1]]

ha·nger[2], n. In vbl senses, esp.: *bell, paper, -h.*; loop &c. by which thing is hung; chain, rod, to which pot is hung in fireplace by pot-hook; stroke with double curve in writing (ʅ), cf. POT-*hook*; short sword, orig. hung from belt; *h.-on*, follower, dependant. [-ER[1]]

ha·nging, n. In vbl senses, esp.: drapery with which walls &c. are hung; *h. committee* (deciding on h. of pictures in exhibition); *a h. matter* (resulting in capital punishment). [-ING[1]]

hank, n. Circular loop or coil, esp. as definite length of cotton yarn (840 yds), worsted (560 yds), &c.; (Naut.) ring of rope, iron, &c., for fixing staysails to stays. [14th c., cf. ON *hōnk* hank, Swed. *hank* string, Da. *hank* handle]

ha·nker, v.i. Crave, long, *after*. Hence **ha·nker**ING[1] n. [etym. dub.; Du. has *hunkeren*]

ha·nky, n. (nursery). Handkerchief. [abbr.; see -Y[3]]

ha·nky-pa·nky, n. Jugglery; underhand dealing. [arbitrary, perh. on *hocus-pocus*]

Hanover. *House of H.*, British sovereigns from George I to Victoria.

Hans (-z), n. (Nickname for) German or Dutchman. [G & Du. f. L *Johannes* John]

Ha·nsardize, v.t. Confront (M.P.) with his former utterances recorded in Hansard (official report of proceedings in Parliament). [-IZE]

Hanse (-s), n. (hist.). Guild of merchants; political and commercial league of Germanic towns, whence **Hansĕ**A·TIC a.; entrance-fee of guild. [OF, f. OHG *hansa* company]

han·som (cab), n. Two-wheeled cabriolet for two inside, with driver mounted behind and reins going over roof. [*Hansom*, patentee, 1834]

Ha·nwell, n. (Used for) H. Lunatic Asylum for county of London.

hap[1], n. (archaic). Chance, luck, lot; (w. pl.) chance occurrence. [ME, f. ON *happ*]

hap[2], v.t. (archaic). Come about by chance; happen (*to* do). [ME *happe(n)*, f. prec.]

hă·pax legŏ·menon, n. (pl. *-ena*). Word of which only one use is recorded. [Gk, = once said]

ha·pha·zard (-p-h-), n., a., & adv. Mere chance, esp. *at, by, h.*; casual(ly). [HAP[1] + HAZARD]

ha·pless, a. Unlucky. Hence **ha·pless**LY[2] adv. [-LESS]

haplo·graphy, n. The mistake of writing once what should be written twice (e.g. *philogy* for *philology*), cf. DITTOGRAPHY. [f. Gk *haplous* single + -GRAPHY]

ha·ply, adv. (archaic). By chance; perhaps. [HAP[1] + -LY[2]]

ha'p'orth. See HALFPENNY.

ha·ppen, v.i. Come to pass (by chance or otherwise), whence **ha·ppen**ING[1] n. (usu. pl.); chance, have the fortune, *to* (do); come *upon* (person, thing) by chance. [ME (HAP[1] + -EN[6])]

ha·ppy, a. (Of person or circumstance) lucky, fortunate; contented with one's lot; *I shall be h.* (pleased) *to assist*; *h. dispatch*, = foll.; *h.* FAMILY; apt, felicitous (of language or conduct); *h.-go-lucky*, haphazard (adj.). Hence **ha·ppi**LY[2] adv., **ha·ppi**NESS n. [f. HAP[1] + -Y[2]]

hara-kī·rī (hah-), n. Suicide by disembowelment, as practised by higher classes in Japan when in disgrace or sentenced to death, happy dispatch. [Jap. (vulg.), f. *hara* belly + *kiri* cut]

hara·ngue (-ng), n., & v.i. & t. Speech to an assembly; loud or vehement address; (v.i.) make h.; (v.t.) make h. to. [(vb f. F *haranguer*) f. OF *arenge* f. med.L *harenga* (It. *aringa*, cf. *aringo* arena)]

hă·ras (*or* ahrah·). Breeding station for horses. [f. OF *haraz*, etym. dub.; now usu. treated as F]

hă·rass, v.t. Vex by repeated attacks; trouble, worry. Hence **ha·rass**MENT n. [f. F *harasser*, perh. f. OF *harer* set a dog on]

har·binger (-j-), n., & v.t. One who announces another's approach, forerunner; (formerly) one sent to purvey lodgings for army, royal train, &c.; (v.t.) announce approach of. [(vb f. n.) f. OF *herbergere* f. *herberge* lodging f. OHG *heriberga* (*hari* army + *-berga* shelter f. *bergen* protect)]

har·bour, n., & v.t. & i. Place of shelter for ships; shelter; *h.-master*, officer in charge of harbour; (v.t.) give shelter to (esp. vermin, criminal, evil thoughts); (v.i.) come to anchor in h. Hence **har·bour**LESS a. [(vb f. n.) ME *hereberge* (*here* army + *beorg* shelter)]

har·bourage, n. (Place of) shelter. [-AGE]

hard, a., n., & adv. Firm, unyielding to touch, solid; *h. cash*, specie, as opp. to paper currency; *h. facts* (not disputable like opinions &c.); difficult (*to* do; *h. nut to crack*, h. problem, person h. to make out or influence); *h. of hearing*, somewhat deaf; difficult to understand or explain, as *h. words, question*; (of person or conduct) unfeeling, harsh; involving undue or unfair suffering (*h. cases make good law*); stingy; difficult to bear, as *h. life, times,* LINES; *h.* (severe) *winter*; *a h. bargain* (without concession); harsh, unpleasant, to eye or ear; *h. water* (unfit for washing owing to its mineral salts); (of markets and prices) high, unyielding; (Phonetics) *k, t, and p, are h. as opposed to g, d, & b, c is h. in cat, g is h. in go*; strenuous, as *h. fight, h. labour* (imposed on some criminals), *h. row to hoe* (difficult task), *h. worker*; *h. swearing*, (euphem. for) unabashed perjury; (n.) sloping roadway across foreshore; (slang) = h. labour (*got 2 years h.*); (adv.) strenuously, severely, as *try h., raining h., freezing h., h. pressed* (closely pursued); with difficulty, as *h.-earned* (cf. HARDLY), *h.-baked, -boiled* (so as to be h.); *be h. put to it*, be in difficulties; *die h.* (only after h. struggle); *it will go h. with him* (prove to his disadvantage); *it shall go h. but* (short of overpowering difficulties) *I will find them*; *h. by*, close by; *h.* (*up*)*on*, too severe in criticism or treatment (*don't be too h. on him*), (of circumstances) bearing with undue severity on; *h. upon*, close to; *run* (person) *h.*, pursue him closely; *h. & fast*, (of rules) strict; *h.-bake*, almond toffee; *h.-bitten*, tough in fight; *h.-favoured, -featured*, of harsh or ugly features; *h.-fisted*, stingy; *h.-headed*, practical, not sentimental; *h.-hearted*, unfeeling, so *h.-heartedly, -ness*; *h. hit*, severely troubled; *h.-laid*, (of string, fabric, &c.) tightly twisted or woven; *h.-mouthed*, (of horse) not easily controlled by bit (also fig.); *h. set*, set so as to be h., (of egg) that has been subjected to incubation, (of person) hungry; *hardshell*, having a h. shell, (fig.) rigid, uncompromising, esp. (U.S.) *Hardshell Baptists*; *h. tack*, ship-biscuit; *h. up*, in want (esp. of money), at a loss *for*, (Naut., adv., of tiller) as far as possible to windward; *hardware*, ironmongery; *hardwareman*, dealer in this; *hardwood*, wood of deciduous trees as opposed to pines and firs. Hence **har·d**NESS n. [com.-Teut. adj.: OE *heard*, Du. *hard*, G *hart*, cf. Gk *kratus* strong; OE adv. *hearde*]

har·den, v.t. & i. Make or become hard, callous (esp. in p.p.), or robust. [-EN[6]]

har·dihood, n. Boldness, audacity. [f. HARDY a. + -HOOD]

har·dly, adv. In a hard manner; with difficulty; harshly; scarcely; *h.-earned*, earned with difficulty or (facet.) ease. [-LY[2]]

har·dship, n. Hardness of fate or circumstance; severe suffering or privation. [-SHIP]

har·dy[1], a. Bold, audacious, whence **har·di**LY[2] adv.; robust, capable of endurance; (Hort., of plants) able to grow in the open air all the year, *half h.*, requiring shelter in winter only, *h. annual* one that may be sown, or sows itself, in the open, (fig.) subject that comes up yearly. Hence **har·di**NESS n. [f. F *hardi* p.p. of *hardir* f. WG *hardjan* make HARD]

har·dy[2], n. Blacksmith's bar of hard iron for cutting metal on &c. [prob. f. prec. or HARD]

hare, n. Rodent quadruped with long ears, short tail, & divided upper lip; *mad as a March h.* (h. in breeding season); (prov.) *first catch your h.* (*then cook him*); *hold* (or *run*) *with the h. & run* (or *hunt*) *with the hounds*, keep in with both sides; *h. & hounds*, paper-chase; *harebell*, round-leaved bell-flower, also (see BLUE[1]*-bell*) wild hyacinth; *h.-brained*, rash, wild; *h.-lip*, fissure of upper lip; *h.'s-foot*, species of clover, (also) corkwood tree, (also) h.'s foot used for applying rouge &c. to face. [com.-Teut.: OE *hara*, Du. *haas*, G *hase*]

hā·rem, -am, n. Women's part of Mohammedan dwelling-house; its occupants; (usu. *-am*) Mohammedan sacred place; *h. skirt* (slang), woman's loose trousers like skirt. [f. Arab. *haram, -im,* prohibited f. *harama* prohibit; also *haree·m -im* (-ēm)]

hă·ricot (-kō), n. Ragout (usu. of mutton); *h.* (*bean*), French bean. [F, etym. dub.]

hark, v.i. & t. Listen (usu. *to*, rarely trans.; also abs. in imper.); (as call to hounds) go *forward, away, off,* &c.; *h. back,* (of hounds) retrace course to find scent, (fig.) revert (*to* subject), (trans.) recall (hounds). [ME *herkien,* cf. MDu. *horken,* G *horchen*]

harl(e), n. Barb, fibre, of feather. [prob. =MLG *herle, harle,* fibre of flax or hemp]

Harlei·an (-lē-), a. Of (the library of) Robert Harley Earl of Oxford, d. 1724. [-EAN]

har·lequin, n. Character in Italian comedy; mute character in English pantomime, invisible to clown & pantaloon, usu. wearing particoloured tights; buffoon; (also *h. duck*) northern duck with variegated plumage. [F, f. It. *arlecchino,* etym. dub.]

harlequinā·de, n. Part of pantomime in which harlequin plays chief part. [f. F *arlequinade* (as prec., see -ADE)]

Har·ley Street, n. London street associated with fashionable physicians.

har·lot, n., & v.i. Prostitute; (v.i.) play the h. Hence **har·lot**RY(4) n. [(vb f. n.) orig. masc. =vagabond, knave, f. OF (*h*)*arlot,* lad, knave, vagabond, =It. *arlotto* hedge-priest; etym. dub.]

harm, n., & v.t. Damage, hurt, (*out of h.'s way,* in safety). Hence **har·m**FUL, **har·m**LESS (doing no h.), aa., **har·mful**LY[2], **har·mless**LY[2], advv., **har·mful**NESS, **har·mless**NESS, nn. [(vb f. OE *hearmian* f. n.) com.-Teut.: OE *hearm,* G *harm,* Da. *harme*]

harma·ttan, n. Parching land-wind on coast of Upper Guinea in Dec., Jan., & Feb. [f. W.-Afric. *haramata*]

harmŏ·nic, a. & n. Harmonious, concordant; relating to harmony; *h. tones* (produced by vibration of aliquot parts of strings &c.); *h. quantities* (whose reciprocals are in arithmetical progression, as ½, ⅓, ¼, or as 12, 15, 20), *h. progression,* series of these; (n.) h. tone. Hence **harmo·**NICALLY adv. [f. L f. Gk *harmonikos* (as HARMONY, see -IC)]

harmŏ·nica, -con, nn. Names of several musical instruments. [(*-ca*) L fem., (*-con*) Gk neut., adj. as prec.]

harmō·nious, a. Concordant, forming a consistent or agreeable whole; free from dissent; sweet-sounding; singing, playing, tunefully. Hence **harmō·nious**LY[2] adv. [f. F *harmonieux* (as HARMONY)]

har·monist, n. Person skilled in harmony; musician; collator of parallel narratives, whence **harmoni·s**TIC a.; harmonizer. [f. HARMONIZE, see -IST]

harmō·nium, n. Keyboard instrument in which tones are produced by metal reeds. [F, as HARMONY]

har·monize, v.t. & i. Bring into, be in, harmony (*with*); make, be, agreeable in artistic effect; add notes to (melody) to form chords. Hence **harmoniz**A·TION n. [f. F *harmoniser* (as HARMONY, see -IZE)]

harmono·meter, n. Instrument measuring harmonic relations of notes. [f. F *harmonomètre* (as foll., see -METER)]

har·mony, n. Agreement; *pre-established h.* (between body & soul before their creation); agreeable effect of apt arrangement of parts; combination of simultaneous notes to form chords (cf. MELODY); sweet or melodious sound; collation of parallel narratives &c., esp. of the four Gospels. [f. F *harmonie* f. L f. Gk *harmonia* (*harmo-* join)]

har·ness, n., & v.t. Gear of draught horse or other animal; (fig.) working equipment; *in h.,* in the routine of daily work; apparatus in loom for shifting warp-threads; (Hist.) defensive armour; *h.-cask* (with rimmed cover, for keeping salt meat on board ship); (v.t.) put h. on (horse &c.), (fig.) utilize (river, waterfall, natural forces) for motive power. [(vb f. OF *harneschier*) f. OF *harneis* (It. *arnese*), etym. dub.]

harp[1], n. Stringed musical instrument, roughly triangular, played with the fingers. [com.-Teut.: OE *hearpe,* Du. *harp,* G *harfe*]

harp[2], v.i. Play on harp, whence **har·p**ER[1], **har·p**IST, nn.; dwell tediously *on* (subject). [OE *hearpian* (as prec.)]

harpoo·n, n., & v.t. Spear-like missile with rope attached, for catching whales &c.; *h.-gun* (for firing this); (v.t.) strike, spear, with h. [(vb f. n.) f. F *harpon* (*harpe* clamp f. L f. Gk *harpē* sickle)]

har·psichord (-k-), n. Keyboard instrument with strings plucked by quill or leather points, used 16th–18th c. [f. obs. F *harpechorde* (LL *harpa* harp + *chorda* string)]

har·py, n. (Gk & L Myth.) rapacious monster with woman's face & body & bird's wings & claws; rapacious person; *h.-eagle,* S.-Amer. bird of prey. [f. L f. Gk *harpuiai* pl. (cf. *harpazō* snatch)]

har·quebus, ar-, n. (hist.). Early type of portable gun, supported on tripod by hook or on forked rest. So **harquebus**IER· n. [f. F *harquebuse* f. It. *arcobugio* corrupt. (as if =*arco* bow + *bugio* hollow) of MHG *hakenbühse* (*haken* hook + *bühse* gun)]

ha·rridan, n. Haggard old woman, vixen. [perh. f. F *haridelle* old jade]

ha·rrier[1], n. One who harries. [-ER[1]]

ha·rrier[2], n. Hound used for hunting hare; (pl.) pack of these with huntsmen (also as name of hare-&-hounds club); kind of falcon. [perh. =prec.]

Ha·rris tweed, n. Kind made in Harris in the Hebrides.

Harrō·vian, a. & n. (Member) of Harrow school; (inhabitant) of Harrow. [-IAN]

ha·rrow[1], n. Heavy frame with iron teeth for breaking clods on ploughed land, covering seed, &c.; *under the h.*, in distress. [ME *harwe*, etym. dub.]

ha·rrow[2], v.t. Draw harrow over (land); lacerate, wound, (lit., & fig. the feelings &c.), whence **ha·rrow**ING[2] a. [f. prec.]

ha·rrow[3], v.t. Harry, spoil, (chiefly in phr. *h. hell*, of Christ). [var. of foll.]

ha·rry, v.t. Ravage, waste, spoil, (land, or abs.); despoil (person); harass, worry. [OE *hergian* f. OTeut. *harjôjan* (*harjo-* army)]

harsh, a. Rough to the touch, taste, eye, or ear; repugnant to feelings or judgement; cruel, unfeeling. Hence **har·sh**LY[2] adv., **har·sh**NESS n. [ME *harsk*, cf. Swed. *härsk*, Da. *harsk*, rank, G *harsch* harsh]

hart, n. Male of (esp. red) deer, esp. after fifth year; *h. of ten* (branches on horns); *h.'s-tongue*, fern with long undivided fronds. [OE *heort* f. OTeut. *herut-* perh. conn. w. Gk *kerat-* horn]

har·tal, n. Form of boycott in India.

har·t(ĕ)beest, n. S.-African kind of antelope. [S.-Afr. Du.]

har·tshorn (-s-h-), n. Substance got from horns of hart, formerly chief source of ammonia; (*spirit of*) *h.*, aqueous solution of ammonia; *salt of h.*, smelling salts.

hār·um-scār·um, a. & n. Reckless (person, conduct). [arbitrary]

har·vest, n., & v.t. (Season for) reaping & gathering in of grain or other products; corncrop; season's yield of any natural product; (fig.) product of any action; *h.-bug*, mite troublesome during h.; *h. festival*, thanksgiving service for h.; *h. home*, close of harvesting, festival of this; *h. moon* (full within fortnight of Sep. 22 or 23); *h. mouse*, small species, nesting in stalks of growing grain; (v.t.) reap & gather in (crop, or abs.), lay up, husband. [(vb f. n.) OE *hærfest* f. OTeut. *harbistoz* (*harb-* =L *carpere* pluck)]

har·vester, n. Reaper; reaping-machine (esp. sheaf-binding one); harvest-bug. [-ER[1]]

has. See HAVE.

hash[1], v.t. (Also *h. up*) cut (meat, also fig.) in small pieces. [f. F *hacher* (*hache* HATCHET)]

hash[2], n. Dish of hashed meat; old matter served up in new form; medley; *make a h. of*, spoil in dealing with; *settle a person's h.*, make an end of, do for, him. [f. prec.]

hă·shish, -eesh, n. Top leaves & tender parts of hemp, dried for smoking or chewing, in Arabia, Egypt, Turkey, &c. (cf. BHANG). [Arab. *hashish* dry herb]

hā·slet, har·slet, n. Piece of meat to be roasted, esp. pig's fry. [f. OF *hastelet* (*haste* spit f. L *hasta* spear, -LET)]

hasp, n., & v.t. Fastening contrivance, esp. clasp passing over staple & secured by padlock; hank, skein, of yarn; (v.t.) fasten with h. [(vb f. OE *hæpsian* f.) OE *hæpse*, cf. OHG *haspa* reelful of yarn, MHG *haspe* hinge]

ha·ssock, n. Cushion for kneeling; tuft of matted grass &c.; (in Kent) soft calcareous sandstone. [OE *hassuc*, etym. dub.]

hă·stāte, a. Spear-shaped. [f. L *hastatus* (*hasta* spear, see -ATE[2])]

hāste, n., & v.i. Urgency of movement; hurry, precipitancy, as *more h., less speed*; *make h.*, be quick (*to* do, *&* do); (v.i.) make h. (*to* do, or abs.). [(vb f. OF *haster*) f. OF *haste* f. WG **haisti-* violence]

hā·sten (-sn), v.t. & i. Cause (person) to make haste; accelerate (work &c.); make haste; come or go in haste (*to* &c.). [-EN[6]]

hā·sty, a. Hurried; speedy; rash, inconsiderate; quick-tempered; *h. pudding* (of flour stirred to thick batter in boiling milk or water). Hence **ha·sti**LY[2] adv., **ha·sti**NESS n. [f. OF *hasti*, for *-if* (as HASTE[1], see -IVE)]

hat, n., & v.t. Man's, woman's, outdoor head-covering, usu. with brim (cf. BONNET, CAP); *top, high, chimney-pot, h.*, cylindrical silk h.; *opera h.* (cylindrical compressible); *cardinal's* or *red h.*, (fig.) office of cardinal; *h. in hand*, servile(ly); *send round the h.*, solicit contributions; *talk through* one's *h.* (slang), boast or bluff or exaggerate; *as black as my h.*, quite black; *hatband* (put round h.); *h.-block* (for moulding h. on); *h. trick* (Cricket), taking 3 wickets by successive balls; *bad h.* (slang), immoral or dishonourable person; (v.t.) cover, furnish, with h. Hence **ha·t**FUL, **ha·tt**ER[1] (3; *as mad as a hatter*), nn., **ha·t**LESS a. [(vb f. n.) OE *hæt* f. OTeut. *hattuz* (*had-, hôd-*, whence HOOD)]

hatch[1], n. Lower half of divided door; aperture in door, wall, floor, or deck; (Naut.) hatchway, trap-door covering this; *under hh.*, below deck, (fig.) down out of sight, brought low, dead; floodgate; *hatchway*, opening in ship's deck for lowering cargo. [OE *hæc, hec*, cf. Du. *hek*, Da. *hekke*]

hatch[2], v.t. & i., & n. Bring forth (young birds &c., or abs.) from egg; incubate (egg); emerge from egg; (of egg) produce young; contrive & develop (plot &c.); (n.) hatching, brood hatched, (*hh., catches, matches, & dispatches*, newspaper list of births, engagements, marriages, & deaths). [(n. f. vb) ME *hacchen*, etym. dub.]

hatch[3], v.t., & n. Engrave (usu. parallel) lines on (surface); (Arch.) *hatched moulding* (with two crossing sets of parallel lines); (n.) engraved line. [(n. f. vb) f. F *hacher* (as HATCHET)]

ha·tchery, n. Place for hatching fish. [-ERY]

ha·tchet, n. Light short-handled axe; *h.-* (narrow, sharp) *face*; BURY *the h.*; *throw the h.*, exaggerate; *throw the helve after the h.*, add new loss to that already incurred. [f. F *hachette* dim. of *hache* f. OHG **happja* sickle]

ha·tchment, n. Escutcheon; tablet with deceased person's armorial bearings, affixed to front of his house. [corrupt. of ACHIEVEMENT]

hate¹, n. (chiefly poet.). Hatred; (army slang) *morning* &c. *h.*, German bombardment customary at dawn &c. [OE *hete* f. OTeut. *hatoz*]

hate², v.t. Have strong dislike of; bear malice to. Hence **hā·TABLE** a. [OE *hatian* (root *hat-*, whence prec.)]

ha·teful, a. Exciting hatred. Hence **ha·tefulLY²** adv., **ha·tefulNESS** n. [-FUL]

hā·tred, n. Active dislike; enmity, ill-will. [ME (HATE¹ + *-red* = OE *rǣden* condition)]

ha·tti, n. Turkish edict made irrevocable by Sultan's mark. [in full *hattishĕri·f* (-ēf), *hattihumayun* (-hōōmah·ūn), f. Pers. *khattisherif, -humayun*, sacred writing]

hau·berk, n. Coat of mail. [f. OF *hauberc* f. OHG *halsberg* (*hals* neck + *-bergan* cover)]

haugh (hahch, hahf), n. Piece of flat alluvial land by river. [perh. f. OE *healh* corner]

haugh·ty (haw-), a. Proud, arrogant; dignified. Hence **haugh·tiLY²** adv., **haugh·tiNESS** n. [extension of older *haught* a. f. F *haut* f. L *altus* high, -Y²]

haul, v.t. & i., & n. Pull, drag, forcibly; pull *at, upon,* (rope &c.); (Naut.) turn ship's course; *h. upon the wind*, bring ship round to sail closer to wind; (of wind) shift; (n.) hauling, (fig.) amount gained, acquisition. Hence **hau·lAGE(3)** n. [(n. f. vb) var. of HALE v.]

hau·lier, n. One who hauls (esp. tubs in coal-mine to bottom of shaft); jobbing carter. [f. prec., see -YER]

ha(u)lm (hawm, hahm), n. Stalk, stem; (collect. sing.) stems, stalks, of peas, beans, potatoes, &c., without the pods &c. [OE *healm*, cf. G & Da. *halm*, Gk *kalamos* reed]

haunch (haw-, hah-), n. Part of body (of men & quadrupeds) between last ribs & thigh; leg & loin of deer &c. as food; side of arch between crown & piers. [f. OF *hanche* = med. L *hancha* prob. of G orig., cf. OHG *ancha* joint, leg]

haunt (haw-), v.t. & i., & n. Frequent (place); frequent company of (person); (of thoughts &c.) visit (person) frequently; (p.p.) visited, frequented, by ghosts; stay habitually (*in, about,* place, *with* person); (n.) place of frequent resort, usual feeding-place of animals, den frequented by criminals. [(n. f. vb) f. F *hanter*, etym. dub.]

haut·boy (hō-), **ho·boy, o·boe** (-oi), n. High-pitched wooden wind instrument; reed-stop on organ; tall species of strawberry. [f. F *hautbois* (*haut* high + *bois* wood)]

hauteur (hōter·), n. Haughtiness of manner. [F]

haut-goût (hōgōō·), n. Taint, high flavour. [F, = seasoning, lit. high flavour]

Havă·na, n. Cigar made at Havana or in Cuba.

hăve¹, v.t. & i. & auxil. (Pres.: *I have*, archaic *thou hast, he has, we, you, they, have*; past *had*, archaic 2nd sing. *hadst*; p.p. *had*; abbr. *I've, we've*, &c., *I'd, we'd*, &c., *'s = has*; colloq. neg. *haven't, hasn't, hadn't*). Hold in possession; experience the existence of (persons &c. in various relations), as *I h. two sons, no uncle, no equals*; possess, contain, as appendage, part, quality, &c., as *June has 30 days, trees h. leaves, it has its advantages*; enjoy, suffer, as *I had that pleasure, a toothache, no fear*; permit (person) to, as *I will not h. you say such things*; know, as *he has no Greek*; be burdened with, as *I had my work to do*; be obliged, as *I had to do my work*; retain, as *h. this in mind*; entertain, as *h. no doubt*; show by action &c. that one possesses, as *h. the impudence to say*; engage in, carry on, as *had some conversation, h. a game, h. a try* (make an attempt); *he will h. it* (maintains) *that*; *as Plato has* (expresses) *it*, obtain, receive, take (food), as *we had news, h. an egg*; *the Ayes h. it* (h. the advantage); *let him h. it*, punish or reprimand him; *I had him there* (gained advantage over him); (slang) *you h. been had* (cheated); *h. him* (cause him to be) *shot*; *h. him up*, cause him to be brought before court of justice; *I had my leg broken* (experienced such breakage); *h. it your own way* (form of refusal to argue further); *h. at*, make attack upon; *h. done*, stop; *h. on*, be wearing (clothes); *h. it out*, settle dispute (*with* person) by discussion &c., (also) get tooth extracted; (in past subj., = would h.) *had rather* (would prefer to) *go*, *had better go*, would act more wisely in going; (auxiliary) *I have, had, shall have, packed*, my packing is, was, will be, complete, *had I* (if I had) *known* &c. [com.-Teut.: OE *habban*, Du. *hebben*, G *haben*, perh. conn. w. L *habēre*]

have², n. *Haves & have-nots*, rich & poor; (slang) a swindle, take-in. [f. prec.]

hā·ven, n. Harbour, port; (fig., often *h. of rest*) refuge. [OE *hæfen*, cf. Du. *haven*, G *hafen*; perh. f. root of HAVE or HEAVE]

hă·versack, n. (Soldier's) stout canvas bag for provisions. [f. F *havresac* f. G *habersack* (*haber* oats + SACK)]

hă·vildar, n. Sepoy officer corresponding to sergeant. [f. Pers. *ḥawalar* (Arab. *ḥawalah* charge + Pers. *dar* holder)]

ha·ving, n. In vbl senses; also, property, belongings, (often pl.). [-ING¹]

hă·voc, n., & v.t. (-ocking, -ocked). Devastation, destruction, as *make h. of, play h. among*; *cry h.*, give signal to army to seize spoil (now fig.); (v.t.) devastate (often abs.). [(vb f. n.) f. AF *havok* f. OF *havot*, prob. of Teut. orig.]

haw¹, n. (Fruit of) hawthorn; (Hist.) hedge, enclosure; *hawbuck*, country bumpkin; *hawfinch*, common grosbeak. [OE *haga*, cf. Du. *haag* hedge, G *hag* hedge, bush]

haw², n. Third eyelid of horse, dog, &c., cartilage within inner corner of eye. [?]

haw-haw¹, int. & n. Boisterous laugh. Hence **haw-haw** v.i. [imit.]

haw·-haw², =HA-HA.

hawk¹, n., & v.i. & t. Bird of prey used in falconry, with rounded wings shorter than falcon's; *know a h. from a handsaw* (perh. corrupt of HERNSHAW), have ordinary discernment (see *Haml.* II. ii. 397); rapacious person; *h.-eyed*, keen-sighted; *h.-moth*, sphinx-moth; *h.-nosed*, with aquiline nose; *h.'s-bill*, kind of turtle; (v.i.) hunt game with h.; (v.i. & t.) *h.* (*at*), attack as h. does, (of swallows &c.) hunt insects. Hence **haw·kISH¹**, **haw·kLIKE**, aa. [(vb f. n.) OE *habuc*, cf. Du. *havik*, G *habicht*, perh. f. root *haf-* seize]

hawk², v.t. Carry (goods) about for sale (often fig.). [prob. f. HAWKER]

hawk³, v.i. & t. Clear the throat noisily; bring (phlegm &c.) *up* from throat. [prob. imit.]

hawk⁴, n. Plasterer's square board with handle. [?]

haw·ker, n. One who hawks goods about. [prob. f. MLG *hoker* (G *höker*, Du. *heuker*) perh. f. *hocken* carry on one's back]

hawse (-z), n. Part of ship's bows in which *h.-holes* are cut for cables; space between head of anchored vessel & anchors; situation of cables before ship's stem when moored with two anchors out from forward, one on starboard, other on port bow. [16th c. *ha(u)lse*, prob. f. ON *hals* neck]

haw·ser (-s-), n. (naut.). Large rope, small cable, now often of steel. [prob. f. OF *haucier* hoist f. LL **altiare* (*altus* high)]

haw·thorn, n. Thorny shrub, with white, red, or pink blossom & small dark red berry, the HAW¹. [OE *hagathorn* (as HAW¹, see THORN)]

hay, n., & v.t. & i. Grass mown & dried for fodder; *Burgundian h.*, Lucerne; *look for a needle in a* BOTTLE³ (or *bundle*) *of h.*; *make h.*, turn it over for exposure to sun; *make h. of*, throw into confusion; *make h. while the sun shines*, seize opportunities; *haybox* (stuffed with h., in which heated food is left to continue cooking); *haycock*, conical heap of h.; *h. fever*, summer disorder usu. with asthmatic symptoms, caused by pollen or dust; *h.-fork* (for turning over or loading h.); *haymaker*, one who lifts, tosses, & spreads h. after mowing, instrument for shaking & drying h.; *hayrick, haystack*, regular pile of h. with pointed or ridged top; (v.t.) put (land) under h., make into h.; (v.i.) make h. [(vb f. n.) com.-Teut.: OE *hieg*, Du. *hooi*, G *heu*, f. st. of HEW]

hay·ward (-ord), n. Officer of parish &c. in charge of fences & enclosures. [obs. *hay* hedge (as HAW¹)+WARD]

hă·zard (-erd), n., & v.t. Game at dice, with complicated chances; chance; danger; *at all hh.* (risks); each of winning openings in tennis-court; (Billiards) *winning h.*, striking object ball into pocket, *losing h.*, pocketing own ball off another; (Golf) any kind of bad ground; (in Ireland) cab-stand; (v.t.) expose to h., run the h. of, venture on (action, statement, guess). [(vb f. F *hasarder*) f. OF *hasard*, prob. of Arab. orig.]

ha·zardous, a. Risky; dependent on chance. Hence **ha·zardousLY²** adv. **ha·zardousNESS** n. [-OUS]

haze¹, n., & v.t. Obscuration of atmosphere near earth, often arising from heat; (fig.) mental obscurity or confusion; (v.t.) make hazy. [?]

haze², v.t. (naut.). Harass with overwork, (U.S.) bully. [cf. OF *haser* harass, worry]

hā·zel, n. Bush whose fruit is the *h.-nut*; (stick of) its wood; reddish-brown colour (esp. of eyes); WYCH-*h.* Hence **ha·zellY²** a. [OE *hæsel*, cf. Du. *hazel*, G *hasel*]

ha·zy, a. Misty; vague, indistinct; slightly drunk. Hence **ha·zILY²** adv. **ha·zINESS** n. [etym. dub.; known earlier than HAZE¹]

he¹, pron. (obj. *him*, poss. *his*, pl. *they*, obj. *them*, poss. *their*) & n. (pl. *hes*). (Pron.) the male person in question; (n.) male; (attrib. esp. of animals) *he-goat* &c.; *he-man* (U.S.), masterful or virile man. [OE, cogn. w. OFris. *hi, he*; other Teut. langg. use st. *i-*]

he², int. expr. amusement or derision (often repeated, *h. h.*). [in many langg.]

head¹ (hĕd), n. Anterior part of body of animal, upper part of man's body, containing mouth, sense-organs, and brain; (as measure) *taller by a h.*, (Horse-racing) *won by a h.*; *cannot make h. or tail of* (understand); seat of intellect or imagination; life, as *it cost him his h.*; image of h., esp. on one side of coin (opp. to *tail*), as *hh. I win, tails you lose, King's* or *Queen's h.*, (slang) postage stamp; antlers of deer, as *deer of the first h.* (when antlers are first developed); person, as *crowned hh.*, *some hot h.* (hasty person); individual, as *twopence a* or *per head*, esp. of cattle, as *every h. of cattle, twenty h.*; *large h.* (number) *of game*; *good h.*

(stock) *of shell*; thing like h. in form or position, e.g. cutting or striking part of tool, knobbed end of nail &c.; (of plants) compact mass of leaves or flowers at top of stem; foam on top of liquor; cream on top of milk; top (of mast, staircase, page, &c.); maturated part of boil &c.; upper end; end of lake at which river enters it; end of bed at which one's head rests; FOUNTAIN-*h.*; body of water kept at height for mill &c.; pressure (per unit of area) of confined body of steam &c.; front (of procession, army, &c.); front part of plough, holding the share; bows of ship, as *by the h.*, with h. lower in water than stern, (fig.) slightly drunk; promontory, as *Beachy H.*; underground passage for working coal mine; ruler, chief, (often attrib.); master of college; head master of school; position of command, as *at the h. of*; main division in discourse; category; culmination, crisis, as *come to a h.*; (Naut.) seamen's latrine in ship's bows; *old h. on young shoulders*, wisdom in the young; *put* thing *out of* one's *h.*, cease to think of it, give up the idea of it; *put* thing *out of* person's *h.*, make him forget it (*something put it out of my h.*); *off* one's *h.*, crazy; *on* one's *h.* (of vengeance falling, guilt resting, on person); (*stand* &c.) *on* one's *h.*, with feet in air (*could do it on my h.* slang, find it quite easy); *out of* one's *own head*, from one's own invention, *over* one's *h.*, above one, esp. fig. of danger impending &c., (also) beyond one's comprehension, as *he talks over our hh.*, (also) *person is promoted over another's h.* (who has prior claim); *by the h. & ears*, forcibly (esp. of dragging in a story); *over h. &* EARS; *from h. to foot*, all over the person; *h. of hair*, the hair on the h., esp. when copious; *h. over heels*, topsy-turvy; *by h. & shoulders*, =by h. & ears, (also) considerably (*taller*, & fig. of mental or moral stature); *keep* one's *h.*, keep calm; *keep* one's *h. above water*, (fig.) keep out of debt; *lose* one's *h.*, be beheaded, (also) become confused; *make h.*, press forward; *make h. against*, resist successfully; *put* (thing) *into* person's *h.*, suggest it to him; *h. first* or *foremost*, with the h. foremost (of plunge &c.), (fig.) precipitately; *give* (horse) *his h.*, let him go freely; *lay* (*our* &c.) *hh. together*, consult together; *talk* person's *h. off*, weary him with talk; *beat* person's *h. off*, outdo him thoroughly; (prov.) *two hh.* (minds) *are better than one*; *headache*, continuous pain in h.; *headachy*, suffering from, producing, this; *h. & front*, essence (*of* offence &c.; but cf. *Oth.* I. iii. 80), (pop.) leader, ringleader; *headband*, band worn round h.; *headborough* (hist.), petty constable; *h.-dress*, covering (esp. woman's ornamental attire) for the h.; *headfast*, rope at h. of vessel to make her fast to wharf &c.; *h.-gear*, hat, cap, h.-dress; *headland*, promontory, (also) strip left unploughed at end of field; *h.-line*, line at top of page containing title &c., title or sub-title in newspaper; *headman*, chief man, chief of tribe &c.; *h. master*, *mistress*, principal master, mistress, of school; *h.-money* (paid for or by each person); *h.-phones*, telephone or wireless receiver attachable to the listener's ears; *h.-piece*, helmet, (also) intellect, man of intellect, (also) ornamental engraving at h. of chapter &c. in book; *headquarters*, (Mil.) commander-in-chief's residence, (gen.) centre of operations; *headspring*, main source of stream (also fig.); *h.-stall*, part of bridle or halter that fits round h.; *headstock*, bearings of revolving parts in machine; *headstone*, gravestone; *h. stone*, chief stone in foundation (also fig.); *h.-voice*, one of higher registers of voice in singing or speaking; *headway*, progress, (of ship) rate of progress, (Arch.) height of arch &c.; *h. wind* (meeting one directly in front); *h.-work*, mental work. Hence (-)**head**ED[2], **hea·d**LESS, aa. [com.-Teut.: OE *héafod*, Du. *hoofd*, G *haupt*; connexion w. L *caput* doubtful]

head[2] (hĕd), v.t. & i. Furnish with head; (also *h. down*) lop off head of (plant, tree); be, form, the head of; place name &c., (of name &c.) be placed, at the head of (chapter, list, &c.); come to a head, develop; be, put oneself, at the head of (a company &c.); lead; excel; oppose; go round the head of (lake &c.); *h. back, off*, get ahead of so as to turn back, aside; (intr.) front (in named direction); (of ship) make *for* (place, point). [f. prec.]

-head, -hood, suff. forming nn. of condition or quality on nn. & aa. An independent noun appearing in Goth. as *haiduz* manner, way, gives OHG *-heit* & the E suff. (1) *-head*, ME *-hēde*, *-hēd*, first joined to aa. but extended to nn. & finally giving place to *-hood* exc. in a few wds such as *godhead*, *maidenhead*, (distinct in meaning f. *godhood*, *maidenhood*). (2) *-hood*, ME *-hod*, OE *-hád*, orig. noun =person, personality, condition, quality; then as suf. to nn. & later to adjj., both in new formations & to replace *-head*.

hea·der, n. One who puts heads on casks &c.; brick, stone, laid at right angle to face of wall (cf. STRETCHER); plunge head first. [-ER[1]]

hea·ding, n. In vbl senses; also or esp.: (Footb.) striking ball with head; title &c. at head of page &c.; horizontal passage in preparation for tunnel. [-ING[1]]

hea·dlong, adv. & a. Head foremost (in falling &c.); precipitate(ly); impetuous(ly). [earlier *headling* (HEAD[1] + -LING[2]), assim. to -LONG]

hea·dmost, a. Foremost.

hea·dsman, n. Executioner; man in

command of whaling boat. [HEAD[1] + -ES + MAN]

hea·dstrong, a. Violently self-willed. Hence **hea·dstrong**NESS n. [=strong in head]

hea·dy, a. (Of person, thing, action) impetuous, violent; (of liquor &c.) apt to intoxicate. Hence **hea·di**LY[2] adv., **hea·di**NESS n. [-Y[2]]

heal (hēl), v.t. & i. Restore (person, wound) to health (lit. & fig.); cure (person *of* disease); (of wound) become sound or whole; *h.-all,* universal remedy (pop. name of various plants). Hence **hea·l**ER[1] n. (*time is a great healer*). [com.-Teut.: OE *hǽlan,* Du. *heelen,* G *heilen,* cogn. w. HALE, WHOLE]

health (hĕl-) n. Soundness of body (also fig.); condition of body, as *good, bad, h.*; *h.-officer, officer of h.,* (charged with administering h. laws &c.); toast drunk in person's honour; BILL[4] *of h.* [OE *hǽlth,* cogn. w. HALE, see -TH[1]]

hea·lthful, a. Health-giving; conducive to moral or spiritual welfare. Hence **hea·lthful**LY[2] adv., **hea·lthful**NESS n. [-FUL]

hea·lthy, a. Having good health (lit. & fig.); conducive to good health. Hence **hea·lthi**LY[2] adv., **hea·lthi**NESS n. [HEALTH + -Y[2]]

heap[1], n. Group of things lying one on another; (colloq.) large number, as *a h. of people, hh. of times,* (adv.) *he is hh. better*; (colloq.) *struck all of a h.,* mentally prostrated. [OE *héap,* cf. Du. *hoop,* Da. *hob,* G *haufe*; also L *cumbere, cubare,* lie]

heap[2], v.t. Pile (things *up, together,* &c.) in a heap; load (cart, person, &c. *with* goods, benefits, &c.); accumulate (insults &c. *upon*). [OE *héapian,* as prec.]

hear (hēr), v.t. & i. (*heard* pron. herd). Perceive (sound &c. or intr.) with the ear; as *I heard a groan, I h. him groaning, I heard him groan* (but *he was heard to groan*); listen, give audience, to, *as h. him out* (to the end), *h. him his lesson, h. a sermon*; listen judicially to (case, plaintiff, &c.); grant (prayer); *he will not h.* (entertain the notion) *of it*; *you will h. of this* (be reprimanded for it); be informed (*that, of, about*); *h. from,* receive letter or message from; *h. tell of* (archaic), be told about; (as form of cheering, often iron.) *h.! h.!.* Hence **hear·**ABLE a., **hear·**ER[1] n. [com.-Teut.: OE *hieran,* Du. *hooren,* G *hören*]

hear·ing, n. In vbl senses, esp.: perception by ear, as *hard of h.,* deaf; *within, out of, h.,* near enough, too far off, to be heard; *give him a fair h.,* listen impartially to him. [-ING[1]]

hearken (har-), **har-,** v.i. Listen (*to*). [OE *hercnian* (as HARK, w. suf. *-n-*)]

hear·say, n. What one hears (but does not know to be true), gossip, (often attrib., as *h. evidence*).

hearse (hers), n. Car for carrying coffin at funeral; (formerly) framework supporting pall at funeral, often adapted for carrying tapers. [f. F *herse,* f. L *hirpicem* (nom. *-ex*) rake, harrow]

heart (hart), n. Hollow organ keeping up circulation of blood by contracting & dilating; *right, left, h.* (side of h.); *smoker's h.* (h. disorder due to smoking); breast; mind; soul (*h. to h.,* with candour; so *h.-to-h. talks*); *after* one's (*own*) *h.* (desire); seat of the emotions, esp. of love, as *give, lose,* one's *h. to, win the h. of,* (person), *union of hh.* (depending on affection, not constraint); sensibility, as *he has no h.*; courage, as *pluck up* or *take, lose, h.*; (as term of endearment to person) *dear, sweet, h.*; (Naut.) *my hh.* (brave fellows); central part, esp. of tree, as (fig.) *h. of oak,* courageous man; vital part, essence, (*the h. of the matter*); (of land) fertility, as *out of h.,* in poor condition; h.-shaped thing; (Cards, pl.) suit marked with hh.; *at h.,* in one's inmost feelings; *by h.,* in, from, memory, as *learn, say, by h.*; *from* one's *h.,* sincerely; *in* one's *h.,* secretly; *in h.,* in good spirits; *near*(*est*) one's *h.,* dear(est) to one; *out of h.,* in low spirits; *with all* one's *h.,* sincerely, with the utmost goodwill; *find in* one's *h.,* (esp. w. neg.) prevail on oneself (*to* do); *have* thing *at h.,* be deeply interested in it; *lay* thing *to h.* think it over seriously; *searchings of h.,* misgivings; *take* thing *to h.,* be much affected by it; *break* person's *h.,* overwhelm him with sorrow; *cry* one's *h. out,* cry violently, *eat* one's *h. out,* pine away from vexation &c.; *have the h.,* (esp. w. neg.) be hard-hearted enough (*to* do); *h. & hand,* enthusiastically; *in* one's *h. of hh.* (inmost feelings); *h. & soul,* with all one's energy; *have* one's *h. in* one's *mouth,* be violently alarmed or startled; *his h. is in the right place,* he means well; *take h. of grace,* pluck up courage; *wear* one's *h. upon* one's *sleeve,* lack proper reserve; *it does my h. good,* it rejoices me; *h.-ache,* mental anguish; *h.-beat,* pulsation of h., (fig.) emotion; *h.('s)-blood,* life-blood, life; *h.-break,* overwhelming distress; *h.-breaking, -broken,* causing, crushed by, this; *heartburn,* burning sensation in lower part of chest; *h.-burning,* jealousy, grudge; *h.-disease* (of h.); *h.-felt,* sincere (*emotion* &c.); *h.-rending,* distressing; *heartsease,* pansy; *h.-sick,* despondent; *h.-sore,* grieved at h.; *h.-strings,* (fig.) heart, deepest affections; *h.-whole,* undismayed, with the h. unengaged, sincere. Hence **-heart**ED[2] a. [com.-Teut.: OE *heorte,* Du. *hart,* G *herz*; cf. L *cor -dis,* Gk *kardia*]

hear·ten (har-), v.t. & i. Inspirit, cheer (often *up,* also *on*); (intr.) cheer *up.* [f. archaic vb *heart* (OE *hiertan,* as prec.) + -EN[6]]

hearth (har-), n. Floor of fireplace; *h.-rug* (laid before fireplace); *hearthstone*, flat stone forming h., (also) stone &c. for whitening hh. [OE *heordh*, cf. Du. *haard*, G *herd*]

hear·tily, adv. With goodwill, courage, or appetite; very, as *h. sick of it*. [HEARTY, -LY²]

hear·tless, a. Unfeeling, pitiless, cruel. Hence **hear·tless**LY² adv., **hear·tless**NESS n. [-LESS]

hear·ty (har-), a. & n. Cordial, genial; (of feelings) sincere; vigorous; (of meals) abundant; (n., as address to sailors) *my hh.* Hence **hear·ti**NESS n. [-Y²]

heat¹, n. Hotness; sensation, perception, of this; *red, white*, &c., *h.*, at which metals &c. are red, white, &c.; (Physics) kinetic & potential energy of the invisible molecules of bodies, capable of transmission by conduction or radiation (formerly held an elastic material fluid); *latent h.*, h. required to convert a solid into liquid or vapour, or a liquid into vapour; *specific h.*, h. required to raise temperature of a given substance to given extent (usu. one degree), usu. calculated relatively to water; hot weather; inflamed state of body; pungency of flavour; *prickly h.*, skin disease common in hot climates; single effort, esp. *at a h.*; *(trial) hh.*, races, contests, the winners of which compete in *final (h.)*; warmth of feeling, anger; violent stage (of debate &c.); sexual excitement of animals during breeding season (*on, in, at, h.*, of females); *h.-spot*, freckle, (also) point of the skin at which heat can be felt; *h.-wave*, wave of radiant h., (also) access of great h. in atmosphere regarded as passing from place to place. [OE *hǣtu*, cf. MDu. *heete*; also G *hitze*, Du. *hitte*]

heat², v.t. & i. Make hot; inflame (blood &c.); inflame with passion, whence **hea·ted**LY² adv.; (intr.) become hot (lit. & fig.). Hence **hea·t**ER¹(2) n. [com.-Teut.: OE *hǣtan*, Du. *heten*, G *heizen*; cogn. w. HOT]

heath, n. Bare flat waste tract of land, esp. if covered with shrubs; name of such shrubs, esp. of genus *Erica*; *h.-bell*, flower of h. & other plants; *h.-berry*, bilberry, crowberry, & other berries; *h.-cock*, blackcock. Hence **hea·th**Y² a. [OE *hǣdh*, cf. Du. & G *heide*]

hea·then (-dh-), a. & n. (One who is) neither Christian, Jewish, nor Mohammedan; (n. pl. collect.) *the h.*; unenlightened person; *the h.* CHINEE. Hence **hea·then**DOM, **hea·then**ISM(2), **hea·then-ish**NESS, **hea·then**RY, nn., **hea·then**ISH¹ a., **hea·thenish**LY² adv., **hea·then**IZE(3) v.t. & i. [OE *hǣdhen*, cf. Du. *heiden*, G *heide*; Goth. has *haithnô* heathen woman, perh. f. *haithi* heath]

hea·ther (hĕdh-), n. Various species of genus *Erica* (called in the North *Ling*); *h.-bell*, (flower of) species of Erica; *h. mixture*, (fabric) of mixed hues supposed to resemble h. Hence **hea·ther**Y² a. [ME *hathir* etym. dub., now assim. to *heath*]

heave¹, v.t. & i. (past & p.p. *heaved* or *hove*). Lift (heavy thing); (of vein or stratum) displace (another); utter (groan, sigh) with effort; (Naut. & colloq.) throw; (Naut.) haul up, haul, by rope; rise, swell up; rise with alternate falls, as waves; pant; retch; pull (*at* rope, &c.); *h. down*, turn (ship) over on one side for cleaning &c.; *h. to*, bring (sailing-ship, or abs.) to a standstill; *h. in sight*, become visible; *h. ho* (cry of sailors in heaving anchor up). [com.-Teut.: OE *hebban*, Du. *heffen*, G *heben*, cf. L *capere* take]

heave², n. Heaving; *h. of the sea*, force exerted by swell of sea on ship's course; horizontal displacement of vein or stratum; (pl.) disease of horses, broken wind. [f. prec.]

hea·ven (hĕ-), n. Sky, firmament, (in prose now usu. pl.); region of the atmosphere in which clouds float, winds blow, & birds fly; (formerly) each of the heavenly SPHERES; habitation of God & his angels, usually placed beyond sky (cf. HELL); *seventh h., h. of hh.*, highest of seven hh. recognized by Jews, abode of God; God, Providence, as *it is H.'s will*; (in asseverations & exclamations) *by h.!, good hh.!*; place, state, of supreme bliss; *h.-born*, of divine origin. Hence **hea·ven**WARD a., **hea·ven**WARD(S) adv. [OE *hefen*, later *heofone*, cf. LG *heben*; etym. dub.]

hea·venly, a. Of heaven, divine, (*the H. City*, Paradise); of the sky, as *h. bodies*, *the H. Twins*, = GEMINI; of superhuman excellence; (colloq.) *what h.* (excellent) *figs!*; *h.-minded*, holy, devout. Hence **hea·venli**NESS n. [OF *heofonlic* (as prec., see -LY¹)]

hea·vy (hĕ-), a., n., & adv. Of great weight; of great specific gravity; weighty because abundant, as *a h. crop*; laden *with*; (of ordnance of the larger kind) *h. guns, metal, artillery*, (fig.) *h. metal*, formidable opponent(s); (Mil.) carrying h. arms; striking, falling, with force, as *h. storm, sea*; (of ground) clinging, difficult to travel over; (of bread &c.) dense from not having risen; (of food) hard to digest; (of horse) *h. in* or *on hand*, bearing or hanging on bit, (fig.) dull, hard to entertain; (of sky) overcast, gloomy; clumsy in appearance or effect; (of persons) intellectually slow; unwieldy; (of artistic or literary productions) dull, tedious; (Theatr.) serious, sombre, as *h. villain*; oppressive, grievous, as *a h. fate*; sad, as *h. news*; despondent; doleful; drowsy; *it lies h.* (makes its weight felt); *time hangs h.* (passes slowly); (n. pl.) *the Hh.*, Dragoon

Guards, (also) h. artillery; (adv.) = heavily (now chiefly in compounds; as *h.-buying, -laden, -pulling*); *h.-armed*, bearing h. arms or armour; *h.-hearted*, melancholy, doleful; *h. spar*, barytes; *h.-weight*, jockey &c. of more than average weight, boxer over 11 st. 4. Hence **hea·vILY**² adv., **hea·vINESS** n., **hea·vyISH**¹ a. [OE *hefig* (*hefe* weight, cogn. w. HEAVE), cf. Du. *hevig*]

he·bdomad, n. Week (esp. in reference to *Dan.* ix. 27). [f. L f. Gk *hebdomas -ados* (*hepta* seven, see -AD)]

hebdŏ·madal, a. Weekly; (Oxf. Univ.) *H. Council*, board meeting weekly. [f. L *hebdomadalis* (as prec., see -AL)]

Hē·bē, n. (Gk. Myth.) goddess of youth, cupbearer of Olympus; (facet.) waitress, barmaid. [Gk]

hĕ·bĕtate, v.t. & i. Make, become, dull. [f. L *hebetare* (*hebes -etis* blunt), see -ATE³]

Hēbrā·ic, a. Of Hebrew or the Hebrews. Hence **Hebra·ICALLY** adv. [f. LL f. Gk *Hebraïkos* (as HEBREW, see -IC)]

Hē·brāism, n. Attribute of the Hebrews; Hebrew system of thought or religion; Hebrew idiom or expression. So **he·braIZE**(3) v.t. & i., **hebrai·stIC** a., **hebrai·stICALLY** adv. [f. F *hébraïsme* f. late Gk *Hebraïsmos* (as prec., see -ISM)]

Hē·brāist, n. Hebrew scholar; adherent of Hebrew thought or religion. [as prec., -IST]

Hē·brew, n. & a. Israelite, Jew; *Epistle to the Hh.*, book in N.T.; language of the ancient Hebrews; (colloq.) unintelligible speech (cf. GREEK); (adj.) of Hebrew, of the Jews; *H.-wise*, (of writing) from right to left. [f. OF *Ebreu* f. med.L *Ebreus* f. L f. Gk *Hebraios* f. Aram. *'ebrai* = Heb. *'ibri* one from the other side (*'abar* cross over)]

hĕ·catomb (-ŏm), n. (Gk ant.). Great public sacrifice (prop. 100 oxen). [f. L f. Gk *hekatombē* (*hekaton* hundred + *bous* ox)]

heck, n. Frame obstructing passage of fish in river. [OE *hec*, see HATCH¹]

he·ckle, v.t., & n. (Dress *flax, hemp*, with) HACKLE¹; catechize severely. [= HACKLE¹]

hectare (hĕ·ktār, ĕktar·r), n. (In metric system) superficial measure of 100 ares (2·471 acres). [f. HECTO- + ARE¹]

he·ctic, a. & n. *H. fever*, that which accompanies consumption and similar diseases, attended with flushed cheeks and hot skin; consumptive; morbidly flushed (lit. & fig.); (slang) exciting, wild, impassioned, (*for a h. moment*); (n.) h. fever, patient, flush. [f. LL f. Gk *hektikos* habitual, hectic, (*hexis* habit of body, f. *ekhō* hold, be; see -IC)]

hecto- in comb. = Gk *hekaton* hundred, as: *-graph*, apparatus for multiplying copies, (v.t.) multiply with this; (Metric system) *-gram(me)*, weight of 100 grammes (3·52 oz), *-litre, -liter*, (-lēter), 100 litres (3·531 cub. ft), *-metre, meter*, 100 metres (328·089 ft); cf. CENTI-.

he·ctor, n., & v.t. & i. Bluster(er), bully. [(vb f. n.) f. Gk *Hektōr*, son of Priam and Hecuba, Trojan hero in *Iliad*]

he·ddles, n. pl. Small cords or wires through which warp is passed in loom before going through the reed. [?]

hedge¹, n. Fence of bushes or low trees, living (*quickset h.*) or dead (*dead h.*), or of turf, stone, &c. (*doesn't grow on every h.*, is rare); line of things or persons forming barrier; (fig.) barrier; (Betting) act, means, of hedging; *h.-priest*, illiterate priest of low status; *hedgerow*, row of bushes forming h.; *h.-school*, low-class school, (formerly) open-air school esp. in Ireland; *h.-sparrow*, common British and European bird, one of the Warblers. [OE *hecg*, cf. Du. *hegge*, G *hecke*; cogn. w. HAW¹]

hedge², v.t. & i. Surround with hedge (lit. & fig.); fence *off*; hem *in*; make, trim, hedges, whence **he·dgER**¹ n.; secure oneself against loss on (bet, speculation, or abs.) by compensating transactions on the other side; (intr.) avoid committing oneself. [f. prec.]

he·dgehog, n. Spiny insectivorous quadruped, rolling itself up into ball for defence; name of various animals armed with spines; prickly seed-vessel of some plants; person hard to get on with, whence **he·dgehoggY**² a., [HEDGE (from its habits) + HOG (from its snout)]

hēdŏ·nic, a. & n. Of pleasure; (n. pl.) doctrine of pleasure. [f. Gk *hēdonikos* (foll., -IC)]

hē·donism, n. Doctrine that pleasure is the chief good. So **he·donIST** n., **hedoni·stIC** a. [f. Gk *hēdonē* pleasure + -ISM]

heed, v.t. (Sc. & literary), & n. Concern oneself about, take notice of; (n.) careful attention, as *take h., pay* or *give h. to.* Hence **hee·dFUL, hee·dLESS,** aa., **hee·dfulLY**², **hee·dlessLY**², advv., **hee·dfulNESS, hee·dlessNESS,** nn. [(n. prob. f. vb) OE *hēdan*, cf. Du. *hoeden*, G *hüten* (*hut* guard)]

hee·-haw·, n. Ass's bray; loud laugh. [imit.]

heel¹, n. Hinder part of human foot below ankle (*h. of Achilles*, only vulnerable spot, weak point); (Anat.) corresponding part of hind limb in quadruped, often raised above ground; (pop., of quadruped) hinder part of hoof, (pl.) hind feet; part of stocking that covers h.; part of boot that supports h.; thing like h. in shape or position, as handle end of violin bow, crook in head of golf club, after end of ship's keel; *at h., at, on, upon*, one's *hh.*, close behind one; *down at h.*, (of shoes) with h. part crushed down, (of person) wearing such shoes, slovenly; *to h.*, (of dog) close behind, under control; *h.-&-toe* WALK¹*ing*; *hh. over head*, (usu.) *head over hh.*, upside down, in a somersault; *kick* one's *hh.*, stand waiting;

COOL one's *hh.*; *lay, clap, by the hh.*, imprison; *show a clean pair of hh.*, *take to* one's *hh.*, run away; *have the hh. of*, outrun; *turn on* one's *h.*, turn sharply round; *be carried with the hh. foremost* (as a corpse); (Cribbage) *his hh.*, knave if turned up by dealer, scoring two (cf. NOB); *h.-ball*, shoemaker's polishing mixture of hard wax and lamp black; *h.-tap*, a thickness of leather in h., liquor left at bottom of glass. [OE *hēla*, cf. Du. *hiel*, Da. *hæl*]

heel², v.i. & t. Touch ground with heel, e.g. in dancing; furnish (boot &c.) with heel; chase or follow closely; (Football) pass ball *out* at back of scrummage with the heels; (Golf) strike (ball) with heel of club. [f. prec.]

heel³, v.i. & t. (Of ship &c.) lean over owing to pressure of wind or uneven load; cause (ship) to do this. [corrupt. of obs. *heeld*, OE *hieldan* (*heald* sloping), cf. Du. *hellen*]

heel⁴, n. (naut.). Inclination of heeling ship (cf. LIST³). [f. prec.]

heft, n., & v.t. (dial., U.S.). Weight; (dial.) lift, push, (v.t.) lift, esp. to judge weight. [(vb prob. f. n.) 16th c., f. HEAVE v., cf. *weave weft*]

he·fty, a. Sturdy, stalwart, (*a battalion of h. fellows*). [prec., -Y²]

hegemŏ·nic (hĕjĭ-, hēgĭ-), a. Ruling, supreme. [f. Gk *hēgemonikos* (as foll., see -IC)]

hē·gemony (-g-, -j-; *also* -ĕ·m-), n. Leadership, esp. of one State of a confederacy. [f. Gk *hēgemonia* (*hēgemōn* leader)]

hē·gīra (-j)-, **-jira**, n. Mohammed's flight from Mecca to Medina; Mohammedan era reckoned from this (622 A.D.). [med. L, f. Arab. *hijrah* departure from one's country (*hajara* separate)]

hei·fer (hĕf-), n. Young cow that has not had calf. [OE *heahfore*, etym. dub.]

heigh (hā), int. expr. encouragement or inquiry; *h.-ho*, int. expr. boredom, disappointment, &c.

height (hīt), n. Measurement from base to top; elevation above ground or recognized (esp. sea) level; considerable elevation, as *situated at a h.*; high point; top; *the h.* (utmost degree) *of folly* &c.; rising ground; *at its h.* (highest degree). [OE *hiehtho* (as HIGH, see -TH¹)]

heigh·ten (hī-), v.t. & i. Make high(er); intensify; inflate (description, story); (intr.) rise (usu. fig.). [prec. + -EN⁶]

hei·nous (hā-), a. (Of crime or criminal) odious, atrocious. Hence **hei·nous**LY² adv., **hei·nous**NESS n. [f. F *haineux* (*haine* hatred f. *haïr* hate, cf. Goth. *hatjan*; see -OUS)]

heir (ār), n. Person receiving or entitled to receive property or rank as legal representative of former owner; (fig.) one to whom something (joy, punishment, &c.) is morally due; *h.* APPARENT; *h.-at-law* (by right of blood); *h. in tail* (to entailed estate); *h. male*, male h. tracing descent wholly through males; *h.* PRESUMPTIVE. Hence **heir·**DOM, **heir·**ESS¹, **heir·**SHIP, nn., **heir·**LESS a. [OF, f. LL *herem* = L *heredem* (nom. *heres*)]

heir·loom (ār-), n. Chattel that follows devolution of real estate; piece of personal property that has been in family for generations (also fig. of qualities). [prec. + LOOM¹]

hejira. See HEGIRA.

held. See HOLD¹.

helī·acal, a. *H. rising, setting*, of star (when it first emerges from sun's rays and becomes visible before sunrise, or is last visible after sunset before being lost in sun's rays). [f. Gk *hēliakos* (*hēlios* sun, see -AC) + -AL]

hēlia·nthus, n. Genus including common sunflower. [f. Gk *hēlios* sun + *anthos* flower]

hĕ·lical, a. Spiral. Hence or cogn. **he·li·cal**LY² adv., **he·lic**OID, **helicoi·d**AL, aa. [as HELIX + -AL]

Hĕ·licon, n. Boeotian mountain, sacred to Muses; source of poetic inspiration. So **Helicō·**NIAN a. [L, f. Gk *Helikōn*]

hĕ·licopter, n. Flying-machine that should rise vertically by airscrews revolving horizontally. [f. Gk *helix -ikos* screw, *pteron* wing]

hēlio- in comb. = Gk *hēlios* sun, as: *-ce·ntric*, as viewed from centre of sun, taking sun as centre; *-chromy*, photographic representation in natural colours; *-gram*, message by heliograph (3); *-graph*, n., (1) engraving obtained by exposure to light, (2) apparatus for photographing sun, (3) signalling apparatus reflecting flashes of sunlight; *-graph*, v.t., send (message) by heliograph, photograph by heliography; *-gra·phic*, of heliography; *-graphy*, description of the sun, engraving process, signalling by heliograph; *-gravure·*, photogravure; *-meter*, instrument for finding angular distance between two stars (orig. for measuring diameter of sun); *-scope*, apparatus for observing sun without injury to eye; *-the·rapy*, use of sun-baths in treating disease; *-trŏ·pic*, *-tropism*, (of plants) turning, property of turning, in particular way under influence of light; *-type*, picture obtained from gelatine film exposed to light.

hēliō·sis, n. (Bot.) spots on leaves caused by concentration of sun's rays through glass &c.; sunstroke. [Gk *hēliōsis* (*hēlios* sun, see -OSIS)]

hĕ·liotrope, n. Plant with fragrant purple flowers; colour, scent, of these; bloodstone. [f. L f. Gk *hēliotropion* plant turning flowers to the sun (*hēlios* sun + *-tropos* f. *trepō* turn)]

hē·lium, n. A transparent gas, inferred as existing in sun's atmosphere in 1868, first obtained in 1895. [f. Gk *hēlios* sun]

hĕ·lix, n. (pl. *-icēs*). Spiral (like corkscrew, or in one plane like watch-spring); (Arch.) spiral ornament; rim of external ear; genus including common snail. [Gk *helix*]

hell, n. Abode of the dead; abode of condemned spirits; place, state, of wickedness or misery; *a h. of a* (considerable) *noise*; den for captives in Prisoner's Base & other games; gaming-house; (in imprecations) *h.!, what the h. do you want?*; *h.-cat,* spiteful or furious woman; *h. for leather,* at top riding-speed (usu. *ride h. f. l.*); *h.-hound,* fiend; *h.-weed,* name of various plants. Hence **he·llish**[1] a., **he·llishly**[2] adv., **he·llishness** n., **he·llward** adv. & a. [OE *hel(l)*, cf. Du. *hel*, G *hölle*, f. root *hel-* hide]

he·llĕbore, n. Ancient name of various plants supposed to cure madness; (Bot.) species including Christmas Rose. [f. L f. Gk *helleboros*]

He·llēne, n. Ancient Greek of genuine Greek race; subject of modern kingdom of Greece. So **Hellē·nic** a. [f. Gk *Hellēn*]

He·llenism, n. Greek idiom or construction; imitation of the Greeks; Grecian culture; Greek nationality. So **He·llenize**(3) v.t. & i. [f. Gk *Hellēnismos* (as prec., see -ISM)]

He·llenist, n. One who used the Greek language but was not a Greek, whence **Helleni·stic** a.; Greek scholar. [f. Gk *Hellēnistēs* (as prec., see -IST)]

he·llo, n. & v. =HALLO.

helm[1], n. (Archaic) helmet; (also *h.-cloud*) cloud forming over mountain before or during storm. Hence **helmed**[2] a. [com.-Teut.: OE, Du., G; f. *kel-* cover]

helm[2], n., & v.t. Tiller, wheel, by which rudder is managed; space through which h. is turned, as *more, little, h.*; *down* (*with the*) *h., up* (*with the*) *h.,* place h. so as to bring rudder to windward, to leeward; *weather, lee, h.,* h. put up, down; (fig.) government, guidance, (*take the h.,* assume control); *helmsman,* steersman; (v.t.) steer (usu. fig.). [(vb f. n.) OE *helma*, cf. ON *hjálm*]

he·lmet, n. Defensive head-cover of soldiers, firemen, &c.; felt or pith hat for hot climates; upper part of retort; (Bot.) arched upper part of corolla in some flowers; shell of a genus of molluscs. Hence **he·lmeted**[2] a. [obs. F, dim. of *helme* HELM[1]]

he·lminth, n. Worm (usu. intestinal). Hence **helmi·nthic, helmi·nthoid,** aa., **helmintho·logy** n. [f. Gk *helmins -inthos* maw-worm]

hĕ·lot, n. (*H-*) one of a class of serfs in ancient Sparta; *drunken H.* (made drunk as warning to Spartan youth); serf. Hence **he·lotism**(2), **he·lotry**(1, 2), nn., **he·lotize**(3) v.t. [f. L *Helotes* f. Gk *Heilōtes* (pl. of *Heilōs*) taken as=inhabitant of *Helos*, Laconian town]

help[1], v.t. (archaic past *hōlp* & p.p. *hōlpen*). Aid, assist, as *h. me, h. me to lift it, h. me to an answer, h. the work on* or *forward, h. me over the stile, h. me out* (*of* a difficulty); *h.* person *on, off, with* coat &c., h. him to put it on, take it off; *h.* (person) *to,* serve him with (food); distribute (food at meal); remedy, prevent, as *it can't be helped, I can't h. that, don't be longer than you can h.* (cannot); (w. neg.) refrain from or avoid doing (*cannot h. hoping that* —); (in invocation or oath) *so h. me God* (as I keep my word, as I speak the truth, &c.). [com.-Teut.: OE *helpan*, Du. *helpen*, G *helfen*]

help[2], n. Assistance, as *we need your h., she, it, is a great h., by h. of*; (U.S.) domestic servant; *lady h.,* assistant & companion to mistress of house; *mother's h.,* superior nursemaid; remedy or escape, as *there is no h. for it*; helping (of food). [OE & MDu., cf. Du. *hulp*, G *hülfe*]

he·lpful, a. (Of person or thing) useful, serviceable. Hence **he·lpfully**[2] adv., **he·lpfulness** n. [-FUL]

he·lping, n. In vbl senses, esp. portion of food served. [-ING[1]]

he·lpless, a. Lacking help; unable to help oneself. Hence **he·lplessly**[2] adv., **he·lplessness** n. [-LESS]

he·lpmate, n. Helpful companion or partner (usu. husband or wife). [HELP + MATE]

he·lpmeet, n. =prec. [formed by misunderstanding of *Gen.* ii. 18, 20]

he·lter-ske·lter, adv., a., & n. (In) disordered haste. [imit.]

helve, n. Handle of weapon or tool; *throw the h. after the* HATCHET. [OE *hielfe*, cf. MDu. *helf, helve*; f. same root as HALTER]

Helvē·tian (-shn), a. & n. Swiss. [f. L *Helvetius* + -AN]

hem[1], n. Border, edge, of cloth &c., esp. border made by turning in edge & sewing it down. [OE, cf. NFris. *heam*]

hem[2], v.t. Turn down & sew in edge of (cloth &c., or abs.); *h. in, about, round,* enclose, confine. [f. prec.]

hem[3], int., n., & v.i. Int. calling attention or expressing hesitation; (n.) utterance of this; (v.i.) utter sound *h.,* clear throat, hesitate in speech. [imit.]

hematic &c. See **haem-.**

hĕmi-, pref. in wds f. Gk or on Gk elements, =half-, affecting one half, &c., as *-ano·psia,* half-blindness, *he·micycle,* half-moon figure, *-demisemiqua·ver,* half a demisemiquaver, *-he·dral* (cryst.), having half proper number of planes, *-meta·bola,* insects undergoing incomplete metamorphosis, *-plē·gia,* paralysis of one side. [Gk *hēmi-* =L *semi-*]

hĕ·misphere, n. Half sphere; half the celestial sphere, esp. as divided by the equinoctial or by the ecliptic; half the earth, containing (*Eastern h.*) Europe, Asia, & Africa, or (*Western h.*) America;

Northern, Southern, hh., halves of the earth as divided by equator; *Magdeburg hh.*, pair of brass hh. exhausted of air to show atmospheric pressure by their cohesion. Hence **hemisphe·**RIC(AL) aa. [f. OF *emispere* f. Gk HEMI(*sphaira* SPHERE)]

hĕ·mistich (-k), n. Half of line of verse. [f. LL f. Gk HEMI(*stikhion* f. *stikhos* verse)]

he·mlock, n. Poisonous umbelliferous plant, used as powerful sedative; poisonous potion got from this. [OE *hymlic(e)*, etym. dub.]

hemorrhage &c. See **haem-.**

hemp, n. Annual herbaceous plant, native of India; its cortical fibre, used for rope & stout fabrics; (facet.) rope for hanging; = BHANG, HASHISH; name of various other plants yielding fibre. Hence **he·mp**EN[5] a. [OE *henep*, cf. Du. *hennep*, G *hanf*; cogn. w. Gk *kannabis*]

he·m-stitch, v.t., & n. (Hem *cloth* &c. with) kind of ornamental stitch.

hen, n. Female of common domestic fowl (cf. COCK[1]); second element in name of other female birds, as *guinea-h., pea-hen*; *like a h. with one chicken*, absurdly fussy; *h. & chickens*, name of a compound daisy & other plants; *henbane*, narcotic & poisonous plant, drug got from this; *h.-coop* (for keeping poultry in); *h. crab, lobster*, female; *h.-harrier*, blue hawk, a bird of prey; *h.-hearted*, pusillanimous; *h.-party*, (of women only); *h.-pecked*, domineered over by one's wife; *h.-roost*, place where fowls roost at night. [OE *henn* (fem. of *hano* cock) cf. Du. *hen*, G *henne*]

hence, adv. (Archaic) from here, from this, (often pleonast. *from h.*); (poet., rhet.) *h.!*, go away, *h. with*, away with, take away, *go h.*, die; *henceforth, henceforward*, from this time forward; *five years h.*, in five years' time from now; as a result from this; as an inference from this (*h. it appears that*), therefore. [ME *hennes* (*henne* adv. f. root of HE + -ES)]

he·nchman, n. (Hist.) squire, page of honour; chief attendant of Highland chief; trusty follower; political supporter. [14th c.; OE *heng(e)st* male horse, cf. Du. & G *hengst*, + MAN]

hendeca- in comb. = Gk *hendeka* eleven, as *hendĕ·cagon*, plane rectilineal figure of eleven sides, *-sylla·bic* a. & n., (verse) of eleven syllables, *-sy·llable*, such a verse (esp., in Latin: ⏓– (or –⏑) –⏑⏑–⏑–⏑–⏓).

hendī·adȳs, n. Expression of a complex idea by two words connected with *&* (e.g. *in goblets & gold* for *in golden goblets*). [med. L, f. Gk *hen dia duoin* one thing by two]

He·ndon, n. Town in Middlesex associated with aviation.

He·nley, n. (Used for) annual regatta at H.-on-Thames.

he·nna, n. Egyptian privet; its shoots & leaves used as a dye for the body. [Arab. *henna'*]

he·nny, a. & n. Hen-like; (n.) hen-like cock. [HEN + -Y[2]]

hĕ·notheĭsm, n. Belief in one God without asserting that he is the only God (cf. MONOTHEISM). [f. Gk *heis henos* one + *theos* god + -ISM]

hepă·tic, a. Of, good for, the liver; liver-hued. [f. L f. Gk *hēpatikos* (HEPATO-, -IC)]

hĕ·patize, v.t. Convert (lungs) into liver-substance. Hence **hepatiz**A·TION n. [as foll. + -IZE]

hĕpato- in comb. = Gk *hēpar -atos* liver, as *-genous*, originating in the liver.

He·pplewhite, n. A delicate style of furniture. [G. *H.*, d. 1786]

hepta- in comb. = Gk *hepta* seven, as: *-chord*, 7-stringed instrument, 7-note scale; *-glot* a. & n., (book) in seven languages; *-gon*, plane rectilineal figure of seven sides, so *-gonal* a.; *-he·dron*, solid of seven faces; *-sylla·bic*, of seven syllables; *-teuch*, first seven books of Bible.

he·ptad, n. Set, group, of seven. [f. Gk *heptas -ados* set of seven (*hepta*)]

he·ptarchy, n. Government by seven rulers; seven kingdoms of Angles & Saxons in Britain. So **heptar·chi**C(AL) aa. [f. HEPTA- + Gk *-arkhia* government]

her[1], pron. Objective case of SHE; colloq. also subjective, as *Was that her?*. [OE *hire*, dat. of *hio, heo*, SHE]

her[2], pron. & a. Possessive case of, & adj. corresp. to, SHE, with absolute form *hers*, as *it is her hat, it is hers, hers is best, my father & hers suffer(s) for it, her* (vulg. *hers*) *& my* (common) *father, her* (vulg. *hers*) *& my* (respective) *father(s)*. [OE *hi(e)re*, genitive as prec.]

hĕ·rald[1], n. Officer who made state proclamations, bore messages between princes, officiated in the tourney, arranged various state ceremonials, regulated use of armorial bearings, settled questions of precedence, & recorded names & pedigrees of those entitled to armorial bearings; *Heralds' College*, corporation (now) recording pedigrees & granting bearings; messenger (often as title of newspaper); forerunner. [f. OF *heraut*, prob. of Teut. orig.]

he·rald[2], v.t. Proclaim the approach of; usher in. [f. OF *herauder* (as prec.)]

hera·ldic, a. Of heraldry. [-IC]

he·raldry, n. Science of a herald; CANT[3]-*ing h.*; armorial bearings; heraldic pomp. [-RY]

herb, n. Plant whose stem is not woody or persistent; plant of which leaves &c. are used for food, medicine, scent, flavour, &c.; *h. beer*, drink made from hh.; *h. bennet*, yellow-flowered species of Avens [prob. f. OF *herbe beneite* = L *herba benedicta* blessed herb]; *h.-tea, -water*, medicinal infusion of herbs. So **herb**A·CEOUS (*-aceous border* in gardens, one devoted to

perennial flowering plants), **herbi·**FEROUS, **herbi·**VOROUS, **her·b**LESS, aa. [f. OF *erbe* f. L *herba* grass]
her·bage (-ij), n. Herbs collectively; succulent parts of herbs; (Law) right of pasture on another's ground. [OF, f. med. L *herbaticum* (as prec., see -AGE)]
her·bal, a. & n. (Book with descriptions) of herbs. [f. L *herbalis* (as prec., see -AL)]
her·balist, n. One skilled in herbs (now of early botanical writers); dealer in medicinal herbs. [prec. + -IST]
herbār·ium, n. (Book, case, room, for) collection of dried plants. [LL (HERB, -ARIUM)]
her·borize, v.i. Gather herbs, botanize. So **herboriz**A·TION, **her·bor**IST, nn. [f. F *herboriser* (*herbe* HERB, confused w. L *arbor* tree); correct forms *herbalize, -arize,* are archaic]
her·by, a. Abounding in herbs; of the nature of a herb. [-Y[2]]
Hercū·lĕan, a. Of Hercules; strong as Hercules; difficult as his labours. [f. L *Herculeus* (as foll.) + -AN]
Her·culēs, n. (Gk & Rom. Myth.) hero of prodigious strength, who performed 12 immense labours; *Pillars of H.*, rocks on either side of Strait of Gibraltar, (fig.) ultimate limit; strong man; *H. beetle* (S.-Amer., 5 in. long); a northern constellation; *H. powder*, explosive used in mining. [L, f. Gk *Hēraklēs*]
herd[1], n. Company of animals, esp. cattle, feeding or travelling together; large number of people (contempt.), esp. *the, the common, the vulgar, h.*; *the h. instinct*, gregariousness & mutual influence as a psychological factor; *h.-book*, pedigree-book of cattle or pigs; *herdsman*, keeper of hh. [com.-Teut.: OE *heord*, G *herde*, Da. *hjord*]
herd[2], n. Keeper of herds, herdsman, esp. w. word prefixed, as *cowh., swineh.* [com.-Teut.; OE *hirde*, G *hirte*, Da. *hyrde*]
herd[3], v.i. & t. Go in a herd (*together, with* others; esp. fig. of persons); tend (sheep, cattle). [f. HERD[1, 2]]
here (hēr), adv. & n. In this place; (answering roll-call) *h.!*, I am present; (calling attention to person's presence) *my son h. will show you*; (in drinking healths) *here's* (a health) *to*; in this life (esp. *h. below*); at this point (in discourse &c.); in this matter; to this place; *look h.* (in this direction; esp. in bespeaking attention or making protest); *I don't belong h.* (to this place); *h. & there*, in various places; *h., there, & everywhere*, everywhere, all about; *neither h. nor there*, not to the point, of no importance; (colloq., to announce commencement of bold act) *h. goes!*; (n.) this place or point, as *from, to, near, h.*; *hereabout(s)*, somewhere near h.; *hereafter*, in future, later on, in the world to come, (n.) the future, the world to come; *hereat* (archaic), at this; *hereby*, by this means, as a result; *herein*, in this point, book, &c.; *hereinafter*, below (in document &c.); *hereof* (archaic), of this; *hereto* (archaic), to this matter; *heretofore*, formerly; *hereunder*, below (in book &c.); *hereupon*, after this, in consequence of this; *herewith*, with this (esp. of enclosure in letter &c.). [com.-Teut.: OE *hér*, cf. Du. & G *hier*; prob. f. HE]
herĕ·ditable, a. That may be inherited. So **hereditab**I·LITY n. [f. obs. F *héréditable* f. L *hereditare* inherit (*heres -edis* heir), see -ABLE]
hĕrĕdĭ·tament (*or* hĕrĕ·-), n. Property that can be inherited; real property; inheritance. [f. med. L *hereditamentum* (as prec., see -MENT)]
hĕrĕditār·ian, n. One who holds the doctrine of heredity. [-ARIAN]
herĕ·ditary, a. Descending by inheritance; (of diseases, instincts, &c.) transmitted from one generation to another; like, the same as, that one's parents had, as *h. creed, hatred*; of, holding position by, inheritance. Hence **here·ditari**LY[2] adv., **here·ditari**NESS n. [f. L *hereditarius* (as HEREDITY, see -ARY[1])]
herĕ·dity, n. Tendency of like to beget like. Hence **herĕ·dit**ISM(3) n. [f. F *hérédité* f. L *hereditatem* heirship (as HEIR, see -TY)]
herĕ·siarch, n. Leader, founder, of a heresy. [f. LL (*-cha*) f. Gk *hairesiarkhēs* (as foll. + *-arkhēs* ruler)]
hĕ·resy, n. Opinion contrary to the orthodox doctrine of the Christian Church, or to the accepted doctrine on any subject. Hence **he·resio·**LOGIST, **he·resio·**LOGY, nn. [f. OF *eresie* f. L **heresia* for *haeresis* f. Gk *hairesis* choice, sect (*haireomai* choose)]
hĕ·retic, n. Holder of an unorthodox opinion (orig. in the matter of religion). So **herĕ·tic**AL a. [f. F *hérétique* f. eccl. L f. Gk *hairetikos* (as prec., see -IC)]
hĕ·riot, n. (law). Render of best live beast or dead chattel, or money payment, to lord on decease of tenant (now only of manorial tenures). [OE *heregeatwa* (*here* army + *geatwa* trappings)]
hĕ·ritable, a. That passes to heirs-at-law (opp. to movable property); transmissible from parent to child; capable of inheriting. Hence **he·ritab**LY[2] adv. [f. F *héritable* (*hériter*, see HEREDITABLE)]
hĕ·ritage, n. What is or may be inherited; (fig.) portion allotted to any one; (bibl.) the ancient Israelites, the Church; inherited lot. [OF (as prec., see -AGE)]
hĕ·ritor, n. One who inherits. [f. OF *heritier* (as HEREDITARY), assim. to wds in -OR]
herl. See HARL.
hermă·phrodite (-īt), n. & a. Human being, animal, combining characteristics of both sexes; (Zool.) animal having

normally both male & female sexual organs, e.g. earth-worm; (Bot.) plant in which same flower has stamens & pistils; person, thing, combining opposite qualities; ship having characters of two kinds of craft; (adj.) combining both sexes or opposite characteristics. Hence **hermaphro-di·tic(al)** aa., **herma·phroditism** n. [f. L f. Gk *Hermaphroditos*, who became one with the nymph Salmacis]

hermeneu·tic, a. & n. Of interpretation; (n. pl.) interpretation, esp. of Scripture. So **hermeneu·tical** a. [f. Gk *hermēneutikos* (*hermēneuō* interpret, see -IC)]

Her·mēs, n. (Gk Myth.) son of Zeus & Maia, messenger of the gods, god of science, eloquence, &c.; *H. Trismegistus* (Thrice-Great), Neo-platonist name of Egyptian god Thoth, as author of mysterious doctrines, secrets of alchemy, &c. [L f. Gk *Hermēs*]

hermĕ·tic, a. Of alchemy, as *h. art*; *h. seal*, air-tight closure by fusion &c. (also fig.), whence **herme·tically** adv. [f. med. L *hermeticus* irreg. f. HERMES *Trismegistus*]

her·mit, n. Early Christian recluse; person living in solitude; *h.-crab*, kind that lives in mollusc's cast-off shell to protect its shell-less hinder parts. [f. OF *ermite* f. L (*-ta*) f. Gk *erēmitēs* (*erēmia* desert, see -ITE[1])]

her·mitage, n. Hermit's abode; solitary abode; French wine from hill near Valence (with ruined h. on top). [OF (as prec., see -AGE)]

hern. See HERON.

her·nia, n. (path.). Rupture. Hence **her·nial, her·niary**[1], aa., **hernio·tomy** n. [L]

hernshaw. See HERON (etym.).

hēr·o, n. (pl. *-oes*). (Gk Ant.) man of superhuman qualities favoured by the gods, demigod; illustrious warrior, (Rhet) one who has fought for his country (*homes for hh.*, housing for ex-service men); man admired for achievements & noble qualities; chief man in poem, play, or story; *h.-worship(per)*, worship(per) of the ancient hh. or of some great man or men. [f. L f. Gk *hērōs*]

hĕrō·ic, a. & n. (Of acts or qualities) of, fit for, a hero; (of persons) having the qualities of a hero; *the h. age* (of Greece, before return from Troy); (of poetry) dealing with heroes; *h. verse*, that used in h. poetry (Gk & L hexameter, E five-foot iambic, F Alexandrine); (of language) grand, high-flown; bold, attempting great things; (n.) h. verse; (n. pl.) high-flown language or sentiments. Hence **hero·ically** adv. [f. L f. Gk *hērōikos* (as prec., see -IC)]

hĕrōi-cŏ·mic, a. Combining the heroic with the comic. [HERO + -I- + COMIC]

hĕrō·ify, v.t. Make a hero of. [as prec. + -FY]

hero·in, n. A sedative drug prepared from morphia. [?]

hĕ·roine (-ĭn), n. Demigoddess; heroic woman; chief woman in poem, novel, &c. [f. L f. Gk *hērōinē*, fem. of *hērōs* HERO]

hĕ·rōism, n. Heroic conduct or qualities. [f. F *héroïsme* (*héros* HERO, see -ISM)]

hĕ·rōize, v.t. & i. Make a hero of; make heroic; play the hero. [-IZE]

hĕ·ron, hern, n. Long-legged wading bird. [f. OF *harion* f. pop. L **hagironem* (nom. *-ro*) f. OHG *heiger*; OF dim. *heronceau* gives *heronsew, -shew, -shaw, hernshaw*, now dial.]

he·ronry, n. Place where herons breed. [-RY]

her·pēs, n. Skin disease, with patches of distinct vesicles. Hence **herpĕ·tic** a. [L, f. Gk *herpēs, -ētos* shingles (*herpō* creep)]

herpeto·logy, n. Zoology of reptiles. So **herpeto·logist** n. [f. Gk *herpeton* reptile (*herpō* creep) + -LOGY]

Herr (hār), n. (pl. *Herren*). German equivalent of *Mr.* German gentleman.

he·rring, n. North Atlantic fish, much used for food, coming near coast in large shoals to spawn; *kippered h.*, = KIPPER; RED *h.*; *h.-bone*, stitch resembling bones of h., (Arch.) zigzag arrangement of stones or tiles, (v.t.) work with h.-bone stitch, mark with h.-bone pattern; *h.-pond*, (facet.) North Atlantic. [OE *hǣring*, cf. Du. *haring*, G *hering*]

Herrnhuter (hār·nhōōter), n. One of the sect of Moravians. [f. *Herrnhut*, their first German settlement]

hers. See HER.

herse·lf, pron. Emphatic & reflexive form corr. to SHE, as *she said it h., she has hurt h., ask the woman h.*; *she is not h.* (in her normal state of body or mind). [OE *hire self*]

Her·tzian, a. *H. waves*, electric waves (so called from the discoveries of H. R. Hertz, German physicist, d. 1894); *H. telegraphy*, wireless. [-IAN]

hĕ·sitant, a. Hesitating; irresolute. So **he·sitance, -ancy,** nn. [as foll., see -ANT]

hĕ·sitate (-z-), v.i. Show, speak with, indecision; scruple, be reluctant, *to* (do). Hence or cogn. **he·sitatingly**[2] adv., **hesita·tion** n., **he·sitative** a. [f. L *haesitare* frequent. of *haerēre haes-* stick fast, see -ATE[3]]

Hespē·rian, a. (poet.). Western. [f. L f. Gk *Hesperios* (as HESPERUS) + -AN]

he·speris, n. Genus including Rockets & Dame's Violet. [L, f. Gk *Hesperis* of evening, of the West (as foll.)]

hesperor·nis, n. American genus of fossil birds. [as foll. + Gk *ornis* bird]

He·sperus, n. Evening star. [L, f. Gk *hesperos* a. & n., western, evening (star)]

He·ssian (-shn), a. & n. Of Hesse in Germany; *H.* (*boot*), high boot first worn by H. troops; *H. fly*, fly whose larva destroys wheat; (n.) strong coarse cloth of hemp or jute. [-IAN]

hest, n. (archaic). Behest. [OE *hǽs* (*hátan*, see HIGHT), assim. to OE nn. in *-t*]

hĕtaer·a (-tēra), **-air·a** (-īra), n. (pl. *-rae*). Courtesan, harlot. [Gk *hetaira*, fem. of *hetairos* companion]

hetaer·ism, -air·ism (-īr-), n. Open concubinage; communal marriage in a tribe. [f. Gk *hetairismos* (as prec., see -ISM)]

hĕtero- in comb. (before vowel *heter-*) = Gk *heteros* other, different, as: *-chrō·mous*, of different colours; *-dyne, -dyning*, (in wireless reception) pulsation due to simultaneous sounding of waves that are nearly in unison; *-gamous*, irregular as regards stamens & pistils; *-graphy*, incorrect or inconsistent spelling; *-mor·phic*, of dissimilar forms; *-mor·phism*, diversity of form; *-nomous*, subject to different laws (of growth &c.), subject to an external law (cf. AUTONOMOUS); *-nomy*, presence of a different law, subjection to external law; *-pă·thic*, = ALLOPATHIC, also, differing in effect; *-phy·llous*, bearing leaves of different forms on same plant; *-taxy*, abnormal disposition of organs or parts.

hĕ·teroclite, a. & n. Irregularly declined; (n.) h. noun. [f. F *hétéroclite* f. L f. Gk HETERO(*klitos* f. *klinō* inflect)]

hĕ·terodox, a. (Of person or opinion) not orthodox. So **he·terodox**Y[1] n. [f. Gk HETERO*doxos* (*doxa* opinion)]

hĕterogĕ·neous, a. Diverse in character; composed of diverse elements; (Math.) incommensurable because of different kinds. Hence or cogn. **heterogenē·**ITY, **heteroge·neous**NESS, nn., **heteroge·neous**LY[2] adv. [f. scholastic L *heterogeneus* f. Gk HETERO(*genēs* f. *genos* kind) + -OUS]

hĕterogĕ·nesis, n. Birth of a living being otherwise than from parent of same kind, esp. spontaneous generation from inorganic matter. So **heterogen**E·TIC a. [HETERO-]

heterozȳ·gote, n. (Mendelism). Zygote resulting from fusion of unlike gametes. So **heterozy·go**US a. [HETERO-]

he·tman, n. Polish military commander (retained as title among Cossacks). [Polish]

heuri·stic, a. Serving to discover. [irreg. f. Gk *heuriskō* find, see -IC]

hew (hū), v.t. & i. (p.p. *hewn* or *hewed*). Chop, cut, (thing *down, away, off, asunder, to pieces*, &c.) with axe, sword, &c.; cut into shape; *h.* one's *way*, make a way for oneself by hewing; deal cutting blows *at, among*, &c. [com.-Teut.: OE *hēawan*, Du. *houwen*, G *hauen*]

hew·er, n. One who hews; man who cuts coal from seam; *hh. of wood & drawers of water*, drudges (*Joshua* ix. 21). [-ER[1]]

hexa- in comb. (before vowel, & in some mod. words before consonant, *hex-*) = Gk *hex* six, as: *-chord*, diatonic series of six notes with semitone between third & fourth; *-gon, -gonal*, (figure) having six sides; *-gram*, figure formed by two intersecting equilateral triangles (the angular points coinciding with those of a hexagon), figure of six lines; *-he·dral* a., *-he·dron* n., (figure) having six faces; *-pod*, n. & a., (animal) with six feet; *-pody*, line of verse of six feet; *-style* a. & n., (portico) of six columns; *-sylla·bic*; *-teuch*, first six books of Bible.

he·xad, n. A six (uses as PENTAD). [f. Gk *hexas -ados* (*hex* six, -AD)]

hexă·meter, n. Line of six metrical feet, esp. *dactylic h.* (five dactyls & trochee or spondee, any of first four feet, & rarely the fifth, being replaced by spondee). Hence **hexame·tr**IC a., **hexa·metr**IST n. [L, f. Gk HEXA(*metros* f. *metron* measure)]

he·xapla, n. Six-fold text in parallel columns, esp. of Old or New Testament. [Gk, neut. pl. of HEXA(*ploos* -fold)]

hey (hā), int. calling attention, or of joy, surprise, or interrogation; *h. for —!* (expr. applause or exultant appreciation); *h. presto* (conjuror's phrase of command, hence used to announce surprising transformation &c.). [ME ,Du., G]

hey·-day[1], int. expr. joy, surprise, &c. [*hey* prob. = prec.; *day* unexpl.]

hey·day[2] (hā-), n. Full bloom, flush, (of youth, vigour, prosperity, &c,). [?]

heyduck (hī·do͝ok), n. Hungarian of an ennobled military class; Polish liveried retainer. [f. Pol. *hajduk* brigand]

hī, int. calling attention. [parallel form to HEY]

hīa·tus, n. (pl. *-uses*). Break, gap, esp. in a series, account, or chain of proof; break between word ending, and another beginning, with a vowel. [L, vbl n. f. *hiare* gape]

hī·bernate, v.i. Spend the winter (of animals) in torpid state, (of persons) in mild climate; (fig.) remain inactive. So **hi·bern**ANT a., **hibern**A·TION n. [f. L *hibernare* (*hibernus* wintry), see -ATE[3]]

Hīber·nian, a. & n. (Native) of Ireland. [f. L *Hibernia* Ireland, corrupt. of *Iverna* f. Gk *Iernē* f. OCelt. **Iveriu*, whence *Erin*; see -AN]

Hiber·nicism, n. Irish idiom, expression, or bull. [as prec., on *Anglicism* &c.]

hi·ccup, n., & v.i. & t. Involuntary spasm of respiratory organs,with sudden closure of glottis & characteristic sound; (v.i.) make h.; (v.t.) say, bring *out*, with hh. [(vb f. n.) earlier *hicket*, imit.; *hiccough* due to pop. etym.]

hĭc jă·cĕt, n. Epitaph. [L, = here lies]

hick, H-, n. (U.S. colloq.). Countryman, farmer, provincial. [?]

hi·ckory, n. N.-Amer. tree allied to walnut, with tough heavy wood; wood, stick, of this. [f. native Virginian *pohickery*]

hid, hidden. See HIDE[2].

hida·lgo, n. Spanish gentleman. [Sp., f. *hijo dalgo* (L *filius de aliquo*) son of something]

hide[1], n., & v.t. Animal's skin, raw or dressed; (facet.) human skin, as *to save his own h.*; *hide-bound*, (of cattle) with skin clinging close as result of bad feeding, (fig.) narrow-minded; (v.t., colloq.) flog. Hence **(-)hid**ED[2] a. [OE *hȳd*, cf. Du. *huid*, G *haut*, & L *cutis*, Gk *kutos*]

hide[2], v.t. & i. (past *hid*, p.p. *hidden*, *hid*). Put, keep, out of sight (*h.* one's *light under a* BUSHEL); keep (fact) secret (*from*); keep (thing) from view without that intention; *h.* one's *head*, keep out of sight from shame &c.; (intr.) conceal oneself; *h.-&-seek*, children's game (also fig. of dealings with evasive person or thing). [OE *hȳdan*, cf. MDu. *hûden*; cogn. w. Gk *keuthō*]

hide[3], n. (hist.). Measure of land, as much as would support one free family & dependants (perh. about 120 acres). [OE *hīd*, *hīgid* (*hīw-* household)]

hi·dĕous, a. Frightful, repulsive, revolting, to senses or mind, as *h. crime*, *noise*, *pattern*. Hence **hi·deous**LY[2] adv., **hi·deous**NESS n. [f. OF *hidos* (*hisde* fear, etym. dub., -OUS)]

hi·ding[1], n. Thrashing. [f. HIDE[1] + -ING[1]]

hi·ding[2], n. In vbl senses of HIDE[2], esp.: *be in h.*, remain hidden; *h.-place*, place of concealment. [-ING[1]]

hie, v.i. (poet.). Go quickly (*to* &c.); (with pers. pron. used reflexively, orig. dat.) *h. thee, he hied him.* [OE *hīgian* strive, pant, cf. Du. *hijgen*, G *heichen*]

hī·erarch (-k), n. Chief priest; archbishop. [f. med. L (*-cha*) f. Gk *hierarkhēs* (*hieros* sacred + *-arkhēs* ruler)]

hī·erarchy, n. Each of three divisions of angels; the angels; priestly government; organized priesthood in successive grades; any graded organization. Hence **hierar·chic**(AL) aa., **hī·erarch**ISM(3) n. [f. OF *ierarchie* f. LL (*ier-*) f. Gk *hierarkhia* (as prec.)]

hierā·tic, a. Of the priests (esp. of ancient Egyptian writing, & of Egyptian & Greek traditional styles of art); priestly. [f. L f. Gk *hieratikos* f. *hieraomai* be a priest (*hiereus*), -IC]

hīero- in comb. = Gk *hieros* sacred, holy, as: *-cracy*, priestly rule; *-gram*, *-graph*, sacred inscription or symbol; *-latry*, worship of saints; *-logy*, sacred literature or lore.

hī·eroglyph, n. Figure of an object standing for a word, syllable, or sound, as used in ancient Egyptian & other writing; writing of this kind; secret symbol; writing difficult to make out. [f. foll.]

hierogly̆·phic, a. & n. Of, written in, hieroglyphs; symbolical; (n. pl.) hieroglyphs. Hence **hierogly·phic**AL a., **hierogly·phical**LY[2] adv. [f. LL f. Gk HIERO(*gluphikos* f. *gluphē* carving, see -IC)]

hī·erophant, n. (Gk Ant.) initiating priest; expounder of sacred mysteries. Hence **hieropha·nt**IC a. [f. LL f. Gk HIERO(*phantēs* f. *phainō* show)]

hi·ggle, v.i. Dispute about terms; chaffer. [prob. conn. w. HAGGLE]

hi·ggledy-pi·ggledy (-gldĭ), adv., a., & n. (In) utter confusion. [?]

high (hī), a. (n.) & adv. Of great or specified upward extent, as *a h. hill*, *one inch h.*; situated far above ground, sea level, &c.; upper, inland, as *H. Asia*, *H. Dutch*, *German*; (of physical actions) extending to or from, performed at, a height, as *h. jump*, *h. flying*; of exalted rank; *the Most H.*, God; of exalted quality, as *h. art*, *h. minds*; *h. spirit* (courageous, enterprising); *a h.* (very favourable) *opinion of*; *h. life*, that of the upper classes; *h.* (luxurious) *feeding*; (of meat or game) slightly tainted; great, intense, extreme, as *in h. favour*, *h. pressure*, *h. temperature*, *how is that for h.?* (slang appeal to wonder); *h. latitude* (far from equator); *h. colour*, (esp.) red complexion, flush, blush; expensive, as *corn is h.*; (of time) far advanced, as *h. noon*, *it is h. time to go*; (of sounds) acute in pitch, shrill; *h.* (angry) *words*; extreme in opinion, as *a h. Tory*; *h.* (elated, hilarious) *spirits*; *h. & dry*, (of ship) out of the water, (fig.) out of the current of events, of the old High Church before the Oxford movement; (of officers &c.) chief, as *H. Admiral*, *Chancellor*; *with a h.* HAND; *on the h.* HORSE; *h. & low*, (people) of all conditions, (adv.) everywhere (esp. *search h. & l.*); *h. & mighty*, arrogant; *on the h. ropes*, (colloq.) elated, disdainful, enraged; *on h.*, in, to, heaven; *from on h.*, from heaven or a high place; (adv.) far up, aloft; in, to, a h. degree; at a h. price; (of sounds) at, to, a h. pitch; *play h.*, play for h. stakes, play card of h. value; *run h.*, (of sea) have strong current with h. tide (also fig. of feelings); *h.* (chief) *altar*; *h.-blower*, horse that flaps nostrils noisily; *h.-born*, of noble birth; *h.-brow*, a. & n. (U.S. slang), (person) of detached intellectual views on politics &c. (*h.-browed*, of h.-b. kind); *H. Church* n. & a., (party, principles) giving a h. place to authority of Episcopate and priesthood, saving grace of sacraments, &c.; *H.-Churchman*, holder of these principles; *H. Court*, supreme court (usu. = H. Court of Justice); *h. day*, festal day; *h. falu·tin(g)* a. & n. [etym. dub.], bombast(ic); *h.-flown*, extravagant, bombastic; *h.-flyer*, *-flier*, (fig.) ambitious person, one who has high-flown notions; *h.-flying*, fig. ambitious; *h.-handed*, overbearing, arbitrary; *h.* JINKS; *highlands*, mountainous or elevated country, esp. (Sc. pron. hē·lants) N. part of Scotland; *Highlander*, inhabitant of (esp. the Scotch) highlands; *h.-lows* (archaic), boots reaching over ankles; *h.* MASS[1]; *h.-minded*, of morally lofty character, (archaic) proud (*Lord, I am not h.-m.*); *h.-mindedness*, one of these qualities; *h.-pitched,* (of sound) acute in pitch, (of roof &c.) steep, (fig.) of lofty character; *h. priest,* chief priest, esp. of the Jews; *h. priori road,* resort to assumption (see A PRIORI) in preference to reasoning; *h. road,* main road; *h.* SEAS; *h.-spirited,* of lofty or courageous spirit; *h.-stepper,* horse that lifts its feet high in walking & trotting (also fig.); *H. Street* (often proper name of principal street in town, at Oxford usu. *the H.*); *h.-strung,* in h. state of vigour or sensitiveness; *h. table* (for the fellows of college, colloq. *the h.*); *h. tea,* tea at which meat is served; *h.* TIDE; *h.* TREASON; *h. water,* state of tide when water is highest, time when tide is at the full; *h. watermark,* level reached at h. water, (fig.) recorded maximum in any fluctuation; *highway,* public road (often *the king's h.-w.*), main route by land or water, (fig.) ordinary direct course (of action &c.); *high·wayman,* man (usu. mounted, cf. FOOT*pad*) who robs passengers on highway. [com.-Teut.: OE *héah,* Du. *hoog,* G *hoch*]

hīgh·ly, adv. In a high degree, as *h. amusing, h. polished, commend, esteem, h.*; *h. paid* (at a high price); honourably, favourably, as *think, speak, h. of*; *h. descended* (of noble parentage). [OE *héalíce* (as prec., see -LY[2])]

hīgh·ness, n. Title of various British and other princes &c., as *His, Her,* (*Royal, Serene, Imperial*) *H.*; (used where *height* is not idiomatic) *the h. of his character, of the poor-rate, fell from sheer h. of* (but *reached the height of his*) *ambition.* [OE *héanes* (as prec., see -NESS)]

hight (hīt), p.p. (archaic, poet., facet.). Called, named. [irreg. p.p. of OE *hátan,* com.-Teut., cf. Du. *heeten,* G *heissen*]

hī·jacker, n. (U.S. slang). Person who preys on bootleggers, appropriating & profiting by their illicit liquor. [?]

hijra. =HEGIRA.

Hi·lary, n. *H. term,* legal or university term beginning in Jan. [*Hilarius,* d. 367, w. festival 13 Jan.]

hilār·ious, a. Mirthful, joyous. Hence or cogn. **hilar·ious**LY[2] adv., **hilār·ious**NESS, **hilă·**RITY, nn. [f. L *hilaris* + -OUS]

hill, n., & v.t. Natural elevation of earth's surface, small mountain; *the hh.* (Anglo-Ind.), a h.-station as health-resort &c.; heap, mound, however raised, as *ant-, dung-, mole-, h.*; (v.t.) form into h., bank *up* (plants) with soil. Hence **hi·lly**[2] a., **hilli**NESS n. [(vb f. n.) OE *hyll,* cf. MDu. *hil, hul*; also L *collis* hill, *celsus* high, *culmen* top]

hillo·, -loa· (-lō), (*or* hĭ·-), int. used to hail distant person or to express surprise at meeting. [cf. HALLO]

hi·llock, n. Small hill or mound. [-OCK]

hilt, n., & v.t. Handle of sword or dagger; *prove &c. up to the h.,* completely; (v.t.) furnish with h. [(vb f. n.) OE & MDu.]

hī·lum, n. (bot.). Point of attachment of seed to seed-vessel. [L, =little thing, trifle]

him, pron. Objective case of HE; colloq. also subjective, esp. after *than,* as *that's h., you are worse than h.* [OE, dat. of HE & IT]

himse·lf, pron. Emphatic & reflexive form corr. to HE, as *he did it h., I saw the man h., he hurt h.*; *he is not h.* (not in normal state of body or mind. [HIM + SELF]

hīnd[1], n. Female of (esp. red) deer, esp. in and after third year. [OE, cf. Du. & G *hinde*]

hīnd[2], n. Farm servant, esp. (in Scotland & northern England) married & skilled farm-workman, having charge of two horses, & provided with cottage on the farm; steward; rustic, boor. [ME *hine,* prob. f. OE *hína, hígna,* genit. pl. of *hígan, híwan,* domestics]

hīnd[3], a. Situated at the back, posterior, (less usu. than *hinder* exc. of things in pairs, front & back, as *h. leg, quarters, wheel*). [ME, perh. back formation f. OE *hinder* adv. =Goth. *hindar,* G *hinter,* taken as compar. adj., or a shortening of *behindan* BEHIND]

hī·nder[1]. See prec.

hĭ·nder[2], v.t. Impede, obstruct, prevent, as *you will h. him, h. his work, h. its completion, h. him from working* (or abs.). [OE *hindrian,* cf. G *hindern*; f. *hindar* adv., see HIND[3]]

Hi·ndi (-ē), a. & n. (Aryan vernacular language) of N. India. [Hind. (*hind* India)]

hī·ndmost, a. Furthest behind; most remote. [HIND[3]]

hĭ·ndrance, n. Obstruction, prevention; obstacle. [f. HINDER[2] + -ANCE]

Hindu· (-dōō), **-doo·,** (*or* hĭ·-), n. & a. Aryan of N. India who (also, any one who) professes Hinduism; (adj.) of the Hh., that is a H., (loosely) Indian. [Pers., f. *hind* India =Skr. *Sindhu* river (esp. the Indus)]

Hi·nduism, -dooism, n. Polytheistic religion of the Hindus. [-ISM]

Hi·nduize, -dooize, v.t. Render Hindu in religion, customs, &c. [-IZE]

Hindusta·ni, -doosta·nee, (-ŏŏstahnē), a. & n. Of Hindustan; (n.) Hindu, Mohammedan, of Upper India; language of Mohammedan conquerors of Hindustan, Urdu (Hindi mixed with Arabic, Persian, &c.). [Pers. (-*i*), =of *Hindustan* country of the Hindus (HINDU + -*stan* place)]

hinge (-j), n., & v.t. & i. Movable joint or mechanism like that by which door is hung on side post; natural joint doing similar work, as that of bivalve shell; *off the hh.,* in disordered state of body or mind; (fig.) central principle, critical point, on which all turns; (v.t.) attach (as) with h.; (v.i., of door &c. or fig.) hang & turn *on* (post, principle, &c.). Hence **hinge**ED[2], **hi·nge**LESS, aa. [(vb f. n.) ME *heng*, cf. Du. *henghe*, conn. w. HANG]

hi·nny[1], n. Offspring of she-ass by stallion. [f. L *hinnus*, cf. Gk *hinnos*, *ginnos*]

hi·nny[2], **-nie.** See HONEY.

hint, n., & v.t. & i. Slight indication, covert or indirect suggestion; (v.t.) suggest slightly (thing, *that*); (v.i.) *h. at*, give a h. of. [(vb f. n.) prob. f. obs. *hent* lay hold of, etym. dub.]

hi·nterland, n. District behind coast or river's banks. [G]

hip[1], n. Projection of pelvis & upper part of thigh-bone, in men & quadrupeds; *have* (person) *on the h.* (at a disadvantage); *smite h. & thigh* (unsparingly); (Arch.) arris of roof from ridge to eaves; *h.-bath* (in which one sits immersed to the hh.); *h.-disease* (of h.-joint, with fungous growth). Hence (-)**hipp**ED[2] a. [OE *hype*, cf. Du. *heup*, G *hüfte*]

hip[2], **hep**, n. Fruit of (esp. wild) rose. [OE *héope*, *híope*, cf. OHG *hiufo*, *hiafo*]

hip[3], **hyp**, n. Morbid depression, the blues. [=*hyp*(*ochondria*)]

hip[4], v.t. Make low-spirited. [f. prec.]

hip[5], int. introducing united cheer, as *h., h., hurrah.*

hipe, v.t., & n. Throw (antagonist in wrestling) in a particular manner; (n.) such throw. [?]

hi·ppo, n. (colloq.). Hippopotamus. [abbr.]

hippo- in comb. = Gk *hippos* horse, as: *-centaur*, = CENTAUR; *-phagy*, practice of eating horse-flesh; -PHIL; -PHOBIA.

hippoca·mpus, n. (pl. *-pī*). Genus of small fishes, sea-horse; (Anat.) *h. major, minor*, eminences on floor of each lateral ventricle of brain. [f. LL f. Gk HIPPO-(*kampos* sea-monster)]

hi·ppocrăs, n. (hist.). Wine flavoured with spices. [f. OF *ipocras* f. *Hippokratēs* Gk physician of 5th c. B.C., prob. because strained through filter called *Hippocrates's sleeve*]

Hi·ppocrene (-ēn), n. Fountain on Mount Helicon sacred to the Muses. [L f. Gk (*hippos* horse, *krēnē* fountain, as having been produced by stroke of Pegasus's hoof)]

hi·ppodrōme, n. (Gk & Rom. Ant.) course for chariot races &c.; circus. [F, f. L f. Gk HIPPO(*dromos* race, course)]

hi·ppogriff, -gryph, n. Fabulous griffin-like creature with body of horse. [f. F *hippogriffe* f. It. *ippogrifo* (HIPPO- + *grifo* GRIFFIN)]

hippopŏ·tamus, n. (pl. *-muses, -mī*). Large African pachydermatous quadruped inhabiting rivers &c. [f. LL f. Gk HIPPO(*potamos* river)]

hir·cine, a. Goat-like. [f. L *hircinus* (*hircus* goat, see -INE[1])]

hire[1], n. Payment by contract for use of thing or for personal service; engagement on these terms; (fig.) reward; *h.-purchase, h.-system*, (by which hired thing becomes hirer's after certain number of payments); *on h.*, ready to be hired. [OE *hýr*, cf. Du. *huur*, G *heuer*]

hire[2], v.t. Employ (person) for wages; procure, grant (also *h. out*), temporary use of (thing) for stipulated payment. Hence **hīr·**ABLE a. [OE *hýrian*, cf. Du. *huren*, G *heuern*]

hire·ling, n. One who serves for hire (usu. contempt.). [OE *hýrling* (as HIRE[1], see -LING[1])]

hir·sute, a. Hairy, shaggy; untrimmed. Hence **hir·sute**NESS n. [f. L *hirsutus*, cf. *hirtus* shaggy]

his (-z), a. & pron. Possessive case of, & adj. corr. to, HE, also in absolute use, as *h. hat, it is h.* [OE, genit. of HE & IT]

hi·spid, a. (bot., zool.). Shaggy; bristly. [f. L *hispidus*]

hiss, v.i. & t., & n. (Of person, snake, goose, liquid poured on fire, &c.) (make) sharp spirant sound of *s*, esp. as sign of disapproval or derision; express disapproval of (person &c.) thus; *h. off* (the stage), *away, down*, &c., drive off &c. by hh.; utter (quoted words) with angry h. [imit.]

hist, int. used to call attention, enjoin silence, or incite dog &c.

histo- in comb. = Gk *histos* web, tissue, in biol. wds, as: *-ge·nesis, -geny*, production of organic tissues; *-genĕ·tic*, concerned with this; *-logy*, science of organic tissues, whence *-lo·gical, -logist.*

histor·ian, n. Writer of history (esp. in higher sense, as opp. to mere annalist or compiler). [f. F *historien* f. L as HISTORY + -AN]

histor·iated, a. (Of ornamental letters &c.) decorated with figures of men or animals. [f. med. L *historiare* (as HISTORY), see -ATE[2]]

histŏ·ric, a. Noted in history; (Lat. & Gk Gram.) *h. tenses*, those normally used of past events (cf. PRIMARY), *h. present* (used for past), *h. infinitive* (used for indicative); = foll. [f. L f. Gk *historikos* (as HISTORY, see -IC)]

histo·rical, a. Of history, as *h. evidence, principles*; belonging to history, not legend; *h. method* (of investigation), that based on history; in connexion with history, from the historian's point of view (*of purely h. interest*), belonging to the past, not of the present; (of novel, picture, &c.) dealing with h. events; = prec. Hence **histo·rical**LY[2] adv. [-AL]

histori·city, n. Historical character, genuineness, of alleged event &c. [-ITY]

historio·grapher, n. Writer of history, esp. official historian of a court &c. [f. LL *historiographus* (as HISTORY, see -GRAPHER)]

historio·graphy, n. Writing of history. Hence **historiogra·phic(al)** aa. [f. Gk *historiographia* (as foll., see -GRAPHY)]

hi·story, n. Continuous methodical record of public events; (no pl.) study of growth of nations; whole train of events connected with nation, person, thing, &c.; eventful past career, as *this knife has a h.*; (no. pl.) aggregate of past events, course of human affairs; *ancient h.* (usu. to A.D. 476), (facet.) thing that is out of date; *medieval, modern, h.* (to, from, 15th c.); systematic account of natural phenomena &c., esp. NATURAL[1] *h.*; historical play. [f. L f. Gk *historia* inquiry, h., (*histōr* learned man f. *id-* know)]

hi·strion, n. Stage-player (usu. contempt.). [F, f. L *histrionem* (nom. *-io*)]

histriŏ·nic, a. & n. Of actors or acting; stagy, hypocritical, whence **hi·strion-ism, histrio·nicism,** nn.; (n. pl.) theatricals, theatrical art, pretence. Hence **histrio·nically** adv. [f. LL *histrionicus* (as prec., see -IC)]

hit[1], v.t. & i. (hit). Strike with blow or missile; direct blow *at*; (of moving body) strike; (intr.) strike *against, upon*; deliver (blow, person &c. a blow); (fig.) affect sensibly, wound, as *hard h.* (e.g. by money losses); (also *h. upon*) light upon, get at, (thing aimed at); (also *h. off*) imitate to a nicety; fall in with, suit; *h. below the belt*, play foul in boxing & fig.; *h. it, h. the (right) nail on the head*, guess right, express the exact truth; *h. it off*, agree (*with, together*); *h. out*, deal vigorous blows. [OE *hyttan*, cf. Sw. *hitta*, Da. *hitte*]

hit[2], n. Blow, stroke; stroke of sarcasm &c. (*at*); stroke of good luck; successful attempt. [f. prec.]

hitch[1], v.t. & i. Move (thing) with jerk; shift; *h. up*, lift with jerk; contrive to bring (thing *into* story &c.); fasten with loop, hook, &c.; become so fastened (*in, on to*, &c.); *h.* one's WAGGON *to a star*. [?]

hitch[2], n. Jerk, abrupt pull or push; (Naut.) noose, knot, of various kinds, as *half h.* (formed by passing end of rope round its standing part & then through the bight); temporary stoppage; impediment. [f. prec.]

hi·ther (-dh-), adv. & a. To, towards, this place (now usu. *here*); *h. & thither*, in various directions, here & there; (adj.) situated on this side, *the* nearer (of two); *hitherto*, up to this time; *hitherward* (archaic), in this direction. [OE *hider*, f. stem of HE, HERE, + suf. seen in L *citra* on this side]

hive, n., & v.t. & i. (Also *beeh.*) artificial habitation for bees; (fig.) busy swarming place; hiveful of bees; swarming multitude; h.-shaped thing; (v.t.) place (bees) in h., house (persons &c.) snugly, hoard up; (v.i.) enter h., live together like bees. [OE *hȳf*, prob. conn. w. ON *húfr* hull & L *cupa* tub]

hīves, n. pl. Skin eruption; inflammation of bowels, larynx, &c. [?]

h'm. = HEM[3], HUM[2].

hō, int. expr. surprise, admiration, triumph, derision; calling attention; added to other intt. as *heigh-ho, what ho*, or (Naut.) to name of destination &c., as *westward ho.* [not in OE]

hoar, a. & n. Grey-haired with age; greyish white; *h.-frost*, white frost, frozen dew; (of things) grey with age; *h.-stone*, ancient boundary stone; (n.) hoariness, h.-frost. [OE *hár*, cf. OHG *hêr* old, G *hehr* august]

hoard, n., & v.t. Stock, store, (esp. of money laid by; amassed stock of facts &c. (V.t.) amass (money &c. or abs.) & put away, store *up*; treasure up in the heart; overstock oneself with food &c. in war-time. [(vb OE *hordian*) OE *hord*, cf. OS *hord*, Goth. *huzd*, treasure]

hoar·ding, n. Fence of boards round building during erection or repairs, often used for posting bills. [f. obs. *hoard* ult. f. OF *hurt* f. OHG *hurt* hurdle, + -ING[1]]

hoarhound. See HOREHOUND.

hoarse, a. (Of voice) rough, husky, croaking; having such a voice. Hence **hoar·sely**[2] adv., **hoar·sen**[6] v.t. & i., **hoar·seness** n. [OE *hás*, **hárs*, ME *hōrs*, cf. MDu. *hees*]

hoar·y, a. (Of hair) grey, white, with age; having such air, venerable; (Bot., Entom.) covered with short white hairs. Hence **hoar·iness** n. [-Y[2]]

hoax, v.t., & n. Deceive, take in, (person) by way of joke; (n.) humorous or mischievous deception. [f. 18th c.; perh. conn. w. HOCUS]

hob, n. Side casing of fireplace, having surface level with top of grate; peg, pin, as mark in quoits &c.; shoe of sledge; = HOBNAIL. [?]

ho·bble[1], v.i. & t. Walk lamely, limp; (fig.) proceed haltingly in action or speech; (of verse) have halting rhythm; cause to h.; tie together legs of (horse &c.) to prevent it from straying &c.; tie (legs) thus. [14th c.; prob. cogn. w. Du. *hobbelen* rock from side to side, stammer]

ho·bble[2], n. Uneven or infirm gait; awkward situation; rope, clog, &c., for hobbling horse &c.; *h. skirt* (so narrow at foot as to impede wearer in walking). [f. prec.]

ho·bbledehoy, hobbad-, hobbĕd-, n. Awkward youth, between boyhood & manhood. Hence **hobbledehoy·hood, hobbledehoy·ism,** nn., **hobbledehoy·ish**[1] a. [?]

ho·bby[1], n. Favourite subject or occupation that is not one's main business; (archaic) small horse; (Hist.) early type of velocipede. [f. OF *hobin, hobi*, prob. var. of name *Robin*]

ho·bby[2], n. A small falcon. [f. OF *hobé*]

ho·bby-horse, n. Wicker horse used in

morris-dance &c.; child's stick with horse's head; rocking-horse; horse on merry-go-round; (now rare) = HOBBY[1].

ho·bgoblin, n. Mischievous imp; bogy; bugbear. [f. *hob* for *Rob(in)* + GOBLIN]

ho·bnail, n. Heavy-headed nail for boot-soles.

ho·bnailed, a. Furnished or set with hobnails; *h. liver* (studded with projections like nail-heads). [-ED[2]]

ho·b-nob, v.i. (-bb-). Drink together; hold familiar intercourse (*with*). [f. *hob or nob* = give & take, earlier *hab nab*, perh. = have or not have]

hō·bo, n. (U.S.). Wandering workman or tramp. [?]

hock[1], n. Joint of quadruped's hind-leg between true knee & fetlock. [southern by-form of HOUGH]

hock[2], n. German white wine (prop. that of Hochheim). [earlier *hockamore* f. G *Hochheimer*]

ho·ckey, n. Game played with ball & curved clubs between goals. [?]

hō·cus, v.t. (-ss-). Take in, hoax; stupefy (person) with drugs; drug (liquor). [f. obs. n. *hocus* = foll.]

hō·cus-pō·cus, n., & v.i. & t. (-ss-). Jugglery, deception; typical conjuring formula; (v.i.) juggle; (v.t.) play tricks on. [17th-c. sham L]

hod, n. Builder's light open trough on staff for carrying mortar &c.; *hodman*, labourer who carries h., (fig.) mechanical worker, literary hack. [prob. = obs. *hot* f. OF *hotte* panier, of G orig.]

ho·dden, n. (Sc.). Coarse woollen cloth; *h. grey*, grey h., typical rustic garb. [?]

Hodge, n. Typical English agricultural labourer. [changed from *Roger*]

ho·dge-po·dge, n. = HOTCH-POTCH. [assim. to prec.]

hŏdier·nal, a. Of the present day. [f. L *hodiernus* (*hodie* to-day) + -AL]

hŏdŏ·meter, od-, n. Instrument for measuring distance travelled by wheeled vehicle. [f. Gk *hodos* way, see -METER]

hoe (hō), n., & v.t. & i. Tool for loosening soil, scraping up weeds, &c.; *Dutch h.*, kind pushed forward by user; (v.t.) weed (crops), loosen (ground), dig *up*, cut *down*, with h.; (v.i.) use h. [(vb f. n.) f. F *houe* f. OHG *houwâ* (*houwan* HEW)]

hog[1], n. Swine, esp. castrated male reared for slaughter; (dial.) young sheep before first shearing; (fig.) coarse, gluttonous, or filthy person; = ROAD[1]-*h.*; *go the whole h.*, do the thing thoroughly; *hogback*, *h.'s-back*, crested hill-ridge; *h.-fish*, fish with bristles on head; *h. in armour*, stiff clumsy person; *h. mane*, horse's mane cut short; *h.'s pudding*, h.'s entrail variously stuffed; *h.-wash*, kitchen swill &c. for hh. Hence **ho·ggish**[1], **ho·glike**, aa., **ho·ggishly**[2] adv., **ho·ggishness**, **ho·gling**[1], nn. [ME, etym. dub.]

hog[2], v.t. & i. Raise (back &c.), rise, arch-wise in the centre; cut (mane) short. [f. prec.]

ho·gget, n. Yearling sheep. [HOG[1] + -ET[1]]

ho·ggin, n. Sifted gravel. [?]

ho·gmanay, n. (Sc.). Last day of year; gift of cake &c. demanded by children on that day. [f. OF *aguillanneuf* (mod. Norman *hoguignettes*, Guernsey *hoginono*) etym. dub., prob. containing *l'an neuf* the new year]

ho·gshead (-z-h-), n. Large cask; liquid measure, 52½ imperial gallons (abbr. *hhd*). [f. HOG[1] (unexpl.) + HEAD]

hoi(c)k, v.t. & i. Force (aeroplane) to turn abruptly upwards; h. aeroplane. [cf. dial. *hike* swing, toss]

hoick(s), int. used to incite hounds (also *yoicks*). [?]

hoi pollοi. See POLLOI.

hoist[1], v.t. & n. Raise aloft (esp. flags); raise by means of tackle &c. (N.) hoisting, shove up; elevator, lift. [(n. f. vb) corrupt. of obs. *hoise*, earlier *hysse*, cf. Da. *hisse*, Du. *hijschen*, F *hisser*, etym. dub.]

hoist[2], p.p. *H. with his own petard*, blown up by his own bomb, ruined by his own devices against others. [p.p. of *hoise*, see prec.]

hoi·ty-toi·ty, n., a., & int. Riotous or giddy conduct; (adj.) frolicsome; haughty; petulant; (int.) expr. surprised protest at undue assumption &c. [prob. f. obs. *hoit* v. romp, etym. dub.]

hō·key-pō·key, n. = HOCUS-POCUS; cheap ice-cream sold by street vendors. [f. HOCUS-POCUS; second sense perh. of diff. orig.]

hōld[1], v.t. & i. (*held*; also archaic p.p. *holden* in formal reports of meetings &c.). Keep fast, grasp (*held!* at Rugby football, claim that ball being held by opponent as well as runner must be put down); keep (*oneself*, one's head, &c.) in particular attitude; (of vessel) contain; possess, be the owner or holder or tenant of, (property, stocks, land); (Mil.) keep possession of (place); occupy (place, person's thoughts, &c.); engross (person, his attention); keep (person &c.) in specified place, condition, &c., as *h. him at bay*, *in suspense*; *h.* thing *over* one, threaten him constantly with it; make (person) adhere *to* (terms, promise); observe, celebrate, conduct, (festival, meeting, conversation); use (insolent &c. language); *h. to* (bind by) *bail*; restrain, as *h. your noise*, *tongue*, (*h.* one's *hand*, refrain from punishing or other action; *there is no holding* him &c., he &c. is restive or in high spirits or determined); think, believe, (thing, *that*, person &c. *to* be; *h. it good*, think it advisable *to* do); (of judge or court) lay down, decide (*that*); entertain specified feeling towards, as *h. him in esteem*, *contempt*, *h.* thing *cheap* (not value it), *h. dear* (regard with affection);

(intr.) remain unbroken, not give way; *h. by, to,* adhere to (choice, purpose, &c.); *h. with,* approve of; (of laws &c., also *h. good, true*) be valid, apply; keep going, esp. *h. on* one's *way*; (archaic) *h.!*, stop, wait; *h.* one's *hand,* forbear; *h.* one's *head high,* behave proudly; *h. up* one's *head,* not be downcast; *h.* one's *ground,* or one's *own,* not give way; *h. water,* (fig.) be sound, bear examination; *h. aloof,* avoid communication with persons &c.; *h. back,* (trans.) restrain, (intr.) hesitate, refrain *from*; *h. forth,* speak publicly (usu. contempt.); *h. hard,* stop (imperative); *h. in,* confine, keep in check; *h. off,* (intr.) delay; *h. on,* keep one's grasp on something, (colloq. imper.) stop; *h. out,* (trans.) stretch forth, offer (inducement &c.), (intr.) endure, persist; *h. over,* postpone; *h. together* t. & i., (cause to) cohere; *h. up,* support, sustain, (lit. & fig.), exhibit, display, (esp. *to* derision &c.), arrest progress of, obstruct, (U.S.) stop & rob on highway, (of horse) keep up, not fall; *h.-all,* portable case for clothes &c.; *h.-back,* hindrance; *holdfast,* firm grasp, staple or clamp securing object to wall &c. [com.-Teut.: OE *haldan,* MDu. *houden,* G *halten*]

hold², n. Grasp (lit. & fig.), esp. *take, get, keep, h. of*; opportunity of holding, thing to hold by; (fig.) *h.* (*on*), influence (over). [f. prec.]

hōld³, n. Cavity in ship below deck, where cargo is stowed. [corrupt. of HOLE]

ho·lder, n. In vbl senses, esp.: temporary occupant of office &c.; contrivance for holding something, as *cigar, pen, -h.* [-ER¹]

ho·lding, n. In vbl senses, esp.: tenure of land; land held; stocks &c. held. [-ING¹]

hole¹, n. Hollow place in solid body; deep place in stream &c.; animal's burrow; small mean abode; cavity into which ball &c. must be got in various games; (Golf) point scored by player who gets ball from one h. to another with fewest strokes; perforation; (slang) awkward situation (*am in rather, a devil of, a hole*); *pick hh. in,* find fault with; *make a h. in,* use large amount of; *round* (*square*) *peg in square* (*round*) *h.,* person not fitted for his place; *h.-&-corner,* secret, underhand. Hence **ho·ley**² a. [OE & Du. *hol*; orig. neut. adj.]

hole², v.t. & i. Make holes in; (Naut.) pierce side of (ship); make (shaft, tunnel); (Mining, intr.) dig through from one working to another; put into hole; drive (golf-ball, or abs.) into hole. [OE *holian,* as prec.]

hŏ·liday (-dĭ), n. Day of cessation from work or of recreation; (usu. pl.) period of this, vacation; BANK³ *h.*; BLIND¹ *man's h.*; *make h., take a h.,* cease from work; *h.* (gay) *clothes*; *h. task* (to be done by schoolboy during hh.); =HOLY-*day.* [OE *hālig-dæg,* see HOLY & DAY]

hō·lily, adv. In a holy manner. [-LY²]

hō·liness, n. Sanctity; *H., his H.,* title of Pope. [OE *hálignes* (HOLY, -NESS)]

hŏlism, n. (philos.). Tendency in nature to form wholes that are more than the sum of the parts by creative evolution. [as HOLO- + -ISM]

ho·lla, int. See HOLLO. [f. F *holà*]

Ho·lland, n. Province of northern Netherlands, kingdom of the Netherlands, whence **Ho·llander**¹(4) n.; a linen fabric; *brown H.,* this unbleached. [Du., f. *holt* wood + *-lant* land]

Ho·llands, n. A grain spirit. [f. Du. *hollandsch genever,* Holland gin]

ho·llo¹, int. calling attention; (n.) the cry h. [conn. w. HOLLA]

ho·llo², **-low**¹, **-la, -loa,** v.i. & t. Shout (i. & t.); call to hounds. [as prec.]

ho·llow², a., n., & adv. Having a hole, not solid; *h.* SQUARE; empty, hungry; (of sound) not full-toned; (fig.) empty, insincere, false; (n.) h. place, hole, valley, basin; (adv.) *beaten h.* (completely); *h.-eyed,* with eyes deep sunk; *h.-hearted,* insincere; *h. race* &c., feebly contested. Hence **ho·llowly**² adv., **ho·llowness** n. [ME *holg, holch, holu,* a., OE *holh* n., prob. = *hol* HOLE]

ho·llow³, v.t. (Also *h. out*) excavate; bend into hollow shape. [f. prec.]

Ho·lloway, n. (Used for) H. prison (for women awaiting trial & convicted debtors).

ho·lly, n. Evergreen shrub with prickly leaves, small green flowers, & red berries. [OE *hole(g)n,* cf. Du. & G *hulst*]

ho·llyhock, n. Tall plant with large flowers of many varieties of colour. [f. HOLY + obs. *hock* mallow, OE *hoc,* etym. dub.]

Ho·llywood, n. (Used for) moving pictures of American type, chiefly made at H. in California.

holm,¹ **-me,** (hōm), n. Islet, esp. in river or near mainland; flat ground by river, submerged in time of flood. [f. ON *holmr*]

holm² (hōm), n. (Usu. *h.-oak*) evergreen oak, ilex. [corrupt. of OE *holen* HOLLY (from resemblance in foliage) + OAK]

hŏlo- in comb. = Gk *holos* whole, as: *-graph* a. & n., (document) written wholly by person in whose name it appears; *-he·dral,* (of crystal) having full number of planes for perfect symmetry; *-meta·bola* n. pl., insects undergoing complete metamorphosis; *-phote,* apparatus for making available all the light of a lamp (in lighthouse &c.).

ho·locaust, n. Whole burnt-offering; wholesale sacrifice (fig.) or destruction. [f. F *holocauste* f. LL f. Gk HOLO(*kauston* burnt f. *kaiō*)]

holothūr·ian, a. & n. (Animal) of the genus *Holothuria,* sea-slug. [f. mod. L *Holothuria,* n. pl. f. Gk *holothourion,* a zoophyte]

holpen. See HELP[1].

ho·lster, n. Leather case for pistol, fixed to saddle or worn on belt. [17th-c. E & Du., cf. Icel. *hulstr* case, Sw. *holster*]

hōlt, n. (Poet.) wood, copse; wooded hill. [OE, cf. Du. *hout* timber, G *holz* wood, a wood]

hō·ly, a. & n. Consecrated, sacred; morally & spiritually perfect; belonging to, commissioned by, devoted to, God; of high moral excellence; (n.) *h. of hh.*, inner chamber of sanctuary in Jewish temple, separated by veil from *h. place* or outer chamber, (fig.) innermost shrine; *h. cross* (of Christ); *H.* CITY; *H. Cross day*, festival of Exaltation of the Cross, Sep. 14; *h. day*, religious festival; *H.* FAMILY; *H. Ghost, Spirit*, third person of the Godhead; *H.* GRAIL; *h. Joe* (naut. slang), pious person; *H. Land*, W. Palestine, esp. Judaea; *H.* OFFICE; *h.* ORDERS; *H.* ROMAN *Empire*; *h. terror* (slang), formidable person, embarrassing child, bore; *H. Thursday*, (prop.) Ascension Day, (pop.) Thursday in H. Week; *H. Saturday* (in H. Week); *h. water*, water dedicated to h. uses, or blessed by a priest; *H. Week* (before Easter Sunday); *H. Writ*, h. writings collectively, esp. the Bible. [OE *hálig* (*hál* whole, see -Y[2]), cf. Du. & G *heilig*]

hō·lystone, n., & v.t. (Scour with) soft sandstone used for scouring decks. [?]

hōm, n. Sacred plant of ancient Persians & Parsees; its juice. [Pers.]

hŏ·mage, n. (Feud.) formal public acknowledgement of allegiance; acknowledgement of superiority, dutiful reverence, as *pay, do, h. to* (person, his qualities). [f. OF *ommage* f. LL *hominaticum* (*homo -minis* man, see -AGE)]

home[1], n., a., & adv. Dwelling-place; fixed residence of family or household; native land; *long* or *last h.*, the grave; place where thing is native or most common; institution of refuge or rest for destitute or infirm persons; (in games) goal; *at h.*, in one's own house or native land, at one's ease, familiar *with* or *on* or *in* (subject &c.), accessible to callers (esp. *not at h.*), (n.) see AT-HOME; (adj.) of, connected with, h.; carried on at h.; proceeding from h.; in the neighbourhood of h.; *h. counties*, those nearest to London, Middlesex, Surrey, Kent, Essex, & somet. Hertford & Sussex; carried on, produced, in one's own country, as *h. industries, products*; *the h. trade* or *market* (inland; opp. *foreign*); treating of domestic affairs; *H. Office*, department of Secretary of State for H. Affairs, building used for this; that comes h. to one, as *h. question, truth, thrust*; (adv.) to one's h. or country, as *come, go, h.*; arrived at h., as *he is h.*; to the point aimed at, as *the thrust went h.*; *bring charge h. to person*, convict him of it; *come h. to*, affect intimately; *h.-born*, native; *h.-bred*, bred at h.; *h.-brewed* a. & n., (beer &c.) brewed at h.; *h.-coming*, arrival at home; *h.-felt*, felt intimately; *h.-keeping* a., stay-at-home; *h.-made*, made at h. or for h. consumption; *H. Rule*, government of a country (esp. Ireland) by its own citizens; *h.-sick(ness)*, depressed, depression, as result of absence from h. Hence **ho·me**LESS, **ho·me**LIKE, aa. [com.-Teut.: OE *hám*, Du. *heem*, G *heim*; (adv.) accus. case of this]

home[2], v.i. & t. Go home (esp. of pigeons); furnish (person &c.) with a home. [f. prec.]

ho·mely, a. Simple, plain; primitive; unpretending; (of persons or features) uncomely, plain. Hence **ho·meli**NESS n. [-LY[1]]

homeo-. See **homoeo-.**

hō·mer, n. Homing pigeon. [-ER[1]]

Homĕ·ric, a. Of, in the style of, Homer or the poems ascribed to him; *H. laughter* (like that of Homer's gods as they watched lame Hephaestus hobbling). [f. L f. Gk *homērikos* (*Homēros*, traditional author of *Iliad* & *Odyssey*, see -IC]

ho·mespun, a. & n (Cloth made of yarn) spun at home; (anything) plain, homely.

ho·mestead, n. House with outbuildings; farm. [OE *hámstede* (HOME, STEAD)]

ho·meward, adv. & a., **-wards,** adv. (Going, leading) towards home; *h.*-BOUND[5], (esp. of ship) preparing to go, or on the way, home. [-WARD(S)]

hŏ·micīde, n. 1. One who kills a human being. 2. Killing of a human being. Hence **homicī·d**AL a. [F, f. L (1) *homicida*, (2) *homicidium* (*homo* man, see -CIDE)]

homilĕ·tic, a. & n. Of homilies; (n. pl.) art of preaching. [f. Gk *homilētikos* (*homileō* hold converse, consort, as foll.; see -ETIC)]

hŏ·mily, n. Sermon (*Books of Hh.*, for use in parish churches of the Ch. of England, published in 1547 & 1563); tedious moralizing discourse. [f. F *omelie* f. eccl. L f. Gk *homilia* f. *homilos* crowd (*homou* together + *ilē* crowd)]

ho·ming, a. That goes home; (of pigeons) trained to fly home. [part. of HOME[2]]

hŏ·miny, n. Coarsely ground maize boiled with water or milk. [of Amer.-Ind. orig.]

hō·mo, n. (zool.). Man; *H. sapiens* (L = wise), man regarded as a species. [L]

hŏ·mo- in comb. = Gk *homos* same, as: *-ce·ntric*, having same centre; *-gamous*, (Bot.) having all florets hermaphrodite or of same sex; *-gene·tic*, having common descent or origin; *-geny*, similarity due to common descent; *-mor·phic, -mor·phous*, of same or similar form; *-nomous*, having same law of growth; *-phone*, word having same sound as another, but of different meaning or origin (e.g. *gait, gate*), (also) symbol denoting same sound as another; *-phŏ·nic*, (Mus.) of same pitch, in unison; *-phonous*, (of music) in unison, (of symbols) denoting same sound; *-phony*, unison; *-pla·stic*, similar in structure; *-type*, part, organ, like another in structure; *-zȳ·gote* (Mendelism), zygote of like gametes (cf. HETEROZYGOTE), & so *homozy·gous* a.

hŏ·moeopath (-mĭ-), n. One who practises homoeopathy. [f. foll.]

hōmoeo·pathy, n. Hahnemann's treatment of disease by drugs (usu. in minute doses) that in healthy person would produce symptoms like those of the disease. So **homoeopă·thic** a. (often facet., = minute), **homoeopa·thically** adv., **homoeo·pathist** n. [f. Gk *homoios* like + *-patheia* f. *pathos* suffering; first used by Hahnemann (G *homöopathie*)]

homogĕ·neous, a. Of the same kind; consisting of parts all of the same kind, uniform. Hence or cogn. **homogenē·ity**, **homoge·neousness**, nn., **homoge·neously**[2] adv. [f. schol. L *homogeneus* f. Gk HOMO(*genēs* f. *genos* kind) + -OUS]

hŏmoiou·sian (-ow-), a. & n. (One who held that Father & Son in the Godhead were) of like substance (cf. HOMOOUSIAN). [f. Gk *homoiousios* (*homoios* like + *ousia* essence) + -AN]

homŏ·logate, v.t. (Sc.). Acknowledge, admit; confirm. So **homologa·tion** n. [f. med. L *homologare* f. Gk HOMO(*logeō* f. *logos* word), see -ATE[3]]

homŏ·logize (-j-), v.i. & t. Be homologous, correspond; make homologous. [as foll. + -IZE]

homŏ·logous, a. Having the same relation, relative position, &c.; corresponding. [f. med. L f. Gk HOMO(*logos* ratio)]

hŏ·mologue (-ŏg), n. Homologous thing. [F, f. Gk (neut. adj.) as prec.]

homŏ·logy, n. Correspondence, sameness of relation. Hence **homolo·gical** a., **homolo·gically**[2] adv. [f. LL f. Gk *homologia* (as prec.)]

hŏ·monym, n. Word of same form as another but different sense (e.g. POLE[1], POLE[2]); namesake. So **homonȳ·mic**, **homo·nymous**, aa. [f. LL f. Gk *homōnumon*, neut. adj. (HOMO- + *onoma* name)]

hŏmōou·sian, hŏmou·s-, (-ow-), a. & n. (One who held the persons of the Trinity to be) of the same substance (cf. HOMOIOUSIAN). [f. med. L f. Gk HOMO(*ousios* f. *ousia* essence) + -AN]

homu·ncule, -cle, n. Little man, manikin. [f. L *homunculus* (*homo -minis* man, see -CULE)]

ho·my, a. Suggesting home, home-like. [-Y[2]]

hone, n., & v.t. Whetstone, esp. for razors; various stones as material for this; (v.t.) sharpen on h. [(vb f. n.) OE *hān*, cf. ON *hein*, Da. *heen*]

ho·nest (ŏ-), a. Fair & upright in speech & act, not lying, cheating, or stealing; sincere; (of act or feeling) showing uprightness; (of gain &c.) gained by fair means, as *turn, earn, an h. penny*; (of things) unadulterated, unsophisticated; (archaic, of woman) chaste, virtuous; *make an h. woman of*, marry (seduced woman); (patronizing or facet.) good, worthy; *h. Injun* (= Indian), slang phr. questioning (*h.I.?*) or confirming statement. Hence **ho·nestly**[2] adv. [f. OF *honeste* f. L *honestus* honourable, handsome (*honos* HONOUR)]

ho·nesty (ŏ-), n. Uprightness; truthfulness; *h. is the best policy* (maxim of self-interested morality); plant with purple flowers & semi-transparent pods. [f. OF *oneste* f. L *honestatem* (prec., -TY)]

ho·ney (hŭ-), n. Sweet viscid yellow fluid, the nectar of flowers collected by bees & other insects; (fig.) sweetness; (also Sc. & North. *hinnie, -ny*) sweetheart, darling; *h.-bee*, common hive-bee; *h.-buzzard*, bird of prey feeding on larvae of bees & wasps; *h.-dew*, sweet sticky substance found on leaves & stems, held to be excreted by aphides, ideally sweet substance, tobacco sweetened with molasses; *honeysuckle*, woodbine, climbing shrub with fragrant yellow flowers; *h.-sweet*, sweet as h. Hence **ho·neyed**[2], **-nied,** a. [OE *hunig*, cf. Du., G, *honig*]

ho·neycōmb (-m), n., & v.t. Bees' wax structure of hexagonal cells for honey & eggs; cavernous flaw in metal, esp. guns; ornamental or other work hexagonally arranged; (v.t.) fill with cavities, undermine, mark with h. pattern. [(vb f. n.) OE *hunigcamb*, see prec. and COMB]

ho·neymoon, n., & v.i. Holiday spent together by newly married couple; (v.i.) spend h. (*in, at*, place). [(vb f. n.) HONEY + MOON, reference being orig. to waning affection, not to period of a month]

hong, n. (In China) set of buildings used as factory &c.; foreign trading establishment in China or Japan. [f. Chin. *hang* row, rank]

honk, n., & v.i. Wild goose's cry; sound of motor horn; (vb) emit or give h. [imit.]

honorār·ium (hŏ-, ŏ-), n. (pl. *-ums, -a*). Fee for professional services. [LL as foll.]

ho·norary (ŏ-), a. Conferred as an honour (without the usual requirements, functions, &c.); holding h. title or position; *h. secretary, treasurer*, &c., serving without pay (abbr. *hon.*); (of obligations) depending on honour, not legally enforceable. [f. L *honorarius* (as HONOUR, see -ARY[1])]

honori·fic (ŏ-), a. & n. (Expression) implying respect (esp. of Oriental forms of speech). [f. L *honorificus* (as foll., see -FIC)]

honour[1] (ŏ·ner), n. High respect; glory; reputation, good name; nobleness of mind; allegiance to what is right or to conventional standard of conduct; (of woman) chastity, reputation for this; exalted position (*your, his, H.*, said to or of County-Court judge, & in rustic speech to or of any person of rank); thing conferred as distinction; (Golf) right of driving off first as having won last hole (*it is my h.*); (pl.) civilities rendered to guests &c., esp. *do the hh. of* (the table, a house, the town, &c.); *last, funeral, hh.*, observances of respect at funeral; *military hh.*, marks of respect paid by troops at burial of officer, to royalty, &c.; *hh. of war*, privileges granted to capitulating force, as that of marching out with colours flying &c.; (Univv., pl.) special distinction for proficiency beyond that required to pass examination; person, thing, that reflects h. on (*to*) another, as *he is an h. to his profession*; (in Whist) ace, king, queen, knave, of trumps (in Bridge the ten also); (Commerc.) *acceptance* (of protested bill by third party) *for the h. of* (to save the credit of) drawer or indorser; *in h.* (celebration) *of*; *bound in h.* (as a moral duty) *to* (do); *be on* one's *h.* (under moral obligation) *to* (do); (forms of asseveration) *upon my h.*, (colloq.) *h. bright*; *code, law, of h.*, rules forming conventional standard of conduct; AFFAIR, DEBT, LEGION, MAID, POINT, WORD[1], *of h.* [f. OF *onor* f. L *honorem* (nom. *-or*) repute, office, beauty]

ho·nour[2], v.t. Respect highly; confer dignity upon; (Commerc.) accept, pay, (bill) when due. [f. OF *honorer* f. L *honorare* (as prec.)]

ho·nourable, a. Worthy of honour; bringing honour to its possessor; consistent with honour; upright; person's *intentions* (in courting woman) *are h.*, he has marriage in view; title (abbr. *Hon.*) of children of peers below rank of Marquis, Maids of Honour, Justices of High Court, Lords of Session, members of Government or Executive Councils in India & Colonies; *Most H.*, title of Marquises, Order of Bath, & Privy Council; *Right H.*, title of peers below rank of Marquis, Privy Councillors, & others. Hence **ho·nourab**LY[2] adv. [f. OF *honorable* f. L *honorabilis* (as prec., see -BLE)]

hooch (-tsh), n. (U.-S. slang). Alcoholic liquor. [abbr. of *hoochinoo* an Amer.-Ind. name for spirit]

hŏŏd, n., & v.t. Covering for head & neck, whether part of cloak &c. or separate; (Univv.) badge worn over gown &c. to indicate degree; leather covering for hawk's head; thing like h. in shape or use; (v.t.) cover with h. Hence **hoo·d**ED[2] a. [(vb f. n.) OE *hód*, cf. Du. *hoed*, G *hut* hat]

-hŏŏd. See -HEAD.

hoo·die, -dy, n. (Also *h. crow*) Hooded or Royston Crow. [HOOD[1] + -Y[3]]

hōō·dlum, n. (U.S.). Street rowdy, young ruffian. [?]

hoo·dman-blind, n. Old name for BLIND-MAN'S-BUFF.

hoo·dwink, v.t. Deceive, humbug; blindfold. [HOOD n. + WINK v.]

hōōf, n. (pl. *-fs, -ves*), & v.t. & i. Horny casing of foot of horse & other animals; CLOVEN *h.*; (facet.) human foot; *h.-pad*, pad to prevent one foot from striking the other; *h.-pick* (for removing stones from h.); (v.t.) strike with h., (slang, of person) kick (another) *out* &c.; (v.i.) go on foot. Hence (-)**hoof**ED[2] a. [(vb f. n.) com.-Teut.: OE *hóf*, Du. *hoef*, G *huf*]

hŏŏk[1], n. Piece of metal or other material bent back or having sharp angle, for catching hold or for hanging things upon; (also *fish-h.*) bent piece of wire, usu. barbed, for catching fish; (fig.) trap, snare; stroke (see foll.) in cricket or golf; curved cutting instrument, esp. *reaping-h.*; *h. & eye*, small metal h. & loop as dress-fastening; sharp bend, e.g. in river; projecting point of land, esp. *H. of Holland*; =POT-*h.*; *by h. or by crook*, by fair means or foul; *drop off the hh.*, (slang) die; (slang) *on* one's *own h.* (account); *take* one's *h.* (slang), =*h. it* (see foll.); *h.-nose*(*d*), (having) aquiline nose. [OE *hóc*, cf. Du. *hoek* corner, point of land]

hook[2], v.t. & i. Grasp with hook; secure with hook(s); *h. on, in, up*, &c., attach with hook; *h. on* intr., take person's arm; steal; catch (fish) with hook (also fig., esp. husband); (Golf) drive (ball) widely to left; (Cricket) play (ball) round from off to on side without hitting it at the pitch; *h. it* (slang), make off, run away. [f. prec.]

hōō·kah (-*ka*), n. Smoking-pipe with long flexible tube, smoke being drawn through water in vase to which tube and bowl are attached. [f. Arab. *ḥuqqah*, casket, hookah-bottle]

hooked, a. Hook-shaped; furnished with hook(s). [-ED[1,2]]

hōō·ker, n. Kinds of small Dutch & Irish sailing ship (*the old h.*, said scornfully or fondly of any ship). [prob. f. Du. *hoeker* (*hoek* hook)]

hōō·lee, **hō·li** (-lē), n. Hindu festival in honour of Krishna & the milkmaids. [Hind. (-*i*)]

hōō·ligan, n. One of gang of young street roughs. Hence **hoo·ligan**ISM(3) n. [name]

hōōp[1], n., & v.t. Circular band of metal, wood, &c., esp. for binding staves of casks &c.; wooden or iron circle trundled along by child; circle of elastic material for expanding woman's skirt; iron arch used in croquet; *h. petticoat* (expanded by hh.); (v.t.) bind with hh., surround as h. does. [(vb f. n.) OE *hóp*, cf. Du. *hoep*]

hoop[2], v.i., & n. Utter the cry *h.*: *hooping-cough*, contagious disease, esp.

of children, with short violent cough followed by long sonorous inspiration; (n.) the cry h., sound heard in hooping-cough. [(n. f. vb) f. F *houper* (*houp*, imit.); *whoop* is late spelling]

hōō·poe (-ōō), n. S.-European bird with variegated plumage & large erectile crest. [earlier *hoop* f. F *huppe* tuft, crest, bird, f. pop. L *ūpŭpa* = L *ŭpŭpa* hoopoe]

hōōsh, n. (slang). Hotchpotch or stew in Arctic travel. [?]

hōōt, v.i. & t., & n. Make loud sounds, esp. of disapproval (*at* or abs.); assail (person &c.) with derisive shouts; drive (person) *out, away,* &c. by hooting; (of owl) utter cry; (of steam whistle or motor car or driver) sound (intr.); (n.) inarticulate shout, esp. of derision or disapprobation; owl's cry; *not care, not worth, a h.* (U.S. slang, = anything at all). [(n. f. vb) ME *huten*, perh. imit.]

hōōt(s), int. (Sc. & north.) expr. dissatisfaction or impatience. [cf. Sw. *hut* begone, W *hwt* away, Ir. *ut* out, all in similar sense]

hoo·ter, n. In vbl senses, esp.: siren, steam whistle, esp. as signal for work to begin or cease. [-ER[1]]

hōōve, n. Disease of cattle, with inflation of stomach, usu. caused by green fodder. [f. OE *hof-*, a stem of HEAVE]

hop[1], n., & v.t. & i. Climbing perennial plant, cultivated for the cones borne by the female; (pl.) ripe cones of this, used for giving bitter flavour to malt liquor &c.; *h.-bind, -bine,* climbing stem of h.; *h.-fly,* aphis destructive to hh.; *h.-garden,* field for cultivation of hh.; *h.-picker,* labourer, machine, employed to pick hh.; *h.-pillow* (stuffed with hh., to produce sleep); *h.*-POCKET; *h.-pole* (on which h. plant is trained); (v.t.) flavour with, bear, hh.; (v.i.) gather hh. [(vb f. n.) earlier *hoppe*, MDu., etym. dub.]

hop[2], v.i. & t. Spring (of person) on one foot, (of animals) with all feet at once; (trans.) h. over (ditch &c.); (slang) *h.* (*the twig* or *stick*), depart suddenly, die, *h.* (*it*), go away, *h. off,* (of aeroplane) start; *hop-o'-my-thumb,* dwarf, pygmy; *hopscotch,* child's game of hopping on one foot & with it pushing flat stone &c., over *scotches* (lines) marked on ground. [OE *hoppian*, cf. Sw. *hoppa*, Da. *hoppe*, G *hopfen*]

hop[3], n. Hopping (*on the h.,* colloq., bustling about); spring; (colloq.) dance; *h., skip* (or *step*), *& jump,* exercise consisting of these three movements in sequence. [f. prec.]

hope[1], n. Expectation & desire combined (*of* thing, *of* doing, *that*); feeling of trust; ground of h., probability, (*hoping against h.,* clinging to a mere possibility); person, thing, that h. centres in; FORLORN HOPE. [OE *hopa*, cf. Du. *hoop*, G *hoffe*]

hope[2], v.i. & t. Look with expectation & desire (*for* thing or abs.); expect & desire (thing, *that, to* do.) [OE *hopian*, cf. Du. *hopen*]

ho·peful, a. & n. Feeling hope; inspiring hope, promising, often iron. as (n.) *young h.* (of boy or girl). Hence **ho·peful**LY[2] adv., **ho·peful**NESS n. [HOPE[1] + -FUL]

ho·peless, a. Feeling no hope; admitting no hope, as *a h. case.* Hence **ho·peless**LY[2] adv., **ho·peless**NESS n. [-LESS]

ho·plite, n. Heavy-armed foot-soldier of ancient Greece. [f. Gk *hoplitēs* (*hoplon* weapon, see -ITE[1])]

ho·pper[1], n. One who hops; hopping insect, esp. flea or cheese-maggot; inverted pyramid or cone (orig. with hopping motion) through which grain passes in mill; similar contrivance in various machines; barge carrying away mud &c. from dredging-machine & discharging it; *h.-light* or *-casement* (hinged below with opening at top for ventilation). [HOP[2] + -ER[1]]

ho·pper[2], n. Hop-picker. [HOP[1] + -ER[1]]

ho·pple, v.t., & n. Fasten together legs of (horse &c.); (n.) apparatus for this. [(n. f. vb) etym. dub.; earlier than *hobble* in this sense]

hōr·ary, a. Of the hours; occurring every hour. [f. med. L *horarius* (*hora* hour, see -ARY[1])]

Horā·tian (-shn), a. Of, like, (the poems of) Horace (Q. Horatius Flaccus, d. B.C. 8). [f. L *Horatianus* (*Horatius*, see -AN)]

horde, n. Troop of Tartar or other nomads; gang, troop, (usu. in contempt). [ult. f. Turki *orda*, see URDU]

hore·hound, hoar-, n. Herb with bitter aromatic juice used for coughs &c. (also *common, white, h.*); other allied herbs. [OE *hāre hūne* (*hār* hoar + *hūne*, a plant)]

horī·zon, n. Line at which earth & sky appear to meet; *apparent, sensible, visible, h.,* circle of contact with earth's surface of a cone whose vertex is at observer's eye; *celestial, rational, true, h.,* great circle of the celestial sphere, plane of which passes through centre of earth & is parallel to that of sensible h. of a place; (fig.) limit of mental perception, experience, interest, &c. [f. OF *orizonte* f. LL *horizontem* (nom. *-on*) f. Gk *horizōn* (*kuklos*) bounding (circle), part. of *horizō* (*horos* boundary, -IZE)]

horizo·ntal, a. & n. Of, at, the horizon; parallel to the plane of this, at right angles to the vertical; level, flat; (of machinery &c.) having its parts working in h. direction; (n.) h. line, bar, &c. Hence **horizonta·l**ITY n., **horizo·ntal**LY[2] adv. [f. L as prec. + -AL]

hor·mone, n. (physiol.). Kinds of internal secretion that pass into the blood & stimulate organs to action. [f. Gk *hormōn* part. of *hormaō* impel, with *-e* to mark sound of ō]

horn[1], n. Non-deciduous excrescence, often curved & pointed, on head of cattle, sheep, goats, & other mammals, found in pairs, single, or one in front of another; *take the* BULL[1] *by the hh.*; each of two deciduous branched appendages on head of deer; projection on head of other animals, as snail's tentacles, insect's antennae, crest of horned owl; *draw in* one's *hh.*, restrain one's ardour, draw back; substance of which hh. consist; *h.-shavings* (used as manure); thing made of h., as SHOE-*h.*; drinking-vessel, powder-flask, made of h.; *h. of plenty*, = CORNUCOPIA; wind instrument (not now made of h.), as *hunting-h.*, *French h.* (of trumpet class), *English h.* (kind of oboe); h.-shaped projection; extremity of moon or other crescent; arm, branch, of bay, river, &c.; either alternative of a dilemma; *the H.*, Cape Horn; *h.-bar*, cross-bar of carriage; *hornbeam*, small tough-wooded tree used in hedges; *hornbill*, bird with h.-like excrescence on bill; *h.-book* (hist.), paper containing alphabet, Lord's Prayer, &c., mounted on wooden tablet with handle, & protected by thin plate of h.; *h.-mad* (archaic), stark mad (orig. of horned beasts); *h.-plate*, axle-guard of railway carriage; *h.-rimmed* (of spectacles or their wearers); *hornstone*, brittle siliceous rock. Hence **hor·n**FUL n., **hor·n**LESS a. [com.-Teut.: OE & ON *horn*, Goth. *haurn*, cogn. w. L *cornu*, Gk *keras*]

horn[2], v.t. & i. Furnish with horns (esp. in p.p.); gore with the horns; adjust (frame of ship) at right angles to line of keel; *h. in* (U.S.), intrude, interfere. [f. prec.]

hor·nblende (-d), n. Dark-brown, black, or green mineral, a constituent of granite & many rocks, composed chiefly of silica, magnesia, & lime. [G (*horn* + BLENDE)]

hor·ner, n. Maker of horn spoons, combs, &c.; one who blows a horn. [HORN[1] + -ER[1]]

hor·net, n. Large insect of wasp family, inflicting serious sting; *bring hornets' nest about* one's *ears*, stir up host of enemies. [OE *hyrnet(u)*, cf. MDu. *hornete*, LG *hornt*, G *hornisse*]

hor·npipe, n. Obsolete wind instrument; (music for) lively dance, usu. of single person (esp. associated with merry-making of sailors).

hor·ny, a. Of, like, horn; abounding in horns; hard as horn, callous, as *h.-handed*. Hence **hor·ni**NESS n. [-Y[2]]

hŏ·rolŏge (-j), n. Time-piece, dial, clock. So **horo·log**ER[1](3), **horo·log**IST(3), nn. [f. OF *orloge* f. L f. Gk *hōrologion* (*hōra* time + *-logos* -telling)]

horŏ·logy, n. Art of measuring time or making clocks. So **horolo·gic**(AL) aa. [f. Gk *hōra* time + -O- + -LOGY]

horo·pter, n. Aggregate of points seen single in any given position of eyes. [f. Gk *horos* limit + *optēr* one who looks]

hŏ·roscope, n. (astrol.). Observation of sky & planets at certain moment, esp. at person's birth; scheme showing disposition of the heavens at particular moment; *cast a h.*, erect such scheme by calculating degree of ecliptic on eastern horizon at person's birth &c. So **horosco·pic**(AL) aa., **horo·scop**Y[1] n. [F, f. L f. Gk *hōroscopos* (*hōra* time + *skopos* observer)]

hŏ·rrent, a. (poet.). Bristling. [f. L *horrēre* bristle, shudder at, see -ENT]

hŏ·rrible, a. Exciting, fit to excite, horror; hideous, shocking; (colloq.) excessive, unpleasant, as *h. noise, bore, weather.* Hence **ho·rrible**NESS n., **ho·rribl**Y[2] adv. [OF, f. L *horribilis* (as prec., see -BLE)]

hŏ·rrid, a. Terrible, frightful; (poet., archaic) rough, bristling; (colloq.) as prec. Hence **ho·rrid**LY[2] adv., **ho·rrid**NESS n. [f. L *horridus* (as prec., see -ID[1])]

hŏ·rrify, v.t. Excite horror in; shock, scandalize. So **horri·f**IC a., **horri**FICA·TION n. (facet.). [f. L *horrificare* (as HORRENT, see -FY)]

hŏ·rror, n. Terrified shuddering; intense dislike (*of*); (Med.) shuddering, as symptom of disease; *the hh.*, fit of h. or depression, esp. as in delirium tremens; *h.-struck* or *-stricken*, shocked; horrifying thing; *Chamber of Hh.*, place full of hh. (orig. room of criminals &c. in Tussaud's waxwork exhibition). [f. OF *orror* f. L *horrorem* (as prec., see -OR[1])]

hors (F), adv. & prep. Outside, as *h. concours*, (of exhibit) not competing for prize; *h. de combat* pred. a., out of fight, disabled; *h.-d'œuvre* (pl. usu. *-s*), extra dish served as relish at beginning or in interval of meal.

horse[1], n. Solid-hoofed quadruped with flowing mane & tail, used as beast of burden & draught, & for riding on (*you may take a h. to the water, but you can't make him drink*, prov.); (esp.) adult male h., stallion or gelding, (cf. MARE, COLT); (collect. sing.) cavalry; *light h.*, lightly armed mounted soldiers; SEA-*h.*; vaulting block in gymnasium; frame (often with legs) on which something is supported, as *clothes-h.*; (Naut.) rope, bar, in various uses; (Mining) obstruction in vein; *to h.*, (as command) mount your hh.; FLOG *a dead h.*; *grin through a h.-collar*, practise elementary humour; *look a gift h. in the mouth*, find fault with a gift; *mount, ride, the high h.*, put on airs; DARK, WILLING, *h.*; *put the* CART *before the h.*; *eat, work, like a h.* (much); *on horse-back*, mounted on a h.; *h. artillery* (of mounted soldiers); *h.-block*, small platform of stone or wood for mounting h.; *h.-box*, closed vehicle for taking h. by rail or for slinging h. into ship, (facet.) large pew; *h.-breaker*, one who breaks in hh.; *h.-chestnut*, large tree with conical clusters of white or pink flower, fruit of this (like edible chestnut, but of coarse bitter taste); *h.-cloth* (used to cover h., or as part of trappings); *h.*-COPER; *h.-flesh*, flesh of h., esp. as food, horses collectively; *h.-fly*, insect (of various kinds) troublesome to hh.; *H. Guards*, cavalry brigade of English Household troops, esp. (*Royal H.G.*) second regiment of it, (also) headquarters of such cavalry, esp. a building opposite Whitehall, (also) military authorities at head of army; *horse-hair*, hair from mane or tail of h. (often attrib.); *h. latitudes*, belt of calms at northern edge of N.E. trade-winds; *h.-laugh*, loud coarse laugh; *h.-leech*, large kind of leech, insatiable person, (*daughters of the h.-leech, Prov.* xxx. 15); *horseman*, (skilled) rider on horseback; *horsemanship*, art of riding, skill in riding, on horseback; *h.-marines*, imaginary corps of mounted marines, as type of men out of their element, (prov.) *tell that* (nonsense) *to the h.-marines*; *h.-mushroom*, coarse but edible variety with hollow stem; *h.-play*, boisterous play; *h.-pond* (for watering & washing horses, prov. as ducking-place for obnoxious persons); *h.-power*, machine by which work of h. is made to drive other machinery, (Mech.) unit of rate of doing work, =550 foot-pounds per second (abbr. *h.p.*); *h.-race* (between hh. with riders); *h.-radish*, plant whose pungent root is scraped or grated as condiment; *h. sense* (colloq.), plain rough sagacity; *horseshoe*, iron shoe for h., thing of this shape (often attrib., as *h.-s. table*); *h.-tail*, tail of h. (used in Turkey as standard, or as ensign denoting rank of pasha), genus of cryptogamous plants like h.'s tail; *horse-whip*, whip for h., (v.t.) chastise (person) with this; *horsewoman*, woman who rides on horseback. Hence **hor·se**LESS a. [com.-Teut.: OE *hors*, OHG *hros*, Du. *ros*, G *ross*]

horse[2], v.t. & i. Provide (person, vehicle) with horse(s); carry (person) on one's back; place person on man's back to be flogged; (intr.) mount, go, on horseback. [f. prec.]

Hor·sey pouch, n. Rubber tobacco-pouch with one half folding into the other. [inventor's name]

hor·sy, a. Concerned with, addicted to, horses or horse-racing; affecting dress & language of groom or jockey. Hence **hor·si**LY[2] adv., **hor·si**NESS n. [f. HORSE[1] + -Y[2]]

hor·tative, a. Tending, serving, to exhort. So **hor·tat**ORY a. [f. L *hortativus* (*hortari* exhort, see -IVE)]

hor·ticulture (-tsh*er*), n. Art of garden cultivation. Hence **horticu·tur**AL a., **horticu·lltur**IST n. [f. L *hortus* garden + CULTURE]

hor·tus si·ccus, n. Arranged collection of dried plants. [L, =dry garden]

hō·sanna (-z-), n. Cry of *h.*, shout of adoration. (*Matt.* xxi. 9, 15, &c.). [LL f. Gk *hōsanna* f. Heb. *hosha'na* for *hoshi'-ahnna* save, pray!]

hose (-z), n., & v.t. (Collect. as pl.) stockings, *half-h.*, socks, (now chiefly shop); (w. pl. *hoses*) flexible tube for watering plants &c.; *h.-tops* (Sc., pron. hō·tŏps), footless stockings; (v.t.) provide with h., drench or water with h. [(vb f. n.) OE *hosa*, cf. Du. *hoos*, G *hose*]

hō·sier (-zh*er*), n. Dealer in hose & frame-knitted or woven underclothing. Hence **ho·si**ERY(1) n. [f. HOSE[1] + -IER]

hŏ·spice, n. House of rest for travellers, esp. one kept by religious order; home for the destitute or sick. [F, f. L *hospitium* (as HOST[2])]

hŏ·spitable, a. Giving, disposed to give, welcome & entertainment to strangers or guests. Hence **ho·spitab**LY[2] adv. [F, f. med.L *hospitare* entertain, as prec., -ABLE]

hŏ·spital, n. Institution for care of the sick or wounded; charitable institution (in proper names, as *Christ's H.*, public school formerly in London); (Hist.) hospice, establishment of Knights Hospitallers; *h. fever* (typhus arising from exhalations from diseased bodies); *H. Saturday, Sunday*, days on which money is collected in streets &c. (*Saturday*), in churches (*Sunday*), for the local hh. [OF, f. med. L *hospitale* neut. adj. place for guests (as HOST[2], see -AL)]

ho·spitalism, n. (Hygienic imperfections of) the hospital system. [-ISM]

hospita·lity, n. Friendly & liberal reception of guests or strangers; *afford me the h. of your columns*, put my letter in. [f. OF *hospitalité* f. L *hospitalitatem* (as HOSPITAL, see -TY)]

ho·spital(l)er, n. Member of charitable religious order; (in some London hospitals) chaplain; *Knights Hh.*, order of military monks founded c. 1048. [f. OF *hospitalier* f. med. L *hospitalarius* (as prec., see -ARY[1])]

hŏ·spodar, n. Lord (formerly title of governors of Wallachia & Moldavia). [Roumanian, of Slav. orig.]

hōst[1], n. Large number (*of*; person *is a h. in himself*, can do as much as a number of ordinary persons); (archaic) army; (bibl.) *Lord* (*God*) *of hh.* (armies), *host(s) of heaven*, sun, moon, & stars, (also) angels. [OF, f. L *hostis* stranger, enemy]

hōst[2], n. One who lodges another; landlord of inn; *reckon without* one's *h.*, overlook difficulty, opposition, &c.; (Biol.) animal, plant, having parasite or commensal. [f. OF *oste* f. L *hospitem* (nom. *-pes*) host, guest]

hōst[3], n. Bread consecrated in the Eucharist. [f. OF *oiste* f. L *hostia* victim]

hŏ·stage, n. Person given to another as

pledge; pledge, security; *h. to fortune*, person, thing, that one may lose. Hence **ho·stage**SHIP n. [OF, f. L *obses -idis* hostage, see -AGE]

hŏ·stel, n. (Archaic) inn; house of residence for students or other special class. [OF (as HOSPITAL)]

hŏ·stelry, n. (archaic). Inn. [f. OF *ostelerie* (*ostelier* innkeeper, f. med. L as HOSPITALLER, see -ERY)]

hō·stess, n. Woman who entertains guests; mistress of inn. [f. OF *ostesse* (HOST², -ESS¹)]

hŏ·stīle, a. Of an enemy; unfriendly; opposed. Hence **ho·stile**LY² adv. [f. L *hostilis* (as HOST¹, see -IL)]

hosti·lity, n. Enmity; state of warfare; (pl.) acts of warfare; opposition (in thought &c.). [f. LL *hostilitas* (as prec., see -TY)]

hostler (ŏ·sl*er*), n. = OSTLER.

hot¹, a. & adv. Of a high temperature; very warm; communicating or feeling heat; producing the sensation of heat, as *h. fever, blush*; (of pepper &c.) pungent, biting; ardent, passionate; angry; excited; exciting; (Hunt., of scent) strong; (fig., of news &c.) fresh, recent; BLOW¹ *h. & cold*; *h. & h.*, (of food) served as soon as cooked; *give it him h.*, chastise, reprimand, him severely; *make it, the place, too h.* (uncomfortable, by persecution) *for, to hold, him*; (adv.) hotly, eagerly, angrily; *h. air*, (slang) excited or boastful talk; *h. & strong*, vehement(ly); *hotbed*, bed of earth heated by fermenting manure, (fig.) place favourable to growth *of* (vice &c.); *h. blast* (of heated air forced into furnace); *h.-blooded*, ardent, passionate; *h.-brained, -headed*, excitable; *h. cockles* (hist.), rustic game in which blindfolded person guessed who struck him; *h.-foot*, in h. haste; *hothead*, impetuous person; *hothouse*, heated building with glass roof & sides for growing plants out of season or in colder climate; *h.-pot*, mutton, beef, with potatoes &c. cooked in oven in tight-lidded pot; *h.-press*, press of glazed boards & hot metal plates for smoothing paper or cloth, (v.t.) press (paper &c.) in this; *h.-short*, (of iron) brittle in its h. state; *hotspur*, rash person (surname of Sir H. Percy, d. 1403); *h. stuff* (slang), person of high spirit, vigour, skill, or strong will or passions; *h. water*, (fig.) trouble, disgrace, scrape; *h. well*, spring of naturally h. water, reservoir in condensing steam-engine. Hence **ho·t**LY² adv., **ho·t**NESS n. [com.-Teut.: OE *hát*, Du. *heet*, G *heiss*, cf. HEAT]

hot², v.t. (vulg.). Heat, warm *up*. [f. prec.]

Ho·tchkiss, n. A kind of machine gun. [inventor's name]

ho·tchpotch, -pot, n. Dish of many mixed ingredients, esp. mutton broth with vegetables; (Law) blending of properties for purpose of securing equal division (esp. of property of intestate parent); mixture, medley. [f. F *hochepot* (*hocher* shake + POT); *-potch* by assim.]

hōtĕ·l (*or* ō-), n. House for entertainment of travellers &c., (usu. large) inn. [F *hôtel*, later form of HOSTEL]

Ho·ttentŏt, n. Member of S.-African race formerly occupying region near the Cape; (fig.) person of inferior intellect or culture. [Du., perh. = stammerer]

hough (hŏk), n., & v.t. Joint of quadruped's hind leg between true knee & fetlock; (v.t.) hamstring, whence **hou·gh**ER¹ n. [(vb f. n.) f. 14th c.; = OE *hóh* human heel, cogn. w. HEEL¹]

hound¹ (how-), n. Dog for chase, esp. one hunting by scent; *the hh.*, pack of fox-hh.; MASTER *of hh.*; despicable man; player who follows scent in HARE *& hh.*; *h.'s-tongue*, genus of plants of the borage family. Hence **hou·nd**ISH¹ a. [com.-Teut.: OE & G *hund*, Du. *hond*, perh. cogn. w. Gk *kuōn kunos*, L *canis*]

hound², v.t. Chase (as) with hound; set (hound, or fig. person) *at* (quarry &c.); urge (person) *on*. [f. prec.]

hour (owr), n. Twenty-fourth part of day, 60 minutes; short time; *the* time o'clock; (pl.) fixed time for daily work &c., as *office hh. are 10 to 3*; *at the eleventh h.*, at a late stage (*Matt.* xx); *small hh.*, 1, 2, &c., *a.m.*; *good* or *early, bad* or *late, regular, hh.*, (time for getting up & going to bed); *the question of the h.* (present time); *in a good, evil, h.*, (un)luckily; (prayers to be said at) seven stated times of day appointed for prayer; (Astr.) 15° of longitude; *h.-circle*, meridian (24 of which are usu. marked on globe); *h.-glass*, sand-glass running for an hour; *h.-hand* (showing h. on clock &c.). [f. OF *ure* f. L f. Gk *hōra* season, hour]

houri (hoor·ĭ, howr·ĭ), n. Nymph of Mohammedan Paradise; voluptuously beautiful woman. [F, f. Pers. *huri* f. Arab. *ḥaura* (*ḥawira* have eyes like gazelle's)]

hour·ly (owr-), a. & adv. (Occurring, done, reckoned) every hour; continual(ly), frequent(ly). [HOUR + -LY¹·²]

house¹ (hows), n. (*pl. pron.* -zĭz). Building for human habitation or (usu. w. defining prefix) occupation, as ALMS*h.*, BAKE*h.*, LIGHT¹*h.*, SUMMER*h.*; *h. of God*, church, place of worship; inn; *bow down in the h. of Rimmon*, sacrifice one's principles for the sake of conformity (2 *Kings* v. 18); ALE, COFFEE, EATING, *-h.*; PUBLIC, TIED, *h.*; building for keeping animals or goods, as *hen-h.*, STORE*h.*, WARE¹*h.*; (place of abode of) religious fraternity; (Oxf. Univ.) *the H.*, Christ Church; = (boys in) BOARDING*-h.*; (building used by) an assembly, as *H. of* COMMONS, LORDS, *Hh. of* PARLIAMENT; *make a H.*, secure presence of 40 members in H. of Commons; *the H.*, (colloq.) Stock

Exchange, (euphem.) workhouse, (Pol.) H. of Commons or Lords; CLEARING, CUSTOM, *-h.*; COUNTING-HOUSE; (audience in) theatre (*full h.*, with all seats engaged); household, family, dynasty (*the H. of Windsor*, British Royal family); merchantile firm; (Astrol.) twelfth part of heavens; a game of chance playable by large numbers with no apparatus but pencil & paper; (attrib. of animals) kept in, frequenting, infesting, the h., as *h.-cat, -fly*, &c.; *h. of call*, h. where carriers call for commissions, where person may be heard of, &c.; *h. of ill fame*, brothel; *h. & home*, (emphatic) home; *h.-to-h.*, carried on from h. to h.; BRING *down the h.*; *keep h.*, maintain, provide for, a household; *keep open h.*, provide general hospitality; *keep the h.*, not go outdoors; *like a h. on fire*, vigorously, fast; *h.-agent* (for sale & letting of hh.); *h.-boat*, boat fitted up for living in; *housebreaker*, person entering another's h. by day (cf. BURGLAR) with felonious intent, man employed in demolishing old houses; *h. dinner*, (at clubs) specially appointed dinner for members & guests; *h.-dog* (kept to guard h.); *h.-flag*, that flown by a firm's ship; *h.-flannel* (coarse, for cleaning floor &c.); *housekeeper*, woman managing affairs of household, (also) person in charge of h., office, &c.; *housekeeping*, (*good, bad, liberal*, &c.) domestic economy; *houseleek*, herb with pink flowers growing on walls & roofs; *housemaid*, female servant in charge of reception & bed rooms; *housemaid's knee*, inflammation of knee-cap due to kneeling; *housemaster* (of school boarding-h.); *h. of cards* (built by child out of playing-cards; often fig. of insecure scheme &c.); *H. of Keys*, branch of Manx legislature; *h. party* (of guests staying at country house &c.); *h.-place*, living-room in farmhouse &c.; *h.-room*, accommodation in h. (*would not give it h.-r.*, take it as a gift); *h.-surgeon, -physician*, residing in hospital; *h.-top*, esp. *proclaim from the h.-tops*, publicly; *h.-warming*, celebration of entrance into new h.; *housework*, cleaning, cooking, &c. Hence **hou·se**FUL(2) n., **hou·se**LESS a. [com.-Teut.: OE *hús*, Du. *huis*, G *haus*]

house[2] (-z), v.t. & i. Receive (person &c.), store (goods), in house or as house does; (Naut.) place (gun &c.) in secure position, lower (upper masts); take shelter (as) in house; provide hh. for (population; esp. *the housing problem*). [OE *húsian* (as prec.), cf. Du. *huizen*, G *hausen*]

hou·sehold, n. Inmates of house; domestic establishment; (pl.) second quality of flour; *h. troops* (employed to guard sovereign's person); *h. gods*, (Rom. Ant.) Lares & Penates, (fig.) essentials of home life; *h. word*, familiar saying or name. [HOUSE[1] + HOLD[2]]

hou·seholder, n. One who occupies house as his own dwelling (esp. formerly as entitled to franchise); head of household. [HOUSE[1] + HOLDER]

housewife, n. Mistress of family, (*good, bad*) domestic economist, (how·swīf); (hŭ·zĭf) case for needles, thread, &c. Hence **hou·sewife**LY[1] a. [ME *hus(e)wif* (HOUSE[1], WIFE)]

hou·sewifery (-wĭfrĭ), n. Domestic economy, housekeeping. [prec. + -RY]

hou·sing (-z-), n. Horse's cloth covering, for protection or ornament. [obs. *house* f. OF *huche* housing, etym. dub., + -ING[1]]

Houyhnhnm (hwĭ·nĭm), n. Horse with human characteristics (*Gulliver's Travels*). [imit. of horse's neigh; made by Swift]

Hō·va, n. One of ruling tribe in Madagascar. [native]

hove. See HEAVE.

hovel (hŏ·vl, hŭ-), n. Open shed, outhouse; mean dwelling; conical building enclosing kiln. [?]

hoveller (hŏ·vler, hŭ-), n. Unlicensed pilot or boatman, esp. one who goes out to wrecks. [?]

hŏ·ver (*or* hŭ-), v.i., & n. (Of bird &c.) hang in the air (*over, about*, spot); loiter *about* (person, place); (n.) hovering, state of suspense. [(n. f. vb) perh. f. obs. *hove*, etym. dub.]

how, adv. (n.). (In direct or indirect question) in what way, as *h. does he do it?*, *ask him h. he does it*, *tell him h. to do it*, (with intensive addition) *h. the deuce, devil, dickens, h. ever. h. on earth*; *h. are you?*, *h. do you do?*, what is your state of health?; *h. is that for high, queer*, &c.? (colloq. invitation to wonder); (colloq.) *h.-d'ye-do*, embarrassing situation; (Crick.) *h.'s that?*, is he out or not?; *h. now?*, what is the meaning of this?; *h.* (can you show that to be) *so?*; *h.* (at what price) *is corn?*; (in indirect statement, rhet. for) that (*told us how God was almighty*); (in question or exclamation) to what extent as *h. far is it?*, *h. far it is!*, *h. many are there?*, *h. many there are!*, *h. would you like it?*, *h. he snores!*; (n.) *the h.*, the way in which; (in relative clause) in whatever way, as, as *do it h. you can*; *howbē·it* (archaic), nevertheless; *however*, in whatever way, to whatever extent, nevertheless, (archaic) in any case; *h.* EVER; *howsoever, how — soever*, in whatsoever manner, to what extent soever; *h. much?*, (slang) what? (as request to person to repeat his remark or a particular word; *he plays the saxtuba. Plays the how much?*). [OE *hú*, cf. Du. *hoe*; f. stem of WHO]

howdah (how·da), Seat for two or more, usu. with canopy, on elephant's back. [f. Pers. *haudah* f. Arab. *haudaj* litter]

how·itzer, n. Short gun for high-angle firing of shells at low velocities. [earlier *howitz* f. G *haubitze* f. Boh. *houfnice* catapult]

howl[1], v.i. & t. (Of animals) utter long loud doleful cry; (of persons) utter long cry of pain, derision, &c.; utter (words) with howling. [ME *houlen*, cf. Du. *huilen*, G *heulen*, also Gk *hulaō*, L *ululare*]

howl[2], n. Long doleful cry of dog, wolf, &c.; loud cry of pain; yell of derision; (Broadcast) whining noise in receiver during tuning-in, often affecting other listeners. [f. prec.]

how·ler, n. In vbl senses; esp.: S.-Amer. monkey; (slang) glaring blunder; (slang) *come a h.*, come to grief. [-ER[1]]

how·let, n. (dial.). Owl. [prob. f. F *hulotte* (as OWL)]

how·ling, a. That howls; *h.* DERVISH; (bibl.) *h.* (dreary) *wilderness*; (slang) extreme, glaring, as *a h. shame*. [-ING[2]]

hoy[1], n. Small vessel, usu. rigged as sloop, carrying passengers & goods esp. for short distances. [prob. f. MDu. *hoei*, etym. dub.]

hoy[2], int. used to call attention, drive beasts, & (Naut.) hail or call aloft. [natural cry]

hoy·a, n. Genus of climbing plants with pink, white, or yellow flowers, known as *wax-flowers*. [T. *Hoy*, gardener, d. 1821]

hoy·den, n. Boisterous girl. Hence **hoy·den**HOOD, **hoy·den**ISM, nn., **hoy·den**ISH[1] a. [?]

hub[1], n. Central part of wheel, rotating on or with axle, & from which spokes radiate; nave; (fig.) central point of interest &c. (esp. *h. of the universe*). [?]

hub[2], **hu·bby**, n. (colloq.). Husband. [abbr.]

hu·bble-bubble, n. Form of hookah; bubbling noise; confused talk. [imit.]

hu·bbub, n. Confused din; disturbance, riot; confused yelling of war-cry. [of Ir. orig.; cf. Gael. *ubub* int. of contempt, Ir. *abu*, a war-cry]

hū·bris, n. Insolent pride or security. So **hubri·stic** a. [Gk; prop. *hy-*]

hu·ckaback, n. Stout linen fabric with rough surface, for towels &c. [?]

hu·ckle, n. Hip; haunch; *h.-back(ed)*, hump-back(ed); *h.-bone*, hip, haunch, -bone, (also) knuckle-bone of quadruped. [dim. of obs. *huck* hip, etym. dub.]

hu·ckleberry, n. (Fruit of) low berry-bearing shrub common in N. Amer. [perh. corrupt. of *hurtleberry* WHORTLEBERRY]

hu·ckster[1], n. Pedlar, hawker; mercenary person. Hence **hu·ckst**ERY(2) n. [earlier than obs. *huck* v. higgle; see -STER]

hu·ckster[2], v.i. & t. Bargain, haggle; carry on petty traffic in (lit. & fig.); adulterate. Hence **hu·ckster**ER[1], **hu·ckster**ESS[1], nn. [f. prec.]

hu·ddle, v.t. & i., & n. Heap together confusedly; crowd (things &c.) promiscuously *together*, *up*, *into*, *out of*, &c.; coil one*self up*; hurry *over*, *through*, botch *up*, (work &c.); (intr.) nestle closely *together*. (N.) confused mass; confusion, bustle. [(n. f. vb) perh. f. Teut. root *hud-* cover + -LE(3)]

Hūdibră·stic, a. In the metre or manner of Butler's *Hudibras*, mock-heroic poem 1663–78. [after *fantastic* &c.]

hue[1] (hū), n. Colour, tint; variety of colour caused by admixture of another. Hence **-hu**ED[2] a. [OE *hīw*, cf. Goth. *hiwi* form, appearance, also Skr. *chawi* hide, skin, beauty]

hue[2] (hū), n. *H. & cry*: clamour of pursuit or assault; outcry (*against*); proclamation for capture of criminal; (formerly) police gazette with particulars of offenders wanted &c. [f. OF *hu*, *hui*, outcry, f. *huer* shout, imit.]

huff[1], v.t. & i. Bully, storm at; bully (person *into*, *out of*, thing or do*ing*); offend; take offence; (Draughts) remove (opponent's man) from board as forfeit (orig. after blowing on the piece). [imit. f. sound of blowing; v. & n. f. 16th c.]

huff[2], n. Fit of petulance, esp. *in a h.*, *take h.*; (Draughts) act of huffing. Hence **huff**ISH[1], **hu·ff**Y[2], aa., **hu·ffi**LY[2], **hu·ffish**LY[2], advv., **hu·ffi**NESS, **hu·ffish**NESS, nn. [see prec.]

hug, v.t., & n. Squeeze tightly in one's arms, usu. with affection; (of bear) squeeze (man &c.) between its forelegs; delight in, cling to, (prejudices &c.); exhibit fondness for (person); congratulate one*self* (*on*, *for*); keep close to (shore, &c.); *h.-me-tight*, woollen wrap; (n.) strong clasp, grip in wrestling, esp. *Cornish h.* [?]

huge, a. Very large; enormous; (of immaterial things) great. Hence **hu·ge**NESS n. [prob. f. OF *ahuge*, etym. dub.]

hu·gely, adv. Enormously, very much. [prec. + -LY[2]]

hu·geous (-jus), a. (usu. facet.). Huge. Hence **hu·geous**LY[2] adv., **hu·geous**NESS n. [-OUS; f. 1529]

hu·gger-mu·gger, n., a., adv., & v.t. & i. Secrecy; secret(ly); confusion; confused(ly); (v.t.) conceal, hush *up*; (v.i.) proceed in secret or muddled fashion. [?]

hu·ggery, n. Practice (on part of barrister &c.) of courting attorney &c. for employment. [f. HUG[1] + -ERY]

huguenot (hū·genŏt), n. (hist.). French Protestant. [F, perh. assim. of G *eidgenosz* confederate to F pers. name *Hugues*]

hulk, n. Body of dismantled ship, used as store vessel &c. or (pl., hist.) as prison; unwieldy vessel; (fig.) big person or mass. [OE *hulc*, cf. OF *hulke*, Du. *hulk*, perh. f. Gk *holkas* towed ship, ship of burden (*helkō* draw)]

hu·lking, a. Bulky; clumsy. [prec. + -ING[2]]

hull[1], n., & v.t. Outer covering of fruit, esp. pod of peas & beans; (fig.) covering; (v.t.) remove h. of. [OE *hulu* (*helan* cover), cf. G *hülle* covering]

hull², n., & v.t. Frame of ship; *h. down*, far away, so that h. is invisible; (v.t.) strike (ship) in h. with cannon shot. [perh. = prec.]

hu·llabaloo·, n. Uproar. [prob. redupl. f. HULLO; f. 18th c.]

hullo·, -loa (-lō), int. used to call attention, express surprise, or answer call, esp. on telephone. [cf. HALLO]

hum¹, v.i. & t. Make continuous murmuring sound, as of bee, spinning top, &c.; make low inarticulate vocal sound, esp. (usu. *h. & ha*) of hesitation; sing with closed lips; (colloq.) be in state of activity, as *make things h.*; (trans.) utter, sing, with closed lips. [imit.]

hum², n. Humming sound esp. of hesitation (usu. *hh. & ha's*), applause, surprise, &c. [imit.]

hum³, int. expr. hesitation, dissent, &c.

hum⁴, n. (slang). Sham, hoax. [= HUMBUG]

hū·man, a. (n.). Of, belonging to, man, as *h. nature*; that is a man or consists of men, as *h. race, creature*; of man as opp. to God, as *h. affairs*; having, showing, the qualities distinctive of man, as *more, less, than h.*; (n., facet.) h. being. Hence **hu·man**NESS n. [f. F *humain* (12th c.) f. L *humanus* (*homo* man, see -AN)]

hūma·ne, a. Benevolent, compassionate; *H. Society* (for rescue of drowning persons); (of branches of study) tending to refinement, elegant. Hence **huma·ne**LY² adv., **huma·ne**NESS n. [differentiated f. prec. after 1700]

hu·manism, n. Devotion to human interests; system concerned with human (not divine) interests, or with the human race (not the individual); Religion of HUMANITY; literary culture, esp. that of the Humanists. [-ISM]

hu·manist, n. Student of human nature or human affairs; student (esp. in 14th–16th cc.) of Roman & Greek literature & antiquities, whence **humani·st**IC a. [f. F *humaniste* (as HUMAN, see -IST)]

humănitār·ian, n. & a. One who professes humanism (Religion of Humanity), visionary philanthropist; (adj.) holding, concerned with, the views of hh. Hence **humanitar·ian**ISM n. [f. foll. + -ARIAN]

humă·nity, n. Human nature; (pl.) human attributes; the human race; humaneness, benevolence; (pl.) benevolent acts; *Religion of H.* (rejecting the supernatural & concerned chiefly or wholly with the advancement of man's welfare); *the hh.*, polite scholarship, esp. of Latin & Greek classics. [f. F *humanité* f. L *humanitatem* (as HUMAN, see -TY)]

hu·manize, v.t. & i. Make human, give human character to; make, become, humane. Hence **humaniz**A·TION n. [f. F *humaniser* (as HUMAN, see -IZE)]

hu·mankind, n. Mankind.

hu·manly, adv. In a human manner; by human means; from human point of view; with human feeling. [-LY²]

hu·mble, a. (*comp. & sup. pron.* -bler, -blist), & v.t. Having, showing, low estimate of one's own importance; (formally, esp. in subscribing letter) *your h. servant*; of lowly condition; (of things) of modest pretensions, dimensions, &c.; *eat h. pie*, make h. apology, submit to humiliation; *H. Plant*, common sensitive plant; (v.t.) make h., bring low, abase (one*self* &c.). Hence **hu·mble**NESS n., **hu·mb**LY² adv. [(vb f. n.) OF, f. L *humilis* lowly (*humus* ground, -IL)]

hu·mble-bee, n. Bumble-bee. [f. 15th c.; cf. G *hummel* large wild bee, Du. *hommel* drone bee]

hu·mbug, n., & v.t. & i. (-gg-). Fraud, sham; deception; (as int.) nonsense!; impostor; (v.t.) delude (person *into, out of*, thing or do*ing*); (v.i.) be, behave like, a h. Hence **humbu·gg**ERY n. [(vb f. n.) f. 1750 etym. dub.]

hu·mdrum, a. & n., & v.i. (-mm-). Commonplace(ness), dull(ness); (v.i.) proceed in h. way. Hence **hu·mdrum**NESS n. [f. 1550; prob. redupl. f. HUM v.]

hū·merus, n. (anat.). Bone of the upper arm in man; corresponding bone in other vertebrates. Hence **hu·mer**AL a. [L, = shoulder]

hū·mid, a. Moist, damp. So **humi·di**FY v.t., **humi·d**ITY n. [f. L (*h*)*umidus* (*umēre* be moist, see -ID¹)]

humi·liate, v.t. Lower the dignity or self-respect of; mortify. Hence or cogn. **humi·liat**ING² a., **humili**A·TION n. [f. LL *humiliare* (as HUMBLE¹, see -ATE³)]

humi·lity, n. Humbleness, meekness; humble condition. [f. F *humilité* f. L *humilitatem* (as HUMBLE¹, see -TY)]

hu·mming, a. In vbl senses; also or esp.: (colloq.) vigorous, energetic. as *a h. knock on the head*; *h.-bird* (of several species that make h. sound by vibration of wings); *h.-top* (h. when it spins). [f. HUM v. + -ING¹]

hu·mmock, n. Hillock, knoll; rising ground, esp. in marsh; hump or ridge in icefield. Hence **hu·mmock**Y² a. [orig. naut.; etym. dub.]

hū·moral, a. (med.). Of the bodily humours; *h. pathology*, doctrine referring all disease to state of the humours, whence **hu·moral**ISM, **hu·moral**IST, nn., **humorali·st**IC a. [F, f. L as HUMOUR, see -AL]

hu·morist, n. Facetious person; humorous talker, actor, or writer. Hence **humori·st**IC a. [f. F *humoriste* f. med.L *humorista* (as prec., see -IST)]

hu·morous, a. Full of humour; facetious, funny. Hence **hu·morous**LY² adv., **hu·morous**NESS n. [-OUS]

hū·mour¹ (*or* ū-), n. State of mind, mood; inclination, as *in the h. for fighting*; facetiousness, comicality; faculty of perceiving this; jocose imagination (less intellectual & more sympathetic than wit), whence **hu·mour**LESS a.; *out of h.*, displeased; *good, ill, h.* (temper), whence **-humour**ED[2] a.; *cardinal hh.* (hist.), four chief fluids of the body (blood, phlegm, choler, melancholy), determining person's physical & mental qualities; *aqueous, vitreous, h.*, transparent fluid parts of the eye. [AF, f. L *(h)umorem* moisture (as HUMID, see -OR[1])]

hū·mour[2], v.t. Gratify, indulge, (person, taste, temper, &c.); adapt oneself to, make concessions to. [f. prec.]

hu·moursome, a. Capricious; peevish. Hence **hu·moursome**NESS n. [-SOME]

hump, n., & v.t. Protuberance, esp. on the back, as deformity or (in camel &c.) as normal feature; rounded boss of earth &c.; (slang) fit of depression or vexation, as *it gives me the h.*; *humpback*, (person having) back with a h.; *h.-backed*, having such a back. (V.t.) make h.-shaped; annoy, depress; (Austral.) hoist up, shoulder, (one's pack, swag, or *bluey*). Hence **hump**ED[2], **hu·mp**LESS, **hu·mp**Y[2], aa. [f. 1680, *h.-backed* replacing *crump-backed*; Du. *homp* = thick piece (cut off)]

humph (hmf), int., & v.i. Int. expr. doubt or dissatisfaction; (v.i.) utter this.

hu·mpty-du·mpty, n. Short dumpy person; (from nursery rhyme in which *H.* is taken to mean an egg) person, thing, that once thrown down cannot be restored. [for *humpy-dumpy*]

hu·mpy, n. Australian hut. [native *oompi*]

hū·mus, n. Vegetable mould. [L, = ground]

Hun, n. One of an Asiatic nomad race who invaded & ravaged Europe in 4th & 5th cc.; (contempt.) German, Austrian, or esp. Prussian. Hence **Hu·nn**ISH[1] a. [OE *Húne* f. med. L *Hunni*]

hunch[1], v.t. Bend, arch, convexly; thrust *out, up*, to form a hump. [?]

hunch[2], n. Hump; thick piece; *h.-back(ed)*, hump-back(ed); (U.-S. slang) *have a h. that*, conceive the idea, suspect, rather think, that. Hence **hu·nch**Y[2] a. [?]

hu·ndred, n. & a. (Cardinal number) ten times ten (100, C), as *a, one, six, several, h. men, a, one, six h. of them* or *of my friends, hh. of men, hh. of them, some, several, hh. of* &c.; (ordinal, in compds) *the h.-&-first, six-h.-&-ninth*; (also *h. & one*) large number; *not a h. miles from* (facet.), at or close to; *a h. per cent efficient*, doing the utmost in practice that it theoretically should; h. pounds (of money); (chiefly hist.) subdivision of county or shire, having its own court; CHILTERN HUNDREDS; *great, long, h.*, 120; *h., of* BRICK[1]S; *hundredweight*, 112lb. avoirdupois (abbr. *cwt*), (U.S.) 100lb.; *hh. & thousands*, sweets like small shot used chiefly for decorating cakes &c. Hence **hu·ndred**FOLD n., **hu·ndred**TH[2] a. & n. (*Old Hundredth*, hymn 'All people that . . .', version of Ps. C, or its tune). [OE *(hund* hundred + *-red* = Goth. *-rath* number)]

hung. See HANG v.

hu·nger[1] (-ngg-), n. Uneasy sensation, exhausted condition, caused by want of food; (fig.) strong desire (*for, after*, &c.); *h.-strike*, prisoner's refusal to take food in order to procure release. [OE *hungor*, cf. Du. *honger*, G *hunger*]

hu·nger[2] (-ngg-), v.i. & t. Feel hunger; have craving (*for, after*); (p.p., archaic) hungry; (trans.) starve (*into* submission, *out of* place &c.). [OE *hyngran*, f. prec.]

hu·ngry (-ngg-), a. Feeling hunger (*h. as a hunter*); showing hunger, as *a h. look*; inducing hunger, as *a h. air*; *h. rice*, W.-African grain allied to millet; (fig.) eager, greedy; (of soil) poor, barren. Hence **hu·ngri**LY[2] adv., **hu·ngri**NESS n. [OE *hungrig* (as HUNGER[1], see -Y[2])]

hunk, n. Large piece cut off; clumsy piece; hunch. [19th c.; cf. WFlem. *hunke*]

hunks, n. Close-fisted man, miser. [?]

Hunnish. See HUN.

hunt[1], v.i. & t. Pursue wild animals or game; (trans.) chase (these) for food or sport; seek *after, for*; drive *away, out*; scour (district) in pursuit of game; use (horse, hounds) in hunting; *h. down*, bring to bay; *h. out*, track out, find by search; *h. up*, search for; *h. in* COUPLES; *h. the hare, slipper, squirrel*, games. [OE *huntian* f. *hunta* hunter, cogn. w. Goth. *hinthan* seize]

hunt[2], n. Hunting (lit. & fig.); persons hunting with a pack; hunting district; *h. ball* (given by members of h., men wearing pink). [f. prec.]

hu·nter, n. One who hunts; (fig.) *fortune, place*, &c., *-h.*; horse for hunting; watch with hinged cover protecting glass or (*half-h.*) outer part of it. Hence **hu·nt**RESS[1] n. [-ER[1]]

hu·nting, n. In vbl senses; *h.-box*, small house for use during h.-season; *h.*-COG[1]; *h.*-CROP; *h.-ground*, place where one hunts (often fig.); *happy h.-ground(s)*, the future state (prop. as expected by Amer. Indians), good place for h. (fig.); *h.-horn*, horn used in h., second pommel on near side of side-saddle. [-ING[1]]

hu·ntsman, n. Hunter; man in charge of (esp. fox-) hounds.

hur·dle, n., & v.t. Portable rectangular frame strengthened with withes or wooden bars, for temporary fence &c.; wooden frame to be jumped over in *h.-race*; (Hist.) frame on which traitors were dragged to execution; (v.t.) fence *off* &c. with hh. [(vb f. n.) OE *hyrdel*; cf. Du. *horde*, G *hürde*, also L *cratis* hurdle, Gk *kurtia* wickerwork]

hur·dler, n. One who makes hurdles, or runs in hurdle-races. [-ER[1]]

hur·dy-gurdy, n. Musical instrument

with droning sound, played by turning handle, orig. one with rosined wheel turned by left hand & played by right. [prob. imit.]

hurl, v.t., & n. Throw violently from some position (lit. & fig.); throw (missile &c., also fig.); (n.) hurling, violent throw. [cf. LG *hurreln*; prob. imit.]

hur·ley, n. (Ir.). Hockey; hockey-stick. [as prec.]

Hur·lingham, n. (Used for) H. Park, Fulham, head-quarters of H. Polo Club.

hur·ly, n. (archaic). Commotion. [as HURL]

hur·ly-bur·ly, n. Commotion, tumult. [f. 1540; redupl. f. HURL v.]

hurrah· (hu-, hōō-), **-ray·**, int., n., & v.i. Int. expr. exultation or approbation; (n.) this cry; (v.i.) shout h. [replaces *huzza*; cf. Swed. & Da. *hurra*, Du. *hoera*]

hu·rricane (-kan), n. Storm with violent wind, esp. W.-Indian cyclone (also fig.); *h.-bird*, frigate-bird; *h. deck*, light upper deck; *h. lamp* (designed to resist wind). [f. Sp. *huracan*, of Carib orig.]

hu·rry¹, n. Undue haste; eagerness to get a thing done quickly; eagerness (*to* do, *for* thing); (w. neg. or interrog.) need for haste; (colloq.) *you will not beat that in a h.* (easily), *shall not ask again in a h.* (willingly); *h.-scurry* adv., adj., & n., (in) disorderly haste, (v.i.) proceed thus. [f. 16th c.; imit., cf. HURL]

hu·rry², v.t. & i. Carry, drive, (person &c. *away, along, into, into* do*ing*, &c.) with undue haste; move, act, with great or undue haste; *h. up*, make haste. Hence **hu·rried**LY² adv., **hu·rried**NESS n. [as prec.]

hurst, n. Hillock; sandbank in sea or river; wooded eminence; wood. [OE *hyrst*, cf. G dial. *horst* sandbank, MDu. *horst* thicket]

hurt¹, n. Wound, material injury; harm, wrong. Hence **hur·t**FUL, **hur·t**LESS, aa., **hur·tful**LY² adv., **hur·tful**NESS n. [prob. f. OF *hurte*, as foll.]

hurt², v.t. & i. (hurt). Cause bodily injury or pain to; damage; inflict injury upon; distress, wound, (person, his feelings &c.); (colloq.) suffer injury or pain. [prob. f. OF *hurter* (mod. *heurter*) knock, etym. dub.]

hur·tle, v.t. & i., & n. (archaic). Strike against; hurl swiftly; strike *against*; move with clattering sound; come with a crash; (n.) hurtling, clashing sound. [(n. f. vb) prob. f. HURT v. + -LE(3)]

hu·sband¹ (-z-), n. Man joined to woman by marriage; *h.'s tea*, weak & cold; (archaic) *good, bad, h.* (economist). Hence **hu·sband**HOOD, **hu·sband**SHIP, nn., **hu·sband**LIKE a. [OE *húsbonda* master of house (*hús* house + *bónda* f. ON *bóndi* freeholder f. *búa* dwell)]

hu·sband², v.t. Manage thriftily, economize; (archaic) till (ground), cultivate (plants); (poet., facet.) provide with husband; (rare) marry (woman). [f. prec.]

hu·sbandman, n. Farmer.

hu·sbandry, n. Farming; (*good, bad*) economy; careful management. [-RY]

hush¹, n. Stillness; silence; *h.-money*, paid to prevent exposure. [f. foll.]

hush², v.t. & i. Silence, quiet; *h. up*, suppress (affair); be silent, esp. (as int.) *h.!*; *hushabȳ*, int. used to lull child; *h.-ship* (of great length, speed, & gun-power, secretly built in the great war; cf. Q-*ship*). [back formation f. obs. adj. *husht* f. *husht, hust*, intt. (imit.)]

husk, n., & v.t. Dry outer covering of some fruits or seeds; (fig.) worthless outside part of anything; disease of cattle; (v.t.) remove h. from. [late ME *huske*, etym. dub.]

hu·sky¹, a. Of, full of, husks; dry as a husk; (of voice or person) dry, hoarse, whence **hu·ski**LY² adv., **hu·ski**NESS n. [-Y²]

hu·sky², n. Eskimo dog; (*H*-) Eskimo person or language. [prob. = ESKIMO]

hussar· (-z-), n. Soldier of light cavalry regiment (orig. Hungarian light horseman of 15th c.). [f. Hung. *huszar* f. OSerb. *husar* f. It. *corsaro* CORSAIR]

Hu·ssite, n. Follower of John Huss, Bohemian religious reformer of 15th c. [-ITE]¹

hu·ssy, -zzy, n. Woman of light or worthless character; pert girl. [f. HOUSEWIFE]

hu·stings, n. Platform from which (before 1872) candidates for Parliament were nominated; election proceedings; court (now rarely) held in Guildhall of London. [OE *hústing* f. ON *hústhing* house-assembly]

hu·stle (-sl), v.t. & i., & n. Push roughly, jostle; thrust (person &c. *into, out of*, &c.); impel unceremoniously (*into* thing or do*ing*); (intr.) push roughly *against*; push one's way; hurry, bustle; (n.) hustling. [(n. f. vb) f. Du. *husselen* shake, toss]

hut, n., & v.t. & i. Small mean house of rude construction; (Mil.) temporary wooden house for troops; (v.t.) place (troops &c.) in hh.; (v.i.) lodge in h. Hence **hu·t**MENT n., h. encampment. [(vb f. F *hutter*) f. F *hutte* f. G *hütte*]

hutch, n. Box-like pen for rabbits &c.; hut, cabin, small house; truck used in mining &c. [ME & F *huche* f. med. L *hutica*, etym. dub.]

huzza· (-ah), int., n., & v.i. & t. Int. of exultation, encouragement, or applause; (make, greet with) the cry *h.* [imit.]

hȳ·acinth, n. Genus of bulbous plants with bell-shaped flowers of various colours, esp. purplish blue, so (esp. as Homeric epithet of doubtful sense for *locks, hair*) **hyaci·nth**INE² a.; this colour; precious stone, orange variety of zircon. [earlier *jacynth*, ult. f. L f. Gk *huakinthos*, flower & gem, also name of youth loved by Apollo]

Hy̆·adēs, n. pl. Group of stars near Pleiades. [f. Gk *Huades* (acc. to pop. etym., f. *huō* rain, but perh. f. *hus* swine)]

hyaena. See HYENA.

hȳ·aline, a. & n. Glass-like, vitreous (chiefly techn.); (n., poet.) smooth sea, clear sky, &c. [f. L f. Gk *hualinos* (*hualos* glass, see -INE[2])]

hȳ·alite, n. Colourless variety of opal. [f. Gk *hualos* glass, see -ITE]

hȳ·aloid, a. & n. (anat.). Glassy; *h.* (*membrane*), thin transparent membrane enveloping vitreous humour of eye. [f. F *hyaloïde* f. L f. Gk *hualoeidēs* (as prec., see -OID)]

hȳ·brid, n. & a. Offspring of two animals or plants of different species or varieties; person of mixed nationality; (fig.) thing, word, composed of incongruous elements; (adj.) crossbred, mongrel; heterogeneous; *h. bill* in Parliament, one combining characteristics of public & private bill, & referred to a *h. committee*. Hence **hy-bri·d**ITY n. [f. L *hybrida* offspring of tame sow & wild boar; etym. dub.]

hȳ·bridism, n. Fact, condition, of being hybrid; cross-breeding. [prec. + -ISM]

hȳ·bridize, v.t & i. Subject (species &c.) to cross-breeding; produce hybrids; (of animal or plant) interbreed. Hence **hy·bridiz**ABLE a., **hybridiz**A·TION n. [HYBRID + -IZE]

hȳ·datid, n. (path.). Cyst containing watery fluid, morbid formation in animal bodies, esp. that of tape-worm larva. [f. Gk *hudatis -idos* watery vesicle (*hudōr -atos* water, -ID[2])]

Hyde Park, n. A London park, a fashionable resort, and of late years the scene of many political and other demonstrations.

hy·dra, n. (Gk Myth.) snake whose many heads grew again when cut off; (fig.) thing hard to extirpate; water-snake; a fresh-water polyp. [L, f. Gk *hudra* water-snake]

hȳdră·ngea (-jya), n. Genus of shrubs with globular clusters of white, blue, or pink flowers. [f. Gk *hudōr* water + *aggos* vessel]

hȳ·drant, n. Pipe (esp. in street) with nozzle to which hose can be attached, for drawing water from main. [U.S. (HYDRO-, -ANT)]

hȳ·drate[1] (-at), n. (chem.). Compound of water with another compound or an element. [f. Gk *hudōr* water, see -ATE[1]]

hȳ·drate[2], v.t. (chem.). Combine with water. Hence **hydr**A·TION n. [f. prec.]

hȳdrau·lic, a. & n. Of water conveyed through pipes or channels; operated by water-power, as *h. lift*; *h. ram*, automatic pump in which kinetic energy of descending column of water raises some of the water above its original level; hardening under water, as *h. cement*; *h. press*, hydrostatic press; (n. pl.) science of conveyance of liquids through pipes &c., esp. as motive power. Hence or cogn. **hydrau·li**CALLY adv., **hydrauli**·CIAN n. [f. L f. Gk *hudraulikos* (*hudōr* water + *aulos* pipe, see -IC)]

hȳ·dric, a. (chem.). Of, containing, hydrogen. So **hy·dr**IDE n. [f. HYDROGEN + -IC]

hȳ·dro, n. = HYDROPATHIC. [colloq. abbr.]

hȳdro- in comb. = Gk *hudro-* comb. form of *hudōr* water, (1) in miscell. terms, w. sense 'having to do with water', (2) in names of diseases, w. sense 'dropsical' or 'affected with accumulation of serous fluid', (3) in chem. terms, usu. w. sense 'combined with hydrogen'; as: *-a·eroplane* (now rare), a SEAplane; *-car·bon*, compound of hydrogen & carbon; *-ce·phalus*, water on the brain; *-cepha·lic*, *-ce·phalous*, affected with this; *-chlor·ic*, containing hydrogen & chlorine; *-cyă·nic*, containing hydrogen & cyanogen, esp. *h. acid*, prussic acid; *-dyna·mic(al)*, of the forces acting on or exerted by liquids; *-dyna·mics*, science of these forces; *-ele·ctric*, developing electricity by friction of water or steam; *-grapher*, person skilled in, *-gra·phic(al)* having to do with, hydrography; *-graphy*, scientific description of the waters of the earth; *-kinĕ·tic(s)*, (science) of the motion of liquids; *-logy*, science of the properties, laws, &c., of water; *-lysis*, decomposition of water in which the two constituents are fixed in distinct compounds; *-mā·nia*, craving for water; *-mecha·nics* (of liquids); *-meter*, instrument for finding specific gravity of liquids (sometimes also of solids); *-me·tric*, *-metry*, concerned with, determination of, specific gravity of liquids; *-phane*, opal that absorbs water & becomes transparent on immersion; *-phone*, instrument for detection of sound by water; *-phyte*, aquatic plant; *-plane*, fin-like device enabling submarine to rise or fall; *-pneuma·tic*, involving combined action of water & air; *-quĭ·none*, (Phot.) preparation from quinone, used as developer; *-sphere*, waters of the earth's surface; *-stat*, electrical device for detecting presence of water; *-therapeu·tic*, *-the·rapy*, hydropathic, hydropathy; *-ther·mal*, of the action of heated water on earth's crust; *-thor·ax*, dropsy of the chest; *-tropism*, (of plants) tendency to turn to or from moisture; *-zo·a* n. pl., class of coelenterate animals chiefly marine, including jelly-fish & fresh-water hydra.

hȳ·drogen, n. Colourless invisible odourless gas, an element, the lightest substance known, forming two-thirds in volume of water. Hence **hydro·gen**OUS a. [f. F HYDRO(*gène* -GEN)]

hȳdro·genate, v.t. Charge, cause to combine, with hydrogen. So **hydro·gen**IZE v.t. [prec. + -ATE[3]]

hȳ·droid, a. & n. (zool.). (Animal) like, allied to, the hydra (polyp). [-OID]
hȳ·dromĕl, n. Mixture of honey & water; *vinous h.* (also *mead*), this fermented. [L, f. Gk *hudromeli* (*meli* honey, see HYDRO-)]
hȳdropă·thic, a. & n. Of, concerned with, hydropathy; (n.) h. establishment. [f. foll. + -IC]
hȳdrŏ·pathy, n. Medical treatment by external & internal application of water. So **hydro·path**IST n. [HYDRO- + -PATHY]
hȳdrophō·bia, n. Aversion to water, esp. as symptom of rabies in man; rabies, esp. in man; (facet.) dread of water. So **hȳdrophō·b**IC a. [L, f. Gk *hudro*PHOBIA, see HYDRO-]
hȳdrŏ·pic, a. Dropsical. [ME, f. OF *ydropique* f. L f. Gk *hudrōpikos* (as foll., see -IC)]
hȳ·dropsy, n. (archaic or med.). Dropsy. [ME, f. OF *ydropisie* f. med. L *hydropisia* (for L *-sis*) f. Gk *hudrōps* (*hudōr* water)]
hȳdrostă·tic, a. & n. Of the equilibrium of liquids & the pressure exerted by liquids at rest; *h. paradox*, principle that any quantity of a perfect liquid, however small, may be made to balance any other quantity; *h. press* (also *hydraulic, Bramah's, press*), machine in which pressure of a body of water is multiplied by transmission from small to larger cylinder; (n. pl.) science of the pressure & equilibrium of liquids at rest. Hence **hydrosta·tic**AL a., **hydrosta·tical**LY[2] adv. [HYDRO- + STATIC; Gk had *hudrostatēs* hydrostatic balance]
hȳ·drous, a. (chem., mineral.). Containing water. [f. Gk *hudōr* water- + OUS]
hyē·na, hyae·na, n. Carnivorous quadruped allied to dog tribe; *striped h.*, variety whose howl is compared to fiendish laughter; cruel, treacherous, or rapacious person; Tasmanian tiger; *h.-dog*, S.-African canine quadruped like h. [L (*-ae-*) f. Gk *huaina* fem. f. *hus* pig]
hȳeto- in comb. = Gk *huetos* rain, as *-graphy*, mapping of rainfall, *-meter*, rain-gauge.
Hȳgei·a (-jē·*a*), n. Goddess of health; health personified. Hence **hygēi·**AN a. [f. Gk *Hugeia* late for *Hugieia* (*hugiēs* healthy)]
hȳ·giene (-jīēn), n. Principles of health; sanitary science. Hence **hygiĕ·n**IC(AL) aa., **hygie·nical**LY[2] adv., **hygie·n**ICS, **hy·gien**IST, nn. [f. F *hygiène* f. Gk *hugieinē* (*tekhnē* art) of health, f. *hugiēs* healthy]
hygro- in comb. = Gk *hugros* wet, fluid, as: *-deik* (dīk), form of hygrometer; *-logy*, study of the humidity of atmosphere &c.; *-meter*, instrument for measuring humidity of air or gas; *-me·tric, -metry*, concerned with, measurement of, humidity; *-scope*, instrument indicating but not measuring humidity of air; *-sco·pic*, of the hygroscope, (of bodies) sensitive to moisture.
Hȳ·ksōs, n. pl. The shepherd kings of Egypt (about 2000 B.C.). [Gk *Huksōs*]
hȳ·lic, a. Of matter, material. [f. med. L f. Gk *hulikos* (*hulē* matter, see -IC)]
hylo- in comb. = Gk *hulē* matter, as: *-morphism*, doctrine that primordial matter is first cause of the universe; *-theism*, doctrine that God & matter are identical; *-theist, -thei·stic*, holder of, concerned with, this doctrine; *-zo·ism, -zoist(ic), -zo·ic*, materialism, -ist(ic).
Hȳ·mĕn[1], n. (Gk & Rom. myth.). God of marriage. So **hȳmenē·**AL a., **hymene·al**LY[2] adv. [L, f. Gk *Humēn*]
hȳ·mĕn[2], n. (anat.). Virginal membrane, stretched across external orifice of vagina. [f. Gk *humēn* membrane]
hymeno- in comb. = Gk *humēn* membrane, as: *-ptera* n. pl., large order of insects with four membranous wings, so *-pteral, -pterous*, aa.
hymn (-m), n., & v.t. & i. Song of praise to God, esp. metrical composition sung in religious service; song of praise; *h.-book* (of hh.); (v.t.) praise (God &c.) in hh., express (praise &c.) in h.; (v.i.) sing hh. Hence **hy·mn**IC (-mn-) a., **hy·mn**IST (-mn-) n. [(vb f. n.) f. L f. Gk *humnos*]
hy·mnal (-mn-), a. & n. Of hymns; (n.) hymn-book, so **hy·mn**ARY[1] n. [HYMN + -AL]
hy·mnody (-mn-), n. Singing of hymns; composition of hymns, whence **hy·mnod**IST n.; hymns collectively. [f. L f. Gk *humnōdia* (*humnos* hymn + *ōdē* song, ODE]
hymno·grapher, n. Composer of hymns. [f. Gk *humnographos* (as prec., see -GRAPHER)]
hymno·logy (-mn-), n. Composition, study, of hymns; hymns collectively. So **hymnolo·g**IC a., **hymno·log**IST n. [HYMN + -O- + -LOGY]
hȳ·oid, a. & n. (anat.). *H. bone*, tongue-bone between chin & thyroid cartilage; pertaining to this; (n.) h. bone. [f. F *hyoïde* f. Gk *huoeidēs* shaped like letter U]
hȳoscȳ·amīne, hȳ·oscīne, nn. Alkaloids contained in henbane and used in medicine. [f. Gk *huoskuamos* henbane (*hus huos* pig, *kuamos* bean), -INE[5]]
hyp. See HIP[3].
hȳpae·thral, -pē·thral, a. Open to the sky, roofless; open-air. [f. L f. Gk *hupaithros* (*aithēr* air, see HYPO-)]
hȳpă·llage (-jī), n. (gram.). Reversal of natural relations of two elements in a proposition (e.g. *apply the wound to water* for *apply water to the wound*). [L, f. Gk *hupallagē* (*allassō* exchange, see HYPO-)]
hȳper-, pref. = Gk *huper* in senses 'over', 'above', 'exceeding', 'excessive'.
hyperaesthē·sia, n. (Path.) morbid sensitiveness of nerves; excessive sensibility. So **hyperaesthĕ·t**IC a. [HYPER- + Gk *-aisthēsia* f. *aisthanomai* perceive]

hyper·baton, n. Inversion of normal order of words, esp. for sake of emphasis. [L, f. Gk *huperbaton* (*bainō* step, see HYPER-)]

hyper·bola, n. (geom.). Curve produced when cone is cut by plane making larger angle with base than side of cone makes (cf. ELLIPSE). Hence **hyperbŏ·lic** a. [mod. L, f. Gk *huperbolē* f. *huperballō* exceed (*ballō* throw, see HYPER-)]

hyper·bole (-lĭ), n. (rhet.). Exaggerated statement not meant to be taken literally. Hence **hyperbŏ·lical** a., **hyperbo·lically**[2] adv., **hyper·bolism**, **hyper·bolist**, nn. [f. Gk as prec.]

hyperbor·ean, a. & n. (Inhabitant) of the extreme north of the earth or (colloq.) of a country; (Gk Myth.) one of a race living in land of sunshine & plenty beyond north wind. [f. LL *hyperboreanus* (L *-boreus*) f. Gk *huperboreos* (*Boreas* north wind, see HYPER-)]

hypercatale·ctic, a. (pros.). (Of verse) having extra syllable after last complete dipody. [f. LL HYPER(*catalecticus* CATALECTIC)]

hypercri·tical, a. Too critical, esp. of small faults. Hence **hypercri·tically**[2] adv., **hypercri·ticism** n., **hypercri·ticize** v.t. & i. [HYPER- + CRITICAL]

hyperme·tric(al), aa. (Of verse) having a redundant syllable; (of syllable) redundant. [f. Gk *hupermetros* (*metron* metre, HYPER-)]

hypermetrō·pia, n. Morbidly long sight. Hence **hypermetrŏ·pic** a. [as prec. + Gk *ōps* eye + *-ia* -Y[1]]

hyperphy·sical, a. Supernatural. [HYPER-]

hy·persthene (-ēn), n. Greenish mineral allied to hornblende. [f. F HYPER(*stène* f. Gk *sthenos* strength, from its hardness)]

hyper·trophy, n. Enlargement (*of* organ &c.) due to excessive nutrition. Hence or cogn. **hypertrŏ·phic**, **hyper·trophied**[2], aa. [HYPER- + Gk *-trophia* nourishment f. *trephō*]

hypethral. See HYPAETHRAL.

hȳ·phen, n., & v.t. Sign (-) used to join two words together, to join separated syllables of word broken at end of line, or to divide word into parts; short pause between syllables in speaking; (v.t.) join (words) with h., write (compound word) with h. [(vb f. n.) LL, f. Gk *huphen* together (*hupo* under + *hen* one)]

hy·phenate, v.t. = prec. vb (*hyphenated Americans*, German-Americans, Irish-Americans, &c.). [prec., -ATE[3]]

hypno- in comb. (before vowel *hypn-*) = Gk *hupnos* sleep, as: *-ge·nesis, -genĕ·tic*, induction of, inducing, the hypnotic state; *-logy*, science of the phenomena of sleep.

hypnō·sis, n. Artificially produced sleep; hypnotic state. [f. Gk *hupnoō* make sleep, -OSIS]

hypnŏ·tic, a. & n. Of, producing, hypnotism; thing that produces sleep; person under influence of hypnotism. [f. F *hypnotique* f. LL f. Gk *hupnōtikos* (as prec., see -OTIC)]

hy·pnotism, n. (Artificial production of) a state resembling deep sleep, in which the subject acts only on external suggestion. So **hy·pnotist** n.; **hy·pnotize** v.t. [f. prec. + -ISM]

hȳ·po, n. (photog.). Hyposulphite of soda, used in fixing. [abbr.]

hypo- in comb. (before vowel *hyp-*) = Gk *hupo* under, below, slightly; (Chem.) forming names of oxygen compounds lower in the series than those with the simple name. Exx.: *-blast*, inner layer of cells in blastoderm; *-bra·nchial* situated under the gills; *-cȳ·cloid*, curve traced by point in circumference of circle rolling round interior circumference of another circle; *-ga·strium*, lowest region of abdomen; *-gē·al, -gē·an*, aa., underground; *-gene*, (of rocks) formed under the surface; *-ge·um*, pl. *-gea*, underground chamber; *-glo·ssal* (*nerve*), motor nerve of tongue; *-gynous* (bot.), situated below pistils or ovary; *-năsty* (bot.), tendency in plant-organs to grow more rapidly on under side; *-pho·sphite*, salt of hypophosphorous acid; *-style*, (hall &c.) with roof supported on pillars; *-trache·lium* (-kē-), lower part of capital of column.

hȳ̆·pocaust, n. (Rom. antiq.). Hollow space under floor in which heat from furnace was accumulated for heating house or bath. [f. LL f. Gk *hupokauston* place heated from below (*kaiō, kau-*, burn, see HYPO-)]

hȳ̆pocho·ndria (-k-), n. Morbid state of depression for which there is no real cause. So **hypochondrī·asis** n. [f. LL f. Gk (*ta*) *hupokhondria* soft parts of body below costal cartilages (*khondros* cartilage, see HYPO-)]

hȳ̆pocho·ndriac, a. & n. Of, affected by, hypochondria; (n.) h. person. Hence **hypochondrī·acal** a., **hypochondri·acally**[2] adv. [f. F *hypochondriaque* f. med. L f. Gk *hupokhondriakos* (as prec., see -AC)]

hȳ̆po·crisy, n. Simulation of virtue or goodness; dissimulation, pretence. [f. OF *ypocrisie* f. eccl. L f. Gk *hupokrisis* lit. acting of a part f. *hupokrinomai* (*hupo-* HYPO- + *krinō* decide, judge)]

hȳ̆·pocrite, n. Person guilty of hypocrisy; dissembler, pretender. So **hypocri·tical** a., **hypocri·tically**[2] adv. [f. OF *ypocrite* f. eccl. L (*-ta*) f. Gk *hupokritēs* actor (as prec.)]

hȳ̆poder·mic, a. (Med., of drugs &c.) introduced beneath the skin, as *h. injection*; (Anat.) lying under the skin. Hence **hypoder·mically** adv. [f. HYPO- + Gk *derma* skin + -IC]

hȳ̆po·stasis, n. (pl. *-asēs*). (Med.) Excess of blood in organs of body; (Metaphys.) underlying substance, opp. to attributes or to what is unsubstantial; (Theol.) personality (of Christ), person (of the Godhead). So **hypostă·tic(al)** aa., **hyposta·ticalLY²** adv., **hypo·stasIZE(3)**, **hypo·statIZE(3)**, vv.t. (metaphys.). [f. LL f. Gk *hupostasis* (*hupo-* HYPO- + *stasis* standing, state)]

hўpŏ·tenuse, n. Side opposite right angle of triangle. [f. LL f. Gk *hupoteinousa* (*grammē*) subtending line (*hupo-* HYPO- + *teinō* stretch); also (improp.) *-thenuse*]

hў·pothec (-ĭk), n. (Rom. & Sc. Law). Security established by law over thing belonging to debtor. So **hypo·thecARY¹** a. [f. LL f. Gk *hupothēkē* f. *hupotithēmi* place under, deposit as pledge (*hupo-* HYPO- + *tithēmi* place)]

hypŏ·thecate, v.t. Pledge, mortgage. Hence **hypothecA·TION** n. [f. LL *hypothecare* (as prec.), see -ATE³]

hўpo·thesis, n. (pl. *-thesēs*). Supposition made as basis for reasoning, without reference to its truth, or as starting-point for investigation; groundless assumption. So **hypothe·tic(al)** aa., **hypothe·ticalLY²** adv. [f. Gk *hupothesis* foundation (as HYPOTHEC)]

hypo·thesize, v.i. & t. Frame a hypothesis; (trans.) assume. [f. prec. + -IZE]

hypso- in comb. = Gk *hupsos* height, as: *-graphy*, department of geography dealing with altitudes; *-meter*, *-me·tric(al)*, *-metry*, instrument for, concerned with, science of, measuring altitudes.

hўr·ax, n. Genus of small rabbit-like quadrupeds, including Syrian rock-rabbit and S.-Afr. rock-badger. [f. Gk *hurax* shrew-mouse]

hў·son (-sn), n. Kind of green tea from China. [f. Chin. *hsi-ch'un* lit. bright spring]

hy-spy, I spy, n. Kind of hide-&-seek.

hy·ssop, n. Small bushy aromatic herb, formerly used medicinally; (bibl.) plant whose twigs were used for sprinkling in Jewish rites, bunch of this used in purification. [f. L f. Gk *hussōpos*, prob. of eastern orig.]

hystēr·ia, n. Functional disturbance of nervous system (esp. of women), characterized by anaesthesia, convulsions, &c., & usu. attended with disturbance of moral & intellectual faculties (formerly thought to be due to disturbance of womb); morbid excitement. [mod. medical L, on foll.]

hystĕ·ric, a. & n. = foll.; (n. pl.) hysterical fits or convulsions. [f. L f. Gk *husterikos* of the womb (*hustera*, see -IC)]

hystĕ·rical, a. Of, affected with, hysteria; morbidly emotional. Hence **hyste·ricalLY²** adv. [prec. + -AL]

hystero- in comb. = Gk *hustera* womb, as: *-gĕ·nic*, *-geny*, productive, production, of HYSTERIA; *-logy*, treatise on the uterus; *-tomy*, operation of cutting into the uterus.

hў·sterŏn prŏ·terŏn, n. (Gram.) figure of speech in which what should come last is put first; inversion of natural order. [LL, f. Gk *husteron proteron* latter (put in place of) former]

I

I¹, i, (ī), letter (pl. *Is*, I's). As Roman numeral I or i = 1, as i 1, ii 2, iii 3, iv (rarely iiii) 4, vi 6, viii 8, ix (rarely viiii) 9, xi 11, xiv 14, li 51, cii 102, miv 1,004.

Abbreviations (1): (I.): Idaho; Jesus, **I.N.R.I.** (*Nazarenus Rex Judæorum*, of Nazareth King of the Jews), see also IHS; Imperial, **I.S.O.** (Service Order); Independent, **I.L.P.** (Labour Party); Indian, **I.C.S.** (Civil Service); industrial, **I.W.W.** (workers of the world); Irish, **I.R.A.**, **I.R.B.**, (republican army, brotherhood); Island; Isle, **I. of M.** (Man), **I.W.** (of Wight). (i.): *id*, **i.e.** (*est*); *idem*, **i.q.** (*quod*); indicated, **i.h.p.** (horse power).

Abbreviations (2): **Ia**, Iowa; **ib.** (*idem*), **ibid.**(*em*); **id.**(*em*); **IHS** (see dict. place); **Ill.**(inois); **in.**(ches); **incl.**(usive); **incog.**(nito); **Ind.**(iana); **Ind.**(ian) **T.**-(erritory); **inf.**(ra); **init.**(*io*); **inst.**(ant); **inv.**(*enit*); **IOU** (see dict. place); **Is.**(aiah.)

I², pron. & n. Subjective case of 1st pers. pron. (objective *me*, poss. *my*; pl. *we*, obj. *us*, poss. *our*); (n., metaphys.) *the I*, the ego, subject or object of self-consciousness. [OE *ic*, cf. Du. *ik*, G *ich*, also L *ego*, Gk *egō*]

-i, suf. forming pl. of L nn. in *-us* & *-er* of 2nd decl. & of Ital. wds in *-o*, *-e*; retained in E in wds of scientific or learned use, as *cirri, foci, dilettanti, literati*; also freq. in mod. L names of groups or orders in Nat. Hist., as *acanthopterygii, acrocarpi.*

-i-, connecting vowel in L, being stem vowel, as in *omnivorus*, weakened representative of this, as in *herbivorus* (*herba*), *granivorus* (*grano-*), or merely connective, as in *graminivorus* (*gramin-*); used in E in compds formed on L models, as *hydriform, setiform.* Cf. -O-.

-ia¹, suf., f. L & Gk *-ia*, forming abstract nn. &c., as *hydrophobia, mania, militia*; freq. in mod. L terms of pathology (*cephalalgia, hysteria*); of bot. (classes, as *Cryptogamia*, & personal names, as *dahlia, fuchsia*); in names of countries, as *Australia*; & in names of alkaloids, as *morphia, strychnia*, (in more recent nomenclature *-ine*). F *-ie* f. *-ia* gives -Y¹.

-ia², suf. forming pl. of Gk nn. in *-ion* & L nn. in *-ium*, as *paraphernalia, regalia*; freq. in mod. L names of classes &c. in Zool., as *mammalia, reptilia.*

-ial, suf. repr. L *-ialis*, in adjj. f. n.-stems in *-io-*, *-ia-*, as *curialis, tibialis*; much used in med. L, F, & E, to form adjj. f. L adjj. in *-is* & *-ius*, as *celestial, dictatorial* (L *-tis*, *-rius*).

ī·amb, n. =IAMBUS. [f. F *iambe*, as IAMBUS]

ia·mbic, a. & n. (pros.). Of, containing, based on, iambuses; (n.) i. verse. [f. F *iambique* f. L f. Gk *iambikos* (as foll., see -IC)]

ia·mbus, n. (pl. *-buses, -bī*). The metrical foot ⏑–. [L, f. Gk *iambos* iambus, lampoon (*iaptō* assail)]

-ian, suf. of aa. & nn. =L *-anus* -AN added to stems in *-i-*, as *Italian, Virgilian*, or w. connective *-i-*, as *Christian*; esp. forming aa. on proper names, as *Addisonian, Bostonian*, (varying in place-names with *-er*, as *Londoner*, & often added to Latinized stems, as *Mancunian, Glaswegian, Oxonian, Liverpudlian*).

Ibē·rian (ī-), a. & n. Of ancient Iberia; of Spain & Portugal as one country; (n.) inhabitant, language, of ancient Iberia. [f. L *Iberia* f. Gk *Ibēres* Spaniards + -AN]

ī·bex, n. (pl. *-exes*). Wild goat of Alps & Apennines, with large recurved horns. [L]

ibī·dem, adv. In the same book, chapter, passage, &c. (abbr. *ib., ibid.*). [L, = in same place (*ibi* there + demonstr. suf. *-dem*)]

ī·bis, n. (pl. *ibises*). Stork-like bird found in lakes & swamps of warm climates; *Sacred I.*, kind venerated by ancient Egyptians. [L f. Gk]

-ible, suf. f. L *-ĭbilis*, i.e. *-bilis* -BLE as appended to p.p. stems, 3rd conj. vbs, & some 2nd conj. (*terrible*), or f. L *-ībilis* (*-bilis* with 4th conj.); also in mod. formations, as *avertible*. Displaced by *-able* in many wds taken thr. F or formed really or apparently on E vbs. Meaning: 'that can be —d'.

-ic, suf. (1) forming adjj. (often thr. F *-ique*) f. L *-icus*, sometimes of L orig., as in *classicus, publicus, domesticus*, but usu. f. Gk *-ikos*, as in *grammaticus, poeticus*. E adjj. in *-ic* are direct f. Gk, or on Gk elements, or (esp. scientific terms) on wds f. L or other langg., as *carbonic, Byronic*. (Chem.) *-ic* in names of oxygen acids &c. indicates higher degree of oxidation than *-ous*, as in *chloric, sulphuric*. (2) Gk adjj. in *-ikos* were used as nn. in 3 ways: in masc. sing., as *kritikos* man able to discern, critic; in fem. sing., as *mousikē* (*tekhnē*) art of the muses, music; in neut. pl., as *ta oikonomika* things pertaining to management, economics. In L the last two both became *-ica*, whence much fluctuation in med. L as to grammatical treatment. The Rom. langg. usu. had fem. sing. for names of arts and sciences, but F occas. had pl., as *les mathématiques*. E wds before 15th c. were sing., as still *arithmetic, music, magic, logic, rhetoric*; later, *-ics* became usu. form for names of sciences, as *acoustics, conics, dynamics*, (treated as sing.), & of practical matters, as *athletics, politics, tactics*, (pl.). Besides this spec. use, other adjj. in *-ic* become nn., as *epic, emetic, cosmetic, rustic, mechanic*.

-ical, suf. (*-ic* + *-al*) forming adjj. f. nn., as *musical*, or more commonly secondary adjj. f. adjj. as *comical, historical*. Many adjj. have both the *-ic* & *-ical* form, often with distinction in meaning (see -AL)]

-ically, suf. (*-ical* + -LY²) forming advv. corr. to adjj. in *-ic, -ical*, advv. in *-icly*, as *publicly, politicly*, being rare.

ice¹, n. Frozen water; *break the i.*, (fig.) make a beginning, break through reserve or stiffness; CUT² *no i.*; (w. pl.) frozen confection, i.-cream, water-i.; *i.-age*, glacial period; *i.-axe*, (used by Alpine climbers for cutting steps); *iceblink*, luminous appearance on horizon, caused by reflexion from i.; *i.-boat*, boat mounted on runners for travelling on i., (also *i.-breaker*) boat used for breaking i. on river &c.; *i.-cream*, flavoured cream or custard congealed in freezing-mixture; *coco-nut* &c. *i.*, slabs of sugar flavoured with coco-nut &c.; *i.-fall*, steep part of glacier like frozen waterfall; *i.-field*, expanse of i., esp. in Polar regions; *i.-foot*, belt of i. along coast in Arctic regions; *i.-house*, building often partly or wholly underground for storing i.; *iceman*, man skilled in traversing i., (also) maker of ii.; (*i.*-)PACK¹; *i.-pick*, stiletto for splitting up table i.; *i. pudding*, a frozen confection; *i.-run*, artificial tobogganing track of i.; *i.-wool* (glossy kind used in crochet &c.). [com.-Teut.: OE *īs*, Du. *ijs*, G *eis*]

ice², v.t. Freeze; cover (as) with ice; cool (wine) in ice; cover (cake &c.) with concretion of sugar whence **i·cING¹** n. [f. prec.]

-ice, suf., OF, f. L *-itia* in abstract nn. (*justice, avarice, malice, notice*, & F formations *cowardice, jaundice*) & f. L *-itius, -itium*, (*novice, precipice, service*). But E *-ice* has freq. diff. orig., as in *apprentice, bodice, practice*, where *-ice* is partly due to assim.

i·ceberg, n. Floating mass of ice often of great height above water, detached portion of Arctic glacier; (fig.) unemotional person. [prob. f. Du. *ijsberg* (*ijs* ice + *berg* hill)]

I·celand, n. Large island between Norway and Greenland; *I. lichen, moss*, edible species; *I. poppy*, yellow Arctic poppy; *I. spar*, transparent variety of calcite. Hence **I·celandER¹**(4) n. [f. ON *Island* (*iss* ice + -LAND)]

Icela·ndic, a. & n. (Language) of Iceland. [-IC]

ichneu·mon (ĭknū-), n. Small brown weasel-like quadruped allied to mongoose, noted for destroying crocodiles' eggs; (also *i. fly*) small parasitic hymenopterous insect depositing eggs in or on larva of another insect. [L, f. Gk *ikhneumōn* spider-hunting wasp f. *ikhneuō* track (*ikhnos*)]

ichno- in comb. = Gk *ikhnos* track, trace, as: *-gra·phic(al)*, *-graphy*, (of) the drawing of ground-plans; *-lite* (also *ichnite*), fossil footprint; *-logy*, study of fossil footprints.

i·chor (ĭk-), n. (Gk Myth.) fluid flowing like blood in veins of gods; (Path.) watery acrid discharge from wounds &c. Hence **i·chor**OUS a. [Gk *ikhōr*]

ichthyo- (ĭk-) in comb. (before vowel *ichthy-*) = Gk *ikhthus* fish, as: *-grapher*, *-graphy*, writer on, description of, fishes; *-latry*, worship of a fish-god; *-lite*, fossil fish; *-logy*, natural history of fishes, whence *-lo·gical*, *-logist*; *-phagi*, *-phagist*, fish-eater(s); *-phagous*, fish-eating; *ichthyornis*, extinct genus of toothed birds.

i·chthyoid, a. & n. Fish-like; (n.) vertebrate of fish type. [as prec. + -OID]

ichthyosau·rus, n. Extinct marine animal with huge head, tapering body, four paddles, & long tail. [ICHTHYO- + Gk *sauros* lizard]

ichthyō·sis, n. Disease in which epidermis becomes dry & horny. So **ichthyŏ·**TIC a. [f. Gk *ikhthus* fish + -OSIS]

-ician, suf. (= F *-icien*), spec. form of -IAN added to names of arts or sciences in *-ic(s)* to form personal designations (= one skilled in or concerned with), as *arithmetician*, *logician*, *optician*, *politician*; sometimes used when there is no corresp. n. (& even no adj.) in *-ic*, as *academician*, *algebrician*, *Hebrician*.

ī·cicle, n. Tapering ice-formation, produced by freezing of successive drops trickling from the point of attachment. [OE has *ises gicel* (*is* ICE + *gicel*, cogn. w. ON *jokull* icicle, glacier)]

i·ckle, a. (nursery). Little. [corrupt.]

ī·cŏn, n. Image, statue; (Eastern Church) painting, mosaic, &c., of sacred personage, itself regarded as sacred. [LL, f. Gk *eikōn* image (**eikō* be like)]

īcŏ·nic, a. Of (the nature of) an image or portrait; (of statues) following a conventional type. [f. LL f. Gk *eikonikos* (as prec., see -IC)]

icono- in comb. = Gk *eikōn* image, as: *-graphy*, illustration of subject by drawings or figures, book whose essence is pictures, treatise on pictures or statuary, so *-grapher*, *-gra·phic*; *-later*, *-latry*, worshipper, worship, of images; *-logy*, study of icons (in any sense); *-machy*, war against use of images in connexion with worship; *-stasis*, (Eastern Church) screen separating sanctuary from main body of church, & on which icons are placed.

icŏ·noclasm, n. Breaking of images (lit. & fig.). [prec. + Gk *klasma* (*klaō* break, -M)]

ico·noclast, n. Breaker of images, esp. one who took part in movement in 8th & 9th cc. against use of images in religious worship in churches of the East; (fig.) one who assails cherished beliefs. Hence **icŏnocla·s**TIC a. [f. LL f. Gk *eikonoklastēs* (*eikōn* ICON + *klastēs* f. *klaō* break)]

ī·cosahĕ·dron, n. Solid contained by twenty plane faces. [f. Gk *eikosaedron* (*eikosi* twenty + *hedra* base)]

-ics. See -IC(2).

i·ctus, n. (pros.). Rhythmical or metrical stress. [L, = blow, f. *icere* strike]

i·cy, a. Abounding in, covered with, ice; very cold (lit., & fig. as *i. manners*). Hence **i·ci**LY[2] adv., **i·ci**NESS n. [-Y[2]]

id, n. (Biol.) a unit of germ-plasm or idioplasm; (Psycho-anal.) *the* instinctive impulses of the individual. [first sense, abbr. IDIOPLASM; second, perh. new application of same]

-id[1], suf. f. F *-ide* f. L *-idus*, which forms adjj. chiefly f. vbs w. *-ē-* stems, as *acidus* acid f. *acēre*, but also f. vbs w. *-i-* or consonant stem, as *fluidus* fluid f. *fluĕre*, & f. nn., as *morbidus* morbid f. *morbus*. Earlier E wds come thr. F, others f. L direct.

-id[2], suf. of nn. (= F *-ide*) f. L f. Gk *-id-* (nom. *-is*), as *chrysalid*, *pyramid*. In bot., *amaryllid*, *orchid*, &c., should denote plants amaryllis, orchis, &c., but in fact denote members of the order of which these are typical genera (*amaryllideae*, *orchidaceae*).

-id[3], suf. of nn. & aa. (zool.). 1. Through F f. L names of families in *-idae* pl. of *-ides* f. Gk *-idēs* son of, as *Araneid*, member of the family *Araneidae*. 2. f. L names of classes in *-ida* taken as neut. pl. of *-ides* (= Gk *-idēs*), as *Arachnid*, member of the class *Arachnida*.

-id[4], suf. Early spelling of -IDE, now chiefly U.S.

ide, n. Fish allied to carp. [f. Swed. *id*]

-ide, suf. (chem.) forming names of simple compounds of an element with another element or radical, the suf. *-ide* being added to the name (usu. abbrev.) of the more electro-negative element, as *bromine chloride*, *sulphur bromide*, *carbon sulphide*, *boron carbide*; first used in *oxide* from *oxygen*.

idea (īdē·*a*), n. Archetype, pattern, as distinguished from its realization in individuals; (Platonic) eternally existing pattern of which individual things in any class are imperfect copies; conception, plan, of thing to be aimed at, created, &c.; plan of action; notion conceived by the mind; way of thinking (*the young i.*, the child's mind); vague belief, fancy, as *the i. of his doing such a thing*, *I had no i. you were there*; (Descartes, Locke) immediate object of thought or mental perception; (Kant) conception of reason transcending all experience. Hence **idea'd,** **idea**ED[2], (-ĭad), **idea·**LESS, aa. [LL f. Gk, = form, kind, f. *id-* see]

īdē·al, a. & n. Answering to one's highest conception; embodying an idea; existing only in idea; visionary; relating to, consisting of, (Platonic) ideas; (n.) perfect type; actual thing as standard for imitation. Hence **idē·al**LY² adv. [f. F *idéal* f. LL *idealis* (as prec., see -AL)]

idē·alism, n. Representation of things in ideal form, imaginative treatment, (cf. REALISM), so **idēaliz**A·TION n., **idē·al**IZE v.t. & i.; (Philos.) system of thought in which the object of external perception is held to consist of ideas (cf. REALISM). So **idē·al**IST n.; **idēali·st**IC a. [-ISM]

idea·lity, n. Quality of being ideal; (Phrenol.) imaginative faculty. [-ITY]

idē·ate, v.t. & i. Imagine, conceive; form ideas. Hence **idēa**·TION n., **idēa·tion**AL a. [f. IDEA + -ATE³]

idée fixe (ēdāfē·ks), n. Idea that dominates the mind, monomania. [F, lit. fixed idea]

idem, n. or adv. (abbr. *id.*). (In) the same author (ĭ-); the same word (ĭ-); *ĭ. quod,* the same as. [L *īdem* masc., *ĭdem* neut., same]

īde·ntic, a. (Diplom.) *i. note,* simultaneous & uniformly worded expression of opinion from several powers to another; = foll. [f. schol. L *identicus* (cf. IDENTITY)]

ide·ntical, a. (Of one thing viewed at different times) the very same; (of different things) agreeing in every detail (*with*); (Logic, Math.) expressing an identity (*i. proposition,* of the type *Man is man*). Hence **ide·ntical**LY² adv. [-AL]

ide·ntify, v.t. Treat (thing) as identical (*with*); associate one*self* inseparably *with* (party, policy, &c.); establish identity of. Hence **ide·ntifi**ABLE a., **identi**FICA·TION n. (*identification* or *identity disk,* of rubber &c. hung from soldier's neck on active service & bearing his name &c.). [f. LL *identificare* (as foll., see -FY)]

ide·ntity, n. Absolute sameness; individuality, personality, (*i. disk,* see prec.); (Alg.) equality of two expressions for all values of the literal quantities, equation expressing this, e.g. $(x+1)^2 = x^2 + 2x + 1$. [f. F *identité* f. LL *identitas,* irreg. f. *idem* same (see -TY)]

ĭdeo- in comb. =IDEA, as: *-gram, -graph,* character symbolizing the idea of a thing without expressing its name (e.g. Chinese characters), whence *-gra·phic(al), -graphy; i·deologue,* theorist, visionary; *-logy,* science of ideas, (also) visionary speculation, whence *-lo·gical, -logist.*

ides, n. pl. (Rom. antiq.). Eighth day after nones (15th of March, May, July, October, 13th of other months). [F, f. L *Idūs*]

ĭd est (abbr. *i.e.*). That is to say. [L]

ĭ·diocy, n. Extreme mental imbecility. [f. Gk *idiōteia* (as IDIOT) or f. *idiot* + -CY; *idiotcy* is irreg. form]

i·diom, n. Language of a people or country; specific character of this; form of expression peculiar to a language. [f. L f. Gk *idiōma -matos* (*idioomai* make one's own f. *idios,* see -M)]

idiomă·tic, a. Characteristic of a particular language; vernacular; colloquial. Hence **idioma·t**ICALLY adv. [f. Gk *idiōmatikos* (prec., -IC)]

idiŏ·pathy, n. (path.). Disease not preceded or occasioned by another. Hence **idiopa·th**IC a., **idiopa·th**ICALLY adv. [f. Gk *idiopatheia* (*idios* own, see -PATHY)]

ĭ·dioplasm, n. (biol.). Portion of PLASM that determines an organism's nature. [Gk *idios* own, PLASM]

ĭdiosy·ncrasy, n. Mental constitution, view, feeling, peculiar to a person; mode of expression peculiar to an author; (Med.) physical constitution peculiar to a person. So **idiosyncra·t**IC a. [f. Gk *idiosugkrasia* (*idios* own + *sun* together + *krasis* mixture f. *kerannumi* mix]

ĭ·diot, n. Person so deficient in mind as to be permanently incapable of rational conduct; utter fool. So **idiŏ·t**IC, a. **idio·t**ICALLY adv. [F, f. L (*-ta*) f. Gk *idiōtēs* private person, 'layman', ignorant person, f. *idios* own, private]

ī·dle, a. (-er, -est), & v.i. & t. (Of action, thought, word) ineffective, worthless, vain; groundless; useless; unoccupied; lazy, indolent; (v.i.) be i.; (v.t.) pass (time &c.) *away* in idleness; *i. wheel,* safety wheel coming into operation in case of breakdown, (also) intermediate wheel between two geared wheels. Hence **i·dle**NESS, **i·dl**ER¹, nn., **i·d**LY² adv. [(vb f. a.) OE *īdel,* cf. Du. *ijdel,* G *eitel*; orig. sense prob. 'empty']

ī·dlesse, n. Idleness. [sham archaic, -ESS²]

idol (ī·dl), n. Image of deity used as object of worship; false god; person, thing, that is the object of excessive devotion; phantom; (Logic) false mental conception, *ii. of the tribe, cave, market, theatre,* (L *idola tribus, specus, fori, theatri*), four classes of fallacies (Bacon, *Nov. Org.* I. xxxix) referable respectively to limitations of human mind, prejudices of idiosyncrasy, influence of words, philosophical & logical prepossessions. [f. OF *idole* f. L f. Gk *eidōlon* phantom (*eidos* form)]

īdŏ·later, n. Worshipper of idols; devoted admirer (*of*). So **ido·latr**ESS¹, **ido·latr**Y¹ (*honour* one *on this side idolatry,* short of making a god of him), nn., **ido·latr**OUS a., **ido·latrous**LY² adv. [f. OF *idolatre* shortened f. eccl. L f. Gk *eidōlolatrēs* (IDOL, -LATRY); F had also *idolâtre* by confus. w. suf. *-âtre* -ASTER, whence earlier E *idolatrer*]

i·dolize, v.t. & i. Make an idol of; venerate, love, to excess; practise idolatry. Hence **idoliz**A·TION n. [-IZE]

idō·lum, n. (pl. *-la*). Mental image, idea; (Logic) fallacy (see IDOL). [L, as IDOL]

ĭ·dyll, -yl, n. Short description in verse or (*prose i.*) in prose of picturesque scene or incident, esp. in rustic life; episode suitable for such treatment. Hence **idy·ll**IC a., **idy·ll**ICALLY adv., **i·dyll**IST n., **i·dyll-**

IZE(1) v.t. [f. L f. Gk *eidullion* (*eidos* form)]

-ier, suf. forming personal nn. denoting occupation &c.; there are two sets, ME wds w. unaccented *-ier*, as *collier* (see -ER[2]), & later wds f. 16th c. w. *-ier* usu. accented, as *cavalier* (but *fina·ncier*), and often spelt *-eer*. The latter, & perh. usu. the former, f. F *-ier*, -EER.

if, conj. (n.). On the condition or supposition that, as *i. you are* (now) *tired we will sit down, i. you* (hereafter) *see him give him the message, i. he has found it he will send it, i. he had fair warning he has nothing to complain of, i. he had been warned he has* (or *had*) *nothing to complain of*, (w. past tense implying that condition is not fulfilled) *i. I knew what to do I should do it, i. he had been warned he would have* (or *would have had*) *nothing to complain of*; whenever, as *i. I feel any doubt I inquire, i. I felt any doubt I inquired, i. I had been badly treated I complained*; whether, as *ask, see, try, i. you can turn the handle*; (when *if* is omitted, order of verb & subject is inverted, as) *were I* (if I were) *in your place, would, could, should, might, had, he* (if he would, could, &c.), (poet.) *loved I not honour more*; (without apodosis) *i. I only knew!*, I wish I knew, *i. I haven't lost my watch!* (I have, to my surprise or disgust); *as i.*, as the case would be if, as *it seems as i. he meant* (vulg. *means*) *to compromise, he talks as* (he would) *i. he were drunk*; *as i. you didn't know*, you know quite well; (n.) condition, supposition, as *i. ifs & ans were pots & pans*. [OE *gif*, cf. Du. *of* if, G *ob* whether; perh. cases of a noun (OHG *iba*) meaning 'doubt']

i·gloo, n. Eskimo dome-shaped hut. [native, = house]

i·gneous, a. Of fire, fiery; produced by volcanic agency. [f. L *igneus* (*ignis* fire) + -OUS]

i·gnis fă·tuus, n. Will-o'-the-wisp, phosphorescent light (now rarely) seen on marshy ground, supposed due to spontaneous combustion of gas from decaying organic matter; delusive hope or gain. [med. or mod. L, = foolish fire]

igni·te, v.t. & i. Make intensely hot; (Chem.) heat to the point of combustion or chemical change; set fire to; take fire. Hence or cogn. **igni·t**ABLE a., **ignĭ·t**ION n. [f. L *ignire -it-* (*ignis* fire)]

igno·ble, a. (-er, -est). Of low birth, position, or reputation; mean, base, dishonourable. Hence **igno·ble**NESS n., **igno·b**LY[2] adv. [F, f. L *ignobilis* (*in*- not + (*g*)*nobilis* NOBLE)]

i·gnominy, n. Dishonour, infamy; infamous conduct. So **ignomi·ni**OUS a. (now usu. in less damnatory sense, = humiliating), **ignomi·nious**LY[2] adv. [f. F *ignominie* f. L *ignominia* (*in*- not + (*g*)*nomen* name)]

ignorā·mus, n. (pl. *-muses*). Ignorant person. [L, = we do not know, (legal) we take no notice of (bill); mod. sense perh. f. Ruggle's *Ignoramus* (1615) exposing lawyers' ignorance]

i·gnorance, n. Want of knowledge (*of* thing, or in general; *where i. is bliss, 'tis folly to be wise*). [F, f. L *ignorantia* (as foll., see -ANCE)]

i·gnorant, a. Lacking knowledge; uninformed (*of, in*, subject, *of* fact). Hence **i·gnorant**LY[2] adv. [F, f. L, as IGNORE see -ANT]

ignorā·tio (-shĭō) ***ele·nchi*** (-kī), n. (logic). Argument that appears to refute opponent while actually disproving something not advanced by him. [L]

ignore·, v.t. Refuse to take notice of; (of Grand Jury) reject (bill) as unfounded. [f. F *ignorer* f. L *ignorare* not know, ignore (*in*- not + *gno*- know)]

ignō·tum per igno·tius. (Explanation of) the unknown by the still less known. [L]

igua·na (-wah-), n. Large W.-Ind. & S.-Amer. arboreal lizard. [Sp., f. Carib *iwana*]

igua·nodŏn (-wăn-), n. Huge herbivorous lizard, found fossil. [f. prec. + Gk *odous odontos* tooth, after *mastodon* &c.]

IHS, abbr. repr. Gk *Iēsous* Jesus (Gk cap. *ē* being like H); often taken to mean *Jesus Hominum Salvator* (Saviour of men) *In Hoc Signo* (*vinces*) in this sign (thou shalt conquer), *In Hac* (*cruce*) *Salus* in this (cross) is salvation.

il-, pref. = IN[1,2] before *l*.

il-, -ile, suf. of adjj. & sometimes nn., repr. L *-ĭlis* or when added to *-i-* stems *-īlis* (*civilis*). In OF *-īlis* appeared as *-il*, but *-ĭlis* lost *i*, tonic accent falling on prec. syllable (*humble* L *humilem*, *frêle* L *fragilem*). L wds adopted early in OF took *-il* masc., *-ile* fem. (*civil, -ile*); later wds have *-ile* for both genders (*agile, facile*). Few E wds have *-il* (*civil, fossil, utensil*); & the tendency is to pronounce *-ile* of either origin with *ī*.

i·lex, n. (pl. *-exes*). Holm-oak; (Bot.) genus including common holly. [L]

ĭ·liac, a. Of the flank(-bone), as *i. artery*; *i. passion*, painful affection due to intestinal obstruction. [f. F *iliaque* f. LL *iliacus* (*ilium*, class. L only in pl. *ilia* flanks; but orig. the adj. corr. to L *ileus* f. Gk *eileos* colic)]

I·liad (ĭ-), n. Epic poem attributed to Homer & describing siege of Troy; (fig.) *I.* (long series) *of woes*. [f. L f. Gk *Ilias* (*poiēsis*) (poem) of Ilium or Troy]

ĭ·lium, n. (pl. *-ia*). Hip-bone. [L, see ILIAC]

ilk, a. (Sc.). *Of that i.*, of the same, as *Guthrie of that i.*, Guthrie of Guthrie; (vulg.) *that i.*, that family, class, or set. [OE *ilca* same, prob. f. pronominal st. *i*- (cf. Goth. *is* he) + *-lic* LIKE]

ill, a., n., & adv. Out of health, sick, as *he is i., was taken i.*, (*of* or *with* disease, *with* anxiety &c.); (of health) unsound, disordered; morally bad, as *i. fame*, disrepute, *i. blood, i. will*, animosity, strife, *i. nature*, churlishness, *i.* (morose) *humour, temper*; harmful, as (prov.) *i. weeds grow apace; do an i. turn to person*, harm him or his interests; wretched, disastrous, as (prov.) *it's an i. wind that blows nobody good*; (archaic) difficult, as *i. to please*; faulty, unskilful, as *i. management*; (of manners or conduct) improper; *i.* (imperfect) *success*. (N.) evil, the opposite of good; harm, injury; *speak i.* (something unfavourable) *of*; (pl.) misfortunes. (Adv.) badly, as *behaved i.*; *take* (thing) *i.*, take offence at it; unfavourably, as *it would have gone i. with him*; imperfectly, scarcely, as *i. provided, it i. became him to speak*; *i. at ease*, embarrassed, uneasy; *i.-advised, -visĕdly*, imprudent(ly); *i.-affected*, not well disposed; *i.-bred*, badly brought up, rude; *i. breeding*, bad manners; *i.-conditioned*, of evil disposition, (also) in bad condition; *i.-disposed*, disposed to evil, malevolent, (also) unfavourably disposed (*towards*); *i.-fated*, destined to, bringing, bad fortune; *i.-favoured*, uncomely, (also) displeasing, objectionable; *i.-gotten*, gained by evil means; *i.-humoured*, bad-tempered; *i.-judged*, unwise; *i.-mannered*, unmannerly, rude; *i.-natured(ly)*, churlish(ly); *i.-omened*, attended by bad omens; *i.-starred*, born under an evil star, unlucky; *i.-tempered*, morose, peevish; *i.-timed*, unseasonable; *i.-treat, -use*, treat badly. [early ME, f. ON *illr*, etym. dub.]

illa·tion, n. Deduction, conclusion; thing deduced. [f. LL *illatio* (as INFER, see -ION)]

illa·tive, a. (Of words) stating, introducing, an inference, as *i. particles*; inferential. Hence **illa·tive**LY[2] adv. [f. LL *illativus* (as prec., see -IVE)]

illē·gal, a. Not legal; contrary to law. Hence or cogn. **illega·li**TY n., **ille·gal**LY[2] adv. [f. med. L IL(*legalis* LEGAL)]

illĕ·gible, a. Not legible. Hence **illegi**BI·LITY n., **ille·gib**LY[2] adv. [IL-]

illegi·timate[1] (-*at*), a. & n. Not authorized by law; improper; not born in lawful wedlock, bastard; wrongly inferred; abnormal; (n.) one whose position is i., esp. bastard. Hence **illegi·tim**ACY n., **illegi·timate**LY[2] adv. [IL-]

illegi·timāte[2], v.t. Declare illegitimate. Hence **illegitim**A·TION n. [f. prec.]

illi·beral, a. Not befitting a free man; without liberal culture; vulgar, sordid; narrow-minded; stingy. Hence or cogn. **illibera·li**TY n., **illi·beral**LY[2] adv. [f. F *illibéral* f. L IL(*liberalis* LIBERAL)]

illi·cit, a. Unlawful, forbidden. Hence **illi·cit**LY[2] adv. [f. F *illicite* f. L IL(*licitus* p.p. of *licēre* be allowed)]

illi·mitable, a. Boundless. Hence **illimitab**I·LITY, **illi·mitable**NESS, nn., **illi·mitab**LY[2] adv. [IL-]

illi·terate (-*at*), a. & n. Ignorant of letters; unlearned; unable to read; (n.) i. person. Hence **illi·ter**ACY, **illi·terate**NESS, nn. [f. L IL(*litteratus* LITERATE)]

i·llness, n. Unhealthy condition of body, sickness. [-NESS]

illo·gical, a. Devoid of, contrary to, logic. Hence **illogica·li**TY n., **illo·gical**LY[2] adv. [IL-]

illth, n. (rare). Evil state. [-TH[1]]

illu·me, v.t. (poet.). Light up, make bright, (lit. & fig.). [for ILLUMINE, cf. F *allumer*]

illu·minate (-ōō-, -ū-), v.t. Light up, whence **illu·min**ANT a. & n.; give spiritual or intellectual light to; throw light upon (subject); shed lustre upon; decorate (buildings &c.) profusely with lights as sign of festivity; decorate (initial letter in manuscript &c.) with gold, silver, & brilliant colours. So **illu·mina·**TION, **illu·minat**OR[2], nn., **illu·minat**IVE a. [f. L IL(*luminare* f. *lumen -minis* light), see -ATE[3]]

illuminā·tī (*or* -ahtē), n. pl. Secret society founded by Weishaupt in 1776, holding deistic & republican principles, & organized like freemasons; persons claiming to possess special enlightenment. So **illu·min**ISM(3), **illu·min**IST(2), nn. [L (as prec., see -ATE[2]) or It., whence occasional sing. -*ato*]

illu·mine, v.t. Light up; enlighten spiritually; brighten. [f. F *illuminer* (as ILLUMINATE)]

illu·sion (-zhn), n. Deception, delusion; sensuous perception of an external object involving a false belief; a transparent tulle. [F, f. L *illusionem* f. IL(*ludere lus-* play), see -ION]

illu·sionist, n. One who disbelieves in objective existence, so **illu·sion**ISM n.; one who produces illusions, esp. conjurer. [-IST]

illu·sive (-s-), a. Deceptive. Hence or cogn.: **illu·sive**LY[2], **illu·sori**LY[2], advv., **illu·sive**NESS, **illu·sori**NESS, nn., **illu·s**ORY a. [as ILLUSION, see -IVE]

i·llustrate, v.t. Make clear, explain; make clear by examples; elucidate (description &c.) by drawings; ornament (book, newspaper, &c.) with designs. Hence **i·llustrat**OR[2] n. [f. L IL(*lustrare* light up, prob. f. st. of *lumen* light)]

illustra·tion, n. Illustrating; example; drawing &c. illustrating book or article in paper. [F, f. L *illustrationem* (prec., -ATION)]

illu·strative, a. Serving as explanation or example (*of*). Hence **illu·strative**LY[2] adv. [as ILLUSTRATE, see -IVE]

illu·strious, a. Distinguished, renowned. Hence **illu·strious**LY[2] adv., **illu·strious**NESS n. [f. L IL(*lustris* see ILLUSTRATE) + -OUS]

im-[1, 2], pref. =IN-[1, 2] before *b*, *m*, *p*.
i·mage[1] (-ij), n. Artificial imitation of the external form of an object, e.g. statue (esp. of saint &c. as object of veneration); optical counterpart produced by rays of light reflected from mirror, refracted through lens, &c.; form, semblance; counterpart, as *he is the very i. of his father*; type; simile, metaphor; idea, conception. Hence **i·mage**LESS a. [F, f. L *imaginem* (nom. *-go*) prob. f. same root as IMITATE]
i·mage[2], v.t. Make an image of, portray; reflect, mirror; picture (thing *to* one*self*); describe vividly; typify. Hence **i·mage**ABLE a. [f. prec.]
i·magery, n. Images; statuary, carving; figurative illustration. [f. OF *imagerie* (as IMAGE[1], see -ERY)]
ima·ginable, a. That can be imagined, as *the greatest difficulty i., took all the trouble i.* Hence **ima·ginab**LY[2] adv. [f. LL *imaginabilis* (as IMAGINE, see -BLE)]
imă·ginal, a. (entom.). Of an insect imago. [f. L as IMAGE[1] + -AL]
imă·ginary, a. Existing only in imagination; (Math.) having no real existence, but assumed to exist for a special purpose (e.g. square root of negative quantity). Hence **ima·ginari**LY[2] adv. [f. L *imaginarius* (as prec., see -ARY[1])]
imagina·tion, n. Imagining; mental faculty forming images of external objects not present to the senses; fancy; creative faculty of the mind. [F, f. L *imaginationem* (as IMAGINE, see -ATION)]
ima·ginative, a. Of, given to using, having or showing in a high degree, the faculty of imagination. Hence **ima·ginative**LY[2] adv., **ima·ginative**NESS n. [OF (*-if*, *-ive*), f. LL *imaginativus* (as prec., see -ATIVE)]
imă·gine, v.t. Form mental image of; conceive (thing, thing *to* be or do, *that* it is, *how, what*, &c.); guess, as *cannot i. what he is doing*; suppose, be of opinion, (*that*); take into one's head (idea, *that*). [f. F *imaginer* f. L *imaginari* (as IMAGE[1])]
imā·gō, n. (pl. *-gĭnēs, -gos*). Final & perfect stage of insect after all metamorphoses, e.g. butterfly. [mod. L sense of *imago* IMAGE]
ima·m, imau·m, (-ahm), n. Officiating priest of mosque; title of various Mohammedan leaders. Hence **ima·m**ATE[1] n. [Arab. (*-am*) f. *amma* go before]
i·mbecile (-ēl, -ĭl), a. & n. Mentally weak, stupid, idiotic; physically weak; (n.) person of weak intellect. Hence or cogn. **i·mbecile**LY[2] adv., **imbeci·l**ITY n. [f. F *imbécille* (now *-ile*) f. L *imbecillus* etym., dub.]
imbi·be, v.t. Drink in, assimilate, (ideas &c.); drink (liquid); inhale (air &c.); absorb (moisture &c.). So **imbibi·t**ION n. [(partly thr. F *imbiber*) f. L IM[1](*bibere bibit-* drink) conceive (opinions), drink]
i·mbricate, v.t. & i. Arrange (leaves, scales of fish, &c.), be arranged, so as to overlap like tiles. So **i·mbric**ATE[2] (*-at*), **i·mbricat**IVE, aa., **imbric**A·TION n. [f. L *imbricare* form like a tile (*imbrex -icis* f. *imber* shower), -ATE[3]]
imbro·glio (-ōlyō), n. Confused heap; complicated (esp. political or dramatic) situation. [It., f. *broglio*, cf. BROIL[1]]
imbrue· (-ōō), v.t. Stain (one's hand, sword, &c., *in, with*, blood, slaughter, &c.). [f. OF *embreuver* moisten for EM-(*beuvrer* f. L **biberare* f. *bibere* drink])
imbru·te, em-, v.t. Brutalize. [IM-[1]]
imbue·, v.t. Saturate (*with*); dye (*with*); permeate, inspire, (*with* feelings &c.); = IMBRUE. [f. L IM[1](*buere* cogn. w. *bibere* drink)]
i·mitate, v.t. Follow example of; mimic; be (consciously or not) like. So **imita**BI·LITY, **i·mitat**OR[2], nn., **i·mit**ABLE a. [f. L *imitari*, see -ATE[3]]
imita·tion, n. Imitating (*i. is the sincerest flattery*); copy; counterfeit (often attrib., as *i. leather*); (Mus.) repetition of melody &c., usu. at different pitch, in another part or voice. [f. L *imitatio* (prec., -ATION)]
i·mitative, a. Following model or example (*of*); *i. arts*, painting & sculpture; *i. word*, one that reproduces a natural sound (e.g. *fizz*) or whose sound is thought to correspond to appearances &c. of object described; counterfeit. Hence **i·mitative**LY[2] adv., **i·mitative**NESS n. [f. LL *imitativus* (as prec., see -ATIVE)]
immă·culate (-*at*), a. Pure, spotless; faultless (often iron.); *I. Conception* (of Virgin Mary, as born free from taint of original sin); (Nat. Hist.) not spotted. Hence **imma·cul**ACY, **imma·culate**NESS, nn., **imma·culate**LY[2] adv. [f. L IM[1](*maculatus* f. *macula* spot)]
i·mmanent, a. Indwelling, inherent, (*in*); (of God) permanently pervading the universe. Hence **i·mman**ENCE, -ENCY, nn. [f. LL IM[1](*manēre* remain), see -ENT]
immatē·r·ial, a. Not material, incorporeal; unimportant. Hence **immateria·l**ITY n., **immater·ial**IZE(3) v.t. [f. med. L IM[2](*materialis* MATERIAL)]
immatē·r·ialism, n. Doctrine that matter does not exist in itself apart from perception. So **immater·ial**IST n. [-ISM]
immature·, a. Not mature. So **immatur·**ITY n. [f. L IM[2](*maturus* MATURE)]
immea·surable, a. Not measurable, immense. Hence **immeasura**BI·LITY, **immea·surable**NESS, nn., **immea·surab**LY[2] adv. [IM-[2]]
immē·diate (-*at*), a. (Of person or thing in its relation to another) not separated by any intervening medium; (of relation or action) direct, without intervening medium; (Logic) *i. inference* (from single premiss, without intervention of middle term); nearest, next, as *my i. neighbour*;

occurring at once, without delay, as *an i. reply*. Hence **imme·diACY, imme·diateNESS**, nn., **imme·diateLY**² adv. [f. med. L IM²(*mediatus* MEDIATE)]

immemor·ial, a. Ancient beyond memory; very old. Hence **immemor·ialLY**² adv. [f. med. L IM(*memorialis* MEMORIAL)]

immen·se, a. Vast, huge; (slang) very good. Hence or cogn. **imme·nseNESS, imme·nsITY**, nn. [F, f. L IM²(*mensus* p.p. of *metiri* measure) immeasurable]

imme·nsely, adv. In an immense degree; (colloq.) very much. [-LY²]

immer·se, v.t. Dip, plunge, (*in* liquid); put overhead in water, esp. baptize thus; bury, imbed, (*in*); involve deeply, absorb, (*in* debt, difficulties, thought, &c.). [f. L IM(*mergere mers-* dip)]

immer·sion, n. Immersing; baptism by plunging whole person in water (cf. AFFUSION); (fig.) absorption (*in* thought &c.); (Astr.) disappearance of celestial body behind another or in its shadow. [f. LL *immersio* (prec., -ION)]

i·mmigrate, v.i. & t. Come as settler (*into* foreign country); bring in (person) as settler. So **i·mmigrANT** a. & n., **immigrA·TION** n. [f. L IM(*migrare* MIGRATE)]

i·mminent, a. (Of events, esp. dangers) impending, soon to happen. Hence or cogn. **i·mminENCE** n., **i·mminentLY**² adv. [f. L IM(*minēre* see EMINENT) overhang, see -ENT]

immi·scible, a. That cannot be mixed. Hence **immisciBI·LITY** n., **immi·scibLY**² adv. [f. IM-² + L *miscēre* mix, see -BLE]

immi·tigable, a. That cannot be softened or toned down. Hence **immi·tigabLY**² adv. [f. L IM²(*mitigabilis*, see MITIGATE)]

immi·xture, n. Mixing up; being involved (*in*). [f. L IM(¹*miscēre mixt-* mix) + -URE]

immō·bile, a. Immovable; not mobile; motionless. So **immoBI·LITY** n. [F, f. L IM²(*mobilis* MOBILE)]

immō·bilize, v.t. Fix immovably; make (troops) incapable of being shifted; withdraw (specie) from circulation. Hence **immobilizA·TION** n. [f. F *immobiliser* (as prec., see -IZE)]

immo·derate, a. Excessive, wanting in moderation. Hence **immo·derateLY**² adv. [f. L IM²(*moderatus* MODERATE)]

immo·dest, a. Indecent, indelicate; forward, impudent. Hence **immo·destLY**² adv., **immo·destY**¹ n. [f. L IM²(*modestus* MODEST)]

i·mmolate, v.t. Kill (victim) as sacrifice; (fig.) sacrifice (thing &c. *to* another). So **immolA·TION, i·mmolatOR**², nn. [f. L IM¹*molare* sprinkle with meal (*mola*), sacrifice, -ATE³]

immŏ·ral, a. Opposed to morality; morally evil; vicious, dissolute. Hence **immoraLITY** n., **immo·ralLY**² adv. [IM-²]

immor·tal, a. & n. Undying; divine; unfading, incorruptible; famous for all time; (colloq.) constant, long-lasting. (N.) i. being, esp. (pl.) gods of antiquity; person esp. author of enduring fame, member of French Academy; (pl.) royal bodyguard of ancient Persia. So **immorta·lITY** n. [f. L IM²(*mortalis* MORTAL)]

immor·talize, v.t. Confer enduring fame upon; endow with endless life; perpetuate. Hence **immortalizA·TION** n. [-IZE]

immor·tally, adv. Eternally; (colloq.) infinitely, very. [-LY²]

immorte·lle (-ĕl), n. Composite flower of papery texture retaining colour after being dried, often used to adorn graves. [F, fem. of *immortel* IMMORTAL]

immo·vable (-mōō-), a. & n. That cannot be moved; motionless; not subject to change; *i.* FEAST; steadfast, unyielding; emotionless; (Law, of property) consisting of land, houses, &c. (also as n. pl.). Hence **immovaBI·LITY, immo·vableNESS**, nn., **immo·vabLY**² adv. [IM-²]

immu·ne, a. & n. Having immunity (*from, against, to*, poison, contagion, &c.); (n.) i. person. [f. L IM²*munis* exempt from public burden (*munus*)]

immu·nity, n. (Law) exemption (*from* taxation, jurisdiction, &c.); freedom (*from*); being proof against contagion &c. (*from*). [f. L *immunitas* (as prec., see -TY)]

i·mmūnize, v.t. Render immune (*against* contagion). Hence **immunizA·TION** n. [-IZE]

immure· (-ūr), v.t. Imprison; shut one*self* up. Hence **immure·MENT** n. [f. med. L IM¹(*murare* f. *murus* wall)]

immu·table, a. Unchangeable; not subject to variation in different cases. Hence **immutaBI·LITY** n., **immu·tabLY**² adv. [f. L IM²(*mutabilis* MUTABLE)]

imp¹, n. Child of the devil; little devil; mischievous child; (archaic) child. [OE *impa* young shoot, scion, conn. w. foll.]

imp², v.t. *Imp the wings of* (bird), strengthen its flight; (rare) enlarge, eke *out*. [OE *impian* graft, prob. f. Gk *emphuō*, cf. F *enter* (for **empter*)]

i·mpact¹, n. Striking (*on, against*), collision. [f. L *impingere -pact-* IMPINGE]

impa·ct², v.t. Press, fix, firmly (*into, in*). So **impa·ctION** n. [prob. back formation f. *impacted* f. L p.p. as prec. + -ED¹]

impair·, v.t. Damage; weaken. So **impair·MENT** n. [f. OF *empeirer* f. L *IM¹-(*pejorare* f. *pejor* worse) make worse]

impa·le, v.t. Transfix (body &c. *upon, with*, stake &c., esp. as form of capital punishment); (Herald.) combine (two coats of arms) by placing side by side on one shield separated by vertical line down middle; (rare) fence in with stakes. So **impa·leMENT** n. [f. F *empaler* f. med. L IM¹(*palare* f. *palus* stake)]

impa·lpable, a. Imperceptible to the touch; not easily grasped by the mind, intangible. Hence **impalpabi·lity** n., **impa·lpably**² adv. [f. med. L IM²-(*palpabilis* PALPABLE)]

impă·lūdism, n. Morbid state, with tendency to intermittent fevers & enlargement of spleen, found in dwellers in marshes. [f. IM-¹ + L *palus -udis* marsh + -ISM]

impā·nate (*or* ĭ·mpa-), a. (Of the body of Christ) contained in the bread after consecration. So **impana·tion** n. [f. med. L IM¹(*panare* f. *panis* bread), see -ATE²]

impanel. See EMPANEL.

impă·radise, em-, (-is), v.t. Bring into state of supreme happiness; ravish; make a paradise of (place, state). [IM-¹]

impărisylla·bic, a. & n. (Gk & Lat. Gram.). (Noun) that has more syllables in genitive than in nominative. [f. L IM²(*par* equal) + SYLLABIC]

impar·k, v.t. Enclose (beasts) in park; enclose (land) for park. Hence **imparka·tion** n. [f. OF EM(*parquer* f. *parc* PARK)]

impar·t, v.t. Give share of (thing *to* person &c.); communicate (news &c. *to*). Hence **imparta·tion, impar·tment,** nn. [f. OF *empartir* f. L IM¹(*partire* PART)]

impar·tial (-shl), a. Not partial, unprejudiced, fair. Hence **impartia·lity** (-shĭ-) n., **impar·tially**² adv. [IM-²]

impar·tible, a. (Of estate) not divisible. [f. LL IM²(*partibilis* PARTIBLE)]

impa·ssable, a. That cannot be traversed Hence **impassabi·lity, impa·ssableness,** nn. [IM-²]

impasse (ĭmpă·s, -pah·s, *or as F*). Blind alley; position from which there is no escape. [F (IM-² + *passer* PASS)]

impă·ssible, a. Incapable of feeling or emotion; incapable of suffering injury; not subject to suffering. Hence **impa·ssibi·lity, impa·ssibleness,** nn., **impa·ssibly**² adv. [f. eccl. L IM²(*passibilis* PASSIBLE)]

impă·ssion, v.t. Stir the passions of, excite strongly, (chiefly in p.p.). [f. It. IM¹(*passionare* f. *passione* PASSION)]

impă·ssive, a. Deficient in feeling or emotion; serene; without sensation; not subject to suffering. Hence **impa·ssively**² adv., **impa·ssiveness, impassi·vity,** nn. [IM-²]

impā·ste, v.t. Enclose (as) with paste; make into a paste; paint by laying on colours thickly. [f. It. IM¹(*pastare* f. *pasta* PASTE)]

impă·sto, n. (paint.). Laying on of colour thickly. [It., as prec.]

impā·tient (-shnt), a. Not enduring with composure; intolerant *of*; restlessly desirous (*for* thing, *to* do). Hence or cogn. **impa·tience** n., **impa·tiently**² adv. [OF, f. L IM²(*patientem* part. of *pati* suffer)]

impaw·n, v.t. Put in pawn; (fig.) pledge, plight. [IM-¹]

impay·able (or as F), a. Beyond price; (colloq.) going beyond ordinary limits. [F (IM-²)]

impea·ch, v.t. Call in question, disparage, (character &c.); accuse (person) *of*, charge (*with*); find fault with (thing); accuse of treason or other high crime before competent tribunal. Hence **impea·chable** a. [f. OF *empechier* impede f. LL IM¹(*pedicare* f. *pedica* fetter, f. *pes pedis* foot) entangle]

impea·chment, n. Calling in question; accusation, esp. (facet.) *the soft i.* (Sheridan, *Rivals* v. 3); accusation & prosecution for treason &c. [f. OF *empechement* (as prec., see -MENT)]

impe·ccable, a. Not liable to sin; (of things) faultless. Hence or cogn. **impeccabi·lity** n., **impe·ccably**² adv., **impe·ccant** a. [f. LL IM²(*peccabilis* f. *peccare* sin, see -BLE)]

impecū·nious, a. Having no money. Hence **impecunio·sity** n. [f. IM-² + obs. *pecunious* f. L *pecuniosus* (*pecunia* money f. *pecu* cattle, see -OUS)]

impē·dance, n. (electr.). Virtual resistance due to self-induction in electrified body. [f. foll. + -ANCE]

impē·de, v.t. Retard, hinder. [f. L IM¹-(*pedire* f. *pes* foot) lit. shackle the feet of]

impĕ·diment, n. Hindrance, obstruction; *i.* (*in* one's *speech*), stammer; (pl., also L *impedime·nta*) baggage, esp. of army. Hence **impedime·ntal** a. [f. L *impedimentum* (as prec., see -MENT)]

impe·l, v.t. (-ll-). Drive, force, (person &c. *to* action, *to* do); drive forward, propel. So **impe·llent** a. & n. [f. L IM¹-(*pellere puls-* drive)]

impe·nd, v.i. Hang, be suspended, (*over*); (fig., of danger) hang threateningly (*over*); be imminent. So **impe·ndence, -ency,** nn., **impe·ndent** a. [f. L IM¹(*pendēre* hang)]

impĕ·netrable, a. That cannot be penetrated; inscrutable, unfathomable; impervious (*to, by,* ideas &c.); (Nat. Philos.) having that property in virtue of which two bodies cannot occupy same place at same time. So **impenetrabi·lity, impe·netrableness,** nn., **impe·netrably**² adv. [f. F *impénétrable* f. L IM²(*penetrabilis* PENETRABLE)]

impe·netrate, v.t. Penetrate deeply. [IM-¹]

impe·nitent, a. Not penitent. Hence or cogn. **impe·nitence, -ency,** nn., **impe·nitently**² adv. [f. L IM²(*paenitens* PENITENT)]

impĕ·rative, a. & n. (Gram.) expressing command; commanding, peremptory; urgent; obligatory; (n.) i. mood, whence **imperatival** a. Hence **impe·ratively**² adv., **impe·rativeness** n. [f. LL *imperativus* f. IM¹-(*perare* = *parare* make ready) command, -IVE]

imperā·tor, n. (Rom. hist.). Commander (title conferred by salutation of soldiers on victorious general, under the Republic); emperor. So **imperator·**IAL a. [L (as prec., see -OR[2])]

imperce·ptible, a. That cannot be perceived; very slight, gradual, or subtle. Hence **imperce·ptib**LY[2] adv. [F, f. med. L IM[2](*perceptibilis* PERCEPTIBLE)]

imperci·pient, a. Lacking perception. [IM-[2]]

i·mperence, n. (Form, ascribed to illiterate speakers, of) impudence. [corrupt.]

imper·fect, a. & n. Not fully formed or done, incomplete; faulty; (Gram.) *i. tenses*, those that denote action going on but not completed (e.g. *he is, he will be, singing*, but usu. of past time, as *he was singing*); (n.) i. tense. Hence **imper·fect**LY[2] adv. [f. F *imparfait* f. L IM[2](*perfectus* PERFECT), refash. on L]

imperfe·ction, n. Incompleteness; faultiness; fault, blemish. [f. L *imperfectio* (as prec., see -ION)]

imper·forate (-*at*), a. Not perforated, esp. (Anat.) lacking the normal opening (also of sheet of postage-stamps or single stamp). [IM-[2]]

impēr·ial, a. & n. Of an empire or sovereign state ranking with an empire; of Great Britain, as dist. from its constituent kingdoms &c.; *i. federation*, proposed adjustment of British Empire, giving colonies share in control & cost of measures taken for joint interest; *I. Institute*, building in London devoted to promoting trade between parts of the Empire; *i. preference*, taxing of imports from parts of the Empire at lower rates than those from foreign countries; of an emperor; supreme in authority; majestic, august; magnificent; (of weights & measures used by statute in U.K.) *i. gallon, acre*, &c.; (of paper) 22 × 32 in. (N.) small part of beard left growing beneath lower lip (from Napoleon III); trunk for luggage, adapted for roof of coach; Russian tsarist gold coin = 15 silver roubles. Hence **imper·ial**LY[2] adv. [OF, f. L *imperialis* (IMPERIUM, see -AL)]

impēr·ialism, n. Rule of an emperor; extension of British Empire where trade requires protection of the flag; union of different parts of British Empire for purposes of warlike defence, internal commerce, &c.; belief in value of colonies & dependencies (cf. LITTLE *Englandism*). So **impērialì·st**IC a., **impēr·ial**IZE(3) v.t. [-ISM]

impēr·ialist, n. Adherent of an emperor, esp. (1600–1800) of German Emperor; advocate of imperial rule, esp. adherent of Bonaparte family; advocate of (British) imperialism. [-IST]

impě·ril, v.t. (-ll-). Bring into danger. [IM-[1]]

impēr·ious, a. Overbearing, domineering; urgent, imperative. Hence **impēr·ious**LY[2] adv., **impēr·ious**NESS n. [f. L *imperiosus* (as IMPERIUM, see -OUS)]

impě·rishable, a. That cannot perish. Hence **impe·rishab**I·LITY, **impe·rishable**NESS, nn., **impe·rishab**LY[2] adv. [IM-[2]]

impě·rium (*or* -ēr-), n. Absolute power; empire; *i. in imperio*, supreme authority within jurisdiction of another authority. [L, = command, dominion]

imper·manent, a. Not permanent. Hence **imper·man**ENCE, -ENCY, nn. [IM-[2]]

imper·měable, a. That cannot be passed through; (Physics) that does not permit passage of fluids. Hence **impermea**BI·LITY n. [f. LL IM[2](*permeabilis* PERMEABLE)]

impermi·ssible, a. Not permissible. [IM-[2]]

imperscri·ptible, a. Not backed by written authority. [f. IM-[2] + L PER-(*scribere script-* write) register, see -BLE]

imper·sonal, a. (Gram.) *i. verb*, one used only in 3rd sing. (e.g. *it rains*); having no personality or personal reference or tone. Hence **impersona·**LITY n., **imper·sonal**LY[2] adv. [f. LL IM[2](*personalis* PERSONAL)]

imper·sonate, v.t. Represent in bodily form, personify; play the part of, personate; act (character). Hence **imperson**A·TION, **imper·sonat**OR[2], nn., **imper·sonat**IVE a. [f. IM-[1] + L *persona* PERSON + -ATE[3]]

imperso·nify, v.t. Personify. [IM-[1]]

imper·tinent, a. Insolent, saucy; intrusive; out of place, absurd; not to the point. Hence or cogn. **imper·tin**ENCE n., **imper·tinent**LY[2] adv. [f. L IM[2](*pertinens* PERTINENT)]

impertur·bable, a. Not excitable, calm. Hence **imperturb**ABI·LITY, **impertur·bable**NESS, nn., **impertur·bab**LY[2] adv. [IM-[2]]

imper·vious, a. Not affording passage (*to*); (fig.) *i.* (deaf) *to argument* &c. Hence **imper·vious**LY[2] adv., **imper·vious**NESS n. [f. L IM[2](*pervius* PERVIOUS)]

impetī·go, n. Pustular disease of skin. So **impetī·gin**OUS a. [L, gen.-*ginis*, f. IM[1](*petere* seek) assail, cf. *vertigo*]

i·mpetrate, v.t. (Theol.) obtain by request; (rare) ask for. So **impetr**A·TION n., **i·mpetrat**ORY a. [f. L IM[1](*petrare* = *patrare* bring to pass), see -ATE[3]]

impě·tuous, a. Moving violently or rapidly; acting with rash or sudden energy. Hence or cogn. **impetuo·**SITY, **impe·tuous**NESS, nn., **impe·tuous**LY[2] adv. [f. F *impétueux* f. L *impetuosus* (as foll., see -OUS)]

i·mpetus, n. (pl. -*uses*). Force with which a body moves; (fig.) moving force, impulse. [L, = assault, force, f. IM[1](*petere* seek) assail]

i·mpeyan, a. *I. pheasant*, E.-Indian

pheasant, with crested head & brilliant plumage. [Sir Elijah *Impey*, 1787]

i·mpi, n. Body of Kafir warriors. [Zulu]

impī·ety, n. Ungodliness; want of dutifulness or reverence. [f. L IM²(*pietas* PIETY)]

impi·nge (-j), v.i. & t. Make impact (*on, upon*); (trans.; archaic) make (thing) do this. Hence **impi·nge**MENT n. [f. L IM¹(*pingere* = *pangere* fix, drive) drive (thing) at)]

i·mpious, a. Not pious, wicked, profane. Hence **i·mpious**LY² adv. [f. L IM²(*pius* PIOUS)]

i·mpish, a. Of, like, an imp. Hence **i·mpish**LY² adv., **i·mpish**NESS n. [-ISH¹]

impi·teous, a. (poet.). Pitiless. [IM-²]

implā̆·cable, a. That cannot be appeased. Hence or cogn. **implaca**BI·LITY n., **impla·cab**LY² adv. [F, f. L IM²(*placabilis* PLACABLE)]

implace·ntal, a. With no placenta. [IM-²]

impla·nt, v.t. Insert, infix, (*in*); instil (principle, idea, &c., *in* mind &c.); plant. Hence **implant**A·TION n. [f. F IM¹(*planter* PLANT)]

imple·dge, v.t. Put in pledge, pawn. [IM-¹]

i·mplement¹ (-ent), n. Article of furniture, dress, &c., (pl.) equipment of these; tool, instrument, (esp. in pl.); (Sc. Law) full performance. [prob. f. L *implementum*, in sense 'that which serves to stock a house &c.' f. IM¹(*plēre* fill), see -MENT]

i·mplemĕnt², v.t. (chiefly Sc.). Complete (contract &c.); fulfil (engagement); fill up, supplement. [f. prec.]

imple·tion, n. Filling; fullness. [f. LL *impletio* f. IM¹(*plēre plet-* fill), see -ION]

i·mplicate¹ (-*a*t), n. Thing implied. [f. L IM¹(*plicare plicat-* or *plicit-* fold), see -ATE²]

i·mplicāte², v.t. Entwine, entangle; involve, imply, as inference, so **i·mplicat**IVE a.; involve (person *in* charge, crime, &c.); (pass.) be affected *in* (a thing's operation). So **implic**A·TION n. [as prec., see -ATE³]

implĭ·cit, a. Implied though not plainly expressed; virtually contained (*in*); *i. faith* (not independently reached by the individual, but involved in general belief of Church, absolute, unreserved, cf. EXPLICIT). Hence **impli·cit**LY² adv., **impli·cit**NESS n. [(perh. thr. F) as IMPLICATE¹]

implore·, v.t. Beg earnestly for; entreat (person *to* do). Hence **implor·ing**LY² adv., **implor·ing**NESS n. [f. L IM¹(*plorare* weep)]

implu·vium (-plōō-), n. (Rom. ant.). Square basin in middle of atrium receiving rain-water from open space in roof. [L, f. IM¹(*pluere* rain)]

imply·, v.t. Involve the truth of (thing not expressly asserted, *that*); mean; insinuate, hint. Hence **implī·ĕd**LY² adv. [f. OF *emplier* (as IMPLICATE, cf. EMPLOY)]

impo·licy, n. Bad policy; inexpediency. [IM-²]

i·mpolī·te, a. (-est). Uncivil, rude. Hence **impoli·te**LY² adv., **impoli·te**NESS n. [f. L IM²(*politus* POLITE)]

impŏ·litic, a. Not politic; inexpedient. Hence **impo·litic**LY² adv. [IM-²]

impo·nderable, a. & n. (Physics) having no weight; very light; not to be estimated by physical weight (of mind, qualities, electricity, &c.); (n.) i. thing. [IM-²]

impō·nent, a. & n. (Person) that imposes a duty &c. [f. L IM¹(*ponere* place) lay on, see -ENT]

impor·t¹, v.t. Bring, introduce, (thing, esp. goods from foreign country, *into*), whence **impor·t**ABLE a., **importa**BI·LITY, **import**A·TION, **impor·t**ER¹, nn.; imply, indicate, mean, (thing, *that*); express, make known, (*that*); be of consequence to, as *questions that i. us nearly, it imports us to know*. [f. L IM¹(*portare* carry) bring in, in med. L = be of consequence]

i·mport², n. What is implied, meaning; importance; (usu. pl.) commodity imported; importation. [f. prec.]

impor·tance, n. Being important; weight, significance; personal consequence, dignity; pompousness (usu. *self-i.*). [F, f. med. L *importantia* (as IMPORT¹, see -ANCE)]

impor·tant, a. Carrying with it great consequence (*to* person concerned or purpose &c.), weighty, momentous; consequential, pompous. Hence **impor·tant**LY² adv. [F, f. med. L as IMPORT¹, see -ANT]

impor·tunate (-*a*t), a. Persistent, pressing, in solicitation; (of affairs) urgent. Hence or cogn. **impor·tunate**LY² adv., **importu·n**ITY n. [f. L IM²(*portunus* f. *portus* port) inconvenient, -ATE²]

importū·ne (*or* impor·t-), v.t. Solicit pressingly (person or abs.). [f. F *importuner* f. med. L *importunari* (as prec.)]

impo·se (-z), v.t. & i. (Archaic) place (thing) *upon*; (Print.) lay (pages of type) in proper order & secure them in a chase; lay (tax, duty, charge, obligation, *upon*); palm off (thing *upon* person); exert influence (*on* person) by striking character or appearance, whence **impo·sing**LY² adv., **impo·sing**NESS n.; *i. upon*, take advantage of (person); practise deception (*upon*). [f. F IM¹(*poser*, cf. COMPOSE)]

impo·sition, n. In vbl senses of IMPOSE; also or esp.: laying on of *hands* (in ordination &c.); impost, tax, duty; piece of deception or overcharge; work set as punishment at school (colloq. abbr. *impo, impot*). [f. L *impositio* f. IM¹(*ponere posit-* place), -ION]

impo·ssible, a. Not possible (often w. *it* as subj., as *it is i. to alter them*); (loosely) not easy, not convenient; (colloq.) outrageous, intolerable, as *an i. hat, person*. Hence or cogn. **impossi**BI·LITY n.,

impo·ssibly[2] adv. [f. L IM[2](*possibilis* POSSIBLE)]
i·mpōst[1], n. (Hist.) tax, duty, tribute; (Racing slang) weight horse carries in handicap. [OF f. med. L IM[1](*ponere pos(i)t-* place)]
i·mpōst[2], n. Upper course of pillar, bearing arch. [f. F *imposte* f. It. *imposta* (as prec.)]
impŏ·stor, n. One who assumes a false character or passes himself off for some one else; swindler. Hence **impo·strous** a. [f. F *imposteur* f. LL *impostor* (as IMPOST[1], see -OR[2])]
impo·stume, -thume, n. (now rare). Purulent swelling, abscess, (lit. & fig.). [f. OF *empostume* f. Gk APO(*stēma* f. *sta-* stand, -M)]
impo·sture (-tsher), n. Fraudulent deception. [F, f. LL *impostura* (IMPOST[1], -URE)]
impot. See IMPOSITION.
i·mpotent, a. Powerless; helpless, decrepit; (of males) wholly lacking in sexual power. Hence or cogn. **i·mpotence, -ency,** nn., **i·mpotently**[2] adv. [F, f. L IM[2](*potens* POTENT)]
impou·nd, v.t. Shut up (cattle) in pound; shut up (person, thing) as in pound; take legal possession of; confiscate. [IM-[1]]
impŏ·verish, v.t. Make poor; exhaust strength of. So **impo·verishment** n. [f. OF EM(*poverir* f. *povre* POOR), see -ISH[2]]
impra·cticable, a. Impossible in practice; (of persons or things) unmanageable; (of roads &c.) impassable. Hence **impracticabi·lity, impra·cticableness,** nn., **impra·cticably**[2] adv. [IM-[2]]
i·mprecate, v.t. Invoke, call down, (evil *upon* person &c.). So **impreca·tion** n. (esp., spoken curse), **i·mprecatory** a. [f. L IM[1](*precari* pray)]
imprĕ·gnable, a. (Of fortress &c.) that cannot be taken by arms; (fig.) proof against attack. Hence **impregnabi·lity** n., **impre·gnably**[2] adv. [f. F IM[2]-(*prenable* f. *prendre* take f. L *prehendere*); *-g-* in imit. of *reign, deign,* &c.]
impre·gnate[1] (-*a*t), a. Pregnant (lit. & fig.); permeated (*with*). [f. LL IM[1]-(*praegnare* be pregnant), see -ATE[2]]
impre·gnāte[2], v.t. Make (female) pregnant; (Biol.) fecundate (female reproductive cell or ovum); fill, saturate, (*with*); imbue, fill, (*with* feelings, moral qualities, &c.). Hence **impregna·tion** n. [as prec., see -ATE[3]]
imprĕsar·io (-zar-), n. Organizer of public entertainments, esp. manager of operatic or concert company. [It. (*impresa* undertaking, as EMPRISE, see -ARY[1])]
imprescri·ptible, a. Not subject to prescription, that cannot be legally taken away, esp. *i. right.* [F (IM-[2])]
i·mpress[1], n. Stamping; mark made by seal, stamp, &c.; (fig.) characteristic mark. [f. foll.]
impre·ss[2], v.t. Apply (mark &c.) with pressure, imprint, stamp, (*on*); imprint, enforce, (idea &c., *that, what,* &c., *on* person, his mind); mark (thing *with* stamp &c. lit. & fig.); affect, influence, deeply, whence **impre·ssible** a., **impressibi·lity** n.; affect (person) strongly (*with* idea &c.). [f. L IM[1](*primere* = *premere* PRESS[2])]
impre·ss[3], v.t. Force (men) to serve in army or navy; seize (goods &c.) for public service; enlist, make use of, (thing) in argument &c. Hence **impre·ssment** n. [IM-[1] + PRESS[3]]
impre·ssion, n. Impressing (of mark); mark impressed; print taken from type or engraving; (printing of) number of copies forming one issue of book, edition, (also, unaltered reprint from standing type or plates, as opp. to *edition*); effect produced (esp. on mind or feelings); notion, (vague) belief, impressed on the mind, as *that is my i., I was under the i. that.* [F, f. L *impressio* (as IMPRESS[2], see -ION)]
impre·ssionable, a. Susceptible of impressions, easily influenced. Hence **impressionabi·lity** n. [F (*impressionner,* as prec., see -ABLE)]
impre·ssionism, n. Method of painting or writing so as to give general tone & effect without elaborate detail, or (in painting, opp. *pre-Raphaelitism*) with details so treated as to be apprehended simultaneously, and not successively with changes of focus. So **impre·ssionary**[1], **impressioni·stic,** aa., **impre·ssionist** n. [-ISM]
impre·ssive, a. (Of language, scenes, &c.) able to excite deep feeling. Hence **impre·ssively**[2] adv., **impre·ssiveness** n. [-IVE]
i·mprest, n. Money advanced to person to be used in State business. [earlier *prest* n. & v.; It. has IM[1](*prestare* = L *praestare* be surety for, fulfil) lend, *impresto* loan]
imprīmā·tur, n. Official licence to print (now usu. of works sanctioned by R.-C. Church); (fig.) sanction. [mod. L, = let it be printed]
imprī·mis, adv. In the first place. [L, = *in primis* among the first things]
i·mprint[1], n. Impression, stamp, (lit. & fig.); *publisher's, printer's, i.* (name, place &c., on title-page or at end of book). [f. F *empreinte* stamp (as foll.)]
impri·nt[2], v.t. Stamp (figure &c. *on*); impress (idea &c. *on, in,* mind &c.); impress (quality &c. *on, in*); stamp (thing *with* figure). [f. OF *empreinter* f. *empreindre* f. pop. L IM[1](*premere* press)]
impri·son (-zn), v.t. Put into prison; (fig.) confine, shut up. So **impri·sonment** n. [f. OF EM(*prisoner* f. PRISON)]
impro·bable, a. Not likely to be true or to happen. Hence **improbabi·lity** n., **impro·bably**[2] adv. [f. L IM[2](*probabilis* PROBABLE)]

imprŏ·bity, n. Wickedness; dishonesty. [f. L *improbitas* f. IM²(*probus* honest), see -TY]

impro·mptū, adv., n., & a. Extempore (performance, composition); musical composition having character of improvisation. [=L *in promptu* in readiness (*promere,* see PROMPT)]

impro·per, a. Inaccurate, wrong; *i. fraction* (greater than 1, with numerator greater than denominator); unseemly, indecent. Hence **impro·per**LY² adv. [IM-²]

imprō·priāte, v.t. Annex (ecclesiastical benefice) to corporation or person as property; place (tithes, ecclesiastical property) in lay hands. So **impro·pri**ATE² (-*at*) a., **impropri**A·TION n. [f. med. or mod. L IM¹(*propriare* f. *proprius* own), see -ATE³]

imprō·priātor, n. One to whom benefice is impropriated. [as prec., see -OR²]

impropri·ety, n. Incorrectness; unfitness; indecency. [f. L IM²(*proprietas* PROPRIETY)]

impro·vable, a. That can be improved; adapted for cultivation. Hence **improv**ABI·LITY, **impro·vable**NESS, nn. [-ABLE]

impro·ve (-ōōv), v.t. & i. Make, become, better; *i. away,* get rid of by improvements; make good use of (*the occasion, the opportunity*); *i. upon,* produce something better than; preach on (*the occasion*) with a view to edification. So **impro·ve**MENT n. [f. AF EM(*prower* f. OF *prou* profit, =L *pro* prep. used as n.)]

impro·ver, n. In vbl senses; also or esp.: one who works at trade for low wage or none to improve his skill; =DRESS-*i.* [-ER¹]

imprŏ·vident, a. Unforeseeing; heedless; thriftless. Hence or cogn. **impro·vid**ENCE n., **impro·vident**LY² adv. [IM-²]

imprŏ·visātor (-z-), ***improv(v)isator·e*** (-vēzahtōrĕ), n. (It. pl. *-ori,* pron. -ōrē). One who improvises or composes extempore. So **improv(v)isatric·e** (-trētshā) [-TRIX] n. [It. (-*e*), as IMPROVISE, see -OR²]

improvi·se (-īz), v.t. Compose, utter, (verse, music, &c., or abs.) extempore; provide, get up, extempore. Hence **imprŏvis**A·TION n., **imprŏvisator**·IAL, **improvi·sat**ORY, aa. [f. F *improviser* f. It. *improv(v)isare* f. *improv(v)iso* f. L IM²(*provisus* p.p. as PROVIDE)]

impru·dent, a. Rash, indiscreet. Hence or cogn. **impru·d**ENCE n., **impru·dent**LY² adv. [f. L IM²(*prudens* PRUDENT)]

i·mpudent, a. Shamelessly forward; unblushing; insolently disrespectful. Hence or cogn. **i·mpud**ENCE n., **i·mpudent**LY² adv. [f. L IM²*pudens* (*pudēre* be ashamed, -ENT)]

impudi·city, n. Shamelessness, immodesty. [f. F *impudicité* f. L IM(*pudicus* as prec.), -TY]

impūg·n, v.t. Assail by word, call in question, (statement, action). Hence **impūg·n**ABLE a., **impūg·n**MENT n. [f. F *impugner* f. L IM¹(*pugnare* fight) assail]

impū·issant, a. Impotent, weak. So **impu·iss**ANCE n. [F (IM-² + PUISSANT)]

i·mpulse, n. Impelling, push; (Dynam.) indefinitely large force enduring inappreciably short time but producing finite momentum, e.g. blow of hammer, (also) product of average value of force multiplied by time during which it acts; mental incitement; sudden tendency to act without reflection; impetus. [f. L *impulsus* -*ūs* (as IMPEL)]

impu·lsion, n. Impelling, push; mental impulse; impetus. [F, f. L *impulsio* (as IMPEL, see -ION)]

impu·lsive, a. Tending to impel; (of persons, conduct, &c.) apt to be moved, prompted, by sudden impulse. Hence **impu·lsive**LY² adv.; **impu·lsive**NESS n. [f. med. L *impulsivus* (as prec., see -IVE)]

impū·nity, n. Exemption from punishment, esp. *with i.*; exemption from injury as consequence of act. [f. L *impunitas* f. IM²(*punis* f. *poena* penalty), see -TY]

impure·, a. Dirty; unchaste; mixed with foreign matter, adulterated, (lit. & fig.); (of colour) mixed with another colour. Hence or cogn. **impure·**LY² adv., **impūr·**ITY n. [f. L IM²(*purus* PURE)]

impū·te, v.t. Attribute, ascribe, (fault &c., rarely good quality &c., *to* person &c.); (Theol.) ascribe (righteousness, guilt, *to* person) by vicarious substitution. So **imput**ABI·LITY, **imput**A·TION, nn., **impu·t**ABLE, **impu·tat**IVE, aa., **impu·tative**LY² adv. [f. F *imputer* f. L IM¹(*putare* reckon) enter in the account]

in¹, prep. expr. inclusion or position within limits of space, time, circumstance, &c.; as: *i. Europe, England, London* (so of any large city or of town &c. in which speaker lives, cf. AT), *i. the house, a box, a cab, a pond, a crowd*; (of dress &c.) *i. muslin, mourning, white, brown boots*; *i.* (the works of) *Thackeray*; (of part affected) *blind i. one eye*; (of ratio) *not one i. a hundred*; (of body &c. to which one belongs &c.) *i. the army, shares i. a company*; (of non-physical regions) *i. politics, fancy, my opinion*; (of situation, often idiomatic) *i.* CLOVER, HOT *water, fetters, leading-strings, the* DARK², *health, hope (of), sorrow,* CALF, *i.* (supplied with) *cash, i.* (under influence of) *liquor*; (of occupation) *i. search of, i. pursuance of, i.* (while) *crossing the river*; (of form or arrangement) *packed i. dozens, sold i. building-plots, falling i. folds, i.* ORDER¹ (2) *to* or *that*; (of instrument or material) *drank his health i. a cup of ale, the coat was i. green velvet*; (of purpose) *i. reply to, i. quest of, i. honour of*; (of time) *i.* (during) *the day, i.* (within the space of) *three months*; *i. itself,* apart from all else, absolutely; (of person's capacity &c.) *as* *far as i. me lies, did not think he had it i. him* (was capable of it); *not i. it,* not in the running, not a serious competitor; *nothing, little, not much, in it,* (racing slang) no decided advantage as yet gained by any competitor, no guessing who will win; (with vbs of motion or change) *put it i. your pocket, cut it i. half, throw it i. the fire*: (expr. relation of vb to indirect object), *believe i., trust i., share i., engage i., rejoice i.*; (so with adjj. & nn.) *weak i.* (as regards) *algebra, wanting i. courage, your trust i. him, a change i. the constitution*; (of number or dimension) *seven i. number, four feet i. width*; (forming adv. phr.) *i. fact, i. truth, i. honour, i. any case*; *i. so* (or *as*) *far as,* in such measure as; *i. that,* since, because. [com.-Teut.: OE, OSax., OHG, Goth., *in,* Swed., Da., *i*; cogn. w. L *in,* Gk *en*]

in[2], adv. expr. position bounded by certain limits or motion to a point enclosed by them, as: *come i., send him i., walk i.,* (into house, enclosed ground, &c.), *put a notice i.* (into a paper), *lock him i., he is i.* (the house &c., esp. = at home); *i. with it,* put, take, it i.; *throw i. the harness* (to the bargain, in addition); *a coat with the woolly side i.* (nearest the body); *the Liberals were i.* (office); (Crick.) *before he had been i.* (batting) *five minutes*; *keep the fire i.* (burning); *train, boat, summer, is i.* (arrived); (with trans. vbs) *burn, cut, rub,* (thing) *i.* (so as to penetrate into another), *hem, cover, wall,* (thing) *i.* (so as to enclose it); *i. for,* involved in, committed to, (usu. something unpleasant, esp. *it*), also, engaged in competition for (race, prize, &c.); *be, keep, i.* (on friendly terms) *with*; *breed i. & i.* (repeatedly within same stock); *i. & out,* now i., now out, to & fro, with alternation or oscillation. [com.-Teut.: OE, OSax., OHG]

in[3], a. Internal, living &c. inside, as *i. patient, i.-patient,* one who remains in hospital while under treatment. [prec. used attrib.]

in[4], n. (Pl.) political party in office; *ins & outs,* turnings to & fro (usu. fig.), details (*of* procedure &c.). [f. IN[2]]

in[5], prep. (L). *In arti·culo mortis,* in the instant of death; *in* CAMERA; *in comme·ndam,* as a charge or trust (of benefice pending appointment of regular incumbent, or of its revenue enjoyed by layman &c.); *in esse,* in actual existence, cf. *in posse*; *in exte·nso,* at full length; *in extrē·mis,* at the point of death; *in flagra·ntĕ deli·cto,* in the very act of committing an offence; *in formā paup·eris,* as poor person not liable to costs; *in lō·cō pare·ntis,* in place of a parent; *in mē·diās rēs,* into the thick of it; *in memor·iăm,* in memory of; *in nū·bibus,* in the clouds, vague, speculative; *in partibus (infidē·lium),* (of Rom. Cath. titular bishop) in a heretical country; *in posse,* potentially, opp. to *in esse*; *in prō·priā persō·nā,* in his (her) own person; *in puris naturā·libus,* stark naked; *in* RE; *in si·tū,* in its (original) place; *in stā·tū pūpillār·ī,* under guardianship; *in stā·tū quō,* in the same state (as formerly); *in terror·em,* as a warning; *in tō·tō,* completely.

in-[1], pref. = L *in* in, on, into, towards, against (becoming *il-* before *l, im-* before *b, m, p, ir-* before *r*). In OF *in-, im-,* became *en-, em-*; E has usu. *in-, im-,* in wds obviously of L orig., whether thr. F or otherwise. Words that still retain both forms are given in this dictionary under the more usual form.

in-[2], pref. = L *in-* (*il-* &c. as prec.), cogn. w. Gk *a, an-,* com.-Teut. *un-,* prefixed to adjj. & their derivatives to express negation. As living E pref., *in-* often interchanges with *un-,* which is preferred in wds not obviously answering to L types (*unavailing, uncertain, undevout*).

-in, suf. (chem.) forming names of neutral substances such as glycerides, glucosides, proteids, &c. (*albumin, casein, fibrin, gelatin*) to distinguish them from names of alkaloids & basic substances in -INE[5]. Some wds of this class were formerly spelt *-ine,* & are still so spelt in pop. use (*margarine, gelatine*).

-ina[1], L fem. suf. found in *regina,* extended in It. or Sp. & used in E to form fem. titles (*czarina*) & proper names (*Georgina*); occurring also in names of musical instruments (*concertina, seraphina*).

-ina[2], suf., neut. pl. of (often mod.) L adjj., used, in agreement with *animalia* animals understood, to form names of groups of animals related to some typical genus, as *Bombycina* (genus *Bombyx*).

inabi·lity, n. Being unable; lack of power or means. [IN-[2]]

inacce·ssible, a. That cannot be reached; (of persons) not open to advances, unapproachable. Hence **inaccessi**BI·LITY n., **inacce·ssib**LY[2] adv. [F, f. LL IN[2](*accessibilis* ACCESSIBLE)]

ina·ccurate, a. Not accurate. Hence **ina·ccur**ACY n., **ina·ccurate**LY[2] adv. [IN-[2]]

ina·ction, n. Absence of action; sluggishness, inertness. So **ina·ct**IVE a., **ina·ctive**LY[2] adv., **inacti·**VITY n. [IN-[2]]

inadaptabi·lity, n. Want of adaptability. [IN-[2]]

ina·dequate, a. Not adequate (*to* purpose, *to* do); insufficient. Hence **ina·dequ**ACY n., **ina·dequate**LY[2] adv. [IN-[2]]

inadhe·sive, a. Not adhesive. [IN-[2]]

inadmi·ssible, a. That cannot be admitted or allowed. Hence **inadmissi**BI·LITY n. [IN-[2]]

inadver·tent, a. Not properly attentive; negligent; (of actions) unintentional. Hence or cogn. **inadver·t**ENCE, -ENCY, nn., **inadver·tent**LY[2] adv. [IN-[2] + obs. *advert*ENT ADVERT)]

inā·lienable, a. Not alienable. Hence **inalienaBI·LITY** n., **ina·lienabLY**[2] adv. [IN-[2]]

ina·lterable, a. Unalterable. Hence **inalteraBI·LITY** n., **ina·lterabLY**[2] adv. [IN-[2]]

inămora·tō (-rah-), n. (fem. *-ta*). Lover. [It. (now *inn-*) f. IN[1](*amorare* f. *amore* f. L *amor* love) enamour]

inā·ne, a. & n. Empty, void, silly; senseless; (n.) *the i.*, vacuity, infinite space. Hence or cogn. **ina·neLY**[2] adv., **inā·NITY** n. [f. L *inanis* empty, vain]

ina·nimate (-*at*), a. Destitute of life; not endowed with animal life, as *i. nature* (outside the animal world); spiritless, dull. Hence or cogn. **ina·nimateLY**[2] adv., **inanimA·TION** n. [f. LL IN[2](*animatus* ANIMATE[1])]

inani·tion, n. Emptiness, esp. from want of nourishment. [f. L *inanitio* f. *inanire* make empty (as INANE), see -ION]

inappea·sable, a. Not appeasable. [IN-[2]]

inappe·llable, a. Not to be appealed against. [f. IN-[2]+L *appellare* APPEAL+-BLE]

ina·ppetence, n. Want of appetence. [IN-[2]]

ina·pplicable, a. Not applicable, unsuitable, (*to* case, purpose). Hence **ina·pplicaBI·LITY** n., **ina·pplicabLY**[2] adv. [IN-[2]]

ina·pposite, a. Not apposite, out of place. Hence **ina·ppositeLY**[2] adv. [IN-[2]]

inapprē·ciable, a. Imperceptible, not worth reckoning; that cannot be appreciated. Hence **inappre·ciabLY**[2] adv. [IN-[2]]

inapprecia·tion, n. Failure to appreciate. So **inappre·ciatIVE** a. [IN-[2]]

inapprehe·nsible, a. That cannot be grasped by senses or intellect. [IN-[2]]

inapproa·chable, a. Unapproachable. [IN-[2]]

inappro·priate, a. Not appropriate. Hence **inappro·priateLY**[2] adv., **inappro·priateNESS** n. [IN-[2]]

ina·pt, a. Unfit, unskilful. Hence **ina·ptiTUDE, ina·ptNESS,** nn., **ina·ptLY**[2] adv. [IN-[2]]

inar·ch, v.t. Graft by connecting growing branch without separation from parent stock. [IN-[1]+ARCH v.]

inar·m, v.t. (poet.). Embrace. [IN[1]+ARM[1]]

inarti·culate, a. Not jointed; (of speech) not articulate; unable to speak distinctly; dumb. Hence **inarti·culateLY**[2] adv., **inarti·culateNESS** n. [f. L IN[2](*articulatus* ARTICULATE)]

inartifi·cial, a. Lacking in art, inartistic; artless, natural. Hence **inartifi·ciaLLY**[2] adv. [f. L IN[2](*artificialis* ARTIFICIAL)]

inarti·stic, a. Not following the principles of art; unskilled in art. Hence **inarti·stICALLY** adv. [IN-[2]]

inasmuch, adv. *I. as*, since, because; (archaic) in so far *as*. [orig. three wds]

inatte·ntion, n. Want of attention, heedlessness; neglect to show courtesy. So **inatte·ntIVE** a., **inatte·ntiveLY**[2] adv., **inatte·ntiveNESS** n. [IN-[2]]

inau·dible, a. That cannot be heard. Hence **inaudiBI·LITY** n., **inau·dibLY**[2] adv. [f. L IN[2](*audibilis* AUDIBLE)]

inau·gūral, a. Of inauguration. [F, f. *inaugurer* (as foll.)]

inau·gūrate, v.t. Admit (person) to office &c. with ceremony; enter with ceremony upon (undertaking &c.); initiate public use of (building &c.). Hence or cogn. **inaugurA·TION, inau·guratOR**[2], nn., **inau·guratORY** a. [f. L IN[1](*augurare* take omens, f. *augur*), see -ATE[3]]

inauspi·cious, a. Not of good omen; unlucky. Hence **inauspi·ciousLY**[2] adv., **inauspi·ciousNESS** n. [IN-[2]],

i·nboard, adv. & a. (naut.). (Situated) within sides of or towards centre of ship. [IN[1]]

i·nborn, a. Implanted by nature. [IN[2]]

inbrea·the, v.t. Breathe (thing) in (lit. & fig.). [IN[2]]

i·nbred, a. Innate, inherent by nature. [IN[2]]

i·nbreeding, n. Breeding in-&-in, breeding from animals closely related. [IN[2]]

I·nca, n. Emperor or king of Peru before Spanish conquest; one of royal race of Peru. [Peruv.]

inca·lculable, a. Too great for calculation; that cannot be reckoned beforehand; (of person, character, &c.) uncertain. Hence **incalculaBI·LITY** n., **inca·lculabLY**[2] adv. [IN-[2]]

incande·sce (-ĕs), v.i. & t. Glow, cause to glow, with heat. [f. L IN[1](*candescere* incept. of *candēre* be white)]

incande·scent, a. Glowing with heat; shining brightly; (of electric & other light) produced by glowing of filament &c. Hence **incande·scENCE** n. [as prec., see -ENT]

incanta·tion, n. (Use of) magical formula; spell, charm. [F, f. L *incantationem* f. IN[1](*cantare* chant) bewitch, see -ION]

inca·pable, a. Not capable (*of* conduct &c., *of* do*ing*; often in good sense, =too honest &c. to do); not susceptible (*of* improvement &c.); lacking in ordinary powers, as *drunk & i.* Hence **incapaBI·LITY** n., **inca·pabLY**[2] adv. [f. med. L IN[2](*capabilis* CAPABLE)]

incapa·citate, v.t. Render incapable or unfit (*for* work &c., *for, from,* do*ing*). Hence **incapacitA·TION** n. [f. foll.+-ATE[3]]

incapa·city, n. Inability (*for* do*ing*, *for* work &c., *to* do, or abs.); legal disqualification. [f. F IN[2](*capacité* CAPACITY)]

incar·cerate, v.t. Imprison (lit. & fig.). Hence or cogn. **incarcerA·TION, incar·ceratOR**[2], nn. [f. med. L IN[1](*carcerare* f. *carcer* prison), see -ATE[3]]

incar·nadine, a., & v.t., (poet.). (Dye)

flesh-coloured, crimson. [vb f. a.) F (*-in, -ine*) f. It. *incarnadino* (for *-tino*) f. *incarnato* INCARNATE¹[

incar·nate¹ (*-at*), a. (Of person, spirit, quality, &c.) embodied in flesh, esp. in human form, as *he is an i. fiend, Liberty i.*; (as p.p. of Christ) *was i. by the Holy Ghost.* [f. L IN¹(*carnare* f. *caro carnis* flesh), see -ATE²]

i·ncarnāte², v.t. Embody in flesh; put (idea &c.) into concrete form, realize; (of person &c.) be living embodiment of (quality). [as prec., see -ATE³]

incarna·tion, n. Embodiment in (esp. human) flesh, esp. *the I.* (of Christ); impersonation, living type, (*of* quality &c.). [F, f. LL *incarnationem* (as prec., see -ION)]

incau·tious, a. Rash. Hence **incau·tious**LY² adv., **incau·tious**NESS n. [IN-²]

ince·ndiary, a. & n. Of, guilty of, the malicious setting on fire of property (*i. shell,* filled with material for causing fires instead of explosive); (fig.) tending to stir up strife, inflammatory; (n.) i. person (lit. & fig.). Hence **ince·ndiar**ISM n. [f. L *incendiarius* f. *incendium* conflagration f. IN(*cendere cens-* = **candĕre* cause to glow, cf. *candēre* glow), see -ARY¹]

i·ncense¹, n. Gum, spice, producing sweet smell when burned; smoke of this, esp. in religious ceremonial; (fig.) praise, flattery. [f. OF *encens* f. eccl. L *incensum* thing burnt, incense, neut. p.p. as prec.]

i·ncense², v.t. Fumigate (person, thing) with incense; burn incense to (deity &c.); suffuse with fragrance. Hence **incen**SA·TION n. [f. F *encenser* (as prec.)]

ince·nse³, v.t. Enrage, make angry (*incensed against, with, at, by*). [f. OF *incenser* f. L *incendere* (see INCENDIARY)]

i·ncensory, n. Vessel for burning incense, censer. [f. med. L *incensorium* (INCENSE¹, -ORY)]

ince·ntive, a. & n. Tending to incite; (n.) incitement (*to* action, *to* do, *to doing*), provocation, motive. [f. L *incentivus* setting the tune f. IN¹(*cinere cent-* = *canere* sing) sing to, blow on instrument; -IVE]

ince·pt, v.i. & t. (Camb. Univ.) commence the taking (completed later by creation) of Master's or Doctor's degree, so **ince·pt**OR² n.; (Biol.) take in. [f. L IN¹(*cipere cept-* = *capere* take) begin]

ince·ption, n. Beginning; (Camb. Univ.) incepting. [f. L *inceptio* (as prec., see -ION)]

ince·ptive, a. & n. Beginning; initial; (Gram.) *i. verb,* one that denotes the beginning of an action; (n.) i. verb. [obs. F (*-if, -ive*), as INCEPT, see -IVE]

incer·titude, n. Uncertainty. [F, f. L IN²(*certus* CERTAIN), see -TUDE]

ince·ssant, a. Unceasing, continual, repeated. Hence **ince·ss**ANCY, **ince·ssant**NESS, nn., **ince·ssant**LY² adv. [F, f. LL IN²(*cessantem* part. of *cessare* cease)]

i·ncest, n. Sexual commerce of near kindred. [f. L *incestus -ūs* or IN²(*cestum* neut. adj. = *castum* chaste)]

ince·stuous, a. Involving, guilty of, incest. Hence **ince·stuous**LY² adv. [f. L *incestuosus* (as prec., see -OUS)]

inch¹, n., & v.t. & i. Twelfth part of (linear) foot; *square, cubic, i.,* area equal to square, content equal to cube, whose side is an i.; (as unit of rainfall) quantity that would cover surface to depth of an inch; (of atmospheric or other pressure) amount that balances weight of column of mercury 1 in. high in mercurial barometer; small amount; *by ii.,* bit by bit; *every i.,* entirely; (pl.) stature (*a man of your ii.*); *give him an i. & he'll take an* ELL; *flog* person *within an i. of* his *life,* almost to death; *an i. of cold iron,* stab with a dagger &c.; (v.t. & i.) move by ii., edge *in, forward,* &c. [(vb f. n.) OE *ynce* f. L *uncia* twelfth part, inch]

inch², n. Small (esp. Scotch) island. [f. Gael. *innis*]

-incher, n. *Six* &c. *-i.,* thing of six inches in length, diameter, &c. [-ER¹]

i·nchoate¹ (-kōat), a. Just begun; undeveloped. [f. L IN¹(*cohare, choare*), see -ATE²]

i·nchōāte² (-k-), v.t. Begin; originate. So **incho**A·TION n., **i·nchoāt**IVE (*or* -kō·*a*-) a. [prec., -ATE³]

i·ncidence, n. Falling on, contact with, a thing; *what is the i. of the tax?,* on whom will it fall?; (Physics) falling of line, or of thing moving in a line, upon a surface; *angle of i.,* that which the incident line, ray, &c., makes with the perpendicular to the surface at point of i.; range, scope, extent, of influence. [F (as foll., see -ENCE)]

i·ncident¹, n. Subordinate or accessory event; event, occurrence; detached event attracting general attention; distinct piece of action in play or poem; (Law) privilege, burden, &c., attaching to estate &c. [F (as foll.)]

i·ncident², a. Apt to occur, naturally attaching, (*to*); (Law) attaching *to* (cf. prec.); (of light &c.) falling, striking, (*upon*). [F, f. L IN¹(*cĭdere* = *cadere* fall), see -ENT]

incide·ntal, a. Casual, not essential; liable to happen *to*; *i. images, colours* (perceived as consequence of impressions no longer present). Hence **incide·ntal**LY² adv. [INCIDENT¹ + -AL]

inci·nerate, v.t. Reduce to ashes; consume (body &c.) by fire. Hence or cogn. **inciner**A·TION, **inci·nerat**OR²(2), nn. [f. med. L IN¹(*cinerare* f. *cinis -eris* ashes), see -ATE²]

inci·pient, a. Beginning; in an initial stage. Hence **inci·pi**ENCE, -ENCY, nn., **inci·pient**LY² adv. [f. L as INCEPT, see -ENT]

i·ncipit, sent. (Here) begins (book &c.). [L]

inci·se (-z), v.t. Make a cut in; engrave. [f. F *inciser* f. L IN[1](*cīdere cis-* =*caedere* cut)]
inci·sion (-zhn), n. Cutting into a thing; cut, gash, notch. [F, f. L *incisionem* (prec., -ION)]
incī·sive (-s-), a. Cutting, penetrating; (fig.) mentally sharp; acute, trenchant. Hence **inci·sive**LY[2] adv., **inci·sive**NESS n. [f. med. L *incisivus* (as INCISE, see -IVE)]
incī·sor (-z-), n. Any tooth between the canine teeth in either jaw. [med. L, = cutter (as INCISE, see -OR[2])]
inci·te, v.t. Urge, stir up, (person &c. *to* action, *to* do). Hence or cogn. **incit**A·TION, **inci·te**MENT, nn. [f. F *inciter* f. L IN[1](*citare* rouse frequent. of *ciēre cit-*)]
incivi·lity, n. Rudeness, discourtesy. [f. F *incivilité* f. LL IN[2](*civilitatem* CIVILITY)]
i·ncivism, n. Want of good citizenship, esp. of loyalty to French Revolution principles. [f. F IN[2](*civisme* f. L *civis* citizen)]
i·n-clearing, n. The cheques &c. collectively payable by a bank & received through clearing-house for settlement. [IN adv.]
incle·ment, a. (Of weather or climate) severe, esp. cold or stormy. So **incle·m**ENCY n. [f. L IN[2](*clemens* CLEMENT)]
inclī·nable, a. Inclined, disposed, (*to* thing, *to* do); favourable (*to*). [f. OF *enclinable* (as INCLINE, see -ABLE)]
inclina·tion, n. Leaning, slope, slant; difference of direction of two lines, esp. as measured by angle between them; disposition, propensity, (*to, for,* thing, *to* do); liking, affection, (*for*). [F, f. L *inclinationem* (foll., -ATION)]
incli·ne[1], v.t. & i. Bend (head, body, oneself) forward or downward; *i.* one's *ear,* listen favourably (*to* person, prayer, &c.); dispose (mind, heart, person, *to* do), as *i. our hearts to keep this law, I am inclined to think*; be disposed, as *I i. to think*; lean, cause to lean, from the vertical &c.; *inclined* (sloping) *plane,* one of the MECHANICAL *powers*; tend (*to* corpulence &c.). [f. OF *encliner* f. L IN[1](*clinare* bend)]
incli·ne[2] (*or* ĭ·n)-, n. Inclined plane; slope. [f. prec.]
inclinŏ·meter, n. Instrument measuring vertical intensity of earth's magnetic force as shown by dip of magnetic needle, or for measuring slope. [INCLINE + -O- + -METER]
inclu·de, v.t. Comprise, embrace, (thing &c.) as part of a whole; (part. in abs. constr.) if we i., as *seven were killed, including the guard*; treat, regard, as so comprised; (p.p.) shut in. [f. L IN[1](*cludere clus-* =*claudere* shut)]
inclu·sive (-s-), a. Including, comprising, (*of,* or abs.); (abbr. *incl.*) *pages 7 to 26 i.* (including pages 7 & 26); including much or all, as *i. terms* (at hotel &c.). Hence or cogn. **inclu·s**ION (-zhn) n., **inclu·sive**LY[2] adv., **inclu·sive**NESS n. [f. med. L *inclusivus* (as prec., see -IVE)]
inco·gnitō, a. & n. (pl. *-ti* pron. -tē, fem. *-ta,* pron. -tă, pl. *-te,* pron. -tā), & adv. (abbr., spoken & written, *inco·g*). (Person) concealed under disguised character; (adv.) with one's name, character, &c., concealed, as *travel, do good, i.* [It., = unknown, f. L IN[2](*cognitus* p.p. of *cognoscere* get to know)]
inco·gnīzable (-kŏgn-, -kŏn-), a. That cannot be apprehended by senses or intellect. [IN-[2]]
inco·gnizant (as prec.), a. Unaware, unconscious *of.* So **inco·gniz**ANCE n. [IN-[2]]
incohēr·ent, a. Not coherent (lit. & fig.). So **incohēr·**ENCE n., **incohēr·ent**LY[2] adv. [IN-[2]]
incohē·sive, a. Not cohesive. [IN-[2]]
incombu·stible, a. That cannot be consumed by fire. Hence **incombusti**BI·LITY n. [f. med. L IN[2](*combustibilis* COMBUSTIBLE)]
income (ĭ·ngk*u*m), n. Periodical (usu. annual) receipts from one's business, lands, work, investments, &c.; *i.-tax* (levied on this). [IN[2]]
i·nco·mer (-kŭ-), n. One who comes in; immigrant; intruder; successor. [IN adv.]
i·nco·ming[1] (-kŭ-), n. Entrance, arrival; (usu. pl.) revenue, income. [IN adv.]
i·ncoming[2] (-kŭ-), a. Succeeding; immigrant; (of profit) accruing. [IN adv.]
incomme·nsurable, a. (Of magnitudes) having no common measure integral or fractional (*with* another); irrational, surd; not comparable in respect of magnitude; not worthy to be measured *with.* Hence **incommensura**BI·LITY n., **incomme·nsurab**LY[2] adv. [f. med. L IN[2](*commensurabilis* COMMENSURABLE)]
incomme·nsurate (-*a*t), a. Out of proportion, inadequate, (*with, to*); =prec. Hence **incomme·nsurate**NESS n. [IN-[2]]
incommo·de, v.t. Trouble, annoy; hinder. [f. F *incommoder* f. L IN[2](*commodare* f. *commodus* COMMODIOUS)]
incommo·dious, a. Not affording good accommodation, uncomfortable. Hence **incommo·dious**NESS n. [IN-[2]]
incommu·nicable, a. That cannot be shared; that cannot be told. Hence **incommunica**BI·LITY, **incommu·nicable**NESS, nn., **incommu·nicab**LY[2] adv. [IN-[2]]
incommu·nicative, a. Not communicative. Hence **incommu·nicative**LY[2] adv., **incommunicative**NESS n. [IN-[2]]
incommu·table, a. Unchangeable; not commutable. Hence **incommu·tab**LY[2] adv. [f. L IN[2](*commutabilis* COMMUTABLE)]
incompa·ct, a. Not compact (esp. fig.). [IN-[2]]
inco·mparable, a. Matchless; not to be compared (*with, to*). Hence **inco·mparable**NESS n., **inco·mparab**LY[2] adv. [F, f. L IN[2](*comparabilis* COMPARABLE)]

incompă·tible, a. Opposed in character, discordant; inconsistent (*with*). So **incompatiBI·LITY** n. [f. med. L IN²(*compatibilis* COMPATIBLE)]
inco·mpetent, a. Not qualified or able (*to* do); not legally qualified. Hence or cogn. **inco·mpetENCE**, -ENCY, nn., **inco·mpetentLY²** adv. [f. F *incompétent* f. LL IN²(*competentem* COMPETENT)]
incomple·te, a. Not complete. Hence **incomple·teLY²** adv., **incomple·teNESS** n. [f. L IN²(*completus* COMPLETE)]
incomprehe·nsible, a. That cannot be understood; (Athanas. Creed) boundless (also as n., *three ii.*). Hence **incomprehensiBI·LITY**, **incomprehe·nsibleNESS**, nn., **incomprehe·nsibLY²** adv. [f. L IN²(*comprehensibilis* COMPREHENSIBLE)]
incomprehe·nsion, n. Failure to understand. [IN-²]
incompre·ssible, a. That cannot be compressed. Hence **incompressiBI·LITY** n. [IN-²]
incompu·table, a. That cannot be computed. [IN-²]
inconcei·vable, a. That cannot be imagined; (pop.) very remarkable. Hence **inconceivaBI·LITY** n., **inconcei·vabLY²** adv. [IN-²]
inconclu·sive, a. (Of argument, evidence, action) not decisive or convincing. Hence **inconclu·siveLY²** adv., **inconclu·siveNESS** n. [IN-²]
inconde·nsable, a. That cannot be condensed, esp. that cannot be reduced to liquid or solid condition. [IN-²]
inco·ndīte, a. (Of literary composition &c.) ill constructed; crude, unpolished. [f. L IN²(*conditus* p.p. of *condere* put together)]
inconfor·mity, n. Dissimilarity, want of conformity, (*to, with*); =NONCONFORMITY. [IN-²]
inco·ngruous, a. Disagreeing, out of keeping, (*with*); out of place, absurd. Hence or cogn. **incongru·ITY**, **inco·ngruousNESS**, nn., **inco·ngruousLY²** adv. [f. L IN²(*congruus* CONGRUOUS)]
inconse·cutive, a. Wanting in sequence, inconsequent. Hence **inconse·cutiveLY²** adv., **inconse·cutiveNESS** n. [IN-²]
inco·nsequent, a. Not following naturally, irrelevant; wanting in logical sequence; disconnected. Hence or cogn. **inco·nsequENCE** n., **inconseque·ntIAL** a., **inconseque·ntialLY²**, **inco·nsequentLY²**, advv. [f. L IN²(*consequens* CONSEQUENT)]
inconsi·derable, a. Not worth considering; of small size, value, &c. [f. F IN²(*considerable* CONSIDERABLE)]
inconsi·derate (-*at*), a. (Of person or action) thoughtless, rash; lacking in regard for feelings &c. of others. Hence or cogn. **inconsi·derateLY²** adv., **inconsi·derateNESS**, **inconsiderA·TION**, nn. [f. L IN²(*consideratus* CONSIDERATE)]
inconsi·stent, a. Not in keeping, discordant, incompatible, (*with*); (of single thing) having i. parts; acting at variance with one's own principles or former conduct. Hence **inconsi·stENCY** n., **inconsi·stentLY²** adv. [IN-²]
inconso·lable, a. (Of person, his grief, &c.) that cannot be consoled. Hence **inconso·labLY²** adv. [f. L IN²(*consolabilis* CONSOLABLE)]
inco·nsonant, a. Not harmonizing (*with, to*). Hence **inco·nsonANCE** n. [IN-²]
inconspi·cuous, a. Not conspicuous; (Bot., of flowers) small, pale, or green. Hence **inconspi·cuousNESS** n. [f. LL IN²(*conspicuus* CONSPICUOUS)]
inco·nstant, a. (Of person) fickle, changeable; variable, irregular. Hence or cogn. **inco·nstancY** n., **inco·nstantLY²** adv. [F, f. L IN²(*constantem* CONSTANT)]
inconsu·mable, a. That cannot be consumed by fire &c.; (Pol. Econ.) not meant to be consumed in use. [IN-²]
inconte·stable, a. That cannot be disputed. Hence **inconte·stabLY²** adv. [F (IN-²)]
inco·ntinent, a. Wanting in self-restraint (esp. in regard to sexual appetite); unable to hold in something (*of* secrets, tongue, urine, &c.). So **inco·ntinENCE** n. [F, f. L IN²(*continentem* CONTINENT)]
inco·ntinently, adv. At once, immediately. [archaic *incontinent* adv. (thr. F) f. LL *in continenti* (*tempore*) in continuous time, + -LY²]
incontrover·tible, a. Not to be disputed. Hence **incontrover·tibLY²** adv. [IN-²]
inconve·nience, n. Want of adaptation to personal requirement or ease; instance of this; (v.t.) put (person &c.) to i., incommode. [(vb f. n.) OF, f. LL *inconvenientia* (as foll., see -ENCE)]
inconve·nient, a. Unfavourable to ease or comfort, awkward, troublesome. Hence **inconve·nientLY²** adv. [f. 13th-c. F *inconvénient* f. L IN²(*convenientem* CONVENIENT)]
inconver·tible, a. Not convertible (esp. of paper money). Hence **inconvertiBI·LITY** n., **inconver·tibLY²** adv. [IN-²]
inconvi·ncible, a. Not to be convinced. [IN-²]
incōordina·tion, n. Want of coordination. [IN-²]
incor·porate¹ (-*at*), a. (Of company &c.) formed into a corporation; (of persons) united in a corporation. [as foll., see -ATE²]
incor·porāte², v.t. & i. Unite (*in* one body, *with* another thing); combine (ingredients) into one substance; constitute as a legal corporation; become incorporated (*with*). Hence or cogn. **incorporA·TION**, **incor·poratOR²**, nn. [f. LL IN¹(*corporare* f. *corpus -oris* body), -ATE³]
incorpor·eal, a. Not composed of mat-

ter; of immaterial beings; (Law) having no material existence, esp. *i. hereditament.* Hence **incorpor·eal**LY[2] adv., **incorporē·**ITY n. [f. L IN[2](*corporeus* f. *corpus -oris* body) + -AL]

incorre·ct, a. Not in accordance with fact; (of style &c.) improper, faulty; (of book) not properly corrected for press. Hence **incorre·ct**LY[2] adv., **incorre·ct**NESS n. [f. L IN[2](*correctus* CORRECT)]

incŏ·rrigible, a. (Of person or habit) incurably bad or depraved. Hence **incorrigi**BI·LITY n., **inco·rrigib**LY[2] adv. [F, f. L IN[2](*corrigibilis* CORRIGIBLE)]

incorru·ptible, a. That cannot decay, so **incorr·uption** n. (bibl.); eternal; that cannot be corrupted, esp. bribed. Hence or cogn. **incorruptibi·lity** n., **incorru·ptib**LY[2] adv. [f. LL IN[2](*corruptibilis* CORRUPTIBLE)]

incra·ssate (-*at*), a. (bot., zool.). Of thick or swollen form. [f. L IN[1](*crassare* f. *crassus* thick), see -ATE[2]]

increa·se[1] (-s), v.i. & t. Become greater; grow in numbers, esp. by propagation; advance (*in* quality, attainment, &c.); make greater or more numerous; intensify (quality). Hence **increa·sing**LY[2] adv. [f. OF *encreistre* (st. *-eiss-*) f. L IN[1](*crescere* grow)]

i·ncrease[2], n. Growth, enlargement; growth in numbers, multiplication (of men, animals, or plants); *on the i.*, increasing; increased amount; (archaic) crops. [f. prec.]

incrĕ·dible, a. That cannot be believed; (colloq.) hard to believe, surprising. So **incredi**BI·LITY n., **incre·dib**LY[2] adv. [f. L IN[2](*credibilis* CREDIBLE)]

incrĕ·dulous, a. Unbelieving (*of* or abs.). Hence or cogn. **incredū·**LITY n., **incre·dulous**LY[2] adv. [f. L IN[2](*credulus* CREDULOUS)]

i·ncrĕment, n. Increase; amount of this; profit; UNEARNED *i.*, see UN-[2](1); (Math.) small amount by which variable quantity increases. [f. L *incrementum* (as INCREASE, see -MENT)]

incri·minate, v.t. Charge with crime; involve in accusation. Hence **incri·minat**ORY a. [f. med. L IN[1](*criminare* CRIMINATE)]

incrusta·tion, n. Encrusting; crust, hard coating; facing of marble &c. on building; (fig.) accretion of habit; scab. [f. LL *incrustatio* (as ENCRUST, see -ATION)]

i·ncūbate, v.t. & i. Hatch (eggs) by sitting on them or otherwise; sit on eggs, brood. [f. L IN[1](*cubare cubit-* or *cubat-* lie), see -ATE[3]]

incuba·tion, n. Hatching; *artificial i.* (by artificial heat); (of the Holy Ghost) brooding; (Path.) phase through which germs of disease pass before development of first symptoms. So **i·ncubat**IVE, **i·ncubat**ORY, aa. [f. L *incubatio* (as prec., see -ATION)]

i·ncubator, n. Apparatus for hatching birds, rearing children born prematurely, or developing bacteria. [L (as prec., see -OR[2])]

i·ncūbus, n. Evil spirit supposed to descend on sleeping persons; nightmare; person, thing, that oppresses like nightmare. [LL, = L *incubo* nightmare (as INCUBATE)]

i·nculcate, v.t. Urge, impress, (fact, habit, idea) persistently (*upon* or *in* person, mind). So **inculc**A·TION, **i·nculcat**OR[2], nn. [f. L IN[1](*culcare* = *calcare* tread f. *calx -lcis* heel), -ATE[3]]

i·nculpate, v.t. Accuse, blame; involve in charge. Hence **inculp**A·TION n., **incu·lpat**ORY a. [f. L IN[1](*culpare* f. *culpa* fault), -ATE[3]]

incu·lt, a. (rare). Untilled; unpolished, rude; (of person or manners) coarse. [f. L IN[2](*cultus* p.p. of *colere* till)]

incu·mbency, n. Office, tenure, sphere, of an incumbent. [f. foll., see -ENCY]

incu·mbent[1], n. Holder of ecclesiastical benefice or (rare) of any office. [as foll.]

incu·mbent[2], a. Lying, pressing, (*on*); resting (*up*)*on* (person) as duty, as *it is i. on you to warn them.* [f. L IN[1](*cumbere* lie), -ENT]

incūnă·būla, n. pl. Early stages of thing; (w. sing. *-um*) books printed early, esp. before 1500. [L, = swaddling-clothes, f. *cunae* cradle]

incur·, v.t. (-rr-). Fall into, bring on oneself, (danger, blame, punishment, &c.). [f. L IN[1](*currere curs-* run)]

incūr·able, a. & n. (Person) that cannot be cured. Hence **incūra**BI·LITY, **incūr·able**NESS, nn., **incūr·ab**LY[2] adv. [OF, f. L IN[2](*curabilis* CURABLE)]

incūr·ious, a. Devoid of curiosity; heedless, careless; uninteresting (usu. *not i.*). Hence **incurio·**SITY n., **incur·ious**LY[2] adv. [f. L IN[2](*curiosus* CURIOUS)]

incur·sion, n. Hostile invasion; sudden attack. So **incur·**SIVE a. [f. L *incursio* (as INCUR, see -ION)]

incur·ve, v.t. Bend into a curve; curve inwards (esp. in p.p.). So **incurv**A·TION n. [f. L IN[1](*curvare* CURVE)]

i·ncus (-*us*), n. Bone of ear receiving vibrations from MALLEUS. [L, = anvil (as foll.)]

incu·se[1] (-z), a. & n. (Of impression on coin &c.) hammered or stamped in; (n.) such impression. [f. L IN[1](*cudere cus-* forge)]

incu·se[2] (-z), v.t. (esp. in p.p.). Impress (figure &c.) by stamping; mark (coin &c.) with such figure. [as prec.]

indĕb·ted, a. Owing money (*to*); owing gratitude (*to* person, or fig. *to* thing, *for* benefit &c.). Hence **indeb·ted**NESS n. [f. OF *endetté* p.p. of EN(*detter* f. *dette* DEBT)]

indē·cent, a. Unbecoming; immodest,

obscene. Hence or cogn. **inde·**CENCY n., **inde·cent**LY[2] adv. [f. L IN[2](*decens* DECENT)]
indeci·duous, a. Not deciduous. [IN-[2]]
indeci̅·pherable, a. That cannot be deciphered. [IN-[2]]
indeci·sion, n. Want of decision, hesitation. [f. F IN[2](*décision* DECISION)]
indeci̅·sive, a. Not decisive; undecided, irresolute. Hence **indeci·sive**LY[2] adv., **indeci·sive**NESS n. [IN-[2]]
indecli̅·nable, a. That cannot be declined, having no inflexions. [f. F IN[2](*déclinable* DECLINABLE)]
indēcompo·sable, a. That cannot be decomposed or resolved into constituents. [IN-[2]]
indecor·ous, a. Improper; in bad taste. Hence **indecor·ous**LY[2] adv., **indecor·ous**NESS n. [f. L IN[2](*decorus* DECOROUS)]
indecor·um, n. Lack of decorum; improper proceeding. [L, neut. adj. as prec.]
indee·d, adv. In truth, really, as *he was, i., a remarkable man*; (intensifying) *I shall be very glad i., this is quick work i., yes, i.!, no, i.!*; (echoing last speaker's words with approval or iron.) *who is this Mr Smith?—who is he, i.!* (=you may well ask, or, can you ask?); (concessive) *there are i. exceptions*; (interrog.) really? is it so?; as int., expr. irony, contempt, incredulity, &c. [IN prep. + DEED]
indefă·tigable, a. (Of persons, qualities, &c.) that cannot be tired out, unremitting. Hence **indefatiga**BI·LITY n., **indefa·tigab**LY[2] adv. [f. obs. F *indéfatigable* f. L IN[2](*defatigabilis* f. DE*fatigare* wear out, see -BLE)]
indefea·sible, a. That cannot be forfeited or done away with, esp. *i. right.* Hence **indefeasi**BI·LITY n., **indefea·sib**LY[2] adv. [IN-[2]]
indefe·ctible, a. Unfailing, not liable to defect or decay; faultless. [IN-[2] + DEFECT + -IBLE]
indefe·nsible, a. Admitting of no defence (by force of arms or by argument). Hence **indefensi**BI·LITY n., **indefe·nsib**LY[2] adv. [IN-[2]]
indefi̅·nable, a. That cannot be defined. Hence **indefi·nab**LY[2] adv. [IN-[2]]
indĕ·finite, a. Vague, undefined; unlimited; (Gram., of adjj., pronouns, &c.) not determining the person, thing, time, &c., to which they refer, esp. *i. article* (a, an); (of tenses) denoting an action without specifying whether it is continuous or complete (e.g. Greek aorist, English past). Hence **inde·finite**LY[2] adv., **inde·finite**NESS, **indefi̅·ni**TUDE, nn. [f. L IN[2](*definitus* DEFINITE)]
indehi·scent, a. (bot.). Not dehiscent. [IN-[2]]
indĕ·lible, a. (Of mark, stain, ink, &c., & fig. of disgrace &c.) that cannot be blotted out. Hence **indeli**BI·LITY n., **inde·lib**LY[2] adv. [f L IN[2](*delebilis* f. *delēre* blot out, see -BLE)]
indĕ·licate (-*a*t), a. Coarse, unrefined; immodest; tactless. Hence **inde·lic**ACY n., **inde·licate**LY[2] adv. [IN-[2]]
inde·mnify, v.t. Protect, secure, (person *from, against,* harm or loss); secure (person) against legal responsibility (*for* actions); compensate (person *for* loss, expenses incurred, &c.). Hence **indemni**FICA·TION n. [f. L IN[2](*demnis* f. *damnum* loss), see -FY]
inde·mnity, n. Security against damage or loss; legal exemption from penalties &c. incurred; compensation for loss incurred; sum paid for this, esp. sum exacted by victorious belligerent as one condition of peace. [f. F *indemnité* f. LL *indemnitas* (as prec., see -TY)]
indemo·nstrable, a. That cannot be proved (esp. of primary truths). [IN-[2]]
inde·nt[1], v.t. & i. Make tooth-like notches in; form deep recesses in (coast-line &c.); divide (document drawn up in duplicate) into two halves with zigzag line, draw up (document) in exact duplicate; (Print.) set back (beginning of line) further from margin to mark new paragraph; (intr.) make requisition (prop. written order with duplicate) *upon* (person *for* thing); order (goods) by an indent. [f. F *endenter* f. L *IN[1](*dentare* f. *dens -ntis* tooth)]
inde·nt[2] (*or* i̅·n-), n. Indentation; indenture; official requisition for stores; order for goods (esp. to England from abroad). [f. prec.]
inde·nt[3], v.t. Make a dent in; impress (mark &c.). [IN[1]]
i·ndent[4], n. Dent, depression. [f. prec.]
indenta·tion, n. Indenting; cut, notch; zigzag; deep recess in coast-line &c. [INDENT[1,3] + -ATION]
inde·ntion, n. Indenting of line in printing; =prec. [irreg. f. INDENT[1] + -ION]
inde·nture (-tsh*e*r), n., & v.t. Indented document (see INDENT[1]); any sealed agreement or contract, esp. that which binds apprentice to master; *take up* one's *ii.*, receive them back on completion of service; formal list, certificate, &c.; indentation; bind (person) by ii. esp. as apprentice. [(vb f. n.) f. OF *endenteure* (as INDENT[1], see -URE)]
indepe·ndence, -ency, nn. (-*ce*) being independent (*on, of,* or abs.); independent income; (-*cy*) =CONGREGATIONALISM; (-*cy*) independent State. [f. foll., see -ENCE, -ENCY]
indepe·ndent, a. & n. Not depending on authority (*of,* or abs.); (*I*-) =CONGREGATIONAL; not depending on something else for its validity, efficiency, &c., as *i. proof, research, observer*; not needing to earn one's livelihood; *i. income* (dispensing one from earning livelihood); unwilling to be under obligation to others. (N.) person who acts (in politics &c.) independently

of any party; Congregationalist; (as title of paper) *New York I.* &c. Hence **inde·pe·ndent**LY[2] adv. [IN-[2]]

indescri·bable, a. Vague, indefinite; too great, beautiful, bad, &c., to be described. Hence **indescriba**BI·LITY n., **indescri·b-ab**LY[2] adv. [IN-[2]]

indestru·ctible, a. That cannot be destroyed. Hence **indestructi**BI·LITY n., **indestru·ctib**LY[2] adv. [IN-[2]]

indeter·minable, a. That cannot be ascertained; (of disputes &c.) that cannot be settled. [f. L IN[2](*determinabilis* DETERMINABLE)]

indeter·minate (-*at*), a. Not fixed in extent, character, &c.; vague; left doubtful; *i. sentence*, one that leaves prisoner's release dependent on his conduct & on probability of amendment; *i. vowel*, sound in *a*go, mom*e*nt, cous*i*n, *o*pine, s*u*pport, cert*ai*n; (Math., of quantity) not limited to fixed value(s). Hence **indeter·minate**LY[2] adv., **indeter·minate**NESS n. [f. L IN[2](*determinatus* DETERMINATE)]

indeter·mination, n. Want of determination; being indeterminate. [IN-[2]]

indeter·minism, n. Theory that human action is not wholly determined by motives. So **indeter·mini**ST n. [IN-[2]]

i·ndex, n. (pl. *-exes, -icēs*), & v.t. Forefinger; (on instruments) pointer showing measurements &c.; guiding principle; alphabetical list, usu. at end of book, of subjects &c. with references; (R.C.) *the I.*, list of books forbidden to Roman Catholics, or to be read only in expurgated editions (in full, *I. librorum prohibitorum*); *i. expurgatorius*, list of passages to be expunged in books otherwise permitted (in fig. use often confused with last); (Alg.) exponent; (v.t.) furnish (book) with i. (esp. in p.p.), enter (word &c.) in i. Hence **i·ndex**LESS a. [(vb f. n.) L (gen. *-icis*), =forefinger, informer, sign, f. IN-[1] + *dic-* point out]

I·ndia, n. Country of S. Asia east of river Indus & south of Himalayas; *Further I.*, country between this & China; *Indiaman*, ship engaged in Indian trade; *I. Office*, department of British Government dealing with Indian affairs; *I. paper*, soft absorbent kind imported from China, used for proofs of engravings (*Oxford I. p.*, thin tough opaque printing-paper); *I. proof* (on I. paper); *indiarubber*, coagulated juice of certain plants, used for tires, rubbing out pencil marks, &c. [L, f. Gk (*Indos* Indus, f. Pers. *hind* =Skr. *sindhu* river, -IA[1])]

I·ndian, a. & n. (Native) of India; (one) of the original inhabitants of America & W. Indies; European, esp. Englishman, formerly resident in India; *Red I.*, one of aboriginal race of N. America; *I. civilian*, member of I.C.S.; *I. club* (bottle-shaped, for use in gymnastics); *I. corn*, maize, N. American graminaceous plant; *I. file*, single file; *India(n) ink*, black pigment made in China & Japan; *I. meal* (made from I. corn); *I. summer*, period of calm dry hazy weather in late autumn in North. U.S.; *I. weed*, tobacco. Hence **I·ndian**IZE(3) v.t. [-AN]

i·ndicate, v.t. Point out, make known, show; (Med.) suggest, call for, (treatment); state briefly; be a sign of, betoken, (thing, *that*, &c.; *indicated horsepower* (shown by indicator; abbr. *i.h.p.*). So **indica**·TION n. [f. L IN[1](*dicare* make known), see -ATE[3]]

indi·cative, a. & n. (Gram.) stating a thing as a fact, not as conception, wish, &c., of speaker; (*also* ĭ·ndĭcătĭv) suggestive, giving indications, *of*; (n.) i. mood. Hence **indi·cative**LY[2] adv. [F (*-if, -ive*), f. L *indicativus* (prec., -IVE)]

i·ndicator, n. Person, thing, that points out, esp. recording instrument attached to apparatus &c. Hence **i·ndicat**ORY a. [LL (as prec., see -OR[2])]

indĭ·cium (-shĭ-), n. (pl. *-ia*). Indication, sign, (now rare). [L (as INDEX)]

indī·ct, v.t. Accuse (person *for* riot &c., *as* a rioter, *on* charge), esp. by legal process. [f. AF *enditer* indict f. OF *enditer* make known f. LL *IN[1](*dictare* DICTATE)]

indī·ctable, a. Liable, (of action) rendering one liable, to be indicted. [-ABLE]

indi·ction, n. Fiscal period of 15 years instituted by Constantine & reckoned from Sep. 1st, 312; assessment of property-tax by Roman Emperors at beginning of each 15 years; this tax; proclamation. [f. L *indictio* f. IN[1](*dicere dict-* say), see -ION]

indī·ctment, n. Formal accusation; legal process in which this is preferred to & presented by Grand Jury; document containing charge; *bill of i.*, written accusation as preferred to Grand Jury. [f. AF *enditement* (as INDICT, see -MENT)]

I·ndies, n. pl. (Also *East I.*) India, Further India, & the islands beyond; *West I.*, group of islands lying at mouth of Gulf of Mexico. [pl. of *Indy* f. L *India*]

indi·fference, n. Absence of interest or attention (*to, towards*, or abs.); neutrality; unimportance, esp. *a matter of i.*, so **indi·ffer**ENCY n. [f. L *indifferentia* (as foll., see -ENCE)]

indi·fferent, a. & n. Impartial, neutral; having no inclination for or against (*to*); neither good nor bad; rather bad, esp. *very i.*; neutral in chemical, electrical, or magnetic quality; unimportant (*to*); (n.) neutral person, esp. in religion or politics. Hence **indi·fferent**LY[2] adv. [f. L IN[2](*differens* DIFFERENT)]

indi·fferentism, n. Spirit of indifference, professed or practised, esp. in religious matters. So **indi·fferent**IST n. [-ISM]

i·ndigene, n. Native. [f. F *indigène* f. L *indigena* (*indu-* =IN-[1] + *gen-* be born)]

indi·genous, a. Native, belonging naturally, (*to* soil &c., also fig.). Hence **indi·genous**LY[2] adv. [f. LL *indigenus* (as prec.) + -OUS]

i·ndigent, a. Needy, poor. So **i·ndig**ENCE n. [F, f. L *indigēre* (*indu-* =IN-[1] + *egēre* want), see -ENT]

indige·sted, a. Shapeless; not thought out; not digested in stomach. [f. obs. *indigest* a. f. L IN[2](*digestus* p.p. as DIGEST) + -ED[1]]

indige·stible, a. Not digestible (lit. & fig.). Hence **indigesti**BI·LITY n. [f. L IN[2](*digestibilis* DIGESTIBLE)]

indige·stion, n. Difficulty in digesting food, dyspepsia; undigested condition (lit. & fig.). [F, f. L IN[2](*digestionem* DIGESTION)]

indige·stive, a. Suffering from, tending to, indigestion. [IN-[2]]

indig·n, a. (archaic). Unworthy. [f. F *indigne* f. L IN[2](*dignus* worthy)]

indi·gnant, a. Moved by mingled anger & scorn or feeling of injured innocence (*at* thing, *with* person, or abs.). Hence **indi·gnant**LY[2] adv. [f. L *indignari* (as prec.), see -ANT]

indigna·tion, n. Anger excited by meanness, injustice, wickedness, or misconduct (*at* thing, *against*, *with*, person); *i.-meeting* (to express public i.). [f. L *indignatio* (prec., -ATION)]

indi·gnity, n. Unworthy treatment; slight, insult. [f. L *indignitas* (as INDIGN, see -TY)]

i·ndigo, n. Blue powder from plants of genus *Indigofera*, used as dye; *i. blue*, blue-violet (often attrib.); *i.-bird*, N.-Amer. species of painted finch; *i. white*, reduced or deoxidized i., a white crystalline powder.. Hence **indigŏ·tic** [-*t*- euphon.] a. [f. L f. Gk *indikon* Indian (dye)]

indire·ct, a. (Of road &c.) not straight; not going straight to the point; (Pol. Econ., of taxes) not direct, paid by consumer in the form of increased price for the taxed goods; (Gram.) *i. speech*, reported speech, with necessary changes of pronouns, tenses, &c. (e.g. *I will help you*, he said *he would help me*), *i. object*, person, thing, affected by verbal action but not primarily acted on (e.g. *him* in *give him the book*), *i. passive*, passive having for subject the i. object of the active (e.g. *I* in *I was told it*); not directly aimed at, as *an i. result*. Hence **indire·ct**LY[2] adv., **indire·ct**NESS n. [f. L IN[2](*directus* DIRECT)]

indire·ction, n. Round-about means, esp. *by i.* (after Shak. *Ham.* II. i. 66); deceit, trickery. [prec. + -ION]

indiscer·nible, a. & n. (Thing) that cannot be discerned or distinguished from another; *identity of ii.*, doctrine that things cannot exist together as separate entities unless they have different attributes. Hence **indiscer·nib**LY[2] adv. [IN-[2]]

indiscer·ptible, a. Incapable of, not destructible by, dissolution of parts. Hence **indiscerpti**BI·LITY n. [IN-[2]]

indi·scipline, n. Want of discipline. So **indi·sciplin**ABLE a. [IN-[2]]

indiscree·t, a. Injudicious, unwary. Hence **indiscree·t**LY[2] adv. [f. L IN[2](*discretus* DISCREET)]

indi·screte, a. Not divided into distinct parts. [IN-[2]]

indiscrĕ·tion, n. Injudicious conduct; accidental or (*calculated i.*) supposed accidental revelation of official secret &c.; imprudence; transgression of social morality. [f. F *indiscrétion* f. LL IN[2](*discretionem* DISCRETION)]

indiscri·minate (-*at*), a. Confused, promiscuous; making no distinctions. Hence **indiscri·minate**LY[2] adv., **indiscri·minate**NESS, **indiscrimina**A·TION, nn., **indiscri·minat**IVE a. [IN-[2]]

indispe·nsable, a. That cannot be dispensed with, necessary; (of law, duty, &c.) that cannot be set aside. Hence **indispensa**BI·LITY, **indispe·nsable**NESS, nn., **indispe·nsab**LY[2] adv. [f. med. L IN[2](*dispensabilis* DISPENSABLE)]

indispo·se, v.t. Render unfit or unable (*for* thing, *to* do); make averse (*towards*, *from*, thing, *to* do); (esp. in p.p.) put out of health. [IN-[2]]

indisposi·tion, n. Ill health, ailment, (esp. of passing kind); disinclination (*to* thing, *to* do); aversion (*to*, *towards*). [IN-[2]]

indi·sputable, a. That cannot be disputed. Hence **indisputa**BI·LITY, **indi·sputable**NESS, nn., **indi·sputab**LY[2] adv. [f. LL IN[2](*disputabilis* DISPUTABLE)]

indi·ssoluble (*or* ĭndĭsŏ·l-), a. Lasting, stable, as *an i. bond*; that cannot be dissolved or decomposed. Hence **indissolu**BI·LITY n., **indi·ssolub**LY[2] adv. [f. L IN[2](*dissolubilis* DISSOLUBLE)]

indisti·nct, a. Not distinct; confused, obscure. Hence **indisti·nct**LY[2] adv., **indisti·nct**NESS n. [f. L IN[2](*distinctus* DISTINCT)]

indisti·nctive, a. Not distinctive. Hence **indisti·nctive**LY[2] adv. [IN-[2]]

indisti·nguishable, a. Not distinguishable. Hence **indisti·nguishab**LY[2] adv. [IN-[2]]

indistri·butable, a. That cannot be distributed. [IN-[2]]

indi·te, v.t. Put into words, compose, (poem, speech, &c.); (usu. facet.) write (letter &c.). [f. OF EN(*diter* f. L *dictare* DICTATE)]

indiver·tible, a. That cannot be turned aside. Hence **indiver·tib**LY[2] adv. [IN-[2] + DIVERT + -IBLE]

indivi·dual, a. & n. Single; particular, special, opp. to *general*; having distinct character; characteristic of particular person; single member of class; single human being, opp. to *society*, *family*, &c.; (vulg.) person, as *an i. of somewhat pre-*

possessing appearance. [f. med. L *individualis* f. IN²(*dividuus* f. *dividere* DIVIDE), see -AL]

indivi·dualism, n. Self-centred feeling or conduct, egoism; social theory favouring free action of individuals (cf. SOCIALISM). So **indivi·dualIST** n., **individuali·stic** a. [-ISM]

individua·lity, n. Separate existence; individual character, esp. when strongly marked; (pl.) individual tastes &c. [-ITY]

indivi·dualize, v.t. Give individual character to; specify. Hence **individualizA·TION** n. [-IZE]

indivi·dually, adv. Personally, in an individual capacity; in a distinctive manner; one by one, not collectively; *i. different*, different as individuals though perhaps identical in species. [-LY²]

indivi·duate, v.t. Individualize, form into an individual. So **individuA·TION** n. [f. med. L *individuare* (as INDIVIDUAL), see -ATE³]

indivi·sible, a. & n. Not divisible; (n.) infinitely small particle or quantity. Hence **indivisiBI·LITY** n., **indivi·sibLY²** adv. [f. LL IN²(*divisibilis* DIVISIBLE)]

Indo- in comb. = Indian, as: *-Aryan*, Aryan of or in India; *-Chinese*, of Further India; *-European*, *-Germanic*, of the family of languages spoken over greater part of Europe & Asia as far as N. India; *-nē·sian*, of the East Indian islands. [f. L f. Gk *Indos*]

indō·cile (*or* -dŏsīl), a. Not docile. Hence **indoci·lITY** n. [f. L IN²(*docilis* DOCILE)]

i·ndolent, a. Slothful, lazy; (Med.) causing no pain, as *i. tumour*. Hence or cogn. **i·ndolENCE** n., **i·ndolentLY²** adv. [f. LL *indolens* (IN-² + *dolēre* grieve, see -ENT)]

indŏ·mitable, a. Unyielding; stubbornly persistent. Hence **indo·mitabLY²** adv. [f. LL IN²(*domitabilis* f. *domitare* tame, see -BLE)]

i·ndoor, a. Situated, carried on, within doors or under cover, as *i. games*; within workhouse, as *i. relief*. [IN prep.]

indoor·s, adv. Within a house; under cover. [earlier *within doors*]

indorsa·tion, n. Endorsement. [f. *indorse* var. of ENDORSE + -ATION]

indorsee·, n. One in whose favour note or bill is endorsed. [as prec., see -EE]

i·ndraught (-ahft), **-draft,** n. Drawing in; inward flow or current. [IN adv.]

i·ndrī, n. Babacoote, lemurine animal of Madagascar. [f. Malagasy *indry* behold, mistaken for its name]

indū·bitable, a. That cannot be doubted. Hence **indu·bitabLY²** adv. [f. L IN²(*dubitabilis* f. *dubitare* doubt, see -BLE)]

indu·ce, v.t. Prevail on, persuade, (*to* do, now rarely *to* action &c.; *nothing shall i. me to*, I will never); bring about, give rise to; (Electr.) produce (current) by induction; infer, derive as an induction. [f. L IN¹(*ducere duct-* lead)]

indu·cement, n. What induces; attraction that leads one on (*to*). [-MENT]

indu·ct, v.t. Introduce formally into possession (*to* benefice); install (*into* seat, room, &c.); introduce, initiate, (*to*, *into*). [as INDUCE]

indu·ctīle, a. Not ductile. [IN-²]

indu·ction, n. Inducting; (archaic) preamble, prologue, introduction; production (*of* facts) to prove general statement; inferring of general law from particular instances (cf. DEDUCTION); *mathematical i.*, proving universal truth of theorem by showing (1) that if true of any particular case it is true of the next case in a series, (2) that it is true of a particular case; (Electr., Magnet.) bringing about of electric or magnetic state in a body by proximity (without contact) of electrified or magnetized body; *i.-coil*, apparatus for producing electric currents by i. [f. L *inductio* (as INDUCE, see -ION)]

indu·ctive, a. (Of reasoning &c.) of, based on, induction; of electric or magnetic induction. Hence **indu·ctiveLY²** adv., **indu·ctiveNESS** n. [f. L *inductivus* (as INDUCE, see -IVE)]

indu·ctor, n. One who inducts clergyman; any part of electric induction apparatus. [L, as INDUCE, see -OR²]

indu·lge, v.t. & i. Gratify (person, oneself, *in* wish, matter, &c.); gratify (person *with* thing given); give free course to, entertain, (desire &c.); (intr.) take one's pleasure freely *in* (strong language, bicycling, a cigar). Hence **indu·lgENT** a., **indu·lgentLY²** adv. [f. L *indulgēre, -dult-*, etym. dub.]

indu·lgence, n. Indulging (*in*, t. & i.); (also *self-i.*) habitual indulging of one's desires; privilege granted; *Declaration of I.*, proclamation of religious liberties, esp. those of Charles II in 1672 & of James II in 1687; (R.-C. Ch.) remission of punishment still due to sin after sacramental absolution. [f. L *indulgentia* (as prec., see -ENCE)]

indu·lgenced, a. (R.-C. Ch.). (Of prayers, material objects, &c.) procuring indulgence to the user. [-ED²]

indu·lt, n. Pope's licence for thing not sanctioned by common law of Church. [F, f. L *indultum*, neut. p.p. as INDULGE]

i·ndūrate, v.t. & i. Make, become, hard; make callous or unfeeling; become inveterate. Hence or cogn. **indurA·TION** n., **i·nduratIVE** a. [f. L IN¹(*durare* f. *durus* hard), see -ATE³]

indū·sium, n. (pl. *-ia*). Membranous shield covering fruit-cluster of fern; collection of hairs enclosing stigma of some flowers; case of larva. [L, = tunic, f. *induere* ENDUE]

indu·strial, a. & n. Of industries (*i. maintenance*, system by which each industry should provide for its own unemployed; *the i. revolution*, changes in the relation between employers & employed brought about in the late 18th & early 19th cc. esp. by mechanical inventions); *i. school,* one where neglected children are taught a trade besides ordinary subjects; (n.) one engaged in i. pursuits; (n. pl.) shares in joint-stock i. enterprise. Hence **indu·strial**ISM(3), **indu·strial**IST(3), nn., **indu·strial**IZE(3) v.t., **indu·strial**LY[2] adv. [as INDUSTRY, see -AL]

indu·strious, a. Diligent, hard-working. Hence **indu·strious**LY[2] adv. [f. L *industriosus* (as foll., see -OUS)]

i·ndustry, n. Diligence; habitual employment in useful work; branch of trade or manufacture. [f. L *industria,* etym. dub.]

indwe·ll, v.t. & i.(indwelt). (Usu. fig., of spirit, principle, &c.) inhabit, occupy; (intr.) be permanently present *in.* Hence **indwe·ll**ER[1] n. [IN prep.]

-ine[1], suf. of adjj., repr. L *-īnus,* w. sense 'pertaining to, of the nature of'; appearing in F as *-in* masc., *-ine* fem., in E formerly as *-in,* now usu. as *-ine* (*asinine, divine, marine, supine*); a previous suf. is sometimes blended, as in *clandestine, vespertine.* On model of proper names f. L, adjj. like *Florentine, Caroline,* are formed in E. Nat. Hist. forms adjj. on names of genera (*bovine, equine, caprine, feline*); these have (-īn) unstressed; others have (-īn) stressed or not (*divi·ne, A·lpine*), (-ĭn) unstressed (*fe·minine*), or (-ēn) stressed (*mari·ne*).

-ine[2], suf. of adjj., repr. L *-ĭnus* f. Gk *-ĭnos* in names of minerals, plants, &c. (*adamantine, hyacinthine*); also repr. orig. L *-īnus* (*pristine*). Normal pronunc. (-ĭn) is giving place to (-īn).

-ine[3], suf. forming fem. nn., repr. F *-ine* f. L *-īna* f. Gk *-īnē* (*heroine*). E represents in same way *-in* in G *markgräfin* &c. (*margravine*).

-ine[4], suf. of nn., repr. F *-ine* f. L *-īna* (*-inus*), orig. = -INE[1] used in L to form abstract nn. f. vbs (*rapina* rapine, *ruina* ruin), f. agent nouns (*disciplina, doctrina, medicina*), & f. other sources (*resina, urina*). L adjj. in *-inus, -ina,* were also used as nn. (*concubina, lupinus*), esp. in prop. names (*Antoninus, Agrippina*). For *-ina,* E has *-ine,* sometimes *-in* (*resin*); for *-inus,* E has *-in* (*Crispin, Justin*) or *-ine* (*lupine, Constantine*). E further forms (thr. F) names of derivative products (*dentine, brilliantine, nectarine*). Fem. names of Rom. orig. also often take *-ine* (-ĭn), as *Carolĭne, Cathar̆ine.*

-ine[5], suf. (chem.), offshoot of prec., in names of derived substances, orig. used unsystematically, & interchangeable with -IN; now confined to alkaloids & basic substances (*aconitine, cocaine, nicotine*) & (less freq.) Hofmann's names of hydrocarbons; also retained in the four elements *chlorine, fluorine, iodine, bromine.*

inē·briate[1] (*-at*), a. & n. Drunken; (n.) i. person, esp. habitual drunkard. [f. L IN[1](*ebriare*) f. *ebrius* drunk), see -ATE[2]]

inē·briāte[2], v.t. Make drunk, intoxicate (lit. & fig.). So **inebri**A·TION n. [as prec., -ATE[3]]

inēbrī·ety, n. (Habit of) drunkenness. [IN-[1]]

inĕ·dible, a. Not edible. Hence **inedi**BI·LITY n. [IN-[2]]

inĕ·dited, a. Not published; published without editorial alterations. [IN-[2]]

ine·ffable, a. Unutterable, too great for words. Hence **ine·ffab**LY[2] adv. [F, f. L IN[2](*effabilis* f. EF*fari* speak, utter, see -BLE)]

ineffa·ceable, a. That cannot be effaced. Hence **ineffaceа**BI·LITY n., **ineffa·ceab**LY[2] adv. [IN-[2]]

ineffe·ctive, a. Not producing the desired effect; (of person) inefficient; lacking artistic effect. Hence **ineffe·ctive**LY[2] adv., **ineffe·ctive**NESS n. [IN-[2]]

ineffe·ctual, a. Without effect, fruitless. Hence **ineffe·ctual**LY[2] adv., **ineffe·ctual**NESS n. [IN-[2]]

inefflca·cious, a. (Of remedy &c.) not efficacious. [IN-[2]]

ineffi·cient (-shnt), a. (Of person) not fully capable, not well qualified; ineffective. Hence **ineffi·ci**ENCY n., **ineffi·cient**LY[2] adv. [IN-[2]]

inela·stic, a. Not elastic; unadaptable, unyielding. Hence **inelăsti·**CITY n. [IN-[2]]

inĕ·legant, a. Ungraceful; unrefined; (of style) unpolished. Hence **ine·leg**ANCE n., **ine·legant**LY[2] adv. [f. F IN[2](*élégant* ELEGANT)]

inĕ·ligible, a. Not eligible (esp. of men unfit for military service). Hence **ineligi**BI·LITY n., **ine·ligib**LY[2] adv. [IN-[2]]

inelu·ctable, a. That cannot be escaped from. [f. L IN[2](*eluctabilis* f. E*luctari* struggle out, see -BLE)]

ine·pt, a. Out of place; absurd, silly. Hence or cogn. **ine·pti**TUDE, **ine·pt**NESS, nn., **ine·pt**LY[2] adv. [f. L IN[2](*eptus* = *aptus* APT)]

inequa·lity (-ŏl-), n. Want of equality in magnitude, quality, rank, circumstances, &c.; variableness; (of surface) irregularity; (Astr.) deviation from uniformity in motion of heavenly body. [f. OF *inequalité* f. med. L IN[2](*aequalitatem* EQUALITY)]

inēquilă·teral, a. Of unequal sides. [IN-[2]]

inĕ·quitable, a. Unfair, unjust. Hence **ine·quitab**LY[2] adv. [IN-[2]]

inĕ·quity, n. Unfairness. [IN-[2]]

inerā·dicable, a. That cannot be rooted out. Hence **inera·dicab**LY[2] adv. [IN-[2]]

inĕ·rrable, a. Not liable to err. Hence or cogn. **inerra**BI·LITY, **ine·rr**ANCY, nn., **ine·rrab**LY[2] adv., **ine·rr**ANT a. [f. L IN[2](*errabilis* f. *errare* ERR, see -BLE)]

iner·t, a. Without inherent power of action, motion, or resistance; without active chemical or other properties; sluggish, slow. Hence **iner·t**LY[2] adv., **iner·t**NESS n. [f. L IN[2](*ers -ertis* f. *ars* ART)]

iner·tia (-shĭa), n. (Physics) property of matter by which it continues in its existing state of rest or uniform motion in straight line, unless that state is changed by external force (also *vis inertiae* force of i.); inertness, sloth. [L, as prec.]

inesca·pable, a. Not to be escaped. [IN-[2]]

inesse·ntial, a. Not indispensable. [IN-[2]]

ine·stimable, a. Too great, intense, precious, &c., to be estimated. Hence **ine·stimab**LY[2] adv. [f. F IN[2](ESTIMABLE)]

inĕ·vitable, a. Unavoidable, sure to happen, esp. *the i.*; (colloq.) tiresomely familiar (*the i. Derby dog*); (Critics' slang, of character-drawing, development of plot, &c.) so true to nature &c. as to preclude alternative treatment or solution, convincing. Hence **inevitab**I·LITY, **ine·vitable**NESS, nn., **ine·vitab**LY[2] adv. [f. L IN[2](*evitabilis* f. E*vitare* avoid, see -BLE)]

inexa·ct, a. Not exact. Hence **inexa·cti**TUDE, **inexa·ct**NESS, nn., **inexa·ct**LY[2] adv. [IN-[2]]

inexcū·sable, a. (Of person, action, &c.) that cannot be justified. Hence **inexcu·sab**LY[2] adv. [f. L IN[2](*excusabilis* EXCUSABLE)]

inexe·cutable, a. That cannot be carried out. [IN-[2]]

inexhau·stible, a. That cannot be exhausted. Hence **inexhausti**BI·LITY n., **inexhau·stib**LY[2] adv. [IN-[2]]

ine·xorable, a. Relentless. Hence **inexora**BI·LITY n., **ine·xorab**LY[2] adv. [f. L IN[2](*exorabilis* f. EX*orare* entreat, -ABLE)]

inexpe·ctant, a. Not expectant. [IN-[2]]

inexpē·dient, a. Not expedient. Hence **inexpe·di**ENCY n. [IN-[2]]

inexpe·nsive, a. Cheap. Hence **inexpe·nsive**LY[2] adv., **inexpe·nsive**NESS n. [IN-[2]]

inexpēr·ience, n. Want of experience. So **inexpēr·ience**D[2] a. [f. F IN[2](*expérience* EXPERIENCE)]

inexper·t, a. Unskilled. Hence **inexper·t**LY[2] adv. [OF, f. L IN[2](*expertus* EXPERT)]

ine·xpiable, a. (Of offence) that cannot be expiated; (of resentment &c.) implacable. Hence **ine·xpiab**LY[2] adv. [f. L IN[2](*expiabilis* EXPIABLE)]

ine·xplicable, a. That cannot be explained or accounted for. Hence **inexplica**BI·LITY n., **ine·xplicab**LY[2] adv. [F, f. L IN[2](*explicabilis* EXPLICABLE)]

inexpli·cit, a. Not definitely or clearly expressed. Hence **inexpli·cit**LY[2] adv., **inexpli·cit**NESS n. [IN-[2]]

inexplō·sive, a. Not explosive. [IN-[2]]

inexpre·ssible, a. & n. That cannot be expressed in words; (n. pl., facet.) trousers. Hence **inexpre·ssib**LY[2] adv. [IN-[2]]

inexpre·ssive, a. Not expressive; (archaic) inexpressible. Hence **inexpre·ssive**LY[2] adv., **inexpre·ssive**NESS n. [IN-[2]]

inexpu·gnable, a. Impregnable, invincible, (lit. & fig.). [F, f. L IN[2](*expugnabilis* f. EX*pugnare* storm, see -BLE)]

inexte·nsible, a. Not extensible. [IN-[2]]

inexti·nguishable, a. Unquenchable (lit. & fig.). [IN-[2]]

ine·xtricable, a. (Of place, state, &c.) that cannot be escaped from; (of knot, problem &c.) that cannot be unravelled or solved. Hence **ine·xtricab**LY[2] adv. [f. L IN[2](*extricabilis* EXTRICABLE)]

infa·llibilism, n. Principle of the Pope's infallibility. So **infa·llibil**IST n. [-ISM]

infa·llible, a. Incapable of erring; (of method, test, proof, &c.) unfailing. Hence **infallib**I·LITY n. (esp. as attribute of the Pope speaking *ex cathedrâ,* decreed 1870 by the Vatican Council), **infa·llib**LY[2] adv. [f. med. L IN[2](*fallibilis* FALLIBLE)]

i·nfamize, v.t. Render infamous. [f. L IN[2](*famis* f. *fama* fame) infamous, see -IZE]

i·nfamous, a. Of ill fame, notoriously vile; abominable; (Law) deprived of all or some rights of citizen on account of i. crime. Hence or cogn. **i·nfamous**LY[2] adv., **i·nfam**Y[1] n. [f. med. L *infamosus* =L *infamis* (see prec.)]

i·nfancy, n. Early childhood, babyhood; (Law) minority (to end of one's 21st year); early stage of development. [f. L *infantia* (foll., -ANCY)]

i·nfant, n. Babe; child under 7 years of age; minor (under 21); *i.-school* (for children, usu. under 7). [f. OF *enfant* f. L IN[2](*fans -ntis* part. of *fari* speak)]

infa·nta, n. Daughter of king & queen of Spain or Portugal (usu. eldest daughter who is not heir to throne). So **infa·ntĕ** n. (second son). [Sp., Port., f. L as prec.]

infa·nticide, n. Murder of infant after birth, esp. with mother's consent; custom of killing new-born infants. Hence or cogn. **infa·nti**CIDE(1) n., **infa·nticī·d**AL a. [f. LL *infanticidium* (as INFANT, see -CIDE(2))]

i·nfantīle, a. Of, as of, infants (*i. paralysis,* a form of spinal meningitis); in its infancy. So **i·nfant**INE[1] a. [f. LL *infantilis* (INFANT, -IL)]

i·nfantry, n. Foot-soldiers; *mounted i.* (mounted for transit but fighting on foot); *infantryman* (-an), soldier of i. regiment. [f. F *infanterie* f. It. *infanteria* (*infante* youth, foot-soldier, as INFANT, see -ERY)]

infă·tuate, v.t. Affect (person) with extreme folly; inspire with extravagant passion. Hence **infa·tuated**LY[2] adv., **infatu**A·TION n. [f. L IN[1](*fatuare* f. *fatuus* foolish), see -ATE[3]]

infe·ct, v.t. Fill (air &c.) with noxious corruption or germs; affect (person, body, mind, *with* disease &c. lit. & fig.); imbue (person *with* opinion &c.). So **infe·ctive** a., **infe·ctiveness**, **infecti·vity**, nn. [f. L IN[1](*ficere fect-* =*facere* make) taint]

infe·ction, n. Communication of disease, esp. by agency of atmosphere or water (cf. CONTAGION); moral contamination; diffusive influence of example, sympathy, &c. [F, f. LL *infectionem* (as INFECT, see -ION)]

infe·ctious, a. Infecting with disease, pestilential; (of disease) liable to be transmitted by air or water (cf. CONTAGIOUS); (of emotions &c.) apt to spread, catching. Hence **infe·ctiously**[2] adv., **infe·ctiousness** n. [prec., -IOUS]

infelici·fic, a. Producing unhappiness. [IN-[2]]

infeli·citous, a. Not felicitous. [IN-[2]]

infeli·city, n. Unhappiness; misfortune; inaptness of expression &c. [f. L IN[2](*felicitas* FELICITY)]

infer·, v.t. (-rr-). Deduce, conclude, (thing, *that, when,* &c.; *from* fact &c.); imply. Hence **i·nferable** a. [f. L IN[1](*ferre* bring)]

i·nference, n. Inferring; thing inferred. Hence **infere·ntial** a., **infere·ntially**[2] adv. [f. med. L *inferentia* (as prec., see -ENCE)]

infēr·ior, a. & n. Situated below (*i.* LIMIT[1]); lower in rank, quality, &c. (*to,* or abs.); of poor quality; (of planets) whose orbit lies within that of the earth; (Bot., of calyx) below ovary, (of ovary) below calyx; (Print.) placed at bottom of ordinary letters (e.g. H_2, C_n); (n.) person i. to another esp. in rank (*kind to ii.*). Hence **inferio·rity** n. (*inferiority complex,* abnormal reactions, such as assertiveness or megalomania, from suppressed sense of inferiority), **infer·iorly**[2] adv. [L, comp. of *inferus* low]

infer·nal, a. Of hell; hellish, fiendish; (colloq.) abominable, confounded; *i. machine,* apparatus (usu. disguised) for producing explosion destructive of life or property. Hence **inferna·lity** n., **infer·nally**[2] adv. [F, f. L *infernalis* (*infernus* situated below, see -AL)]

infer·no, n. Hell (esp. w. reference to Dante's *Divine Comedy*); scene of horror. (It., f. L *infernus,* see prec.]

infer·rable, a. =INFERABLE.

infer·tile, a. Not fertile. So **inferti·lity** n. [F, f. LL IN[2](*fertilis* FERTILE)]

infe·st, v.t. (Of vermin, pirates, diseases, &c.) haunt, swarm in or about, (place). So **infesta·tion** n. [f. L *infestare* assail (*infestus* hostile)]

infeuda·tion, n. Enfeoffment; *i. of tithes,* granting of tithes to laymen. [f. med. L *infeudatio* f. IN[1](*feudare* f. *feudum* fee), see -ATION]

infibula·tion, n. Fastening of sexual organs with clasp to prevent copulation. [f. rare *infibulate* v. f. L IN[1](*fibulare* f. FIBULA), -ATION]

i·nfidel (-dl), n. & a. Disbeliever in religion; (Hist.) adherent of religion opposed to Christianity; (from Jewish or Mohammedan point of view) disbeliever in the true religion; (gen.) unbeliever, (adj.) unbelieving, of unbelievers. Hence **i·nfidelize**(3) v.t. & i. [f. OF *infidèle* f. L IN[2](*fidelis* faithful f. *fides* faith)]

infidě·lity, n. Disbelief in Christianity; disloyalty, esp. (also *conjugal i.*) to husband or wife. [f. L *infidelitas* (as prec., see -TY)]

i·nfield, n. Farm land around or near homestead; arable land; land regularly manured & cropped. [IN[3]]

i·nfigh·ting, n. Boxing at closer quarters than arm's length. [IN[2]]

infi·ltrate, v.t. & i. Introduce (fluid) by filtration (*into, through*); permeate (t. & i.) by filtration. Hence **infiltra·tion** n. (esp., Mil. & Pol., gradual unobserved occupation of ground or territory by detached parties or settlers). [IN-[1]]

i·nfinite, a. & n. Boundless, endless; very great; (w. pl. noun) innumerable, very many; (Gram., of verb parts) not limited by person or number, e.g. infinitive, gerund, supine (cf. FINITE); (n.) *the I.,* God, *the i.,* i. space. Hence **i·nfinitely**[2] adv. [f. L IN[2](*finitus* FINITE)]

infinitě·simal, a. & n. Infinitely or very small (amount); *i. calculus,* the differential & integral calculuses conceived as one. Hence **infinite·simally**[2] adv. [as prec. on CENTESIMAL &c.]

infi·nitive, a. & n. (gram.). (Verb-form) that expresses the verbal notion without predicating it of any subject (e.g. *see, to see*). Hence **infiniti·val** a. [f. L IN[2](*finitivus* f. *finire -it-* define, see -IVE)]

infi·nitude, n. Boundlessness; boundless number or extent (*of*). [as INFINITE, -TUDE]

infi·nity, n. =prec.; (Math.) infinite quantity (symbol: ∞). [f. F *infinité* f. L *infinitas* (as INFINITE, see -TY)]

infir·m, a. Physically weak, esp. through age; (of person, mind, judgement, &c.) weak, irresolute (often *i. of purpose*). Hence **infir·mity** n., **infir·mly**[2] adv. [f. L IN[2](*firmus* FIRM)]

infir·mary, n. Hospital; sick-quarters in school, workhouse, &c. [f. med. L *infirmaria* (as prec., see -ARY[1])]

infi·x[1], v.t. Fix (thing *in* another); impress (fact &c. *in* mind); (Gram.) insert (formative element) in body of word. [IN adv.]

i·nfix[2], n. (gram.). Modifying element infixed in word. [IN-[1], after *prefix, suffix*]

infla·me, v.t. & i. Set ablaze; light up (as) with flame; excite passionately (*-ed with, by*); raise (body, blood, &c.) to morbid heat; aggravate; catch fire; become excited; become morbidly inflamed. [f. OF *enflammer* f. L IN[1](*flammare* f. *flamma* flame)]

infla·mmable, a. & n. Easily set on fire; easily excited; (n.) i. substance. Hence **inflammab**ɪ·ʟɪᴛʏ, **infla·mmable**ɴᴇss, nn. [f. L as prec., see -ʙʟᴇ]

inflamma·tion, n. Inflaming (lit. & fig.); morbid process affecting a part of the body with heat, swelling, pain, & redness. [f. L *inflammatio* (as prec., see -ᴀᴛɪᴏɴ)]

infla·mmatory, a. Tending to inflame with desire or passion (usu. in bad sense); of, tending to, inflammation of the body. [f. L as ɪɴғʟᴀᴍᴇ, see -ᴏʀʏ]

infla·te, v.t. Distend with air or gas; puff up (person *with* pride &c.); (Finance) resort to inflation of (the currency, or abs.); raise (price) artificially; (p.p., of language) bombastic. So **infla·t**ɪᴏɴ n. (in vbl senses, & esp.) abnormal increase of the currency, e.g. by the issue of inconvertible legal-tender notes; **infla·t**ᴏʀ[2] n. [f. L ɪɴ[1](*flare* blow), see -ᴀᴛᴇ[3]]

infle·ct, v.t. Bend inwards, curve; (Gram.) vary termination of (word) to express grammatical relation; (Mus.) flatten, sharpen, (note) by a chromatic semitone. [f. L ɪɴ[1](*flectere flex-* bend)]

inflection, = ɪɴғʟᴇxɪᴏɴ.

infle·ctive, a. (gram.). Of inflexion. [-ɪᴠᴇ]

infle·xible, a. Unbendable; (fig.) unbending, rigid. Hence **inflexi**ʙɪ·ʟɪᴛʏ n., **infle·xib**ʟʏ[2] adv. [f. L ɪɴ[2](*flexibilis* ғʟᴇxɪʙʟᴇ)]

infle·xion, n. Inflecting; inflected form of word; suffix &c. used to inflect; modulation of voice; (Geom.) change of curve from convex to concave. Hence **infle·xion**ᴀʟ, **infle·xion**ʟᴇss, aa. [f. L *inflexio* (as ɪɴғʟᴇᴄᴛ, see -ɪᴏɴ)]

infli·ct, v.t. Lay on (stroke, wound, *upon*); impose (suffering, penalty, one*self*, one's company, &c., *upon*). Hence or cogn. **infli·ct**ᴀʙʟᴇ a., **infli·ct**ɪᴏɴ n. (esp., troublesome or boring experience), **infli·ct**ᴏʀ[2] n. [f. L ɪɴ[1](*fligere flict-* dash)]

inflore·scence, n. (bot.). Arrangement of flowers of plant in relation to axis & to each other; collective flower of plant; flowering (also fig.). [f. L ɪɴ[1](*florescere* come into flower f. *flos floris*), see -ᴇsᴄᴇɴᴛ, -ᴇɴᴄᴇ]

i·nflow, n. Flowing in. So **i·nflow**ɪɴɢ[1, 2] n. & a. [ɪɴ adv.]

i·nfluence, n., & v.t. (Astrol.) flowing from stars of ethereal fluid affecting character & destiny of man (also fig. of personal power); action insensibly exercised (*upon*); ᴜɴᴅᴜᴇ *i.*, see ᴜɴ-[2](1); ascendancy, moral power, (*over, with,* person &c.); thing, person, exercising (usu. non-material) power; (Electr.) = ɪɴᴅᴜᴄᴛɪᴏɴ; (v.t.) exert i. upon, have effect upon. [(vb f. n.) F, f. LL *influentia* f. L ɪɴ[1](*fluere* flow), see -ᴇɴᴄᴇ]

i·nfluent, a. & n. Flowing in (lit. & fig.); (n.) tributary stream. [f. L as prec., see -ᴇɴᴛ]

influe·ntial, a. Having great influence. Hence **influe·ntial**ʟʏ[2] adv. [ɪɴғʟᴜᴇɴᴄᴇ, -ᴀʟ]

influe·nza, n. Contagious febrile disorder, usu. with rapid prostration & severe catarrh; (also *i. cold*) severe catarrh; (fig.) mental or commercial epidemic. [It., as ɪɴғʟᴜᴇɴᴄᴇ]

i·nflux, n. Flowing in, esp. of stream &c. (*into* river &c.), or of persons or things (*into* place &c.). [f. LL ɪɴ[1](*fluxus* ғʟᴜx)]

infor·m, v.t. & i. Inspire, imbue, (person, heart, thing, *with* feeling, principle. quality, &c.); tell (person *of* thing, *that, how,* &c.), so **infor·m**ᴀɴᴛ n.; bring charge (*against* person). [f. OF *enformer* f. L ɪɴ[1](*formare* f. *forma* form) give shape to, fashion]

infor·mal, a. Not according to due form; without formality. Hence **informa·l**ɪᴛʏ n., **infor·mal**ʟʏ[2] adv. [ɪɴ-[2]]

informa·tion, n. Informing, telling; thing told, knowledge, items of knowledge, news, (*on, about*); (Law) charge, complaint, lodged with court or magistrate (*against*). Hence **informa·tion**ᴀʟ a. [f. OF *enformacion* f. L *informationem* (as ɪɴғᴏʀᴍ, see -ᴀᴛɪᴏɴ)]

infor·mative, a. Giving information, instructive. So **infor·mat**ᴏʀʏ a. [-ᴀᴛɪᴠᴇ]

infor·med, a. Instructed, knowing the facts, educated, intelligent, esp. *well, ill, -i.* [-ᴇᴅ[1]]

infor·mer, n. One who informs against another, esp. (also *common i.*) one who makes it his business to detect offenders and lay information against them. [-ᴇʀ[1]]

i·nfra (-*a*), adv. (abbr. *inf.*) Below, lower down, further on, (in book), as *vide i.*, see below. [L, = below]

infra- in comb. = L *infra* below; used esp. in anat. terms in sense 'below, under, some part', as *-re·nal, -sca·pular, -ster·nal,* beneath the kidneys, shoulder-blade, breast-bone.

infra·ction, n. Violation, infringement. [f. L *infractio* (as ɪɴғʀɪɴɢᴇ, see -ɪᴏɴ)]

i·nfra dig., pred. a. Beneath one's dignity, unbecoming. [abbr. L *infra dignitatem*]

i·nfralapsār·ian, n. & a. Calvinist who held that God's election of some was consequent to his prescience of the Fall, or that it contemplated man as already fallen (cf. sᴜʙʟᴀᴘsᴀʀɪᴀɴ, sᴜᴘʀᴀʟᴀᴘsᴀʀɪᴀɴ); (adj.) of these views. [f. ɪɴғʀᴀ- + L *lapsus* fall + -ᴀʀɪᴀɴ]

infrē·quent, a. Not frequent. Hence or cogn. **infre·qu**ᴇɴᴄʏ n., **infre·quent**ʟʏ[2] adv. [f. L ɪɴ[2](*frequens* ғʀᴇǫᴜᴇɴᴛ)]

infri·nge (-j), v.t. Transgress, violate, (law, oath, &c.). Hence **infri·nge**ᴍᴇɴᴛ n. [f. L ɪɴ[1](*fringere fract-* = *frangere* break)]

infru·ctuous, a. Unfruitful; (fig.) fruitless. [ɪɴ-[2] + ғʀᴜᴄᴛᴜᴏᴜs]

infundi·bular, a. Funnel-shaped. [f. L *infundibulum* funnel (used in E of parts of body) f. ɪɴ[1](*fundere* pour)]

infŭr·iate, v.t. Fill with fury, enrage. [f. med. L IN[1](*furiare* f. *furia* FURY), see -ATE[3]]

infu·se (-z), v.t. & i. Pour (thing *into*); (fig.) instil (grace, spirit, life, &c., *into*); steep (herb, tea, &c.) in liquid to extract its soluble properties, whence **infu·**SER[1] (2) n.; (v.i.) undergo infusion (*let it i. for five minutes*). [f. L IN[1](*fundere fus-* pour)]

infu·sible (-z-), a. That cannot be fused or melted. Hence **infusi**BI·LITY n. [IN-[2]]

infu·sion (-zhn), n. Infusing (lit. & fig.); liquid extract thus obtained; infused element, admixture. [f. L *infusio* (as INFUSE, see -ION)]

infusor·ia (-s-), n. pl. Class of protozoa found in infusions of decaying animal or vegetable matter. Hence **infusor·**IAL a., **infusor·**IAN, **infu·**SORY, aa. & nn. [mod. L (INFUSE, -ORY)]

-ing[1], suf. forming vbl nn., OE *-ung, -ing*, f. OTeut. *-unga*. *-ing* orig. formed mere nn. of action (*asking*), but came in ME to acquire partly vbl (gerundial) character, being qualified by adv. (*the habit of speaking loosely*) or governing an object (*the idea of building him a house*). This use, peculiar to E, led to introduction of perf., fut., & pass. forms (*having killed, being killed*). The substantival nature of *-ing* is marked by the possess. case or adj. that often precedes it (*after John's behaving so badly, upon my granting the request*); but mod. tendency is to drop the possess. sign exc. with pronn. or single nn. Meanings: (1) vbl action (*bicycling, forebodings*), esp. as occupation (*banking*) or as inflicted (*thrashing*), also perh. f. nn. (*soldiering*); (2) thing produced by vbl action (*carving, filings, building*); (3) material for (*sacking*), whether f. n. or vb (*fencing* = what fences or serves as fence); (4) what is used to do vbl action (*binding*, dentist's *filling*); (5) what is to be operated on (*washing, darning*); (6) set or arrangement of (*colouring, feathering*).

-ing[2], suf. of pres. part. (often used as adj., as *charming*, sometimes as prep. or adv., as *during*). OE *-ende* (cf. OHG *-anti*, L *-ent-*, Gk *-ont-*, Skr. *-ant-*) was weakened to *-inde* & thus confused with *-inge* -ING[1], which became the regular form in 14th c. As result of the confusion, some constructions gerundial in orig. now appear participial, as *he went hunting* (i.e. on hunting, vbl n.), *the ark was building* (on building). On the other hand, some wds in *-ing* that might be explained as attrib. nouns in -ING[1] are perh. better regarded as quasi-pass. participles (*washing* tie, *cooking* apple, *breech-loading* gun). Compds are formed with advv. & adjj. (*well-meaning, fair-seeeming*; for stress cf. -ED[2]), & with objective nn. (*cheese-paring heart-breaking*; stressed on first component).

-ing[3], suf. (*-ing, -ung*, in other Teut. langg.) forming nn. w. sense 'one belonging to', 'one having the quality of'; also used as patronymic & dim. Exx.: *Atheling, king, shilling, farthing, Riding, gelding, herring, whiting.*

i·ngathering, n. Gathering in, harvest.

inge·minate (-j-), v.t. Repeat, reiterate, (esp. *i. peace*, constantly urge it). [f. L IN[1](*geminare* f. *geminus* twin)]

ingē·nious (-j-), a. Clever at contriving; cleverly contrived. Hence **inge·nious**LY[2] adv. [f. L *ingeniosus* (*ingenium* cleverness, see -OUS)]

ingénue (F), n. Artless girl, esp. as stage type.

ingenū·ity, n. Skill in contriving. [f. L *ingenuitas* ingenuousness (as foll., see -TY); E meaning by confusion of INGENIOUS w. foll.]

ingĕ·nuous (-j-), a. Open, frank; innocent, artless. Hence **inge·nuous**LY[2] adv., **inge·nuous**NESS n. [f. L IN[1](*genuus* f. *gen-* beget) free-born, frank]

inge·st (-j-), v.t. Take in (food) to the stomach. So **inge·st**ION n., **inge·st**IVE a. [f. L IN[1](*gerere gest-* carry)]

i·ngle, n. Fire burning on hearth; *i.-nook*, chimney-corner. [Sc.; etym. dub.]

inglor·ious, a. Shameful, ignominious; obscure. Hence **inglor·ious**LY[2] adv. [f. L IN[2](*gloriosus* GLORIOUS)]

i·ngōing, a. & n. Going in.

ingot (ĭ·nggot), n. Mass (usu. oblong) of cast metal, esp. of gold, silver, or steel. [perh. f. IN adv. + *goten* p.p. of OE *geótan* cast]

ingrain (ĭ·n- before noun, -grā·n after n. or in pred.), a. Dyed in grain; inherent, inveterate, ingrained. [orig. two wds]

ingrained (as prec.), a. Deeply rooted, inveterate; thorough. Hence **ingrai·nĕd**LY[2] adv. [prob. var. of *engrained*]

ingra·te, a. & n. (archaic). Ungrateful; ungrateful person. [f. L IN[2](*gratus* grateful)]

ingrā·tiate (-shĭ-), v.t. Bring one*self* into favour *with*. Hence **ingra·tiating**LY[2] adv. [prob. f. 16th-c. It. *ingratiare* f. L *in gratiam* into favour, see -ATE[3]]

ingră·titude, n. Want of gratitude. [F, f. LL *ingratitudo* (as INGRATE, see -TUDE)]

ingrave·scent, a. (med.). (Of disease &c.) growing worse. So **ingrave·**SCENCE n. [f. L IN[1](*gravescere* f. *gravis* heavy), see -ENT]

ingrē·dient, n. Component part, element, in a mixture. [f. L IN[1](*gredi gress-* = *gradi* step) enter, see -ENT]

i·ngress, n. Going in; right of entrance. [f. L *ingressus -ūs* (as prec.)]

i·ngrowing, a. Growing inwards, esp. (of nail) growing into the flesh. So **i·ngrowth** n. [IN adv.]

i·nguinal (-gw-), a. Of the groin. [f. L *inguinalis* (*inguen -inis* groin, see -AL)]

ingur·gitate (-jĭ-), v.t. Swallow greedily; (fig.) engulf. So **ingurgit**A·TION n. [f. L

IN[1](*gurgitare* f. *gurges -itis* whirlpool), see -ATE[3]]

inhă·bit, v.t. (Of men or animals) dwell in, occupy, (region, town, house; also fig.). Hence or cogn. **inha·bit**ABLE, a., **inha·bit**ANT, **inhabit**A·TION, nn. [f. OF *enhabiter,* f. L IN(*habitare* dwell, see HABIT)]

inha·bitancy, n. Residence as inhabitant, esp. during specified period, so as to acquire rights &c. [-ANCY]

inha·le, v.t. Breathe in (air, gas, &c., or abs.), take (esp. tobacco-smoke or abs. of this) into the lungs (also fig.). Hence **inhal**A·TION, **inha·l**ER[1](2), nn. [f. L IN[1](*halare* breathe)]

inharmŏ·nic, a. Not harmonic. [IN-[2]]

inharmō·nious, a. Not harmonious. Hence **inharmo·nious**LY[2] adv. [IN-[2]]

inhere·, v.i. (Of qualities &c.) exist, abide, *in*; (of rights &c.) be vested *in* (person &c.). So **inhēr·**ENCE n., **inhēr·**ENT a., **inhēr·ent**LY[2] adv. [f. L IN[1](*haerēre haes-* stick)]

inhĕ·rit, v.t. Receive (property, rank, title) by legal descent or succession; derive (quality, character) from one's progenitors; (abs.) succeed as heir. Hence **inhe·rit**OR[2], **inhe·rit**RESS[1], **inhe·rit**RIX, nn. [f. OF EN(*heriter* put in possession as heir f. LL *hereditare* f. *heres -edis* heir)]

inhe·ritable, a. Capable of inheriting or of being inherited (lit. & fig.). Hence **inheritab**I·LITY n. [AF (as prec., see -ABLE)]

inhe·ritance, n. Inheriting; what is inherited (lit. & fig.). [f. AF *enheritance* (as prec., see -ANCE)]

inhē·sion (-zhn), n. Inhering. [f. LL *inhaesio* (as INHERE, see -ION)]

inhĭ·bit, v.t. Forbid, prohibit, (person &c. *from doing*; esp. in Eccl. Law); forbid (ecclesiastic) to exercise clerical functions; hinder, restrain, (action, process). So **inhibi·t**ION n., (in vbl senses, & esp., Psychol.) instinctive or induced habitual shrinking from some action as a thing forbidden; **inhi·bit**ORY a. [f. L IN[1](*hibēre hibit- =habēre* hold)]

inho·spitable, a. Not hospitable; (of region, coast, &c.) not affording shelter &c. Hence **inho·spitable**NESS n., **inho·spitab**LY[2] adv. [OF (IN-[2])]

inhospita·lity, n. Being inhospitable. [f. L IN[2](*hospitalitas* HOSPITALITY)]

inhū·man, a. (Of person or conduct) brutal, unfeeling, barbarous, so **inhumă·n**ITY n., **inhū·man**LY[2] adv.; not of the ordinary human type. [f. L IN[2](*humanus* HUMAN)]

inhu·me, v.t. Bury. Hence **inhum**A·TION n. [f. L IN[1](*humare* f. *humus* ground)]

inĭ·mical, a. Hostile (*to*); harmful (*to*). Hence **ini·mical**LY[2] adv. [f. LL *inimicalis* f. IN[2](*imicus =amicus* friend), see -AL]

inĭ·mitable, a. That defies imitation. Hence **ini·mitable**NESS n., **ini·mitab**LY[2] adv. [f. L IN[2](*imitabilis* IMITABLE)]

inĭ·quity, n. Unrighteousness, wickedness; gross injustice. Hence **ini·quit**OUS a., **ini·quitous**LY[2] adv. [f. OF *iniquité* f. L *iniquitatem* f. IN[2](*iquus =aequus* just), see -TY]

inĭ·tial (-shl), a. & n., & v.t. (-ll-). Of, existing or occurring at, the beginning, as *i. stage, expenses, difficulties*; *i. letter* (standing at beginning of word), esp. (n. pl.) first letters of person's name & surname; (v.t.) mark, sign, with ii. Hence **ini·tial**LY[2] adv. [(vb f. n.) f. L *initialis* f. *initium* f. IN[1](*ire it-* go), see -AL]

inĭ·tiāte[1] (-shĭ-), v.t. Begin, set going, originate; admit (person), esp. with introductory rites or forms, (*into* society, office, secret, *in* mysteries, science, &c.). So **initi**A·TION, **ini·tiāt**OR, **ini·tia**TRIX, nn., **ini·tiat**ORY (-sha-) a. [f. L *initiare* (as INITIAL), see -ATE[3]]

ini·tiate[2] (-at), a. & n. (Person) who has been initiated. [as prec., see -ATE[2]]

ini·tiative (-shya-), n. & a. First step, origination; *take the i.*, take the lead (*in doing*); *have the* (power, right, to take the) *i.*, (Mil.) be able to make enemy conform to one's movements; right of citizen(s) outside legislature to originate legislation (as in Switzerland); (adj.) beginning, originating. [(as noun, f. F) as prec., see -IVE]

inĭ·tio (-shĭō), adv. At the beginning (in reference to passage in book &c.; abbr. *init.*). [L]

inje·ct, v.t. Drive, force, (fluid, medicine, *into* cavity &c.) as by syringe; fill (cavity &c. *with*) by injecting. Hence **inje·ct**OR[2] n. [f. L IN[1](*jicĕre ject- =jacĕre* throw)]

inje·ction, n. Injecting; liquid or solution injected; *i.-engine*, one in which steam is condensed by injection of jet of cold water. [f. L *injectio* (as prec., see -ION)]

injudi·cious (-shus), a. Unwise, ill-judged. Hence **injudi·cious**LY[2] adv., **injudi·cious**NESS n. [IN-[2]]

inju·nction, n. Authoritative admonition or order; judicial process restraining person from wrongful act or compelling restitution &c. to injured party, whence **inju·nct** v.t. (colloq.). [f. LL *injunctio* f. *injungere* ENJOIN, see -ION]

i·njure (-jer), v.t. Do wrong to; hurt, harm, impair. [back formation f. INJURY]

i·njured, a. Wronged; showing sense of wrong, offended, as *in an i. voice.* [p.p. of prec.]

injur·ious (-oor-), a. Wrongful; (of language) insulting, calumnious; hurtful. Hence **injur·ious**LY[2] adv., **injur·ious**NESS n. [f. F *injurieux* f. L *injuriosus* (as foll., see -OUS)]

i·njury, n. Wrongful action or treatment; harm, damage. [f. L IN[2](*juria* f. *jus juris* right) wrong]

inju·stice, n. Want of equity, unfairness; unjust act; *you do him an i.* (judge him unfairly). [F, f. L IN[2](*justitia* JUSTICE)]

ink, n., & v.t. Fluid (black, red, &c.) for writing with pen; MARKING-*i.*; (*printer's i.*) viscous paste similarly used in printing; black liquid ejected by cuttle-fish &c. from bladder (*i.-bag*) to assist its escape; *i.-bottle, -pot* (for holding i.); *i.-horn,* small vessel of horn formerly used for holding i.; *i.-pad* (for inking rubber stamp &c.); *inkstand,* stand for one or more i.-bottles, often with pen-tray &c.; *i.-well* (pot fitted into hole in desk); (v.t.) mark (*in, over,* &c.) with i., cover (types &c.) with i. so as to print from them. Hence **i·nki**NESS n., **i·nk**LESS, **i·nk**Y², aa. [(vb f. n.) f. OF *enque* f. LL *encau·stum* f. Gk *e·gkauston* (as ENCAUSTIC) purple ink used by Roman emperors for signature; It. *inchiostro* follows L accent]

i·nker, n. Telegraph instrument recording message in ink; (Print. &c.) inking-roller. [-ER¹]

i·nkling, n. Hint, slight knowledge or suspicion, (*of*). [f. obs. or dial. *inkle* hint, get a notion of, etym. dub.]

i·nland (-*a*nd, -ănd), n., a., & adv. Interior of country; placed in this, remote from sea or border; carried on within limits of a country, as *i. trade, i. duty* (on i. trade), *i. revenue* (consisting of taxes & i. duties); (adv.) in, towards, the interior. Hence **i·nland**ER¹(4) n., **inla·nd**ISH¹ a. [IN³]

inlay·¹, v.t. (*inlaid*). Embed (thing *in* another) so that their surfaces are even; ornament (thing with another inlaid); insert (page, plate, cut) in space cut in larger stouter page. [IN²]

i·nlay² (*or* ĭnlā·), n. Inlaid work. [f. prec.]

i·nlet, n. Small arm of sea, creek; piece inserted. [IN adv. + LET v.]

i·nlier, n. (geol.). Underlying formation completely covered by overlying one. [IN adv.]

i·nly, adv. (poet.). Inwardly, in the heart; intimately. [OE *innlice* (IN¹, see -LY²)]

i·nlȳing, a. Lying inside. [IN adv.]

i·nmate, n. Occupant (*of* house &c.), esp. one of several. [IN adv.]

i·nmōst (*or* -*o*st), a. Most inward; (fig.) deepest, most intimate. [OE *innemest* (IN adv., see -MOST)]

inn, n. Public house for lodging &c. of travellers; *innkeeper,* one who keeps an i.; *Ii. of Court,* (buildings in London belonging to) four legal societies having exclusive right of admitting persons to practise at bar (*Inner Temple, Middle Temple, Lincoln's I., Gray's I.*); *Ii. of Chancery,* buildings in London formerly used for residence of law students, societies occupying these. [OE, f. IN adv.]

inna·te (*or* ĭ·n-), a. Inborn, natural. Hence **inna·te**LY² adv., **inna·te**NESS n. [f. LL IN¹(*natus* p.p. of *nasci* be born)]

innă·vigable, a. Not navigable. [f. L IN²(*navigabilis* NAVIGABLE)]

i·nner, a. & n. Interior, internal; *the i. man,* man's soul or mind, (facet.) stomach, as *refreshed his i. man*; (n.) division of target next outside bull's-eye, shot that strikes this. Hence **i·nner**MOST a. [OE *innera* a., compar. of IN²]

inner·vate, v.t. Supply (organ &c.) with nerve-force or nerves. Hence **innerva·**TION n. [f. IN-¹ + NERVE + -ATE³]

i·nnings, n. (pl. same, colloq. -*es*). (Cricket &c.) portion of game played by either side while in or batting, play of one batsman during his turn; (fig.) tenure of office, dominance, of political party, cause, &c. [orig. pl.; f. IN adv. + -ING¹]

i·nnocent, a. & n. Free from moral wrong, sinless; not guilty (*of* crime &c.); (colloq.) *windows i. of* (without) *glass*; simple, guileless; harmless. (N.) i. person, esp. young child; *Innocents' Day,* Dec. 28, festival of the slaughter of children by Herod (*Matt.* ii. 16); (Parl. slang) *massacre of the ii.,* sacrifice of measures at end of session for want of time; simple person; idiot. Hence or cogn. **i·nnoc**ENCE, -ENCY (rare), nn., **i·nnocent**LY² adv. [F, f. L IN²(*nocentem* part. of *nocēre* hurt)]

innŏ·cūous, a. Not injurious, harmless (esp. of snakes). Hence **innocū·**ITY, **inno·cuous**NESS, nn., **inno·cuous**LY² adv. [f. L IN²(*nocuus* as prec.) + -OUS]

innŏ·minate (-*a*t), a. Unnamed; (Anat.) *i. bone,* hip-bone (made up of three original bones). [f. L IN²(*nominatus,* as NOMINATE)]

i·nnovate, v.i. Bring in novelties; make changes *in.* Hence or cogn. **innova·**TION, **i·nnovat**OR², nn., **i·nnovat**ORY a. [f. L IN¹(*novare* make new f. *novus*), see -ATE³]

inno·xious, a. Harmless. Hence **inno·xious**LY² adv., **inno·xious**NESS n. [f. L IN²(*noxius* NOXIOUS)]

innuĕ·ndo, n. (pl. -*oes*), & v.i. Oblique hint, allusive remark (usu. depreciatory); (v.i.) make ii. [(vb f. n.) L, gerund of IN¹(*nuere* nod), = by nodding, i.e. by way of explanation, as 'he, innuendo the plaintiff')]

innū·merable, a. Countless. [f. L IN²(*numerabilis* NUMERABLE)]

innutri·tion, n. Lack of nutrition. [IN-²]

innutri·tious, a. Not nourishing. [IN-²]

inobser·vance, n. Inattention; non-observance (*of* law &c.). [F, f. L IN²(*observantia* OBSERVANCE)]

inoccupa·tion, n. Want of occupation. [IN-²]

inŏ·culate, v.t. Impregnate (person, animal, *with* virus or germs of disease) to induce milder form of it & so safeguard person against its attacks; implant (disease &c.) thus (*on, into,* person &c.); insert (bud, scion) in plant, treat (plant) thus. Hence or cogn. **inocula·**TION, **ino·culat**OR², nn., **ino·culat**IVE a. [f. L IN¹(*oculare* f. *oculus* eye, bud) engraft, see -ATE³]

inō·dorous, a. Having no odour. [f. L IN²(*odorus* ODOROUS)]

inoffe·nsive, a. Unoffending; not objectionable. Hence **inoffe·nsive**LY[2] adv., **inoffe·nsive**NESS n. [IN-[2]]

inoffi·cious, a. Without office or function; (Law) not in accordance with moral duty. [f. L IN[2](*officiosus* dutiful, see OFFICIOUS)]

inŏ·perative, a. Not working or taking effect. [IN-[2]]

ino·pportūne, a. Unseasonable. Hence **ino·pportune**LY[2] adv., **ino·pportune**NESS n. [f. LL IN[2](*opportunus* OPPORTUNE)]

inor·dinate (-*at*), a. Immoderate, excessive; intemperate; disorderly. Hence **inor·dinate**LY[2] adv. [f. L IN[2](*ordinatus* p.p. of *ordinare* f. *ordo -dinis* order)]

inorga·nic, a. Having no organized physical structure; (Chem., of compounds &c.) not entering into composition of organized bodies; *i. chemistry,* that of mineral substances; not arising by natural growth, extraneous. [IN-[2]]

inorganiza·tion, n. Lack of organization. [IN-[2]]

inorna·te, a. Not ornate. [IN-[2]]

ino·sculate, v.i. & t. (Of blood-vessels &c.) join, have terminal connexion, (*with*); (of fibres &c.) unite closely, be interwoven; (trans.) unite (fibres &c.) closely. Hence **inoscul**A·TION n. [f. IN-[1] + L *osculare* furnish with mouth (*osculum* dim. of *os* mouth), -ATE[3]]

i·npouring, a. & n. Pouring in.

i·nquest, n. Legal or judicial inquiry to ascertain matter of fact; =CORONER'S *i.*; *great, last, i.,* last Judgement; coroner's jury; *grand i.,* grand jury (*g.i. of the nation,* House of Commons). [f. OF *enqueste* f. med. L *inquesta* as INQUIRE]

inquī·etude, n. Uneasiness of mind or body. [f. LL (-*do*) f. IN[2](*quietus* QUIET), -TUDE]

inquire·, en-, v.i. & t. Make search (*into* matter); seek information (*of* person, *about, after,* thing &c.); *i. after, for, him* (how he is); ask *for* (goods in shop &c.); ask to be told (person's name, business, &c., *whether, how,* &c.). Hence **inquīr·ing**LY[2] adv. [ME *enquere* f. OF *enquerre* f. com.-Rom. *inquerere -quest-* = L IN[1](*quirere quisit-* =*quaerere* seek); wholly (*in-*) or partly (*en-*) refash. on L]

inquīr·y, en-, n. Asking; question; investigation; *make ii.,* ask (*about* &c.); *court of i.* (investigating charge against officer or soldier). [f. prec. + -Y[4]]

inquisi·tion (-z-), n. Search, investigation; judicial or official inquiry; (Rom. Cath.) *the I.,* ecclesiastical tribunal for suppression of heresy, the Holy Office. Hence **inquisi·tion**AL a. [OF, f. L *inquisitionem* (as INQUIRE, see -ION)]

inquĭ·sitive (-z-), a. Inquiring, curious; prying. Hence **inqui·sitive**LY[2] adv., **inqui·sitive**NESS n. [OF (-*if, -ive*), f. LL *inquisitivus* (as prec., see -IVE)]

inquĭ·sitor (-z-), n. Official investigator; officer of the Inquisition; *Grand I.,* director of court of Inquisition in some countries; *I. General,* head of this in Spain. [f. OF *inquisiteur* f. L *inquisitorem* (as INQUIRE, see -OR[2])]

inquisitor·ial, a. Of, like, an inquisitor; offensively prying. Hence **inquisitor·ial**LY[2] adv. [f. med. L *inquisitorius* (as prec., see -ORY) + -AL]

i·nroad, n. Hostile incursion, raid; (fig.) forcible encroachment. [IN adv. + ROAD n. in sense ' riding ']

i·nrush, n. Rushing in. [IN adv.]

insă·līvate, v.t. Mix (food) with saliva. Hence **insaliv**A·TION n. [f. IN-[1] + SALIVA + -ATE[3]]

insalu·brious, a. (Of climate or place) unhealthy. So **insalu·br**ITY n. [f. L IN[2](*salubris* SALUBRIOUS)]

insa·ne, a. Mad; senseless; *i. asylum* (for i. persons). Hence or cogn. **insa·ne**LY[2] adv., **insă·n**ITY n. [f. L IN[2](*sanus* SANE)]

insă·nitary, a. Not sanitary. [IN-[2]]

insā·tiable (-sh*a*-), a. That cannot be satisfied; inordinately greedy (*of*). Hence **insatia**BI·LITY n., **insa·tiab**LY[2] adv. [f. L IN[2](*satiabilis,* as SATIATE, see -BLE)]

insa·tiate (-shy*at*), a. Never satisfied. [f. L IN[2](*satiatus,* as prec.)]

inscri·be, v.t. Write (words &c. *in, on,* stone, metal, paper, &c.); enter name of (person) on list; (esp. in p.p.) issue (loan) in form of shares with registered holders, as *inscribed stock*; mark (sheet, tablet, &c., *with* characters); (Geom.) trace (figure) within another so that some particular points of it lie in the boundary of that other, whence **inscrī·b**ABLE a. [f. L IN[1](*scribere script-* write)]

inscri·ption, n. Words inscribed, esp. on monument, coin, &c., so **inscri·ption**AL, **inscri·pt**IVE, aa.; inscribing (*of* loan). [f. L *inscriptio* (as prec., see -ION)]

inscru·table (-rōō)-, a. That cannot be penetrated (fig.), wholly mysterious. Hence **inscruta**BI·LITY, **inscru·table**NESS, nn., **inscru·tab**LY[2] adv. [f. LL IN[2](*scrutabilis* f. *scrutari* search, see -BLE)]

i·nsect, n. Small invertebrate animal, usu. with body divided into segments & several pairs of legs, esp. (Zool.) one with body divided into three regions (head, thorax, abdomen), six legs upon thorax, & (usu.) two or four wings; (fig.) insignificant person or creature; *i.-powder* (for killing or driving away ii.). Hence **insectĭ·**VORA n. pl., **inse·cti**VORE n., **insecti·**VOROUS a. [f. L *insectum* (*animal*) notched animal. f. IN[1](*secare sect-* cut)]

insectār·ium, n. Place for keeping insects. [-ARIUM]

inse·cticide, n. Insect-killer, esp. preparation used for killing insects. Hence **insecticī·d**AL a. [-CIDE]

insecto·logy, n. Science of insects, esp. in their economic relations to man. [f. F *insectologie* (as INSECT, see -O- & -LOGY)]

insecure· (-ūr), a. Unsafe; (of ice, ground, &c.) liable to give way. Hence or cogn. **insecure·**LY[2] adv., **insecūr·**ITY n. [f. L IN[2](*securus* SECURE)]

insĕ·minate, v.t. Sow (seed &c., lit. & fig., *in*). Hence **insemin**A·TION n. [f. L IN[1](*seminare* f. *semen -minis* seed), see -ATE[3]]

inse·nsate (-*a*t), a. Without sensibility, unfeeling; stupid; without physical sensation. Hence **inse·nsate**LY[2] adv. [f. LL IN[2](*sensatus* f. *sensus* SENSE, see -ATE[2])]

insensibi·lity, n. Lack of mental feeling or emotion; indifference (*to*); unconsciousness, swoon. [f. LL *insensibilitas* (as foll., see -TY)]

inse·nsible, a. Too small or gradual to be perceived, inappreciable, whence **inse·nsib**LY[2] adv.; unconscious, as *he fell down & was long i.*; unaware (*of, to, how*, &c.); emotionless, callous. [f. L IN[2](*sensibilis* SENSIBLE)]

inse·nsitive, a. Not sensitive (*to* touch, sight, light, mental or moral impressions). Hence **inse·nsitive**NESS n. [IN-[2]]

inse·ntient (-shĭ-), a. Inanimate. [IN-[2]]

insĕ·parable, a. & n. That cannot be separated; (Gram.) *i. prefix*, one that cannot be used as separate word (e.g. *dis-, mis-, un-*); (n., usu. pl.) i. person or thing, esp. friend. Hence **insepara**BI·LITY n., **insep·arab**LY[2] adv. [f. L IN[2](*separabilis* SEPARABLE)]

inser·t, v.t. Place, fit, thrust, (thing *in, into*, another, *between* edges &c.); introduce (letter, word, article, *in, into*, written matter, newspaper, &c.). [f. L IN[1](*serere sert-* join)]

inser·tion, n. Inserting; thing inserted, esp. in writing or print; ornamental needlework &c. inserted into plain material, as *lace i.*; (Anat.) mode of attachment of muscle, organ, &c. [f. L *insertio* (as prec., see -ION)]

i·nset[1], n. Extra page(s) inserted in sheet or book; small map &c. inserted within border of larger; piece let into dress; pair of white slips worn as edging to waistcoat opening. [IN[2] + SET n.]

inse·t[2], v.t. (*inset* or *-tted*). Put in as an inset. [IN adv. + SET v. or f. prec.]

i·nshore·, adv. & a. Close to shore; *i. of*, nearer to shore than. [IN[1]]

inside, n., a., adv., & prep. (Pron. ĭ·nsī·d) inner side or surface, (of path) side next to wall or away from road; (ĭ·nsī·d) inner part, interior; (ĭnsī·d) stomach & bowels (colloq.); *the i·nsi·de* (middle part) *of a week*; (ĭnsī·d) passenger travelling i. coach &c.; *turned i·nside out*, so that inner side becomes outer; (adj., ĭ·nsīd) situated on or in, derived from, the i. (*i. information*, not accessible to outsiders); (adv., ĭnsī·d) on or in the i.; (colloq.) *i. of* (in less than) *a week*; (prep. ĭ·nsī·d) on the inner side of, within. [IN a. + SIDE]

insi·der, n. One who is in some society, organization, &c. (cf. OUTSIDER); one who is in the secret. [f. prec. + -ER[1]]

insi·dious, a. Treacherous, crafty; proceeding secretly or subtly, as *i. disease*. Hence **insi·dious**LY[2] adv., **insi·dious**NESS n. [f. L *insidiosus* cunning f. IN[1](*sidiae* f. *sedēre* sit) ambush, see -OUS]

i·nsight, n. Penetration (*into* character, circumstances, &c.) with the understanding. [IN adv. + SIGHT]

insi·gnia, n. pl. Badges, distinguishing marks, (*of* office, honour, &c.). [L, neut. pl. of IN[1](*signis* f. *signum* SIGN) distinguished]

insigni·ficant, a. Unimportant, trifling; contemptible; meaningless. Hence **insigni·fic**ANCE, -ANCY, nn., **insigni·ficant**LY[2] adv. [IN-[2]]

insincere·, a. Not sincere, disingenuous. Hence **insincere·**LY[2] adv., **insincĕ·**RITY n. [f. L IN[2](*sincerus* SINCERE)]

insĭ·nuate, v.t. Introduce (thing, one*self*, *into* place; one*self*, person, *into* favour, office, &c.) gradually or subtly; convey indirectly, hint obliquely, (idea, *that*). Hence **insi·nuating**LY[2] adv., **insinu**A·TION, **insi·nuat**OR[2], nn., **insi·nuat**IVE a. [f. L IN[1](*sinuare* f. *sinus -ūs* curve), see -ATE[3]]

insi·pid, a. Tasteless; wanting in flavour; lifeless, dull, uninteresting. Hence **insipĭ·d**ITY, **insi·pid**NESS, nn., **insi·pid**LY[2] adv. [f. LL IN[2](*sipidus* = *sapidus* well-tasting, f. *sapere* taste, be wise, see -ID[1])]

insi·st, v.i. & t. Dwell long or emphatically (*on*), as *i. on this point, on his unpunctuality*; maintain positively, as *i. on his innocence, i.* (*on it*) *that he is innocent*; make a stand *on* as essential (*I i. on being present, on your being present, on your presence, on it that you shall be present*). Hence **insi·st**ENCE, -ENCY, nn., **insi·st**ENT a., **insi·stent**LY[2] adv. [f. L IN[1](*sistere* stand)]

insobrī·ety, n. Intemperance, esp. in drinking. [IN-[2]]

insola·tion, n. Exposure to sun's rays, for purposes of bleaching &c., as medical treatment, or as cause of disease. [f. L *insolatio* f. IN[1](*solare* f. *sol* sun), see -ATION]

i·nsolent, a. Offensively contemptuous, insulting. Hence or cogn. **i·nsol**ENCE n., **i·nsolent**LY[2] adv. [f. L IN[2](*solens* part. of *solēre* be accustomed), see -ENT]

insŏ·lūble, a. That cannot be solved; that cannot be dissolved. Hence **insolu**BI·LITY, **inso·luble**NESS, nn., **inso·lub**LY[2] adv. [f. L IN[2](*solubilis* SOLUBLE)]

inso·lvent, a. & n. (Debtor) unable to pay debts; relating to ii., as *i. laws*. Hence **inso·lv**ENCY n. [IN-[2]]

inso·mnia, n. Sleeplessness. [L, f. IN[2](*somnis* f. *somnus* sleep) sleepless]

insomu·ch, adv. To such an extent *that*.

insou·ciant (-sōō-, or as F), n. Careless,

unconcerned. So **insou·ci**ANCE n. [F (IN-[2] + *souciant* part. of *soucier* care f. L *sollicitare* disturb)]

inspa·n, v.t. (S.-Afr.; -nn-). Yoke (oxen &c.) in team to vehicle; harness (wagon). [f. Du. IN[1](*spannen* span, put horses to)]

inspe·ct, v.t. Look closely into; examine officially. So **inspe·ct**ION, **inspe·ct**OR[2] (esp., police officer below superintendent and above sergeant), **inspe·ctor**SHIP, nn., **inspe·ctor**AL, **inspector·**IAL, aa. [f. L IN[1](*spicere spect-* look)]

inspe·ctorate (-*at*), n. Office of inspector; body of inspectors; district under inspector, esp. in Greenland. [-ATE[1]]

inspira·tion, n. Drawing in of breath; inspiring; divine influence, esp. that under which books of Scripture are held to have been written, whether *verbal i.* (dictating every word), *plenary i.* (covering all subjects treated), or *moral i.* (confined to moral & religious teaching), whence **inspira·tion**ISM(3), **inspiration**IST(2), nn.; thought &c. inspired, prompting; sudden happy idea; inspiring principle. Hence **inspira·tion**AL a. [OF, f. L *inspirationem* (as INSPIRE, see -ATION)]

i·nspirator, n. Apparatus for drawing in air or vapour. [L (as foll., see -OR[2])]

inspire·, v.t. Breathe in, inhale, (air &c. or abs.), whence **inspīr·at**ORY a.; infuse thought or feeling into (person; esp. of divine or supernatural agency; often in p.p.); animate (person &c. *with* feeling); infuse (feeling *into* person &c.), create (feeling *in* person); *an inspired article* (in journal), one secretly suggested by or emanating from influential person &c. [f. OF *enspirer* f. L IN[1](*spirare* breathe)]

inspi·rit, v.t. Put life into, animate; encourage (person *to* action, *to* do). Hence **inspi·rit**ING[2] a. [IN-[1] + SPIRIT n.]

inspi·ssate (*or* ĭ·n-), v.t. Thicken, condense. So **inspiss**A·TION n. [f. LL IN[1](*spissare* f. *spissus* thick), see -ATE[3]]

instabi·lity, n. Lack of stability (usu. fig. of moral qualities &c.). [f. F *instabilité* f. L *instabilitatem* f. IN[2](*stabilis* STABLE), see -TY)]

insta·ll (-awl), v.t. Place (person *in* office or dignity) with ceremonies, whence **insta·ll**ANT (-awl-) a. & n.; establish (person, one*self*, *in* place, condition, &c.); place (heating or lighting apparatus &c.) in position for use. So **install**A·TION n. [f. med. L IN[1](*stallare* f. *stallum* STALL)]

insta·lment (-awl-), n. Each of several parts, successively falling due, of a sum payable; each of several parts supplied &c. at different times. [f. obs. IN[1](*stall* v. arrange, fix) + -MENT]

i·nstance[1], n. Fact illustrating a general truth, example; particular case (*in your, this, i.*); *for i.*, for example; *at the i.* (request, suggestion) *of*; (Law) process, suit, as *court of first i.* (primary jurisdiction); *in the first i.*, in the first place, at the first stage of a proceeding. [F, f. L *instantia* presence, urgency, pleading, objection to general statement, instance to the contrary (as INSTANT[1], see -ANCE)]

i·nstance[2], v.t. Cite (fact, case) as an instance; (usu. pass.) exemplify. [f. prec.]

i·nstancy, n. Urgency. [as prec., -ANCY]

i·nstant[1], a. Urgent, pressing; (abbr. *inst.*) of the current month, as *the 6th inst.* (cf. PROXIMO, ULTIMO); immediate. [F, f. L IN[1](*stare* stand) be present, press upon, see -ANT]

i·nstant[2], n. Precise (esp. the present) point of time, moment, as *come this i.*, *I went that i.* or *on the i.*; *I told you the i.* (as soon as) *I knew*; short space of time, moment. [prec. as n.]

instantané (F), n. Snap-shot, (fig.) short sketch in a few sentences.

instantā·neous, a. Occurring, done, in an instant; (Dynam.) existing at a particular instant. Hence **instanta·neous**LY[2] adv., **instanta·neous**NESS n. [prec. + -ANEOUS, after *momentaneous*]

insta·nter, adv. Immediately, at once, (now usu. facet.). [L, f. *instans* INSTANT[1]]

i·nstantly, adv. At once. [INSTANT[1] + -LY[2]]

instaura·tion, n. Restoration, renewal. So **i·nstaurat**OR[2] n. [f. L *instauratio* f. IN[1](*staurare*, see RESTORE & -ATION)]

instea·d (-ĕd), adv. As a substitute or alternative; in place *of*, as *i. of this, i. of going, you should be out i. of (sitting) in on this fine day*, (also *in his, my, our*, STEAD). [IN prep. + STEAD n.]

i·nstep, n. Upper surface of foot between toes & ankle; part of shoe &c. fitting this; i.-shaped thing. [f. 16th c.; etym. dub.]

i·nstigate, v.t. Urge on, incite, (person *to* action, *to* do usu. something evil); bring about (revolt, murder, &c.) by persuasion So **instig**A·TION, **i·nstigat**OR[2], nn. [f. L IN[1](*stigare*, cf. Gk *stizō* prick, root *stig-*), see -ATE[3]]

insti·l(l), v.t. (-ll-). Put in (liquid *into* thing) by drops; infuse, (feeling, ideas, &c. *into* person, mind, &c.) gradually. Hence or cogn. **instill**A·TION, **insti·l**MENT, nn. [f. L IN[1](*stillare* drop)]

i·nstinct[1], n. Innate propensity, esp. in lower animals, to certain seemingly rational acts performed without conscious design; innate impulse; intuition, unconscious skill. Hence **insti·nct**IVE a., **insti·nctive**LY[2] adv. [f. L *instinctus -ūs* f. IN[1](*stinguere stinct-* prick) incite]

insti·nct[2], pred. a. Imbued, charged, (*with* life, beauty, force, &c.). [f. L p.p. as prec.]

i·nstitute[1], n. Society, organization, for promotion of scientific or other object; building used by this; (pl.) digest of elements of a subject, esp. of jurisprudence, as *Ii. of Justinian.* [f. L neut. p.p. as foll.]

i·nstitute[2], v.t. Establish, found; set on foot (inquiry &c.); appoint (person *to*, *into*, benefice). [f. L IN[1](*stituere -tut-* = *statuere* set up)]

institu·tion, n. Instituting; establishment (*of* person) in cure of souls; established law, custom, or practice; (colloq., of person &c.) familiar object; organization for promotion of some public object; building used by this. Hence **institu·tion**AL a. [OF, f. L *institutio* (as prec., see -ION)]

instru·ct, v.t. Teach (person &c. *in* subject); inform (person *that, when,* &c.); (of client, solicitor) give information to (solicitor, counsel); direct, command, (person *to* do). Hence or cogn. **instru·ct**OR[2], **instru·ctr**ESS[1], nn. [f. L IN[1](*struere struct-* pile up) build, teach]

instru·ction, n. Teaching; (pl.) directions, orders; (pl.) directions to solicitor or counsel. Hence **instru·ction**AL a. [OF, f. L *instructionem* (as prec., see -ION)]

instru·ctive, a. Tending to instruct, conveying a lesson. Hence **instru·ctive**LY[2] adv., **instru·ctive**NESS n. [-IVE]

i·nstrument, n., & v.t. Thing used in performing an action; person so made use of; tool, implement, esp. for delicate or scientific work; (also *musical i.*) contrivance for producing musical sounds by vibration of strings &c. (*stringed* &c. *ii.*) or of body of air in pipe &c. (*wind ii.*); formal, esp. legal, document; (v.t.) arrange (music) for ii. [(vb f. n.) F, f. L *instrumentum* (as INSTRUCT, see -MENT)]

instrume·ntal, a. Serving as instrument or means (*to* purpose, *in* work, *in* doing); of, arising from, an instrument, as *i. errors*; (of music) performed on instruments (cf. VOCAL), whence **instrume·ntal**IST(3) n.; (Gram.) *i. case* (denoting the instrument). Hence **instrume·ntal**LY[2] adv. [F, f. med. L *instrumentalis* (as INSTRUMENT, see -AL)]

instrumenta·lity, n. Agency, means, esp. *by the i. of.* [-ITY]

instrumenta·tion, n. Arrangement of music for instruments; operation with surgical or other instrument; instrumentality. [F, f. *instrumenter* (as INSTRUMENT), see -ATION]

insubor·dinate (-*at*), a. Disobedient, rebellious. Hence **insubordin**A·TION n. [IN-[2]]

insubsta·ntial, a. Not real; lacking solidity or substance. Hence **insubstantia·l**ITY n. [f. LL IN[2](*substantialis* SUBSTANTIAL)]

insu·fferable, a. Unbearably arrogant, conceited, &c. Hence **insu·fferab**LY[2] adv. [IN-[2]]

insuffi·cient, a. Not sufficient, inadequate. Hence or cogn. **insuffi·ci**ENCY n., **insuffi·cient**LY[2] adv. [OF, f. L IN[2](*sufficientem* SUFFICIENT)]

i·nsufflate, v.t. Blow, breathe, (air, gas, &c.) into cavity of the body &c.; treat (nose &c.) thus. Hence **i·nsufflat**OR[2](2) n. [f. L IN[1](SUF*flare* blow upon), see -ATE[3]]

insuffla·tion, n. Blowing on or into; breathing on person as rite of exorcism. [f. L *insufflatio* (as prec., see -ION)]

i·nsular, a. Of (the nature of) an island; of, like, islanders, esp. narrow-minded, whence **i·nsular**ISM n. Hence **insulă·**RITY n., **i·nsular**LY[2] adv. [f. L *insularis* (as foll., see -AR[1])]

i·nsulate, v.t. Make (land) into an island; detach (person, thing) from surroundings, isolate; isolate (thing) by interposition of non-conductors, to prevent passage of electricity or heat. Hence **insul**A·TION, **i·nsulat**OR[2](2), nn. [f. L *insula* island + -ATE[3]]

i·nsulin, n. A specific for diabetes extracted from the islets of Langerhans in the pancreas of animals. [f. L *insula* islet + -IN]

i·nsult[1], n. Insulting speech or action, affront. [f. LL IN[1](*sultus* = *saltus* leap, as foll.)]

insu·lt[2], v.t. Treat with scornful abuse, offer indignity to; (of person or thing) affront. Hence **insu·lting**LY[2] adv. [f. L IN[1](*sultare* = *saltare*, frequent. of *salire salt-* leap)]

insū·perable, a. (Of barriers &c. & fig. of difficulties &c.) that cannot be surmounted or overcome; (rare) unsurpassable. Hence **insupera**BI·LITY n., **insu·perab**LY[2] adv. [f. L IN[2](*superabilis* f. *superare* overcome, -BLE)]

insuppor·table, a. Unbearable. Hence **insuppor·tab**LY[2] adv. [F (IN-[2])]

insur·ance, (-shoor-), n. Insuring; sum paid for this, premium; *National I. Act*, that of 1911 requiring wage-earners to make weekly payments supplemented by their employers in return for which they receive State assistance in sickness, unemployment, &c. [earlier *en-*, f. OF *enseurance* (as ENSURE, see -ANCE)]

insur·ant, n. Person to whom insurance policy is issued. [f. foll. + -ANT]

insure· (-shoor), v.t. Secure payment of sum of money in event of loss of or damage to (property, life; cf. ASSURANCE) by payment of premium; secure payment of (sum of money) thus (said of owner of the property or of insurance company); *the insured*, the person to whom such payment is secured. Hence **insur·**ABLE a. [earlier ENSURE]

insur·er, n. One who insures property in consideration of premium, underwriter. [-ER[1]]

insur·gent, a. & n. Rising in active revolt; (of sea &c.) rushing in; (n.) rebel. Hence **insur·g**ENCY n. [f. L IN[1](*surgere surrect-* rise), see -ENT]

insurmou·ntable, a. Not to be surmounted. Hence **insurmou·ntab**LY[2] adv. [IN-[2]]

insurre·ction, n. Rising in open resistance to established authority; incipient rebellion. Hence **insurre·ction**AL, **insurre·ction**ARY[1], aa., **insurre·ction**IST (3) n. [F, f. rare L *insurrectionem* (as INSURGENT, see -ION)]

insusce·ptible, a. Not susceptible (*of* treatment, *to* agency &c.). Hence **insuscepti**BI·LITY n. [IN-[2]]

inta·ct, a. Untouched; entire; unimpaired. [f. L IN[2](*tactus* p.p. of *tangere* touch)]

intăg·liated, a. Carved on the surface. [f. It. *intagliato* p.p. of IN[1](*tagliare* cut f. LL *taleare* f. *talea* twig) + -ED[1]]

intăg·lio, n., & v.t. Engraved design; carving in hard material; gem with incised design (cf. CAMEO); (v.t.) engrave (material, design) thus. [(vb f. n.) It. (as prec.)]

i·ntake, n. (chiefly Sc.). Place where water is taken into channel or pipe from river &c.; airway in mine; abrupt narrowing in pipe, stocking, &c.; land reclaimed from moor. [IN adv. + TAKE v.]

inta·ngible, a. That cannot be touched; impalpable; that cannot be grasped mentally. Hence **intangi**BI·LITY n., **inta·ngib**LY[2] adv. [f. med. L IN[2](*tangibilis* TANGIBLE)]

i·ntegĕr, n. Whole number, undivided quantity, (cf. FRACTION); thing complete in itself. [L, adj. = untouched, whole (IN-[2] + *tag-* root of *tangere* touch)]

i·ntegral, a. & n. Of, necessary to the completeness of, a whole; whole, complete; (Math.) of, denoted by, an integer, involving only integers; *i. calculus* (dealing with finding & properties of ii. of functions, cf. DIFFERENTIAL); (n.) quantity of which a given function is the differential coefficient. Hence or cogn. **integra·**LITY n., **i·ntegral**LY[2] adv. [f. LL *integralis* (as prec., see -AL)]

i·ntegrant, a. (Of parts) component, making up a whole. [as foll., see -ANT]

i·ntegrate[1] (-*a*t), a. Made up of parts; whole, complete. [as foll., see -ATE[2]]

i·ntegrāte[2], v.t. Complete (imperfect thing) by addition of parts; combine (parts) into a whole; (Math.) find the integral of; indicate mean value or total sum of (area, temperature, &c.), whence **i·ntegrat**OR[2](2) n. Hence or cogn. **integr**A·TION n., **i·ntegrat**IVE a. [f. L *integrare* make whole (INTEGER), see -ATE[3]]

intĕ·grity, n. Wholeness; soundness; uprightness, honesty. [f. L *integritas* wholeness, purity, (INTEGER, see -TY)]

intĕ·gument, n. Skin, husk, rind, or other (usu. natural) covering. Hence **integume·nt**ARY[1] a. [f. L *integumentum* f. IN[1](*tegere* cover), see -MENT]

i·ntellect, n. Faculty of knowing & reasoning; understanding; person, persons collectively, of good understanding. [f. L *intellectus* -*ūs* (as INTELLIGENT)]

intelle·ction, n. Action, process, of understanding, esp. as opp. to *imagination*. So **intelle·ct**IVE a. [f. LL *intellectio* (as INTELLIGENT, see -ION)]

intelle·ctual, a. & n. Of, appealing to, requiring the exercise of, intellect; (person) possessing a good understanding, enlightened person, esp. *the ii.* (*of* a country &c.). Hence or cogn. **intellectua·**LITY, **intellectualiz**A·TION, nn., **intelle·ctual**IZE(3) v.t. & i., **intelle·ctual**LY[2] adv. [f. L *intellectualis* (as INTELLECT, see -AL)]

intelle·ctualism, n. Doctrine that knowledge is wholly or mainly derived from pure reason. So **intelle·ctual**IST(2) n. [-ISM]

inte·lligence, n. Intellect, understanding, whence **intellige·nt**IAL a.; quickness of understanding, sagacity, (of person or animal); rational being; information, news, (*I. Department*, engaged in collecting information esp. for mil. purposes). [F, f. L *intelligentia* (as INTELLIGENT)]

inte·lligencer, n. Bringer of news, informant; secret agent, spy. [f. prec. + -ER[1]]

inte·lligent, a. Having or showing (usu. a high degree of) understanding. Hence **inte·lligent**LY[2] adv. [f. L *intelligere* understand (INTER- + *legere* gather, pick out, read), -ENT]

intellige·ntzia, -sia, n. The part of a nation (esp. the Russian) that aspires to independent thinking. [Russ. *intelligentsiya* f. It. *intelligenza* f. L as INTELLIGENCE]

inte·lligible, a. That can be understood, comprehensible *to*; (Philos.) that can be apprehended only by the intellect, not by the senses. Hence **intelligi**BI·LITY n., **inte·lligib**LY[2] adv. [f. L *intelligibilis* (as prec., see -BLE)]

inte·mperate (-*a*t), a. (Of person or conduct) immoderate, unbridled, violent; excessive in the indulgence of an appetite; addicted to drinking. Hence or cogn. **inte·mper**ANCE n., **inte·mperate**LY[2] adv. [f. L IN[2](*temperatus*, as TEMPER v.)]

inte·nd, v.t. Purpose, design, as *we i. to go, we i. no harm, we i. that it shall be done today, was this intended* (done on purpose)?; design, destine, (person, thing) for a purpose, as *we i. our son for the bar, i. him to go, i. it as a stop-gap, this bun is intended for you* (to eat), *this daub is intended for* (meant to represent) *me*; mean, as *what exactly do you i. by the word?*. [f. F *entendre* f. L IN[1](*tendere tent-* or *tens-* stretch, tend) strain, direct, purpose]

inte·ndant, n. Superintendent, manager, of public business &c. (chiefly as foreign title). Hence **inte·ndan**CY n. [F, f. L as prec., -ANT]

inte·nded, n. (colloq.). Affianced lover, as *your, his, her, i.* [p.p. of INTEND as n.]

inte·ndment, n. True meaning as fixed by

law. [f. F *entendement* meaning (as INTEND, see -MENT)]

inte·nse, a. (-er, -est). (Of quality &c.) existing in a high degree, violent, vehement; having some quality in high degree; (of feeling or action) eager, ardent; feeling, apt to feel, i. emotion. Hence **inte·nse**LY[2] adv., **inte·nse**NESS, **intensi**FICA·TION, **inte·nsi**TY, nn., **inte·nsi**FY, v.t. & i. [F, as INTENT[2]]

inte·nsion, n. Intensity, high degree, of a quality, opp. to *extension*; strenuous exertion of mind or will. [f. L *intensio* (INTEND, -ION)]

inte·nsive, a. Of, relating to, intensity as opp. to extent; producing intensity; (Gram.) expressing intensity, giving force; concentrated, directed to a single point or area or subject, (*i. bombardment, study*); (Econ.) serving to increase production of given area, as *i. methods, agriculture*; (Med.) *i. inoculation* (in which intensity of matter introduced is increased in successive operations). Hence **inte·nsive**LY[2] adv. [F (*-if, -ive*), f. L as INTEND, see -IVE]

inte·nt[1], n. Intention, purpose, esp. *with i. to* (defraud &c.), *with malicious, good,* &c., *i.*; (pl.) to *all ii. & purposes*, practically, virtually. [ME & OF (1) *entent* f. L *intentus -ūs*, (2) *entente* f. pop. L *intenta* fem. p.p., both as INTEND]

inte·nt[2], a. Resolved, bent, (*on doing, on* object); sedulously occupied (*on*); (of faculties, looks, &c.) earnest, eager. Hence **inte·nt**LY[2] adv., **inte·nt**NESS n. [f. L as INTEND; doublet of *intense*, L *-tens-* having chiefly the physical, *-tent-* the mental senses]

inte·ntion, n. Intending; thing intended, purpose, whence (-)**inte·ntion**ED[2] a.; ultimate aim; (pl., colloq.) purposes in respect of proposal of marriage; (Med.) *second i.*, healing of wound by granulation, *first i.*, healing without this by immediate re-union of parts; (Logic) conception, as *first ii.*, primary conceptions of things (e.g. a tree, an oak), *second ii.*, secondary conceptions (e.g. difference, identity, species); (Theol.) *special, particular, i.*, special object for which mass is celebrated &c. [OF, f. L *intentionem* (as INTEND, see -ION)]

inte·ntional, a. Done on purpose. Hence **inte·ntional**LY[2] adv. [f. med. L *intentionalis* (as prec., see -AL)]

inter·[1], v.t. (-rr-). Deposit (corpse &c.) in earth, tomb, &c.; bury. [f. OF *enterrer* f. pop. L IN[1](*terrare* f. *terra* earth)]

i·nter[2], prep. (L). Between, among, as *i. ălia*, amongst other things, *i. nōs, se*, between ourselves, themselves, *i. vi·vōs*, between the living (esp. of gift as opp. legacy).

inter-, pref. = prec. Besides wds given in their alphab. place, *inter-* is used freely to form (1) vbs, nn., & aa., expr. mutual or reciprocal action or relation, or with sense 'among', 'between', as: *-be·d*, embed (thing) between others; *-ce·nsal*, between two censuses; *-collē·giate*, carried on &c. between colleges; *-colu·mnar*, placed, existing, between two columns; *-columnia·tion*, placing of columns at intervals, such interval; *-conne·ct*, connect by reciprocal links; *-conver·tible*, interchangeable; *-cro·ss*, t. & i., lay, lie, across each other, (cause to) propagate with each other; *-flow* n. & v.i., flow into each other; *-grada·tion*, gradual approximation; *-grade*, (v.i.) pass into another form by intervening grades, (n.) such grade; *-grow·th*, growing of things into each other; *-ja·culatory*, expressed in parenthetical ejaculations; *-kni·t*, intertwine; *-la·p*, overlap; *-li·nk*, link together (things, one *with* another); *-ocea·nic*, between, connecting, two oceans; *-plai·t*, plait together; *-provi·ncial*, situated, carried on, between provinces; *-pu·nction*, punctuation; *-pu·nctuate*, punctuate; *-ra·cial*, existing between different races; *-shoo·t*, shoot or glance (t. & i.) at intervals, variegate (thing *with* colours &c., esp. in p.p. *-shot*); *-space*, interval of space or time; *-ta·ngle*, tangle together, whence *-ta·nglement* n.; *-te·xture*, interweaving; *-tri·bal*, existing between different tribes; *-twi·st*, twist together; *-vei·n*, intersect (as) with veins; *-wor·k*, (trans.) interweave lit. & fig., (intr.) work upon each other; *-wrea·the*, wreathe together. (2) Scientific, esp. anat., wds w. sense 'between', chiefly adjj., as: *-arti·cular*, between contiguous surfaces of a joint; *-co·stal*, between the ribs (of body or ship), (n. pl.) i. parts; *-di·gital*, between fingers or toes; *-di·gitate*, interlock like fingers of clasped hands, so *-digita·tion* n.; *-fa·cial*, included between two faces of crystal or other solid; *-fe·moral*, between the thighs; *-folia·ceous*, placed alternately between a pair of opposite leaves; *-gla·cial*, between glacial periods; *-lo·bular*, between lobes; *-node*, (Bot.) part of stem between two of the knots from which leaves arise, (Anat.) slender part between two joints, esp. bone of finger or toe; *-o·sseous*, between bones; *-parī·etal*, between right & left parietal bones of skull; *-se·ptal*, between partitions; *-spi·nal, spi·nous*, between spines or spinous processes; *-ste·llar*, between stars; *-stratifica·tion, -stra·tified*, interspersion, interspersed, (*with* strata).

i·nteract[1], n. Interval between two acts of play; interlude. [INTER-, after F ENTR'ACTE]

intera·ct[2], v.i. Act reciprocally, act on each other. Hence **intera·ct**ION n., **intera·ct**IVE a. [INTER-]

For other words in *inter-* see INTER-.

interble·nd, v.t. & i. Mingle (things, one *with* another); (intr.) blend with each other. [INTER-]

interbree·d, v.t & i. Cross-breed; (intr., of animals of different race or species) breed with each other. [INTER-]

inter·calary, a. (Of day or month) inserted in calendar to harmonize calendar with solar year; (of year) having such additions; interpolated, intervening. [f. L *intercalarius* (as foll., see -ARY[1])]

inter·calate, v.t. Insert (intercalary day &c., or abs.); interpose (anything out of ordinary course, esp. in p.p. of strata). So **intercal**A·TION n. [f. L INTER(*calare* proclaim), see -ATE[3]]

interce·de, v.i. Interpose on behalf of another, plead (*with* one person *for* another). [f. L INTER(*cedere cess-* go) intervene]

interce·pt, v.t. Seize, catch, (person &c.) on the way from place to place; cut off (light &c. *from*); check, stop; (Math.) mark off (space) between two points &c. Hence or cogn. **interce·pt**ION, **interce·pt**OR[2], nn., **interce·pt**IVE a. [f. L INTER(*cipere cept-* = *capere* take)]

interce·ssion, n. Interceding, esp. by prayer. So **interce·ss**OR[2] n., **intercessor·**IAL, **interce·ss**ORY, aa. [f. L *intercessio* (as INTERCEDE, see -ION)]

i·nterchange[1], n. Reciprocal exchange (*of* things) between two persons &c.; alternation. [f. OF *entrechange* (as foll.)]

intercha·nge[2], v.t. (Of two persons) exchange (things) with each other; put each of (two things) in the other's place; alternate. Hence or cogn. **interchange**ABI·LITY, **intercha·ngeable**NESS, nn., **intercha·nge**ABLE a., **intercha·ngeab**LY[2] adv. [f. OF *entrechangier* (*entre-* INTER- + *changier* CHANGE)]

intercolō·nial, a. Existing, carried on, between different colonies. [INTER-]

intercommū·nicate, v.i. Have mutual intercourse; have free passage to each other. So **intercommunic**A·TION n. [INTER-]

intercommū·nion, n. Intimate intercourse; mutual action or relation. [INTER-]

intercommū·nity, n. Being common to various parties; having things in common. [INTER-]

i·ntercourse, n. Social communication, dealings, between individuals; communion between man & God; communication for trade purposes &c. between different countries &c.; sexual connexion. [f. OF *entrecours* f. *entrecorre* run between f. L INTER(*currere curs-* run)]

intercu·rrent, a. (Of time or event) intervening; (of disease) occurring during progress of another, (also) recurring at intervals. Hence **intercu·rr**ENCE n. [f. L as prec., -ENT]

interdepe·nd, v.i. Depend on each other. So **interdepe·nd**ENCE, -ENCY, nn., **interdepe·nd**ENT a., **interdepe·ndent**LY[2] adv. [INTER-]

i·nterdict[1], n. Authoritative prohibition; (Sc. Law) = INJUNCTION; (R.-C. Ch.) sentence debarring person or place from ecclesiastical functions &c. [f. OF *entredit* f. *entredire* f. L INTER(*dicere dict-* say)]

interdi·ct[2], v.t. Prohibit (action); forbid use of; restrain (person *from doing*); forbid (thing *to* person). So **interdi·ct**ION n., **interdi·ct**ORY a. [ME *entrediten* (as prec.), refash. on L]

i·nterest[1], n. Legal concern, title, right, (*in* property); pecuniary stake (*in* commercial undertaking &c.); VEST*ed ii.*; advantage, profit, as *it is* (*to*) *your i. to go, I do it in your i., in the i.* (or *ii.*) *of truth*; thing in which one is concerned; principle in which a party is concerned; party having a common i., as *the brewing i.*; selfish pursuit of one's own welfare; *make i.*, bring personal interest to bear (*with* person); concern, curiosity, or quality exciting them (*take an i., no i., in*; *this has no i. for me*); money paid for use of money lent or for forbearance of debt (*with i.* transf., with increased force &c., as *returned the blow, his kindness, w. i.*); *simple i.* (reckoned on principal only, & paid at fixed intervals); *compound i.* (reckoned on principal & on accumulations of i.). [L, = it matters, 3rd sing. pres. of INTER(*esse* be); earlier *interess* f. L inf. in sense compensatory payment]

i·nterest[2], v.t. Cause (person) to take personal interest or share (*in*); (p.p.) having a private i., not impartial or disinterested, as *-ed parties, motives*; excite curiosity or attention of, whence **i·nterest**ING[2] (-teres-) a., **i·nteresting**LY[2] adv. Hence **i·nterested**LY[2] adv. [earlier *interess* (vb f. n.) as prec.]

interfere·, v.i. (Of things) come into collision or opposition (*with*); (of person) meddle (*with* or abs.), whence **interfēr·**ING[2] a.; intervéne, take part, (*in*); (Physics, of waves of light &c.) strike against each other; (of horse) knock one leg against another. Hence **interfēr·**ENCE n. [f. OF *s'entreférir* strike each other (*entre-* INTER- + *férir* f. L *ferire* strike)]

inter·fluent, a. Flowing into each other. [f. L INTER(*fluere* flow), see -ENT]

interfu·se (-z), v.t. & i. Intersperse, mix, (thing *with*); blend (things) together; (of two things) blend with each other. So **interfu·s**ION (-zhn) n. [f. L INTER(*fundere fus-* pour)]

i·nterim, adv., n., & a. (Archaic) meanwhile (adv.); intervening time; *the I.* (eccl.), truce pending a General Council between

For other words in *inter-* see INTER-.

German Protestants & the Papacy in 16th c.; intervening; provisional, temporary; *i. dividend* (paid between two annual &c. balances & not in pursuance of a published balance-sheet). [L (INTER + adv. suf. *-im*)]

intēr·ior, a. & n. Situated within; inland, remote from coast or frontier; internal, domestic, opp. to *foreign*; existing in mind or soul, inward. (N.) i. part, inside; inland region; inside of building or room, picture of this; inner nature, soul; (department dealing with) home affairs of a country, as *Minister of the I.* Hence **intēr·ior**LY² adv. [L, compar. adj. f. INTER²]

interjā·cent, a. Lying between, intermediate. [f. L INTER(*jacēre* lie), see -ENT]

interje·ct, v.t. Throw in, interpose, (remark &c.) abruptly; remark parenthetically. [f. L INTER(*jicĕre ject-* = *jacĕre* throw)]

interje·ction, n. Ejaculation, exclamation; natural ejaculation viewed as part of speech (e.g. *ah!, whew!*). Hence or cogn. **interje·ction**AL, **interje·ct**ORY, aa., **interje·ctional**LY² adv. [F, f. L *interjectionem* (prec., -ION)]

interla·ce, v.t. & i. Bind together intricately, entangle; interweave (often fig.); mingle (two things, one *with* another); cross each other intricately. Hence **interla·ce**MENT n. [f. F *entrelacer* (*entre-* INTER- + *lacer* LACE)]

interlar·d, v.t. Mix (writing, speech, *with* foreign words &c.). [f. F *entrelarder* (*entre-* INTER- + *larder* LARD)]

i·nterleaf, n. (pl. *-ves*). Extra leaf (usu. blank) between leaves of book. [INTER-]

interlea·ve, v.t. Insert (usu. blank) leaves between leaves of book, (also fig.). [f. prec.]

interli·ne, v.t. Insert words between lines of (document &c.); insert (words) thus. So **interlinĕ**A·TION n. [prob. f. med. L INTER(*lineare* f. *linea* LINE)]

interli·near, a. Written, printed, between the lines. [f. med. L INTER(*linearis* LINEAR)]

interlo·ck, v.i. & t. (Intr.) engage with each other by overlapping &c.; (trans., usu. pass.) lock, clasp, within each other; (Railways) connect (levers for signals &c.) by bolts &c. to ensure uniformity of movement. [INTER-]

interlŏ·cūtor, n. One who takes part in dialogue or conversation; *my i.*, the person in conversation with me. Hence or cogn. **interlocu·**TION, **interlo·cutr**ESS¹, **interlo·cu**TRIX, nn., **interlo·cut**ORY a. [f. L INTER(*loqui locut-* talk), see -ION]

i·nterloper, n. Intruder, one who (esp. for profit) thrusts himself into others' affairs; (Hist.) unauthorized trader. So **interlo·pe** v.i. [INTER- + *loper* f. *lope* dial. form of LEAP]

i·nterlude, n. Pause between acts of play; what fills this up; (Mus.) instrumental piece played between verses of psalm or hymn &c.; intervening time or space of different character; event, amusing incident, &c., interposed; (Hist.) dramatic or mimic representation between acts of mystery-plays or moralities. [f. med. L INTER(*ludium* f. *ludus* play)]

interma·rriage, n. Marriage between members of different families, castes, tribes, &c., or (loosely) between near relations. [INTER-]

interma·rry, v.i. (Of tribes, nations, families, &c.) become connected by marriage (*with* other tribes &c.). [INTER-]

interme·ddle, v.i. Concern oneself (*with, in*, esp. what is not one's business). [f. OF *entremesler* (*entre-* INTER- + *mesler* MEDDLE)]

intermē·diary, a. & n. Acting between parties, mediatory; intermediate; (n.) i. person, thing, esp. mediator. [f. INTERMEDIUM, -ARY¹]

intermē·diate¹ (-*at*), a. & n. Coming *between* two things, as regards time, place, or order; (n.) i. thing. Hence **interme·diate**LY² adv. [f. med. L *intermediatus* f. L INTER(*medius* middle), -ATE²]

intermē·diate², v.i. Act between others, mediate, (*between*). Hence **intermedi**A·TION, **interme·diat**OR², nn. [INTER-]

intermē·dium, n. (pl. *-ia, -iums*). Intermediate thing, medium, esp. one serving to transmit energy through space. [L, neut. adj. as INTERMEDIATE¹]

inter·ment, n. Burial. [INTER¹ + -MENT]

interme·zzo (-dzō), n. Short light dramatic or other performance between acts of drama or opera, short movement connecting main divisions of large musical work. [It., pop. form of *intermedio* (as INTERMEDIATE¹)]

intermigra·tion, n. Reciprocal migration. [INTER-]

inter·minable, a. Endless; tediously long. Hence **inter·minable**NESS n., **inter·minab**LY² adv. [f. LL IN²(*terminabilis* f. *terminare* TERMINATE, see -BLE)]

intermi·ngle, v.t. & i. Mix together (two things, one *with* another); (intr.) mingle (*with*). [INTER-]

intermi·ssion, n. Pause, cessation, esp. *without i.* [f. L *intermissio* (as foll., see -ION)]

intermi·t, v.t. & i. (-tt-). Suspend, discontinue; stop for a time (esp. of fever, pain, &c., or of pulse). Hence or cogn. **intermi·tt**ENCE n., **intermi·tt**ENT a., **intermi·ttent**LY² adv. [f. L INTER(*mittere miss-* send)]

interm·ix, v.t. & i. Mix together. So **intermi·xt**URE n. [first in p.p., see MIX]

inter·n, v.t. Oblige to reside within limits of country &c. Hence **intern**EE· n., **inter·n**MENT n. (*-ment camp*, for prisoners of war & aliens). [f. F *interner* f. L *internus* internal (*in* + suf. *-ternus*)]

inter·nal, a. & n. Of, situated in, the inside of a thing; of the inner nature of a thing, intrinsic; *i. evidence*, derived from what is contained in the thing itself (cf. EXTERNAL); of the domestic affairs of a country; of the mind or soul, inward, subjective; (n. pl.) intrinsic qualities. Hence **interna·lITY** n., **inter·nalLY**² adv. [f. late med. L *internalis* (as prec., see -AL)]

internă·tional, a. & n. Existing, carried on, between different nations; of the I. Working Men's Associations (for promoting joint political action of working classes in all countries). (N.) one who takes part in **i.** (usu. athletic) contests; *first, second, third, I.*, three Associations as above (1st, Marxist, 1862–73; 2nd, French socialist, 1889 —; 3rd, Russian communist, abbr. *Comintern*, 1918—); member of any of these. Hence **internationa·lITY** n., **interna·tionalLY**² adv. [INTER-]

internationa·le (-shonahl, *or as* F), n. *The i.*, a French socialistic hymn sung at demonstrations; =*International Association* (see prec.). [F]

internă·tionalist, n. One who advocates community of interests between nations, esp. supporter of Association named in prec., so **interna·tionalISM** n.; one versed in international law. [-IST]

internă·tionalize, v.t. Make international, esp. bring (territory &c.) under combined protection &c. of different nations. Hence **internationalizA·TION** n. [-IZE]

internē·cine, a. Mutually destructive; (orig.) deadly, as *i. war*. [f. L *internecinus* f. INTER(*necare* kill) destroy, see -INE¹]

internu·ncial, a. (Of nerves) communicating between different parts of the system. [f. L as foll. + -AL]

internŭ·ncio (-shĭō), n. Ambassador of Pope when or where no nuncio is employed; (Hist.) minister representing (esp. Austrian) government at Ottoman Porte. [f. It. *internunzio* f. L INTER(*nuntius* messenger)]

intero·sculate, v.i. Intermingle with each other; form connecting link. Hence **interosculA·TION** n. [INTER-]

interpa·ge, v.t. Print, insert, on intermediate pages. [INTER-]

interpe·llate, v.t. (In foreign, esp. French, Chamber) interrupt order of day by demanding explanation from (Minister concerned). So **interpellA·TION**, **interpella·tOR**², nn. [f. L INTER(*pellare* var. of *pellere* drive), see -ATE³]

interpe·netrate, v.t. & i. Penetrate thoroughly, pervade; penetrate reciprocally; (intr., of two) penetrate each other. So **interpenetra·TION** n., **interpe·netratIVE** a. [INTER-]

i·nterplay, n. Reciprocal play; operation of two things on each other. [INTER-]

interplea·d, v.i. Litigate with each other in order to settle a point in which a third party is concerned. [INTER-]

inter·polate, v.t. Make insertions in (book &c.), esp. so as to give false impressions as to date &c.; introduce (words) thus; (Math.) insert (intermediate term) in series. So **interpolA·TION**, **inter·polatOR**², nn. [f. L INTER(*polare* cogn. w. *polire* POLISH) furbish up, -ATE³]

interpo·se (-z), v.t. & i. Insert, make intervene, (*between*); put forth, introduce, (veto, objection, authority, &c.) by way of interference; intervene (*between* disputants &c.); say (quoted words) as an interruption; make an interruption. Hence **interpo·SAL** n. [f. F INTER(*poser*, see COMPOSE)]

interposi·tion, n. Interposing; thing interposed; interference. [F, f. L *interpositionem* f. INTER(*ponere posit-* place)]

inter·pret, v.t. & i. Expound the meaning of (abstruse words, writings, &c.); make out the meaning of; bring out the meaning of, render, by artistic representation or performance; explain, understand, in specified manner, as *this we i. as a threat*; act as interpreter. Hence or cogn. **inter·pretABLE**, **inter·pretATIVE**, aa., **interpretA·TION** n. [f. F *interpréter* f. L *interpretari* f. INTER(*pres -pretis* cogn. w. Skr. *prath-* spread abroad) explainer, interpreter]

inter·preter, n. One who interprets; one whose office it is to translate orally in their presence the words of persons speaking different languages. Hence **inter·preterSHIP**, **inter·pretrESS**¹, nn. [f. OF *interpreteur* f. LL *interpretatorem* (as prec., see -OR²)]

interre·gnum, n. (pl. *-na, -nums*). Period during which State has no normal ruler, esp. between end of king's reign & accession of successor; interval, pause. [L INTER(*regnum* REIGN)]

interrela·tion, n. Mutual relation. [INTER-]

interrela·tionship, n. Mutual relationship. [INTER-]

intĕ·rrogate, v.t. Ask questions of (person &c.), esp. closely or formally. So **inte·rrogatOR**² n. [f. L INTER(*rogare* ask), see -ATE³]

intĕrroga·tion, n. Asking questions; question; *point, mark, note, of* (used to express) *i.* (?). [F, f. L *interrogationem* (as prec., see -ATION)]

interrŏ·gative, a. & n. Of, having the form or force of, a question; of inquiry, as *an i. tone*; (Gram., of words) used in asking question, as *i. pronouns* (*who?, which?*, &c.) Hence **interro·gativeLY**² adv. [f. LL *interrogativus* (as prec., see -IVE)]

interrŏ·gatory, a. & n. Of inquiry, as *an*

For other words in *inter-* see INTER-.

i. tone; (n.) question, set of questions, esp. (Law) one formally put to accused person &c. [f. LL *interrogatorius* (as prec., see -ORY)]

interru·pt, v.t. Break in upon (action, process, speech, person speaking, &c., or abs.); obstruct (view &c.); break the continuity of. Hence or cogn. **interru·pted**LY[2] adv., **interru·pt**ER[1], **interru·pt**ION, nn., **interru·pt**ORY a. [f. L INTER(*rumpere rupt-* break)]

interse·ct, v.t. & i. Divide (thing) by passing or lying across it; (of lines &c.) cross, cut, each other. [f. L INTER(*secare sect-* cut)]

interse·ction, n. Intersecting; point, line, common to intersecting lines, planes. Hence **interse·ction**AL a. [f. L *intersectio* (as prec., see -ION)]

intersper·se, v.t. Scatter, place here & there (*between, among*); diversify (thing) *with* (others so scattered). So **intersper·s**ION n. [f. L INTER(*spergere spers-* = *spargere* scatter)]

i·nterstate, a. (U.S.). Existing, carried on, between States. [INTER-]

inter·stice (*or* ĭ·n-), n. Intervening space; chink, crevice. [f. L *interstitium* f. INTER(*sistere stit-* stand)]

intersti·tial (-shl), a. Of, forming, occupying, interstice(s). [as prec. + -AL]

intertwi·ne, v.t. & i. Entwine (things, one *with* another); become entwined. Hence **intertwi·ne**MENT n. [INTER-]

i·nterval, n. Intervening time or space; pause; break, gap; *at ii.*, here & there, now & then; (Mus.) difference of pitch between two sounds, in melody or harmony; distance between persons or things in respect of qualities. Hence **interva·ll**IC a. [f. L INTER(*vallum* rampart) space between ramparts, interval]

interve·ne, v.i. Come in as something extraneous; occur in the meantime; (of person or thing) come between, interfere, so as to prevent or modify result &c. (*between* persons, *in* affair); (Law) interpose in lawsuit to which one was not an original party (esp. of King's Proctor in divorce cases), whence **interve·n**ER[1] n.; lie, be situated, *between*. So **intervē·ni**ENT a., **interve·nt**ION n. [f. L INTER(*venire vent-* come)]

i·nterview, n., & v.t. Meeting of persons face to face, esp. for purpose of conference; meeting between person employed by newspaper & some one from whom he seeks to get statements for publication; (v.t.) have an i. with (person), esp. with a view to publication of his statements. Hence **i·nterview**ER[1] n. [(vb f. n.) f. F *entrevue* f. *s'entrevoir* (*entre-* INTER- + *voir* f. L *vidēre* see)]

intervo·lve, v.t. Wind, roll up, (things) within each other. [f. INTER- + L *volvere* roll]

interwea·ve, v.t. Weave together, interlace, (things, one *with* another); blend (things) intimately. [INTER-]

interwi·nd, v.t. & i. Wind together. [INTER-]

inte·state (-*a*t), a. & n. (Of person) not having made a will, as *he died i.*; (n.) i. person. Hence **inte·sta**CY n. [f. L IN[2](*testatus* p.p. of *testari* make will f. *testis* witness)]

inte·stine[1], n. (Usu. pl.) lower part of alimentary canal from pyloric end of stomach to anus; *small, large, i.*, parts of this. So **inte·stin**AL (*or* -ī·nal) a. [f. L neut. adj. as foll.]

inte·stine[2], a. (Of wars &c.) internal, domestic, civil; *i. motion* (entirely within a body). [f. L *intestīnus* internal (*intus* within)]

i·ntimate[1] (-*a*t), a. & n. Close in acquaintance, familiar, as *i. friend(ship)*; *i.* (close) *connexion*; *i. knowledge* (resulting from familiarity); essential, intrinsic; (of diary) recording emotions &c.; (n.) i. friend. Hence **i·ntima**CY n., **i·ntimate**LY[2] adv. [foll., -ATE[2]]

i·ntimāte[2], v.t. Make known, state, (fact, wish, *that*); imply, hint. So **intima·t**ION n. [f. LL *intimare* (*intimus* inmost), -ATE[3]]

inti·midate, v.t. Inspire with fear, cow, esp. in order to influence conduct. Hence **intimida·t**ION, **inti·midat**OR[2], nn. [f. med. L IN[1](*timidare* f. *timidus* TIMID), see -ATE[3]]

inti·mity, n. Inwardness; privacy. [f. L *intimus* inmost, see -TY]

inti·nction, n. Dipping of the Eucharistic bread in the wine, to enable the communicant to receive both kinds. [f. LL *intinctio* f. IN[1](*tingere tinct-* TINGE)]

inti·tūle, v.t. Entitle (Act of Parliament, usu. p.p.). [f. OF *intituler* f. LL IN[1](*titulare* f. *titulus* TITLE)]

i·nto (as TO), prep. expr. motion or direction to a point within a thing, lit. & fig., as: *come i. the garden, throw it i. the fire, look i. the box, the matter, inquire i. it, get i. trouble, come i.* (acquire) *property, watching far on i. the night*; expr. change, condition, result, as: *turn stones i. gold, collect them i. heaps, divide them i. three classes, flogged i. submission.* [IN + TO]

i·n-toed (-ōd), a. Having the toes turned inwards. [IN adv. + TOE + -ED[2]]

into·lerable, a. That cannot be endured. Hence **into·lerable**NESS n., **into·lerab**LY[2] adv. [f. L IN[2](*tolerabilis* TOLERABLE)]

into·lerant, a. Not tolerant (*of*, esp. religious opinions differing from one's own). Hence or cogn. **into·ler**ANCE n., **into·lerant**LY[2] adv. [f. L IN[2](*tolerans* TOLERANT)]

i·ntonate, v.t. = INTONE. [-ATE[3]]

intona·tion, n. Reciting in singing voice; (Church Mus.) opening phrase of plainsong melody; utterance, production, of musical tones; modulation of voice, accent. [as foll., see -ATION]

into·ne, v.t. Recite (psalm, prayer, &c.,

or abs.) in singing voice; utter with particular tone. [f. L IN[1](*tonare* f. *tonus* TONE)]

into·xicant, a. & n. Intoxicating (liquor). [as foll., see -ANT]

into·xicate, v.t. Make drunk; excite, exhilarate, beyond self-control (*intoxicated with, by*). Hence **into·xicat**ING[2] a., **intoxica**·TION n. [f. med. L IN[1](*toxicare* smear with poison f. *toxicum* f. Gk *toxikon* f. *toxa* arrows), see -ATE[3]]

i·ntra- in comb. = L *intra* on the inside, within, as: *-cra·nial*, within the skull; *-mur·al*, existing, done, within walls; *-national*, (not inter)national.

intra·ctable, a. Not docile, refractory; (of things) not easily dealt with. Hence **intractab**I·LITY, **intra·ctable**NESS, nn., **intra·ctab**LY[2] adv. [f. L IN[2](*tractabilis* TRACTABLE)]

intrā·dŏs, n. (arch.). Interior curve of arch (cf. EXTRADOS). [F (INTRA- + *dos* back)]

intra·nsigent, a. & n. Uncompromising in politics; (n.) uncompromising republican. [f. F *intransigeant* f. Sp. *los intransigentes* extreme republicans f. IN-[2] + L TRANS(*igere* = *agere* act) come to an understanding, see -ENT]

intra·nsitive, a. & n. (Verb) that does not take a direct object (cf. TRANSITIVE). Hence **intra·nsitive**LY[2] adv. [f. L IN[2](*transitivus* TRANSITIVE)]

i·ntrant, n. One who enters a college, association, &c. [f. L *intrare* enter, see -ANT]

intrĕ·pid, a. Fearless, brave. Hence **intrepi·d**ITY n., **intre·pid**LY[2] adv. [f. L IN[2](*trepidus* alarmed)]

i·ntricate (-*at*), a. Perplexingly entangled; involved; obscure. Hence **i·ntric**ACY n., **i·ntricate**LY[2] adv. [f. L IN[1](*tricare* f. *tricae* tricks), see -ATE[2]]

i·ntrig(u)ant (-gant), n. (fem. *intrig(u)a·nte*, pron. -ahnt, -ănt, or as F). Intriguer. [F (*-guant*), part. as foll.]

intri·gue[1] (-ēg), v.i. & t. Carry on underhand plot; employ secret influence (*with*); have a liaison (*with*); (as journalistic gallicism, v.t.) rouse the interest or curiosity of. [f. F *intriguer* (as INTRICATE)]

intri·gue[2] (-ēg), n. Underhand plotting or plot; secret amour, liaison. [F, f. It. *intrigo* f. *intrigare* (as INTRICATE)]

intri·nsic, a. Belonging naturally, inherent, essential, esp. *i. value* (cf. EXTRINSIC). Hence **intri·ns**ICALLY adv. [f. F *intrinsèque* f. med. L *intrinsecus* (adj. f. L adv.), cf. EXTRINSIC]

intro- in comb. = L *intro* to the inside, as: *-fle·xion*, inward bending; *-gre·ssion*, going or coming in; *-susce·ption*, (Physiol., Biol.) = INTUSSUSCEPTION.

introdu·ce, v.t. Bring in; place in, insert; bring into use (custom, idea, improvement, &c., *into* place, system, &c.); usher in, bring forward, (matter &c.); (of conjunctions &c.) open (sentence); make known, esp. in formal manner (person *to* another); bring (young lady) out, into society; draw attention of (person *to* subject &c.); bring (bill &c.) before Parliament. So **introdu·ct**ORY a. [f. L INTRO(*ducere duct-* lead)]

introdu·ction, n. Introducing; preliminary matter prefixed to book; (as title) introductory treatise; formal presentation of one person to another; *letter of i.* (given by one person to another & introducing him to a third). [F, f. L *introductionem* (as prec., see -ION)]

intrō·it, n. (eccl.). Psalm, antiphon, sung while priest approaches altar to celebrate mass or Holy Communion. [f. F *introït(e)* f. L *introitus -ūs* f. INTRO(*ire it-* go)]

intromi·t, v.t. (archaic). (-tt-). Let in, admit, (*into*); insert. So **intromi·ss**ION n., **intromi·tt**ENT a. [f. L INTRO(*mittere miss-* send)]

introspe·ct, v.i. Examine one's own thoughts & feelings. Hence **introspe·c**TION, **introspe·ction**IST, **introspe·ctive**NESS, nn., **introspe·ct**IVE a., **introspe·ctive**LY[2] adv. [f. L INTRO(*spicere spect-* look)]

introver·t, v.t. Turn (mind, thought) inwards upon itself; (esp. Zool.) withdraw (organ &c.) within its own tube or base, as finger of glove, whence **introver·s**IBLE a. Hence **introver·s**ION n., **i·ntrovert** n., person given to introversion, **introver·s**IVE, **introver·t**IVE, aa. [f. L INTRO(*vertere vers-* turn)]

intru·de, v.t. & i. Thrust, force, (thing *into*); force (thing *upon* person); come uninvited, thrust oneself in, (*into* place, company, &c., *upon* person, his privacy, &c.). Hence **intru·d**ER[1] n. [f. L IN[1](*trudere trus-* thrust)]

intru·sion (-zhn), n. Intruding; forcing in; forcing oneself in (*into, upon*); (Geol.) influx of rock in state of fusion between strata &c.; settlement of minister of Church of Scotland without consent of congregation, whence **intru·sion**IST(2) n. So **intru·s**IVE (-s-) a., **intru·sive**LY[2] adv., **intru·sive**NESS n. [OF, f. med. L *intrusionem* (as prec., see -ION)]

i·ntubate, v.t. (med.). Insert tube into (larynx &c.) to keep it open. Hence **intuba**·TION n. [f. IN-[2] + L *tuba* tube + -ATE[3]]

i·ntūit, v.t. & i. Know by intuition; receive knowledge by direct perception. [f. L IN[1](*tuēri tuit-* look)]

intui·tion (-shn), n. Immediate apprehension by the mind without reasoning; immediate apprehension by sense; immediate insight. Hence **intui·tion**AL a. [F, f. med. L *intuitionem* (as prec., see -ION)]

intui·tionalism, n. Doctrine that the perception of truth is by intuition. So **intui·tional**IST n. [-ISM]

intui·tionism, n. Doctrine that in perception external objects are known immediately, without intervention of vicarious phenomenon; = prec. So **intui·tionIST** n. [-ISM]

intū·itive, a. Of, possessing, perceived by, intuition. Hence **intu·itiveLY**[2] adv., **intu·itiveNESS** n. [f. med. L *intuitivus* (INTUIT, -IVE)]

intū·itivism, n. Doctrine that ethical principles are matters of intuition. So **intu·itivIST** n. [-ISM]

intume·scent (-snt), a. Swelling up. So **intume·SCENCE** n. [f. L IN[1](*tumescere* incept. of *tumēre* swell), see -ENT]

i·ntussusce·ption, n. (Physiol.) taking in of foreign matter by living organism, & its conversion into organic tissue; taking in (*of* ideas &c.); withdrawal of one portion of intestine within another. [f. L *intus* within + *susceptio* f. SUS(*cipere* = *capere* take) take up, see -ION]

inu·nction, n. Smearing, rubbing, with oil. [f. L *inunctio* f. IN[1](*unguere unct-* anoint), see -ION]

i·nundate, v.t. Overflow, flood, (land &c. *with* water, also fig.). So **inundA·TION** n. [f. L IN[1](*undare* flow f. *unda* wave), see -ATE[3]]

inurbā·ne, a. Not urbane, discourteous. Hence **inurbă·NITY** n. [f. L IN[2](*urbanus* URBANE)]

inure·, en-, (-ūr), v.t. & i. Accustom, habituate, (person &c. *to* thing, *to* do), whence **inure·MENT** n.; (intr., chiefly Law; often *en-*) come into operation, take effect. [IN-[1] + obs. *ure* work f. F *œuvre* f. L *opera*]

inur·n, v.t. Put (ashes of cremated body) in an urn. [IN-[1]]

inū·tile, a. Useless. So **inuti·lITY** n. [F, f. L IN[2](*utilis* useful); long out of use, but recently revived]

inva·de, v.t. Make hostile inroad into (country &c.); (fig. of sounds, diseases, feelings, &c.) assail; encroach upon (rights &c.). Hence **inva·dER**[1] n. [f. L IN[1](*vadere vas-* go)]

invă·ginate, v.t. Put in a sheath; introvert (tubular sheath). Hence **invaginA·TION** n. [f. IN-[1] + L *vagina* sheath + -ATE[3]]

i·nvalid[1] (-ēd), a. & n. (Person) enfeebled or disabled by illness or injury. Hence **i·nvalidHOOD, i·nvalidISM**(3), nn. [f. L IN[2](*validus* VALID), pronunc. after F *invalide*]

invali·d[2] (-ēd, *also* ĭ·n-), v.t. & i. Lay up, disable, (person) by illness (usu. pass.); treat as an invalid, remove from active service, send *home* &c., as an invalid; (intr.) become an invalid, go on the sick-list. [f. prec.]

invă·lid[3], a. Not valid, esp. having no legal force. Hence **inva·lidLY**[2] adv. [as INVALID[1], without assim. to F]

inva·lidate, v.t. Make INVALID[3]. Hence **inva·lidA·TION** n. [prec. + -ATE[3]]

invali·dity, n. Want of validity; bodily infirmity. [INVALID[3,1] + -ITY]

inva·luable, a. Above price, priceless. [IN-[2]]

invār·iable, a. Unchangeable; always the same; (Math.) constant, fixed. Hence **invariaBI·LITY, invar·iableNESS,** nn., **invar·iabLY**[2] adv. [IN-[2]]

invā·sion (-zhn), n. Invading; encroachment. So **inva·SIVE** (-s-) a. [F, f. L *invasionem* (as INVADE, see -ION)]

inve·ctive, n. Violent attack in words; abusive oratory. [F, f. med. L *invectiva* (*oratio*) f. LL *invectivus* (as foll., see -IVE)]

inveigh· (-ā), v.i. Speak violently, rail loudly, *against*. [f. L IN[1](*vehi* pass. of *vehere vect-* carry) go into, assail]

invei·gle (-vē-, -vā-), v.t. Entice, seduce, (*into* place, conduct, &c., *into* doing). Hence **invei·gleMENT** n. [16th-c. *envegle* prob. f. F *aveugler* blind f. *aveugle* adj. f. pop. L AB(*oculus* eye); taken as *a-vegle*, & so changed to *envegle*]

invē·nit, invenēr·unt, (abbr. *inv.*), v. sing. & pl. 3rd pers. (So-&-so) designed this work (used with artist's signature). [L, perf. of *invenio*, see foll.]

inve·nt, v.t. Devise, originate, (new method, instrument, &c.); fabricate (false story &c.). Hence or cogn. **inve·ntIVE** a., **inve·ntiveLY**[2] adv., **inve·ntiveNESS, inve·ntOR**[2] (esp. in Law, patentee of INVENTION), **inve·ntrESS**[1], nn. [f. L IN[1](*venire vent-* come) find, contrive]

inve·ntion, n. Inventing; thing invented, contrivance, (Law) any new manufacture the subject of letters patent; fictitious story; inventiveness; *I. of the Cross,* (festival, May 3, commemorating) finding of the Cross by Helena mother of Constantine, A.D. 326. [OF, f. L *inventionem* (as prec., see -ION)]

i·nventory (-vn-), n., & v.t. Detailed list (of goods, furniture, &c.); stock of goods in this; (v.t.) enter (goods &c.) in i., make i. of. [(vb f. n.) f. med. L *inventorium* (as INVENT, see -ORY)]

inveră·city, n. Untruthfulness. [IN-[2]]

Inverne·ss, n. Town in Scotland; *I. cloak, coat,* or *i.* as n., man's sleeveless cloak with removable cape.

inver·se (*or* ĭ·n-), a. & n. Inverted in position, order, or relations; *i. ratio, proportion* (between two quantities one of which increases as the other decreases); (n.) inverted state, thing that is the direct opposite (*of* another). Hence **inver·seLY**[2] adv. [f. L as INVERT]

inver·sion, n. Turning upside down; reversal of position, order, or relation, esp. (Gram.) of order of words; reversal of a ratio. So **inver·SIVE** a. [f. L *inversio* (as foll., see -ION)]

inver·t[1], v.t. Turn upside down (*inverted commas*, those above the line before & after quotations, the first single or double comma being inverted, as *what is a* '*German peace*' or "*German peace*"?); reverse position, order, or relation, of;

(Mus.) change relative position of notes of (chord, interval) by placing lowest note higher. [f. L IN¹(*vertere vers-* turn)]
i·nvert², n. Inverted arch, as at bottom of sewer. [f. prec.]
inver·tebrate (-*at*), a. & n. Not having backbone or spinal column; (fig.) wanting in firmness; (n.) i. animal or (fig.) person. [f. IN-² + L *vertebra* joint of spine + -ATE²]
inve·st, v.t. & i. Clothe (person &c. *in, with*); cover as garment; clothe, endue, (person &c. *with* qualities, insignia of office, rank, &c.); lay siege to; employ (money *in* stocks &c.); (intr.) *i. in*, put money into (stocks), (colloq.) lay out money on, as *i. in a bun*. Hence **inve·stor**² n. [f. L IN¹(*vestire* clothe)]
inve·stigate, v.t. Examine, inquire into. Hence or cogn. **investigA·TION, inve·stigatOR²**, nn., **inve·stigatIVE, inve·stigatORY**, aa. [f. L IN¹(*vestigare* track), see -ATE³]
inve·stiture, n. Formal investing of person (*with* office); enduing (*with* attributes). [f. med. L *investitura* (as INVEST, see -URE)]
inve·stment, n. Investing of money; money invested; property in which money is invested; investiture; clothing. [-MENT]
invĕ·terate (-*at*), a. Long-established; (of disease, habit, prejudice, &c.) deep-rooted, obstinate. Hence **inve·terACY** n., **inve·terateLY²** adv. [f. L IN¹(*veterare* make old f. *vetus -eris* old), see -ATE³]
invi·dious, a. (Of conduct &c.) giving offence, esp. by real or seeming injustice &c.; (of thing) likely to excite ill feeling against the possessor. Hence **invi·diousLY²** adv., **invi·diousNESS** n. [f. L *invidiosus* (*invidia* ENVY, see -OUS)]
invi·gilate, v.i. Watch over students at examination. Hence **invigilA·TION, invi·gilatOR²**, nn. [f. L IN¹(*vigilare* watch), -ATE³]
invi·gorate, v.t. Make vigorous; animate. Hence **invi·gorATIVE** a., **invi·goratOR²** n. [f. IN-¹ + L *vigor* VIGOUR + -ATE³]
invi·ncible, a. Unconquerable (lit. & fig.). Hence **invinciBI·LITY** n., **invi·ncibLY²** adv. [F, f. L IN²(*vincibilis* f. *vincere* conquer, -BLE)]
invī·olable, a. Not to be violated; (of laws, persons, places, &c.) to be kept sacred from infraction, profanation, &c. Hence **inviolaBI·LITY** n., **invi·olabLY²** adv. [f. L IN²(*violabilis*, as foll., see -BLE)]
invī·olate (-*at*), a. (Of laws, places, &c.) not violated; unbroken; unprofaned. Hence **invi·olACY, invi·olateNESS**, nn., **inviolateLY²** adv. [f. L IN²(*violatus* p.p. as VIOLATE)]
invĭ·sible (-z-), a. & n. That cannot be seen; not to be seen at particular time, as *when I called she was i.*; too small to be seen; *i. exports*, shipping services, foreign investments, & other items that account for the apparent excess of a country's imports over exports; *i. ink* (visible only after heating &c.); *the i.*, the unseen world, God. Hence or cogn. **invisiBI·LITY, invi·sibleNESS**, nn., **invi·sibLY²** adv. [F, f. L IN²(*visibilis* VISIBLE)]
invi·te, v.t., & n. Request courteously to come (*to* dinner, *to* one's house, *in*, &c.); request courteously (*to* do what is presumably agreeable); solicit courteously (suggestions, opinion, confidences); bring on, tend to bring on, (thing) unintentionally; (of thing) present inducements, attract, whence **invi·tingLY²** adv., **invi·tingNESS** n.; (n., colloq.) invitation. So **invītA·TION** n., **invī·tatORY** a. [(n. f. vb) f. F *inviter* f. L *invitare*]
invoca·tion, n. Invoking, calling upon God &c. in prayer; *the i.*, (esp.) the words 'In the name of the Father' &c. as used by preacher before sermon (cf. ASCRIPTION); appeal to Muse for inspiration or assistance in poem. So **invŏ·catORY** (*or* ĭ·nvokā-) a. [OF, f. L *invocationem* (as INVOKE, see -ATION)]
i·nvoice, n., & v.t. List of goods shipped or sent, with prices & charges; (v.t.) make an i. of (goods). [(vb f. n.) prob. orig. *invoyes* pl. of *invoy* as ENVOY¹]
invo·ke, v.t. Call on (God &c.) in prayer or as witness; appeal to (person's authority &c.); summon (spirit) by charms; ask earnestly for (vengeance, help, &c.). [f. F *invoquer* f. L IN¹(*vocare* call)]
i·nvolucre (-*ker*), n. Covering, envelope, (esp. anat.); (Bot.) whorl of bracts surrounding inflorescence. [F, f. L *involucrum* (as INVOLVE)]
invo·luntary, a. Done without exercise of the will, unintentional. Hence **invo·luntariLY²** adv., **invo·luntariNESS** n. [f. L IN²(*voluntarius* VOLUNTARY)]
i·nvolute, a. & n. Involved, intricate; curled spirally; (Bot.) rolled inwards at edges; (n., geom.) locus of point in a straight line that rolls without sliding on a curve in the plane of that curve (cf. EVOLUTE). [as INVOLVE]
involu·tion, n. Involving; entanglement; intricacy; curling inwards; part so curled; (Math.) raising of quantity to any power. [f. L *involutio* (as foll., see -ION)]
invo·lve, v.t. Wrap (thing *in* another); wind spirally; entangle (person, thing, *in* difficulties, mystery, &c.); implicate (person *in* charge, crime); include (*in*); imply, entail. [f. L IN¹(*volvere volut-* roll)]
invo·lvement, n. Involving; financial embarrassment; complicated affair. [-MENT]
invu·lnerable, a. That cannot be wounded or hurt (esp. fig.). Hence **invulneraBI·LITY** n., **invu·lnerabLY²** adv. [f. L IN²(*vulnerabilis* VULNERABLE)]
i·nward (-*erd*), a. & n. Situated within; mental, spiritual; directed towards the

inside; (n. pl.) entrails. [OE *innanweard* (*innan* in adv., see -WARD)]

i·nwardly, adv. On the inside; (of speaking) not aloud; in mind or spirit. [-LY^{2}]

i·nwardness, a. Inner nature, essence; quality of being inward; spirituality. [-NESS]

i·nward(s), adv. (Of motion or position) towards the inside; within mind or soul. [prec.]

inwea·ve, en-, v.t. Weave in (thing *with* another, lit. & fig.). [IN-^{1}]

i·nwrought, a. & (ĭnraw·t) p.p. (Of fabric) decorated (*with* pattern); (of pattern) wrought (*in, on,* fabric); (fig.) intimately blended (*with*). [IN + *wrought* p.p. of WORK]

inya·la (-ah-), n. S.-Afr. antelope. [native]

ī·odine, n. Non-metallic element resembling chlorine & bromine in chemical properties, used in medicine & photography. Hence **iŏ·d**IC a., **i·od**ISM(5) n., **i·od**IZE(5) v.t. [f. F *iode* f. Gk *iōdēs* violet-like (*ion* violet, see -OID), from colour of its vapour, + -INE^{3}]

iō·doform, (*or* ī·o-), n. Compound of iodine analogous to chloroform, used as antiseptic &c. [f. prec. + -O-, see CHLOROFORM]

ī·olite, n. Silicate of aluminium, iron, & magnesium, of blue or violet colour. [f. Gk *ion* violet, see -LITE]

ī·on, n. Either of the elements that pass to the poles in electrolysis, particle of moving matter carrying a unit(ary) charge of positive or negative electricity (the + a *cation*, the − an *anion*). Hence **i·on**IZE v.t., convert into ii., **ioniz**A·TION n. [Gk *ion* neut. part. of *eimi* go]

-ion, suf., mainly thr. F *-ion* f. L *-ionem* (nom. *-io*) forming nouns of condition or action f. adjj. & nn. (*communio*), f. vb stems (*legio*), but esp. f. p.p. stems, producing the compd suff. *-tion, -sion, -xion, -ation, -ition, -son.*

Iō·nian, a. & n. Of Ionia; (Mus.) *I. mode,* (1) effeminate mode in ancient Greek music, (2) ecclesiastical mode corresp. to modern major diatonic scale; (n.) member of part of the Hellenic race which occupied Attica, western Asia Minor, &c. [f. L f. Gk *Iōnios* + -AN]

Iŏ·nic, a. Of Ionia, as *I. dialect,* that of which Attic was a development; *I.* ORDER (characterized by two lateral volutes of the capital); (Pros.) *i. ā major·ĕ,* metrical foot – – ⌣ ⌣, *i. ā minor·ĕ,* ⌣ ⌣ – –. [f. L f. Gk *Iōnikos*]

-ior^{1}, suf., later spelling of -IOUR, as in *warrior.*

-ior^{2}, suf. = L *-ior* of comparatives, as in *senior, ulterior.*

īō·ta, n. Greek letter (Ι, ι, = I); atom, jot, (after *Matt.* v. 18). [Gk *iōta*]

iō·tacism, n. Excessive use of iota; pronunciation of other Greek vowels like iota (ē), cf. ITACISM. [f. L f. Gk *iōtakismos*]

Ī Ō Ū·, n. Signed document bearing these letters followed by specified sum, constituting formal acknowledgement of debt. [= I owe you]

-iour, suf. = *-i-* representing some formative or stem element + *-our* -OR^{2}, as *saviour* f. *salvatorem* thr. OF *salve(d)or,* AF *sauveour.*

-ious, suf. repr. L *-iosus,* F *-ieux,* = *-i-* (part of another suf.) + -OUS, w. sense 'characterized by, full of'. L has *-iosus* (1) in adjj. f. derivative nn. in *-ia, -ies, -ius, -ium,* (*invidiosus, perniciosus, odiosus,* & by false anal. *curiosus* f. *cura*), (2) in adjj. f. nn. in *-ion-* (nom. *-io*), as *ambitiosus, captiosus, religiosus.* E tends to use *-ious* for any noun in *-ion* (*rebellious, cautious, contradictious*). E also forms adjj. in *-ious* by adding -OUS to stem of L adjj. in *-ius* (*various*); see also -ITIOUS & -OUS.

ĭpĕcăcūă·nha (-n*a*), n. Root of a S.-Amer. shrub, used as emetic & purgative. [Port., f. native *ipekaaguene*]

i·pse di·xit, n. Dogmatic statement resting on bare authority. [L, = he himself (the master) said it]

i·pso fa·cto, adv. By that very fact. [L]

ir-^{1,2}, (ĭ-r), preff. = IN-^{1,2} before *r.*

ĭra·dĕ (-ah-), n. Written decree of Sultan of Turkey. [Turk., f. Arab. *iradah* will]

Ira·k, 'Ira·q, n. Arab kingdom including Mesopotamia administered by British Empire as mandatary. So **Ira·ki, -qi,** (-ahkĭ) a.

Irā·nian (īr-), a. & n. Persian; (of languages) of the Asiatic family comprising Zend, Old Persian, & their modern descendants; (n.) member of I. race. [Pers. *iran* Persia, -IAN]

ĭra·scible (-sĭ-), a. Irritable, hot-tempered. Hence **irasci**BI·LITY n. [F, f. L *irascibilis* (*irasci* grow angry, see -BLE)]

īrā·te, a. Angry. [f. L *iratus* p.p. as prec.]

ire, n. (poet.). Anger. Hence **ire·**FUL a., **ire·ful**LY^{2} adv. [OF, f. L *ira*]

irē·nic(al), aa. Aiming or aimed at peace. [f. Gk *eirēnikos* (*eirēnē* peace) + -AL]

irenicon. See EIRENICON.

īridā·ceous (-sh*u*s), a. Of the iris kind. [-ACEOUS]

ĭride·scent (-snt), a. Showing colours like those of rainbow; changing colour with position. Hence **iride·sc**ENCE n. [as IRIS + -ESCENT]

īrĭ·dium, n. White metal of platinum group, like polished steel. [as IRIS + -IUM]

īr·is, n. Flat circular coloured membrane in aqueous humour of eye, with circular opening (PUPIL) in centre; genus of plants, chiefly with tuberous roots, sword-shaped leaves, & showy flowers; kind of rock-crystal reflecting prismatic colours. [Gk *iris -idos* (goddess of) rainbow, iris]

Ir·ish (īr-), a. & n. Of Ireland; *I.* BULL^{4}; *I. Free State,* part of Ireland separated from the U.K. & established as a British

Dominion 1922; *I.* STEW; (n.) I. language; (as pl.) *the I.* (people); *Irishman, -woman,* native of Ireland. Hence **Ir·ish**ISM(4) n., **Ir·ish**IZE(3) v.t. [f. *Ir-* st. of OE *Iras* n. pl. + -ISH[1]]

irk, v.t. (archaic). Disgust, tire, bore, esp. *it irks* (*me, him,* &c.). [ME *irken,* etym. dub.]

ir·ksome, a. Tedious, tiresome. Hence **ir·ksome**LY[2] adv., **ir·ksome**NESS n. [-SOME]

iron[1] (īrn), n. & a. Metal largely used for tools &c. (*wrought i., cast i.,* STEEL), often fig. as type of hardness, as *a man of i., rod of i.*; preparation of i. as tonic; tool made of i., as *curling, grappling, -i.*; branding tool; golf-club with i. head laid back to loft the ball; i. tool for smoothing out linen &c.; (usu. pl.) fetters (esp. *in ii.,* handcuffed); *the i. entered into his soul* (*Ps.* cv. 18, L mistranslation of Heb. ' his person entered into the iron ', i.e. fetters); (Provv.) *strike while the i. is hot* (at a good opportunity), *have* (*too*) *many ii. in the fire* (many undertakings, also, many expedients); (adj.) of i., very robust, firm, unyielding, merciless; *i. age,* age of cruelty, oppression, &c. (cf. BRAZEN[1]), (also, cf. BRONZE, STONE, *age*) era of iron implements; *i.-bark,* species of eucalyptus with solid bark; *i.-bound,* bound with i., (of coast) rock-bound, (fig.) rigorous, hard & fast; *iron-clad,* clad in, protected with, i., (n.) ship cased with plates of i.; *I. Duke,* Duke of Wellington; *i.-grey* a. & n., (of) the colour of freshly broken i.; *i. horse,* locomotive steam-engine, also, bicycle or tricycle; *iron-master,* manufacturer of i.; *i.-mould,* spot caused by i.-rust or ink-stain, (v.t. & i.) stain, be stained, with this; *i. rations,* soldier's modicum of food to be touched only in emergency; *Ironsides,* man of great bravery, esp. (pl.) Cromwell's troopers; *i.-stone,* name of various hard i.-ores; *ironwork,* work in i., things made of i.; *ironworks* (sing. or pl.), place where i. is smelted or i. goods are made. [OE (1) *īsern, īsen,* n. & a., cf. Du. *ijzer,* G *eisen,* (2) OE *īren* n., not paralleled in other langg.]

iron[2] (īrn), v.t. Furnish, cover, with iron; shackle with irons; smooth (linen &c.) with flat-iron &c. [f. prec.]

īrŏ·nic(al), aa. Of, using, said in, addicted to, irony. Hence **īrŏ·nical**LY[2] adv. [f. L f. Gk *eirōnikos* (as IRONY[1], see -IC)]

īr·onist, n. One who uses irony. [f. Gk *eirōn* dissembler + -IST]

ir·onmonger (īrn-), n. Dealer in iron goods. Hence **ir·onmonger**ERY(1, 2, 3) n.

irony[1] (īr·onĭ), n. Expression of one's meaning by language of opposite or different tendency, esp. simulated adoption of another's point of view for purpose of ridicule; ill-timed or perverse arrival of event or circumstance in itself desirable, due to the feigned good will & actual malice *of* (Fate, circumstance, &c.); use of language that has an inner meaning for a privileged audience and an outer meaning for the persons addressed or concerned (sometimes including speaker, cf. TRAGIC *i.*); *Socratic i.,* simulation of ignorance as means of confuting adversary. [f. L f. Gk *eirōneia* simulated ignorance]

irony[2] (īr·nĭ), a. Of, like, iron. [-Y[2]]

irrā·diant, a. Shining brightly. So **irra·di**ANCE n. [as foll., see -ANT]

irrā·diate, v.t. Shine upon; (fig.) throw light on (subject); light up (face &c. *with* joy &c.). Hence **irra·diat**IVE a. [f. L IR[1](*radiare* f. *radius* RAY), see -ATE[3]]

irrādia·tion, n. Shining, illumination, (lit. & fig.); apparent extension of edges of illuminated object seen against dark ground. [F (as prec., see -ATION)]

irră·tional, a. & n. Unreasonable, illogical, absurd; not endowed with reason; (Math., of roots &c.) not rational, not commensurable with the natural numbers (e.g. non-terminating decimal); (n.) i. number, surd. Hence **irrationa·l**ITY n., **irra·tional**IZE(3) v.t., **irra·tional**LY[2] adv. [f. L IR[2](*rationalis* RATIONAL)]

irreclai·mable, a. Not to be reclaimed or reformed. Hence **irreclai·mab**LY[2] adv. [IR-[2]]

irre·cognizable, a. Unrecognizable. [IR-[2]]

irre·concīlable, a. & n. Implacably hostile; (of ideas &c.) incompatible; (n.) implacable opponent of political measure &c. Hence **irreconcila**BI·LITY, **irre·concilable**NESS, nn.; **irre·concilab**LY[2] adv. [IR[2]-]

irreco·verable (-kŭ-), a. That cannot be recovered or remedied. Hence **irreco·verab**LY[2] adv. [IR-[2]]

irrecū·sable, a. That must be accepted. f. LL IR[2](*recusabilis* f. *recusare* refuse, see -BLE)]

irredee·mable, a. (Of government annuities) not terminable by repayment; (of paper currency) for which issuing authority does not undertake to pay coin; irreclaimable, hopeless, whence **irredee·mab**LY[2] adv. [IR-[2]]

ĭrrede·ntist, n. (It. politics) advocate of recovery to Italy of all Italian-speaking districts; Greek, Pole, Serbian, &c., of similar views. So **irrede·nt**ISM n. [f. It. *irredentista* f. (*Italia*) *irredenta* unredeemed (Italy)]

irredū·cible, a. That cannot be brought (*to* desired condition); that cannot be reduced, as *i. minimum*; that cannot be simplified. Hence **irreduci**BI·LITY n. [IR-[2]]

irrĕ·fragable, a. (Of statement, argument, person) indisputable, unanswerable. Hence **irre·fragab**LY[2] adv. [f. LL IR[2](*refragabilis* f. RE*fragari* etym. dub., see -BLE)]

irrefra·ngible, a. Inviolable; (Opt.) incapable of being refracted. [IR-[2]]

irre·fūtable, a. Not to be refuted. Hence **irrefuta**BI·LITY n., **irre·futab**LY[2] adv. [f. L IR[2](*refutabilis* REFUTABLE)]

irrĕ·gular, a. & n. Not regular, contrary to rule; abnormal; not of symmetrical form; (of surface) uneven; disorderly; uneven in duration, order, &c.; (Gram., of part of speech) not normally inflected; (of troops) not in regular service; (n. pl.) i. troops. Hence or cogn. **irregulă·**RITY n., **irre·gular**LY[2] adv. [f. OF *irreguler* f. med.L IR[2](*regularis* REGULAR)]

irrĕ·lative, a. Unconnected, unrelated, (*to*); having no relations, absolute. Hence **irre·lative**LY[2] adv. [IR-[2]]

irrĕ·levant, a. Not to the point; that does not apply (*to* matter in hand). Hence **irre·lev**ANCE, -ANCY, nn., **irre·levant**LY[2] adv. [IR-[2]]

irreli·gion, n. Hostility to, disregard of, religion. Hence or cogn. **irreli·gion**IST(2) n., **irreli·gi**OUS a., **irreli·gious**LY[2] adv. [f. L IR[2](*religio* RELIGION)]

irremē·diable, a. That cannot be remedied. Hence **irreme·diab**LY[2] adv. [f. L IR[2](*remediabilis* REMEDIABLE)]

irremi·ssible, a. Unpardonable; unalterably binding. Hence **irremi·ssib**LY[2] adv. [f F *irrémissible* f. L IR[2](*remissibilis*, as REMIT, see -BLE)]

irremo·vable (-ōō-), a. That cannot be removed, esp. from office. Hence **irremova**BI·LITY n., **irremo·vab**LY[2] adv. [IR-[2]]

irrĕ·parable, a. (Of injury, loss, &c.) that cannot be rectified or made good. Hence **irre·parable**NESS n., **irre·parab**LY[2] adv. [f. F *irréparable* f. L IR[2](*reparabilis* REPARABLE)]

irreplā·ceable, a. Of which the loss cannot be supplied. [IR-[2]]

irrepre·ssible, a. & n. Not to be repressed or restrained; (n., colloq.) i. person. Hence **irrepre·ssib**LY[2] adv. [IR-[2], REPRESS, -IBLE]

irreproa·chable, a. Free from blame, faultless. Hence **irreproacha**BI·LITY n., **irreproa·chab**LY[2] adv. [f. F IR[2](*réprochable*, as REPROACH v., see -ABLE)]

irresi·stible, a. Too strong, convincing, charming, &c., to be resisted. Hence **irresisti**BI·LITY n., **irresi·stib**LY[2] adv. [f. LL IR[2](*resistibilis*, as RESIST, see -BLE)]

irrĕ·solute, a. Undecided, hesitating; wanting in resolution. Hence or cogn. **irre·solute**LY[2] adv., **irre·solute**NESS, **irresolu·t**ION, nn. [f. L IR[2](*resolutus* RESOLUTE)]

irreso·lvable, a. That cannot be resolved into parts; (of problem) that cannot be solved. [IR-[2]]

irrespe·ctive, a. *I. of*, not taking into account, without reference to, (often quasi-adv., as *the posts were filled i. of nationality*). Hence **irrespe·ctive**LY[2] adv. [IR-[2]]

irrespo·nsible, a. Not responsible for conduct; acting, done, without due sense of responsibility. Hence **irresponsi**BI·LITY n., **irrespo·nsib**LY[2] adv. [IR-[2]]

irrespo·nsive, a. Not responsive (*to*). Hence **irrespo·nsive**NESS n. [IR-[2]]

irrete·ntion, n. Failure to retain (esp. the urine). [IR-[2]]

irrete·ntive, a. Not retentive. Hence **irrete·ntive**NESS n. [IR-[2]]

irretrie·vable, a. That cannot be retrieved. Hence **irretrieva**BI·LITY n., **irretrie·vab**LY[2] adv. [IR-[2]]

irrĕ·verent, a. Wanting in reverence. Hence or cogn. **irre·ver**ENCE n., **irrevere·nt**IAL a., **irre·verent**LY[2] adv. [f. L IR[2](*reverens* REVERENT)]

irrever·sible, a. Unalterable; not reversible. Hence **irreversi**BI·LITY n., **irrever·sib**LY[2] adv. [IR-[2]]

irrĕ·vocable, a. Unalterable; gone beyond recall. Hence **irrĕvoca**BI·LITY n., **irre·vocab**LY[2] adv. [f. L IR[2](*revocabilis* REVOCABLE)]

i·rrigate, v.t. (Of streams &c.) supply (land) with water; water (land) with channels &c.; (Med.) supply (wound &c.) with constant flow of liquid; (fig.) refresh as with moisture. Hence or cogn. **i·rrig**ABLE, **i·rrigat**IVE, aa., **irrig**A·TION, **i·rrigat**OR[2](1, 2), nn. [f. L IR[1](*rigare* moisten), see -ATE[3]]

i·rritable, a. Quick to anger, touchy, whence **i·rritab**LY[2] adv.; (of organ &c.) very sensitive to contact &c.; (Physiol., of muscles & nerves) capable of being excited to vital action by physical stimulus. So **irrita**BI·LITY n. [f. L *irritabilis* (as IRRITATE[1], see -BLE)]

i·rritancy[1], n. Irritation, annoyance. [as IRRITANT, see -ANCY]

i·rritancy[2], n. (law). Making, being, null & void. [as IRRITATE[2], see -ANCY]

i·rritant, a. & n. Causing (usu. physical) irritation; (n.) i. substance or agency (also fig.). [as foll., see -ANT]

i·rritate[1], v.t. Excite to anger, annoy, vex, (*-ed at, by, with, against*), whence **i·rritating**LY[2] adv.; excite, produce uneasy sensation in, (bodily organ &c.); (Physiol.) stimulate (organ) to vital action. Hence or cogn. **irrit**A·TION n., **i·rritat**IVE a. [f. L *irrītare*, see -ATE[3]]

i·rritate[2], v.t. (law). Make null & void. [f. L *irrĭtare* f. IR[2](*ritus* = *ratus* established) invalid, see -ATE[3]]

irru·ption, n. Invasion; violent entry. [f. L *irruptio* f. IR[1](*rumpere rupt-* break), see -ION]

Irvingite (er·vĭngīt), n. Member of a religious body called by its members the Catholic Apostolic Church. [E. *Irving*, minister of Ch. of Scotland, d. 1834]

is. See BE.

Isabe·lla, I·sabel, (Iz-), a. & n. Greyish yellow. Hence **isabe·ll**INE a. [female name; history unknown]

īsagŏ·gic (-jĭk), a. & n. Introductory;

(n. pl.) study of literary & external history of Bible. [f. L f. Gk *eisagōgikos* f. *eisagōgē* introduction (*eis* into + *agōgē* leading f. *agō*), see -IC]

ī·satin, n. (chem.). Crystalline reddish substance got from indigo by oxidation. [f. L f. Gk *isatis* woad + -IN]

ischiă·tic, -dic, (-k-), a. Of the hip, sciatic. [(f. med.L *ischiaticus*) f. L f. Gk *iskhiadikos* f. *iskhias -ados* pain in hip (*iskhion*), see -IC]

-ise, suf. of nn., = OF *-ise*, prop. f. L *-ītia*, but also (in learned formations) f. L *-ĭcia, -ĭtia, -ĭcium, -ĭtium* (OF *justise, juise, servise*, f. L *justitia, judicium, servitium*). In wds f. L, later F changed *-ise* to *-ice*, which E adopted; but in native wds F & E retain *-ise* (*franchise, merchandise*; E also has *exercise*, F *-ice*).

-ish[1], suf. of adjj., = OE *-isc* of com.-Teut. orig. (cf. Du. & G *-isch*), cogn. w. Gk *-iskos* dim. suf. of nn. In old formations, prec. vowel was modified, as still in *English, French, Welsh*. (1) OE chiefly formed aa. f. national names (*British, Danish*), with a few in sense 'belonging to, of the nature of' (*heathenish, outlandish*); later aa. have usu. not the neutral sense (*boyish, girlish*), but that of 'having the bad qualities of' (*foppish, monkish, swinish*, f. names of things *bookish, hellish*, f. vbs & advv. *snappish, standoffish, uppish*). (2) Sense peculiar to E is 'somewhat' (*stiffish*).

-ish[2], suf. of vbs repr. F *-iss-* seen in some parts of some vbs in *-ir* (*périssant, finissais*), f. L inceptive suf. *-isc-*, used in It. & F to form vbs without incept. sense to correspond to L vbs in *-ire, -ĕre*. In a few wds F *-iss-* became in E *-ise* (*chastise, advertise*); on the other hand, other F endings have become *-ish* (ADMONISH, LAVISH, RELISH).

I·shmăĕl, n. Outcast, one at war with society. Hence **I·shmael**ITE[1] n. [*Gen.* xvi. 12]

i·singlass (īzĭngg-), n. Whitish semi-transparent substance, a form of gelatin, got from some fresh-water fish, esp. sturgeon, & used in making jellies, glue, &c. [perh. corrupt. of obs. Du. *huisenblas* sturgeon's bladder]

I·slam (ĭz-), n. Mohammedanism; the Mohammedan world. Hence **Islă·m**IC, **Islami·t**IC, aa., **I·slam**ISM(3), **I·slam**ITE[1] (1), nn. [Arab., = surrender, n. f. *aslama* he surrendered f. *salama* he became safe, whence also *salaam, Moslem, Mussulman*]

īs·land, n., & v.t. Piece of land surrounded by water; (fig.) anything detached or isolated, esp. woodland surrounded by prairie, street REFUGE; (Physiol.) detached portion of tissue or group of cells; (v.t.) make into an i., isolate, dot as with ii. Hence **is·land**ER[1] (4) n. [(vb f. n.) OE *igland* (*ieg* isle, cf. ON & OFris. *ey*, + LAND); *-s-* by confus. w. *isle*]

isle (īl), n. Island (in prose usu. only with proper name, as *I. of Wight, British Ii.*, & usu. of small islands). [ME & OF *i(s)le* f. L *insula* island (IN-[1], see CONSUL)]

īs·let, n. Little island; isolated tract or spot. [f. F *islette* (as prec., see -ET[1])]

i·sm, n. Any distinctive doctrine or practice. [foll. used as n.]

-ism, suf. forming abstract nn.: (1) of action on vbs in -IZE, as *baptism*; (2) of typical conduct or condition on class nouns, as *heroism, barbarism*; (3) of system or principle on name of subject or founder or connected catchword, as *conservatism, Arianism, jingoism*; (4) of peculiarity in manner or language, as *Gallicism, archaism*; (5) of morbid condition induced by excessive use of drug, as *alcoholism*. [= F *-isme* f. L f. Gk *-ismos* or *-isma* f. *-izō* -IZE]

isn't. See BE.

īso- in comb. = Gk *isos* equal, as: *-bar* n., *-bă·ric* a., (line on map) connecting places at which barometric pressure is the same (at given time or on the average); *-cheim* (kīm) n., *-chei·mal, -chī·menal*, aa. & nn., (line on map) connecting places of same mean winter temperature; *-chroma·tic*, of same colour; *-chronous*, occupying equal time, vibrating uniformly, as pendulum; *-clī·nal*, showing equal magnetic inclination; *-cracy* n., *-cra·tic* a., (polity) in which all have equal political power; *-dynă·mic*, indicating equal magnetic force; *-ge·otherm*, line connecting points in interior of earth having same temperature; *-gŏ·nic*, indicating equal angles (of magnetic variation); *-mĕ·ric*, composed of same elements in same proportions, & having same molecular weight, but differently grouped; *-me·tric(al)*, of equal measure; *-mor·phism, -mor·phous*, (property of) crystallizing in same or closely related geometric forms; *-nomy*, equality of political rights; *-perime·trical*, having equal perimeters; *-sei·smal*, connecting points at which earthquake-shock is of same intensity; *-theral* a. & n., (line) connecting places of same mean summer temperature; *-therm* n., *-ther·mal* a. & n., (line) connecting places of same mean annual temperature.

ī·solate, v.t. Place apart or alone; (Chem.) free (substance) from its combinations; (Electr.) = INSULATE; subject (person &c.) to quarantine. Hence **isol**A·TION, **i·solat**OR[2](2), nn. [orig. in p.p., f. F *isolé* f. It. *isolato* (as INSULATE)]

-ison, suf. of nn., f. OF *-aison, -eison, -ison*, f. L *-ationem, -etionem, -itionem*; later formations took -ATION, -ITION. For exx. see -SON.

ī·sopŏd, n. Crustacean with seven pairs of equal & similarly placed thoracic legs. [ISO- + Gk *pous podos* foot]

isŏ·scelēs (-sel-), a. (Of triangle) having two sides equal. [LL, f. Gk ISO(*skelēs* f. *skelos* leg)]

I·sraĕl (iz-), n. The Jewish people, whence **I·sraelITE**[1](1) n., **I·sraelītISH**[1] a.: (fig.) God's elect. [L, f. Gk *Israēl* f. Heb. *yisrael* striver with God (*Gen.* xxxii. 28)]

i·ssue[1], n. Outgoing, outflow; termination (*of* matter &c.); discharge of blood &c., incision to procure this; way out, outlet; mouth of river; progeny, children, as *without male i.*; result, outcome; *in the i.*, as things turn out; point in question, esp. (Law) between contending parties in action, as *i. of fact* (when fact is denied), *i. of law* (when application of the law is contested); *at i.*, (of persons) at variance, (of things) in dispute; *join i.*, proceed to argue (*with* person *on* point agreed upon as basis of dispute), (Law) submit an i. jointly for decision, (of one party) accept the i. tendered by the other; giving out, issuing, (*of* bills of exchange, notes, stamps, &c.); number of coins, notes, copies of newspaper, &c., issued at one time. Hence **i·ssueLESS** a. [OF, f. pop. L **exūta*=L *exitus* -*ūs* f. EX(*ire it-* go), whence OF *issir*]

i·ssue[2], v.i. & t. Go or come out (often *out, forth*); emerge from a condition; be derived, spring, (*from*); result (*from*); end, result, (*in*); come out, be published; send forth; publish, put into circulation, (notes, newspaper), whence **i·ssuABLE** a., **i·ssuANCE** n.; (Mil.) supply (soldier) *with* article of equipment. [f. prec.]

-ist, suf. forming personal nn.: (1) of agent, corresp. to Gk vbs in *-izō* or possible E vbs in -IZE, as *antagonist, plagiarist*; (2) of adherent of creed &c. in -ISM, as *atheist, ventriloquist, Darwinist, fatalist*; (3) of one concerned with any subject (apart from *-ism, -ize*), as *dentist, tobacconist, balloonist*, esp. as player of musical instrument (*violinist*). [=F *-iste*, It. & Sp. *-ista*, f. L *-ista* f. Gk *-istēs* (*-izō* -IZE + *-tēs* agent-suf.); *tobacconist, accompanist* are formed irreg.]

-ister, suf. of nn., f. OF *-istre*, by-form of *-iste* -IST, perh. by false anal. f. *ministre* (L *minister*) &c.; in E prob. associated with -ER[1]. Exx.: *chorister, palmister, sophister.*

i·sthmus, n. (pl. *-muses*). Neck of land; (Anat., Bot.) narrow part connecting two larger parts. Hence **i·sthmIAN** a. [L, f. Gk *isthmos*]

i·stle (-tlĭ), n. Fibre used for cord, nets, &c., got from species of agave &c. [f. Mex. *ixtli*]

it, pron. (poss. *its*; pl. *they*, obj. *them*, poss. *their*). The thing in question; the person in question, as *who is it* (that knocks)?, *it* (the person that knocks) *is I*, (archaic poet.) *it* (what occupies my mind) *is the miller's daughter, & she is grown so dear*, (nursery sympathetic) *has it lost its rattle then?* (have you, your); (as subject of impers. vb) *it rains, it is cold*; *it* (the season) *is winter, it* (the day) *is Ash Wednesday, it is Ash Wednesday today, it* (the distance) *is 6 miles to Oxford*; *it says in the Bible* (the Bible says) *that all men are liars*; *I would go if it were not* (would go but) *for the expense*; (as subject, anticipating deferred virtual subject in more or less conscious apposition) *it is absurd talking* (or *to talk*) *like that, it is incredible that he should refuse, it is a dirty business, this meat-canning*; (anticipating deferred subject introduced by *that* conj., separated from *it* by adv. predicate) *it is seldom that he fails, it is in vain that you quibble, it is to him that you must apply*; (as antecedent to relative of either number & any gender, separated by predicate) *it was a purse that he dropped, it was the Russians that began it*; (as indef. obj. w. trans. or intr. vb) *face it out, carry it with a high hand, deuce take it, run for it, lord it over him, cab it* (go habitually or on the particular occasion in cab), *give it him* (*hot*), *have done it* (blundered); (slang) the ne plus ultra (*for barefaced lying you really are* it). [OE *hit* nom. & acc. f. (orig. demonstr.) stem *hi-* (nom. masc. HE); OE gen. *his*, dat. *him*; OE *hit* corresponds to Du. *het* & in form to Goth. *hita* this]

i·tacism (ē-), n. Pronunciation of Greek ē like English ē, cf. ETACISM; substitution in MS. of Greek iota for other vowels. [f. Gk *ēta* the letter ē, spelt *ita* to indicate the pronunc. (ēta)]

Ită·lian (ĭt-), a. & n. Of Italy; *I. cloth*, satin-faced linen cloth for linings; *I. handwriting*, that now current in England, Italy, France, &c., opp. to Gothic; *I. iron* (cylindrical, with rounded end, for crimping lace &c.); *I. warehouse(man)*, for supply of I. groceries, fruits, olive oil, &c.; (n.) language, native, of Italy. Hence **Ita·lianISM**(2, 4) n., **Ita·lianIZE**(3) v.t. & i. [f. L *Italianus* (*Italia* Italy, see -AN)]

Ită·lic, a. & n. Of ancient Italy, esp. as apart from Rome; *i. type*, sloping type introduced by Aldus Manutius of Venice (c. 1500); (n. pl.) letters thus sloping, now used for emphasis or distinction, e.g. to indicate foreign word (cf. ROMAN). [f. L f. Gk *Italikos* (*Italia* Italy, see -IC)]

ita·licize, v.t. Print (words) in italics, usu. for emphasis or distinction. [-IZE]

Ită·liot (-ot), **-ōte,** n. & a. (Inhabitant) of Greek colonies in S. Italy. [f. Gk *Italiōtēs* (*Italia* Italy, see -OT[2])]

itch[1], n. Irritation in the skin; contagious disease accompanied by this & caused by the *i.-mite*, which burrows in the skin; restless desire, hankering, (*for* thing, *to* do). Hence **i·tchINESS** n., **i·tchY**[2] a. [OE *gicce*, as foll.]

itch[2], v.i. Feel irritation in skin; *scratch where it itches* (where there is an itching);

(of person or his *fingers*) crave uneasily (*for* thing, *to* do). [OE *gicc(e)an*, cf. Du. *jeuken*, G *jucken*]

-ite[1], suf. of adjj. & nn., = F *-ite* f. L *-ita* f. Gk *-itēs* (also used in E, as *pyrites*), w. sense '(one) belonging to or connected with'; (1) in names of persons, in mod. formation often contempt. (*Stagirite, Sybarite, Durhamite, Shelleyite, Preraphaelite*); (2) in names of fossil organisms (*ammonite, belemnite*); of mineral species, often superseding *-ane, -in*, &c. (*anthracite, haematite, graphite, darwinite*); of constituent parts of body or organ (*somite, cerite*, segment of body, of horn); of some saccharine substances, glucoses, &c. (*dulcite, pinite*); of explosives (*cordite, dynamite*); of commercial products (*ebonite, vulcanite*); of salts of acids denominated by aa. in *-ous* (*nitrite, sulphite*).

-ite[2], suf. formed in adjj. f. L p.p. in *-ītus* (*erudīte, composīte*) & similar vbl nn. (*appetīte*), & in vbs formed on L p.p. stem in *-īt-* (*expedīte, unīte*); but vbs f. L p.p. st. *-ĭt-* usu. end in *-it* (*deposit, merit*).

ī·tĕm, n. & adv. Article, unit, included in enumeration; entry of this in account &c.; detail of news &c. in newspaper &c.; (adv.) likewise, also, (introducing mention of i.). [L, adv., = in like manner, also, (*is* he + *-tem* adv. suf.)]

ĭ·terate, v.t. Repeat (quoted words &c.); make (charge, assertion, objection, &c.) repeatedly. Hence or cogn. **i·ter**ANCE, -ANCY, **itera·**TION, nn., **i·terat**IVE a. [f. L *iterare* (*iterum* again), see -ATE[3]]

-ites. See -ITE[1].

Ithūr·iel's spear, n. Infallible test of genuineness. [Milt. *Par. Lost*, iv. 810]

ĭthȳpha·llic, a. & n. Of the phallus carried in Bacchic festivals; in the metre used for Bacchic hymns; (n.) poem in this metre, licentious poem. [f. L f. Gk *ithuphallikos* (*ithus* straight + *phallos* PHALLUS, see -IC)]

ītī·nerant, a. Travelling from place to place; (of justices) travelling on circuit; (of Wesleyan ministry) preaching in a circuit. Hence **iti·ner**ACY, **iti·ner**ANCY, nn. [as ITINERATE, see -ANT]

ītī·nerary, n. & a. Route; record of travel; guide-book; (adj.) of travelling, of roads. [f. LL *itinerarius* a., *-um* n. (also used in E), f. *iter itineris* journey, see -ARY[1]]

ītī·nerate, v.i. Travel from place to place; (of Wesleyan) preach within circuit. Hence **itinera·**TION n. [f. L *itinerari* (as prec.), see -ATE[3]]

-ition, suf., = -ION appended to L 3rd or 4th conj. p.p. stems (*perdition, sortition*).

-itious[1], suf. of adjj., f. L *-icius* + -OUS (*-t-* by confus. of *c* & *t* in LL MSS.), formed usu. on L p.p. stems (*factitious*); E wds in *-icious*, on the other hand, often repr. L stems with *-it-* + -IOUS (*avaricious*) as well as those in *-ic-* + -IOUS (*suspicious*).

-itious[2], suf. (in appearance compd) in which -IOUS is appended to L stems in *-ĭt-* (*ambitious, nutritious*, cf. *supposititious*[1]), sometimes also disguised as *-icious* (*malicious*).

-ītis, suf. forming esp. names of inflammatory diseases (*appendicitis, bronchitis*), f. Gk *-itis* adj., fem. of *-itēs*, w. *nosos* disease understood.

-itous, suf. of adjj., = -IT(Y) + -OUS, corresp. to L *-itosus* for *-itatosus* (*calamitosus* calamitous).

its, poss. a. See IT. [replaces HIS in 16th c.]

itse·lf, pron. Emphatic & reflexive form corresp. to IT; *by i.*, automatically, apart from its surroundings; *in i.*, apart from its surroundings, viewed in its essential qualities &c. [IT + SELF, but often treated as ITS + *self*, cf. *its own self*]

-ity. See -TY.

-ium, suf. forming names of metals, after *sodium* (*soda*), *potassium* (*potassa*); *aluminum* is changed to *-minium* to conform to the type, but some later metals have names in *-um*, the L termination for metals.

-ive, suf. forming adjj. w. sense 'tending to, having the nature of', f. F *-if* (fem. *-ive*) f. L *-ivus* added to p.p. stem (*activus, passivus*), pres. stem (*cadivus*), or noun (*tempestivus*). Most E wds are of mod. formation, chiefly in *-sive, -tive*, & esp. *-ative*, which tends to become living suf. (*talkative*). Some are formed immed. on vb stems (esp. in *-s, -c, -t*), as *amusive, coercive*. COSTIVE is not an ex.

ī·vory, n. Hard white substance composing main part of tusks of elephant, hippopotamus, walrus, narwhal, & (*fossil i.*) mammoth; *vegetable i.*, hard albumen of seed of S.-Amer. palm (*i.-nut*); *black i.*, African negro slaves; colour of i.; (slang, pl.) dice, billiard-balls, piano-keys; (slang, sing. or pl.) teeth; *i. black*, black pigment from calcined i. [f. OF *yvoire* f. L *eboreus* a. (*ebur -oris*)]

ī·vy, n. Climbing evergreen shrub, with dark-green shining leaves, usu. five-angled; *i. geranium*, i.-leaved pelargonium. Hence **i·vi**ED[2] a. [OE *ifig*, etym. dub.]

i·xia, n. Genus of S.-Afr. iridaceous plants, with large showy flowers. [Gk]

Ixi·on's wheel, n. (Gk myth.). Wheel on which Ixion was condemned to revolve eternally in Hades.

i·zard, n. Capriform antelope of Pyrenees, allied to chamois. [f. F *isard*, etym. dub.]

-ize, -ise, suf. of vbs, = F *-iser* f. LL *-izare* f. Gk *-izō*; in Gk either intr., 'act like', as *hellenizō*, speak, act as a, Greek, or trans., as *katharizō* clean; Christian Gk vbs, as *euaggelizō* evangelize, were first Latinized, & *-izare* so established as L for Gk vbs (cf. G *-iren* for Rom. vbs); F extended *-iser* to form vbs from names

&c., whence the mod. use. *-ize* is the better spelling for all wds, mod. or f. Gk, that contain the Gk suf. (*advertise, surprise*, &c., do not). Meanings: (1) trans., treat in such a way (*catechize*); (2) intr., follow, have, such a practice or feeling (*apostatize, sympathize*); (3) t. & i., bring, come, into such a state (*pulverize, anglicize, cicatrize*); (4) t. & i., act like, treat on system of, (*Calvinize, Bowdlerize*); (5) trans., impregnate &c. with (*oxidize*). Nn. are formed in *-izer, -ization*, as well as -IST, -ISM.

i·zzard, n. (archaic). The letter z (*from A* to *I*.). [var. of ZED]

J

J, j, (jā), letter (pl. *J*s, J's). *J* (*pen*), broad-pointed pen stamped with J.

Abbreviations (1): Judge; Justice, in **J.P.** (of Peace).

Abbreviations (2): **Jam.**(aica); **Jam.**(es, Epistle of); **Jan.**(uary); **Jas**, James; **Jer.**(emiah); **Jno.**, John; **Josh.**(ua); **Jud.**(ith); **Judg.**(es, O.-T. book); **jun.**-(ior).

jā·al-goat (*or* yah-), n. Wild goat of Sinai, Upper Egypt, &c. [f. Heb. *ya'el* wild goat]

jab, v.t. & n. Poke roughly; stab; thrust (thing) abruptly (*into*); (n.) abrupt blow with pointed thing or fist; (Mil.) supplementary bayonet thrust delivered without full withdrawal from previous one. [prob. imit.]

ja·bber, v.i. & t., & n. Speak volubly & with little sense; utter (words) rapidly & indistinctly; chatter, as monkeys &c.; (n.) jabbering, gabble, gibberish. [(n. f. vb) prob. imit., with -ER[5]]

jă·biru (-ōō), n. Tropical American bird of stork family. [native]

jăbora·ndi, n. Dried leaflets of Brazilian plant with diuretic & sudorific properties. [f. native *jaburandi*]

jabōt· (zh-), n. Ornamental frill on woman's bodice; (Hist.) frill on man's shirt-front. [F, etym. dub.]

jă·cinth, n. Reddish-orange gem, variety of zircon. [f. OF *iacinte*, as HYACINTH]

jack[1], n. (*J*-) familiar form of name *John*, esp. as type of the common people, as *J. & GILL*; *every man j.*, every individual; =j. tar; labourer, man who does odd jobs, &c.; CHEAP *J.*; STEEPLE-*j.*; (Cards) knave; machine for turning spit in roasting meat; machine for lifting heavy weights; (also *carriage-j.*) machine for lifting axle off ground while cleaning wheel; BOOT[1]-*j.*; parts of various machines &c.; pike, esp. young or small one; *J. Frost*, frost personified; *before you could say J. Robinson*, very quickly or suddenly; *J.-a-dandy*, dandy; *jackass*, male ass, dolt, blockhead; *laughing jackass*, Giant Kingfisher of Australia; *j.-boot*, large boot coming above knee; *jackdaw*, thievish small crow haunting church towers; *J. in office*, fussy official; *j.-in-the-box*, toy figure that springs out of box when opened, (also) kind of firework; *J.-in-the-green*, man or boy enclosed in framework covered with leaves in May-day sports; *J. Johnson* (army slang), German large-calibre shell; *J. Ketch*, common hangman; *j.-knife*, large clasp-knife for the pocket; *J. of all trades*, one who can turn his hand to anything; *j.-o'-lantern*, will-o'-the-wisp (often fig.); *j.-plane* (for coarse work); *j. pudding*, buffoon, clown; *j.-snipe* (small species); *j. tar*, common sailor; *j.-towel* (endless, hung from roller). [prob. conn. w. *John*, but perh. f. F *Jacques* James f. L f. Gk *Iakōbos* Jacob]

jack[2], v.t. Hoist with jack; *j. up*, abandon (attempt &c., or abs.). [first sense f. prec.; for second cf. *chuck*]

jack[3], n. Ship's flag, smaller than ensign, esp. one flown from *j.-staff* at bow, indicating nationality, as *British, French, j.*; single flag flown on foremast as signal for pilot (Brit. pilot's j., union j. with white border); UNION *J.*; *j.-staff*, (also) stick on which flag is bent that is to show above mast-head. [prob. = JACK[1]]

jack[4], n. (archaic). Foot-soldier's sleeveless tunic; (also *black j.*) vessel for liquor, usu. of waxed leather coated with tar &c. [f. F *jaque*, etym. dub.]

jack[5], n. E.-Ind. fruit, like bread-fruit but coarser. [f. Port. *jaca* f. Malayalam *chakka*]

ja·ckal (-awl), n., & v.i. (-ll-). Animal of dog kind, of size of fox, formerly supposed to hunt up lion's prey for him; (fig.) person who does preparatory drudgery &c., (vb) act as j. (*for*). [f. Turk. *chakal* f. Pers. *shagal*, cogn. w. Skr. *s'rgala*]

ja·ckanapes, n. (Archaic) monkey; pert fellow; coxcomb; pert child. [earlier *Jack Napes*, first found of William de la Pole, Duke of Suffolk (d. 1450), whose badge was a clog & chain, such as was used for tame ape]

ja·cket, n., & v.t. Sleeved outer garment for man or woman; NORFOLK, ETON, DINNER, *j.*; *dust his j.*, beat him; outer covering round boiler &c. for protection, keeping in heat, &c.; loose special cover in which book is shown for sale; animal's coat; *potatoes boiled in their jj.* (skins); (v.t.) cover with j. [(vb f. n.) f. OF *jaquet*, dim. as JACK[4]]

Jā·cob, n. *J.'s ladder*, plant with corymbs of blue or white flowers, & leaves suggesting ladder, (Naut.) rope ladder with wooden rungs, esp. one slung from a boom to the water; *J.'s staff*, surveyor's iron-shod rod used instead of tripod, (also) instrument for measuring distances & heights. [f. L f. Gk *Iakōbos* f. Heb. *ya'aqob*]

Jăcobē·an, a. Of the reign of James I; of St James the Less. [f. LL *Jacobaeus* (*Jacobus* as prec., whence *James*), see -AN]

Jă·cobin[1], n. Dominican friar [from convent near to church of S. Jacques]; member of extreme democratic club established in Paris in old J. convent (1789), sympathizer with its principles, extreme radical, whence **Jacobi·nic**(AL) aa., **Ja·cobinism**(3) n., **Ja·cobinize**(3) v.t. [F, f. med.L *Jacobinus* (JACOB, -INE[1])]

jă·cobin[2], n. Pigeon with reversed feathers on back of neck, suggesting cowl. [f. F *jacobine*, fem. as prec.]

Jă·cobīte, n. Adherent of James II after his abdication, or of his son the Pretender. Hence **Jăcobĭ·tical** a., **Jă·cobītism**(3) n. [f. L *Jacobus* James + -ITE[1]]

jacō·bus, n. English gold coin struck in reign of James I, worth 20–24*s*. [as prec.]

jă·conet, n. Cotton cloth of medium thickness, esp. dyed waterproofed kind for poulticing &c. [f. Hind. *Jagannathi* f. place-name]

jacquerie (zhăkkerē·), n. Rising of peasantry, esp. that of 1357–8 in France. [F (*Jacques* James, peasant, see -ERY)]

jactita·tion, n. (Law) *j. of marriage*, offence of falsely claiming to be a person's wife or husband; (Med.) restless tossing of body in illness; twitching of limb or muscle. [f. med.L *jactitatio* f. L *jactitare* toss, boast, (*jacĕre jact-* throw), see -ATION]

jade[1], n., & v.t. Inferior, wearied, or worn-out horse; (in reprobation, usu. playful) woman; (v.t., esp. in p.p.) wear out with hard work. [?]

jade[2], n. A silicate of lime & magnesia, a hard green, blue, or white stone, a variant of hornblende; (also **ja·d**(e)**ite**) silicate of sodium & aluminium like this in appearance. [f. F *le jade* for *l'ejade* f. Sp. (*piedra de*) *ijada* (stone of) the colic, f. L *ilia* pl. flank]

jaeger (yā·ger), n. Kinds of woollen clothing-material from which vegetable fibres are excluded as unwholesome. [*J.*, inventor]

jag[1], n. Sharp projection, e.g. point of rock. Hence **ja·ggy**[2] a. [prob. imit.]

jag[2], v.t. Cut, tear, in uneven manner; make indentations in, whence **ja·gger**[1] (2) n. Hence **ja·ggĕdly**[2] adv., **ja·ggĕdness** n. [f. prec.]

jäger. = YAGER.

ja·guar (-war, -ūar), n. Large carnivorous spotted quadruped of cat kind, in some wooded parts of America. [f. native *yaguara*]

Jah, n. Jehovah. [repr. Heb. *Yah* shortened form of *Yahweh* JEHOVAH]

jail &c. See GAOL &c.

Jain, n. & a. (Member) of a non-Brahminical E.-Ind. sect, with doctrines like those of Buddhism. Hence **Jai·nism** n. [f. Hind. f. Skr. *jaina* of a Buddha (*jina* f. root *ji* conquer)]

jă·lap, n. Purgative drug got esp. from tuberous roots of a Mexican climbing plant. [F, f. Sp. *jalapa* f. *Xalapa*, *Ja-*, Mexican city, f. Aztec *Xalapan* (*xalli* sand + *atl* water + *pan* upon)]

jalousie (zhă·lōōzē), n. Blind, shutter, with slats sloping upwards from without. [F, as JEALOUSY]

jam[1], v.t. & i., & n. Squeeze (thing) between two surfaces; cause (part of machine) to be fixed so that it cannot work; squeeze (things) together in compact mass; thrust (thing) violently (*into* space); block, fill up, (passage &c.) by crowding into it; become tightly wedged; (Wireless) make (message, instrument) unintelligible by operating elsewhere; (n.) crush, squeeze, stoppage (of machine &c.) due to this, crowded mass; *j.-stroke*, = PENDULUM *stroke*. [prob. imit.]

jam[2], n. Conserve of fruit, made by boiling it with sugar to a pulp; (slang) *real j.*, a real treat. [perh. f. prec.]

Jamai·ca, n. *J.* (*rum*), rum made in J.

jamb (-m), n. Side post of doorway, window, &c., esp. (pl.) stone sides or cheeks of fireplace. [f. F *jambe* leg f. LL *gamba* hoof, perh. f. Celt. *camb-* crooked]

jamboree·, n. (slang). Celebration, merrymaking. [U.-S.]

ja·ngle, v.i. & t., & n. (Make) harsh noise; cause (bell &c.) to do this; speak, utter, in discordant or noisy way; (archaic) dispute, wrangle, (n. & vb). [(n. f. vb) f. OF *jangler*, etym. dub.]

jă·nitor, n. Doorkeeper. [L, f. *janua* door]

ja·nizary, -nissary, (jă-, yă-), n. (Hist.) one of body of Turkish infantry forming Sultan's guard (abolished in 1826); Turkish soldier; (fig.) personal instrument of tyranny. [ult. f. Turk. *yeñi-tsheri* (*yeñi* new + *tsheri* soldiery)]

Ja·nsenist, n. Member of party in Rom. Cath. Church holding with Cornelius Jansen (d. 1638) the perverseness & inability for good of the natural human will. So **Ja·nsenism** n., **Janseni·stic** a. [-IST]

Jă·nūary, n. (abbr. *Jan.*). First month of year. [f. L *Januarius* (*mensis* month) of JANUS, see -ARY[1]]

Jā·nus, n. Ancient Italian god, guardian of doors & gates, represented with faces on front & back of head. [L]

Jap, a. & n. (colloq.). Japanese.

japa·n[1], n. (*J-*) insular empire on east of Asia, whence **Jăpanese·** a. & n., **Japanesque·** a.; hard varnish, esp. kind brought orig. from J.; work in Japanese style. [prob. f. Malay *Japung* f. Chin. *Jih-pun* sunrise (*jih* sun + *pun* origin)]

japa·n[2], v.t. (-nn-). Lacquer with japan; make black & glossy as with japan. [f. prec.]

jape, v.i., & n. Jest. [f. 14th c.; etym. dub.]

Japhĕ·tic, a. Of, descended from, Japheth son of Noah; Indo-European. [-IC]

japŏ·nic, a. Japanese. [F *Japon* JAPAN, -IC]

japŏ·nica, n. Kinds of Japanese plant, esp. ornamental variety of pear or quince. [mod.L fem. adj. as prec.]

jar[1], n. Sound, vibration, esp. harsh one; thrill of nerves or feelings, shock; want of harmony, disagreement; quarrel. [as foll.]

jar[2], v.i. & t. Sound discordantly, make grating impression (*upon* person, his ear, nerves, &c.); strike with grating sound (*upon, against*, object); (of body affected) vibrate, resound, discordantly; (of opinion, statement, action) be at variance, disagree, (*with*); dispute, wrangle; cause (thing) to j.; send shock through (nerves). Hence **jar·ring**LY[2] adv. [prob. imit.]

jar[3], n. Earthenware, stoneware, or glass vessel with or without handle(s), usu. cylindrical; LEYDEN *j.* Hence **jar·**FUL(2) n. [f. F *jarre* f. Arab. *jarrah*]

jar[4], n. (colloq.). *On the, on a, on, j.*, ajar. [corrupt. of AJAR]

jardinière (zhardĭnyār·), n. Ornamental pot or stand for display of growing flowers in room, on window-sill, &c. [F]

jar·gon[1], n. Unintelligible words, gibberish; barbarous or debased language; mode of speech full of unfamiliar terms, as *critics' j., metaphysical j.*; twittering of birds. Hence **jar·gon**IZE(2, 3) v.t. & i. [OF, etym. dub.]

jar·gon[2], **jargoo·n,** n. Translucent, colourless, or smoky variety of zircon found in Ceylon. [F, perh. ult. f. ZIRCON]

jargone·lle, n. Kind of pear that ripens early. [F, dim. of prec.]

jarl (y-), n. (hist.). Old Norse or Danish chief. [ON, orig. man of noble birth; = EARL]

jă·rrah, n. (Durable timber of) W.-Austral. mahogany gum-tree. [f. native *jerrhyl*]

jar·vey, n. Hackney-coachman; driver of Irish car. [by-form of surname *Jarvis*]

jā·sey, n. (old slang). Wig, esp. of worsted. [?]

ja·smin(e), je·ssamin(e), n. Genus of shrubs with white or yellow salver-shaped flowers, esp. *common* or *white j.*, climbing shrub with fragrant flowers. [f. Arab. f. Pers. *yasmin*; F has *jasmin, jessemin*]

ja·sper, n. Opaque variety of quartz, usu. red, yellow, or brown. [f. OF *jaspre* f. L f. Gk *iaspis*, of oriental orig., =any bright chalcedony except carnelian; cf. Heb. *yashpeh*]

Jat, n. Member of a people widely distributed in N.W. India & varying in religion & occupation. -

jau·ndice (jah-, jaw-), n., & v.t. Morbid state caused by obstruction of bile, & marked by yellowness of skin, fluids, & tissues, constipation, & loss of appetite; disordered vision (usu. fig.), as characteristic of this; (v.t.) affect with j., (fig. esp. in p.p.) affect (person, his judgement &c.) with envy or jealousy. [(vb prob. back formation f. *jaundic*ED[2]) f. F *jaunice* (*jaune* yellow f. L *galbinus* f. *galbus*, -ICE)]

jaunt (jaw-, jah-), v.i., & n. (Take) excursion, journey, esp. for pleasure; *jaunting-car*, light two-wheeled vehicle popular in Ireland. [?]

jau·nty (jaw-, jah-), a. & n. Having or affecting easy sprightliness, airy self-satisfaction; (n., naut.) head of ship's police. Hence **jau·nti**LY[2] adv., **jau·nti**NESS n. [earlier *jantee* f. F *gentil* GENTEEL]

Ja·van (jah-), **Jăvane·se,** aa. & nn. (Native) of Java; (*-ese*) language of central Java. [-AN, -ESE; the needless *-ese* prob. on false anal. of *Japanese*]

jă·velin (-vl-), n. Light spear, dart. [f. F *javeline*, perh. of Celt. orig.]

jaw, n. *Lower, upper, j.*, two bones or sets of bones forming framework of mouth & masticating apparatus in vertebrates; *j.-bone*, each of the two bones forming lower jaw in most mammals, these two combined into one in others; (pl.) bones of mouth including teeth, mouth; (pl.) narrow mouth of valley, channel, &c.; (pl.) seizing members of machine, e.g. vice; (colloq.) loquacity, as *hold your j.*, stop talking, (also) sermonizing talk, lecture; *j.-breaker* (colloq.), word hard to pronounce; (v.i.) speak esp. at tedious length; (v.t.) lecture. [(vb f. n.) perh. cogn. w. CHEW]

jay, n. Noisy chattering European bird of brilliant plumage; genus to which this belongs; (fig.) impertinent chatterer, simpleton. [OF, perh. f. OHG *gâhi* quick]

jazz, n., a., & v.i. Syncopated music, & dancing, of U.-S. negro origin; noisy or grotesque proceedings; (adj.) discordant, loud in colour &c., rude, burlesque; *j. band* (of such combinations as piano, violin, saxophone, banjo, & drums); (vb) play, dance, indulge in, j. [?]

jea·lous (jĕl-), a. Solicitous for preservation *of* (rights &c.); apprehensive of being displaced in the love or good-will *of* (wife, husband, lover, friend; also *of* the supposed rival); envious (*of* person, his advantages, &c.); (bibl., of God) intolerant of unfaithfulness; (of inquiry, supervision, &c.) suspiciously vigilant. Hence **jea·lous**LY[2] adv. [f. OF *gelos* f. LL *zelosus* (as ZEAL, see -OUS)]

jea·lousy, n. Quality, state, of being jealous. [f. OF *gelosi* (as prec., see -Y[1])]

jean (jān), n. Twilled cotton cloth, kind of fustian. [prob. =ME *Gene* f. med.L *Janua* Genoa]

jeer[1], n. (naut.). (Usu. pl.) tackle for hoisting & lowering lower yards. [?]

jeer[2], v.i. & t., & n. Scoff derisively (*at*); deride; (n.) gibe, taunt. [?]

jehad. See JIHAD.

Jehō·vah, n. Principal name of God in O.T. [repr. Heb. *yahaveh*, perh. f. *hawah* be, exist]
Jeho·vist, n. Author(s) of those parts of the Hexateuch in which God is called *Jehovah* (cf. ELOHIST). Hence **Jehovi·stic** a. [-IST]
Jē·hū, n. (facet.). Furious driver; driver. [2 *Kings* ix. 20]
jeju·ne, a. Meagre, scanty; (of land) barren; unsatisfying to the mind. Hence **jeju·ne**LY[2] adv., **jeju·ne**NESS n. [f. L *jejunus* fasting]
Jĕ·kyll & Hyde, n. Single person in whom two personalities alternate. [*Dr J. & Mr H.*, by Stevenson]
je·lly, n., & v.t. & i. Soft stiff semi-transparent food, consisting chiefly of gelatin, got from skin, bones, &c., by boiling & cooling; similar preparation of juice of fruit &c.; *j.-bag* (for straining j.); *j.-fish*, pop. name of medusa or sea-nettle; (vb) (cause to) set as j., congeal. [(vb f. n.) f. F *gelée* frost f. L *gelata* (*gelare* freeze, see -Y[4])]
jemi·mas, n. pl. (colloq.). Elastic-sided boots; goloshed cloth over-boots.
je·mmy, n. Crowbar used by burglars, usu. made in sections; sheep's head as a dish. [fam. form of *James*]
je ne sais quoi (zhenesākwah·), n. An indescribable something. [F, =I know not what]
je·nnet, n. Small Spanish horse. [f. F *genet* f. Sp. *jinete* light horseman, etym. dub.]
je·nneting, n. Kind of early apple. [prob. f. F name *Jeannet* + -ING[3]]
je·nny, n. Locomotive crane; =SPINNING-*j.*; a stroke at billiards; *j. wren*, (pop. & nursery name for) wren. [fam. form of *Janet*]
jeo·pardize, v.t. Endanger. [foll., -IZE]
jeo·pardy (jĕp-), n. Danger. [ME *iuparti* f. OF *iu* (or *ieu*) *parti* divided (i.e. even) game, f. L *jocus* game + *partitus* p.p. of *partiri* divide f. *pars -rtis* part]
jequi·rity, n. Indian twining shrub with parti-coloured seeds used for ornament & in medicine. [f. F *jéqwirity* f. native *jekiriti*]
jerbō·a (*or* jer·b-), n. Small rodent of African deserts, with long hind legs & great jumping powers. [f. Arab. *yarbu'* flesh of loins, jerboa]
jeremī·ad, n. Lamentation, doleful complaint. [f. F *jérémiade* f. *Jérémie* f. L *Jeremias* Jeremiah, see -AD]
Jĕremi·ah, n. Doleful prophet or denouncer of the times. [*Lamentations of J.*, O.-T. bk]
Je·richo (-kō), n. Town in Palestine; *go to J.* (to the devil).
jeri·d (-ēd), **-eed,** n. Javelin used by Persian, Turkish, & Arabian horsemen; game in which this is used. [f. Arab. *jarid*]
jerk[1], n. Sharp sudden pull, twist, &c.; involuntary spasmodic contraction of muscle; (pl.) spasmodic movements of limbs or face, esp. in religious excitement; PHYSICAL *jj.* Hence **jer·ki**LY[2] adv., **jer·ki**NESS n., **jer·ky**[2] a. [prob. imit.]
jerk[2], v.t. & i. Pull, thrust, twist, &c., with a jerk; throw with suddenly arrested motion; (intr.) move with a jerk. [as prec.]
jerk[3], v.t. Cure (esp. beef) by cutting in long slices & drying in sun. [f. Amer. Sp. *charquear* (*charque* f. Peruv. *ccharqui* dried flesh)]
jer·kin, n. (hist.). Man's close-fitting jacket, often of leather. [?]
Jĕrobō·ăm, n. Wine-bottle of 8–12 times ordinary size. ['A mighty man of valour' 'who made Israel to sin'—1 *Kings* xi. 28, xiv. 16]
jĕ·rry, n. *J.-builder, -building*, builder, building, of unsubstantial houses with bad materials; *j.-built*, so built; (also *j.-shop*) low beer-shop; (slang) chamber-pot; (army slang, *J-*) German soldier, the Germans. [prob. fam. form of *Jeremiah*]
jer·sey (-zĭ), n. (*J-*) one of the Channel Islands (often attrib.); close-fitting woollen knitted tunic, esp. as worn in athletic exercises; similar garment worn as under-vest; woman's close-fitting knitted jacket; J. cow.
Jeru·salem, n. City in Palestine; *J.* (*pony*), donkey; *J.* ARTICHOKE.
jess, n., & v.t. Short strap of leather, silk, &c., round legs of hawk used in falconry; (v.t.) put jj. on (hawk). [(vb f. n.) f. OF *ges* nom. of *get* f. L *jactus -ūs* throw f. *jacĕre jact-*]
jessamine. See JASMINE.
Je·ssĕ, n. *J. window* (with Christ's descent from J. represented). [*Is.* xi. 1, *Matt.* i. 6, 16]
jest[1], n. Piece of raillery or banter; taunt, jeer; joke; fun, esp. *in j.*, not seriously; object of derision, as *a standing j.*; *j.-book*, book of jj. [orig. = exploit, f. OF *geste* f. L *gesta*, neut. pl. p.p. of *gerere* do]
jest[2], v.i. Joke; jeer; speak, act, in trifling manner, whence **je·sting**LY[2] adv. [f. prec.]
je·ster, n. One who jests, esp. professed maker of amusement maintained in court or noble household. [-ER[1]]
Jĕ·sūit (-z-), n. Member of Society of Jesus, Rom. Cath. order founded by Ignatius Loyola in 1533; dissembling person, prevaricator; *Jesuits'* (Peruvian) *bark*. Hence **Jesui·tic**AL a., **Jesui·tical**LY[2] adv., **Je·suit**ISM(2), **Je·suit**RY(4), nn., **Je·suit**IZE(3) v.t. & i. [f. mod.L *Jesuita* (*Jesus*, see -ITE[1])]
jet[1], n. & a. Hard black lignite taking brilliant polish; (of) colour of this, deep glossy black, (also *j.-black*). [f. OF *jaiet* f. L f. Gk *gagatēs*, acc. to Pliny f. *Gagae* town in Lycia]
jet[2], n. Stream of water, steam, gas, &c.,

shot forward or upwards esp. from small opening; spout, nozzle, for emitting water &c. thus. [f. foll. & f. F *jet* as foll.]

jet[3], v.t. & i. Spurt forth in jets. [f. F *jeter* throw f. LL *jectare* = L *jactare* frequent. of *jacĕre jact-* throw]

je·tsam, n. Goods thrown overboard from ship to lighten it, & (in mod. use) washed ashore (cf. FLOTSAM). [= foll.]

je·ttison, n., & v.t. Throwing of goods overboard, esp. to lighten ship in distress; throw (goods) overboard thus. [(vb f. n.) f. AF *getteson* (OF *getaison*) f. L *jactationem* (*jactare* throw, see JET[3] & -ATION)]

je·tton, n. Counter with stamped or engraved device. [F *jeton* (*jeter*, see JET[3])]

je·tty[1], n. Mole running out to defend harbour or coast; landing-pier. [f. OF *jetee* (mole) thrown out, fem. p.p. as JET[3]]

je·tty[2], a. Jet-black. [JET[1], -Y[2]]

jeu (zher), n. (pl. *jeux* pron. zher). *J. de mots* (mō), play on words, pun; *j. d'esprit* (ĕsprē·), witty or humorous (usu. literary) trifle. [F]

jeunesse dorée (F), n. The gilded youth, young swells.

Jew[1], n. Person of Hebrew race; (transf., colloq.) extortionate usurer, driver of hard bargains; *rich as a J.*; *unbelieving J.*, incredulous person; *tell that* (an unlikely tale) *to the Jj.*; *J.-baiting*, persecution of Jj.; *J.'s-ear*, edible cup-shaped fungus; *J.'s-harp*, small lyre-shaped musical instrument, played by holding frame between teeth & striking metal tongue. Hence **Jew·**ESS[1] n., **Jew·**ISH[1] a. [f. OF *giu* f. L f. Gk *Ioudaios* f. Aramaic *y'hudai* = Heb. *y'hudi* f. *y'hudah* Judah]

Jew[2], v.t. (colloq.). Cheat, overreach. [prec.]

jew·el, n., & v.t. (-ll-). Ornament containing precious stone(s), worn for personal adornment; precious stone; highly prized person or thing; *the J.-house*, room in Tower of London in which crown jj. are kept; hence or cogn. **jew·ell**ER[1], **jew·el**LERY(1), **jew·el**RY, nn., **jew·ell**Y[2] a. (Vb) adorn, furnish, with jj., fit (watch) with jj. for the pivot-holes. [(vb f. n.) f. AF *juel* = OF *joel*, perh. ult. f. L *gaudium* joy, or cogn. w. F *jeu* play f. L *jocus*]

jew·ing, n. Wattles at base of beak in some domestic pigeons. [*Jew* (from resemblance to hooked nose) + -ING[1]]

Jewry (joor·ĭ), n. The Jews; (Hist.) Jews' quarter in town &c. [f. OF *juerie* (JEW, -ERY)]

Jĕ·zebel, n. Impudent or abandoned woman; woman who paints her face. [*J.*, wife of Ahab]

jib[1], n. Triangular stay-sail from outer end of jibboom to fore-topmast head in large ships, from bowsprit to masthead in smaller ones; *cut of his j.*, his personal appearance; *jibboom*, spar run out from end of bowsprit; projecting arm of crane. [perh. abbr. of GIBBET]

jib[2], v.t. & i. (naut.). Pull (sail, yard) round from one side of ship to the other; (intr., of sail &c.) swing round thus. [Da. has *gibbe* (hard *g*) in same sense]

jib[3], v.i. (Of horse &c.) stop & refuse to go on, move backwards or sideways instead of going on, whence **ji·bb**ER[1] n.; (fig.) refuse to proceed in some action; *j. at*, show repugnance to (course, person). [?]

ji·bba(h), ju-, dj-, n. Mohammedan's long cloth coat. [Arab. (*ju-*)]

jib door, n. Door flush with wall in which it stands, usu. painted &c. so as to be indistinguishable. [?]

jibe. See GIBE.

ji·ff(y), n. Very short time, as *in a j.*, (*wait*) *half a j.* [?]

jig[1], n. Lively dance; music for this. [etym. dub.; mod. F *gigue* jig is prob. f. this, not f. OF *gigue*, kind of fiddle]

jig[2], v.i. & t. Dance a jig; move (t. & i.) up & down rapidly & jerkily; separate coarser & finer portions of (ore) by shaking it under water in box with perforated bottom; *j.-saw* (U.S.), machine fretsaw (*j.-s. puzzle*, picture pasted on board & cut in irregular pieces with j.-s.). [as prec.]

ji·gger[1], n. (Naut.) small tackle consisting of a double & single block with rope; small sail, small smack with this; (slang) rest for cue; one who jigs ore; *j.-mast*, aftermost mast in four-master. [partly f. prec. + -ER[1]]

ji·gger[2], n. = CHIGOE. [corrupt.]

ji·gger[3], v.t. (only in pass.). (As substitute for oath) *I'm jiggered* &c. [?]

ji·ggle, v.t. Rock or jerk lightly. [f. JIG[2] + -LE(3)]

jiha·d, je-, (-ahd), n. Religious war of Mohammedans against unbelievers; (fig.) crusade for or against a doctrine &c. [Arab. (*ji-*)]

Jill. See GILL[4].

jilt, n., & v.t. Woman who capriciously casts off lover after giving him encouragement; (rarely) man who treats woman thus; (v.t.) play the j. towards, be faithless to. ([vb f. n.) prob. f. obs. *gillot*, prob. dim. of name GILL]

Jim Crow, n. (U.S.). Negro (*J.-C. car*, to which Negroes are restricted on railroads). [nickname]

jiminy, int. (archaic). = GEMINI.

jimp, a. (Sc.). Slender, graceful; scanty. [?]

ji·ngle, n., & v.i. & t. Mingled noise like that of small bells, links of chain, &c.; repetition of same or similar sounds in words, esp. if designed to catch the attention; Irish & Australian covered two-wheeled car; (vb) make, cause (keys &c.) to make, a j., (of writing) be full of alliterations, rhymes, &c. [imit.]

ji·ngo, int., n. (pl. *-oes*), & a. (In asseveration) *by* (*the living*) *j.!*; supporter of bellicose policy, blustering patriot (esp. supporter of Lord Beaconsfield's policy in 1878, f. use of *by j.* in popular song); (adj.) vulgarly dashing. Hence **ji·ngo**ISM(2), **ji·ngo**IST(2), nn., **jingoi·stic** a. [orig. conjurer's gibberish]

jinks, n. *High j.*, boisterous sport, merry-making. [prob. imit. of nimble motion]

jinnee·, n. (pl. *jinn*, often used as sing.; fem. *jinnee·yeh*). (In Mohammedan demonology) spirit, lower than angels, able to appear in human & animal forms, & having supernatural power over men (also GENIE). [f. Arab. *jinni*]

jinri·cksha, -ri·kisha, n. Light two-wheeled hooded vehicle drawn by man or men, first used in Japan c. 1870. [Jap. (*-kisha*), f. *jin* man + *riki* power + *sha* vehicle]

jiu-jitsu. See JU-JUTSU.

jŏb[1], n. Piece of work, esp. one done for hire or profit; transaction in which duty is sacrificed to private advantage; anything one has to do (*on the j.*, slang, in action, alert); *do* person's *j.*, ruin him; *bad j.*, thing on which labour is wasted, failure; *good, bad, j.* (state of affairs); *j. lot*, lot of goods bought as speculation; *jobmaster*, one who lets out horses & carriages by the j.; *j.-work*, done & paid for by the j. [?]

jŏb[2], v.i. & t. Do jobs; hire (horse, carriage) for definite time or job, let out on hire thus; buy & sell (stock, goods) as broker; deal in stocks; turn position of trust to private advantage; deal corruptly with (matter), whence **jo·bb**ERY (4) n. Hence **jo·bb**ER[1] n. [f. prec.]

job[3], v.t. & i., & n. Prod, stab slightly; hurt (horse) with bit; (intr.) thrust *at* (thing); (n.) prod, thrust, jerk at bit. [prob. imit.]

Jōb[4], n. Patriarch whose story forms *Book of J.* in O.T. (*would try the patience of J.*, is vexatious); *J.'s comforter*, one who under guise of comforter aggravates distress; *J.'s tears*, seeds of a grass used as beads.

jōba·tion, n. Reprimand, esp. lengthy one. [f. obs. *jobe* reprove f. prec. + -ATION)]

jo·bbernowl (-ōl), n. Stupid head; stupid person. [prob. f. obs. (& F) *jobard* fool (*jobe* silly) + NOLL]

Jock, n. (army slang). Highland soldier. [= Jack]

jo·ckey[1], n. Professional rider in horse-races (also colloq. *jock*); *J. Club*, club established at Newmarket, the body controlling horse-racing; lad, under-strapper. Hence **jo·ckey**DOM, **jo·ckey**SHIP(3), nn. [f. Sc. *Jock* Jack + -Y[3]]

jo·ckey[2], v.t. & i. Outwit, cheat; get (person &c.) *away, out, in*, &c., by trickery; cheat (person *into, out of*, doing); (intr.) cheat. [f. prec. in obs. sense 'cheat']

jo·cko, n. Chimpanzee. [F, made by Buffon f. Gaboon *engeco* (prop. *ncheko*)]

joco·se, a. Playful; waggish. Hence **joco·se**LY[2] adv., **joco·se**NESS, **jocŏ·s**ITY, nn. [f. L *jocosus* (*jocus* jest, see -OSE[1])]

jŏ·cular, a. Mirthful; humorous. Hence or cogn. **joculă·r**ITY n., **jo·cular**LY[2] adv. [f. L *jocularis* (*joculus* dim. of *jocus* jest, -AR[1])]

jŏ·cund, a. Merry, sprightly; pleasant. Hence or cogn. **jocu·nd**ITY n., **jo·cund**LY[2] adv. [OF, f. LL *jocundus* f. L *jucundus* (*juvare* please), influenced by assoc. w. *jocus* jest]

Jodhpurs (jŏdpoor·z), n.pl. Long breeches for riding &c., tight from knee to ankle. [*Jodhpur* in India]

Joe, n. *Not for J.* (i.e. me)!, slang refusal.

Joe Mi·ller, n. Stale joke, chestnut. [f. *Joseph M.*, comedian, d. 1738]

jō·ey, n. Young kangaroo; young animal. [f. native Austral. *joè*]

jog, v.t. & i., & n. Shake with push or jerk; nudge (person), esp. to arouse attention; stimulate (person's, one's own, memory); move up & down with unsteady motion; proceed laboriously, trudge, (often *on, along*); go on one's way, depart, as *we must be jogging*; proceed, get through the time, as *we must j. on somehow, matters j. along*; *j.-trot*, slow regular trot, (fig.) monotonous progression (often attrib.); (n.) shake, push, nudge, slow walk or trot. [prob. imit.]

jo·ggle[1], v.t. & i., & n. Shake, move, (as) by repeated jerks; (n.) slight shake. [prob. f. prec. + -LE(3)]

jo·ggle[2], n., & v.t. Joint of two pieces of stone or timber, contrived to prevent their sliding on one another; notch in one of two pieces, projection in the other, or small piece let in between both, for this purpose; (v.t.) join by means of a j. [(vb f. n.) perh. cogn. w. JAG]

Jōha·nnīne, a. Of the apostle John. [f. L as JOHN, see -INE[1]]

Joha·nnisberger, n. Fine white wine from Johannisberg in the Rheingau. [G]

John (jŏn), n. Masculine Christian name; *J.* BARLEY*corn*; *J. Bull*, English nation, typical Englishman, whence **John-Bu·ll**ISM n.; *J. Chinaman*, = CHINA*man*; *J.* COMPANY; *J. Doe*, fictitious character in law; *J.* DORY[1]; *J.-o'-Groat's* (*-House*), north of Scotland (*from J.-o'-G. to Land's End*, through Gt Britain). [= OF *Jehan* f. L f. Gk *Iōannēs* f. Heb. *yokhanan*]

Jōh·nian, a. & n. (Member) of St John's College, Cambridge. [-IAN]

jŏh·nny, n. Fellow, esp. fashionable idler; *J. Armstrong* (naut. slang), hand-power; *J. Raw*, novice; *j.-cake*, cake of (U.S.) maize-meal or (Austral.) wheat-meal. [f. JOHN, -Y[3]]

Johnsō·nian (jŏn-), a. Of, like, Samuel Johnson, man of letters & lexicographer (d. 1784), esp., abounding in Latin-derived words. So **Johnson**E·SE n. [-IAN]

join, v.t. & i., & n. Put together, fasten,

unite, (things, one *to* another); connect (two points) by straight line; unite (persons, one *with* or *to* another) in marriage, friendship, alliance, &c.; (intr.) come together, be united, (*with, to*, or abs.); take part with others (*in doing*); come into the company of (person); become member of (club &c.); take, resume, one's place in (regiment, ship, company, &c.); come into connexion with, as *the Cherwell joins the Thames below Oxford*; *j. battle*, begin fighting; *j. hands*, clasp one's hands together, clasp each other's hands, (fig.) combine in action or enterprise; *j.* ISSUE¹; (n.) point, line, of junction. [(n. f. vb) f. OF *joindre* (st. *joign-*) f. L *jungere junct-* join, cogn. w. Gk *zug-*, E *yoke*]

joi·nder, n. (rare exc. law). Joining, union. [f. F *joindre* JOIN taken as noun, cf. -ER⁴]

joi·ner, n. In vbl senses, esp.: one who makes furniture, house fittings, & other woodwork lighter than carpenter's, whence **joi·n**ERY(1, 2) n. [f. OF *joigneor* (*joigner* JOIN)]

joint¹, n. Place at which two things are joined together; structure in animal body by which two bones are fitted together; *out of j.*, (of bone) dislocated, (fig.) out of order; *put* (person's) NOSE *out of j.*; part of stem from which leaf or branch grows; point at which, contrivance by which, two parts of artificial structure are joined, rigidly or so as to allow of movement; (Geol.) fissure in mass of rock; one of the parts of which a body is made up; one of the parts into which butcher divides carcass, esp. as served at table; (slang, esp. U.S.) illicit opium-den or drinking-saloon; *j.-stool* (orig. *joined*), one made of parts fitted by a joiner. Hence **joi·nt**LESS a. [OF, p.p. as JOIN]

joint², a. Held or done by, belonging to, two or more persons &c. in conjunction, as *j. action, opinion, estate*; (of persons) sharing (*with* others in possession, action, state, &c.), as *j. owners*; *during their j. lives*, while they are all alive; *j. stock*, capital divided into shares, common fund, (attrib.) holding, formed on basis of, a j. stock, as *j.-stock bank, company*. Hence **joi·nt**LY² adv. [F, as prec.]

joint³, v.t. Connect by joints; fill up joints of (masonry &c.) with mortar &c., point; prepare (board &c.) for being joined to another by planing its edge; divide (body, member) at a joint or into joints. [f. JOINT¹]

joi·nter, n. In vbl senses, esp.: plane for jointing; mason's tool for pointing; workman employed in jointing esp. electric wire. [-ER¹]

joi·ntress, n. Widow who holds a jointure. [f. obs. *jointer* joint possessor + -ESS¹]

joi·nture, n., & v.t. Sole estate limited to wife, to be employed by her after husband's death for her life; (v.t.) provide (wife) with j. [(vb f. n.) F, f. L *junctura* (as JOIN¹, see -URE)]

joist, n. One of parallel timbers stretched on edge from wall to wall for ceiling laths or floor boards to be nailed to. Hence **joi·st**ED² a. [f. OF *giste* (*gesir* lie f. L *jacēre*)]

joke¹, n. Thing said or done to excite laughter; witticism, jest; ridiculous circumstance; *practical j.*, trick played on person in order to have laugh at his expense; *it is no j.* (a serious matter). Hence **jo·k**Y² a. [f. 17th c., prob. f. L *jocus* jest]

joke², v.i. & t. Make jokes; poke fun at, banter. Hence **jo·king**LY² adv. [f. prec. or f. L *jocari* as prec.]

jo·ker, n. One who jokes; (slang) fellow, chap; (Cards) odd (often blank) card in some games, counting as (highest) trump. [-ER¹]

jokul, *jökull*, (yō·ko͝ol, yer-), n. Snow-mountain in Iceland. [Icel. (*jö-*), = icicle, glacier, dim. of *jaki* piece of ice]

jo·llify̆, v.i. & t. Make merry, esp. tipple; make jolly. Hence **jolli**FICA·TION n. [-FY]

jo·llity, n. Merrymaking, festivity. [f. OF *jolivete* (as JOLLY, see -TY)]

jo·lly, a., adv., & n. Joyful; slightly drunk; festive, jovial; *the j. god*, Bacchus; (colloq., of person or thing) very pleasant, delightful, (often iron., as *he must be a j. fool to do it*), whence **jo·lli**LY² adv.; (adv., colloq.) very, as *he will be j. savage, you will j. well have to*; (n., Nav. slang) royal marine. [ME & OF *joli(f)* gay, pretty, etym. dub.]

jo·lly-boat, n. (Also *jolly*) clinker-built ship's boat, smaller than cutter. [?]

jōlt, v.t. & i., & n. Shake (person &c.) with jerk from seat &c., esp. in locomotion; (of vehicle) move along with jerks, as on rough road; (n.) such jerk. Hence **jō·lt**Y² a. [?]

jō·lterhead, n. Clumsy head; stupid person. [extension of obs. *jolthead*, etym. dub.]

Jō·nah, n. Person who brings, or is sacrificed lest he bring, ill luck. [see *Jonah*, O.T. book]

Jŏ·nathan, n. (*Brother*) *J.*, personified people of, typical citizen of, United States. [perh. f. *J.* Trumbull, governor of Connecticut]

jongleur (F), n. (hist.). Itinerant minstrel. [var. of *jingleur* JUGGLER]

jŏ·nquil (*or* jŭ-), n. Species of narcissus, rush-leaved daffodil; j. colour, pale yellow. [ult. dim. of L *juncus* rush; F *jonquille* &c.]

jor·dan, n. (not in polite use). Chamber-pot. [?]

Jor·dan al·mond, n. Fine almond esp. from Malaga. [prob. f. F *jardin* garden]

jor·um, n. Large drinking-bowl; its contents, esp. punch. [?]

jō·seph (-z-), n. (*J-*) chaste man; woman's long riding-cloak of 18th c. [see *Gen.* xxxix, xxxvii. 3]

jo·skin, n. Country bumpkin, dolt. [cf. dial. *joss* bump, -KIN]

joss, n. Chinese idol; *j.-house*, Chinese temple; *j.-stick* (of fragrant tinder mixed with clay, as incense). [prob. f. Port. *deos* f. L *deus* god]

jo·sser, n. (slang). Fool; fellow. [?]

jo·stle (-sl), v.i. & t., & n. Knock, push, *against*; struggle *with* (person *for* thing); push against, elbow; push (person *away*, *from*, &c.); (n.) jostling, encounter. [(n. f. vb) earlier *justle*, f. *just* JOUST + -LE(3)]

jot[1], n. (Usu. w. negative expressed or implied) small amount, whit. [f. L f. Gk *iōta* letter *i*]

jot[2], v.t. Write (usu. *down*) briefly or hastily. [prob. f. prec.]

jounce (jow-), v.t. & i. Bump, bounce, jolt. [?]

jour·nal (jer-), n. (In bookkeeping by double entry) book in which each transaction is entered, with statement of accounts to which it is to be debited & credited; daily record of events; (Parl.) *the Jj.*, record of daily proceedings; (Naut.) log-book; daily newspaper, other periodical; part of shaft or axle that rests on bearings (hist. unexpl.); *j.-box* (enclosing j. & bearings). [OF as DIURNAL]

jour·nalist, n. One whose business it is to edit or write for a public journal. Hence or cogn. **journal**E·SE, **jour·nal**ISM, nn., **journali·stic** a. [-IST]

jour·nalize, v.t. & i. (Bookk.) enter in journal; record in, keep, private journal. [-IZE]

jour·ney (jer-), n., & v.i. Distance travelled in specified time, as *a day's*, *4 days'*, *j.*; expedition to some distance, round of travel (usu. by land, cf. VOYAGE), as *take*, *undertake*, *perform*, *a j.*; *journeyman*, qualified mechanic or artisan who works for another, (fig.) mere hireling, (Astr.) *j.-m.(clock)*, secondary clock in observatory; *j.-work*, work of a journeyman (esp. fig.); (v.i.) make a j. [(vb f. OF *journéer*) f. OF *jornee* day, day's work or journey, f. pop. L *diurnata* (*diurnus* DIURNAL, see -ADE)]

joust (jōōst), **jŭst,** v.i., & n. (Engage in) combat between two knights &c. on horseback with lances. [(n. f. OF *juste*) f. OF *juster* f. pop. L *juxtare* approach (*juxta* near)]

Jōve, n. Jupiter, esp. *by J.!* [f. L *Jovem* (nom. *Jupiter*)]

jō·vial, a. Merry; convivial. Hence or cogn. **jovia·l**ITY n., **jo·vial**LY[2] adv. [F, f. L *jovialis* of Jupiter (*Jupiter Jovis*, see -AL)]

Jō·vian, a. Of, like, Jove; of the planet Jupiter. [f. L as prec., see -AN]

jowl, n. Jawbone, jaw; cheek, esp. *cheek by j.*; external throat or neck when prominent, dewlap of cattle, crop of bird; head & shoulders of salmon & other fish. [(1) OE *ceafl* jaw, cf. Du. *kevel* gum; (2) OE *ceolur* throat, cf. Du. *keel*, G *kehle*; the ME forms (1) *jowle* (2) *cholle*, both of unexplained development, were ult. confused]

joy[1], n. Vivid emotion of pleasure, gladness; thing that causes delight; *j.-bells* (rung on festive occasions); *j.-ride* (slang), stolen or other pleasure-ride in motor &c.; *joystick* (slang), control lever of aeroplane. Hence or cogn. **joy·**FUL, **joy·**LESS, **joy·**OUS, aa., **joy·ful**LY[2], **joy·less**LY[2], **joy·ous**LY[2], advv., **joy·ful**NESS, **joy·less**NESS, **joy·ous**NESS, nn. [f. OF *joie* f. pop. L **gaudia* fem. f. L *gaudia* pl. of *gaudium*]

joy[2], v.i. & t. (chiefly poet.). Rejoice; gladden. [f. OF *joir* rejoice ult. f. L *gaudēre* rejoice]

ju·bilāte[1] (jōō-), v.i. Exult, make demonstrations of joy. Hence or cogn. **ju·bi**LANCE, **jubil**A·TION, nn., **ju·bil**ANT a., **ju·bilant**LY[2] adv. [f. L *jubilare* (*jubilum* shout), see -ATE[3]]

Jubilatĕ[2] (jōōbĭlah·tĭ *or* yōō-), n. Hundredth psalm as canticle in Anglican service; outburst of triumph. [L, = shout ye (its first word)]

ju·bilee (jōō-), n. (Jewish Hist.) year of emancipation & restoration, kept every 50 years, acc. to *Lev.* xxv; (R.-C. Ch.) year of remission from penal consequences of sin, granted formerly at various intervals, now at any time; fiftieth anniversary; *silver j.*, twenty-fifth anniversary; *Diamond J.*, sixtieth year of reign of Queen Victoria; season of rejoicing; exultant joy. [f. F *jubilé* f. LL *jubilaeus* (*annus* year) of jubilee f. Gk *iōbēlaios* (*iōbēlos* f. Heb. *yobel* ram, ram's-horn trumpet, jubilee) by assoc. w. native L *jubilum* shout]

Judā·ic (jōō-), a. Jewish. [f. L f. Gk *Ioudaïkos* (*Ioudaios* JEW[1], see -IC)]

Ju·dāize, v.i. & t. Follow Jewish customs or rites; make Jewish. So **Ju·dā**ISM, **Ju·dā**IST, nn. [f. LL *judaizare* f. Gk *ioudaïzō* (as prec., see -IZE)]

ju·das (jōō-), n. (*J-*) disciple who betrayed Christ, infamous traitor; peephole in door; (of beard &c.) *J.-colour(ed)*, red; *J. kiss* (see *Matt.* xxvi. 48); *J.-tree* (with purple flowers appearing before the leaves).

Ju·denhetze (yōō-, -ze), n. Systematic persecution of Jews. [G]

judge[1], n. Public officer appointed to hear & try causes in court of justice; (of God) supreme arbiter; (Heb. Hist.) officer having temporary authority in Israel in period between Joshua & the kings; (pl., abbr. *Judg.*) book of O.T.; person appointed to decide dispute or contest; person who decides a question; person who is qualified to decide on merits of thing or question, as *am no j. of that, good j. of claret*; *J. Advocate General*, civil officer in supreme control of courts martial; *j.-made law*, principles based on judges' decisions. Hence **ju·dge**SHIP(1, 2) n. [f. OF *juge* f. L *judicem* (nom. *-dex*) f. *jus* right + *-dicus* speaking]

judge[2], v.t. & i. Pronounce sentence on (person) in court of justice; try (cause); decide (question); decide, decree, (*that* &c.); form opinion about, estimate, (person &c. *by* his deeds &c.); criticize, censure; conclude, consider, suppose, (thing *to be, that*, &c., *from* or *by* data); act as judge; form a judgement (*of* thing &c.). [f. OF *jugier* f. L *judicare* (as prec.)]

judgemă·tic(al), aa. (colloq.). Judicious, discerning. Hence **judgema·tical**LY[2] adv. [f. JUDGE, on *dogmatic* &c.]

ju·dgement, -gment, n. Sentence of court of justice; *the last j.* (by God at end of world); misfortune viewed as sign of divine displeasure, as *it is a j. on you for getting up late*; criticism; opinion, estimate, as *in my j.*; critical faculty, discernment; good sense; *j.-day* (of God's final j.); *j. debt* (for payment of which a j. has been given); *j. creditor, debtor* (for, against, whom j. has been given); *j. summons* (for failure to pay j. debt); *j.-seat*, judge's seat, tribunal. [f. F *jugement* (as prec., see -MENT)]

ju·dicature (jōōd-), n. Administration of justice; *Supreme Court of J. in England* (uniting former Courts of Chancery, King's Bench, Common Pleas, Exchequer, &c.); judge's (term of) office; body of judges; court of justice. [f. med. L *judicatura* (as JUDGE[2], -URE)]

judi·cial (jōō-), a. Of, done by, proper to, a court of law; *j. murder*, legal but unjust death sentence; inflicted as a divine judgement (esp. *j. blindness*, punitive infatuation); having the function of judgement, as *a j. assembly*; of, proper to, a judge; expressing a judgement, critical; impartial. Hence **judi·cial**LY[2] adv. [f. L *judicialis* (as foll., -AL)]

judi·ciary (-ĭsharĭ), n. The judges of a State collectively. [f. L *judiciarius* (med. L *-aria* fem. as n.) of judgement (*judicium*, see foll.)]

judi·cious (jōō-), a. Sensible, prudent; sound in discernment. Hence **judi·cious**LY[2] adv., **judi·cious**NESS n. [f. F *judicieux* f. L *judicium* judgement (as JUDGE[1]), see -OUS]

jug[1], n. Deep vessel for holding liquids, with handle & often with spout, whence **ju·g**FUL(2) n.; (slang, also *stone-j.*) prison. [?]

jug[2], v.t. Stew, boil, (hare, rabbit) in jug or jar (usu. in p.p.); (slang) imprison. [f. prec.]

jug[3], v.i. (Of nightingale or other bird) utter sound *jug*. So **jug, jug-jug**, nn. [imit.]

jugate (jōō·gat), a. (bot.). Having leaflets in pairs. [f. L *jugare* join (*jugum* yoke), see -ATE[2]]

Ju·ggernaut, n. (Hind. Myth.) Krishna, eighth avatar of Vishnu, his idol at Puri, annually dragged in procession on huge car, under wheels of which devotees are said to have formerly thrown themselves; (fig., also *J. car*) institution, notion, to which persons blindly sacrifice themselves or others. [f. Hind. *Jagannath* f. Skr. *Jagannatha* (*jagat* world + *natha* lord)]

ju·ggins, n. (slang). Simpleton. [?]

ju·ggle, v.i. & t., & n. Play conjuring tricks; *j. with*, deceive (person), misrepresent (facts); cheat, (person &c. *out of* thing); bring, get, change, (*away, into*, &c.) by trickery; (n.) piece of juggling, fraud. [(n. f. vb) f. OF *jogler* f. LL *joculare* (L *-ri*) jest (*joculus* dim. of *jocus* jest)]

ju·ggler, n. Conjurer; trickster, impostor. So **ju·ggl**ERY(2, 4) n. [f. OF *jogleor, jougleur* (whence var. JONGLEUR), f. L *joculatorem* (as JUGGLE, see -OR[2])]

Jugo-Slav (ū·goslahv), a. & n. (Inhabitant) of the new State, including Serbia & the southern Slavs of the former Austrian Empire, called *Jugo-Slavia*. [Serb., = south Slav]

jŭ·gular (*or* jōō-), a. & n. Of the neck or throat; *j. veins*, great veins of neck, conveying blood (*external j.*) from superficial parts of head, (*internal j.*) from inside of skull; (of fish) having the ventral fins in front of the pectoral; (n.) j. vein. [f. L *jugulum* collar-bone, see -AR[1]]

jŭ·gulate (*or* jōō-) v.t. Kill, esp. (fig.) arrest course of (disease &c.) by powerful remedy &c. [f. L *jugulare* (as prec.), see -ATE[3]]

juice (jōōs), n. Liquid part of vegetables or fruits; fluid part of animal body or substance, esp. *the jj.*, the bodily humours, *gastric j.*; (fig.) essence, spirit, of anything; (slang) petrol or electricity used in engine &c. Hence **jui·ce**LESS a. [f. F *jus* f. L *jus* broth, juice]

jui·cy, a. Full of juice, succulent; (of weather) wet; (colloq.) of rich intellectual quality, interesting; (Art slang) of rich colouring suggestive of moisture. Hence **jui·ci**NESS n. [-Y[2]]

ju-ju (jōō·jōō), n. (W.-Afr.). Charm or fetish; ban effected by this. [perh. f. F *jou-jou* toy]

ju·jube (jōō-), n. Edible berry-like drupe of certain plants; lozenge of gelatin &c. flavoured with or imitating this. [F, f. med. L *jujuba* f. Gk *zizuphon*]

ju-jutsu, jiu-jitsu, (jōōjutsōō·), n. Japanese art of wrestling &c. [Jap. (*ju*-)]

ju·lep (jōō-), n. Sweet drink, esp. as vehicle for medicine; medicated drink as stimulant &c.; (U.S.) iced or spiced spirit & water. [F, f. Arab. *julab* f. Pers. *gulab* (*gul* rose + *ab* water)]

Ju·lian (jōō-), a. Of Julius Caesar; *J. calendar* (introduced by him, cf. GREGORIAN). [f. L *Julianus* (*Julius*, see -AN)]

julienne (F), n. Soup of vegetables cooked in meat broth.

Julȳ· (jōō-), n. Seventh month of year, called after Julius Caesar. [ME & OF *Jule* f. L *Julius*; 18th-c. pron. jōō·lĭ, mod. pron. irreg. & unexpl.]

ju·mbal, -ble³, n. Kinds of crisp thin sweet cake. [?]

ju·mble¹, v.i. & t. Move (t. & i.) about in disorder; mix *up*, confuse. [prob. imit.]

ju·mble², n. Confused assemblage; muddle; jolting; *j.-sale* (of miscellaneous cheap articles at bazaar &c.); *j.-shop* (where miscellaneous goods are sold). Hence **ju·mbl**Y² a. [f. prec.]

ju·mbo, n. Big clumsy person, animal, or thing, esp. (*J-*) famous elephant in London Zool. Gardens; notably successful person. [?]

jump¹, n. Leap, bound, spring from ground; *long, high, j.*, athletic competitions; start caused by shock or excitement, esp. (slang) *the jj.*, delirium tremens; abrupt rise in amount, price, value, &c.; sudden transition, gap in series, argument, &c. Hence **ju·mpi**NESS n., **ju·mp**Y² a. [f. foll.]

jump², v.i. & t. Spring from ground &c. by flexion & sudden muscular extension of legs or (of fish) tail; move suddenly with leap or bound (*up* from seat &c., *out*, &c.); *j. in*, get quickly into carriage &c.; start with sudden jerk from excitement, shock, &c., esp. *j. for joy*; rise suddenly in price &c.; come *to*, arrive *at*, (conclusion) hastily; *j. at*, (fig.) accept (offer, bargain) eagerly; *j.* (*up*)*on*, attack (offender &c.) crushingly with word or act; agree, coincide, (*together*, one *with* another); pass over (gate &c.) by leap; (of railway carriage) leave (line); help (child &c.) to j. *down* &c.; cause (thing) to j.; startle (person, nerves); cook (potatoes &c.) in frying-pan, occasionally shaking them (usu. in p.p.); pounce upon (thing); steal a march upon; (Colon.) take summary possession of (claim abandoned or forfeited by former occupant); skip over (subject, part of book, &c.; drill (rock, hole in rock) with jumper; *j. down* person's *throat*, answer, interrupt, him violently; *j. out of* one's *skin*, j. with surprise; *j. over the* BROOM*stick*. Hence **ju·mp**ABLE a. [f. 1500; prob. imit.]

ju·mper¹, n. In vbl senses, esp.: member of Welsh Methodist body (or later sects) who jump(ed) as part of worship; jumping insect, e.g. flea; rope made fast to keep yard, mast, &c., from jumping; heavy chisel-ended iron bar for drilling blasting-holes. [-ER¹]

ju·mper², n. Loose outer jacket of canvas &c. worn by sailors &c.; woman's loose outer garment of any material slipped on over head & reaching hips. [prob. f. obs. *jump* short coat perh. f. F *juppe*]

ju·mping, a. In vbl senses, esp. in names of j. animals, as *j.-deer*, N.-Amer. black-tailed deer; *j.-bean*, seed of Mexican plant j. owing to movements of enclosed larva; *j.* CAT¹. [-ING²]

ju·nction, n. Joining; joint, meeting-place; station where railway lines meet & unite (often in proper names, as *Clapham J.*). [f. L *junctio* (as JOIN¹, see -ION)]

ju·ncture (-tsh*er*), n. Joining; place where things join; concurrence of events, state of affairs, as *at this j.* [f. L *junctura* (JOIN, -URE)]

June, n. Sixth month of year. [(partly thr. F *juin*) f. L *Junius*]

ju·ngle, n. Land overgrown with underwood or tangled vegetation, esp. in India (often attrib. of animals inhabiting j., as *j.-bear, -cat, -fowl*); wild tangled mass; (slang) W.-African share market; *j. fever* (caused by miasma of j.). Hence **ju·ngl**ED², **ju·ngl**Y², aa. [f. Hind. *jangal* desert, forest]

ju·nior (jōō-), a. & n. The younger (esp. of son having same name as father, as *John Smith j.*, or of younger of two boys of same surname in school; abbr. *jun.,jr*); of less standing, of lower position, as *j. partner*; (n.) j. person, as the *jj.*, *is my j.* Cf. SENIOR. Hence **juniŏ·r**ITY n. [L, compar. of *juvenis* young]

ju·niorate (-*a*t), n. (In Society of Jesus) two-years' course attended by junior members before entering priesthood. [-ATE¹]

ju·niper (jōō-), n. Genus of coniferous evergreen shrubs, esp. *common j.*, shrub with prickly leaves & dark berries yielding *oil of j.* used in medicine & in making gin. [f. L *juniperus*]

junk¹, n., & v.t. Old cable cut up for oakum &c.; discarded material; lump, chunk; (Naut.) salt meat; lump of tissue in sperm-whale, containing spermaceti; *j.-shop*, marine store; (v.t.) divide into jj. [?]

junk², n. Flat-bottomed sailing vessel used in Chinese seas. [prob. f. Javanese *djong*]

ju·nker (yŏŏngk-), n. Young German noble; member of exclusive aristocratic party in Prussia. [G, earlier *junkher* (YOUNG, HERR)]

ju·nket, n., & v.i. Dish of sweetened curds & whey, usu. with scalded cream on top; feast; (v.i.) feast, picnic. Hence **ju·nket**ING¹ n. [(vb f. n.) prob. f. ONF *jonquette* rush-basket (for making j.) f. *jonc* rush f. L *juncus*]

Ju·no (jōō-), n. Wife of Jupiter; woman of stately beauty; third of the asteroids. [L]

jŭ·nta, n. Deliberative or administrative council in Spain or Italy; =foll. [Sp., f. L *juncta*, fem. p.p. as JOIN¹]

jŭ·nto, n. Clique, faction, political or other combination of persons. [erroneous f. prec.]

jupe (F), n. Woman's skirt.

Ju·piter (jōō-), n. (Rom. Myth.) king of gods; *J. Pluvius* (plōō-), god of rain; largest planet of solar system. [L]

jur·al (joor-), a. Of law, of (moral) rights & obligations. [f. L *jus juris* right + -AL]

jura·ssic (joor-), a. Of the Jura mountains between France & Switzerland; marked like these by prevalence of oolitic limestone. [f. F *jurassique* after *liassic, triassic*]

jurat (joor·*a*t), n. Municipal officer like alderman; life magistrate in Channel Is. [f. med. L *juratus* (*jurare* swear)]

jurĭ·dical (joor-), a. Of judicial proceedings; legal. [f. L *juridicus* (*jus juris* right + -*dicus* f. *dicere* say) + -AL]

jur·isconsu·lt (joor-), n. One learned in law, jurist. [f. L *jurisconsultus* (*jus juris* law + p.p. as CONSULT)]

jurisdi·ction, n. Administration of justice; legal or other authority; extent of this, territory it extends over. Hence **jurisdi·ction**AL a. [f. L *jurisdictio* (as prec., see DICTION)]

jurispru·dence, n. Science, philosophy, of human law, whence **jurisprude·nt**IAL a.; skill in law, so **jurispru·d**ENT a. & n. [f. L *jurisprudentia* (as prec., see PRUDENCE)]

jur·ist (joor-), n. One versed in law; legal writer; student of, graduate in, law. Hence **juri·st**IC(AL) aa., **juri·stical**LY² adv. [f. F *juriste* f. med. L *jurista* (*jus juris* law, see -IST)]

jur·or (joor-), n. Member of jury; one who takes an oath (cf. NON-*juror*). [f. OF *jureor* f. L *juratorem* (*jurare* swear, see -OR²)]

jury (joor·ĭ), n. Body of men sworn to render verdict on question submitted to them in court of justice; *grand j.* (of from 12 to 23 men appointed to inquire into indictments before they are submitted to trial j.); *trial, common, petty, j.* (of 12 men, who try final issue of fact in civil or criminal cases & pronounce unanimous verdict); *special j.* (of persons of certain station in society); CORONER'*s j.*; *j. of matrons* (in case where pregnancy is pleaded in stay of execution); body of persons selected to award prizes in competition; *j.-box*, enclosure for j. in court; *juryman*, member of j. [f. OF *jurée* oath, inquiry, f. med. L *jurata* (*jurare* swear, cf. -Y⁴)]

jur·y-mast (joor-), n. Temporary mast in place of broken or lost one. [?]

ju·ssive, a. (gram.). Expressing a command. [f. L *jubēre juss-* command]

just¹, a. (Of person or conduct) equitable, fair, (*to* person &c.); (of treatment &c.) deserved, as *a j. reward*; (of feelings, opinions, &c.) well-grounded, as *j. resentment, fear*; right in amount &c., proper. Hence **ju·st**LY² adv., **ju·st**NESS n. [f. L *justus* (*jus* right)]

just², adv. Exactly, as *j. at that spot, j. there, j. then, j. three o'clock, j. as you say, j. so, that is j. it* (precisely the point in question), (U.S.) *j. how many there are remains to be seen*; barely, as *I j. managed it*; exactly at that moment, (loosely) not long before, as *I have j.* (a moment, or not long, ago) *seen him pass*; *j. now*, at this moment, (also) a little time ago; (colloq.) positively, quite, as *it is j. splendid, not j. yet*; (as slang emphasizer) *Won't I j. give it him!*, '*Did he swear? Didn't he, j.!*' [f. prec.]

just³. See JOUST.

ju·stice, n. Just conduct; fairness; exercise of authority in maintenance of right; *poetical j.* (ideal, as shown in poem &c.); judicial proceedings, as *Court of J.*; magistrate; judge, esp. (in England) of Supreme Court of Judicature, whence **ju·stice**SHIP n.; *J. of the Peace*, inferior magistrate appointed to preserve peace in county, town, &c.; *do j. to*, treat fairly, show due appreciation of; *do oneself j.*, perform worthily of one's abilities. [OF (*-ice, -ise*), f. L *justitia* (as JUST, see -ICE)]

justi·ciable (-shy*a*-), a. Subject to jurisdiction; (n.) person subject to jurisdiction (*of* another). [OF, f. *justicier* bring to trial f. med. L *justitiare* (as prec.), see -ABLE]

justi·ciar (-shy-), n. Chief political & judicial officer under Norman & early Plantagenet kings. [as foll., see -AR²]

justi·ciary (-shy-), n. & a. Administrator of justice; = prec.; (adj.) of the administration of justice. [f. med. L *justitiarius* (JUSTICE, -ARY¹)]

ju·stifȳ, v.t. Show the justice or rightness of (person, act, &c.); vindicate, (of circumstances) be such as to j.; (Theol.) declare (person) free from penalty of sin on ground of Christ's righteousness or (Rom. Cath.) of the infusion of grace; make good (statement &c.); adduce adequate grounds for (conduct, claim, &c.); *j. bail*, show by oath of person furnishing bail that he is pecuniarily qualified. Hence or cogn. **justifia**BI·LITY, **justi**FICA·TION, nn., **ju·stifi**ABLE, **ju·stificat**IVE, **ju·stificat**ORY, aa., **ju·stifiab**LY² adv. [f. F *justifier* f. LL *justificare* (as JUST¹, see -FY)]

jut, n., & v.i. Projection; protruding point; (v.i.) project (often *out, forth*). [var. of JET², ³]

jute¹, n. Fibre from bark of certain plants, chiefly imported from Bengal, used for canvas, cordage, &c. [f. Bengali *jhoṭo* f. Skr. *juṭa* = *jaṭa* braid of hair]

Jute², n. One of Low German tribe invading Britain in 5th & 6th cc. [Baeda has *Jutae* pl., OE *Eotas* = Icel. *Iotar* people of Jutland]

juvene·scence, n. (Transition from infancy to) youth. So **juvene·scENT** a. [f. L *juvenescere* reach age of youth (*juvenis* young), see -ENCE]

ju·venīle (jōō-), a. & n. Young, youthful; suited to, characteristic of, youth; (n.) young person. Hence or cogn. **ju·venile**LY[2] adv., **juvenī·l**ITY n. [f. L *juvenilis* (as prec., -IL)]

juxtapo·se (-z), v.t. Place (things) side by side. [f. F *juxtaposer* (L *juxta* next + *poser*, see COMPOSE)]

juxtaposi·tion, n. Placing, being placed, side by side. [F (L *juxta* next, POSITION)]

K

K, k, (kā), letter (pl. *K*s, K's).

Abbreviations (1): King's, as **K.B., K.C.,** (Bench, Counsel); Knight, as **K.G.** (of the Garter), **K.G.C.B.** (Grand Cross of the Bath), **K.P.** (of the Order of St Patrick), **K.T.** (of the Order of the Thistle); Knight Commander, **K.B.E.** (of British Empire); **K.C.,** Knight Commander, as **K.C.B.** (of the Bath), **K.C.I.E.** (of the Indian Empire), **K.C.M.G.** (of the Order of St Michael & St George), **K.C.S.I.** (of the Star of India), **K.C.V.O.** (of the Royal Victorian Order).

Abbreviations (2): **Kan.**(sas); **kg.,** kilogramme; **kl.,** kilolitre; **km.,** kilometre; **Knt, Kt,** knight; **Ky,** Kentucky.

kaama (kah·*ma*), n. Hartebeest. [S. Afr.]

kabbalah. = CABBALA.

ka·ddish, n. Jewish mourner's prayer; the *Magnificat* in the synagogue service. [f. Aram. *qaddish* holy]

kadi. See CADI.

Kă·f(f)ir, Ca·ffre, n. Member of a S.-Afr. race of Bantu family; native of Kafiristan in Asia; (pl.) S.-Afr. mine shares. [Arab. *kafir* infidel]

ka·go (kah-), n. Japanese basket-work palanquin slung on pole. [f. Jap. *kango* of Chin. orig.]

kail(yard). See KALE.

kai·nīt(e) (kī-), n. Hydrouschlorosulphate of magnesium & potassium, used as fertilizer. [G (*-it*) f. Gk *kainos* new, see -ITE[1]]

kai·ser (kīz-), n. Emperor; German Emperor; Emperor of Austria; (Hist.) head of Holy Roman Empire. Hence **kai·ser**SHIP n. [ult. f. L *Caesar*]

kaja·wah (-jah-, *or* kă·ja-), n. Camel-litter for women. [Hind. & Pers.]

kale, kail, n. Kinds of cole or cabbage, esp. borecole, kind with wrinkled leaves; *Scotch k.,* kind with purplish leaves; broth made of this or other vegetables; *k.-yard,* kitchen-garden; *k.-yard school,* writers of fiction describing, with unsparing use of the vernacular, common life in Scotland. [northern form of COLE]

kalei·doscope (-lī-), n. Tube through which are seen symmetrical figures, produced by reflections of pieces of coloured glass, & varied by rotation of the tube; (fig.) constantly changing group of bright objects. Hence **kaleidoscŏ·pic**(AL) aa., **kaleidosco·pical**LY[2] adv. [f. Gk *kalos* beautiful + *eidos* form + -SCOPE]

kalends. See CALENDS.

kă·li, n. Prickly saltwort, from which soda-ash was obtained. [f. Arab. *qali* ALKALI]

kalian, -lioun, (kahlyah·n, -yōōn), n. Persian form of hookah. [Pers. (*-an*), f. Arab. *qalyan, -un*]

Ka·lmuck, -myk, a. & n. (Member, language) of a Mongolian race living on the Caspian.

ka·long (kah-), n. Malay frugivorous fox-bat, largest known bat. [Malay]

ka·lpa, n. Great age of the world, day of Brahma, (4,320,000,000 years). [Skr.]

kămera·d (-ahd), int. of German soldier offering to surrender. [G, f. F as COMRADE]

ka·mī (kah-), n. Japanese title of governors &c.; divinity, god, in Japanese native religion.

kamptū·licon, n. Floor-cloth of mixed rubber, gutta-percha, & cork, mounted on canvas. [f. Gk *kamptos* flexible + *oulos* thick + *-ikon* -IC]

kă·naka, n. Native of South Sea Islands, esp. one employed in Queensland on sugar plantations. [Hawaiian, = man]

kangaroo· (-ngg-), n. Marsupial mammal with strongly developed hindquarters & great leaping-power, native of Australia, Tasmania, &c.; *k. rat,* small Australian marsupial; (slang, pl.) W.-Australian mining shares, dealers in these; *k. bicycle,* one with sloping back, early form of safety; *k. closure* (when chairman in committee selects some amendments for discussion and excludes others). [perh. native Austral.]

kanoo·n, n. Kind of harp with fifty to sixty strings. [f. Pers. or Arab. *qanun*]

Kă·ntian, a. Of Immanuel Kant, German philosopher, d. 1804. So **Ka·nt**ISM n. [-IAN]

ka·olin (kah-, kā-), n. Fine white clay produced by decomposition of feldspar, used in making porcelain. Hence **ka·olin**IZE(3) v.t. [F, f. Chin. *kao-ling,* name of mountain (*kao* high + *ling* hill)]

kape·llmeister (-mī-), n. Leader or conductor of orchestra or choir. [G]

ka·pok (kah-), n. Fine cotton wool surrounding seeds of certain tree, used for stuffing cushions &c. [f. Malay *kapog*]

ka·ppa, n. Greek letter k (K, κ).

Kar·aīte, n. Member of Jewish sect that rejects Rabbinical tradition & interprets scriptures literally, found chiefly in Crimea. [f. Heb. *q'raim* (*qara* read) + -ITE[1]]

kar·ma, n. (Buddh.). Sum of person's actions in one of his successive states of existence, viewed as deciding his fate in the next; destiny. [Skr., = action, fate]

kar(r)oo·, n. Elevated plateau of clayey

soil in S. Africa, waterless in dry season; *the Great K.* (in Cape Colony). [of Hottentot orig.]

karŏ·ss, n. Mantle of animals' skins with the hair on, used by S.-African natives. [f. S.-Afr. *karos*, perh. of Du. orig.]

kar·tel, n. Wooden bed in S.-African ox-wagon. [S.-Afr. Du., prob. f. Port. *catel* f. Tamil *kaṭṭil* bedstead]

karte·ll. See CARTEL.

kă·sha, n. Ladies' dress-fabric. [?]

kată·bolism, n. (biol.). Destructive METABOLISM. [f. Gk *katabolē* throwing down (*kataballō* throw down) + -ISM]

kā·tydid, n. Large green orthopterous insect abounding in America. [imit. of the sound the insect produces]

kauri (kowr·ĭ), n. Coniferous tree of N. Zealand, furnishing valuable timber & a resin, *k.-gum.* [Maori]

ka·va (kah-), n. (Intoxicating beverage from roots of) a Polynesian shrub. [native]

kava·ss, n. Armed constable, servant, or courier, in Turkey. [f. Turk. *qawwas* bow-maker (*qaws* bow)]

kay·ak (kī-), n. Eskimo canoe of light wooden framework covered with seal-skins. [Eskimo]

kea (kā·*a*), n. Green Alpine parrot of N. Zealand which destroys sheep for their kidney-fat. [Maori, imit.]

keck, v.i. Make sound as if about to vomit; *k. at*, reject (food &c.) with loathing. [imit.]

kedge, v.i. & t., & n. Change position of ship by winding in hawser attached to small anchor at some distance; (of ship) move thus; move (ship) thus; *k.(-anchor)*, small anchor for this purpose. [perh. var. of CADGE]

ke·dgeree, n. Indian dish of rice, split pulse, onions, eggs, &c.; European dish of fish, rice, eggs, &c. [f. Hind. *khichri*, Skr. *k'ṛsara*]

keel[1], n., & v.t. Lowest longitudinal timber of vessel, on which framework of the whole is built up; combination of iron plates serving same purpose in iron vessel; (poet.) ship; *false k.* (attached to bottom of true k. to protect it); *k.-blocks* (on which k. rests in building &c.); *kee·l-haul*, haul (person) under k. as punishment; (v.t.) turn (ship) k. upwards, *k. over*, upset, capsize, (person &c.). Hence **kee·l**LESS a. [(vb f. n.) prob. f. ON *kjolr*, cf. Sw. *kōl*)]

keel[2], n. Flat-bottomed vessel, esp. of kind used on Tyne &c. for loading colliers; amount carried by this. [prob. f. MDu. *kiel*, cogn. w. OE *céol*]

keelson. See KELSON.

keen[1], n. Irish funeral song accompanied with wailing. [f. Ir. *caoine*, as foll.]

keen[2], v.i. & t. Utter the keen; bewail (person) thus; utter in wailing tone. [f. Ir. *caoinim* wail]

keen[3], a. Having sharp edge or point; (of edge &c.) sharp; (of sound, light, &c.) penetrating, vivid, strong; (of cold) intense; (of pain &c.) acute, bitter; (of person, desire, interest) eager, ardent, (colloq. *on* thing, *on* doing; *k. as mustard*, enthusiastic, w. pun on *Keene's* mustard); (of eyes, sight, smell) sharp, highly sensitive; intellectually acute; *k.-set*, hungry, eager, (*for*). Hence **kee·n**LY[2] adv., **kee·n**NESS n. [com.-Teut.: OE *céne*, Du. *koen*, G *kühn*, bold]

keep[1], v.t. & i. (kept). Pay due regard to, observe, stand by, (law, promise, faith, treaty, appointment; *k. the* PEACE); celebrate (feast, ceremony, &c.); guard, protect, (person, as *God k. you!*, fortress, town, &c., goal at football &c.); have charge of; retain possession of, not lose; maintain (house &c.) in proper order (*k. open house*, entertain all comers) carry on (shop &c.); maintain (diary, accounts, books) by making requisite entries; provide for sustenance of (family, one*self*, &c.); own & manage (cows, bees, &c.); maintain (woman) as mistress; have (commodity) habitually on sale; *k.* COMPANY[1], PACE, STEP, LOOK[1] *out*, TIME, WATCH[1], WICKET; maintain in proper or specified condition (often in spec. senses, as *k. the* BALL[1] *rolling*, POT *boiling*, one's HAIR *on*, one's HEAD[1]; *k.* one's *balance*, not lose it, lit. & fig.); detain (person *in prison*, *in custody*, &c.); restrain (person, thing, one*self*, *from* doing, *from* thing); refrain *from*; reserve (thing *for* future time &c.); conceal, as *k.* one's COUNSEL[1], *a secret*; continue to follow (way, course; *k. track of*, follow the course or development of); remain in (one's bed, room, house); retain one's place in (the saddle, the field, the stage, one's ground, &c.) against opposition; *k.* HOUSE; remain (indoors &c.); (colloq., esp. Camb. Univ.) reside, as *where do you k.?*; remain in specified condition, as *k. in good health*, *k. in* TOUCH *with*, *k. cool*, *k. friends*; continue in specified direction, course, or action, as *k. straight on for two miles*, *he keeps giggling*; (of food &c.) remain in good condition, (fig., of news &c.) admit of being reserved for later occasion; *k.* (work, cause to work, persistently) *at*; *k.* (abstain) *from*; *k. to*, adhere to (course, promise), confine oneself to; *k.* (thing &c.) *to* one*self*, refuse to share it with others; *k.* one*self to* one*self*, avoid society; *k. away*, avoid coming, prevent from coming; *k. back*, hold back, retard progress of, conceal; *k. down*, hold in subjection, k. low in amount, (Mil.) lie low in skirmishing; *k. in*, confine, restrain, (feelings &c.), confine (schoolboy) after hours, k. (fire) burning, (intr.) remain indoors, remain on good terms *with*; *k*, one's *feet*, not fall; *k.* one's HAND *in*; *k. off*, ward off, avert, (intr.) stay at a distance; *k. on*, continue to hold, use, show, &c., (intr.) continue (do*ing*); *k. out*, not let enter; *k. together*, remain, cause to remain, together; *k. under*, hold in subjection; *k. up*, prevent (one's spirits, prices, &c.) from sinking, maintain (*k.* one's END[1] *up*; *k. it up*, not slacken), k. in repair, in efficient or proper state, &c., as *k. up appearances, k. up your Greek*, carry on (correspondence &c.), cause (person) to sit up at night, (intr.) bear up, not break down, proceed at equal pace *with*. [late OE *cēpan*, etym. dub.]

keep[2], n. (Hist.) tower, stronghold; maintenance, food required for this, as *you don't earn your k.*; *for keeps* (U.S. slang), in permanence. [f. prec.]

kee·per, n. In vbl senses, esp.: =GAME[1]-*keeper*; lunatic's attendant; ring that keeps another, esp. wedding-ring, on the finger. [-ER[1]]

kee·ping, n. In vbl senses, also or esp.: custody, charge, as *in safe k., in his k.*; agreement, harmony, (orig. esp. of painting) as *in, out of, k.* (*with*); (attrib., or intr. part.) fit for k., as *k. apples*; *k.-room* (chiefly U.S.), sitting-room usually occupied. [-ING[1]]

kee·psake, n. Thing kept for sake, or in remembrance, of giver; (attrib.) namby-pamby, like certain literary annuals of early 19th c. called kk. [KEEP[1]+SAKE]

kĕf, keif (kīf), ***kief*** (kēf), n. Drowsy state produced by bhang &c.; enjoyment of idleness; Indian hemp &c. smoked to produce k. [f. Arab. *kaif*, colloq. *kef*, well-being]

keffi·yeh (-fēyā), n. Bedouin Arab's kerchief worn as head-dress. [f. Arab. *kaffiyah, kuffiyeh*, perh. f. LL *cofea* COIF]

kĕ·fir, n. Effervescent liquor like koumiss, used for invalids. [Caucas.]

keg, n. Small barrel, usu. of less than 10 gals. [earlier *cag*, cf. Icel. *kaggi*, Sw. *kagge*]

kelp, n. Large kinds of seaweed; calcined ashes of seaweed used for the sake of carbonate of soda, iodine, &c. contained, formerly used in making soap & glass. [ME *culp*, etym. dub.]

ke·lpie, -py, n. (Sc.). Water-spirit, usu. in form of horse, reputed to delight in the drowning of travellers &c. [?]

ke·lson, kee·lson, n. Line of timber fastening ship's floor-timbers to keel. [f. KEEL; *-son* unexpl., cf. Du. *kolzwijn*, G *kielschwein*]

Kelt &c. See CELT &c.

kemp, n. Coarse hair in wool. Hence **ke·mpy**[2] a. [prob. f. ON *kampr* beard, whisker, &c.]

ken[1], n. Range of sight or knowledge, esp. *in, out of, beyond*, one's *k.* [f. foll.]

ken[2], v.t. (now Sc. or north.; kent). Recognize at sight; know (person, thing, fact, *that* &c.). [com.-Teut.: OE *cennan*, Du. & G *kennen*]

kennel[1], n., & v.i. & t. (-ll-). House for shelter of house-dog or hounds; mean dwelling; (v.i.) live in, go to, k.; (v.t.) put into, keep in, k. [(vb f. n.) prob. f. ONF **kenil* (F *chenil*) f. pop. L *canile* (*canis* dog)]

ke·nnel[2], n. Gutter. [earlier *cannel* f. OF *canel* CHANNEL]

kenō·sis, n. (theol.). Renunciation of divine nature, at least in part, by Christ in the incarnation. So **kenŏ·tic** a., **keno·ticism**(3) n. [Gk *kenōsis* (*kenoō* vb empty f. *kenos*, see -OSIS)]

Ke·ntish, a. Of Kent; *K. fire*, prolonged volley of applause or demonstration of dissent; *K. man* (born W. of Medway, opp. *man of Kent* born E.); *K. rag*, hard limestone found in Kent. [OE *Centisc* (*Cent* f. L *Cantium*, see -ISH[1])]

ke·ntledge (-lĭj), n. (naut.). Pig-iron used as permanent ballast. [?]

kĕ·pĭ, n. French military cap with horizontal peak. [f. F *képi* f. G-Swiss *käppi* dim. of *kappe* cap]

kept. See KEEP[1].

kĕ·ratose, a. & n. Of horny substance; (n.) horn-like substance forming part of some sponges. [f. Gk *keras -atos* horn + -OSE[1]]

kerb, n. Stone edging to pavement or raised path; *k.-stone*, one of stones forming this. [var. of CURB n.]

ker·chief (-ĭf), n. Cloth used to cover head; (poet.) handkerchief. Hence **ker·chiefed**[2] a. [ME *curchef, ker-*, f. OF *couvrechief, cuevre-*, (*covrir* COVER + *chief* head f. L *caput*)]

kerf, n. Slit made by cutting, esp. with saw; cut end of felled tree. [OE *cyrf*, f. st. of CARVE]

ker·mes (-ĭz), n. Pregnant female of an insect, formerly taken for a berry, feeding on *k. oak*, an evergreen oak of S. Europe & N. Africa; red dye-stuff consisting of dried bodies of these; amorphous trisulphide of antimony, of brilliant red. [f. Arab. & Pers. *qirmiz*]

ker·mis, n. Periodical fair in Holland &c., with much noisy merrymaking. [Du., orig. = mass on anniversary of dedication of church, when yearly fair was held (KIRK + *mis* MASS[1])]

kern(e), n. (hist.). Light-armed Irish foot-soldier; peasant, boor. [f. Ir. *ceithern*]

ker·nel, n. Softer (usu. edible) part within hard shell of nut or stone fruit; body of seed within husk &c., e.g. grain of wheat; nucleus, centre of formation (often fig.). [OE *cyrnel*, dim. of CORN]

kĕ·rosene, n. Lamp-oil obtained by distillation of petroleum & from coal & bituminous shale, paraffin. [irreg. f. Gk *kēros* wax + -ENE]

Ke·rry, n. attrib. *K. blue*, a breed of terrier.

ker·sey (-zĭ), n. Kind of coarse narrow cloth woven from long wool, usu. ribbed. [perh. f. *K.* in Suffolk]

ker·seymere, n. Twilled fine woollen

cloth; (pl.) trousers of this. [corrupt. of *cassimere*, var. of CASHMERE, assim. to prec.]

ke·strel, n. Species of small hawk. [ME *castrel*, prob. = OF *cresserelle*, etym. dub.]

ketch, n. Small two-masted or cutter-rigged coasting vessel. [earlier *cache*, *catch*, f. CATCH v.]

ke·tchup, n. Sauce made from juice of mushrooms, tomatoes, &c. [prob. f. Chin. *kôe-chiap* brine of pickled fish]

ke·ttle, n. Vessel, usu. of metal with spout & handle, for boiling water; FISH¹-*k.*; *a pretty k. of fish*, awkward state of affairs; *ke·ttle-drum(mer)*, (player of) hollow brass or copper hemisphere, over edge of which parchment is stretched & tuned to definite note; *k.-drum*, (also) large afternoon tea-party; *k.-holder*, piece of cloth &c. to protect hand from heat of k. handle. Hence **ke·ttle**FUL(2) n. [com.-Teut.: OE *cetel*, Du. *ketel*, G *kessel*]

kĕ·vel, n. (naut.). Peg, cleat, usu. fixed in pairs, to which certain ropes are belayed. [f. ONF *keville* (F *cheville*) f. L *clavicula* dim. of *clavis* key]

Kew Gardens, n. pl. National botanical gardens at Kew.

key¹ (kē), n. Instrument, usu. of iron, for moving bolt of lock forwards or backwards; *get, have, the k. of the street*, be shut out for the night, homeless; MASTER¹ *k.*; *House of Kk.*, elective branch of legislature of I. of Man; *St Peter's kk.*, cross kk. borne in Papal arms; what gives or precludes opportunity for or access to something; *golden, silver, k.*, money used as bribe; (pl.) ecclesiastical authority as transmitted to the Pope, esp. *power of the kk.*; place that from its position gives control of sea, territory, &c.; solution, explanation, translation of foreign book; book of solutions of mathematical problems &c.; (Mus.) system of notes definitely related to each other & based on particular note, (fig.) tone, style, of thought or expression; *k.-note*, note on which a k. is based, (fig.) prevailing tone or idea; piece of wood or metal inserted between others to secure them; part of first coat of wall plaster passing between laths & so securing the rest; lever pressed by finger in playing organ, piano, &c.; similar lever in typewriter &c.; instrument for grasping screws, pegs, nuts, &c., esp. one for winding clock or watch; *keyboard*, set of kk. on piano &c.; *k.-bugle* (fitted with kk. to increase number of sounds); *keyhole* (by which k. is put into lock); *k. industry*, one essential to the carrying on of others, e.g. coal-mining, dyeing; *k. map* (in bare outline, to simplify use of full map); *k.-ring* (for keeping kk. on); *keystone*, stone at summit of arch locking the whole together, (fig.) central principle &c. on which all depends. Hence **key·**LESS a. [OE *cǽg*, etym. dub.]

key², v.t. Fasten (often *in, on*, &c.) with pin, wedge, bolt, &c.; regulate pitch of strings of (piano &c.); (fig.) *k. up*, stimulate (person *to* do, *to* condition &c.), raise the tone or standard of, brace up, raise (offer, demand, endeavour). [f. prec.]

key³, (kē) n. Low island or reef. [f. Sp. *cayo*, see QUAY]

khakan (kahkah·n), n. = KHAN¹. [f. Turk. *khaqan* king, emperor]

kha·ki (kah-), a. & n. Dust-coloured, dull-yellow; (n.) k. fabric of twilled cotton or wool, used in Brit. army; *k. election* (so timed as to exploit war-enthusiasm & secure majority for general purposes). [Hind., = dusty (*khak* dust)]

kha·lifa, kha·lifat, nn. = CALIPH(ATE).

kha·msin, n. Hot S. or S.E. wind in Egypt for about 50 days in March, April, & May. [Arab. (*khamsun* fifty)]

khăn¹ (*or* kahn), n. Title of rulers & officials in Central Asia, Afghanistan, &c.; (Hist.) supreme ruler of Turkish, Tartar, & Mongol tribes, & emperor of China, in middle ages. Hence **kha·n**ATE¹(1) n. [Turk., perh. as KHAKAN]

khăn² (*or* kahn), n. Caravanserai. [Arab., = inn]

khe·da (kā-), ***ke·ddah***, n. Enclosure used in Bengal &c. to catch elephants. [Hind. (*-da*)]

Khedi·ve (-ēv), n. Title of viceroy of Egypt, accorded to Ismail Pasha by Turkish Government in 1867. Hence **Khedi·v**(I)AL aa. [f. F *khédive* f. Turk. *khediv*]

khi·dmutgar, n. Male servant who waits at table (in India). [f. Hind. *khidmatgar* (*khidmat* service + *-gar* suf.)]

khi·lafat, n. = KHALIFAT; *k. agitation*, anti-British movement in India based on Moslem resentment of the loss of power by Islam in & after the great war, & contemporary Hindu discontents.

kibble¹, n. Iron hoisting-bucket used in mines. [prob. f. G *kübel*]

ki·bble², v.t. Grind coarsely. [?]

kibe, n. Ulcerated chilblain, esp. on heel; *tread on* one's *kk.*, hurt his feelings. [?]

kibi·tka, n. Tartar's circular tent covered with felt; Tartar household; Russian hooded sledge. [Russ.]

ki·blah, n. Point to which Mohammedans turn at prayer, i.e. temple at Mecca. [f. Arab. *qiblah* (*qabala* be opposite)]

kibo·sh (*or* ki·-), n. (slang). Nonsense, humbug; *put the k. on*, do for, knock on the head. [?]

kick¹, n. Act of kicking; (colloq.) reacting-power, resilience, (*has no k. left*); DROP¹-, PLACE-, *k.*; *more kk.* (harshness) *than halfpence* (kindness); recoil of gun when discharged; (Footb.) *good, bad*, &c., *k.* (kicker), *k.-off*, k. with which game is started; *k.-starter*, lever on motor-cycle by kicking which it can be started. [f. foll.]

kick[2], v.i. & t. Strike out with the foot; *k. against the pricks,* resist to one's own hurt; show annoyance, dislike, &c. (*against, at,* proposal, treatment); strike with foot; (slang) *k. the bucket,* die; *k.* one's HEELS; drive, move, (thing) by kicking; (Footb.) score (goal) by a k.; drive forcibly & contemptuously (*out, downstairs,* &c.; *k.* one *upstairs* fig., shelve him by giving him peerage or titular promotion); *k. off,* throw off (shoes) by kicking, (Footb.) give first kick; *k. up,* raise (dust), create (fuss, noise), *k. up* its *heels* (of horse in play); *kicking-strap* (arranged to prevent carriage-horse from kicking; also joc. in pl. of soldier's valise straps). [ME *kike,* etym. dub.]

kick[3], n. Indentation in bottom of glass bottle. [?]

ki·cker, n. In vbl senses, esp. horse given to kicking. [-ER[1]]

ki·ckshaw, n. Fancy dish in cookery (usu. contempt.); toy, trifle. [f. F *quelque chose* something]

kid[1], n., & v.t. & i. Young of goat; leather from skin of this, used for gloves & boots; *the Kk.* or *K.*, pair of small stars in Auriga; (slang) child, whence **kidd**Y[3] n.; *k.-glove* (adj.), over-dainty, avoiding everyday work &c.; (v.t.) give birth to (k.); (v.i.) give birth to k. [(vb f. n) ME *kide,* cf. ON *kidh,* G *kitz*]

kid[2], v.t., & n., (slang). Hoax, humbug, (vb often abs.). [perh. f. prec.]

kid[3], n. Small wooden tub, esp. sailor's mess-tub. [perh. var. of KIT[1]]

Ki·dderminster, n. Town in Worcestershire; *K. carpet* (with pattern formed by intersection of two cloths of different colours).

ki·ddle, n. Barrier in river with opening fitted with nets &c. to catch fish; arrangement of stake-nets on sea-beach. [f. OF *quidel, gu-*]

ki·dnap, v.t. (-pp-). Steal (child); carry off (person) by illegal force. Hence **ki·dnapp**ER[1] n. [KID[1]+obs. *nap* seize, cf. NAB]

ki·dney, n. One of pair of glandular organs in abdominal cavity of mammals, birds, & reptiles, serving to excrete urine & so remove effete nitrogenous matter from blood; k. of sheep, cattle, & pigs, as food; temperament, nature, as *a man of that k., of the right k.*; (also *k. potato*) oval kind of potato; *k. bean,* (1) dwarf French bean, (2) scarlet-runner. [?]

kief. See KEF.

kie-kie (kē·kē), n. N.-Zealand climbing plant with leaves used for baskets &c. [Maori]

kier (kēr), n. Vat in which cloth is boiled for bleaching &c. [cf. ON *ker,* Da. &c. *kar*]

Kikuyu· (-ŏŏyōō), n. (Used for) the controversy in the Anglican Church on the admissibility to Holy Communion of members of other Christian Churches. [*K.* in Brit. E. Africa, a conference at which in 1913 gave rise to the controversy]

ki·lderkin, n. Cask for liquids &c., containing 16 or 18 gal.; this as measure. [corrupt. of Du. *kindeken* (*kind* child, see -KIN)]

kill[1], v.t. & i. Put to death, slay (*k. two birds with one stone,* effect two purposes at once); (of disease, grief, shock, drink, poison, &c.) cause the death of; *k. off,* get rid of (number of persons &c.) by killing; (abs., esp. Sport.) perform act of killing, do execution; (intr., quasi-pass.) yield good or much meat when killed, as *pigs do not k. well at that age*; represent in fiction &c. as dead, as *k. your villain in the last chapter*; destroy vitality of (plant, disease, &c.); destroy, put an end to, (feelings &c.); neutralize (colour &c.) by contrast; consume (time) for the sake of doing so; overwhelm (person) with admiration, amusement, &c. (*got up to k.,* fascinatingly dressed), whence **ki·ll**ING[2] a., **ki·lling**LY[2] adv.; (Lawn Tennis) strike (ball) so that it cannot be returned; (Footb.) stop (ball) dead; totally defeat (bill in Parliament); *k.* (fatally harm) *with* (mistaken) *kindness*; *k.-devil,* artificial bait made to spin in water; *k.-joy,* one who throws gloom over social enjoyment; *k.-time,* n. & a. (occupation) intended to k. time. [?]

kill[2], n. Act of killing; animal killed, esp. by sportsman. [f. prec.]

kiln, n. Furnace, oven, for burning, baking, or drying, esp. (*lime-k.*) for calcining lime, or (*brick-k.*) baking bricks; *k.-dry* v.t., dry in k. [OE *cylene* f. L *culina* kitchen]

kilo- in comb., arbitrary representative (f. F) of Gk *khilioi* 1,000, as: *-cycle,* unit of frequency (1,000 alternations per second) used instead of wave-length metres in distinguishing sound-waves; *-gram(me),* weight of 1,000 grammes (2·205lb. avoird.); *-gra·mmetre,* energy that will raise one kilogramme to the height of one metre; *-litre, -liter,* measure of 1,000 litres (35·31 cub. ft); *-metre, -meter,* measure of 1,000 metres (3280·89 ft), whence *-me·tric(al)* aa.; *-watt,* 1,000 watts.

kilt[1], v.t. Tuck up (skirts) round body; gather in vertical pleats (esp. in p.p.). [prob. of Scand. orig., cf. Da. *kilte*]

kilt[2], n. Skirt, usu. of tartan cloth, reaching from waist to knee, part of Highland male dress; hence **ki·ltie** (-Y[3]) n., kilted Highland soldier. [f. prec.]

kin, n. & a. Ancestral stock, family, as *comes of good k.*; one's relatives; KITH *& k.*; (pred. adj.) related, as *we are k., he is k. to me*; *of k.,* akin, related by blood ties or (fig.) in character; *near of k.,* closely related; NEXT *of k.* Hence **ki·n**LESS a.

[com.-Teut.: OE *cyn(n)*, Du. *kunne*, Da. & Sw. *kön*, f. root *kin, kan, kun*; cogn. w. Gk *genos* race, L *genus* kind]

-kin, suf. form. dimm., corresp. to MDu. *-kijn, -ken*, G *-chen*; chiefly in wds f. Du. or of doubtful orig., *lambkin* being the only E formation of real currency; ME had proper names, as *Malkin, Perkin, Simkin.*

ki·nchin, n. (cant). Child; *k. lay*, practice of stealing money from children sent on errands. [prob. f. G *kindchen* (*kind* child, see prec.)]

ki·ncŏb (-ngk-), n. Rich Indian stuff embroidered with gold or silver. [f. Hind. *kimkhab*]

kind[1], n. Race, natural group, of animals, plants, &c., as *human k., the rabbit k.*; class, sort, variety, as *of what kind is it?, of a different k., something of the k.*, something like the thing in question, *nothing of the k.*, not at all like it, (contempt.) *we had coffee of a k.* (that scarcely deserved the name); (in transposed constr.) *what k. of tree is this?*, of what k. is this tree?, *this is the k. of thing I meant* (a thing of the kind I meant); (colloq.) *these k. of men* (men of this k.) *annoy me*; (implying looseness, vagueness, exaggeration, &c., in the term used) *he is a k. of stockbroker, of millionaire, felt a kind of compunction*; (colloq.) *I k. of* (to some extent) *expected it*; (archaic) nature in general, as *the law of k.*; (archaic) way, fashion, natural to person &c., as *they act after their k.*; character, quality, as *they differ in k.* (not merely in degree); *in k.*, (of payment) in goods or natural produce, not in money, (of repayment, esp. fig.) *repay his insolence in k.* (with insolence). [OE *gecynde* (*ge-* Y- + **cynde* f. root. *kun-* see KIN)]

kind[2], a. Of gentle or benevolent nature; friendly in one's conduct *to* (person &c.); (archaic) affectionate; *k.-hearted*, having a k. heart. Hence **ki·ndly**[1] adv. (often politely in requests, or ironically in commands), **ki·nd**NESS n. [OE *gecynde* (as prec.); orig. = natural, native]

ki·ndergarten, n. School for developing minds of children by object-lessons, toys, games, &c. Hence **ki·ndergarten**ISM n. [G, = children's garden]

ki·ndle, v.t. & i. Set on fire, light, (flame, fire, substance); (fig.) inflame, inspire, (passion &c.), stir up (person *to* emotion &c., *to* do); (intr.) catch fire, burst into flame; (fig.) become animated, glow with passion &c.; make, become, bright, (cause to) glow (often *up*); hence **ki·nd**LING[1] n., (esp., sing. or pl.) small wood for lighting fires. [prob. f. ON *kynda* kindle + -LE(3)]

ki·ndly[2] (for *k.*[1] see KIND[2]), a. Kind; (of climate &c.) pleasant, genial; (archaic) native-born, as *a k. Scot.* Hence **ki·ndli**LY[2] adv., **ki·ndli**NESS n. [OE *gecyndelic* (as KIND[2], see -LY[1])]

ki·ndred, n. & a. Blood relationship; (fig.) resemblance in character; one's relatives; (adj.) related by blood, (fig.) allied, connected, similar, as *frost & k. phenomena.*) [f. KIN + *-red*, OE *rǣden* condition, reckoning]

kine. See COW.

kīne·ma, var. of CINEMA.

kīnēmă·tic, a. & n. Of motion considered abstractly without reference to force or mass; (n. pl.) science of this. Hence **kinema·tic**AL a. [f. Gk *kinēma -matos* motion (*kineō* move, see -M) + -IC]

kinematograph, -ic, -y. = CINEMATOGRAPH &c.

kīnē·tic, a. & n. Of, due to, motion; *k.* ENERGY; *k. theory of heat, of gases* (that heat, the gaseous state, is due to motion of particles); (n. pl.) science of the relations between the motions of bodies & the forces acting on them. [f. Gk *kinētikos* (*kineō* move, see -ETIC)]

king[1], n. Male sovereign (esp. hereditary) ruler of independent state (*k. sends his carriage*, i.e. BLACK[1] *Maria*); *K. Baby*, baby as household idol; *K. Emperor* (of U.K. & India); *K. Log, K. Stork*, rulers going to extremes of laissez faire, oppression (w. ref. to fable of the frogs); *K. of kk.*, God, (also) title assumed by many Eastern kk.; *K. of Terrors*, Death; *K. Charles's* SPANIEL; *K.'s* BENCH, BOUNTY, COLOUR[1], COUNSEL[1], ENGLISH, EVIDENCE[1], HEAD[1], HIGHWAY, PIPE[1], SHILLING, WEATHER; *K. of the Castle*, child's game; great merchant &c., as *fur, railway, -k.*; *k. of beasts, birds*, lion, eagle; best kind (*of* fruits, plants, &c.); (Chess) piece that has to be protected from checkmate, *k.'s bishop, knight, rook* (placed on k.'s side of board at beginning); (Cards) card bearing representation of k., & usu. ranking next below ace; *k.-bird*, kind of bird of paradise, (also) American tyrant flycatcher; *k.-bolt*, main or large bolt; *k.-crab*, large arachnid or crustacean animal with horseshoe-shaped carapace; *k.-craft*, skilful exercise of royalty; *k.-cup*, buttercup, (also) marsh marigold; *kingfisher*, small bird with long cleft beak & brilliant plumage, feeding on fish it captures by diving; *k.-maker*, one who sets up kk., esp. Earl of Warwick in reign of Henry VI; *K.-of-Arms*, any of five chief heralds of College of Arms, *Garter, Clarenc(i)eux, Norroy*, (Scotland) *Lyon*, (Ireland) *Ulster*; *k.-post*, upright post from tie-beam to rafter-top; *k.'s evil*, scrofula, formerly held to be curable by k.'s touch; *k.'s peg*, drink of champagne & brandy; *K.'s Roll* (of employers pledged to employ at least a fixed proportion of ex-service men). Hence **ki·ng**LESS, **ki·ng**LIKE, **ki·ng**LY[1], aa., **ki·ngli**NESS, **ki·ng**SHIP(1), nn. [com.-Teut.: OE *cyni(n)g*, Du. *koning*, G *könig*, f. same root as KIN]

king[2], v.i. & t. Act the king, govern, esp. *k. it*; make (person) a king. [f. prec.]

ki·ngdom, n. Monarchical State; *United K.*, Great Britain & (Northern) Ireland; territory subject to king; spiritual reign of God, sphere of this, exp. *the k. of heaven*; domain; province of nature, esp. *animal, vegetable, mineral, k.*; (slang) *k.-come*, the next world (echo of *thy k. come* in Lord's Prayer). Hence **ki·ngdom**ED[2] a. [OE *cyningdóm* (as KING[1], see -DOM)]

ki·nglet, n. Petty king (usu. contempt.), so **ki·ng**LING[1] n.; golden-crested wren. [-LET]

kink, n., & v.i. & t. Back-twist in wire or chain or rope such as may cause obstruction or a break; (fig.) mental twist, crotchet; (v.i., of rope &c.) form a k.; (v.t.) cause (rope) to do this. Hence **ki·nk**Y[2] a. [(vb) prob. f. Du. *kinken*; (n.) Du., G, Da., Sw., f. root **kik* bend]

ki·nkajou (-ōō), n. Animal allied to racoon, with prehensile tail & nocturnal habits. [f. F *quincajou* f. N. Amer. Ind.]

ki·nnikini·c, n. Mixture of dried sumach-leaves, bark of willow, &c., as substitute for tobacco, or mixed with it; any plant used for this. [Algonquin]

ki·no (kē-), n. Gum of various trees, resembling catechu, & used in medicine & tanning as astringent. [prob. of W.-Afr. orig.]

ki·nsfolk (-ōk), n. pl. (literary). Relations by blood. So **ki·ns**MAN, **ki·ns**WOMAN, nn. [f. KIN + FOLK]

ki·nship, n. Blood relationship; similarity, alliance, in character. [-SHIP]

ki·ntal, early form of QUINTAL.

kio·sk, n. Light open pavilion in Turkey & Persia; *Yildiz K.*, Turkish Sultan's palace; (in France & Belgium) structure for sale of newspapers, band-stand, &c. [f. Turk. *kiushk*]

kip[1], n. Hide of young or small beast as used for leather. [?]

kip[2], n. (slang). Common lodging-house; lodging; bed. [cf. Da. *keppi* mean hut or alehouse]

ki·pper[1], n. Male salmon in spawning season; kippered fish, esp. herring. [?]

ki·pper[2], v.t. Cure (salmon, herring, &c.) by splitting open, cleaning, rubbing with salt, pepper, &c., & drying in open air or smoke. [perh. f. prec.]

Kirghiz (kẽrgē·z), a. & n. (Member, language) of a Mongolian race living on the Caspian, N.E. of the Kalmucks.

kirk, n. (Sc. & north.) church; (in E use) *K. of Scotland*, Church of Scotland as opp. to Church of England or to Episcopal Church in Scotland; *kirkman*, member of K. of Scotland; *k. session*, lowest court in K. of Scotland & other Presbyterian Churches, composed of ministers & elders. [north. form of CHURCH]

kirsch(wasser) (kẽr·shvahser), n. Spirit distilled from fermented liquor of wild cherries. [G (*kirsche* cherry + *wasser* water)]

kir·tle, n. (archaic). Woman's gown or outer petticoat; man's tunic or coat. [OE *cyrtel*, cf. Da. & Sw. *kjortel*, perh. f. L *curtus* short]

ki·smet, n. Destiny. [Turk., f. Arab. *qisma(t)* f. *qasama* divide]

kiss[1], n. Caress given with lips; (Billiards) impact between moving balls; kind of sugar-plum. [OE *coss*, cf. Du. *kus*, G *kuss*]

kiss[2], v.t. Touch with the lips, esp. as sign of affection, greeting, or reverence; (abs., of two persons) *k. & be friends*, &c.; (Billiards, of ball) touch (ball) with KISS[1] (also abs. of two balls); *k. away*, remove (tears &c.) with kisses; *k. the book* (Bible, in taking oath); *k. the dust*, yield abject submission, (also) be slain; *k. the ground*, prostrate oneself in token of homage, (fig.) be brought low; *k.* one's *hand to*, wave a k. to; *k. hands* or *the hand* (of sovereign &c. as ceremonial salutation or on appointment to office); *k. the rod*, accept chastisement submissively; *k.-in-the-ring*, game for young people in which one pursues & kisses another of opposite sex; *k.-me-quick*, kinds of plant, small bonnet standing far back on head, curl worn on forehead. Hence **ki·ss**ABLE a., **ki·ssab**LY[2] adv. [OE *cyssan*, cf. Du. *kussen*, G *küssen*]

ki·ssing[1], a. In vbl senses; *k.-crust*, soft crust where loaf has touched another in baking. [-ING[2]]

ki·ssing[2], n. In vbl senses; *k.-gate* (hung in U or V shaped enclosure); *k. kind*, on affectionate terms. [-ING[1]]

kit[1], n. Wooden tub for various purposes; (articles carried in) soldier's valise or knapsack; personal equipment, esp. as packed for travelling; workman's, esp. shoemaker's, outfit; *k.-bag* (for carrying soldier's or traveller's k.). [prob. f. MDu. *kitte* wooden bowl, etym. dub.]

kit[2], n. Abbr. of KITTEN.

kit[3], n. (now rare). Small fiddle used by dancing-master. [perh. ult. as CITHERN]

ki·t-cat, n. *K. Club*, club of Whig politicians founded under James II; member of this; *k. (portrait)*, portrait of less than half-length, but including hands. [f. *Kit Cat(ling)*, keeper of pie-house where club met]

ki·tchen, n. Part of house where food is cooked; *k. garden* (for fruit & vegetables); *k.-maid*, servant employed in k., usu. under cook; *k.* MIDDEN; *k. physic*, good & plentiful food; *k.-stuff*, k. requisites, esp. vegetables. [OE *cycene*, cf. Du. *keuken*, G *küche* f. vulg. L *cucina* var. of *coquina* (*coquere* cook)]

ki·tchener, n. Cooking-range; person in charge of monastery kitchen. [-ER[1]]

kite, n., & v.i. & t. Bird of prey of same family as falcon, with long wings, usu. forked tail, & no tooth in bill; rapacious person, sharper; toy consisting of light wooden frame, usu. in form of isosceles triangle with circular arc as base, with paper stretched over it, flown in strong wind by string; *fly a k.*, (fig.) make experiment to gauge public opinion &c.; (Commerc. slang) accommodation bill (*fly a k.*, raise money by this); (pl.) highest sails of ship, set only in light wind; *k. balloon*, sausage-shaped captive balloon for military observation; (v.i.) soar like k.; (v.t.) cause to do this, (Commerc.) convert into k. [(vb f. n.) OE *cȳta*]

kith (-th), n. *K. & kin*, acquaintance & kinsfolk. [OE *cȳthth*, orig. = knowledge, known country, cogn. w. *cunnan* CAN]

ki·tten, n., & v.t. Young of cat; skittish young girl; (v.t.) bring forth (kk., or abs.). Hence **ki·tten**ISH[1] a. [(vb f. n.) ME, prob. f. OF *chitoun* var. of *chaton* kitten, see CAT]

kitteree·n, n. W.-Ind. one-horse chaise. [?]

ki·ttiwake, n. Genus of sea-gulls. [imit.]

ki·ttle, a. Ticklish, difficult to deal with, esp. *k. cattle* (usu. fig. of persons or things). [f. ME vb *kytylle* tickle, puzzle; prob. imit.]

kittu·l (-ōōl), **kitoo·l,** n. Kind of palm; strong black fibre from leaf-stalks of this. [f. Cingalese *kitul*]

ki·tty, n. Pet name for kitten. [f. KIT[2] + -Y[3]]

ki·wi (kē-), n. = APTERYX. [Maori]

klepht, n. One of the Greeks who after Turkish conquest of Greece in 15th c. maintained independence in mountains; brigand. [f. mod. Gk *klephtēs* f. Gk *kleptēs* thief]

kleptomā·nia, n. Irresistible tendency to theft in persons not tempted to it by needy circumstances. Hence **klepto**MA·NIAC n. [f. Gk *kleptēs* thief + -O- + -MANIA]

kli·pspringer (-nger), n. Small S.-Afr. antelope. [S.-Afr. Du. (*klip* rock + *springer* springer)]

klōōf, n. Ravine, deep narrow valley, in S. Africa. [Du., = cleft]

knack, n. Acquired faculty of doing a thing adroitly; ingenious device; trick, habit, of action, speech, &c. Hence **kna·ck**Y[2] a. [?]

kna·cker, n. One who buys & slaughters useless horses, whence **kna·ck**ERY(3) n.; one who buys old houses, ships, &c., for the materials. [?]

knag, n. Knot in wood, base of a branch. Hence **kna·gg**Y[2] a. [ME, = G *knagge*]

knap[1], n. (dial.). Crest of hill, rising ground. [OE *cnæp(p)*, perh. cogn. w. ON *knapper* knob]

knap[2], v.t. Break (flints for roads) with hammer, whence **kna·pp**ER[1](1, 2) n.; (bibl., dial.) knock, rap, snap asunder. [imit.]

kna·psack, n. Soldier's or traveller's canvas or leather bag, strapped to back & used for carrying necessaries. [LG, prob. f. *knappen* bite + SACK]

kna·pweed, n. Common weed with hard stem & light purple flowers on dark globular head. [earlier *knopweed* (KNOP + WEED)]

knar, n. Knot in wood, esp. protuberance covered with bark on trunk or at root of tree. [ME *knarre* = LG *knarre(n)*, Du. *knar*]

knāve, n. Unprincipled man, rogue, whence **kna·**VERY(4), **kna·vish**NESS, nn., **kna·**VISH[1] a., **kna·vish**LY[2] adv.; (Cards) lowest court card of each suit. [OE *cnafa* boy, servant, knave, cf. G *knabe*]

knead (nēd), v.t. Work up (moist flour or clay) into dough or paste; make (bread, pottery) thus; (fig.) blend, weld together; operate on (muscles &c.) as if kneading, massage. Hence **knead·**ABLE a., **knea·d**ER[1](1, 2) n. [OE *cnedan*, cf. Du. *kneden*, G *kneten*]

knea·ding, n. In vbl senses; *k.-trough*, wooden trough in which dough is kneaded. [-ING[1]]

knee[1], n. Joint between thigh & lower leg in man, corresponding joint in animals; *give a k. to*, support (pugilist) on one's knee between rounds, act as second to; *on* one's *kk.*, kneeling, esp. in supplication, worship, or submission; *bring* (person) *to his kk.*, reduce him to submission; *is on the kk. of the gods*, is yet uncertain; part of garment covering the k.; thing like k. in shape or position, esp. piece of wood or iron with angular bend; *k.-breeches* (reaching down to or just below k.); *k.-cap*, convex bone in front of k.-joint, (also) protective covering for k.; *k.-deep*, so deep as to reach the kk.; *k.-hole* (*table*), (writing-table with) hole between drawer pedestals to admit kk.; *k.-joint*, joint of k., joint of two pieces hinged together; *k.-pan*, k.-cap; *k.-swell*, (in Amer. organ &c.) lever worked by k., for producing crescendo & diminuendo effects. [com.-Teut.: OE *cnéow*, Du. & G *knie*, cf. L *genu*, Gk *gonu*, Skr. *janu*]

knee[2], v.t. Touch with the knee; fasten (framework &c.) with knees; (colloq.) cause (trousers) to bulge at knees. [f. prec.]

kneel, v.i. (knelt). Fall, rest, on the knee(s) esp. in prayer or reverence (*to* person). [ME *cneolen* f. OE *cnéowlian* (as KNEE[1])]

knell[1], n. Sound of bell, esp. of one rung solemnly after death or at funeral; (fig.) announcement, event, &c., regarded as an omen of death or extinction. [OE *cnyll* (as foll.)]

knell[2] v.i. & t. (archaic). (Of bell) ring, esp. at death or funeral; give forth doleful sound; (fig.) sound ominously; (trans.) proclaim as by a knell. [OE *cnyllan*, cf. MHG *erknellen*]

kn-: pronounce n-.

knelt. See KNEEL.

knew. See KNOW[1].

kni·ckerbocker, n. (*K*-) New Yorker; (pl.) loose-fitting breeches gathered in at knee. [*K*., pretended author of W. Irving's *History of New York*]

kni·ckers, n. pl. Knickerbockers (colloq.); woman's drawers of knickerbocker shape. [abbr. of prec.]

kni·ck-knack, ni·ck-nack, n. Light dainty article of furniture, dress, or food; trinket, gimcrack. Hence **(k)ni·ck-(k)nack**ERY(2, 5) n., **(k)ni·ck-(k)nack-**ISH[1] a. [redupl. of KNACK in obs. sense 'trinket']

knife, n. (pl. *knives*), & v.t. (-fed). Blade with sharpened longitudinal edge fixed in handle either rigidly, as in *table, carving, -k.*, or with hinge, as in *pocket-k.*, used as cutting instrument or as weapon; (of malicious or vindictive person) *get a k. into* (person); *war to the k.*, relentless war; blade forming part of machine, as in turnip-cutter &c.; *the k.*, surgical operations, as *have a horror of the k.*; *before you can say k.*, very quickly or suddenly; *play a good k. & fork*, eat heartily; *k.-board* (on which kk. are cleaned), (transf.) double bench placed lengthways on the top of omnibus; *k.-boy* (employed to clean table-kk.); *k.-edge*, edge of k., steel wedge on which pendulum &c. oscillates, =ARÊTE; *k.-grinder*, itinerant sharpener of kk. &c., one who grinds kk. &c. in process of making; *k.-machine* (for cleaning kk.); *k.-rest*, metal or glass support for carving k. or fork at table; (v.t.) cut, stab, with k. [(vb f. n.) late OE *cnif*, cf. Du. *knijf*, G *kneif*]

knight (nit), n., & v.t. Military follower, esp. one devoted to service *of* (lady) as attendant or champion in war or tournament; person, usu. one of noble birth who had served as page & squire, raised to honourable military rank by king or qualified person; one on whom corresponding rank is conferred as reward for personal merit or services to crown or country; (Hist., also *k. of the shire*) person representing shire or county in parliament; (Rom. Ant.) one of the class of equites, orig. the cavalry of Roman army; (Gk Ant.) citizen of second class at Athens; piece in game of chess, usu. with horse's head; *k.* BACHELOR, COMMANDER, COMPANION[1], HOSPITALLER, TEMPLAR; *k.-errant*, medieval k. wandering in search of chivalrous adventures, (fig.) person of chivalrous or of quixotic spirit; *k.-errantry*, practice, conduct, of a k.-errant (lit. & fig.); *k.-heads*, two vertical timbers supporting bowsprit; *k. of the post*, one who got his living by giving false evidence; *k.-service* (hist.), tenure of land by military service. (V.t.) confer k.-hood on. Hence **knigh·t**HOOD n., **knigh·t**LIKE, **knigh·t**LY[1], aa., **knigh·t**LY[2] adv. (poet.). [com.-WG.: OE *cniht*, Du. & G *knecht* lad, servant, soldier]

knigh·tage, n. Whole body of knights; list & account of knights. [-AGE]

knit, v.t & i. (*knitted* or *knit*). Form (close texture, garments &c. of this) of interlooping yarn or thread; contract (brow) in wrinkles; make, become, close or compact (esp. in p.p., as *a well-k. frame*); (fig.) unite (t. & i.) intimately by means of common interests, marriage, &c., (often *together*); *k. up*, repair by knitting, (fig.) close up, conclude, (argument &c.). [OE *cnyttan*, cf. MDu. *knutten*, G *knütten*]

kni·tting, n. In vbl senses, esp. work in process of k.; *k.-needle*, slender rod of steel, wood, ivory, &c., two or more of which are used together in k. [f. prec. + -ING[1]]

kni·ttle, n. (naut.). Small line made of yarn. [f. KNIT + -LE]

knob, n., & v.t. & i. Rounded protuberance, esp. at end or on surface of thing; handle of door (often *door-k.*) or drawer; small lump (of sugar, coal, &c.); (slang) head (usu. *nob*); *kno·bkerrie* [after Cape Du. *knopkirie*], short stick with knobbed head as weapon of S.-Afr. tribes; *knob-stick*, knobbed stick, esp. as weapon, (also) workman who works during strike; (v.t.) furnish with kk.; (v.i.) bulge *out*. Hence **kno·bb**Y[2] a., **kno·bb**INESS n. [(vb f. n.) ME, cf. G *knobbe*]

kno·bble, n. Small knob. Hence **kno·b-bl**Y[2] a. [f. KNOB + -LE]

knock[1], v.t. & i. Strike with hard blow; strike door, strike *at the door*, to gain admittance; (slang) make strong impression on, as *what knocks me is his impudence*; *k.* (person &c.) *on the head*, stun, kill, him by blow on head, (fig.) put an end to (scheme &c.); *k.* one's *head against*, (fig.) come into unpleasant collision with (unfavourable facts or conditions); *k. head* vb, kotow; drive (thing) *in, out, off*, &c., by striking (see also below); *k. into a* COCK[2]*ed hat*; *k.* one *into the middle of next week*, send him flying; *k. the bottom out of*, render (argument &c.) invalid; *k. about*, strike repeatedly, treat roughly, (intr.) wander, lead irregular life; *k. against*, collide with, come across casually; *k. down*, strike (person &c.) to ground with blow, (fig.) cause to succumb, (at auction) dispose of (article *to* bidder) by knock with hammer, (colloq.) call upon (person *for* a song &c.), (colloq.) lower (prices), (commerc.) take (machinery &c.) to pieces to save space in transport; *k. off*, strike off with blow, leave off work, leave off (work), (colloq.) dispatch (business) or rapidly compose (verses &c.), deduct (sum from price, bill, &c.), *k.* person's *head off*, (fig.) surpass him easily; *k. out*,

kn-: pronounce n-.

empty (one's pipe) by tapping, disable (pugilist) so that he cannot respond to call of ' Time ', (fig.) vanquish, (colloq.) make (plan &c.) hastily; *k. together*, put hastily together; *k. under*, submit, knuckle under; *k. up*, drive upwards with blow, make or arrange hastily, score (runs) at cricket, arouse (person) by knocking at door, exhaust, become exhausted; *k.-about* n. & a., boisterous, noisy (performance in music-hall &c.), wandering irregularly, (of clothes) suitable for rough use; *k.-down* a. & n., (of blow, lit. & fig.) overwhelming, (of price at auction) reserve, minimum, (n.) free fight; *k.-knees* (that k. together in walking); *k.-kneed*, having k.-knees; *k.-out*, (blow) that knocks boxer out, (n.) one of gang who join at auction to buy goods at low price, afterwards reselling among themselves, this practice, such sale. [late OE *cnocian*, cf. ON *knoka*, prob. imit.]

knock², n. Blow; rap esp. at door; (slang) innings at cricket; *k.-up*, practice or casual game at cricket, fives, &c. [prec.]

kno·cker, n. In vbl senses, esp.: appendage, usu. of iron or brass, so hinged to door that it may be struck against metal plate to call attention (*up to the k.*, slang, to perfection); goblin held to dwell in mines & indicate presence of ore by knocking. [-ER¹]

knōll¹, n. Small hill, mound. [OE *cnoll*, cf. Du. *knol* clod, ball, MHG *knolle* clod]

knōll², v.t. & i. (archaic). Ring (bell); (of bell) sound; toll out (hours); summon by sound of bell. [var. of KNELL]

knop, n. (archaic). Knob; bud of flower. [ME & Du., cf. G *knopf*]

knot¹, n. Intertwining of parts of one or more ropes, strings, &c., to fasten them together; GRANNY'*s*, REEF¹-, SLIP-, WEAVER'*s*, *k.*; ribbon &c. so tied as ornament or adjunct to dress, as SHOULDER, SWORD, TOP, TRUE-*love*, -*k.*; (Naut.) division marked by kk. on log-line, as measure of speed, (loosely) nautical mile (6,080 ft); difficulty, problem; GORDIAN *k.*; central point in problem or plot of story &c.; *marriage, wedding, -k.* (bond); hard lump in animal body; excrescence in stem, branch, or root, of plant; (hard mass formed in trunk at insertion of branch, causing) round cross-grained piece in board; node on stem of plant; group, cluster, of persons or things; (usu. *porter's k.*) double shoulder-pad used for carrying loads; *k.-grass*, common weed with intricate creeping stems & pale pink flowers; *knotwork*, ornamental work representing or consisting of intertwined cords, (also) kind of fancy needlework. Hence **kno·t**LESS a. [OE *cnotta*, cf. Du. *knot*, G *knoten*]

knot², v.t. & i. Tie (string &c.) in knot; make knots for fringes, (trans.) make (fringe) thus, whence **kno·tt**ING¹ n.; knit (one's brows); unite closely or intricately; entangle. [f. prec.]

kno·tty, a. Full of knots; (fig.) puzzling, hard to explain, as *k. subject, question, point.* Hence **kno·tti**NESS n. [f. KNOT¹ + -Y²]

knout (nowt, nōōt), n., & v.t. (Flog with) scourge formerly used in Russia, often fatal in its effects. [(vb f. n.) F, f. Russ. *knut*]

know¹ (nō), v.t. & i. (*knew*, pron. nū, *known*). Recognize, identify, as *I knew him at once, knew him for an American, shall you k. him again?*; be able to distinguish (*don't k. him from Adam*; *k. one from another, a* HAWK¹ *from a handsaw*); be acquainted with (thing, place, person) *by sight, to speak to*, &c. (*k. by name*, have heard the name of, be able to give the name of); have personal experience of (fear, pain, &c.); be on intimate terms with; be aware of (fact), be aware (*that, how, what*, &c.); *k.* (person &c.) *to be* (that he is); be versed in (language, science, &c.); *he would do it if he knew how* (knew the way); *all one knows*, all one can, (adv.) to the utmost of one's power; *k. about*, have information about; *I k. better* (*than that*), I am too well informed of the facts to believe that; *k. better than*, be too discreet *to* do; *k. of*, be aware of; *not that I k. of*, not so far as I k.; *k.* one's *own mind*, not vacillate; *k. what's what*, have proper knowledge of the world & of things in general; *don't you k.* (esp. as parenthetic expletive in various contexts; *it's such a bore, don't you k.*); *k. the* ROPES; *k.-nothing*, ignorant person, (also) agnostic, whence *know-nothingism.* Hence **knowabi·lity, know·able**NESS, nn., **know·**ABLE a. [com.-Teut. (retained only in E) & Aryan: OE (*ge*)*cnāwan*, OHG *-cnâan*, L & Gk *gnō-*, Skr. *jna-*]

know², n. (colloq.). *In the k.*, knowing (about) the thing in question or what is not generally known. [f. prec.]

know·ing, a. In vbl senses, esp.: cunning, wide-awake; (colloq.) stylish, smart, as *a k. hat.* Hence **know·ing**NESS n. [-ING²]

know·ingly, adv. In a knowing manner; consciously, intentionally, as *I have never k. injured him.* [-LY²]

knowledge (nŏ·lij), n. Knowing, familiarity gained by experience, (*of* person, thing, fact); person's range of information, as *it came to my k.* (became known to me), *not to my k.*, not so far as I know, *he had to my* (*certain*) *k. been bribed* (I know he had); theoretical or practical understanding (*of* subject, language, &c.); the sum of what is known, as *every branch of k.* Hence **know·ledge**ABLE, a. (colloq.), well-informed, intelligent. [ME *knaulage*, century later than obs. vb *knowledge* confess (KNOW, *-ledge* unexpl.)]

knu·ckle, n., & v.t. & i. Bone at finger-joint, esp. at root of finger; projection of carpal or tarsal joint of quadruped; joint of meat consisting of this with parts above & below it; *k.-bone,* bone forming k., esp. of sheep or the like, (pl.) game played with such bones; *k.-duster,* metal instrument protecting kk. from injury in striking; (v.t.) strike, press, rub, with kk.; (v.i.) place kk. on ground in playing at marbles, *k. down, under,* give in, submit (*to*). [(vb f. n.) ME *knokel,* cf. Du. *kneukel,* G *knöchel,* prob. dim. of wd appearing in MLG as *knoke* bone]

knur(r), n. Hard excrescence on trunk of tree; hard concretion; wooden ball in north-country game like trap-ball. [ME *knorre,* cf. Du. *knor,* G *knorre(n)*]

knurl, n. Knot, knob (esp., that by which typewriter platen is turned); bead or ridge in metal work, whence **knurl**ED[2] a. [prob. f. prec.]

knut, joc. spelling of NUT used of youths.

kō·a n. An acacia in Sandwich Is. [native]

kō·bold, n. (Germ. Myth.). Familiar spirit, brownie; underground spirit in mines, &c. [G, etym. dub.]

kō·dăk, n., & v.t. Kind of photographic camera with continuous roll of sensitized film; (v.t.) photograph with k., (fig.) seize quickly, describe vividly, (scene, view). [trade name]

kō·el, n. Indian & Australian kinds of cuckoo. [f. Hind. *kóil* f. Skr. *kokila*]

kō·h-i-noor (-hĭ-), n. Famous Indian diamond, property of British Crown since 1849; anything superb (*of* its class). [f. Pers. *kohi nur* (*koh* mountain + *nur* light)]

kohl (kōl), n. Powder, usu. antimony, used in East to darken eyelids &c. [f. Arab. *koh'l,* see ALCOHOL]

kohlra·bĭ (-rah-), n. Cabbage with turnip-shaped stem, used in England as food for cattle. [G, f. It. *cavoli rape* pl. (see COLE & RAPE)]

kola. See COLA.

koo·doo, kudu (kōō·dōō), n. Large white-striped spiral-horned S.-Afr. antelope. [native]

koo·lah, n. Arboreal mammal of Australia, like sloth in form. [native]

kopec(k), -peek, -pek, = COPECK.

kŏ·pje (-pĭ), n. (S.-Afr.). Small hill. [Du., dim. of *kop* head]

Kōr·an (*or* korah·n), n. Sacred book of the Mohammedans, collection of Mohammed's oral revelations, written in Arabic. Hence **koră·n**IC a. [f. Arab. *qoran* recitation (*qara'a* read)]

kō·sher, a. & n. (Of food or shop where food is sold or used) fulfilling requirements of Jewish law; (n.) k. food or shop. [f. Heb. *kasher* right]

kōtow· (-ow), n., & v.i. Chinese custom of touching ground with forehead as sign of worship or absolute submission; (v.i.) perform the k., act obsequiously (*to* person &c.). [(vb f. n.) f. Chin. *k'o-t'ou* (*k'o* knock + *t'ou* head)]

kou·miss (kōō-), n. Fermented liquor prepared from mare's milk. [f. Tartar *kumiz*]

kour·bash (koor-), **koor-,** n. Hide whip as instrument of punishment in Turkey & Egypt. [f. Arab. *qurbash* f. Turk. *qirbach*]

kraal (krahl), n. S.-African village of huts enclosed by fence; enclosure for cattle or sheep. [colon. Du., f. Port. CORRAL]

kra·ken (krah-, krā-), n. Mythical sea-monster appearing off coast of Norway. [Norw.]

krăn(t)z, n. (S.-Afr.). Precipitous or overhanging wall of rocks. [S.-Afr. Du., = Du. *krans* coronet]

kre·mlin, n. Citadel within Russian town, esp. that of Moscow containing imperial palace &c. [F, f. Russ. *kreml*]

kreu·tzer (kroi-), n. Small silver & copper coins formerly current in Germany & Austria. [f. G *kreuzer* (*kreuz* cross)]

kriegspiel (krē·gspēl), n. War-game in which blocks representing troops &c. are moved about on maps. [G]

kris. See CREESE.

Kri·shnaism (-aĭ-), n. Worship of Krishna, great deity of later Hinduism, worshipped as incarnation of Vishnu. [-ISM]

krome·sky, n. Minced chicken &c. rolled in bacon & fried. [f. Russ.]

krō·ne (-*e*), n. Silver coin of Denmark, Norway, & Sweden, worth 1*s.* 1½*d.*; Austrian pre-war silver coin (10*d.*); German 10-mark gold piece. [G & Da. *krone,* Sw. *krona,* crown]

Kroo, Krou, Kru, (-ōō), n. & a. (Member) of negro race on coast of Liberia, skilful as seamen (often, for the n., *K.-boy, K.-man*). [W.-Afr.]

kry·pton, n. (chem.). A rare gas discovered by Ramsay in 1898. [f. Gk *krupton* hidden, neut. adj. f. *kruptō* hide]

kū·dŏs, n. (slang). Glory, renown. [Gk]

Kufic. See CUFIC.

Ku·-Klux(-Kla·n), n. (U.S.). Secret society hostile to Negroes formed in southern States after civil war; similar organization throughout U.S. to combat alien influences after great war. [arbitrary]

ku·krĭ (kŏŏ-), n. Curved knife broadening towards point, used by Gurkhas of India. [Hind.]

kultur (kŏŏltoor·), n. Civilization as conceived by the Germans. [G, = culture]

kultur·kampf (kŏŏltoor-), n. Conflict between German imperial government and Pope for control of schools and church appointments (1872–87). [G]

kü·mmel (G), n. Cumin-flavoured liqueur.

Kurd (koord), n. Native of Kurdistan.
kursaal (koor·zahl), n. Building for use of visitors esp. at German health resort. [G]
kvass, n. Russian rye-beer. [f. Russ. *kvas*]
kȳ·anize, v.t. Treat (wood) with solution of corrosive sublimate to prevent decay. [f. J. H. *Kyan,* inventor, + -IZE]
ky·lin (kē-), n. Fabulous composite animal figured on Chinese & Japanese pottery. [f. Chin. *ch'i-lin* (*ch'i* male + *lin* female)]
kȳ·loe (-ō), n. One of small breed of long-horned Scotch cattle. [?]
kȳ·mograph, n. Instrument recording curves of pressure, pulsations, sound-waves, &c. [Gk *kuma* wave + -O- + -GRAPH(2)]
Kyrie eleison (kēr·ĭi ĭlā·ĭson), n. Words of short petition used in Eastern & Roman Churches, esp. at beginning of Mass, musical setting of these; response to commandments in Communion Service in Anglican Church. [f. Gk *Kurie eleēson* Lord, have mercy]

L

L (ĕl), letter (pl. *Ls,* L's). Thing shaped like L (*L-iron,* = ANGLE[1]*-iron*); rectangular joint of pipes &c.; Roman numeral = 50, as CL 150, XL 40, lx 60, lv 55, (LXX, the Septuagint).

Abbreviations (1): L., lance, **L.-Corp.-**(oral); least, **L.C.M.** (common multiple); left; libra(e), **L.S.D.** (solidi, denarii;) licentiate, as **L.D.S.** (of dental surgery), **L.R.C.P., L.R.C.S.** (of Royal college of physicians, surgeons); lira(s); local, **L.G.B.** (government board); London, **L.A.C.** (athletic club), **L.C.C.** (county council), **L.M.S.** (missionary society, also Midland & Scottish), **L.N.E.R.** (& north-eastern railway), **L.R.C.** (rowing club); lord, **L.C.J.** (chief justice), **L.J.** (justice; pl. **LL. JJ.**); low, **L.G.** (German); LL., legum, **LL.B.** (baccalaureus), **LL.D.** (doctor). **£,** libra(e), **£. s. d.** (see dict. place), **£E** (Egyptian), **£T** (Turkish). l., leg, **l.b.w.** (before wicket); libra(e); line (pl. **ll.**); litre(s); loco, **l.c.** (citato); lower, **l.c.** (case).

Abbreviations (2): **La,** Louisiana; **Lam.**(entations); **Lancs.,** Lancashire; **lat.**(itude); **lb.,** libra(e); **Leics.,** Leicestershire; **Lev.**(iticus); **Lieut.**(enant); **Lincs.,** Lincolnshire; **lit.**(erally); **lit.**(*erae*) **hum.**(*aniores*); **Lit.**(*erarum*) **D.**(*octor*); **loc.**(*o*) **cit.**(*ato*); **log.**(arithm); **London.** (also **-in.**), Bishop of London; **long.** (itude); **loq.**(*uitur*); **Lt,** lieutenant; **Ltd,** limited.

la (lah), n. (mus.). Sixth note of octave. [first syl. of L *labii,* see GAMUT]
laa·ger (lahg-), n., & v.t. & i. Camp, encampment, esp. in circle of wagons. (Vb) form (wagons) into l.; encamp (persons) in l.; encamp. [S.-Afr. Du., & G, *lager,* Du. *leger,* see LEAGUER[1]]
lă·barum, n. Constantine the Great's imperial standard with Christian added to Roman-military symbols; symbolic banner. [L, f. Gk *labaron* etym. dub.]
labdacism. See LAMBDACISM.
lăbefa·ction, n. Shaking, weakening, downfall. [f. L *labefacere* (*labare* totter, *facere* make), see -FACTION]
lā·bel (-bl), n., & v.t. (-ll-). Slip of paper, card, linen, metal, &c., for attaching to object & indicating its nature, owner, name, destination, &c.; (fig.) short classifying phrase or name applied to persons &c.; adhesive stamp; (Archit.) dripstone. (Vb) attach l. to; assign to a category (*as,* obj. & compl., or abs.). [OF, = ribbon, fillet, etym. dub.]
lā·bial, a. & n. Of the lips; (Anat., Zool.) of, like, serving as, a lip, lip-like part, or labium; (Mus.) *l. pipe,* in organ, one furnished with lips, flue-pipe; (Phonet.) (sound) requiring closure or approximation of lips (*p, b, m, f, v, w,* & vowels in which lips are rounded, as *o*), whence **la·bial**ISM(1), **labializa·**TION, nn., **la·bial**-IZE(3) v.t. [f. med. L *labialis* (LABIUM, -AL)]
la·biate (-at), a. & n. (Bot.) with corolla or calyx divided into two parts suggesting lips (n., such plant); (Bot., Zool.) like lip or labium. [LABIUM + -ATE[2]]
lā·bile, a. (physics, chem.). Unstable, liable to displacement or change. [f. L *labilis* (*labi* to LAPSE[2], -IL)]
la·bio-, comb. form of foll. = of the lip(s) & —, as *-dental,* made with lip & teeth.
lā·bium, n. (pl. *-ia*). (Anat.; usu. pl.) lip(s) of female pudendum; floor of mouth of insects, crustaceans, &c.; inner lip of univalve shell; lip, esp. the lower, of labiate corolla. [L, = lip]
lă·boratory (*or* labŏ·-), n. Room or building used for experiments in natural science, esp. chemistry, or for manufacturing chemicals &c. (also fig., *l. of the mind, of ideas,* &c.). Hence **laborator·i**AL a. [f. med. L *laboratorium* (*laborare* LABOUR[2], -ORY)]
labor·ious, a. Hard-working; toilsome; (of style &c.) showing signs of toil, not facile or fluent. Hence **labor·ious**LY[2] adv., **labor·ious**NESS n. [f. L *laboriosus* (foll., -IOUS)]
lā·bour[1], n. Bodily or mental toil, exertion, (HARD *l.*; *lost l.,* fruitless efforts; *l. of love,* task one delights in); toil tending to supply wants of community, body of those who contribute by toil to production, labourers, (opp. CAPITAL[2], often *L-*) the working classes as a political force; task (*l. of Hercules, Herculean l.,* one needing enormous strength &c.); pains of childbirth, travail, (*in l.*); *L. Exchange,* local office under State for directing l. to places requiring it; *L. leader,*

(esp.) trade-union official; *l.-market*, supply of unemployed **l.** with reference to demand on it; *L. Party*, that representing wage-earners, M.P.s elected by it. [f. OF *labor* f. L *laborem* nom. *-or*]

la·bour[2], v.i. & t. Use l., exert oneself, work hard; strive *for* end or *to* do; advance with difficulty (*wheels l. in the sand*); be troubled (*her labouring heart*) or impeded, suffer *under* mistake &c.; (of ship) roll or pitch heavily; (archaic or poet.) till (ground); elaborate, work out in detail, treat at length, (*I will not l. the point*; *laboured*, much elaborated, showing signs of l., not spontaneous); *labouring man*, labourer. [f. F *labourer* f. L *laborare* (*labor* LABOUR[1])]

la·bourer, n. In vbl senses; esp., man doing for wages work that requires strength or patience rather than skill or training. [-ER[1]]

lā·bourite, n. Member, adherent, of Labour Party. [-ITE[1](1)]

Lă·brador, n. attrib. *L. dog, retriever*, breed of retriever.

lā·bret, n. Piece of shell, bone, &c., inserted in lip as ornament. [L *labrum* lip, -ET[1]]

labur·num, n. Small tree with racemes of bright yellow flowers. [L]

lă·byrinth n. Complicated irregular structure with many passages hard to find way through or about without guidance, maze; intricate or tortuous arrangement; (Anat.) complex cavity of internal ear; entangled state of affairs. Hence **labyri·nth**ĪNE[2] a. [f. L f. Gk *laburinthos* etym. dub.]

labyri·nthodon, n., **-dont**, n. & a. (Kinds of large fossil amphibian) with labyrinthine teeth. [*-dont* f. *-don* mod. L, f. Gk as prec. + *odous -ontos* tooth]

lac[1], n. Dark-red resin used in East as scarlet dye; ware coated with this. [f. Hind. *lakh* f. Skr. *laksha*]

lac[2], **lakh**, n. (Anglo-Ind.). A hundred thousand (usu. *l. of rupees*). [Hind. (*-kh*) f. Skr. *laksha*]

lace[1], n. Cord or leather strip for fastening or tightening opposite edges of boots, stays, &c., by help of eyelets or hooks; braid for trimming men's coats &c. (usu. *gold* or *silver l.*); fine open fabric of linen, cotton, silk, woollen, or metal threads usu. with inwrought or applied patterns; *l.-glass*, Venetian with l.-like designs; *l.-pillow*, laid on lap of woman making l. Hence **la·**CY[2] a. [f. OF *laz, las*, f. L *laqueus* noose]

lace[2], v.t. & i. Fasten or tighten (boot, stays, &c.) with l.; compress waist of by drawing stay-ll. tight, (intr.) compress one's waist; interlace or embroider (fabric) *with* thread &c.; pass (cord &c.) *through*; trim with l.; diversify (flower *with* streaks of colour); lash, beat, (also intr. as *l. into* person); flavour, fortify, (milk, beer, &c.) *with* spirit. Hence **la·**CING[1](1, 3, 6) n. [f. OF *lacier* as prec.]

lă·cerate, v.t. Mangle, tear, (esp. flesh or tissues); afflict, distress, (heart, feelings). Hence or cogn. **la·cer**ABLE, **la·cer**ATE[2] (*-at*), **la·cer**ATIVE, aa., **lacer**A·TION n. [f. L *lacerare* (*lacer* torn), -ATE[3]]

lacer·tian, -tine, aa. Of lizards; lizard-like. [f. L *lacerta* lizard + -IAN, -INE[1]]

lace·t (*la-*), n. Work made of braid or tape shaped into a design with lace stitches. [-ET[1]]

lā·ches (-tshĭz), n. (Law) negligence in performing a legal duty, delay in asserting right, claiming privilege, &c.; culpable negligence. [f. OF *laschesse* (*lasche* f. *lascher* f. L *laxare* f. *laxus* LAX, -ESS[2])]

la·chryma Chri·stī (lăk-), n. Strong sweet red S.-Ital. wine. [L, = Christ's tear]

lă·chrymal (-k-), a. & n. Of, for, tears (*l. vase*, or *l.* as n., to hold tears; *l. canal, duct, gland, sac*, in Anat.; also *ll.* as n., these organs). [med. L (*-alis*), f. L *lacrima* tear cf. Gk *dakru*]

lachryma·tion, n. Flow of tears. [f. L *lacrimatio* (*lacrimare* as prec., -ATION)]

la·chrymatory, a. & n. Of, causing, tears (*l. shell*, emitting gas that disables by making eyes water); phial of kind found in anc.-Roman tombs & conjectured to be tear-bottles. [f. *lacrimare* see prec. + -ORY]

la·chrymose, a. Tearful, given to weeping. Hence **lachrymo·se**LY[2] adv. [f. L *lacrimosus* (*lacrima* tear, -OSE[1])]

lacĭ·niate (*-at*), **-āted**, aa. (bot., zool.). Cut into deep irregular segments, slashed, jagged, fringed. [f. L *lacinia* lappet, -ATE[2]]

lack, n., & v.i. & t. Deficiency, want, need, *of* (*no l.*, plenty *of*; *for l.*, owing to want or absence *of*). (Vb) be wanting (only in part. forms, as *money was lacking, is lacking in courage*); be without, not have, be deficient in; *lackland*, (person) having no land; *la·ck-lustre*, (of eye &c.) dull. [cf. MLG *lak*, MDu. *lac*, deficiency, blame, fault]

lackadai·sical (-z-), a. Languishing, affected, given to airs & graces, feebly sentimental. Hence **lackadai·sical**LY[2] adv., **lackadai·sical**NESS n. [f. archaic *lackaday, -daisy*, int. (ALACK) + -ICAL]

lacker. See LACQUER.

la·ckey, la·cquey (-kĭ), n., & v.t. Footman, man-servant (usu. liveried); obsequious person, parasite; (vb) dance attendance on, behave servilely to. [f. F *laquais* (in OF also *alacays* pl.), etym. dub.]

lacŏ·nic, a. Brief, concise, sententious; given to such speech or style. Hence **laco·**NICALLY adv., **laco·nic**ISM(2) n. [f. Gk *lakōnikos* (*Lakōn* Spartan, -IC)]

lă·conism, n. Brevity of speech; short pithy saying. [f. Gk *lakōnismos* (*lakōnizō* behave like Spartan or *Lakōn*, -ISM)]

la·cquer (-ker), **la·cker**, n., & v.t. Gold-coloured varnish of shellac dissolved in alcohol used esp. as coating for brass; kinds of resinous varnish (esp. *Japanese l.*) taking hard polish & used for wood &c., articles so coated; (vb) coat with l. [f. obs. F *lacre* sealing-wax perh. f. Port. *lacca* LAC[1]]

lacquey. See LACKEY.

lacrim-, lacrym-. See **lachrym-.**

lacrosse (lahkraw·s, -ŏs), n. N.-Amer. game like hockey, but with ball driven by & carried in CROSSE. [F *la* the + CROSSE]

lacta·tion, n. Suckling; secreting of milk. [f. L *lactare* suckle (*lac -tis* milk) + -ATION]

la·ctēal, a. & n. Of milk; conveying chyle or other milky fluid (n. pl., vessels of mesentery doing this). [f. L *lacteus* (*lac* see prec.) + -AL]

lacte·scence, n., **lacte·scent,** a. Milky (appearance); (yielding) milky juice. [f. L *lactescere* (*lactēre* be milky, see prec.), -ENCE, -ENT]

la·ctic, a. (chem.). Of milk; *l. acid*, formed in sour milk, whence **la·ct**ATE[1](3) n. [f. L *lac -tis* milk + -IC]

lacti·ferous, a. Yielding milk or milky fluid. [f. L *lactifer* (prec., -FEROUS)]

lacto-, comb. form (-I-, -O-) of L as prec.; *-protein*, albuminous constituent of milk; -METER, -SCOPE, instruments for testing purity of milk.

lacto·se, n. Saccharine substance in, sugar of, milk. [as prec. + -OSE[2]]

lacu·na, n. (pl. *-ae, -as*). Hiatus, blank, missing portion, empty part; cavity in bone, tissue, &c. Hence **lacu·**NAL, **lacu·**NAR, **lacu·**NARY, **lacu·**NOSE[1], aa. [L (*lacus* LAKE[1])]

lacu·strine, a. Of, dwelling or growing in, lake(s); *l. age*, of LAKE[1]-dwellings. [f. L *lacus -ūs* LAKE[1] on anal. of L *palustr-* f. *palus -udis* marsh + -INE[1]]

lad, n. Boy, youth, young fellow; fellow. Hence **la·ddie** [-Y[3]] n. [ME *ladde*; earlier sense *serving-man*; perh. orig. p.p. of LEAD[2]]

la·dder, n., & v.i. Set of steps (called *rungs*) inserted usu. in two uprights of wood or metal or in two cords to serve as (usu. portable) means of ascending building &c.; (transf.) vertical flaw in stocking &c. like that caused by dropping a stitch in knitting (v.i., develop l.), whence *la·dder*PROOF[2] a.; (fig.) means of rising in the world or attaining object (*kick down l.*, abandon friends or occupation that have helped one to rise); *l.-dredge*, with buckets carried round on l.-like chain; *l.-stitch*, crossbar stitch in embroidery. [OE *hlǣder* cf. G *leiter* cogn. w. LEAN[2] & Gk *klimax* CLIMAX]

lade, v.t. (p.p. *laden*). Put cargo on board (ship); ship (goods) as cargo (BILL[4] *of lading*), whence **la·**DING[1](3) n.; (p.p., of vehicle, beast of burden, person, tree, branch, table, &c.) loaded (*with*); (p.p.) painfully burdened *with* sin, sorrow, &c. [com.-Teut.; OE *hladan*, cf. Du. & G *laden*]

la-di-da· (lah-, -ah), a. & n. (Person given to) swagger or pretension in manners & pronunciation; pretentious in this way. [imit. of pronunciation used]

Ladi·n (-ēn), n. RHAETO-ROMANIC of the Engadine. [f. It. *Ladino* f. L LATIN*us*]

lā·dle, n., & v.t. Large spoon with cup bowl & long handle for transferring liquids; hence **la·dle**FUL(2) n.; (vb) transfer (liquid) with l. from one receptacle to another. [OE *hlædel* f. *hladan* LADE in obs. sense to bale + -LE(1)]

lā·dy, n. Ruling woman (poet. exc. in *l. of the manor, our sovereign l.*); woman to whom man is devoted, mistress, love; *Our L.*, Virgin Mary; woman belonging to, or fitted by manners, habits, & sentiments, for, the upper classes (corresp. to GENTLEMAN; *l. of bedchamber, l.-in-waiting*, l. attending sovereign; FINE[3] *l.*); (courteously for) woman (as voc., only poet. or vulg. in sing., but usu. form of address in pl.); (title used as less formal prefix for) Marchioness, Countess, Viscountess, Baroness, (also prefixed to Christian name of) daughter of duke, marquis, or earl, (or to husband's Christian name of) wife of holder of courtesy title *lord* William &c., (or to surname of) wife of baronet or knight, (also in the compound title) *L. Mayoress*, wife of Lord Mayor; *my l.*, form of address used chiefly by servants &c. to holders of title *l.*; *my dear* or *good l.* (address in ord. use); wife (archaic or vulg., exc. of those who hold the title *l.*); *your good l.*, your wife; *ll. & gentlemen* (voc. in addressing company of both sexes); *painted l.*, kind of butterfly; (with *clerk, doctor, president, dog*, &c.) female; (with *cook, parlourmaid, help*, &c.) claiming to be treated as l.; *Ladies* (as sing. n.), women's public lavatory &c.; *Ladies' chain*, figure in quadrille; *Ladies' gallery*, in House of Commons reserved for ll.; *L.-altar* (in L.-chapel); *la·dy-bird*, coleopterous insect, usu. reddish-brown with black spots; *L. Bountiful*, lady playing the part of Providence in a village &c. (character in Farquhar's *Beaux's Stratagem*); *l.-chair*, made by two persons' interlaced hands to carry wounded man &c.; *L.-chapel*, in large church usu. east of high altar & dedicated to Virgin; *l.-clock, -cow*, lady-bird; *L.-Day*, Feast of Annunciation 25th March, one of the quarterdays; *l.-fern*, tall slender kind; *l. help*, l. employed as domestic; *l.-killer*, man devoting himself to making conquests of ll.; *l.-love*, sweetheart; *L.'s* BED[1]*straw*; *l.'s companion*, roll containing cottons &c.; *L.'s cushion*, mossy saxifrage; *L'.s finger*, kidney vetch; *L.'s laces*, kind of striped grass; *l.'s-maid*, in charge of l.'s toilet; *l.'s man*, *ladies' man*, (fond of female society); *L.s' mantle*, rosaceous herb; *L.-smock*, cuckoo-flower; *L.'s slipper*, orchidaceous wild & garden plant with usu. yellow bag or slipper shaped flowers, calceolaria; *L.'stresses*, kind of orchis. Hence **la·dy**HOOD **n.** [OE *hlǣfdige*(*hlāf* LOAF, *dīg-* knead cf. DOUGH); in *l.-altar, -bird, -chapel, -clock, -cow, -day, -smock*, *l.* is old genit. = (Our) Lady's]

la·dyfȳ, -ify, v.t. Make lady of; call lady; (p.p.) having the airs of a fine lady. [-FY]

la·dylike, a. With manners &c. of a lady; (of man) effeminate; befitting a lady. [-LIKE]

la·dyship, n. Being a lady; *her, your, l., their ll.*, she, you, they, (in respectful mention of or address to titular lady). [-SHIP]

l(a)evo-, comb. form of L *laevus* left, esp. in terms concerned with chem. property of causing plane of polarized light ray to rotate to left (opp. DEXTRO-); so *-gyr·ous, -ro·tatory*, of substances having this; *-compound*, chemical compound having it; *-glucose*, = foll.

l(a)e·vulose, n. (chem.). Laevo-rotatory form of glucose, fruit-sugar. [prec., -UL-, -OSE²]

lag¹, v.i., & n. Go too slow, not keep pace, fall behind (often *behind* adv. & prep.); (n., physics) (amount of) retardation in current or movement (*l. of tide*, interval by which it falls behind mean time in 1st & 3rd quarters of moon, cf. PRIMING²). Hence **la·gg**ARD n. & a., **la·gg**ER¹ n., **la·gg**ING² a. [n. f. vb; vb perh. f. obs. n. = hindmost person, which is perh. corruption of *last* in children's games, (*fog, seg, l.*, = 1st, 2nd, last, in diall.)]

lag², v.t., & n., (slang). Send to penal servitude; apprehend, arrest; (n.) convict. [?]

lag³, n., & v.t. (Piece of the) non-conducting cover of boiler &c.; (vb) case with ll., whence **la·gg**ING¹(3) n. [f. ON *logg* barrel-rim]

lă·gan, n. (legal). Goods or wreckage lying on bed of sea. [OF, perh. f. Teut. LIE³, LAY³])

la·ger (beer) (lahg-), n. Light kind of (orig. German) beer. [f. G *lager-bier* (*lager* store)]

lagoo·n, -une, n. Stretch of salt water parted from sea by low sand-bank; enclosed water of atoll. [F (*-une*), f. It. & Sp. *laguna* f. L LACUNA]

lā·ic, a. & n. Non-cleric(al), lay(man), secular, temporal. So **la·ic**AL a., **la·ical**LY² adv. [f. LL f. Gk *laikos* (*laos* people, -IC)]

la·icize, v.t. Make lay; commit (school &c.), throw open (office), to laymen. Hence **laiciz**A·TION n. [prec., -IZE]

laid. See LAY³.

lain. See LIE³.

lair, n., & v.i. & t. Place where animals lie down; shed or enclosure for cattle on way to market, whence **lair·**AGE(1, 3) **n.**; wild beast's lying-place; (vb) go to, rest or place in, l. [OE *leger* bed, also Du., cf. G *lager*; cogn. w. LIE³]

laird, n. (Sc.). Landed proprietor in Scotland. Hence **lair·d**SHIP **n.** [Sc. form of LORD w. changed sense]

Lā·is, n. Accomplished or beautiful courtesan. [name of two celebrated Greek hetaerae]

laissez-aller (lā·sā ă·lā, *or as F*), n. Unconstrained freedom, absence of constraint. [F]

lai·ssez-faire (lā·sā fār, *or as F*), n. Government abstention from interference with individual action esp. in commerce. [F, = let act]

lā·ity, n. Being a layman; laymen; unprofessional people, those outside any particular learned profession. [f. F *lai* LAY² + -TY]

lake¹, n. Large body of water entirely surrounded by land; *the Great L.*, Atlantic ocean; *the Great Ll.*, Superior, Huron, Michigan, Erie, & Ontario, forming boundary of U.S. & Canada; *l.-country, l.-land, the Ll.*, region of English ll. in Westmorland, Cumberland, & Lancs.; *l.-dweller*, prehistoric inhabitant of *l. dwelling*, built on piles driven into bed of l.; *l. poets*, Coleridge, Southey, & Wordsworth, who lived in lake-land. Hence **la·ke**LESS a., **la·ke**LET n. [f. OF *lac* f. L *lacus*]

lake², n. Crimson pigment, orig. made from lac, now from various combinations. [var. of LAC¹]

lakh. See LAC².

lalla·tion, n. LAMBDACISM. [f. L *lallare* sing lullaby + -ATION]

lam, v.t. & i. (slang). Thrash, hit (t., & i. with *into*) hard with cane &c. [perh. cogn. w. LAME]

la·ma¹ (lah-), n. Thibetan or Mongolian Buddhist priest (*Dalai* or *Grand L.*, chief l. of Thibet, *Teshu L.*, of Mongolia). Hence **la·ma**ISM, **la·ma**IST, nn. [Thibetan *blama*]

lama². See LLAMA.

Lamar·ckian, a. & n. (Follower) of Lamarck or his theory of organic evolution by inheritable modifications produced in the individual by habit &c. [*Lamarck*, F botanist & zoologist, d. 1829, + -IAN]

lama·sery (-mah-), n. Monastery of lamas. [f. F *lamaserie* irreg. f. LAMA¹]

lamb (-m), n., & v.t. & i. Young of sheep (***as well be hanged for a sheep as for a l.***, sin boldly, go the whole hog; ***like a l.***, unresistingly; ***wolf, fox, in l.'s skin***, hypocrite); its flesh as food; young member of church flock; innocent, weak, or dear person; ***The L.*** (***of God***), Christ; ***l.'s-fry***, product of l.'s castration; ***lamb-skin***, with wool on, or as leather; ***l.'s-tails***, hazel catkins; *l.'s-wool*, used in hosiery; hence **la·mb**HOOD, **la·mb**KIN, nn., **la·mb**LIKE a. (Vb): (Pass.; of ll.) be brought forth; bring forth l., yean; tend (lambing ewes), whence **la·mb**ER[1] (-*mer*) n. [OE; com.-Teut., cf. Du. *lam*, G *lamm*]

lambā·ste, v.t. (dial.). Thrash, beat. [perh. = LAM + BASTE[3]]

la·mbda, n. Greek letter L (Λ λ); *l. moth*, with l. on wings. [Gk, also *labda*]

la·(m)bdacism, n. Pronunciation of *r* as *l*. [prec., -ISM]

la·mbdoid, lambdoi·dal, aa. Lambda-shaped (*l. suture*, connecting two parietal bones with occipital). [f. F *lambdoïde* f. Gk *lambdoeidēs* (LAMBDA, -OID) + -AL]

la·mbent, a. (Of flame or light) playing on surface without burning it, with soft radiance; (of eyes, sky, &c.) softly radiant; (of wit &c.) gently brilliant. Hence **la·mb**ENCY n., **la·mbent**LY[2] adv. [f. L *lambere* lick, -ENT]

La·mbeth, n. (Used for) Archbishop of Canterbury's palace at L., the Archbishop as representing the Church, &c.

la·mbrequin (-kĭn), n. Short piece of drapery over top of door or window, or hung from mantelpiece. [F, etym. dub.; orig. scarf worn over helmet]

lame, a., & v.t. Crippled by injury or defect in a limb, esp. foot or leg, limping or unable to walk, (of person, limb, steps, &c.; *l. of* or *in a leg* &c.); (of argument, story, excuse) imperfect, unsatisfactory; (of metre) halting; *l.* DUCK[1]; hence **lā·m**ISH[1](2) a., **la·me**LY[2] adv., **la·me**NESS n. (Vb) make l., cripple, (lit. & fig.). [OE *lama*, cf. Du. *lam*, G *lahm*]

lamé (F), a. & n. (Material) with gold or silver thread inwoven.

lame·lla, n. (pl. *-ae*). Thin plate, scale, layer, or film, esp. of bone or tissue. Hence **lame·ll**AR[1], **lă·mell**ATE[2], **-ated**, **lame·ll**OSE[1], aa., **lame·lli**- comb. form. [L, dim. of LAMINA]

lame·nt, n., & v.t. & i. Passionate expression of grief; elegy, dirge. (Vb) express or feel grief for or about, be distressed at, regret, (also intr. with *for* or *over*, or abs.); (p.p.) mourned for (esp. conventionally of the dead, as *the late lamented* —). [f. L n. *lamentum* & vb *lamentari*]

lă·mentable, a. Mournful (archaic); (of events, fate, condition, character, &c.) deplorable, regrettable. Hence **la·ment·ab**LY[2] adv. [f. L *lamentabilis* (prec., -ABLE)]

lămenta·tion, n. Lamenting, lament; *Ll.* (*of Jeremiah*), O.-T. book (abbr. *Lam.*). [f. L *lamentatio* (LAMENT, -ATION)]

lā·mia, n. Monster in woman's shape preying on human beings & sucking children's blood. [L f. Gk]

lă·mina, n. (pl. *-ae*). Thin plate, scale, layer, or flake, of metal, bone, membrane, stratified rock, vegetable tissue, &c. Hence **la·min**AR[1], **la·min**OSE[1], aa., **la·mini**- comb. form. [L]

la·minate, v.t. & i. Beat or roll (metal) into thin plates; split (t. & i.) into layers or leaves; overlay with metal plates; manufacture by placing layer on layer. Hence or cogn. **la·min**ATE[2] (-*at*) a., **lamina·**TION n. [prec. + -ATE[3]]

La·mmas, n. First of August, formerly observed as harvest festival (*latter L.*, non-existent date, day that will never come, cf. *Greek* CALENDS). [OE *hláfmæsse* (LOAF, MASS[1])]

la·mmergeyer (-gī-), n. Bearded Vulture, largest European bird of prey. [f. G *lämmergeier* (*lämmer* lambs, *geier* vulture)]

lamp, n., & v.i. & t. Vessel with oil & wick for giving light; glass vessel enclosing candle, gas-jet, incandescent wire, or other illuminant (*smell of the l.*, betray nocturnal study, be laborious in style &c.; with allusion to ancient-Greek torch-race, *pass, hand, on the l.*, do one's part in advancing knowledge, a cause, &c.); SAFETY *l.*; SPIRIT *l.*; (fig.) sun, moon, star; source of spiritual or intellectual light, hope, &c.; *l.-black*, pigment made from soot; *l.-chimney*, glass cylinder making draught for l.-flame; *lamplight*, given by l. or ll.; *l.-lighter*, man who lights street ll. (*like a l.-l.*, with speed); *l.-post*, usu. of iron supporting street l.; hence **la·mp**LESS a. (Vb) shine; supply with ll.; illuminate. [f. F *lampe* f. L f. Gk *lampas* (*lampō* shine)]

la·mpas[1], n. Horse-disease with swelling in roof of mouth. [F, earlier = disease producing thirst, etym. dub.]

la·mpas[2], n. Kind of flowered silk orig. from China. [F, etym. dub.]

la·mpion, n. Pot of usu. coloured glass with oil & wick used in illuminations. [F, f. It. *lampione* (*lampa* LAMP, -OON)]

lampoo·n, n., & v.t. Virulent or scurrilous piece of satire; hence **lampoo·n**IST (1) n.; (vb) write l. or ll. against, whence **lampoo·n**ER[1] n. [f. F *lampon* perh. f. *lampons* let us drink]

la·mprey, n. Eel-like fish with sucker mouth, pouch gills, & seven spiracles on each side, & fistula on top, of head. [f. OF *lamproie* f. med. L *lampreda* perh. = *lampetra* taken as f. L *lambere* lick, *petra* stone w. ref. to use of sucker]

Lanca·strian, a. & n. (Inhabitant) of Lancashire or Lancaster; (adherent) of family descended from John of Gaunt Duke of Lancaster, or of the Red-rose party fighting for it in Wars of the Roses. [*Lancaster*, -IAN]

lance[1], n. Weapon with long wooden shaft & pointed steel head used by horseman in charging; similar implement for spearing fish or killing harpooned whale; (pl., w. numbers) = lancers; *l.-corporal* (&, slang, *l.-jack*), N.C.O. acting as corporal with private's pay; *l.-sergeant* (as l.-corporal); *l.-fish*, launce; *l.-snake*, venomous Amer. kind; *lancewood*, tough elastic W.-Ind. kind used for carriage-shafts, fishing-rods, &c. [F, f. L *lancea*; *l.-corporal* on anal. of obs. *lancepesade* f. It. *lancia spezzata* broken lance, i.e. veteran]

lance², v.t. Fling, launch, (poet.); (Surg.) prick or cut open with lancet; pierce with l. [poet. sense f. OF *lancier* f. L *lanceare* (*lancea* LANCE¹); other senses f. prec.]

la·ncelet, n. A fish, the lowest true vertebrate. [LANCE¹, -LET]

la·nceolate (-*at*), a. Shaped like spear-head, tapering to each end. [f. L *lanceolatus* (*lanceola* dim. of *lancea* lance, -ATE²)]

la·ncer, n. Soldier of cavalry regiment armed with lances; (pl.) kind of quadrille, music for it. [f. F *lancier* (LANCE¹, -IER)]

la·ncet, n. Surgical instrument usu. with two edges & point for bleeding or lancing; (also *l. arch, light, window*, &c.) arch or window with pointed head, whence **la·ncet**ED² a. [f. OF *lancette* (LANCE¹, -ETTE)]

la·ncinating, a. (Of pain) acute, shooting. [part. of rare *lancinate* f. L *lancinare* rend]

land¹, n. Solid part of earth's surface (opp. *sea, water*; *travel by l.*; *how the l. lies*, what is the state of affairs); ground, soil, expanse of country; country, nation, State, (*l. of promise*, Canaan; *l. of* CAKE¹*s*; *l. of the leal*, heaven; *l. of the living*, present life); landed property, (pl.) estates; strip of plough or pasture land parted from others by water furrows, any of the divisions between the rifling-grooves in guns. *L.-agent, -ncy*, steward(ship) of estate, agent, agency, for sale &c. of estates; *l.-bank*, issuing notes on security of landed property; *l.-breeze*, blowing seaward from l.; *l.-carriage*, transport by l.; *l.-crab*, kinds that live on l. but breed in sea; *landfall* (naut.), approach to land esp. for first time on voyage (*good, bad, landfall*, according, not according, to calculation); *l.-force(s)*, military, not naval; *l.-girl* (doing farm-work, as in the great war); *l.-grabber*, (esp.) man who takes Irish farm after eviction of tenant; *landholder*, proprietor or (usu.) tenant of l.; *l.-hunger, -gry*, eager(ness) to acquire l.; *l.-jobber*, speculator in l.; *landlady*, woman keeping inn, boarding-house, or lodgings, also woman having tenants; *l.-law* (usu. pl.), law(s) of landed property; *L. League*, Irish association 1879–81 for reducing rents, introducing peasant-proprietorship, &c.; *l.-locked*, almost or quite enclosed by l.; *landlord*, person of whom another holds any tenement (opp. *tenant*), keeper of inn, lodgings, &c.; *l.-lubber* (naut.), person ignorant of the sea & ships; *landmark*, object marking boundary of country, estate, &c., conspicuous object in district &c., object or event or change marking stage in process or turning-point in history; *landowner*, owner of l.; *landrail*, corncrake; *Land's-end*, western point of Cornwall (see JOHN-*o'-Groat's*); *l.-service*, military; *l.-shark*, one who lives by preying on seamen ashore; *l.-sick* (naut.; of ship), impeded in movement by nearness of l.; *l.-slide* (U.S.), overwhelming political defeat; *landslip*, sliding down of mass of land on cliff or mountain; *landsman*, non-sailor; *l.-swell*, roll of water near shore; *l.-tax*, assessed on landed property; *l.-tie*, rod, beam, or piece of masonry, securing or supporting wall &c. by connecting some part of it with the ground; *l.-wind*, =l.-breeze. Hence **la·nd**LESS a., **la·nd**WARD a. & adv., **la·nd**WARDS adv. [com.-Teut.; OE, Du., G, Sw., & Da., *land*]

land², v.t. & i. Set or go ashore (p.p. = having come ashore, see -ED¹(2), esp. in comb. as *newly-landed*), disembark (*at*); set down from vehicle; bring to, reach or find oneself in, a certain place, stage, or position; deal (person blow &c.; *landed him one in the eye*); bring (fish) to l., (fig.) win (prize &c.); (trans. of jockey, intr. of horse) bring or come in (*first* &c., or abs. =first); alight after jump &c. [f. prec.]

la·ndau, n. Four-wheeled carriage with top of which front & back halves can be independently raised & lowered. [*L.* in Germany]

landaule·t, n. Coupé with landau top. [-LET]

la·nddrōst, n. Kind of magistrate in S. Africa. [S.-Afr. Du.]

la·nded, a. Possessed of land (*the l. interest*, owners & holders of land); consisting of land (*l. estate, property*). [LAND¹ +ED²]

la·ndgrave, n. (fem. *-gravine*, pr. -ēn). Title of certain German potentates. [f. MHG *lantgrâve* (LAND¹, G *graf* count)]

la·nding, n. In vbl senses; also: (also *l.-place*) place for disembarking; platform between two flights of stairs; *l.-net*, for landing large fish when hooked; *l.-stage*, platform, often floating, on which passengers & goods are disembarked. [-ING¹]

la·ndlordism, n. System by which land is owned by landlords receiving fixed rents from tenants (esp. depreciatively of Irish system); advocacy of this. [-ISM]

lando·cracy, n. The landed class. So **la·ndo**CRAT n. [-CRACY]

la·ndscape, n. (Picture representing, art reproducing, or actual piece of) inland scenery; *l.-gardening, -ener*, laying, layer, out of grounds in imitation of natural scenery; *l.-marble*, kind with treelike markings; *l.-painter*, who paints ll., also **la·ndscāp**IST(1) n. [f. Du. *landschap* (LAND¹, -SHIP)]

la·ndsturm (-oorm), n. (In Germany &c.) general levy in war, of men outside army, navy, & landwehr. [G]

la·nd-tag (-ahch), n. Legislative body, diet, of a German State. [G]

la·ndwehr (-vār), n. (In Germany &c.) militia serving continuously only during war. [G]

lane, n. Narrow road usu. between hedges (*it is a long l. that has no turning,* change is sure to come), narrow street; passage made or left between rows of persons; course prescribed for ocean steamers; *red l.,* throat; *the L.,* Drury L. (theatre). [OE; cf. OFris. *lana,* Du. *laan*]

la·ngrage, -idge (-ngg-), n. Case-shot with irregular pieces of iron formerly used to damage rigging. [?]

lang syne, adv. & n. (In) the old days. [Sc., =long since]

la·nguage (-nggwĭj), n. A vocabulary & way of using it prevalent in one or more countries (DEAD *l.*), (transf.) method of expression (*finger l.,* talk by conventional signs with fingers; *l. of flowers,* symbolic meanings attached to various kinds); words & their use; faculty of speech; person's style of expressing himself (*bad l.,* or vulg. *l.,* oaths & abusive talk; *strong l.,* expressing vehement feelings); professional or sectional vocabulary; literary style, wording; *l.-master,* teacher of (usu. mod. foreign) l. or ll. [f. F *langage* (L *lingua* tongue, -AGE)]

langue d'oc, langue d'oïl, nn. (F). Medieval French as spoken south, north, of the Loire, the latter the staple of modern French. [OF, f. L *lingua* tongue, *de* of, *hoc* this, *hoc illud* this (is) that (*oc* & *oïl* being the respective forms for *yes*)]

la·nguid (-nggw-), a. Inert, lacking vigour, indisposed to exertion, spiritless, apathetic, not vivid, dull, uninteresting, sluggish, slow-moving, faint, weak. Hence **la·nguid**LY[2] adv., **la·nguid**NESS n. [f. L *languidus* (foll., -ID[1])]

la·nguish, v.i. Grow or be feeble, lose or lack vitality; live *under* enfeebling or depressing conditions; grow slack, lose intensity; droop, pine (*for*); put on languid look, affect sentimental tenderness, whence **la·nguishing**LY[2] adv. Hence **la·nguish**MENT n. [f. F *languir* (-ISH[2]) f. L *languēre* cf. LAX*us*]

la·nguor (-gger), n. Faintness, fatigue; lassitude, inertia, want of alertness; soft or tender mood or effect; slackness, dullness, drooping state; (of sky &c.) oppressive stillness. So **la·nguor**OUS a., **la·nguorous**LY[2] adv. [OF, f. L *languorem* nom. *-or* (prec., -OR[2])]

lă·niary, a. & n. (Tooth) adapted for tearing, canine. [f. L *laniarius* (*lanius* butcher f. *laniare* tear, -ARY[1])]

lani·ferous, -gerous, aa. Wool-bearing. [f. L (*-fer, -ger*) f. *lana* wool, -FEROUS, -GEROUS]

lank, a. Shrunken, spare; tall & lean; (of grass &c.) long & flaccid; (of hair) straight & limp, not wavy. [OE *hlanc*; excl. E.; perh cogn. w. G *lenken* to bend]

lanky, a. Ungracefully lean & long or tall (of limbs, person). Hence **la·nki**NESS n. [-Y[2]]

la·nner, la·nneret, nn. Kind of falcon, female of it, (*-er*); (*-et*) male of it. [f. F *lanier* prob. f. OF *lanier* cowardly]

lă·nolin, n. Extract from sheep's wool as basis of ointments. [f. L *lana* wool + -OL[2] + -IN]

la·nsquenet (-ke-), n. Card-game of German origin. [F, f. G *landsknecht* 17th-c. mercenary (lit., servant of country)]

la·ntern, n. Transparent case protecting flame of candle &c. (BULL[1]'*s-eye,* CHINESE, DARK[1], MAGIC, *l.*); *parish l.,* the moon; =magic l., whence **la·ntern**IST(3) n.; light-chamber of lighthouse; erection on top of dome or room with glazed sides to admit light; luminous proboscis of *l.-fly*; *l. jaws,* long & thin, giving hollow look to face, whence **lantern-jaw**ED[2] a. [f. F *lanterne* f. L *lanterna* perh. f. Gk *lamptēr* (*lampō* shine) w. assim. to L *lucerna*]

la·nthanum, n. (chem.). Rare element belonging to earth-metal group, discovered 1839–41. [f. Gk *lanthanō* lurk (w. ref. to lateness of discovery) + -UM]

la·nthorn (-tern), n. Lantern. [pop. assim. of *lantern* to *horn,* common former material]

la·nyard, n. (naut.). Short rope or line attached to something to secure it or serve as handle. [f. F *lanière,* w. assim. to *yard*]

Lāodicē·an, a. & n. (Person) lukewarm esp. in religion or politics. [*Rev.* iii. 15, 16]

lap[1], n. Hanging part or flap of garment, saddle, &c.; lobe of ear; front part of skirt held up to contain something; waist to knees of one sitting, with dress, as place on which child is nursed or object held (*in Fortune's l., in the l. of luxury,* &c.), whence **la·p**FUL(2) n.; hollow among hills; *l.-dog,* small pet dog; *lapstone,* shoemaker's stone held in l. to beat leather on. [OE *lappa,* cf. G *lappen*]

lap[2], v.t. & i. Coil, fold, wrap, (garment &c. *about, round,* advv. or prepp.); enfold, swathe, *in* wraps &c.; (of influences &c.) surround, encircle, (often *round*), enfold caressingly (esp. pass., *lapped in luxury*); make (valve, roof-slate, &c.) overlap; project *over* something (also *l. over* adv. = *overlap* intr.); (Racing) pass (competitor) by one or more ll. [prob. f. prec.]

lap[3], n. Amount of overlapping, overlapping part (*half-l.,* joining of rails, shafts, &c., by halving thickness of each at end); layer or sheet (of cotton &c. being made) wound on roller; single turn of rope, silk, thread, &c., round drum or reel; one circuit of race-track; *l.-joint,* = *half-l.* above; *l.-streak,* clinker-built boat. [f. prec.]

lap[4], n., & v.t. Rotating disk for polishing

gem or metal; (vb) polish with l. [perh. f. prec.]

lap[5], v.i. & t., & n. Take up liquid, drink (*up* liquid), by scooping with tongue; consume (liquid) greedily (usu. *up* or *down*); (of water) move, beat upon (shore), with sound of lapping. (N.) liquid food for dogs; (slang) weak beverage, also alcoholic liquor; single act of lapping, amount taken up by it; sound of wavelets on beach &c. [OE *lapian* cf. OHG *laffan*; cf. G *löffel* spoon, L *lambere*, Gk *laptō*, lick]

lăpar(o)-, comb. form of Gk *lapara* flank, in anat. & surg. terms: *la·parocele* lumbar hernia, *lapare·ctomy* excision of part of intestine at side, *laparo·tomy* cutting of abdominal walls.

lape·l, n. Part of coat-breast folded back. Hence **lape·ll**ED[2] a. [LAP[1], -EL]

lă·picide, n. Cutter of stones or inscriptions on stone. [f. L *lapicida* for *lapidicida* (*lapis -idis* stone + *caedere* cut, kill, cf. -CIDE)]

lă·pidary, a. & n. Concerned with stones (esp. *l. bee*, building in stone walls &c.); engraved on stone, (of style) suitable for inscriptions, monumental; (n.) cutter, polisher, or engraver, of gems. [f. L *lapidarius* (*lapis -idis* stone, -ARY[1])]

lă·pidate, v.t. Stone, stone to death. So **lapid**A·TION n. [f. L *lapidare* (prec.), -ATE[3]]

lapi·dify, v.t. Make into stone. Hence **lapidi**FICA·TION n. [f. F *lapidifier* f. med. L *lapidificare* (prec., -FY)]

lă·pis lă·zūlī, n. A silicate containing sulphur, bright blue pigment from it; its colour. [L, = stone of AZURE]

Lapp, n. & a. One of dwarfish race of northern Scandinavia; (also **La·pp**ISH[1] n.) their language; *Lapland*, their country, whence **La·pland**ER[1](4) n.; (also **La·pp**ISH[1] a.) of the Ll. or their language. [f. Sw. *Lapp*, perh. term of contempt, cf. MHG *lappe* simpleton]

la·ppet, n. Flap, fold, loose or overlapping piece, of garment, flesh, membrane, &c.; lobe of ear &c.; = lapel; streamer of lady's head-dress. Hence **la·ppet**ED[2] a. [LAP[1] + -ET[1]]

Lappō·nian, a. & n. = LAPP. [f. med. L *Lappo -onis* + -IAN]

lapse[1], n. Slip of memory, tongue, or pen, slight mistake; weak or careless deviation from right, moral slip; falling away *from* faith or *into* heresy; decline to lower state; termination of right or privilege through disuse; (of water) gentle flow; passage or interval *of* time. [f. L *lapsus -ūs* (*labi laps-* glide)]

lapse[2], v.i. Fail to maintain position or state for want of effort or vigour, fall *back* or *away*, (often *into* inferior or previous state); (of benefice, estate, right, &c.) fall in, pass away, become void, revert *to* some one, by failure of conditions, heirs, &c.; glide, flow, subside, pass *away*; (p.p.) that has lapsed, see -ED[2](2). [f. L *lapsare* frequent. (prec.)]

la·psus, n. (pl. *-ūs*). Slip (usu. in *l. linguae*, pr. -gwē, of the tongue, *l. călamī* of the pen). [L]

Lapū·tan, a. & n. (Inhabitant) of Laputa; chimerical, visionary, absurd. [*Laputa* in *Gulliver's Travels* + -AN]

la·pwing, n. Bird of plover family, peewit. [OE *hlēapwince* (*hlēapon* LEAP[1], WINK, w. ref. to manner of flight) assim. to LAP, WING]

lar, n. (Pl. *lā·rēs*) ancient-Roman household deity (usu. pl.; *Ll.*, *Ll. & Penates*, the home); (pl. *lars*) white-handed Burmese gibbon. [L]

lar·board (-berd), n. & a. (naut.). (Older term now replaced, to save confusion with *starboard*, by) PORT[5]. [ME *lade-*, *lathe-*, *borde*; *lade-* (etym. dub.) changed to *lar-* by assim. to STARBOARD]

lar·ceny, n. (Law) felonious taking away of another's personal goods with intent to convert them to one's own use (*petty l.*, formerly, of property below value of 12*d.*); theft. Hence **lar·cen**ER[1], **lar·cen**IST(1), nn., **larcen**OUS a., **lar·cenous**LY[2] adv. [f. F *larcin* f. L *latrocinium* (*latro* robber) + -Y[1]]

larch (-tsh), n. Bright-foliaged coniferous tree yielding Venetian turpentine, tough timber, & bark used in tanning; its wood. [f. G *lärche* f. L *larix -icis*]

lard[1], n. Internal fat of abdomen of pigs esp. when rendered & clarified for use in cooking & pharmacy. Hence **lar·d**Y[2] a. [OF, = bacon, f. L *lardum* perh. cogn. w. Gk *larinos* fat, *laros* pleasant to taste]

lard[2], v.t. Insert strips of bacon in (meat &c.) before cooking (*larding-needle*, *-pin*, instruments for doing this); garnish (talk, writing) *with* metaphors, technical terms, foreign words, &c. [f. F *larder* (prec.)]

larda·ceous, a. (med.). Lardlike (esp. of degeneration of tissue or of patient suffering from it). [-ACEOUS]

lar·der, n. Room or closet for meat &c. [f. OF *lardier* f. med. L *lardarium* (LARD, -ARY[1])]

lar·don, lardoo·n, n. Strip of bacon or pork used to lard meat. [F (*-on*); LARD[1], -OON]

lar·dy-dar·dy, a. (slang). Affected, languidly foppish. [cf. LA-DI-DA]

lares. See LAR.

large, a. & n. (Archaic) liberal, generous, kindly, munificent, unprejudiced, (still in *l. views*, *l. charity*, *l. tolerance*, *l.-minded*, whence **large-mi·nded**NESS n., *l.-hearted*, whence **large-hear·ted**NESS n., &c.); of wide range, comprehensive, (*l. powers*, *discretion*); (of artistic treatment) free, sweeping, broad; of considerable or relatively great magnitude (less colloq. than *big*, & without emotional implications of *great*; seldom used of persons except as in *l. of limb* = with l. limbs &c.); (with agent nouns) on a large scale (*l. & small farmers*); hence **lar·gish**[1](2) a., **lar·geness** n., **lar·gen**[6], v.i. & t. (poet.). (N.; only now with *at, in*); *at l.*: at liberty, free; (of narration &c.) at full length, with details; as a body or whole (*popular with the people at l.*); without particularizing, without definite aim, (*scatters imputations at l.*; *gentleman at l.*, gentleman attached to the court without special duties, person who has no occupation); *in l.*, on l. scale (opp. *in little*). [F, f. fem. of L *largus* copious]

lar·gely, adv. In adj. senses; also, to a great or preponderating extent (*is l. due to*). [-LY[2]]

lar·gess(e), n. (archaic). Money or gifts freely bestowed esp. by great person on occasion of rejoicing; generous or plentiful bestowal. [F (-*e*), f. L *largus* copious, -ESS[2]]

lă·riat, n. Rope for picketing horses &c.; lasso. [f. Sp. *la reata* f. *reatar* tie again (RE-, L *aptare* fit)]

lark[1], **lă·verock**, n. Kinds of small bird with sandy-brown plumage & long hind-claws, esp. the SKY*lark* (*Crested, Horned, Red, Shore, L.*, other kinds); *rise with the l.*, get up early; *if the sky fall, we shall catch ll.* (comfort for alarmists); *l.-heel*, larkspur, also Indian cress or garden nasturtium; *larkspur*, plant with spur-shaped calyx. [OE *lāferce*, cf. Du. *leeuwerik*, G *lerche*, etym. dub.]

lark[2], n., & v.i. Frolic, spree, amusing incident (*what a l.!*, how amusing!); hence **lar·ky**[2] a.; (vb) play tricks, frolic. [f. 1811; etym. dub.]

la·rrikin, n. (Usu. young) street rowdy, hooligan. [orig. Australian; etym. dub.]

lă·rum, n. (Now rare for) ALARUM.

lar·va, n. (pl. -*ae*). Insect from time of leaving egg till transformation into pupa, grub; immature form of other animals that undergo some metamorphosis. Hence **lar·val** a., **lar·vi-** comb. form. [L, = ghost, mask]

lary·ngoscope, n. Mirror apparatus for examining larynx. [LARYNX, -SCOPE]

lăryngo·tomy, n. Cutting into larynx from without, esp. to provide breathing-channel. [foll., -TOMY]

lă·rynx, n. Cavity in throat holding vocal cords. Hence **lary·ngĕal**, **lary·ngic**, aa., **lăryngi·tis** n., (-j-), **lary·ngo-** comb. form, **laryngo·logy** n. [f. Gk *larugx -ggos*]

La·scar (*or* -ar·), n. E.-Indian sailor. [perh. incorrect use of Hind. *lashkar* army]

lasci·vious (lasĭ-), a. Lustful, wanton; inciting to lust. Hence **lasci·viously**[2] adv., **lasci·viousness** n. [f. LL *lasciviosus* (L *lascivia* f. *lascivus* sportive, -OSE[1])]

lash[1], v.i. & t. 1. Make sudden movement of limb, tail, &c.; pour, rush, vehemently, whence **la·shings** (-ING[1](2)) n. pl. (slang), plenty (*of*); strike violently *at*; hit or (of horse) kick *out*; break *out* into excess, strong language, &c. 2. Beat with l., flog; (of waves) beat upon; castigate in words, rebuke, satirize; urge as with ll. (*l. oneself into a fury*, work up a rage); hence **la·shing**[1](1) n. 3. Fasten (*down, on, together, to* something) with cord, twine, &c., whence **la·shing**[1](4) n. [sense 1 perh. imit.; sense 2 f. foll.; sense 3 prob. separate wd, etym. dub.]

lash[2], n. Stroke with thong, whip, &c.; flexible part of whip (*the l.*, punishment of flogging); = EYE-*l.*, whence **la·shless** a.; goading influence. [f. prec. in sense 1]

la·sher, n. In vbl senses; esp. (water rushing over) weir, pool below weir. [-ER[1]]

la·shkar, n. Body of armed Indian tribesmen. [Hind., = army]

la·spring, n. Young salmon. [perh. corruption of obs. *lax-pink* (obs. *lax*, OE *leax*, see LAX[2], cf. G *lachs*, salmon)]

lasque (-k), n. Flat, ill-formed, or veiny diamond. [perh. f. Pers. *lashk* piece]

lăss, n. Girl; sweetheart. Hence **la·ssie** [-Y[3]] n. [ME *lasce*, cf. MSw. *lösk* (*kona*) unmarried (woman)]

lă·ssitude, n. Weariness, languor, disinclination to exert or interest oneself. [F, f. L *lassitudo* (*lassus* tired, -TUDE)]

la·sso (*also pron.* lasōō·), n., & v.t. Sp.-Amer. noosed rope of untanned hide for catching cattle &c.; (vb) catch with l. [f. Sp. *lazo* LACE[1]]

last[1], n. Shoemaker's wooden model for shaping shoe &c. on (*stick to* one's *l.*, not meddle with things one does not understand, w. ref. to L prov. *ne sutor ultra crepidam*). [OE *lāst* footstep, *lǣst* boot, cf. G *leiste* last, *geleise* track, perh. cogn. w. L *lira* furrow]

last[2], n. Commercial measure of weight, capacity, or quantity, varying with place & goods (*l. of wool*, 12 sacks or 4,368 lb.; *l. of malt*, 10 qrs or 80 bushels). [OE *hlæst*, cf. G *last*, load]

last[3], a., n., & adv. After all others, coming at the end, (*the l. two* &c. = the l. & l. but one &c., *the two* &c. *l.* being now usu. held incorrect in this sense; *l. but not least*, l. in order of mention or occurrence but not of importance); belonging to the end, esp. of life or the world (*the four l. things*, death, judgement, heaven, hell; *l. day*, Day of Judgement; *on* one's *l.* LEGS); next before expressed or implied point of time, latest up to date, most recent, (*in the l. fortnight*, *l. Christmas*, *l. Tuesday* or *Tuesday l.*; *l. evening* or *night* or *week* or *month* or *year* used as adverbs, but not *l. morning, day,* or *afternoon*; also ellipt. as n. for l. letter, joke, baby, &c., *as I said in my l.*, *have you heard —'s l.?*, *Mrs —'s l.*); lowest, of least rank or estimation; only remaining (*l. crust, resource*); latest *to be* (*was the l. to be consulted*); least likely, willing, suitable, &c. *to* or *to be* (*should be the l. to do it*; *is the l. thing to try*); conclusive, definitive, (*has said the l. word on the matter*); utmost, extreme, (*is of the l. importance*). (N.) l.-mentioned person or thing (*the, this, which, l.*); l. day or moments, death, (*the* or *his* &c. *l.*); l. performance of certain acts (*breathe, look,* one's *l.*); l. mention (*shall never hear the l. of it*); *at l.*, (also) *at long l.*, in the end, after much delay; *to, till, the l.*, to the end, esp. till death. (Adv.) after all others (often in comb., as *l.-made, -mentioned*); on the l. occasion before the present (*when did you see him l.?*); (in enumerations) in the l. place, finally, also **la·st**LY[2] adv. [OE *latost* superl. of *læt* a., *late* adv.; cf. G *letzt*, & for dropping of *-t-* BEST]

last[4], v.i. & t., & n. Go on, remain unexhausted or adequate or alive; suffice (*will l. me eight months*); *l. out*, continue esp. in vigour or use at least as long as; (n.) staying power, stamina. [OE *lǣstan* fulfil, cf. G *leisten*]

la·sting, a. & n. Enduring, permanent (*no l. benefit*); durable; hence **la·sting**LY[2] adv., **la·sting**NESS n.; (n.) kind of durable cloth. [-ING[2]]

Lătaki·a (-ēa), n. Kind of Turkish tobacco chiefly used in mixtures. [*L.* (anc. *Laodicea*), a Syrian port]

latch, n., & v.t. Door or gate fastening made of small bar falling into catch & lifted by lever &c. from outside; small spring-lock of outer door catching when door is closed & worked by *l.-key* from outside (*l.-k. vote*, LODGER franchise as tested by possession of l.-k.); *on the l.*, fastened by l. only; (vb) fasten with l. [perh. f. OF *lache* LACE[1]; or f. obs. *latch*, OE *læccan*, to grasp]

la·tchet, n. (bibl.). Thong for fastening shoe. [f. OF *lachet* (LACE[1], -ET[1])]

late[1], a. (comp. *later*, LATTER; superl. *latest*, LAST), & n. After the due or usual time (*was l. for dinner*; *it is too l. to go*; with agent nouns, as *l.-comer* = one who comes l.); backward in flowering, ripening, &c.; far on in day or night (*l. dinner*, in evening; *l. hours*, after usual time for rising or going to bed), or in time (*on Wednesday at latest*, then if not before); far on in a period, development, &c. (*l. stained glass, l.* LATIN); no longer alive, no longer having specified status &c., that was recently so-&-so, (*the l. prime minister*, dead or resigned; *my l. husband, residence*); of recent date (*the l. floods, war*; *of l. years*, in the last few; also as n. in *of l.*, recently); *l. fee*, on letter posted after ordinary collection time. Hence **la·te**N[6] v.t. & i., **la·te**NESS n., **la·**TISH[1](2) a. & adv. [com.-Teut.; OE *læt*, cf. Du. *laat*, G *lass*, sluggish, cogn. w. L *lassus* tired]

late[2], adv. (-er, -est, LAST). After proper time (*better l. than never*), far on in time, (*this happened later on*; *sooner or later, early or l., soon or l.*, some time or other); at or till l. hour (*we sat l.*); (Poet.) recently, lately, (*I sent thee l. a rosy wreath*); formerly but not now (*his own room, l. the chaplain's*); at l. stage of development &c. (*traces remained as l. as the Stuart times*; *l. in the day*, (colloq.) at a l. stage, esp. unreasonably l. in the proceedings &c. [OE, f. *læt* see prec.]

latee·n, a. *L. sail*, triangular on long yard at angle of 45° to mast; (of ship &c.) so rigged. [f. F (*voile*) *latine* Latin (sail), named as common in Mediterranean]

la·tely, adv. Not long ago, recently, in recent times. [OE *lætlice* (LATE[1], -LIKE)]

lā·tent, a. Hidden, concealed; existing but not developed or manifest; dormant; *l.* HEAT. Hence **la·t**ENCY n., **la·tent**LY[2] adv. [f. L *latēre* be hidden, -ENT]

-later, suf. See -LATRY.

lă·teral, a. & n. Of, at, towards, from, the side, side-, (*l. branch* of family, descended from brother or sister of person in direct line); (n.) side part, member, or object, esp. l. shoot or branch. Hence **la·teral**LY[2] adv. [f. L *lateralis* (*latus -eris* side, -AL)]

Lă·teran, n. & a. *The L., St John L.*, cathedral church of St John L. (*Sancti Joannis in Laterano*) in Rome; *L. Council*, one of five general councils of Western Church there held. [f. L *Laterana, -um*, named f. ancient-Roman family of Plautii Laterani]

lā·tex, n. (bot.). Milky juice of plants; (commerc.) crude rubber. [L, = liquid]

lath, n. (-th, *pl.* -dhz), & v.t. Thin narrow strip of wood esp. for use as support for slates or plaster or as material for trellis or Venetian blind (*as thin as a l.*, of persons, whence **la·th**Y[2] a.; *l. & plaster*, material for interior wall-faces, ceilings, partitions, &c.); (vb) provide (wall, ceiling) with ll., whence **la·th**ING[1](3) n. [ME *laththe*, cf. G *latte*, perh. cogn. w. G *laden* shop-counter; cf. also OE *lætt*]

lāthe[1] (-dh), n. One of (now five) administrative districts of Kent. [OE *lǣth* estate]

lāthe[2] (-dh), n. (Also *turning-l.*) machine for turning wood, metal, ivory, &c., by rotating article against tools used; (also *potter's l.*) machine with horizontal revolving disk for throwing & turning pottery; *l.-bearer, -carrier, -dog*, appliance connecting object with l. centres or holders; *l.-bed*, lower framework of l. with slot from end to end for adjustment. [prob. cogn. w. Da. *-lad* structure, frame, & LADE; or perh. modification of LATH]

lă·ther (-dh-), n., & v.t. & i. Froth of soap & water; frothy sweat of horse; hence **la·ther**Y[2] a. (Vb) cover (esp. chin &c. for shaving) with l.; (of horse) become covered with l.; (of soap) form l.; beat, thrash, whence **la·ther**ING[1](1) n. [n. f. OE *léathor* washing soda cogn. w. Gk *loetron* bath, L *lavare* wash; vb f. OE *léthran* f. same root]

lātifu·ndia, n. pl. Large estates, esp. as characterizing a country's social system. [L (sing. *-um*), f. *latus* broad, *fundus* farm]

Lă·tin, a. & n. Of Latium or ancient Latins or Romans; of, like, in, the language of the ancient Romans, whence **La·tin**ISM(4) n.; of the Roman Catholic Church; *Latin* (see WESTERN) *Church*; (of peoples) inheriting Roman customs &c., speaking one of the languages descended from Latin, Romance, (*the L. peoples*, France, Spain, Portugal, Italy, &c.). (N.) the L. language (*old L.*, before about 75 B.C., preclassical; *classical L.*, that of great writers of late republican & early imperial Rome, about 75 B.C. to 175 A.D.; *late L.*, about 175 to 600 A.D.; *medieval L.*, about 600 to 1500 A.D.; *modern L.*, since 1500 A.D.; *low L.*, =medieval, or late & medieval; SILVER[1] *L.*; *thieves' L.*, secret language of thieves &c.; DOG *L.*), whence **La·tin**LESS a., **La·tin**IST(3) n.; inhabitant of Latium, (Rom. Ant.) Italian with special franchise. [f. L *Latinus* (*Latium* Roman district, -INE[1])]

Lati·nē, adv. In Latin (giving Latin equivalent of word &c.). [L]

Lati·nity, n. Way person writes Latin, quality of Latin style or grammar. [f. L *Latinitas* (prec., -TY)]

la·tinize, v.t. & i. Give Latin form to (word), put into Latin; make conformable to ideas, customs, &c., of the ancient Romans, Latin peoples, or Latin Church; use Latin forms, idioms, &c. Hence **latiniz**A·TION, **la·tiniz**ER[1], nn. [f. L *latinizare* (LATIN, -IZE)]

lă·titude, n. (Joc.) breadth (*hat with great l. of brim*); (rare) scope, full extent, (*understood, taken, in its proper l.*); freedom from narrowness, liberality of interpretation, tolerated variety of action or opinion, whence (esp. of religious matters) **latitudin**AR·IAN a. & n., **latitudinar·ian**ISM(3) n.; (Geog.) angular distance on a meridian (*degree, minute, &c., of l.*), place's angular distance on its meridian N. or S. of equator (in l. 40° N. &c.), (usu. pl.) regions, climes, esp. w. ref. to temperature (*high ll.*, far N. or S.; *low ll.*, near equator); (Astron.) angular distance of heavenly body from ecliptic. So **latitu·din**AL a. (geog.). [f. L *latitudo -inis* (*latus* broad, -TUDE)]

latri·ne (-ēn), n. Privy, esp. in camp, barracks, hospital, &c. [F, f. L *latrina* for *lavatrina* (*lavare* wash, -INE[4])]

-latry, suf. f. Gk *latreia* worship, in wds f. an existing Gk original (*idolatry*), & mod. formations on same model (*angelolatry*, *Mariolatry*). In (humorous) hybrid formations -o- is added to the initial component as *lordolatry*, *babyolatry*. Corresponding personal nn. (-worshipper) are formed in -(o)*later* f. Gk *-latrēs*.

la·tten, n. & a. (archaic). (Of) a mixed yellow metal like (or the same as) brass. [f. OF *laton* perh. f. Teut. (LATH)]

la·tter, a. (Archaic) later, second, (*l. grass*, aftermath); belonging to end of period, world, &c. (*in these l. days*, at this late period of the world's history; *l. end*, death); second-mentioned (opp. *former*; also *the l.* ellipt. =second-mentioned thing or person); *l.-day*, modern (*l.-day saints*, Mormons). [OE *lætra* comp. of *læt* LATE[1], *later* being a new formation]

la·tterly, adv. Towards the end of life or some period; nowadays, of late. [f. prec.]

la·ttice, n. Structure of cross laths with interstices serving as screen, door, &c.; (also *l.-work*) laths so arranged; *l. bridge*, made with l. girders; *l. frame* or *girder*, girder made of two flanges connected by iron l.-work; *l. window*, one having l., also one with small panes set in diagonal lead-work. Hence **la·ttic**ED[2] a., **la·tti·c**ING[1](6) n. [f. OF *lattis* (*latte* LATH)]

La·tvian, a. & n. (Inhabitant) of the Republic of Latvia on the Gulf of Riga, proclaimed 1918. [f. *Latvi* see LETTISH + -AN]

laud, n.,& v.t. Praise (rare exc. in hymns); (pl.) first of day-hours of church; hymn of praise. (Vb) praise, celebrate; so **laud**A·TION, **lauda·tor**[2], nn., **lau·d**ATIVE, **lau·dat**ORY, aa. [n. f. OF *laude*, vb f. L *laudare*, f. L *laudem* nom. *laus* praise]

lau·dable, a. Commendable, praiseworthy; (Med., of secretions) healthy, sound. Hence or cogn. **laud**ABI·LITY n., **lau·dab**LY[2] adv. [f. L *laudabilis* (prec., -ABLE)]

lau·danum (lŏdn-), n. Alcoholic tincture of opium. [name given by Paracelsus to a costly panacea or elixir, later transferred to preparations containing opium; perh. var. of L *ladanum* or med. L *labdanum* a gum-resin, or f. L *laudare* praise]

laudā·tor te·mporis a·cti, n. One who prefers the good old days. [L]

laugh (-ahf, -ăf), v.i. & t., & n. Make the sounds & movements of face & sides by which lively amusement, sense of the ludicrous, exultation, & scorn, are instinctively expressed, have these emotions, (*l. in* one's *sleeve*, be secretly amused; *laughing* HYENA, JACKASS; *l. on wrong side of mouth*, have revulsion from joy or amusement to tears or vexation; *he laughs best who laughs last*, warning against premature exultation); (of water, landscape, corn, &c.) be lively with play of movement or light; utter laughingly; hold up *to scorn*; *l. at*, make fun of, ridicule, also look pleasantly or smile at; get (person) *out of* habit, belief, &c., by ridicule (*l.* person, opinion, &c., *out of* *court*, deprive of a hearing by ridicule); *l. away*, dismiss (subject) with a l., while away (time) with jests; *l. down*, silence with laughter; *l. off* (embarrassment &c.), get rid of with a jest; *l. over*, discuss with laughter; hence **lau·gh**ER[1] n., **lau·gh**ING[2] a., **lau·ghing**LY[2] adv. (N.) sound made in, act of, laughing (*join in the l.*, esp. of person taking banter good-humouredly; *have, get, the l. of*, turn the tables on assailant, also *have the l. on* one's *side*); person's manner of laughing. [com.-Teut.; OE *hlehhan*, cf. Du. & G *lachen*; prob. imit.]

lau·ghable, a. Exciting laughter, amusing. Hence **lau·ghab**LY[2] adv. [prec. n. or v. + -ABLE]

lau·ghing, n. In vbl senses; esp.: *no l. matter*, serious thing, not a fit subject for l.; *l.-gas*, nitrous oxide, with intoxicating effect when inhaled, used as anaesthetic; *l.-stock*, person or thing generally ridiculed. [-ING[1]]

lau·ghter, n. Laughing (*Homeric l.*, loud & general, such as Homer attributes to spectators of ludicrous incident). [OE *hleahtor* cf. G *gelächter* (*lachen* LAUGH)]

launce (lahns, lăns), n. Sand-eel. [perh. var. of LANCE[1]]

launch[1] (lah-, law-), v.t. & i., & n. Hurl, discharge, send forth, (missile, blow, censure, threat, decree); burst (usu. *out*) *into* expense, strong language, &c. (also *l. out* abs., spend money freely, expatiate in words); set (vessel) afloat; send off, start, (person, enterprise) on a course; go *forth, out*, on an enterprise; (n.) process of launching ship. [f. ONF *lancher* = OF *lancier* LANCE[2]]

launch[2] (as prec.), n. Man-of-war's largest boat, rather flat-bottomed & usu. sloop-rigged; large electric or steam boat for passengers, pleasure trips, &c. [f. Sp. *lancha* pinnace perh. f. Malay *lancharan* (*lanchar* swift)]

lau·ndress, n. Woman who washes & gets up linen; caretaker of chambers in Inns of Court. [f. (now rare) *launder* vb f. obs. *launder* n. washer of linen f. OF *lavandier* f. LL *lavandarius* (*lavanda* neut. pl. gerundive of L *lavare* wash, -ARY[1]) + -ESS[1]]

lau·ndry, n. Establishment for washing linen. [as prec., -RY]

lau·reate (-ĭat), a. & n. Wreathed with, (of wreath) consisting of, laurel; worthy of laurels as poet (*poet l.*, or *l.* as n., poet receiving stipend as writer of Court odes, whence **lau·reate**SHIP n.), or for eloquence &c. [f. L *laureatus* (*laurea* laurel-wreath f. *laurus* laurel, -ATE[2])]

lau·rel (lŏ-), n., & v.t. (-ll-). Kinds of glossy-leaved shrub; foliage of bay-tree as emblem of victory or distinction in poetry (collect. sing. or pl.; *reap, win, ll.*; *rest on* one's *ll.*, cease to strive for further glory; *look to* one's *ll.*, beware of losing pre-eminence); *l.-bottle*, filled with l.-leaves for killing insects; (vb) wreathe with l. [f. F *laurier* f. OF *lor* f. L *laurus*; *-l* by dissim.]

laurustī·nus, -res-, n. Evergreen flowering shrub. [mod. L, prop. two wds (L *laurus* laurel, *tinus* a plant, perh. the l.)]

la·va (lah-), n. Matter flowing from volcano, solid substance it cools into; (w. pl.) kind, bed, of l. [It. (*lavare* It. & L wash)]

lavā·bo, n. (pl. *-ōs*). Ritual washing of celebrant's hands at offertory, towel or basin used for this; monastery washing-trough; wash-basin, (pl.) lavatory, (after F). [L, = I will wash, first wd of *Ps.* xxvi. 6]

lava·tion, n. Washing. [f. L *lavatio* (*lavare* wash, -ATION)]

lă·vatory, n. Vessel for washing (archaic); room &c. for washing hands & face, often provided also with water-closets &c. [f. L *lavatorium* f. *lavare* wash, -ORY(2)]

lave, v.t. (poet.). Wash, bathe; (of stream &c.) wash against, flow along. [repr. both OE *lafian* pour (water) cf. G *laben* refresh, & F *laver* f. L *lavare* = Gk *louō* wash, cf. LATHER]

la·vement, n. (med.). Injection, enema. [F (prec., -MENT)]

lă·vender, n., & v.t. Small lilac-flowered narrow-leaved shrub cultivated for perfume; its flowers & stalks laid among linen &c. (*lay up in l.*, often fig., put aside for future use); pale blue colour with trace of red; *l.-water*, perfume of distilled l., alcohol, & ambergris; (vb) put l. among (linen). [f. AF *lavendre* f. med. L *lavendula, livendula*, perh. f. L LIVIDus]

lā·ver[1], n. Kinds of marine algae, esp. the edible species. [L]

lā·ver[2], n. (Bibl.) large brazen vessel for Jewish priests' ablutions; (archaic) washing or fountain basin, font. [f. OF *laveoir* LAVATORY]

laverock. See LARK[1].

lă·vish, a., & v.t. Giving or producing without stint, profuse, prodigal, (*of* money &c., *in* giving); very or over abundant; hence **la·vish**LY[2] adv., **la·vish**NESS n. (Vb) bestow or spend (money, effort, blood, admiration, &c.) profusely; hence **la·vish**MENT n. [f. obs. *lavish* profusion f. OF *lavache* deluge of rain]

law[1], n. Body of enacted or customary rules recognized by a community as binding, this personified, (*the l. forbids, allows*; often *the l. of the land*; *the l. of the Medes & Persians*, unalterable l., see *Dan.* vi. 12; *lay down the l.*, talk authoritatively, hector); one of these rules; their controlling influence, l.-abiding state of society, (often *l. & order*; *necessity knows no l.*, over-rides its sanctity; *be a l. unto oneself*, take one's own line, disregard convention), the ll. as a system (COURT *of l.*; so SON-*in-l.* &c.) or science (*learned in the l.*; *read l.*, study the ll.), jurisprudence; binding injunctions (*give the l. to*, impose one's will upon); (with defining word) one of the branches of the study of l., the ll. concerning specified department, (*commercial l.*; *the l. of evidence*; CANON, CIVIL, COMMON[1], MARTIAL, *l.*; *international l.*, *l. of nations*, regulating relations between States); the statute & common l. (opp. EQUITY); (in pred. use, of decisions, opinions, &c.; also *good, bad*, &c., *l.*) borne out, or not, by the relevant ll. (*it may be common sense, but it is not l.*); the legal profession (usu. *the l.*; *bred to the l.*); legal knowledge; judicial remedy, l.-courts as providing it, litigation, (*go to l.*; *have, take, the l. of* person; *take the l. into* one's *own hands*, redress one's wrong by force); *the L.-Courts*, (esp.) the ROYAL *Courts of Justice*; (also *l. of Moses*) precepts of Pentateuch, Mosaic dispensation; rule of action or procedure, esp. in an art, department of life, or game; (also *l. of nature* or *natural l.*) correct statement of invariable sequence between specified conditions & specified phenomenon (*ll. of motion*, three propositions formulated by Newton; *Gresham's l.*, that bad money drives out good; *Kepler's ll.*, three propositions on planetary motions; *Grimm's, Verner's, l.*, on consonant changes in Germanic languages); laws of nature, regularity in nature (*where they saw chance, we see l.*); *L. of Nature* (see also above) or *Reason*, principles of conduct recognized as pleasing to God or as intrinsically reasonable; (Sport) allowance, start, given to hunted animal or competitor in race, (whence gen.) time of grace, respite. *L.-abiding*(*ness*), obedient, obedience, to l.; *l. calf*, unstained used for binding l.-books; *l.*-COURT[1]; *l. French*, the Anglo-Norman terms used in l.-books & l.; *law giver*, one who makes (esp. code of) ll.; *l.-hand*, handwriting used in legal documents; *l. Latin*, barbarous Latin of early English statutes; *l.-lord*, member of House of Lords qualified to assist in its legal work; *l.-maker*, legislator; *l. merchant*, ll. regulating trade & commerce, differing in some respects from Common L.; *l.-officer*, legal functionary, esp. Attorney or Solicitor General; *l.-stationer*, selling stationery needed by lawyers & taking in documents to be engrossed; *lawsuit*, prosecution of claim in l.-court; *l.-term*, word or expression used in l., also period appointed for sitting of l.-courts; *l.-writer*, writer on l., also engrosser of legal documents. [OE *lagu* f. ON, orig. sense *thing laid*, cogn. w. LAY[3]]

law[2], **laws**, int. (vulg.) expressing astonishment. [var. of LO, or earlier *la*, or *lor'* for *Lord*]

law·ful, a. Permitted, appointed, qualified, or recognized, by law, not illegal or (of child) illegitimate. Hence **law·ful**LY[2] adv., **law·ful**NESS n. [-FUL]

lawk(s), int. (vulg.) expressing astonishment; *lawk-a-mussy* (vulg.), = Lord have mercy. [for ALACK or *Lord*]

law·less, a. (Of country &c.) where law is non-existent or inoperative; regardless of, disobedient to, uncontrolled by, law, unbridled, licentious. Hence **law·less**NESS n. [-LESS]

lawn[1], n. Kind of fine linen used esp. for bishop's sleeves; *l. sieve*, fine sieve of l. or silk. Hence **law·n**Y[2] a. [prob. f. *Laon* in France]

lawn[2], n. Glade (archaic); (extent of) grass-covered land; close-mown turf-covered piece of pleasure-ground or garden, whence **law·n**Y[2] a.; *l.-mower*, machine with revolving spiral knives for mowing ll.; *l.-sprinkler*, machine with revolving pipe-end for watering ll.; *l. tennis*, modification of tennis played on l., asphalt, &c. [earlier *laund* f. OF *launde* f. OCelt. (W *llan*), cogn. w. LAND[1]]

law·yer, n. Member of legal profession, esp. attorney, solicitor; person versed in law (*good, no*, &c., *l.*); *Penang l.*, walking-stick of Penang palm (perh. f. native tree name). [-YER]

lax[1], a. Loose, relaxed, not compact, porous, (rare); negligent, careless, not strict, vague. Hence or cogn. **la·x**ITY n., **la·x**LY[2] adv. [f. L *laxus* cogn. w. *languēre* LANGUISH]

lax[2], n. Swedish or Norwegian salmon. [OE *leax* salmon, cf. Da., Swed., &c., *lax*; now only as an alien word]

la·xative, a. & n. (Medicine) tending to loosen the bowels. [F (*-if, -ive*) f. L *laxativus* (*laxare*, see prec., -ATIVE)]

lay[1], n. Short lyric or narrative poem meant to be sung; (loosely) song, poem, song of birds. [f. OF *lai* perh. f. Teut. (OHG *leich* melody); not cogn. w. G *lied*]

lay[2], a. Non-clerical, not in orders; of, done by, layman or laity; non-professional, not expert, (esp. w. ref. to law or medicine); (Cards) other than trump (*l. suit, card*); *l. brother, sister*, person who has taken habit & vows of religious order but is employed in manual labour & excused other duties; *l. clerk*, singing man in cathedral or collegiate church, parish clerk; *l. communion*, membership of church as layman, also communicating of laity in eucharist; *l. deacon*, man in deacon's orders but also following secular employment; *l. lord*, peer who is not LAW[1]-*lord*; *layman*, one of the laity, non-expert in regard to some profession, art, or science (esp. law or medicine); *l. reader*, layman licensed to conduct religious services. [f. F *lai* f. eccl. L f. Gk *laikos* LAIC]

lay[3], v.t. & i. (laid), & n. Prostrate (*l. low*, bring down, humble); (of wind or rain) beat down (crops); cause (sea, wind, dust, misgivings, ghost) to subside. Deposit; place in recumbent posture (*l. to sleep* or *rest*, lit., & fig. =bury; *l.* one's *bones*, be buried *in* specified place); (of hen) produce (egg, or abs.); put down (amount, one's head or life, &c.) as wager, stake, (abs.) announce readiness to bet (*that* —). Place, set, apply, (*l. to* HEART; *l. heads together*, confer; *laid a spark to the train*; *l. hounds on scent*; *l. hold on* or *of*, seize, grasp, & *fig.* make capital *of* opponent's weak point &c.; *l.* one's *hopes on*; *l. great store upon*, value highly; *l. snare, trap, ambush*; *l.* WAIT²; *l. siege to*, besiege, importune); locate (scene; *scene of tale is laid in London*); put (limb &c.) in certain position (*horse laid his ears back*; *l. hands on*, seize, appropriate, also do violence to, esp. one*self* =commit suicide, also find, as *cannot l. my hands upon it*, also confirm or ordain by imposition of hands); aim (cannon); (with compl.) put into specified state (*l. land fallow, under water*; *l.* person *under obligation*, oblige him, *under necessity*, compel him, *under contribution*, make him contribute; *l. bare*, denude, reveal; *l. waste*, ravage; *l. open*, reveal, explain, also break skin of; *l. fast, by the heels*, confine or imprison; *l.* ABOARD). Present, put forward, (esp. *claim to* something; *l. an information*, bring indictment in legal form), place (facts, question) for consideration *before* person; (Parl.) *Foreign Secretary* &c. *will l. papers* (i.e. on the table, to give information to the H. of Commons); (of suitor) fix (damages) *at* certain sum; (archaic) impute (fault) *to* person or (mod.) *to* his *charge*, *at* or *to* his *door*; represent (evil) as consequent *on* some cause. Impose (penalty, command, obligation, burden, tax), cast (blame), (*up*)*on* (*l. stress, weight, emphasis, on*, emphasize, treat as important); bring (stick &c.) down *on* (also *l. blows* or *it on* adv.; & abs. *l. into* slang, belabour, *l. about* one, *hit* out on all sides). Dispose, arrange, esp. horizontally (foundation, floor, bricks, submarine cable; *l. table, cloth*, or *breakfast* &c., prepare table for meal; *l. the fire*, put fuel ready for lighting); make (strand, rope) by twisting yarn or strands; fix outlines of, devise (plan, plot; *l.* one's ACCOUNT²); put (colour &c.) on a surface in layers; cover, coat, strew, (surface) *with* carpet, metal, straw, &c.; *laid paper* (having ribbed surface owing to wires used in making). (Vulg., also Naut.) =LIE². *L. aside* or *by*, put away, cease to use or practise or think of, abandon, save (money &c.) for future needs; *l. down*, put on the ground &c. (*l. d.* one's *arms*, surrender), relinquish (office, hopes), pay or wager (money), sacrifice (one's life), (begin to) construct (ship, railway), formulate (rule, principle, course; *l. d. the* LAW¹), set down (chart) &c.) on paper, convert (land) into pasture (*in, to, under, with*, grass, clover, &c.), store (wine) in cellar; *l. in*, provide oneself with stock of, (also, colloq.) shower blows; *l. on*, impose (tax, command, penalty), deal blows, inflict (blows), ply (lash &c.), apply coat of (paint &c.; *l. it on thick* or *with a trowel*, use obvious flattery), put (hounds) on scent, provide pipes &c. supplying (gas, water, electricity); *l. out*, spread, expose to view &c., prepare (body) for burial, (slang) kill, expend (money), (refl.) take pains *to* do, dispose (grounds, garden) according to a plan; *l. up*, store, put by, put (ship) out of commission, save (money, or abs.), (pass.) be confined to bed or house. (N.) line of business, job, pursuit, (slang); direction or amount of twist in rope-strands; way, position, or direction, in which something (esp. country) lies, lie; *l.-out*, disposing or arrangement of ground &c. [OE *lecgan*, cf. Du. *leggen*, G *legen*, & see LIE³]

lay⁴. See LIE³.

lay·er, n., & v.t. & i. In vbl senses; also: stratum, thickness of matter (esp. one of several) spread over surface; (Gardening) shoot fastened into earth to strike root while attached to parent plant (v.t., propagate thus); (pl.) patches of laid corn (v.i., of corn, be laid flat by weakness of growth); oyster-bed; *good, bad*, &c., *l.* (of hens); *ll.* & *backers*, persons betting against, on, individual horse &c.; *l.-stool*, root from which ll. are produced. Hence **lay·er**ED² a. [LAY³, -ER¹]

laye·tte, n. Clothes, toilet articles, & bedding, needed for newborn child. [F]

lay figure, n. Jointed wooden figure of human body used by artists for arranging drapery on &c.; unimportant person, nonentity; unreal character in novel &c. [*lay* f. obs. *layman* lay figure f. Du. *leeman* (*led* joint)]

lay·lock, n. (Dial. for) LILAC.

lay·stall, n. Refuse heap. [LAY³, STALL]

lă·zar, n. (archaic). Poor & diseased person, esp. leper; *l.-house*, =foll. [f. med. L *lazarus* f. proper name (*Luke* xvi. 20)]

lazare·t(to), n. Hospital (chiefly in foreign countries) for diseased poor, esp. lepers; building or ship for performing quarantine in; after part of ship's hold used for stores. [F (*-et*), f. It. *lazzaretto* (*lazzaro* LAZAR)]

Lă·zarus, n. Beggar, poor man, (esp. in contrasts, *L. & Dives* &c.). [see LAZAR]

laze, v.i. & t., & n., (colloq.). Be lazy; pass (time) *away* in laziness; (n.) lazy time. [back formation f. LAZY]

lă·zūlī, n. =LAPIS LAZULI.

la·zy, a., & v.i. & t. Averse to labour, indolent, slothful; appropriate to or inducing indolence; *l.-bed*, bed for potato-growing about 6 ft wide with trench on each side; *l.-bones*, l. person; *l. pinion*, serving as transmitter of motion between other pinions or wheels; *l.-tongs*, arrangement of zigzag levers for picking up

distant objects; hence **la·zɪʟʏ**[2] adv., **la·zɪɴᴇss** n. (Vb) = ʟᴀᴢᴇ. [earlier *laysy*, perh. f. ʟᴀʏ[2] + *-sy* as in *tipsy, tricksy*]

lazzaro·nĕ (lăts-), n. (pl. *-ni*, pr. -nē). Neapolitan street-lounger living by odd jobs & begging. [It. (ʟᴀᴢᴀʀ, -ᴏᴏɴ)]

'ld, abbr. of *would* (now rare, cf. 'ᴅ).

-le, -el, suf. (1) f. ME *-el, -le*, f. OE *-el, -ela*, -(*e*)*le* in nn., *-ol, -ul, -el*, in adjj.; after *ch*, soft *g, n, r, sh, th, v, -el* is retained, & after *m* the suf. becomes *-ble*. Nn. formed on n. stems have dim. sense (*bramble*), or that of tool, appliance, (*thimble, handle*); nn. formed on vb stems express agent (*beadle*), instrument (*bridle, girdle*), or less definite relations (*bundle*); adjj., formed on vb stems have the sense *apt or liable to the vbl action* (*brittle, nimble*). (2) f. ME *-el, -elle*, in nn. f. F *-el* f. L *-ellum* (*castle, mantle*) or L *-ale* (*cattle*); f. F *-aille* f. L *-alia* see -ᴀʟ (*battle*), or F *-eille* f. L *-icula* (*bottle*); f. L *-ulus, -ula, -ulum*, (*angle, calcycle*); *-el* in some mod. sci. wds on L anal. (*carpel*). (3) verbal, f. ME -(*e*)*len* f. OE *-lian* f. OTeut. *-ilôjan*, w. freq. or dim. sense (*nestle, twinkle, wrestle, crumple, dazzle*).

lea[1], n. (poet.). Tract of open ground, esp. grass land. [OE *lēah*, cf. OHG *lôh* grove]

lea[2], n. Measure of yarn (300, 200, 120, & 80 yds in different districts &c.). [perh. f. F *lier* f. L *ligare* to bind]

leach, v.t. Make (liquid) percolate through some material; subject (bark, ore) to action of percolating fluid; purge (soluble matter) *away* &c. by such means. [prob. f. OE *leccan* to water]

lead[1] (lĕd), n., & v.t. & i. Heavy easily fusible soft malleable base metal of dull pale bluish-grey colour (*red l.*, red oxide of l. used as pigment, minium; *white l.*, mixture of l. carbonate & hydrated l. oxide used as pigment, ceruse; = ʙʟᴀᴄᴋ[1]*-l.*, whence *l.* is used, w. pl., for the small stick of graphite in pencil or pencil-case; *ounce of l.*, bullet); lump of l. used in sounding water (*cast, heave, the l.*; *arm the l.*, fill hollow in it with tallow, to learn nature of bottom; *swing the l.*, nav. & mil. slang, malinger or scrimshank); (pl.) strips of l. used to cover roof, piece of (esp. horizontal) l.-covered roof, l. frames or cames holding glass of lattice or painted window; (Print.) metal strip for widening space between lines; *l. comb*, made of l. & used to darken hair; *l. pencil*, of graphite usu. enclosed in cedar; *l.-poisoning*, acute or chronic poisoning by taking of l. into system; *leadsman*, sailor who heaves the l.; *l.-work*, plumber's or glazier's work; *l.-works*, place where l.-ore is smelted; hence **lea·dʟᴇss** a. (Vb) cover, weight, frame, (panes) with l.; (Print.) separate lines of (printed matter) with ll.; (of gun-barrel) become foul with coating of l. [OE *lēad*, cf. Du. *lood*, G *lot*]

lead[2] (lēd), v.t. & i. (led). Force to go with one (*l. captive*, take away as prisoner); conduct, guide, esp. by going in front (of person, also of motive, circumstance, &c.; *curiosity, chance, led him to Rome*; *l.* one *a dance*, give him much trouble to secure his end; *l.* one *a life*, worry him constantly; *l. the way*, go first, take the l. in course lit. or fig.); (of commander) direct movements of; conduct (person) by the hand or contact, (animal) by halter &c., (*led horse*, spare horse led by groom &c.; *led captain*, hanger-on, toady, parasite; *l.* woman *to altar*, marry), guide by persuasion (*is easier led than driven*; *l. astray*, esp. tempt to sin &c.; *l. by the nose*, induce to do unconsciously all one wishes); guide actions or opinions of, bring by argument &c. *to* conclusion, induce *to* do (*l.* one *to suppose* &c., deceive him into thinking); (of road &c.) conduct (person, or usu. abs.) *to* place (*all roads l. to Rome*; also fig. = have as result, *this led to confusion*); make (rope, water, &c.) go through pulley, channel, &c.; pass, go through, spend, (life &c., esp. w. epithet as *l. a miserable existence, a double life*); have first place in (*l. the dance, van*), (abs.) go first (*l. off*, begin intr.), be first at some point in race; direct by example (*l. orchestra, band, chorus*, &c.), set (fashion), be official director or spokesman of (party, esp. in Houses of Parliament), act as leading counsel in (case, or usu. abs.); (Cards) play as first card, be first player, in trick (*lead up to*, play so as to elicit specified card), play one of (suit) when leading. *L. away*, (usu. in pass.) induce to follow unthinkingly; *l. off*, begin (dance, conversation, or abs.); *l. on*, entice into going further than was intended; *l. up to*, form preparation for, serve to introduce, direct conversation towards, (subject). Hence **lea·dᴀʙʟᴇ** a. [com.-Teut.; OE *lǣdan*, cf. Du. *leiden*, G *leiten*, cogn. w. ʟᴏᴀᴅ, ʟᴏᴅᴇ]

lead[3], n. Direction given by going in front, example, (*follow the l. of*; *give* one *a l.*, encourage him by doing thing, esp. leaping fence in hunting, first); leading place, leadership, (*take the l.*); artificial water-course, esp. leading to mill; (Electr.) conductor conveying current from source to place of use; channel in ice-field; string &c. for leading dog; (Cards) act or right of playing first (*return l.*, l. from suit already led by partner); (Theatr.) (player of) chief part; *l.-off*, commencement. [f. prec.]

leaden (lĕ·dn), a. (As) of lead (*sleep's l. sceptre*, stupefying power; *l. sword*, useless); heavy, slow, burdensome, (*l. limbs*); inert, deadening, (*l. rule*); lead-coloured. [-ᴇɴ[1]]

Lea·denha·ll (lĕd-), n. (Used for) L. meat and poultry market in London.

lea·der, n. In vbl senses of LEAD² (FOLLOW *my l.*); also or esp.: *l. of House of Commons,* member of Government with official initiative in business; counsel who leads in case, also K.C., also senior counsel of circuit; front horse in team or tandem (opp. WHEELER); shoot growing at apex of stem or principal branch; tendon; = LEADING² *article*; (Print.) line of dots or dashes to guide eye. Hence **lea·der**LESS a., **lea·der**SHIP(1, 3) n. [-ER¹]

leadere·tte, n. Short editorial paragraph in same type as leading article. [prec., -ETTE]

lea·ding¹, n. In vbl senses; esp.: *men of light & l.,* of deserved influence; *l.-business,* parts usu. taken by l. actor; *l.-rein,* to lead horse with; *l.-staff,* attached to ring in bull's nose; *l.-strings,* with which children were formerly taught to walk (*in l.-s.,* in state of pupilage). [-ING¹]

lea·ding², a. In vbl senses; *l. article,* large-type editorial expression of opinion at full length in newspaper, (Commerc). article of trade sold at low price to attract custom for other things; *l. case,* (Law), serving as precedent for deciding others; *l. lady, man,* taking chief part in play; *l. motive,* transl. of LEITMOTIV; *l. question,* prompting desired answer. [-ING²]

leaf¹, n. (pl. *-ves*), & v.i. Expanded organ (usu. green) of plant springing from side of stem or branch or direct from root; (pop.) petal (esp. *rose-l.*); foliage (*fall of the l.,* autumn; *in l.,* with ll. out), leaves of tobacco or tea; single thickness of folded paper, esp. (=2 pages) in book (*take l. out of* person's BOOK¹; *turn over new l.,* mend one's ways); very thin sheet of metal, esp. gold or silver, or horn, marble, talc, &c.; hinged part or flap of door, shutter, table (also used of slab inserted in expansible table), bridge (= bascule), or rifle-sight; tooth of pinion; *l. brass,* brass foil; *l.-mould* (mixed with decaying ll.); hence **lea·f**AGE(1) n., **(-)leaf**ED², **lea·f**LESS, aa., **lea·fless**NESS n., **lea·f**Y² a., **lea·fi**NESS n. (Vb) put forth ll. [OE *léaf,* cf. Du. *loof,* G *laub*]

leaf², n. (nav. & mil. slang). Leave of absence, furlough. [=LEAVE¹]

lea·flet, n. (Bot.) one division of compound leaf; young leaf; small leaf of paper, or sheet folded but not stitched, with printed matter, esp. for gratuitous distribution. [-LET]

league¹ (lēg), n. Varying measure of road-distance, usu. about three miles. [f. LL *leuga* perh. f. Gaulish]

league² (lēg), n., & v.t. & i. Compact for mutual protection & assistance or prosecution of common interests, parties (whether States or individuals) to such compact, (*Solemn L. & COVENANT*; PRIMROSE *l.*; *in l. with,* allied with); *L. football* (in which clubs forming a l. play each other for championship); *L. of Nations* (established by the treaty of peace 1919 for prevention of war); (vb) join (t. & i.) in l. (esp. in p.p. *leagued together* or *with*). [f. F *ligue* f. It. *liga, lega,* (L *ligare* bind)]

leaguer¹ (lē·ger), n. (archaic). (Camp, esp. for purpose of) siege. [f. Du. *leger,* see LAIR]

lea·guer², n. Member of LEAGUE¹. [-ER¹]

leak, n., & v.i. Hole caused by injury, wear, &c., through which liquid makes way into or out of vessel that is immersed in or contains it (*spring a l.,* be found to have one). (Vb) let liquid, (of liquid) pass, out or in through l.; (of secrets &c.) transpire, come *out* gradually; hence **lea·k**AGE(3) n., what leaks out or in, transpiring of secrets, unexplained disappearance of money pointing to embezzlement &c. [vb prob. f. ON *leka* drip; relation of n. & vb doubtful]

lea·ky, a. Having leak(s); incontinent of urine; given to letting out secrets. Hence **lea·ki**NESS n. [-Y²]

leal (lēl), a. (Sc. & literary). Loyal, honest, (LAND¹ *of the l.*). [f. OF *leel* (cf. LOYAL) f. L *legalis* lawful (*lex legis* law, -AL)]

lean¹, a. & n. (Of persons) thin, not plump; meagre, of poor quality, innutritious, (*l. crops, diet*; *l. years,* of scarcity); unremunerative; (of meat) consisting chiefly of muscular tissue, not of fat (n., muscular part of meat). Hence **lea·n**NESS n. [OE *hlǽne* etym. dub.

lean², v.i. & t. (past & p.p. *leaned,* or *leant* pr. lĕnt), & n. Incline one's body against something for support, support oneself (of thing, be supported in sloping position) *against* or *on* (Mil., *l. upon,* have as protection on flank); rely or depend (*up*)*on*; incline body *back, forward, over, towards,* &c.; stand obliquely, out of the perpendicular; have tendency *to* mercy &c., be partial *to* cause, opinion, or person, whence **lea·n**ING¹(1) n.; place (thing) in leaning position; *l.-to,* building with rafters resting against side of another, pent-house; (n.) inclination, slope, (*has a decided l. to the right*). [OE *hleonian, hlinian,* cf. Du. *leunen,* G *lehnen,* cogn. w. LADDER, & w. CLIMAX & Gk *klinō* bend, & L *inclinare*]

leap¹, v.i. & t. (past & p.p. *leapt* pr. lĕpt, or *leaped*). =JUMP (still in poet., literary, & dignified use; LOOK¹ *before you l.*); *l.-frog,* (n.) game in which players vault with parted legs over others bending down, (vb) perform such vault (*over*). Hence **lea·p**ER¹ n. [com.-Teut.; OE *hléapan,* cf. Du. *loopen,* G *laufen* run]

leap², n. Jump (by which wd it is now replaced in ordinary use; *l. in the dark,* hazardous attempt of doubtful issue; *by ll. & bounds,* with startlingly rapid progress); thing to be jumped; *l.-day,* 29th Feb.; *l.-year,* year with intercalary day (perh. because fixed festivals after February in leap-year fall two weekdays, instead of as usual one, later than in the preceding year), *l.-year proposal* (of woman to man, allowable only in l.-year). [OE *hlýp* f. root of prec.]

learn (lern), v.t. & i. (past & p.p. *learnt, learned* pr. -nd). Get knowledge of (subject) or skill in (art &c.) by study, experience, or being taught (*from, of*); commit to memory (esp. *l. by heart* or *rote*); become aware *that, how*, &c. (*I am* or *have yet to l.*, do not know, usu. with implication of disbelief), be informed of, ascertain; receive instruction; (archaic, joc., or vulg.) teach. Hence **lear·n**ABLE a., **lear·n**ER[1] n. [OE *leornian*, cf. G *lernen*]

lear·nĕd, a. Deeply read, erudite; showing profound knowledge; (in conventionally courteous mention of lawyer in House of Commons, lawcourts, &c.) l. in the law (esp. *my l. friend* or *brother*); (of language, profession, &c.) pursued or studied by, (of words in a language) introduced by, l. men. Hence **lear·ned**LY[2] adv. [f. prec. in obs. sense (still in vulg. use) *teach*, + -ED[1]]

lear·ning, n. In vbl senses; esp. (possession of) knowledge got by study, esp. of language or literary or historical science (*the new l.*, studies, esp. of Greek, introduced into England in 16th c., renaissance). [-ING[1]]

lease[1], n., & v.t. Contract by which lessor, usu. in consideration of rent, conveys land or tenement to lessee for specified time (*put out to l.*; *by* or *on l.*; *a new l. of life*, prospect of living due to recovered health or removal of anxiety &c.); *leasehold(er)*, (person having) tenure, real property held, by l.; (vb) grant or take l. of. [f. AF *les(ser)*, cf. F *laisser*, f. L *laxare* (LAX) to loose]

lease[2], n. Crossing of warp-threads in loom; =foll. (weaving). [prob. var. of foll.]

leash, n., & v.t. Thong in which hounds or coursing-dogs are held (*hold in l.*, control); set of three hounds, hares, &c.; (Weaving) cord with eye to receive warp-thread extending between parallel laths of loom-heddle; (vb) connect, hold in, with l. [f. OF *lesse* perh. f. fem. of L LAX*us*]

lea·sing (-z-), n. (bibl.). Lying, lie. [OE *léasung* (*léasian* f. *léas* false, destitute of, =-LESS)]

least, a., n., & adv. Smallest, slightest, (*the l.*, esp. after neg., any however small; *l. common* MULTIPLE; *line of l.* RESISTANCE). (N.) l. amount (*to say the l. of it*, to put the case moderately; *l. said soonest mended*, discussion will only make things worse); *at l.*, at all events, even if a wider statement is disputable, (also *at the l.*) at the lowest computation; (*in*) *the l.*, in the smallest degree, at all. (Adv.) in the l. degree. [OE *lǣst* superl. of LESS]

lea·stways (vulg.), **lea·stwise** (rare), advv. Or at least, or rather. [-WAYS, -WISE]

leat, n. Open water-course conducting water to mill &c. [OE *-gelǣt* (Y- + root of LET[2])]

lea·ther (lĕdh-), n., & v.t. Skin prepared for use by tanning or similar process (*patent l.*, with fine black varnished surface; *American l.*, kind of oilcloth; *l. & prunella*, a difference in clothes only, see Pope, *Essay*, iv. 304; *nothing like l.*, one's own goods will serve all purposes; vb, cover or arm with l.); article, or part of one, made of l., piece of l. for polishing, thong (esp. *stirrup-l.*; vb, beat with strap, whence **lea·ther**ING[1](1) n.), (slang) cricket-ball (*l.-hunting*, fielding) or football, (pl.) leggings or breeches; (slang) one's skin (*lose l.*, suffer abrasion); *l.-back*, kind of turtle; *l.-head*, blockhead; *l.-jacket*, kinds of fish, crane-fly grub; *l.-neck*, (sailor's name, w. ref. to l. stock formerly worn, for) soldier; *l.-wood*, kinds of tough-barked tree. Hence **leather**E·TTE(2) n., **lea·thern** (-EN[5]), **lea·ther**Y[2] (esp. of meat &c., tough), aa. [OE *lether*, cf. Du. & G *leder*]

lea·theroid, n. Cotton paper chemically treated & resembling raw hide. [-OID]

leave[1], n. Permission (*to* do; *by your l.*, apology, often iron., for taking liberty, making unwelcome statement, &c., esp. as porter's formula for asking person to make way for him & his load; *without a 'with your l.' or 'by your l.'* colloq., without even asking l.); (in army, navy, offices, schools) *l.* (*of absence*), permission to be absent from duty, period for which this lasts, (*on l.*, absent thus; *l.-breaker*, sailor remaining away beyond the period; TICKET *of l.*); *take* (one's) *l.* (*of*), bid farewell (to; *t.l.o.* one's *senses*, go mad), whence **lea·ve-taking**[1](1) n.; FRENCH *l.* [OE *léaf* prob. =orig. pleasure or approval, cogn. w. LOVE, LIEF]

leave[2], v.t. (left), & n. Cause to or let remain, depart without taking, (*leaves a wife & three sons*; *six from seven leaves one*; *leaves much* &c. *to be desired*, is unsatisfactory; *has left a soreness behind*), bequeath; abstain from consuming or dealing with, (pass.) remain over; let remain in specified state (*this leaves me cool*, does not excite me; *l. it at that* colloq., abstain from comment or further action; *be well* &c. *left*, provided for by legacy &c.; *l. undone, unsaid*, &c.); commit, refer, *to* another agent &c. than oneself (*l. it to you, sir*, fix my pay yourself; *nothing was left to accident*; *l. him to himself*, do not try to control); allow (person, thing) *to* do something without interference; deposit, entrust, (thing, instructions, message), station (person), to be seen to, delivered, &c., or to discharge function, in one's absence (*l. card on* person, as equivalent of formal call); quit, go away from, (*left him quite well an hour ago*; *l. this* or *here*; *l. the track, room*), (abs.) depart (*we l. tomorrow*, often *for* destination); pass (object) so as to put it in specified relative direction (*l. the church on the left*); cease to reside at (place), belong to (school, society), or serve (employer), (also abs., as *I am leaving at Christmas*); abandon, forsake (esp. *l. in the lurch*; *get left* colloq., be deserted or worsted). *L. alone*, not interfere with; *l. behind*, go away without, l. as consequence or trace, pass; *l. go* (vulg.), relax one's hold; *l. hold of*, cease holding; *l. off*, cease to wear, discontinue (habit, *doing, work*), come to or make an end; *l. out*, omit; *l. over*, let stand over for the time. (N., billiards) position in which player leaves the balls. Hence (usu. pl.) **lea·**VING[1](2) n. [OE *lǽfan*, cf. MHG *leiben*; cogn. w. obs. *lave* remainder, & w. G *bleiben* (MHG *belîben*) remain]

(-)leaved, a. Having leaves (rare); having — leaves (*one-l. table*; *red-l.*). [f. LEAF + -ED[2]]

leaven (lĕ·vn), n., & v.t. Substance added to dough to produce fermentation, esp. fermenting dough reserved for purpose; (fig.) spreading & transforming influence (*Matt.* xiii. 33), tinge or admixture *of* some quality; *the old l.*, traces of unregenerate state (1 *Cor.* v. 6, 7). (Vb) ferment (dough) with l.; permeate & transform, modify *with* tempering element. [f. F *levain* f. L *levamen* (*levare* lift, -MEN)]

leaves. See LEAF.

lĕ·cher (-tsh-), n. (archaic). Fornicator, debauchee. So **le·cher**OUS a., **le·cherous**LY[2] adv., **le·ch**ERY(4) n. [f. OF *lecheor* (*lechier* live in debauchery or gluttony f. OHG *leccôn* LICK)]

le·ctern, n. Reading or singing desk in church, esp. that for the lessons. [ME & OF *lettrun* f. LL *lectrum* (*legere lect-* read)]

le·ctionary, n. Book containing, list of, portions of Scripture appointed to be read at divine service. [f. eccl. L *lectionarium* (*lectio* reading, see prec., -ARY[1])]

le·cture (-tsh*e*r), n., & v.i. & t. Discourse before audience or class on given subject, usu. by way of instruction; admonition, reproof, (*read* one *a l.*, reprove him). (Vb) deliver l. or ll. (*on* subject); instruct or entertain (class &c.) by l.; admonish, reprimand; hence **le·ctur**ER[1] n. [vb f. n., f. L *lectura* (*legere lect-* read, -URE)]

le·ctureship, n. Office of lecturer. [prec. + -SHIP (unusual formation)]

led. See LEAD[2].

ledge, n. Narrow horizontal surface projecting from wall &c.; shelf-like projection on side of rock or mountain; ridge of rocks, esp. below water; (Mining) stratum of metal-bearing rock. Hence **le·dg**Y[2], **ledg**ED[2], aa. [perh. f. ME *legge* LAY[3]]

le·dger (-j-), n. & a. Principal book of the set used for recording trade transactions, containing debtor-&-creditor accounts; horizontal timber in scaffolding, parallel to face of building; flat grave-stone; (also *l.-bait*) bait fixed in one place (so *l.-hook, -line*); *l.-blade*, stationary blade in cloth-shearing machine acting with revolving spiral blade; (adj.; Mus.) *l. line*, short line added above or below stave for outside notes (perh. attrib. use of n. in scaffolding sense). [perh. f. LIE[3], LAY[3], + -ER[1] in imit. of Du. *ligger, legger*]

lee, n. Shelter given by neighbouring object (*under the l. of*); (also *l. side*) sheltered side, side away from wind, (opp. *windward, weather side*; often attrib., *lee* or *lee-*, = belonging to ship's l. side, or to leeward of other object, whence **lee·**MOST a.); *l.-board*, plank frame fixed to side of flat-bottomed vessel & let down into water to diminish l.-way; *l. shore*, shore to leeward of ship; *lee·way*, lateral drift of ship to leeward of course (*make up l.-w.* fig., struggle out of bad position, often *much l.-w. to make up*). [OE *hléo*, cogn. w. OFris. *hli*, ON *hlý* shelter, warmth]

leech[1], n. (archaic, poet., or joc.). Physician, healer; *leechcraft*, art of healing. [OE *lǽce*, cf. OHG *lâhhi*]

leech[2], n. Kinds of aquatic bloodsucking worm, esp. that used medicinally for bleeding (*stick like a l.*, persistently); person who sucks profit out of others. [OE *lǽce*, cf. MDu. *lake*]

leech[3], n. Perpendicular or sloping side of sail. [cf. Du. *lijk*, G *liek*]

leek, n. Culinary herb like onion, but with cylindrical bulb, this as Welsh national emblem (cf. ROSE; *eat the l.*, pocket affront, see Shak. *Hen. V*, v. i.) [OE *léac*, cf. Du. *look*, G *lauch*]

leer[1], v.i., & n. Glance (esp. sideways) with sly, lascivious, or malign expression. Hence **leer·ing**LY[2] adv. [n. f. vb, perh. f. obs. *leer* cheek (= look over one's cheek), cf. MDu. *liere*]

leer[2], n. Annealing-furnace for glass. [?]

leer·y, a. (slang). Knowing, sly. [perh. f. LEER[1] n. + -Y[2]]

lees, n. pl. Sediment of wine &c. (*drink, drain, to the l.*, lit. & fig.); basest part, refuse. [earlier *lee* sing. also, f. F *lie* f. Gaulish L *lia*]

leet, n. (hist.). Yearly or half-yearly court of record (also *court l.*) holdable by lords of certain manors; its jurisdiction, its district. [perh. f. OE *lǽth lathe*[1]]

leew·ard (lū)-, a., n., & adv. On, towards, the sheltered side (opp. *windward*); (n.) this direction (*to l., on the l. of*). Hence **leew·ard**MOST a. [LEE + -WARD]

leew·ardly, a. (Of ship) apt to fall to leeward (opp *weatherly*). [-LY[1]]

left[1], a., adv., & n. Belonging to the side of a person's body that is westward when he faces N. or that has normally the less used hand, having corresponding relation to front of any object (*l. wing* or *flank* of army; *l. bank* of river, assuming it to face the way it flows); situated nearer to or more directly in front of observer's or speaker's l. hand than his right; *l. hand*, lit., & = region or direction nearer the l. hand, (*on the l. h. of*, in that direction relatively to; *marry with the l. h.*, morganatically; *l.-h. blow*, delivered with it; *l.-h. man*, standing next one on l.; *l.-h. rope*, twisted counter-clockwise); *over the l.* (*shoulder* now rare), slang phr. denoting that what is said is to be interpreted by contraries; *l. turn*, that brings one's front to face as one's l. side did before; hence **le·ft**MOST a., **le·ft**WARD a. & adv., **le·ft**WARDS adv. (Adv.) on or to the l. side. (N.) l. hand (lit. in pugilism, as *got in one with his l.*; *cannon to l. of them*); l. wing of army; (Pol., orig. of continental legislatures) more democratic section of legislative chamber seated on president's l., advanced or innovating section of philosophical school, religious sect, &c. [OE, orig. sense *weak, worthless*, cf. EFris. *luf*]

left[2]. See LEAVE[2].

left-handed, a. Having left hand more serviceable than right, using it by preference; awkward, clumsy; ambiguous, double-edged, of doubtful sincerity or validity, (esp. *l. compliment*; also sometimes of marriage = fictitious, cf. correct sense below); (archaic) ill-omened, sinister; (of marriage) morganatic (from German custom by which bridegroom gave left hand in such marriages); adapted for use of, (of blow) delivered with, left hand. Hence **left-ha·nded**LY[2] adv., **left-ha·nded**NESS n. [-ED[2]]

left-ha·nder, n. Left-handed person or blow. [-ER[1]]

leg, n., & v.i. Organ of support & locomotion in animal, esp. human, body, part of this from hip to ankle, (*all ll.*, overgrown; BOOT[2] *is on other l.*; *pull* one's *l.* colloq., befool him; *give* one *a l. up*, help him to mount or get over obstacle material or other; BONE *in* one's *l.*; *have the ll. of*, be able to go faster than; *put* BEST[1] *l. foremost*; *shake a l.*, dance; *stretch* one's *ll.*, take walking exercise; *take to* one's *ll.*, run away; *on* one's *ll.*, also joc. *hind ll.*, standing esp. to make speech, also well enough to go about, also in prosperous or established state, esp. *set* one *on* his *ll.*; *stand on* ones' *own ll.*, be self-reliant or independent; FALL[1] *on* one's *ll.*; *has not a l. to stand on*, cannot support thesis by any facts or sound reasons; *on* one's *last ll.*, near death or end; *walk* &c. one *off* his *ll.*, tire him out in walking &c.; *feel, find*, one's *ll.*, get power of standing or walking; *keep* one's *ll.*, not fall; *l. before wicket*, abbr. *l.b.w.*, illegal stopping of cricket ball by batsman's l.; SEA-*ll.*); l. of animal as food (*l. of mutton*; *l.-of-m. sail, sleeve*, so shaped); obeisance made by drawing back one l. (usu. *make a l.*; archaic); swindler (for BLACK[1]-*l.*); (Cricket) part of field to right rear of batsman in position (*l. stump*, stump nearest this; *long, short, square, l.*, fielders variously posted in it; *hit to l.*); artificial l. (*cork, wooden*, &c., *l.*); part of garment covering l.; support, pole, prop, of machine &c.; support of chair, table, bed, &c.; one branch of forked object; side of triangle other than base; (Naut.) run made on single tack (usu. *long, short, l.*); *give l.-bail*, decamp; *l.*-BYE; *l.-guard*, pad for ankle, shin, & knee, in cricket; *l.-rest*, support for seated invalid's l. Hence (-)**legged**[2], **le·g**LESS, aa. (Vb) *l. it*, walk or run hard; propel (boat) through canal-tunnel by pushing with ll. against tunnel sides, whence **le·gg**ER[1] n. [f. ON *leggr* limb, perh. cogn. w. Gk *laktizō* kick, L *lacertus* arm]

lĕ·gacy, n. Sum of money or article given by will; material or immaterial thing handed down by predecessor; *l.-hunter*, person who pays court to another to secure l. [f. OF *legacie* legateship (LEGATE, -ACY)]

lē·gal, a. Of, based on, falling within province of, occupied with, law; required or appointed by law (*l. tender*, money that creditor is bound to accept in payment); recognized by law as distinguished from equity; lawful, whence **le·gal**IZE(3) v.t., **legaliz**A·TION n.; (Theol.) of the Mosaic law, of salvation by works not faith. Hence **le·gal**LY[2] adv. [f. L *legalis* (*lex legis* law, -AL) cf. LEAL, LOYAL]

le·galism, n. (Theol.) preference of the Law to the Gospel, doctrine of justification by works; exaltation of law or formula, red tape. So **le·gal**IST(2) n. [-ISM]

legă·lity, n. Legalism; lawfulness. [f. F *légalité* (LEGAL, -ITY)]

lĕ·gate[1] (-*at*), n. Ecclesiastic deputed to represent Pope (*l. ā lă·tĕrĕ*, one of highest class & full powers), whence **le·gat**INE[1] (-ĭn) a.; (archaic) ambassador, delegate. Hence **le·gate**SHIP n. [f. OF *legat* f. L *legatus* p.p. of *legare* commission]

lega·te[2], v.t. Bequeath (often *give & l.*). So **lega·tor**[2] n. [f. L *legare* (prec.), -ATE[3]]

legatee·, n. Recipient of legacy. [prec., -EE]

lega·tion, n. Sending of legate or deputy; body of deputies, diplomatic minister & his suite (esp. when he does not rank as ambassador), his official residence; legateship. [f. L *legatio* (LEGATE[2], -ION)]

lega·to (-ah-), mus. direction. Smoothly, without breaks. [It., = bound (L *ligare* bind)]

lĕ·gend, n. Collection of lives of saints or similar stories, esp. *the* (*Golden*) *L.*, particular 13th-c. collection (hist.); traditional story popularly regarded as historical, myth, such literature or tradition (so *in l.*), whence **le·gend**ARY[1] a.; inscription or motto, esp. on coin or medal. Hence **le·gend**RY(5) n. [f. F *légende* f. med. L *legenda* what is read (L *legere* read)]

lĕ·gerdĕmai·n, n. Sleight of hand, conjuring tricks, juggling; trickery, sophistry. [f. F *léger de main* light of hand]

le·gging, n. (usu. pl.). Outer covering of leather &c. for leg usu. up to knee. [-ING[1]]

le·ggy, a. Lanky-legged (esp. of boy, colt, puppy). Hence **le·ggi**NESS n. [-Y[2]]

leghorn (lĭgor·n), n. Kind of straw plaiting for hats &c.; kind of domestic fowl. [imported f. *L.* (now *Livorno*) in Italy]

lĕ·gible, a. (Of handwriting or print) clear, easily read. Hence **legi**BI·LITY n., **le·gib**LY[2] adv. [f. LL *legibilis* (*legere* read, -IBLE)]

lē·gion (-jn), n. Division of 3,000–6,000 men, including complement of cavalry, in ancient Roman army; *British L.*, national association of ex-service men formed 1921 & incorporated 1925 by Royal Charter; *foreign l.*, body of foreign volunteers in modern, esp. French, army; vast host, multitude, or number (*their name is L.*, they are numberless, see *Mark* v. 9); *L. of Honour*, French order of distinction. [OF, f. L *legionem* nom. *-o* (*legere* choose)]

le·gionary, a. & n. (Soldier) of (a) legion(s). [f. L *legionarius* (prec., -ARY[1])]

le·gioned, a. (poet.). In legions. [-ED[1]]

lĕgisla·tion, n. (Enacting of) laws. Hence **le·gisl**ATIVE a., **le·gislative**LY[2] adv. [f. LL *legislatio* (*lex legis* law, *latio* proposing f. *lat-* part. st. of *ferre* bring, -ION)]

le·gislator, n. Lawgiver, member of legislative body. Hence **le·gislate** (by back formation) v.i., **legislator·**IAL a. (rare), **le·gislatr**ESS[1] n. [L (as prec., -OR[2])]

le·gislāture (-tsh*e*r), n. Legislative body of a State. [after prec., -URE]

lē·gist, n. Person versed in law. [f. F *légiste* f. med. L *legista* (L *lex legis* law, -IST)]

legi·timate[1] (-*a*t), a. Born in lawful wedlock (also said of parent, birth, descent, &c.); lawful, proper, regular, conforming to standard type (*the l. drama*, body of plays, Shaksperian or other, of recognized merit, also ellipt., slang, *the l.*); (of sovereign's title) based on strict hereditary right; logically admissible. Hence **legi·tim**ACY n., **legi·timate**LY[2] adv., **legi·timat**IZE(3) v.t. [as foll., -ATE[2]]

legi·timāte[2], v.t. Make l. by decree, enactment, or proof; justify, serve as justification for. Hence **legitim**A·TION n. [f. med. L *legitimare* (L *legitimus* lawful f. *lex legis* law), -ATE[3]]

legi·timism, n. Adherence to sovereign or pretender whose claim is based on direct descent (esp. in Spanish & French politics). So **legi·tim**IST(2) n. & a. [f. F *légitimisme* (*légitime* f. L see prec., -ISM)]

legi·timize, v.t. Legitimatize (see LEGITIMATE[1]). Hence **legitimiz**A·TION n. [as LEGITIMATE[2], -IZE]

lē·gum, n. genit. pl. (*abbr.* LL.). Of laws (in degrees, see L). [L (*lex* law)]

lĕ·gume, legū·men, n. Fruit, edible part, pod, of leguminous plant; vegetable used for food. [F (*légume*), f. L (*-en*) f. *legere* pick]

legu·minous, a. Of, like, of the botanical order of, pulse. [LEGUMEN *-inis*, -OUS]

Leibni·tzian (līb-), a. & n. (Follower) of G. W. Leibnitz (d. 1716) or his philosophy. [-IAN]

lei·ster (lēs-), n., & v.t. Pronged salmon-spear; (vb) spear with this. [f. ON *ljóstr* (*ljósta* to strike)]

leisure (lĕ·zh*e*r), n. (Opportunity *to* do, *for*, afforded by) free time, time at one's own disposal (*wait* &c. one's *l.*, wait till he has l.; *at l.*, not occupied, also deliberately, without hurry; *at* one's *l.*, when one has time). Hence **lei·sur**ED[2], **lei·sure**LESS, aa. [f. OF *leisir* n. use of infin. f. L *licēre* be allowed; see -URE]

lei·surely, a. & adv. Having, acting or done at, leisure, deliberate; hence **lei·sureli**NESS n.; (adv.) deliberately, without haste. [-LY[1,2]]

leit-motiv, -if (lī·tmōtē·f), n. (mus.). Theme associated throughout piece with some person, situation, or sentiment. [G (LEAD[2], MOTIVE)]

lĕ·man, n. (archaic). Lover, sweetheart; unlawful lover or (usu., in mod. archaistic use) mistress. [ME *leofmon* (LIEF, MAN)]

lē·mma, n. (pl. *-ta*). Assumed or demonstrated proposition used in argument or proof; argument or subject of literary composition, dictionary article, annotation, &c., prefixed as heading; motto appended to picture &c. [Gk (*-ē-*) f. *lambanō* take, see -M]

le·mming, n. Small arctic rodent resembling field-mouse. [Norw.]

lĕ·mon[1], n. Pale-yellow oval acid-juiced fruit used for flavouring & for making the beverage **lemon**A·DE(1) n.; SALT *of l.*, an oxalate used in removing ink-stains; tree bearing it; pale-yellow colour; *l.-drop*, sugar-plum flavoured with l.; *l. kālī*, effervescing drink of tartaric acid, soda bicarbonate, & water; *l.-plant*, l.-scented verbena; *l. pudding* (flavoured with l.); *l. squash*, drink of l.-juice & soda-water; *l.-squeezer*, instrument for pressing juice out. Hence **le·mon**Y[2] a. [f. F *limon* f. Oriental source (Arab. *laimun*, Pers. *limun*), cf. LIME[2]]

lĕ·mon², n. (Usu. *l. dab, l. sole*) kind of plaice resembling sole. [f. F *limande*]

lĕ·mur, n. Kinds of nocturnal mammal esp. of Madagascar, allied to monkeys but with pointed muzzle. Hence **lĕ·mūr**INE¹ a., **lĕ·mūr**OID a. & n. [f. L *lemures* pl. spirits of the dead]

lend, v.t. (lent). Grant (person) use of (thing) on understanding that it or its equivalent shall be returned; let out (money) at interest, (books &c.; so *lending-library*) for hire; bestow, contribute, (something of temporary service or effect, as *enchantment, aid, dignity*; *l. ear, an ear,* one's *ears,* listen; *l. a hand* or *helping hand,* help; archaic, *l.* person *a box on the ear*); accommodate one*self to* some policy or purpose (thing *lends itself to,* is serviceable for). Hence **le·nd**ABLE a., **le·nd**ER¹, **le·nd**ING¹(1, 4), nn. [earlier *len,* OE *lǣnan* (cf. Du. *leenen,* G *lehnen*) f. *lǣn* LOAN]

length, n. Thing's measurement from end to end, greatest of body's three dimensions (*know l. of* person's FOOT); extent in, of, or with regard to, time (*a stay of some l.*; *the l. of a book, speech,* &c.); distance thing extends (*at arm's l.,* as far away as an arm can reach; *keep* one *at arm's l.,* avoid intimacy with him; *ships a cable's l. apart*; *horse, boat, wins by three* &c. *ll.,* i.e. of itself); (with *go*) degree of thoroughness in action (*prepared to go all ll., went to great ll., will not go the l. of asserting*); (Pros.) vowel's or syllable's quantity; (Cricket) distance from wicket at which ball pitches (*bowler keeps a good l.*; *l.* or *good-l. ball,* that pitches at right l.); long stretch or extent; piece of cloth &c. of certain l.; *at l.,* in detail or without curtailment (also *at full, great, some, l.*), at last or after a long time; *at full l.* (see above; also) lying with body fully extended. Hence **le·ngth**WAYS adv., **le·ngth**WISE adv. & a. [OE *lengthu,* cf. Du. *lengte,* (LONG)]

le·ngthen, v.t. & i. Make or become longer; (Pros.) make (vowel) long. [-EN⁶]

le·ngthy, a. (Of speech, writing, style, speaker, &c.) of unusual length, prolix, tedious. Hence **le·ngthi**LY² adv., **le·ngthi**NESS n. [-Y²; orig. an Americanism]

lē·nient, a. Emollient (archaic); tolerant, gentle, indisposed to severity; (of punishment &c.) mild. Hence **le·ni**ENCE, **le·ni**ENCY, nn., **le·nient**LY² adv. [f. L *lenire* soothe (*lenis* gentle), -ENT]

lĕ·nitive, a. & n. Soothing (drug, appliance), palliative. [f. med. L *lenitivus* (prec., -IVE)]

lĕ·nity, n. Mercifulness; mercy shown. [f. L *lenitas* (*lenis* gentle, -TY)]

lē·no, n. Kind of cotton gauze for caps, veils, curtains, &c. [perh. f. F *linon*]

lens (-z), n. (pl. *-ses*). Lentil-shaped glass with both sides (or one only) curved for concentrating or dispersing light-rays; combination of lenses in photography; (Anat.) = CRYSTALLINE *l.,* also one facet of compound eye. Hence **lens**ED², **le·ns**LESS, aa. [L *lens lentis* lentil]

lent¹, n. Period from Ash Wednesday to Easter Eve of which the 40 week-days are devoted to fasting & penitence in commemoration of Christ in the wilderness; (pl., at Cambridge) l.-term boatraces; *l. lily,* daffodil; *l. term,* university term in which l. falls. [f. LENTEN]

lent². See LEND.

-lent, suf. in adjj. f. L, = -FUL; the L suf. is normally preceded by *-u-* (*turbulentus*); but *pestilentus, violentus.*

le·nten, a. Of, in, or appropriate to, lent (*l. fare,* without meat; *l. face,* dismal look). [prop. n., of which the attrib. use is now regarded as adj. = LENT¹ + -EN⁵; orig. sense *spring,* now obs. in E, but the only sense in cogn. Teut. wds; OE *lencten,* cf. G *lenz,* prob. f. same root as LONG perh. w. ref. to lengthening of day in spring]

lenti·cular, a. Shaped like lentil or lens, double-convex; of the lens of the eye. [f. LL *lenticularis* (foll., -AR¹)]

le·ntil, n. (Seed of) leguminous plant grown for food. [F (*-lle*) f. L *lenticula* (LENS, -CULE)]

le·ntisk, n. The mastic tree. [f. L *lentiscus*]

le·ntitude, n. Sluggishness. [f. L *lentitudo* (*lentus* slow, -TUDE)]

le·ntoid, a. Lens-shaped. [LENS, -OID]

Le·o, n. Zodiacal constellation the Lion; fifth sign of the zodiac. [L, = LION]

Le·onid, n. One of the meteors that seem to radiate from Leo. [f. L *leo -onis,* -ID²]

le·onine¹, a. Lionlike, of lions. [f. L *leoninus* (prec., -INE¹)]

Le·onine², a. & n. Of, made or invented by, person (esp. one of the Popes) called Leo; *L. City,* part of Rome round Vatican fortified by Leo IV; *L. verse,* line (also *L.* as n.) or lines of medieval Latin verse in hexameter or elegiac metre with internal rhyme (e.g. *Daemon languebat, monachus tunc esse volebat*). [as prec.; inventor of L. verse unknown]

leo·pard (lĕp-), n. Large African & S.-Asiatic carnivorous quadruped with dark-spotted yellowish-fawn coat, panther, (*black l.,* black-coated kind; *American l.,* jaguar; *hunting l.,* cheetah; *snow l.,* ounce; *can the l. change his spots?,* character persists); (Her.) lion passant guardant as in arms of England; (in names of animals &c.) *l.-,* spotted like l. Hence **leo·pard**ESS¹ n. [OF, f. LL f. late Gk *leopardos* (LION, PARD)]

lĕ·per, n. Person with leprosy. [perh. attrib. use of obs. *leper* leprosy f. OF *lepre* f. L f. Gk *lepra* fem. of *lepros* scaly (*lepos* scale)]

lĕpido·pterous, a. Of the *Lepidoptera,*

order of insects with four membranous scale-covered wings including butterflies & moths. So **lepido·pterIST**(3) n. [f. Gk *lepis -idos* scale, *pteron* wing, -OUS]

lĕ·porīne, a. Of the hare kind. [f. L *leporinus* (*lepus -oris* hare, -INE[1])]

leprechau·n (-ch-), n. (Irish). Sprite. [perh. f. OIr. *luchorpán* (*lu* small, *corp* body)]

le·prosy, n. (In mod. Path.) an endemic chronic constitutional disease, *Elephantiasis Graecorum,* varying in manifestations as the skin, nerves, or other tissues, are affected; (pop., partly by confusion with *psoriasis,* formerly *Lepra Graecorum*) loathsome disease eating body slowly away & forming silvery scales on skin, (fig.) moral corruption or contagion. [foll., -Y[1]]

le·prous, a. Having, like, (as) of, leprosy. [OF, f. LL *leprosus* (*lepra* see LEPER, -OSE[1])]

lepto-, comb. form of Gk *leptos* fine, small, thin, delicate, in zool. & bot. terms, as *-cepha·lic* narrow-skulled, *-da·ctyl* n. & a. (bird) with long slender toes.

Le·sbian (-z-), a. Of Lesbos (*L. vice,* SAPPHISM). [L f. Gk *Lesbios* (*Lesbos*), -AN]

lèse-majesté (F), n. =foll. (in frequent use about foreign States, & joc. of presumptuous conduct on the part of inferiors &c.).

lese-ma·jesty (lēz-), n. (civil law). Treason. [f. F *lèse-majesté* f. L *laesa majestas* injured majesty (of the sovereign people)]

lē·sion (-zhn), n. Damage, injury, esp. (Path.) morbid change in functioning or texture of organs. [f. F *lésion* f. L *laesionem* nom. *-o* (*laedere laes-* injure, -ION)]

less, a., prep., n., & adv. (Of abstracts expressing measurement, as *size, degree, duration, number*) smaller (opp. *greater*; *in a l. degree, of l. magnitude* or *importance*); of smaller quantity, not so much, not so much of, (opp. *more*; *find l. difficulty*; *eat l. meat*; *of two evils choose the l.*; *may your shadow never be l.*, may you not grow thin); of lower rank &c. (rare; *no l. a person than*; *James the L.*). (Prep.) minus, deducting, (*a year l. three days*). (N.) smaller amount, quantity, or number (*cannot take l.*; *in l. than no time* joc., very quickly or soon; often *far, little, much, nothing, something, l.*; *expected nothing l. than an attack,* expected an attack & no milder procedure, but see under the adv.). (Adv.) to smaller extent, in lower degree, (often *none the, no, not the, l.*; *l. known* &c. or *l.-known* &c.; *do not suspect him of equivocation, still l.* or *much l. of lying*; *nothing l.*, anything rather; *expected nothing l. than an attack,* did not expect attack at all, but see the now usu. sense under n.). [OE *lǽs* adv., *lǽssa* adj., cf. OFris. *lês* & *lêssa*]

-less, suf. f. OE *léas* (used both as separate adj. in sense *free from, devoid of,* & as suf.) forming adjj. (*guileless, homeless*) & advv. (*doubtless*) f. nn. On anal. of compds in which the component n. was of same form as the corr. vb (*countless, dauntless, numberless*) & the sense was *unable, -less* has been appended to vbs (*resistless, describeless, tireless*).

lessee·, n. Holder of, tenant (*of* house, theatre, &c.) under, lease. Hence **lessee·SHIP** n. [f. OF *lessé* (LEASE[1], -EE)]

le·ssen, v.i. & t. Decrease, diminish. [-EN[6]]

le·sser, a. (attrib. only). Not so great as the other or the rest, minor, (*the L. Bear*; *the l. evils of life*). [double comparat.; LESS + -ER[3]]

le·sson, n., & v.t. One of two readings from O.T. (*first l.*) & N.T. (*second l.*) at morning & evening prayer (PROPER *l.*); thing to be learnt by pupil; amount of teaching given at one time, time assigned to it, (pl.) systematic instruction *in* subject (*give, take, ll. in*); occurrence, example, rebuke, or punishment, that serves as encouragement or warning; (vb) admonish, rebuke, discipline. [f. OF *lecon* (now *leçon*) f. L *lectionem* (*legere lect-* read, -ION)]

le·ssor (-or), n. Person who lets on lease. [AF (LEASE[1], -OR[2])]

lest, conj. In order that — not, for fear that; (after *fear* vb or n., & similar words) that. [OE *thý lǽs the* whereby less; *thý* was dropped in ME, & *les the* became *les te* by normal change]

let[1], v.t. (archaic; *letted* or *let*), & n. Hinder, obstruct. (N.) stoppage, hindrance, (archaic); (Rackets &c.) obstruction of ball or player in certain ways, requiring round to be played again. [OE *lettan,* cf. OHG *lezzan*]

let[2], v.t. & aux. (let), & n. 1. v.t.: Allow (liquid, air) to escape (*l.* BLOOD); grant use of for rent or hire (also intr. in pass. sense, as *the rooms l. well*; *to l.*, offered for rent; noun, letting, as *cannot get a l. for the rooms*); allow to, suffer to, (*we let them go*; *I was let see him*; pass. now rare, & sometimes followed by *to*); cause to (only in *l.* one *know,* inform him). *L. alone,* not interfere with, attend to, or do (*l.* WELL[3] *a.*; *l.* one *a. to* do, he may be trusted to; *l. a.* imperat., not to mention, far less or more); *l. be,* not interfere with, attend to, or do; *l. down,* lower, fail (friend) at need, disappoint (*l. him d. gently,* avoid humiliating abruptly), (n.) disappointment; *l.* DRIVE[1]; *l. fall,* drop (lit., & fig. hint, significant word) intentionally or by accident, (Geom.) draw (perpendicular) from outside point (*up*)*on* line; *l.* FLY[2]; *l. go,* release, set at liberty, lose hold of, lose or relinquish hold *of,* dismiss from thought, cease to restrain (*l. oneself go,* give way to enthusiasm, impulse, &c.); *l. in,* admit or open door to (*l. in a flood of* *light*; *this would l. in all sorts of evils*; *l. oneself in*, with latchkey &c.), insert into surface of something, involve in loss or difficulty (often *for*); *l.* (trans). *into*, admit to, insert into surface of, make acquainted with (secret &c.); *l.* (intr. or abs.) *into*, assail with blows or words; *l. loose*, release or unchain (dog, fury, maniac, &c.); *l. off* adv., discharge (gun, & fig. joke &c.), not punish or compel, punish *with* light penalty, allow or cause (fluid &c.) to pass away, (n., *l.-o.*) being allowed to escape something (esp. in cricket, not being caught &c. when there is a chance); *l. off* prep., excuse (person penalty); *let on* slang, peach, reveal secret, betray fact; *l.* (trans.) *out*, open door for exit to, allow (person &c., secret) to escape (*l. cat out of* BAG[1]), make (garment) looser, put out to hire esp. to several tenants, divulge (often *that*); *l.* (intr. or abs.) *out*, strike out with fist, lash out with heels, use strong language; *l. slip*, loose from leash, miss (opportunity). 2. v. aux. supplying 1st & 3rd persons of imperat. in exhortations (*l. us pray*; *l. you & me try now*), commands (*l. it be done*, *l. him do it, at once*), assumptions (*l. AB be equal to CD*), & permissions (*l. him do his worst*). [com.-Teut.; OE *lǣtan*, cf. G *lassen*, cogn. w. LATE & L *lassus* tired]

-let, suf. forming nn. usu. dim. (*ringlet*, *streamlet*), but somet. denoting articles of attire or ornament (*armlet*, *frontlet*); *-let* appears to come f. wrong division of wds taken f. OF diminutives in which *-et(e)* is added to nn. in *-el* (f. L *-ellus*, *-ella*, *-ellum*, dim. suff., or L *-ale* neut. adj. used as n.), as *chaplet*, *hamlet*, f. OF *chapelet*, *hamelet*, dimm. of *chapel*, *hamel*, mod. F *chapeau*, *hameau*.

lē·thal, a. Causing, sufficient or designed to cause, death (*l. chamber*, for killing animals painlessly). [f. L *let(h)alis* (*letum* death, -AL)]

lĕ·thargy (-er-), n. Morbid drowsiness, prolonged & unnatural sleep; torpid, inert, or apathetic state, want of interest & energy. So **lethar·gic** a., **lethar·gically** adv., **le·thargize**(3) v.t. [f. L f. Gk *lēthargia* (*lēthargos* forgetful f. *lēth-*, *lanthanō* forget), -Y[1]]

Lē·thē, n. (River in Hades producing) forgetfulness of the past. So **Lethe·an** a. [L, use of Gk *lēthē* forgetfulness, see prec.]

lē·thĕon, n. Sulphuric ether as anaesthetic. [irreg. f. prec.]

Lett, n. Member of a people living about the Baltic; =LETTISH n. [see LETTISH]

le·tter, n., & v.t. Character representing one or more of the simple or compound sounds used in speech, one of the alphabetic symbols, (*capital l.*, of the large form A, B, &c., opp. *small*, a, b, &c.; ROMAN, ITALIC, *l.*;) (Print.) type, fount of type; (pl.) lettering, inscription, (now only in PROOF[1] *before ll.*); missive, epistle, (*l. of advice*, notifying dispatch of goods, drawing of bill, &c.; *l. of attorney*, = POWER *of attorney*); (pl.) epistle of legal or formal kind for various purposes (*ll.* PATENT, *of* ADMINISTRATION, &c.; *ll. of business*, royal authority to Convocation to deal with a matter); precise terms of statement (*to the l.*, with adherence to every detail), strict verbal interpretation (opp. SPIRIT; esp. *in l. & in spirit*, in form & substance); (pl.) literature, acquaintance with books, erudition, (*man of ll.*, scholar, author; *commonwealth* or *republic of ll.*, authors as a body; *the profession of ll.*, authorship), whence **le·ttered**[2] a.; *l.-balance*, for ascertaining postage of ll.; *l.-book*, in which copies of correspondence are kept; *l.-bound*, too subservient to the l.; *l.-box*, in which ll. are posted; *l.-card*, folded card with gummed edge for use as postal missive; *l.-case*, pocket-book for holding ll.; *l.-lock*, kind of padlock opened by making out of certain ll. on it a word known to owner; *l.-paper*, quarto-sized paper for ll.; *l.-perfect* (Theatr.), knowing one's part perfectly; *letterpress*, contents of illustrated book other than the illustrations, printed matter relating to illustration; *l.-weight*, =l.-balance, also thing used to keep papers still on table; *l.-worship*, undue devotion to the l.; *l.-writer*, lit., also as title for manuals of l.-writing; hence **le·tterless** a. (Vb) impress title &c. on (book-cover); classify with ll.; hence **le·ttering**[1](1, 6) n. [f. OF *lettre* f. L *littera* l. of alphabet, (pl.) epistle]

Le·ttic, a. & n. =foll.; (of) the group of languages comprising Lettish, Lithuanian, & Old Prussian; of these peoples. [as foll., -IC]

Le·ttish, a. & n. (Language) of the Letts. [*Lett* f. G *Lette* f. native *Latvi* + -ISH[1]]

le·ttuce (-tĭs), n. Garden herb with crisp leaves much used as salad (*cabbage*, COS, *l.*, kinds of it). [f. L *lactuca* (*lac lactis* milk, w. ref. to milky juice of root)]

leuco-, comb. form of Gk *leukos* white, as *-cyte* colourless corpuscle of blood or found in lymph &c., *-pathy* albinism, *-rrhoe·a* mucous discharge from female genitals, the whites.

Leva·nt[1], n. Eastern part of Mediterranean with its islands & neighbouring countries; *L.* MOROCCO. [F, part. of *lever* rise, used as n. =sunrise, east, f. L *levare* lift (*lĕvis* light)]

leva·nt[2], v.i. Abscond, bolt, esp. with betting or gaming losses unpaid. Hence **leva·nter**[1] (-ER[1]) n. [perh. f. Sp. *levantar el campo* break up camp (*levar* f. L *levare* lift)]

leva·nter[2], n. Inhabitant of Levant; strong Mediterranean easterly wind. [LEVANT[1], -ER[1]]

Leva·ntine, a. & n. Of, trading to, inhabitant of, the Levant. [-INE[1]]

leva·tor, n. (Also *l.-muscle*) muscle that raises organ. [LL (L *levare* lift, -OR[2])]

lĕ·vee[1] (-ĭ), n. (Formerly) reception of visitors on rising from bed; assembly held by sovereign or his representative at which men only are received; assembly of visitors. [f. F *levé* var. of *lever* see LEVANT[1]]

levee[2] (lĭvē·, lĕ·vĭ), n. (U.S.). Embankment against river floods. [f. F *levée* fem. p.p. of *lever* raise, see LEVANT[1]]

lĕ·vel (-vl), n., a., & v.t. (-ll-). Instrument giving line parallel to plane of horizon for testing whether things are horizontal; horizontal line or plane (*on a l. with,* in same horizontal plane as; *find* one's *l.*, reach right place with regard to others; *water finds its l.*, its surface in communicating receptacles will be at same l. unless they have no common l.); plane or standard in social, moral, or intellectual matters; more or less l. surface; flat country. (Adj.) horizontal, perpendicular to the plumb-line; on a l. or equality (*with,* or abs.; *l. race,* in which leading competitors are close together; *l.* CROSSING); even, equable, uniform, well-balanced, in quality, style, temper, judgement, &c. (*l.-headed*; *do* one's *l. best,* not be remiss, take all possible pains); hence **le·vel**LY[2] adv. (rare), **le·vel**NESS n. (Vb) make l., even, or uniform; place on same l., bring *up* or *down* to a standard; raze, lay low, (*to* or *with the ground, in the dust,* or abs.), (rarely) knock (person) down; abolish (distinctions); aim (missile, or abs.), lay (gun), direct (satire, accusation, or abs.), (*at* or *against*); *levelling-screw,* for adjusting parts of machine &c. to exact l. [f. OF *livel* (now *niveau*) f. L *libella* dim. of *libra* balance]

le·veller, n. In vbl senses; esp., person who would abolish social distinctions, advocate of equality. [-ER[1]]

lē·ver, n., & v.i. & t. Bar used to prize up heavy or fixed object; (Mech.) straight bar or other rigid structure of which one point (*fulcrum*) is fixed, another is connected with the force (*weight*) to be resisted or acted upon, & a third is connected with the force (*power*) applied (*l. of first order* with fulcrum, *of second order* with weight, *of third order* with power, between the other two); piece by which barrel of breechloader is opened; =l. watch; *l.-*, acting as or worked by l.; *l. escapement,* with connexion between pallet & balance made by two ll.; *l. watch,* with l. escapement. (Vb) use l.; lift, move, act on, with l. (often *along, away, out, over, up,* &c.). [f. OF *leveour* (*lever* see LEVANT[1]), -OR[2]]

le·verage (-ĭj), n. Action of, way of applying, lever; set or system of levers; power, mechanical advantage gained by use, of lever; means of accomplishing a purpose, power, influence. [-AGE]

lever de rideau (F), n. CURTAIN[1]-raiser.

lĕ·veret, n. Young (esp. first-year) hare. [f. OF *levrete* (*levre* f. L *leporem* nom. *-us* hare, -ET[1])]

levī·athan, n. Sea monster (bibl.); huge ship; anything very large of its kind; person of formidable ability, power, or wealth. [L, f.Heb. *livyathan* etym. dub.]

lĕ·vigate, v.t. Reduce to fine smooth powder; make smooth paste of. Hence **levig**A·TION n. [f. L *levigare* (*lēvis* smooth), -ATE[3]]

lĕ·vin, n. (poet.). (Flash of) lightning. [ME *leven,* etym. dub.]

lē·vĭrate (-*at*), n. Jewish &c. custom by which dead man's brother or next of kin had to marry his widow. Hence **leviră·t**IC(AL) aa. [f. L *levir* brother-in-law + -ATE[1]]

lĕ·vitate, v.i. & t. (Make) rise & float in air (w. ref. to spiritualism). Hence **levit**A·TION n. [f. L *lĕvis* light, after GRAVITATION]

Lē·vite, n. One of tribe of Levi, esp. of that part of it which provided assistants to priests in worship of Jewish temple. [f. L f. Gk *leuitēs* (*Leui* f. Heb. *Levi*)]

Levĭ·tical, a. Of Levites or tribe of Levi; of Levites' ritual; of Leviticus. So **levi·tic**ISM(3) n. [f. LL f. Gk *leuitikos* (prec., -IC) + -AL]

Levi·ticus, n. (abbr. *Lev.*). Third book of Pentateuch with Levitical law & ritual. [prec.]

lĕ·vity, n. Lightness of weight (rare); want of thought, frivolity, unseasonable jocularity, inconstancy; light behaviour. [f. OF *levité* f. L *levitatem* (*lĕvis* light, -TY)]

levulose. See LAEVULOSE.

lĕ·vy, n., & v.t. Collecting of assessment, tax, &c. (*capital l.*, appropriation by the State of a fixed proportion of all the wealth in the country); enrolling of men for war &c. (*l. in mass,* of all able-bodied men); amount or number levied, body of men enrolled (also pl.). (Vb) raise (contribution, taxes), impose (rate, toll), whence **le·vi**ABLE a.; raise (sum) by legal execution or process *on* person's goods; extort (*l. blackmail*); enlist, enrol, (soldiers, army); collect men & munitions for, proceed to make, (war; usu. *upon, against*). [f. F *levée* (*lever* see LEVANT[1], -Y[4])]

lewd, a. Base, worthless, (bibl.); lascivious, unchaste, indecent, whence **lew·d**LY[2] adv., **lew·d**NESS n. [OE *lǣwede*; earlier senses *lay, unlearned*; perh. as LAY[2] + -ED[2]]

lew·is (lōō-), n. Iron contrivance for gripping heavy blocks of stone for lifting. [?]

Lew·is gun, n. Kind of machine gun. [*Lewis,* inventor]

le·xical, a. Of the words of a language (opp. *grammatical*); (as) of a lexicon.

Hence **le·xical**LY² adv. [f. Gk *lexikos*, & LEXICON, + -AL]

lexico·graphy, n. Dictionary-making. So **lexico·**GRAPHER n., **lexico**GRA·PHICAL a. [foll., -GRAPHY]

le·xicon (-kn), n. Dictionary, esp. of Greek, Hebrew, Syriac, or Arabic. [Gk (*-kon*), neut. of *lexikos* (*lexis* word f. *legō* speak, -IC)]

lexi·graphy, n. System of writing in which each character represents a word. [*lexis*, see prec., -GRAPHY]

lex tāliō·nis, n. The law of retaliation, an eye for an eye. [L]

Ley·den (lī-), n. Dutch city (*L. jar*, kind of electrical condenser invented 1745 at L.; *L. battery*, of several L. jars).

liabi·lity, n. Being liable (*limited l.*, being responsible only to limited amount for debts of trading company; so *l.-l. company*, or ellipt. *limited company*); what one is liable for, (pl.) debts or pecuniary obligations. [foll., -BILITY]

li·able, a. Legally bound, answerable *for*, subject or amenable *to* tax or penalty, under obligation *to* do; exposed or open *to*, apt *to* do or suffer, something undesirable (*difficulties are l. to occur*). [perh. f. L **ligabilis* (*ligare* bind, -ABLE)]

liai·son (-zn, *or as F*), n. Illicit intimacy between a man & a woman; sounding of ordinarily silent final consonant before vowel or mute *h* in French; (Mil.) connexion, touch, (*l. officer*, acting as go-between for allied forces). [F, f. L *ligationem* (*ligare* bind, -ATION)]

lia·na (-ah-), **lia·ne** (-ahn), n. Kinds of climbing & twining tropical-forest plant. [F (*-e*), perh. f. *lier* bind f. L as prec.; *-a* form a Latinization of *-e*]

li·ar, n. Teller (esp. habitual) of lie(s). [OE *lēogere* (LIE², -AR³)]

li·as, n. Blue limestone rock of some S.-W. counties; (Geol.) lower strata of jurassic series, blue argillaceous limestone rich in fossils. Hence **lia·ssic** a. [f. OF *liois* etym. dub.]

liba·tion, n. (Pouring of) drink-offering to god; (joc.) potation. [f. L *libatio* (*libare* pour a little of, -ATION)]

li·bel, n., & v.t. (-ll-). (Civil & Eccl. Law) plaintiff's written declaration; (Law) published statement damaging to person's reputation, act of publishing it (*the greater the truth, the greater the l.*); (pop.) false & defamatory statement, (transf.) thing that brings discredit *on* by unsuccessful portrayal &c. (*the portrait is a l. on him*; *the book, play, is a l. on human nature*); hence **li·bell**IST(1) n., **li·bell**OUS a., **li·bellous**LY² adv. (Vb) defame by libellous statements, accuse falsely & maliciously, (Law) publish l. against, whence **li·bell**ER¹ n.; (Eccl. & Admiralty Law) bring suit against, whence **li·bel**LANT(1), **libell**EE·, nn. [vb f. n., OF, f. L *libellus* dim. of *liber* book]

li·beral, a. & n. Fit for a gentleman (now rare exc. in *l. education*, i.e. directed to general enlargement of mind, not professional or technical); generous, open-handed, not sparing *of*; ample, abundant; not rigorous or literal, open-minded, candid, unprejudiced, (Pol.) favourable to democratic reforms & abolition of privilege (esp. *l. party*; opp. CONSERVATIVE; *l. conservative*, member of conservative party not ill-disposed to reforms; *l. unionist*, member of section that seceded from l. party in 1886 on Home Rule), whence **li·beral**ISM(3) n., **li·beral**IST(2) n. & a., **liberali·s**TIC a., **li·beral**IZE(3) v.t. & (rarely) i., **li·beraliz**A·TION n.; hence **li·beral**LY² adv. (N.) member of (esp. the British) l. party. [OF, f. L *liberalis* (*līber* free (man), -AL)]

libera·lity, n. Free giving, munificence; freedom from prejudice, breadth of mind. [f. OF *liberalité* f. L *liberalitatem* (prec., -TY)]

li·berate, v.t. Set at liberty, release *from* (in Chem., from combination). Hence **li·berat**OR² n. [f. L *liberare* (*līber* free), -ATE³]

libera·tion, n. Releasing, release; *L. Society*, advocating church disestablishment, whence **libera·tion**ISM(3) n., **libera·tion**IST(2) n. & a. [f. L *liberatio* (prec., -ATION)]

libertā·rian, n. & a. Believer, believing, in free will (opp. *necessitarian*); advocate of liberty. Hence **libertar·ian**ISM(3) n. [-ARIAN]

liber·ticide, n. & a. Destroyer, destructive, of liberty. [F (LIBERTY, -CIDE)]

li·bertine, n. & a. Free thinker on religion; licentious (man); free-thinking, antinomian; *chartered l.*, person allowed to do as he pleases (Shak. *Hen. V*, I. i. 48). Hence **li·bertin**ISM(2) & (in same sense) **li·bertin**AGE, nn. [f. L *libertinus* freedman (*libertus* made free cogn. w. *līber* free)]

li·berty, n. Being free from captivity, imprisonment, slavery, or despotic control (CAP¹ *of l.*; *natural l.*, state in which there are no laws; *civil l.*, natural l. limited only by laws established on behalf of community; *l. of conscience*, system allowing all members of State to follow what form of religion seems good to them; *l. of the press*, system by which any one may print & publish what he pleases without previous permission, but not without liability to penalties for publishing libellous or criminal matter); right or power to do as one pleases or *to* do something, (Philos.) freedom from control of fate or necessity; a setting aside of rules, licence, (*take the l. to* do, *of doing*, presume or venture to; *take ll.*, be unduly familiar *with* person or abs., deal freely *with* rules or facts); freedom from despotic rule personified; (pl.) privileges, immunities, or rights, enjoyed by prescription or grant; *at l.*, free (*set at l.*, liberate), having the right *to* do, disengaged; *l.* HALL; *l. man*, sailor with leave to go ashore. [f. F *liberté* f. L *libertatem* (*līber* free, -TY)]

libĭ·dinous, a. Lustful. Hence **libi·dinous**LY² adv. [f. L *libidinosus* (*libīdo -inis* lust, -OUS)]

lī·bra, n. (pl. *-ae*). Pound weight (used only in abbr. *lb.*, as 1 lb., 10 lb.); pound sterling (used only in abbrr. *£ s. d.*, see L, & *l.* placed after figure as 50*l.*); (Astron.; *L-*) zodiacal constellation the Scales, seventh sign of zodiac. [L]

librār·ian, n. Custodian of library. Hence **librar·ian**SHIP(1) n. [f. L as foll. + -AN]

lī·brary, n. Room or building containing books for reading or reference; writing & reading room in house; collection of books for use by the public, some part of it, or members of some society, public institution charged with care of such collection, (*lending l.*, from which books may be taken away with or without payment; *reference l.*, in which books may be consulted; *free l.*, used by public without payment & usu. supported by rates; *circulating l.*, letting out use of books for profit); person's book-collection; series of books issued by publisher in similar bindings as connected in some way; books used by or familiar to an author; *walking l.*, person of erudition; *l. edition*, of good size & print fit for ll. [f. F *librairie* bookshop (L *librarius* of books f. *līber -bri* book, orig. bark, -ARY¹, + Y¹)]

lībra·te, v.i. Oscillate, be poised, balance, sway, quiver. Hence **lī·brat**ORY a. [f. L *librare* (*libra* balance), -ATE³]

libra·tion, n. Librating (*l. of moon*, apparent oscillation by which parts near edge of disk are alternately visible & invisible). [f. L *libratio* (prec., -ATION)]

lĭbre·tto, n. (pl. *-ti*, pr. -tē). Book or words of an opera or long musical work. Hence **libre·tt**IST(1) n. [It., dim. of *libro* book f. L *līber -bri*]

Li·byan, a. & n. (Inhabitant) of ancient Libya; (poet.) African; (of) the Berber language or the group of mod. Hamitic languages to which it belongs. [f. L f. Gk *Libuē* + -AN]

lice. See LOUSE.

lī·cence¹, n. Leave, permission, (*Have I your l. to remove the fence?*); permit from government &c. to marry, print something, preach, carry on some trade (esp. that in alcoholic liquor), &c.; university certificate of competence in some faculty; liberty of action esp. when excessive, abuse of freedom, disregard of law or propriety; licentiousness; writer's or artist's irregularity in grammar, metre, perspective, &c. (usu. *poetic l.*). [F, f. L *licentia* (*licēre* be lawful, -ENCE)]

lī·cense, -ce², v.t. Allow (person *to* do, thing to be done; rare); (in p.p.) allow complete freedom to (*a licensed satirist*); grant permit (see prec.) to (person; *licensed* VICTUALLER); authorize use of (premises) for certain purpose; authorize publication of (book &c.) or performance of (play). Hence **licens**EE· n. [f. prec.; *-se* on anal. of *practise, prophesy*, vv., cf. *practice, prophecy*, nn.; the distinction perh. comes by imit. of spelling in pairs like *advise, advice*, where the sound differs]

lī·censer, n. In vbl senses; esp. *l. of the press, l. of plays*, officials licensing publication or performance when satisfied that law, morals, & decency, are not outraged. [-ER¹]

lice·ntiate (-shĭat), n. Holder of university licence or attestation of competence from collegiate or examining body (chiefly in abbr. L. as part of title, see L); licensed preacher not yet having appointment esp. in Presbyterian Church. [f. med. L *licentiare* (LICENCE¹), -ATE³)]

lice·ntious (-sh*us*), a. Disregarding accepted rules esp. of grammar or style; lascivious, libertine, lewd. Hence **lice·ntious**LY² adv., **lice·ntious**NESS n. [f. med. L *licentiosus* (LICENCE¹, -OSE¹)]

lich, lȳch, (-tsh), **lȳke**, n. (obs.). Corpse; *-ch-gate*, roofed gateway of churchyard where coffin awaits clergyman's arrival; *-ch-house*, mortuary; *-ch-owl*, screech-owl (boding death); *-ch-stone*, to place coffin on at l.-gate; *lyke-wake*, watch kept at night over corpse. [OE *līc*, cf. G *leiche*; orig. sense prob. *form*, cf. LIKE]

lī·chen (-k-), n. Kinds of cellular cryptogamic plant (prob. fungus parasitic on alga) usu. of green, grey, or yellow tint growing on & colouring rocks, tree-trunks, &c., whence **li·chen**ED² a., **licheno·**LOGY n.; skin-disease with reddish eruption. Hence **li·chen**OUS a. [f. L f. Gk *leikhēn*]

lĭ·cit, a. Not illicit. Hence **li·cit**LY² adv. [f. L *licitus* (*licēre* be lawful)]

lick, v.t. & i., & n. Pass tongue over to taste, moisten, clean, &c. (*l.* one's *chops* or *lips*, in relish or anticipation of food; *l. into shape*, mould, make presentable or efficient; *l.* one's *shoes*, show servility to him; *l. the dust*, fall, be vanquished); take *up* or *off*, make *clean*, by licking; (of waves, flame, &c.) play lightly over, (of flame) swallow *up* in passing; (slang) thrash (person, fault *out of* person), beat in fight or competition, excel, (*licks creation*, is beyond everything), whence **li·ck**ING¹(1) n.; (slang) surpass comprehension of (*this licks me*); (slang) go, hasten, (*as hard as he could l.*); ***li·ckspittle***, toady. (N.) act of licking with tongue; (also *salt-l.*) spot to which animals resort for salt; smart blow with stick &c.; (slang) pace (*at a great l.*, *full* or *at full l.*).

[OE *liccian*, cf. G *lecken*; cogn. w. Gk *leikhō*, L *linguere*]

li·ckerish, li·quorish (-ker-), a. Fond of dainty fare; greedy, longing; lecherous. [earlier *lickerous* var. through ONF of *lecherous* see LECHER & retaining its obs. orig. sense]

licorice. See LIQUORICE.

licorous. Var. of *lickerous*, LICKERISH.

li·ctor, n. Officer attending ancient-Roman consul (12 ll.) & dictator (24 ll.), bearing fasces, & executing sentence on offenders. [L, perh. f. st. of *ligare* bind]

lid, n. Hinged or detached cover for aperture, esp. for opening at top of vessel; *with the l. off*, with all horrors &c. exposed to view; *put the l. on* (slang), be the culmination (of), surpass all; =EYE[1]-*lid*; (Bot., Conch.) operculum. Hence (-)**lid**DED[2], **li·d**LESS, aa. [OE *hlid*, cf. Du. *lid*, G (*augen*)*lid*]

lie[1], n. Intentional false statement (*tell a l.*, make this; *act a l.*, deceive without verbal lying; *white l.*, excused or justified by its motive; *give* one *the l.*, accuse him of lying; *give the l. to* supposition &c., serve to show its falsity, belie it); imposture, false belief, mistaken convention, (*worship, maintain, a l.*). [OE *lyge*, cf. G *lug* & see foll.]

lie[2], v.i. & t. (lying). Speak falsely, tell lie(s), (*you l. in your teeth, throat*, archaic or facet. forms of accusation; *lies like a gas-meter*, freely); take *away* (reputation &c.), get (*oneself*, person) *into, out of*, by lying; (of things) deceive (part., deceptive). [com.-Teut.; OE *léogan*, cf. Du. *liegen*, G *lügen*, as prec.]

lie[3], v.i. (*lying*; past *lay*; p.p. *lain* & bibl. *li·en*). 1. Of persons or animals: Have one's body in more or less horizontal position along ground or surface (often *asleep, sick*, &c.; *l.* DOGGO; *let sleeping dogs l.*, avoid mooting debatable questions; *l. on the bed* one *has made*, endure consequences of past acts), have sexual intercourse *with*; (of the dead) be in the grave *at* or *in*, *l. in* STATE; assume lying position (usu. *down, back*, &c.); be kept or remain in specified state (*l. in prison, at the mercy of, helpless, idle*, CLOSE[1], LOW[1], PERDU, *in ambush, in* WAIT[2]; *l. out of* one's *money*, remain unpaid); (of game-birds) not rise; (of troops) be encamped *at, in, near*, a place. 2. Of things: Be at rest, usu. more or less horizontally, on surface (*l. in ruins* or *the dust*, be fallen; *l. heavy*, be a weight *on* one's *stomach* or *conscience*); be stored up in specified place (*money lying at the bank*), remain in specified state esp. *waste, hid, barren*, be situated (*land lying high, to the east, round*; *find out how the land lies* fig., how affairs stand), be spread out to view (*lies on the surface, before us, open*), (of road) lead *through, by, along, among*, &c.; (of ship) float in berth or at anchor; (of abstracts) exist, be to be found, reside, be arranged or related, in some position or manner (*the choice lies between* —; *his acquaintance lay among* —; *knows where his interest lies*; *how do they lie to each other?*; *as far as in me lies*, to best of my power; *lies with you to* do, is your business or right; *the remedy lies in education*; *her strength lay in her weakness*; *lies in a* NUT*shell*); (Law) be admissible or sustainable (*action, appeal, objection, will not l.*). 3. With advv.: *l. by*, be unused, keep quiet or retired; *l. down* in part., behaving in abject manner, not standing up to opponent &c., (*take* defeat, chastisement, & esp. *it, lying down*); *l. in*, be brought to bed in childbirth (*lying-in hospital*); *l. off* (naut.), stand some distance from shore or other ship; *l. over*, be deferred; *l. to* (naut.), come almost to a stop with head near wind by backing or shortening sail; *l. up*, go into or be in retirement, take to one's bed or room, (of ship) go into dock or be out of commission. *Lie·-abed*, late riser. [com.-Teut.; OE *licgan*, cf. Du. *liggen*, G *liegen*, cogn. w. Gk *lekhos*, L *lectus*, bed]

lie[4], n. Way, direction, or position, in which thing lies; *l. of the land*, (fig.) posture of affairs; place where beast, bird, or fish, is accustomed to l. [f. prec.]

Lie·big('s extract of beef) (lē-), n. Concentrated preparation of beef without albumen, gelatin, or fat. [Baron von *Liebig*, 1873, inventor]

lied (lēd), n. (pl. *-der*). German song or poem of ballad kind. [G]

lief, adv. (comp. *-er*, rare). Gladly, willingly, (usu. *I would as l.* do something out of the question *as*). [prop. adj. (earlier construction being *I had as l.*, i.e. should find it as pleasant, now corrupted to *would*); OE *léof* dear, cf. G *lieb*, cogn. w. LOVE]

liege, a. & n. (Of superior) entitled to receive, (of vassal) bound to give, feudal service or allegiance (*l. lord*, feudal superior, sovereign; *liegeman*, sworn vassal, faithful follower). (N.) l. lord (esp. *my l.* voc.); vassal, subject, (usu. *the ll.*). [f. OF *lige*, perh. f. OHG *ledig* free]

li·en[1] (lē·en), n. Right to keep possession of property till debt due in respect of it is discharged (usu. *a. l. on* or *upon*). [F, f. L *ligamen* (*ligare* bind, -MEN)]

lien[2]. See LIE[3].

lier·ne, n. Short rib connecting bosses & intersections of vaulting-ribs. [F, etym. dub.]

lieu (lū), n. *In l.*, in the place, instead, *of*. [F, f. L *locus* place]

lieutĕ·nant (lĕft-, left-, *in navy* let-), n. (*abbr.* Lieut. *& in comb.* Lt-). Deputy, substitute, vicegerent, acting for a superior (still as formal title in *L. of the Tower*, acting commandant of Tower of London; & see LORD *L.*); *l.*, *l. colonel*, *l.*

commander, l. general, OFFICERS of navy & army; *l.-governor(ship)*, (position of) actual governor of district &c. in subordination to governor general. Hence **lieute·n**ANCY n. [F (prec., TENANT)]

life, n. (pl. *-ves*). State of ceaseless change & functional activity peculiar to organized matter, & esp. to the portion of it constituting an animal or plant before death, animate existence, being alive, (*a matter of l. & death,* something on which it depends whether one shall live or die; NECESSARY, STAFF, *of l.*; *come, bring, to l.*, recover (i. & t.) from swoon; *lose, save, lay down,* one's *l.*; *safe in, escape with, l. & limb*; SELL one's *l. dearly*; *great sacrifice of l.*, many killed; *have no regard for human l.*, kill men or let them die recklessly; *for* one's, *for dear, l.*, to escape death; *cannot for the l. of me* &c. by exag., could not if my l. depended on it; *'pon my l.*, asseveration); energy, liveliness, vivacity, animation; vivifying influence (*was the l.*, or *l. & soul, of the party*; *my l.*, voc. of affection); living things & their motions (*very little l. to be seen*); the living form or model, l.-size figure &c., (*taken from the l.*; *as large as l.*, l.-size, also facet. as *here he is as l. as l.*, i.e. in person; *portray* &c. *to the l.*, with fidelity to the original), whence **li·fe**LIKE a.; period from birth to death, birth to present time, or present time to death (*have done it all my l.*; *have the time of* one's *l.*, slang, enjoy oneself as never before; *l. sentence, rent, annuity,* to continue for rest of person's l.; *lease for three* &c. *ll.*, to terminate with last of three &c. named persons' ll.; *l.* ASSURANCE; INSURE one's *l.*; *expectation of l.*, average period that person at specified age may expect to live; *a good, bad, l.*, person likely to pass, fall short of, this average; *new* LEASE[1] *of l.*); fresh start after narrowly escaped lit. or metaph. death (*cat has nine ll.*, is hard to kill; *batsman was given a l.*, not put out on giving a chance; *pool-player has three ll.*, successive chances); individual's actions & fortunes, manner of existence, (*with all the pleasure in l.*, greatest possible; *nothing in l.*, at all; *this l.*, that on earth; *the other, future, eternal, everlasting, l.*, state of existence after death; *the* SIMPLE *l.*; *has led a good* &c. *l.*), written story of these, biography; active part of existence, business & pleasures of the world, (*see life,* mix freely with others; *high, low, l.*, social customs of upper, lower, classes); (Theol.) salvation, regenerate condition, (also *eternal, everlasting, l.*, see above also). *L.-belt,* of buoyant material to support body in water; *l.-blood,* blood necessary to l., vitalizing influence, involuntary twitching of lip or eyelid; *l.-boat,* of special construction for saving l. in storms; *l.-breath,* inspiring influence, sustaining principle; *l.*-BUOY[1]; *l. estate,* property that one holds for l. but cannot dispose of further; *l.-giving,* that gives, sustains, or restores, physical or spiritual l.; *l.-guard,* body-guard of soldiers; *L. Guards,* regiment of household cavalry; *L.-Guardsman,* soldier of L. Guards; *l. interest,* right to l. estate; *l.-jacket,* as *l.-belt*; *l.-line,* rope used for l.-saving, e.g. that attached to l.-buoy; *lifelong,* continued for a lifetime; *l.-office,* for l.-assurance; *l. peer(age)*, with title lapsing at death; *l.-preserver,* short stick with heavily loaded end; *l.-spring,* source of l.; *l.-strings,* hold on l. (*l.-s. are cut* or *broken,* person dies); *l.-table,* statistics of expectation of l.; *lifetime,* duration of person's l.; *l.-work,* task pursued through l. Hence **li·fe**LESS a., **li·feless**LY[2] adv., **li·feless**NESS n., **(-)lī**VED[2] a. (esp. *long-, short-*). [OE *līf*, cf. OFris. *līf* life, body, Du. *lijf* & G *leib* body, cogn. w. LIVE & LEAVE[2], f. Aryan *leip-, loip-, lip-*, endure, cf. Gk *liparēs* persistent]

li·fer, n. (slang). One sentenced to, sentence of, penal servitude for life. [-ER[1]]

lift, v.t. & i., & n. Raise to higher position, take up, hoist, (often *up, off, out*), elevate to higher plane of thought or feeling, give upward direction to (eyes, face), (*l. up* or *l.* one's *hands* or *heart,* in prayer &c.; *l.* one's *hand,* to take oath; *l. a hand,* make the slightest effort, usu. *to* do; *never lifted a hand against* one, struck him; *l. up* one's *head,* recover vigour after prostration, *l. up* another's *head* bibl., restore to liberty or dignity; *l. up* one's *heel,* kick; *l. up* one's *horn,* be ambitious or proud; *l. up a cry,* one's *voice,* cry out); hold or have on high (*church lifts its spire*); steal (esp. cattle), take (passage, information) in the way of plagiarism; remove (tents &c.); dig up (potatoes); hit (cricket-ball) into air; (of ship afloat) rise on wave; yield to a l. (*window will not l.*); (of cloud, fog, darkness) rise, disperse; (of floor) swell upwards, bulge. (N.) lifting (DEAD *l.*; *give* one *a l.*, take him up into vehicle for part of way, also fig. give him helping hand); one layer of leather in boot-heel; apparatus for raising & lowering people or things to other floor of house, elevator, hoist; rise in the ground. [f. ON *lypta* (*lopt* air, sky, cf. G *luft*, obs. E *lift*, & LOFT)]

li·gament, n. Tie, bond of union, (archaic); (Anat.) short band of tough flexible fibrous tissue binding bones together, (loosely) any membranous fold keeping organ in position, similar part in lower organisms. Hence **ligame·nt**AL, **ligame·nt**ARY[1], **ligame·nt**OUS, aa. [f. L *ligamentum* (*ligare* bind, -MENT)]

liga·te, v.t. (surg.). Tie up (bleeding artery &c.). Hence **lig**A·TION n. [f. L *ligare*, -ATE[3]]

li·gature (-tsher), n., & v.t. Thing used in tying, esp. band or cord used to tie up bleeding artery, strangulate tumour, &c. (vb, bind with l.); thing that unites, bond; tying, ligation; (Mus.) slur, tie; (Print.) two or more letters joined (fi &c.). [f. L *ligatura* (prec., -URE)]

light[1] (līt), n. The natural agent that stimulates the sense of sight; medium or condition of space in which sight is possible (opp. *darkness*); appearance of brightness (NORTHERN *ll.*; ZODIACAL *l.*; *saw a distant l.*); sensation peculiar to optic nerve; amount of illumination in place (*in a good l.*, easily visible), one's fair or ordinary share of this (*stand in* one's *l.*, deprive him of this, *fig.* prejudice his chances); vivacity in person's eyes; favouring aspect (*l. of* one's *countenance*, his favour, approving presence, or sanction, often iron.); sun's direct or diffused or reflected rays, daylight, (*see the l.*, be born); being visible or exposed (*come, bring, to l.*, be revealed, reveal); (Poet.) eyesight, (slang, pl.) eyes; object from which brightness emanates (*l. of* one's *eyes*, beloved person), sun or other heavenly body, ignited candle or lamp or the like, (collect.) lamps &c. illuminating place, beacon lamp esp. of ship or lighthouse, lighthouse, (fig.) eminent person or luminary (often *shining l.*); mental illumination, elucidation (*throw, shed, l. upon*, help to explain), enlightenment (*by the l. of nature*, without aid of revelation or teaching; *men of l. &* LEADING[1]), (pl.) facts or discoveries serving to explain subject (*we have many new ll. upon it since then*), (pl.) one's natural or acquired mental powers (usu. *do* one's *best* &c. *according to* one's *ll.*), (sing.) aspect in which thing is viewed (*in the l. of these facts*, with the help given by them; *appeared in the l. of a scoundrel*, seemed to be one; *place thing in a good l.*, represent it favourably), (in acrostic puzzles) one of the words whose initial & final letters make up the answer; (Theol.) brightness of heaven, illumination of soul by divine truth; window or opening in wall for admission of l., perpendicular division of mullioned window, glazed compartment of side or roof in greenhouse; (Paint.) illuminated surface, part of picture represented as lighted up; (Law) light falling on windows, the obstruction of which by neighbour is illegal (*Ancient Ll.*, inscription giving notice of this); flame or spark serving to ignite (*strike a l.*, produce this with match &c.), thing used for igniting, spill, taper, match; *l. due, duty*, toll on ships for maintenance of *lighthouses* (tower or other structure) & *lightships* (moored or anchored) containing beacon ll. for warning or guiding ships at sea. Hence **ligh·t**LESS a. [OE *lēoht*, cf. Du. & G *licht*, f. Aryan *leuk-* whence Gk *leukos* white, L *lux* light]

light[2], a. Well provided with l., not dark; pale-coloured (often prefixed to adjj. & nn. of colour, as *a l.-blue ribbon, I prefer l. blue*; *the l.* BLUE[2]*s*). [as prec.]

light[3], v.t. & i. (*lit* or *lighted*; as attrib. adj., *lighted* is usu.). Set (lamp &c., fire, combustible) burning (often *up*; *l. up* abs., begin to smoke pipe &c., also kindle the ll. in street or room at dusk), (of fuel, lamp, &c.) take fire, begin to burn; give l. to (room, street, &c.; *l. up*, l. brightly or make conspicuous by l.); brighten (t. & i., with *eyes, face*, &c., as obj. or subj.) with animation; show (person his) way or surroundings with a l. Hence **(-)ligh·ter**[1], see -ER[1](1, 2), n. [OE *lihtan* (LIGHT[1, 2])]

light[4] (līt), a. & adv. Of little weight, not heavy, (*l.-armed*, with l. equipment & weapons); deficient in weight (*l. coin, gold*, &c.); of small specific gravity; having or intended for a small load (*l. ship*, unladen; *l. waterline* &c., that of ship when l.; *l. engine*, with no train attached; *l. railway*, for l. traffic; *l. porter*; *l. horse*, l.-armed cavalry, & so *l. horseman, l. infantry*; *l. marching order*, in which only arms & ammunition are taken), (of ship, cart, &c.) made lightly for small loads & quick movement; (of building) not looking heavy, graceful, elegant; acting gently, applied delicately, not violent, (*l. hand*, lit., & fig. = tactful management, whence **light-hand**ED[2] a., **light-ha·nded**LY[2] adv., **light-ha·nded**NESS n.; *l. touch, blow, wind, step*, &c.); not dense or tenacious; porous, friable, (*l. soil, bread*); easy of digestion; (of wine or beer) not strong; (of syllable) unemphatic; not important (*make l. of*, treat as of no consequence), slight, trivial, venial, not grave, jesting, thoughtless, frivolous (whence **light-mind**ED[2] a., **light-mi·nded**NESS n.); wanton, unchaste, (esp. of women or their conduct); nimble, quick-moving, (*l. of foot*; *l. heels*, whence **light-heel**ED[2] a.; *l. movements*; *l. rhythm*; *l. fingers*, good at stealing, whence **light-finger**ED[2] a.); fickle, inconstant; easily borne (*l. punishment, taxation, rule, expense*) or done (*l. work, task*); aimed or aiming at entertainment merely (*l. literature, writer, comedy, comedian*); (of sleep) easily disturbed, not profound, (so *l. sleeper*); free from sorrow, cheerful, sanguine, (*l. heart* only; *did it with a l. heart*, sanguinely, *often* rashly; so **light-heart**ED[2] a., **light-hear·ted**LY[2] adv., **light-hear·ted**NESS n.); delirious (now only in **light-head**ED[2] a., **light-head·ed**NESS n.); *l.*-BOB[5]; *light-foot*, springy, nimble; *l.-o'-love*, fickle woman, harlot; *l.-skirts*, woman of l. character; *l.-weight* a., *l. weight* n., (man or animal) below average weight, esp. in boxing not over 10 st.; hence **ligh·tLY**[2] adv., **ligh·tNESS** n. (Adv.) in l. manner (esp. *tread, sleep, l.*; *l. come l. go*, what is easily gained is soon lost). [OE *léoht*, cf. Du. *licht*, G *leicht*, also Skr. *laghu*, Gk *elaphros* light & *elakhus* small]

light[5], v.t. & i. (*lit* or *lighted*). (Naut.) lift (rope &c.) along, lend a hand in hauling ropes &c.; (archaic) alight, descend, come down; chance, come by chance, (*up*)*on*. [orig. sense *make l.*, intr. meanings coming from idea of relieving horse &c. of weight; OE *lihtan* (prec.)]

ligh·ten[1], v.t. & i. Reduce load of (ship &c.), (of ship) have her load reduced; relieve (heart &c.), (of heart &c.) feel relief; reduce weight of, (fig.) mitigate; grow lighter. [LIGHT[4] + -EN[6]]

ligh·ten[2], v.t. & i. Shed light upon, make bright; (of face, eyes, sky, &c.) grow bright, shine, flash; (of sky, clouds, or *it*) emit lightning (also fig. of scorn &c.). [LIGHT[2] + -EN[6]]

ligh·ter[2] (for *l.*[1] see LIGHT[3]), n., & v.t. Boat, usu. flat-bottomed, for unloading & loading ships not brought to wharf & for transporting goods in harbour; (vb) remove (goods) in l. Hence **lighterAGE**(4) n. [LIGHT[5] + -ER[1]]

ligh·tish[1, 2], aa. Somewhat LIGHT[2]; somewhat LIGHT[4]. [-ISH[1](2)]

ligh·tning, n. Visible electric discharge between clouds or cloud & ground (*forked, chain,* or *chained l.*, l.-flash in form of zigzag or divided line; *sheet l.*, l. flash of diffused brightness; *summer, heat, l.*, sheet l. without audible thunder, result of distant storm; *like l.*, with greatest conceivable speed; *with l. speed*); *l.-rod* or *-conductor*, metal rod or wire fixed to exposed part of building or to mast to divert l. into earth or sea; *l. strike*, labour strike at short notice by way of surprise. [differentiated form of *lightening* vbl n. of LIGHTEN[2]]

lights, n. pl. Lungs of sheep, pigs, bullocks, &c., used as food esp. for cats & dogs. [n. use of LIGHT[4], cf. LUNG]

ligh·tsome[1], a. Light, graceful, elegant, in appearance; light-hearted, merry; nimble. Hence **ligh·tsomeLY**[2] adv., **ligh·tsomeNESS** n. [LIGHT[4], -SOME]

ligh·tsome[2], a. (rare). Light-giving, luminous; well lighted, bright. [LIGHT[1], -SOME]

ligh·twood, nn. Kinds of tree with light wood; kinds of tree with wood that burns with bright flame. [LIGHT[4, 1]]

lign-aloes (linā·lōz), n. The drug aloes; aloes-wood, an aromatic Mexican wood. [f. LL *lignum aloes* wood of the ALOE]

li·gneous, a. (Of plants) woody (opp. *herbaceous*). [f. L *ligneus* (foll.) + -OUS]

ligni-, comb. form of L *lignum* wood. Hence **ligni·FEROUS**, **li·gniFORM**, aa., **li·gniFY** v.t. & i., **ligniFICA·TION** n.

li·gnite, n. Brown coal showing traces of ligneous structure. [F, see prec., -ITE[1](2)]

li·gnum vī·tae, n. Guaiacum. [L, = wood of life]

li·gūlate, a. (bot.). With strap-shaped fillet(s). [L *ligula* strap (*lingua* tongue, -ULE), -ATE[2]]

like[1], a. (often governing noun like trans. part.; *more, most*, rarely or poet. *-er, -est*), prep., adv. (archaic), conj. (vulg.), & n. Similar, resembling something or each other or the original, (*in l. manner* or *wise*; *on this & the l. subjects*; *the two letters are very l.*; *as l. as two peas*; *l. father l. son, l. master l. man*, as the one is so will the other be; *the picture is not l.*; in Alg., *l. signs*, both positive or both negative, *l. quantities*, expressed by same letters; sometimes with *with*, as *beings of l. passions with us*; now rarely, & chiefly in comp. *-er*, with *to*, as *liker to God than man*); resembling, such as, (*nothing l.* LEATHER, as good as; *what is he, it, l.?*, what sort of person or thing is he or it?; *look l.*, have appearance of; *l. that*, of the kind just seen or referred to; *a critic l. you*, of the class that you exemplify; *something l. £1,000*, nearly, about; *something like a day*, with stress on *like*, remarkably fine or otherwise satisfactory; so abs., *this is something like*; *nothing l. as good*, not nearly); characteristic of (*that is l. your impudence*; *it was l. him to think of himself last*); in promising state or right mood for doing (*looks l. lasting*; *feel l. working* or *stopping work*; also *looks l.* with n. = promise the finding or suggest the agency of, as *looks l. rabbits*); (archaic) likely, (archaic & colloq.) likely *to* (*had,* = was, *l. to have* done, narrowly escaped doing); *l.-minded*, having same tastes, views, &c. (Prep.) in the manner of, to the same degree as, (*cannot do it l. you*; *do not talk l. that*; *l. a shot*, without demur, willingly, regardless of consequences; *l. fun, blazes, one o'clock, anything,* MAD, &c., vigorously); (in proverbial or facet. pseudo-proverbial phrr.; emphasizing vbs) *blush l. a peony, drink l. a fish, fit l. a glove, get on l. a house on fire, smoke* i.e. tobacco *l. a chimney, spread l. wildfire, swear l. a trooper, swim l. a duck*; less usu. w. noun in objective relation, *hate* person &c. *l. poison, scatter them l. chaff*). (Adv.) in the same manner *as* (archaic); probably (now only in *very l., l. enough*, usu. parenthetic); (vulg.) so to speak (*by way of argument l.*). (Conj.; for archaic *l. as*; vulg. & colloq.) as (*cannot do it l. you do*; *snow is falling l. in January*). (N.) counterpart, equal, l. thing or person, (*mix with your ll.*; *shall not see his l. again*; *did you ever see the l. of it?*; *l. cures l.*; *the ll. of me* colloq., persons so humble as I; *the ll. of you* colloq., persons so distinguished as you); (Golf) stroke that equalizes number of strokes played by each side; (ellipt. use of adj. with pl. *l.*) thing(s) of the same kind (*will never do the l. again*; *& the l.* often as pl. = etcetera, as *music, painting, & the l.*; *or the l.*, or other thing(s) of the kind). [ME *lich* f. OE *gelic*, cf. G *gleich* & see ALIKE, f. OTeut. *galīko-* (*ga-* with, *līko-* body cf. LICH)]

like², v.t. & i., & n. Be pleasing to (archaic or facet.; chiefly impers., *it likes me not, well*, &c.); thrive (obs. exc. in *well-liking*); find agreeable, congenial, or satisfactory, feel attracted by, wish for, (*I l. you, the offer, his visits*, iron. *his impudence, her to be within reach, to see them now & then*; *do not l. such subjects discussed*; *should much l. to come*; *should l. to know* or *see* iron., think you will find it hard to tell me, am not likely to see; *should l. time to consider it*; *how do you l. it?*, do you l. it much or little or dislike it?), whence **li·kABLE** a., **li·kableNESS** n.; *if you l.* (expr. consent to request, as you *will come i. y. l.*, or limited assent, as *I am* shy *i. y. l.*, i.e. but not misanthropic, or emphatic selection, as I *am shy i. y. l.*, i.e. but someone else is not); suit (only in *I l. it*, i.e. kind of food, *but it does not l. me*); (n., usu. pl.) liking(s), predilection(s) (esp. *ll. & dislikes*). [OE *līcian* cf. Du. *lijken* (prec.)]

-like, suf. (i.e. LIKE a. & adv. in comp.). (1) Appended to nn. *-like* forms adjj. (*godlike, womanlike, plumbago-like*); advv. of similar form are perh. archaic, & in mod. use possible advv. can usu. be explained as adjj. (*he, cowardlike, refused*). (2) Appended to adjj. it forms adjj. chiefly Sc. (*humanlike, auldlike*) & Sc. advv.

li·kelihŏŏd, n. Being likely, probability, (esp. *in all l.*, probably). [-HOOD]

li·kely, a. & adv. (more, most, -ier, -iest). Probable, such as might well happen, or be or prove true, or turn out to be the thing specified, (*a l. story*, often iron.; *it is not l. he will come*; *his most l. halting-place is* —), to be expected *to* (*he, this, is* or *was not l. to come, happen*); promising, apparently suitable *for* purpose or *to* do or be, capable-looking, (*called at every l. house*; *six l. young fellows*; *the likeliest place for smugglers* or *to find him in*); (adv.) *most* or *very* probably. [f. ON *líkligr* (LIKE¹, -LY¹)]

li·ken, v.t. Find or point out resemblance in (thing) *to*, (rarely) make like *to* (*its arbitrary character likens it to a despotism*). [-EN⁶]

li·keness, n. Being like, resemblance (*between, to*); semblance (*enemy in l. of friend*); representation, copy, portrait (*take* one's *l.*, portray him), person or thing having the exact appearance *of* another. [-NESS]

li·kewise, adv. & conj. Similarly (bibl.); also, moreover, too. [for *in like wise*]

likin (lē·kē·n), n. Provincial transit duty in China. [Chin.]

li·king, n. What one likes, one's taste (*is it to your l.?*); regard, fondness, taste, fancy, *for* (*have a l. for him, for precise statement, no l. for flattery*). [OE *līcung* (LIKE², -ING¹)]

lil, U.S. dial for LITTLE.

li·lac (-*a*k), n. & a. Shrub with fragrant pale pinkish violet, or white, blossoms; (of) pale pinkish violet colour. [F f. Sp., f. Pers. *līlak* var. of *nīlak* (*nīl* blue)]

lilia·ceous, a. Of the lily kind. [f. L *liliaceus* (LILY, -ACEOUS)]

Lillibullē·ro, n. Song popular at end of 17th c., often referred to by writers. [part of refrain]

Lillipū·tian (-shn), a. & n. Native of Lilliput, diminutive (person or thing). [*Lilliput* in *Gulliver's Travels*, -IAN]

lilt, v.t. & i., & n. Sing melodiously or rhythmically; (song with) marked rhythmical cadence or swing. [n. f. vb, ME *lulte* etym. dub.]

li·ly, n. (Flower of) kinds of bulbous plant bearing large showy white or reddish or purplish flowers on tall slender stem, esp. the White or Madonna L. (*orange, tiger, turk's cap*, &c., *l.*); kinds of plant allied to these (*belladonna, calla, Guernsey, lent, water*, &c., *l.*); *l. of the valley*, spring flower with two large leaves & racemes of white bell-shaped fragrant flowers; person or thing of special whiteness or purity (*ll. & roses*, fair complexion); heraldic fleur-de-lis (*the ll.*, arms of old French monarchy, Bourbon dynasty); (attrib.) delicately white (*l. maid, hand*, &c.), pallid; *l.-iron*, harpoon with detachable head for killing swordfish; *l.-livered*, cowardly; *l.-white*, as a l. Hence **li·liED**² a. [OE *lilie* f. L *lilium* f. Gk *leirion*]

limb¹ (-m), n., & v.t. Leg, arm, or wing (*escape with life & l.*, without grave injury); (orig. *l. of the devil* or *Satan*) mischievous child, so *l. of the law*, lawyer, policeman, &c.; main branch of tree, one of four branches of cross, clause of sentence, spur of mountain; hence **(-)limbED**² (-md), **li·mbLESS** (-ml-), aa.; (vb) disable l. of (person or animal), dismember (body). [OE *lim*, cf. ON *limr*]

limb² (-m), n. (scient.). Edge of surface; graduated edge of quadrant &c.; edge (*eastern, lower*, &c., *l.*) of sun, moon, &c.; expanded part of petal, sepal, or leaf. [f. L *limbus* hem]

li·mbate (-*a*t), a. (biol., bot.). Having distinct or different-coloured border. [f. LL *limbatus* (prec., -ATE²)]

li·mbec, n. (archaic). = ALEMBIC.

li·mber¹, n., & v.t. Detachable front of gun-carriage (two wheels, axle, pole, & ammunition-box); (vb) attach l. to (gun), fasten together two parts of (gun-carriage; also abs.), (usu. *up*). [earlier *lymor*, perh. f. F *limonière* shafts & framework (*limon* shaft)]

li·mber², n. (naut.). One of the holes cut in floor-timbers for drainage to pump-well. [perh. f. F *lumière* light, so used]

li·mber³, a. Flexible; lithe, nimble. [f. 16th c.; etym. dub.]

li·mbo, n. Region on border of hell where pre-Christian just men & unbaptized infants are confined; prison, durance; condition of neglect or oblivion. [f. L phr. *in limbo* (LIMB²)]

lime¹, n., & v.t. Sticky substance made from holly bark for catching small birds (usu. *bird-lime*); white caustic alkaline earth (calcium oxide) got by burning *limestone*, kinds of rock chiefly carbonate of l., & used for making mortar, as manure, &c. (also *quick-l.*; *slaked l.*, this after combination with water, hydrate of l.), whence **li·me**LESS, **li·my**², aa.; *l.-burner*, maker of l.; *l.-cast*, outer layer of l. on building; *l.-kiln*, for burning limestone; *limelight*, intense white light got by heating cylinder of l. in oxyhydrogen flame (*the l.-l.* fig., w. ref. to use in theatre, full glare of publicity); *l.-pit*, for steeping hides to remove hair; *l.-twig*, smeared with birdlime. (Vb) smear (twigs), catch (bird), with birdlime (also fig.); treat, dress (land), with l.; steep (skins) in l. & water. [OE *lim*, cf. Du. *lijm*, G *leim*, cogn .w. L *limus* mud, *linere* smear, & w. LOAM]

lime², n. Round fruit smaller & more acid than lemon; *l.-juice*, used as drink & esp. as antiscorbutic. [F, f. Arab. as LEMON]

lime³, n. Ornamental tree with heart-shaped leaves & small fragrant yellowish blossom (often *l.-tree*). [prob. var. of *lind* LINDEN]

lī·mĕn, n. (psychol.). Limit below which given stimulus ceases to be perceptible, minimum of nerve-excitation required to produce sensation. Hence **li·min**AL a. [L (genit. *-inis*), = threshold, representing G *schwelle*]

Li·merick, n. Kind of nonsense verse (now usu. applied to the five-line form seen in Lear's nursery rhymes). [said to be f. chorus 'Will you come up to L.?' sung after extempore verses contributed each by member of party]

li·me-wort, li·mp-, n. = BROOK¹-*lime*. [OE *hleomece*]

li·mit¹, n. Bounding line, terminal point (*superior, inferior, l.*, earliest & latest possible date, largest & smallest possible or permissible amount), bound that may not or cannot be passed, (*without l.*, unlimited; *is the l.* slang, is the last straw, intolerable &c.; *l. man*, receiving longest start allowed in handicap, opp. *scratch*). Hence **li·mit**LESS a. [f. F *limite* f. L *limitem* nom. *-mes*]

li·mit², v.t. Confine within ll., set (usu. immaterial) bounds to, restrict *to*; serve as l. to; (p.p.) scanty; *limited company*, see LIABILITY; *limited mail*, taking only limited number of passengers; *limited monarchy* &c., subject to constitutional restrictions (opp. *absolute*). So **li·mit**ATIVE a. [f. F *limiter* f. L *limitare* (prec.)]

limitār·ian, n. & a. (Holder) of doctrine that only a limited part of mankind is to be saved. [LIMIT¹, -ARIAN]

li·mitary, a. Subject to restriction; of, on, serving as, limit. [f. L *limitaris* (LIMIT¹, -ARY²)]

limita·tion, n. Limiting; limited condition, disability or inability, (*has his ll.*, is not talented in all directions); limiting rule or circumstance; legally specified period beyond which action cannot be brought, estate or law is not to continue, &c. (*statute of ll.*, any that fixes such period). [f. L *limitatio* (LIMIT², -ATION)]

li·mitrophe (-ōf), a. (Of district &c.) on frontier, adjacent *to*. [F (L *limes* LIMIT¹, Gk *-trophos* -feeding) orig. of lands set apart for support of frontier troops]

limn (-m), v.t. (archaic). Paint (picture); depict, portray. Hence **li·mn**ER¹ (-mn-) n. [f. obs. *lumine* illuminate (MSS.) f. OF *luminer* (L *lumen -inis* light)]

limno·logy, n. Study of physical phenomena of lakes; study of pond-life. [Gk *limnē* lake, -O-, -LOGY]

li·mousine (-ōōzēn), n. Motor-car with closed body & roof over driver. [F, fem. adj. = of Limoges]

limp¹, v.i., & n. Walk lamely, (of verse) halt; (n.) lame walk. Hence **li·mping**LY² adv. [cf. MHG *limphin*]

limp², a. Not stiff, flexible, (of book-bindings) not stiffened with mill-board; (fig.) wanting in energy. Hence **li·mp**LY² adv., **li·mp**NESS n. [f. 18th c.; etym. dub.]

li·mpet, n. Gasteropod mollusc with tent-shaped shell sticking tightly to rocks; (fig.) person, esp. State employee, who clings to office. [OE *lempedu* f. LL *lampreda* limpet, LAMPREY]

li·mpid, a. Pellucid, clear, not turbid, (of liquids, atmosphere, eyes, literary style). Hence or cogn. **li·mpid**LY² adv., **limpi·d**ITY, **li·mpid**NESS, nn. [f. L *limpidus* prob. cogn. w. *lympha* LYMPH]

li·mpkin, n. Kinds of bird between cranes & rails. [LIMP¹, -KIN, from their movements]

limp-wort. See LIME-WORT.

li·nage (-ĭj), n. Number of lines in printed matter; payment according to this. [-AGE]

li·nchpin, n. Pin passed through axle-end to keep wheel on. [OE *lynis*, cf. G *lünse*, PIN]

Li·ncoln green (-kn), n. Bright green stuff made at Lincoln.

li·nden, n. Lime-tree. [orig. adj. (obs. *lind* lime cf. G *linde* cogn. w. Gk *elatē* fir + -EN⁵)]

line[1], n. Fine long flax separated from the tow. [OE *līn* flax, cf. G *lein-* perh. cogn. w. L *linum* & Gk *linon*]

line[2], n. (Order of main senses) 1. Cord; 2. Long narrow mark; 3. Row; 4. Series; 5. Direction. 1. Piece of rope (esp. naut., e.g. for sounding; so prob. *hard ll.*, bad luck, hardship; also =CLOTHES-*l.*); wire or cable for telegraph or telephone (*lineman*, charged with keeping wire &c. in repair), route traversed by this; cord bearing fish-hook(s) (*l.-fishing*, opp. *net-fishing*; *give* one *l. enough*, let him go his own way for a time in order to secure or detect him later); cord for measuring, levelling, &c. (PLUMB-*l.*; *by rule & l.*, with precision), (pl.) one's lot in life (*Ps.* xvi. 6, w. ref. to marking out land); rule or canon (obs. exc. in *l. upon l.*, see *Is.* xxviii. 10, with slow & regular progress). 2. Long narrow mark traced on surface; use of these in draughtsmanship (*boldness, purity, of l.*; *translate life* &c. *into l. & colour*; *l.-drawing*, done with pen or pencil; *l.-engraving*, done with incised lines, as opp. *etching* & *mezzotint*; *l.-work*, with pen or pencil not wash &c.; *l. of beauty*, l. with two opposite curves like elongated S); (Games) mark limiting court or ground or special parts of them; thing resembling traced mark, band of colour, seam, furrow, wrinkle (*l. of life, fortune*, &c., folds in palm of hand significant in palmistry); (Math.) straight or curved continuous extent of length without breadth, track of moving point, (with defining word, as *isothermal l.*) curve connecting all points having specified common property; *the* equator; straight l. (*l. of* FIRE[1], *force*, &c., *picture hung on the l.*, exhibited with its centre about level of spectator's eye; *go as straight as a l.*); contour, outline, lineament (*the savage ll. of his mouth*), (pl.) plan or draft (esp. of ship in horizontal, vertical, & oblique sections) or manner of procedure (*on conservative, political, the same*, &c., *ll., on the ll. laid down by* someone); (as measure) 1/12 inch; limit, boundary, (DRAW[1] *the l.*; so *dividing l.*; *on the l.*, not clearly one thing or the other). 3. Row of persons or things (*come, bring, into l.*, agree or co-operate, induce to do so; *toe the l.*, fig. accept party programme &c.); (Mil., pl.) connected series of field-works (GO[1] *up the l.*), also row of tents or huts in camp; (Naut.) *l. abreast*, number of parallel ships ranged on line crossing keels at right angles, *l. ahead*, ships following in a string, *l. of* BATTLE[1], *ship of the l.* or *l.-of-*BATTLE[1] *ship*; (Mil.) double row (front & rear ranks) of men ranged side by side, also arrangement of companies side by side (opp. COLUMN; *drawn up in, form, wheel into, l.*; *all along the l.*, at every point, often fig. of success &c.; *l.-firing*, by body of men in l.); (Army) *the l.*, regular & numbered regiments (not Guards, Engineers, or Artillery, & sometimes understood to exclude Cavalry); row of words in page or newspaper column (*read between the ll.*, detect hidden meaning in document, speech, &c.; *l.-filling*, flourish or ornament in blank space at end of l. in MS.), (by exag.) short letter (*just a l. to tell you that* —), single verse of poetry, (pl.) piece of poetry (often *upon* subject or *to* person), (pl.) specified amount (*100* &c. *ll.*) of usu. Latin verse to be written out as school punishment, (pl., also *marriage ll.*) certificate of marriage, (pl.) words of actor's part. 4. Series or regular succession of steamers, omnibuses, &c., plying between certain places; connected series of persons or things following one another in time (*can show a long l. of heroes*), esp. several generations of family (*male, female, direct*, &c., *l.*), family, lineage, stock (*comes of a good l.*). 5. Direction, course, track, (*l. of march, communication*, &c.); (Railways) single track of rails (*up, down, l.*, to, from, chief terminus esp. London), one branch of system (*main, branch, loop, l.*) or whole system under one management (*Southern* &c. *l.*); course followed in riding to hounds (*take, keep to*, one's *own l.*, often also fig.); course of procedure, conduct, thought, &c.; department of activity, province, branch of business, (*something in, out of*, one's *l.*, that interests or concerns one, or not; *in the banking, oil-&-colour*, &c., *l.*); (Commerc.) class of goods, order for or stock of this. [partly thr. OE *līne*, cf. G *leine* cord, partly thr. F *ligne*, f. L *linea* line orig. fem. of *lineus* of linen (*linum* flax)]

line[3], v.t. & i. Mark *in, off, out*, with ll. on paper &c.; cover with ll. (*a face lined with pain*); *l. through*, cross out; draw (men or objects) *up* in l.; come *up* or spread (t. & i.) *out* in l.; post troops &c. along (road, hedge, &c.), (of troops) form open or close l. along (pass &c.), (of things) stand at intervals along (wall &c.). [f. prec.]

line[4], v.t. Apply layer of (usu. different) material to inside of (garment, box, vessel, bag, &c.); fill (purse, pocket, stomach, &c.); serve as lining for. Hence **li·**NING[1](4) n. (*every cloud has a silver lining*, there is good in every evil). [f. LINE[1], w. ref. to use of linen for linings]

line[5], v.t. Copulate with, cover, (bitch). [f. F *ligner*]

li·neage (-ĭĕj), n. Lineal descent, ancestry, pedigree. [f. OF *lignage* (L *linea* LINE[2], -AGE)]

li·nĕal, a. In the direct line of descent or ancestry (opp. *collateral*); (rare) of, in, line(s), linear. Hence **li·neal**LY[2] adv. [f. F *linéal* f. LL *linealis* (LINE[2], -AL)]

li·nĕament, n. (Usu. pl.) distinctive feature(s), or characteristic(s) esp. feature(s) of face, (sing. chiefly in *every l.*).

[f. F *linéament* f. L *lineamentum* (*lineare* in unrecorded sense *draw lines* f. *linea* LINE[2])]

li·nĕar, a. Of, in, line(s) (*l.* PERSPECTIVE); (Math., Physics) involving measurement in one dimension only (*l. equation*, of first degree); long, narrow, & of uniform breadth. Hence **li·near**LY[2] adv. [f. L *linearis* (LINE[2], -AR[1])]

lĭnea·tion, n. Drawing of, marking with, arrangement of, lines. [f. L *lineatio* (LINEAMENT, -ATION)]

lĭ·nen, a. & n. Made of flax (*l. cloth*). (N.) cloth woven from flax, (with pl.) particular kind of this; (collect.) shirts, sheets, cloths, &c., of l., calico, &c. (*wash* one's *dirty l. at home, in public*, keep, not keep, quiet about domestic quarrels &c.); *l.-draper*, dealer in l., calico, &c.; hence **linen**E·TTE(2) n. [OE *līnen* (LINE[1], -EN[5])]

lī·ner, n. Ship, usu. steamer, belonging to line of passenger ships. [-ER[1]]

lī·nesman, n. Soldier of line regiment; (Lawn tennis, Football) official assisting umpire or referee by deciding whether or where ball touches or crosses line. [*line's* (LINE[2])]

ling[1], n. Long slender N.-Europ. sea-fish used (usu. cured) for food. [cf. Du. & G *leng* prob. cogn. w. LONG[1]]

ling[2], n. Kinds of heather. Hence **li·ng**Y[2] (-ngĭ) a. [f. ON *lyng*]

-ling[1], suf. forming nn.; com.-Teut., arising f. addition of *-ingoz* -ING[3] to n. stems w. suf. *-ilo-* -LE. (1) in OE, ME, & mod. E, *-ling* is added to nn. to form nn. denoting person or thing connected w. primary n. (*hireling, nursling, sapling*), & to adjj. to form nn. (*grayling, darling, youngling*); so also, f. adv., *underling*. On anal. of *nursling* &c., where first component is ambiguous, *shaveling, starveling*, are formed on vv. (2) in ON *-ling* had dim. force; instances of this appear in E in 14th & 15th cc. (*codling, gosling, duckling*); in this use alone (esp. in formation of contemptuous dimm., as *lordling, princeling*) the suf. is a living one.

-ling[2], **-lings,** suf. forming advv.; Teut. *-ling, -lang, -lung*, (+-ES) used in OE added to nn. to form advv. of direction, as *bæcling* back, *andlang* ALONG, *grundlunga* to ground; in other wds the suf. forms advv. of condition or situation (*darkling*), usu. now dial. only.

li·nger (-ngg-), v.i. & t. Put off departure esp. from reluctance to go; stay about, not depart or arrive at expected or right time; dally *round* place or *over* or (*up*)*on* subject; drag *on* a feeble existence (of invalids & moribund customs); be protracted (*lingering disease, agonies*); be tardy, delay; throw (time) *away* in delays. Hence **li·nger**ER[1] n., **li·ngering**LY[2] adv. [f. obs. *leng* OE *lengan* lengthen, linger, cf. G *längen*, (LONG[1]) + -ER[5]]

lingerie **(F),** n. (Stock of) linen articles.

li·ngo, n. (pl. *-oes*). (Contempt. for) foreign language, vocabulary of special subject or class of people. [prob. corrupt. of LINGUA (FRANCA)]

-lings. See -LING[2].

li·ngua fra·nca (-nggwa), n. Mixture of Italian, French, Greek, & Spanish, used in Levant; any mixed jargon serving as medium between different peoples (also fig. of common ideas &c.). [It., = Frankish tongue]

li·ngual (-gw-), a. & n. (Anat.) of the tongue; (Phonet.) formed by the tongue (n., l. sound; both a. & n. now rare), whence **li·ngual**IZE(3) v.t.; of speech or languages (*l. studies*). [f. med. L *lingualis* (L *lingua* tongue, -AL)]

li·nguiform (-gw)-, a. (bot., anat., zool.). Tongue-shaped. [prec., -I-, -FORM]

li·nguist (-gw-), n. Person skilled in foreign languages (*good, bad, no, l.*). [as prec., -IST]

lingui·stic, a. Of the study of languages; of language, lingual. Hence **lingui·sti**CALLY adv. [prec., -IC]

li·ngūlate (-*a*t), a. Tongue-shaped. [f. L *lingula* dim. of *lingua* tongue, -ATE[2]]

li·nguo-, comb. form of L *lingua* tongue (-O-), as *-de·ntal* made with tongue & teeth (of sounds).

lĭ·niment, n. Liquid usu. made with oil used in rubbing body for rheumatism &c., embrocation. [f. L *linimentum* (*linire* smear, -MENT)]

link[1], n., & v.t. & i. One ring or loop of chain (as measure, 1/100 of surveying chain or 7.92 in.); =SLEEVE-*l.*; loop in knitting &c.; connecting part, thing or person that unites others, filler of gap, member of series (MISSING *l.*). (Vb) connect, join, (things, persons) *together* or (thing, person) *to*; clasp (hands); hook (arm *in* or *through* another's, or arms); attach oneself *on* or *in* to system, company, &c.; *linked battalions*, two, of which one at home supplies drafts for other on foreign service. Hence **li·nk**AGE(1, 3) n. [f. ON (Icel. *hlekkr*, Sw. *länk*) cogn. w. G *gelenk* joint, & w. FLANK]

link[2], n. Torch of pitch & tow formerly used for lighting people along streets; *l.-boy, link-man*, employed to carry ll. [perh. f. prec. in sense *segment* of the material]

links, n. pl. Level or undulating sandy ground near sea shore, with turf & coarse grass (Sc.); ground on which golf is played, often resembling that of prec. sense (also *a links* as sing.). [OE *hlinc* perh. cogn. w. LEAN[2]]

linn, n. (chiefly Sc.). Waterfall; pool below this; precipice, ravine. [perh. mixture of OE *hlynn* torrent & Gael. *linne*]

Linn(a)e·an, a. & n. (Follower) of Linnaeus or his system of classifying plants & animals. [*Linnaeus* latinized name of C. Linné Swedish naturalist + -AN]

li·nnet, n. Common brown or warm-grey song-bird. [f. OF *linette* (*lin* flax, f. its food)]

lino·lēum, n. (also **li·no** abbr.). Floorcloth of canvas with thick coat of oxidized linseed oil. Hence **lino·leum**ED² a. [L *linum* flax, *oleum* oil]

li·notype, n. Machine for producing stereotyped lines of words as substitute for type-setting, much used in printing newspapers. [=*line o' type*]

li·nsang, n. Civet cat of Borneo & Java. [Javanese]

li·nseed, n. Seed of flax; *l. cake,* l. (with the *l. oil* pressed out) as cattle-food; *l. meal,* ground l.; *l. poultice,* of l. or l. meal. [LINE¹]

li·nsey-wōō·lsey (-zĭ-, -zĭ), n. Dress material of coarse inferior wool woven on cotton warp (orig. of wool & flax). [from 1483; *linsey,* perh. a coarse linen (LINE¹ perh. +obs. *say* silk); *woolsey*=*wool* w. jingling termination]

li·nstock, n. (hist.). Match-holder used in old gunnery. [f. Du. *lontstock* (*lont* match)]

lint, n. Soft material for dressing wounds made by scraping linen cloth on one side. [cogn. w. LINE¹; perh. f. F *linette* linseed (*lin* linen)]

li·ntel (-tl), n. Horizontal timber or stone over door or window. Hence **li·ntell**ED² a. [OF,=threshold, f. pop. L **limitale* or **limitellum* see LIMIT¹, -LE(2)]

li·ny, a. Marked with lines; wrinkled; (Art) using line too much. Hence **li·ni**NESS. [-Y²]

li·on, n. Large powerful tawny African & S.-Asiatic carnivorous quadruped with tufted tail & (in the male) flowing shaggy mane (*l. in the way* or *path,* obstacle, esp. imaginary; *l.'s mouth,* perilous position; *l.'s share,* largest or best part; *l. & unicorn,* supporters of royal arms; *l.'s skin,* false assumption of courage; *twist l.'s tail,* of foreign, esp. U.-S., journalists or orators defying or insulting England); courageous person, so **lion-heart**ED² a.; (pl.) sights worth seeing in town &c. (from custom of showing country visitors the ll. in Tower of London; *see, show, the ll.*); person of literary or other celebrity sought after to be shown off at social gatherings (*l.-hunter,* host or hostess depending much on ll.), whence **li·on**HOOD, **li·on**SHIP, nn.; national emblem of Great Britain (*the British L.,* the nation personified); constellation & zodiacal sign LEO. Hence **lion**E·SQUE, **li·on**LIKE, aa., **li·on**ESS¹, **li·on**ET¹, nn. [f. AF *leun* f. L *leonem* nom. *leo* f. Gk *leōn leontos*]

li·onize, v.t. & i. See or show the sights (see prec.) of (place); show these to (visitor); see the sights; treat (person) as celebrity, make a lion (see prec.) of, whence **li·on**ISM(1) n. [-IZE]

lip, n., & v.t. One of the fleshy edges of the opening of the mouth (*upper, lower* or *under, l.*; *bite* one's *l.,* in vexation or to repress emotion, stifle laugh, &c.; *stiff upper l.,* fortitude or obstinacy; *curl* one's *l.,* in scorn; *hang* one's *l.,* in humiliation; *lick, smack,* one's *ll.,* in enjoyment or anticipation of food or fig.; *hang on* one's *ll.,* listen to his every word in reverence; *word* &c. *escapes* one's *ll.,* is uttered thoughtlessly); saucy talk, impudence, (slang, esp. *none of your l.!*); edge of cup, vessel, cavity, wound, &c.; *lip-,* from the ll. only, professed, not heartfelt or sincere, (*l.-homage, -religion, -Christian, -service, -worship*); *l.-deep,* superficial, insincere; *l.-language, -reading, -speaking,* use & interpretation of silent motions of ll. by & with the deaf or dumb; *lipsalve,* ointment for sore lips, fig. flattery; *lipstick,* stick of cosmetic for rouging ll.; hence **(-)lipp**ED², **li·p**LESS, aa. (Vb) touch with ll., apply ll. to; (of water) just touch, lap; murmur, utter softly. [OE *lippa,* cf. Du. *lip,* G *lippe,* cogn. w. L *labium, labrum*]

lipo·graphy, n. =HAPLOGRAPHY. [f. Gk *lip-* st. of *leipō* omit, -GRAPHY]

li·pper, n. (naut.). Rippling or ruffled motion, surface roughness, of sea. [prob. cogn. w. LAP⁵+-ER⁵]

liqua·te, v.t. Separate or purify (metals) by liquefying. Hence **liqua·**TION n. [f. L *liquare* melt, cogn. w. LIQUOR, -ATE³]

li·quefȳ, v.t. & i. Bring (solid or gas) or come into liquid condition. Hence or cogn. **lique**FA·CIENT a. & n., **lique**FA·CTION n., **li·quefact**IVE, **li·quefi**ABLE, aa., **li·quefi**ER¹(1, 2) n. [f. F *liquéfier* f. L *liquefacere* (*liquēre* be LIQUID, -FY)]

lique·scent (-snt), a. Becoming, apt to become, liquid. [f. L *liquescere* (prec., -ESCENT)]

liqueur· (-kūr, *or as F*), n. Strong alcoholic liquor sweetened & flavoured with aromatic substances & usu. drunk in small quantities; mixture of sugar & alcohol or wines used to flavour champagne, whence **liqueur·** v.t.; *l. brandy,* of special quality for drinking as l.; *l.-glass,* very small for ll.; *l.-frame, -stand,* for holding l.-bottles. [F,=LIQUOR]

li·quid, a. & n. (Substance that is) incompressible but offering no resistance to change of shape, neither solid nor gaseous, resembling water or oil in normal state, in fluid but not gaseous condition (*l. air,* reduced to l. state by intense cold; *l. fire,* projected from flame-thrower in war); watery; having the transparence, translucence, or brightness, of water or wine (*l. lustre, eyes, sky, air, blue*); (of sounds) flowing clear, fluent, pure, not grating or discordant, not guttural, vowel-like, (*blackbird's l. notes*; *in his l. Italian*; n., one of the letters l, r, & sometimes m, n); not fixed, unstable, (*has very l. convictions* or *principles*); (of assets, securities, &c.) easily convertible into cash. Hence or cogn. **liqui·d**ITY, **li·quid**NESS, nn., **li·quid**IZE(3) v.t., **li·quid**LY[2] adv. [f. OF *liquide* f. L *liquidus* (*liquēre* be liquid cf. LIQUATE, LIQUOR)]

li·quidate, v.t. & i. Pay, clear off, (debt); wind up, ascertain liabilities & apportion assets of, (company, firm), whence **li·quidat**OR[2] n.; (intr., of company) have this done. Hence **liquid**A·TION n. (*go into l.*, of company, have its affairs wound up, become bankrupt). [f. LL *liquidare* make LIQUID, -ATE[3]]

li·quor (-ker), n., & v.t. & i. Liquid part of secretion or product of operation; liquid used as wash &c.; water used in brewing; liquid (usu. fermented or distilled) for drinking (*malt l.*, ale, beer, porter, &c.; *spirituous l.*, spirits; DISGUISED *with l.*; *in l.*, *the worse for l.*, more or less drunk; *a l.* or *l.-up* slang, taking of l. as refreshment); water in which food has been boiled; (Pharmacy, pr. lī·kwor) solution of specified drug in water (*l. ammoniae* &c.). (Vb) dress (leather, shoes) with grease or oil; steep (malt &c.) in water; (slang) *l. up* or *l.*, have a drink of alcoholic l. [earlier & OF *licur* (now *liqueur*) f. L *liquor* (*liquēre* see LIQUID, -OR[1]) to which spelling has been assimilated]

li·quorice (-ker-), **li·corice,** n. (Black substance used in medicine & as sweetmeat made from) root of *Glycyrrhiza glabra*; the plant. [f. AF *lycorys* f. LL. *liquiritia* f. Gk *glukurrhiza* (*glukus* sweet, *rhiza* root)]

li·quorish, a. Fond of, indicating fondness for, liquor. Hence **li·quorish**LY[2] adv., **li·quorish**NESS n. [misuse of LICKERISH]

lira (lēr·*a*), n. (pl. *lire* pr. -ā, *liras*; abbr. *L.*). Italian monetary unit (pre-war value as silver coin, about 10*d.*). [It., f. L LIBRA]

lisle thread (līl), n. Fine hard-twisted thread made orig. at Lisle (now Lille) in France.

lisp, v.i. & t., & n. Substitute one of the sounds of *th* for sibilants in speaking; (of child) speak with imperfect pronunciation; say with a l. (often *out*); hence **li·sping**LY[2] adv. (N.) lisping pronunciation; rippling of waters, rustling of leaves. [f. OE *wlisp* a. lisping, cf. Du. *lispen*, G *lispeln*, to lisp]

li·ssom(e), a. Lithe, supple, agile. Hence **li·ssom(e)**NESS n. [contr. of LITHE*some*]

list[1], n., & v.t. & i. 1. Selvage or edge of cloth, usu. of different material, whence **li·st**ING[1](3) n.; such edges torn off & used as a material (*l. slippers*; *line edges of door with l.*, to keep out draughts; vb, fasten l. round edges of, as *have listed my doors*); (pl.) palisades enclosing tilting-ground, (fig.) scene of contest (*enter the ll. against*, challenge or accept challenge of, usu. to controversy). 2. Roll or catalogue of names, of persons or things belonging to a class, of articles with prices, of things to be done, &c. (*active l.*, of officers in army or navy liable to be called on for service; *free l.*, of persons to be admitted free to theatre &c., also of duty-free articles; ARMY, CIVIL, SICK, *-l.*); (vb) enter in a l., (now rare or vulg.) go as soldier, enlist. [sense 1 f. OF *liste*, cf. Du. *lijst*, G *leiste*; sense 2 f. F *liste* f. Teut. as in 1]

list[2], v.t. (archaic; 3 sing. pres. *list* or *listeth*, past *list* or *listed*). Be pleasing to (*shall do what him listeth*; *did as him list*); desire, choose, (*to* do or abs.; *ye who l. to hear*; *wind bloweth where it listeth*). [OE *lystan*, cf. Du. *lusten*, G *lüsten*, cogn. w. LUST]

list[3], n., & v.i. Lean(ing) over to one side (of ship, owing to leak, shifting cargo, subsidence, &c., cf. HEEL[3]; also of building, fence, &c.). [vb f. n., perh. transf. use of obs. *list* pleasure, inclination, f. prec.]

list[4], v.i. & t. (archaic). Listen, listen to. [OE *hlystan* (*hlyst* sense of hearing) cf. G *lüstern* & *lauschen* f. Aryan *klus-* (*klu-* see LOUD)]

li·sten (-sn), v.i. & t. Make effort to hear something, hear person speaking with attention, give ear to or now usu. *to* (person or sound or story), yield *to* temptation or request; *l. in*, tap telephonic communication, use broadcast receiver; *listening-post*, point near enemy's lines for detecting his movements by sound. Hence **li·sten**ER[1] (-sn-), n. (*good —er*, one who habitually listens with interest or sympathy). [ONorthumb. *lysna*, cf. OE *hlosnian* & *hlyst*, see prec.]

li·sterine, n. A particular antiseptic solution. [Lord *Lister*, -INE[4]]

li·sterize, v.t. Treat (wound) on the antiseptic methods introduced by Lord Lister. So **listēr·**IAN a. [-IZE]

li·stless, a. Languid, indifferent, uninterested, disinclined for exertion. Hence **li·stless**LY[2] adv., **li·stless**NESS n. [f. obs. *list* inclination (LIST[2]) + -LESS]

lit. See LIGHT[3], LIGHT[5].

li·tany, n. Series of petitions for use in church services or processions recited by clergy & responded to usu. in repeated formula(s) by people (*the L.*, that contained in the Common Prayer Book); *l.-desk, -stool*, at which reciter of l. kneels. [f. med. L f. Gk *litaneia* prayer (*litaneuō* pray f. *litanos* suppliant f. *litē* prayer)]

litchi (lētshē·), n. Fruit(-tree) orig. from China grown in Bengal. [f. Chin. *li-chi*]

-lite, suf. forming names of minerals, F, f. Gk *lithos* stone; usu. preceded by -o-.

li·teracy, n. Ability to read & write. [LITERATE, -CY]

li·terae humānior·ēs, n. (abbr. *Lit. Hum.*). Polite letters, esp. as name of classical school or examination for B.A. degree at Oxford. [L]

li·teral, a. & n. Of, in, expressed by, letter(s) of alphabet (*l. error*, also *l.* as n., misprint); following the letter, text, or exact or original words (*l. translation, transcript*, &c.), whence **li·teral**ISM(4) n.; taking words in their usual or primary sense & applying the ordinary rules of grammar, without mysticism or allegory or metaphor, (*l. interpretation*; *I hear nothing in the l. sense of the word*, with the ears as opp. other means of getting news), whence **li·teral**ISM(3), **li·teral**IST(2), nn.; (of persons) prosaic, matter-of-fact; so called without exaggeration (*l. decimation*; often incorrectly used, as *a l. flood of pamphlets*). Hence **litera·**LITY, **li·teral**NESS, nn., **li·teral**LY[2] adv. [OF, f. L *litteralis* (LETTER, -AL)]

li·teralize, v.t. Take (metaphor &c.) in literal sense. [-IZE]

literā·rum do·ctor, n. Doctor of literature (as University degree). [L]

li·terary, a. Of, constituting, occupied with, literature, polite learning, or books & written composition esp. of the kind valued for form (*l. history of a thing*, of its treatment in literature; *l. property*, exclusive right of publication, books &c. subject to this; *l. man*, man of LETTERS); (of word or idiom) uncolloquial, affected by writers. Hence **li·terari**LY[2] adv., **li·terari**NESS n. [f. L *litterarius* (LETTER, -ARY[1])]

li·terate (-*at*), a. & n. (Person) having some acquaintance with literature or (now usu.) able to read & write; man admitted to Anglican orders without university degree. [f. L *litteratus* (LETTER, -ATE[2])]

literā·ti, n. pl. Men of letters, the learned class. [L, as prec.]

literā·tim, adv. Letter for letter, textually, literally. [L]

li·terātor, n. Literary man. [L (LITERATE, -OR[2]) elementary teacher, grammarian, sciolist]

li·terature (-tsh*er*, -tūr), n. Literary culture (archaic); literary production (*engaged in l.*), the literary profession (*l. was represented by* —); realm of letters, writings of country or period; writings whose value lies in beauty of form or emotional effect (LIGHT[4] *l.*); *the* books treating *of* a subject; (colloq.) printed matter. [f. L *litteratura* (LITERATE, -URE)]

-lith, suf. repr. Gk *lithos* stone (*aerolith, monolith*); cf. -LITE.

li·tharge (-j), n. Protoxide of lead. [f. OF *litarge* f. Gk *litharguros* (*lithos* stone, *arguros* silver) so called as by-product in separation of silver from lead]

lithe (-dh), a. Flexible, supple. Hence **li·the**NESS n., **li·the**SOME a. [OE *lithe* soft, cf. G *lind*, cogn. w. L *lentus*]

li·thia, n. Oxide of lithium; *l.-water*, used for gout. [changed f. earlier *lithion* f. Gk neut. of *litheios* (*lithos* stone) after *soda, potassa*, &c.]

li·thic[1], a. Of the stone or calculus; of stone. [f. Gk *lithikos* (prec., -IC)]

li·thic[2], a. (chem.). Of lithium. [foll., -IC]

li·thium, n. Metallic element of alkaline group. [LITHIA, -IUM]

lith(o)-, comb. form of Gk *lithos* stone, esp. in wds having ref. either to the treatment of stone in the bladder or kidneys, or to the use of stone in printing.

li·thograph, n., & v.t. Lithographic print; (vb) print by lithography. [prec., -GRAPH]

litho·graphy, n. Drawing or writing on kind of yellow slaty limestone (*lithographic stone*) so that impressions in ink can be taken. So **litho·**GRAPHER n., **litho**GRA·PHIC a. [LITHO-, -GRAPHY]

litho·logy, n. Science of the nature & composition of stones & rocks, whence **litholo·**GICAL a.; department of medical science dealing with calculus. [LITHO-, -LOGY]

li·thontri·ptic, a. & n. (Medicine) that breaks up stone in bladder. [f. F *lithontriptique* f. Gk *lithōn thruptika* (drugs) comminutive of stones]

li·thophyte, n. (Zool.) polyp whose substance is calcareous, as some corals; (Bot.) plant that grows on stone. [LITHO-, Gk *phuton* plant (*phuō* grow)]

litho·tomy, n. Operation of cutting for stone in bladder. Hence or cogn. **litho·to·mic**(AL) aa., **litho·tom**IST(1) n., **litho·tom**IZE(1) v.t. [f. LL f. Gk *lithotomia* (LITHO-, -TOMY)]

litho·trity, n. Operation of crushing stone in bladder into small particles that can be passed through urethra. Hence **litho·trit**IST(1) n., **litho·trit**IZE(1) v.t. [f. LITHONTRIPTIC, by change of *lithōn* to LITHO- & confusion of *-tript-* (already transferred f. Gk *thruptō* comminute to Gk *tribō* wear) with L *terere trit-* wear]

Lithūā·nian, a. & n. (Language or native) of Lithuania. [-AN]

li·tigate, v.i. & t. Go to law, be party to lawsuit; contest (point) at law, whence **li·tig**ABLE a. Hence **li·tig**ANT(1) n. & a., **litig**A·TION n. [f. L *litigare* (*lis litis* lawsuit), -ATE[3]]

liti·gious (-jus), a. Given to litigation, fond of going to law; disputable at law, offering matter for lawsuit; of lawsuits. Hence **liti·gious**LY[2] adv., **liti·gious**NESS n. [f. F *litigieux* f. L *litigiosus* (*litigium* litigation cf. prec.)]

li·tmus, n. Blue colouring-matter got from lichens that is turned red by acid & restored to blue by alkali; *l.-paper*, unsized & stained with l. as test for acids. [f. MDu. *leecmos* (LAC[1], *moes* pulp)]

li·totēs, n. Ironically moderate form of speech (as *'scoundrel' is* rather *a rude word*), esp. the expressing of an affirmative by the negative of its contrary, as *no small* for *great*. [Gk (*-ēs*) f. *litos* plain, meagre]

litre (lē·ter), n. Unit of capacity in metric system, = cube of 1/10 metre, about 1¾ pints. [F, from 1793, prob. f. LL f. Gk *litra* pound]

li·tter, n., & v.t. & i. Vehicle containing couch shut in by curtains & carried on men's shoulders or by beasts; framework with couch for transporting sick & wounded; straw, rushes, &c., as bedding esp. for animals; straw & dung of farmyard; odds & ends, leavings, state of untidiness, disorderly accumulation of papers &c., whence **li·tter**Y² a.; the young brought forth at a birth. (Vb) provide (horse &c.) with l. as bed (usu. *down*); spread l. or straw on (floor, stable; usu. *down*); make (place) untidy (of objects lying about, or of person *with* these or simply); scatter & leave lying; bring forth (whelps &c., or abs.). [f. OF *litiere* f. med. L *lectaria* (L *lectus* bed, -ARY¹)]

litterae, -rarum. See **lite-.**

littérateur (F), n. Literary man.

li·ttle, a. (LESS, LESSER, LEAST; also *smaller, smallest*), n., & adv. (LESS, LEAST). Small (often with emotional implications not given by *small*, cf. GREAT), not great or big (the idiomatic antitheses are *great & l., big & l., great & small, large & small*, not *large & l.* nor *big & small*); (as distinctive epithet) of smaller or smallest size &c. (*the L. Auk, L. Malvern, the L.* BEAR¹, *the l. finger* or *toe*); young (*the l. Joneses*, Jones's children; *l. man* or *woman*, boy or girl, esp. as voc.; *his, her, its, our, l. ones*, children or cubs &c.); as of a child, evoking tenderness, patronage, amusement, &c., (*her poor l. efforts to please; we know his l. ways; so that is your l. game*, what you are hoping to do undetected); short in stature, distance, or time (*a l. man; the l. people*, fairies; *will go a l. way with you; wait a l. while*); trivial, unimportant, (*every l. difficulty*); mean, paltry, contemptible, (*with the l. cunning of l. minds*); not much (*gained l. advantage from it*; often *but* or *very l.*); *a l.*, some though not much, even a small amount of, (prob. f. the n. use with ellipse of *of*; *give me a l. butter; a l. care would have prevented it*); (abs.) *the l.*, persons of l. power or importance, what is l., *in l.*, on a small scale; *l.-Englander, -dism*, (holder of) principle that Great Britain should contract her responsibilities for colonies & dependencies (opp. IMPERIALIST, -ISM); *l.-go* colloq., first examination for B.A. degree at Cambridge; *l. Mary* (colloq.), the stomach; *L. Masters*, group of 16th-c. German engravers, followers of Dürer, named from small size of their prints; hence **li·ttle**NESS n. (N.) not much, only a small amount, a mere trifle, (*l. or nothing*, hardly anything; *did not a l. for the cause*, much; *got but, very, rather, l. out of it; a l. makes us laugh; gives me l. of his company; did what l. he could; the l. of his work that remains*); a certain but no great amount (*knows a l. of everything; a l.*, rather, somewhat; *not a l.*, extremely); (for a) short time or distance (*after, for, a l.; leave me here a l.; l. by l., by l. & l.*, by degrees). (Adv.) to a small extent only (*I like him l.; l. known authors; is l. more than a cento*); not at all (*he l. knows, dreams*, &c.). [OE *lȳtel, lytel*, prob. cogn. w. *lūtan* bow down]

li·ttoral, a. & n. Of, on, the shore; region lying along the shore. [f. L *lit(t)oralis* (*litus -oris* shore, -AL)]

li·turgy, n. Communion office of Eastern Church; form of public worship, set of formularies for this; *the* Book of Common Prayer; (Gk Ant.) public office or duty performed gratuitously by rich Athenian. Hence **litur·g**ICAL a., **litur·gical**LY² adv. [f. med. L f. Gk *leitourgia* (*leitourgos* public servant prob. f. *leōs* people, *-ergos* -working)]

li·vable, a. (Of house, room, climate, &c.) fit to live in; (of life) worth living; companionable, easy to live with. Hence **li·vable**NESS n. [LIVE², -ABLE; cf. RELIABLE]

live¹, a. (attrib.). That is alive, living, (joc.) actual not pretended or pictured or toy (*a real l. burglar, steam engine, mountain*); full of power, energy, or importance, not obsolete or exhausted, (*make the question a l. issue*); glowing (*l. embers*); (of shell, match, wire) unexploded, unkindled, charged with electricity; (of rock) not detached, seeming to form part of the earth's frame; (of wheels &c. in machinery) moving or imparting motion; *l.-bait*, living fish or worm as fishing-bait; *l.-oak*, Amer. evergreen tree; *l.-stock*, animals kept or dealt in for use or profit. [=ALIVE used attrib.]

live², v.i. & t. Be alive, have animal or vegetable life; subsist (*up*)*on* (*l. on fruit*), depend (*up*)*on* for subsistence (*lives upon his wife, wife's earnings*, &c.; *living* WAGE¹), (fig.) sustain one's position or repute (*up*)*on* (*lives on his name*), get livelihood *by* one's wits &c. or *by* doing, (*l. & let l.*, wink at others' incompetence or deficiencies to secure the same treatment for oneself; *l. from* HAND¹ *to mouth*); conduct oneself *honestly, viciously, like a saint*, &c. (*l. up to* one's *principles, faith*, &c., put them in practice); arrange one's habits, expenditure, feeding, &c. (*l.* FAST⁴, *in* CLOVER; *l. well*, on dainty food; *l. on air*, (appear to) take no food; *l. in a small way*, cheaply & quietly; *l. close*, stingily; *l. a double life*, (esp.) sustain two different characters, act two different parts, in life; *l. to oneself*, in isolation); (with cogn. obj.) spend, pass, experience, (*l. a virtuous life; he lived what he narrated*); wear *down* (scandal, prejudice, effect of past guilt) by blameless course of life; express in one's life (*l. a lie*); enjoy life intensely; continue alive, have one's life prolonged, (*patient cannot l.*; *lived to see his children's children*; *l. & learn!*, way of greeting new fact; *l. out the night*, remain alive through it), (of things) survive (*his memory lives*), (of ship) escape destruction (*nothing could l. afloat*); dwell (*l. in, out*, of shop-assistants residing on premises or not), spend daytime *in* room (*room does not seem to be lived in*). [com.-Teut.; OE *libban* cf. Du. *leven*, G *leben*, cogn. w. LIFE]

lī·velihōōd, n. Means of living, sustenance. [OE *liflād* (LIFE, *lād* course, see LOAD[1]) gradually assimilated to obs. *livelihood* liveliness]

lī·velong, a. (poet., rhet.). Whole length of (*the l. day, night, summer*, with implication of weariness or delight.) [earlier *lefe long* (LIEF)]

lī·vely, a. Lifelike, realistic, (*a. l. description*; *give a l. idea of*); full of life, vigorous, energetic, brisk, vivid, interesting; (joc.) exciting, dangerous, difficult, (*police had a l. time*; *press is making it* or *things l. for* —); (of colour) bright; gay, vivacious; (of boat &c.) rising lightly to waves. Hence **lī·veli**LY[2] adv., **lī·veli**NESS n. (*a certain -iness* slang, some heavy firing). [OE *liflic* (LIFE, -LY[1])]

lī·ven, v.t. & i. Brighten, cheer, (usu. *up*). [LIFE, -EN[6]]

lī·ver[1], n. Large glandular organ in vertebrates secreting bile & purifying venous blood; (also *l.-complaint*) diseased state of l., whence **lī·ver**ISH[1] a.; (also *l.-colour*) dark reddish brown; flesh of some animals' l. used as food; (archaic) l. as seat of emotion (*hot l.*, passionate or amorous temperament; *white* or *lily l.*, cowardice, whence **-liver**ED[2] a.); *l.-line*, one of lines of palm significant in palmistry; *l. wing*, right wing of cooked fowl, under which l. is tucked, (joc.) right arm; *liverwort*, kinds of plant with l.-shaped parts or used in l. disease. Hence **lī·ver**LESS a. [OE *lifer* cf. Du. *lever*, G *leber*]

lī·ver[2], n. One who lives in specified way (*clean, loose, l.*; *good l.*, virtuous person, also one given to *good* LIVING[1]). [-ER[1]]

Liverpū·dlian, a. & n. (Inhabitant) of Liverpool. [facet. formation]

lī·very[1], n. Provision of food or clothing served out to retainers &c. (hist.); allowance of provender for horses (*at l.*, of horse, kept for owner & fed & groomed for fixed charge); distinctive clothes worn by member of city company or person's servant (*in, out of, l.* of servant, so attired or in plain clothes; also fig., *birds in their winter l.*, *the l. of grief*, *of other men's opinions*, &c.), whence **lī·veri**ED[2] a.; membership of city company (*take up* one's *l.*, become liveryman); (Law) legal delivery of property (*sue* one's *l.*, bring suit as heir in court of wards to get possession), writ allowing this; *l. company*, one of London City companies that had formerly distinctive costume; *l. fine*, payment for becoming member of l. company; *liveryman*, member of l. company, keeper of or attendant in l. stable; *l. servant*, wearing l.; *l. stable*, where horses are kept at l. or let out for hire. [f. F *livrée* (*livrer* see DELIVER, -Y[4])]

lī·very[2], a. Of the consistence or colour of liver; (of soil) tenacious; having a disordered liver, feeling out of sorts, irritable. [-Y[2]]

lī·vid, a. Of bluish leaden colour; discoloured as by bruise. Hence or cogn. **livi·**DITY n., **lī·vid**LY[2] adv. [f. L *lividus*]

lī·ving[1], n. In vbl senses; also or esp.: livelihood, maintenance, (*make* one's *l.*); (Eccl.) benefice; *good l.*, luxurious feeding; *plain l. & high thinking*, frugal & philosophic life; *l.-room* (for general day use); *l. wage*, on which it is possible for worker to live. [-ING[1]]

lī·ving[2], a. In vbl senses; esp.: contemporary, now existent, (*no man l. could do better*; *the greatest l. master of irony*; *the first of l. artists*; *the l.*, those now alive; *in the land of the l.*, alive); (of likeness) exact, whence **lī·ving**LY[2] adv.; *l. water*, perennially flowing; *l. rock, coal*, = LIVE[1]; *l. language*, still in vernacular use; *l. death*, state of hopeless misery; *within l. memory*, that of persons still l. [-ING[2]]

livre (lē·vr), n. Old French money of account (20 sous, about = pre-war franc). [F, f. L LIBRA]

lixi·viate, v.t. Separate (substance) into soluble & insoluble constituents by percolation of water. Hence **lixivia·**TION n. [f. L *lixivius* made into lye (*lix*), -ATE[3]]

li·zard, n. Kinds of reptile having usu. long body & tail, four legs, & scaly or granulated hide; fancy variety of canary. [f. OF *lesard* f. L *lacertus* w. assim. to -ARD]

'll, contr. of WILL in *I'll, he'll, that'll*, &c.

lla·ma (lah-, lyah-), n. S.-Amer. ruminant allied to camel but smaller, humpless, & woolly-haired, used as beast of burden; (material made of) its wool. [Sp., prob. f. Peruvian]

Lloyd's (loidz), n. Incorporated society of marine underwriters in London; *L. list*, newspaper devoted to maritime intelligence; *L. register*, annual alphabetic list of ships assigned to various classes. [orig. 17th-c. coffee-house established by Edward *Lloyd*]

lo, int. (archaic). Look!, see!, behold! (usu. *lo and behold!*, as joc. introduction of surprising fact). [mixture of OE *lā* int. & ME *lo* = *loke*, LOOK[1]]

loach (lōtsh), n. Small edible freshwater fish. [f. F *loche*]

load[1], n. What is (to be) carried, burden; amount usu. carried (*cart-l.* &c.), recognized unit in measure or weight of certain substances; material object or force acting as weight or clog, resistance of machinery worked to motive power, pressure of superstructure on arch &c.; burden of responsibility, care, grief, &c. (*take a l. off* one's *mind*, relieve him of anxiety); (pl., colloq.) plenty, superabundance, heaps, lots, *of*; *l.-displacement, -draught*, of ship when laden; *loadstone, lodestone*, magnetic oxide of iron, piece of it used as magnet, thing that attracts, (=way stone, see etym.); *l.-(water)line*, ship's flotation line when laden, Plimsoll's mark. [OE *lád* way, journey, conveyance, cf. G *leite*, cogn. w. LEAD²]

load², v.t. & i. Put l. on or aboard (person, vehicle, ship, &c.), (of ship, vehicle, person responsible for these, or person) take load aboard &c. (often *up*); place (l., cargo) aboard ship, on vehicle, &c.; add weight to, be burden upon, oppress *with* (*stomach loaded with food*), weight with lead (*a loaded cane*; *loaded dice*, so weighted as to fall with a certain face up), strain bearing-capacity of (*table loaded with food*); adulterate with something to increase weight or (of wines) strength; supply or assail overwhelmingly *with* (*loaded her with gifts, praise, abuse*; *air loaded with carbon*); charge (fire-arms; *am loaded*, have my gun &c. charged); (Stock-Exch.) buy heavily of stock (*loaded up with*, having large amounts of in hand as security); (Life-insurance) add extra charge or **loa·d**ING¹ n. to (premium) for special reasons. [f. prec.]

loa·der, n. In vbl senses; esp.: attendant loading sportsman's guns; loading-machine; *-l.*, gun loaded in specified way (*breech, muzzle, single, -l.*), so **-loadi**NG² a. [-ER¹]

loaf¹, n. (pl. *-ves*). Piece of bread baked alone or as separate or separable part of batch, usu. of some standard weight as 1lb., 2lb., or 4lb. (COTTAGE, *household, tinned, l.*, various shapes; QUARTERN *l.*; *brown l.*, of BROWN bread; *white l.*, of FIRSTS; *ll. & fishes*, personal profit as inducement to religious profession or public service, see *John* vi. 26; *half a l. is better than no bread*, motto of compromise, opp. *all or nothing*); (also *sugar-l.*) conical moulded mass of sugar (*l. sugar*, this as whole or cut into lumps); solid roundish head of cabbage or lettuce, whence **loav**ED² a. [com.-Teut.; OE *hláf*, cf. G *laib*, etym. dub.]

loaf², loave, v.i. (Of cabbage &c.) form a l. or head. [f. prec.]

loaf³, v.i. & t., & n. Spend time idly; saunter; *l.* (time) *away*, spend in loafing; hence **loa·f**ER¹ n.; (n.) loafing (*going to have a, on the, l.*). [etym. dub.; *l.* may be back-form. f. *loafer*]

loam, n. Paste of clay & water, composition of moistened clay & sand with chopped straw &c. used in making bricks, plastering, &c.; fertile soil chiefly of clay & sand with admixture of decayed vegetable matter, whence **loa·m**Y² a. [OE *lám*, cf. Du. *leem*, G *lehm*, cogn. w. LIME¹]

loan, n., & v.t. Thing, esp. sum of money, lent to be returned with or without interest; word, custom, &c., adopted by one people from another (so *l.-god, -myth, -word*); lending or being lent (*on l.*; *may I have the l. of —?*, may I borrow it?); money contribution from individuals or public bodies to State expenses acknowledged as debt; arrangement or contract by which a government receives advances of money usu. for stipulated interest; *l.-collection*, of pictures &c. lent by owners for exhibition; *l.-holder*, person holding debentures or other acknowledgements of l., mortgagee; *l.-office*, for lending money to private borrowers, also for receiving subscriptions to government l.; *l.-society*, of periodical subscribers to fund from which members may have ll.; (vb, now chiefly U.S.) grant l. of, whence **loa·n**ABLE a., **loan**EE·, **loan**ER¹, nn. [OE *lán*, cf. Du. *leen*, G *lehn*, cogn. w. Gk *leipō* leave, & OE *léon* lend]

lo(a)th, a. Disinclined, reluctant, unwilling, (usu. *to* do or abs.; also *for* person *to* do, or *that*; *nothing l.*, quite willing or willingly); *l.-to-depart*, tune played as farewell. [OE *láth*, cf. Du. *leed*, also G *leid* sorrow, f. OTeut. *laitho-* whence F *laid* ugly]

loathe (-dh), v.t. Regard with disgust, abominate, detest. Hence **loa·th**ING¹(1) n., **loa·thing**LY² adv. [OE *láthian* (prec.)]

loa·thly (-dh-), a. (Archaic & literary for) loathsome. Hence **loa·thli**NESS n. [OE *láthlic* (LOATH, -LY¹)]

loa·thsome (-th-, -dh-), a. Exciting nausea or disgust, offensive to the senses, sickening, repulsive, odious. Hence **loa·thsome**LY² adv., **loa·thsome**NESS, n. [LOATH, -SOME]

loaves. See LOAF¹.

lob, v.i. & t., & n. Walk, run, or move, heavily or clumsily or slowly (often *along*); toss, bowl, or send, (ball) with slow or high-pitched motion; (n.) ball bowled underhand at cricket or sent high in air at lawn tennis. [f. obs. *lob* n. fowl's wattle &c.]

lō·bate, a. (nat. hist.). Having lobe(s). Hence **lob**A·TION n. [LOBE, -ATE²]

lo·bby, n., & v.t. & i. Porch, anteroom, entrance-hall, corridor; (in House of Commons &c.) large hall open to public used esp. for interviews between members & outsiders, (also *division l.*) one of two corridors to which members retire to vote. (Vb, chiefly U.S.) influence (members of legislature), get (bill &c.) *through*, by l. interviews &c.; frequent l. of legislature, solicit members' votes, whence **lo·bby**IST(1) n. [f. med. L *lobia* LODGE¹]

lobe, n. Roundish & flattish projecting or

pendulous part, often one of two or more such parts divided by fissure (so *l. of liver* or *lungs*; *ll. of brain*; *l. of ear*, lower soft pendulous external part). Hence **lo·bed**², **lo·beless**, aa. [f. LL f. Gk *lobos* lobe, pod, cogn. w. LEGUME]

lobē·lia, n. Kinds of herbaceous plant with blue, scarlet, or purple flowers having deeply cleft corolla without spur. [M. de *Lobel*, -IA¹]

loblo·lly man, boy, nn. (naut.). Surgeon's mate, attendant. [f. obs. *loblolly* gruel, prob. imit. of bubbling]

lo·bscouse (-ows), n. Sailor's dish of meat stewed with vegetables & ship's biscuit. [?]

lo·bster, n. Large marine stalk-eyed ten-footed long-tailed edible crustacean with large claws formed by first pair of feet, bluish black before & scarlet after boiling; its flesh as food; (contempt.) British soldier, also (*blue* or *raw l.*) marine of R.M.A., (*red* or *boiled l.*) marine of R.M.L.I.; *l.-eyed*, with protruding eyes; *l. joint* (adaptable kind in pipe or tube); *l.-pot*, basket in which ll. are trapped. [OE *lopustre* corrupt. of L *locusta* LOCUST, (orig.) lobster, cf. F *langouste*; ending assim. to -STER]

lŏ·bule, n. Small lobe. Hence **lo·bular**¹ a. [LOBE, -ULE]

lo·bworm, n. Large earthworm used as fishing-bait; marine worm (also *lug*) similarly used. [f. obs. *lob* n., see LOB]

lŏca·l¹(e), (-ahl), n. Scene or locality of operations or events. [F (*-l*), abs. use of adj. = foll.; *-e* is E respelling to indicate stress, cf. MORALE]

lō·cal², a. & n. In regard to place (*l. habitation*, position in space as test of thing's material existence; *London is a l. name*; *l. adverb*); belonging to, existing in, or peculiar to certain place(s) (*l. time*, reckoned from sun's transit over place's meridian; *the l. lawyer*; *globe-flower is very l.*, not generally distributed; *l. government*, administration of town &c. by inhabitants, decentralization, *L. Government Board*, State department now absorbed by MINISTRY *of Health*; *l. examination*, held in various places under university board & giving certificates to boys & girls; *l. preacher*, Methodist layman authorized to preach in his own district; *l. option, veto*, system by which inhabitants of district may prohibit sale of liquor in it; *l. colour*, details characteristic of the scene or time represented in novel or other literary work inserted to give actuality, & see below); affecting, of, a part & not the whole (*l. disease, pain, remedy*; *l. colour* in picture, that of separate objects apart from general colour-scheme, & see above); (Math.) of a locus; (Post.; written on cover of letter as warning to P.O. officials) for delivery in this town or district; hence **lo·cally**² adv. (N.) inhabitant of, professional man practising in, particular district; l. preacher; (item of) l. news in newspaper; postage-stamp current in limited district; train serving stations of district; (pl.) l. examination(s). [F, f. L *localis* (*locus* place, -AL)]

lo·calism, n. Attachment to a place; limitation of ideas &c. resulting; favouring of what is local; a local idiom, custom, &c. [-ISM]

locă·lity, n. Thing's position, place where it is; site or scene of something; faculty of remembering & recognizing places, finding one's way, &c. [f. F *localité* f. LL *localitatem* (LOCAL², -TY)]

lo·calize, v.t. Invest with the characteristics of a particular place; restrict to particular place; attach to districts, decentralize; concentrate (attention) *upon*; (rare) = LOCATE. Hence **lo·calizable** a., **localiza·tion** n. [-IZE]

Locar·no, n. *Pact of L.*, set of treaties concluded at L. in 1925, with France, Germany, & Belgium, as chief parties, & Great Britain & Italy as guarantors, intended to secure inviolability of the frontiers & other safeguards of peace; *the spirit of L.*, renunciation of ancient enmities, esp. of that between France & Germany. [*L.* in Switzerland]

loca·te, v.t. Establish in a place, (pass.) be situated, (U.S.); state locality of; discover exact place of (*l. the enemy's camp*). Hence **loca·tion** n. [f. L *locare* (*locus* place), -ATE³]

lŏ·cative, a. & n. (gram.). (Case) denoting place where. [prec., -IVE]

lŏch (-ch), n. Scotch lake or narrow or landlocked arm of the sea. [Gael.]

lock¹, n. Portion of hair that hangs together, tress, (pl.) hair of head; tuft of wool or cotton. Hence **-locked**² a. [OE *loc* masc., cf. Du. *lok*, G *locke*, prob. cogn. w. Gk *lugos* withy]

lock², n. Appliance for fastening door, lid, &c., with bolt that requires key of particular shape to work it (*under l. & key*, locked up); appliance to keep wheel from revolving or slewing; mechanism for exploding charge of gun (*l., stock, & barrel*, whole of thing, completely); confined section of canal at point where level changes for raising & lowering boats by use of sluiced gates; ante-chamber to chamber in which engineering work is done in compressed air; interlocking, e.g. block or jam of carriages in street; extent to which fore-wheel's can be made to cross hind-wheel's plane; (also *L. Hospital*) hospital for venereal disease; *lockfast*, secured with l.; *l.-keeper*, = *locksman*; *lockman*, coroner's summoner in I. of Man; *locksman*, keeper of canal l.; *locksmith*, maker & mender of ll. Hence **lo·ckless** a. [OE *loc* neut., cf. G *loch* hole, Da. *laag* lid]

lock³, v.t. & i. Fasten (door, box, &c.) with l., shut *up* (house &c.) by fastening doors thus, (of door &c.) admit of being so fastened, have a l.; shut (person, thing) *up*, *in*, or *into*; *l. the stable door after the horse has been stolen*, take precautions too late; (of land, hills, &c.) hem in (usu. in pass.); (fig.) store (*up* or *away*) inaccessibly (*facts locked up in hieroglyphics*; *capital locked up in land*), imprison (*senses locked in sleep*); keep (person) *out* by locking door (esp. of employer coercing workmen by refusing them work; *l.-out* n., this procedure, cf. STRIKE); bring or come into rigidly fixed position, engage, (make) catch, fasten by interlacing or fitting of corresponding parts, entangle, (p.p.) joined in hostile or other embrace; (Mil., of rear rank) march so close to front rank that feet overlap; (of vehicle or wheels) (have fore-wheels that) admit of being slewed into different planes from those of hind-wheels; provide (canal, &c.) with ll., convey (boat) *up* or *down* through l., go through l.; *l.-chain*, for locking wheels of vehicle; *l.-jaw*, *locked-jaw*, (pop. name for) trismus, variety of tetanus, tonic spasm of muscles of mastication causing jaws to remain rigidly closed; *l.-nut*, extra nut screwed over another to prevent its starting; *l.-spring*, closing watch-case; *l.-stitch*, sewing-machine stitch by which two threads are firmly locked together; *l.-up*, (time of) locking up school &c. for night, unrealizable state of invested capital or amount of capital locked up, house or room for temporary detention of prisoners, (attrib.) that can be locked up (*l.-up coach-house*). [f. prec.]

lo·ckage, n. Amount of rise or fall effected by canal locks; toll for use of lock; use or number of locks. [-AGE]

lo·cker, n. In vbl senses; also, small cupboard, esp. one of many reserved each for individual's use in public room, e.g. cricket pavilion or schoolroom; (Naut.) chest or compartment for clothes, stores, ammunition, &c. (*not a shot in the l.*, no money in one's pocket; DAVY JONES'S LOCKER). [-ER¹]

lo·cket, n. Metal plate or band on scabbard; small gold or silver case holding portrait, lock of hair, &c., & usu. hung from neck. [f. OF *locquet* (*loc* latch f. Teut. cogn. w. LOCK², -ET¹)]

Lo·ckian, a. Of John Locke or his philosophy or followers. So **Lo·ck**IST(2) n.

lo·co, n. Locomotive engine. [abbr.]

lō·co cĭta·to, adv. (abbr. *l.c.*). In the passage already quoted. [L]

lō·comote, v.i. (biol.). Move from place to place. [back formation f. foll.]

lōcomō·tion, n. (Power of) motion from place to place; travel, way (esp. artificial) of travelling. [f. L *loco* see foll., *motio* MOTION]

lo·comōtive, a. & n. Of locomotion (*l. faculty, power*), (joc.) of travel (*in these l. days*); having power of or given to locomotion, not stationary, (*the l. bivalves*; *a l. person* joc., constantly travelling; *l. engine*, that goes from place to place by its own power, esp. steam-engine for drawing train along rails); effecting locomotion (*the l. organs*). (N.) l. engine; (slang, pl.) legs (*use your ll.*); l. animal. [f. L *loco* abl. of LOCUS, MOTIVE a.; suggested by scholastic phr. *in loco moveri* move in space]

lo·comōtor, n. & a. Locomotive person or thing; (adj.) of locomotion (*l.* ATAXY). [as prec., MOTOR]

lo·comōtory, a. Of, having, locomotion. [as prec., MOTORY]

lŏ·cūlus, n. (zool., anat., bot.; pl. *-lī*). One of a number of small separate cavities. Hence **lo·cul**AR¹ a. [L, dim. of LOCUS]

lō·cum tē·nens (also colloq. **locum**), n. Deputy acting esp. for clergyman or doctor. Hence **locum-te·nen**CY n. [med. L, (one) holding place TENANT, (foll.)]

lō·cus, n. (pl. *-ci* pr. -sī). Locality or exact place of something; (Math.) curve &c. made by all points satisfying particular equation of relation between coordinates, or by point, line, or surface, moving according to mathematically defined conditions; *l. classicus*, best known or most authoritative passage on a subject; *l. in quo*, scene of event; *l. poenitentiae*, opportunity allowed for receding until decisive step has been taken; *l. standi*, recognized position, right to intervene, appear in court, &c. [L, = place]

lō·cust, n. Kinds of African & Asiatic winged edible insect migrating in swarms & consuming vegetation of districts; person of devouring or destructive propensities; fruit of carob-tree; cassia pod; (also *l.-tree*) kinds of tree, esp. carob & pseudo-acacia; *l.-bird*, *-eater*, kinds of bird feeding on ll. [f. L *locusta* lobster, locust]

locu·tion, n. Style of speech; word or phrase considered in regard to style, idiom, (*a barbarous l.*; *to use the Greek l.*). [f. L *locutio* (*loqui locut-* speak, -ION)]

lŏ·cutory, n. Parlour or conversation-room in monastery; grille for interviews between inmates of monastery & outsiders. [f. med. L *locutorium* (prec., -ORY)]

lode, n. Watercourse, open drain in fens; vein of metal ore; *lodestar*, *loadstar*, star that is steered by, esp. the pole-star, (fig.) guiding principle, object of pursuit; *lodestone*, see LOAD¹*stone*. [var. of LOAD¹]

lodge¹, n. Small house; cottage at gates of park or grounds of large house, occupied by gardener or other servant; porter's room at gate of college, factory, or house of chambers or flats; (Freemasonry &c.) (place of meeting for) members of branch, *grand l.*, governing body of freemasons & societies imitating them; residence of head of college at Cambridge; beaver's or otter's lair; N.-Amer. Indian's tent or wigwam. [f. OF *loge* f. med. L *lobia* (LOBBY) f. Teut. (G *laube* arbour, prob. cogn. w. LEAF)]

lodge[2], v.t. & i. Provide with sleeping quarters; receive as guest or inmate; establish as resident *in* house or room(s), (pass.) be *well, ill,* &c., accommodated in regard to house-room; serve as habitation for, contain, (pass.) be contained *in*; leave *in* place or *with* person for security; deposit in court or with official a formal statement of (complaint, information), (pop.) allege (objection &c.); place (power &c.) *in, with, in the hands of,* (person); (of wind) lay (crops) flat; (make, let) stick or remain in place without falling or going further (*lodged bullet, bullet lodged, in his brain; tide lodges mud in the cavities*); reside, be situated; be inmate paying for accommodation in another's house, whence **lo·dg**ER[1] n. (*-er franchise,* right to vote at election of M.P. enjoyed by a class of lodgers before the 1918 extension). [f. OF *logier* (prec.)]

lo·dging, n. In vbl senses; esp.: accommodation in hired rooms; dwelling-place, abode, (pl.) room(s) hired elsewhere than in hotel for residing in; *l.-house,* in which ll. are let (*common l.-h.,* usu. one with dormitory in which bed can be had for the night). [-ING[1]]

lo·dgement, -gment, n. (Mil.) temporary defensive work on captured part of enemy's works; stable position gained, foothold, (*make, effect, a l.*); (Law) deposit(ing) of money; accumulation of matter intercepted in fall or transit. [f. F *logement* (prec., -MENT)]

lŏ·ess (or as G), n. Deposit of fine yellowish-grey loam in Rhine & other river valleys. [G *löss*]

loft (law-, lŏ-), n., & v.t. Attic; room over stable; pigeon-house; flock of pigeons; gallery in church or hall; (Golf) backward slope in club-head, lofting stroke. (Vb) hit (golf-ball) high up, clear (obstacle) thus; keep (pigeons) in l. [ON, = sky, air, loft, cf. G *luft*]

lo·fter, n. Golf-club for lofting. [-ER[1]]

lo·fty, a. Of imposing height, towering, soaring, (*l. mountain, flight, stature*; not of persons); haughty, consciously superior or dignified, (*l. contempt, good humour*); exalted, distinguished, high-flying, high-flown, elevated, sublime, grandiose. Hence **lo·fti**LY[2] adv., **lo·fti**NESS n. [-Y[2]]

log[1], n., & v.t. Unhewn piece of felled tree or similar rough mass of wood (*in the l.,* unhewn; *float, lie, fall, like a l.,* in helpless or stunned state; *roll my l. & I'll roll yours,* applied to mutual help, esp. to unprincipled political combinations & puffing of each other's works by author-reviewers, whence **lo·g-roll** v.i., **lo·g-roll**ING[1,2] n. & a.; *King L.,* fainéant ruler, w. ref. to fable of Jupiter & the frogs, cf. STORK); float attached to line wound on reel for gauging speed of ship, other apparatus for same purpose, (*heave, throw, the l.,* use this; *sail by the l.,* calculate ship's position by it); =l.-book; table by which journeyman-tailor's work-time is assessed; *l.-board,* on which entries are made for transcription into *l.-book,* book with permanent record daily made of all events occurring in ship's voyage including rate of progress shown by l., (also) traveller's diary &c.; *l. cabin,* hut built of ll.; *l.-line,* to which float of ship's l. is attached; *logwood,* (wood of) Amer. tree used in dyeing. (Vb) cut into ll.; enter (distance made &c.) in ship's l.-book, (of ship) make (distance); enter (seaman's name with offence committed) in l.-book, fine (offender). [ME *logge,* etym. dub.; cf. CLOG]

log[2], = LOGARITHM of (prefixed to number or algebraic symbol).

lō·ganberry, n. Fruit got by cross between raspberry & blackberry. [*Logan,* surname]

lŏ·gan(-stone), n. Poised heavy stone rocking at a touch. [=*logging* (dial. *log* to rock)]

lŏgaoe·dic (*-aē-*), a. & n. (Line) in metre composed of dactyls & trochees. [f. LL f. Gk *logaoidikos* combining prose & poetry (*logos* speech, *aoidē* song, -IC)]

lŏ·garithm, n. One of a class of arithmetical functions tabulated for use in abridging calculation & enabling computer to substitute addition & subtraction for multiplication & division, & the latter two for involution & evolution; index of power to which fixed number (the *base*) must be raised to produce given number (*the l. of 1,000 is 3*; *common ll.,* whose base is 10). Hence **logari·thm**IC a., **logari·thm**ICALLY adv. [f. Gk *logos* reckoning, ratio, *arithmos* number]

loge (F), n. Box in theatre &c.

-loger, suf. repr. L *-logus* or Gk *-logos. Astrologer,* the oldest wd of the type, may be either f. L *astrologus* + -ER[1] (afterwards a common type of formation) or f. *astrology* + -ER[1] (cf. -GRAPHER). As living suf., *-loger* was used to form personal nn. corresp. to wds in -LOGY, but is now superseded by -LOGIST.

lo·ggerhead, n. Blockhead, fool, (archaic; *We three ll. be,* inscription under two wooden heads on inn-sign); iron instrument with ball at end heated for melting pitch &c.; post built into boat for catching turn of rope to; kinds of large-headed turtle & bird; *at ll.* (*with*), disagreeing or disputing (with) (prob. f. notion of trying whose head is harder). [f. dial. *logger* block of wood for hobbling horse]

loggia (lŏ·jya, *or as It.*), n. (pl. -s or *loggie* pr. -ā). Open-sided gallery or arcade. [It.]

lŏ·gic, n. Science of reasoning, proof, thinking, or inference; particular scheme of or treatise on this; chain of reasoning, correct or incorrect use of argument, ability in argument, arguments (CHOP[4] *l.*), (*argues with great learning & l.*; *is not governed by l.*); (with purposely perverted sense) converting-power, compulsion, (*the l. of events, facts, necessity, grape-shot, war,* &c.). So **logi·**CIAN n. [f. F *logique* f. med. L f. Gk *logikē* (*tekhnē* art) of reason f. LOGOS, -IC(2)]

-logic, -logical. See -LOGY.

lŏ·gical, a. Of logic or formal argument; not contravening the laws of thought, correctly reasoned; deducible, defensible on ground of consistency, reasonably to be believed or done; capable of correct reasoning. Hence **logica·l**ITY n., **lo·gical**LY[2] adv. [-AL]

lō·gie (-gĭ), n. Zinc ornament looking like jewel used in theatres. [perh. inventor's name]

lŏ·giŏn (-g-), n. (pl. *-ia*). Saying of Christ not recorded in Gospels but preserved elsewhere. [Gk, = oracle (LOGOS)]

-logist, suf. forming nn. meaning *one versed in -logy,* f. -LOGY, -IST.

logi·stics (-j-), n. pl. Art of moving & quartering troops (cf. STRATEGY, TACTICS). [f. F *logistique* (*loger* LODGE[2], -IC)]

lŏ·gogram, n. Sign or character representing a word in shorthand. [LOGOS, -GRAM]

lo·gograph, n. =prec.; =LOGOTYPE. [LOGOS, -GRAPH]

logo·grapher, n. (Gk ant.). One of the Greek prose historians before Herodotus; ancient-Greek professional speech writer. [f. Gk *logographos* (LOGOS, -GRAPHER)]

lo·gogriph, n. Kind of anagrammatic word-puzzle. [f. F *logogriphe* (LOGOS, Gk *griphos* riddle)]

logo·machy (-kĭ), n. Dispute about words, controversy turning on merely verbal points. [f. Gk *logomakhia* (LOGOS, *-makhia* -fighting)]

lŏ·gos, n. (no pl.). The Word or Second Person of the Trinity. [Gk, = word, reason, f. *legō* speak, used in mystic sense by Hellenistic & Neo-Platonist philosophers & in St John]

lo·gotype, n. Word, or more letters than one, cast in one piece but not as ligature, for use in printing. [prec., TYPE]

-logue (lŏg), suf. repr. Gk *-logos, -logon,* chiefly in wds f. F (*catalogue, dialogue*). Personal nn. = *one skilled in* -LOGY (*ideologue*) are now rare, -LOGER or -LOGIST being usu. preferred.

-logy, suf. f. Gk *-logia* (in early instances, thr. F *-logie* f. med. L *-logia*). (1) In most wds *-log-* is the *o* form of Gk *leg-* speak, *-logia* indicating the character, action, or branch of knowledge, of a person (Gk *-logos* n. or a.) who speaks in a certain way (*brachylogy, tautology, eulogy*) or treats of a certain subject (*theology, astrology*). E compounds of the latter kind, in which first component is alw. n., take -O- with some exceptions (*petralogy, mineralogy*). *Sociology, terminology,* are hybrids. (2) In a few wds *-log-* is the Gk *logos* discourse (*trilogy, tetralogy*).—Mod. formations in *-logy* may alw. have correl. adjj. in *-logical* (rarely *-logic*), & nn. in *-logist* (somet. -LOGER).

loin, n. (Pl.) part of body on both sides of spine between false ribs & hip-bones (*gird up* one's *ll.*, prepare for journey or effort; *fruit, child,* &c., *of, sprung from,* &c., one's *ll.*, one's begotten offspring); joint of meat that includes the l. vertebrae; *l.-cloth,* worn for decency & fastened round ll. Hence **-loin**ED[2] a. [f. OF *loigne* (L *lumbus*) cogn. w. Du. *lende*]

loir, n. The Fat Dormouse. [F, f. L *glirem* nom. *glis*]

loi·ter, v.i. & t. Linger on the way, hang about; travel indolently & with frequent pauses; pass (time &c.) *away* in loitering. Hence **loi·ter**ER[1] n., **loi·tering**LY[2] adv. [f. MDu. *loteren* wag about]

lŏll, v.t. & i. Hang (one's tongue) *out,* (of tongue) hang (usu. *out*); stand, sit, or recline, in lazy attitude; let (one's head or limbs) rest lazily on something. Hence **lo·lling**LY[2] adv. [prob. imit.; cf. LULL]

Lŏ·llard, n. One of the 14th-c. heretics who followed Wyclif or held opinions like his. Hence **Lo·llard**ISM(3) n. [f. MDu. *lollaerd* (*lollen* mumble, -ARD)]

lo·llipop, n. (usu. pl.). Sweetmeat(s), sugar-plum(s). [?]

lo·llop, v.i. (colloq.). Flop about; move or proceed in a lounging or ungainly way. [extension of LOLL]

Lo·mbard (lŭ-, lŏ-, *-erd*), n. & a. One of the Germanic 6th-c. conquerors of Italy; native of Lombardy; (adj.) of the Ll. or Lombardy, Lombardic; *L. street,* a London street formerly occupied by L. bankers, & still containing many of chief London banks, (transf.) the money market, financiers as a body (*L. Street to a china orange,* virtual certainty, long odds). [F, f. It. *Lombardo* f. LL *Longobardus* (LONG[1], L *Bardi* name of the people)]

Lŏmbar·dic, a. Of the Lombards or Lombardy (esp. of N.-Ital. 7th–13th-c. architecture & 15th–16th-c. painting). [f. med. L *Lombardicus* (prec., -IC)]

lō·ment, n. (bot.). Kind of pod that breaks up when mature into one-seeded joints. Hence **loment**A·CEOUS a. [f. L *lomentum* bean-meal (orig. cosmetic) f. *lo-, lavare,* wash, -MENT]

Lo·ndon (lŭ-), attrib. a. *L. clay,* geological formation in lower division of eocene tertiary in S.-E. England; *L. ivy,* fog or smoke of L.; *L. particular* colloq., kind of fog peculiar to L.; *L. pride,* kind of saxifrage; *L. smoke,* dull grey colour. So **Lo·ndon**ER[1](4), **Lo·ndon**ISM(4), nn., **Lo·ndon**IZE(3) v.t.

lone, attrib. a. Solitary, companionless, unfrequented, uninhabited, lonely,(poet. or rhet., exc. in *l. hand,* hand played or player playing against the rest at quadrille & euchre, also fig.); feeling or making feel lonely, whence **lo·ne**SOME a., **lo·nesome**LY[2] adv., **lo·nesome**NESS n.; (of woman) single or widowed. [attrib. form of ALONE, cf. LIVE[1]]

lo·nely, a. Solitary, companionless, isolated; unfrequented. Hence **lo·neli**NESS n. [-LY[1]]

long[1], a. & n. Measuring much from end to end in space or time (*l. line, distance, journey*; *l. life,* whence **long-liv**ED[2] a.; *make a l. arm,* reach out for something esp. at table; *has a l. arm,* can make his power felt far; *l. face,* dismal; *l. head,* of more than average length, fig. shrewdness or foresight, whence **longhead**ED[2] a., **long-hea·ded**NESS n., lit. & fig.; *make a l. nose,* cock SNOOK; *l. tongue,* loquacity; *two* &c. *l. miles* &c., more than that; *by a l.* CHALK[1]; *grievance* &c. *of l. standing,* not recent); (prefixed to name; colloq.) tall (*L. Tom,* gun of great length or range); far-reaching, acting at a distance, involving great interval or difference, (*l. sight,* that sees distant objects, fig. penetration, whence **long-sight**ED[2] a., **long-sigh·ted**NESS n., lit. & fig.; *little* PITCHERS *have l. ears*; *take l. views,* consider remote effects; *l. odds* in betting, very uneven; *l. bowls,* fighting at l. range, opp. *close quarters*; *l. date,* distant date for maturing of bill &c., whence **long-dat**ED[2] a.; *l. waist* in dress, made far down); (usu. appended to measurement) having specified length or duration (*tail 6 in. l.*; *vacation is two months l.*; *as* BROAD *as it is l.*); of elongated shape; remarkable for or distinguished by or concerned with length or duration (*l. clay,* churchwarden pipe; *l.* DIVISION; *l. drink,* one served in tall glass; *l. ears,* stupidity as of ass, whence **long-ear**ED[2] a.; *l. finger,* the second; *l. jump,* measured along ground, opp. *high jump*; *l. measure,* miles, yards, inches, &c.; *l. metre,* hymn-stanza of four eight-syllable lines; *L. Parliament,* that elected 1640 & dissolved 1660; *l.* PRIMER; *l. robe,* legal attire, esp. *gentleman of the l. r.,* lawyers; *in the l. run,* in the end after vicissitudes; *l. service,* system of military enlistment for many e.g. 12 years; *l. vacation,* summer vacation of law-courts & universities; *l.* WHIST[3]; *l. wind,* capacity for running far without rest, or fig. for talking or writing at tedious length, whence **long-wind**ED[2] a., **long-wi·nded**NESS n.); expressed by many ciphers or consisting of many individuals (*l. figure* or *price,* heavy cost; *l. family,* of many children; *l. bill,* of many items; *l. suit,* many cards of one suit in a hand); lengthy, prolix, tedious; of more than the usual numerical amount (*l.* DOZEN, HUNDRED); lasting, going far back or forward, (*a l. custom, memory, farewell*); (Phonet., Pros.; of vowel or syllable) (prop.) having the greater of the two recognized durations, (pop.) stressed, (also, of vowel) having the pronunciation shown in its name (e.g., *pate* & *lucre* have long, *pat* & *put* or *but* short a & u); *l.-bill,* kinds of bird, esp. snipe; *l.-boat,* sailing-ship's largest boat (cf. LAUNCH[2]); *l.-bow,* drawn by hand & discharging long feathered arrow (cf. CROSS-BOW), *draw the l.-b.,* tell exaggerated or invented stories; *l. butt,* cue for reaching billiard-ball beyond range of half butt; *l. cloth,* kind of calico made in l. pieces; *l.-clothes,* & archaic *-coats,* clothes of baby in arms; *l. field,* l. off or on (see below), also part of ground behind bowler; *l.* FIRM[1]; *longhand,* ordinary writing (opp. SHORT*hand*); *l. hop,* short-pitched ball in cricket; *l. off, on,* man fielding at bowler's left, right, rear; *l. pig,* sailors' transl. of cannibals' name for human flesh; *longshanks,* stilt or long-legged plover; *longstop,* man fielding straight behind wicket-keeper, (vb) field there; hence **lo·ng**ISH[1](2) a., **lo·ng**WAYS, **lo·ng**WISE, advv. (N. or abs. adj.) l. interval or period (*shall see you before l.*; *shall not be away for l.*; *will not take l.*; *it is l. since I saw him*; so *at longest,* to mention the most distant date possible); recital at length (*the l. & the short of it,* all that can or need be said, the total upshot); l. syllable (*ll. & shorts,* verse esp. Latin); (Arch.) *ll. & shorts,* l. & short blocks placed alternately; =l. vacation. [com.Teut.; OE & Du. & G *lang,* cogn. w. L *longus* & perh. Gk *dolikhos*]

long[2], adv. (-er, -est). For a l. time (*have l. thought so*; *nor wants that little l.*; *so* or *as l. as* transf., provided that, if only; *be l. doing,* &, prob. by confusion of the adv. w. the adj., *in doing,* take a l. time, be slow, to do, as *he was l. finding it out, the chance was l. in coming*; *not be l. for this world,* have short time to live; *l.-liver,* one who lives l.); by a l. time (*l. before, after, since, ago*); (appended to nn. of duration) throughout specified time (*all day l., his life l.*); (comp., with *no, any, much,* &c.) after implied point of time (*shall not wait any longer*; *no longer,* not henceforth as formerly); *l.-ago* a. & n., (belonging to) the distant past; *l.-drawn(-out),* unduly prolonged; *l.-standing,* that has l. existed; *l.-suffering* n. & a., bearing provocation patiently. [OE *lange* (prec.)]

long[3], v.i. Yearn, wish vehemently, *for* thing or *to* do. Hence **lo·ngING**[1](1) n., **lo·ngingLY**[2] adv. [OE *langian* seem LONG[1] to]

-long, suf., f. LONG[1], has ousted -LING[2] in *sidelong, headlong. Endlong* f. ON *endlangr* adj. orig. meaning *extending from end to end* was used in E as adv. meaning *endwise*, & *-long* thus came to be regarded as var. of *-ling.*

longanĭ·mity (-ngg-), n. (rare). Long-suffering, forbearance. [f. LL *longanimitas* (*longanimus* f. *longus* long, *animus* spirit, -TY)]

lo·ngeron (-j-), n. (usu. in pl.). Longitudinal member of aeroplane's fuselage or nacelle. [F, = girder]

longē·val, -gae- (-j-), a. Long-lived. [f. L *longaevus* (*longus* long, *aevum* age, -AL)]

longĕ·vity (-j-), n. Long life. [f. L *longaevitas* (prec., -TY)]

longi- (-jĭ-), comb. form of L *longus* long in scientific terms, as *-cau·date* long-tailed, *-corn* kinds of beetle with long threadlike antennae.

lo·ngitude (-j-), n. Length (now facet.); (Geol.) angular distance east or west from a standard meridian, as that of Greenwich, to the meridian of any place, reckoned to 180° E. or W. (*abbr.* long.); (Astron.) angular distance eastward on ecliptic from vernal equinoctial point to foot of body's or point's circle of latitude. [f. L *longitudo -inis* (prec., -TUDE)]

longitu·dinal, a. Of or in length; running lengthwise; of longitude. Hence **longitu·dinalLY**[2] adv. [-AL]

Lo·ngobard, n. =LOMBARD (1st sense).

lo·ng-shore, a. Existing, found, or employed, on, frequenting, the shore; *l.-man*, landsman employed in loading ships, shore-fishing, &c. [for *along shore*]

longue haleine (F), n. *Work* &c. *of* (or *de*) *l.* (requiring long persistent effort; esp. of books). [F, = long wind]

loo, n., & v.t. Round card-game with penalties paid to the pool; (having to pay) this penalty; *unlimited l.*, in which penalty is = amount already in pool; *l.-table*, (trade name for) kind of round table; (vb) subject to the penalty. [abbr. of obs. *lanterloo* f. F *lanturelu* refrain of a song]

loo·by, n. Silly fellow. [cf. LUBBER]

loo·fah, n. Pod of *luffa Aegyptiaca* used as flesh-brush. [f. Arab. *lufah* the plant]

lŏŏk, v.i. & t., & n. Use one's sight, turn eyes in some direction, direct eyes *at*, (*fair* &c. *to l. at*, in outward appearance; *l. before you leap*, avoid precipitate action; *to l. at him* &c., judging by his &c. ll.; *will not l. at*, refuses to take, rejects, scorns); stare, show surprise; contemplate, examine, (*looked me through & through*; *l. gift* HORSE[1] *in mouth*; *l.* one, *death*, &c., *in the face*, face him &c. boldly or at close quarters); express, threaten, show, by one's ll. (*l. compassion, death, daggers*, &c.); ascertain or observe by sight *who, how, whether*, &c.; (fig.) make mental search (*let him l. at home*), inquire (*when one looks deeper*), aim one's attention *at* & consider (*way of looking at things*; *what I l. at is the comfort of it*), take care or make sure *that*, expect *to* do, (*l. you* imperat., observe, mind; *l. here* imperat., formula for demanding attention or expostulating; *l. sharp*, orig., keep strict watch, now, lose no time, bestir oneself); (of things) face, be turned, have or afford outlook, in some direction (*towards, on to, into, down*, &c.), (of facts) tend, point; have certain appearance, seem, (*l. grave* &c., whence **-lookING**[2] a.; *l. a fool, every inch a king*, BLACK[1], BLUE; *l. small*, be exposed as mean &c.; *l. alive* imperat., make haste; *l. well* or *ill*, in good or bad health, also of things, seem to be going so; *looks to be*, seems; *l. as if*, suggest by appearance the belief that; *l. like*, seem to be, also threaten or promise, as *it looks l. rain, he looks like biting* or *winning*), seem to be (*looks his age*, seems as old as he really is; *l. oneself again*, seem recovered); *l.-in*, informal call or visit, (Sport) *will have a l.-in*, come near winning & perhaps win; *loo·king-glass*, mirror, quicksilvered glass for mirrors; *l.-out*, watch, looking out, (*keep a good l.-o.*; *on the l.-o. for* or *to* do), post of observation, man or party or boat stationed to l. out, view over landscape, prospect of luck (*it's a bad l.-o. for him*), person's own concern (*that is his l.-o.*, he must see to that himself). (With prepp.) *l. about* one, examine one's surroundings, take time to form plans; *l. after*, follow with the eye, seek for, attend to, take care of; *l. down* one's *nose at* (colloq.), regard with covert displeasure; *l. for*, expect, hope or be on the watch for, search for (*l. for* TROUBLE); *l. into*, examine the inside of (box &c.), dip into (book), investigate; *l. on*, regard *as*, regard *with* distrust &c.; *l. over*, inspect, overlook or pardon; *l. through*, direct eyes through (window &c.), penetrate (veil &c.) with sight or (pretence or pretender) with insight, be visible through (*his greed looks through his eyes*), glance through (book &c.); *l. to*, consider, take care of, be careful about (*l. to your manners*; *l. to it that*), keep watch over, rely on (person or thing) *for*, expect, count upon, aim at; *l. towards* colloq., drink health of; *l. upon*, regard *with* specified feeling (also with adv., as *favourably*), regard *as*. (With advv.) *l. about*, be on the watch, be in search *for*, let one's eyes rove; *l. ahead*, (of rower) turn round to see where he is going (esp. imperat.); *l. back*, be half-hearted about enterprise one has begun, turn one's thoughts *upon* or *to* something past, cease to progress (usu. w. neg.); *l. down*, subdue with a l., (commerc.) sink in price, *l. d.* (*up*)*on*, consider oneself superior to; *l. forward to*, anticipate (usu. with pleasure); *l. in*, make short visit or call; *l. on*, be mere spectator, whence **look**ER[1]**-o·n** n.; *l. on with*, read from book &c. at same time as (another person); *l. out*, direct eyes or put head out of window &c., be vigilant, keep one's eyes open *for* expected person, be prepared *for* squalls &c., have or afford outlook *on*, *over*, &c., select by inspection; *l. over*, inspect one by one or part by part; *l. round*, esp. examine the possibilities &c. with a view to deciding on a course; *l. through*, survey with searching glance (*looked him through*), inspect exhaustively or successively; *l. up*, (esp. commerc.) improve in price or prosperity, search for (esp. word in dictionary or facts in book of reference), call on (person), raise eyes (*l. up to*, respect, venerate), *l.* one *up & down*, scrutinize him keenly or contemptuously. (N.) act of looking, direction of eyes, glance (*a kind, scornful, l.*); (sing. or pl.) appearance of face, expression, personal aspect, (*good ll.*, beauty); (of things) appearance (*the place has a European l.*). [OE *lócian*]

lōōm[1], n. Machine for weaving yarn or thread into fabric; (inboard part of) shaft of oar. [earlier sense *tool*, OE *gelóma* (Y- + *lóma* as in *andlóman* pl. apparatus)]

lōōm[2], v.i., & n. Appear indistinctly, be seen in vague & often magnified or threatening shape, (lit. & fig.; often *l. large* &c.); (n.) vague first appearance of land at sea &c. [cf. EFris. *lômen* move slowly, MHG *luomen* be weary]

lōōm[3], n. Kinds of guillemot & diver. Hence **loo·m**ERY(3) n. [f. ON *lómr*]

loon[1], n. (Sc. & archaic). Scamp, idler, boor; lad. [earlier *lowne*; etym. dub.]

loon[2], n. Kinds of water-bird, esp. of diver & grebe. [perh. = LOOM[3] w. assim. to prec.]

loo·ny, lu-, n. & a. (slang). Lunatic. [-Y[3]]

loop[1], n., & v.t. & i. Figure produced by a curve, or bent string or withe, that crosses itself; attachment or ornament formed of cord, thread, &c., so crossed & fastened at crossing; ring or curved piece of metal as handle &c.; (also *l.-line*) railway or telegraph line that diverges from main line & joins it again; circuit in centrifugal railway along top of which passenger travels head downwards (*looping the l.*, bicyclist's or airman's similar feat); (Skating) curve crossing itself made on single edge. (Vb) form (string &c.) into loop(s); form l. (esp. of LOOPER larvae); enclose (as) with l.; fasten (*up*, *back*) or join (*together*) with loop(s). [cf. Ir. & Gael. *lub*]

loop[2], n. (rare). = LOOP-HOLE. [prob. cogn. w. MDu. *lûpen* to peer]

loo·per, n. Caterpillar of geometer moths, progressing by arching itself into loops; contrivance in sewing-machine &c. for making loops. [-ER[1]]

loo·p-hole, n., & v.t. Narrow vertical slit in wall for shooting or looking through or to admit light or air; outlet, means of evading rule &c.; (vb) make ll. in (wall &c.). [LOOP[2]]

loose[1], a. Released from bonds or restraint; detached or detachable from its place (*come, get, l.*; *play* FAST[3] *& l.*; (Chem.) free, uncombined; hanging partly free (esp. *l. end*; *at a l. end*, without definite occupation); not rigidly fixed, apt to shift, (*have a* SCREW *l.*); slack, relaxed, not tense or tight, (*with a l. rein*, lit. of riding, & fig. indulgently; *l. tongue*, given to blabbing; *l. bowels*, tending to diarrhoea; *l. clothes*; *l. build* or *make*, ungainly figure); not compact, dense, or serried (*l. soil, fabric*; *l. order*, military arrangement with wide intervals; *l. handwriting*, straggling; *l. play* or *game* in football, in which players do not lock together); (of statements, ideas, &c.) inexact, indefinite, vague, incorrect, (of translation) not close or faithful, (of style) ungrammatical, (of agent) doing the act loosely (*l. thinker*); (Cricket) *l. bowling*, inaccurately pitched, *l. fielding*, careless or bungling; morally lax, dissolute, wanton in speech or act, (*l. fish*, dissolute person; *on the l.*, having a spree); *l.* BOX[2]; *loose-*, loosely, as *l.-flowing*, *-fitting*. Hence **loo·se**LY[2] adv., **loo·se**NESS n., **loo·**SISH[1](2) a. [f. ON *lauss* = OE *léas*, cf. G *los*, cogn. w. Gk *luō* undo]

loose[2], v.t., & n. Release, set free, free from constraint (*wine loosed his tongue*); untie, undo, (knot, fetters, seal, hair of head); detach from moorings; discharge (arrow), (abs.) discharge gun (*at*); relax (now only in *l. hold*); (n.) vent, free expression, (*give l.* or *a l. to* one's *feelings* &c.). [f. prec.]

loo·sen, v.t. & i. Loose (person's tongue); make or become less tight or compact or firm; relieve (bowels) from costiveness or (cough) from dryness; relax (discipline &c.). [-EN[6]]

loo·sestrife (-s-s-), n. Two kinds of herbaceous plant (*Golden* or *Yellow*, & *Red* or *Purple* or *Spiked*, *L.*). [mistransl. of LL f. Gk *lusimakhion* (Gk pers. name *Lusimakhos*) as if directly f. *luō* undo, *makhē* battle]

loot, n., & v.t. & i. Goods taken from enemy, spoil, booty; illicit gains made by official. (Vb) plunder, sack, (city &c., or abs.); carry off as booty. Hence **loo·t**ER[1] n. [f. Hind. *lūṭ*]

lop[1], n., & v.t. & i. Smaller branches & twigs of trees (*l. & top*, *l. & crop*, trimmings of tree). (Vb) cut off branches & twigs & rarely top of (tree); strip tree of (branches &c.; often *off*, *away*), whence

lo·ppings [-ING[1](2)] n. pl.; cut off (person's limb or head); make lopping strokes *at*. [vb prob. f. n.; etym. dub.]

lop[2], v.i. & t., & n. Hang limply; let (ears) hang; slouch, dawdle, hang *about*; =LOPE; *l.-ears*, drooping ears, whence **lo·p-ear**ED[2] a.; *l.-ear*, kind of rabbit; hence **lo·ppy**[2] a.; (n.) lop-eared rabbit. [prob. imit.]

lop[3], v.i., & n. (Of water) break in short lumpy waves; (n.) such motion of water. [imit.]

lope, v.i., & n. (Run with) long bounding stride (esp. of animals). [f. ON *hloupa* cogn. w. LEAP]

lŏpho-, comb. form of Gk *lophos* crest, in scientific wds as *-dont* (animal) with transverse ridges on crowns of molars, *-bra·nchiate* with gills disposed in tufts.

lop-si·ded, a. With one side lower or smaller than the other, unevenly balanced. Hence **lop-si·ded**LY[2] adv., **lopsi·ded**NESS n. [f. LOP[2]]

loqua·cious, a. Talkative; (of birds, water) chattering, babbling. Hence or cogn. **loqua·cious**LY[2] adv., **loqua·cious**NESS, **loquă·city**, nn. [L *loquax* (*loqui* talk), -ACIOUS]

lō·quat, n. Chinese & Japanese fruit(-tree) naturalized in S. Europe, Australia, &c. [f. Chin. *luh kwat* rush orange]

lŏ·quitur, v.i. 3 sing. pres. (abbr. *loq.*). Speaks (with speaker's name added, as stage-direction or notice to reader). [L]

lor, lor', form of LORD used (vulg.) as int.

lor·al, a. Of the LORE[2]. [-AL]

lor·cha (-tsha), n. Ship with hull of European shape but Chinese rig. [Port., etym. dub.]

lord, n. & int., & v.i. & t. Master, ruler, chief, prince, sovereign, (*our sovereign l. the King*; *ll. of creation*, mankind, also joc. men as opp. women), (poet.) owner (*l. of few acres*; cf. *landlord*); magnate in some trade (*the cotton ll.*; cf. *king*); feudal superior (MESNE *l.*; *l. of the* MANOR; *l.* PARAMOUNT); (poet. & joc.) husband (also *l. & master*); (Astrol.) dominant planet; (usu. *the L.* exc. in voc.; also with *God*) God (*L. knows who, how*, &c., I cannot guess who &c., some one &c. or other; *L. have mercy*, *L. bless me* or *us* or *my soul* or *you*, excll. of surprise &c.; also *Lord!* alone as excl.), Christ (*the* or more usu. *our L.*; *in the year of our L.*, anno domini; *L.'s prayer*, the *Our Father*; *L.'s supper*, Eucharist; *L.'s table*, Christian altar, Eucharist; *L.'s day*, Sunday); nobleman, peer of the realm or person entitled by courtesy to the prefix *L.* (see below) as part of his ordinary style (*live, treat, like a l.*, fare, entertain, sumptuously; *drunk as, swear like, a l.*, excessively; *L. in waiting, of the Bedchamber*, nobleman attending sovereign, called by former title if queen is reigning, by latter if king); (pl., *the Ll.*) temporal & spiritual peers of Parliament (*House of Ll.*, upper legislative chamber of United Kingdom, also committee of specially qualified members of this appointed as ultimate judicial appeal court); (pl.; also in full *Ll. Commissioners*) members of board performing duties of high State office put in commission (*Ll. of the Admiralty, Treasury*, &c.; *First L.*, president of such board; *Civil L.*, civilian member of Admiralty board, opp. *Naval Ll.*); *Ll. of Session*, judges of Scotch *Court of* SESSION; first word of many official titles (*L.* CHAMBERLAIN, CHANCELLOR, *Chief Justice, High Commissioner*; *L. Justice General, L. Justice Clerk*, president, vice-president, of Scotch Court of Justiciary; *L. Lieutenant*, viceroy of Ireland till 1922, chief executive authority & head of magistracy in each county, whence **lord-lieute·nan**CY n.; *L. Rector*, triennially elected honorary head of a Scotch university court; *L. Mayor*, mayor of London, York, Dublin, & some great towns; *L. Bishop*, any bishop in ceremonious mention); (prefixed as part of personal designation) marquis, earl, viscount, or baron (whether peer, or peer's eldest son holding his second title by courtesy; with suppression of *of*, e.g. *Earl of*, or *Lord, Derby*; *l.* is invariable instead of *baron*, which is used as prefix only in foreign titles), (followed by Christian & family name) younger son of duke or marquis; *mў l.* (voc.), respectful or polite formula for addressing nobleman below duke, bishop, l. mayor, or judge of supreme court; *ll. & ladies*, wild arum; hence **lor·d**LESS a., **lor·d**LING[1](2), **lordo·**LATRY, nn. (Vb) play the l. *over* (usu. in pass., *will not be lorded over*; or with *it*, as *lording it over his household*; ennoble, confer title of *l.* upon. [OE *hláford* orig.= bread-keeper (LOAF[1], WARD)]

lor·dly, a. Haughty, imperious, lofty, disdainful; grand, magnificent, fit for or belonging to a lord. Hence **lor·dli**NESS n. [OE *hláfordlic* (prec., -LY[1])]

Lord's, n. (Used for) Lord's cricket ground in London, headquarters of the M.C.C. and English cricket. [Thomas *Lord*, maker of successive grounds named after him]

lor·dship, n. Dominion, rule, ownership *of* or *over*; domain, estate, manor; lord's personality (*your l., his l.*, you, he, in speaking deferentially to or of a lord, also facet. to or of other persons or animals). [-SHIP]

lore[1], n. Doctrine (archaic); erudition, scholarship, (archaic); body of traditions & facts on a subject (*ghost, bird, animal, fairy*, &c., *l.*). [OE *lár* cf. Du. *leer*, G *lehre*, cogn. w. LEARN]

lore[2], n. (nat. hist.). Strap-like surface, in birds between eye & upper mandible, in snakes between eye & nostril. [f. L *lorum* strap]

Lŏretto·nian, a. & n. (Member) of Loretto School in Scotland.

lorgne·tte (lornyĕ·t), n. Pair of eye-glasses usu. held by long handle; opera-glass. [F]

lŏ·ricate (-*a*t), a. (zool.). Having defensive armour of bone, plates, scales, &c. [f. L *loricatus* (*lorica* cuirass f. *lorum* strap, -ATE[2])]

lŏ·riner, n. (hist.). Bit-maker, spurrier, (now only in title of a livery company). [f. OF *lorenier* (*lorain* harness-strap f. L *lorum* thong]

lor·is, n. Small slender tailless nocturnal climbing quadrumanous Cingalese mammal; kinds of lemur. [F]

lorn, a. (poet. & joc.). Desolate, forlorn, (often *lone l.*). [p.p. of obs. *leese* LOSE, OE *-léosan* cf. G *verlieren*]

lo·rry, n. Long low flat sideless wagon; truck used on railways & tramways. [?]

lor·y, n. Kinds of bright-plumaged parrot-like bird. [f. Malay *luri*]

lose (lōōz), v.t. & i. (*lost* pr. law- *or* lŏ-). Be deprived of, cease by negligence, misadventure, separation, death, &c., to possess or have, (property, life, quality, limb, father, friend, &c.; *doctor loses patient,* fails to keep him alive, also is left by him for another doctor; *l. patience,* one's *temper,* become impatient, angry; *l.* one's HEAD[1]; *l.* one's HEART; *l.* HEART; *l. ground,* fail to keep position, recede, decline; *have lost my cold,* got rid of it; *l. interest,* of person, cease to be interested, of thing, cease to interest), (pass.) disappear, perish, die or be dead, (*letter-writing is a lost art*; *the ship & all hands were lost*; *lost to sense of duty, shame,* &c., no longer affected by them; *lost soul,* damned); suffer loss or detriment, incur disadvantage, be the worse off in money or otherwise *by* transaction &c., (*the publisher lost by it*; *the army lost heavily*; *story does not l. in the telling,* is if anything exaggerated); become unable to find, fail to keep in sight or follow or mentally grasp, (*l. a document,* one's *way, the thread of a discourse, a person* &c. *under observation*); spend (time, opportunities, pains) to no purpose, waste, (pass., *be lost upon,* fail to influence or draw the attention of); fail to obtain, catch, see, or hear (*l.* one's *train, a legacy, a word* or *remark, a fox*); forfeit (stake), be defeated in (*game, battle, lawsuit,* or abs.; *losing game,* in which defeat seems inevitable; *cannot play a losing game,* loses heart or temper in it); fail to carry (motion); cause person the loss of, cost, (*will l. you your place*); (refl. & pass.) go astray, become merged or engrossed (*in*), be obscured (*in*); *losing* HAZARD. Hence **lo·**SABLE **a.** [OE *losian* (*los* LOSS) intr., the trans. senses being f. the cogn. obs. *leese*]

lō·sel (-zl), n. (archaic). Profligate, rake, ne'er-do-well. [prob. f. *losen* p.p. of obs. *leese* LOSE]

lo·ser, n. In vbl senses; esp.: *be a l. by,* suffer loss by; *good l.,* person not dejected or angered by losing game &c.; person, horse, &c., that loses race &c.; (Billiards) losing HAZARD. [-ER[1]]

loss (laws, lŏs), n. Losing or being lost (see LOSE); person, thing, or amount lost (CUT[2] *a* or *the l.*); detriment, disadvantage, resulting from loss (person &c. *is a great, no, little,* &c., *l.,* the l. of him is a serious &c. blow); *at a l.* (*for, to discover,* &c.), puzzled, at fault. [prob. partly f. OE *los* (cf. ON *los*) dispersion, rout, & partly back formation f. *lost* p.p. of LOSE]

löss (G), n. =LOESS.

lost. See LOSE.

lot, n., & v.t. One of a set of objects used to secure a chance decision in dividing goods, selecting officials, &c. (now only in *draw, cast, ll.,* usu. *between, for, who,* &c., & in *throw* or *cast in* one's *l. with,* share fortunes of), this method of deciding (*the l.*; *by l.*), choice resulting from it (*the l. fell upon me*); what falls to person by l., share (*have no part nor l. in*), person's destiny, fortune, condition, (*the l. falls to me, it falls to my l., it falls to me as my l., to* do); tax, due, (*scot & l.*); plot or allotment of land; article or set of articles offered separately at sale, item at auction, (*bad l.,* disreputable or vicious person); number or quantity of persons or things of same kind or somehow associated (*the l.,* the whole number or quantity); (colloq.) considerable number or amount, *a* good or great deal (also in pl., as *has ll. of friends*). (Vb) divide (land, usu. *out,* or goods for sale) into ll. [OE *hlot,* cf. Du. *lot,* cogn. w. G *loos*]

loth. See LOATH.

Lothār·io, n. Libertine, rake. [character in Rowe's *Fair Penitent*]

lō·tion (-shn), n. Liquid preparation used externally to heal wound, cure skin-disease, clear complexion, &c.; (slang) alcoholic drink. [f. L *lotio* (*lavare lot-* wash, -ION)]

lo·ttery, n. Arrangement for distributing prizes by chance among purchasers of tickets; *l.-wheel,* wheel with box used for shuffling numbers corresponding to those on tickets; (fig.) thing that defies calculation (*life, marriage, is a l.*). [f. It. *lotteria* (LOT, LOTTO)]

lo·tto, n. Game of chance with drawing of numbers as in lottery. [It., f. Teut. (LOT)]

lō·tus, n. Plant represented in ancient Greek legend as inducing luxurious dreaminess & distaste for active life (*l.-eater,* person given to indolent enjoyment; so *l.-eating* a. & n.); Egyptian & Asiatic water-lily; kinds of plant, esp. Bird's-foot Trefoil; *l.-land,* place of indolent enjoyment. [L, f. Gk *lōtos*]

loud (lowd), a. & adv. Strongly audible, sonorous (*l. speaker*, wireless receiver l. enough to be heard without head-phones); clamorous, noisy; (of colour, dress, pattern, manners) obtrusive, conspicuous, flashy; hence **lou·d**EN[6] v.i., **lou·d**ISH[1](2) a., **lou·d**LY[2] adv., **lou·d**NESS n.; (adv.) loudly (*don't talk so l.*; *laughed l. & long*); *l.*-SPOKEN. [com.-WG; OE *hlúd*, cf. Du. *luid*, G *laut*; cogn. w. Gk *kluō* hear, L *cluēre* be famed]

lough (lŏch), n. (Anglo-Ir.). Lake, arm of sea. [perh. f. ONorthumb. *luh* f. Gael. & Ir. LOCH]

Louis (lōō·ĭ, *or as F*), n. (pl. *Louis* pr. -z or as F). Name of many French kings (*l.* or *l.-d'or*, French gold coin of about 20 fr. from L. XIII to L. XVI; *L. Treize, Quatorze, Quinze, Seize*, used adj. of furniture &c. in styles prevalent in those reigns).

lounge (lownj), v.i. & t., & n. Go lazily, saunter; loll, recline; idle (intr., & *l. away* time &c.); hence **lou·ng**ER[1] n., **lou·nging**LY[2] adv. (N.) spell of lounging, saunter, stroll; place where one can l., esp. entrance-hall or gallery furnished for the purpose (*l.-lizard* slang, professional dance-partner at hotel l.-dances); sofa or deep chair. [?]

lour, lower, (lowr), v.i., & n. Frown, scowl, look sullen, (*on, upon, at*); (of clouds, sky, storm) look dark & threatening; hence **lour·ing**LY[2], **lower-**, adv. (N.) scowl; gloominess of sky &c., whence **lour·**Y[2] a. [ME *louren*, cf. Du. *loeren* frown, G *lauern* watch; spelling *lower* prob. due to confusion w. LOWER[1]]

louse (lows), n. (pl. *lice*). Parasitic insect infesting human hair & skin; kinds of parasite of mammals, birds, fish, & plants. Hence **lou·s**Y[2] (-z-) a., **lou·si**NESS n. [com.-Teut.; OE *lús*, cf. Du. *luis*, G *laus*]

lout[1] (lowt), n. Awkward fellow, bumpkin, clown. Hence **lou·t**ISH[1] a., **lou·tish**LY[2] adv., **lou·tish**NESS n. [?]

lout[2] (lowt), v.i. (archaic). Bow, make obeisance. [OE *lútan*, cf. ON *lúta*]

lou·ver (lōō-), n. Domed turret-like erection on medieval hall-roof &c. with side openings to let smoke out or air in; (pl., also *l.-boards*) arrangement of overlapping boards or slips of glass to admit air but exclude rain. Hence **lou·ver**ED[2] a. [f. OF *lover*, cf. med. L *lodium*]

Louvre (F), n. *The L.*, former royal palace, now art museum, in Paris.

lo·vable (lŭ-), a. Deserving love, amiable. Hence **lo·vab**LY[2] adv., **lo·vable**NESS n. [LOVE[2], -ABLE]

lovage (lŭ·vĭj), n. Kinds of herb. [ME *loveache* f. OF *levesche* f. LL *levisticum* perh. f. L *ligusticum* Ligurian; assim. to *love, ache*]

love[1] (lŭv), n. Warm affection, attachment, likeness, or fondness, paternal benevolence, affectionate devotion, (*of, for, to,* or *towards* person, *for* or *to* thing; *give l. to*, convey affectionate message to, *send* one's *l. to*, get this done; *for the l. of*, for sake or in name of, esp. in adjurations; *for l. or money*, by any means, esp. *cannot get it* &c. *f. l. o. m.*; *labour of l.*, that one delights in, or that one does for l. of some one; *there's no l. lost between them*, they dislike each other; *play for l.*, for the pleasure of it, not for stakes); sexual affection or passion or desire, relation between sweethearts, this feeling as a literary subject, a personified influence, or a god (also representation of Cupid, or of naked winged child, or in pl. children, symbolizing l.), (*in l.*, possessed by this; *in l. with*, enamoured of, also transf. fond of a pursuit, thing, &c.; *fall in l.*, become enamoured; *all's* FAIR[2] *in l. & war*; *l. in a cottage*, marriage on insufficient means; *make l.*, pay amorous attentions *to* or abs., whence **lo·ve-mak**ING[1] n.); beloved one, sweetheart, (esp. of woman, cf. LOVER; hence **lo·ve**Y[3] n.; *my l.*, common form of address between husband & wife), (colloq.) delightful person or pretty thing (*he is an old l., what ll. of teacups !*); (Games) no score, nothing, nil, (*l. all*, neither side has yet scored; *l. game*, in which loser has not scored); *l.-affair*, amour; *l.-apple*, (old name for) tomato; *l.-begotten*, illegitimate; *l.-bird*, small bird of parrot kind said to pine away at death of its mate; *l.-child*, illegitimate; *l.-feast*, meal in token of brotherly l. among early Christians, religious service among Methodists &c. imitating this; *l.-in-a-mist*, Fennel-flower; *l.-in-idleness*, Heart's-ease; *l.-knot*, peculiarly interlaced bow of ribbon; *l.-letter*, between sweethearts & concerned with l.; *l.-lies-bleeding*, garden plant with long drooping spike of purple-red bloom; *lovelock*, tress or curl worn on temple or forehead; *l.-lorn*, pining with l., deserted by one's love(r); *l.-match*, marriage made for l.'s sake only; *l.-philtre*, philtre; *lovesick*, languishing with l.; *l.-song*, about or expressing l.; *l.-story*, novel &c. of which main theme is l., facts of a wooing &c.; *l.-token*, thing given in sign of l. Hence **lo·ve**WORTHY a., **lo·veworthi**NESS n. [OE *lufu*, cogn. w. G *lieben*, Du. *lieven*, to love; also w. LIEF, LEAVE[1], BELIEVE]

love[2], v.t. & i. Hold dear, bear l. to, be in l. with, be fond of, (*l. me, l. my* DOG[1]; *Lord l. you !*, excl. of surprise at person's mistake &c.; *l.* one's *l. with an A, a B*, &c., formula in game of forfeits); be in l.; cling to, delight in, enjoy having, be addicted to, admire or be glad of the existence of, (life, honour, comfort, golf, do*ing*, virtue, man who knows his own mind, &c.); (w. inf.) be (habitually) inclined (*children l. to ape their elders*); (colloq.) like, be delighted, (*he simply loves* *to find mistakes*; *Will you come?* — *I should l. to*). [OE *lufian* (prec.)]

Lo·velace (lŭvl-), n. Libertine, accomplished rake. [character in *Clarissa Harlowe*]

lo·veless, a. Unloving; unloved. Hence **lo·veless**LY[2] adv., **lo·veless**NESS n. [-LESS]

lo·vely (lŭ-), a. Attractively or admirably beautiful; (colloq.) delightful, very pleasing, intensely amusing. Hence **lo·veli**LY[2] adv. (rare), **lo·veli**NESS n. [OE *luflic* (LOVE[1], -LY[1])]

lo·ver, n. Woman's sweetheart or suitor, (pl.) pair in love; paramour, gallant; admirer, devotee, *of* thing, action, or idea; *lovers' knot*, LOVE[1]-knot. Hence **lo·ver**LESS a., **lo·ver**LIKE, **lo·ver**LY[1], [2], aa. & advv. [-ER[1]]

lo·ving, a. That loves, affectionate, (*our l. subjects*, formula in royal proclamation; *your l. friend* &c., formula in concluding letter); manifesting or proceeding from love (*l.-cup*, large drinking vessel passed round at banquet; *l.-kindness*, tender consideration). Hence **lo·ving**LY[2] adv., **lo·ving**NESS n. [-ING[2]]

low[1] (lō), a. & adv. (*-er*, *-est*, as aa. & advv.). Not reaching far up, not high or tall, (*l. house, forehead, stature*; not used of persons; *l. dress*, leaving neck & part of shoulders & breast exposed, so *l. neck*; *l. relief*, bas-relief); not elevated in geographical &c. position (*L. Countries*, Netherlands; *L.* GERMAN[2], DUTCH; *Lower Egypt* &c.; *l. moon* &c., near horizon; *l. tide* or *water*, level of ebbed sea, time of extreme ebb; *l.-water mark*, lowest point reached by ebb-tide, & fig.; *in l. water*, out of funds &c.); of or in humble rank or position (*the lower orders* or *classes*; *l. birth*; *high & l.*, every one); not exalted or sublime, commonplace, undignified, little civilized, not highly organized; abject, mean, degraded, coarse, vulgar, (*l. cunning*); ill-nourished, not nourishing, indicative of ill nutrition, wanting in vigour, depressed, not intense, (*l. condition, diet, fever*; *l. spirits*, whence **low-spi·rit**ED[2] a.); of small amount as measured by a scale or degrees (*l. price, wages, rates, temperature, power*; *have l. opinion of*, do not estimate highly; *at lowest*, to mention the least possible amount &c.; *l. latitudes*, near equator); (of sounds) not shrill or high up, produced by slow vibrations, (also) not loud; (of liquid, receptacle, supply of anything, esp. fig. of purse or money) nearly exhausted or empty (often *run l.*); recent (*belongs to a lower date*); (also *l.-church*) giving l. place to authority of bishops & priests, inherent grace of sacraments, ecclesiastical organization, & ritual, not sacerdotal, approximating to protestant non-conformity, (*L. Church*, party in Church of England thus minded; *L. Churchman*, member of it); *bring l.*, depress, reduce, in health, wealth, or position; *lay l.*, overthrow; *lie l.*, crouch, be prostrate or dead or abased, (slang) keep quiet or out of the way, say nothing, bide one's time; BURN[2] *l.*; *l.-browed*, lit., also (of rocks) beetling, (of building &c.) with low entrance, gloomy; *l. celebration* of Eucharist, without choir or assistant ministers; *l. comedian*, actor in *l. comedy*, in which subject & treatment border on farce; *l.-down*, abject, mean, dishonourable; *lower boy*, in lower school at public schools; *lower* CASE[2]; *lower chamber*, = *lower House*; *lower critic*(*ism*), of the verbal or textual kind; *lower deck*, immediately over hold (*the l. d.*, petty officers & men of the Navy or of a ship); *lower Empire*, later Roman Empire, usu. from Constantine; *lower House*, lower branch of legislative assembly, e.g. House of Commons; *lower school* in public schools, usu. forms below fifth; *lower world*, the earth, (also) hell; *lowland*, (usu. pl.) lowlying country, (adj.) of or in this; *Lowlands*, S.-E. part of Scotland, whence **Low·land**ER[1](4) n., *Lowland* (adj.) of or in this; *l.* LATIN; *l. life*, that of the lower classes, whence **low-lived**[2] a.; *l.* MASS[1]; *l. pitch*, l. key or tone, also slight angular elevation of roof, whence **low-pitch**ED[2] a.; *l.* PRESSURE; *L. Sunday, Week*, after Easter Day & Week; hence **low·er**MOST, **low·ish**[1](2) aa., **low·**NESS n. (Adv.) in or to l. or mean position (*hangs l.*; *aim* or *shoot l.* or *lower*; *collar l.* in football, catch at or below waist; *bowed l.*; *never fell so l. as that*); on poor diet (*live l. for a time*); for small stakes (*play l.*); in l. tone, on or to l. note, (*talk l.*; *cannot get so l.*); (of date) late (*find it as low as the 18th century*); *l.-born*, of humble birth; *l.-bred*, of vulgar manners; *l. down*, far down, also in mean or ungenerous way (esp. *play it l.d.*, or *l., upon*, treat scurvily). [ME *lah* f. ON *lágr* cogn. w. LIE[3]]

low[2] (lō), v.i. & t., & n. Utter cry (as) of cow, moo; say, utter *forth*, with lowing sound; (n.) cow's cry. [com.-Teut.; OE *hlówan*, cf. OHG *hluojen*, Du. *loeien*, cogn. w. L *clamare*]

low·er[1] (lō-), v.t. & i. Let or haul down; (Naut., abs.) let down boat, haul down sail, &c.; diminish height of; sink, descend, slope downwards; diminish (price &c.), (of price &c.) come down; diminish (t. & i.) in intensity or pitch; degrade, disgrace; reduce bodily condition of (*a lowering diet*). [f. *lower* comp. of LOW[1]]

lower[2]. See LOUR.

low·ly (lō-), a. & adv. Humble in feeling, behaviour, or condition, modest, unpretending; (adv.) in l. manner. Hence **low·li**LY[2] adv., **low·li**NESS n. [LOW[1], -LY[1], [2]]

loxodrŏ·mic, a. & n. Of oblique sailing

or sailing by the RHUMB; (n.) l. line or table. Hence **loxodro·mICS** n. [f. Gk *loxos* oblique, *dromos* course, -IC]
loy·al, a. & n. True, faithful, to duty, love, or obligation (*to*); faithful in allegiance to sovereign, government, or mother-country; enthusiastically devoted to sovereign's person & family; exhibiting loyalty; hence **loy·alISM**(3), **loy·alIST**(2), nn., **loy·alIZE**(3) v.t., **loy·alLY**[2] adv.; (n.) person who remains l. in time of disaffection. [F, f. L *legalis* LEGAL]
loy·alty, n. Loyal temper or conduct. [f. OF *loialté* (prec., -TY)]
lŏ·zenge (-j), n. RHOMB, diamond figure, esp. as bearing in heraldry; l.-shaped shield for spinster's or widow's arms; l.-shaped facet of cut gem; small tablet (orig. l.-shaped) of flavoured sugar, medicine, meat essence, &c., to be dissolved in mouth; l.-shaped pane in casement. [f. OF *losenge*, cf. Pr. *lausa* tombstone perh. ult. f. L *lapis* stone]
lo·zenged, a. With lozenges of alternate colours; with lozenge panes. [-ED[2]]
£.s.d. (ĕ·lĕsdē·), n. Pounds, shillings, & pence; money, riches; *L. S. De·ism*, money-worship. [see L, LIBRA]
'lt. See WILL[1].
lu·bber, n. Big clumsy stupid fellow, lout; clumsy seaman. Hence **lu·bberLIKE** a., **lu·bberLY**[1], [2] a. & adv., **lu·bberliNESS** n. [prob. f. or cogn. w. LOB]
lu·bricate (lōō-, lū-), v.t. Make slippery or smooth by applying fluid or unguent; minimize friction of (machinery) with grease &c. (also fig.). Hence **lu·bricANT** (2) a. & n., **lu·bricatOR**[2](1, 2), **lubricA·TION**, nn. [f. L *lubricare* (*lubricus* slippery cogn. w. SLIP), -ATE[3]]
lubri·city, n. Slipperiness, smoothness, oiliness, (lit. & fig.); lewdness, wantonness. So **lubri·ciOUS**, **lu·bricOUS**, aa. [f. L *lubricitas* (prec., -TY)]
Lu·can (lōō-, lū)-, a. Of St Luke. [f. L *Lucas* Luke, -AN]
luce (lōōs, lūs), n. Pike fish, esp. when full-grown. [f. OF *lus* f. LL *lucius*]
lu·cent (lōō-, lū-), a. Shining, luminous; translucent. Hence **lu·CENCY** n. [f. L *lucēre* shine (*lux lucis* light), -ENT]
lucer·n(e) (lōō-, lū-), n. Cloverlike plant used for fodder. [f. F *luzerne* etym. dub.]
Luciă·nic (lōōsĭ-), a. After the manner of Lucian, witty & scoffing. [f. L f. Gk *Loukianos*, writer of Greek dialogues c. 160 A.D., -IC]
lu·cid (lōō-, lū-), a. Bright (poet.); (Entom., Bot.) with smooth shining surface; clear, pellucid, (usu. fig. of reasoning, literary style, &c.); *l. interval*, period of sanity between attacks of madness, or of quiet between disturbances. Hence or cogn. **luci·dITY** n., **lu·cidLY**[2] adv. [f. L *lucidus* (LUCENT)]
Lu·cifer (lōō-, lū-), a. (Planet Venus as) morning star; (supposed name, see A.V. & R.V. of *Isa.* xiv. 12, of) the chief rebel angel, Satan, the devil, (*as proud as L.*); *l. match* or *l.*, friction match (now rare in educated use). [L, light-bringing, morning star, (*lux lucis* light, *-fer* f. *ferre* bring)]
luci·fugous, a. (nat. hist.). Shunning daylight. [f. L *lucifugus* (prec., *fugere* flee), -OUS]
luck, n. (Chance as bestower of) good or ill fortune, fortuitous events affecting one's interests, person's apparent tendency to be (un)fortunate, supposed tendency of chance to bring a succession of (un)favourable events, (*bad l. to him* &c.!, form of imprecation; *as l. would have it*, fortunately or unfortunately; *down on* one's *l.*, dispirited by misfortune, temporarily unfortunate; *try* one's *l.*, make a venture at gaming-table or in anything; *just my l.*, usu. = I am unlucky as usual; *worse l.* parenth., more's the pity, unfortunately for me or us); good fortune, success due to chance, (*have the l.*, be fortunate enough *to*; *for l.*, to bring good l.; *in, out of, l.*; *have no l.*), whence **lu·ckLESS** a., **lu·cklessNESS** n.; *l.-money, -penny*, piece of money kept for l., also sum returned by seller to buyer esp. in live-stock sale. [f. LG *luk*, short for *geluk* cf. G *glück* etym. dub.]
lu·ckily, adv. (As ordinary adv.) by luck (rare); (as qualification of sentence or clause) which is &c. a fortunate thing, thank goodness, (*l. for me I was wrong*; *on a snow-slope which was l. in good order*). [foll., -LY[2]]
lu·cky[1], a. Constantly attended by good luck, enjoying it on a particular occasion, having as much success or happiness as one deserves & more, (*you're a l. dog*, form of congratulation esp. to accepted lover; *l. beggar!*, *l. bargee!*, of or to person in luck); right by luck, of the nature of a fluke, (*l. guess, hit, shot*), coming in the nick of time; presaging, bringing, worn &c. for, good luck, well-omened, (*l. penny, stone, day*); *l.-bag, -tub*, at bazaars &c. containing articles of more or less value for one of which payer of small sum may dip. Hence **lu·ckiNESS** n. [-Y[2]]
lu·cky[2], n. (slang). *Cut* one's *l.*, decamp, make off. [?]
lu·crative (lōō-, lū-), a. Yielding gain, profitable. Hence **lu·crativeLY**[2] adv., **lu·crativeNESS** n. [f. L *lucrativus* (*lucrari* to gain, see foll., -ATIVE)]
lucre (lōō·ker, lū-), n. Pecuniary profit as motive; FILTHY *l.* [f. L *lucrum*, cogn. w. Gk *apolauō* enjoy, G *lohn* reward]
Lucrē·tia (-sha), n. Model of chastity, woman preferring honour to life. [see Livy i. 57–8]
lu·cūbrate (lōō-, lū-), v.i. Express one's meditations in writing; produce lucubra-

tions. Hence **lu·cubrat**OR[2] n. [f. L *lucubrare* work by lamplight (*lux lucis* light), -ATE[3]]

lucubra·tion, n. Nocturnal study or meditation; literary work esp. of pedantic or elaborate character. [f. L *lucubratio* (prec., -ATION)]

lu·cŭlent (lōō-, lū-), a. (rare). Clear, convincing, lucid, (*l. proof, instance, explanation*). Hence **lu·culent**LY[2] adv. [f. L *luculentus* (*lux lucis* light, -LENT)]

lu·cus ă non luce·ndo (lōō-, lū-), n. Paradoxical derivation; (transf.) reference of effect to paradoxical cause, explanation by contraries. [L, = *lucus* (grove) is derived from *lucēre* (shine) because it does not shine there]

lud. *My l.*, = my lord in representations of counsel's pronunciation in addressing judge.

Lu·ddite, n. & a. (Member) of band of mechanics (1811–16) who raised riots for destruction of machinery. [origin doubtful; leaders were called *Captain Ludd*]

lu·dicrous (lōō-, lū-), a. Absurd, ridiculous, exciting or deserving derision. Hence **lu·dicrous**LY[2] adv., **lu·dicrous**NESS n., **ludicro-** comb. form. [f. L *ludicrus* prob. f. *ludicrum* stage-play (*ludere* play)]

lues (lōō·ēz), n. Plague, contagious disease, contagion, (*l. Boswelliana*, biographer's tendency to magnify his subject, see BOSWELL); (also *l. venerea*) syphilis, whence (irreg.) **lue**·TIC a. [L, genit. *luis*]

luff, n., & v.i. & t., (naut.). Side of fore-&-aft sail next mast or stay; broadest part of ship's bow where sides begin to curve in. (Vb) bring ship's head, bring head of (ship), nearer wind, turn (helm) so as to secure this; (Yacht-racing) get windward side of (opponent; *luffing-match*, struggle for this). [prob. f. F *lof* some contrivance for altering ship's course, cf. Du. *loef*]

lug[1], n. Large marine worm used as bait. [perh. cogn. w. LOG[1]]

lug[2], n. = LUG-SAIL.

lug[3], v.t. & i., & n. Drag or tug (heavy object) with effort or violence; (intr.) pull hard *at*; bring (subject &c.) irrelevantly *in* or *into*; force (person) *along*; (n.) hard or rough pull. [cf. Sw. *lugga* pull person's hair (*lugg* forelock)]

lug[4], n. (Sc.) ear; (Mech.) projection from a casting &c. by which it may be fixed in place. [?]

luge (as F), n., & v.i. Short raised toboggan used in Switzerland; (vb) toboggan in this.

lu·ggage (-ĭj), n. Traveller's baggage, portmanteaus, boxes, &c. [LUG[3], -AGE]

lu·gger, n. Small ship with four-cornered sails set fore & aft. [prob. f. foll.]

lu·g-sail (-sl), n. Four-cornered sail bent on yard slung at a third or quarter of its length from one end. [?]

lugū·brious (lōō-, lū-), a. Doleful, dismal, mournful. Hence **lugu·brious**LY[2] adv., **lugu·brious**NESS n. [f. L *lugubris* (*lugēre* mourn), -OUS]

lukewarm (lōō·kworm, lū-), a. & n. Moderately warm, tepid; not zealous, indifferent, (n., l. person). Hence **lu·kewarm**LY[2] adv., **lu·kewarm**NESS n. [f. obs. *luke* tepid, cf. obs. *lew*, & ON *hlýr* warm]

lull, v.t. & i., & n. Soothe or send to sleep by sounds or caresses, quiet (suspicion &c.) usu. by deception; (usu. pass.) quiet (sea, storm); (of storm or noise) lessen, fall quiet; hence **lu·lling**LY[2] adv.; (n.) intermission in storm lit. or fig. [imit. of sounds used in lullaby]

lu·llabȳ, n., & v.t. Soothing refrain or song to put child to sleep; (vb) sing to sleep. [prec., *-by* as in BYE-BYE]

lumbā·go, n. Rheumatic affection in loins. Hence **lumbā·gin**OUS (-j-), a. [L (*lumbus* loin)]

lu·mbar, a. & n. (Artery, vein, nerve, or vertebra) of or in loin. [prec., -AR[1]]

lu·mber[1], v.i. Move in clumsy blundering noisy way (*along, past, by*, &c.). Hence **lu·mber**ING[2] a., **lu·mbering**LY[2] adv., **lu·mber**SOME a. [ME *lomere* perh. f. LAME]

lu·mber[2], n., & v.t. & i. Disused articles of furniture &c. taking up room (*l.-room*, in which such things are kept), useless or cumbrous material; superfluous fat; roughly prepared timber (*l.-carrier*, boat in l.-trade; *l.-mill*, for sawing l.; *lumberman*, feller, dresser, or conveyer of l.; *l.-scaler*, one who measures l.). (Vb) fill up inconveniently, obstruct, (room, place; often *up, over*); heap together, treat, as l.; cut & prepare forest timber, whence **lu·mber**ER[1] n. [prob. f. prec.; or f. obs. *lumber* pawnbroker's shop (LOMBARD)]

lumbo-, comb. form of L *lumbus* loin, as *-abdo·minal* of loins & abdomen.

lu·mbrical, a. & n. *L. muscle* or *l.*, one of the muscles flexing fingers or toes. [f. L *lumbricus* earthworm, w. ref. to the shape]

Lumière (lōō·mīār). *L. process*, a colour-photography method; so *L. plate*. [Brothers *L.*, inventors]

lu·minary (lōō-, lū-), n. Natural light-giving body, esp. sun or moon; person of intellectual, moral, or spiritual eminence, person of light & leading. [f. F *luminaire* f. med. L *luminarium* (L *lumen -inis* light, -ARY[1])]

lumini·ferous, a. Producing or transmitting light. [prec., -FEROUS]

lu·minous (lōō-, lū-), a. Emitting or full of light, bright, shining, (*l. paint*, phosphorescent kind making thing conspicuous at night), whence **lumino·**SITY n.; (of writers &c.) throwing light upon subject. Hence **lu·minous**NESS n., **lu·minous**LY[2] adv. [f. L *luminosus* (*lumen -inis* light, -OUS)]

lu·mme, int. (vulg.) of surprise or emphasis. [=(Lord) love me]

lump[1], n., & v.t. & i. Compact shapeless or unshapely mass (*l. in throat*, feeling of pressure caused by emotion; *is a l. of selfishness*, is selfish through & through); great quantity, lot, heap; mass of clay or dough ready for moulding or baking; protuberance, excrescence, swelling, bruise; heavy dull person; *in the l.*, taking things as a whole, in gross, wholesale; *l. sugar*, loaf sugar broken or cut into ll. or cubes; *l. sum*, covering number of items, also paid down at once (opp. *instalments*). (Vb) put together in one l., mass together, treat as all alike, disregard differences between or among, (*together, with, in with, under* title &c.); lay whole of (sum) *on* horse, event, &c.; rise or collect (intr.) into ll.; go heavily *along*, sit heavily *down*. [cf. Du. *lomp* rag]

lump[2], n. Uncouth spiny-finned leaden-blue fish clinging tightly to objects by sucking-disk on belly. [cf. MLG *lumpen*, MDu. *lompe*; perh. f. prec., but the G & Du. forms are found earlier]

lump[3], v.t. Be displeased at, put up with ungraciously, (now only in *if you don't like it you may l. it*). [earlier =sulk; prob. imit.]

lu·mper, n. Labourer employed in (un)loading cargoes; small contractor taking work in the lump & giving it out in the piece; classifier who avoids minute subdivision. [LUMP[1], -ER[1]]

lu·mping, a. (colloq.). Big, plentiful, (*l. weight*, good weight). [LUMP[1], -ING[2]]

lu·mpish, a. Heavy & clumsy; stupid, lethargic. Hence **lu·mpish**LY[2] adv., **lu·mpish**NESS n. [LUMP[1], -ISH[1]]

lu·mpy, a. Full of or covered with lumps; (of water) cut up by wind into small waves. Hence **lu·mpi**LY[2] adv., **lu·mpi**NESS n. [-Y[2]]

lu·nacy (lōō-, lū-), n. Being a lunatic, insanity (formerly of the intermittent kind attributed to changes of moon), (Law) such mental unsoundness as interferes with civil rights or transactions (*Commission of l.*, authorization of inquiry into person's sanity; *Commissioner in l.*, member of board of ten for inspecting asylums &c.; *Master in l.*, officer investigating cases of alleged lunacy); great folly. [LUNATIC, -ACY]

lu·nar (lōō-, lū-), a. & n. Of, in, as of, the moon (*l.* CYCLE; *l. distance*, of moon from sun, planet, or star, used in finding longitude at sea; *l. month*, interval between new moons about 29½ days, *pop.* period of four weeks; *l. nodes*, at which moon's orbit cuts ecliptic; *l. observation*, finding of longitude by l. distance; *l. politics*, unpractical questions; *l. rainbow*, made by moon's rays); (of light, glory, &c.) pale, feeble; crescent-shaped, lunate, (esp. *l. bone* in wrist); of or containing silver (from alchemists' use of *luna* moon for silver; *l. caustic*, nitrate of silver fused). (N.) l. distance or observation; l. bone. [f. L *lunaris* (*luna* moon, -AR[1])]

lunār·ian, n. Inhabitant of moon; astronomer or navigator with special knowledge of the moon. [prec., -IAN]

lu·nate (lōō-, lū-), a. (nat. hist.). Crescent-shaped. [f. L *lunatus* (*luna* moon, -ATE[2])]

lu·natic (lōō-, lū-), a. & n. Insane (person; see LUNACY), mad(man); (of actions &c.) outrageously foolish, frantic, mad; eccentric, foolish, (person); *l. asylum*, hospital for reception & treatment of ll. [f. LL *lunaticus* (*luna* moon, -ATIC)]

luna·tion, n. Time from one new moon to next. [f. med. L *lunatio* (prec., -ATION)]

lunch (-tsh), n., & v.i. & t., **lu·ncheon** (-tshn), n., (*-ch* now usu. exc. in formal or ceremonious use.) (With late diners) midday meal; (with midday diners) light refreshment taken between breakfast & dinner. (Vb; *-ch*) take l.; provide l. for. [etym., & relation between forms, doubtful; both had earlier sense *lump* (of bread, meat, &c.), & *lunch* may be related to it as *hunch, bunch*, to *hump, bump*]

lune (lōōn, lūn), n. (geom.). Figure formed on sphere or plane by two arcs enclosing space. [F, f. L *luna* moon]

lune·tte (lōō-, lū-), n. Arched aperture in concave ceiling to admit light; crescent-shaped or semicircular space in dome or ceiling decorated with painting &c.; (Fortif.) work larger than redan, with two faces & two flanks; watch-glass of flattened shape; hole for neck in guillotine. [F (prec., -ETTE)]

lung, n. Either of the pair of breathing-organs in man & most vertebrates (*good ll.*, strong voice; *ll. of London* &c., open spaces in or close to great city; *ll. of oak*, lungwort; *l.-fish*, having ll. as well as gills; *l.-power*, power of voice; *lungwort*, plant of borage kind with white-spotted leaves likened to diseased l., (also *ll. of oak*) kind of lichen supposed to be good for l.-disease. Hence **-lung**ED[2], **lu·ng**LESS, aa. [OE *lungen*, cf. Du. *long*, G *lunge*, cogn. w. Gk *elaphros* LIGHT[4] (named from lightness of substance), & see LIGHTS]

lunge[1], **longe,** (-j), n., & v.t. Long rope with which horse-breaker holds horse while he makes it canter in circle; circular exercise-ground for training horses; (vb) exercise (horse) with or in l. [F *longe* halter (L *longus* long)]

lunge[2] (-j), n., & v.i. Thrust with sword &c. esp. in fencing; sudden forward movement, plunge, rush. (Vb) make l. in fencing, deliver blow from shoulder in boxing, (*at*; *out*); (of horse) kick *out*; drive (weapon, sting, &c.) violently in some direction; rush, make sudden start in some direction. [f. earlier *allonge*, F, f. *allonger* lengthen (*à* to, L *longus* long)]

luniso·lar (lōō-, lū-), a. Of sun & moon (*l. period*, of 532 years between agreements of solar & lunar cycles; *l. year*, with divisions regulated by changes of moon, & average length made to agree with sun's revolution). [f. L *luna* moon, -I-, L *sol* sun, -AR[1]]

lu·nkah (-ngka), n. Kind of strong Indian cheroot. [f. Hind. *lanka* islands (of delta where the tobacco is grown)]

luny. See LOONY.

lu·pin(e[1]) (lōō-, lū-), n. Kinds of garden & fodder plant with long tapering spikes of blue, purple, white, or yellow flowers; (usu. pl.) seed of these. [f. L *lupinus*]

lu·pine[2] (lōō-, lū-), a. Of wolf or wolves, wolf-like. [f. L *lupinus* (*lupus* wolf, -INE[1])

lu·pus (lōō-, lū-), n. Ulcerous disease of skin. Hence **lu·poid**, **lu·pous**, aa. [L, = wolf]

lurch[1] (-tsh), n. *Leave in the l.*, desert (friend, ally) in difficulties. [formerly = state of score in some games in which winner was far ahead of loser, f. F *lourche* game like backgammon, also bad defeat in this]

lurch[2] (-tsh), n., & v.i. Sudden lean to one side, stagger; (vb) make lurch(es), stagger. [?]

lur·cher (-tsh-), n. Petty thief, swindler; spy; cross-bred dog between collie or sheep-dog & greyhound, used esp. by poachers. [f. obs. *lurch* vb var. of LURK]

lure (lūr), n., & v.t. Falconer's apparatus for recalling hawk (bunch of feathers, within which it finds its food while being trained, attached to thong); something used to entice; enticing quality *of* a pursuit &c. (Vb) recall (hawk) with l.; entice (person, animal; usu. *away* or *into*). [f. OF *leurre*, cf. It. *logoro* bait, prob. f. Teut. (G *luder* bait)]

lūr·id, a. Ghastly, wan, glaring, unnatural, stormy, terrible, in colour or combination of colours or lights (of complexion, landscape, sky, lightning, thunder-clouds, smoky flame, glance, &c.; *casts a l. light on* facts or character, explains or reveals them in a tragic or terrible way); (Bot. &c.) of dingy yellowish brown. Hence **lur·idly**[2] adv., **lur·idness** n. [f. L *luridus* pale-yellow]

lurk, v.i., & n. Be hidden *in*, *under*, *about*, &c.; escape notice, exist unobserved, be latent; (n.) *on the l.*, spying; *lurking-place*, hiding-place. [perh. cogn. w. LOUR; cf. LG *lurken* shuffle along, Norw. *lurka* loiter in work]

lŭ·scious (-shus), a. Richly sweet in taste or smell; sickly sweet, cloying; (of language or literary style) over-rich in sound, imagery, or voluptuous suggestion. Hence **lu·sciously**[2] adv., **lu·sciousness** n. [ME *luci- licious*, perh. = DELICIOUS]

lush[1], a. Luxuriant & succulent (of plants, esp. grass). [?]

lush[2], n., & v.t. & i., (slang). Liquor, drink. (Vb) ply with liquor; drink. [?]

lu·shy, a. (slang). Drunk. [-Y[2]]

lust, n., & v.i. (Bibl., Theol.) sensuous appetite regarded as sinful; animal desire for sexual indulgence, lascivious passion, whence **lu·stful** a., **lu·stfulness** n.; passionate enjoyment or desire *of* (*l. of battle, conquest, accumulation, applause*); (vb) have strong or excessive desire (usu. *after* or *for*). [com.-Teut.; so Du. & G]

lu·stral, a. Of, used in, ceremonial purification. [f. L *lustralis* (LUSTRUM, -AL)]

lustra·te, v.t. Purify by expiatory sacrifice, ceremonial washing, or other such rite. So **lustra·tion** n. [f. L *lustrare* (LUSTRUM), -ATE[3]]

lu·stre[1] (-ter), n., & v.t. Gloss, refulgence, shining surface, brilliance, bright light, radiant beauty, whence **lu·streless**, **lu·strous** aa., **lu·strously**[2] adv.; splendour, glory, distinction, (*add l. to, throw* or *shed l. on*); (prismatic glass pendant of) chandelier; thin dress-material with cotton warp, woollen woof, & lustrous surface; kind of wool with lustrous surface; (vb) put l. on (cloth, pottery, &c.). [F (L *lustrare* illumine, prob. f. *lux lucis* light)]

lu·stre[2] (-ter), n. = LUSTRUM.

lu·strine, n. Glossy silk fabric. [LUSTRE[1]]

lu·strum, n. (pl. *-a, -ums*). Period of five years. [L, orig. purificatory sacrifice after quinquennial census, prob. f. *luere* wash]

lu·sty, a. Healthy & strong; vigorous, lively. Hence **lu·stihood**, **lu·stiness**, nn., **lu·stily**[2] adv. [-Y[2]]

lu·sus natūr·ae (lōō-, lū-), n. Freak of nature, strikingly abnormal natural production, sport. [L]

lu·tanist (lōō-, lū-), n. Lute-player. [f. med. L *lutanista* (*lutana* LUTE[1], -IST)]

lute[1] (lōōt, lūt), n. Guitar-like instrument used in 14th–17th centuries (RIFT *within the l.*). [f. F *lut* f. Arab. *al'ud* (*al* the, *'ud* lute, orig wood)]

lute[2] (lōōt, lūt), n., & v.t. Clay or cement used to stop hole, make joint airtight, coat crucible, protect graft, &c.; (vb) apply l. to. Hence **lu·ting**[1](3) n. [f. OF *lut* f. L *lutum* mud]

luteo- (lōō-, lū-), comb. form of L *luteus* orange-coloured (*lutum* weld), as *-fu·lvous* orange-tawny.

lu·tēous, a. (nat. hist.). Of deep orange yellow. [prec., -OUS]

lu·testring (lōō-, lū-), n. Glossy silk fabric. [perh. assim. of obs. *lustring* var. of LUSTRINE to *lute, string*]

Lutē·tian (lōō-, lū-), a. Parisian. [f. L *Lutetia* ancient name of Paris, -AN]

Lu·theran (lōō-, lū-), a. & n. (Follower) of Martin Luther, (member) of Church accepting the Augsburg confession. Hence **Lu·theranism**(3) n., **Lu·theranize**(2) v.i., (3) v.t. [-AN]

luxa·te, v.t. Dislocate (joint &c.). Hence **luxa·tion** n. [f. L *luxare* (*luxus* dislocated f. Gk *loxos*), -ATE[3]]

luxe (F), n. *De l.*, of unusual sumptuousness (*édition de l.*) or comfort (*train de l.*).

luxūr·iant, a. Prolific (lit., & of imagination &c.); profuse of growth, exuberant, rank; (of literary or artistic style) florid, richly ornamented. Hence **luxur·iance** n., **luxuri·antly**[2] adv. [f. L *luxuriare* grow rank (*luxuria* LUXURY), -ANT]

luxūr·iāte, v.i. Revel, enjoy oneself, *in* or *on*; take one's ease, be luxurious. [prec., -ATE[3]]

luxūr·ious, a. Given, contributing, to luxury, self-indulgent, voluptuous, very comfortable. Hence **luxur·iously**[2] adv., **luxur·iousness** n. [f. OF *luxurius* f. L *luxuriosus* (foll., -OUS)]

lu·xury (-ksheri), n. (Habitual use of) choice or costly food, dress, furniture, &c.; thing that one enjoys; thing desirable but not indispensable; luxuriousness. [f. OF *luxurie* f. L *luxuria* (*luxus* abundance)]

-ly[1], suf. f. OE *-lic*, cf. OHG *-lîk*, G *-lich*, f. OTeut. *-lîko-* (*lîkom* form). The suf. forms adjj. f. nn. w. sense *having the qualities of* (*kingly, scholarly, soldierly*), or w. sense of recurrence (*daily, hourly*).

-ly[2], suf. forming advv., f. OE *-lice* (cf. OHG *-lîchô*, G *-lich*) f. OTeut. *-lîko-* (prec.) + adv. suf. *-ô*. In OTeut. an adv. in *-ly* implies the existence of an adj. in *-ly*[1]; but even in OE the suf. (in the form *-lice*) was added to other adjj., & later became the usu. ending for advv. Down to 17th c. adv. *-ly* was added even to adjj. in *-ly*, the orig. *-lîkô* being thus doubly represented; these advv. in *-lily* are now avoided as awkward, & as the adv. use of the adj. (*to live godly*) is also avoided, adjj. in *-ly* have in ordinary use no corr. adv. *Partly* is a solitary formation on n. Wds in *-le* have *-ly* for *-lely* (*feebly, supply*, not *feeblely, supplely*).

lȳca·nthropy, n. Transformation of witch into a wolf; form of madness in which patient imagines himself some beast & exhibits depraved appetites, change of voice, &c. [f. Gk *lukanthrōpia* (*lukos* wolf, *anthrōpos* man, -Y[1])]

lycée (lē·sā), n. State secondary school in France. [F]

Lȳcē·um, n. Garden at Athens in which Aristotle taught, his philosophy & followers (cf. ACADEMY, GARDEN, PORCH, TUB); literary institution, lecture-hall, teaching-place. [L, f. Gk *Lukeion* neut. of *Lukeios* epithet of Apollo (from whose neighbouring temple the L. was named)]

lych. See LICH.

ly·chnis (lĭk-), n. Genus of plants including Campion & Ragged Robin. [L, f. Gk *lukhnis* red flower (*lukhnos* lamp)]

lȳ·copod, -pō·dium, n. Clubmoss; (*-ium* only) fine powder from kind of l. used as absorbent in surgery, & in making stage-lightning. [*-d* anglicized f. *-ium* mod. L (Gk *lukos* wolf, *pous podos* foot)]

ly·ddite, n. High explosive chiefly of picric acid used in shells. [*Lydd* in Kent, -ITE[1]]

Lȳ·dian, a. & n. (Language, inhabitant) of Lydia, ancient division of Asia Minor; *L.* MODE, of effeminate plaintive character. [f. L f. Gk *Ludios*, -AN]

lye (lī), n. Water alkalized by lixiviation of vegetable ashes, any strong alkaline solution esp. for washing, any detergent. [OE *léog* cf. Du. *loog*, G *lauge*, prob. cogn. w. LATHER]

ly·ing[1], n. In vbl senses of LIE[2, 3]; also: place to lie (*soft, dry, l.*); *l.-in*, being in childbirth (also attrib., as *l.-in hospital*). [-ING[1]]

ly·ing[2], a. In vbl senses of LIE[2, 3]; esp.: deceitful, false, whence **ly·ingly**[2] adv.; *-l.*, placed, as *low-l. land*. [-ING[2]]

ly·ke-wake, n. Watch kept at night over dead body. [LICH, WAKE[2]]

ly·me-grass, n. Kind of grass planted on sand to keep it from shifting. [perh. f. LIME[1] w. ref. to its binding effect]

lymph, n. Pure water (poet.); (Physiol.) colourless alkaline fluid from tissues or organs of body, like blood but without red corpuscles; exudation from sore &c., (also *vaccine l.*) matter taken from cow-pox vesicles & used in vaccination, other morbid matter used for similar purpose. Hence **ly·mphous** a. [f. L *lympha* water prob. cogn. w. LIMPID*us*]

lymphă·tic, a. & n. Of, secreting, conveying, lymph, (*l. gland, vessel*; *l. system*, these glands & vessels); (of persons or temperament) flabby-muscled, pale-skinned, sluggish, (qualities formerly attributed to excess of lymph); (n.) vein-like vessel conveying lymph. [f. L *lymphaticus* mad (*lympha* see prec.; the L sense perh. due to supposed connexion w. Gk *numphē* nymph, which affected spelling of *lympha*) as though = of water]

lynce·an, a. Lynx-eyed, keensighted. [f. L f. Gk *lugkeios* (*lugx* lynx), -AN; often also w. ref. to *Lynceus* the keen-sighted Argonaut]

lynch, n., & v.t. *L. law* (*L-* or *l-*), procedure of self-constituted illegal court that summarily executes person charged with flagrant offence; *Judge L.*, imaginary authority to whom sentences are attributed; (vb) execute (person) thus. [orig. U.S., earlier *Lynch's law*, doubtfully referred to Charles *L.*, J.P. in Virginia, indemnified 1782 for illegally punishing persons]

lynx, n. Kinds of animal of the cat tribe with tufted ear-tips, short tail, spotted fur, & proverbially keen sight; l. fur; *l.-eyed*, sharp-sighted. [L, f. Gk *lugx*, cf. G *luchs*, prob. cogn. w. Gk *leussō* see]

Ly·on, n. (Also *L. King of Arms*) chief

herald of Scotland. [archaic for *lion*; named f. lion on royal shield]

Lȳr·a, n. Northern constellation. [L, f. Gk *lura* LYRE]

Lȳr·aid, Lȳr·id, n. (usu. pl.). Meteor(s) radiating from Lyra about 20 Apr. [-ID²]

lȳr·ate, a. (nat. hist.). Lyre-shaped. [-ATE²]

lyre, n. Obsolete instrument of harp kind but of size fit for holding up in left hand, & with strings supported by two symmetrically curved horns, chiefly used for accompanying voice; *l.-bird,* Australian bird with l.-shaped tail. So **lyr·**IST(3) n. [f. L f. Gk *lura*]

lў·ric, a. & n. Of or for the lyre, meant to be sung; of the nature of, expressed or fit to be expressed in, song (*l. drama, the l. stage,* opera); (of poem) expressing writer's own thoughts & sentiments usu. at no great length & in stanzas or strophes, (of poet) writing in this manner; (n.) l. poem, (pl.) l. verses. Hence **ly·rico-** comb. form. [f. L f. Gk *lurikos* (prec., -IC)]

ly·rical, a. = prec. (now rare); resembling, couched in or using language appropriate to, lyric poetry. Hence **ly·rical**LY² adv. [-AL]

ly·ricism, n. Lyric character or (w. pl.) expression; high-flown sentiments. [-ISM]

M

M, m, (ĕm), letter (pl. *M*s, M's). (As numeral) 1,000, as MMCI 2,101, MCMLI 1,951; (Print., m), = EM.

Abbreviations (1): (M.): mark (coin); Marylebone, **M.C.C.** (cricket club); Master, as **M.A.** (of Arts), **M.C.** (of Ceremonies), **M.F.H.** (of Foxhounds), **M.R.** (of the Rolls); mean, **M.S.L.** (sea level); medical, **M.O.(H).,** officer (of health); *Medicinae,* of medicine, as **M.B.** (*Baccalaureus* Bachelor), **M.D.** (Doctor); Member, as **M.B.E.** (of Order of British Empire), **M.I(nst).C.E.** (of institute of civil engineers), **M.P.** (of Parliament), **M.P.S.** (pharmaceutical soc.), **M.R.C.P., M.R.C.S., M.R.C.V.S.** (of Royal college of physicians, surgeons, veterinary surgeons), **M.V.O.** (Victorian Order); metropolitan, **M.A.B.** (asylums board), **M.W.B.** (water board); middle, **ME.** (English); military, **M.C.** (cross), **M.M.** (medal); Monsieur, pl. **MM.,** Messieurs; mounted, **M.I.** (infantry). (m.): machine, **m.g.** (gun); masculine; metre(s); mile(s), **m.p.h.** (per hour); minute(s).

Abbreviations (2): **Macc.**(abees); **Mal.**-(achi); **Man(it).,** Manitoba; **Mass.**-(achusetts); **matric.**(ulation); **Matt.**-(hew); **Md,** Maryland; **Me,** Maine; **Me,** *Maître* (F advocate's title); **mem.**-(ento); **memo.**(randum); **Messrs,** see MR; **meton.**(ymy); ***mf.,*** mezzo forte; **mg.,** milligram(s); **Mgr,** Monsignor, pl. **Mgrs**; **Mic.**(ah); **Mich.**(igan); **Minn.**-(esota); **Miss.**(issippi); **Mk,** mark (coin); **ml.,** millilitre(s); **Mlle,** Mademoiselle, pl. **Mlles**; **mm.,** millimetre(s); **Mme,** Madame, pl. **Mmes**; **Mo.,** Missouri; **Mon.**(mouthshire); **Mont.**(ana); ***mp.,*** mezzo piano; **Mr, Mrs,** see MR, MRS; **MS(S).,** manuscript(s); **Mt,** Mount; **Mus.**(*icae*) **Bac.**(*calaureus*), **Doc.,** Bachelor, Doctor, of Music; **Mx,** Middlesex.

-m, -ma, -me, suf. in nn. taken f. Gk (*-ma -matos*), usu. expr. result of verbal action; as *phlegm, poem, comma, coma, scheme, theme.* Adjj. formed on these show the *-at-* of the Gk stem (*phlegmatic, comatose*).

ma (mah), n. (vulg.). = MAMMA¹.

ma'am (mahm, măm, m'm), n. Madam (esp. used at Court in addressing Queen or royal princess, pr. mahm, or by servants, pr. m'm).

maca·bre (-ahbr), a. *Danse m.,* dance of death; grim, gruesome. [F, perh. corrupt. of OF *Macabé* Maccabee]

macā·co¹, n. Monkey of genus Macacus. [Port., = monkey]

macā·co², n. Kinds of lemur. [?]

macă·dam, a. & n. (Of roads) made in the manner & with the materials advocated by J. L. McAdam (d. 1836), i.e. with successive layers of broken stone of nearly uniform size, each subjected to pressure before next is laid; such material. Hence **maca·dam**IZE v.t., **macadamiz**A·TION n.

macarō·ni, n. Wheaten paste formed into long tubes, used as food; *m. cheese,* savoury pudding of m. & cheese baked; (Hist.) 18th-c. exquisite affecting continental tastes, whence **macaro·n**ISM n. [f. It. *maccaroni,* etym. dub.]

macarŏ·nic, a. & n. pl. (Verses) of burlesque form containing Latin (or other foreign) words & vernacular words with Latin &c. terminations; medley. [f. prec. + -IC]

macaroo·n, n. Small cake or biscuit of ground almonds, white of egg, sugar, &c. [f. F *macaron* (as MACARONI)]

macar·tney, n. Kind of pheasant. [George, Earl *M.,* d. 1806]

maca·ssar, a. & n. *M.* (*oil*), kind of hair oil. [f. *Mangkasara,* in island of Celebes]

macaw·¹, n. Kinds of parrot. [f. Port. *macao,* etym. dub.]

macaw·², n. Kinds of palm. [prob. Carib]

Maccabē·an, a. Of the *Maccabees,* Jewish princes who freed Judaea from tyranny of Antiochus Epiphanes, c. 166 B.C. [f. L f. Gk *Makkabaios*]

ma·ccaboy, -baw, n. Kind of snuff, usu. scented with attar of roses. [f. *Macouba,* district in Martinique]

mace¹, n. (Hist.) heavy usu. metal-headed & spiked club; staff of office resembling this; *m.-bearer,* official carrying this staff; stick used in bagatelle. [OF, f. L *mattea whence matteola (prob.) = mallet]

mace², n. Dried outer covering of nutmeg, as spice. [f. F *macis*, etym. dub.]

mă·cédoine (-ĕdwahn), n. Fruit or vegetables in jelly as a dish or as cook's material. [F]

mă·cerate, v.t. & i. Soften by soaking; waste away by fasting. So **macerA·TION** n. [f. L *macerare*, perh. cogn. w. Gk *massō* knead, see -ATE³]

mache·tĕ (-tshā-), see MATCHET.

Mă·chiavĕl (-k-), n. Unscrupulous schemer; one who practises duplicity in statecraft, whence **Machiave·llIAN** a., **Machiave·llISM** n. [f. Niccolò *Machiavelli*, Florentine statesman, author of work *del Principe*, in which unscrupulous statecraft is advocated]

machĭ·colate (-tsh-), v.t. Furnish (parapet &c.) with openings between supporting corbels for dropping stones &c. on assailants. Hence **machicolA·TION** n. [f. med. L *machicolare* = OF *machecoller*, conn. w. foll.]

machicoulis (mahshĭkōō·lĭ), n. Machicolation. [f. F *mâchicoulis*]

mă·chinate (-k-), v.t. Lay plots, intrigue. So **machinA·TION**, **ma·chinatOR²**, nn. [f. L *machinari* contrive (as foll.), see -ATE³]

machi·ne (-shēn), n., & v.t. & i. Apparatus for applying mechanical power, having several parts each with definite function (the kind often being specified, as *sewing*, *printing*, *-m.*); bicycle, tricycle; *bathing-m.* (see BATHE¹); person who acts mechanically & without intelligence, or with unfailing regularity; (Mech.) instrument that transmits force or directs its application, as *simple m.*, one without parts, e.g. lever; controlling political organization (esp. in U.S.); *m.-gun*, mounted gun mechanically loaded & fired, delivering continuous fire; *m.-made*, made by m.; (vb) make or operate on with m. (esp. of sewing & printing); use m. [F, f. L *machina* f. Gk *mēkhanē* f. *mēkhos* contrivance, cogn. w. MAY¹]

machi·nery (-shē-), n. Machines; work of a machine, mechanism; contrivances, esp. supernatural persons & incidents, used in literary work. [f. prec. + -ERY]

machi·nist (-shē-), n. One who makes or controls machinery; one who works (esp. sewing-) machine. [f. prec. + -IST]

ma·ckerel, n. Sea-fish used as food & approaching shore in shoals in summer to spawn; *m. breeze, gale* (strong, & so favourable to m.-catching); *m. sky* (dappled with small white fleecy clouds). [f. OF *makerel*, etym. dub.]

ma·ckintosh, n. Waterproof material of rubber & cloth for garments, esp. that patented by C. Macintosh (d. 1843); cloak, coat, of this.

mă·cle, n. Twin crystal; dark spot in mineral. [F, f. MACULA]

macŏ·nochie (-kĭ), n. Tinned stew as part of army rations. [maker]

macra·mé (-rahmĭ), n. Fringe, trimming, of knotted thread or cord. [prob. f. Turk. *magrama* towel]

măcro- in comb. = Gk *makros* long, large, as: *-cepha·lic*, long, large, -headed; *-cosm*, the great world, the universe, (cf. MICROCOSM), any great whole; *-meter*, instrument for measuring distant objects; *-sco·pic*, visible to naked eye.

mă·cron, n. Mark placed over vowel (ā) to show that it is long. [Gk, neut. adj. as prec.]

mă·cūla, n. (pl. *-ae*). Dark spot in sun; spot in mineral; spot, esp. permanent one, in skin, whence **ma·cūlAR¹** a., **maculA·TION** n. [L]

mad¹, a. Out of one's mind, insane; (of person or conduct) wildly foolish; *like m.*, furiously, violently, as *I ran like m.*; wildly excited, infatuated, (*after, about, for, on*, thing, subject, &c.); (colloq.) annoyed, as *I was rather m. at missing my train*; (of animals) rabid; (Prov.) *m. as a March* HARE, *as a hatter*; extravagant, wild, in gaiety; *madcap*, wildly impulsive person; *m.-doctor* (treating the m.); *madhouse*, lunatic asylum; *madman, -woman*, m. person; *m. minute* (army slang), rapid fire in class-firing. Hence **ma·dLY²** adv., **ma·dNESS** n. [OE *gemǣd(e)d*, p.p. of *gemǣdan* make mad (*gemád* mad, cf. OS *gimêd* foolish, OHG *gameit*, & L *mutare* change)]

mad², v.t. & i. (rare). Make mad; be mad, act madly, as *the madding crowd* (as quot. from Gray's *Elegy*, now often taken as = distracting). [f. prec.]

mă·dam, n. Polite formal address to woman. [f. OF *ma* DAME my lady]

madame (madah·m, mă·dam; pl. *mesdames* pr. mādah·m). F form of prec. as title or form of address; *M. Tussaud's* (tōō·sōz), show in London of waxwork figures of celebrated & notorious persons (often w. ref. to the chamber of HORRORS in it). [as prec.]

mădapo·llam, n. A cotton cloth, orig. of Indian make. [f. *M.* in Madras]

ma·dden, v.t. & i. Make, become, mad; irritate. Hence **ma·ddeningLY²** adv. [f. MAD¹ + -EN⁶]

ma·dder, n. Herbaceous climbing plant with yellowish flowers; dye got from this. [OE *mædere*, cf. Sw. *madra*, Norw. *modra*]

made, a. P.p. of MAKE. Special uses: *m. dish* (of several ingredients); *m. gravy* (artificially compounded); *a m. man*, one whose success in life is assured; (of person &c.) *well, stoutly, loosely, powerfully, -m.* (built, formed).

Madeir·a (-ēra), n. Island in Atlantic Ocean; white wine there produced; *M. cake*, kind of sponge-cake. [Port., f. L *materia* MATTER, timber, from its thick woods]

mademoiselle (mădamazĕ·l, or *as F*), n. (pl. *mesdemoiselles*, pron. mā-). Unmarried Frenchwoman; French governess. [F]

mā·dia, n. Plant allied to Sunflower; *m. oil* (got from its seed, & made into cake for cattle). [f. Chil. *madi*]

mado·nna, n. (Picture, statue, of) Virgin Mary; *M. lily* (white, as in pictures of M.). [It. (*ma* =*mia* my +*donna* lady f. L *domina*)]

madră·sah (-*a*), ***medre·sseh*** (-ā), n. Mohammedan college. [Arab. (-*sah*) f. *darasa* v. study]

mă·drĕpore, n. Genus of perforate corals; animal producing these. Hence **madrepŏ·RIC, madrepor·IFORM,** aa. [f. It. *madrepora* (*madre* mother +*poro*, coral-like but porous substance)]

mă·drigal (-gl), n. Short amatory poem; part-song for several voices, prop. with elaborate contrapuntal imitation & without instrumental accompaniment. Hence **madrigā·LIAN** a. [f. It. *madrigale*, etym. dub.]

Maecē·năs, n. Generous patron of literature or art. [*M.*, patron of Horace & Virgil]

mae·lstrom (māl-), n. Whirlpool on W. coast of Norway; great whirlpool (lit. & fig.). [Du. (*malen* grind +*stroom* stream)]

mae·nad, n. Bacchante. [f. L f. Gk *mainas -ados* f. *mainomai* rave]

maĕsto·so (mah-), adv. (mus.). Majestically. [It.]

maĕ·stro, n. Great musical composer, teacher, or conductor. [It.]

ma·ffick, v.i. Exult riotously. [back formation f. *Mafeking* (relief of which in 1900 was celebrated extravagantly in London &c.), treated as gerund]

mafi·a (-ēa), n. Hostility to law & its ministers among Sicilian population, often shown in crimes; those who share in this. [Sicil.]

mag, n. (slang). Halfpenny. [?]

magazi·ne (-zēn), n. Store for arms, ammunition, & provisions, in time of war; store for gunpowder or other explosives; *m. gun* (with chamber containing supply of cartridges fed automatically to the breech); periodical publication containing articles by various writers. [f. F *magasin* f. Arab. *makhasia* pl. of *makhzan* storehouse (*khazana* store up)]

Ma·gdalĕn, -lene (-ĕn), n. Reformed prostitute. [Mary *Magdalene* of Magdala (*Luke* viii. 2) identified with the sinner of *Luke* vii. 37]

Magdalē·nian, a. (archaeol.). Of the (latest) palaeolithic period represented by remains found at La *Madeleine*, Dordogne, France.

mage, n. (archaic). Magician; learned person. [f. MAGUS]

mage·nta, n. Brilliant crimson aniline dye, discovered soon after battle at *M.* in N. Italy (1859).

ma·ggot, n. Larva, esp. of cheese-fly & bluebottle; *red m.*, larva of wheat-midge; whimsical fancy, esp. *m. in* one's *head.* Hence **ma·ggotY**[2] a. [prob. conn. w. ME *madhek* in same sense]

Magi. See MAGUS.

Mā·gian, a. & n. (One) of the Magi; magician. Hence **Ma·gianISM**(3) n. [-IAN]

mă·gic, a. & n. (Of) the pretended art of influencing course of events by occult control of nature or of spirits, witchcraft; *black, white, natural, m.* (involving invocation of devils, angels, no personal spirit); inexplicable or remarkable influence producing surprising results; *m. square*, one divided into smaller squares containing each a number, so arranged that sum of a row, vertical, horizontal, or diagonal, is always same; *m. lantern*, optical instrument throwing magnified image of glass picture on white screen in dark room; *m. mirror* (in which future or distant scenes are presented to spectator). Hence **ma·gicAL** a., **ma·gicalLY**[2] adv. [f. F *magique* a. & n. f. L f. Gk *magikos* (as MAGUS, see -IC)]

magĭ·cian (-shn), n. One skilled in magic, wizard. [f. F *magicien* (as prec., see -ICIAN)]

magi·lp. See MEGILP.

magistēr·ial, a. Of, conducted by, a magistrate; invested with authority; dictatorial; (of opinions) authoritative. Hence **magister·ialLY**[2] adv. [f. med. L *magisterialis* f. LL *magisterius* (as MASTER)]

magi·stral, a. Of a master or masters, as *the m. staff* (of a school); (Pharm., of remedy &c.) devised by physician for particular case, not included in the pharmacopoeia (cf. OFFICINAL). [f. L *magistralis* (as MASTER, see -AL)]

mă·gistrate (-*at*), n. Civil officer administering law; JUSTICE of the peace. Hence or cogn. **ma·gistrACY, ma·gistrateSHIP, ma·gistratURE,** nn. [f. L *magistratus -ūs* (orig. office of) magistrate (as prec., see -ATE[1])]

ma·gma, n. (pl. *-ta, -s*). Crude pasty mixture of mineral or organic matters; one of supposed fluid strata under solid crust of earth. [L f. Gk (*massō* knead, root *mag-*, see -M)]

Ma·gna C(h)arta (k-), n. Great charter of English personal & political liberty obtained from John in 1215. [med. L]

magnă·nimous, a. High-souled, above petty feelings. Hence or cogn. **magnani·MITY** n., **magna·nimousLY**[2] adv. [f. L *magnanimus* (*magnus* great +*animus* soul) + -OUS]

ma·gnāte, n. Great man; wealthy or eminent man. [f. LL *magnas -atis* (*magnus* great)]

magnē·sia (-sha), n. Oxide of magnesium; (pop.) hydrated magnesium carbonate, white powder used as antacid & cathartic. Hence **magne·siAN** a. [med.

L, f. Gk *magnēsia* (*lithos* stone) of Magnesia, (1) loadstone, (2) perh. talc]

magnē·sium (*or* -shyum), n. Chemical element, base of magnesia; *m. light*, blinding light got by burning m. wire. [f. prec., see -IUM]

ma·gnet, n. Piece of iron or ore having the properties of attracting iron & of pointing north & south when suspended, natural (as in loadstone) or induced by contact with a m., by induction, or by electric current; *horse-shoe m.* (in shape of bar bent till ends nearly meet); = LOAD[1]*stone*; (fig.) thing that attracts. [f. L f. Gk *Magnēs -ētos* (*lithos* stone) of Magnesia]

magnĕ·tic, a. & n. Having properties of magnet; producing, produced by, acting by, magnetism; *m. equator*, ACLINIC line; *m.* NEEDLE, NORTH; capable of receiving properties of, or being attracted by, loadstone; (fig.) very attractive; mesmeric; (n. pl.) science of magnetism. Hence **magne·**TICALLY adv. [-IC]

ma·gnetism, n. Magnetic phenomena; natural agency producing these; *terrestrial m.*, magnetic properties of the earth as a whole; *animal m.*, = MESMERISM; (fig.) attraction, personal charm. So **ma·gnet**IST(3) n. [-ISM]

ma·gnetite, n. Magnetic iron oxide. [-ITE]

ma·gnetize, v.t. Give magnetic properties to; attract (lit. & fig.) as magnet does; mesmerize. Hence **magnetiz**A·TION n. [-IZE]

magnē·to, n. (pl. *-os*). A magneto-electric machine (esp. as name for the igniting-apparatus of internal-combustion engines). [abbr.]

magnē·to- in comb. = magnetic, as: *-electri·city* (generated by relative movement of electric conductors & magnets); *-graph*, instrument recording movements of *-meter* (instrument measuring magnetic forces, esp. terrestrial magnetism).

magnĭ·fic(al), aa. (archaic). Magnificent, sublime. [f. F *magnifique* f. L *magnificus* (*magnus* great, see -FIC) + -AL]

magnĭ·ficăt, n. Hymn of Virgin Mary in *Luke* i. 46–55, used as canticle, & beginning thus. [L, 3rd sing. of *magnificare* MAGNIFY]

magnĭ·ficent, a. Splendid, stately; sumptuously constructed or adorned; splendidly lavish; (colloq.) fine, excellent. Hence or cogn. **magni·fic**ENCE n., **magni·ficent**LY[2] adv. [OF, f. L *magnificent-* stem seen in comp. & sup. of *magnificus* MAGNIFIC]

magnĭ·fico, n. Venetian magnate; grandee. [It., as MAGNIFIC]

ma·gnify, v.t. Increase apparent size of (thing), as with lens or microscope; exaggerate; (rare) increase; (archaic) extol. Hence or cogn. **magni**FICA·TION, **ma·gnifi**ER[1](2), nn. [f. L *magnificare* (*magnus* great, see -FY)]

magni·loquent, a. Lofty in expression; boastful. Hence **magni·loqu**ENCE n., **magni·loquent**LY[2] adv. [f. L *magniloquus* (*magnus* great + *-loquus* -speaking) + -ENT]

mag·nitude, n. Largeness; size; importance; *first, seventh*, &c., *m.*, classes of fixed stars arranged according to degree of brilliancy, (fig.) *of the first m.* (importance). [f. L *magnitudo* (*magnus* great, see -TUDE)]

magnō·lia, n. Genus of large trees cultivated for foliage & flower. [f. P. *Magnol*, botanist (d. 1715)]

ma·gnum, n. (Bottle containing) two quarts (of wine or spirits). [L, neut. of *magnus* great]

ma·gnum bō·num, n. Large yellow cooking plum; kind of potato. [L wds = large good]

magnum opus. See OPUS.

ma·gpie, n. European bird with long pointed tail & black-&-white plumage; idle chatterer; variety of pigeon; (rifle shot that strikes) outermost division but one of target. [f. *mag* abbr. of *Margaret* +PIE[1]]

mā·gus, n. (pl. *-gi*, pron. -jī). Member of ancient Persian priestly caste; sorcerer; *the (three) Magi*, the 'wise men' from the East who brought offerings to infant Christ. [L, f. Gk *magos* f. OPers. *magus*]

Ma·gyar (mŏdy-), n. & a. (Member, language) of the Mongoloid race now predominant in Hungary. [native]

Mahabharata (mahhahbah·rata), n. An ancient Hindu epic. [Skr.]

Mahara·ja(h) (mah-h-), n. Title of some Indian princes. [Hind. (*maha* great + RAJAH)]

Maharanee (mah-harah·nī), n. Maharajah's wife. [Hind. (*maha* great, *rani* queen)]

Maha·tma (-h-), n. (esoteric Buddhism). One of a class of persons with preternatural powers, supposed to exist in India & Tibet. [f. Skr. *mahatman* (*maha* great + *atman* soul)]

Mah·di, n. Spiritual & temporal leader expected by Mohammedans (often applied to leaders of insurrection in Soudan), whence **Mah·d(i)**ISM(3) n. [f. Arab. *mahdiy* he who is guided right, p.p. of *hada* guide]

mah-jongg, n. A Chinese game for four played with 144 pieces called tiles, recently adopted in Europe & America.

mahlstick. See MAULSTICK.

mahŏ·gany (-h-), n. Wood of a tropical American tree, much used for furniture, & taking high polish; the tree; dining-table (*have* one's *knees under* person's *m.*, be dining with him); the colour of m., reddish-brown, (often attrib.). [?]

Mahŏ·metan. See MOHAMMEDAN.

Mahou·nd (-hōō-), n. (archaic, facet.). Mohammed. [f. OF *Mahun* short for *Mahomet*]

mahou·t (-owt), n. Elephant-driver. [f. Hind. *mahaut*]

Mahra·tta (marā-), n. Member of a warlike Indian race. [Hind. *Marhaṭṭa*]

maid, n. Girl; young unmarried woman; spinster; *old m.*, elderly spinster, (also) round game at cards; (also *maidservant*) female servant, as *house-, nurse-, lady's-, m., m.-of-all-work*; *m. of honour*, unmarried lady attending on queen or princess, (also) kind of cheesecake. Hence **mai·**DISH[1] a., **mai·**DY[3] n. [f. MAIDEN; not same as OE *mægedh*, G *magd*]

maidan (mīdah·n), n. (Anglo-Ind.). Parade-ground. [Pers.]

mai·den, n. & a. Girl; spinster; (Hist.) kind of guillotine used at Edinburgh; = *m. over*. (Adj.) unmarried; *m. name* (before marriage); (of female animals) uncoupled; (of horse) that has never won prize, (of race) open to such horses; (of plant) grown from seed; (of soldier, sword, &c.) untried; *m. assize*, one at which there are no cases for trial; (Crick.) *m. over* (in which no runs are scored); *m. speech*, M.P.'s first speech in the House; *maidenhair*, kinds of fern with fine hair-like stalks & delicate fronds; *maidenhead*, virginity. Hence **mai·den**HOOD n., **mai·den**ISH[1], **mai·den**LIKE, **mai·den**LY[1], aa. [OE *mægden* dim. corresp. to OE *mægedh*, Du. *maagd*, G *magd*, see -EN[2]]

maieu·tic (māū-), a. (Of Socratic mode of inquiry) obstetric, serving to bring out a person's latent ideas into clear consciousness. [f. Gk *maieutikos* f. *maieuomai* act as midwife (*maia*), see -IC]

mail[1], n. Armour composed of rings or chain-work, or of plates fastened on a groundwork, as *chain, plate, ring, -m.* [f. F *maille* f. L *macula* spot, mesh]

mail[2], v.t. Clothe (as) with mail; *the mailed fist*, (fig.) physical force. [f. prec.]

mail[3], n., & v.t. Bag of letters for conveyance by post; this system of conveyance, the post, (esp. for foreign letters); *the m.*, all that is so conveyed on one occasion; *m. (train)*, train carrying this; *m.-cart*, cart for carrying m. by road, (also) light vehicle for carrying children; *m.-coach*, (now) = m.-cart, (formerly) stage-coach for entire conveyance of m.; (v.t.) send (letters &c.) by post. [(vb f. n.) f. OF *male* bag, of Teut. orig.]

maim, v.t. Mutilate, cripple, (lit. & fig.). [ME *maynhe* f. OF *mahaignier*, etym. dub.]

main[1], n. (In game of hazard) number (5, 6, 7, 8, or 9) called by caster before dice are thrown; match between cocks. [?]

main[2], n. Physical force (only in *with might & m.*); SPANISH *m.*; (poet.) high sea; *in the m.*, for the most part; principal channel, duct, &c., for water, sewage, &c. [OE *mægen*, see MAY v.]

main[3], a. Exerted to the full, as *by m. force*; chief in size or extent, as *the m. body* (of army &c.); principal, most important, as *the m. point* (in argument), *m. line* (of railway), whence **mai·n**LY[2] adv.; *have an eye to the m. chance* (one's own interests); (Naut.) *m. brace* (attached to m. yard, esp. in slang phr. *splice the m. brace*, drink freely), *m. deck*, (in man-of-war) deck next below spar deck, (in merchantman) upper deck between poop & forecastle, *mainmast*, principal mast, *mai·nsail* (-sāl, -sl), (in square-rigged vessel) sail that is bent to the m. yard, (in fore-&-aft rigged vessel) sail set on after part of mainmast, *mai·nstay*, stay from maintop to foot of foremast, (fig.) chief support, *m.-top*, platform above head of lower mainmast, *m. yard*, yard on which mainsail is extended; *mai·nland*, extent of land including greater part of a country; *mainspring*, principal spring of watch, clock, &c. [prob. partly as prec., partly f. cogn. ON *megenn* strong]

maintai·n, v.t. Carry on, keep up, (war, contest, action at law, condition, position, attitude, relations, correspondence); cause (person &c.) to continue *in* (condition, possession of thing, &c.); support (life, one's state in life) by nourishment, expenditure, &c.; furnish (*oneself*, children) with means of subsistence; keep (road &c.) in repair; back up (cause, party); assert as true (opinion, statement, *that*). Hence **maintai·n**ABLE a. [f. F *maintenir* f. L phr. *manu tenēre* hold in the hand]

mai·ntenance, n. Maintaining; enough to support life; *cap of m.*, cap, hat, worn as symbol of official dignity or carried before sovereign &c.; (Law) offence of aiding a party in litigation without lawful cause. [F (as prec., see -ANCE)]

maize, n. Indian corn, its grain. [f. Sp. *maiz*, of Cuban orig.]

maizē·na, n. Maize starch prepared for use as food. [f. prec.]

maje·stic, a. Possessing grandeur, imposing. Hence **maje·st**ICALLY adv. [f. foll. + -IC]

mă·jesty, n. Impressive stateliness of aspect, bearing, language, &c.; sovereign power; (in speaking to or of sovereign) (*Your, His, Her, M.*, you, he, she, as *Your M. forgets that with the best of intentions it is scarcely in your M.'s* (or *your*) *power to miss your train*; representation of God (the Father or Son) enthroned within aureole. [f. F *majesté* f. L *majestatem* (as MAJOR[2], see -TY)]

majŏ·lica, maio- (-yŏ-), n. Kinds of ornamented Italian ware; modern imitation of these. [It. (*mai-*), perh. f. *Marjorca, -olica*]

mā·jor[1], n. Officer next below lieutenant-colonel & above captain (also in army slang for *sergeant m.*). Hence **ma·jor**SHIP n. [F, short for *sergent-major*]

mā·jor², a. & n. Greater (not foll. by *than*) of two things, classes, &c.; *m.* PROPHETS; *m. epilepsy*, epilepsy proper; (Log.) *m. term* (that enters into predicate of conclusion of syllogism), *m. premiss* (containing m. term); *m. axis* of conic section (passing through the foci); (Mus., of intervals) greater by chromatic semitone than minor intervals, as *m. third*, (of keys) in which scale has a m. third; *m. part*, majority (*of*); (Mil.) *m. general* (see OFFICER), SERGEANT *m.*, *bugle, drum, pipe, trumpet, m.* (head bugler &c. of unit); (in schools) *Brown, Smith, m.* (the elder or first to enter school); of full age; (n.) person of full age; (Log., ellipt. for) m. term or premiss (*I deny your m.*); *m.-dōmo*, chief official of Italian or Spanish princely household, (loosely) house-steward. [L, compar. of *magnus* great]

majŏ·rity, n. Greater number or part (*of*); *the m.*, the dead, esp. *join the m.*, die; *absolute m.* of votes, more than half number of electors or actual voters; number by which votes cast on one side exceed those on other; full age, as *attained his m.*; office of MAJOR¹. [f. F *majorité* f. med. L *majoritatem* (as prec., see -TY)]

maju·scule, a. & n. (palaeogr.). Large (letter), whether capital or uncial. Hence **maju·sculAR¹** a. [F, f. L *majuscula* (*littera* letter, dim. of MAJOR)]

make¹, v.t. & i. (made). Construct, frame, as *God made man* (*a rational creature*), *bees m. cells of wax, you were made for this work*; *pipes are made* (consist) *of clay*; *m.* GOOD, SURE; compose, draw up, (book, will, document); prepare (tea, coffee, beds); *m.* HAY; *m.* (arrange & light materials for) *a fire*; cause to exist, bring about, (disturbance, sport, noise, one's mark in the world, a corner in wheat); *m. no* BONES; *m. fun, game, of*, trifle with, treat with ridicule; *m.* (conclude treaty of) *peace*; *m.* (give) *place, room, way* (*for* others); *m. way*, progress; result in, as *it makes a difference*; '*find*' *makes* (becomes) *in the past tense* '*found*'; establish, enact, (distinctions, rules, laws); *m.* FRIENDS; get together (a HOUSE¹, quorum); *m. a bag*, kill number of game; *m. a book*, arrange series of bets on same event; *m.* WATER¹; *m. a habit of it*, cause it to become one, so *m. an* EXAMPLE¹, *exhibition, fool, beast* (*of* oneself, person); *m. a night of it*, carry it (festivity &c.) on through the night; *m. of*, conclude to be the meaning or character of (*can you m. anything of it?*; *what am I to m. of your behaviour?*); *m. much, little, the best*, &c., *of*, derive much &c. advantage from, (also) attach much &c. importance to, so *m.* LIGHT⁴ *of*; *m. a* HASH² *of*; entertain, feel, (doubt, scruple, *of, about*); *m.* HEAD¹ *or tail of*; (Naut.) discern, come in sight of, (also) arrive at; amount to, as *2 & 2 m. 4*; constitute, as *one swallow does not m. a summer*; form, be counted as, as *this makes the tenth time, will you m. one of the party?*; serve for, as *this makes pleasant reading*; become, turn out to be, as *she will m. a good wife*; gain, acquire, (money, a living, one's fortune); (Cards) win (trick), play (card) to advantage, (also) shuffle (cards, or abs.); proceed (*towards* &c.); *m. sail*, set sail, (also) spread additional sail; secure the advancement of, cf. MADE; *m. or mar*, cause success or ruin of; cause to be, as *m. it* HOT, *m.* one*self a martyr*, *m.* one*self* SCARCE, *m. him a duke*; convert *into*; consider to be, as *what do you m. the time?*, *I m. it 5 miles*; cause, compel, (without *to* in act.), as *m. him repeat it*, but *he was made to repeat it*; *m. believe*, pretend (*to* do, *that*); *what bird do you m.* (consider) *that to be?*, *he makes Richard die* (represents him as having died) *in 1026*; wage (war); execute (bodily movement, bow, FACE¹, LEG); perform (journey &c., & with many nn. expr. vbl action, as *acquisition, attempt, blunder, start, venture*); *m.* (eat) *a good breakfast*; *m.* HEAD¹, LOVE; accomplish (distance, knots per hour, &c.); *m. as if one had*, pretend one has; *m.* BOLD, FREE¹, MERRY; (of flood or ebb tide) begin to flow or ebb; *m. after* (archaic), pursue; *m. against*, be unfavourable to; *m.* (hasten) *away*; *m. away with*, get rid of, kill, squander; *m. for*, conduce to (happiness &c.), confirm (view), proceed towards, assail; *m. off*, run away, decamp, (often *with* stolen goods &c.); *m. out*, draw up, write out, (list, document, cheque), get together with difficulty, as *articles put in to m. out a volume*, (try to) prove, as *how do you m. that out?*, *you m. me out* (*to be*) *a hypocrite*, understand, as *I can't m. him out, can't m. out what he wants*, decipher (handwriting &c.), distinguish by sight, as *I made out a figure in the distance*; *m. over*, transfer possession of (thing *to* person), esp. by formal agreement; *m. up*, supply (deficiency), complete (amount, party), compensate, as *m. up lost ground, m. up for lost time, we must m. it up to* (compensate) *him somehow*, compound, put together, (medicine, hay *into* bundles, butter, &c.), sew together (coat &c.), get together (company, sum of money), arrange (type) in columns or pages, compile (list, account, document), concoct (story), (of parts) compose (whole), prepare (actor) for his part by dressing, false hair, &c., arrange (marriage &c.), settle (dispute), *m. it up*, be reconciled, *m. up* one's *mind to*, decide *to* (do), resolve upon (course); *m. up to*, court, curry favour with; *make-bate* (archaic), breeder of strife; *m.-believe*, pretence; *makepeace*, peacemaker; *makeshift*, temporary substitute or device; *m.-up*, disguise of actor, cosmetics &c.

used for this, made-up story; *makeweight*, small quantity added to m. up weight, esp. small candle, (also fig. of persons), (fig.) unimportant point added to make case seem stronger. [com.-WG: OE *macian*, Du. *maken*, G *machen*]

make², n. (Of natural or manufactured thing) style of structure or composition; mental or moral disposition; *American m.*, made in America, *is this your own m.* (made by you)?; *on the m.* (slang), intent on gain; (Electr.) making of contact, position in which this is made, esp. *at m.* [f. prec.]

ma·ker, n. In vbl senses, esp. *the, our*, &c., *M.*, the Creator. [-ER¹]

ma·king, n. In vbl senses, esp.: *be the m. of*, ensure success or favourable development of; (pl.) earnings, profits; (pl.) essential qualities, as *he has the mm. of a general.* [-ING¹]

măl-, pref. = F *mal* f. L *male* badly, in sense (1) bad(ly), as *maltreat*, (2) un-, as *maladroit*.

Mala·cca, n. Town & district on Malay peninsula; *M. cane*, rich-brown walking-cane, from stem of a palm.

mă·lachite (-k-), n. Hydrous carbonate of copper, green mineral taking high polish. [f. OF *melochite* (Gk *malakhē* mallow, see -ITE¹)]

mălaco- in comb. = Gk *malakos* soft, as: *-derm*, soft-skinned animal (esp. of sea-anemones & of one division of reptiles); *-logist, -logy*, student, science, of molluscs; *-ptery̆·gian* a. & n., soft-finned (fish); *malaco·stracan*, member of one order of crustaceans.

maladju·stment, n. Faulty adjustment. [MAL-]

maladministra·tion, n. Faulty administration. [MAL-]

mă·ladroi·t, a. Clumsy, bungling. Hence **ma·ladroi·tLY²** adv., **ma·ladroi·tNESS** n. [F (MAL- + ADROIT)]

mă·lady, n. Ailment, disease, (lit. & fig.). [f. F *maladie* f. *malade* sick f. LL *male habitus* (*male* ill + *habitus* p.p. of *habēre* have)]

mā·la fī·dē, adv. & a. (Acting, done) in bad faith. [L]

Mă·laga, n. Seaport in S. Spain; white wine from this.

Mălagă·sy, a. & n. (Language, inhabitant) of Madagascar. [used in native lang., but prob. of foreign orig.]

mă·laise, n. Bodily discomfort, esp. without development of specific disease. [F (OF *mal* bad + *aise* EASE)]

mă·landers, ma·llen-, n. pl. Scabby eruption behind knee in horses. [f. F *malandre* f. L *malandria*]

mă·lapert, a. & n. (archaic). Impudent, saucy, (person). [OF (MAL- + *appert* = *espert* EXPERT)]

mă·laprŏp(ism), n. Ludicrous misuse of word, esp. in mistake for one resembling it (e.g. *a nice derangement of epitaphs* for *arrangement of epithets*). Hence **malaprŏ·PIAN** a. [f. Mrs *Malaprop* in Sheridan's *Rivals*]

mălăpropōs·, adv., a., & n. (Thing) inopportunely (said, done, or happening). [f. F *mal à propos* (*mal* ill, see APROPOS)]

mā·lar, a. & n. (Bone) of the cheek. [f. L *mala* jaw, see -AR¹]

malār·ia, n. Kinds of intermittent & remittent fever caused by bite of mosquito, which conveys the germs; unwholesome atmosphere caused by exhalations of marshes, to which these fevers were formerly referred. Hence **malar·IAL, malar·IAN, malar·IOUS**, aa. [f. It. *mal' aria* bad air]

Malay·, a. & n. (Language, member) of race predominating in Malacca & Eastern Archipelago; *M. fowl*, large domestic variety. Hence **Malay·AN** a. & n. [f. native *malayu*]

Mălaya·lam (-yah-), n. Language of Malabar. [native]

ma·lcontent, a. & n. Discontented (person), (one) inclined to rebellion. [OF (MAL-)]

male, a. & n. Of the sex that begets offspring or performs the fecundating function (used of persons or animals, & of plants whose flowers contain only fecundating organs, also of plants to which sex was once attributed on account of colour &c., as *m. fern*); of men or male animals; (of parts of machinery &c.) designed to enter or fill the corresponding FEMALE part, as *m. screw*; *m.* (masculine) *rhyme*; (n.) m. person or animal. [OF, f. L *masculus* (*mas* male, see -CULE)]

malĕ- in comb. = L *male* ill.

maledi·ction, n. Curse. So **maledi·ctORY** a. [f. L *maledictio* f. MALE(*dicere dict-* speak), see -ION]

ma·lefactor, n. Criminal; evil-doer, esp. opp. to *benefactor*. So **malefa·ctION** n. [L, f. MALE(*facere fact-* do), see -OR²]

malĕ·fic, a. (Of magical arts &c.) harmful, baleful. [f. L MALE(*ficus* -FIC)]

malĕ·ficent, a. Hurtful (*to*); criminal. So **male·fiCENCE** n. [f. L altered stem of *maleficus* MALEFIC]

malĕ·volent, a. Desirous of evil to others. Hence or cogn. **male·volENCE** n., **male·volentLY²** adv. [f. OF *malivolent* f. L MALE(*volens* part. of *velle* wish)]

malfea·sance (-ēz-), n. (law). Evil-doing, esp. official misconduct. So **malfea·SANT** a. & n. [f. OF MAL(*faisant* part. of *faire* do f. L *facere*), see -ANCE]

malforma·tion, n. Faulty formation. So **malfor·MED¹** a. [MAL-]

mā·lic, a. (chem.). *M. acid* (derived from apple & other fruits). [f. F *malique* f. L *malum* apple, see -IC]

mă·lice, n. Active ill-will; desire to tease; *bear m.* (*to*), cherish vindictive feelings (against); (Law) wrongful intention, esp.

as increasing guilt of certain offences, esp. murder; *m.* PREPENSE. So **mali·cious** a., **mali·ciously**[2] adv. [F, f. L *malitia* (*malus* bad, see -ICE)]

malig·n[1], a. (Of things) injurious; (of diseases) = MALIGNANT; (rare) malevolent. Hence **malig·nly**[2] adv. [f. OF *maligne* f. L *malignus* (*malus* bad, cf. BENIGN)]

malīg·n[2], v.t. Speak ill, of slander. [f. OF *malignier* f. L *malignare* contrive maliciously, as prec.]

mali·gnant, a. & n. (Of disease) very virulent or infectious (now usu. denoting definite variety of disease, as *m. cholera*); harmful; feeling or showing intense ill-will; (Hist.) supporter of, supporting, Charles I against Parliament. Hence **mali·gnancy** n., **mali·gnantly**[2] adv. [f. LL part. as prec.]

mali·gnity, n. Deep-rooted ill-will; (of diseases) malignant character. [f. OF *malignité* f. L *malignitatem* (as MALIGN, see -TY)]

mali·nger (-ngg-), v.i. Pretend, produce, or protract, illness in order to escape duty (esp. of soldiers & sailors). Hence **mali·ngerer**[1] n. [f. F *malingre* sickly, etym. dub.]

mā·lism, n. Doctrine that it is a bad world. [f. L *malus* bad + -ISM]

mă·lison (-sn, -zn), n. (archaic). Curse. [f. OF *maleison* MALEDICTION]

mall (mawl), n. Sheltered walk as promenade, esp. *the M.* in St James's Park, London, orig. alley for game of PALL-MALL; (Hist.) this game, alley for it, mallet for it. [= MAUL[1]]

mă·llard, n. Wild drake or duck; its flesh. [f. OF *mal(l)art*, etym. dub.]

mă·llĕable, a. (Of metals &c.) that can be hammered or pressed out of form without tendency to return to it or to fracture; (fig.) adaptable, pliable. Hence **malleabi·lity** n. [OF, f. L *malleare* hammer (*malleus*), see -BLE]

mă·llet, n. Hammer, usu. of wood; implement for striking croquet or polo ball. [f. F *maillet*, dim. as MAUL[1]]

mă·lleus, n. Bone of ear transmitting vibrations of tympanum to incus. [L, = hammer]

mă·llow, n. Wild plant with hairy stems & leaves & purple flowers; garden varieties of this. [OE *mealuwe* f. L *malva*, prob. conn. w. Gk *malakhē*]

mal·m (mahm), n. Soft chalky rock; loamy soil from disintegration of this. [OE *mealm*, cf. Icel. *málmr*, Da. *malm*, f. *mal-* grind]

mălmai·son (-zn), n. Kind of carnation. [*M.*, palace of empress Josephine]

malmsey (mah·mzĭ), n. Strong sweet wine from Greece, Spain, &c. [f. med. L *malmasia* corrupt. of Gk *Monembasia*, Napoli di Monemvasia, in the Morea]

malnutri·tion, n. Insufficient nutrition. [MAL-]

malō·dorous, a. Evil-smelling. [MAL-]

malpra·ctice, n. Wrong-doing; (Law) physician's improper or negligent treatment of patient; (Law) illegal action for one's own benefit while in position of trust. [MAL-]

malt[1] (mawlt), n. Barley or other grain prepared for brewing or distilling; *extract of m.* (as food for invalids); *m. liquor* (made from m. by fermentation, not distillation, e.g. beer, stout); *m.-house* (for preparing & storing m.); *m.-worm*, (fig.) toper. [com.-Teut.: OE *mealt*, Du. *mout*, G *malz*, cogn. w. OHG *malt* soft]

malt[2], v.t. & i. Convert (grain) into malt; (of seeds) come to condition of malt from germination's being checked by drought. [f. prec.]

Ma·lta (maw-), n. Island in Mediterranean; *M. fever*, complicated fever common in M.

Malte·se, a. & n. (pl. same). (Language, native) of Malta; *M. cat, dog*, fancy kinds; *M.* CROSS[1]. [-ESE]

mă·ltha, n. Cement of pitch & wax or other ingredients. [L f. Gk]

Malthū·sian, a. & n. (Follower) of T. R. Malthus (d. 1835) who advocated moral restraint (pop. understood as abstention from marriage) as means of checking increase of population. Hence **Malthu·sianism** n. [-IAN]

ma·lting (maw-), n. In vbl senses; also, malt-house. [-ING[1]]

ma·ltose, n. (chem.). Sugar produced from starch-paste by action of malt. [F (MALT + -OSE[2])]

măltrea·t (-ēt), v.t. Ill-treat. So **maltrea·tment** n. [f. F MAL(*traiter* TREAT)]

ma·ltster, n. One who makes malt. [-STER]

malvā·ceous, a. Of the genus Mallow. [f. LL *malvaceus* (as MALLOW, -ACEOUS)]

malversa·tion, n. Corrupt behaviour in position of trust; corrupt administration (*of* public money &c.). [F, f. *malverser* f. L *male* badly + *versari* behave frequent. of *vertere vers-* turn, see -ATION]

mă·melon, n. Rounded eminence. [F, = nipple f. *mamelle* breast f. MAMILLA]

Mă·mĕluke, n. (hist.). Member of military body (orig. Caucasian slaves) that seized throne of Egypt in 1254; (in Mohammedan countries) slave. [ult. f. Arab. *mamluk* slave (*malaka* possess)]

mami·lla, n. Nipple of female breast; nipple-shaped organ &c. So **mă·millary**[1], **mă·millate**[2](2), **mă·millated**[1], **mami·lliform,** aa. [L, dim. of MAMMA[2]]

mam(m)a·[1] (-ah), n. Mother (used esp. by children). [instinctive]

mă·mma[2], n. (pl. *-ae*). Milk-secreting organ of female in mammals; corresponding structure in males. Hence **ma·mmary**[1], **mammi·ferous, ma·mmiform,** aa. [L]

ma·mmal, n. One of foll. class. [f. foll.]

mammā·lia, n. pl. Class of animals hav-

ing mammae for nourishment of young. Hence **mammā·lian** a. & n., **mammă·logist**, **mammă·logy**, nn. [neut. pl. of LL *mammalis* (as MAMMA², see -AL)]
mammali·ferous, a. (geol.). Containing mammalian remains. [f. prec. + -FEROUS]
ma·mmee, n. Tropical American tree with large yellow-pulped fruit. [f. Sp. *mamey* f. Haytian]
ma·mmon, n. Wealth regarded as idol or evil influence; the worldly rich; *the m. of unrighteousness*, wealth ill used or ill gotten. Hence **ma·mmonish**¹ a., **ma·mmonism**, **ma·mmonist**, **ma·mmonite**, nn. [f. LL *mamona* f. Gk *mamōnas* f. Aram. *mamon* riches; see *Matt.* vi. 24, *Luke* xvi. 9–13]
ma·mmoth, n. & a. Large extinct elephant; (adj.) huge. [f. Russ. *mammot*, etym. dub.]
ma·mmy, n. Child's word for mother; (U.S.) coloured woman in charge of white children. [f. *mam* (instinctive) + -Y³]
man¹, n. (pl. *men*). Human being (*a man & a brother*, fellow man); in indefinite or general application) person, as *any, no, m., some, few, men*; *(all) to a m.*, all without exception; the human race, as *m. wants but little here below*; *inner, outer, m.*, spiritual, material, parts of m., (facet.) interior, esp. stomach, exterior, of m.; NEW, OLD, *m.*; adult male, opp. to *woman*, *boy*, or both; *m. & boy* (adv.), from boyhood upwards; (as impatient or lively vocative) *nonsense, m.!, hurry up, m. (alive)!*; (jocular or endearing) *little m.*, young boy; one, as *what can a m. do in such a case?*; individual (male) person, as *m. for m., between m. & m., 5/- per m.*; *as a m.*, viewed simply in regard to his personal character; *if you want noise, he is your m.* (can supply you); *I'm your m.* (accept your offer &c.); *be* one's *own m.*, be free to act, (also) be in full possession of one's faculties, senses, &c.; *every m.* JACK¹; (in comb., denoting one who follows profession, uses implement, trades in article, &c.) *clergym., postm., brake-m., penm., rag-&-bone-m.*; BEST¹, HANDY, *m.*; m. eminently endowed with manly qualities, as *be a, play the, m.*; husband, in *m. & wife*; (Hist.) vassal; manservant, valet; workman, as *the masters locked out the men*; (usu. pl.) soldiers, esp. common soldiers; piece in game of chess, draughts, &c.; *m. of* STRAW; (in comb.) ship, as *m.-of-war*, armed ship belonging to a country's navy, INDIAm., MERCHANTm.; *m. of the* WORLD; *m. Friday*, servile follower, factotum, (name given by Robinson Crusoe to his servant); *m. about town*, London society idler; *m.-at-arms*, soldier, esp. heavy-armed & mounted; *m.-* (male) *child*; *m.-eater*, cannibal, biting horse, m.-eating shark or tiger; *m.-handle*, move by force of man alone, (slang) handle roughly; *m.-hole*, opening in floor, sewer, &c., for m. to pass through; *m. in the moon*, semblance of m. in moon, esp. as type of imaginary person; *the m. in the street*, the ordinary m. (esp. as opp. experts on the matter in question); *m.-*MILLINER; *m. of Kent* (see KENTISH); *m. of* LETTERS; *m.-power*, amount of men available for military or other service; *manslaughter*, slaughter of human beings, (Law) criminal homicide without malice aforethought; *m.-trap* (for catching men, esp. trespassers). Hence **ma·nless** a. [com.-Teut.: OE & Du. *man*, G *mann*]
man², v.t. Furnish (fort, ship, &c.) with men for service or defence; (Naut.) place men at (part of ship); fill (post); fortify spirits or courage of (esp. *oneself*). [OE *mannian*, as prec.]
mă·nacle, n. (usu. pl.), & v.t. Fetter (prop. for the hand; also fig.); (v.t.) fetter with mm. [f. OF *manicle* handcuff f. L *manicula* dim. of *manus* hand]
mă·nage¹, n. (archaic). Training of horse; trained movements of horse, esp. short gallop; riding-school. [f. It. *maneggio*, as foll.]
mă·nage² (-ĭj), v.t. & i. Handle, wield, (tool &c.); conduct (undertaking &c.); control (household, institution, State); take charge of (cattle &c.); subject (person, animal) to one's control; gain one's ends with (person &c.) by flattery &c., whence **ma·naging**² a.; contrive (*to* do, often iron., as *he managed to muddle it*); succeed in one's aim (often *with* inadequate material &c.); (with *can* or *be able to*) cope with, make proper use of, as *can you m. another slice?*. Hence **manageabi·lity**, **ma·nageableness**, nn., **ma·nageable** a., **ma·nageably**² adv. [f. It. *maneggiare* f. vulg. L **manidiare* (*manus* hand)]
ma·nagement, n. In vbl senses; also or esp.: trickery, deceitful contrivance; *the m.*, governing body, board of directors, &c. [-MENT]
ma·nager, n. Person conducting a business, institution, &c.; member of either House of Parliament appointed with others for some duty in which both Houses are concerned; *good, bad*, &c., *m.* (of money, household affairs, &c.); (Law) person appointed, usu. by Court of Chancery, to manage a business for benefit of creditors &c. Hence **ma·nageress**¹, **ma·nagership**, nn., **managēr·ial** a. [-ER¹]
mănatee·, n. Large aquatic herbivorous mammal, sea-cow. [f. Sp. *manati* f. Carib *manattoui*]
mană·v(i)lins, n. pl. (slang). Odds & ends, esp. of food. [?]
Manchester. *M. School*, adherents of the doctrines of free trade & *laissez-faire*. [name given by Disraeli to Cobden & Bright & their followers]
manchinee·l, n. W.-Ind. tree with

poisonous milky sap & acrid fruit. [f. F *mancenille* f. Sp. *manzan(ill)a* f. L *matiana* kind of apple f. Roman gens *Matia*]

ma·nciple, n. Officer who buys provisions for college, inn of court, &c. [OF, f. L *mancipium* = (in med. L) office of *manceps* buyer (*manus* hand + *capere* take)]

Mancū·nian, a. & n. (Inhabitant) of Manchester; (member) of Manchester Grammar School. [f. L *Mancunium* Manchester, -AN]

-mancy, suf. f. OF *-mancie* f. LL f. Gk *manteia* divination, = divination by —.

Mandae·an, a. & n. (Member, language) of a gnostic sect surviving in Mesopotamia. [f. Aram. *mandā* knowledge]

mandā·mus, n. Judicial writ issued from King's Bench Division as command to inferior court. [L, = we command]

ma·ndarin¹, n. Chinese official in any of 9 grades; party leader who lags behind the times; nodding toy figure in Chinese costume. [f. Port. *mandarim* f. Malay f. Hind. *mantri* f. Skr. *mantrin* counsellor]

ma·ndarin², -ine (-ēn), n. Small flat deep-coloured orange; colour of this (got from coal-tar); a liqueur. [F (*-ine*); perh. f. *m.*¹ w. ref. to his yellow robes]

ma·ndatary, n. (law). One to whom a mandate is given (for spec. sense see **foll.**). [f. L *mandatarius* (foll., -ARY¹)]

ma·ndate¹ (-*at*), n. Judicial or legal command from superior; commission to act for another, esp. one from League of Nations to a State (the *mandatary*) to govern a people not qualified for independence; (poet.) command; papal rescript; (Law) contract by which mandatary undertakes to perform gratuitously some service in respect of thing committed to him; (after F *mandat*) political instructions supposed to be given by electors to (member of) parliament. [f. L *mandatum*, neut. p.p. of *mandare* command (*manus* hand + *dare* give)]

manda·te², v.t. Commit (State &c. *to* mandatary). [back formation f. MANDATARY]

ma·ndatory, a. & n. Of, conveying, a command; (n.) = MANDATARY. [f. LL *mandatorius* (as prec., see -ORY)]

ma·ndible, n. Jaw, esp. lower jaw in mammals & fishes; upper or lower part of bird's beak; (in insects) either half of upper pair of jaws. So **mandi·bul**AR¹, **mandibul**ATE²(2), aa. [f. LL *mandibula* (*mandere* masticate)]

mando·la, -dor·a, n. Large kind of mandolin. [It., var. of PANDORA²]

ma·ndolin(e), n. Musical instrument with 4 to 6 metal strings stretched on deeply-rounded body. [F (*-ine*), f. It. *mandolino* dim. of prec.]

mandră·gora, n. = foll., esp. as type of narcotic (Shak. *Othello* III. iii. 330). [LL, f. Gk *mandragoras*]

ma·ndrake, n. Poisonous plant with emetic & narcotic properties, with root thought to resemble human form & to shriek when plucked. [ME *mandrag(g)e*, shortened f. prec.]

ma·ndrel, -il, n. (In lathe) axis to which work is fixed while turned; cylindrical rod round which metal or other material is forged or shaped; (dial.) miner's pick. [?]

ma·ndrill, n. Large, hideous, & ferocious baboon. [prob. MAN¹ + DRILL³]

ma·ndūcate, v.t. Chew, eat. So **man-duca**·TION n., **ma·nducat**ORY a. [f. L *manducare* (*mandere* chew), see -ATE³]

mane, n. Long hair on neck of horse, lion, &c. (also fig. of person). Hence (**-**)**man**ED², **ma·ne**LESS, aa. [OE *manu*, cf. Du. *mane*, G *mähne*, f. OTeut. *manâ* neck]

manè·ge, -ege, (-āzh), n. Riding-school; movements of trained horse; horsemanship. [F (*-ège*), as MANAGE¹]

mā·nes (-ēz), n. pl. Deified souls of departed ancestors; shade of departed person, as object of reverence. [L]

ma·nful, a. Brave, resolute. Hence **ma·nful**LY² adv., **ma·nful**NESS n. [MAN¹ + -FUL]

ma·ngabey (-ā), n. African genus of monkey. [*M.*, region of Madagascar]

ma·nganese, n. Black mineral used in glass-making &c.; metallic element of which this is the oxide. Hence **man-gane·**SIAN, **mangă·nic**, aa. [f. F *manganèse*, corrupt. of MAGNESIA]

mā·nge, n. Skin disease in hairy & woolly animals, caused by an arachnidan parasite; (loosely) dirty condition of skin. [ME *manjewe* f. OF *manjue* itch f. *manjuer* (mod. *manger*) eat (as MANDUCATE)]

mă·ngel (-wur·zel) (-nggl-), **ma·ngold-** (-nggold), n. Large kind of beet, used as cattle food. [G (*-gold*, corrupt. *-gel*), f. *mangold* beet + *wurzel* root]

mā·nger (-j-), n. Box, trough, in stable &c. for horses or cattle to eat from; DOG *in the m.* [f. F *mangeoire* f. vulg. L **manducatoria* (as MANDUCATE, see -ORY)]

ma·ngle¹, n., & v.t. Machine of two or more cylinders for rolling & pressing washed clothes; press (clothes) in m. [(vb f. n.) f. Du. *mangel* f. Gk as MANGONEL]

ma·ngle², v.t. Hack, lacerate, by blows; cut roughly so as to disfigure; spoil (quotation, text, &c.) by gross blunders, disguise (words) by mispronouncing. [f. AF *mahangler*, prob. frequent. of *mahaignier* MAIM]

mă·ngo (-nggō), n. (Indian tree bearing) fleshy fruit with turpentine flavour, eaten ripe or used green for pickles &c.; *m.-fish*, golden-coloured Indian fish; *m. trick* (in which m.-tree appears to spring up & bear fruit in few hours). [f. Port. *manga* f. Tamil *mankay* (*man* m.-tree + *kay* fruit)]

mangold (-wurzel). See MANGEL.

ma·ngonel, n. (hist.). Military engine for casting stones &c. [OF, dim. f. LL *mango -onis* f. Gk *magganon*]

ma·ngosteen, n. (E.-Indian tree bearing fruit with thick red rind & white juicy pulp. [f. Malay *mangustan*]

ma·ngrove, n. Tropical tree or shrub, bark of which is used in medicine & tanning. [?]

mā·ngy (-ji), a. Having the mange; squalid, shabby. Hence **ma·ngi**LY[2] adv., **ma·ngi**NESS n. [f. MANGE + -Y[2]]

ma·nhood, n. State of being a man (in any sense); *m. suffrage* (granted to all male citizens of lawful age not disqualified by crime, insanity, &c.); manliness, courage; the men of a country. [MAN[1] + -HOOD]

mā·nia, n. Mental derangement marked by excitement, hallucination, & violence; great enthusiasm (*for* thing, do*ing*). [L f. Gk, = madness (*mainomai* be mad, st. *man*-)]

-māniа, suf. denoting scientifically a special type of madness (*kleptomania, megalomania*); also (pop.) eager pursuit (*bibliomania*) or admiration (*Anglomania*). Hence personal suf. *-maniac* (cf. -PHOBE, -PHOBIA). [as prec.]

mā·niăc, a. & n. (Person) affected with mania, raving mad(man). Hence **manī·-a**CAL a., **mani·acal**LY[2] adv. [f. LL *maniacus* (as MANIA, see -AC)]

-māniac, suf. See -MANIA.

Mānichee· (-k-), n. Adherent of religious system (3rd to 5th c.) that represented Satan as coeternal with God. Hence **Manich(a)e·**AN a. & n., **Ma·nich(a)**EISM n. [f. LL f. Gk *Manikhaios,* founder of sect, living in Persia]

mă·nicure, n., & v.t. (One who undertakes) treatment of hands & finger-nails as profession; (v.t.) apply m. treatment to (hands, person). [(vb f. n.) F (L *manus* hand + *cura* care)]

mă·nifest[1], n. List of cargo for use of Customs officers. [f. F *manifeste* (as MANIFEST[3])]

mă·nifest[2], a. Clear, obvious, to eye or mind. Hence **ma·nifest**LY[2] adv. [f. L *manifestus,* perh. f. *manus* hand + **festus* struck f. root of DEFEND]

mă·nifest[3], v.t. & i. Show plainly to eye or mind; be evidence of, prove; display, evince, (quality, feeling) by one's acts &c.; (of thing) reveal *itself*; record in ship's manifest; (of government or political party) take measures, hold public meeting, &c., as public expression of opinion; (of ghost) appear. So **manifest**A·TION n., **manife·stat**IVE a. [f. F *manifester* f. L *manifestare* (as prec.)]

manife·sto, n. Public declaration by sovereign, state, or body of individuals, making known past actions & motives of actions announced as forthcoming. [It., as MANIFEST[2]]

mă·nifōld[1], a. & n. Having various forms, applications, &c.; performing several functions at once; many & various, as *m. vexations*; *m. writer,* carbon copying-apparatus; (n., mech.) pipe or chamber with several openings. Hence **ma·nifold**LY[2] adv., **ma·nifold**NESS n. [com.-Teut.: OE *manigfeald,* MDu. *menichvout,* G *mannigfalt*; (MANY + -FOLD)]

ma·nifold[2], v.t. Multiply copies of (letters &c.) as by MANIFOLD[1] writer. [OE *manigfealdian* multiply, as prec.,]

mă·nikin, n. Little man, dwarf; artist's lay figure; anatomical model of the body; small tropical American bird. [f. Du. *manneken,* dim. of MAN[1]]

mani·lla[1], n. Metal bracelet used by African tribes as medium of exchange. [Sp.; dim. of L *manus* hand or f. L *monilia* pl. of *monile* collar]

Mani·lla[2], **-ī·la,** n. Capital of Philippine islands; (also *M. hemp*) fibrous material for ropes, matting, &c.; cheroot made in M. [native (*-ila*)]

mani·lle (-il), n. Second best trump or honour in quadrille & ombre. [corrupt. of Sp. *malilla* dim. of *mala* bad f. L *malus*]

mă·nioc, n. Plant cassava; meal made from it. [f. Tupi *mandioca*]

mă·niple, n. (Rom. Ant.) subdivision of legion, containing 120 or 60 men; Eucharistic vestment, strip about 3 feet long hanging from left arm. [OF, f. L *manipulus* (*manus* hand + *pl-* weak form of root *ple-* fill)]

mani·pulate, v.t. Handle, treat, esp. with skill (material thing, question); manage (person) by dextrous (esp. unfair) use of influence &c. Hence or cogn. **manipul**A·TION, **mani·pulat**OR[2](1, 2) nn., **mani·pulat**IVE, **mani·pulat**ORY, aa. [prob. back formation f. *manipulation* (F, f. *manipuler* f. L as prec.)]

mă·nitou (-ōō), n. (Amer. Ind.). Good or evil spirit; thing having supernatural power. [f. Algonquin *manito, -tu*]

mankind, n. (-kī·nd) human species; (mă·n-) male sex. [MAN[1] + KIND n.]

ma·nlike, a. Having good or bad qualities of a man; (of woman) mannish. [-LIKE]

ma·nly, a. Having a man's virtues, courage, frankness, &c.; (of woman) having a man's qualities; (of things, qualities, &c.) befitting a man. Hence **ma·nli**NESS n. [-LY[1]]

ma·nna, n. Substance supplied as food to Israelites (*Exod.* xvi.); spiritual nourishment, esp. the Eucharist; sweet juice from *m.-ash* & other plants, used as gentle laxative (*m. in tears, in sorts,* superior, inferior, kinds of this); *m.-croup,* coarse granular wheat meal [Russ. *krupa* groats]. [LL f. Gk, f. Heb. *man,* explained as = *man hu?* what is it, but perh. = Arab. *mann* exudation of *Tamarix gallica*]

ma·nnequin, n. Person employed by dressmakers &c. to wear & show off costumes. [F, = lay figure, f. Du. as MANIKIN]

ma·nner, n. Way a thing is done or happens, as *in, after, this m.*; (archaic) *in* *a m. of speaking*, so to speak; (Gram.) *adverb of m.*, one that asks or tells how; *to the m. born*, (Shak. *Ham.* I. iv. 15) destined by birth to be subject to the custom, (pop.) naturally fitted for the position &c.; (pl.) modes of life, conditions of society; outward bearing; *the grand m.*, old-fashioned dignity; (pl.) *good, bad*, &c. behaviour in social intercourse, habits indicating good breeding, as *he has no mm.*, whence **ma·nner**LESS a.; style in literature or art; mannerism; (archaic) kind, sort, as *what m. of man is he?*; *all m. of*, every kind of; *no m. of right*, no right at all; *in a m.*, in some sense, to some extent. [f. OF *manière* f. pop. L *man(u)aria* fem. adj. as n. =mode of handling (*manus* hand, -ARY[1])]

ma·nnered, a. *Ill, well, rough, -m.*, having bad &c. manners; (of style, artist, writer) showing mannerism. [-ED[2]]

ma·nnerism, n. Excessive addiction to a distinctive manner in art or literature; trick of style. Hence **ma·nner**IST n., **manneri·st**IC(AL) aa. [-ISM]

ma·nnerly, a. Well-mannered, polite. Hence **ma·nnerli**NESS n. [-LY[1]]

ma·nnish, a. (Of woman) masculine; characteristic of man as opp. to woman, as *what a m. way to thread a needle!*. Hence **ma·nnish**NESS n. [-ISH[1]]

ma·nnite, n. (Also *m.-sugar*) substance obtained from manna. Hence **ma·nni**TOSE[2] n. [f. MANNA + -ITE[1]]

manœu·vre[1] (-nōōver, -nū-), n. Planned movement of troops or ships of war; deceptive or elusive movement; skilful plan; MASS[2] *of m.* [F, f. LL *manopera*, as foll.]

manœu·vre[2] (as prec.), v.i. & t. Perform, cause (troops) to perform, manœuvres; employ artifice; force, drive, (person, thing, *into, out, away*, &c.) by contrivance; manipulate adroitly. Hence **manœu·vr**ER[1] n. [f. F *manœuvrer* f. LL *manoperare* =L *manu operari* work by hand (*opus -eris* work)]

manŏ·meter, n. Instrument showing elastic force of gases. Hence **manome·tr**IC a. [f. F *manomètre* (Gk *manos* thin, see -METER)]

ma non tro·ppo, mus. direction appended to another. But not to excess. [It.]

mă·nor, n. English territorial unit, orig. of nature of feudal lordship, now consisting of lord's demesne & of lands from whose holders he can exact certain fees &c.; *lord of the m.*, person, corporation, having rights of this; *m.-house*, his mansion. Hence **manor·**IAL a. [f. OF *manoir* (vb as n.) f. L *manēre* remain]

manqué (F), a. (after its n.). That might have been but is not, that has missed being, (*a Napoleon, comic actor, m.*).

ma·nsard, n. (Usu. *m. roof*) curb roof in which each face has two slopes, lower one steeper than upper. [f. F *mansarde* (F. *M.*, architect, d. 1666)]

manse, n. Ecclesiastical residence, esp. Scotch parish minister's house. [f. med. L *mansus, -sa, -sum*, house (*manēre mans-* remain)]

ma·nsion, n. Large residence (in pl. often of large buildings divided into flats); *m.-house*, house of lord of manor or landed proprietor, official residence, esp. (*the M.-house*) of Lord Mayor of London. [OF, f. L *mansionem* (as prec., see -ION)]

ma·nsuetude (-swĭ-), n. (rare). Meekness, docility. [f. L *mansuetudo* (*mansuetus* tame f. *manus* hand, *suesco* be used)]

ma·ntel, n. (Now usu. *mantelpiece*) structure of wood, marble, &c., above & around fireplace; (usu. *mantelshelf*) shelf projecting from wall above firěplace; *m.-board*, wooden shelf (usu. draped) fixed upon this; *m.-tree*, beam across opening of fireplace. [var. of MANTLE]

ma·nt(e)let, n. Kinds of short mantle; bullet-proof screen for gunners. [OF (*-el-*), dim. as MANTLE[1]]

ma·ntic, a. Of divination. [f. Gk *mantikos* (*mantis* prophet, see -IC)]

manti·lla, n. Large veil covering woman's hair & shoulders; small cape. [Sp., dim. of *manta* MANTLE]

ma·ntis, n. Orthopterous insect; *praying m.*, kind that holds forelegs in position suggesting hands folded in prayer. [Gk, =prophet]

manti·ssa, n. Decimal part of logarithm. [L]

ma·ntle[1], n. Woman's loose sleeveless cloak; (fig.) covering; fragile lace-like tube fixed round gas-jet to give incandescent light; outer fold of skin enclosing mollusc's viscera. [(1) OE *mentel*, (2) f. OF *mantel*, both f. L *mantellum* cloak]

ma·ntle[2], v.t. & i. Clothe (as) in mantle; cover, conceal, envelop; (of liquids) become covered with coating or scum; (of blood) suffuse cheeks, (of face) glow, with blush. [f. prec.]

mantlet. See MANTELET.

ma·ntūa, n. Woman's loose gown in 17th–18th cc.; *m.-maker*, dressmaker. [corrupt. of *manteau* (F, as MANTLE[1])]

mă·nūal, a. & n. Of, done with, the hands, as *m. labour*; (Mil.) *m.* (*exercise*), drill in handling rifle; *m. fire-engine* (worked by hand, not steam); *m.* (finger) *alphabet*; SIGN[1] *m.* (N.) small book for handy use, handbook; organ keyboard played with hands; (Hist.) book of the forms to be used by priests in the administration of the Sacraments. Hence **ma·nual**LY[2] adv. [f. L *manualis* (*manus* hand, see -AL)]

manufa·ctory, n. Factory, workshop. [f. L as foll., see -ORY]

manufa·cture[1] (-tsh*er*), n. Making of articles by physical labour or machinery, esp. on large scale; branch of such industry, as *woollen m.*; *of home, English*, &c., *m.*, made at home &c.; (contempt.) mechanical production (of literature &c.).

[F, f. L *manu* by hand + *facere fact-* make, see -URE]
manufa·cture[2] (-tsher), v.t. Work up (material) for use; produce (articles) by labour, esp. on large scale (contempt. of literary work &c.); invent, fabricate, (story). Hence **manufa·cturER**[1] n. [f. prec.]
mănūmi·t, v.t. (hist.). Set (slave) free. So **manumi·SSION** n. [f. L *manumittere* (*manus* hand + *mittere miss-* send)]
manure·[1], n. Dung, compost, spread over or mixed with soil to fertilize it. Hence **manur·IAL** a. [f. foll.]
manure·[2], v.t. Apply manure to (land, or abs., also fig.). [f. AF *maynoverer*, as MANŒUVRE[2]]
mă·nūscript, a. & n. (abbr. *MS.*, pl. *MSS.*). (Book, document) written by hand, not printed. [f. med. L *manuscriptus* (*manu* by hand + *scriptus* p.p. of *scribere* write)]
ma·nward, a. Tending, directed, towards man. [-WARD]
Manx, a. & n. Of the Isle of Man, as *M. cat*, tailless variety; *Ma·nxman*, inhabitant of I. of Man; (n.) M. cat, language, (as pl., *Manx*) M. people. [f. ON *manskr* of Man]
ma·ny (mĕ-), a. & n. Numerous, as *m. times*, (poet., rhet.) *m. a time* (*& oft*), *m. & m. a time*, *m. people wish*, *m. wish*, *m. of us wish*, *how m.* (*of them*) *can I have?*, *as m. as you like*, (pred., rare) *his reasons were m. and good*, *six mistakes in as m.* (six) *lines*; *m.'s the*, there are m. that (*m.'s the tale he has told us*); *m.'s the time*, often (*m. t. t. I have seen you do it*); *the m.*, the multitude; *one too m.*, not wanted, in the way; *he was* (*one*) *too m. for us* (outwitted, baffled, us); *a good, great, m.*, fair, large, number; *m.-headed beast, monster*, the populace; *manyplies* (mĕ·nĭplīz), (dial. for) *third* STOMACH; *m.-sided*, having m. sides, aspects, capabilities, &c., so *m.-sidedness*. [com.-Teut.: OE *manig*, Du. *menig*, G *manch*]
Maori (mowr·ĭ), n. Member, language, of brown race in N. Zealand. [native]
map[1], n. Representation on paper &c. of (part of) earth's surface, showing physical & political features &c., or of the heavens. Hence **ma·PLESS** a. [f. L *mappa* napkin; med. L has *mappa mundi* map of world]
map[2], v.t. Represent on map; *m. out*, plan out, arrange in detail (course of conduct, one's time, &c.). [f. prec.]
mā·ple, n. Genus of trees & shrubs grown for shade, ornament, wood, or sugar; wood of these; *m.-leaf*, emblem of Canada. [OE has *mapeltréow* m.-tree, cf. OSax. *mapulder*, MLG *mapeldora*]
mar, v.t. Impair fatally, ruin, esp. *make* (or *mend*) *or m.*; *mar-plot*, one who hinders undertaking by officiousness. [com.-Teut.: OE *merran*, OFris. *meria* hinder, MDu. *merren* hinder]
mă·rabou (-ōō), n. Large W.-Afr. stork; tuft of down from its wings or tail as trimming for hat &c. [F, prob. f. vulg. Arab. use of foll.]
mă·rabout (-ōōt), n. Mohammedan hermit or monk, esp. in N. Africa; shrine marking m.'s burial-place. [f. Arab. *murabiṭ*]
măraschi·no (-kē-), n. Liqueur from a small black cherry. [It. (*marasca* small black cherry, for *amarasca* f. *amaro* bitter f. L *amarus*)]
mara·smus, n. Wasting away of body. Hence **mara·smIC** a. [f. Gk *marasmos* (*marainō* wither)]
Mă·rathon, n. *M.* (*race*), a race of abnormal length (w. ref. to Phidippides, who ran 150 miles to secure Spartan aid in the battle of M.).
marau·d, v.i. & t. Make plundering raid (*on*); go about pilfering; (trans.) plunder. Hence **marau·dER**[1] n. [f. F *marauder* (*maraud* rogue)]
mărave·di (-vā), n. (hist.). Spanish coins, gold worth 14*s.*, copper ⅛*d.* [Sp. f. Arab. *Murabiṭin* MARABOUTS, Moorish dynasty at Cordova]
mar·ble, n., & v.t. Limestone in crystalline (also, in granular) state & capable of taking polish, used in sculpture & architecture; this as type of hardness or smoothness (often attrib.); (pl.) collection of sculptures, as *Elgin mm.*; small ball of m., clay, glass, &c., as toy; (v.t.) stain, colour, (paper, edges of book, soap) to look like variegated m. (esp. in p.p.). Hence **mar·blY**[2] a. [(vb f. n.) f. F *marbre* f. L *marmor*, cogn. w. Gk *marmaros* (*marmairō* sparkle)]
marc, n. Refuse from pressed fruit. [F, perh. f. *marcher* MARCH[5] in sense 'crush']
mar·casite, n. (Usu. white iron) pyrites. [f. med. L *marcasita*, etym. dub.]
marce·l. *M. wave* n., kind of artificial wave in hair; *m.-wave* v.t., produce m. w. in. [*M.*, inventor of method]
marce·scent, a. (Of parts of plant) withering but not falling. Hence **marce·SCENCE** n. [f. L *marcescere* frequent. of *marcēre*, see -ENT]
March[1] (-tsh), n. (abbr. *Mar.*). Third month of year; *M.* HARE. [OF, f. L *Martius* (*mensis* month) of Mars]
march[2] (-tsh), n. (hist.). Boundary, frontiers, (often pl., esp. of borderland between England & Scotland or Wales); tract of (often debatable) land between two countries. [f. F *marche* f. Teut. *markâ* MARK[1]]
march[3], v.i. (Of countries, estates, &c.) border *upon*, have common frontier *with*. [f. OF *marchir* (as prec.)]
march[4], n. (Mil.) marching of troops; *line* (route) *of m.*; long toilsome walk; progress (*of events, time, intellect, mind*); distance covered by troops in a day; FORCED *m.*; uniform step of troops &c., as

QUICK, SLOW, *m.*; *m. past*, m. of troops in line past saluting-point at review; (Mus.) composition meant to accompany m., as DEAD *m.* [f. F *marche* (as foll.)]

march[5] (-tsh), v.i. & t. Walk *away, forth, past* (reviewing officer or sovereign), *out*, &c., in military manner with regular and measured tread; walk, proceed, steadily; *marching orders*, direction for troops to depart for war &c.; (as gallicism) make progress; (trans.) cause to go *on, off*, &c. [f. F *marcher*, etym. dub.]

mar·chioness (-shonĭs), n. Wife, widow, of marquis; lady holding in her own right position equal to that of marquis. [f. med. L *marchionissa* f. *marchio -onis* MARCH[2]-captain (*marca*)]

mar·chpane (-tsh-), **mar·zipăn**, n. Paste of pounded almonds, sugar, &c., made up into small cakes &c.; such cake. [cf. F *massepain*, G *marzipan*, &c., etym. dub.]

marcō·ni, n., & v.t. & i. =foll.; send m., send (message) thus. [see foll.]

marcō·nigram, n. Message sent by Marconi's system of wireless telegraphy. [-GRAM]

mār·e[1], n. *M. clausum*, sea under jurisdiction of particular country; *m. lī·berum*, sea open to all nations. [L]

mare[2], n. Female of equine animal, esp. horse; GREY[1] *m.*; SHANKS'*s m.*; *m.'s-nest*, illusory discovery; *m.'s-tail*, kinds of aquatic plant, long straight streaks of cirrus. [OE *mere*, cf. Du. *merrie*, G *mähre* jade]

mare·mma, n. Low marshy unhealthy country by sea shore. [It.]

mar·garine (*or* -ēn), n. Legal name for all substances made in imitation of butter. [F, misapplication of a chem. term, f. Gk *margaron* pearl, see -IN]

mar·gay, n. S.-Amer. tiger-cat. [F, f. native *mbaracaia*]

marge, n. (poet.). =foll. [F, as foll.]

mar·gin, n., & v.t. Edge, border, of surface, whence **mar·gin**ATE[2](2), **-ated**, aa.; condition near the limit below or beyond which a thing ceases to be possible &c.; extra amount (of time, money, &c.) over & above the necessary; (Commerc.) sum deposited with stockbroker to cover risk of loss on transaction of account; space round main body of printed matter on page; (v.t.) furnish with m. or marginal notes, deposit m. on (stock). [(vb f. n.) f. L *margo -ginis*]

mar·ginal, a. Of, written in, the margin; having marginal notes; of, at, the edge; close to the limit. Hence **mar·ginal**LY[2] adv. [-AL]

margină·lia, n. pl. Marginal notes. [mod. L neut. pl., as MARGIN[1], see -AL]

mar·grave, n. (hist.). German title of some princes of Holy Roman Empire, orig. of military governor of border province. [f. MDu. *markgrave* border count (MARK[1] + *grave* count)]

mar·gravine, n. Margrave's wife. [f. Du. *markgravin* (as prec., see -INE[3])]

mar·guerite (-gerēt), n. Ox-eye daisy. [F, f. LL (*-ta*) f. Gk *margaritēs* (*margaron* pearl, see -ITE[1])]

mariage de convenance (F), n. Marriage contracted from prudential motives.

Mār·ian, a. & n. Of the Virgin Mary, Mary Queen of England, or Mary Queen of Scots; (n.) adherent of the last. [f. L *Maria* Mary + -AN]

mă·rid, n. Jinn of most powerful class. [Arab., part. of *marada* rebel]

mă·rigold, n. Kinds of plant with golden or yellow flowers; MARSH *m.* [f. *Mary* (prob. the Virgin) + *gold*]

mărina·de, n., & (also *-te*) v.t. Pickle of wine, vinegar, & spices; fish, meat, thus pickled; pickle with m. [(vb f. n.) F, f. Sp. *marinada* (*marinar* pickle in brine, as foll., -ADE)]

mari·ne (-ēn), a. & n. Of, found in, produced by, the sea; of shipping or naval matters, as *m. insurance*; *m. stores*, old ships' materials & similar odds & ends as merchandise; for use at sea; (of soldiers) serving on board ship. (N.) country's shipping, fleet, or navy, esp. *mercantile m.*; soldier on man-of-war (*blue, red, mm.*, artillery, light infantry); *tell that to the* (HORSE[1]) *mm.* [f. F *marin* (fem. *-ine*) f. L *marinus* (*mare* sea, -INE[1])]

mă·riner, n. Sailor, seaman; *master m.*, captain of merchant ship. [AF, f. med. L *marinarius* (as prec., see -ARY[1])]

Mari·nism (-ēn-), n. Affected style of It. poet Marini (d. 1625). So **Mari·**NIST n. [-ISM]

Mārio·latry, n. Idolatrous worship of Virgin Mary. [f. Gk *Maria* Mary + -LATRY]

mărione·tte, n. Puppet worked by strings, representing person &c. [f. F *marionnette* (*Marion* dim. of *Marie* Mary, -ETTE)]

mă·rish, n. & a. (poet.). Marsh(y). [ME & OF *mareis* f. med. L *mariscus* MARSH]

Mār·ist, n. Member of Rom. Cath. Society of Mary. [f. F *Mariste* (*Marie* Mary, see -IST)]

mă·rital (*or* marī·t-), a. Of a husband; of marriage. Hence **marital**LY[2] adv. [f. L *marītalis* (*marītus* husband, see -AL)]

mă·ritime, a. Living, found, near the sea; connected with the sea, as *m. insurance*. [f. L *maritĭmus* (*mare* sea; for suf. cf. *ultimus*)]

mar·joram, n. Genus including *Sweet M.*, aromatic herb used in cookery. [f. OF *majorane* f. med. L *majorana*, etym. dub.]

mark[1], n. Target or other object to be aimed at; *beside, wide of, the m.*, not hitting it, (fig.) not to the point; (Boxing) pit of stomach; desired object, as *hit, miss, the m.*; sign, indication, (*of* quality, character, &c.), esp. *m. of mouth*, depression in horse's tooth indicating age;

affixed or impressed sign, seal, &c.; EAR[1], HALL, TRADE, *-m.*; cross &c. made in place of signature by illiterate person; written symbol; this as sign of *good* or *bad* conduct; unit of numerical award of merit in examination, as *he gained 46 mm.*; line &c. serving to indicate position; *Plimsoll's m.*, line showing how far ship may legally be submerged when loaded; *below, up to,* &c., *the m.* (standard); (Footb.) heel-m. on ground made by player who has obtained fair catch; stain, scar, &c.; *make* one's *m.*, attain distinction; (as apology for mentioning anything horrible &c.) (*God*) *save the m.*; *of m.*, noteworthy; (Hist.) tract of land held by Teutonic village community. [OE *mearc*, cf. Du. & G *mark*, f. OTeut. *markâ*]

mark[2], v.t. Make a mark on (thing) by stamping, cutting, writing, &c.; put identifying mark or name on (linen); attach figures indicating prices to (goods); (pass.) have natural marks, as *marked with silver spots*; *m. out*, trace out boundaries for (ground), plan (course), destine, as *marked out for slaughter*; *m. off*, separate (thing *from* another, lit. & fig.) by boundary; indicate (place on map, length of syllable) by signs or marks; record (points gained in games); manifest (one's displeasure &c. *by*); (pass.) *this tendency is strongly marked* (noticeable), *a marked difference*, whence **mar·kĕd**LY[2] adv., **mar·kĕd**NESS n.; accompany, be a feature of, as *no triumph marks her manner*; *m. time*, move feet as in marching, but without advancing (often fig.); see, notice; observe mentally, as *m. my words*; *a marked man*, one whose conduct is watched with suspicion or hostility; (also *m. down*) note & remember spot to which (grouse &c.) has retired; (Footb.) keep close to (opponent) so as to hamper him if he receives ball. [OE *mearcian*, cf. Du. & G *merken*, (as prec.)]

mark[3], n. Denomination of weight for gold & silver, usu. 8 oz (now only of continental weights); German coin corresp. to shilling; (Hist.) English money of account, 13/4. [com.-Teut. & Rom., etym. dub.]

mar·ker, n. In vbl senses, esp.: one who marks down game; one who records score, esp. in billiards; =BOOK[1]-*m.* [MARK[2] + -ER[1]]

mar·ket[1], n. Gathering of people for purchase & sale of provisions, livestock, &c.; time of this; *bring* one's *eggs* or *hogs to a bad m.*, fail in one's schemes; open space or covered building in which cattle &c. are exposed for sale; *make a m. of*, (fig.) barter away; demand (*for* commodity); *the corn m.*, the trade in corn; *come into the m.*, be offered for sale; *put on the m.*, offer for sale; MONEY-*m.*; rate of purchase & sale, m. value, as *the m. fell*; seat of trade; *m. cross* (erected in m.-place); *m.-day* (on which m. is held); *m. garden* (in which vegetables are grown for m.); *m.-place*, square, open space, where m. is held; *m.-town* (where m. is held). [ONF, f. L *mercatus* (*mercari* trade, see MERCANTILE)]

mar·ket[2], v.i. & t. Buy or sell in market; sell (goods) in market, whence **mar·ket**ABLE a., **mar·ketab**LY[2] adv. [f. prec.]

mar·king, n. In vbl senses, esp. colouring of feathers, skin, &c.; *m.-ink* (indelible, for m. linen). [MARK[2] + -ING[1]]

mar·ksman, n. One skilled or practised in aiming at mark, esp. one who attains certain standard of proficiency in rifle practice. Hence **mar·ksman**SHIP(1, 3) n. [MARK[1] + -ES + MAN]

Mark Ta·pley, n. Invincibly cheery person. [character in Dickens's *Martin Chuzzlewit*]

marl, n., & v.t. Soil consisting of clay and carbonate of lime, a valuable fertilizer; (v.t.) apply m. to (ground). Hence **mar·l**Y[2] a. [(vb f. n.) f. OF *marle* f. LL *margila* dim. of L *marga*]

Mar·lborough House (mawl-), n. Royal Palace used as London residence of Princes of Wales.

Marlbūr·ian (mawl-), n. & a. (Member) of Marlborough College. [-IAN]

mar·līne, n. (naut.). Small line of two strands; *m.-spike, marlinspike*, pointed hard-wood or iron tool for separating strands of rope in splicing. [f. Du. *marlijn* (*marren* bind + *lijn* LINE)]

mar·lite, n. Kind of marl that resists action of air. [-ITE[1]]

mar·malade, n. Preserve of oranges or specified fruit. [f. F *marmelade* f. Port. *marmelada* f. *marmelo* quince f. L f. Gk *melimēlon* (*meli* honey + *mēlon* apple) see -ADE]

mar·molite, n. Laminated serpentine of pale green colour. [irreg. f. Gk *marmairō* shine, see -LITE]

marmor·eal, a. (poet.). Of, like, marble. [f. L *marmoreus* (as MARBLE) + -AL]

mar·moset (-z-), n. Small tropical American monkey with bushy tail. [f. OF *marmouset* grotesque image, etym. dub.]

mar·mot, n. Rodent of squirrel family; kind of bathing-cap. [f. F *marmotte* prob. f. Roumansch *murmont* f. L *murem* (nom. *mus*) *montis* mouse of the mountain]

mă·rocain, n. A dress-fabric made in silk (or other materials). [F, = Moroccan]

Mă·ronite, n. One of a sect of Syrian Christians dwelling in Lebanon. [f. LL *Maronita* (*Maron* founder, see -ITE[1])]

maroo·n[1], n. & a. (Of) brownish-crimson colour; firework exploding with loud report. [f. F *marron* chestnut f. It. *marrone*]

maroo·n[2], n. One of class of negroes, orig. fugitive slaves, in mountains & forests of Dutch Guiana & W. Indies;

marooned person. [f. F *marron* perh. corrupt. of Sp. *cimarron* wild (*cima* mountain-top perh. ult. f. Gk *kuma* wave)]

maroo·n[3], v.t. & i. Put (person) ashore & leave him on desolate island or coast as punishment; idle, hang about. [f. prec.]

marque (-k), n. *Letter(s) of m.* (*& reprisal*), licence to fit out armed vessel & employ it in capture of enemy's merchant shipping, (sing.) ship carrying such licence. [F, f. Prov. *marca* f. *marcar* seize as pledge, perh. conn. w. MARK[1]]

marquee· (-kē), n. Large tent. [f. MARQUISE taken as pl. n.]

mar·quetry, -terie, (-ke-), n. Inlaid work. [F (*-ie*), f. *marqueter* variegate (MARK[1])]

mar·quis, -quess, n. Noble ranking between duke & earl or (in foreign countries) count. Hence **mar·quis**ATE[1](1) n. [f. OF *marchis* = It. *marchese* ruler of MARCH[2], -ESE]

marqui·se (-kēz), n. (Of foreign nobility) marchioness; finger-ring set with oval pointed cluster of gems; (archaic) tent. [F, fem. of *marquis*]

mar·quois (-kwoiz), n. *M. scale*, apparatus for drawing equidistant parallel lines. [prob. blunder for F *marquoir* marker (MARK[1])]

mă·rram, n. A shore grass that binds sand. [f. ON *maralm-r* (*mar-r* sea, HAULM)]

ma·rriage (-rĭj), n. Relation between married persons, wedlock; *give, take, in m.* (as husband or wife); *communal m.*, system by which all the men in small community are married to all the women; *companionate m.* (U.S.), probationary union of man & woman; act, ceremony, of marrying; *civil m.* (performed by civil official without religious ceremony); (fig). intimate union; (Cards) declaration of king & queen of same suit; *m. articles*, antenuptial agreement respecting rights of property & succession; *m.-bed*, (fig.) marital intercourse; *m.* LICENCE[1]; *m. lines*, certificate of marriage; *m. market*, supply & demand of eligible partners for m.; *m. settlement*, arrangement securing property to wife & sometimes to children. [f. F *mariage* f. pop. L **maritaticum* (*maritus* husband, see -AGE)]

ma·rriageable (-ĭja-), a. Of an age to marry; (of age) fit for marriage. [-ABLE]

ma·rried, a. United in wedlock; of person(s) so united, as *m. life*. [p.p. of MARRY]

marron glacé (F), n. Chestnut iced with sugar as sweetmeat.

ma·rrow[1], n. Soft fatty substance in cavities of bones, often a type of rich food or of vitality (*chilled to the m.*, right through); *spinal m.*, substance forming spinal cord; essential part, as *pith & m.*; *vegetable m.*, kind of gourd; *marrowbone*, bone containing edible m., (pl., facet.) knees; *marrow(fat)*, kind of large pea; *m.-spoon* (for getting m. from bones). Hence **ma·rrow**LESS, **ma·rrow**Y[2], aa. [com.-Teut.: OE *mearg*, Du. *merg*, G *mark*]

mă·rrow[2], n. (dial.). Mate, consort, match, very image *of*. [?]

ma·rry[1], v.t. & i. (Of priest &c.) join (persons, one *to* another) in wedlock; (of parent or guardian) give (son, daughter, &c.) in marriage; (of either contracting party) take in marriage; (fig.) unite intimately; (intr.) take husband or wife. [f. F *marier* f. L *maritare* f. *maritus* husband (*mas maris* male)]

ma·rry[2], int. (archaic) expr. surprise, asseveration, indignation, &c.; *m. come up* (expr. indignant or contemptuous surprise). [= (the Virgin) *Mary*]

Mars (-z), n. Roman god of war; warfare; planet fourth in order of distance from sun. [L]

Marsa·la (-sah-), n. White wine like light sherry, from M. in Sicily.

Marseillai·se (-selāz, *or as F*), n. National song of French Republic, first sung by Marseilles patriots. [F, fem. adj. f. *Marseille*, -ESE]

Marsei·lles (-sālz), n. Seaport in S. France; stiff cotton fabric like piqué.

marsh, n. Low land flooded in winter & usu. watery at all times; *m. gas*, light carburetted hydrogen; *m. mallow*, (confection made from root of) shrubby herb growing near salt marshes; *m. marigold*, golden-flowered ranunculaceous plant growing in moist meadows. Hence **mar·shi**NESS n., **mar·sh**Y[2] a. [OE *mersc* f. WG **marisk-* (whence med. L *mariscus*) f. OTeut. *mari-* sea, see -ISH[1]]

mar·shal[1], n. EARL-*m.*; officer of highest rank in some foreign armies; PROVOST-*m.*; FIELD-*m.*, *m. of the* AIR[1], AIR[1]-*m.*; (Hist.) *knight m.*, officer of royal household with judicial functions; (*judge's*) *m.*, official accompanying judge on circuit, with secretarial duties; officer arranging ceremonies &c. Hence **mar·shal**SHIP n. [f. OF *mareschal* f. Frank. L *mariscalcus* f. OHG *marahscalh* (OTeut. *marhoz* horse + *skalkoz* servant)]

mar·shal[2], v.t. & i. (-ll-). Arrange in due order (persons at feast &c., soldiers, facts, &c.); (Her.) combine (coat of arms); conduct (person) ceremoniously (*into* &c.). [f. prec.]

mar·shalsea, n. (hist.). Court held, prison in Southwark controlled by, knight marshal. [f. obs. *marshalcy* (MARSHAL[1] + -CY)]

marsū·pial, a. & n. (anat., zool.). Of, like, a pouch, as *m. muscle*; (animal) of the class of mammals characterized by having a pouch in which to carry their young, born imperfect. [f. L f. Gk *marsupion* pouch dim. of *marsipos* purse + -AL]

mart, n. (Poet.) market-place; auction

room; trade centre. [f. Du. *markt*, f. L as MARKET]

marte·llo, n. *M. tower*, small circular fort, usu. on coast to prevent hostile landing. [corrupt. of Cape *Mortella* in Corsica]

mar·ten, n. Animal like weasel, with valuable fur. [f. OF *martrine* (*peau* skin) of the marten (*martre* f. OTeut. *marthuz*)]

mar·tial (-shl), a. Of, suitable for, appropriate to, warfare, whence **mar·tial**IZE v.t.; *m. law*, military government, by which ordinary law is suspended; brave; fond of fighting; (*M*-) of the planet Mars. Hence **mar·tial**LY[2] adv. [F, f. L *martialis* of MARS, see -AL]

Mar·tian (-shn), n. Inhabitant of Mars. [f. L *Martius* of MARS + -AN]

mar·tin, n. *St M.*, bishop of Tours in 4th c.; *Martinmas, St M.'s day*, Nov. 11; *St M'.s summer*, fine season about this time; (also *house-m.*) bird of swallow family building mud nest on house walls &c. [F, f. L *Martinus*]

martine·t, n. Strict (esp. military or naval) disciplinarian. Hence **martinĕ·t-t**ISM n., **martine·tt**ISH[1] n. [*M.*, French drill-master in reign of Louis XIV]

mar·tingale (-ngg-), n. Strap, set of straps, fastened at one end to nose-band, at other end to girth, of horse to prevent rearing &c.; (Naut.) rope for guying down jibboom; gambling system of doubling stakes in hope of eventual turn of luck. [F, etym. dub.]

marti·ni (-ēnē), n. The M.-Henry rifle. [*M.*, inventor of its breech action]

mar·tlet, n. Swift; (Herald.) footless bird. [f. F *martelet* prob. f. *martinet* dim. f. MARTIN]

mar·tyr, n., & v.t. One who undergoes penalty of death for persistence in Christian faith or obedience to law of Church, or undergoes death or suffering for any great cause; *m. to* (constant sufferer from) *gout* &c.; *make a m. of one-self*, (pretend to) sacrifice one's inclinations, for sake of credit thus gained; (v.t.) put to death as m., torment. [(vb f. n.) eccl. L f. late Gk *martur* = Gk *martus -uros* witness]

mar·tyrdom, n. Sufferings & death of martyr; torment. [-DOM]

mar·tyrize, v.t. Make a martyr of (one-*self*, person). [f. med. L *martyrizare* (MARTYR, -IZE)]

martyro- in comb. = of martyrs, as: *-latry*, worship of martyrs; *-logy*, list, register, history, of martyrs, whence *-lo·gical.*

mar·tyry, n. Shrine, church, erected in honour of martyr. [f. med. L f. Gk *marturion* (as MARTYR[1])]

mar·vel[1] (-vl), n. Wonderful thing; wonderful example *of* (quality); (archaic) astonishment. [f. OF *merveille* f. L *mirabilia* neut. pl. of *mirabilis* (*mirari* wonder at, see -BLE)]

mar·vel[2], v.i. (literary; -ll-). Be surprised (*at, that*); wonder (*how, why*, &c.). [f. OF *merveillier* (as prec.)]

mar·vellous, a. Astonishing; extravagantly improbable, esp. *the m.* Hence **mar·vellous**LY[2] adv., **mar·vellous**NESS n. [f. OF *merveillos* (as prec.)]

Mar·xian, a. & n. (Adherent) of the doctrines of the German socialist Karl Marx (1818–83). [-IAN]

marzipan. See MARCHPANE.

ma·scot, n. Person, thing, that brings luck. [f. provincial F *mascotte*, perh. cogn. w. Pr. *masco* witch]

ma·sculine, a. & n. Of the gender to which names of males normally belong; *m. rhyme* (in French verse, between words ending in stressed syllables, not *e* mute), *m. ending*, ending of line with stressed syllable; of the male sex; manly, vigorous; (of woman) having qualities appropriate to man; (n.) m. gender, word. Hence **ma·sculine**NESS, **masculi·n**ITY, nn. [f. F *masculin* (fem. *-ine*) f. L *masculinus* (as MALE, see -INE[1])]

mash[1], n. Malt mixed with hot water to form wort; mixture of boiled grain, bran, &c., given warm to horses &c.; soft pulp made by crushing, mixing with water, &c.; (slang) mashed potatoes (*sausage & m.*); confused mixture; *m.-tub* (in which malt is mashed). [OE *māsc-*, cf. G *meisch* crushed grapes, malt, Da. *mask* grains for pigs, perh. cogn. w. MIX]

mash[2], v.t. Mix (malt) with hot water; crush, pound, to pulp; reduce (potatoes &c.) to uniform mass by crushing. [f. prec.]

mash[3], v.t., & n. (slang). Excite sentimental admiration in (one of opposite sex); *be mashed on*, have such admiration for; person on whom one of opposite sex is mashed. [?]

ma·sher, n. Fop posing as lady-killer. [?]

ma·shie, -y, n. Short-headed iron golf club with straight sole & face. [perh. corrupt. of F *massue* club]

ma·sjid (mŭ-), n. Mosque. [Arab.]

mask[1], n. Covering, usu. of velvet or silk, for concealing face at balls &c., or of wire, gauze, &c., for protection; hollow figure of human head worn by Greek & Roman actors; clay or wax likeness of person's face, esp. (also *death-m.*) one made by taking mould from face; (fig.) disguise, as *throw off the m.*; masked person; face, head, of fox. [f. F *masque* f. Sp. *máscara*, or f. med. L *mascus*, etym. dub.]

mask[2], v.t. Cover (face) with mask; (pass.) be disguised with mask; (Mil.) conceal (force) &c. from enemy's view, hinder (army &c.) from action by watching with adequate force, hinder (friendly force) by standing in line of its fire; disguise (feelings &c.); *masked ball* (at which masks are worn). [f. prec.]

m·asker, -quer, n. One who takes part in masquerade or masque. [prec. + -ER[1]]

maskino·nge (-j, -jĭ), n. Large pike in great lakes of N. America. [Odjibwa]

mā·son, n., & v.t. Worker in stone; freemason, whence **masŏ·nic a.**; (v.t.) build, strengthen, with masonry. [(vb f. F *maçoner*) f. OF *maçon*; med. L *machio* etym. dub.]

ma·sonry, n. Mason's work, stonework. [f. F *maçonnerie* (as MASON, see -ERY)]

Mas(s)or·a(h), n. Body of traditional information on text of Hebrew Bible. [f. Heb. *masoreth* perh. = bond]

Mă·s(s)orete, -ite, n. Jewish scholar contributing to the Masora. Hence **mas(s)orĕ·tic** a. [(*-ete*) corrupt. of Heb. as prec.; (*-ite*) prec. + -ITE[1]]

masque (-k), n. Amateur histrionic entertainment, orig. in dumb show, later including dialogue &c.; dramatic composition for this. [as MASK[1]]

masquerā·de[1] (-ke-), n. Masked ball; false show, pretence. [f. Sp. *mascarada* (*máscara* mask, see -ADE)]

masquerā·de[2] (-ke-), v.i. Appear in disguise; assume false appearance. [f. prec.]

măss[1], n. (A) celebration (now usu. Rom. Cath.) of the Eucharist, as *m. was said, we attend, go to, hear, m., mm. were said for his soul*; liturgy used in this; musical setting of parts of this; *high m.* (with incense, music, & assistance of deacon & subdeacon); *low m.* (with no music & minimum of ceremony). [OE *mæsse* f. vulg. L *messa* f. eccl. L *missa* (*mittere miss-* send); sense history doubtful]

măss[2], n., & v.t. & i. Coherent body of matter of indefinite shape; dense aggregation of objects, as *a m. of fibres*; large number (*of*); *he is a m. of* (covered with) *bruises*; unbroken expanse (*of* light &c.); *the* (*great*) *m.*, the majority (*of*); *the mm.*, the lower orders, cf. CLASSes; *in the m.*, in the aggregate; (Physics) quantity of matter a body contains; *m. meeting*, large (usu. political) assembly of people; *m. of manœuvre*, body of troops kept free for strategic needs; (vb) gather (t. & i.) into m., (Mil.) concentrate (troops). [(vb f. F *masser*) f. F *masse* f. L *massa* prob. f. Gk *maza* barley-cake (*massō* knead)]

mă·ssacre (-ker), n., & v.t. General slaughter, carnage, (of persons, occas. of animals); (v.t.) make a m. of, murder cruelly or violently. [(vb f. F *massacrer*) F; OF *maçacre*, etym. dub.]

măssa·ge (-ahzh), n., & v.t. Rubbing, kneading, &c., of muscles & joints of the body with the hands, to stimulate their action, &c.; (v.t.) treat (part, person) thus. [(vb f. n.) F (*masser* treat with massage, perh. f. Port. *amassar* knead, f. *massa* dough, see -AGE)]

massé (-ā), n. (billiards). Stroke made with cue held perpendicular. [F, p.p. of *masser* make such stroke (as MACE[1])]

masseur· (-er), n. (fem. *-euse*, pron. -erz). One who practises massage. So **ma·sser**[1], **ma·ssor**[2], nn. [F (as MASSAGE, see -OR[2])]

mă·ssif, n. Mountain heights forming a compact group. [F (see MASSIVE) in n. use]

ma·ssive, a. Large & heavy or solid; (of features, head, &c.) largely moulded; (fig.) solid, substantial; (Psych.) of sensation &c.) having large volume or magnitude. Hence **ma·ssively**[2] adv., **ma·ssiveness** n. [F (*-if, -ive*), as MASS[2], see -IVE]

ma·ssy, a. Solid; weighty. Hence **ma·ssiness** n. [MASS[2] + -Y[2]]

mast[1], n. Long pole of timber, iron, &c., set up on ship's keel to support sails; BEFORE *the m.*; HALF-*m. high*; hence (of ship) **-masted**[2] a., **-master**[1] n.; *m.-head*, highest part of m., esp. of lower mast as place of observation or punishment, (v.t.) send (sailor) to this, raise (sail) to its position. [com.-Teut.: OE *mæst*, Du. & G *mast*]

mast[2], n. Fruit of beech, oak, & other forest-trees, esp. as food for swine. [com.-WG: OE *mæst*, G *mast*]

ma·ster[1], n. Person having control; (Naut.) captain of merchant vessel; employer; owner of dog, horse, &c.; male head of household, as *m. of the house*; *be m. of*, have at one's disposal; *be* one's *own m.*, be independent or free to do as one will; *make* one*self m. of*, acquire thorough knowledge of or facility in using; one who has or gets the upper hand, as *we will see which of us is m.*; teacher, tutor, esp. (also *schoolm.*) in school; HOUSE[1]-*m.*; teacher in philosophy &c.; *The M.*, Christ; *M. of Arts* (abbr. *M.A.*), holder of university degree orig. giving authority to teach in university; skilled workman, or one in business on his own account, as *m. carpenter*; great artist, esp. *old m.* (esp. of painters of 13th-17th cc.), picture &c. by a m.; head of some colleges; (as title of legal functionaries) *M. in Chancery* &c.; *M. of Ceremonies* (see CEREMONY), MISRULE, ROLLS; *M.* (organizer, leader, esp. in Royal Household & Inns of Court) *of the revels*; *M. of the Horse*, official in English royal household; *M.* (one who has control) *of foxhounds* (abbr. *M.F.H.*), *beagles*, &c.; (prefixed, esp. by servants, to name of young gentleman) *M. Tom, M. Jones*; (attrib.) *a m.* (commanding, superior) *mind*; *m.-at-arms*, police officer on man-of-war; *m.-key* (opening many locks, each also opened by separate key); *m. mason*, (as above, also) freemason who has passed third degree; *masterpiece*, consummate piece of workmanship; *m.-stroke*, surpassingly skilful act (of policy

&c.). Hence **ma·sterDOM, ma·sterHOOD,** nn., **ma·sterLESS** a. [OE *mægester* (partly also f. OF *maistre*) f. L *magister* cogn. w. *magis* more]

ma·ster[2], v.t. Overcome, defeat; reduce to subjection; acquire complete knowledge of (subject) or facility in using (instrument &c.); rule as a master. [f. prec.]

ma·sterful, a. Self-willed, imperious. Hence **ma·sterfulLY**[2] adv., **ma·sterfulNESS** n. [-FUL]

ma·sterly, a. Worthy of a master, very skilful. Hence **ma·sterliNESS** n. [-LY[1]]

ma·stership, n. Dominion, control; office, function, of master, esp. in school. [-SHIP]

ma·stery, n. Sway, dominion; *the* upper hand; masterly skill; masterly use or knowledge (*of* instrument, subject). [f. OF *maistrie* (as MASTER[1], see -Y[1])]

mă·stic, n. Gum or resin exuding from bark of certain trees, used in making varnish; trees yielding this; kinds of cement; liquor flavoured with m., used in Turkey & Greece; m. colour, pale yellow. Hence **masti·CIC** a. (chem.). [F, f. LL *mastichum* f. L f. Gk *mastikhē*, etym. dub.]

ma·sticate, v.t. Grind (food) with teeth, chew. Hence or cogn. **masticaBI·LITY, mastica·TION, ma·sticatoR**[2](1, 2), nn., **ma·sticatoRY** a. [f. LL *masticare* (perh. as prec.), -ATE[3]]

ma·stiff, n. Large strong dog with drooping ears & pendulous lips. [f. OF *mastin* f. pop. L **mansuetinus* (*mansuetus* tame f. *manus* hand + *suescere suet-* grow accustomed, see -INE[1])]

măstī·tis, n. Inflammation of female breast. [f. Gk *mastos* breast, see -ITIS]

mă·stodon, n. Large extinct mammal like elephant, with nipple-shaped tubercles on crowns of molar teeth. Hence **mastodo·ntIC** a. [f. Gk *mastos* breast + *odous odontos* tooth]

mă·stoid, a. (anat.). Shaped like female breast. [f. Gk *mastos* breast, see -OID]

mă·sturbate, v.i. Practise self-abuse. Hence **masturba·TION** n. [f. L *masturbari*, etym. dub., see -ATE[3]]

mat[1], n. Coarse fabric of plaited rushes, straw, &c., for lying upon, packing furniture, &c.; piece of this for wiping shoes upon, esp. *door-m.* [OE *matt* f. LL *matta*]

mat[2], v.t. & i. Cover, furnish, with mats; entangle (often *together*) in thick mass (esp. in p.p., as *matted hair*); become matted. [f. prec.]

mat[3], a., n., & v.t. (Of colours, surfaces, &c.) dull, without lustre. (N.) border of dead gold round framed picture; appearance of unburnished gold; roughened or frosted groundwork. (V.t.) make (gilding &c.) dull; frost (glass). [(vb f. F *mater*) F, f. med. L *mattus* f. Arab. *mat* helpless]

mă·tador, n. Man appointed to kill bull in bull-fight; principal card in some games. [Sp., f. L *mactatorem* (*mactare* kill, -OR[2])]

match[1], n. Person able to contend with another as an equal, as *find, meet,* one's *m.*, *be* (*more than*) *a m. for*; person equal to another in some quality, as *we shall never see his m.*; person, thing, exactly like or corresponding to another; contest of skill &c. in which persons are matched against each other, as *cricket-m.*; matrimonial alliance; *make a m.*, bring this about; person viewed in regard to his or her eligibility for marriage, esp. as to rank or fortune, as *he is an excellent m.*; *m.-board*, one with tongue cut along one edge & groove along another, so as to fit into similar boards; *match-maker*, one fond of scheming to bring about marriages. [OE *gemæcca*, cogn. w. MAKE]

match[2], v.t. & i. Join (person *with* another) in marriage; prove a match for; place (person &c.) in conflict *against* another; *well matched*, fit to contend with each other, live together, &c., on equal terms; place (person, thing) in competition *with*; be equal, correspond in quantity, quality, colour, &c., to (thing &c.; also intr. *with*) as *the carpets m. the wall-paper, these ribbons do not m., do not m. with your hat, trimmed with velvet to m.*; find material &c. that matches with (another), as *can you m. me this silk?*. [f. prec.]

match[3], n. Short piece of wood, wax taper, &c., tipped with composition that bursts into flame when rubbed on rough or (*safety m.*) specially prepared surface; piece of wick, cord, &c., designed to burn at uniform rate, for firing cannon &c.; *m.-box* (for holding mm.); *match-lock*, (gun with) lock in which m. is placed for igniting powder; *matchwood*, wood suitable for mm., minute splinters, (*make m.-w. of*, utterly smash). [f. OF *mesche* (F *mèche* wick), etym. dub.]

ma·tchet (*or* -ĕ·t), n. Broad heavy knife used in America &c. as tool & weapon. [f. Sp. *machete*]

ma·tchless, a. Without an equal, peerless. Hence **ma·tchlessLY**[2] adv. [MATCH[1] + -LESS]

mate[1], n. & v.t. (chess). = CHECKMATE; *fool's m.* (in which first player is mated at opponent's second move); STALE[1] *m.* [see CHECKMATE]

mate[2], n. (In working-classes) companion, fellow worker, (also as general form of address); one of a pair, esp. of birds; fitting partner in marriage; (Naut.) officer on merchant ship who sees to execution of master's commands & takes command in his absence, (also) assistant to some functionary, as *cook's, gunner's, surgeon's, m.* Hence **ma·teLESS** a. [prob. f. MLG *mate* for *gemate* f. OTeut. *gamaton* messmate (*ga-* Y- + *mat-* MEAT)]

mate[3], v.t. & i. Join (two persons, one *with* another) in marriage; marry (*with*, or abs.); pair (birds), (of birds) pair; keep company (*with*). [f. prec.]

mă·té (-ā), n. (Vessel for) infusion of leaves of a shrub, Paraguay tea; the shrub. [f. Sp. *mate* f. native *mati*]

matelot (mă·tlō), **mă·tlo**, n. (naut. slang). Sailor. [F (*-elot*)]

mă·telote (-ot), n. Dish of fish &c. with sauce of wine, onions, &c. [F, f. *matelot* sailor]

mā·ter, n. (School slang) mother; DURA MATER, PIA MATER; *mā·terfamĭ·liăs*, mother of household. [L]

matēr·ial, a. & n. Concerned with the matter, not the form, of reasoning; of matter, corporeal; *m. theory* of heat (that it is a m. substance); (of conduct, point of view, &c.) unspiritual; concerned with bodily comfort &c., as *m. well-being*; important, essential, (*to*, or abs.). (N.) matter from which thing is made, as *raw* (unmanufactured) *m.*; elements, constituent parts, (*of* substance, *for* historical composition &c.); stuff, fabric; *writing-mm.* (requisites). Hence **materia·l**ITY n., **mater·ial**LY[2] adv. [f. LL *materialis* (as MATTER, see -AL)]

matēr·ialism, n. Opinion that nothing exists but matter & its movements & modifications, also, that consciousness & will are wholly due to material agency; (Art) tendency to lay stress on material aspect of objects. So **mater·ial**IST n., **materiali·st**IC a., **materiali·st**ICALLY adv. [-ISM]

matēr·ialize, v.t. & i. Make, represent as, material; cause (spirit) to appear, (of spirit) appear, in bodily form; (chiefly U.S.) become actual fact; make materialistic. Hence **materializ**A·TION n. [-IZE]

matēr·ia mĕ·dica, n. Remedial substances used in practice of medicine. [med. L]

matérĭĕ·l (F), n. Stock-in-trade, available means (opp. *personnel*). [F, as MATERIAL]

mater·nal, a. Of mothers; motherly; related on the mother's side, as *m. uncle*, mother's brother; (facet.) one's mother's. Hence **mater·nal**LY[2] adv. [f. F *maternel* f. L *maternus* (*mater* mother), see -AL]

mater·nity, n. Motherhood; motherliness; *m. bag* (of child-birth requisites, provided by parish for the needy); *m. hospital* (for women during confinement). [f. F *maternité* f. L *maternitatem* (prec., -TY)]

măthemă·tical, a. Of mathematics; (of proofs &c.) rigorously precise. Hence **mathema·tical**LY[2] adv. [f. L f. Gk *mathēmatikos* (*mathēma* science f. *manthanō*, root *math-*, learn, see -IC)]

mathemă·tics, n. pl. (usu. treated as sing.). (Also *pure m.*) abstract science of space & number; (also *mixed, applied, m.*) this applied to branches of physical research, e.g. astronomy. So **mathemati**·CIAN n. [as prec., see -ICS]

mati·co (-tē-), n. Peruvian shrub; its leaves used as styptic. [Sp., dim of *Mateo* Matthew]

mă·tin, n. (Pl.) one of canonical hours of breviary, prop. a midnight office, but also recited at daybreak; (pl.) morning prayer in Church of England (often *mattins*); (poet., sing. or pl.) morning song of birds. [f. F *matines* f. eccl. L *matutinas*, acc. fem. pl. adj. as n. (*Matuta* goddess of morning, see -INE[1])]

mă·tinée (-nā), n. Afternoon theatrical or musical performance (*the m. hat*, ladies' hats obstructing, also hat designed not to obstruct, view of stage). [F, = what occupies a morning (*matin* morning, -ADE)]

ma·tlo. See MATELOT.

mă·trass, n. Long-necked glass vessel with round or oval body, used for distilling &c. [f. F *matras*, etym. dub.]

mā·triarch, n. Woman corresponding in status to patriarch (usu. facet.). [f. L *mater* mother on false anal. of *patriarch*]

mā·triarchy, n. Social organization in which mother is head of family. So **matriar·ch**AL a. [prec. + -Y[1]]

mā·tricide, n. One who kills his, killing of one's, own mother. So **ma·tricid**AL a. [f. L *matricida* (MATER, see -CIDE)]

matrĭ·culate, v.t. & i. Admit (student) to privileges of university; (intr.) be thus admitted. Hence **matricul**A·TION n., **matri·culat**ORY a. [f. LL *matricula* register, dim. of MATRIX, + -ATE[3]]

mă·trimony, n. Rite of marriage; state of being married; a card game; combination of king & queen of trumps in some card games. So **matrimō·ni**AL a., **matrimo·nial**LY[2] adv. [f. OF *matremoine* f. L *matrimonium* (*mater -tris* mother, see -MONY)]

mā·trix, n. (pl. *-icēs, -ixes*). Womb; place in which thing is developed; formative part of animal organ; mass of rock &c. enclosing gems &c.; (Biol.) substance between cells; mould in which type &c. is cast or shaped. [L, prob. f. *mater* mother]

mā·tron, n. Married woman; woman managing domestic affairs of hospital, school, &c. Hence **ma·tron**AGE(1, 2), **ma·tron**HOOD, **ma·tron**SHIP, nn., **ma·tron**AL, **ma·tron**LY[1], aa. [f. F *matrone* f. L *matrona* (*mater* mother)]

ma·ttamore, n. Subterranean dwelling or storehouse. [f. F *matamore* f. Arab. *maṭmurah* (*ṭamara* store up)]

ma·tter[1], n. Substance(s) of which a physical thing is made; purulent discharge, whence **ma·tter**Y[2] a., purulent, festering; physical substance in general, as opp. to spirit, mind, &c.; (Logic) particular content of proposition, distinguished from its form; material for thought or expression; substance of book speech, &c. (often opp. to *manner*);

occasion (*of, for*, complaint, regret, &c.); thing(s), as *printed m., postal m.*, all that may be sent by post; *no m.*, it is of no importance (*when, how*, &c., or abs.); *what m.?*, that need not disquiet us; affair; thing (of a kind specified esp. by vbl n.), as *a hanging m., no laughing m., money mm.*; *that is a m.* (case, question) *of habit* &c.; *for that m.*, so far as that is concerned; *a m. of* (about) *40 years*; *what is the m.?*, what is amiss (*with*)? (*w. i. t. m. w.* —, slang, surely — will do); *in the m. of*, as regards; *m. of course* (also as adj., w. hyphens), thing to be expected in natural course; *m. of fact*, what pertains to the sphere of fact, (opp. to *opinion* &c.), esp. *as a m. of fact*, (Law) part of judicial inquiry concerned with truth of alleged facts (opp. to *m. of law*), (adj., with hyphens) unimaginative, prosaic. [f. OF *matere* f. L *materia* timber, stuff]

ma·tter[2], v.i. Be of importance, signify, (*to* person &c. *how, when*, &c.; esp. w. neg.); secrete or discharge pus. [f. prec.]

ma·tting, n. In vbl senses (MAT[2]), esp.: fabric of hemp, bast, grass, &c. as covering &c., as *coco-nut m.* [-ING[1]]

mattins. See MATIN.

ma·ttock, n. Tool of PICK[1] shape, with an adze & a chisel edge as ends of head. [OE *mattuc*, etym. dub.]

ma·ttoid, n. Person of erratic mind, compound of genius & fool. [f. It. *mattoide* (*matto* mad)]

ma·ttress, n. Canvas case stuffed with hair, straw, &c., as bed or support for bed; (usu. *spring m.*) similar appliance of springs stretched in frame. [f. OF *materas* f. It. *materasso* prob. f. Arab. *almaṭraḥ* place, cushion (*ṭaraḥa* throw)]

mă·tūrate, v.i. (med.). (Of pustule &c.) come to maturation. [as MATURE[2], -ATE[3]]

matūra·tion, n. Ripening of morbific matter; causing of this, whence **matūr·a**TIVE a.; ripening of fruit; maturing, development. [F, f. L *maturationem* (as MATURE v., see -ATION)]

mature[1], a. Complete in natural development; with fully developed powers of body & mind; *m.* (careful) *deliberation, m. plans* (formed after this); (of bill) due. So **mature·**LY[2] adv., **mature·**NESS, **matūr·**ITY, nn. [f. L *maturus* ripe]

mature[2], v.t. & i. Develop fully; ripen; perfect (plan &c.); come to maturity; (of bill) become due. [f. obs. F *maturer* f. L *maturare* (as prec.); & f. prec.]

mătūtī·nal, a. Of, occurring in, the morning; early. So **ma·tutine** a. [f. L *matutinalis* (*matutinus* f. *Matuta* goddess of dawn]

maud, n. Scotch shepherd's grey striped plaid; travelling-rug like this. [?]

mau·dlin, a. & n. Mawkishly sentimental, esp. of tearful stage of drunkenness; (n.) mawkish sentiment. [(adj. f. n.) f. OF *Madelaine* MAGDALEN]

mau·gre (-ger), prep. (archaic). In spite of. [f. OF *maugré* (*mal* bad f. L *malus* + *gré* f. L *gratus* pleasing)]

maul[1], **mall**, n. Kinds of special hammer, commonly of wood. [f. F *mail* f. L *malleus* hammer]

maul[2], v.t. Beat & bruise; handle (material thing, subject, quotation) roughly or carelessly; damage by criticism. [f. prec.]

mau·ley, n. (slang). Fist, hand. [prob. f. prec.]

mau·lstick, n. Light stick held by painter in left hand as support for right, with padded leather ball at one end. [f. Du. *maalstok* (*malen* paint + *stok* stick)]

mau·nder, v.i. Move, act, listlessly; talk in dreamy or rambling manner. [?]

mau·ndy, n. (In R.-C. countries) ceremony of washing the feet of poor people; (in English use) distribution of *m. money* by royal almoner to the poor on *M. Thursday* (next before Easter). [f. OF *mandé* f. L *mandatum* MANDATE (*John* xiii. 14)]

Mau·ser (mowz-), n. Kind of military rifle. [inventor's name]

mausolē·um, n. Magnificent tomb, orig. that of Mausolus king of Caria erected by his queen Artemisia in 4th c. B.C. [L, f. Gk *Mausōleion* (*Mausōlos*)]

mauvais (mōvā·), a. *M. sujet*, black sheep, rogue; *m. quart d'heure*, short but unpleasant experience, interview, &c. [F]

mauvaise honte (F), n. False shame; painful diffidence. [F, = ill shame]

mauve (mōv), n. & a. Bright but delicate purple dye from coal-tar aniline; of the colour of this. [F, f. L *malva* MALLOW]

mā·vis, n. (poet.). Song-thrush. [f. F *mauvis* = Sp. *malviz*, etym. dub.]

maw, n. Stomach (only facet. of men), esp. last of ruminant's four stomachs; *mawworm*, intestinal worm, also [f. *M.*, character in Bickerstaffe's play *The Hypocrite*] hypocrite. [com.-Teut.: OE *maga*, Du. *maag*, G *magen*]

maw·kish, a. Of faint sickly flavour; feebly sentimental. Hence **maw·kish**LY[2] adv., **maw·kish**NESS n. [f. obs. *mawk* maggot f. ON *madkr* + -ISH[1]]

maw·seed, n. Seed of opium poppy. [f. G *mohsamen* (*moh* poppy + *samen* seed)]

maxi·lla, n. (pl. *-ae*). Jaw(bone), esp. upper jaw in animals & most vertebrates. Hence **maxi·lla**RY[1], **maxi·lli**FORM, aa. [L]

ma·xim[1], n. A general truth drawn from science or experience; principle, rule of conduct. [f. F *maxime* f. L *maxima*, fem. adj., greatest]

Ma·xim[2], n. Single-barrelled quick-firing machine gun, with water-casing to keep parts cool; *M.-Nordenfelt gun*, modification of this. [Sir Hiram S. *M.*, inventor]

ma·ximalist, n. Person who holds out for the maximum of his demands & rejects compromises (esp. as variety of Russian socialist). [*maximum*, -AL, -IST]

ma·ximize, v.t. Increase, magnify, to the utmost; interpret (doctrine &c.) vigorously. Hence **maximiza·tion** n. [f. L *maximus* greatest + -IZE]

ma·ximum, n. (pl. usu. *-ma*). Highest possible magnitude or quantity (often attrib.); *m. price* (that may not be exceeded); *m. thermometer* (recording highest temperature within given period). [L, neut. as prec.]

ma·ximus, a. (In schools) eldest of the name, as *Jones m.* [see MAXIMIZE]

may[1], v. auxil. (3rd sing. *may*; past *might*), expr. possibility, as *it may be true* (neg. *it cannot be*), *it may not be* (perhaps is not) *true, you may walk miles without seeing one, he may* or *might* (perhaps will) *lose his way, I was afraid he might* (perhaps would) *lose his way, afraid he might have* (perhaps had) *lost it*; expr. permission, as *you may* (neg. MUST[4] *not* or *cannot*) *go, I wish I might*; *you might* (I request you to) *call at the baker's*; *you might* (ought to, yet do not) *offer to help, you might* (ought to) *have offered*; (in final clauses, & after *wish, fear*, &c.) *take, took, such a course as may, might, avert the danger, I hope he may, hoped he might, succeed*; (expr. wish) *may you live to repent it!*; (in questions, emphasizing uncertainty) *who may you be?*; *may·be* (also archaic *mayhap*), perhaps; *might-have-been*, a past possibility. [com.-Teut.: OE *mæg*, past *meahte*, Du. *mag*, *mocht*, G *mag*, *mochte*]

may[2], n. (poet.). Maiden. [OE has *mǽg* kinswoman]

May[3], n. Fifth month of year; (fig.) bloom, prime; *Queen of* (*the*) *M.*, girl chosen to be queen of games on May-day; hawthorn (blossom); (Camb. Univ., pl.) M. examination, M. boat-races held during *M.-week* (late in M. or early in June); *M.-day*, May 1 (*maying*[1], keeping this, picking m.); *Mayfair*, fashionable London district enclosed by Park lane, Oxford street, Regent street, & Piccadilly (named from fair formerly held in May); *m.-fly*, an ephemeral insect; *M.-games*, on M.-day; *may-pole*, pole painted & decked with flowers, for dancing round on M.-day; *M. meetings* (of religious & philanthropic societies held during M. in London). [f. F *mai* f. L *Maius*]

ma·ya (mah-), n. (Hind. philos.) Illusion. [Skr.]

Ma·yan, (mah-), a. Of the ancient culture of the Mayas before their conquest by the TOLTECS.

mayonnai·se (-z), n. (*Salmon, chicken*, &c., *m.*, dish with) creamy dressing of egg-yolk &c. [F]

mayor (mār), n. Head of municipal corporation of city or borough; LORD *m.*; *m. of the palace*, nominal subordinate to whom the power of his titular superior has passed (see ROI *fainéant*). Hence **may·oral** a. [f. F *maire*, as MAJOR[2]]

mayoralty (mār·altĭ), n. Mayor's (period of) office. [f. OF *mairalté* (as prec., see -AL & -TY)]

mayoress (mār·ĭs), n. Mayor's wife. [-ESS[1]]

mă·zard, n. (archaic). Head, face; (perh. different wd) small black cherry. [prob. f. obs. *mazer* f. OF *masere* of Teut. orig.]

măzari·ne (-ēn), n. & a. Deep rich blue. [?]

Ma·zdaism, n. Zoroastrianism. [f. Avestic *mazda*, good principle in Persian theology]

maze, n., & v.t. Complex network of paths, labyrinth; confused mass &c.; (v.t.) bewilder, confuse, (esp. in p.p.). Hence **ma·zily**[2] adv., **ma·ziness** n., **ma·zy**[2] a. [?]

mazur·ka, n. Lively Polish dance like polka, music for this in triple time. [Polish, = woman of province Mazovia]

me (mē, mĭ), pron., objective case of I (& colloq. subjective, as *it's only me*); (archaic & poet., reflexive) myself, *I laid me down*; (in intt.) *ah me!*, *dear me!*. [OE had (1) *me*, cf. Du. *mij*, L *me*, Gk (*e*)*me*; (2) *mec* (lost in ME), cf. G *mich*, Gk *emege* me at least]

mead[1] (mēd), n. Alcoholic liquor of fermented honey & water. [com.-Teut. & Aryan; OE *meodu*, Du. *mede*, G *met*; cf. Skr. *madhu* honey, sweet drink, Gk *methu* wine]

mead[2] (mēd), n. (poet.). =foll. [see foll.]

meadow (mĕ·dō), n. Piece of grass land, esp. one used for hay; low well watered ground, esp. near river; *m.-sweet*, rosaceous plant common in moist mm., with creamy-white heads & fragrant flowers. Hence **mea·dowy**[2] a. [OE *mǽdwe* oblique case of *mǽd* (whence prec.) f. Teut. root *me-*, whence MOW]

meagre (mē·*ger*), a. (Of persons &c.) lean, thin; poor, scanty; (of literary composition, ideas, &c.) wanting in fullness. Hence **mea·grely**[2] adv., **mea·greness** n. [f. OF *maigre* f. L *macer -cri*, cogn. w. Gk *makros* long]

meal[1], n. Edible part of any grain or pulse (usu. exc. FLOUR) ground to powder; WHOLE *m.* [com.-Teut.: OE *melo*, Du. *meel*, G *mehl*, f. Teut. root *mel-*, cogn. w. L *molere* grind]

meal[2], n., & v.i. Customary (also, any) occasion of taking food; food so taken (*make a m. of*, consume); quantity of milk given by cow at a milking; *m.-time*, usual time of eating; (v.i.) eat a m. [(vb f. n.) com.-Teut.: OE *mǽl* mark, fixed time, meal, Du. *maal*, G *mal* time, *mahl* meal]

mealie, n. (S.-Afr.). Maize (usu. pl.). [f. Cape Du. *milje* f. Port. *milho* MILLET]

mea·ly, a. Of, like, containing, meal; (of boiled potatoes) dry & powdery; *m.-bug*, insect infesting vines &c.; *m. primrose* (mauve-flowered with powdery stem); (of horses) spotty; (of complexion) pale; (usu. *m.-mouthed*) apt to mince matters, soft-spoken. Hence **mea·li**NESS n. [MEAL[1] + -Y[2]]

mean[1], n. Condition, quality, course, equally removed from two opposite (usu. blamable) extremes, esp. *the golden, happy, m.*; (Math.) term between first & last terms of arithmetical, geometrical, &c., progression; (pl., often treated as sing., as *a mm.*) that by which a result is brought about, as *it has been the mm. of extending our trade, by fair mm.*, WAYS *&* *mm., mm. of grace* (sacraments &c.); pecuniary resources, as *he lives beyond his, on his own, mm.*; wealth, as *a man of mm.*; *by all* (*manner of*) *mm.*, in every possible way, at any cost, certainly; *by no* (*manner of*) *mm.*, not at all, certainly not; *by mm.* (the instrumentality) *of* (person, thing, doing). [f. foll.]

mean[2], a. (Math.) equally far from two extremes, as *5 is the m. quantity between 2 & 8*; *m. sea level* (half way between those of high and low water); *m. sun*, fictitious sun moving in celestial equator at m. rate of real sun; *m. proportional*, second of three quantities of which first is to it as it to third; *in the m.* (intervening) *time, while*; *meantime, meanwhile*, advv., in the m. time. [f. OF *men, moien*, f. LL *medianus* (*medius* mid, see -AN)]

mean[3], a. (Of capacity, understanding, &c.) inferior, poor; (Hist.) *m. white*, landless white man in S. United States; not imposing in appearance, shabby; *he is no m.* (a good) *scholar*; ignoble, small-minded; stingy. Hence **mea·n**LY[2] adv., **mea·n**NESS n. [OE *gemǣne* common, cf. Du. *gemeen*, G *gemein*, cogn. w. L *communis* COMMON]

mean[4], v.t. (*meant*, pron. mĕnt). Purpose, have in mind, (*mischief, business, to* do); design, destine, for an object &c., as *m. it to be used, m. it for a stopgap, he was meant* (by parents &c., also, by Providence) *for a soldier*; *I m. you to* (am determined that you shall) *go*; *m. well to, by*, be kindly disposed towards; intend to convey (specified sense) or indicate (object), as *I m. that he is stingy, I m. his father*; (of words) signify, import, (thing, *that*); *what do you m. by* (how do you justify) *it?*. [com.-WG: OE *mǣnan*, Du. *meenen*, G *meinen*]

meă·nder, n., & v.i. (Pl.) sinuous windings of river; (pl.) winding paths; (usu. pl.) circuitous journey; ornamental pattern of lines winding in & out; (v.i.) wander at random, (of stream) wind about. [(vb f. n.) L, f. Gk *Maiandros*, river in Phrygia]

meă·ndrine, a. Full of windings (esp. of genus of corals with surface like human brain). [MEANDER[1] + -INE[1]]

mea·ning[1], n. What is meant; *with m.*, significantly. Hence **mea·ning**LESS a. [-ING[1]]

mea·ning[2], a. Expressive, significant, whence **mea·ning**LY[2] adv.; *well-m.*, having good intention. [-ING[2]]

mea·sles (-z-), n. pl. Infectious disease of man, marked by red pustules; such pustules; disease in swine; GERMAN[2] *m.* [ME *maseles*, cf. Du. *mazelen*, cogn. w. OHG *masala* blood-blister]

mea·sly, a. Of, affected with, measles; (slang) contemptible, worthless. [f. prec. + -Y[2]]

measure[1] (mĕ·zh*er*), n. Size, quantity, found by measuring, whence **mea·sure**LESS a., beyond m., infinite; *short, full, m.*, less, not less, than professed amount; *clothes made to m.* (in accordance with measurements taken); *take* (person's) *m.*, measure him for clothes &c., (fig.) gauge his character &c.; degree or extent or amount (esp. *in a* or *some m.*, partly); vessel of standard capacity for dealing out liquids &c., as *pint m.*; rod, tape, &c., for measuring, as *tape-m., yard-m.*; unit of capacity, e.g. bushel, as *20 mm. of wheat*; system of measuring, as *liquid, linear, m.*; that by which a thing is computed, as *a chain's weakest link is the m. of its strength*; quantity contained in another an exact number of times; *greatest common m.* (greatest that divides each of given quantities); prescribed extent or quantity, as *set mm. to*, limit, *beyond m.*, excessively; poetical rhythm, metre; time of piece of music; (archaic) dance, as *tread a m.*; suitable action, as *take mm.*; legislative enactment. [f. F *mesure* f. L *mensura* (*metiri mens-* measure, -URE)]

measure[2] (mĕ·zh*er*), v.t. Ascertain extent or quantity of (thing) by comparison with fixed unit or with object of known size; ascertain size & proportions of (person) for clothes; look (person) up & down *with* one's *eye*; mark off or *off* (line &c. of given length); *m.* one's *length*, fall prostrate; *m. swords*, (of duellists) see that swords are of equal length, (fig.) try one's strength *with* (person); *it measures 7 inches* (is 7 inches long); estimate (immaterial thing, person's character, &c.) by some standard or rule; deal *out* (thing *to* person); bring (one's strength &c.) into competition *with* (another's); (poet.) traverse (distance). Hence **mea·sur**ABLE a. (*within measurable distance of* ruin &c., getting near it), **mea·surab**LY[2] adv., **mea·sure**MENT n. (esp., pl., detailed dimensions). [f. F *mesurer* (as prec.)]

mea·sured, a. In vbl senses, also: rhythmical, regular in movement, as *m. tread*; (of language) carefully weighed. [p.p. of prec.]

meat, n. Animal flesh as food, usu. (also *butcher's m.*) excluding fish & poultry; *green m.*, grass, green vegetables, as food; (archaic) food of any kind (*as full as an egg is of m.*, quite full; *one man's m. is another man's poison*); *this was m. &*

drink (a great pleasure) *to him*; (archaic) meal, as *before, after, m.*; *m.-safe,* cupboard for storing m., usu. of wire gauze &c.; (bibl.) *m.-offering* (R.V. *meal-*), sacrifice of flour & oil. Hence **mea·tLESS** a. [OE *meta*, cf. Sw. *mat*, Da. *mad*]

meā·tus, n. (anat.; pl. *-ūs, -uses*). Channel, passage, in the body, as *auditory m.*, channel of the ear. [L, f. *meare* flow, run]

mea·ty, a. Full of meat, fleshy; (fig.) full of substance; of or like meat. [-Y²]

Me·cca, n. Mohammed's birthplace; (fig.) place one aspires to visit, (also) birthplace of a faith, policy, pursuit, &c. [f. Arab. *makkah*]

mechă·nic (-k-), n. Handicraftsman; skilled workman, esp. one who makes or uses machinery; (pl.) branch of applied mathematics treating of motion & tendencies to motion, (also) science of machinery. [f. L f. Gk *mēkhanikos* adj. (as MACHINE, see -IC)]

mecha·nical (-k-), a. Of machines or mechanism; *the m. powers*, lever, wheel & axle, pulley, inclined plane, wedge, screw; of the nature of handicraft; working, produced, by machinery; *m. drawing* (done with compasses &c.); *m. transport* (abbr. M.T.), motor branch of R.A.S.C.; (of persons or actions) like machines, automatic, lacking originality; (of agencies, principles, &c.) belonging to mechanics, often opp. to *chemical*, as *air is a m. mixture, not a chemical compound*; (of theories &c.) explaining phenomena by assumption of mechanical action, whence **mecha·nicalISM** n.; of mechanics as a science. Hence **mecha·nicalLY²** adv., **mecha·nicalNESS** a. [as prec., see -AL]

mechani·cian (-ĭshn), n. One skilled in constructing machinery. [MECHANIC + -IAN]

mĕ·chanism, n. Structure, adaptation of parts, of machine (lit. & fig.); system of mutually adapted parts working together (as) in machine; (Art) mechanical execution, technique. [f. MECHANIC + -ISM]

me·chanist, n. Machinist (now rare); mechanician, expert in mechanics; (Philos.) one who holds that all biological phenomena admit of mechanico-chemical explanation (opp. VITALIST), whence **mechani·stIC** a. [as prec. + -IST]

mĕ·chanize, v.t. Give mechanical character to. Hence **mechanizA·TION** n. (esp., Mil., resort to tanks, aircraft, &c., in war). [-IZE]

Mĕ·chlin (-k-), n. (Also *M. lace*) lace made at *M.* in Belgium.

mecŏ·nic, a. *M. acid*, white crystalline acid obtained from opium. [f. Gk *mēkōn* poppy + -IC]

mĕ·dal, n. Piece of metal, usu. in form of coin, struck or cast with inscription & device to commemorate event &c., also awarded as distinction to soldier, student, &c., for services rendered, proficiency, &c.; *the reverse of the m.*, other side of question. Hence **me·dallED²**, **meda·llIC,** aa. [f. F *médaille* f. pop. L **metallea* (as METAL)]

medă·llion, n. Large medal; thing so shaped, e.g. decorative panel or tablet, portrait, &c. [f. F *médaillon* (as prec., see -OON)]

me·dallist, n. Engraver, designer, of medals; recipient of medal, as *gold m.* [-IST]

me·ddle, v.i. Busy oneself unduly *with*, interfere *in*. Hence **me·ddlER¹**, **me·ddlesomeNESS,** nn., **me·ddlesome** a. [f. OF *medler* = *mesler* f. pop. L **misculare* (*miscēre* mix)]

mē·dia, n. (pl. *-ae*). Voiced or soft mute (*b, d, g*), cf. TENUIS; middle membrane of artery or vessel. [L, fem. of *medius* middle]

mĕdiē·val, -diaeval, a. Of, imitating, the middle ages. Hence **medi(a)e·valISM**(2), **medi(a)e·valIST**(3), nn., **medi(a)e·valIZE**(2, 3) v.t. & i., **medi(a)e·valLY²** adv. [f. L *medius* middle + *aevum* age + -AL]

mē·dial, a. Situated in the middle; of average dimensions. Hence **me·dialLY²** adv. [f. LL *medialis* (as prec., see -AL)]

mē·dian, a. & n. Situated in the middle; (n., Anat.) m. artery, vein, nerve, &c. [f. L *medianus* (as prec., see -AN)]

mē·diant, n. (mus.). Third of any scale. [f. It. *mediante* (as MEDIATE², see -ANT)]

mēdiastī·num, n. (anat.). Membranous middle septum, esp. between lungs. Hence **mediasti·nAL** a. [med. L, neut. adj., = middle, f. L *medius*]

mē·diate¹ (-*a*t), a. Connected not directly but through some other person or thing; involving intermediate agency. Hence **me·diateLY²** adv. [as foll., see -ATE²]

mē·diāte², v.i. & t. Form connecting link between; intervene (*between* two persons) for purpose of reconciling them; be the medium for bringing about (result) or conveying (gift &c.). So **mediA·TION** n. [f. LL *mediare* (*medius* middle), see -ATE³]

mē·diatize, v.t. Annex (principality) to another State, leaving former sovereign his title & some rights of government. Hence **mediatizA·TION** n. [f. F *médiatiser* (*médiat*, as MEDIATE¹, see -IZE)]

mē·diator, n. One who mediates, esp. Christ. Hence or cogn. **mediator·IAL,** **me·diatORY,** aa., **mediā·TRIX** n. [f. F *médiateur* f. LL *mediatorem* (as MEDIATE², see -OR²)]

mĕ·dicable, a. Admitting of remedial treatment. [f. L *medicabilis* (as MEDICATE, see -BLE)]

mĕ·dical, a. & n. Of the healing art; *m. man*, physician or surgeon; of medicine as opp. to surgery, obstetrics, &c.; requiring m., not surgical, treatment; *m.*

jurisprudence, the legal knowledge required of a doctor; (n., colloq.) m. student. Hence **me·dical**LY[2] adv. [f. F *médical* f. LL *medicalis* (*medicus* physician, see -AL)]

medi·cament (*or* mĕ·d-), n. Substance used in curative treatment. [f. F *médicament* f. L *medicamentum* (as MEDICATE, see -MENT)]

mĕ·dicaster, n. Quack. [f. L *medicus* physician, see -ASTER]

mĕ·dicate, v.t. Treat medically; impregnate with medicinal substance. Hence or cogn. **medica·tion** n., **me·dicative** a. [f. L *medicari* (as prec.), see -ATE[3]]

Medicē·an, a. Of the Medici family, rulers of Florence in 15th c. [f. med. L *Mediceus* + -AN]

medi·cinal, a. Of medicine; having healing properties. Hence **medi·cinal**LY[2] adv. [f. L *medicinalis* (as foll., see -AL)]

medicine (mĕ·dsn), n., & v.t. Art of restoring & preserving health, esp. by means of remedial substances & regulation of diet &c., as opp. to surgery & obstetrics; substance, esp. one taken internally, used in this; (among savages) spell, charm, fetish, as *m.-man*, magician; (v.t.) give m. to, cure with m. [(vb f. OF *medeciner*) f. OF *medecine* f. L *medicina* (*medicus* physician)]

mĕ·dico, n. (facet.; pl. *-os*). Doctor. [It.]

medico- in comb. = L *medicus* physician, medical-, as *-bota·nical*, *-galva·nic*, *-judi·cial*.

medieval. See MEDIAEVAL.

mē·diōcre (-*ker*), a. Of middling quality, indifferent, neither good nor bad. So **mĕdiŏ·crity** n. (in adj. senses, & esp. m. person). [f. F *médiocre* f. L *mediocris* of middle degree (*medius* middle)]

mĕ·ditate, v.t. & i. Plan mentally, design; (intr.) exercise the mind in (esp. religious) contemplation (*on*, *upon*, subject). Hence or cogn. **medita·tion**, **me·ditator**[2], **me·ditative**NESS, nn., **me·ditative** a., **me·ditative**LY[2] adv. [f. L *meditari*, f. root *med-*, cf. Gk *mēdomai* think about]

mĕditerrā·nean, a. & n. (Of land) remote from coast; (of water surfaces) landlocked; *M.* (*Sea*), that which separates Europe from Africa. [f. L *mediterraneus* (*medius* middle + *terra* land) + -AN]

mē·dium, n. & a. (pl. *-a*, *-ums*). Middle quality, degree, &c. (*between* extremes, or abs.); intervening substance through which impressions are conveyed to senses &c., e.g. air; (fig.) conditions of life; agency, means, as *by*, *through*, *the m. of*; *m. of circulation*, what serves as instrument of commercial transactions, e.g. coin; liquid vehicle with which pigments are mixed, e.g. oil, water; person claiming ultraphysical perception and revealing its results to others, whence **me·dium**ISM n., **me·diumi·stic** a., **me·dium**IZE(3) v.t.; (adj.) intermediate between two degrees or amounts, average, moderate; *m. bowler* (neither fast nor slow). [L, neut. of *medius* middle]

me·dlar, n. (Tree with) fruit like small brown apple, eaten when decayed. [f. OF *medler* f. L f. Gk *mespilē*]

me·dley, n., a., & v.t. Heterogeneous mixture; mixed company; literary miscellany; (adj.) mixed, motley; (v.t.) make a m. of, intermix. [(vb & a. f. n.) f. OF *medlee* (as MEDDLE)]

Médŏ·c (mē-), n. Red wine from *M.*, district in S.-W. France.

medu·lla, n. Marrow of bones; spinal marrow; *m.* (*oblongata* prolonged) hindmost segment of brain; central parts of some organs, esp. kidney; pith of mammalian hair; soft internal tissue of plants. So **medu·llary**[2] a. [L, = pith, marrow, prob. cogn. w. *medius* middle]

Medū·sa, n. (Gk Myth.) one of the three Gorgons, with snakes for hair; (Zool.) jellyfish, whence **medu·sal**, **medu·san**, aa., **medu·soid** a. & n. [L, f. Gk *Medousa*]

meed, n. (poet.). Reward; merited portion (*of* praise &c.). [OE *méd*, cf. MDu. *miede*, G *miete*, cogn. w. Gk *misthos* reward, Skr. *midha* prize]

meek, a. Piously humble & submissive; submitting tamely to injury &c.; (provv.) *as m. as a lamb*, *as Moses*. Hence **mee·k**LY[2] adv., **mee·k**NESS n. [ME *meoc* f. ON *miukr* soft, gentle]

meer·schaum (-shm), n. Hydrous silicate of magnesium, found in soft white masses; tobacco-pipe with m. bowl. [G, = sea-foam (*meer* sea + *schaum* foam)]

meet[1], n. Meeting of hounds & men for hunt or of cyclists &c. [f. foll.]

meet[2], v.t. & i. (met). Come face to face with (person coming from opposite direction); go to place to receive (person, train, &c.) on arrival; make the acquaintance of (imperat., U.-S. form of introduction, as *m. Dr Smith*); *m.* (person) *half-way*, respond to friendly advances of, come to compromise with; (of line, road, &c.) reach point of contact with (another line &c.); *m. the eye*, *ear*, be visible, audible; *m.* person's *eye*, see he is looking at one, (also) return his gaze; oppose in battle or duel; grapple with (evils &c.); come by accident or design into the company of; come into conformity with (person, his wishes); satisfy (demand; *m. the case*, be adequate); pay (bill) at maturity; (intr., of two persons) come face to face; come *together*, as *they had* or *were met together*; come into contact (*waistcoat won't m.*, is too small); (of qualities) unite in same person; *m. with*, come across (person, obstacle, &c.), experience (treatment &c.). [OE *mētan*, cf. Du. *moeten*, Da. *möde*, cogn. w. MOOT n.]

meet[3], a. (archaic). Suitable, fit, proper, (*for* thing, *to* do, *to* be done); *it is m.*

(proper) *that*. Hence **mee·tly**[2] adv., **mee·tness** n. [ME *mête* prob. repr. OE **gemǽte* f. OTeut. *gamǽtje* (*ga-* Y- +*mæta* measure)]

mee·ting, n. In vbl senses, esp.: duel; race-m.; assembly of people for entertainment &c.; assembly for worship; persons assembled, as *address the m.*; *m.-house*, place of worship (usu. disparaging exc. of Quakers); *m.-place* (appointed for m.). [MEET[2] + -ING[1]]

mĕga- in comb. = Gk *megas* great, as: *-cephă·lic*, large-headed; *-lith*, large stone, esp. as monument; *-li·thic*, made of, marked by use of, large stones; *-phone*, instrument for carrying sound a long distance, large speaking-trumpet (v.t., announce with m.-p.); *-pōde, -pŏd*, genus of mound-building birds (lit. large-footed); *-scope*, kind of magic lantern; *-sco·pic*, visible to naked eye; *-thēr·ium*, extinct genus of huge herbivorous sloth-like animals.

mĕ·galo- in comb. = Gk *megas* (fem. *megalē*) great, as: *-ma·nia*, insanity of self-exaltation, passion for big things; *-saur·us*, extinct genus of huge carnivorous lizards.

megă·ss, n. Fibrous residue after expression of sugar from cane. [?]

megi·lp (-g-), n. Vehicle (usu. linseed oil & turpentine) for oil colours. [?]

mē·grim, n. Severe headache usu. on one side only; whim, fancy; (pl.) low spirits, vapours; (pl.) staggers, vertigo, in horses &c. [f. F *migraine* f. L f. Gk HEMI(*krania* f. *kranion* skull)]

meiō·sis (mī-), n. = LITOTES. [Gk *meiōsis* (*meioō* lessen, f. *meiōn* less, see -OSIS)]

mei·stersinger (mī-), n. pl. German lyric poets of 14th–16th cc. organized in guilds & having elaborate technique. [G (*master*)]

melanchō·lia, n. Emotional mental disease marked by depression & ill-grounded fears. [LL, see MELANCHOLY]

melanchŏ·lic, a. Melancholy; liable to melancholy. [f. LL f. Gk *melagkholikos* (as foll., see -IC)]

mĕ·lancholy, n. & a. (Habitual or constitutional tendency to) sadness & depression; pensive sadness; (adj., of persons) sad, gloomy; (of things) saddening, depressing. [(adj. f. n.) OF (*-lie*) f. L f. Gk *melagkholia* (*melas* black *kholē* bile)]

mélange (F), n. Mixture, medley. [F (*mêler* mix, as MEDDLE)]

mĕ·lanism, n. Darkness of colour resulting from abnormal development of black pigment in epidermis, hair, &c. [f. Gk *melas -anos* black + -ISM]

melanŏ·chrōi, n. pl. (anthrop.). Smooth-haired class of men with dark hair & pale complexion. [f. Gk *melanokhroos* (*melas* black + *khroa* skin)]

melanō·sis, n. Morbid deposit, abnormal development, of black pigment in tissue; black cancer. Hence **melanŏ·tic** a. [Gk *melanōsis* f. *melanoō* blacken (*melas* black), see -OSIS]

mêlée (mĕ·lā), n. Mixed fight, skirmish; lively debate. [F, as MEDLEY]

mĕ·lic, a. (Of poem, esp. Gk lyric) meant to be sung. [f. Gk *melikos* (*melos* song, -IC)]

mĕ·linite, n. An explosive of French invention. [f. F *mélinite* f. Gk *mēlinos* (*mēlon* apple), see -ITE[1]]

mē·liorate, v.t. & i. Improve. Hence **meliora·tion** n. [f. LL *meliorare* (as foll.), -ATE[3]]

mē·liorism, n. Doctrine that the world may be made better by human effort. So **me·liorist** n. [L *melior* better + -ISM]

me·llay, n. (archaic). = MÊLÉE.

melli·ferous, a. Yielding, producing, honey. [f. L *mellifer* (*mel* honey, see -FEROUS)]

melli·fluous, a. (Of voice, words) sweet as honey. So **melli·fluence** n., **melli·fluent** a. [f. L *mellifluus* (*mel* honey, *fluere* flow) + -OUS]

me·llow, a. (-er, -est), & v.t. & i. (Of fruit) soft, sweet, & juicy; (of wine) well-matured; (of earth) rich, loamy; (of character) softened by age or experience; (of sound, colour, light) full & pure without harshness; genial, jovial; partly intoxicated; (v.t. & i.) make, become, m. Hence **me·llowly**[2] adv., **me·llowness** n. [(vb f. adj.) perh. f. OE *melo* MEAL[1]]

melō·deon, -dion, -dium, n. Early form of American organ; kind of accordion. [f. MELODY]

melō·dious, a. Of, producing, melody; sweet-sounding. Hence **melo·diously**[2] adv., **melo·diousness** n. [f. OF *melodieus* (as MELODY, see -OUS)]

mĕ·lodist, n. Singer; composer of melodies. [f. MELODY + -IST]

mĕ·lodize, v.i. & t. Make melody; make melodious. [f. MELODY + -IZE]

mĕlodra·ma (-rah-), n. Sensational dramatic piece with violent appeals to emotions & happy ending; language, behaviour, suggestive of this; (formerly) play with songs interspersed. Hence **melodramă·tic** a., **melodrama·tically** adv., **melodră·matist** n., **melodră·matize** v.t. [earlier *-drame* f. F *mélodrame* (Gk *melos* music + F *drame* DRAMA)]

mĕ·lody, n. Sweet music; musical arrangement of words; arrangement of single notes in musically expressive succession; principal part in harmonized music, air. [f. OF *melodie* f. LL f. Gk *melōidia* f. *melōidos* musical (*melos* song + *-aoidos* singing f. *aeidō* sing)]

mĕ·lon, n. Kinds of gourd, esp. WATER *m.* [F, f. LL *melonem* (nom. *-lo*), prob. shortened f. L (*-po*) f. Gk *mēlopepōn* (*mēlon* apple + *pepōn* gourd f. *pepōn* ripe)]

Melpŏ·mенē, n. The muse of tragedy. [Gk]

melt[1], n. Melted metal; amount melted at a time. [f. foll.]

melt², v.i. & t. (p.p. *melted, mōlten*). Become liquefied by heat; *m. away*, disappear thus: (colloq., of person) suffer extreme heat; (of tender food) *it melts* (is easily dissolved) *in the mouth*; (of clouds) break *into rain*; (of person, heart, feelings) be softened by or *with* pity or love, dissolve *into tears*, esp. *the melting mood*, whence **me·lting**LY² adv.; dwindle *away*; (of sound) be soft & liquid; pass imperceptibly *into* (another form); reduce (metal &c.) to liquid condition by heat; *m. down* (plate &c., to use the metal as raw material); *go into the melting-pot* (fig.), be revolutionized; soften (person, feelings). [OE (1) *meltan* intr. (2) *mieltan* trans.; cf. ON *melta* digest]

me·lton, n. Kind of cloth for men's clothes; *M. Mowbray pie*, kind of pasty. [*M. Mowbray*, in Leics.]

me·mber, n. Part, organ, of body, esp. limb; *unruly m.*, tongue; (fig.) *m. of Christ*, Christian; constituent portion of complex structure; person belonging to a society &c.; *M.* (one formally elected to take part in proceedings) *of Parliament* (abbr. *M.P.*); part, branch, of political body; division, clause, of sentence; group of figures, part of numerical expression. Hence **(-)member**ED², **me·mber**LESS, aa. [f. F *membre* f. L *membrum* limb]

me·mbership, n. Being a member; number of members; (vulg.) members. [-SHIP]

me·mbrāne, n. Pliable sheet-like connective tissue or lining in animal or vegetable body; morbid formation in some diseases; skin of parchment, forming part of a roll. So **membran**A·CEOUS, **membrā·**NEOUS, **me·mbran**OUS, aa. [f. L *membrana* m., parchment, as prec.]

me·mbrum virī·lĕ, n. =PENIS. [L, =male member]

meme·nto, n. (pl. *-oes, -os*). Object serving as reminder or warning, or kept as memorial of person or event; *m. mori* (=remember you must die), warning or reminder of death (e.g. skull). [L, imperat. of *meminisse* remember]

memoir (mĕ·mwar), n. Record of events, history written from personal knowledge or special sources of information; (auto)-biography; essay on learned subject specially studied by the writer. [f. F *mémoire* masc., spec. use of *mémoire* fem. MEMORY]

me·morabĭ·lia, n. pl. Memorable things. [L, neut. pl. as foll.]

mĕ·morable, a. Worth remembering, not to be forgotten. Hence **memora**BI·LITY n., **me·morab**LY² adv. [f. L *memorabilis* (*memorare* bring to mind f. *memor* mindful, -BLE)]

memora·ndum, n. (pl. *-da, -dums*; abbr. *memo.*). Note to help the memory; record of events &c. for future use; (Law) document recording terms of contract &c.; informal letter without signature &c., usu. on paper headed *M.* [L, neut. sing. gerundive as prec.]

memor·ial, a. & n. (Of statue, festival, &c.) serving to commemorate; of memory; m. object, custom, &c.; record, chronicle, (usu. pl.); informal State paper of various kinds; statement of facts as basis of petition &c. Hence **memor·ial**IST n. [OF, f. L *memorialis* (as MEMORY, see -AL)]

memor·ialize, v.t. Commemorate; address memorial to (person). [prec. + -IZE]

memor·ia te·chnica, n. System, contrivance, used to assist memory. [L, =artificial memory]

me·morize, v.t. Put on record; (U.S.) commit to memory. [f. foll. + -IZE]

mĕ·mory, n. Faculty of remembering; this in an individual, as *a good, bad, m.* (*convenient* or *accommodating m.*, that retains only what it is to one's interest to remember); recollection; *in m. of*, as a record of, to keep alive the m. of; posthumous repute, as *his m. has been censured, of blessed, happy*, &c., *m.* (used esp. of deceased princes &c.); length of time over which m. extends, as *beyond, within, the m. of men, within living m.* [f. OF *memoire* f. L *memoria* (*memor* mindful f. root *mer-* remember)]

mem-sahib (-sah·ib), n. (In India) European married lady. [f. MA'AM + SAHIB]

-men, suf. in L wds, often side by side with L *-mentum* -MENT & w. same meaning, as *fundamen-tum*. Many wds of slightly technical or learned use, as *acumen, stamen, gravamen, albumen, cognomen, regimen, specimen*; cf. *crime*, shortened in F f. L *crimen*.

mĕ·nace¹, n. (literary). Threat. [OF, f. L *minacia* (*minax -acis* f. *minari* threaten)]

mĕ·nace², v.t. Threaten. Hence **me·nacing**LY² adv. [f. F *menacer* f. pop. L **minaciare* (as prec.)]

ménage (mĕnah·zh), n. Household management; domestic establishment. [f. OF *manaige* f. pop. L **mansionaticum* (as MANSION, see -AGE)]

menă·gerie (-jerĭ), n. Collection of wild animals in cages &c. [f. F *ménagerie* (as prec., see -ERY)]

mend¹, n. Repaired hole in material &c.; *on the m.*, improving in health or (of affairs &c.) condition. [f. foll.]

mend², v.t. & i. Restore to sound condition, repair, (broken articles, clothes, roads, &c.); *m.* (correct) one's *ways*; *least said soonest mended* (rectified); *m.* (add fuel to) *fire*; cut to required shape (quill pen); (intr.) regain health; *m.* (improve state of) *matters*; *m.* (quicken) one's *pace*; *m. or end*, improve or abolish. Hence **me·nd**ABLE a. [f. AMEND v., but found earlier]

mendā·cious, a. Lying, untruthful.

Hence or cogn. **menda·cious**LY² adv., **mendă·**CITY n. [f. L *mendax* f. root of *mentiri* lie, see -ACIOUS]

Me·ndelism, n. A theory of heredity tending to reduce to numerical law the recurrence of inherited characters. So **Mendē·lian** a. & n. [G. J. *Mendel,* 1822–84]

me·ndicant, a. & n. Begging; *m. friars* (living solely on alms); (n.) beggar. Hence or cogn. **me·ndic**ANCY, **mendĭ·**CITY, nn. [f. L *mendicare* (*mendicus* beggar), see -ANT]

menhā·den, n. Fish of herring family, used for manure, & yielding valuable oil. [Amer. Ind. *munnawhatteaug*]

mĕ·nhir (-ēr), n. Tall upright monumental stone found in Europe, Africa, & Asia. [f. Breton *men hir* long stone]

mē·nial, a. & n. (Of service) servile; (of servant, usu. contempt.) domestic; (n.) m. servant. Hence **mē·nial**LY² adv. [AF, f. OF *mesnie* household (obs. E *meinie*) f. pop. L **mansionata* (as MANSION, see -ADE)]

mē·ninx, n. (usu. in pl. *meni·ngēs*). Any of three membranes enveloping brain & spinal cord (*dura mater, arachnoid, pia mater*). Hence **meni·nge**AL a., **meningi·**TIS, **meni·ngo**CELE, nn. [Gk *mēninx*]

meni·scus, n. Lens convex on one side, concave on the other; (Math.) figure of crescent form. [f. Gk *mēniskos* crescent (*mēnē* moon)]

mēno- in comb. Of the menses, as: *-pause* final cessation, *-rrhā·gia,* excessive flow, *-rrhoe·a,* ordinary flow, of the menses. [f. Gk *mēn* month]

mēno·logy, n. Calendar, esp. that of Greek Church, with biographies of saints. [f. late Gk *mēnologion* (*mēn* month + *logos* account)]

me·nsēs, n. pl. Flow of blood from mucous coat of uterus of female, occurring normally at intervals of lunar month. [L, pl. of *mensis* month]

Me·nshevik, n. Russian socialist of the more moderate party (cf. BOLSHEVIK). [Russ., = minority party, cf. BOLSHEVIK]

mens sā·na in cor·porĕ sā·no, L phr. = sound mind in sound body, used esp. as expressing the ideal of education.

me·nstrual, a. Of the menses, so **me·nstru**OUS a.; (Astr.) monthly. [f. F *menstruel* f. L *menstrualis* (as MENSTRUUM, see -AL)]

me·nstruate, v.i. Discharge the menses. Hence **menstru**A·TION n. [f. L *menstruare* (as foll.), see -ATE³]

me·nstruum, n. (pl. *-a*). Solvent (lit. & fig.). [neut. of L *menstruus* monthly (*mensis* month), named as analogue of menses]

me·nsurable (-sher-), a. Measurable, having fixed limits; (Mus.) having fixed rhythm. [F, f. LL *mensurabilis* (*mensurare* f. *mensura* MEASURE, see -BLE)]

me·nsural, a. Of measure; (Mus.) = prec. [f. med. L *mensuralis* (as MEASURE, see -AL)]

mensura·tion, n. Measuring; (Math.) rules for finding lengths, areas, & volumes. [f. LL *mensuratio* (as MENSURABLE, see -ATION)]

-ment, suf. forming nn. expr. result or means of vbl action (*atonement*); some formed in L (*fragment*), some in F (*abridgement*), some in E on L, F, or E vbs; a few are on adjj. (*oddment*; *funniment,* perh. on anal. of *merriment,* which is really f. obs. vb *merry*); *-y* of first element is changed to *-i-*. [OF, f. L *-mentum*]

me·ntal¹, a. Of the mind; done by the mind, as *m. arithmetic* (performed without use of written figures); *m. patient* (under care for disordered mind); *m.* RESERVATION. Hence **me·ntal**LY² adv. [F, f. LL *mentalis* (*mens -ntis* mind, see -AL)]

me·ntal², a. Of the chin. [F, f. L *mentum* chin, see -AL]

menta·lity, n. The being mental or in or of the mind; (degree of) intellectual power; (loosely, in recent use) mind, disposition, character. [f. MENTAL¹ + -ITY]

menta·tion, n. Mental action; state of mind. [f. L *mens -ntis* mind, see -ATION]

me·nthol, n. Camphor-like substance got from oil of peppermint &c.; *m. pencil* &c., piece of m. & spermaceti for relief of facial neuralgia. [G, f. L *mentha* mint, see -OL(2)]

me·ntion¹, n. Mentioning, naming, (*of* thing); *honourable m.,* award of merit to candidate in examination, work of art, &c., not entitled to prize. [F, f. L *mentionem* (*men-* root of *mens* mind, see -ION)]

me·ntion², v.t. Refer to, remark upon, specify by name, (esp. thing not obviously essential to context, as *this was expressly mentioned*; *that*); (in deprecation of apology or thanks) *don't m. it*; (introducing fact or thing of secondary or, as rhet. artifice, of primary importance) *not to m.* [f. F *mentionner* (as prec.)]

me·ntor, n. Experienced & trusted adviser. [F, f. Gk *Mentōr* adviser of Telemachus (root *men-* think)]

mĕ·nu (-ōō, *or as F*), n. Bill of fare. [F adj. = small, n. = detailed list]

Mephistŏ·phelēs, n. Evil spirit to whom Faust, in German legend, sold his soul; fiendish person. Hence **Mephistophele·**AN, **Mephistophē·**LIAN, aa. [G, etym. dub.]

mephī·tis, n. Noxious emanation, esp. from the earth; noisome or poisonous stench. So **mephi·**TIC a. [L]

mer·cantile, a. Of trade, commercial; *m. theory* (that money is the only wealth); *m. marine,* shipping employed in commerce; mercenary, fond of bargaining.

Hence **mer·cantil**ISM, **mer·cantil**IST, nn. [F, f. It. *mercantil* (as MERCHANT)]

Merca·tor. See PROJECTION.

mer·cenary, a. & n. Working merely for money or other reward; hired (soldier). Hence **mer·cenari**NESS n. [f. L *mercenarius* (*merces -edis* reward, see -ARY¹)]

mer·cer, n. Dealer in textile fabrics, esp. silks & other costly materials. Hence **mer·c**ERY(1) n. [f. F *mercier* f. pop. L **merciarius* (*merx mercis* goods, -ARY¹)]

mer·cerize, v.t. Prepare (cotton goods) for dyeing by use of chemicals; (p.p.) having silky gloss due to mercerizing. [J. *Mercer*, patentee, + -IZE]

mer·chandise (-z), n. Commodities of commerce, goods for sale. [f. F *marchandise* (as foll., see -ISE)]

mer·chant, n. & a. Wholesale trader, esp. with foreign countries; *m. prince*, wealthy *m.*; LAW¹ *m.*; *m. ship, merchantman*, (ship conveying merchandise); *m.* (mercantile marine) *service*; *-m.* (slang), one given to — (*speed-m.*, reckless motorist; *lob-m.*, slow bowler). [f. OF *marchant* f. pop. L *mercatare* frequent. of *mercari* trade (*merx mercis* merchandise), see -ANT]

mer·chantable, a. Salable, marketable. [f. *merchant* v. (now rare) f. OF *marcheander* (as prec.) + -ABLE]

mer·ciful, a. Having, showing, or feeling mercy. Hence **mer·ciful**LY² adv., **mer·ciful**NESS n. [-FUL]

mer·ciless, a. Pitiless, showing no mercy. Hence **mer·ciless**LY² adv., **mer·ciless**NESS n. [-LESS]

mercūr·ial, a. & n. Sprightly, ready-witted, & volatile, whence **mercuria·l**ITY n.; of, containing, mercury; (*M-*) of the planet Mercury; (n.) m. drug, whence **mercur·ial**ISM(5) n., **mercur·ial**IZE(5) v.t. Hence **mercur·ial**LY² adv. [f. F *mercuriel* (as MERCURY, see -AL)]

mer·cury, n. (*M-*) Roman god of eloquence, skill, thieving, &c., & messenger of gods, messenger (joc., & often in newspaper titles); (*M-*) planet nearest to sun; a white normally liquid metal usu. got from cinnabar & used in barometers, thermometers, amalgams, & mirrors (*the m. is rising*, weather or temper is improving), quicksilver, whence **mercūr·**IC, **mer·cur**OUS, aa. (chem.); (fig.) liveliness (*has no m. in him*). [f. L *Mercurius*, prob. f. *merx -rcis* merchandise]

mer·cy, n. Compassion shown by one to another who is in his power & has no claim to kindness (*have m. on* or *upon*, *show m. to*; *m.!*, *m. on* or *upon us!*, appeals, or excll. usu. playful of terror or surprise); compassionateness; *at the m. of*, wholly in the power of, liable to danger or harm from; *that is a m.* (blessing, thing to be thankful for); (facet.) *left to the tender mm. of*, exposed to probable rough handling by; *m.-seat*, golden covering of Ark of Covenant, throne of God. [f. F *merci* f. L *mercedem* (nom. *-ces*) reward, (LL) pity]

mere¹ (mēr), n. Lake, pond. [OE, cf. Du. & G *meer* sea, cogn. w. L *mare* sea]

mere² (mēr), a. That is solely what the noun implies, as *a m. swindler, the merest buffoonery*; (Law) *m. right* (without possession). Hence **mere·**LY² adv. [f. L *merus* unmixed]

mĕrĕtrĭ·cious (-shus), a. Of, befitting, a harlot; (of ornament, literary style, &c.) showily attractive. Hence **meretri·cious**LY² adv., **meretri·cious**NESS n. [f. L *meretricius* f. *meretrix* harlot (*mereri* earn, see -TRIX) + -OUS]

merga·nser, n. Diving fish-eating duck. [f. L *mergus* diver + *anser* goose]

merge, v.t. & i. Lose, cause (thing) to lose, character or identity *in* (another), esp. sink (title, estate, *in* greater one). Hence **mer·g**ENCE n. [f. law F *merger* f. L *mergere mers-* dip]

mer·ger, n. Merging; combine. [-ER⁴]

merĭ·dian, n. & a. Circle passing through celestial poles & zenith of any place on earth's surface; circle lying in the plane of this & passing through the place & the poles, as *m. of Greenwich* (of longitude 0° in British maps); point at which sun or star attains highest altitude; prime, full splendour; *calculated for the m.* (to suit the tastes &c.) *of* (place, people); (adj.) of noon, (fig.) of the period of greatest splendour, vigour, &c. [(n. f. adj.) f. OF *meridien* f. L *meridianus* (*meridies* midday f. *medius* middle + *dies* day, see -AN)]

merĭ·dional, a. & n. Of (the inhabitants of) the south of Europe; of a meridian; (n.) inhabitant of the south (esp. of France). [f. F *méridional* f. LL *meridionalis* (irreg. as prec., -AL)]

meri·ngue (-ăng), n. Confection of sugar, white of eggs, &c., small cake of this. [F]

meri·no (-rē-), n. (Also *m. sheep*) kind of sheep with fine wool; soft woollen or wool-&-cotton material like French cashmere, orig. of m. wool; fine woollen yarn. [Sp., prob. f. L *majorinus* of a larger kind (*major* greater, see -INE¹)]

mĕ·rit, n., & v.t. Quality of deserving well; excellence, worth; (usu. pl.) thing that entitles to reward or gratitude; *make a m. of*, view, represent, (one's own conduct) as meritorious; *the mm.*, intrinsic rights & wrongs (of case &c., esp. Law); *judge* (proposal &c.) *on its mm.* (with only its intrinsic excellences &c. in view); (v.t.) deserve (reward, punishment). [(vb f. F *mériter*) f. OF *merite* f. L *meritum* neut. p.p. of *merēri* earn, deserve]

mĕritor·ious, a. (Of person or act) deserving reward, praise, or gratitude (often as term of limited praise, = well-meant, well-meaning). Hence **meritor·ious**LY² adv., **meritor·ious**NESS n. [f. L *meritorius* (*merērimerit-* earn, see -ORY) + -OUS]

merle, n. (archaic, Sc.). Blackbird. [F, f. L *merulus, -la*]

mer·lin, n. Kind of falcon. [f. AF *merilun* f. OF *esmerillon* f. com.-Rom. **smerillo* (med. L *smerillus*), perh. of Teut. orig.]

mer·lon, n. Part of embattled parapet between two embrasures. [F, f. It. *merlone* (*merlo* battlement, perh. f. *mergola* dim. f. L *mergae* pitchfork; see -OON)]

mer·maid, n. Half-human being, with head & trunk of woman & tail of fish. So **mer·**MAN n. [f. MERE¹ + MAID]

mĕro- in comb. = Gk *meros* part, in senses 'partly', 'partial', as: *-blast*, ovum that is only partly germinal; *-hē·dral*, (of crystal) having less than full number of faces admissible.

-merous, suf. (bot.) = having so many parts, as *dimerous, 5-merous*. [f. Gk as prec. + -OUS]

Mĕrovi·ngian (-j-), a. & n. (King) of the Frankish line founded by Clovis & reigning in Gaul & Germany c. 500–750. [f. F *Merovingien* f. med. L *Merovingi* of Germanic orig.]

me·rriment, n. Hilarious enjoyment, mirth, fun. [f. obs. vb *merry* be merry + -MENT]

me·rry¹, n. Kind of black cherry. [f. F *merise* etym. dub., prob. taken as pl.]

me·rry², a. Joyous, mirthful; *m.* (pleasant) *England*; *the m. monarch*, Charles II; slightly tipsy; *make m.*, be festive; *make m. over*, make fun of; *m. andrew*, mountebank's assistant, clown, buffoon, (also fig.); *m.* DANCERS; *m.-go-round*, revolving machine with wooden horses or cars; *m.-making*, festivity; *me·rry-thought*, forked bone between neck & breast of bird. Hence **me·rri**LY² adv., **me·rri**NESS n. (rare). [OE *myr(i)ge*, whence *myrgdh* MIRTH, cf. MDu. *merchte* mirth; perh. f. OTeut. *murgjo-* short, prob. cogn. w. Gk *brakhus*]

mĕsalliance (F), n. Marriage with person of inferior social position.

mesdames, mesdemoiselles. See MADAME, MADEMOISELLE.

mesee·ms, v.i. (archaic). It seems to me. [*me* dat. + SEEMS]

mesembria·nthemum, n. Fig-marigold. [f. Gk *mesēmbria* noon + *anthemon* flower]

mĕ·sentery, n. Fold of peritoneum attaching some part of intestinal canal to posterior wall of abdomen. Hence **mesente·r**IC a., **mesenter**I·TIS n. [f. med. L f. Gk *mesenterion* (MESO- + *enteron* intestine)]

mesh¹, n. Open space, interstice, of net; (pl.) network, (fig.) snare; (Physiol., pl.) interlaced structure; (of teeth of wheels) *in m.*, engaged. [cogn. w. OE *max* net]

mesh², v.t. & i. Catch in net (lit. & fig.); (of teeth of wheel) be engaged (*with* others). [f. prec.]

me·sial (mĕz-, mĕs-), a. Of, in, directed towards, middle line of a body. Hence **me·sial**LY² adv. [irreg. f. Gk *mesos* middle + -IAL]

me·smerism (mĕz-), n. Hypnotic state, usu. involving insensibility to pain & muscular rigidity, produced on patient by operator's influence over will & nervous system; doctrine concerning, influence producing, this. Hence **mesmĕ·r**IC a., **me·smer**IST, **mesmeriz**A·TION, nn., **me·smer**IZE(4) v.t. [F. A. *Mesmer*, Austrian physician, d. 1815, + -ISM]

mesne (mēn), a. Intermediate, as *m. profits* (received from estate by wrongful tenant between two dates); *m. process*, proceedings in suit intervening between primary & final process; (Feud.) *m. lord* (holding of superior lord). [law F, = MEAN²]

mĕso- in comb. = Gk *mesos* middle, intermediate, as: *-ga·ster*, membrane attaching stomach to dorsal wall of abdomen; *-li·thic*, of stone age between palaeolithic & neolithic; *-phyll*, inner tissue of leaf; *-zo·ic*, of second geological period (cf. CAINOZOIC, PALAEO*zoic*).

Me·spot, slang abbr. of *Mesopotamia.*

me·squit(e) (-kēt), n. N.-Amer. leguminous tree; (also *m.-grass*) kinds of grass growing near this. [f. Mex. Sp. *mezquite*]

mess¹, n. Portion of liquid or pulpy food; *m. of pottage*, material comfort &c. for which something higher is sacrificed (*Gen.* xxv. 29–34); liquid or mixed food for hounds &c.; concoction, medley; dirty or untidy state of things; *make a m. of*, bungle (undertaking); company of persons who take meals together, esp. (Army, Navy) each of several parties into which regiment or ship's company is divided; meal so taken, as *at m., go to m.* (often attrib., as *m.-jacket*, coat worn at m.); *messmate*, one of the same (usu. ship's) m. Hence **me·ss**Y², a. (*-y floor, food, job*), **me·ssi**LY² adv., **me·ssi**NESS n. [f. OF *mes* f. LL *missum*, p.p. of *mittere* send]

mess², v.t. & i. Make a mess of, dirty, (thing); muddle (business); potter *about*; take one's meals (*with* or abs.). [f. prec.]

me·ssage¹ (-ĭj), n. Oral or written communication sent by one person to another; prophet's inspired communication. [F, f. pop. L **missaticum* (*mittere miss-* send, see -AGE)]

me·ssage², v.t. Send as a message; transmit (plan &c.) by signalling &c. [f. prec.]

me·ssenger, n. One who carries a message; paper sent up string from flier to kite; endless rope passing from capstan to cable to haul it in. [f. F *messager* (as prec., see -ER¹); for *-n-* cf. *passenger*]

Messi·ah, n. Promised deliverer of Jews; Christ as this; liberator of oppressed people or country. Hence **Messi·ah**SHIP n. [f. F *Messie* f. L f. Gk *Messias* f. Heb. *mashiaḥ* anointed (*mashaḥ* anoint)]

messiă·nic, a. Of the, inspired by hope of or belief in a, Messiah. [prec., -AN, -IC]

messieurs· (-yer), n. pl. Pl. of MONSIEUR or (in abbr. form *Messrs*, pron. mĕ·sserz) of Mr, used esp. as prefix to name of firm, or introducing list of gentlemen.

me·ssuage (-swĭj), n. (law). Dwelling-house with outbuildings & land assigned to its use. [AF, prob. corrupt. of *mesnage* MENAGE]

mesti·zo (-tē-), n. (pl. *-os*). Spanish or Portuguese half-caste, esp. child of Spaniard & Amer.-Indian. [Sp., f. pop. L *mixticius* (*miscēre* MIX)]

mĕta- in comb. (before vowel *met-*, before aspirate *meth-*) = Gk *meta* with, after; sometimes w. sense 'change'.

metă·bolism, n. Process, in organism or single cell, by which nutritive material is built up into living matter (*constructive m.*) or protoplasm is broken down into simpler substances (*destructive m.*). So **metabŏ·l**IC a., **meta·bol**IZE(3) v.t. [f. Gk *metabolē* change f. META(*ballō* throw) change + -ISM]

metacar·pus, n. Part of hand between wrist & fingers. [f. META- + Gk *karpos* wrist]

mē·tage(-ĭj), n. Official measuring of load of coal &c.; duty paid for this. [f. METE + -AGE]

metagĕ·nesis, n. Alternation between sexual & asexual reproduction. So **metagen**E·TIC a. [META- + GENESIS]

mĕ·tal, n., & v.t. (-ll-). Any of a class of substances represented by gold, silver, copper, iron, lead, & tin, but containing many substances that have few of the characteristics of these; BELL[1], BRITANNIA, GUN, WHITE, YELLOW, *m.*; HEAVY *m.*; material used for making glass, in molten state; (also *road-m.*) broken stone for macadam roads or railway; (pl.) rails of a railway line (*train leaves the mm.*, is derailed); (v.t.) furnish, fit, with m., mend (road) with m. [(vb f. n.) OF, f. L f. Gk *metallon* mine, perh. cogn. w. *metallaō* seek after]

metă·llic, a. Of metal(s); *m. currency*, gold, silver, copper, &c., cf. PAPER; characteristic of metals, as *m. lustre* (peculiar sheen of metals), *m. sound*. So **me·tal**LINE[1] a. [f. L f. Gk *metallikos* (as METAL, see -IC)]

me·tallize, v.t. Render metallic; vulcanize (rubber). Hence **metalliz**A·TION n. [f. METAL + -IZE]

metallo·graphy, n. Descriptive science of internal structure of metals. [f. Gk *metallographia* (as METAL, see -GRAPHY)]

me·talloid, a. & n. Having form or appearance of metal; non-metallic element. [-OID]

meta·llurgy, n. Art of working metals, esp. of extracting metals from their ores. Hence **metallur·g**IC(AL) aa., **meta·llurg**IST n. [f. Gk *metallourgos* metal-worker (*metallon* METAL + *-ergos* -worker), see -Y[1]]

me·tamere (-ēr), n. (zool.). One of several similar segments of a body. [f. META- + Gk *meros* part]

metamĕ·ric, a. (Chem.) having same composition & molecular weight, but different chemical properties; (Zool.) of metameres. So **meta·mer**ISM n. (chem., zool.). [as prec. + -IC]

metamor·phic, a. Of, marked by, metamorphosis; (Geol., of rock) that has undergone transformation by natural agencies, whence **metamor·ph**ISM n. [irreg. f. META- + Gk *morphē* form + -IC]

metamor·phose (-ōz), v.t. Change in form, turn (*to, into*, new form); change nature of. [f. F *métamorphoser* (*métamorphose*, as foll.)]

metamor·phosis, n. (pl. *-osēs*). Change of form (by magic or by natural development &c.); changed form; change of character, conditions, &c. [L, f. Gk *metamorphōsis* f. META(*morphoō* f. *morphē* form)]

me·taphor, n. Application of name or descriptive term to an object to which it is not literally applicable (e.g. *a glaring error*); instance of this; *mixed m.*, combination of inconsistent mm. Hence **metaphŏ·r**ICAL a., **metapho·rical**LY[2] adv. [f. F *métaphore* f. L f. Gk *metaphora* f. META(*pherō* bear) transfer]

me·taphrase (-z), n., & v.t. Translation, esp. word-for-word; (v.t.) put into other words. So **metaphra·st**IC a. [(vb f. n.) f. Gk *metaphrasis* f. META(*phrazō* show) translate]

metaphy·sical, a. Of metaphysics; based on abstract general reasoning; over-subtle; incorporeal; supernatural; visionary. Hence **metaphys·ical**LY[2] adv. [-AL]

metaphy·sics, n. pl. (often treated as sing.). Theoretical philosophy of being & knowing; philosophy of mind; (pop.) abstract or subtle talk, mere theory. So **metaphysi**·CIAN n., **metaphy·sic**IZE(2) v.i. [earlier *-ic*; med. L has *metaphysica* fem. sing. & neut. pl., f. med. Gk *metaphusika* f. Gk *ta meta ta phusika* the works (of Aristotle) placed after the PHYSICS]

me·taplasm, n. (biol.). Part of protoplasm that contains formative material. [META- + *-plasm* as in PROTOPLASM]

metapo·litics, n. pl. Abstract political science (often contempt.). Hence **metapoli·tic**AL a., **metapoliti**·CIAN n. [META-, after METAPHYSICS]

meta·stasis, n. Transference of bodily function, disease, &c., from one part or organ to another; transformation of chemical compounds into others in process of assimilation by an organism. So **metastă·t**IC a. [LL f. Gk, = change, f. *methistēmi* remove (META- + *histēmi* place)]

metatar·sus, n. (anat.). Group of five long bones of foot between tarsus & toes. Hence **metatar·s**AL a. [META-]

meta·thesis, n. (Gram.) transposition of sounds or letters in word; (Chem.). interchange of atoms between two molecules. [LL f. Gk, f. META(*tithēmi* place) transpose]

métayage (mĕ·tāyahzh), n. Land tenure in which farmer pays part (usu. half) of produce as rent to owner, who furnishes stock & seed. [F, irreg. as foll., see -AGE]

métayer (mĕ·tāyā), n. Holder of land on prec. system. [F, f. med. L *medietarius* (*medietas* MOIETY, see -ARY¹)]

mete¹, n. Boundary, boundary stone, esp. (Law) *mm. & bounds.* [OF, f. L *meta* goal]

mete², v.t. (literary). (Poet.). measure; portion *out*, allot, (punishment, reward); *mete-wand, -yard,* (fig.) standard of estimation. [com.-Teut.: OE *metan,* Du. *meten,* G *messen*]

metempi·ric, n. (Also *-ics*) philosophy of things outside the sphere of experience; believer in this. Hence **metempi·ric**AL a., **metempi·ric**IST n. [f. META- + EMPIRIC, after *metaphysics*]

metempsȳchō·sis, n. Transmigration of soul of human being or animal at death into new body of same or different species. Hence **metempsycho·**SIST(2) n. [LL f. Gk (META- + *en* in + *psukhē* soul + -OSIS)]

mē·teor, n. (Any atmospheric phenomenon, esp.) shooting star, small mass of matter from celestial space rendered luminous by collision with earth's atmosphere. [f. Gk *meteōros* lofty, (neut. pl.) atmospheric phenomena (META- + *aeirō* raise)]

mēteŏ·ric, a. Of the atmosphere; dependent on atmospheric conditions; of meteors; (fig.) dazzling, rapid. [prec. + -IC]

mē·teorite, n. Fallen meteor, meteoric stone. So **mē·teoro**LITE n. [METEOR + -ITE¹]

mē·teorograph, n. Apparatus recording meteorological phenomena. [METEOR, -GRAPH]

mē·teoroid, n. Body moving through space, of same nature as those which by passing through atmosphere become visible as meteors. Hence **meteoroi·d**AL a. [-OID]

meteoro·logy, n. Study of motions & phenomena of atmosphere, esp. for weather forecast; atmospheric character (*of* region). Hence or cogn. **meteoro·lo·gi**C(AL) aa., **meteorolo·gical**LY² adv., **meteoro·log**IST n. [f. Gk *meteōrologia* (as METEOR, -LOGY)]

mē·ter, n. Person, thing, that measures, esp. *gas, water,* &c., *-m.,* instruments for recording volume of gas &c. supplied. [f. METE + -ER¹, prob. after wds w. foll. suf., as *gasometer*]

-meter, suf. in names of measuring instruments on Gk nn. (but not on Gk anal.), as *barometer,* L nn., as *calorimeter,* mod. wds as if Gk or L, as *gasometer,* or without assim. to Gk or L, as *ammeter.* [f. Gk *metron* measure]

methe·glin, n. (hist., dial.). Spiced kind of mead. [f. W *meddyglyn* (*meddyg* healing f. L *medicus* + *llyn* liquor)]

methi·nks, v.i. (archaic; past *methought* pron. -awt). It seems to me. [ME dat. + THINKS]

mĕ·thod, n. Special form of procedure esp. in any branch of mental activity, whence **methodo·**LOGY n.; orderly arrangement of ideas; orderliness, regular habits; *there's m. in his &c. madness,* (joc.) his conduct or proposal is not so mad as it seems; (Nat. Hist.) scheme of classification. Hence or cogn. **metho·d**ICAL a., **metho·dical**LY² adv. [f. L f. Gk *methodos* (META- + *hodos* way)]

me·thodist, n. (*M-*) member of any of several religious bodies originating in the evangelistic movement of Charles & John Wesley & George Whitefield, whence **methodi·st**IC(AL) aa., **methodi·stical**LY² adv.; (contempt.) person of strict religious views; one who follows a method, esp. in Nat. Hist. Hence **me·thod**ISM n. [-IST]

me·thodize, v.t. Reduce to order, arrange in orderly manner. [-IZE]

methought. See METHINKS.

mĕ·thyl, n. The base of wood-spirit, formic acid, & many organic compounds. Hence **methȳ·l**IC a. [f. F *méthyle* (Gk *methu* wine + *hulē* wood)]

me·thylate, v.t. Mix, impregnate, (esp. spirit of wine, to make it unfit for drinking, so as to exempt it from duties) with methyl, as *methylated spirit.* [-ATE³]

meti·culous, a. Over-scrupulous about minute details. Hence **meti·culous**LY² adv. [f. L *meticulosus* (*metus* fear, see -CULE, -OUS)]

métier (mĕ·tyā), n. One's trade, profession, or line. [F]

mē·tis, n. Offspring of white & American Indian, esp. in Canada. [f. F *métis* (as MESTIZO)]

metŏ·nymy, n. Substitution of the name of an attribute for that of the thing meant (e.g. *crown* for *king*). Hence **metonȳ·m**ICAL a., **metony·mical**LY² adv. [f. LL f. Gk *metōnumia* (META- + *onoma* name)]

mĕ·tope (-opĭ, -ōp), n. (Arch.). Square space between triglyphs in Doric frieze. [f. L f. Gk *metopē* (META- + *opē* hole for beam)]

mē·tre¹ (*-er*), n. Any form of poetic rhythm, determined by character & number of feet; metrical group, esp. pair of feet in iambic & other rhythms. Hence **metri·**CIAN, **mĕ·tr**ICS, **mĕ·tr**IST, nn. [f. L f. Gk *metron* measure]

mē·tre² (*-er*), n. Unit of length in metric system (39·37 in.). [f. F *mètre* (as prec.)]

mĕ·tric, a. Of the METRE²; *m. system,* decimal measuring-system with the metre, & the litre & gramme determined by it, as units of length, capacity, & weight (the prefixing to *metre* &c. of the Greek-derived *deca-*, *hecto-*, *kilo-*, denotes multiplication by 10, 100, 1,000, as *kilometre* 1,000 metres; that of the Latin-derived *deci-*, *centi-*, *milli-*, division by 10, 100, 1,000, as *decilitre* tenth of a litre). [-IC]

mĕ'trical, a. Of, composed in, metre; of, involving, measurement, as *m. geometry*. Hence **me'trical**LY[2] adv. [f. LL f. Gk *metrikos* (as METRE[1], see -IC) + -AL]

metrŏ'logy, n. Science, system, of weights & measures. Hence **metrolo'gical** a. [as METRE[1] + -LOGY]

mĕ'tronōme, n. (mus.). Instrument marking time by means of pendulum. Hence **metronŏ'mic** a. [as METRE[1] + Gk *nomos* law]

metrŏ'polis, n. Chief city of a country; capital; *the m.*, London; metropolitan bishop's see; centre of activity. [L, f. Gk *mētropolis* parent State (*mētēr -tros* mother + *polis* city)]

metropŏ'litan, a. & n. Of a or the metropolis; of an ecclesiastical metropolis; *m.* (*bishop*), bishop having authority over bishops of a province, in the West equivalent to archbishop, in Greek church ranking above archbishop & below patriarch, whence **metropo'litan**ATE[1] (-*at*) n.; inhabitant of a metropolis. [f. LL *metropolitanus* f. Gk *mētropolitēs* (as prec., -ITE[1]), see -AN]

-metry, suf. in names of systems corresp. to instruments in -METER on anal. of Gk *geōmetria* GEOMETRY, but also in hybrids, as *alkalimetry*. [f. Gk *-metria* (*-metrēs* measurer, as METRE[1])]

me'ttle, n. Quality of disposition; natural ardour; spirit, courage; *be on* one's *m.* (incited to do one's best). Hence (-)**mettl**ED[2], **me'ttle**SOME, aa. [var. of METAL n.]

mē'um, n. *M. & tuum*, mine & thine (used to express rights of property). [L, neut. of *meus*]

mew[1], n. (Also *sea-m.*) gull, esp. common gull. [OE *mæw*, cf. Du. *meeuw*, G *möwe*]

mew[2], n., & v.t. Cage for hawks, esp. while moulting; (v.t.) put (hawk) in m., (fig.) shut *up*, confine. [(vb f. n.) f. F *mue* (as foll.)]

mew[3], v.t. (archaic). (Of hawk) moult, shed, (feathers). [f. F *muer* f. L *mutare* change]

mew[4], v.i., & n. (Of cat, sea-birds) utter sound *mew*; this sound, esp. of cat. [imit.]

mewl, mule, v.i. Cry feebly, whimper; mew like cat. [imit., cf. MIAUL]

mews, n. Set of stabling round open yard. [pl. (now used as sing.) of MEW[2]; orig. of royal stables on site of hawks' mews]

me'zzanine (-ēn), n. Low storey between two higher ones (usu. between ground & first floors); (Theatr.) floor beneath stage. [F, f. It. *mezzanino* dim. of *mezzano* f. L *medianus* (*medius* middle, see -AN)]

me'zzo (-dz-), adv. (Mus.) half, moderately, as *m.* FORTE[2], PIANO[1]; *m.-rilie'vo* (-lyāvō), half-relief, in which figures project half their true proportions; *m.-soprano*, (person with, part for) voice between soprano & contralto. [It., f. L *medius* middle)]

me'zzotint (-dz-), n., & v.t. Method of engraving in which plate is roughened uniformly, lights & half-lights being given by scraping away the nap thus produced, deep shadows by leaving it; print produced by this; (v.t.) engrave in m. [(vb f. n.) f. It. *mezzotinto* (also used in E) f. *mezzo* half + *tinto* TINT]

mi (mē), n. (mus.). Third note of octave. [first syllable of L *mira*, see GAMUT]

miaow (mĭow'), n., & v.i. (Make) cry of cat. [imit.]

mia'sma, n. (pl. *-ta*, *-s*). Infectious or noxious emanation, esp. malaria. Hence **mia'sm**AL, **miasma'tic**, aa. [Gk(*miainō* pollute, see -M)]

miau'l, v.i. Cry like cat. [f. F *miauler*, imit.]

mī'ca, n. Any of several minerals composed of silicate of aluminium with other silicates, found in small glittering scales in granite &c., or in crystals; *m.-schist*, *-slate*, slaty rock of quartz & m. Hence **mica'ceous** a. [L, = crumb]

Micaw'ber, n. *M.*, *Mr M.*, *Wilkins M.*, sanguine idler trusting that something good will turn up. Hence **Micaw'ber**ISM(3) n. [person in Dickens's *David Copperfield*]

Mī'chael (-kel), n. An archangel; *Order of St M. & St George*, English civil order of knighthood; *Michaelmas* (mĭ-), feast of St M., Sep. 29, a quarter-day. [f. Heb. *mikhael* who is like God?]

mi'ckle, mu'-, a. & n. (archaic, Sc.). Much, great; a large amount (in prov. *many a little*, or *pickle*, *makes a m.*). [com.-Teut.: OE *micel*, Sw. *mycken*, Da. *meget*, cogn. w. Gk *megas* great]

micro-[1] in comb. = Gk *mikros* small, as: *-cephă'lic* a. & n., (person) with abnormally small head, so *-cĕ'phalous* a.; *-li'thic*, constructed of small stones, marked by monuments so constructed; *-logy*, hair-splitting; *-meter*, instruments for measuring small objects or (Astr.) distances, so *-me'trical*, *-metry*; *-phone*, instrument for intensifying small sounds, esp. the transmitting disk in a telephone receiver; *-pho'tograph* (of microscopic object on magnified scale;) *-phyte*, microscopic plant, esp. bacterium; *-seism* (-sīzm), faint earthquake tremor, whence *-sei'smic*, *-sei'smograph*, *-seismo'logy*; *-spore*, parasitic fungus with small spores, small spore; *-tome*, instrument for cutting thin sections for microscope; *-zyme*, zymotic microbe.

mīcro-[2] (etym. as prec.) prefixed in Physics to unit-names = the millionth part of the unit; *micro-ampere, -coulomb, -farad, -gramme, -litre, -metre, -millimetre, -ohm, -volt.*

mī·crobe, n. Minute living being, plant or animal (esp. of bacteria causing diseases & fermentation). Hence **micrō·bi**AL a., **microbio·**LOGY n. [F (MICRO-[1] + Gk *bios* life)]

mī·crocosm, n. Man viewed as epitome of the universe; any community or complex unity so viewed; miniature representation (*of*). Hence **microco·smi**C a. [f. F *microcosme* f. med. L MICRO [1](*cosmus* f. Gk *kosmos* world)]

mī·cron, n. The millionth of a metre. [f. Gk neut. of *mikros* small]

mi·croscope, n. Instrument magnifying objects by means of lens(es) so as to reveal details invisible to naked eye. [MICRO- + -SCOPE]

microscŏ·pic, a. Of the microscope, whence **microsco·pic**AL a.; too small to be visible (in detail) without microscope. Hence **microsco·pical**LY[2] adv. [-IC]

micro·scopy, n. Use of the microscope. So **micro·scop**IST n. [-Y[1]]

micturi·tion, n. Morbidly frequent desire to make water; (improp.) making water. [f. L *micturire -it-*, desiderative f. *mingere mict-* make water, see -ION]

mid[1], a. (sup. *mi·dmost*). The middle of (usu. after *in*, as *in m. air, career, Channel, course, stream, winter*; also with *from, to*, &c., as *from m. June to m. August*; & in attrib. compounds, as *a m.-winter day*); that is in the middle, medium, half, (*m. iron*, golf iron with medium loft; *m. off, m. on*, = midwicket off, on; *mi·drib*, central rib of leaf; *midway·* adv., in middle of distance between places; *mi·dwicket off* or *on*, fielder near bowler on off, on, side). [com.-Teut.: OE *midd*, OFris. *midde*, OHG *mitti*, cogn. w. Gk *mesos*, L *medius*]

mid[2], prep. (poet.). = AMID.

mi·dday (-d-d-), n. Noon (often attrib.). [OE *middæg*, see MID[1] & DAY]

mi·dden, n. (dial.). Dunghill; *kitchen m.*, prehistoric refuse heap, chiefly of shells & bones. [of Scand. orig.]

mi·ddle[1], a. (not pred.; rare sup. *middlemost*) & n. (Of member of group) so placed as to have same number of members on each side; equidistant from extremities; intermediate in rank, quality, &c.; *m. course, way*, compromise between two extremes; (Gram.) a voice in (esp. Greek) verbs that is passive in form but reflexive or active in sense, cf. DEPONENT; *M.* ENGLISH; *m. age*, between youth & old age; *m.-aged*, of such age; *the M. Ages* (about 1000–1400, or in a wider sense 600–1500); *m. article*, brief essay of literary kind in weekly or other journal often placed between political articles & book-reviews; *m. class*, class of society between upper & lower (often attrib., *m.-class*); *m.* (second) *finger*; *M. Kingdom*, China (orig. of Honan as central & sovereign State); *m. life*, the m. part of life, m. age; *in the m. of*, while (do*ing*), during (process); (Log.) *m.* (*term*), term common to both premisses, *principle of excluded m.* (that anything must be included either under a given term or under its negative); *middleman*, any of the traders through whose hands commodity passes from producer to consumer; *m. weight* (boxing), from 11 st. 4 to 10 st.; (n.) m. point or part (*of*), waist. [OE & Du. *middel*, G *mittel*, f. OTeut. *midjo-* MID]

mi·ddle[2], v.t. (Footb.) return (ball or abs.) from wing to mid field in front of goal; (techn.) place in the middle; (Naut.) fold in the middle. [f. prec.]

mi·ddling, a. & adv. (Commerc., of goods) of the second of three grades, so **mi·ddlings** n. pl. (also in spec. senses, flour of medium fineness, & comminuted bran); moderately good; second-rate; (adv.) moderately, as *m. good*; (colloq.). fairly well (in health), as *I am only m.* Hence **mi·ddling**LY[2] adv. [prob. of Sc. orig., f. MID[1] + -LING[1] & [2] (confused)]

mi·ddy n. See MIDSHIP.

mi·dge, n. Kinds of gnat-like insect; small person. [OE *mycg*, cf. Du. *mug*, G *mücke*]

mi·dget, n. Extremely small person, esp. when exhibited as curiosity; photograph of very small size. [f. prec. + -ET[1]]

mi·dland, n. & a. Middle part of country; (pl.) *the* middle counties of England; (adj.) of, in, the m. or mm. [MID + LAND]

mi·dnight, n. The middle of the night, 12 o'clock; intense darkness (often attrib.). [OE *midniht* (MID + NIGHT)]

mi·drăsh, n. (pl. *-shim*). Ancient Jewish commentary on part of Hebrew Scriptures. [Heb.]

mi·driff, n. Diaphragm. [OE *midhrif* (*midd* MID + *hrif* belly)]

mi·dship, n. Middle part of ship or boat; *mi·dshipman* (abbr. *middy*), rank between naval cadet & sub-lieutenant; *midships*, = AMIDSHIPS. [MID + SHIP]

midst, n., adv., & prep. *In the m. of*, among; *in our, your, m.*, among us, you; (adv., only in phr.) *first, m., & last*; (prep., poet.) in the m. of. [(1) MID + *-st*, see -ES, (2) sup. of MID]

mi·dsummer, n. Period of summer solstice, about June 21; *M. day*, June 24, a quarter-day; *m.* (the height of) *madness*. [MID]

mi·dwife, n. (pl. *-wives*). Woman who assists other women in childbirth. Hence **mi·dwif**ERY(2) (mĭ·dĭfrĭ, mĭ·dwĭfrĭ) n. [MID (or obs. prep. *mid* with, cf. G *mit*) + WIFE]

mien (mēn), n. (literary). Air, bearing, of person, as showing character or mood.

[prob. shortened f. *demean* n., assim. to F *mine* expression, etym. dub.]

miff, n., & v.i. & t. (colloq.). Petty quarrel; huff; (v.i.) take offence *with* or *at*; (v.t.) put out of humour. [perh. imit.; cf. G *muff*, exclamation of disgust]

might[1] (mīt), n. Great (bodily or mental) strength; power to enforce one's will opp. *right*); *with m. & MAIN*[2]. [OE *miht*, cf. Du. & G *macht*, f. OTeut. *mag-* MAY[1]]

might[2]. See MAY[1].

mīgh·ty, a. & adv. Powerful, strong, in body or mind; (bibl.) *m. works*, miracles; massive, bulky; (colloq.) great, considerable; HIGH *& m.*; (adv., colloq.) very, as *that is m. easy*. Hence **migh·ti**LY[2] adv., **migh·ti**NESS n. (esp. in *your* &c. *high mightiness* as burlesque title). [OE *mihtig* (as MIGHT[1], see -Y[2])]

mignon (F), a. Small & delicately formed.

mignone·tte (mĭnyo-), n. Plant with fragrant flowers; colour of these, greyish green; kinds of lace & fine net. [f. F (*-onn-*), dim. of prec.]

migrai·ne, n. =MEGRIM (first sense). [as MEGRIM]

mīgra·te (*or* mī·-), v.i. Move from one place (country, town, college, house) to another; (of birds & fishes) come & go with the seasons. Hence or cogn. **mi·gr**ANT a. & n., **migr**A·TION, **migra·t**OR[2], nn., **mi·grat**ORY a. [f. L *migrare*, see -ATE[3]]

mika·do (-kah-), n. Emperor of Japan. [Jap. *mi* august + *kado* door]

mike, v.i., & n., (slang). Shirk work, idle; (n.) idling (*on the m.*). [cf. dial. *miche* app. f. OF *muchier* to skulk]

mil, n. A thousand (*per m.*, as *per cent*); (Pharm., short for) MILLIlitre; proposed coin =£$\frac{1}{1000}$ (*pound & m. scheme*); unit measure for diameter of wire &c., =$\frac{1}{1000}$ in. [f. L *mille* thousand, *millesimum* thousandth]

mi·lage (-lĭj), n. Miles travelled, used, &c.; expenses per mile. [-AGE]

Milan·ese (-ēz), a. & n. (pl. same). (Native) of Milan, chief city of Lombardy; *the M.*, territory of old duchy of Milan. [It. (*Milano* Milan), -ESE]

milch, a. (Of domestic mammals) giving, kept for, milk; *m. cow*, (fig.) source of profit, esp. person from whom money is easily drawn. [ME *mielch*, f. OTeut. *melukjo-* (*meluk-* milk)]

mild, a. Gentle & conciliatory; (of rule, punishment, &c.) not severe; (of weather) calm & warm; (of medicine) operating gently; (of food, tobacco, &c.) not sharp or strong in taste &c.; (of beer) not strongly flavoured with hops, opp. to *bitter*; tame, feeble, lacking in energy or vivacity; *m. steel*, containing small percentage of carbon, strong & tough, but not readily tempered. Hence **mī·ld**EN[6] v.t. & i., **mi·ld**LY[2] adv., **mi·ld**NESS n. [com.-Teut.: OE *milde*, Du. & G *mild*]

mi·ldew, n., & v.t. & i. Destructive growth of minute fungi on plants; similar growth on paper, leather, &c., exposed to damp; (vb) taint, be tainted, with m. Hence **mi·ldew**Y[2] a. [(vb f. n.) OE *meledéaw*, f. OTeut. **melith* honey + *dauwo-* DEW]

mile, n. Unit of lineal measure, in England now 1,760 yards (orig. Roman measure of 1,000 paces, about 1,618 yards); *geographical, nautical, m.*, one minute of great circle of earth, fixed by British Admiralty at 6,080 feet; race extending over a m.; *not 100 mm. from*, in or at or close to (as sham-mysterious indication); *milestone*, pillar set up on road to mark mm., (fig.) stage, event, in life. [OE *mīl*, ult. f. L *mil(l)ia* pl. of *mille* thousand]

mī·ler, n. (colloq.). Man, horse, qualified or trained specially to run a mile; also in comb., as *two-m.* [-ER[1]]

Milē·sian, a. & n. Irish(man). [f. *Milesius* fabulous Spanish king whose sons are said to have conquered Ireland c. 1300 B.C., + -AN]

mi·lfoil, n. Common yarrow & other plants. [ME & OF, f. L *millefolium* (*mille* thousand + *folium* leaf)]

mĭ·liary, a. (path.). Like millet-seed in size or form, as *m. gland, tubercle*; *m. fever* (marked by rash like measles, with vesicles of form of millet-seed). [f. L *miliarius* (as MILLET, -ARY[1])]

milieu (F), n. Environment, state of life, social surroundings.

mi·litant, a. Engaged in (esp. spiritual) warfare, as *the Church m.*; combative. Hence **mi·lit**ANCY n., **mi·litant**LY[2] adv. [F, as MILITATE, see -ANT]

mi·litarism, n. Spirit, tendencies, of the professional soldier; undue prevalence of military spirit or ideals. So **militariz**A·TION n., **mi·litar**IZE(3) v.t. [f. F *militarisme* (as MILITARY, see -ISM)]

mi·litarist, n. Student of military science; one dominated by military ideas. [-IST]

mĭ·litary, a. & n. Of, done by, befitting, soldiers; *m. fever*, enteric; *m. chest*, treasury of army; *m. testament*, soldier's nuncupative will; (n.) *the* soldiery (also vulg. without *the*, = some soldiers, as *m. had been seen in the vicinity*). Hence **mi·litar**ILY[2] adv. [f. F *militaire* f. L *militaris* (*miles -itis* soldier, see -ARY[2])]

mĭ·litate, v.i. Take part in warfare (usu. fig.); (of facts, evidence) have force, tell, (*against*, rarely *in favour of*, conclusion &c.). [f. L *militare* (*miles -itis* soldier), see -ATE[3]]

mili·tia (-sha), n. Military force, esp. citizen army; branch of British military service formerly raised by the several counties, usu. by voluntary enlistment; *militiaman*, member of the m. [L (as prec.)]

milk[1], n. Opaque white fluid secreted by female mammals for nourishment of their young; (fig.) *m. for babes*, simple forms of literature, doctrine, &c., opp. to *strong meat*; CONDENSED*d m.*; *m. & honey,* abundant means of enjoyment; *m. of human kindness,* kindness natural to humanity; *no use crying over spilt m.* (irremediable loss or error); m.-like juice of plants; m.-like preparation of herbs, drugs, &c., as *m. of almonds*; *m. & water,* feeble or mawkish discourse or sentiment (attrib. *m.-&-w.*); *m.-crust,* skin-eruption in infants; *m. fever,* (occurring to women shortly after childbirth); *m.-leg,* swelling, esp. of legs, after childbirth; *m.-float,* light low horse-cart used in delivering m.; *milkmaid,* woman who milks or works in dairy; *milkman,* man who sells m.; *m. pudding* (of rice, sago, tapioca, &c., baked with m. in dish); *m. punch,* drink made of spirits & m.; *mi·lksop,* spiritless man or youth; *m.-tooth,* temporary tooth in young mammals; *mi·lkweed,* kinds of wild plant with milky juice; *m.-white* (as m.); *mi·lkwort,* kinds of plant. [com.-Teut.: OMercian *milc,* Du. *melk,* G *milch,* f. OTeut. *meluks* (*melk* vb, cogn. w. Gk *amelgō,* L *mulgēre* to milk]

milk[2], v.t. Draw milk from (cow, ewe, goat); *m. the ram* or *bull,* engage in hopeless enterprise; get money out of, exploit, (person); (slang) steal message from (telegraph or telephone wire); extract juice, virus, &c., from (snake &c.). [OE *milcian* (as prec.)]

mi·lky, n. Of, like, mixed with, milk; (of liquid) cloudy, not clear; effeminate, weakly amiable; *M. Way,* luminous band of countless stars encircling the heavens. Hence **mi·lki**NESS n. [-Y[2]]

mill[1], n. Building fitted with machinery for grinding corn (often *watermill, windmill*; *put, go, through the m.,* subject to, undergo, training or experience; *the mm. of God grind slowly,* retribution is often delayed); any mechanical apparatus for grinding corn; apparatus for grinding any solid substance to powder or pulp, as *coffee, pepper, paper, -m.*; any machine, or building fitted with machinery, for manufacturing processes &c., as *saw, cotton, silk, -m.* (*m.-hand,* factory worker); pugilistic encounter; *millboard,* stout pasteboard for bookbinding &c.; *m.-dam,* dam put across stream to make it available for m.; *m.-pond,* water retained by this (*like a m.-p.,* said of calm sea), (joc.) =HERRING-*pond*; *m.-race,* current of water that drives m.-wheel; *millstone,* one of pair of circular stones for grinding corn, as NETHER *millstone, see far into a millstone,* (usu. iron.) be extraordinarily acute, *between upper & nether m.-s.,* subject to irrestible pressure; *millstone grit,* a hard siliceous rock; *m.-wheel,* one (esp. water-wheel) used to drive m.; *millwright,* one who designs or erects mm. [OE *mylen* f. LL *molinum, -na* (*mola* mill f. root of *molere* grind)]

mill[2], v.t. & i. Thicken (cloth &c.) by fulling; grind (corn), produce (flour), in mill; produce regular markings on edge of (coin, esp. in p.p.); beat (chocolate) to froth; beat, strike, fight, (person); (of cattle) move round & round in a mass. [f. prec.]

mill[3], n. (U.S.). One-thousandth of a dollar, money of account. [f. L *millesimum* thousandth part, on anal. of CENT]

millenār·ian, a. & n. Of the millennium; (person) believing in this. Hence **millenar·ian**ISM n. [as foll. + -AN]

mi·llenary, a. & n. (Period) of 1,000 years; of, (person) believing in, the millennium. [f. L *millenarius* consisting of a thousand (*milleni* a thousand each f. *mille* thousand, -ARY[1])]

mille·nnium, n. Period of a thousand years, esp. that of Christ's reign in person on earth (*Rev.* xx. 1–5). Hence **mille·nni**AL a. [f. L *mille* thousand + *annus* year, on anal. of *biennium* two years' space]

mi·llepede (-ĭpēd), n. Genera of myriapods, with numerous legs usu. placed on each segment in double pairs; kinds of terrestrial crustacean, esp. common woodlouse & armadillo. [f. L *millepeda* woodlouse (*mille* thousand + *pes pedis* foot)]

mi·ller, n. Proprietor, tenant, of corn-mill; one who works any mill; kinds of white or white-powdered insect; cockchafer; *m.'s thumb,* bull-head & other fishes. [MILL[1] + -ER[1]]

millĕ·simal, a. & n. Thousandth (part); consisting of thousandths. [f. L *millesimus* (*mille* thousand + -AL)]

mi·llet, n. Graminaceous plant, native of India, bearing large crop of small nutritious seeds; its seed; *m.-grass,* a tall handsome grass. [F, dim. of *mil* f. L *milium*]

mi·lli- in comb. = one-thousandth of a — (in metric system), as: *-gramme* (·0154 of English grain), *-litre* (·061 cub. in.), *-metre* (·0393 in.). [L *mille* thousand, -I-]

mi·lliard, n. A thousand millions. [F (*mille* thousand)]

mi·lliner, n. Person (usu. woman) who makes up hats & other female headgear; *man m.,* (fig.) man busied in trifling occupations. Hence **mi·llin**ERY(1) n. [f. *Milan* + -ER[1]; orig. = vendor of Milan goods]

mi·llion, n. & a. A thousand thousand (things, *of* things, or abs.); a m. pounds or (U.S.) dollars; *the m.,* bulk of the population. Hence **mi·llion**FOLD a. & adv., **mi·llion**TH[2] a. & n. [F, f. It. *millione* (*mille* thousand + *-one* -OON)]

millionaire· (-ār), n. Person possessing a million pounds, dollars, francs, &c.; person of great wealth. [f. F *millionnaire* (prec., -ARY[1])]

Mills bomb, n. Oval hand-bomb much used in the great war. [inventor]

milor(d) (mēlor·), n. French word for English lord or wealthy Englishman. [f. E *my lord*]

mi·lreis (-āĭs), n. Portuguese gold coin worth 4*s.* 5½*d.* [Port. (*mil* thousand + REIS)]

milt, n., & v.t. Spleen in mammals; analogous organ in other vertebrates; roe of male fish; (v.t.) impregnate (roe of female). [(vb f. n.) OE *milte*, cf. Du. *milt*, G *milz*, perh. cogn. w. MELT]

mi·lter, n. Male fish in spawning time. [-ER¹]

Miltŏ·nic, a. Of, in the style of, Milton. So **Miltō·**NIAN a. [-IC]

mime, n., & v.i. (Gk or Rom. Ant.) simple farcical drama marked by mimicry; performer in this; pantomimist, buffoon; (v.i.) act with mimic gesture, usu. without words. [(vb f. n.) f. L f. Gk *mimos*]

mĭ·mĕograph, n. Apparatus for making stencils of written pages, from which many copies may be taken. [irreg. f. Gk *mimeomai* imitate, see -GRAPH]

mīmē·sis, n. (biol.). Close external resemblance between animal & another animal or inanimate object. [Gk, = imitation (as prec.)]

mīmĕt·ic, a. Of, addicted to, imitation, mimicry, or mimesis. Hence **mime·t**IC-ALLY adv. [f. Gk *mimētikos* (as prec., see -ETIC)]

mĭ·mic¹, a. & n. Apt to imitate; imitative as opp. to *real*; person skilled in ludicrous imitation. [f. L f. Gk *mimikos* (as MIME¹, see -IC)]

mĭ·mic², v.t. (-cking, -cked). Ridicule by imitating (person, manner, &c.); copy minutely or servilely; (of things) resemble closely. [f. prec.]

mi·micry, n. Mimicking; thing that mimics another; (Zool.) = MIMESIS. [MIMIC¹ + -RY]

mĭ·miny-pĭ·miny, a. Over-refined, finicking. [imit.]

mimō·sa (-*za*, -*sa*), n. Genus of leguminous shrubs, including common Sensitive Plant. [f. L as MIME + -*osa* fem. suf., see -OSE¹]

mĭ·mūlus, n. Genus of flowering plants, esp. monkey-flower. [prob. dim. as prec.]

mī·na¹, n. Greek denomination of money, about £4; ancient unit of weight in Greece, Egypt, &c., about 1lb. [L, f. Gk *mna*]

mī·na², n. Kinds of eastern passerine bird. [f. Hind. *maina*]

minā·cious, a. Threatening. Hence **mina·cious**LY² adv., **mină·**CITY n. [f. L *minax* (*minari* threaten), see -ACIOUS]

minar·, n. Lighthouse; turret. [f. Arab. *manar* f. root of *nar* fire]

mĭ·naret, n. Slender turret connected with mosque, from which muezzin calls people to prayer. [f. Arab. *manarat* (as prec.)]

mĭ·natory, a. Threatening. [f. OF *minatoire* f. LL *minatorius* (*minari* threaten, -ORY)]

mince¹, a. Minced meat; *mincemeat*, mixture of currants, raisins, sugar, apples, candied-peel, &c., for *m. pie* (small round pie containing this), *make m.-m. of*, destroy (person, argument, &c.). [f. foll.]

mince², v.t. & i. Cut (meat &c.) small; (usu. w. negative) *m. matters*, express oneself politely in condemnation; restrain (one's words) within bounds of politeness; utter (words), walk, with affected delicacy, whence **mi·ncing**LY² adv. [f. OF *mincier* f. pop. L **minutiare* (as MINUTIA)]

Mi·ncing Lane, n. (Used for) the wholesale trade in tea & similar imports. [London street]

mīnd¹, n. Remembrance, as *have* or *keep in m.*, *bring* or *call to m.*, remember, *go* or *pass out of m.*, be forgotten; TIME¹ *out of m.*; candid opinion, as *speak* one's *m.*, *tell* (person) one's *m.*, *give* him *a piece of* one's *m.*; *be of* (person's) *m.*, agree in opinion with him; *to my m.*, as I think; *be of a* or *one m.*, agree; *know* one's *own m.*, form & adhere to decision; *make up* one's *m.*, resolve (*to* do, *to* a course &c., or abs.), reconcile oneself to fact as inevitable (*the crop is ruined, we must make up our mm. to that*); *change* one's *m.*, alter one's purpose; *have a good* or *great m.*, *half a m.*, be strongly, somewhat, disposed (*to* do); *be in two mm.*, vacillate, be irresolute; MONTH'*s m.*; direction of thoughts or desires, as *set* one's *m. on*, desire to attain, *give* one's *m.* (attention) *to*; *to* one's *m.*, as one would have it; way of thinking & feeling, as *frame, state, of m.*; seat of consciousness, thought, volition, & feeling; soul, opp. to *body*; *m.'s eye*, mental view; person, as embodying mental qualities; intellectual powers, opp. to will & emotions, whence **mi·nd**LESS a.; ABSENCE, PRESENCE, *of m.*; *m.-stuff* (philos.), supposed rudimentary form of psychical existence regarded as the reality of which matter is an aspect. [ME *mynd*, cf. OHG *gemund* f. OTeut. *gamundiz* (*ga*- Y- + *mun*- think, intend, cogn. w. L *mens* mind, Gk *menos* rage)]

mīnd², v.t. & i. Bear in mind (chiefly in imperat.); give heed to, as *never m. the expense*; concern oneself (*never m.* imperat., take comfort, also as refusal to answer question); apply oneself to (business &c.; *m. your own business*, leave other people's alone); (chiefly in neg. or quasi-neg. sentences) object to, as *would you m. ringing?*, *I should not m.* (should like) *a cup of tea, if you don't m.* (have no objection); remember & take care (*that* thing is done, or omit *that*); *m. you* or *m.* (parenth. imperat.), please to observe (*but I have no objection, m. you*; *now m., not a word till I give the signal*); (slang) *m.*

your eye, be on the lookout; *m.* one's *P's & Q's*, be careful as to one's words or behaviour; be on one's guard against or about, as *m. the step* (remember there is one); have charge of. [f. prec.]

mī·nded, a. Disposed (*to* do); having (specified) mind, as *high, small, -m.* [-ED[2]]

mi·ndful, a. Taking thought or care (*of*, or abs.). Hence **mi·ndful**LY[2] adv., **mi·ndful**NESS n. [MIND[1] + -FUL]

mine[1], n. Excavation in earth for metal, coal, salt, &c.; (fig.) abundant source (*of* information &c.); iron ore; (Mil.) subterranean gallery in which explosive is placed to blow up fortifications, (formerly) subterranean passage under wall of besieged fortress; (Nav.) receptacle filled with explosive & sunk esp. at entrance to harbour (*m.-field*, area of sea beset with floating or submarine mm.; *m.-layer, -sweeper*, ship used for laying mm., for clearing away enemy mm.) [F, etym. dub.]

mine[2], v.t. & i. Burrow in (earth); make (hole) underground; make subterranean passages under; (fig.) undermine; (Mil.) Nav.) lay mines under or in; obtain (metal &c.) from mine; dig in (earth &c.) for ore &c. [f. F *miner* (prec.)]

mine[3], poss. pron. & a. corresponding in pred. & elliptical uses to MY, as *it is m., I have lost m., me & m.* (my relations), *is a friend of m.*; also used (archaic, poet.) before noun beginning with vowel or *h*, as *m. eyes.* [com.-Teut.: OE *mīn*, Du. *mijn*, G *mein*]

mī·ner, n. One who works in a mine; soldier whose duty it is to lay mines; SAPPERS *& mm.* [f. OF *minour* (as MINE[2], see -OR[2])]

mi·neral, a. & n. (Substance) obtained by mining; (belonging to) any of the species into which inorganic substances are classified; *m.* KINGDOM; *m. water*, water found in nature impregnated with mineral substance, artificial imitation of this, esp. soda-water, also, other effervescent drink, e.g. ginger-beer. Hence **mineraliz**A·TION n., **mi·neral**IZE(3) v.t. & i. [f. F *minéral* f. med. L *mineralis* (*minera* mine f. com.-Rom. **mina*, see -AL)]

mineră·logy, n. Science of minerals. Hence **mineralo·gi**CAL a., **mineralo·gical**LY[2] adv., **minera·log**IST n. [f. prec. + -LOGY]

Miner·va, n. Roman goddess of wisdom; *M. press*, printing-press in London, ultra-sentimental novels issued from it c. 1800. [L]

mi·never, -iver, n. Kind of fur used in ceremonial costume. [f. F *menu vair* (*menu* small, as MINUTE; VAIR kind of fur, as VARIOUS)]

mi·ngle, v.t. & i. Mix, blend; *m. their* &c. *tears*, weep together; *m. with*, go about among. [ME *mengel* f. obs. *meng* f. OE *mengan*, cf. Du. & G *mengen*, see -LE(3)]

mi·niate, v.t. Paint with vermilion; illuminate (manuscript). [f. L *miniare* (*minium* native cinnabar, red lead), see -ATE[3]]

mi·niature, n. & a., & v.t. Picture in illuminated manuscript; small-scale minutely finished portrait, usu. on ivory or vellum; this branch of painting, as *portrait in m.*; reduced image; *in m.*, on a small scale; (adj.) represented on small scale, small-scale; (v.t.) represent in m. Hence **mi·niatūr**IST n. [(vb f. n.) f. It. f. L *miniatura* (as prec., see -URE)]

mi·nifȳ, v.t. Represent as smaller or less important than it is; lessen in size or importance. [irreg. f. L *minor* less, see -FY]

mi·nikin, n. & a. Diminutive (creature); affected, mincing. [f. Du. *minneken* (*minne* love + *kijn* -KIN)]

mi·nim, n. (Mus.) note half the value of SEMIbreve; single down-stroke of pen; creature of the smallest size or importance; sixtieth part of fluid drachm. [f. L *minimus* smallest]

mi·nimal, a. Very minute; the least possible, minimum. [as prec., see -AL]

mi·nimalist, n. Person ready to accept a minimum provisionally (opp. MAXIMALIST). [prec., -IST]

mi·nimize, v.t. Reduce to, estimate at, smallest possible amount or degree. Hence **minimiz**A·TION n. [as prec., see -IZE]

mi·nimum, n. (pl. *-ma*). Least amount attainable, usual, &c.; *m. thermometer* (automatically recording lowest temperature within period); *m. wage* (than which, by law or agreement, less is not to be offered). [L, neut. as foll.]

mi·nimus, a. (In schools) youngest of the name, as *Jones m.* [L, = least]

mi·nion, n. Favourite child, servant, animal, &c. (contempt.); slave; *mm. of the law*, gaolers, police, &c.; (Print.) size of TYPE. [f. F *mignon*, etym. dub.]

mi·nish, v.t. & i. (archaic). Diminish (t. & i.); reduce in power &c. [f. OF *menusier* f. vulg. L **minutiare* (as MINUTE[3])]

mi·nister[1], n. Person employed in execution *of* (purpose, will, &c.); person administering department of State; PRIME *m.*; political agent accredited by one State to another; clergyman (now rare of Anglican); (also *m. general*) superior of some religious orders. [f. OF *menestre* f. L *minister* servant (*minus* less)]

mi·nister[2], v.i. & t. Render aid or service (*to* person, cause, &c.; *-ing angel*, w. ref. to *Mark* i. 13, esp. of sick-nurse &c.); be helpful, contribute, (*to* result); (archaic) furnish, supply, (help &c.). [f. OF *ministrer* f. L *ministrare* (prec.)]

ministēr·ial, a. Concerned with the execution of law; subsidiary, instrumental; of a minister of religion or his office; of minister of State; siding with the Ministry against Opposition, whence **minister·ial**IST(2) n. Hence **minister·ial**LY[2] adv. [f. F *ministériel* f. L *ministerialis* (as MINISTRY, see -AL)]

ministra·tion, n. Ministering, esp. in religious matters; supplying (*of*). So **mi·nistrANT** a. & n., **mi·nistratIVE** a. [f. L *ministratio* (as MINISTER², see -ATION)]

mi·nistry, n. Ministering; *the* body of ministers of State or in religion; State department, as *M. of Health* (set up in 1919 with powers of old L.G.B., see L, & others), also *Air M., M. of Agriculture & Fisheries, of Labour, of Transport.* [f. L *ministerium* (as MINISTER¹)]

mi·niver, see MINEVER.

mink, n. Small semi-aquatic stoat-like animal; its fur. [Sw. has *menk*]

mi·nnĕsinger, n. German lyrical poet & singer in 12–14th cc. [G (*minne* love)]

Mi·nnie, n. (army slang). Trench mortar. [abbr. of G *minenwerfer* mine-thrower]

mi·nnow, n. Small freshwater fish (loosely used of several kinds, esp. stickleback); *Triton among the mm.*, one who seems great from insignificance of others. [prob. =OHG *munewa*; OE has *myne*]

Mino·an, a. (archaeol.). Of the Cretan civilization (3000–1500 B.C.) named from king Minos. [f. Gk *Minōs* + -AN]

mī·nor, a. & n. Lesser (not followed by *than*), as *m.* PROPHETS; *m. canon*, clergyman assisting in daily cathedral service, not member of chapter; comparatively unimportant, as *m. poet*; (Log.) *m. term*, subject of conclusion of categorical syllogism, *m. premiss* (containing this); (Mus.) *m. interval*, see MAJOR², *m. key* (in which scale has m. third), (fig.) *conversation in a m. key* (doleful); (in schools) *Jones minor* (the younger); (n.) Franciscan friar; m. term or premiss; person under age. [L, = less]

Minor·ca, n. One of the Balearic Isles; *M. (fowl)*, black variety brought from Spain. [f. Sp. *Menorca*]

minŏ·rity, n. State of being under age, period of this; smaller number or part, esp. smaller party voting together against majority; number of votes cast for this. [f. med. L *minoritas* (as MINOR, see -TY)]

Mī·notaur, n. *The M.*, fabulous monster, half bull half man, fed with human flesh. [f. Gk *Minōtauros* (*Minōs*, king of Crete, husband of M.'s mother, +*tauros* bull)]

mi·nster, n. Church of a monastery; large or important church, cathedral. [OE *mynster* (as MONASTERY)]

mi·nstrel, n. Mediaeval singer or musician, who sang or recited (often his own) poetry; (Hist.) person who entertained his patrons with singing, buffoonery, &c.; (pl.) band of public entertainers, with blacked faces &c., performing songs & music ostensibly of negro origin. [f. OF *menestral* (as MINISTERIAL)]

mi·nstrelsy, n. Minstrel's art; minstrels; minstrel poetry. [f. OF *menestralsie*, as prec.]

mint¹, n. Place where money is coined, usu. under State authority; (fig.) source of invention &c.; vast sum *of money*; *m.-mark*, mark placed on coin to show at what m. it was struck (also fig.); *m.-master*, superintendent of coinage at m. [OE *mynet* f. L *moneta* MONEY]

mint², v.t. Make (coin) by stamping metal; invent, coin, (word, phrase, &c.). Hence **mi·ntAGE**(3, 4) n. [f. prec.]

mint³, n. Aromatic plant, much used in cookery; *m. sauce* (of finely chopped mint with vinegar & sugar, eaten with roast lamb), also, with pun on *mint¹*, money. [OE *minte* = OHG *minza* f. L *menta* f. Gk *minthē*]

minuĕ·t, n. Slow stately dance for two in triple measure; music for this, music in same rhythm & style. [f. F *menuet*, dim. of *menu* (as MINUTE a.)]

mī·nus, quasi-prep. & a. With the deduction of (symbol –), as *7 m. 4 is equal to 3*; (colloq.) deprived of, as *he came back m. an arm*; *a m.* (negative) *quantity*. [L, neut. of MINOR]

minu·scule, a. & n. (Of kind of cursive script developed in 7th c.) small; (n.) small letter. [F, f. L *minusculus* dim. of MINOR]

mi·nute¹ (-ĭt), n. Sixtieth part of hour; short time, instant; exact point of time, as *the m. (that)*, as soon as; sixtieth part of degree (in angles); rough draft, memorandum; (pl.) brief summary of proceedings of assembly, committee, &c.; official memorandum authorizing or recommending a course, as *a Treasury m.*; *m.-book* (for writing mm. in); *m.-gun* (fired at intervals of a m.); *m.-hand* (indicating mm. on watch or clock); *m.-mark* (′, cf. SECOND-*mark*). [F, f. L *minuta* fem. as MINUTE³]

mi·nute² (-ĭt), v.t. Find the exact time of; draft (document, scheme); record in minutes; *m. down*, make a note of. [f. prec.]

minū·te³, a. Very small; trifling, petty; (of inquiry, inquirer, &c.) accurate, precise. Hence **minu·teLY²** adv., **minu·teNESS** n. [f. L *minutus*, p.p. of *minuere* lessen]

mi·nutely (-nĭt-), a. Occurring every minute. So **mi·nuteLY²** adv. [MINUTE¹ + -LY¹]

minū·tia (-shĭa), n. (usu. in pl. *-ae*). Precise or trivial detail. [L (as MINUTE³)]

minx, n. Pert girl, hussy, flirt. [?]

mī·ocene (-sēn), a. (geol.). Of the middle division of tertiary strata. [irreg. f. Gk *meiōn* less + *kainos* new]

mi·racle, n. Marvellous event due to some supernatural agency; remarkable occurrence; remarkable specimen (*of* ingenuity, impudence, &c.); *to a m.*, surprisingly well; (also *m. play*) dramatic representation in Middle Ages, based on life of Christ or saints. [OF, f. L *miraculum* (*mirari* wonder f. *mirus* wonderful)]

mirăʹcūlous, a. Supernatural; surprising. Hence **miraʹculous**LY[2] adv., **miraʹculous**NESS n. [f. F *miraculeux* f. med. L *miraculosus* (as prec., see -OUS)]
miraʹge (-ahzh), n. Optical illusion, esp. illusive appearance of sheet of water in desert &c. (also fig.). [F, f. (*se*) *mirer* look at oneself in mirror, be reflected, f. L *mirari* wonder at]
mire[1], n. Swampy ground, bog; *stick, find* oneself, *in the m.* (in difficulties); mud, dirt. [ME, f. ON *mýrr*, cogn. with MOSS]
mire[2], v.t. Plunge in mire; (fig.) involve in difficulties; defile, bespatter. [f. prec.]
miʹrror, n., & v.t. Polished usu. glass surface reflecting image, looking-glass; (fig.) what gives faithful reflection or true description of thing; (v.t.) reflect in as m. [(vb f. n.) f. OF *mirour* f. pop. L **miratorium* (*mirare* look at, f. L *mirari* wonder at, see -ORY)]
mirth, n. Merriment. Hence **mirʹth**FUL, **mirʹth**LESS, aa., **mirʹthful**LY[2] adv., **mirʹthful**NESS n. [OE *myrigth*, cogn. w. MERRY]
mīrʹy, a. Muddy; vile. [f. MIRE[1] + -Y[2]]
mirʹza, n. (In Persia) title added to name of prince or prefixed to that of official or man of learning. [Pers.]
mis-[1], pref. added freely to vbs & vbl nn. w. sense 'amiss', 'badly', 'wrongly', 'unfavourably', or intensifying unfavourable meaning contained in vb (*misdoubt*). [OE, cf. Du. *mis-*, G *miss-* f. OTeut. *misso-* (1) divergent (2) mutual]
mis-[2], pref. to vbs, adjj., & nn., derived f. F, in same sense as prec. [f. OF *mes-* f. MINUS, used in com.-Rom. as pref.]
misadveʹnture, n. (Piece of) bad luck; (Law) *homicide by m.* (accident). [f. OF *mesaventure* (see MIS-[2] & ADVENTURE)]
misallīʹance, n. Improper alliance, esp. marriage. [MIS-[1], after MESALLIANCE]
mĭʹsanthrope, n. Hater of mankind; one who avoids human society. Hence or cogn. **misanthrŏʹpic**(AL) aa., **misaʹnthrop**IST, **misaʹnthropy**[1], nn., **misaʹnthrop**IZE(2) v.i. [f. Gk *misanthrōpos* (*miseō* hate + *anthrōpos* man)]
misapplicaʹtion, n. Wrong application, wrong use (esp. of funds). [MIS-[1]]
misapplyʹ, v.t. Apply wrongly. [MIS-[1]]
misappreheʹnd, v.t. Misunderstand (words, person). So **misappreheʹnsion** n., **misappreheʹnsive** a. [MIS-[1]]
misaproʹpriate, v.t. Apply (usu. another's money) to wrong (esp. one's own) use. So **misappropriaʹtion** n. [MIS-[1]]
misbecoʹme (-ŭm), v.t. Suit ill, be unbecoming to. [MIS-[1]]
misbegoʹtten, a. Illegitimate, bastard, (often as general term of opprobrium). [MIS-[1] + *begotten* p.p. of BEGET]
misbehāʹve, v.t. Behave (one*self*, or abs.) improperly. So **misbehāʹviour** n. [MIS-[1]]
misblieʹf (-ēf), n. Wrong religious belief; false opinion. So **misbelieʹver** n., **misbelieʹving** a. [MIS-[1]]
misbeseeʹm, v.t. Misbecome. [MIS-[1]]
miscaʹlculate, v.t. & i. Calculate (amount, results, &c., or abs.) wrongly. So **miscalculaʹtion** n. [MIS-[1]]
miscaʹll (-awl), v.t. Call by a wrong name; (dial.) call (person) names. [MIS-[1]]
miscaʹrriage, n. Failure (of letter) to reach destination; *m.* (failure of court to attain the ends) *of justice*; untimely delivery (of woman), abortion; failure (of scheme &c.). [MIS-[1]]
miscaʹrry, v.i. (Of person or business) fail, be unsuccessful; (of woman) be delivered prematurely (*of* child); (of letter) fail to reach destination. [MIS-[1]]
miscaʹsting, n. Wrong addition (of accounts). [MIS-[1]]
miscegenaʹtion (mĭsĭj-), n. Mixture of races, esp. sexual union of whites with negroes. [irreg. f. L *miscēre* mix + *genus* race + -ATION]
miscellāʹnĕa (-sel-), n. Literary miscellany. [L, neut. pl. as foll.]
miscellāʹneous (-sel-), a. Of mixed composition or character; (w. pl. noun) of various kinds; (of persons) many-sided. Hence **miscellaʹneous**LY[2] adv., **miscellaʹneous**NESS n. [f. L *miscellaneus* (*miscellus* mixed f. *miscere* mix, see -ANEOUS)]
misceʹllany (*or* mĭʹs-), n. Mixture, medley; collection of treatises &c. in one volume; such volume. Hence **misceʹllan**IST(3) n. [prob. f. F *miscellanées* fem. pl. (as MISCELLANEA)]
mischaʹnce, n. (Piece of) bad luck, esp. *by m.* [f. OF *mesch(e)ance* (MIS-[2], CHANCE n.)]
miʹschief (-ĭf), n. Harm, injury, wrought by person or other agent (*do one a m.*, vulg., wound or kill him); *make m.*, create discord, so *m.-maker, -making*; *the m.* (annoying part) *of it is that* &c.; worker, source, of harm or annoyance; vexatious conduct, esp. of children; pranks, scrapes, (*get into, keep out of, m.*); playful malice, archness, satire, (*eyes full of m.*); *where the m.* (devil) *have you been?*. [f. OF *meschief* (MIS-[2], *chief* end, CHIEF)]
miʹschievous (-ĭv-), a. (Of things) having harmful effects; (of persons, conduct, &c.) disposed to acts of playful malice or annoyance. Hence **miʹschievous**LY[2] adv., **miʹschievous**NESS n. [f. AF *meschevous* (prec., -OUS)]
miʹscible (-sĭ-), a. That can be mixed (*with*). Hence **misci**BIʹLITY n. [f. L *miscēre* mix, -BLE]
misconceiʹve, v.i. & t. Have a wrong conception (*of*, or abs.); misunderstand

For words in *mis-* not given see MIS-[1].

(word, person). So **misconce·ption** n. [MIS-¹]

misco·nduct, n. Improper conduct, esp. adultery; bad management. So **miscondu·ct,** v.t. & refl. [MIS-¹]

misco·nstrue, v.t. Put wrong construction on (word, action); mistake meaning of (person). So **misconstru·ction** n. [MIS-¹]

miscou·nt, n., & v.t. & i. (Make) wrong count, esp. of votes; count (things) wrongly. [MIS-¹]

mi·screant, a. & n. (Archaic) heretical; depraved; (n., archaic) heretic; vile wretch. [f. OF *mescreant* (MIS-² + *creant* f. L *credere* believe, see -ANT)]

miscreā·ted, a. Ill-formed (often as abusive epithet). So **miscrea·tion** n. [MIS-¹]

mis-cue· (-ū), n. (billiards). Failure to strike ball properly with cue. [MIS-¹ or MISS v.)]

misda·te, v.t. Date wrong. [MIS-¹]

misdea·l, v.t. & i. Make mistake in dealing (cards, but usu. abs.). So **misdea·l** n. [MIS-¹]

misdee·d, n. Evil deed; crime. [OE *misdǣd* (see MIS-¹ & DEED)]

misdee·m, v.t. & i. (archaic, poet.). Have wrong opinion of; mistake (person, thing *for* another); form wrong judgement (*of*). [MIS-¹]

misdemea·nant, n. Person convicted of misdemeanour or guilty of misconduct; *first, second, -class m.* (to be treated with more, less, indulgence). [f. archaic *misdemean* (MIS-¹ + DEMEAN) + -ANT]

misdemea·nour, n. (Law) indictable offence less heinous than felony; offence, misdeed. [MIS-¹]

misdire·ct, v.t. Direct (person, blow, &c.) wrongly. So **misdire·ction** n. [MIS-¹]

misdo·ing (-dōō-), n. Misdeed. [MIS-¹]

misdoub·t, v.t. (archaic). Have doubts as to the truth or existence of; have misgivings, be suspicious, about; suspect (*that*). [MIS-¹]

mise (mēz, mīz), n. (Hist.) settlement by agreement, as *M. of Lewes* (between Henry III & barons, 1264); *mise en scène* (F), scenery & properties of acted play, (fig.) surroundings of an event. [OF fem. p.p. of *mettre* put f. L *mittere miss-* send, used as n.]

mī·ser¹ (-z-), n. One who hoards wealth & lives miserably; avaricious person. [L, = wretched]

mī·ser² (-z-), n. Boring instrument for well-sinking. [?]

mi·serable (-z-), a. Wretchedly unhappy; (of events &c.) causing wretchedness; contemptible, mean, as *a m. hovel.* Hence **mi·serab**LY² adv. [f. F *misérable* f. L *miserabilis* (*miserari* pity f. *miser* wretched, -BLE)]

mīserēr·ĕ (-z-), n. Fifty-first psalm (*M. mei Deus*); cry for mercy; (improp.) = foll. (last sense). [L, = have mercy (*miserēri* as MISER¹)]

misĕ·ricord, n. Apartment in monastery in which some indulgences were permitted; dagger for giving the *coup de grâce*; shelving projection on under side of hinged seat in choir stall, serving when seat was turned up to support person standing. [f. OF *misericorde* f. L *misericordia* f. *misericors* compassionate (stem of *miserēri* pity + *cors -rdis* heart)]

mī·serly, a. Like a miser, stingy. Hence **mī·serli**NESS a. [-LY¹]

mi·sery, n. Wretched state of mind or of outward circumstances; (Cards, colloq. for F *misère*) declaration by which caller undertakes not to take trick. [f. OF *miserie* f. L *miseria* (as MISER¹)]

misfea·sance (-z-), n. (Law) transgression, esp. wrongful exercise of lawful authority (also gen., esp. facet.). [f. OF *mesfaisance* f. *mesfaire* misdo (MIS-², *faire* do f. L *facere*), -ANCE]

misfi·re, v.i., & n. (Of gun, motor engine, &c.) fail(ing) to go off or start action. [prob. for MISS² *fire*]

misfi·t, n. Garment &c. that does not fit the person it is meant for. [MIS-¹]

misfor·tune, n. Bad luck (*more his m. than his fault*). [MIS-¹]

misgi·ve, v.t. (Person's) *mind misgives him*, fills him with suspicion or foreboding (*about* thing, *that*). [MIS-¹]

misgi·ving, n. Feeling of mistrust or apprehension. [f. prec. + -ING¹]

misgo·vern, v.t. Govern (State &c.) badly. So **misgo·vernment** n. [MIS-¹]

misgui·de, v.t. (chiefly in p.p.). Mislead, cause to err in thought or action. Hence **misgui·ded**LY² adv. [MIS-¹]

misha·ndle, v.t. Handle (person, thing) roughly or rudely, ill-treat. [MIS-¹]

misha·p, n. Unlucky accident. [MIS-¹]

mishear·, v.t. Hear amiss or imperfectly. [MIS-¹]

mi·shmash, n. Confused mixture. [redupl. f. MASH n.]

mi·shna(h), n. Collection of precepts forming basis of Talmud. Hence **mi·sh**NIC a. [post-bibl. Heb., = repetition, instruction, (*shanah* repeat)]

misinfor·m, v.t. Give wrong information to, mislead. So **misinforma·tion** n. [MIS-¹]

misinter·pret, v.t. Give wrong interpretation to, make wrong inference from. So **misinterpreta·tion** n. [MIS-¹]

misju·dge, v.t. & i. Judge wrongly (person &c., or abs.); have wrong opinion of. [MIS-¹]

mislay·, v.t. Put (thing) by accident where it cannot readily be found. [MIS-¹]

mislea·d, v.t. Lead astray, cause to go wrong, in conduct; give wrong impression to. [OE *mislǣdan*, see MIS-¹ & LEAD²]

misli·ke, v.t. (archaic). Dislike. [OE *mislician*, see MIS-¹ & LIKE v.]

mismă·nage, v.t. Manage badly or wrongly. So **misma·nagement** n. [MIS-[1]]
misna·me, v.t. Call by wrong name. [MIS-[1]]
misnō·mer, n. Use of wrong name, wrong use of term. [f. OF *mesnommer* (*mes*-MIS-[2] + *nommer* vb name f. L *nominare*)]
miso- in comb. = Gk *miso-* comb. form of *miseō* hate, = 'hater, hatred, of', as: *-logist, -logy*, hater, hatred, of reason or of learning; *-nē·ism, -ne·ist*, hatred, hater, of novelty.
misŏ·gamy, n. Hatred of marriage. So **miso·gamIST** n. [f. Gk MISO(*gamos* marriage), -Y[1]]
miso·gynist (-j-, -g-), n. Hater of women. So **misogў·nIC** a. [f. Gk MISO(*gunēs* f. *gunē* woman) + -IST]
mispla·ce, v.t. Put in wrong place or hands; set (affections) on wrong object; place (confidence) amiss; time (words, action) badly. So **mispla·ceMENT** n. [MIS-[1]]
mispri·nt, n. Mistake in printing. So **mispri·nt** v.t. [MIS-[1]]
mispri·sion[1] (-zhn), n. (law). Wrong action or omission, esp. *m. of treason* or *felony*, (now restricted to) concealment of one's knowledge of treasonable designs &c. [f. OF *mesprison* mistake (see MIS-[2] & PRISON)]
mispri·sion[2] (-zhn), n. (archaic). Contempt; failure to appreciate the value (*of*). [f. foll., after prec.]
mispri·ze, v.t. Despise; fail to appreciate. [f. OF *mespriser* (see MIS-[2] & PRIZE)]
mispronou·nce, v.t. Pronounce wrongly. So **mispronuncia·tion** n. [MIS-[1]]
misquo·te, v.t. Quote wrongly. So **misquota·tion** n. [MIS-[1]]
misrea·d, v.t. (*-read* pron. -rĕd). Read or interpret wrongly. [MIS-[1]]
misreprese·nt, v.t. Represent wrongly, give false account of. So **misrepresenta·tion** n. [MIS-[1]]
misru·le, n. Bad government; (Hist.) *Lord, Abbot, Master, of M.*, person presiding over Christmas revels. [MIS-[1]]
miss[1], n. Failure to hit or attain; *a m. is as good as a mile*, failure or escape is what it is, however narrow the margin; (Billiards) *give a m.*, avoid hitting object ball so as to leave one's own in safe position. [f. foll.]
miss[2], v.t. & i. (Of person or missile) fail to hit (mark &c., or abs.); fail to find, get, or meet; let slip (opportunity); fail to catch (train); fail to hear or understand (remark &c.); (also *m. out*) leave out (words &c. in reading, writing, &c.); fail to keep (appointment) or perform; notice esp. with regret the absence of, feel the want of; *m. fire*, (of gun) fail to go off, (fig.) fail in one's object; (Naut.) *m. stays*, fail in attempt to go about from one tack to another. [OE *missan*, cf. Du. & G *missen*]
miss[3], n. (As title of unmarried woman or girl) *M. Smith*, (pl. *the M. Smiths, the Misses Smith*; *M.* 1928 or current year, the modern girl); (usu. contempt. or playful) girl, esp. schoolgirl, as *a pert m.*, whence **mi·ssISH**[1] a., **mi·ssishNESS** n.; (Voc., in servants' or trade use) young lady. [abbr. of MISTRESS]
mi·ssal, n. Book containing service of Mass for whole year; (loosely) Rom. Cath. book of prayers, esp. illuminated one. [f. eccl. L *missale* (as MASS[1], see -AL)]
mi·ssel, n. (Usu. *m.-thrush*) kind of thrush that feeds on mistletoe berries. [OE *mistel* basil, mistletoe, cf. Du. & G *mistel*]
mis-shā·pen, a. Ill-shaped, deformed. [MIS-[1] + *shapen* p.p. of SHAPE]
mi·ssīle, a. & n. (Object, weapon) suitable for throwing or for discharge from machine or engine (or, rarely, gun). [f. L *missĭlis* (*mittere miss-* send, see -IL)]
mi·ssing, a. In vbl senses; also: wanting, not in its place, as *there is a page m., a page is m.*; *the m.*, soldiers neither present after battle &c. nor known to have been killed or wounded; *m. link*, thing lacking to complete series, (Zool.) hypothetical intermediate type, esp. between man & anthropoid apes. [MISS[2] + -ING[2]]
mi·ssion (-shn), n. Body of persons sent to foreign country to conduct negotiations &c.; body sent by religious community to convert heathen; field of missionary activity; missionary post; organization in a district for conversion of the people; course of religious services &c. for this purpose; errand of political or other mission; person's vocation or divinely appointed work in life. [f. L *missio* (*mittere miss-* send, -ION)]
mi·ssionary, a. & n. Of, concerned with, religious missions; *m.-box* (for contributions to m. work); person who goes on m. work; person attached to police-court to influence or help offenders or applicants. [-ARY[1]]
mi·ssioner, n. Missionary; person in charge of parochial mission. [-ER[1]]
mi·ssis, -us, n. (As used by servants) the mistress; (vulg., facet.) *the m.*, one's own or another's wife. [corrupt. of MISTRESS]
mi·ssive, a. & n. *Letter(s) m.*, letter from sovereign to dean & chapter nominating person to be elected bishop; letter, esp. official one. [F, f. med. L *missivus* (as MISSION, -IVE)]
mis-spe·ll, v.t. (-spelt). Spell wrongly. [MIS-[1]]
mis-spe·nd, v.t. (-spent). Spend amiss or wastefully (esp. in p.p.). [MIS-[1]]
mis-sta·te, v.t. State wrongly. Hence **mis-sta·teMENT** n. [MIS-[1]]
mi·ssy, n. (Affectionate, playful, or con-

tempt.) = MISS[3] (not followed by name). [-Y[3]]

mist, n., & v.i. & t. Water vapour descending in fine drops smaller than raindrops; *Scotch m.*, thick m. frequent on Scottish hills; filmy appearance before eyes caused by disorders of body or by tears; (vb) cover, be covered, as with m. Hence **mi·st**FUL a., **mi·st**LIKE a. & adv. [(vb f. OE *mistian*) OE & Du., cogn. w. Gk *omikhlē*]

mista·ke[1], n. Misunderstanding of a thing's meaning; error, fault, in thought or action; (emphasizing preceding statement) *and*, or *make, no m.*, undoubtedly. [f. foll.]

mista·ke[2], v.t. & i. Misunderstand meaning or intention of (person, statement, purpose); err in opinion; (p.p.) wrong in opinion, (of action &c.) ill-judged, as *you are mistaken, mistaken kindness*, whence **mista·ken**LY[2] adv., **mista·ken**NESS n.; *m. A for* (think he is) *B*; *there is no mistaking*, no one can help recognizing (person, fact). Hence **mista·k**ABLE a. [f. ON *mistaka* (MIS-[1] + *taka* TAKE)]

mi·ster, n., & v.t. Title prefixed to man's name or to designation of office &c. (written *Mr*), as *Mr Jones, Mr Secretary, Mr Speaker*; *Mr Right*, destined husband; (alone as voc., vulg.) = *sir*; the word *m.* as title, as *please don't call me m.*; untitled person, as *be he prince or mere m.*; (v.t.) address as Mr, as *don't m. me.* [(vb f. n.) weakened form of MASTER]

mi·stigris, n. (cards). (Blank card in) a variety of poker. [f. F *mistigri* knave of spades]

misti·me, v.t. Say, do, (thing) out of season (esp. in p.p.). [MIS-[1]]

mi·stletoe (-zltō, -sltō), n. Parasitic plant growing on apple & other trees, & bearing glutinous fruit used in making birdlime; *kiss under the m.* (w. ref. to the custom permitting a girl standing below m. used as Christmas decoration to be kissed by the finder). [OE *mistiltán* (as MISSEL + *tán* twig)]

mi·stral (*or* -trah·l), n. Cold N.W. wind in Mediterranean provinces of France &c. [F & Pr., f. L as MAGISTRAL]

mistransla·te, v.t. Translate incorrectly. So **mistransla·tion** n. [MIS-[1]]

mi·stress, n. Woman in authority over servants; female head of household; woman who has power to control or dispose *of*, as *you are m. of the situation, you are your own m.*, (fig. of countries) *m. of the world* &c.; woman who has thorough knowledge (*of* subject); woman loved & courted by a man; woman illicitly occupying place of wife; female teacher in school or of special subject, as *music-m.*; *M. of the Robes*, lady charged with care of Queen's wardrobe; (as title) see MRS. Hence **mi·stress-**SHIP n. [f. OF *maistresse* (*maistre* MASTER[1], see -ESS[1])]

mistri·al, n. Trial vitiated by error. [MIS-[1]]

mistru·st, v.t. Feel no confidence in (person, one*self*, one's powers, &c.). So **mistru·st** n., whence **mistru·st**FUL a., **mistru·stful**LY[2] adv., **mistru·stful**NESS n. [MIS-[1]]

mi·sty, a. Of, covered with, mist; indistinct in form; (fig.) obscure, vague, as *a m. idea.* Hence **mi·sti**LY[2] adv., **mi·sti**NESS n. [OE *mistig* (as MIST, see -Y[2])]

misundersta·nd, v.t. (-stood). Take (words &c., or abs.) in wrong sense; misinterpret words or actions of (person, esp. in p.p.). So **misundersta·nding** n. [MIS-[1]]

misu·se (-z), v.t. Use wrongly, apply to wrong purpose; ill-treat. So **misu·se** (-s) n. [MIS-[1]]

mite, n. (Orig.) Flemish copper coin of small value; (pop.) half-farthing (as in *Mark* xii. 43); modest contribution, the best one can do, as *let me offer my m. of comfort*; (colloq.) *not a m.*, not at all; small object, esp. child; *a m. of a* (a tiny) *child* &c.; [OE *mite*, perh. different wd] kinds of arachnid, esp. *cheese-m.* (found in cheese), whence **mī·ty**[2] a. [f. MDu. *mîte*, cf. G *meite* small thing]

Mī·thrăs, -ra, n. Persian god identified with sun. Hence **Mithrā·ic** a., **Mi·thra**ISM, **Mi·thra**IST(2), nn. [L f. Gk (*-as*) f. OPers. (*-a*)]

mithrĭ·datize, v.t. Render proof against poison by gradually increasing doses of it. So **mithridă·**TIC a., **mi·thridat**ISM n. [f. *Mithridates VI*, king of Pontus, + -IZE]

mi·tigate, v.t. Appease (anger &c.); alleviate (pain, grief); reduce severity of (punishment); moderate (heat, cold, severity, &c.). So **mitig**A·TION n., **mi·tigat**ORY a. [f. L *mitigare* (*mitis* mild), see -ATE[3]]

mitrailleu·se (-trahyerz), n. Many-barrelled breech-loading machine gun discharging small missiles simultaneously or in rapid succession. [F, fem. agent-n. f. *mitrailler* (*mitraille* small missiles, OF small money, f. *mite* MITE)]

mi·tral, a. & n. Of, like, a mitre; *m.* (*valve*), a valve of the heart. [F (as foll., see -AL)]

mi·tre[1] (*-er*), n. Bishop's tall cap, deeply cleft at top, esp. as symbol of episcopal office, whence **mi·tr**ED[2] a.; [perh. different wd] joint of two pieces of wood &c. at angle of 90°, such that line of junction bisects this angle; angle of 45°; *m.-block, -board, -box*, guide for saw in cutting m.-joints; *m.-wheels*, pair of bevelled cog-wheels with teeth set at 45° & axes at right angles. [F, f. L f. Gk *mitra* girdle, turban]

mi·tre[2], v.t. Bestow mitre on; join with mitre; shape off (end of wood &c.) to a mitre; *mitring-machine* (for doing this.) [f. prec.]

mi·tten, mitt, n. (*Mitten*) kind of glove with thumb but no fingers, for warmth or protection in hedgers' work &c.; (now usu. *mitt*) woman's lace or knitted glove covering forearm & part of hand, but not fingers; *give, get, the mitten,* dismiss (lover), be dismissed, (gen.) be dismissed from office &c. Hence **mi·tten**ED[2] a. [f. F *mitaine,* etym. dub.]

mi·ttimus, n. Warrant committing person to prison; (colloq.) dismissal from office, as *get* one's *m.* [L, = we send]

mix, v.t. & i. Put together (two or more substances or groups, one *with* another) so that the particles or members of each are diffused among those of the others (also of immaterial things); prepare (compound) by mixing ingredients;(intr.) join, be mixed, as *oil will not m. with water, they* (persons) *do not m. well* (get on together); have intercourse *with*; *m. up,* mix thoroughly, also, confuse esp. in thought; *be mixed up,* be involved (*in, with,* shady dealings &c.). [back formation f. foll., taken as E p.p.]

mixed, a. In vbl senses, esp.: of diverse qualities or elements; (of company) not select, containing persons of doubtful status; (colloq.) mentally confused, muddled; for persons of both sexes, as *m. school, bathing*; *m.* MATHEMATICS. Hence **mi·xed**NESS n. [earlier *mixt* f. F *mixte* f. L *mixtus* p.p. of *miscēre* mix]

mi·xen, n. (dial.). Dung-hill. [OE (*meox* dung, cf. Fris. *miux,* + -EN[3])]

mi·xture (-tsh*er*), n. Mixing; what is mixed,esp.medicinalpreparation; HEATHER *m.*; mechanical mixing of two substances, involving no change in their character, opp. to *chemical combination.* [f. L *mixtura* (as prec., see -URE)]

Mi·zpah. *M. ring,* one inscribed *M.* w. ref. to *Gen.* XXXI. 49 & given as love-token.

mi·z(z)en, n. (naut.). (Also *m.-sail*) lowest square sail (rarely set, SPANKER being usual) of full-rigged ship's *m.-mast* (aftermost mast of three-masted ship); *m. yard* (on which m. is extended). [f. F *misaine* perh. f. It. *mezzana* m.-sail, fem. adj., see MEZZANINE]

mi·zzle[1], v. impers. Drizzle. Hence **mi·zzle** n., **mi·zzly**[2] a. [cogn. w. Du. dial. *miezelen* & LG *misig* drizzly]

mi·zzle[2], v.i. (slang). Go, decamp. [?]

mnemŏ·nic (n-), a. & n. Of, designed to aid, the memory; (n. pl.) art of, system for, improving memory. Hence **mnē·mo**NIST n. [f. Gk *mnēmonikos* (*mnēmōn* mindful f. *mna-* remember, see -IC)]

mnemote·chny, (n-) n. =prec. (n. pl.). Hence **mnemote·chn**IC a. [f. Gk *mnēmē* memory + *tekhnē* art]

mo, abbr. (vulg. & joc.) for *moment* (esp. *wait, in, half a mo*).

moan[1], n. Long low murmur of physical or mental suffering; (archaic) *make* (one's) *m.,* complain. Hence **moa·n**FUL a. [cogn. w. OE *mǣnan,* obs. *mean,* vb, replaced by foll.]

moan[2], v.i. & t. Make moan(s); utter (specified words) with moans; lament (misfortune &c.); lament for (dead person &c.). [f. prec.]

moat, n., & v.t. Deep wide ditch surrounding town, castle, &c., usu. filled with water; (v.t.) surround (as) with m. [(vb f. n.) ME & OF *mote* mound prob. of Teut. orig.]

mob[1], n. The lower orders; rabble, tumultuous crowd; promiscuous assemblage of persons; *m. law* (imposed, enforced, by m.); *swell m.,* class of stylishly dressed pickpockets. Hence **mo·bb**ISH[1] a., **mobŏ·**CRACY n. [earlier *mobile vulgus,* L, = excitable crowd (MOBILE)]

mob[2], v.t. & i. (Of mob) attack, molest; assemble in a mob. [f. prec.]

mob-cap, n. Woman's indoor cap covering whole head, worn in 18th & early 19th cc. [f. obs. *mob* in same sense, cf. Du. *mop* woman's coif, *mopmuts* woman's nightcap]

mō·bĭle, a. Movable, not fixed, free to move; (of person or mind) easily, too easily, changing; (of troops) that may be easily moved from place to place. So **mobi·l**ITY n. [F, f. L *mobilis* (*movēre* move, see -BLE)]

mō·bilize, v.t. Render movable, bring into circulation; prepare (army, navy) for active service (also quasi-pass. of army). So **mo·biliz**ABLE a., **mobiliza·**TION n. [f. F *mobiliser,* as prec.]

mo·ccasin, n. Foot-gear of deerskin &c. worn by N.-Amer. Indians, trappers, &c. [f. native *mockasin*]

mō·cha[1] (-k-), n. Kind of chalcedony. [?]

mō·cha[2] (-k-), n. (Also *M. coffee*) fine quality of coffee, orig. from *M.,* Arabian port at entrance of Red Sea.

mock[1], n. (archaic). Derision; thing deserving scorn; imitation, counterfeit. [f. MOCK[3]]

mock[2], a. (not pred.). Sham; *m. sun, moon,* = PARHELION, PARASELENE; *m. duck, goose,* pork with duck stuffing; *m.-turtle soup* (usu. of calf's head, to imitate turtle); *m.-heroic* a. & n., burlesquely imitating, burlesque imitation of, heroic style. [prec. & foll.]

mock[3], v.t. & i. Hold up to ridicule; defy contemptuously; impose upon; ridicule by imitation; scoff *at*; *mocking-bird,* American song-bird that mimics notes of other birds, other birds that do this. Hence **mo·cking**LY[2] adv. [f. OF *mocquer,* etym. dub.]

mo·ckery, n. Derision; subject, occasion, of this; counterfeit representation (*of*); ludicrously or insultingly futile action &c. [f. F *moquerie* (as prec., see -ERY)]

mō·dal, a. Of mode or form as opp. to substance; *m. legacy* (with directions as to mode in which it is to be applied);

(Gram.) of the mood of a verb, (of particle) denoting manner; (Logic) *m. proposition*, one in which predicate is affirmed of subject under some qualification, (also) one that involves affirmation of possibility, impossibility, necessity, or contingency. Hence or cogn. **moda·**LITY n. (esp. in pl. = method laid down for discharge of obligation &c.), **mo·dal**LY[2] adv. [f. med. L *modalis* (as foll., see -AL)]

mode, n. Way, manner, in which thing is done; prevailing fashion or custom; (archaic) *the m.*, the fashion in dress &c.; (Mus.) each of the two (MAJOR[2], MINOR) classes of keys, (in ancient & mediaeval music) form of scale, as DORIAN, LYDIAN, IONIAN, AUTHENTIC, PLAGAL, *m.*; (Logic) character of modal proposition. [(partly F) f. L *modus* measure, manner]

mŏ·del[1] (-dl), **n.** Representation in three dimensions of proposed structure &c.; *working m.* (imitating movements of machine it represents); figure in clay, wax, &c., to be reproduced in other material; design, style of structure; person, thing, proposed for imitation; person who poses for artists; woman in draper's shop wearing clothes &c. to show their effect to customers; *The New M.*, plan for reorganization of Parliamentary army 1644–5; (attrib.) exemplary, ideally perfect. [f. OF *modelle* f. It. *modello* dim. of *modo* (as MODE)]

mŏ·del[2] **(-dl),** v.t. (-ll-). Fashion, shape, (figure) in clay, wax, &c.; give shape to (document, argument, &c.); form (thing) *after, on, upon*, a model. [f. prec.]

mŏ·dena, n. Deep purple. [*M.*, Italian city]

mŏ·derate[1] (-*a*t), a. & n. Avoiding extremes, temperate in conduct or expression; fairly large or good; *m. prices*, low (in advertisements &c., as *prices strictly m.*); (n.) one who holds m. opinions in politics &c., whence **mo·derat**ISM n. Hence **mo·derate**LY[2] adv., **mo·derate**NESS n. [f. L *moderari* f. st. *modes-* (cf. MODEST) cogn. w. *modus* MODE, -ATE[2]]

mŏ·derāte[2], v.t. & i. Render less violent, intense, vigorous, &c.; (of fury, storm, &c.) become less vehement; act as moderator. [as prec., see -ATE[3]]

modera·tion, n. Moderating; moderateness; *in m.*, in a moderate manner or degree; (Oxf. Univ., pl.) first public examination for degree of B.A. (abbr. *mods*). [f. F *modération* f. L *moderationem* (as MODERATE[1], see -ATION)]

mŏ·derātor, n. Arbitrator; mediator; presiding officer; one of two officers presiding over mathematical tripos at Cambridge; examiner for moderations; Presbyterian minister presiding over any ecclesiastical body; *m. lamp* (with contrivance for regulating flow of oil). Hence **mo·derator**SHIP n. [f. F *modérateur* f. L *moderator* (as prec., see -OR[2])]

mŏ·dern, a. & n. Of the present & recent times; *m. school, side*, in schools, division in which subjects other than ancient languages are taught; new-fashioned, not antiquated; (n.) person living in m. times. Hence or cogn. **moder·**NITY, **mo·dern**NESS, **moderniza·**TION, nn., **mo·dern**IZE(3) v.t. & i., **mo·dern**LY[2] adv. [f. LL *modernus* (*modo* just now)]

mo·dernism, n. Modern view(s) or method(s), esp. tendency in matters of religious belief to subordinate tradition to harmony with modern thought; so **mo·dern**IST(2) **n.**; modern term or expression. [-ISM]

mŏ·dest, a. Having a humble estimate of one's own merits; retiring, bashful; (of women) decorous in manner & conduct, scrupulously chaste; (of demands, statements, &c.) not excessive; (of things) unpretentious in appearance, amount, &c. Hence or cogn. **mo·dest**LY[2] adv., **mo·dest**Y[1] n. [f. F *modeste* f. L *modestus* (see MODERATE[1])]

mŏ·dicum, n. Small quantity (*of* food &c.). [L, neut. of *modicus* moderate (*modus* measure)]

mŏ·dify̆, v.t. Make less severe or decided, tone down; make partial changes in; (Gram.) qualify sense of (word &c.); change (vowel) by umlaut. Hence or cogn. **modifia**BI·LITY, **modi**FICA·TION, nn., **mo·difi**ABLE, **mo·dificat**ORY, aa. [f. F *modifier* f. L *modificare* (as MODE, see -FY)]

modi·llion, n. (archit.). Projecting bracket under corona of cornice in Corinthian & other orders. [f. It. *modiglione*, etym. dub.]

mō·dish, a. Fashionable. Hence **mo·dish**LY[2] adv., **mo·dish**NESS n. [f. MODE + -ISH[1]]

mŏdi·ste (-ēst), n. Milliner, dressmaker. [F (as MODE, see -IST)]

mŏ·dulate, v.t. & i. Regulate, adjust; vary (thing) conformably *to*; attune (voice) to certain pitch; (Mus.) pass, make transition, (*from* key *to* key). So **modula·**TION, **mo·dulat**OR[2], nn. [f. L *modulari* measure, adjust, (as foll.), see -ATE[3]]

mŏ·dule, n. Standard, unit, for measuring; (Arch.) unit of length for expressing proportions, usu. semidiameter of column at base. [F, as foll.]

mŏ·dulus, n. (pl. *-li*). Constant multiplier esp. for converting Napierian into common logarithms; constant indicating relation between amount of physical effect & that of force producing it. [L, = measure, dim. of foll.]

mō·dus, n. *M. operandi*, way a person goes to work, way a thing operates; *m. vivendi*, mode of living, i.e. arrangement between disputants pending settlement of debate; money payment in lieu of tithe (orig. *m. decimandi*). [L, = MODE]

mofe·tte, **n.** (Fissure in earth from which issues) exhalation of mephitic gas. [F]

mofu·ssil, n. (Anglo-Ind.). Rural localities as opp. to chief station. [f. Hind. *mufaççil* f. Arab. *mufaççal* p.p. of *faççala* divide]

Mogŭ·l, n. & a. Mongolian; *the* (*Great* or *Grand*) *M.*, emperor of Delhi; (pl.) playing cards of best quality. [f. Pers. *mugul* f. MONGOL]

mō·hair, n. (Fine camlet, yarn, from) hair of Angora goat. [ult. f. Arab. *mukhayyar*, lit. = choice, select, (*khayyara* choose)]

Moha·mmedan, n. & a. (Follower) of Mohammed, founder of the Moslem religion. Hence **Moha·mmedan**ISM(3) n., **Moha·mmedan**IZE(3) v.t. [*Mohammed* f. Arab. *Muhammad* + -AN]

Mō·hawk, n. One of a tribe of N.-Amer. Indians; their language; (Skating) step from either edge in one direction to same edge on other foot in opposite direction (cf. CHOCTAW). [native]

Mō·hock, n. (hist.). One of a class of aristocratic ruffians infesting London streets at night in 18th c. [f. prec.]

mō·hur, n. (Also *gold m.*) gold coin of British India, worth 15 rupees. [f. Pers. *muhr* seal]

moi·der, v.t. (dial.). To perplex, confuse, worry (esp. in p.p.). [?]

moi·dore, n. Portuguese gold coin worth, sum of, 27*s*. [f. Port. *moeda d'ouro* (*moeda* MONEY + *ouro* f. L *aurum* gold)]

moi·ety, n. Half, esp. in legal use; (loosely) one of two parts into which thing is divided. [f. OF *moit(i)é* f. L *medietatem* middle point (as MEDIUM, see -TY)]

moil, v.i. Drudge, esp. *toil & m.* [f. OF *moillier* moisten, paddle in mud, f. L *mollis* soft]

moire (mwahr), n. (Also *m. antique*) watered fabric, usu. silk, orig. mohair. [F, perh. f. MOHAIR]

moiré (mwah·rā), a. & n. (Of silk) watered; (of metals) having clouded appearance like watered silk; (n.) this appearance. [F, p.p. of *moirer* give moiré appearance to]

moist, a. Slightly wet, damp; (of season &c.) rainy; (of disease) marked by discharge of matter &c. Hence **moi·st**NESS n. [f. OF *moiste*, etym. dub.]

moi·sten (-sn), v.t. & i. Make moist; become moist. [-EN⁶]

moi·sture (-tsh*er*), n. Water or other liquid diffused in small quantity as vapour, condensed on surface, &c. Hence **moi·sture**LESS n. [f. OF *moistour* (as MOIST, see -OR¹)]

moke, n. (slang). Donkey. [?]

mō·ko, n. Maori system of tattooing. [Maori]

mō·lar¹, a. & n. (Usu. of mammal's back teeth) serving to grind; (n.) m. tooth. [f. L *molaris* (*mola* millstone, see -AR¹)]

mō·lar², a. Of mass; acting on or by means of large masses. [f. L *moles* mass, see -AR¹)]

mola·sses, n. pl. (treated as sing.). Uncrystallized syrup drained from raw sugar; syrup got from sugar in process of refining, treacle. [f. Port. *melaço* f. LL *mellaceum* must (*mel mellis* honey, see -ACEOUS)]

mole¹, n. Spot, blemish, on human skin. [OE *mál*, cf. OHG *meil*]

mole², n. Small burrowing animal with (usu. blackish) velvety fur & very small eyes, other mammals of same family; *blind as a m.* (quite); *m.-hill*, small mound thrown up by m. in burrowing (*make mountains out of m.-hh.*, exaggerate obstacles &c.); *moleskin*, skin of mole as fur, kind of cotton fustian with surface shaved before dyeing, (pl.) clothes, esp. trousers, of this. [ME *mulle, molle*, cf. MDu. *mol*]

mole³, n. Massive structure, usu. of stone, as pier, breakwater, or junction between places separated by water; artificial harbour. [f. F *môle* f. L *moles* mass]

molĕ·cular, a. Of molecules; acting, inherent, in the molecules of a substance; *m. weight* of substance (of one of its molecules relatively to one of hydrogen). Hence **moleculă·**RITY n., **mole·cular**LY² adv. [-AR¹]

mŏ·lĕcule, n. (Physics, Chem.) one of the minute groups of atoms of which material substances are conceived to consist, smallest portions into which substance can be divided without losing chemical identity; (loosely) small particle. [f. F *molécule* dim. of L *moles* mass]

mole·st, v.t. (Usu. after neg.) meddle hostilely or injuriously with (person). So **mŏlest**A·TION n. [f. OF *molester* f. L *molestare* (*molestus* troublesome, perh. cogn. w. *moles* mass)]

Mŏ·linism, n. Doctrine of Luis Molina (d. 1600), that efficacy of grace depends on the will that freely accepts it; doctrine of Miguel de Molinos (d. 1696), quietism. Hence **Mo·lin**IST n. [f. *Molina, Molinos*, + -ISM]

mo·llify̆, v.t. Appease, soften. So **molli**FICA·TION n. [f. F *mollifier* f. L *mollificare* (*mollis* soft, see -FY)]

mo·llusc, n. Animal belonging to the *Mollusca*, sub-kingdom of soft-bodied & usu. hard-shelled animals, including limpets, snails, cuttle-fish, oyster, mussel, &c. Hence **mollu·sc**AN, **mollu·sc**OUS, aa., **mollu·sc**OID a. & n. [f. L *molluscus* (*mollis* soft)]

mo·lly, n. Effeminate man or boy, milksop; *m.-coddle*, (n.) milksop, (v.t.) coddle, cocker up. [pet form of *Mary*]

Mō·loch (-k), n. Canaanite idol to whom children were sacrificed (often fig.); thorn-lizard, a hideous Australian reptile. [L f. Gk, f. Heb. *molek*]

molo·ssus, n. Metrical foot – – –. [Gk *molossos*]

mo·lten. See MELT.

mŏ·lto, adv. Very (preceding mus.

direction, as *m. espressivo*). [It., f. L *multus* much]

mō·ly, n. Fabulous herb with white flower & black root, endowed with magic properties; wild garlic & other plants. [L, f. Gk *mōlu*]

mō·ment, n. Minute point of time, instant; *one m.*, *half a m.*, (ellipt.) wait a m.; *come here this m.* (at once); *came the very m.* (as soon as) *I heard of it*; *timed to the m.* (with absolute accuracy); *the m.* (time that affords an opportunity); *am, was, busy at the m.* (just now, then), so *men of* (important at) *the m.*; (Mech.) *m. of a force about a point*, measure of its power in causing rotation; importance, as *of great, little, no, m.*, whence **mome·nt**OUS a., **mome·ntous**LY² adv., **mome·ntous**NESS n. [f. MOMENTUM]

mō·mentary, a. Lasting only a moment; short-lived, transitory. Hence **mo·mentari**LY² adv., **mo·mentari**NESS n. [f. L *momentarius* (as prec., see -ARY¹)]

mō·mently, adv. From moment to moment; every moment; for a moment. [-LY²]

mome·ntum, n.(pl. *-ta*). (Mech.) quantity of motion of moving body, product of its mass by its velocity; (pop.) impetus gained by movement (lit. & fig.). [L (as MOVE, see -MENT)]

Mō·mus, n. Greek god of ridicule; fault-finder. [L, f. Gk *Mōmos*]

mŏ·nac(h)al, a. Monastic. So **mo·na·ch**ISM (-k-), n. [f. eccl. L *monachalis* (MONK, -AL)]

mŏ·nad, n. The number one, unit; ultimate unit of being (e.g. a soul, an atom, a person, God), esp. in philosophy of Leibnitz, whence **mo·nad**ISM(3) n.; (Biol.) simple organism assumed as first term in genealogy of living beings; (Chem.) element, radical, with combining power of one atom of hydrogen. Hence **monă·d**IC a. [f. L f. Gk *monas -ados* unit (*monos* alone)]

mŏnade·lphous, a. (bot.). (Of stamens) having filaments united into one bundle; (of plants) with m. stamens. [f. Gk *monos* one + *adelphos*, brother + -OUS]

mona·ndrous, a. (bot.). Having a single stamen. [f. Gk *monandros* (*monos* one + *anēr andros* male) + -OUS]

mona·ndry, n. Custom of having only one husband at a time. [as prec. + -Y¹]

mŏ·narch (*-erk*), n. Sovereign with title of king, queen, emperor, empress, or equivalent; supreme ruler (often fig.); large red & black butterfly. Hence **monar·ch**AL, **monar·ch**IC(AL), aa., **monar·chal**LY², **monar·ch**ICALLY, advv. [f. L (*-cha*) f. Gk *monarkhēs* (*monos* alone + *arkhō* rule)]

mo·narchism, n. Principles of, attachment to, monarchy. So **mo·narch**IST n. [-ISM]

mo·narchy, n. (State under) monarchical government; *constitutional, limited, m.* (subject to constitutional restrictions). [f. F *monarchie* f. L f. Gk *monarkhia* (MONARCH, -Y¹)]

mŏ·nastery, n. Residence of community (usu. of monks) living secluded under religious vows. [f. eccl. L f. late Gk *monastērion* (*monazō* live alone f. *monos*)]

monă·stic, a. Of monks or monasteries; (Bookbind.) finished by tooling without gold (also *antique*). Hence **mona·st**ICALLY adv., **mona·stic**ISM(3) n., **mona·stic**IZE(3) v.t. [f. med. L f. late Gk *monastikos* (as prec., see -IC)]

Mo·nday (mŭ-), n. Second day of week; *Black M.* (school slang), first day of term; *St M.*, M. as day of little work (w. ref. to saint's-day holidays). [OE *Mónan dæg* (*móna* moon + *dæg* DAY)]

mo·ndayish, a. (Of clergy) indisposed as result of Sunday work; (of others) slack as result of Sunday holiday. [-ISH¹]

monde (F), n. The fashionable world, society; the set in which one moves.

mo·netary (mŭ-, mŏ-), a. Of the coinage; of money. [f. L *monetarius* (as MONEY, see -ARY¹)]

mo·netize (mŭ-, mŏ-), v.t. Put (metal) into circulation as money. Hence **mone·tiz**A·TION n. [f. L *moneta* MONEY + -IZE]

mo·ney (mŭ-), n. Current coin; coin & promissory documents representing it (*paper m.*), esp. government & bank notes; (w. pl.) particular coin; (pl., archaic, legal) sums of money; *m. of* ACCOUNT²; CONSCIENCE *m.*; property viewed as convertible into m.; coin in reference to its purchasing power, as (prov.) *m. makes the mare to go, time is m., for* LOVE¹ *or m.*; *make m.*, acquire wealth, *coin m.*, do this rapidly; *not every man's m.*, not worth its price to every one; *m.-bag*, bag for m., (pl.) wealth; *m.-bags*, wealthy or avaricious person; *m.-box*, closed box into which savings or contributions are dropped through slit; *m.-changer*, one whose business it is to change m. at fixed rate; *m.-grubber*, person sordidly intent on amassing m., *-grubbing* a. & n., (given to) this practice; *m.-lender*, one whose business it is to lend m. at interest; *m.-market*, sphere of operation of dealers in stocks &c.; *m.* ORDER¹3; *m.-spinner*, small spider thought to bring good luck; *money-wort*, plant with round glossy leaves; *m.'s-worth*, anything recognized as equivalent to m. Hence **mo·ney**LESS a. [f. OF *moneie* f. L *moneta* mint, money, orig. goddess in whose temple at Rome m. was coined]

mo·neyed, a. Rich; consisting of money, as *m. resources, assistance*; *m. interest*, the class concerned in money as a possession. [-ED²]

mo·nger (mŭngg-), n. Dealer, trader, (chiefly in comb., as *cheesem.*, *fishm.*, *ironm.*, *costerm.*, & fig. *scandal-m.* &c.). [OE *mangere* (*mangian* to traffic f. L *mango* dealer)]

Mŏ·ngol, n. & a. (Member) of Asiatic race now inhabiting Mongolia, between China & Siberia. [native, perh. f. *mong* brave]

Mongō·lian, a. & n. =prec.; (Anthrop.) of the yellow-skinned straight-haired type of mankind; of a class of idiots like Mm. [-IAN]

mŏ·ngoose, mŭ·ngoose, (-ngg-), n. An ichneumon, common in India, & able to kill venomous snakes unharmed; kind of lemur. [f. native *mangus*]

mo·ngrel (mŭngg-), n. & a. Dog of no definable breed; animal, plant, resulting from crossing of different breeds or kinds; person not of pure race; (adj.) of mixed origin, nature, or character. Hence **mo·ngrel**ISM(2) n., **mo·ngrel**IZE(3) v.t., **mo·ngrel**LY[1] a. [prob. f. root *mang-, mong-*, mix, + -REL]

mō·nial, n. Mullion. [OF, etym. dub.]

monĭ·liform, a. Suggesting necklace or string of beads. [f. L *monile* necklace, -FORM]

mŏ·nism, n. Doctrine that only one being exists; any of the theories that deny the duality of matter & mind. Hence **mo·n**IST n., **moni·st**IC a. [f. Gk *monos* one, -ISM]

moni·tion, n. Warning (*of* danger); formal notice from bishop or ecclesiastical court admonishing person to refrain from some offence; (in courts that use civil law process) summons. [f. L *monitio* (*monēre monit-* warn, -ION)]

mŏ·nitor, n. (Archaic) one who admonishes; senior pupil in school with duties of keeping order &c., whence **monitor·**IAL a., **mo·nitor**SHIP n.; lizard supposed to give warning of approach of crocodiles; ironclad heavily gunned & armoured for coast defence. Hence **mo·nitr**ESS[1] n. [L (as prec., -OR[2])]

mŏ·nitory, a. & n. Warning, admonitory; (n.) bishop's or pope's letter of admonition. [f. L *monitorius* (as prec., see -ORY)]

monk (mŭ-), n. Member of community living apart under vows of poverty, chastity, & obedience; *m.'s-hood,* kinds of plant. Hence **mo·nk**HOOD, **mo·nk**SHIP, nn. [OE *munuc* f. pop. L *monicus* =L f. Gk *monakhos* solitary (*monos* alone)]

mo·nkery (mŭ-), n. Monastic life; monastery; monks; monkish practices. So **mo·nk**DOM n. [-ERY]

mo·nkey (mŭ-), n., & v.t. & i. Mammal of a group closely allied to & resembling man, ranging from anthropoid apes to marmosets; (as term of playful contempt, to or of person) *young m.* &c.; machine hammer for pile-driving &c.; globular earthenware water-vessel with straight upright neck; *put his m. up,* enrage him, *get* one's *m. up,* become angry; (slang) £500; *m.-bread,* fruit of baobab tree; *m.-cup,* pitcher-plant; *m.-jacket,* short close-fitting one worn by sailors &c.; *m.-nut,* peanut; *m.-puzzle, puzzle-m.,* Chili pine, prickly tree of genus *Araucaria*; *m.-wrench,* one with movable jaw; (v.t.) mimic, mock; (v.i.) play mischievous tricks. Hence **mo·nkey**ISH[1] a., **mo·nkey-ish**NESS n. [?]

mo·nkish, a. Of monks, monastic; characteristic of monks (usu. in bad sense). [-ISH[1]]

mŏ·no- in comb. (before vowels *mon-*) =Gk *monos* alone, sole, single; as: (1) *-bā·sic* (Chem.), having one base or atom of a base; *-car·pic, -car·pous,* bearing fruit only once; *-cĕ·phalous* (Bot.), having only one head; *-cli·nal,* (of strata) dipping in one & the same direction; *-cotylē·don(ous),* (plant with) single cotyledon; *monŏ·cracy,* government by single person; *monŏ·cular,* with, adapted to, one eye; *-cycle,* velocipede with one wheel; *-da·ctylous,* having one finger, toe, or claw; *-drama,* piece for one performer; *monoe·cious* (-nē-), (Bot.) with male & female organs on same plant, (Zool.) hermaphrodite; *-ge·nesis,* development of all beings from single cell, so *-genĕ·tic* a.; *monŏ·geny,* descent of mankind from one pair of ancestors; *-glot* a. & n., (one) who uses only one language; *monŏ·gy̆nous,* with only one pistil or stigma; *monŏ·gyny,* usage of mating with only one female; *mono-idē·ism,* concentration on single idea, esp. as form of monomania; *monŏ·latry,* worship of one god without denying that others may exist; *-mā·nia,* insanity on one subject only, so *-mā·niăc* n., *-manī·acal* a.; *-me·tallism,* standard of currency based on one metal, so *-meta·llic* a.; *-mor·phic, -mor·phous,* not changing form during development; *-pĕ·talous,* having corolla in one piece, or petals united into tube; *-phthong,* single vowel sound; *-plane,* aeroplane with one plane; *-psy·chism,* theory that all souls are one; *-rail,* railway of one rail; *-rhyme,* poem in which all lines have same rhyme; *-sper·mous* (Bot.), having one seed; *monŏ·stichous* (-k-) (Bot., Zool.), arranged in, consisting of, one layer or row; *-stro·phic,* consisting of repetitions of one strophic arrangement; *-tint,* representation, picture, in only one colour; *mo·notreme,* member of lowest order of mammals with one vent for urinary, genital, & digestive organs; *-type,* composing-machine that casts & sets up type; *-ty̆·pic,* represented by only one type. (2) chem. wds denoting presence of a single atom or combining equivalent, as *-bro·mide, -car·bon, -chlor·ide, mono·xide.*

mo·nochord (-k-), n. Instrument for determination of musical intervals. [f. F *monocorde* f. L f. Gk MONO(*khordon* f. *khordē* CHORD)]

monochromă·tic, a. (Of light) presenting one colour only; executed in monochrome. [MONO- + CHROMATIC]

mo·nochrome, n. & a. Painting executed in different tints of one colour; representation in one colour; (adj.) having only one colour. [ult. f. Gk MONO(*khrōmatos* f. *khrōma* colour)]

mŏ·nocle, n. Single eye-glass. [F, f. LL *monoculus* one-eyed being (MONO- + *oculus* eye)]

mŏ·nody, n. Ode sung by single actor in Greek tragedy; poem in which mourner bewails some one's death. Hence or cogn. **monŏ·dic** a., **mo·nodist** n. [f. L f. Gk *monōidia* f. *monōidos* singing alone (MONO- + *ōid-*, *aoid-*, f. *aeidō* sing)]

monŏ·gamy, n. Practice, circumstance, of being married to one at a time; (rare) practice of marrying only once; (Zool.) habit of having only one mate. Hence or cogn. **mono·gamist** n., **mono·gamous** a. [f. F *monogamie* f. L f. Gk MONO(*gamia* f. *gamos* marriage)]

mo·nogram, n. Two or more letters, esp. person's initials, interwoven. So **monogrammă·tic** a. [f. LL *monogramma* f. late Gk MONO(*grammon*, neut. adj. as -GRAM)]

mo·nograph, n., & v.t. Separate treatise on single object or class of objects; (v.t.) write a m. on. Hence **mono·grapher**[1], **mono·graphist,** nn., **monogra·phic** a., **momogra·phically** adv. [MONO- + -GRAPH]

mo·nolith, n. Single block of stone, esp. shaped into pillar or monument. Hence **monoli·thic** a. [f. L f. Gk MONO(*lithos* stone)]

mo·nologue (-ŏg), n. Scene in drama in which one person speaks by himself; dramatic composition for single performer; long speech by one person in a company; soliloquy. Hence **monolo·gical** a., **mono·logist, mo·nologuist,** nn., **mono·logize**(2) v.i. [F, = one who loves to hear himself talk, f. Gk MONO(*logos* -LOGUE)]

monō·mial, n. & a. (alg.). (Expression) consisting of one term. [MONO-, on *binomial*]

Monŏ·physite, n. One who holds there is only one nature in the person of Christ. [f. eccl. L (*-ta*) f. eccl. Gk MONO(*phusitēs* f. *phusis* nature, see -ITE[1])]

mono·polist, n. One who favours monopoly; one who assumes monopoly (*of*). [-IST]

mono·polize, v.t. Obtain exclusive possession or control of (trade, commodity, the conversation, person's attention, &c.). Hence **monopoliza·tion** n. [f. foll. + -IZE]

monŏ·poly, n. Exclusive possession of the trade in some commodity; this conferred as privilege by State; exclusive possession, control, or exercise (*of*); thing that is monopolized. [f. LL f. Gk MONO(*pōlion* f. *pōleō* sell)]

monopŏ·lylogue (-ŏg), n. Entertainment in which sole performer plays many parts. [MONO- + POLY- + -LOGUE]

monosy·llable, n. Word of one syllable; *speak in mm.*, answer little but Yes or No, with intentional curtness. Hence or cogn. **monosyllă·bic** a., **monosylla·bically** adv., **monosy·llabism**(2) n., **monosy·llabize**(3) v.t. [f. LL MONO(*syllabus* SYLLABLE)]

mo·notheĭsm, n. Doctrine that there is only one God. Hence **mo·notheist** n., **monothei·stic** a. [f. MONO- + Gk *theos* god + -ISM]

mo·notone, a. & n., & v.t. (Utterance of successive syllables) without change of pitch, whence **monotŏ·nic** a. (mus.); sameness of style in writing; (v.t.) recite, speak, sing, in unvaried tone. [(vb f. n.) f. late Gk MONO(*tonos* TONE)]

monŏ·tonous, a. (Of sound or utterance) without variation in tone or cadence; lacking in variety, wearisome through sameness. Hence or cogn. **mono·tonize** (3) v.t., **mono·tonously**[2] adv., **mono·tonousness, mono·tony**[1], nn. [as MONOTONE + -OUS]

Monroe·ism (mŭ-), n. Monroe DOCTRINE. So **Monroe·ist** n. [-ISM]

monseigneur (F), n. (pl. *messeigneurs*). French title given to eminent persons, esp. princes, cardinals, archbishops, & bishops.

monsieur (mesyer·, *or as F*), n. (pl. *messieurs*). French equivalent of MR, but also used by itself as substitute for name, as *did M. ring?*; Frenchman; (Hist.) title of second son or next younger brother of French king.

***mŏnsignor·*(ĕ)** (-sēny-), n. Title of prelates, officers of Papal court, & others. [It., after MONSEIGNEUR]

monsoo·n, n. Wind in S. Asia, esp. in Indian Ocean, blowing from S.W. in summer (*wet m.*) & N.E. in winter (*dry m.*); rainy season; other winds with periodic alternations. [f. Du. *monssoen* f. Port. *monção* perh. f. Arab. *mausim*, lit. season, (*wasama* mark)]

mo·nster, n. & a. Mis-shapen animal or plant, abortion; imaginary animal compounded of incongruous elements, e.g. centaur, sphinx, griffin; inhumanly wicked person, inhuman example *of* (cruelty &c.); animal, thing, of huge size; (adj.) huge. [f. OF *monstre* f. L *monstrum* portent, monster (*monēre* warn)]

mo·nstrance, n. (R.-C. Ch.). Open or transparent vessel of gold or silver in which the host is exposed. [OF, f. med. L *monstrantia* (*monstrare* show, see -ANCE)

monstrŏ·sity, n. Monstrousness; abortion, imaginary monster; outrageous thing. [f. LL *monstrositas* (as foll., see -TY)]

mo·nstrous, a. & adv. Abnormally formed, of the nature of a monster; huge; outrageously wrong or absurd; atrocious;

(adv., archaic) extremely, as *m. good friends.* Hence **mo·nstrous**LY[2] adv., **mo·nstrous**NESS n. [f. OF *monstreux* f. LL *monstrosus* (MONSTER, -OUS)]

mo·ntane, a. Of, inhabiting, mountainous country. [f. L *montanus* (as MOUNT, see -ANE)]

mo·ntĕ, n. Spanish game of chance, played with 45 cards; *three-card m.*, game of Mexican origin. [Sp., = mountain, heap of cards]

Montenē·grin, n. & a. (Inhabitant) of Montenegro. [-INE[1]]

mo·nth (mŭ-), n. Any of the twelve portions into which the year is divided (also *calendar m.*); *lunar m.*, period in which moon makes complete revolution; space of time from a day in one month to corresponding day in next; space of 28 days; *m. of Sundays*, indefinite period; *this day m.*, a month from to-day; *m.'s mind*, mass &c. in commemoration of deceased person a month after death, (also) inclination, liking. [com.-Teut.: OE *mónadh*, Du. *maand*, G *monat*, cogn. w. MOON]

mo·nthly (mŭ-), a. & n. Done, recurring, payable, &c., once a month; *m. nurse* (attending woman during first month after childbirth); *m. rose*, China rose, supposed to flower monthly. (N.) magazine &c. published each month; (pl.) menses. So **mo·nth**LY[2] adv. [-LY[1]]

mo·nticule, n. Small hill; small mound caused by volcanic eruption; minute eminence on surface of animal &c. [F, f. LL *monticulus* (*mons* MOUNT, see -CULE)]

mŏ·nument, n. Written record; anything that serves to commemorate, esp. structure, building; *The M.*, column in London commemorating fire of London in 1666; stone or other structure placed over grave or in church &c. in memory of the dead. [f. L *monumentum* (*monēre* remind, see -MENT)]

monume·ntal, a. Of, serving as, a monument; (of literary works) massive & permanent; stupendous, as *m. ignorance.* Hence **monume·ntal**LY[2] adv. [f. LL *monumentalis* (as prec., see -AL)]

monume·ntalize, v.t. Record, commemorate, as by monument. [prec., + -IZE]

-mony, suf. = L *-monia, -monium*, which formed nn. f. aa. (*acrimonia*), nn. (*patrimonium*), & vbs (*alimonium*), adopted in E thr. F or direct; in E the *-a* & *-um* forms are alike; in F *-um* gave *-moine, -a -monie*, (*patrimoine, parcimonie*).

moo, v.i. (Of cow or ox) low, make the sound *moo.* Hence **moo** n. [imit.]

mooch, mouch, (mōō-), v.i. & t. (slang). Loiter *about*, slouch *along*; (trans.) steal. [perh. f. OF *muchier* hide, skulk]

mōōd[1], n. State of mind or feeling; *in the m., in no m.*, inclined, disinclined, (*for* thing, *to* do). [com.-Teut.: OE *mód*, Du. *moed*, G *mut*]

mōōd[2], n. (Gram.) any of the groups of forms in conjugation of verb that serve to indicate its function, as *indicative, imperative, subjunctive, m.*; (Mus.) = MODE; (Log.) any of the classes into which each of the figures of valid categorical syllogism is subdivided. [var. of MODE, by assoc. w. prec.]

mōō·dy, a. Gloomy, sullen. Hence **moo·di**LY[2] adv., **moo·di**NESS n. [OE *módig* (see MOOD[1] & -Y[2])]

moollah. See MULLAH.

mōōn[1], n. Satellite of the earth, revolving round it monthly, & deriving light from sun & reflecting it to earth; this in particular month, regarded as a distinct object from that visible in other months, as *age of the m., new m.* (at beginning of revolution), *full m.* (with disk entirely illuminated; (Poet.) month (*where summer is but three mm. long*); *once in a* BLUE[1] *m.*; *old m. in new m.'s arms*, m. during first quarter, when dark part of orb is made faintly luminous by earthlight; *moonbeam*, ray of moonlight; *mooncalf*, born fool; *m.-flower*, ox-eye daisy; *moonlight*, light of m. (often attrib.); *moonlight flitting*, removal of household goods by night to avoid paying rent; *moonlighter*, one who in Ireland perpetrated outrages by night on tenants who incurred hostility of Land League; *moonlit*, lit up by m.; *moonshine*, visionary talk or ideas, (also) smuggled spirits; *moonshiner*, (U.S. slang) illicit distiller, spirit-smuggler; *moonshiny*, lighted by m., (also) visionary; *moonstone*, feldspar of pearly appearance; *moonstruck*, deranged in mind. Hence **moo·n**LESS a. [com.-Teut.: OE *móna*, Du. *maan*, G *mond*, cogn. w. L *mensis*, Gk *mēn*, month]

moon[2], v.i. & t. Move, look, listlessly (*about, around*, &c.); pass *away* (time) in listless manner. [f. prec.]

mōō·nshee, n. Native secretary or language-teacher in India. [f. Hind. *munshi* f. Arab. *munshi'* (*ansha'a* compose)]

moo·ny, a. Of, like, the moon; listless, stupidly dreamy. [MOON[1, 2] + -Y[2]]

moor[1], n. Tract of open waste ground, esp. if covered with heather; (in Cornwall) waste land where tin is found; *m. game*, red (rarely, black) grouse; *m.-cock*, male of this; *m.-hen*, female of this, (also) water-hen; *moorland*, country abounding in heather; *moorstone*, kind of granite. Hence **moor·**ISH[1], **moor·**Y[2], aa. [OE *mór*, cf. Du. *moer*, G *moor*]

Moor[2], n. One of a Mohammedan race, mixed Berber & Arab, inhabiting N.W. Africa. Hence **Moor·**ISH[1] a. [f. F *More* f. L f. Gk *Mauros* inhabitant of Mauretania, region of N. Africa]

moor[3], v.t. Attach (boat or other floating thing) to moorings. Hence **moor·**AGE(3, 4) n. [OE has *mǣrels* mooring-rope, cf. MDu. *mâren* moor)]

moor·ing, n. (Usu. pl.) permanent anchors & chains laid down for ships to be moored to, what a floating object is moored to; (pl.) place where vessel is moored. [-ING[1]]

mōōse, n. N.-Amer. animal closely allied to or same as European elk. [f. native *moos*]

mōōt, n., a., & v.t. (Hist.) assembly; (Law) students' discussion of hypothetical case for practice; (adj.) debatable; (v.t.) raise (question) for discussion. [(vb f. OE *mótian*, adj. f. n.) OE *(ge)mót*, cf. Du. *gemoet*, cogn. w. MEET v.]

mop[1], n. Bundle of coarse yarn or cloth fastened at end of stick, for cleaning floors &c.; similar instruments for various purposes; *m.-head*, (fig.) thick head of hair like m., person with this. Hence **mo·ppy**[2] a. [15th c. *mappe* ult. f. L *mappa* napkin]

mop[2], v.t. Wipe, clean, (as) with mop; wipe tears, sweat, &c., from (brow &c.); (slang) *m. the floor with*, have & use overwhelming advantage of (combatant); *m. up*, wipe up (as) with mop, (slang) absorb (profits &c.), dispatch, make an end of. [f. prec.]

mop[3], v.i., & n. *M. & mow*, make grimaces; *mm. & mows*, grimaces. [perh. imit.; cf. Du. *moppen* pout]

mope, v.i. & t., & n. Abandon oneself to listless condition; (refl. or pass.) make one*self*, be, the victim of ennui; (n.) one who mopes, *the mm.*, depression of spirits. Hence **mō·pish**[1] a., **mo·pishly**[2] adv., **mo·pishness** n. [?]

mō·poke, more·pork, n. In N. Zealand, an owl; in Tasmania, night-jar; in Australia, various birds. [imit. of bird's note]

moque·tte (-k-), n. Material of wool & hemp or linen, used for carpets. [F, etym. dub.]

mŏ·r(r)a, n. Italian game in which player guesses number of fingers held up simultaneously by another. [It. *mora*, etym. dub.]

morai·ne, n. Débris carried down & deposited by glacier. [F]

mŏ·ral, a. & n. Concerned with character or disposition, or with the distinction between right & wrong; *m. sense*, power of distinguishing right & wrong; (of literary work &c.) dealing with regulation of conduct, as *m. science*; *m. philosophy*, ethics; *m. law*, the requirements to which right action must conform; (of rights &c.) founded on m. law; capable of m. action; *m. victory*, defeat, indecisive result, that eventually produces the m. effects of victory; *m. courage*, courage to encounter odium, contempt, &c., rather than abandon right course; morally good, conforming to rules of morality; virtuous as regards general conduct; *m. certainty*, probability so great as to admit of no reasonable doubt. (N.) the m. teaching of a fable, story, event, &c. (*draw the m.*, show what it is); moral maxim or principle (*point a m.*, illustrate or apply it); (vulg.) *the very m.* (exact likeness) *of*; (pl.) m. habits, esp. sexual conduct; = foll. Hence **mo·rally**[2] adv. [f. L *moralis* (*mos* custom, pl. *mores* morals, -AL)]

mora·le (-ahl), n. Moral condition, esp. (of troops) as regards discipline & confidence. [f. F *moral* respelt to preserve pronunciation, cf. LOCAL(E), CHORAL(E), DIPLOMAT]

mŏ·ralism, n. Natural system of morality, religion reduced to moral practice. [-ISM]

mŏ·ralist, n. One who practises or teaches morality; man who is merely moral. Hence **morali·stic** a. [MORAL + -IST]

mora·lity, n. Moral science; (pl.) moral principles, points of ethics; particular system of morals, as *commercial m.*; moral conduct (esp. good); moralizing; (Hist.) kind of drama inculcating moral lesson, popular in 16th c. [f. F *moralité* f. L *moralitatem* (MORAL, -TY)]

mŏ·ralize, v.i. & t. Indulge in moral reflection or talk (*on* subject); interpret morally, point the moral of; improve the morals of. So **moraliza·tion** n. [f. F *moraliser* f. LL *moralizare* (as MORAL, see -IZE)]

morā·ss, n. Bog, marsh. [f. Du. *moeras* f. MDu. *marasch* f. OF as MARISH]

mor·at, n. (hist.). Drink made of honey flavoured with mulberries. [f. med. L *moratum* (*morus* mulberry, see -ATE[1])]

mŏrator·ium, n. Legal authorization to debtors to postpone payment. [neut. of LL *moratorius* (L *morari* delay, -TORY)]

Morā·vian, a. & n. (Inhabitant) of Moravia; (one) of Protestant sect holding Hussite doctrines, founded in Saxony by M. emigrants. [f. *Moravia*, now part of Czecho-Slovakia, -AN]

mor·bid, a. (Of mind, ideas, &c.) unwholesome, sickly; given to m. feelings; (Med.) of the nature, or indicative, of disease; *m. anatomy* (of diseased organs &c.). Hence **mor·bidly**[2] adv., **mor·bidness** n. [f. L *morbidus* (*morbus* disease f. root of *mori* die)]

morbid·ezza (-ĕtsa), n. (painting). Lifelike delicacy in flesh-tints. [It. (*morbido* MORBID)]

morbi·dity, n. Morbidness; prevalence of disease (in a district). [-ITY]

morbi·fic, a. Causing disease. [f. F *morbifique* (L *morbus* disease, see -FIC)]

morceau· (-sō), n. Short literary or musical composition. [F (as MORSEL)]

mor·dant, a. & n. (Of sarcasm &c.) caustic, biting, so **morda·cious** a., **mordă·city, mor·dancy,** nn.; pungent, smarting; (of acids) corrosive or cleansing (n., such acid); (substance) serving to fix colouring-matter or gold-leaf. [F, part. of *mordre* bite f. L *mordēre*]

mor·dent, n. (mus.). Grace consisting in rapid alternation of written note with one immediately below it. [G, f. It. *mordente* part. of *mordere* bite, as prec.]

more, a. & adv. Existing in greater quantity, amount, or degree, as *there is m. truth in it than you think, 10 is 2 m. than 8, bring some m. water*; (abs.) greater quantity, as *m. is meant than meets the ear, hope to see m. of you*; *what is m.* (m. important); *m. than one person has* (not *have*) *found it it so*; (adv.) in greater degree, as *you must attend m. to details, m. in sorrow than in anger, m. frightened than hurt*; (forming compar. of most adjj. of more than one syllable & most advv.) *m. absurd(ly), m. curious, m. easily, m. truly*; *m. & m.*, in an increasing degree; *m. or less*, in greater or less degree; THE *m.*; *be no m.*, be dead; again, as *once, twice, never, m.*; *neither m. nor less than* (simply, literally) *absurd* &c. [com.-Teut. adj.: OE *mára*, MDu. *mêre*, f. OTeut. *maizon-* f. *maiz* adv. whence obs. *mo* more (OE *má*) adv.]

moree·n, n. Stout woollen or woollen & cotton material for curtains &c. [?]

more·l[1], n. Kinds of nightshade. [f. OF *morele* prob. fem. f. It. *morello* dark-coloured perh. f. L *morum* mulberry]

more·l[2], n. An edible fungus. [f. F *morille*, etym. dub.]

more·llo, n. Bitter kind of cherry. [?]

moreō·ver, adv. Further, besides, (introducing new statement). [MORE + OVER]

morepork. See MOPOKE.

More·sque (-k), a. Moorish in style or design. [F, f. It. *moresco* (*Moro* Moor, see -ESQUE)]

morgană·tic, a. *M. marriage*, one between man of exalted rank & woman of lower rank, who remains in her former station, the issue having no claim to succeed to possessions or title of father; *m. wife* (so married). Hence **morgana·tically** adv. [f. med. L phr. *matrimonium ad morganaticam*, prob. f. *morganaticum* f. OHG **morgangeba* morning gift from husband to wife the morning after consummation of marriage (the m. wife's only claim on husband's possessions)]

***morgue*[1]** (-g), n. Building (esp. one formerly in Paris) in which bodies of persons found dead are exposed for identification. [F]

***morgue*[2]** (-g), n. Haughty demeanour, esp. (*m. anglaise*) as English characteristic. [F]

mŏ·ribund, a. At the point of death (lit. & fig.). [f. L *moribundus* (*mori* die)]

mŏ·rion, n. (hist.). Helmet without beaver or visor. [F, etym. dub.]

Mori·sco, a. & n. Moorish; Moor, esp. in Spain; morris dance. [Sp. (*Moro* MOOR)]

Mor·mon, n. Member of religious body founded in 1830 by Joseph Smith in New York on basis of supposed Divine revelations in *Book of M.* (imaginary author); person who practises polygamy (regarded as chief feature of the sect). Hence **Mor·monism** n.

morn, n. (poet.). Morning. [OE *morgen, myrgen, margen*, cf. Du. & G *morgen*, perh. f. root **mergh-* twinkle]

mor·ning, n. Early part of day-time, ending at noon, or at hour of midday meal; *good m.*, form of salutation; (poet.) dawn; (attrib. of clothes) meant to be worn in the m., as *m. coat*, tail-coat with front sloped away; *m. call*, visit paid during afternoon; *m. draught*, liquor taken before breakfast; *m. gift* (see MORGANATIC, etym.); *m. performance*, matinée; *m. prayer*, Anglican service of matins; *m.-room*, sitting-room for the m.; *m. star*, Venus (or other planet or bright star) seen in E. before sunrise; *m. watch* (naut.) 4–8 A.M. [ME *morwening* (*morwen* MORN, + -ING[1])]

moro·cco, n. Leather made (orig. in Morocco, now also in Europe) from goatskins tanned with sumac; *French m.*, inferior small-grained kind; *Levant m.*, high-grade large-grained kind. [f. native *Marrakesh*]

mōr·on, n. Adult whose mental development is arrested at the stage normal in a 7-year child. [neut. of Gk *mōros* dull]

moro·se, a. Sullen, gloomy, & unsocial. Hence **moro·sely**[2] adv., **moro·seness** n. [f. L *morosus* (*mos moris* manner, see -OSE[1])]

Mor·pheus (-fūs), n. God of dreams or sleep; *in the arms of M.*, asleep. [L]

mor·phĭa, -phine, nn. Alkaloid narcotic principle of opium, largely used to alleviate pain. Hence **mor·phinism**(5) n. [(*-ine* f. G *morphin*, see -INE[5]) f. prec.]

morpho·logy, n. (Biol.) study of the form of animals & plants; (Philol.) study of the form of words. Hence **morpholo·gical** a., **morpholo·gically**[2] adv., **morpho·logist** n. (biol.). [f. Gk *morphē* form + -LOGY]

mo·rris, a. & n. *M.*(*-dance*), grotesque dance by persons in fancy costume, usu. as characters in Robin Hood legend (medieval, & as modern revival); *m.-pike* (hist.), form of pike supposed to be of Moorish origin. [f. *morys*, var. of MOORISH]

mo·rris tube, n. Small-bore rifle barrel insertable in rifle for practice on miniature range. [R. *Morris*, inventor]

mo·rrow, n. (literary). *The m.*, the following day; (fig.) *on the m. of* (time following on) *a long war* &c. [ME *morwe*, shortened f. *morwen* MORN]

morse[1], n. Walrus. [f. Lapp. *morsa*]

Morse[2], n. Of the recording telegraph invented by S. F. B. Morse (d. 1872), as *M. alphabet, code* (in which letters are represented by variations on two signs, e.g. dot & line, long & short flash, or two flags).

morse[3], n. Clasp, often jewelled &c., of cope. [f. OF *mors* f. L *morsus* bite, catch]

mor·sel, n. Mouthful, small piece, (*of* food &c.); fragment. [OF, dim. of *mors* a bite f. L *mordēre mors-* bite]

mort[1], n. Note sounded on horn at death of deer. [F, f. L *mortem* (nom. *mors*) death]

mort[2], n. Salmon in third year. [?]

mort[3], n. (dial.). A great amount or number of (*a m. of*). [?]

mor·tal, a. & n. Subject to death; causing death, fatal, (*to*, often fig.); (of battle) fought to the death; (of enemy) implacable; (of pain, fear, &c.) deadly; (of sin) entailing spiritual death, deadly; accompanying death, as *m. agony*; (slang) very great, as *in a m. hurry*; (slang) long & tedious, as *for two m. hours*; (n.) m., esp. human, being; (facet.) person, as *a thirsty m.* Hence **mor·tal**LY[2] adv. [f. OF *mortel* f. L *mortalis* (*mors -rtis* death, see -AL)]

morta·lity, n. Mortal nature; loss of life on large scale; number of deaths in given period &c.; death-rate. [f. F *mortalité* f. L *mortalitatem* (as prec., see -TY)]

mor·tar, n., & v.t. Vessel of hard material, e.g. marble, in which ingredients are pounded with pestle; short piece of ordnance for throwing shells at high angles; contrivance for firing shells in pyrotechnic displays; mixture of lime, sand, & water, for joining stones or bricks, whence **mor·tar**LESS, **mor·tar**Y[2], aa.; *m.-board*, board for holding m., (pop.) square college cap; (v.t.) plaster, join, with m. [(vb f. n.) f. F *mortier* f. L *mortarium*, etym. dub.]

mortgage[1] (mor·gĭj), n. Conveyance of property by debtor (*mortgager, -or*) to creditor (*mortgagee*) as security for debt, with proviso that it shall be reconveyed on payment of debt within certain period; deed effecting this. [OF, = dead pledge (*mort* f. L *mortuus* dead + GAGE[1])]

mort·gage[2], v.t. Make over (property) by mortgage; pledge (*oneself*, one's powers &c., *to* object &c.). Hence **mortgag**EE·, **mort·gag**ER[1], **mortgag**OR·[2] (-jor), nn. (see prec.). [f. prec.]

mor·tify, v.t. & i. Bring (body, passions, &c.) into subjection by self-denial or discipline; cause (person) to feel humiliated, wound (feelings), whence **mor·tify**ING[2] a.; (intr., of flesh) be affected by gangrene or necrosis. So **mortifi**CA·TION n. [f. F *mortifier* f. L *mortificare* (*mors -rtis* death, see -FY)]

mor·tise, -ice, n., & v.t. Hole in a framework designed to receive the end of some other part esp. a TENON; *m. chisel* (with stout blade, for cutting mm.); (v.t.) join (things *together*, one *to* or *into* another) securely, esp. by tenon & m. [(vb f. n.) f. F *mortaise*, etym. dub.]

mor·tmain, n. (law). Condition of lands or tenements held inalienably by ecclesiastical or other corporation; (fig.) *in m.*, under posthumous control. [f. OF *mortemain* f. med. L *mortua manus* dead hand, prob. in allusion to impersonal ownership]

mor·tuary, a. & n. Of death or burial; building in which dead bodies are kept for a time. [f. L *mortuarius* (*mortuus* dead, see -ARY[1])]

mosā·ic[1] (-z-), a., n., & v.t. (-cking, -cked). (Form or work of art) in which pictures &c. are produced by joining together minute pieces of glass, stone, &c., of different colours (also fig. of any diversified whole); *m. disease* (in plants, esp. tobacco, maize, & sugarcane); *m. woolwork* (producing effect like that of m.); *m.gold*, a disulphide of tin, also alloy of copper & zinc used in cheap jewellery &c.; (v.t.) adorn with mm.; combine (as) into m. Hence **mosa·ic**IST(3) n. [(vb f. n.) f. F *mosaïque* f. med. L *mosaicus, mu-*, as if f. a Gk *mousaïkos* of the Muses (*mousa* MUSE, see -IC)]

Mosā·ic[2] (-z-), a. Of Moses, esp. *M. Law* (in Pentateuch). [f. L *Moses* + -IC]

mosasau·rus, n. Large extinct marine reptile, first found near Maestricht on Meuse. [L *Mosa* Meuse + Gk *sauros* lizard]

moschate·l (-k-), n. Small plant with pale-green flowers & musky smell. [f. F *moscatelle* f. It. *moscatella* (*moscato* MUSK)]

mose·lle (-z-), n. Dry white wine produced near the river M.

Mo·ses (-ĭz), n. (Nickname for) Jewish moneylender.

Mŏ·slem, Mŭ·slim, (-z-, -s-), a. & n. (pl. *-ms, -min*). Mohammedan. Hence **Mo·slem**ISM n. [Arab. (*-im*), part. of *aslama* whence ISLAM]

mo·sque (-k-), n. Mohammedan place of worship. [16th-c. *mosquee* f. F *mosquée* f. It. *moschea* f. Arab. *masgid* (*sagada* vb worship])

mosqui·to (-kē-), n. Kinds of gnat, female of which punctures skins of animals with long proboscis & sucks their blood; *m.-net, -curtain* (to keep off mm.); *m.-craft*, small light vessels for rapid manœuvring. [Sp., dim. of *mosca* f. L *musca* fly]

mŏss, n., & v.t. Wet spongy soil; peat-bog; kinds of small herbaceous cryptogamous plant, some growing in bogs, others on surface of ground, trees, stones, &c., in crowded masses, whence **mo·ssi**NESS n., **mo·ss**Y[2] a.; *rolling stone gathers no m.*, one who constantly changes his place or employment will not grow rich; *mo·ssbunker*, = MENHADEN; *m.-grown*, overgrown with m.; *m.-hag*, broken ground from which peat has been taken; *m.-rose*, garden variety of cabbage rose, with m.-like growth on calyx & stalk; *m.-trooper*, border freebooter of 17th c.; (v.t.) cover with m. [(vb f. n.) OE *mos*, cf. Du. *mos*, G *moos*]

mōst, a. & adv. Existing in greatest quantity or degree, as *you have made m. mistakes, see who can make m. noise*, (abs., quasi-noun) *this is the m. I can do, make the m. of it*, employ it to the best advantage, (also) represent it at the best or worst; the majority, as *m. people think so*, (quasi-n.) *m. of them are broken*; *for the m. part*, in the main, usually, whence **mo·stLY**[2] adv.; (adv.) in the highest degree, as *what m. annoys me*, (forming superl. of most adjj. of more than one syllable & most advv.) *m. ludicrous(ly)*, *m. certain(ly)*, *m. callous(ly)*; *ten at m.*, not more than ten, *this is at m.* (is no more than) *a makeshift*. [com.-Teut.: OE *mǣst*, Du. *meest*, G *meist*, f. OTeut. *maisto-* (*maiz* MORE, see -EST)]

-most, suf. forming superl. adjj. formed not on adjj. but on prep. or demonstr. stems (*afterm.*, *forem.*, *inm.*, *utm.*) & later on wds indicating position in place, time, or order, (*backm.*, *topm.*, *centrem.*, & the compar. *upperm.*, *utterm.*, *furtherm.*, &c.); also in *bettermost*; altered form of OE *-mest*, combining two superl. suff., *-mo-* & *-isto-* -EST; in late OE *-mest* was confused with MOST (see prec.), whence usu. mod. pronunc. (mōst) for the unstressed (most).

mot (mō), n. (pl. *mots* pron. mōz). Witty saying; *mot juste* (F), the expression that conveys a desired shade of meaning with more precision than any other. [F, =word, f. pop. L **mottum* =L *muttum* (*muttire* murmur)]

mote, n. Particle of dust; *m. in* (another's) *eye*, trifling fault if compared to one's own (see *Matt.* vii. 3). [OE *mot*, perh. cogn. w. Du. *mot* dust, sawdust]

mote·t, n. (mus.). Vocal composition in harmony, usu. to words from Scripture, for church use. [F, dim. of MOT]

mŏth, n. (Also *clothes-m.*) small nocturnal lepidopterous insect breeding in cloth &c., on which its larva feeds (*m.*, *the m.*, collect., mm.), whence **mo·thY**[2] a.; one of two great divisions of Lepidoptera including this, distinguished from butterflies by not having clubbed antennae, & apt to scorch themselves by fluttering about light, (fig.) person hovering around temptation; *m.-eaten*, destroyed by mm., (fig.) antiquated, time-worn. [OE *moththe* cf. MDu. & G *motte*]

mo·ther[1] (mŭdh-), n. Female parent; quality, condition, &c., that gives rise to another, as *necessity is the m. of invention*; head of female religious community (often *M. Superior*); (term of address for) elderly woman of lower class; (also *artificial m.*) apparatus for rearing chickens; (archaic, f. obs. sense *womb*) hysteria; *M. Carey's* CHICKEN; *M. Church* (as of maternal authority); *M.-Church* (whence others have sprung); *m. country*, country in relation to its colonies; *m.-craft*, skill in treatment of offspring; *m. earth*, earth as m. of its inhabitants &c., (facet.) the ground; *M. Hubbard*, person in nursery rhyme, kind of cloak; *m.-in-law*, one's wife's or husband's m.; *m. of pearl*, smooth shining iridescent substance forming inner layer of some shells (often attrib., w. hyphens); *m. of thousands* or *millions*, ivy-leaved toad-flax; *m. ship* (in charge of torpedo-boats, seaplanes, &c.); *m.'s son*, man, esp. *every m.'s son of* (*you* &c.); *m. tongue*, one's native tongue, (also) tongue from which others spring; *m. wit*, native wit, common sense. Hence **mo·therHOOD** n., **mo·therLESS**, **mo·therLIKE**, aa. [com.-Teut.: OE *mōdor*, Du. *moeder*, G *mutter*, cogn. w. Gk *mētēr*, L *mater*]

mo·ther[2], v.t. Give birth to (usu. fig.); protect as a mother; acknowledge or profess oneself the mother of (child, lit. & fig.); *mothering Sunday*, Mid-lent Sunday, with old custom of visiting parents with gifts. [f. prec.]

mo·ther[3] (mŭdh-), n. (Also *m. of vinegar*) mucilaginous substance produced in vinegar during fermentation by mould-fungus. Hence **mo·therY**[2] a. [prob. =MOTHER[1]; cf. MDu. *moeder*, G *mutter*]

mo·therly, a. Having, showing, the good qualities of a mother. Hence **mo·therliNESS** n. [OE *mōdorlic* (see MOTHER[1] & -LY[1])]

mōti·f (-ēf), n. Constituent feature, dominant idea, in artistic composition; ornament of lace &c. sewn separately on dress. [F, as MOTIVE a.]

mō·tile, a. (zool., bot.). Capable of motion. Hence **moti·LITY** n. [as MOVE, see -IL]

mō·tion[1] (-shn), n. Moving, change of place; manner of moving the body in walking &c.; change of posture; gesture; *in m.*, moving, not at rest; *put in m.*, set going or working; formal proposal in deliberative assembly; (Law) application by party &c. for rule or order of court; evacuation of bowels; piece of moving mechanism. Hence **mo·tionAL**, **mo·tionLESS**, aa. [F, f. L *motionem* (as MOVE, -ION)]

mō·tion[2] (-shn), v.t. & i. Direct (person *to*, *towards*, *away*, &c., *to* do) by sign or gesture; make gesture (*to* person) directing him (*to* do). [f. prec.]

mō·tive[1], a. & n. Tending to initiate movement, whence **moti·VITY** n.; *m. power*, moving or impelling power, esp. form of mechanical energy used to drive machinery, e.g. steam, electricity; concerned with movement; (n.) what induces a person to act, e.g. desire, fear, circumstance, whence **mo·tiveLESS** a.; = MOTIF. [f. F *motif* f. med. L *motivus* (MOVE, -IVE)]

mo·tive[2], **mō·tivate**, vv.t. Supply a motive to, be the motive or motif of. Hence **motivA·TION** n. [f. prec. n.]

mo·tley, a. & n. Diversified in colour; of varied character, as *m. assembly*; (n.) incongruous mixture; (Hist.) fool's parti-coloured dress, esp. *wear m.*, play the fool. [f. 14th c., etym. dub.]

mō·tor, n., a., & v.i. & t. What imparts motion; machine supplying motive power for carriage or vessel, esp. internal-combustion engine, as (attrib). *m. bicycle, cab, (omni)bus, boat, ship*; motor-car; *m.-car*, carriage propelled by m. for use on ordinary roads, whence **mo·tor**IST(3) n.; *m. cycle*, bicycle &c. worked by m. engine; (Anat.) muscle designed to move a part of the body; (nerve) designed to excite muscular activity, whence **motor·**IAL, **mo·**TORY, aa.; (vb) go or convey in m.-car. [L (MOVE, -OR²)]

mo·ttle, n., & v.t. Arrangement of spots or confluent blotches of colour; such spot; variegated woollen yarn; (v.t.) mark (esp. soap) with mm. (esp. in p.p.). [prob. f. MOTLEY]

mo·tto, n. Sentence inscribed on some object & expressing appropriate sentiment; maxim adopted as rule of conduct; verses &c. in paper cracker; quotation prefixed to book or chapter; (Mus.) recurrent phrase. [It., as MOT]

mou·fflon (mōō-), n. Wild mountain sheep of S. Europe. [f. F *mouflon* f. LL *mufron*]

moujik, muzhik, (mōō·zhĭk), n. Russian peasant; lady's loose fur cape. [f. Russ. *muzhiku* peasant]

mould¹ (mōld), n. Loose earth; upper soil of cultivated land; *man of m.*, mere mortal; *m.-board*, board in plough that turns over the furrow-slice. [OE *molde*, cf. Du. *moude*, G dial. *molt*, f. OTeut. *mul-* grind, cf. MEAL¹]

mould² (mōld), n. Pattern, templet, used by masons, bricklayers, &c., as guide in shaping mouldings; hollow form into which molten metal &c. is cast to cool into required shape; metal or earthenware vessel used to give shape to puddings &c., pudding &c. so shaped; (fig.) *cast in heroic* &c. *m.*, of such character; form, shape, esp. of animal body; (Arch.) group of mouldings; *m. candle* (made in a m.); *m.-loft*, room on floor of which plans of ship are drawn full size. [ME *mold(e)* prob. f. OF *modle* f. MODULUS]

mould³, v.t. Produce (object) in certain shape, *out of* (elements), or *upon* (pattern), lit. & fig.; bring into certain shape; shape (bread) into loaves. [f. prec.]

mould⁴ (mō-), n. Woolly or furry growth of minute fungi on things that lie for some time in moist warm air. [prob. f. obs. *mould* a., p.p. of *moul* grow mouldy, cf. Swed. *mögla*]

mou·lder¹, n. One who moulds, esp. workman making moulds for casting. [-ER¹]

mou·lder² (mō-), v.i. Decay to dust, rot *away*, (often fig.). [perh. MOULD¹ + -ER⁵]

mou·lding (mō-), n. In vbl senses, esp. moulded object, esp. ornamental variety of outline in cornices &c. of building, woodwork, &c.; *m.-board* (on which dough is kneaded). [MOULD³ + -ING¹]

mou·ldy¹ (mō-), a. Overgrown with mould; (fig.) stale, out-of-date; (slang) dull, tiresome, boring. Hence **mou·ldi**NESS n. [MOULD⁴ + -Y²]

mou·ldy² (mō-), n. (naut. slang). Torpedo. [?]

moulin (F), n. Nearly vertical shaft in glacier, formed by surface water falling through crack in ice. [F, lit. = mill]

moult (mō-), v.t. & i., & n. (Of birds) shed (feathers), shed feathers, in changing plumage (also fig.); (n.) moulting. [(n. f. vb) ME *mouten* f. OE **mutian* f. L *mutare* change; *-l-* on false anal. of *fault* &c.]

mound¹ (mow-), n. Ball of gold &c. representing earth, surmounting crown &c., & used in heraldry. [f. F *monde* f. L *mundus* world]

mound² (mow-), n., & v.t. Elevation of earth or stones, esp. of earth heaped on grave; hillock; *m.-builder*, one of prehistoric Indian race in N. America who erected mm., (also) kinds of bird depositing eggs in a heap; (v.t.) enclose with, heap up in, mm. [?]

mount¹ (mow-), n. Mountain, hill, (abbr. *Mt*, preceding name, as *Mt Ephraim*); (Palmistry) fleshy prominence on palm of hand. [OE *munt* f. L *mons -ntis*]

mount² (mow-), v.i. & t. Ascend (hill &c. or abs.); proceed upwards; (of blood) rise into cheeks; rise to higher level of rank, power, intensity, &c.; (also *m. up*) rise in amount; get *on* horse &c. for purpose of riding; get on (horse &c. or abs.); put (person) on horse &c.; furnish (person) with horse; raise (guns) into position; put (loom &c.) in working order; put (picture &c.) in a MOUNT³; fit (gems &c.) in gold &c.; fix (object) on microscope slide; put (play) on stage; display (article of costume); *m.* (go on duty as) *guard* (*over* thing or abs.). [f. OF *munter* f. pop. L **montare* (as prec.)]

mount³ (mow-), n. Margin surrounding picture, card on which drawing is mounted; ornamental metal parts of thing; horse for person's riding; chance of riding, esp. as jockey. [f. prec.]

mou·ntain (-tĭn), n. Natural elevation of earth's surface, large or high hill; *Mahomet & the m., Mahomet will go to the m.*, phrases applied to the pretender who is not abashed under exposure (w. ref. to the story told in Bacon's Essay on Boldness); *waves ran mm.* (very) *high, m.-high*; large heap or pile; (also *m. wine*) Malaga wine from m. grapes; *the M.*, extreme party in first French Revolution, occupying elevated position in chamber of assembly; *m. ash*, tree with delicate pinnate leaves & scarlet berries; *m. chain*, series of mm.; *m. sickness*, malady caused by rarefied m. air. [f. OF *montaigne* f. pop. L *montanea* f. **montaneus* = L *montanus* (*mons -ntis* mountain, -AN)]

mountaineer·, n. Dweller amongst mountains; one skilled in mountain climbing, whence **mountaineer·**ING[1] n. [-EER]

mou·ntainous, a. Abounding in mountains; huge. [f. OF *montagneux* (MOUNTAIN, -OUS)]

mou·ntĕbank (mow-), n. Itinerant quack who held forth to audience from platform; charlatan. Hence **mou·ntebank**ERY(4) n. [f. It. *montambanco* = *monta in banco* mount on bench]

mourn (mōrn), v.i. & t. Feel sorrow or regret (*for, over,* dead person, lost thing, loss, misfortune, &c.); show conventional signs of grief for period after person's death; sorrow for (dead person, thing). [com.-Teut.: OE *murnan,* OHG *mornên* be anxious, ON *morna* pine]

mour·ner, n. One who mourns, esp. who attends funeral of friend or relation; person hired to attend funeral. [-ER[1]]

mour·nful, a. Doleful, sad, sorrowful. Hence **mour·nful**LY[2] adv., **mour·nful**NESS n. [MOURN + -FUL]

mour·ning, n. In vbl senses, also or esp.: (wearing of) black clothes as sign of m.; DEEP[1], HALF, *m.*; *complimentary m.* (worn as tribute to unrelated dead); *in m.,* wearing such garments, (of the eye) blacked in fighting &c., (of finger-nails) dirty; *m.-coach* (attending funeral); *m.-paper,* note-paper with black edge; *m.-ring* (worn as memorial of deceased person). [-ING[1]]

mouse[1] (mows), n. (pl. *mice*). Animal of any of the smaller species of a genus of rodents, esp. *house, field-, harvest-, m.*; (slang) black eye; *m.-colour,* dark grey with yellow tinge; *m.-ear,* hawkweed & other plants; *mousetrap* (for catching mice). Hence **mou·s**Y[2] a. [com.-Teut.: OE *mús,* Du. *muis,* G *maus,* cf. L & Gk *mus*]

mouse[2] (-z), v.i. (Of cat or owl) hunt for or catch mice, whence **mou·s**ER[1] n.; search industriously, prowl *about* in search of something. [f. prec.]

mousse (mōōs), n. Dish of flavoured cream whipped & frozen (*chestnut, chocolate, &c., m.*). [F, = froth]

mousseline (mōōslē·n), n. French muslin; *m.-de-laine,* dress material of wool & cotton; *m.-de-soie* (swah), thin silk fabric of muslin-like texture. [F, see MUSLIN]

moustache (mustah·sh), n. Hair on either side or both sides of a man's upper lip; similar hair round mouths of some animals; *m.-cup* (with partial cover to protect m. when drinking). [F, f. It. *mostaccio* f. Gk *mustax -akos*]

Moustĕr·ian (mōō-), a. (archaeol.). Of the palaeolithic epoch represented by remains found in the Moustier cave in France. [-IAN]

mouth[1] (mowth), n. External orifice in head, with cavity behind it containing apparatus of mastication & organs of vocal utterance; (slang) impudent talk, cheek; (of horse, with reference to his readiness to feel & obey pressure of bit) *good, bad, hard, m.*; *m. waters at* (food; referring to flow of saliva caused by anticipation); *useless m.,* one who does no work but must be fed; *this sounds strange in your m.* (when said by you); *put words into his m.,* tell him what to say; *put* (speech) *into* person's *m.,* represent him as having made it; *take the words out of* person's *m.,* say what he was about to say; (of dog) *give m.,* bark, bay; *down in the m.,* dejected; *laugh on wrong side of* one's *m.,* lament; *make a wry m.,* grimace in sign of disapproval &c.; opening of bag, cave, furnace, &c.; outfall of river; *m.-filling,* bombastic, inflated; *m.-organ,* pan-pipe & other musical instruments; *mouthpiece,* part of pipe, musical instrument, &c., placed between lips, (also) one who speaks for others. Hence **(-)mouth**ED[2] (-dhd), **mou·th**LESS, aa., **mou·th**FUL n. [com.-Teut.: OE *múth,* Du. *mond,* G *mund,* cogn. w. L *mentum* chin]

mouth[2] (-dh), v.t. & i. Utter (words or abs.) pompously or very distinctly; take (food) in, touch with, the mouth; train mouth of (horse); grimace. [f. prec.]

mou·thy (-dhĭ), a. Railing, ranting; bombastic. [MOUTH[1] + -Y[2]]

mo·vable (mōō-), a. & n. That can be moved; (of property) that can be removed, personal as opp. to *real*; *m. feast,* one that varies its date, (facet.) meal taken at no regular time; (n.) article of furniture that may be removed from the house, opp. to *fixture*; (pl.) personal property. Hence **mova**BI·LITY, **mo·vable**NESS, nn. [OF (as MOVE[2], see -ABLE)]

move[1] (mōōv), n. Moving of a piece in chess & other games; player's turn to do this; device, step taken to secure object; *on the m.,* moving about; *make a m.,* go, esp. rise & go from dinner-table &c.; *get a m. on* (slang), hurry up, bestir oneself. [f. foll.]

move[2] (mōōv), v.t. & i. Change position of; change position of (piece) in chess &c.; put, keep, in motion, shake, stir; *m. heaven & earth,* make every effort (*to* do); change posture of (one's body, limbs, &c.); cause (bowels) to act; provoke (laughter, anger, &c., *in* person, person *to* these); affect (person) with (usu. tender) emotion, whence **mo·v**ING[2] a., **mo·ving**LY[2] adv.; prompt, incline, (person *to* action, *to* do); *the spirit* (orig. in Quaker use, = Holy Spirit) *moves me,* I feel inclined (*to* do); make formal application to (court &c. *for*); propose (question, resolution, *that* thing be done) in deliberative assembly; go, pass, (*about, away,* &c.) from place to place; make progress, as *the work moves slowly*; make a move at chess &c.; change one's abode; *m. about,* do this often; *m. in*, take possession of new abode; *m. on* (policeman's order to person who stands too long in one place), (trans.) cause person to m. on by giving this order; (of person or part of body) change posture; (of inanimate things) suffer change of position; (of bowels) be moved; make request or application (*for*); take action, proceed, (*in* matter). Hence **mo·ve**LESS a. (rare). [f. OF *movoir* f. L *movēre mot-*]

mo·vement, n. Moving; military evolution; moving parts of machine, particular group of these; mental impulse; development of poem, story, &c.; (Mus.) mode of progression as regards speed or rhythm, (also) principal division of a musical work; series of actions & endeavours of a body of persons for special object, as *the* OXFORD *m.*; activity in market for some commodity. [OF, f. med. L *movimentum* (as prec., see -MENT)]

mo·ver, n. In vbl senses, esp.: one who moves proposal; *prime m.*, initial source (natural or mechanical) of motive power, (also) author of fruitful idea. [-ER[1]]

mo·vies (mōō-), n. pl. (slang). Cinema pictures; *mo·vietone*, form of SOUND[2]*-film*. [=*moving pictures*]

mow[1] (mow), n. Stack of hay, corn, peas, &c.; place in barn where hay &c. is heaped; *mow-burnt*, spoilt by becoming overheated in the m. [OE *múga*, cf. ON *múge*, Sw. & Norw. *muga*]

mow[2] (mō, mow), n., & v.i. See MOP[3]. [(vb f. n.) f. OF *moue* mouth, lip, pout, etym. dub.]

mow[3] (mō), v.t. (mowed, mown). Cut down (grass &c. or abs.) with scythe or machine; cut down produce of (field) thus; destroy sweepingly, cut *off* or *down* in great numbers. Hence **mow·**ER[1] (1, 2) n. [com.-WG: OE *máwan*, Du. *maaien*, G *mähen*]

mo·xa, n. Down from dried leaves of a plant, used for burning on skin as counter-irritant for gout; anything so used. [f. Jap. *mokusa* (*moe kusa* burning herb)]

moy·a, n. Volcanic mud. [?]

Moză·rab, n. (hist.). Christian owning allegiance to Moorish king but allowed his own religion. Hence **Moza·rab**IC a. [f. Sp. *Mozárabe* f. Arab. *musta'rib* would-be Arab (*'arab*)]

Mpret, n. Albanian ruler. [f. L *imperator* emperor]

Mr (mĭ·ster). See MISTER.

Mrs (mĭ·sĭz), n. Title prefixed to surname of married woman who has no superior title; *Mrs Grundy* (see GRUNDYISM). [abbr. of MISTRESS]

mu, n. Greek letter M (M, μ). [Gk]

mŭch, a. & adv. Existing in great quantity, as *m. trouble, too m. noise, not m. rain*, (abs., quasi-n.) *I have stood m., m. of what you say is true*; *too m.* (more than a match) *for*; THINK, MAKE, *m. of*; *he is not m. of a* (not a good) *scholar*; (adv.) in a great degree (qualifying vb or p.p., cf. VERY), as *I m. regret the mistake, was m. annoyed*; (qualifying compar. or superl. adj.) *m. better, m. the most likely*; pretty nearly, as *m. of a size*, about the same size. Hence **mu·ch**LY[2] adv. (facet.). [f. OE *micel* MICKLE]

mu·chness, n. Greatness in quantity or degree; *much of a m.*, very nearly the same or alike. [prec. + -NESS]

mū·cilage (-ĭj), n. Viscous substance from various plants; gum; viscous fluid in animal bodies, e.g. mucus. So **muci-lă·gin**OUS a. [F, f. LL *mucilago -ginis* (MUCUS)]

muck[1], n. Farm-yard manure; dirt; (colloq.) anything disgusting; (colloq.) untidy state; *m.-rake* (for collecting m., usu. fig.); *muckworm*, worm that lives in m., (fig.) money-grubber, street arab. Hence **mu·ck**Y[2] a. [ME *muk*, prob. of Scand. orig.]

muck[2], v.t. & i. Make dirty; (slang) bungle (job); (slang) go aimlessly *about*. [f. prec.]

mu·cker, n. (slang). Heavy fall (lit. & fig.); *come a m.*, experience this; *go a m.*, plunge into extravagance (*on, over*, purchase). [-ER[1]]

muckle. See MICKLE.

mu·cous, a. Of, covered with, mucus, as *m. membrane*, internal prolongation of the skin so covered. So **mucŏ·s**ITY n. [f. L *mucosus* (as MUCUS, see -OUS)]

mū·cro, n. (bot., zool.). Pointed part or organ. Hence **mu·cron**ATE[2](2) a. [L, =point]

mū·cus, n. Slimy substance secreted by mucous membrane; gummy substance found in all plants; slimy substance exuded by some animals, esp. fishes. [L, cogn. w. *emungere* blow the nose, & Gk *mussomai*]

mud, n. Wet soft earthy matter, mire; (fig.) what is worthless or polluting; *fling, throw, m.*, make disgraceful imputations; STICK *in the m.*; *m.-bath* (in m. of mineral springs, for rheumatism &c.); *mudguard*, piece of metal attached to wheel of cycle &c. to protect rider from mud; *mudlark*, one who dabbles, works, or lives, in m., esp. street arab; *m. pie*, m. shaped like pie by child; *m. volcano* (discharging m.). [ME *mode*, cf. Du. *modden*, dabble in m., G dial. *mott* bog]

mudar·, ma- (*ma*-), n. E.-Ind. shrub, of which root-bark is used in medicine & inner bark yields silky fibre (yercum). [Hind. (*ma*-)]

mu·ddle[1], n. Disorder; *make a m. of*, bungle; *muddle-headed(ness)*, stupid(ity). [f. foll.]

mu·ddle[2], v.t. & i. Bewilder, esp. with drink; mix (things *up, together*) blunderingly; bungle (affair); busy oneself in confused & ineffective way; *m. on*, get on in haphazard way; *m. through*, attain one's end by no skill of one's own. [f. MUD + -LE(3)]

mu·ddy, a., & v.t. Like, abounding in, covered with, mud; (of light) dull; (of voice) thick; mentally confused; obscure; (v.t.) make m. Hence **mu·ddi**LY[2] adv., **mu·ddi**NESS n. [(vb f. adj.) f. MUD + -Y[2]]

Mū·die's, n. (Used for) M.'s circulating library. [name of London firm]

mudir (mōōdēr·), n. Governor of Turkish village or of Egyptian province. [Turk. f. Arab., part. of *adara* govern]

muĕ·zzin (mōō-), n. Mohammedan crier who proclaims hours of prayer from minaret. [f. Arab. *mu'adhdhin* (*adhana* proclaim)]

muff[1], n. Woman's fur or other covering (usu. cylindrical) into which both hands are thrust from opposite ends to keep them warm; *foot-m.*, contrivance serving same end for feet. [prob. f. Du. *mof* f. F as MUFFLE[2]]

muff[2], n., & v.t. Person who is awkward or stupid, orig. in some athletic sport; failure, esp. to catch ball at cricket &c.; (v.t.) bungle, miss (catch, ball, &c.). Hence **mu·ff**ISH[1] a. [?]

muffetee·, n. Worsted cuff worn on wrist. [prob. irreg. f. MUFF[1]]

mu·ffin, n. Light flat round spongy cake, eaten toasted & buttered; *m.-bell* (rung by *m.-man*, seller of mm.). [?]

muffineer·, n. Small castor for sprinkling salt or sugar on muffins. [-EER]

mu·ffle[1], n. Thick part of upper lip & nose of ruminants & rodents. [f. F *mufle*, etym. dub.]

mu·ffle[2], n. Leather glove for lunatics who tear clothes &c.; mitten; receptacle placed within furnace, in which substances may be heated without contact with products of combustion; chamber in kiln for baking pottery. [f. F *moufle* mitten f. med. L *muffula*]

mu·ffle[3], v.t. Wrap, cover *up*, (one*self*, one's throat &c., or abs.) for warmth; wrap up head of (person) to prevent his speaking; wrap up (oars, bell, drum, horse's hoofs) to deaden sound; repress, deaden, sound of (curse &c., usu. in p.p.). [prob. as prec.]

mu·ffler, n. Wrap, scarf, worn for warmth; boxing-glove; thick glove; thing used to deaden sound, esp. felt pad between hammer & string of piano. [f. prec. + -ER[1]]

mŭ·fti. n. Mohammedan priest or expounder of law, esp. official head of religion in Turkey; plain clothes worn by one who has right to wear uniform, esp. *in m.* [Arab., part. of *afta* decide point of law]

mug[1], n. Drinking-vessel, usu. cylindrical, with or without handle; its contents; a cooling drink; [perh. diff. wd] (slang) face, mouth. [?]

mug[2], n. (slang). Simpleton, muff. [?]

mug[3], v.i. & t., & n., (slang). Study hard (*at* subject or abs.); (also *m. up*) get up (subject); (n.) one who studies hard, examination. [?]

mu·gger, n. Broad-nosed Indian crocodile. [f. Hind. *magar*]

mu·ggins, n. Simpleton; children's game of cards; game of dominoes. [perh. the surname *M.*, w. allusion to MUG[2]]

Muggletō·nian, a. & n. (Member) of sect founded by, & believing in personal inspiration of, L. Muggleton & John Reeve, c. 1650. [-IAN]

mu·ggy, a. (Of weather, day, &c.) damp & warm; stifling, close. Hence **mu·ggi**NESS n. [f. dial. *mug* drizzle, cf. ON *mugga*, + -Y[2]]

mu·gwump, n. (U.S.). Great man, boss; one who holds aloof from party politics. [f. native *mugquomp* great chief]

Muhammadan. See MOHAMMEDAN.

mūla·tto, n. & a. Offspring of European & Negro; (adj.) of m. colour, tawny. [f. Sp. *mulato* young mule, mulatto, irreg. f. *mulo* MULE]

mu·lberry, n. Genus of tree, leaves of which are much used for feeding silkworms: its fruit; *m. bush*, children's game with ditty *Here we go round the m. bush.* [ult. f. OHG *mûlberi* (*mûr* f. L *morum* mulberry + *beri* berry)]

mulch (-tsh), n., & v.t. Mixture of wet straw, leaves, &c., spread to protect roots of newly planted trees; (vb) treat with m. [prob. f. obs. adj. *mulch* soft, cf. dial. *melch* (OE *melsc*) & G dial. *molsch* soft]

mulct, n., & v.t. Fine imposed for offence; (v.t.) punish (person) by fine (*in* amount, or with amount as second object), deprive (person &c. *of*). [(vb f. L *mulctare*) f. L *mul(c)ta*]

mule[1], n. Offspring of he-ass & mare, or (pop.) of she-ass & stallion (prop. *hinny*), used as beast of draught & burden & noted for obstinacy; stupid or obstinate person; hybrid plant or animal; *m. canary*, cross between canary & other finch; kind of spinning-machine. Hence **mu·lish**[1] a., **mu·lish**LY[2] adv., **mu·lish**NESS n. [f. OE *mūl*, & f. OF *mul(e)*, f. L *mulus*, *-la*]

mule[2], v.i. = MEWL.

mūlĕteer·, n. Mule-driver. [f. F *muletier* (*mulet* dim. of OF *mul* mule, see -EER)]

mull[1], n. Thin variety of plain muslin. [shortened f. *mulmull* f. Hind. *malmal*]

mull[2], n., & v.t. Muddle, mess, esp. *make a m. of*; (v.t.) make a m. of (catch &c.). [?]

mull[3], v.t. Make (wine, beer) into a hot drink with sugar, spices, yolk of egg, &c. [?]

mŭ·llah, mōō·llah, n. Mohammedan learned in theology & sacred law. [f. Pers., Turk., Hind., *mulla* f. Arab. *maula*]

mu·llein (-lĭn), n. Kinds of herbaceous

plant with woolly leaves & yellow flowers. [f. AF *moleine*, perh. f. F *mol* soft f. L *mollis*]

mu·ller, n. Stone used for grinding powders &c. on slab. [perh. f. OF *moldre* grind f. L *molere*]

mu·llet, n. Two genera of fishes of which *Red & Grey M.* are the types. [f. OF *mulet* dim. f. L *mullus* red m.]

mulligataw·ny, n. (Also *m. soup*) E.-Ind. highly seasoned soup; *m. paste*, curry paste used for this. [f. Tamil *milagu-tannir* pepper-water]

mu·lligrubs, n. pl. Depression of spirits; stomach-ache. [arbitrary]

mu·llion, n. Vertical bar dividing lights in window. Hence **mu·llion**ED[2] a. [prob. var. of MONIAL]

mu·llock, n. (Austral.) rock containing no gold, also, refuse from which gold has been extracted; (dial.) rubbish. [f. dial. *mull* dust, rubbish, f. Teut. root *mul* grind, + -OCK]

multa·ngular, a. Many-angled. [f. MULTI- + ANGULAR]

multē·ity, n. Manifoldness. [f. L *multus* many]

mu·lti- in comb. (before vowel sometimes *mult-*) = L *multus* many, as: *-colour(ed)*, of many colours; *-fid* (bot., zool.) cleft into many parts; *-flor·ous*, (of stalk) bearing more than three flowers; *-foil* (arch.), ornament consisting of more than 5 foils; *-form*, having many forms, of many kinds, so *-for·mity* n.; *-lă·teral*, having many sides; *-millionaire·*, person with fortune of several millions; *-nō·mial* a. & n. (alg.), (expression) of more than two terms; *multĭ·parous*, bringing forth many young at a birth, (of woman) who has borne more than one child; *-par·tite*, divided into many parts; *-valve* a. & n., (shell, animal with shell) of many valves; *multĭ·vocal* a. & n., (word) susceptible of many meanings; *multŏ·cular*, having many eyes; *multu·ngulate* a.& n.,(animal) with more than two functional hoofs.

multifār·ious, a. Having great variety; (w. pl. n.) many & various. Hence **multifar·ious**LY[2] adv., **multifar·ious**NESS n. [f. LL MULTI(*farius* f. L *-fariam* adv.) + -OUS]

mu·ltiple, a. & n. Of many parts, elements, or individual components (*m. shop*, with branches in various places); (w. pl. n.) many & various; quantity that contains another some number of times without remainder, as *14 is a m. of 7*; *least common m.* (abbr. L.C.M.) least quantity that contains two or more given quantities exactly. [F, f. LL *multiplus* = foll.]

mu·ltiplex, a. Manifold, of many elements. [L (MULTI- + *-plex* -fold)]

mu·ltiplicable, a. Multipliable. [f. L *multiplicabilis* (as MULTIPLY, see -ABLE)]

multiplică·nd, n. Quantity to be multiplied, cf. MULTIPLIER. [f. L as MULTIPLY, see -ND[1]]

multiplica·tion, n. Multiplying, esp. the arithmetical process (*symbol of m.*, ×, as in 2 × 3); *m. table*, table of products of factors taken in pairs. So **mu·ltiplica**TIVE a. [F, f. L *multiplicationem* (as MULTIPLY, see -ATION)]

multipli·city, n. Manifold variety; *a, the, m.* (great number) *of*. [f. L *multiplicitas* (as MULTIPLEX, see -TY)]

mu·ltiplier, n. In vbl senses, esp.: quantity by which MULTIPLICAND is multiplied; (Electr., Magn.) instrument for multiplying intensity of force, current, &c., so as to make it appreciable. [f. foll. + -ER[1]]

mu·ltiply, v.t. & i. Produce large number of (instances &c.); breed (animals),propagate (plants); (intr.) increase in number by procreation; (Math.) substitute for (given number, the *multiplicand*) a number (the *product*) equal to a given number (the *multiplier*) of times its value, as *m. 6 by 4 & the product is 24*, or *6 multiplied by 4 is 24.* Hence **mu·ltipli**ABLE a. [f. OF *multiplier* f. L *multiplicare* (MULTIPLEX)]

mu·ltitude, n. Numerousness; great number (*of*); large gathering of people, crowd; *the m.*, the common people. Hence **multitu·din**OUS a., **multitu·dinous**LY[2] adv., **multitu·dinous**NESS n. [f. L *multitudo -dinis* (*multus* many, see -TUDE)]

multitu·dinism, n. Principle that prefers interests of multitudes to those of individuals. So **multitu·din**IST n. [as prec. + -ISM]

mu·ltum in par·vo, n. Much in small compass; (attrib., w. hyphens) small but comprehensive. [L]

mu·lture (-tsh*er*), n. Toll of grain or flour paid to miller. [f. OF *molture* f. med. L *molitura* (*molere -it-* grind, see -URE)]

mum[1], int. & a. Silence !, esp. *m.'s the word*; (adj.) silent. [imit., cf. G *mumm*]

mum[2], v.i. Act in dumb show; *mumchance* (archaic), silent, tongue-tied. [f. prec.]

mum[3], n. (hist.). Kind of beer orig. brewed in Brunswick. [f. G *mumme*]

mum[4], n. (nursery). = MUMMY[2].

mu·mble, v.i. & t., & n. Speak indistinctly; utter indistinctly; bite, chew, (as) with toothless gums; (n.) indistinct utterance. [(n. f. vb) ME *momele*, as MUM[1], -LE(3)]

Mu·mbo Ju·mbo, n. Grotesque idol said to have been worshipped by some tribes; (fig.) object of senseless veneration. [?]

mu·mmer, n. (Contempt.) play-actor; (Hist.) actor in dumb show. [f. OF *momeur* (*momer* MUM[2])]

mu·mmery, n. Performance of mummers; ridiculous (esp. religious) ceremonial. [f. OF *mommerie* (as prec., see -ERY)]

mu·mmifȳ, v.t. Preserve (body) by embalming & drying; shrivel, dry up, (tissues &c., esp. in p.p.). Hence **mum-**

miFICA·TION n. [f. F *momifier* (as foll., see -FY)]

mu·mmy[1], n. Body of human being or animal embalmed for burial; dried-up body; pulpy substance or mass, esp. *beat* (thing) *to a m.*; rich brown pigment. [f. F *momie* f. med. L *mumia* f. Arab. *mumiya* (*mum* wax)]

mu·mmy[2], n. Mother. [nursery form of MAMMA]

mump[1], v.i. Be silent & sullen; assume demure expression, whence **mu·mp**ING[2] a. [conn. w. MUMPS]

mump[2], v.i. Beg, go about begging. [prob. f. Du. *mompen* cheat]

mumps, n. pl. (treated as sing.). Contagious disease with swelling of parotid & salivary glands; sulks, whence **mu·mp**ISH[1] a. [imit.]

munch, v.t. & i. Eat (food, or abs.) with much action of jaws, as cattle chew fodder. [prob. imit.]

Munchausen (muntshow·zn), n. *Baron M.*, hero of extravagant book of adventures written in English by R. E. Raspe, a German (1785); extravagantly mendacious story.

mu·ndāne, a. Of this world; of the universe. Hence **mu·ndane**LY[2] adv., **mu·ndane**NESS n. [f. F *mondain* f. L *mundanus* (*mundus* world, see -AN)]

mundu·ngus (-ngg-), n. (archaic). Bad-smelling tobacco. [f. Sp. *mondongo* tripe]

mu·ngo (-nggō), n. Cloth like SHODDY, but of better quality. [?]

mūni·cipal, a. Of, under, local self-government or corporate government of city or town, whence **muni·cipal**ISM(2), **muni·cipal**IST(2, 3), nn., **muni·cipal**IZE (3) v.t.; carried on &c. by a municipality (*m. debt, kitchen, trading, undertaking*); *m. law*, that of particular State, opp. to law of nations. Hence **muni·cipal**LY[2] adv. [f. L *municipalis* f. *municeps -cipis* citizen of city that had privileges of Roman citizens (*munia* civic offices + root of *capere* take), see -AL]

munĭcipa·lity, n. Town, district, having local self-government; governing body of this. [f. F *municipalité* (as prec., see -TY)]

mūni·ficent, a. Splendidly generous, bountiful. Hence or cogn. **muni·fic**ENCE n., **muni·ficent**LY[2] adv. [f. L *munificent-*, var. stem of *munificus* (*munus* gift, see -FIC)]

mū·niment, n. (usu. pl.). Document kept as evidence of rights or privileges. [OF, f. L *munimentum* defence (*munire* fortify, -MENT)]

mūni·tion, n., & v.t. (Pl. exc. in comb.) military weapons, ammunition, equipment, & stores (*Ministry* &c. *of mm.*; *m.-factory*); (archaic) *m.*, or *mm.*, *of war*; hence **muni·tion**ER[1] n. (esp. worker in m.-factory). (Vb) supply with mm. [(vb f. n.) F, f. L *munitionem* fortification (as prec., see -ION)]

munnion. =MULLION.

mŭ·ntjăk, n. Small Asiatic deer. [f. native *minchak*]

mŭntz, n. *M.* (*metal*), copper alloy used for sheathing ships &c. [G. F. *Muntz*, inventor]

mūr·age, n. (hist.). Tax levied for building or repairing walls of town. [OF, f. med. L *muragium* (*murus* wall, see -AGE)]

mūr·al, a. Of, like, on, a wall, as *m. paintings*; (Rom. Ant.) *m. crown*, garland given to soldiers who first scaled wall of besieged town). [F, f. L *muralis* (*murus* wall, see -AL)]

Mūrator·ian, a. Of Muratori, Italian scholar, d. 1750; *M. fragment* or *canon*, earliest Western canon of N.T. [-AN]

mur·der[1], n. Unlawful killing of human being with malice aforethought; JUDICIAL *m.*; (prov.) *m. will out* (cannot be hidden); *the m. is out*, the secret is revealed or mystery explained; (as int. of alarm) *m.!*; *cry blue m.*, make extravagant outcry. [OE *mordhor*, cf. Goth. *maurthr*, cogn. w. L *mori* die, Gk *brotos* mortal]

mur·der[2], v.t. Kill (human being) unlawfully with malice aforethought; kill wickedly or inhumanly; spoil by bad execution, mispronunciation, &c. Hence **mur·der**ER[1], **mur·der**ESS[1], nn. [OE *myrdhrian*, cf. OHG *murdran*, Goth. *maurthrjan*, & see prec.]

mur·derous, a. (Of person, weapon, action, &c.) capable of, bent on, involving, murder. Hence **mur·derous**LY[2] adv. [-OUS]

mure, v.t. Confine as in prison; shut *up*. [f. F *murer* f. L *murare*, see IMMURE]

mūr·ex, n. (pl. *-ĭcēs*, *-exes*). Shell-fish yielding purple dye. [L, prob. cogn. w. Gk *muax* sea mussel]

mūr·iate (-*at*), n. (now commerc.). Chloride. [F, f. *muriatique*, as foll.]

muriă·tic, a. (now commerc.). *M.*(hydrochloric) *acid*. [f. L *muriaticus* (*muria* brine, see -ATIC)]

murk, mirk, a. (archaic, poet.). (Of night, day, place, &c.) dark; misty, dense. [OE *mirce* cf. Sw. *mörk*]

mur·ky, a. Dark, gloomy; (of darkness) thick. Hence **mur·ki**LY[2] adv., **mur·ki**NESS n. [f. *murk* n. darkness, cogn. w. prec., + -Y[2]]

mur·mur[1], n. Subdued continuous sound, as of waves, brook, &c.; subdued expression of discontent; softly spoken word or speech. Hence **mur·mur**OUS a., **mur·murous**LY[2] adv. [f. F *murmure* (as foll.)]

mur·mur[2], v.i. & t. Make low continuous sound; complain in low tones, grumble, (*at, against*); utter (words) in low voice. [f. F *murmurer* f. L *murmurare* (*murmur*)]

mur·phy, n. (slang). Potato. [Irish surname]

mŭ·rrain (-ĭn), n. Infectious disease in cattle; (archaic) *a m.* (plague) *on you!*.

[f. F *morine*, cf. Sp. *morriña*, perh. f. L *mori* die]

mu·rrey, a. & n. (archaic). (Of) the colour of a mulberry, purple-red. [f. OF *moré* f. med. L *moratus* (*morum* mulberry)]

mu·rrhine, a. *M. glass*, modern delicate ware from the East, made of fluor-spar. [f. L *murr(h)inus* (*murra*, substance of which precious vases &c. were made, see -INE[1])]

mu·scadine, n. Musk-flavoured kinds of grape. [prob. f. Pr. as MUSCAT]

mu·scardine, n. Disease of silkworms caused by vegetable parasite. [F, f. It. *mosca(r)dino* musk-lozenge (ult. as MUSK)]

mu·scat, muscate·l, -de·l, nn. Muscadine; strong sweet wine from muscadines; (*-tel*) raisin from muscadine. [(*-at*) F f. Pr., f. It. *moscato* musk-flavoured f. L *muscus* MUSK; (*-tel, -del*) OF, dim.]

mu·scle (-sl), n. Any of the contractile fibrous bands or bundles that produce movement in animal body; *not move a m.*, be perfectly motionless; that part of the animal body which is composed of mm., the chief constituent of flesh. Hence **mu·scle**LESS a. [f. L *musculus* dim. of *mus* mouse]

musco·logy, n. Study of mosses. So **musco·**LOGIST n. [f. L *muscus* moss, -LOGY]

muscova·do (-vah-), n. Unrefined sugar got from juice of sugar-cane by evaporation & draining off molasses. [f. Sp. *mascabado* of lowest quality]

mu·scovite[1], n. Common mica (earlier *Muscovy glass*). [as foll.]

Mu·scovite[2], n. & a. (archaic). Russian. [f. foll. + -ITE[1]]

Mu·scovy, n. (Archaic) Russia; *M. duck*, MUSK-duck. [f. F *Muscovie* f. Russ. *Moskova* Moscow]

mu·scŭlar, a. Of, affecting, the muscles; having well-developed muscles; *m.Christianity*, ideal of religious character exhibited in writings of C. Kingsley. Hence **muscŭlă·r**ITY n. [as MUSCLE, see -AR[1]]

mu·sculature (-tsher), n. Muscular system of body or organ. [F, as MUSCLE, see -URE]

muse[1] (-z), n. *The Mm.*, nine goddesses, daughters of Zeus & Mnemosyne, inspirers of poetry, music, &c.; *the m.*, poet's inspiring goddess, poet's genius; (poet.) poet. [F, f. L f. Gk *Mousa* f. root *men-, mon-*, think, remember]

muse[2] (-z), v.i., & n. Ponder, reflect, (*on, upon*); gaze meditatively (*on* scene &c.); (n., archaic) fit of abstraction. [f. F *muser*, prob. f. OF *muse* MUZZLE, orig. w. sense 'sniff the air when in doubt about scent']

mūse·tte (-z), n. Kind of bagpipe; soft pastoral air imitating bagpipe's sound; dance for which this served; reed stop on organ. [F, dim. of OF *muse* bagpipe]

mūsē·um, n. Building used for storing & exhibition of objects illustrating antiquities, natural history, art, &c. [L, f. Gk *mouseion* seat of the Muses (*Mousa*)]

mush[1], n. Soft pulp; (N.-Amer.) kind of porridge. Hence **mu·shi**NESS n., **mu·sh**Y[2] a. [prob. var. of MASH]

mush[2], n. (slang). Umbrella; small cab-proprietor. [shortened f. foll.]

mu·shroom, n., & v.i. Edible kind of fungus, proverbial for rapid growth (*m. growth* &c., sudden development or thing suddenly developed); (fig.) upstart; (colloq.) lady's straw hat with down-curved brim; (v.i.) gather mm., (of bullet) expand & flatten. [(vb f. n.) f. F *mousseron*, perh. f. *mousse* moss]

mū·sic, n. Art of combining sounds with a view to beauty of form & expression of emotion; sounds so produced; pleasant sound, e.g. song of bird, murmur of brook, cry of hounds; *set* (poem &c.) *to m.*, provide it with m. to which it may be sung; written or printed score of musical composition; *face the m.*, face one's critics &c., not shirk; *rough m.*, noisy uproar, esp. with vexatious intention; *m.-hall* (used for singing, dancing, & other entertainments); *m.-stool* (with adjustable seat, for piano-player). [f. F *musique* f. L f. Gk *mousikē* (*tekhnē* art) of the Muses (*Mousa* Muse, see -IC)]

mu·sical, a. Of music; (of sounds, voice, &c.) melodious, harmonious; fond of, skilled in, music; set to, accompanied by, music; *m.-box*, mechanical musical instrument played by causing toothed cylinder to work in comb-like metal plate; *m. chairs*, drawing-room game in which *n* players circulate round *n*—1 chairs till piano ceases, when the one who finds no seat is eliminated, and a chair is removed before the next round; *m. glasses*, kinds of musical instrument in which tones are produced by glass bowls or tubes. Hence **musica·l**ITY, **mu·sical**NESS, nn., **mu·sical**LY[2] adv. [F, f. med. L *musicalis* (*musica* MUSIC, see -AL)]

musica·le (-ahl), n. (U.S.). Musical party. [F, for *soirée* or *matinée m.*]

musi·cian (-shn), n. Person skilled in science or practice of music. [f. F *musicien* (as MUSIC, see -ICIAN)]

musk, n. Odoriferous reddish-brown substance secreted in gland by male m.-deer, used for perfumes & as stimulant &c.; kinds of plant with musky smell; *m.-deer*, small hornless ruminant of Central Asia; *m.-duck* (also *Muscovy duck*), tropical American variety, (also) Australian variety male of which has musky smell; *m. melon*, common melon; *m.-ox*, ruminant found in Arctic America, with strong musky smell; *m.-rat* (also *musquash*), large N.-Amer. aquatic rodent, its fur; *m.-rose*, rambling rose with large fragrant white flowers; *m.-tree, -wood*, trees with musky smell. Hence

mu·sky² a. [f. F *musc* f. LL *muscus* f. late Gk *mosk(h)os* perh. ult. f. Skr. *muska* scrotum]

mu·sket, n. Infantry soldier's hand-gun (now usu. of obsolete kinds, cf. RIFLE); *m.-shot,* shot fired from m., range of m. [f. F *mousquet* f. It. *moschetto* sparrow-hawk]

musketeer·, n. Soldier armed with musket. [-EER]

mu·sketry, n. Muskets; art of using, troops armed with, muskets; (Mil., in mod. use) instruction, practice, in rifle-shooting. [f. F *mousqueterie* (as MUSKET, see -ERY)]

Muslim. See MOSLEM.

mu·slin (-z-), n. Kinds of delicately woven cotton fabric for ladies' dresses, curtains, &c.; (colloq.) *bit of m.,* woman, girl; *m.-de-laine,* see MOUSSELINE. Hence **mu·slin**ED² a. [f. F *mousseline* f. It. *mussolina* (*Mussolo,* town in Mesopotamia whence m. came, see -INE¹)]

musline·t, n. Thick kind of muslin. [-ET¹]

mu·smon, n. =MOUFFLON. [f. L *musimo(n)* f. late Gk *mousmōn*]

mu·squash (-ŏsh), n. (Fur of) MUSK-rat. [f. Algonkin *muskwessu*]

mussa·l (-ahl), n. (Anglo-Ind.). Torch; (also *mussa·lchu*) torch-bearer. [f. Arab. *mas'al*]

mu·ssel, n. Kinds (*Sea, Fresh-water, M.*) of bivalve mollusc; *m. plum,* dark purple plum. [OE *muscle* f. LL *muscula,* fem. as MUSCLE]

Mu·ssulman, n. & a. (pl. *-mans*). Mohammedan. [f. Pers. *musulmān* (as MOSLEM)]

must¹, n. New wine; grape-juice before fermentation is complete. [f. L *mustum* neut. of *mustus* new]

must², n. Mustiness, mould. [prob. back formation f. MUSTY]

must³, a. & n. (Of male elephants & camels) in state of frenzy; (n.) this state. [f. Hind. f. Pers. *mast* intoxicated]

must⁴, v. auxil. (3rd sing. *must*; past *must,* only as below). Be obliged to (do), as *you m.* (neg. *need not,* see below & cf. MAY¹) *find it, it m. be found,* (w. necessity less emphasized) *we m. see what can be done, I m. ask you to retract that, you m. know* (I now tell you); be certain to (do), as *you m. lose, whichever happens*; *you m. be* (surely are) *aware of this*; *he must be* (clearly is) *mad*; (as past tense, reporting reflection made at the time) *it was too late now to retreat, he m. make good his word or incur lasting disgrace*; (past or historic present, w. reference to perverse destiny) *just as I was getting better, what m. I do but break my leg?, just as I was busiest, he m. come worrying*; *m. have* done, (1) surely did, as *you m. have known quite well what I meant,* (2) necessarily would have done, as *you m. have caught it if you had run*; (w. negative belonging in sense to dependent vb, cf. MAY¹) *you m. not infer* (m. avoid the inference), *you m. never contradict.* [OE *móste,* past of *mót* (later *mote*) may, be permitted to, cf. Du. *moet,* G *muss*]

musta·chio (-ahshō), n. (archaic). Moustache. [(partly f. Sp. *mostacho*) f. It. as MOUSTACHE]

mu·stang, n. Wild horse of Mexico & California; *m.* (small red Texas) *grape.* [f. Sp. *mestengo,* perh. f. *mesta* company of graziers]

mu·stard, n. Kinds of plant, esp. *black & white m.,* seeds of which are ground, made into paste, & used as condiment or for poultice or *m. plaster*; *grain of m. seed,* small thing capable of vast development (*Matt.* xiii. 31); *m. & cress* (used in seed-leaf for salad); *French m.* (mixed with vinegar); *m.-pot* (for table m.). [orig. of the condiment; f. OF *moustarde* f. com.-Rom. *mosto* MUST¹]

mu·ster¹, n. Assembling of men for inspection &c. (*pass m.,* be accepted as adequate), assembly, collection; *m.-book,* (for registering military forces); *m.-roll,* official list of officers & men in army or ship's company (also fig.). [f. OF *mostre* f. L *monstrare* show]

mu·ster², v.t. & i. Collect (orig. soldiers) for inspection, to check numbers, &c.; collect, get together, (t. & i.); summon (courage, strength, &c.; often *up*). [f. OF *mostrer* f. L as prec.]

mu·sty, a. Mouldy; of mouldy or stale smell or taste; (fig.) stale, antiquated. Hence **mu·sti**NESS n. [?]

mū·table, a. Liable to change; fickle. Hence **muta**BI·LITY n. [f. L *mutabilis* (*mutare* change, see -BLE)]

muta·tion, n. Change, alteration; (Biol.) change resulting in production of new species. [F, f. L *mutationem* (as prec., see -ATION)]

mutā·tis muta·ndis, adv. With due alteration of details (in comparing cases). [L]

mutch, n. (Sc.). Woman's or child's linen cap. [f. MDu. *mutse,* cf. G *mütze*]

mute¹, a. & n. Silent; not emitting articulate sound; (Law) *stand m. of malice,* refuse deliberately to plead; (of person or animal) dumb; (of hounds) not giving tongue; not expressed in speech, as *m. appeal, adoration*; temporarily bereft of speech; (of consonant) produced by entire interruption of passage of breath or complete closure of organs of mouth, stopped, (usu. applied to *b p ph d t th k g*); (of letter) not pronounced, as *the* e *in late is m.*; (n.) m. consonant; dumb person; actor whose part is in dumb show; dumb servant in Oriental countries; hired mourner; clip for deadening resonance of strings of violin &c., pad for deadening sound of wind instrument. Hence **mu·te-**

LY[2] adv., **mu·te**NESS n. [f. F *muet* f. pop. L **mutettus* dim. of L *mutus*]
mute[2], v.t. Deaden, muffle, the sound of (esp. musical instrument). [f. prec.]
mute[3], v.i. & t. (Of birds) void the faeces, discharge thus. [f. OF *muetir* etym. dub.]
mu·tilate, v.t. Deprive (person &c.) of limb or organ; cut off, destroy the use of, (limb &c.); render (book &c.) imperfect by excision &c. So **mutil**A·TION, **mu·tilat**OR[2], nn. [f. L *mutilare* (*mutilus* maimed), see -ATE[3]]
mūtineer·, n. One who mutinies. [f. F *mutinier* (*mutin* rebellious ult. f. L as MOVE)]
mū·tinous, a. Rebellious. Hence **mu·tinous**LY[2] adv. [f. obs. *mutine* f. F *mutin* (see prec.) + -OUS]
mū·tiny, n., & v.i. Open revolt against constituted authority, esp. of soldiers or sailors against officers; *Indian M.*, revolt of Bengal native troops, 1857–8; *M. Act* (dealing with offences against military & naval discipline, now embodied in Army Act, 1881); (v.i.) revolt (*against* or abs.). [(vb f. n.) as prec. + -Y[1]]
mu·tism, n. Muteness; silence; dumbness. [f. F *mutisme* f. L as MUTE[1], see -ISM]
mūto-, comb. form (irreg.) of L *mutare* change, as: *-graph*, apparatus for taking series of photographs of moving objects, (v.t.) portray with this; *-scope*, apparatus for exhibiting scene recorded by mutograph, so *-sco·pic* a.
mu·tter, v.i. & t., & n. Speak low in barely audible manner; murmur, grumble, (*against, at*); utter (words &c.) in low tone; (fig.) say in secret; (n.) muttering, muttered words. [prob. imit., w. suf. -ER[5]]
mu·tton, n. Flesh of sheep as food; (facet.) sheep (*to our mm.*, gallicism = let us come back to our subject); *dead as m.*, quite dead; *eat* one's *m.*, dine *with*; *m. chop*, piece of m. (usu. rib & half vertebra to which it is attached) for frying &c., side whisker shaped like this. Hence **mu·tton**Y[2] a. [f. OF *moton* f. med. L *multonem* nom. *-to*, cf. OIr. *molt* ram]
mū·tūal, a. (Of feelings, actions, &c.) felt, done, by each to(wards) the other, as *m. affection, benefit, suspicion*; standing in (specified) m. relation, as *m. well-wishers*; *m. admiration society*, set of persons who overestimate each other's merits; (Commerc.) *m. terms* (by which exchange of services takes the place of money payments); (improp.) common to two or more persons, as *our m. friend*. Hence **mutua·l**ITY n., **mu·tual**LY[2] adv. [f. F *mutuel* f. L *mutuus* borrowed (cf. *mutare* change), see -AL]
mū·tualism, n. Doctrine that mutual dependence is necessary to well-being. So **mu·tual**IST n. [-ISM]
mū·tule, n. (archit.). Modillion proper to cornice in Doric order. [F, f. L *mutulus*]
muzhik. See MOUJIK.
muzz, v.t. (slang). Make muzzy. [?]
mu·zzle[1], n. Projecting part of animal's head including nose & mouth; open end of fire-arm; contrivance of strap or wire put over animal's head to prevent its biting, eating, &c.; *m.-loader*, gun that is loaded at the m. [f. OF *musel* f. med. L *musellum* dim. of *musus*]
mu·zzle[2], v.t. Put muzzle on (animal, its mouth, &, fig., a person); impose silence upon; take in (sail). [f. prec.]
mu·zzy, a. Dull, spiritless; stupid from drinking. Hence **mu·zzi**LY[2] adv., **mu·zzi**NESS n. [?]
my (mī, unstressed often mĭ), poss. adj. of 1st pers. sing. (with abs. form MINE); (prefixed to some terms of address) *my boy, friend, man, son, daughter*, (not colloq. w. other terms of relationship), *dear, darling, love*; *my* (vulg. *mine*) *& her* (common) *father, my* (vulg. *mine*) *& her* (respective) *father(s)*; (in ejaculations) *my! my eye!*, &c. [ME *mī*, reduced f. OE *mīn* MINE[3]]
mȳ·alism, n. Kind of sorcery practised esp. in W. Indies. [prob. of W.-Afr. orig.]
mȳ·all, n. Austral. acacia, with scented wood used for pipes. [f. native *maial*]
mȳa·lgia, n. (path.). Muscular rheumatism. [Gk *mus* muscle, *algos* pain, -IA[1]]
mȳcē·lium, n. (bot.). Mushroom spawn. Hence **myce·li**AL a. [f. Gk *mukēs* mushroom + Latin ending]
Mȳcēnae·an, a. (archaeol.). Of the prehellenic or Achaean culture illustrated by remains at Mycenae in Greece, & by Homer. [f. L f. Gk *Mukēnaios* + -AN]
mȳcetō·ma, n. Fungoid disease of foot or hand. [as prec., see -M]
mȳcŏ·logy, n. Study of fungi. So **myco·lo**GIST n. [irreg. f. Gk as prec., see -LOGY]
mycō·sis, n. Presence of, disease caused by, parasitic fungi. [as prec., see -OSIS]
mȳeli·tis, n. Inflammation of spinal cord. [f. Gk *muelos* marrow, see -ITIS]
mȳ·lodon, n. Extinct genus of gigantic sloths with cylindrical teeth. [f. Gk *mulē* mill + *odous -ontos* tooth]
myna, = MINA[2].
mȳnheer·, n. Dutchman. [f. Du. *mijnheer* Mr, sir, (*mijn* my + *heer* master)]
mȳo- in comb. = Gk *mus muos* muscle, as: *-car·dium*, muscular substance of heart, whence *-cardI·TIS*; *-logy*, science of muscles.
mȳ·ōpe, n. Short-sighted person. Hence or cogn. **myō·p**IA[1], **my·op**Y[1], nn., **myŏ·p**IC a. [F, f. LL f. Gk *muōps* (*muō* shut + *ōps* eye)]
myō·sis, n. Contraction of pupil of eye. So **myŏ·**TIC a. [f. Gk *muō* shut, see -OSIS]
mȳ·osōte, n. Forget-me-not. [f. foll.]
mȳosō·tis, n. Genus of small plants with blue, pink, or white flowers. [L, f. Gk *muosōtis* (*mus muos* mouse + *ous ōtos* ear)]

mў·riad, a. & n. (poet., rhet.). Ten thousand; (of) indefinitely great number. [f. LL f. Gk *murias -ados* (*murioi* 10,000)]

mў·riapod, a. & n. (Animal) with many legs, of the class comprising centipedes & millepedes. [as prec. + Gk *pous podos* foot]

mўriora·ma (-rah-, -ră-), n. Entertainment consisting of series of views. [f. Gk *murios* countless + *horama* view (*horaō* see)]

myr·midon (mer-), n. (*M-*) any of a warlike Thessalian race who followed Achilles; hired ruffian; base servant, as *m. of the law*, policeman, bailiff, &c. [f. L f. Gk *Murmidones* pl.]

mўrŏ·balan, n. Astringent plum-like fruit used in dyeing, tanning, &c. [f. L *myrobalanum* f. Gk *myrobalanos* (*muron* unguent + *balanos* acorn)]

myrrh[1] (mer), n. Gum resin used in perfumery & medicine, & in incense. Hence **myr·rh**IC, **myr·rh**Y[2], aa. [OE *myrra*, f. L f. Gk *murra*]

myrrh[2] (mer), n. Sweet Cicely, an aromatic plant. [f. LL f. Gk *murris*]

myr·tle, n. Genus of plants, esp. *Common M.*, shrub with shiny evergreen leaves & white scented flowers, sacred to Venus. **myrt**A·CEOUS a., of N.O. *Myrtaceae* (m. &c.). [f. OF *myrtille*, dim. f. L f. Gk *murtos*]

mўse·lf, pron. Emphatic & reflexive form corresp. to *I*, as *I saw it m.*, *I m.* (for my part) *am doubtful*, *I have hurt m.*; *I am not m.* (in my normal state of body or mind). [f. ME + SELF; *my-* perh. on anal. of *herself*]

my·stagogue (-ŏg), n. Teacher of mystical doctrines, esp. (Gk Ant.) to candidates for initiation in Eleusinian & other mysteries. So **mystagŏ·gic**(AL) aa. [f. L f. Gk *mustagōgos* (*mustēs* one initiated into mysteries, f. *muō* close eyes or lips, + *-agōgos* -leading f. *agō* lead)]

mystē·rious, a. Full of, wrapt in, mystery; (of persons) delighting in mystery. Hence **mysteri·ous**LY[2] adv., **myster·i·ous**NESS n. [f. foll. + -OUS]

my·stery[1], n. Hidden or inexplicable matter; *make a m. of*, treat as a secret; secrecy, obscurity, as *is wrapt in m.*; (practice of) making a secret of (unimportant) things; religious truth divinely revealed, esp. one beyond human reason; religious rite, esp. (pl.) Eucharist; (pl.) secret religious rites of Greeks, Romans, &c.; miracle-play; *m.-ship*, war-ship disguised as tramp steamer &c. to decoy submarines in the great war. [f. OF *mistere* f. L f. Gk *mustērion* (*muō* close lips or eyes)]

my·stery[2], n. (archaic). Handicraft, trade, esp. (in indentures) *art & m.* [f. med. L *mi(ni)sterium* (MINISTER), confused w. prec.]

my·stic, a. & n. Spiritually allegorical; occult, esoteric; of hidden meaning, mysterious; mysterious & awe-inspiring; one who seeks by contemplation & self-surrender to obtain union with or absorption into the Deity, or who believes in spiritual apprehension of truths beyond the understanding, whence **my·sti**CISM n. (often contempt.). Hence **my·sti**CAL a., **my·stical**LY[2] adv., **my·stic**IZE(3) v.t. [f. OF *mystique* f. L f. Gk *mustikos* (as MYSTERY[1], -IC)]

my·stify, v.t. Hoax, play on credulity of; bewilder; wrap up in mystery. So **mysti**FICA·TION n. [f. F *mystifier* (irreg. as prec., -FY)]

mўth, n. Purely fictitious narrative usu. involving supernatural persons &c. & embodying popular ideas on natural phenomena &c.; fictitious person or thing. Hence **mў·th**IC(AL) aa., **my·thical**LY[2] adv. [f. Gk *muthos*]

mў·thicize, v.t. Treat story (&c.) as a myth, interpret mythically. So **my·thi**CISM, **my·thic**IST, nn. [MYTHIC + -IZE]

mўtho- in comb. = Gk *muthos* myth, as: *-grapher*, writer of myths; *-graphy*, representation of myths in plastic art; *-pœic* (-pē·ĭk), *-poĕ·tic*, making, productive of, myths; *-po·et*, *-po·etry*, poetical writer, writing, of myths.

mўtho·logy, n. Body of myths, esp. relating to particular person or subject; study of myths. Hence or cogn. **mytho·log**ER[1], **mytho·log**IST, nn., **mytholo·gic**(AL) aa., **mytholo·gical**LY[2] adv., **mytho·log**IZE(2, 3) v.t. & i. [f. Gk *muthologia* (see prec., & -LOGY)]

mўthus, n. Myth. [mod. L, as MYTH]

N

N (ĕn), letter (pl. *N*s, N's). (Print.) *n* (also *en*) unit of measurement; (Math.) indefinite number (*to the nth*, to any required power, also fig. to any extent, to the utmost); *N-rays*, *N*[1]*-rays*, forms of radiation.

Abbreviations (1): N.: National, as **N.L.C.** (Liberal Club), **N.L.F.** (Liberal Federation), **N.S.P.C.C.** (Society for Prevention of Cruelty to Children); Natural, **N.O.**(rder); New, as **N.E.D.** (English dictionary: original title, still often used, of the O.E.D.), **N.F.**(oundland), **N.H.**-(ampshire), **N.J.**(ersey), **N.Mex.**(ico), **N.S.**(tyle), **N.S.W.**(South Wales), **N.T.**-(estament), **N.Y.**(ork), **N.Z.**(ealand); non, **N.C.O.**(-commissioned officer); North, as **N.B.**(ritain), **N.C.**(arolina), **N.Dak.**-(ota), **N.** & **N.E.**(ast) & **N.W.**(est) as points of compass & (exc. N.E.) London postal districts, **N.W.Prov.**(inces); not, **N.S.**(ufficient); *Nota*, **N.B.**(*ene*); Nova, **N.S.**(cotia). n.: neuter; no, **n.d.**(ate); noon; noun.

Abbreviations (2): **Nah.**(um); **Nebr.**-(aska); **Neh.**(emiah); **nem.**(*ine*) **con.**-(*tradicente*); **nem.**(*ine*) **dis.**(*sentiente*);

Nev.(ada); **No, Nos**, number(s); **non-com.**(missioned officer); **Northants.**, Northamptonshire; **Northumb.**(erland); **Norvic.**, bishop of Norwich; **Notts.**, Nottinghamshire; **Num.**(bers, O.-T. book).

nab, v.t. (slang). Apprehend, arrest; catch in wrong-doing. [?]

nā·bŏb, n. (Hist.) Mohammedan official or governor under Mogul empire; wealthy luxurious person, esp. one returned from India with fortune. [= NAWAB]

Nā·both's vineyard, n. Possession that one will stick at nothing to secure. [see 1 *Kings* xxi]

na·carăt, n. Bright orange-red colour. [F, perh. f. Sp. & Port. *nacarado* (NACRE)]

nace·lle, n. Body of pusher aeroplane; car of airship. [F, f. LL *navicella* dim. of L *navis* ship]

nā·cre (-ker), n. Pinna or sea-pen; (shell-fish yielding) mother-o'-pearl. Hence **nā·cre**ous (-rĭ-), **nā·cr**ous, aa. [F, = Sp. & Port. *nacar* etym. dub.]

nā·dir, n. Point of heavens directly under observer (opp. ZENITH); (transf.) lowest point, place or time of greatest depression &c. [f. Arab. *nadir* (*es-semt*) opposite to (zenith)]

nag[1], n. Small riding horse or pony; horse (colloq.). [?]

nag[2], v.i. & t. Find fault or scold (intr.) persistently (*at* person); annoy thus. Hence **na·gg**ING[1] n. [cf. Norw. & Sw. *nagga* gnaw]

nā·gor, n. Senegal antelope. [wd made by Buffon]

nai·ad (nī-), n. Water-nymph. [f. L f. Gk *naias -ados* (*naō* flow)]

naïf (nah-ē·f), a. (rare). = NAÏVE. [F]

nail[1], n. Horny covering of outer tip of finger & upper tip of toe (*n.-brush, -scissors*, for cleaning & paring nn.; TOOTH *& n.*), whence **-nail**ED[2] a.; claw, talon; hard excrescence on some soft-billed birds' upper mandible; small metal spike usu. with point & broadened head driven in with hammer to hold things together or as peg or ornament (*hit n.*, or *right n., on head*, give true explanation, propose or do right thing, hit the mark; *n. in* one's COFFIN; *on the n.*, without delay, esp. of payment; *hard as nn.*, in fine training; *right as nn.*, quite right); *n.-head*, architectural ornament. Hence **nai·l**LESS a. [OE *nægel* cf. Du. & G *nagel*, cogn. w. L *unguis*, Gk *onux*]

nail[2], v.t. Fasten with nn. (*on, to, together, down, in*, &c.; *n. colours to mast*, persist; *n. to counter, barndoor*, expose as spurious, vile; *n. up*, close, affix at height, with nn.; *nailed-up drama*, ill-constructed, loosely put together); fix or keep fixed (person, attention, &c.); secure, catch, engage, succeed in getting hold of, (person or thing). [OE *næglan* cf. prec.]

nai·ler, n. Nail-maker, whence **nai·l**ERY(3) n.; (slang) excellent specimen, person very skilful *at*. [-ER[1]]

nai·ling, a. In vbl senses; also (slang) splendid, excellent (*a n.*, or *n. good, race*). [-ING[2]]

nainsōō·k, n. Fine cotton fabric, orig. Indian. [f. Hind. *nainsukh* (*nain* eye, *sukh* pleasure)]

naïve (nah-ē·v), **naive** (nāv), a. Artless, unaffected; amusingly simple. Hence **naï·**VELY[2], **nai·vely**, adv., **naïveté** (nah-ē·vtā), **naïve**TY (naē·vtĭ), **nai·vety** (nāv-), n. [F, fem. of *naïf* f. L *nativus* NATIVE]

nā·ked, a. Unclothed, nude, (*as n. as my mother bore me*); defenceless; unsheathed; plain, undisguised, (*the n. truth*; *n. facts*; *in its n. absurdity*), exposed for examination (*his n. heart*); devoid *of*; treeless, leafless, barren; (of rock) exposed; (of rooms) unfurnished; without ornament; (of candles &c.) exposed to air; without pericarp, leaves, hairs, scales, shell, &c.; without addition, comment, support, evidence, &c. (*n. faith, quotations, word, assertion*); unassisted (*n. eye*, without telescope &c.); *N. Lady, N. Boys*, meadow saffron. Hence **na·ked**LY[2] adv., **na·ked**NESS n. (*the —ness of the land*, person's or institution's or State's lack of resources or openness to attack, see *Gen.* xiii. 9). [OE *nacod, næcad*, cf. Du. *naakt*, G *nackt*, cogn. w. L *nudus*]

nā·ker, n. (hist.) Kettledrum. [f. OF *nacre*, f. Arab. & Pers. *naqāra*(*h*)]

na·mby-pa·mby, a. & n. Insipidly pretty, mildly sentimental; (n.) talk of this kind. [formed on name of Ambrose Philips pastoral writer d. 1749]

name[1], n. Word by which individual person, animal, place, or thing, is spoken of or to (*mention* person *by n.*; *Tom by n., by n. Tom*, called; *know by n.*, individually, also by hearsay only; *of* or *by the n. of*, called; *put* one's *n. down for*, apply as candidate &c.; *keep* one's *n. on, take* one's *n. off, the books*, remain, cease to be, member of college, club, &c.); word denoting any object of thought, esp. one applicable to many individuals (*call* person *nn.*, describe him by uncomplimentary nn.; *give it a n.* colloq., mention the drink, present, &c., that you wish); person as known, famed, or spoken of (*adore the n. of God*; *Nelson himself & many great nn. were there*); all who go under one n., family, clan, people; reputation (*has an ill, a good, n.*; *has a n. for honesty, the n. of being honest*; *win oneself a n.*; *bequeath a great n.*; *persons of n.*; one's *good n.*); merely nominal existence, practically non-existent thing, (opp. *fact, reality, deed*; *virtuous in n.*; *honour had become a n.*); *in* person's *n., in the n. of*, invoking, relying upon, calling to witness, (*in God's n.*; *in the n. of goodness, fortune, common sense*), acting as deputy for or in the interest of (*in* one's *own name*, independently, without authority); *n.-child*, one named after another (*my* &c. *n.-c.*); *n.-day*, day of saint after whom person is named (esp. of continental sovereigns); *n.-part*, that after which play is named, title-role; *namesake*, person or thing with same n. as another (*his* &c. *namesake*) [prob. f. phr. *for the n.'s sake*]. [Aryan; OE *nama*, cf. Du. *naam*, G *name*, Skr. *naman*, L *nomen*, Gk *onoma*]

name[2], v.t. Give n. to (*after*, *from*), call so-&-so; call (person, thing) by right n.; nominate, appoint (*to* office &c.); mention, specify, (*not to be named on* or *in same day with*, quite inferior to; *n. your price*); (of Speaker) mention (M.P.) as disobedient to Chair (*name!*, vb or n., appeal to do this, or to give n. of some person alluded to in speech); cite as instance; specify as something desired (*n. the day*, of woman fixing date for wedding). Hence **na·m**ABLE a. [OE (*ge*)*namian* as prec.]

na·meless, a. Obscure, inglorious; not mentioned by name, left unnamed on purpose (esp. *who shall be n.*); anonymous, unknown; having no name, bearing no name-inscription; inexpressible, indefinable; too bad to be named, abominable, loathsome, (esp. *n. vices*). [-LESS]

na·mely, adv. That is to say, viz. [NAME[1], -LY[2]]

nammet, var. of NUMMET.

nankee·n, n. Kind of cotton cloth orig. made of naturally yellow cotton; (pl.) trousers of this; yellow or pale buff colour. [f. *Nankin(g)* in China]

na·nny, n. *N.* (*-goat*) she-goat (cf. BILLY); child's nurse. [f. the female name]

Năntz, n. (archaic). Brandy (often *right N.*). [f. *Nantes* in France]

nap[1], v.i., & n. Sleep lightly or briefly (*catch napping*, find asleep, take unawares, detect in negligence or error); (n.) short sleep, doze, esp. by day (often *take a n.*). [n. f. vb, OE *knappian*, cf. OHG (*h*)*naffez-*]

nap[2], n., & v.t. Surface given to cloth by raising & then cutting & smoothing the short fibres, pile, whence **na·p**LESS a.; soft or downy surface; (vb) raise n. on (cloth). [f. MDu. or MLG *noppe(n)*]

nap[3], n. A card-game (*n. hand* fig., position that justifies confident expectation of winning if one takes a risk; *go n.*, risk attempting highest form of win in n, also fig.); (Betting) the putting of all one's money on one chance, a tipster's choice for this. [abbr. of *Napoleon*]

nape, n. Back of or usu. *of* neck. [?]

nā·pery, n. (Sc. & archaic). Household, esp. table, linen. [f. obs. F *naperie* (NAPKIN, -ERY)]

na·phtha (-fth-), n. Kinds of inflammable oil got by dry distillation of organic substances, as coal, shale, or petroleum. [L, f. Gk, = inflammable volatile liquid issuing from earth]

na·phthalene, -ine, n. White crystalline substance got in distilling coal-tar & used as disinfectant. Hence **na·phthal**IZE(5) v.t. [prec. + *-l-* + -ENE, -INE[5]]

na·pkin, n. (Also *table-n.*) square piece of linen for wiping lips or fingers with at meals, or serving fish &c. on; small towel esp. for nursery purposes; *lay up* &c. *in a n.*, make no use of (*Luke* xix. 20); *n.-ring*, to distinguish person's table-n. [prob. f. F *nappe* f. L *mappa* table-cloth + -KIN]

napō·leon, n. French gold twenty-franc piece of Napoleon I (*double n.*, forty-franc piece); kind of top-boot; the game NAP[3]. [f. name of French emperor]

Napōleŏ·nic, a. Of, like, &c., Napoleon I. Hence or cogn. **Napoleo·n**ICALLY[2] adv., **Napo·leon**ISM(3), **Napo·leon**IST(2), nn., **Napo·leon**IZE(4) v.t. & i. [as prec., -IC]

napōō· (nah-), int. (army slang). Vanished!, lost!, done!, finished!, no go!. [f. F (*il n'y e*)*n a plus* there is no more of it]

na·ppy, a. (archaic). (Of ale &c.) foaming, heady, strong. [perh. f. NAP[2], -Y[2]]

napu (nah·pōō), n. Musk-deer of Java & Sumatra. [Malay]

nar·cēine, n. Alkaloid got from opium sometimes used instead of morphia. [f. Gk *narkē* numbness + -INE[1]]

narci·ssism, n. (pyscho-anal.). Tendency to self-worship, absorption in one's own personal perfections. Hence **narcissi·st**IC a. [Gk *Narkissos* youth who fell in love with his reflection in water, -ISM]

narci·ssus, n. (pl. *-ssuses*, *-ssī*). Kinds of bulbous plant, esp. one bearing heavily scented single white flower with undivided corona edged with crimson & yellow. [L, f. Gk *narkissos* perh. as NARCEINE w. ref. to narcotic effect]

nar·colepsy, n. Disease with fits of somnolence. [f. Gk *narkē* numbness + (EPI)-LEPSY]

narco·sis, n. Operation or effects of narcotics; state of insensibility. [f. Gk *narkōsis* (*narkoō* benumb)]

narcŏ·tic, a. & n. (Substance) inducing drowsiness, sleep, stupor, or insensibility; (fig.) soporific (a. & n.); of narcosis. Hence **nar·co·t**ICALLY adv., **nar·cot**IZE(3, 5) v.t., **narcotiz**A·TION, **nar·cot**ISM(5), **nar·cot**IST(2), nn. [f. Gk *narkōtikos* (prec., -IC)]

nard, n. (Plant yielding) aromatic balsam of ancients. [f. L f. Gk *nardos* f. Oriental wd]

nar·ghile (-gilĕ), n. Oriental tobacco-pipe with smoke passed through water, hookah. [f. Pers. *nargileh* (*nargil* coconut)]

nark, n. (slang). Police decoy or spy. [Romany *nak* nose]

narra·te (na-), v.t. Relate, recount, give continuous account of, (abs.) utter or write narrative. Hence or cogn. **narra·tion**, **narra·tor**[2], **narrā·tress**[1], nn.

[f. L *narrare* perh. f. *gnarus* aware cogn. w. KNOW, -ATE[3]]

na·rrative, n. & a. Tale, story, recital of facts; kind of composition or talk that confines itself to these; (adj.) in the form of, concerned with, narration, whence **na·rrative**LY[2] adv. [f. L *narrativus* a. (prec., -IVE)]

na·rrow, a. (-er, -est) & n., & v.i. & t. Of small width in proportion to length, wanting in breadth, constricted, (*the n. way*, righteousness see *Matt.* vii. 14; *n. vowels*, made with tongue & uvula tense); of small size, confined or confining, (*the n. bed, cell, house*, grave; *within n. bounds* &c.); of limited scope, restricted, (*in the narrowest sense*; *n. circumstances*, poverty); with little margin (*a n. majority, escape*); lacking in breadth of view or sympathy, illiberal, prejudiced, exclusive, self-centred, whence **narrow-mind**ED[2] a., **narrow-mi·nded**LY[2] adv., **narrow-mi·nded**NESS n.; searching, precise, exact, (*after a n. examination*); *n. cloth*, under 52 in., of single width usu. about a yard; *n. goods*, ribbons, braid, &c.; *n.* GAUGE on railway, any of less than 4ft 8½in. (formerly, the gauge of 4ft 8½in.); *n. seas*, English & Irish channels; hence **na·rrow**ISH[1] a., **na·rrow**LY[2] adv., **na·rrow**NESS n. (N., usu. pl.) n. part of a sound, strait, river, pass, or street. (Vb) make or become narrower, diminish, lessen, contract. [OE *nearu*, cf. Du. *naar* dismal]

nar·thex, n. Railed-off western portico or ante-nave in early Christian churches for women, penitents, & catechumens. [Gk (-*ēx*), orig. name of a plant = FERULA]

nar·whal (-wal), n. Arctic delphinoid cetacean with straight horn(s) developed from one or both of its two teeth. [f. Da. *narhval* cf. ON *náhvalr* (perh. *ná-r* corpse w. allusion to its colour, WHALE)]

nā·sal (-zl), a. & n. Of the nose (*n. organ* facet., nose); (of letters or sounds) requiring the nose passage to be open (n., such a letter &c., e.g. *m, n, ng*), (of voice or speech) having the twang described as speaking through the nose, whence **na·sal**IZE(2, 3) v.i. & t., **nasaliz**A·TION n. Hence **nasa·l**ITY n., **na·sal**LY[2] adv. [f. med. L *nasalis* (L *nasus* nose, -AL)]

na·scent (-snt), a. In the act of being born, just beginning to be, not yet mature. So **na·sc**ENCY n. [f. L *nasci* be born, -ENT]

na·seberry (-z-), n. W.-Ind. tree yielding Sapodilla plum. [f. Sp., Port., *néspera* medlar]

nāso-, comb. form of L *nasus* nose, as *-fro·ntal* of nose & forehead.

nastur·tium (-shm), n. (Bot.) genus of pungent-tasted cruciferous plants including watercress; trailing garden plant with bright orange flowers, Indian cress. [L, derived by Pliny f. *nasus* nose, *torquēre tort-* pain]

na·sty, a. Disgustingly dirty, filthy; obscene, delighting in obscenity; disagreeable to smell or taste, unpalatable lit. & fig., annoying, objectionable; (of weather &c.) foul, wet, stormy; hard to deal with or get rid of, serious, (*a n. sea, fence, blow, illness*; *a n. one*, rebuff, snub, disabling blow, &c.); ill-natured, spiteful *to*. Hence **na·sti**LY[2] adv., **na·sti**NESS n. [from 1400; etym. dub.; cf. Du. *nestig* dirty]

nā·tal, a. Of, from, one's birth. [f. L *natalis* (NATION, -AL)]

nata·lity, n. Birth-rate. [F (-*té*), as prec., -TY]

nata·tion, n. Swimming. [f. L *natatio* (*natare* swim, -ATION)]

nātator·ial, na·tatory, aa. Swimming, of swimming. [LL *natatorius* (prec.), -ORY, -AL]

nā·tēs, n. pl. (anat.) Buttocks; anterior pair of optic lobes in brain. [L]

nā̆·th(e)less, adv. (archaic). Nevertheless. [f. OE *ná* (*ne* not, *á* ever) + THE + LESS]

na·tion, n. Distinct race or people having common descent, language, history, or political institutions (*most favoured n.* diplom., to which State accords lowest scale of import duties); (in medieval & some Scotch univv.) body of students from particular country or district; LAW *of nn.* Hence **na·tion**HOOD n. [F, f. L *nationem* nom. -*o* (*nasci nat-* be born, -ION)]

nă·tional, a. & n. Of a or the nation, common to the whole nation; peculiar to or characteristic of a particular nation; *n. anthem*, 'God save the King' & corresponding hymns of other peoples; *n.* DEBT; *N. Gallery, N. Portrait Gallery*, buildings in London in which pictures, portraits, owned by the nation are permanently exhibited; *N.* INSURANCE; *N. Liberal Club*, club in close connexion with the Liberal party (cf. CARLTON); *N. Society*, founded 1811 to promote education of the poor; *Grand N.* (*Steeplechase*), chief steeplechase of year, at Aintree in March; (n. pl., diplomatic) one's fellow-countrymen (*consul's powers over his own nn.*). Hence **na·tional**LY[2] adv. [F (prec., -AL)]

na·tionalism, n. Patriotic feeling, principles, or efforts; policy of national independence, esp. in Ireland; policy of nationalizing industry. So **na·tional**IST(2) n. [-ISM]

nationa·lity, n. Being national, national quality; patriotic sentiment; one's nation (*what is his n.?*); a nation (*men of all nn.*); existence as a nation; race forming part of one or more political nations. [-ITY]

na·tionalize, v.t. Make national; make into a nation; naturalize (foreigner); convert (land, railways, manufactures, &c.) into national property or undertakings. Hence **nationaliz**A·TION n. [-IZE]

na·tive[1], n. One born, or whose parents are domiciled, in a place (*of*); (Austral.) white born in Australia; member of non-European or uncivilized race; indigenous animal or plant; oyster reared wholly or partly in British waters, esp. in artificial beds. [f. med. L *nativus* n. (L *nativus* a., see foll.)]

na·tive[2], a. Belonging to a person or thing by nature, innate, inherent, natural *to*, whence **na·tive**LY[2] adv.; unadorned, simple, artless; of one's birth, where one was born; belonging to one by right of birth; (of metals &c.) found in pure or uncombined state (*n. rock*, in its original place); born in a place (esp. of non-Europeans), indigenous, not exotic; of the nn. of a place. [f. L *nativus* (NATION, -IVE)]

na·tivism, n. (philos.). Doctrine of innate ideas. So **na·tiv**IST(2) n. [-ISM]

nati·vity, n. Birth of Christ, the Virgin, or St John Baptist; picture of the N. of Christ; festival of Christ's N., Christmas, or of birth of Virgin (8 Sep.) or St John (24 June); birth; (Astrol.) horoscope. [f. F *nativité* f. L *nativitatem* (NATIVE, -TY)]

nā·tron, n. Native SESQUIcarbonate of soda. [F f. Sp., f. Arab. *natrun* f. Gk *nitron* NITRE]

na·tterjack, n. British species of toad with yellow stripe down back. [?]

na·tty, a. Spruce, trim, daintily tidy; deft-handed; showing deftness. Hence **na·tti**LY[2] adv., **na·tti**NESS n. [?]

nă·tural (-tshōō-, -tshr-), a. & n. Based on the innate moral sense, instinctive, (*n. law, justice*); constituted by nature (*n.* DAY, *year*; in Mus., *n. note* or *key*, not sharp or flat, so *B n.*, *F n.*, &c., *n. scale*, without accidentals; in Sci., *n. classification, orders* with abbr. N.O., &c., esp. in Bot. of Jussieú's arrangement of species according to likeness as opp. Linnaeus's sexual system); normal, conformable to the ordinary course of nature, not exceptional or miraculous or irregular, (*n. magic*; *n. death*, by age or disease, not accident, poison, or violence); not enlightened or communicated by revelation (*the n. man*; *n. religion, theology*); physically existing, not spiritual or intellectual or fictitious, concerned with physical things, (*the n. world*; one's *n. life*, duration of one's life on earth; *n. law*); existing in or by nature, not artificial, innate, inherent, self-sown, uncultivated; life-like; unaffected, easy-mannered, not disfigured or disguised; not surprising, to be expected; consonant or easy *to* (*comes n. to him*); destined to be such by nature (*n. enemies, antithesis*); so related by nature only, illegitimate, (*n. son, child, brother*, &c.); dealing with nature as a study (*n. history*, study of animal life, esp. as set forth for popular use, also aggregate of facts about the natural objects or the characteristics *of* a place or class; *n. historian*, writer on n. history; *n. philosophy*, physics; *n. philosopher*, physicist; *n.* SCIENCE); *n.-born*, having the character or position by birth; hence **na·tural**NESS n. (N.) person half-witted from birth; (Mus.) n. note, white key in piano; hand making 21 as first dealt in vingt-et-un. [f. L *naturalis* (NATURE, -AL)

na·turalism, n. Action based on natural instincts; moral or religious system on purely natural basis; (Philos.) view of the world that excludes the supernatural or spiritual; realistic method, adherence to nature, in literature & art; indifference to conventions. [prec., -ISM]

na·turalist, n. & a. One who believes in or practises naturalism; student of animals or plants; (shop) dealer in cage animals, dogs, &c.; (shop) taxidermist; (adj.) = foll. [-IST]

naturali·stic, a. Of, according to, naturalism; of natural history. Hence **naturali·st**ICALLY adv. [-IC]

na·turalize, v.t. & i. Admit (alien) to citizenship; adopt (foreign word, custom, &c.); introduce (animal, plant) into another country; become naturalized; free from conventions, make natural; free from the miraculous, place on naturalistic basis; pursue natural history. Hence **naturaliz**A·TION n. [f. F *naturaliser* (NATURAL, -IZE)]

na·turally, adv. In adj. senses; esp., as might be expected, of course. [-LY[2]]

na·ture (-tsh*er*, -tūr), n. Thing's essential qualities, (*in* or *by* or *from the n. of the case* or *of things*, inevitably considering these qualities), person's or animal's innate character (whence **-nature**ED[2] a.; *by n.*, innately; GOOD, ILL, SECOND, *n.*), general characteristics & feelings of mankind (often *human n.*; TOUCH[2] *of n.*), specified element of human character (*the rational, animal, moral, n.*), person of specified character (*sanguine nn. do not feel this*; *there are nn. who can never*—); kind, sort, class, (*things of this n.*; *is in* or *of the n. of a command*), (of guns or shot) size (*100 of each n. of case-shot*); inherent impulses determining character or action (*against n.*, unnatural, immoral); vital force or functions or needs (*n. is exhausted*; *such a diet will not support n.*; *ease n.*, evacuate bowels or bladder); resin or sap in wood (esp. *full of n.*, still resinous); physical power causing phenomena of material world, these phenomena as a whole, (*N-*, these personified; *N.'s engineering*; *all n. looks gay*; *N. is the best physician*; LAW[1] *of n.*; *in the course of n.*, in the ordinary course; *debt of n.*, death; *in n.*, actually existing, also anywhere, at all; *against* or *contrary to n.*, miraculous, miraculously); naturalness or fidelity in art; *state of n.*, unregenerate condition (opp. *state of* GRACE[1]), condition of man before society is organized, uncultivated or undomesticated state of plants or animals, bodily nakedness; *n.-printing*, method of producing print of leaves &c. by pressing them on prepared plate. [F, f. L *natura* (*nasci nat-* be born, -URE)]

naught (nawt), n. & pred. a. (archaic). Nothing, nought, (*set at n.*, or NOUGHT); (Arith.) cipher, nought; (adj.) worthless, useless. [OE *náwuht* (*ná* see NATHLESS, WIGHT)]

naugh·ty, a. (used of, to, or by children, or in imit. of childish speech). Wayward, disobedient, badly behaved; wicked, blameworthy, indecent. Hence **naugh·ti**LY[2] adv., **naugh·ti**NESS n. [prec., -Y[2]]

nau·sĕa, n. Feeling of sickness; sea-sickness; loathing. [L, f. Gk *nausia* (*naus* ship)]

nau·sĕate, v.t. & i. Reject (food, or fig.) with loathing; affect with nausea, whence **nau·seat**ING[2] a.; feel sick (*at*), loathe food, occupation, &c. [f. L *nauseare* (prec.), -ATE[3]]

nau·seous, a. Causing nausea; offensive to taste or smell, nasty; disgusting, loathsome. Hence **nau·seous**LY[2] adv., **nau·seous**NESS n. [NAUSEA, -OUS]

nautch, n. E.-Indian exhibition of professional dancing-girls (*n.-girl*, one of these). [f. Hind. *nach*]

nau·tical, a. Of sailors or navigation, naval, maritime. Hence **nau·tical**LY[2] adv. [L f. Gk *nautikos* (*nautēs* sailor f. *naus* ship), -AL]

nau·tilus, n. (pl. *-li*). *Paper n.*, small cephalopod of which the female has very thin shell & webbed sail-like arms; *pearly n.*, cephalopod with chambered shell having nacreous septa. [f. L f. Gk *nautilos* sailor (prec.)]

nā·val, a. Of, in, for, &c., ships or (usu.) the or a navy (*n. stores*, all materials used in shipping; *n. officer*, in navy); fought, won, &c., by or consisting of or based on ships of war. Hence **nav·al**LY[2] adv. [f. L *navalis* (*navis* ship, -AL)]

nave[1], n. Central block of wheel holding axle & spokes, hub. [OE *nafu*, cf. Du. *naaf*, G *nabe*, & see NAVEL]

nave[2], n. Body of church from inner door to chancel or choir, usu. separated by pillars from aisles. [f. L *navis* ship]

nā·vel, n. Depression in front of belly left by severance of umbilical cord; central point of anything; *n. orange*, large orange with n.-like formation at top; *n.-string*, structure connecting foetus & placenta, umbilical cord; *n.-wort*, kinds of plant. [OE *nafela*, cf. Du. *navel*, G *nabel*, derivatives of st. of NAVE[1], cogn. w. Skr. *nabhila*, Gk *omphalos*]

navi·cular, a. & n. Boat-shaped (of shrines, & of parts of plants or body; esp. *n. bone* in hand or usu. foot; *n. disease*, or *n.* as noun, disease in horse's n. bone). [f. LL *navicularis* (L *navicula* dim. of *navis* ship, -AR[1])]

nă·vigable, a. (Of river, sea, &c.) affording passage for ships; seaworthy (*in n. condition*); (of balloon) steerable, dirigible. Hence **naviga**BI·LITY n. [f. L *navigabilis* (foll., -ABLE)]

nă·vigate, v.i. & t. Voyage, sail ship; sail over or up or down (sea, river); manage, direct course of, (ship or aircraft). [f. L *navigare* (*navis* ship, *agere* drive), -ATE[3]]

naviga·tion, n. Navigating (*inland n.*, communication by canals & rivers; *aerial n.*, of airship or aeroplane); methods of determining ship's position & course by geometry & nautical astronomy, seamanship; voyage; *n.-coal*, steam-coal. [f. L *navigatio* (prec., -ATION)]

na·vigator, n. One charged with or skilled in navigation; sea explorer; (now rare) navvy. [L (NAVIGATE, -OR[2])]

na·vvy, n. Labourer employed in excavating &c. for canals, railways, roads, &c.; (also *steam-n.*) mechanical excavator. [abbr. of prec.]

nā·vy, n. Fleet (poet.); whole of State's ships of war with their crews & all the organization for their maintenance; officers & men of n.; *n. bill*, issued by Admiralty in lieu of cash payment; *n. blue* n., *n.-blue* a., (of) the dark blue used in naval uniform; *n. league*, association founded to rouse national interest in n.; *n. list*, official book with all naval officers' names & other information. [f. OF *navie* fleet (L *navis* ship, -Y[1])

nawab (na-waw·b), n. Native governor or nobleman in India; (rare) rich retired Anglo-Indian, nabob. [f. Hind. *nawwab*, orig. pl. f. Arab. *nā'ib* deputy]

nay, particle equivalent to negative sentence, & n. =NO[4] (archaic); why, well, (vaguely introducing comment on another's statement &c.; archaic); or rather, & even, & more than that, (*weighty, nay, unanswerable*). (N.) the word *n.* (*will not take n.*, disregards refusals; *yea & n.*, shilly-shally; *say n.*, utter denial or usu. refusal, = refuse or contradict, as *cannot say him n.*). [f. ON *nei* (*ne* not, *ei* ever)]

Năzare·ne, n. & a. Native of Nazareth; (in Jewish, Moham., use) Christian; member of early Jewish-Christian sect (adj., of this sect). [f. L f. Gk *Nazarēnos* (*Nazaret* Nazareth)]

Nă·zarite[1], n. Native of Nazareth. [f. L *Nazaraeus* f. Gk *Nazōraios* + -ITE[1](1)]

Nă·zarite[2], n. Hebrew who had taken certain vows of abstinence (*Numb.* vi). [f. L *Nazaraeus* f. Heb. *nazir* (*nazar* separate oneself) + -ITE[1](2)]

naze, n. Promontory, headland, ness. [=NESS]

-nd[1], suf. of nn. & adjj. formed f. L gerundive (*-andus, -endus, -undus*) = (thing) to be treated in such a way, as *deodand, reverend, dividend*; also in the full L form, as *memorandum, agenda*; & an element in *-bund* (*moribund*), *-cund* (*fecund, rubicund*).

-nd[2], suf. forming nn. as *fiend* (hating), *friend* (loving) = the old part. termination *-and*.

neap, a. & n., & v.t. & i. *N.-tide* or *n.*, tide soon after moon's first & third quarters in which high-water level is at lowest. (Vb): (of tides) tend towards n.; (of tide) reach highest point of n.-tide; (pass., of ship) be prevented from getting off by neaping of tides. [OE *népflód* etym. dub.]

Nēapŏ·litan, a. & n. (Inhabitant) of Naples (*N. ice*, ice-cream made in strata of different colours & flavours, sweetmeat of similar appearance; *N. violet*, double sweet-scented kind of viola). [f. L *Neapolitanus* (*Neapolites* f. L f. Gk *Neapolis* f. *neos* new, *polis* city, -AN)]

near[1], adv. & prep. (*-er, -est*, also as advv. & prepp.). To, at, a short distance, in(to) proximity in space or time, (*far & n.*, everywhere; *n. at hand*, within easy reach, not far in the future; *n. by*, chiefly U.S., not far off; *n. upon*, not far in time from); almost, nearly, *not* nearly or anything like, (now usu. *nearly*; *was n. dead with fright*; *lasted n. a century*; so *n. upon*; *not n. so numerous*); closely (*as n. as one can guess*; *the nearer it resembles him the less I like it*); parsimoniously (*lives very n.*); *go n. to* do, *come* or *go n.* doing, nearly do &c. (Prep.) n. in space, time, condition, or resemblance, to (*comes no nearer the end*; *lies n. his heart*, affects him deeply; *the time draws n. Christmas*; *sun is n. setting*; *hope came n. fulfilment*; *who comes nearest him in wit?*). [f. ON *nǽr* orig. comp. of *ná-* = OE *néah* NIGH]

near[2], a. (often governing n. in pred. use; so also in comp. & superl.). Closely related (*n. relation*; *is n. akin to*; *is n. me in blood*; *n. & dear*), intimate (*a n. friend*); (of parts of animals or vehicles, or horses &c. in team) left (opp. *off*; *the n. fore leg, wheel*; *the n. wheeler*); close at hand, close to, in place or time (also, esp. U.S., *n.-by*; *the nearest man*; *on a n. day*; *the man n.* or *nearest you*; *is nearer to*, or *nearer, us*; *n. work*, that must be done with the eye close to it; *the n. distance*, part of scene between background & foreground; *the n. prospect of reward*); (of road or way) direct; close, narrow, (*a n. guess, resemblance, translation, race, escape*); niggardly; *n.-sighted*, short-sighted. Hence **near·**ISH[1](2), a., **near·**NESS n. [f. prec.]

near[3], v.i. & t. Draw n. (to), approach. [f. NEAR[1, 2]]

Nēar·ctic, a. (zool.). Of arctic & temperate parts of N. America. [f. Gk *neos* new (w. ref. to the New World), ARCTIC]

near·ly, adv. Closely (*examine it n.*; *n. related*; *concerns me n.*; *approached the place n.*; *correspond, resemble, n.*); almost; *not n.*, nothing like. [NEAR[2], -LY[2]]

neat[1], n. (sing. & collect. as pl.). Any animal of ox kind; (collect.) cattle; *n.-herd*, cowherd; *n.-house*, cattle-shed; *n.'s-foot, n.'s-tongue*, used as food; *n.'s-leather*, ox-hide. [OE *néat*, cf. ON *naut*, cogn. w. OE *néotan* possess]

neat[2], a. (Of liquor, esp. alcoholic) undiluted; of elegant simplicity in form or arrangement, nicely made or proportioned; (of language, style, sayings) brief, clear, & pointed, cleverly phrased, epigrammatic; deft, dextrous, cleverly done; tidy, methodical; *n.-handed*, dextrous. Hence **nea·t**LY[2] adv., **nea·t**NESS n. [AF *neit* = F *net* f. L *nitidus* shining (*nitēre* shine)]

neath, prep. (poet.). Beneath. [f. BENEATH]

neb, n. (Sc.). Beak or bill; nose; snout; tip, spout, point. [OE *nebb* cf. Du. *nebbe*]

nĕ·būla, n. (pl. *-lae*). Clouded speck on cornea causing defective sight; (Astron.) luminous patch made by cluster of distant stars or by gaseous or stellar matter outside solar system. [L, = mist, cf. Gk *nephelē*, G *nebel*]

ne·bular, a. Of nebula(e); *n. theory* or *hypothesis*, that solar & stellar systems were developed from nebulae. [-AR[1]]

nebū·lium, n. Element known only as producing green line in spectrum of gaseous nebulae. [-IUM]

ne·bulous, a. (Astron.) of, like, nebula(e), *n. star*, small cluster of indistinct stars, or star in luminous haze; cloud-like; hazy, vague, indistinct, formless; clouded, turbid. So **nebulo·**SITY n. [f. L *nebulosus* (NEBULA, -OUS)]

necessār·ian, n. & a. = NECESSITARIAN. Hence **necessar·ian**ISM(3) n. [L *necesse* NECESSARY, -ARIAN]

ne·cessarily, adv. As a necessary result, inevitably. [-LY[2]]

nĕ·cessary, a. & n. Indispensable, requisite, (*to* or *for* person &c.; *it is n. that, to* do), requiring to, that must, be done; determined by predestination or natural laws, not by free will, happening or existing by necessity, (of concept or mental process) inevitably resulting from nature of things or the mind, inevitably produced by previous state of things, (of agent) having no independent volition. (N.) thing without which life cannot be maintained (often *the nn. of life*); (loosely) desirable thing not generally regarded as a luxury; (abs. use of adj.) *the n.* (slang), money or action needed for a purpose (*provide, find, do, the n.*). [f. L *necessarius* (*necesse* needful, -ARY[1])]

necessitār·ian, n. & a. (Person) denying free will & maintaining that all action is determined by antecedent causes. Hence **necessitar·ian**ISM (3) n. [NECESSITY, -ARIAN]

nece·ssitate, v.t. Force, compel, (person)

to do (now rare); render necessary, involve as condition or accompaniment or result. [f. med. L *necessitare* (NECESSITY), -ATE[3]]

nece·ssitous, a. Poor, needy. [foll., -OUS]

nece·ssity, n. Constraint or compulsion regarded as a law prevailing through the material universe & governing all human action (often *physical n.*; *logical n.*, compulsion to believe that of which the opposite is inconceivable; *absolute, moral, natural,* &c., *n.*); constraining power of circumstances, state of things compelling to certain course, (*of n.*, unavoidably; *make a virtue of n.*, claim credit for doing what one cannot help doing, do thing with a good grace; *am under the n. of doing*; *n. knows no law*, absolves from any offence); imperative need (*for*; *n. is the mother of invention*); indispensability (*the n. of protecting life & property*); indispensable thing, necessary; (usu. pl.) want, poverty, hardship, pressing need. [f. F *nécessité* f. L *necessitatem* (*necesse* needful, -TY)]

neck[1], n. Part of body that connects head with shoulders (*break one's n.*, dislocate vertebrae of this, be killed so; *break n. of* task &c., get hardest part of it over; *save* one's *n.*, escape hanging; *n. & crop*, headlong, bodily; *get it in the n.* slang, suffer fatal or severe blow; *n. or nothing*, desperately, staking all on success, *it is* a case for desperate attempts; *n. & n.*, running even in race); flesh of animal's n. as food (esp. *n. of mutton*); part of shirt &c. that touches n.; narrow part *of* vessel, esp. of bottle near mouth, or *of* passage, pass, or channel; pass, narrow channel, isthmus; narrow connecting part between two parts of thing; (Arch.) lower part of capital; *n.-band*, part of garment round n.; *neckcloth*, cravat; *ne·ckerchief*, kerchief worn round n.; *necklace*, ornament of precious stones or metal, or beads &c., worn round n.; *n.-tie*, band of silk &c. securing or seeming to secure shirt-collar; *n.-verse*, Latin verse (usu. beginning of *Ps.* li) printed in black letter by reading which person claiming benefit of clergy might save his n.; *n.-wear* (shop), collars & ties. Hence (-)**neck**ED[2] a. [OE *hnecca*, cf. Du. *nek*, G *nacken*]

neck[2], n. Last sheaf of corn cut. [?]

ne·cking, n. (archit.). Part of column between shaft & capital. [NECK[1], -ING[1]]

ne·cklet, n. Ornament or fur protector for neck. [-LET]

nĕcr(o)-, comb. form of Gk *nekros* corpse, dead body, as *-ge·nic* produced by contact with dead bodies, *-phore* burying beetle, *-bio·sis* decay in tissues of body, -LATRY, *-logy* death-roll or obituary notice, *-phagous* feeding on carrion, *-polis* cemetery, *-psy* or *-scopy*, post-mortem examination.

ne·cromancy, n. Art of predicting by means of communication with the dead; magic, enchantment. So **ne·cromanc**ER[1] n., **necroma·ntic** a. [f. OF *nygromancie* f. med. L *nigromantia* changed by assoc. w. L *niger* black f. L f. Gk *nekromanteia* (prec., -MANCY)]

necro·sis, n. (path.). Death of circumscribed piece of tissue, esp. mortification of bones. Hence **necrŏ·tic** a., **ne·crot**IZE (3) v.i. [f. Gk *nekrōsis* (*nekroō* kill, see NECRO-)]

ne·ctar, n. (Gk myth.) drink of the gods (cf. AMBROSIA); any delicious drink; sweet fluid or honey produced by plants; kind of aerated water. Hence or cogn. **nectār·**EAN, **nectār·**EOUS, **ne·ctar**ED[2], **nectari·**FEROUS, **ne·ctar**OUS, aa. [f. Gk *nektar* etym. dub.]

ne·ctarine, n. Kind of peach with thin downless skin & firm flesh. [n. use of obs. or rare adj. (NECTAR, -INE[1])]

ne·ctary, n. Flower's or plant's honey-secreting organ. [f. NECTAR, prob. on false anal. of *ovary* (-ARY[1]) for *nectarary*]

Ne·ddy, n. Donkey. [dim. of Edward; -Y[3]]

née (nā), a. Born (used in adding woman's maiden name, as *Mrs Smith, n. Jones*). [F]

need[1], n. Circumstances requiring some course (*if n. be* or *were*, *there is no* &c. *n.*, *to* do or abs.; *have n.*, require *to*; *had n.*, ought to, as *had n. remember*); imperative demand for presence or possession *of* (*the n. of further securities*; *have n. of*, require, want); emergency, crisis, time of difficulty, (*a friend in n. is a friend indeed*; *good at n.*; *failed him in his n.*); destitution, lack of necessaries, poverty, whence **nee·d**Y[2] a., **nee·d**INESS n.; thing wanted, respect in which want is felt, requirement, (*my nn. are few*); (pl.) offices of nature (*do* one's *nn.*); *nee·dfire*, fire got from dry wood by friction. [com.-Teut.: OE *nied, néod*, cf. Du. *nood*, G *not*]

need[2], v.i. & t. (3 sing. pres. *needs*, & *need* as specified below). Be necessary (archaic; *it needs not*, it is needless; *there needs*, so-&-so is required; *more than needs*, than is necessary; *what need* or *needs?*, why should one?); stand in n. of, require, (intr.) be needy; be under necessity or obligation to (do &c.) or *to* do (3 sing. *need*, & *to* omitted, in neg. & interrog. forms; *he n. not trouble himself*; *it needs to be done with care*; *why n. he have come tonight?*; *n. not have done* &c., usu. form = did not n. to do &c.; often ellipt., as *don't be longer away than you n.*). [OE *néodian* (prec.)]

nee·dful, a. Requisite, necessary, indispensable, (*to, for*, or abs.; *it is n. to* do, or *that*; *the n.*, what is necessary, esp. slang, the money required, also *do the n.* in football, convert try into goal.) Hence **nee·dful**NESS n. [-FUL]

nee·dle, n., & v.t. & i. Thin round long piece of steel pointed at one end & with eye for thread at other used in sewing (*knitting, darning, packing, crochet*, &c., *-n.*, shapes or modifications of it for different purposes; *sharp as a n.*, lit., & fig. acute, observant; *look for n. in* BOTTLE[3] &c. *of hay*; PINS & *nn.*; *n.'s eye*, least possible aperture, esp. w. ref. to *Matt.* xix. 24); piece of magnetized steel used as indicator on dial of compass & magnetic & electric apparatus, esp. in telegraphy; strip of standard gold or silver used for comparison in assaying with touchstone; pointed etching instrument; pointed surgical instrument used in soft cataract; end of hypodermic syringe; steel pin exploding cartridge of breechloader; obelisk; sharp rock, peak; beam used as temporary support during under-pinning; n.-shaped crystal; leaf of fir or pine; (slang) *the n.*, fit of nervousness; *n.-bath*, shower-bath with fine spray; *n.-book*, book-shaped *n.-case*; *n.-fish*, kinds of fish, esp. garfish; *nee·dleful*, length of cotton &c. put into n. at once; *n.-gun*, in which cartridge is exploded by impact of n.; *n.-lace*, made with nn. not bobbins; *n.-point*, fine sharp point, also point-lace made with nn.; *needlewoman*, sempstress, also *good* or *bad* user of n.; *needlework*, sewing or embroidery. (Vb) sew, pierce, or operate on, with n.; thread (one's way) between or through things; under-pin with n.-beams; form n.-shaped crystals; thread one's way. [OE *nǽdl*, cf. G *nadel*, Da. *naal*, prob. cogn. w. L *nēre* spin, Gk *nēsis* spinning & *nēma* thread]

nee·dless, a. Unnecessary, uncalled for, (*n. to say* used parenth., as I need not tell you). Hence **nee·dless**LY[2] adv., **nee·dless**NESS n. [-LESS]

nee·dments, n. pl. Things needed, esp. personal necessaries carried on journey. [NEED n. or v., -MENT]

needs, adv. Of necessity (now only after or before *must*; *n. must* do, cannot help or avoid or get out of doing; *must n.* do, sometimes =*n. must* do, usu. foolishly insists or insisted on doing). [OE *nýdes* (NEED[1], -ES)]

ne'er (nār), adv. (Poet.) never (not used ellipt. for sentence like *never*); *n. a*, not a single; *n.-do-well*, *-weel*, good-for-nothing (person). [contr. of NEVER]

nefar·ious, a. Wicked, iniquitous. Hence **nefar·ious**LY[2] adv., **nefar·ious**NESS n. [f. L *nefarius* (*nefas* wrong), -OUS]

nega·te, v.t. Nullify, deny existence of, imply or involve non-existence of, be the negation of. [from 1835 only, f. L *negare* deny, -ATE[3]]

nega·tion, n. Denying; negative statement or doctrine; refusal, contradiction, denial *of*; (Log.) affirmation of difference or exclusion; absence or opposite of something actual or positive; negative or unreal thing, nonentity. So **nĕ·gat**ORY a. [f. L *negatio* (prec., -ATION)]

nega·tionist, n. One who denies accepted beliefs without proposing substitutes. [-IST]

nĕ·gative[1], a. Expressing or implying denial, prohibition, or refusal (*n. proposition* in logic, asserting difference or discrepancy; *n. statute, vote, answer*; *n. voice*, right of veto); wanting, consisting in the want of, positive attributes (*n. virtue*, abstention from wrongdoing; *n. instance, evidence*, of non-occurrence of something; *n. causes of dissatisfaction*, sins of omission); (Alg.) denoting quantities to be subtracted from others or from zero (*n. sign*, —), (colloq., facet.) *n. quantity*, nothing; (Electr.) of the kind produced by friction on resin &c. (opp. *positive*, on glass), containing or producing such electricity; of opposite nature to thing regarded as positive (*debt is n. capital, & capital n. debt*); (Photog.) having lights & shadows of the actual object or scene reversed. Hence **ne·gative**LY[2] adv., **ne·gative**NESS, **negati·**VITY, nn. [f. LL *negativus* (NEGATE, -IVE)]

ne·gative[2], n. N. statement, reply, or word (*it is hard to prove a n.*; *he returned a n.*, answered 'no' &c; *two nn. make an affirmative*); right of veto; *in the n.*, negative(ly) (esp. in ministerial answers in Parliament, *the answer is in the n.*, no; *it was decided in the n.*, proposal was rejected); n. quality, want of something, (*his character is made up of nn.*); (Alg.) n. or minus quantity; (Photog.) print on glass &c. with reversed lights & shadows from which positive pictures are taken; n. plate or metal in voltaic battery. [f. prec.]

ne·gative[3], v.t. Veto, reject, refuse to accept or countenance; disprove (inference, hypothesis); contradict (statement); neutralize (effect). [as prec.]

ne·gativism, n. Attitude of NEGATIONIST. So **ne·gativ**IST(2) n. [-ISM]

negle·ct, v.t., & n. Slight, not pay attentions to; leave uncared-for; leave undone, be remiss about; omit *to* do or do*ing*; hence **negle·ct**ABLE a. (rare). (N.) neglecting or being neglected; disregard *of*; negligence; hence **negle·ct**FUL a., **negle·ctful**LY[2] adv., **neglect·ful**NESS n. [(n. f. L *neglectus* *-ūs*) f. L *neglegere -lect-* (*neg-* not, *legere* pick up)]

né·gligé (-zhā), n. Free & easy or unceremonious attire. [F, p.p. of *négliger* (prec.)]

ne·gligeable, a. (rare). Negligible. [f. F *négligeable* (prec., -ABLE)]

ne·gligence, n. Want of proper care or attention, (piece of) carelessness; *contributory n.*, n. on a person's part that has helped to bring about the injury that he has suffered; freedom from restraint or artificiality in literature or art. So **ne·gli**GENT a. (*of* duty &c.), **ne·gligent**LY[2] adv. [f. L *neglegentia* (NEGLECT, -ENCE)]

ne·gligible, a. That need not be regarded (esp. *n. quantity*). [as prec., -IBLE]

negō·tiate (-shĭ-), v.i. & t. Confer (*with* another) with view to compromise or agreement; arrange (affair), bring about (desired object), by negotiating; transfer (bill) to another for a consideration, convert into cash or notes, get or give value for (bill, cheque) in money; clear, get over, dispose of, (fence, obstacle, difficulty). Hence or cogn. **nego·ti**ABLE(-sha-) a., **nego·ti**ANT(1) (-shĭ-) n., **negoti**A·TION (-sĭ-, -shĭ-), **nego·tiāt**OR[2] (-shĭ-), **nego·tia**-TRESS[1] (-sha-), **nego·tia**TRIX (-sha-), nn. [f. L *negotiare* (*negotium* business f. *neg*-not, *otium* leisure), -ATE[3]]

negri·llo, n. Small Negro; one of dwarf negro race in Central & S. Africa. [Sp., dim. of NEGRO]

negri·to (-rē-), n. One of small negroid race in the Malayo-Polynesian region. [as prec.]

Nē·gro, n. (fem. *Negress*) & a. Member, esp. male, of black-skinned woolly-haired flat-nosed thick-lipped African race. (Adj.) of this race, black-skinned, (*n. minstrels*, troupe of real or sham Nn. performing n. songs & dances); occupied by, connected with, Nn.; black or dark (*n. ant, bat, monkey*, dark species). *N.-head*, strong black plug tobacco, also inferior indiarubber; *Negroland*, part of Africa inhabited by Nn. Hence **ne·gro**ID a. & n., **negroi·d**AL a., **ne·gro**PHIL a. & n., **ne-grō·phil**ISM n., **negro**PHO·BIA n. [Sp., f. L *nigrum* nom. *niger* black]

Nē·gus[1], n. Ruler of Abyssinia. [native]

nē·gus[2], n. Hot sweetened wine & water. [Col. F. *N.*, d. 1732]

neigh (nā), v.i., & n. (Utter) cry (as) of horse. [OE *hnǣgan*, cf. MHG *nêgen*, imit.]

neighbour (nā·ber), n., & v.t. & i. Dweller next door, near, in same street or village or district, or in adjacent country (*my n. Jones*; *are next-door nn.*; *his nearest n. is 12 miles off*; *our nn. across the Channel*), esp. regarded as one who should be friendly (*good, bad, nn.*; **neigh·bour**LY[1] a., **neigh·bourli**NESS n.) or as having claim on others' friendliness (*duty to* one's *n.*, to any fellow man); person or thing near or next another (*my n. at dinner*; *falling tree brought down its n.*); (attrib.) neighbouring; hence **neigh·bour**LESS a., **neigh·bour**SHIP n. (Vb) adjoin, border upon, border *upon*, (chiefly now in **neigh·bour**ING[2] a.). [OE *nēahgebūr* (NIGH, BOOR), cf. G *nachbar*]

neigh·boured, a. Having neighbours or surroundings of specified kind (*ill n.*; *a beautifully n. town*). [-ED[2, 1]]

neigh·bourhōōd, n. Neighbourly feeling or conduct (usu. *good n.*); nearness, vicinity *of* (*in the n. of £100*, about); neighbours, people of a district, district. [-HOOD]

nei·ther (nīdh-, nēdh-), adv., conj., a., & pron. Adv.: (introducing word, clause, &c., that is to be negatived equally with a following one attached to it by *nor*) not either, not on the one hand, (*n. knowing nor caring*; *n. you nor I know*, *n. he nor I know*, *n. I nor he knows*; also often irreg., *n. he nor she know*; *n. does cowardice ensure nor courage preclude defeat*; *n.* HERE *nor there*); (placed at end to emphasize preceding negative) either, any more than something else, (*I don't know that n.*); (in apodosis after negative protasis) not either (*if you do not go, n. shall I*); (bibl.) not even (*but n. so did their witness agree*). Conj. (archaic): nor, nor yet, (*I know not, n. can I guess*). Adj. & pron.: not either, not the one nor the other, (*n. accusation*, *n. of the accusations, is true*; *n. of them knows*, often also irreg. *know*); (loosely) none of any number of specified things. [ME *naither*, *neyther*, assim. of OE *nawther* contr. of *nahwæther* (*ná* not, WHETHER) to EITHER]

nĕk, n. (S.-Afr.). =COL. [Du., = NECK]

ne·lly, n. Largest kind of petrel. [perh. the feminine name]

nĕmato-, comb. form of Gk *nēma -atos* thread in scientific terms (=filamentous, having filament, thread-like), as *-cyst* cell in jelly-fish &c. containing coiled thread that can be projected as sting, *ne·matode* & *ne·matoid* aa. & nn. (worm) of slender cylindrical shape.

Nĕ·mesis, n. Goddess of retribution; retributive justice, downfall that satisfies this. [Gk (*nemō* give what is due)]

nē·minĕ, abl. of L *nemo* no one; *n. contradicente* or *dissentiente* (abbr. *nĕm. con.* or *diss.*) unanimously (or without objection raised).

nĕ·nuphar, n. Water-lily. [med. L, ult. f. Skr. *nilotpala* (*nil* blue, *utpala* lotus)]

nē·o-, comb. form of Gk *neos* new, used as living pref. to adjj. & nn., & adding the notions *new, modern, later, recast, lately found* or *invented* (*n.-Ca·tholic*, *n.-pa·ganism*; *n.-Pla·tonism*, 3rd-cent. mixture of Platonic ideas with Oriental mysticism; *n.-Malthu·sianism*, use of preventives against conception; *n.-He·llenism*, revival of Greek ideals; *n.-Ca·mbrian* geol., of the later Cambrian period; *ne·odoxy*, new doctrine or view; *neonto·logy*, study of extant animals; *neozo·ic* geol., of later period of geological history, post-palaeozoic).

neolĭ·thic, a. Of the later stone age, when ground or polished stone weapons & implements prevailed. [prec., Gk *lithos* stone, -IC]

neolō·gian, a. & n. Of, inclined to, marked by, neologism in theology; (n.) neologist in theology. [NEOLOGY, -AN]

neo·logism, neo·logy, nn. Coining or using of new words, new-coined word; tendency to or adoption of novel or rationalistic religious views. So **neo·lo**GIST(1) n., **neo·log**IZE(2) v.i. [f. F *néologie, néologisme* (NEO-, -LOGY)]

ne·on, n. (chem.). Lately discovered atmospheric gas. [neut. of Gk *neos* new]

ne·ophron, n. White Egyptian vulture & allied birds. [name of man turned to vulture in *Metamorphoses* of Antoninus Liberalis]

ne·ophyte, n. New convert esp. among primitive Christians or Roman Catholics; newly ordained R.-C. priest; novice of religious order; beginner, novice, tiro. [f. eccl. L f. Gk *neophutos* newly planted (NEO-, *phuō* plant)]

neotĕ·ric, a. Recent, new-fangled, modern. [f. LL f. Gk *neōterikos* (*neōteros* comp. of *neos* new, -IC)]

neotrŏ·pical, a. Of, found in, tropical & S. America. [NEO-, TROPICAL]

nepe·nthē(s) (-z), n. Drug producing forgetfulness of grief (poet.); (*-s*) genus of plants with pitcher-shaped leaves, Pitcher-plant. [(*-s*) L f. Gk, neut. of *nēpenthēs* griefless (*nē-* not, *penthos* grief)]

nĕ·phew (-v-), n. Brother's or sister's son. [f. OF *neveu* f. L *nepotem* nom. *-pos* grandson, nephew, cogn. w. OE *nefa*, G *neffe*]

nepho·logy, n. Study of the clouds. [f. Gk *nephos* cloud, -LOGY]

nephrĭ·tic, a. Of or in the kidneys, renal. [f. LL f. Gk *nephritikos* (foll., -IC)]

nephrī·tis, n. Inflammation of the kidneys. [LL f. Gk (*nephros* kidney, -ITIS)]

nĕphr(o)-, comb. form (prec.) = kidney-, *-e·ctomy* excision of kidney, -LOGY, -TOMY.

ne plus u·ltra, n. Prohibition of advance, impassable obstacle; furthest point attained or attainable; highest pitch or form *of*, acme, culmination. [L, = not more beyond, supposed inscription on Pillars of Hercules]

nē·potism, n. Undue favour from holder of patronage to relatives (orig. from Pope to illegitimate sons called nephews). So **ne·pot**IST(1) n. [f. It. *nepotismo* (*nepote* NEPHEW, -ISM)]

Ne·ptune, n. (God of) the sea (*N.'s cup*, kinds of coral & sponge); farthest planet of solar system. [f. L *Neptunus*]

Neptu·nian, a. & n. (Geol.) produced by water action; (person) maintaining aqueous origin of certain rocks, so **Ne·ptun**IST(2) n. (opp. *Vulcanist*); of planet Neptune. [f. L *Neptunius* (prec.), -AN]

Nēr·ĕid, n. Sea-nymph; (Zool.) long sea-worm or centipede. [f. L f. Gk *Nērēis -idos* daughter of sea-god Nereus]

ner·o anti·co (năr-, -tē-), n. Kind of black marble found in Roman ruins. [It.]

nēr·olĭ, n. Essential oil from orange-flowers used in perfumery. [It., inventor's name]

Nerō·nian, a. Of, as of, the emperor Nero or his times, cruel, licentious, tyrannical. [f. L *Neronianus* (*Nero -onis*, -IAN)]

ner·vāte, a. (bot.). (Of leaves) having ribs. So **nerva·**TION n. [foll., -ATE²]

nerve, n., & v.t. Sinew, tendon, (now poet., exc. in *strain every n.*, make all possible efforts; also in pl. fig., as *good laws are the nn. of a State*); vigour, energy, well-strung state; (Bot.) rib, esp. mid-rib, of leaf; (Anat.) fibre or bundle of fibres connecting & conveying impulses of sensation & motion between brain or spinal cord or ganglionic organ & some part of body; (pl.) bodily state in regard to physical sensitiveness & interaction between brain & other parts, disordered state in these respects, exaggerated sensitiveness, nervousness, (*does not know what nn. are*, is normal in sensation; *a fit of nn.*, nervous state; *get on* one's *nn.*, be a worry or annoyance to him; *has iron nn.*, *nn. of steel*, &c., is not easily upset or frightened); nervous fibre; coolness in danger, boldness, assurance, (*lose* one's *n.*, become timid or irresolute); *n.-centre*, group of closely connected ganglion-cells; *n.-knot*, ganglion; hence **(-)nerv**ED² a., **ner·vo-** comb. form. (Vb) give strength, vigour, or courage, to; collect one*self* to face danger or suffering. [f. L *nervus*, cf. Gk *neuron*]

ner·veless, a. Inert, wanting in vigour or spirit, listless; (of style) flabby, diffuse; (Bot., Entom.) without nervures; (Anat., Zool.) without nerves. Hence **ner·veless**LY² adv., **ner·veless**NESS n. [-LESS]

ner·vīne, a. & n. (med.). (Medicine) relieving nerve-disorders. [NERVE¹, -INE¹]

ner·vous, a. Sinewy, muscular; (of literary style) vigorous, terse; full of nerves; of the nerves (*n. system*, nerves & nerve-centres as a whole); acting on the nerves; having disordered or delicate nerves, excitable, highly strung, easily agitated, timid. Hence **ner·vous**LY² adv., **ner·vous**NESS n. [f. L *nervosus* (NERVE¹, -OSE¹)]

ner·vure, n. One of the tubes framing insect's wing; principal vein of leaf. [F (NERVE¹, -URE)]

ner·vy, a. Sinewy, strong, (poet.); (slang) cool, confident, impudent; jerky, nervous; (slang) trying to the nerves. [-Y²]

nĕ·science (-shĭ-, -sĭ-), n. Not knowing, absence of knowledge *of*. [f. LL *nescientia* f. L *nescire* not know (*ne-* not, *scire* know), -ENCE]

ne·scient, a. & n. Ignorant (*of*); agnostic (a. & n.). [prec., -ENT]

ness, n. Promontory, headland, cape. [OE *næs* cf. *naus* nose]

-ness, suf. appended freely to adjj. (*bitterness*), participles (*lovingness*, *tiredness*), compd adjj. (*tongue-tiedness*), & adj. phrr. (*up-to-dateness*) to form nn. expressing state or condition. [OE *-nes(s)*, *-nis(s)*, *-nys(s)*, cf. Du. *-nis*, G *-niss*; the *n* is not orig. part of suf. (*-assus*, *-assi*, f. vbs in *-atjan*) but an accretion f. stem]

nest, n., & v.t. & i. Structure or place made or chosen by bird for laying eggs & sheltering young (*it's an ill bird that fouls its own n.*, one should not speak ill of home &c.; FEATHER² one's *n.*), animal's or insect's abode or spawning or breeding place; snug or secluded retreat, lodging, shelter, bed, receptacle; haunt *of* robbers &c.; fostering-place *of* vice &c.; brood, swarm; collection, series, *of* similar objects; small chest *of drawers*; *n.-egg*, real or imitation egg left in n. to induce hen to go on laying there, sum of money kept as reserve or nucleus; hence **ne·st**FUL(2) n., **ne·st**LIKE a. (Vb) make or have n. in specified place; take to n.-building; (p.p.) established (as) in n., (of boxes &c.) packed one inside another; take bird's nn. [OE, Du., & G, cogn. w. L *nidus* (*ni*-down, cf. NETHER, *sed*- sit)]

ne·stle (-sl), v.i. & t. =prec. vb (sense 1; now rare); settle oneself, be settled, comfortably *down*, or *in*, *into*, *among*, &c., leaves, wraps, chair, &c.; press oneself affectionately *close to*, *to*, person; lie half-hidden or embedded; push (head, face, shoulder, &c.) affectionately or snugly *in*; hold embraced (usu. in p.p.). [OE *nestlian*, cf. Du. *nestelen*, see NEST, -LE(3)]

ne·stling (-sl-, -stl-), n. Bird too young to leave nest. [NEST n. + -LING[1], or prec., + -ING[3]]

Ne·stor, n. Wise old man, senior *of* company &c. [name of character in Homer]

Nestor·ian, a. & n. (Adherent) of doctrine of Nestorius patriarch of Constantinople A.D. 428 asserting that Christ had distinct divine & human persons. Hence **Nestor·ian**ISM(3) n. [f. L *Nestorianus* (-AN)]

net[1], n., & v.t. & i. Meshed fabric of twine, cord, hair, &c.; piece of this used for catching fish &c. (*beach, casting, trawl, herring, lark, clap*, &c., *-n.*), or for covering, confining, protecting, carrying, &c. (*fruit, hair, tennis, cricket*, &c., *-n.*); moral or mental snare; spider's web; reticulation, network; *network*, arrangement with intersecting lines & interstices recalling those of n., complex system *of* railways, rivers, canals, &c., ramification; hence **ne·t**FUL(2) n. (Vb) cover, confine, catch, with net(s); fish (river &c.) with nn., set nn. in (river); make netting; make (purse, hammock, &c.) by netting; (usu. in p.p.) mark with netlike pattern, reticulate. [com.-Teut.; OE, Du., Da., *net*, cf. G *netz*]

net[2], a., & v.t. Free from deduction, remaining after necessary deductions, (*n. profit*, true profit, actual gain after working expenses have been paid, opp. GROSS; *n. price*, real price off which discount is not allowed, opp. *nominal, publisher's, price*); (vb) gain or yield (sum) as n. profit. [F, see NEAT[2]]

nē tĕ·mere (-ĭ), n. The papal decree of 1907 under which marriages between Roman Catholics and others are not valid unless solemnized by R.-C. bishop or his deputy. [initial L words, = lest at random]

nĕ·ther (-dh-), a. (archaic or facet.). Lower (*n. lip* or *jaw*; *n. garments* &c., trousers; *n. man* or *person*, legs &c.; *n. millstone*, simile for hard heart &c.; *n. world*, rarely the earth, usu. hell, also *n. regions*). Hence **ne·ther**MOST a. [com.-Teut.; OE *neothera*, cf. Du. *neder*-, G *nieder*]

Nĕ·therlander, n., **Ne·therlandish,** a. (Native) of the Netherlands. [f. Du. *Nederlander*, *-landsch*, (*Nederland*, -ER[1], -ISH[1])]

ne·tsuke (-sōōkā), n. Carved buttonlike ornament worn by Japanese. [Jap.]

ne·tting, n. In vbl senses; also: netted string, thread, or wire; piece of this used for various purposes. [-ING[1]]

ne·ttle, n., & v.t. Genus of plants including *Great* or *Common N.* & *Small N.*, two species growing profusely on waste land & having leaf-hairs that sting; other plants resembling these, esp. DEAD-*n.*; *n.-rash*, eruption on skin in patches like those made by n. stings. (Vb) beat with nn.; get one*self* stung with nn.; irritate, provoke, annoy. [com.-Teut.; OE *netele*, cf. Du. *netel*, G *nessel*]

neum(e) (nūm), n. (mus.). Group of notes sung to single syllable in plainsong. [F (*-e*), f. med. L *neuma* f. Gk *pneuma* breath (*pneō* breathe, -M)]

neur·al (nūr-), a. Of the nerves, of the central nervous system. [f. Gk *neuron* nerve, -AL]

neura·tion, n. Distribution of nervures. [irreg. f. foll., -ATION]

neur(o)-, comb. form of Gk *neuron* nerve; *neura·lgia*, affection of nerve(s) usu. of head or face causing intense intermittent pain, so *-a·lgic* a.; *neurasthē·nia*, nervous debility, so *-thĕ·nic* a.; *neure·ctomy*, excision of nerve; *neur·ine*, nerve-tissue; *neur*I·TIS n.; *neuro*·LOGY, *-log*IST, *-lo·g*ICAL; *neuro-mu·scular*, of nerves & muscles; *neur·opăth*, person of abnormal nervous sensibility or affected by nervous disease, so *-pa·th*IC a., *-patho*·LOGY, *-path*Y[1]; *neuro·pathist*, specialist in neuropathy; *neurophysio·logy*, physiology of nervous system; *neuro-psy·chic*, of nervous & psychic functions; *neuro·pterous*, of the *Neuroptera*, order of insects having four naked membranous transparent wings with reticulate neuration; *neuro·tomy*, cutting of nerve to produce sensory paralysis; *neurypno·logy*, science of hypnotism.

neuro·ma, n. (pl. *-ta*). Tumour on nerve or in nerve-tissue. [f. Gk *neuron* nerve, -M]

neuro·sis, n. Functional derangement due to disorders of nervous system; change in nerve-cells of brain prior to psychic activity. [as prec., -OSIS]

neurŏ·tic, a. & n. (Drug) affecting nervous system; (person) affected with nervous disorder, of abnormal sensibility. [as prec., -OTIC]

neu·ter, a. & n. (Gram.) neither masculine nor feminine (cf. COMMON[1], EPICENE), (of verb) intransitive; neutral, not taking or assisting either side, in war, argument, opinion, &c. (esp. *stand n.*, remain neutral, declare neutrality); (Bot.) without pistils & stamens, asexual; (Entom.) sexually undeveloped, sterile. (N.) n. noun, adjective, verb, or gender; person standing n.; sexually undeveloped female insect, esp. bee or ant; castrated animal. [L, =neither (*ne-* not, *uter* either)]

neu·tral, a. & n. Not assisting either of two belligerent States, belonging to a State that thus stands aloof, exempted or excluded from active or passive hostilities; taking neither side in dispute or difference of opinion, indifferent, impartial; not distinctly marked or coloured, indefinite, vague, indeterminate, (*n. tint*, grey or slate-colour, whence **neutral-tint**ED[2] a. lit. & fig.); (Chem.) neither acid nor alkaline; (Electr.) neither positive nor negative; (Entom., Bot.) sexually undeveloped, asexual; hence or cogn. **neutra·l**ITY n., **neu·tral**LY[2] adv. (N.) n. State or person; subject of n. State. [f. L *neutralis* of neuter gender (prec., -AL)]

neu·tralize, v.t. Counterbalance, render ineffective by opposite force or effect; exempt or exclude (place) from sphere of hostilities. Hence **neutraliz**A·TION n. [f. med. L *neutralisare* (prec., -IZE)]

névé (nĕ·vā, *or as F*), n. Expanse of granular snow not yet compressed into ice at head of glacier. [F (L *nix nivis* snow, -ATE[2])]

nĕ·ver, adv. At no time, on no occasion, not ever, (often *n. before, since, after, yet*; also repeated for emphasis; NOW *or n.*; *n. is a long word* or *day*, comment on rash renunciation or despair or negative prophecy; *it is n. too late to mend*, reformation is always possible); (colloq. expressing surprise or incredulity in sentence or ellipt.) surely not, you do not mean it, (*you n. left the key in the lock!*; *'He ate the whole turkey.'—'Never!'*; *I n. did!*, *Well, I never!*, i.e. heard of such a thing &c.); not at all (*n. fear*; *n. mind*, do not be troubled); *n. a*, not a, no — at all; *n. a one*, none; (in condit. clauses) *n. so*, to unlimited extent, ever so; (with compar.) *n. the*, none the; (with participles &c.) *n.-enough-to-be-regretted*, *n.-to-be-forgotten*, *n.-ceasing*, *-dying*, *-ending*, *-failing*, *-fading*; *nevermore*, at no future time; *Never Never (Land)*, north Queensland; *nevertheless* adv. & conj., for all that, but for all that, notwithstanding, all the same. [OE *næfre* (*ne* not, EVER)]

new[1], a. Not existing before, now first made, brought into existence, invented, introduced, known or heard of, experienced, or discovered, (*N.* TESTAMENT); unfamiliar *to*; renewed, fresh, further, additional; different, changed, (*a n. morality*; *n. man* theol., one converted to Christianity, *put on the n. m.*, show conversion by amendment; *a n. fashion*, whence **new-fashion**ED[2] a.; *my n. tailor*; *lead a n. life*; *n.* STYLE; *turn over n.* LEAF); (with *the*, as distinctive epithet implying difference of character) later, modern, newfangled, (*the n.* LEARNING, MODEL, COMEDY; *the n. diplomacy, journalism, theology*, &c., advanced in method or doctrine, usu. contempt.; *the n. poor, rich*, classes impoverished, enriched, by the great war; *the n. woman*, women who aspire to freedom & independence & reject convention; *the N. World*, America); of recent origin, growth, arrival, or manufacture, now first used, not worn or exhausted, (*n. red sandstone*; *n. potatoes, wine, cheese*; *n. furniture, clothes*; *n. countries, soil*; *a heart, pleasures, ever n.*; *n.* CHUM; *n. members* of Parliament &c.); not yet accustomed *to*, fresh *from*; (of family or person) lately risen in position; *n. comer*, person lately arrived; *N. Englander*, inhabitant of *N. England*, six N.-E. States of U.S.A.; *new-fangled* [f. obs. *newfangle* a. in same sense (*-fangel* inclined to take f. OE st. *fang-*, infin. *fón* take)], fond of novelty (now rare), different from the good old fashion, objectionably novel; *n. moon*, moon when first seen as crescent after conjunction with sun, time of such appearance, (bibl.) Hebrew festival; *n. year*, coming or lately begun year, first few days of year (*n.-year's gift, wishes*, &c.; *n.-year's day*, 1st Jan.; *n.-year's eve*, 31 Dec.); *N. Zealander*, Maori, also European settler in N. Zealand. Hence **new·**ISH[1] a., **new·**NESS n. [Aryan; OE *niwe*, cf. G *neu*, Gk *neos*, L *novus*]

new[2], adv. (preceding, & now usu. hyphened with, qualified word). Newly, recently, just, (*n.-blown*, having just come into bloom, lit. & fig.; *n.-born*, & see below; *n.-built*, & see below; *n.-coined*, esp. of words; *n.-come*, lately arrived; *n.-fallen snow*; *n.-fledged*; *n.-found*; *n.-laid eggs*; *n.-made*; *n.-mown hay* or *lawn*); anew, afresh, re-, (*n.-born*, regenerated, & see above; *n.-build*, rebuild, & see above; *n.-create*; *n.-front*, put n. front to; *n.-furnish*; *n.-model*, recast). [f. prec.]

new·el, n. Centre pillar of winding stair (*open* or *hollow n.*, central well of winding stair); post supporting stair-handrail at top or bottom. [f. OF *nouel* (L *nux nucis* nut, -AL)]

Newfou·ndland, n. Island at mouth of St Lawrence (*N. dog* or *N.*, also *Newfoundlander*, large breed of spaniel kind noted for swimming powers). Hence **New-fou·ndland**ER[1](4) n.

New·gate (-ĭt), n. Celebrated London prison (*N. Calendar*, publication with accounts of N. prisoners; *N. fringe, frill*, beard grown below chin while face is shaven; *N. knocker*, curl worn by costermongers &c.).

new·ly, adv. Recently (usu. with p.p. =NEW[2] in sense 1 & often now preferred; hyphened w. attrib. part.; *the n.-discovered country; a guest n. arrived*); in new manner. [-LY[2]]

New·market, n. Town noted for horse-races (*N. coat* or *N.*, close-fitting overcoat for men or women); a card-game.

news, n. pl. (usu. followed by sing. vb). Tidings, new information, fresh events reported, (*have you heard the, this,* or rarely *these, n.?; ill n. flies apace; no n. is good n.; that is no n.*, already well known; *is there any, what is the, n.?*); (*N-*) part of newspaper title, as *Evening N.*; *n.-agent*, dealer in newspapers &c.; *n.-boy, -man*, selling newspapers in streets; *n.-letter* (hist.), letter sent out periodically with the n. to country towns &c.; *newsmonger*, gossip; *newspaper*, printed publication usu. daily or weekly containing the n., advertisements, & literary matter; *n.-print*, paper for printing newspapers on; *n.-room*, reserved for newspaper-reading; *n.-sheet*, simple form of newspaper; *n.-stand*, stall for sale of newspapers; *n.-vendor*, newspaper-seller. Hence **new·s**LESS, **new·sy**[2], aa., **new·si**NESS n. [pl. of NEW[1] after med. L *nova* neut. pl. of L *novus* new]

newt, n. Small tailed amphibian allied to salamander, eft. [for *ewt* (*a newt = an ewt*, cf. NICKNAME) var. of *evet* EFT]

Newtō·nian, a. & n. Of Newton or his theory of the universe; devised &c. by Newton. (N.) follower of Newton; N. telescope or reflector. [Sir Isaac *Newton* (1642–1727), -IAN]

next, a.(sometimes governing noun), adv., prep., & n. (Adj.) lying, living, being, nearest or nearest *to* or nearest to (*in the n. house; my n. neighbour; lives n. door*, in the n. house; *n.-door neighbours; n.-door to felony, to blasphemous*, almost; *n. to nothing, none, impossible*, almost; *the chair n. the fire; the skin with the flesh n. it; the shop n. to the corner*); soonest come to, first ensuing, immediately following, coming nearest in order &c. *to*, immediately *before*, (*will ask the n. man I see, the n. policeman; shall return next year, n. Friday, on Friday n.; what is the n. article?*, shopman's formula; *the Sunday n. before Easter; what is true one day may be false the n.; not till n. time*, facet. addition to promise of abstention; *the n. town to London in size; n.-best*, second-best; *the person n. him*, or *n. to him*, in rank). (Adv., often indistinguishable f. pred. use of adj.) in the n. place or degree, on the n. occasion, (*in the week n. ensuing; n. came a strange figure; what n.?*, can anything follow to beat this for absurdity &c.?; *placed his chair n. to hers; New York is the largest city n. to London; when I n. saw him he was lame*). (Prep., often indistinguishable f. pred. adj. governing noun) in or into the n. place, on the n. occasion, in the n. degree, to (*I was standing n. him; placed his chair n. hers; loves him n. her own child; wear flannel n. your skin*). (N., or ellipt. use of adj.) n. person or thing (*n. of kin*, person nearest of kin to some one; *will tell you in my n.*, i.e. letter; *to be continued in our n.*, i.e. issue of magazine &c.; *her n.*, i.e. husband, *was a greengrocer*, i.e. child, *was a girl; n. please*, ask your n. question, let the n. man come, &c.). [OE *néahst* (NIGH, -EST)]

ne·xus, n. Bond, link, connexion, (fig.); *the cash n.* (consisting in money payments). [L (*nectere nex-* bind)]

Nīă·gara, n. Cataract, torrent, din, (*shoot N.*, run fearful risks). [N.-Amer. waterfall]

nib, n., & v.t. Point of quill pen; metal or quill pen-point for insertion in penholder; point of tool &c.; (pl.) fragments of crushed cocoa-beans; (vb) make, mend, insert n. of, (pen). [=Sc. *neb* nose, OE *nebb*, cf. ON *nef*, Du. *neb*]

ni·bble, v.t. & i., & n. Take small bites at; bite (t. & i.) gently or cautiously or playfully (esp. of fish with bait, or rabbits; often *n. at*, lit., & fig. of dallying with temptation, bargain, &c.); carp *at*, make trifling criticisms. (N.) act of nibbling, esp. of fish at bait; enough (grass &c.) to n. at. [cf. LG *nibbelen*]

ni·blick, n. Golf-club with small round heavy head. [?]

nibs, n. (slang). *His* &c. *n.*, burlesque title after *his Grace* &c. [?]

nice, a. & adv. Fastidious, dainty, hard to please, of refined or critical tastes; precise, punctilious, scrupulous, particular, (*must not be too n. about the means*); requiring precision, care, tact, or discrimination (*a n. experiment, question, point, negotiation*); minute, subtle, (*a n. distinction, shade of meaning*); attentive, close, (*a n. inquiry, observer*); delicately sensitive, discriminative, or deft (*a n. ear, judgement, hand; weighed in the nicest scales*, lit. or fig.); (colloq.) agreeable, attractive, delightful, well-flavoured, satisfactory, kind, friendly, considerate, generally commendable (often iron., as *here is a n. mess*); *n.* (*and*), satisfactorily, as *the house stands n. & high, car is going n. & fast, this is a n. long one; n.-looking*, pretty or of engaging appearance. Hence **ni·ce**LY[2] adv., **ni·ce**NESS n., **ni·c**ISH[1](2) a. [earlier senses, *stupid, wanton*; OF, f. L *nescius* ignorant (NESCIENCE)]

Nice·ne (*or* nī·-), a. Of Nicaea (*first & second N. councils*, held A.D. 325, 787, to settle the Arian controversy & the question of images; *N. Creed*, formal statement of Christian belief based on that adopted at first N. council). [f. LL *Nicenus* (L f. Gk *Nikaia*)]

ni·cĕty, n. Punctiliousness; precision, accuracy, (*to a n.*, exactly); intricate or

subtle quality (*a point of great n.*); minute distinction, subtle or unimportant detail, (pl.) minutiae. [f. OF *niceté* (NICE, -TY)]
niche (-tsh), n., & v.t. Shallow recess in wall to contain statue, vase, &c.; (fig.) place destined for person's occupation, esp. *n. in the temple of fame*, right to be remembered for one's achievements. (Vb) place (statue &c.) in n. (usu. in p.p.); ensconce, settle, (esp. one*self*, or in p.p.) in some hollow or corner. [F, f. It. *nicchia* etym. dub.]
nick[1], n. Notch serving as catch, guide, mark, &c.; certain throws in hazard; *in the n.* (*of time*), just at the right moment. [?]
nick[2], v.t. & i. Make nick(s) in, indent; make incision at root of (horse's tail; also with *horse* &c. as obj.) to make him carry it higher; hit upon, guess rightly, (*n. it, the truth*, &c.); just catch (the time, a train, &c.); catch, nab, (criminals &c.); make (certain winning throws) at hazard; cut *in* by short cut, at corner, &c., in hunting or racing; (of breeding stocks) mingle *well* &c. with others. [?]
ni·ckel (-kl), n., & v.t. (-ll-). Hard silvery-white lustrous malleable ductile metal much used esp. in alloys; U.S. five-cent. piece or kinds of Continental coin corresponding to English & French coppers; *n. silver*, alloy like German silver; *n. steel*, alloy of iron with n.; (vb) coat with n. [abbr. of G *kupfernickel* copper-coloured ore f. which n. was first got (*kupfer* copper, *nickel* demon, w. ref. to disappointing nature of ore, which yielded no copper)]
ni·ck-nack. See KNICK-KNACK.
ni·ckname, n., & v.t. Name added to or substituted for person's, place's, or thing's proper name; abbreviation or familiar form of Christian name. (Vb) call (person or thing a n.), give n. to, (*some people are never nicknamed; they n. patience cowardice; Cumberland, nicknamed Butcher*). [earlier *neke-*, orig. *an* EKE[1]*-name*, cf. NEWT]
nicō·tian (-shĭ-), a. & n. Of tobacco; (n.) smoker. [foll., -IAN]
ni·cotine (-ēn), n. Poisonous alkaloid extracted as oily liquid from tobacco. Hence **ni·cotin**ISM(5) n., **ni·cotin**IZE(5) v.t. [F (*Nicot*, introducer of tobacco into France, -INE[5])]
ni·ctate, ni·ctitate, vv.i. Close & open the eyes, wink, chiefly in *nict(it)ating membrane*, third or inner eyelid of many animals. Hence **nict**A·TION, **nictit**A·TION, nn. [f. (med. L *nictitare* frequent. of) L *nictare*, -ATE[3]]
ni·cy, n. (nursery). Sweet, lollipop. [NICE, -Y[3]]
nīdame·ntal, a. Serving as receptacle for ova in molluscs &c. (*n. gland, capsule, ribbon*). [f. L *nidamentum* (NIDUS, -MENT)]
ni·d(d)ering, n. & a. (pseudo-archaic). Base or cowardly (person). [misreading (in early printed text of William of Malmesbury) of obs. *nithing* f. ON *nithingr* (*nith* satire, cf. G *neid* envy); given currency by Scott]
ni·ddle-no·ddle, a., & v.i. & t. Nodding, quivering, unsteady; keep nodding (head, or intr.), totter, sway. [redupl. f. NOD, -LE(3)]
nide, n. Brood of pheasants. [f. L NIDUS]
ni·dificate, ni·difȳ, vv.i. Build nest(s). Hence **nidific**A·TION n. [f. L *nidificare* (NIDUS, -FY), -ATE[3]]
nid-nod, v.i. & t. Keep nodding. [reduplicated f. NOD]
nī·dus, n. (pl. *-dī, -duses*). Place in which insects &c. deposit eggs; place in which spores or seeds develop; place of origin or development for disease, or for some quality, doctrine, &c.; natural receptacle; collection of eggs, tubercles, &c. [L, see NEST[1]]
niece (nēs), n. One's brother's or sister's daughter. [f. F *nièce* (L *neptis* cogn. w. obs. E *nift*, G *nichte*)]
nie·llo, n. (pl. *-li* pr. -lē, *-lōs*). Black composition for filling engraved lines in silver or other metal; (specimen of) such ornamental work. Hence **nie·llo**ED[2] a. [It., f. neut. of L *nigellus* dim. of *niger* black]
Nier·steiner (nērstī-), n. A white hock. [G]
ni·ggard, n. & a. Stingy person, grudging giver *of*; (adj., rhet. & poet.) = foll. [etym. dub.; cf. obs. *nig, nigon*; prob. of F orig.]
ni·ggardly, a. & adv. Parsimonious, stingy, sparing, scanty, giving or given grudgingly or in small amounts; hence **ni·ggardli**NESS n.; (adv.) in **n.** manner. [-LY[1], [2]]
ni·gger, n. Negro (usu. contempt.; *n. in the woodpile* or *fence* U.S. slang, suspicious circumstance, something that spoils a good thing); (loosely) member of any dark-skinned race, e.g. E.-Indian, native Australian; black turnip caterpillar; *n. minstrel*, see NEGRO; *n. melody, song*, &c., such as prevail among American Negroes; *niggerhead*, = NEGRO*-head*. Hence **ni·gger**DOM n. [earlier *neger* f. F *nègre* f. Sp. NEGRO]
ni·ggle, v.i. Spend time, be over-elaborate, on petty details. [cf. Norw. *nigla*]
ni·ggling, a. Trifling, petty, lacking in breadth, largeness, or boldness of effect; (of handwriting) cramped. [-ING[2]]
nigh (nī), adv., prep., & a., (comp. & sup. formerly *near, next*, now *nigher, nighest*, also as advv., prepp., & aa., cf. NEAR[1], [2]). = NEAR[1, 2] (archaic, poet., or dial.). [com.-Teut.; OE *néah*, cf. Du. *na*, G *nah*; the adv. use is the orig.; *nigher, -est*, have been formed since the relation of *near, next*, to *nigh* was obscured]
night (nīt), n. Dark period between day & day, time from 6 p.m. to 6 a.m. or from sunset to sunrise, darkness then prevail-

ing, the dark, (also *nightfall*) end of daylight, weather or experiences or occupation of a n., (*black, dark, as n.*; *went forth into the n.*; *the n. of ignorance* or *barbarism*; *stayed three nn. with them*; *a dirty n.*, stormy or rainy; *have a good, bad, n.*, sleep well or ill, be comfortable or in pain, cf. GOOD-*n.*; *make a n. of it*, spend n. in festivity; *n. out*, festive evening, also evening on which servant is allowed out; *n. & day*, always, without cessation; *all n., all n. long*, for the whole n.; *by n.*, during, under cover of, the n.; *at n.*, at nightfall, in the evening, also added to the hours from 6 p.m. to midnight, cf. *in the morning* of hours 1–6 a.m.; *cannot sleep o' nn. for thinking of*); *night-*, by, like, during, appropriate to, employed for, active in, the n. (*-veiled, -black, -walking, -haunted, -brawl, -attire, -lamp, -porter, -moth*); *n.-bird*, esp. owl or nightingale, also person esp. of disreputable character who goes about by n.; *n.-blindness*, nyctalopia; *n.-boat*, passenger-boat crossing by n.; *n.-cap*, worn in bed, also alcoholic drink taken before going to bed; *n.-cellar*, underground drinkshop of low class; *n.-chair*, = n.-stool; *n.-clothes*, worn in bed; *n.-club* (open to members for dancing, supper, &c.); *n.-dress, n.-gown* (also **nigh·t**Y[3] n.), woman's or child's n. attire; *n.-flower*, that opens at n. & closes in the day; *n.-glass*, short telescope for n. use at sea; *n.-hag*, female demon riding the air at n., nightmare; *n.-hawk*, thieving or other nocturnal prowler; *nightjar*, the GOAT*sucker*; *n.-light*, short thick candle giving dim light through n. for invalids &c.; *n.-line*, left with baited hooks to catch fish by n.; *n.-long*, lasting through the n.; *nightman*, employed to remove n.-soil; *nigh·tmare*, female monster sitting upon & seeming to suffocate sleeper, incubus, oppressive or paralysing or terrifying or fantastically horrible dream (whence **nigh·tmār**ISH[1] a.), also haunting fear or thing vaguely dreaded; *n.-piece*, (painting of) n. scene or landscape; *n.-school*, providing instruction for workmen afterdays' work; *n. season*, = n.-time (poet., rhet.); *n.-shirt*, boy's or man's long shirt for sleeping in; *n.-soil*, contents of cesspools &c. removed at n.; *n.-stool*, close-stool or commode for use at n.; *n.-suit*, set of pyjamas; *n.-time*, n. as a state of things or opportunity (*in the n.-t.*, by n.); *n.-watch*, (person or party keeping) watch by n., Hebrew or Roman division (one of three or four) of the n. (*in the n.-ww.*, during the anxious, wearisome, wakeful, &c., n.); *n.-work*, done, that must be done, by n. Hence **nigh·t**LESS a. [Aryan; OE *niht*, cf. G *nacht*, L *nox -ctis*, Gk *nux -ktos*, Skr. *nakta*]

nigh·tingale (-ngg-), n. Small reddish-brown migratory bird singing melodiously & powerfully both by night & in the day. [OE *nihtegale* (NIGHT, *galan* sing), cf. G *nachtigall*]

nigh·tly[1], a. Happening, done, existing, &c., in the night; happening every night; (poet.) of or suiting night. [OE *nihtlic* (NIGHT, -LY[1])]

nigh·tly[2], adv. Every night. [-LY[2]]

nigh·tshade, n. Kinds of plants, esp. *Black N.* with white flowers & black poisonous berries, *Woody N.* with purple flowers & bright red berries, & *Deadly N.* or belladonna. [OE *nihtscada*, cf. Du. *nachtschade*, G *nachtschatte*, prob. f. NIGHT, SHADE, w. ref. to its poison]

nīgre·scent, a. Blackish. So **nigre·s**CENCE n. [f. L *nigrescere* (*niger* black), -ENT]

nĭ·gritude, n. Blackness (lit. & fig.). [f. L *nigritudo* (prec., -TUDE)]

nĭ·hil ad rem, pred. a. Irrelevant. [L]

nīh·ilism (*or* nĭ·h-), n. Negative doctrines, total rejection of current beliefs, in religion or morals; (Philos.) scepticism that denies all existence; doctrines of extreme revolutionary party in 19th-c. Russia finding nothing to approve of in the constituted order of things. Hence **nih·i**LIST(2) n., **nihili·st**IC a. [f. L *nihil* nothing, -ISM]

nīhĭ·lity (-h-), n. Non-existence, nothingness; mere nothing, trifle, nullity. [f. med. L *nihilitas* (prec., -TY)]

nil, n. Nothing, no number or amount, (esp. in scoring at games &c., as *three goals to n.*); *n. admirari* [L], attitude of being surprised at, or admiring, nothing, nonchalance. [L]

nill, v.i., 3rd sing. pres. condit. *Will he n. he*, whether he likes it or not (now usu. *willy-nilly*). [obs. *ne* not, WILL[1]]

Nīlo·meter, n. Graduated pillar &c. showing height to which Nile rises. [f. Gk *Neilometrion* (-METER)]

Nīlŏ·tic, a. Of the Nile or Nile region or its inhabitants. [f. L f. Gk *Neilōtikos* (*Neilos* Nile, -OT[2], -IC)]

ni·mble, a. Quick in movement, agile, swift, (*the n. shilling*, or *ninepence* archaic, circulating quickly); (of the mind &c.) versatile, clever, quick to apprehend, dextrous. Hence **ni·mble**NESS n., **ni·mb**LY[2] adv. [f. OE *numol* f. *niman* take, -LE (1)]

ni·mbus, n. (pl. *-bī*). Bright cloud or halo investing deity or person or thing; bright disk or aureole round or over head of saint &c. in picture; (Meteorol.) rain-cloud. Hence **ni·mbus**ED[2] a. [L, = cloud]

nimĭ·ety, n. (rare). Excess, too much. [f. LL *nimietas* (L *nimius* excessive f. *nimis* too much, -TY)]

nĭ·miny-pĭ·miny, a. Affected, mincing, prim. [imit.]

Ni·mrod, n. Great hunter or sportsman. [see *Gen.* x. 8, 9]

ni·ncompōōp (-kom-), n. Simpleton, person without sense or character, ninny. [?]

nine, a. & n. One more than eight, 9, IX, (often agreeing with understood noun, as *n. of the men, n. of them, n. o'clock* or *n., cost n. & six, will be n. next birthday; n.-o'clock wind,* blowing from rifleman's left hand; *twenty-n.* &c. or, not beyond *n. & ninety, n. & twenty* &c.; *the N.*, the Muses; *n. days' wonder,* novelty that attracts much attention but is soon forgotten; *n. times out of ten,* generally; *possession is n.* POINTS *of the law*; *cat has n. lives,* see LIFE); *ninepins,* kind of skittles; *n. tenths,* nearly the whole; hence **ni·ne**FOLD a. & adv. (N.) the number n.; card of n. pips; *to the nn.*, to perfection (esp. *dressed up to the nn.*, elaborately). [Aryan; OE *nigon,* cf. G *neun,* Skr. *návan,* Gk *ennea,* L *novem*]

nī·netee·n, a. & n. One more than eighteen, 19, XIX, (*is nearly n.*, years old; *twice n. is 38*; *a n.-&-sixpenny pair of shoes*; *n. to the* DOZEN). Hence **ninetee·n**TH[2] a. (*-th hole* joc., golf-club's bar) & n. [-TEEN]

ni·nety, a. & n. Nine times ten, 90, XC, (*n.-one* &c., or *one* &c. *& n.*; *n.-first* &c.; *n.-nine out of a hundred,* nearly all); hence **ni·netie**TH[2] a. & n. (N.) the number n.; (pl.) *the nn.*, degrees on thermometer &c., years of century or life, between 89 & 100. [-TY[2]]

Nī·nĕvite, n. Inhabitant of Nineveh. [f. L *Ninivita* (*Ninive,* -ITE[1])]

ni·nny, n. Simpleton, fool, person of weak character or mind. [perh. for INNOCENT]

nīnth, a. & n. Next after eighth (*on the n.*, day of month; *n. part,* one of nine equal parts into which thing may be divided; *n. part of a man,* tailor). (N.) n. part; (Mus.) interval of octave & second. [NINE, -TH[2]]

nī·nthly, adv. In the ninth place (in enumerations). [-LY[2]]

Nī·obĕ, n. Inconsolable bereaved woman. Hence **Niobē·**AN a. [Gk (-ē), woman turned to stone while weeping for slain children]

niō·bium, n. (chem.). A metallic element. Hence **niō·bi**C (chem.), **niō·bo**US (chem.), aa. [prec., -IUM; named 1845]

nip[1], v.t. & i., & n. Pinch, squeeze sharply, bite; pinch *off* (bud &c.); check growth of (esp. *n. in the* BUD[1]; lit. & fig.) (of cold) affect injuriously, pain, whence **ni·pp**ING[2] a., **ni·pping**LY[2] adv.; take *up, out,* &c., hurriedly or unobserved; (slang) step &c. nimbly *in(to), out, up,* whence **ni·pp**Y[2] a. (N.) pinch, sharp squeeze, bite; sharp saying, sarcasm; (check to vegetation caused by) coldness of air. [cf. Du. *nijpen* nip, Du. & G *nippen* sip, Du. *nippen* wrangle]

nip[2], n., & v.i. & t. Small quantity of spirits &c. as pick-me-up; (vb) take nn., take nn. of. [prob. for obs. *nipperkin* small measure of ale &c., etym. dub., prob. of Du. orig.]

ni·pa (nē-, nī-), n. Kind of E.-Indian palm. [f. Malay *nipah*]

ni·pper, n. In vbl senses of NIP[1, 2]; also or esp.: kinds of fish; boy, lad, esp. costermonger's assistant or street arab; (pl.) implement with jaws for gripping or cutting, forceps, pinchers, pliers, (often *pair of nn.*); (pl.) pince-nez; horse's incisor tooth; crustacean's claw. [-ER[1]]

ni·pple, n. Small projection in which mammary ducts terminate in mammal of either sex, teat, esp. on woman's breast; cover for protecting woman's teat while child sucks; teat of nursing-bottle; n.-like protuberance on skin, glass, metal, &c.; small rounded elevation on mountain; perforated projection of musket-lock on which percussion-cap is placed; *nipplewort,* yellow-flowered weed. [?]

nirva·na (-vah-), n. Buddhist beatitude, i.e. extinction of individuality & absorption into the supreme spirit. [Skr. (*nirva* to blow)]

nī·sī, conj. (legal). Unless (*decree, order, rule,* &c., *n.*, decree &c. valid unless cause is shown for rescinding it before appointed time at which it is 'made absolute'; *n. prius,* hearing of civil causes by judges of assize, court-business of this kind). [L; *n. prius,* unless before that, words from writ directing sheriff to provide jury on certain day unless judges come sooner]

nit, n. Egg of louse or other parasitic insect. [OE *hnitu,* cf. Du. *neet,* G *niss*]

nī·trate[1] (-*at*), n. Salt given by combination of nitric acid with base, or compound made by interaction of nitric acid & alcohol; (short for) *potassium* or *sodium n.* [NITRE, -ATE[1](3)]

nītra·te[2], v.t. Treat, combine, or impregnate, with nitric acid. Hence **nitra·**TION n. [foll., -ATE[3]]

nī·tre (-*er*), n. Saltpetre, potassium nitrate; *cubic n.*, sodium nitrate. [F, f. L f. Gk *nitron* perh. of Oriental orig.]

nī·tric, a. Of nitre; *n. acid,* clear colourless pungent highly corrosive & caustic liquid, aquafortis. [f. F *nitrique* (prec., -IC)]

nī·trifȳ, v.t. & i. Turn into nitre, make or become nitrous. So **nitri**FICA·TION n. [f. F *nitrifier* (NITRE, -FY)]

nī·trite, n. Compound of base or alcohol with nitrous acid. [NITRE, -ITE[1](2)]

nītr(o)-, comb. form of Gk *nitron* NITRE, = of, containing, made with or by use of, nitric acid or nitroxyl or nitre or nitrogen; *nitro-a·cid,* compound of nitric with organic acid; *nitro-co·mpound* (made by action of nitric acid); *nitro-explo·sive* (prepared by means of nitric acid); *nitro-gly·cerin(e),* yellowish oily violently explosive liquid made by adding glycerine to mixture of nitric & sulphuric acids; *nitro-pow·der,* gunpowder made with nitric acid; *nitro-sulphūr·ic,* formed by mixture of nitric & sulphuric acids; *nitro·xyl,* chemical grouping of nitrogen & oxygen.

nī·trogen, n. Colourless tasteless scentless permanent gas forming four-fifths of atmosphere. Hence **nitrŏ·gen**ous a. [f. F *nitrogène*, see NITRE, -GEN(1)]

nī·trous, a. Of, like, impregnated with, nitre (*n. acid*, containing less oxygen than nitric acid; *n. oxide*, gas used as anaesthetic, laughing-gas). [f. L *nitrosus* (NITRE, -OUS)]

nix[1], int. (slang) giving warning to confederates &c. that master &c. is approaching. [?]

nix[2], n. (fem. *nixie*). Water-elf. [G (fem. *nixe*), cf. OE *nicor*, Du. *nikker*, perh. cogn. w. Gk *nizō* wash]

nix[3], n. (slang). Nothing. [f. G *nichts*]

Niza·m (-ahm), n. Ruler of Hyderabad; (man, men, of) Turkish regular army. [Hind. & Turk., f. Arab. *nidam* order, arrangement]

no[1], a. Not any (*no circumstances could justify it*; *no date*, abbr. *n.d.*, = undated, in library lists &c.; *no song no supper*, you must sing first; *no* END[1]; *by no* MEAN[1]*s*); not a, quite other than a, (*service of no honourable kind*; *is no part of my plan*; *is no genius*), hardly any (*is no distance*; *did it in no time*), *there is* &c. *no —ing*, none is &c. possible (*there's no accounting for tastes*; *there was no mistaking what he meant*); imperfect substitute for, absence of, (often *no-*; *these opinions or rather no opinions*; *his faith or no-faith*); (in ellipt. sentences) we will not have any, let there not be any, there is not any, (*no Popery, surrender*, &c., whence *no-Popery riots, a no-confidence vote*, &c.; *now no mistake*, understand me clearly; *& no* MISTAKE[1]; *no cards, no flowers*, invitations to funeral are not being sent out, floral tributes are not desired; *no* DOUBT[1]; *no* FEAR[1]; *no* WONDER[1]); *no ball*, unlawfully delivered ball in cricket, umpire's announcement of this, (vb, *no-b.*) pronounce (bowler) to have bowled n. b.; *no-being*, non-existence; *no·body*, no person (*everybody's* BUSINESS *is nobody's business*; *nobody ever did his*, or irreg. *their, work better*), (w. pl.) person of no importance, authority, or position; *no bon* (army slang), no good; *no* GO[2]; *no·how*, in no way, by no means, (usu. w. *can, -able*, &c.), *be, feel, look*, &c., *nohow*, out of order, out of sorts; *no man*, no person (*no man's land*, piece of waste, unowned, or debatable ground, esp. Mil. the space between opposed trenches); *no meaning*, nonsense; *no one*, no person, (also, as adj.) no single (*n. o. man could lift it*); *no thoroughfare*, notice that path, street, &c., is closed at other end, or that entrance is not permitted, (also) such path; *no·way(s)*, *no·wise*, in no manner, not at all; *no·whence, no·whither*, from, to, no place; *no whit*, not at all (usu. w. compar.). [for NONE, orig. only before consonants]

no[2], adv. (Alw. as alternative after *or*) not (usu. *whether or no*, in either case, also *tell me whether or no*; *pleasant or no, it is true*); *no compree·* (army slang), do not understand. [prob. f. prec. by extension of adj. use as in *whether there be any church or no* (*church*)]

no[3], adv. (Alw. with compar.) by no amount, not at all, (*no better than before*; *is no better than she should be*, is not quite respectable; *no sooner had he said it than*, as soon as he had said it; *no sooner said than done*; *no* LONG[1]*er*); *no less* (*than*), as much (n., a., adv.) or many (as) (*gave me £50, no less, no less than £50*; *no less than ten people have told me*; *did it no less for my warning*; *is no less than a scandal*; *a no less fatal victory*); *no more*, (n.) nothing further (*have no more to say*; *want no more of it*; often ellipt. for *say no more* or *let us have no more of it*), (adj.) not any more (*no more wine?*), (adv.) no longer (*is no more*, is dead or passed away), never again, to no greater extent (*is no more a lord than I am, could no more help laughing than I could fly*), just as little, neither, (*you did not come, no more did he*). [OE *ná* see NATHLESS]

no[4], particle equivalent to negative sentence, & n. (pl. *noes*). The answer to your question is negative, your request or command will not be complied with, the statement made or course intended or conclusion arrived at is not correct or satisfactory, (*no, nor*, form for substituting stronger phrase, as *A man could not lift it, no, nor half a dozen*). (N.) the word *no*, a denial or refusal, (*two noes make a yes*; *will not take no for an answer*, persists in spite of refusals); (pl.) voters against a motion (*the nn. have it*, are in a majority). [as prec.]

Noā·chian, Noā·chic, (-k-), aa. Of Noah or his time. [*Noach* = Noah, -IAN]

No·ah, n. Hebrew patriarch; *N.'s ark*, in which Noah, his family, & animals, were saved (*Gen.* vi), imitation of it as child's plaything, large or cumbrous or old-fashioned trunk or vehicle, small bivalve, detached fragment of flying cloud; *N.'s nightcap*, the plant eschscholtzia (w. ref. to conical bud-sheaths).

nob[1], n., & v.t., (slang). Head; (Cribbage) knave of same suit as turn-up (*one for his n.*, point scored by holder of this); (vb, boxing) hit on the head. [perh. var. of KNOB]

nob[2], n. (slang). Member of upper classes. [perh. for *nobleman*, but Sc. form is *knabb*]

no·bble, v.t. (slang). Tamper with (racehorse) to prevent its winning; secure partiality of by underhand means; get hold of (money &c.) dishonestly; catch (criminal). [?]

no·bby, a. (slang). Suitable for a NOB[2], smart, elegant. [-Y[2]]

nobi·liary, a. Of (the) nobility (*n. particle*, preposition, as French *de*, German *von*,

prefixed to title; *n. pride, rank,* &c.). [f. F *nobiliaire* (NOBLE, -ARY)]
nobi·lity, n. Noble character, mind, birth, or rank; *the* or *a* class of nobles. [f. L *nobilitas* (foll., -TY)]
nō·ble, a. & n. Illustrious by rank, title, or birth, belonging to the nobility; of lofty character or ideals (so **noble-minded**ED[2] a., **noble-mi·ndedness** n.); showing greatness of character, magnanimous, morally elevated; splendid, magnificent, stately, imposing, impressive, in appearance; excellent, admirable, (*a n. horse, cellar,* &c.); *nobleman,* peer; *no·blewoman,* woman of n. birth or rank; hence **no·ble**NESS n., **no·b**LY[2] adv. (N.) nobleman; obsolete coin, usu. 6/8. [F, f. L *nobilis* (*noscere* KNOW, -BLE)]
noble·sse (-ĕs), n. The class of nobles (esp. of a foreign country; *n. obli·ge* (-ēzh), privilege entails responsibility. [F]
nock[1], n., & v.t. Notch at ends of bow for holding string; notch(ed horn tip) of arrow for receiving bowstring; (vb) set (arrow) on string. [perh. = foll.; prob. not conn. w. NOTCH]
nock[2], n. Forward upper corner of some sails. [f. Du. *nok*]
noct(i)-, comb. form of L *nox noctis* night =by night, as *nocta·mbulant* night-walking, *noctiflor·ous* night-flowering, *-lu·ca* phosphorescent animalcule, *-vagant, -vagous,* night-wandering.
no·ctule, n. Largest British species of bat. [F, f. It. *nottola* bat]
noctur·nal, a. Of, in, done by, active in, the night. [f. LL (*-alis*) f. L *nocturnus* (NOCT-), -AL]
no·cturne, n. Dreamy musical piece; (Paint.) night-scene. [F, cf. prec.]
nod, v.i. & t., & n. Incline head slightly & quickly in salutation (*nodding acquaintance,* very slight one *with* person or subject), assent, or command; let head fall forward in drowsiness, be drowsy, make sleepy mistake (*Homer sometimes nods,* the best of us may be dull or make a slip); (of buildings &c., also fig.) incline from perpendicular (esp. *nods to its fall*); (of plumes) dance up & down; incline (head); signify (assent &c.) by n. (N.) nodding of the head; this as sign of absolute power (*the empire was at* or *dependent on his n.*); *land of Nod,* sleep (with ref. to phr. in *Gen.* iv. 16). [excl. E; from 14th c.; etym. dub.]
no·ddle[1], n. (colloq.). Head, pate. [?]
no·ddle[2], v.t. Nod or wag (head). [NOD, -LE(3)]
no·ddy, n. Simpleton, noodle; tropical sea-bird. [perh. f. obs. *noddy* foolish (perh. NOD, -Y[2])]
node, n. Knob on root or branch; point at which leaves spring; hard tumour esp. on gouty or rheumatic joint; intersecting point of planet's orbit & ecliptic or of two great circles of celestial sphere, whence **nō·d**ICAL a.; point or line of rest in vibrating body; central point in system; point at which curve crosses itself. Hence **nō·d**AL a. [f. L NODUS]
nodo·se, a. Knotty, knobbed. [f. L *nodosus* (NODUS, -OSE[1])]
nodŏ·sity, n. Knottiness; knot, protuberance. [f. L *nodositas* (prec., -TY)]
nŏ·dule, n. Small rounded lump of anything; small node in plant; small knotty tumour, ganglion. Hence **no·dul**AR[1], **no·dulāted** [-ATE[2]], **no·dul**OSE[1], **no·dul**OUS, aa., **nodul**A·TION n. [f. L *nodulus* (foll., -ULE)]
nō·dus, n. (pl. *-dī*). Knotty point, difficulty, complication in plot of story &c. [L, = knot, w. spec. ref. to *dignus vindice nodus* complication requiring divine intervention]
Nōĕ·l, = NOWEL.
noĕ·tic, a. & n. Of the intellect; purely intellectual or abstract; given to intellectual speculation; (n., sing. or pl.) science of the intellect. [f. Gk *noētikos* (*noētos* f. *noeō* apprehend, -IC)]
nog[1], n., & v.t. Pin, peg, small block, of wood; snag or stump on tree. (Vb) secure with nn.; build in form of (*brick-, concrete-, stone-*)**no·gg**ING[1] n., i.e. brickwork &c. in timber frame. [?]
nog[2], n. Kind of strong beer brewed in E. Anglia. [?]
no·ggin, n. Small mug; small measure, usu. ¼ pint, of liquor. [?]
noil, n. (Sing. or pl.) short wool-combings. [?]
noise (-z), n., & v.t. & i. Loud outcry, clamour, shouting, din of voices & movements; any sound, esp. loud or harsh one, whence **noi·se**LESS a., **noi·seless**LY[2] adv., **noi·seless**NESS n.; *make a n.,* lit., also talk or complain much *about,* also be much talked of, attain notoriety *in the world.* (Vb) make public, spread *abroad,* (person's fame, fact; *it was noised abroad that* —); (rare) make n. [F, cf. Pr. *noysa, nosa, nausa,* etym. dub.]
noisette[1] (nwahzĕ·t), n. Kind of rose, cross between China & musk. [*N.,* grower, 1817]
noise·tte[2] (as prec.), n. (Usu. pl.) small piece(s) of meat cooked in certain way. [F]
noi·some (-sum), a. Harmful, noxious; ill-smelling; objectionable, offensive. Hence **noi·some**NESS n. [obs. *noy* for ANNOY n., -SOME]
noi·sy, a. Clamorous, turbulent; full of, making much, noise; (of colour, costume, literary style) loud, conspicuous, violent, glaring. Hence **noi·si**LY[2] adv., **noi·si**NESS n. [-Y[2]]
nō·lens vō·lens (-ĕnz), adv. Willy-nilly, perforce. [L partt. =unwilling, willing]
nō·lī mē ta·ngerĕ (-j-), n. Erosive ulcer(s), lupus; warning against meddling or approach (*carries a* n. m. t. *in his face*; *a*

n.-m.-t. *manner*); picture of Christ as he appeared to Magdalen at sepulchre (*John* xx. 17). [L, = touch me not]

nŏll, n. (now dial.). (Crown of) head. [OE *knoll*, cf. OHG *knol*]

no'llĕ prŏ'sequī, n. (legal). Relinquishment by plaintiff or prosecutor of (part of) his suit, stay of proceedings, entry of it on record. [L, = to refuse to pursue]

nō'lo episcopār'ī, n. (Formula expressing) avoidance of responsible office. [L, = I do not wish to be a bishop]

nŏ'mad, -ade (now rare), (*-ad*), n. & a. (Member of tribe) roaming from place to place for pasture; wanderer, wandering. Hence or cogn. **nomă'dɪc** a., **noma'dɪcally** adv., **no'madɪsm**(2) n., **no'madɪze** (2) v.i. [f. L f. Gk *nomas -ados* (*nemō* to pasture)]

nom de guerre (F), n. Pseudonym, sobriquet, assumed name under which person fights, plays, writes, &c. [F, = war-name]

nom de plume (as F), n. Writer's pseudonym, title or initials or borrowed name under which he writes. [formed in E of F words = pen-name on anal. of prec.]

nō'menclātor, n. Slave or client in ancient Rome charged with naming persons met, usher assigning places at banquet, (also in mod. use with ref. to these senses); giver or inventor of names, esp. in nat.-hist. classification. [L (*nomen* name, *calare* call, -OR[2])]

no'menclature (-ātsher), n. Catalogue, register, (now rare); person's or community's system of names for things; terminology of a science &c.; systematic naming. So **no'menclATIVE** a. [f. L *nomenclatura* (prec., -URE)]

nŏ'minal, a. Of, as, like, a noun (*n. & verbal roots*); of, in, names (*n. & essential distinctions*; *n. definition*, statement of all marks connoted in name of concept); existing in name only, not real or actual, (*n. & real price, ruler*; *n. sum, rent*, &c., virtually nothing), whence **no'minalLY**[2] adv.; consisting of, giving, the names (*n. list of officers* &c.). [f. L *nominalis* (*nomen -inis* name f. *noscere* KNOW, -MEN)]

no'minalism, n. (philos.). Doctrine that universals or abstract concepts are mere names (opp. *realism*). So **no'minalIST**(2) n., **nominali'stIC** a. [f. F *nominalisme* (prec., -ISM)]

no'minate, v.t. Call by the name of, mention by name, name or appoint (date, place), (now rare); appoint, propose for election, to office (*a board of six nominated & six elected members*; *the candidates were nominated to-day*), whence or cogn. **no'minatOR**[2], **nominEE'**, nn. [f. L *nominare* (NOMINAL), -ATE[3]]

nomina'tion, n. In vbl senses; also, right of nominating for appointment (*have a n. at your service*). [f. L *nominatio* (prec., -ATION)]

no'minative, a. & n. (Case) used as or in agreement with subject of verb (*n. absolute*, construction like Latin ablative absolute, as *this being so, I did nothing*); of this case (*n. ending, form*); word in this case, (loosely) subject (*of* verb); hence **nominati'vAL** a. Of, appointed by, nomination (*the n. & the elective principles, members*). [f. L *nominativus* (NOMINATE, -IVE)]

nŏn, Latin adv. = not, forming part of phrases: *n. assumpsit* (he did not undertake), plea that defendant made no promise; *n. compos* (*mentis*), (not master of his mind), lunatic, mad, (legal, & in gen. use); *n. esse*, (not to be) non-existence; *n. est inventus* (he has not been found), *n. est*, or *n. inventus*, sheriff's statement, in returning writ, that defendant is not to be found in his bailiwick (legal, & transf. in gen. use); *n. liquet* (it is not clear), jury's verdict in doubtful case deferring matter to another day; *n. nobis* (not unto us; *Ps.* cxv), formula attributing victory &c. not to oneself but to God, song of rejoicing; *n. plăcet* (it does not please), negative vote in ecclesiastical or university assemblies (also as v.t., throw out); *n. plus ultra*, = NE PLUS ULTRA; *n. possumus* (we cannot), statement of inability, refusal to act or move; *n. sequitur* (it does not follow), illogical inference, paradoxical result.

non-, pref. (AF *noun-* f. OF *non-*, *nom-*, *num-*, *nun-*, f. prec.) now freely prefixed (1) usu. to vbl n., giving neg. vbl n. corresp. to *not* w. parent vb, = failure to do, abstention from doing, or rarely to other n. giving neg. abstract n. corresp. to *not* w. connected adj.; *n.-acceptance*; *n.-a'ccess*, impossibility of access for sexual intercourse (in questions of paternity); *n.-acquai'ntance*; *n.-appear'ance* (esp. in court as party or witness); *n.-atte'ndance*; *no'n-claim*, failure to make claim within legal time; *n.-commi'ttal*, avoidance of committing oneself to definite course or either side (usu. attrib., as *n.-c. answer*); *n.-compli'ance*; *n.-fea'sance* (legal), omission of act that ought to have been done; *n.-interfer'ence*, *-interve'ntion*, principle or practice, esp. in politics & international affairs, of keeping aloof from others' disputes; *n.-intru'sion* (Church of Scotland), principle that patron shall not thrust unacceptable minister on congregation; *n.-joi'nder* (legal), omission of partner &c. to join another as party to suit; *n.-pay'ment*; *n.-perce'ption*; *n.-perfor'mance*; *n.-resi'stance* (hist.), 17th-c. principle that authority must not be resisted even if unjustly exercised; *n.-succe'ss*; *n.-u'sage*; *n.-u'se*; *n.-u'ser* (legal), neglect to use a right, by which it may become void. (2) to n. of designation, giving n. (somet. w. derivatives) = person, thing, or all, that is not the thing specified;

n.-abstai·ner, one who does not abstain (esp. from liquor); *n.-e·go* (metaphys.), all that is not the conscious self, the object as opposed to the subject; *n.-me·mber* (so *n.-me·mbership*); *n.-me·tal* (esp. chem. = element that is not a metal; so *n.-meta·llic*). (3) to attrib. n., giving n. (somet. w. derivatives) that can only be used attributively, = unconnected with, not involving; *n.-jur·y*, tried without jury; *n.-par·ty*, that may be dealt with irrespective of political partisanship; *n.-ski·d*, of tires, safe against skidding; *n.-soci·ety*, *-u·nion* (also *n.-unionist*), not belonging to a workman's society or trade union. (4) to adj. (usu. participial in *-ant*, *-ent*, *-ing*, *-ate*, *-ed*), giving adj. (& somet. n. or derivatives) =not-; *n.-colle·giate*, (student) not belonging to a college, (of universities) without colleges; *n.-co·mbatant*, (person, esp. in the fighting services, e.g. surgeon, chaplain, ambulance man) who has not to fight, civilian; *n.-commi·ssioned*, not holding commission (esp. of army officers such as *sergeant*, *corporal*. abbr. N.C.O. or *non-com.*); *n.-commu·nicant*, (person) who does not attend the communion service; *n.-conde·nsing* (of steam-engine), discharging used steam into atmosphere instead of using condenser; *n.-condu·cting*, that will not conduct heat or electricity (so *n.-condu·ctor*, n.-conducting medium or substance; *n.-conductibility*); *no·n-content*, voter against motion in House of Lords; *n.-esse·ntial* a. & n.; *n.-Euclidē·an*, denying or dispensing with any of the assumptions of Euclid's geometry; *n.-exi·stent*, *-ence*; *n.-flammable*, (of flannelette &c.) not inflammable; *n.-jur·ing*, *-jur·or*, (hist.), (beneficed clergyman) who refused oath of allegiance to William & Mary; *n.-o·ffice-holding* &c.; *n.-provi·ded*, (of schools) other than PROVIDED. (5) to adj. requiring a neutral negative form free from some special sense, usu. of condemnation, attached to the compd in *in-*, *un-*, = not coming under the description of, not; *n.-effe·ctive*, (soldier, sailor) not qualified for active service (cf. INEFFECTIVE); *n.-hu·man*, not belonging to human race (cf. INHUMAN); *n.-lo·gical*, proceeding by other means than logic (cf. ILLOGICAL); *n.-mo·ral*, unconcerned with morality (cf. IMMORAL); *n.-na·tural*, deviating from the natural order (cf. UNNATURAL). (6) to adv., as *n.-conte·ntiously*.

nŏ·nage (-ĭj), n. Being under age, minority; immaturity, early stage. [OF (prec., AGE)]

nŏnagenār·ian, a. & n. (Person) between 89 & 100 years old. [f. L *nonagenarius* (*nonageni* 90 each, -ARY[1]), -IAN]

nō·nary, a. & n. (Arith., of SCALE[3] of notation) having nine as basis; (n.) group of nine. [f. L *nonarius* (*nonus* ninth, -ARY[1])]

non avenu (F), a. (Regarded as) not having happened.

nonce, n. Time being, present occasion, (only in *for the n.*); *n.-word*, coined for one occasion. [ME *to*, **for*, *than anes* =(for) the ONCE, cf. NEWT]

no·nchalant (-shalant), a. Unexcited, unmoved, cool, indifferent. Hence **no·nchal**ANCE n., **no·nchalant**LY[2] adv. [F, part. of *nonchaloir* (NON-, L *calēre* be warm)]

nonconfor·mist, n. One who does not conform to doctrine or discipline of an established Church, esp. member of sect dissenting from Anglican Church (usu. not including Roman Catholics), protestant dissenter (*the n. conscience*, opinions as to right & wrong prevalent among nn. esp. as affecting their political attitude). [NON-(2)]

nonconfor·mity, n. Principles, practice, the body, of nonconformists, protestant dissent; failure to conform (*to* rule &c.); want of correspondence between things. [NON-(2)]

no·ndescript, a. & n. (Person, thing) not easily classified, neither one thing nor another, hybrid. [NON-(4), L *descriptus* (DESCRIBE)]

none (nŭn), pron., a., & adv. Not any *of* (*n. of them came*; *n. of them is*, or *are*, acc. to sense required; *n. of this concerns me*; *n. of your impudence !*); no person, no one, (now rare; *n. can tell*); no persons (*n. but fools have ever believed it*). (Adj.; rarely with noun; usu. ellipt. = *no* with reference defined by noun previously used or shortly to follow) no, not any, not to be counted in specified class, (*make of n. effect* archaic; *you have money & I have n.*; *he is n. of my friends*, *n. of your canting hypocrites*; *his understanding is n. of the clearest*; *this is n. other but the house of God*; *seeking rest & finding n.*; *if a linguist is wanted, I am n.*; *would rather have a bad reputation than n. at all*; *poetry we have almost n.*). (Adv.) by no amount, not at all, (w. *the* & comparat., *so*, or *too*; *am n. the better for it*; *n. the less*, = NEVER*theless*; *are n. so fond of him*; *the pay is n. too high*). [OE *nán* (*ne* not, ONE)]

none·ntity, n. Non-existence, non-existent thing, figment, (nŏn-); person or thing of no importance, cipher, (non-). [NON-(2)]

nones, n. pl. (Rom. Ant.) ninth day by inclusive reckoning before IDES, i.e. 7th of Mar., May, July, Oct., & 5th of other months; (Eccl.) daily office orig. said at ninth hour or 3 p.m. [Rom.-Ant. sense f. L *nonae*, eccl. sense pl. of rare *none* f. L *nona*, (*nonus* ninth); cf. NOON]

nonesuch. See NONSUCH.

nōne·t, n. (mus.). Composition for nine instruments or voices. [f. It. *nonetto* (*nono* ninth f. L *nonus*)]

noni·llion (no-), n. Ninth power of million, 1 with 54 ciphers. [see NONARY, BILLION]

nō·nius, n. Contrivance for graduating mathematical instruments, of which the VERNIER is an improved form. [Latinized from *Nuñez*, Portuguese inventor]

nonparei·l (-rĕl), a. & n. Unrivalled or unique (person, thing); (Print.) size of TYPE; kinds of comfit, apple, bird, wheat, moth, &c. [F (NON-, L *par* equal, *-cul*dim.)]

nonplŭ·s, n., & v.t. (-ss-). State of perplexity, standstill, (usu. *at a n.*, perplexed, *reduce* &c. *to a n.*); (vb) reduce to hopeless perplexity. [f. L *non plus* not more]

non-re·sident, a. & n. (Clergyman) not residing where his duties require him, absentee (incumbent); (person) sojourning in place only for short time or residing elsewhere. So **non-re·sid**ENCE n. [NON-]

no·nsense, n. & int. Absurd or meaningless words or ideas, foolish or extravagant conduct, arrangement &c. that one disapproves of, (int., = you are talking or proposing n., it surely cannot be true, &c.); *n.-book*, meant to amuse by absurdity; *n. verses*, having no sense or an absurd one. Hence **nonse·nsi**CAL a., **nonse·nsical**LY[2] adv. [NON-(2)]

no·nsuch, none-, n. Person or thing that is unrivalled, paragon; kind of lucerne. [NONE, SUCH, usu. now assim. to NON-]

no·nsuit (-ūt), n., & v.t. Stoppage of suit by judge when plaintiff fails to make out legal case or bring sufficient evidence; (vb) subject to n. [NON-(2)]

nonus. See PRIMUS[1].

noo·dle, n. Simpleton. Hence **noo·dle**DOM n. [?]

nŏŏk, n. Out-of-the-way corner, recess, secluded place. [?]

nōōn, n. Twelve o'clock in the day, midday; *noonday, noontide*, midday. [OE *nón* f. L *nona* (*hora*) ninth hour; orig. =3 p.m.]

noose, n., & v.t. Loop with running knot, tightening as string is pulled, esp. in snare, lasso, or hangman's halter; the marriage tie; snare or bond. (Vb) capture with n., ensnare; make n. on (cord); arrange (cord) in n. *round* neck &c. [cf. OF *nous* f. L *nodus* knot]

nō·pal, n. American cactus grown in plantations for breeding cochineal. Hence **no·pal**RY(3) n. [Sp., f. Mex. *nopalli* cactus]

nor, adv. & conj. (Archaic) neither (as the first *nor* in *n. gold n. silver*); (conj.) & not, & no more, neither, & not either, (*had neither arms n. provisions*; *not a man n. a child was to be seen*; *I said I had not seen it, n. had I*; *all that is true, n. must we forget*; also poet. & archaic w. omission of preceding *neither* or *n.*, as *thou nor I have made the world*). [prob. f. obs. *nother* (OE *nā* see NATHLESS, WHETHER)]

nor'-. See NORTH.

Nor·denfelt, n. Kind of machine-gun. [Swedish inventor]

Nor·dic, a. (ethnol.). Of the tall blond dolichocephalic race found esp. in Scandinavia & northern Britain (of more limited application than *Teutonic*). [G *nord* north + -IC]

Nor·folk (-ok), n. English county (*N. capon*, red herring; *N. dumpling, turkey*, inhabitant or native of N.; *N. Howard* slang, bed-bug; *N. jacket*, man's loose jacket with waistband; *N. plover*, stone-curlew).

nor·land, n. Northern region. [for *north-*]

norm, n. Standard, pattern, type. [f. L *norma* carpenter's square]

nor·mal, a. & n. (Geom.) standing at right angles, perpendicular; conforming to standard, regular, usual, typical; *n. school*, for training teachers; hence **norma·l**ITY (also irreg. **nor·malc**Y) n., **nor·mal**IZE(3) v.t., **normaliza·**TION n., **nor·mal**LY[2] adv. (N.): (Geom.) n. line; (Physics) average or mean of observed quantities; usual state, level, &c., n. temperature (98·4°) of human body. [f. L *normalis* (prec., -AL)]

Nor·man, n. & a. Inhabitant or native of Normandy, descendant of mixed Scandinavian & Frankish race there established; =*N.-French* below; =*N. style* below. (Adj.) of the Nn. (*N. Conquest*, of England by Nn. 1066; *N. English*, English as spoken or influenced by Nn.; *N. French*, French as spoken by Nn. or later in English law-courts; *N.* STYLE in architecture, whence **Normane·**SQUE a.); hence **Nor·man**ISM(2, 4) n., **Nor·man**IZE(3, 4) v.t. & i., **Normaniza·**TION n. [f. OF *Normans* pl. f. Teut. NORTH*man*]

Norn, n. One of the female fates of Scandinavian mythology. [ON, etym. dub.]

No·rroy, n. Third KING *of Arms*, with jurisdiction north of the Trent. [f. AF *nor-* NORTH, *roy* king]

Norse, n. & a. The Norwegian language (*Old N.*, language of Norway & its colonies down to 14th c.); (adj.) Norwegian, of Norway, so *Nor·seland, Nor·seman.* [prob. f. Du. *noorsch* (*noord* NORTH, -ISH[1])]

Norsk, n. & a. =prec. [Scand.]

north, adv., n., & a., (abbr. N.; in compp. & derivv. often shortened to *nor'*-). Towards or in the region lying to right of observer on equator at equinox who faces setting sun (*n.* BY *east* &c.; *n. of*, further n. than; DUE[1] *n.*; *lies* &c. *n. & south*, lengthwise along line running between n. & south); *n.-ea·st, n.-we·st*, advv., nn., & aa., (regions) midway between n. & east, west, *n.-n.-east, n.-n.-west*, advv., nn., & aa., (regions) midway between n. & n.-east, n.-west, (with uses & derivatives corresponding to those of *north*; so esp. *n.-ea·sterly, -we·sterly, -ea·stern, -we·stern, -ea·stward, -we·stward, -ea·stwardly,-we·st-*

wardly, see NORTHERLY &c.; *n.-east, n.-west, passage*, passages for ships along northern coasts of Europe & Asia, northern coast of America, formerly thought of as possible routes to E., & from Atlantic to Pacific; *the N.-west*, = N.-W. territories of Canada); hence **nor·th**WARD adv., n., & a., **nor·th**WARDS adv. & n. (Noun) cardinal point lying n. (*magnetic n.*, point indicated by n. end of compass-needle); northern part of England (beyond Humber), Great Britain, Scotland, Ireland, or Europe; (U.S.) northern States in which slavery did not exist; northern part *of* any country; n. wind. (Adj.) situated, dwelling, in or more towards the n. (*N. Germany, Wales, America*; *the N. Germans*; *n. latitude*; *n.* POLE[2], whence **north-po·l**AR a.; *n. transept*); facing n. (*n. window, aspect*); coming from the n. (*n. wind*; *n. light*, esp. as desired by painters); *N. Britain, Briton*, Scot(land); *N. Country*, n. part of England or Great Britain (*N.-cou·ntryman*, native of northern England; *n.-cou·ntry*, from or characteristic of *N. c.*); *Nor·thland* (poet.), northern lands, northern part of a country; *north light*, Aurora Borealis; *Northman*, native of Norway or Scandinavia; *N. Sea*, between Britain, Netherlands, Germany, & Scandinavia; *N. star*, POLE[2]*-star*. [com.-Teut.; OE *north*, cf. Du. *noord*, G *nord*]

north-ea·ster, n. N.-E. wind. [-ER[1]]

nor·ther (-th-), n. (U.S.). Strong cold north wind blowing in autumn & winter over Texas, Florida, & Gulf of Mexico. [-ER[1]]

nor·therly (-dh-), a. & adv. =foll. (rare); (of direction) towards the north; (of wind) blowing from the north or thereabouts. [f. NORTH as EASTERLY]

nor·thern (-dh-), a. & n. Living or situated in, coming from, the north esp. of England or Europe, (U.S.) of the NORTH; (of wind) northerly (rare); characteristic of the north (*a pallid n. day*); *n. lights*, Aurora Borealis; hence **nor·thern**ER[1](4) n., **nor·thern**MOST a. (N.) northerner. [-ERN]

nor·thing (-th-), n. Northward progress or deviation in sailing or travelling (*two miles n.*; *have made very little n.*). [-ING[1]]

Northu·mbrian, a. & n. (Native, dialect) of ancient Northumbria (England N. of Humber) or modern Northumberland. [*Northumber*, person living beyond Humber, + -IAN]

nor·thwardly, adv. & a. Northwards; (of wind) northerly. [-LY[2]]

north-we·ster, n. N.-W. wind. [-ER[1]]

nor·ward(s). =NORTH*ward(s)*.

Norwē·gian, a. & n. (Native, language) of Norway. [f. med. L *Norvegia* + -AN, w. assim. to *Norway*]

nor'-we·ster, n. North-wester; glass of strong liquor; oilskin hat, sou'-wester. [NOR'-]

nose (nōz), n., & v.t. & i. Member of face or head placed above mouth containing nostrils & serving as organ of smell (*parson's n.*, rump of cooked fowl; *n. of wax*, person or thing easily influenced or moulded; *make* LONG[1] *n.*; *keep n. to* GRINDSTONE; *as plain as the n. in your face*, easily seen; *count* or *tell nn.*, count supporters &c., decide question by mere numbers; *follow* one's *n.*, go straight forward, be guided by instinct; *poke, thrust*, &c., one's *n.*, pry or intrude *into* something; *turn up* one's *n. at*, show disdain for; *cut off* one's *n. to spite* one's *face*, indulge pique at one's own expense; *put* one's *n. out of joint*, supplant or disconcert or frustrate him; *bite* or *snap* one's *n. off*, answer him snappishly; *pay through the n.*, be overcharged, have to pay exorbitant prices; *speak through* one's *n.*, pronounce with nasal twang; LEAD[1] *by the n.*; *under* one's *n.*, straight before him, regardless of his displeasure); sense of smell (*has a good n.*, esp. of dogs, & fig. of detectives &c.); odour, perfume, of hay, tea, &c.; open end or nozzle of pipe, tube, bellows, retort, &c.; prow; projecting part; *n.-ape*, proboscis-monkey; *n.-bag*, containing fodder for hanging to horse's head; *n.-band*, lower band of bridle passing over n. & attached to cheek-straps; *n.-dive*, aeroplane's downward plunge (v.i., make this); *n.-flute*, musical instrument blown with n. among Siamese, Fijians, &c.; *nosegay* [GAY in obs. n. use = toy], bunch of (esp. sweet-scented) flowers; *n.-monkey*, proboscis-monkey; *n.-piece*, = n.-band, also part of microscope to which object-glass is attached; *n.-pipe*, piece of piping used as nozzle; *n.-rag* (slang), pocket-handkerchief; *n.-ring*, fixed in n. of bull &c. for leading, also ornament worn by savages; *n.-warmer* (slang), short pipe; hence **(-)nos**ED[2], **no·se**LESS, aa. (Vb) perceive smell of, discover by smell, (fig.) detect (*noses a job in everything*), smell *out*; rub with the n., thrust n. against or into; sniff (*at, about* adv. & prep.), pry or search (*after, for*); push one's way, push (one's *way*), with the n. (esp. of ship); (of strata &c.) dip *in*, basset *out*. [OE *nosu*, cf. MLG *nose*, Du. *neus*, also NESS]

no·ser, n. Strong head wind (esp. *dead n.*). [prec., -ER[1]]

no·sing, n. Rounded edge of step, moulding, &c., or metal shield for it. [NOSE, -ING[1]]

nŏso-, comb. form of Gk *nosos* disease, as -GRAPHY, systematic description of diseases; -LOGY, (branch of medical science dealing with) classification of diseases (so -LO·GICAL, -LOGIST).

nosta·lgia, n. Home-sickness as a disease. Hence **nosta·lg**IC a. [f. Gk *nostos* return home, Gk *algos* pain, -IA[1]]

no·stoc, n. Kinds of gelatinous unicellular algae. [name invented by Paracelsus]

Nostradā·mus, n. Prediction-monger, professed seer. [Latinized f. M. de *Nostredame,* French physician who made prophecies 1555]

no·stril, n. Either opening in nose admitting air to lungs & smells to olfactory nerves (*stink in* one's *nn.*, be offensive to him). Hence **(-)nostrill**ED² a. [OE *nosthyrl* (NOSE, obs. *thirl* f. OE *thyrel* hole cf. THRILL)]

no·strum, n. Medicine prepared by person recommending it, quack remedy, patent medicine; pet scheme for political or social reform, special device. [L, neut. of *noster* our, my]

no·sy (-zĭ), a. & n. Large-nosed (person; esp. of Duke of Wellington); ill-smelling (esp. of heated corn, mouldy hay, &c.); fragrant (of tea); sensitive to bad smells; (slang) inquisitive (esp. *N. Parker,* busybody). [-Y²]

not, n't (see below), adv. negativing & following ordinary verbs (archaic for usu. neg. form with *do*; *I know n.*; *I doubt n.*; *say n. so*; *fear n.*; *saidst thou n.?*); (often *n't* joined to word) negativing auxiliaries & vb *be,* & following them or (in questions having *not* in full) their subjects (*I cannot* or *can't say*; *he will n.* or *won't,* or archaic *he'll n., come*; *she is n., isn't,* or vulg. *aint, here*; *do n.,* or usu. *don't, stir*; *didn't you,* or formally *did you n., tell me?*; *am I n.,* or *aint I, aren't we, smart?*); negativing & preceding participles & infinitives (*n. knowing, I cannot say*; *begged him n. to move*); used elliptically for negative sentence or verb or phrase (*Are you ill? N. at all. N. so. If it clears we will go out*; *if n., n. Popular or n., it is right. I would as soon do it as n.*); preceding *that* with sense *it is not to be inferred, however, that,* or *but what* or (formal) *but that* or (archaic) *but* with sense *all the same* or *nevertheless* (*If he said so—n. that he ever did—he lied. I cannot do it*; *n. but what* &c. *a stronger man might*); preceding word &c. that is to be rejected for one that follows with *but* or to emphasize by contrast one already used (*He is n. my son, but yours,* or *but my nephew. He is your son, n.* or *& n. mine*); preceding emphatic appended pronoun (*the Chinese will not fight, n. they*); preceding *a* with sense *n. one* (*not a hair of your head shall be touched*); preceding in litotes or periphrasis a word of opposite sense to that required (*n. a few, n. seldom*; *n. once* or or *nor twice,* many times; *n. unconnected with*; *n. reluctant,* only too glad); *n. at* HOME; *n.-being,* non-existence; *n. half* (adv., slang), very, very much, ('*Was he annoyed?*' '*N. half*', i.e. yes, exceedingly); *n.* OUT; *n.-self,* = NON-*ego*; *n. sufficient,* or usu. *N.S.*, banker's mark on dishonoured cheque. [contr. of NOUGHT]

nōta bĕ·nĕ (-ta), vb imperat. (*abbr.* N.B.). Observe what follows, take notice, (usu. drawing attention to a qualification of what has preceded). [L, = note well]

nōtabi·lity, n. Prominent person, (rare) notable object or thing worth seeing; worthiness of notice (*names of no historical n.*); (archaic) housewifely skill. [foll., -BILITY]

nō·table, a. & n. Worthy of note, remarkable, striking, eminent; (Chem.) perceptible (*a n. quantity of*); (of women; *often pr.* nŏt-) capable, bustling, housewifely; hence **no·tab**LY² adv.; (n.) eminent person (esp. *Assembly of Nn.*, irregular council serving as temporary parliament in emergencies). [F, f. L *notabilis* (NOTE², -ABLE)]

nō·tary, n. Person publicly authorized to draw up or attest contracts &c., protest bills of exchange &c., & perform other formalities (chiefly used about foreign countries; also *n. public*). Hence **notār·**IAL a., **notar·ial**LY² adv. [f. L *notarius* secretary (NOTE¹,², -ARY¹)]

nota·tion, n. Representing of numbers, quantities, &c., by symbols, any set of symbols used for this, esp. in Arith., Alg., & Mus.; SCALE³ *of n.* [f. L *notatio* (NOTE², -ATION)]

notch, n., & v.t. V-shaped indentation in edge or on convex surface; nick made on stick &c. by way of keeping count, (now rare) run scored at cricket; (U.S.) defile, pass; *n.-wing,* kinds of moth; hence **no·tch**Y², **notch**ED² (bot., zool.), aa. (Vb) make nn. in; make *into* saw &c. by notching; score (items &c.; often *up, down*) by nn.; make (number of runs) at cricket; secure or insert (steps in staircase &c.) by nn. [f. F *hoche* with (*a*)*n* prefixed, cf. NEWT]

note¹, n. Written sign representing pitch & duration of a musical sound; key of pianoforte &c.; single tone of definite pitch made by musical instrument, voice, &c.; (single tone in) bird's song or call; significant sound or way of expressing oneself (*there is a n. of self-complacency in his voice*; *sound the n. of war*; *change* one's *n.*, become suddenly more, or less, aggressive, humble, &c.). Sign, token, characteristic, distinguishing feature, proof of genuineness, guarantee consisting *of,* (*these are the nn. of Neo-paganism*; *catholicity is one n. of the true Church*; *has the n. of catholicity*); stigma, mark of censure, (*on which the law has set a n. of infamy*); mark *of exclamation* or *admiration, interrogation.* Brief record of facts, impressions, or topics for speech or article (usu. pl.; *make* or *take a n. of, nn.*; COMPARE¹ *nn.*; *preaches from nn.*; *spoke for an hour without a n.*); annotation appended to passage in book &c.; short or informal letter; formal diplomatic communication; (usu. *n. of hand*) written promise to pay sum by certain time; BANK³-*n.*; CIRCULAR *n.* Eminence (*critic, philosopher, person,* *of n.*, distinguished); notice, attention, (*worthy of n.*; *take n. of*), whence **no·te-**WORTHY a. *N.-book*, for entering memoranda in; *n.-paper*, kinds used for (esp. private) correspondence. Hence **no·te-**LESS a., **no·te**LET n. [OF, f. L *nota* mark]

note², v.t. Observe, notice, give attention to; set down, set *down*, as thing to be remembered or observed; annotate (book &c.); (p.p.) celebrated, well known *for*. [f. OF *noter* f. L *notare* (prec.)]

no·thing (nŭ-), n. & adv. No thing (with adj. following, as *n. great is easy*); not anything, nought, (*has n. in him*, is insignificant or without individuality; *there is n. in it*, it is untrue or unimportant, & see IN¹; *n. doing*, slang announcement of failure or refusal of request; *n. venture n. have*, excuse for or encouragement to bold action; *n. like* LEATHER; NECK *or n.*; *dance on n.*, be hanged; *fade away* &c. *to n.*, disappear gradually; *no n.* colloq., conclusion of negative list, as *no bread, no butter, no cheese, no n.*; *n. else than* or *but, n. but, force* &c., merely force &c., force &c. alone, unmistakable force &c.; *there is n. for it but to*, no alternative; *n. if not critical* &c., critical as leading characteristic; *get thing for n.*, gratis; *have endured it for n.*, to no purpose; so *it was not for n. that he read Plato*; *that is n. to you*, not your concern; *make n. of*, treat as trifle; *make n. of doing*, do without hesitation or as ordinary matter; *can make n. of*, cannot understand, find solution of, use, develop, or deal with; *come to n.*, turn out useless, fail, not amount to anything; *have n. to do with*, not be concerned with, avoid dealing with or society of; *all to n.*, longest odds); trifle, very inferior thing, (*that is n.*, i.e. in comparison with what I am going to tell you; *he is n. without his money*; *learning is n. to*, i.e. compared with, *genius*); (Arith.) no amount, nought, (*multiply 6 by n., & the result is n.*); non-existence, what does not exist; (with *a* & pl.) trifling thing, event, remark, or person (*the little nn. of life*; *whisper soft nn.*; *the new commander-in-chief was a n.*); (of religious belief) *be n.*, belong to no denomination, be an atheist or agnostic, whence **nothing**ĀR·IAN n. (Adv.) not at all, in no way, (*differs n. from*; *is n. less than monstrous*, positively; *helps us n.*; *avails n.*; *is n. like as* or *so good* &c.; *is n. near so extensive*; *n.*LO(A)TH. [NO¹, THING]

no·thingness, n. Non-existence, the non-existent; worthlessness, triviality, unimportance, insignificance, trifles. [-NESS]

nō·tice, n., & v.t. Intimation, intelligence, warning, (*give, have, n.*; *at short, ten minutes'*, &c., *n.*, with such time for preparation); placard &c. conveying information or directions; formal intimation of something or instructions *to* do something (*n. to* QUIT; *till* FURTHER¹ *n.*), announcement by party to agreement that it is to terminate at specified time (esp. between landlord & tenant or employer & employed; *give a week's* &c. *n.*); heed, attention, cognizance, observation, (*come into n.*, attract attention; *takes no n. of it*, does not observe it, or takes no action in consequence of it; *brought it to his n.*; *take n. that*, I warn you that; baby *takes n.*, shows signs of intelligence); paragraph or article upon something in newspaper, esp. review of book, play, &c.; *n.-board*, bearing n. or provided for nn. to be posted on. (Vb) remark upon, speak of; perceive, take n. of; treat with politeness or condescension; serve with n., give n. to, (*was noticed to quit*); hence **no·tice-**ABLE a., **no·ticeab**LY² adv. [F, f. L *notitia* (*notus* p.p. of *noscere* know, -ICE)]

nō·tifiable, a. (Of diseases) that must be notified to public-health authorities. [-ABLE]

nō·tify̆, v.t. Make known, announce, report; inform, give notice to, (person *of, that*, or abs.). Hence **noti**FICA·TION n. [f. F *notifier* f. L *notificare* (NOTICE¹, -FY)]

nō·tion (-shn), n. General concept under which particular thing may be classed (in Philos., *first, second, n.*, = *first, second,* INTENTION); idea, conception, (*the n. of my doing it is absurd*; *what he means I have not the haziest n.*); view, opinion, theory, (*has a n. that*; *such is the common n.*); faculty, capability, or intention *of* (*has no n. of obeying, obedience, discipline, letting himself be made a fool of*); (U.S.) something in the way of miscellaneous wares, esp. cheap useful ingenious article; (pl.) traditional special vocabulary of Winchester College. [f. L *notio* (NOTICE, -ION)]

no·tional, a. (Of knowledge &c.) speculative, not based on experiment or demonstration, whence **no·tional**IST(2) n., **no·tional**LY² adv.; (of things, relations, &c.) existing only in thought, imaginary; (of persons) fanciful. [f. med. L *notionalis* (prec., -AL)]

nōto-, comb. form of Gk *nōton* back, in scientific terms, as *-bra·nchiate* having dorsal gills, *-chord* cartilaginous band forming basis of spinal column, *-ne·cta* [Gk *nēktēs* swimmer] water-beetle swimming on back, the boat-fly.

Nōtogae·a (-jēa), n. Zoological region comprising Australian, New-Zealand, & neotropical regions. [f. Gk *notos* south, *gaia* land]

notor·ious (no-), a. (Of facts) well or commonly known (esp. *it is n. that*); (with designations of persons, conduct, &c., that imply condemnation) undisguised, talked of, generally known to deserve the name, (*n. smuggler, offender, vice*); unfavourably known (*for* some quality or conduct, or abs.; *a ship n. for ill-luck*; *the n. Titus Oates*). Hence or cogn.

nōtorī·ety n., **notor·ious**LY[2] adv. [f. med. L *notorius* (NOTICE, -ORY), -OUS]

Notre-Dame (F), n. The Cathedral of Paris. [F, = our Lady]

notwithsta·nding, prep., adv., & conj. In spite of, not the less for, (*n. his resistance; this n.* The second order is the orig., the prep. having been developed f. a part. abs.); (adv.) nevertheless, all the same; (conj., developed from prep. or part. abs. with *that*, still sometimes retained) although, in spite of the fact (*that*), (archaic). [NOT, WITHSTAND, -ING[2]]

nougat (nōō·gah), n. Sweetmeat of sugar, nuts, &c. [F (L *nux nucis* nut, -ATE[2])]

nought (nawt), n. Nothing (poet., archaic, & arith.; *come, bring, to n.*, be ruined or fail, ruin or baffle; *set at n.*, disregard, ridicule); figure 0, cipher, (*nn. & crosses*, child's game). [OE *nówiht* (*ne* not, see AUGHT, NAUGHT)]

nou·menon (now-), n. (pl. *-ena*). Object of intellectual intuition devoid of all phenomenal attributes. Hence **nou·men**AL a., **nou·menal**LY[2] adv. [f. Gk *nooumenon* neut. pres. part. pass. of *noeō* apprehend, taken by Kant as antithesis to *phenomenon*]

noun (nown), n. (gram.). Word used as name of person or thing, substantive; (formerly) substantive or adjective (*n. substantive*, n.; *n. adjective*, adjective). Hence **nou·n**AL a. (rare). [AF, f. OF *nun, nom*, f. L *nomen* name (*noscere* KNOW, -MEN)]

nou·rish (nŭ-), v.t. Sustain with food (lit. & fig.), whence **nou·rish**ING[2] a.; foster, cherish, nurse, (feeling, hope, &c.) in one's heart. [f. OF *norir* (-ISH[2]) f. L *nutrire*]

nou·rishment, n. Sustenance, food; nourishing. [f. OF *nourissement* (prec., -MENT)]

nous (nows), n. (Gk philos.) mind, intellect; (colloq.) common sense, gumption. [Gk]

nŏ·vel[1], n. One of the tales in such a collection as Boccaccio's *Decameron*; fictitious prose narrative of sufficient length to fill one or more volumes portraying characters & actions representative of real life in continuous plot, *the n.*, this type of literature, whence **novel**E·SE n.; (Rom. law) new decree supplementary to the Codex. [f. It. *novella* f. L neut. pl. as foll.]

nŏ·vel[2], a. Of new kind or nature, strange, hitherto unknown. [OF, f. L *novellus* dim. of *novus* new]

novele·tte, n. Short novel, story of moderate length; (Mus.) piano piece of free form with several themes. [-ETTE]

no·velist, n. Novel-writer. Hence **novel·i·stic** a. [-IST]

no·velize, v.t. Convert (drama, facts) into a novel. Hence **noveliza·tion** n. [-IZE]

no·velty, n. New or unusual thing or occurrence; novel character *of* something. [f. OF *novelté* (NOVEL[2], -TY)]

Nove·mber, n. Eleventh month. [L (*novem* nine); cf. DECEMBER]

nover·cal, a. Stepmotherly. [f. L *novercalis* (*noverca* stepmother, -AL)]

nŏ·vice, n. Person received in religious house on probation before taking the vows; new convert; inexperienced person, beginner, tiro. [OF, f. L *novicius* (*novus* new, -ITIOUS[1])]

novi·ciate, -iti-, (-shĭat), n. Novice's probationary period or initiation or apprenticeship; novice; quarters assigned to novices. [f. F *noviciat* f. med. L *novitiatus* (prec., -ATE[1])]

nŏ·vocaine, n. (pharm.). A regional anaesthetic. [proprietary name, f. L *novus* new + (CO)CAINE]

now, adv., conj., & n. At the present time; by this time; under the present circumstances (*I cannot n. ever believe you again; n. that I know you, it is different*); immediately (*must go n.*); in the immediate past (*just n.*, & archaic *even, but, n.*); (in narrative) then, next, by that time, (*Caesar now marched east; it was n. clear*); (*every*) *n. & then* or *again*, from time to time, intermittently; *n. — n., n. — then, n. — & again*, at one moment — at another; *n. or never!*, this is the nick of time; (without temporal force, giving various tones, soothing, reproving, explanatory, threatening, &c., to sentence) pray, I beg, I insist, I warn you, & yet, you must know, it must be admitted, surely, (*N. what do you mean by it?. Oh, come n.!. No nonsense n.!. You have revealed the secret; n. you were paid to keep it. Now Barabbas was a robber. N. this was bad enough, but —. N. then, what mischief are you at?. You don't mean it, n.*). (Conj.; orig., as often still, *now* adv. followed by *that*) consequently upon or simultaneously with the fact that (*N. I am a man I think otherwise. N. you mention it, I do remember*). (N.) this time, the present, (chiefly after prepp.; *is there by, ere, till, n., from n. till*, &c.; *read the future in the n.*). [Aryan; OE *nu*, also in all older Teut. langg., cf. Skr. *nu*, Gk *nun*, L *nunc*]

now·aday, a. Of nowadays. [f. foll.]

now·adays, adv. & n. (At) the present day, (in) these advanced or newfangled times. [NOW adv., A[2], DAY, -ES]

Nowel (nōĕ·l), int. expr. joy in Christmas carols. [f. OF *noel* f. L NATAL*is*]

no·where (-hwār, -wār), adv. In, at, to, no place (*n. near*, not nearly; *be, come in, n.*, not be placed in race or competition). [NO, WHERE]

no·xious (-kshus), a. Harmful, unwholesome. Hence **no·xious**LY[2] adv., **no·xious**NESS n. [f. L *noxius* (*noxa* harm), -OUS]

noyade (nwahyah·d), n. Execution by

drowning, esp. wholesale as in France in 1794. [F]

noyau (nwahyō·), n. Liqueur of brandy flavoured with fruit-kernels. [F (L *nux nucis* nut, -AL)]

no·zzle, n. Spout, mouth-piece, end fitted to hose &c. [NOSE, -LE(1)]

-n't. See NOT.

nū·ance (or as F), n. Delicate difference in or shade of meaning, feeling, opinion, colour, &c. [F, f. *nuer* to shade, ult. f. L *nubes* cloud]

nub, nu·bble, nn. Small knob or lump, esp. of coal. Hence **nu·bbl**Y[2] a. [= KNOB]

nū·bĭle, a. Marriageable (esp. of women). Hence **nubi·l**ITY n. [f. L *nubilis* (*nubere* become wife)]

nū·chal (-kl), a. Of nape of neck. [f. med. L *nucha* spinal cord, of Arab. orig.]

nūci-, comb. form of L *nux nucis* nut, as -FEROUS, -FORM, -VOROUS.

nū·cleole, n. (biol.). Nucleus of or within a nucleus. Hence **nu·cleol**AR[1], **nu·cleola·ted** [-ATE[2]], aa., **nucleolo**- comb. form. [f. L *nucleolus* dim. of foll.]

nū·clĕus, n. (pl. *-eī*). (Astron.) condensed part of comet's head; central part or thing round which others are collected, kernel of aggregate or mass, beginning meant to receive additions, central part of ovule, seed, plant-cell, animal cell, &c., portion of medullary matter from which nerves spring, (*the n. of a sun-spot, community, library, story, empire,* &c.). Hence **nu·cle**AL, **nu·cle**AR[1], **nu·cle**ARY, aa., **nu·cleo**- comb. form. [L, f. *nucula* dim. of *nux nucis* nut]

nude, a. & n. Naked, bare, unclothed, undraped, (*n. contract* in law, lacking a consideration & therefore void unless under seal); so **nudi**- comb. form (zool.), **nu·d**ITY n.; (as colour adj., esp. of stockings) flesh-coloured. (N.) n. figure in painting or sculpture; *the n.,* the undraped figure, undraped state. [f. L *nudus*]

nudge, v.t., & n. Push slightly with elbow to draw attention privately, (fig.) draw attention of; (n.) such push. [?]

nū·gae (-gē, -jē), n. pl. Trifles, learned triflings, profitless minutiae. [L]

nū·gatory, a. Trifling, worthless, futile; inoperative, not valid. [f. L *nugatorius* (*nugari* trifle f. prec., -ORY)]

nu·ggar, n. Large broad-beamed boat used on upper Nile. [native]

nu·gget, n. Rough lump of native gold. [?]

nui·sance (nūs-), n. Anything injurious or obnoxious to the community or member of it for which legal remedy may be had (*commit no n.,* notice to passengers not to defile place); obnoxious person, offensive object, annoying action, anything disagreeable. [OF (*nuire nuis-* f. L *nocēre* hurt, -ANCE)]

null, a. & n. Not binding, invalid, (often *n. & void*); without character or expression; non-existent, amounting to nothing, (rare); (n.) dummy letter in a cipher. [f. L *nullus* (*ne* not, *ullus* any)]

nu·lla bō·na, n. Sheriff's return stating that party has no goods to be distrained upon. [L, = no goods]

nu·llah, n. (Anglo-Ind.). Stream, watercourse, ravine. [f. Hind. *nala*]

nu·llifȳ, v.t. Cancel, neutralize. So **nulli**FICA·TION n. [f. LL *nullificare* (NULL, -FY)]

nu·llipore, n. Kind of marine vegetation. [f. L *nullus* no + PORE[1]]

nu·llity, n. Being null, invalidity, (esp. *n. of marriage*; *n. suit,* for this); act, document, &c., that is null; nothingness; a mere nothing; a nonentity. [f. med. L *nullitas* (NULL, -ITY)]

numb (-m), a., & v.t. Deprived of feeling or power of motion (*n. with cold* &c.; *n. hand* slang, clumsy person); *n.-fish,* the Electric Ray or Torpedo; *n.-skull,* NUMSKULL; hence **nu·mb**LY[2] (-mlĭ) adv., **nu·mb**NESS n.; (vb) make n., (fig.) stupefy, paralyse. [earlier *num* p.p. of obs. *nim* take, com.-Teut., cf. G *nehmen,* prob. cogn. w. Gk *nemō* occupy]

nu·mber[1], n. (written N°, for *numero* = in number, with pl. N^os^, before distinguishing figure, as *bedroom N° 15,* N°s 1–10). Tale, count, sum, company, or aggregate, of persons (also *of*) or things (also *of*) or abstract units, symbol or figure representing such aggregate, ticket &c. bearing such figure, person or thing (esp. single issue of magazine, or part of opera &c.) whose place in series is indicated by such figure, (*the n. of fools is infinite*; *Numbers,* abbr. *Num.,* O.T. book containing census; *the greatest n. on record is 59 persons*; *to the n. of 80,* as many as; GOLDEN *n.*; *science of nn.,* arithmetic; *took the cabman's n.*; *sleeps in N° 5*; *N° 9 (pill),* army doctors' reputed panacea; *N° 10 Downing Street, N° 10,* (used for) Prime Minister's official residence (when he is also First Lord of the Treasury); *lose the n. of* one's *mess,* die; one's *n. goes up,* he dies; *n. one,* oneself, esp. in *take care of n. one,* also (Nav. slang) first lieutenant; *story issued in nn.,* in parts successively published bearing nn.; *back n.,* earlier issue of magazine, fig. anything out of date; *is not of our n.,* included among us; *is now added to the n. of my enemies*); (sing. or pl.) *large, small,* &c., or large, collection or company *of* or abs. (*were present in great, only in small,* or *in, nn.*; *saw a great,* or *a, n. of birds*; *a small n. came*; *there are nn. who live by begging*); (pl.) numerical preponderance (*won by nn. or force of nn.*); numerical reckoning (*the laws of n. & proportion pervade Nature*; *without n.,* innumerable, also **nu·mber**LESS a.; *in n.,* when counted or estimated, numerically, as *one people exceeds another in n.*); (Gram.) class of word-forms including all singular, all plural, or all dual &c. words (*Greek has three nn.*; *'things' is of the plural n.*);

rhythm; (pl.) groups of musical notes, metrical feet, verses. [f. OF *nombre* f. L *numerus*]

nu·mber², v.t. Count, ascertain n. of; (pass.) be restricted in n. (*his days* or *years are numbered*, he has not long to live); include, regard as, *among, in,* or *with* some class; assign a n. to, distinguish with a n.; have lived, live, (so many years); be able to show (so many inhabitants &c.); amount to (specified n.). [f. OF *nombrer* f. L *numerare* (prec.)]

nū·merable, a. That can be numbered. [f. L *numerabilis* (prec., -ABLE)]

nū·meral, a. & n. (Word, figure, group of figures) denoting a number; of number. [f. LL *numeralis* (NUMBER¹, -AL)]

nūmera·tion, n. Method or process of numbering or computing; calculation; assigning of numbers; (Arith.) expression in words of number written in figures, *n. table,* showing value of figures according to their place in system of notation. [f. L *numeratio* (NUMBER², -ATION)]

nū·merātor, n. Number above line in vulgar fraction showing how many of the parts indicated by the denominator are taken; person who numbers. [LL (NUMBER², -OR²)]

nūmĕ·ric, n. What is either a number, a proper or improper fraction, or an incommensurable ratio. [f. L *numerus* number, -IC]

nume·rical, a. Of, in, denoting, &c., number. Hence **nume·rical**LY² adv. [-AL]

nū·merous, a. Comprising many units (*a n. acquaintance, library, family, army, class*); coming from many individuals (*the n. voice of the people; a n. hum*); (archaic) thronged (*a n. country, university, dinner*); (of verse or prose) rhythmic, harmonious. Hence **nu·merous**LY² adv. [f. L *numerosus* (NUMBER¹, -OUS)]

nūmismă·tic (-z-), a. Of coins or coinage. So **numisma·**TICALLY adv., **numisma·**TICS, **numi·smat**IST(3), **numismato·**LOGY nn. [F (*-ique*), f. L (*num-*) f. Gk *nomisma -atos* coin (*nomizō* use currently f. *nomos* custom), -IC]

nu·mmary, nu·mmūlary, aa. Of, in, coin. [f. L *nummarius* (*nummus* coin, -ARY¹), & *nummulus* dim. + -ARY¹]

nu·mmet, n. (dial.). Lunch. [=*noon meat*]

nu·mmūlite, n. Disk-like fossil shell of Tertiary strata. [*nummulus* (see NUMMARY), -ITE¹(2)]

nu·mnah, n. Saddle-cloth, pad placed under saddle. [Anglo-Ind. *numdah* felt f. Hind. *namda* f. Pers. *namad* carpet]

nu·mskull, n. Dolt or his head. [NUMB]

nun, n. Woman living in convent usu. under vow of poverty, chastity, & obedience; kinds of bird & moth; *n.'s cloth,* thin woollen stuff; *n.'s thread,* fine white sewing cotton; *n.'s veiling,* thin dress-stuff. Hence **nu·n**HOOD, **nu·nn**ERY(3), **nu·n**SHIP, nn., **nu·n**LIKE, **nu·nn**ISH¹, aa. [OE *nunne* f.eccl. L *nonna* fem. of *nonnus* monk, orig. = old man, gaffer]

nu·n-buoy, n. Buoy circular in middle & tapering to each end. [f. obs. *nun* spinning-top, perh. f. prec.]

nunc dĭmi·ttis, n. The canticle *Lord, now lettest thou* (*sing n. d.*, be willing to depart from life &c.). [L, = now lettest thou go]

nu·nciature (-shatūr), n. (Tenure of) office of papal nuncio. [f. It. *nunziatura* (foll.)]

nu·ncio (-shĭō), n. Pope's ambassador at foreign court. [It., f. L *nuncius* messenger]

nu·ncūpate, v.t. Declare (will, testament) orally, not in writing. So **nuncupa·**TION n., **nu·ncup**ATIVE a. [f. L *nuncupare* name (*nomen* name, *capere* take), -ATE³]

nunna·tion, n. Addition of final *n* in declension of (orig. Arabic) nouns. [f. Arab. *nun* the letter *n* + -ATION]

nū·phar, n. Yellow water-lily. [for NENUPHAR]

nu·ptial (-shl), a. & n. Of marriage or wedding; (n., usu. pl.) wedding. [f. L *nuptialis* (*nuptiae* wedding f. *nubere nupt-* become wife)]

nurse¹, n. Woman employed to suckle & take charge of infant (usu. *wet-n.*), or having charge of young children (also *dry-n.*); country &c. that fosters some quality &c. (*the n. of liberty*); nursing or being nursed (*at n., put out* or *put to n.*, of child, & fig. of estate); person, usu. woman, charged with or trained for care of the sick or decrepit; (Forestry) tree planted as shelter to others; (Entom.) sexually imperfect bee, ant, &c., caring for the young brood, worker; (Zool.) individual in a sexual stage of metagenesis; *n.-child,* foster-child; *n.-frog,* kind of which male carries eggs till hatched; *n.-maid,* girl having charge of child(ren); *n. ship* (Nav.), = MOTHER¹ ship. Hence **nur·se**Y³ n. [earlier & OF *norice* f. LL *nutricia* fem. of *nutricius* f. L *nutrix -icis* (*nutrire* nourish)]

nurse², v.t. & i. Suckle (child), give suck, act as wet-n.; act as n.-maid to, have charge of; (pass.) be brought up (*in* luxury, certain place, &c.); foster, tend, promote development of, (the arts, hatred, &c.); manage (plants, estate) with solicitude; cherish (grievance &c.); wait upon (sick person), try to cure (sickness), be sick-n.; hold or clasp (baby, one's knees or foot) caressingly; sit close over (fire); keep (constituency) in good humour by attentions; (Billiards) keep (balls) together for series of cannons; keep close to (rival omnibus to interfere with its custom, or horse in race to impede it); *nursing home,* house for surgical operations, reception of invalids, &c.; *nursing father, mother,* foster-. [earlier *nursh* f. NOURISH]

nurse³, n. Kinds of dog-fish or shark. [prob. f. obs. *huss* dog-fish etym. dub., w. adherent (*a*)*n*, cf. NEWT, & assim. to prec.]

nur·sery, n. Room assigned to children & their nurses (*n. governess*, one combining duties of nurse & governess); practice, institution, sphere, place, in or by which qualities or classes of people are fostered or bred; plot of ground in which young plants are reared for transplantation (*nurseryman*, owner of this); fish-rearing pond; place where animal life is developed; (Billiards) grouped balls (see NURSE²; esp. in *n. cannon*). [-ERY(3)]

nur·s(e)ling, n. Infant, esp. in relation to its nurse; *n. of*, person or thing bred in or fostered by. [NURSE¹, -LING¹]

nur·ture (-tsher), n., & v.t. Bringing up, training, fostering care; nourishment; (vb) nourish, rear, foster, train, educate. [f. OF *nourture* f. L *nutrire* nourish, -URE]

nut, n., & v.i. Fruit consisting of hard or leathery shell enclosing edible kernel (see also EARTH-*n.*, PEA-*n.*; DEAF *n.*; *can't shoot* &c. *for nn.* slang, do thing even tolerably well; *hard n. to crack*, difficult problem, person or thing hard to deal with or get the better of; *be nn. to* slang, please greatly, delight; *be nn.* or *dead nn. on* slang, delight in, be skilful at); (slang) head (*off* one's *n.*, drunk or mad); (slang) showy young man; small toothed projection on spindle engaging with cog-wheel, small spur-wheel; small block usu. of metal pierced with female screw for securing or adjusting bolt; holder that tightens or relaxes horse-hair of fiddle-bow &c.; (pl.) small lumps of coal; *n.-brown*, coloured like ripe hazel-n. (esp. of girl's complexion, & of ale); *n.-butter*, food like butter made from nn.; *n.-cracker*, (usu. pl.) instrument for cracking nuts, prominent chin & nose with points naturally, or by loss of teeth, near each other (also used attrib. in sing., as *a n.-c. face*), (sing.) common European but rare British bird; *n.-gall*, gall found on dyer's oak used as dye-stuff; *nu·thatch*, small creeping bird feeding on nn. [HATCH⁴]; *n.-oil*, got esp. from hazel-nn. & walnuts, & used in paints & varnishes; *n.-palm*, Australian bearing nn.; *nu·tshell*, hard exterior covering of n., tiny receptacle or dwelling, briefest possible way of expressing, epitome, (*can give it you in a nutshell*); *n.-tree*, bearing nn., esp. hazel; *n.-weevil*, beetle laying eggs in green hazel & filbert nn. (Vb) seek or gather nn. (usu. in gerund, *went nutting* &c.). [com.-Teut.; OE *hnutu*, cf. Du. *noot*, G *nuss*]

nū·tate, v.i. (bot.). Nod, droop. So **nu·tANT** a. [f. L *nutare* frequent. of *nuere* nod, -ATE³]

nuta·tion, n. Nodding; (Astr.) oscillation of earth's axis making motion of pole of equator round pole of ecliptic wavy; oscillation of spinning top; curvature in stem of growing plant. [f. L *nutatio* (prec., -ION)]

nu·tmeg, n. Hard aromatic spheroidal seed got from fruit of evergreen E.-Indian tree (*n.-tree*), used as spice & in medicine; *n.-apple*, fruit of n.-tree yielding mace & nn.; *n.-liver*, diseased state of liver, red atrophy. [partial transl. of OF *nois mugede*, = med. L *nux muscata* musky nut]

nū·tria, n. Skin or fur of the S.-Amer. coypu, an aquatic rodent. [Sp., = otter f. L *lutra*]

nū·trient, a. Serving as or providing nourishment. [f. L *nutrire* nourish, -ENT]

nu·triment, n. Nourishing food (lit. & fig.). Hence **nutrime·ntAL** a. (rare). [f. L *nutrimentum* (prec., -MENT)]

nutri·tion, n. (Supplying or receiving of) nourishment, food. [as NUTRIENT, -ION]

nutri·tious, a. Nourishing, efficient as food. Hence **nutri·tiousLY**² adv., **nutri·tiousNESS** n. [f. L *nutritius* (NURSE¹, -ITIOUS²)]

nu·tritive, a. & n. Serving as food; concerned in nutrition; (n.) article of food. [F (*-if, -ive*) f. med. L *nutritivus* (NUTRIENT, -IVE)]

nu·tty, a. Abounding in nuts; tasting like nuts, of rich mellow flavour; (slang) amorous or enthusiastic (*upon*). [-Y²]

nux vŏ·mica, n. Seed of E.-Ind. tree yielding the poison strychnia. [med. L (L *nux* nut, *vomere* vomit, -IC)]

nu·zzle, v.i. & t. Nose, burrow or press or rub or sniff with the nose, press nose or press (nose) *into* or *against*; nestle, lie snug, (also refl.). [NOSE¹, -LE(3)]

nyctalō·pia, n. Night-blindness or recurrent loss of vision after sunset; inability to see clearly except at night. [LL (Gk *nuktalōps* f. *nukt-* night, *alaos* blind, *ōps* eye, -IA¹); incorrect second sense due to overlooking of *-al-*]

nyctitrŏ·pic, a. (bot.). Turning in certain direction at night. [f. Gk *nux nuktos* night, -I-, Gk *tropos* turn, -IC]

nȳ·lghau (-gaw), n. Short-horned Indian antelope. [f. Pers. *nilgaw* (*nil* blue, *gaw* ox)]

nymph, n. One of class of mythological semi-divine maidens inhabiting sea, rivers, fountains, hills, woods, or trees, or attending superior deities, whence or cogn. **nymphē·AN**, **ny·mphISH**¹, **ny·mphLIKE**, aa.; (Poet.) young & beautiful woman; pupa. [f. F *nymphe* f. L f. Gk *numphē*]

ny·mpholepsy, n. Ecstasy or frenzy caused by desire of the unattainable. [foll., *epilepsy*]

ny·mpholept, n. Person inspired by violent enthusiasm esp. for an ideal. Hence **nympholeptIC** a. [f. Gk *numpholēptos* nymph-caught (NYMPH, *lambanō* take)]

nymphomā·nia, n. (path.). Morbid & uncontrollable sexual desire in women. [f. Gk *numphē* bride, -O-, -MANIA]

nўsta·gmus, n. Eye-disease common among miners, with continual oscillation of eyeballs. [f. Gk *nustagmos* nodding (*nustazō* nod)]

O

O[1] (ō), letter (pl. *O*s, O's, Oes). O-shaped mark, circle, (esp. *round O*).

Abbreviations (1): observation, **O.Pip**; officer(s'), as **O.B.E.** (of British Empire), **O.C.** (commanding), **O.T.C.** (training corps); Ohio, **O.**; old, as **O.S.**(tyle), **O.T.**-(estament), **OE**(nglish), **OHG** (high German) **OF**(rench), **ON**(orse), **O.P.**(lay-goers' club); on, **O.H.M.S.** (his *or* her majesty's service); opposite, **o.p.**(rompter); order, as **O.B.E.** (of British Empire), **O.M.** (of merit), **O.F.M.** (of Friars Minor), **O.P.** (of Preachers), **O.S.** (of Servites), **O.S.A., B., D., F.** (of St Augustine, Benedict, Dominic, Francis); ordinary, **O.S.**(eaman); out, **O.P.** (of print); over, **o.p.**(roof); (facet.) all, **O.K.**(correct); Oxford, **O.E.D.** (English Dictionary, =N.E.D.), **O.U.B.C., D.S.** (University Boat Club, Dramatic Society).

Abbreviations (2): **ob.**(*iit*); **Obad.**(iah, O.T. book); **Oct.**(ober); **oct.**(avo); **Okla.**(homa); **Ol.**(ympiad); **Ont.**(ario); **op.**(*us*); **op. cit.** (*opere citato*=in the work quoted); **Ore.**(gon); **Oxon.,** Oxfordshire, bishop of Oxford; **oz,** ounce(s).

O[2], **oh,** int. prefixed to vocative name (O), or expressing various emotions (usu. *oh* if separated by punctuation, otherwise *O*. *O dear me!*; *O for a breathing-space!*; *Oh, what a lie!*; *Oh, is that so?*); *O yes!*, =OYEZ. [ME. prob. f. L]

O'[1], pref. of Irish names, as *O'Connor*. [Ir. *ó*, *ua*, descendant]

o'[2], prep. short for *of, on,* still in some phrases, as (=*of*) *o'clock, Jack-o'-lantern, Will-o'-the-wisp, man-o'-war,* (=*on*) *cannot sleep o' nights.*

-o-, letter used to adapt first part of double-barrelled word for connexion with second; prop. used in Gk compounds, *-i-* being usu. in L, but now extended to many scientific & other terms made of non-Gk wds (*occipito-frontal, joco-serious*; &, in meaning, expressing not merely modification of second element by first (*Franco-German* = essentially German with some French characteristics), but equal or any other relations (*Franco-German war*); used also in forming true derivatives w. Gk endings as *-cracy, -logy,* & perh. taken for part of the suf., whence 'ologies' &c.

oaf, n. (pl. *-s, oaves*). Elf's child, changeling, (archaic); misbegotten, deformed, or idiot child; awkward lout. Hence **oa·fISH**[1] a. [var. of obs. *auf* f. ON *álfr* ELF]

oak, n. Kinds of tree & shrub, of which the best known is a forest tree yielding hard timber & acorns & having jagged leaves (*Dyer's, Holm, Scarlet,* &c., *o.,* other species; *Dwarf, Ground,* &c., *o.,* plants named from some resemblance to o.); wood of the o. (HEART *of o.*), (poet.) wooden ships; (Univv.) outer door of set of rooms (*sport* one's *o.,* shut this to exclude visitors); leaves of o. (*o. is still worn on 29th May*); colour of young o. leaves; *the Oaks,* race at Epsom for three-year-old fillies [f. name of estate]; (attrib., =, but now more usual than) oaken; *o.-apple, -fig, -gall, -plum, -potato, -spangle, -wart,* kinds of excrescence produced on oo. by gall-flies; *o.-apple day,* 29th May (Charles II restored 1660) on which o.-aa. are worn in memory of the ROYAL-*o.* incident; *o.-beauty, -egger, -hook-tip, -lappet, -moth,* kinds of moth bred on or resembling leaf &c. of o.; *o.-fern,* smooth three-branched Polypody; *o.-tree,* o.; *o.-wood,* forest, copse, &c., of oo., also o. timber. Hence **oa·kEN**[5] a., **oa·kLET, oa·kLING**[1](2), nn. [com.-Teut.; OE *ác,* cf. Du. *eik,* G *eiche*]

oa·kum (ōk-), n. Loose fibre got by picking old rope to pieces & used esp. in caulking (*pick o.,* make this, esp. as formerly common task of convicts & paupers). [OE *ácumbe* lit. off-combings (*ǽ-* off, *cemban* cf. G *kämmen* COMB[2])]

oar, n., & v.t. & i. Pole with blade used (usu. in even numbers) to propel boat by leverage, esp. one worked by single rower (cf. SWEEP) with both hands (cf. SCULL), or to steer (*chained to the o.,* constrained to work hard & long, with allusion to galley-slaves; *pair-o., four-o.,* &c., boat with two, four, &c., oo.; *pulls a good o.,* is good oarsman; *put in* one's *o.,* interfere; *have an o. in every man's boat,* be a meddler; *rest on* one's *oo.,* cease work for a time); *good, bad, young, practised,* &c., oarsman; (fig.) wing, fin, arm used in swimming, &c.; *oarsman, -woman,* rower, whence **oar·smanSHIP**(3) n.; hence **oar·AGE**(1) n. (poet.), **(-)oarED**[2], **oar·LESS, oar·Y**[2](poet.), aa. (Vb) row (t. & i.; poet.; *o. boat, water, air,* one's *way*; *o.* one's *arms* or *hands,* move them as in swimming). [OE (& ON) *ár,* perh. cogn. w. Gk *eretēs* rower].

ōā·sis, n. (pl. *oasēs*). Fertile spot in desert (lit. & fig.). [L f. Gk, prob. of Egypt. orig.]

oast, n. Hop-drying kiln; *o.-house,* building containing this. [OE *ást,* cf. Du. *eest,* cogn. w. L *aedes* house, *aestus* heat, *aestas* summer, Gk *aithos* heat]

oat, n. (Pl.) (grain yielded by) hardy cereal grown in cool climates as food for men & horses; (sing., rare exc. in comb.) o.-plant, variety of oo.; *Wild O.,* tall grass resembling oo. (*sow* one's *w. oo.,* indulge in youthful follies before becoming steady); (poet.) o.-stem used as musical pipe by shepherds &c., pastoral or bucolic poetry; *oatcake,* thin unleavened cake made esp.

in Scotland & N. of *oatmeal*, meal from oo. used esp. in oatcake & porridge. Hence **oa·t**EN[5] a. [OE *áte* excl. E, etym. dub.]

oath, n. (pl. pr. ōdhz). Solemn appeal to God or revered or dreaded person or object in witness that statement is true or promise shall be kept (*take an, make, swear an, o.*, bind oneself thus; *on o.*, having thus sworn, made or stated or given by sworn person; BIBLE, CORPORAL[1], *o.*), (form of words containing) statement or promise so corroborated (*o. of allegiance, office, supremacy*, &c.); name of God &c. used as expletive to give emphasis or express anger &c., piece of profanity in speech, curse. [com.-Teut.; OE *áth*, cf. Du. *eed*, G *eid*]

ob-, (before *c*-) **oc-**, (before *f*-) **of-**, (before *p*-) **op-**, pref. f. L *ob* in the way of, occurring chiefly in wds already compounded in L, w. senses (1) exposure, openness, (*object, obnoxious, obtrude, obverse*); (2) meeting (*occasion, occur, offend*), facing (*observe, obstetric, obviate, obvious, opportune*), direction (*oblation, oblique, oblong, obsecrate, obtest, offer*), spontaneity or friendliness (*obey, obsequious, office*); (3) opposition or hostility (*objurgate, obloquy, obstreperous, oppose, oppress, opprobrium, oppugn*) or resistance (*obdurate, obmutescent, obstinate, obtuse*); (4) hindrance, blocking, veiling, (*obbligato, obese, obfuscate, oblige, obliterate, obnubilate, obscure, obsess, obstacle, obstruct, obturate, occlude, occult, oppilate*); (5) finality or completeness (*obiit, oblivion, obsolete, obtain, obtruncate, occident, occupy*); (6, in mod. sci. wds) inversely, in direction or manner contrary to the usual (*obconical, obcordate, oblanceolate, obovate*, shaped like cone, heart, spike, egg, with thick end presented).

obbliga·to (-ah-), a. & n. (mus.). (Of accompaniment or part) inseparable, forming integral part of the composition, (opp. *ad libitum*); (n.) such part or accompaniment. [It., f. L *obligatus* (OBLIGE)]

o·bdūrate (*or* -ūr·-), a. Hardened, impenitent, stubborn. Hence **o·bdur**ACY n., **o·bdurate**LY[2] adv., (*or* -ūr·-). [f. L OB-(*durare* harden f. *durus* hard), -ATE[2]]

ō·beah, ō·bi, n. Kind of sorcery practised by Negroes. [W. Afr.]

obē·dience, n. Obeying as act or practice or quality, submission to another's rule, compliance with law or command, (*in o. to*, actuated by or in accordance with; *passive o.*, surrender of one's will to another's without cooperation, also compliance with commands irrespective of their nature); (Eccl., esp. R. C.) being obeyed, (sphere of) authority, district or body of persons bound to o., (*return to the o. of the Pope*; *not belonging to either the Roman or the Byzantine o.*). [f. F *obédience* f. L *obedientia* (OBEY, -ENCE)]

obe·dient, a. Submissive to or complying with superior's will, dutiful, (*your o. servant*, phrase spoken formerly in courtesy, now only ironically, in taking leave, & written as concluding formula in letters of official or public character). Hence **obe·dient**LY[2] adv. [f. OF *obédient* (OBEY, -ENT)]

obēdie·ntiary (-sh*a*-), n. Holder of any office under superior in monastery or convent. [f. med. L *obedientiarius* (OBEDIENCE, -ARY[1])]

obei·sance (obā-), n. Gesture, esp. bow or curtsy, expressing submission, respect, or salutation (archaic; *make an, do, pay, o.*); deference, homage, submission, (*do, make, pay, o.*). [f. F *obéissance* (OBEY, -ANCE)]

ŏ·belisk, n. Tapering usu. monolithic shaft of stone square or rectangular in section with pyramidal apex; o.-shaped mountain, tree, &c.; (also *obelus*) mark used in ancient MSS. to indicate that word or passage is spurious &c. (—, ÷); (also *obelus*) mark of reference to note in margin &c. (†; *double o.*, ‡). [f. L f. Gk *obeliskos* dim. of *obelos* spit]

ŏbelize, v.t. Mark with the obelisk as spurious &c. [f. Gk *obelizō* (*obelos* see prec., -IZE)]

obelus. See OBELISK.

obe·se, a. Corpulent. So **obē·**SITY n. [f. L OB(*esus* p.p., = having eaten, of *ĕdere* eat)]

obey· (-ā), v.t. & i. Perform bidding of, be obedient to; execute (command); be actuated by (force, impulse); do what one is bidden. [f. F *obéir* f. L OB(*edire* = *audire* hear)]

o·bfuscate, v.t. Darken, obscure, (mind &c.); stupefy, bewilder. So **obfusc**A·TION n. [f. L OB(*fuscare* f. *fuscus* dark), -ATE[3]]

ŏ·biit, v.i. 3rd sing. past (abbr. *ob.*). Died (with date of death). [L, f. OB(*ire it-* go) die]

ŏ·bit, n. (archaic). Memorial service esp. in institution on anniversary of founder's or benefactor's death. [f. L *obitus* death, as prec.]

o·biter, adv. By the way, in passing, (usu. *o. dictum*, pl. *-ta*, judge's expression of opinion uttered in arguing point or giving judgement but not essential to his decision & therefore without binding authority; also gen., incidental remark). [L, = *ob iter* by the way]

obi·tuary, n. & a. Notice of death(s) esp. in newspaper, brief biography of deceased person; hence **obi·tuar**IST(1) n.; (adj.) recording a death, concerning deceased person. [f. med. L *obituarius* (L *obitus* death, see OBIIT, -ARY[1])]

o·bject[1], n. Thing placed before eyes or presented to sense, material thing, thing observed with optical instrument or represented in picture; person or thing of pitiable or ridiculous aspect; person or thing to which action or feeling is directed, subject *of* or *for*, (*the Bible had been the o. of his study*; *he is a proper o. of* or *for charity*); thing aimed at, end, purpose; *no o.*, formula in advertisements &c. announcing that the other party may make his own terms in the specified respect (*money, time, distance*, &c., *no o.*); (Metaphys.) thing thought of or apprehended as correlative to the thinking mind or subject, external thing, *the* non-ego; (Gram.) noun or noun-equivalent governed by active transitive verb or by preposition (*direct, indirect, o.*, that primarily, secondarily, affected by action, as *shilling, him*, in *I gave him a shilling*); *o.-ball*, at which player aims his in billiards &c.; *o.-finder*, contrivance for registering position of o. on mounted microscopic slide so as to find it again; *o.-glass* or *-lens*, lens in telescope &c. nearest the o.; *o.-lesson*, instruction about a material o. that is present for inspection, (fig.) striking practical illustration of some principle; *o.-plate*, on which o. is placed for microscopic examination; *o.-staff*, surveyor's levelling staff. Hence **o·bject**LESS **a.** [f. med. L *objectum* thing presented to the mind, neut. p.p. of L OB(*jicere ject-* throw)]

obje·ct², v.t. & i. Adduce (quality, fact) as objection (*to* theory &c.); state (usu. *that*-clause) as damaging fact *to* or *against* person &c.; state objection, feel or express disapproval, have objection or dislike *to* (*I o. to being*, & incorrectly *to be, treated like this*; *I o.*, words used in House of Commons in announcing intention to oppose a motion &c. & so shelve it as not unopposed business). Hence **obje·ct**OR² n. (*conscientious -or*, excused compulsory service, vaccination, &c., on pleading conscience). [f. L *object-* (prec.)]

obje·ctify̆, v.t. Present as object of sense, make objective, express in concrete form, embody. Hence **objecti**FICA·TION n. [OBJECT¹, -I-, -FY]

obje·ction, n. Objecting, thing objected, adverse reason or statement; expression or feeling of disapproval or dislike. [F, f. L *objectio* (OBJECT¹, -ION)]

obje·ctionable, a. Open to objection; undesirable, unpleasant, offensive, disapproved of. Hence **obje·ctionab**LY² adv. [prec., -ABLE]

obje·ctive, a. & n. (Philos.) belonging not to the consciousness or the perceiving or thinking subject but to what is presented to this or the non-ego, external to the mind, real; (of person, writing, picture, &c.) dealing with outward things & not with thoughts or feelings, exhibiting actual facts uncoloured by exhibitor's feelings or opinions, (Med., of symptoms) observed by another & not only felt by patient, whence **obje·ctive**NESS, **objecti·**VITY, nn.; (Gram.) constructed as, appropriate to, the object (*o. case* in English, that governed by transitive verb or preposition, distinguished in form from the subjective only in some personal pronouns, as *him* cf. *he*; *o. genitive*, as in 'the fear *of God*', cf. SUBJECTIVE *genitive*); (Mil.) *o. point*, towards which advance of troops is directed, (transf.) point aimed at; hence **obje·ctive**LY² adv. (N.) = OBJECT¹-*glass*, (Gram.) o. case; (Mil. & transf.) o. point. [f. med. L *objectivus* (OBJECT¹, -IVE)]

obje·ctivism, n. Tendency to lay stress on the objective; doctrine that knowledge of non-ego is prior & superior to that of ego. [-ISM]

o·bjurgate, v.t. Chide, scold. Hence **objurg**A·TION n., **o·bjurgāt**ORY (*or* -er·*ga*-) a. [f. L OB(*jurgare* quarrel), -ATE³]

ŏ·blate¹, n. Person dedicated to monastic or religious life or work. [f. (med. L sense of) L OB(*latus* p.p. of *ferre* bring)]

obla·te² (*or* ŏ·-), a. (geom.). (Of spheroid) flattened at poles (cf. PROLATE). [as prec.; sense of *ob-* doubtful]

obla·tion, n. (Presenting of bread & wine to God in) Eucharist; thing offered to God, sacrifice, victim; donation for pious uses. Hence **obla·tion**AL, **ŏ·blat**ORY, aa. [OF, f. LL *oblationem* (OBLATE¹, -ION)]

o·bligate, v.t. Bind (person, esp. legally) *to* do (chiefly in p.p.). [f. L (OBLIGE, -ATE³)]

obliga·tion, n. Binding agreement esp. one enforceable under legal penalty, written contract or bond; constraining power of a law, precept, duty, contract, &c. (*of o.*, obligatory); one's bounden duty, a duty, burdensome task; (indebtedness for) service or benefit (*be, put, under an o.*; *repay an o.*). [OF, f. L *obligationem* (OBLIGE, -ATION)]

obli·gatory (*or* ŏ·blĭgā-), a. Legally or morally binding, imperative & not merely permissive; constituting an obligation. [f. LL *obligatorius* (foll., -TORY)]

oblī·ge, v.t. Bind (person, one*self*) by oath, promise, contract, &c., *to* person or *to* do (archaic, legal; also with *oath* &c. as subj.); be binding on; make indebted by conferring favour, gratify *by* do*ing* or *with*; (colloq.) make contribution to entertainment (*with* song &c., or abs.); (pass.) be bound (*to* person) by gratitude (*for* small service); constrain, compel, *to* do. [f. OF *obliger* f. L OB(*ligare* bind)]

oblīgee·, n. (Law) person to whom another is bound by contract or to whom bond is given (cf. OBLIGOR); (rare) person who has received a favour. [prec., -EE]

obli·ging, a. Courteous, accommodating, ready to do kindness, complaisant. Hence **obli·ging**LY² adv., **obli·ging**NESS n. [-ING²]

o·bligor, n. (legal). One who binds himself to another or gives bond. [OBLIGE, -OR²]

obli·que (-ēk), a., & v.i. Slanting, declining from the vertical or horizontal, diverging from straight line or course; (Geom.) (of line, plane figure, surface) inclined at other than right angle, (of angle) acute or obtuse, (of cone, cylinder, &c.) with axis not perpendicular to plane of base; (Anat.) neither parallel nor perpendicular to body's or limb's long axis; (Bot., of leaf) with unequal sides; not going straight to the point, roundabout, indirect; (Gram.) *o. case,* other than nominative or vocative, *o. oration* or *narration* or *speech,* speaker's words with the changes of person, tense, &c., usual in reports, indirect speech; hence or cogn. **obli·que**LY[2] adv., **obli·qu**ITY (-kw-) n.; (vb, esp. mil.) advance obliquely. [f. L OB(*liquus* cf. *licinus* bent upward)]

obli·terate, v.t. Blot out, efface, erase, destroy, leave no clear traces of. So **obliter**A·TION n. [f. L OB(*literare* f. *litera* letter)]

obli·vion, n. Having or being forgotten, disregard, unregarded state, (*Act, Bill, of O.,* amnesty; *fall into o.,* be forgotten or disused). [OF, f. L *oblivionem* f. OB(*livisci* cf. *livēre* be black & blue) forget, -ION]

obli·vious, a. Forgetful, unmindful, (*of*); (poet.) of, inducing, oblivion. Hence **obli·vious**LY[2] adv., **obli·vious**NESS n. [f. L *obliviosus* (*oblivium* forgetfulness as prec., -OSE[1])]

o·blong, a. & n. Deviating from square or circular form by having one long axis, (of spheroid) prolate, (Geom.) rectangular with adjacent sides unequal; (of paper, book, rectangular postage stamp or panel, &c.) greater in breadth than height; hence **oblong**o-(-nggō) comb. form(bot.). (N.) o. figure or object. [f. L OB(*longus* long); sense of *ob-* doubtful]

o·bloquy, n. Abuse, detraction; being generally ill spoken of. [f. LL *obloquium* f. L OB(*loqui* speak) gainsay]

obmute·scence, n. Obstinate silence. So **obmute·sc**ENT a. [f. L OB(*mutescere* f. *mutus* dumb, -ESCENT, -ENCE)]

obno·xious (-kshus), a. Liable *to* harm or evil or attack (now rare); offensive, objectionable, disliked, whence **obno·xious**LY[2] adv. Hence **obno·xious**NESS n. [f. L *obnoxius* (*ob* in the way of, *noxa* harm), -OUS]

ō·boe (-oi), n. Wooden double-reed wind-instrument giving treble to bassoon; organ reed-stop of pentrating tone. Hence **o·bō**IST(3) n. [It., f. F as HAUTBOY]

obol (ŏ·bl), n. Ancient-Greek silver coin =about 1½*d.* [f. L f. Gk *obolos*]

obsce·ne (-sēn), a. Repulsive, filthy, loathsome, (archaic); indecent, lewd. Hence or cogn. **obsce·ne**LY[2] adv., **obsce·n**ITY n. [f. L *obsc(a)enus* etym. dub.]

obscūr·ant, n. Opponent of inquiry, enlightenment, & reform. Hence **obscur·ant**ISM(3) n., **obscur·ant**IST(2) n. & a. [G, f. L (OBSCURE[2], -ANT)]

obscure·, a. & n., & v.t. Dark, dim, (*o. rays,* invisible heat-rays of solar spectrum); (of colour) dingy, dull, indefinite; indistinct, not clear; hidden, remote from observation; unnoticed; unknown to fame, humble; unexplained, doubtful; not perspicuous or clearly expressed; hence or cogn. **obscure·**LY[2] adv., **obscur·**ITY n. (N.) obscurity, indistinctness. (Vb) make o., dark, indistinct, or unintelligible; dim glory of, outshine; conceal from sight; so **obscur**A·TION n. [a. f. OF *obscur* f. L OB(*scurus* f. *scu-* cover, cf. *scutum* shield, Gk *skeuē* attire); vb f. adj. or f. L *obscurare*]

obsecra·tion, n. Earnest entreaty; Litany petition beginning with *By.* [f. L *obsecratio* f. OB(*secrare* = *sacrare* f. *sacer* sacred) entreat]

o·bsequies, n. pl. Funeral rites, a funeral. Hence **obsē·qui**AL a. [pl. of obs. *obsequy* f. OF *obseque* f. med. L *obsequiae* mixture of L *exsequiae* funeral with *obsequium* see foll.]

obsē·quious, a. Obedient, dutiful, (archaic); servile, fawning. Hence **obse·quious**LY[2] adv., **obse·quious**NESS n. [f. L *obsequiosus* f. OB(*sequium* f. *sequi* follow) compliance]

obser·vance, n. Keeping or performance of (also *of*) law, duty, custom, ritual, &c.; act of religious or ceremonial character, customary rite; the rule of a religious order; paying of deference or respect (archaic), also **obser·v**ANCY n. [F, f. L *observantia* (OBSERVE, -ANCE)]

obser·vant, a. & n. Attentive in observance; acute or diligent in taking notice; hence **obser·vant**LY[2] adv. (N.) member of branch of Franciscan order that observes the strict rule. [F (OBSERVE, -ANT)]

observa·tion, n. Noticing or being noticed, perception, faculty of taking notice, (*post, attitude, of o.,* favourable for watching from or in (*o. car,* in train esp. in U.S., so built as to afford good views); (Mil.) watching of fortress or hostile position or movements (*army* &c. *of o.,* so engaged; *o. post,* abbr. *O. Pip* slang, esp. for watching effect of artillery fire); accurate watching & noting of phenomena as they occur in nature (cf. *experiment*) with regard to cause & effect or mutual relations; taking of sun's or other heavenly body's altitude to find latitude or longitude; remark or statement, esp. one of the nature of comment. Hence **observa·tion**AL a., **observa·tional**LY[2] adv. [f. L *observatio* (OBSERVE, -ATION)]

obser·vatory, n. Building &c. whence natural, esp. astronomical, phenomena may be observed. [f. L *observare* see foll., -TORY]

For words in *ob-* not given see OB-.

obser·ve (-z-), v.t. & i. Keep, follow, adhere to, perform duly, (law, command, appointed time, method, principle, *silence*, rite, anniversary, &c.); perceive, mark, watch, take notice of, become conscious of, (*the observed of all observers*, person &c. on whom &c. attention is concentrated); examine & note (phenomena) without aid of experiment; say, esp. by way of comment; make remark(s) *on*. Hence **obser·**VABLE a., **obser·**VER[1] n. (esp., interested spectator, person carried in aeroplane to note enemy's position &c.; *O-*, as newspaper title), **obser·ving**LY[2] adv. [f. F *observer* f. L OB(*servare* keep)]

obse·ss, v.t. (Of evil spirit, delusion, or fixed idea) haunt, harass, preoccupy, fill mind of, (*-ed by, with*). So **obse·s**SION n. [f. L OB(*sidēre sess-* =*sedēre* sit) besiege]

obsĭ·dian, n. Dark vitreous lava or volcanic rock like bottle-glass. [f. L *obsidianus*, erron. for *Obsianus* (*Obsius* personal name, -AN)]

obsole·scent, a. Becoming obsolete, going out of use or date; (Biol., of organ once more fully developed) gradually disappearing. So **obsole·sc**ENCE n. [f. L OB(*solescere* f. *solēre* be accustomed, see -ESCENT), -ENT]

o·bsolete, a. & n. Disused, discarded, antiquated; (Biol.) less developed than formerly or in cognate species, rudimentary; hence **o·bsolete**NESS, **o·bsolet**ISM (3, 4), nn. (N.) o. person or thing. [f. L *obsoletus* p.p. as prec.]

o·bstacle, n. Hindrance, impediment, (*o.-race*, in which artificial or natural oo. have to be passed). [OF, f. L *obstaculum* f. OB(*stare* stand) impede]

obstĕ·tric(al), aa. Of midwifery, of childbirth & its antecedents & sequels, as branch of medicine & surgery. Hence **obste·tr**ICS, **obstetri·**CIAN, nn. [irreg. by confusion with -IC f. L *obstetricius* f. *obstetrix* midwife f. OB(*stare* or *sistere* stand), -TRIX]

o·bstinate (-*at*), a. Stubborn, inflexible, self-willed, refractory. Hence or cogn. **o·bstin**ACY n., **o·bstinate**LY[2] adv. [f. L *obstinatus* p.p. of OB(*stinare* deriv. form of *stare* stand) persist]

obstrĕ·perous, a. Noisy, vociferous; turbulent, unruly, noisily resisting control. Hence **obstre·perous**LY[2] adv., **obstre·perous**NESS n. [f. L *obstreperus* f. OB(*strepere* make noise), -OUS]

obstru·ct, v.t. & i. Block up, fill with impediments, make impassable or difficult of passage; prevent or retard progress of, impede; practise (esp. Parliamentary) obstruction. [f. L OB(*struere struct-* build)]

obstru·ction, n. Blocking or being blocked, making or becoming more or less impassable; hindering, esp. of Parliamentary business by talking against time, whence **obstru·ction**ISM(3), **obstru·ction**IST(2), nn.; obstacle (*o.-guard*, bar fixed before locomotive to remove oo. from rails). [f. L *obstructio* (prec., -ION)]

obstru·ctive, a. & n. Causing, intended to produce, obstruction; hence **obstru·ctive**LY[2] adv., **obstru·ctive**NESS n. (N.) o. person, esp. in House of Commons. [OBSTRUCT, -IVE]

obtai·n, v.t. & i. Acquire, secure, have granted one, get, whence **obtai·n**MENT n. (rare), **obtai·n**ABLE a.; be prevalent or established or in vogue. [f. F *obtenir* f. L OB(*tinēre* =*tenēre* hold) keep]

obte·cted, a. (entom.). (Of pupa) having limbs &c. indistinctly discernible through outer covering. [f. L OB(*tegere tect-* cover) + -ED[1]]

obte·st, v.t. & i. (archaic). Adjure, supplicate, call to witness; protest. So **obtest**A·TION n. [f. L OB(*testari* f. *testis* witness)]

obtru·de, v.t. Thrust forward (*upon* or *on* person or his attention) importunately. So **obtru·**SION (-zhn) n., **obtru·**SIVE (-s-) a., **obtru·sive**LY[2] adv., **obtru·sive**NESS n. [f. L OB(*trudere trus-* push)]

obtru·ncate, v.t. Cut off head of, top. [f. L OB(*truncare* f. *truncus* maimed), -ATE[3]]

obtu·nd, v.t. (med.). Blunt, deaden, (sense or faculty). [f. L OB(*tundere tus-* beat)]

o·btūrate, v.t. Stop up, close, seal, (orifice in body, breech of gun, &c.). Hence or cogn. **obtur**A·TION, **o·bturat**OR[2](2), nn. [f. L *obturare*, -ATE[3]]

obtu·se (-s), a. Of blunt form, not sharp-pointed or sharp-edged; (Geom., of angle) greater than one & less than two right angles; (of pain, the senses) dull, not acute; stupid, slow of perception. Hence **obtu·se**LY[2] adv., **obtu·se**NESS n., **obtu·si-** comb. form. [f. L p.p. of OBTUND*ere*]

o·bverse, a. & n. Narrower at base or point of attachment than at apex (esp. in Nat. Hist., including as general term OB*ovate*, OB*lanceolate*, &c.); answering as counterpart to something else; hence **obver·se**LY[2] adv. (N.) side of coin or medal bearing the head or principal design (cf. REVERSE); face of anything meant to be presented, front; counterpart of a fact or truth. [f. L *obversus* p.p. (foll.)]

obver·t, v.t. (log.). Infer another proposition with contradictory predicate by changing quality of (proposition). So **obver·**SION n. [f. L OB(*vertere vers-* turn)]

o·bviate, v.t. Clear away, get rid of, get round, neutralize, (danger, inconvenience, &c.). [f. L OB(*viare* f. *via* way) withstand]

o·bvious, a. Open to eye or mind, clearly perceptible, palpable, indubitable. Hence **o·bvious**LY[2] adv., **o·bvious**NESS n. [f. L *obvius* (*ob viam* in the way), -OUS]

oc-, pref. See OB-.

ŏcari·na (-rē-), n. Egg-shaped terra-cotta or metal musical instrument. [It. (*oca* goose, -INA[1])]

occa·sion (-āzhn), n., & v.t. Juncture suitable for doing something, opportunity, (*take o.*, avail oneself of opportunity *to* do; *take o. by the* FORELOCK[1]); reason, ground, justification, incitement, need, (*there is no o. to be angry*; *avoid all oo. of quarrel*; *King has no o. for services of* officer, formula of dismissal; *gave o. to a burst of laughter*); subsidiary, incidental, or immediate cause (*the cause of a revolution may be obscure while its o. is obvious*); (pl.) affairs, business, (esp. *go about* one's *lawful oo.*); (particular time marked by) special occurrence (*on this festive o.*; *on the o. of his marriage*; *celebrate the o.*; *rise to the o.*, show requisite energy &c.; *this is a great o.*); (*up*)*on o.*, whenever need arises, now & then; (vb) be the o. or cause of, bring about esp. incidentally, cause (action &c., or person or thing *to* do). [f. L *occasio* f. OC(*cidere cas-* =*cadere* fall), -ION]

occa·sional, a. Arising out of, made or meant for, acting on, special occasion(s); happening irregularly as occasion presents itself; coming now & then, not regular or frequent; *o. cause*, secondary cause, occasion, also apparent cause (see foll.); *o. licence* (to sell liquor only at specified times & places). Hence **occasiona·li**TY n., **occa·sionally**[2] adv. [-AL]

occa·sionalism, n. Doctrine of some Cartesians that volition & sensation are connected with the following & preceding material phenomena not causally but as separate productions of God on the same occasion. So **occa·sional**IST(2) n. [-ISM]

O·ccident (ŏks-), n. (poet., rhet.). The west; western Europe; Europe; Europe & America; America; European as opposed to Oriental civilization, whence **occide·ntal**ISM(3) n., **occide·ntal**IZE(3) v.t., **occide·ntal**IST(2, 3) n. Hence **occide·nt**AL a., **occide·ntal**LY[2] adv. [F, f. L *occident-* setting (OCCASION, -ENT)]

o·cciput (ŏks-), n. Back of head. Hence **occi·pit**AL a., **occi·pito-** comb. form. [L OC(*ciput -itis* =*caput* head)]

occlu·de, v.t. (sci.). Stop up, close, obstruct, (pores, orifice); (Chem.) absorb & retain (gases). So **occlu·**SION, **occlu·**SOR[2] (2), nn. [f. L OC(*cludere -clus-* =*claudere* shut)]

occu·lt[1], a. Kept secret, esoteric; recondite, mysterious, beyond the range of ordinary knowledge; involving the supernatural, mystical, magical, whence **occu·lt**ISM(3), **occu·lt**IST(2, 3), nn. Hence **occu·lt**LY[2] adv., **occu·lt**NESS n. [f. L OC(*culere -cult-* cf. *celare* hide)]

occu·lt[2], v.t. & i. Conceal, cut off from view by passing in front, (usu. astron., & applied only when concealing body is of much greater apparent size than concealed); *occulting light* in lighthouses, one that is cut off at regular intervals. Hence **occult**A·TION n. [f. L *occultare* frequent. as prec.]

o·ccupant, n. Person holding property, esp. land, in actual possession; one who occupies, or resides or is in, a place; one who establishes title to unowned thing by taking possession. Hence **o·ccup**ANCY n. [f. L as OCCUPY, -ANT]

occupa·tion, n. Occupying or being occupied; taking or holding possession, esp. of country or district by military force (*army of o.*, left to hold occupied region till regular government is set up), tenure, occupancy; what occupies one, means of filling one's time, temporary or regular employment, business, calling, pursuit; *o. franchise*, right to vote as tenant; *o. bridge, road*, &c., private for use of occupiers of land. [F, f. L *occupationem* (OCCUPY, -ATION)]

o·ccupier, n. Person in (esp. temporary or subordinate) possession esp. of land or house, holder, occupant. [foll., -ER[1]]

o·ccupȳ, v.t. Take possession of (country, region, town, strategic position) by military force or settlement; hold (office), reside in, tenant; take up or fill (space, time), reside or be in (place, position); busy, keep engaged, (esp. in pass. & refl.; *occupied, o.* one*self, with* or *in*). [irreg. f. F *occuper* f. L OC(*cupare* cf. *capere* take) seize; *o.* & *obtain*, as compared w. L origg., have exchanged senses; in 17th & 18th cc., *o.* almost disappeared, being avoided owing to now obs. sense *cohabit*]

occur·, v.i. (-rr-). Be met with, be found, exist, in some place or conditions; come into one's mind (esp. *it occurs* or *occurred to me that* —); take place, befall, happen. [f. L OC(*currere* run) go to meet]

occŭ·rrence, n. Happening (*is of frequent o.*, often occurs); incident, event. [f. obs. or rare *occurrent* (prec., -ENT), -ENCE]

ocean (ō·shn), n. Great body of water surrounding the land of the globe; one of the main areas into which geographers divide this (usu. reckoned as five, the *Atlantic, Pacific, Indian, Arctic, & Antarctic, Oo.*; *German O.*, = NORTH *Sea*); *the* sea; immense expanse or quantity of anything (often *oo. of*); *o. greyhound*, swift ship, esp. passenger liner; *o. lane*, track prescribed for steamers; *o. tramp*, cargo-carrying steamer not engaged in single trade. Hence **oceano·**GRAPHY (ōsha-) n., **oceano**GRA·PHIC(AL) (osēa-, ōsha-) aa., **o·cean**WARD(S) adv. [f. L f. Gk *ōkeanos* stream encircling earth's disk, Atlantic]

Ocĕā·nia (ōsh-, ōs-), n. Islands of Pacific & adjacent seas. [f. F *Océanie* (prec., -IA[1])]

Ocea·nian, a. & n. (Native) of Oceania. [-AN]

ocĕă·nic, O-, (ōsh-, ōs-), a. Of, like, &c., the ocean; of Oceania. [-IC]

Ocēanid (os-), n. (pl. *-s* or *-ănīdēs*). Ocean nymph of Greek mythology. [f. Gk *Ōkeanis -idos* daughter of Ocean]

oce·llus, n. (pl. *-ī*). One of simple as opposed to compound eyes of insects; facet of compound eye; spot of colour surrounded by ring of other colour, whence **ŏ·cell**ATE², **-ated**, aa. [L, dim. of *oculus* eye]

ō·cēlot, n. Feline quadruped of S. & Central America, resembling leopard. [F, abridged by Buffon f. Mex. *tlal*(*ocelotl* jaguar) of the field, & applied to different animal]

och (ŏch), int. =*oh, ah*, used in Ireland.

ochlo·cracy (ŏk-), n. Mob-rule. Hence **o·chlo**CRAT n., **ochlo**CRA·TIC a. [f. F *ochlocratie* f. Gk *okhlokratia* (*okhlos* mob, -CRACY)]

ochre (ō·ker), n. Kinds of native earth consisting of clay & hydrated oxide of iron used as pigments varying from light yellow to brown; pale brownish yellow. Hence **o·chre**ISH (-er-) **ochr**A·CEOUS, **o·chre**OUS (-rĭ-), **o·chr**OUS, **o·chr**Y², aa., **o·chre**o- (-rĭ-) comb. form. [f. F *ocre* f. L f. Gk *ōkhra* yellow ochre fem. of *ōkhros* yellow]

-ock, suf. forming nn. orig. w. dim. sense (*hillock, bittock, bullock*, perh. *paddock*), which many of them have lost (*paddock, bullock, pollock*); *hassock, bannock, mattock*, are prob. of different orig.

o'clock. See CLOCK¹.

oct-. =OCTA-, OCTO-, before vowel.

octa-, comb. form of Gk *oktō* eight. Hence **octă·**MEROUS a.

o·ctachord (-ak-), a. & n. Eight-stringed (musical instrument); series of eight notes, e.g. the diatonic scale. Hence **octachor·d**AL a. [f. LL f. Gk *oktakhordos* (prec., CHORD)]

o·ctad, n. Group of eight; (Chem.) element or radical with combining-power of eight units. [f. L f. Gk *oktas* f. *oktō* eight, -AD(1)]

o·ctagon, n. & a. Plane figure with eight angles & sides, object or building of such section; hence **octă·gon**AL a., **octa·gonal**LY² adv.; (adj.) octagonal. [f. L f. Gk *oktagōnos* (OCTA-, *gōnia* angle)]

octahĕ·dron, n. Solid figure contained by eight plane faces, & usu. by eight triangles (*regular o.*, by equal & equilateral triangles); body, esp. crystal, of regular octahedral form. So **octahe·dr**AL a. [f. Gk *oktaedron* (OCTA-, *hedra* seat)]

o·ctant, n. Arc of circle =1/8 of circumference; 1/8 of circular area contained within two radii & arc; one of eight parts into which three planes intersecting (esp. at right angles) at point divide space round it; (Astron.) point in planet's apparent course 45° distant from given point, esp. point at which moon is 45° from conjunction or opposition with sun; graduated eighth of circle used in astronomy & navigation. [f. LL *octans* (L *octo* eight, cf. QUADRANT)]

o·ctarchy (-kĭ), n. Aggregate of eight petty kingdoms (substituted by some historians for HEPTARCHY). [OCTA-, cf. HEPTARCHY]

octaroon. See OCTOROON.

o·ctastyle, a. & n. (Portico or building) with eight columns at end or in front. [f. LL f. Gk *oktastulos* (OCTA-, *stulos* pillar)]

o·ctateuch (-k), n. First 8 O.-T. books. [f. LL f. Gk OCTA*teukhos*, cf. PENTATEUCH]

o·ctave (-ĭv), n. The day week of a festival, eight days including festival & its day week; group or stanza of eight lines, octet; (Mus.) note produced by twice or half the vibration-rate of given note & eight diatonic degrees above or below it (*second o.*, o. of the o. in same direction; so *third* &c. *o.*), interval between note & its o., series of notes filling this, note & its o. sounding together; group of eight; a fencing position; wine-cask holding 13½ gal.; *o.-coupler*, device connecting organ-keys an o. apart; *o.-flute*, piccolo, also organ flute-stop an o. higher than the ordinary. [F, f. L *octava dies* eighth day by inclusive reckoning (*octavus* f. *octo* eight)]

octā·vo, n. (*abbr.* 8vo, oct.). (Size of) book or page given by folding sheets three times or into eight leaves. [f. L IN⁵ *octavo* (prec.)]

octā·vus. See PRIMUS¹.

octe·nnial, a. Lasting, recurring every, eight years. [f. L OCT(*ennium* f. *annus* year) period of eight years, -AL]

octe·t(te), n. (Composition for) eight singers or players; group of eight lines, esp. the first eight of sonnet. [f. L *octo* eight after DUET]

octi·llion, n. Eighth power of million (1 followed by 48 ciphers). Hence **octillion**TH² a. & n. [F (now =ninth power of thousand) as prec. after MILLION]

octingentē·nary, n. 800th anniversary. [f. L *octingenti* 800, after CENTENARY]

octo-, oct-, comb. form of L *octo*, & sometimes (=OCTA-) of Gk *oktō*, eight.

Octo·ber, n. Tenth month; beer brewed in O. (archaic). [L (prec.), cf. DECEMBER]

Octo·brist, n. & a. (Member) of moderate party in Russian Duma. [*Oct.* 30, 1905, date of Imperial Constitutional Manifesto]

octocentē·nary (*or* -ĕ·nt-), **octocente·nnial**, nn. (Irreg. for) OCTINGENTENARY.

octodĕ·cimo, n. (*abbr.* 18mo). (Size of) book or page given by folding sheets into eighteen leaves. [for IN⁵ *o.* f. L OCTO-(*decimus* tenth) eighteenth, cf. OCTAVO]

octogenār·ian, a. & n. Eighty-year-old (person); of such person. [f. L *octogenarius* (*octogeni* eighty each, -ARY¹), -AN]

o·ctonal, a. Proceeding by eights (of coinage, numeral system, &c.). [f. L *octoni*, see foll., -AL]

octonār·ian, a. & n. (pros.). Eight-foot (line). [f. L *octonarius versus* eight-foot line (*octoni* eight each f. *octo* eight, -ARY[1]), -AN]

o·ctonary, a. & n. =OCTONAL; (n.) group of eight, eight-line stanza (esp. of divisions of *Ps.* 119). [see prec.]

octō·pus, n. (Genus of) cephalopod mollusc with eight suckered arms round mouth; organized & usu. harmful ramified power or influence. [f. Gk *oktōpous* eight-footed (OCTO-, *pous* foot)]

octoroo·n, -ta-, n. Offspring of quadroon & white, person of one-eighth negro blood. [irreg. f. OCTO- after QUADROON]

octosyllă·bic, a. & n. Eight-syllable (verse). [f. LL OCTO(*syllabus* f. *syllaba* SYLLABLE), -IC]

octosy·llable, n. & a. =prec.; word of eight syllables. [see prec.]

o·ctroi (-rwah), n. Duty levied in some continental countries on goods entering town; place where, officials by whom, it is levied. [F (*octroyer* grant, as AUTHORIZE)]

o·ctūple, a., n., & v.t. Eightfold; (n.) product after multiplication by eight *of*; (vb) multiply by eight. [f. L *octuplus* a. (*octo* eight, cf. DOUBLE)]

ŏ·cular, a. & n. Of, for, by, with, &c., the eye(s) or sight, visual, (*o. demonstration*, proof appealing to the eyes); (n.) eyepiece of optical instrument. Hence **o·cular**LY[2] adv. [f. L *ocularis* (*oculus* eye, -AR[1])]

o·cularist, n. Maker of artificial eyes. [f. F *oculariste* (prec., -IST)]

ŏ·culate(d), a. =OCELLATE. [f. L *oculus* eye, -ATE[2]]

ŏ·culist, n. Eye-doctor. Hence **oculi·st**IC a. [f. F *oculiste* (L *oculus* eye, -IST)]

ŏ·culo-, comb. form of L *oculus* eye, as *-na·sal* of eye & nose.

od, n. Power assumed to pervade nature & account for magnetism, crystallization, chemical action, mesmerism, &c. [arbitrary formation of Baron v. Reichenbach 1788–1869]

ō·dalisque (-k), n. Eastern female slave or concubine, esp. in Turkish Sultan's seraglio. [f. Turk. *odaliq* (*odah* chamber, *-liq* function)]

odd, a. & n. Left over when the rest have been divided into two numerically equal sets (*the o. man*, to whom casting-vote falls in uneven-numbered committee &c.; *the o. trick* in whist, thirteenth when each side has won six; *o. man out*, way of selecting one of three persons by tossing coins till only two agree); (of number) not divisible by two (*o. & even*, a game of chance), (of things or persons numbered consecutively) bearing such number; (appended to number, sum, weight, &c.) with something over of lower denomination &c. (*forty o.*, between 40 & 50; *sixty thousand o.*, with some extra hundreds, tens, or units; *sixty o. thousand*, between 60 & 70 thousand; *twelve pounds o.*, with some shillings or pence); by which round number, given sum, &c., is exceeded (*Here is a sovereign; pay the bill & keep the o. money. There are 1006; what shall we do with the o. six?*); additional, casual, beside the reckoning, unconnected, unoccupied, incalculable, (*picks up o. jobs; do it at o. moments; in some o. corner; o. numbers, volumes*, belonging to incomplete sets of magazines &c.); extraordinary, strange, queer, remarkable, eccentric, whence **o·dd**ISH[1](2) a., **o·dd**LY[2] adv.; *o·dd-come-short*, remnant, odd remainder, (pl.) odds & ends; *o.-come-shor·tly*, some near day (esp. *one of these o.-c.-shortlies*, before long); *o·ddfellow*, member of friendly society of Oddfellows with rites imitative of freemasonry; hence **o·dd**NESS n. (N., golf) advantage given to weaker player by deduction of one, two (*two oo.*), &c., from his strokes for each hole. [f. ON *odda* in *odda-*(*mathr* man) with casting-vote (*oddi* angle, triangle, cogn. w. OE *ord* tip)]

o·ddity, n. Strangeness; peculiar trait; queer person; fantastic object, strange event. [-ITY]

o·ddments, n. pl. Odds & ends. [-MENT]

odds, n. pl. (formerly always, & still in phrases as below, treated as sing.). Inequalities (*make o. even*, do away with these); difference (*what's the o.?*, what does it matter?); variance, strife, (*are at o. with fate*); balance of advantage (*the o. are in our favour; have fought against longer o.*); equalizing allowance to weaker competitor (*give, receive, o.*); ratio between amounts staked by parties to bet (*lay, give, o. of three to one*, said of party offering the advantage; *take o.*, accept the advantage); chances or balance of probability in favour of some result (*it is o. that* or *but, the o. are that, he will do it*); *o. & ends*, remnants, stray articles, (perh. alteration of earlier *odd ends*). [prob. pl. of ODD used as n.]

ode, n. (Orig.) poem meant to be sung (*choral o.*, song of chorus in Greek play &c.); (mod.) rhymed or rarely unrhymed lyric often in form of address, usu. of exalted style and enthusiastic tone, often in varied or irregular metre, & usu. between 50 & 200 lines in length. [F, f. LL *oda* f. Gk *ōidē* contr. of *aoidē* (*aeidō* sing)]

-ode, suf. forming nn. w. sense *thing of the nature of* (*geode, phyllode*); *anode, cathode, electrode*, are not examples. [f. Gk *-ōdēs* adj. ending (-o-, *-eidēs* -like)]

ōdē·um, n. (pl. -*s*, -*ēa*). Building for musical performances, esp. among ancient Greeks & Romans. [f. Gk *ōideion* (ODE)]

ŏ·dic, a. Of OD. [-IC]

o·dious, a. Hateful, repulsive. Hence **o·dious**LY[2] adv., **o·dious**NESS n. [f. OF *odieus* f. L *odiosus* (ODIUM, -OSE[1])]

ō·dium, n. General or wide-spread dislike or reprobation incurred by person or attaching to action (*exposed me to o.*; *the o. of the transaction*); *o. theologicum,* bitterness notoriously characterizing theologians who disagree. [L, = hatred]

odometer. See **hod-.**

odo·nt(o)-, comb. form of Gk *odous odontos* tooth, as *odontorhy·ncous* having toothlike serrations in the bill, *-glo·ssum* genus of orchids with large beautifully coloured flowers, *odo·nt*OID, *ŏdonto·*LOGY.

ōdori·ferous, a. Diffusing (usu. agreeable) scent, fragrant. Hence **odori·ferous**LY[2] adv. [f. L *odorifer* (ODOUR, -FEROUS)]

ō·dorous, a. (chiefly poet.). = prec. Hence **o·dorous**LY[2] adv. [foll., -OUS]

ō·dour (*-er*), n. Pleasant or unpleasant smell, whence **o·dour**LESS a.; fragrance; (archaic, usu. pl.) substance(s) emitting sweet scent, perfume(s); (fig.) savour, trace, (*no o. of intolerance attaches to it*); *good* or *bad* or *ill* repute or favour (*is in bad o. with the nonconformists*); *o. of sanctity,* reputation for holiness (orig. lit., sweet o. exhaled by dying or exhumed saint). [f. OF *odor* f. L *odorem* (-OR[1])]

ŏ·dyl, n. = OD.

O·dyssey (ŏ-), n. (pl. *-eys*). One of two great ancient-Greek national epics (cf. ILIAD) describing adventures of Odysseus or Ulysses returning from siege of Troy; any of the 24 books of this (*in the fourth* &c. *O.*); series of wanderings, long adventurous journey. [f. L f. Gk *Odusseia* (*Odusseus,* -IA[1])]

oe·cist (ēs-), n. Founder of (esp. ancient-Greek) colony. [f. Gk *oikistēs* (*oikizō* settle f. *oikos* house, -IST)]

oeco·logy (ē-), n. Branch of biology dealing with living organisms' habits, modes of life, & relations to their surroundings. [f. Gk *oikos* house, -LOGY]

oecūmĕ·nical, (ē-) a. Of or representing the whole Christian world or universal church, general, universal, catholic, (of general councils of early, & of mod. R.-C., Church); world-wide. So **oecumeni·**CITY n. [f. L f. Gk *oikoumenikos* f. *hē oikoumenē* the inhabited (earth) f. *oikeō* inhabit, -AL]

oedē·ma (ē-), n. (path.; no pl.). Swollen state of tissue &c. with serous fluid, local dropsy. Hence **oedema·t**IC, **oede·matose**[1], **oede·mat**OUS, aa., **oede·matous**LY[2] adv. [f. Gk *oidēma -atos* (*oideō* swell, -M)]

Oe·dipus (ē-), n. Solver of riddles; *O. complex,* a sexual complex held by psychoanalysts of the Freudian school to influence the child in regard to the parent of opposite sex. [f. Gk *Oidipous,* who guessed the Sphinx's riddle, & in ignorance married his mother]

o'er (ŏr), adv. & prep. = OVER (poet.).

oesŏ·phagus (ē-), n. (pl. *-i* pr. -jī, *-guses*). Canal from mouth to stomach, gullet. Hence **oesophă·gĕ**AL (-j-), **oeso·phago-** comb. form. [f. Gk *oisophagos* etym. dub.]

oe·strum, oe·strus, (ē-), n. Gadfly; stimulus, vehement impulse, frenzy. [f. Gk *oistros*]

of (ŏv, ov), prep. connecting its noun with preceding n., adj., adv., or vb, & indicating the relations roughly classified as follows: Removals, separation, point of departure, privation, (*north, within a mile, upwards, have the advantage, of*; *back of* U.S., behind; *wide of the mark*; *heal, rid, ease, brought to* BED[1], *of*; *destitute, empty, free, bare, of*; *take* LEAVE[1] *of*; *balk, cheat, defraud, deprive, disappoint, of*; *independently, guiltless, irrespective, of*); origin, derivation, cause, agency, authorship, (*be, come, descend, spring, of*; *borrow, buy, win, receive, hire, of*; TAKE *it ill of*; *have comfort, wish* one *joy, of*; *ask, demand, learn, expect, of*; *of* one's *own* ACCORD[2]; *of* COURSE[1], *of* RIGHT, *of* NECESSITY; *of* oneself, spontaneously; *die of*; *smell, savour, smack, of*; *tired, ashamed, afraid, glad, proud, of*; *sick of measles,* laid up with; *sick of delays,* disgusted by; *warned of God, forsaken of God & man,* by; *it was kind, foolish, naughty, clever, cruel, well done, of you to say so*; *has the approval of his master*; *the works of Shakspere, Iliad of Homer*); material, substance, closer definition, identity (*house of cards*; *built of brick*; *make a* FOOL[1], *the* BEST[1], *of*; MAKE[1] *much of*; *a family of eight*; *the name of Jones*; *the class of idiots*; *city of Rome, vice of drunkenness*; *a fool of a man, her scamp of a husband, the worst liar of any man I know*; *had a bad time, troublesome journey, of it*); concern, reference, direction, respect, (*think well of him*; *never heard of it*; *was informed of the fact*; *is true of every case*; *repent, beware, of*; *cannot conceive, accept, approve,* THINK, *of*; *does not admit* or *allow of*; *accuse, convict, suspect, of*; *avail, bethink,* oneself *of*; SHORT, *guilty, certain, sure, confident, fond, of*; *swift of foot, blind of an eye, hard of heart,* HARD *of hearing*; *at 30 years of age*); objective relation (*the levying of taxes*; *love of virtue*; *in search of knowledge*; *great eaters of pork*; *redolent, productive, fruitful, lavish, prodigal, sparing, capable, sensible, careful, observant, desirous, impatient, characteristic, destructive, indicative, of*); description, quality, condition, (*man of tact, person of consequence, farm of 100 acres, the hour of prayer, potatoes of our own growing*; *girl of ten years,* or, with mixed construction, *of ten years old*); partition, classification, inclusion, selection, (*no more of that*; *some, five, of us,* = *a.* a portion, or five, of us who are more numerous, or by extension *b.* we, being several or five persons; so *any part,* or *the whole, of it*; *the most dangerous of enemies*; *he of all men,* he most or least of all; *is the one thing of all others that*, illog. for *of all that*; *song of songs, holy of holies*, those best deserving the name; *is one of a, ten, thousand*, such as occurs only in one among 1,000, 10,000, cases; *a friend of mine, of the vicar's*, i.e. orig. in the number of my, the vicar's, friends, but extended to illog. contexts, as *that long nose of his, this only son of the the vicar's*; *drink deep of flattery, partake of food*; *was sworn of the Council*, admitted as member; *his temper is of the quickest*, belongs to the quickest class; *a sort of thud*; *comes in of an evening*, at some time in the evenings; *of old, yore, late years, late*, somewhere in the specified periods); belonging, connexion, possession, (*we of the middle class*; *companions of his exile*; *articles of clothing*; *the manners of to-day*; *a thing of the past*; *the master of the house*; *the widow of the man who was killed*; *a topic of conversation*; esp. with words that naturally require supplementing, as *the cause, result, counterpart, opposite, image, of*;) BECAUSE, *by* MEAN[1]*s*, *for* FEAR[1], *for the* SAKE, *in* BEHALF, *in* CASE[1], *in* FACE[1], *in* RESPECT, *in* SPITE, INSTEAD, *on* ACCOUNT[2], *on* BEHALF, *on the* POINT, *of*. [OE, unaccented form of *æf*, cf. Du. *af* & G *ab* off adv., Gk *apo* & L *ab* from; *of* & *off* are one word, differentiated in 14th–16th cc.]

of-, pref. See OB-.

off (awf, ŏf), adv., prep., a., n., & v.t. Away, at or to a distance, (*rode o.*; *beat o. the attack*; *keep assailant o.*; *ward o. disaster*; *take* oneself, *be, make, o.*, depart; *o. with you!*, go; *o. with his head!*, behead him; *fall, go, o.*, deteriorate; of ship, *fall o.*, become less close to wind; *the bullet glanced o.*; *go o.*, fall asleep; *is far, three miles, two years, o.*); (so as to be) out of position, not on or touching or dependent or attached, loose, separate, gone, (*my hat is o.*; *take his clothes o.*; *cut, break, shake*, &c., *o.*; *throw o. reserve*, become open or candid; *be o. with the old love*, have severed connexion; *get* one's *daughters, stock, o.*, disposed of by marriage, sale; *the gilt is o.*, disillusionment has come; *we are o. now*, just started, starting, or about to start); so as to break continuity or continuance, discontinued, stopped, not obtainable, (*broke o.*, ceased to speak; *leave o. work*; *the engagement, bargain, negotiation, is o.*; *declare o.*, refuse or rescind engagement; *cut o. supplies*; *the gas, asparagus, is o.*, no longer to be got); to the end, entirely, so as to be clear, (*clear, drink, pay, polish, work, o.*); BUY, COME, DASH[1], GET, MARK[2], PALM, PASS, RATTLE, SHOW, TAKE, *o.*; RIGHT, STRAIGHT, *o.*; *well, badly, comfortably*, &c., *o.*, so circumstanced or supplied with money; *o. & on*, intermittently, waveringly, now & again; *o.-load, o.-saddle*, S.-Afr. for *un-*. (Prep.) from, away or down or up from, disengaged or distant from, (so as to be) no longer on, (*drove them o. the seas*; *is o. the beaten track*; *fell o. a ladder*; *take cover o. dish*; *eats o. silver plate*; *take thing, matter, o.* one's *hands*, relieve him of it; *had borrowed £20 o. plaintiff* vulg.; *o.* one's HEAD[1], FEED[2]; *o. colour*, out of condition, indisposed; *took something o. the price*; *is o. duty* or *work*; *cut a slice o., dine o., the joint*; *was only a yard o. me*; *keep ship two points o. the wind*; *o. the point*, irrelevant(ly); *o. the map* slang, vanished, no longer existing; *in a street o. the Strand*, turning out of it; *from o.* archaic, poet., or vulg., = *o.*; *o.-hand*, extempore, without premeditation, unceremoniously, whence **offha·nd, offha·nd**ED[2], aa., **offha·nded**LY[2] adv., **offha·nded**NESS n.; *o. shore*, a short way out to sea; so *o.-shore fisheries*; *o.-shore wind*, blowing seawards; *anchored o. the point, cape*, &c., opposite & a short way from it; *o. side* in football, between ball & opponents' goal (so *o.-side play, rule*). (Adj.) farther, far, (*on the o. side of the wall*); (of horses &c. or vehicles) right (opp. NEAR[2], w. ref. to side at which rider usu. mounts; *the o. leader, front wheel, hind leg, side*); (Cricket) towards, in, or coming from, that half of the field as divided by line through two middle stumps in which playing batsman does not stand (opp. ON[2], LEG; *an o. drive*, whence **offdri·ve** v.t.; *o. stump*; LONG[1] *o.*; *an o. break*); subordinate, divergent, (*in an o. street*; fig. of argument &c., *that is an o. issue*); contingent, improbable, (*there is an o. chance that*); disengaged (*will do it on my next o. day*); *o.-licence*, to sell beer &c. for consumption o. the premises; *o.-print*, separatum, printed copy of article &c. that was orig. part of larger publication. (N.; cricket) the o. side. (Vb; colloq.) announce intention of abandoning or annulling (negotiation, agreement, undertaking), withdraw from negotiation or engagement with (person). [see prec.]

ŏ·ffal, n. Refuse, waste stuff, scraps, garbage; parts cut off as waste from carcase meant for food, esp. entrails, also head, tail, &c.; carrion, putrid flesh; low-priced fish (e.g. plaice as opp. sole or other prime fish); bran or other by-product of grain (often pl.); offscourings, dregs, *o. milk, wheat, wood*, &c., inferior. [= *off-fall* or what falls off]

offe·nce, n. Stumbling-block, occasion of unbelief &c., (now rare); attacking, aggressive action, taking the offensive, (*the most effective defence is o.*); wounding of the feelings, wounded feeling, annoyance, umbrage, (*no o. was meant*; *too quick to take o.*; *give o. to*; *cannot be done without o.*); transgression, misdemeanour, illegal act, (esp. *commit an o. against*). Hence **offe·nce**LESS a. [ME & OF *offens* f. L *offensus, -ūs* annoyance, & ME & F *offense* f. L *offensa* a striking against, both f. OF(*fendere fens-* strike)]

offe·nd, v.i. & t. Stumble morally, do amiss, transgress, (*against* law, decency, person, &c.); whence **offe·nder**[1] n. (esp. FIRST *-er*), **offe·nding**[2] a.; wound feelings of, anger, cause resentment or disgust in, outrage, (*am sorry you are offended*; *offended at* or *by* thing, *with* or *by* person; *o. her delicacy, my sense of justice*), whence **offe·ndedly**[2] adv. [f. OF *offendre* f. L as prec.]

offe·nsive, a. & n. Aggressive, intended for or used in attack, (*o. arms, movement*; opp. DEFENSIVE); meant to give offence, insulting, (*o. language*); disgusting, ill-smelling, nauseous, repulsive; hence **offe·nsively**[2] adv., **offe·nsiveness** n. (N.) attitude of assailant, aggressive action, (*take, act on, abandon, the o.*); an attack, o. campaign or stroke, (*the long-expected German o.*). [f. med. L *offensivus* (OFFENCE, -IVE)]

ŏ·ffer[1], v.t. & i. Present (victim, first-fruits, prayer) to deity, revered person, &c., by way of sacrifice, give in worship or devotion, whence **o·ffering**[1](4) n.; hold out in hand, or tender in words or otherwise, for acceptance or refusal (*offered me his hymn-book to look over*; TAKE*n & offered*; *was offered a free pardon*; *o. an opinion, a few remarks*, &c.; *o. no apology*); make proposal of marriage; show for sale; give opportunity to enemy for *battle*; express readiness *to* do if desired; essay, try to show, (violence, resistance, &c., often *to*); show an intention *to* do (*offered to strike me*); (of things) present to sight or notice (*each age offers its characteristic riddles*); present itself, occur, (*as opportunity offers*; *the first path that offered.*) [OE *offrian* in religious sense f. L OF(*ferre* bring); other senses f. F *offrir* of same orig.]

o·ffer[2], n. Expression of readiness to give or do if desired, or to sell on terms (*on o.*, for sale at certain price), proposal esp. of marriage; bid. [f. F *offre* (prec.)]

ŏ·ffertory, n. Part of mass or communion service at which offerings are made, the offering of these, the gifts offered; collection of money at religious service. [f. eccl. L *offertorium* (LL *offert-* for L *oblat-* p.p. st. of *offerre* OFFER[1], -ORY) offering]

ŏ·ffice, n. Piece of kindness, attention, service, (*ill o.*) disservice, (*owing to, by, the good* or *ill oo. of*); duty attaching to one's position, task, function, (*it is my o., the o. of the arteries, to*); position with duties attached to it, place of authority or trust or service esp. of public kind (*was given an o. under Government*), tenure of official position esp. that of minister of State (*take, enter upon, hold, leave, resign, o.*; JACK[1] *in o.*); ceremonial duty (esp. *perform the last oo. to*, rites due to the dead); (Eccl.) authorized form of worship, daily service of R.-C. breviary (also *divine o.*; *say o.*, recite this), Anglican morning & evening prayer, (introit at beginning of) mass or communion service, any occasional service such as the *O. for the Dead*; place for transacting business (*goes down to the o. at 9 a.m.*), room &c. in which the clerks of an establishment work, counting-house, (with qualification) room &c. set apart for business of particular department of large concern (*booking, inquiry, goods, lost-property, -o.* in railway station) or local branch of dispersed organization (*our Manchester o.*; *a post, telegraph, -o.*) or company for specified purpose (*insurance, fire* or *fire-insurance, -o.*); (*O-*) quarters or staff or collective authority of a Government department (*the* FOREIGN, WAR[1], POST[2], *o.*); *Holy O.*, the inquisition; (pl.) parts of house devoted to household work, storage, &c.; (slang) *give, take, the o.*, hint, private intimation, signal; *o.-bearer*, official or officer. [OF, f. L OF(*ficium* f. *facere* do) service]

ŏ·fficer, n., & v.t. Holder of public, civil, or ecclesiastical office, king's servant or minister, appointed or elected functionary, (usu. with qualification, as *o. of* HEALTH, *of the Household*, or *public, medical, o.*; *relieving o.*, see RELIEVE); president, treasurer, secretary, &c., of society; bailiff, catchpole, (rare) constable; person holding authority in navy, army, air force, or mercantile marine, esp. with commission in army or navy (GENERAL, STAFF, COMMISSION[1]*ed*, FIELD[1], COMPANY[1], BREVET, WARRANT[1], NON-*commissioned*, *o.* in army; FLAG[4], COMMISSION[1]*ed*, WARRANT[1], PETTY, *o.* in navy; *Naval oo.*: Admiral of the Fleet, Admiral, Vice Adm., Rear Adm., Commodore, Captain, Commander, Lieut. Commander, Lieutenant, Sub-lieut., Midshipman: *Army oo.*: Field Marshal, General, Lieut. Gen., Major Gen., Brigadier Gen. or Colonel Commandant, Colonel, Lieut. Col., Major, Captain, Lieutenant, Second Lieut.: AIR[1] *Force oo.*); *Officers' Training Corps* (abbr. O.T.C.; orig. for the Territorial Force, & multiplied for the great war); (vb, usu. in p.p.) provide with oo., act as commander of. [f. OF *officier* f. med. L *officiarius* (prec., -ARY[1])]

offi·cial (-shl), a. & n. Of an office, the discharge of duties, or the tenure of an office; holding office, employed in public capacity; derived from or vouched for by person(s) in office, properly authorized, (Med.) according to the pharmacopoeia, officinal; usual with persons in office (*o. solemnity, red tape*, &c.); hence **offi·cially**[2] adv., **offi·cialize**(3) v.t. (N.) presiding officer or judge of archbishop's, bishop's, or esp. archdeacon's court (usu. *o. principal*); person holding public office or engaged in o. duties, whence **offi·cial-**

DOM, **offi·cial**ISM(2), nn. [f. L *officialis* (OFFICE, -AL)]

offi·ciate (-shĭ-), v.i. Discharge priestly office, perform divine service, so **offi·ci**ANT(1) n.; act in some official capacity, esp. on particular occasion (usu. *as* host, best man, &c.). [f. med. L *officiare* perform divine service (OFFICE), -ATE³]

offi·cinal, a. (Of herb or drug) used in medicine or the arts; (of medical preparation) kept ready at druggists', made from pharmacopoeia recipe (now usu. OFFICIAL), (of name) adopted in pharmacopoeia. Hence **offi·cinal**LY² adv. [f. med. L *officīnalis* f. L *officīna* contr. of *opificīna* workshop (*opifex* workman), -AL]

offi·cious (-shus), a. (Given to) offering service that is not wanted, doing or undertaking more than is required, intrusive, meddlesome, whence **offi·cious**NESS n.; (Diplom., opp. *official*) informal, unofficially friendly or candid, not binding. Hence **offi·cious**LY² adv. [f. L *officiosus* obliging (OFFICE, -OUS)]

o·ffing (ŏ-, aw-), n. Part of visible sea distant from shore or beyond anchoring ground (*was seen in the o.*); position at distance from shore (*gain, keep,* &c., *an o.*). [OFF, -ING¹]

o·ffish (aw-, ŏ-), a. (colloq.). Inclined to aloofness, distant or stiff in manner. Hence **o·ffish**NESS n. [OFF, -ISH¹; cf. UPPISH]

o·ffscourings (aw-, ŏ-), n. pl. Refuse, filth, dregs, (usu. *of*; lit., & fig. of persons as *the o. of humanity*). [OFF, SCOUR, -ING¹(2)]

o·ffset (aw-, ŏ-), n. Start, set-off, outset, (rare); short side shoot from stem or root serving for propagation, (transf. & fig.) offshoot, scion, mountain-spur; compensation, set-off, consideration or amount diminishing or neutralizing effect of contrary one; (Surv.) short distance measured perpendicularly from main line of measurement; (Archit.) sloping ledge in wall &c. where thickness of part above is diminished; bend made in pipe to carry it past obstacle. [OFF, SET¹]

o·ffshoot (aw-, ŏ-), n. Side shoot or branch (lit. & fig.), derivative. [OFF, SHOOT]

ŏ·ffspring (*or* aw-), n. Progeny, issue, (fig.) result. [OE *ofspring* (OF, OFF, SPRING)]

oft (aw-, ŏ-), adv. Often (archaic except in comb. with p.p. or part., as *o.-told, -recurring*; *many a time & o.*, often); *o.-times,* often (archaic). [com.-Teut.: OE & ON, cf. G, *oft*]

often (aw·fn, ŏ·fn; *vulg.* -ten), adv. & a. (-er, -est). Frequently, many times, at short intervals, (with singular generalized subject) in a considerable proportion of the instances (*the victim o. dies of it*); *o. & o.*, emphatic form; *oftentimes*, o. (archaic); (adj.; archaic) frequent (*by o. study of it*). [extended f. prec.]

o·gdoăd, n. The number, a set of, eight. [f. LL f. Gk *ogdoas* (*oktō* eight, -AD)]

ogee (ōjē·), n. & a. (Moulding) showing in section a double continuous curve, concave below passing into convex above; S-shaped (line); *o. arch, doorway, window,* with two o. curves meeting at apex. Hence **ogee·'d** (-ED²) a. [prob. f. F OGIVE, being the usu. moulding in groin-ribs]

ŏ·g(h)am, n. Ancient British and Irish alphabet of twenty characters; inscription in this; one of the characters. [OIr. *ogam,* referred to *Ogma* supposed inventor]

ogive (ō·jīv, ōjī·v), n. Diagonal groin or rib of vault; pointed or Gothic arch, whence **ogi·**VAL a. [F, etym. dub.]

ō·gle, v.i. & t., & n. Cast amorous glances; eye amorously; hence **ō·gl**ER¹ n. (N.) amorous glance. [prob. f. LG *oegeln* or G *äugeln* dim. of *augen* look about (*auge* an eye)]

ogre (ō·g*er*), n. Man-eating giant. Hence or cogn. **o·gre**ISH¹, **o·gr**ISH¹, aa., **o·gr**ESS¹ n. [F, first used by Perrault 1697, etym. dub.]

Ogy·gian (ogĭj-), a. Of obscure antiquity, prehistoric. [f. L f. Gk *Ōgugios* of *Ōgugēs* mythical king of Attica or Boeotia]

oh (ō), int. See O².

ohm (ōm), n. Unit of electrical resistance; *o.-ammeter,* instrument measuring electrical current & resistance. Hence **oh·m**METER n. [G. S. *Ohm,* German physicist 1787-1854]

oho·, int. expressing surprise or exultation. [O², HO]

oh yes. See OYEZ.

-oid, suf. forming adjj. & nn. w. sense *(something) having the form of, resembling*; chiefly on Gk (*rhomboid*), rarely L (*fucoid*) or other (*alkaloid*) stems; adjj. as *thyroid, simioid*, nn. as *asteroid, amygdaloid*; for the nn. an adj. in *-oidal* is formed as *cycloidal.* [f. mod. L *-oīdes* f. Gk *-oeidēs* (-o- + *-eidēs* like) f. which also -ODE]

oil¹, n. (Kinds of) liquid viscid unctuous inflammable chemically neutral substance lighter than & insoluble in water & soluble in alcohol & ether (there are three classes: *fatty* or *fixed* oo. of animal or vegetable origin, greasy & non-distillable, subdivided into *drying* oo., which by exposure harden into varnish, & *non-drying* oo., which by exposure ferment, the latter used as lubricants, illuminants, soap constituents, &c.; *essential* or *volatile* oo. chiefly of vegetable origin, acrid, limpid, & distillable, giving plants &c. their scent, used in medicine & perfumery; *mineral* oo. used as illuminants. Particular kinds are named from source with *of*, as *o. of almonds*, or with source or use preceding, as *cod-liver, olive, salad, hair, o. Pour o. on the flame* &c., aggravate passion &c.; *pour o. on the waters*, smooth matters over; *smell of o.*, bear marks of study;

burn the midnight o., read or work far into the night; *strike* o. lit., find petroleum by sinking shaft, fig., attain prosperity or success; *o. & vinegar*, type of dissimilar or irreconcilable things; *strap* &c. *-o.*, flogging with strap &c.); =o.-colour (often pl.); =oil-skin (usu. pl.); *o.-bird, -nut, -palm, -plant, -seed, -tree*, kinds of bird &c. from which o. is got; *o.-bush*, o.-filled socket for upright spindle [BUSH[3]]; *oil-cake*, mass of compressed linseed &c. left when o. has been expressed, used as cattle food or manure; *o.-can*, containing o., esp. long-nozzled for oiling machinery; *oil-cloth*, fabric waterproofed with o., oil-skin, canvas coated with drying o. & used to cover table or floor; *o.-coat*, of oilskin; *o.-colour*, paint made by grinding pigment in o. (usu. pl.); *o.-field*, district yielding mineral o.; *o.-gauge*, hydrometer measuring specific gravity of oo.; *o.-gilding, -gold*, goldleaf laid on linseed-o. mixed with yellow pigment; *o.-gland*, secreting o.; *o.-hole*, in machinery to receive lubricating o.; *oilman*, maker or seller of oo.; *o.-meal*, ground linseed cake; *o.-paint*, =o.-colour; *o.-painting*, art of painting, picture painted, in o.-colours; *o.-paper*, made transparent or waterproof by soaking in o.; *o.-press*, apparatus for pressing o. from seeds &c.; *oilskin*, cloth waterproofed with o., garment or (pl.) suit of this; *o.-spring*, yielding mineral o.; *oil-stone*, (fine-grained stone used with o. as) whetstone. Hence **oi·l**LESS a. [f. ONF *olie* f. L *oleum* (*olea* olive)]

oil[2], v.t. & i. Apply o. to, lubricate, (*o. the wheels*, lit., & fig. make things go smoothly by courtesy, bribery, &c.; o. one's *hand* or *o.* one, bribe him; o. one's *tongue*, say smooth things, flatter); (with *butter, grease*, &c., as subj. or obj.) turn (t. & i.) into oily liquid; impregnate or treat with o. (*oiled sardines*; *oiled silk*, waterproofed with o.). [f. prec.]

oi·ler, n. In vbl senses; esp. oilcan for oiling machinery, (slang) unctuous person. [-ER[1]]

oi·ly, a. Of, like, covered or soaked with, oil; (of manner &c.) fawning, insinuating, unctuous. Hence **oi·li**LY[2] adv., **oi·li**NESS n. [-Y[2]]

oi·ntment, n. Unctuous preparation applied to skin to heal or beautify, unguent. [f. OF *oignement* (L UNGUENT*um*, -MENT)]

Oireachtas (ĕr·achthăs), n. Legislature of the Irish Free State, the King & two Houses, Dáil Eireann (Chamber of Deputies) & Seanad Eireann (Senate). [Ir.]

oka·pi (-ah-), n. Bright-coloured partially striped Central-Afr. ruminant discovered 1900 with likeness to giraffe, deer, & zebra. [native]

-ol, chem. suf. (1) Termination of *alcohol* used in names of alcohols in the wider sense or analogous compounds (*methol, phenol*). (2) =L *oleum* oil (*furfurol*).

ōld, a. (ELDER[1], *-est*, in particular uses; ordinarily *older, -est*), & n. Advanced in age, far on in natural period of existence, not young or near its beginning, (*the o.*, aged people; *young & o.*, every one; *o. age*, later part of life; *o.-age pensions*, weekly payments under Acts of 1908–1925 to those over 70 or over 65 variously qualified; *O. Lady of Threadneedle Street*, Bank of England; *o. man of the sea*, person who cannot be shaken off; *o. man, woman, party*, &c.; *o. man*, also as name for southernwood, & naut. slang for ship's captain; *my* &c. *o. man* colloq., husband; *o. man's beard*, kind of moss, also TRAVELLER'S *Joy*; *my* &c. *o. woman* colloq., wife; *o. woman*, fussy or timid man, whence **old-wo·man**ISH[1], **old-wo·man**LY[1], aa., **old-wo·manish**NESS, **old-wo·manli**NESS, nn.; *my* &c. *o. bones*, I or me &c. who am o.; *the century grows o.*); having characteristics, experience, feebleness, &c., of age (*o. head on young shoulders*, wisdom beyond one's years; *child has an o. face*; *o. buffer, fogy*, &c.; *a man is as o. as he feels*), worn, dilapidated, shabby, (*o. clothes* &c.); (appended to period of time) of age (*is ten years o., a ten-year-o. boy, a boy* OF *ten years o., could read Greek at ten years o.*; also ellipt. *four* &c. *-year-o.*, person or animal, esp. racehorse, of that age, w. pl. *-olds*); practised or inveterate *in* action or quality or as agent &c. (*o. in crime, folly, cunning, diplomacy*; *an o. campaigner, offender*; *o. bird*, person on his guard against snares; *o. hand*, practised workman, person of experience in something, *at doing*; o. STAGER; *o. bachelor*, man confirmed in bachelorhood; *o. maid*, elderly spinster, whence **old-mai·d**ISH[1] a., also precise & tidy & fidgety man, also a round card game); dating from far back, made long ago, long established or known or familiar or dear, ancient, not new or recent, primeval, (*o. Ocean, Night*, &c.; *o. red* SAND*stone*; *of o. standing*, long established; so *o.-established*; *o. as the hills*; *o. countries*, long inhabited or civilized; *o. friends*; *an o. debt, grudge*, o. SCORES; *an o. name, family*; *o. wine*, matured with keeping; so *O. Tom*, kind of gin; *o. gold*, colour of tarnished gold; o. CATHOLIC; *the o.*, what is not new; o. TESTAMENT; *o. boy, chap, fellow, man*, esp. in voc., intimate or person treated as such, also in mod. slang *o. bean, egg, fruit, thing, top*; *O. England*; *O. Glory*, the Stars & Stripes; *the o. one* or *gentleman, O. Harry, Nick, Scratch*, &c., the devil; *good o.* with name, slang exclamation in real or ironical commendation of person's or thing's performance; *have a fine, good, high*, &c., *o. time* &c. slang, be well amused or entertained; *any o. thing* slang, anything no matter what); belonging only or chiefly to the past, obsolete or obsolescent, out of date, antiquated, antique, concerned with antiquity, not modern, bygone, only lingering on, former, quondam, (*the good o. times*, customs &c. of earlier generations; *o. annals*; *o. fashions*, that have gone or are going out, whence **old-fashion**ED[2] a., **old-fa·sh-ioned**NESS n., opp. *new-fangled* &c.; *am old-fashioned enough to think*, used in ironical self-depreciation; *of the o. school*, o.-fashioned; *the o. country, home*, &c., used by colonists or colonials of mother-country; *call up o. memories*; *the o. order changeth*; *have lost my o. beliefs*; *o. boy*, former member of school; so *o. Etonian* &c.; *the O.* COMEDY, HUNDREDTH; *O. Masters*, Royal Academy's winter exhibition at Burlington House; *o. London, Paris, England*, &c., London &c. as it once was, or the extant relics of its former state; *the o. man*, one's unregenerate self; *the O. World*, Eastern hemisphere; *o.-world*, not American, also belonging to o. times, & so *o.-time* attrib.; *O.* STYLE, abbr. O.S.; *the o. year*, just ended or about to end; *o. clothes*, discarded; *o.-clothes-man*, dealer in these); hence **o·ld**ISH[1](2) a., **o·ld**NESS n. (rare). (N.) o. time (only in *of o.* adj. & adv., as *the men of o., of o. there were giants*; *have heard it of o.*, from long ago). [com.-Teut.; OE *ald*, cf. Du. *oud*, G *alt*, f. OTeut. *al-* grow, nourish, cf. L *alere* feed]

o·lden[1], **a.** (archaic and literary). Old-time, of a former age, (esp. *the o. time*). [-EN[5]]

o·lden[2], v.t. & i. Make or grow feeble &c. as with age. [-EN[6]]

o·ldster, n. One who is no longer a youngster (usu. antithetically to *youngster*). [-STER]

ōlĕă·ginous, a. Having properties of or producing oil, oily, fatty, greasy. [f. F *oléagineux* f. L *oleaginus* (*olea* olive)]

ōlĕa·nder, n. Evergreen poisonous Levantine shrub with leathery lanceolate leaves & fine red & white flowers. [med. L, etym. dub.]

ōlĕa·ster, n. The wild olive; small yellow-flowered tree like it. [L (*olea* olive, -ASTER)]

ōleo-, comb. form of L *oleum* oil, as *-graph*, picture printed in oils, so -GRAPHY; *-mar·garine*, fatty substance extracted from beef fat & serving as constitutent of margarine; *-meter*, instrument determining density & purity of oils; *-re·sin*, natural mixture of volatile oil & resin, balsam, also artificial mixture of fixed or volatile oil & resin &c.

olfa·ction, n. Smelling, sense of smell. So **olfa·ct**IVE a. [f. L *olfacere* v.t. smell for *olefacere* (*olēre* v.i. smell, *facere fact-* make)]

olfa·ctory, a. & n. Concerned with smelling (*o. organ*, nose; *o. nerves*); (n., usu. pl.) o. organ. [prec., -ORY]

oli·banum, n. Aromatic gum resin used as incense. [med. L, f. Gk *libanos* frankincense (*o-* perh. f. L *oleum* oil, Gk *ho* the, or Arab. *al* the)]

ŏ·lid, a. Rank-smelling, fetid. [f. L *olidus* (*olēre* smell, -ID[1])]

ŏ·ligarch (-k), n. Member of oligarchy. [f. Gk *oligarkhēs* (*oligoi* few, *arkhō* rule)]

o·ligarchy, n. Government, State governed, by the few; members of such government. So **oligar·ch**·IC(AL) aa., **oligar·chical**LY[2] adv. [f. Gk *oligarkhia* (prec., -Y[1])]

ŏlig(o)-, comb. form of Gk *oligos* small, *oligoi* few, as *-car·pous*, having few fruits; *o·ligocene* geol., between MIOCENE & EOCENE.

ō·lio, n. Mixed dish, hotchpotch, stew of various meats & vegetables; medley, farrago, miscellany. [f. Sp. *olla* stew f. L *olla* jar]

ŏliva·ceous, a. (nat. hist.). Olive-green, of dusky yellowish green. [L *oliva* olive, -ACEOUS]

ŏ·livary, a. (anat.). Olive-shaped, oval. [f. L *olivarius* (foll., -ARY[1])]

ŏ·live, n. & a. (Also *o.-tree*, evergreen tree with narrow leaves hoary below & axillary clusters of small white flowers, bearing) small oval drupe with hard stone & bitter pulp, of dusky yellowish green when unripe & bluish black when ripe, yielding oil, & pickled unripe for eating as relish; leaf, branch, or wreath of o. as emblem of peace (also *o.-branch*, often fig.; *hold out the o.-b.*, make overtures, show disposition, for reconciliation); wood of the o. (also *o.-wood*); o.-shaped kinds of gasteropod mollusc; (pl.) slices of beef or veal rolled up with herbs & stewed (usu. *beaf, veal, oo.*); o.-shaped bar or button for fastening garment by insertion in corresponding loop, whence **o·liv**ET[1] or **oliv**E·TTE n.; o. colour; *o. crown*, garland of o. as sign of victory; *o.-branch*, see above, also (usu. pl., w. ref. to *Ps.* **cxxviii.** 3) child(ren); *o.-oil*, extracted from oo. (Adj.) coloured like the unripe o. (also *o.-green*); (of complexion) yellowish-brown. [F, f. L *oliva*]

ŏ·liver[1], n. Tilt-hammer attached to axle & worked by treadle for shaping nails &c. [?]

Oliver[2]. See ROLAND.

o·livin(e), n. Kind of chrysoprase, chiefly olive-green. [L *oliva* olive, -INE[4]]

o·lla podri·da (-rē-), rarely **o·lla**, n. = OLIO. [Sp., = lit. rotten pot (OLIO, L PUTRID*us*)]

(-)ology, suf. = -O- + -LOGY, & n. used facetiously = any science, w. pl. = the sciences, mere theory.

oly·mpiăd, n. Period of four years between celebrations of Olympic games, used by ancient Greeks in dating events (abbr. Ol.), 776 B.C. being first year of first O. [f. F *olympiade* f. L f. Gk *olumpias -ad-* (*Olumpios* see foll., -AD)]

Oly·mpian, a. & n. Of Olympus, celestial;

(of manners &c.) magnificent, condescending, superior; =foll. (N.) dweller in Olympus, one of the greater ancient-Greek gods; person of superhuman calmness & detachment. [f. LL *Olympianus* (L f. Gk *Olumpios* f. *Olumpos*, -AN)]

Oly·mpic, a. Of or at Olympia (*O. games*, held there every four years by ancient Greeks with athletic, literary, & musical competitions; also, modern quadrennial international athletic meeting at various places, the first at Athens 1896). [f. L f. Gk *Olumpikos* of Olympus (*Olympia* being named from the games in honour of Zeus of Olympus)]

Oly·mpus, n. Thessalian mountain on which dwelt the chief Greek gods, divine abode, heaven. [L, f. Gk *Olumpos*]

o·mbre (-ber, *or as F*), n. Card-game popular in 17th–18th cc. [f. Sp. *hombre* f. L *hominem* nom. *homo* man, perh. thr. F (*h*)*ombre*]

ombro-, comb. form of Gk *ombros* rain, as -LOGY, -METER.

ō·mega, n. Last letter (Ω, ω) of Greek alphabet, long o; last of series; final development &c. (ALPHA *& o.*). [Gk, =great o]

omelet(te) (ŏ·mlet), n. Whipped eggs fried & folded & often flavoured with or containing herbs, cheese, chopped ham, jam, &c. (*savoury o.*, with herbs &c.; *sweeet o.*, with sugar or jam; *cannot make an o. without breaking eggs*, end necessitates means). [F (*-te*), earlier *amelette* by metath. f. *alemette* var. of *alemelle* thin plate prob. f. L LAMELLA]

ō·mĕn, n., & v.t. Occurrence or object portending good or evil, prognostic, presage; prophetic signification (*is of good* &c. *o.*); (vb) foreshow, give presage of. [L, earlier *osmen* perh. f. *audire* hear, -MEN]

ome·ntum, n. (anat.; pl. *-a*). Fold of peritoneum connecting stomach with other viscera, caul. Hence **ome·nt**AL a. [L]

omi·cron, n. Greek letter (O, o) =ŏ. [Gk, =small o]

ŏ·minous, n. Giving or being an omen (*of* good or evil, or abs.), portentous, (rare); of evil omen, inauspicious, foreshowing disaster, threatening. Hence **o·minous**LY[2] adv. [f. L *ominosus* (OMEN *-inis*, -OUS)]

omi·ssion (-shn), n. Omitting, non-inclusion; non-performance, neglect, duty not done, (*sins of o. & commission*, negative & positive). So **omi·ss**IVE a. [f. L *omissio* (foll., -ION)]

omi·t, v.t. (-tt-). Leave out, not insert or include; leave undone, neglect do*ing*, fail *to* do. So **omi·ss**IBLE a. [f. L *omittere -iss-* (*o-* for OB-, *mittere* send]

omnĭ-, comb. form of L *omnis* all, in compounds taken f. L or formed chiefly w. L elements, w. sense *all-*, *of all things*, *in all ways* or *places*, as *omnico·mpetent*, having jurisdiction in all cases; *omnifār·ious*, of all sorts; *omnĭ·fic* all-creating; *omni·genous*, of all kinds; *omni·potence*, infinite power, also God, also great influence; so *omni·potent* a. (*the O.*, God), *omni·potent*LY[2] adv.; *omnipre·sence*, ubiquity, also being widespread or constantly met with; so *omnipre·sent* a.; *omni·science* (-shĭ-) infinite knowledge, also God, also wide information or the affectation of it; so *omni·scient* a. (*the O.*, God), *omni·scient*LY[2] adv.; *omni·vorous*, feeding on anything that offers (esp. fig. of reading); so *omni·vorous*LY[2] adv., *omni·vorous*NESS n.

o·mnibus, n. (pl. *-uses*) & a. (Also & usu. *bus*) four-wheeled public vehicle usu. covered & with seats on roof as well as inside plying on fixed route & taking up & setting down passengers at fixed, or at any, points in this; (also *hotel o.*) vehicle conveying guests between hotel & railway station; (also *private* or *family o.*) vehicle provided by railway company for conveying party & luggage to or from station. (Adj.) serving several objects at once, comprising several items, (*an o. bill, resolution, clause*, &c.; *o. box* in theatre, box on pit tier appropriated to number of subscribers; *o. train*, stopping at all stations; *o. bar, wire*, &c. in electricity, through which whole current passes). [f. L dat. pl. of *omnis* =for all]

o·mnium gă·therum, n. Miscellaneous assemblage of persons or things, queer mixture, party to which every one is invited. [mock L (L *omnium* of all, GATHER)]

ō·moplate, n. Shoulder-blade, scapula. [f. Gk *ōmoplatē* (*ōmos* shoulder, *platē* blade)]

omphalo- (*-a-*), comb. form of Gk *omphalos* NAVEL, chiefly in surg. & med. wds as -CELE; -TOMY, dividing of umbilical cord.

o·mphalos, n. (Gk Ant.) boss on shield, conical stone at Delphi supposed to be central point of earth; centre, hub, (*the centre & o. of a world-wide empire*). [see prec.]

on[1] (ŏn, on), prep. (So as to be) supported by or attached to or covering or enclosing (*sat on the table*; *floats on the water*; *is on the horns of a dilemma*; *lives on the continent, on annuity*; *have you a match on you?*, about your person; *is, gets, falls, on his* LEGs, *knees*, &c.; *travels on foot, wheels, the wing, the wings of the wind*; *tread on air*, one's *foes*; *dropped it, threw him, on the floor*; *had, put, a ring, gloves, on his finger, hands*; *put a notice on the board*; *hangs on the wall*; *walks on the ceiling*; *has a blister on the sole of his foot*; *a scholar on the foundation*; *a colonel on half-pay*; *went on board*; *is on the jury, committee, general staff*; *a writer on the press*; *dog is on the chain*; *on the* BENCH, BOARD[1]s, CARD[2]s, FENCE[1], MARKET[1], NAIL[1], PARISH, RACK[3],

SHELF, SPOT[1], STREETS, STUMP, TURF, WAY; *on* CHANGE[1], HAND[1], one's HAND[1]*s*, one's *own* HOOK[1], one's KNEE[1]*s*, TENTER*hooks*; *on a* LEVEL[1], *an* EQUALITY, *a* PAR); with axis, pivot, basis, motive, standard, confirmation, or guarantee, consisting in (*turn on* one's *heel*; *works on a peg*; *based on fact*; *imprisonment on suspicion*; *on my conscience*; *swear on the bible*; *had it on good authority*; *decided on no evidence*; *did it on purpose, deliberation*; *got it on good terms*; *on account of*; *on the average, whole*; *on penalty of death*; *charged him on his life to do it*; *a tax on paper*; *borrowed money on his jewels*; *interest on* one's *capital*; *profit on sales*); (so as to be) close to, in the direction of, touching, arrived at, against, just at, (*house is on the shore, road*; *on the right, North, far side, both sides, of*; *Burton on Trent*; *marched on London*; *hit him on the head*; *a box on the ear*; *left a card on him*; *serve a notice, writ, on*; *lay hold, seize, on*; *bowling is on the wicket*, straight; *drew his knife on me*; *smile, frown, turn* one's *back, on*; *make an attack on*; *put* one *on inquiring* or *inquiry*, induce him to inquire; *curse, plague, &c., on him, it!*; *rose on their oppressors*; *on* HIGH; *on side* in football, not OFF *side*; *ship is driving on shore*; *an on-shore wind*); (of time) during, exactly at, contemporaneously with, immediately after, as a result of, (*happened on the morning* &c. *of 29th Feb.*, *on Christmas eve, on the next day*; *on the instant*, immediately; *on time, the minute, &c.*, punctually; *on arriving, my return, analysis, examination, I found*); in manner specified by adj. (*on the cheap, sly*, SQUARE) or state or action specified by noun (*on fire*, TAP, *loan, lease, sale, strike, guard*; *on the look-out, move, run, wane, watch*; *on* one's *best behaviour*); concerning, about, while engaged with, so as to affect, (*keen, mad, bent, determined, set, on*; *gone on* slang, enamoured of; *court martial was held on him*; *my opinion on free trade*; *writes, speaks, lectures, on finance*; *a book, an essay, on grammar*; *meditating on vanity*; *take vengeance on person*; *did it on my way*; *was, went, on an errand*; *is not binding on us*; *work tells severely on him*; *title was conferred on him*; *draw cheque on bank*; *condoled with him on his loss*); added to (*ruin on ruin, heaps on heaps*). [OE *an, on*, cf. Du. *aan*, G *an*, Gk *ana*; hence also A[2]]

ŏn[2], adv., a., & n. (So as to be) supported by, attached to, covering, enclosing, or touching, something (*has, drew, his boots on*; *put the tablecloth on*; *keep your* HAIR *on*; *on with your coat*, put it on); in some direction, towards something, further forward, towards point of contact, in advanced position or state, with continued movement or action, in operation or activity, (LOOK[1], LOOK[1]*er, on*; *getting on for two o'clock*; *broadside, stem, end, on*, with that part forward; ellipt. for imperat. of *go* or *come on*, as *on, Stanley, on!*; *send on*, in front of oneself; MOVE[2] *on*; *happened later on*; *from that day on*; *was well on in the day*; *is rather on* slang, half-drunk; *speak, work, wait, &c., on*, continue to do so; so *struggle on to the end*, cf. *on to* below; *slow bowler is, went, on*, is, began, bowling; *Macbeth is on*, being performed; *gas, water, is on*, lit. running, or procurable by turning tap; *get, be, on*, make, have made, bet; *drove Jones on for 4* in cricket, to the on); CARRY, CATCH[1], COME[1], GET[1], GO[1], HOLD[1], KEEP[1], PUT, TAKE, TRY, *on*; *on & off*, = OFF *& on*; *on to*, compound prep. (corresponding to *on* as *into* to *in*, but usu. written as two words, & avoided in writing though common in speech; to be distinguished from the use in which each word has independent force as in *went on to the next*), to a position on (*jumped on to the landing-stage*). (Adj.) towards or in part of field to left front of playing batsman's wicket (cf. OFF, LEG; MID *on*; *an on drive*, whence **on-dri·ve** v.t.); *on licence*, for selling beer &c. to be drunk on premises. (N.) the on side in cricket (*a fine drive to the on*). [f. prec.]

on-, pref. used with attrib. participles, gerunds, verbal nouns, agent-nouns in -ER[1], & other derivative nn., f. vv. followed idiomatically by ON[2] (sometimes alternatively with the reverse order): *o·ncoming* n. & a., approach(ing); *o·nfall* n., assault; *o·nflow*, onward flow; *o·ngoings* or *goings-o·n*, (usu. strange or improper) proceedings; *o·nhanger*, HANGER[2]-*on*; *o·n-looker* or LOOK[1]*er-o·n*; *o·nrush* n., *o·nrushing* a.; ONSET.

ŏ·nager, n. (pl. *-s, -grī*). Kinds of wild ass. [L, f. Gk *onagros* (*onos* ass, *agrios* wild)]

ō·nanism, n. Self-abuse, masturbation. [*Onan* (*Gen.* xxxviii. 9), -ISM]

once (wŭns), adv., conj., & n. For one time or on one occasion only, multiplied by one, by one degree, (*have read it more than o.*; *shall die o.*; *o. or twice, o. & again*, a few times; *o. more, again*, another time; *o. for all*, in final manner, definitively; *o. in a while* or *way*, very rarely; *o. & away*, = o. for all, o. in a way; *o. bit twice shy*, pain, loss, &c., teaches caution; *o. nought is nought*; *second cousin o.* RE-MOVE*d*); (in negative or conditional or indefinite clause &c.) ever, at all, even for one or the first time, (*if we o. lose sight of him*; *when o. he understands*; *have not seen him o.*; *o. within call, we are safe*); on a certain but unspecified past occasion (also *o. upon a time*), at some period in the past, former(ly), (*o. there was a giant*; *a o.-famous doctrine, o.-loved friend*; *my o. master, ally*); *at o.*, immediately, without delay, at the same time, (*do it at o., please*; *don't all speak at o.*, lit., & as iron. deprecation inviting offers &c. from reluctant party; *at o. stern & tender*); *for, this* or *that, o.*, on one occasion by way of exception. (Conj.) as soon as, if o., when o., (*o. he hesitates, we have him*). (N.) one time, performance, &c. (*o. is enough for me*). [ME *ânes, ônes*, (ONE, -ES)]

on dit (F), n. Piece of hearsay.

one (wŭn), a., n., & pron. (Num. adj.) single & integral, neither none nor fractional nor plural, numbered by the first or lowest integer, half of two, a, (*o. man o. vote*, principle of equality in voting; *o. vote o. value*, principle of equal constituencies; *o.-&-twenty* &c., or usu. *twenty* &c. *-o.*; *o.-&-twentieth* &c., twenty &c. -first; *o. dozen, hundred*, &c., precise or formal for *a*; *o. man in ten, a thousand*, &c., relatively few; *some o. man must direct*; *for o. thing, he drinks*; *o. or two people*, a few; *God is o.*); (adj. with secondary senses developed from the numeral) *the* only, single, forming a unity, united, identical, the same, unchanging, a particular but undefined, to be contrasted with another, (*the o. way to do it*; *no o. man is equal to it*; *is o. & undivided*; *cried out with o. voice*; *were made o.*, married; *become o.*, coalesce; *remains for ever o.*, always the same; *all in o. direction*; *met him o. night*; *will take you there o. day*; *o. man's meat is another man's poison*); (numeral noun, with *a* & pl.; often used as substitute for repetition of previously expressed or implied noun) the number o., thing numbered with it, written symbol for it, a unit, unity, a single thing or person or example, (*o. is half of two*; *in the year o.*, long ago; *Aeneid, book o.*, first book of; *number o.*, oneself, esp. as centre of selfish care; *write down a o., three oo.*; *came by oo. & twos*; *sell scores where they sold oo.*; *never a o.*, none; *will you make o.?* archaic, join the party; *ten* &c. *to o.*, long odds, high probability; *all in o.*, combined; *the all & the o.*, totality & unity; *at o.*, reconciled, in agreement; *I lose a neighbour & you gain o.*; *pick me out a good o., some good oo.*; *which, what kind of, o.* or *oo. do you like?*; *that o., the o. in the window, will do*); (adj. used ellipt. for itself or *a* with noun elsewhere expressed or customarily omitted & to be supplied with more or less of certainty) single person or thing of the kind implied (*o. of them lost his* or *her hat*; *o. of the richest men in England*; *shall see you again o. of these fine days*; *at o. o'clock* or *o.*, i.e. hour; *o. & sixpence*, i.e. shilling; *gave him o. in the eye, owe him o., that was a nasty o.*, blow lit. or fig.; *at o.-&-twenty*, years of age; *I for o. do not believe it*; *go o. better*, bid, offer, risk, more by o. point; *is o. too many for him*, too hard &c. for him to deal with by o. degree; *it is all o. to me*, the same thing, indifferent; *o. & all*, all jointly & severally; *o. by o., o. after another*, singly, successively; *o. with another*, on the average; *o.* or *the o.*, — *the other*, formula distinguishing members of pair, as *o. is immoral, the other nonmoral*, also with pl. constr., as *sheep & goats, of which the o. are the good* &c.; *o. another*, formula of reciprocity with *o.* orig. subjective & *another* objective or possessive, as *struck o. another, write to o. another, buy o. another's goods*); (pronoun) a particular but unspecified person (archaic; *o. came running*; *o. said it pleased him not*), a person of specified kind (ANY, EVERY, SOME, NO[1], SUCH *a, o.*; *many a o.* rhet., many people; LITTLE, *dear, loved, oo.*; *the Holy O., O. above*, God; *the Evil O.*, the devil; *behaves like o. frenzied*; *what a o. he is to make excuses!* colloq.; *bought it from o. Stephens*), any person, esp. the speaker, spoken of as representing people in general (possessive *one's*, objective *o.*, reference-form *o.*, refl. *oneself*, formerly *his, him, he* & *him, himself*, or ungrammatically *their, them, they* & *them, themselves*; *if o. cuts off o.'s nose, o. hurts only oneself*; *it offends o. to be told o. is not wanted*; also incorrectly for *I*, as *o. let it pass, for o. did not want to seem mean*); *o.-eyed*, having only, blind of, o. eye; *o.-handed*, having, done &c. with, o. hand only; *o.-horse*, drawn or worked by single horse, (fig.) petty, poorly equipped; *o.-idea'd, -ideaed*, possessed by single idea, narrow-minded; *o.-legged*, having only o. leg, (fig.) o.-sided, unequal; *o.-man*, requiring, consisting of, done or managed by, o. man; *o.-pair*, room or set of rooms on first floor (above one pair or flight of stairs; *o.-p. back, front*, such room in back or front of house); *oneself*, reflexive, & emphatic appositional, form of *o.* as generalizing pronoun (*to starve oneself is suicide*; *to do right oneself is the great thing*); *o.-sided*, having, occurring on, o. side only (*a o.-s. street*, with houses on o. side only; *a o.-s. plant*, with leaves or flowers all on o. side of stem), larger &c. on o. side, partial, unfair, prejudiced; so *o.-si·ded*LY[2] adv., *o.-si·ded*NESS n. Hence **o·ne**FOLD a. [com.-Teut.; OE *ân*, cf. Du. *een*, G *ein*, cogn. w. Gk *oinos, oinē*, ace, L *unus* one; *an, a*, are weakened forms]

-one (ōn), chem. suf. (1) used unsystematically as in OZONE; (2) in names of hydrocarbons (see -ANE). [f. Gk *-ōnē* fem. patronymic]

oneiro- (onīro), comb. form of Gk *oneiros* dream: -MANCY; *-cri·tic*, interpreter of dreams; so *-cri·tic*AL a., *-cri·tic*ISM n.

o·neness (wŭ-), n. Being one, singleness; singularity, uniqueness; wholeness, unity, union, agreement, concord; identity, sameness, changelessness. [-NESS]

o·ner (wŭ-), n. Remarkable or pre-eminent person or thing (slang; *a o. at*, expert in; *gave him a o.*, severe blow); (colloq.) stroke &c. counting one, esp. one-run hit at cricket. [-ER[1]]

ŏ·nerous, a. Burdensome, causing or requiring trouble, (*o. property* in law, accompanied with obligations). Hence **o·nerous**LY² adv., **o·nerous**NESS n. [f. OF *onereus* f. L *onerosus* (*onus oneris* burden, -OUS)]

onion (ŭ·nyun), n., & v.t. (Plant with) edible rounded bulb of many concentric coats & pungent smell & flavour, much used in cooking or eaten pickled; (slang) native of Bermuda; *o.-couch* or *-grass* or *-twitch*, kind of wild oat; *o.-shell*, kinds of mollusc; hence **o·niony**² a. (Vb) rub (eyes) with o. to make them water. [f. F *oignon* f. L *unionem* nom. *-o* large pearl, onion]

ō·nly¹, a. That is (or are) the one (or all the) specimen(s) of the class, sole, (*the o. way is to die*; *the o. child of his parents*; *the o. instances known*; *was an o. son*; *one o. object was visible*; *my one & o. hope*; *motley's the o. wear*, best or o. one worth considering). [OE *ánlic* (ONE, -LY¹)]

o·nly², adv. & conj. Solely, merely, exclusively, & no one or nothing more or besides or else, & that is all, (*is right because it is customary o.*, *is right o. because it is customary*, *is o. right because it is customary*; *o. you* or *you o. can guess*, no one else can; *you can o. guess* or *guess o.*, can do no more; *I o. thought I would do it*, formed the design & did not execute it, or did it without external instigation; *I not o. heard it, but saw it*; *if o.*, assuming merely that, also as wishing formula, as *if o. some one would leave me a legacy!*; *o. not*, all but; *has o. just come*, *came o. yesterday*, no longer ago; *o. too glad*, *true*, &c., glad &c. & not, as might be expected, the opposite). (Conj.) it must however be added that, but then, (*he makes good resolutions, o. he never keeps them*); with the exception, were it not, *that* (*he does well, o. that he is nervous at the start*; *o. that you would be bored, I should* —). [ONE, -LY²]

ŏ·nomatŏp(e), n. Onomatopoeic word. [shortened f. foll.]

onŏ·matopoe·ia (-pēa, -pēya), n. Formation of names or words from sounds that resemble those associated with the object or action to be named, or that seem naturally suggestive of its qualities; word so formed (e.g. *cuckoo*). So **onomatopoe·**IC, **onomatopŏē·**TIC, aa., **onomatopoe·**ICALLY, **onomatopoe·**TICALLY, advv. [f. L f. Gk *onomatopoiia* word-making (*onoma- atos* name, *poieō* make)]

o·nset, n. Attack, assault, impetuous beginning, (esp. *at the first o.*). [f. *to* SET *on*]

o·nslaught (-awt), n. Onset, fierce attack. [perh. f. Du. *aanslag* or G *anschlag* (*an* on, *schlagen* strike) w. assim. to *draught* &c.]

o·nto, prep. See ON² *to*.

onto-, comb. form of part. of Gk *eimi* be: *ontogĕ·nesis*, origin & development of the individual being (cf. PHYLOGENESIS), whence *ontogenĕ·tic* a., *ontogene·tically* adv.; *onto·geny*, = ontogenesis, also embryology; *onto·logy*, department of metaphysics concerned with the essence of things or being in the abstract, so *ontolo·gical* a., *ontolo·gically* adv., *onto·logist* n.

ō·nus, n. (no pl.). Burden, duty, responsibility; *o. probandi*, obligation to prove resting on maker of assertion or claim. [L]

o·nward, adv. & a., **o·nwards**, adv. Further on, towards the front, with advancing motion; (adj.) directed o. [ON², -WARD(S)]

ŏ·nymous, a. Not anonymous. [f. Gk *onuma* name + -OUS after *anonymous*]

ŏ·nyx, n. Kind of quartz allied to agate with different colours in layers; (Path.) opacity of lower part of cornea; *o. marble*, of banded onyx-like structure. [L, f. Gk *onux* nail, onyx]

oo- (ōo), **o-**, comb. form of Gk *ōion* egg, ovum, in scientific usu. biol. wds, as *ooge·nesis*, production or development of ovum; *ooe·cium* (ōē-), budlike sac for receiving & fertilizing ova in polyzoa; *ōŏ·gamous*, reproducing by union of male & female cells; *ōŏ·logy*, study, collecting, of birds' eggs, so -LO·GICAL, -LOGIST; *o·o-sperm*, fertilized ovum or female cell.

ōōf, n. (slang). Money, pelf, cash; *o.-bird*, source of money, rich person. Hence **oof·**Y² a. [for *oof-tish* Yiddish = G *auf dem tische* on the table]

o·olite, n. Granular limestone, each grain being a calcareous particle in carbonate of lime, roe-stone; (Geol.) series of fossiliferous rocks of this formation lying between Chalk, or Wealden, & Lias. Hence **ooli·**TIC a. [f. F *oölithe* (OO-, -LITE)]

oom, n. (S.-Afr.). Uncle (esp. *O. Paul* = President Kruger). [Du.]

-ōōn, suf. formerly used in borrowing F wds in *-on* (*dragoon*) except when the final syl. was not accented (*baron*); esp. for F *-on* f. It. *-one* f. L *-onem* nom. *-o* (*balloon*, *buffoon*, *cartoon*); rarely in native wds (*spittoon*); F wds now taken have *-on* in E (*chignon*); the L expresses humorous or contemptuous description (*Naso* Nosey), the It. bigness or coarseness, the F (exc. in It. borrowings) small size; in E the suf. has no definite meaning.

ōōnt, n. (Anglo-Ind. slang). Camel.

ooze¹, n. 1. Wet mud, slime, esp. in riverbed or estuary or on ocean bottom. 2. Tanning liquor, infusion of oak-bark &c.; *o.-calf*, calf-skin through which dye has been forced. 3. Exudation, sluggish flow, something that oozes. Hence **oo·zy**² a., **oo·zi**LY² adv., **oo·zi**NESS n. [1 f. OE *wáse* cogn. w. ON *veisa* puddle; 2 f. OE *wós* juice, sap; 3 f. foll.]

ooze², v.i. & t. (Of moisture) pass slowly through the pores of a body, exude, percolate; (of substance) exude moisture; (fig.) leak *out* or *away* (*the secret oozed out*;

my courage is oozing away); emit (moisture, information, encouragement). [f. prec. 2]

op-. See OB-.

opă·city, n. Being opaque, quality of not allowing passage to or (rarely) of not reflecting light, non-transparency, obscurity; obscurity of meaning, obtuseness of understanding. [f. F *opacité* f. L *opacitatem* (OPAQUE, -TY)]

ō·pah, n. Rare brilliant-coloured large N.-Atlantic fish of mackerel family, kingfish, moon-fish. [W.-Afr. name]

ō·pal, n. Amorphous quartz-like form of hydrous silica some kinds of which show changing colours (e.g. *common o.*, milk-white or bluish with green, yellow, & red reflexions), whence **opal**E·SCENT, **opal**E·SQUE, aa., **opale·sc**ENCE n.; (Commerc.) semi-translucent white glass. [f. L *opalus* f. Skr. *upala* gem]

o·paline, a. & n. Opal-like, opalescent, iridescent; (n.) semi-translucent white glass. So **o·pal**IZE(3) v.t. [prec., -INE[1]]

opa·que (-āk), a. (-er, -est), & n. Not reflecting (rare) or transmitting light, not shining (rare), impenetrable to sight; not lucid, obscure; obtuse, dull-witted; (n.) *the o.*, darkness. Hence **opa·que**LY[2] adv., **opa·que**NESS n. [f. L *opacus* shaded; earlier *opake*, now assim. to F]

ope, v.t. & i. (Poet. for) OPEN[2]. [after obs. adj. *ope* reduced f. *open* on anal. of p.p. (cf. *awake, wove*, f. *awaken, woven*)]

open[1] (ō·pn), a. (-er, -est), & n. Not closed or blocked up, allowing of entrance or passage or access, having gate or door or lid or part of boundary withdrawn, unenclosed, unconfined, uncovered, bare, exposed, undisguised, public, manifest, not exclusive or limited, (*o. gate, passage, church, drawer, box, field, grave, carriage, hostilities, scandal, contempt*; *o. air*, outdoors; *door flew o.*; *o. boat*, undecked; *lay o.*, expose esp. by cutting skin &c. of; *o. ears*, eagerly attentive, whence **open-ear**ED[2] a.; *o. mouth*, in voracity, frankness, &c., & esp. in gaping stupidity or surprise, whence **open-mouth**ED[2], pr. -dhd, a.; *o. mind*, accessibility to new ideas, unprejudiced or undecided state, whence **open-mind**ED[2] a., **open-mi·nded**LY[2] adv., **open-mi·nded**NESS n.; *is o. to conviction, offers*, &c.; *keep o. doors* or *house*, entertain all comers, be hospitable; *the o. door*, free admission of foreign nations to country for trade; *force an o. door*, demand from willing giver; *the exhibition is now o.*, admitting visitors; *shop, show, court, is o. at such hours*; *o. heart*, frankness, unsuspiciousness, kindliness, cordiality, whence **open-heart**ED[2] a., **open-hear·ted**LY[2] adv., **open-hear·ted**NESS n.; *o. champion, scholarship*, successful, won, after unrestricted competition; *race is o. to all*; *position is o. to attack*; *o. time*, what is not CLOSE[1] time; *river, harbour, is o.*, free of ice; *o. weather, winter*, not frosty; *bowels are o.*, not constipated; *o. country*, free of fences; *there are three courses o. to us*; *o. question*, matter on which differences of opinion are legitimate; *o.* VERDICT); expanded, unfolded, outspread, spread out, not close, with intervals, porous, communicative, frank, (*o. book, flower*; *o. letter*, esp. protest &c. printed in newspaper &c. but addressing individual; *o. country*, affording wide views; *o. order* mil. & nav., formation with wide spaces between men or ships; *o. harmony*, of chord with wide intervals; *o. ice*, through which navigation is possible; *receive with o. arms*, heartily, whence **open-arm**ED a.; *with o. eyes*, not unconsciously or under misapprehension, also in eager attention or surprise, whence **open-ey**ED[2] a.; *has an o. hand*, gives freely, whence **open-hand**ED[2] a., **open-ha·nded**LY[2] adv., **open-ha·nded**NESS n.; *o. face*, ingenuous-looking, whence **open-fac**ED[2] a.; *o. work* or *o.-work*, pattern with interstices in metal, lace, &c.; *will be o. with you*, speak frankly); (Mus., of note) produced from unstopped pipe or string or without slide, key, or piston; (Phonet., of vowel) produced with relatively wide opening of mouth, (cf. CLOSE[1]), (of syllable) ending in vowel; hence **o·pen**NESS n. (N.) *the o.*, o. space or country or air, public view. [com.-Teut., cf. Du. *open*, G *offen*; f. root of UP]

o·pen[2], v.t. & i. Make or become OPEN[1] or more o. (*o.* SESAME; *shops o. at 9.0 a.m.*; *o. a business, shop, account, campaign*, &c., start or establish it or set it going; *o. fire*, begin shooting; abs. for *o. book*, as *opened at p. 12*; *o. ground*, break up with plough &c.; *o. bowels*, cause evacuation; *opens a prospect* lit. or fig., brings it to view; *o. the door to*, give opportunity for; *o.* one's *designs*, reveal or communicate them; *o.* one's *eyes*, show surprise; *o.* another's *eyes*, undeceive or enlighten him; *o. the mind, heart*, &c., expand or enlarge it; *not o. lips*, remain silent; *o. the* BALL[2]; *o.* PARLIAMENT; *o. the case* of counsel in lawcourt, make preliminary statement before calling witnesses; *o. the debate*, begin it, be first speaker; *door, room, opens into passage, on to lawn*, &c.; *the wonders of astronomy were opening to him*, becoming known; *o.* one's *shoulders* in cricket, of batsman's attitude in driving); commence speaking (*opened upon the fiscal question, with a compliment*, &c.); make a start (*lard opened active*, was in demand at once; *session opened yesterday*); (of hounds, & contempt. of men) begin to give tongue; (Naut.) get view of by change of position, come into full view, (*take care not to o. the obelisk*; *the harbour light opened*); *o. out*, unfold, develop, expand, (t. & i.), become communicative; *o. up*, make accessible, bring to notice, reveal. Hence **o·pen**ABLE a., **(-)o·pen**ER[1] (1, 2) n. [f. prec.]

o·pening[1] (ōpn-), n. In vbl senses; also or esp.: gap, passage, aperture; commencement, initial part; counsel's preliminary statement of case; (Chess) recognized sequence of moves for beginning game; opportunity, favourable conjuncture *for*. [-ING[1]]

o·pening[2] (ōpn-), a. In vbl senses; esp., initial, first, (*his o. remarks*). [-ING[2]]

o·penly, adv. Without concealment, publicly, frankly. [-LY[2]]

ŏ·pera, n. Dramatic performance or composition of which music is an essential part, branch of art concerned with these, (*grand o.*, without spoken dialogue; *comic o.*, or *opéra comique* F, of light character & usu. with spoken dialogue; *o. bouffe* pr. bōōf, of farcical character); *o.-cloak, -hood,* lady's for wearing at o. or going to evening parties; *o.-glass(es)*, small binocular for use at o. or theatre; *o.-hat*, man's tall collapsible hat; *o.-house*, theatre for performance of oo. [It. f. L, = labour, work]

ŏ·perate, v.i. & t. Be in action, produce an effect, exercise influence, (*the tax operates to our disadvantage*); play (*up*)*on* person's fears &c., try to act (*up*)*on*; (of medicines &c.) have desired effect, act; perform surgical or other operation (whence, of cases, **o·perable** a.), (try to) execute purpose, (Mil.) carry on strategic movements, (of stockbroker &c.) buy & sell esp. with view of influencing prices; bring about, accomplish, (*energy operates changes*); manage, work, conduct, (chiefly U.S.); *operating-room, -table*, for use in surgery; *operating-theatre*, room for surgical operations done before students. So **o·perāt**OR[2] n. [f. L *operari* work (*opus -eris* work), -ATE[3]]

operă·tic, a. Of, like, opera. Hence **opera·ti**CALLY adv. [as OPERATIZE, DRAMATIC]

opera·tion, n. Working, action, way thing works, efficacy, validity, scope, (*is in, comes into, o.*; *its o. is easily explained*; *must extend its o.*, make it valid for longer time or in wider sphere); active process, activity, performance, discharge of function, (*the o. of breathing, thinking, pruning*, &c.); financial transaction; (Surg.) thing done with hand or instrument to some part of body to remedy deformity, injury, disease, pain, &c.; strategic movement of troops, ships, &c.; (Math.) subjection of number or quantity to process affecting its value or form, e.g. multiplication. [OF, f. L *operationem* (OPERATE, -ION)]

o·perative (-*a*t-), a. & n. Having effect, in operation, efficacious; practical, not theoretical or contemplative, (*the o. part of the work*); of surgical operations; hence **o·perative**LY[2] adv. (N.) worker, artisan, mechanic, workman, mill-hand. [f. LL *operativus* (OPERATE, -IVE)]

o·peratize, v.t. Put into operatic form. [irreg. after DRAMATIZE, cf. OPERATIC]

oper·cūlum, n. (pl. *-la*). Fish's gill-cover; lid or valve closing aperture of shell when tenant is retracted; similar lidlike structure in plants &c. Hence **oper·cul**AR[1], **oper·cul**ATE[2], **oper·culated,** aa., **oper·-culi-** comb. form. [L (*operire* cover, -CULE)]

opere·tta, n. One-act or short light opera. [It. (OPERA, -ETTE)]

ŏ·perose, a. Requiring or showing or taking great pains, laborious. Hence **opero·se**LY[2] adv., **opero·se**NESS n. [f. L *operosus* (*opus -eris* work, -OSE[1])]

ŏ·phicleide (-īd), n. Keyed wind-instrument consisting of tapering brass tube bent double serving as bass or alto to key-bugle; (also *tuba*) powerful organ reed-pipe. [f. F *ophicléide* (Gk *ophis* serpent, *kleis -dos* key)]

ophi·dian, a. & n. (Member) of the *Ophidia* or order of reptiles including snakes. [mod. L *ophidia* pl., prob. irreg. f. Gk *ophis* snake, -AN]

ophio-, comb. form of Gk *ophis* snake, as -LATER, -LATRY, serpent-worship(per), -LOGY.

ŏ·phite, n. Serpentine, serpentine marble. Hence **ophi·t**IC a. [f. L f. Gk *ophitēs* f. *ophis* snake, -ITE[1](2)]

ophtha·lmia, n. Inflammation of the eye. [LL f. Gk (*ophthalmos* eye)]

ophthal·mic, a. & n. Of the eye; affected with ophthalmia; (remedy) good for eye-disease. [f. L f. Gk *ophthalmikos* (prec., -IC)]

ophthalm(o)-, comb. form of Gk *ophthalmos* eye, as *ophthalmi*·TIS, *ophthalmo*·LOGY, -LOGIST, -TOMY; *ophtha·lmo*SCOPE, instrument for inspecting retina.

ō·piate[1] (-*a*t), a. (archaic), & n. Containing opium, narcotic, soporific; (n.) drug containing opium & easing pain or inducing sleep. [f. med. L *opiatus* (OPIUM, -ATE[2])]

ō·piāte[2], v.t. Mix with opium. [prob. f. med. L **opiare* (OPIUM), -ATE[3]]

opi·ne, v.t. Express or hold the opinion (*that*, or abs. in parenthesis). [f. L *opinari*]

opi·nion (-yon), n. Judgement or belief based on grounds short of proof, provisional conviction, view held as probable, (*in my o.*, as it seems to me; *am of o. that*, believe; *a matter of o.*, disputable point); (also *public o.*) views or sentiment, esp. on moral questions, prevalent among people in general; what one thinks on or *on* a particular question, a belief, a conviction, (*the* COURAGE *of, act up to*, one's *oo.*); formal statement by expert when consulted of what he holds to be the fact or the right course, professional advice, (*you had better have another o.*); estimate (*have, formed, a very high, low, favourable, o. of him*), (with neg.) favourable estimate (*have no o. of Frenchmen*). [F, f. L *opinionem* (OPINE, -ION)]

opi·nionāted, a. Obstinate in opinion, dogmatic; self-willed. Hence **opi·nionated**NESS n. [f. obs. *opinionate* in same sense, perh. latinized form of obs. *opinion*ED²]

opi·nionātive, a. =prec. [OPINION + -ATIVE, cf. TALKATIVE]

o. pip. See OBSERVATION, PIP⁵.

ŏpisō·meter, n. Instrument for measuring curved lines as on map, made of wheel running on screw. [f. Gk *opisō* backwards, -METER]

ō·pium, n., & v.t. Reddish-brown heavy-scented bitter drug prepared from juice of kind of poppy, smoked or eaten as stimulant, intoxicant, or narcotic, & used as sedative (LAUDANUM) in medicine; *o. den*, haunt of o.-smokers; *o. habit*, of taking o.; hence **o·pium**ISM(5) n., **o·pium**IZE(5) v.t. (Vb) drug or treat with o. [L, f. Gk *opion* poppy-juice (*opos* juice)]

opode·ldoc, n. Kinds of soap liniment. [wd used & prob. made by Paracelsus for kinds of medical plaster]

opŏ·panax, n. A fetid gum resin formerly used in medicine; a gum resin used in perfumery. [L f. Gk, f. *opos* juice, *panax* (*pas pantos* all, *akos* cure) name of plant]

opo·ssum, n. Kinds of American small arboreal or aquatic nocturnal marsupial mammal with thumbed hind-foot (see also POSSUM); (Austral.) = PHALANGER. [Amer.-Ind.]

o·ppidan, a. & n. (Inhabitant) of a town (now rare); (at Eton) non-colleger, boy in boarding-house in town. [f. L *oppidanus* (*oppidum* town, -AN)]

o·ppilate, v.t. (med.). Block up, obstruct. Hence **oppil**A·TION n. [f. L OP(*pilare* ram)]

oppo·nency, n. (rare). Antagonism, opposition. [foll., -ENCY]

oppo·nent, a. & n. Opposing, contrary, opposed, (now rare; *o. muscle*, opposing thumb or lateral digit to other digit); (n.) adversary, antagonist. [f. L OP(*ponere* place), -ENT]

o·pportune (*-or-*; *also* -ū·n), a. (Of time) suitable, well-selected or as favourable as if chosen; (of action or event) well-timed, done or occurring by design or chance at favourable conjuncture. Hence **o·pportune**LY² adv., **o·pportune**NESS n., (*also* -ū·n-). [f. F *opportun* f. L OP(*portunus* f. *portus -ūs* harbour)]

opportu·nism, n. Allowing of due or undue weight to circumstances of the moment in determining policy; preference of what can to what should be done, compromise, practical politics, adaptation to circumstances; putting of expediency before principle or place before power, political time-serving. So **opportu·n**IST (2) n. [f. prec. after It. (*-ismo*) & F (*-isme*)]

opportu·nity, n. Opportuneness (rare); favourable juncture, good chance, opening, (*of doing*, *to* do, *for* action, or abs.; *find, make, get, seize, give, afford, an o.*). [f. F *opportunité* f. L *opportunitatem* (OPPORTUNE, -TY)]

oppose (opō·z), v.t. Place or produce or cite (thing, person) as obstacle, antagonist, counterpoise, or contrast, *to*, represent (things) as antithetical, (*to fury let us o. patience*; *you are opposing things that are practically identical*; *to Plato I o. Aristotle*; *opposed himself to it with all his power*; *the thumb can be opposed to any of the fingers*, placed against it front to front, whence **oppo·**SABLE a., **opposa**BI·LITY n.); set oneself against (person, thing), withstand, resist, obstruct, propose the rejection of (resolution, motion, &c.), (abs.) act as opponent or check (*it is the duty of an opposition to o.*); (p.p.) contrary, opposite, contrasted, (*characters strongly opposed*; *black is opposed to white*), (of persons) hostile, adverse, (*is firmly opposed to protection*). [f. F OP(*poser* POSE¹)]

oppo·seless, a. (poet.). Irresistible. [-LESS]

o·pposite (-ozĭt), a. (often governing n. by ellipse of *to*), n., adv., & prep. Contrary in position (to), facing, front to front or back to back (with), (*on o. sides of the square*; *came from, went in, o. directions*; *the tree o. to* or *o. the house*; *o. leaves* &c. in bot., placed at same height on o. sides of stem, or placed straight in front of other organ, opp. *alternate*; *o. number*, person or thing similarly placed in another set &c. to the given one); of contrary kind, diametrically different *to* or *from*, *the* other of a contrasted pair, (*of an o. kind to, from, what I expected*; *much liked by the o. sex*); hence **o·pposite**LY² adv. (chiefly bot.), **o·pposite**NESS n. (N.) o. thing or term (*you are cold-blooded, she is the o.*; *the most extreme oo. have some qualities in common*). (Adv. & prep.) in o. place, position, or direction (to) (*there was an explosion o.*, in the house across the street; *o. prompter* in theatre, abbr. *o.p.*, to actor's left; *happened o. the Mansion House*). [F, f. L OP(*positus* p.p. of *ponere* place)]

oppŏsiti- (-z-), comb. form f. L as prec. in bot. wds as *-fo·lious* opposite-leaved, *-se·palous* (of stamen) placed straight in front of sepal.

opposi·tion (-zĭshn), n. Placing opposite (*o. of the thumb*, cf. OPPOSE); diametrically opposite position (esp. astron., of two heavenly bodies when their longitude differs by 180°, opp. CONJUNCTION; *planet is in o.*, opposite sun); contrast, antithesis; (Log.) relation between two propositions with same subject & predicate but differing in quantity or quality or both; antagonism, resistance, being hostile, (*offer a determined o.*; *did it in o. to public opinion*; *was in o. at the time*, belonging to the o. in next sense); *the o., His Majesty's o.*, chief parliamentary party opposed to that in office (*the leader of the o.*; *the o. whips, benches*, &c.); any party opposed to some proposal. Hence **oppo·si·tion**AL a. (rare), **opposi·tion**IST(2) n. & a. (rare). [f. L OP(*positio* POSITION)]

oppŏ·sitive, a. (rare). Adversative, antithetic; fond of opposing. [prec., -IVE]

oppre·ss, v.t. Overwhelm with superior weight or numbers or irresistible power; lie heavy on, weigh down, (spirits, imagination, &c.); govern tyrannically, keep under by coercion, subject to continual cruelty or injustice. So **oppre·ss**ION (-shn), **oppre·ss**OR², nn., **oppre·ss**IVE a., **oppre·ssive**LY² adv., **oppre·ssive**NESS n. [f. OF *oppresser* f. med. L OP(*pressare* frequent. of L *premere* press)]

opprō·brious, a. Conveying reproach, abusive, vituperative. Hence **oppro·brious**LY² adv. [f. OF *opprobrieux* (foll., -OUS)]

opprō·brium, n. Disgrace attaching to some act or conduct, infamy, crying of shame. [L, f. OP(*probrare* f. *probrum* disgraceful act)]

oppūg·n, v.t. Controvert, call in question, whence **oppug·n**ER¹ n.; (rare) attack, resist, be in conflict with, (so **oppŭ·gn**ANT a. & n., **oppŭ·gn**ANCE, **oppŭ·gn**ANCY, **oppugn**A·TION, nn., all rare). [f. L OP(*pugnare* fight) attack, besiege]

o·psimath, n. (rare). One who learns late in life. So **opsi·math**Y¹ n. [f. Gk *opsimathēs* (*opse* late, *manthanō* learn)]

opsŏ·nic, a. Having the effect on bacteria of making them easier of consumption by phagocytes (*o. action, power*; *o. index*, numerical expression of the phagocytic power of the serum of a patient under anti-bacterial injections as below). So **o·pson**IN n., the substance produced in patient's blood by injection of dead cultures of the bacteria of his disease. [f. Gk *opsōnion* provisions (*opson* cooked meat), -IC]

opt, v.i. (rare). Exercise an option, make choice, (*between* alternatives or *for* alternative). [f. F *opter* f. L *optare* choose, wish]

optā·tive, a. & n. (gram.). Expressing wish (*o. mood*, set of verbal forms of this kind, distinct chiefly in Greek and Sanskrit; *o. use of subjunctive*); hence **opta·tive**LY² adv. (N.) o. mood, verbal form belonging to it. [F (*-if, -ive*), f. LL *optativus* (prec., -ATIVE)]

o·ptic, a. & n. (Anat.) of the eye or sense of sight (*o. nerve, neuritis*, &c.; *o. angle*, between lines from extremities of object to eye, or from two eyes to one point). (N.) eye (now usu. facet.); (pl., with sing. constr.) science of sight & esp. of the laws of its medium, light. [f. F *optique* f. med. L f. Gk *optikos* (*optos* seen f. *op-*, cf. *opsomai* fut. of *horaō* see, -IC)]

o·ptical, a. Visual, ocular, (*o. illusion*, produced by too implicit confidence in the evidence of sight); of sight or light in relation to each other, belonging to optics, constructed to assist sight or on the principles of optics. Hence **o·ptical**LY² adv. [prec., -AL]

opti·cian (-shn), n. Maker or seller of optical instruments. [f. F *opticien* (OPTIC, -ICIAN)]

optime. See WRANGLER.

o·ptimism, n. Doctrine, esp. as set forth by Leibnitz, that the actual world is the best of all possible worlds; view that good must ultimately prevail over evil in the universe; sanguine disposition, inclination to take bright views. So **o·ptimi**ST(2) n. & a., **optimi·st**IC a., **optimi·st**ICALLY adv., **o·ptim**IZE(2) v.i. [f. F *optimisme* (L *optimus* best, -ISM)]

o·ption, n. Choice, choosing, thing that is or may be chosen, (*make* one's *o.*; *none of the oo. is satisfactory*); liberty of choosing, freedom of choice, (LOCAL² *o.*; *imprisonment without the o. of a fine*; *have no o. but to*, must); (Stock Exch. &c.) purchased right to call for or make delivery within specified time of specified stocks &c. at specified rate. [F, f. L *optionem* (st. of *optare* choose, -TION)]

o·ptional, a. Not obligatory. [prec., -AL]

o·ptophone, n. Instrument converting light into sound, & so enabling the blind to read print &c. by ear. [see OPTIC, -O-, PHONO-]

ŏ·pūlent, a. Rich, wealthy; abounding, abundant, well stored. Hence or cogn. **o·pul**ENCE n., **o·pulent**LY² adv. [f. L *opulens* or *-lentus* (*opem* accus. quantity, -ULENT)]

ŏ·pus, n. (no pl.). Musician's separate composition of any kind (used esp. in citing it from among his works by number; abbr. *op.*; *Beethoven op. 15*); *magnum o., o. magnum*, or *o.*, great literary undertaking, writer's or other artist's chief production. [L, = work]

opu·scule, ***opu·scūlum*** (pl. *-la*), n. Minor musical or literary composition. [(*-ule* F) f. L (*-um*) dim. of prec. (-CULE)]

or¹, n. (herald.). Gold or yellow in armorial bearings. [F, f. L *aurum* gold]

or², prep. & conj. (archaic). Before, ere, (chiefly now in *or ever, or e'er*, poet.). [OE *ár* adv. early, w. sense of its compar. *ǽr* ERE]

or³, conj. introducing second of two alternatives (*white or black*), all but the first (*white or grey or black*) or only the last (*white, grey, or black*) of any number, the second of each of several pairs (*white or black, red or yellow, blue or green*), or (poet.) each of two (*or in the heart or in the head*). An alternative introduced by *or* may be (1) on equal footing with preceding (*shall you be there or not?*; *any Tom, Dick, or Harry*), (2) true of other instances (*ripe tomatoes are red or yellow*), (3) mere synonym (*common or garden*), (4) indication that preceding is doubtfully accurate (*one or two, five or six, &c.*, a few), (5) explanation of preceding (*saw a dug-out or hollowed-tree boat*), (6) statement of only remaining possibility or choice given (often after *either*; *a thing must surely be or not be*; *for goodness' sake either take it or leave it*), (7) statement of result of rejection &c. of preceding (often with *else*; *she must weep or she must die*; *make haste, or else you will be late*), (8) second &c. member of indirect question or conditional protasis after *whether* (*ask him whether he was there or not*; *must do it whether I like or dislike it*). In syntax, a set of alternatives with *or* is sing. if each member is sing. (*man or woman, boy or girl, goes unmolested*; not *go*); if the members differ in number &c., the nearest prevails (*were you or he, was he or you, there?*; *either he or you were, either you or he was*), but some forms (e.g., *was I or you on duty?*) are avoided; forms in which difference of gender in the members causes difficulty with pronouns (*a landlord or landlady expects their, his or her, his, rent*) are usually avoided, *their rent* or *the rent due to them* being ungrammatical, *his or her rent* or *the rent due to him or her* clumsy, & *his rent* or *the rent due to him* slovenly. [f. obs. *other* conj., prob. modif. of OE *oththe* or (cf. G *oder*, earlier *eddo, ode*, &c.) on anal. of alternative &c. wds in -THER]

-or[1], suf. varying with *-our* (ME), f. AF *-our* f. OF *-or, -ur*, F *-eur*, in wds f. L nn. of condition in *-or -oris* mostly f. vbs in *-ēre*, as *liquor* (ME *licour*), *ardour*; all corrected in U.S. to *-or*; in England many retain *-our*.

-or[2], suf. (varying with *-er*, see below) in nn. expressing (1) personal agent (*possessor*), (2) thing that acts, instrument, machine, &c., (*extensor*), f. L *-or -oris* appended to p.p. stems. L *-or* was always preceded by *-t-* or *-s-*, which remains in all E recent adoptions (mis-spelt in *author* f. *auctor*) taken direct or thr. F *-teur, -seur*; but L wds in *-ator, -etor, -itor*, taken f. OF have lost *-t-* & usu. the preceding vowel; thus L *donator(em)*, OF *doneor, doneur*, AF *donour*, E *donor*; *saviour* retains trace of *-at-* (see -IOUR) in *-i-*; some E agent nn. were formed orig. in F on this anal., as *surveyor, warrior*. In E, *-or*, pronounced like -ER[1], [2], has been displaced by it in some wds, as *barber* (ME & AF *barbour* f. L *barbatorem*), & has displaced it in others, as *sailor* (perh. on anal. of *tailor*), *chancellor*. When *-er* & *-or* coexist, *-or* has sometimes a more legal or professional sense.

ŏ·rach (-ĭtsh), n. Kitchen-garden plant, Mountain Spinach. [earlier *arache* f. F *arroche* f. L *atriplicem* nom. *-ex* f. Gk *atraphaxus*]

ŏ·racle, n. Place at which ancient Greeks &c. were accustomed to consult their deities for advice or prophecy (*work the o.*, secure desired answer by tampering with priests &c., also fig. bring secret influence to bear in one's favour); response, often ambiguous or obscure, given at such place; holy of holies or mercy-seat in Jewish temple; (vehicle, personal or other, of) divine inspiration or revelation; person or thing serving as infallible guide, test, or indicator; authoritative, profoundly wise, or mysterious adviser or advice, judge or judgement, prophet or prophecy. Hence (esp. w. ref. to obscurity) **orā·cul**AR[1] a., **ora·cular**LY[2] adv., **oraculă·**RITY n. [f. L *oraculum* (*orare* speak, *-culo-* instr. suf.)]

or·al, a. Spoken, verbal, by word of mouth; (Anat.) of the mouth. Hence **or·al**LY[2] adv. [f. L *os oris* mouth, -AL]

ŏ·range[1] (-ĭnj), n. & a. (Evergreen tree bearing) large roundish many-celled juicy acid or sweet fruit enclosed in bright reddish-yellow tough rind (*squeeze the o.*, take all the good from anything; *squeezed o.*, thing from which no more good can be got; *China o.*, former name of common o.; *mock o.*, the shrub Syringa; *oo. & lemons*, nursery game, also kind of toad-flax; *Blenheim o.*, kind of apple); (also *o.-colour*) reddish-yellow (*o.* adj., of this colour); *o.-blossom*, flowers of o., worn by brides at wedding; *o.-fin*, kind of trout; *o.* MARMALADE; *o.-tip*, kind of butterfly. Hence **o·range**RY(3) n. [OF, ult. f. Arab. *nāranj*]

Orange[2] (ŏ·rĭnj), n. Town on Rhone from which *Princes of O.* took title (*William of O.* in Eng. hist., King William III); (attrib. & in comb.) connected with Irish ultra-protestant party (prob. f. the *orangemen*, political society formed 1795 for protestant ascendancy in Ireland, prob. named after O. lodge of freemasons in Belfast, prob. named after William), whence **o·rang**ISM(3) n. [F, f. L *Arausionem* nom. *-o*]

orangea·de (-jād), n. Effervescent or still drink of orange juice &c. [-ADE]

ora·ng - outa·ng (-ōō-), **or·ang - u·tan** (-ōō-), n. Large long-armed arboreal anthropoid ape of Borneo & Sumatra. [Malay (*-utan*) = man of the woods]

ora·te, v.i. (joc.). Make speech, hold forth, play the orator. [back form. f. foll.]

orā·tion (-shn), n. Formal address or harangue or discourse esp. of ceremonial kind; (Gram.) language, way of speaking (*direct, indirect* or *oblique, o.*, person's words as actually spoken, or with the changes of person, tense, &c., usual in reporting). [f. L *oratio* (*orare* speak, -ATION)]

ŏ·rator (-*ater*), n. Maker of a speech; eloquent public speaker; *Public O.*, official at Oxford & Cambridge speaking for university on state occasions. Hence

o·ratress[1] n. [f. OF *orateur* f. L *oratorem* (prec., -OR[2])]

ŏrator·io, n. Semi-dramatic musical composition on sacred theme performed by soloists, chorus, & orchestra, without action, scenery, or costume. [It., orig. of musical services at oratory of St Philip Neri]

ŏ·ratorize, v.i. =ORATE. [-IZE]

ŏ·ratory[1], n. Small chapel, place for private worship; R.-C. religious society of simple priests without vows founded in Rome 1564 to give plain preaching & popular services, also any branch of this in England &c., whence **orator·ian** a. & n. [f. L *oratorium* neut. of *oratorius* (*orare* pray, speak, -TORY)]

o·ratory[2], n. (Art of making) speeches, rhetoric; highly coloured presentment of facts, eloquent or exaggerating language. Hence **oratŏ·rical** a., **orato·rically**[2] adv. [f. L *oratoria* (*ars* art) of speaking, fem. as prec.]

orb, n., & v.t. & i. Circle, circular disk, ring, (now rare); sphere, globe; heavenly body; eyeball, eye, (poet.); globe surmounted by cross as part of regalia; organized or collective whole; hence **or·bless** a. (Vb) enclose in, gather (t. & i.) into, o. [f. L *orbis* ring]

orbi·cūlar, a. Circular, discoid, ring-shaped (*o. muscle*, sphincter); spherical, globular, rounded, (fig.) forming complete whole. Hence or cogn. **orbicula·rity** n., **orbi·cularly**[2] adv., **orbi·culate**[2] a. (nat. hist.). [f. L *orbicularis* (*orbiculus* dim. as prec., -AR[1])]

or·bit, n. Eye-socket, whence **or·bito-** comb. form; border round eye of bird or insect; curved course of planet, comet, satellite, or binary star. Hence **or·bital** a. [f. L *orbita* track of wheel or moon (*orbis* ring)]

orc, n. Kinds of cetacean; sea or other monster. [f. F *orque* f. L *orca* kind of whale]

Orcā·dian, a. & n. (Native) of Orkney. [f. L *Orcades* Orkney Islands, -IAN]

or·chard (-tsh-), n. Enclosure with fruit-trees; *orchardman*, fruit-grower, also **or·chardist**(3) n. [OE *ortegeard* prob. f. L *hortus* garden, YARD[2]]

orchĕ·stic (-k-), a. Of dancing. Hence **orche·stics** n. [f. Gk *orkhēstikos* (*orkhēstēs* dancer, see foll.)]

or·chestra (-k-), n. Semicircular space in front of ancient-Greek theatre-stage where chorus danced & sang; part of modern theatre or concert-room assigned to band or chorus; instrumental performers, or concerted music performed by them, in theatre or concert-room, whence **orche·stral** a. [L, f. Gk *orkhēstra* (*orkheomai* dance)]

or·chestrate, v.t. & i. Compose (t. & i.), arrange, or score, for orchestral performance. Hence **orchestra·tion** n. [-ATE[3]]

orchestri·na (-ēna), n. Elaborate kind of barrel-organ meant to give orchestra-like effect. [-INA[1]]

or·chid, or·chis, (-k-), n. Member of large order of monocotyledonous herbs (*-is* is usu. of wild English kinds, *-id* of exotics or in bot. use), of which English kinds are terrestrial with tuberous root & erect fleshy stem with spike of usu. red or purple flowers, & many exotic kinds have flowers of fantastic shapes & brilliant colours. Hence **orchida·ceous** a., **or·chidist**(3) n. [(*-id* made 1845 by Lindley, see -ID[2]) f. L f. Gk *orkhis -ios* testicle, orchis, (w. ref. to shape of tuber)]

or·chido-, comb. form of prec., as -MA·NIA, -LOGY. [irreg. for *orchio-* f. Gk as prec.]

or·chil (-tsh-), n. Red or violet dye from lichen. [f. OF *orchel* etym. dub.]

or·cin, n. (chem.). Colourless crystalline substance extracted from lichens & yielding various dyes when compounded. [f. mod. L *orcina* (prec., -IN)]

ordai·n, v.t. (Eccl.) appoint ceremonially to Christian ministry, confer holy orders (esp. those of deacon or priest) on (*was ordained priest, elder*, &c., or abs.); (of God, fate, &c.) destine, appoint, (*has ordained the time, death as our lot, us mortal, us to die, that we should live*); appoint authoritatively, decree, enact, (*what the laws o.; o. that* —). [f. OF *ordener* f. L *ordĭnare* (*ordo -inis* order)]

ordai·nment, n. (rare). Decree(ing). [-MENT]

ordē·al (*or* -dēl), n. Ancient Teutonic mode of deciding suspected person's guilt or innocence by subjecting him to physical test such as plunging of hand in boiling water, safe endurance of which was taken as divine acquittal; experience that tests character or endurance, severe trial. [com.-Teut.; OE *ordāl,-ēl*, cf. Du. *oordeel*, G *urteil*, judgement; n. f. compd vb (OHG *artailan*, OE *adǣlan*, deal out)]

or·der[1], n. (Main senses) 1. Rank, row, class. 2. Sequence, arrangement. 3. Mandate. 1. Tier (now rare; *o. on o. of sculptured figures*); social class or rank, separate & homogeneous set of persons, (*esp. the higher, lower, oo.; all oo. & degrees of men; the o. of baronets; the clerical, military, o.*); kind, sort, (*talents of a high, considerations of quite another, o.*); any of the nine grades of angels (seraphim, cherubim, thrones, dominations, principalities, powers, virtues, archangels, angels); grade of Christian ministry (*holy oo.* in Anglican church, those of bishop, priest, & deacon, in R.-C., these & subdeacon; *minor oo.* in R.-C. Church, those of acolyte, exorcist, reader, & doorkeeper), (pl.) status of clergyman (*take oo.*, be ordained; *in oo.*, ordained; often in these phrr., & always elsewhere, *holy oo.*); fraternity of monks or friars, or formerly of knights, bound by common rule of life (*the Fran-*

ciscan o.; *the Teutonic o.*; *the o. of Templars*); company usu. instituted by sovereign to which distinguished persons are admitted by way of honour or reward (*o. of the Garter, the Bath, Merit,* &c.), insignia worn by members of this (*sent him, wears, the o. of the Golden Fleece*); (Archit.) mode of treatment with established proportions between parts (esp. one of the five *classical oo.*, Tuscan, Doric, Ionic, Corinthian, & Composite, each of which is superior to the preceding in height, lightness, & decoration, of pillar & capital; Tuscan & Composite were Roman developments of the others, which were Greek); (Math.) degree of complexity (*line, equation, fluxion, of the first* &c. *o.*); (Nat. Hist.) classification-group below CLASS[1] & subdivided into genera or families (*natural o.* in bot., abbr. N.O., of plants allied in general structure, not merely agreeing in single characteristic as in Linnaean system). 2. Sequence, succession, manner of following, (*in alphabetical, chronological,* &c., *o.*; *out of o.*, not systematically arranged; *follow the o. of events*; *inverts the natural o.*; *take them in o.*, one after another according to some principle); regular array, condition in which every part or unit is in its right place, tidiness, normal or healthy or efficient state, (*drew them up in o.*; *are scattered without any o.*; *love of o.*; *is in bad, out of, o.*, not working rightly; *is in o.* or *good o.*, fit for use); (archaic) suitable action, measures, (*take o. to* do; *take o. with*, arrange, dispose of); constitution of the world, way things normally happen, collective manifestations of natural forces or laws, natural or moral or spiritual system with definite tendencies, (esp. *the o. of nature* or *things* or *the world*; *the old o. changeth*; *whether there is a moral o. or not*); stated form of divine service (*the o. of confirmation*); principles of decorum & rules of procedure accepted by legislative assembly or public meeting, or enforced by its president (*Speaker called him to o.*; *O.! O.!*, protest against infringement of it; *rise to o.* or *a point of o.*, interrupt debate &c. with inquiry whether something being said or done is *in* or *out of o.*; *o. of the day*, programme, business set down for treatment, whence, in gen. use, prevailing state of things, as *industry, thunder, cricket, is the o. of the day*; *o.-paper*, written or printed o. of the day; *o.-book*, in which motions to be submitted to the House of Commons must be entered); prevalence of constituted authority, law-abiding state, absence of riot, turbulence, & violent crime, (often *law & o.*; *o. was restored*; *keep o.*, enforce it); *marching, review,* &c., *o.* (mil.), the regulation uniform & equipment carried by the soldier in marching, at review, &c. (cf. MARCH[5]*ing orders*); (Mil.) *the o.*, position of company &c. with arms ordered (see foll.); *in o. to* do, with a view to, for the purpose of, doing; *in o. that*, with the intention or to the end that. 3. Mandate, injunction, authoritative direction or instruction, (often pl.; *gave oo., an o., the o., for* something *to be* done, *that* it *should be* done, &c.; *is obedient to oo.*; *O. in Council*, sovereign order on some administrative matter given by advice of Privy Council; *by o.*, according to direction of the proper authority; *judge gave, made, refused, an* or *the o.*); (Banking &c.) instruction to pay money or deliver property signed by owner or responsible agent (*o. cheque, cheque to* person's *o.*, one requiring payee's endorsement before being cashed; *postal, money* or pop. *post-office, o.*, kinds of Post-Office cheque for remitting money, the latter non-transferable); (Commerc.) direction to manufacturer, tradesman, &c., to supply something (*made to o.*, according to special directions, to suit individual measurements, &c., opp. *ready-made*; *grocer has sent for oo.*; *is on o.*, has been ordered but not yet supplied; *a large o.* colloq., difficult job; *o.-book*, in which tradesman enters oo.; *o.-clerk*, with duty of entering oo.; *o.-form*, skeleton o. to be filled in by customer); pass admitting bearer gratis, cheap, or as privilege, to theatre, museum, private house, &c. [f. OF *ordre* f. L *ordinem* nom. *-o*]

or·der[2], v.t. Put in o., array, regulate, (archaic; *ordered his troops*; *o.* one's *affairs*; *has ordered his life well*); (Mil.) *o. arms*, stand rifles butt on ground & hold them close to right side; (of God, fate, &c.) ordain (*so we hoped, but it was otherwise ordered*); command, bid, prescribe, (*o. a retreat*, thing *to be* done, person *to* do, *that* person or thing *should*; *ordered him a mustard plaster*); command or direct (person &c.) to go *to, away, home,* &c. (*was ordered to Egypt*; *o. about*, send hither & thither, domineer over); direct tradesman, servant, &c., to supply (*o. dinner*, settle what it shall consist of). [f. prec.]

or·derly, a. & n. Methodically arranged or inclined, regular, obedient to discipline, not unruly, well-behaved, whence **or·derliness** n.; (Mil.) of, charged with conveyance or execution of, orders (*o. book*, regimental or company book for entry of orders; *o. officer*, officer of the day; *o.-room*, in barracks for company's business); *o. bin*, street box for refuse. (N.) soldier in attendance on officer to carry orders &c.; attendant in (esp. military) hospital. [-LY[1]]

or·dinal, a. & n. (Number) defining thing's position in series (*first, twentieth,* &c., *are oo.* or *o. numbers*; cf. CARDINAL); of a nat.-hist. order; (n.) service-book used at ordinations. [f. LL *ordinalis* (ORDER[1], -AL)]

or·dinance, n. Authoritative direction, decree (SELF-*denying o.*); religious rite; (rare) collocation of parts in literary work or architecture. [f. OF *ordenance* (ORDAIN, -ANCE)]

or·dinary, a. & n. Regular, normal, customary, usual, not exceptional, not above the usual, commonplace, (*in o.* appended to *physician* &c., by permanent appointment, not temporary or extraordinary; *in an o. way I should refuse*, if the circumstances were not exceptional; *something out of the o.*; *o. seaman*, abbr. O.S., lower rating than *able*; *in o.* of ships, laid up, not in commission), whence **or·dinari**LY[2] adv., **or·dinari**NESS n.; (authority) having immediate or *ex officio* & not deputed jurisdiction (*the O.*, archbishop in province, bishop in diocese; *O.* or *Lord O.* in Scotland, one of five judges of Court of Session constituting Outer House); rule or book laying down order of divine service; public meal provided at fixed time & price in tavern &c.; (Herald.) charge of earliest, simplest, & commonest kind (esp. chief, pole, bend, fess, bar, chevron, cross, saltire); ungeared bicycle (opp. *safety*). [f. L *ordinarius* (ORDER[1], -ARY[1])]

or·dinate (-*a*t), n. (geom.). Any of series of parallel chords of conic section in relation to bisecting diameter (esp. used of half the chord, from curve to diameter), straight line from any point drawn parallel to one coordinate axis & meeting the other. [f. L (*linea*) *ordinate* (*applicata*) line applied parallel]

ordina·tion, n. Arrangement in ranks, classification; conferring of holy orders, admission to church ministry; decreeing, ordainment. [f. L *ordinationem* (ORDAIN, -ATION)]

ordinee·, n. Newly ordained deacon. [ORDAIN, -EE]

or·dnance, n. Mounted guns, cannon; branch of public service dealing esp. with military stores & materials (*Army O. Department*, formerly with wider powers *Board of O.*; *o. survey*, Government survey of Great Britain & Ireland; *o. datum*, sea level as defined for o. survey). [var. of ORDINANCE]

or·dure (-dūr, -j*er*), n. Excrement, dung; obscenity, foul language. [F (*ord* foul f. L HORRID*us*, -URE)]

ore, n. Native mineral from which precious or useful metal may be profitably extracted; (poet.) metal, esp. gold. [prob. f. OE *ár* brass (cf. L *aes aeris*, Skr. *ayas* metal) with sense changed to that of OE *óra* unwrought metal (cf. Du. *oer*), which would itself have given a mod. *oor*, not *ore*]

or·ĕăd, n. (L & Gk mythol.). Mountain nymph. [f. L *oreas -ados* f. Gk *oreias* f. *oros* mountain, -AD(1)]

ore·ctic, a. (philos., med.). Of desire or appetite, appetitive. [f. Gk *orektikos* (*oregō* stretch out, -IC)]

or·ĕide, n. Kind of brass resembling gold used in imitation jewellery. [f. F *oréide* (*or* f. L *aurum* gold)]

orfe, n. Kind of gold-fish. [G & F, f. Gk *orphos* sea perch]

or·gan, n. Musical instrument of pipes supplied with wind by bellows, sounded by keys, & distributed into sets or stops having special tone, which in turn form groups or partial **oo.** (*great, choir, swell, solo, pedal, o.*) each with separate keyboard, whence **or·gan**IST(3) n.; =BARREL[1]-o. (*o.- grinder*, player of this); keyboard wind-instrument with metal reeds, harmonium, (*American o.*, with wind drawn inwards to reeds); *mouth o.*, child's toy reed instrument; part of animal or vegetable body adapted for special vital function (*oo. of speech, perception, digestion, generation*, &c.; NASAL *o.*); person's voice with reference to its quality or power (*has a magnificent o.*); medium of communication, mouthpiece of opinion, esp. newspaper or magazine or review representing a party, cause, sect, pursuit, &c.; *o.-blower*, person or mechanism working o. bellows; *o.-builder*, of musical oo.; *o.-loft*, gallery in church or concert-room for o.; *o. piano*, with mechanism giving sustained tones as in o.; *o.-screen*, ornamental screen often between choir & nave on which o. is placed in cathedral &c.; *o.-stop*, set of pipes of similar tone in o., handle of mechanism that brings it into action. Hence **or·gan**LESS a. [f. L f. Gk *organon* tool (*erg-* WORK)]

or·gandie, n. Kind of very fine translucent muslin. [f. F *organdi* etym. dub.]

orgă·nic, a. (Physiol.) of the bodily organs, vital, (Path., of disease) affecting structure of an organ (opp. *functional*); having organs or organized physical structure, of animals or plants, (opp. *inorganic*); (Chem., of compound substances &c.) existing as constituent of organized bodies or formed from bodies so existing, of hydrocarbons or their derivatives (*o. chemistry*, dealing with these); constitutional, inherent, fundamental, structural; organized or systematic or coordinated (*o. unity*; *an o. whole*). Hence **orga·ni**CALLY adv. [f. L f. Gk *organikos* (ORGAN, -IC)]

or·ganism, n. Organized body with connected interdependent parts sharing common life, (material structure of) individual animal or plant; whole with interdependent parts compared to living being. [ORGANIZE, -ISM]

organiza·tion, n. In vbl senses of foll.; also, organized body or system or society. [f. med. L *organizatio* (foll., -ATION)]

or·ganize, v.t. & i. Furnish with organs, make organic, make into living being or tissue, (usu. in p.p.), (intr.) become organic; form into an organic whole (with constituents or resulting whole as obj.); give orderly structure to, frame & put into working order, make arrangements for or get up (undertaking involving co-operation). Hence **or·ganiz**ABLE a., **or·ganiz**ER[1] n. [f. med. L *organizare* (ORGAN, -IZE)]

or·ganon, or·ganum, n. Instrument of thought, system of or treatise on logic. [Gk (*-on*), & L (*-um*), see ORGAN; *-on* was title of Aristotle's logical writings, & *novum* (new) *organum* that of Bacon's]

or·ganzine (-ēn), n. Silk thread in which the main twist is in contrary direction to that of the strands. [f. F *organsin* f. It. *organzino*]

or·gasm (-zm), n. Violent excitement, rage, paroxysm; venereal excitement in coition. So **orga·stic** a. [f. Gk *orgaō* swell, *-sm* as in SPASM, -ISM]

or·gĕăt (*or* -zhah), n. Cooling drink made from barley or almonds & orange-flower water. [F (*orge* f. L *hordeum* barley, -ADE)]

orgia·stic, a. Of the nature of an orgy. [f. Gk *orgiastikos* (*orgiastēs* agent n. f. *orgiazō* celebrate ORGY)]

or·gy (-jĭ), n. (Gk & Rom. Ant.; usu. pl.) secret rites in worship of various gods, esp. in that of Bacchus celebrated with wild dancing, drinking, and singing; drunken or licentious revel, (pl.) revelry or debauchery. [earlier pl. only, f. F *orgies* f. L f. Gk *orgia* pl.]

or·iel, n. Large windowed polygonal recess projecting usu. from upper storey & supported from ground or on corbels; (also *o. window*) window of o., projecting window of upper storey. [f. OF *oriol*, etym. dub.]

or·ient[1], n. & a. (Poet.) *the* eastward part of sky or earth; *the* East or countries E. of Mediterranean & S. Europe; o. pearl; peculiar lustre of pearl of best quality. (Adj.) oriental (poet.); (of precious stones esp. pearls, of finest kinds, as coming anciently from the East) lustrous, sparkling, precious; (of sun, daylight, &c., or fig.) rising, nascent. [F, f. L *orientem* nom. *-ens* rising sun, east, (*oriri* rise, -ENT)]

ŏrie·nt[2], **ŏ·rientate,** (*or* or-), vv.t. & i. Place (building &c.) so as to face E., build (church) with chancel end due E., bury with feet eastward; place or exactly determine position of with regard to points of compass, settle or find bearings of, (fig.) bring into clearly understood relations (*o. oneself*, determine how one stands); (intr.) turn eastward or in specified direction. Hence **orient**A·TION n. [f. F *orienter* (prec.)]

ŏrie·ntal (*or* or-), a. & n. Easterly (archaic); (inhabitant) of the East or countries E. of Mediterranean & S. Europe, esp. Asiatic, occurring in or coming from or characteristic of the civilization &c. of the East, whence **orie·ntal**ISM(2, 4), **orie·ntal**IST(3), nn., **orie·ntal**IZE(2, 3) v.i. & t.; (of pearls &c.) orient; *o. stitch*, close kind of herringbone stitch. Hence **orie·ntal**LY[2] adv. [F, f. L *orientalis* (ORIENT[1], -AL)]

ŏ·rifice, n. Aperture, mouth of cavity, perforation, vent. [F, f. LL *orificium* (*os oris* mouth, *-ficere* = *facere* make)]

ŏ·riflamme (-ăm), n. Sacred banner of St Denis, banderole of red silk on lance received by early French kings from abbot of St Denis on starting for war; (fig.) anything material or ideal serving as rallying-point in struggle; bright conspicuous object, blaze of colour, &c. [F (L *aurum* gold, *flamma* flame)]

ŏ·rigan, ori·ganum, n. Wild Marjoram, & kinds of allied plant. [L (*-um*), f. Gk *origanon*]

ŏ·rigin, n. Derivation, beginning or rising from something, person's extraction, source, starting-point. [f. F *origine* f. L *originem* nom. *-go* (*oriri* rise)]

ori·ginal, a. & n. Existent from the first, primitive, innate, initial, earliest, (*o. sin*, innate depravity common to all human beings in consequence of the fall); that has served as pattern, of which copy or translation has been made, not derivative or dependent, first-hand, not imitative, novel in character or style, inventive, creative, thinking or acting for oneself, (*where is the o. picture?*; *what does the o. Greek say?*; *where hooping-cough is o.*; *is it an o. drawing or a woodcut?*; *made a very o. remark*; *has an o. mind*; *o. people do o. things*); hence or cogn. **origina·l**ITY n., **ori·ginal**LY[2] adv. (N.) derivation, descent, origin, (rare); pattern, archetype, thing from which another is copied or translated, (*several transcripts from the same o.*; *reads Don Quixote in the o.*); eccentric person. [F, f. L *originalis* (prec., -AL)]

ori·ginate, v.t. & i. Give origin to, initiate, cause to begin, whence **ori·gin**ATIVE a.; have origin, take rise, (usu. *from* or *in* thing or place, *with* or *from* person. So **origin**A·TION, **ori·ginat**OR[2], nn. [ORIGIN, -ATE[3]]

ōrinā·sal (-zl), a. & n. Of, sounded with, both mouth & nose (esp. of French nasalized vowels); (n.) o. vowel. [L *os oris* mouth, -I-, L *nasus* nose, -AL]

or·iole, n. (Also *Golden o.*) bird with black & yellow plumage visiting British Isles in summer; other old-world birds of same genus; kinds of bird of similarly coloured American genus. [f. med. L *oriolus* f. L *aureolus* dim. of *aureus* golden (*aurum* gold)]

Ori·on, n. (astron.). Brilliant constellation S. of zodiac, figured as hunter with belt & sword (*O.'s belt*, three bright stars in short line across O.; *O.'s hound*, Sirius). [L, f. Gk *Ōriōn*]

Orī·onid, n. (astron.). One of meteor-system with radiant point in Orion. [prec., Gk *-is -idos* fem. patronymic]

ŏ·rison (-zn), n. (archaic). A prayer (usu. in pl.). [F, f. L *orationem* speech (*orare* speak, pray, -ATION, -SON)]

Or·lĕans, n. Kind of plum; fabric of cotton warp & worsted weft. [name of French city]

or·lop, n. Lowest deck of ship with three or more decks. [f. Du. *overloop* covering (*overloopen* run over, see OVER, LEAP¹)]

or·mer, n. Edible univalve mollusc, the Sea-ear. [Channel-I. F, f. F *ormier* contr. of *oreille-de-mer* ear of sea]

or·molu (-ōō), n. & a. Gilded bronze used in decorating furniture; gold-coloured alloy of copper, zinc, & tin; articles made of or decorated with these; (adj., Nav. slang) gorgeous, luxurious. [f. F *or moulu* ground gold (for use in gilding)]

or·nament¹ (-ent), n. (Eccl., usu. pl.) accessories of a church or the worship in it (e.g. vestments, plate, organ, bells; *o. rubric*, that immediately before Order for Morning & Evening Prayer in prayer-book); thing used or serving to adorn, quality or person whose existence or presence confers grace or honour, (*mantelpiece crowded with oo.*; *the o. of a quiet spirit*; *was an o. to his country* or *age*); (sing. only) adorning, being adorned, embellishment, features or work added for decorative purposes, (*a tower rich in o.*; *by way of o.*). Hence **ornament·al** a., **ornament·ally²** adv., **ornament·alist** (3), **ornament·alism**(3), nn. [f. OF *ornement* f. L *ornamentum* equipment (*ornare* equip, -MENT)]

or·namĕnt² (*or* -ĕ·nt), v.t. Adorn, beautify. Hence **ornamentA·TION** n. [f. prec.]

orna·te, a. Elaborately adorned; (of literary style) embellished with flowers of rhetoric &c. Hence **orna·teLY²** adv., **orna·teNESS** n. [f. L *ornatus* p.p. (prec.)]

ornith(o)-, comb. form of Gk *ornis -īthos* bird, in many scientific wds, as *or·nithOID* approaching birds in structure (of some reptiles); *ornitho·*LOGY, -LO·GICAL, -LOGIST; *orni·thoMANCY*; *ornithorhy·ncus* Australian duck-billed platypus, an aquatic mammal with dark-brown fur, webbed feet, & duck's bill, & laying eggs; *ornitho·scopy*, augury.

ŏro·graphy, ŏrĕo·-, n. Branch of physical geography dealing with mountains; hence **oroGRA·PHIC(AL)** aa. So **or(e)o·LOGY** n., **or(e)oLO·GICAL** a., **or(e)o·LOGIST** n. [Gk *oros -eos* mountain, -GRAPHY]

ŏrohi·ppus, n. Fossil quadruped held to be ancestral form of horse. [Gk *oros* mountain, *hippos* horse]

or·oide, n. Gold-coloured alloy of copper & zinc. [F *or* gold f. L *aurum*, Gk *eidos* form]

ōr·otund, a. (Of utterance or phrasing) swelling, mouth-filling, imposing, dignified, pompous, magniloquent, pretentious. [f. L *ore rotundo* (Hor. *A.P.* 323) with round mouth]

or·phan (-fn), n. & a., & v.t. (Child) bereaved of parent(s); hence **or·phanHOOD** n., **or·phanIZE**(3) v.t.; (vb) bereave of parent(s). [f. LL f. Gk *orphanos* bereaved]

or·phanage (-ĭj), n. Orphanhood; institution for orphans' education &c. [-AGE]

Or·phic, a. Of Orpheus or the mysteries or doctrines associated with his name, oracular, mysterious; like Orpheus's music, melodious, entrancing. [f. Gk *Orphikos* (*Orpheus*, -IC)]

or·phrey, or·fray, n. Ornamental often richly embroidered border of ecclesiastical vestment. [earlier sense *embroidery*, f. OF *orfreis* f. L *auriphrygium* gold embroidery (*aurum* gold, *Phrygius* Phrygian); *-s* dropped as though pl. sign, cf. PEA]

or·piment, n. A mineral, trisulphide of arsenic, used as yellow dye. [OF, f. L *auripigmentum* (*aurum* gold, PIGMENT)]

or·pin(e), n. Succulent herbaceous fleshy-leaved purple-flowered plant common in cottage gardens. [F (*-n*), prob. corrupt. of prec., orig. of yellow-flowered species of same genus]

Or·pington, n. A breed of poultry. [village in Kent]

o·rrery, n. Clockwork model of the planetary system. [named after Earl of *O.* c. 1700]

o·rris¹, n. Kind of iris, flower-de-luce, (now rare); *o.-root*, fragrant root of three species of iris used in perfumery & medicine; *o.-powder*, powdered o.-root. [prob. corrupt. of IRIS]

o·rris², n. Kinds of gold or silver lace or embroidery. [prob. cogn. w. ORPHREY]

Or·son, n. Rough valiant person. [tale of *Valentine & O.*]

ort, n. (dial. & archaic; usu. pl.). Refuse scrap(s), leavings. [15th-c. *ortys* pl., cf. Du. *oor-aete* remains of food (*oor-* not, *etan* eat)]

orth(o)-, comb. form of Gk *orthos* straight, in many scientific wds w. senses *straight, rectangular, upright, right, correct*: *orthocephălic*, with breadth of skull from $\frac{3}{4}$ to $\frac{4}{5}$ of length, between brachycephalic & dolichocephalic; *orthochroma·tic*, giving correct relative intensity to colours in photography; *or·thoclase*, common feldspar in crystals with two cleavages at right angles; *ortho·epy*, science of correct pronunciation, whence *orthoĕ·PIC*, *ortho·epIST*(3); *orthogĕ·nesis*, a view of evolution according to which variations follow a defined direction & are not merely sporadic & fortuitous; *ortho·gnathous*, upright-jawed, not prognathous; *ortho·gonal*, of or involving right angles; *ortho·pterous*, of the insect order *Orthoptera* with straight narrow fore-wings including cockroaches, crickets, grasshoppers, &c.; *ortho·ptic*, of straight or correct seeing, esp. used as n. or a. of opaque perforated eyeglass assisting aim in rifle-shooting; *or·thotone*, (word) having independent accent, not enclitic or proclitic.

or·thodox, a. Holding correct or the currently accepted opinions esp. on religious doctrine, not heretical or independent-minded or original; generally accepted as right or true esp. in theology, in harmony with what is authoritatively established, approved, conventional; *the O. Church*, the Eastern or Greek recognizing Patriarch of Constantinople as head & the national Churches of Russia, Roumania, &c., in communion with it. Hence **or·thodox**LY[2] adv. [f. Gk ORTHO(*doxos* f. *doxa* opinion)]

or·thodoxy, n. Being orthodox. [f. Gk *orthodoxia* (prec., -Y[1])]

ortho·graphy, n. Correct or conventional spelling; spelling with reference to its correctness (*his o. is shocking*); perspective projection used in maps & elevations in which the point of sight is supposed infinitely distant so that the rays are parallel, map &c. so projected. So **ortho-gra·phi**C(AL) aa., **orthogra·phical**LY[2] adv. [f. OF *ortografie* f. L f. Gk ORTHO-(*graphia* -GRAPHY)]

or·thopaedy (-pē-), n. The curing of deformities in children or others, surgery directed to this. So **orthopae·di**C a. [f. F ORTHO(*pédie* f. Gk *paideia* rearing of children f. *paideuō* train f. *pais* child)]

or·tolan, n. The garden bunting, small bird esteemed as table delicacy. [F, f. It. *ortolano* orig. gardener f. L *hortulanus* (*hortulus* dim. of *hortus* garden, -AN)]

-ory, suf. (1) of adjj., originating in ONorm. F *-ori* masc., *-orie* fem., & repr. (sometimes thr. F *-oir*, *-oire*) L in *-orius*, *-oria*, *-orium*, = agent termination -OR[2] added to p.p. stems + *-ius* adj. suf. As every L vb could form agent n. in *-or*, E has adjj. in *-ory* corr. to L vbs even when L has neither adj. in *-orius* nor agent n. in *-or* (*compulsory, dispensatory, illusory*), or when the L vb is not itself represented in E (*amatory, perfunctory*). As alternatives to *-ory*, E often has *-orial* (*-ory* + -AL), *-orious* (*-ory* + -OUS). (2) of nn., chiefly f. L neut. adjj. in *-orium* (*dormitory, factory, laboratory*). In a few wds *-ory* is -Y[1] added to agent termination -OR[2] (*rectory, oratory*). In some technical wds L *-orium* is preserved, as *auditorium, crematorium, sensorium*, (also *-ory*).

ō·ryx, n. (Genus of) large straight-horned African antelope. [L, f. Gk *orux*]

o·sborne, n. Plain kind of sweet biscuit. [trade name]

O·scan, a. & n. (Of, in) the language, allied to Latin, of the Osci, Opsci, or Opici, a primitive people of Campania. [L *Osci*, -AN]

o·scillate (ŏsĭ-), v.i. & t. Swing (i., rarely t.) like pendulum, move to & fro between two points; vacillate, vary between extremes of opinion, action, condition, &c. Hence or cogn. **oscill**A·TION, **o·scillat**OR[2] (1, 2), nn., **o·scillat**ORY a. [f. L *oscillare*, -ATE[3]]

ŏscita·tion, n. (rare). Yawning, inattention, negligence. [f. L *oscitatio* (*oscitare* gape f. *os* mouth, *citare* move, -ATION)]

o·scŭlar, a. Of the mouth, of kissing; (Math.) that osculates. [f. L *osculum* mouth, kiss, (*os* mouth, -CULE), -AR[1]]

o·sculate, v.i. & t. Kiss (i. & t., rare, usu. facet.); (Nat. Hist., of species &c.) have contact through intermediate species &c., have common characters *with* another or with each other; (Math., of curve or surface) have contact of higher order with, coincide in three or more points. Hence or cogn. **o·scul**ANT a. (esp. nat. hist.), **oscul**A·TION n., **o·sculat**ORY a. (esp. math.). [f. L *osculari* kiss (prec.), -ATE[3]]

-ose[1], suf. f. L *-osus* abounding in; chiefly in adjj. of a technical kind, adjj. in ordinary use having -OUS; but there are *bellicose, jocose, grandiose*, & a few others. Nn. are formed from them usu. in *-osity*, also in *-oseness*.

-ose[2], suf. in chem. wds formed on *glucose* (mod. F adoption of Gk *gleukos* must) giving names for the related carbohydrates saccharose & cellulose & isomeric substances.

osier (ō·zher), n. (Shoot of) species of willow used in basket-work; *o.*-BED[1]; (attrib.) of oo. [F, cf. LL *ausaria, os-*, willow-bed]

-ōsis, suf. forming nn. of process or condition on Gk & sometimes L stems; names of diseases or pathological states (*amaurosis, trichinosis*); a few rhetorical terms (*meiosis*); & some in gen. use (*metamorphosis, apotheosis*). [f. Gk *-ōsis*, n. suf. usu. f. vbs in *-oō*]

-ŏsity, suf. See -OSE[1], -OUS.

Osma·nlĭ, a. & n. = OTTOMAN[1]. [Turk., native wd for which *Ottoman* is the usu. E form]

o·smium (ŏs-, ŏz-), n. A metal of the platinum group. [f. Gk *osmē* smell, -IUM, named from pungent smell of volatile acid formed by it with oxygen]

o·smose, osmo·sis, (ŏs-, ŏz-), n. (physics). (Tendency to) percolation & intermixture of fluids separated by porous septa. Hence **osmŏ·**TIC a., **osmo·ti**CALLY adv. [irreg. f. Gk *ōsmos* push (*ōtheō* push) + -OSIS]

o·smund (ŏz-, ŏs-), n. The Flowering Fern; any fern of genus *Osmunda*. [?]

o·sprey (-ā, -ĭ), n. Large bird preying on fish, the sea-eagle, fishing-eagle, or sea-hawk; (milliner's name for) egret-plume on hat or bonnet. [prob. f. L *ossifraga* (*os ossis* bone, *frangere* break) perh. the lammergeyer]

o·ssĕous, a. Consisting of bone, ossified; having bony skeleton (*o. & cartilaginous fishes*); abounding in fossil bones. [f. L *osseus* (*os ossis* bone) + -OUS]

o·ssicle, n. (anat.). Small bone, small piece of bony or chitinous or calcareous substance in animal framework. [f. L *ossiculum* (prec., -CULE)]

o·ssifrage (-ĭj), n. = OSPREY. [OSPREY]

o·ssifÿ, v.i. & t. Turn (i. & t.) into bone, harden, make or become rigid or callous or unprogressive. Hence **ossi·**FIC a., **ossi**FICA·TION n. [L *os ossis* bone, -FY]

o·ssūary, n. Receptacle for bones of dead, charnel-house, bone-urn; cave in which ancient bones are found. [f. LL *ossuarium* (irreg. f. *os* see prec., -ARY[1])]

oste·nsible, a. Professed, for show, put forward to conceal the real, (*his o. errand was to* —). Hence **oste·nsib**LY[2] adv. [F (L *ostendere -ens-*, -IBLE)]

oste·nsory, n. Receptacle for displaying Host to congregation, monstrance. [f. med. L *ostensorium* as prec., + -ORY(2)]

ostenta·tion, n. Pretentious display esp. of wealth or luxury, showing off, attempt or intention to attract notice. Hence **ostenta·**TIOUS a., **ostenta·tious**LY[2] adv. [F, f. L *ostentationem* (*ostentare* frequent. of *ostendere -ent-* show, -ATION)]

oste(o)-, comb. form of Gk *osteon* bone in many med. & anat. terms, as *ostĕ*I·TIS; *osteoge·nesis*, formation of bone; *osteo·graphy*, scientific description of the bones; *o·steo*ID a.; *osteo·logy*, anatomy dealing with bones, animal's bony structure; *osteomala·cia*, softening of bone by loss of earthy salts; *osteo·pathy*, manipulative surgery as a profession (legally recognized in Canada & U.S.), *o·steopath*, practitioner of it.

o·stler (-sl-), n. Stableman at inn. [earlier *hostler* (HOSTEL, -ER[1])]

o·stracize, v.t. (Gk Ant.; at Athens) banish (dangerously powerful or unpopular citizen) for ten or five years by peculiar voting-system, name of person to be ostracized being written on potsherd; (mod.) exclude from society, favour, or common privileges, send to Coventry, &c. Hence **o·strac**ISM(1) n. [f. Gk *ostrakizō* (*ostrakon* potsherd)]

o·strĕi-, o·streo-, comb. forms of L *ostrea*, *ostreum*, & Gk *ostreon*, oyster, as *o·streiculture* oyster-breeding; *ostreo·phagous* eating oysters.

o·strich (-tsh), n. Large swift-running African & Arabian bird with wing & tail feathers valued as ornaments, swallowing hard substances to assist working of gizzard, & reputed to bury its head in sand when pursued in the belief that it cannot be seen (*has the digestion of an o.*; *o. policy, belief*, &c., depending on self-delusion); *o.-farm*, breeding oo. for feathers; *o.-plume*, feather, or bunched feathers, of o.; *o.-tip*, tip of o.-feather. [f. OF *ostruce* f. pop. L *avis struthio* (*avis* bird, LL f. Gk *strouthiōn* ostrich f. *strouthos* sparrow, ostrich)]

-ot[1], suf. = F *-ot*, orig. dim., but often not so now; *ballot, chariot, parrot.*

-ot[2], -ote, suf. giving nativity in ancient Gk names, as *Epirot*, & in mod. names from places near Greece, as *Suliote*; also in a few Gk derivatives of other meanings (*idiot, helot, patriot, zealot*). [= F *-ote* f. L *-ota* f. Gk *-ōtēs*]

o·ther (ŭdh-), a., n. or pron., & adv. Not the same as one or more or some already mentioned or implied, separate in identity, distinct in kind, alternative or further or additional, *the* &c. only remaining, *every* second, different *than* or *from*, (for sing. use with *an*, see ANOTHER; *we have o. evidence*; *o. people think otherwise*; *it must be decided by quite o. considerations*; *have no o. place to go to*; *o. things being equal*, if the conditions are or were, in everything but the point in question, alike, as *o. t. b. e., I should prefer you to him, but he is rich & you are poor*; *a few o. examples would be useful*; *give me some o. ones*; *now open the, your, o. eye*; *happens every o. day*, on alternate days, as often as not; *any person o. than yourself*; *do not wish him, them, o. than he is, they are*; *a world far o. from ours*; *on the o. hand*, used to introduce fact or argument making against or contrasted with previous one; *the o. day* adv., a few days ago; *some time or o.* adv., one day &c.; *some one or o.*, a person unknown; *some idiots or o. have been shouting all night*; *it was none o. than Jones*, = no o. one or person; *the o. world*, future life, *o.-world*, concerned with or thinking of this only, whence **other-wor·ldly**[1] a., **other-wor·ldli**NESS n.; often ellipt. with numerals, as *another, the o. two*, i.e. person or persons, thing or things, of kind not needing specification); *otherguess* a. [corrupt. of *othergates* adv. (GATE[2], -ES) in another way], of very different kind (archaic & colloq.); *o·therwhence*, from elsewhere; *o·therwhere(s)*, elsewhere (poet.); *o·therwhile(s)*, at other times. (N. or pron.; orig. elliptic use of adj., & often indistinguishable from this in sing., but now distinguished in pl. by -s, cf. *the o. six, the six oo.*) o. person, thing, specimen, &c. (*give me another, some oo.*; *do good to oo.*; *if this soap is, these candles are, too soft, have you any o., oo.?*; *one or o. of us will be there*; *let oo. talk, I act*; *I can do no o.* archaic, nothing else; *you are the man of all oo. for the work*; *one neutralizes the o.*; *they neutralize* EACH *o.* OR ONE *another*; *in oo. of his sermons*). (Adv.) otherwise (*o. than cursorily*). [Aryan; OE *ōther*, cf. Du. & G *ander*, Skr. *ántaras*, L *alter*; see -THER]

o·therness, n. (rare). Being other, diversity, difference; thing or existence that is not the thing mentioned or the thinking subject. [-NESS]

o·therwise, adv. In a different way (*could not have acted o.*; *Judas, o. called,* or *o., Iscariot*; sometimes preceded by *any, no,* with reminiscence of its etym., as *could do it no o., does not influence him any o. than by example*); if circumstances are or were different, else, or (*seize the chance, o. you will regret it*); in other respects (*he is unruly, but not o. blameworthy*; also qualifying the adj. sense in n., as *his o. dullness*); in different state (*how can it be o. than fatal?*; *should not wish it o.*); *& o., or o.,* ungrammatical substitute for *&* or *or* followed by the negation or opposite of a noun or adj. or by *other* (*the merits or o. of the Bill,* i.e. *or demerits* usu. omissible; *additions automatic & o.,* i.e. *& other*); *o.-minded,* having different, or jarring, inclinations or views, averse to current opinions. [OE *on othre wisan* (OTHER, WISE[2])]

-ōtic, suf. forming adjj. corr. to nn. in -OSIS, in sense *affected with* or *producing* or *resembling -osis*; so *neurotic, hypnotic, narcotic*; *Quixotic, exotic, erotic,* are not exx. [f. Gk *-ōtikos* f. nn. in *-ōtēs* formed on same stems as -OSIS]

otiose (ōshīō·s), a. At leisure, lazy, unoccupied, (rare); sterile, futile, (rare); not required, serving no practical purpose, functionless. Hence **otio·se**LY[2] adv., **otio·se**NESS n. [f. L *otiosus* (*otium* leisure, -OSE[1])]

o·tium cum dignitā·tĕ (ōshĭ-), n. Dignified ease. [L]

ōt(o)-, comb. form of Gk *ous ōtos* ear, as *oto·*LOGY, science of ear diseases, anatomy, &c.; *o·to*SCOPE, instrument for examining cavity of ear, or for auscultation of sounds in it.

otta·va ri·ma (-tah-, rē-), n. Stanza of eight lines, 11-syllabled in Italian, 10-syllabled in English, with rhymes as abababcc (as in Byron's *Don Juan*). [It.]

o·tter, n. Furred aquatic fish-eating mammal with fin-like legs, webbed feet, & long flattened tail; its fur; kinds of fishing-tackle (also as name for the paravane when used on non-naval craft); *o.-dog, -hound,* breed used in o.-hunting; *o.-spear,* used in o.-hunting. [com.-Teut.; OE *otr,* cf. Du. & G *otter,* also Skr. *udrás*; cogn. w. Gk *hudōr* water, & w. WATER]

o·tto, n. *O. of roses,* = ATTAR. [f. *attar*]

O·ttoman[1], a. & n. Of the dynasty of Othman I, his branch of the Turks, or the empire ruled by his descendants, Turkish; (n.) O. person, Turk. [F, f. Arab. name of *Othman* (pronounced in Turk. *osman,* whence OSMANLI)]

o·ttoman[2], n. Cushioned seat like sofa or chair without back or arms, often a box with cushioned top. [f. prec. (cf. DIVAN)]

ou·bit (ōō-), n. =WOOBUT.

oublie·tte (ōō-), n. Secret dungeon with entrance only by trapdoor. [F (*oublier* forget)]

ouch (owtsh), n. (archaic). Clasp or buckle often jewelled; setting of precious stone. [f. OF *nouche* (cf. ADDER) f. LL *nusca* f. OHG *nuscha* prob. f. Celt.]

ought[1] (awt), n. (vulg.). Figure denoting nothing, nought. [perh. f. *an ought* for *a nought,* cf. ADDER]

ought[2] (awt), v. aux. (the only form in use, except archaic *oughtest* or *oughtst,* is *ought* serving as present or past finite) expressing duty, rightness, shortcoming, advisability, or strong probability; the past sense (except when merely due to sequence of tenses in reporting &c.) is indicated by a following perf. infin. Exx.: *we o. to love our neighbours*; *it o. not to be allowed*; *you o. to know better*; *you o. to go to Pinafore*; *Eclipse o. to win*; *it o. to be done at once, have been done long ago*; *I told you it o. to be, have been, done*; *I said it, & still think I o. to have said it.* [OE *áhte* past of *ágan* OWE; the mod. uses represent the imperf. subj. = would owe]

ought[3], var. of AUGHT.

ounce[1] (ow-), n. (abbr. *oz*). Unit of weight, 1/12 lb. in Troy weight, 1/16 lb. in avoirdupois (also fig., as *an o. of practice* &c. *is worth a pound of theory* &c.). [f. OF *unce* f. L *uncia* twelfth of pound or foot (cf. INCH[1])]

ounce[2] (ow-), n. (Poet. &c.) lynx or other vaguely identified medium-sized feline beast; (Zool.) the mountain panther or snow leopard smaller than leopard but marked like it. [f. OF *once,* cf. It. *lonza,* f. L *lyncea* (LYNX); for *once* f. *l'once* by mistake for *lonce* cf. ADDER]

our (owr), a. Of or belonging to us (see WE), that we are concerned with or speaking or thinking of, (*is in o. midst*; *acting on o. behalf*; *have done o. share*; *O. Father,* the creator of us men; *O. Saviour, Lady,* of us Christians, Christ, the Virgin; *given under O. seal,* of Us the king or queen, emperor or empress; *a worthless book in o. opinion,* of us the present spokesman of a newspaper &c.). [com.-Teut.; OE *úre* orig. genit. pl. of first pers. pron. = of us, afterwards inflected as adj.; cf. G *unser,* OSax. *úser*]

-our, suf. in *colour* &c.; see -OR[1].

ours (owrz), pron. & pred. a. The one(s) belonging to us (*o. is a large family*; *I like o. better*; *let me give you one of o.*; *look at this garden of o.,* this our garden); our regiment or corps (*Jones of o.*); (pred. a.) belonging to us (*became o. by purchase*). [OUR, -ES; double possessive for the emphatic abs. use]

ourse·lf, pron. (pl. *-ves,* which is the usu. form, the sing. being used similarly when *We* represents a sovereign, & alternatively with the pl. when *we* represents a newspaper writer or the average man). (Emphat.; usu. pl.) we or us in person, in particular, in our normal condition, & not others, or alone, (usu. in apposition with *we*, & either next after it or later, rarely substituted for it; usu. substituted for *us*, rarely after it in apposition; *we oo. will see to it*; *we will see to it oo.*; *oo. are first to be thought of*; *it was good for the others, if not for oo.*; *let us do it oo.*; *we were not oo. for some time*; *what touches us o. shall be last served*; *can we imagine a world in which o. does not exist?*); (Refl.; usu. pl., always in objective case) the person(s) previously described as *we* (*we shall only harm, do harm to, oo.*; *we cannot persuade o.* or *oo. that the Government is in earnest*; *we shall give oo. the pleasure of calling*). [OUR, SELF]

-ous, suf. forming adjj.; f. L *-osus*, cf. -OSE[1], abounding in, thr. OF *-os, -us*, & OE *-ús*, written after 1300 *-ous* (ōōs) & gradually weakened in sound to ŭs; familiarized in L & F wds f. OF, *-ous* has now become the established anglicizer for many L adjj., esp. in *-eus, -ius, -er, -ax -acis, -ox -ocis, -endus, -ulus*, & *-vorus* (*igneous, dubious, adulterous, capacious, ferocious, tremendous, bibulous, herbivorous*); *righteous, courteous, gorgeous*, are by false anal.; (Chem.; of acids &c.) with larger proportion of the element indicated by the stem than those in -IC (*chlorous acid*). Nn. f. adjj. in *-ous* have usu. *-ousness*, sometimes *-osity* (*curiosity*), cf. -OSE[1].

ousel. See OUZEL.

oust (ow-), v.t. Put out of possession, eject, deprive *of*, expel *from*, drive out, force oneself or be put into the place of. Hence **ou·st**ER[4] n. (legal). [f. OF *oster* (now *ôter*) take away, etym. dub.]

out (owt), adv., prep., n., & a., (for spec. uses of the adv. in comb. with vbs see the vbs). Away from or not in or at a place, the right or normal state, the fashion, &c., (*is o.*, not at home; *keep him o.*; *go o. for a walk*; *has her Sundays o.*; *arm is o.*, dislocated; *Tories are o.*, not in office; *her son is o. in Canada*; *anchored some way o.*; *on the voyage o.*; *batsman is o.*, no longer in possession of wicket; *all o.*, side's innings over; *o., not o.*, umpire's decision against, for, batsman in answer to claim of opponents; *miners are o.*, not at work, on strike; *candle, fire, is o.*, not burning; *crinolines are o.*, not in fashion; *was o. in my calculations*, incorrect; *o. with*, no longer on friendly terms with; also as interj., *o. with him* &c., turn him o.); in(to) the open, publicity, existence, notice, hearing, sight, clearness, &c. (*book, rose, chicken, secret, girl, is o.*, published, open, hatched, revealed, introduced to society; *is the best game o.*; *tell him right o.*; *the eruption is o. all over him*; *o. for, o. to* do, colloq., engaged in seeking, as *is o. for kudos, to capture the market*; *all o.* slang, showing one's utmost pace or effort; *o. at* ELBOW[1]*s*; *o. & about*, able to leave bed or house & appear; also ellipt. for *come o.*, as *murder will o.*); to or at an end, completely, (*she had her cry o.*; *tired o.*; *before the week is o.*; *o. & away*, by far; *o. & o.*, thorough, -ly, surpassing, -ly, whence **out-&-ou·t**ER[1] n. slang); *out of* compd prep., from within, not within, from among, beyond range of, (so as to be) without, from, owing to, by use of (material), at specified distance from (town &c.), beyond, transgressing rules of, (*come o. o. the house*; *happened o. o. England*; *o. o. doors*, in or into the open air, so *o.-of-door* as adj.; *must choose o. o. these*; *is o. o. sight*; *was swindled o. o. his money*; *is o. o. breath, his mind, work, brown sugar, &c.*; *get money o. o. him*; *a filly got by Persimmon o. o. Lutetia*; *asked o. o. curiosity*; *what did you make it o. o.?*; *is seven miles o. o. Liverpool*; *o. o. wedlock*, without marriage; *times o. o. number*, beyond counting; *o. o. doubt*, undoubtedly; *is o. o. drawing*, incorrectly drawn; *o. o. it*, not included, forlorn, at a loss, wrongly informed or mistaken; *o. o.* DATE[2], CHARACTER[1], HAND[1], one's *own* HEAD[1], KEEPING, TEMPER, *the* WOOD, SORTs, *the* WAY). (Prep.) = o. of (only now in *from o.*, as *from o. the dungeon came a groan*). (N.; pl.) *the* party o. of office; *the* IN[1]*s & outs*. (Adj.) *o. match*, played away from home ground; *o. size*, beyond the ordinary. [com.-Teut.; OE *út*, cf. Du. *uit*, G *aus*]

out-, pref. = prec. prefixed adverbially or adjectivally or prepositionally to vbs or nn.

(1) to any vb, making equivalent of same vb followed by *out*; chiefly in poet. & rhet. use. So *outbla·ze, outbra·nch, outspea·k, outsprea·d*.

(2) Vbs that are followed in other parts by *out* often form partt. & gerunds with prefixed *out*; the meaning is often a specialized one. So *ou·tcast* a. & n., (person) cast out from home & friends, homeless & friendless (vagabond); *ou·t-clearing* n., sending out of bills & cheques to Clearing-house for settlement; *ou·tfighting*, boxing at arm's length, opp. *infighting*; *ou·tlying* a., situated far from a centre, remote; *ou·tspoken* (*or* -pō·-) a., frank, given to plain speaking, whence *outspo·ken*LY[2] adv., *outspo·ken*NESS n.; *ou·tspread*; *ou·tstanding* a., prominent, still unsettled; *ou·tstretched*; *ou·tworn*.

(3) Nn. are formed f. vbs that can be followed by *out*, either with the simple vb form or with a derivative n.; the meaning, which is often specialized, may be.

a. the verbal action or its occurrence. So *ou·tbreak*, a breaking out of emotion esp. anger, hostilities, disease, volcanic energy, &c., outcrop, an insurrection; *ou·tburst*, explosion of feeling esp. expressed by vehement words, volcanic eruption, outcrop; *ou·tcrop,* emergence of stratum, vein, or rock, at surface (also b.); *ou·tcry* (also c.); *ou·tflow*; *ou·tgoing* (also b.); *ou·tlook* (also c.); *ou·trush* (also b.); *ou·tsight,* perception of external things (only as antithesis to *insight*); *ou·tthrust,* outward pressure of some part in architecture.

b. that which does the action. So *ou·tcome,* issue, result; *ou·tcrop* (also a.); *ou·tfit,* complete equipment material or mental; *ou·tfitter,* supplier of equipment; *ou·tflow* (also a.); *ou·tgo, ou·tgoings* (also a. in sing.), expenditure, outlay; *ou·tgrowth,* offshoot, natural product; *ou·tlier,* detached part of something; *ou·tpour*; *ou·trush* (also a.).

c. that which is made or done by or suffers the action. So *ou·tcry* (also a.), clamour, uproar; *ou·tlay,* what one spends, expenses; *ou·tlook,* what one sees on looking out, view, prospect, esp. fig. of what seems likely to happen; *ou·tpouring,* effusion, verbal or literary expression of emotion; *ou·tput, ou·t-turn,* amount produced by manufacture, mining, labour, &c.; *ou·t-throw,* amount ejected.

d. the place or time of occurrence. So *ou·tfall,* outlet of river &c.; *ou·tlet,* means of exit or escape, vent, way out; *ou·tset,* start, commencement, (usu. *at* or *from the o.*).

(4) *out-* is prefixed w. adj. force to nn., meaning.

a. external. So OUTLINE, OUTSIDE.

b. connected but separate, subordinate & detached, not at the centre, some way off. So *ou·tbuilding,* outhouse; *ou·tfield,* outlying land of farm, outlying region of thought &c., (Cricket) part remote from wickets; *ou·thouse,* house or building or shed belonging to & near or built against main house; *outla·ndish* a. [f. obs. *ou·tland* foreign countries], foreign looking or sounding, unfamiliar, bizarre, uncouth; *ou·t-patient, -pensioner,* receiving aid from institution &c. without being lodged in it; *ou·tpost,* detachment on guard at some distance from army to prevent surprise; *o.-relief,* outdoor relief (5); *ou·trider,* mounted attendant riding before, behind, or with carriage, also commercial traveller; OUTRIGGER; *ou·trunner,* running attendant on carriage, horse in traces outside shafts, dog acting as guide to sledge-team; *ou·tsentry,* man stationed as outpost; *ou·tskirts,* outer border, fringe, of city, district, &c., or subject; *ou·tstation,* at distance from head-quarters; *ou·tvoter,* non-resident parliamentary elector; *ou·twork,* advanced or detached part of fortification, also work done outside shop or house; *ou·tworker,* one who does outwork.

(5) *out-* is prefixed to & governs nn. with the force of *out of,* forming adjj. or advv. f. which vbs or nn. may be secondary formations. So *ou·tboard* a. & adv. (naut.), on or towards or nearer than something else to ship's outside; *ou·tcaste* a. & n., (person) having lost or been expelled from his or not belonging to a caste; *outca·ste* v.t., expel from caste; *ou·t-college* a., not residing in or not belonging to a or the college; *ou·tdoor* a., done or existing or used outdoors (*o. relief,* given to person not resident in workhouse or institution; *o. agitation* &c., conducted outside Parliament); *outdoor·s* adv., in the open air; *ou·tlaw* n. & v.t. [OE *útlaga* n. f. *útlag* a. outlawed], person deprived of the protection of the law, banished or exiled person, (vb) proscribe, declare outlaw, whence *ou·tlaw*RY, condition of or condemnation as outlaw.

(6) *out-* with general sense of excess is prefixed

a. to simple vbs capable of taking the same object, adding the idea of more than, or successfully, doing the action. So *outba·lance,* weigh down; *outbra·ve,* defy; *outfa·ce,* look out of countenance; *outfigh·t*; *out-he·ctor*; *outla·st* (*will not o. six months*; also b.); *outma·tch*; *outmea·sure*; *outri·val*; *outsco·ld*; *out-tru·mp,* at cards.

b. to any vb, or n. such as *general* used for the nonce as vb, enabling it to take as obj. a person or thing that the subj. surpasses or defeats by doing the action more, better, or longer. So *out-a·ct, -ar·gue, -be·llow*; *outbi·d,* bid higher than at auction, promise more than, surpass in exaggeration or anecdote; *out-bla·ze, -bra·g, -da·nce, -dare·*; *outdo·,* surpass; *out-ea·t*; *out-figh·t,* fight better than (also a.); *outfly·*; *out-ge·neral,* defeat by superior generalship; *outgo·,* go faster than, (fig.) surpass; *outgrow·,* grow faster or get taller than (also c.); *out-he·ctor,* be more formidable at hectoring than (also a.); *out-jo·ckey,* overreach; *out-ju·ggle*; *out-ju·mp*; *outla·bour*; *outla·st,* last longer than (another; also a.); *outli·ve* (also c.); *out-manœuvre, -mar·ch, -pai·nt, -prea·ch, -rea·ch, -rea·son, -ri·de, -row·* (-ō); *outru·n* (*o. the* CONSTABLE; also c.); *outsai·l*; *outsco·ld* (also a.); *outshi·ne* lit. & fig.; *outshoot·*; *outsi·ng*; *outsi·t,* stay longer than (other guests); *outspar·kle, -spe·nd, -stare·*; *outstay·* (also c.); *out-sti·nk, -swi·m, -tal·k, -thi·nk, -thu·nder, -toi·l, -tra·de, -tra·vel*; *outvie·,* surpass in competition; *out-vo·te, -wal·k*; *outwa·tch,* keep awake longer than (also c.); *outwee·p*; *outweigh·,* exceed in weight, value, importance, or influence; *out-wor·k, -wra·ngle, -ye·ll.*

c. to vb, enabling it to take as obj. something in the nature of a limit or amount that is exceeded. So *outgrow·,* get too big for (clothes), get rid of (childish habit or ailment or taste) with advancing age, (also b.); *outli·ve,* live beyond (a century, the ordinary span, &c.), come safely through (accident &c.), get over effect of (disrepute &c.), (also b.); *outri·de*, (of ship) keep afloat through (storm; also b.); *outru·n*, pass the limit of (*his imagination outruns the facts*; also b.); *outstay·* (*never o. your welcome*; also b.); *outste·p*, pass limit of (*outsteps the truth*); *outwa·tch*, keep awake beyond the end of (the night &c.; also b.); *outwear·*, pass away (time) by endurance.

d. to n., forming vb expressing that subj. surpasses obj. in this respect. So *outcla·ss*, belong to higher class than; *out-di·stance*, get far ahead of; *outfla·nk*, have flank overlapping that of (enemy); *outnu·mber*; *outpa·ce*, go faster than; *outra·nge*, (of gun or its user) have longer range than; *outspee·d*; *outva·lue*; *outvoi·ce*, speak louder or more effectively or persuasively than; *outwi·t*, prove too clever for, overreach, take in.

e. to name of person noted for some quality, forming vb (w. the name usu. repeated as obj.) indicating that subj. surpasses even him in it. So *out-he·rod Herod*, *out-zo·la Zola*, be more blustering, realistic, than Herod or Zola.

outba·lance v.t., see OUT- 6 a.; **outbi·d** v.t. (-dd-), see OUT- 6 b; **ou·tboard** a. & adv., OUT- 5; **outbra·ve** v.t., OUT- 6 a; **ou·tbreak** n., OUT- 3 a; **ou·tbuilding** n., OUT- 4 b; **ou·tburst** n., OUT- 3 a; **ou·tcast** a. & n., OUT- 2; **ou·tcaste** a. & n., **outca·ste** v.t., OUT- 5; **outcla·ss** v.t., OUT- 6 d; **ou·tclearing** n., OUT- 2; **ou·tcollege** a., OUT- 5; **ou·tcome** n., OUT- 3 b; **ou·tcrop** n., OUT- 3 a b; **ou·tcry** n., OUT- 3 a c; **out-di·stance** v.t., OUT- 6 d; **outdo·** v.t., OUT- 6 b; **ou·tdoor** a., **outdoor·s** adv., OUT- 5.

ou·ter, a. & n. Farther from centre or inside, relatively far out, external, of the outside; objective, physical, not subjective or psychical; *the o. man*, personal appearance, dress; *the o. world*, people outside one's own circle; hence **ou·ter**MOST a. (N.) part of rifle-target outside circles surrounding bull's-eye. [14th-c. formation substituted for & differentiated f. UTTER as compar. of OUT]

outfa·ce, v.t., see OUT- 6 a; **ou·tfall** n., OUT- 3 d; **ou·tfield** n., OUT- 4 b; **ou·tfighting,** OUT- 2; **ou·tfit, ou·tfitter,** nn., OUT- 3 b; **outfla·nk** v.t., OUT- 6 d; **ou·tflow** n., OUT- 3 a; **outge·neral** v.t., OUT- 6 b; **outgo** n., OUT- 3 b, vb, OUT- 6 b; **ou·tgoing(s)** n., OUT- 3 a b; **outgrow·** v.t., OUT- 6 b c; **ou·tgrowth** n., OUT- 3 b; **out-he·rod** v.t., OUT- 6 e; **ou·thouse** n., OUT- 4 b.

ou·ting, n. Pleasure-trip, holiday away from home. [f. obs. *out* vb put or go out, -ING[1]]

out-jo·ckey, v.t., see OUT- 6 b; **outla·ndish** a., OUT- 4 b; **outla·st** v.t., OUT- 6 a b; **ou·tlaw** n. & v.t., **ou·tlawry** n., OUT- 5; **ou·tlay** n., OUT- 3 c; **ou·tlet** n., OUT- 3 d; **ou·tlier** n., OUT- 3 b.

ou·tline, n., & v.t. (Sing. or pl.) lines enclosing the apparently plane figure presented by any object to sight, contour, external boundary; sketch containing only contour lines & no shading (*in o.*, so sketched); rough draught, verbal description of essential parts only, summary, (pl.) main features, general principles. (Vb) draw or describe in o.; mark o. of in decorating &c. [OUT- 4 a]

outli·ve, v.t., see OUT- 6 b c; **ou·tlook** n., OUT- 3 c; **ou·tlying** a., OUT- 2; **outmanœu·vre** v.t., OUT- 6 b; **outmar·ch** v.t., OUT- 6 b; **outma·tch** v.t., OUT- 6 a.

ou·tmost, a. =OUTER*most*.

ou·tness, n. Externality, objectivity. [-NESS]

outnu·mber, v.t., see OUT- 6 d; **outpa·ce** v.t., OUT- 6 d; **ou·t-patient** n., OUT- 4 b; **ou·tpost** n., OUT- 4 b; **ou·tpouring** n., OUT- 3 c; **ou·tput** n., OUT- 3 c.

ou·trage, n. (-ĭj), & v.t. (-āj). Forcible violation of others' rights, sentiments, &c. (*never safe from o.*); deed of violence, gross or wanton offence or indignity (*an o. upon decency, justice* &c.). (Vb) do violence to, subject to o., injure, insult, violate, ravish; infringe (law, morality, &c.) flagrantly. [f. OF *ultrage* (L *ultra* beyond, -AGE)]

outrā·geous (-jus), a. Immoderate, extravagant, extraordinary; violent, furious; grossly cruel, immoral, offensive, or abusive. Hence **outra·geous**LY[2] adv., **outra·geous**NESS n. [f. OF *outrageus* (prec., -OUS)]

outra·nge, v.t. See OUT- 6 d.

outré (o͞otrā), a. Outside the bounds of propriety, eccentric, outraging decorum. [F]

ou·t-relief, n., see OUT- 4 b; **outri·de** v.t., OUT- 6 b c; **ou·trider** n., OUT- 4 b.

ou·trigged, a. Having outriggers. [f. OUT-, RIG, -ED[1], after foll.]

ou·trigger, n. Beam, spar, framework, rigged out & projecting from or over ship's side for various purposes; similar projecting beam &c. in building; extension of splinter-bar enabling extra horse to be harnessed outside shafts, such horse; iron bracket bearing rowlock attached to boat's side to increase leverage of oar, boat with these. [OUT-, RIG, -ER[1]]

outrigh·t, adv. & a. Altogether, entirely, once for all, not by degrees or instalments or half & half, (*kill, buy, o.*); without reservation, openly; (adj.) downright, direct, thorough, whence **outrigh·t**NESS **n.** [OUT, RIGHT]

outri·val, v.t. (-ll-), see OUT- 6 a; **outru·n** v.t., OUT- 6 b c; **ou·trunner** n., OUT- 4 b; **ou·tset** n., OUT- 3 d; **outshi·ne** v.t., OUT- 6 b.

outsi·de, n., adj., adv., & prep. External surface, outer parts, (*knows only the oo. of books*; *ride on the o. of an omnibus*); external appearance, outward aspect; all that is without, *the* world as distinguished from the thinking subject, (*impressions from the o.*); position without (*open the door from o.*); highest computation (*there were a hundred, it is a mile, at the o.*); (pl.) outer sheets of ream of paper; o. passenger on coach &c.; *o. in,* = INSIDE *out.* (Adj.) of, on, nearer, the o., outer, (*o. edge* in skating, progression on outer edge of one skate; *o. seat,* nearer the end; *o. work,* done off the premises; *o. porter,* conveying luggage from station); not belonging to some circle or institution (*o. opinion,* esp. of people not in Parliament; *o. broker,* not member of Stock Exchange); greatest existent or possible or probable (*quote the o. prices*). (Adv.) on or to the o., the open air, open sea, &c., not within or enclosed or included, (*come o.,* out from room or house, esp. as challenge to fight; *is black outside & in*; *o. of,* = o. prep.; *o. of a horse* slang, mounted; *get o. of* slang, eat or drink; *o. of his own family no one will speak to him*). (Prep.) external to, not included in, beyond the limits of, not in, to the o. of, at or to the exterior of, (*natural forces are o. morality*; *cannot go o. the evidence*). [OUT- 4 a, SIDE¹]

outsi·der, n. Non-member of some circle, party, profession, &c., unitiated person, layman, person without special knowledge, breeding, &c., or not fit to mix with good society; horse or person not known to have a chance in race or competition. [-ER¹]

ou·tsight, n., see OUT- 3 a; **outsi·t** v.t., OUT- 6 b; **ou·tskirts** n. pl., OUT- 4 b.

ou·tspan, v.i. & t. (-nn-), & n., (S. Afr.). Unyoke, unharness; (n.) act, time, or place of outspanning. [f. Du. *uitspannen* (OUT, SPAN)]

outspoken, a., see OUT- 2; **ou·tspread** a., OUT- 2; **ou·tstanding** a., OUT- 2; **outstay·** v.t., OUT- 6 b c; **outste·p** v.t., OUT- 6 c; **ou·tstretched** a., OUT- 2.

outstri·p, v.t. (-pp-). Pass in running &c.; surpass in competition or relative progress or ability. [OUT- 6 b, STRIP in obs. sense *run fast*]

ou·t-thrust, n., see OUT- 3 a.; **outva·lue** v.t., OUT- 6 d; **outvie·** v.t., OUT- 6 b; **outvoi·ce** v.t., OUT- 6 d; **outvo·te** v.t., OUT- 6 b; **ou·tvoter** n., OUT- 4 b.

ou·tward, a., adv., & n. Outer (archaic); directed towards the outside; bodily, external, material, visible, apparent, superficial, (*the o. eye,* opp. *mind's eye*; *o. form,* appearance; *o. man* in Theol., body, opp. *soul,* also facet. = clothing &c.; *to o. seeming,* apparently; *o. things,* the world around us); hence **ou·twardLY²** adv. (Adv.) = OUTWARDS (*o.-bound* of ship or passenger, going away from home). (N.) o. appearance; (pl.) o. things, externals. [OE *útweard* (OUT, -WARD)]

ou·twardness, n. External existence, objectivity; interest or belief in outward things, objective-mindedness. [-NESS]

ou·twards, adv. In an outward direction, towards what is outside. [-WARDS]

outwa·tch, v.t., see OUT- 6 b c; **outwear·** v.t., OUT- 6 c; **outweigh·** v.t., OUT- 6 b; **outwi·t** v.t. (-tt-), OUT- 6 d; **ou·twork** n., OUT- 4 b; **outwor·k** v.t., OUT- 6 b; **ou·tworker** n., OUT- 4 b.

ouzel, -s-, (ōō·zl), n. Kinds of small bird (*Ring, Water, Brook, o.*). [OE *ósle,* cf. G *amsel*]

ova. See OVUM.

ō·val, a. & n. Egg-shaped or ellipsoidal; having the outline of an egg or elliptical; hence **o·valLY²** adv., **o·valNESS** n. (N.) closed curve with one axis considerably longer than the other, like ellipse or outline of egg; thing with o. outline; *the O.,* the Surrey County cricket ground, Kennington O. in S. London. [OVUM, -AL]

ō·vary, n. Either of two reproductive organs in which ova are produced in female animals, whence **ovārio·TOMY, ovarI·TIS,** nn.; lower part of pistil, consisting of one or more carpels, seed-vessel, germen. Hence **ovār·IAN** a., **ovārio-** comb. form. [OVUM, -ARY¹]

ō·vate, a. (nat. hist.). Egg-shaped as solid or in outline, oval. Hence **ova·to-** comb. form. [f. L *ovatus* (OVUM, -ATE²)]

ova·tion, n. (Rom. Ant.) lesser triumph; enthusiastic reception, spontaneous applause. [f. L *ovatio* (*ovare* exult, -ATION)]

oven (ŭ·vn), n. Brick or stone or iron receptacle for baking bread or other food in (*Dutch o.,* metal box of which open side is turned towards ordinary fire); small furnace or kiln used in chemistry, metallurgy, &c.; *o.-bird,* kinds making domed or o.-shaped nests. [com.-Teut.; OE *ofn,* cf. Du. *oven,* G *ofen,* Gk *ipnos*]

ō·ver, o'er (ōr; *poet.*) adv., n., & prep. (Adv.) outward & downward from brink or from erect position (*lean, fall, jump, knock,* &c., *o.*); so as to cover or touch whole surface (*brush, paint, it o.*); with motion above something, so as to pass across something, (*climb, look, boil, o.*); so as to produce fold or reverse position, upside down, (*bend it o.*; *turn o.,* turn other side of leaf up; *turn him o. on his face*; *roll o. & o.,* so that same point comes uppermost repeatedly), (Cricket, as umpire's direction) change ends for bowling &c. (n., number of balls, i.e. 4, 5, or 6, allowed between two such calls, & the play that results; MAIDEN *o.*); across a street or other space or distance (*take this o. to the post-office*; *asked him o.,* to come as visitor from some place not far off; *is o. in, am going o. to, America*; *o. against,* in opposite situation to, in contrast with); with transference or change from one hand, party, &c., to another (*malcontents went o. to the enemy*; *handed o. the seals*; *made o. the balance to a charity*; GIVE[1] *o.*); too, in excess, in addition, besides, more, apart, (*o. anxious* &c., more than is right, see OVER-; *not o. well* &c., rather badly &c.; *shall have something o.*; *20 lb. & o.*; *that can stand o.*, not be dealt with now; *o. & above*, moreover, into the bargain); from beginning to end, with repetition, with detailed consideration, (*read, count, o.*; *did it six times o., o. & o., o. again, o. & o. again*; *talk, think, the matter o.*); at an end, done with, settled, (*the struggle is o.*). (Adj.) upper, outer, superior, excessive, (usu. written as one word with n., see OVER-). (Prep.) above, on, at all or various points upon, to & fro upon, all through, round about, concerning, engaged with, (*an umbrella o. his head*; *projects o. the street*; *doubt hangs o. the question*; *o. our heads*, beyond our comprehension, also without consulting us; HAND[1] *o. hand*; *writing o. the signature X.*; *o. head & ears*, completely immersed lit. & fig.; *o. shoes o. boots*, no half measures; *with his hat o. his eyes*; *draw a veil o. it*; *a change came o. him*; *blush spread o. his face*; *rice is grown all o. India*; *you may travel o. Europe* or *Europe o.*; *all the world o.*, in all countries &c.; *went o. his notes*; *sitting o. the fire, a cheerful glass*, &c.; *pause o. the details*; *laugh o. the absurdity of it*; *go to sleep o.* one's *work*); with or so as to get or give superiority to, beyond, more than, (*is king, reigns, has jurisdiction, o. twenty millions*; *was victor, won the victory, was victorious, o.*; *set him o. the rest*; *has no command o. herself*; *give me the preference o. him*; *cost o. £50*; *o. & above*, besides, not to mention); out & down from, down from edge of, so as to clear, across, on or to the other side of, throughout, through duration of, till end of, (*fell o. the edge, precipice*; *stumble o.*, be tripped up by; *jumped o. the brook*; *o. the bags* or *top*, of troops emerging from trench to attack; *looking o. the hedge*; *spoke o. her shoulder*; *coursing o. the plain*; *a pass o. the company's line*; *the house o. the way*, opposite; *the King o. the water*, Jacobite phr. for exiled king; *if we can tide o. the next month*; *payments spread o. a series of years*; *will not live o. today*; *can you stay o. Wednesday?*). [Aryan; OE *ofer*, cf. Du. *over*, G *über*, *ober*, Gk *huper*, Skr. *upari*; cogn. w. ABOVE, & having compar. termin.]

o·ver-, pref. = prec. 1. Used as adj. in agreement with second part of compound, =upper, outer, of higher kind, upside down, extra, to or in higher position. So *o·vercoat*, worn outside another; *o·verdress*, outer part of gown made to resemble one dress worn over & showing parts of another of different colour &c.; *o·verfault* geol., reverse fault with inclination towards upthrow side; *o·verfold* geol., fold of strata so complete that middle part is upside down; *o·verhand* a. & adv., with hand above object held, with hand above shoulder (*o. bowling*; *bowls o.*), out of water (*o. stroke* in swimming), &c.; *o·verlord*, supreme lord, suzerain, whence *overlor·d*SHIP n.; *o·vermăn* philos., also *superman*, the ideal man, beyond good & evil, or superior to moral restrictions, of Nietsche's philosophy; *o·verplus*, surplus, superabundance; *o·vershoe*, of rubber or felt worn outside another; *o·versleeve*, for pulling on over sleeve to protect it; *o·versoul*, God as animating the universe & including all human souls; *o·verthrust* geol., thrust of strata on one side over those of other side of fault; *o·vertime*, during which workman works beyond regular hours; *o·vertone* n. mus., harmonic; *o·verweight*, preponderance, excessive weight.

2. As prep. governing second component & making with it n., a., or adv. So *ov·erall* n., woman's loose work-garment, (pl.) outer trousers or leggings or combination suit for dirty work, (Mil., pl.) officer's full-dress tight trousers; *o·verboard* adv., from within ship into water (usu. *fall, throw, o.*; *throw o.* fig., abandon, discard); *o·verdoor* n., ornamental woodwork above door; *o·verfront* n., armflap of Inverness cape &c.; *o·verground* a., raised above ground, not underground; *overhea·d* adv., on high, in the sky, in the storey above; *o·verhead* a., placed overhead (esp. *o. wires*; *o. charges* &c. commerc., those due to office expenses, management, interest on capital, & other general needs of a business); *o·verhouse* a., (of wires) supported on housetops instead of poles; *o·verknee* a., reaching above knee; *overla·nd* adv., by land & not sea; *o·verland* a., entirely or partly by land (esp. of route by Mediterranean to India, or from Atlantic to Pacific across continent); *overlea·f* adv., on other side of leaf (of book); *o·vermantel* n., ornamental shelves &c. over mantelpiece; *overnigh·t* adv., on the preceding evening with a view to, or as regarded from, the next day; *o·vernight*, a., done &c. overnight; *o·verproof* a., containing more alcohol than proof spirit; *oversea·(s)* adv., *o·versea* a., across or beyond sea; *oversi·de* adv., *o·verside* a., (of loading & unloading ship) over the side into or out of lighters; *overti·me* adv., beyond regular hours of work; *o·verweight* a., beyond weight allowed (esp. *o. luggage*).

3. As prep. prefixed to verbs, but itself governing case independently, often with specialized sense; also in abs. uses of, or in derivatives from, such vbs. So *overbri·m* v.t. & i. (*water overbrimmed the cup*; also said of the vessel); *overco·me* v.t. & i.,

prevail over, master, get the better of, be victorious, (p.p.) exhausted, made helpless, deprived of self-possession, (*with* or *by* emotion &c.; *o. with liquor*, drunk); *overcrow·* v.t., exult or triumph over (rival), outswagger; *o·verflow* n., what overflows or is superfluous (*o. meeting*, of those who have not found room at a demonstration &c. & meet elsewhere); *overflow·* v.t. & i., flow over (brim &c.), flood (surface), (fig., of crowd &c.) extend beyond limits of (room &c.), (of receptacle &c.) be so full that contents o., (of kindness, harvest, &c.) be very abundant, whence *overflow*ING[1, 2] a. & n. (esp. *full to o.*), *overflow·ing*LY[2] adv.; *overgrow·* v.t. (of creeping plants); *o·vergrowth* n., plants that have grown over anything, (fig.) accretion; *overha·ng* v.t. & i. (-hung), jut out over, jut out, (fig.) impend over, impend; so *o·verhang* n., fact or amount of overhanging; *overla·p* v.t., partly cover, cover & extend beyond, (reciprocally of pl. subj.) partly coincide (*the great difficulty in classification is the overlapping of species*); *overlea·p* v.t., leap over, surmount, omit, ignore; *overlie·* v.t., lie on top of, smother (child) thus; *overloo·k* v.t., have prospect of or over from above, be higher than, fail to observe, take no notice of, condone, superintend, oversee, bewitch with the evil eye; *overpa·ss* v.t. & i., pass over, across, beyond, &c., get to the end of, surmount, surpass; *overri·de* v.t., ride over (enemy's country) with armed force, trample (person) under one's horse's hoofs, (fig.) trample under foot, set aside, refuse to comply with, have or claim superior authority to, (Surg., of fractured bone) overlap; *overru·n* v.t., flood, harry & spoil (enemy's country), (of vermin, weeds, &c.) swarm or spread over, exceed (limit); *oversai·ling*, (of masonry course &c.) projecting beyond the one below; *oversee·* v.t., look at from above (rare), superintend or look after (workmen, execution of work, &c.), whence *o·verseer* (-sēr) n. (*o. of the poor*, parish officer charged with poor-relief & other duties); *overshoo·t* v.t., send missile, go, beyond (mark &c. lit. & fig.; *o. the mark*, also *o. oneself*, go too far, exaggerate, overdo something; *o·vershot wheel*, turned by water flowing above it); *o·versight* n., supervision (rare), omission to notice, mistake of inadvertence; *overspread·d* v.t., become diffused over, cover or occupy surface of; *overste·p* v.t., pass beyond (boundary lit. or fig.).

4. As adverb in local senses (above, by way of cover, down from above or from erectness, past, beyond, in addition) modifying vb or derived n. without itself governing object. So *overar·ch* v.t. & i.; *overba·lance* v.i. & t., lose balance & fall, cause to do this; *overbear·* v.t., bear down or upset by weight or force, put down or repress by power or authority, surpass in importance &c., outweigh; *overbear·ing* a., domineering, masterful, whence *overbear·ing*LY[2] adv., *overbear·ing*NESS n.; *overblow·n* p.p., (of storm &c.) passed; *overca·nopy* v.t.; *overclou·d* v.t.; *overcru·st* v.t.; *o·verfall* n., turbulent stretch of sea &c. caused by set of tide or current over submarine ledge or meeting of currents, overflow opening to keep water of lock or canal up or down to required level; *overfi·lm* v.t.; *overgi·ld* v.t.; *overhau·l* v.t., pull to pieces for purposes of examining, examine condition of, (esp. Naut.) catch up, come up with; *overhear·* v.t., hear as an eavesdropper or as an unperceived or unintended listener; *overlay·* v.t., cover surface of *with* coating &c., (incorrectly) overlie; *o·verlay* n., thing laid over something, coverlet, small tablecloth, &c.; *overpa·ssed, -pa·st*, a., gone by, past; *o·versew* v.t., sew (two edges) with every stitch passing in same direction through both, the inter-stitch parts of thread lying across & outside united edge; *oversha·dow* v.t., shelter from sun, protect from attack (rare), cast into the shade, diminish conspicuousness of by outshining; *o·verspill* n., what is spilt, surplus population &c.; *overspread·d* v.t., cover *with* (chiefly pass.; *heaven was o. with clouds*); *o·verstrung* a., (of piano) with strings in sets crossing each other obliquely; *overta·ke* v.t., come up with, catch up, (person &c. who has start, or arrears of work), (of storm, misfortune, &c.) come suddenly upon (*overtaken in drink*, drunk); *overthrow·* v.t., upset, knock down, cast out from power, vanquish, subvert, put an end to (institution &c.); *o·verthrow* n., defeat, subversion, (Cricket) fielder's return not stopped near wicket & so allowing further run(s); *overtur·n* v.t. & i., upset, (cause to) fall down or over, overthrow, subvert, abolish; *o·verturn* n., upsetting, revolution; *overwhe·lm* v.t., bury beneath superincumbent mass, submerge utterly, crush, bring to sudden ruin, overpower with emotion &c., deluge *with* inquiries &c.; *overwhe·lming* a., irresistible by numbers, amount, &c., whence *overwhe·lming*LY[2] adv.

5. As adv. with trans. vb, adding sense of *effectually, completely, into submission.* So *overawe·* v.t.; *overcloy·* v.t.; *overjoy·ed* p.p., transported with joy (*at*); *overma·ster* v.t.; *overpersua·de* v.t., persuade in spite of reluctance.

6. As adv. or adj. prefixed to vb, adj., adv., or n., adding notion of excess over the desirable, the truth, or a definite limit. So *over-abou·nd* v.i.; *over-abu·ndant* a.; *over-abu·ndantly* adv., *over-abu·ndance* n.; *over-a·ct* v.t. & i., act (part, emotion, &c.), act part, with exaggeration; *over-a·ctive* a.; *over-acti·vity* n.; *over-a·nxious* a.; *over-a·nxiously* adv.; *over-anxi·ety* n.; *over-*

-*blow·* v.t. (mus.), blow (pipe &c.) with such force as to produce harmonic instead of fundamental note; *overblow·n* a., (of flowers) too fully open, past prime; *overbo·ld* a.; *overbur·den* v.t., & n.; *overbur·densome,* a.; *overbu·sy* a., too much occupied, officious; *overbuy·* v.i., buy more than enough to meet demand; *over-ca·pitalize* v.t., fix or estimate capital of (company &c.) too high; *over-care·* n.; *over-care·ful* a.; *over-cau·tion* n.; *over-cau·tious* a.; *over-cau·tiously* adv.; *overchar·ge* v.t., put too much explosive or electricity or the like into, put exaggerated details or too much detail into (description, picture, &c.), charge too high a price for (thing) or to (person), charge (specified sum) beyond right price; *o·vercharge* n., excessive charge (of explosive, or in money, see prec.); *over-co·lour* v.t., exaggerate (details of description &c.); *over-co·nfident* a.; *over-co·nfidently* adv.; *over-co·nfidence* n.; *over-cre·dulous* a.; *over-credu·lity* n.; *overcro·p* v.t., exhaust (land) by continuous cropping; *overcrow·d* v.t.; *overcu·nning* n., cunning that overreaches itself; *over-cur·ious* a., too inquisitive, too careful or precise or fastidious; *over-cur·iously* adv.; *over-curio·sity* n.; *over-de·licacy* n.; *over-de·licate* a.; *over-deve·lop* v.t. (photog.); *overdo·* v.t., carry to excess, go too far in, cook too much (esp. in p.p.), overtax strength of (esp. in p.p.); *overdo·se* v.t.; *o·verdo·se* n.; *o·verdraft* n., overdrawing of bank account, amount by which draft exceeds balance; *overdraw·* v.t. & i., draw cheque in excess of (one's account) or in excess of one's account, exaggerate in describing; *over-dre·ss* v.t. & i.; *overdri·ve* v.t., drive (horse &c.), work (person), to exhaustion; *over-ea·ger* a.; *over-ea·gerly* adv.; *over-ea·gerness* n.; *over-ear·nest* a.; *over-e·stimāte* v.t., put value or amount of too high; *over-e·stimate* (-at) n.; *over-exci·te* v.t.; *over-exer·tion* n.; *over-expo·se* v.t., *over-expo·sure* n., (photog.); *over-fati·gue* v.t., & n.; *overfi·sh* v.t., fish (stream &c.) to depletion; *overfo·nd* a.; *over-go·vern* v.t., subject to needless restrictions & regulations; *overgo·vernment* n.; *overgrow·th* n., growth too great for health &c.; *over-ha·ste* n.; *over-ha·sty* a.; *over-ha·stily* adv.; *over-hea·t* v.t.; *over-housed* (-zd) a., living in too large a house; *over-indu·lge* v.t. & i.; *over-indu·lgence* n.; *over-i·ssue* v.t., issue (notes, shares, &c.) beyond authorized amount or ability to pay; *over-i·ssue* n., things or amount so issued; *over-la·bour* v.t., elaborate to excess; *over-la·den* a.; *overlar·ge* a.; *overloa·d* v.t.; *o·verloa·d* n.; *overlo·ng* a.; *over-ma·ny* a.; *overma·sted* a., with too tall or heavy masts; *o·ver-mea·sure* n., amount beyond the due or sufficient; *over-mo·dest* a.; *overmu·ch* a., n., & adv. (*be not righteous o.*); *over-ni·ce* a., too fastidious; *over-ni·ceness, over-ni·cety,* nn.; *overpay·* v.t., recompense (person, service) too highly; *over-peo·pled* a., overstocked with people; *overpi·tch* v.t., bowl (cricket ball) so that it pitches too near wicket; *over-po·pulated* a., too thickly populated; *over-popula·tion* n., overpopulated condition; *overpo·t* v.t., plant in too large a pot; *overprai·se* v.t., & n.; *over-pre·ssure* n., pressing or being pressed too hard, esp. overwork; *over-pri·nt* v.t. (photog.); *over-produ·ce* v.i. & t., produce too much of (commodity, or usu. abs.) for the demand; *over-produ·ction* n.; *over-pu·nish* v.t.; *overra·te* v.t., have too high an opinion of, assess too high for rating purposes; *over-rea·d* v.i., do too much reading; *over-refi·ne* v.i., make too subtle distinctions; *over-ri·de* v.t., exhaust (horse) by riding; *over-ri·pe* a.; *over-scru·pulous* a.; *overse·ll* v.t. & i., sell more of (commodity, stock, or abs.) than one can deliver; *over-se·nsitive* a.; *over-se·nsitiveness* n.; *over-soli·citous* a.; *over-soli·citude* n.; *overstat·e* v.t., state too strongly, exaggerate; *over-sta·tement* n.; *oversto·ck* v.t.; *o·verstock* n.; *overstrai·n* v.t., damage by exertion, make too much of (scruples &c.; esp. in p.p.); *o·verstrai·n* n., overstraining or being overstrained; *overstru·ng* a., (of person, his nerves, &c.) intensely strained or wound up; *overstu·dy* v.i., & n.; *over-su·btle* a.; *over-supply·* n.; *over-swo·llen* a.; *overta·sk* v.t., give or be too heavy a task to or for; *over-ta·x* v.t., make excessive demand on (person's strength &c.), burden with excessive taxes; *over-tire·* v.t.; *overtoi·l* n.; *overto·ne* v.t. (photog.); *overtrai·n* v.t. & i., subject to or undergo too much athletic training, with injury to condition; *overu·se* v.t.; *o·ver-u·se* n.; *overva·lue* v.t.; *overwee·ning* a., arrogant, presumptuous, conceited, self-confident; *overweigh·ted* a., unduly loaded *with*; *overwi·nd* v.t., wind (watch &c.) beyond proper stopping-point; *overwor·k* v.t. & i., (cause to) work too hard, weary or exhaust with work; *overwor·k* n., excessive work; *over-wrough·t* a., overexcited, suffering reaction from excitement, too elaborate; *over-zea·l* n.; *over-zea·lous* a.; *over-zea·lously* adv.

7. Prefixed to vb & enabling it to take *self* as obj., or be used in p.p., with sense *damage oneself by doing action to excess*; many of these compounds can also be used abs. in same sense. So *overdri·nk, overea·t, overfee·d* (also trans.), *overgrow·* (in p.p., that has overgrown himself &c.); *overju·mp* one*self*, strain sinew &c. in jumping; *overrea·ch* one*self*, strain oneself by reaching too far, (of horse) injure fore-foot by striking it with hind-hoof; *overprea·ch, over-ru·n*; *oversleep·p* one*self*, miss intended hour of rising by sleeping too long; *oversmo·ke*; *overspe·nd* (one*self* or abs.), spend money beyond one's

means; *overtoi·led* p.p.; *overwa·lk*; *overwa·tched* p.p., exhausted by keeping awake; *overwri·te* one*self*, damage one's style by writing too much.

8. Prefixed to vb or deriv., or adj., with added sense of *more than*. So *overba·lance* v.t., outweigh lit. & fig.; *o·verbalance* n., (amount of) excess; *overdue·* a.; *overfi·ll* v.t.; *overfu·ll* a.; *overma·tch* v.t., be too strong &c. for, defeat; *overma·tch* n.; *overpoi·se* v.t., outweigh; *oversubscri·be* v.t., subscribe more than amount of (loan &c.; usu. in p.p.).

9. As prefix making trans. vb out of intr. vb, or vb not taking same obj., or n., usu. with sense of *exceeding*. So *overbui·ld*, build too closely on (land); *overca·st*, cover (sky &c.) with clouds or darkness (usu. p.p.), stitch over (edge) to prevent unravelling, esp. with blanket or buttonhole stitch; *overli·ve*, live beyond (other person, specified age, &c.); *overpow·er*, reduce to submission, subdue, master, make (thing) ineffective or imperceptible by greater intensity, (of heat, emotion, &c.) be too intense for, overwhelm; *overpow·ering* a., irresistible; *overpow·eringly* adv.; *overrea·ch*, circumvent, outwit, get the better of by cunning or artifice; *overre·nt*, charge too high a rent for (land &c.) or to (farmer &c.); *overru·le*, set aside (decision, argument, proposed course) by superior authority, annul decision or reject proposal of (person); *oversta·y*, stay beyond (one's welcome &c.); *overto·p*, be or become higher than; *overtru·mp*, play higher trump than.

overact, v.t. & i., see OVER- 6; **overall** n., OVER- 2; **overarch** v.t. & i., OVER- 4; **overawe** v.t., OVER- 5; **overbalance** v.i. & t., & n., OVER- 4, 8; **overbear** v.t., **overbearing** a., OVER- 4; **overblow** v.t., OVER- 6; **overblown** a., OVER- 4, 6; **overboard** adv., OVER- 2; **overbrim** v.t. & i., OVER- 3; **overbuild** v.t., OVER- 9; **overburden** v.t., **overbusy** a., **overbuy** v.i., OVER- 6; **overcanopy** v.t., OVER- 4; **over-capitalize** v.t., **overcare** n., OVER- 6; **overcast** v.t., OVER- 9; **over-caution** n., **overcharge** v.t., & n., OVER- 6; **overcloud** v.t., OVER- 4; **overcloy** v.t., OVER- 5; **overcoat** n., OVER- 1; **overcolour** v.t., OVER- 6; **overcome** v.t., OVER- 3; **over-confidence** n., **over-credulity** n., **overcrop** v.t., OVER- 6; **overcrow** v.t., OVER- 3; **overcrowd** v.t., OVER- 6; **overcrust** v.t., OVER- 4; **over-cunning** n., **over-curious** a., **over-delicacy** n., **over-develop** v.t., **overdo** v.t., OVER- 6; **overdoor** n., OVER- 2; **overdose** v.t. & n., **overdraft**, n., **overdraw** v.t. & i., OVER- 6; **overdress**, n. OVER- 1, v.i. OVER- 6; **overdrink** v. refl. & i., OVER- 7; **overdrive** v.t., OVER- 6; **overdue** a., OVER- 8; **overeat** v. refl. & i., OVER- 7; **over-estimate** v.t., & n., **over-expose** v.t., **over-exposure** n., OVER- 6; **overfall** n., OVER- 4; **over-fatigue** v.t., & n., OVER- 6; **overfault** n., OVER- 1; **overfeed** v.t. & i., OVER- 7; **overfill** v.t., OVER- 8; **overfilm** v.t., OVER- 4; **overfish** v.t., OVER- 6; **overflow** v.t. & i., & n., **overflowing** n. & a., OVER- 3; **overfold** n., OVER- 1; **overfront** n., OVER- 2; **overfull** a., OVER- 8; **overgild** v.t., OVER- 4; **over-govern** v.t., **over-government** n., OVER- 6; **overground** a., OVER- 2; **overgrow**, v.t. OVER- 3, v. refl. & i. OVER- 7; **overgrowth** n., OVER- 3, 6; **overhand** adv. & a., OVER- 1; **overhang** v.t. & i., & n., OVER- 3; **overhaul** v.t., OVER- 4; **overhead** adv. & a., OVER- 2; **overhear** v.t., OVER- 4; **over-house** a., OVER- 2; **overhoused** a., **over-indulgence** n., **over-issue** v.t., & n., OVER- 6; **overjoyed** a., OVER- 5; **overjump** v. refl., OVER- 7; **overknee** a., OVER- 2; **overlabour** v.t., **overladen** a., OVER- 6; **overland** adv. & a., OVER- 2; **overlap** v.t. & i., OVER- 3; **overlay** v.t., & n., OVER- 4; **overleaf** adv., OVER- 2; **overleap** v.t., **overlie** v.t., OVER- 3; **overlive** v.t., OVER- 9; **overload** v.t., & n., OVER- 6; **overlook** v.t., OVER- 3; **overlord, overlordship, overman**, nn., OVER- 1; **overmantel** n., OVER- 2; **over-many, overmasted**, aa., OVER- 6; **overmaster** v.t., OVER- 5; **overmatch** v.t., & n., OVER- 8; **over-measure** n., **over-much** a., adv., & n., **over-nice** a., **over-niceness, over-nicety**, nn., OVER- 6; **overnight** adv. & a., OVER- 2; **overpass** v.t., OVER- 3; **overpassed, -past**, a., OVER- 4; **overpay** v.t., **overpeopled** a., OVER- 6; **over-persuade** v.t., OVER- 5; **overpitch** v.t., OVER- 6; **overplus** n., OVER- 1; **overpoise** v.t., OVER- 8; **over-population** n., **overpot** v.t., OVER- 6; **overpower** v.t., **overpowering** a., OVER- 9; **overpraise** v.t., & n., OVER- 6; **over-preach** v. refl. & i., OVER- 7; **overpressure** n., **overprint** v.t,. **over-produce** v.t. & i., **over-production** n., OVER- 6; **over-proof** a., OVER- 2; **overrate** v.t., OVER- 6; **overreach**, v. refl. & i. OVER- 7, v.t. OVER- 9; **over-read** v.i., **over-refine** v.i., OVER- 6; **over-rent** v.t., OVER- 9; **override** v.t., OVER- 3, 6; **over-ripe** a., OVER- 6; **overrule** v.t., OVER- 9; **overrun** v.t., OVER- 3, 7; **oversailing**, OVER- 3; **oversea** a. & adv., **overseas** adv., OVER- 2; **oversee** v.t., **overseer** n., OVER- 3; **oversell** v.i. & t., OVER- 6; **oversew** v.t., OVER- 4; **overshadow** v.t., OVER- 4; **overshoe** n., OVER- 1; **overshoot** v.t., **overshot** a., OVER- 3; **overside** adv. & a., OVER- 2; **oversight** n., OVER- 3.

o·verslaugh (-aw), n. (mil.). Passing over of one's turn of duty in consideration of another duty that takes precedence of it. [f. Du. *overslag* (*overslaan* omit f. OVER, *slaan* strike)]

oversleep, v. refl. & i., see OVER- 7; **oversleeve** n., OVER- 1; **oversmoke** v. refl. & i., OVER- 7; **oversoul** n., OVER- 1; **over-**

spend v. refl. & i., OVER- 7; **overspill** n., OVER- 4; **overspread** v.t., OVER- 3, 4; **overstate** v.t., **overstatement** n., OVER- 6; **overstay** v.t., OVER- 9; **overstep** v.t., OVER- 3; **overstock** v.t., & n., **overstrain** v.t., & n., OVER- 6; **overstrung** a., OVER- 4, 6; **overstudy** v.i., & n., OVER- 6; **over-subscribe** v.t., OVER- 8; **over-supply** n., **overswollen** a., OVER- 6.

over·t, a. Openly done, unconcealed, patent; *market o.*, open displaying of goods for sale to all comers. Hence **over·tLY**[2] adv. [OF, p.p. of *ovrir*, now *ouvrir*, open, f. L *aperire*]

overtake, v.t., see OVER- 4; **overtask** v.t., **overta·x** v.t., OVER- 6; **overthrow** v.t., & n., OVER- 4; **overthrust** n., OVER- 1; **overtime,** adv. OVER- 2, n. OVER- 1; **overtire** v.t., OVER- 6; **overtoil** n., OVER- 6; **overtoiled** a., OVER- 7; **overtone** v.t., OVER- 6; **overtone** n., OVER- 1; **overtop** v.t., OVER- 9; **overtrain** v.t. & i., OVER- 6; **overtrump** v.t., OVER- 9.

ō·verture (-tsher, -tūr), n. Opening of negotiations with another, formal proposal or offer, (usu. pl., esp. *make oo. to*); (Mus.) orchestral piece opening opera, oratorio, &c.; beginning of poem &c. [OF (OVERT, -URE)]

overturn, v.t. & i., & n., see OVER- 4; **over-use** v.t., & n., **over-value** v.t., OVER- 6; **over-walk** v. refl. & i., **over-watched** a., OVER- 7; **overweening** a., OVER- 6; **overweight,** n. OVER- 1, adj. OVER- 2; **overweighted** a., OVER- 6; **overwhelm** v.t., **overwhelming** a., OVER- 4; **overwind** v.t., **overwork** v.t. & i., & n., OVER- 6; **overwrite** v. refl. & i., OVER- 7; **overwrought** a., OVER- 6.

ōvi-[1], **ōvo-**, comb. forms of OVUM; *o·viduct*, n., canal through which ova pass from ovary esp. in oviparous animals; *o·viform*, a., egg-shaped; *ovi·parous*, a., producing young by means of eggs expelled from body before being hatched (opp. VIVIPAROUS); *ovipo·sit*, v.i., lay egg(s), esp. with *ovipo·sitor*, n., pointed tubular organ with which female insect deposits eggs; *ovorhomboi·dal* &c., between rhomboid &c. & oval; *ovo·logy*, n., science of the formation of animals' ova; *ovovivi·parous*, a., producing young by eggs hatched within body.

ŏvi-[2], comb. form of L *ovis* sheep; *ovibo·vine*, a. & n., (animal) having characters intermediate between sheep & ox, musk-ox; *o·vicide*, n. (facet.), sheep-killing.

Ovi·dian, a. (As) of Ovid or his poetry. [L *Ovidius* Ovid, -IAN]

ō·vīne, a. Of, like, sheep. [f. L *ovinus* (*ovis* sheep, -INE[1])]

ō·void, a. & n. Solidly or superficially egg-shaped, oval with one end more pointed; (n.) o. body or surface. [OVUM, -OID]

ō·volo, n. Convex moulding of quarter-circle or quarter-ellipse section, receding downwards. [It. (now *uovolo*), dim. of *uovo* egg f. L OVUM]

ō·vule, n. Rudimentary seed, female germ-cell, unfertilized ovum. Hence **o·vulAR**[1] a. [F (foll., -ULE)]

ō·vum, n. (pl. *-a*). Female germ in animals, capable of developing into new individual when fertilized by male sperm, egg esp. of mammals, fish, or insects. [L, =egg]

owe (ō), v.t. & i. Be under obligation to (re)pay (person money, money *to* person, money) or render (person honour &c., gratitude &c. *to* person), be in debt (*for* thing, with creditor in dat.; *he owes not any man*; *I o. you for your services, owed for all my clothes*); *o.* one *a grudge*, cherish resentment against him; be indebted for *to* person (or with dat.; *we o. to Newton the principle of gravitation*; *I o. him much*). [com.-Teut.; OE *ágan*, cf. OHG *eigan*, Da. *eie* own; earlier past tense, OUGHT[2], OE *áhte*]

Ow·enism (ō-), n. Communistic cooperation advocated by Robert Owen (d. 1858). [-ISM]

ow·ing (ō-), pred. a. Yet to be paid, owed, due, (*paid all that was o.*); *o. to*, attributable to, caused by, (*all this was o. merely to ill luck*), (as prep.) on account of (*o. to the drought, crops are short*). [OWE, -ING[2]]

owl (owl), n. Kinds of large-headed small-faced hook-beaked large-eyed soft-plumaged nocturnal bird of prey (esp. *Barn O.*, *Tawny O.*, & *Long-eared* or *Horned O.*, each with other names, as *Church*, *Screech*, *Hooting*, &c., *O.*; *fly with the o.*, have nocturnal habits; *oo. to Athens*, = COAL[1]s *to Newcastle*); solemn person, wise-looking dullard, whence **ow·lISH**[1] a., **ow·lishLY**[2] adv.; (also *o. pigeon*) fancy variety of pigeon; *o.-light*, dusk, twilight. Hence **ow·lERY**(3) n. [com.-Teut.; OE *úle*, cf. G *eule*; prob. imit., cf. L *ulula* owl, *ululare* HOWL[1]]

ow·let, n. Owl, young owl. [earlier HOWLET]

own[1] (ōn), a. (Appended to possessive adj. or case) in full ownership, proper, peculiar, individual, & not another's, (*saw it with my o. eyes*; *has a value all its o.*; *let them* STEW[2] *in their o. juice*; *loves truth for its o. sake*; *be* one's *o. man*, independent, free; *God's o. heaven*; *may I have it for my o.* or *my very o.?*; *my o. sweetheart* &c., or abs. *my o.*, esp. in voc. expressing affection; often also used to emphasize not the ownership, but the personality of the subject &c., as *cooks her o. meals, every man his o. lawyer, am my o. master*; also used abs. = private property, kindred, &c., as *May I not do what I will with my o.?, And his o. received him not, The* DEVIL[1]*'s o.*; *of* one's *o.*, belonging to one, as *I have nothing of my o., will give you one of my o.*; *hold* one's *o.*, maintain position, not be defeated; *on* one's *o.*

slang, independently, on one's o. account or responsibility or resources); (without preceding possessive) *o. brother, sister,* with both parents the same, *o. cousin,* first. [OE *ǽgen, ágen,* p.p. of OWE (in obs. sense *possess*); cf. Du. & G *eigen*]

own[2], v.t. & i. Have as property, possess, whence **ow·ner**[1], **ow·nership**(1), nn., **ow·nerless** a.; acknowledge authorship, paternity, or possession, of (*child, pamphlet, hat, that nobody will o.*); admit as existent, valid, true, &c. (*owns his deficiencies, himself indebted, he* or *that he did not know*); confess *to* (*owns to a sense of shame, to having done*); *o. up* colloq., make frank confession; submit to (person's sway &c.) without protest; *the owner* (Nav. slang), captain of the ship. [OE *ágnian* (*ágen* OWN[1])]

ox, n. (pl. *oxen*). Any bovine animal, individual of kinds of large usu. horned cloven-footed ruminant quadruped used when domesticated for draught, for supplying milk, and for eating as meat, (esp.) castrated male of domestic species, (*the black ox has trod on* one's *foot,* misfortune or old age has come upon him); *ox-bird,* kinds of small bird, esp. the dunlin; *ox-eye,* large human eye, whence **o·x-eyed**[2] a., kinds of plant esp. (*Yellow O.-e.*) Corn Marigold, (*White O.-e.*) Ox-eyed Daisy; *ox-fence* or **o·xer**[1] n., strong cattle-fence of railing & hedge & sometimes ditch; *ox-gall* (used for cleansing, & in painting & pharmacy); *oxherd,* cowherd; *oxhide,* skin of ox; *oxlip,* hybrid plant between primrose & cowslip; *oxtail,* tail of ox, much used for soup-making. [com.-Teut.; OE *oxa,* cf. Du. *os,* G *ochse,* also W *ych,* Skr. *ukshán* pl.]

ox-, comb. form (chem.) = OXY-, as *oxace·tic* or *oxyace·tic,* or = OXAL-, as *oxa·mic.*

oxal(o)-, comb. form of *oxalic acid,* whence **o·xalate**[1](3) n.; *oxalo-ni·trate* &c.

oxă·lic, a. (chem.). Derived from wood-sorrel (*o. acid,* a highly poisonous & sour acid found in wood-sorrel & other plants). [f. F *oxalique* (L f. Gk *oxalis* kinds of plant including wood-sorrel, -IC)]

O·xford, n. University town in England; *O. bags,* very wide trousers; *O. blue* (dark with purple tinge); *O. clay,* deposit of stiff blue clay underlying coral rag in midland counties; *O. frame,* picture-frame of which sides cross each other at corners & project; *O. man,* educated at O. Univ.; *O. mixture,* dark-grey cloth; *O. movement,* for revival of Catholic doctrine & observance in Church of England begun c. 1833; *O. shirting,* kind of shirt or dress material; *O. shoes,* low shoes lacing over instep; *O. Tracts,* the TRACTS for the times.

o·xide, n. Compound of oxygen with another element or with organic radical. [F, after *acide* acid (OX- = OXY-, -IDE)]

o·xidize, v.t. & i. Cause to combine with oxygen; cover (metal) with coating of oxide, make rusty; take up or enter into combination with oxygen, rust; *oxidized silver,* (incorrect name for) silver with dark coating of silver sulphide. Hence **o·xidizable** a., **oxidiza·tion, oxidi·zer**[1] (2), nn. [prec., -IZE]

Oxo·nian, a. & n. (Past or present member) of University of Oxford. [*Oxonia* latinized name of *Ox(en)ford,* -AN]

oxy-, comb. form of Gk *oxus* sharp: (1) in gen. senses, as *oxycar·pous* with pointed fruit; *oxyō·pia,* abnormal keenness of vision; OXYGEN; OXYMORON; OXYTONE; (2) in chem. wds as comb. form of *oxygen,* (a) denoting presence or admixture of oxygen; *o.-hou·se-gas, o.-pa·raffin,* &c., used attrib. of flame produced by mixing the vapour of the gas &c. with oxygen; *o.-calcium light,* limelight; *o.-hydrogen blow-pipe, flame, light,* &c.; *oxya·cid* (& see b.); *o·xysalt,* containing oxygen; (b) loosely used for *hydroxy-,* denoting compound of organic substance having atom of hydroxyl substituted for one of hydrogen, as *oxya·cid* (& see a.).

o·xygen, n. Colourless tasteless scentless gas, one of the non-metallic elements, existing in air & combined in water & most minerals & organic substances, & being essential to animal & vegetable life. Hence **oxy·genous** a. [f. F *oxygène* acidifying principle, see OXY-(1), -GEN; it was at first held to be the essential principle in formation of acids]

oxy̆·genate, v.t. Supply, treat, or mix, with oxygen, oxidize; charge (blood) with oxygen by respiration. Hence **oxy·genant**(2), **oxygena·tion,** nn. [f. F *oxygéner* (prec.), -ATE[3]]

oxy·genize, v.t. = prec. [-IZE]

o·xymel, n. Syrup of honey & vinegar. [L f. Gk *oxumeli* (OXY-, *meli* honey)]

oxymō̆r·on, n. (rhet.). Figure of speech with pointed conjunction of seeming contradictories (e.g. *faith unfaithful kept him falsely true*). [Gk (-*mō*-) f. OXY-(1), *mōros* foolish]

o·xytone (-*on*), a. & n. (Gk gram.). (Word) with acute accent on last syllable. [f. Gk *oxutonos* f. OXY-(1), *tonos* TONE]

oy·er, n. Criminal trial under the writ of *o. & terminer* or commission to judges on circuit to hold courts. [f. AF *oyer et terminer* (L *audire* hear, *terminare,* determine), -ER[4]]

ōye·z ! (-s), **ōye·s !, o ye·s !,** int. uttered, usu. thrice, by public crier or court officer to bespeak silence & attention. [OF (-*z*), imperat. of *oir* hear = L *audiatis* (*audire* hear)]

oy·ster, n. Kinds of edible bivalve mollusc usu. eaten alive; o.-shaped morsel of meat in fowl's back; *o.-bank, -bed,* part of sea-bottom where oo. breed or are bred; *o.-bar,* tavern where oo. are served; *o.-catcher,* wading sea-bird; *o.-farm,* sea bottom used for breeding oo.; *o.-knife*, of shape adapted for opening oo.; *o. patty*, piece of pastry containing cooked oo. [f. OF *oistre* f. L *ostrea* f. Gk *ostreon*]

ozŏ·cerīte, ozŏ·kerit, n. Wax-like fossil resin used for candles, insulating, &c. [G (*-kerit*), irreg. f. Gk *ozō* smell, *kēros* wax]

ō·zone (*or* ŏdz-), n. Condensed form of oxygen with three atoms to molecule having pungent refreshing odour, (fig.) exhilarating influence. Hence **ozŏ·n**IC, **ozoni·**FEROUS, aa., **o·zon**IZE(3, 5) v.t., **o·zoniz**ER[1](2), **ozono·**METER, nn. [F (Gk *ozō* smell, -ONE)]

P

P, p, (pē), letter (pl. *Ps*, P's). *Mind* one's *P's & Q's*, be careful of propriety.

Abbreviations (1): (P.): parish, **P.P.** (priest); Peninsular, **P. & O.** (Oriental); Please, **P.T.O.** (Turn Over); Police, **P.C.** (Constable); Post, **P.O.** (Office); *Post*, **P.S.** (*Scriptum*), postscript; Postal, **P.O.** (Order); President, as **P.R.A.** (of the Royal Academy); prime, **P.M.** (Minister); Privy, **P.C.** (Council, -lor); Prize, **P.R.** (Ring). (p.): page (of book &c.); past, **p.p.** (participle); per, **p.p.** = per pro. (see 2); perch (measure); *post*, **p.m.** (*meridiem*); *pour*, **p.p.c.** (*prendre congé*, to take leave); prompt, **p.s.** (side).

Abbreviations (2): **Pa**, Pennsylvania; **per pro.**(*curationem*), by proxy; **Petriburg.**, (signature of) Bishop of Peterborough; **Ph.**(*ilosophiae*) **D.**(*octor*), Doctor of Philosophy; **Phil.**(ippians); **Philem.**(on); **pnxt**, *pinxit*; **pop.**(ulation); **pp.**, pages; **Preb.**(endary); **Prof.**(essor); **pro tem.**(*pore*), for the time; **Prov.**(erbs); **prox.**(*ime*) **acc.**(*essit, -esserunt*); **prox.**-(imo); **Ps.**(alms); **Pte**, Private (soldier).

pa (pah), n. (colloq.). =PAPA.

pă·bŭlum, n. Food (often fig., as *mental p.*). [L (*pascere* feed)]

pă·ca, n. Genus of large rodents in Central & South America. [native]

pace[1], n. Single step in walking or running; space traversed in this (about 30 in.); space between successive stationary positions of same foot in walking (about 60 in.); mode of walking or running, gait; any of various gaits of (esp. trained) horse, mule, &c.; =AMBLE; (fig.) *put* person *through his pp.*, test his qualities in action &c.; speed in walking or running; rate of progression (often fig.); *keep p.*, advance at equal rate *with*; *go the p.*, go at great speed, (fig.) indulge in dissipation; *p.-maker*, rider, runner, &c., who sets p. for another in race &c.; *p.-stick*, drill-sergeant's adjustable two-legged appliance for measuring length of p. Hence **-pac**ED[2] a. [ME, f. OF *pas* f. L *passus* (*pandere pass-* stretch)]

pace[2], v.i. & t. Walk with slow or regular pace; traverse thus; measure (distance) by pacing; (of horse) amble; set pace for (rider, runner, &c.). [f. prec.]

pā·ce[3] (-sĭ), prep. *P. tūā*, *p. Smith*, (in announcing contrary opinion) with all deference to you, to Smith. [L, abl. of PAX]

pa·cer, n. In vbl senses, esp. horse that paces. [-ER[1]]

pacha, &c. See PASHA &c.

pachi·si (-tshēsĭ), n. Four-handed Indian game with cowries for dice. [Hind., =of 25]

pă·chўderm (-k-), n. Thick-skinned quadruped, esp. one of Cuvier's order *Pachydermata* (hoofed quadrupeds that do not chew cud, e.g. elephant, horse, &c.); (fig.) thick-skinned person. So **pachyder·mat**OUS a. [f. F *pachyderme* f. Gk *pakhudermos* (*pakhus* thick + *derma -matos* skin)]

paci·fic, a. & n. Tending to peace; of peaceful disposition; *The P.* (*Ocean*), that between America & Asia. Hence **paci·fi**CALLY adv. [f. L *pacificus* (*pax pacis* peace, see -FIC)]

pacifica·tion, n. Pacifying; treaty of peace. So **paci·ficat**ORY a. [F, f. L *pacificationem* (as foll., see -FICATION)]

pacĭ·ficism, pă·cifism, n. The doctrine that the abolition of war is both desirable & possible. Hence **pacĭ·fic**IST, **pă·cif**IST, n. [PACIFIC, -ISM; the *-fism, -fist,* forms are barbarous but usual]

pă·cifў, v.t. Appease (person, anger, excitement, &c.); reduce (country &c.) to state of peace. [f. L *pacifier* f. F *pacificare* (as PACIFIC, see -FY)]

pack[1], n. Bundle of things wrapped up or tied together for carrying, parcel, esp. pedlar's bundle or soldier's knapsack; a measure of various goods; lot, set, (*p. of fools, lies, nonsense,* &c.); number of hounds kept together for hunting, or of beasts (esp. wolves) or birds (esp. grouse) naturally associating; (Rugby footb.) a side's forwards; set of playing-cards; large area of large pieces of floating ice in polar sea; quantity of fish, fruit, &c., packed in a season &c.; *p.-drill*, military punishment of walking up and down in full *marching* ORDER[1](2); *p.-horse* (for carrying pp.); *packman*, pedlar; *p.-saddle* (adapted for supporting pp.); *packthread*, stout thread for sewing or tying up pp. [ME *packe*, cf. Du. *pak*, G *pack*]

pack[2], v.t. & i. Put (things) together into bundle, box, bag, &c., for transport or storing (often *p. up*, esp. abs.); (of things) admit of being packed *well, easily,* &c.; prepare & put up (meat, fruit, &c.) in tins &c. for preservation; put closely together; (Naut.) *p.* (put) *on all sail*; form (hounds) into pack; place (cards) together in pack; (intr.) crowd together, (of animals) form into pack; cover (thing) with something pressed tightly round; (Med.) wrap (body &c.) in wet cloth; fill (bag, box, &c.) with clothes &c.; cram (space &c. *with*); load (beast) with pack; (intr.) take oneself off with one's belongings; *send* (person) *packing*, dismiss him summarily; *p.* (person) *off*, send him away; [prob. diff. wd] select (jury &c.) so as to secure partial decision. [f. prec.]

pa·ckage, n. Bundle of things packed, parcel; box &c. in which goods are packed. [-AGE]

pa·cker, n. In vbl senses, esp.: one who packs meat, fruit, &c., for market; machine for packing. [-ER[1]]

pa·cket, n. Small package; *p.*(*-boat*), mail-boat. [PACK[1] + -ET[1]]

pa·cking, n. In vbl senses; *p.-needle*, large needle for sewing up packages; *p.-sheet*, (1) sheet for packing goods in, (2) wet sheet used in hydropathy. [-ING[1]]

pact, n. Compact; *P. of* LOCARNO, PEACE *P.* [OF, f. L *pactum*, neut. p.p. of *paciscere* agree]

pad[1], n. (Slang) road, esp. *gentleman, knight, squire, of the p.*, highwayman; (also *p.-nag*) easy-paced horse. [Du., cogn. w. PATH]

pad[2], v.t. & i. Tramp along (road &c.) on foot; travel on foot; *p. it, p. the hoof*, slang, go on foot. [cogn. w. prec.]

pad[3], n. Soft stuffed saddle without tree; part of double harness to which girths are attached; cushion, stuffing, used to diminish jarring, fill out hollows, &c.; guard for parts of body in cricket &c.; number of sheets of blotting-, writing-, or drawing-paper fastened together at edge; fleshy cushion forming sole of foot in some quadrupeds; paw of fox, hare, &c.; socket of brace, tool-handle. [?]

pad[4], v.t. Furnish with a pad, stuff; fill out (sentence &c.) with superfluous words; *padded cell*, room in lunatic asylum with padded walls. Hence **pa·d-d**ING[1](4) n. [f. prec.]

pad[5], n. Open pannier used as measure of fruit &c. [?]

pa·ddle[1], n. Small spade-like implement with long handle; short broad-bladed oar used without rowlock; *double p.* (with blade at each end); one of the boards fitted round circumference of p.-wheel; p.-shaped instrument; (Zool.) fin or flipper; *p.-wheel*, wheel for propelling ship, with boards round circumference so as to press backward against water; *p.-box*, casing over upper part of this. [?]

pa·ddle[2], v.i. & t., & n. Move on water, propel canoe, by means of paddles; *p.* one's *own canoe*, (fig.) depend on oneself alone; row gently; (n.) action, spell, of paddling. [f. prec.]

pa·ddle[3], v.i. Dabble with the feet in shallow water; toy with the fingers (*in, on, about*, thing); (of child) toddle. [?]

pa·ddock[1], n. Small field, esp. as part of stud farm; turf enclosure near race-course, where horses are assembled before race. [prob. var. of *parrock*, OE *pearroc*, cf. G *pferch* fold, Du. *perk* pen, PARK]

pa·ddock[2], n. (archaic, dial.). Frog or toad. [f. OE *pade*, cf. Du. *pad*, toad + -OCK]

Pa·ddy[1], n. (Nickname for) Irishman. [pet-form of *Padraig, Patrick*]

pa·ddy[2], n. Rice in the straw or in the husk. [f. Malay *padi*]

pa·ddy[3], **pa·ddywhack**, nn. (colloq.). A rage, fit of temper. [PADDY[1]; *-whack* unexpl.]

Pa·dishah, Pa·dshah, (pah-), n. Title in Persia of the Shah, in Europe usu. of the Sultan of Turkey, in India of British sovereign. [Pers.(*pati* master + *sah* SHAH)]

pa·dlock, n.,& v.t. Detachable lock hanging by pivoted hoop on object fastened; (v.t.) secure with this. [*pad*, etym. dub., + LOCK]

padre (pah·drā), n. (mil. & nav. slang). Chaplain. [Port. &c., = father, priest]

padrō·nĕ, n. Master of Mediterranean trading-vessel; Italian employer of street musicians, begging-children, &c., whence **pă·dron**ISM(3) n.; proprietor of Italian inn. [It.]

pă·dūasoy, n. Strong corded silk fabric much worn in 18th c. (cf. POULT-DE-SOIE). [corrupt. f. F *pou-de-soie*, etym. dub., by assoc. with *Padua*]

pae·an, n. Chant of thanksgiving for deliverance (orig.) addressed to Apollo or Artemis; song of praise or triumph. [L, f. Gk *paian* hymn to Apollo under name of Paian]

pae·derasty, pē·d-, n. Sodomy. [f. Gk *paiderastia* (*pais paidos* boy + *erastēs* lover]

paedo-, pēdo-, in comb. = Gk *pais paidos* child, as *-ba·ptism*, infant baptism, *-ba·ptist*, adherent of this.

pae·on, n. Metrical foot of one long syllable placed first, second, third, or fourth (*first* &c. *p.*) & three short. Hence **paeŏ·n**IC a. [L, f. Gk *paiōn*, Attic form of *paian* PAEAN]

pā·gan, n. & a. Heathen; unenlightened person. Hence **pa·gan**DOM, **pa·gan**ISM (2), nn., **pa·gan**ISH[1] a., **pa·gan**IZE(3) v.t. & i. [f. L *paganus* (*pagus* country district, -AN)]

page[1], n. Boy, usu. in livery, employed to attend to door, go on errands, &c.; *p. of honour, of the presence*, &c., titles of various officers of royal household; boy employed as personal attendant of person of rank; (Hist.) boy in training for knighthood & attached to knight's service. Hence **pa·ge**HOOD, **pa·ge**SHIP, nn. [OF, etym. dub., cf. It. *paggio*]

page[2], n. One side of leaf of book &c.; (fig.) episode fit to fill a p. in history &c. [F, f. L *pagina* (*pangere* fasten)]

page[3], v.t. Put consecutive numbers on pages of (book &c.). [f. prec.]

pă·geant (-jnt; *also* pā-), n. Brilliant

spectacle, esp. procession, arranged for effect; tableau, allegorical device, &c., on fixed stage or moving car; (fig.) empty or specious show. [etym. dub., perh. f. *pagina* PAGE²]

pa·geantry, n. Splendid display; empty show. [prec. + -RY]

Pă·gett, M. P., n. Traveller who expects to know all there is to know of a country in a few months. [character in Kipling]

pă·ginal, a. Of pages; page for page. So **pa·ginARY¹** a. [f. LL *paginalis* (PAGE², -AL)]

pă·ginate, v.t. Page (book &c.). Hence **paginA·TION** n. [f. L *pagina* PAGE² + -ATE³]

pagō·da, n. Sacred building, esp. tower usu. of pyramidal form, in India, China, &c.; ornamental imitation of this; gold coin once current in S. India; *p.-tree,* kinds of Indian & Chinese tree, (fig.) tree feigned to produce pagodas (coin), esp. *shake the p.-tree,* make rapid fortune in India. [f. Port. *pagode* of Ind. orig.]

pagūr·ian, a. & n. (Of) the hermit-crab. [f. L f. Gk *pagouros,* kind of crab, + -IAN]

pah¹, int. expr. disgust. [natural]

***pah*²,** n. Native fort in New Zealand. [f. Maori *pà* (*pà* vb, block up)]

paid. See PAY.

pail, n. Vessel, usu. round, of wood or metal for carrying liquids &c.; amount contained in this, as *half a p. of milk.* Hence **pai·lFUL** n. [OE has *pægel* gill; OF has *paelle* frying-pan, bath, &c., f. L *patella* dim. of *patina* dish]

paillasse, palliasse, (pălyă·s *or* pă·lyas), n. Straw mattress. [F (*pai-*), f. *paille* straw f. L *palea*]

paillette (pălyĕ·t), n. Piece of bright metal used in enamel painting; spangle. [F (dim. as prec.)]

pain¹, n. Suffering, distress, of body or mind, whence **pai·nFUL, pai·nLESS,** aa., **pai·nfulLY², pai·nlessLY²,** advv., **pai·nfulNESS, pai·nlessNESS,** nn.; (pl.) throes of childbirth; (pl.) trouble taken, esp. *take pp., be at the pp. of* (doing), *get* (a thrashing &c.) *for* one's *pp.*; punishment, now only in *pp. & penalties, on* or *under p. of* (death or other punishment to be incurred); *p.-killer,* medicine for alleviating p.; *painstaking,* careful, industrious. [f. OF *peine* f. L *poena* penalty]

pain², v.t. Inflict pain upon. [f. OF *pener* f. med. L *poenare* (as prec.)]

paint¹, n. Solid colouring-matter, suspended in liquid vehicle so as to impart colour to a surface; LUMINOUS *p.*; colouring-matter for face &c., rouge &c. [f. foll.]

paint², v.t. Portray, represent, (object, or abs.) in colours; adorn (wall &c.) with painting; (fig.) represent (incident &c.) in words vividly as by painting; *not so black as he is painted* (represented); cover surface of (object) with paint; apply paint of specified colour to, as *p. the door green,* (slang) *p. the town red,* cause commotion by riotous spree &c.; apply rouge to (face, often abs.); *p. out,* efface with paint; *Painted Lady,* butterfly of orange-red colour with black & white spots. Hence **pai·ntING¹** (1, 2) n. [f. OF *peindre* f. L *pingere pict-* paint]

pai·nter¹, n. One who paints pictures; workman who colours woodwork &c. with paint; *p.'s colic,* form of colic to which pp. who work with lead are liable. So **pai·ntrESS¹** n. [f. AF *peintour* f. com.-Rom. *pinctorem* = L *pictorem* (as prec., see -OR²)]

pai·nter², n. Rope attached to bow of boat for making it fast to ship, stake, &c.; *cut the p.,* (fig., usu. of colony) effect a separation. [?]

pai·nty, a. Of paint; (of picture) overcharged with paint. [-Y²]

pair¹, n. Set of two, couple, (esp. *of* things that usu. exist or are used in couples, as gloves, shoes, sculls, heels, eyes); *p. royal,* set of three cards of same denomination or of three dice turning up same number; article consisting of two corresponding parts not used separately, as *p. of scissors, tongs, trousers*; engaged or married couple; mated couple of animals; *p.* (*of horses*), two horses harnessed together; (Parl.) two voters on opposite sides absenting themselves from division by mutual agreement, person willing to act thus (*cannot find a p.*); the other member of a p. (*where is the p. to this sock?*); *p.* (flight) *of stairs, of steps* (*one, two, three, -p. front* or *back,* room on the first &c. floor or its occupant); *another p. of* SHOES; *p.-horse* a., for a p. of horses; *p.-oar,* boat rowed by p. of oars. [f. F *paire* f. L *paria* neut. pl. of *par* equal]

pair², v.t. & i. Arrange (persons, things), be arranged, in couples; unite (t. & i.) in love or marriage; (of animals) mate; unite (*with* one of opposite sex); *p. off,* put two by two, (intr.) go off in pairs, (Parl.) make a pair, (colloq.) marry (*with*). [f. prec.]

pajamas. See PYJAMAS.

păl, n., & v.i., (slang). Comrade, mate; (v.i., usu. *p. up*) associate (*with*). [E Gipsy]

pă·lace (-*as*), n. Official residence of sovereign, archbishop, or bishop; stately mansion; spacious building for entertainment, refreshment, &c.; GIN-*p.*; *p. car,* luxurious railway-carriage. [f. OF *palais* f. L *Palatium,* hill in Rome, house of Augustus built on this]

pă·ladin, n. Any of the Twelve Peers of Charlemagne's court, of whom Count Palatine was the chief; knight errant. [F, as PALATINE¹]

pălaeo-, pălēo-, in comb. (before vowel *palae-*) = Gk *palaios* ancient (cf. NEO-), as: *-ar·ctic,* of northern part of Old World; *-cry·stic,* of ancient ice, frozen from remote ages; *-graphy*, study of ancient writing & inscriptions, so *-grapher*, *-gra·phic*; *-li·thic*, marked by use of primitive stone implements; *-onto·logy*, study of extinct organized beings, so *-ontolo·gical*, *-onto·logist*; *-there* (-ēr), extinct genus of tapir-like mammal; *-zō·ic*, of, containing, ancient forms of life, of the first geological period (cf. CAINOZOIC, MESO*zoic*).

palae·stra, palĕs-, n. Wrestling-school, gymnasium. [L, f. Gk *palaistra* (*palaiō* wrestle)]

pă·lafitte (-ĭt), n. Prehistoric hut on piles over lake in Switzerland or N. Italy. [F, f. It. *palafitta* pile-fence (*palo* stake + *fitto* fixed)]

palankee·n, -nquin (-kēn), n. Covered litter for one, in India & the East, carried usu. by four or six men; (loosely) closed carriage in the East. [f. Port. *palanquin*, cf. Malay *palangki*, Hind. *palki*]

pă·latable, a. Pleasant to the taste; (fig.) agreeable to the mind. Hence **pa·latab**LY² adv. [f. PALATE + -ABLE]

pă·latal, a. & n. Of the palate; (sound) made by placing tongue against (usu. hard) palate, whence **pa·latal**IZE(3) v.t. [F (foll., -AL)]

pă·late (-*a*t), n. Roof of the mouth in vertebrates; *bony* or *hard*, *soft*, *p.*, its front, back, part; *cleft p.* (see CLEAVE¹); sense of taste; mental taste, liking. [f. L *palatum*]

palā·tial (-shl), a. Like a palace; splendid. [f. L as PALACE + -AL]

pală·tinate (-*a*t), n. Territory under a count palatine; *The* (*Rhine*) *P.*, State of old German Empire, under rule of Count Palatine of the Rhine. [f. foll. + -ATE¹]

pă·latine¹, a. & n. (*Count*) *P.*, count having within the territory jurisdiction such as elsewhere belongs only to sovereign (in Eng. Hist. also *Earl P.*); *County P.*, his territory (still in England of Lancashire and Cheshire); (n.) woman's fur tippet. [F (*-in*, *-ine*), f. L *palatinus* of the PALACE, see -INE¹]

pă·latine², a. & n. Of the palate; (n. pl., also *p. bones*) two bones forming hard palate. [F (*-in*, *-ine*), as PALATE, see -INE¹]

pala·ver (-lah-), n., & v.i. & t. Conference, discussion, esp. between African or other uncivilized natives & traders &c.; profuse or idle talk; cajolery; (v.i.) talk profusely; (v.t.) flatter, wheedle. [vb f. n. f. Port. *palabra* word f. L as PARABLE]

pale¹, n. Pointed piece of wood for fence &c., stake; boundary, esp. (fig.) *within*, *beyond*, &c., *the p.*; (Hist.) *the* (*English*) *P.*, part of Ireland under English rule; (Herald.) vertical stripe in middle of shield. [f. F *pal* f. L *pālŭs*]

pale², a. (Of person or complexion) of whitish or ashen appearance; (of colours) faint; faintly coloured; of faint lustre, dim; *p.-face*, supposed N.-Amer.-Ind. name for white man. Hence **pa·le**LY² adv., **pa·le**NESS n. [f. OF *pal(l)e* f. L *pallidus* (*pallēre* be pale)]

pale³, v.i. & t. Grow pale; (fig.) become pale in comparison (usu. *before* or *beside*); make pale. [f. OF *palir* (as prec.)]

paled, a. Having palings. [PALE¹, -ED²]

pă·letot (-*e*tō), n. Loose cloak for man or woman. [F, etym. dub.]

pă·lette (-ĭt), n. Artist's flat tablet for mixing colours on; colours used by particular artist or on particular occasion; *p.-knife*, thin steel blade with handle for mixing colours. [F, dim. of *pale* shovel f. L *pala*]

pa·lfrey (paw-, pă-), n. (archaic, poet.). Saddle-horse for ordinary riding, esp. for ladies. [f. OF *palefrei* f. LL *palafredus*, *paraveredus* (Gk *para* beside, extra, + *veredus* light horse, whence G *pferd*)]

Pa·li (pah-), n. Language used in canonical books of Buddhists. [for *pali-bhasa* (*pali* canon + *bhasa* language)]

pă·likar, n. Member of band of Greek or Albanian military chief, esp. during War of Independence. [f. mod. Gk *palikari* lad (Gk *pallax -akos* youth)]

pă·limpsĕst, n. & a. Writing-material, manuscript, original writing on which has made room for a second; (adj.) so treated. [f. L f. Gk *palimpsēstos* (*palin* again + *psaō* rub smooth)]

pă·lindrome, n. & a. (Word, verse, &c.) that reads the same backwards as forwards. Hence **palindrŏ·mi**C a. [f. Gk *palindromos* running back again (*palin* again + *drom-* run)]

pā·ling, n. (Fence of) pales. [PALE¹, -ING¹]

pălingĕ·nesis (-j-), n. Regeneration (lit. & fig.); revival; (Biol.) exact reproduction of ancestral character, whence **palingenĕ·ti**C a. [f. Gk *palin* again + GENESIS]

pă·linode, n. Poem in which author retracts thing said in former poem; recantation. [f. L f. Gk *palinōidia* (*palin* again + *ōidē* song)]

pălisa·de, n., & v.t. Fence of pales or of iron railings; (Mil.) strong wooden stake; (v.t.) furnish, enclose, with palisade. [f. F *palissade* (*palisser* enclose with pales, as PALE¹, see -ADE)]

pā·lish, a. Somewhat pale. [-ISH¹]

pall¹ (pawl), n. Cloth, usu. of black or purple or white velvet, spread over coffin, hearse, or tomb; woollen vestment worn by Pope & some metropolitans or archbishops; (fig.) mantle, cloak; *p.-bearer*, person holding up corner of p. at funeral. [OE *pæll*, f. L *pallium* cloak]

pall² (pawl), v.i. & t. Become insipid (now only fig.), esp. *p. on* (person, mind, taste); satiate, cloy. [prob. aphetic f. APPAL]

Pallā·dian, a. (archit.). In the pseudo-classical style of the 16th-c. Italian Palladio. [-AN]

pallā·dium¹, n. Image of Pallas on which

safety of Troy was held to depend; safeguard. [L, f. Gk *palladion*]

pallā·dium[2], n. Hard white metal of platinum group. [f. *Pallas*, an asteroid + -IUM]

pă·llet[1], n. Straw bed; mattress. [ME & dial. F *paillet* (*paille* straw f. L *palea*)]

pă·llet[2], n. Flat wooden blade with handle, used by potters &c.; artist's PALETTE; projection on a part of a machine, serving to change mode of motion of wheel; valve in upper part of wind-chest of organ. [f. PALETTE]

palliasse. See PAILLASSE.

pă·lliate, v.t. Alleviate (disease) without curing; extenuate, excuse. So **pallia·tion** n. [f. L *palliare* cloak (PALLIUM), see -ATE[3]]

pa·lliative (-*at*-), a. & n. (Thing) that serves to palliate. [F (-*if*, -*ive*), as prec., see -IVE]

pă·llid, a. Pale. Hence **pa·llidly**[2] adv., **pa·llidness** n. [f. L as PALE]

păllium, n. Man's large rectangular cloak, esp. among the Greeks; archbishop's PALL[1]; integumental fold of mollusc, whence **pa·llial** a. [L]

pall-mall (pĕ·lmĕ·l), n. Game in which ball was driven through iron ring suspended in long alley; *P.M.*, street in London developed from such an alley, & noted for clubs. [f. obs. F *pallemaille* f. It. *pallamaglio* (*palla* ball + *maglio* mallet f. L *malleus*)]

pa·llor, n. Paleness. [L (*pallēre* be pale, see -OR[1])]

palm[1] (pahm), n. Large family of trees, chiefly tropical, usu. with upright unbranched stem & head of large pinnate or fan-shaped leaves; branch of p.-tree as symbol of victory; supreme excellence, prize for this, esp. *bear, yield, the p.*; branch of various trees substituted for p. in northern countries, esp. in celebrating *P. Sunday*; *p.-oil* (got from various pp.; also, with pun on *palm*[2], bribe-money); *P. Sunday*, Sunday before Easter, on which Christ's entry into Jerusalem is celebrated by processions, in which branches of p. are carried. Hence **pălma·ceous** a. [OE, f. L *palma*]

palm[2] (pahm), n. Part of hand between wrist & fingers, esp. its inner surface; part of glove that covers this; breadth (about 4 in.), length (about 8 in.), of hand as measure; *grease* person's *p.*, bribe him. Hence (-)**palmed**[2] a., **pal·mful** n. [ME & F *paume* f. L *palma*]

palm[3] (pahm), v.t. Impose fraudulently, pass *off* (thing *on* person); conceal (cards, dice, &c.) in hand; touch with palm; bribe. [prec.]

Pă·lma Chri·stī, n. Castor-oil plant. [med. L, = palm of Christ, from handlike shape of leaves]

pă·lmar, a. Of, in, the palm of the hand. [f. L *palmaris* (as PALM[2], see -AR[1])]

pă·lmary, a. Bearing the palm, preeminent. [f. L *palmarius* (as PALM[1], see -ARY[1])]

pă·lmate (-*at*), **-āted,** a. PALM[2]-shaped. [f. L *palmatus* (as PALM[1], see -ATE[2])]

pal·mer (pah-), n. Pilgrim returning from Holy Land with palm branch or leaf; itinerant monk under vow of poverty; (also *p.-worm*) destructive hairy caterpillar; hairy artificial fly. [AF (as PALMARY)]

pălme·tto, n. Kinds of small palm, esp. dwarf fan-palm. [f. Sp. *palmito* dim. of *palma* PALM[1], refash. on It. wds in -*etto*]

pă·lmipĕd, -pēde, a. & n. Web-footed (bird). [f. L *palmipes -pedis* (as PALM[2] + *pes pedis* foot)]

pal·mistry (pah-), n. Divination from palm of hand. So **pal·mist**(3) n. [ME (PALM[2] + -*estry*, -*istry*, unexpl.)]

pal·my (pah-), a. Of, like, abounding in, palms; triumphant, flourishing, esp. *p. days*. [PALM[1] + -Y[2]]

palmȳr·a, n. Kind of palm grown in India & Ceylon, with fan-shaped leaves used for matting &c. [f. Port. *palmeira*]

pălp, pă·lpus (pl. -*pī*), nn. Jointed sense-organ in insects &c., feeler. Hence **pa·lpal** a. [L (-*pus*)]

pă·lpable, a. That can be touched or felt; readily perceived by senses or mind. Hence **palpabi·lity** n., **pa·lpably**[2] adv. [f. LL *palpabilis* (as foll., see -BLE)]

pă·lpāte, v.t. Handle, esp. in medical examination. So **palpa·tion** n. [f. L *palpare*, -ATE[3]]

pă·lpebral, a. Of the eyelids. [f. L *palpebralis* (*palpebra* eyelid, see -AL)]

pă·lpitate, v.i. Pulsate, throb; tremble (*with* fear, pleasure, &c.). [f. L *palpitare* frequent. as PALPATE, see -ATE[3]]

palpita·tion, n. Throbbing; increased activity of heart due to exertion, agitation, or disease. [f. L *palpitatio* (as prec., see -ATION)]

pa·lsgrave (pawl-), n. Count palatine. [f. Du. *paltsgrave* = G *pfalzgraf* (*pfalenza* palace + *grâvo* count)]

pa·lstave (pawl-), n. Celt of bronze &c. shaped to fit into split handle. [f. Da. *paalstav* f. Icel. *pálstafr* (*páll* hoe)]

palsy (paw·lzĭ), n., & v.t. Paralysis; (fig.) cause, condition, of utter helplessness. (v.t.) paralyse (usu. fig.). [ME, f. OF *paralisie* as PARALYSIS]

pa·lter (pawl-), v.i. Shuffle, equivocate, (*with* person); haggle (*with* person *about* thing); trifle (*with* subject). [?]

pa·ltry (pawl-), a. Worthless, petty, contemptible. Hence **pa·ltriness** n. [perh. attrib. use of dial. *paltry* rubbish (Fris., MDu., & E dial. *palt* rubbish + -RY)]

palū·dal (*or* pă·l-), a. Of a marsh; malarial. [f. L *pălūs -udis* marsh + -AL]

pā·ly, a. (poet.). Somewhat pale. [-Y[2]]

pam, n. Knave of clubs, esp. in five-card loo. [Sc. has *Pamphie*, F *Pamphile*, prob. f. Gk name *Pamphilos*]

pa·mpa, n. (usu. pl., pron. *-az, -as*). Large treeless plain in S. America south of the Amazon; *p.-grass,* gigantic grass introduced into Europe from S. America. [Sp., f. Peruv. *bamba* steppe, flat]

pa·mper, v.t. Over-indulge (person, tastes, &c.); *pampered menial,* flunkey. [prob. frequent. of obs. *pamp* cram, cf. G *pampen*; see -ER[5]]

pampē̆r·o, n. Cold wind blowing from Andes to Atlantic. [Sp., as PAMPA]

pa·mphlet, n. Small unbound treatise, esp. on subject of current interest. [prob. f. *Pamphilet,* familiar name of 12th-c. Latin amatory poem *Pamphilus seu de Amore,* see -ET[1]]

pamphleteer·, n., & v.i. Writer of pamphlets; (v.i.) write pamphlets. [-EER]

pan[1], n. Metal or earthenware vessel, usu. shallow, for domestic purposes; STEW, WARM[2]*ing, -p.*; p.-like vessel in which substances are heated &c.; part of lock that held the priming in obsolete types of gun; hollow in ground, as SALT-*p.*; (also *hard-p.*) hard substratum of soil; BRAIN-*p.*; *pancake,* thin flat batter-cake fried in p., esp. *flat as a p.,* quite flat (v.i. slang, of aeroplane, descend vertically in level position). Hence **pa·nFUL** n. [OE *panne,* cf. Du. *pan,* G *pfanne*]

pan[2], v.t. & i. *P. off, out,* wash (gold-bearing gravel) in pan; (intr.) *p. out,* yield gold, (fig.) succeed, work, (*well* &c.). [f. prec.]

Pan[3], n. Greek rural god; the spirit of nature, paganism, the pre-Christian or the non-moral world. [Gk]

pan- in comb. = Gk *pas pantos* all, as: *-A·frican,* of, for, all Africans; *-A·nglican,* of the Anglican Church & its branches, (*p.-A. conference*); *-co·smism,* doctrine that material universe is all that exists; *-ge·nesis,* theory that each unit of an organism reproduces itself; *-Ger·man,* of all the Germans in political union; *-he·llenism,* political union of all Greeks, so *-helle·nic* a.; *-i·slam,* union of Mohammedan world, so *-islă·mic* a.; *-logi·stic,* (of Hegel's philosophy) treating only the rational as real, so *-logism*; *-sla·vism* (-lah-), movement for political union of all Slavs; *-sper·matism, -sper·my,* theory that the atmosphere is full of minute germs that develop in favourable environment.

pănacē·a, n. Universal remedy. [L, f. Gk *panakeia* f. PAN(*akēs* f. *akos* remedy)]

pana·che (-ahsh, -ăsh), n. Tuft, plume, of feathers esp. as head-dress or on helmet; (fig.) display, swagger. [F, f. It. *pennachio* (*penna* feather)]

pana·da (-nah-), n. Bread boiled to pulp & flavoured. [Sp., = It. *panata* (*pane* bread f. L *panis,* see -ADE)]

Pănama· (-ah). *P. hat* or *p.,* hat of fine pliant strawlike material made (orig. in Ecuador) from leaves of the screw-pine.

pancră·tic, a. Of the pancratium; (Opt., of eyepiece) extensively adjustable. [f. foll. + -IC]

pancrā·tium (-shĭum), n. (Gk ant.). Athletic contest combining wrestling & boxing. So **pancrā·tiAST, pa·ncratIST,** nn. [L, f. Gk *pagkration* (PAN- + *kratos* strength)]

pa·ncrĕăs, n. Gland near stomach discharging a digestive secretion (pancreatic juice) into duodenum, sweetbread. So **pancreă·tIC** a. [f. Gk *pagkreas* (PAN- + *kreas -atos* flesh)]

pa·nda, n. Indian racoon-like animal, red bear-cat. [native]

Pandē·an, -aean, a. Of PAN[3]; *P. pipe,* = PAN-PIPE. [irreg. f. Gk *Pan*]

pa·ndect, n. (usu. pl.). Compendium in 50 books of Roman civil law made by order of Justinian in 6th c.; complete body of laws. [f. F *pandecte* f. L f. Gk PAN(*dektēs* f. *dekhomai* receive) all-receiver]

pandĕ·mic, a. & n. (Disease) prevalent over the whole of a country or over the world; *p.,* or *pandemian,* VENUS. [f. Gk PAN(*dēmos* people) + -IC]

pandemō·nium, n. Abode of all demons; place of lawless violence or uproar; utter confusion. [mod. L (Milton) f. PAN- + DEMON]

pa·nder, n., & v.i. & t. Go-between in clandestine amours, procurer; one who ministers to evil designs; (v.i.)minister (*to* base passions, evil designs); (v.t.) act as p. to (person's lust). [vb f. n. f. *Pandare,* character in Chaucer's *Troilus & Criseyde* & in Boccaccio, f. L f. Gk *Pandaros*]

pandit. See PUNDIT.

pandor·a, -dore·, n. Stringed instrument of cither type. [It., f. L f. Gk *pandoura,* prob. of foreign orig.]

Pandor·a's box, n. The box in which Hope alone remained when by its rash opening all objects of desire were dispersed to play havoc among mankind. [Gk Myth., see Hesiod, *Op.,* 50–105]

pa·ndour (-oor), **-oor,** n. (Pl.) force of rapacious & brutal soldiers raised by Baron Trenck in 1741 & afterwards enrolled in Austrian army. [f. Serbo-Croatian *pàndur* f. med. L *banderius* follower of a BANNER]

pane[1], n. Single sheet of glass in compartment of window; rectangular division of chequered pattern &c. Hence **pa·neLESS** a. [f. F *pan* f. L *pannus* piece of cloth]

pane[2], v.t. Make up (garment &c.) of strips of different colours (chiefly in p.p.). [f. prec.]

pănĕgȳ·ric (-j-), n. & a. Laudatory discourse (*upon*); (adj.) laudatory. Hence **panegy·ricAL** a. [f. F *panégyrique* f. L f. Gk *panēgurikos* f. PAN(*ēguris* = *agora* assembly), see -IC]

For words in *pan-* not given see PAN-.

pă·nĕgyrize, v.t. Speak, write, in praise of, eulogize. So **pa·negyr**IST n. [f. Gk *panēgurizō* (as prec., see -IZE)]

pă·nel[1], n. Stuffed lining of saddle; kind of saddle; slip of parchment; list of jury; jury; list of the doctors registered in a district as accepting Insurance-Act patients (*on the p.*, so registered); distinct compartment of surface, esp. of wainscot, door, &c., often sunk below or raised above general level; piece of stuff of different kind or colour inserted in woman's dress; large size of photograph, with height much greater than width. [ME & OF, f. med. L *pannellus* dim. as PANE[1]]

pa·nel[2], v.t. (-ll-). Saddle (beast) with panel; fit (wall, door, &c.) with panels; ornament (dress &c.) with panel(s). Hence **pa·nell**ING[1](2) n. [f. prec.]

pang, n. Shooting pain; sudden sharp mental pain. [?]

pangō·lin (-ngg-), n. Scaly ant-eater. [f. Malay *peng-goling* roller (from habit of rolling itself up)]

pă·nic,[1] n. Genus of grasses including Italian millet. [f. L *panicum*]

pă·nic[2], a. & n. (Of terror) unreasoning, excessive; (n.) infectious fright, sudden alarm (e.g., in commerce) leading to hasty measures; *p.-monger*, one who fosters a p. Hence **pa·nick**Y[2] a. (colloq.). [f. F *panique* f. Gk *panikos* of god Pan, reputed to cause p.]

pă·nicle, n. (bot.). Loose irregular type of compound inflorescence, as in oats. [f. L *panicula*, dim. of *panus* swelling, ear of millet]

pănifica·tion, n. Bread-making. [F, f. L *panis* bread, see -FICATION]

panja·ndrum, n. Mock title of exalted personage; pompous official or pretender. [arbitrary]

pa·nnage, n. (Right of, payment for) pasturage of swine; acorns, beech-mast, &c., as food for swine. [f. OF *pasnage* f. LL *pastionaticum* (*pastio* pasture f. *pascere past-*, -AGE)]

panne, n. A soft long-napped cloth used as dress-material. [F, etym. dub.]

pa·nnier[1], n. Basket, esp. one of those carried, usu. in pairs, by beast of burden or on the shoulders; covered basket for surgical instruments & medicines for ambulance; part of skirt looped up round hips. [f. F *panier* f. L *panarium* bread-basket (*panis* bread, see -ARY[1])]

pa·nnier[2], n. (colloq.). Robed waiter in Inner Temple. [?]

pa·nnikin, n. Small metal drinking-vessel; its contents. [f. PAN[1] + -KIN]

pă·noply, n. Complete suit of armour (often fig.). Hence **pa·nopli**ED[2] a. [f. G PAN(*oplia* f. *hopla* arms)]

păno·pticon, n. Bentham's proposed circular prison with cells round warders' well in centre. [f. PAN- + Gk *optikos* of sight (*op-* see)]

panora·ma (-rah-, -ră-), n. Picture of landscape &c. arranged on inside of cylindrical surface or successively rolled out before spectator; continuous passing scene; unbroken view of surrounding region (often fig.). Hence **panoră·m**IC a., **panoră·m**ICALLY adv. [f. PAN- + Gk *horama* view (*horaō* see)]

pa·n-pipe, n. Musical instrument made of series of reeds, mouth-organ. [*Pan*, Greek rural god, + PIPE]

pa·nsy (-zĭ), n. Wild & garden plant with flowers of various colours, heartsease. [f. F *pensée* thought, pansy, f. *penser* think f. L *pensare* frequent. of *pendere pens-* weigh]

pant, v.i. & t., & n. Gasp for breath; (fig.) yearn (*for*, *after*, thing, *to* do); throb violently; utter gaspingly; (n.) gasp, throb. [n. f. vb, prob. cogn. w. OF *pantoisier* pant f. pop. L *phantasiare* be oppressed with nightmare (as PHANTASY)]

pant- in comb. = PANTO- before vowels.

pantagru·elism, n. Extravagant coarse humour like that of Pantagruel, a character in Rabelais. So **pantagruĕ·l**IAN a., **pantagru·el**IST n. [-ISM]

pantale·t(te)s, n. pl. Woman's drawers, cycling knickerbockers, &c. [f. foll., see -ETTE]

pantalōō·n, n. (*P-*) character in Italian comedy wearing pp., (now) clown's butt & abettor in pantomime; (Hist., pl. or sing.) garment of breeches & stockings in one piece, close-fitting breeches down to ankle as transition from knee-breeches to trousers; (pl., chiefly U.S., & being ousted by *pants*) trousers. [f. F *pantalon* f. It. *pantalone*, Venetian character in Italian comedy, perh. f. *San Pantaleone*, favourite Venetian saint]

pante·chnicon, n. Furniture warehouse (orig. name of a bazaar); *p. van* (for removing furniture). [f. PAN- + Gk *tekhnikon* of art (*tekhnē*, see -IC)]

pa·ntheism, n. Doctrine that God is everything & everything God; heathen worship of all gods. So **pa·nthe**IST n., **panthei·st**IC(AL) aa. [f. PAN- + Gk *theos* god + -ISM]

panthē·on (*or* pă·n-), n. Temple dedicated to all the gods, esp. circular one at Rome; deities of a people collectively; building in which illustrious dead are buried or have memorials; building in London opened for public entertainment in 1772. [L, f. Gk PAN(*theion* holy f. *theos* god)]

pa·nther, n. Leopard. Hence **pa·nther**ESS[1] n. [f. OF *pantère* f. L *panthera* f. Gk *panthēr* etym. dub.]

pa·ntile, n. Roof tile transversely curved to ogee shape, one curve being much larger than the other. [PAN[1] + TILE]

For words in *pan-* not given see PAN-.

pantiso·cracy, n. Community in which all are equal & all rule. [PANT- + ISO- + -CRACY]

panto- in comb. (before vowels *pant-*) = Gk *pas pantos* all, as: *-lo·gic, -logy,* (of) universal knowledge; *-mor·phic,* taking all shapes; *-pragma·tic* a. & n., (person) meddling in everything; *-scŏ·pic,* with wide range of vision.

pa·ntograph, n. Instrument for copying plan &c. on any scale. Hence **panto-gra·phic** a. [f. PANTO- + Gk *-graphos* writing]

pa·ntomime, n., & v.t. & i. (Hist.) Roman actor performing in dumb show, mimic actor; English dramatic performance ending with transformation scene followed by broad comedy of clown & pantaloon & dancing of harlequin & columbine; dumb show; (v.t. & i.) express (thing), express oneself, by dumb show. Hence or cogn. **pantomĭ·mic** a., **pa·ntomīmist**(3) n. [f. L f. Gk PANTO-(*mimos* mimic)]

pa·ntry, n. Room in which bread & other provisions or (*butler's, housemaid's, p.*) plate, table linen, &c., are kept; *pantry-man,* butler or his assistant. [f. OF *paneterie* f. med. L *panetaria* bread-shop (*panis* bread, see -ARY[1])]

pants, n. pl. (vulg.). (Chiefly U.S.) trousers; (Shop) long tight drawers. [abbr. of PANTALOON]

pap[1], n. (archaic). Nipple of woman's breast; corresponding part of man; (pl.) conical hilltops side by side. [imit. of sound made by infant in feeding]

pap[2], n. Soft or semi-liquid food for infants or invalids; mash, pulp. Hence **pa·ppy**[2] a. [imit., cf. prec.]

papa· (-ah), n. Father (used chiefly by children). [F f. L; imit.]

pā·pacy, n. Pope's (tenure of) office; papal system. [f. med. L *papatia* (*papa* pope, -ACY)]

pā·pal, a. Of the pope or his office. Hence **pa·palism**(3), **pa·palist**(2), nn., **pa·palize**(3) v.t. & i., **pa·pally**[2] adv. [F, f. eccl. L *papalis* (as prec., see -AL)]

papā·verous, a. Like, allied to, the poppy. So **papavera·ceous** a. [f. L *papaver* poppy + -OUS]

papaw·, n. (Fruit of) palm-like S.-Amer. tree of which stem, leaves, & fruit, contain a milky juice that makes meat tender; (U.S.) N.-Amer. tree with purple flowers & oblong edible fruit. [f. Sp. *papaya,* of Carib orig.]

pā·per[1], n. Substance used for writing, printing, drawing, wrapping up parcels, &c., made of interlaced fibres of rags, straw, wood, &c.; *commit to p.,* write down; *put pen to p.,* begin writing; negotiable documents, e.g. bills of exchange; (also *p. money*) bank-notes &c. used as currency, opp. to coin, so *p. currency* (cf. METALLIC); (slang) free passes to theatre &c.; (pl.) documents proving person's or ship's identity, standing, &c.; *send in* one's *pp.,* resign; set of questions in examination; = NEWS*paper*; essay, dissertation, esp. one read to learned society; *p. war(fare)* (carried on in books or news-pp.); *on p.,* hypothetically, to judge from statistics, &c., as *on p. he is the better man,* so (attrib.) *p. profits* (hypothetical); *p.-bag cookery,* method of cooking food of various kinds by enclosing it in buttered p.-bag before putting it in moderately hot oven; *p.-chase,* cross-country run in which a trail of torn-up p. is laid by one or more runners to set a course for the rest; *p.-hangings, wall-p.,* p. for covering walls of room &c.; *p.-hanger,* one who covers walls with these; *p.-knife* (of ivory, wood, &c., for cutting open leaves of book &c.); *p.-mill* (in which p. is made); *p.-stainer,* one who stains p. or makes p.-hangings; *p.-weight,* small heavy object for securing loose pp. from being displaced. Hence **pa·pery**[2] a. [f. OF *papier* f. PAPYRUS]

pa·per[2], v.t. Enclose in paper; decorate (wall &c.) with paper; furnish with paper; (slang) fill (theatre &c.) by means of free passes. [f. prec.]

papier mâché (pă·pyā mă·shā), n. Moulded paper pulp used for boxes, trays, &c. [F, = chewed paper]

papĭ·lionā·ceous, a. (bot.). With corolla like a butterfly. [f. L *papilio -onis* butterfly, see -ACEOUS]

papi·lla, n. (pl. *-ae*). Small nipple-like protuberance in a part or organ of the body; (Bot.) small fleshy projection on plant. Hence or cogn. **pă·pillary**[1], **pa·pillate**[2](2), **pa·pillose**[1], aa. [L, = nipple, dim. of PAPULA]

pā·pist, n. Advocate of papal supremacy; Roman Catholic (usu. in hostile sense). Hence **papi·stic(al)** aa., **papi·stically**[2] adv., **pa·pistry** n. [f. 16th-c. L *papista* (*papa* pope, see -IST)]

papoo·se, n. N.-Amer.-Indian young child. [native]

papoo·sh, -ouche (-ōōsh), n. = BABOUCHE. [f. Pers. *paposh* (*pa* foot + *posh* covering)]

pa·ppus, n. (bot.). Downy appendage on seeds of thistles, dandelions, &c. Hence **pappo·se**[1] a. [mod. L, f. Gk *pappos*]

pă·pula, -ule, nn. (pl. *-lae, -les*). Pimple; small fleshy projection on plant. Hence **pa·pular**[1], **papulo·se**[1], **pa·pulous,** aa. [L (*-la*)]

păpÿrā·ceous, a. (nat. hist.). Of the nature of, thin as, paper. [f. PAPYRUS, see -ACEOUS]

papÿro- in comb. = Gk *papuros* usu. in sense 'paper', as: *-graph,* apparatus for copying documents by means of paper-stencil; *-graphy, -type,* copying processes in which picture &c. is transferred from paper to zinc plate &c.

papÿr·us, n. Aquatic plant of sedge

family, paper reed; ancient writing material prepared by Egyptians &c. from stem of this; MS written on this. [L, f. Gk *papuros*]

par[1], n. Equality, equal footing, esp. *on a p.* (*with*); *p. of exchange*, recognized value of one country's currency in terms of another's; (of stocks, shares, &c.) *at p.*, at face value, *above p.*, at a premium, *below p.*, at a discount; average or normal amount, degree, or condition, as *on a p.*, on an average, *above, below, up to, p.* [L, a. & n., = equal(ity)]

par[2], n. (colloq.). Paragraph.

para-[1] in comb. = Gk *para* in senses 'beside', 'beyond', 'wrong, irregular'.

para-[2] in comb. = It. *para* imperat. of *parare* ward off, shelter, as *parasol*.

pară·basis, n. (pl. *-basēs*). Part sung by chorus in Greek comedy, addressed to audience in the poet's name. [Gk, f. PARA[1](*bainō* go) go aside, step forward]

pă·rable, n. Fictitious narrative used to typify moral or spiritual relations; allegory; (archaic) enigmatical saying, proverb; (archaic) *take up* one's *p.*, begin to discourse. [f. F *parabole*, as foll.]

pară·bola, n. Plane curve formed by intersection of cone with plane parallel to its side. [f. L f. Gk PARA[1](*bolē* throw, f. *ballō*) placing side by side, comparison, parable, &c.]

parabŏ·lic(al), aa. Of, expressed in, a parable, whence **parabo·lICALLY** adv.; of, like, a parabola. [f. LL f. late Gk *parabolikos* (as prec., see -IC)]

pară·boloid, n. Solid some of whose plane sections are parabolas, esp. (also *p. of revolution*) that generated by revolution of parabola about its axis. [-OID]

pară·chronism, n. Error in chronology. [f. PARA-[1] + Gk *khronos* time + -ISM]

pă·rachute (-sh-), n. Umbrella-like apparatus for descending safely from a height, esp. from aircraft, whence **pa·rachutISM**, **pa·rachutIST**, nn.; natural or artificial contrivance serving this purpose. [F (PARA-[2] + *chute* fall)]

pă·raclete, n. Advocate (as title of the Holy Spirit, see *John* xiv. 16, 26, &c.). [f. F *paraclet* f. L f. Gk PARA[1](*klētos* f. *kaleō* call)]

parā·de[1], n. Display, ostentation, esp. *make a p. of* (one's virtues &c.); muster of troops for inspection, esp. one held regularly at set hours; ground used for this; public square or promenade (often as name of street). [F, = show, f. It. *parata* f. L *parare* prepare, furnish, see -ADE]

parā·de[2], v.t. & i. Assemble (troops) for review or other purpose; display ostentatiously; march through (streets &c.) with display; (intr.) march in procession with display. [f. prec.]

pă·radigm (-īm), n. Example, pattern, esp. of inflexion of noun, verb, &c. So **paradigmă·tIC** (-ĭg-) a. [f. F *paradigme* f. L f. Gk *paradeigma* f. PARA[1](*deiknumi* show), see -M]

pă·radise (-s), n. (Also *earthly p.*) garden of Eden; heaven; region, state, of supreme bliss; FOOL'S *p.*; park in which animals are kept; BIRD *of p.* Hence or cogn. **paradisā·IC(AL)** [irreg. on *Mosaic* &c.], **paradĭ·seAN**, **paradĭ·siAC(AL)**, **paradĭ·siAL**, **paradĭ·siAN**, **paradĭ·sIC(AL)**, aa. [f. F *paradis* f. L f. Gk *paradeisos* f. OPers. *pairidaeza* park (*pairi* around + *diz* mould)]

pă·rados, n. Elevation of earth behind fortified place to secure from reverse attack or fire, esp. the mound along back of trench. [F (PARA-[2] + *dos* back f. L *dorsum*)]

pă·radox, n. Statement contrary to received opinion; seemingly absurd though perhaps really well-founded statement; self-contradictory, essentially absurd, statement; person, thing, conflicting with preconceived notions of what is reasonable or possible; HYDROSTATIC *p.* Hence or cogn. **pa·radoxER**[1](3), **pa·radoxIST**(3), **paradoxica·lITY**, **pa·radoxY**[1], nn., **parado·xICAL** a., **parado·xicalLY**[2] adv. [f. L f. Gk *paradoxon* neut. adj. (PARA-[1] + *doxa* opinion)]

părado·xure, n. Palm-cat, animal with remarkably long curving tail. [f. Gk *paradoxos* (see prec.) + *oura* tail]

pă·raffin, n., & v.t. Colourless tasteless inodorous fatty substance got by dry distillation from wood, coal, petroleum, &c., & used for making candles &c.; (also *p. oil*) oil so obtained & used as illuminant or lubricant; (v.t.) treat with p. [f. L *parum* little + *affinis*, from small AFFINITY it has for other bodies]

păragō·ge (-jĭ), n. Addition of letter or syllable to a word. Hence **paragŏ·gIC** a. [L, f. Gk *paragōgē* leading past (PARA-[1] + *agōgē* f. *agō* lead)]

pă·ragon, n., & v.t. Model of excellence; supremely excellent person or thing, model (*of* virtue &c.); perfect diamond of more than 100 carats; (v.t., poet.) compare (thing *with*). [OF, f. It. *paragone*, etym. dub.]

pă·ragraph (-ahf, -ăf), n., & v.t. Distinct passage or section in book &c., marked by indentation of first line; symbol (usu. ¶) formerly used to mark new p., now as REFERENCE mark; detached item of news &c. in newspaper, without heading, whence **pa·ragraphER**[1](3), **pa·ragraphIST**(3), **pa·ragraphY**[1], nn.; (v.t.) write p. about (person, thing), arrange (article &c.) in pp. Hence **paragră·phIC** a., **paragra·phICALLY** adv. [f. F *paragraphe* f. LL f. Gk PARA[1](*graphos* f. *graphō* write) short stroke marking break in sense]

pă·raguay (-gwā, -gwī), n. = MATÉ. [name of S.-Amer. river & republic]

paraheliŏ·tropism, n. Tendency in plants to turn leaves parallel to incidence of light-rays. So **paraheliotrŏ·pic** a. [PARA-[1] + HELIOTROPISM]

pă·rakeet, -oquet (-kĕt), n. Small (esp. long-tailed) kinds of parrot. [f. OF *paroquet* prob. f. It. *parrochetto* dim. of *parroco* parson, or f. It. *parrucchetto* dim. of *parrucca* peruke]

pă·rakite, n. 1. Kite acting like parachute. 2. Tailless kite for scientific purposes. [1. f. PARACHUTE + KITE. 2. PARA-[1]]

părali·psis, -leipsis (-lī-), n. Trick of securing emphasis by professing to omit all mention of subject, e.g., *I say nothing of his antecedents, how from youth upwards &c.* [f. Gk PARA[1](*leipsis* f. *leipō* leave) passing over]

pă·rallax, n. (Angular amount of) apparent displacement of object, caused by actual change of point of observation. So **paralla·ctic** a. [f. F *parallaxe* f. Gk *parallaxis* change f. *parallassō* (PARA-[1] + *allassō*)]

pă·rallel[1], a. & n. (Of lines &c.) continuously equidistant, (of line) having this relation *to*; *p. bars,* pair of p. bars supported on posts for gymnastic exercises; *p. ruler,* two rulers connected by pivoted cross-pieces, for drawing parallel lines; (fig.) precisely similar, analogous, or corresponding. (N.) *p.* (*of latitude*), each of the p. circles marking degrees of latitude on earth's surface in map, as *the 49th p.*; (Mil.) trench p. to general face of works attacked; person, thing, precisely analogous to another; p. position; comparison, as *draw a p. between* (two things); two p. lines (‖) as REFERENCE-mark. [f. F *parallele* f. L f. Gk *parallēlos* (PARA-[1] + *allēlous* one another)]

pă·rallel[2], v.t. (-ll-). Represent as similar, compare, (things, one *with* another); find, mention, something parallel or corresponding to; be parallel, correspond, to. [f. prec.]

părallelĕ·pipĕd, n. Solid contained by parallelograms. [f. Gk *parallēlepipedon,* as PARALLEL[1] + EPI(*pedon* ground) plane surface]

pă·rallelism, n. Being parallel (lit. or fig.); comparison or correspondence of successive passages, esp. in Hebrew poetry. [f. Gk *parallēlismos* f. *parallēlizō* place side by side (as PARALLEL[1], see -IZE)]

parallĕ·logram, n. Four-sided rectilineal figure whose opposite sides are parallel; *p. of forces,* (p. illustrating) theorem that if two forces acting at a point be represented in magnitude & direction by two sides of a p., their resultant is represented by diagonal drawn from that point. [f. F *parallélogramme* f. Gk *parallēlogrammon* (as PARALLEL[1] + *grammē* line)]

pară·logism, n. Illogical reasoning (esp. of which reasoner is unconscious, cf. SOPHISM); fallacy. So **para·logize**(2) v.i. [f. F *paralogisme* f. LL f. Gk *paralogismos* f. *paralogizomai* f. PARA[1](*logos* reason) contrary to reason]

pă·ralyse (-z), v.t. Affect with paralysis; (fig.) render powerless, cripple. Hence **paralysa·tion** n. [prob. f. F *paralyser,* as foll.]

pară·lȳsis, n. Nervous affection marked by impairment or loss of motor or sensory function of nerves; (fig.) state of utter powerlessness. [L, f. Gk *paralusis* f. PARA[1](*luō* loose) disable]

paralȳ·tic, a. & n. (Person) affected with paralysis (lit. or fig.). Hence **paraly·tically** adv. [f. F *paralytique* f. L f. Gk *paralutikos* (as prec., see -IC)]

paramagne·tic, a. Capable of being attracted by poles of magnet (cf. DIAMAGNETIC). So **parama·gnetism** n. [PARA-[1] + MAGNETIC]

parama·tta, n. Light dress fabric of merino wool & silk or cotton. [f. *Par(r)amatta,* town in N.S. Wales]

pară·meter, n. (math.). Quantity constant in case considered, but varying in different cases. [f. PARA-[1] + Gk *metron* measure]

pă·ramo, n. (pl. *-os*). High treeless plateau in tropical parts of S. America. [f. Sp. *paramo,* prob. of native orig.]

pă·ramount, a. Supreme; *lord, lady, p.* (in supreme authority); pre-eminent, as *of p. importance*; superior (*to*). Hence **pa·ramountcy** n., **pa·ramountly**[2] adv. [f. AF *paramont* f. OF *par* by + *amont* above f. L *ad montem* to the hill]

pă·ramour, n. Illicit partner of married man or woman. [f. OF *par amour* by love]

par·ang, n. Malay heavy sheath-knife. [Malay]

păranoi·a, -noe·a (-nē*a*), n. Mental derangement, esp. when marked by delusions of grandeur &c. [Gk (*-noia*) f. PARA[1](*noos* mind) distracted]

pă·rapet (-ĭt), n. Low wall at edge of balcony, roof, &c., or along sides of bridge &c.; (Mil.) defence of earth or stone to conceal & protect troops, esp. mound along front of trench (cf. *parados*). Hence **pa·rapeted**[2] a. [f. It. PARA[2](*petto* breast f. L *pectus*)]

pă·raph, n. Flourish after a signature, orig. as precaution against forgery. [f. F *paraphe* f. med. L *paraphus* for *paragraphus* PARAGRAPH]

paraphernā·lia, n. pl. Personal belongings; mechanical accessories, appointments, &c.; (formerly) articles of personal property that law allowed married woman to keep & treat as her own. [L, neut. pl. adj. f. L f. Gk PARA[1](*pherna* f. *phernē* dower), see -AL]

pă·raphrase (-z), n., & v.t. Free rendering or amplification of a passage, expression of its sense in other words; any of a collection of metrical pp. of passages of Scripture used in Church of Scotland &c.;

(v.t.) express meaning of (passage) in other words. So **paraphră·stic** a., **paraphra·stically** adv. [(n.) F, f. L f. Gk *paraphrasis* f. PARA¹(*phrazō* tell); (vb) f. F *paraphraser*]

păraplē·gia (-j-), n. Paralysis of lower limbs & part or whole of trunk. So **paraplē·gic** a. [Gk (-ē-) f. PARA¹(*plēssō* strike)]

pă·rasang, n. Ancient-Persian measure of length, about 3¼ miles. [f. L (-*ga*) f. Gk *parasaggēs*, of Pers. orig.]

păraselē·nē, n. Bright spot on lunar halo, mock-moon. [PARA-¹ + Gk *selēnē* moon]

pă·rasīte, n. Interested hanger-on, toady; animal, plant, living in or upon another & drawing nutriment directly from it (cf. COMMENSAL); (loosely) plant that climbs about another plant, wall, &c. Hence or cogn. **parasi·tic(al)** aa., **pă·rasītism**(2), **parasīto·logy**, nn. [f. L f. Gk PARA¹(*sitos* food)]

parasi·ticide, n. Agent that destroys parasites. [as prec. + -CIDE]

pa·rasītize, v.t. Infest as a parasite (chiefly in p.p.). [as prec. + -IZE]

părasŏ·l (*or* pă·r-), n. Sunshade. [F, f. It. PARA²(*sole* sun f. L *sol*)]

părasy·nthesis, n. (philol.). Derivation from a compound. So **parasynthĕ·tic** a. [PARA-¹ + SYNTHESIS]

părata·xis, n. (gram.). Placing of clauses &c. one after another, without words to indicate co-ordination or subordination. So **parata·ctic** a., **parata·ctically** adv. [f. Gk PARA¹(*taxis* arrangement f. *tassō*)]

paratȳ·phoid, n. Kinds of fever distinguishable from typhoid only by bacteriological examination, & not confined to man. [PARA-¹]

pă·ravane, n. Instrument towed at a depth regulated by its vanes or planes to cut the moorings of submerged mines. [PARA-²]

par·boil, v.t. Boil partially; (fig.) overheat. [f. OF *parboillir* f. LL PER(*bullire* boil) boil thoroughly, by confus. w. *part*]

par·buckle, n., & v.t. Rope for raising or lowering casks & cylindrical objects, the middle being secured at the upper level, & both ends passed under & round the object & then hauled or let slowly out; (v.t.) raise (*up*) or lower (*down*) thus. [?]

par·cel¹ (-sl), n. & adv. (Archaic) part, esp. PART¹ *& p.*; piece of land, esp. as part of estate; goods &c. wrapped up in single package; *p. post*, branch of postal service concerned with pp.; (Commerc.) quantity dealt with in one transaction; (adv., archaic) partly, as *p. blind, drunk*; *p. gilt*, partly gilded, esp. (of cup &c.) with inner surface gilt. [f. F *parcelle* f. L **particella*, dim. as PARTICLE]

par·cel², v.t. (-ll-). Divide (usu. *out*) into portions; (Naut.) cover (caulked seam) with canvas strips & pitch, wrap (rope) with canvas strips. [f. prec.]

par·celling, n. In vbl senses, esp. (Naut.) strip of canvas, usu. tarred, for binding round rope. [-ING¹]

par·cenary, n. Joint heirship. [f. AF *parcenarie* = OF *parçonerie* (as foll., see -ERY)]

par·cener, n. Coheir. [AF, = OF *parçonier* f. med. L *parti(ti)onarius* (PARTITION, -ER²)]

parch, v.t. & i. Roast (pease &c.) slightly; (of sun, thirst, &c.) make (person &c.) hot & dry; become hot & dry. [?]

par·chment, n. Skin, esp. of sheep or goat, prepared for writing, painting, &c.; manuscript on this; p.-like skin, esp. husk of coffee-bean. Hence **par·chmenty**² a. [f. F *parchemin* f. L *pergamena* (*charta* paper) of *Pergamum*, city in Asia Minor]

pard¹, n. (archaic.) Leopard. [OF, f. L f. Gk *pardos*]

pard², n. (slang, esp. U.S.). Partner. [abbr.]

par·don¹, n. Forgiveness; (Eccl.) = INDULGENCE, festival at which this is granted; (Law) remission of legal consequences of crime; *general p.* (for offences generally, or to number of persons not named individually); courteous forbearance, esp. *I beg your p.* (apology for thing done, for dissent or contradiction, or for not hearing or understanding what was said). [f. OF *perdun*, as foll.]

par·don², v.t. Forgive (person, offence, person his offence); make allowance for, excuse, (person, fault, person *for doing*). So **par·donable** a., **par·donableness** n., **par·donably**² adv. [f. OF *pardoner* f. LL PER(*donare* give) concede, remit]

par·doner, n. (hist.). Person licensed to sell pardons or indulgences. [PARDON¹ + -ER²]

pare, v.t. Trim (thing) by cutting away irregular parts &c.; cut away skin, rind, &c. of (fruit &c.); *p.* (nails &c.) *to the quick* (so deep as to reach sensitive parts); (fig.) diminish little by little (often *away, down*); shave, cut, *off, away*, (edges &c.). Hence **pār·er**¹(2), **pār·ing**¹(1, 2), nn. [f. F *parer* f. L *parare* prepare]

părĕgŏ·ric, a. & n. *P.* (*elixir*), camphorated tincture of opium flavoured with aniseed & benzoic acid. [f. LL f. Gk *parēgorikos* soothing (PARA-¹ + -*agoros* speaking f. *agora* public assembly)]

pareir·a (-āra), n. Drug from root of Brazilian shrub, used in urinary disorders. [f. Port. *parreira* vine trained against wall]

pare·nchȳma (-k-), n. (Anat.) proper substance of gland, organ, &c., as distinguished from flesh & connective tissue; (Bot.) tissue of cells of about equal length & breadth placed side by side (cf. PROSENCHYMA), usu. soft & succulent, found esp. in softer parts of leaves, pulp of fruits, &c. Hence **pare·nchymal**, **pă-**

renchy̆·matous, aa. [f. Gk *paregkhuma* something poured in beside (PARA-[1] + *egkhuma* f. *egkheō* pour in f. *en* in + *kheō* pour)]

pār·ent, n. Father or mother; forefather, esp. *our first pp.*, Adam & Eve; animal, plant, from which others are derived, (often attrib., as the *p. bird, tree*); (fig.) source, origin, (*of* evils &c.). So **pare·ntAL** a., **pare·ntalLY**[2] adv. [OF, f. L *parens* (*parere* beget, see -ENT)]

pār·entage, n. Descent from parents, lineage, as *his p. is unknown.* [F, as prec., see -AGE]

pare·nthesis, n. (pl. *-thesēs*). Word, clause, sentence, inserted into a passage to which it is not grammatically essential, and usu. marked off by brackets, dashes, or commas; (sing. or pl.) round brackets ( ) used for this; (fig.) interlude, interval. [med. L, f. Gk *parenthesis* f. *parentithēmi* put in beside (PARA-[1] + EN-(2) + *tithēmi* place)]

pare·nthesize, v.t. Insert (words &c., or abs.) as parenthesis; put between marks of parenthesis. [f. prec., see -IZE]

părenthĕ·tic, a. Of, inserted as a, parenthesis; (fig.) interposed. Hence **parenthe·ticAL** a., **parenthe·ticalLY**[2] adv. [f. med. L *parentheticus* (as PARENTHESIS, see -ETIC)]

pă·resis, n. (med.). Partial paralysis, affecting muscular motion but not sensation. So **parE·TIC** a. [f. Gk *paresis* f. *pariēmi* let go (PARA-[1] + *hiēmi* let go)]

par excellence (F), adv. By virtue of special excellence, above all others that may be so called, as *Mayfair was the fashionable quarter p. e.*

par·get (-j-), v.t., & n. Plaster (wall &c.); (n.) plaster. [prob. f. OF *pargeter, por-*, f. L PRO(*jectare* = *jactare* frequent. of *jacĕre jact-* throw)]

parhē·lion (par-h-), n. Spot on solar halo at which light is intensified, mock sun. Hence **parhēlī·ACAL, parhē·lIC,** aa. [f. L f. Gk *parēlion* (PARA-[1] + *hēlios* sun)]

pār·iah (*or* par-), n. Member of a low caste in S. India; member of low or no caste; (fig.) social outcast; *p.-dog*, yellow vagabond dog of low breed in India &c. [f. Tamil *paṛaiyar* pl. of *paṛaiyan* drummer (*paṛai* drum)]

Pār·ian, a. & n. Of the island of Paros, famed for white marble; (n.) fine white kind of porcelain. [f. L *Parius* of Paros + -AN]

parī·etal, a. Of the wall of the body or of any of its cavities; *p. bones*, pair forming part of sides & top of skull; (Bot.) of the wall of a hollow structure &c. [f. F *pariétal* f. L *parietalis* (*paries -etis* wall, see -AL)]

pari mutuel (F), n. Form of betting in which those who have staked on winning horse divide the stakes on the rest. [= mutual stake]

pā·rī pă·ssū, adv. With equal pace; simultaneously & equally. [L]

Pă·ris, n. Capital of France; *P. blue*, kinds of pigment; *P. doll*, dressmaker's lay figure; *P. green*, poisonous chemical used as pigment & insecticide; *P. white*, fine whiting used in polishing.

pă·rish, n. Subdivision of county, having its own church & clergyman; (also *civil p.*) district constituted for administration of Poor law &c., as *go on the p.*, receive parochial relief; the inhabitants of a p.; *p. clerk*, official performing various duties connected with the church, esp. (formerly) leading responses; *p. council*, local administrative body in rural civil p.; *p.* LANTERN; *p. register*, book recording christenings, marriages, & burials, at p. church. [f. OF *paroche* f. LL *parochia* f. L f. Gk *paroikia* district round (a church) f. *paroikos* (PARA-[1] + *-oikos* -dwelling f. *oikeō* dwell)]

parī·shioner (-shoner), n. Inhabitant of parish. [f. OF *paroissien* (*paroisse* f. pop. L **parocia* as prec., see -AN) + -ER[1]]

Parī·sian (-z-), a. & n. (Native, inhabitant) of Paris. [f. F *parisien* f. med. L *parisianus* (*Parisii* Paris, see -AN)]

părisyllă·bic, a. (Of Gk & L nouns) having same number of syllables in nominative as in oblique cases of singular. [f. L *par* equal + SYLLABIC]

pă·rity, n. Equality, esp. among members or ministers of church; parallelism, analogy, as *p. of reasoning*; (Commerc.) equivalence in another currency, being *at* PAR[1]. [f. L *paritas* (as prec., see -TY)]

park[1], n. Large enclosed piece of ground, usu. with woodland & pasture, attached to country house &c.; enclosure in town ornamentally laid out for public recreation; *The P.*, (now) Hyde P., (formerly) St James's P.; large tract of land kept in natural state for public benefit; (space occupied by) artillery, stores, &c., in encampment, area assigned for motor-cars &c. to wait in; *oyster-p.*, enclosed area for oyster-breeding, overflowed by sea at high tide. Hence **par·kISH**[1] a. [ME, f. OF *parc* f. WG **parruk*, whence OE *pearroc*, dial. *parrock*, PADDOCK]

park[2], v.t. Enclose (ground) in or as park; (Mil.) arrange (artillery &c.) compactly in a park; leave (car &c.) in p. [f. prec.]

Par·khurst, n. *P.* (*prison*), a convict prison.

par·kin, n. (north). Cake of oatmeal & treacle. [?]

par·ky, a. (slang). Chilly (of air, morning, &c.). [?]

par·lance, n. Way of speaking, as *in common, legal,* &c., *p.* [OF (*parler* speak f. LL *parabolare* talk, as PARABLE, see -ANCE)]

par·ley[1], n. Conference for debating of points in dispute, esp. (Mil.) discussion of terms, as *beat, sound, a p.*, call for it by drum or trumpet. [f. F *parler*, see prec.]

par·ley², v.i. & t. Discuss terms (*with* enemy &c.); speak (esp. foreign language). [f. or as prec.]

parleyvoo·, n., & v.i., (facet.). French; Frenchman; (v.i.) speak French. [f. F *parlez-vous (français)?* do you speak (French)?]

par·liament (-lam-), n. Council forming with the Sovereign the supreme legislature of United Kindgom, consisting of House of Lords (Spiritual & Temporal) & House of Commons (representatives of counties, cities, &c.); (of King) *open P.*, declare it open with ceremonial; corresponding legislative assembly in other countries; *the P. Act*, that of 1911 depriving the Lords of their veto on money bills & making their veto on other bills merely suspensory; LONG¹ *P.* (met Nov. 3rd, 1640, dissolved March 1660); *Short P.* (sat from Apr. 13 to May 5, 1640); (also *p.-cake*) thin crisp cake of gingerbread. [f. OF *parlement* speaking (as PARLANCE, see -MENT)]

parliamentār·ian, n. & a. Skilled debater in parliament; adherent of Parliament in Civil War of 17th c.; (adj.) = foll. [foll., -AN]

parliame·ntary (-lam-), a. Of parliament (*old p.* HAND¹); *p. agent* (charged with interests of party concerned in private legislation of Parliament); enacted, established, by Parliament; *p. train* (carrying passengers at rate not above 1*d.* per mile); (of language) admissible in Parliament, (colloq.) civil. [-ARY¹]

par·lour (-*er*), n. Ordinary sitting-room of family in private house; room in inn for private conversation; *p. boarder*, boarding-school pupil living in principal's family; *p. car* (U.S.), luxuriously fitted railway carriage; *p.-maid*, maid who waits at table. [f. OF *parleor* f. med. L *parlatorium* (*parlare* talk, see PARLANCE & -ORY)]

par·lous, a. & adv. (archaic, facet.). Perilous; hard to deal with; surprisingly clever &c.; (adv.) extremely. [= PERILOUS]

Parmesă·n (-z-), a. & n. *P. (cheese)*, kind of cheese made at Parma & elsewhere. [F, f. It. *parmegiano* of Parma]

Parnă·ssus, n. Mountain in central Greece, anciently sacred to Muses. So **Parna·ss**IAN a. & n., (esp., member) of a later 19th-c. school of French poets. [L, f. Gk *Parna(s)sos*]

Par·nellism, n. Policy of Irish Home-Rule party led by C. S. Parnell from 1880 to 1891. So **Par·nell**ITE¹ n. [-ISM]

parō·chial (-k-), a. Of a parish; (fig., of affairs &c.) confined to narrow area. Hence **paro·chial**ISM, **parōchia·l**ITY, nn., **paro·chial**IZE(3) v.t., **paro·chial**LY² adv. [OF, f. LL *parochialis* (as PARISH, see -AL)]

pă·rody, n., & v.t. Composition in which an author's characteristics are ridiculed by imitation; feeble imitation, travesty; (v.t.) make (literary work, manner, &c.) ridiculous by imitation. So **pa·rod**IST(3) n. [(vb f. n.) f. Gk *parōidia* (PARA-¹ + *ōidē* song, ODE)]

paro·le (-ōl), n., & v.t. (Also *p. of honour*, F *p. d'honneur*) word of honour, esp. (Mil.) prisoner's promise that he will not attempt escape, or will return to custody if liberated, or will refrain from taking up arms against captors for stated period; *on p.*, (liberated) on this understanding; (Mil.) password used only by officers or inspectors of guard (cf. COUNTERSIGN); (v.t.) put (prisoner) on p. [(vb f. n.) F, = word, as PARABLE]

păronomā·sia (-z-, -s-), n. Word-play, pun. [L, f. Gk *paronomasia* (PARA-¹ + *onomasia* f. *onomazō* f. *onoma* name)]

paroquet. See PARAKEET.

parō·tid, a. & n. Situated near the ear, esp. *p. gland* (in front of ear, with *p. duct*, opening into mouth); (n.) p. gland. [f. F *parotide* f. L f. Gk *parōtis, -idos* (PARA-¹ + *ous ōtos* ear)]

paroti·tis, n. Mumps. [f. prec. + -ITIS]

pă·roxysm, n. Fit of disease; fit (*of* rage, laughter, &c.). Hence **paroxy·sm**AL a. [f. F *paroxysme* f. L f. Gk *paroxusmos* f. *paroxunō* exasperate (PARA-¹ + *oxunō* sharpen f. *oxus* sharp)]

paro·xytone (-tn), a. & n. (Gk gram.). (Word) with acute accent on last syllable but one. [f. Gk *paroxutonos* (PARA-¹, OXYTONE)]

par·pen, n. Stone passing through wall from side to side, with two smooth vertical faces. [f. OF *parpain*, etym. dub.]

parquĕ·t (-k-), n., & v.t. Wooden flooring of pieces of wood, often of different kinds, arranged in pattern; (v.t.) floor (room) thus. So **par·quet**RY(1) n. [F, = small compartment, floor, dim. of *parc* PARK]

par(r), n. Young salmon. [?]

pă·rricide, n. 1. One who murders his father or near relative or one whose person is held sacred; person guilty of treason against his country. 2. Any of these crimes. So **părrici·d**AL a. [F, f. L (1) *parricida* (2) *-cidium*; etym. dub., see -CIDE]

pă·rrot, n., & v.t. Genus of birds, of which many species have beautiful plumage, & some can be taught to repeat words; person who repeats another's words or imitates his actions unintelligently; (v.t.) repeat (words, or abs.) mechanically, drill (person &c.) to do this, whence **pa·rrot**RY(4) n.; *p.-fish*, kinds with brilliant colouring or mouth like p.'s bill. [?]

pa·rry, v.t., & n. Ward off, avert, (weapon, blow, awkward question); (n.) warding off. [f. F *parer* f. It. & L *parare* prepare]

parse (-z, -s), v.t. Describe (word) grammatically, stating inflexion, relation to sentence, &c.; resolve (sentence) into its component parts & describe them. [prob. f. L *pars* part]

Parsee·, n. Adherent of ZOROASTRIANism, descendant of Persians who fled to India from Mohammedan persecution in 7th & 8th cc., whence **Parsee·**ISM(3) n.; language of Persia under Sassanian kings. [f. Pers. *Parsi* Persian (*Pars* Persia)]

Par·seval, n. Type of non-rigid German airship. [inventor's name]

par·simony, n. Carefulness in employment of money &c. or (fig.) of immaterial things; stinginess; *law of p.* (that no more causes or forces should be assumed than are necessary to account for the facts). So **parsimō·ni**OUS a., **parsimo·nious**LY[2] adv., **parsimo·nious**NESS n. [f. L *parsimonia, parci-, (parcere pars-* spare, see -MONY)]

par·sley, n. Biennial umbelliferous plant with white flowers & aromatic leaves, used for seasoning & garnishing dishes. [(partly thr. OF *peresil*) f. LL *petrosilium* f. L f. Gk *petroselinon* (*petra* rock + *selinon* parsley)]

par·snip, n. (Plant with yellow flowers &) pale yellow root used as culinary vegetable; *fine words* BUTTER[2] *no pp.* [ME *passenep*, ult. f. L *pastinaca* (*pastinum* digging-fork)]

par·son, n. Rector; vicar or any beneficed clergyman; (colloq.) any clergyman; *p.-bird*, N.-Zealand bird with dark plumage & white neck; *p.'s nose*, rump of fowl &c. Hence **parsŏ·n**IC a. [ME & OF *persone* f. L *persona* PERSON, (med. L) rector]

par·sonage (-ĭj), n. Rector's or other incumbent's house. [var. of PERSONAGE]

part[1], n. & adv. Some but not all of a thing or number of things, as (*a*) *p. of it was spoilt*, (*a*) *p. of them have arrived*, (*a*) *great part of this is true*, *most p.* (the majority) *of them failed*; division of books &c., esp. as much as is issued at one time; portion of animal body; *the* (privy) *pp.*; each of several equal portions of a whole, as *three pp.* (quarters), *19 pp.* (twentieths), *take 3 pp. of sugar, 5 of flour, 2 of ground rice*, &c.; portion allotted, share, esp. *have neither p. nor lot* (no concern) *in*; ART[2] *& p.*; person's share in action, his duty, as *I have done my p., it was not my p. to interfere*; character assigned to actor on stage; words spoken by actor on stage; copy of these; (fig.) *play a noble, an unworthy, p.*, behave nobly &c.; *play a p.*, act deceitfully; (Mus.) each of the successions of notes that make up a harmony, melody assigned to particular voice or instrument; (pl., archaic) abilities, as *a man of* (*good*) *pp.*; (pl.) region (*a stranger in these pp.*); side in dispute; *p. & parcel*, essential p.; *p. of speech*, each of the grammatical classes of words (noun, adjective, pronoun, verb, adverb, preposition, conjunction, interjection); *for the most p.*, in most cases, mostly; *take p.*, assist (*in doing, in* discussion &c.); *take the p. of*, support, back up; *for my p.*, as far as I am concerned; *in p.*, partly; *take* (words, action) *in good p.*, not be offended at; *on the p. of*, proceeding from, done &c. by, as *there was no objection on my p.*; *p.-owner*, one who owns in common with others; *p.-song*, song for three or more voice-parts, usu. without accompaniment, & in simple harmony; (adv.) in p., partly (*made p. of iron & p. of wood*; *a lie that is p. truth*). [OE, f. L *pars partis*]

part[2], v.t. & i. Divide (t. & i.) into parts, as *the crowd parted & let him through, an islet parts the stream, the cord parted* (broke); separate (hair of head) with comb; separate (combatants, friends, &c.); *p. company*, dissolve companionship (*with*); *p.* BRASS *rags with*; quit one another's company, as *let us p. friends, the best of friends must p.*; *p. from* or *with*, say goodbye to; *p. with*, give up, surrender, (property &c.); (colloq.) p. with one's money, pay, (*if I know him, he won't p.*); (archaic) distribute (thing) in shares. [f. F *partir* f. L *partiri* (prec.)]

parta·ke, v.t. & i. Take a share in; take a share (*in* or *of* thing, *with* person); take, esp. eat or drink some or (colloq.) all *of*, as *he partook of our lowly fare, partook of a bun*; have some (*of* quality &c.), as *his manner partakes of insolence.* [back formation f. *partaker* = part-taker]

par·tan, n. (Sc.). Crab. [Celt.]

parterre· (-ār), n. Level space in garden occupied by flower-beds; part of ground-floor of auditorium of theatre, behind orchestra. [F, = *par terre* on the ground]

parthenogĕ·nesis, n. (biol.). Reproduction without sexual union. So **partheno-gen**E·TIC a. [f. Gk *parthenos* virgin]

Par·thian, a. Of Parthia, ancient kingdom of W. Asia; *P. shaft, glance*, &c., remark, glance, &c., reserved for the moment of departure, like missile shot backwards by flying P. horseman. [-AN]

parti· (-ē), n. Person regarded as eligible &c. in the marriage market (*is quite a, a desirable, an unsuitable, p.*). *p. pris* (-ē), preconceived view, bias. [F]

par·tial (-shl), a. Biased, unfair; *p. to*, having a liking for (person), thing; forming only a part, not complete, as *a p. success*; *p. eclipse* (in which part only of the luminary is covered or darkened). Hence **par·tial**LY[2] adv. [f. OF *parcial* f. LL *partialis* (as PART[1], see -AL)]

partia·lity (-shĭ-), n. Bias, favouritism; fondness (*for*). [f. OF *parcialité* f. med. L *partialitas* (as prec., see -TY)]

par·tible, a. That can or must be divided (*among*; esp. of heritable property). [f. LL *partibilis* f. L as PART[2], -IBLE]

parti·cipate, v.t. & i. Have share in

(thing *with* person); have share (*in* thing *with* person); have something *of*, as *his poems p. of the nature of satire.* So **par·ti·cip**ANT, **particip**A·TION, **parti·cipa·tor**[2], nn. [f. L *participare* (as PART[1] + *cip-* = *cap-* st. of *capere* take)]

par·ticiple, n. Verbal adjective qualifying noun but retaining some properties of verb, e.g. tense & government of object. So **par·ticipled a.** (slang substitute for *damned* &c.), **partici·pi**AL a., **partici·pi·al**LY[2] adv. [OF, f. L *participium* sharing, participle, (as prec.)]

par·ticle, n. Minute portion of matter; smallest possible amount, as *has not a p. of sense*; minor part of speech, esp. short indeclinable one; common prefix or suffix such as *un-*, *out-*, *-ness*, *-ship*. [f. L *particula* (PART[1], -CULE)]

par·ticoloured, par·ty-, a. Partly of one colour, partly of another. [prob. f. PARTY[2]]

parti·cŭlar, a. & n. Relating to one as distinguished from others, special; *P. Baptists*, body holding doctrines of *p. election* & *p. redemption* (i.e. of only some of the human race); one considered apart from others, individual, as *this p. tax is no worse than others*; worth notice, special, as *took p. trouble, for no p. reason*; minute, as *full & p. account*; scrupulously exact; fastidious (*about, what* or *as to what* one eats &c.); *in p.*, especially, as *mentioned one case in p.*; (n.) detail, item, (pl.) detailed account. Hence or cogn. **particulă·**RITY n., **parti·cular**LY[2] adv. [f. OF *particuler* f. L *particularis* (as PARTICLE, see -AR[1])]

parti·cularism, n. Doctrine of PARTICULAR election or redemption; exclusive devotion to a party, sect, &c.; principle of leaving political independence to each State in an empire &c. So **parti·cular**IST n. [-ISM]

parti·cularize, v.t. Name specially or one by one, specify, (often abs.). Hence **particulariz**A·TION n. [f. F *particulariser* (as PARTICULAR, see -IZE)]

par·ting, n. In vbl senses, esp.: leave-taking (often attrib., as *p. injunctions*); dividing line of combed hair; *p. of the ways*, point at which road divides into two or more (often fig. of choice between courses). [-ING[1]]

partisă·n[1] (-z-), **-zan,** (*or* par·t-), n. Adherent of party, cause, &c., esp. unreasoning one (often attrib., as *in a p. spirit*); (hist.) member of light irregular troops employed in special enterprises. Hence **partisa·n**SHIP n. [F, f. It. *partigiano* (*parte* PART, see -AN)]

par·tisan[2] (-z-), **-zan,** n. (hist.). Long-handled spear like halberd. [f. F *partizane* f. It. *partesana*, etym dub.]

par·tite, a. (bot., entom.). Divided (nearly) to the base. [f. L *partiri -it-* PART[2]]

partĭ·tion, n., & v.t. Division into parts; such part; structure separating two such parts, esp. slight wall, whence **par·ti·tion**ED[2] a.; (Law) division of real property between joint tenants &c.; (v.t.) divide into parts; *p. off*, separate (part of room &c.) by a p. [(vb f. n.) F, f. L *partitionem* (as prec., see -ION)]

par·titive, a. & n. (Word) denoting part of a collective whole (e.g. *some, any*); *p. genitive*, that used to indicate a whole divided into parts, expressed in English by *of*. Hence **par·titive**LY[2] adv. [f. L *partitivus* (PARTITE, -IVE)]

Par·tlet, n. used as proper name for a hen, esp. *Dame P.*, also applied to women. [f. OF *Pertelote*, female proper name]

par·tly, adv. With respect to a part; in some degree. [-LY[2]]

par·tner, n., & v.t. Sharer (*with* person, *in* or *of* thing); person associated with others in business of which he shares risks & profits; SLEEP[2]*ing p.*; *predominant p.*, England (among constituents of United Kingdom); wife, husband; companion in dance; player associated with another in whist, tennis, &c.; (Naut., pl.) timber framework round hole in deck through which mast, pump, &c., passes; (v.t.) associate (persons, one *with* another) as pp., (also) be p. of. Hence **par·tner**LESS a., **par·tner**SHIP n. [prob. var. of *parcener*, see CO-PARCENER]

par·tridge, n. Kinds of game-bird, esp. *Common* or *Grey P.*; *p.-wood*, hard red wood used for cabinet work &c., (also) speckled effect produced on wood by certain fungus. [ME *pertrich*, ult. f. L f. Gk *perdix -dikos*]

partūr·ient, a. About to give birth (often fig. of the mind &c.). [f. L *parturire* be in labour (*parere part-* bear), see -ENT]

parturi·tion, n. Childbirth (also fig.). [f. L *parturitio*, as prec., see -ION]

***partūr·iunt mo·ntes* (*,nascē·tur rĭ·di·cŭlus mŭs*),** sent. (As comment on fiasco) the mountains are in labour (,the product a poor mouse). [Hor., *A.P.* 139]

par·ty[1], n. Body of persons united in a cause, opinion, &c.; system of taking sides on public questions; *p. spirit*, zeal for a p., so *p.-spirited*; body of persons travelling or engaged together, as *fishing, reading, -p.*; social gathering, esp. of invited guests at private house, as *dinner, tea, p.*; each of the two or more persons making the two sides in legal action, contract, marriage, &c.; accessory (*to* action; (now vulg. or facet.) person, as *an old p. with spectacles*; *p.-coloured*, see PARTI-COLOURED; *p. wall*, wall shared by each of the occupiers of the two buildings &c. that it separates. [f. F *partie* (*partir* f. L as PART[2])]

par·ty[2], a. (herald.). Divided into parts of different tinctures. [f. F *parti*, as prec.]

par·venū (or as F), n. Person of obscure

origin who has gained wealth or position, upstart, (often attrib.). [F, p.p. of *parvenir* arrive f. L PER(*venire* come)]

par·vis, n. Enclosed area in front of cathedral, church, &c. [F, f. OF *pare(v)is* f. L *paradisus* PARADISE, court in front of St Peter's, Rome]

pas (pah), n. Precedence, esp. *dispute, give, take, the p.*; step in dancing, as *p. seul* (serl), *p. de deux* (der), dance for one, two. [F, = step]

pa·schal (-kl), a. Of the Jewish Passover; of Easter. [f. F *pascal* f. LL *paschalis* (*pascha* f. Gk *pashka* f. Heb. *pesakh* Passover f. *pasakh* pass over, see -AL)]

pa·sha, -cha, (pah·sha, pă·sha, pashah·), n. Turkish officer of high rank, e.g. military commander, governor of province, &c.; *p. of three, two, tails, of one tail,* (of first, second, third, grade; from number of horse-tails displayed as symbol in war.) [Turk. (*-sha*)]

pa·shalic, -ch-, (*or* pashah·-), n. Jurisdiction of pasha. [f. Turk. *pashalik*]

pa·shm, n. Under-fur of hairy quadrupeds in Tibet &c., esp. that of goats as used for Cashmere shawls. [Pers., = wool]

pa·sque-flower (-k-), n. Anemone with bell-shaped purple flowers. [orig. *passe-flower*, f. F *passefleur* (surpassing flower) w. assim. to obs. *Pasque* Easter (PASCHAL)]

pasquinā·de (-kw-), n. Lampoon, satire, orig. one affixed to public place. [f. It. *pasquinata* (*Pasquino*, statue at Rome on which Latin verses were annually posted, see -ADE)]

pass[1], v.t. & i. (p.p. *passed* or as adj. *past*). 1. intr. Move onward, proceed, (*along, down, over, on,* &c.); circulate, be current; *p. for,* be accepted as; *p.* (be currently known) *by the name of*; be transported from place to place; change (*into* something, *from* one state *to* another); die (now usu. *p. hence, p. from among us,* &c.); go by, as *saw the procession p., time passes rapidly, remarks p. unnoticed*; come to an end, as *kingdoms & nations p.*; get through, effect a passage; go uncensured, be accepted as adequate; (of bill in Parliament, proposal, &c.) be sanctioned; (of candidate) satisfy examiner; happen, be done or said, as *I saw* or *heard what was passing*; adjudicate (*upon*); (of judgement) be given (*for* plaintiff &c.); (Cards) forgo one's opportunity, e.g. of making trump, (also) throw up one's hand. 2. trans. Leave (thing &c.) on one side or behind as one goes (*has passed the chair*, been chairman, president, mayor, &c.); go across (sea, frontier, mountain range); (of bill) be examined & approved by (House of Commons &c.); reach standard required by (examiner, examination); *p.* MUSTER[1]; outstrip; surpass; be too great for, as *it passes my comprehension*; transport (usu. w. prep. or adv.); move, cause to go, as *passed his hand across his forehead, p. your eye* (glance) *over this letter, p. a rope round it, p.*(=*hand*) *in* one's CHECK[1]*s*; cause to go by, as *p.* (troops) *in review*; cause, allow, (measure in Parliament, candidate for examination, &c.) to proceed after scrutiny; spend (*time, the winter,* &c.); hand round, transfer, as *read this & p. it on*; give currency to (coin, esp. base coin); pledge (one's word, oath, &c.); utter (criticism, judicial sentence, *upon*); *p. the* TIME *of day*; *p. water*, void urine. 3. Spec. senses w. advv. & prepp.: *p. away*, die, come to an end; *p. by* (adv. or prep.), omit, disregard, walk &c. past; *p. off*, (of sensations &c.) fade away, (of proceedings) be carried through (*without a hitch* &c.), (trans.) palm off (thing *upon* person *for* or *as* what it is not), distract attention from (awkward situation or allusion); *p. over* (adv. or prep.), omit, make no remark upon, as *p. over his subsequent conduct, p. it over in silence*; *p. through*, experience. [f. F *passer* f. L *passus* PACE]

pass[2], n. Passing, esp. of examination; (Univv.) attainment of standard that satisfies examiners but does not entitle to honours; *bring to p.*, accomplish, carry out; *come to p.*, happen; critical position as *things have come to a* (*strange*) *p.*; written permission to pass into or out of a place, or to be absent from quarters (*on p.*, away thus); (usu. *free p.*) ticket authorizing holder to travel free on railway &c.; thrust in fencing; juggling trick; passing of hands over anything, esp. in mesmerism; *p.-book*, book supplied by bank to person having current or deposit account, showing all sums deposited & drawn; *p.-key*, private key to gate &c. for special purposes, (also) master-key; *pa·ssman*, one who takes p. degree at university; *pa·ssword*, selected word or phrase distinguishing friend from enemy. [partly f. prec., partly f. F *passe* as prec.]

pass[3], n. Narrow passage through mountains; (Mil.) such passage viewed as key to a country (*sell the p.* fig., betray a cause); navigable channel, esp. at river's mouth; passage for fish over weir. [f. F *pas* f. L *passus* PACE]

pa·ssable, a. In vbl senses, esp. that can pass muster, fairly good, whence **pa·ssabLY**[2] adv. [-ABLE]

pă·ssage[1] (-ĭj), n. Passing, transit (BIRD *of p.*); transition from one state to another; liberty, right, to pass through; voyage, crossing, from port to port; right of conveyance as passenger by sea; passing of a measure into law; way by which one passes; corridor &c. giving communication between different rooms in house; (pl.) what passes between two persons mutually, interchange of confidences &c.; *p.* (*of* or *at arms*), fight (often fig.); part of a speech or literary work taken for quotation &c. [F (as PASS[1], see -AGE)]

pă·ssage[2] (-ij), v.i. & t. (Of horse or rider) move sideways, by pressure of rein on horse's neck & of rider's leg on opposite side; make (horse) do this. [f. F *passager*, earlier *passéger* f. It. *passeggiare* (*passeggio* walk f. L *passus* PACE)]

pa·ssant, a. (herald.). Walking, & looking to dexter side, with three paws on ground & dexter fore-paw raised. [F, part. as PASS[1]]

passé (F), a. (fem. *-sée*). Past the prime, esp. (of woman) past the period of greatest beauty; behind the times. [F, p.p. as PASS[1]]

passementerie (F), n. Trimming of gold or silver lace, braid, beads, &c. [F (*passement* gold lace &c. as PASS[1], see -MENT & -ERY)]

pă·ssenger (-j-), n. Traveller in public conveyance by land or water; *foot-p.*, traveller on foot; *p.-pigeon*, wild pigeon of N. America, capable of long flight. [ME & F (n. & a.) *passager* (PASSAGE, see -IER)]

passe-partout (pahspartōō·), n. Master-key; mount for photograph &c. [F, =pass everywhere]

pa·sser, n. In vbl senses; *p.-by*, one who passes, esp. casually. [-ER[1]]

pă·sserīne, a. & n. (Bird) of the order of *Passeres* or Perchers; of the size of a sparrow. [f. L *passer* sparrow + -INE[1]]

pă·ssible, n. (theol.). Capable of feeling or suffering. So **passi**BI·LITY n. [OF, f. LL *passibilis* (*pati pass-* suffer, see -BLE)]

pă·ssim, adv. (Of allusions, phrases, &c., to be found in specified author or book) in every part, as *this occurs in Milton p.* [L, = scatteredly (*pandere pass-* spread)]

pa·ssing[1], n. In vbl senses; *p.-bell* (rung in moment of person's death); *p.-note* (not belonging to the harmony but interposed to secure smooth transition). [-ING[1]]

pa·ssing[2], a. & adv. In vbl senses, esp.: transient, fleeting; cursory, incidental; (adv., archaic) very (esp. *p. rich*). [-ING[2]]

passion[1] (pă·shn), n. Strong emotion; outburst of anger; sexual love; strong enthusiasm (*for* thing, *for* doing); (*the P.*) sufferings of Christ on cross, (musical setting of) narrative of this from Gospels; *p.-play*, mystery-play representing Christ's P.; *p.-flower*, genus of (chiefly climbing) plants, flower of which was supposed to suggest instruments of Christ's P.; *P. Sunday*, fifth Sunday in Lent; *P.* (also *Holy*) *Week*, week before Easter. Hence **pa·ssion**LESS a., **pa·ssionless**LY[2] adv., **pa·ssionless**NESS n. [OF, f. L *passionem* (*pati pass-* suffer, see -ION)]

pa·ssion[2], v.i. (poet.). Feel or express passion. [f. OF *passionner*, as prec.]

pa·ssional[1], n. Book of the sufferings of saints & martyrs. [f. med. L *passionale* neut. adj. as n. (as foll.)]

pa·ssional[2], a. Of, marked by, passion. [f. LL *passionalis* (as PASSION[1], see -AL)]

pa·ssionate (-at), a. Easily moved to anger; dominated by, easily moved to, strong feeling; due to, (of language &c.) showing, passion. Hence **pa·ssionate**LY[2] adv., **pa·ssionate**NESS n. [f. med. L *passionatus* (as PASSION[1], see -ATE[2])]

Pa·ssionist, n. Member of an order pledged to do their utmost to keep alive the memory of Christ's Passion. [-IST]

pa·ssive, a. & n. Suffering action, acted upon; (Gram.) *p. voice* (comprising those forms of transitive verbs that attribute the verbal action to the person &c. to whom it is directed, cf. ACTIVE); offering no opposition, submissive; *p.* RESISTANCE; not active, inert; *p. debt* (on which no interest is paid); (n.) p. voice or form of verb. Hence **pa·ssive**LY[2] adv., **pa·ssive**NESS, **passi·**VITY, nn. [f. L *passivus* (*pati pass-* suffer, see -IVE)]

pa·ssōver, n. Jewish feast commemorating passing over of Israelites' houses when Egyptians were smitten (*Exod.* xii), held on 14th day of month Nisan; Paschal lamb, (fig.) Christ (1 *Cor.* v. 7).

pa·ssport, n. Document issued by competent authority permitting person specified in it to travel in the country & entitling him to protection; (fig.) thing that ensures admission, as *flattery is the sole p. to his favour.* [f. F *passeport* (*passer* PASS[1] + PORT[1])]

past[1], a. & n. As p.p. or adj. in vbl senses of PASS[1], esp.: gone by in time, as *his prime is p., our p. years*; just gone by, as *the p. month, for some time p.*; (Gram.) expressing p. action or state, as *p. tense, p. participle*; *p. master*, one who has been master in guild, freemasons' lodge, &c., (also) thorough master (*in, of,* a subject). (N.) p. time, esp. *the p.*; what has happened in p. time, as *cannot undo the p.*; person's p. life or career, esp. one that will not bear inquiry, as *a woman with a p.*

past[2], prep. & adv. Beyond in time or place, as *stayed till p. two o'clock, half p. three, old man p. seventy, ran p. the house*; beyond the range or compass of, as *p. endurance, bearing, praying for*; (adv.) so as to pass by, as *hastens p.* [prob. f. misuse of *am past* with object, *past* being then mistaken for prep., e.g. *I was now p. the house*]

pāste[1], n. Flour moistened & kneaded, with butter, suet, &c., as cooking material; kinds of sweet confection; relish of pounded fish, as *anchovy p.*; cement of flour & water; any soft plastic mixture; hard vitreous composition used in making imitation gems; *pasteboard*, stiff substance made by pasting together sheets of paper, (attrib., fig.) unsubstantial, flimsy, (slang) visiting-card, railway-ticket. [OF, f. com.-Rom. *pasta* perh. f. Gk *pastē* (*pastos* sprinkled)]

păste[2], v.t. Fasten with paste; stick *up* (playbill &c.) on wall with paste; cover (thing *with* paper &c.) by pasting. [f. prec.]

pă·stel, n. Woad; blue dye from this; dry paste made by compounding pigments with gum-water, used for crayons; drawing in p., whence **pa·stel(l)**IST n. [F, f. It. *pastello* woad, dim. of *pasta* PASTE[1]]

pă·stern, n. Part of horse's foot between fetlock & hoof. [f. OF *pasturon* f. OF *pasture* (perh. as PASTURE)]

Pa·steurism (-*er*-), n. Prevention or cure of diseases esp. hydrophobia by successive inoculations. [f. L *Pasteur*, French scientist (1822–1895) + -ISM]

Pa·steurize, v.t. Subject (milk &c.) to Pasteur's method of partial sterilization; treat by Pasteurism. Hence **Pasteuriza·tion** n. [-IZE]

păsti·ccio (-ĭtshō), **păsti·che** (-ēsh), nn. Medley, esp. musical composition, picture, made up from various sources; (usu. *-iche*) literary or other work of art composed in the style of a known author. [F (*-iche*) f. It. (*-iccio*), f. *pasta* PASTE[1]]

pă·stil, pasti·lle (-ēl), n. Small roll of aromatic paste burnt as fumigator &c.; lozenge. [F (*-le*), f. L *pastillus* small roll, etym. dub.]

pa·stime, n. Recreation; game, sport. [f. PASS[1] + TIME]

pa·stor, n. Minister in charge of church or congregation, whence **pa·stor**SHIP n.; person exercising spiritual guidance; kind of starling. [OF, f. L *pastorem* shepherd (*pascere past-* feed, see -OR[2])]

pa·storal, a. & n. Of shepherds; (of land) used for pasture; (of poems &c.) portraying country life, whence **pa·storal**ISM n.; of a pastor, as *p. epistles* (of Paul to Timothy & Titus, dealing with pastor's work). (N.) p. play, poem, poetry, or picture; letter from pastor, esp. bishop, to clergy or people. Hence **pastora·l**ITY n., **pa·storal**LY[2] adv. [f. L *pastoralis* (as prec., see -AL)]

pastora·le (-ahlĭ), n. (pl. *-ali*, pron. -lē, or *-ales*). Musical composition dealing with pastoral subject. [It., as prec.]

pa·storate (-*at*), n. Pastor's (tenure of) office; body of pastors. [f. med. L *pastoratus* (as PASTOR, see -ATE[1])]

pā·stry, n. Baked flour-paste; articles of food made wholly or partly of this; *p.-cook*, one who makes p., esp. for public sale. [prob. f. PASTE[1] + -RY]

pa·sturage (-ĭj), n. Pasturing; herbage for cattle &c.; pasture-land. [OF, as foll., see -AGE]

pa·sture (-tsh*e*r), n., & v.t. & i. Herbage for cattle; (piece of) land covered with this; (v.t.) lead, put, (cattle) to p., (of sheep &c.) eat down (grass-land), (of person) put sheep &c. on (land) to graze, whence **pa·stur**ABLE a.; (v.i.) graze. [F, f. LL *pastura* (as PASTOR, see -URE)]

pa·sty[1] (pah-, pă-), n. Pie of venison &c. enclosed in paste & baked without dish. [f. OF *pastée* f. com.-Rom. *pasta* PASTE, cf. -ADE]

pā·sty[2], a. Of, like, paste; (also *p.-faced*) of pale complexion. [-Y[2]]

pat[1], n. Stroke, tap, esp. with hand as caress &c.; small mass (esp. of butter) formed by patting; sound made by striking lightly with something flat. [prob. imit.]

pat[2], v.t. & i. Strike (thing) gently with flat surface; *p.-ball*, lawn tennis (contempt.); flatten thus; *p.-a-cake*, first words of nursery rhyme, connected child's game; strike gently with inner surface of fingers, esp. to mark sympathy, approbation, &c.; (fig.) *p.* (person, one*self*) *on the back*, express approbation of; beat lightly *upon*. [w. prec.]

pat[3], adv. & a. Apposite(ly), opportune(ly), as *story came p. to his purpose*; ready for any occasion, as *has the story p.* [prob. as prec.]

Pat[4], n. (Nickname for) Irishman. [abbr. of *Patrick*]

pătagī·um, n. (zool.; pl. *-ia*). Wing-membrane of bat or similar animal. [L, f. Gk *patageion* gold edging on gown, etym. dub.]

pătavi·nity, n. Dialectal characteristics of Patavium (Padua) as seen in Livy's style; provincialism. [f. L *patavinitas* (*Patavinus* of Padua, see -INE[1] & -ITY)]

patch[1], n. Piece of cloth, metal, &c., put on to mend hole or rent; piece of plaster &c. put over wound; pad worn to protect injured eye; *not a p. on*, not comparable to, nothing to; small piece of black silk or plaster worn esp. in 17th & 18th cc. to show off complexion; large or irregular spot on surface; piece of ground; number of plants growing on this, as *a p. of beans*; scrap, remnant; *patchwork*, work made up of fragments of different kinds & colours (often fig. & attrib.). Hence **pa·tch**ERY(1), **pa·tchi**NESS, nn., **pa·tchi**LY[2] adv., **pa·tch**Y[2] a. [ME, etym. dub.]

patch[2], v.t. Put patch(es) on; *p. up*, repair with patches; (of material) serve as patch to; (fig., usu. *p. up*) repair, set to rights (matter, trouble, quarrel); (usu. *p. up*) put together hastily; piece (things) together (lit. or fig.); appear as patches on (surface). [f. prec.]

pa·tchouli (*or* patshōō·-), n. Odoriferous Indian plant; perfume got from p. [native]

pate, n. (now colloq.). Head, often as seat of intellect. Hence **-pat**ED[2] a. [?]

pâté (pă·tā), n. Pie, patty; *p. de foi gras* (fwah grah), pie &c. of fatted goose liver. [F, f. OF *pasté*, cf. PASTY]

pate·lla, n. Knee-cap, whence **pate·llAR**[1], **pa·tellATE**[2](2), aa.; (Rom. Ant.) small pan. [L, dim. as foll.]

pă·ten, n. Shallow dish used for bread at eucharist; thin circular plate of metal. [f. OF *patene* f. L *patena, -ina*]

pă·tent[1], a. *Letters p.*, open letter from sovereign &c. conferring right, title, &c., esp. sole right for a term to make, use, or sell, some invention; conferred, protected, by this; *p.* LEATHER; (fig.) to which one has proprietary claim; (colloq.) such as might be patented, ingenious, well-contrived; (of door &c.) open, (fig.) plain, obvious, whence **pa·tENCY** n., **pa·tentLY**[2] adv. [(partly thr. F) f. L *patēre* lie open, see -ENT]

pă·tent[2], n. =*letters* PATENT[1]; government grant of exclusive privilege of making or selling new invention; invention, process, so protected; (fig.) sign that one is entitled to something, possesses a quality, &c., as *a p. of gentility*; *p. office* (from which pp. are issued); *p.-roll* (containing pp. issued in Great Britain in a year). [short for *letters patent*]

pă·tent[3], v.t. Obtain patent for (invention). [f. prec.]

pătentee·, n. Taker-out or holder of a patent, person for the time being entitled to the benefit of a patent. [-EE]

pā·ter, n. (slang). Father; *P., peccavi*, =PECCAVI. [L, = father]

pă·terfami·liăs, n. (Rom. Law & facet.) head of family. [L]

pater·nal, a. Of a father; fatherly; related through the father, as *p. grandmother*, father's mother; *p. government, legislation*, &c. (that limits the freedom of the subject by well-meant needless regulations). Hence **pater·nalLY**[2] adv. [f. L *paternus* (*pater* father), + -AL]

pater·nity, n. Fatherhood; one's paternal origin; (fig.) authorship, source. [f. F *paternité* f. L *paternitatem* (as prec., see -TY)]

pă·ternŏ·ster, n. The Lord's Prayer, esp. in Latin; *black, white, p.*, forms of words said as charms &c.; *devil's p.*, muttered imprecation; bead in rosary indicating that p. is to be said; *p. line*, weighted fishing-line with hooks at intervals. [f. L *pater noster* our father]

path, n. (pl. pron. -dhz). Footway, esp. one merely beaten by feet, not specially constructed (also *pathway*); track laid for foot or cycle racing, esp. *cinder-p.*; line along which person or thing moves. Hence **pa·thLESS** a. [com.-WG: OE *pæth*, Du. *pad*, G *pfad*]

Patha·n (-tahn), n. Member of the Afghan tribes settled in India or on its N.W. frontier. [f. PUSHTOO]

pathĕ·tic, a. & n. Exciting pity or sadness; of the emotions (*p. fallacy*, crediting nature with human emotion); (n. pl.) study of, indulgence in, demonstration of, these. Hence **pathe·tICALLY** adv. [f. LL f. Gk *pathētikos* (*path-*, root of *paskhō* suffer, see -ETIC)]

pă·thic, n. =CATAMITE. [f. L f. Gk *pathikos* passive (PATHOS, -IC)]

pătho- in comb. =Gk *pathos* suffering, disease, passion, as: *-ge·nesis, -geny*, production of disease, so *-genĕ·tic, -gĕ·nic, -genous*, aa.; *-gnomŏ·nic*, characteristic of particular disease; *-gnomy* (-gn-), study of the emotions, so *-gnŏ·mic* a.; *-logy*, science of (usu. bodily) diseases, so *-lo·gical* a., *-lo·gically* adv., *-logist* n.

pā·thŏs (*or* pă-), n. Quality in speech, writing, events, &c., that excites pity or sadness. [f. Gk *pathos* suffering, see PATHETIC]

-pathy, suf. repr. Gk *-patheia* suffering, feeling, in *homoiopatheia* suffering or feeling alike, extended to ALLOPATHY & (w. sense curative treatment) to other compds, as *hydropathy, kinesipathy, electropathy*.

pā·tience (-shns), n. Calm endurance of pain or any provocation; perseverance; *have no p. with*, be irritated by, be unable to endure, (person, his conduct, &c.); *out of p. with*, no longer able to endure; *the p. of Job*, the utmost limits of p. (*would try the p. o. J.*); game of cards, usu. for one; *p.-dock*, kinds of plant. [OF, f. L *patientia* (as foll., see -ENCE)]

pā·tient (-shnt), a. & n. Having, showing patience; *p. of*, enduring with patience, (also) admitting of or compatible with (*the facts are p. of two interpretations*); (n.) person under medical treatment. Hence **pa·tientLY**[2] adv. [OF, f. L *pati* suffer, see -ENT]

pă·tina, n. Incrustation, usu. green, on surface of old bronze, esteemed as ornament. Hence **pa·tinated** [-ATE[2]], **pa·tinOUS**, aa., **patinA·TION** n. [f. F *patine* etym. dub.; L has *patina* dish]

pa·tio (pah-), n. Inner court open to sky in Spanish or Span.-Amer. house. [Sp.]

pă·tois (-wah), n. Dialect of common people in a district, differing materially from the literary language. [F, etym. dub.]

pā·triarch (-k), n. Father & ruler of family or tribe; (pl.) sons of Jacob, (also) Abraham, Isaac, & Jacob, & their forefathers; (in early & Eastern Churches) bishop, esp. of Antioch, Alexandria, Constantinople, Jerusalem, or Rome; (in R. C. Church) bishop ranking next above primates & metropolitans; founder of an order, science, &c.; venerable old man; *the* oldest living representative (*of* a class &c.). Hence **patriar·chAL** a. [f. OF *patriarche* f. L (*-cha*) f. Gk *patriarkhēs* (*patria* family f. *patēr* father + *-arkhēs* ruler)]

pa·triarchate (-kat), n. Office, see, residence, of ecclesiastical patriarch; rank of tribal patriarch. [f. med. L PATRIARCH-*atus* (-ATE[1])]

pa·triarchy, n. Patriarchal system of society, government, &c. So **pa·triarch**ISM n. [f. Gk *patriarkhia* (as PATRIARCH, see -Y[1])]

patri·cian (-shn), n. & a. Ancient Roman noble (cf. PLEBEIAN); member of a noble order in later Roman Empire; officer representing Roman Emperor in provinces of Italy & Africa; nobleman (cf. PLEBEIAN), esp. (hist.) in some Italian republics; (adj.) noble, aristocratic, esp. of the ancient Roman nobility. Hence **patri·cian**SHIP n. [f. L *patricius* (*pater -tris* father, pl. senators, nobles) + -AN]

patri·ciate (-shyat), n. Patrician order, aristocracy; rank of patrician. [f. med. L *patriciatus* (as prec., see -ATE[1])]

pă·tricide, n. Parricide (less correct & less usual than *parricide*, but sometimes preferred in the narrower sense of murder(er) of one's father). Hence **patrici·dal** a. [PATER, -CIDE]

pă·trimony, n. Property inherited from one's father or ancestors, heritage (often fig.); endowment of church &c. So **patrimō·ni**AL a. [f. F *patrimoine* f. L *patrimonium* (*pater -tris* father, see -MONY)]

pā·triot (-ot), n. One who defends or is zealous for his country's freedom or rights. Hence or cogn. **patriŏ·t**IC a., **patrio·t**ICALLY adv., **pa·triot**ISM n. [f. F *patriote* f. LL (*-ta*) f. Gk *patriōtēs* (*patrios* of one's fathers f. *patēr -tros* father, see -OT[2])]

patri·stic, a. Of (the study of the writings of) the Fathers of the Church. [f. L *pater -tris* father + -IST + -IC]

patrō·l, n., & v.i. & t. (-ll-). Going the rounds of garrison, camp, &c.; perambulation of town &c. by police; detachment of guard, police constable(s), told off for this; detachment of troops sent out to reconnoitre; (v.i.) act as p.; (v.t.) go round (camp, town, &c.) as p. [n. (thr. F *patrouille*) & vb f. F *patrouiller*, orig. = paddle in mud, earlier *patouiller*, cf. OF *patoueil* pool]

pā·tron, n. One who countenances, protects, or gives influential support to (person, cause, art, &c.); (Shop) regular customer; (also *p. saint*) tutelary saint; (Rom. Ant.) former owner of manumitted slave, (also) protector of a CLIENT; one who has right of presentation to benefice. So **pā·tron**ESS[1] n. [OF, = patron, PATTERN, f. L *patronus* (*pater -tris* father)]

pă·tronage (-ĭj), n. Support, encouragement, given by patron; right of presentation to benefice or office, as *has a great deal of p. in his hands*, (attrib.) *P. Secretary* (of the Treasury); patronizing airs; customer's support. [F (as prec., see -AGE)]

pā·tronal, a. Of a patron saint (*the p. festival* &c.). [-AL]

pă·tronize, v.t. Act as patron towards, support, encourage, (person, practice, &c.); treat condescendingly, whence **pa·tronizing**LY[2] adv. [-IZE]

patronȳ·mic, a. & n. (Name) derived from that of a father or ancestor. [f. L f. Gk *patrōnumikos* f. *patrōnumos* (*patēr -tros* father + *onoma* name), see -IC]

patrōō·n, n. (U.S., hist.). Possessor of landed estate with manorial privileges (abolished c. 1850) under Dutch governments of New York & New Jersey. [var. of PATRON]

pa·tten, n. Overshoe with wooden sole on iron ring &c., for raising wearer's shoes out of mud &c. [ME, f. F *patin*, etym. dub.]

pa·tter[1], n. Lingo of a profession or class; speechifying; rapid speech introduced into song; words of song, comedy, &c. [f. foll.]

pa·tter[2], v.t. & i. Repeat (prayers &c.) in rapid mechanical way; talk glibly. [f. PATERNOSTER]

pa·tter[3], v.i. & t., & n. Make rapid succession of taps, as rain on window-pane; run with short quick steps; cause (water &c.) to p.; (n.) succession of taps. [f. PAT[2] + -ER[5]]

pa·ttern, n., & v.t. Excellent example, as *she is a p. of domestic virtues*; (attrib.) perfect, ideal, model, (esp. of persons, as *p. wife, father*); model from which thing is to be made; sample (of tailor's cloth &c.); decorative design as executed on carpet, wall-paper, cloth, &c.; marks made by shot from gun on target; *p.-room, -shop*, part of foundry &c. in which pp. are prepared; (v.t.) model (thing *after, upon*, design &c.), decorate with p. [(vb f. n.) f. ME PATRON]

pa·tty, n. Little pie or pasty; *pattypan* (for baking p. in). [f. F *pâté* PASTY[1]]

pă·tulous, a. Open, expanded; (of boughs &c.) spreading. Hence **pa·tulous**LY[2] adv., **pa·tulous**NESS n. [f. L *patulus* (*patēre* be open) + -OUS]

pau·city, n. Smallness of number or quantity. [f. L *paucitas* (*paucus* few, see -TY)]

Paul, n. *Rob* PETER[1] *to pay P.*; *P. Pry*, inquisitive person (character in comedy by J. Poole 1825).

Pau·line, a. & n. Of St Paul, as *the P. epistles*; (n.) member of St Paul's School in London. [-INE[1]]

paulo-post-fu·ture, n. (Gk Gram.) tense expressing state resulting from future act, future-perfect; (facet.) immediate future. [L, = future a little after]

paunch (paw-, pah-), n., & v.t. Belly, stomach; ruminant's first stomach; (Naut., perh. diff. wd) thick strong mat, (*rubbing p.*) wooden shield on mast, to prevent chafing; (vb) disembowel. [f. ONF *panche* f. L *pantex -icis*]

pau·per, n. Person without means of livelihood, beggar; recipient of poor-law relief; person who may sue IN[5] *forma* *pauperis*. Hence **pau·per**DOM, **pau·per**ISM(2), **pauperiz**A·TION, nn., **pau·per**IZE(3) v.t. [L, = poor]

pause (-z), n., & v.i. Interval of inaction or silence, esp. from hesitation; *give p. to*, cause (person) to hesitate; break made in speaking or reading; (Mus.) mark (𝄐 or 𝄑) over or under note or rest that is to be lengthened indefinitely; (v.i.) make a p., wait; linger *upon* (word &c.). [(vb f. n.) F, f. L *pausa* f. Gk *pausis* (*pauō* stop)]

pā·vage, n. Paving; tax, toll, towards paving of streets. [F (as PAVE, see -AGE)]

pă·van, n. Stately dance in which dancers were elaborately dressed. [f. F *pavane* f. It. or Sp. *pavana*, etym. dub.]

pāve, v.t. Cover (street, floor, &c.) with or as with pavement (often fig., as *paved with flowers, with good intentions*); (fig.) *p.* (prepare) *the way* (*for, to*, reform &c.). Hence **pa·v**ER[1], **pa·v**IOUR [perh. after *saviour*], nn. [f. F *paver* f. L *pavire* beat, ram]

pă·vé (-ā), n. Pavement; setting of jewels placed close together. [F, p.p. as prec.]

pa·vement, n. Covering of street, floor, &c., made of stones, tiles, wooden blocks, asphalt, &c., esp. paved footway at side of road (*crazy p.*, of irregular flat stones for garden paths &c.); *p.-artist*, one who draws coloured figures on p. to get money from passers-by; (Zool.) p.-like formation of close-set teeth &c. [OF, f. L *pavimentum* (as PAVE, see -MENT)]

pavĭ·lion, n., & v.t. Tent, esp. large peaked one; light ornamental building, esp. one attached to cricket or other ground for spectators & players; projecting (usu. highly decorated) subdivision of building; part of cut gem-stone below girdle; (v.t.) enclose in, furnish with, p. [f. F *pavillon* f. L *papilionem* (nom. *-io*) butterfly, tent]

pavona·zzo (pah-, -ătsō), a. & n. (Marble) with peacock-coloured markings. [It.]

pă·vonine, a. Of, like, a peacock. [f. L *pavoninus* (*pavo -onis* peacock, see -INE[1])]

paw[1], n. Foot of beast having claws or nails, opp. to HOOF; (colloq.) hand, person's handwriting. [f. OF *powe*, prob. of Frank. orig.]

paw[2], v.t. & i. Strike with paw; (of horse) strike (ground), strike ground, with hoofs; (colloq.) handle awkwardly or rudely. [f. prec.]

paw·ky, a. (Sc., dial.). Sly, arch. Hence **paw·ki**LY[2] adv., **paw·ki**NESS n. [*pawk* trick, etym. dub., + -Y[2]]

pawl, n., & v.t. Lever with catch for teeth of wheel or bar; (Naut.) short bar used to prevent capstan, windlass, &c., from recoiling; (v.t.) secure (capstan &c.) with p. [?]

pawn[1], n. Piece of smallest size & value in chess (often fig. of persons). [f. AF *poun* f. L *pedonem* (nom. *-o*) foot-soldier (*pes pedis* foot)]

pawn[2], n. Thing, person, left in another's keeping as security, pledge, (now chiefly fig.); state of being pledged, esp. *in, at, p.*; *pawnbroker*, one who lends money upon interest on security of personal property pawned; *pawnbroking*, his occupation; *pawnshop*, his place of business. [f. OF *pan*, prob. = OFris. & Du. *pand*, G *pfand*]

pawn[3], v.t. Deposit (thing) as security for payment of money or performance of action; (fig.) pledge (one's life, honour, word). [prec.]

pawnee·, n. Person with whom pawn is deposited. [-EE]

pax, n. Tablet with representation of Crucifixion &c. kissed at Mass by priests & congregation, osculatory; the kiss of peace as liturgical form at High Mass; *p. Romana, Britannica*, abstention from war enforced on States subject to the Roman, British, empire; *p. vobis*, peace to you; (School slang, as int.) peace!, truce!. [L, = peace]

pa·xwax, n. (dial., colloq.). Stout tendon extending from dorsal vertebrae to occiput in man & other mammals. [earlier *faxwax*, prob. f. OE *feax* hair + **weax* growth]

pay[1], n. Payment; *in the p.* (employment) *of*; wages; *p.-day*, day on which payment is (to be) made, (Stock Exch.) day on which transfer of stock has to be paid for; *pay·master*, official who pays troops, workmen, &c. (often fig.), *paymaster general*, officer at head of a department of Treasury. [f. OF *paie*, as foll.]

pay[2], v.t. & i. (paid). Give (person) what is due in discharge of debt or *for* services done or goods received; *p. off*, p. in full & discharge or be quit of (ship's crew, creditor, &c.); (fig.) reward, recompense; *p.* (person) *out*, punish him; *p. him in his own* COIN; recompense (work); hand over (money owed *to* person, or w. double object); hand over the amount of (debt, wages, ransom, tithes); *p. in*, p. to one's own or another's banking account; *p. one's way*, not get into debt; *p. through the* NOSE, *p. the* PIPER; *p. up*, p. full amount of (arrears, or abs.); render, bestow, (attention, respect, court, compliment, *to*); (of business &c.) yield adequate return, yield adequate return to (person); *p. for*, hand over the price of, bear the cost of (*p. f.* one's WHISTLE), (fig.) be punished for (fault &c.); *p. off*, (of ship) fall off to leeward when helm is put up; (Naut.) *p. out, away*, let out (rope) by slackening it. Hence **pay**EE·, **pay·**ER[1], nn. [f. F *payer* f. L *pacare* appease (*pax pacis* peace)]

pay[3], v.t. (naut.). Smear with pitch, tar, &c., as defence against wet. [f. ONF *peier* f. L *picare* (*pix picis* pitch)]

pay·able, a. That must be paid, due; that may be paid; (of mine &c.) profitable. [-ABLE]

pay·ment, n. Paying; amount paid; (fig.) recompense. [f. F *paiement* (PAY²)]

pay·nim, n. (archaic). Pagan, esp. Mohammedan (often attrib.). [f. OF *paienime* f. LL *paganismus* (PAGAN, see -ISM)]

pay·nize, v.t. Impregnate (wood) with certain preservatives. [*Payne,* inventor, -IZE]

paysa·ge (-zahzh), n. Rural scene, landscape; landscape painting, so **pay·sag**IST (-*a*j-) n. [F]

pea (pē), n. Leguminous plant whose seeds are used for food; its seed, as *green pp.* (gathered unripe for food); SWEET *p.*; *as like as two pp.*, undistinguishable; *peanut,* (plant whose fruit is a pod containing) seed used as food & yielding oil; *p.-shooter,* tube from which dried pp. are shot; *p.-soup* (made from esp. dried pp.); *p.-souper* (colloq.), thick yellow fog; *p.-soupy,* (of fog) thick & yellow. [back formation f. PEASE taken as pl.]

peace, n. Freedom from, cessation of, war, as *p. with honour, p. at any price, make* (bring about) *p.*; *a* treaty of p. between two powers at war; freedom from civil disorder; *the* (*king's*) *p.*, general p. of the realm as secured by law, as *commission,* JUSTICE, *of the p., be sworn of the p.* (made a magistrate); quiet, tranquillity; (in & after bibl. use) *p. be with you, p. to his ashes!*; mental calm, as *p. of mind, conscience*; *at p.*, in state of friendliness, not at strife (*with*); *hold* one's *p.*, keep silence; *keep the p.*, prevent, refrain from, strife; *make* (person's, one's) *p.*, bring person, oneself, back into friendly relations (*with*); *peacemaker,* one who brings about p., (facet.) revolver, warship, &c.; *p.-offering,* propitiatory gift, (bibl.) offering presented as thanksgiving to God; *P. Pact,* renunciation of war drawn up by U.S. & signed by 15 Powers in Paris 1928; *p.-pipe,* tobacco-pipe as token of p. among N.-Amer. Indians. [f. OF *pais* f. L *pacem* (nom. *pax*)]

pea·ceable, a. Disposed, tending, to peace; free from disturbance, peaceful. Hence **pea·ceable**NESS n., **pea·ceab**LY² adv. [f. OF *paisible* (as prec., see -BLE)]

pea·ceful, a. Characterized by, belonging to a state of, peace. Hence **pea·ceful**LY² adv., **pea·ceful**NESS n. [-FUL]

peach¹, n. Large fruit, usu. round, with downy white or yellow skin flushed with red, highly flavoured sweet pulp, & rough stone; (also *p.-tree*) tree bearing this; *p.-blow,* (glaze of) delicate purplish-pink colour; *p. brandy,* spirituous liquor from p. juice; *p.-colour(ed),* (of) soft pale red. [f. OF *pesche* f. LL *persica* f. L *persicum* (*malum*), lit. Persian apple]

peach², v.i. (now slang). Turn informer; inform (*against, upon,* accomplice). [earlier *appeach* f. OF *empechier* IMPEACH]

pea·-chick, n. Young pea-fowl.

pea·chy, a. Like a peach, esp. (of cheeks) in colour & softness. Hence **pea·chi**NESS n. [-Y²]

pea·cock, n., & v.t. & i. Bird with splendid plumage & tail that can be expanded erect like fan (often as type of ostentatious display; *proud as a p.*); *p. blue,* lustrous blue of p.'s neck; *p. butterfly,* European butterfly with ocellated wings; *p. coal* (iridescent); *p.-fish,* fish with brilliant green, blue, red, & white colouring; (v.refl.) plume one*self,* make display; (v.i.) strut about ostentatiously, whence **pea·cock**ERY (4) n. Hence **pea·cock**ISH¹, **pea·cock**LIKE, aa. [(vb f. n.) f. OE *péa, pawa,* f. L *pavo,* + COCK]

pea·fowl, n. Peacock or peahen. [see prec.]

pea·hen, n. Female of the peacock. [see PEACOCK]

pea·-jacket, n. Sailor's short overcoat of coarse woollen cloth. [f. obs. *pee* f. MDu. *pîe* (now *pij*) pea-jacket + JACKET]

peak¹, n. Projecting part of brim of cap; (Naut.) narrow part of ship's hold esp. (also *forepeak*) at bow, (also) upper outer corner of sail extended by gaff; pointed top, esp. of mountain; point e.g. of beard; highest point in curve or record of fluctuations (*p.-load,* maximum of electric power, traffic, &c.). Hence **peak**ED², **pea·k**Y², aa. [f. 16th c., var. of PIKE]

peak², v.i. Waste away, esp. (Shakspere) *p. & pine*; (p.p.) sharp-featured, pinched. So **peak**Y² a., sickly, puny. [?]

peak³, v.t. & i. (naut.). Tilt (yard) vertically; place (oars) APEAK; (of whale) raise (tail, flukes), raise tail or flukes, straight up in diving vertically. [f. APEAK]

peaky. See PEAK¹, PEAK².

peal, n., & v.i. & t. Loud ringing of bell(s), esp. series of changes on set of bells; set of bells; loud volley of sound, esp. of thunder or laughter; (v.i.) sound forth in a p.; (v.t.) utter sonorously; *p. bells,* ring them in pp. [(vb f. n.) perh. short for APPEAL]

pear (pār), n. A fleshy fruit, tapering towards stalk; *p.-shaped*; *p.-tree*; PRICKLY *p.* [OE *pere* f. LL *pira* f. L *pirum*]

pearl¹ (perl), n. Concretion, usu. white or bluish-grey, formed within shell of *p.-oyster* & other bivalve molluscs, having beautiful lustre & highly prized as gem; MOTHER¹-*of-p.*; SEED *p.*; precious thing, finest example (*of* its kind); *cast pp. before swine,* offer good thing to one incapable of appreciating it; p.-like thing, e.g. dew-drop, tear, tooth; size of TYPE; small fragment of various substances; *p.-ash,* potassium carbonate; *p.-barley, -sago,* &c. (reduced by attrition to small rounded grains); *p.-diver,* one who dives for p.-oysters; *p.-fisher,* one who fishes for pp.; *p.-fishery,* his occupation, place of this; *p.-powder, -white,* cosmetic used to whiten skin; *p.-shell,* mother of-p. as naturally found. Hence **pearl**ED², **pear·l**Y², aa.,

pear·liness n. [f. F *perle*, med. L *perla*, etym. dub.]

pearl², v.t. & i. Sprinkle with pearly drops; make pearly in colour &c.; reduce (barley &c.) to small pearls; form pearl-like drops; fish for pearls. [f. prec.]

pearl³, n. One of a row of fine loops forming decorative edging on pillow-lace &c. [prob. var. of PURL]

pear·lies (per·līz), n. pl. Costermongers' dress with many pearl buttons.

pear·main (pār-), n. Kind of apple. [f. OF *permain* prob. f. L **parmanus* of Parma]

pea·sant (pĕz-), n. Countryman, rustic. [AF *paisant* f. L *pagensis* of a canton (*pagus*)]

pea·santry, n. (Set of) peasants. [-RY]

pease (-z), n. Peas, esp. in *p.-pudding*; (archaic) *peasecod*, pea-pod. [OE *pise* pea, pl. *pisan*, f. LL *pisa* f. L *pisum* f. Gk *pison*; cf. PEA]

peat¹, n. (Cut piece of) vegetable matter decomposed by water & partly carbonized, used for fuel; *p.-bog*, *-moss*, bog composed of p.; *p.-reek*, smoke of, whisky distilled over, p.-fire. Hence **pea·t**ERY(3) n., **pea·t**Y² a. [13th c. *pete*, etym. dub.]

peat², n. (archaic). Girl, belle, (esp. *proud p.*). [?]

pe·bble, n. Small stone worn & rounded by action of water; colourless transparent rock-crystal used for spectacles, lens of this; kinds of agate or other gem. Hence **pe·bbl**Y² a. [?]

pébrine (pĕbrē·n), n. Epidemic disease of silkworms characterized by black spots. [F, f. Pr. *pebrino* (*pebre* PEPPER)]

pe·ccable, a. Liable to sin. Hence **pecca**BI·LITY n. [f. med. L *peccabilis* (*peccare* sin, see -BLE)]

peccadi·llo, n. Trifling offence. [f. Sp. *pecadillo*, dim. of *pecado* sin, as foll.]

pe·ccant, a. Sinning; (Med.) morbid, inducing disease. So **pe·cc**ANCY n. [f. L *peccare* sin, see -ANT]

pe·ccary, n. American gregarious quadruped allied to swine. [f. native *pakira*]

peccā·vi, sent. & n. I have sinned, esp. *cry p.*; (n.) this confession. [L]

peck¹, n. Measure of capacity for dry goods, =2 gallons; vessel used for this; *a p.* (large number, amount) *of troubles*, *of dirt*. [ME & OF *pek*, etym. dub.]

peck², v.t. & i., & n. Strike (thing) with beak; *p. out*, pluck out thus; make (hole &c.) thus; aim *at* (thing) with beak, (fig.) carp *at*; (colloq.) eat (food or abs.), esp. in nibbling fashion; break (ground, wall, &c., *up*, *down*, &c.) with pointed tool; (n.) stroke with beak, mark made with this, (slang) victuals. [prob. var. of PICK²]

peck³, v.t. & i. (slang). Throw (stone), throw stones (*at*). [dial. var. of *pitch*²]

pe·cker, n. Bird that pecks (chiefly in comb., esp. WOOD*p.*); kind of hoe; (slang) *keep your p.* (spirits, perh. orig. = beak) *up*. [-ER¹]

pe·ckish, a. (colloq.). Hungry. [-ISH¹]

Pecksniff, n. Unctuous hypocrite prating of benevolence &c. [in *Martin Chuzzlewit*]

pe·cten, n. (zool.). Comb-like structure of various kinds in animal bodies, so **pe·c·tin**ATE², **-ated**, aa., **pectin**A·TION n.; scallop. [L, gen. *-tinis*, = comb]

pe·ctin, n. (chem.). White neutral substance formed in fruits from pectose by ripening. So **pe·ct**IC a. [f. Gk *pēktos* congealed (*pēgnumi* make solid) + -IN]

pe·ctoral, n. & a. Ornamental breastplate, esp. that of Jewish high priest. (Adj.) of, for, good for diseases of, the breast or chest; worn on the breast (*p. cross*, by bishops). [(partly thr. F) f. L *pectoralis* a., *-le* n. (*pectus -oris* breast, see -AL)]

pe·ctose, n. (chem.). Insoluble substance related to cellulose & found with it in unripe fruits &c. [as PECTIN, see -OSE²]

pĕ·culate, v.t. & i. Embezzle (money, or abs.). So **pecul**A·TION, **pe·culat**OR², nn. [f. L *peculari* (as foll.), see -ATE³]

pecū·liar, a. & n. Belonging exclusively *to*; belonging to the individual, esp. one's *own p.* (character &c.); particular, special, as *a point of p. interest*; strange, odd, as *a p. flavour, he has always been a little p.*; *p. people*, the Jews, (in wider sense) God's elect, (*P. People*) modern religious sect having no church organization & relying on prayer alone for cure of disease. (N.) p. property, privilege, &c.; (Hist.) parish, church, exempt from jurisdiction of diocese in which it lies, (*P-*) one of the P. People. [f. L *peculiaris* of private property (*peculium* f. *pecu* cattle, see -AR¹)]

peculia·rity, n. Being peculiar; characteristic; oddity. [-ITY]

pecu·liarly, adv. As regards oneself alone, individually, as *does not affect him p.*; especially, more than usually, as *p. annoying*; oddly, as *they dress p.* [-LY²]

pecū·niary, a. (Consisting) of money, as *p. aid, considerations*; (of offence) having p. penalty. Hence **pecu·niari**LY² adv. [f. L *pecuniarius* (*pecunia* money f. *pecu* cattle, see -ARY¹)]

pĕ·dagogue (-ŏg), n. Schoolmaster, teacher, (usu. contempt. implying pedantry). Hence or cogn. **pedago·g**IC(AL) (-g-, -j-) aa., **pedago·gical**LY² adv., **pe·dagog(u)**ISM(1) n. [OF, f. L f. Gk *paidagōgos* (*pais paidos* boy + *-agōgos* f. *agō* lead)]

pe·dagŏgy (-gĭ, -jĭ), n. Science of teaching. So **pedago·g**ICS n. [f. F *pédagogie* f. Gk *paidagōgia*, as prec.]

pĕ·dal¹, n., & v.i. & t. (-ll-). (In organ) each of the wooden keys played upon by the feet, (also) foot-lever for drawing out several stops at once or other purposes; (in piano) foot-lever for making the tone fuller (*loud p.*) or softer (*soft p.*); foot-lever in various machines, esp. bicycle or tricycle; (Mus.) note sustained in one part, usu. bass, through successive harmonies some of which are independent of it; (v.i.) play on organ pp., work bicycle pp.; (v.t.) work (bicycle) thus. [prob. f. F *pedale* f. It. *pedale* f. L as foll.]

pĕ·dal[2], a. (zool.). Of the feet or foot (esp. of mollusc). [f. L *pedalis* (*pes pedis* foot, see -AL)]

pĕ·dant, n. One who overrates or parades book-learning or technical knowledge or insists on strict adherence to formal rules; one who is possessed by a theory, doctrinaire. Hence or cogn. **peda·ntic** a., **peda·nticALLY** adv., **pe·dantIZE**(2, 3) v.t. & i., **pedantŏ·CRACY**, **pe·dantRY**(1, 4, 5), nn. [(perh. thr. F *pédant*) f. It. *pedante*, perh. cogn. w. PEDAGOGUE]

pĕ·date (-*at*), a. (Zool.) footed; (Bot., of leaf) having divisions like toes or bird's claws. [f. L *pedatus* (*pes pedis* foot, see -ATE[2])]

pe·ddle, v.i. & t. Follow occupation of pedlar; busy oneself with trifles; deal out in small quantities, retail, (usu. fig.). [?]

pĕ·destal, n., & v.t. (-ll-). Base supporting column in construction; base of statue &c.; each of two supports of kneehole table; foundation (lit. & fig.); movable cupboard for chamber-pots; (v.t.) set, support, on p. [f. F *piédestal* f. It. *piedestallo* foot of stall (*piè* foot f. L *pes pedis* + *di* of + *stallo* STALL)]

pede·strian, a. & n. Going, performed, on foot; of walking; prosaic, dull, uninspired; (n.) one who walks, esp. as athletic performance, whence **pede·strianISM**(2) n., **pede·strianIZE**(2) v.i. [f. L *pedester -tris* + -IAN]

pĕ·dicel, pe·dicle, nn. (bot., zool.). Small (esp. subordinate, cf. PEDUNCLE) stalk-like structure in plant or animal. Hence **pe·dicellATE**[2], **pedi·culATE**[2], (-*at*) aa. [f. L (-*cel*) *pedicellus* double dim., (-*cle*) *pediculus* dim., f. *pes pedis* foot, see -CULE]

pedi·cular, -lous, aa. Lousy. So **pediculo·SIS** n. [f. L *pedicularis*, *-losus* (*pediculus* louse, see -AR[1], -OUS)]

pĕ·digree, n. Genealogical table; ancestral line (of man or animal); derivation (of word); ancient descent; (attrib.) having known line of descent, as *p. cattle.* Hence **pe·digreED**[2] a. [earlier *pedegru* prob. f. F *pié de grue* crane's foot, mark denoting succession in pp. (*pied* foot f. L *pes pedis* + *de* of + *grue* crane f. L *grus*)]

pĕ·diment, n. Triangular part crowning front of building in Grecian style, esp. over portico; similarly placed member of same or other form in Roman & Renaissance styles. Hence **pedime·ntAL, pe·dimentED**[2], aa. [earlier *peremint*, perh. corrupt. of PYRAMID]

pe·dlar, n. Travelling vendor of small wares usu. carried in pack; (fig.) retailer (*of* gossip &c.); *p.'s French*, thieves' cant. Hence **pe·dlaRY** n. [prob. f. Sc. *pedder* prob. f. *ped* basket, etym. dub.; found long before PEDDLE]

pedŏ·meter, n. Instrument for estimating distance travelled on foot by recording number of steps taken. [f. F *pédomètre* f. L *pes pedis* foot + -O- + -METER]

pedu·ncle, n. (Bot.) stalk of flower, fruit, or cluster, esp. main stalk bearing solitary flower or subordinate stalks (*pedicels*); (Zool.) stalklike process in animal body. Hence **pedu·nculAR**[1], **pedu·nculATE**[2] (-*at*), aa. [f. L *pes pedis* foot + -UNCLE]

peek, v.i. Peep, peer, (*in, out*, &c.); *p.-a-boo* (now U.S.), = BO-PEEP. [ME *pike*, etym. dub.]

peel[1], n. (hist.). Small square tower built in 16th c. in border counties of England & Scotland. [earlier = palisade, ult. f. L *palus* stake]

peel[2], n. Shovel, esp. baker's for thrusting loaves &c. into oven. [f. OF *pele* f. L *pala*]

peel[3], v.t. & i., & n. Strip the peel, rind, bark, &c., from (orange, potato, tree, &c.); take *off* (skin, peel, &c.); (archaic, from *Isa.* xviii. 2, perh. mistransl.) *scattered & peeled* (pillaged); (intr., of tree, animal body, &c.) become bare of bark, skin, &c., (of bark, surface, &c.) come off or *off* like p., (of person, now slang) strip for exercise &c.; (n.) rind, outer coating, of fruit, *candied p.* (usu. of citron). Hence **pee·ler**[1] [-ER[1](1, 2)] n., **pee·LING**[1] (2) n. (esp. *potato peelings*). [= PILL[2], orig. in all senses]

pee·ler[2], n. (Colloq.) policeman; (Hist.). member of Irish constabulary, founded under Peel's secretaryship. [Robert *Peel*, cf. BOBBY, + -ER[1]]

Pee·lite, n. Conservative siding with Sir R. Peel when he introduced measure for repeal of Corn-laws in 1846. [-ITE[1]]

peep[1], v.i., & n. (Make) feeble shrill sound of young birds, mice, &c., chirp, squeak. [(n. f. vb) var. of PIPE[2]]

peep[2], v.i. Look through narrow aperture (*at, into*, &c.); look furtively (*peeping Tom*, type of prurient curiosity, in tale of Godiva); (of daylight, flower, distant object) come cautiously or partly into view, emerge, (often *out*); (fig., of qualities &c.) show itself unconsciously. [f. 15th c., cf. PEEK]

peep[3], n. Furtive or peering glance; first appearance, esp. *of dawn, of day*; *p.-of-day boys*, Protestant organization in Ireland (1784–95) searching opponents' houses at daybreak for arms; *p.-hole*, small hole to peep through; *p.-show*, small exhibition of pictures &c. viewed through lens in small orifice (also fig.); *p. sight*, aperture sight of some rifles. [f. prec.]

pee·per, n. One who peeps; (slang) eye. [PEEP[2] + -ER[1]]

peer[1], n. An equal in civil standing or rank; equal in any respect, as *you will* *not easily find his p.*, whence **peer·**LESS a., **peer·less**LY[2] adv., **peer·less**NESS n.; member of one of the degrees (duke, marquis, earl, viscount, baron) of nobility in United Kingdom, whence **peer·**ESS[1] n.; *pp. of the realm* or *United Kingdom* (all of whom may sit in House of Lords), *pp. of Scotland, of Ireland,* (represented in H. of Lords by 16 elected to each parliament, by 28 elected for life); noble (of any country). [ME & OF *per* f. L *par* equal]

peer[2], v.t. & i. Rank with, equal; rank as equal *with*; make (man) a peer. [f. OF *perer* f. L *pariare* (*par* equal)]

peer[3], v.i. Look narrowly (*into, at,* &c.); appear, peep out; come in sight. [?]

peer·age (-ĭj), n. The peers; nobility, aristocracy; rank of peer; book containing list of peers with genealogy &c. [-AGE]

peeved, a. (slang). Irritated. [PEEV(ISH), -ED[1]]

pee·vish, a. Querulous, irritable. Hence **pee·vish**LY[2] adv., **pee·vish**NESS n. [?]

peewit. See PEWIT.

peg[1], n. Pin, bolt, of wood, metal, &c., usu. round & slightly tapering, for holding together parts of framework &c., stopping up vent of cask, hanging hats &c. on, holding ropes of tent, marking cribbage score, &c.; *round peg in square* HOLE[1]; CLOTHES-*p.*; (fig.) *a p. to hang* (discourse &c.) *on*, (occasion, pretext, theme); a drink, esp. of brandy & soda-water; *take* (person) *down a p. or two*, humble him; *p.-top*, pear-shaped spinning-top with metal p., *p.-top trousers* (wide at hips, narrow at ankles). [prob. of LG orig., cf. dial. Du. *peg*]

peg[2], v.t. & i. Fix (thing *down, in, out,* &c.) with peg; *p. down*, restrict (*to* rules &c.); (Stock Exch.) prevent price of (stock &c.) from falling (rising) by freely buying (selling) at given price; strike, pierce, aim *at*, with peg, (slang) throw (stone), throw stones &c., (*at*); mark (score) with pegs on cribbage-board; mark *out* boundaries of (mining claim &c.); *p.* (*away*), work persistently (*at*); drive pp. into (cricket-bat); *p. out*, (Croquet) hit peg with ball as final stroke in game, (slang) die, be ruined. [f. prec.]

pĕ·gamoid, n. Kind of imitation leather used in coach-building &c. [?]

Pĕ·gasus, n. Winged horse that with stroke of hoof caused fountain Hippocrene to flow on Mt Helicon, (fig.) poetic genius. [L, f. Gk *Pēgasos* (*pēgē* fount)]

peignoir (pā·nwar, *or as F*), n. Woman's loose dressing-gown worn while hair is combed or on coming out of bath. [F (*peigner* comb)]

peine forte et dure (F), n. Severe & hard punishment, i.e. pressing to death, inflicted on person charged with felony who refused to plead.

pē·jorative (*or* pĭjŏ·r-), a. & n. Depreciatory (word), as *the p. suffix -aster.* [f. L *pejorare* make worse (*pejor*), see -ATIVE]

pĕ·kan, n. N.-Amer. carnivorous beast of weasel family, valued for fur. [f. native *pékané*]

peke, n. PEKINESE dog. [abbr.]

pē·ki·n (-ĭn, -ĭng), n. Kind of silk stuff; [f. F *pékin* as used by Napoleon I's soldiers] civilian. [f. F *pékin* f. Chin. *Pe-king* northern capital]

Pēkinē·se (-z), n. & a. (Inhabitant) of Pekin; Chinese pug-dog with long silky hair. [-ESE]

pĕ·koe (-ō), n. Superior kind of black tea. [f. Chin. *pek-ho* (*pek* white + *ho* down), leaves being picked young with down on them]

pĕ·lage (-ĭj), n. Fur, hair, wool, &c., of quadruped. [F (OF *pel* hair + -AGE)]

Pelā·gian[1], a. & n. (Follower) of the monk Pelagius (4th–5th c.), who denied doctrine of original sin. Hence **Pela·gian**ISM n. [-AN]

pelā·gian[2], a. & n. Of, inhabiting, inhabitant of, the open sea. [f. L *pelagius* (*pelagus* sea f. Gk *pelagos*) + -AN]

pelă·gic, a. Of, performed on, the open sea, esp. *p. sealing.* [f. L *pelagicus* (as prec., -IC)]

pĕlargō·nium n. Genus of plants with showy flowers & fragrant leaves (pop. called *geranium*). [f. Gk *pelargos* stork]

Pela·sgic (-zj- *or* -zg-), a. Of the Pelasgians, an ancient race on coasts & islands of Eastern Mediterranean & Aegean; *P. architecture*, oldest form of masonry found in Greece. [f. L *Pelasgicus* (*Pelasgi* f. Gk *Pelasgoi*, see -IC)]

pĕ·lerine (or -ēn), n. Woman's long narrow cape or tippet. [f. F *pèlerine*, fem. of *pèlerin* PILGRIM]

pelf, n. Money, wealth, (usu. contempt.). [f. OF *pelfre*, etym. dub.]

pĕ·lican, n. Large water-fowl with pouch for storing fish, fabled to feed its young with its own blood. [f. LL *pelicanus* f. Gk *pelekan*, cf. *pelekas* woodpecker perh. f. *pelekus* axe]

peli·sse (-ēs), n. Woman's mantle with armholes or sleeves, reaching to ankles; child's outdoor garment worn over other clothes; hussar officer's fur-trimmed undress jacket. [F, f. L *pellicia* (*vestis* garment) of fur (*pellis* skin)]

pellā·gra, n. Disease frequent in Lombardy, marked by cracking of skin & often ending in insanity. So **pella·gr**OUS a. [perh. f. It. *pelle agra* rough skin]

pe·llet, n., & v.t. Small ball of paper, bread, &c.; pill; small shot; circular boss in coins &c.; (vb) hit with (esp. paper) pp. [f. F *pelote* f. med. L *pelota* f. L *pila* ball]

pe·llicle, n. Thin skin; membrane; film. Hence **pelli·cul**AR[1] a. [f. L *pellicula*, dim. of *pellis* skin]

pe·llitory, n. 1. (*P. of Spain*) plant with pungent-flavoured root, used as local irritant &c. 2. (*P. of the wall*) low bushy plant with greenish flowers growing on or at foot of walls. [1. earlier *pelleter* f. L f. Gk *purethron* feverfew, cf. *puretos* fever. 2. f. L *parietaria* (*paries -etis* wall)]

pe·ll-me·ll, adv., a., & n. In disorder, promiscuously; headlong, recklessly; (adj.) confused, tumultuous; (n.) confusion, medley, mêlée. [f. F *pêle-mêle* (*pêle* etym. dub. +*mêle* prob. f. *mêler* mix f. LL *misculare* f. L *miscēre*)]

pellū·cid, a. Transparent, clear; clear in style or expression; mentally clear. Hence or cogn. **pelluci·dɪᴛʏ** n., **pellu·cidʟʏ**[2] adv. [f. L *pellucidus* f. ᴘᴇʀ(*lucēre* shine), see -ɪᴅ[1]]

Pĕ·lmanism, n. A 20th-c. memory-training system. [?]

pelō·ta, n. Basque game like tennis, played with ball & wicker racket. [Sp., =ball, f. *pella* f. L *pila* ball]

pelt[1], n. Skin of sheep or goat with short wool on; raw skin of sheep &c. stripped of wool or fur, so **pe·ltʀʏ**(1) n. [cogn. w. obs. *pell* skin f. OF *pel* f. L *pellis*]

pelt[2], v.t. & i., & n. Assail with missiles (also fig.); (intr., of rain &c.) beat with violence; strike repeatedly with missiles, go on firing *at*; (n.) pelting; (*at*) *full p.* (speed). [?]

pe·lta, n. (pl. *-ae*). Small light shield of ancient Greeks, Romans, &c.; (Bot.) shield-like structure, so **pe·ltᴀᴛᴇ**[2](2) a. [L, f. Gk *peltē*]

pe·lvis, n. (anat.). Basin-shaped cavity formed in most vertebrates by haunch-bones with sacrum & other vertebrae, whence **pe·lvɪᴄ** a.; basin-like cavity of kidney. [L, =basin]

Pe·mbroke (-ŏŏk), n. Town in Wales; *P. table, p.*, table on four fixed legs with hinged flaps that can be spread out & supported on other legs.

pe·mmican, n. N.-Amer.-Ind. cake of dried & pounded meat mixed with melted fat; beef so treated & flavoured with currants &c. for travellers; (fig.) condensed literary matter. [f. native *pimecan* (*pime* fat)]

pe·mphigus, n. (path.). Formation of watery vesicles or eruptions on skin of body. Hence **pe·mphigᴏɪᴅ, pe·mphigᴏᴜs,** aa. [f. Gk *pemphix -igos* bubble]

pen[1], n. Small enclosure for cows, sheep, poultry, &c., or for other purposes; (W.-Ind.) farm, plantation. [OE *penn*, etym. dub.]

pen[2], v.t. Enclose, shut *up*, shut *in*; shut up (cattle &c.) in pen. [prob. f. prec.]

pen[3], n., & v.t. Quill-feather with quill pointed & split into two sections, for writing with ink; similar instrument of steel, gold, &c., fitted into rod of wood &c. (*penholder*); writing, style of this, as *made a living with his p., wields a formidable p.*; ꜰᴏᴜɴᴛᴀɪɴ-*p.*; *p. & ink*, instruments of writing, writing; *p.-&-ink* a., drawn, written, with these; *p.-feather*, quill-feather of bird's wing; *penknife*, small knife usu. carried in pocket; *pe·nman* (-an), one who writes a (*good, bad, &c.*) hand, author; *penmanship*, skill in writing, style of handwriting, action or style of literary composition; *p.-name*, literary pseudonym; *penwiper*, appliance usu. of small pieces of cloth for wiping p. after use; (v.t.) write, compose & write, (letter &c.). Hence **pe·nꜰᴜʟ** n. [(vb. f. n.) f. OF *penne* f. L *penna* feather]

pen[4], n. Female swan. [?]

pē·nal, a. Of punishment; concerned with inflicting this, as *p. laws*; (of offence) punishable, esp. by law; inflicted as punishment, as *p. servitude*, imprisonment with hard labour; used as place of punishment, as *a p. colony*. Hence **pe·nalʟʏ**[2] adv. [f. F *pénal* f. L *penalis* (*poena* penalty f. Gk *poinē* fine, see -ᴀʟ)]

pē·nalize, v.t. Make, declare, (action) penal; (Sport.) subject (competitor, also fig.) to penalty or comparative disadvantage. [-ɪᴢᴇ]

pĕ·nalty, n. Punishment, esp. (payment of) sum of money, for breach of law, rule, or contract; *the p. of*, disadvantage resulting from (quality &c.); (Sport.) disadvantage imposed on competitor for breaking rule or winning previous contest. [ult. f. med. L *poenalitas* (as ᴘᴇɴᴀʟ, see -ᴛʏ)]

pĕ·nance, n., & v.t. (Rom. & Gk churches) a sacrament including contrition, confession, satisfaction, & absolution; act of self-mortification as expression of penitence, esp. one imposed by priest; *do p.*, perform such act; (v.t.) impose p. on. [f. OF *peneance* f. L *paenitentia* (as ᴘᴇɴɪᴛᴇɴᴛ, see -ᴀɴᴄᴇ)]

Penā·tēs, n. pl. (Rom. myth.). Household gods. [L, perh. f. *penus* sanctuary]

pence. See ᴘᴇɴɴʏ.

penchant (F), n. Inclination, liking, (*for*). [F, part. of *pencher* slope f. L **pendicare* (*pendēre* hang)]

pe·ncil[1] (-sl), n. (Archaic) artist's paint-brush (still tech. of small brushes, esp. in comb., as *sable-, camelhair, p.*); (fig.) painter's art or style; instrument for drawing or writing, esp. of black lead enclosed in cylinder of wood or in metal case with tapering end; (Optics) set of rays meeting at a point; (Geom.) figure formed by set of straight lines meeting at a point; p.-shaped object; *p.-case*, holder, usu. of metal, for p. or p.-lead. [f. OF *pincel* ult. f. L *penicillum* dim. of *peniculus* brush dim. of ᴘᴇɴɪs]

pe·ncil[2] (-sl), v.t. (-ll-). Tint or mark (as) with lead pencil; jot down with pencil; enter (horse's name) in betting-book, whence **pencilʟᴇʀ**[1] **n.** (slang), book-maker's clerk at race-meetings; (esp. in p.p.) mark delicately with thin concentric lines of colour or shading. [f. prec.]

pe·ndant[1], **-ent**[1], n. Hanging ornament,

esp. one attached to necklace, bracelet, etc.; (Naut., also *pennant*) short rope hanging from head of mast &c. with eye at lower end for receiving hooks of tackles, (also) tapering flag, esp. that flown at mast-head of vessel in commission, *broad p.*, short swallow-tailed p. distinguishing commodore's ship in squadron; shank & ring of watch by which it is suspended; (also pron. as F) match, parallel, companion, complement, (*to*). [F (*-ant*), f. *pendre* hang f. L *pendēre*, see -ANT]

pe·ndent², -ant², a. Hanging; overhanging; undecided, pending, whence **pe·nd**ENCY n.; (Gram.) of which the construction is incomplete. [as prec.]

pende·ntĕ lī·tĕ, adv. Pending the suit. [L]

pende·ntive, n. (arch.) Each of spherical triangles formed by intersection of dome by two pairs of opposite arches springing from the four supporting columns. [F (*-if, -ive*), adj., as PENDANT¹ + -IVE]

pe·nding, a. & prep. Undecided, awaiting decision or settlement, as *a suit, a treaty, was then p.*; (prep.) during, as *p. these negotiations* (orig. = while these negotiations are p.), until, as *p. his return*. [after F PENDANT², -ING²]

pendrā·gon, n. Ancient British or Welsh prince. [W, = chief leader (*pen* head + DRAGON standard)]

pe·ndūlate, v.i. Swing like a pendulum; (fig.) be undecided. [as foll. + -ATE³]

pe·ndūline, a. (Of nest) suspended; (of bird) building such nest. [F (as foll. + -INE¹)]

pe·ndūlous, a. Suspended, hanging down, (esp. of bird's nest, flower, &c.); oscillating. Hence **pe·ndulous**LY² adv. [f. L *pendulus* (*pendēre* hang) + -OUS]

pe·ndūlum, n. Body suspended so as to be free to swing, esp. rod with weighted end regulating movement of clock's works; *swing of the p.*, alternation of power between political parties; COMPENSATION *p.*; person, thing, that oscillates (lit. & fig.); (Billiards) *p. cannon* or *stroke*, succession of cannons off two balls jammed in pocket-mouth. [f. L neut. adj. as prec.]

Penĕ·lope (-ĭ), n. Chaste wife. [f. Gk *Pēnelopē, -peia*, wife of Odysseus]

pĕnĕtrā·lia, n. pl. Innermost shrine or recesses. [L, pl. of *penetral*, cogn. w. foll.]

pĕ·nĕtrate, v.t. & i. Find access into or through, pass through; (of sight) pierce through (darkness, thicket, &c.); permeate; imbue (person, thing, *with*); (fig.) see into, find out, discern, (person's mind, meaning, design, the truth); (intr.) make a way (*into, through, to*); (part.) gifted with or suggestive of insight, (of voice &c.) easily heard through or above other sounds. Hence or cogn. **penetra**BI·LITY, **penetr**A·TION, **pe·netrat**OR², nn., **pe·netra**BLE, **pe·netrat**IVE, aa., **pe·netrating**LY², **pe·netrative**LY², advv. [f. L *penetrare*, cogn. w. *penitus* interior, see -ATE³]

pe·nguin (-gw-), n. Sea-fowl of southern hemisphere with wings represented by scaly paddles with which it swims under water. [?]

pē·nial, a. Of the penis. [-AL]

pĕ·nicillate (-*at*), n. (nat. hist.). Furnished with, forming, small tuft(s); marked with streaks as of pencil or brush. [as PENCIL, -ATE²]

peni·nsūla, n. Piece of land almost surrounded by water or projecting far into the sea; *the P.*, Spain & Portugal. [f. L *paeninsula* (*paene* almost + *insula* island)]

peni·nsular, a. & n. Of (the nature of) a peninsula; of the Peninsula or of the war there carried on between French & English &c. (1808–14); (n.) inhabitant of a peninsula, (*P-*) soldier of the P. war. [-AR¹]

peni·nsulate, v.t. Make (land) into a peninsula. [-ATE³]

pē·nis, n. (pl. *-nēs*). Copulatory organ of male animal. [L, = tail, penis]

pĕ·nitent, a. & n. That repents, contrite; (n.) repentant sinner, person doing penance under direction of confessor, (pl.) various R.-C. orders associated for mutual discipline &c. Hence or cogn. **pe·nit**ENCE n., **pe·nitent**LY² adv. [f. F *pénitent* f. L *paenitēre* repent, -ENT]

penite·ntial, a. Of penitence or penance; *the p. psalms* (vi, xxxii, xxxviii, li, cii, cxxx, cxliii). Hence **penite·ntial**LY² adv. [f. med. L *paenitentialis* (*paenitentia* penitence, as prec., see -ENCE & -AL)]

penite·ntiary, n. & a. Office in papal court deciding questions of penance, dispensations, &c.; *Grand P.*, cardinal presiding over this; asylum for prostitutes resolving on amendment; reformatory prison; (adj.) of penance, of reformatory treatment of criminals.

pe·nnant, n. = PENDANT¹ (naut.); = PENNON. [compromise between *pendant & pennon*]

pe·nniform, a. (nat. hist.). Having the form or appearance of a feather. So **penni·**FEROUS a. [f. L *penna* feather, see -FORM]

pe·nniless, a. Having no money; poor, destitute. [f. PENNY + -LESS]

pe·nnill, n. (pl. *-illion*). (Stanza of) improvised verse sung to harp at Eisteddfod &c. [Welsh, f. *penn* head]

pe·nnon, n. Long narrow flag, triangular or swallow-tailed, esp. as military ensign of lancer regiments; long pointed streamer of ship; flag. Hence **pen·non**ED² a. [f. OF *penon* prob. f. L *penna* feather, see -OON]

pe·nny, n. (pl. *pence* exc. as below). English bronze coin worth 1/12 of shilling (in pl. *pence* combined with numbers from 2 to 11 & 20, pron. without stress, as ***si·x-***

pence but *eigh·teen pe·nce*; after numeral written *d.* = DENARIUS, as *6d.*; pl. *pennies* of individual coins as such, as *gave me my change in pennies, doled it out in single pennies*); (bibl.) = DENARIUS; *a pretty p.*, a good sum of money; PETER'S *p., pence*; *a p. for your thoughts* (said to person absorbed in thought); *in for a p., in for a pound*, thing once begun must be concluded at all costs; *take care of the pence*, be sparing in small outlays; *turn an honest p.*, make something by an odd job; *a p. plain & twopence coloured* (jeer at cheap showiness); *p.-a-line* a., (of writing) cheap, superficial, *p.-a-liner*, hack writer; *p.-in-the-*SLOT; *p. post* (for conveyance of letters at ordinary charge of 1*d.*); *pe·nny-weight* (abbr. *dwt*), measure of weight, 24 grains, 1/20 of an ounce Troy; *penny wise*, (over-) careful in small expenditures, esp. *p. wise & pound foolish*, careful in small, wasteful in large matters; *pe·nny-wort* (-wert), (also *wall p.-w.*) plant with rounded concave leaves growing in crevices of rocks & walls, (*marsh* or *water p.-w.*) small herb with rounded leaves growing in marshy places; *pennyworth, penn'orth*, (pĕ·nĭwerth, pĕ·nerth), as much as can be bought for a penny, *not a p.-w.*, not the least bit, *a good, bad, p.-w.* (bargain); *fivep., tenp.*, &c., *nail*, sizes of nail orig. costing 5*d.* &c. per 100. [OE *pening*, cf. Du. *penning*, G *pfennig*]

pennyroy·al, n. Kind of mint cultivated for supposed medicinal virtues. [prob. = earlier *pulyole ryale* f. OF *poliol* thyme f. L *pulegiolum* dim. of *pulegium* + ROYAL]

pēno·logy, n. Study of punishment & of prison management. Hence **penolo·gi**CAL a., **peno·log**IST n. [f. Gk *poinē* fine + -O- + -LOGY]

pe·nsile, a. Hanging down, pendulous; (of bird &c.) that constructs p. nest. [f. L *pensilis* (*pendĕre pens-* hang, see -IL)]

pe·nsion (-shn), n., & v.t. Periodical (usu. annual) payment made esp. by government, company, or employer, in consideration of past services or of relinquishment of rights &c. (*Ministry of Pp.*, department necessitated by the great war); such payment to person who is not a professed servant for good will, secret service, &c., or to artists, scientists, &c., to enable them to carry on work of public interest; *old-age p.*, weekly or monthly payment by government to workmen, poor persons, or every one, after specified age; consultative assembly of members of Gray's Inn; (pron. as F) boarding-house at fixed rate, *live en p.* (as boarder); (v.t.) grant p. to, buy over with p.; *p. off*, dismiss with p. Hence **pe·nsion**LESS a. [(vb. f. n.) F, f. L *pensionem* payment (*pendĕre pens-* pay, -ION)]

pe·nsionable, a. Entitled, (of services &c.) entitling person, to pension. [-ABLE]

pe·nsionary, a. & n. (Recipient) of a pension; creature, hireling; (Hist.) *Grand P.*, first minister of Holland & Zealand (1619-1794). [f. med. L *pensionarius* (as PENSION, see -ARY[1])]

pe·nsioner, n. Recipient of pension; hireling, creature; (Camb. Univ.) undergraduate who is not a scholar on the foundation or a sizar but pays for his own commons &c. [f. OF *pensionnier* (as prec.)]

pe·nsive, a. Plunged in thought; melancholy. Hence **pe·nsive**LY[2] adv., **pe·nsive**NESS n. [F (*-if, -ive*), f. *penser* think f. L *pensare* frequent. of *pendĕre pens-* weigh]

pe·nstock, n. Sluice, flood-gate. [PEN[1] in sense 'mill-dam' + STOCK]

pent, a. Closely confined, shut *in* or *up*. [p.p. of *pend* var. of PEN[2]]

penta- in comb. (before vowel *pent-*) = Gk *pente* five, as: *pe·ntachord*, musical instrument of 5 strings, series of 5 notes; *penta-da·ctyl* a. & n., (person, animal) with 5 toes or fingers on each limb, so *-dacty·lic* a., *da·ctylism* n.; *pentă·gynous*, with 5 pistils; *pentahē·dron* solid figure of 5 faces, so *-hē·dral* a.; *pentă·merous*, (Bot., also written *5-merous*) having parts of flower-whorl 5 in number, (Zool.) consisting of 5 joints; *penta·ndrous*, with 5 free stamens; *pentape·talous*, with 5 petals; *pentă·pody*, verse, sequence in verse, of 5 feet; *pe·ntastich* (-k), group of 5 lines in verse; *pentatŏ·mic*, having 5 atoms of some substance in the molecule; *pentato·nic*, of 5 notes; *pentă·valent*, with combining power of 5 atoms of hydrogen &c.

pe·ntacle, n. Figure used as symbol, esp. in magic, prob. = PENTAGRAM. [f. med. L *pentaculum*, prob. = PENTA- + -CULE]

pe·ntad, n. The number, group of, five; (Chem.) element, radical, with combining power of five. [f. Gk *pentas -ados* (*pente* five, -AD)]

pe·ntagon, n. Five-sided (usu. plane rectilineal) figure. Hence **pentă·gon**AL a. [f. L f. Gk PENTA(*gōnon* f. *gōnia* angle)]

pe·ntagrăm, n. Five-pointed star formed by producing sides of pentagon both ways till they intersect, formerly used as mystic symbol. [f. Gk PENTA(*grammon* f. *grammē* line)]

pentă·meter, n. (Gk & Lat. Pros.) form of dactylic verse composed of two halves each of two feet (dactyls in second half, dactyls or spondees in first) & long syllable, chiefly used alternately with hexameters to form elegiac verse; English iambic verse of ten syllables. [L, f. Gk PENTA(*metros* f. *metron* measure)]

pe·ntane, n. Paraffin hydrocarbon occurring as a colourless fluid in petroleum &c. [f. Gk *pente* five + -ANE(2)]

pe·ntateuch (-tūk), n. First five books of O.T., traditionally ascribed to Moses. Hence **pentateu·ch**AL a. [f. L f. Gk PENTA(*teukhos* implement, in late Gk, book) of five books]

Pe·ntĕcŏst, n. Jewish harvest festival, on fiftieth day from the wave offering on second day of Passover (*Levit.* xxiii. 15,16), (later) synagogue anniversary of giving of Law on Sinai; (archaic) Whit Sunday. Hence **penteco·stAL** a. [f. eccl. L f. Gk *pentēcostē* (*hēmera*) fiftieth (day), f. *pentēkonta* fifty]

pe·nthouse (-t-h-), (archaic) **pe·ntice,** n. Sloping roof, esp. as subsidiary structure attached to wall of main building; awning, canopy, or the like. [ME *pentis*, prob. f. OF *apentis, -dis*, f. LL *appendicium* appendage (APPEND)]

Pe·ntonville, n. London prison associated with the principle of confinement in separate cells, to suit which and to serve as a model it was designed.

pentste·mon, n. Bright-flowered garden plant. [irreg. f. PENTA- + Gk *stēmōn* warp (cf. STAMEN)]

penu·lt(imate), a. & n. Last but one; (n.) last syllable but one. [(*-ult* abbr.) f. L *paene* almost + ULTIMATE after L *paenultimus*]

penu·mbra, n. Partly shaded region around shadow of opaque body, esp. round total shadow of moon or earth in eclipse; lighter outer part of sun-spot; partial shadow. Hence **penu·mbrAL** a. [f. L *paene* almost + *umbra* shadow]

penūr·ious, a. Poor, scanty; stingy, grudging, whence **penur·iousLY**[2] adv., **penur·iousNESS** n. [f. med.L *penuriosus* (foll., -OUS)]

pĕ·nury, n. Destitution, poverty; lack, scarcity, (*of*). [f. L *penuria*, cogn. w. Gk *peina* hunger, *penia* poverty, *spanis* want]

pē·on (-on, *or* pūn), n. (In India) foot-soldier, native constable, footman; (Span. Amer.) day-labourer; (Mex.) enslaved debtor. [OF, Sp., f. L as PAWN[1]]

pe·onage (-ĭj), n. Employment, service, of peons. [-AGE]

pe·ony, n. Plant with large globular red or white flowers, in cultivation often double. [OE *peonie* f. L f. Gk *paiōnia* (*Paiōn*, physician of the gods)]

people (pē·pl), n., & v.t. Persons composing community, race, or nation, as *the English p.*, *English-speaking pp.*, *a warlike p.*, (treated as sing.); the persons belonging to a place or forming a company or class &c. (*the p. of the western counties were in revolt, the p. here are furious*), subjects of king &c., congregation of parish priest &c., (as pl.); armed followers, retinue, workpeople, &c., (as pl.); one's parents or other relatives, as *his p. are sure to hear of it*; *the* commonalty (as pl.); *the* body of enfranchised or qualified citizens (as sing. or pl.); persons in general, as *p. don't like to be kept waiting*; *P.'s Palace,* East London institution with library, entertainments, educational classes &c., for the use of the working class; (v.t.) fill with p., populate, fill (place *with* animals &c.), (of persons, animals, &c.) inhabit, occupy, fill, esp. in p.p., as *a thickly peopled country*. [f. OF *pople, poeple*, &c., f. L *populus*]

pep, n. (U.S. slang). Vigour, go, spirit. [abbr. *pepper*]

pĕperi·no (-rē-), n. Light porous (usu. brown) volcanic rock formed of sand, cinders, &c. [It., f. *pepere* PEPPER, see -INE[1]]

pe·pper[1], n. Pungent aromatic condiment got from dried berries of certain plants used whole (*peppercorns*) or ground into powder; *Black P.*, plant chiefly used for this; *black, white, p.* (from unripe, ripe, berries); CAYENNE *p.*; (fig.) anything pungent; *p.-&-salt*, cloth of dark & light wools woven together, showing small dots of dark & light intermingled; *p.-box*, small usu. round box with perforated lid for sprinkling p., irregular buttress in Eton fives-court; *p.-castor, -er*, = p.-box (1st sense); *peppercorn*, dried berry of Black P., esp. as nominal rent ; *peppermint*, kind of mint grown for its essential oil, this oil, lozenge flavoured with peppermint; *p.-pot*, = *p.-castor*, (also) W.-Ind. dish of meat &c. stewed with red p. &c. (also, as nickname) Jamaican. [OE *pipor*, f. L *piper* = Gk *peperi* of oriental orig.]

pe·pper[2], v.t. Sprinkle, treat, with pepper; besprinkle as with pepper; pelt with missiles (lit. or fig.); punish severely. [f. prec.]

pe·ppery, a. Of, like, abounding in, pepper; (fig.) pungent, stinging, hot-tempered. [-Y[2]]

pe·psin, n. A ferment contained in gastric juice, converting proteids into peptones in presence of weak acid. [f. Gk *pepsis* digestion (*pep-* cook) + -IN]

pe·ptic, a. & n. Digestive; *p. glands* (secreting gastric juice); (n. pl., facet.) digestive organs. [f. Gk *peptikos* (as prec., see -IC)]

pe·ptone, n. Class of albuminoid substances into which proteids are converted by action of pepsin &c. Hence **pe·ptonIZE**(3) v.t. [f. G *pepton* f. Gk *pepton* cooked]

per, prep. Through, by, by means of. 1. In L phrr.; *p. annum*, (so much) by the year, yearly; *p. contra* adv. & n., (on) the opposite side (of an account &c.); *p. diēm, mensĕm*, (so much) by the day, month; *p. mille*, in or to the thousand; *p. procurātiō·nĕm* (abbrr. *per pro(c)., p.p.*), by proxy, by the action of (person signing document); *p. săltum*, without intermediate steps, all at once; *p. se*, by or in itself, intrinsically. 2. As E prep.; by, by means or instrumentality of, as *p. post, rail, steamer, bearer*; (facet.) *as p. usual*, as usual; for each, as *a shilling p. man, 5 p. cent.* [L]

per- in comb. = prec. 1. In L senses; through, all over, (*perforate, pervade*);

completely, very (*perturb*); to destruction, to the bad, (*pervert, perdition*). 2. Chem. denoting maximum of some element in combination; in names of binary compounds in *-ide* (formerly *-uret*), as *-chloride, -iodide, -oxide, -sulphide*; in adjj. in *-ic* naming oxides, acids, &c., as *-chloric, -iodic, -manganic*, in names of salts of these &c., as *-chlorate, -iodate, -manganate, -sulphate*.

pĕradve·nture, adv. & n. (archaic). Perhaps; *if, lest, p.*, if, lest, it chance that; (n.) uncertainty, chance, conjecture; *beyond, without, (all) p.* (doubt). [f. OF *per* or *par aventure* by chance (PER + *aventure* ADVENTURE)]

pĕrai· (-rahĭ, -rī), **-ra·ya** (-rahya), n. Voracious Amer. fresh-water fish. [native (*-ya*)]

pera·mbūlate, v.t. Walk through, over, or about; travel through & inspect (territory); formally establish boundaries of (parish &c.) by walking round them. Hence or cogn. **perambulA·TION** n., **pera·mbulatORY** a. [f. L PER(*ambulare* walk), see -ATE[3]]

pera·mbulator, n. Hand carriage for one or two children, with three or four wheels, pushed from behind (colloq. abbr. *pram*). [f. prec. + -OR[2]]

perca·le (-āl, -ahl), n. A closely woven cotton fabric. [F, etym. dub.]

percei·ve (-ēv), v.t. Apprehend with the mind, observe, understand, (circumstance, *that, how*, &c.); apprehend through one of the senses, esp. sight. [f. OF *perçoivre*, **-ceivre*, f. L PER(*cipere cept-* = *capere* take) seize thoroughly]

perce·ntage, n. Rate, proportion, per cent; (loosely) proportion, as *only a small p. of books are worth reading*. [-AGE]

per·cept, n. (philos.). Object of perception; mental product, as opp. to action, of perceiving. [as PERCEIVE]

perce·ptible, a. That can be perceived by senses or intellect. Hence **perceptiBI·LITY** n., **perce·ptibLY**[2] adv. [f. LL *perceptibilis* (as prec., see -BLE)]

perce·ption, n. Act, faculty, of perceiving; intuitive recognition (*of* truth, aesthetic quality, &c.); (Philos.) action by which the mind refers its sensations to external object as cause; (Law) collection (of rents &c.). Hence **perce·ptionAL**, **perce·ptIVE**, aa., **perce·ptiveLY**[2] adv., **perce·ptiveNESS, percepti·VITY**, nn. [OF, f. L *perceptionem* (as PERCEIVE, see -ION)]

perch[1], n. European spiny-finned freshwater fish, used as food. [f. F *perche* f. L f. Gk *perkē*]

perch[2], n. Horizontal bar for bird to rest upon; anything serving for this, as *bird takes its p.* (alights); (fig.) elevated or secure position; *hop the p.*, die, *knock* (person) *off* his *p.*, vanquish, destroy, him; centre pole of some fourwheeled vehicles; (also *pole, rod*) measure of length esp. for land, 5½ yds, *square p.*, 30¼ sq. yds. [f. F *perche* f. L *pertica* pole]

perch[3], v.i. & t. Alight, rest, as bird (*upon* bough &c.); (of person &c.) settle, alight, (*upon*); place (as) upon perch (esp. in p.p., as *town perched on a hill*). [f. F *percher*, as prec.]

percha·nce, adv. By chance (archaic); possibly, maybe. [f. AF *par chance* (*par* by + CHANCE)]

percheron (F), n. Strong & swift horse bred in le Perche, district of France.

percĭ·pient, a. & n. Perceiving, conscious; (n.) one who perceives esp. (Telepathy) something outside range of senses. Hence **perci·pIENCE** n. [f. L as PERCEIVE, see -ENT]

per·colate, v.i. & t. (Of liquid) filter, ooze, through (also fig.); (trans.) ooze through, permeate; (rare, of person or strainer) strain (liquid, powder) through pores &c. Hence or cogn. **percolA·TION, per·colatOR**[2](2), nn. [f. L PER(*colare* strain f. *colum* strainer), -ATE[3]]

percu·ss, v.t. (med.). Tap gently with finger or instrument for purposes of diagnosis &c. [f. L PER(*cutere cuss-* = *quatere* shake) strike]

percu·ssion, n. Forcible striking of one (usu. solid) body against another; (Med.) percussing; (Mus.) *instrument of* (played by) *p.*; *p. cap*, small copper cap or cylinder in fire-arm, containing fulminating powder and exploded by p. of a hammer. So **percu·ssIVE** a. [f. L *percussio* (as prec., see -ION)]

percŭtā·neous, a. Made, done, through the skin. [PER- + CUTANEOUS]

perdi·tion, n. Eternal death, damnation. [f. OF *perdiciun* f. L *perditionem* f. PER(*dere dit-* = *dare* give) destroy, see -ION]

perdū·, -due·, a. (Mil.) placed as an outpost in hiding, esp. *lie p.*; (often as F, with fem. *-due*) hidden. [F, p.p. of *perdre* lose, as prec.]

perdūr·able, a. Permanent; eternal; durable. Hence or cogn. **perdurABI·LITY** n., **perdur·abLY**[2] adv. [OF, f. L PER(*durabilis* DURABLE)]

père (pār), n. Father (appended to surname to distinguish father from son, cf. FILS). [F]

pĕ·rĕgrĭnate, v.i. (now facet.). Travel, journey. So **peregrinA·TION, pe·regrinatOR**[2], nn. [f. L *peregrinari* (as foll.), see -ATE[3]]

pĕ·rĕgrĭn(e), a. & n. (Archaic) foreign, imported from abroad, outlandish; *p.* (*falcon*), kind esteemed for hawking. [f. L *peregrinus* (*peregre* abroad, f. PER + *ager* field, see -INE[1])]

pĕ·remptory, a. Decisive, final, esp. (Law) *p. mandamus* (in which the command is absolute), *p. writ* (enforcing defendant's appearance without option); (of statement or command) admitting no denial or refusal; absolutely fixed, essential; (of person &c.) dogmatic, imperious, dictatorial. Hence **pe·remptori**LY[2] adv., **pe·remptori**NESS n. [f. L *peremptorius* destructive f. PER(*imere empt-* = *emere* take, buy) destroy, cut off, see -ORY]

pere·nnial, a. & n. Lasting through, (of stream) flowing through all seasons of, the year; lasting long or for ever; (of plant) living several years (cf. ANNUAL); (n.) p. plant. Hence **perennia·**LITY n., **pere·nnial**LY[2] adv. [f. L PER(*ennis* f. *annus* year) + -AL]

per·fect[1], a. & n. Complete, not deficient; faultless; (of lesson) thoroughly learned; thoroughly trained or skilled (*in* duties &c.); exact, precise, as *a p. square, circle*; entire, unqualified, as *a p. stranger, p. nonsense*; (Gram., of tense) denoting completed event or action viewed in relation to the present (*future p.,* giving sense *will have done*); (Bot.) having all four whorls of the flower; (Mus.) *p. concord* or *consonance* (of unison, fifth, & octave, & sometimes fourth), *p. interval* (of fourth, fifth, & octave in their normal form), *p. chord* (=*common* CHORD[2]). (N.) p. tense. Hence **per·fect**LY[2] adv., **per·fect**NESS n. [f. OF *parfit* f. L PER(*ficere fect-* = *facere* do) complete]

perfe·ct[2] (*or* per·f-), v.t. Complete, carry through; make perfect; improve. Hence **perfecti**BI·LITY n., **perfe·cti**BLE a. [f. prec.]

perfe·ction, n. Completion; making perfect; full development; faultlessness; (loosely) comparative excellence; perfect person or thing; highest pitch, extreme, perfect specimen or manifestation, (*of* quality &c.); (w. pl.) accomplishment. [OF, f. L *perfectionem* (as PERFECT[1], see -ION)]

perfe·ctionist, n. One who holds that religious or moral perfection may be attained; (*P-*) member of communistic community of Oneida Creek, N.Y. So **perfe·ction**ISM n. [-IST]

perfer·vid, a. Very fervid. [PER-]

per·fidy, n. Breach of faith, treachery, Hence or cogn. **perfi·dious** a., **perfi·dious**LY[2] adv., **perfi·dious**NESS n. [f. F *perfidie* f. L *perfidia* f. PER(*fidus* f. *fides* faith) treacherous]

perfō·liate (-*at*), a. (bot.). Having the stalk apparently passing through the leaf. [f. PER + L *folium* leaf + -ATE[2]]

per·forate, v.t. & i. Make hole(s) through, pierce, esp. make rows of holes in (sheet) to separate stamps, coupons, &c., make an opening into; pass, extend, through; (intr.) penetrate (*into, through,* &c.). Hence or cogn. **perfora**·TION, **per·forator**[2](2), nn., **per·forat**IVE a. [f. L PER(*forare* bore), see -ATE[3]]

perfor·ce, adv. & n. Of necessity; (n., rare) necessity, esp. *of, by, p.* [f. OF *par force* by FORCE]

perfor·m, v.t. & i. Carry into effect (command, promise, task, operation, &c.); go through, execute, (public function, play, piece of music, &c.); (intr.) act in play, play, sing, &c.; (of trained animals) execute tricks &c. at public show &c., whence **perfor·**MING[2] a. Hence **perfor·**MABLE a. **perfor·**MER[1] n. [OF (*par-* PER- + *former* FORM, or perh. corrupt. of *parfournir* f. *fournir* FURNISH)]

perfor·mance, n. Execution (*of* command &c.); carrying out, doing; notable feat; performing of play or public exhibition, as *there are two pp. a day, the afternoon p.* [-ANCE]

per·fume[1], n. Odorous fumes of burning substance; sweet smell; smell; fluid containing essence of flowers &c., scent. Hence **per·fume**LESS a. [f. F *parfum,* as foll.]

perfu·me[2], v.t. Impart sweet scent to, impregnate with sweet smell, (esp. in p.p.). [f. F *parfumer* (PER- + L *fumare* smoke)]

perfu·mer, n. Maker, seller, of perfumes. Hence **perfu·mery**(1, 2, 3) n. [-ER[1]]

perfu·nctory, a. Done merely for sake of getting through a duty, acting thus, superficial, mechanical, as *a p. inspection, inquirer, in a p. manner.* Hence **perfu·nctori**LY[2] adv., **perfu·nctori**NESS n. [f. LL *perfunctorius* f. PER(*fungi funct-* perform), see -ORY]

perfu·se (-z), v.t. Besprinkle (*with* water &c.); cover, suffuse, (*with* radiance &c.); pour (water &c.) through or over. Hence or cogn. **perfu·**SION (-zhn) n., **perfu·**SIVE (-s-) a. [f. L PER(*fundere fus-* pour)]

pergamē·neous, a. Of or like parchment. [f. L as PARCHMENT + -EOUS]

per·gola, n. Arbour, covered walk, formed of growing plants trained over trellis-work. [It., f. L *pergula* projecting roof (*pergere* proceed)]

pergu·nnah, -ga·na (-gŭ-), n. Division of territory in India, group of villages. [f. Pers. & Hind. *parganah* district]

perha·ps (*colloq.* prăps), adv. It may be, possibly, as *p. he has lost it, he has p. lost it, p. you would like to see it?.* [PER + HAPS (pl.)]

pēr·ĭ, n. (Pers. Myth.) fairy, good (orig. evil) genius; beautiful or graceful being. [Pers.]

pĕrĭ- in comb. = Gk *peri* round, about, as: *-anth,* floral envelope; *car·dium,* membranous sac enclosing the heart, so *-car·diac, -car·dial,* aa.; *-carp,* seed-vessel, wall of ripened ovary of plant; *-cho·ndrium* (-k-), membrane enveloping cartilages (except at joints); *-clī·nal* (geol.), sloping in all directions from central point; *-gy̆nous,* (of stamen) situated around pistil or ovary; *-ŏ·stĕum,* mem-

For other words in *peri-* see PERI-.

brane enveloping the bones, so *-o·steal* a., *-ostī·tis* n.; *-pteral,* (of temple) surrounded by single row of pillars; *-scope,* kind of photographic object-glass, (also) tube-&-mirror apparatus by which observer in submarine or trench can see things above water or parapet; *-sco·pic,* enabling one to see distinctly for some distance round axis of vision; *-sperm,* mass of albumen outside embryo-sac in some seeds; *-stome,* (Bot.) fringe of small teeth around mouth of capsule in mosses, (Zool.) parts around mouth in various invertebrates; *-tўphlī·tis,* inflammation of some part around the caecum, e.g. appendicitis.

pĕ·riapt, n. Thing worn about the person as charm, amulet. [f. F *périapte* f. Gk PERI(*apton* f. *haptō* fasten)]

pe·riclase, n. Mineral consisting of magnesia & protoxide of iron, found esp. at Vesuvius. [f. PERI- (in sense 'very') + Gk *klasis* breaking, from its perfect cleavage]

pĕri·copē, n. Short passage, paragraph; portion of Scripture read in public worship. [f. LL f. Gk PERI(*kopē* cutting f. *koptō* cut)]

pericrā·nium, n. Membrane enveloping skull; (facet.) skull, brain, intellect. [f. Gk PERI(*kranion* CRANIUM)]

pĕ·ridŏt, n. (Jeweller's name for) olivine, kind of chrysolite. [f. F *péridot,* etym. dub.]

pe·rigee (-jē), n. That point in planet's (esp. moon's) orbit at which it is nearest to earth (cf. APOGEE). Hence **perigē·**AN a. [f. F *périgée* f. LL f. late Gk PERI(*geion* f. *gē* earth)]

perihē·lion, n. That point in planet's orbit at which it is nearest to sun (cf. APHELION). [f. PERI- + Gk *hēlios* sun]

pĕ·ril, n., & v.t. (-ll-). Danger; *in p. of* (in danger of losing) one's *life* &c.; *you do it at your p.,* you take the risk; *keep off at your p.* (take the risk if you do not); (v.t.) expose to danger, imperil. Hence or cogn. **pe·ril**OUS a., **pe·rilous**LY[2] adv., **pe·rilous**NESS n. [(vb f. n.) f. F *péril* f. L *periculum* (*-periri* try)]

peri·meter, n. Circumference, outline, of closed figure; length of this; instrument for measuring the field of vision. [f. L f. Gk PERI(*metros* f. *metron* measure)]

perinē·um, n. (anat.). Region of the body between anus & scrotum or vulva. Hence **perinē·**AL a. [LL, f. Gk *pĕrinaios,* cf. *pēris -inos* scrotum]

pēr·iod, n. Round of time marked by recurrence of astronomical coincidences; time of planet's revolution; time during which disease runs its course; (pl.) menses; indefinite portion of history, life, &c.; any portion of time; *the p.,* the present day (*the girl, costume, catchwords,* &c., *of t. p.*); complete sentence, esp. one of several clauses; (pl.) rhetorical language; full pause at end of sentence, full stop (.) marking this, (*put a p. to,* bring to an end); set of figures marked off in large number, as in numeration, recurring decimals, &c. [f. F *période* f. L f. Gk PERI(*odos* = *hodos* way)]

pēriŏ·dic, a. Of revolution of heavenly body, as *p. motion*; recurring at regular intervals, so **periodi·**CITY n.; recurring at intervals; expressed in (rhetorical) periods. [f. F *périodique* f. L f. Gk *periodikos* (as prec., see -IC)]

perio·dical, a. & n. = prec. (not in last sense); (magazine, miscellany) published at regular intervals, e.g. monthly. Hence **periŏ·dical**LY[2] adv. [-AL]

peripatĕ·tic, a. & n. (*P-*) Aristotelian (a. & n.; so called from Aristotle's custom of walking in Lyceum while teaching); walking from place to place on one's business, itinerant, whence **peripate·ti**CALLY adv.; (n., chiefly facet.) itinerant dealer. Hence **peripate·tic**ISM(2, 3) n. [f. F *péripatétique* f. L f. Gk *peripatētikos* f. PERI(*pateō* walk), see -IC]

peripetei·a (-īa), **-tīa,** n. Sudden change of fortune in drama or in life. [Gk PERI(*peteia* f. *pet-* fall)]

peri·phery, n. Bounding line esp. of round surface; external boundary or surface. Hence **peri·pher**AL a., **peri·pheral**LY[2] adv. [f. OF *periferie* f. LL f. Gk PERI(*phereia* f. *pherō* bear) circumference]

peri·phrasis, n. (pl. *-asēs*). Roundabout way of speaking, circumlocution; roundabout phrase. Hence or cogn. **periphra·st**IC a., **periphra·st**ĪCALLY adv. [L f. Gk, f. PERI(*phrazō* declare, vbl adj. *-phrastos*); also anglicized *pe·riphrase* (pl. pron. -ĭz)]

peri·que (-ēk), n. Dark Louisiana tobacco of a choice kind. [?]

pĕ·rish, v.i. & t. Suffer destruction, lose life, come to untimely end (by the sword &c.); (of cold or exposure) reduce to distress or inefficiency (usu. in pass.; *we were perished with cold*; *in perishing cold*; *the heat had perished all vegetation*), whence **pe·rishing**LY[2] adv.; *we were perished* (much incommoded) *with cold, hunger,* &c. [f. OF *perir* (see -ISH[2]) f. L PER(*irego*) perish]

pe·rishable, a. & n. Liable to perish; subject to speedy decay; (n. pl.) things (esp. foodstuffs in transit) subject to this. Hence **pe·rishable**NESS n. [-ABLE]

pe·rispome, perispō·menon, a. & n. (Gk gram.). (Word) with circumflex accent on last syllable. [abbr. of Gk *perispōmenon* (also used in E) neut. part. of PERI(*spaō* draw) draw round, mark with circumflex]

peri·stalith, n. (archaeol.). Ring of standing stones round burial-mound &c. [irreg. f. Gk PERI(*statos* standing) + -LITH]

perista·lsis, n. (physiol.). Automatic muscular movement consisting of wave-like contractions in successive circles, by which contents of alimentary canal &c. are propelled along it. Hence or cogn.

perista·ltic a., **perista·ltically** adv. [Gk f. PERI(*stellō* send)]
peristerō·nic, a. Of pigeons. [prob. f. Gk *peristerōn* dovecot (*peristera* dove)]
pe·ristyle, n. Row of columns surrounding temple, court, cloister, &c.; space so surrounded. [f. F *péristyle* f. L f. Gk PERI(*stulon* f. *stulos* pillar)]
peritonē·um, -naeum, n. (anat.). Double serous membrane lining cavity of abdomen. Hence **peritonē·al** a., **peritoni·tis** n. [L, f. Gk PERI(*tonaion* f. *ton-* stem of *teinō* stretch)]
pe·riwig, n. Wig. Hence **pe·riwigged**[2] a. [earlier *perwyke* f. F as PERUKE]
pe·riwinkle[1], n. Genus of plants, esp. *Lesser* & *Greater P.*, evergreen trailing shrubs with light-blue flowers; *p.* (*blue*), colour of pp. [OE *pervince* f. L *pervinca*]
pe·riwinkle[2], n. Gastropod mollusc much used for food. [OE has *pinewinclan, wine-*]
per·jure (-j*er*), v. refl. *P.* one*self*, forswear oneself; (p.p.) guilty of perjury. So **per·jurer**[1] n. [f. OF *parjurer* f. L PER(*jurare* swear)]
per·jury, n. Swearing to statement known to be false; wilful utterance of false evidence while on oath; breach of oath. So **perjur·ious** (-joor-) a., **perjur·iously**[2] adv. [f. AF *perjurie* f. L *perjurium* as prec.]
perk, v.i. & t., & a. (Also *p. up*) lift one's head, thrust oneself forward, briskly or impudently; (trans.) smarten *up*; hold *up* (head, tail) self-assertively; (adj., rare) perky. [?]
per·ky, a. Self-assertive, saucy, pert. Hence **per·kily**[2] adv., **per·kiness** n. [prec. + -Y[2]]
per·lite, n. Obsidian or other vitreous rock in form of enamel-like globules. [F, as PEARL, see -ITE[1]]
per·manent, n. Lasting, intended to last, indefinitely (cf. TEMPORARY); *p. set*, condition of metal after being subjected to the strain of use; *p. way*, finished road-bed of railway. Hence or cogn. **per·manence, per·manency** (esp. = p. thing or arrangement), nn., **per·manently**[2] adv. [f. L PER(*manēre* remain), -ENT]
per·mēāte, v.t. & i. Penetrate, pervade, saturate; diffuse itself *through, among*, &c. Hence or cogn. **permeabi·lity, per·meance, permea·tion,** nn., **per·meable, per·meant,** aa. [f. L PER(*meare* run), see -ATE[3]]
Per·mian, a. Of the uppermost division of the Palaeozoic series of strata, consisting chiefly of red sandstone & magnesian limestone. [*Perm*, E.-Russian province, + -IAN]
permi·ssible, a. Allowable. Hence **permi·ssibly**[2] adv. [OF, prob. f. med. L *permissibilis* (as PERMIT[1], see -BLE)]
permi·ssion, n. Leave, licence, (*to* do). [f. L *permissio* (as PERMIT, see -ION)]
permi·ssive, a. Giving permission; *p. legislation* (giving powers, but not enjoining their use). Hence **per·missively**[2] adv., **permi·ssiveness** n. [OF (*-if, -ive*), as foll., see -IVE]
permi·t[1], v.t. & i. (-tt-). Allow, as *p. me to remark, appeals are permitted, p. it to be altered, weather permitting*; (intr.) admit *of* (alteration &c.). [f. L PER(*mittere miss-* let go)]
per·mit[2], n. Written order giving permission esp. for landing or removal of dutiable goods &c.; (*also* permi·t) permission. [f. prec.]
permuta·tion, n. (Math.) variation of the order of a set of things lineally arranged, any one such arrangement; (rare) alteration. [f. OF *permutacion* f. L *permutationem* (foll., -ION)]
permu·te, v.t. Alter the order of. [f. L PER(*mutare* change)]
pern, n. HONEY-buzzard. [irreg. f. Gk *pternis*, kind of hawk]
perni·cious, a. Destructive, ruinous, fatal. Hence **perni·ciously**[2] adv., **perni·ciousness** n. [f. F *pernicieux* f. L *perniciosus* (*pernicies* ruin f. PER- + *nex necis* death, see -OUS)]
perni·ckety, a. (colloq.). Fastidious; ticklish, requiring careful handling. [?]
pernocta·tion, n. Passing the night; (Eccl.) all-night vigil. [f. L *pernoctatio* f. PER(*noctare* f. *nox noctis* night), see -ATION]
pě·rorate, v.i. Sum up & conclude speech, whence **perora·tion** n.; speak at length. [f. L PER(*orare* speak)]
perpe·nd, v.t. (archaic). Ponder, consider, (matter, or abs.). [f. L PER(*pendĕre* weigh)]
perpendi·cular, a. & n. At right angles to plane of horizon; (loosely, of ascent &c.) very steep; erect, upright; (facet.) in standing position; (Geom.) at right angles (*to* given line, plane, or surface); *p.* STYLE. (N.) plumb-rule or other instrument for showing p. line, (pl.) two datum-lines used in designing ship & fixing its nominal length (*between pp.*); p. line; *the p.*, p. line or direction (*is out of p.* or *the p.*, not straight up and down); (slang) meal &c. at which guests stand. Hence **perpendiculă·rity** n., **perpendi·cularly**[2] adv. [f. OF *perpendiculer* f. L *perpendicularis* (*perpendiculum* plumb-line, as prec., see -AR[1])]
per·petrate, v.t. Perform, commit, (crime, blunder, pun or other thing viewed as outrageous). So **perpetra·tion, per·petrator**[2], nn. [f. L PER(*petrare* = *patrare* effect), -ATE[3]]
perpě·tual, a. Eternal; permanent during life; applicable, valid, for ever or for indefinite time; *p. motion* (of machine that should go on for ever unless stopped by external force or worn out); continuous;

For other words in *peri-* see PERI-.

(colloq.) frequent, repeated, as *this p. nagging*. Hence **perpe·tual**LY² adv. [f. F *perpétuel* f. L *perpetualis* f. *perpetuus* (perh. f. PER- + *petere* seek), see -AL]

perpe·tuate, v.t. Make perpetual; preserve from oblivion. Hence or cogn. **perpe·tu**ANCE, **perpetu**A·TION, **perpe·tuat**OR², nn. [f. L *perpetuare* (as prec.,) see -ATE³]

perpetū·ity, n. Quality of being perpetual; *in, to, for, p.*, for ever; perpetual possession or position; perpetual annuity. [f. F *perpétuité* f. L *perpetuitatem* (as PERPETUAL, see -TY)]

perple·x, v.t. Bewilder, puzzle, (person, his mind); complicate, confuse, (matter); entangle, intertwine, (esp. in p.p.). Hence **perple·xĕd**LY², **perple·xing**LY², advv. [f. obs. *perplex* a. f. L PER(*plexus* p.p. of *plectere* plait)]

perple·xity, n. Bewilderment; what causes this; entangled state. [f. LL *perplexitas* (as prec., see -TY)]

per·quisite, (-z-) n. Casual profit, esp. (Law) that coming to lord of manor beyond regular revenue; thing that has served its primary use and to which subordinate or servant has then a customary right, as *remains of the daily commons are among the pp. of college scouts*; customary gratuity. [f. L PER(*quirere quisit-*, = *quaerere* seek) search narrowly for]

pĕ·rron, n. Platform in front of door of church or other large building, ascended by steps. [F, f. L *petra* stone, see -OON]

pe·rry, n. Drink from juice of pears fermented. [f. OF *peré* f. LL *pera* = L *pirum* pear]

perse, a. & n. (archaic). Bluish-grey, bluish grey. [ME, f. OF *pers* f. LL *persus* etym. dub.]

per·secute, v.t. Pursue with enmity and injury (esp. holder of opinion held to be heretical); harass, worry; importune (person *with* questions &c.). So **persecu·**TION n. (*-tion mania*, insane delusion that one is persecuted), **per·secut**OR² n. [f. F *persécuter* f. L PER(*sequi secut-* follow) pursue]

persevēr·ance, n. Steadfast pursuit of an aim, constant persistence, so **persever·**ANT a. (rare); (Theol.) continuance in state of grace. [f. F *persévérance* f. L *perseverantia* (as foll., see -ANCE)]

persevere·(-ēr), v.i. Continue steadfastly, persist, (*in* course, *in doing, with* task, or abs.). Hence **persever·ing**LY² adv. [f. F *persévérer* f. L *perseverare* f. PER(*severus* SEVERE)]

Per·sian (-shn), a. & n. (Inhabitant) of Persia, as *P. carpet, cat* (with long silky hair & thick tail). [-AN]

persie·nnes(-ĕnz), n. pl. Outside window-blinds of light horizontal laths. [F, = Persian (fem. pl. adj.)]

persiflage(per·sĭflahzh), n. Light raillery, banter. [F, f. PER(*sifler* = *siffler* f. L *sibilare* whistle), see -AGE]

persi·mmon, n. American date-plum, yellow fruit becoming sweet when softened by frost. [corrupt. of native name]

persi·st (-sĭ-), v.i. Continue firmly or obstinately (*in* opinion, course, *doing*) esp. against remonstrance &c. Hence or cogn. **persi·st**ENCE, **persi·st**ENCY, nn., **persi·st**ENT a. (esp., in Zool. & Bot., of horns, hair, leaves, &c.) permanent (opp. DECIDUOUS), **persi·stent**LY² adv. [f. L PER(*sistere* stand)]

per·son (-sn), n. Individual human being; (contempt.) *who is this p.?*; *young p.*, young man or (usu.) woman; living body of human being, as *he had a fine p., attracted by her fortune not her p.*; *acting, appearing, in his own* (*proper*) *p.* or *in p.* (himself, personally); *found a friend in* (*the p. of*) *his landlord*; (Law) human being (*natural p.*) or body corporate (*artificial p.*) with recognized rights & duties; character in play or story; *the three pp.* (modes of being) *of the Godhead*, Father, Son, Holy Spirit; (Gram.) each of the three classes of personal pronouns &c. denoting respectively the p. &c. speaking (*first p.*), spoken to (*second p.*), & spoken of (*third p.*); (Zool.) individual of a compound or colonial organism. [f. OF *persone* f. L *persona* player's mask, character in play, (LL) human being, perh. cogn. w. PER(*sonare* sound)]

persō·na, n. Person, as: *p. grāta*, acceptable person; IN⁵ *propriā personā*. [L]

per·sonable, a. Handsome, comely. [-ABLE]

per·sonage, n. Person of rank or importance; person; character in play &c. [OF, = med. L *personaticum* (as PERSON, see -AGE)]

per·sonal, a. One's own, individual, private, as *to suit his p. convenience, this is p. to myself*; done, made, &c., in person, as *p. service, acquaintance, interview*; directed, referring, (esp. hostilely) to an individual, as *p. abuse, remarks*; making, given to making, p. remarks, as *do not let us become p.*; (Law) *p. property, estate*, chattels or chattel interests in land, all property except land and those interests in land that pass to one's heir, (cf. REAL); (Gram.) of, denoting, one of the three persons, esp. *p. pronouns*. [OF, f. L *personalis* (PERSON, -AL)]

persona·lity, n. Being a person; personal existence or identity; distinctive personal character; person; (of remarks) fact of being aimed at an individual, (usu. pl.) such remark(s); (rare) = PERSONALTY. [f. OF *personalté* f. med. L *personalitatem* (as prec., see -TY)]

per·sonalize, v.t. Personify. Hence **personaliz**A·TION n. [PERSONAL + -IZE]

per·sonally, adv. In person, in one's own person, as *he conducted them p., a p.-conducted tour* (conducted by some one in person), *writ was served on them p.*; *a God* *existing p.* (as a person); for one's own part, as *p. I see no objection.* [-LY[2]]

per·sonalty, n. Personal estate. [f. AF *personaltie* PERSONALITY]

per·sonate[1] (-*at*), a. (bot.). Having the opening of the lips closed by upward projection of the lower, as in snapdragon. [f. L *personatus* masked (as foll., see -ATE[2])]

per·sonāte[2], v.t. Play the part of (character in drama, also fig.); pretend to be (person) esp. for fraudulent purpose. Hence **persona·tion**, **per·sonator**[2], nn. [f. LL *personare* (as PERSON), see -ATE[3]]

persŏnifica·tion, n. Personifying; person, thing, viewed as striking example or embodiment *of* (quality &c.). [f. foll., see -FICATION]

persŏ·nify, v.t. Attribute personal nature to (abstraction); symbolize (quality) by figure in human form; embody (quality) in one's own person, exemplify typically, (esp. in p.p.). [prob. f. F *personnifier,* see PERSON & -FY]

personne·l, n. Body of persons engaged esp. in public institution. [F, =PERSONAL, adj. as n.]

perspe·ctive, n. & a. Art of delineating solid objects on plane surface so as to give same impression of relative positions, magnitudes, &c., as the actual objects do when viewed from particular point; picture so drawn; apparent relation between visible objects as to position, distance, &c.; *linear p.* (concerned with apparent form, magnitude, & position, of objects); (fig.) relation in which parts of subject are viewed by the mind; view, prospect, (lit. & fig.); *in* (drawn according to rules of) *p.*; (adj.) of, in, p., whence **perspe·ctively**[2] adv. [f. med. L *perspectiva* (*ars* art) f. PER(*spicere spect*- look), see -IVE]

perspicā·cious, a. Having mental penetration or discernment. Hence or cogn. **perspica·ciously**[2] adv., **perspică·city** n. [f. L *perspicax* (as prec., see -ACIOUS)]

perspi·cūous, a. Easily understood, clearly expressed; (of person) clear in expression. Hence or cogn. **perspicū·ity**, **perspi·cuousness**, nn., **perspi·cuously**[2] adv. [f. L *perspicuus* (as prec.), + -OUS]

perspīr·able, a. Allowing the passage of perspiration; that can be thrown off in perspiration. [f. PERSPIRE + -ABLE]

perspira·tion, n. Sweating; sweat. So **perspīr·atory** a. [F (as foll., -ATION)]

perspire·, v.i. & t. Sweat; (trans.) give off (liquid) through pores in form of vapour or moisture. [f. L PER(*spirare* breathe) breathe, (of wind) blow]

persua·de (-swād), v.t. Convince, (person, one*self*, *of* fact, *that* thing is so); induce (person *to* do, *into* action); (p.p.) convinced (*of* thing, *that*). Hence or cogn. **persua·dable**, **persua·sible**, aa., **persuasibi·lity** n. [f. L PER(*suadēre suas*- advise)]

persua·der, n. Person or thing that persuades, esp. (pl., slang) spurs (*clap in the pp.*, spur horse). [-ER[1]]

persua·sion (-swāzhn), n. Persuading; persuasiveness; conviction, as *it is my private p. that he is mad*; religious belief; sect holding this, as *he is of the Roman Catholic p.*; (facet.) race, kind, sort, as *a man of the Jewish p.* (Jew), *no one of the male p. was there.* [f. L *persuasio* (as prec. see -ION)]

persua·sive, a. & n. Able to persuade, winning; (n.) motive, inducement. Hence **persua·sively**[2] adv., **persua·siveness** n. [f. med. L *persuasivus* (as PERSUADE, see -IVE)]

pert, a. Forward, saucy, in speech or conduct. Hence **per·tly**[2] adv., **per·tness** n. [earlier (& OF) *apert* f. L (1) *apertus* p.p. of *aperire* open (2) *expertus* EXPERT]

pertai·n, v.i. Belong as part, appendage, or accessory, *to*; be appropriate *to*; have reference, relate, *to*. [f. OF *partenir* f. L PER(*tinēre* =*tenēre* hold)]

pertinā·cious, a. Stubborn, persistent, obstinate. Hence or cogn. **pertina·ciously**[2] adv., **pertina·ciousness**, **pertină·city**, nn. [f. L PER(*tinax* =*tenax* TENACIOUS)]

per·tinent, a. & n. Pertaining, relevant, apposite, (*to* matter in hand &c.); to the point; (n., usu. pl.) appurtenance(s). Hence or cogn. **per·tinence**, **per·tinency**, nn., **per·tinently**[2] adv. [f. L as PERTAIN, see -ENT]

pertur·b, v.t. Throw into (physical) confusion; disturb mentally, agitate. So **perturba·tion** n., **pertur·bative** (*or* per·t-) a. [f. L PER(*turbare* disturb)]

peru·ke (-o͝ok), n. Wig. [f. F *perruque* f. It. *perruca, parrucca,* perh. ult. f. L *pilus* hair]

peru·se (-o͞oz), v.t. Read thoroughly or carefully; read; (fig.) examine (person's face &c.) carefully. Hence **peru·sal** (-zl), n. ([in earlier sense 'use up'] PER- + USE]

Peru·vian (-o͞o-), a. Of Peru; *P. bark* (of CINCHONA tree). [f. mod. L *Peruvia* Peru + -AN]

perva·de, v.t. Spread through, permeate, saturate, (often fig. of influences &c.). Hence or cogn. **perva·sion** (-zhn), **perva·siveness** (-s-), nn., **perva·sive** a., **perva·sively**[2] adv. [f. L PER(*vadere vasgo*)]

perver·se, a. Persistent in error; different from what is reasonable or required; wayward; peevish; perverted, wicked; (of verdict) against weight of evidence or judge's direction. Hence or cogn. **perver·sely**[2] adv., **perver·seness**, **perver·sity**, nn. [F (*-rs, -rse*), f. L as foll.]

perver·t[1], v.t. Turn aside (thing) from its proper use; misconstrue, misapply, (words &c.); lead astray (person, mind) from right opinion or conduct or esp. religious belief. Hence or cogn. **perver·**-

SION n., **perver·sIVE** a. [f. F *pervertir* f. L PER(*vertere vers-* turn)]

per·vert², n. Perverted person, apostate. [f. prec., cf. CONVERT²]

per·vious, a. Affording passage (*to*); permeable; (fig.) accessible (*to* reason &c.). Hence **per·viousNESS** n. [f. L PER(*vius* f. *via* way) + -OUS]

pese·ta (-sā-), n. Spanish silver coin worth about 10*d*. [Sp.]

Peshi·to, -itta, (-shē-), n. Principal ancient Syriac version of O. & N.T. [f. Syriac *p'shiṭ(t)â, -ô,* simple]

peshwa (pā·shwah), n. (hist.). Hereditary sovereign (earlier, chief minister) of the Mahratta State. [Pers., = chief]

pe·sky, a. (U.S. slang). Troublesome, confounded, annoying, plaguy. [?]

peso (pā·sō), n. Silver coin worth about 4*s*., used in most S.-Amer. republics. [Sp.]

pe·ssary, n. (med.) Instrument worn in the vagina to prevent uterine displacements. [f. med. L *pessarium* f. L f. Gk *pessos* oval stone used in game like draughts]

pe·ssimism, n. Tendency to look at the worst aspect of things (cf. OPTIMISM); doctrine that this world is the worst possible, or that all things tend to evil. So **pe·ssimIST** n., **pessimi·stIC** a., **pessimi·stICALLY** adv. [f. L *pessimus* worst + -ISM]

pest, n. Troublesome or destructive person, animal, or thing; (now rare) pestilence; *p.-house,* hospital for plague &c. [f. F *peste* f. L *pestis* plague]

pe·ster, v.t. Trouble, plague. [perh. f. F EM(*pestrer* f. L *pastorium* tether, as PASTOR)]

pesti·ferous, a. Noxious, pestilential; (fig.) bearing moral contagion, pernicious. [f. L *pestifer* (as PEST, see -FEROUS)]

pe·stilence, n. Any fatal epidemic disease, esp. bubonic plague. So **pestile·ntIAL** a. [F, f. L *pestilentia* (as foll., see -ENCE)]

pe·stilent, a. Destructive to life, deadly; (fig.) injurious to morals &c.; (colloq.) troublesome, plaguy. Hence **pe·stilentLY**² adv. [f. L *pestilens* (also *-lentus*) f. *pestis* plague]

pe·stle (-sl), n., & v.t. & i. Club-shaped instrument for pounding substances in a mortar; kinds of appliance for pounding &c.; (v.t.) pound (as) with p.; (v.i.) use p. [f. OF *pestel* f. L *pistillum* (*pinsere pist-* pound)]

pet¹, n., & v.t. Animal tamed & kept as favourite or treated with fondness; darling, favourite, (often attrib.); one's *p. aversion,* what one specially dislikes; *p.-cock,* small stop-cock for draining, letting out steam, &c.; *p. name,* one expressing fondness or familiarity; (v.t.) treat as a p., fondle. [?]

pet², n. Offence at being slighted, ill-humour, esp. *take* (usu. *the*) *p., be in a p.* [?]

pĕ·tal, n. Each of the divisions of the corolla of a flower. Hence **pe·talINE** (-ĭn), (-)**pe·tal(l)ED**², **pe·talOID,** aa. [f. Gk *petalon* thin plate, leaf, (*pet-* spread)]

pĕ·talŏn, n. Gold plate on mitre of Jewish high priest. [as PETAL]

petar·d, n. Small engine of war formerly used to blow in door &c.; kind of firework, cracker; HOIST² *with his own p.* [f. F *pétard* (*péter* break wind ult. f. L *pedere,* see -ARD)]

pĕ·tasus, n. Ancient Greek low-crowned broad-brimmed hat, esp. as worn by Hermes; winged hat of Hermes. [L, f. Gk *petasos*]

petaur·ist, n. Genus of marsupials most of which have a patagium enabling them to take flying leaps. [f. Gk *petauristēs* performer on spring-board (*petauron*)]

Pe·ter¹, n. A male Christian name; *St P.,* one of Christ's disciples; *rob P. to pay Paul,* take away from one to give to another, discharge one debt by incurring another; BLUE *P.*; *P.'s fish,* haddock or other fish with marks supposed to have been made by St P.'s thumb & finger; *P.-penny, P.'s-penny* or *pence,* (Hist.) annual tax of penny paid to papal see, (since 1860) voluntary payments to papal treasury. [f. L f. Gk *Petros* stone]

pe·ter², v.i. (slang). (Of stream, vein of ore, & fig.) *p. out,* give out, come to an end. [?]

pē·tersham (-sh-), n. Thick ribbed or corded silk ribbon; heavy overcoat or breeches formerly worn; cloth for these. [Viscount *P.*, c. 1812]

pĕ·tiole, n. (bot.). Leaf-stalk. Hence **pe·tiolAR**¹, **pe·tiolATE**²(2), aa. [f. L *petiolus* little foot, stalk]

petit (petē·), a. *Petits-chevaux* (-vō), a gambling game; *p.-maître* (mātr), dandy, coxcomb; *p. mal,* mild form of epilepsy; *p. souper* (sōōpā), informal supper for a few intimates; *petits soins,* small attentions; *p. verre* (vār), glass of liqueur. [F, = little]

petite (F), a. (Of woman) of small dainty make. [fem. of prec.]

peti·tio (-tĭshĭō, -tĭtĭō), n. *P. principii,* begging the question. [L, as foll.]

peti·tion (-tĭshn), n., & v.t. & i. Asking, supplication, request; formal written supplication from one or more persons to sovereign &c.; (Hist.) *P. & Advice,* Parliament's remonstrance to Cromwell 1657, *P. of Right,* parliamentary declaration of rights & liberties of the people assented to by Charles I in 1628; (Law) kinds of formal written application to a court; (v.t.) make p. to (sovereign &c. *for* thing, *to* do); (v.i.) ask humbly (*for* thing, *to* be allowed to do &c.). So **peti·tionARY**¹ a., **peti·tionER**¹ n. (esp., plaintiff in divorce suit). [f. F *pétition* f. L *petitionem* (*petere -tit-* seek, see -ION)]

pĕ·trel, n. (Also *storm-p., stormy p.*) small sea-bird with black & white plumage & long wings. [perh. f. St *Peter* + -REL]

petrifa·ction, n. Petrifying; petrified substance or mass. [irreg. f. foll., see -FACTION; the reg. *petrification* is now rare]

pĕ·trify̆, v.t. & i. Convert into stone; (fig.) paralyse, stupefy, with astonishment, terror, &c. (*-fied with fear* &c.); deprive (mind, doctrine, &c.) of vitality, stiffen; (intr.) turn into stone (lit. & fig.). [f. F *pétrifier* f. L f. Gk *petra* rock, see -FY]

petro- in comb. = Gk *petra* rock, as: *-glyph*, rock-carving; *-graph*, rock-inscription; *-graphy*, scientific description of formation & composition of rocks, so *-grapher* n., *-gra·phic(al)* aa.; *-logy*, study of origin, structure, &c., of rocks, so *-lo·gic(al)* aa., *-lo·gically* adv., *-logist* n.

pĕ·trol, n., & v.t. Refined petroleum as used in motor-cars &c.; (v.t.) supply (motor) with this. [f. F *pétrole* f. foll.]

petrō·leum, n. Mineral oil found in rocks or on surface of water, used for illumination & mechanical power. [med. L (L & Gk *petra* rock + L *oleum* oil)]

pétroleur (pĕtrōler·), n. (fem. *-euse* pron. -erz). Incendiary who uses petroleum. [F]

petrŏ·lic, a. Of petrol or petroleum. [-IC]

pe·trolin, n. Oil got from petroleum; substance got from Rangoon petroleum. [-IN]

pe·tronel, n. (hist.). Large pistol used esp. by horse-soldiers in 16–17th cc. [f. F *petrinal* (*poitrine* chest, ult. f. L *pectus -oris*, see -AL); the butt end rested against chest in firing]

pĕ·trous, a. Of, like, rock, esp. (Anat.) applied to hard part of the temporal bone. [f. L *petrosus* (L & Gk *petra* rock, see -OUS)]

pe·tticoat, n. Woman's (under-)garment fastened round waist & hanging loose usu. inside a skirt (*have known him since he was in pp.*, a small child); *she is a Cromwell in pp.* (in all but sex); woman, girl, (pl.) female sex; (attrib.) feminine, esp. *p. government*, predominance of woman in the home or in politics. Hence **pe·tticoat**ED², **pe·tticoat**LESS, aa. [earlier *petty coat*]

pe·ttifog, v.i. Practise legal chicanery; quibble, wrangle, about petty points. [prob. back formation f. foll.]

pe·ttifogger, n. Inferior legal practioner; rascally attorney; petty practitioner in any department. Hence **pe·ttifogg**ERY(4) n., **pe·ttifogg**ING² a. [f. PETTY; *-fogger* unexpl.]

pe·ttish, a. Peevish, petulant, easily put out. Hence **pe·ttish**LY² adv., **pe·ttish**NESS n. [f. PET² + -ISH¹]

pe·ttitoes, n. pl. Pig's trotters. [?]

pe·tto, n. *In p.*, in one's own breast, in secret. [It., f. L *pectus*]

pe·tty, a. Unimportant, trivial; little-minded; minor, inferior, on a small scale, as *p. princes, farmers*; *p. cash*, small cash items of receipt or expenditure; *p. officer*, in navy corresponding in rank to N.C.O.; *p.* JURY, LARCENY, SESSION. Hence **pe·tti**LY² adv., **pe·tti**NESS n. [earlier *petit* f. F *petit* etym. dub.]

pĕ·tulant, a. Peevishly impatient or irritable. Hence or cogn. **pe·tul**ANCE n., **pe·tulant**LY² adv. [f. F *pétulant* f. L *petulantem* (**petulare* dim. of *petere* seek, see -ANT)]

petū·nia, n. Plant with white, purple, or violet flowers of funnel shape; dark violet, purple, (esp. attrib.). [f. F *petun* f. S.-Amer. *pety* tobacco]

petu·ntsĕ (-ŏŏn-, -ŭn-), n. White earth used in China for making porcelain. [f. Chin. *pai-tun-tze* (*pai* white + *tun* stone + suf. *-tze*)]

pew (pū), n., & v.t. Place (often enclosed & raised) in church appropriated to a family (*family p.*) or others; fixed bench with back in church; *p.-rent* (for p. or seats in church); (v.t.) furnish with pp., enclose in p. Hence **pew·**AGE(4) n., **pew·**LESS a. [ME *puwe* prob. f. OF *puye* balcony f. L *podia* pl. of *podium* f. Gk *podion* pedestal (*pous podos* foot)]

pewit, peewit, (pē·wit, pū·it), n. Lapwing; its cry; *p.* (*gull*), black-headed gull. [imit.]

pew·ter (pū-), n. Grey alloy of tin & lead or other metal; utensils of this; p. pot; (slang) prize-money. [ME & OF *peutre*, It. *peltro*, etym. dub.]

pfe·nnig, -ing, n. Small German copper coin worth $\frac{1}{8}$ of English penny. [G, cogn. w. PENNY]

phaeton (fā·ĭtn, fā·tn), n. Light four-wheeled open carriage usu. drawn by pair of horses. [f. Gk *Phaethōn*, son of Helios (Sun-god) and famous for bad driving of sun chariot]

phăged(a)e·na (-j-, -g-), n. Spreading ulcer. So **phagedae·n**IC, **-dĕn**IC, a. [L, f. Gk *phagedaina* (*phag-* eat)]

phă·gocyte, n. Leucocyte capable of guarding the system against infection by absorbing microbes. [f. Gk *phag-* eat + -O- + -CYTE]

-phagous in comb. = Gk *-phagos* -eating + -OUS.

phă·lange (-j), n. See PHALANX.

phala·ngeal, a. (anat.). Of a phalanx. [-AL]

phala·nger (-j-), n. Kinds of Australian marsupial of arboreal habits, e.g. flying squirrel or opossum. [f. Gk *phalaggion* spider's web (PHALANX), from webbed toes of hind feet]

phă·lanstery, n. (Buildings of) socialistic PHALANX. Hence **phalanstē̆r·**IAN a. & n. [f. F *phalanstère* f. foll. after *monastère*]

phă·lanx, n. (pl. *pha·lanxes, phala·ngēs*). (Gk Ant.) line of battle, esp. body of Macedonian infantry drawn up in close order; set of persons banded together for common purpose; socialistic community of about 1800 persons as proposed by Fourier; (Anat., also *pha·lange*) each bone of finger or toe; (Bot.) bundle of

stamens united by filaments. [L, f. Gk *phalagx -ggos*]
phă·larope, n. Kinds of small wading and swimming bird allied to snipe. [F, irreg. f. Gk *phalaris* coot + *pous* foot]
pha·llus, n. (pl.) *-ī*. Image of the penis, venerated in religious systems as symbolizing generative power in nature. Hence or cogn. **pha·llIC** a., **pha·ll(ic)ISM**(3) nn. [L, f. Gk *phallos*]
phană·riot, n. Resident in the Phanar quarter of Constantinople; member of the Greek official class under the Turks. [f. mod. Gk *phanariōtēs* (*phanari* lighthouse f. Gk *phanarion*, see -OT[2])]
phă·nerogam, n. (bot.). Plant that has stamens & pistils, flowering plant, (cf. CRYPTOGAM). So **phanerogă·mIC, phanerŏ·gamOUS** a. [f. F *phanérogame* f. Gk *phaneros* visible + *-gamos* -married]
pha·nsigar, n. Thug. [Hind. (*phansi* noose)]
pha·ntasm (-zm), n. Illusion, phantom; illusive likeness (*of*); (Physics) supposed vision of absent (living or dead) person. Hence **phanta·smAL, phanta·smIC,** aa., **phanta·smalLY**[2] adv. [f. F *fantasme* f. L f. Gk *phantasma* (*phantazō* make visible f. *phan-* stem of *phainō* show, see -M)]
phantasmagor·ia, n. Exhibition of optical illusions in London in 1802; shifting scene of real or imagined figures. Hence **phantasmagŏ·rIC** a. [f. prec. + Gk *agora* assembly]
phantasy. See FANTASY (the *ph-* form is used esp. for the first sense there given).
pha·ntom, n. Apparition, spectre; image (*of*); vain show, form without substance or reality; mental illusion; (attrib.) apparent, illusive, as *p. tumour*, temporary swelling. [ME & OF *fantosme* PHANTASM]
Phār·aoh (-rō), n. Generic name of ancient Egyptian kings; *P.'s serpent*, chemical toy fusing in serpentine form. [f. L f. Gk *Pharaō* ult. f. Egypt. *pr'o* great house]
Phă·risee, n. One of ancient Jewish sect distinguished by strict observance of traditional & written law & pretensions to sanctity; self-righteous person, formalist, hypocrite. Hence or cogn. **Pharisā·IC(AL)** aa., **Pharisa·icalLY**[2] adv., **Pha·risāISM** n. [f. L f. Gk *Pharisaios* ult. f. Heb. *parush* separated]
pharmaceu·tical (-sū-, -kū-), a. Of, engaged in, pharmacy; of the use or sale of medicinal drugs. Hence or cogn. **pharmaceu·ticalLY**[2] adv., **pharmaceu·tICS** n. [f. L f. Gk *pharmakeutikos* (*pharmakeutēs* druggist f. *pharmakon* drug) + -AL]
pharmaco·logy, n. Theory of pharmacy. Hence **pharmaco·logIST** n. [f. Gk *pharmakon* drug + -LOGY]
pharmacopoe·ia (-pēa), n. Book (esp. one officially published) containing list of drugs with directions for use; stock of drugs. Hence **pharmacopoe·iAL** a. [f. Gk *pharmakopoiia* (as prec. + *-poiia* making f. *poieō* make)]
phar·macy, n. Preparation & (esp. medicinal) dispensing of drugs; drug-store, dispensary. [f. OF *farmacie* f. LL f. Gk *pharmakeia* practice of the druggist (*pharmakeus* f. *pharmakon* drug)]
phār·ŏs, n. Lighthouse or beacon to guide mariners. [L f. Gk *Pharos*, island off Alexandria, lighthouse on this]
pharyngo- in comb. = foll., as: *-cele*, abnormal enlargement at base of pharynx; *-tomy*, incision into pharynx.
phă·rynx, n. Cavity, with enclosing muscles & mucous membrane, behind & communicating with nose, mouth, & larynx. Hence **phary·ngAL, phary·ngeAL** (-j-), aa., **pharyngI·TIS** (-j-) n. [f. Gk *pharugx -ggos*]
phase (-z), n. Aspect of moon or planet, according to amount of illumination (esp. applied to new moon, first quarter, full moon, last quarter); stage of change or development. Hence **phā·sIC** a. [f. Gk *phasis* appearance (*phan-* show), also in E w. pl. pron. -sēz]
phea·sant (fĕz-), n. A game-bird naturalized in Britain & other parts of Europe; *p.-eyed*, (of flowers) marked like p.'s eye. [AF *fesant*, f. L f. Gk *Phasianos* (bird) of the river *Phasis*]
phen(o)- in comb. = Gk *phainos* shining (*phan-* show), in chem. names of substances derived from coal-tar (orig. in manufacture of illuminating gas), as: *phena·cetin*, an anti-pyretic; *phē·nol*, carbolic acid; *phĕ̄·nyl*, radical found in benzene, phenol, &c.
pheno·logy, n. Study of the times of recurring natural phenomena esp. in relation to climatic conditions. So **phēnolo·gICAL** a. [f. PHENOMENON + -LOGY]
phenŏ·menal, a. Of the nature of a phenomenon; cognizable by, evidenced only by, the senses; concerned with phenomena; remarkable, prodigious. Hence **pheno·menalLY**[2] adv., **pheno·menalIZE** v.t., make, or represent as, p. [-AL]
pheno·men(al)ism, n. Doctrine that phenomena are the only objects of knowledge. So **pheno·men(al)IST** n., **phenomen(al)i·stIC** a. [prec. + -ISM]
phenŏ·menon, n. (pl. *-ena*). Thing that appears or is perceived, esp. thing the cause of which is in question; (Philos.) that of which a sense or the mind directly takes note, immediate object of perception; remarkable person, thing, occurrence, &c. [f. LL f. Gk *phainomenon* neut. part. of *phainomai* appear]
phew, int. expr. impatience or disgust.
phī, n. Greek letter (Φ, φ) = ph. [Gk]
phī·al, n. Small glass bottle, esp. for liquid medicine. [f. F *fiole* f. L f. Gk *phialē* broad flat vessel]
phil- in comb. = PHILO- before vowel or *h*.
-phil, -phīle, suf. forming nn. w. sense

'lover of' & adjj. = '-loving', as *biblio-phil(e)*, *Russophil(e)*, *gastrophil(e)*; repr. Gk *philos* dear, in Gk found as suf. only in personal names w. sense 'dear to' (*Diphilos* dear to Zeus), the sense 'loving' being given in Gk by PHILO-. Hence **-philous** adj. suf.

phila·nder, v.i. Make love esp. in trifling manner, dangle after woman. Hence **phila·nderER**[1] n. [f. *philander* n. f. Gk PHIL(*andros* f. *anēr* man) prop. = fond of men, taken in sense 'lover']

phi·lanthrōpe, n. = PHILANTHROPIST. [f. Gk PHIL(*anthrōpos* man)]

philanthrŏ·pic, a. Loving one's fellow men, benevolent, humane. Hence **philanthro·pICALLY** adv. [f. F *philanthropique* (as prec., see -IC)]

phila·nthropist, n. Lover of mankind; one who exerts himself for the well-being of his fellow men. So **phila·nthropISM** n. [f. PHILANTHROPY + -IST]

phila·nthropize, v.i. & t. Practise philanthropy; make (persons) objects of this; make philanthropic. [-IZE]

phila·nthropy, n. Love, practical benevolence, towards mankind. [f. LL f. Gk *philanthrōpia* (as PHILANTHROPE)]

philă·tely, n. Stamp-collecting. Hence **philatĕ·lIC** a., **philă·telIST** n. [f. F PHIL(*atélie* f. Gk *ateleia* exemption from payment f. *a-* not + *telos* toll, tax)]

philharmŏ·nic, a. & n. (Person) fond of music. [f. F PHIL(*harmonique* HARMONIC)]

phi·lhellene (-ēn), a. & n. (Person) loving or friendly to the Greeks or supporting the cause of Greek independence. So **philhellĕ·nIC** a., **philhe·llenISM**, **philhe·llenIST**, nn. [f. Gk PHIL(*ellēn* = *Hellēn* Greek)]

Phili·ppī. *Thou shalt see me at P., meet at P.*, phrases threatening retribution (w. ref. to Shaksp., *J.C.*, IV. iii. 283). [battle at *P.*, 42 B.C.]

phili·ppic, n. (Pl.) orations of Demosthenes against Philip of Macedon, Cicero's orations against Antony; bitter invective. [f. L f. Gk *philippikos* (*Philippos* Philip, see -IC)]

philippi·na (-pē-), **-pi·ne** (-ēn), **philopoe·na,** n. Almond or other nut with double kernel, the finding of which at dessert &c. & sharing it with another person involves the giving or receiving of a present at next meeting; the present; the custom. [perh. f. G *vielliebchen* darling (*viel* much + *liebchen* dim. of *lieb* dear)]

Phi·listīne, n. & a. One of an alien warlike people in S. Palestine who harassed the Israelites; (facet.) enemy into whose hands one may fall, e.g. bailiff, critic, &c.; (in German univv., after G *philister*) non-student, outsider; uncultured person, one whose interests are material & commonplace, whence **Phi·listinISM** n.; (adj.) uncultured, commonplace, prosaic. [f. F *Philistin* f. LL f. Gk *Philistinos* = *Palaistinos* f. Assyr. *Palastu*, *Pilistu*]

phĭlo- in comb. (before vowel or *h*, *phil-*) = Gk *philos*, lover of, friend of, in wds f. Gk & mod. formations, as: *-bi·blic*, fond of books; *-gy̆nist* (-j-), lover of women; *-math*, lover of learning, esp. of mathematics; *-proge·nitive*, prolific, (Phrenol.) loving one's offspring, whence *-proge·nitiveness*; *-te·chnic*, fond of (esp. the industrial) arts.

philo·logy, n. Science of language; (now rare) love of learning & literature. Hence **philo·logER**[1], **philolō·gIAN**, **philo·logIST**, nn., **philolo·gICAL** a., **philo·logicalLY**[2] adv., **philo·logIZE**(2) v.i. [f. L f. Gk PHILO(*logia* f. *logos* word, speech) love of learning]

Phi·lomel, Philomē·la, nn. (poet.). The nightingale. [f. F *philomèle* f. L f. Gk PHILO(*mēla* f. *melos* song or *mēlon* apple), cap. *P* in reference to myth of P. transformed into nightingale]

philopoe·na. See PHILIPPINA.

philo·sopher, n. Lover of wisdom; *natural, moral, p.*, student of natural, moral, philosophy; one who regulates his life by the light of philosophy; one who shows philosophic calmness in trying circumstances; *philosophers'* (not *-er's*) *stone*, supreme object of alchemy, substance supposed to change other metals into gold or silver. [var. of OF *filosofe* f. L f. Gk *philosophos* (as PHILOSOPHY)]

philoso·phic(al), aa. Of, consonant with, philosophy; skilled in, devoted to, philosophy (often in titles of societies); wise; calm; temperate. Hence **philoso·phicalLY**[2] adv. [f. LL *philosophicus* f. Gk as prec., see -IC]

philo·sophism, n. Philosophizing system (usu. contempt., esp. of the French Encyclopaedists). So **philo·sophIST** n. [f. F *philosophisme* (as PHILOSOPHER, see -ISM)]

philo·sophize, v.i. & t. Play the philosopher; speculate, theorize; moralize; render philosophic. [as PHILOSOPHER + -IZE]

philo·sophy, n. Love of wisdom or knowledge, esp. that which deals with ultimate reality, or with the most general causes & principles of things; *natural p.*, study of natural objects & phenomena; *moral p.*, study of principles of human action or conduct; (w. pl.) philosophical system; system for conduct of life; serenity, resignation. [f. OF *filosofie* f. L f. Gk PHILO(*sophia* wisdom f. *sophos* wise)]

phi·ltre, -ter, n. Love-potion. [F (*-tre*) f. L f. Gk *philtron* (*phileō* love + *-tron* suf. of instrument)]

phiz, n. (colloq.). Face; expression of face. [abbr. of PHYSIOGNOMY]

phlebī·tis, n. Inflammation of walls of vein. Hence **phlebĭ·tIC** a. [f. Gk as foll. + -ITIS]

phlĕ·bo- in comb. = Gk *phleps phlebos*

vein, as: *-lite, -lith,* morbid calcareous concretion in vein, so *-li·t(h)ic* a.

phlebo·tomize, v.i. & t. Practise phlebotomy; bleed (person, part of body). So **phlebo·tom**IST n. [f. F *phlébotomiser* (foll., -IZE)]

phlebo·tomy, n. Blood-letting as medical operation. [f. OF *flebothomie* f. L f. Gk *phlebotomia* f. PHLEBO(*tomos* -cutter f. *temnō* cut)]

phlegm (-ĕm), n. Thick viscid (semi)fluid substance secreted by mucous membranes (formerly regarded as one of the four HUMOURS) esp. when morbid or excessive & discharged by cough &c., whence **phlĕg·m**Y[2] a.; coolness, sluggishness, apathy, (supposed to result from predominance of p. in constitution), so **phlegmă·**TIC (-gm-) a., **phlegma·**TICALLY adv. [f. OF *fleume* f. LL f. Gk *phlegma -matos* inflammation, phlegm (*phlegō* burn, see -M)]

phle·gmon, n. Inflammatory tumour, boil. Hence **phlegmŏ·**NIC, **phle·gmon**OUS, aa. [ME f. L, f. Gk *phlegmonē* (*phlegō* burn)]

phlō·ĕm, n. (bot.). Bast with associated tissues. [f. Gk *phloos* bark + *-ēma* (see -M)]

phlogi·stic (-j-, -g-), a. Of phlogiston; (Med.) inflammatory. [-IC]

phlogi·ston (-j-, -g-), n. Principle of inflammability formerly supposed to exist in combustible bodies. [Gk, f. *phlogizō* set on fire (*phlox phlogos* flame, see -IZE)]

phlorī·zin (*or* flŏ·rĭ) n. (chem.) Bitter substance got from bark of root of apple & other trees. [f. Gk *phloos* bark + *rhiza* root + -IN]

phlox, n. Genus of plants with clusters of salver-shaped flowers of various colours. [L f. Gk *phlox* (lit. flame), a plant]

-phobe, suf. forming aa. & nn., = -fearing, -fearer, f. F *-phobe* f. L f. Gk *-phobos,* adj. suf. f. *phobos* fear, as in *hydrophobe, Anglophobe, Russophobe.*

-phobia, suf. f. L f. Gk *-phobia,* forming abstract nn. f. adjj. in -PHOBE, as *hydrophobia, Anglophobia.*

Phoe·bus (fēb-), n. The Greek sun-god; (poet.) the sun. [L, f. Gk *Phoibos*]

Phoenĭ·cian (-shn), a. & n. (Inhabitant) of Phoenicia (ancient name for part of coast of Syria) or its colonies; Carthaginian. [f. F *phénicien* f. L *Phoenicia* f. Gk *Phoinikē* + -AN]

phoe·nix, phē-, n. (Myth.) bird, the only one of its kind, that after living five or six centuries in Arabian desert burnt itself on funeral pile & rose from the ashes with renewed youth to live through another cycle; paragon. [L, f. Gk *phoinix* Phoenician, purple, phoenix]

pho·nate, v.i. Utter vocal sound (usu. opp. to *articulate*). Hence **phon**A·TION n., **phō·nat**ORY a. [f. Gk *phōne* voice + -ATE[3]]

phonau·tograph, n. Apparatus for automatically recording vibrations of sound. [as prec. + AUTO- + -GRAPH]

phone[1], n., & v.i. & t., (colloq.). Telephone.

phone[2], n. Simple vowel or consonant sound. [f. Gk *phōnē* voice]

phone·ndoscope, n. Apparatus for making small sounds (esp. in human body) distinctly audible. [as prec. + Gk *endon* within + -SCOPE]

phonĕ·tic, a. & n. Representing vocal sounds, esp. (of systems of spelling) using always same letter for same sound, whence **phone·tic**ISM, **phone·tic**IST, nn., **phone·tic**IZE(3) v.t.; of vocal sounds; (n. pl.) (study of) p. phenomena of a language. Hence **phone·**TICALLY adv., **phō-neti·**CIAN n. [f. Gk *phōnētikos* (*phōneō* speak, see -ETIC)]

phō·netist, n. Person versed in phonetics; advocate of phonetic spelling. [-IST]

phŏ̄·nic, a. Of sound, acoustic; of vocal sounds. [f. Gk *phōnē* voice + -IC]

phōno- in comb. = Gk *phōnē* sound, as: *-lite,* kinds of volcanic rock ringing when struck; *-logy,* science of vocal sounds, system of sounds in a language, so *-lo·gic(al)* aa., *-lo·gically* adv., *-logist* n.; *-meter,* instrument recording number or force of sound-waves; *-pore,* apparatus for transmitting telephone messages along telegraph wire without interfering with the current transmitting telegraph messages [Gk *poros* passage], so *-pŏ·ric* a.; *-scope,* apparatus for testing musical strings, (also) instrument for representing sound-vibrations in visible form; *-type,* phonetic print, character used in this, so *-ty·pic(al)* aa., *-typist, -typy,* nn.

phō·nogram, n. Symbol representing spoken sound, esp. in Pitman's phonography; sound-record made by phonograph. [PHONO-, -GRAM]

pho·nograph, n., & v.t. Instrument automatically recording & reproducing sounds; (v.t.) record, reproduce, by p. [PHONO- + -GRAPH]

phono·graphy, n. Pitman's phonetic shorthand, whence **phono·graph**ER[1], **phono·graph**IST, nn.; automatic recording of sounds, as by phonograph. Hence **phonogra·ph**IC a., **phonogra·ph**ICALLY adv. [PHONO- + -GRAPHY]

-phore, suf. = bearer, f. F *-phore* f. Gk *-phoros* (*pherō* bear), used to form technical wds, as *carpophore, semaphore.* Hence **-phorous,** adj. suf., = *-phore* + -OUS, synonymous w. -FEROUS, but prop. used only in wds f. Gk as *carpophorous.*

pho·sgene, n. A poison gas, carbon oxychloride, used in the great war. [f. Gk *phōs* light + -GEN(1), w. ref. to its orig. production by action of sunlight on chlorine & carbonic oxide]

pho·sphate (-*at*), n. A salt of phosphoric acid, esp. (pl.) of lime or iron & alumina as constituents of cereals &c. Hence **phosphă·tic** a. [F (PHOSPHO- + -ATE[1])]

pho·sphene, n. Appearance of rings of light produced by pressure on eyeball, due to irritation of retina. [irreg. f. Gk *phōs* light + *phainō* show]

pho·sphide, n. (chem.). Combination of phosphorus with other element or radical. [f. PHOSPHO- + -IDE]

pho·sphite, n. (chem.). A salt of phosphorous acid. [F (PHOSPHO- + -ITE[1])]

phosph(o)- in comb. = PHOSPHORUS.

pho·sphorate, v.t. Combine, impregnate, with phosphorus. [-ATE[3]]

phosphore·sce, v.i. Emit luminosity without combustion, or by gentle combustion without sensible heat. So **phosphore·scence** n., **phosphore·scent** a. [f. PHOSPHORUS + L *-escere* of inceptive vbs]

pho·sphorite, n. A non-crystallized variety of phosphate of lime. [f. PHOSPHORUS + -ITE[1]]

phosphoro- in comb. = phosphorus, as: *-gĕ·nic,* causing phosphorescence; *-graph,* evanescent picture on phosphorescent surface, so *-gra·phic* a., *-graphy* n.; *-scope,* apparatus for measuring duration of phosphorescence, (also) toy containing various phosphorescent substances glowing with different coloured lights.

pho·sphorus, n. A non-metallic element, a yellowish wax-like substance undergoing slow combustion at ordinary temperatures & hence appearing luminous in the dark; *p. necrosis* (colloq. *phossy jaw*), gangrene of jawbone due to p. fumes esp. in match-making. Hence or cogn. **phosphŏ·ric, pho·sphorous,** aa., **pho·sphorism**(5) n. (path.). [L, = morning star, f. Gk *phōsphoros* (*phōs* light + *-phoros* -bringing f. *pherō*)]

pho·sphuret(t)ed, a. Combined chemically with phosphorus. [f. obs. *phosphuret* phosphide + -ED[2]]

pho·ssy. See PHOSPHORUS.

phō·tism, n. Hallucinatory sensation or vision of light. [f. Gk *phōtismos* (*phōtizō* shine f. *phōs phōtos* light, see -ISM)]

phō·to, n. (pl. *-os*), & v.t. = PHOTOGRAPH.

photo- in comb. = Gk *phōs phōtos* light (sometimes = photographic), as: *-chromy,* colour-photography; *-gen,* kind of paraffin oil; *-gĕ·nic,* producing or emitting light; *-glyph, -glyphy,* engraved plate produced by action of light, art of producing such plates; *-meter,* instrument for measuring intensity of light, so *-me·tric, -metry*; *-pho·bia* (path.), dread of light; *-phone,* apparatus in which sounds are transmitted by light; *-sphere,* luminous envelope of sun or star from which its light & heat radiate, so *-sphĕ·ric* a.; *-tele·graphy,* electric reproduction of pictures, writing, &c., at a distance (cf. TELEPHOTOGRAPHY); *-type,* plate for printing from produced by photographic process, picture &c. printed from this; *-zinco·graphy,* photographic production of design on zinc plate.

pho·tograph, n., & v.t. Picture, likeness, taken by means of chemical action of light on sensitive film on basis of glass, paper, metal, &c.; (v.t.) take p. of (person &c., or abs.); (quasi-pass.) *I always p. badly* (come out badly in p.). Hence **photo·grapher**[1], **photo·graphy**[1], nn., **photogra·phic** a., **photogra·phically** adv. [(vb f. n.) PHOTO- + -GRAPH]

photogravure· (-ūr), n., & v.t. Picture produced from photographic negative transferred to metal plate & etched in; this process; (v.t.) reproduce thus. [F (PHOTO- + *gravure* engraving)]

phrase (-z), n., & v.t. Mode of expression, diction, as *in simple p., felicity of p.*; an idiomatic expression; small group of words usu. without predicate, esp. preposition with the word(s) it governs, equivalent to adjective, adverb, or noun (e.g. the house *on the hill,* I refuse *to do it*); short pithy expression; (pl.) mere words, as *we have had enough of pp.*; (Mus.) short & more or less independent passage forming part of longer passage or of whole piece; *p.-monger,* person addicted to fine-sounding phrases; (v.t.) express in words, as *thus he phrased it.* [(vb f. n.) f. LL f. Gk *phrasis* (*phrazō* tell)]

phrā·sĕogram, n. Written symbol representing a phrase esp. in shorthand. [as prec. + -O- + -GRAM]

phra·seograph, n. Phrase for which there is a phraseogram. [as prec. + -GRAPH]

phraseo·logy, n. Choice or arrangement of words; mode of expression. Hence **phraseolo·gical** a., **phraseolo·gically**[2] adv. [as prec. + -LOGY]

phrā·try, n. (Gk Hist.) a kinship unit, esp. (in Athens) each of three sub-divisions of the (*phyle* or) tribe; tribal division among primitive races. [f. Gk *phratria* (*phratēr, -tōr,* clansman, cogn. w. BROTHER)]

phrenĕ·tic, a. Frantic; fanatic. [f. OF *frenetike* f. L f. late Gk *phrenētikos* = Gk *phrenitikos* (*phrenitis* delirium, as foll., see -ITIS & -IC)]

phrĕ·nic, a. (anat.). Of the diaphragm. [f. Gk *phrēn phrenos* diaphragm, mind, see -IC]

phreno·logy, n. Study of external conformation of cranium as index to development & position of organs belonging to the various mental faculties. Hence **phrenolo·gical** a., **phrenolo·gically**[2] adv., **phreno·logist** n. [as prec. + -LOGY]

phro·ntistery, n. (facet.). Place for thinking in, thinkery. [f. Gk *phrontistērion* (*phrontizō* think f. *phrontis* thought)]

Phrȳ·gian, a. Of Phrygia, ancient country in Asia Minor; (Mus.) *P. mode,* ancient Greek mode of warlike character; *P. cap,* ancient conical peaked cap now identified with cap of liberty. [f. L *Phrygianus* (*Phrygia*, see -AN)]

phthi·sis (fth-, th-), n. Progressive wasting disease, esp. pulmonary consumption. So (through OF *tisike*) **phthi·sical** (tĭz-) a., of, having, phthisis. [Gk (*phthinō* decay)]

phut, n. & adv. The sound of a bladder collapsing, a bullet passing, &c.; (adv., esp.) *go p.*, collapse (also fig. of scheme &c.). [prob. imit.]

phўla·ctery, n. Small leather box containing Hebrew texts on vellum, worn by Jews to remind them to keep the law (*make broad* one's *p.* or *pp.*, make a display of righteousness); (usu. ostentatious) religious observance; amulet, charm. [f. L f. Gk *phulaktērion* amulet (*phulassō* guard)]

phȳlĕ·tic, a. (biol.). Of a phylum, racial. [f. Gk *phuletikos* (*phuletēs* tribesman f. *phulē* tribe, see -IC)]

phyllo- in comb. = Gk *phullon* leaf, as: *-phagan*, animal that feeds on leaves, so *-phagous* a.; *-pod* a. & n., leaf-footed (crustacean); *-stome*, leaf-nosed bat; *-ta·xis*, arrangement of leaves on axis or stem; *-xēr·a* [f. Gk *xēros* dry], genus of plant-lice, vine-pest.

phȳlo- in comb. = Gk *phulon* race, tribe, in biol. wds, as: *-ge·nesis*, *-geny*, racial evolution of animal or plant type, history of this, so *-gene·tic*, *-ge·nic*, aa., *-gene·tically* adv.

phȳ·lum, n. (biol.; pl. *-la*). Race of organisms descended from common ancestral form. [mod. L f. Gk *phulon* race]

phў·sic (-z-), n., & v.t. (-ck-). Art of healing; medical profession; (colloq.) medicine, as *a dose of p.*; (n. pl.) sciences treating of properties of matter & energy or of action of different forms of energy on matter in general (excluding chemistry & biology); (v.t.) dose with p. (lit. & fig.). [(vb f. n.) f. OF *fisique* f. L f. Gk *phusikē* (*epistēmē* knowledge) of nature (*phusis*, see -IC)]

phy·sical, a. Of matter, material, as *p. force* (opp. to *moral*); of, according to laws of, natural philosophy, as *p. explanations of miracles, a p. impossibility*; belonging to physics; bodily, as *p. exercise, strength, beauty, drill* (also slang *p. jerks*); *p. geography* (dealing with natural features). Hence **phy·sical**LY[2] adv., **phy·sico-** comb. form. [f. med. L *physicalis* (as prec., see -AL)]

physi·cian (-shn), n. One who practises the healing art including medicine & surgery; one legally qualified in medicine as well as in surgery; (fig.) healer. [f. OF *fisician* (as PHYSIC, see -ICIAN)]

phy·sicist, (-sĭst), n. Student of physics or of natural science in general; believer in the material origin of vital phenomena (cf. VITALIST), so **phy·sic**ISM n. [PHYSIC + -IST]

phy·sicky, a. Suggestive of physic. [-Y[2]]

phўsio- in comb. = Gk *phusis* nature, as *-cracy*, government according to natural order; *-crat*, advocate of this, esp. member of Quesnay's school in France in 18th c.; *-geny*, genesis of vital functions; *-latry*, nature-worship.

physiŏg·nomy (*or* -ŏ·gn-), n. Art of judging character from features of face or form of body, whence **physiog·nom**IST (3) (*or -ŏgn-*) n.; cast of features, type of face; (vulg.) face; external features of country &c.; characteristic (moral or other) aspect. Hence or cogn. **physiog-nŏ·m**IC(AL) aa., **physiogno·mical**LY[2] adv., (-on-, -ogn-). [ME *fisnomye* f. med. L *phisonomia* f. Gk *phusiognōmonia* judging of a man's nature (by his features) f. *phusis* nature + *gnōmōn* judge f. *gnō-* know]

physio·graphy, n. Description of nature, of natural phenomena, or of a class of objects; physical geography. Hence **physio·graph**ER[1] n., **physiogra·phi-c**(AL) aa. [PHYSIO- + -GRAPHY]

physio·logy, n. Science of normal functions and phenomena of living things (comprising *animal* and *vegetable p.*). Hence or cogn. **physiolo·g**IC(AL) aa., **physiolo·gical**LY[2] adv., **physio·log**IST n. [f. L f. Gk *phusiologia*, see PHYSIO- and -LOGY]

physique (-ēk), n. Bodily structure, organization, and development. [F, n. f. adj. (as PHYSIC)]

-phyte, suf. repr. Gk *phuton* plant, denoting a vegetable organism, as *protophyte, saprophyte*. See also ZOOPHYTE.

phўto- in comb. = Gk *phuton* plant, as: *-ge·nesis*, *-geny*, generation or evolution of plants; *-graphy*, descriptive botany; *-mer*, plant unit; *-phagous*, feeding on plants; *-tomy*, dissection of plants; *-zō·on* (pl. *-zo·a*) plant-like animal or zoophyte.

pī[1], n. Greek letter p (Π, π), esp. (Math., π) as symbol of ratio of circumference of circle to diameter (3·14159).

pī[2], a. (school slang). = PIOUS; *pi jaw*, sermonizing, moral lecture. [abbr.]

piă·cular, n. Expiatory. [f. L *piacularis* (*piaculum* expiation f. *piare* appease, see -AR[1])]

pia·ffe, v.i. (Of horse &c.) move as in trot, but slower. [f. F *piaffer*, etym. dub.]

piă·ffer, n. Movement of piaffing. [as prec.]

pī·a mā·ter, n. (anat.). Innermost MENINX. [med. L transl. of Arab. *umm raqiqah* tender mother]

piane·tte, n. Low pianino. [PIANO, -ETTE]

piani·no (-nē-), n. Small upright piano. [It., dim. of PIANO]

piani·ssimo, adv. & n. (mus.). (Passage to be played) very softly. [It., superl. of PIANO[1]]

pi·anist (pē-) n. Player on piano. [f. F *pianiste* (also in E, usu. as fem.), see -IST]

pia·no[1] (pyah-), adv. & n. (mus.). (Passage to be played) softly. [It., f. L *planus* flat, (LL) soft]

pĭă·no[2], **pĭă·nofortĕ** (*or* -t), nn. Musical instrument with metal strings struck by hammers worked by levers from a keyboard (vibration being stopped by dampers), and usu. furnished with pedals for regulating volume; *grand p.*, large harp-shaped p. with horizontal strings; *upright p.*, p. with vertical strings; *cottage p.*, low upright p. with strings ascending obliquely; *p. organ*, mechanical p. constructed like barrel-organ; *p.-player*, contrivance for playing p. mechanically. [It., earlier *piano e forte* soft and strong]

piano·la, n. Kind of mechanical piano-player. [trade name]

pĭă·stre, -ter, n. Spanish silver coin, about 4/2; small Turkish coin worth 2*d.* to 6*d.* [F (*-tre*), f. It. *piastra*, ult. as PLASTER]

pia·zza (-ăza), n. Public square or market-place esp. in Italian town; (U.S.) verandah of house. [It., ult. f. L *platea* f. Gk *plateia* (*hodos*) broad (street)]

pibroch (pē·broch), n. Series of variations for bagpipe, chiefly martial. [f. Gael. *piobaireachd* (*piobair* piper f. *piob* f. E PIPE)]

pi·ca, n. Size of TYPE. [earlier sense, collection of rules about Easter and other movable feasts, f. med. L *pica*, perh. = L *pica* magpie, hist. unexpl.]

pĭcador·, n. Mounted man with lance in bull-fight. [Sp. (*picar* prick)]

pi·camar, n. Bitter oil got from wood-tar. [f. L *pix picis* pitch + *amarus* bitter]

pĭcare·sque (-k), a. (Of a style of fiction) dealing with adventures of rogues. [f. Sp. *picaresco* (*picaro* rogue, etym. dub., -ESQUE)]

picaroo·n, n., & v.i. Rogue; thief; pirate; pirate ship; (v.i.) play the pirate or brigand. [f. Sp. *picaron* (as prec., see -OON)]

pi·ccalilli, n. Pickle of chopped vegetables & hot spices. [?]

pi·ccaninny, pi·ck-, n. & a. Child, esp. of Negroes or S.-African or Australian natives; (adj.) very small, baby. [f. Sp. *pequeño* or Port. *pequeno*, dim. *-nino*, small]

pi·ccolo, n. Small flute, octave higher than the ordinary. [It., = small (flute)]

pīce, n. E.-Ind. copper coin, ¼ of anna. [f. Hind. *paisa*]

pichiciā·go (pĭtsh-), n. Small burrowing animal of Chili, allied to armadillos. [f. Sp. *pichiciego* perh. f. native *pichey* + Sp. *ciego* blind f. L *caecus*]

pick[1], n. Tool consisting of iron bar usu. curved with point at one end & point or chisel-edge at other, with wooden handle passing through middle perpendicularly, used for breaking up hard ground &c.; instrument for picking; TOOTH*p.* [prob. = PIKE]

pick[2], v.t. & i. Break surface of (ground &c.) with or as with pick; make (hole &c.) thus; (fig.) *p.* HOLES *in*; probe (teeth &c.) with pointed instrument to remove extraneous matter; clear (bone, carcass) of adherent flesh, pluck, gather, (flower, fruit, &c.) from stalk &c.; (of birds) take up (grains &c.) in bill; (of persons) eat (food, or meal, or abs.) in small bits, (colloq.) eat (t. & i.); select carefully, as *p.* one's *words, way, steps, p. & choose,* select fastidiously; *p.* (contrive) *a quarrel with*; *p.* (person's) *pocket*, steal its contents; (intr.) *p. & steal*, pilfer; *p. a lock*, open it (esp. with intent to rob) with pointed instrument, skeleton key, &c.; pull asunder, esp. *p. oakum*; *p. to pieces*, pull asunder, (fig.) criticize (person &c.) hostilely; *p. off*, pluck off, (also) shoot (persons &c.) deliberately one by one; *p. out*, select, distinguish from surrounding objects, relieve (ground colour *with* another), make out (meaning of passage &c.), play (tune) by ear on piano &c.; *p. up*, break up (ground &c.) with pick, lay hold of & take up, raise one*self* from a fall &c., gain, acquire (livelihood, profit, tricks, information), take (person, or thing overtaken) along with one, esp. *train stops to p. up passengers*, regain (lost path &c., *flesh, spirit*), (intr.) recover health, make acquaintance *with*, (Games) select sides by alternate choosing (*p.-up* n., game between such sides); *picklock*, person who picks locks, instrument used for this; *p.-me-up*, stimulating drink (also fig.); *pickpocket*, one who steals from pockets; *pick-thank* (archaic), sycophant; *p.-up*, picking up (esp. of ball in cricket). [OE has *pīken, pikken*, hist. dub., cf. prec. & F *piquer* prick]

pick[3], n. Picking; selection; *the* best part *of*. [f. prec.]

pi·ck-a-back, adv. On shoulders or back like a bundle (of the way person or thing is carried). [?]

pi·ckax(e), n., & v.t. & i. = PICK[1]; (v.t.) break (ground &c.) with p.; (v.i.) work with p. [ME & OF *picois* cogn. w. OF *pic* PIKE, assim. to AXE]

pi·ckelhaube (-howbe), n. German spiked helmet. [G, = spike cap]

pi·cker, n. One who picks, gathers, or collects, as *hop, rag, -p.*; kinds of instrument for picking (in var. senses). [-ER[1]]

pi·ckerel, n. Young pike. [PIKE[1], -REL]

pi·cket, n., & v.t. & i. Pointed stake or peg driven into ground to form palisade, tether horse, &c.; (Hist.) (stake with pointed top on which person stood as) form of military punishment; (Mil., also *piquet, picquet*) small body of troops sent out (*outlying p.*) to watch for enemy, or (*inlying p.*) held ready in quarters, party of sentinels, outpost, (in mod. use, chiefly) camp-guard doing police duty in garrison town &c.; (usu. pl.) men stationed in a body or singly by trade-union to dissuade men from work during strike &c.; (vb) secure (place) with stakes, tether, post (men) as p., beset (workmen) with pp., act as p. [(vb f. n.) f. F *piquet* pointed stake f. *piquer* prick]

pi·cking, n. In vbl senses, esp.: *p. & stealing*; (pl.) gleanings, remaining scraps; (pl.) pilferings. [-ING[1]]

pi·ckle, n., & v.t. Brine, vinegar, or similar liquor in which flesh, vegetables, &c., are preserved; ROD *in p.*; food, esp. (pl.) vegetables preserved in p.; acid solution for cleaning purposes &c.; *sad, sorry, nice,* &c. *p.* (plight); mischievous child; (v.t.) preserve in p. (esp. in p.p.), treat with p., (Naut.) rub salt or vinegar on (person's back) after flogging. [prob. f. MDu. *pekel* etym. dub.]

pi·cksome, a. Fastidious. [PICK[2] + -SOME]

pi·ckwick, n. Cheap kind of cigar. [f. Mr *P.* in Dickens]

Pickwi·ckian, a. (facet.). (Of words) *used in a P.* (technical, constructive, or esoteric) *sense*. [see Dickens *Pickwick* i]

pi·cnic, n., & v.i. (-ck-). Pleasure party including meal out of doors; (v.i.) take part in this. Hence **pic·nicker**[1] n., **pi·cnicky**[2] a. (colloq.). [(vb f. n.) f. F *piquenique* etym. dub.]

picot· (-kō), n. Small loop of twisted thread in edging to lace &c. [F, dim. of *pic* peak, point]

picotee·, n. Carnation of which flowers have light ground with darker edging to petals. [f. F *picoté* p.p. of *picoter* prick, as prec.]

picquet. See PICKET.

pi·cric, a. *P. acid,* yellow very bitter substance used in dyeing & surgery, & in explosives. [f. Gk *pikros* bitter + -IC]

Pict, n. One of an ancient people in N. Britain. Hence **Pi·ctish**[1] a. [LL has *Picti* perh. f. *pingere pict-* paint]

pi·ctograph, n. Pictorial symbol; primitive record consisting of these. Hence **pictogra·phic** a., **picto·graphy**[1] n. [f. L *pingere pict-* paint + -GRAPH]

pictor·ial, a. & n. Of, expressed in, picture(s); illustrated; picturesque; (n.) journal of which pictures are main feature. Hence **pictor·ially**[2] adv. [f. LL *pictorius* (*pictor* painter, as foll.) + -AL]

pi·cture (-tsher), n., & v.t. Painting, drawing, of objects esp. as work of art; portrait, beautiful object, as *her hat is a p.*; scene, total visual impression produced, (fig.) conjuncture or affair (*out of, come into, the p.*, irrelevant, become interesting &c.); *she looks the very p.* (a perfect type) *of health*; *p.-book* (for children, consisting chiefly or wholly of pp.); *p.-card,* court-card; *p.-gallery,* (hall &c. containing) collection of pp.; *p. hat,* lady's wide-brimmed hat usu. black with ostrich-feathers as in pp. of Reynolds & Gainsborough; *p. postcard* (with p. on back); *p.-writing,* mode of recording events &c. by pp., as in early hieroglyphs &c.; *moving pp.* or ellipt. *the pp.* (cinematographic); *p.-palace, -theatre, -drome,* building &c. in which moving pp. are shown; (v.t.) represent in p., describe graphically, imagine (*to oneself*). Hence **pi·cturize** v.t., = FILM v. [(vb f. n.) f. L *pictura* (*pingere, pict-* paint, see -URE)]

picture·sque (-k), a. Like, fit to be the subject of, a striking picture; (of language &c.) strikingly graphic, vivid. Hence **picture·squely**[2] adv., **picture·squeness** n. [f. F *pittoresque* f. It. *pittoresco* (*pittore* painter, as PICTORIAL, see -ESQUE)]

pi·ddle, v.i. (Archaic) work, act, in trifling way; (colloq. or childish) make water. [?]

pi·ddock, n. Bivalve mollusc used for bait. [?]

pi·dgin, pi·geon (-jen), a. *P. English,* jargon chiefly of English words used between Chinese & Europeans. [corrupt. of *business*]

pie[1], n. = MAGPIE; *French, rain-, wood-, p.* kinds of woodpecker; SEA-*p.* [OF, f. L *pica*]

pie[2], n. Dish of meat, fruit, &c., enclosed in or covered with paste & baked; APPLE-*p.* (fig.); *have a finger in the p.,* be (esp. officiously) concerned in the matter; *bran p.,* tub of bran with toys &c. hidden in it to be drawn at random at Christmas festivities &c.; MUD *p.*; *piecrust,* baked paste of p., (prov.) *promises are like piecrust, made to be broken*; *pieman* (-an), vendor of pp. [perh. = prec., f. miscellaneous contents compared to piebald appearance of magpie]

pie[3], n., & v.t. (print.). (Also *printers' p.*) confused mass of type; (fig.) chaos; (v.t.) mix (type). [perh. as prec.]

pie[4], n. (Anglo-Ind.). Copper coin, twelfth part of anna. [f. Hind. *pa'i* f. Skr. *pad* quarter, prob. orig. same as PICE]

pie·bald, a. Of two colours irregularly arranged, esp. black & white (usu. of animal, esp. horse); (fig.) motley, mongrel. [PIE[1] + BALD]

piece[1], n. One of the distinct portions of which thing is composed; *in pp.,* broken; *break to pp.* (fragments); *pick up the pp.* (said to fallen child &c.); enclosed portion *of* (land); detached portion (*of* a substance); *a p. of* one's *mind,* one's candid opinion, rebuke; definite quantity (*of* wall-paper = 12 yds, *of* muslin = 10 yds, &c.) in which thing is made up; cask (*of* wine &c.) varying in capacity; *p.* (product) *of work*; example, specimen, as *a p. of impudence, fine p. of painting, cricket,* &c.; *p. of* GOODS; cannon, gun, pistol; man at chess, draughts, &c.; coin, as *crown, penny, p.*; *p. of eight* (i.e. REAL[1]s), Spanish dollar; picture; literary or musical composition, usu. short; drama; *paid* *by the p.* (according to amount done; *of a piece*, uniform, consistent, in keeping (*with*); *p.-goods*, textile fabrics (esp. Lancashire cotton goods) woven in recognized lengths; *p.-work* (paid for by the p.). [ME & OF *pece*, cf. It. *pezza*, *-zo*, &c., etym. dub.]

piece², v.t. Put together, form into a whole; join threads in spinning, whence **pie·cer¹** n.; fit *on* (thing *to* another); eke *out*; make *out* (story, theory, chain of evidence) by combination of parts; join *together*; patch *up*. [f. prec.]

pièce de résistance (F), n. Most substantial dish at meal (also fig.).

pie·cemeal, adv., a., & n. (Also *by p.*) piece by piece, part at a time; (adj.) done &c. p. [ME (PIECE, OE *-mǣlum* suf. f. instr. pl. of *mǣl* MEAL²)]

pied (pīd), a. Particoloured. [PIE¹, -ED²]

pied à terre (pyā·dahtār·), n. Rest for the sole of one's foot, somewhere to stay. [F]

pier (pēr), n. Breakwater, mole; structure of iron or wood open below running out into sea & used as promenade & landing-stage, whence **pier·age**(4) n.; support of spans of bridge; pillar; solid masonry between windows &c.; *p.-glass*, large mirror orig. used to fill up this. [12th c. *per* f. med. L *pera* etym. dub.]

pierce (pērs), v.t. & i. (Of sharp instrument &c., also fig. of cold, pain, grief, glance, discernment, discerning person, shriek, &c.) penetrate; prick (substance *with* pin &c.); make hole in (cask &c.); force one's way through or into; penetrate *through*, *into*, &c. Hence **pier·cingly²** adv. [f. OF *percer* etym. dub.]

Pīer·ian (*or* -ĕ·rĭ-), a. Of Pieria in N. Thessaly, reputed home of Muses. [f. L *Pierius* + -AN]

pierrot (pyēr·ō, pyĕ·rō), n. (fem. *pierrette*). French pantomine character; itinerant minstrel with whitened face & loose white dress. [F, dim. of *Pierre* PETER]

pietà (pyā·tah), n. Picture, sculpture, of Virgin Mary holding dead body of Christ on her lap. [It., f. L as PIETY]

pi·etism, n. Spener's movement for revival of piety in Lutheran Church in 17th c.; pious sentiment, exaggeration or affectation of this. So **pi·etist** n., **pieti·stic(al)** aa. [f. G *pietismus* (as PIETY, see -ISM)]

pi·ety, n. Quality of being pious. [f. OF *piete* f. L *pietatem* (as PIOUS, see -TY)]

pīĕzŏ·meter, n. Kinds of instrument for measuring pressure or the sense of it. [f. Gk *piezō* press + -O- + -METER]

pi·ffle, v.i., & n., (slang). Talk or act feebly, trifle; (n.) twaddle. Hence **pi·ffler¹** n., **pi·ffling** a., trivial, worthless. [?]

pig, n., & v.i. & t. Swine, hog; flesh of (usu. young or sucking) p. as meat, esp. *roast p.*; GUINEA-*p.* (lit. & fig.); (colloq.) greedy, dirty, sulky, obstinate, or annoying person, whence **pi·ggish¹** a., **pi·ggishly²** adv., **pi·ggishness** n.; oblong mass of metal (usu. iron) from smelting-furnace, esp. *p.-iron*; segment of orange; *buy a p. in a poke*, buy thing without seeing it or knowing its value; *bring* one's *pp. to a fine, a pretty, the wrong, market*, fail in a venture; *pp. might fly*, wonders might happen; *please the pp.*, joc. substitute for *please God*; *pi·gheaded*, obstinate, stupid, whence *pigheadedly* adv., *pigheadedness* n.; *p.-jump*, (of horse) jump sportively from all four legs not brought together as in buck-jumping; *pignut*, a tuber, kind of EARTH-*nut*; *pigskin*, (leather made of) p.'s skin, (slang) saddle; *pi·gsticking*, hunting of wild boar with spear, butchering of swine, so **pi·gsticker** n. (also, long-bladed pocket-knife); *pigstȳ*, sty for pp., (fig.) dirty hovel; *p.'s wash*, *pigwash*, swill of brewery or kitchen given to pp.; *pigweed*, kinds of herb eaten by pp.; (v.i. & t.) bring forth (pigs or abs.); (v.i.) herd together like pigs (also *p. it*). Hence **pi·glet**, **pi·gling¹**, nn. **pi·glike** a. [ME *pigge*, etym. dub.]

pĭ·geon (-jn), n., & v.t. Bird with many varieties, wild, domesticated, produced by fancy breeding, trained to carry missives, &c., the dove, (now preferred to *dove* exc. in poet. & rhet. contexts, or of the turtle-dove); *carrier-p.*, *homing p.*, (trained to carry home messages tied to its neck &c.); simpleton, gull, as PLUCK² *a p.*; *clay p.*, clay saucer thrown into air from trap as mark for shooting; *p.-breast*, deformed human chest laterally constricted, so *p.-breasted*; *pi·geongram*, message carried by p.; *p. English*, see PIDGIN; *p.-hole*, small recess for p. to nest in, one of a set of compartments for papers &c. in cabinet &c., (v.t.) deposit (document) in this, put aside (matter) for future consideration, assign (thing) to definite place in memory; *p. pair*, boy & girl twins, or boy & girl as sole children; *p.'s milk*, partly-digested food with which pp. feed their young, imaginary article for which children are sent on fool's errand; (v.t.) cheat (person *of* thing). [f. OF *pijon* f. LL *pipionem* (nom. *-io*) young cheeping bird (*pipire* cheep)]

pi·geonry, n. Pigeon-house. [-RY]

pi·ggery, n. Pig-breeding establishment; pigsty; dirty place; piggishness. [-ERY]

pi·ggy, n. Little pig; (nursery) *p.-wiggy*, little pig, dirty child; game of tip-cat. [-Y³]

pi·gment, n. Colouring-matter used as paint or dye; natural colouring-matter of a tissue. Hence **pigme·ntal**, **pi·gmentary¹**, aa. [f. L *pigmentum* (*pig-* root of *pingere* paint, -MENT)]

pigmy. See PYGMY.

pi·gtail, n. Tobacco twisted into thin roll; plait of hair hanging from back of head, esp. as worn by Chinese under the Manchus, by young girls, & formerly by soldiers & sailors. Hence **pi·gtailed²** a.

pike[1], n., & v.t. Long wooden shaft with steel or iron head, infantry weapon superseded by the bayonet; (dial.) pickaxe, spike; [perh. diff. wd of Norse orig.] peaked top of hill (in names of hills in Lake district); [prob. abbr. of *p.-fish*, from its pointed snout] large voracious freshwater fish, jack; (v.t.) thrust through, kill, with p.; *pikeman*, miner who uses pickaxe. [(in first sense f. F *pique*, cf. F *piquer* prick, *pic* pickaxe, cogn. w.) OE *pic*, etym. dub.]

pike[2], n. Toll-bar; toll; turnpike road; *pikeman*, keeper of turnpike. [abbr. of TURNPIKE]

pi·kelet, n. Kind of teacake. [f. W (*bara*) *pyglyd* pitchy (bread)]

pi·kestaff, n. Wooden shaft of pike; *plain as a p.* [orig. *packstaff*, smooth staff used by pedlar], quite plain. [PIKE[1] + STAFF]

pilă·ster, n. Rectangular column, esp. one engaged in wall. [f. F *pilastre* f. It. *pilastro* f. med. L *pilastrum* (L *pila* pillar, see -ASTER)]

pilau·, -aw, (-ow, -aw, -ō), **-aff**, n. Oriental dish of rice with meat, spices, &c. [Pers. (*-aw*)]

pilch, n. Triangular flannel wrapper for infant. [OE *pylece*, as PELISSE]

pi·lchard, n. Small sea-fish allied to herring. [?]

pi·lcorn, n. Kind of oat in which husk does not adhere to grain. [= *pilled corn*]

pile[1], n., & v.t. Pointed stake or post; heavy beam driven vertically into bed of river &c. as support for bridge &c.; *p.-driver*, machine for driving pp.; (v.t.) furnish with pp., drive pp. into. [OE *pil* f. L *pilum* javelin]

pile[2], n. Heap of things laid more or less regularly upon one another; (*funeral*) *p.*, heap of combustibles on which corpse is burnt; (colloq.) heap of money, fortune, as *make a p.*, *make* one's *p.* (as much as one wants); lofty mass of buildings; series of plates of dissimilar metals laid one upon another alternately for producing electric current. [F, f. L *pila* pillar]

pile[3], v.t. Heap up (often *up*, *on*); *p. arms*, place (usu. four) rifles with butts on ground & muzzles interlocked; *p. up* naut., run (ship) on rocks or aground; (colloq.) *p. up* (or *on*) *the agony*, intensify painful description &c., *p. it on*, exaggerate; load (table &c. *with*). [f. prec.]

pile[4], n. (archaic). Reverse of coin; *cross or p.*, heads or tails. [as PILE[2], orig. = under iron of minting apparatus]

pile[5], n. Soft hair, down, wool of sheep; nap on cloth, esp. on velvet, plush, &c., or on carpet, as *two, three, -p. carpet.* Hence **pī·ly**[2] a. [f. L *pilus* hair]

pile[6], n. (Pl.) haemorrhoids, disease marked by tumours of veins of lower rectum; (sing.) such tumour; *pilewort*, lesser celandine (from reputed efficacy against pp.). [f. L *pila* ball]

pi·lfer, v.t. & i. Steal (thing, or abs.) esp. in small quantities. Hence **pi·lfer**AGE(3), **pi·lfer**ER[1], nn. [ult. f. OF *pelfre* PELF]

pilgar·lic, n. (archaic). Bald head; bald-headed man; poor creature. [= *pilled* or *peeled garlic*]

pi·lgrim, n., & v.i. One who journeys to sacred place as act of religious devotion; person regarded as journeying to a future life (*The P.'s Progress*); traveller; *The Pp. of Gt Britain, of the U.S.*, societies fostering Anglo-American friendship by mutual hospitality &c.; *P. Fathers*, English Puritans who founded colony of Plymouth, Massachusetts, in 1620; (v.i.) wander like a p. Hence **pi·lgrim**IZE(2) v.i. [ME *pelegrim* f. OF **pelegrin* f. L *peregrinus* stranger f. PER(*egre* f. *ager* field) abroad, -INE[1]]

pi·lgrimage (-ĭj), n., & v.i. Pilgrim's journey, esp. *go on* (*a*) *p.*; (fig.) mortal life viewed as a journey; (v.i.) go on a p. [f. OF *pelerinage* f. *peleriner* go as a pilgrim (as prec.)]

pilĭ·ferous, a. Having hair (esp. in Bot.). So **pĭ·li**FORM a. [f. L *pilus* hair, see -FEROUS]

pill[1], n., & v.t. Small ball of medicinal substance for swallowing whole (*a p. to cure an earthquake*, half measures); (fig.) something that has to be done, a humiliation &c., (*swallow the p., a bitter p.*, &c.); *p.-box*, shallow cylindrical box for holding pp., (facet.) small vehicle or building, (Mil.) small isolated chiefly underground concrete fort; GILD[1] *the p.*; (slang or facet.) ball, e.g. cannon-ball, tennis-ball, (pl.) billiards; *pillwort*, kinds of plant with small globular involucres; (v.t., slang) blackball, defeat. [f. L *pilula* dim. of *pila* ball]

pill[2], v.t. (archaic). Pillage, plunder; (dial.) = PEEL[3]. [prob. f. L *pilare* make bare of hair (*pilus*), cf. PEEL[3]]

pi·llage (-ĭj), n., & v.t. Plunder, esp. as practised in war; (v.t.) sack, plunder, (place, person, or abs.). Hence **pi·llag**ER[1] n. [(vb f. n.) F, f. *piller* as prec., see -AGE]

pi·llar, n., & v.t. Vertical structure of stone, wood, metal, &c., slender in proportion to height, used as support or ornament; post, pedestal; (fig.) person who is a main supporter, as *a p. of the faith*; upright mass of air, water, &c.; (Mining) solid mass of coal &c. left to support roof of the working; *driven from p. to post* (to & fro, from one resource to another); *p.-box*, hollow p. about 5 ft high in which letters may be posted; (v.t.) support (as) with pp. Hence **pi·llar**ET[1] n. [f. OF *piler* f. late pop. L *pilare* (*pila* pillar, see -AR[1])]

pi·llion, n. (Hist.) woman's light saddle, cushion attached to hinder part of saddle for second rider, usu. woman; (mod.) seating for passenger behind motorcyclist &c. [prob. of Celt. orig., ult. f. L *pellis* skin]

pi·lliwinks, n. (hist.). Instrument of torture for squeezing fingers. [?]

pi·llory, n., & v.t. Wooden framework with holes for head & hands of offender exposed to public ridicule &c.; (v.t.) put in the p., (fig.) expose to ridicule. [f. OF *pellori*, etym. dub.]

pi·llow, n., & v.t. & i. Cushion of linen &c. stuffed with feathers &c. as support for head in reclining esp. in bed; *take counsel of* one's *p.*, take a night to reflect; (techn.) p.-shaped block or support; *p.-case,* (shop) *-slip*, washable case of linen &c. for p.; *p.-fight*, = BOLSTER[2]*-fight*; (v.t.) rest, prop up, on p.; (v.i.) rest on p. Hence **pi·llow**Y[2] a. [OE *pyle, pylu*, cf. Du. *peluw*, G *pfühl*]

pī·lose, -ous, aa. Covered with hair. Hence **pilŏ·**SITY n. [f. L *pilosus* (*pilus* hair, -OSE[1])]

pī·lot, n., & v.t. Person qualified to take charge of ships entering or leaving a harbour (*drop the p.*, abandon trusted adviser); steersman (archaic); (Aeronaut.) person navigating aircraft or qualified to do so; (fig.) guide, esp. in hunting-field; *p.-cloth*, blue woollen cloth for great-coat &c.; *p. engine* (clearing the way for another); *p.-jacket*, = PEA-JACKET; *p.-fish*, small fish said to act as p. to shark; (v.t.) conduct as p. (lit. & fig.), act as p. on (way, piece of water). Hence or cogn. **pi·lot**AGE(3, 4) n., **pi·lot**LESS a. [f. F *pillotte* f. It. *pilota* perh. f. It. *pedota*, cf. It. *pedoto* rudder perh. f. Gk *pēdon* oar, (pl.) rudder]

pi·lūle, pill-, n. Pill; small pill. Hence **pi·lul**AR[1], **pi·lul**OUS, aa. [F, as PILL[1]]

pi·melode, n. Cat-fish. [f. Gk *pimelōdēs* fatty (*pimelē* fat, see -ODE)]

pime·nto, n. Dried aromatic berries of a certain tree, Jamaica pepper; the tree. [f. Sp. *pimienta* f. L *pigmentum* PIGMENT, (med. L) spice]

pimp, n., & v.i. Pander. [etym. dub.; F has *pimpant* seductive in appearance]

pi·mpernel, n. Small annual found in cornfields & waste ground, with scarlet (also blue or white) flowers closing in cloudy or rainy weather. [f. OF *pimprenele* f. med. L *pipinella* perh. corrupt. of *bipinnella* double dim. of BI(*pennis* f. *penna* feather) two-winged]

pi·mping, a. Small, mean; sickly. [?]

pi·mple, n. Small solid round tumour of the skin, usu. inflammatory. Hence **pi·mpl**ED[2], **pi·mpl**Y[2], aa. [?]

pin[1], n. Thin piece of (usu. tinned brass or iron) wire with sharp point & round flattened head for fastening together parts of dress, papers, &c.; peg of wood or metal for various purposes (*split p.*, metal cotter to be passed through hole & held there by the gaping of its split end); each of the pegs round which strings of musical instrument are fastened; THOLE, BELAY*ing*, DRAWING, *-p.*, HAIR*p.*, NINEPIN; *don't care a p.* (at all); (pl., colloq.) legs, as *quick on his pp.*; *pp. & needles*, tingling sensation in limb recovering from numbness; small cask of 4½ gal.; *pi·ncushion*, small cushion for sticking pp. in to keep them ready for use; *p.-feather*, ungrown feather; *p.-fire cartridge* (exploded by means of p.); *p.-head*, (fig.) minute thing; *p.-hole* (made by p. or into which peg fits); *p.-money*, annual allowance to woman for dress expenses &c., allowance settled on wife for private expenditure; *p.-prick*, (fig.) trifling irritation; *pintail*, kinds of duck & grouse with pointed tail; *p.-wheel*, small catharine-wheel. [com.-LG: OE *pinn*, Du. *pin*, G *pin(ne)*; perh. f. L *pinna* point]

pin[2], v.t. Fasten (thing *to* another, *up*, &c., things *together*) with pin(s); *p. up* (archit.), = UNDERPIN; transfix with pin, lance, &c.; *p.* one's *faith* (rely implicitly) *on* (person &c.); seize & hold fast (*against* wall &c.); bind (person &c., often *down*) *to* (promise, arrangement); enclose by bars &c. [f. prec.; last sense perh. f. obs. *pind* impound]

pi·nafore, n. Child's washable covering worn over frock to protect it from dirt. Hence **pi·nafore**D[2] n. [PIN[2] + AFORE]

pīnă·ster, n. A pine indigenous to S.W. Europe. [L, = wild pine (*pinus*, -ASTER)]

pince-nez (F), n. Pair of eyeglasses with spring to clip nose. [F, lit. = pinch-nose]

pi·ncers, n. pl. (Also *a pair of pp.*) gripping tool made of two limbs pivoted together forming pair of jaws with pair of handles to press them together with; similar organ of crustaceans &c. [ME *pinsours* (as PINCH v., see -OR[2])]

pincette (F), n. Small pincers, tweezers.

pinch[1], n. Nip, squeeze; (fig.) stress (*of* poverty &c.); *at a p.* (critical juncture); as much as can be taken up with tips of finger & thumb, as *a p. of snuff, salt.* [f. foll.]

pinch[2], v.t. & i. Nip, squeeze, esp. between tips of finger & thumb (also fig. of cold, hunger, &c., esp. *-ed with cold*); *that is where the shoe pinches*, that is the difficulty or trouble; extort (money &c. *from, out of*, person &c.); stint (person &c. *in, of, for*, food &c.); be niggardly; urge (horse esp. in race); sail (ship) close-hauled; (slang) steal (thing), rob (person), arrest, take into custody. [f. ONF **pinchier* (F *pincer*), etym. dub.]

pi·nchbeck, n. & a. Gold-like alloy of copper & zinc used in cheap jewellery &c.; counterfeit, sham. [f. C. *P.*, watchmaker, d. 1732]

Pindar·i (-ē), n. Mounted marauder in India in 17th & 18th cc. [f. Hind. *pindari*]

Pindă·ric, a. & n. Of, like, the Greek poet Pindar; (n., usu. pl.) P. ode(s), metre, verse(s). [f. L f. Gk *Pindarikos* (*Pindaros* see -IC)]

pine[1], n. Genus of trees with evergreen needle-shaped leaves growing in sheathed clusters of two or more (cf. FIR), many species of which afford timber, tar, & turpentine; *p.-apple*, large collective fruit of the ananas, so called from resemblance to p.-cone; *p.-beauty, p. carpet*, moths whose larvae feed on p.-trees; *p.-cone*, fruit of the p. [OE *pin* f. L *pinus*]

pine[2], v.i. Languish, waste away, from grief, disease, &c.; long eagerly (*for, after, to* do). [OE *pinian* f. obs. *pin* pain f. L *poena* punishment, pain]

pi·neal, a. (anat.). Shaped like a pine-cone; *p. gland*, gland of unknown function behind third ventricle of brain. [f. F *pinéal* f. L *pinea* PINE-cone, see -AL]

pi·nery, n. Place in which pine-apples are grown; plantation of pines. [-ERY]

pi·nfold, n., & v.t. Pound for stray cattle &c.; (v.t.) confine in this. [OE *pundfald* (**pund* POUND[2] + *fald* FOLD[1])]

ping, n., & v.i. Abrupt ringing sound as of rifle bullet flying through air; (v.i.) make, fly with, this. [imit.]

pi·ng-po·ng, n. Game like lawn-tennis played on table with celluloid balls & (usu.) parchment bats. [imit. f. sound of bat]

pi·nguid (-gw-), a. (usu. facet.). Fat, oily, greasy. [f. L *pinguis* fat + -ID[1]]

pi·nguin (-gw-), n. W.-Ind. plant allied to pine-apple; its fruit. [?]

pi·nion[1], n. Terminal segment of bird's wing; (poet.) wing; any flight-feather of wing; (in carving) part of wing corresponding to forearm. [f. OF *pignon* f. L *penna* feather, -OON]

pi·nion[2], v.t. Cut off pinion of (wing, bird) to prevent flight; bind the arms of (person), bind (arms); bind (person &c.) fast *to* (thing). [f. prec.]

pi·nion[3], n. Small cog-wheel engaging with larger one; cogged spindle engaging with wheel. [f. F *pignon* f. OF *penon* battlement f. L *pinna* battlement, see -OON]

pink[1], n. & a. Garden plant with sweet-smelling white, pink, crimson, or variegated flowers; *the p.* (embodied perfection) *of elegance* &c.; *the p.* (most perfect condition) *of health* &c. (also, slang, *in the p.* abs., quite well); (of a) pale red slightly inclining to purple; fox-hunter's red coat, cloth of this; fox-hunter; (adj.) of pale red colour of various kinds, as *rose, salmon,-p.*, whence **pi·nk**ISH[1], **pi·nk**Y[2], aa., **pi·nk**NESS n.; *p.-eye*, contagious fever of horse, contagious ophthalmia in man. [?]

pink[2], n. Yellowish pigment made by combining vegetable colouring matter with some white base (*Brown, French, Dutch*, &c. *p.*). [?]

pink[3], n. (hist.). Sailing-vessel esp. with narrow stern (orig. small & flat-bottomed). [prob. f. MDu. *pincke* etym. dub.]

pink[4], v.t. Pierce with sword &c.; (also *p. out*) ornament (leather &c.) with perforations; adorn, deck. [cf. LG *pinken* strike, peck, perh. var. of *picken* PICK[2]]

pink[5], n. Young salmon; (dial.) minnow. [also in dial. G]

pi·nna, n. (pl. *-ae*). Broad upper part of external ear; primary division of pinnate leaf; fin, fin-like structure. [L, = *penna*]

pi·nnace (*-as*), n. Man-of-war's double-banked (usu. eight-oared) boat; (Hist.) small usu. two-masted vessel. [f. F *pinasse* prob. f. L *pinus* PINE[1]]

pi·nnacle, n., & v.t. Small ornamental turret usu. ending in pyramid or cone, crowning a buttress, roof, &c.; natural peak; (fig.) culmination, climax; (v.t.) set (as) on p., form the p. of, furnish with pp. [ME & OF *pinacle* f. LL *pinnaculum* (*pinna* wing, see -CULE)]

pi·nnate (*-at*), a. (Bot., of compound leaf) with series of leaflets on each side of common petiole; (Zool.) with branches, tentacles, &c., on each side of an axis. Hence **pi·nnated** [-ATE[2]] a., **pi·nnate**LY[2] adv. [f. L *pinnatus* feathered (PINNA, see -ATE[2])]

pi·nner, n. In vbl senses; also: coif with two long side-flaps pinned on. [f. PIN v. + -ER[1]]

pinni- in comb. = PINNA fin, as: *-grade, -ped*, aa. & nn., fin-footed (animal).

pi·nnothere, -tere, (-ēr), n. Genus of small crabs commensally inhabiting shells of oyster, mussel, &c. [f. L f. Gk *pinnotērēs* (*pina* bivalve mollusc, + *tēreō* guard)]

pi·nnule, n. (Bot.) secondary division of pinnate leaf; (Zool.) part, organ, like small wing or fin; sight at end of index of astrolabe &c. Hence **pi·nnul**AR[1] a. [f. L *pinnula* dim. of PINNA]

pi·nny, n. Childish abbr. of PINAFORE.

pi·nocle, n. (U.S.). Game like bezique. [?]

pino·le, n. (U.S.). Meal made from parched corn-flour mixed with sweet flour, sugar, &c. [Amer.-Sp., f. Aztec *pinolli*]

pīnt, n. Measure of capacity for liquids &c., ⅛th of gallon. [f. F *pinte*, etym. dub.]

pinta·do (-ah-), n. (Now usu. *p. bird, petrel*) kind of petrel; guinea-fowl. [f. Port. *pintado* painted p.p. of *pintar* f. L *pingere *pinct-* for *pict-*]

pi·ntle, n. Kinds of pin or bolt, esp. one on which some other part turns. [OE *pintel* penis, etym. dub., cf. Du. & G *pint* penis]

pi·nxit, pinxē·runt, v.t. (So-&-so) painted it (in signature to picture, as FECIT). [L]

pī·ny, a. Of, like, abounding in, pines. [-Y[2]]

piolet (pyōlā·) n. Alpinist's ice-axe. [F]

pīoneer·, n., & v.i. & t. (Mil.) one of body of foot-soldiers marching in advance with spades &c. to prepare road for main body; beginner of enterprise, original explorer, &c.; (v.i.) act as p.; (v.t.) open up (road &c.) as p., act as p. to, conduct. [(vb f. n.) f. F *pionnier* foot-soldier, pioneer, (*pion*, f. L as PAWN[1], -IER)]

pious, a. Devout, religious; *p. founder* (of college &c. for glory of God & good of man); (archaic) dutiful; *p.* FRAUD. Hence **pi·ous**LY[2] adv. [f. L *pius* dutiful, pious, -OUS]

pip[1], n. Disease of poultry, hawks, &c., marked by thick mucus in throat & often by white scale on tip of tongue (also facet. of various human diseases). [prob. f. MDu. *pippe* f. pop. L *pipita* corrupt. of *pituita* phlegm]

pip[2], n. Each spot on playing-cards, dice, or dominoes, or star on officer's shoulder; single blossom of clustered inflorescence; rhomboidal segment of surface of pine-apple. [earlier *peep*, etym. dub.]

pip[3], v.t. (colloq.). Blackball; defeat; hit with shot. [f. prec. or foll.]

pip[4], n. Seed of apple, pear, orange, &c. Hence **pi·p**LESS a. [prob. abbr. of PIPPIN]

pip[5], signallers' letter P, as in *p. emma, o.p.*

pipe[1], n. Tube of wood, metal, &c., esp. for conveying water, gas, &c.; musical wind-instrument consisting of single tube; each of the tubes by which sound is produced in organ; (pl.) = BAG[1]*pipes*; boatswain's whistle, sounding of this; voice, esp. in singing; song, note, of bird; tubular organ, vessel, &c., in animal body; cylindrical vein of ore; channel of decoy for wild fowl; (also *tobacco-p.*) narrow tube of clay, wood, &c., with bowl at one end for drawing in smoke of tobacco, quantity of tobacco held by this, as *light, smoke, a p.*; PEACE-*p.*; *King's* or *Queen's p.*, furnace at London Docks used formerly for burning contraband tobacco; *put that in your p. & smoke it*, digest that fact &c. if you can; cask for wine, esp. as measure usu. = 105 gal.; *p.-clay*, fine white clay used for tobacco-pp. & (esp. by soldiers) for cleaning white breeches, belts, &c., (fig.) excessive attention to minutiae of dress &c. in regiment, (v.t.) whiten with p.-clay; *p.-light*, spill for lighting p.; *p. major*, N.C.O. commanding regimental pipers; *p.-rack* (for tobacco-pp.); *p.-line* (esp. for conveying petroleum to a distance); *p.-stone*, hard red clay used by Amer. Indians for tobacco-pp. Hence **pi·pe**FUL n., **pi·pe**LESS, **pi·p**Y[2], aa. [OE *pipe*, cf. Du. *pijp*, G *pfeife*, ult. f. L as foll.]

pipe[2], v.i. & t. Play (tune &c., or abs.) on pipe; lead, bring, (person, &c.) by sound of pipe; summon (crew *up, to* meal, work, &c.) by sounding whistle (*p. away*, give signal for boat to start); whistle; utter in shrill voice; *p. up*, begin to play or sing; *p.* one's *eye(s)*, weep; propagate (pinks &c.) by cuttings taken off at joint of stem; trim (dress), ornament (cake &c.), with PIPING[1]; furnish with pipes. [OE *pipian* f. L *pipare* pipe, chirp]

pip e·mma, adv. (slang). Post meridiem. [signallers' names for letters P, M]

pi·per, n. One who plays on pipe, esp. strolling musician; bagpipe-player; *pay the p.* (*& call the tune*), bear the cost (& have control) of a proceeding &c.; kinds of fish; broken-winded horse; decoy-dog. [OE *pipere* (PIPE[1] + -ER[1])]

pĭpe·tte (-ĕt), n. Slender tube for transferring &c. small quantities, esp. in chemistry. [F, dim. of PIPE[1]]

pī·ping[1], n. In vbl senses, also: ornamentation of dress by means of cord enclosed in pipe-like fold; ornamental cord-like lines of sugar on cake. [f. PIPE[2] + -ING[1]]

pi·ping[2], a. In vbl senses; *the p. time(s) of peace* (marked by piping as opp. to martial music); *p.* (hissing) *hot.* [f. PIPE[2] + -ING[2]]

pĭpistre·l(le), n. Small kind of bat. [F (*-le*) f. It. *pipistrello, vip-*, f. L *vespertilio* bat (*vesper* evening)]

pi·pit, n. Bird like lark. [prob. imit.]

pi·pkin, n. Small earthenware pot or pan. [?]

pi·ppin, n. Kinds of apple. [ME & OF *pepin* seed, etym. dub.]

pip-squeak, n. (army slang). Shell that emits sound so described. [imit.]

piquant (pē·kant), a. Agreeably pungent, sharp, appetizing; (fig.) pleasantly stimulating or disturbing to the mind. Hence **pi·qu**ANCY n., **pi·quant**LY[2] adv. [F (as foll., see -ANT); F fem. *-te* also as E fem., pron. pēkah·nt or as F]

pique[1] (pēk), v.t., & n. Irritate, wound the pride of; arouse (curiosity, interest); plume one*self on*; (n.) ill-feeling, enmity, resentment, as *in a fit of p., took a p. against me.* [f. F *piquer* vb prick, irritate, *pique* n., cf. PICK[2]]

pique[2] (pēk), n., & v.t. & i. Winning of 30 points at piquet before opponent begins to count; (v.t.) score a p. against; (v.i.) score a p. [(vb f. n.) f. F *pic* etym. dub.]

piqué (pē·kā), n. Stiff ribbed cotton fabric. [F, p.p. of *piquer*, see PIQUE[1]]

pique·t[1] (-kĕt, *or* pĭ·k-), n. Card game for two players with pack of 32 cards. [F, etym. dub.]

piquet[2]. See PICKET.

pirā·gua, peria·gua, (-wa), n. Long narrow canoe made from single tree-trunk; two-masted sailing-barge. [Sp., f. Carib, = dug-out]

pīr·ate (-at), n., & v.t. & i. (Ship used by) sea-robber; marauder; one who infringes another's copyright; bus that encroaches on recognized routes or overcharges or preys on passengers; (v.t.) plunder, (also) reproduce (book &c.) without leave for one's own profit; (v.i.) play the p. Hence or cogn. **pīr·**ACY n., **pirā·**TIC(AL) aa., **pira·tical**LY[2] adv. [(vb f. n.) f. L (*-ta*) f. Gk *peiratēs* (*peiraō* attempt, assault)]

pĭro·gue (-ōg), n. = PIRAGUA. [F]

pirouе·tte (-ŏŏĕt), n., & v.i. Ballet-dancer's spin round on one foot or on point of toe; dance thus. [(n.) F, = top, cf. It.

piruolo top, *pirone* iron peg; vb f. F *pirouetter*]

pis aller (pēzahlā·), n. Course &c. taken for want of a better. [F (*pis* worse + *aller* go)]

pi·scary, n. *Common of p.*, right of fishing in another's water in common with owner (& others). [f. med. L *piscaria* neut. pl. of *piscarius* fishing (*piscis* fish, see -ARY[1])]

pi·scatory, a. Of fishers or fishing, whence **piscator·IAL** a.; addicted to fishing. [f. L *piscatorius* (*piscator* fisher f. *piscis* fish)]

Pi·sces (-sēz), n. pl. The Fishes, 12th zodiacal constellation; 12th sign of zodiac. [L, pl. of *piscis* fish]

pi·sciculture (-sĭ-), n. Artificial rearing of fish. Hence **piscicu·lturAL** a., **piscicu·lturIST** n. [f. L *piscis* fish + CULTURE]

pisci·na (-sē-, -sī-), n. (pl. *-ae, -as*). Fish-pond; ancient Roman bathing-pond; (Eccl.) perforated stone basin for carrying away water used in rinsing chalice &c. [L, f. *piscis* fish]

pi·scine[1] (*or* -ēn), n. Bathing-pool. [F, f. prec.]

pi·scīne[2], a. Of fish. [f. L *piscis* fish, -INE[1]]

pisci·vorous, a. Fish-eating. [as prec. + -VOROUS]

pisé (pē·zā), n. Rammed clay or earth (& gravel) as building-material. [F, p.p. of *piser* pound f. L *pi(n)sare* pound]

Pi·sgah (-z-), n. Mountain whence Moses viewed the Promised Land (*Deut.* iii. 27); (fig.) *P. glance, prospect,* &c. [Heb.]

pish, int. expr. contempt, impatience, or disgust; (v.i.) say p. [natural]

pisho·gue (-ōg), n. (Ir.). Sorcery; charm, spell. [f. Ir. *pis(r)eog*]

pi·siform (pīs-, pīz-), a. Pea-shaped; *p. bone,* small bone of upper row of carpus. [f. L *pisum* pea + -FORM]

pi·smire (-s-), n. Ant. [f. foll. (from smell of anthill) + obs. *mire* ant, cf. Du. *mier*]

piss, v.i. & t., & n., (not now in polite use). Make water; discharge (blood &c.) with the urine; wet with urine; (p.p., slang) drunk; (n.) urine. [(n. f. vb) f. OF *pissier* etym. dub.]

pista·chio (-āshĭō, -āshō, -ătshō), n. (Tree yielding) nut with greenish edible kernel; colour of this. [f. It. *pistacchio* & Sp. *pistacho* f. L f. Gk *pistakion*]

pi·stil, n. Female organ of flower, comprising ovary, style, & stigma. Hence **pi·stillARY**[1], **pi·stillATE**[2](2), **pistilli·FEROUS, pi·stillINE**[1], aa. [as PESTLE]

pi·stol (-tl), n., & v.t. (-ll-). Small fire-arm held & fired by one hand; *within, beyond, p.-shot* (range of p.); (v.t.) shoot with this; *p.-grip,* handhold of p.-butt shape below gunstock. [f. obs. F *pistole* prob. shortened f. *pistolet* dagger, pistol, dim. f. It. *pistolese* (dagger) made at *Pistoia*]

pisto·le, n. (hist.). Foreign gold coin, esp. Spanish worth about 18*s*. [F, prob. shortened f. *pistolet,* etym. dub., perh. as prec.]

pi·stolgraph, n. (Apparatus for obtaining) instantaneous photograph. [-GRAPH]

pi·ston, n. Disk or short cylinder of wood, metal, &c., fitting closely within tube in which it moves up & down, used in steam-engine, pump, &c., to impart or receive motion by means of *p.-rod*; sliding valve in cornet &c. [F, f. It. *pistone* var. of *pestone* PESTLE]

pit[1], n. Natural hole in ground; hole made in digging for mineral &c. or for industrial purposes, as *chalk, clay, gravel, coal, saw, tan, -p.*; covered hole as trap for wild beasts or (esp. bibl.) for enemies (*dig a p. for* fig., try to ensnare); *the p.* (*of hell*), hell; COCKPIT; hollow in animal or plant body or on any surface; *p. of the stomach,* depression between cartilage of false ribs; depressed scar, as after small-pox; that part of auditorium of theatre which is on floor of house, now usu. the part of this behind stalls; people occupying this; *pitfall,* covered p. as trap for animals &c., (fig.) unsuspected snare or danger; *pitman,* collier, (U.S.) connecting rod in machinery; *p. pony* (kept underground in coal-mines). [OE *pytt,* cf. Du. *put,* G *pfütze,* f. L *puteus* well]

pit[2], v.t. & i. Put into a pit (esp. vegetables &c. for storage); set (cock, dog, &c.) to fight in pit (*against* another), (fig.) match (person *against*); make pits, esp. scars, in (esp. in p.p.); (Path., of flesh &c.) retain impression of finger &c. when touched. [f. prec.]

pi·t-(a-)pat, adv. & n. With the sound p., palpitatingly, falteringly, as *his heart, feet, went p.*; (n.) the sound p. [imit.]

pitch[1], n., & v.t. Black or dark-brown tenacious resinous substance, semi-liquid when hot, hard when cold, got from distillation of tar or turpentine, used for caulking seams of ships &c. (*p. black, p. darkness,* with no light at all); *p.-blende,* native oxide of uranium, found in p.-like masses; *p.-cap,* cap lined with p., used as instrument of torture; *p.-pine,* specially resinous kinds of pine; *pitchstone,* old volcanic rock looking like p.; (v.t.) cover, coat, smear, with p. [(OE *pician* vb f.) OE *pic* f. L *pix picis*]

pitch[2], v.t. & i. Fix & erect (tent, camp); (abs.) encamp; (Crick.) *p. wickets,* fix stumps in ground & place bails; fix, plant, (thing) in definite position; expose (wares) for sale in market &c.; pave (road) with set stones; *pitched battle* (of set kind, not casual); (Mus.) set at particular pitch, (fig.) express in particular style; throw, fling; (in games) throw (flat object) towards a mark; (slang) tell (tale, yarn); fall heavily (*on* one's head, *into,* &c.); (of ship) plunge in longitudinal direction (cf. ROLL[2]); *p. in* (colloq.), set to work vigorously; *p. into* (colloq.), assail forcibly with blows, words, &c., make vigorous attack on, (person, food, &c.);

p. upon, happen to select; *p.-&-toss,* game of skill & chance in which coins are pitched at a mark; *p.-farthing,* = CHUCK[3]-*farthing.* [ME *pichen,* etym. dub., perh. cogn. w. PICK[2]]

pitch[3], n. Pitching (e.g. of ship); mode of delivering cricket-ball in bowling; quantity of commodity pitched in market; place at which one (e.g. street performer, bookmaker) is stationed; (Crick.) place between & about wickets; height to which falcon &c. soars before swooping on prey, as *fly a high* &c. *p.* (also fig.); height, degree, intensity, (*of* quality &c.); (Mus.) degree of acuteness or graveness of tone; degree of slope; steepness of roof's slope; (Mech.) distance between success-points or lines, e.g. between successive teeth of cog-wheel; *p.-pipe,* small pipe blown by mouth to set p. for singing or tuning; *p.-wheel,* toothed wheel engaging with another. [f. prec.]

pi·tcher[1], n. Large usu. earthenware vessel with handle or two ears & usu. a lip, for holding liquids; *little pp. have long ears,* children are apt to overhear; (Bot.) modified leaf in p. form, *p.-plant* (with such leaves). Hence **pi·tcher**FUL(2) n. [f. OF *pichier* f. med. L *picarium, bic-,* BEAKER]

pi·tcher[2], n. In vbl senses of PITCH[2], esp.: player who delivers ball, esp. in baseball; street vendor who pitches stall in fixed place; stone used for paving. [-ER[1]]

pi·tchfork, n., & v.t. Long-handled fork with two sharp prongs for pitching hay &c.; (v.t.) cast (as) with p., (fig.) thrust (person) forcibly (*into* position, office, &c.). [earlier *pickfork,* prob. f. PICK[1] + FORK, assoc. w. PITCH[2]]

pi·tchy, a. Of, like, dark &c. as, pitch. [-Y[2]]

pi·tĕous, a. Calling for pity, deplorable. Hence **pi·teous**LY[2] adv., **pi·teous**NESS n. [ME *pitous* f. OF *pitos* f. L **pietosus* (as PIETY, see -ITOUS)]

pith, n., & v.t. Spongy cellular tissue in stems & branches of dicotyledonous plants; similar tissue lining rind of orange &c.; spinal cord; (fig.) essential part, quintessence, (often *p. & marrow of*); physical strength, vigour; force, energy; *of p.* (importance) *& moment* (Shaks. *Ham.* III. i. 86); (v.t.) slaughter (animal) by severing spinal cord. Hence **pi·th**LESS a. [(vb f. n.) OE *pitha,* cf. MDu. *pitte,* Da. *pit*]

pĭtheca·nthrope (-ĭk-), n. Ape-man, hypothetical link between ape & man. [f. Gk *pithēkos* ape + *anthrōpos* man]

pithē·coid, a. Ape-like. [as prec., see -OID]

pi·thy, a. Of, like, abounding in, pith; condensed & forcible, terse. Hence **pi·thi**LY[2] adv., **pi·thi**NESS n. [-Y[2]]

pi·tiable, a. Calling for pity or contempt. Hence **pi·tiable**NESS n., **pi·tiab**LY[2] adv. [OF (as PITY, see -ABLE)]

pi·tiful, n. Compassionate; (of things) calling for pity; contemptible. Hence **pi·tiful**LY[2] adv., **pi·tiful**NESS n. [-FUL]

pi·tiless, a. Showing no pity. Hence **pi·tiless**LY[2] adv., **pi·tiless**NESS n. [-LESS]

pi·tpan, n. Central American dug-out boat. [perh. native]

pi·ttance, n. (Hist.) pious bequest to religious house for extra food &c.; allowance, remuneration, esp. scanty one, as *a mere p.*; small number or amount. [f. OF *pitance*; OF has also *pitance* pity (as PIETY + -ANCE)]

pi·ttite, n. Person occupying seat in pit of theatre. [-ITE[1]]

pitū·itary, a. Of or secreting phlegm, mucous. So **pitu·itous** a. [f. L *pituitarius* (*pituita* phlegm, see -ARY[1])]

pi·ty, n., & v.t. Feeling of tenderness aroused by person's distress or suffering, as *cannot help feeling p. for him, felt no p. for him, in p. of his fate*; *take p. on,* feel or act compassionately towards; (as form of entreaty) *for p.'s sake*; regrettable fact, ground for regret, as *what a p.!, more's the p.* (so much the worse), *it is a thousand pp. you did not mention it,* (archaic) *it is* or *was p. of them,* one feels sorry for them; (v.t.) feel (often contemptuous) p. for, as *he is much to be pitied, I p. you if you think that.* Hence **pi·tying**LY[2] adv. [(vb f. n.) f. OF *pitet* f. L as PIETY]

pi·vot, n., & v.t. & i. Short shaft or pin on which something turns or oscillates; (Mil.) man on whom body of troops wheels; (fig.) cardinal or central point; (v.t.) furnish with, attach by, p.; (v.i.) turn as on p., hinge (*upon,* often fig.). Hence **pi·vot**AL a. [F, etym. dub.]

pi·xy, -xie, n. Being akin to fairy. [?]

pizzicato (pĭtsĭkah·tō), adv., a., & n. (mus.). (Played) by plucking string of violin &c. with finger instead of using bow; (n.) passage, note, so played. [It.]

pi·zzle, n. (now vulg.). Penis of animal esp. that of bull formerly used as flogging instrument. [16th c., cf. Du. *pees*]

plă·cable, a. Easily appeased, mild, forgiving. Hence or cogn. **placabi·lity** n., **pla·cab**LY[2] adv. [OF, f. L *placabilis* (*placare* appease, see -BLE)]

plă·card (*or* -ar·d), n., & v.t. Document printed on one side of single sheet for posting up, poster; (v.t.) set up pp. on (wall &c.), advertise (wares &c.) by pp., display (poster &c.) as p. [OF, f. *plaquier* vb plaster f. Du. *plakken* glue, prob. imit., see -ARD]

placa·te (*or* plă·cāt), v.t. Pacify, conciliate, (now chiefly U.S. of purchasing the connivance &c. of opponents). [f. L *placare,* see -ATE[3]]

place[1], n. Particular part of space; part of space occupied by person or thing, as *it has changed its p.*; city, town, village, &c.; (in names of groups of buildings) *Ely* &c. *P.*; residence, dwelling; country-house with surroundings; building, spot, devoted to specified purpose, as *p. of amusement, worship, bathing-p.*; (H. of Commons) *another p.*, H. of Lords; particular spot on surface &c., as *a sore p. on his wrist*; sore; passage of book &c.; rank, station, as *servants must know their p., keep him in his p.*; (Racing) position among placed competitors; position of figure in series as indicating its value in decimal or similar notation, as *calculated to 50 decimal pp.*; step in progression of argument, statement, &c., as *in the first, second, p.*; proper or natural position, as *take your pp., there in no p. for doubt, is in* or *out of* (*its, his*) *p.*; space, seat, accommodation, for person &c. at table, in conveyance, &c., as *take two pp. in the coach, always a p. for you at our table*; *in p. of*, instead of; *take the p. of*, be substituted for; office, employment, esp. government appointment; duties of office &c., as *it is not my p. to inquire into that*; *in, out of, p.*, (un)suitable, (in)appropriate; *give p. to*, make room for, be succeeded by; *take p.*, happen; *p. brick* (imperfectly burnt from being on windward side of kiln); *p.(-kick)* (Footb.), kick made when ball is previously placed by another player for that purpose on ground; *placeman*, holder of public office, esp. one appointed from motives of interest. [F, f. L f. Gk *plateia* (*hodos*) broad (way)]

place[2], v.t. Put (thing &c.) in particular place; arrange (set of things) in their proper places; appoint (person, esp. clergyman) to post; find situation, living, &c., for; invest (money); dispose of (goods) to customer; put (order for goods &c.) into hands of firm &c.; repose (confidence &c. *in, on*); assign rank to; locate; state position of (usu. any of first 3 horses or runners) in race, *be placed*, be among first three; get (goal) by PLACE[1]*-kick*. [prec.]

place·nta, n. Flattened circular spongy vascular organ in higher mammals, expelled in parturition after nourishing foetus, which is attached to it by umbilical cord; (Bot.) part of carpel to which ovules are attached. Hence **place·nt**AL a. [f. L *placenta* = Gk *plakoeis -entos* flat cake f. root of *plax plakos* flat plate]

plā·cer, n. Deposit of sand, gravel, &c., in bed of stream &c. containing valuable minerals in particles. [Amer. Sp., cogn. w. *placel* sandbank f. *plaza* PLACE[1]]

plă·cĕt, sentence & n. (Univv.). *P., non p.*, it pleases me (not) (forms used in voting for or against measure); (n.) such vote. [L]

plă·cid, a. Mild; peaceful; serene. Hence or cogn. **placi·d**ITY n., **pla·cid**LY[2] adv. [f. L *placidus* (*placēre* please, see -ID[1])]

pla·cket, n. Pocket, esp. in woman's skirt; *p.-hole*, opening in outer skirt giving access to this. [perh. var. of PLACARD]

plă·coid, a. (Of scales) plate-shaped; (of fish) with p. scales. [f. Gk *plax plakos* plate, -OID]

plafond (F), n. Ceiling, esp. one enriched with paintings; such painting.

plā·gal, a. (mus.). (Of ecclesiastical modes) having their sounds comprised between the dominant & its octave; *p. cadence* (in which chord of subdominant immediately precedes that of the tonic). Cf. AUTHENTIC. [f. med. L *plagalis* f. *plaga* p. mode, prob. f. med. L f. Gk *plagios* oblique, (med. Gk) plagal, f. *plagos* side]

plā·giarize (-j-), v.t. Take and use another person's (thoughts, writings, inventions, or abs.) as one's own. So **pla·giar**ISM, **pla·giar**IST, nn. [f. foll. + -IZE]

pla·giary, n. = PLAGIARISM; = PLAGIARIST. [f. L *plagiarius* kidnapper (*plagiare* kidnap)]

plă·gio- (-j-) in comb. = Gk *plagios* oblique, as: *-cepha·lic*, having anterior part of skull more developed on one side, posterior on the other; *-cla·stic* (Min.), having oblique cleavage; *-stome*, fish with mouth placed transversely beneath snout, as sharks & rays.

plāgue, n., & v.t. Affliction, esp. as divine punishment; (colloq.) nuisance, trouble; pestilence, esp. *the* (oriental or bubonic) *p.*; (as imprecation) *p. on it!* &c.; *p.-spot*, spot on skin characteristic of p., locality infected with p., (fig.) source or symptom of moral corruption; (v.t.) afflict with p., (colloq.) annoy, bother, whence **pla·gue**SOME a. (colloq.). [ME & OF *plage* f. L *plaga* stroke (*plag-* root of *plangere* beat breast, cf. Gk *plēgē* stroke, *plēssō* strike)]

plā·guy (-gĭ), a. & adv. (colloq.). Annoying(ly); exceeding(ly), as *was p. glad to get back again.* Hence **pla·gui**LY[2] adv. [f. prec. + -Y[2]]

plaice, n. European flat-fish much used as food. [f. OF *plaïz* f. LL *platessa* perh. f. Gk *platus* broad]

plaid (plăd), n. Long piece of twilled woollen cloth, usu. with chequered or tartan pattern, outer article of Highland costume; cloth used for this. Hence **plai·d**ED[2] a. [cf. Gael. *plaide*, Ir. *ploid*, etym. dub.]

plain[1], a., adv., & n. Clear, evident; simple, readily understood, as *p. words, English*; not intricate, as *p. sewing*; unembellished, (of drawings &c.) not coloured; (of food) not rich or highly seasoned; not luxurious, as *p. living*; outspoken, straightforward, (esp. *be p. with*, tell home truths to); unsophisticated, as *I am a p. man*; of homely manners, dress, or appearance; ugly, as *a pity the poor girl is so p.*; *p. as a* PIKESTAFF; (adv.) clearly, as *learn to speak p.*; *p. cards* (not court-cards); *p.-chant*, = *p.-song*; *p. clothes*, unofficial dress; *p. dealing* candour, straightforwardness; *p. sailing*, sailing in a p. course, (fig.) simple course of action; *plai·n-song*, vocal music composed in medieval modes & in free rhythm depending on accentuation of the words, and sung in unison; *p.-spoken*, outspoken; *p. suit* (not trumps); *p. tile*, flat roofing-tile; (n.) level tract of country; *plainsman*, inhabitant of a p. Hence **plai·n**LY[2] adv., **plai·n**NESS n. [OF, f. L *planus* a., *-num* neut. adj. as n.]

plain[2], v.i. (archaic, poet.). Mourn; complain; emit plaintive sound. [f. OF *plaindre* (st. *plaign-*) f. L *plangere planct-* beat breast]

plaint, n. (Law) accusation, charge; (poet.) lamentation, complaint. [ME & OF (1) *plaint* f. L *planctus -ūs*, (2) *plainte* f. med. L *plancta* fem. p.p. as n.; both as prec.]

plai·ntiff, n. Party who brings suit into court of law, prosecutor. [OF, as foll.]

plai·ntive, a. Expressive of sorrow; mournful. Hence **plai·ntive**LY[2] adv., **plai·ntive**NESS n. [OF (*-if, -ive*), f. L as PLAIN[2], see -IVE]

plait (-ăt), n., & v.t. (Now usu. PLEAT) fold, crease, esp. flattened fold in cloth made by doubling it upon itself, (v.t.) fold (cloth &c.) thus; (now rarely PLAT[2]) contexture of three or more interlaced strands of hair, ribbon, straw, &c., (v.t.) form (hair, straw, &c.) into p. [(vb. f. n.) f. OF *pleit, ploit*, f. L *plicare plicitum* fold]

plan, n., & v.t. Drawing, diagram, made by projection on flat surface (cf. ELEVATION), esp. one showing relative position of parts of (one floor of) a building; large-scale detailed map of town or district; table indicating times, places, &c., of intended proceedings &c.; scheme of arrangement; project, design; way of proceeding, as *the better p. is to peel them after boiling*; *p. of* CAMPAIGN; (Perspective) any of the imaginary planes, perpendicular to line of vision, passing through objects shown in picture; (v.t.) make a p. of (ground, existing building), design (building to be constructed &c.), scheme, arrange beforehand, (procedure &c.). Hence **pla·n**LESS a. [(vb f. n.) F, f. L as PLAIN[1]]

planch (-sh), n. Slab of metal, stone, &c., esp. of baked fire-clay used in enamelling. [f. F *planche* PLANK]

pla·nchet, n. Plain disk of metal of which coin is made. [prec. + -ET[1]]

planchette (plănshĕ·t *or as F*), n. Small usu. heart-shaped board supported by two castors & pencil, which when person's fingers rest lightly on board is said to trace letters &c. without conscious direction. [F, dim. of *planche* PLANK[1]]

plane[1], n. Genus of tall spreading trees with broad angular palmately-lobed leaves; *p.-tree* (of this genus). [F, f. L f. Gk *platanos* (*platus* broad)]

plane[2], n., & v.t. Tool for smoothing surface of woodwork by paring shavings from it, consisting of wooden or metal stock from smooth bottom of which projects a steel blade; similar tool for smoothing metal; *smoothing-p.* (used to finish surface, cf. JACK[1]- & TRY*ing-p.*); *moulding-p.* (for making mouldings); (v.t.) smooth (wood, metal) with p., pare *away* or *down* (irregularities) with p., (archaic) level, esp. *p. the way*. [(n.) F, f. LL *plana*, (vb) f. F *planer*; both f. L *planare* (as PLANE[4])]

plane[3], n., & v.i. Surface such that the straight line joining any two points in it lies wholly in it; imaginary surface of this kind in which points or lines in material bodies lie; level surface; flat thin object such as table-top, supporting part of aeroplane, (esp. in pl.) aeroplane(s); INCLINE[1]*d p.*; each of the natural faces of a crystal; main road in mine; (fig.) level (*of* thought, knowledge, &c.), as *his superstition places him on the same p. as the savage*; *p. sailing*, art of determining ship's place on the theory that she is moving on a p., (fig., now usu. PLAIN[1] *sailing*) simple course; (v.i.) travel, glide (*down* &c.), in aeroplane. [f. L *planum* neut. as foll.]

plane[4], a. Perfectly level, as a PLANE[3]; (of angle, figure, &c.) lying in a plane; *p. chart* (on which meridians & parallels of latitude are represented by equidistant straight lines, used in PLANE[3] sailing); *p.-table*, surveying instrument used for measuring angles in mapping, (v.t.) survey (area) with this. [f. L *planus* flat, level, refash. f. PLAIN a.]

plă·net[1], n. (Hist.) heavenly body distinguished from fixed stars by having apparent motion of its own (Moon, Mercury, Venus, Sun, Mars, Jupiter, Saturn), esp. (Astrol.) with reference to its supposed influence on persons & events; (Astron.) *primary pp.*, heavenly bodies revolving in approximately circular orbits round sun (*major pp.*, Mercury, Venus, Earth, Mars, Jupiter, Saturn, Uranus, Neptune; *minor pp.*, the asteroids, whose orbits lie between those of Mars & Jupiter), *secondary pp.* (also *satellites*), those that revolve round primary; SUN-*&-p.*; *p.-struck, -stricken*, bewildered, terrified. [ME & OF *planete* f. LL f. Gk *planētēs* wanderer, planet, f. *planaomai* wander]

plă·net[2], n. Chasuble. [f. med. L *planeta* perh. as prec.]

plănĕtār·ium, n. Orrery, model of planetary system. [as foll.]

plă·netary, a. Of planets, as *p. influence, motions*; *p. hour*, twelfth part of natural day or night; *p.* (solar) *system*; terrestrial, mundane; wandering, erratic. [f. LL *planetarius* (as PLANET[1], see -ARY[1])]

plă·netoid, n. Minor PLANET[1]. [-OID]

pla·ngent, (-j-), a. (Of sound) thrilling, vibrating, moaning, insistent. Hence **pla·ng**ENCY n. [f. L *plangere* beat the breast, see -ENT]

plani- in comb. =L *planus* level, smooth, plane, as: *-meter*, instrument for mechanically measuring area of irregular plane figure; *-metry*, measurement of plane surfaces, so *-me·tric(al)* aa.; *-pe·talous*, with flat petals; *-sphere*, map formed by projection of (part of) sphere or plane, (*revolving p.*, device for showing the part of the heavens visible at given time & place), so *-sphĕ·ric* a.

plă·nish, v.t. Flatten (sheet metal &c.) with smooth-faced hammer or otherwise; flatten out (coining-metal) between rollers; polish (photograph &c.) with roller &c. Hence **pla·nish**ER[1] (1, 2) n. f. obs. F *planir* smooth (*plan* a. as PLANE[4]), see -ISH[2]]

plank[1], n. Long flat piece of smoothed timber, 2 to 6 in. thick, 9 or more in. wide (cf. BOARD[1]); item of political or other programme (cf. PLATFORM); *walk the p.*, (of pirates' captive &c.) walk blindfold into sea along p. laid over side of ship; *p. bed* (of boards, without mattress, used as prison discipline &c.). [f. ONF *planke* f. LL *planca* prob. f. root of Gk *plax placos* flat plate]

plank[2], v.t. Furnish, cover, floor, with planks, whence **pla·nk**ING[1] (2, 3) n.; (slang) put *down*, esp. pay (money, or abs.) *down* on the spot. [f. prec.]

pla·nktŏn, n. (biol.). The forms of drifting or floating organic life found at various depths in the ocean, taken collectively. [G, f. Gk *plagktos* wandering (*plazomai*)]

plāno- in comb. =L *planus* level, flat, as: *-co·ncave, -co·nvex*, (of lens &c.) with one surface plane & the other concave, convex; *-meter*, flat plate, usu. of cast iron, as gauge for plane surfaces.

plant[1], n. Living organism capable of living wholly on inorganic substances & having neither power of locomotion nor special organs of sensation or digestion, member of the vegetable kingdom (often restricted to the smaller pp., excluding trees and shrubs); crop; growth, as *in p.*, growing, *lose p.*, die off, *miss p.*, fail to spring from seed; mode of planting oneself, pose; fixtures, implements, machinery, &c., used in industrial process, (fig.) machinery of intellectual work &c.; (slang) planned swindle or burglary, hoax; (slang) detective, picket of these; *p.-louse*, kinds of insect that infest pp., esp. aphis. Hence **pla·nt**LET n., **pla·nt**LIKE a. [OE *plante* f. L *planta* slip, cutting; partly also f. foll.]

plant[2], v.t. Place (tree, shoot, bulb, seed, crop, &c.) in ground that it may take root & grow; deposit (young fish, spawn, oysters) in river &c.; *p. out*, transfer (plant) from pot or frame to open ground, set out (seedlings) at intervals; fix firmly (*in, on*, ground &c.); station (person), esp. as spy; *p. oneself*, take up a position; establish, found, (community, city, church); settle (person) in a place as colonist &c.; cause (idea &c.) to take root *in* (mind); furnish (land *with* plants, district *with* settlers, &c.); deliver (blow, thrust) with definite aim; (slang) conceal (stolen goods &c.); (slang) bury; (slang) place (gold-dust, ore) in mining claim to encourage prospective buyer, cf. SALT v.; (slang) devise (fraudulent scheme); abandon, as *there I was, fairly planted.* Hence **pla·nt**ABLE a. [OE *plantian* f. L *plantare*, cf. prec.]

Planta·genet, n. & a. (Member) of the family founded by Geoffrey of Anjou, esp. any of the English kings from Henry II to Richard III. [surname, f. sprig of broom (L *planta* plant, *genesta* broom) worn as cognizance]

plă·ntain[1] (-tĭn), n. Genus of plants, esp. *Greater P.*, low herb with broad flat leaves spread out close to ground & seeds much used for cage-birds. [ME & OF, f. L *plantaginem* (nom. *-go*) prob. f. *planta* sole of foot, from its prostrate leaves]

plă·ntain[2] (-tĭn), n. Tree-like tropical herbaceous plant allied to banana and bearing similar fruit; its fruit. [16th-c. *pla(n)tan* f. Sp. *pla(n)tano*; Sp. has also *plá(n)tano* PLANE[1]-tree (obs. E *plantain*)]

plă·ntar, a. (anat.). Of the sole of the foot. [f. L *plantaris* (*planta* sole, see -AR[1])]

planta·tion, n. Assemblage of planted growing plants, esp. trees; estate on which cotton, tobacco, &c., are cultivated (formerly by servile labour); *p. song* (of the kind sung by Negroes on American pp.); (Hist.) colonization, colony. [f. L *plantatio* (as PLANT[2], see -ATION)]

pla·nter, n. Cultivator of soil; (in Ireland) English settler on forfeited lands in 17th c., (19th c.) person settled in evicted tenant's holding; occupier of plantation, esp. in (sub-)tropical countries, as *coffee, cotton, sugar, tobacco, -p.*; machine for planting, as *corn, potato, -p.* Hence **pla·nter**SHIP n. [PLANT[2] + -ER[1]]

plă·ntigrade, a. & n. (Animal) that walks on its soles (cf. DIGITIGRADE); (of human being) placing whole sole on ground at once in walking. [F, f. L *planta* sole + *-gradus* -walking]

planto·cracy, n. Dominant class of planters in W. Indies &c. [irreg. f. PLANTER + -O- + -CRACY]

pla·nxty, n. (Ir. mus.) Animated harp-tune moving in triplets. [?]

plaque (-ahk), n. Ornamental tablet of metal, porcelain, &c., plain or decorated; small tablet as badge of rank in honorary order; (Path.) patch of eruption &c. So **plaqu**E·TTE n. [F, f. Flem. *placke*, small coin, whence Sc. *plack*]

plash[1], n. Marshy pool; puddle. Hence **pla·sh**Y[2] a. [OE *plæsc*, cf. Du. *plas*, prob. imit.]

plash[2], v.t. & i., & n. Strike surface of (water) so as to break it up; splash (t. &

i.); (n.) splash, plunge. Hence **pla·sh**Y² a. [cf. Du. *plassen*, G *platschen*, prob. imit.]

plash³, v.t. Bend down and interweave (branches, twigs) to form hedge; make, renew, (hedge) thus. [f. OF *plaissier* ult. f. L *plectere* plait; cf. PLEACH]

plasm (-zm), n. Living matter of a cell, protoplasm, esp. general body of this as distinct from nucleus. [f. foll.]

pla·sma (-z-), n. Green variety of quartz; colourless coagulable part of blood, lymph, or milk, in which the corpuscles or oil-globules float, so **plasmă·t**IC a.; =prec., whence **pla·sm**IC a. [LL & Gk (gen.-*matos*), =thing moulded (*plassō* mould, see -M)]

pla·smin, n. (chem.). A proteid obtained from the plasma of the blood. [f. F *plasmine* (as prec., see -IN)]

plasmo- in comb. =PLASM, as: *-gen*, true or formative protoplasm; *-geny, -gony*, mode of spontaneous generation, when the organism arises in an organic formative fluid; *-logy*, study of ultimate corpuscles of living matter; *-lysis*, contraction of protoplasm of vegetable cell under action of certain reagents, so *-lyse* v.t., subject to this, *-lў·tic* a.

plasmō·dium, n. (biol.; pl. *-ia*). Mass of naked protoplasm formed by fusion or aggregation of amoeboid bodies; parasitic organism found in blood of patients with recent malaria &c. [mod. L, f. PLASMA + *-odium*, see -ODE]

pla·ster¹, n. Curative application consisting of some substance spread upon muslin &c. & capable of adhering at the temperature of the body, as COURT¹, MUSTARD, *sticking-, p.*; soft plastic mixture, esp. of lime, sand, & hair, for spreading on walls &c. to form smooth surface; *p. of Paris*, fine white p. of gypsum used for making moulds & as cement &c. [prepared from gypsums of Montmartre, Paris]. Hence **pla·ster**Y² a. [OE, f. pop. L *plastrum* f. L f. Gk *emplastron* for *emplaston* thing daubed on f. EM(*plassō* mould)]

pla·ster², v.t. Cover (wall &c.) with plaster or the like, whence **pla·ster**ER¹ n.; coat, bedaub, (fig.) load to excess (*with* praise &c.); apply medical plaster to, (facet.) give compensation for (blow, wound); stick, fix, (thing) like plaster upon surface; treat (wine) with gypsum &c. to neutralize acidity. [f. prec.]

plă·stic, a. Moulding, giving form to clay, wax, &c.; *p. arts*, those concerned with modelling, e.g. sculpture, ceramics; *p. surgery* (repairing deficiency of structure); causing growth of natural forms, formative of immaterial things; produced by moulding; capable of being (easily) moulded; *p. clay* (Geol.), middle group of Eocene beds; (fig.) pliant, supple; (Biol.) capable of forming living tissue, (also) accompanied by this process, as *p. bronchitis*. Hence **pla·st**ICALLY adv., **plasti·**CITY n. [f. L f. Gk *plastikos* (*plassō* mould, see -IC)]

pla·sticine, n. Proprietary name for a plastic substance used esp. in schools as substitute for modelling clay. [-INE⁴]

plă·stron, n. Fencer's leather-covered breast-plate; breast-covering of facings-cloth worn by lancers; ornamental front to woman's bodice; man's starched shirt-front; ventral part of shell of tortoise or turtle, corresponding part in other animals; (Hist.) steel breast-plate. [F, f. It. *piastrone* (*piastra* breastplate, as PLASTER; see -OON)]

plat¹, n. Patch, plot, of ground, as *grass-p.* [collat. form of PLOT]

plat², n., & v.t. =PLAIT (2nd sense).

plat³ (plah), n. Dish of food. [F, see PLATE¹]

plă·tan, n. Oriental plane-tree. [f. L *platanus* plane-tree]

plate¹, n. Flat thin usu. rigid sheet of metal &c. of even surface and more or less uniform thickness; this as part of mechanism; smooth piece of metal &c. for engraving; impression from this; = BOOK¹-*p.*; piece of metal with name or inscription for affixing to something, as *coffin, door, name,-p.*; thin sheet of metal, glass, &c., coated with sensitive film for photograph (*whole-p.*, $8\frac{1}{2} \times 6\frac{1}{2}$ in., *half-p.*, $6\frac{1}{2} \times 4\frac{3}{4}$, *quarter-p.*, $4\frac{1}{4} \times 3\frac{1}{4}$); stereotype or electrotype cast of page of composed movable types, from which sheets are printed; horizontal timber laid along top of wall to support ends of joists or rafters, or at top or bottom of a framing, as *roof, wall, window, p.*; (also *p.-rail*) early form of railroad; (collective sing.) table & domestic utensils of silver, gold, or other metal, as *pewter p., electro-p.*; silver or gold cup as prize for (orig. horse-) race, such race; *selling p.*, horse-race winner of which must be sold at fixed price; shallow usu. circular vessel, now usu. of earthenware or china, from which food is eaten, as *dessert, dinner, soup, -p.*; contents of this, as *a p. of strawberries*; similar vessel used for collection in churches &c., as *put a shilling in the p.*; (U.S.) *home, pitcher's, p.*, stations of batter, pitcher, in baseball; *p.-basket* (for spoons, forks, &c.); *p. glass*, thick glass of fine quality cast in pp. for shop windows &c.; *p.-layer*, man employed in fixing & repairing railway; *p.-mark*, = HALL-*mark*; *p.-powder* (for cleaning silver); *p.-rack* (in which pp. are kept or placed to drain). Hence **pla·te**FUL(2) n., **pla·te**LESS a. [ME & OF, fem. of *plat* flat, perh. ult. f. Gk *platus* broad]

plate², v.t. Cover (esp. ship) with plates of metal for protection, ornament, &c.; cover (other metal) with thin coat of silver, gold, or tin; make a plate of (type) for printing. [f. prec.]

plateau· (-tō), n. (pl. *-x*, *-s*, pron. -z). Tableland; ornamented tray or dish; decorative plaque; woman's hat with level top. [F, f. OF *platel* dim. of PLAT[3]]

plă·ten, -tt-, n. Plate in printing-press by which paper is pressed against type; corresponding part in type-writers &c. [f. OF *platine* flat piece (*plat*, see PLATE[1])]

plā·ter, n. One who plates with silver &c.; one who makes or applies plates in ship-building; inferior race-horse, competing chiefly for plates. [-ER[1]]

pla·tform, n., & v.t. & i. Raised level surface, natural or artificial terrace; raised surface of planks &c. along side of line at railway station; raised flooring in hall or open air from which speaker addresses audience, (fig.) *the p.*, p. oratory; (fig.) political basis of party &c., esp. (U.S.) declaration issued by representatives of party assembled to nominate candidates for election; (v.t.) place (as) on p.; (v.i.) speak on p. [f. F *plateforme* ground-plan, lit. flat form (as PLATE[1] + *forme* FORM)]

pla·ting, n. In vbl senses; also or esp.: coating of gold, silver, &c.; plate-racing. [f. PLATE[2] + -ING[1]]

plă·tinize, v.t. Coat with platinum. [-IZE]

pla·tinode, n. Negative plate or pole of voltaic cell, often consisting of platinum (cf. ZINCODE). [f. PLATINUM + Gk *hodos* path]

pla·tinoid, n. Alloy of nickel, zinc, copper, &c., with some qualities of platinum; kinds of metal found associated with platinum. [-OID]

pla·tinotype, n. Process of photographic printing in platinum black. [f. foll. + -O- + -TYPE]

plă·tinum, n. White heavy ductile malleable metal unaffected by simple acids & fusible only at very high temperature; *p. black*, p. in form of powder like lamp-black; *p. metals*, platinoids. Hence **plati·nic**, **platini·ferous**, **pla·tinous**, aa. [f. Sp. (& earlier E) *platina* dim. of *plata* silver, see PLATE[1]]

plă·titude, n. Commonplaceness; commonplace remark, esp. one solemnly delivered. Hence **platitu·dinize**(2) v.i. **platitu·dinous** a., **platitu·dinously**[2] adv. [F, f. *plat* (see PLATE[1]) after *lati*TUDE &c.]

platitudinār·ian, n. & a. Dealer in platitudes; (adj.) of the nature of platitude. [-ARIAN]

Platŏ·nic, a. Of Plato the Greek philosopher (d. circ. 347 B.C.) or his doctrines; *P. love* purely spiritual love for one of opposite sex (*platonics*, p. lovers' talk or relation); (pop.) confined to words or theory, not issuing in action, harmless; *P. year*, cycle in which heavenly bodies were supposed to go through all their possible movements & return to original positions. So **Plato·nically** adv., **Plā·tonism**, **Pla·tonist**, nn., **Pla·tonize**(2, 3) v.i. & t. [f. L f. Gk *Platōnikos* (*Platōn* Plato, see -IC)]

platōō·n, n. (Hist.) small infantry detachment, esp. a unit for volley-firing &c., volley fired by it; (in mod. use) a half-company, one of four parts of a double company, as a tactical unit commanded by a lieutenant. [f. F *peloton* small ball (as PELLET, see -OON)]

pla·tter, n. (chiefly archaic). Flat dish or plate, often of wood. [ME & OF *plater* (PLAT[3])]

plăty- in comb. = Gk *platus* broad, flat, as: *-pus*, Australian duck-mole, ornithorhynchus; *-(r)rhine*, (of monkeys) with nostrils far apart & directed forwards or sideways.

plau·dit, n. (usu. in pl.). Round of applause; emphatic expression of approval. [shortened f. L *plaudite* applaud (also as E noun) pl. imperat. of *plaudere plaus-* applaud, said by Roman actors at end of play]

plau·sible (-z-), a. (Of arguments, statements, &c.) specious, seeming reasonable or probable; (of persons) fair-spoken (usu. implying deceit). Hence or cogn. **plausibi·lity** n., **plau·sibly**[2] adv. [f. L *plausibilis* (as prec., see -BLE)]

play[1], v.i. & t. Move about in lively or capricious manner, frisk, flit, flutter, pass gently (*around, about*, &c.), strike lightly (*upon* &c.), alternate rapidly, as *bees p. about flowers, tresses p. on her neck, smile played on his lips, wind plays on water, his fancy played round the idea*; (of part of mechanism &c.) have free movement; wield freely, as *p. a good knife & fork*, eat heartily, *p. a good stick*, fence well; allow (fish) to exhaust itself by pulling against line; discharge (guns &c. *on*), discharge guns (*on*), (intr., of guns) be fired (*on*); direct (light *on, over, along*, &c.), (intr., of light) pass (*over, along*, &c.); perform, execute, (trick, prank, joke, *on* person, or with double object); amuse oneself, sport, frolic; *p. with*, amuse oneself with, trifle with, treat lightly; *p. upon words*, pun; (dial., esp. of workmen on strike) abstain from work; employ oneself in the game of (cricket, whist, &c., or abs.); *played out*, exhausted of energy or vitality or usefulness (*our horses were, I felt, Free Trade is, p.o.*); *p. up*, put all one's energy into the game &c.; *p.* DUCK[1]*s & drakes, p.* FAST[3] *& loose*; (in Cricket, Lawn Tennis, &c., as bowler's warning to batsman &c.) *p.!*; pretend for fun (*that we are gipsies* &c.); (Crick., of ground) *p. well* &c., be in good &c. condition for play; *p.-or-pay bet* (holding good whether horse runs or not); game, gamble; *p. fair, foul*, p. or (fig.) act (un)fairly; *p.* (observe the rules of) *the game* (also fig. of keeping to code of honour); *p. into the hands of*, act so as to give advantage to (opponent or partner); (slang) *p. it on, p. it low on, p.* (*low*) *down on*, take mean advantage of (person); *p. upon the* SQUARE; *p. at*, engage in (game), (fig.) engage in (fighting &c.) in trivial or half-hearted way; contend against (person) in game; employ (person) to play in game, include in team; *p.* BOOTY; move (piece in chess &c.); take (playing-card) from one's hand & lay it face upwards on table in one's turn, (fig.) *p.* one's *cards well*, make good use of opportunities; (Crick. &c.) strike (ball) in specified esp. defensive manner; (Crick.) *p. on* (abs.), p. the ball on to one's own wicket and so put oneself out; *p. off*, oppose (person *against* another) esp. for one's own advantage, (also) cause (person) to exhibit himself disadvantageously, (also) pass (thing) off as something else; perform on (musical instrument, or abs.); perform (*on* instrument); perform (music *on* instrument); *p.* (congregation &c.) *in, out*, p. on organ &c. as they come in, go out; *p.* (*up*)*on*, make use of (person's fears, credulity, &c.); *p. first, second,* FIDDLE; perform (drama, or abs.) on stage; act (*in* drama); act (part) in drama, as *p. Shylock*, (fig.) act in real life the part of (*the* DEUCE[2] or *devil, the fool, the man, truant*, &c., also *p.* one's *part well* &c.); *p. up to*, act in drama so as to support (another actor), (fig.) back up, flatter, toady. Hence **play·**ABLE a. [OE *plegan, plagian, plægian*, cf. MDu. *plegen* dance, be glad, cogn. w. Du. *plegen*, G *pflegen*, be wont, take charge of]

play[2], n. Brisk, light, or fitful movement; activity, operation, as *lively p. of fancy, other forces come into p., are in full p., are brought* or *called into p., make p.,* act effectively, esp. (Racing, Hunting) exercise pursuers or followers; freedom of movement, space for this, scope for activity, as *bolts should have half an inch of p., allow full p. to curiosity*; amusement, as *at p.*, engaged in playing; *said it only in p.* (not seriously); *p. of words*, trifling with words, *p. on words*, pun; playing of game; manner, style, of this; (Crick., Footb., &c.) *ball is in p.* (being used in ordinary course of p.), *is out of p.* (temporarily removed from p. according to rules), so *p.*, part of ground within definite boundaries; CHILD'*s-p.*; FAIR[2], FOUL, *p.*; cessation from work (of workmen on strike &c.); dramatic piece, drama; gaming, gambling; *p.-actor* (usu. contempt.); *p.-bill*, bill, placard, announcing theatrical p.; *p.-club* (Golf), driver; *p.-day*, school holiday, week-day on which miners &c. do not work; *p.-debt* (incurred in gaming); *play·fellow*, companion in (usu. children's) p.; *playgame*, experience that falls short of another (*is a p.-g. in comparison*) or of grim reality (e.g. sham fight); *play·goer*, frequenter of theatre; *play·ground*, piece of ground used for p., esp. at school (*the p.-g. of Europe*, Switzerland); *play·house*, theatre; *play·mate*, playfellow; *play·thing*, toy, (fig.) person &c. treated as mere toy; *play·time*; *play·wright*, dramatist. [OE *plega* as prec.]

play·er, n. In vbl senses, esp.; person engaged at the time, person skilful, in a game; professional p. at cricket &c.; actor; (Pool, Croquet) ball that after present p. has finished break &c. will play on him. [-ER[1]]

play·ful, a. Frolicsome, sportive; humorous, jocular. Hence **play·ful**LY[2] adv., **play·ful**NESS n. [-FUL]

play·ing, n. In vbl senses; *p.-cards*, set or pack of cards used in games. [-ING[1]]

plea, n. Pleading, argument, excuse; (Law) formal statement by or on behalf of defendant, defence, *special p.* (alleging new fact); *Court of* COMMON[1] *Pp.*; (Hist.) action at law. [ME & OF *plaid* f. L *placitum* decree, neut. p.p. of *placēre* please]

pleach (-ētsh), v.t. Entwine, interlace; esp. = PLASH[3] [ME *pleche*, as PLASH]

plead (-ēd), v.i. & t. Address court as advocate on behalf of either party, so **plea·d**ER[1] n.; maintain (cause) in court; allege formally as plea, (fig.) allege as excuse &c., as *I can only p. inexperience*, so **plea·d**ABLE a.; *p.* (*not*) *guilty*, deny, confess, liability or guilt; *p. with*, make earnest appeal to (person *for* person, *for, against*, thing, decision, &c.), whence **plea·ding**LY[2] adv. [f. OF *plaidier* (as PLEA)]

plea·ding, n. In vbl senses, esp.: formal (now usu. written) statement of cause of action or defence; SPECIAL *p.* [-ING[1]]

pleasance (plĕ·zans), n. (archaic). Pleasure, enjoyment; pleasure-ground, esp. one attached to mansion (now chiefly surviving in proper names). [f. OF *plaisance* (as foll., see -ANCE)]

pleasant (plĕ·znt), a. Agreeable to mind, feelings, or senses, as *a p. breeze, flavour, discovery, companion, has a p. manner, spent a p. evening*; (archaic) jocular, facetious. Hence **plea·sant**LY[2] adv., **plea·sant**NESS n. [f. OF *plaisant* (as PLEASE, see -ANT)]

plea·santry (plĕz-), n. Jocularity; humorous speech, jest. [f. F *plaisanterie* (prec., -ERY)]

please (plēz), v.t. Be agreeable to, as *meant only to p. the eye, his last book will p. you*; *p. yourself*, do as you like; *be pleased with*, derive pleasure from: *I shall* (vulg. *will*) *be pleased* (glad) *to* (do, esp. as polite form of consent or offer); think fit, as *take as many as you p.*; (in formal or iron. deference) *His Majesty has been graciously pleased to confer* &c., *your lordship was pleased to doubt my veracity*; (with *it* as subject, expressed or omitted, representing a prec. or foll. infinitive, clause, or sentence, now chiefly as in last use) *it has never pleased him to explain*, (*may it*) *p. your honour, there was no moon that night, the matter will be cleared up* *some day, p. God* (or, facet., *p. the pigs*); (abs.) *was anxious to p.*; (as polite form of request esp. for trifling services) *if you p.* with your permission, as *I will take another cup, if you p.*, (with iron. implication that nothing could be more reasonable) *& now, if you p., he expects me to pay for it!*; (imperat., orig. = may it please you) *ring the bell, p., may I come in, p.?, coffee for two, p., p.* (*to*) *return it soon, p. don't* (or *p. not to*) *forget the key.* Hence **pleas**ED[1], **plea·s**ING[2], aa., **plea·s-ing**LY[2] adv. [ME *plaise* f. OF *plaisir* (F *plaire*) f. L *placēre*]

plea·surable (plĕzh-), a. Affording pleasure. Hence **plea·surable**NESS n., **plea·s-urab**LY[2] adv. [f. foll. + -ABLE]

pleasure (plĕ·zher), n., & v.t. & i. Enjoyment, delight; sensuous enjoyment as chief object of life, as *a life given up to p., man of p.*, profligate; will, desire, as *shall not consult his p., can be postponed during our p., can be altered at p.*; (royal formula) *it is our p. to*, we are graciously pleased to, (vulg.) *it is our p. to submit* (we have p. in submitting) *balance sheet* &c.; *to converse with him is a* (source of) *p.*; *do me the p. of* (gratify me by) *dining with me*; *he takes* (*a*) *p. in* (likes) *contradicting* or *contradiction*; (archaic) *are now taking their p.* (enjoying themselves) *at Bath*; *p.-boat* (used for p., not business); *p.-ground* (laid out for p.); (v.t.) give p. to; (v.i.) take p. (*in* thing, *in* doing). [(vb f. n.) ME & OF *plesir, plaisir*, PLEASE used as n.]

pleat (-ēt), n., & v.t. =PLAIT (1st sense). [collateral form of PLAIT]

plĕb, n. (slang). Plebeian, person of lower classes. [abbr.]

plēbei·an (-bēan), n. & a. Commoner in ancient Rome (cf. PATRICIAN); commoner; (adj.) of low birth, of the common people, coarse, base, ignoble. Hence **plebei·an-**NESS n., **plebei·an**IZE(3) v.t. [f. L *plebeius* (*plebs* common people) + -AN]

plĕ·biscite (-sĭt), n. (Rom. Hist.) law enacted by commonalty in *comitia tributa*; (mod.) direct vote of all electors of State on important public question; public expression of community's opinion, with or without binding force. So **plebi·scit**ARY[1] a. [f. F *plébiscite* f. L *plebiscitum* (*plebs plebis* commons + *scitum* decree f. *sciscere* vote for)]

plĕ·ctrum, n. Small instrument of ivory, quill, &c., for plucking strings of zither &c. [L, f. Gk *plēktron* (*plēssō* strike)]

pledge[1], n. Thing handed over to person as security (cf. REPLEVIN) for fulfilment of contract, payment of debt, &c., & liable to forfeiture in case of failure; thing put in pawn; (fig.) one's child; thing given as token of favour &c. or of something to come; drinking of a health, toast; promise, as *under p. of secrecy*; solemn engagement to abstain from intoxicants, as *take, sign, keep, the p.*; (Pol.) leader's public promise (not) to adopt some course; state of being pledged, as *goods lying in p., taken out of p.* [ME & OF *plege* &c., prob. f. med. L *plevire* warrant, engage, of G orig., cf. PLIGHT]

pledge[2], v.t. Deposit as security, pawn; (fig.) plight (one's honour, word, &c.); drink to the health of. Hence **ple·dge-**ABLE a. [f. prec.]

pledgee·, n. One with whom pledge is deposited, pawnee. So **ple·dg**ER[1] n. [-EE]

ple·dget, n. Small wad of lint &c. [?]

Plei·ad (plī-), n. (pl. *-ads, -adēs*). (Pl.) cluster of small stars in Taurus, usu. spoken of as 7; (fig., sing.) brilliant group of (usu. 7) persons or things. [f. L *Plēias* f. Gk *Pleias -ados*]

plei·stocene (plī-), a. & n. (geol.). (Of) the division immediately overlying the pliocene formation. [f. Gk *pleistos* most + *kainos* new]

plē·nary, a. Entire, absolute, unqualified; (of assembly) fully attended; *p.* INSPIRATION. Hence **ple·nari**LY[2] adv. [f. LL *plenarius* (*plenus* full, see -ARY[1])]

plĕ·nipote·ntiary, a. & n. (Person) invested with full power, esp. as ambassador deputed to act at discretion; (of power) absolute. [f. med. L *plenipotentiarius* f. LL *plenipotens* (*plenus* full + *potens* POTENT), see -ARY[1]]

plĕ·nitude, n. Fullness, completeness; abundance. [OF, f. L *plenitudo* (*plenus* full, see -TUDE)]

ple·nteous, a. (chiefly poet.). Plentiful. Hence **ple·nteous**LY[2] adv., **ple·nteous-**NESS n. [ME & OF *plentivous* (PLENTY, -IVE, -EOUS)]

ple·ntiful, a. Abundant, copious. Hence **ple·ntiful**LY[2] adv., **ple·ntiful**NESS n. [f. foll. + -FUL]

ple·nty, n. & adv. Abundance, as much as one could desire, (*of* thing, or abs.), as *p. of cake, here is cake in p., we are in p. of time*; *horn of p.*, cornucopia; (adv., colloq.) *p.* (quite) *large* &c. *enough.* [f. OF *plentet* f. L *plentitatem* (*plenus* full, see -TY)]

plē·num, n. Space filled with matter (*p. system*, of ventilation by forcing air in); full assembly. [L, neut. of *plenus* full]

plē·onasm, n. (gram.). Redundancy of expression, e.g. *hear with* one's *ears, a false lie.* So **pleona·st**IC a., **pleona·sti-**CALLY adv. [f. L f. Gk *pleonasmos* (*pleonazō* add superfluously f. *pleon* more]

plē·siosau·rus, n. Extinct marine reptile with long neck, short tail, & four large paddles. [f. Gk *plēsios* near + *sauros* lizard]

plĕ·thora (*or* plĕthō·r*a*), n. Morbid condition marked by excess of red corpuscles in the blood; (fig.) unhealthy repletion. Hence or cogn. **plethŏ·r**IC a., **pletho·ric-**ALLY adv. [med. L, f. Gk *plēthōrē* (*plēthō* become full)]

pleura (ploor·*a*), n. Either of the two serous membranes lining the thorax & enveloping the lungs in mammals; part of the body-wall in invertebrates. Hence **pleur·**AL a. [Gk, = side of body, rib]

pleur·isy, n. Inflammation of the pleura, usu. caused by chill, & marked by pain in chest or side, fever, &c. So **pleuri·ti**CA. [f. OF *pleurisie* f. LL *pleurisis* altered f. Gk *pleuritis* (as prec., see -ITIS), also used in E]

pleuro- in comb. (before vowel *pleur-*) = Gk *pleura*, side, pleura, rib, as: *pleurody·nia*, pain in side caused by rheumatism in muscles of chest; *pleuro-pneumo·nia*, pneumonia complicated with pleurisy, esp. as contagious disease of horned cattle.

plexi·meter, n. (med.). Thin plate of ivory &c. placed on part of the body & struck with plexor in medical percussion. [f. Gk *plēxis* stroke (*plēssō* strike) + -METER]

ple·xor, n. (med.). Small hammer used with pleximeter. [irreg. as prec. + -OR²]

ple·xus, n. (Anat.) network of fibres or vessels in animal body, as *gastric, pulmonary, p.*; network, complication. Hence **ple·xi**FORM a. [L, gen. *-ūs*, f. *plectere plex-* plait]

pli·able, a. =foll. Hence **plia**BI·LITY n., **pli·ab**LY² adv. [F (*plier* bend f. L *plicare*)]

pli·ant, a. Bending, supple; (fig.) yielding, compliant. Hence **pli·**ANCY n., **pli·ant**LY² adv. [F (as prec., see -ANT)]

plĭ·ca, n. (pl. *-ae*). Fold, as of skin or membrane; *p.* (*polo·nica* Polish), matted filthy condition of hair due to disease. [med. L, as foll.]

plĭ·cate (*-at*), a. (bot., zool., geol.). Folded. So **plĭca·t**ED¹ a. [f. L *plicare* fold, -ATE²]

plĭca·tion, n. Folding; fold; folded condition. [OF (as prec., see -ATION)]

pli·ers, n. pl. Pincers having long jaws with parallel surfaces, for bending wire &c. [f. (dial. *ply* bend (see PLIABLE) + -ER¹]

plight¹ (plīt), v.t., & n. Pledge (one's troth, faith, promise, esp. in p.p.); engage one*self* (*to* person, esp. in p.p. as *plighted lovers*); (n.) engagement. [OE (*plihtan* vb f.) *pliht* danger, cf. Du. *pligt*, G *pflicht*, responsibility, duty, f. WG *plegan* take risk of]

plight² (plīt), n. Condition, state, esp. *a sorry, evil, hopeless,* &c. *p.* [ME *plit*, doublet of PLAIT]

plim, v.t. & i. (dial.). Swell, fill *out*, make or grow plump. [also *plum*, perh. cogn. w. PLUMP¹]

Pli·msoll, a. & n. *P. line, P.'s* MARK¹; (n. pl.) cheap rubber-soled canvas shoes, [S. *P.*, agitator for Merchant Shipping Act of 1876]

plinth, n. Lower square member of base of column; projecting part of wall immediately above ground. [f. L (= plinth) f. Gk *plinthos* tile, brick]

pli·nthite, n. Kind of brick-red clay. [as prec. + -ITE¹]

pli·ocene (-ēn), a. & n. (geol.). (Of) the newest division of Tertiary formation. [f. Gk *pleiōn* more + *kainos* new]

plod, v.i. & t., & n. Walk laboriously, trudge, (*on, along,* &c.); drudge, slave, (*at* &c.); make (one's way) laboriously; (n.) laborious walk or work. Hence **plo·dd**ER¹ n., **plo·dding**LY² adv. [prob. imit.]

plo·mbé (-awmbā), a. Officially lead-sealed. [F]

plop, n., adv., & v.t. & i. Sound as of smooth object dropping into water without splash; act of falling with this; (adv.) with a p.; (v.i. & t.) (cause to) fall thus. [imit.]

plot¹, n. Piece (usu. small) of ground; plan of play, poem, novel, &c., whence **plo·t**LESS a.; conspiracy; sly plan. [?]

plot², v.t. Make plan or map of (existing object, place or thing to be laid out, constructed, &c.); plan, contrive, (evil object, or abs.). Hence **plo·tt**ER¹ n. [f. prec.]

plough¹ (-ow), n. Implement for cutting furrows in soil & turning it up, consisting of cutting blade (*ploughshare*) fixed in frame drawn by horses &c. & guided by man (*ploughman*); *put* one's *hand to the p.*, undertake task (*Luke* ix. 62); ploughed land; kinds of instrument resembling p., as *ice-p.* (for cutting up blocks of ice), *snow-p.* (for clearing away snow); *the P.*, CHARLES'S WAIN; [f. foll.] rejection of candidate in examination; *p.-beam*, central beam of p.; *p.-boy*, boy who leads p.-horses &c.; *p.-land* (hist.), as much land as could be ploughed by one team of 8 oxen in the year, unit of assessment in N. & E. counties of England (cf. HIDE³); *P. Monday* (first after Epiphany), *p.-shoe*, appliance for protecting or supporting ploughshare; *p.-staff* (ending in small spade, used to clear coulter &c. from earth &c.); *p.-tail*, rear of p., (fig.) farm-labour, as *at the p.-tail*. [late OE *plóh*, cf. Du. *ploeg*, G *pflug*]

plough², v.t. & i. Turn up (earth, or abs.) with plough, esp. before sowing (*p. the sand* or *sands*, labour uselessly); root *out*, cast *up*, thrust *down*, (roots, weeds) with plough; furrow, scratch, (surface) as with plough; produce (furrow, line) thus; produce wrinkles in (brow &c.); advance laboriously (*through* snow &c., *through* book &c.); (of ship &c.) cleave (surface of water, its way, &c.); (slang) reject (candidate) in examination. [f. prec.]

plo·ver (plŭ-), n. Kinds of gregarious grallatorial bird, esp. *Golden, Grey, P.*, & (pop.) lapwing (whose eggs are sold as p.'s); *p.-page, p.'s-page*, dunlin & other birds said to follow golden p. [f. OF *plovier* f. LL **plovarius* (*pluvia* rain, reference unexpl., see -ARY¹)]

ploy, n. (north.) Expedition, undertaking, occupation, job. [perh. f. *employ*]

pluck¹, n. Plucking, twitch; rejection,

failure, in examination; heart, liver, & lungs, of beast as food; courage, spirit, whence **(-)pluck**ED², **plu·ck**LESS, **plu·ck**Y², aa., **plu·ck**ILY² adv., **plu·ck**INESS n.; (Photog. slang) boldness of effect. [f. foll.]

pluck², v.t. & i. Pull off, pick, (flower, feather, hair); (archaic) pull, drag, snatch, (*away, off,* &c.); pull at, twitch; tug, snatch, *at*; strip (bird) of feathers; CROW¹ *to p.*; plunder, swindle, as *p. a* PIGEON; reject (candidate) in examination; *p. up* one's *heart, spirits, courage,* take courage. [com.-WG; OE *ploccian, pluc-*, MDu. & MG *plocken*]

plug¹, n. Piece of wood &c. fitting tightly into hole, used to fill gap or act as wedge (in various techn. uses); natural or morbid concretion acting thus; kinds of stopper for vessel or pipe; FIRE¹-*p.*; tobacco pressed into cake or stick, piece of this cut off for chewing. [prob. f. MDu. *plugge*, etym. dub.]

plug², v.t. & i. Stop (hole &c., often *up*) with plug; (slang) shoot; (slang) strike with fist; (colloq.) plod (*away at* work &c.). [f. prec.]

plum, n. Roundish fleshy fruit with sweet pulp & flattish pointed stone; (also *p.-tree*) tree bearing this; dried grape or raisin as used for cakes &c.; SUGAR-*p.*; *French p.*, fine kind of prune; (fig.) good thing, best of a collection, prize in life &c.; (slang) £100,000; *p. cake* (containing raisins, currants, &c.); *p. duff*, plain flour pudding with raisins or currants; *p. pudding*, boiled pudding of flour, bread-crumbs, suet, raisins, currants, eggs, spices, &c., eaten at Christmas, (also) ordinary suet-pudding with raisins, *p.-pudding* (Dalmatian or Spotted Coach) *dog, p.-pudding stone* (geol.), conglomerate of flint or other pebbles. [OE *plūme* cf. G *pflaume*, Du. *pruim*, f. LL *pruna* (L *prunum*) f. late Gk *prounon* (Gk *proumnon*)]

plumage (ploo·mij), n. A bird's feathers. Hence **(-)plumag**ED² a. [OF (PLUME, -AGE)]

plumassier (ploomasēr·), n. One who trades or works in ornamental feathers. [F (*plumasse* augment. of PLUME, see -IER)]

plumb¹ (-m), n., a., & adv. Ball of lead, esp. that attached to mason's *p.-line* (string for testing perpendicularity of wall &c., also fig.); *out of p.*, not vertical; sounding-lead, plummet; *p.-rule*, mason's p.-line attached to board; (adj.) vertical, (fig.), downright, sheer, as *p. nonsense*, (Crick., of wicket) level, true; (adv.) vertically, (fig.) exactly, as *points p. in the same direction*; (U.-S. slang) quite, utterly, (*p. crazy*, clean mad). [(adj. & adv. f. n.) f. F *plomb* f. L *plumbum* lead]

plumb² (-m), v.t. & i. Sound (sea), measure (depth, lit. & fig.), with plummet, whence **plu·mb**LESS a.; make vertical; (intr.) work as plumber. [f. prec.]

plumbā·go (-mb-), n. Black lead, graphite, a form of carbon used for pencils &c. & mixed with clay for making crucibles; leadwort, plant with p.-coloured flowers. Hence **plumbă·gin**OUS a. [L, gen. *-ginis*, f. *plumbum* lead]

plu·mbeous (-mb-), a. Of, like, lead; lead-glazed. [f. L *plumbeus* (as prec.) + -OUS]

plu·mber (-mer), n. Artisan who fits & repairs pipes, cisterns, &c., with lead, zinc, or tin. So **plu·mb**ERY(2, 3) n. [f. OF *plummier* f. L *plumbarius* (as prec., see -ARY¹)]

plu·mbic (-mb-), a. (Chem.) combined with lead, so **plumbi·**FEROUS a.; (Path.) due to presence of lead, so **plu·mb**ISM(5) n. [f. L *plumbum* lead + -IC]

plume¹, n. Feather, esp. large one used for ornament; (fig.) *borrowed pp.* (referring to fable of jackdaw in peacock's pp.); ornamental feather or bunch of feathers or horsehair, esp. as attached to helmet or hat, or worn in hair, as *court p.* (of ostrich feathers); (Zool.) feather-like part or formation. Hence **plu·me**LESS, **plu·me**LIKE, aa., **plu·me**LET n. [OF, f. L *pluma* down]

plume², v.t. Furnish with plume(s); dress one*self* with borrowed plumes; pride one*self* (*on* esp. something trivial or to which one has no claim); (of bird) trim, dress, (feathers). [f. prec.]

plu·mmer-block, n. (mech.). Metal case for supporting revolving shaft, with movable cover giving access to bearings. [?]

plu·mmet, n. (Weight attached to) plumb-line; sounding-lead; (fig.) oppressive or obstructive weight; weight attached to fishing-line to keep float upright. [ME & OF *plommet* dim. as PLUMB¹]

plu·mmy, a. Of, abounding in, plums; (colloq.) rich, good, desirable. [-Y²]

plumo·se, a. Feathered; featherlike. [f. L *plumosus* (as PLUME¹, see -OSE¹)]

plump¹, a., & v.t. & i. (Esp. of person or parts of body) full, rounded, fleshy, filled out; (v.t.) make p., fatten *up*; (v.i.) become p., swell *out* or *up*. Hence **plu·mp**LY² adv., **plu·mp**NESS n., **plu·mp**Y² a. [cf. Du. *plomp* blunt]

plump², v.i. & t., n., adv., & a. Drop or plunge (t. & i.) with abrupt descent (*down upon* &c.); vote *for* (one candidate alone, when one might vote for two); (n.) abrupt plunge, heavy fall; (adv.) with sudden or heavy fall, as *came p. into the river*, (also) flatly, bluntly, as *I told him p., I lied p.*; (adj.) direct, unqualified, as *answer with a p. No.* [com.-LG: Du. *plompen*, G *plumpen*, prob. imit.]

plump³, n. (archaic). Company, troop, esp. *p. of spears* (spearmen); cluster. [?]

plu·mper¹, n. Ball, disk, carried in mouth to fill out hollow cheeks. [PLUMP¹ + -ER¹]

plu·mper², n. In vbl senses, esp.: (vote of) one who plumps for candidate; downright lie. [PLUMP² + -ER¹]

plu·mule (ploo-), n. Rudimentary stem of embryo plant, whence **plu·mul**AR¹ a.; little feather of down whence **plumul**A·CEOUS a. [f. L *plumula*, dim. as PLUME¹]

plu·my, a. Plume-like; feathery; adorned with plumes. [-Y²]

plu·nder, v.t., & n. Rob (place, person) forcibly of goods, esp. as in war; rob systematically; steal, embezzle, (goods or abs.); (n.) violent or dishonest acquisition of property; property so acquired; (slang) profit, gain. Hence **plu·nder**ER¹ n. [(n. f. vb) f. G *plündern* (*plunder, bl-*, bed-clothes &c.)]

plu·nderage (-ĭj), n. Plundering, esp. embezzling of goods on shipboard; spoil thus obtained. [-AGE]

plunge, v.t. & i., & n. Thrust violently (*into* liquid, cavity, &c.); (fig.) thrust (person &c. *into, in*, condition, action, &c.); sink (pot containing plant) in ground; throw oneself, dive, (*into* water, difficulty, discussion, &c.); enter impetuously (*into* room, *up, down*, stairs, &c.); (of horse) throw itself violently forward; (of ship) pitch; (slang) gamble deeply, run into debt; *plunging fire* (from guns at higher level); (n.) plunging, dive, (*p.-bath*, large enough to dive into), (fig.) critical step, as *take the p.* [f. OF *plunjer* f. LL **plumbicare* heave the lead (*plumbum*)]

plu·nger, n. In vbl senses, esp.: parts of mechanism that work with plunging motion; (slang) cavalryman; (slang) gambler, speculator. [-ER¹]

plu·per·fect, a. & n. (Tense) expressing action completed prior to some past point of time specified or implied (expr. in E by *had* with p.p. as *he had called*). [f. L *plus quam perfectum* more than perfect]

plur·al (ploor-), a. & n. (Form of noun, verb, &c.) denoting more than one (or, in languages with dual, more than two); more than one in number; *p. vote, voter, voting* (of one person in more than one constituency). Hence **plur·al**LY² adv. [f. L *pluralis* (*plus pluris* more, see -AL)]

plur·alism, n. Holding of more than one office, esp. benefice, at a time; (Philos.) system that recognizes more than one ultimate principle (cf. MONISM). So **plur·al**IST n., **plurali·st**IC a. [-ISM]

plurǎ·lity, n. State of being plural; large number, multitude; holding of two or more benefices or offices; benefice, office, held with another; majority (*of* votes &c.). [f. OF *pluralite* f. LL *pluralitas* (as PLURAL, see -TY)]

plu·ralize, v.t. & i. Make plural, express in the plural; hold more than one benefice. [f. F *pluraliser* (as PLURAL, see -IZE)]

pluri- in comb. = L *plus pluris* more, as; *-li·teral* (Heb. Gram.), having more than 3 letters in the root; *-pre·sence*, presence in more than one place at same time; *-ser·ial, -ser·iate*, consisting of several series.

plŭs, prep., a., & n. (As oral rendering of symbol +) with the addition of, as *3 p. 4* (cf. MINUS); *p. 4* (or other number), golfer's handicap (*plus-fours*, long wide knickerbockers worn first by golfers); (adj.) additional, extra, (Math.) positive, (Electr.) positive, positively electrified; (n.) the symbol (+), additional quantity, positive quantity. [L, = more]

plush, n. Kind of cloth of silk, cotton, &c., with nap longer & softer than that of velvet; (pl.) footman's p. breeches. Hence **plu·sh**Y² a. [f. F *pluche* shortened f. *peluche* f. LL **piluceus* (cf. OSp. *peluza*) f. *pilus* hair]

plu·tarchy (ploo-, -kĭ), n. Plutocracy. [f. Gk *ploutos* wealth + *-arkhia* -rule]

pluto·cracy, n. Rule of the wealthy; ruling class of wealthy persons. So **plu·to**CRAT n., **plutocra·t**IC a. [f. Gk *ploutokratia* (as prec., see -CRACY)]

pluto·latry, n. Worship of wealth. [as prec., see -LATRY]

Plutŏ·nic, a. & n. Of Pluto, infernal; (Geol.) igneous, as *P. rocks, P. theory* (attributing most geological phenomena to action of internal heat, whence **Plu·ton**ISM(3), **Plu·ton**IST(2), nn.); (n.) P. rock. So **Plutō·n**IAN a. [f. Gk *Ploutōn* 'Pluto, god of infernal regions, + -IC]

pluto·nomy, n. Political economy. Hence **plutonŏ·m**IC a., **pluto·nom**IST n. [f. Gk *ploutos* wealth + *-nomia* arrangement]

plu·vial (ploo-), a. & n. Of rain, rainy, so **plu·vi**OUS a.; (Geol.) caused by rain; (n., Eccl.Hist.) long cloak as ceremonial vestment. [(adj.) f. L *pluvialis* (*pluvia* rain, see -AL); (n.) f. med. L *pluviale* rain-cloak]

pluvio·meter, n. Rain-gauge. Hence **pluviome·tr**IC(AL) aa. [f. L *pluvia* rain + -O- + -METER]

ply¹, n. Fold, thickness, layer, of cloth &c.; strand of rope &c.; *two, 2, 3, -p.*, having 2 &c. thicknesses or strands; (fig.) turn, tendency, esp. *take a p.*; *p.-wood*, strong thin board made by gluing layers with the grains crosswise. [f. F *pli* fold f. OF *ploi* f. *ployer* (F *plier*) f. L *plicare* fold]

ply², v.t. & i. Use, wield vigorously, (tool, weapon); work at (one's business, task); supply (person &c.) persistently *with* (*food* &c.); assail vigorously (person *with* questions, arguments); (Naut.) work to windward; (of vessel or its master, coach, &c.) go to & fro *between* (places); (of boatman, porter, cabman) attend regularly for custom (*at* place). [aphetic form of APPLY]

Plȳ·mouth, n. *P. Brethren*, religious body that arose at Plymouth c. 1830, with no formal creed & no official order of ministers, whence **Ply·mouth**ISM(3), **Ply·mouth**IST(2), **Ply·mouth**ITE¹, nn.;

P. Rock, large breed of domestic fowl of Amer. origin.

pneumă·tic (n-), a. & n. Of, acting by means of, wind or air; *p. tire* (inflated with air); *p. dispatch*, conveyance of parcels &c. along tubes by compression or exhaustion of air; *p. trough* (for collecting gases in jars over surface of water or mercury); containing, connected with, air-cavities esp. in bones of birds; spiritual; (n.) p. tire, cycle with such tires; (n. pl.) science of mechanical properties of air or other elastic fluids or gases. Hence **pneuma·tic**ALLY adv., **pneumati·c**ITY n. [f. L f. Gk *pneumatikos* (*pneuma* wind f. *pneō* breathe, see -IC)]

pneumato- in comb. = Gk *pneuma -matos* air, breath, spirit, as: *-cyst*, air-sac in body of bird &c.; *-logy*, theory of spiritual beings, doctrine of the Holy Spirit, psychology, so *-lo·gical* a.; *-meter*, instrument for measuring amount of air breathed at each inspiration; *-phore*, part of some compound hydrozoa containing air-cavity.

pneumoga·stric, a. Of lungs & stomach, esp. *p. nerves*, tenth pair of cerebral nerves. [irreg. f. Gk *pneumōn -monos* lung + GASTRIC]

pneumō·nia (n-), n. Inflammation of the substance of one (*single p.*) or both (*double p.*) lungs. So **pneumŏ·n**IC a. **pneumoni·t**IS n. [f. Gk *pneumonia* (*pneumōn -monos* lung f. *pneō* breathe)]

po. See POT[1].

poach[1], v.t. Cook (egg) by dropping it without shell into boiling water. Hence **poa·ch**ER[1](2) n. [f. OF *pochier* (*poche* POKE[1])]

poach[2], v.t. & i. Thrust (stick, finger, &c. *into* &c.); trample, cut *up* (turf &c.) with hoofs; (of land) become sodden by being trampled; encroach, trespass, (*on* person's *preserves* often fig., lands, &c.), whence **poa·ch**ER[1] n.; trespass on (land, &c.), capture (game, fish) by illicit or unsportsmanlike methods; obtain (advantage, start, in race) by unfair means; (Lawn Tennis) strike (ball, or abs.) in partner's court. [prob. = POKE v.]

pŏ·chard (-tsh-, -k-), n. European diving-bird with bright reddish-brown head & neck. [?]

pock, n. Eruptive spot esp. in small-pox. [OE *poc*, cf. Du. *pok*, G *pocke*; see also POX]

po·cket[1], n. Bag, sack, esp. as measure of hops (168 lb.) or wool (= half sack); small bag inserted in garment for carrying purse &c., as *coat, waistcoat, trouser, watch, ticket, -p.*; (fig.) pecuniary resources, as *he will suffer in his p.*; *empty p.*, person without money; *be prepared to put your hand in your p.* (spend some money); *put* one's *pride in* one's *p.*, submit to doing something that mortifies it; *out-of-p. expenses*, actual outlay incurred; *am 5s. in p.*, have 5s. available; *am 5s.* in *p.*, *out of p., by the transaction* (have gained, lost); *has him in her p.* (completely under control); pouch at each corner & on each side of billiard-table into which balls are driven; cavity in earth filled with gold or other ore, whence **po·cket**Y[2] a.; cavity in rock esp. (Geol.) filled with foreign matter; = AIR[1]*-p.*; (attrib.) of suitable size or shape for carrying in p.; *p.-book*, note-book, book-like case for papers &c. carried in p.; *p. borough* (under control of one person or family); *p.* (small personal) *expenses*; *p. handkerchief* (carried in p.) *p.-money* (for occasional expenses, esp. that allowed to children); *p.-piece*, lucky coin carried in p. as charm; *p.-pistol*, (facet.) p. spirit-flask. Hence **po·cket**FUL n., **po·cket**LESS a. [ME *poket* f. Anglo-Norman *pokete* dim. f. F *poche* POKE[1]]

po·cket[2], v.t. Put into one's pocket; confine as in pocket; hem in (competitor) in race; appropriate, usu. dishonestly; submit to (affront, injury); conceal, suppress, (feelings); (Billiards) drive (ball) into pocket. Hence **po·cket**ABLE a. [f. prec.]

pock-pudding, see POKE[1].

pōcōcura·nte (-koorahntā, -kūrăntĭ), a. & n. Indifferent (person). Hence **pococura·nt(ĕ)**ISM n. [It., = caring little]

pod[1], n. Socket of brace & bit. [?]

pod[2], n., & v.i., & t. Long seed-vessel esp. of leguminous plants; cocoon of silkworm; case of locust's eggs; narrow-necked eel-net; (v.i.) bear pp.; (v.t.) shell (peas &c.) [?]

pod[3], n., & v.t. Small herd of seals or whales; (v.t.) drive (seals) into a p. [?]

pŏ·dagra (*or* podă·g-), n. (med.). Gout, esp. in feet. Hence or cogn. **po·dagr**AL, **poda·gr**IC, **po·dagr**OUS, aa. [L, f. Gk *podagra* (*pous podos* foot + *agra* catching]

po·dded, a. Bearing pods; growing in pod; (fig.) well-off, snug. [-ED[2]]

pŏdĕstà· (-ah), n. Magistrate in Italian municipalities; (Hist.) chief magistrate in medieval Italian towns. [It., f. L *potestatem* power (*potis* able, see -TY)]

podge, n. Short fat person. Hence **po·dg**Y[2] a. [var. of PUDGE]

pō·dium, n. (pl. *-ia*). Continuous projecting base or pedestal; raised platform round arena of amphitheatre; continuous bench round room. [L, f. Gk *podion* (*pous podos* foot)]

pŏdophy·llin, n. (chem.). Yellow bitter resin of cathartic properties got from root of wild mandrake. [f. bot. L *podophyllum*, may-apple, wild mandrake, (Gk *pous podos* foot + *phullon* leaf) + -IN]

pō·ĕ-bird, n. = PARSON-bird. [f. Otaheitan wd for 'ear-rings', from tufts under throat]

pō·em (-ĭm), n. A metrical composition, esp. of elevated character; elevated composition in prose or verse, as *prose p.*;

(fig.) something (other than a composition of words) akin or compared to a p., *as their lives are a p.* [f. F *poème* f. L f. Gk *poēma* = *poiēma* (*poieō* make)]

pō·esy, n. (archaic). Art, composition, of poetry; poems collectively. [f. OF *poesie* f. L f. Gk *poēsis* = *poiēsis* making, poetry, (as prec.)]

pō·et, n. Writer of poems; writer in verse, esp. one possessing high powers of imagination, expression, &c.; *Poets' Corner,* part of Westminster Abbey containing graves & monuments of several poets, (facet.) part of newspaper devoted to poetry. Hence **po·et**ESS[1] n. [f. OF *poete* f. L (*-ta*) f. Gk *poētēs* = *poiētēs* maker, poet, (as prec.)]

pōetă·ster, n. Paltry poet. So **pōĕ·tic**ULE n. [-ASTER]

pōĕ·tic(al), aa. Of, proper to, poets or poetry; (usu. *-ic*) having the good qualities of poetry; (usu. *-ical*) written in verse, as *p. works*; *p.* JUSTICE, LICENCE[1]. Hence **poe·tic**ALLY adv., **poe·tic**S n. [f. F *poétique* f. L f. Gk *po(i)ētikos* (as POET, see -IC & -AL)]

pōĕ·ticize, v.t. Make (theme) poetic. [-IZE]

pō·etize, v.i. & t. Play the poet, compose poetry; treat poetically; celebrate in poetry. [f. F *poétiser* (as POET, see -IZE)]

pō·etry, n. Art, work, of the poet; elevated expression of elevated thought or feeling in metrical form; poems; quality (in any thing) that calls for poetical expression; *prose p.*, prose having all the qualities of poetry except metre. [f. OF *poetrie* f. LL *poetrīa* (as POET)]

po·go, n. Toy like stilt with spring, used to jump on. [?]

pogro·m, n. Organized massacre of a body or class in Russia. [Russ.]

poig·nant (poin-), a. Sharp, pungent, in taste or smell; painfully sharp, as *p. hunger, regret, sarcasm*; pleasantly piquant. Hence **poig·n**ANCY n., **poig·nant**LY[2] adv. [OF, part. of *poindre* prick f. L *pungere*]

poilu (F), n. French soldier (nickname, cf. TOMMY). [F, lit. hairy, unshaven]

poinse·ttia, n. Plant with large scarlet floral leaves & small yellowish flowers. [f. J. R. *Poinsett,* discoverer]

point[1], n. Small dot on a surface; stop or punctuation-mark (chiefly now in *full p.*, full stop); dot, small stroke, used in Semitic languages to indicate vowels or distinguish consonants; dot separating integral from fractional parts in decimals, as *four p. six* (4·6); single item, detail, particular, as *we differ on these pp., it is a p. of conscience,* STRETCH *a p.*; (Mus.) important phrase or subject, (archaic) *p. of war,* short phrase sounded on instrument as signal; *possession is nine pp. of the law* (nine-tenths, almost the whole); *give pp.* (odds) *to* (opponent in game), (fig.) be superior to; unit in appraising qualities of exhibit in show; unit (of varying value) in quoting price of stocks &c.; (Print.) unit of measurement for type bodies, esp. *Didot p.*, 1/72 of French inch; (Geom.) that which has position but not magnitude, e.g. *p. of intersection of two lines*; precise place or spot, as *p. of contact*; (Hunt.) spot to which straight run is made, such run, *p.-to-p. race* (over course defined only by certain landmarks); (Herald.) any of nine particular spots on shield used for determining position; stage, degree, in progress or increase, esp. of temperature, as *boiling, freezing, -p.* (at which thing boils &c.); precise moment for action &c., as *when it came to the p., he declined*; exact moment (*of* death &c.); distinctive trait, characteristic, as *singing is not his strong p.*; *the* essential thing, *the* thing under discussion, as *that is just the p., come to the p.*; *to the p.*, relevant(ly) to the purpose; *make a p. of,* regard, treat, as essential; *carry* one's *p.*, secure one's object; *make a p.*, establish proposition, prove contention; (also *p. lace*) thread lace made wholly with needle, (improp.) pillow lace imitating this; sharp end of tool, weapon, pin, pen, &c. (*not to put too fine a p. upon it,* to speak bluntly); tip (*the p. of the jaw* or *the p.*, in boxing, tip of chin as spot for knock-out blow); tip; promontory, esp. in names, as *Start P.*; (Mil.) small leading party of advanced guard; (pl.) extremities of horse, as *bay with black pp.*; sharp-pointed tool, e.g. etching-needle; tine of deer's horn; (on railway) tapering movable rail by which train is directed from one line to another; tapered division on backgammon board; (Hist.) tagged lace for lacing bodice, attaching hose to doublet, &c.; (Naut.) short piece of cord at lower edge of sail for tying up a reef; *pp. of the compass,* 32 equidistant pp. on compass (N, N by E, NNE, NE by N, NE, NE by E, ENE, E by N, E, E by S, ESE, SE by E, SE, SE by S, SSE, S by E, S, S by W, SSW, SW by S, SW, SW by W, WSW, W by S, W, W by N, WNW, NW by W, NW, NW by N, NNW, N by W), at angular intervals of 11° 15′; salient feature of story, joke, &c., as *don't see the p.*; pungency, effectiveness, as *his remarks lack p.*; (Crick.) (position of) fieldsman placed more or less in line with popping-crease a short distance on off-side of batsman; (of dog) act of pointing, esp. *make, come to, a p.*; *potatoes & p.*, potatoes to eat & bacon &c. to look at; *at all pp.*, in every part; *at the p.* (on the verge) *of death* &c.; *in p.*, apposite, as *the case you take is not in p.*; *in p.* (as a matter) *of fact*; *(up)on the p. of,* on the very verge of (action, doing); *p. of* (thing that vitally affects one's) *honour,* esp. *the p. of honour* (obligation to demand satisfaction, esp. by duel); *p. of view,* position from which thing is viewed, (fig.) way of looking at a matter;

p.-duty (of constable stationed at particular p. to regulate traffic &c.); *poi·ntsman,* man in charge of railway pp., constable on p.-duty. [(partly thr. F *point, pointe,* & f. foll.) f. L *punctum,* neut. p.p. of *pungere* prick]

point[2], v.t. & i. Sharpen (pencil &c.); punctuate (now rare); mark (Psalms &c.) with points for chanting; give point to (words, actions), as *pointing his remarks with apt illustrations, to p. a moral*; fill in joints of (brickwork &c.) with mortar or cement smoothed with trowel; prick *in* (manure), turn *over* (soil), with point of spade; direct attention (*to, at,* lit. & fig.); *p. out,* indicate, show, (thing, fact, *that* &c.); (of hound) indicate presence of (game, or abs.) by standing looking rigidly towards it; direct (finger, weapon, &c., *at*); direct attention of (person *to*); aim *at,* tend *towards.* [f. OF *pointer,* as prec.]

poi·nt-bla·nk, a. & adv. (Of shot) fired horizontally, level; *p. distance* (within which gun may be fired horizontally); (adv.) with direct aim, horizontally, in direct line, (fig.) directly, flatly, as *told him p. it would not do,* offhand, as *refused it p.* [prob. f. prec. + BLANK, i.e. white spot in centre of target]

point-devi·ce, a. & adv. (archaic). Perfectly correct, extremely neat or precise; (adv.) in p. manner. [ME *at point devis* prob. f. OF *à point devis* to the point arranged, or arranged to the proper point (see POINT[1] & DEVICE)]

poi·nted, a. Having, sharpened to, a point; (of remark &c.) having point, penetrating, cutting; emphasized, made evident. Hence **poi·nted**LY[2] adv., **poi·nted**NESS n. [-ED[1,2]]

poi·nter, n. In vbl senses, esp.: index hand of clock, balance, &c.; rod used for pointing to words &c. on blackboard, map, &c.; dog that on scenting game stands rigidly, with muzzle stretched towards it & usu. one foot raised; (pl.) two stars in Great Bear, straight line through which points nearly to pole-star. [-ER[1]]

poi·nting, n. In vbl senses, esp.: punctuation; filling up joints of brickwork &c. with cement, facing thus given to the joints. [-ING[1]]

poi·ntless, a. Without a point, blunt; without point, meaningless; not having scored a point. Hence **poi·ntless**LY[2] adv., **poi·ntless**NESS n. [-LESS]

poise (-z), v.t. & i., & n. Balance; hold suspended or supported; carry (one's head &c. in specified way); be balanced; hover in air &c.; (n.) equilibrium (lit. & fig.), carriage (*of* head &c.); state of indecision, suspense. [(vb) f. OF *peser* (st. *pois-*) f. LL *pesare* f. L *pensare* weigh frequent. of *pendĕre pens-* weigh; (n.) f. OF *pois* f. pop. L *pesum* f. L *pensum* weight]

poi·son (-zn), n., & v.t. Substance that when introduced into or absorbed by a living organism destroys life or injures health, esp. (pop.) one that destroys life by rapid action & when taken in small quantity; *slow p.* (of which repeated doses are injurious); *hate each other like p.* (bitterly); (fig.) baneful principle, doctrine, &c.; *p.* GAS; *p.-tree, -wood,* kinds of tree or plant with poisonous properties. (V.t.) administer p. to (man, animal), kill or injure thus, whence **poi·son**ER[1] n.; produce morbid effects in (blood &c.), whence **(-)poi·son**ING[1] n.; infect (air, water, &c.) with p., smear (weapon) with p. (esp. in p.p.); corrupt, pervert, (person, mind), destroy, spoil, (person's pleasure &c.); render (land, furnace, &c.) foul & unfit for its purpose by noxious application &c. Hence **poi·son**OUS a., **poi·son**OUSLY[2] adv. [(n.) ME & OF *puison* (as POTION, see -SON); (vb) f. OF *poisonner* f. the n.]

poissar·de (pwŏs-), n. Parisian market-woman leading riots during first revolution; French fishwife. [F]

poke[1], n. Bag, sack, (now dial. exc. *buy a* PIG *in a p.*); (Sc.) *p.-pudding* (also *pock-*), corpulent or gluttonous person, Englishman. [ME, cf. F *poche,* Icel. *poki,* & perh. obs. E *pough* (OE *pohha*)]

poke[2], v.t. & i. Thrust, push, (thing *in, up, down,* &c.) with hand, arm, point of stick, &c.; stir (fire) with poker; (colloq.) shut (one*self* &c.) *up* in poky place; produce (hole &c. *in* thing) by poking; make thrusts with stick &c. (*at* &c.); thrust forward, esp. obtrusively, as (fig.) *don't p. your nose into my affairs*; *p. about, p. & pry,* be inquisitive; *p.* one *in the ribs,* nudge him with finger or elbows; *p. fun at,* assail with ridicule; pry (*into*); *p.* one's *head,* carry head thrust forward, stoop. [ME & Du. *poken,* cf. Du. *pook* dagger, & POACH[2]]

poke[3], n. Poking; thrust, nudge; device fastened on cattle &c. to prevent their breaking through fences; projecting brim or front of woman's bonnet or hat; *p.* (*-bonnet*), bonnet with this, esp. as worn by Salvation Army women. [f. prec.]

po·ker[1], n., & v.t. Stiff metal rod with handle, for poking fire; (of person's carriage or manner) *as stiff as a p.*; (Oxf. & Camb.) bedell carrying mace or stave before Vice-Chancellor; kinds of instrument used in p.-work; *red-hot p.,* plant with spikes of scarlet or yellow flowers; (facet. asseveration) *by the holy p.*; *p.-work,* burning of designs on white wood with heated implement; (v.t.) execute (design) in, adorn (thing) with, p.-work. [-ER[1]]

po·ker[2], n. American card-game for two or more persons, each of whom if not bluffed into declaring his hand bets on its value. [?]

po·ky, a. (Of place, room, &c.) confined, mean, shabby; (of occupation &c.) pottering, petty. [f. POKE[2] + -Y[2]]

pola·cre (-ahk*er*), **-ă·cca,** n. Three-masted Mediterranean merchant vessel. [f. F *polacre -aque,* Polish, Pole, hist. unexpl.]

pō·lar, a. & n. Of, near, either pole of the earth or of the celestial sphere; *p.* (white) *bear, hare*; *p. circles* (parallel to equator at distance of 23° 28′ from the poles); *p. distance,* angular distance of point on sphere from nearer pole; having polarity, magnetic; having positive & negative electricity; (of molecules) symmetrically arranged in definite direction; (Geom.) relating to a pole, *p. curve* (related in particular way to given curve & to fixed point called pole); (fig.) analogous to the pole of the earth or to the pole-star; (fig.) directly opposite in character; (n.) p. curve. Hence **po·lar**LY[2] adv. [f. med. L *polaris* (as POLE[2], see -AR[1])]

polari- in comb. = prec., as: *polari·meter, pola·riscope,* instruments for showing polarization of light, so *-me·tric, -sco·pic,* aa., *-metry* n.

polă·rity, n. Tendency of lodestone, magnetized bar, &c., to point with its extremities to the magnetic poles of earth; tendency of a body to place its mathematical axis in particular direction; possession of two poles having contrary qualities (also fig.); electrical condition of body as positive or negative; (fig.) magnetic attraction towards an object. [-ITY]

po·larize, v.t. & i. Modify the vibrations of (light, radiant heat, &c.) so that the ray exhibits different properties on different sides, opposite sides being alike & those at right angles showing maximum difference; (Magn., Electr.) give polarity to (bar, coil); (fig.) give arbitrary direction, special meaning, &c., to (word &c.), (also) give unity of direction to. Hence or cogn. **po·lariz**ABLE a., **polariz**A·TION, **po·lariz**ER[1](2), nn. [(partly thr. F) f. POLAR, see -IZE]

pŏlatou·che (-ōōtsh), n. Small flying squirrel. [F, f. Russ. *poletuchii* flying]

pō·lder, n. Piece of low-lying land reclaimed from sea or river in Netherlands. [Du.]

pole[1], n., & v.t. Long slender rounded tapering piece of wood or (rarely) metal esp. as support for tent, telegraph wires, &c.; wooden shaft fitted to fore-carriage of vehicle & attached to yokes or collars of the horses &c.; *under bare pp.* (naut.), with no sail set; *up the p.* (slang), in a fix; (as measure) rod, perch, 5½ yds; *p.-jumping* (with help of p. held in hands); (v.t.) furnish with pp., push, move, (*off* &c.) with p. [(vb f. n.) OE *pál,* cf. Du. *paal,* G *pfahl,* f. L *palus* stake]

pole[2], n. *North, South, p.,* the two points in the celestial sphere about which the stars appear to revolve, (also) N. & S. extremities of earth's axis; (Geom.) *pp. of a circle of a sphere,* the two points in which axis of that circle cuts surface of sphere, (also) fixed point to which others are referred; each of the two opposite points on surface of magnet at which magnetic forces are manifested; each of two terminal points (*positive, negative, p.*) of electric cell, battery, &c.; (Biol.) extremity of main axis of any spherical or oval organ; (fig.) each of two opposed principles &c.; *p.-star,* a star of Ursa Minor, now about 1¼° distant from N. pole of heavens, (fig.) thing serving as guide, lodestar, centre of attraction. Hence **po·le**WARD a., **po·le**WARD(S) adv. [f. L f. Gk *polos* pivot, axis, sky]

Pole[3], n. Native of Poland. [G, f. Pol. *Poljane* lit. field-dwellers (*pole* field)]

po·le-ax(e), n., & v.t. Battle-axe; axe formerly used in naval warfare as weapon & for cutting ropes &c.; halbert; butcher's axe with hammer at back, (vb) slaughter (beast) with this. [ME *pollax* (POLL[1] + AXE)]

po·lecat, n. Small dark-brown fetid carnivorous quadruped of weasel family, native of Europe. [ME *polcat* (*pol-* etym. dub. + CAT)]

pŏ·lĕmarch (-k), n. (Gk Hist.). Military commander-in-chief with varying civil functions; (in Athens) third archon orig. with military functions. [f. Gk *polemarkhos* (*polemos* war + *-arkhos* -ruler)]

polĕ·mic, a. & n. Controversial, disputatious; (n.) controversial discussion, (pl.) practice of this, esp. in theology, (also) controversialist. Hence **pole·mic**AL a., **pole·mical**LY[2] adv., **pŏ·lem**IZE(2) v.i. [f. Gk *polemikos* (*polemos* war, see -IC)]

pole·nta, n. Italian porridge made of barley, chestnut meal, &c. [It.]

poli·ce (-ēs), n., & v.t. Civil administration, public order; department of government concerned with this; civil force responsible for maintaining public order; (as pl.) members of this, as *the p. are on his track*; *p.-court* (of summary jurisdiction, dealing with charges preferred by the p.); *p.-magistrate* (presiding in p.-court); *poli·ceman,* member of p. force; *p.-office,* headquarters of p. in city or town; *p.-officer,* policeman; *p.-station,* office of local p. force; (v.t.) control (country &c.) by means of p., furnish with p., (fig.) administer, control. [F, f. med. L *politia* = L *politia* POLICY[1]]

policlĭ·nic, n. Clinic in private houses, not in hospital; out-patients' department of hospital. [f. G *poliklinik* (Gk *polis* city, CLINIC)]

pŏ·licy[1], n. Political sagacity; statecraft; prudent conduct, sagacity; craftiness; course of action adopted by government, party, &c.; (Sc.) park round country seat &c.; *Court of P.,* legislative council in British Guiana. [f. OF *policie* f. L f. Gk *politeia* citizenship, polity (*politēs* citizen f. *polis* city); in Sc. sense (earlier =

improvement of estate) confused w. L *politus* polished]

po·licy[2], n. (In full, *p. of assurance, insurance p.*) document containing contract of assurance or insurance. [f. F *police* bill of lading, contract of insurance, prob. f. med. L *apodissa* f. L f. Gk *apodeixis* demonstration, proof, f. APO(*deiknumi* show)]

pŏ·ligar, n. Feudal chief in S. India; predatory follower of such chief; *p.-dog* (variety from the p. country). [ult. f. Tamil *palaiyakkaran* (*palaiyam* feudal estate)]

pŏ·lish[1], v.t. & i. Make, become, smooth & glossy by friction; (fig.) make elegant or cultured, refine, (esp. in p.p.); smarten *up*; *p. off*, finish off quickly. Hence **po·lish**ABLE a., **po·lish**ER[1] (1, 2) n. [f. F *polir* (see -ISH[2]) f. L *polire -it-*]

pŏ·lish[2], n. Smoothness, glossiness, produced by friction; such friction; substance used to produce smooth surface, as FRENCH *p.*, FURNITURE, *brass, -p.*; (fig.) refinement. [f. prec.]

Pō·lish[3], a. Of Poland or the Poles. [-ISH[1]]

pŏ·litarch (-k), n. (hist.). Governor of some Oriental cities, e.g. Thessalonica, under Romans. [f. Gk *politarkhēs* (*politēs* citizen + *-arkhēs* ruler)]

poli·te, a. Of refined manners, courteous; cultivated, cultured; well-bred; (of literature &c.) refined, elegant, as *p. letters.* Hence **poli·te**LY[2] adv., **poli·te**NESS n. [f. L as POLISH[1]]

pŏ·litic, a. & n. (Of person) sagacious, prudent, (of actions &c.) judicious, expedient; scheming, crafty; BODY[1] *p.*; (n. pl.) science & art of government, political affairs or life, political principles, as *what are his pp.?, talk pp., is not practical pp.* (is too remote to be worth discussing). Hence **po·litic**LY[2] adv. [f. F *politique* f. L f. Gk *politikos* (as POLICY[1], see -IC)]

poli·tical, a. & n. Of the State or its government; of public affairs; of politics; (of person) engaged in civil administration, as *p. agent, resident,* (in India) government official advising ruler of native State; having an organized polity; belonging to, taking, a side in politics; *p.* ECONOMY; *p. geography* (dealing with boundaries & possessions of States); *p. verse,* modern Greek verse composed by accent, not quantity, with accent on last syllable but one; (n.) p. agent. Hence **poli·tical**LY[2] adv. [-AL]

politi·cian (-shn), n. One skilled in politics, statesman; one interested or engaged in politics, esp. as profession; (U.S.) one who makes a trade of politics. [f. POLITIC, see -ICIAN]

poli·ticize, v.i. & t. Act the politician; engage in, talk, politics; give political character to. [-IZE]

poli·tico- in comb. = politically, political & —, as *-economical, -geographical, -moral, -social; -religious,* (usu.) pertaining to politics as influenced by religion. [as POLITIC]

pŏ·lity, n. Condition of civil order; form, process, of civil government; organized society, state. [f. obs. F *politie*, as POLICY[1]]

pōlk, v.i. Dance polka. [f. F *polker* as foll.]

pō·lka, n. Lively dance of Bohemian origin in binary time; music for this; woman's tight-fitting jacket, usu. knitted. [F & G, etym. dub.]

pōll[1], n. (Now dial. or facet.) human head; part of this on which hair grows, as *grey, flaxen, p.*; counting of voters esp. at parliamentary or other election; voting at election, as *exclusion of women from the p.*; number of votes recorded, as *heavy, light, p.*; *p.-tax* (levied on every person). [ME & obs. Du. *polle* top of head, cf. Da. *puld*, Sw. dial. *pull*]

pōll[2], v.t. & i. (Archaic) crop the hair of; cut off top of (tree, plant), esp. make a pollard of; cut off horns of (cattle, esp. in p.p.); take the votes of, (pass.) have one's vote taken; (of candidate) receive (so many votes); give (vote); give one's vote. Hence **po·ll**ABLE a. [f. prec.]

pōll[3], a. & n. (Adj. in comb.) hornless, as *p.-beast, -ox*; (n.) p.-beast, esp. one of a breed of hornless oxen. [short for p.p. of prec.]

pōll[4], n. (*P-*) conventional proper name of parrot; *p. parrot*, parrot, user of conventional phrases & arguments. [altered f. *Moll* familiar equivalent of *Mary*]

pōll[5], n. (Camb. Univ. slang). *The P.*, the passmen; *go out in the P.*, take pass degree; (attrib.) *p. degree, man.* [perh. f. POLLOI]

pŏ·llack, -ock, n. Sea-fish allied to cod. [?]

pŏ·llam, n. Feudal estate of poligar. [f. Tamil *palaiyam*]

pŏ·llan, n. Irish fresh-water fish. [cf. Gael. *pollag*, Ir. *pollóg*, perh. f. Ir. *poll* inland lake]

pŏ·llard, n., & v.t. Animal that has cast or lost its horns; ox, sheep, goat, of hornless variety; tree polled so as to produce close rounded head of young branches; bran sifted from flour, (techn.) fine bran containing some flour; (v.t.) make a p. of (tree). [POLL[1] + -ARD]

pŏ·llen, n., & v.t. Fine powdery substance discharged from anther of flower, male element that fertilizes ovules; (v.t.) convey p. to, cover with p. Hence **po·llen**LESS, **polli·**NIC, **pollini·**FEROUS, aa. [L, gen. *-inis*, = fine flour, dust]

pollicita·tion, n. (civil law). Promise not yet formally accepted, & therefore revocable. [f. L *pollicitatio* (*pollicitari* frequent. of *pollicēri* promise, see -ATION)]

po·llinate, v.t. Besprinkle with pollen, shed pollen upon. Hence **pollin**A·TION n. [-ATE[3]]

pŏ·lloi, n. pl. *Hoi p.*, most people, the majority, the rabble. [Gk, lit. the many]

pollu·te, v.t. Destroy the purity or sanctity of; make (water &c.) foul or filthy. So **pollu·**TION n. [f. L *polluere -lut-* (*pol-* =*pro* forth + *luere* wash)]

pō·lō, n. Game of Eastern origin like hockey played on horseback; *p.-stick*, long-handled mallet used; WATER-*p*. [native]

pŏlonai·se (-āz), n. Woman's dress consisting of bodice with skirt open from waist downwards; (music for) slow dance of Polish origin. [F, fem. (as n.) of *polonais* Polish]

polō·nium, n. A highly RADIO-*active* element. [f. med. L *Polonia* Poland, discoverer's country, -IUM]

polō·ny, n. (Also *P. sausage*) sausage of partly cooked pork. [perh. f. med. L *Polonia* Poland, or f. *Bologna*]

pŏ·ltergeist (-gīst), n. Spirit announcing its presence by raps or other sound. [G]

pō·lt-foot, n. & a.(archaic). Club-foot(ed). [*polt* pestle, club, etym. dub., + FOOT]

pŏltroo·n, n. Spiritless coward. So **poltroo·**NERY(4) n. [f. F *poltron* f. It. *poltrone* (*poltro* sluggard, lazy, f. obs. *poltro* bed perh. f. OHG *polstar* bolster, see -OON)]

pŏly- in comb. = Gk *polus* many, as: *-ade·lphous*, with stamens united in 3 or more bundles; *-a·ndrist*, woman with several husbands; *a·ndrous*, of, practising, polyandry, (Bot.) with numerous stamens; *-andry*, plurality of husbands; *-archy*, government by many; *-atŏ·mic*, containing many (esp. replaceable hydrogen) atoms; *-auto·graphy*, lithography; *-bā·sic* (chem.), having more than two bases or atoms of a base; *-car·pellary*, *-car·pous*, having several carpels; *-chaete* (kēt) a. & n., *-chae·tan*, *-chae·tous*, aa., (worm) with many bristles on the foot-stumps; *-chrō·ite*, colouring matter of saffron, exhibiting various colours under various reagents; *-da·ctyl* a. & n., (animal) with more than normal number of fingers or toes; *-dae·monism*, belief in many supernatural powers; *-ga·stric*, with many stomachs; *-ge·nesis*, origination of a race or species from several independent ancestors or germs, so *-genĕ·sic*, *-genĕ·tic*, aa.; *-ge·nic*, (Chem.) forming more than one compound with hydrogen &c., (Geol.) = *-genous*; *-genism*, theory of polygeny; *-genist*, holder of this, so *-geni·stic* a.; *-genous*, (Geol.) composed of various kinds of rock, (Chem.) = *-genic*; *-geny*, origination of mankind from several independent pairs of ancestors; *-gram*, many-lined figure or design; *-graph*, kinds of copying apparatus, (also) writer of many or various works, so *-gra·phic* a., *-graphy* n.; *-gy̆nous*, of, practising, polygyny, (Bot.) with many pistils, styles, or stigmas; *-gyny*, plurality of wives; *-hē·dron*, many (usu. more than six)-sided solid, so *-hē·dral*, *-hē·dric*, aa.; *-mĕ·ric*, (of compounds) composed of same elements in same proportions, but differing in molecular weight; *-merism*, condition of being polymeric or polymerous; *-merize*, render polymeric or polymerous; *-merous* (nat. hist.), composed of many parts; *-mor·phic*, *-mor·phous*, multiform, esp. (Nat. Hist., Biol.) varying in individuals, passing through successive variations, so *-mor·phism* n.; *-nō·mial* a. & n. (alg.), = MULTI*nomial*; *-ŏ·nymous*, called by several different names; *-o·nymy*, use of different names for same thing; *-ō·pia*, affection of the eyes in which one object appears as two or more; *-pe·talous*, having separate petals; *-phagous*, voracious, (Zool.) feeding on various kinds of food; *-phone*, letter, symbol, standing for different sounds; *-phŏ·nic*, *-phonous*, many-voiced, (Philol.) standing for different sounds, (Mus.) contrapuntal; *-phony*, quality of being polyphonic, (Mus.) counterpoint; *-phylĕ·tic*, = *-genetic*; *-phy·llous*, *-sĕ·palous*, having separate perianth-leaves, sepals; *-stome* a. & n., (animal) with many mouths or suckers, so *-stomous* a.; *-synthĕ·tic*, (of languages) combining several words of a sentence (e.g. verb & object) into one; *-thă·lamous* (nat. hist.), many-chambered; *-type*, kind of stereotype, copy of engraving &c. made from this; *-zō·a*, class of compound invertebrates, so *-zō·ic* a.; *-zō·nal*, (of lighthouse lens) composed of several annular segments.

polya·nthus, n. Kinds of cultivated primula. [f. POLY- + Gk *anthos* flower]

polychromă·tic, a. Many-coloured. [POLY-]

po·lychrome, a. & n. Painted, printed, decorated, in many colours; work of art in several colours, esp. coloured statue; varied colouring. Hence **polychrō·**MIC, **po·lychrom**OUS, aa. [F, f. Gk *polukhrōmos* (POLY-, *khrōma* colour)]

po·lychrōmy, n. Art of painting in several colours, esp. as applied to ancient pottery &c. [f. F *polychromie* (as prec., see -Y[1])]

polycli·nic, n. Clinic devoted to various diseases; general hospital. [POLY-; altered in sense & form f. POLICLINIC]

poly̆·gamous, a. Having more than one wife or (less usu.) husband at once, so **polygă·**MIC a., **poly·gam**IST, **poly·gam**Y[1], nn.; (Zool.) having more than one mate; (Bot.) bearing some flowers with stamens only, some with pistils only, some with both, on same or on different plants. [f. late Gk *polugamos* (*polu-* POLY- + *-gamos* marrying)]

po·lyglot, a. & n. Of many languages;

For other words in *poly-* see POLY-.

(person) speaking or writing several languages; (book, esp. Bible) written in several languages. Hence **polyglo·tt**AL, **polyglo·tt**IC, aa., **po·lyglott**ISM n. [f. Gk *poluglōttos* (*polu-* POLY- + *glōtta* tongue)]

po·lygon, n. Figure (usu. plane rectilineal) with many (usu. more than four) angles or sides; *p. of forces*, p. illustrating theorem relating to number of forces acting at a point. Hence **poly·gon**AL a., **poly·gonal**LY[2] adv. [f. L f. Gk *polugōnon* neut. adj. as n. (*polu-* POLY- + *-gōnos* -angled)]

polў·gonum, n. Genus of plants including knotgrass, snakeweed, &c. [f. Gk *polugonon* (*polu-* POLY- + *gonu* knee)]

polyhi·stor, n. Man of varied learning, great scholar. [f. Gk *poluistōr* (*polu-* POLY- + *histōr*, see HISTORY)]

po·lymath, n. = prec. So **poly·mathy**[1] n. [f. Gk *polumathēs* (*polu-* POLY- + *math-* st. of *manthanō* learn)]

Polynē·sia, n. Small islands in Pacific Ocean east of Australia. Hence **Polyne·si**AN a. [f. POLY- + Gk *nēsos* island]

polў·nia, n. Space of open water in midst of ice, esp. in arctic seas. [f. Russ. *poluinya* (*pole* field)]

pŏ·lўp(e), n. Kinds of animal of low organization, e.g. hydra; individual of some compound organisms. [F (*-pe*), as POLYPUS]

po·lypary, n. Common stem or supporting structure of a colony of polyps. [*-ary* = -ARIUM]

polў·pidom (*or* pŏl-), n. = prec. [f. POLYPUS + L *domus* house]

po·lypite, n. Individual polyp. [-ITE[1]]

po·lypod, a. & n. (Animal) with many feet. [f. F *polypode* f. Gk as POLYPUS]

po·lypŏdy, n. Genus of ferns, esp. (*common p.*) species growing on moist rocks, walls, &c. [f. L f. Gk *polupodion*, as POLYPUS]

po·lypoid, a. Of, like, a polyp or a polypus. So **po·lyp**OUS a. [-OID]

po·lypus, n. (pl. *-pī*). Kinds of tumour, usu. with ramifications like tentacles. [L, f. Gk *polupous* cuttle-fish, polypus in nose (*polu-* POLY- + *-pous -podos* footed)]

polysyllă·bic, a. (Of word) having many syllables; marked by polysyllables. Hence **polysylla·bi**CALLY adv. [f. med. L f. Gk *polusullabos* (as foll.) + -IC]

polysy·llable, n. Polysyllabic word. [f. med. L *polysyllaba* (*vox* word), see POLY- & SYLLABLE]

polyte·chnic, a. & n. Dealing with, devoted to, various arts, as *p. school*; *P.* (*Institution*), technical school, esp. one in London orig. opened 1838. [f. F *polytechnique* f. Gk *polutekhnos* (*polu-* POLY- + *tekhnē* art), see -IC]

po·lythēism, n. Belief in, worship of, many gods or more than one god. So **po·lythe**IST n., **polythei·st**IC a. [f. F *polythéisme* f. Gk *polutheos* of many gods (*polu-* POLY- + *theos* god), see -ISM]

pom, abbr. for *Pomeranian dog.*

pomace (pŭ·mĭs), n. Mass of crushed apples in cider-making before or after juice is pressed out; any pulp; refuse of fish &c. after oil has been extracted, used as fertilizer. [ult. f. L *pomum* apple]

pomā·de (*or* -ahd), n., & v.t. Scented ointment (perh. orig. from apples) for hair & skin of head; (v.t.) anoint with p. [f. F *pommade* (*pomme* apple, POME, + -ADE)]

pŏ·mander (*or* pomă·n-), n. (hist.). Ball of mixed aromatic substances carried in box, bag, &c., as preservative against infection; ball of gold, silver, &c., in which p. was carried. [earlier *pomamber* f. OF *pomme d'ambre* (*pomme* apple, see prec., + *ambre* AMBER)]

pomard·, pomm-, n. A red Burgundy wine. [*P.*, village in France]

pomā·tum, n., & v.t. = POMADE. [f. L *pomum* apple + *-atum* -ATE[1]]

***pŏ·mbĕ*,** n. Intoxicating drink from various kinds of grain & fruit in Africa. [native]

pome, n. (Bot.) succulent INFERIOR fruit with firm fleshy body enclosing carpels forming the core, e.g., apple, pear, quince, so **pomi·**FEROUS a.; (poet.) apple; metal ball. [OF, f. L *poma* pl. of *pomum* fruit, apple]

pomegranate (pŏmgră·nat, pŏ·m-, pŭm-). Fruit of a tree native to N. Africa & W. Asia, a large red berry about size of orange with tough golden or orange rind & acid reddish pulp enveloping seeds; the tree. [f. OF POME *grenate* f. L *granata* seeded (GRAIN, -ATE[2])]

Pŏmerā·nian, a. & n. Of Pomerania on S. coast of Baltic; *P.* (*dog*), small dog with long silky hair, pointed muzzle, & pricked ears. [-AN]

pŏ·mfret, n. Fish found in Indian & Pacific Oceans, used as food. [prob. ult. f. Port. *pampo*]

po·mfret-cake (pŭ-), n. Liquorice cake made at Pontefract (earlier Pomfret) in Yorks.

pō·miculture, n. Fruit-growing. [f. L *pomum* fruit + CULTURE]

po·mmel (pŭ-), n., & v.t. (-ll-). Rounded knob esp. at end of sword-hilt; upward projecting front part of saddle; (v.t.) strike or beat (as) with p., beat with fists. [(vb f. n.) f. OF *pomel* f. LL **pomellum* dim. as POME]

pomo·logy, n. Science of fruit-growing. Hence **pomolo·gi**CAL a., **pomo·log**IST n. [as POME + -LOGY]

Pomō·na, n. (Rom. Myth.) goddess of fruits; *P. green* (in which yellow predominates). [L]

pomp, n. Splendid display, splendour; (pl.) *the pp. & vanity of this wicked world.* [f. F *pompe* f. L f. Gk *pompē* procession, pomp, (*pempō* send)]

po·mpano, n. Kinds of W.-Ind. & N.-

Amer. fish esteemed for food. [f. Sp. *pampano*]

po·mpier, a. *P. ladder,* fireman's scaling ladder. [F, = fireman (as PUMP, see -IER)]

po·m-pom, n. Long-range Maxim automatic quick-firing gun. [imit.]

po·mpon (or as F), n. Ornamental tuft or bunch of ribbon, flowers, &c., on women's & children's hats & shoes; round tuft on soldier's cap, front of shako, &c. [F, etym. dub.]

po·mpous, a. Magnificent, splendid; self-important, consequential, (of language) inflated, so **pompo·SITY** n. Hence **po·mpousLY**² adv., **po·mpousNESS** n. [f. LL *pomposus* (as POMP, see -OUS)]

ponceau (F), n. Poppy colour, bright red.

po·ncho (-tshō), n. S.-Amer. cloak, oblong piece of cloth with slit in middle for head; cape for bicycling &c. on same plan. [native]

pond, n., & v.t. & i. Small body of still water artificially formed by hollowing or embanking; (facet.) the sea; cf. HERRING-*p.*; *p.-life,* animals esp. invertebrates that live in pp.; *po·ndweed,* kinds of aquatic herb growing in still water; (v.t.) hold *back,* dam *up,* (stream); (v.i., of water) form a pool or p. [prob. var. of POUND²]

po·ndage (-ĭj), n. Capacity of pond; storage of water. [-AGE]

po·nder, v.t. & i. Weigh mentally, think over, (matter, *how,* &c.); think *on,* muse *over.* Hence **po·nderingLY**² adv. [f. OF *ponderer* f. L *ponderare* (*pondus -eris* weight)]

po·nderable, a. Having appreciable weight (lit. & fig.). Hence **ponderaBI·LITY** n. [f. LL *ponderabilis* (as prec., see -BLE)]

pondera·tion, n. Weighing, balancing, (lit. & fig.). [f. L *ponderatio* (as prec., see -ATION)]

po·nderous, a. Heavy; unwieldy; laborious; (of style) dull, tedious. Hence or cogn. **pondero·SITY, po·nderousNESS,** nn., **po·nderousLY**² adv. [f. F *pondéreux* f. L *ponderosus* (*pondus -eris* weight, see -OUS)]

pō·nĕ¹, n. Leader('s partner) in some card games. [L, 2nd sing. imperat. of *ponere* place]

pōne², n. Maize bread, esp. as made by N.-Amer. Indians; fine light bread made with milk, eggs, &c.; cake, loaf, of this. [native]

pongee (pŭnjē·), n. Soft unbleached kind of Chinese silk. [perh. f. Chin. *pun-chi* own loom]

po·ngo, n. (Early name for) a large anthropoid African ape; (improp.) orang-outang. [native]

pŏ·niard, n., & v.t. Dagger; (v.t.) stab with p. [f. F *poignard* (*poing* fist f. L *pugnus,* -ARD)]

pons, n. *P. asinorum,* bridge of asses, i.e. 5th proposition of 1st book of Euclid, hence, anything found difficult by beginners; *P.* (*Varolii*), band of nerve-fibres in brain [f. *Varoli,* Italian anatomist]. [L, = bridge]

po·ntifex, n. (pl. *-fĭcēs*). (Rom. Ant.) member of principal college of priests in Rome, *P. maximus,* head of this; = foll. [L, f. *pons -ntis* bridge or Osc.-Umbr. *puntis* sacrifice + *-fex -ficis* f. *facere* make]

po·ntiff, n. (Also *sovereign p.*) the Pope; bishop; chief priest. [f. F *pontife* f. prec.]

ponti·fical, a. & n. Of, befitting, a pontiff; (n.) office-book of Western Church containing forms for rites to be performed by bishops; (n. pl.) vestments & insignia of bishop. Hence **ponti·ficalLY**² adv. [f. L *pontificalis* (as PONTIFEX, see -AL)]

pontificā·lia, n. pl. Pontificals. [L, neut. pl. as prec.]

pontificate (-*a*t), n. Office of pontifex, bishop, or pope; period of this. [f. L *pontificatus* (as PONTIFEX, see -ATE¹)]

po·ntify, v.i. Play the pontiff, assume airs of infallibility. [f. F *pontifier* f. L *pontificare* (as PONTIFEX), see -FY]

pŏnt-lĕ·vis (or as F), n. Drawbridge.

pontoneer·, -ier, n. One who has charge of pontoons or of construction of a pontoon-bridge. [f. F *pontonnier* f. med. L *pontonarius* (as foll., see -EER)]

pontoo·n, n., & v.t. Flat-bottomed boat used as ferry-boat &c.; one of several boats, hollow metal cylinders, &c. used to support temporary bridge; = CAISSON (last two senses); (v.t.) cross (river) by means of pp. [f. F *ponton* f. L *ponto -onis* (*pons -ntis* bridge, see -OON)]

pō·ny, n. Horse of any small breed, esp. not more than 13 or (pop.) 14 hands; (slang) £25. [f. Sc. *powney* prob. f. OF *poulenet* little foal dim. of *poulain* f. LL *pullanus* (*pullus* foal)]

pōōd, n. Russian weight, 36 lb. avoirdupois. [f. Russ. *pudu* f. Norse *pund* POUND]

pōō·dle, n., & v.t. Kinds of pet dog with long curling hair often clipped & shaved fantastically; clip & shave (dog) thus. [f. G *pudel*(*hund*) f. *pudeln* splash in water, cf. *pudel* PUDDLE]

pooh (pōō, pōōh), int. expr. impatience or contempt. [imit. f. sound of blowing a thing away]

Pooh-Bah·. n. Holder of many offices at once. [person in W. S. Gilbert's *The Mikado*]

pooh-pooh·, v.t. Express contempt for, make light of, as *he pooh-poohed the idea.* [f. prec.]

pōō·ka, ph- (ph-), n. Hobgoblin. [Ir. *púca*]

pōō·koo, puku (pōō·kōō), n. Red antelope of S. Central Africa. [f. Zulu *mpuku*]

pōōl¹, n., & v.t. Small body of still water, usu. of natural formation; puddle of any liquid; deep still place in river; (v.t.) make (hole) for insertion of wedge in quarrying, undermine (coal). [(vb f. n.) OE *pól*, cf. Du. *poel*]

pool[2], n., & v.t. (Cards) collective amount of players' stake & fines; receptacle for these; game on billiard-table in which each player has ball of different colour with which he tries to pocket the others in fixed order, winner taking the whole stakes; collective stakes in betting &c.; arrangement between competing parties by which prices are fixed & business divided to do away with competition; common fund, e.g. of the profits of separate firms; (v.t.) throw into common fund, (of competing railway companies &c.) share (traffic, profits). [(vb f. n.) prob. f. F *poule* hen (perh. in sense 'booty'), in E early assoc. with prec.]

pōōn, n. E.-Indian tree; *p.-oil*, oil from seeds of this, used in medicine & for lamps. [f. Cingalese *puna*]

pōō·nah, a. *P. painting* (on rice or other thin paper in imitation of oriental work); *p. brush, paper* (used for this). [*P.*, Indian city]

pōōp[1], n., & v.t. Stern of ship; aftermost & highest deck; (v.t., of wave) break over stern of (ship), (of ship) receive (wave) over stern. Hence **(-)poo·p**ED[2] **a.** [f. OF *pupe* f. LL *puppa* f. L *puppis*]

poop[2]. See POPE[3].

poop[3], n. (slang). Foolish insignificant person. [abbr. NINCOMPOOP]

poor, a. Wanting means to procure comforts or necessaries of life, needy, indigent; ill supplied, deficient, (*in* a possession or quality); (of soil) unproductive; scanty, inadequate, less than is expected, as *the crop was p.*, *a p. three weeks' holiday*; paltry, sorry, as *that is a p. consolation*; spiritless, despicable, as *he is a p. creature*; humble, insignificant, (often iron. or facet. as *in my p. opinion*); (expr. pity or sympathy) unfortunate, hapless, as *p. fellow!*, *the p. child is inconsolable*; *the p.*, (esp.) those dependent on charitable or parochial relief; *p.-box*, money-box esp. in church for relief of the p.; *p.-house*, workhouse; *p.-law* (relating to support of paupers); *p. man's weather-glass*, pimpernel; *p.-rate*, rate, assessment, for relief or support of the p.; *p.-spirited*, timid, cowardly. [ME & OF *pov(e)re, poure*, f. L *pauper*]

poor·ly, adv. & pred. a. Scantily, defectively; with no great success; meanly, contemptibly; (pred. a.) unwell, as *he is (looking) very p.* [prec. + -LY[2]; pred. a. prob. orig. adv.]

poor·ness, n. Defectiveness; lack of some good quality or constituent. [POOR + -NESS]

pop[1], v.i. & t. Make small quick explosive sound as of cork when drawn; let off (fire-arm &c.); fire gun (*at* bird &c.); put (thing *in, out, down,* &c.) quickly or suddenly; move, go, come, (*in* &c.) thus; put (question) abruptly, esp. (colloq.) *p. the question*, propose marriage; (slang) pawn; (slang) *p. off (the hooks)*, die; (U.S.) parch (maize) till it bursts open, *p.-corn*, maize so parched; *p.-gun*, child's toy gun shooting pellets by compression of air with piston, (contempt.) inefficient fire-arm; *p.-shop*, pawnbroker's shop. [imit.]

pop[2], n., adv., & int. Abrupt explosive sound; dot, spot, esp. in marking sheep &c.; (colloq.) effervescing drink, esp. ginger-beer or champagne; (slang) pawning, esp. *in p.*, in pawn; (int. or adv.) *heard it go* (make the sound) *p.!*, *p. goes the weasel*, country dance in which dancer darted under arms of others to his partner. [as prec.]

pop[3], n. (colloq.). Popular concert, as *Saturday pp.* [abbr.]

Pop[4], n. Social & debating club at Eton. [f. L *popina* cookshop (orig. meeting-place)]

pop[5]. See POPPA.

pope[1], n. Bishop of Rome as head of Roman Catholic Church; (fig.) person assuming or credited with infallibility &c.; *P. Joan*, fabulous female p., a card-game; *p.'s eye*, lymphatic gland surrounded with fat in middle of leg of mutton; *p.'s head*, round long-handled broom; *p.'s nose*, = PARSON'*s nose*. Hence **po·pe**DOM n., **po·pe**LESS a. [OE *pápa* f. eccl. L *papa* f. late Gk *papas* = Gk *pappas* father, cf. PAPA]

pope[2], n. Parish priest of Greek Church in Russia &c. [f. Russ. *popu* f. Gk as prec.]

pope[3], **pōōp**, n., & v.t. Place in thigh on which blow is painful or paralysing, esp. *take* person's *p.*, strike this; (v.t.) take the p. of. [?]

pō·pery, n. Papal system, Roman Catholic religion, (in hostile use). [f. POPE[1] + -ERY]

pŏ·pinjay, n. (Archaic) parrot; (Hist.) figure of parrot on pole as mark to shoot at; conceited person; (dial.) green woodpecker. [f. OF *papingay* &c., cf. med. Gk *papagas*, Arab. *babagha*, prob. imit. & of Afr. orig.]

pō·pish, a. Of popery, papistical. Hence **po·pish**LY[2] adv. [f. POPE[1] + -ISH[1]]

po·plar, n. Genus of large trees of rapid growth (often w. allusion to straightness of trunk); *trembling p.*, aspen. [f. OF *poplier* f. L *pōpulus* + -IER]

po·plin, n. Woven fabric of silk warp & worsted weft with corded surface, now made chiefly in Ireland. [f. F *popeline* f. It. *papalina* PAPAL, from the papal town Avignon where it was made]

poplĭ·tĕal, a. Of the ham, of the hollow at back of knee, as *p. artery, p. tendons* (hamstrings). [f. L *poples -itis* ham, see -AL]

po·p(pa), n. (U.S.). Papa. [f. *papa*]

po·ppet, n. (Now dial.) small person, esp. as term of endearment; lathe-head; (Naut.) short piece of wood for various purposes; *p.-head*, lathe-head, (Mining) frame at top of shaft supporting pulleys for ropes used in hoisting. [earlier form of PUPPET]

po·pping, n. In vbl senses; (Crick.) *p.-crease* [perh. = striking-crease], line 4 feet in front of & parallel to wicket within which batsman must stand. [-ING[1]]

po·pple, v.i., & n. (Of water) tumble about, toss to & fro; (n.) rolling, tossing, ripple. Hence **po·ppl**Y[2] a. [prob. imit.]

po·ppy, n. Genus of herbs having milky juice with narcotic properties & showy flowers of scarlet or other colour; *opium p.*, species from which opium is obtained; *Flanders pp.* (sacred to dead of great war; also as name of those made for & sold on *Poppy Day*, 11 Nov.); *p.-head*, seed capsule of p., (Arch.) ornamental top to end of church seat. Hence **po·ppi**ED[2] a. [OE *popæg, papoeg*, ult. f. L *papaver*]

po·psy(-wopsy), n. An endearing appellation for a girl. [prob. f. *pop* abbr. of POPPET, with dim. suf.]

pŏ·pulace (-*as*), n. The common people; the rabble. [F, f. It. *popolaccio* (*popolo* PEOPLE + -*accio* pejorative suf. as -ACEOUS)]

pŏ·pular, a. Of, carried on by, the people, as *p. election, meetings, tumult*; adapted to the understanding, taste, or means, of the people, as *in p. language, p. science, at p.* (low) *prices*; liked, admired, by the people or by people generally or *with* specified class, as *p. teachers, the p. hero, is p. with his men*, so **populă·**RITY n.; prevalent among the people, as *p. fallacies.* Hence **po·pular**LY[2] adv. [f. L *popularis* (as PEOPLE, see -AR[1])]

po·pularize, v.t. Make popular, cause (person, principle, &c.) to be generally known or liked; extend (suffrage &c.) to the common people; present (technical subject &c.) in popular form. Hence **populariz**A·TION n. [-IZE]

pŏ·pulate, v.t. Inhabit, form the population of, (country, town, &c.); supply with inhabitants, as *a densely populated district.* [f. LL *populare* (as PEOPLE)]

popula·tion, n. Degree in which place is populated; total number of inhabitants, the people of a country &c. (*an A1*, a *C3, p.*, of highest, lowest efficiency, w. ref. to military classification of men in categories ranging from A1 to C3); *the* inhabitants of a place (*the p. turned out to welcome him*). [f. LL *populatio* (as prec., see -ATION)]

pŏ·pulist, n. Adherent of U.S. political party aiming at public control of railways, graduated income-tax, &c., formed 1892; adherent of Russian political party advocating collectivism. So **po·pul**ISM n., **populi·st**IC a. [f. L *populus* PEOPLE + -IST]

po·pulous, a. Thickly inhabited. Hence **po·pulous**NESS n. [f. L *populosus* (as PEOPLE, see -OUS)]

por·beagle, n. Mackerel-shark. [Cornish dial., etym. dub.]

por·celain (-slĭn, -sĭlăn), n. Fine kind of earthenware with translucent body & transparent glaze; thing made of this; (fig., attrib.) delicate, fragile; *p.-shell*, cowrie; *p. clay*, kaolin. Hence or cogn. **por·celain**OUS (-slĭn-), **porcĕllā·n**EOUS, **porcĕllă·n**IC, **porcĕ·llan**OUS, aa. [f. F *porcelaine* Venus shell, porcelain, f. It. *porcellana* (*porcella* dim. of *porco* hog f. L *porcus*, from resemblance of the shell to hog's back)]

por·celainize, v.t. Convert (clay, shale, &c.) into porcelain or similar substance. [-IZE]

porch, n. Covered approach to entrance of building; *the P.*, colonnade at Athens to which Zeno & his disciples resorted, (hence) Stoic school or philosophy (cf. ACADEMY, GARDEN, LYCEUM). Hence **porch**ED[2], **por·ch**LESS, aa. [f. L *porche* f. L *porticus*]

por·cīne, a. Of or like swine. [F (-*in*, -*ine*), f. L *porcinus* (*porcus* hog, see -INE[1])]

por·cūpine, n. Rodent quadruped with body & tail covered with erectile spines; kinds of machine with many spikes or teeth, e.g. for heckling flax &c.; (attrib., applied to animals with spines &c.) *p. ant-eater, crab, fish, grass.* Hence **por·cupīn**ISH[1], **por·cupīn**Y[2], aa. [f. OF *porc espin* ult. f. L *porcus* hog + *spina* thorn; earlier also *porkenpick* f. F *porc-épic* (L *spicus* = *spica* spike) & *porpentine*]

pore[1], n. Minute opening (esp. in skin of animal body) through which fluids may pass. [F, f. L f. Gk *poros* passage, pore]

pore[2], v.i. & t. *P. over*, be absorbed in studying (book &c.), (fig.) meditate, think intently upon, (subject); (archaic) look intently *at, on, over*; *p.* one's *eyes out*, tire them by close reading. [ME *puren*, etym. dub.]

porge, v.t. (Jew. ritual). Make (slaughtered beast) ceremonially clean by removing sinews &c. Hence **por·g**ER[1] n. [prob. f. L as PURGE]

por·ism (*or* pŏ·r-), n. (math.). Proposition concerned with the conditions that will render a given problem capable of innumerable solutions; corollary. So **porismă·t**IC, **pori·st**IC, aa. [f. L f. Gk *porisma -matos* (*porizō* deduce f. *poros* way, see -M)]

pork, n. Flesh (esp. fresh) of swine used as food; *p.-butcher*, one who slaughters pigs for sale; *p. pie* (of minced &c. p.); *p.-pie hat* (with flat crown & brim turned up all round). [f. F *porc* f. L *porcus* hog]

por·ker, n. Pig raised for food; young fattened hog, so **por·k**ET[1] n. [prec. + -ER[1]]

por·kling, n. Young or small pig. [-LING[1]]

por·ky, a. Of, like, pork, esp. (colloq.) fleshy, fat. [-Y[2]]

porno- in comb. = Gk *pornē* harlot, as: -*cracy*, dominant influence of harlots, esp. in government of Rome in 10th c.;

-graphy, description of manners &c. of harlots, treatment of obscene subjects in literature, such literature, so *-grapher* n., *-gra·phic* a.

por·oplă·stic (*or* pŏ·r-), a. (surg.). (Of felt) both porous & plastic. [as PORE + PLASTIC]

por·ous, a. Full of pores (lit. & fig.). Hence or cogn. **porŏ·**SITY, **por·ous**NESS, nn. [-OUS]

por·phyry, n. Hard rock anciently quarried in Egypt, composed of crystals of white or red feldspar in red ground-mass; (Geol.) unstratified or igneous rock having homogeneous base in which crystals of one or more minerals are disseminated. [ult. f. Gk *porphuros* purple]

por·poise (*-us*), n. Cetaceous mammal five feet long with blunt rounded snout. [f. OF *porpeis* f. L *porcus* hog + *piscis* fish]

porra·ceous (-sh*us*), a. Leek-green. [f. L *porraceus* (*porrum* leek, see -ACEOUS)]

porre·ct, v.t. (Nat. Hist.) stretch out (part of body); (Eccl. Law) tender, submit, (document). [f. L *porrigere -rect-* (*por-* PRO- + *regere* direct)]

pŏ·rridge, n. Soft food made by stirring oatmeal or other meal or cereal in boiling water or milk; *keep* one's *breath to cool* one's *p.*, keep one's advice &c. for one's own use. [altered f. POTTAGE]

pŏrrī·go, n. (path.). Scaly eruption of scalp. So **porri·gin**OUS a. [L, gen. *-ginis*]

pŏ·rringer, n. Small basin from which soup &c. is eaten esp. by children. [earlier *potager* (as PORRIDGE, see -ER[1]); for *-n-* cf. *passenger, messenger*]

port[1], n. Harbour (lit. & fig.); town, place, possessing harbour, esp. one where customs officers are stationed; (in proper names) *P. Arthur, Said,* &c.; *P. of London Authority*, corporate body set up by P.-of-London Act 1908 for control of p. & docks; *free p.*, one open for merchants of all nations to load & unload in, (also) exemption for imports or exports; *close p.* (lying up river); CINQUE PORTS; *p. admiral* (in command of naval p.). [OE, f. L *portus*]

port[2], n. Gate, gateway, esp. of walled town (chiefly Sc.); (Naut.) opening in side of ship for entrance, loading, &c., (also) = *p.-hole*; (Mech.) aperture for passage of steam, water, &c.; curved mouthpiece of some bridle-bits; *p.-hole*, aperture in ship's side for admission of light & air, or (formerly) for pointing cannon through. [f. F *porte* f. L *porta* gate]

port[3], n. External deportment, carriage, bearing. [F, as foll.]

port[4], v.t. (mil.). Carry (rifle, sword) diagonally across & close to the body, with barrel or blade opposite middle of left shoulder, esp. *p. arms!*. [f. F *porter* f. L *portare* carry]

port[5], n., & v.t. & i., (naut.). (Also *larboard*) left-hand side of ship looking forward (cf. STARBOARD), as *put the helm to p.* or *a-p.*; (attrib.) *on your p.* (left) *bow* &c.; (v.t.) turn (helm or abs.) to left side of ship; (v.i., of ship) turn to her p. side. [etym. dub.; perh. f. PORT[1]; vb earlier than n.]

port[6], n. Strong sweet dark-red wine of Portugal. [shortened f. *Oporto*, city of Portugal]

por·table, a. Movable, convenient for carrying, as *p. furnace, railway*. Hence **porta**BI·LITY n. [F, f. L *portabilis* (*portare* carry, -BLE)]

por·tage (-ĭj), n., & v.t. Carrying, carriage; cost of this; *mariner's p.*, space allowed to mariner for own venture or to be let by him for freight in lieu of wages; carrying of boats or goods between two navigable waters, place at which this is necessary, (v.t.) convey (boat, goods) over a p. [F, as PORT[4], see -AGE]

por·tal[1], n. Door(way), gate(way), esp. elaborate one. [obs. F, f. med. L *portale* neut. adj. as n. (*porta* gate, see -AL)]

por·tal[2], a. (anat.). Of the *porta* or transverse fissure of the liver, as *p. vein* (conveying blood to liver). [f. med. L *portalis* as prec.]

portame·nto, n. (mus.). Gliding continuously from one pitch to another. [It.]

por·tative, a. Serving to carry or support. [F (*-if, -ive*), f. L *portare* carry, see -IVE]

portcu·llis, n. Strong heavy grating sliding up & down in vertical grooves at sides of gateway in fortress &c. Hence **portcu·llis**ED[2] a. [f. OF *porte coleïce* sliding door (*porte* door f. L *porta*, see COULISSE)]

Porte, n. *The* (*Sublime* or *Ottoman*) *P.* (hist.), Ottoman court at Constantinople, Turkish government to 1923. [F (*la Sublime P.*), transl. of Turk. title of central office of Ottoman government]

porte- in comb. = F *porte-* imperat. of *porter* carry in wds meaning '-case', '-holder', as: *port(e)-crayon*, metal tube or other holder for crayon; *portefeuille*, portfolio; *porte-monnaie*, flat leathern purse or pocket-book.

porte-cochère (F), n. Gateway & passage for vehicles through house into courtyard.

porte·nd, v.t. Foreshow, foreshadow, as an omen; give warning of, as *this portends a renewal of the conflict*. [f. L *portendere -tent-* (*por-* PRO- + *tendere* stretch)]

por·tent, n. Omen, significant sign; prodigy, marvellous thing. So **porte·nt**OUS a., **porte·ntous**LY[2] adv. [f. L *portentum* as prec.]

por·ter[1], n. Gate-keeper, door-keeper. [ME & AF, f. LL *portarius* (*porta* door, see -ER[2])]

por·ter[2], n. Person employed to carry burdens, esp. servant of railway company who handles luggage, whence **por·ter**AGE (4) n.; dark brown bitter beer brewed from charred or browned malt [perh. orig. made esp. for porters]; (U.S.) *p.-house,* house at which p. &c. were retailed, (also) one where steaks, chops, &c., were served (*p.-house steak,* choice cut of beef from region of undercut); *p.'s knot,* pad resting on shoulders & secured to forehead used by pp. in carrying loads. [f. OF *porteour* f. L *portatorem* (*portare* carry, see -OR[2])]

por·tfire, n. Device for firing rockets, igniting explosives in mining, &c. [f. PORTE- + FIRE]

portfō·lio, n. Case for keeping loose sheets of paper, drawings, &c.; (fig.) office of minister of state. [f. It. *portafogli* (*porta* imperat. of *portare* carry + *foglio* leaf f. L *folium*)]

por·tico, n. Colonnade, roof supported by columns at regular intervals, usu. attached as porch to a building. [It., f. L *porticus* (*porta* door)]

portière (portyār·), n. Curtain hung over door(way). [F, f. med. L *portaria* fem. adj. as n. (*porta* door, see -ARY[1])]

por·tion, n., & v.t. Part, share; dowry, whence **por·tion**LESS a.; one's destiny, one's lot; *a p.,* some (*of* anything); (v.t.) divide (thing) into shares, distribute *out,* assign (thing *to* person) as share, give dowry to. [(vb f. F *porcionner*) f. OF *porcion* f. L *portionem* (nom. *-io*) cogn. w. *pars* PART]

Por·tland, n. (Used for) P. prison.

por·tly, a. Bulky, corpulent; of stately appearance. Hence **por·tli**NESS n. [PORT[3], -LY[1]]

portma·nteau (-tō), n. (pl. *-s, -x,* pr. -z). Leather trunk for clothes &c. opening into two equal parts; (fig.) factitious word blending the sounds & combining the meanings of two others (e.g. *slithy* = lithe & slimy). [f. F PORTE-(*manteau* MANTLE)]

portola·no (-lah-), n. (hist.). Book of sailing directions with description of harbours &c. [f. It. (*porto* PORT[1])]

por·trait (-ĭt), n. Likeness of person or animal made by drawing, painting, photography, &c.; (fig.) type, similitude; verbal picture, graphic description. [F, p.p. as PORTRAY]

por·traitist, n. One who paints or takes portraits. [-IST]

por·traiture, n. Portraying; portrait; graphic description. [OF (PORTRAIT + -URE)]

portray·, v.t. Make likeness of; describe graphically. Hence **portray·**AL(2) n. [f. OF *pourtraire* f. L PRO(*trahere tract-* draw)]

por·treeve, n. (Hist.) chief officer of town or borough; (now) officer inferior to mayor in some towns. [OE *port-geréfa* (*port* town, = PORT[1] or [2] + REEVE]

por·tress, n. Female PORTER[1]. [-ESS[1]]

Portūgue·se (-gēz), a. & n. (Native, language) of Portugal. [f. Port. *portuguez* f. med. L *portugalensis* (see -ESE)]

pose[1] (-z), v.t. & i., & n. Lay down (assertion, claim, &c.); propound (question); place (artist's model &c.) in certain attitude; assume an attitude, esp. for artistic purposes; set up, give oneself out, *as* (connoisseur &c.); (Dominoes) place first domino on table; (n.) attitude of body or mind, esp. one assumed for effect, as *his philanthropy is a mere p.,* (Dominoes) posing, right to p. [(n. f. F *pose*) f. F *poser* f. L *pausare* PAUSE; some senses by confus. w. L *ponere* place, cf. COMPOSE]

pose[2] (-z), v.t. Puzzle (person) with question or problem. [short for OPPOSE]

po·ser, n. In vbl senses of prec., esp. puzzling question or problem. [-ER[1]]

poseur· (-zer), n. Affected person. [F]

posh, a. (slang). Smart, tiptop. [?]

pŏ·sit (-z-), v.t. Assume as fact, postulate; put in position, place, as *posited by natural agency.* [f. L *ponere posit-* place]

posi·tion (-zĭshn), n., & v.t. Proposition, laying down of this; bodily posture; *eastward p.* (of priest at eucharist standing in front of altar & facing east); mental attitude, way of looking at question; place occupied by a thing; *in, out of, p.* (proper place); (Mil.) place where troops are posted for strategical purposes (*the p. was stormed*), the being advantageously placed (*manœuvring for p.*); *in a p. to do, state,* &c., enabled by circumstances or resources or information to; situation of vowel in syllable, esp. (Gk & L Pros.) of short vowel before two consonants, making the vowel metrically long; (fig.) situation in relation to other persons or things, as *difficult for a person in my p.*; rank, status, (*people of p.,* esp. upper & upper-middle classes); official employment; (v.t.) place in p., determine p. of. Hence **posi·tion**AL a. [F, f. L *positionem* (as prec., see -ION)]

po·sitive, a. & n. Formally laid down, artificially instituted, (opp. to *natural*), as *p. laws*; explicitly laid down, definite, admitting no question, as *p. assertion, have no p. proof, here is proof p.*; (of person) convinced, confident in opinion, cocksure; (Gram.) *p.* (*degree of*) *adjective,* primary form expressing simple quality without comparison (cf. COMPARATIVE, SUPERLATIVE); absolute, not relative; (colloq.) downright, out-&-out, as *he is a p. nuisance*; dealing only with matters of fact, practical, as *p. philosophy*; marked by presence, not absence, of qualities (cf. NEGATIVE); (Alg., of quantity) greater than zero (cf. NEGATIVE), *p. sign* (+); tending in the direction naturally or arbitrarily taken as that of increase or progress, as *clockwise rotation is p.*; *p. electricity* (of the kind produced by rubbing glass with silk, vitreous); *p. pole,* (of magnet) north-seeking pole, (of earth) south pole; (Photog.) showing lights & shades as seen in nature; *p. organ,* small (orig. portable) organ used to supplement large one in church; (n.) p. degree, adjective, quantity, &c. Hence **po·sitive**LY[2] adv., **po·sitive**NESS, **positi·**VITY, nn. [F (*-if, -ive*), f. L *positivus* (as POSIT, see -IVE)]

po·sitivism, n. Philosophical system of Auguste Comte, recognizing only positive facts & observable phenomena; religious system founded on this. So **po·sitiv**IST n., **positivi·st**IC a. [f. F *positivisme* (as prec., see -ISM)]

posŏ·logy (-s-), n. Study of the quantities in which drugs should be administered; (Bentham's word for) mathematics. Hence **posolo·g**ICAL a. [f. F *posologie* f. Gk *posos* how great, see -LOGY]

pŏ·ssĕ, n. Body (*of* constables); strong force or company; *p. cŏmita·tus*, body of men above age of 15 in a county, whom sheriff may summon to repress riot &c.; IN[5] *p.* [L, = to be able, (med. L) power]

posse·ss (-z-), v.t. Hold as property, own; have (faculty, quality, &c.), as *they p. a special value for us*; maintain (one-*self*, one's mind, soul, *in* patience &c.); (of demon or spirit) occupy, dominate, (person &c.), as *possessed by a devil, you are surely possessed*, (fig.) *he is possessed by* or *with this idea, what possesses you to think of such a thing?*; *p.* one*self of*, take, get for one's own; *be possessed of*, own, have. So **posse·ss**OR[2] n., **posse·ss**ORY a. [f. OF *possess(i)er* f. L *possidēre -sess-* (**port-* towards + *sedēre* sit)]

posse·ssion (poz-), n. Possessing; actual holding or occupancy; (Law) visible power of exercising such control as attaches to (but may exist apart from) lawful ownership; *in p.*, (of thing) possessed, (of person) possessing; *p. is nine* POINTS *of the law*; *in p. of*, having in one's p. (*am in p. of a fine specimen*); *in the p. of*, held by (*the specimen is in the possession of the present writer*); *rejoice in the possession of*, be so fortunate as to possess; thing possessed; (pl.) property, wealth; subject territory, esp. foreign dominions; SELF-*p.* [OF, f. L *possessionem* (as prec., see -ION)]

posse·ssive (poz-), a. & n. Of possession; (Gram.) indicating possession, as *p. pronoun* (e.g. *my, mine, his, ours*), *p. case* (e.g. *John's, the baker's*); (n.) p. case or word. Hence **posse·ssive**LY[2] adv., **posse·ssive**NESS n. [f. L *possessivus* (as POSSESS, see -IVE)]

po·sset, n. Drink made of hot milk curdled with ale, wine, &c., often flavoured with spices &c., formerly much used as remedy for colds &c. [ME *poshote*, etym. dub.]

possi·bilist, n. Member of (esp. Spanish republican or French socialist) political party aiming at those reforms only that are immediately practicable. [f. F *possibiliste* (as POSSIBLE, see -IST)]

possibi·lity, n. State, fact, of being possible, as *the p. of miracles, cannot by any p. be in time, there is no p. of his coming, it is within the range of p.*; thing that may exist or happen, as *what are the pp.?, there are three pp.* [f. F *possibilité* f. L *possibilitatem* (POSSIBLE, -TY)]

po·ssible, a. & n. That can exist, be done, or happen, as *that is quite p., it is scarcely p. to say, it is p.* (*that*) *he knows* or *may know, there are three p. excuses* (that may be made), *provide against a p. loss of men* (that may occur), *get all the assistance p.*; *come if* (it is) *p.*, *come as early as p.* (as you can); tolerable to deal with, reasonable, intelligible, &c., as *only one p. man among them*; (n.) highest p. score esp. in rifle practice, as *scored a p. at 800 yds*; *do* one's *p.*, do all one can (imit. of F *faire son p.*). [F, f. L *possibilis* (*posse* be able, -BLE)]

po·ssibly, adv. In accordance with possibility, as *cannot p. do it, how can I p.?*; perhaps, maybe, for all one knows to the contrary. [f. prec. + -LY[2]]

po·ssum, n. (colloq.). = OPOSSUM; *play p.*, pretend to be ill (from p.'s habit of feigning death when attacked).

pōst[1], n., & v.t. Stout piece of timber usu. cylindrical or square & of considerable length placed vertically as support in building; stake, stout pole, for various purposes; BED[1], DOOR, GOAL, KING, LAMP, SIGN, *-p.*; *starting, winning, -p.*, p. that marks starting, finishing, point in race; thick compact stratum of sandstone &c.; vertical mass of coal left as support in mine; (v.t.) stick (paper &c., usu. *up*) to p. or in prominent place, advertise (fact, thing, person) by placard; (in colleges) place in list that is posted up the names of (unsuccessful students); publish name of (ship) as overdue or missing; placard (wall &c.) with bills. [(vb f. n.) OE, f. L *postis*]

pōst[2], n. & adv. (Hist.) one of a series of men stationed with horses along roads at intervals, the duty of each being to ride forward with letters to next stage; (Hist.) courier, letter-carrier, mail-cart; a single dispatch of letters, letters so dispatched; letters taken from p.-office or pillar-box on one occasion, as *I missed the morning p.*; letters delivered at one house on one occasion, as *the p. has come, had a heavy p. today*; official conveyance of letters, parcels, &c., as *send it by p.*; GENERAL, PARCEL, PENNY, *p.*; p. office or postal letter box, as *take it to the p.*; *by return of p.*, (Hist.) by same courier who brought the dispatch, (mod.) by next mail in opposite direction; (as title of newspaper) *Morning P.* &c.; sizes (about 20 × 16 in.) & kinds of writing-paper; (adv.) with p.-horses, express, with haste, as *ride p.*; *p.-bag*, mail-bag; *p.-boat*, mail-boat, (also) boat conveying travellers between certain points; *p.-boy*, letter-carrier, (also) postilion; *po·stcard*, card of regulation size for conveyance by p.; *p.-chaise* (-sh-),

(Hist.) travelling carriage hired from stage to stage or drawn by horses so hired; *p.-free,* carried free of charge by p., or with postage prepaid; *p.-haste,* n. (archaic) & adv., (with) great expedition; *p.-horse* (kept at inns &c. for use of p. or travellers); *po·stman,* one who delivers or collects letters; *po·stmark,* (n.) official mark stamped on letter, esp. one giving place, date, & hour, of dispatch or arrival, & serving to deface stamp, (v.t.) mark (envelope &c.) with this; *po·stmaster*[1], official in charge of a p.-office, *p.-m. general,* administrative head of postal service; *po·stmastership,* office of postmaster; *po·stmistress,* woman in charge of p.-office; *p.-office,* public department for conveyance of letters &c. by p., house or shop where postal business is carried on (GENERAL *P.-O.*, *p.-o.* ORDER, *savings-bank,* see SAVE[1]); *p.-paid,* on which postage has been paid; *p.-town* (with p.-office, esp. one that is not sub-office of another). [f. F *poste* fem. f. It. f. LL *posta* = *posita* fem. p.p. of *ponere posit-* place]

pōst[3], v.i. & t. Travel with relays of horses; travel with haste, hurry; put (letter &c.) into post-office or letter-box for transmission; (Book-keep.) carry (entry) from auxiliary book to more formal one, esp. from day-book or journal to ledger, (also *p. up*) complete (ledger &c.) thus, (fig., also *p. up*) supply (person) with full information. [f. prec.]

pōst[4], n., & v.t. Place where soldier is stationed, (fig.) place of duty; position taken by body of soldiers, force occupying this; fort; (also *trading-p.*) place occupied for purposes of trade esp. in uncivilized country; situation, employment; (Naval, hist.) commission as officer in command of vessel of 20 guns or more, *p. captain,* holder of such commission (not of courtesy title or inferior command); (Mil.) *first, last, p.*, bugle-call giving notice of hour of retiring for night (*last p.* also blown at mil. funerals); (v.t.) place, station, (soldiers &c.), (Mil., Nav.) commission (person) as captain. [(vb f. n.) f. F *poste* masc. f. It. *posto* f. L neut. p.p. as POST[2]]

pōst- in comb. = L *post* after, behind, in wds f. L; & as living E prefix, as: *-cla·ssical,* occurring later than the classical period of (esp. Greek & Roman) language, literature, or art; *-commu·nion,* part of eucharistic office following act of communion; *-cŏ·stal,* behind a rib; *-da·te,* (v.t.) affix, assign, a later than the actual date to (document, event, &c.), (n., pō·st-) such date; *-dilu·vian,* a. & n., (person) existing, occurring, after the Flood; *-e·ntry,* late or subsequent entry (for race, in book-keeping, &c.); *-exĭ·lian, -exĭ·lic,* subsequent to the Babylonian exile; *-fi·x,* (v.t.) append (letters) at end of word, (n., pō·st-) suffix; *-glā·cial,* subsequent to the glacial period; *-grǎ·duate,* (of course of study) carried on after graduation; *-impre·ssionism,* artistic aims & methods (so named as a reaction from IMPRESSIONISM) directed to expressing rather the individual artist's than the ordinary observer's presumable conception of the objects represented; *-mille·nnial,* of the period following the millennium; *-mille·nnialism,* doctrine that second Advent will follow the millennium, so *-mille·nnialist* n.; *-nā·tal,* occurring after birth; *-nu·ptial,* subsequent to marriage; *-or·al,* situated behind the mouth; *-plī·ocene,* of the formation immediately overlying the pliocene; *-ter·tiary,* of the formations subsequent to the tertiary.

pō·stage (-ĭj), n. Amount charged for carriage of letter &c. by post, now usu. prepaid by *p. stamp,* adhesive label to be affixed, or stamp embossed or impressed on envelope &c., having specified value. [-AGE]

pō·stal, a. Of the POST[2]; *p.* ORDER[1](3); *p. union,* union of governments of various countries for regulation of international postage. [F (*poste* POST[2], see -AL)]

pō·ster, n. (Also *bill-p.*) one who posts bills; placard displayed in public place; (Rug. ftb.) attempt at goal that passes straight over a post. [POST[1], -ER[1]]

poste restante (F), n. Department in post-office in which letters are kept till applied for. [F, prop. = remaining post]

pŏstēr·ior, a. & n. Later, coming after in series, order, or time, so **posterīŏ·rITY** n.; hinder, whence **poster·iorLY**[2] adv., as viewed from behind; (n. sing. or pl.) the buttocks. [L, compar. of *posterus* (*post* after)]

pŏste·rity, n. The descendants of any person; all succeeding generations, as *deserves the gratitude of p.* [f. F *postérité* f. L *posteritatem* (as prec., see -TY)]

pŏ·stern, n. Back door; side way or entrance; (attrib.) *p. door, gate.* [f. OF *posterne, -rle,* f. LL *posterula* dim. f. *posterus* coming after (*post*)]

pōst hŏc er·gō prŏ·pter hŏc, L phr. (after this, therefore on account of this) ridiculing the tendency to confuse sequence with consequence.

pŏ·sthumous (-tū-), a. (Of child) born after death of its father; (of book &c.) published after author's death; occurring after death. Hence **po·sthumousLY**[1] adv. [f. L *postumus* last (*post* after), in LL *posth-* by assoc. w. *humus* ground, + -OUS]

pŏstī·cous, a. (bot.). Posterior, hinder. [f. L *posticus* (*post* behind) + -OUS]

pŏ·stil, n. (hist.). Marginal note, comment, esp. on text of Scripture; commentary. [f. F *postille* f. med. L *postilla* etym. dub.]

posti·lion, -llion, (po-), n. One who rides the near horse of the leaders, or near horse when one pair only is used & there is no driver on box. [f. F *postillon* f. It. *postiglione* (*posta* POST[2] + compd suf.)]

pōstli·miny, n. (Rom. Law) right of banished person or captive to resume civic privileges on return; (Internat. Law) restoration to their former state of persons & things taken in war, when they come again into the power of the nation they belonged to. [f. L POST(*liminium* f. *limen -minis* threshold)]

pō·stmaster[2] (for *p.*[1] see POST[2]), n. Scholar of Merton College, Oxford. Hence **po·stmaster**SHIP n. [?]

post merī·dĭĕm, adv. (usu. abbr. *P.M.*, pron. pē ĕm). After midday, as *3.20 P.M.* [L]

pōst mor·tem, adv., **post-mor·tem,** a. & n. After death; (examination) made after death. [L]

pōst-ō·bit, a. & n. Taking effect after death; (n.) bond securing to lender a sum to be paid on death of specified person from whom borrower has expectations. [f. L *post* after + *obitus -ūs* decease f. OB(*ire* go) die]

pōstpo·ne, v.t. & i. Put off, defer; treat (thing) as inferior in importance (*to* another); (intr., Path., of ague &c.) be later in coming on. Hence **postpo·ne**MENT n. [f. L POST(*ponere posit-* place)]

postposi·tion, n. Particle, word, placed after another, usu. as enclitic, (e.g. *-wards*). Hence **postposi·tion**AL, **postpŏ·sit**IVE, aa. [as prec., see -ION]

pōstpra·ndial, a. (usu. facet.). After-dinner, as *p. oratory, eloquence.* [f. POST- + L *prandium* lunch + -AL]

pōst·script, n. (abbr. P.S.). Additional paragraph esp. at end of letter after signature. [f. L *postscriptum* neut. p.p. of POST(*scribere* write)]

pŏ·stūlant, n. Candidate esp. for admission into religious order. [F (as foll., see -ANT)]

po·stulate[1] (-*at*), n. Thing claimed or assumed as basis of reasoning, fundamental condition; pre-requisite; (Geom.) claim to take for granted the possibility of simple operation, e.g. of drawing straight line between any two points. [as foll., see -ATE[2]]

po·stulāte[2], v.t. & i. Demand, require, claim, take for granted (thing, *that, to* do); stipulate *for*; (Eccl. Law) nominate or elect subject to superior sanction. So **postula·tion**, **po·stulat**OR[2], nn. [f. L *postulare* demand, -ATE[3]]

pŏ·sture, n., & v.t. & i. Carriage, attitude of body or mind; condition, state, (*of* affairs &c.); *p.-maker,* acrobat, contortionist; *p.-master,* teacher of callisthenics; (v.t.) dispose the limbs of (person) in particular way; (v.i.) assume p. (lit. & fig.). Hence **po·stur**AL a., **po·stur**ER[1] n. [(vb f. n.) F, f. L *positura* (*ponere posit-* place, see -URE)]

pō·sy (-zĭ), n. (archaic). Short motto, line of verse &c., inscribed within ring (*p.-ring*) &c.; nosegay. [= POESY]

pot[1], n. Rounded vessel of earthenware, metal, or glass, for holding liquids or solids, as GLUE, *ink, jam,* WATER[2]*ing, -p.*; such vessel for cooking; drinking vessel of pewter &c.; contents of p., as a *p. of porter, honey*; COFFEE-*p.*; TEA*p.*; (also, childish, *pō*) = CHAMBER-*p.*; = FLOWER-*p.*; vessel, usu. of silver, as prize in athletic sports, (slang) any prize in these; *p. paper* or *p.* (also *pott*), writing or printing paper 15½ in. × 12½, named from the orig. watermark of a p.; LOBSTER-*p.*; CHIMNEY-*p.*; large sum, as *made a p.* or *pp. of money*; (Racing slang) large sum staked or betted, as *put the p. on,* (also) favourite; *big p.*, important person; *the p. calls the kettle black,* person blames another for fault he too has; *go to p.* (vulg.), be ruined or destroyed; *make the p. boil,* make a living; *keep the p. boiling,* make a living, keep anything going briskly; *watched p. never boils* (proverb against worrying); *p.-ale,* completely fermented wash in distillation; *p.-belly,* (person with) protuberant belly; *p.-boiler,* work of literature or art done merely to make a living, writer or artist who does this; *p.-bound,* (of plant) whose roots fill flower-p. & want room to expand (also fig.); *p.-boy, potman,* publican's assistant; *p. hat,* bowler; *p.-herb,* any of those grown in kitchen-garden; *p.-hole* (geol.), deep cylindrical hole worn in rock; *p.-hook,* hook over fireplace for hanging p. &c. on or for lifting hot p., curved stroke in handwriting esp. as made in learning to write (cf. HANGER[2]); *p.-house,* ale-house; *p.-hunter,* sportsman who shoots anything he comes across, person who takes part in contest merely for sake of prize, so *p.-hunting* n. & a.; *p. lead,* black-lead esp. as used for hull of racing-yacht; *p. luck,* whatever is to be had for a meal, as *come & take p. luck with us*; *p.-metal,* stained glass coloured in melting-p. so that the colour pervades the whole; *p.-shot,* shot taken at game merely to provide a meal, shot aimed at animal &c. within easy reach; *p.-still,* kind of STILL[2] (opp. *patent still*) in which heat is applied directly & not by steam-jacket; *potstone,* granular variety of soapstone; *p.-valiant,* valiant because drunk, so *p. valour*; *potwall(op)er,* householder voter (before 1832), (naut., *-oper*) cook's assistant. [f. *wall(op)* boil]. Hence **po·t**FUL n. [late OE *pott,* cf. Du. *pot,* G *pott,* F *pot,* perh. cogn. w. L *potus* drinking]

pot[2], v.t. & i. Place (butter, fish, minced meat, &c., usu. salted or seasoned) in pot or other vessel to preserve it (esp. in p.p., as *potted ham*); plant (plant) in pot; (Billiards) pocket; bag (game), kill (animal) by pot-shot; (intr.) shoot (*at* or abs.); seize, secure. [f. prec.]

pō·table, a. & n. (usu. facet.). Drinkable; (n. pl.) drinkables. [F, f. LL *potabilis* (*potare* drink, see -BLE)]
potă·mic, a. Of rivers. So **potamo·**LOGY n. [f. Gk *potamos* river + -IC]
pŏ·tăsh, (archaic) **potă·ss** (*or* pŏ·t-), n. An alkaline substance, crude form of potassium carbonate, orig. got by lixiviating vegetable ashes & evaporating the solution in iron pots; *caustic p.*, hydroxide or hydrate of potassium; *permanganate of p.*, a disinfectant; *p.-water,* an aerated drink. [early mod. E *pot-ashes,* prob. f. Du. *pot-asschen*]
pota·ssium, n. One of the elements, the basis of potash, a lustrous white metal with slight tinge of pink. Hence **pota·ssic** a. [-IUM]
pota·tion, n. Drinking; (usu. pl.) tippling; draught. So **pō·tat**ORY a. [OF, f. L *potationem* (*potare* drink, see -ATION)]
potā·to, n. (pl. *-oes*). Plant with farinaceous tubers used for food; its tuber; *sweet, Spanish, p.*, tropical plant with tuberous roots used for food; *pp.* & POINT[1]; (slang) *quite the p.* (proper thing); (slang) *p.-box, -trap,* mouth; *p.-ring,* Irish (usu. silver) ring used as stand for bowl &c. [f. Sp. *patata* var. of native Amer. *batata*]
potee·n, -theen, n. Irish whisky from illicit still. [f. Ir. *poitin* dim. of *pota* pot]
pō·tent, a. (Chiefly poet. or rhet.) powerful, mighty; (of reasons &c.) cogent; (of drugs &c.) strong. Hence or cogn. **po·t**ENCE, **po·t**ENCY, nn., **po·tent**LY[2] adv. [f. L *potens* part. of *posse* be able]
pō·tentāte, n. Monarch, ruler. [f. L *potentatus -ūs* (as prec., see -ATE[1])]
pote·ntial (-shl), a. & n. Capable of coming into being or action, latent; (Mod.) *p. cautery, corrosive* (agent producing same effect on skin as an actual one); (Gram.) *p. mood,* subjunctive expressing possibility; (Physics) *p. function* (by differentiation of which the force at any point in space arising from any system of bodies &c. can be expressed); *p. energy* (existing in p. form, not as motion); (rare) powerful. (N.) p. mood, (amount of energy or quantity of work denoted by) p. function; possibility, as *reached its highest p.* Hence or cogn. **potentia·l**ITY n., **pote·ntial**LY[2] adv. [f. LL *potentialis* (*potentia,* as POTENT, see -AL)]
pote·ntialize, v.t. Make potential; convert (energy) into potential condition. [-IZE]
pote·ntiate (-shĭ-), v.t. Endow with power; make possible. [f. L as foll. + -ATE[3]]
potentio·meter, n. Instrument for measuring differences of electrical potential. [f. L *potentia* power (POTENT) + -O- + -METER]
po·ther (pŏdh-, pŭdh-), n., & v.t. & i. Choking smoke or cloud of dust; noise, din; verbal commotion, as *made a p. about it*; display of sorrow; (v.t.) fluster, worry; (v.i.) make a fuss. [etym. dub.; prob. not connected w. *powder*]
pŏtichoma·nia (-sh-), n. (Craze for) imitation of Japanese porcelain by covering inner surface of glass vessels with designs on paper &c. [f. F *potichomanie* (*potiche* oriental porcelain, see -MANIA)]
pō·tion (-shn), n. Dose, draught, of liquid medicine or of poison. [OF, f. L *potionem* (*potus* drunk, see -ION)]
po·tlatch, -lach(e), n. Tribal feast of N.-Amer. Indians given by aspirant to chiefship. [native]
pot-pourri (pōpŏŏrē·), n. Mixture of dried petals & spices kept in jar for its perfume; musical or literary medley. [F, lit. rotten pot]
po·tsherd, n. (archaic). Broken piece of earthenware. [POT[1] + SHERD]
pott, var. of POT[1] as applied to paper.
po·ttage (-ĭj), n. (archaic). Soup, stew; (fig.) MESS[1] *of p.* [f. F *potage* (POT[1] + -AGE)]
po·tter[1], n. Maker of earthenware vessels; *p.'s wheel,* horizontal revolving disk in *p.'s lathe* (machine for moulding clay); *p.'s asthma, bronchitis,* &c. (caused by dust in the pottery industry). [OE *pottere* (-ER[1])]
po·tter[2], v.i. & t. Work in feeble or desultory manner (*at, in,* subject or occupation); dawdle, loiter, (*about* &c.); trifle *away* (one's time &c.). [prob. f. obs. *pote* push, OE *potian,* etym. dub., + -ER[5]]
po·ttery, n. Earthenware; potter's work or workshop; *the Pp.*, district in N. Staffordshire, seat of p. industry. [f. F *poterie* (POT[1], -ERY)]
po·ttle, n. (Archaic) measure for liquids, half gallon, pot &c. containing this; small wicker or chip basket for strawberries &c. [ME & OF *potel* (POT[1], see -LE)]
po·tto, n. W.-Afr. lemur; kinkajou. [native]
po·tty, a. (slang). Insignificant, trivial, (often *p. little*; *p. little State, details*; *p. questions* in examination paper, easy to answer). [?]
pouch[1] (powtsh), n. Small bag or detachable outside pocket; (archaic) purse; soldier's leathern ammunition bag; bag-like receptacle of marsupials &c.; bag-like cavity, esp. seed-vessel, in plant. Hence **pouch**ED[2], **pou·ch**Y[2], aa. [f. ONF *pouche* = OF *poche* POKE[1]]
pouch[2], v.t. & i. Put into pouch; take possession of, pocket; (slang) give money to, tip; make (part of dress) hang like pouch, (intr., of such part) hang thus. [f. prec.]
poudrette (pŏŏdrĕ·t), n. Manure of night-soil mixed with charcoal &c. [F, dim. of *poudre* POWDER]
pouf (pŏŏf), n. Woman's high roll or pad of hair; part of dress gathered up in bunch; soft stuffed couch. [F]

poulp(e) (poo-), n. Octopus or other cephalopod. [F (*-pe*), as POLYPUS]
poult (pōlt), n. Young of domestic fowl, turkey, pheasant, &c. [as PULLET]
poult-de-soie (poodeswah·), n. Fine corded (now usu. coloured) silk. [F, etym. dub.]
pou·lterer (pō-), n. Dealer in poultry. [f. earlier *poulter* (still in City Company's name) f. OF *pouletier* (as PULLET, see -ER[2]) + -ER[1]]
pou·ltice (pō-), n., & v.t. Soft mass of bread, linseed, &c., usu. made with boiling water & spread on muslin &c. & applied to sore or inflamed part; (v.t.) apply p. to. [ult. f. L *puls -ltis* thick pap &c.]
pou·ltry (pō-), n. Domestic fowls, e.g. barn-door fowls, ducks, geese, turkeys. [f. OF *pouletrie* (as PULLET, see -ERY)]
pounce[1] (pow-), n., & v.t. & i. Claw, talon, of bird of prey; pouncing, sudden swoop, esp. *make a p.*; (v.t.) swoop down upon & seize; (v.i.) make sudden attack *upon*, (fig.) seize eagerly *upon* (blunder &c.). [?]
pounce[2] (pow-), n., & v.t. Fine powder used to prevent ink from spreading on unsized paper &c.; powdered charcoal &c. dusted over perforated pattern to transfer design to object beneath; (v.t.) smooth (paper, surface of hat, &c.) with pumice or p., transfer (design) by use of p., dust (pattern) with p. [(vb f. F *poncer*) f. F *ponce* PUMICE]
pou·ncet-box (pow-), n. (archaic). Small box with perforated lid for perfumes. [in Shakspere; f. prec., hist. unexpl.]
pound[1] (pow-), n., & v.i. (Abbr. *lb.* = L *libra*) measure of weight, 16 oz avoirdupois, 12 oz Troy; *p. of flesh* (see Shak. *Merchant of Venice*, IV. i); (also *p. sterling*) a money of account, 20 shillings, now represented by gold sovereign, as *five pp.* (written £5 or 5*l.*), *five p. ten* (*shillings*); (Hist.) *p. Scots*, 1s. 8*d.*; *pay* 5s. *in the p.* (for each p. owing); PENNY *wise & p. foolish*; *p., five-p., note*, bank-note for one p., five pp.; *p.-cake*, rich cake containing a p. (or equal weight) of each of chief ingredients; *p.-day* (on which a charity &c. receives contributions from all comers of a p. of anything, e.g. £1, 1lb. of tea, &c.); (v.i.) test the weight of coins by weighing the number that ought to weigh a p. [(vb f. n.) OE *pund*, cf. Du. *pond*, G *pfund*, f. L *pondo* p. weight, orig. abl. of **pondus -di* = *pondus -eris* weight]
pound[2] (pow-), n., & v.t. Enclosure for detention of stray cattle or of distrained cattle or goods till redeemed; enclosure for animals; (fig.) place of confinement, (Hunt.) difficult position; *p.-lock* (with two gates, opp. *flash-lock* with one); (v.t.) shut (cattle &c., often *up*) in p., (Hunt.) *p. the field*, (of barrier) be impassable, (of rider) clear fence that others cannot. [(vb f. n.) OE *pund(fold)*, etym. dub.]
pound[3] (pow-), v.t. & i. Crush, bruise, as with pestle; thump, pummel, with fists &c.; knock, beat, (thing *to pieces, into a jelly*, &c.); deliver heavy blows, fire heavy shot, (*at, on, away at*); walk, run, ride, make one's way, heavily (*along* &c.). [OE *púnian*, cf. LG *pün* chips of stone, Du. *puin* rubbish]
pou·ndage (-ij), n. Commission, fee, of so much per pound sterling; percentage of total earnings of a business, paid as wages; payment of so much per pound weight; TONNAGE & *p.* [-AGE]
pou·nder[1], n. In vbl senses, esp. instrument for pounding with or in, pestle, mortar. [POUND[3] + -ER[1]]
pou·nder[2], n. Thing that, gun carrying shot that, weighs a pound or (*-p.*) so many pounds, as *a three-p.*; (*-p.*) thing worth, person possessing, so many pounds sterling. [POUND[1], -ER[1]]
pour (pōr), v.t. & i., & n. Cause (liquid, granular substance, light, &c.) to flow, discharge copiously, as *p. hot water over it, p. out the tea, river pours itself into the sea*; *p. oil upon troubled waters*, (fig.) calm disturbance with soothing words &c.; *p. cold water on*, (fig.) discourage (person, zeal, plan); discharge (missiles, crowd from building, &c., often *forth, out*) copiously or in rapid succession; send *forth* or *out* (words, music, &c.); (intr., of liquids &c.) flow (usu. *forth, out, down*) in stream, (of rain) descend heavily, whence **pour·ing**[2] a.; *it never rains but it pours*, (fig.) events esp. misfortunes always come together; (fig.) come *in, out*, &c., abundantly, as *letters p. in from all quarters*; (n.) heavy fall of rain, downpour, (Found.) amount of molten metal &c. poured at a time. [(n. f. vb) ME *pouren*, etym. dub.]
pourboire (poorbwar·), n. Gratuity, tip. [F, = *pour boire* (money) for drinking]
pourparler (poor·parlā·), n. (usu. in pl.). Informal discussion preliminary to negotiation. [F]
pour·point (poor-), **pur-**, n. (hist.). Stuffed & quilted doublet. [OF (*pour-*) p.p. of *pourpoindre* perforate (*pour* PRO- substituted for *par* PER- + *poindre* prick f. L *pungere*)]
poussette (poose·t), v.i., & n. Dance round & round with hands joined, as couple in country dance; (n.) this action. [(vb f. n.) F, dim. of *pousse* PUSH]
pou stō (pow), n. Standing-place, basis of operation. [Gk *pou stō* where I may stand]
pout[1] (powt), n. Kinds of fish, as *whiting, eel, horn, -p.* [OE *-púta*, cf. Du. *puit*, G *-putte*]
pout[2] (powt), v.t. & i., & n. Protrude (lips), protrude lips, (of lips) protrude, esp. as sign of displeasure, whence **pou·tingly**[2] adv.; (n.) such protrusion; *in the pp.*, sulky. [(n. f. vb) perh. cogn. w. prec., cf. Da. *pude* cushion, Sw. *puta* pad, dial. *puta* be inflated]

pou·ter, n. In vbl senses, esp.: kind of pigeon with great power of inflating crop; (also *whiting-pout*) kind of fish. [-ER[1]]

pŏ·verty, n. Indigence, want; scarcity, deficiency, (*of*); deficiency *in* (a property); inferiority, poorness, meanness; *p.-stricken*, poor, esp. fig., as *a p.-stricken language.* [f. OF *poverté* f. L *paupertatem* (as PAUPER, see -TY)]

pow·der, n., & v.t. Mass of dry particles or granules, dust; medicine in the form of p.; cosmetic p. applied to face, skin, or hair; =GUN*p.*, as *smell of p.*, experience of fighting, FOOD *for p.*; *not worth p. and shot*, not worth shooting, or fighting or striving for; (Games &c.) force put into a blow or stroke (*no p. behind the ball*; *put more p. into it*); (v.t.) sprinkle p. upon, cover (*with* powder &c.), apply p. to (hair, or abs. in same sense), decorate (surface) with spots or small figures; (esp. in p.p.) reduce to p. (*powdered sugar*); *p. blue*, powdered smalt esp. for use in laundry, deep blue colour of this (also attrib.); *p.-down*, down-feathers found in definite patches on some birds; *p.-flask*, case for carrying gunp.; *p.-horn*, p.-flask orig. & esp. of horn; *p.-magazine*, place where gunp. is stored; *p.-monkey*, boy employed on board ship to carry p. to guns; *p.-puff*, soft pad usu. of down for applying p. to skin. Hence **pow·deri**NESS n., **pow·dery**[2] a. [(vb f. F *poudrer*) f. F *poudre* f. OF *polre* f. L *pulvis -eris*]

pow·er, n. Ability to do or act, as *will do all in my p.*, *has the p. of changing its colour*; particular faculty of body or mind, as *taxes his pp. to the utmost*, *man of varied pp.*; vigour, energy, as *more p. to your elbow!* (formula of encouragement or approval); active property, as *has a high heating p.*; government, influence, authority, (*over*); *in* one's *p.*, under one's control; personal ascendancy (*over*); political ascendancy as *the party now in p.*; authorization, delegated authority, as *a bill to extend & define their pp.*; *p. of* ATTORNEY[2]; influential person, body, or thing, as *the press had not become a p. in the State*; *the pp. that be*, constituted authorities; State having international influence; deity, as *merciful pp.!*; sixth ORDER[1] of angels; (vulg.) large number or amount, as *saw a p. of people*, *did a p. of work*; (Math.) *third, tenth*, &c., *p.* of a number, product obtained by multiplying the number into itself three, ten, &c., times, as, *the third p. of 2 is 8*; instrument for applying energy to mechanical purposes, esp. *the* MECHANICAL *pp.*, the simple MACHINES; mechanical energy as opp. to hand-labour, esp. attrib., as *p.-lathe, -loom, -mill*; *p.-station* (in which electric p. is generated for distribution); capacity for exerting mechanical force esp., HORSE[1]-*p.*, whence **(-)power**ED[2] a.; magnifying capacity of lens. [ME & OF *poër* (vb inf. as n.) f. LL *potēre*=L *posse* be able (*potis*)]

pow·erful, a. Having great (physical or other) power or influence as *p. grasp, horse, mind, ally, book, speech, odour.* Hence **pow·erful**LY[2] adv. [-FUL]

pow·erless, a. Without power; wholly unable (*to* help &c.). Hence **pow·erless**LY[2] adv., **pow·erless**NESS n. [-LESS]

pow·wow, pawaw·, n., **powwow·,** v.i. & t. N.-Amer.-Indian medicine-man or sorcerer; magic ceremonial, conference, of N.-Amer. Indians, (U.S.) political or other meeting; (v.i.) practise medicine or sorcery, hold a p., (U.S.) confer, discuss, (*about* &c.); (v.t.) doctor, treat with magic. [f. native *powwaw, powah*]

pox, n. Syphilis; CHICKEN-*p.*; COWPOX; SMALL-*p.* [=POCKS]

pozz(u)olana (pŏtsolah·na, -tswo-), n. Volcanic ash found near Pozzuoli, much used for hydraulic cement. [It.]

po·zzy, n. (army slang). Jam. [?]

praam. See PRAM[1].

pra·cticable, a. That can be done, feasible; (of road, passage, food) that can be used or traversed; (Theatr., of windows &c.) real, that can be used as such. Hence **practica**BI·LITY. **pra·cticable**NESS, nn., **pra·cticab**LY[2] adv. [f. F *practicable* (*pratiquer* PRACTISE, -ABLE)]

pra·ctical, a. Of, concerned with, shown in, practice (cf. THEORETICAL), as p. *agriculture, philosophy*; *p.* JOKE[1]; available, useful, in practice; engaged in practice, practising; inclined to action rather than speculation, as *does not appeal to p. minds*; that is such in effect though not nominally, virtual, as *a p. atheist, has p. control.* Hence **practica·**LITY, **pra·ctical**NESS, nn. [f. obs. *practic* n. & a. f. obs. F *practique* f. LL f. Gk *praktikos* (*prassō* do, see -IC) + -AL]

pra·ctically, adv. In a practical manner; virtually, almost, (*p. nothing*). [-LY[2]]

pra·ctice, n. Habitual action or carrying on, as *naval p., the p. of advertising, makes a p. of cheating*; method of legal procedure; habit, custom, (*has been the regular p.*); repeated exercise in an art, handicraft, &c., as *p. makes perfect, in, out of, p.* (lately, not lately, practised in thing), *is good p.* (improves skill), (also) spell of this (*ball, target, p.*); professional work, business, or connexion, of lawyer or doctor, as *has a large p., sold his p.*; (archaic) scheming, (usu. underhand) contrivance, artifice, (esp. in pl., & cf. SHARP[1] *p.*); (Arith.) mode of finding value of given number of articles, or of quantity of commodity at given price, when quantity or price or both are in several denominations; *in p.*, in the realm of action, as *quite useless, would never work, in p.*; *put* (plan, method) *in(to) p.*, carry it out. [earlier *practize* prob. f. PRACTISE, replacing earlier *practic* (as PRACTICAL)]

practi·cian (-shn), n. Worker, practitioner. [f. obs. F *practicien* (as PRACTICAL, see -ICIAN)]

pra·ctise, v.t. & i. Perform habitually, carry out in action, as *p. the same method, p. what you preach*; exercise, pursue, (profession; *practising doctor, barrister,* &c., engaged in actual practice, not retired nor merely qualified); exercise oneself in or on (art, instrument, or abs.), as *p. the flute, the piano, music, running*; exercise (person, one*self, in* action or subject), whence **pra·ctis**ED[1] a.; (archaic) scheme, contrive, as *when first we p. to deceive*; *p. (up)on,* impose upon, take advantage of, (person, his credulity &c.). [f. OF *pra(c)tiser, -tiquer,* f. med. L *practicare* (as PRACTICAL)]

practi·tioner (-shoner), n. Professional or practical worker, esp. in medicine; *general p.* (in both medicine & surgery; abbr. G.P.). [erron. f. PRACTICIAN + -ER[1]]

prae-, pref., the L form of PRE-, kept only in a few wds.

praecō·cial (-shal), a. (Of birds) whose young can feed themselves as soon as hatched. [as PRECOCIOUS, see -AL]

praemūnīr·e, n. (law). Writ charging sheriff to summon person accused of asserting or maintaining papal jurisdiction in England; *Statute of p.* (of 16th Richard II, on which the writ is based). [med. L, = L PRAE(*monēre* warn), the wds *p. facias* warn (so-&-so to appear) occurring in the writ]

praeno·men, n. (Rom. ant.). First or personal name (e.g. *Marcus* Tullius Cicero). [PRAE-, cf. COGNOMEN]

praepo·stor, pre-, n. (pub. school). = PREFECT, MONITOR. [syncop. f. *praepositor* f. L PRAE(*ponere posit-* place) set over, see -OR[2]; irreg. altered f. L p.p. *-tus*]

prae·tor, n. (Rom. hist.). (Orig.) Roman consul as leader of army; (later) annually elected magistrate performing some duties of consul. Hence **praetor·**IAL a., **prae·tor**SHIP n. [L, f. PRAE(*ire it-* go)]

praetor·ian, pre-, a. & n. Of a praetor; of the body-guard of Roman general or emperor; (n.) man of p. rank, soldier of p. guard. [f. L *praetorianus* (as prec., see -AN)]

pragmă·tic(al), aa. Meddlesome; dogmatic; of pragmatism; (*-ic*) treating facts of history with reference to their practical lessons; (*-ic*) of the affairs of a State (*p. sanction,* imperial or royal ordinance issued as fundamental law, esp. that of Charles VI in 1724 settling Austrian succession). Hence **pragmatica·**LITY n., **pragma·tical**LY[2] adv. [f. F *pragmatique* f. L f. Gk *pragmatikos* (*pragma -matos* deed f. *prassō* do), -IC, -AL]

pra·gmatism, n. Officiousness; pedantry; matter-of-fact treatment of things; (Philos.) doctrine that estimates any assertion solely by its practical bearing upon human interests. So **pra·gmat**IST n., **pragmati·s**TIC a. [f. Gk *pragma,* see prec. & -ISM]

pra·gmatize, v.t. Represent as real; rationalize (myth). [as prec., see -IZE]

prair·ie, n. Large treeless tract of level or undulating grass-land; *p.-chicken, -hen,* N.-Amer. kind of grouse; *p.-dog,* N.-Amer. rodent with bark like dog's; *p. oyster,* raw egg swallowed whole. [F, f. Rom. **prataria* (L *pratum* meadow, see -ARY[1])]

praise (-z), v.t., & n. Express warm approbation of, commend the merits of, (person, thing); glorify, extol the attributes of, (God &c.); (n.) praising, commendation, as *won high p., was loud in his pp.* Hence **prai·se**FUL a., **prai·seful**NESS n. [(n. f. vb) f. OF *preisier* price, prize, praise, f. LL *preciare, pret-,* (*pretium* price)]

prai·seworthy, a. Worthy of praise, commendable, (often patronizing). Hence **prai·seworthi**LY[2] adv., **prai·seworth**INESS n.

Pra·krit (prah-), n. Any of the dialects of N. & Central India existing alongside of or growing out of Sanskrit. [f. Skr. *prakṛta* unrefined]

pra·line (-ah-), n. Sweetmeat made by browning nuts in boiling sugar. [F (*Praslin,* surname)]

pram[1], ***praam,*** (prahm), n. Flat-bottomed boat used in Baltic &c. for shipping cargo &c.; flat-bottomed boat mounted with guns; Scandinavian ship's boat corresp. to dinghy. [Du. (*-aam*)]

prăm[2], n. (colloq.). Perambulator; milkman's hand-cart. [abbr. of PERAMBULATOR]

prance, v.i. & t., & n. (Of horse) rise by springing from hind legs; cause (horse) to do this; (fig.) walk, behave, in elated or arrogant manner (esp. *prancing proconsuls*); (n.) prancing, prancing movement. [?]

pra·ndial, a. (facet.). Of dinner. [f. L *prandium* lunch, see -AL]

prank[1], n. Mad frolic, practical joke; (fig., of machinery &c.) erratic action. Hence **pra·nk**FUL, **pra·nk**ISH[1], aa., **pra·nkish**NESS n. [?]

prank[2], v.t. & i. Dress, deck, (person, one*self,* thing, often *out*); adorn, spangle, (field *with* flowers &c.); (v.i.) show oneself off. [cf. Du. *pronken,* G *prunken,* show off, & obs. E adj. *prank* smart, showy]

prate, v.i. & t., & n. Chatter; talk too much; blab; tell, say, (thing) in prating manner; (n.) prating, idle talk. Hence **pra·**TER[1] n., **pra·**TING[2] a. [(n. f. vb) f. 15th c., cf. Du. *praten,* Sw. *prata,* Da. *prate*]

prā·ties, n. (Anglo-Ir. colloq.). Potatoes. [corrupt.]

prā·tincole, n. Bird like swallow in appearance & habits, & allied to plover. [f. L *pratum* meadow + *incola* inhabitant]

pră·tique (-ĭk, *or* pratē·k), n. Licence to hold intercourse with port, granted to ship after quarantine or on showing clean bill of health. [F, = PRACTICE, intercourse]

pră·ttle, v.i. & t., & n. Talk in childish or artless fashion; say (thing) thus; (n.) childish chatter, small talk. Hence **pra·ttl**ER[1] n., **pra·ttl**ING[2] a. [(n. f. vb) f. PRATE + -LE(3)]

pră·vity, n. (rare). Depravity; badness, corruptness, (of food &c.). [f. L *pravitas* (*pravus* crooked, bad, see -TY)]

prawn, n., & v.i. Crustacean like large shrimp; (v.i.) fish for pp., so **praw·n**ING[1] n. [ME *pra(y)ne*, etym. dub.]

pra·xis, n. Accepted practice, custom; (Gram.) set of examples for practice. [Gk, = doing, f. *prassō* do]

pray, v.t. & i. Make devout supplication to (God, object of worship); beseech earnestly (God, person, *for* thing, *to* do, *that*); ask earnestly for (permission &c.) engage in prayer, make entreaty, (*to* God, *to* person, *for* thing, *for* or *on behalf of* person, *to* do, *that*); *p.* (I beg you to) *consider* &c., *what is the use of that, p.* (tell me)*?*; *p. in aid of* (archaic; *in* adv., not prep.), summon to one's support. [f. OF *preier* f. LL *precare* (L *-ri*)]

prayer[1] (prār), n. Solemn request to God or object of worship; formula used in praying, e.g. LORD'*s p.*; form of divine service consisting largely of pp., as *morning p., evening p., family pp.*; action, practice, of praying; entreaty to a person; thing prayed for; *p.-book,* book of forms of p., esp. Book of Common P., public liturgy of Church of England; *p.-meeting,* religious meeting at which several persons offer p.; *p.-wheel,* revolving cylindrical box inscribed with or containing pp., used esp. by Buddhists of Tibet. Hence **prayer·**FUL, **prayer·**LESS, aa., **prayer·ful**LY[2], **prayer·less**LY[2], advv., **prayer·ful**NESS, **prayer·less**NESS, nn. [ME & OF *preiere* f. med. L *precaria* fem. sing. (orig. neut. pl.) adj. as n. (as PRECARIOUS)]

pray·er[2], n. One who prays. [-ER[1]]

pre-, pref., = med. L *pre-*, L *prae-*, before (in time, place, order, degree, or importance). Besides wds of L orig. *pre-* as living E pref. forms unlimited vbs & vbl nn., only the more important of which are given in their alphabetical place. In secondary wds such as those here classified, the pron. is (prē-) & the hyphen is usu. written. 1. Vbs & vbl nn. w. sense 'do, doing, thing done, beforehand', as: *-acquai·nt*; *-admi·ssion*; *-admo·nish, -admoni·tion*; *-advi·se*; *-annou·nce(ment)*; *-appoi·nt(ment)*; *-arra·nge(ment)*; *-au·dience,* right (of lawyer at Bar) to be heard before another; *-ca·lculable, -ca·lculate, -calcula·tion*; *-compo·se*; *-concer·t*; *-conde·mn*; *-condi·tion,* prior condition, one that must be fulfilled beforehand; *-consi·der, -considera·tion*; *-contra·ct* v.i., *-co·ntract* n.; *-decea·se,* (v.t.) die before (person), (n.) such death; *-defi·ne*; *-dige·st* render food easily digestible before introduction into stomach, *-dige·stion,* this process; *-doo·m* v.t., *-ele·ct, -ele·ction* (see also in 2); *-enga·ge(ment)*; *-esta·blish*; *-e·stimāte* v.t., *-e·stimate* (-at) n.; *-exi·st* v.i., *-exi·stence* n., so *-exi·stent* a.; *-i·ndicate*; *-i·ntimāte* v.t.; *-li·mit* v.t.; *-mo·tion,* motion given beforehand, esp. divine act as determining the will of the creature; *-ordai·n,* appoint beforehand, foreordain; *-perce·ption.* 2. Adjj. & nn. w. sense '(person &c.) existing, dating from, before the time of—', as: *-adă·mic* a., *-a·damite* n. & a., (one of supposed race) existing before the time of Adam; *-Chri·stian,* before Christ(ianity); *-cla·ssical,* before the classical age (usu. of Greek & Roman literature); *-co·nqueror, -co·nquest,* before the Norman conquest; *-co·nscious,* antecedent to consciousness; *-ele·ction,* done, given, before election, as *p. promises*; *-exĭ·lian, -exĭ·lic,* before (usu. the Babylonian) exile; *-glā·cial,* before the glacial period; *-hu·man,* existing before man existed; *-mille·nnial(ism),* (belief that Christ's Second Advent will occur) before the millennium, so *-millenar·ian, -mille·nnialist*; *-na·tal,* existing, occurring, before birth; *-pra·ndial,* before-dinner; *-scienti·fic,* before the rise of modern science; *-war·* adj. (as *p.-w. prices*) & (vulg.) adv. (as *that happened p.-w.*), before the great war. 3. Adjj., chiefly anat. & zool., w. sense 'situated in front of', as: *-cor·dial,* in front of or about the heart; *-co·stal,* in front of the ribs; *-dor·sal,* anterior to the dorsal region; *-frŏ·ntal,* in front of frontal bone of skull, in fore part of frontal lobe of brain; *-maxi·llary,* in front of the upper jaw; *-o·cular,* in front of the eye.

preach (-ētsh), v.i. & t., & n. Deliver sermon or religious address, deliver (sermon); give moral advice in obtrusive way; proclaim, expound, (the Gospel, Christ, *that,* &c.) in public discourse; advocate, inculcate (quality, conduct, principle, &c.) thus; *p. up,* extol, commend; *p. down,* disparage, put down by preaching or speaking; (n., colloq.) preaching, sermon, lecture. Hence or cogn. **prea·ch**ABLE a., **prea·ch**ER[1], **prea·cher**SHIP, **prea·ch**MENT (usu. contempt.), nn. [f. OF *prechier* f. L PRAE(*dicare* proclaim)]

prea·chify, v.i. Preach, moralize, hold forth, tediously. [-FY]

prea·chy, a. (colloq.). Fond of preaching or holding forth. Hence **prea·chi**NESS n. [-Y[2]]

prēă·mble, n., & v.i. Preliminary statement in speech or writing; introductory

For other words in *pre-* see PRE-.

part of statute, deed, &c.; (v.i.) make p. [(vb f. n.) f. F *préambule* f. med. L *praeambulum* f. L *praeambulus* going before f. PRAE(*ambulare* walk)]

prē·bend, n. Part of revenue of cathedral or collegiate church granted to canon or member of chapter as stipend; portion of land or tithe from which this stipend is drawn; =foll. So **pre·bend**AL a. [f. OF *prebende* f. med. L *praebenda* pension, neut. pl. gerund. of L *praebēre* grant, = PRAE(*hibēre* = *habēre* have, hold)]

prē·bendary, n. Holder of prebend; *p.-stall*, p.'s stall in cathedral. Hence **pre·bendary**SHIP n. [f. med. L *praebendarius* (as prec., see -ARY[1])]

precār·ious, a. Held during the pleasure of another, as *p. tenure*; question-begging, taken for granted, as *a p. assumption*; dependent on chance, uncertain, as *makes a p. living*; perilous, as *the p. life of a fisherman.* Hence **precar·ious**LY[2] adv., **precar·ious**NESS n. [f. L *precarius* obtained by entreaty (*precem* prayer, see -ARY[1]) + -OUS]

prĕ·catory, a. (Gram., of word or form) expressing entreaty; (in wills) *p. words* (requesting that a thing be done), *p. trust*, p. words that are held to be binding. So **pre·cat**IVE a. [f. LL *precatorius* (*precari* pray, see -ORY)]

precau·tion (prĭ-), n. Prudent foresight, measure taken beforehand to ward off evil or ensure good result. Hence **precau·tion**ARY[1] a. [f. F *précaution* f. med. L *praecautionem* f. L PRAE(*cavēre caut-* beware of), see -ION]

prece·de (prĭ-), v.t. & i. (Of person or thing) go before in rank or importance, as *such duties p. all others, sons of barons p. baronets*; come before (thing &c. or abs.) in order, as *the words that p.* (*this paragraph*); walk in front of, as *preceded by our guide*; come before in time, as *in the years preceding his accession*; cause (thing) to be preceded by, as *must p. this measure by milder ones.* [f. F *précéder* f. L PRAE(*cedere cess-* go)]

prĕ·cedence (*or* prĭsē·d-), (rarely) **-cy,** nn. Priority in time or succession; superiority, higher position, as *takes p. of* (is recognized as superior to) *all others*; right of preceding others in ceremonies & social formalities. [prob. f. PRECEDENT[2], see -ENCE, -ENCY]

prĕ·cedent[1], n. Previous case taken as example for subsequent cases or as justification, as *there is no p. for this, it is without p., do not take this as a p.*; (Law) decision, procedure, &c., serving as rule or pattern. [as foll.]

precē·dent[2] (prĭ-, *or as prec.*), a. (now rare). Preceding in time, order, rank, &c., as *condition p.* Hence **prece·dent**LY[2] adv. [f. F *précédent* a. & n. f. L as PRECEDE, see -ENT]

prĕ·cedented, a. Having, supported by, precedent. [-ED[2]]

prece·nt (prĭ-), v.i. & t. Act as precentor; lead (psalm &c.) in singing. [back form. f. foll.]

prece·ntor (prĭ-), n. One who leads the singing of choir or congregation, esp. (in cathedrals of old foundation) member of chapter ranking next to dean, whose duty as p. is now usu. performed by succentor, (in those of new foundation) minor canon or chaplain. Hence or cogn. **prece·ntor**SHIP, **prece·ntrix**, nn. [f. LL *praecentor* f. L PRAE(*cinere cent-* = *canere* sing)]

prē·cept, n. Command, maxim, so **prece·pt**IVE a.; moral instruction, as *example is better than p.*; divine command; writ, warrant; written order to arrange for & hold election; order for collection or payment of money under a rate. [f. L *praeceptum* neut. p.p. of PRAE(*cipere cept-* = *capere* take) instruct]

prece·ptor (prĭ-), n. Teacher, instructor. Hence or cogn. **prēceptor·**IAL a., **prece·ptor**SHIP, **prece·ptress**[1], nn. [f. L *praeceptor* (as prec., see -OR[2])]

prece·ptory, n. (hist.). Subordinate community of Knights Templars; estate, buildings, of this. [f. med. L *praeceptoria* fem. adj. as n. (as prec., see -ORY)]

prece·ssion (prĭ-), n. *P. of the equinoxes*, (earlier occurrence of the equinoxes in each successive sidereal year, due to) retrograde motion of equinoctial points along ecliptic. Hence **prece·ssion**AL a. [f. LL *praecessio* (as PRECEDE, see -ION)]

prē·cinct, n. Space enclosed by walls or other boundaries of a place or building, esp. of place of worship; (pl.) *the* environs *of*; boundary. [f. med. L *praecinctum* neut. p.p. of PRAE(*cingere* gird)]

prĕ·cious (-shus), a. & adv. Of great price, costly; *p. metals*, gold, silver, (sometimes) platinum; *p. stone*, gem; of great non-material worth, as *p. words, privilege, knowledge, blood of Christ*; affectedly refined in language, workmanship, &c., so **precio·**SITY (-shĭ-) n.; (colloq., as intensive) *made a p. mess of it, a p. sight more than you think*; (ellipt.) *my p.* (dear &c.); (adv., colloq. intensive) *took p. good care of that, p. little of it.* Hence **pre·cious**LY[2] adv., **pre·cious**NESS n. [ME & OF *precios* f. L *pretiosus* (*pretium* price, see -OUS)]

prĕ·cipice, n. Vertical or steep face of rock, cliff, mountain, &c. [f. L *praecipitium* falling headlong, precipice (as PRECIPITOUS)]

preci·pitate[1] (-*at*), n. (Chem.) body precipitated from solution, so **preci·pit**ABI·LITY, **preci·pit**ANT(2), nn., **preci·pit**ABLE a.; (Physics) moisture condensed from vapour by cooling & deposited, e.g. rain, dew. [as foll.]

preci·pitate[2] (-*at*), a. Headlong, violently hurried, as *p. flight*; (of person or act) hasty, rash, inconsiderate. Hence or cogn. **preci·pit**ANCE, **preci·pit**ANCY, **pre-**

ci·pitateNESS, nn., **preci·pitate**LY[2] adv. [as foll., see -ATE[2]]

preci·pitāte[3], v.t. Throw down headlong; (fig.) hurl, fling, (person &c. *into* condition &c.); hurry, urge on, (course of events &c.); hasten the occurrence of, as *served to p. his ruin*; (Chem.) cause (substance in solution) to be deposited in solid form; condense (vapour) into drops & so deposit. So **precipit**A·TION (esp., Meteorol., fall of rain, sleet, snow, or hail), **preci·pitat**OR[2], nn. [f. L *praecipitare* (as foll.), -ATE[3]]

preci·pitous, a. Of, like, a precipice; steep; (rare) = PRECIPITATE[2]. Hence **preci·pitous**LY[2] adv., **preci·pitous**NESS n. [f. obs. F *precipiteux* f. L PRAE(*ceps -cipitis* f. *caput* head) headlong, see -OUS]

précis (prĕ·sē), n. Summary, abstract. [F, = foll.]

precī·se (-s), a. Accurately expressed, definite, exact; punctilious, scrupulous in observance of rules &c.; *the p.* (exact, identical) *moment* &c. Hence **preci·se**NESS n. [f. F *précis, -ise,* f. L PRAE(*cīdere cis-* = *caedere* cut) cut short]

preci·sely, adv. In precise manner; (in emphatic or formal assent) quite so. [-LY[2]]

preci·sian (-zhn), n. One who is rigidly precise or punctilious, esp. in religious observance. Hence **preci·sian**ISM n. [-IAN]

precĭ·sion (-zhn), n. Accuracy; *arm of p.*, fire-arm fitted with sights or other mechanical aids. Hence **preci·sion**IST n. [f. L *praecisio* (as PRECISE, see -ION)]

preclu·de (prĭ-), v.t. Exclude, prevent, make impracticable, as *so as to p. all doubt.* So **preclu·**SIVE a. [f. L PRAE(*cludere clus-* = *claudere* shut)]

precō·cious (-shus), a. (Of plant) flowering or fruiting early; (of person) prematurely developed in some faculty; (of actions &c.) indicating such development. Hence or cogn. **preco·cious**LY[2] adv., **preco·cious**NESS, **precŏ·**CITY, nn. [f. L *praecox -cocis* f. PRAE(*coquere* cook) + -OUS]

prēcogni·tion, n. Antecedent knowledge; (Sc. Law) preliminary examination of witnesses &c., esp. in order to know whether there is ground for trial. [f. LL *praecognitio* f. PRAE(*cognoscere,* cf. RECOGNIZE), see -ION]

prēconcei·ve, v.t. Conceive beforehand, anticipate in thought. So **prēconce·ption** n. (esp. = *prejudice*). [PRE-]

prē·conize, v.t. Proclaim publicly; commend publicly; summon by name; (Rom. Cath., of pope) approve publicly the appointment of (bishop). So **preconiz**A·TION n. [f. med. L *praeconizare* (L *praeco -onis* herald, see -IZE)]

precur·sor (prĭ-), n. Forerunner, harbinger, esp. John the Baptist; one who precedes in office &c. [f. L *praecursor* f. PRAE(*currere curs-* run), see -OR[2]]

precur·sory, a. Preliminary, introductory, serving as harbinger (*of*). So **precur·**SIVE a. [f. L *praecursorius* (as prec.; see -ORY)]

preda·cious, a. (Of animals) naturally preying on others, predatory; pertaining to such animals, as *p. instincts.* So **predă·**CITY n. [as PREDATORY, see -ACIOUS]

prēda·te, v.t. Antedate. [PRE-]

prĕ·datory, a. Of, addicted to, plunder or robbery; (of animal) preying upon others. [f. L *praedatorius* (*praedari* plunder f. *praeda* booty, see -ORY)]

prē·decessor, n. Former holder of any office or position, as *my, William's, pp., his immediate p.*; thing to which another has succeeded, as *will share the fate of its p.*; forefather. [f. LL PRAE(*decessor,* see DECEASE, -OR[2])]

prede·lla, n. (Painting on vertical face of) altar-step; (painting, sculpture, on) raised shelf at back of altar. [It., = stool, prob. f. OHG *pret* board + *-ella* dim. suf.]

predestinār·ian (prĭ-), n. & a. (Holder of the doctrine) of predestination. [-ARIAN]

prede·stināte, v.t. (Of God) foreordain (person) to salvation or *to* (any fate), *to* (do); determine beforehand. So **prede·stin**ATE[2] (-*a*t) a. [f. L PRAE(*destinare* DESTINE), see -ATE[3]]

predestina·tion, n. God's appointment from eternity of some of mankind to salvation & eternal life; God's foreordaining of all that comes to pass; fate, destiny. [f. LL *praedestinatio* (as prec., see -ION)]

prede·stine (prĭ-), v.t. Determine beforehand, appoint as if by fate; (Theol.) = PREDESTINATE. [as PREDESTINATE]

prēdeter·mine, v.t. Decree beforehand, predestine, so **predeter·min**ATE[2] (-*a*t) a.; (of motive &c.) impel (person &c. *to* thing, *to* do) beforehand. Hence **predetermin**A·TION n. [f. LL PRAE(*determinare* DETERMINE)]

prē·dial, a. & n. Of land or farms; rural, agrarian; (of slaves) attached to the land; (n.) p. slave. [f. med. L *praedialis* (L *praedium* farm, see -AL)]

prĕ·dicable, a. & n. That may be predicated or affirmed, so **predica**BI·LITY n.; (n.) p. thing, esp. (pl.) Aristotle's classes of predicates viewed relatively to their subjects (viz. genus, definition, property, accident). [f. F *prédicable* (as PREDICATE[2], see -BLE)]

predĭ·cament (prĭ-), n. Thing predicated, esp. (pl.) Aristotle's ten categories, whence **prēdicame·nt**AL a.; unpleasant, trying, or dangerous situation. [f. LL *praedicamentum* (as foll., see -MENT)]

prĕ·dicant, a. & n. (Of religious order, esp. Dominicans) engaged in preaching; (n.) = PREDIKANT. [as foll., see -ANT]

prē·dicate[1] (-*at*), n. (Logic) what is predicated, what is affirmed or denied of the subject by means of the copula (e.g. *a fool* in *he is a fool*); (Gram.) what is said of the subject, including the copula (e.g. *is a fool* in prec. ex.); quality, attribute. [as foll., see -ATE[2]]

prē·dicāte[2], v.t. Assert, affirm, as true or existent, as *many truths may be predicated about humanity, we p. goodness or badness of a motive, p. of a motive that it is good or bad*; (Logic) assert (thing) about subject. So **predica·tion** n. [f. L PRAE(*dicare* declare) proclaim, see -ATE[3]]

predi·cative, a. Making a predication; (Gram., of adj. or n., opp. *attributive*) forming part or the whole of the predicate, as in 'This is *absurd*', cf. 'an *absurd* notion'. Hence **predi·cative**LY[2] adv. [as prec. see -IVE]

prē·dicatory, a. Of, given to, marked by, preaching. [f. LL *praedicatorius* (prec., -ORY)]

predi·ct (prĭ-), v.t. Foretell, prophesy, (thing, *that, who*, &c.). Hence or cogn. **predictabi·lity, predi·ction, predi·ctor**[2], nn., **predi·ctable, predi·ctive,** aa., **predi·ctive**LY[2] adv. [f. L PRAE(*dicere dict-* say])

prĕdika·nt (-ahnt), n. Minister of Dutch Protestant church, esp. in S. Africa. [Du., as PREDICANT]

prēdile·ction, n. Mental preference, partiality, (*for*). [f. F *prédilection* f. med. L PRAE(*diligere*), see DILIGENT & -ION]

prēdispo·se, v.t. Render liable, subject, or inclined (*to* feeling, disease, &c., *to* do). [PRE-]

prēdisposi·tion, n. State of mind or body favourable *to* (mercy, malaria, &c.). [PRE-]

predŏ·minate (prĭ-), v.i. Have or exert control (*over* person &c.), be superior; be the stronger or main element, preponderate, as *garden in which dahlias p.* Hence or cogn. **predo·minance** n., **predo·minant** a., **predo·minant**LY[2], **predo·minating**LY[2], advv. [f. med. L *PRAE(*dominare* DOMINATE)]

prē-ĕ·minent, a. Excelling others; distinguished beyond others in some quality. Hence or cogn. **pre-e·minence** n., **pre-e·minent**LY[2] adv. [f. L PRAE(*eminens* EMINENT)]

prē-e·mpt, v.t. Obtain by pre-emption; (U.S.) occupy (public land) so as to have right of pre-emption; (fig.) appropriate beforehand. [back formation f. foll.]

pre-e·mption (-shn), n. Purchase by one person &c. before opportunity is offered to others; right so to purchase. So **pre-e·mptive** a. [f. med. L PRAE(*emere empt-* buy), -ION]

preen, v.t. Trim (feathers) with beak; (of person) trim one*self*. [prob. var. of PRUNE[3], assoc. w. Sc. & obs. E *preen* prick, pin]

prĕ·face (-*as*), n., & v.t. & i. Introduction to book stating subject, scope, &c.; preliminary part of a speech; introduction to central part of eucharistic service; (v.t.) furnish (book &c.) with p., introduce (act, speech, *with*), as *prefaced his remarks with a snort*, (of event &c.) lead up to (another); (v.i.) make preliminary remarks. So **prefator·ial, pre·fatory,** aa. [f. F *préface* prob. f. med. L *prefatia* for L *praefatio* f. PRAE(*fari* speak), see -ION]

prē·fect, n. (Rom. Ant.) title of various officers, civil & military; chief administrative officer of French department; *p. of police*, head of Paris police; (in some public schools) senior pupil authorized to maintain discipline. So **prefe·ctoral, prefector·ial,** aa. [OF, f. L *praefectus* f. PRAE(*ficere fect-* =*facere* make) set over]

prē·fecture, n. (Period of) office, official residence, district under government, of a prefect. Hence **prefe·ctural** a. [f. L *praefectura* (as prec., see -URE)]

prefer·, v.t. (-rr-). Promote (person *to* office), whence **prefer·ment** n.; bring forward, submit, (statement, information, &c., *to* person in authority &c., *against* offender &c.); choose rather, like better, as *gentlemen p. blondes, p. water to wine, p. to leave it alone, p. that it should be left* (*than* is unidiomatic after *p.* unless *rather* is inserted, as *preferred to die rather than pay*), so **prĕ·ferable** a., **prĕ·ferably**[2] adv. [f. F *préférer*. f L PRAE(*ferre lat-* bear)]

prĕ·ference, n. Liking of one thing better than another (*of* A *to* or *over* B); thing one prefers; prior right esp. to payment of debts; *p. bond, share, stock*, (on which dividend is paid before any is paid on ordinary stock); favouring of one person or country before others in business relations, esp. favouring of a country by admitting its products at lower import duty. [f. F *préférence* f. med. L *praeferentia* (prec., -ENCE)]

prefere·ntial, a. Of, giving, receiving, preference; (of duties &c.) favouring particular countries, esp. favouring trade between Great Britain & her colonies, whence **prefere·ntialism, prefere·ntialist,** nn. Hence **prefere·ntial**LY[2] adv. [as prec. + -AL]

prefer·red (-erd), a. In vbl senses; *p. shares, stock*, &c., preference shares &c. [-ED[1]]

prefi·gure (-*ger*), v.t. Represent beforehand by figure or type; picture to oneself beforehand. Hence or cogn. **prefigūra·tion, prefi·gurement** (-*ger*-), nn., **prefi·gūrative** a. [f. LL PRAE(*figurare* FIGURE)]

prē·fix[1], n. Verbal element placed at beginning of word to qualify meaning or (in some languages) as inflexional formative; title placed before name, e.g. *Mr, Mrs, Sir, Dr.* [f. L PRAE(*figere* FIX)]

prefi·x[2] (prĭ-), v.t. Add (chapter, paragraph, &c., *to* book &c.) as introduction; join (word, verbal element) as prefix (*to* word), so **prefi·x**ION, **pre**FI·XTURE, nn. [f. OF PRE(*fixer* FIX[1])]

prēfor·m, v.t. Form beforehand. [PRE-]

prēforma·tion, n. Previous formation; (Biol.) *theory of p.* (that all parts of the perfect organism exist in the germ & are merely developed). [PRE-]

prefor·mative, a. & n. Forming beforehand; (syllable, letter) prefixed as formative element. [PRE-]

pre·gnable, a. Not impregnable. [ME & F *prenable*, see IMPREGNABLE]

pre·gnant, a. (Of woman or female animal) with child, gravid; teeming with ideas, imaginative, inventive; fruitful in results, big *with* (consequences &c.); (of words or acts) having a hidden meaning, significant, suggestive, whence **pre·gnant**LY[2] adv.; (Gram.) *p. construction* (in which more is implied than the words express). Hence **pre·gn**ANCY n. [f. L *praegnans -ntis* perh. f. PRAE- + *gna-* root of (*g*)*nasci* be born; but older L has *praegnas -atis*]

prehe·nsĭle, a. (zool.). (Of tail or limb) capable of grasping. Hence **prehensi·l**ITY n. [f. F *préhensile* f. L PRE(*hendere hens-* cogn. w. Gk *khandanō* grasp), see -ILE]

prehe·nsion, n. Grasping, seizing; mental apprehension. [f. L *prehensio* (prec., -ION)]

prēhisto·ric, a. Of the period antecedent to history. Hence **prehistŏ·r**ICALLY adv. [PRE-]

prehi·story, n. Prehistoric matters or times. [PRE-, after prec.]

prēju·dge, v.t. Pass judgement on (person) before trial or proper inquiry; form premature judgement upon (person, cause, action, &c.). So **prēju·dge**MENT, **prejudic**A·TION, nn. [f. F *préjuger* f. L PRAE(*judicare* JUDGE)]

prĕ·judĭce, n., & v.t. Preconceived opinion, bias, (*against, in favour of*, person or thing), as *divest your mind of p., has a p. against foreigners, has a p. in our favour, this is mere p.*; injury that results or may result from some action or judgement, as *to the p. of*; *without p.*, without detriment to existing right or claim; (v.t.) impair the validity of (right, claim, statement, &c.), cause (person) to have a p. (*against, in favour of*), esp. in p.p. [(vb f. F *préjudicier*) f. F *préjudice* f. L PRAE(*judicium* judgement f. *judex* JUDGE) preceding judgement, precedent, damage]

prĕjudi·cial (-shl), a. Causing prejudice, detrimental, (*to* rights, interests, &c.). Hence **prejudi·cial**LY[2] adv. [f. L as prec., see -AL]

prĕ·lacy, n. Office, rank, see, of a prelate; *the* prelates; church government by prelates (usu. hostile for EPISCOPACY). [f. AF *prelacie* f. med. L *praelatia* (as foll., see -ACY)]

prĕ·late (-*at*), n. High ecclesiastical dignitary, e.g. (arch)bishop, metropolitan, patriarch, (hist.) abbot or prior. Hence **prelă·t**IC(AL) aa., **prela·tical**LY[2] adv. [f. OF *prélat* f. L *praelatus* (as PREFER)]

prĕ·latess, n. Abbess, prioress; (facet.) prelate's wife. [-ESS[1]]

prĕ·latize, v.t. Bring (church) under prelatical government. [f. PRELATE + -IZE]

prĕ·lature, n. Office of prelate; *the* prelates. [f. F *prélature* f. med. L *praelatura* (as PRELATE, see -URE)]

prele·ct (prĭ-), v.i. Discourse, lecture, (*to* audience *on* subject, esp. in univv.). So **prele·ct**ION, **prele·ct**OR[2], nn. [f. L PRAE(*legere lect-* read)]

prēlība·tion, n. Foretaste (usu. fig.). [f. LL PRAE(*libatio* LIBATION)]

prelĭ·minary (prĭ-), a. & n. Introductory, preparatory; (n.) p. arrangement (usu. in pl.). Hence **preli·minari**LY[2] adv. [f. L PRAE- + *limen -minis* threshold, see -ARY[1]]

prĕ·lūde[1], n. Performance, action, event, condition, serving as introduction (*to* another); (Mus.) introductory movement esp. one preceding fugue or forming first piece of suite. Hence **prelu·di**AL a., **pre·lud**IZE(2) v.i. [f. F *prélude* f. LL *praeludium*, as foll.]

prĕ·lude[2] (*or* prĭlū·d), v.t. & i. Serve as prelude to, introduce, foreshadow; introduce with a prelude; be, give, a prelude *to*; (Mus.) play a prelude. So **prelu·s**ION (-zhn) n., **prelu·s**IVE (-s-) a. [f. L PRAE(*ludere lus-* play)]

prĕmature· (-tūr; *also* prĕ·m-), a. Occurring, done, before the usual or proper time, too early, hasty, as *p. decision, decay*. Hence or cogn. **premature·**LY[2] adv., **premature·**NESS, **prematūr·**ITY, nn. [f. L PRAE(*maturus* MATURE)]

premĕ·ditate (prĭ-), v.t. Think out, design, (action &c.) beforehand (esp. in p.p.). Hence or cogn. **preme·ditated**LY[2] adv., **premedit**A·TION n. [f. L PRAE(*meditari* MEDITATE)]

prĕ·mier (*or* prē-), a. & n. (Now chiefly slang) first in position, importance, order, or time, as *secured p. place* (in race); (n.) prime minister of Great Britain or British colony. Hence **pre·mier**SHIP n. [F, = first, f. L as PRIMARY]

premĭère· (-ār), n. First performance of play. [F, fem. adj. as prec.]

prĕ·mise[1], **-ss** (as below), n. (Logic, often *-ss*) previous statement from which another is inferred, esp. MAJOR[2], MINOR, *p.* in syllogism; (pl.) the aforesaid, the foregoing, esp. (Law) the aforesaid houses, lands, or tenements; (pl.) house, building, with grounds & appurtenances, as *to be* *drunk on the pp.* [f. F *prémisse* f. med. L *praemissa* (*propositio* proposition) set in front f. L PRAE(*mittere miss-* send)]

premi·se (prĭ-, -z), v.t. Say, write, (thing, *that*) by way of introduction. [f. prec.]

prē·mium, n. Reward, prize, (chiefly now in *put a p.* on, provide or act as incentive to, as *you, this, will put a p. on fraud*); amount to be paid in consideration of contract of insurance; sum additional to interest, wages, &c., bonus; fee for instruction in profession &c.; charge for changing one currency into another of greater value, agio; *at a p.*, at more than nominal value (cf. DISCOUNT¹), (fig.) in high esteem. [f. L *praemium* booty, reward, f. PRAE- + *emere* buy, take]

prēmoni·tion (-shn), n. Forewarning. So **premŏ·nitor**² n., **premo·nitorily**² adv., **premo·nitory** a. [f. obs. F *premonicion* f. LL *praemonitio* f. L PRAE(*monēre -it-* warn), -ION]

Premonstrate·nsian (prĭ-), a. & n. (Member) of order of regular canons founded at Prémontré in 1119, or of corresponding order of nuns. [f. med. L *Praemonstratensis* (*Praemonstratus* Prémontré, see -ESE) + -AN]

premor·se (prĭ-), a. (bot., entom.). With the end abruptly truncate. [f. L PRAE-(*mordēre mors-* bite) bite off in front]

pre·ntice, n., & v.t. (archaic). = APPRENTICE, esp. *p.* (tiro's) *hand*. Hence **pre·nticeship** n. (archaic). [aphetic]

preoccūpa·tion (prĭ-), n. Prepossession, prejudice; occupation of a place beforehand; occupation, business, that takes precedence of all others; mental absorption. [f. L *praeoccupatio* (foll., -ATION)]

preo·ccupy (prĭ-), v.t. Engage beforehand, engross, (mind &c.); (p.p., esp.) distrait, with thoughts elsewhere, whence **preo·ccupiedly**² adv.; appropriate beforehand. [f. L PRAE(*occupare* OCCUPY)]

prep, n. (school slang). Preparation. [abbr.]

prĕpara·tion, n. Preparing; (usu. pl.) thing(s) done to make ready (*for*); *make pp.*, prepare (*for*); (abbr. *prep*) p. of lessons as part of school routine; substance, e.g. food or medicine, specially prepared; (Mus.) preparing of a discord. [f. F *préparation* f. L *praeparationem* (as PREPARE, see -ION)]

prepă·rative (prĭ-), a. & n. Preparatory; (n.) p. act, (Mil., Naut.) signal on drum, bugle, &c., as order to make ready. Hence **prepa·ratively**² adv. [F (*-if, -ive*), f. med. L *praeparativus* (as PREPARE, see -IVE)]

prepă·ratory, a. & n. Serving to prepare, introductory (*to*); *p.* (*school*), where pupils are prepared for higher school; (quasi-adv.) *am packing it up p. to sending it by post*. Hence **prepa·ratorily**² adv. [f. med. L *praeparatorius* (as foll., see -ORY)]

prepare (prĭpār·), v.t. & i. Make (person, thing) ready (*for*); make ready (food, meal) for eating; make (person) mentally ready or fit (*for* news, *to* hear, &c.); get (lesson, speech, sermon) ready by previous study; get (person) ready by teaching (*for* college, examination, the army, &c.); make preparations (*for, to* do, &c.); *be prepared*, be ready or willing (*to* do); make (chemical product &c.) by regular process; (Mus.) lead up to (discord) by sounding the dissonant note in it as consonant note in preceding chord. [f. F *préparer* f. L PRAE(*parare* make ready)]

prēpay·, v.t. Pay (charge) beforehand; pay (postage of parcel), pay postage of (parcel), beforehand e.g. by affixing stamp. Hence **prepay·able** a., **prepay·ment** n. [PRE-]

prepe·nse (prĭ-), a. Deliberate, intentional, chiefly in *malice p.*, intention to injure, *of malice p.*, with intent to injure. Hence **prepe·nsely**² adv. [earlier *prepensed* p.p. of obs. *prepense* altered f. earlier *purpense* f. OF PUR(*penser*, see PENSIVE)]

prepo·nderate (prĭ-), v.i. Weigh more, be heavier; *p. over*, exceed in number, quantity, &c.; be of greater moral or intellectual weight; be the chief element, predominate; (of scale of balance) sink. So **prepo·nderance** n., **prepo·nderant** a., **prepo·nderantly**² adv. [f. L PRAE(*ponderare* PONDER), -ATE³]

prĕposi·tion (-shn), n. Indeclinable word serving to mark relation between the noun or pronoun it governs & another word (e.g. the italic wds in: found him *at* home, wait *in* the hall, what did you do it *for*?, the bed (that) he slept *on*, won *by* waiting, came *through* the roof, that is what I was thinking *of*). Hence **preposi·tional** a., **preposi·tionally**² adv. [f. L *praepositio* f. PRAE(*ponere posit-* place)]

prepŏ·sitive (prĭ-), a. (gram.). (Of word, particle, &c.) proper to be placed before or prefixed. [f. LL *praepositivus* (as prec., see -IVE)]

prepo·sitor. See PRAEPOSTOR.

prēposse·ss, v.t. Imbue, inspire, (person *with* notion, feeling, &c.); (of idea &c.) take possession of (person, usu. pass.); prejudice, usu. favourably, whence **preposse·ssing**² a., **preposse·ssingly**² adv., **preposse·ssingness**, **preposse·ssion**, nn. [PRE-]

prepo·sterous (prĭ-), a. Contrary to nature, reason, or common sense; perverse, foolish; absurd. Hence **prepo·sterously**² adv., **prepo·sterousness** n. [f. L PRAE(*posterus* coming after) reversed, absurd]

prepō·tent (prĭ-), a. Very powerful; more powerful than others; (Biol.) having stronger fertilizing influence or power of transmitting hereditary qualities. So **prepo·tence**, **prepo·tency**, nn. [f. L *praepotens* part. of PRAE(*posse* be able)]

prē-pre·ference, a. (Of shares, claims, &c.) ranking before preference shares &c. [PRE-]

prē·pūce, n. Foreskin, loose integument covering end of penis. So **prepū·tIAL** (-shl), a. [f. L PRAE(*putium* perh. = Gk *posthion* penis)]

Prē-Ră·phăēlīte, n. Artist who aims at producing work in the spirit that prevailed before the time of Raphael; *P. Brotherhood* (abbr. *P.R.B.*), group of English artists including Holman-Hunt, Millais, D. G. Rossetti. So **pre-Ra·phael** a., **Pre-Ra·phael(īt)ISM** n. [PRE- + *Raphael* + -ITE¹]

prērĕ·quisite, a. & n. (Thing) required as previous condition. [PRE-]

prerŏ·gative, n. & a. (Also *royal p.*) right of the sovereign, theoretically subject to no restriction; peculiar right or privilege, as *it is our p. to* (do), *we have the p. of* (doing), *the p. of* (right to show) *mercy*; natural or divinely-given advantage, privilege, or faculty, as *it is the p. of man to drink without thirst*; (pedantic) right of giving first vote and thus influencing those that follow; (Hist.) *p. court*, archbishop's court for probate of wills &c.; (adj.) privileged, enjoyed by privilege, (Rom. Hist.) having the right to vote first. [adj. f. L PRAE(*rogativus* f. *rogare* ask, see -IVE) asked first; n. f. F *prérogative* f. L *praerogativa* previous choice, prognostic, privilege, fem. adj. as n.]

prĕ·sage¹ (-ĭj), n. Omen, portent; presentiment, foreboding. Hence **presā·geFUL** a. [f. F *présage* f. L *praesagium* f. PRAE(*sagus* predicting)]

presa·ge²(prĭ-),v.t. Portend, foreshadow; give warning of (event &c.) by natural means, as *such ideas are held to p. insanity*; (of person) predict, (also) have presentiment of. [f. F *présager*, as prec.]

presbyŏ·pia (-s-, -z-), n. Form of long-sightedness incident to old age. Hence **presbyŏ·pIC** a. [f. Gk *presbus* old man + *ōps ōpos* eye]

pre·sbyter (-s-, -z-), n. (In early Church) one of several officers managing affairs of local church; (in Episcopal church) minister of second order, priest; (in Presbyterian church) elder. Hence or cogn. **presbў·terAL, presbytēr·IAL,** aa., **presby·terATE**¹ (-at), **pre·sbyterSHIP,** nn. [LL, f. Gk *presbuteros* elder]

Presbytēr·ian, a. & n. *P. church*, one governed by elders, all (including ministers) of equal rank; *United P. church*, that formed in 1847 by union of United Secession & Relief churches, now embodied in the United Free church of Scotland; (n.) adherent of P. system, member of P. church. Hence **Presbyter·ianISM** n., **Presbyter·ianIZE**(3) v.t. [f. L as foll. + -AN]

pre·sbytery, n. Eastern part of chancel beyond choir, sanctuary; body of presbyters, esp. court next above KIRK-session, district represented by this; (R.-C. Ch.) priest's house. [f. OF *presbiterie* f. LL f. Gk *presbuterion* (as PRESBYTER)]

prĕ·scient (-shĭ-), a. Having foreknowledge or foresight. Hence or cogn. **pre·sciENCE** n., **pre·scientLY**² adv. [F, f. L PRAE(*scire* know), see -ENT]

prescind (prĭsĭ·nd), v.t. & i. Cut off (part *from* whole) esp. prematurely or abruptly; *p. from*, leave out of consideration. [f. L PRAE(*scindere* cut)]

prescri·be (prĭ-), v.t. & i. Lay down or impose authoritatively, as *do not p. to me what I am to do or how to do it, the statutes p. the practice*; (Med.) advise use of (medicine &c., or abs.; *to* or *for* patient, *for* complaint; also fig.); assert prescriptive right or claim (*to, for,* thing). [f. L PRAE(*scribere script-* write) direct in writing, (Law) bring exception against]

prē·script, a. Ordinance, law, command. [as prec.]

prescri·ption, n. Prescribing; physician's (usu. written) direction for composition & use of medicine; (Law) (*positive*) *p.*, uninterrupted use or possession from time immemorial or for period fixed by law as giving title or right, such title or right, *negative p.*, limitation of the time within which action or claim can be raised; (fig.) ancient custom viewed as authoritative, claim founded on long use. [f. L *praescriptio* (as prec., see -ION)]

prescri·ptive, a. Prescribing; based on prescription, as *p. right*; prescribed by custom. Hence **prescri·ptiveLY**² adv. [f. LL *praescriptivus* (as PRESCRIBE, see -IVE)]

prĕ·sence (-z-), n. Being present, as *your p. is requested, in the p. of a large company*; REAL² *p.*; place where person is, as *admitted to, banished from, his p., in this* (*august* &c.) *p.*, in the p. of this (&c.) person; *the p.*, ceremonial attendance on person of high esp. royal rank, as *remained in, retired from, the p.*; carriage, bearing, as *a man of* (*a*) *noble p.*; *p. of mind*, calmness & self-command in sudden emergencies; *p.-chamber* (in which great personage receives guests &c.). [OF, f. L *praesentia* (as foll., see -ENCE)]

prĕ·sent¹ (-z-), a. Being in the place in question (chiefly pred.), as *no one else was p.* (*in* place, *at* proceedings &c.); being dealt with, discussed, &c., as *no excuse in the p. case, the p. volume* (the book you are reading or I am reviewing), *the p. writer* (I) *could not verify this*; *p. to* (felt, remembered, by) *the mind, the imagination*; (archaic) ready at hand, ready with assistance, as *a very p. help in trouble*; existing, occurring, being such, now, as *the p. Duke of York, in the p. fashion*; *the p. worth of* (sum that with compound interest dating from now will amount to) *£100 in 12 years*; (Gram.) *p. tense* (denoting action &c. now going on). [OF, f. L *praesens -ntis* part. of PRAE(*esse* be) be at hand]

pre·sent[2], **n.** *The* present time, the time now passing; *at p.*, now, as *do not want any more at p.*, *is at p. in Egypt*; *for the p.*, just now, as far as the p. is concerned, as *that will do for the p.*; =*p. tense*; (*know all men* &c.) *by these pp.*, by this document (now legal or facet.). [prec.]

pre·sent[3], **n.** Gift; *make a p. of*, present (thing *to* person). [OF (as prec.). orig. in phr. *mettre une chose en p. à quelqu'un*, put a thing into the presence of a person]

prese·nt[4] (prĭ-), v.t. & i., & n. Introduce (person *to* another); introduce (person) to sovereign at court; *p. oneself*, appear esp. as candidate for examination &c.; (of theatr. manager) cause (actor) to take part in play, produce (play); recommend (clergyman) to bishop for institution (*to* benefice); exhibit (thing *to* person &c.), as *p. a ragged appearance, presented its front to me*; show (quality &c.), as *cases that p. some difficulty*; (Mil.) hold (fire-arm) in position for taking aim, (also *p. arms*) hold fire-arm &c. in deferential position in saluting; (of idea &c.) offer, suggest it*self*; (Law) bring formally under notice, submit, (complaint,offence,*to* authority); aim (weapon *at*), hold out (weapon) in position for aiming (also abs. *p.!* as word of command; offer, give, (thing *to* person) as present; offer (compliments, regards, *to*); deliver (bill &c. *to* person &c.) for acceptance &c.; *p.* person *with* thing, p. it to him; (n.) act of aiming weapon esp. fire-arm, position of weapon when aimed, position of 'P. arms' in salute. [(n. f. vb) f. OF *presenter* f. L *praesentare* (as PRESENT[1])]

prese·ntable, a. Of decent appearance, fit to be introduced or go into company; suitable for presentation as a gift &c. Hence **presenta**BI·LITY n.,**prese·ntab**LY[2] adv. [-ABLE]

presenta·tion, n. Presenting; *p.* (gratis) *copy of book* &c.; exhibition, theatrical representation, &c.; formal introduction esp. at court; (Metaphys.) all the modification of consciousness directly involved in the knowing or being aware of an object in a single moment of thought, whence **presenta·tion**AL a. [f. LL *praesentatio* (as PRESENT[4], see -ATION)]

presenta·tionism, n. (metaphys.). Doctrine that in perception the mind has immediate cognition of the object. So **presenta·tion(al)**IST nn. [prec. + -ISM]

prese·ntative, a. (Of benefice) to which patron has right of presentation; serving to present an idea to the mind; (Metaphys.) of (the nature of) presentation. [-ATIVE]

prĕsentee·, n. Clergyman presented to benefice; person recommended for office; person presented at court; recipient of present. [AF (as PRESENT[4], see -EE)]

prese·ntient (prĭs-), a. Having a presentiment (*of* event &c. or abs.). [f. L PRAE(*sentiens* SENTIENT)]

prese·ntiment (prĭz-, -s-), n. Vague expectation, foreboding, (*of* coming event esp. evil). [f. obs. F PRE(SENTIMENT)]

prese·ntive (prĭz-), a. (Of word) presenting an object or conception directly to the mind (opp. to *symbolic*). [-IVE]

prĕ·sently, adv. Soon, after a short time; (archaic) as direct result, necessarily, as *it does not p. follow that he knew.* [PRESENT[1] + -LY[2]]

prese·ntment, n. (Law) statement on oath by jury of fact within their knowledge; formal complaint of offence made by parish authorities to bishop or archdeacon at his visitation; theatrical representation; delineation, portrait; statement, description, (*of*); act, mode, of presenting to the mind. [f. OF *presentement* (as PRESENT[4], see -MENT)]

prĕserva·tion (-z-), n. Preserving, being preserved, from injury or destruction; state of being well or ill preserved, as *in an excellent state of p.*, *in* (*a state of*) *fair p.* [f. F *préservation* f. med. L *praeservatio* (as PRESERVE, see -ATION)]

preser·vative (prĭz-), a. & n. (Drug, measure, &c.) tending to preserve; chemical substance for preserving perishable food-stuffs, whence **preser·vat**IZE(5) v.t. [f. F *préservatif* f. med. L *praeservativus* (as prec., see -ATIVE)]

preser·ve[1] (prĭz-), n. Jam; ground set apart for protection of game (often fig.); piece of water for fish; (pl.) goggles used as protection from dust &c. [f. foll.]

preser·ve[2] (prĭz-), v.t. Keep safe (*from* harm &c.); keep alive (name, memory, &c.); maintain (state of things); retain (quality, condition); prepare (fruit, meat, &c.) by boiling with sugar, pickling, &c., to prevent decomposition or fermentation; keep from decomposition by chemical treatment &c.; keep (game, game-run, river, or abs.) undisturbed for private use; *well preserved* (of elderly person), showing little sign of age. Hence **preser·v**ABLE a., **preser·v**ER[1] n. [f. F *préserver* f. LL PRAE(*servare* keep)]

presi·de (prĭz-), v.i. Occupy chair of authority at meeting of society or company (often *over*); sit at head of table; exercise control, sit or reign supreme, (often fig.); *p. at the organ, piano*, &c. act as organist &c. [f. F *présider* f. L PRAE(*sidēre* = *sedēre* sit)]

prĕ·sidency (-z-), n. Office of president; period of this; district administered by president, esp. division of E. India Company's territory (*Bengal, Madras, Bombay, P.*; not now official). [f. med. L *praesidentia* (prec., -ENCY)]

prĕ·sident (-z-), n. Head of temporary or permanent body of persons, presiding over their meetings & proceedings; head of some colleges; person presiding over meetings of academy, literary or scientific society, &c.; (U.S.) person presiding over proceedings of bank or company; head of advisory council, board, &c., as *P. of the Board of Agriculture, Trade,* &c.; *Lord P. of the Council,* English crown officer presiding at meetings of Privy Council; elected head of government in U.S. & other modern republics; (Hist.) governor of province, colony, &c. Hence or cogn. **pre·side·nt**IAL a., **preside·ntial**LY[2] adv., **pre·sident**SHIP n. [f. F *président* f. L as PRESIDE, see -ENT]

pre·sidentess, n. Female president; wife of president. [-ESS[1]]

presĭ·diary (prĭs-), a. Of, having, serving as, a garrison. [f. L *praesidiarius* (*praesidium* garrison, as PRESIDE, see -ARY[1])]

presĭ·dio (prĭs-), n. (In Spain & Sp. America) fort, garrison town. [Sp., as prec.]

press[1], n. Crowding; crowd (*of* people &c.); throng, crush, in battle; pressure, hurry, of affairs, as *the p. of modern life*; pressing, as *give it a slight p.*; (Naut.) *p. of sail, canvas* (as much as wind &c. will allow); kinds of instrument for compressing, flattening, or shaping, or for extracting juice &c.; (also *printing-p.*) machine for printing; printing-house or establishment; *the* art, practice, of printing; *in the p.*, being printed, *send, go, come, to* (*the*) *p.* (to be printed), *correct the p.* (errors in printing); *freedom of the p.*, right to print & publish anything without censorship; *the* newspapers generally, as *favourably noticed by the p.* (*have a good* &c. *press*, receive such notice); *the* GUTTER, YELLOW, *p.*; *p. campaign* or *stunt*, prosecution of political or other aims by newspaper letters & articles; (as name of newspaper) *Liverpool* &c. *P.*; large usu. shelved cupboard for clothes, books, &c., esp. in recess in wall; *p.-box*, shelter for newspaper reporter at cricket match &c.; *p.* CUTTING; *p.-gallery* (for reporters esp. in House of Commons); *pre·ssman*, journalist, operator of printing-p.; *p.-mark*, mark, number, in book showing its place in library. [ME & F *presse*, as foll.]

press[2], v.t. & i. Exert steady force against (thing in contact), as *let a heavy weight p. it, p. it under* or *with a stone, p. the two plates together*; *p. the button*, set electric machinery in motion, (fig.) take decisive initial step; (as sign of affection &c.) *he pressed my hand, pressed her to his side*; move (thing *up, down, against*, &c.) by pressing; exert pressure, bear with weight or force, (*on, against*, &c.); squeeze (juice &c. *out of, from*, &c.); compress, squeeze, (thing) to flatten or shape or smooth it, or to extract juice &c., as *pressed beef*; (of enemy, attacking force, &c.) bear heavily on, esp. in p.p. *hard pressed*; weigh down, oppress, (feelings, mind, spirits); (pass.) *am pressed for* (have barely enough) *space, time, funds*, &c.; produce strong mental or moral impression, esp. weigh heavily, (*up*)*on* (mind, person); be urgent, demand immediate action, as *time presses, nothing remains that presses*; urge, entreat, (person *to* do, person or without object *for* answer &c.); insist on strict interpretation of (words, metaphor); urge (course, opinion, *upon* person); force (offer, gift, &c. *upon*); (intr). crowd, throng, (*up, round*, &c.); hasten, urge one's way, *on, forward*, &c. [f. OF *presser* f. L *pressare* frequent. of *premere press-*)

press[3], v.t., & n. Force (man, or abs.) to serve in army or navy (also fig., esp. *p.* thing *into the service of*); take (horses, boats, &c.) for royal or public use; (n., Hist.) compulsory enlistment in navy or (less usu.) army; *p.-gang*, body of men employed to p. men. [earlier *prest* f. OF *prest* loan, advance, f. *prester* lend f. L PRAE(*stare* stand) vouch for, furnish]

pre·ssing, a. In vbl senses, esp.: urgent, as *p. need, danger*; importunate, persistent, as *a p. invitation, since you are so p.* Hence **pre·ssing**LY[2] adv. [PRESS[2] + -ING[2]]

pre·ssure (-sh*er*), n. Exertion of continuous force, force so exerted, upon or against a body by another in contact with it; amount of this, expressed by the weight upon a unit area; *atmospheric p.* (of the ATMOSPHERE; *high, low, p.*, local atmospheric condition sending barometer up, down); *blood-p.*, varying tension, now measured for diagnosis &c., of blood-vessels; affliction, oppression; trouble, embarrassment, as *financial p.*; urgency, as *wrote hastily & under p.*; constraining influence, as *p. must be brought to bear upon him*; *high p.*, (orig.) p. higher than atmospheric (now indefinite, used esp. of compound engines in which steam is used at different pp. in different cylinders, so *low p.*), (fig.) high degree of activity, speed, &c., as *working at high p., high-p. work.* [obs. F, f. L *pressura* (as PRESS[2], see -URE)]

Pre·ster John, n. Alleged Christian priest & king in Abyssinia or some eastern country in Middle Ages. [f. OF *prestre* (as PRESBYTER) *Jehan* priest John]

prestidi·gitator (-j-), n. Juggler, conjurer. So **prestidigita·tion** n. [f. F *prestidigitateur* (*preste*, as PRESTO + L *digitus* finger, see -OR[2])]

For other words in *pre-* see PRE-.

presti·ge (-ēzh, *or* prĕ·stij), n. Influence, reputation, derived from past achievements, associations, &c. [F, = illusion, glamour, f. L *praestigium* (for *-strig-*) f. PRAE(*stringere* bind) blindfold, dazzle]

presti·ssimo, a., adv., & n. (mus.). Very quick (piece, movement). [It., superl. as foll.]

pre·sto[1], a., adv., & n. (mus.). Quick (piece, movement). [It., f. LL *praestus* f. L *praesto* ready]

pre·sto[2], adv. & a. (In conjurer's formulae) quickly, as *hey p.*, *pass!*; (adj.) rapid, juggling. [=prec.]

presū·me (prĭz-), v.t. & i. Take the liberty, venture, (*to* do); assume, take for granted, as *I p. that he has seen them, I p. this decision to be final, you had better p. no such thing*, whence **presu·mABLE** a., **presu·mabLY**[2], **presu·mĕdLY**[2], advv.; *p.* (*up*)*on*, take advantage of, make unscrupulous use of, (person's good nature, one's acquaintance with him, &c.), whence **presu·mingLY**[2] adv. [f. L PRAE(*sumere sumpt-* take)]

presu·mption, n. Arrogance, assurance; taking for granted, thing taken for granted, as *this was a mere p.*; *the* (only natural) *p. is that he had lost it*; ground for presuming, as *there is a strong p. against its truth*; (Law) *p. of fact*, inference of fact from known facts, *p. of law*, (1) assumption of truth of thing until the contrary is proved, (2) inference established by law as universally applicable to certain circumstances. [f. OF *presumpcion* f. L *praesumptionem* (as prec., see -ION)]

presu·mptive, a. Giving grounds for presumption, as *p. evidence*, whence **presu·mptiveLY**[2] adv.; *heir p.* (whose right of inheritance is liable to be defeated by birth of nearer heir, cf. APPARENT) [f. F *présomptif* f. LL *praesumptivus* (as PRESUME, see -IVE)]

presu·mptuous, a. Unduly confident, arrogant, forward. Hence **presu·mptuousLY**[2] adv., **presu·mptuousNESS** n. [f. OF *presuntueux* f. LL *praesumptuosus* =L *praesumptiosus* (as PRESUME, see -IOUS)]

prēsuppo·se, v.t. Assume beforehand (thing, *that*); involve, imply, as *effects p. causes.* [f. F *présupposer* (see PRE- & SUPPOSE)]

prēsupposi·tion, n. Presupposing; thing assumed beforehand as basis of argument &c. [f. med. L PRAE(*suppositio* SUPPOSITION)]

prete·nce (prĭ-), n. Claim (*to* merit &c.); ostentation, display, as *devoid of all p.*; false profession of purpose, pretext, as *under the p. of helping, on the slightest p.*; pretending, makebelieve. [f. late AF *pretensse*, as foll.]

prete·nd, v.t. & i. Feign, give oneself out, (*to* be or do), as *does not p. to be a scholar*; make believe (*to* do, *that*) in play; profess falsely to have, as *you should p. illness*; allege falsely (*that*); venture, aspire, presume, (*to* do); lay claim *to* (right, title, &c.); *p. to*, try to win (person, person's hand) in marriage; *p. to*, profess to have (quality &c.). Hence **prete·ndedLY**[2] adv. [f. L PRAE(*tendere tent-* later *tens-* stretch)]

prete·nder, n. One who makes baseless pretensions (*to* title &c., or abs.); *Old, Young, P.*, son, grandson, of James II as claimants to British throne. Hence **prete·ndersHIP** n. [-ER[1]]

prete·nsion (-shn), n. Assertion of a claim (*to* thing or abs.); justifiable claim (*to* thing, *to* be or do), as *he has no pp. to the name, has some pp. to be chosen as the site, what p. has he?*; pretentiousness. [prob. f. med. L *praetensio, -tio*, (as PRETEND, see -ION)]

prete·ntious, a. (Of person, book, speech, &c.) making claim to great merit or importance; ostentatious. Hence **prete·ntiousLY**[2] adv., **prete·ntiousNESS** n. [f. F *prétentieux* f. L **praetentiosus* (as prec., see -IOUS)]

prēter-, pref. = L *praeter* past, beyond, in senses 'beyond, outside the range of, more than', as: *-ca·nine*, more than canine; *-hu·man*, beyond what is human, superhuman; *-na·tural*, outside the ordinary course of nature, (also) supernatural, whence *-na·turally* adv.; *-na·turalism*, system, doctrine, of the preternatural; *-se·nsual*, beyond the domain of the senses.

prĕ·terite, -it, a. & n. (Gram.) *p.* (*tense*), one expressing past action or state, *p.-present* (*tense*), one originally p. but now used as present (e.g. *can, may, shall*); (facet.) past, bygone, whence **pre·teriteNESS** n. [f. L *praeteritus* p.p. of *praeterire* pass (*ire it-* go, see prec.)]

prēteri·tion (-shn), n. Omission, disregard, (*of*); (Theol.) passing over of the non-elect. [f. LL *praeteritio* (as prec., see -ION)]

prētermi·t, v.t. (-tt-). Omit to mention (fact &c.); omit to do or perform, neglect; leave off (custom, continuous action) for a time; (improp.) leave off. So **preter·mi·ssION** n. [f. L *praetermittere* (*mittere miss-* let go, see PRETER-)]

prē·text[1], n. Ostensible reason, excuse; *on* or *under*, or *upon, the p. of* or *that*, professing as one's object &c. [f. L PRAE(*texere text-* weave)]

prete·xt[2] (prĭ-), v.t. Allege (thing, *that*) as pretext. [f. F *prétexter*, as prec.]

prē·tone, n. Syllable, vowel, preceding the stressed syllable. So **prētŏ·nIC** a. [PRE-]

pretor &c. See PRAETOR &c.

pre·ttifȳ, v.t. Make pretty, represent with finicking prettiness. [-FY]

pre·ttily, adv. In a way that pleases the eye, ear, or aesthetic sense, as *p. dressed*; (Nursery) *eat, ask, behave, p.* (in the approved manner). [f. PRETTY + -LY[2]]

pre·ttiness, n. Beauty of a dainty or childish kind; pretty thing, ornament, &c.; affected or trivial beauty of style in literature or art, so **pre·tty**ISM n. [-NESS]

pre·tty (prĭ-), a. & adv. (Of woman or child) beautiful in dainty or diminutive way; attractive to eye, ear, or aesthetic sense, as *p. cottage, song, scene, story*; *the p.*, fluted or cut part of wine-glass or tumbler, *as fill it up to the p.*; fine, good of its kind, as *has a p. wit, very p. sport*, (iron.) *a p. mess you have made*; (archaic) fine. stout, as *a p. fellow*; (archaic) considerable in amount or extent, as *earned a p. sum*; (ellipt.) *my p.* (one, child); (adv.) fairly, moderately, as *am p. well, find it p. difficult, that is p. much* (very nearly) *the same thing*; *pretty-pretty*, overdoing the p., aiming too much at prettiness, (n. pl.) *pretty-pretties*, ornaments, knick-knacks. Hence **pre·tty**ISH[1] a. [OE *prættig* (*prætt* trick, cf. Du. *part, pret*, Norw. *pretta*, see -Y[2])]

pre·tzel, b-, n. Crisp knot-shaped biscuit flavoured with salt, used esp. by Germans as relish with beer. [G]

preux chevalier (F), n. Gallant knight.

prevai·l (prĭ-), v.i. Gain the mastery, be victorious, (*against, over*); *p.* (*up*)*on*, persuade (*to* do); be the more usual or prominent, predominate; exist, occur, in general use or experience, be current, whence or cogn. **prevai·ling**LY[2], **prĕ·valent**LY[2], advv., **pre·val**ENCE n., **pre·val**ENT a. [f. L PRAE(*valēre* have power)]

prevă·ricate (prĭ-), v.i. Speak, act, evasively; quibble, equivocate. So **pre·varica**·TION, **preva·ricat**OR[2], nn. [f. L PRAE(*varicari* straddle f. *varicus* straddling f. *varus* bent) walk crookedly, deviate, practise collusion]

prevē·nient (-prĭ-), a. Preceding, previous; having in view the prevention (*of*); (Theol.) *p. grace* (preceding repentance & predisposing the heart to seek God). [as foll., see -ENT]

preve·nt (prĭ-), v.t. Hinder, stop, as *this may p. him from writing, p. his* (pop. *him*) *writing, wish to p. all dispute*; (archaic) meet, deal with, (wish, question, &c.) before it is expressed &c.; (Theol.) *God prevents* (goes before, guides) *us with His grace.* Hence or cogn. **preve·nt**ABLE, **preve·nt**IBLE, aa., **preve·nt**ION n. [f. L PRAE(*venire vent-* come) come before, hinder]

preve·nter, n. In vbl senses, also; (Naut.) rope, chain, bolt, &c., used to supplement another. [-ER[1]]

preve·ntive, a. & n. Serving to prevent, esp. (Med.) to keep off disease; *P.* (Coastguard) *Service*; (n.) p. agent, measure, drug, &c. Hence or cogn. **preve·nt**ATIVE a. & n., **preve·ntive**LY[2] adv. [-IVE]

prē·vious, a. & adv. Coming before in time or order; prior *to*; (slang) done or acting hastily, as *you have been a little too p.*, whence **pre·vious**NESS n.; (Parl.) *p. question*, question whether vote shall be taken on main question (put to avoid putting of main question); *P. Examination*, = LITTLE-*go*; (adv.) *had called p. to* (before) *writing*, &c. Hence **pre·vious**LY[2] adv. [f. L PRAE(*vius* f. *via* way) + -OUS]

previ·se (prĭvī·z), v.t. Foresee, forecast, (event &c. or abs.). So **previ·**SION (-zhn) n., **previ·sion**AL a., **previ·sional**LY[2] adv. [f. L PRAE(*vidēre vis-* see)]

prey[1] (prā), n. Animal hunted or killed by carnivorous animal for food (also fig.); *beast, bird, fish, of p.*, kinds that kill & devour other animals; (bibl). what one brings away safe from contest &c. (*Jer.* xxi. 9); person, thing, that falls a victim (*to* enemy, disease, fear, &c.). [f. OF *preie, proie*, f. L *praeda*]

prey[2] (prā), v.i. *P. upon*, seek, take, (animal &c.) as prey, plunder (persons); (of disease, emotion, &c.) exert baneful or wasteful influence *upon*. [f. OF *preer* f. LL *praedare* as prec.]

prī·apism, n. Licentiousness; (Path.) persistent erection of penis. [f. LL f. Gk *priapismos* (*Priapos*, god of procreation, see -ISM)]

price, n., & v.t. Money for which thing is bought or sold, as *what is the p. of this?, try our superb tea, p. 2s. per lb., offered at reduced pp.*; *p. current, p.-list*, list of current pp. of commodities; LONG[1], COST[1], *p.*; *above, beyond, without, p.*, so valuable that no p. can be stated; *set p. on* person's *head*, offer reward for his capture or death; (Betting) odds, as *the starting p. of a horse*; (fig.) what must be given, done, sacrificed, &c., to obtain a thing, as *must be done at any p.*; *every man has his p.* (can be won over by some inducement); *would not have it, do it, &c., at any p.*, on any terms, for any consideration; *what p. the Concert of Europe* &c.? (slang), taunting allusion to the failure of something vaunted; (archaic) preciousness, value; (v.t.) fix, inquire, the p. of (thing for sale), (fig.) estimate the value of. [(n.) f. OF *pris* f. L *pretium*; ME *pris* became *prise* to secure ī, and *price* to avoid z sound of *s* between vowels; (vb) earlier *prise* PRIZE[1]; *price, prize, praise*, are all variants of same wd]

priced (-ist), a. To which a price is assigned, esp. in comb., as *high, low, -p.*; *p. catalogue* &c. (in which prices are named). [-ED[1], [2]]

prī·celess, a. Invaluable; (slang) most amusing, incredibly absurd. Hence **pri·celess**NESS n. [-LESS]

prick[1], n. Pricking, puncture; (fig.) *pp.* (stinging reflections) *of conscience*; mark made by pricking; (archaic) goad for

For other words in *pre-* see PRE-

oxen, esp. fig. *kick against the pp.*, hurt oneself by useless resistance (*Acts* ix. 5); *p.-ears*, erect pointed ears of some dogs &c., conspicuous ears of person, esp. of Roundheads, *p.-eared*, having such ears. [OE *prica, -ce*, cf. Du. & Da. *prik*, Sw. *prick*, cogn. w. foll.]

prick², v.t. & i. Pierce slightly, make minute hole in; *p. a* or *the bladder* or *bubble*, show the emptiness of a person or thing that has passed for important; (fig.) cause sharp pain to, as *my conscience pricked me*; make a thrust (*at, into*, &c.); (archaic) spur, urge on, (horse), (intr.) advance on horseback; mark off (name &c. in list) with a prick, select (sheriff) thus; mark (pattern *off, out*) with dots; *p. in, out, off*, plant (seedlings &c.) in small holes pricked in earth; *p. up* one's *ears*, (of dog) erect the ears when on the alert, (fig., of person) become suddenly attentive. [late OE *prician*, cf. Du. *prikken*, Da. *prikke*]

pri·cker, n. In vbl senses, esp., pricking instrument, e.g. awl. [-ER¹]

pri·cket, n. Buck in second year, with straight unbranched horns; *p.'s sister*, female fallow deer in second year; spike to stick candle on. [prob. f. med. L *prikettus* f. PRICK, see -ET]

pri·ckle¹, n., & v.t. & i. Thorn-like process developed from, & capable of being peeled off with, epidermis of plant; (pop.) small thorn; hard-pointed spine of hedgehog &c.; (v.t. & i.) affect, be affected, with sensation as of pricks, whence **pri·ckl**ING¹ n., **pri·ckl**ING² a. [OE *pricel* f. stem of PRICK, cf. Du. *prikkel*]

pri·ckle², n. Kinds of wicker basket or measure. [?]

pri·ckly, a. Armed with prickles (esp. in names of plants & animals); tingling; *p. heat*, inflammation of sweat glands with eruption of vesicles & p. sensation, common in hot countries; *p. pear*, (p. plant bearing) pear-shaped edible fruit. Hence **pri·ckli**NESS n. [-Y²]

pride, n., & v. refl. Overweening opinion of one's own qualities, merits, &c., a deadly SIN, often personified, as *P. will have a fall*; arrogant bearing or conduct; *p. of place*, exalted position, consciousness of this, arrogance; (also *proper p.*) sense of what befits one's position, preventing one from doing unworthy thing, *false p.*, mistaken feeling of this kind; feeling of elation & pleasure, as *take a p. in*, be proud of (person, thing, do*ing*); object of this feeling, as *he is his mother's p.*, esp. in names of plants, as LONDON *p.*; (Herald.) *peacock in his p.* (with tail expanded and wings drooping); best condition, esp. *p. of* GREASE¹; *p. of the morning*, mist or shower at sunrise; (vb) *p.* one*self* (*up*)*on*, be proud of (thing, quality, do*ing*). Hence **pri·de**FUL (chiefly Sc.), **pri·de**LESS, aa., **pri·deful**LY² adv. [(vb) ME *prīden*, (n.) OE *prȳto, -tu, -te* (*prūt* PROUD]

prie-dieu (prē·dyer·), n. Kneeling-desk; (also *p. chair*) chair with tall sloping back for use in praying. [F, lit. pray God]

priest (prēst), n., & v.t. (Now usu. *clergyman*, exc. in official use) clergyman, esp. one above deacon & below bishop with authority to administer sacraments & pronounce absolution; (fig.) *p. of nature, science*, &c.; minister of the altar, esp. officiant at Eucharist; HIGH *p.*; official minister of non-Christian religion, whence **prie·st**ESS¹ n.; mallet used to kill fish when spent (chiefly in Ireland); *prie·stcraft*, ambitious or worldly policy of pp.; *p.'s hood, p.-in-the-pulpit*, wild arum; *p.-ridden*, held in subjection by pp.; *p. vicar*, minor canon in some cathedrals; (v.t.) make (person) a p. Hence **prie·st**HOOD, **prie·st**LING¹, nn., **prie·st**LESS, **prie·st**LIKE, aa. [(vb f. n.) OE *prēost*, ult. as PRESBYTER]

prie·stly, a. Of, like, befitting, a priest; (O. T. criticism) *p. code*, one of the constituent elements in the Hexateuch, *p. writer* (of this). Hence **prie·stli**NESS n. [-LY¹]

prig, n., & v.t. Precisian in speech or manners, conceited or didactic person, whence **pri·gg**ERY(2), **pri·ggish**NESS, **pri·gg**ISM, nn., **pri·gg**ISH¹ a., **pri·ggish**LY² adv.; (slang) thief; (v.t., slang) steal. [orig. cant, etym. dub.]

prim, a., & v.i. & t. (Of persons, manner, speech, &c.) formal, demure; (v.i.) assume p. air; (v.t.) form (face, lips, &c.) into p. expression. Hence **pri·m**LY² adv., **pri·m**NESS n. [f. 17th c., orig. cant]

pri·ma (prē-), a. First, chief; as: *p. buffa* (bŏŏ-), chief female comic singer or actress; *p. donna*, (pl. *-ma -nas, -me -ne* pron. prē·mā dŏ·nā), chief female singer in opera. [It., fem. adj.]

prī·macy, n. Office of a primate; pre-eminence. [f. OF *primacie* f. med. L *primatia* (as PRIMATE, see -ACY)]

prī·ma fă·cie (-shĭē), adv. & a. (Arising) at first sight, (based) on the first impression, as *has* p. f. *a good case, see a* p. f. *reason for it*. [L]

prī·mage¹, n. Percentage addition to freight, paid to owners or freighters of vessels. [med. L *primagium*, etym. dub.]

prī·mage², n. Amount of water carried off suspended in steam from boiler. [f. PRIME v. + -AGE]

prī·mal, a. Primitive, primeval; chief, fundamental. Hence **pri·mal**LY² adv. [f. med. L *primalis* (as PRIME a., see -AL)]

prī·mary, a. & n. Earliest, original; of the first rank in a series, not derived, as *the p. vowel sounds, p. meaning of a word*; of the first importance, chief; (Geol.) of the lowest series of strata; (Biol.) belonging to first stage of development; *p. amputation* (performed before inflammation supervenes); *p. education*, that which begins with the rudiments of knowledge, esp. that provided for children liable to compulsory attendance, so *p. school, scholar* (cf. SECONDARY); (Gram.) *p. tenses*, present, future, perfect, & future perfect, (cf. HISTORIC); *p. assembly, meeting* (for selection of candidates for election); *p.* COLOUR; *p. planets* (revolving directly round sun as centre); *p. battery* (in which current is produced); (n.) p. planet, meeting, &c. Hence **pri·mari**LY[2] adv. [f. L *primarius* (as PRIME a., see -ARY[1])]

prīma·te (-*at*), n. Archbishop; *p. of England*, archbishop of York, *p. of all England*, archbishop of Canterbury; (Zool.) sing. of foll. Hence **prima·t**IAL (-āshl) a. [f. LL *primas -atis* (as PRIME a.)]

prīmā·tēs, n. pl. (zool.; for sing., see prec.). Highest order of mammals, including man, monkeys, lemurs, & (in Linnaean order) bats. [as prec.]

prime[1], n. State of highest perfection, as *in the p. of life, manhood*, &c.; *the* best part (*of* thing); beginning, first age, of anything; a canonical hour of the divine office, appointed for first hour of day (i.e. 6 a.m. or sunrise), (archaic) this time; (archaic) GOLDEN number; prime number; (Chem.) single atom as unit in combination; a position in fencing. [partly abs. use of foll.; OE has *prīm*, the canonical hour, f. L *prima* (*hora*) first (hour)]

prime[2], a. Chief, most important, as *p. agent, motive*; first-rate (esp. of cattle & provisions), excellent, whence **pri·me**LY[2] adv., **pri·me**NESS n.; primary, fundamental; (Arith., of a number) having no integral factors except itself and unity (e.g. 2, 3, 5, 7, 11), (of numbers) having no common measure but unity; *p.* COST[1], MOVER; *p. vertical* (*circle*), great circle of the heavens passing through E. & W. points of horizon & through zenith, where it cuts meridian at right angles; *p. minister*, principal minister of any sovereign or State (now official title of first minister of State in Great Britain). [f. L *primus* first]

prime[3], v.t. & i. (Hist.) supply (fire-arm, or abs.) with gunpowder for firing charge; wet (pump) to make it start working; equip (person *with* information &c.); fill (person *with* liquor); cover (wood &c.) with first coat of paint or with oil &c. to prevent paint from being absorbed; (of engine boiler) let water pass with steam into cylinder in form of spray. [?]

prĭ·mer[1], n. Elementary school-book for teaching children to read (-ĭ-); small introductory book (-ī-), as *P. of Evolution, Latin P.*; (Hist.) prayer-book for use of laity esp. before Reformation (-ĭ-); *great, long, p.*, sizes of TYPE (-ĭ-). [f. med. L *primarius* adj. (as PRIME[2], see -ER[2](2)]

prī·mer[2], n. In vbl senses of PRIME[3], esp. cap, cylinder, &c., used to ignite powder of cartridge &c. [-ER[1]]

primē̆r·o, n. (hist.). Gambling card-game fashionable in 16th & 17th cc. [f. Sp. *primera* fem. of *primero*, as PRIMARY]

primeur (prēmer·), n. First-fruits; fruit &c. before its season; early news. [F; affected by E journalists]

primē·val, -aeval, a. Of the first age of the world; ancient, primitive. Hence **prime·val**LY[2] adv. [f. L *primaevus* (*primus* first + *aevum* age) + -AL]

prī·ming[1], n. In vbl senses of PRIME[3]; also or esp.: gunpowder placed in pan of fire-arm; train of powder connecting fuse with charge in blasting &c.; mixture used by painters for preparatory coat; preparation of sugar added to beer; hasty imparting of knowledge, cramming. [-ING[1]]

prī·ming[2], n. Acceleration of the tides taking place from neap to spring tides (cf. LAG[1]). [f. rare vb *prime* f. PRIME a.]

prīmi·parous, a. Bearing child for the first time. [f. L *primipara* p. woman (also used in E) f. *primus* first + *parere* bring forth]

pri·mitive, a. & n. Early, ancient, as *the P. Church* (Christian Church in its earliest times); old-fashioned, simple, rude; original, primary; (Gram., of words) radical, not derivative; (Math., of line, figure, &c.) from which another is derived, from which some construction begins, &c.; (of colours) primary; (Geol.) of the earliest period; (Biol.) appearing in earliest or very early stage of growth &c.; *P. Methodist Connexion*, society of Methodists founded 1810 by Hugh Bourne by secession from main body, *P. Methodist, Methodism*, member, principles, of this; (n.) painter of period before Renascence, picture by such painter, p. word, line, &c., P. Methodist. Hence **pri·mitive**LY[2] adv., **pri·mitive**NESS n. [ME & F *primitif* f. L *primitivus* (as PRIME a.)]

pri·mo[1] (-ē-), n. (mus.). First or principal part in duet &c. [It.]

prī·mo[2], adv. *P., secundo, tertio*, in the first, second, third, place (written 1°, 2°, 3°). [L]

prīmogĕ·nitor, n. Earliest ancestor; (loosely) ancestor. [med. L, f. L *primo* (at) first + *genitor* begetter (*gignere genit-* bring forth, see -OR[2]), after L *primogenitus* first-born]

prīmogĕ·niture, n. Fact of being the first-born of the children of the same parents; (*right of*) *p.*, right of succession belonging to the first-born, esp. feudal rule by which whole real estate of intestate passes to eldest son. So **primoge·nit**AL, **primoge·nit**ARY[1], aa. [f. med. L *primogenitura* (as prec., see -URE)]

prīmor·dial, a. Existing at or from the beginning, primeval; original, fundamental. Hence **primordia·l**ITY n., **primor·dial**LY[2] adv. [f. LL *primordialis* (L *primordium* f. *primus* first + *ordiri* begin, see -AL)]

pri·mrose (-z), n. Plant bearing pale yellow flowers in early spring; flower of this; (attrib.) of the colour of this flower; *the p. path*, the pursuit of pleasure (w. ref. to *Haml.* I. iii. 50); *P. Day, League*, anniversary of the death (Apr. 19th, 1881) of, Conservative association formed in memory of, Benjamin Disraeli Earl of Beaconsfield, *P. dame, knight, habitation*, (of the P. League); *p. peerless*, two-flowered narcissus, (formerly) any species of narcissus. Hence **pri·mrosy**[2] a. [late ME *primerose* f. med. L *prima rosa* lit. first rose, sense unexpl.]

pri·mūla, n. Kind of herbaceous perennial with yellow, white, pink, or purple flowers. [med. L, fem. adj. as n., dim. as PRIME[2]]

pri·mum mō·bĭlĕ, n. Outermost sphere added in Middle Ages to Ptolemaic system, supposed to revolve round earth in 24 hours carrying with it the contained spheres; (fig.) prime source of motion or action. [med. L, lit. first moving thing]

pri·mus[1], a. & n. (In boys' school) eldest (or of longest standing) of the name, as *Jones p.* (usu. written *Jones* i.; similarly *secundus* ii., *tertius* iii., *quartus* iv., *quintus* v., *sextus* vi., *septimus* vii., *octā·vus* viii., *nōnus* ix., *dĕ·cimus* x.); (L) *p. inter pār·ēs*, first among equals, senior or spokesman of a board of colleagues; (n.) presiding bishop in Scottish Episcopal Church. [L, = first]

pri·mus[2], n. Kind of stove burning vaporized oil for cooking &c. [trade name]

prince, n. (Now rhet.) sovereign ruler; *P. of Peace*, Christ; *p. of darkness, the air, the world*, &c., Satan; ruler of small State, actually or nominally feudatory to king or emperor; male member of royal family, esp. (in Great Britain) son or grandson of king or queen (also *p. of the blood*); *P. of Wales*, heir apparent to British throne (*P. o. W.'s feathers*, triple ostrich plume); *P. Consort*, husband of reigning female sovereign being himself a p.; *P. of Denmark*, Hamlet (*Hamlet without the P. of D.*, thing robbed of its essence); (as English rendering of foreign titles) noble usu. ranking next below duke; (as courtesy title in some connexions) duke, marquis, earl; (title of cardinal) *p. of the (Holy Roman) Church*; (fig.) chief. greatest, (*of* novelists, liars, &c.); *p. bishop*, bishop who is also a p.; *P. Regent*, p. who acts as regent, e.g. George (afterwards IV); *p. royal*, eldest son of reigning monarch; *P. Rupert's drops*, pear-shaped lumps of glass bursting to pieces when thin ends are broken off; *p.'s feather*, kinds of plant, esp. tall plant with feathery spikes of small red flowers; *p.'s metal*, alloy of copper & zinc. Hence **pri·ncedom**, **pri·ncekin**, **pri·ncelet**, **pri·nceling**[1](2), **pri·nceship**, nn., **pri·ncelike** a. [F, f. L *princeps -cipis* first, prince, (*primus* first + *-cipere* = *capere* take)]

pri·ncely, a. (Worthy) of a prince; sumptuous, splendid. Hence **pri·nceliness** n. [-LY[1]]

pri·ncess (*or* -ĕ·s *exc. when followed by name*), n. (Archaic) queen; wife of prince; (also *p. of the blood*) daughter, granddaughter, of sovereign; *p. royal*, (title conferrable on) sovereign's eldest daughter; *P. Regent*, p. acting as regent, (also) wife of prince regent; *p. dress*, lady's robe of which the lengths of bodice & skirt are cut in one piece. Hence **pri·ncessship** n. [ME & F *princesse* (as PRINCE, see -ESS[1])]

pri·ncipal, a. & n. First in rank or importance, chief, as *their p. food is potatoes, the p. town of the district, the p. persons concerned*; main, leading, as *a p. cause of his failure*; (of money) constituting the original sum invested or lent; (Gram.) *p. sentence, clause*, one to which another is subordinate, *p. parts* of verb, those from which the others can be derived; (n.) head, ruler, superior; head of some colleges (*lady p.*, female head), whence **pri·ncipalship** n.; person for whom another acts as agent &c., as *I must consult my p.*; person directly responsible for crime, either (*p. in the first degree*) as actual perpetrator or (*p. in the second degree*) as aiding; person for whom another is surety; combatant in duel; any of the main rafters on which rest the purlins that support the common rafters; capital sum as distinguished from interest or from income; an organ-stop. [f. L *principalis* adj. (as PRINCE, see -AL)]

principa·lity, n. Government of a prince; State ruled by a prince; *the P.*, Wales; (pl.) an ORDER[1]1 of angels. [f. OF *principalite* f. LL *principalitatem* (as prec., see -TY)]

pri·ncipally, adv. For the most part, chiefly. [-LY[2]]

pri·ncipate (-at), n. (Rom. hist.) rule of early emperors while some republican forms were retained; State ruled by a prince. [f. L *principatus* (as PRINCE, see -ATE[1])]

pri·nciple, n. Fundamental source, primary element, as *held water to be the first p. of all things*; fundamental truth as basis of reasoning &c., as (*first*) *pp. of political economy*; (Physics) general law (often with discoverer's name, as *Pascal's p.*); general law as guide to action, as *moral, conservative, pp., a dangeraus p.*, whence **-principled**[2] a.; (pl. & collect. sing.) personal code of right conduct, as *a man of high p., has ability but no pp., p. is everything*; *on p.*, from settled moral motive, as *I refuse on p.* (not from selfish motive &c.); law of nature seen in working of machine &c., as *in all these instruments the p. is the same*; (Chem.) constituent of a substance, esp. one giving rise to some quality &c., as *bitter, colouring, p.* [f. L *principium* beginning, as PRINCE]

prink, v.t. & i. Make (one*self* &c.) spruce; dress one*self up*; (of bird) trim (feathers); dress oneself up. [cogn. w. PRANK[2]]

print[1], n. Indentation in surface preserving the form left by pressure of some body, as *finger-p., footp.*, whence **pri·nt**LESS a.; printed cotton fabric, as (attrib.) *p. dress*; language embodied in printed form, printed lettering, as *large, small, clear, p.*; state of being printed; *book is in p.*, (1) in printed form, (2) on sale, not *out of p.* (sold out); (of writer) *rush into p.*, publish book, write to newspaper &c., on insufficient grounds; (chiefly U.S.) printed publication, esp. newspaper; picture, design, printed from block or plate; (Photog.) picture produced from negative; *p. hand, letters* (imitating p.); *p.-seller*, dealer in engravings &c.; *p.-shop*, his shop; *p.-works*, factory where cotton fabrics are printed. [ME *prent* f. OF *priente, -nt*, p.p. of *preindre* press f. L *premere*]

print[2], v.t. Impress, stamp, (surface, e.g. pat of butter, *with* seal, die, &c.; a mark or figure *on, in*, yielding or other surface); (fig.) impress (idea, scene, &c., *on* mind, memory); produce (book, picture, &c., or abs.) by applying inked types, blocks, or plates, to paper, vellum, &c.; (of author or editor) cause (book, MS.) to be so printed; express, publish, in print, as *not bound to p. every opinion you hold*; write (words, or abs.) in imitation of typography; mark (textile fabric) with decorative design in colours; transfer (coloured design) from paper &c. to unglazed surface of pottery; (Phot., also *p. out, off*) produce (picture) by transmission of light through negative. Hence **pri·nt**ABLE a. [ME *prenten*, prob. f. prec.]

pri·nter, n. In vbl senses, esp.: one who prints books; owner of printing business; printing instrument; *Printers' Bible* (with *Pp.* for *Princes*, Ps. cxix. 161); *p.'s* DEVIL[1]; *p.'s mark* (device, trade-mark); *p.'s pie*, =PIE[3] n. [-ER[1]]

pri·nting, n. In vbl senses; *p.-ink, p.-press*, (for p. on paper &c. from types &c.). [-ING[1]]

pri·or[1], n. Superior officer of religious house or order, (in abbey) officer next under abbot, so **pri·or**ESS[1] n.; (Hist.) chief magistrate in some Italian republics. Hence or cogn. **pri·or**ATE[1](1), **pri·or**SHIP, nn. [OE as foll.]

pri·or[2], a. & adv. Earlier; antecedent in time, order, or importance, (*to*); (adv.) *existing p. to his appointment*, &c. So **priŏ·r**ITY n. [L, f. OL *pri* before]

pri·ory, n. Monastery, nunnery, governed by prior(ess); *alien p., p. alien*, (dependent on abbey in foreign country). [f. AF *priorie* f. med. L *prioria* (as prec., see -Y[1])]

prise. See PRIZE[3].

pri·sm (-zm), n. Solid figure whose two ends are similar, equal, & parallel rectilineal figures, & whose sides are parallelograms; transparent body of this form, usu. triangular, with refracting surfaces at acute angle with each other; (loosely) spectrum produced by refraction through p., (pl.) prismatic colours; PRUNE[1]*s & p.* Hence **pri·sm**AL a. [f. LL f. Gk *prisma -matos* thing sawn (*prizō* saw, see -M)]

prismă·tic, a. Of, like, a prism; *p. powder*, gunpowder whose grains are hexagonal prisms; (of colours) formed, distributed, &c., by transparent prism, (also) brilliant, so **pri·smy**[2] a.; *the p. colours*, seven into which ray of light is separated by prism. Hence **prisma·ti**CALLY adv. [as prec., see -IC]

pri·smoid, n. Body like prism, with similar but unequal parallel polygonal ends. Hence **prismoi·d**AL a. [-OID]

pri·son (-zn), n., & v.t. Place in which person is kept in captivity, esp. building to which person is legally committed while awaiting trial or for punishment; custody, confinement, as *lie, put* (person), *in p.*; *p.-bird*, = GAOL-bird; *p.-breaking*, breaking out of lawfully confined person from p., so *-breaker*; *p. editor*, editor of newspaper who takes legal responsibility for its contents & serves terms of imprisonment entailed by conviction; *p.-house* (usu. rhet.), p.; (v.t., poet., rhet.) imprison. [(vb f. n.) ME & OF *prisun, -on*, f. L *prensionem* (*pre(he)ndere prens-* seize, see -ION, -SON)]

pri·soner (-zn*er*), n. Person kept in prison; *p. at the bar*, person in custody on criminal charge & on trial; *p. of State, State p.*, (confined for political reasons); (also *p. of war*) one who has been captured in war; *take* (person) *p.*, seize & hold as p.; (fig.) *am a p.* (confined by illness &c.) *to my room* or *chair, made her hand a p.* (secured it); *prisoners' bars, base*, game played by two parties of boys &c., each occupying distinct base or home. [f. F *prisonnier*, as prec., see -ER[2](2)]

pri·stine, a. Ancient, primitive, good old. [f. L *pristinus*, cf. *priscus* ancient, *primus* first]

prĭ·thee (-ĭ), int. (archaic). Pray, please, as *tell me, p.* [=(I) pray thee]

prī·vacy, n. Being withdrawn from society or public interest, as *lived in absolute p.*, *must disturb your p.*; avoidance of publicity, as *in such matters p. is impossible.* [PRIVATE, -ACY]

privat-docent, -zent, (prēvah·t dōtsĕ·nt), n. (In German univv.) private teacher or lecturer recognized by university but not on salaried staff. [G]

prī·vate (-ĭt), a. & n. (Of person) not holding public office or official position; *p.* (*soldier*), ordinary soldier without rank or distinction; *p. member* of House of Commons (not member of Ministry); kept, removed, from public knowledge, as *the matter was kept p., had p. reasons*; not open to the public, as *p. door, news, came through p. channels, p. boarding-house, carriage, hotel, theatricals, p. view* (of exhibition of pictures esp. before it is opened to the public); *p. house*, dwelling-house of p. person (opp. to his shop or office, to public house, or to public building); *p. parts*, genitals (*p.-protector*, guard worn at cricket &c.); *p. school* (carried on for owner's profit, cf. PUBLIC; *p. schoolmaster*, of or in this); one's own, as *my p. goods, property*; individual, personal, not affecting the community, as *motives of p. malice*; (Parl.) *p. bill, act* (affecting individual or corporation only); confidential, as *asked for some p. conversation*; *this is for your p. ear* (confidential); (of place) retired, secluded; (archaic, of person) given to retirement; *in p.*, privately, in p. company or life; (n. pl.) = *p. parts*. Hence **pri·vate**LY[2] adv. [f. L *privatus*, orig. p.p. of *privare* deprive]

prīvateer·, n. Armed vessel owned & officered by private persons holding commission from government (*letters of* MARQUE) & authorized to use it against hostile nation esp. in capture of merchant shipping, whence **privateer**·ING[1](1) n.; commander, (pl.) crew, of this. [f. prec. + -EER, prob. after *volunteer*]

prīva·tion, n. Loss, absence, (*of* quality), as *cold is the p. of heat*; want of the comforts or necessaries of life, as *died of p., suffered many pp.* [F, f. L *privationem* (PRIVATE, -ATION)]

pri·vative, a. Consisting in, marked by, the loss or removal or absence of some quality or attribute, as *cold is merely p.* (cf. prec.); (of terms) denoting privation or absence of quality &c.; (Gram., of particles &c.) expressing privation, as (Gk Gram.) *alpha p.* (*a-* = not-). Hence **pri·vative**LY[2] adv. [f. L *privativus* (as PRIVATE, see -IVE)]

pri·vet, n. Bushy evergreen shrub with small white flowers & small shining black berries, much used for hedges; *p.-hawk*, large species of moth depositing eggs on p. [?]

pri·vilege (-ĭj), n., & v.t. Right, advantage, immunity, belonging to person, class, or office (*p. of Parliament*, those of either House or its members; *breach of p.*, esp., infringement of any of these); special advantage or benefit, as *to converse with him was a p.*; *p.* (BENEFIT[1]) *of clergy*; *bill of p.*, petition of peer demanding to be tried by his peers; *writ of p.*, writ to deliver privileged person from custody when arrested in civil suit; monopoly, patent, granted to individual, corporation, &c.; *p. cab* (admitted to stand for hire in private places esp. railway station); (v.t.) invest with p., allow (person *to* do) as p., exempt (person *from* burden &c.). Hence **pri·vileg**ED[1] a. [(vb f. F *privilégier* f. med. L *privilegiare*) f. L *privilegium* bill, law, affecting an individual (*privus* private + *lex legis* law)]

pri·vity, n. (Law) any relation between two parties that is recognized by law, e.g. that of blood, lease, service; being privy (*to* designs &c.). [f. OF *priveté* f. L *privus* private, see -TY]

pri·vy, a. & (archaic exc. in law) n. (Of things, places, &c.) hidden, secluded; *p. parts*, external organs of sex; (of action) secret, whence **pri·vi**LY[2] adv.; *p. to*, in the secret of (person's designs &c.); *P. Council*, sovereign's private counsellors, (in Great Britain) body of advisers chosen by sovereign (now chiefly as personal dignity, most functions being performed by Cabinet, committees, &c.) together with princes of blood, archbishops, &c.; *p. counsellor, -cillor*, private advisor, esp. (abbr. *P.C.*) member of P. Council; *p. purse*, allowance from public revenue for monarch's private expenses, keeper of this; *p. seal*, seal affixed to documents that are afterwards to pass, or that do not require, the Great Seal, *Lord* (keeper of the) *P. Seal*; (n.) private place of ease, latrine, (Law) person having a part or interest in any action, matter, or thing. [f. F *privé* PRIVATE]

prize[1], n., & v.t. Reward given as symbol of victory or superiority to students in school or college who excels in attainments, to competitor in athletic contest, to exhibitor of best specimen of manufactured products, works of art, &c., in exhibition; (fig.) anything striven for or worth striving for, as *many pp. in the Church, missed all the great pp. of life*; money or money's worth offered for competition by chance, in lottery, &c.; (attrib.) *p. ox, poem*, &c. (to which p. is adjudged in show, competition, &c.); *p. fellowship* (given as reward for eminence in examination), *p. fellow*, holder of this; *p.-fight*, boxing-match for money, so *-fighter, -fighting*, nn.; *pri·zeman*, winner of (often specified) p., as *Smith's prizeman*, winner of Smith's P.; *p.-ring*, enclosed area (now usu. square) for, (fig.) practice of, p.-fighting; (v.t.) value highly, as *we p. liberty more than life*. Hence **pri·ze**LESS a. [(n.) differentiation of PRICE; (vb) f. OF *prisier, preisier*, PRAISE]

prize[2], n., & v.t. Ship, property, captured at sea in virtue of rights of war; *p.-court*, department of admiralty court concerned with pp.; *p.-money* (realized by sale of p.); *make p. of* (cargo, ship, &c.), seize thus; *become* (*lawful* &c.) *p.*, be thus seized; (fig.) find or windfall (*see what a p. I have found!*); (v.t.) make p. of. [(vb f. n.) f. F *prise* taking, capture, f. Rom. *prensa* f. L *pre(he)ndere -hens-* seize]

prize[3], **-se**, v.t., & n. Force (lid &c. *up, out*, box &c. *open*) by leverage; (n.) leverage, purchase. [(vb f. n.) as prec.]

pro[1], prep. *P. formā* adv. & a., (done) for form's sake; *p. hăc vĭcĕ*, for this occasion only; *p. rātā* adv. & a., proportional(ly); *p. rē nātā* adv. & a., for an occasion as it arises, as *a meeting held p. r. n., a p. r. n. meeting*; *p. tănto*, so far, to that extent; *p. te·mporĕ* adv. & a. (abbr. *pro tem.*), for the time, as *made secretary pro tem., the pro tem. secretary*. [L]

pro[2], n. (pl. *pros*). Colloq. abbr. of PROFESSIONAL.

pro-[1], pref. (before vowel somet. in earlier form *prod-*) = L *pro* in front of, for, on behalf of, instead of, on account of. As living E pref. (1) in sense 'substitute(d) for', as *-cathe·dral* a. & n., (church) used as substitute for cathedral, *-pro·ctor*, assistant or deputy proctor in univv., *-re·ctor*, vice-rector in univv. &c.; *-leg*, fleshy abdominal limb of larvae of some insects, e.g. caterpillars. (2) in sense '(person) favouring or siding with' (cf. ANTI-) as *-Boer* a. & n., *-British, -educational, -negro* a. & n., *-papist* a. & n., *-slavery, -tariff-reform.*

pro-[2], pref. = Gk *pro* before (in time, place, order, &c.) in wds f. Gk & in mod. scientific wds.

prō·a, n. Malay boat, esp. a type of sailing boat. [f. Malay *pra(h)u*, also used in E]

pro & con, adv. & n. (Of arguments or reasons) for & against, on both sides; *pros & cons*, reasons for & against. [f. L *pro et contra*]

probabi·liorism, n. (R.C. casuistry). Doctrine that the side on which evidence preponderates ought to be followed (cf. foll.). So **probabi·liorIST** n. [f. L *probabilior* more PROBABLE- + ISM]

prŏ·babilism, n. Doctrine that where authorities differ any course may be followed for which recognized doctor of the Church can be cited (cf. prec.); theory that there is no certain knowledge, but may be grounds of belief sufficient for practical life. So **pro·babilIST** n. [as PROBABLE + -ISM]

probabi·lity, n. Quality of being probable; *in all p.*, most likely; *there is no p.* (likelihood) *of his coming*; (most) probable event, as *what are the pp.?, the p. is that he will come*; (Math.) likelihood of an event, measured by the ratio of the favourable cases to the whole number of cases possible, as *from a bag containing 3 red balls & 7 white the p. of a red ball's being drawn first is 3/10*. [f. F *probabilité* f. L *probabilitatem* (as foll., see -TY)]

prŏ·bable, a. That may be expected to happen or prove true, likely, as *reckon the p. cost, it is p. that he forgot, gives a p. account of the matter.* Hence **pro·babLY**[2] adv. [f. L *probabilis* (*probare* PROVE, see -BLE)]

prō·bang, n. Surgeon's strip of whalebone with sponge, button, &c., at end for introducing into throat. [altered f. inventor's wd *provang* (etym. dub.), perh. on *probe*]

prō·bate (-*at*), n. Official proving of will; verified copy of will with certificate as handed to executors; *p. duty*, tax on personal property of deceased testator, now merged in estate duty. [f. L *probatum* neut. p.p. of *probare* PROVE]

proba·tion, n. Testing of conduct or character of person esp. of candidate for membership in religious body &c. (*on p.*, undergoing it before full admission &c.); moral trial or discipline; system of releasing young criminals esp. first offenders on suspended sentence during good behaviour under supervision of person (*p. officer*) acting as friend & adviser. [f. OF *probacion* f. L *probationem* (as PROVE, see -ATION)]

proba·tionary, a. Of, serving for, done in the way of, probation, so **proba·tionAL** a.; undergoing probation. [-ARY[1]]

proba·tioner, n. Person on probation, e.g. novice in religious house; offender under PROBATION. Hence **proba·tionership** n. [-ER[1]]

prō·bative, a. Affording proof, evidential. [f. L *probativus* (as PROVE, see -IVE)]

probe, n., & v.t. Blunt-ended surgical instrument usu. of silver for exploring wound &c.; (v.t.) explore (wound, part of body) with p., penetrate (thing) with sharp instrument, (fig.) examine closely, sound, (person, motive, report, &c.). [(vb f. n.) f. LL *proba* PROOF]

prŏ·bity, n. Uprightness, honesty. [f. L *probitas* (*probus* good, see -TY)]

prŏ·blem, n. Doubtful or difficult question, as *how to prevent it is a p., the p. of ventilation*; (attrib.) *p. play, novel* (in which social or other p. is treated); thing hard to understand, as *his whole conduct is a p. to me*; (Geom.) proposition in which something has to be done (cf. THEOREM); (Log.) the question (usu. only implied) involved in a syllogism; (Physics, Math.) inquiry starting from given conditions to investigate a fact, result, or law, as *Kepler's p.*; (Chess) arrangement of pieces on the board in which player is challenged to accomplish specified result, often under prescribed conditions. [f. F *problème* f. L f. Gk *problēma -matos* f. PRO[2](*ballō* throw), see -M]

problemă·tic(al), aa. Doubtful, questionable, as *its success is p., the whole question is p.*; (Log.) enunciating or supporting what is possible but not necessarily true. Hence **problema·ticalLY**[2] adv. [f. F *problématique* f. LL f. Gk *problēmatikos* (as prec., see -IC)]

pro·blem(at)ist, nn. One who studies or composes (esp. chess) problems. [-IST]

prŏbŏsci·dean, -ian, aa. & nn. Having a proboscis; of, like, a proboscis; (mammal) of the order *Proboscidea*, containing elephant & extinct allies. [f. mod. L *Proboscidea* + -AN]

probo·scis, n. Elephant's trunk; long flexible snout of tapir &c.; elongated part of mouth of some insects; sucking organ in some worms; (facet.) human nose; *p.-monkey* (with nose projecting far beyond mouth). So **proboscidi·**FEROUS, **probosci·di**FORM, aa. [L, gen. *-cidis*, f. Gk *proboskis* f. PRO[2](*boskō* feed)]

procē·dure (-*yer*), n. Proceeding; mode of conducting business (esp. in parliament) or legal action. [f. F *procédure* (as foll., see -URE)]

procee·d, v.i. Go on, make one's way, (*to* place); go on (*with, in*, action, investigation, remarks, &c., *to* another subject, *to* do); adopt course of action, as *how shall we p.?*; take legal proceedings *against* person; (abs.) go on to say, as '*in either case*' *he proceeded* '*our course is clear*'; *p. to* (take) *the degree of M.A.*, *p.* (take degree of) *M.A.*; (of action) be carried on, take place, as *the case, the play, will now p.*; come forth, issue, originate, as *sobs heard to p. from next room, volumes p. from the Pitt Press, exertions p. from a false hope.* [f. F *procéder* f. L PRO[1](*cedere cess-* go)]

procee·ding, n. In vbl senses, esp.: action, piece of conduct, as *a high-handed p.*; *legal pp.*, (steps taken in) legal action, as *shall institute legal pp.* (go to law); (as title) *Pp. of Royal Society* &c. [-ING[1]]

prō·ceeds, n. pl. Produce, outcome, profit, as *the pp. will be devoted to charity.* [f. PROCEED v.; sing. now obs.]

prŏceleusmă·tic, a. & n. (prosody). *P.* (*foot*), metrical foot of four short syllables. [f. LL f. Gk *prokeleusmatikos* f. *prokeleusma* incitement f. PRO[2](*keleuō* command), see -M & -IC]

prŏcellār·ian, a. & n. (Bird) of the genus or family to which petrels belong. [f. L *procella* storm, see -ARIAN]

prō·cess[1], n., & v.t. Progress, course, esp. *in p. of construction* &c., being constructed &c., *in p. of time*, as time goes on; course of action, proceeding, esp. method of operation in manufacture, printing, photography, &c.; natural or involuntary operation, series of changes; (print from block produced by) method other than simple engraving by hand; action at law, formal commencement of this, summons or writ (*p.-server*, sheriff's officer); (Anat., Zool., Bot.) outgrowth, protuberance; (v.t.) institute legal p. against (person), treat (material), preserve (food), reproduce (drawing), by a p. [(vb partly thr. OF *processer*) f. F *procès* f. L *processus -ūs*, as PROCEED]

proce·ss[2], v.i. (colloq.). Walk in procession. [back formation f. foll.]

proce·ssion, n., & v.i. & t. Proceeding of body of persons (or of boats &c.) in orderly succession, esp. as religious ceremony or on festive occasion, as *go, walk, in p.*; body of persons doing this; (fig.) ill-contested race; (Theol.) emanation of the Holy Ghost; *p. caterpillars*, kinds that go in p., so *p. moth*, whence **proce·ssion**ARY[1] a.; (v.i.) go in p.; (v.t.) walk along (street) in p. [(vb f. n.) F, f. L *processionem* (as PROCEED, see -ION)]

proce·ssional, a. & n. Of processions; used, carried, sung, in processions; (n.) p. hymn, (Eccl.) office-book of p. hymns &c. [f. med. L *processionalis* a., *-le* n., (as prec., see -AL)]

proce·ssionist, n. One who goes in procession. So **proce·ssion**IZE v.i. [-IST]

procès-verbal (prŏsāvārbah·l), n. (pl. *-baux* pron. -bō). Written report of proceedings, minutes; (Fr. Law) written statement of facts in support of charge. [F]

prō·chronism, n. Referring of event &c. to an earlier than the true date, as *races held in June & called by a p. the Mays.* [f. PRO-[2] on ANACHRONISM]

proclai·m, v.t. Announce publicly & officially (thing, *that*); declare (war, peace); announce officially the accession of (sovereign); declare (person, thing) officially to be a (traitor &c.); declare publicly or openly (thing, *that*); place (district &c.) under legal restrictions, prohibit (meeting &c.), by declaration, as *the whole county is proclaimed.* So **prŏclam**A·TION n., **proclă·mat**ORY a. [f. L PRO[1](*clamare* cry out)]

procli·tic, a. & n. (Gk gram.). (Monosyllable) closely attached in pronunciation to following word & having itself no accent. [f. PRO-[2] on ENCLITIC]

procli·vity, n. Tendency (*to, towards*, action or habit, esp. bad one, *to* do). [f. L *proclivitas* f. PRO[1](*clivis* f. *clivus* slope), see -TY]

prōco·nsul, n. (Rom. Hist.) governor of Roman province, in later republic usu. an ex-consul; (under empire) governor of senatorial province; (rhet.) governor of modern colony &c.; (*pro-consul*) deputy consul. Hence or cogn. **proco·nsul**AR[1] a., **proco·nsul**ATE[1](1), **proco·nsul**SHIP, nn. [L, earlier *pro consule* (one acting) for consul]

procră·stinate, v.i. & t. Defer action, be dilatory; (rare) postpone (action). Hence or cogn. **procra·stinating**LY[2] adv., **procrastin**A·TION, **procra·stinat**OR[2], nn., **procra·stinat**IVE, **procra·stinat**ORY, aa. [f. L PRO[1](*crastinare* f. *crastinus* of tomorrow f. *cras*), see -ATE[3]]

prō·crēate, v.t. Beget, generate, (offspring, or abs.). Hence or cogn. **pro·cre**ANT, **pro·creat**IVE, aa., **procre**A·TION n. [f. L PRO[1](*creare* CREATE)]

Procru·stēan, a. Tending to produce uniformity by violent methods. [f. Gk *Prokroustēs*, lit. stretcher, name of fabulous robber who fitted victims to his bed by stretching or mutilation, see -AN]

pro·ctor, n. (Univv.) each of two officers (*senior, junior, p.*) appointed annually & charged with various functions esp. discipline of persons *in statu pupillari*; (Law) person managing causes in court (now chiefly eccl.) that administers civil or canon law, *King's, Queen's, P.*, official who has right to intervene in probate, divorce, & nullity cases when collusion or suppression of facts is alleged. Hence **proctor·**IAL a., **pro·ctor**SHIP n. [syncop. of PROCURATOR]

pro·ctorize, v.t. Exercise proctor's authority on (undergraduate &c.). Hence **proctoriz**A·TION n. [-IZE]

procu·mbent, a. Lying on the face, prostrate; (Bot.) growing along the ground. [f. L PRO¹(*cumbere* lay oneself) fall forwards, -ENT]

prŏcura·tion, n. Procuring, obtaining, bringing about, so **procur·**AL(2), **procur·**ANCE, nn.; function, authorized action, of attorney; (Eccl.) provision of entertainment for bishop or other visitor by incumbent &c., now commuted to money payment; (fee for) negotiation of loan; procurer's trade or offence. [F, f. L *procurationem* (as PROCURE, see -ATION)]

prŏ·curator, n. (Rom. Hist.) treasury officer in imperial province; agent, proxy, esp. one who has power of attorney; magistrate in some Italian cities; *p. fiscal*, public prosecutor of district in Scotland. Hence or cogn. **procurator·**IAL a., **pro·curator**SHIP n. [L, as PROCURE, see -OR²]

prŏ·curatory, n. Authorization to act for another, esp. *letters of p.* [f. LL *procuratorium* neut. adj. (as PROCURE, see -ORY)]

prŏ·curātrix, n. Inmate of nunnery managing its temporal concerns. [L, as foll., -TRIX]

procūre·, v.t. & i. Obtain by care or effort, acquire, as *must p. a copy, cannot p. employment*; (archaic) bring about, as *procured his death by poison*; act as procurer or procuress. Hence **procur·**ABLE a., **procure·**MENT n. [f. F *procurer* f. L PRO¹(*curare* see to)]

procur·er, n. In vbl senses, esp. man or woman who procures women for gratification of another's lust. So **procur·**ESS¹ n. [ME & AF *procurour* f. L as PROCURATOR]

prod, v.t., & n. Poke with pointed instrument, end of stick, &c.; (fig.) goad, irritate; (n.) poke, thrust, pointed instrument. [?]

prōdēli·sion (-zhn), n. (prosody). Elision of initial vowel (as in *I'm* for *I am*). [f. L *prod* = PRO-¹ + ELISION]

prŏ·digal (-gl), a. & n. Recklessly wasteful (person); lavish *of*; *p. son* (*Luke* xv. 11–32). Hence or cogn. **prodiga·**LITY n., **pro·digal**LY² adv. [obs. F, f. L *prodigus* f. *prodigere* squander (*prod* PRO-¹ + *agere* drive), -AL]

pro·digalize, v.t. Spend lavishly. [-IZE]

prodi·gious (-jus), a. Marvellous, amazing; enormous; abnormal. Hence **prodi·gious**LY² adv., **prodi·gious**NESS n. [f. L *prodigiosus* (as foll., see -OUS)]

prŏ·digy (-jĭ), n. Marvellous thing, esp. one out of the course of nature; wonderful example *of* (some quality); person endowed with surprising qualities, esp. precocious child, as (attrib.) *a p. violinist.* [f. L *prodigium* portent (*prod-* PRO-¹, cf. ADAGE)]

prŏ·drome (-om), n. Preliminary book or treatise (*to* another); (Med.) premonitory symptom (*of*), whence **pro·drom**AL, **prodrŏ·m**IC, aa. [f. mod. L *prodromus*, pl. *-mī*, also in E, f. Gk PRO²(*dromos* running, -er) a. & n.; E has also in med. sense *prodroma* n. pl. & (improp.) n. sing. with pl. *-mata*]

prŏ·duce¹, n. Amount produced, yield, esp. in assay of ore; (also *raw p.*) agricultural & natural products collectively; result (*of* labour, efforts, &c.); (of ordnance or military or naval stores) *brought to p.*, broken up & assorted into classes to be disposed of. [f. foll.]

produ·ce², v.t. Bring forward for inspection or consideration, as *will p. evidence, witnesses, reasons, p. your tickets*; bring (play, performer, book, &c.) before the public; (Geom.) extend, continue, (line *to* a point); manufacture (goods) from raw materials &c.; bring about, cause, (a sensation &c.); (of land &c.) yield (produce); (of animal or plant) bear, yield, (offspring, fruit). So **produci**BI·LITY n., **produ·**CIBLE a. [f. L PRO¹(*ducere duct-* lead)]

produ·cer, n. In vbl senses, esp. (Pol. Econ.) one who produces article of consumption (cf. CONSUMER). [f. prec. + -ER¹]

prŏ·duct, n. Thing produced by natural process or manufacture; result, as *the p. of his labours*; (Math.) quantity obtained by multiplying quantities together; (Chem.) compound not previously existing in a body but formed during its decomposition. [as PRODUCE²]

produ·ction, n. Producing; thing produced, esp. literary or artistic work. [F, f. L *productionem* (as prec., see -ION)]

produ·ctive, a. Producing, tending to produce, as *p. of figs, p. of great annoyance*; (Pol. Econ.) producing commodities of exchangeable value, as *p. labour(er)*; producing abundantly, as *a p. soil, mine, writer*. Hence **produ·ctive**LY² adv., **produ·ctive**NESS, **prōducti·**VITY, nn. [f. med. L *productivus* (as PRODUCE², see -IVE]

prō·em (-ĭm), n. Preface, preamble, to book or speech; beginning, prelude. Hence **proē·m**IAL a. [f. OF *proeme* f. L f. Gk PRO²(*oimion* f. *oimos* way or *oimē* song)]

profa·ne¹, v.t. Treat (sacred thing) with irreverence or disregard; violate, pollute, (what is entitled to respect). So **prŏfan**A·TION n. [f. L *profanare*, as foll.]

profa·ne[2], a. Not belonging to what is sacred or biblical, as *p. history, literature, writer*; not initiated into religious rites or any esoteric knowledge; (of rites &c.) heathen; irreverent, blasphemous, so **profă·nity** n. Hence **profa·nely**[2] adv., **profa·neness** n. [f. obs. F *prophane* f. L PRO[1](*fanus* f. *fanum* temple) before i.e. outside the temple]

profe·ss, v.t. & i. Lay claim to (quality, feeling,) pretend (*to* be or do), as *they p. extreme regret, does not p. to be a scholar*; openly declare, as *they p. themselves quite content, I p.* (*that*) *this is news to me*; affirm one's faith in or allegiance to (religion, God, Christ); make (law, medicine, flute-playing, the flute, &c.) one's profession or business; teach (subject) as professor; perform duties of a professor. [f. L PRO[1](*fitēri fess-* =*fatēri* confess)]

profe·ssed (-st), a. Self-acknowledged, as *a p. Christian*; alleged, ostensible, whence **profe·ssĕdly**[2] adv.; claiming to be duly qualified, as *a p. anatomist*; *p. monk, nun* (that has taken vows of religious order). [p.p. of prec.]

profe·ssion, n. Declaration, avowal, as *in practice if not in p., accept my sincere pp. of regard, spare me these pp.*; declaration of belief in a religion; vow made on entering, fact of being in, a religious order; vocation, calling, esp. one that involves some branch of learning or science, as *the learned pp.* (divinity, law, medicine), *the military p., a carpenter by p.*, whence **profe·ssionless** a.; *the* body of persons engaged in this, esp. (Theatr. slang) actors, as *lets apartments to the p.* [F, f. L *professionem* (as PROFESS, see -ION)]

profe·ssional, a. & n. Of, belonging to, connected with, a profession, as *p. men, etiquette, jealousy*; *p. politician, agitator*, &c. (making a trade of politics &c.); *p. cricketer, golfer;* &c. (playing for money, cf. AMATEUR); (n.) p. man, esp. (abbr. *pro*) p. cricketer, golfer, &c. Hence **profe·ssionally**[2] adv. [-AL]

profe·ssionalism, n. Qualities, stamp, of a profession; practice of employing professionals. So **profe·ssionalize**(3) v.t. [-ISM]

profe·ssor, n. One who makes profession (*of* a religion); public teacher of high rank, esp. holder of a chair in university (prefixed as title, abbr. *Prof.*), whence **profe·ssorate**[1](1), **profe·ssoress**[1], **prŏfessor·iate**[1](1), **profe·ssorship**, nn., **prŏfessor·ial** a., **professor·ially**[2] adv.; (as grandiose title) *P. Smith's Boxing Dormice* &c.; (slang) professional. [L (as PROFESS, see -OR[2])]

pro·ffer, v.t., & n., (literary). Offer (gift, services, &c., archaic *to* do; esp. in p.p.); (n.) offer. [(n. f. AF *profre*) f. AF *proffrir* (PRO-[1] + *offrir* OFFER)]

profi·cient (-shnt), a. & n. Adept, expert, (*in, at*, an art &c., *in doing*). Hence **profi·ciency** n., **profi·ciently**[2] adv. [f. L as PROFIT[1], see -ENT]

prō·file (-ēl), n., & v.t. Drawing, silhouette, or other representation, of side view esp. of human face, whence **pro·filist** n.; *drawn* &c. *in p.* (as seen from one side); side outline esp. of the human face; (Fortif.) transverse vertical section of fort, comparative thickness of earthwork &c.; flat outline piece of scenery on stage; (v.t.) represent in p., give a p. to. [(n. f. It. *profilo* now *proff-*) f. It. (now *proff-*) PRO[1](*filare* spin f. L *filare* f. *filum* thread)]

prŏ·fit[1], n. Advantage, benefit, as *have studied it to my p., no p. in such pursuits*; pecuniary gain, excess of returns over outlay, (usu. pl.); (Bookkeep.) *p. & loss account*, account in which gains are credited & losses debited so as to show net p. or loss at any time; *p.-sharing* (of pp. esp. between employer & employed). Hence **pro·fitless** a., **pro·fitlessly**[2] adv., **pro·fitlessness** n. [OF, f. L *profectus -ūs* f. PRO[1](*ficere fect-* =*facere* do) advance]

prŏ·fit[2], v.t. & i. (Of thing) be of advantage to (person &c., orig. indirect object), as *it will not p. him, what will it p. him?*; be of advantage; (of person &c.) be benefited or assisted, as *hope to p. by your advice, profited by his confusion to make my escape.* [f. F *profiter* as prec.]

pro·fitable, a. Beneficial, useful, as *p. conservation*; yielding profit, lucrative, as *a p. speculation.* Hence **pro·fitableness** n., **pro·fitably**[2] adv. [F (PROFIT[1] + -ABLE)]

prŏfiteer·, v.i., & n. Make inordinate profits out of the State's or the consumer's straits (esp. of contractors & traders in war-time); (n.) profiteering person. [PROFIT, -EER]

prŏ·fligate (-*at*), a. & n. Licentious, dissolute; recklessly extravagant; (n.) p. person. Hence **pro·fligacy** n., **pro·fligately**[2] adv. [f. L PRO[1](*fligare* =*fligere* strike down) overthrow, ruin, see -ATE[3]]

profou·nd (-ow-), a. & n. Having, showing, great knowledge or insight, as *p. statesman, inquiry, treatise*; demanding deep study or thought, as *p. doctrines*; (of state or quality) deep, intense, unqualified, as *fell into a p. sleep, take a p. interest, simulated a p. indifference*; having, coming from, extending to, a great depth, as *p. crevasses, a p.* (deep-drawn) *sigh, p.* (deep-seated) *gangrene*; (n., poet.) *the* vast depth (*of* ocean, futurity, the soul, &c.). Hence or cogn. **profou·ndly**[2] adv., **profou·ndness**, **profu·ndity**, nn. [f. OF *profund* f. L PRO[1](*fundus* bottom) deep]

profu·se (-s), a. Lavish, extravagant, (*in, of*, gifts, promises, expenditure, &c.); (of things) exuberantly plentiful. Hence or cogn. **profu·sely**[2] adv., **profu·seness**, **profu·sion** (-zhn), nn. [f. L PRO[1](*fundere fus-* pour)]

prog[1], n. (slang). Food, esp. for journey or excursion. [?]

prog[2], **pro·ggins**, nn. & vv.t. (slang). Proctor at Oxford or Cambridge; (v.t.) proctorize. [abbr.]

proge·nitive, a. Capable of, connected with, the production of offspring. [as foll., -IVE]

progĕ·nitor (-j-), n. Ancestor of person, animal, or plant; (fig.) political or intellectual predecessor, original of a copy. Hence **progenitor·IAL** a., **proge·nitorSHIP**, **proge·nitrESS**[1], nn. [f. obs. F *progeniteur* f. L *progenitorem* f. PRO[1](*gignere genit-* beget), see -OR[2]]

proge·niture, n. (Begetting of) offspring. [as prec., see -URE]

prŏ·geny, n. Offspring of person, animal, or plant; descendants; (fig.) issue, outcome. [f. obs. F *progenie* f. L *progenies* f. PRO[1](*gignere* beget)]

proggins. See PROG[2].

proglo·ttis, n. (pl.*-idēs*). Sexually mature segment of tapeworm. [f. Gk PRO[2](*glōssis* f. *glōssa, -tta*, tongue), from its shape]

prŏ·gnathous, a. With projecting jaws; (of jaws) projecting. So **prognă·thIC** a., **pro·gnathISM**(2) n. [f. PRO-[2] + Gk *gnathos* jaw + -OUS]

prŏgnō·sis, n. (pl. *-osēs*). Prognostication, esp. (Med.) forecast of course of disease. [L, f. Gk PRO[2](*gnōsis* f. *gnō-* know)]

prŏgnŏ·stic, n. & a. Pre-indication, omen, (*of*); prediction, forecast; (adj.) foretelling, predictive, (*of*). [(n. f. OF *pronostique*) f. med. L f. Gk *prognōstikos* f. PRO[2](*gignōskō* learn), -IC]

progno·sticate, v.t. Foretell (event, *that*); (of things) betoken. Hence or cogn. **progno·sticABLE**, **progno·sticatIVE**, **prognos·ticatORY**, aa., **prognosticA·TION**, **progno·sticatOR**[2], nn. [f. med. L *prognosticare* (as prec.), see -ATE[3]]

prō·gram(me), n., & v.t. Descriptive notice of series of events, e.g. of course of study, concert, &c.; definite plan of intended proceedings; (colloq.) *what is the p. for* (what are we going to do) *to-day?*; *p.-music* (intended to suggest series of scenes or events); (v.t.) make a p. or definite plan of. [f. L f. Gk *programma* f. PRO[2](*graphō* write) write publicly, see -M; *-me* now usu., but cf. *diagram, telegram*, &c.]

prŏ·gress[1], n. Forward or onward movement in space, as *made slow p., continued his p.*; *an inquiry is now in p.* (going on); advance, development, as *made no p. in his studies, the p. of civilization, disease made rapid p.*; (archaic) state journey, official tour, esp. *royal p.* [ult. f. L PRO[1](*gredi gress-* = *gradi* walk)]

progre·ss[2], v.i. Move forward or onward; be carried on, as *the controversy still progresses*; advance, develop, as *we p. in knowledge, science progresses.* [f. prec.; Amer. revival of obs. E]

progre·ssion (-shn), n. Progress, as *mode of p.*; (Math.) ARITHMETICAL, GEOMETRICAL, HARMONIC, *p.*; (Mus.) passing from one note or chord to another. Hence **progre·ssionAL** a. [F, f. L *progressionem* (as PROGRESS[1], see -ION)]

progre·ssionist, n. Advocate of progress e.g. in political or social matters (also **prŏ·gressIST** n.); one who holds that life on the earth has been marked by gradual progression to higher forms. [-IST]

progre·ssive, a. & n. Moving forward, as *p. motion*; proceeding step by step, successive; *p. whist* &c. (played by several sets of players at different tables, certain players passing after each round to next table); advancing in social conditions, character, efficiency, &c., as *a p. nation*; (of disease) continuously increasing; favouring progress or reform, as *p. principles, party*, whence **progre·ssivISM** n.; (n.) advocate of p. policy. Hence **progre·ssiveLY**[2] adv., **progre·ssiveNESS** n. [F (*-if, -ive*), as PROGRESS[1], see -IVE]

prohĭ·bit, v.t. Forbid, debar, (action, thing, person *from* do*ing*). Hence or cogn. **prohibitER**[1], **prohi·bitOR**[2], nn. [f. L PRO[1](*hibēre hibit-* = *habēre* hold)]

prohibi·tion, n. Forbidding; edict, order, that forbids; forbidding by law of sale of intoxicants for common consumption, whence **prohibi·tionIST** n. (Law) writ from High Court of Justice forbidding inferior court to proceed in suit as being beyond its cognizance. [F, f. L *prohibitionem* (as prec., see -ION)]

prohi·bitive, a. Prohibiting; serving to prevent the (ab)use of a thing, as *p. tax, published at a p. price.* Hence or cogn. **prohi·bitiveLY**[2] adv., **prohi·bitiveNESS** n., **prohi·bitORY** a. [F (*-if, -ive*), as PROHIBIT, see -IVE]

proje·ct[1], v.t. & i. Plan, contrive, (scheme, course of action, &c.); cast, throw, impel, (body *into* space &c.); *p. oneself*, go out of oneself *into* another's feelings, the future, &c., (Spirit.) make a phantom of oneself visible to a distant person; (Chem.) cast (substance *into, on*, &c.); cause (light, shadow) to fall on surface &c.; (fig.) cause (idea &c.) to take shape; (Geom.) draw straight lines from a centre through every point of (given figure) to produce corresponding figure on a surface by intersecting it, draw (such lines), produce (such corresponding figure); make projection of (earth, sky, &c.); (intr.) protrude. [f. L PRO[1](*jicĕre ject-* = *jacĕre* throw)]

prŏ·ject[2], n. Plan, scheme. [as prec.]

proje·ctile, a. & n. Impelling, as *p. force*; capable of being projected by force, esp. from cannon; (n.; *also* prŏ·j-) p. missile. [as prec. + -ILE]

proje·ction, n. Throwing, casting; transmutation of metals, as *powder of p.*, alchemists' powder of philosophers' stone; planning; protruding; protruding thing; thrusting forward; (Geom.) projecting of a figure (see PROJECT[1]), *p. of a point*, line joining point in original figure to one in derived figure; representation on plane surface of (any part of) surface of earth or of celestial sphere, as *Mercator's p.* (in which points of compass preserve same direction all over the map); mental image viewed as objective reality. [f. L *projectio* (as prec., see -ION)]

proje·ctive, a. (Geom.) of, derived by, projection, *p. property* of a figure (unchanged after projection); mentally projecting or projected, as *p. imagination*. Hence **proje·ctive**LY[2] adv. [as prec., see -IVE]

proje·ctor, n. One who forms a project; promoter of bubble companies; apparatus for projecting rays of light. [as prec., see -OR[2]]

prola·pse, v.i., & n., (path.). Slip forward or down out of place; (n.) = foll. [f. L PRO[1](*labi laps-* slip)]

prola·psus, n. (path.). Slipping forward or down of part of organ esp. of uterus or rectum. [L, gen. *-ūs*, as prec.]

prō·lāte, a. (Geom., of spheroid) lengthened in direction of polar diameter (cf. OBLATE); growing, extending, in width; (fig.) widely spread; (Gram.) = foll. Hence **pro·late**LY[2] adv. [f. L PRO[1](*ferre lat-* carry) prolong]

prola·tive, a. (gram.). Serving to extend or complete predication, as *in ' you can go ' go is a p. infinitive.* [f. LL *prolativus* (prec., -IVE)]

prōlegŏ·menon, n. (usu. in pl. *-ena*). Preliminary discourse or matter prefixed to book &c. Hence **prolego·men**ARY[1], **prolego·men**OUS, aa. [Gk *prolegomenon* neut. pass. part. of PRO[2](*legō* say)]

prolĕ·psis, n. Anticipation; (Gram.) anticipatory use of adjectives, as in *So those two brothers & their* murdered *man Rode past fair Florence.* Hence or cogn. **prolĕ·pt**IC a., **prole·pt**ICALLY adv. [Gk *prolēpsis* f. PRO[2](*lambanō* take)]

prŏlĕtaire· (-ār), n. = foll. n. Hence **proletair·**ISM(2) n. [f. F *prolétaire*, as foll.]

prŏlĕtār·ian, a. & n. (Member) of the proletariate; *p. dictatorship* (as in SOVIET Russia). Hence or cogn. **proletar·ian**ISM(2) n., **pro·let**ARY[1] a. [f. L *proletarius* one who served the State not with property but with offspring (*proles*), see -ARY[1] & -AN]

prōlĕtār·iat(e) (*-at*), n. (Rom. Hist.; & mod., often contempt.) lowest class of community; (Pol. Econ.) indigent wage-earners, labouring classes. [f. F *prolétariat* (as prec., see -ATE[1])]

prō·licide, n. Killing of offspring, esp. before or soon after birth. Hence **prolici·d**AL a. [f. L *proles* offspring + -CIDE]

proli·ferate, v.i. & t. Reproduce itself, grow, by multiplication of elementary parts; produce (cells &c.) thus. So **prolifer**A·TION n., **proli·ferat**IVE a. [back formation f. *proliferation* f. F *prolifération* (as foll., see -ATION)]

proli·ferous, a. (Bot.) producing leaf or flower buds from leaf or flower, (also) producing new individuals from buds; (Zool.) multiplying by budding; (Path.) spreading by proliferation. [f med. L *prolifer* (*proles* offspring), see -FEROUS]

proli·fic, a. Producing (much) offspring; abundantly productive *of*, abounding *in*. Hence **proli·fic**ACY [irreg.], **prolifi·**CITY, **proli·fic**NESS, nn. [f. med. L *prolificus* (as prec., see -FIC)]

proli·gerous, a. Bearing offspring, generative. [as prec. + L *-ger* -bearing + -OUS]

proli·x (*or* prō·-), a. Lengthy, wordy, tedious, as *p. speech, writer.* Hence or cogn. **proli·x**ITY n., **proli·x**LY[2] adv. [f. L PRO[1](**lixus* p.p. of *liquēre* be liquid)]

prŏ·locūtor (*or* prolŏ·-), n. Chairman esp. of lower house of convocation of either province of Church of England. Hence **prolo·cutor**SHIP n. [L, f. PRO[1](*loqui locut-* speak), -OR[2]]

prŏ·logize (-j-), **-guize** (-gīz), vv.i. Write, speak, a prologue. [(*-gize*) f. Gk *prologizō* as foll., (*-gu-*) f. foll. + -IZE]

prŏ·logue (-ŏg), n., & v.t. Preliminary discourse, poem, &c., esp. introducing play (cf. EPILOGUE); (fig.) act, event, serving as introduction (*to*); (v.t.) introduce, furnish, with a p. [(vb f. n.) F, f. L f. Gk PRO[2](*logos* speech)]

prolo·ng, v.t. Extend (action, condition, &c.) in duration; extend in spatial length; lengthen pronunciation of (syllable &c.). So **prolo·ng**ABLE (-nga-) a., **prōlong**A·TION (-ngg-), n. [f. OF *prolonguer* f. LL PRO[1](*longare*, as LONG[1])]

prolu·sion (-zhn), n. Preliminary essay, article, or attempt. So **prolu·s**ORY (-s-) a. [f. L *prolusio* f. PRO[1](*ludere lus-* play) practise beforehand]

prŏmĕna·de (-ahd, -ād), n., & v.i. & t. Walk, ride, drive, taken for exercise, amusement, or display, or as social ceremony; place, esp. paved public walk, for this; *p. concert* (at which audience walk about); (v.i.) make a p., whence **promena·d**ER[1] n.; (v.t.) make a p. through (place), lead (person) about a place esp. for display. [(vb f. n.) F, f. *promener* take for walk f. LL PRO[1](*minare* threaten) drive (beasts), -ADE]

prŏ·mĕrops, n. S.-Afr. genus of birds, esp. *Cape p.*, small bird with long curved bill & very long tail. [PRO-[2] + Gk *merops* bee-eater]

Promē·thēan, a. Of, like, Prometheus in his skill or punishment. [f. Gk *Promētheus* (demigod who made man from clay, stole fire from Olympus & taught men the use of it & various arts, & was chained by Zeus to rock in Caucasus), see -AN]

prŏ·minent, a. Jutting out, projecting; conspicuous; distinguished. Hence or cogn. **pro·min**ENCE, **pro·min**ENCY, nn., **pro·minent**LY[2] adv. [f. L PRO[1](*minēre*, see EMINENT)]

promi·scuous, a. Of mixed & disorderly composition, as *a p. mass*; (w. pl. n.) of various kinds mixed together; indiscriminate, as *p. massacre, hospitality*; *p. bathing* (of both sexes together); *p. sexual relations* (unrestricted by marriage or cohabition); (colloq.) casual, as *took a p. stroll*; (vulg., facet.) *p.-like*, casually, for no particular reason. Hence or cogn. **prŏmiscū·**ITY n., **promi·scuous**LY[2] adv. [f. L PRO[1](*miscuus* f. *miscēre* mix) + -OUS]

prŏ·mise[1] (-s), n. Assurance given to a person that one will do or not do something or will give or procure him something; thing promised, as *I claim your p.*; BREACH[1] *of p.*; *land of p.* (see foll.); (fig.) ground of expectation of future achievements or good results, as *book, writer, of great p.* [f. L *promissum* p.p. of PRO[1](*mittere* send) put forth, promise]

prŏ·mise[2] (-s), v.t. & i. Make (person) a promise to give or procure him (thing). as *I p. you a fair hearing*; make (person) a promise (*to* do, *that* thing shall be done &c.); (abs.) *cannot positively p.*; *p. oneself*, look forward to (a pleasant time &c.); (colloq.) *I p.* (assure) *you, it will not be so easy*; (fig.) afford expectation of, as *these discussions p. future storms*, seem likely (*to* do); (abs.) *p. well* &c., hold out good &c. prospect; *promised land* (also *land of promise*), Canaan (*Gen.* xii. 7 &c.), heaven, any place of expected felicity. Hence **pro·mis**ER[1] n. [f. prec.]

prŏmisee·, n. (law). Person to whom promise is made. So **pro·mis**OR[2] n. [-EE]

pro·mising, a. Likely to turn out well, hopeful, full of promise, as *p. boy, sky, beginning*. Hence **pro·mising**LY[2] adv. [-ING[2]]

prŏ·missory, a. Conveying or implying a promise; (rare) full of promise (*of*); *p. note*, signed document containing written promise to pay stated sum to specified person or to bearer at specified date or on demand. [f. med. L *promissorius* (as PROMISE[1], see -ORY)]

prŏ·montory, n. Point of high land jutting out into sea &c., headland; (Anat.) kinds of protuberance in the body. Hence **pro·montori**ED[2] a. [f. med. L *promontorium* altered (on *mons -ntis* mount) f. L *promunturium* (perh. as PROMINENT)]

promo·te, v.t. Advance, prefer, (person *to* position, higher office; *was promoted archbishop, to be archbishop, to the archbishopric*, not *to archbishop*); help forward, encourage, (process, result); support actively the passing of (law), take necessary steps for passing of (local or private act of parliament); (Chess) raise (pawn) to rank of queen &c. Hence or cogn. **promo·**TION n., **promo·**TIVE a. [f. L PRO[1](*movēre mot-* move)]

promo·ter, n. In vbl senses, esp. (also *company-p.*) one who promotes formation of joint-stock company (esp. in opprobrious sense, whence **promo·ter**ISM n.). [-ER[1]]

prompt[1], a. & n. Ready in action, acting with alacrity, as *a p. assistant*, made, done, &c., readily or at once, as *p. reply, decision, payment*, whence or cogn. **pro·mpti**TUDE, **pro·mpt**NESS, nn., **pro·mpt**LY[2] adv.; *for p. cash* (on the spot); (Commerc., of goods) for immediate delivery & payment, as *p. iron*, (n.) time limit for payment of account, stated on *p.-note*, as *what is the p.?*. [(n. f. adj.) f. L *promere prompt-* produce (PRO-[1] + *emere* take)]

prompt[2], v.t., & n. Incite, move, (person &c. *to* action, *to* do); supply (actor, reciter, or abs.) with the words that come next, assist (hesitating speaker) with suggestion; inspire, give rise to, (feeling, thought; action); (n.) thing said to help the memory esp. of actor; *p.-book*, copy of play for prompter's use; *p.-* (prompter's) *box* on stage; *p. side* of stage (to actor's right; abbr. *p.s.*). [(n. f. vb) f. prec.]

pro·mpter, n. One who prompts, esp. (Theatr.) person stationed out of sight of audience to assist actor's memory. [-ER[1]]

pro·mpting, n. In vbl senses, esp. *the pp. of conscience* &c. [-ING[1]]

prŏ·mulgate, v.t. Make known to the public, disseminate (creed &c.), proclaim (decree, news). Hence or cogn. **promulga·**TION, **pro·mulgat**OR[2], nn. [f. L *promulgare* perh. corrupt. of PRO[1](*vulgare* publish f. *vulgus* the people). see -ATE[3]]

promu·lge, v.t. (archaic). = prec. [as prec.]

pronā·ŏs, n. (Gk ant.). Space in front of body of temple, enclosed by portico & projecting side walls. [L f. Gk PRO[2](*naos* temple)]

prō·nate, v.t. (physiol.). Put (hand, fore limb) into prone position (cf. SUPINATE). So **pron**A·TION n. [f. LL *pronare* (as PRONE), see -ATE[3]]

pronā·tor, n. (anat.). Muscle that effects or helps pronation. [med. L (as prec., see -OR[2])]

prōne, a. Having the front or ventral part downwards, lying face downwards, (loosely) lying flat, prostrate, as *fell p.*, whence **pro·ne**LY[2] adv.; (of ground) having downward aspect or direction, (loosely) steep, headlong; disposed, liable, (*to* quality, action, or condition, *to* do). Hence **pro·ne**NESS n. [f. L *pronus*]

prōneur· (-er), n. Extoller, eulogist. [F]

prong, n., & v.t. Forked instrument, e.g. hay-fork; each pointed member of fork, whence **(-)prong**ED[2] a.; (v.t.) pierce, stab, turn up (soil &c.), with p.; *p.-buck*,

-horn, -horned antelope, N.-Amer. deer-like ruminant. [?]

pronŏ·minal, a. Of (the nature of) a pronoun. Hence **prono·minal**LY² adv. [f. LL *pronominalis* f. L PRO¹(*nomen -minis* noun), see -AL]

prō·noun, n. Word used instead of (proper or other) noun to designate person or thing already mentioned or known from context or forming the subject of inquiry (used also to include pronominal & other adjectives, see below); *personal pp.* (I, we, thou, you, he, she, it, they); *interrogative pp.* (who, what, which); *relative pp.* (who, that, which); *possessive pp.*, adjectives representing possessive case (*my, her, our,* &c., with absolute forms *mine, hers, ours*); *demonstrative pp.* (this, that); *distributive pp.* (each, every, either, &c.); *indefinite pp.* (any, some, &c.). [PRO-¹]

pronou·nce (-ow-), v.t. & i. Utter, deliver, (judgement, sentence, curse, &c.) formally or solemnly, state, declare, as one's opinion, as *I p. the pears unripe, cannot p. him* (or *that he is*) *out of danger,* whence **pronou·nce**MENT n.; pass judgement, give one's opinion, (*on, for, against, in favour of*); utter, articulate, (words, or abs.), as *p. more distinctly,* esp. with reference to different modes, as *how do you p. 'fulsome'?, cannot p. French,* whence **pronou·nce**ABLE a. [f. OF *pronuncier* f. LL PRO¹(*nuntiare* announce f. *nuntius* messenger)]

pronou·nced, a. In vbl senses, also: strongly marked, decided, as *p. tendency, magenta, flavour.* Hence **pronou·ncĕd**LY² adv. [-ED¹]

pronou·ncing, n. In vbl senses; (attrib.) *p. dictionary* (in which pronunciation is indicated). [-ING¹]

pronŭnciame·nto (-sĭ-), n. Proclamation, manifesto, esp. (in Spanish-speaking countries) one issued by insurrectionists. [f. Sp. *pronunciamiento,* also used in E, f. L as PRONOUNCE, see -MENT]

pronunciation (-sĭ-), n. Mode in which a word is pronounced; a person's way of pronouncing words, as *his p. is often faulty.* [f. L *pronuntiatio* (as PRONOUNCE, see -ATION)]

prōōf¹, n. Evidence sufficing or helping to establish a fact, as *this requires no p., as a p. of his esteem, p. positive of his intention* or *that he intended,* whence **proo·f**LESS a.; spoken or written legal evidence; proving, demonstration, as *not capable of p., in p. of my assertion*; (Sc. law) trial before judge instead of by jury; test, trial, as *must be brought to the p., will stand a severe p., the p. of the pudding is in the eating*; (place for) testing of firearms or explosives; (archaic) proved impenetrability, as *armour of p.*; standard of strength of distilled alcoholic liquors; (*first*) *p.*, trial impression taken from type, in which corrections &c. may be made (cf. REVISE), *p.-reader, -reading,* (person employed in) reading & correcting pp., *p.-sheet,* sheet of p.; each of a limited number of careful impressions made from engraved plate before printing of ordinary issue & usu. (also *p. before letters*) before inscription is added, *artist's, engraver's, p.* (taken for examination or alteration by him), *signed p.*, early p. signed by artist; test-tube; rough edges left to some leaves of book to show it has not been cut down; *p.-plane,* conductor fixed on insulating handle & used in measuring electrification of a body. [f. OF *prueve* f. LL *proba,* as PROVE]

prōōf², a., & v.t. (Of armour) of tried strength; impenetrable, as *p. against the severest weather, the pricks of conscience,* esp. in comb., as *bomb, bullet, fire, rain, sound, burglar, thief, weather, -p.*, WATER¹-*p.*; (v.t.) make (thing) p., esp. make (fabric &c.) waterproof. [(vb f. adj.) f. prec.]

prop¹, v.t. & i. Rigid support, esp. one not forming structural part of thing supported, e.g. pole; CLOTHES-*p.*; (fig.) person &c. who upholds institution &c.; (v.t.) support (as) by prop (lit. & fig.), hold *up* thus; (v.i., of horse &c.) come to a dead stop with forelegs rigid. [(vb prob. f. n.) cf. Du. *proppe,* etym. dub.]

prop². See PROPOSITION.

prōpaedeu·tic (-dū-), a. & n. (Subject, study) serving as introduction to higher study; (n. pl.) preliminary learning. Hence **propaedeu·tic**AL a. [f. Gk PRO²(*paideuō* teach f. *pais paidos* child), see -IC]

prŏpaga·nda (-*a*), n. (*Congregation, College, of*) *the P.*, committee of cardinals in charge of foreign missions; association, organized scheme, for propagation of a doctrine or practice; (improp. as pl.) efforts, schemes, principles, of propagation. [It., f. mod. L *congregatio de propaganda fide* congregation for propagation of the faith]

propaga·ndist, n. Member, agent, of a propaganda, whence **propaga·nd**ISM n., **propagandi·st**IC a., **propaga·nd**IZE(2, 4) v.i. & t.; proselytizer; missionary, convert, of the Propaganda. [-IST]

prŏ·pagate, v.t. Multiply specimens of (plant, animal, disease, &c.) by natural process from parent stock; (of plant &c.) reproduce (it*self*, or abs.); hand down (quality &c.) from one generation to another; disseminate, diffuse, (statement, belief, practice); extend the operation of, transmit, (vibration, earthquake, &c.). Hence or cogn. **propag**A·TION, **pro·pagat**OR², nn., **pro·pagat**IVE a. [f. L *propagare* multiply plants from layers, f. PRO¹(*pago* perh. f. root of *pangere* fix, set), see -ATE³]

prōparo·xytone (-tn), a. & n. (Gk gram.). (Word) with acute accent on antepenult. [f. Gk PRO²(*paroxutonos* PAROXYTONE)]

prope·l, v.t. (-ll-), Drive forward, give onward motion to, (lit. & fig.). [f. L PRO¹(*pellere puls-* drive)]

prope·llent, a. & n. Propelling (agent); explosive that propels bullet from fire-arm. [-ENT]

prope·ller, n. In vbl senses, esp.: revolving shaft with blades usu. (*screw p.*) set at an angle & twisted like thread of screw, for propelling ship or aircraft. [-ER¹]

prope·nsity, n. Inclination, tendency, (*to* condition, quality, thing, *to* do, *for doing*). [f. now rare *propense* f. L *propensus* inclined, p.p. of PRO¹(*pendĕre* hang) + -ITY]

prŏ·per, a. (Archaic, usu. w. possessive pron. & sometimes w. *own*) own, as *with my own p. eyes*; (Astr.) *p. motion*, that part of the apparent motion of fixed star &c. supposed to be due to its actual movement in space; belonging, relating, exclusively or distinctively (*to*, or abs. as *p. psalms, lessons*, p. to particular day); (Gram.) *p. noun* or *name*, name used to designate an individual person, animal, town, ship, &c. (e.g. Jane, Smith, France, London); accurate, correct, as *in the p. sense of the word*; (usu. foll. its noun) strictly so called, real, genuine, as *within the sphere of architecture p., p. fraction* (less than unity); (colloq.) thorough, complete, as *will be a p. row about this*; (archaic) handsome, as *a p. man*; fit, suitable, right, as *choose the p. time, do it the p. way*; in conformity with demands of society, decent, respectable, as *she is so distressingly p., would it be quite p.?*; (Herald.) in the natural, not conventional, colours, as *a peacock p.* [ME & F *propre* f. L *proprius*]

prō·perispō·menon, a. & n. (Gk gram.). (Word) with circumflex accent on penult. [Gk PRO²(PERISPOMENON)]

pro·perly, adv. Fittingly, suitably, as *do it p. or not at all*; rightly, duly, as *he very p. refused*; with good manners, as *behave p.*; (colloq.) thoroughly, as *puzzled him p.* [-LY²]

pro·perty, n. Owning, being owned, as *p. has its duties*; thing owned, possession(s), as *the book is his p., regards him as her exclusive p., a man of* (great) *p., has a small p.* (estate) *in Norfolk*, PERSONAL, REAL², *p.*; *p. qualification* (based on possession of p.), *p. tax* (levied directly on p.); (Theatr.) article of costume, furniture, &c., used on stage, *p.-man, -master*, man in charge of stage pp.; attribute, quality, as *the pp. of soda, has the p. of dissolving grease*; (Logic) quality common to a whole class but not necessary to distinguish it from others. [f. OF *proprieté* f. L *proprietatem* (as PROPER, see -TY)]

prŏ·phecy̆, n. Faculty of a prophet, as *the gift of p.*; prophetic utterance; foretelling of future events. [f. OF *profecie* f. LL f. Gk *prophēteia* (as PROPHET)]

pro·phesy̆, v.i. & t. Speak as a prophet; foretell future events; (archaic) expound the Scriptures; foretell (event, *that, who*, &c.). [f. OF *profecier*, as prec.]

prŏ·phet, n. Inspired teacher, revealer or interpreter of God's will; *the pp.*, prophetical writers of O.T., *major pp.*, Isaiah, Jeremiah, Ezekiel, Daniel, *the 12 minor pp.*, Hosea to Malachi; *the P.*, Mohammed, (also) Joseph Smith, founder of Mormons; *Saul among the pp.*, person revealing unexpected gifts or sympathies (see I *Sam.* x. 11); spokesman, advocate, (*of* principle &c.); one who foretells events, as *am no weather-p.*, (slang) tipster. Hence **pro·phet**ESS¹, **pro·phet**HOOD, **pro·phet**SHIP, nn. [f. F *prophète* f. L (-*ta*) f. Gk PRO²(*phētēs* speaker f. *phēmi* speak) spokesman]

prophĕ·tic, a. Of a prophet; predicting, containing a prediction *of* (event &c.). Hence **prophe·tic**AL a., **prophe·tical**LY² adv. [f. LL f. Gk *prophētikos* (prec., -IC)]

prŏphy̆la·ctic, a. & n. (Medicine, measure) tending to prevent disease. [f. Gk *prophulaktikos* f. PRO²(*phulassō* guard)]

propi·nquity, n. Nearness in place; close kinship; similarity. [f. obs. F *propinquité* f. L *propinquitatem* (*propinquus* near f. *prope* near, see -TY)]

propi·tiate (-shĭ-), v.t. Appease (offended person &c.); make propitious. [f. L *propitiare* (as PROPITIOUS, see -ATE³)]

propitia·tion, n. Appeasement; atonement; (archaic) gift &c. meant to propitiate, as *he is the p. for our sins.* [f. LL *propitiatio* (as prec., see -ATION)]

propi·tiatory (-shat-), a. & n. Serving, meant, to propitiate, as *a p. smile*; (n.) the mercy-seat (esp. fig. of Christ). Hence **propi·tiatori**LY² adv. [f. LL *propitiatorius* (as PROPITIATE, see -ORY)]

propi·tious (-sh*u*s), a. Well-disposed, favourable, as *the fates were p.*; (of omens &c.) favourable; (of weather, occasion, &c.) suitable *for*, favourable *to*, (purpose). Hence **propi·tious**LY² adv. [f. OF *propicius* f. L *propitius*, -OUS]

prŏ·polis, n. Red resinous substance got by bees from buds to stop up crevices with. [Gk PRO²(*polis* city) suburb, bee-glue]

propō·nent, a. & n. (Person) that puts forward a motion, theory, or proposal. [f. L as PROPOUND, see -ENT]

propor·tion, n., & v.t. Comparative part, share, as *a large p. of the earth's surface, of the profits*; comparative relation, ratio, as *the p. of births to the population, price will be raised in p.* (*to the labour* &c., or abs.); due relation of one thing to another or between parts of a thing, as *windows are in admirable p., his success bore no p. to his abilities*, whence **propor·tion**LESS a.; *was out of* (*all*) *p. to*, too great for; (pl.) dimensions, as *athlete, building, of magnificent pp.*; (Math.) equality of ratios between two pairs of quantities, as

3, 5, 9, & 15 are in p., set of such quantities, (Arith.) RULE of three; (v.t.) make (thing &c.) proportionate *to*, as *must p. the punishment to the crime*, whence **(-)propor·tion**ED[1] a., **propor·tion**MENT n. [(n.) F, f. L PRO(*portionem* PORTION); vb f. OF *proporcioner*]

propor·tional, a. & n. In due proportion, corresponding in degree or amount, as *a p. increase in the expense, resentment p. to his injuries, p.* REPRESENTATION, so **propor·tion**ABLE, **propor·tion**ATE[2], aa., **propor·tionab**LY[2], **propor·tionate**LY[2], advv.; (n.) one of the terms of a proportion, as *5, 3, 10, 6, are pp., 6 is a mean p. between 3 & 12.* Hence or cogn. **proportiona·l**ITY n., **propor·tional**LY[2] adv. [f. L *proportionalis* (as prec., see -AL)]

propor·tionalist, n. One who plans proportions; advocate of proportional representation. [-IST]

propo·sal (-z-), n. Act of proposing something; offer of marriage, as *have had a p.*; scheme of action &c. proposed, as *the p. was never carried out.* [-AL]

propo·se (-z), v.t. & i. Put forward for consideration, propound; set up as an aim, as *the object I p. to myself*; nominate (person) as member of society &c.; offer (person's health, person) as toast; make offer of marriage (*to*); put forward as a plan, as *we p.* (to make) *a change, that a change should be made*; intend, purpose, (*to* do, do*ing*); (abs.) *man proposes, God disposes.* [f. F PRO[1](*poser*, see COMPOSE)]

prŏposi·tion (-z-), n. Statement, assertion, as *a p. too plain to need argument*, esp. (Logic) form of words consisting of predicate & subject connected by copula; (Math., abbr. *prop*) formal statement of theorem or problem, often including the demonstration, as *Euclid, Book I, p. 5*; proposal, scheme proposed; (U.S. commerc., & slang) task, job, problem, objective, occupation, trade, opponent, prospect, &c. Hence **proposi·tion**AL a. [F, f. L *propositionem* (as foll., see -ION)]

propou·nd (-ow-), v.t. Offer for consideration, propose, (question, problem, scheme, matter, &c., *to* person); produce (will) before proper authority in order to establish its legality. Hence **propou·nd**ER[1] n. [earlier *propone* f. L PRO[1](*ponere posit-* place), cf. *compound* &c.]

propraе·tor, n. (Rom. hist.). Ex-praetor with authority of praetor in province not under military control. [L, earlier *pro praetore* (one acting) for praetor]

propri·etary, a. & n. Of a proprietor, as *p. rights*; holding property, as *the p. classes*; held in private ownership, as *p. medicines* (sale of which is restricted by patent &c.); (n.) proprietorship, as *an exclusive p.*, body of proprietors, as *the landed p.* [f. LL *proprietarius* (as PROPERTY, see -ARY[1])]

propri·etor, n. Owner. Hence **proprietor·i**AL a., **proprietor·ial**LY[2] adv., **propri·etor**SHIP, **propri·etr**ESS[1], nn. [altered in 17th c. f. prec.]

propri·ety, n. Fitness, rightness, as *doubt the p. of the term, of refusing him*; correctness of behaviour or morals, as *a breach of p.*, (pl.) details of correct conduct, as *must observe the pp.* [(in earlier senses 'ownership, peculiarity') f. F *propriété* PROPERTY]

prō̆·prio mō·tu (or ***mō·tu prō̆·prio***), n. Form of papal bull without seal & used in the administration of the papal court. [L, = of our own motion, wds included in the formula]

props, n.pl. (slang). Stage properties. [abbr.]

prŏptō·sis, n. (path.). Prolapse, protrusion, esp. of eye. Hence **propto·s**ED[1] a. [LL, f. Gk *proptōsis* f. PRO[2](*piptō* fall)]

propu·lsion, n. Driving or pushing forward; (fig.) impelling influence. So **propu·ls**IVE a. [(F as PROPEL, see -ION)]

prŏpȳlae·um, n. (pl. *-a*). Entrance to temple; *the Pp.*, entrance to Acropolis at Athens. [L, f. Gk PRO[2](*pulaion* f. *pulē* gate)]

prō·pylite, n. Volcanic rock found in some silver-mining regions. Hence **propyli·t**IC a. [f. foll. + -ITE[1], as opening a volcanic epoch]

prō·pylon, n. (pl. *-ons, -a*). = PROPYLAEUM. [L, f. Gk PRO[2](*pulon* f. *pulē* gate)]

prorō·gue (-g), v.t. & i. Discontinue meetings of (British parliament &c.) without dissolving it; (of parliament &c.) be prorogued. So **prōrog**A·TION n. [f. F *proroger* f. L PRO[1](*rogare* ask) prolong (term of office &c.)]

pros- in comb. = Gk *pros* to, towards, in addition.

prōsā·ic, a. Like prose, lacking poetic beauty; unromantic, commonplace, dull, as *a p. life, person, view of things.* Hence **prosa·i**CALLY adv., **prosa·ic**NESS n. [f. med. L *prosaicus* (as PROSE, see -IC)]

prō·sāist, n. Prose author; prosaic person. So **pro·sa**ISM(4) n. [as PROSE, see -IST]

prōscē·nium, n. (pl. *-a*). (In ancient theatre) the stage; (mod.) space between curtain or drop-scene & orchestra, esp. with the enclosing arch. [L, f. Gk PRO[2](*skēnion* f. *skēnē* background of stage)]

proscri·be, v.t. Put (person) out of protection of law; banish, exile, (esp. fig.); reject, denounce, (practice &c.) as dangerous &c. So **proscri·pt**ION n., **proscri·pt**IVE a. [f. L PRO[1](*scribere script-* write)]

prose (-z), n., & v.i. & t. Ordinary non-metrical form of written or spoken language (*Milton's p. works*); (Eccl.) = SEQUENCE; *p. poem*, p. work of poetical style; plain matter-of-fact quality, as *the p. of existence*; tedious discourse; (v.i.) talk prosily (*about* &c.), whence **pro·s**ER[1] n.;

(v.t.) turn (poem &c.) into prose. [F, f. L *prosa* (*oratio*) straightforward (discourse), fem. of *prosus*, earlier *prorsus*, contraction of PRO[1](*versus* p.p. of *vertere* turn)]

prose·ctor, n. One who dissects dead bodies in preparation for anatomical lecture &c. [LL, = anatomist, f. PRO[1](*secare sect-* cut)]

prŏ·secute, v.t. Follow up, pursue, (inquiry, studies); carry on (trade, pursuit); institute legal proceedings against (person), as *trespassers will be prosecuted*, (abs.) *shall not p.* [f. L PRO[1](*sequi secut-* follow)]

prosecu·tion, n. Prosecuting (*of* pursuit &c.); (Law) exhibition of criminal charge before court; carrying on of legal proceedings against person; prosecuting party, as *the p. denied this*; *director of public pp.*, English public prosecutor. [f. LL *prosecutio* (prec., -ION)]

pro·secutor, n. One who prosecutes esp. in criminal court; *public p.*, law officer conducting criminal proceedings in public interest. Hence **prosecu·**TRIX n. (pl. *-trīcēs*). [med. L (as PROSECUTE, see -OR[2])]

prŏ·selyte, n., & v.t. Convert from one opinion, creed, or party, to another, as *made many pp.*; Gentile convert to Jewish faith, *p. of the gate* (not submitting to circumcision &c.); (v.t., now rare) make a p. of (person or abs.). Hence **pro·selyt**ISM(1, 2), **pro·selytiz**ER[1], nn., **pro·selyt**IZE(2) v.t. (often abs.). [(vb f. n.) f. LL f. Gk PROS(*ēlutos* f. st. *eluth-* come) one who has come, convert]

prŏse·nchyma (-k-), n. (bot.) Tissue of elongated cells placed with their ends interpenetrating (cf. PARENCHYMA), esp. fibro-vascular tissue. Hence **prosenchȳ·mat**OUS a. [f. Gk *pros* toward, as PARENCHYMA]

prō·sifȳ (-z-), v.t. & i. Turn into prose, make prosaic; write prose. [-FY]

pro·sit, int. used in drinking person's health, wishing him success, &c., lit. = may it benefit you. [L]

prŏ·sody, n. Science of versification. Hence **prosodī·**ACAL, **prosō·di**AL, **prosŏ·di**C, aa., **pro·sod**IST n. [f. L f. Gk PROS(*ōidia* as ODE)]

prŏsōpopoe·ia (-pēĭa), n. (rhet.). Introduction of pretended speaker; personification of abstract thing. [L, f. Gk *prosōpopoiia* (*prosōpon* person + *poieō* make)]

prŏ·spect, n., & v.i. & t. Extensive view of landscape &c., as *a fine, striking, p.*; mental scene, as *opened a new p. to his mind*; expectation, what one expects, as *offers a gloomy p., his pp. were brilliant, no p. of success, have nothing in p. at present*, whence **pro·spect**LESS a.; (Mining) spot giving pp. of mineral deposit, sample or ore for testing, resulting yield; (v.i.) explore region (*for* gold &c.), so **prospe·ct**OR[2] (*or* prŏ·s-) n., (fig.) look out *for*, (of mine) promise (*well, ill*); (v.t.) explore (region) for gold &c., work (mine) experimentally, (of mine) promise (specified yield). [(vb f. n.) as PROSPECTUS]

prospe·ctive, a. Concerned with, applying to, the future (cf. RETROSPECTIVE), as *the law was held to be exclusively p., implies a p. obligation*; expected, future, some day to be, as *p. peer, bridegroom, profit*. Hence **prospe·ctive**LY[2] adv., **prospe·ctive**NESS n. [f. med. L *prospectivus* (as foll., see -IVE)]

prospe·ctus, n. (pl. *-tuses*). Circular describing chief features of school, commercial enterprise, forthcoming book, &c. [L, gen. *-ūs*, = prospect, f. PRO[1](*spicere* = *specere* look)]

prŏ·sper, v.i. & t. Succeed, thrive, as *cheats never p., nothing will ever p. in his hands*; make successful, as *Heaven p. our attempt*. [f. F *prospérer* f. L *prosperare*, as foll.]

pro·sperous, a. Flourishing, successful, thriving, as *a p. merchant, enterprise*, whence or cogn. **prospĕ·**RITY n., **pro·sperous**LY[2] adv.; auspicious, as *a p. gale, in a p. hour*. [f. obs. F *prospereus* f. L *prosper(us)*, see -OUS]

prŏ·stāte, n. Large gland, each of several small glands, accessory to male generative organs in mammals. Hence **prostă·ti**C a. [f. med. L (*-ta*) f. Gk PRO[2](*statēs* f. *sta-* stand) one who stands before]

prŏ·sthesis, n. (Gram.) addition of letter or syllable at beginning of word; (Surg.) making up of deficiencies (e.g. by false teeth or wooden leg) as a branch of surgery. So **prosthĕ·ti**C a. [L, f. Gk *prosthesis* f. PROS(*tithēmi* put, vbl adj. *thetos*)]

prŏ·stitute, n., & v.t. Woman who offers her body to indiscriminate sexual intercourse esp. for hire; (v.t.) make a p. of one*self*, (fig.) sell for base gain (one's honour &c.), put (abilities &c.) to infamous use. So **prostitu·ti**ON n. [f. L PRO[1](*stituere -ut-* = *statuere* set up, place) offer for sale]

prŏ·strate[1] (-*at*), a. Lying with face to ground, esp. as token of submission or humility; lying in horizontal position; overcome, overthrown, as *had laid the Whig party p.*; physically exhausted; (Bot.) lying flat on ground. [f. L p.p. as foll.]

prostrā·te[2] (*or* prŏ·s-), v.t. Lay (person &c.) flat on ground; cast one*self* down prostrate (*at* shrine, *before* person &c.); (fig.) overcome, make submissive; (of fatigue &c.) reduce to extreme physical weakness. So **prostra·ti**ON n. [f. L PRO[1](*sternere strat-* lay flat)]

prō·style, n. & a. Portico of not more than four columns in front of Greek temple; (adj.) having a p. [f. L (-*os*) f. Gk *PRO[2](*stulos* STYLE[2])]

pro·sy (-zĭ), a. Commonplace, tedious,

dull, as *p. talk(er)*. Hence **pro·sily**[2] adv., **pro·siness** n. [f. PROSE + -Y[1]]

prōtă·gonist (also *-agō·-*), n. Chief person in drama or plot of story; leading person in contest, champion of cause &c. [f. Gk *prōtagōnistēs* (*prōtos* first + *agōnistēs* actor, as AGONIZE)]

prŏ·tasis, n. (pl. *-asēs*). Introductory clause, esp. clause expressing condition (cf. APODOSIS). So **protă·tic** a. [LL, f. Gk PRO[2](*tasis* f. *teinō* stretch) stretching forward, proposition]

prō·tĕan, a. Variable, versatile; of or like PROTEUS. [-AN]

prote·ct, v.t. Keep safe, defend, guard, (person, thing, *from, against,* danger, injury, &c.); (Pol. Econ.) guard (home industry) against competition by imposts on foreign goods; (Commerc.) provide funds to meet (bill, draft); provide (machinery &c.) with appliances to prevent injury from it, as *protected rifles.* Hence **prote·ctive** a., **prote·ctively**[2] adv., **prote·ctiveness** n. [f. L PRO[1](*tegere tect-* cover)]

prote·ction, n. Protecting, defence, as *is safe under your p., affords p. against weather*; patronage, as *book was indebted to your kind p.*; protecting person or thing, as *man, dog, is a great p. against burglars*; safe-conduct; U.S. certificate of American citizenship issued to seamen; (Pol. Econ.) system of protecting home industries, whence **prote·ctionism**(3), **prote·ctionist**(2), nn. [F, f. LL *protectionem* (as prec., see -ION)]

prote·ctor, n. Person who protects; regent in charge of kingdom during minority, absence, &c., of sovereign, *Lord P. of the Commonwealth,* title of Oliver Cromwell (1653–8) & Richard Cromwell (1658–9), whence **prote·ctoral** a., **prote·ctorship** n.; thing, device, that protects, as CHEST-*p.*, *point-p.* (for pencil). Hence **prote·ctress**[1] n. [f. OF *protectour* f. LL *protector* (as PROTECT, see -OR[2])]

prote·ctorate (*-at*), n. Office of protector of kingdom or State; period of this, esp. of the p. of O. & R. Cromwell; protectorship of weak state by stronger one, esp. of territory inhabited by native tribes; such territory. [-ATE[1]]

prote·ctory, n. (Rom. Cath.). Institution for care of destitute or vicious children. [f. LL *protectorius* a. (as PROTECT, see -ORY)]

prŏ·tégé (-ĕzhā), n. (fem. *-gée*). Person to whom another is (usu. permanent) protector or patron. [F, p.p. of *protéger* PROTECT]

prō·tĕid, n. =PROTEIN (1st sense). [-ID[4]]

prō·tĕiform, a. Very changeable in form. [f. PROTEUS + -FORM]

prō·tĕin, n. (chem.). (Now preferred in scient. use to *proteid*) albuminoid; (orig.) supposed basis of albuminoids. Hence **proteina·ceous, proteĭ·nic, protē·inous,** aa. [G, f. Gk *prōteios* primary (*prōtos* first), see -IN]

prŏter(o)- in comb. = Gk *proteros* former, anterior, as: *protera·ndrous, proterŏ·gynous,* having stamens (pistil) mature before pistil (stamens).

prō·test[1], n. Formal statement of dissent or disapproval, remonstrance, as *made a p., paid it under p.*; written statement of dissent from motion carried in H. of Lords signed by any peer of minority; written declaration usu. by notary public that bill has been duly presented & payment or acceptance refused; solemn declaration. [obs. F, as foll.]

prote·st[2], v.t. & i. Affirm solemnly (one's innocence &c., *that,* or abs.); write a protest in regard to (bill, see prec.); make (often written) protest *against* (action, proposal), whence **prote·ster**[1], **prote·stor**[2], nn., **prote·stingly**[2] adv. [f. F *protester* f. L PRO[1](*testari* aver f. *testis* witness)]

prŏ·testant, P-, n. & a. (Member, adherent) of any of the Christian bodies that separated from the Roman communion in the Reformation (16th c.) or their offshoots, whence **Pro·testantism**(3) n., **Pro·testantize**(3) v.t. & i.; (Hist., pl.) those who dissented from decision of Diet of Spires (1529), adherents of reformed doctrines in Germany; (*also* prote·s-) making, maker of, a protest. [F or G (as prec., -ANT)]

prŏtesta·tion, n. Solemn affirmation (*of, that*); protest (*against*). [F, f. LL *protestatio* (as prec., see -ATION)]

Prō·teus (-tūs), n. Changing or inconstant person or thing; (earlier name for) amoeba; kinds of bacteria; kinds of tailed amphibian with eel-like body & four short legs. [L, f. Gk *Prōteus* sea-god taking various shapes]

prōthală·mium, -on, n. Preliminary nuptial song. [(*-on*) made by Spenser on EPITHALAMIUM (PRO-[2])]

prŏ·thesis, n. (Placing of eucharistic elements on) credence-table, part of church where this stands; (Gram.) =PROSTHESIS, so **prothĕ·tic** a. [Gk *prothesis* f. PRO[2](*tithēmi* place)]

proti·sta, n. pl. Kingdom of organized beings not distinguished as animals or plants. [Gk *prōtista,* neut. pl. double superl. f. *prōtos* first]

prōto- in comb. = Gk *prōtos* first. (1) = chief, original, primitive, as; *-A·rabic, -Ce·ltic,* &c., of the original Arabs &c.; *-genĕ·tic, -gĕ·nic,* of first period of formation of growth; *-gine* (-jin), kind of granite found in Alps, assumed to be the most ancient; *-hi·ppus,* extinct quadruped related to horse; *-martyr,* first martyr (esp., of Christians, St Stephen); *-phyta* n. pl., the most simply organized plants, each consisting of single cell, *-phyte,* such plant; *-thēr·ia* n. pl., mammals of the lowest subclass, their hypothetical ancestors; *-zo·a* n.pl., great division of animal kingdom comprising animals of simplest type consisting of single cell & usu. microscopic, *-zo·on,* such animal; *-zo·al* a., *-zo·an* a. & n., (animal) of the protozoa, (of disease) caused by parasitic protozoon; *-zo·ic,* (Geol., of strata) containing earliest traces of living beings (also) = *-zo·al*; *-zoŏ·logy,* study of protozoa. (2) in chem. names of compounds in which the element or radical combines in smallest proportion with another element, as *protochloride, -sulphide, protoxide,* compound containing minimum of chlorine, sulphur, oxygen.

pro·tocŏl, n., & v.i. & t. (-ll-). Original draught of diplomatic document, esp. of terms of treaty agreed to in conference & signed by the parties; formal statement of transaction; (in France) etiquette department of Ministry of Foreign Affairs; official formulas at beginning & end of charter, papal bull, &c.; (v.i.) draw up pp.; (v.t.) record in p. [f. OF *prothocole* f. med. L f. Gk PROTO(*kollon* f. *kolla* glue) fly-leaf glued to book]

pro·ton, n. (physics). Unit of positive electricity, forming part (or, in hydrogen, whole) of the nucleus of the atom (cf. ELECTRON). [neut. of Gk. *prōtos* first]

protono·tary, protho-, (*or* protŏ·n-), n. Chief clerk in some law courts, esp. (Hist.) Chancery, Common Pleas, & King's Bench, (orig. in Byzantine court); *Pp. Apostolic(al),* twelve prelates who register papal acts, direct canonization of saints, &c. [f. LL f. late Gk PROTO(*notarios* NOTARY)]

pro·toplasm, n. Semifluid semitransparent colourless substance consisting of oxygen, hydrogen, carbon, & nitrogen, basis of life in plants & animals. Hence **protoplasmă·tic, protopla·smic,** aa. [f. G PROTO(PLASMA)]

pro·toplast, n. The first created man; original, model; unit or mass of protoplasm. Hence **protopla·stic** a. [f. LL f. Gk PROTO(*plastos* moulded, as PLASMA)]

pro·totype, n. The original thing or person in relation to any copy, imitation, representation, later specimen, improved form, &c. Hence **pro·totўpal, prototў·pic(al),** aa. [F, f. Gk PROTO(*tupon* f. *tupos* TYPE)]

protra·ct, v.t. Prolong, lengthen out, as *protracted their stay for some weeks,* whence **protra·ctedly**[2] adv.; draw (plan of ground &c.) to scale [f. L PRO(*trahere tract-* draw)]

protra·ctile, a. (zool.). (Of organ &c.) that can be extended. [-ILE]

protra·ction, n. Protracting; action of protractor muscle; drawing to scale. [f. LL *protractio* (as PROTRACT, see -ION)]

protra·ctor, n. Instrument for measuring angles, usu. in form of graduated semicircle; muscle serving to extend limb &c. [med. L (as prec., see -OR[2])]

protru·de, v.t. & i. Thrust forth, cause to project; (fig.) obtrude; stick out, project. Hence or cogn. **protru·dent, protru·sible** (-s-), **protru·sive** (-s-), aa., **protru·sion** (-zhn) n. [f. L PRO[1](*trudere trus-* thrust)]

protru·sile (-s-), a. (Of limb &c.) that may be thrust forth. [as prec., see -ILE]

protū·berant, a. Bulging out, prominent (lit. & fig.). Hence **protu·berance** n. [f. L PRO[1](*tuberare* f. *tuber* hump), see -ANT]

prō·tўle, n. (chem.). Supposed original undifferentiated matter of which chemical elements may be composed. [f. PROTO- + -YL]

proud (-owd), a. & adv. Valuing oneself highly or too highly, esp. on the ground *of* (qualities, rank, possessions, &c.); (also *p.-hearted*) haughty, arrogant; feeling oneself greatly honoured, as *am p. of his acquaintance, of knowing him, to know him*; having a proper PRIDE, as *too p. to complain*; (of actions &c.) showing pride; of which one is or may be justly p., as *a p. day for us, a p. sight*; (of things) imposing, splendid; (of waters) swollen, in flood; *p. flesh,* overgrown flesh round healing wound; (adv., colloq.) *you do me p.* (honour me greatly). Hence **prou·dly**[2] adv. [OE *prút, -d,* prob. f. OF *prud* (F *preux*) f. LL **prodis* useful, cf. L *prodesse* be of use]

prove (-ōōv), v.t. & i. (archaic p.p. *-en*). (Archaic) test qualities of, try; subject (gun &c.) to testing process; (Arith.) test accuracy of (calculation); take proof impression of (stereotype plate &c.); make certain, demonstrate, (fact, *the truth of,* thing &c. *to* be, *that*), whence **pro·vable** a., **pro·vableness** n., **pro·vably**[2] adv.; (Sc. Law, as verdict in criminal trial) *not proven*; establish genuineness & validity of (will); (intr.) turn out (*to* be, *to* do), turn out to be, as *will p. (to be) the heir, to know nothing about it.* [f. OF *prover* f. L *probare* test]

provē·ditor, prŏvedore·, nn. (*-tor*) officer of Venetian republic; caterer, purveyor. [f. obs. It. *proveditore,* Port. *provedor,* ult. f. L as PROVIDE, see -OR[2]]

prŏ·venance, n. (Place of) origin, as *vases of doubtful p.* [F. f. *provenir* f. L PRO[1](*venire* come), see -ANCE]

Provençal (F), a. & n. (Inhabitant, language) of Provence. [as PROVINCIAL]

prŏ·vender (-ĭn-), n. Fodder; (facet.) food for human beings. [f.OF *provend(r)e* corrupt. f. L as PREBEND]

provē·nience, n. = PROVENANCE. [f. L as PROVENANCE, see -ENCE]

prŏ·verb, n. Short pithy saying in general use, adage, saw; *ignorant* &c. *to a p.* (notoriously); *their fickleness is a p.* (notorious), *he is a p.* (byword) *for in-*

accuracy; play (usu. French) based on p.; (pl.) kinds of round game; *Book of Pp.* (in O.T.). [f. F *proverbe* f. L PRO[1](*verbium* f. *verbum* word)]

prover·bial, a. Of, expressed in, proverbs, as *p. wisdom*; that has become a proverb, notorious. Hence **proverbia·lity** n., **prover·bially**[2] adv. [f. LL *proverbialis* (as prec., see -AL)]

prŏviant, n. Food supply esp. of army. [G, ult. f. L as PROVENDER]

provi·de, v.i. & t. Make due preparation (*for* person's safety, entertainment, &c., *against* attack &c., rarely *for* undesirable thing); (of person, law, &c.) stipulate (*that*); supply, furnish, (person *with* thing, thing *for* or *to* person); equip with necessaries, as *you must p. yourselves*; make provision, esp. secure maintenance, (*for* oneself, family, &c.); (Hist.) appoint (incumbent *to* benefice), (of pope) appoint (successor *to* benefice not yet vacant); *provi·ding* (*that*) conj., = foll. [f. L PRO[1](*vidēre vis-* see)]

provi·ded, a. & conj. (Adj.) in vbl senses, as *p. school*, public elementary school p. by local authority; (conj.) on the condition or understanding, as *p.* (*that*) *all is safe, p.* (*that*) *he does no harm.* [-ED[1]]

pro·vidence, n. Foresight, timely care; thrift; beneficent care of God or nature, *special p.*, particular instance of this; (*P*-) God. [F, f. L *providentia* (as foll., see -ENCE)]

prŏ·vident, a. Having or showing foresight; thrifty. Hence **pro·vidently**[2] adv. [as PROVIDE, see -ENT]

provide·ntial (-shl), a. Of, by, divine foresight or interposition; opportune, lucky. Hence **provide·ntially**[2] adv. [f. L as PROVIDENCE + -AL]

provi·der, n. In vbl senses; *lion's p.*, jackal (lit. & fig.); *universal p.*, tradesman dealing in all or many kinds of goods &c. [-ER[1]]

prŏ·vince, n. (Rom. Hist.) territory outside Italy under Roman governor; principal division of kingdom &c.; (Eccl.) district under archbishop or metropolitan; *the pp.*, whole of a country outside the capital; sphere of action, business, as (*is not within*) *my p.*; branch of learning &c., as *in the p. of polite letters.* [F, f. L *provincia* official duty, province, etym. dub.]

provi·ncial (-shl), a. & n. Of a province; of the provinces; having the manners, speech, narrow views, &c., prevalent in these, whence **provincia·lity** (-shĭ-) n.; (n.) inhabitant of a province or the provinces (also **provi·ncialist** n.), countrified person, (Eccl.) head of, chief of religious order in, a province. Hence **provi·ncialize** v.t., **provi·ncially**[2] adv. [f. L *provincialis* (as prec., see -AL)]

provi·ncialism, n. Provincial manner, fashion, mode of thought, &c.; word, phrase, peculiar to province(s); attachment to one's province rather than country. [-ISM]

provi·sion (-zhn), n., & v.t. Providing (*for, against*), esp. *make p.*; provided amount *of* something; (pl.) supply of food, eatables & drinkables, whence **provi·sionless** a.; legal or formal statement providing for something, clause of this; (Hist.) appointment to benefice not yet vacant; (Hist.) *Pp. of Oxford*, ordinances for checking king's misrule drawn up by barons under Simon de Montfort in 1258; (v.t.) supply with pp., whence **provi·sionment** n. [F, f. L *provisionem* (as PROVIDE, see -ION)]

provi·sional, a. For the time being, temporary. Hence **provisiona·lity, provi·sionalness,** nn., **provi·sionally**[2] adv. [-AL]

provī·so (-zō), n. (pl. *-oes*). Stipulation; clause of stipulation or limitation in document. [L, neut. abl. p.p., = PROVIDED *that*]

provī·sor (-z-), n. (Hist.) holder of a PROVISION, *Statute of Pp.* (preventing pope from granting provisions); (R.-C. Ch.) vicar general. [f. AF *provisour* f. L *provisorem* (as PROVIDE, see -OR[2])]

provī·sory (-z-), a. Conditional; making provision, as *p. care.* Hence **provī·sorily**[2] adv. [f. prec., see -ORY]

prŏvoca·tion, n. Incitement, instigation, irritation, as *did it under severe p.* [F, f. L *provocationem* (as PROVOKE, see -ATION)]

provŏ·cative, a. & n. (Thing) tending to provocation (*of* curiosity &c.); intentionally irritating. [f. LL *provocativus* (foll., -IVE)]

provo·ke, v.t. Rouse, incite, (person *to* anger, *to* do); irritate; instigate, tempt, allure; call forth (indignation, inquiry, a storm, &c.); cause, as *will p. fermentation.* Hence **provo·king**[2] a., **provo·kingly**[2] adv. [f. L PRO[1](*vocare* call)]

prŏ·vost (*in mil. senses* provō·), n. Head of some colleges at Oxford, Cambridge, &c.; (Hist.) head of chapter or religious community; head of Scotch municipal corporation or burgh (in some cities, *Lord P.*); Protestant clergyman in charge of principal church of town &c. in Germany &c.; *p. marshal*, head of military police in camp or on active service, master-at-arms of ship on which court martial is to be held, chief police official in some colonies, (Hist.) French semi-military officer; *p.-sergeant*, sergeant of military police. Hence **pro·vostship** n. [OE has *profost, pra-* cf. OF *provost, pre-*, G *probst*, ult. f. L *propositus* = *praepositus*, see PRAEPOSTOR]

prow[1], n. Fore-part immediately about stem of boat or ship; (Zool., also *prora*) p.-like projection in front. [f. F *proue* prob. ult. f. L *prora* f. Gk *prō(i)ra*]

prow[2], a. (archaic). Worthy, gallant. [f. OF *prou, prod*, (F *preux*) f. LL as PROUD]

prow·ess, n. Valour, gallantry. [f. OF *proece* (as prec., see -ESS[2])]

prowl, v.i. & t., & n. Go about in search of plunder or prey (also fig.); traverse (streets, place) thus; (n.) prowling, esp. *on the p.* Hence **pro·wl**ER[1] n. [ME *prollen*, etym. dub.]

pro·ximal, a. (anat.). Situated towards centre of body or of point of attachment (cf. DISTAL). Hence **pro·ximal**LY[2] adv. [f. L *proximus* nearest + -AL]

pro·ximate (-*at*), a. Nearest, next before or after (in place, order, time, connexion of thought, &c.); approximate. Hence **pro·ximate**LY[2] adv. [f. LL *proximare* draw near (as prec.), see -ATE[2]]

pro·ximē acce·ssit, sent., & n. (Placed in list after name of candidate for prize &c.) he came very near (the winner); (n.) *I was, he got a, p. a.* (was very near). [L]

proxi·mity, n. Nearness in space, time, &c. (*to*); *p. of blood*, kinship. [f. F *proximité* f. L *proximitatem* (as PROXIMAL, see -TY)]

pro·ximo, a. (abbr. *prox.*). Of next month, as *the 3rd prox.* [L, = in next (*mense* month)]

pro·xy, n. Agency of substitute or deputy, as *married, voted, by p.*; person authorized to act for another, as *made me his p.*; writing authorizing person to vote on behalf of another, vote so given; (attrib.) done, given, made, by p. [f. obs. *procuracy* f. med. L *procuratia* (as PROCURATION, see -ACY)]

prude, n. Woman of extreme (esp. affected) propriety in conduct or speech. Hence or cogn. **pru·d**ERY(4), **pru·dish**NESS, nn., **pru·d**ISH[1] a., **pru·dish**LY[2] adv. [mod. F, f. OF *prude, prode*, good, modest, fem. adj. as PROW[2], as n. perh. back formation f. *prudefemme*]

pru·dent, a. (Of person or conduct) sagacious, discreet, worldly-wise. Hence or cogn. **prud**ENCE n., **pru·dent**LY[2] adv. [f. L *prudens* = *providens* PROVIDENT]

prude·ntial, a. & n. Of, involving, marked by, prudence, as *p. motives, policy*; (n. pl.) p. considerations or matters. Hence **prude·ntial**ISM(2), **prude·ntial**IST(2), nn., **prude·ntial**LY[2] adv. [f. PRUDENCE + -AL]

prud'homme (F), n. Member of French tribunal appointed to decide labour disputes.

pru·inose, a. (nat. hist.). Covered with white powdery substance, frosted. [f. L *pruinosus* (*pruina* hoar-frost, see -OSE[1])]

prune[1], n. Dried plum; colour of its juice, dark reddish purple (esp. attrib.); *pp. & prism* (of mincing way of speaking &c., *Little Dorrit* II. v). [F, f. med. L *pruna* (L -*num*) f. Gk *prou(m)non* plum]

prune[2], v.t. Trim (tree &c., often *down*) by cutting away superfluous branches &c.; lop *off, away* (branches &c.); (fig.) remove (superfluities); *pruning-hook* (used for this purpose); clear (book &c. *of* what is superfluous). [f. OF *prooing(n)ier*, etym. dub.]

prune[3], v.t. (now rare). = PREEN. [?]

prune·lla[1], n. Strong silk or worsted stuff used formerly for barristers' gowns &c. & later for uppers of women's shoes; LEATHER *& p.* [etym. dub.; F has *prunelle*]

prune·lla[2], n. Kinds of fever & of throat disorder; *p. salt*, preparation of fused nitre used for p.; genus of plants including the weed Self-heal used to cure p. [earlier *br-*, dim. of med. L *brunus* brown]

prune·llo, n. Finest kind of prune, made esp. from greengages. [f. obs. It. *prunella* dim. of *pruna* PRUNE[1]]

prunt, n. Piece of (esp. blackberry-shaped) ornamental glass laid on to vase &c., tool for applying this. [perh. dial. form of *print*]

prur·ient (-oor-), a. Given to indulgence of lewd ideas; (rare) having morbid desire or curiosity. Hence **prur·i**ENCE, -ENCY, nn., **prur·ient**LY[2] adv. [f. L *prurire* itch, be wanton, see -ENT]

prurī·go, -ī·tus, (-oor-), nn. (Diseased state of skin marked by) violent itching (*-tus*). So **prurī·gin**OUS (-j-) a. [L (gen. *-ginis, -tūs*), = itching, as prec.]

Pru·ssian, a. & n. (Native, inhabitant) of Prussia; *P. blue*, a deep blue pigment, *P. brown, green* (derived from or allied to this); *P.* (small kind of) *carp*. Hence **Pru·ssian**IZE(3) v.t., (esp.) assimilate to the P. system of sacrificing the individual to the State. [f. med. L *Pruzzi* (also *Borussi* &c.) + -AN]

pru·ssic, a. Of, got from, Prussian blue; *p. acid* (HYDROcyanic). [f. F *prussique* (*Prusse* Prussia, see -IC)]

pry, v.i. Look, peer, inquisitively (often *into, about* adv.); inquire impertinently *into* (person's affairs, conduct, &c.). Hence **pry·**ING[2] a., **pry·ing**LY[2] adv. [ME *prien*, etym. dub.]

prўtanē·um, n. (Gk ant.). Public hall, esp. one in Athens for entertainment of ambassadors, presidents of senate, & specially honoured citizens. [L, f. Gk *prutaneion* (*prutanis* president, member of presiding division of Council)]

psalm (sahm), n. Sacred song, hymn; *the* (*Book of*) *Pp.*, (pop.) the *Pp. of David*, book in O.T.; *p.-book*, book containing the Pp., metrical version of these for public worship. [f. L f. Gk *psalmos* song sung to harp (*psallō* twang, sing to harp)]

psal·mist, n. Author of a psalm (also as title of book of psalmody); *the P.*, David or author of any of the Psalms. [f. LL *psalmista* (as prec., see -IST)]

psal·mody (*also* să·l-), n. Practice, art, of singing psalms, anthems, &c., esp. in public worship, whence **psalmŏ·d**IC (săl-) a., **psal·mod**IST (*or* să·l-) n., **psal·mod**IZE(2) (*or* să·l-) v.i.; arrangement of psalms for singing, psalms so arranged. [f. LL *psalmodia* f. Gk *psalmōidia* singing to harp (as PSALM + *ō(i)dē* song)]

psa·lter (sawl-), n. The Book of Psalms; version of this, as *Latin, English, Prayer-book, Scotch Metrical, P.*; copy of the Psalms esp. for liturgical use. [AF *sauter* f. L f. Gk *psaltērion* instrument played by twanging (*psallō* twang)]

psa·ltery, n. Ancient & medieval instrument like dulcimer but played by plucking strings with fingers or plectrum. [f. OF *saltere* f. L as prec.]

psē·phism (ps-, s-), n. (Gk ant.). Decree enacted by vote of (esp. Athenian) public assembly. [f. Gk *psēphisma* (*psēphizō* vote f. *psēphos* pebble, -M)]

pseu·dechis (-k-), n. (zool.). Genus of venomous snakes, as *p. poisoning*, whence **pseudĕ·chic** a. [f. PSEUDO- + Gk *ekhis* viper]

pseudepi·grapha, n. pl. Spurious writings, esp. Jewish writings ascribed to various O.T. prophets &c. Hence **pseudepi·graphAL, pseudepigra·phIC(AL),** aa. [neut. pl. of Gk PSEUD(*epigraphos*, see EPIGRAPH)]

pseud(o)- (psū-, sū-) in comb. = Gk *pseudo-* false(ly), seeming(ly) or professed(ly) but not real(ly), in compp. f. Gk, & as living pref. (sometimes written separately without hyphen as adj., as *the p. penitent*), as: *pseudo-archa·ic*, artificially archaic in style &c., so *-ar·chaism, -ar·chaist*; *-carp* (bot.), fruit formed from parts other than the ovary; *-ca·tholic*; *-Christ*; *-Chri·stian*; *-cla·ssic*, pretending or wrongly held to be classic; *-Go·thic*, sham Gothic in style; *-mar·tyr*; *-pro·phet.*

pseu·dograph, n. A spurious literary work. [f.LL f.Gk PSEUDO(*graphos* -GRAPH)]

pseudo·loger, n. (facet.). Systematic liar. So **pseudolo·gICAL** a., **pseudo·logIST** n. [f. Gk PSEUDO(*logos*, see -LOGER)]

pseu·domorph, n. False form, esp. (Mineral.) crystal &c. consisting of one mineral with form proper to another. Hence **pseudomor·phIC, pseudomor·phOUS,** aa., **pseudomor·phISM(2), pseudomorpho·SIS,** nn. [f. PSEUDO- + Gk *morphē* form]

pseu·donym, n. Fictitious name, esp. one assumed by author. [f. Gk neut. adj. as foll.]

pseudo·nymous, a. Writing, written, under a false name. Hence **pseudony·mITY** n. [f. Gk PSEUD(*ōnumos* f. *onoma* name) + -OUS]

pseu·doscope, n. Optical instrument making convex object seem concave & vice versa. Hence **pseudoscŏ·pIC** a. [-SCOPE]

pshaw (psh-, sh-), int., n., & v.i. & t. (Int.) expr. contempt or impatience; (n.) this exclamation; (v.i.) say p. (often *at*); (v.t.) show contempt for (thing &c.) thus. [natural]

psī, n. Greek letter (Ψ, ψ) = ps. [Gk]

psīla·nthropism, n. Doctrine that Christ was a mere man. So **psilanthrŏ·pIC** a., **psila·nthropIST** n. [f. eccl. Gk *psilanthrōpos* merely human (*psilos* bare, mere, + *anthrōpos* man) + -ISM]

psīlō·sis, n. (path.). Stripping bare, e.g. of hair or flesh; = SPRUE. [Gk (prec., -OSIS)]

psi·ttacine, a. Of parrots, parrot-like. [f. L *psittacinus* (*psittacus* parrot, see -INE[1])]

psō·ăs, n. *P. magnus, parvus,* two hip muscles. [Gk, acc. pl. of *psoa*, taken as sing.]

psor·a, n. A contagious skin disease, itch. [L, f. Gk *psōra*]

psorī·asis, n. Skin disease marked by red patches covered with scales. [prec., -ASIS]

psyche (psī·kĭ, s-), n. Soul, spirit, mind, (in Gk Myth. personified as beloved of Eros, & represented with butterfly wings); genus of dayflying moths. [f. Gk *psukhē* breath, life, soul]

psychī·ater, n. One who treats mental disease. So **psychiă·trIC(AL)** aa., **psychi·atrIST, psychi·atrY[1],** nn. [f. Gk as prec. + *iatros* physician]

psȳ·chic, a. & n. = foll.; *p. force*, non-physical force assumed to explain spiritualistic phenomena; (n.) person susceptible to p. influence, medium; (n. pl.) psychology. [f. Gk *psukhikos* (as PSYCHE, see -IC)]

psȳ·chical, a. Of the soul or mind, whence **psy·chicalLY[2]** adv.; of the animal life of man; of phenomena & conditions apparently outside domain of physical law, esp. *p. research*, so **psy·chicISM, psy·chicIST,** nn. [-AL]

psȳ·cho- in comb. = Gk *psukhē* soul, mind, as: *psycho-ana·lysis*, the psychology of Freud, Jung, & Adler, dividing the mind into conscious & unconscious elements, & investigating the interactions of these (so *-y·tic* a.); *-dyna·mic(s)*, (science) of the mental powers; *-ge·nesis, -gony*, genesis of soul or mind, so *-gene·tic(al), -go·nical*, aa.; *-gram*, writing supposed to come from a spirit, *-graph*, instrument for writing this; *-graphy*, descriptive branch of psychology, (also) spirit-writing; *-mancy*, occult communication between souls or with spirits; *-metry*, faculty of divining from physical contact or proximity the qualities of an object or of persons &c. that have been in contact with it, so *-me·tric(al)* aa.; *-mo·tor* a., inducing movement by psychic action; *-neuro·sis*, mental disease consisting in loss of balance between instincts & controlling power; *-path*, mentally deranged person, *-pa·thic, -pathist, -patho·logy, -pathy*, of, one who treats, science of, mental disease; *-phy·sics*, science of general relations between mind & body, so *-phy·sical* a., *-phy·sicist* n.; *-physio·logy*, branch of physiology dealing with mental phenomena, so *-physiolo·gical* a., *-physio·logist* n.; *-therapeu·tic, -the·rapy,* (of) treatment of disease by hypnotic influence.

psycholo·gical, a. Of psychology; *p. moment* [f. F mistransl. of G *moment* neut. potent element as *moment* masc. moment of time], the psychologically appropriate moment, (improp., esp. facet.) nick of time. Hence **psycholo·gical**LY² adv. [-ICAL]

psycho·logy, n. Science of nature, functions, & phenomena, of human soul or mind; treatise on, system of, this. So **psycho·log**IST a., **psycho·log**IZE(2, 3) v.t. & i. [-LOGY]

psychō·sis, n. (pl. *-osēs*). Mental derangement esp. one not due to organic lesion or neurosis. [f. late Gk *psukhōsis* (*psukhoō* give life to, as PSYCHE, see -OSIS)]

psychro·meter, n. Wet-&-dry-bulb thermometer. [f. Gk *psukhros* cold + -METER]

ptar·migan (t-), n. Bird of grouse family, with black or grey plumage in summer & white in winter. [=Gaelic *tàrmachan*, etym. dub.; *p-* is pseudo-etym. after Gk wds in *pt-*]

ptĕrido·logy (pt-, t-), n. Study of ferns. So **pteridolo·g**ICAL a., **pterido·log**IST n. [f. Gk *pteris -idos*, a feathery fern (*pteron* wing) + -O- + -LOGY]

ptĕro- (pt-, t-) in comb. = Gk *pteron* wing, as: *-da·ctyl*, extinct winged reptile; *-graphy*, description of feathers, so *-gra·phic(al)* aa.; *-pod*, mollusc with middle part of foot expanded into pair of wing-like lobes; *-saur*, extinct flying saurian reptile.

ptĕ·ropus (pt-, t-), n. (pl. *-pī*). FLYING fox. [f. Gk PTERO(*pous* foot) wing-footed]

ptĕ·rygoid (pt-, t-), a. *P. process*, each of two processes descending from junction of body & great wing of sphenoid bone; connected with these. So **pte·rygo-** comb. form. [f. Gk *pterugoeidēs* wing-like (*pterux -ugos* wing, -OID)]

ptisan (tĭ·zn, tĭză·n), n. Nourishing decoction, esp. barley-water. [f. F *tisane* f. L f. Gk *ptisanē* peeled barley (*ptissō* peel)]

Ptŏlemā·ic (t-), a. Of Ptolemy, Alexandrine astronomer of 2nd c., esp. *P. system* (of astronomy, in which earth was held to be stationary); of the Ptolemies, rulers of Egypt from death of Alexander the Great to Cleopatra. [f. Gk *Ptolemaios* + -IC]

ptō·maīne (*or* tomā·n), n. Kinds of (often poisonous) alkaloid body in putrefying animal & vegetable matter, esp. *p. poisoning*. [f. It. *ptomaina* f. Gk *ptōma* corpse (*piptō* fall), -INE⁵]

ptō·sis, n. Drooping of upper eyelid from paralysis of a muscle. [Gk *ptōsis* falling]

pub, n. (colloq.). Public house. [abbr.]

pū·berty, n. Being functionally capable of procreation; *age of p.* (at which p. begins; in England, legally, 14 in boys, 12 in girls). [f. L *pubertas* (*puber* of the age of p., see -TY)]

pūbe·scence (-sns), n. Arrival at puberty; soft down on leaves & stems of plants, downiness; soft down on parts of animals esp. insects. So **pube·scent** a. [F, f. L *pubescere* become hairy, reach puberty (*pubes* groin, private parts, hair on these), see -ENCE]

pu·blic, a. & n. Of, concerning, the people as a whole, as *p. utility, offence, holiday*, (Parl.) *p. act, bill*; done by or for, representing, the people, as *p. prosecution, prosecutor, assembly*; (Univv.) of, for, acting for, the university, as *p. orator, lecture, examination*; open to, shared by, the people, as *p. baths, library, road*; *p. house*, inn, tavern, providing food & lodging, esp. alcoholic liquors to be consumed on premises; *p. education* (at school, also, at p. school); *p. school*, one under p. management, esp. endowed grammar (usu. boarding-) school preparing pupils chiefly for universities or public services, often maintaining discipline with help of pupils; *p. utility societies*, co-operative or semi-philanthropic companies for dealing with the housing difficulty; open to general observation, done or existing in p., as *made a p. protest, gave it p. utterance*, whence or cogn. **publi·c**ITY n., **pu·blic**LY² adv.; of, engaged in, the affairs or service of the people, as *p. life, a p. man, notary p.*; *p. spirit*, patriotism, so *p.-spirited* a., *-spi·ritedly* adv., *-spi·ritedness* n.; of the nations, international, as *proscribed Napoleon as a p. enemy*. (N.) the (members of the) community in general, as *the p. is the best judge, are the best judges, the British, American, p.*; section of the community, as *the reading p., the most gullible of pp.*; =*p. house*; *in p.*, openly, publicly. [F, f. L *publicus*, earlier *poplicus* (*populus* people, earlier *poplus*, see -IC)]

pu·blican, n. (Rom. Hist., & in N.T.) tax-farmer, tax-gatherer; keeper of public house. [f. F *publicain* f. L *publicanus* (as prec., see -AN)]

publica·tion, n. Making publicly known; issuing of book, engraving, music, &c., to the public; book &c. so issued. [f. L *publicatio* (as PUBLISH, see -ATION)]

pu·blicist, n. Writer on, person skilled in, international law; writer on current public topics, esp. journalist. So **pu·bli**CISM n., **publici·st**IC a. [f. F *publiciste* (PUBLIC, -IST)]

pu·blish, v.t. Make generally known, noise abroad; announce formally, promulgate (edict &c.); ask, read, (banns of marriage); (of author, editor, or publisher) issue copies of (book, engraving, &c.) for sale to the public. Hence **pu·blish**ABLE a. [f. OF *puplier* f. L *publicare* (as PUBLIC), altered on -ISH²]

pu·blisher, n. In vbl senses, esp. one who produces copies of book &c. & distributes them to booksellers or to the public. [-ER¹]

puccoo·n, n. N.-Amer. plant yielding red or yellow dye. [native]

puce, a. Flea-colour, purple-brown. [F, =flea(-colour), f. L *pulicem* (nom. *-ex*)]

puck[1], n. (*P-*) the goblin *Robin Goodfellow* or *Hobgoblin*; any mischievous sprite or (fig.) child. Hence **pu·ck**ISH[1], **pu·ck**LIKE, aa. [OE *púca*, cf. ON *puki*, W *pwca*, Ir. *púca*]

puck[2], n. (Disease in cattle attributed to) nightjar, goatsucker. [?]

puck[3], n. Rubber disk used for hockey on ice in Canada. [?]

pu·cka, *pa·kka* (pŭ-), a. (Anglo-Ind.). Of full weight; genuine; permanent, solidly built. [Hind. (*pak-*), = cooked, ripe]

pu·cker, v.i. & t., & n. Contract, gather, (t. & i. of brow, seam, material, often *up*) into wrinkles, folds, or bulges, intentionally or as fault e.g. in sewing; (n.) such bulge &c. Hence **pu·ckery**[2] a. [prob. cogn. w. POKE[1], -ER[5]]

pud, n. (nursery). Child's hand; fore-foot of some animals. [?]

pu·dding (pŏŏ-), n. Soft or stiffish mixture of animal or vegetable ingredients, esp. mixed or enclosed in flour or other farinaceous food, cooked by boiling, steaming, or baking (*batter, beefsteak, bread-&-butter, currant,* HASTY, *lemon,* MILK[1], PLUM, *suet,* YORKSHIRE, *p.*); intestine of pig &c. stuffed with oatmeal, blood, &c. (BLACK, *hog's, white, p.*); *more praise than p.* (material reward); *the* PROOF[1] *of the p.* &c.; thing of p.-like appearance &c.; (slang) drugged liver &c. given by burglars &c. to dogs; (Naut., also *pu·ddening*) pad, tow binding, to prevent chafing &c.; *p.-cloth,* cloth in which some pp. are tied up for boiling; *p. face,* large fat face; *p.-head,* dolt; *p.-heart,* coward; *p. pie,* forms of pastry; *p.-stone,* composite rock of rounded pebbles in silicious matrix. Hence **pu·dding**Y[2] a. [ME *poding*, prob. conn. w. F *boudin*, etym. dub.]

pu·ddle[1], n. Small dirty pool esp. of rain on road &c.; (colloq.) muddle, mess; clay (& sand) mixed with water as watertight covering for embankments &c. Hence **pu·ddl**Y[2] a. [ME *podel, puddel*, prob. dim. of OE *pudd* ditch, cf. G dial. *p(f)udel*]

pu·ddle[2], v.i. & t. Dabble, wallow, (often *about*) in mud or shallow water; busy oneself in untidy way; make (water, also fig.) muddy; knead (clay & sand) into, make, line (canal &c.) with, PUDDLE[1]; stir about (molten iron) to make it malleable by expelling carbon. Hence **pu·ddl**ER[1] (1, 2) n. [f. prec., & cf. Du. *poedelen*, G *pud(d)eln, butteln*, dabble]

pu·dency, n. Modesty. [f. LL *pudentia* (as foll., see -ENCY)]

pūde·ndum, n. (usu. in pl. *-da*). Privy parts. Hence or cogn. **pude·nd**AL, **pu·d**IC, aa. [L (*pudēre* be ashamed, -ND[1])]

pudge, n. (colloq.). Short thick or fat person, animal, or thing. Hence **pu·dg**Y[2] a. [etym. dub., cf. PODGE]

pu·dsy (-zĭ), a. Plump. [cf. prec. & PUD]

pue·blo (pwĕ-), n. Spanish (-Amer.) town or village, esp. settlement of Indians. [Sp.]

pū·erile, a. Boyish, childish; trivial, whence or cogn. **pu·erile**LY[2] adv., **puerĭ·l**ITY n.; *p. breathing* (with loud pulmonary murmur as in children, usu. sign of disease in adult). [f. L *puerilis* (*puer* boy see -ILE)]

pūer·peral, a. Of, due to, child-birth. [f. L *puerperus* (*puer* child + *-parus* bearing) + -AL]

puff[1], n. Short quick blast of breath or wind; sound (as) of this; small quantity of vapour, smoke, &c., emitted at one p.; round soft protuberant mass of material in dress, of hair of head, &c.; (also *powder-p.*) small pad of down or the like for applying powder to skin; piece, cake, &c., of light pastry esp. of p. paste; unduly or extravagantly laudatory review of book, advertisement of tradesman's goods &c., esp. in newspaper; *p.-adder,* large venomous African viper inflating upper part of body when excited; *p.-ball,* fungus with ball-shaped spore-case; *p.-box* (containing powder & p.); *p. paste,* light flaky paste; *p.-p.* (nursery), steam-engine, train. [ME *puf*, imit.]

puff[2], v.i. & t. Emit puff of air or breath; (of air &c.) come *out, up,* in puffs; breathe hard, pant, esp. *p. & blow*; put out of breath, as *was rather puffed*; *p. out,* utter pantingly; (of steam-engine, person smoking, &c.) emit puffs, move with puffs, as *puffed away at his cigar, puffed out of the terminus*; blow (dust, smoke, light object, *out, up, away,* &c.) with puff; smoke (pipe) in puffs; blow *out, up,* inflate; become inflated, swell *up, out*; *p. up,* elate, make proud, (esp. in p.p., *with* pride &c.); advertise (goods) with exaggerated or false praise; bid at auction to raise price. Hence **pu·ff**ER[1] n. [ME *puffen*, imit.]

pu·ffery, n. Advertisement, puffing; puff frilling, puffs. [-ERY]

pu·ffin, n. N.-Atlantic sea-bird with large furrowed particoloured bill. [?]

pu·ffy, a. Gusty; short-winded; puffed out; corpulent. Hence **pu·ffi**NESS n. [-Y[2]]

pug[1], n. (Also *p.-dog*) dwarf squat-faced breed of dog like bull-dog, whence **pu·gg**ISH[1], **pu·gg**Y[2] a.; *p.-nose(d)*, (with) short squat or snub nose; (among servants) upper servant in large establishment; (quasi-proper name for) fox; small locomotive for shunting &c. [?]

pug[2], n., & v.t. Loam or clay mixed & prepared for brickmaking &c.; prepare (clay) thus, pack (space esp. under floor, to deaden sound) with p., sawdust, &c.; *p.-mill* (for preparing p.). Hence **pu·gg**ING[1](3) n. [?]

pug[3], **n., & v.t.** (Anglo-Ind.). Footprint of beast; (vb) track by pp. [(vb f. n.) f. Hind. *pag*]

pug[4], n. (slang). Pugilist. [abbr.]

pu·gg(a)ree (-rĭ), n. Indian's light turban; thin scarf of muslin &c. worn round hat & sometimes falling down behind to keep off sun. Hence **pu·ggare**ED[2] a. [f. Hind. *pagri* turban]

pū·gilist, n. Boxer, fighter; (fig.) vigorous controversialist. So **pu·gil**ISM n., **pugili·st**IC a., **pugili·st**ICALLY adv. [f. L *pugil* boxer (*pugnus* fist) + -IST]

pugnā·cious, a. Disposed to fight, quarrelsome. Hence or cogn. **pugna·cious**LY[2] adv., **pugnă·**CITY n. [f. L *pugnax* (*pugnare* fight, see -ACIOUS)]

puisne (pū·nĭ), a. & n. *P.* (*judge*), inferior or junior judge in superior courts of common law; (Law) later, subsequent (*to*), as *p. mortgagees, mortgagees p. to the plaintiff.* [OF (*puis* after f. L *postea* + *né* born f. L *natus*)]

pū·issant (*or* pūĭ·snt *or* pwĭ·-), a. (archaic). Having great power or influence, mighty. Hence or cogn. **puiss**ANCE n., **puissant**LY[2] adv. [F, f. Rom. **possentem* part. of L *posse* be able]

puke, v.i. & t., & n. Vomit. [?]

pukka(h). =PUCKA.

pule, v.i. Cry querulously or weakly, whine. Hence **pu·ling**LY[2] adv. [imit., cf. F *piauler*]

pull[1] (pŏŏl), v.t. & i. Exert upon (thing) force tending to draw it to oneself, as *don't p. my hair, p. his ears* or *him by the ear* (as chastisement), *p. his nose* or *him by the nose* (as insult), *p. his sleeve* or *him by the sleeve* (to gain attention), *p. the* (bell-rope or handle to ring the) *bell, p.* person's LEG, *p.* (=*draw*) *the* LONG[1]*-bow, p. the* STRINGS, WIRES; draw (thing &c.) towards oneself or in direction so regarded, as *p. it nearer, p. him into the room, p. your cap over your ears, p. off* one's *hat* (as salutation), *p. on* one's *stockings*; *p.* (thing) *to pieces,* separate its parts forcibly, (fig.) criticize (person, thing) unfavourably; exert pulling force, as *horse pulls well, pulled* (*away*) *at the handle*; proceed with effort (*up* hill &c.); (of horse) strain, esp. habitually, against bit; *p. devil, p.* BAKER; draw, suck, *at* (pipe, tankard); pluck (plant, often *up*) by root; *pulled,* reduced in health or spirits; *pulled bread,* pieces from inside of new loaf, rebaked till crisp; *p. caps, wigs,* scuffle, quarrel; tear, pluck, *at* (thing); print upon (sheet), print (copy, proof), orig. in old hand-press by pulling bar towards one; move boat, move (boat), by pulling oar, (of boat) be rowed, be rowed by (so many oars), as *she pulled in shore, pulls 6 oars*; *p.* (row with effect in proportion to) one's *weight*; (slang) arrest; (slang) make raid on (gambling-house &c.); check (horse) esp. so as to make him lose race; (Crick.) strike (ball, or abs.), strike ball bowled by (bowler), from off to leg; (Golf) drive (ball, or abs.) widely to left; *p. a* FACE[1]; *p. a sanctimonious* &c. *face,* assume such expression; *p. about,* p. from side to side, treat roughly; *p. down,* demolish (building &c.), lower in health, spirits, price, &c.; *p. off,* win (prize, contest); *p. out,* row out, (of train) move out of station; *p. out of the fire,* save (game &c.) when the case seems hopeless; *p.-over* n., sweater; *pull through* adv. & prep., get (person), get oneself, safely through (danger, illness, &c., or abs.); *p.-through* n., cord with which cleaning-rag is drawn through rifle; *p.* one*self together,* rally, recover oneself; *p. together,* work in harmony; *p. up,* cause (person, horse, vehicle) to stop, reprimand, check oneself, advance one's relative position in race &c.; *p.-back,* retarding influence, check, contrivance for pulling fullness of woman's skirt to back. [OE *pullian,* etym. dub.]

pull[2], n. Act of pulling, wrench, tug; force thus exerted; (fig.) means of exerting influence, interest with the powerful; (Print.) rough proof; pulling at bridle to check horse esp. in racing; spell of rowing; (Crick., Golf) pulling stroke; (in public house) supply of beer &c. exceeding that asked for; *have the p.* (advantage) *of* (person); deep draught of liquor; handle &c. by which p. is applied, as BEER[1], BELL[1], *-p.* [f. prec.]

pu·ller, n. In vbl senses, esp.: kinds of instrument or machine for pulling; horse that pulls esp. against bit. [-ER[1]]

pu·llet (pŏŏ-), n. Young fowl, esp. hen from time she begins to lay till first moult. [f. F *poulet* dim. of *poule* f. LL *pulla* fem. of L *pullus* young animal, cogn. w. FOAL]

pu·lley (pŏŏ-), n., & v.t. Grooved wheel(s) for cord &c. to pass over, mounted in block & used for changing direction of power, one of the simple mechanical powers; wheel, drum, fixed on shaft & turned by belt, used esp. to increase speed or power; (v.t.) hoist, furnish, work, with p. [ME & OF *polie* ult. f. Gk **polidion* pivot dim. of *polos* POLE[2]]

pŭ·llicate (-*a*t), n. (Material for) coloured handkerchief, orig. one made at Pulicat on Madras coast.

Pu·llman (pŏŏ-), a. & n. *P.* (*car*), railway saloon carriage usu. arranged for use as sleeping car. [G. M. *P.*, designer]

pŭ·llūlate, v.i. (Of shoot, bud) sprout out, bud; (of seed) sprout; (fig., of doctrines &c.) develop, spring up. Hence **pu·llul**ANT a., **pullul**A·TION n. [f. L *pullulare* sprout (*pullulus* dim. of *pullus* chick), see -ATE[3]]

pu·lly-hau·ly, a. & n. (colloq.). (Of) pulling & hauling. So **pu·lly-haul** v.t. & i. [-Y[2]]

pŭlmo- in comb. =L *pulmo -monis* lung, as: *-bra·nchiate*, with gills modified for air-breathing; *-meter*, instrument measuring capacity of lungs, so *-metry*.

pŭ·lmonary, a. Of, in, connected with, the lungs, as *p. artery*, main artery conveying blood from heart to lungs, *p. disease*; having lungs or lung-like organs, so **pu·lmon**ATE[2] a.; affected with, subject to, lung-disease. So **pulmŏ·n**IC a. [f. L *pulmonarius* (*pulmo -monis* lung, see -ARY[1])]

pŭlp, n., & v.t. & i. Fleshy part of fruit; any fleshy or soft part of animal body, e.g. nervous substance in interior cavity of tooth; soft formless mass, esp. that of linen, wood, &c., from which paper is made; ore pulverized & mixed with water; (v.t.) reduce to p., remove p. from (coffee-beans), whence **pu·lp**ER[1](2) n.; (v.i.) become pulpy. Hence or cogn. **pu·lp**IFY v.t., **pu·lp**INESS n., **pu·lp**LESS, **pu·lp**OUS, **pu·lp**Y[2], aa. [f. L *pulpa*]

pu·lpit (pŏŏ-), n. Raised enclosed platform usu. with desk & seat from which preacher in church or chapel delivers sermon; *the* profession of preaching; preachers; (in title of book) collected sermons; (attrib.) *p. eloquence, orator, style*. [f. L *pulpitum* scaffold, platform]

pulpiteer·, n., & v.i. Professional preacher (usu. contempt.), so **pulpit**AR·IAN a. & n.; (v.i.) preach, whence **pulpiteer·ing**[1] n. [-EER]

pulque (pŏŏ·lkĕ), n. Mexican fermented drink from sap of agave &c.; *p. brandy*, intoxicant made from p. [Sp.-Amer.]

pŭlsa·te (*or* pŭ·l-), v.t. & i. Expand & contract rhythmically, beat, throb (lit. & fig.); vibrate, quiver, thrill; agitate (diamonds) with machine (**pulsa·t**OR[2] n.) to separate them from earth in which they are found. Hence or cogn. **puls**A·TION n., **pu·lsat**ORY a. [f. L *pulsare* push, beat, frequent. of *pellere puls-* drive, see -ATE[3]]

pu·lsatile, a. Of, having the property of, pulsation; (of musical instrument) played by percussion. [as prec. + -ILE]

pulsati·lla, n. The pasque-flower, its extract used in pharmacy. [med. L (dim. of *pulsata* fem. p.p. of *pulso* beat (as quivering in wind)]

pulse[1], n., & v.i. & t. Rhythmical throbbing of arteries as blood is propelled along them esp. as felt in wrists, temples, &c.; *feel* person's *p.* (as indicating by its rate & character his state of health, fig., sound his intentions &c.); each successive beat of arteries or heart; (fig.) throb, thrill, of life or emotion; rhythmical recurrence of strokes e.g. of oars; single beat or vibration of sound, light, &c.; (v.i.) pulsate (lit. & fig.); (v.t.) send *out*, *in*, &c., by rhythmic beats. Hence **pu·lse**LESS a., **pu·lseless**NESS n. [(n.) ME & OF *pous* f. L *pulsus -ūs* f. *pellere puls-* drive; vb as PULSATE]

pŭlse[2], n. (Collective sing., sometimes with pl. vb) edible seeds of leguminous plants e.g. peas, beans, lentils; (with pl.) any kind of these. [f. OF *pols* f. L *puls -ltis* pottage of meal &c.]

pulsi·meter, n. Instrument for measuring rate or force of pulse. [f. PULSE[1] + -I- + -METER]

pulso·meter, n. Steam-condensing vacuum pump, so called from pulsatory action of the steam. [as prec., see -O-]

pŭlta·ceous, a. Of (the nature of) pap or a poultice, soft, pulpy. [as PULSE[2], see -ACEOUS]

pŭ·lverize, v.t. & i. Reduce to powder or dust, divide (liquid) into spray, whence **pu·lverizat**OR[2](2), **pu·lveriz**ER[1](2), nn.; (fig.) demolish, crush, smash; (intr.) crumble to dust. Hence **pu·lveriz**ABLE a., **pulveriz**A·TION n. [f. LL *pulverizare* (*pulvis -eris* dust, see -IZE)]

pulvĕ·rulent (-rŏŏ-), a. Powdery, of dust; covered with powder; (of rock &c.) of slight cohesion, apt to crumble. [f. L *pulverulentus* (*pulvis -eris* dust, see -LENT)]

pu·lvinate (-*at*), **-āted,** aa. (Arch., *-ed*) swelling, esp. (of frieze) with convex face; (Bot., Entom.) cushion-like, having cushion-like swelling. [f. L *pulvinatus* (*pulvinus* cushion), see -ATE[2](2)]

pū·ma, n. =COUGAR. [Sp. f. Peruv.]

pŭ·mice(-stone), n., & v.t. (Piece of) light spongy kind of lava used for removing stains from hands &c., polishing, &c.; (v.t.) rub, clean, with p.; *p. hoof* of horse, made spongy by disease. So **pūmi·cĕ**OUS, a. [ME & OF *pomis* f. LL *pūmicem*, L *pū-* (nom. *-mex*)]

pu·mmel, v.t. (-ll-). Strike repeatedly esp. with fist. [altered f. POMMEL]

pump[1], n. Machine, usu. cylinder in which piston &c. is moved up & down by rod, for raising water; kinds of machine for raising or moving liquids, compressing or rarefying gases, &c. (fig. of heart, insect's suckers, &c.); AIR[1], FORCE[1], STOMACH, *-p.*; *bicycle-p.* (for inflating tires); pumping, stroke of pump; attempt, person skilful, at pumping others; *p.-brake*, handle of ship's p. esp. with transverse bar for several persons to work at; *p.-handle* v.t. (colloq.), shake (person's hand) effusively; *p.-room*, building where p. is worked esp. at spa where medicinal water is dispensed. [ME *pumpe*, cf. Du. *pomp*, etym. dub.]

pump[2], v.i. & t. Work a pump; remove, raise, (water &c., usu. *out, up*) thus; make (ship, well, &c.) *dry* by pumping; *p. up* inflate (pneumatic tire), inflate tires of (bicycle &c.); bring out, pour forth, (abuse &c. *upon*) as by pumping; elicit information from (person), elicit (information, usu. *out of* person), by artful or persistent questions; (of exertion) put completely out of breath (esp. pass.); (of mercury in barometer) rise & fall instantaneously; *pu·mpship* v.i. (not in polite use), make water. Hence **pu·mp**ER[1] n. (esp., rail TROLLEY). [f. prec.]

pump[3], n. Kind of light shoe now usu. of patent leather & without fastening, worn with evening dress & for dancing. [?]

pu·mpernickel (pŏŏ-), n. German wholemeal rye bread. [G, etym. dub.]

pu·mpkin, n. (Cucurbitaceous plant bearing) large egg-shaped or globular fruit with edible layer next to rind, used in cookery & for cattle. [f. earlier *pumpion, po-*, f. obs. F *po(m)pon* f. L *pepo* f. Gk *pepōn* large melon + -KIN]

pun[1], n. & v.i. Humorous use of word to suggest different meanings, or of words of same sound with different meanings, play on words; (v.i.) make pp. (*upon* word, subject). Hence **pu·nning**LY[2] adv. [?]

pun[2], v.t. Consolidate (earth, rubble) by pounding or ramming; work *up* to proper consistency with PUNNER. [dial. = POUND[3]]

pu·na (pōō-), n. High bleak plateau in Peruvian Andes; difficulty in breathing caused by rarefied atmosphere. [Peruv., in first sense]

punch[1], n. Instrument or machine for cutting holes in leather, metal, paper, &c. driving bolt &c., driving bolt &c., out of hole (*starting-p.*), forcing nail beneath surface (*driving-p.*), &c.; tool or machine for impressing design or stamping die on material; *bell-p.*, conductor's ticket-p. with bell to announce punching of ticket. [prob. var. of POUNCE[1], but cf. PUNCHEON[1]]

punch[2], v.t., & n. Strike esp. with closed fist, as *p. his head*; *punching-ball*, inflated ball held by elastic bands &c. & punched as form of exercise; prod with stick &c., esp. (U.S.) drive (cattle) thus; pierce (metal, leather, tram-ticket, &c.) as or with punch; pierce (hole) thus; drive (nail &c. *in, out*) with punch; (n.) blow with fist, as *a p. on the head*; (slang) vigour, momentum, effective force. Hence **pu·nch**ER[1](1, 2) n. [(n. f. vb) as prec.]

punch[3], n. Drink usu. of wine or spirits mixed with hot water or milk, sugar, lemons, spice, &c., as *brandy, rum, milk, p.*; bowl of p.; party at which p. is drunk; *p.-bowl*, bowl in which p. is mixed, round deep hollow in hill(s). [perh. f. Hind. *panch* five, from number of ingredients; or abbr. of PUNCHEON[2]]

punch[4], n. (*Suffolk*) *p.*, short-legged thick-set draught horse; (dial.) short fat man or thing; (*P-*) grotesque hump-backed figure in puppet-show called *P. & Judy*, esp. as title of a London weekly comic paper; *as pleased, as proud, as P.* (much, very). [perh. different wds; in last sense abbr. of PUNCHINELLO]

pu·ncheon[1] (-shn), n. Short post esp. one supporting roof in coal-mine; (now rare) = PUNCH[1]. [f. OF *poinçon* f. LL **punctionem* (*puncta* point f. *pungere punct-* prick, see -ION)]

pu·ncheon[2] (-shn), n. (hist.). Large cask for liquids &c. holding from 72 to 120 gals. [identical in form w. prec. in E & OF]

Punchine·llo, n. Chief character in Italian puppet-show; short stout person. [f. It. *polichinello*]

pu·nctate (-*at*), a. (nat. hist., path.). Marked or studded with points, dots, or spots. So **puncta·tion** n. [f. L as POINT[1], see -ATE[2](2)]

puncti·lio, n. (pl. *-os*). Nice point of ceremony or honour; petty formality. [f. It. *puntiglio* dim. of *punto* POINT[1], cf. F *pointille*]

puncti·lious, a. Attentive to punctilios. Hence **puncti·lious**LY[2] adv., **puncti·liousness** n. [f. F *pointilleux* (as prec., -OUS)]

pu·nctūal, a. Observant of appointed time; in good time, not late; (archaic) punctilious; (Geom.) of a point. Hence **punctua·lity** n., **pu·nctual**LY[2] adv. [f. med. L *punctualis* (*punctus -ūs* POINT[1] see -AL)]

pu·nctuate, v.t. Insert stops in (writing), mark or divide with stops; (fig.) interrupt (speech) *with* exclamations &c.; (improp.) emphasize, accentuate, as *flung it on the ground to p. his refusal.* Hence or cogn. **pu·nctuat**IVE a., **pu·nctuat**OR[2] n. [f. med. L *punctuare* (as prec.), see -ATE[3]]

punctua·tion, n. Insertion of vowel & other points in Hebrew &c.; practice, art, of punctuating. [f. med. L *punctuatio* (prec., -ATION)]

pu·nctum, n. (pl. *-ta*). Speck, dot, spot of colour or elevation or depression on surface. So **pu·nct**ULE n., whence **pu·nctu-late**[2](2) a., **punctula·tion** n. [L, = POINT[1]]

pu·ncture (-tsh*er*), n., & v.t. & i. Pricking, prick, esp. accidental pricking of pneumatic tire; hole thus made; (v.t.) prick, pierce; (v.i. of tire, bicycle &c., rider &c.) experience a p. [(vb f. n.) f. L *punctura* (as POINT[1], -URE)]

pu·ndit, n. Hindu learned in Sanskrit & in philosophy, religion, & jurisprudence, of India; (facet.) learned teacher. [f. Hind. *paṇḍit*]

pu·ngent (-j-), a. (Nat. Hist.) sharp-pointed; (of reproof, satire, &c.) biting, caustic; mentally stimulating, piquant; affecting organs of smell or taste, or skin &c., with pricking sensation, as *p. gas, smoke, sauce.* Hence **pu·ng**ENCY n., **pu·ngent**LY[2] adv. [f. L *pungere* prick, -ENT]

Pū·nic, a. & n. Carthaginian; *P. Wars* (between Rome & Carthage); *P.* FAITH; (n.) P. language. [f. L *Punicus, Poen-*, (*Poenus* f. Gk *Phoinix* Phoenician, see -IC]

pŭ·nish, v.t. Cause (offender) to suffer for offence; chastise; inflict penalty on (offender); inflict penalty for (offence); (colloq.) inflict severe blows on (opponent in boxing), (of race, competitor) tax severely the powers of (competitor), take full advantage of (weak bowling, bowler, stroke at tennis), make heavy inroad on (food &c.), whence **pu·nishING**[2] a. Hence **punishABI·LITY**, **pu·nishER**[1], **pu·nishMENT**, nn., **pu·nishABLE** a., **pu·nishabLY**[2] adv. [f. F *punir* (-ISH[2]) f. L *punire* (*poena* = Gk *poinē* fine)]

pū·nitive, a. Inflicting punishment, retributive, as *p. justice, expedition.* So **pū·nitORY** a. [f. med. L *punitivus* (as prec., see -IVE)]

punk[1], n. (archaic). Prostitute. [?]

punk[2], n. (chiefly U.S.). Rotten wood, fungus growing on wood, used as tinder. [?]

pu·nka(h), n. (E.-Ind.). Portable fan usu. of leaf of palmyra; large swinging cloth fan on frame worked by cord. [f. Hind. *pankha*]

pu·nner, n. Tool for ramming earth about post &c. [f. PUN[2] + -ER[1]]

pu·nnet, n. Small round chip basket for fruit or vegetables. [?]

pu·nster, n. Inveterate maker of puns. [-STER]

punt[1], n., & v.t. Flat-bottomed shallow boat, broad & square at both ends, propelled by long pole thrust against bottom of river &c.; (v.t.) propel (p., boat, or abs.) thus; convey in a p. Hence **pu·nter**[1] [-ER[1]], **pu·ntIST**, nn. [(vb f. n.) OE, f. L *ponto*, kind of Gallic transport]

punt[2], v.t., & n. Kick (football) after it has dropped from the hands & before it reaches ground; (n.) such kick; *p.-about*, kicking about of football for practice, ball so used. [?]

punt[3], v.i., & n. (At faro & other card-games) lay stake against bank; (colloq.) bet on horse &c.; (n.) player who punts, point in faro. Hence **pu·nter**[2] (-ER[1]) n. [f. F *ponte(r)*, etym. dub.]

pu·nty, pŏ-, n. Iron rod used in glass-blowing. [prob. f. F *pontil* prob. f. It. *pontello* dim. of *punto* POINT[1]]

pū·ny, a. Undersized; weak, feeble; petty. Hence **pu·niNESS** n. [= PUISNE]

pup, n., & v.t. & i. Young dog; *in p.*, pregnant; *conceited* &c. *p.* (boy, young man); *sell* person *a pup*, swindle him esp. by selling thing on prospective value; (vb) bring forth (pups, or abs.). [shortened f. PUPPY]

pū·pa, n. (pl. *-ae*). Chrysalis. Hence **pu·pAL** a. [L, = girl, doll]

pū·pate, v.i. Become a pupa. Hence **pupA·TION** n. [-ATE[3]]

pū·pil, n. One who is taught by another, scholar; (Law) person below age of puberty & under care of guardian; *p.-teacher*, boy, girl, teaching in elementary school under head teacher & concurrently receiving general education from him or elsewhere; circular opening in centre of iris of eye regulating passage of light to the retina. So **pu·pil(l)AR**[1], **pu·pil(l)ARY**[2], aa. [f. F *pupille* f. L *pupillus, -la*, ward, minor, (*-la*) p. of eye]

pu·pil(l)age (-ĭj), n. Nonage, minority (fig. of country, language, &c.), so **pupil(l)a·RITY** n. (law); being a pupil. So **pu·pilSHIP** n. [-AGE]

pu·pil(l)ize, v.t. & i. Take pupils; coach (pupil). [-IZE]

pupi·parous, a. (entom.). Bringing forth young already advanced to pupal state. [f. PUPA + L *-parus* -bearing]

pu·ppet, n. Figure, usu. small, representing human being, esp. one with jointed limbs moved by wires &c. in p.-show; person whose acts are controlled by another; *p.-play, -show* (with pp. as characters); *p.-clack, -valve*, disk valve opened by lifting bodily from its seat, not hinged. Hence **pu·ppetRY**(4, 5) n. [ME *popet(te)* = F *poupette* doll dim. f. PUPA]

pu·ppy, n. Young dog (also, childish, *p.-dog*); vain empty-headed young man, coxcomb, whence **pu·ppyISM** n. Hence **pu·ppyDOM**, **pu·ppyHOOD**, nn., **pu·ppyISH**[1] a. [prob. = F *poupée* doll, irreg. f. PUPA]

pur-, pref. AF form of OF *por-, pur-*, f. L *por-*, PRO-[1] (*purchase, purport, pursue*).

pura·na (poorah-), n. Any of a class of Sanskrit sacred poems. Hence **pura·nIC** (-rah-) a. [f. Skr. *puraṇá* of former times (*pura* formerly)]

Pur·beck, a. *P. stone*, hard limestone from P. in Dorset; *P. marble*, finer qualities of this.

pur·blind, a., & v.t. Partly blind, dim-sighted; (fig.) obtuse, dull; (v.t.) make p. Hence **pur·blindNESS** n. [earlier *pur(e) blind*; *pur- perh.* = PURE in sense 'quite' or = PUR- intensive, with changed sense]

pur·chase[1] (-*as*), n. Buying; *p.-money*, price (to be) paid; (Hist.) practice of buying commissions in army; thing bought; annual return from land, as *sold at 20 years' p.*, (fig.) *life is not worth an hour's p.*, cannot be trusted to last an hour; (Law) acquisition of property by one's personal action, not by inheritance; mechanical advantage, leverage, (often fig.); appliance for gaining this, esp. (Naut.) rope, windlass, pulley (*single, double, treble, -p. pulley*, with 1, 2, 3, sheaves). [ME, f. OF *porchas, pur-*, as foll.]

pur·chase[2] (-*as*), v.t. Buy; acquire (victory, freedom, &c., *with* one's blood, toil, &c.); (Naut.) haul up (anchor &c.) by means of pulley, lever, &c. So **pur·chasABLE** a., **pur·chasER**[1], n. [ME, f. AF PUR(*chacer* CHASE[1]) procure, bring about]

pur·dah, n. (E.-Ind.). Curtain, esp. one serving to screen women from sight of strangers; (fig.) Indian system of secluding women of rank; striped material for curtains. [f. Hind. & Pers. *pardah*]

pure, a. Unmixed, unadulterated, as *p. white, air, alcohol, water*; (of sounds) not discordant, esp. (Mus.) perfectly in tune;

of unmixed descent, p.-blooded; *p. mathematics* (not including practical applications, opp. to *applied, mixed*); (Gram., of vowel) preceded by another vowel, (of stem) ending in vowel, (of consonant) not accompanied by another; mere, simple, nothing but, sheer, as *knowledge p. & simple, p. nonsense, prejudice*; not corrupt, as *his taste was severe & p.*; morally undefiled, guiltless, sincere; sexually undefiled. Hence **pure·**LY[2] adv. (rare exc. in senses exclusively, solely, entirely), **pure·**NESS n. [f. OF *pur*, fem. *pure*, f. L *purus*]

purée (F), n. Soup of vegetables, meat, &c., boiled to pulp & passed through sieve.

pur·fle, n., & v.t. (archaic). Border, esp. embroidered edge of garment; (v.t.) adorn (robe) with p., ornament (edge of building *with* crockets &c.), beautify. Hence **pur·fl**ING[1] n., (esp.) inlaid bordering on back & belly of fiddles. [f. OF *porfil(er)*, as PROFILE]

purga·tion, n. Purification; purging of bowels; spiritual cleansing, esp. (R.-C. Ch.) of soul in purgatory; (Hist.) clearing of oneself from accusation or suspicion by oath or ordeal. [f. OF *purgacion* f. L *purgationem* (as PURGE, see -ATION)]

pur·gative, a. & n. Aperient (medicine); serving to purify. [F (*-if, -ive*), f. LL *purgativus* (as PURGE, see -ATIVE)]

pur·gatory, n. & a. Condition, place, of spiritual purging, esp. (R.-C. Ch.) of souls departing this life in grace of God but requiring to be cleansed from venial sins &c.; place of temporary suffering or expiation; (adj.) purifying. So **purgator·**IAL a. [f. LL *purgatorius* a. (med. L *-um* n.), as foll., see -ORY]

purge, v.t., & n. Make physically or spiritually clean (*of, from,* impurities, sin, &c.); remove by cleansing process (lit. & fig., often *away, off, out*); (of medicine) relieve (bowels, or abs.) by evacuation; clear (person, one*self, of* charge, suspicion); (Law) atone for, wipe out, (offence, sentence) by expiation & submission. (N.) purgation, esp. (Hist.) *Pride's P.*, exclusion by Col. Pride of Presbyterian & Royalist members from Long Parliament; aperient. [(n. f. vb) f. OF *purger* f. L *purgare*]

purifica·tion, n. Purifying; ritual cleansing, esp. that of woman after child-birth enjoined by Jewish law, as *the P.* (*of the Virgin Mary*), Feb. 2nd (*Luke* ii. 22). So **pur·ificat**ORY a. [f. L *purificatio* (as PURIFY, see -ATION)]

pur·ificator, n. (eccl.). Cloth used at communion for wiping chalice & paten & fingers & lips of celebrant. [as foll., see -OR[2]]

pūr·ify̆, v.t. Make pure, cleanse, (*of, from,* impurities, sin, &c.); make ceremonially clean; clear of foreign elements, whence **pur·ifi**ER[1](2) n. [f. F *purifier* f. LL *purificare* (as PURE, see -FY)]

Pūr·im, n. Jewish festival commemorating defeat of Haman's plot (*Esth.* ix.) [Heb., pl. of *pur*, perh. = lot]

pūr·ist, n. Stickler for, affecter of, scrupulous purity esp. in language. So **pur·**ISM n., **puri·st**IC(AL) aa. [f. F *puriste* (PURE, -IST)]

Pūr·itan, n. & a. (Hist.) member of the party of English Protestants who regarded reformation of Church under Elizabeth as incomplete & sought to abolish unscriptural & corrupt ceremonies &c.; member of any non-religious purist party; person of or affecting extreme strictness in religion or morals; (adj.) of the Pp., scrupulous in religion or morals. Hence **purită·n**IC(AL) aa., **purita·nical**LY[2] adv., **pur·itan**ISM n., **pur·itan**IZE(2, 3) v.i. & t. [f. foll. + -AN]

pūr·ity, n. Pureness, cleanness, freedom from physical or moral pollution. [ME & OF *purte* f. L *puritatem* (as PURE, see -TY)]

purl[1], n., & v.t. & i. Cord of twisted gold or silver wire for bordering; chain of minute loops, each loop of this, ornamenting edges of lace, ribbon, &c.; (Knitt., also *pearl*) inversion of stitches, producing ribbed appearance; (vb) border (material or abs.) with p., invert (stitches or abs.), invert stitches of (stocking &c.). [in 1st sense prob. = archaic & Sc. *pirl* twist, etym. dub.; other senses perh. different wds]

purl[2], v.i., & n. (Of brook &c.) flow with whirling motion & babbling sound; (n.) such motion or sound. [cf. Norw. *purla* bubble up, & perh. *pirl* (see prec.)]

purl[3], n. (hist.). Ale or beer with wormwood infused; hot beer mixed with gin as morning draught, dog's-nose. [?]

purl[4], v.t. & i., & n., (colloq.). Turn (t. & i.) upside down, upset; (n.) cropper, heavy fall. [prob. var. of *pirl* (see PURL[1])]

pur·ler, n. (colloq.). Throw, blow, that hurls one head foremost. [prec. + -ER[1]]

pur·lieu (-lū), n. Tract on border of forest esp. one earlier included in it & still partly subject to forest laws; one's bounds, limits; (pl.) outskirts, outlying region (lit. & fig.); squalid street or quarter of town. [prob. altered after LIEU f. *pur(a)ley* f. obs. & AF PUR(*alé* ALLEY) perambulation to settle boundaries]

pur·lin, n. Horizontal beam running along length of roof, resting on principals & supporting common rafters or boards. [?]

purloi·n, v.t. Steal, pilfer. Hence **purloi·n**ER[1] n. [f. AF PUR(*loigner* f. *loing* far f. L *longe*) put away, do away with]

pur·ple, n., a., & v.t. & i. (Of) a colour mixed of red & blue in various proportions with some black or white or both; (anciently, also *Tyrian p.*) (of) the colour got from the molluscs *purpura* & *murex*, crimson; *p.-red* &c., red &c. inclining to p.; p. robe, esp. as dress of emperor, king, consul, &c., as *born in the p.*, or of cardinal, as *raised to the p.* (cardinalate); (pl.) swine fever, disease in wheat; *P. Emperor*, a butterfly; (vb) make, become, p. Hence **pur·plish**[1], **pur·ply**[2], aa. [ME *purpel* f. OE *purpur(e)* f. PURPURA]

purpoint. See POURPOINT.

pur·port[1], n. Meaning, sense, tenor, of document or speech; (rare) object, purpose. [AF, as foll.]

purpor·t[2], v.t. (Of document or speech) have as its meaning, convey, state, (fact, *that*); profess, be intended to seem (*to* do), as *a letter purporting to be written by you, to contain your decision.* [f. AF & OF PUR(*porter* f. L *portare* carry) extend, embody]

pur·pose[1] (-us), n. Object, thing intended, as *could not effect my p., this will answer* (or *serve*) *our* (or *the*) *p., what was the p. of this law?*; fact, faculty, of resolving on something, as *honesty of p., is wanting in p.*; *novel with a p., p.-novel,* (written to defend some doctrine &c.); *on p.*, in order (*to* do, *that*), (abs., also *of set p.*) designedly, not by accident, whence **pur·posely**[2] adv.; *to the p.*, relevant, useful for one's p.; *to little, some, no, p.*, with such result or effect. Hence **pur·poseful**, **pur·poseless**, aa., **pur·posefully**[2], **pur·poselessly**[2], advv., **pur·posefulness**, **pur·poselessness**, nn. [f. AF & OF *purpos*, as foll.]

pur·pose[2] (-us), v.t. Design, intend, as *I p.* (*arranging* or *to arrange*) *an interview, p. that an interview shall be arranged*; (archaic) *am purposed,* intend (*to* do, *doing, that*). [f. OF PUR*poser* PROPOSE]

pur·posive, a. Having, serving, done with, a purpose; (of person or conduct) having purpose & resolution. [-IVE]

purpūra, n. Disease marked by purple or livid spots on skin; genus of molluscs including some from which purple dye was derived. [L, f. Gk *porphura* (shell-fish yielding) purple]

purpūr·ic, a. Of purpura, as *p. fever*; *p. acid,* a hypothetical acid the salts of which are purple. [-IC]

pur·pūrin, n. Red colouring matter orig. got from madder. [f. PURPURA + -IN]

purr, v.i. & t., & n. (Of cat or other feline animal, fig. of person) make low continuous vibratory sound expressing pleasure; utter, express,(words, contentment) thus; (n.) such sound. [imit.]

pū·rree, n. Yellow colouring-matter from India & China. Hence **purrē·ic** a. [f. Hind. *peori*]

pur sang (F), adv. (appended to classifying n. or adj.). Of the full blood, without admixture, through & through, genuine, (*is Welsh* or *a Welshman, militarist, a cynic, p.*; *the artist p. is a rarity*]

purse[1], n. Small pouch of leather, &c. for carrying money on the person, orig. closed by drawing strings together; (fig.) money, funds, as *a common p.* (fund), *heavy* or *long p.*, wealth, *light p.*, poverty, *the public p.*, national treasury; PRIVY *p.*; sum collected, subscribed, or given, as present or as prize for contest, as *will any gentleman give* or *put up a p.?*; (in Turk. empire) *p. of silver, gold,* 500 piastres, 10,000 piastres; bag-like natural or other receptacle, pouch, cyst, &c.; *p.-bearer*, one who has charge of another's or a company's money, official carrying Great Seal before Lord Chancellor in p.; *p.-net*, bag-shaped net for catching rabbits &c., mouth of which can be closed with cords; *p.-proud,* puffed up by wealth; *p.-seine*, p.-net for fishing; *p.-strings*, strings for closing mouth of p., *hold the p.-s.*, have control of expenditure, *tighten, loosen, the p.-s.*, be sparing, generous, of money. Hence **pur·seful** n., **pur·seless** a. [OE *purs* prob. f. LL *bursa* purse f. Gk *bursa* hide]

purse[2], v.t. & i. Contract (lips, brow, often *up*) in wrinkles; become wrinkled; (rare) put (often *up*) into one's purse. [f. prec.]

pur·ser, n. Officer on ship who keeps accounts & usu. has charge of provisions. Hence **pur·sership** n. [f. PURSE[1] + -ER[1]]

pur·slane (-ĭn), n. Low succulent herb used in salads & pickled. [f. OF *porcelaine* altered f. L *porcillaca, portulaca,* on PORCELAIN]

pursu·ance, n. Carrying out, pursuing, (*of* plan, object, idea, &c.), esp. *in p. of.* [as foll., see -ANCE]

pursu·ant, a. & adv. Pursuing; (adv.) conformably *to* (*the Act* &c.), whence **pursu·antly**[2] adv. [f. OF *porsuiant* part. as foll.]

pursue· (-ū), v.t. & i. Follow with intent to capture or kill; (fig., of consequences, penalty, disease, &c.) persistently attend, stick to; seek after, aim at, (pleasure &c., one's object); proceed in compliance with (plan &c.); proceed along, continue, (road, inquiry, conduct); follow (studies, profession); go in pursuit (*after*, or abs.). Hence **pursu·able** a. [f. AF PUR*siwer* f. OF *porsievre*, f. L PRO(*sequere, -ire,* pop. varr. of *sequi* follow)]

pursu·er, n. In vbl senses, also: (Civil & Sc. Law) prosecutor. [-ER[1]]

pursui·t (-ūt), n. Pursuing, esp. *in p. of* (animal, person, one's object); profession, employment, recreation, that one follows. [f. AF PUR*seute*, fem. p.p. & n. as PURSUE]

pur·suivant (-sw-), n. Officer of College of Arms below herald; (poet.) follower, attendant. [f. OF *porsivant* (as PURSUE, see -ANT)]

pur·sy[1], a. Short-winded, puffy; corpulent. Hence **pur·siness** n. [earlier *-ive* f. OF *polsif* (*polser* breathe with labour as PULSATE)]

pur·sy[2], a. Puckered. [f. PURSE[1] + -Y[2]]
pur·tenance, n. (archaic). Inwards, pluck, of animal. [earlier form of PERTINENCE]
pū̆r·ulent (-rŏŏ-), a. Of, full of, discharging, pus. Hence or cogn. **pur·ul**ENCE, -ENCY, nn., **pur·ulent**LY[2] adv. [f. L *purulentus* (PUS, see -LENT)]
purvey· (-vā), v.t. & i. Provide, supply, (articles of food) as one's business; make provision, act as purveyor, (*for* person, army, &c.). [f. AF PUR*veier* PROVIDE]
purvey·ance, n. Purveying; right of crown to provisions &c. at fixed price & to use of horses &c. [f. OF *porveance*, as PROVIDENCE]
purvey·or, n. One whose business it is to supply articles of food, esp. dinners &c. on large scale, as *P. to the Royal Household*; (Hist.) officer making purveyance for sovereign. [f. AF *purveour* (as PURVEY, see -OR[2])]
pur·view (-vū), n. Enacting clauses of statute; scope, intention, range, (*of* act, document, scheme, book, occupation, &c.); range of physical or mental vision. [f. AF *purveu* provided, p.p. as PURVEY]
pŭs, n. Yellowish viscid matter produced by suppuration. [L, gen. *puris*]
Pū·seyism (-zĭ-), n. (Hostile term for) TRACTARIANISM. So **Pu·sey**ITE[1] n. [E. B. *Pusey* d. 1882 + -ISM]
push[1] (pŏŏ-), v.t. & i. Exert upon (body) force tending to move it away; move (body *up, down, away, back,* &c.) thus; exert such pressure, as *do not p. against the fence*; (Billiards) make push-stroke; (of person in boat) *p. off*, p. against bank with oar to get boat out into stream &c.; (bibl.) butt (t. & i.) with the horns; (cause to) project, thrust *out, forth,* &c., as *plants p. out new roots, cape pushes out into sea*; make one's way forcibly or persistently, force (one's *way*) thus; exert oneself esp. to surpass others or succeed in one's business &c., whence **pu·sh**ING[2] a., **pu·shing**LY[2] adv.; urge, impel, (often *on, to* do, *to* effort &c.); follow up, prosecute, (claim &c., often *on*); engage actively in making (one's *fortune*); extend (one's *conquests* &c.); *p.* (matter) *through*, bring it to a conclusion; press the adoption, use, sale, &c. of (goods &c.) esp. by advertisement; press (person) hard, as *do not wish to p. him for payment*, esp. in pass., as *am pushed for* (can scarcely find) *time, money*; *p.-pin*, a child's game. Hence **pu·sh**ER[1] (1, 2) n. (*pusher aeroplane*, with air-screw behind, opp. *tractor*). [f. F *pousser* as PULSATE]
push[2], n. Act of pushing, shove, thrust; (Billiards) stroke in which ball is pushed, not struck; exertion of influence to promote person's advancement; thrust of weapon or of beast's horn; vigorous effort, as *must make a p. to get it done, for home*, (Mil.) attack in force; continuous pressure of arch &c.; pressure of affairs, crisis, pinch; enterprise, determination to get on, self-assertion, whence **pu·sh**FUL a.; (slang) gang of thieves, convicts, &c.; *p.-bike* (slang) bicycle worked by pedalling (opp. *motor-bike*). [f. prec.]
pŭ·shtōō, -tu (-ōō), n. Afghan language. [f. Pers. *pashto*]
pūsillă·nimous, a. Faint-hearted, mean-spirited. Hence or cogn. **pusillani·m**ITY n., **pusilla·nimous**LY[2] adv. [f. eccl. L *pusillanimis* (*pusillus* petty + *animus* soul) + -OUS]
puss (pŏŏs), n. Cat (esp. as call-name); (quasi-proper name for) hare, tiger; (colloq.) girl, as *sly p.*; *P. Moth*, large European moth. [cf. Du. *poes*, Norw. *puse*, perh. orig. a call]
pu·ssy, n. (nursery). *P.(-cat)*, cat; (nursery) soft furry thing, e.g. hazel catkin; *pussyfoot, P-*, (slang) liquor-prohibition, advocate of this, (from nickname of a U.-S. prohibitionist). [-Y[3]]
pu·stūlāte, v.t. & i. Form into pustules. So **pu·stul**ATE[2] (-*at*) a., **pustul**A·TION n. [f. LL *pustulare*, as foll.]
pŭ·stule, n. Pimple; *malignant p.*, disease caused by anthrax bacillus; (Bot., Zool.) wart, wart-like excrescence. Hence or cogn. **pu·stul**AR[1], **pu·stul**OUS, aa. [f. L *pustula* (PUS)]
put[1] (pŏŏt), v.t. & i. (put). **1.** Propel, hurl, (*the weight, stone*) from hand placed close to shoulder as athletic exercise; thrust (weapon), send (missile), as *p. a knife into*, stab, *put a bullet through*, shoot; (Naut.) proceed, take one's course, *back, forth, in* (*to* harbour &c.), *off* (*from* shore &c.), *out*, in ship; move (thing &c., lit. & fig.) so as to place it in some situation, as *p. it in your pocket, on the table, up the chimney, down the well, p.* (mark, write) *a tick against his name, your signature to it, p. the horse to* (*the cart*), harness him, *p. bull to cow* or *cow to bull* (for breeding), *p.* (convey) *him across the river, p. the children to bed, p. him in prison, cannot p.* (deliver) *Russian stock at present prices, has p.* (infused) *new life into him, will p.* (present) *the matter clearly before her, p. a* SPOKE *in his wheel, p. the words into his* MOUTH[1], *p.* one's FOOT[1] *in it*, one's SHOULDER *to the wheel, hand to the* PLOUGH[1], *the* LID *on*; (with less or no idea of physical motion in space) bring into some relation or state, as *p. yourself, the matter, in(to) my hands, time he was p.* (began to go habitually) *to school, p. it to* (offer it for) *sale, on the market, p. Othello on* (*the stage*), produce it, *p.* (add) *milk to your tea, should p.* (price) *it at 2/6, puts* (estimates) *the circulation at 60,000, p.* (translate) *it into Dutch, cannot p. it into* (express it in) *words, what a way you have of putting things!, puts* (sets) *no value on my advice, I p.* (base) *my decision on the grounds stated, p.* (apply) *it to a good use, p.*

(imagine) *yourself in his place, p.* (substitute) *the will for the deed, p. a good* FACE[1] *on it, p. an end, period, stop, to it,* stop it, *p. a check* or *stopper on it, a veto on it,* check it, forbid it, *p. an end to* (destroyed) *himself* or *his life, p. the wind up* one (slang, frighten him), *p.* (stake) *money on a horse, p. his money into* (invested it in) *land, p. & take* (name of a gambling game with teetotum), *p.* (submit) *the case to him, to the vote, I p. it* (appeal) *to you, I p. it to you* (invite you to acknowledge) *that you were after no good, dues were p.* (imposed) *on cattle, every insult was p.* (inflicted) *on him, don't be p. upon* (victimized) *by him, p.* (lay) *the blame on me, p. him* (caused him to be) *at his ease, in fear of his life, out of temper, on his guard, on his mettle, p. him* (make him speak) *on* (*his*) *oath, p. the servants on* (allow them) *board wages, p. the proposal into shape, p. his* NOSE[1] *out of joint, p.* thing *out of court* (make it not worth discussing &c.), *p.* thing *out of* one's *head* (forget, make him forget, it), *a few words will p.* (make) *the matter right, always manages to p. me* (make me appear) *in the wrong, p. out of* COUNTENANCE[1], *must have p.* (made) *the clock fast* (by advancing hands), *p. wise* (U.-S. slang), disabuse or enlighten, *p.* (subject) *them to death, torture, ransom, expense, inconvenience, the test* or *trial, the rack, the sword, confusion, shame, land was p. into* or *under* (sown with) *turnips, p.* (set) *him to mind the furnace, what has p. him on meddling* (induced him to meddle)*?, on this wild scheme?, p. my horse to* or *at* (invited him to jump) *the fence,* (of horse & fig. of person) *must be p. through* (made to perform) *his paces, p. him* (make him read) *through a book of Livy, was p.* (forced, driven) *to flight, to his shifts, to the* BLUSH[2], *was p. to* (forced to play) *his trumps, surprising what he can do when he's p. to it* (pressed), *was hard p. to it to* (could scarcely) *keep them off.* 2. Special senses with advv. *P. about*: lay (sailing vessel) on opposite tack, cause (horse, body of men) to turn round, (of vessel) go about; (chiefly Sc.) trouble, distress. *P. away*: (archaic) divorce; lay by (money &c.) for future use; (slang) consume (food, drink); (slang) imprison; (slang) pawn. *P. back*: check the advance of, retard; move back the hands of (clock); restore to former place. *P. by*: evade (question, argument); p. off (person) with evasion; lay aside esp. for future use. *P. down*: suppress by force or authority; take down, snub, put to silence; cease to maintain (expensive thing); account, reckon, as *I p. him down for nine years old, at nine, as a fool, for a fool*; attribute, as *p. it down to his nervousness*; *p.* one's FOOT[1] *down. P. forth*: exert (strength, effort, eloquence); p. in circulation; (of plant) send out (buds, leaves, or abs.). *P. forward*: thrust (one*self* &c.) into prominence; advance, set forth, (theory &c.). *P. in*: install in office &c., as *p. in a caretaker, bailiff,* (hence) *distress, execution*; present formally (document, evidence, plea, claim, bail) as in lawcourt; *p. in* (make) *an appearance*; make a claim (*for* election &c.); interpose (blow, shot, remark, quoted words), *p. in* one's OAR; throw in (additional thing); perform (piece of work) as part of a whole; (colloq.) pass, spend, (time). *P. off*: postpone; postpone engagement with (person); evade (person, demand, often *with* excuse, compromise); hinder, dissuade, *from*; foist (thing *upon* person); remove, take off, (clothes); (of boat, crew, &c.) leave shore; *p.-off* n., evasion, postponement. *P. on*: clothe oneself or another with; (colloq.) *p. it on,* overcharge, simulate exaggerated emotion, suffering, &c.; assume, take on, (character, appearance); develop additional (flesh, weight); add (so much *to* price, runs, &c. *to* score); stake (money *upon* horse &c.); advance the hands of (clock); bring into action, exert, (force, pressure, speed, STEAM, *the* SCREW); appoint, arrange for, (person) to bowl &c., train to run &c. *P. out*: dislocate (shoulder &c.); (Crick.) cause (batsman) to be out; extinguish (candle, gas, fire, &c.); disconcert, confuse; annoy, irritate; p. to inconvenience; exert (strength &c.); lend (money) at interest, invest; give (work) to be done off the premises. *P. through*: carry out (task); place (person) in telephonic connexion with (*to*) another through exchange(s). *P. together*: form (whole) by combination of parts; *p.* TWO *& two together*; *p.* (*our* &c.) *heads together,* consult; (Crick.) compile (score). *P. up*: *p.* person's *back up,* enrage him; *p.* one's HAIR *up*; employ (person) as jockey; produce (play) on stage; cause (game) to rise from cover; raise (price); offer (prayer), present (petition); propose for election; publish (banns); offer for sale by auction or for competition; pack up in parcel, place in receptacle for safe keeping; sheathe (sword); lodge & entertain (man, horse); take up one's lodging (*at* inn &c.); *p. up a* (*good* &c.) *fight,* make a good &c. fight of it; *p. up with* (archaic *p. up*) submit to, tolerate, (insult, annoying person or thing); *p.* (person) *up to,* inform him of, instruct him in, (also) instigate him (*to* do, to do*ing* or action); construct, build; concoct (underhand piece of work); *p.-up* a., fraudulently concocted. Hence **pu·tter**[1] n. [OE *putian* (late), *potian* (late), *pȳtan,* cf. Da. *putte*]

put[2] (pŏŏt), n. Throw, cast, of the weight or stone; option of delivering fixed amount of a stock at fixed price within fixed time. [f. prec.]

pŭt[3], **pŭtt**, v.i. & t., & n. (putted). Strike golf-ball, strike (golf-ball) gently with club to get it into hole on smoooth piece of ground called *putting-green*; (n.) such stroke. Hence **pŭ·tt**ER[1](1, 2) n. [differentiated f. PUT[1, 2]]

pŭt[4], n. (old slang). Duffer, queer person, countryman, &c. [?]

pū·tative, a. Reputed, supposed, as *his p. father*. Hence **pu·tative**LY[2] adv. [f. LL *putativus* (*putare* think, see -ATIVE)]

pute, a. (archaic). *Pure (&) p.*, mere. [f. L *putus* in phr. *purus ac putus*]

pū·tĕal, n. (Rom. ant.). Stone curb round mouth of well. [L (*puteus* well, see -AL)]

pŭ·tlog, -lock, n. Short horizontal timber on which scaffold-boards rest. [?]

pū·trefȳ, v.i. & t. Become putrid, rot, go bad; fester, suppurate; become morally corrupt; (rare) cause to p. So **putre**FA·CTION n., **pu·trefact**IVE a. [f. F *putréfier* f. L *putrefacere* (*putrēre* be rotten, see -FY)]

pūtre·scent, a. In process of rotting; of, accompanying, this process. Hence **putre·s**CENCE n., **putre·s**CIBLE a. [f. L *putrescere* incept. of *putrēre* rot, see -ENT]

pū·trid, a. Decomposed, rotten; foul, noxious; (fig.) corrupt; *p. fever*, typhus; *p. sore throat*, gangrenous pharyngitis, diphtheria. Hence **putri·d**ITY, **pu·trid**NESS, nn., **pu·trid**LY[2] adv. [f. L *putridus* (*putrēre* rot, -ID[1])]

putt. See PUT[3].

pŭ·ttee, n. Long strip of cloth wound spirally round leg from ankle to knee for protection & support. [f. Hind. *paṭṭi* bandage]

pŭ·tty, n., & v.t. (Also *jewellers' p.*) powder of calcined tin (& lead) for polishing glass or metal; (also *plasterers' p.*) fine mortar of lime & water without sand; (also *glaziers' p.*) cement of whiting, raw linseed oil, &c., for fixing panes of glass, filling up holes in woodwork, &c.; *p. medal*, fit reward for small service (*you deserve a p. m.*); (v.t.) cover, fix, join, fill *up*, with p. [f. F *potée* lit. POTful, see -Y[4]]

puy (pwē), n. Small volcanic cone esp. in Auvergne. [F]

pu·zzle[1], n. Bewilderment, perplexity; perplexing question, enigma; problem, toy, contrived to exercise ingenuity & patience, as *Chinese p.*; *p.-head(ed)*, *-pate(d)*, (person) with confused ideas; *p.-peg*, piece of wood so fixed to dog's lower jaw as to prevent him from putting nose close to ground. [?]

pu·zzle[2], v.t. & i. Perplex; be perplexed (*about, over*, problem &c.); make *out* (solution of problem &c.); MONKEY-*p*. Hence **pu·zzle**DOM, **pu·zzle**MENT, **pu·zzl**ER[1](2), nn., **pu·zzling**LY[2] adv. [?]

puzzolana. See POZZOLANA.

pȳae·mia, n. Blood-poisoning marked by formation of pus-foci. Hence **pyae·m**IC a. [f. Gk *puon* pus + *haima* blood + -IA[1]]

pȳcno- in comb. = Gk *puknos* thick, dense, as *-style* a. & n., (building) with close arrangement of columns, i.e. at interval of one diameter & a half.

py·gmy, pi-, n. & a. One of a diminutive race of men said to have inhabited parts of Ethiopia or India; *the Pp.*, a dwarf race in equatorial Africa; dwarf (fig. of intellectual inferiority &c.); elf, pixy; (adj.) of the pp., dwarf. So **pygmae·**AN a. [f. L f. Gk *pugmaios* (*pugmē* length from elbow to knuckles)]

pȳja·mas, pa-, (-jah-), n. pl. Loose silk or cotton trousers tied round waist, worn by both sexes among Mohammedans & adopted esp. for night wear by Europeans; sleeping suit of loose trousers & jacket. [f. Pers. *pae jamah* (*pae, pay*, foot, leg, + *jamah* clothing)]

pȳ·lon, n. Gateway esp. of Egyptian temple; tall compound structure erected as support or boundary or decoration. [f. Gk *pulōn* (*pulē* gate)]

pȳlor·us, n. (anat.). Opening from stomach into duodenum; part of stomach where this is. Hence **pylŏ·r**IC a. [LL, f. Gk *pulōros* gatekeeper (*pulē* gate + *ouros* warder)]

pȳo- in comb. = Gk *puon* pus, as *-ge·nesis* formation of pus; *pyorrhoe·a*, purulent discharge (esp. as a dental disease). So **py·**OID a.

pȳr·acanth, n. Evergreen thorny shrub with white flowers & scarlet berries. [f. L f. Gk *purakantha*, etym. dub.]

pȳ·ramid, n. Monumental (esp. ancient Egyptian) structure of stone &c. with polygonal or (usu.) square base, & sloping sides meeting at apex; solid of this shape with base of three or more sides; p.-shaped thing or pile of things; fruit-tree trained in p. shape; poem whose successive lines increase or decrease in length; (Billiards, pl.) game played with (usu. 15) coloured balls & one cue-ball. Hence or cogn. **pyră·mid**AL a., **pyra·midal**LY[2], **py·ramid**WISE, advv. [f. L f. Gk *puramis -idos*, perh. of Egypt. orig.]

py·ramidist, n. Student of structure & history of Egyptian pyramids. [-IST]

pyre, n. Heap of combustible material, esp. funeral pile for burning corpse. [f. L f. Gk *pura* (*pur* fire)]

pȳrē·thrum, n. Genus of composite plants, feverfew. [L, f. Gk *purethron*]

pȳrĕ·tic (*or* pĭ-), a. Of, for, or producing, fever. [f. Gk *puretos* fever + -IC]

pyre·xia, n. (path.). Fever. Hence **pyre·xi**AL, **pyre·x**IC(AL), aa. [f. Gk *purexis* (*puressō* be feverish, as prec.)]

pyrhēlio·meter (per-), n. Instrument for measuring heat given off by sun. [f. Gk *pur* fire + *hēlios* sun + -METER]

pȳr·idine (*or* pĭ-), n. (chem.). A volatile liquid alkaloid from dry distillation of bone-oil, used for asthma. [f. Gk *pur* fire + -ID[4] + -INE[5]]

pȳrī·tēs, n. (Also *iron p.*) either of two

sulphides of iron; *copper p.*, double sulphide of copper & iron. Hence **pyri·tic**, **pyriti·ferous**, **pyr·itous**, aa., **pyr·itize** v.t., (pĭr-, or pī-). [L, f. Gk *puritēs* of fire (*pur*, see -ITE[1])]

pyro. See PYRO*gallic*.

pȳro- in comb. = Gk *pur* fire, as: *-ele·ctric*, *-electri·city*, (property of) becoming electrically polar when heated; *-ga·llic acid* (abbr. *pyro*), acid used as reducing agent in photography &c.; *-gene·tic*, productive of heat, esp. in the body, or (also *-gĕ·nic*) of fever; *-genous*, (of rock) igneous, (of substance) produced by combustion of another; *-graphy*, = POKER[1] *-work*, so *-graph* v.i., *-grapher*, *-graphist*, nn., *-gra·phic* a.; *-gravure·*, piece of poker-work; *-latry*, fire-worship; *-li·gneous*, produced by action of fire or heat on wood, as *p. acid*; *-ma·nia*, incendiary mania, so *-ma·niac* n., *-manī·acal* a.; *-meter*, instrument for measuring high temperatures, so *-me·tric(al)* aa., *-me·trically* adv., *-metry* n.; *-phorus*, substance that takes fire spontaneously on exposure to air, so *-phŏ·ric*, *-phorous*, aa.; *-pho·tograph*, one burnt in on glass or porcelain, so *-photogra·phic* a., *-photo·graphy* n. Also in scientific wds denoting (Chem.) new substance formed from another by destructive distillation &c., (Min.) minerals &c. showing some property or change under action of heat, or having fiery red or yellow colour.

pȳr·ope, n. A deep-red garnet. [f. OF *pirope* f. L f. Gk *purōpos* gold-bronze, lit. fiery-eyed (*pur* fire + *ōps* eye)]

pȳrote·chnic, a. & n. Of (the nature of) fireworks, as *p. display*; (fig., of wit &c.) brilliant, sensational; (n. pl.) art of making, display of, fireworks (lit. & fig.). Hence or cogn. **pyrote·chnical** a., **pyrote·chnically**[2] adv., **pyrote·chnist**, **pyr·otechny**[1], nn. [f. PYRO- + Gk *tekhnikos* (*tekhnē* art, see -IC)]

pyro·xylin, n. Kinds of explosive, including gun-cotton, produced by treating vegetable fibre with nitric acid &c. Hence **pyroxȳ·lic** a. [f. PYRO- + Gk *xulon* wood + -IN]

Py·rrhic[1], **p-**, n. & a. *P.* (*dance*), war dance of ancient Greeks; the metrical foot ˘˘; (adj.) consisting of such feet. [(in pros. sense f. L f. Gk *purrhikhios*) f. *purrhikhē*, said to be named f. *Purrhikhos*, the inventor]

Py·rrhic[2], a. *P. victory* (gained at too great cost, like that of Pyrrhus king of Epirus over the Romans at Asculum). [f. Gk *purrhikos* (*Purrhos* Pyrrhus, see -IC)]

Pȳ·rrhonism, n. Sceptic philosophy of Pyrrho of Elis (c. 300 B.C.), doctrine that certainty of knowledge is unattainable; scepticism, philosophic doubt. Hence or cogn. **Pyrrhō·nian**, **Pyrrhŏ·nic**, aa. & nn., **Py·rrhonist** n. [f. Gk *Purrhōn* Pyrrho + -ISM]

pȳru·s, n. Genus of rosaceous trees & shrubs including pear & apple, esp. *P. japonica*, scarlet p. [med. L, = L *pirus* pear-tree]

Pȳthăgorē·an, a. & n. (Follower) of Pythagoras, philosopher of Samos (6th c. B.C.) said to have believed in transmigration of souls; *P. proposition*, Euclid I. 47. [f. L f. Gk *Puthagoreios* + -AN]

Pȳ·thian, a. & n. Of (Apollo's oracle & priestess at) Delphi; *the P.*, Apollo, his priestess at Delphi. [f. L f. Gk *Puthios* (*Puthō*, older name of Delphi) + -AN]

pȳ·thon[1], n. (Gk Myth.) huge serpent or monster slain near Delphi by Apollo; large snake that crushes its prey. So **pythŏ·nic**[1] [-IC] a. [f. L f. Gk *Puthōn*]

pȳ·thon[2], n. Familiar spirit; person possessed by this. Hence or cogn. **py·thoness**[1] n., **pytho·nic**[2] [-IC] a. [f. LL (-*o*) f. N. T. Gk *puthōn*; connexion w. prec. unexpl.]

pyx, n., & v.t. (Eccl.) vessel in which consecrated bread is kept; box at Royal Mint in which specimen gold & silver coins are deposited to be tested at the annual *trial of the p.* by jury of Goldsmith's Company; (v.t.) deposit (coin) in p., test (coin) by weight & assay. [(vb f. n.) f. PYXIS]

pyxĭ·dium, n. (bot., pl. *-ia*). Capsule of which the top comes off like lid of box. [f. Gk *puxidion*, dim. as foll.]

py·xis, n. Small box, casket; =prec. [L, f. Gk *puxis* f. *puxos* box-tree]

Q

Q (kū), letter (pl. Qs, Q's). (Skating) change of edge followed by turn (*reverse Q*, turn followed by change of edge); *mind* one's *Ps & Qs*, see P; *Q-boat*, *Q-ship*, = MYSTERY[1]*-ship*; *Q department*, that of Q.M.G.

Abbreviations (1): Q: quarter, **Q.M.** (-master), **Q.M.G.**, **Q.M.S.**, (general, sergeant); Queen's, **Q.B.**, **Q.C.**, (Bench, Counsel); quick, **Q.F.** (-firing; quod, **Q.E.D.**, **Q.E.F.**, **Q.E.I.**, (see QUOD); *q.*: quantum, **q.l.**, **q.p.**, **q.s.**, (see QUANTUM); **q.**(uery); quod, **q.v.** (see QUOD).

Abbreviations (2): **qr**, quarter; **q.t.** (slang), quiet (*on the strict q.t.*, privately, avoiding notice); **qu.**(asi); **Que.**(bec); **qu.**(ery or aere).

quā, conj. As, in the capacity of, (*objects to the Church not q. Church, but q. Establishment*). [L, abl. fem. sing. of *qui* rel. pron.]

quack[1], v.i., & n. (Utter) harsh sound made by ducks; talk loudly & foolishly; *q.-q.* (nursery), duck. [imit.; cf. Du. *kwaken*, G *quacken*]

quack[2], n., & v.i. & t. Ignorant pretender to skill esp. in medicine or surgery, one who offers wonderful remedies or devices, charlatan, (often attrib., as *q. doctor*, *reme-*

dies); hence **qua·ck**ERY(4) n., **qua·ck**ISH[1] a. (Vb) play the q.; talk pretentiously; puff or advertise (cure &c.). [abbr. of foll.]
qua·cksalver, n. (Orig. form, now rare, of) QUACK[2] n. [Du. (QUACK[1], SALVE, -ER[1])]
quad (-ŏd), n. See QUADRANGLE, QUADRAT.
qua·drable (-ŏd-), a. (math.). Capable of being represented by an equivalent square or expressed in finite number of algebraic terms. [as QUADRATE[2], -ABLE]
quadragenār·ian (-ŏd-), a. & n. (Person) forty years old. [f. L *quadragenarius* (*quadrageni* distrib. of *quadraginta* forty, -ARY[1])]
Quadragĕ·sima (-ŏd-), n. (Also *Q. Sunday*) first Sunday in Lent. [med. L (earlier sense, the forty days of Lent), fem. of L *quadragesimus* fortieth (*quadraginta* forty)]
quadrage·simal, a. Lasting forty days (of fast, esp. Lent); Lenten. [f. LL *quadragesimalis* (prec., -AL)]
qua·drangle (-ŏd-), n. Four-sided figure, esp. square or rectangle; so **quadra·ngu**LAR[1] a., **quadra·ngular**LY[2] adv.; (also *quad*) four-sided court (partly) enclosed by parts of large buildings, such court with buildings round it. [F, f. LL *quadrangulum* (QUADRI-, ANGLE)]
qua·drant (-ŏd-), n. Quarter of circle's circumference; plane figure enclosed by two radii of circle at right angles & arc cut off by them; quarter of sphere; thing, esp. graduated strip of metal, shaped like quarter-circle, instrument properly so shaped & graduated for taking angular measurements. Hence **quadra·nt**AL a. [f. L *quadrans -antis* (QUADRI-)]
qua·drat (-ŏd-), n. (Also *quad*) small metal block used by printers in spacing (*em q.*, *en q.*, broader, narrower, size). [var. of foll.]
qua·drate[1] (-*at*), a. & n. Square, rectangular, (chiefly in anat. names, as *q. bone* in birds' & reptiles' heads, *q. muscle* in loins, thigh, forearm, &c.). (N.) rectangular block or plate (rare); q. bone or muscle. [f. L *quadratus* (foll., -ATE[2])]
quadra·te[2] (*or* kwŏ·-), v.t. & i. (rare). Make square; (Math.) square (circle &c.); correspond or conform (*with*, or abs. of pl. subj.); make conform *with* or *to* or abs. [f. L *quadrare* (QUADRI-), -ATE[3]]
quadră·tic, a. & n. Square (rare); (Math.) involving second & no higher power of unknown quantity or variable (esp. *q. equation*). (N.) q. equation; (pl.) branch of algebra dealing with these. [QUADRATE[1], -IC]
qua·drature (-ŏd-, -tsh*er*, -tūr), n. (Math.) finding of square with area precisely equal to that of figure bounded by curve (esp. *q. of the circle*); (Astron.) one of two points in space or time at which moon is 90° from sun, position of heavenly body in relation to another 90° away. [f. L *quadratura* (QUADRATE[2], -URE)]
quadre·nnial, a. Occurring every, lasting, four years. [irreg. f. L *quadriennium* four-year period (foll., *annus* year), -AL]
quadri- (-ŏd-), L comb. form = four-, in a few L words (*quadriduum* period of four days, *quadripartitus* quadripartite), & in many of later L & mod. formation, esp. in scientific use: **qua·drifid,** a., cleft into four divisions or lobes; **quadrila·teral,** a. & n., four-sided (figure or area; *the Q.*, four fortresses in N. Italy & district protected by them); **quadrili·ngual,** a., using, in, four languages; **quadri·llion,** n., fourth power of million (1 followed by 24 ciphers), (U.S.) fifth power of a thousand (cf. BILLION); **quadrinō·mial,** a., consisting of four algebraic terms; **quadripar·tite,** a., consisting of four parts, shared by or involving four parties; **qua·drireme,** ancient galley with four banks of oars; **quadrisylla·bic,** a., four-syllabled; **quadrisy·llable,** n., word of four syllables; **quadri·valent,** a. (chem.), capable of combining with four univalent atoms; **quadri·vium,** n. (hist.), medieval university course of arithmetic, geometry, astronomy, & music (cf. TRIVIUM).
qua·dric (-ŏd-), a. & n. (solid geom.). (Surface) of second degree. [as prec., -IC]
quadrī·ga, n. (pl. *-ae*). Ancient chariot with four horses abreast (as in sculpture or coins). [L (QUADRI-, *jugum* yoke)]
quadri·lle[1] (as foll.), n. Fashionable 18th-c. game for four persons with forty cards. [F, perh. f. Sp. *cuartillo* w. assim. to foll.]
quadri·lle[2] (k*a*-, kw*a*-), n. Square dance for four couples & containing five figures (also *set of qq.*); piece of music for such dance. [F, f. Sp. *cuadrilla* (*cuadra* square) squadron, band]
quadroo·n, n. Offspring of white & mulatto, person of quarter-negro blood; hybrid of similarly proportioned descent between other human, animal, or vegetable stocks. [f. Sp. *cuarteron* (*cuarto* fourth) w. assim. to QUADRI-]
quadru·manous (-rōō-), a. Four-handed, belonging to the order *Quadrumana* of mammals with opposable digit on all four limbs. [after foll. f. L *manus* hand]
qua·druped (-ŏd-), n. & a. Four-footed animal, esp. four-footed mammal; so **quadru·ped**AL (-rōō-) a.; (adj.) four-footed. [f. L *quadrupes -pedis* a. & n. (*quadru-* form of QUADRI- somet. used before p-, *pes* foot]
qua·druple (-ŏd-), a., n., & v.t. & i. Fourfold, consisting of four parts or involving four parties, (*q. algebra*, using four independent units; *Q. Pact*, that of 1922 between Gt Britain, U.S., France, & Japan, on relations in the Pacific; *q. rhythm* or *time*, with four beats to a measure; *q. alliance* &c.); amounting to four times the amount or number *of*, equivalent to fourfold the amount of, superior by four times in amount or number *to*, (*has a*

light & heat q., or *q. of* or *to*, *that of the earth*); hence **qua·drup**LY[2] adv. (N.) number or amount four times greater than another (esp. *the q. of*). (Vb) multiply (t. & i.) by four. [F, f. L *quadruplus* (prec., *-plus* as in *duplus* DOUBLE)]

qua·druplet, n. (Pl.) four children at a birth; four things working together; bicycle for four. [f. prec. after TRIPLET]

quadru·plicate[1] (-rōō-,-*at*), a.& n. Fourfold, four times repeated or copied; (n.) *in q.*, in four exactly similar examples or copies; (pl.) four such copies. [f. L *quadruplicare* (*quadruplex* fourfold, cf. QUADRUPED, DUPLEX), -ATE[2]]

quadru·plicāte[2], v.t. Multiply by four; make in q. Hence **quadruplica**·TION n. [as prec., -ATE[3]]

quadrupli·city, n. Fourfold nature, being fourfold. [f. L (*-tas*), as prec., -TY]

quaere (kwēr·ĭ), v.t. imperat., & n. (abbr. *qu.*). Inquire (imperat.), it is a question, I should like to know, (*most interesting, no doubt; but q., is it true?*); (n.) a question, query. [L, imperat. of *quaerere* ask]

quae·stor, n. Ancient-Roman official, state-treasurer, paymaster, &c. Hence or cogn. **quaestor**·IAL a., **quae·stor**SHIP n. [L (*quaerere quaesit-* seek, -OR[2])]

quaff, v.i. & t. Drink (t. & i.), drain (cup &c.), in copious or long draughts. [?]

quăg, n. Marshy or boggy spot, quaking bog. Hence **qua·gg**Y[1] a. [imit.; cf. WAG, SWAG]

quă·gga, n. S.-Afr. quadruped related to ass & zebra, less striped than latter; Burchell's zebra. [S.-Afr.]

quă·gmire, n. Quaking bog, fen, marsh, slough (lit. & fig.). [prob. f. QUAG, MIRE]

Quai d'Orsay· (kā-), n. (Used for) the French Foreign Office.

quail[1], n. Kinds of migratory bird allied to partridge esteeemed as food; *q.-call*, *q.-pipe*, whistle with note like q.'s for luring. Hence **quai·**LERY(3) n. [f. OF *quaille* prob. f. Teut., cf. OHG *quatala* prob. imit.]

quail[2], v.i. & t. (Of person, or his heart, courage, spirit, or eyes) flinch, be cowed, give way *before* or *to*; (rare) cow, daunt. [etym. dub.; from 1440; common 1520–60; then disappears till revived prob. by Scott]

quaint, a. Attractive or piquant in virtue of unfamiliar, esp. old-fashioned, appearance, ornamentation, manners, &c., daintily odd. Hence **quai·nt**LY[2] adv., **quai·nt**NESS n. [earlier senses *wise, cunning, ingenious*; f. OF *cointe* f. L *cognitus* p.p. of *cognoscere* learn]

quake, v.i. Shake, tremble, rock to & fro, (of earth with earthquake, person usu. *for* or *with* fear or cold, bog when trodden on, &c.); *quaking-grass*, kinds with slender foot-stalks trembling in wind. Hence **qua·king**LY[2] adv., **qua·k**Y[2] a. [OE *cwacian* cf. QUAG]

Qua·ker, n. (Outsiders' name for) member of Society of Friends founded by George Fox 1648–50, & devoted to peace principles, plainness of dress (esp. the use of drab or grey), simplicity of speech (esp. the use of *thee* & avoidance of titles & words, such as the names of the days, suggestive of paganism), & peculiar priestless religious meetings; (U.S.) dummy gun in ship or fort; (also *q.-bird*, *-moth*) kinds of plain-coloured bird & moth; *q.*, or *q.s'*, *-meeting*, religious meeting of Friends, silent till some member is moved by the spirit, (transf.) silent meeting, company in which conversation flags. Hence **qua·ker**DOM, **qua·ker**ESS[1], **qua·ker**ISM (3, 4), nn., **qua·ker**ISH[1], **qua·ker**LY[1], aa. [name given 1650 w. ref. to 'quaking at the Word of the Lord'; -ER[1]]

qualifica·tion (-ŏl-), n. Modification, recognition of contingency, restricting or limiting circumstance, detraction from completeness or absoluteness, (*statement with many qq.*; *hedged about with qq.*; *requires q.*; *his delight had one q.*); quality fitting person or thing (*for* post &c., or abs.); condition that must be fulfilled before right can be acquired or office held (*the q. for citizenship may be a certain income*), document attesting such fulfilment; attribution of quality (*the q. of his policy as opportunist is unfair*). So **qua·li·ficātory** a. [f. med. L *qualificatio* (foll., -FICATION)]

qua·lifȳ (-ŏl-), v.t. & i. Attribute some quality to, describe *as*, (*q. documents as heretical, person as a scoundrel, proposal as iniquitous*; *adjectives q. nouns*); invest or provide with the necessary qualities, make competent, fit, or legally entitled, (*for* being or do*ing*, *to* be or do, *for* post or sphere, or abs.; *qualifying examination*, to ascertain that candidates are not below a fixed standard, often followed by competitive), (intr.) fulfil some condition, esp. pass examination or take oath, to make oneself eligible (*for* office, or abs.); modify (statement, opinion), make less absolute or sweeping, subject to reservations or limitation; moderate, mitigate, make less complete or pleasing or unpleasing; diminish strength or flavour of (spirit &c. with water, also facet. water with spirit). [f. med. L *qualificare* (L *qualis* such as, -FY)]

qua·litative (-ŏl-), a. Concerned with, depending on, quality (opp. QUANTITATIVE; esp. *q. analysis*). [f. LL *qualitativus* (foll., -ATIVE)]

qua·lity (-ŏl-), n. Degree of excellence, relative nature or kind or character, (opp. QUANTITY; *of good, high, poor, &c., q.*; *is made in three qq.*; *q. matters more than quantity*), general excellence (*has q.*, is excellent); faculty, skill, accomplishment, characteristic trait, mental or moral attribute, (*give a taste of* one's *q.*, show what one can do; *has many good qq.*, *the* DEFECTS *of his qq.*, *the qq. of a ruler*, *the q. of inspiring confidence* or *of courage*); (archaic or vulg.) high rank or social standing (*people of*, *the*, *q.*, the upper classes); (Log.; of proposition) being affirmative or negative; (of sound, voice, &c.) distinctive character apart from pitch & loudness, timbre. [f. F *qualité* f. L *qualitatem* (*qualis* of what kind, -TY)]

qualm (-ahm, -awm), n. Momentary faint or sick feeling, queasiness; misgiving, sinking of heart; scruple of conscience, doubt of one's own rectitude in some matter. Hence **qual·m**ISH[1] a. [cf. G *qualm* vapour (dial. swoon)]

quandār·y (-ŏn-; *also* kwŏ·ndarĭ), n. A state of perplexity, difficult situation, practical dilemma, (*am in a q.*). [from 1580; etym. dub.]

quand même (F), adv. Despite consequences, even so, all the same.

quant (-ŏ-), n., & v.t. & i. Punting-pole with disk to prevent its sinking in mud used by E.-coast bargemen &c.; (vb) propel (boat), propel boat, with q. [perh. f. L f. Gk *kontos*]

qua·ntic (-ŏn-), n. (math.). Rational integral homogeneous function of two or more variables. [f. L *quantus* how much, -IC]

qua·ntifȳ, v.t. (Log.) define application of (term, proposition) by use of *all*, *some*, &c.; determine quantity of, measure, express as quantity. Hence **quan·tifī**ABLE a., **quanti**FICA·TION n. [f. med. L *quantificare* (prec., -FY)]

qua·ntitātive (*or* -*ta*-), a. Measured or measurable by, concerned with, quantity (opp. QUALITATIVE; esp. *q. analysis*); of, based on, the quantity of vowels (*q. accent*, *scansion*, *verse*, &c.). Hence **qua·ntitative**LY[2] adv. [f. med. L *quantitativus* (QUANTITY, -ATIVE)]

qua·ntitive, a. =prec. (rare). [foll., -IVE]

qua·ntity (-ŏn-), n. The property of things that is estimable by some sort of measure, the having of size, extension, weight, amount, or number, (*mathematics is the science of pure q.*; *stated in terms of q.*; *the q. of a surface is its area*); amount, sum, (*the q. of the current depends on the size of the plates*); specified or considerable portion or number or amount of something, *the* amount of something present, (*a small q. of blood*; *a q. of baskets*; *buys in large qq.*; *the q. of heat in an animal body*), (pl.) large amounts or numbers, abundance, (*is found in qq. on the shore*); (Pros.) length or shortness of vowel sounds (see LONG[1]; *q.-mark*, put over vowel to indicate q.; FALSE *q.*); (Log.) extension given to subject of proposition; (Math.) thing having q., figure or symbol representing it, (*incommensurable qq. have no aliquot parts*; *unknown q.* transf., person or thing whose action cannot be foreseen; *negligible q.* transf., person &c. that need not be reckoned with). [f. OF *quantité* f. L *quantitatem* (*quantus* how much, -TY)]

quanti·valence (-ŏn-, -ăn-), n. (chem.). Extent to which one of element's atoms can hold other atoms in combination. [f. L *quantus* how much, after *equivalence* see EQUIVALENT]

qua·ntum (-ŏn-, *in L phrr.* -ăn-, -ŏn-), n. (pl. -*a*, rare). Amount; share, portion; required, desired, or allowed amount; *q. libet* or *placet*, abbr. *q.l.*, *q.p.*, as much as is desired (in prescriptions); *q. sufficit*, abbr. *quant. suff*, or *q.s.*, as much as suffices (in prescriptions), (gen.) sufficient quantity, to sufficient extent; *q. theory* (physics), the hypothesis, accounting for the stability of the atom & other phenomena, that in radiation the energy of electrons is discharged not continuously but in discrete amounts or quanta. [L, neut. of *quantus* how much, as much as]

quāquaver·sal (-*av*-), a. (geol.). Pointing in every direction. [f. LL *quaquaversus* (*quaqua* wheresoever, *versus* towards)]

quarantine (kwŏ·rantēn), n., & v.t. (Period of) isolation imposed on voyagers, travellers, sick persons, or infected ship, that might spread contagious disease; (vb) impose such isolation on, put in q. [prob. f. It. *quarantina* forty days (*quaranta* f. L *quadraginta* forty)]

quār·ĕ i·mpedit, n. Writ issued in cases of disputed presentation to benefice against objector. [L, = why does he hinder?]

qua·renden, -der (kwŏ-), n. Kind of Devonshire & Somerset apple. [?]

qua·rrel[1] (kwŏ-), n. (hist.). Short heavy arrow or bolt used in crossbow or arbalest. [OF, cf. It. *quadrello* dim. of *quadro* a square (LL *quadrus* a.)]

qua·rrel[2] (kwŏ-), n. Occasion of complaint against person or his actions (*have no q. against* or *with him*; *find q. in a straw*, be captious; *pick a q.*, invent or eagerly avail oneself of such occasion to commence hostilities; *espouse* one's *q.*, *fight* one's *qq. for him*, assist him in getting redress; *in a good q.*, justly taken up); violent contention or altercation *between* persons, rupture of friendly relations. Hence **qua·rrel**SOME a., **qua·rrelsome**LY[2] adv., **qua·rrelsome**NESS n. [f. OF *querele* f. L *querela* complaint (*queri* complain)]

qua·rrel[3], v.i. (-ll-). Take exception, find fault *with* (*I never q. with Providence*; *q. with* one's *bread & butter*, abandon employment by which one lives); contend violently (*with* person, *about* or *for* thing), fall out, have dispute, break off friendly relations. [f. prec.]

qua·rry[1] (-ŏ-), n. Object of pursuit by bird of prey, hounds, hunters, &c.; intended victim or prey. [f. OF *curée* (*cuir* skin f. L *corium*, Y[4]), orig. sense, parts of deer placed on hide & given to hounds]

qua·rry[2] (-ŏ-), n., & v.t. & i. Excavation made by taking stone for building &c. from its bed, place whence stone, or fig. information &c., may be extracted; floor-tile; *qua·rryman*, worker in q. (Vb) extract (stone) from q.; extract (facts &c.) laboriously from books &c.; expend toil in searching documents &c. (*quarrying in the Harleian MSS.*). [f. med. L *quareia, quadraria*, (L *quadrare* to square)]

quart[1] (-ort), n. Measure of capacity, quarter of gallon or two pints (*put q. into pint pot*, make less contain greater); pot or bottle containing this amount (*q. bottle* of wine or spirit, $\frac{1}{8}$ gal.); (abs. for) q. of beer (*still takes his q.*); *q.-pot*. [F, f. neut. of L *quartus* fourth] .

quart[2] (kart), n., & v.i. & t. A position in fencing, CARTE, (*q. & tierce*, fencing-practice); sequence of four cards in piquet &c. (*q. major*, ace, king, queen, knave). (Vb) use the position q.; draw back (head &c.) in this. [f. F *quarte* f. fem. L as prec.]

quar·tan (-or-), a. & n. (Ague or fever) with paroxysm every third (by inclusive reckoning fourth) day. [f. F (*fièvre*) *quartaine* f. L (*febris*) *quartana* (*quartus* fourth, -AN)]

quarta·tion (-or-), n. Combining of three parts of silver with one of gold as preliminary in purifying gold. [L *quartus* fourth, -ATION]

quarte. Var. of QUART[2] (see etym.)

quar·ter[1] (-or-), n. Fourth part, one of four equal or corresponding parts, fourth part of, (*divide the apples into qq.*; *q. of a century*, any period of 25 years; *second* &c. *q. of the century*, 26th to 50th &c. years of it; *q. of an hour*, any consecutive 15 minutes; *bad q. of an hour*, short unpleasant experience; *can get it at the stores for a q. the* or *of the*, or *for q. the, price*; *is not a q. as good as it should be*; *q. mile, yard*, &c., q. of a mile &c.); (U.S., Can.) 25 cents or q. dollar, as amount or coin; one of four parts, each including leg or arm, into which beast's or bird's carcase is divided (of beast, often *fore, hind, q.*), (pl.) similar parts of traitor quartered after execution, (usu. pl. in, often *hind-qq.*) haunch(es) of living animal or man, (sing.) either side of ship aft of main-chains (*on the q.*, between astern & on beam); (Herald.) one of four divisions of quartered shield (*dexter & sinister chief, dexter & sinister base*), charge occupying q. placed in chief; grain-measure of eight bushels, used in stating large quantities, prices, &c.; (abbr. *qr*) fourth of cwt, 28 lb.; fourth of fathom (*& a q. five*, $5\frac{1}{4}$ fathoms; *a q. less five*, $4\frac{3}{4}$); fourth of year for which payments become due on q.-day, instalment of allowance &c. for the q., (now chiefly Sc.) school term; fourth of lunar period, moon's position between first & second or third & fourth of these; point of time 15′ before or after any hour o'clock (*at a q. to, past, six*; *it is not the q. yet*; *strikes the hours, half-hours, & qq.*; *it has gone the q.*, clock has sounded for it); (Channel I.) unit of property or income, reckoned as £25, for assessment of taxes &c.; (region lying about) point of compass, direction, district, locality, source of supply or help or information, (*wind blows from all four qq. at once*; *what q. is the wind in?* lit., & fig. how are things going? &c.; *flocked in from all qq.*; *no help to be looked for in that q.*; *had the news from a good q.*); division of town, esp. one appropriated to or occupied by special class (*the Jewish, manufacturing, residential*, &c., *q.*); (pl.) lodgings, abode, esp. place where troops are lodged or stationed (HEAD*qq.*; *winter qq.*, occupied, esp. by troops, for winter; *take up* one's *qq.*, lodge *in, with*, &c.; BEAT[1] *up qq. of*; *beat to qq.* naut., summon crew to appointed stations as for action; *at* CLOSE[1] *qq.*); exemption from death offered or granted to enemy in battle who will surrender (*give, receive, q.*; *ask for* or *cry q.*; *no q. to be given*); quarter-mile race or running-distance (*won the q.*; *has done the q. in* 50″). *Q.-bell*, sounding the q.-hours; *q. binding* of book, with narrow leather at back & none at corners, so *q.-bound* a.; *q. butt* in billiards, cue shorter than half butt; *q.-day*, on which quarterly payments are due, tenancies begin & end, &c. (Lady Day 25 Mar., Midsummer Day 24 June, Michaelmas 29 Sep., & Christmas 25 Dec.); *q.-deck*, part of upper deck between stern & after-mast, *the* officers (cf. LOW[1]*er deck*) of ship or navy; *q.-ill*, cattle & sheep disease causing putrefaction in one or more of the qq.; *q. left, right* (mil.), q. of a right angle to left, right; *q.-light*, window in body of closed carriage apart from door-window; *q.-line* (naut.), disposition in which bow of each ship is abaft beam of one in front; *quar·termaster*, (naut.) petty officer in charge of steering, binnacle, signals, hold-stowing, &c., (mil., abbr. Q.M.) regimental officer with duties of assigning qq., laying out camp, & looking after rations, clothing, &c. (*Q.-m. general*, abbr. Q.M.G., staff officer at head of department controlling quartering, equipment, &c.); *q.-miler*, runner whose distance is the q.; *q.-plate*, photographic plate $3\frac{1}{4}$ in. $\times 4\frac{1}{4}$, photograph produced from it; *q. sessions*, court of limited criminal & civil jurisdiction & of appeal held quarterly by justices of peace in counties & by recorder in boroughs; *quar·terstaff*, stout pole 6–8 ft long formerly used by peasantry as weapon; *q.-tone* (mus.) half a semitone; *q.-wind*, blowing on ship's q. (most favourable sailing wind). [OF, f. L *quartarius* fourth part (of a measure) f. *quartus* fourth, see -ER[2](2)]

quar·ter², v.t. Divide into four equal parts, divide (traitor's body) into qq.; (Herald.) place or bear (charges or coats of arms) quarterly on shield, add (another's coat) to one's hereditary arms, place in alternate qq. *with*, divide (shield) into qq. or into divisions formed by vertical & horizontal lines; put (esp. soldiers) into qq., station or lodge in specified place; (of dogs) range or traverse (ground) in every direction. [f. prec.]

quar·terage (-ĭj), n. Quarterly payment, a quarter's wages, allowance, pension, &c. [-AGE]

quar·tering, n. In vbl senses; esp. (herald., pl.) coats marshalled on shield to denote alliances of family with heiresses of others. [-ING¹]

quar·terly, a., n., & adv. Occurring every quarter of a year; (n.) q. review or magazine; (adv.) once every quarter of a year; (Herald.) in the four, or in two diagonally opposite, quarters of shield (*q.-quartered*, with one or more quarters divided in four). [-LY¹,²]

quar·tern (-ort-), n. (Also *q.-loaf*) four-pound loaf. [f. OF *quartron* quarter; orig. sense, quarter of stone or peck]

quarte·t(te) (-or-), n. Musical composition for four voices or instruments, players or singers rendering this; set of four. [F (*-te*), f. It. *quartetto* (*quarto* fourth f. L *quartus*, -ET¹]

quar·to (-or-), n. (also written 4to, 4°). Size given by folding sheet of paper twice; book consisting of sheets so folded; *q. paper*, so folded. [L (*in*) *quarto* (in) fourth (of sheet); abl. of *quartus* fourth]

quartus (kwor-). See PRIMUS¹.

quartz (-orts), n. Kinds of mineral, massive or crystallizing in hexagonal prisms, consisting in pure form of silica or silicon dioxide, & often containing gold. [f. G *quarz* etym. dub.]

quash (-ŏ-), v.t. Annul, make void, reject as not valid, put an end to, (esp. by legal procedure or authority). [f. OF *quasser* (now *casser*) f. L *quassare* frequent. of *quatere* shake]

Qua·shee (-ŏ-), n. Negro (as national nickname). [f. Ashantee or Fantee *Kwasi* common personal name]

quā·sī, conj. & pref. (Introducing etymological explanation, abbr. *qu.*) that is to say, as if it were, (*Earls of Wilbraham, q. Wild boar ham*); (hyphened esp. to noun or adj.) seeming(ly), not real(ly), practical(ly), half-, almost, (*engaged in a q.-war*; *the q.-art of making enemies*; *has a q.-episcopal position*). [L, = as if]

quă·ssia (*or* -ăsha, -ŏsha), n. S.-Amer., esp. Surinam, tree; (wood, bark, or root of this & other trees, yielding) bitter medicinal decoction. [f. name of negro (cf. QUASHEE) who discovered its virtues 1761]

quăter-centē·nary, n. Four-hundredth anniversary. [L *quater* four times]

quater·nary, a. & n. Having four parts, esp. compounded of four chemical elements or radicals; concerned with the number four; (Geol.) belonging to most recent period, subsequent to Tertiary. (N.) set of four things; the number four; *the Pythagorean q.*, 1+2+3+4=10, with mystic significance in Pythagoreanism. [f. L *quaternarius* (*quaterni* distrib. of *quatuor* four, -ARY¹)]

quater·nion, n. Set of four; quire of four sheets folded in two; Pythagorean quaternary, mystic number 4 or 10 (see prec.); (Math.) quotient of two vectors or operator that changes one vector into another (named as depending on four geometrical elements), (pl.) form of calculus of vectors in which this operator is used. [f. LL *quaternio* (prec.)]

quater·nity, n. Set of four, being four, (esp. as analogous to *Trinity*, in describing heresies). [f. LL *quaternitas* (QUATERNARY, -TY)]

quatorzain (kă·terzān), n. Fourteen-line poem, irregular sonnet. [f. F *quatorzaine* (*quatorze* fourteen f. L *quatuordecim*)]

qua·train (-ŏt-), n. Stanza of four lines usu. with alternate rhymes. [F (*quatre* four f. L *quatuor*)]

quatre (kā·ter), n. =CATER¹.

qua·trefoil (kătre-, kāter-), n. Four-cusped figure, esp. as opening in architectural tracery, resembling symmetrical four-lobed leaf or flower. [f. OF *quatre* (QUATRAIN), FOIL¹]

quattroce·ntist, n. & a. (Artist &c.) of the quattrocento. [-IST]

quattroce·nto (-ah-, -tshĕ-), n. Fifteenth century as period in Italian art. [It., lit. 400, but used =1400]

quā·ver¹, v.i. & t. Vibrate, shake, tremble, (esp. of voice or musical sound); use trills in singing; sing (note, song) with trills, say (usu. *out*) in trembling tones. Hence **qua·vering**LY² adv. [f. obs. *quave* cogn. w. QUAKE, QUIVER², + -ER⁵]

qua·ver², n. Trill in singing; tremulousness in speech, whence **qua·very**¹ a.; (Mus.) note equal in length to half crotchet. [f. prec.]

quay (kē), n. Solid stationary artificial landing-place usu. of stone or iron lying alongside or projecting into water for (un)loading ships. Hence **quay·**AGE(1, 4) n. [earlier & OF *kay*, cf. Sp. *cayo* shoal, W *cae* hedge, w. assim. to F *quai*]

quean, n. Impudent or ill-behaved girl, jade, hussy. [OE *cwene* woman, cf. Du. *kween* barren cow; cogn. w. Gk *gunē* woman & w. QUEEN]

quea·sy (-zĭ), a. (Of food) unsettling the stomach, causing or tending to sickness, fulsome; (of person, his stomach, or his conscience) easily upset, weak of digestion, over scrupulous or tender or delicate, in fastidious condition. Hence **quea·si**NESS n. [earlier *coisy*; etym. dub.; cf. OF *coisier* hurt]

queen[1], n. King's wife (also *q. consort* for distinction from next sense; *q. dowager*, wife of late king; *q. mother*, q. dowager who is mother of sovereign, & see next sense; also prefixed as title, as *Q. Alexandra*); female sovereign of kingdom (*q. mother*, q. having child or children; also prefixed as title, as *Q. Victoria*; *Q. Anne is dead*, retort to stale news; *Q. Anne's* BOUNTY; *Q.-Anne*, in the architectural or decorative style of Q. Anne's time; *Q. of Scots*, Mary Stuart); adored female, e.g. the Virgin Mary (*Q. of grace* &c.), ancient goddess (*Q. of heaven*, Juno, *of love*, Venus, *of night*, Diana, &c.), person's sweetheart or wife or mistress; majestic woman; belle, mock sovereign, on some occasion (*Q. of the* MAY[3] &c.); personified best example of anything that can be regarded as fem. (*the q. of watering-places, roses, nurses*); person, country, &c., regarded as ruling over some sphere (*q. of hearts*, any beautiful woman; *q. of the Adriatic*, Venice; *q. of the seas*, Gt Britain; *q. of the meadows*, meadowsweet); (also *q. bee, wasp, ant*) perfect female of bee &c.; piece in chess (*q.'s bishop, knight, pawn*, &c., those placed nearest q. at start; *q.'s* GAMBIT); one of court-cards in each suit; *q.-cake*, small soft currant cake often heart-shaped; *q.-posts*, two upright timbers between tie-beam & rafters of roof (cf. KING-*post*); *Q.'s* BENCH, BOUNTY; *Q.'s Club*, (used for) athletic ground in Kensington at which some inter-University & other sporting events are decided; *Q.'s* COLOUR[1], COUNSEL[1], ENGLISH[1], EVIDENCE, HEAD[1]; *Q.'s omnibus* (slang), = BLACK[1] *Maria*; *q.'s pincushion*, flower of guelder rose; *q.'s* SHILLING; *q.-stitch*, fancy stitch in embroidery; *q.'s-ware*, cream-coloured Wedgwood; *q.'s weather*, sunshine. Hence **quee·n**DOM, **quee·n**HOOD, **quee·n**SHIP, nn., **quee·n**LESS, **quee·n**LIKE, aa. [OE *cwēn*, cf. ON *kvæn*; cogn. w. QUEAN]

queen[2], v.t. & i. Make (woman) q.; *q. it*, play the q.; (Chess) advance (pawn) to opponent's end of board & have it converted to q. or other piece, (intr., of pawn) be converted thus. [f. prec.]

quee·ning, n. Kind of apple. [-ING[3]]

quee·nly, a. Fit for, appropriate to, queen; majestic, queenlike. Hence **quee·nli**NESS n. [-LY[1]]

queer, a., & v.t. (slang). Strange, odd, eccentric; of questionable character, shady, suspect; out of sorts, giddy, faint, (esp. *feel q.*); (slang) drunk; *in Q. street* (slang), in a difficulty, in debt or trouble or disrepute; hence **queer·**ISH[1] a., **queer·**LY[2] adv., **queer·**NESS n. (Vb) spoil, put out of order, (esp. *q. the pitch for* one, spoil his chance beforehand by secret dealings); make feel q. [perh. f. G *quer* crosswise]

quell, v.t. (poet. & rhet.). Suppress, forcibly put an end to, crush, overcome, reduce to submission, (fear, opposition, rebellion, rebels, &c.). Hence **(-)que·ll**ER[1] n. [OE *cwellan*, cf. G *quälen*]

quench, v.t. Extinguish (fire, light, eyesight; chiefly poet. or rhet.); *q. smoking flax*, cut short promising development (see *Is.* xlii. 3); cool, esp. with water (heat, heated thing; poet. or rhet.); stifle, suppress, (desire, speed, motion; poet. or rhet.); slake (thirst); (slang) reduce to silence, shut up, (opponent). Hence **que·nch**ABLE, **que·nch**LESS, aa. [cf. Fris. *kwinka*]

que·ncher, n. In vbl senses; esp. (slang) something to drink (usu. *a modest q.*). [-ER[1]]

quene·lle (ke-), n. Seasoned ball of fish or meat reduced to paste. [F, etym. dub.]

quer̄·ist, n. Person who asks question. [f. L *quaerere* ask, -IST]

quern, n. Hand-mill for grinding corn; small hand-mill for pepper &c.; *q.-stone*, millstone. [OE *cweorn*, cf. Du. *kweern*, Da. *kværn*]

quĕ·rulous (-rōō-), a. Complaining, peevish. Hence **que·rulous**LY[2] adv., **que·rulous**NESS n. [f. LL *querulosus* (L *querulus*, f. *queri* complain, -OSE[1])]

quer̄·y, n., & v.t. & i. (Used abs. to introduce question; abbr. *qu.*) pray, one would like to know, (*Query*, or *qu.*, *was the money ever paid?*); a question, esp. of the nature of objection (*was prepared to suppress all qq.*); mark of interrogation or the word *query* or *qu.* written against statement, or the word *query* interjected in speech, to question accuracy. (Vb) ask, inquire, (*whether, if*, &c.); put a question; call (thing) in question in speech or writing, question accuracy of. [anglicized form of QUAERE]

quest[1], n. Official inquiry or jury &c. making it (now only in vulg. *crowner's q.*, coroner's inquest); seeking or thing sought by inquiry or search, esp. object of medieval knight's pursuit (*in q. of*, seeking). [f. OF *queste* f. pop. L p.p. of *quaerere* seek]

quest[2], v.i. & t. (Of dogs &c.) search for game (often *about*); go (*about*) in search of something; (poet.) search for, seek *out*. [f. OF *quester* (prec.)]

que·stion[1] (-stshon), n. Sentence adapted by order of words, use of interrogative pronoun or stop, or other means, to elicit answer, interrogative sentence, (*put a q. to* one, ask him something; *q. & answer*, alternation of qq. & answers, catechetic procedure; LEADING[2], RHETORICAL, *q.*; *indirect, oblique, q.*, made into dependent clause; *q.-mark* or *-stop*, mark of interrogation); (raising of) doubt about or objection to thing's truth, credibility, advisability, &c. (*allowed it without q.*; *beyond all* or *beyond, out of, past, without, q.*, certainly, undoubtedly; *call in q.*, raise objections to; *make no q. of* fact &c., *but that it is so* &c., admit it; *there is no q. but that . . .*), whence **que·stion**LESS adv. & a.; problem requiring solution, matter or concern depending on conditions *of*, (EASTERN *q.*; *a difficult q.*; BEG *the q.*; *success is merely a q. of time*, will certainly come, but may come sooner or later; *it is only a question of putting enough coffee in*); subject being discussed or for discussion, thing to be voted on, (*the person in q.*, that we are referring to; *come into q.*, be discussed, become of practical importance; *that is not the q.*, is irrelevant; *the q. is*, introducing or recalling exact matter of debate; *Q.!* in public assemblies, used to recall speaker from digression; *the* PREVIOUS *q.*; *out of the q.*, too impracticable to be worth discussing; *put the q.*, require supporters & opponents of proposal to record their votes, divide meeting &c.; OPEN *q.*); (archaic) torture to elicit confession (*was put to the q.*). [OF f. L *quaestionem* (*quaerere* seek, -TION)]

que·stion[2], v.t. Ask qq. of, interrogate, subject to examination, (person); seek information from study of (phenomena, facts); call in q., throw doubt upon, raise objections to, (*q. the honesty, accuracy, fitness, &c., of*; *it cannot be questioned but that* or *but*, it is certain that), whence **que·stion**ABLE a. (esp., doubtfully true, not clearly consistent with honesty or honour or wisdom), **que·stionab**LY[2] adv. Hence **que·stioning**LY[2] adv. [f. OF *questionner* (prec.)]

questionnaire· (kĕstĭ-), **que·stionary** (rare), n. Formulated series of questions, an interrogatory. [(*-aire* F) f. med. L *questionarium*, see QUESTION, -ARY[1]]

que·tzal, n. Beautiful Central-Amer. bird. [Sp., f. Aztec *quetzalli* the bird's tail-feather]

queue (kū), n., & v.t. & i. Hanging plaited tail of hair or wig, pigtail; line of persons, vehicles, &c., awaiting their turn to be attended to or proceed. (Vb) dress (hair) in q.; (of persons &c.) form *up* in, join *on* to, a q. [F, f. L *cauda* tail]

qui·bble, n., & v.i. Play on words, pun; equivocation, evasion, unsubstantial or purely verbal argument &c. esp. one depending on ambiguity of word; (vb) use qq.; hence **qui·bbl**ER[1] n., **qui·bbl**ING[2] a. [perh. dim. of obs. *quib* f. L *quibus* abl. pl. of *qui* who (familiar f. use in legal documents)]

quick, a., n., & adv. Living, alive, (archaic; esp. *the q. & the dead, go down q. into hell*; *q. with child*, orig. *with q. child*, at stage of pregnancy when motion has been felt); vigorous, lively, ready, sensitive, prompt to act, perceive, be affected, learn, think, or invent, (*a q. child*, intelligent; *q. temper*, easily irritated, whence **quicktemper**ED[2] a.; *q. sight*, acute or alert, whence **quicksight**ED[2] a.; *has a q. eye, ear*, &c., whence **quick-ey**ED[2], **quick-ear**ED[2], aa.; *is q. to take offence*; *has q. wits*, is ready at grasping situation, making repartees, &c., whence **quick-witt**ED[2] a.; N.B. these compounds have *quick* stressed when attrib., unstressed when pred.); moving rapidly, rapid, swift, done in short time or with little interval, (*q. succession*; *at a q. trot*; *a q. way of doing it*; *his q. growth*; *be q.*, make haste; *did a q. mile*; *was followed by q. vengeance*), whence **qui·ck**LY[2] adv.; *q.-change* (of actor &c.), quickly changing costume or appearance to play another part; *qui·ck*LIME[1]; *q. march* (mil.), march in q. time (see below; esp. as word of command for starting at usual pace); *qui·cksand*, (bed of) loose wet sand readily swallowing up ships, animals, &c.; *qui·ckset*, (adj., of hedge) formed of living plants esp. hawthorn, (n.) live slips of plants esp. hawthorn set in ground to grow, hedge formed of these; *qui·cksilver*, (n.) mercury, (fig.) mobility of temperament or mood, (v.t.) coat (mirror-glass) with amalgam of tin; *q. step*, step used in *q. time* (mil.), rate of marching reckoned at 128 paces of 33 in. to the minute or four miles an hour, the usual British-army rate. (N.) tender or sensitive flesh below skin or esp. nails, tender part of wound or sore where healthy tissue begins, seat of feeling or emotion, (*bites his nails to the q.*; *probed it to the q.*; *the insult stung him to the q.*; *is a Tory to the q.*, through & through); =*quickset* a. & n. (Adv., with compar. *-er, -est*, always after vb) at rapid rate, in comparatively short time, (*ran as q. as I could*; *who will be there quickest?*); (ellipt. for imperat. of *go, come, be, q.*) make haste; *quick-* (prefixed to partt. esp. in *-ing*) quickly, soon, (*q.-fading, -forgotten*, &c.; *q.-firing gun*, or **quick-fīr·**ER[1] n., gun with special mechanism for firing shots in q. succession). [Aryan; OE *cwicu*, cf. Du. *kwik*, G *keck* pert, Skr. *jivá*, L *vivus*, Gk *bios* life]

qui·cken, v.t. & i. Give or restore natural or spiritual life or vigour to, animate, stimulate, rouse, inspire, kindle, whence **quic·ken**ING[2] a.; receive, come to, life; (of woman or embryo) reach QUICK stage in pregnancy; accelerate, make or (of pace, motion, &c.) become quicker. [-EN[6]]

qui·ckness, n. Readiness or acuteness of perception or apprehension; speed, rapidity, suddenness, (rare; esp. of single gesture or motion); hastiness *of temper*. [-NESS]

quĭcu·nque vult. *The q.*, the Athanasian creed. [initial L wds, = whosoever will]

quid[1], n. (slang; pl. *quid*). A sovereign, £1, (*at two q. a week*). [?]

quid[2], n. Lump of tobacco held in mouth & chewed. [var. of CUD]

qui·ddity, n. Essence of a thing, what makes a thing what it is; quibble, captious subtlety. [f. med. L *quidditas* (L *quid* what, -ITY)]

qui·dnunc, n. Newsmonger, person given to gossip. [f. L *quid* what, *nunc* now]

quid pro quo, n. Blunder made by using or putting one thing for another (now rare); compensation, return made, consideration, (*must get, must find him, a q. p. q.*). [f. L *quid* something *pro* for *quo* something]

quiē·scent (-snt), a. Motionless, inert, silent, dormant. Hence or cogn. **quie·s**CENCE, **quie·s**CENCY, nn., **quie·scent**LY[2] adv. [f. L *quiescere* (*quies* QUIET[1], -ESCENT)]

quī·et[1] (-*et*), n. Undisturbed political condition, public tranquillity; silence, stillness; being free from disturbance or agitation or urgent tasks, rest, repose, peace of mind; unruffled deportment, calm. [f. L *quies -etis*]

quī·et[2] (-*et*), a. (-*er*, -*est*). With no or slight or gentle sound or motion; of gentle or inactive disposition; (of colour, dress, &c.) unobtrusive, not showy; not overt, private, disguised, (*q. resentment*; *had a q. dig at him*; esp. *on the q.*, or slang abbr. *on the q.t.*, secretly); undisturbed, not interfered with or interrupted, free or far from strife or uproar; enjoyed in q.; tranquil, not anxious or remorseful. Hence **qui·et**LY[2] adv., **qui·et**NESS, **qui·e**TUDE, nn. [f. L *quietus* p.p. (QUIESCENT)]

quī·et[3] (-*et*), v.t., & i. Reduce to quietness, soothe, calm; become q. (rare; usu. *q. down*). [f. med. L *quietare* (prec.)]

quie·ten, v.t. & i. =prec. (vulg.). [-EN[6]]

quī·etism, n. Passive attitude towards life with devotional contemplation & abandonment of the will as form of religious mysticism, non-resistance principles. So **qui·et**IST(2) n. & a., **quieti·st**IC a. [f. It. *quietismo* (QUIET[2], -ISM)]

quiē·tus, n. Acquittance, receipt, given on payment of account &c. (now rare); release from life, death, extinction, final riddance, (*got, gave him, his q.*). [f. med. L *quietus* (*est* he is) quit (QUIET[2]) used as receipt form]

quill[1], n. Hollow stem of feather, (also *q.-feather*) whole large feather of wing or tail; pen (also *q. pen*), plectrum, fishing-float, or toothpick, made of this; one of porcupine's spines; bobbin of hollow reed, any bobbin; musical pipe made of hollow stem; curled-up piece of cinnamon or cinchona bark; *q.-coverts*, feathers covering base of q.-feathers; *q.-driver*, clerk or journalist or author. [etym. dub.; cf. LG *quiele*, G *kiel*]

quill[2], v.t. & i. Form into q.-like folds, goffer, whence **qui·ll**ING[1](2) n.; wind thread or yarn on bobbin. [f. prec.]

qui·llet, n. Quibble, nice distinction. [perh. abbr. of obs. *quillity* perh. corrupt. of QUIDDITY]

quilt, n., & v.t. Bed-coverlet made of padding enclosed between two layers of linen &c. & kept in place by cross lines of stitching; any coverlet or counterpane (PATCH-*work q.*). (Vb) cover with padded material; make or join together after the manner of a q.; sew up (coin, letters, &c.) between two layers of garment &c.; compile (literary work) out of extracts or borrowed ideas; (slang) thrash. Hence **qui·lt**ING[1](1, 3) n. [f. OF *cuilte* f. L *culcita* cushion]

quī·nary, a. Of the number five; consisting of five things. [f. L *quinarius* (*quini* distrib. of *quinque* five, -ARY[1])]

quī·nate (-*at*), a. (bot.). (Of leaf) composed of five leaflets. [f. L *quini* (prec.), -ATE[2]]

quince, n. Hard acid yellowish pear-shaped fruit used as preserve or as flavouring, tree bearing it. [orig. pl. of obs. *quine*, *coyn*, f. OF *cooin* f. L *cotoneum* var. of *cydonium* neut. of *Cydonius* of Cydonia in Crete]

quincentenary, irreg. for **quing-.**

qui·ncŭnx, n. (Arrangement of) five objects set so that four are at corners of square or rectangle & the other at its centre (e.g. the five on dice or cards; *plantation is laid out in quincunxes*, in the diagonal cross lines given by combining qq.). So **quincu·ncial** (-shl) a., **quincu·ncial**LY[2] adv. [L, = 5/12 (*quinque* five, *uncia* OUNCE), also q. pattern]

quingentē·nary (*or* -jĕ·n-), a. & n. Of, in, 500th year; (n.) 500th anniversary. [f. L *quingenti* 500 after CENTENARY]

quī·nia, n. (med.). =QUININE. [f. Sp. *quina* f. Peruv. *kina* bark]

quini·ne (-ēn, -in), n. Alkaloid found esp. in cinchona bark & used as febrifuge, tonic, & antiperiodic; (pop.) sulphate of q., the usu. form in which q. is taken. So **quī·n**IZE(4) v.t., **quī·n**ISM(5) n. [as prec., -INE[5]]

quinquagenār·ian, a. & n. (Person) fifty years old. [f. L *quinquagenarius* (*quinquageni* distrib. of *quinquaginta* fifty, -ARY[1]), -AN]

quinquagē·nary (*or* -kwă·j-), a. & n. = prec. a. & n.; fiftieth anniversary. [prec.]

quinquagĕ·sima, n. (Also *Q. Sunday*) Sunday before Lent. [f. med. L *q.* (*dies*) lit. 50th (day), so called either as 50th day before Easter by incl. reckoning, or loosely (cf. *sexagesima*, *septuagesima*) as before QUADRAGESIMA]

quinqu(e)-, comb. form of L *quinque* five, in some wds taken f. L, & in many mod., esp. bot. & zool., formations. So **quinqua·ngular** five-angled; **quinqueco·state** five-ribbed; **quinque·nniad, quinque·nnium** (pl. -*a*), five-year period; **quinque·nnial** five-year-long, five-yearly, whence **quinque·nnial**LY[2] adv.; **quinquelă·teral** a. & n., five-sided (figure or object); **quinquelō·bate** five-lobed; **quinquepar·tite** divided into, consisting of, five parts; **qui·nquereme** ancient galley with five banks of oars; **quinqueva·lvular** five-valved; **qui·nquifid** cleft in five; **quinqui·valent** capable of combining with five univalent atoms.

quinqui·na (kĭnkē·-, kwĭnkwī·-), n. (Kinds of tree producing) Peruvian bark yielding quinine & other febrifuge alkaloids. [f. Peruv. *kinkina* redupl. form as QUINIA]

quĭ·nsy (-zĭ), n. Inflammation of throat, suppuration of tonsils. Hence **qui·nsiED**[2] a. [f. med. L *quinancia* f. Gk *kunagkhē* (*kun-* dog, *agkhō* throttle)]

quint (*in piquet usu.* kĭnt), n. Musical interval of fifth; organ-stop of tone one-fifth above normal; (Piquet) sequence of five of same suit (*q. major,* of ace to ten; *q. minor,* of knave to seven). [f. F *quinte* f. L fem. of *quintus* fifth]

qui·ntain (-tĭn), n. (hist.). (Medieval military exercise of tilting at) post set up as mark & often provided with sandbag to swing round & strike unskiful tilter. [f. OF *quintaine* perh. f. L *quintana* (*quintus* fifth) camp market]

qui·ntal, kin-, n. 100 lb.; 112 lb. or hundredweight; 100 kilograms. [OF, f. Arab. *qinṭar*]

qui·ntan, a. & n. (Ague or fever) with paroxysm every fourth (by incl. reckoning fifth) day. [f. L (*febris*) *quintana* (*quintus* fifth, -AN) fifth-day (fever)]

quinte (as F), n. Fifth fencing thrust or parry. [as QUINT]

quinte·ssence, n. (Ancient Philos.) fifth substance, apart from four elements, composing the heavenly bodies entirely & latent in all things; most essential part of any substance, refined extract; purest & most perfect form, manifestation, or embodiment, *of* some quality or class. Hence **quintesse·ntiAL** a. [f. med. L *quinta essentia*]

quinte·t(te), n. (Performers of) piece for five voices or instruments; set of five. [F (*-te*), f. It. *quintetto* (*quinto* fifth f. L *quintus*)]

quinti·llion, n. Fifth power of million (1 with 30 ciphers). [L *quintus* fifth, BILLION]

qui·ntūple, a., n., & v.t. & i., **qui·ntuply,** adv., **qui·ntuplet,** n., **quintu·plicate** (*-at*), a. & n., (-āt), v.t., **quintuplica·tion** n. Fivefold &c. (for detailed senses see QUADRUPLE & wds in *quadrupl-*, substituting *five* for *four*). [*-uple* F, f. L *quintus* fifth, after QUADRUPLE]

quintus. See PRIMUS[1].

quip, n. Sarcastic remark, clever hit, smart saying, verbal conceit; equivocation, quibble. [var. of obs. *quippy* perh. f. L *quippe* forsooth]

quipu (kē·pōō, kwē-), n. Ancient-Peruvian substitute for writing by variously knotting threads of various colours. [Peruv., = knot]

quire[1] (-īr), n. Four sheets of paper &c. folded to form eight leaves as in medieval MSS.; any collection of leaves one within another in MS. or book (*in qq.*, unbound, in sheets); 24 sheets of writing-paper. [f. OF *quaer,* now *cahier* (L *quaterni* see QUATERNARY)]

quire[2], n., & v.t. & i. See CHOIR.

Qui·rinal, n. (Used for) the Italian Government or Court (esp. as opp. VATICAN). [name of palace]

quirk, n. Quibble, quip; trick of action or behaviour; twist or flourish in drawing or writing; (Arch.) acute hollow between convex part of moulding & soffit or fillet. [etym. dub.; from 16th c.]

quit[1], pred. a. Free, clear, absolved, (archaic; *the others can go q.*; *was q. for a ducking,* got off with that); rid *of* (*glad to be q. of the trouble*); *qui·tclaim,* (n) renunciation of right, (v.t.) renounce claim to, give up (thing) *to*; *quit-rent,* (usu. small) rent paid by freeholder or copyholder in lieu of service. [f. OF *quit(t)e* f. L *quietus* QUIET[2]]

quit[2], v.t. (*quitted,* rarely *quit*). Rid one*self of* (archaic); (refl., usu. w. archaic refl. pron. without *self*) behave, acquit, conduct, oneself *well* &c. (esp. *q. you like men*; archaic); give up, let go, abandon, (*q. hold of,* loose; *q. office* &c.); depart from, leave, (place, person, &c.; *quitted Paris at midnight*; *quitted him in anger*), (abs., of tenant) leave occupied premises (esp. *give, have,* &c., *notice to q.*); (poet.) requite, repay, clear off, (*q. love with hate*; *death quits all scores*). [f. OF *quit(t)er* QUIET[3]]

quī tam, n. (legal). (Action brought by) informer. [L, = who as well (for the King as for himself sues)]

quitch, n. (Also *q.-grass*) COUCH[3]*-grass.* [OE *cwice,* cf. Du. *kweek,* G *queeke*]

quite, adv. Completely, wholly, entirely, altogether, to the utmost extent, nothing short of, in the fullest sense, positively, absolutely, (*q. covers it*; *was q. by myself*; *q. other,* very different; *q. another,* a very different; *is q. a hero, disappointment, good thing*; *I q. like him*; *is q. too delightful* colloq., i.e. to be done justice to in words; *is q. the thing,* fashionable; *not q. proper,* rather improper); *q. so* (& improp. *q.*), I grant the truth of that. [f. obs. *quite* a. = QUIT[1]]

quits, pred. a. On even terms by retaliation or repayment (*will be quits with him yet,* will have revenge; *now we are q.*; *cry q.*, acknowledge that things are now even, agree not to proceed further in quarrel &c.; DOUBLE[2] *or q.*). [perh. abbr. of med. L *quittus* = *quietus* QUIT[1]; or = QUIT[1] + -ES]

qui·ttance, n. (archaic, poet.). Release *from* something; acknowledgement of payment, receipt, (*omittance is no q.*, debt is not annulled by not being pressed); requital. [f. OF *quitance* (*quiter* QUIT[2])]

qui·ver[1], n. Case for holding arrows (*have*

an arrow, shaft, left in one's *q.*, not be resourceless; *q. full of children*, large family, see *Ps.* cxxvii. 5). Hence **qui·ver**FUL(2) n. [f. OF *quivre* f. Teut. (OE *cocer*, cf. G *köcher*)]

qui·ver², v.i. & t., & n. Tremble or vibrate with slight rapid motion (of person, leaf, wing, voice, light, &c.; *with* emotion, *in* the wind &c.); (of birds, esp. skylark) make (wings) q.; hence **qui·vering**LY² adv. (N.) quivering motion or sound. [prob. imit.; cf. QUAVER]

qui vive (kē vēv). *On the* q. v., on the alert, watching for something to happen. [F, =lit. (*long*) *live who?*, i.e. *on whose side are you?*, as sentinel's challenge]

Qui·xote (-ot), n. Enthusiastic visionary, pursuer of lofty but impracticable ideals, person utterly regardless of his material interests in comparison with honour or devotion. Hence **quixŏ·t**IC a. (*quixotics* n. pl., quixotic sentiments), **quixo·t**ICALLY adv., **qui·xot**ISM(2), **qui·xot**RY(4), nn., **qui·xot**IZE(2, 3) v.t. & i. [hero of Cervantes's *Don Q.*]

quiz, n., & v.t. Odd or eccentric person, person of ridiculous appearance, (now rare); person given to quizzing; hoax, ridicule, thing done to expose or burlesque another's oddities, (now rare); hence **qui·zzic**AL a., **qui·zzical**LY² adv. (Vb) make sport of (person or his ways), whence **qui·zz**ABLE a.; regard with mocking air; look curiously at, observe the ways or oddities of, survey through an eye-glass or (now rare) *quizzing-glass*; hence **qui·zzing**LY² adv. [?]

quō·ăd, prep. As regards; *q. hoc*, in this respect, so far as this goes. [L (*quo* whither, *ad* to)]

quŏd¹, n., & v.t., (slang). Prison (*in, out of, q.*); (vb) imprison. [?]

quŏd², neut. of L *qui* which (*q. erat demonstrandum* abbr. *Q.E.D.*, *q. erat faciendum* abbr. *Q.E.F.*, *q. erat inveniendum* abbr. *Q.E.I.*, which was the thing to be proved, made or done, found; formulae in geometrical demonstrations, &, esp. *Q.E.D.*, in gen. use; *quod vide*, abbr. *q.v.*, which see, in cross & other references).

quoin (koin), n., & v.t. External angle of building; stone or brick forming angle, corner-stone, whence **quoi·n**ING¹(3) n.; internal corner of room; wedge for locking type in form, raising level of gun, keeping barrel from rolling, &c.; (vb) secure or raise with qq. [var. of COIN]

quoit (koit), n., & v.t. Heavy flattish sharp-edged iron ring thrown to encircle iron peg or to stick in ground near it in game of *qq.*; (vb; rare) fling like q. [?]

quo·ndăm, adj. That once had but no longer has the specified character, sometime, former, (*a q. friend of mine*). [L, =formerly]

quōr·um, n. Fixed number of members that must be present to make proceedings of assembly or society or board valid. [L, =of whom (we will that you &c. be)]

quō·ta, n. Share that individual person or company is bound to contribute to or entitled to receive from a total. [f. L *quota* (*pars*) how great (a part); fem. of *quotus* how-manyeth (*quot* how many)]

quota·tion, n. (Print.) quadrat used for filling up blanks; quoting, passage quoted; amount stated as current price of stocks or commodities; *q.-marks*, inverted commas & apostrophes, single or double, used to mark beginning & end of quoted passage. [f. med. L *quotatio* (QUOTE, -ATION)]

quō·tative, a. Of quoting; given to quotation. [foll., -ATIVE]

quote, v.t., & n. Cite or appeal to (author, book) in confirmation of some view, repeat or copy out passage(s) from; repeat or copy out (borrowed passage) usu. with indication that it is borrowed, (abs.) make quotations, (*from* author, book, speech, &c.); adduce or cite *as*; state price of (usu. *at* figure); hence **quo·t**ABLE, **quo·te**WORTHY, aa. (N.; colloq.) passage quoted; (usu. pl.) quotation-mark(s). [earlier sense *mark with numbers*, f. med. L *quotare* (QUOTA)]

quōth, v.t. 1st & 3rd pers. past indic. Said *I, he, she*, & rarely *we* or *they* (placed amidst, after, or before the words quoted; *quotha* archaic for *quoth he*, used in quoting contemptuously =forsooth). [past of obs. *quethe*, OE *cwethan* cf. OHG *quedan*]

quotĭ·dian, a. & n. Daily, of every day, (*q. fever, ague*, recurring every day); commonplace, trivial; (n.) q. ague or fever. [f. L *quotidianus* (*quotidie* daily, -AN)]

quō·tient (-shnt), n. Result given by dividing one quantity by another. [erron. f. L *quotiens* how many times, by confusion w. -ENT]

R

R (ar), letter (pl. *R*s, R's). *The* r *months*, those with *r* in their names (Sep.–Ap.) as season for oysters; *the three* Rs, reading, (w)riting, & (a)rithmetic, as basis of elementary education.

Abbreviations (1): R.: railway, **R.T.O.** (transport officer); **R.**(éaumur); refer, **R.D.** (to drawer); regimental, **R.S.M.** (sergeant major); regina, **R.**, **R. et I.** (Imperatrix); religious, **R.T.S.** (tract society); *répondez*, **R.S.V.P.** (*s'il vous plaît*); *requiesca(n)t*, **R.I.P.** (*in pace*); resident, **R.M.**(agistrate); revised, **R.V.**(ersion); *rex*, **R.**, **R. et I.** (Imperator); Rhode, **R.I.** (island); rifle, **R.B.** (brigade); **R.**(iver); Roman, **R.C.**(atholic); Royal, as **R.A.** (academy or academician; artillery), **R.A.C.** (automobile club), **R.A.F.** (air force), **R.A.M.** (academy of music), **R.A.M.C.**, **R.A.O.C.**, **R.A.P.C.**, **R.A.S.C.**,

R.A.V.C., (army medical, ordnance, pay, service, veterinary, corps), **R.B.A.** (British artists, soc. of), **R.C.O.** (college of organists), **R.E.** (engineers), **R.F.** (fusiliers), **R.F.A.** (field artillery), **R.F.C.** (flying corps), **R.G.A.** (garrison artillery), **R.H.A.**, **R.H.G.**, (horse artillery, guards), **R.H.S.** (humane soc.), **R.I.C.** (Irish constabulary, **R.M.** (marines), **R.M.A.** (marine artillery, military academy), **R.M.C.** (military college), **R.M.L.I.** (marine light infantry), **R.M.S.** (mail steamer), **R.N.** (navy), **R.N.A.S.**, **R.N.D.**, **R.N.R.**, **R.N.V.R.**, (naval air service, division, reserve, volunteer reserve), **R.S.P.C.A.** (soc. for prevention of cruelty to animals), **R.W.S.** (watercolours, soc. of painters in), **R.Y.S.** (yacht squadron); Rugby, **R.U.** (union); rural, **R.D.C.** (district council); **r.**(ight).

Abbreviations (2): **Rev.**(elation); **Rev.**-(erend); **Roffen.**, Bishop of Rochester; **Rom.**(ans); **rom.**, roman type; **Rt Hon.**, **Rt Rev.**, (right honourable, reverend); **℞**, recipe; **Rs**, rupees; **Rx**, tens of rupees.

ra·bbet, n., & v.t. Step-shaped reduction cut along edge or face or projecting angle of wood &c. usu. to receive edge or tongue of another piece (vb, join or fix with r., make r. in); elastic beam arranged to give rebound to hammer striking it in ascent. [f. OF *rabat* abatement, recess, (*rabattre* REBATE[1])]

ra·bbī, n. Jewish doctor of the law (as form of address by itself or prefixed to name, or as ordinary noun), esp. one authorized by ordination to deal with law & ritual & perform certain functions; *Chief R.*, ecclesiastical head of the United Synagogue in U.K. [L, f. Gk f. Heb. =my master (*rabh* master + pronom. suf.]

ra·bbin, n. Rabbi (usu. *the rr.*, chief Jewish authorities on law & doctrine, most of them between 2nd & 13th cc.). Hence **ra·bbin**ATE[1], **ra·bbin**ISM(3), **ra·bbin**IST (2, 3), nn., **rabbĭ·n**ICAL a., **rabbi·nical**LY[2] adv. [F (prec.); *-n* perh. originated as supposed Heb. pl. term.]

ra·bbit[1], n., & v.i. Burrowing rodent of hare family, brownish-grey in natural state, also black or white or pied in domestication; *r.-hutch, -warren*; WELSH[1] *r.*; hence **ra·bbit**Y[2] a.; (vb) hunt rr. [cf. Walloon *robett*, Flem. *robbe*]

ra·bbit[2], v.t. (vulg.). *Odd r. it* &c., form of imprecation. [perh. alteration of *-rat* in DRAT]

ra·bble[1], n. Disorderly crowd, mob; contemptible or inferior set of people; *the* lower part of the populace. [etym. dub.; earlier sense *pack* or *string of animals* &c.]

ra·bble[2], n. Iron bar with bent end for stirring molten metal. [f. F *râble* f. L *rutabulum* (*ruere rut-* rake up) fire-shovel]

ra·bblement, n. (now rare). (Tumult as of) a rabble. [-MENT]

Răbelai·sian, -aesian, (-z-), a. & n. Of, like, Rabelais or his writings, marked by exuberant imagination & language & coarse humour & satire; (n.) admirer or student of Rabelais. [*Rabelais*, French humorist, -IAN]

ră·bid, a. Furious, violent, (*r. hate*); unreasoning, insensate, headstrong, (*r. democrat*); (esp. of dog) affected with rabies, mad; of rabies. Hence **rabi·d**ITY, **ra·bid**NESS, nn., **ra·bid**LY[2] adv. [f. L *rabidus* (*rabere* rave)]

rā·biēs (-z), n. Canine madness, hydrophobia. [L (prec.)]

race[1], n. Onward sweep or movement, esp. strong current in sea or river (*tide set with a strong r.*; *the R. of Alderney* &c.); course of sun or moon, course of life, (*ere he had run half his r.*); channel of stream (esp. in comb., as *mill-r.*); channel along which shuttle moves; contest of speed between runners, ships, horses, &c., or persons doing anything, (pl.) series of these for horses at fixed time on regular course (SELL*ing r.*); *r. ball*, dance held in connexion with rr.; *r.-card*, programme of rr.; *ra·cecourse*, ground for horse-racing; *ra·cehorse*, bred or kept for racing; *r.-meeting*, horse-racing fixture. [f. ON *rás*, cf. OE *rǣs* swift motion]

race[2], v.i. & t. Compete in speed *with*; indulge in horse-racing (*a racing man*; *the racing world*, the turf); go at full speed, (of propeller, paddle-wheel, &c.) work violently from diminished resistance when out of the water; have r. with, try to surpass in speed; cause (horse &c.) to r. (*raced his bicycle against a motor-car*), make (person, thing) move at full speed (*raced me along at five miles an hour*; *raced the Bill through the House*); fling (fortune &c.) *away* on horse-racing. [f. prec.]

race[3], n. Group of persons or animals or plants connected by common descent, posterity *of* (person), house, family, tribe or nation regarded as of common stock, distinct ethnical stock (*the Caucasian, Mongolian, &c., r.*), genus or species or breed or variety of animals or plants, any great division of living creatures (*the human, feathered, four-footed, finny, &c., r.*); descent, kindred, (*of noble, Oriental, &c., r.*; *separate in language & r.*); class of persons &c. with some common feature (*the r. of poets, dandies, &c.*). [F, f. It. *razza* etym. dub.]

race[4], n. Root (of ginger). [f. OF *rais* f. L *radicem* nom. *-ix* root]

racē·me, n. (bot.). Flower-cluster with the separate flowers attached by short equal stalks at equal distances along central stem. Hence **ră·cem**OSE[1] a. (bot., also anat. of compound glands). [f. L *racemus* grape-bunch]

ra·cer, n. In vbl senses; esp., racehorse yacht, bicycle, &c., used for racing. [-ER[1]]

rā·chis, rha-, (-k-), n. (pl. *-idēs*). Stem of grasses &c. bearing flower-stalks at short intervals; axis of pinnately compound leaf or frond; vertebral column or cord from which it develops, whence **rachi**(o)- comb. form; feather-shaft, esp. the part that bears the barbs. [f. Gk *rhakhis* spine; the E pl. *-ides* is irreg.]

rachī·tis, n. (Learned form for) RICKETS. [f. Gk *rhakhitis* (prec., -ITIS)]

rā·cial (-shl), a. Of, in regard to, due to, race. Hence **ra·cial**LY[2] adv. [RACE[3], -IAL]

rack[1], n., & v.i. 1. Driving clouds; (vb; of clouds) drive before wind. 2. Destruction (usu. *go to r. & ruin*). [with sense 1 cf. Norw. & Sw. dial. *rak* wreckage; sense 2 perh. var. of WRACK, WRECK]

rack[2], n., & v.t. & i. Fixed or movable frame of wooden or metal bars for holding fodder; framework with rails, bars, pegs, or shelves, for keeping articles on or in (*plate, hat, tool, pipe*, &c., *-r.*); cogged or indented bar or rail gearing with wheel or pinion or worm, or serving with pegs &c. to adjust position of something; *r.-railway*, with cogged rail between bearing rails; *r.-wheel*, cog-wheel. (Vb) fill *up* stable-r. with hay or straw for the night (also trans., *r. up horse*, provide it thus); fasten (horse) *up* to r.; place in or on r. [prob. f. MDu. *rec* (Du. *rek*, cf. G *reck*) rail &c. (*recken* stretch)]

rack[3], v.t., & n. Stretch joints of (person) by pulling esp. with instruments of torture made for the purpose; (of disease or bodily or mental agony) inflict torture on (*a racking headache*; *racked with pain*); shake violently, injure by straining, task severely, (*cough that seemed to r. his whole body*; *r.* one's *brains for something to say, a plan*, &c.); exact utmost possible amount of (rent), oppress (tenants) with excessive rent, exhaust (land) with excessive use; *r.-rent* n., extortionate rent equal or nearly equal to full value of land, v.t., exact this from (tenant) or for (land); *r.-renter*, tenant paying or landlord exacting r.-rent. (N.) instrument of torture, a frame with roller at each end to which victim's wrists & ankles were tied so that his joints were stretched when rollers were turned (*on the r.*, being racked, lit., or fig. of person in distress or under strain.) [prob. f. MDu. *recken* stretch]

rack[4], n. Arrack (esp. *r. punch*). [for ARRACK]

rack[5], n., & v.i. Horse's-gait between trot & canter, both legs of one side being lifted almost at once, & all four feet being off ground together at moments; (vb) progress thus. [?]

rack[6], v.t. Draw off (wine &c.) from the lees (often *off*). [f. Pr. *arracar* (*raca* stems & husks of grapes, dregs)]

ra·cket[1], **ra·cquet** (-kit), n. Cat-gutted bat used in tennis, rackets, &c.; (pl.) ball-game for two or four persons played in plain four-walled court with rr.; snow-shoe resembling r.; *r.-ball*, small hard kid-covered ball of cork & string; *r.-press*, for keeping rr. taut & in shape; *r.-tail*, kinds of small bird with r.-shaped tail. [f. F *raquette* etym. dub.]

ra·cket[2], n., & v.i. Disturbance, uproar, din; social excitement, gaiety, dissipation; (slang) dodge, game, line of business, lay; ordeal, trying experience, (*stand the r.*, come successfully through test, face consequences of action); hence **ra·ckety**[2] a. (Vb) live gay life (often *about*), move about noisily. [prob. imit.]

raconteur (F), n. (fem. *-euse*). Teller of anecdotes (usu. *good, skilful*, &c., *r.*).

rac(c)oo·n (*ra-*), n. Greyish-brown furry bushy-tailed sharp-snouted American nocturnal carnivore. [Algonquin]

ra·cy, a. Having the qualities that characterize the kind in high degree (esp. *r. flavour*); of distinctive quality or vigour, not smoothed into sameness or commonness, retaining traces of origin (esp. *r. of the soil*, of homely directness, spirited, lively, piquant). Hence **ra·ci**LY[2] adv., **ra·ci**NESS n. [RACE[3], -Y[2]]

rad. See RADICAL n.

ra·ddle, n., & v.t. Red ochre. (Vb) paint with r.; plaster with rouge. [var. of RUDDLE]

rā·dial, a. & n. Of, in, rays; arranged like rays or radii, having position or direction of a radius (*r. axle*, maintaining such direction to curve of track as car &c. travels round it); having spokes or radiating lines, whence **ra·dialized** a., **radializa·tion** n.; acting or moving along lines that diverge from a centre; of radium; of the radius of the forearm (*r. artery, vein, nerve*); hence **ra·dial**LY[2] adv. (N.) r. nerve or artery. [RADIUS, RADIUM, -AL]

ra·dian, n. Angle at centre of circle subtending arc whose length is equal to the radius. [RADIUS, -AN]

rā·diant, a. & n. Emitting rays of light, (of eyes or looks) beaming with joy or hope or love, (of light) issuing in rays, (of beauty) splendid or dazzling, whence or cogn. **ra·di**ANCE, **ra·di**ANCY (rare), nn., **ra·diant**LY[2] adv.; operating radially (esp. *r. heat*); (Bot. &c.) extending radially, radiating; *r. point*, from which rays or radii proceed, (Astron.) apparent focal point of meteoric shower. (N.) point or object from which light or heat radiates; (Astron.) r. point. [f. L *radiare* (RADIUS), -ANT]

ra·diate[1] (*-at*), a. Having divergent rays or parts radially arranged. Hence **ra·diate**LY[2] adv. [as foll., -ATE[2]]

ra·diāte[2], v.i. & t. Emit rays of light or heat, (of light or heat) issue in rays; diverge or spread from central point; emit (light or heat) from centre; disseminate (life, love, joy, &c.). Hence or cogn. **radia·**TION n., **ra·di**ATIVE a. [f. L *radiare* (RADIUS), -ATE[3]]

ra·diator, n. In vbl senses; esp., small

chamber heated with hot air or otherwise & radiating warmth into room &c.; engine-cooling apparatus in motor-car. [-OR[2]]

ră·dical, a. & n. Of the root(s); naturally inherent, essential, fundamental, (*r. humour, heat,* &c., in medieval philos. & still joc., moisture, heat, &c., essential to life; *a r. error; the r. rottenness of human nature*); forming the basis, primary, (*the r. idea* or *principles of a system*); affecting the foundation, going to the root, root-&-branch, (*r. change, cure, reform*), (of politicians) desiring such reforms, belonging to extreme section of Liberal party, (of measures &c.) advanced by or according to principles of r. politicians, whence **ra·dical**ISM(2) n., **ra·dical**IZE(3) v.t. & i., **radicaliz**A·TION n.; (Math.) of the root of a number or quantity (*r. sign,* $\sqrt{}$, $\sqrt[3]{}$, $\sqrt[4]{}$, &c., indicating that square, cube, fourth, &c. root of number following is to be extracted); (Philol.) of the roots of words (*r. word,* not analysable into root & other known element); (Mus.) belonging to the root of a chord; (Bot.) of, springing direct from, the root or the main stem close to it; hence **ra·dical**LY[2] adv. (N.): (Philol.) root; fundamental principle; (Math.) quantity forming or expressed as root of another, also the r. sign; (Chem.) element or atom, or group of these, forming base of compound & remaining unaltered during compound's ordinary chemical changes; (Pol.; also colloq. *rad*) person holding r. views or belonging to r. party. [f. LL *radicalis* (*radix -icis* root, -AL)]

ră·dicle, n. Part of plant embryo that develops into primary root; rootlet; (Anat.) rootlike subdivision of nerve or vein; (Chem.) = prec. n. Hence **radĭ·cūl**AR[1] a. [f. L *radicula* (prec., -ULE)]

ra·dio, n., & v.t. & i. Wireless telegraphy & telephony; X-rays, Hertzian rays, & their applications. (Vb) telegraph or broadcast by wireless; photograph by X-rays; treat with radium. [vb f. n., developed (at first in attrib. use) f. foll.]

rādio-, comb. form of L RADIUS & E RADIUM, w. sense *of the radius, of rays* or *radiation,* of *radium,* as *-car·pal,* of radius & wrist; *-a·ctive,* capable of affecting electrometer &c. by radiation, (of radium, uranium, polonium, &c.) having power of emitting invisible rays that penetrate opaque matter & produce electrical effects, so *-acti·vity*; *-graph,* instrument recording intensity & duration of sunshine, also image on sensitive plate given by Röntgen rays, (vb) secure such image of, & so *radio·graphy, radiogra·phic, radiographically*; *-meter,* instrument illustrating conversion of radiant energy into mechanical force; *-phony,* production of sound by radiant light or heat; *-scopy,* examination by Röntgen rays; *-te·legram,* message by wireless telegraphy.

ră·dish, n. (Cruciferous plant with) fleshy pungent root often eaten raw as relish in salads. [f. F *radis* f. L *radicem* nom. *-ix* root]

rā·dium, n. Metal resembling barium, yielded by pitch-blende, discovered 1898 & named from its RADIO-active power. [-IUM]

rā·dius, n. (pl. *-ĭī*). Thicker & shorter bone of fore-arm in man, corresponding bone in beast's foreleg or bird's wing; (Math.) straight line from centre to circumference of circle or sphere, radial line from focus to any point of curve (*r. vector,* variable line drawn to curve from fixed point, esp. in Astron. from sun or planet to path of satellite); any of a set of lines diverging from a point like rr. of circle, object of this kind, e.g. spoke; circular area as measured by its r. (*knows everyone within a r. of 20 miles; the four-mile r.,* that of which Charing Cross is centre, outside which cab-fares are higher); (Bot.) outer rim of composite flowerhead, e.g. daisy, also radiating branch of umbel. [L, = staff, spoke, ray]

rā·dix, n. (pl. *ra·dīcēs, radī·cēs*). Number or symbol used as basis of numeration scale (*ten is the r. of decimal numeration, & of common logarithms*); source or origin *of.* [L, = root]

răff. = RIFF-RAFF.

Raffaelesque. = RAPHAELESQUE.

ră·ffia, n. Kind of palm; fibre from its leaves used for tying up plants &c. [Malagasy]

ra·ffish, a. Disreputable, dissipated, fast-looking. Hence **ra·ffish**LY[2] adv., **ra·ffish**NESS n. [-ISH[1]]

ră·ffle[1], n., & v.i. & t. Sale of article by taking entrance-fee from any number of persons & assigning it by lot to one of them. (Vb) enter one's name in r. *for* article; sell by r. [earlier sense *kind of dice-game* f. F *rafle* etym. dub.]

ră·ffle[2], n. Rubbish, refuse, lumber, debris. [cf. OF *rifle ou rafle* anything whatever]

raft, n., & v.t. & i. Collection of logs, casks, &c., fastened together in the water for transportation; flat floating structure of timber or other materials for conveying persons or things, esp. as substitute for boat in emergencies; floating accumulation of trees, ice, &c.; *raftsman,* worker on r. (Vb) transport as or on r.; form into a r.; cross (water) on raft(s); work r. [f. ON *raptr* RAFTER[2]]

ra·fter[1], n. Man who rafts timber. [-ER[1]]

ra·fter[2], n., & v.t. One of the sloping beams forming framework on which slates &c. of roof are upheld. (Vb): (usu. in p.p.) provide with rr.; plough (land) so that contents of furrow are turned over on same breadth of unploughed ground next it, half-plough. [OE *ræfter,* cf. MLG *rafter,* ON *raptr*]

rag[1], n. Torn or frayed piece of woven material, one of the irregular scraps to which cloth &c. is reduced by wear & tear (*in rr.*, torn), (pl.) tattered clothes (*in rr.*, in old clothes), (usu. with neg.) smallest scrap of cloth or sail (*not a r. to cover him*; *spread every r. of sail*); (collect.) rr. used as material for paper, stuffing, &c.; remnant, odd scrap, irregular piece, (*flying rr. of cloud*; *cooked to rr.*, till it falls to pieces; *not a r. of evidence*); (contempt.) flag, handkerchief, curtain, newspaper, &c.; jagged projection (rare); *r.-baby*, doll made of rr.; *r.-bag*, in which scraps of linen &c. are kept for use; *r.-bolt* n., with barbs to keep it tight when driven in, v.t. join together with these; *r. fair*, old-clothes sale held in Houndsditch; *r. paper*, made of rr.; *ragtag*, *ragtag & bobtail*, the riff-raff, ragged or low or disreputable people; *r.-time*, music with much syncopation as in negro songs, (attrib.) farcical (*a r.-t. army*); *r.-wheel*, with projections catching in links of chain that passes over it, sprocket-wheel; *ragwort*, yellow-flowered ragged-leaved plant. [f. ON *rogg* tuft of fur]

rag[2], n. Large coarse roofing-slate; kinds of hard coarse stone breaking up in thick slabs (esp. CORAL-*r.*, *Kentish*, *Rowley*, *r.*). [?]

rag[3], v.t. & i., & n., (slang). Scold, reprove severely; tease, torment, play rough jokes upon, disarrange (person's room &c.) by way of practical joke; engage in bally-ragging, be noisy & riotous; (n.) noisy disorderly scene. [cf. BALLYRAG]

ră·gamuffin, n. Ragged dirty fellow. Hence **ragamu·ffin**LY[1] a. [prob. f. RAG[1] w. fancy termination]

rage[1], n. (Fit of) violent anger; violent operation of some natural force or some sentiment (*the r. of the wind, of faction*); vehement desire or passion *for* (*has a r. for*, or *for collecting, first editions*), object of widespread temporary enthusiasm or fashion (*Mrs Siddons, the open-air cure, is the* or *all the r.*); poetic or prophetic or martial ardour. [F, f. LL *rabia* f. L RABIES]

rage[2], v.i. & refl. Rave, storm, speak madly or furiously, (*at*, *against*, or abs.), be full of anger; (of wind, sea, passion, feeling, battle, pain, disease, &c.) be violent, be at the height, operate unchecked, prevail, be violent, whence **ra·ging**LY[2] adv.; (refl., esp. of storm &c.) *r.* it*self out*, cease raging. [f. F *rager* (prec.)]

ra·gged, a. Rough, shaggy, hanging in tufts; of broken jagged outline or surface, full of rough or sharp projections; faulty, imperfect, wanting finish or smoothness or uniformity, (*r. rhymes*, *time* in rowing, &c.); rent, torn, frayed, (of persons) in r. clothes; *r. robin*, crimson-flowered wild plant; *r. school*, free school for poor children. Hence **ra·gged**LY[2] adv., **ra·gged**NESS n. [RAG[1], -ED[2]; cf. Norw. *ragget* shaggy]

ragout· (-ōō), n., & v.t. Meat in small pieces stewed with vegetables & highly seasoned; (vb) cook thus. [f. F *ragoût* (*ragoûter* revive taste of, see RE-, GUST)]

ra·hat lakou·m (rah-h-, -ōōm), n. Kinds of Turkish sweetmeat, esp. TURKISH *delight*. [Turk.]

raid, n., & v.i. & t. Military expedition esp. of mounted men, predatory incursion in which surprise & rapidity are usu. relied upon, foray, inroad; sudden descent of police &c. upon suspected premises or illicit goods. (Vb) make r. *into* &c.; make r. on (person, place, cattle); hence **rai·d**ER[1] n. [Sc. form of OE *rād* ROAD]

rail[1], n., & v.t. & i. Horizontal or inclined bar or continuous series of bars of wood or metal used to hang things on, as top of banisters, as part of fence, as protection against contact or falling over, or for similar purpose; any horizontal piece (cf. STILE[2]) in frame of panelled door; iron bar or continuous line of bars laid on ground as one side or half of railway track (*off the rr.*, disorganized, out of order, not working right; *by r.*, by railway), (pl.; St. Exch.) railway shares; *r.-chair*, iron holder, attached to sleeper, in which railway r. rests; *railroad*, railway (esp. now in U.S.); *railway*, road laid with rr. for heavy horse-carts, track or set of tracks of iron or steel rr. for passage of trains of cars drawn by locomotive engine & conveying passengers & goods, (also *railway line*) the tracks of this kind worked by single company or the whole of the organization & persons required for their working, (attrib. in many phrr., as *railway accident*; *railway act*, regulating duties & rights of railway companies; *railway bill*, proposal in Parliament esp. for constructing new railway; *railway bridge, carriage, company, contractor, director, engine, journey, shares*; *at railway speed*, very quickly; *railway rug, station, stock, system, train, travelling, tunnel*), whence **rai·lway**LESS a., *railway* v.i., travel by r.; hence **rai·l**LESS a. (Vb) furnish or enclose (place) with r. (often *in*, *off*), provide (bench &c.) with r., whence **rai·ling**[1] [-ING[1](3, 4)] n.; lay (railway route) with rr.; convey (goods),travel, by r. [f. OF *reille* (L *regula* RULE)]

rail[2], n. Kinds of bird, esp. LAND[1]*r.*, *water-r.* [f. F *râle* etym. dub.]

rail[3], v.i. Use abusive language (usu. *at* or *against*, or archaic *upon*). Hence **rai·l**ER[1] n., **rai·ling**[2] [-ING[1](1)] n., **railing**[3] [-ING[2]] a., **rai·ling**LY[2] adv. [f. F *railler* etym. dub.]

rai·llery, n. (Piece of) good-humoured ridicule, rallying. [f. F *raillerie* (prec., -ERY)]

rai·ment, n. (poet. & rhet.). Clothing, dress, apparel. [f. obs. *arrayment* (ARRAY[1], -MENT)]

rain[1], n. Condensed moisture of atmosphere falling visibly in separate drops, fall of such drops (*r. or shine*, whether it rains or not), (pl.) showers of r., esp. *the rr.*, rainy season in tropical countries, (Naut.) *the Rr.*, rainy region of Atlantic 4–10° N. lat.; (r.-like descent of) falling liquid or solid particles or bodies (*a r. of ashes, frogs, pearls, rice, fire*; also fig. *a r. of melody, kisses, congratulations*); *r.-bird*, kinds of bird, esp. Green Woodpecker; *r.-box*, theatre contrivance imitating sound of r.; *r.-coat*, waterproof; *r.-doctor*, producer of r. by magic; *rai·ndrop*, single drop of r.; *rai·nfall*, shower, quantity of r. falling within given area in given time (usu. in inches of depth per annum); *r.-gauge*, instrument measuring rainfall; *r.-glass*, barometer; *r.-water*, collected from r., not got from wells &c.; *r.-worm*, common earthworm. Hence **rai·n**LESS, **rai·n**PROOF[2], **rai·n**TIGHT, aa. [com.-Teut.; OE *regn, rén*, cf. Du. & G *regen*]

rain[2], v.i. & t. *It rains*, r. comes down (*it rained blood, frogs, invitations, tracts*, &c., there was a shower of them; *it rains cats & dogs*, violently; *it never rains but it pours*, events usu. happen several together; *it rains in*, r. penetrates house &c.; *it has rained itself out*, r. has ceased); *God, the sky, the clouds, r.*, send down r.; fall or send down in showers or like r. (*flowers rained from their hands*; *tears rained down her cheeks*; *blows r. upon him*; *his eyes r. tears*; *r. influence*; *he rained benefits upon us*). [OE *regnian* (prec.)]

rai·nbow (-ō), n. Arch showing prismatic colours in their order formed in sky (or across cataract &c.) opposite sun by reflection, double refraction, & dispersion, of sun's rays in falling drops of rain (*lunar r.*, similar effect from moon's rays, rarely seen; *sea r.*, formed on sea spray; *secondary r.*, additional arch with colours in reverse order formed inside or outside of r. by double reflection & double refraction; *all the colours of the r.*, many colours); (attrib.) many-coloured; *r. trout*, Californian kind. [OE *rénboga* (RAIN[1], BOW[1])]

rai·ny, a. In or on which rain is falling or much rain usually falls (*r. weather, climate, day, month, county*, &c.; *r. day* fig., time of esp. pecuniary need, as *provide against a r. d.*); (of clouds, wind, &c.) laden with, bringing, r. Hence **rai·ni**LY[2] adv., **rai·ni**NESS n. [-Y[2]]

raise (-z), v.t. (often followed by *up* in most senses). Set upright, make stand up, restore to or towards vertical position, rouse, (*raised him from his knees*; *r. the standard of revolt*; *raised pastry, pie*, &c., standing without support of dish at sides; *r.* one *from the dead*, restore him to life; *r. the country, city*, &c., rouse inhabitants in some emergency, often *against* or *upon* enemy &c.; *the danger raised his spirits*; *r. the wind* fig., procure money for some purpose; *r. a dust*, lit., & fig. cause turmoil, also obscure the truth); build up, construct, create, produce, breed, utter, make audible, start, give occasion for, elicit, set up, advance, (*r. palace, large family, blister*, one's *own vegetables, storm, shout, hymn, controversy, prejudice, claim, demand, objection, question*; *a deliverer was raised up*, caused by Providence to appear; *r. a laugh*, cause others to laugh; *no one raised his voice*, spoke); elevate, put or take into higher position, extract from earth, direct upwards, promote to higher rank, make higher or nobler, cause to ascend, make (voice) louder or shriller, (Naut.) come in sight of (land, ship), increase amount of, heighten level of, (*r.* one's *hat*, bow; *r.* one's *glass to*, drink health of; *thousands of tons of coal were raised*; *r.* one's *eyes*, look upwards; *r.* one's *eyebrows*, look supercilious or shocked; *raised him to the see of York*; *trying to r. a degraded class*; *undertook to r. the spirit of King Solomon*, cf. LAY[3]; *r. Cain, hell, the devil, the mischief*, &c., make disturbance; *their voices were raised as in anger*; *r. income-tax from 6d. to 9d.*; *r. cloth*, make nap on it; *r. bread*, cause it to rise with yeast; *r.* one's *reputation*, add to it; *the price of the 4lb. loaf is raised a penny*; *r. colour* in dyeing, brighten it); levy, collect, bring together, procure, manage to get, (*r. tax, loan, subscription, money, army, fleet*); relinquish, cause enemy to relinquish, (siege, blockade). [f. ON *reisa*; causative of RISE[1], cf. BAIT[1], BITE[1]]

rai·sin (-zn), n. Partially dried grape. [f. OF *raizin* f. L as RACEME]

raison d'être (F), n. Purpose &c. that accounts for or justifies or originally caused thing's existence.

rait. See RET.

raj (rahj), n. (Anglo-Ind.). Sovereignty (*the British r. in India*). [Hind.]

ra·ja(h) (rah-), n. Indian king or prince (also as title of petty dignitary or noble in India, or of Malay or Javanese chief). Hence **ra·jah**SHIP n. [Hind. (*-a*), f. *rai* to reign]

Rajpoot, -put, (rah·jpo͞ot), n. Member of Hindu soldier caste claiming descent from Kshatriyas. [Hind. (*-ut*), f. prec., *putra* son]

rake[1], n. Implement consisting of pole with cross-bar toothed like comb at end for drawing together hay &c. or smoothing loose soil or gravel, wheeled implement drawn by horse for same purpose; kinds of implement resembling r. used for other purposes, e.g. by croupier drawing in money at gaming-table. [OE *raca*, cf. Du. *raak*, G *rechen*, (also Goth. *rikan* heap up)]

rake[2], v.t. & i. Collect, draw *together*, gather *up*, pull *out*, clear *off*, (as) with r. (*r. out the fire*; *r. up* or *together all possible* *charges*; *r. off the leaves*); clean or smooth with r.; search (as) with r., ransack, (*has raked all history for proofs*); make *level, clean*, &c., with r.; scratch, scrape; sweep with shot, enfilade, send shot along (ship) from stem to stern, sweep with the eyes, (of window &c.) have commanding view of; use r., search as with r. (*have been raking among* or *in* or *into old records*). [f. ON *raka* cogn. w. prec.]

rake³, n. Dissipated or immoral man of fashion. [for RAKEHELL]

rake⁴, v.i. & t., & n. (Of ship or its bow or stern) project at upper part of bow or stern beyond keel; (of masts or funnels) incline from perpendicular towards stern; give backward inclination to (*bicycle's front forks are raked*); (n.) amount to which thing rakes, raking position or build. [?]

ra·kehell, n. (archaic). =RAKE³. Hence **ra·kehell**Y² a. (archaic). [RAKE², HELL]

rā·kish¹, a. (As) of, like, a RAKE³. Hence **ra·kish**LY² adv., **ra·kish**NESS n. [-ISH¹]

rā·kish², a. (Of ship) smart & fast-looking, seeming built for speed & therefore open to suspicion of piracy. [perh. =prec. with extra association of raking masts (RAKE⁴)]

râle (rahl), n. (path.). Sound additional to that of respiration heard in auscultation of unhealthy lungs. [F, f. *râler* to rattle, etym. dub.]

rallenta·ndo, mus. direction. Gradually slower. [It.]

ră·llicar(t), n. Light two-wheeled driving-trap for four. [*Ralli*, first purchaser, 1885]

ră·lly¹, v.t. & i., & n. Reassemble, get together again, (t. & i.; esp. of army or company) after rout or dispersion, (cause to) renew conflict; bring or come together as support or for concentrated action (*rallied his party, his party rallied, round* or *to him*); revive (faculty &c.) by effort of will, pull oneself together, assume or rouse to fresh energy, throw off prostration of illness or fear. (N.) act of rallying (intr.), reunion for fresh effort; recovery of energy after or in the middle of exhaustion or illness; (in tennis, rackets, &c.) strokes quickly exchanged. [n. f. vb, f. F *rallier* (RE-, ALLY¹)]

ră·lly², v.t. Banter, chaff. Hence **ra·lly-ing**LY² adv. [as RAIL³]

ram¹, n. Uncastrated male sheep, tup; (*R-*) zodiacal sign Aries; =BATTER*ing-r.*; (battleship with) projecting beak at bow for charging side of other ships; falling weight of pile-driving machine; rammer; hydraulic water-raising or lifting machine; piston of hydrostatic press; plunger of force-pump; *r.'s-horn*, lit., also scroll ornament imitated from r.'s head & horns. [OE, also Du. & OHG; perh. cogn. w. ON *rammr* strong]

ram², v.t. Beat down (soil &c.) into solidity with wooden block &c., (abs.) use rammer, make (post, plant, &c.) firm by ramming soil round it; drive (pile &c.) *down, in, into*, by heavy blows; force (charge) home, pack (gun) tight, with ramrod; squeeze or force into place by pressure (*rammed his clothes into a bag, his hat down on his head*; *had the list rammed into me by repetition*; *r. the argument home*, lay sufficient stress on it); cram *with* stuffing &c.; (of ship) strike with r.; dash or violently impel (thing) *against, at, on*, or *into* (*rammed his head against the wall, his horse at a fence*); *ra·mrod*, for ramming home charge of muzzle-loader. Hence **ra·mm**ER¹(2) n. [perh. f. prec.]

ram³, n. (naut.). Boat's length over all. [?]

Rămada·n, n. Ninth month of Mohammedan year, during all daylight hours of which rigid fasting is observed. [Arab. (*ramaḍa* be hot); perh. orig. one of hot months, now passing through all seasons owing to lunar reckoning]

rā·mal, a. (bot.). Of, proceeding from, a branch. [f. L *ramus* branch, -AL]

ra·mble, v.i., & n. Walk (v. & n.) for pleasure & without definite route; wander in discourse, talk or write disconnectedly. [?]

ra·mbler, n. In vbl senses; also, kinds of climbing rose, esp. the Crimson R. [-ER¹]

ra·mbling, a. Peripatetic, wandering; disconnected, desultory, incoherent; (of plants) straggling, climbing; (of house, street, &c.) irregularly planned. Hence **ra·mbling**LY² adv. [-ING²]

ră·mekin, -quin (-kĭn), n. Small quantity of cheese with bread-crumbs, eggs, &c., baked in small mould. [F (*-quin*), etym. dub.]

rămifica·tion, n. Ramifying, (arrangement of) tree's branches; subdivision of complex structure comparable to tree's branches (*the rr. of a river, society, trade, plot, inquiry*, &c.). [foll., -ATION]

ră·mifȳ, v.i. & t. Form branches or subdivisions or offshoots, branch out; (usu. pass.) cause to branch out, arrange in branching manner (*railways were ramified over the country*). [f. F *ramifier* f. med. L *ramificare* (L *ramus* branch, -I-, -FY)]

ra·mmish, a. Rank-smelling. [RAM¹, -ISH¹]

ramo·se, a. Branched, branching. [f. L *ramosus* (*ramus* branch, -OSE¹)]

ramp¹, n. Slope, inclined plane joining two levels of ground esp. in fortification, or of wall-coping; difference in level between opposite abutments of rampant arch; upward bend in stair-rail. [f. F *rampe* (foll.)]

ramp², v.i. & t. (Chiefly of lion) stand on hind-legs with fore-paws in air, assume or be in threatening posture; (now usu. facet.) storm, rage, rush about; (Archit., of wall) ascend or descend to different level; (Archit., Mil.) furnish or build with r. [f. OF *ramper* etym. dub.]

ramp[3], n., & v.i. & t., (slang). Attempt to extort payment of fictitious debt from bookmaker, (transf.) levying of exorbitant prices (*the telephone r.*, increased tariff); (vb) engage in, subject (person &c.) to, r. [?]

rampā·ge, v.i., & n. Behave violently, storm, rage, rush about; (n.) violent behaviour (esp. *be on the r.*). Hence **rampa·geo**US(-jus) a., **rampa·geous**LY[2] adv., **rampa·geous**NESS n. [perh. f. prec.]

ra·mpant, a. (Chiefly of lion, esp. in Herald.) ramping (in Herald., & in allusive imitations, placed after nouns, as *lion r.*, *the snob r.*); violent or extravagant in action or opinion, arrant, aggressive, unchecked, prevailing, (*is a r. theorist*; *popery is r. among us*); rank, luxuriant, (*a rich soil makes nasturtiums too r.*); (of arch &c.) having one abutment higher than the other, climbing. Hence **ra·mp**ANCY n., **ra·mpant**LY[2] adv. [F (RAMP[2], -ANT)]

ra·mpart, n., & v.t. Broad-topped & usu. stone-parapeted defensive mound of earth, (fig.) defence, protection; (vb) fortify or protect (as) with r. [f. F *rempart* (*remparer* fortify, f. RE-, *emparer* take possession of, f. L *ante* before, *parare* secure)]

ra·mpion, n. Kind of bell-flower with white tuberous roots used as salad. [cf. F *raiponce*, It. *ramponzolo*, etym. dub.]

ra·mpire, n., & v.t. (archaic). RAMPART.

ra·mshackle, a. Tumbledown, crazy, rickety, (usu. of house or vehicle; *the r. Empire*, Austria-Hungary). [earlier *-ed*, perh. p.p. of obs. *ransackle* RANSACK]

ra·mson (-sn), n. (Root, eaten as relish, of) broad-leaved garlic. [prop. pl. in *-en* of OE *hramsa*, cf. G *rams*, Gk *kromuon* onion]

ran[1], n. A certain length of twine. [?]

ran[2]. See RUN[1].

rance, n. Kind of red marble with blue & white veins & spots. [?]

ranch (-tsh), n., & v.i. Cattle-breeding establishment in U.S.; (vb) conduct r. [f. Sp. *rancho* mess, persons feeding together]

ră·ncid, a. Smelling or tasting like rank stale fat. Hence **rancĭ·d**ITY, **ra·ncid**NESS, nn. [f. L *rancidus* stinking]

ra·ncour(-ngk-), n. Inveterate bitterness, malignant hate, spitefulness. Hence **ra·nco**rOUS a., **ra·ncorous**LY[2] adv. [OF, f. L *rancorem* nom. *-or* (prec., -OR[1])]

rand, n. Strip of leather between heel & shoe or boot; (S.-Afr.) highlands on either side of river valley (*the R.*, Johannesburg). [OE & Du., = bank, rim]

răndă·n[1], n. Style of rowing for three men, the middle using sculls & the others oars; boat for such use. [?]

randa·n[2], n. Spree (esp. *on the r.*). [var. of RANDOM]

ra·ndem, adv. & n. With three horses harnessed tandem; (n.) carriage or team so driven. [prob. formed on *random* & *tandem*]

random (-om), n. & a. *At r.*, at haphazard, without aim or purpose or principle, heedlessly. (Adj.) made, done, &c., at r.; (of masonry) with stones of irregular size & shape; hence **ra·ndom**LY[2] adv. (rare). [orig. sense *great speed*; f. OF *randon* (*randir* gallop); for *-m* cf. *ransom*]

ra·ndy, a. Loud-tongued, boisterous, lusty, (Sc.); (of cattle &c.; dial.) wild, restive; lustful, in lustful mood. Hence **ra·ndi**NESS n. [prob. f. obs. *rand* var. of RANT, -Y[2]]

ra·nee (rah-), n. Hindu queen. [f. Hind. *rani* f. Skr. *rajni* fem. of RAJAH]

rang. See RING[2].

rānge[1] (-j), v.t. & i. Place or arrange in a row or ranks or in specified situation or order or company (usu. pass. or refl.; *ranged their troops*; *ranged themselves on each side*; *was ranged against, among, on the side of, with, &c.*; *trees ranged in an ascending scale of height*; *r. oneself* imit. F, take up definite position in society, settle down, e.g. by marrying); run in a line, reach, lie spread out, extend, be found or occur over specified district (often *from . . . to*), vary between limits, (*ranges north & south, along the sea*; *nightingale ranges from the Channel to Warwickshire*); be level (*with*; *a 12mo does not r. well with a folio*), rank or find right place *with* or *among* (*ranges with the great writers*); rove, wander, (often *over, along, through, &c.*, district or coast; *his thoughts r. over past, present, & future*; *ranging fancy*, inconstant affections); (of gun) throw projectile over, (of projectile) traverse, (distance; *ranges over a mile*); go all about (place), sail along or about (coast, sea). [f. OF *ranger* (*rang* RANK[1])]

range[2], n. Row, line, tier, or series, of things, esp. of buildings or mountains; lie, direction, (*the r. of the strata is east & west*; *keep the two buoys in r. with the lighthouse*); stretch of grazing or hunting ground; piece of ground with targets for shooting; area over which plant &c. is distributed, area included in or concerned with something, sphere, scope, compass, register, limits of variation, limited scale or series, distance attainable by gun or projectile, distance between gun &c. & objective, (*gives the rr. of all species*; *the thorniest question in the whole r. of politics*; *the r. of her voice is astonishing*; *his reading is of very wide r.*; *the r. of the barometer readings is about 2 in.*; *Hebrew is out of my r.*; *there is a lower r. of prices today*; *the enemy are out of r., have found the r. of our camp*); cooking fireplace usu. with oven(s), boiler(s), & iron top plate with openings for saucepans &c.; *r.-finder*, instrument for estimating distance of object to be shot at. [OF, = row, rank, (prec.)]

rā·nger, n. In vbl senses; also: keeper of a royal park, whence **ra·nger**SHIP n.; (pl.) body of mounted troops (esp. *the Connaught Rr.*, a British regiment). [-ER[1]]

rank[1], n. Row, line, queue, (now chiefly of cabs standing; in chess, row of squares across board, opp. FILE[3]); number of soldiers drawn up in single line abreast (usu. one r. behind another, called *front, rear, r.*; *the rr. were broken*, could not keep the formation; *the rr.* or *the r. & file*, common soldiers, i.e. privates & corporals, & transf. lower classes or ordinary undistinguished people; *rise from the rr.*, said of common soldier or sergeant who is given commission, or of selfmade man); order, array, (*keep r.*, *break r.*, remain, fail to remain, in line); distinct social class, grade of dignity, station, high station, (*people of all rr.*; *persons of r.*, members of nobility; *r. & fashion*, high society; *the pride of r.*); place in a scale. [f. obs. F *ranc* (now *rang*), perh. f. OHG *hrinc* RING[1]]

rank[2], v.t. & i. Arrange (esp. soldiers) in r.; classify, give certain grade to; have r. or place (*ranks among the Great Powers, next to the king*, &c.); (Mil.) march *past* or *off*. [f. prec.]

rank[3], a. Too luxuriant, gross, coarse, over-productive, choked with or apt to produce weeds, (*roses are growing r.*, running too much to leaf; *land too r. to grow corn*); foul-smelling, offensive, rancid; loathsome, indecent, corrupt; strongly marked, unmistakable, flagrant, virulent, gross, (*r. treason, pedantry, poison, nonsense*). Hence **ra·nk**LY[2] adv., **ra·nk**NESS n. [OE *ranc*, cf. LG *rank* long & thin, ON *rakkr* slender, bold]

ra·nker, n. (Commissioned officer who has been) a soldier in the ranks. [-ER[1]]

ra·nkle, v.i. (Of wound, sore, &c.) fester, continue painful, (archaic); (of envy, disappointment, &c., or their cause) be bitter, give intermittent or constant pain. [f. OF *rancler* (*rancle, drancle, draoncle*, festering sore = med. L *dracunculus* dim. of *draco* serpent)]

ra·nsack, v.t. Thoroughly search (place, receptacle, person's pockets, one's conscience, &c.); pillage, plunder, (house, country, &c.). [f. ON *rannsaka* (*rann* house, *sœkja* seek]

ra·nsom, n., & v.t. (Liberation of prisoner of war in consideration of) sum of money or value paid for release (*hold* one *to r.*, be willing to release him for such consideration; *worth a king's r.*, of immense value); blackmail, sum &c. exacted in return for privilege or immunity, (*graduated income-tax & death-duties are no more than a fair r. paid by the rich*); *r.-bill, -bond*, undertaking, esp. on part of captured ship, to pay r.; hence **ra·nsom**LESS a. (Vb) redeem, buy freedom or restoration of; atone for, expiate; hold to r., release for a r.; exact r. from. [f. OF *ranson(ner)* f. L *redemptionem* REDEMPTION]

rant, v.i. & t., & n. Use bombastic language; declaim, recite theatrically; preach noisily, whence (esp. of Primitive Methodists) **ra·nt**ER[1] n. (N.) piece of ranting, tirade; empty turgid talk. [f. obs. Du. *randten* rave, cf. G *ranzen* frolic]

ranu·ncŭlus(ra-), n. (pl. *-luses, -lī*). Genus of plants including the buttercups, crowfoot. Hence **ranuncul**A·CEOUS a. [L, orig. dim. of *rana* frog]

ranz-des-vaches (F), n. Swiss herdsmen's melody made of harmonic notes of Alpine horn. [Swiss dial.]

rap[1], n., & v.t. & i. Smart slight blow (*a r. on the knuckles*, punishment inflicted on child, also fig. reproof); sound made by knocker on door &c., or by some agency on table or floor in spiritualistic seances. (Vb) strike (esp. person's knuckles) smartly; make the sound called a r. (*rapped at the door, on the table*, &c.); *r. out* (oath, pun, &c.), utter abruptly or on the spur of the moment, (v.i.) use strong language; (of spirits) *r. out* (message, word), express by rr. [prob. imit.]

rap[2], n. Skein of 120 yds of yarn. [?]

rap[3], n. An atom, the least bit, (*don't care a r.*). [earlier sense *18th-c. Irish counterfeit halfpenny*; etym. dub.]

rapā·cious, a. Grasping, extortionate, predatory. Hence or cogn. **rapa·cious**LY[2] adv., **rapă·**CITY n. [f. L *rapax* (*rapere* seize, -ACIOUS)]

rape[1], v.t., & n. Take by force (poet.); ravish, force, violate, (woman). (N.) carrying off by force (poet.); ravishing or violation of a woman. [prob. f. L *rapere* seize]

rape[2], n. Any of six administrative divisions of Sussex. [from 1086; etym. dub.]

rape[3], n. Plant grown as food for sheep; plant cultivated for its seed from which oil is made, coleseed; *wild r.*, charlock; *r.-cake*, r.-seed pressed into flat shape after extraction of oil & used as manure; *r.-oil*, made from r.-seed & used as lubricant & in making soap & indiarubber. [f. L *rapum* turnip]

rape[4], n. Refuse of grapes after wine-making used in making vinegar; vessel used in vinegar-making. [f. F *râpe*, cf. Pr. *raspa*, It. *raspo*]

Răphāĕle·sque (-k), **Raff-**, a. In style of Raphael. [*Raphael* (It. *Raffaello*), -ESQUE]

ră·pid, a. & n. Speedy, quick, swift; acting or completed in short time; (of slope) descending steeply; hence or cogn. **rapi·d**ITY n., **ra·pid**LY[2] adv. (N.) steep descent in river-bed, with swift current. [f. L *rapidus* (*rapere* seize)]

rā·pier, n. Light slender sword for thrusting only, small-sword, (*r.-thrust*, often fig. of delicate or witty repartee). [f. F *rapière* etym. dub.]

ră·pine, n. (rhet.). Plundering, robbery. [f. L *rapina* (*rapere* seize, -INE[4])]
rapparee·, n. (hist.). 17th-c. Irish irregular soldier or freebooter. [f. Ir. *rapaire* short pike]
rappee·, n. Coarse kind of snuff. [f. F (*tabac*) *râpé* RASPed (tobacco)]
rappor·t (*or* rapor·), n. Communication, relationship, connexion, (*be in*, or F *en*, *come into*, or F *en*, *r. with*). [F (*rapporter* f. RE-, AP-, *porter* f. L *portare* carry)]
rapprochement (F), n. Re-establishment or recommencement of harmonious relations, esp. between States.
rapscă·llion, n. Rascal, scamp, rogue. [earlier *rascallion*, prob. f. RASCAL]
rapt, p.p., & a. Snatched away bodily or carried away in spirit from earth, from life, from consciousness, or from ordinary thoughts & perceptions (often *away*, *up*, &c.); absorbed, enraptured, intent, (esp. *listen with r. attention*). [f. L *raptus* p.p. of *rapere* seize]
raptor·ial, a. & n. (zool.). (Member) of the *Raptores*, an order of birds of prey; predatory, (as) of predatory birds or animals. [f. L *raptor* (prec., -OR[2]) plunderer + -IAL]
ra·pture (-tsher), n. Mental transport, ecstatic delight, (*be in*, *go into*, *rr.*, be enthusiastic, talk enthusiastically; *rr.*, vehement pleasure or the expression of it). Hence **ra·pturous** a., **ra·pturously**[2] adv. [f. RAPT + -URE]
ra·ptured, a. Enraptured, in ecstasy. [f. obs. *rapture* vb (prec.), -ED[1]]
rār·a ā·vis, n. Rarity, kind of person or thing rarely encountered. [L, = rare bird]
rare, a. Of loosely packed substance, not dense, (*the r. atmosphere of the mountain tops*); few & far between, uncommon, unusual, exceptional, seldom found or occurring, (*it is r. for* person &c. *to* do, or *it is rarely that* he &c. does); of uncommon excellence, remarkably good, very amusing, (*a miracle of r. device*; *had r. fun with him*). Hence **rare·ly**[2] adv., **rare·ness** n. [f. L *rarus*]
rare·bit, n. See WELSH *rabbit*.
rār·ee-show, n. Show carried about in a box; any show or spectacle. [perh. = *rare show* as pronounced by Savoyard showmen]
rār·efȳ, v.t. & i. Lessen density or solidity of (esp. air); purify, refine, (person's nature &c.); make (idea &c.) subtle; become less dense. So **rārĕfa·ction**, **rarefica·tion**, nn., **rar·efactive** a. [f. L *rarefacere* (for *rarifacere* perh. on anal. of *arefacere*) f. *rarus* rare, *facere* make]
rār·ity, n. Rareness (see RARE); uncommon thing, thing valued as being rare. [f. L *raritas* (RARE, -TY)]
ra·scal, n. & a. Rogue, knave, scamp, (often playfully to child &c.; *you lucky r.!*); (adj.) belonging to the rabble (archaic; *the r. rout*, the common people). Hence **ra·scaldom**, **ra·scalism**(2), **rasca·lity** nn., **ra·scally**[1] a. [f. OF *rascaille* rabble, etym. dub.]
rase. See RAZE.
rash[1], n. Eruption of the skin in spots or patches. [cf. OF *rache* scurf, It. *raschia* itch; from 18th c. only]
rash[2], a. Hasty, impetuous, overbold, reckless, acting or done without due consideration. Hence **ra·shly**[2] adv., **ra·shness** n. [cf. Du. & G *rasch* quick]
ră·sher, n. Thin slice of bacon or ham. [perh. f. obs. *rash* to slice, prob. var. of RAZE]
rasp, v.t. & i., & n. (Scrape with) coarse kind of file having separate teeth raised with pointed punch; scrape roughly; grate upon (person or his feelings), irritate; scrape *off* or *away*; make grating sound. [f. OF *raspe(r)*, now *râpe(r)*, perh. f. Teut., cf. OHG *raspôn* scrape together]
ra·spatory, n. Rasp used in surgery. [f. med. L *raspatorium* (*raspare* RASP, -TORY)]
ra·spberry (-zb-), n. (Plant bearing) white, yellow, or usu. red subacid fruit of many small juicy grains arranged on conical receptacle; *r.-canes*, the plants; *r. vinegar*, kind of syrup. [f. *rasp* (now Sc. & north.), *raspis*, etym. dub.]
rasse (ră·sĭ, răs), n. Kind of civet-cat. [f. Javanese *rase*]
rat[1], n., & v.i. Rodent of some larger species of the mouse kind (MUSK, WATER, -*r.*; *black* or *old-English r.*, variety now nearly ousted by common *grey*, *brown*, or *Norway r.*; *smell a r.*, have suspicions; *like a drowned r.*, said of person wet through; *Rats!* slang, nonsense!, incredible!, &c.); (Pol.) person who deserts his party in difficulties as rr. desert doomed house or ship, turncoat; workman who refuses to join strike, takes striker's place, or accepts less than trade-union wages: *r.-catcher* (who rids houses of rr.), (slang) unorthodox hunting dress; *ra·tsbane*, r.-poison (now only in literary fig. use); *r.'s-tail*, thing shaped like r.'s tail, e.g. kind of file; *r.-tail*, (horse with) hairless horse's tail, whence **ra·t-tailed**[2] a. (*r.-t. spoon*, with tail-like prolongation of handle along back of bowl); *r.-trap*, lit., also (cycle pedal) made of two parallel iron plates with teeth; hence **ra·tty**[2] a. (in n. senses, &, slang, snappish, irritable, touchy). (Vb) hunt or kill rr. (of person or dog); play the r. in politics; hence **ra·tter**[1] n. [OE *ræt*, cf. Du. *rat*, G *ratz*, also F *rat*, etym. dub.]
rat[2], v.t. 3rd sing. pres. subj. (vulg.). = DRAT.
rā·ta, n. Large handsome New-Zealand tree with crimson flowers & hard red wood. [Maori]
rā·table, a. Proportional (archaic); liable to payment of municipal rates, whence **ratabi·lity** n. Hence **ra·tably**[2] adv. [RATE[2], -ABLE]

rătafi·a (-ēa), **-fee·**, n. Liqueur flavoured with almonds or kernels of peach, apricot, or cherry; kind of biscuit similarly flavoured; kind of cherry. [F (*-ia*), etym. dub.]

rā·tal, n. Amount on which rates are assessed (also attrib., as *the r. qualification for vestries*). [f. RATE[1], prob. after RENTAL]

rătapla·n, n., & v.t. & i. (-nn-). Drumming sound. (Vb) play (as) on drum; make r. [F, imit.]

ra·tchet, ratch, nn., & vv.t. Set of teeth on edge of bar or wheel by which in combination with a catch motion in one direction may be prevented while possible in the other; (also *r.-wheel*) wheel with rim so toothed; (vb) provide with r., give r. form to. [f. F *rochet* kind of lance-head, cf. ROCKET[2]]

rate[1], n. Statement of numerical proportion prevailing or to prevail between two sets of things either or both of which may be unspecified, amount &c. mentioned in one case for application to all similar ones, standard or way of reckoning, (measure of) value, tariff charge, cost, relative speed, (*going at the r. of six miles an hour*; *can have them at the r. of 1/ - a thousand*; *the death-r. was 19 per mille*; *the r. of interest, wages, &c., is to be regulated*; *the high rr. charged by the railways*; *at that r.* colloq., if this is a fair specimen, if this assumption is true, &c.; *at any r.*, in either or any possible case, even if a stronger statement is doubtfully true, &c.; *the low r. at which you value it*; *sell at a high r.*; *win success at an easy r.*; *went off at a great r.*, speed; *pauperism increases at a fearful r.*); assessment levied by local authorities for local purposes (*rr. & taxes*; *a 1d. r. is raised for the free library*); class (archaic except in FIRST, THIRD, &c., *-r.*); *ra·tepayer*, person liable to have municipal rr. exacted from him. [OF, f. med. L *rata* (L *pro rata parte* according to the proportional share, f. *ratus* p.p. of *rēri* reckon]

rate[2], v.t. & i. Estimate worth or value of (*I do not r. his merits high*; *each offence is rated at a fixed sum by way of penalty*; esp. in *over-r.*, *under-r.*), assign fixed value to (coin, metals) in relation to monetary standard (*the copper coinage is rated much above its real value*); consider, regard as, (*I r. him among my benefactors*); (usu. in pass.) subject to payment of a local r., value for purpose of assessing rr. on, (*we are highly rated for education*, have to pay a high r.; *houses are rated at a sum smaller than the rent*, the sum on which rr. are charged is less); *r. up*, impose higher insurance r. on (persons &c., liable to exceptional risks); (Naut.) class under a certain RATING[1], (intr.) rank or be rated *as*. [f. prec.]

rate[3], v.t. & i. Scold (trans.) angrily; (rare) storm *at*. [?]

rate[4]. See RET.

rā·tel, n. S.-Afr. carnivorous quadruped, honey-badger. [Cape-Du., etym. dub.]

-rā·ter, n. Racing yacht of specified tonnage (*10-r.*, *2½-r.*, &c.). [RATE[1], -ER[1]]

rāthe (-dh), a. (poet.). Coming, blooming, &c., early in the year or day; *r.-ripe*, *răthripe* (-th-), ripening early, precocious, (n.) early kinds of pea, apple, &c. [f. obs. *rathe* adv., OE *hrathe* (*hrad* quick)]

ra·ther (rahdh-), adv. More truly, to a greater extent, as a more accurate description or preferable account of the matter, *or* to be more precise, (*Is r. good than bad. Derived r. from imagination than reason. Orderliness is not the result of law*; *r. it is the cause of it. Late last night, or r. early this morning*), *the r. that*, so much the more because; in a modified way, to some extent, slightly, somewhat, (*I r. think you know him*; *the performance was r. a failure, was r. good, fell r. flat*); by preference, for choice, sooner, as an alternative chosen sooner *than* another of same grammatical form or *than* to (*would much r. not go*; *he would r. have died than refused*; *use soft water r. than hard*; *the desire to seem clever r. than honest*; *he resigned r. than stifle his conscience*; also with *had*, as *I had r. err with Plato than be right with Horace*); (colloq., in answers) most emphatically, yes without doubt, assuredly, (*Have you been here before?—Rather!*). [compar. of obs. *rathe* adv., see prec.]

ră·tify̆, v.t. Confirm or make valid (compact made in one's name) by formal consent, signature, &c. So **ratifica·tion** n. [f. F *ratifier* f. med. L *ratificare* (RATE[1], -FY)]

rā·ting[1], n. In vbl senses of RATE[2]; also or esp.: amount fixed as municipal rate; (Naut.) person's position or class on ship's books, (collect.) all persons of a particular r.; any of the classes into which racing yachts are distributed by tonnage. [RATE[2], -ING[1]]

rā·ting[2], n. Angry reprimand. [RATE[3], -ING[1]]

rā·tio (-shĭō), n. (pl. *-os*). Quantitative relation between two similar magnitudes determined by the number of times one contains the other integrally or fractionally (*are in the r. of three to two* or *3 : 2*; *the rr. 1 : 5 & 20 : 100 are the same*). [L (RATE[1], -ION)]

răˈtiŏ·cinate (*or* -shĭ-), v.i. Go through logical processes, reason formally, use syllogisms. So **ratiocina·tion** n., **ratio·cinative** a. [f. L *ratiocinari* (prec.), -ATE[3]]

ră·tion (-shn), n., & v.t. Fixed daily allowance of food served out for man or animal esp. in army or navy; single portion *of* provisions, fuel, &c.; (pl.) provisions; (vb) limit (persons, food) to fixed r. [f. L RATIO]

ră·tional (-sho-), a. & n. Endowed with reason, reasoning; sensible, sane, moderate, not foolish or absurd or extreme; of, based on, reasoning or reason, rejecting what is unreasonable or cannot be tested by reason in religion or custom, (*r. dress*, esp. of knickerbockers worn by women instead of skirts; *has r. leanings in religion*, has doubts about the truth of revelation, the possibility of miracles, &c.); (Math., of quantity or ratio) expressible without radical signs (opp. SURD); hence or cogn. **rationa·lITY** n., **ra·tionalLY**[2] adv. (N., pl.) r. dress. [f. L *rationalis* (prec., -AL)]

rationā·lē, n. Reasoned exposition, statement of reasons, (now rare); fundamental reason, logical basis, *of*. [L, neut. as prec.]

ra·tionalism, n. Practice of explaining the supernatural in religion in a way consonant with reason, or of treating reason as the ultimate authority in religion as elsewhere; theory that reason is the foundation of certainty in knowledge (opp. *empiricism, sensationalism*). So **ra·tionalIST**(2) n. & a., **rationali·stIC** a., **rationali·stICALLY** adv. [-ISM]

ra·tionalize, v.t. & i. Explain, explain *away*, by rationalism, bring into conformity with reason; be or act as a rationalist; (Math.) clear from surds; (Econ.) reform (an industry) by making production balance consumption, & by co-operation of rival producers & of capital & labour, whence **rationalizA·TION** n. [-IZE]

ră·tite, a. (ornith.). Belonging to the *Ratitae*, a genus including ostrich, emu, cassowary, &c., with keelless breastbone (opp. CARINA*te*). [f. L *ratis* raft, -ITE[2]]

ra·tlin(e), -ling, n. (usu. pl.). (One of) small lines fastened across ship's shrouds like ladder-rungs. [cf. OF *raalingue* small cordage strengthening sail-edge]

ratoo·n, n., & v.i. New shoot springing from sugar-cane root after cropping; (vb) send up rr. [f. Sp. *retoño* sprout]

rat(t)a·n, n. Kinds of E.-Indian climbing palm with long thin many-jointed pliable stems; piece of r. stem used as cane or for other purposes; rr. used as a material in building &c. [f. Malay *rotan* (*raut* pare)]

rat-ta·t, rătata·t, ra·t-tat-ta·t, n. Rapping sound, esp. of knocker. [imit.]

ra·tten, v.t. Molest (workman or employer) by abstracting or injuring tools or machinery &c. in disputes. [?]

ra·ttle[1], v.i. & t. Give out rapid succession of short sharp hard sounds, cause such sounds by shaking something (*he rattled at the door*); talk in lively thoughtless way (often *on, away, along*); move or fall with rattling noise, drive vehicle or ride or run briskly, (usu. *down, along, past*, &c.); (part.) brisk, vigorous, (*a rattling wind, pace*), (preceding *good* &c.) remarkably (*had a rattling good run, dinner*, &c.); make (chain, window, crockery, &c.) r. (*r. the sabre*, threaten war); say or recite (verses, stories, lists, oaths) rapidly (usu. *off, out, over, away*, &c.); stir *up* from dullness; (slang) excite, agitate, fluster, make nervous, frighten; make move quickly (*r. fox*, hunt it close; *r. up the anchor*; *r. bill through the House*). [ME & Du. *ratelen*, cf. G *rasseln*, prob. imit.]

ra·ttle[2], n. Instrument or plaything made to r. esp. in order to give alarm or to amuse babies; set of horny rings in rattlesnake's tail; kinds of plant with seeds that r. in their cases when ripe (esp. *Yellow, Red, r.*); rattling sound, uproar, bustle, noisy gaiety, racket, (*death-r.*, such sound in throat immediately before death; *the rr.*, croup); noisy flow of words, empty chatter, trivial talk; lively incessant talker; *r.-bag, -bladder, -box*, rr. constructed of bag &c. with objects inside to r.; *r.-brain, -head, -pate*, (person with) empty brain &c., whence **ra·ttlebrainED**[2], **ra·ttleheadED**[2], **ra·ttlepaTED**[2], aa.; *rattlesnake*, venomous American snake with rattling apparatus in tail; *rattletrap* n. & a., rickety (vehicle &c.), (pl.) curiosities, odds & ends. [f. prec.]

ra·ttler, n. In vbl senses; esp., remarkably good specimen of anything. [-ER[1]]

ratty. See RAT[1].

rau·cous, a. Hoarse, harsh-sounding. Hence **rau·cousLY**[2] adv. [f. L *raucus*, -OUS]

raughty. See RORTY.

rauque (-k), a. (rare). Raucous. [F(RAUCOUS)]

ră·vage (-ĭj), v.t. & i., & n. Devastate, plunder, (t. & i.), make havoc; (n.) devastation, damage, (esp. pl.) destructive effects *of*. [f. F *ravage(r)*, vb f. n., (*ravir* RAVISH, -AGE)]

rave[1], n. Rail of cart; (pl.) permanent or removable framework added to sides of cart to increase capacity. [also *rathe* dial.; etym. dub.]

rave[2], v.i. & t., & n. Talk wildly or furiously (as) in delirium (often *about, against, at, of, for*; *raving mad*, uncontrollably, so as to r.); (of sea, wind, &c.) howl, roar; speak with rapturous admiration *about* or *of*, go into raptures; utter with ravings (*r.* one's *grief* &c.); *r. oneself hoarse, to sleep*, &c.; *storm raves itself out*, to an end; hence (often pl.) **ra·VING**[1](1) n. (N.) raving sound *of* wind &c. [perh. f. OF *raver* var. of *rêver* dream (REVERIE)]

ră·vel, v.t. & i. (-ll-), & n. Entangle or become entangled, confuse, complicate, (thread &c., or fig. question, problem; esp. in p.p., as *the ravelled skein of life*); fray (i. & t.) *out*, whence **ra·vellING**[1](2) n.; disentangle, unravel, distinguish the separate threads or subdivisions of, (often *out*). (N.) entanglement, knot, complication; frayed or loose end. [prob. f. Du. *ravelen*]

ră·velin (-vl-), n. (fortif.). Outwork of two faces forming salient angle outside main ditch before curtain. [F, f. It. *ravellino* etym. dub.]

ră·ven[1], n. & a. Large black-plumaged hoarse-voiced bird of crow kind feeding chiefly on flesh, often kept tame, & popularly held of evil omen; (adj.) of glossy black (esp. *r. locks*, black hair). [com.-Teut.; OE *hræfn*, cf. Du. *raaf*, G *rabe*]

ră·ven[2], v.i. & t. Plunder (intr.), go plundering *about*, seek *after* prey or booty, prowl for prey; eat (t. & abs.) voraciously; have ravenous appetite (*for*). [f. OF *raviner* ravage (L *rapina* RAPINE)]

ră·venous, a. Rapacious (now rare); voracious (esp. *r. hunger, eagerness*, &c.); famished, very hungry. Hence **ra·venous**LY[2] adv., **ra·venous**NESS n. (rare). [f. OF *ravineux* (prec., -OUS)]

ră·vin, n. (poet., rhet.). Robbery, rapine; seizing & devouring of prey (*beast of r.*, of prey); spoil. [f. F *ravine* (now obs. in this sense) f. L *rapina* RAPINE]

ravi·ne (-ēn), n. Deep narrow gorge, mountain cleft. Hence **ravi·n**ED[2] a. [F, =violent rush, ravine, (prec.)]

ră·vish, v.t. Carry off (person, thing) by force (now rare); (of death, circumstances, &c.) take from life or from sight; commit rape upon, violate, (woman), whence **ra·vish**ER[1] n.; enrapture, charm, entrance, fill with delight, whence **ra·vish**ING[2] a., **ra·vishing**LY[2] adv., so **ra·vish**MENT n. [f. F *ravir* (L *rapere* seize), -ISH[2]]

raw, a., n., & v.t. Uncooked (*r. cream*, got without scalding of milk; *r. brick*, not hardened by fire); in unwrought state, not or not completely manufactured, (*r. silk*, as reeled from cocoons; *r. cloth*, unfulled; *r. hide*, untanned leather, also rope or whip of this; *r. spirit*, undiluted; *r. grain*, unmalted; *r. material*, that out of which any process of manufacture makes the articles it produces, as *the finished product of one industry is the r. material of another, the r. material of an army is men*); artistically crude; inexperienced, untrained, unskilled, fresh to anything, (*is a r. lad*; *r. recruits*); stripped of skin, having the flesh exposed, excoriated, sensitive to a touch from being so exposed; *r. edge* of cloth, without hem or selvage; (of atmosphere, wind, day, &c.) damp & chilly; *r.-boned*, with bones almost exposed, gaunt; *r. head & bloody bones*, nursery bugbear, death's-head & cross-bones, (attrib., of narrative style &c.) crudely horrible; hence **raw·**ISH[1](2) a., **raw·**NESS n. [N.) r. place on person's or esp. horse's skin; *touch* one *on the r.*, wound his feelings on the points on which he is sensitive. (Vb) rub (esp. horse's back) into rawness. [com.-Teut.; OE *hrēaw*, cf. Du. *rauw*, G *roh*; cogn. w. L *cruor* blood, Gk *kreas* flesh]

ray[1], n. Single line or narrow beam of light, (in scientific use) straight line in which radiant energy capable of producing sensation of light is propagated to given point (*Röntgen*, pr. rŭntyen or as G, or *X*, *-rr.*, form of radiation penetrating many substances impervious to ordinary light; *Becquerel rr.*, rr. emitted by RADIOactive bodies); analogous propagation-line of heat or other non-luminous physical energy, (fig.) remnant or beginning of enlightening or cheering influence (*a r., not a r., of hope, truth, genius*, &c.); radius of circle (rare), any of the lines forming a pencil or set of straight lines passing through one point, any of a set of radiating lines or parts or things; (Bot.) marginal part of composite flower, as daisy; radial division of starfish. Hence **ray**ED[2], **ray·**LESS, aa., **ray·**LET n. [f. OF *rai* (nom. *rais* f. L RADIUS)]

ray[2], v.i. & t. (Of light &c., or fig. of thought, hope, &c.) issue, come *forth*, or *off* or *out*, in rr.; radiate (t. & i.; poet.). [f. prec.]

ray[3], n. Kinds of large sea-fish allied to shark, with broad flat body, used as food, esp. the skate. [f. F *raie* f. L *raia*]

Ray·ah (rī-), n. Non-Moslem Turkish subject. [f. Arab. *ra'iyah* flock (*ra'a* feed)]

rayon (F), n. Artificial silk.

raze, rase (-z), v.t. Wound slightly, graze, (rare); erase, scratch *out*, (rare exc. fig. as *r.* person's *name from remembrance*); completely destroy, level with the ground, (town, house, walls, &c.; usu. *to the ground*). [f. F *raser* f. pop. L frequent. of L *radere ras-* scrape]

razee·, n., & v.t. Ship reduced in height by removal of upper deck(s); (vb) turn into a r. [f. F *rasée* fem. p.p. as prec.]

ra·zor, n., & v.t. Instrument used in shaving hair from skin (*safety r.*, kinds with guard to obviate risk of gashing skin); *r.-back*, back sharp as r.'s edge (often attrib., as *r.-b. whale* or RORQUAL, *r.-b. hill*, &c.), whence **ra·zorback**ED[2] a.; *r.-bill*, kinds of bird with *r. bill* (bill shaped like r.), whence **ra·zor-bill**ED[2] a.; *r.-edge*, keen edge, sharp mountain ridge, critical situation, sharp line of division (*keep on the r.-e. of orthodoxy*; *be on a r.-e.* or *r.'s edge* imit. Gk, be in great danger); *r.-fish, -shell*, kinds of bivalve with shell like handle of ordinary r.; *r.-grinder*, lit., also kinds of bird; *r.-strop*. (Vb; rare) use r. upon, shave, cut *down* close. [f. OF *rasor* (prec., -OR[2])]

ra·zzia (-z-), n. Raid, plundering or slave-collecting expedition, esp. as carried out by African Mohammedans. [F, f. Arab. *ghazwah* (*ghasw* make war)]

ra·zzle-dazzle, n. (slang). Excitement, bustle, stir, spree; undulating merry-go-round. [redupl. of DAZZLE]

re[1] (rā), n. Second note of octave; (rare) note D, the second in natural scale of C major. [See GAMUT]

rē², abl. of RES. (As prep.) in the matter of (chiefly in legal & business use as first word of head-line stating matter to be dealt with; also vulg. as substitute for *about, concerning,* in ordinary use); *re infe·ctā,* without having accomplished one's object (esp. *return r. i.*)

re- (see *Pronunciation, **Hyphen, below), pref. f. L *re-, red-,* again, back, un-. *Re-* both forms part of large numbers of. already compounded words borrowed f. L or Rom., & is treated as a living pref. In the latter capacity it may be prefixed for the occasion to any vb or vbl derivative; this is esp. common in such phrr. as *traverse & re-traverse* = traverse again & again, *reckoning & re-reckoning, translation & re-translation;* but many vbs &c. that originated as nonce-wds have become established, often with restriction to one or some only of the simple word's senses; the more common or important words of this class, & others whose simplicity of meaning allows them to be grouped with it, are given with any necessary information under senses 8, 9, below. Those senses are the simple ones, found also in many of the wds compounded before being adopted by E; but in others of the pre-E compds the sense of the pref. has been so developed as to be obscure or unrecognizable, & senses 1-7 are given as a rough classification.

*Pronunciation:—rē in all wds (esp. all given under senses 8, 9) that are historically, or are capable of being taken for, simple modifications of existing E wds by one of those senses (even when a similarly spelt compd exists in senses not capable of being so regarded; so *rēcover* = cover again, cf. RECOVER¹, *rēcount* = count again, cf. RECOUNT¹, *recreation* second or new creation, cf. *recreation* in RECREATE¹); rē before vowels, and before h (exc. in *rehearse*); rē also in *reflex, regress* n., *rescript, retail* n.; rē also in *recalesce, recrudesce, regelate,* & their derivv., & *recantation, retardation, retractation, retractility*: elsewhere, rĭ when the next syllable bears the word-accent (*refle·ct, repo·sitory*), & otherwise rĕ (*recolle·ct, re·vocable*).

**Hyphen:—The hyphen is often used when a writer wishes to mark the fact that he is using not a well-known compd vb, but *re-* as a living prefix (senses 8, 9) attached to a simple vb (*re-pair* = pair again, cf. *repair* mend); also usu. before e (*re-emerge*), & sometimes before other vowels (*re-assure,* usu. *reassure*); also when the idea of repetition is to be emphasized, esp. in such phrr. as *make & re-make.*

1–7: Special senses chiefly in pre-E compds.

1. In return, mutual(ly); *react, reciprocal, recompense, recrimination, rejoinder, remunerate, repartee, repay, requite, result, revenge,* &c.

2. Opposition: *rebel, recalcitrant, recusant, reluctance, remonstrate, repugnant, resist, revolt,* &c.

3. Behind, after: *relic, relinquish, relish, remain, remorse,* REST³,⁴, &c.

4. Retirement, secrecy: *recluse, recondite, recourse, refuge, remote, repository, reticent,* &c.

5. Off, away, down: *rebate, relax, release, relegate, remiss, renounce, repress, repudiate, rescind, reside, resolve, retail,* &c.

6. Frequentative or intensive: *redolent, redouble, redoubtable, redound, reduplicate, refine, refulgent, regard, rejoice, remark, renown, repine, repute, research, respect, resplendent, revere, revile, revolve,* &c.

7. Negative, un-: *reproach, reproof, reprobate, resign, reveal.*

8, 9: Ordinary senses as living prefix.

8. Once more, again, anew, afresh, repeated, (often with implication that previous doing &c. was deficient or erroneous or now requires alteration or improvement or renewal; many wds may be classed indifferently under 8 or 9); *readdre·ss* v.t., change address of (letter); *re-adju·st* v.t.; so *readju·stment* n.; *reaffir·m* v.t.; so *reaffirma·tion* n.; *reappa·rel* v.t.; *rear·m* v.i. & t., esp. provide (troops) with arms of new pattern; so *rear·mament* n.; *rearra·nge* v.t.; so *rearra·ngement* n.; *reasser·t* v.t.; so *reasser·tion* n.; *reasse·ss* v.t.; so *reasse·ssment* n.; *reassig·n* v.t.; *rebapti·ze* v.t., lit., & fig. give new name to; so *reba·ptism* n.; *rebir·th* n., esp. fresh incarnation; so *rebor·n* p.p.; *rebi·te* v.t., (defective parts of etched &c. plate with acid); *rebui·ld* v.t.; *recapi·tulate* v.t., go over headings of, summarize, go quickly through again; so *recapitula·tion* n. (spec. in Biol., reproduction in embryos of successive type-forms in line of development), *recapi·tulative, recapi·tulatory,* aa.; *reca·st* v.t., & n., (put into) new shape, improve(d) arrangement &c. (of); *rechri·sten* v.t., = *rebaptize* above; *reclo·the,* v.t.; *recoa·l* v.t.; *recoa·t* v.t., put new coat of paint on; *recoi·n* v.t.; so *recoi·nage* n.; *reco·lonize* v.t.; so *recoloniza·tion* n.; *reco·lour* v.t.; *recombi·ne* v.t.; so *recombina·tion* n.; *recomme·nce* v.t. & i.; so *recomme·ncement* n.; *recommi·t* v.t., esp. refer back (bill &c.) for further consideration to committee; so *recommi·tment, recommi·ttal,* nn.; *recompo·se* v.t.; *recompou·nd* v.t.; *reconsi·der* v.t.; so *reconsidera·tion* n.; *reconsti·tuent* a. & n., (remedy) that builds up strength or tissue anew; *reco·nstitute* v.t., esp. piece together (past events) into an intelligible whole; so *reconstitu·tion* n.; *reconstru·ct* v.t.; so *reconstru·ction* n., *reconstru·ctive*

a.; *re-cou·nt* v.t., (esp. votes at election as security against error), & see RECOUNT[1]; so *re-cou·nt* n.; *re-co·ver* v.t., (esp. umbrellas &c.), & see RECOVER[1]; *recrea·te* v.t., create over again, & see RECREATE[1]; so *recrea·tion*, & see in RECREATE[1]; *redire·ct* v.t., esp. = *readdress* above; so *redire·ction* n.; *redistri·bute* v.t.; so *redistribu·tion* n., esp. of seats in Parliament or voting-power in elections, *redistri·butive* a.; *redivi·de* v.t.; so *redivi·sion* n.; *redo·* v.t.; *redye·* v.t.; *re-e·dit* v.t.; so *re-edi·tion* n.; *re-enfor·ce* v.t. (cf. REINFORCE); *re-e·ngine* v.t., supply (ship &c.) with new engines; *re-exa·mine* v.t., esp. of opening side's second examination of witness after opponents' cross-examination; so *re-examina·tion* n.; *refa·ce* v.t., put new facing on (building); *refa·shion* v.t.; so *refa·shionment* n.; *refi·t* v.t. & i., restore (ship) by, (of ship) undergo, renewal & repairs; so *refi·t*, *refi·tment*, nn.; *refoo·t* v.t., supply new foot to (stocking); *refur·nish* v.t.; *rege·nesis* n.; *regrow·p* v.t.; *reha·ndle* v.t., esp. = *recast* above; *reha·ng* v.t., (esp. pictures); *reha·sh* v.t., & n., (put) stale materials esp. of literary kind in new shape; *rehear·* v.t., (case in lawcourt); *rehear·ing* n.; *rehou·se* v.t., provide with new house(s); *reincar·nāte* v.t.; so *reincarna·tion* n., *reincar·nate* (-at) a.; *rei·nk* v.t.; *reinsure·* v.i. & t. (esp. of underwriter &c. devolving risk upon another); so *reinsur·ance* n.; *reinter·* v.t.; *reinve·st*[1] (see also sense 9) v.t., shift (money) to other investment; so *reinve·stment* n.; *rei·ssue* v.t.; so *rei·ssuable* a. (esp. of bills or notes), *rei·ssue* n., esp. part of already published edition to be sold with change of form or price; *rei·terate* v.t., say or do over again or several times, repeat; so *reitera·tion* n., *rei·terative* a.; *rela·bel* v.t.; *reli·ve*, v.i. & t.; *reloa·d* v.t.; *rema·ke* v.t.; *rema·n*[1] (see also sense 9) v.t., equip with fresh men; *remar·gin* v.t., (esp. of secondhand bookseller repairing worn book); *rema·rry* v.i. & t.; so *rema·rriage* n.; *rema·st* v.t.; *remi·nt* v.t.; *remo·del* v.t.; *remou·ld* v.t.; *remou·nt* (see also REMOUNT[2]) v.t., esp. provide with fresh horse &c.; *remou·nt* n., supply of fresh horses for regiment &c., fresh horse; *rena·me* v.t.; *renu·mber* v.t., esp. change numbers of series &c.; *reor·ganize* v.t.; so *reorganiza·tion*, *reor·ganizer*, nn.; *repa·per* v.t.; *reparti·tion* v.t.; *reperu·se* v.t.; so *reperu·sal* n.; *repla·nt* v.t.; so *replanta·tion* n.; *repo·t* v.t. (esp. plant into larger pot); *repri·nt* v.t.; *re·print* n., book, article, &c., reprinted; *reprodu·ce* v.t. & i., esp. (trans.) produce copy or representation of, (intr.) multiply by generation; so *reprodu·ction* n., *reprodu·ceable*, *reprodu·cible*, *reprodu·ctive*, aa., *reprodu·ctively* adv., *reprodu·ctiveness* n.; *reprovi·sion* v.t.; *repu·blish* v.t. (esp. book &c.); so *republica·tion* n.; *rerea·d* v.t.; *resea·t* v.t., esp. provide church, theatre, &c., with fresh seats; *resee·k* v.t.; *rese·t* v.t. (esp. gems); *rese·ttle* v.t.; so *rese·ttlement* n.; *resha·pe* v.t.; *reshu·ffle* v.t. (esp. cards); *reso·le* v.t.; *respe·ll* v.t., esp. spell phonetically; *resta·mp* v.t.; *restar·t* v.t. & i., & n.; *resta·te* v.t., esp. put into more intelligible or convincing words; so *resta·tement* n.; *resto·ck* v.t. & i., provide with or take in fresh stock; *resu·mmons* n., renewed legal summons; *resurvey·* v.t.; so *resur·vey* n.; *reta·ste* v.t.; *rete·ll* v.t.; *retou·ch* v.t. (esp. composition, picture, &c.), & n.; *retri·m* v.t.; *retry·* v.t. = *rehear* above; so *retri·al* n.; *retur·f* v.t.; *reur·ge* v.t.; *reva·ccinate* v.t.; so *revaccina·tion* n.; *reva·lue* v.t., assess value of anew; so *revalua·tion* n.; *revic·tual* v.t.; *revi·sit* (*often* ri-) v.t.; *rewor·d* v.t., change wording of; *rewri·te* v.t.

9. Back, with return to previous state after lapse or cessation or occurrence of opposite state or action, (often corresponding to compounds in DIS- or UN-; many words may be assigned indifferently to 9 or 8); *reaffo·rest* v.t.; so *reafforesta·tion* n.; *rea·nimate* v.t.; so *reanima·tion* n.; *reappear·* v.i.; so *reappear·ance* n.; *reappoi·nt* v.t.; so *reappoi·ntment* n.; *reari·se* v.i.; *rearou·se* v.t.; *reasce·nd* v.i. & t.; *reasse·mble* v.i. & t.; *reassu·me* v.t. (now rare, ousted by RESUME); so *reassu·mption* n.; *reassure·* v.t., restore to confidence, dispel apprehensions of; so *reassur·ing* a. (of words, manner, &c.), *reassur·ingly* adv.; *rebar·barize* v.t.; *rebi·nd* v.t. (esp. book); *reca·pture* v.t., & n.; *re-ce·de* v.t.; so *re-ce·ssion* n.; *rechar·ge* v.t.; *rechar·ge* n., amount of substance used in recharging; *reci·vilize* v.t.; so *reciviliza·tion* n.; *reco·mfort* v.t.; *recondu·ct* v.t.; *reco·nquer* v.t.; so *reco·nquest* n.; *reconver·t* v.t.; so *reconver·sion* n.; *recro·ss* v.t.; *redesce·nd* v.i. & t.; *redisco·ver* v.t.; so *redisco·very* n.; *re-ele·ct* v.t.; so *re-ele·ction* n.; *re-e·ligible* a.; *re-embar·k* v.i. & t.; so *re-embarka·tion* n.; *re-emer·ge* v.i.; so *re-emer·gence* n., *re-emer·gent* a.; *re-ena·ble* v.t.; *re-ena·ct* v.t.; so *re-ena·ctment* n.; *re-e·nter* v.i. & t. (part. sometimes = RE-ENTRANT); *re-e·ntrance*, *re-e·ntry*, nn.; *re-esta·blish* v.t.; so *re-esta·blishment* n.; *re-exi·st* v.i.; *re-expor·t* v.t.; *re-e·xport* n., commodity imported & then exported esp. without further manufacture; so *re-exporta·tion* n.; *refi·ll* v.t.; *re·fill* n., = *recharge* above; *refloa·t* v.t. (stranded ship); *re·flux* n., backward flow; *refo·rest* v.t., turn into forest again; so *reforesta·tion* n.; *refur·bish* v.t.; *reger·minate* v.i.; so *regermina·tion* n.; *regi·ld* v.t.; *rehabi·litate* v.t., restore to privileges, reputation, or proper condition; so *rehabilita·tion* n.; *rehu·manize* v.t.; *reigni·te* v.t. & i.; *reimpor·t* v.t., import (same goods) after exporting; so *rei·mport* n.;

reimpo·se v.t.; so *reimposi·tion* n.; *reincor·porate* v.t.; *reingra·tiate* v.t.; *reinser·t* v.t.; so *reinser·tion* n.; *reinve·st*[2] (see also sense 8) v.t., replace *in* office, *with* privilege; so *reinve·stiture* n.; *reinvi·gorate* v.t.; so *reinvigora·tion* n.; *reki·ndle* v.t. & i.; *reli·ne* v.t., renew lining of (esp. garment); *rema·n*[2] (see also sense 8) v.t., restore to manhood or courage; *remigra·te* v.i., esp. return after migrating; so *remigra·tion* n.; *reo·ccupy* v.t.; so *reoccupa·tion* n.; *reo·pen* v.t. & i.; *repa·ganize* v.t.; *repai·nt* v.t., restore paint or colouring of; *repa·ss* v.t. & i., esp. pass again on way back; so *repa·ssage* n.; *repeo·ple* v.t.; *repercu·ssion* n., echo, recoil after impact, indirect effect or reaction *of* event or act; so *repercu·ssive* a.; *repie·ce* v.t., put pieces of together again, reconstruct; *repoi·nt* v.t. (joints of masonry); *repo·lish* v.t.; *repo·pulate* v.t.; *reposse·ss* v.t.; so *reposse·ssion* n.; *repur·chase* v.t., & n.; *repur·ify* v.t.; *requi·cken* v.t.; *resa·ddle* v.t. & abs.; *resa·le* n., esp. sale of thing bought; so *resa·lable* a.; *resei·ze* v.t.; so *resei·zure* n.; *rese·ll* v.t., esp. sell after buying; *reshi·p* v.t. & i., put, go, on board ship again; so *reshi·pment* n.; *restu·ff* v.t.; *reta·ke* v.t.; *retransfer·* v.t.; so *retra·nsfer* n.; *retransfor·m* v.t.; *retransla·te* v.t. (esp. back into the original language); so *retransla·tion* n.; *retrea·d* v.t.; *reuni·te* v.t. & i.; *revi·talize* v.t.; *rewi·n* v.t.

're, colloq. abbr. of *are* appended to *we, you, & they* (*we're, you're, they're*).

reach[1], v.t. & i. Stretch out, extend, (t. & i.; often *out* &c.; *reached out his hand, its branches; a dominion reaching from the Ebro to the Carpathians*); stretch out the hand &c., make reaching motion or effort lit. or fig., (*you must r. out further; mind reaches forward to an ideal; ship reaches ahead in race*); get as far as, attain to, arrive at, (specified point or object of destination; also abs.), succeed in affecting, either simply or with the hand or instrument or missile or missive or influence (*r.* BOTTOM[1]; *reached land; could not r. his enemy*, esp. in fencing, boxing; *how is her conscience to be reached?; libels that the ordinary law reaches; the steps by which you r. the entrance; your letter reached me today; every syllable reached the audience; has reached middle age, its eighth edition; cannot r. so high, far enough, down, up to it*, &c.; *as far as eye could r.; my income will not r. to it*); hand, pass or take with outstretched hand, (*reached him the book; reached down his hat*); *rea·ch-me-down* a. & n. (slang), ready-made (garment). Hence **rea·ch**ABLE a. [OE *rǣcan*, cf. Du. *reiken*, G *reichen*]

reach[2], n. Act of reaching out; extent to which hand &c. can be reached out, influence be exerted, motion be carried out, or mental powers be used, range, scope, compass, (*within, above, out of, beyond*, one's *r.*, possible, impossible, of attainment or performance; *has a wide r.; within easy r. of the railway; no help was within r.*); continuous extent, esp. part of river that can be looked along at once between two bends; (Naut.) tack. [f. prec.]

rea·ct, v.i. Produce reciprocal or responsive effect, act upon the agent, (*they r. upon each other; tyranny reacts upon the tyrant*, has effects upon him as well as upon his victims), (Chem., of substance applied to another) call out activity, cause manifestation, (*nitrous oxide reacts upon the metal*); respond *to* stimulus, undergo change due to some influence; (Mil.) make counter-attack(s); be actuated by repulsion *against*, tend in reverse or backward direction. Hence **rea·ct**IVE a., **reacti·v**ITY n. [RE- 1]

rea·ction, n. Responsive or reciprocal action (esp. *action & r.*); (Chem.) action set up by one substance in another; response of organ &c. to external stimulus; return of previous condition after interval of opposite (e.g. glow felt after cold bath, depression after excitement); (Mil.) counter-stroke; retrograde tendency esp. in politics, whence **rea·ction**ARY[1] a. & (=reactionary person) n., **rea·ction**IST(2) n. & a. [RE- 1]

read (rēd), v.t. & i. (*read*, pr. rĕd), & n. Interpret mentally, declare interpretation or coming development of, divine, (*r. dream, riddle, omen, futurity, men's hearts* or *thoughts* or *faces; r.* person's *hand*, as palmist; *r. the sky*, as astrologist or meteorologist); (be able to) convert into the intended words or meaning (written or printed or other symbols or things expressed by their means, or abs.; *reads* or *can r. hieroglyphs, shorthand, the clock, the Morse system, music, several languages; does not r. or write*); reproduce mentally or (often *aloud, out, off*, &c., or with ind. obj.) vocally, while following their symbols with eyes or fingers, the words of (author, book, tale, letter, &c., or abs.; often *over, through*, advv.; *reads well*, with good intonation &c., expressively; *was reading Plato; r. me off the list; r. it through six times; does he preach extempore or r.?; have no time to r.; the Bible is the most r. of all books; r.* one *a lesson*, admonish him; *the Bill was r. for the first* &c. *time*, was allowed its first &c. READING; invalid *is r. to for several hours daily; seldom reads French*, anything written in it); study (t. & i.) by reading (often *up*; *is reading law; shall not r. for honours; reading man*, who devotes most of his time to study; *has r. much*), (p.p. in active sense as adj. with *well, deeply, slightly, little,* &c.) versed *in* subject by reading, acquainted with literature; find (thing) stated, find statement, in print &c. (*revenge, we r., is wild justice*; *I have r. somewhere that . . ., have r. of it*); interpret (statement, action) in certain sense (*may be read several ways*; *my silence is not to be r. as consent*); assume as intended in or deducible from writer's words, find implications, (*you r. too much into the text*; *in their pleas for reform I r. Protection*; *r. between the lines*, search for or discover hidden meanings); (of editor) give as the word(s) probably used by author (*Bentley reads* peraeque; also facet. in correcting statements, as *for* white *read* black, *& the account may be accepted*); bring into specified state by reading (*r. me to sleep, himself stupid, hoarse,* &c.; *r.* oneself *in* of incumbent, enter upon office by public reading of xxxix articles &c.); (of recording instrument) present (figure &c.) to one reading it (*thermometer reads 33°*); sound or affect hearer or reader *well, ill,* &c., when r. (*play reads better than it acts*; *reads like a threat, translation,* &c.). (N.) time spent in reading (*have a short, long, good, quiet, r.*). [com.-Teut.; OE *rǣdan* consider, discern, cf. Du. *raden*, G *rathen*; cogn. w. Skr. *radh-* accomplish]

rea·dable, a. Interestingly written; (rare) legible. Hence **readabi·lity**, **rea·dableness**, nn., **rea·dably**[2] adv. [-ABLE]

readdress. See RE- 8.

rea·der, n. In vbl senses; also or esp.: person employed by publisher to read & report on offered MSS.; printer's proof-corrector; person appointed to read aloud, esp. (often *lay-r.*) parts of service in church; lecturer in some universities &c. (*r. in Roman law* &c.); book of selections for use by students of a language &c. Hence **rea·dership** n. [-ER[1]]

rea·dily (rĕd-), adv. Without showing reluctance, willingly; without difficulty (*the facts may r. be ascertained*). [READY, -LY[2]]

rea·diness (rĕd-), n. Prompt compliance, willingness; facility, prompt resourcefulness, quickness in argument or action; ready or prepared state (*all is in r.*). [READY, -NESS]

rea·ding, n. In vbl senses; also or esp.: literary knowledge (*a man of vast r.*); *first, second, third, r.*, successive occasions on which Bill must have been presented for acceptance to each House before it is ready for royal assent (*first r.*, permitting introduction; *second*, approving general principle; *third*, accepting details as amended in committee); entertainment at which something is read to audience (*penny r.*, for poor of parish &c.); word(s) read or given by an editor or found in MS. in text of a passage (*the right, true, best, MS.*, &c., *r.*; *various rr.*); (specified quality of) matter to be read (*is good, dull, r.*; *there is plenty of r. in it*); figure &c. shown by graduated instrument (*40° difference between day & night rr.*); interpretation, view taken, rendering, (*what is your r. of the facts?*; *his r. of Iago was generally condemned*); *r.-desk*, for supporting book &c., lectern; *r.-room*, in club &c. for persons wishing to read. [-ING[1]]

readjust &c. See RE- 8.

ready (rĕ·dĭ), a., adv., n., & v.t. With preparations complete, in fit state, with resolution nerved, willing, apt, inclined, about *to*, prompt, quick, facile, provided beforehand, within reach, easily secured, unreluctant, easy, fit for immediate use, (*Are you r.? Go!*, formula for starting race; *Ready, present, fire*, successive orders, the first = make rifle r.; *dinner is r.*; *are r. to march*; *am r. to risk my life*; *is too r. to suspect*; *was r. to swear with rage*; *a bud just r. to burst*; *is r. for death*; *the r.*; *ministers of vengeance*; *is very r. at excuses, has a r. pen, wit,* whence **ready-witted**[2] a., &c.; *gave a r. consent*; *found r. acceptance*; *its r. solubility in water*; *found an instrument r. to hand, a r. source of revenue*; *the readiest way to do it*; *make r.*, prepare i. & t., as *they made r. for the attempt* or *to fight*, or *made everything r.*; *r. money*, actual coin, also payment on the spot); *r. reckoner*, book of r.-reckoned (see adv.) computations of kind commonly wanted in business. (Adv.; chiefly with p.p., usu. hyphened, prop. a pred. use of adj.) beforehand, so as not to require doing when the time comes, (*please pack everything r.*; *boxes are r. packed* or *packed r.*; *r.-built houses*; *r.-made clothes*, made in standard shapes & sizes, not to customer's individual measure; *r.-made shop*, selling these); (rare exc. in comp. & superl.) quickly (*the child that answers readiest*). (N.) position in which rifle is held before the present (*come to the r.* &c.); (slang) r. money (*planked down the r.*). (Vb; racing slang) qualify (horse) for good handicap in race by preventing its winning in another. [ME *rǣdig* perh. f. OE *gerǣde* = MHG *gereit*, cf. G *bereit*, + -Y[2] on false anal.]

reaffirm &c., see RE- 8; **reafforest** &c., RE- 9.

rea·gency, n. Reactive power or operation (see REACT).

rea·gent, n. (Chem.) substance used to detect presence of another by REACTION; reactive substance or force (see REACT).

re·al[1] (rē-, rā-), n. Silver coin & money of account (about 6½*d.*) still used in some Spanish-speaking countries; present Spanish monetary unit (about 2½*d.*,) quarter of peseta. [Sp., n. use of adj. f. L *regalis* REGAL]

re·al[2], a. Actually existing as a thing or occurring in fact, objective, genuine, rightly so called, natural, sincere, not merely apparent or nominal or supposed

or pretended or artificial or hypocritical or affected, (*r. money,* coin, cash; *the r. presence,* of Christ's body & blood in the Eucharist as disputed by theologians; *a r. object & its image; r. & paper roses; effected a r. cure; should like a r. fine day; r. life,* that lived by actual people, opp. fictitious & dramatic imitations; *there is no r. doubt about it; who is the r. manager?; is a r. man,* unaffected, also worthy of the name; *the r. thing,* not a makeshift or inferior article); (Law; cf. PERSONAL) consisting of immovable property such as lands or houses (esp. *r. estate*); (Philos.) having an absolute & necessary & not merely contingent existence; (abs.) *the r.,* what is r., esp. opp. the ideal (also rarely as n. with pl. =r. thing, as *I deal only with rr.*). [f. LL *realis* (*res* thing, -AL])

rĕă·lgar, n. Disulphide of arsenic, red arsenic, red orpiment, used as pigment & in fireworks. [med. L, f. Arab. *rehj algahr* powder of the cave]

re·alism, n. Scholastic doctrine that universals or general ideas have objective existence (cf. *nominalism, conceptualism*); belief that matter as object of perception has real existence (cf. *idealism*); practice of regarding things in their true nature & dealing with them as they are, freedom from prejudice & convention, practical views & policy, (cf. *idealism*); fidelity of representation, truth to nature, insistence upon details. So **re·alIST**(2) n. & a., **reali·stIC** a., **reali·stICALLY** adv. [-ISM]

reă·lity, n. Property of being real; resemblance to original (*reproduced with startling r.*); real existence, what is real, what underlies appearances, (*in r.,* in fact, opp. *in words, in appearance,* &c.); existent thing; real nature *of.* [f. med. L *realitas* (REAL², -TY)]

re·alize, v.t. Convert (hope, plan, &c.) into fact (usu. pass.); give apparent reality to, make realistic, present as real, (*these details help to r. the scene*); conceive as real, apprehend clearly or in detail (noun, *that, how,* &c.); convert (securities, property) into money (often abs., =sell one's property); amass (fortune, specified profit); fetch as price. Hence **re·alizABLE** a., **realizA·TION** n. [-IZE]

really (rĭ·alĭ), adv. In fact, in reality, (often *r. & truly*); positively, indeed, I assure you, I mean what I say, I protest; *r.?,* do you mean it?, is that so?. [-LY²]

realm (rĕlm), n. Kingdom (chiefly rhet., & in some legal phrr., as *the laws of the r., persons who are out of the r.*); sphere, province, domain, (*the rr. of fancy, poetry,* &c.). [f. OF *reaume* f. pop. L **regalimen* (REGAL, -MEN)]

rē·alty, n. Real estate(cf. *personalty*). [-TY]

ream¹, n. Twenty quires or 480 sheets of paper (often 500, to allow for waste; *printers' r.,* 516); (often pl.) large quantity of paper (*wrote rr. & rr. of verse*). [ult. f. Arab. *rizmah* bundle, cf. Du. *riem,* OF *remme,* It. *risma*]

ream², v.t. Widen (hole in metal) with borer or **rea·mER¹**(2) n.; turn over edge of (cartridge-case &c.); (Naut.) open (seam) for caulking. [OE *rýman* (ROOM), cf. G *räumen*]

reanimate &c. See RE- 9.

reap, v.i. & t. Cut (grain or similar crop), cut grain &c., with sickle in harvest; gather in thus or with machine or fig. as harvest (*r. as* one *has sown, sow wind & r. whirlwind, r. the fruits of,* take consequences of one's actions; *r. where* one *has not sown,* profit by others' toil); harvest crop of (field &c.); *reaping-hook,* sickle; *reaping-machine,* for cutting grain & often binding sheaves without manual labour. Hence **rea·pER¹**(1, 2) n. [OE *ripan,* excl. E]

reapparel, see RE- 8; **reappear** &c., **reappoint** &c., RE- 9.

rear¹, n. Hindermost part of army or fleet (*hang on the r. of,* follow with view to attacking); back of, space behind, position at back of, army or camp or person (*bring, close, up the r.,* come last; *take enemy in r.,* attack from behind; *saw them far in the r.,* behind; *was sent to the r. for safety*); back part of anything (*at the r. of,* behind); (colloq.) w.-c. or latrine; *rear-, r.* attrib., hinder, back-; so **rear·MOST** a.; *r.-admiral,* flag-officer below vice-admiral; *r.-guard,* body of troops detached to protect r. esp. in retreats (*r.-g. action,* engagement between r.-g. & enemy); *rear·ward* n. [f. AF *rerewarde*=rear-guard], rear (esp. in prep. phrr., as *to rearward of, in the rearward*); *rear·ward* a. & adv., *rear·wards* adv., towards the rear [-WARD(S).] [shortened f. ARREAR]

rear², v.t. & i. Raise, set upright, build, uplift, hold upwards, (rhet.; *r. a pillar, cathedral,* &c.; *reared his mighty stature; r.* one's *head,* one's *voice, a hand,* &c.); raise, bring up, breed, foster, nourish, educate, cultivate, grow, (cattle, game, children, crops, &c.); (of horse &c.; intr. & rarely refl.) rise, raise it*self,* on hind feet. Hence **rear·ER¹** n. [OE *ræ̆ran,* native form corresp. to & largely ousted by RAISE]

rear·-arch, rere-, n. Inner arch of window or door opening when of different size &c. from the outer. [f. F *arrière* see ARREAR]

rearise, see RE- 9; **rearm** &c., RE- 8; **rearouse,** RE- 9; **rearrange** &c., RE- 8.

rear·-vault, n. Vaulted space connecting arched window or door head with arch in inner face of wall. [as REAR-ARCH]

reascend. See RE- 9.

reason¹ (rē·zn), n. (Fact adduced or serving as) argument, motive, cause, or justification (*give rr. for*; *prove with rr.*; *the woman's r.*, repetition of fact as its own explanation, as in *I love him because I love him*; *for no other reason than that I forgot, but this*; *there is no r. to suppose*; *r. of State*, political justification esp. for immoral proceeding; *the r. of your isolation, of eclipses, is that—*; *failed by r. of its bad organization*; *there was r. to believe*; *I saw r. to suspect him*; *he complains with r.*, not unjustifiably); (Log.) one of premisses of syllogism, esp. minor premiss when given after conclusion; the intellectual faculty characteristic esp. of human beings by which conclusions are drawn from premisses (*whether dogs have r. is really a question of definition*; *there can be no opposition between r. & common sense*); intellect personified (*God & r. are identical*); (as transl. of G *Vernunft* in Kant) faculty transcending the understanding (*Verstand*) & providing *a priori* principles, intuition; sanity (*has lost his, is restored to, r.*); sense, sensible conduct, what is right or practical or practicable, moderation, (*without* RHYME *or r.*; *bring to r.*, induce to cease from vain resistance; *will do anything in r.*, within the bounds of moderation; *it stands to r.*, cannot be denied without paradox, would be generally admitted; *hear* or *listen to r.*, suffer oneself to be persuaded; *as r. was*, as good sense bade; *have r.* archaic or transl. of F, be right; *there is r. in what you say*). Hence **rea·son**LESS a. [f. OF *raisun* f. L *rationem* (*rēri rat-* consider, -ION)]

rea·son[2], v.i. & t. Use argument *with* person by way of persuasion; form or try to reach conclusions by connected thought silent or expressed (*from* premisses; *about, of, upon*, subject), whence **rea·son**ER[1] n.; discuss *what, whether, why*, &c.; conclude, assume as step in argument, say by way of argument, *that* (or parenth.); express in logical or argumentative form (*a reasoned exposition, manifesto, article*; *-ed amendment*, in which reasons are embodied with a view to directing course of debate); persuade by argument *out of, into* (*tried to r. him out of his fears*; *reasoned himself into perplexity*); think *out* (consequences &c.). Hence **rea·son**ING[1](1) n. [f. OF *raisoner* f. LL *rationare* (prec.)]

rea·sonable, a. Endowed with reason, reasoning, (rare); sound of judgement, sensible, moderate, not expecting too much, ready to listen to reason; agreeable to reason, not absurd, within the limits of reason, not greatly less or more than might be expected, inexpensive, not extortionate, tolerable, fair. Hence **rea·sonable**NESS n., **rea·sonab**LY[2] adv. [f. OF *raisonable* (REASON[1], -ABLE)]

reassemble, see RE-9; **reassert, reassess** &c., **reassign**, RE-8; **reassume** &c., **reassure** &c., RE-9.

Réaumur (F), name of French physicist appended (*abbr.* R.) to readings of the thermometer introduced by him with freezing-point 0° & boiling-point 80° (*a temperature of more than 55° R.* or *Réaumur*).

reave, reive, (rēv), v.i. & t. (archaic, poet.; *reft*). Commit ravages (usu. *reive*), whence **rei·**VER[1] n.; forcibly deprive *of* (esp. in p.p.); take by force, carry off, (*away, from*). [com.-Teut.; OE *réafian*, cf. Du. *rooven*, G *rauben*]

rebaptize &c., see RE-8; **rebarbarize**, RE-9.

reba·te[1], v.t. (archaic). Diminish, reduce force or effect of; blunt, dull. [f. OF *rabattre* (RE-5, ABATE)]

reba·te[2], n. Deduction from sum to be paid, discount, drawback. [f. F *rabat* (prec.)]

rebate[3] (ră·bĭt, rĭbā·t), n., & v.t. = RABBET.

rĕ·beck, n. Medieval three-stringed instrument, early form of fiddle. [f. F *rebec* var. of OF *rebebe* f. Arab. *rebab*]

rĕ·bel[1], n. Person who rises in arms against, resists, or refuses allegiance to, the established government; person or thing that resists authority or control; (attrib.) rebellious, of rr., in rebellion. [orig. a. & n.; the pred. a. use now obs.; f. F *rebelle* f. L *rebellis* (RE-2, *bellum* war)

rebe·l[2], v.i. (-ll-). Act as r. (*against*); feel or manifest repugnance to some custom &c. (*against*). [f. F *rebeller* f. L *re*(*bellare* make war) revolt, RE-2]

rebe·llion, n. Organized armed resistance to established government (*the Great R.*, period of English history 1642–60); open resistance to any authority. [f. F *rébellion* f. L *rebellionem* (REBEL[1], -ION)]

rebe·llious (-yus), a. In rebellion, disposed to rebel, insubordinate, defying lawful authority; (of diseases, things) difficult to treat, unmanageable, refractory. Hence **rebe·llious**LY[2] adv., **rebe·llious**NESS n. [as REBEL[1] or prec. + -OUS]

rebe·llow, v.i. & t. Re-echo loudly. [RE-6; after L *re*(*boare* bellow), RE-6]

rebind, see RE-9; **rebirth** &c., **rebite**, RE-8.

re·boant, a. (poet.). Rebellowing, resounding, re-echoing. [f. L *reboare* REBELLOW, -ANT]

rebou·nd[1], v.i. Spring back after impact; have reactive effect, recoil upon agent, (*our evil example will r. upon ourselves*). [f. OF *rebonder* (RE-1, BOUND[3])]

rebou·nd[2], n. Act of rebounding, recoil; reaction after emotion (*take* one *on* or *at the r.*, utilize such reaction to persuade him to contrary action &c.). [f. prec.]

rebu·ff, n., & v.t. Check given to one who makes advances, proffers help or sympathy, shows interest or curiosity, makes request, &c., repulse, snub; (vb) give r. to. [f. obs. F *rebuffe*(*r*) f. It. *ribuffo, ribuffare*, (RE-2, *buffo* puff)]

rebuild. See RE- 8.
rebu·ke, v.t., & n. Reprove, reprimand, censure authoritatively; hence **rebu·kingLY**[2] adv. (N.) rebuking or being rebuked; a reproof. [f. ONF *re(buker* = OF *bucher* beat), RE- 5]
rē·bus, n. Enigmatic representation of name, word, &c., by pictures &c. suggesting its syllables. [prob. = abl. pl. of L *res* thing; origin of sense (in F & E) doubtful]
rebu·t, v.t. (-tt-). Force or turn back, give check to; refute, disprove, (evidence, charge), whence **rebu·ttAL**(2), **rebu·tMENT**, **rebu·ttER**[4] (see SURREBUT), nn. [f. OF *re(buter* BUTT[1]), RE- 9]
recă·lcitrate, v.i. Kick *against* or *at* rules &c., refuse compliance, be refractory. So **reca·lcitrANT**(1) a. & n., **reca·lcitrANCE**, **recalcitrA·TION**, nn. [f. L *re(calcitrare* strike with heel f. *calx -cis* heel), RE-2, -ATE[3]]
rēcale·sce (-ĕs), v.i. Grow hot again (esp. in techn. use of iron allowed to cool from white heat, which recovers heat at certain point for short time). Hence **recale·sCENCE** n. [f. L *re(calescere* grow hot), RE- 9]
reca·ll[1] (-awl), v.t. Summon back from a place or from different occupation, inattention, digression, &c.; cancel appointment of (official sent to distance, esp. overseas); bring back to memory, serve as reminder of, recollect, remember; revive, rescuscitate; revoke, annul, (action, decision), take back (gift). Hence **reca·llABLE** a. [RE- 9]
reca·ll[2], n. Summons to come back; cancelling of appointment abroad; signal to ship &c. to return; possibility of recalling esp. in sense of annulling (esp. *beyond, past, r.*). [RE- 9]
recă·nt, v.t. & i. Withdraw & renounce (opinion, statement, &c.) as erroneous or heretical; disavow former opinion, esp. with public confession of error. Hence **rēcantA·TION** n. [f. L *re(cantare* sing) revoke, RE- 7]
recapitulate &c., see RE- 8; **recapture,** RE-9; **recast,** RE- 8.
rece·de, v.i. Go or shrink back or further off; be left by observer's motion at increasing distance; slope backwards; withdraw (*from* engagement, opinion, &c.); decline in character or value. [f. L *re(cedere* go), RE- 5]
receip·t (-ēt), n., & v.t. = RECIPE; amount of money received; fact or action of receiving or being received into person's hands or possession (*on r. of a postal order for 1/- the goods will be sent*; *beg to acknowledge r. of your book*; *entrusted with the r. of subscriptions*), written acknowledgement of such r. esp. of payment of sum due; (archaic) place where money is officially received, esp. *r. of custom*, custom-house; (vb) write or print r. on (bill). [ME *receit* f. ONF *receite* f. L *recepta* fem. p.p. of *recipere* RECEIVE w. *p* inserted on L]
recei·ve (-ēv), v.t. Accept delivery of, take (proffered thing) into one's hands or possession, (*Lord, r. my soul*, dying man's prayer; *r. stolen goods*, as thief's accomplice; *r.* person's *confession, oath*, consent to hear; *r. a petition*, take it to consider; *r. the sacraments*, eat & drink the bread & wine, also abs. as *attend without receiving*); bear up against, stand force or weight of, encounter with opposition, (*received his body in their hands*; *arch receives weight of roof*; *received the sword-point with his shield*; *prepare to r. cavalry*, order to infantry); admit, consent or prove able to hold, provide accommodation for, submit to, serve as receptacle of, (*had to r. the visits, attentions, of*; *r. an impression, stamp, mark*, &c., be marked lit. or fig. more or less permanently with it; *sensitive paper receives the record of signals*; *the basin that received his blood*; *the house received a new guest*; *hole large enough to r. two men*; *fitted to r. the knowledge of God*; *has received our yoke*; *town receives a French garrison*; *was received into the Church*, admitted to membership); entertain as guest, greet, welcome, give specified reception to, (*shall not be received at my house*; *he that receiveth me receiveth him that sent me*; *you stay here & r. him*; *how did she r. his offer?*; *was received with cries of* Judas; *news was received with horror*; *I r. it as certain, as a prophecy*, regard it in that light), (abs.) r. company, hold reception; give credit to, accept as true, (*an axiom universally received*; *they r. not our report*), whence **recei·vED**[1] a.; acquire, get, come by, be given or provided with, have sent to or conferred or inflicted on one, (*have not yet received my dividend*; *r. a letter, news*; *a window that has not received a frame*; *r. the name of John*; *r. Christ in baptism*, have Christian character conferred; *pleasant to r. sympathy*; *deserves more attention than it receives*; *r. orders to march*; *received many insults, a thrust, a broken jaw, the contents of his pistol*); partake *of*. Hence **recei·vABLE** a. [f. ONF *receivre* f. L *re(cipere* = *capere* take) recover, RE- 9]
recei·ver, n. In vbl senses, esp.: person appointed by court's *receiving-order* to administer property of bankrupt or property under litigation, whence **recei·verSHIP** n.; person who receives stolen goods, fence; receptacle &c. for receiving something in machine or instrument, esp. earpiece of telephone. [-ER[1]]
rece·nsion, n. Revision of, revised, text. [f. L *recensio* f. *re(censēre* review), RE- 8]
rē·cent, a. Not long past, that happened or existed lately, late; not long established, lately begun, modern. Hence

re·cency n., **re·cent**LY² adv., **re·cent-ness** n. [f. L *recens -entis*]

rece·ptacle, n. Containing vessel, place, or space; (Bot.) common base of floral organs, axis of cluster. [f. L *receptaculum* (*recept-* p.p. st. of *recipere* RECEIVE)]

rece·ption (-shn), n. Receiving or being received (rare in gen. sense); receiving esp. of person, being received, into a place or company (*the rooms were prepared for his r.*; *was honoured by r. into the Academy*; *r. order,* authorizing r. of lunatic in asylum); formal or ceremonious welcome (*the r. of the delegates is arranged for Monday next*), occasion of receiving guests, assembly held for this purpose, (*after the review there will be a r.*; *r.-room,* available for receiving company, esp. opp. *bedroom*); receiving of ideas or impressions into the mind (*has a great faculty of r., but little originative power*); (rare) mental acceptance, recognition of something as true or advisable, (*the general r. of the Newtonian hypothesis*); welcome or greeting of specified kind, demonstration of feeling towards person or project, (*warm r.,* vigorous resistance or enthusiastic welcome; *his r. was frigid, all that he could desire*; *proposal, book, had a favourable r.*). [f. L *receptio* (as prec., -ION)]

rece·ptive, a. Able or quick to receive impressions or ideas (*a mind more r. than retentive or creative*); (rare) concerned with receiving. Hence **rece·ptive**LY² adv., **rece·ptive**NESS, **rĕcepti·v**ITY, nn. [f. med. L *receptivus* (as prec., -IVE)]

rece·ss, n., & v.t. Temporary cessation from work, vacation, esp. of Parliament; receding of water, land, glacier, &c., from previous limit, amount by which it recedes, recession, (rare); retired or secret place (*in the inmost rr. of the Alps, of the heart*); receding part of mountain chain &c., niche or alcove of wall; (Anat.) fold or indentation in organ. (Vb) place in a r., set back; provide with recess(es). [f. L *recessus* (*recess-* p.p. st. of RECEDE*re*)]

rece·ssion, n. Receding, withdrawal, from a place or point; receding part of object, recess. So **rece·ss**IVE a. [f. L *recessio* (as prec., -ION)]

rece·ssional, a. & n. *R. hymn* or *r.,* hymn sung while clergy & choir withdraw after service (*the R.,* poem of Kipling in *The Five Nations* sung on imperial occasions); of the parliamentary recess. [-AL]

Rĕ·chabite (-k-), n. Total abstainer. [*Rechab,* see *Jer.* xxxv. 6, -ITE¹(1)]

recharge. See RE- 9.

réchauffé (rĕshōfā·, rĭshō·fā), n. Warmed-up dish; rehash (RE- 8). [F]

recherché (reshār·shā), a. Devised or got with care or difficulty, choice, far-fetched, thought out, (esp. of meals or words). [F]

rechristen. See RE- 8.

reci·divist, n. One who relapses into crime. So **reci·div**ISM n. [f. F *récidiviste* f. L *recidivus* f. *re*(*cidere* = *cadere* fall), RE- 9, -IVE, -IST]

re·cipĕ, n. Medical prescription or remedy prepared from it; statement of ingredients & procedure for preparing dish &c.; expedient, nostrum, device for effecting something. [2nd sing. imperat. as used (*abbr.* ℞.) in prescriptions of L *recipere* RECEIVE]

reci·pient, a. & n. Receptive, whence **reci·pi**ENCY n.; person who receives something. [f. L *recipere* RECEIVE, -ENT]

reci·procal, a. & n. In return (*if I helped him, I had r. help from him*); mutual (*r. love, protection, injuries*); inversely correspondent, complementary, (*I took the chamois for a man, & it made the r. mistake*); (Gram.) expressing mutual action or relation (*'each other' is a r. pronoun*), (formerly also) reflexive; hence **reci·procal**LY² adv. (N., math.) function or expression so related to another that their product is unity (*1/5 is the r. of 5*). [f. L *reciprocus* (prob. f. *re-* back & *pro* forward), -AL]

reci·procate, v.t. & i. (Mech.) go with alternate backward & forward motion (*reciprocating engine* &c., with work done by part that moves thus, opp. *rotatory* see ROTATE²), give such motion to; give & receive mutually, interchange, (influence &c.); return, requite, (affection &c.), make a return (often *with* thing given in return). So **reciproca·**TION n. [f. L *reciprocare* (prec.), -ATE³]

recipro·city, n. Reciprocal condition, mutual action; principle or practice of give-&-take, esp. interchange of privileges between States as basis of commercial relations. [f. F *réciprocité* (RECIPROCAL, -ITY)]

reci·tal, n. Detailed account *of* a number of connected things or facts, relation *of* the facts of an incident &c., a narrative; part of document stating facts; act of reciting; instrumental musical performance by, or of works of, one man. [RECITE, -AL]

recitati·ve (-ēv), n., & v.t. & i. Musical declamation of kind usual in narrative & dialogue parts of opera & oratorio; words, part, given in r.; (vb) perform (t. & i.) in r. [f. It. *recitativo* (foll., -IVE)]

reci·te, v.t. & i. Repeat aloud or declaim (poem, passage) from memory esp. before audience, give recitation (*reciting-note,* that held on for indefinite number of syllables in chanting); (Law) rehearse (facts) in document; mention in order, enumerate. So **recita·**TION n. [f. L *re*(*citare* CITE), RE- 8]

reci·ter, n. Person who recites; book of passages for recitation. [-ER¹]

recivilize &c. See RE- 9.

reck, v.i. & t. (rhet., poet., in neg. & interrog. sentences only). *R. of,* pay heed to, take account of, care about; care, be troubled, concern oneself, (*if, though, that how, whether,* &c., or abs.; also impers. with same construction following, as *what recks it him that . . .?*). [com.-Teut.; OE *reccan,* cf. OHG *ruohen,* ON *rǽkja*]

re·ckless, a. Devoid of caution, regardless of consequences, rash; heedless *of* danger &c. Hence **re·ckless**LY[2] adv., **re·ckless**NESS n. [OE *recceléas* (prec., -LESS)]

re·ckon (-kn), v.t. & i. Ascertain (number, amount), ascertain number or amount of, by counting or usu. by calculation, compute; start *from,* go on *to,* in counting t. & i.; count *up,* sum *up* character of; arrive at as total (*I r. 53 of them*); include in computation, count *in,* place in class *among* or *with* or *in,* take *for,* regard *as,* consider *to be* (or with obj. & compl. as *r. him wise, beyond redemption*); conclude after calculation, be of the confident opinion, (*that*; also, chiefly U.S., parenth., cf. *calculate, guess*); make calculations, cast up account or sum, (*r. without* one's HOST[2]), settle accounts *with* person; rely or count or base plans *upon.* [OE (*ge*)*recenian,* cf. MDu. *rekenen,* G *rechnen*; cogn. w. RECK]

re·ckoner (-kn-), n. In vbl senses; esp., READY *r.* [-ER[1]]

re·ckoning (-kn-), n. In vbl senses; esp.: tavern bill; *day of r.,* time when something must be atoned for or avenged; DEAD *r.*; *out in* one's *r.,* mistaken in a calculation or expectation. [-ING[1]]

reclai·m, v.t. & i., & n. Win back or away from vice or error or savagery or waste condition, reform, tame, civilize, bring under cultivation, whence **reclai·m**ABLE a.; make protest, say in protest, (rare); so **reclam**A·TION n. (N.) reclaiming, reclamation, (rare, chiefly in *past* or *beyond r.*). [f. OF *reclamer* f. L *re*(*clamare* shout) cry out against, RE-2]

réclame (rĕ·klahm), n. Art or practice by which notoriety is secured. [F]

re·clinate (-*a*t), a. (bot.). Bending downwards. [f. L *reclinatus* (foll., -ATE[2])]

recli·ne, v.t. & i. Lay (esp. one's head, body, limbs) in more or less horizontal or recumbent position (p.p., of person, lying thus); assume or be in recumbent position, lie or lean, sit with back or side supported at considerable inclination; (fig.) rely confidently *upon.* [f. L *reclinare* (RE-9), see DECLINE[1]]

reclothe. See RE-8.

reclu·se (-lo͞os), a. & n. (Person) given to or living in seclusion or retirement or isolation, esp. as religious discipline, hermit, anchorite or anchoress. [F (*-us, -use*) p.p. of *reclure* f. L *re*(*cludere* = *claudere* shut), RE-4]

recoal, recoat. See RE-8.

recogni·tion, n. In vbl senses (RECOGNIZE). So **reco·gnit**ORY a. (rare). [f. L *recognitio* (RECOGNIZE, -ION)]

recŏg·nizance, n. Bond by which person engages before court or magistrate to observe some condition, e.g. to keep the peace, pay a debt, or appear when summoned; sum pledged as surety for such observance. [f. OF *reconuissance* (*reconoistre* RECOGNIZE, -ANCE)]

recŏg·nizant, a. Showing recognition (*of* favour &c.), conscious or showing consciousness of something. [as foll., see -ANT]

re·cognize (-gn-), v.t. Acknowledge validity or genuineness or character or claims or existence of, accord notice or consideration to, discover or realize nature of, treat *as,* acknowledge *for,* realize or admit *that*; know again, identify as known before. Hence **re·cogniz**ABLE a., **recogniza**BI·LITY n. **re·cognizab**LY[2] adv. [f. OF *reconuiss-* part. st. of *reconoistre* f. L *re*(*cognoscere -gnitum* learn), RE-8, w. assim. to -IZE]

recoi·l, v.i., & n. Retreat before enemy (now rare); start or spring back, shrink mentally, in fear or horror or disgust; rebound after impact, (of fire-arms) be driven backwards by discharge, kick; (n.) act or fact or sensation of recoiling. [n. f. vb, f. OF *reculer* (RE-9, *cul* the posterior f. L *culus*)]

recoin &c. See RE-8.

recolle·ct, v.t. Succeed in remembering, recall to mind, remember. [f. p.p. st. of L *re*(*colligere* COLLECT[2]), RE-8]

recolle·ction, n. Act, power, of recollecting; thing recollected, reminiscence; person's memory, time over which it extends, (*it is in my r. that,* I remember that; *happened within my r.*). So **recolle·ct**IVE a. [f. med. L *recollectio* (prec., -ION)]

recolonize &c., **recolour, recombine** &c., see RE-8; **recomfort,** RE-9; **recommence** &c., RE-8.

recomme·nd, v.t. Give (one*self,* one's spirit, a child, &c.) in charge *to* God or a person or his care &c.; speak or write of or suggest as fit for employment or favour or trial (*to* person, or with ind. obj. as *can you r. me a cook, a book?*; *as* servant &c.; *for* post); (of qualities, conduct, &c.) make acceptable, serve as recommendation of; advise (course of action or treatment, person *to* do, *that* thing should be done). Hence or cogn. **recommend**A·TION n., **recomme·nd**ABLE, **recomme·ndat**ORY, aa. [f. med. L *re*(*commendare* COMMEND), RE-5]

recommit &c. See RE-8.

re·compense, v.t., & n. Requite, reward or punish, (person, action, person *for* action, action *to* person or with ind. obj.); make amends to (person) or for (another's loss, injury, &c., or rarely one's own misconduct). (N.) reward, requital, atonement or satisfaction given for injury, retribution. [f. OF *recompenser* f. LL, *re(compensare* COMPENSATE), RE-1]

recompose, recompound. See RE-8.

re·concile, v.t. Make friendly after estrangement (persons to one another, person *to* or *with* another, person to oneself); purify (consecrated place &c.) by special service after desecration; make resigned or contentedly submissive (*to* disagreeables, *to* doing, or abs.; usu. in pass.); heal, compose, (quarrel &c.); harmonize, make compatible, show compatibility of by argument or in practice, (apparently conflicting facts, statements, qualities, actions, or one such *with* or *&* or rarely *to* another). Hence or cogn. **re·concilABLE** a., **reconcilABI·LITY, re·concileMENT, reconcilIA·TION,** nn. [f. L *re(conciliare* CONCILIATE), RE-9]

re·condite (*or* -kŏ·-), a. (Of subjects of knowledge) abstruse, out of the way, little known; (of author or style) dealing in r. knowledge or allusion, obscure. Hence **re·conditeLY**[2] adv., **re·conditeNESS** n. [f. L *re(conditus* p.p. of *condere* hide), RE-4]

rēcondi·tion, v.t. Overhaul & refit. [RE-8]

reconduct. See RE-9.

reco·nnaissance (-*isans*), n. Military or naval examination of tract by detachment to locate enemy or ascertain strategic features (*r. in force*, made by strong party); reconnoitring party; preliminary survey made by anyone for any purpose. [F (earlier *-oissance*), as foll., -ANCE]

reconnoi·tre (-*ter*), v.t. & i., & n. Make reconnaissance of (enemy, district), approach & try to learn position & condition &c. of; make reconnaissance; (as n., rare) reconnaissance. Hence **reconnoi·trER**[1] n. [f. F *reconnoître* f. L *recognoscere* RECOGNIZE]

reconquer &c., see RE-9; **reconsider** &c., **reconstitute** &c., **reconstruct** &c., RE-8; **reconvert** &c., RE-9.

recor·d[1], v.t. (Of birds) practise (tune, or abs.) by singing in an undertone; register, set down for remembrance or reference, put in writing or other legible shape, represent in some permanent form, (*his thoughts have been recorded for us by himself, his features by Watts, & his voice by the phonograph*; *recording angel*, who registers men's good & bad actions; *minimum thermometer recorded 10° below zero*). Hence **recor·dABLE** a. [f. OF *recorder* f. L *recordare* (cl. *-ari*) remember (RE-, *cor* heart)]

re·cord[2], n. State of being recorded or preserved in writing esp. as authentic legal evidence (*is on r.*, legally or otherwise recorded; *matter of r.*, something established as fact by being recorded; *court of r.*, whose proceedings are recorded & valid as evidence of fact); official report of proceedings & judgement in cause before court of r., copy of pleadings &c. constituting case to be decided by court (*travel out of, keep to, the r.*, introduce, abstain from introducing, irrelevant matter); (*Public*) *R. Office*, building in London in which State papers and other public documents are stored, calendared, &c.; piece of recorded evidence or information, account of fact preserved in permanent form, document or monument preserving it, object serving as memorial of something, portrait &c., series of marks &c. given by recording instrument or plate &c. containing these (*second-hand gramophone rr. for sale*); facts known about person's past (*has an honourable r. of service*; *his r. is against him*); best performance or most remarkable event of its kind on r. (*break* or *cut* or *beat the r.*, outdo all predecessors), (attrib.) best hitherto recorded (*at r. pace*; *the r. height*). [OF (prec.)]

recor·der, n. In vbl senses; also; city or borough magistrate with criminal & civil jurisdiction & holding court of Quarter sessions, whence **recor·derSHIP** n.; recording-apparatus in instruments; obsolete instrument of flute kind [RECORD[1], 1st sense]. [-ER[2](4), -ER[1]]

recou·nt[1] (-ow-), v.t. Narrate, tell in detail. [f. ONF *re(conter* COUNT[2]), RE-8]

re-cou·nt[2]. See RE-8.

recou·p (-ōōp), v.t. & i. (Law) deduct, keep back, (part of sum due), make such deduction; compensate (person loss, person *for* loss, loss; *r. oneself*, recover what one has expended or lost). Hence **recou·pMENT** n. [f. F *re(couper* cut, see COUP), RE-5]

recour·se (-ōrs), n. Resorting or betaking of oneself *to* possible source of help (*r. to brandy is deprecated*; usu. in phr. *have r. to*, adopt as adviser, helper, or expedient); thing resorted to (rare; *their usual r. is perjury*). [f. F *recours* f. L *re(cursus* COURSE[1]), RE-9]

reco·ver[1] (-kŭ-), v.t. & i., & n. Regain possession or use or control of, acquire or find (out) again, reclaim, (*has recovered his kingdom, his friends' affection, the meaning of the hieroglyphs, the track, health, his appetite, his voice, much land from the sea*; *r. oneself*, regain consciousness or calmness or control of limbs or senses; *horse recovers itself after stumble*; *r. one's legs*, stand up after fall); secure restitution or compensation, secure (damages), by legal process (*plaintiff shall r. according to verdict*; *his remedy is to r. in a court of law*; *an action to r. damages for false imprisonment*); bring or come back to life, consciousness, health, or normal state or position (*he recovered slowly*; *the mention of a bucket of water recovered her*; *I recovered the heat of his body with* *fomentations*; *corpse cannot be recovered to life*; *recovered me from a lingering illness*; *am quite recovered from my cold*; *sat down to r. from his agitation*; *r. sword*, bring it back after thrust &c., or, Mil., hold it upright with hilt opposite mouth); retrieve, make up for, get over, cease to feel effects of, (*must try to r. lost time*; *never recovered the blow, his losses, this* faux pas); make one's way back to (rare; *recovered the shore with difficulty*); hence **reco·ver**ABLE a. (N.) position to which sword &c. is brought back in fencing or drill, act of coming to this. [f. OF *recovrer* f. L *recuperare* RECUPERATE]

re-cover[2]. See RE-8.

reco·very, n. Act or process of RECOVER[1]-ing or being recovered. [f. OF *recovree* (RECOVER[1], -Y[4])]

re·crĕant, a. & n. (rhet., poet.). Craven, coward(ly), apostate. Hence **re·cre**ANCY n., **re·creant**LY[2] adv. [OF, part. of *re(croire* f. L *credere* entrust), RE-6, yield in trial by combat]

re·crĕate[1], v.i. & t. (Of pastime, relaxation, holiday, employment, &c., or refl. of person indulging in them) refresh, entertain, agreeably occupy, (*it recreates him to invent histories for his neighbours*; *recreates himself with cricket, climbing, lying in a hammock, political argument*); amuse oneself, indulge in recreation. Hence **recre**A·TION n., **re·cre**ATIVE a. [f. L *re(creare* CREATE), RE-8, -ATE[3]]

re-create[2] &c. See RE-8.

re·crement, n. Waste product, refuse, (now rare); (Physiol.) fluid separated from blood & again absorbed in it, e.g. saliva, bile. Hence **recrementi**·TIOUS[1] a. [f. L *re(crementum* f. *cernere cret-* sift, RE-5, -MENT)]

recri·minate, v.i. Retort accusation, indulge in mutual or counter charges. So **recrimin**A·TION n., **recri·min**ATIVE, **recri·minā**TORY, aa. [f. med. L *re(criminari* f. *crimen*, CRIME), RE-1]

recross. See RE-9.

rĕcrude·sce, v.i. (Of sore, disease, &c., or fig. of discontent &c.) break out again. Hence **recrud**E·SCENT a., **recrude·sc**ENCE n. [f. L *re(crudescere* f. *crudus* raw, see -ESCENT), RE-8]

recrui·t[1] (-ōōt), n. Newly enlisted & not yet trained soldier; person who joins a society &c.; tiro (often *raw r.*). [earlier sense *reinforcement*, f. obs. F *recrute* = *recrue* fem. p.p. of *re(croître*, OF *creistre*, f. L *crescere* increase), RE-8]

recrui·t, v.t. & i. Enlist rr. for (army, regiment, crew, society, party), enlist (person) as r., get or seek rr. (esp. *recruiting-sergeant*); replenish, fill up deficiencies or compensate wear & tear in, refresh, reinvigorate; (seek to) recover health &c. (*has gone to the country to r.*), whence **recrui·t**AL(2) n. Hence **recrui·t**MENT n. [f. F *recruter* (obs. *recrute*, see prec.)]

re·ctal, a. Of or by the rectum. [-AL]

re·ctangle, n. Plane rectilinear four-sided figure with four right angles, esp. one with adjacent sides unequal. [f. LL *rectiangulus* (*rectus* straight, ANGLE[1]) right-angled]

recta·ngular, a. Shaped, having base or sides or section shaped, like rectangle; placed, having parts or lines placed, at right angles. Hence **rectangulă·**RITY n., **recta·ngular**LY[2] adv. [as prec., -AR[1]]

re·ctifȳ, v.t. Put right, correct, amend, reform, adjust, (method, calculation, statement, position, instrument); abolish, get rid of, exchange for what is right, (abuse, anomaly, error, omission, grievance); (Chem.) purify or refine by renewed distillation or other process; (Geom.) find straight line equal to (curve). Hence or cogn. **re·ctifi**ABLE a., **recti**FICA·TION, **re·ctifi**ER[1](1, 2), nn. [f. F *rectifier* f. LL *rectificare* (L *rectus* right, -FY)]

rectili·near, -li·neal, aa. In or forming a straight line; bounded or characterized by straight lines. Hence **rectilineă·**RITY n., **rectili·near**LY[2] adv. [f. LL *rectilineus* (L *rectus* straight, *linea* LINE[2]), -AR[1], -AL]

re·ctitude, n. Moral uprightness, righteousness; (rare) correctness, rightness. [F, f. LL *rectitudo* (L *rectus* right, -TUDE)]

re·cto, n. Right-hand page of open book; front of leaf (opp. VERSO). [f. L *recto* (*folio*) on the right (leaf)]

re·ctor (*-er*), n. Parson of parish whose tithes are not impropriate (cf. VICAR); head of university, college, school, or religious institution (esp. abroad; in England only of heads of Exeter & Lincoln Colleges, Oxford; in Scotland of head masters of secondary schools &c., & see LORD *rector*), whence **re·ctr**ESS[1] n. Hence **re·ctor**ATE[1], **re·ctor**SHIP, nn., **rector·**IAL a. [L, = ruler (*regere rect-* rule, -OR[2])]

re·ctory, n. Rector's benefice; rector's house. [f. med. L *rectoria* (prec., -Y[1])]

re·ctum, n. Final section of large intestine, terminating at anus. [f. L *rectum* (*intestinum*) straight (intestine)]

recu·mbent, a. Lying down, reclining. Hence **recu·mb**ENCY n., **recu·mbent**LY[2] adv. [f. L *re(cumbere* lie), RE-9, -ENT]

recū·perate, v.t. & i. Restore, be restored or recover, from exhaustion, illness, loss, &c. So **recuper**A·TION n., **recu·per**ATIVE a. [f. L *recuperare*, *recip-*, extended form of *recipere* RECEIVE, -ATE[3]]

recur·, v.i. (-rr-; part. *-ŭ·rring* or *-ur·ring*). Go back in thought or speech *to*; (of idea &c.) come back *to* one's mind &c., return to mind; (of problem &c.) come up again;

occur again, be repeated, (*recurring decimals*, figures in decimal fraction that r. in same order again & again); *recurring curve*, that returns upon itself, e.g. circle. Hence **recu·rrence** n. [f. L *re(currere* run), RE- 9]

recu·rrent, a. & n. (Of nerve, vein, branch, &c.) turning back so as to reverse direction; occurring again or often or periodically; hence **recu·rrently**[2] adv. (N.) r. artery or nerve, esp. one of the two r. laryngeal nerves. [as prec., -ENT]

recur·ve, v.t. & i. Bend backwards. So **recur·vate**[2] a., **recur·vature** n. [f. L *re(curvare* bend), RE- 9]

recu·sant (-z-), n. & a. (Hist.) (person) who refused to attend Church-of-England services; (person) refusing submission to authority or compliance with regulation (*against*). Hence **recu·sance, -ancy,** nn. [f. L *recusare* RECUSE]

recu·se (-z), v.t. (now rare). Reject (person, his authority), object to (judge) as prejudiced. [f. L *recusare* (RE- 2, *causa* cause) refuse]

red, a. & n. Of or approaching the colour seen at least refracted end of spectrum, of shades varying from crimson to bright brown & orange, esp. those seen in blood, sunset clouds, rubies, glowing coals, human lips, & fox's hair, (*r. as a rose* &c.; *blood, fiery, yellowish, deep,* &c., *-r.*; *r. with anger* &c., flushed in face; *with r hands*, bloodstained; *all-r. route, line, cable,* &c., traversing British territory or under British control, w. ref. to r. in maps as British colour; *r. gold* archaic & poet., real gold, money; *r. cent* U.S., smallest coin orig. of copper, esp. *don't care a r. cent*; *r. eyes*, bloodshot, or with lids sore from weeping, also of bird &c. with r. iris; as distinctive epithet with many varieties of animal & plant & mineral, as *r. deer, partridge, mullet, ant,* CURRANT, *campion,* ARSENIC); having to do with bloodshed, burning, violence, or revolution (*r. battle, ruin*; SEE[1] *r.*; *a r. republican, radical, anarchist*); *r.* ADMIRAL; *r. bark*, superior kind of cinchona; *r.-blind*, colour-blind to r.; *r. book* (containing list of nobility & gentry); *r. box*, used by Ministers for official documents; *redbreast*, the robin; *r.-cap*, military policeman; *re·dcoat*, British soldier; *r. cross*, St George's cross or national emblem of England, also Christian side in crusades, also (emblem of) ambulance service organized according to Geneva Convention; *r.* ENSIGN, used by British merchant ships; *r.-eye*, the fish rudd; *r.-fish*, male salmon in spawning season, also (market name for) salmon (opp. *white fish* of all other kinds); *r. flag*, symbol of revolution (*the R.F.*, a modern revolutionary song), signal for battle, danger signal on shooting-ranges & railways; *r. gum*, teething-rash in children, also (kinds of eucalyptus yielding) reddish resin; *r.-handed*, in the act of crime (*take r.-h.*); *r. hat*, cardinal's, (also nickname for) British staff-officer; *r. heat*, being r.-hot lit. & fig., temperature of r.-hot thing; *r. herring*, herring(s) reddened by being cured in smoke (*neither fish, flesh, nor good r.h.*, of ambiguous indefinite nature; *draw a r.h. across the track*, divert attention from subject in hand by starting irrelevant but exciting question, with ref. to use of r.h. in exercising hounds); *r.-hot*, heated to redness, highly excited, enthusiastic, furious; *r.-hot poker*, garden plant with flame-coloured spikes of flower; *r. lamp*, night-sign of doctor or chemist; *r. lane*, (nursery name for) throat; *r. lead*, pigment made from r. oxide of lead (v.t., coat with this); *r.-legged*, with r. legs (of birds &c., esp. the *r.-l.* or French *partridge*); *r.-legs*, kinds of bird, also the plant bistort; *r.-letter*, (of day) marked with r. letter(s) in calendar as saint's day or festival, (fig.) memorable as date of joyful occurrence, (v.t., record as memorable for joy); *r. light*, danger-signal on railways &c. (*see the r.l.*, fig., realize approach of disaster); *r. man*, N.-Amer. Indian; *r. meat*, beef, mutton, &c. (opp. veal & pork & chicken); *r. mass*, at which priest wears r.; *r.-pōll*, kinds of r.-crested bird, esp. male linnet, also (pl.) r.-haired polled cattle; *r. rag*, thing that excites person's rage as r. object enrages bull (*is a r.r. to him*), also kind of rust in grain; *r. rattle*, lousewort; *r. ribbon*, ribbon, membership, of Order of Bath; *r. sanders*, wood of E.-Ind. tree used in dyeing; *redshank*, kind of snipe; *r.-short*, (of iron) brittle while r.-hot; *redskin*, = *r. man* above; *r. snow*, reddened by kind of alga & common in Arctic & Alpine regions; *r. soldier*, (pig affected with) kind of swine fever with redness of skin; *r. spider*, insect infesting hot-house plants esp. vines; *re·dstart*, r.-tailed European songbird [OE *steort* tail]; *r.-streak*, kind of cider apple; *r. tape*, excessive use of or adherence to formalities esp. in public business, whence **red-ta·pery, red-ta·pism, red-ta·pist,** nn.; *r. triangle*, (emblem of) the Y.M.C.A.; *r.-water*, malarial cattle & sheep disease with r. urine; *r. weed*, corn poppy; *r.-wing*, kinds of thrush & other birds; *re·dwood*, kinds of tree; *r. worm*, kind used as fishing-bait; hence **re·dden**[6] v.t. & i., **re·ddish**[1](2), **re·ddy**[2]-, aa., **re·dly**[2] adv. (rare), **re·dness** n. (N.) r. colour; *a* shade of r.; the r. colour in roulette & rouge-et-noir; *the* r. ball at billiards; r. cloth or clothes (*dressed in r.*); one of former three squadrons or divisions (*the r., white, blue*) of British fleet; radical or republican or anarchist. [com.-Teut.; OE *réad*, cf. Du. *rood*, G *rot*; cogn. w. L *rufus, ruber*, Gk *eruthros*, Skr. *rudhirá-*]

red-, pref. =RE-, only in wds of L origin.

reda·ct, v.t. Put into literary form, arrange for publication, edit. So **reda·ctOR**[2] n. [in mod. use a back formation f. foll.]

reda·ction, n. Preparing or being prepared for publication, revision, editing, rearrangement; new edition. [f. F *rédaction* f. L *red(igere -act-* =*agere* bring), RE- 8, -ION]

reda·n, n. Field work with two faces forming salient angle. [F (RE-, *dent* tooth)]

redd, v.t. (Sc.). Clear up, arrange, tidy, put right, settle, compose. [cf. Du. *redden* of same meaning; prob. related to READY]

re·ddle, n., & v.t. Red ochre, ruddle; (vb) colour with r. [var. of RUDDLE]

rede[1], n. (archaic). Counsel, advice; resolve, design; narrative. [OE *rǣd*, cf. Du. *raad*, G *rat*, f. st. of foll. or READ]

rede[2], v.t. (archaic). Advise (person, with inf. with or without *to*, or with imperat.); read (riddle, dream). [var. of READ]

redee·m, v.t. Buy back, recover by expenditure of effort or by stipulated payment, (*r.* one's *rights, position, honour, mortgaged land, pledged goods*); compound for, buy off, (charge or obligation) by payment; perform (promise); purchase the freedom of (another, one*self*), save (one's life) by ransom; save, rescue, reclaim; (of God or Christ) deliver from sin & damnation; make amends for, compensate, counterbalance, (fault, defect; *has one redeeming feature*); save *from* a defect (*the eyes r. the face from ugliness*). Hence **redee·mABLE** a., (esp. of Christ, see above) **redee·mER**[1] n. [f. L *red(imere -empt-* =*emere* buy), RE- 8]

rede·mption, n. REDEEMing or being redeemed, esp. the deliverance from sin & damnation wrought by Christ's atonement (*past, beyond, without, r.*, so that r. is hopeless; *in the year of our r. 1900* &c., A.D. 1900 &c.); thing that redeems (*that blow was* or *proved his r.*); purchase (*became a member of a livery company by r.*). Hence **rede·mptivE** a. [f. L *redemptio* (prec., -ION)]

redescend. See RE- 9.

redi·f, n. (Soldier of) Turkish military reserve. [Turk.]

rĕ·dingote, n. Woman's long double-breasted outer coat with skirts sometimes cut away in front. [F, =kind of (orig. man's) coat, corrupt. of E *riding-coat*]

redi·ntegrate, v.t. Restore to wholeness or unity; renew or re-establish in united or perfect state. So **redintegrA·TION** n. [f. L *red(integrare* INTEGRATE[2]), RE- 9, -ATE[3]]

redirect &c., see RE-8; **rediscover** &c., RE-9; **redistribute** &c., **redivide** &c., **redo**, RE- 8.

re·dolent, a. Fragrant (now rare); having a strong smell, (fig.) strongly suggestive or reminiscent, *of*. Hence **re·dolENCE** n. [f. L *red(olēre* smell), RED- 6, -ENT]

redou·ble (-dŭ-), v.t. & i. Intensify, increase, make or grow greater or more intense or numerous, (*r.* one's *efforts*; *the clamour redoubled*). [f. F *re(doubler* DOUBLE[3]), RE- 6]

redoub·t (-owt), n. (fortif.). Outwork or fieldwork usu. square or polygonal & without flanking defences. [f. F *redoute* f. med. L *reductus* refuge f. p.p. of L REDUCE*re*; *-b-* on false anal. of DOUBT]

redoub·table (-owt-) a. (Of opponent, warrior, controversialist, &c.) formidable. [f. F *redoutable* f. *re(douter* DOUBT[2]) fear, RE- 6]

redoub·ted, a. (archaic). Dreaded, redoubtable. [f. obs. *redoubt* f. F as prec.]

redou·nd (-ow-), v.i. Contribute in the end, make great contribution, *to* one's advantage, credit, &c. (*this procedure will r. to our advantage*; *the tale, fact, redounds to their credit*); come as final result *to*, come back or recoil *upon*, person (*the benefits that r. to us from his self-sacrifice*; *his praises r. upon himself*). [earlier sense *overflow*, f. F *rédonder* f. L *red(undare* f. *unda* wave), RE- 6]

redre·ss, v.t., & n. Readjust, set straight again, (usu. *r. the balance*, restore equality); set right, remedy, make up for, get rid of, rectify, (distress, wrong, damage, grievance, abuse); (n.) reparation for wrong, redressing *of* grievances &c. [n. f. vb, f. F *re(dresser* DRESS), RE- 8]

redu·ce, v.t. Restore to original or proper position, remedy by such restoration, (now only surg.; *had the shoulder, dislocation, reduced*), bring back *to* (*r. person to discipline*); convert physically or mentally *to* other form, subject to such conversion, make suitable or conformable or adapted *to*, bring by classification or analysis *to*, (*r. rule to practice*, act on it; *observations taken at surface must be reduced to centre*; *r. anomalies to rule*, discover formula covering them; *the facts may all be reduced to three heads*; *r. it to English orthography & spell it* employee; *the unwritten customs were reduced to writing*; *r. dissimilar quantities to one denomination, integer to form of fraction*; *can we r. these ripples to their mechanical elements?*; *r. clods to powder, ore to metal, compound to components, surface by harrowing*, or simply *r. clods, compound*, &c.; *r. syllogism of one form to another*); compel *to* do (rare), bring by force or necessity *to* some state or action, subdue, bring back to obedience, (*r. the Crown to submission, the revolted towns, all the other Powers of the continent*; *reduced him to assert* or usu. *asserting an absurdity*; *was reduced to* *despair, to weakness, to borrow* or usu. *borrowing clothes, to borrowing*); bring down, lower, weaken, impoverish, diminish, contract, (*r. Pope to place of chief bishop*; *N.C.O. was reduced to the ranks*, made a private; *is in a very reduced state*, feeble; *r. liquid to two-thirds of its bulk*; *this reduces the temperature*; *the 16 may be reduced to 5*, by omission of 11, or by reclassification &c.; *have reduced our outfit to almost nothing*; *he reduced himself into the least possible compass*; *to be sold at reduced prices*; *reduced circumstances*, poverty after prosperity; *r. the establishment*, dismiss officials or cut down expenses; *reduced officers* &c., dismissed in such reduction). Hence **redu·**CIBLE a. [f. L *re(ducere duct-* bring), RE- 9]

redu·ctio ad absur·dum, n. Reduction to absurdity (see foll.). [L]

redu·ction, n. Reducing or being REDUCEd; also: reduced copy of picture, map, &c.; *r. to absurdity*, proof of the falsity of a principle &c. given by producing a logical consequence of it that is absurd, (loosely) pushing of a principle to unpractical lengths. [f. L *reductio* (REDUCE, -ION)]

reduit (redwē·), n. (fortif.). Keep for garrison to retire to & hold when outworks are taken. [f. F *réduit* REDOUBT]

redu·ndant, a. Superfluous, excessive, pleonastic; copious, luxuriant, full. Hence or cogn. **redu·nd**ANCE, **redu·nd**ANCY, nn., **redu·ndant**LY[2] adv. [f. L as REDOUND, -ANT]

redū·plicate, v.t. Make double, repeat; (Gram.) repeat (letter, syllable), form (tense) by reduplication. So **redu·plica**TIVE a. [f. med. L *re(duplicare* DUPLICATE[2]), RE- 8, -ATE[3]]

reduplica·tion, n. Doubling, repetition; counterpart; (Gram.) repetition of syllable or letter in word-formation, part so repeated. [f. LL *reduplicatio* (prec. -ATION)]

redye. See RE- 8.

ree. =REEVE[2].

re-e·cho, v.i. & t. Echo (t. & i.), echo (t. & i.) again & again, resound. [RE- 6]

reed, n., & v.t. (Tall straight stalk of) kinds of firm-stemmed water or marsh plant (*broken r.*, unreliable person or thing; *lean on a r.*, put trust in weak thing or person), whence **ree·d**ED[2] a.; (collect.) reeds growing in a mass or used as material esp. for thatching, wheat-straw prepared for thatching; (poet.) arrow, musical pipe of r. or straw, pastoral poetry; vibrating part, of various shape & material, inserted in some musical wind-instruments (esp. oboe, bassoon, clarinet, bagpipe, & some organ-pipes) to produce the sound, (usu. pl., cf. *strings, brass*) r. instrument(s); weaver's implement for separating warp-threads & beating up weft; (usu. pl.) set of semicylindrical adjacent mouldings like rr. laid together; *r.-babbler* or *-warbler* or *-wren, r.-bunting* or *-sparrow*, two kinds of bird; *r.-mace*, bulrush; *r.-pheasant*, Bearded Titmouse; *r.-pipe*, musical pipe of r., also reeded organ-pipe; *r.-stop*, organ-stop consisting of r.-pipes. (Vb) thatch with r.; make (straw) into r.; decorate with r.-moulding; fit (musical instrument or organ-pipe) with r. [com.-WG; OE *hréod*, cf. Du. & G *riet*]

re-ē·dify̆, v.t. Rebuild (house &c.); build up again (hopes, wasted tissue, &c.). [RE- 8]

re-e·dit &c. See RE- 8.

ree·dling, n. Bearded Titmouse. [-LING[1]]

ree·dy, a. Abounding with reeds; made of reed (chiefly poet., as *r. pipe, couch*); like a reed in weakness, slenderness, or (of grass &c.) thickness; (of voice) like reed-instrument in tone, scratchy, not round & clear. Hence **ree·di**NESS n. [-Y[2]]

reef[1], n., & v.t. One of three or four strips across top of square & bottom of fore-&-aft sail that can be taken in or rolled up to reduce sail's surface (*take in a r.*, lit., & fig. proceed cautiously); *r.-knot*, consisting of two bights each enclosing the other's parallel-laid shanks, ordinary double-knot made symmetrically (opp. GRANNY). (Vb) take in reef(s) of (sail; *single, double, treble, -reefed*, with 1, 2, 3, rr. taken in); shorten (topmast, bowsprit, also paddles of paddle-wheel by shifting them nearer centre). [ult. f. ON *rif* in same sense, perh. a spec. use of *rif* rib]

reef[2], n. Ridge of rock or shingle or sand at or just above or below surface of water; (Gold-mining) lode of auriferous quartz, also the bedrock. [as prec., prob. through Du. *rif*]

ree·fer, n. One who reefs; (slang) midshipman; REEF[1]-knot; (also *reefing-jacket*) close double-breasted stout jacket. [REEF[1], -ER[1]]

reek[1], n. Smoke (Sc. & literary); vapour, visible exhalation, (chiefly Sc. & lit.); foul or stale odour (*the r. of tobacco*), fetid atmosphere (*amid r. & squalor*). Hence **ree·k**Y[2] a. (chiefly Sc. & literary; *Auld Reekie*, Edinburgh). [com.-Teut.; OE *réc*, cf. Du. *rook*, G *rauch*]

reek[2], v.i. Emit smoke (chiefly of houses after conflagration or object that has been burning in open air); emit vapour, steam, (of hot drink or food, sweating person &c., or shed blood or thing smeared with it); smell unpleasantly (usu. *of*; *reeks of patchouli, tobacco, blood*, or fig. *of murder, affectation*, &c.). [OE *réocan*, cf. Du. *rieken*, G *riechen*, smell, & Du. *rooken*, G *rauchen*, smoke, & see prec.]

reel[1], n., & v.t. & i. Kinds of rotatory apparatus on which thread, silk, yarn, paper, wire, &c., are wound at some stage of manufacture; contrivance for winding up & unwinding cord as required, esp. in cod-fishing (*off the r.* fig., straight off, without hitch or pause, in rapid succession); small cylinder on which sewing-cotton &c. are wound for convenience; revolving part in various machines. (Vb) wind (thread, fishing-line, &c.) on r.; take (cocoon silk &c.) *off*, draw (fish, logline, &c.) *in* or *up*, by use of r.; rattle (story, list, verses) *off* without pause or apparent effort; (of grasshopper &c.) make clicking noise like r. in motion. [vb f. n., OE *hréol*, excl. E]

reel², v.i., & n. (Of eyes, mind, head) be in a whirl, be dizzy, swim; sway, stagger, stand or walk or run unsteadily, be shaken physically or mentally, rock from side to side, swing violently, (*his mind, the front rank, the ship, the tower, reeled under the shock*; *r. to & fro like a drunken man*; *went reeling down the street*; *the State was reeling to its foundations*); seem to shake (*the mountains r. before his eyes*); hence **ree·ling**LY² adv. (N.) reeling motion lit. or fig. (*without a r. or a stagger*; *the r. of vice & folly around us*). [perh. cogn. w. prec.]

reel³, n., & v.i. Lively esp. Scotch dance, usu. of two couples facing & describing figures of 8; (vb) dance r. [perh. f. REEL² n.]

re-elect &c., **re-embark** &c., **re-emerge** &c. See RE- 9.

reen, n. =RHINE¹.

re-enable, re-enact &c., see RE- 9; **re-engine**, RE- 8; **re-enter** &c., RE- 9.

re-e·ntrant, a. & n. (Angle) that points inward (opp. SALIENT; esp. in fortification). [RE- 9, ENTRANT]

re-establish &c. See RE- 9.

reeve¹, n. (Hist.) chief magistrate of town or district; (Canada) president of village or town council. [OE *geréfa* etym. dub.; prob. unconnected w. obs. *grave* steward, *landgrave* &c., G *graf* count]

reeve², **ree**, n. Female of RUFF². [?]

reeve³, v.t. (naut.; past & p.p. *rove* or *reeved*). Thread (rope, rod, &c.) *through* ring or other aperture, (aperture, block, &c.) with rope; fasten (rope, block or other object) *in, on, round, to*, something by reeving; (of ship) thread (shoals, ice-pack). [perh. f. Du. *reven* REEF¹ vb]

re-examine &c., see RE- 8; **re-exist, re-export** &c., RE- 9; **reface, refashion** &c., RE- 8.

refe·ction, n. Refreshment by food or drink (*milk & eggs were offered for our r̄.*); slight meal, repast. [f. F *réfection* f. L *re(fectionem = factionem* FACTION), RE- 8]

refe·ctory (or in monastic use rĕ·fiktorĭ), n. Room used for meals in monasteries &c. [f. med. L *refectorium* f. L *re(ficere -fect- = facere* make) refresh, RE- 8, -ORY]

refer·, v.t. & i. (-rr-). Trace or ascribe *to* person or thing as cause or source, assign *to* certain date or place or class, (*r.* one's *victories to Providence, miraculous tales to ignorance, ill temper to indigestion, the lake-dwellings to the sixth century, the origins of sculpture to Egypt, barnacles to the molluscs*), whence **re·fer**ABLE a.; commit, hand over, (one*self*, question for decision) *to* person &c. (*I r. myself to your generosity*; *let us r. the dispute to Socrates*; *r. to drawer*, abbr. R.D., banker's note suspending payment &c. of cheque); send on or direct (person), make appeal or have recourse, *to* some authority or source of information, (abs.) cite authority or passage, (*ostler referred me to landlord*; *for my proof I r. to the facts of human nature, to 1* Kings *iii. 7*; *referred to his watch for the exact time*); (of statement &c.) have relation, be directed, (of hearer &c.) interpret (statement &c.) as directed, *to* (*these remarks r. only to deliberate, are not to be referred to involuntary, offences*); (of person speaking &c.) make allusion, direct attention, *to* (*he several times referred to the modern increase in expenditure*; *found myself on the peak referred to*). [f. L *re(ferre latum* bring), RE- 9]

referee·, n., & v.i. Arbitrator, person to whom dispute is to be or is referred for decision, umpire esp. in football; (vb) act as r. esp. in football. [-EE]

re·ference, n., & v.t. Referring of matter for decision or settlement or consideration to some authority, scope given to such authority, (*the peerage was allowed without r. to the House of Lords*; *the r. is very wide, strictly limited*; *the Commission must confine itself to, that is a question outside, the r.*); relation, respect, correspondence, *to* (*the parts of a machine all have r. to each other*; *success seems to have little r. to merit*; *in, with, r. to*, regarding, as regards, about; *without r. to*, irrespective of); allusion *to* (*r., a* or *no r., several rr., to a previous conversation was* or *were made*); direction more or less precise to (page &c. of) book &c. where information may be found (*loads his pages with, does not give, rr.*; *cross r.*, to another passage in same book; *r. bible*, with marginal cross rr.; *legislation by r.*, use in bill-drafting of rr. to previous statutes instead of restatement), mark used to refer reader of text to note or to part of diagram (usual r. marks: asterisk *, obelisk †, double obelisk ‡, section §, parallel ||, paragraph ¶); act of looking up passage &c., or of referring another or applying to person, for information (*r.* or *a r. to the dictionary would have enlightened him*; *please give me a r., I should like to make r., to your last employer*; *book of r.*, to be used not for continuous reading but to consult on occasion; *r. library*, where books may be consulted without being taken away), person named by one applying for post or offering goods &c. as willing to vouch for him or them (*who are your rr.?*), (vulg.) testimonial; hence **refere·ntIAL** a. (Vb) provide (book) with rr. to authorities. [-ENCE]

refere·ndary, n. (rare). Referee; assessor to commission; reporting or revising official. [f. med. L *referendarius* (foll., -ARY[1])]

refere·ndum, n. Referring of certain political questions or of such questions under certain circumstances to the electorate for direct decision by a general vote on the single question. [L (REFERre, -ND[1])]

refill. See RE- 9.

refi·ne, v.t. & i. Free from dross or impurities or defects, purify, clarify; make elegant or cultured, imbue with delicacy of taste, polish manners or appearance of; become pure or clear or improved in polish or delicacy; employ subtlety of thought or language, make fine distinctions, discourse subtly (*up*)*on*; improve (*up*)*on* by refinements. Hence **refinĕd-LY**[2] adv. [RE- 6, FINE[2] v.]

refi·nement, n. Refining or being refined; fineness of feeling or taste, polished manners &c.; subtle or ingenious manifestation *of*, piece of elaborate arrangement, (*all the rr. of luxury*; *a countermine was a r. beyond their skill*); piece of subtle reasoning, fine distinction. [-MENT]

refi·ner, n. In vbl senses; esp., person whose business is to refine metal, sugar, &c., whence **refi·nERY**(3) n. [-ER[1]]

refit &c. See RE- 8.

refle·ct, v.t. & i. Fold back (rare; *r. the corner of the paper*); (of surface or body) throw (heat, light, sound, rarely ball &c.) back, cause to rebound, (*shine with reflected light*, not one's own, borrowed); (of mirror &c., or transf.) show image of, reproduce to eye or mind, exactly correspond in appearance or effect to, (*laws r. the average moral attitude of a half century earlier*); (of action, result, &c.) bring back or cause to redound (credit, discredit, &c.), (abs.) bring discredit, (*up*)*on* person or method responsible; go back in thought, meditate, or consult with oneself (*on*, *upon*, or abs.), remind oneself or consider (*that*, *how*, &c.), whence **refle·ctingLY**[2] adv.; make disparaging remarks *upon*. [f. L *re*(*flectere flex-* bend), RE- 9]

refle·ction, -exion, n. (-x- etym. correct but now rare exc. in scientific use). REFLECTing or being reflected (*angle of r.*, made by reflected ray with perpendicular to surface); reflected light, heat, colour, or image; reflex action; (piece of) censure (usu. *on* or *upon*); thing bringing discredit (*up*)*on*; reconsideration (*on r.*, *I doubt whether I was right*); mental faculty dealing with products of sensation & perception; idea arising in the mind, mental or verbal comment, apophthegm, (often *on* or *upon*). Hence **refle·ctionAL, refle·ctionLESS,** aa. [f. LL *reflexio* (prec., -ION) w. assim. to *reflect*]

refle·ctive, a. (Of surface &c.) giving back reflection or image; (of light &c.) reflected (rare); (Gram.) reflexive (now rare); (of action) reflex, reciprocal, (now rare); (of mental faculties) concerned in reflection or thought; (of person, mood, &c.) thoughtful, given to meditation. Hence **refle·ctiveLY**[2] adv., **refle·ctiveNESS** n. [REFLECT, -IVE]

refle·ctor, n. Body or surface reflecting rays, esp. piece of glass or metal usu. concave for reflecting in required direction; (telescope &c. provided with) apparatus for reflecting images; person, book, &c., that gives or affords conscious or unconscious representation *of* prejudices, habits, &c. [-OR[2]]

reflet (F), n. Lustre, iridescence, esp. on pottery.

rē·flex[1], n. Reflected light or colour or glory (*the fame of Greece was a r. from the glory of Athens*), (Paint.) part of picture represented as affected by the light or colour of another part; image or reflection in mirror &c.; reproduction, secondary manifestation, correspondent result, (*legislation should be a r. of public opinion*; *lamb & mint sauce is a popular r. of the passover with bitter herbs*); a r. action (*doctor tested patient's rr.*). [f. LL *reflexus* *-ūs* (REFLECT)]

rē·flex[2], a. Recurved (rare); (of light &c.) reflected (rare); (of thought &c.) introspective, directed back upon itself or its own operations, (of effect or influence) reactive, coming back upon its author or source; (Physiol.) *r. action*, independent of the will, excited as involuntary response to nerve-stimulation; (Gram.) reflexive (now rare). Hence **re·flexLY**[2] adv. [f. L *reflexus* p.p. (REFLECT)]

refle·xed, a. (bot.). Recurved. [f. obs. *reflex* vb = REFLECT]

refle·xible, a. Capable of being reflected. Hence **reflexIBI·LITY** n. [as prec., -IBLE]

reflexion. See REFLECTION.

refle·xive, a. & n. (gram.). (Word, form) implying agent's action upon himself; (verb) indicating identity of subject & object; (pers. pronoun or poss. adjective) referring to subject. Hence **refle·xiveLY**[2] adv. [as prec., -IVE]

refloat. See RE- 9.

re·fluent, a. Flowing back (*r. tide, blood*). Hence **re·fluENCE** n. [f. L *re*(*fluere* flow), RE- 9]

reflux, see RE- 9; **refoot,** RE- 8; **reforest** &c., RE- 9.

refor·m[1], v.t. & i. Make (person, institution, procedure, conduct, *oneself*) or (of person or body of persons) become better by removal or abandonment of imperfections, faults, or errors (*reformed churches,* see REFORMATION); abolish, cure, (abuse, malpractice). Hence **refor·mABLE** a. [f. L *re(formare* FORM²), RE- 8]

refor·m², n. Removal of abuse(s) esp. in politics (*R. Bill, Act*, esp. those of 1831–2 amending parliamentary representation); improvement made or suggested; *R. Club*, former headquarters of the Liberal party (cf. CARLTON, NATIONAL *Liberal*). [f. prec.]

re-for·m³, v.t. & i. Form again. So **re-forma·tion¹** n. [RE- 8]

reforma·tion², n. Reforming or being reformed, esp. radical change for the better in political, religious, or social affairs; *the R.*, 16th-c. movement for reform of abuses in Roman Church ending in establishment of Reformed or Protestant Churches, whence **reforma·tionAL** a. [f. L *reformatio* (REFORM¹, -ATION)]

refor·mative a., **refor·matory** a. & n. Tending or intended to produce reform; (n.) institution to which juvenile offenders are sent for r. purposes. [REFORM¹, -ATIVE, -ORY]

refor·mer, n. In vbl senses; esp.: leader in the 16th-c. REFORMATION; advocate of the REFORM² bill. [-ER¹]

refra·ct, v.t. (Of water, air, glass, &c.) deflect (light) at certain angle when it enters obliquely from another medium of different density (*refracting telescope*, with object-glass converging rays to focus); (Chem.) analyse (nitre) to discover percentage of impurities. Hence or cogn. **refra·ctION** n., **refra·ctionAL**, **refra·ctIVE**, aa. [f. LL *re(fringere -fract- =frangere* break), RE- 5]

refra·ctor, n. Refracting medium or lens or telescope. [-OR²]

refra·ctory, a. Stubborn, unmanageable, rebellious; (of wound, disease, &c.) not yielding to treatment; (of substances) hard to fuse or work. Hence **refra·ctoriLY²** adv., **refra·ctoriNESS** n. [f. L *refractarius* (REFRACT, -ARY¹) w. assim. to -ORY]

refrai·n¹, n. Recurring phrase or line esp. at end of stanzas. [OF, ult. f. pop. L **refrangere =refringere* REFRACT]

refrai·n², v.t. & i. Put restraint upon, curb, (one*self*, one's tears, soul, &c.; archaic); abstain from doing something, abstain *from* act or do*ing*. [f. OF *refrener* f. L *re(frenare* f. *frenum* bridle), RE- 9]

refra·ngible, a. That can be refracted. Hence **refrangiBI·LITY** n. [incorrect for *refringible* (REFRACT, -IBLE)]

refre·sh, v.t. & i. Make cool again (rare); reanimate, reinvigorate, (of food, drink, rest, amusement, &c., or person providing these esp. in *r.* one*self*; *refreshing innocence* &c., interesting to blasé observer); freshen up (memory); restore (fire, electric battery, &c.) with fresh supply; take esp. liquid refreshment. Hence **refre·shingLY²** adv. [f. OF *refrescher*, see FRESH, RE- 9]

refre·sher, n. In vbl senses; esp.: extra fee to counsel in prolonged case; (colloq.) a drink. [-ER¹]

refre·shment, n. Refreshing or being refreshed in mind or body; thing, esp. (usu. in pl.) drink or food, that refreshes (*the sight was a r. to him*; *take some r.* or *rr.*; *r. room* at railway station or *car* on train); *R. Sunday*, 4th in Lent with gospel f. *John* vi. [f. OF *refreschement* (prec., -MENT)]

refri·gerate, v.t. & i. Make, rarely become, cool or cold; expose (provisions) to extreme cold in order to freeze or preserve, whence **refri·geratOR²**(2) n. Hence or cogn. **refri·gerANT**(2) a. & n., **refriger-A·TION** n. [f. L *re(frigerare* f. *frigus -oris* cold), RE- 9, -ATE³]

refri·geratory, n. & a. Cold-water vessel attached to still for condensing vapour; refrigerator; (adj.) refrigerant. [f. L *refrigeratorius* (prec., -ORY)]

reft. See REAVE.

re·fuge, n., & v.t. & i. (Place of) shelter from pursuit or danger or trouble (*seek r.*; *has found a r.*; *take r. in a cave, in lying*; *city of r.*, see *Josh.* xx; *house of r.*, institution for the homeless &c.); person, thing, course, that gives shelter or is resorted to in difficulties (*he is the r. of the distressed*; *books are the r. of the destitute*); raised piece in middle of busy road for crossers to halt on. (Vb, rare) give r. to; taker. [F, f. L *re(fugium* f. *fugere* flee), RE-4]

refugee·, n. Person escaped to foreign country from religious or political persecution. [f. F *réfugié* p.p. of *réfugier* (prec.)]

refu·lgent, a. Shining, gloriously bright. Hence or cogn. **refu·lgENCE** n., **refu·lgentLY²** adv. [f. L *re(fulgēre* shine), RE- 6, -ENT]

refu·nd, v.t. & i., & n. Pay back (money received or taken, expenses incurred by another); reimburse; make repayment; hence **refu·ndMENT** n. (N.) refundment. [earlier sense *pour back*, f. L *re(fundere fus-* pour), RE- 9]

refurbish, see RE- 9; **refurnish**, RE- 8.

refu·sal, n. In vbl senses (*will take no r.*, is importunate); also, right or privilege of deciding to take or leave a thing before it is offered to others (*have, stipulate for, give* person, *the r. of*). [foll., -AL(2)]

refu·se¹ (-z), v.t. & i. Say or convey by action that one will not accept or submit to or give or grant or gratify or consent (*r. offer, gift, chance, office, candidate*, person as husband, &c.; *horse refuses fence* &c., or abs., will not jump, whence **re-fu·SER¹** n.; *r. orders, control*, &c.; *r. obedience, compliance*; *refused me satisfaction, tribute to suzerain, my request*; *r.* one, not grant his request; *have never been refused*, had request rejected; *r. to*

do); make refusal, (whist &c.) not follow suit. Hence **refu·sABLE** a. [f. F *refuser* (L *refundere* see REFUND)]
re·fuse² (-s), a. & n. (What is) rejected as worthless or left over after use. [perh. f. OF *refuse* p.p. as prec.]
re-fu·se³, v.t. Fuse again. [RE- 9]
refu·te, v.t. Prove falsity or error of (statement, opinion, argument, person advancing it), rebut or repel by argument. Hence or cogn. **rĕ·futABLE** a., **re-fu·TAL**(2), **refutA·TION**, nn. [f. L *re(futare* see CONFUTE), RE- 9]
regai·n, v.t. Recover possession of (esp. *r. consciousness*); reach (place) again; recover (one's *feet* or *footing* or *legs*). [f. F *re(gagner* GAIN²), RE- 9]
rē·gal, a. Of or by kings (*r. government, title, office*); fit for a king, magnificent, (*lives in r. splendour*). Hence **re·galLY²** adv. [f. L *regalis* (*rex regis* king, -AL)]
rega·le¹, n. Choice repast lit. or fig., feast *of* some dainty; a dainty (rare); choice flavour (rare; *viands of higher r.*). [f. obs. F *régale* f. It. *regalo* gift, etym. dub.]
rega·le², v.t. & i. Entertain choicely (often iron.) with food or *with* talk &c.; (of beauty, flowers, &c.) give delight to; feed oneself choicely (usu. *on*). Hence **rega·leMENT** n. [f. F *régaler* (prec.)]
regā·lia¹, n. pl. Royal privileges (now rare); insignia of royalty used at coronations; insignia of an order, e.g. of Freemasons. [L, neut. pl. of REGAL*is*]
regā·lia², n. Large cigar of good quality. [f. Sp. *regalia* royal privilege (REGAL, -Y¹)]
rē·galism, n. Doctrine of sovereign's ecclesiastical supremacy. [-ISM]
regă·lity, n. Attribute of kingly power, being king, (*things that touch his r.*); monarchical State, kingdom, (rare); royal privilege. [f. OF *regalité* (REGAL, -ITY)]
regar·d¹, v.t. & i. Gaze upon (usu. with adv. phr. or adv.; *found him regarding me with curiosity, intently*); give heed to, take into account, let one's course be affected by, (esp. in neg. context; *fears not God nor regards man*; *does not r. my advice*), give heed, pay attention, take notice; look upon or contemplate mentally *with* reverence, horror, &c., or with adv. specified sentiment (*I still r. him kindly*); consider (usu. *as* with compl., also *in the light of, under an aspect*, &c., also vulg. with compl. & without *as* = consider; *is to be regarded as a wild beast*; *r. it as madness* or *indispensable, him as among my friends*); (of things) concern, have relation to, (*does not r. me* &c., has nothing to do with; esp. as *regards*, or *regarding* as part. or prep., = about, touching; *as regards wheat, prices are rising*; *considerations regarding peace*; *am innocent regarding the former*). [f. F *re(garder* GUARD²), RE- 6, cf. REWARD]
regar·d², n. Gaze, steady or significant look; respect, point attended to, (*in this* &c. *r.*; esp. *in r. to* or *of, with r. to*, regarding, as touching, about; *in* one's *r.*, concerning or about or towards him); attention, heed, care, (*to, for*; *r. must be had* or *paid to general principles*; *the next object of r. is his conduct*; *act without r. to* or *for decency*; *pays no r. to expostulations* or *adviser*), whence **regar·dFUL** a. (*of*), **regar·dLESS** a. & adv. (*of*; also slang as ellipt. adv. = r. of expense, as *got up r.*, expensively dressed), **regar·dfulLY²** (rare), **regar·dlessLY²**, advv., **regar·dfulNESS** (rare), **regar·dlessNESS**, nn.; esteem, kindly feeling or respectful opinion, (*for*; *have little, a great, r. for him, no, a high, r. for his judgement* or *advice*), (pl.) expression of friendliness in letter &c., compliments, (*kind rr. to you all*; *give him my rr.* or *best* &c. *rr.*). [F (prec.)]
regar·dant, a. (Herald.) looking backward; observant, with steady or intent gaze. [F (REGARD¹, -ANT)]
rega·tta, n. Meeting for boat or yacht races. [It. (earlier sense *contention*), etym. dub.]
rēgela·te, v.i. (Of fragments of ice, heaped snow, &c.) be fused by temporary thawing of surfaces into frozen mass. Hence **regelA·TION** n. [RE- 9, L *gelare* freeze, -ATE³]
rē·gency, n. Rule, control, (rare); office of regent; commission acting as regent; regent's or regency-commission's period of office (*the R.* in Eng. Hist., 1810–20). [REGENT, -ENCY]
regĕ·nerāte, v.t. & i. Invest with new & higher spiritual nature; improve moral condition of, breathe new & more vigorous & higher life into, (person, institution, &c.); generate again, bring or come into renewed existence, (*must r. his self-respect*; *polypus regenerates after extraction*); reform oneself. Hence or cogn. **re-ge·nerATE²** (-at), **rege·nerATIVE** aa., **re-generA·TION** n. [f. L *re(generare* GENERATE), RE- 8]
rege·nerātor, n. In vbl senses; also, fuel-saving fire-brick device in furnaces. [-OR²]
regenesis. See RE- 8.
rē·gent, n. & a. Ruler, ruling principle, (rare); person appointed to administer kingdom during minority, absence, or incapacity of monarch; (adj., following n.) acting as r. (*Queen, Prince*, &c., *r.*). [n. f. a., f. L *regere* rule, -ENT]
regerminate &c. See RE- 9.
rĕ·gicide, n. Killer or participator in killing of a king (*the rr.*, those concerned in trying & executing Charles I); king-killing. Hence **regicī·dAL** a. [L *rex regis* king, -CIDE]
régie (rĕzhē·), n. State monopoly or control of tobacco, salt, &c. [F]
regild. See RE- 9.
régime, regime, (rĕzhē·m), n. Method of government, prevailing system of things, (*ancien régime* F, system of government

in France before the revolution, also transf. any now abolished or past method); *under the r. of purchase, privilege, protection, competition, Whig ascendancy,* &c. [F (*ré-*) f. L REGIMEN]

rĕ·gimen, n. Rule, system of government, régime, (now rare); (Med.) prescribed course of exercise, way of life, & esp. diet; (Gram.) relation of syntactic dependence between words, government. [L (*regere* rule, -MEN)]

rĕ·giment (-jm-), n., & v.t. Rule, government, (now rare); permanent unit of army usu. commanded by (Lieut.) Colonel & divided into several companies or troops & often into two, or in the great war into many, battalions; (often pl.) large array or number, legion, (usu. *of*). (Vb) form (men) into r. or rr.; organize (workers, labour) in groups or according to a system, whence **regimenta·tion** n. [f. LL *regimentum* (prec., -MENT)]

regime·ntal, a. & n. Of a regiment; hence **regime·ntally**[2] adv. (N., pl.) dress worn by regiment, military uniform. [-AL]

Regī·na, n. (abbr. *R.*). Reigning queen (in signatures to proclamations, as *V.R.*, Victoria R., titles of crown law-suits, as R. *v. Jones, R.* versus Jones, &c.). [L (*rex regis* king, -INA[1])]

regī·nal, a. (rare). Queenly, of or befitting a queen. [f. med. L *reginalis* (prec., -AL)]

rē·gion (-jn), n. Tract of country, space, place, of more or less definitely marked boundaries or characteristics (*a desert, fertile, r.; the r. between the Elbe & the Rhine; earth is divided into rr. characterized by different fauna & flora*); separate part of world or universe (often pl.; *lower rr.*, hell, realm of the dead; *upper rr.*, sky, heaven; *the r. beyond the grave*); sphere or realm *of* (*you are getting into the r. of metaphysics*); *upper, middle, lower,* layer of atmosphere or sea; part of the body round or near some organ &c. (the *lumbar, abdominal,* &c., *r.*; *the r. of the eyes.*) Hence **re·gional** a. [f. AF *regiun* f. L *regionem* nom. *-o* direction (*regere* direct, -ION)]

re·gister[1], n. Book in which entries are made of details to be recorded for reference; official or authoritative list kept e.g. of births, marriages, & burials or deaths, of shipping, of qualified voters in constituency (*r. office*, or in mod. use *r.*, a registry); slider in organ controlling set of pipes; compass of voice or instrument, part of voice-compass (*heat, chest, throat, upper, middle, lower, r.*); adjustable plate for widening or narrowing an opening & regulating draught esp. in fire-grate; recording indicator of speed, force, &c.; (Print.) exact correspondence of printed matter on two sides of leaf (*in r.*, so corresponding), (Photog.) correspondence of focussing screen with plate or film. [f. med. L *regestrum* for *regestum* (LL *regesta* things recorded f. RE- 8, L *gerere* carry)]

re·gister[2], v.t. & i. Set down (name, fact, &c.) formally, record in writing, (fig.) make mental note of; enter or cause to be entered in particular r. (*r. letter*, entrust to post-office with special precautions for safety; *r. luggage*, on railway &c.; *r. oneself* or abs., put one's name on electoral r.); (of instrument) record automatically, indicate; (Print. &c.) correspond, make correspond, exactly. Hence or cogn. **re·gistrable** a., **registra·tion** n. [f. med. L *registrare* (prec.)]

re·gistrar, n. Official recorder, person charged with keeping register. Hence **re·gistrarship** n. [prec., -AR[2]]

re·gistrary, n. Registrar of Cambridge University. [REGISTER[1], -ARY[1]]

re·gistry, n. Registration; place, office, where registers are kept; *married at a r.* or *r. office* or *register office*, i.e. without religious ceremony; *servant's registry (office)*, shop &c. where lists of vacant situations & servants seeking them are kept; register (rare). [REGISTER[1], -RY]

Rē·gius, a. *R. professor of Greek* &c., holder of chair at Oxf. or Camb., instituted by Henry VIII or of later one placed on same footing. [L, = royal (*rex regis* king)]

re·gnal, a. Of a reign (*r. year*, beginning with king's accession or an anniversary of it; *r. day*, anniversary of accession). [f. med. L *regnalis* (REIGN, -AL)]

re·gnant, a. Reigning (*Queen R.*, ruling in her own right & not as consort; *Prince R.* &c.); (of things, qualities, opinions, &c.) predominant, prevalent. [f. L *regnare* REIGN[2], -ANT]

regor·ge, v.t. & i. Bring or cast up again, vomit, disgorge; gush or flow back from pit, channel, &c.; swallow again. [RE- 9]

regra·te, v.t. (hist.). Buy up (goods, esp. victuals) with view to retailing at a profit (a practice formerly prohibited). Hence **regra·ter**[1], **regra·tor**[2], nn. [f. OF *regrater* perh. f. RE-, *grater* (now *gratter*) scrape, GRATE[2]]

rē·gress[1], n. Going back; declension, backward tendency. [f. L *regressus* (foll.)]

regre·ss[2], v.i. Move backwards (chiefly astron.). [f. L *re(gredi = gradi gress-* step), RE- 9]

regre·ssion (-ĕshn), n. Backward movement, retreat; return of curve; relapse, reversion. So **regre·ssive** a., **regre·ssively**[2] adv., **regre·ssiveness** n. [f. L *-io* (prec., -ION)]

regre·t, v.t. (-tt-), & n. Be sorry for loss of, wish one could have again; be distressed about or sorry for (event, fact), grieve at, repent (action &c.); be sorry *to* say &c.

or *that* (esp. in polite refusal of invitation &c.); hence **regre·ttABLE** a., **regre·t-tabLY**² adv. (N.) sorrow for loss of person or thing (often *for*); repentance or annoyance concerning thing (left un)done (*has no rr.*; *express r. for*, esp. make apology or ask pardon for); vexation or disappointment caused by occurrence or situation (*hear with r. of* or *that*; *refuse with much r.* or *many rr.*); hence (of person or feeling) **regre·tFUL** a., **regre·tfulLY**² adv. [f. F *regret(ter)*, OF also *regreter*, *regrater*, etym. dub.]

regroup. See RE- 8.

rĕ·gulable, a. Admitting of regulation. [REGULATE, -ABLE]

rĕ·gūlar, a. & n. (Eccl.) bound by religious rule, belonging to religious or monastic order, (cf. SECULAR; *the r. clergy* in R.-C. countries, monks as opp. parish priests &c.); (of shape, structure, arrangement, or objects in these respects) following or exhibiting a principle, harmonious, consistent, systematic, symmetrical, (*r. nomenclature, formation, features, curve, figure, flower*; *the five r. solids*, tetrahedron or triangular pyramid bounded by 4 triangles, hexahedron or cube by 6 squares, octahedron by 8 triangles, dodecahedron by 12 pentagons, & icosahedron by 20 triangles); acting, done, recurring, uniformly or calculably in time or manner, habitual, constant, not capricious or casual, orderly, (*r. working, steps, procedure, sequence, pulse, bowels, salary, orbit, bed-time, employ*; *keep r. hours*, do same thing at same time daily; *a r. life*, lived in orderly manner, esp. without excesses; *r. people*, living r. lives; also vulg. as adv., as *comes, happens, r.*); conforming to a standard of etiquette &c., not transgressing conventions, in order, (*had no r. introduction*; *the attitude of the Foreign Office has been quite r.*); (Gram., of verbs, nouns, &c.) following a normal type of inflection; properly constituted or qualified, not defective or amateur, devoted exclusively or primarily to its nominal function, (*cooks as well as a r. cook*; *has no r. profession*; *r. soldiers*, opp. volunteers or militia or temporary levies; *r. army*, of r. soldiers), (colloq.) complete, thorough, indubitable, (*is a r. rascal, brick, hero*; *a r. royal queen*; *had a r. smash, overhauling*, &c.; also vulg. as adv., as *is r. angry*); hence **regulă·RITY** n., **re·gularIZE**(3) v.t., **re·gularizA·TION** n., **re·gularLY**² adv. (N., usu. in pl.) one of the r. clergy; r. soldier; (colloq.) person permanently employed. [f. L *regularis* (*regula* rule f. *regere* direct, -AR¹)]

re·gūlate, v.t. Control by rule, subject to restrictions, moderate, adapt to requirements; adjust (machine, clock) so that it may work accurately. Hence **re·gulatOR**²(1, 2) n., **re·gulATIVE** a. [f. LL *regulare* (L *regula* rule), -ATE³]

regula·tion, n. Regulating or being regulated; prescribed rule, authoritative direction, (attrib.) fulfilling what is laid down by rr., of correct pattern &c., ordinary, usual, formal, (*of the r. size*; *exceed the r. speed*; *a r. sword, cap*; *the r. mourning*). [prec., -ATION]

rĕ·gūlus, n. (pl. *-li*). Bright star in Leo (*R-*); (Chem.) purer or metallic part of mineral separated by sinking to bottom in crucible, impure metallic product of smelting various ores, whence **re·gulINE**¹ a.; golden-crested wren. [L, dim. of *rex regis* king; chem. sense orig. of metallic form of antimony, perh. as title of honour due to its readiness to combine with gold]

regur·gitate, v.i. & t. Gush back; (of stomach or receptacle) pour or cast up again. Hence **regurgitA·TION** n. [f. med. L *re(gurgitare* f. L *gurges -itis* whirlpool), RE- 9, -ATE³]

rehabilitate &c., see RE- 9; **rehandle, rehang, rehash, rehear,** &c., RE- 8.

rehear·sal (-her-), n. Rehearsing; preparatory performance of play or other entertainment (*dress r.*, such r. in costume, i. e. when practice is far advanced). [-AL (2)]

rehear·se (-ers), v.t. Recite, say over, repeat from beginning to end, give list of, recount, enumerate; have rehearsal of (play &c. or part in it), practise for later public performance. [f. OF *rehercer* prob. f. RE- 8, *hercer* harrow (*herse* harrow f. L *hirpex* rake)]

rehouse, see RE- 8; **rehumanize,** RE- 9.

reichsrat(h) (rī·ksraht), n. Parliament of the late Cisleithan Austria-Hungary. [G]

reichstag (rī·kstahch), n. Parliament of the German empire; parliament of the late Transleithan Austria-Hungary. [G]

rē·ifȳ, v.t. Convert (person, abstract concept) into thing, materialize. So **reifiCA·TION** n. [f. L *res* thing, -I-, -FY]

reign¹ (rān), n. Sovereignty, rule, sway, (*under the r. of Queen Victoria*; *his r. was a gentle one*; *the r. of law in nature*; *night resumes her r.*; *R. of Terror*, period of sanguinary excesses by revolutionaries or reactionaries, & see TERROR); realm, sphere, (rare); period during which sovereign reigns (*in the r. of John*; *during five successive rr.*). [f. OF *regne* f. L *regnum* (*regere* rule)]

reign², v.i. Hold royal office, be king or queen lit. or fig., (*reigned over Great Britain for 60 years*; *a king who desired to rule as well as r.*; *better to r. in hell than serve in heaven*; *reigning beauty*, acknowledged as supreme for the time); hold sway, prevail, (*dissension & improvidence reigned*; *silence reigns*, all is quiet). [f. OF *regner* f. L *regnare* (prec.)]

reignite. See RE- 9.

reimbur·se, v.t. Repay (person who has expended money, out-of-pocket expenses, person expenses). Hence **reimbur·se-**

MENT n. [RE- 9, obs. *imburse* put in purse f. LL *imbursare* (IM-[1], BOURSE)]

reimport, reimpose &c. See RE- 9.

rein (rān), n., & v.t. Long narrow strap with each end attached to bit used to guide or check horse &c. in riding or driving, (fig.) means of control, (often pl. in same senses; *draw r.*, stop one's horse, pull up, abandon effort, retrench expenditure, &c.; *give horse the rr.* or *r.*, let it go its own way; so *throw the rr. to*; *give r.* or *the rr. to* one's *imagination* &c., let it have free scope; *assume, drop, the rr. of government*, enter upon, resign, office); hence **rei·n**LESS a. (Vb) check or manage with rr., (fig.) govern, restrain, control; pull *up* or *back* with rr., hold *in* with rr. or fig. [vb f. n., f. OF *resne*, AF *redne*, cf. It. *redina*, perh. ult. f. L as RETAIN]

reincarnate &c., see RE- 8; **reincorporate**, RE- 9.

rei·ndeer (rā-), n. (collect. sing. usu. for pl.). Subarctic deer used for drawing sledges & kept in herds for its milk, flesh, & hide. [f. ON *hreindýri* (*hreinn* reindeer, DEER)]

reinfor·ce, v.t., & n. Strengthen or support by additional men or material or by increase of numbers, quantity, size, thickness, &c. (*r. fortress, army, provisions, party, the basses* &c. in band or chorus, person's *health* &c. with food &c., one's *argument* with fresh points); *reinforced concrete* (with metal bars, gratings, or wire, embedded in it); (rare) enforce again, re-enforce. (N.) thicker part of gun next breech; strengthening part, band, &c., added to object. [RE- 8, *inforce* = ENFORCE]

reinfor·cement, n. Reinforcing or being reinforced; (often pl.) additional men, ships, &c., for military or naval force; anything that reinforces. [-MENT]

reingratiate, see RE- 9; **reink**, RE- 8.

reins (rānz), n. pl. (archaic). The kidneys; the loins. [OF, f. L *renes*, sing. *ren*]

reinsert &c. See RE- 9.

reinsta·te, v.t. Restore to, replace *in*, lost position, privileges, &c.; restore to health or proper order. Hence **reinstat·**EMENT n. [RE- 9, obs. *instate* (IN-[1], STATE n.)]

reinsure &c., **reinter**, see RE- 8; **reinvest** &c., RE- 8, 9; **reinvigorate** &c., RE- 9.

reis (rās), n. pl. Portuguese money of account (1/20*d.* in Portugal, 1/40*d.* in Brazil). [Port. (sing. REAL[1])]

reissue &c., **reiterate** &c. See RE- 8.

reiver. See REAVE.

reje·ct, v.t. Put aside as not to be accepted, practised, believed, chosen, used, complied with, &c. (*r. doctrine, custom, evidence, candidate, literary contribution, food, request, suitor, vote*; *sorting-machine rejects all defective specimens*); cast up again, vomit, evacuate. Hence or cogn. **reje·ct**ABLE a., **reje·ct**ER[1], **reje·ct**ION, **reje·ct**OR[2], nn. [f. L *re(jicĕre -ject- = jacĕre* throw), RE- 9]

rejectame·nta, n. pl. Refuse, waste matters; things cast up by the sea; excrements. [mod. L (prec., -MENT)]

rejoi·ce, v.t. & i. Cause joy to, make glad, (*the news rejoiced him*; *I am rejoiced to hear it, that it should be so, at it, by it, &c.*); feel great joy, whence **rejoi·cing**LY[2] adv.; be glad *that* or *to* do, take delight *in* or *at*, (*r. in*, be blessed in the possession of, often facet. for *have*); make merry, celebrate some event, whence **rejoi·**CING[1]**s** n. pl. [f. OF *re(joir -iss-* JOY[2]), RE- 6]

rejoi·n[1], v.i. & t. (Law) reply to charge or pleading, esp. to plaintiff's replication; say in answer, retort; join (one's companion, regiment, &c.) again. [f. F *re(joindre* JOIN), RE- 9, or perh. partly as foll.]

re-joi·n[2], v.t. & i. Join (t. & i.) together again, reunite. [RE- 9 + JOIN, or as prec.]

rejoi·nder, n. What is REJOIN[1]ed or said in reply, retort. [as REJOIN[1], -ER[4]]

reju·venate, reju·venize, vv.t. & i. Make or become young again. Hence **rejuve**NA·TION, **reju·venat**OR[2], nn. [RE- 9, L *juvenis* young, -ATE[3], -IZE]

rejuvene·sce (-ĕs), v.i. & t. Become young again; (Biol., i. & t. of cells) get, fill with, fresh vitality. Hence **rejuvene·**SCENT a., **rejuvene·**SCENCE n. [f. LL *re(juvenescere* f. L *juvenis*, -ESCENT), RE- 9]

rekindle. See RE- 9.

-rel, also *-erel*, suf. of dim. & depreciating tendency, somet. repr. OF *-erel*, mod. F *-ereau*, but usu. in native wds of obscure origin.

relabel. See RE- 8.

rela·pse, v.i., & n. Fall back, sink again, into wrong-doing, error, heresy, weakness or illness, quiescence or indolence, (often *into*); (n.) act or fact of relapsing, esp. deterioration in patient's condition after partial recovery. [f. L *re(labi laps-* slip), RE- 9]

rela·te, v.t. & i. Narrate, recount, whence **rela·t**ER[1] n.; bring into relation, establish relation between, (*to, with*, or abs.; *cannot r. the phenomena with* or *to anything we know* or *to each other*), (p.p.) connected, allied, akin by blood or marriage, (*the law extends to several related groups*; *is related to the royal family*), whence **rela·ted**NESS n.; have reference *to*, stand in some relation *to*, (*notices nothing but what relates to himself*; *how parts r. to parts*). [f. L *relat-* (REFER)]

rela·tion, n. Narration, a narrative, (Law) laying of information before Attorney General for him to take action upon (*proceeding at the r. of the Board of Works*); what one person or thing has to do with another, way in which one stands or is related to another, kind of connexion or correspondence or contrast or feeling that prevails between persons or things, (*the rr. primarily expressed by prepositions are those of place & time*; *the outlay seems to bear no r.*, *is out of all r.*, *to the object aimed at*; *the r. between them is that of guardian & ward*; *rr. are rather strained*, cordiality is impaired; *the report has r. to a state of things now past*; *in* or rarely *with r. to*, as regards), whence **rela·tion**AL a., **rela·tional**LY² adv.; (rare, usu. now **rela·tion**SHIP n.) kinship lit. or fig.; kinsman, kinswoman, relative (somet. with mixture of prec. sense, as *is he any, what, r. is he to you?*, *he is no r.*). Hence **rela·tion**LESS a. [f. L *relatio* (prec., -ION)]

re·lative, a. & n. (Gram.) referring, & attaching a subordinate clause, to an expressed or implied antecedent (*r. pronoun*, as in *The man* whom *you saw*; *r. adjective*, as in Which *things are an allegory*; *r. adverb*, as in *The place* where *he died*), (of clause) attached to antecedent by r. word; (rare) having mutual relations, corresponding in some way, related to each other, (*different yet r. designs*); (rare) pertinent, relevant, related to the subject, (*without some more r. proof*); comparative (*what are the r. merits of the two?*; *made the next attempt with r. coolness*), in relation to something else (*their r. positions are the same though they are miles apart*), proportioned to something else (*supply is r. to demand*), implying comparison (heat, speed, strength, *are r. words*), correlative or essentially involving a different but corresponding idea (*the conceptions of husband & wife are r. to each other*), not having absolute existence but conditioned (*she is beautiful to me, but beauty is r. to the beholder's eye*); having reference, relating, *to* (*detailed the facts r. to the matter*; also loosely as adv., as *I wrote to him r. to renewal of the lease*); hence **re·relative**LY² adv. (N.): (Gram.) r. word, esp. pronoun (*the principal rr. are* who, which, that, what), whence **rela·ti·**VAL a.; (Philos.) r. thing or term; kinsman, kinswoman, relation by blood or marriage. [f. L *relativus* (RELATE, -IVE)]

re·lativism, n. Doctrine that knowledge is of relations only. So **re·lativ**IST(2) n. [prec., -ISM]

relati·vity, n. Relativeness; (Philos.) Einstein's theory of the universe, based on the principle that all motion is relative, regarding space-time as a fourth dimension, & invalidating previous conceptions of gravitation, the ether, geometry, & other matters.

rela·tor, n. Relater (now rare); (Law) maker of RELATION (legal sense). [L (RELATE, -OR²)]

rela·x, v.t. & i. Cause or allow to become loose or slack or limp, enfeeble, enervate, mitigate, abate, (*r. the bowels, the muscles*, one's *grasp, discipline, a rule*, one's *attention*, one's *efforts*; *relaxed throat*, form of sore throat; *place has a relaxing climate*, opp. *bracing*); grow less tense or rigid or stern or ceremonious or energetic or zealous (*his hold, hands, severity, features, manner, endeavours, relaxed*; *must not r. in* one's *efforts*). [f. L *re*(*laxare* see LAX), RE- 9]

relaxa·tion, n. Partial remission *of* penalty, duty, &c.; cessation from work, recreation, amusements; diminution of tension, severity, precision, &c. [f. L *relaxatio* (prec., -ATION)]

relay·¹, n., & v.t. & i. Set of fresh horses substituted for tired ones; gang of men, supply of material, &c., similarly used (*r.-race*, between teams of which each person does part of the distance, the 2nd &c. members of teams starting when the 1st &c. end); (Teleg.) instrument reinforcing long-distance current with local battery. (Vb) arrange in, provide with, replace by, get, relay(s). [f. OF *relais* n., *relayer* vb, etym. dub.]

re-lay·² v.t. Lay again. [RE- 8]

relea·se¹, v.t. (Law) remit, surrender, make over to another, (debt, right, property), whence **relea**SEE·, **relea·**SOR², nn.; set free, liberate, deliver, unfasten, (*from*); (Cinemat.) exhibit (film &c.) for the first time. Hence **relea·**SABLE a. [f. OF *relesser* f. L RELAX*are*]

relea·se², n. Deliverance, liberation, from trouble, sorrow, life, duty, confinement, or fixed position; written discharge, receipt; legal conveyance of right or estate to another, document effecting this; handle, catch, &c., that releases part of machine &c. [f. OF *reles* (prec.)]

re·legate, v.t. Banish *to* some place of exile; consign or dismiss *to* some usu. inferior position, sphere, &c.; transfer (matter) for decision or execution, refer (person) for information &c., *to*. Hence **re·leg**ABLE a., **relega·**TION n. [f. L *re*(*legare* send), RE- 5, -ATE³]

rele·nt, v.i. Relax severity, become less stern, abandon harsh intention, yield to compassion. Hence **rele·nting**LY² adv., **rele·nt**LESS a., **rele·ntless**LY² adv., **rele·ntless**NESS n. [ult. f. RE- 9, L *lentus* soft; cf. F *ralentir*]

re·levant, a. Bearing upon, pertinent *to*, the matter in hand. Hence **re·lev**ANCE, **re·lev**ANCY, nn., **re·levant**LY² adv. [f. L *relevare* RELIEVE, -ANT; from 16th c.]

reli·able, a. That may be relied upon, of sound & consistent character or quality. Hence **reliabi·**LITY, **reli·able**NESS, nn., **reli·ab**LY² adv. [RELY, -ABLE; from 16th c.; an established wd avoided by purists as of irreg. formation]

reli·ance, n. Trust, confidence, (usu. *upon, on, in*; *have, place, feel, r. upon* &c.; *my r. is upon God*); thing depended upon (*the well is our chief r.*). So **reli·**ANT a. [RELY, -ANCE]

re·lic, n. Part of holy person's body or belongings kept after his death as object of reverence; memento, souvenir; (pl.) dead body, remains, of person; (pl.) what has survived destruction or wasting, remnant, residue, scraps; surviving trace or memorial *of* a custom, belief, period, people, &c.; object interesting for age or associations. [f. F *relique* f. RELIQUIAE]

re·lict, n. Widow (usu. *his* &c. *r.*, or *r. of*); (rare) = prec. [f. p.p. of L *re(linquere -lict-* leave), RE- 3]

relie·f[1], n. Alleviation of or deliverance from pain, distress, anxiety, &c. (*the medicine brought r.*; *it is a r. to come across an optimist*); feature &c. that diversifies monotony or relaxes tension (*a blank wall without r.*; *a comic scene follows by way of r.*); assistance given to the poor esp. under the Poor Law (*recipients of public r. shall not be eligible*) or to persons in special danger or difficulty (*a r. fund for the earthquake victims*; *r.-works*, building &c. operations started to give work to the unemployed); reinforcement & esp. raising of siege *of* besieged town; (replacing of person or persons on duty by) person(s) appointed to take turn of duty; redress of hardship or grievance. [OF (*relever* RELIEVE)]

relie·f[2], n. Method of moulding or carving or stamping in which design stands out from plane or curved surface with projections proportioned & more or less (*high, low, r.*) closely approximating to those of objects imitated (*the profile of Julius in r.*); piece of sculpture &c. in r.; appearance of being done in r. given by arrangement of line or colour or shading, distinctness of outline lit. or fig., vividness, (*stands out in r.*; *bring out the facts in full r.*). [f. It. *rilievo* (*rilevare* raise f. L as RELIEVE)]

relie·ve, v.t. Bring, give, be a, RELIEF[1] to (*town was relieved*; *am much relieved to hear it*; *devotes himself to relieving distress* or *the distressed*; *relieving officer*, parish or union official charged with care of the poor; *relieving arch*, built in substance of wall to r. part below from weight; *r.* one's *feelings*, by strong language or some ebullition; *r. nature*, evacuate bladder or bowels; *a black bodice relieved with white lace*; *r. guard*, come & take one's turn on guard; *you shall be relieved at 10.30*; *r.* one *of load*, take it off him, also facet., as *a tramp relieved him of his purse*); bring into RELIEF[2], exhibit with appearance of solidity or detachment, (esp. in p.p., often *against* background). Hence **relie·**VABLE a. [f. OF *relever* f. L *re(levare* f. *levis* light), RE- 9]

relie·vo, n. = RELIEF[2] esp. in lit. senses (ALTO, BASSO, MEZZO, *-r.*). [f. It. *rilievo* RELIEF[2] w. anglicized spelling & pronunc.]

reli·gion (-ĭjn), n. Monastic condition, being monk or nun, (*enter into, be in, r.*), (rare) a monastic order; (rare) practice of sacred rites; one of the prevalent systems of faith & worship (*the Christian, Mohammedan, r.*; *established r.*, that of established CHURCH[1]; NATURAL, REVEAL[1]*ed, r.*; *all rr. are the same to him*); human recognition of superhuman controlling power & esp. of a personal God entitled to obedience, effect of such recognition on conduct & mental attitude, (*get r.* vulg. or facet., be converted to such belief); action that one is bound to do (*make a r. of doing*). Hence **reli·gion**LESS a. [f. L *religio* perh. connected w. *re(ligare* bind), RE- 9]

reli·gioner, n. Member of monastic order; person zealous for religion. [-ER[1]]

reli·gionism, n. Excessive religious zeal. So **reli·gion**IST(2) n. [-ISM]

reli·gionize, v.t. & i. Convert to or imbue with religion; exhibit religious zeal. [-IZE]

reli·giōse, a. Morbidly religious. [as RELIGIOUS, -OSE[1]]

religiŏ·sity, n. Being religious or religiose. [f. LL *religiositas* (foll., -ITY)]

reli·gious (-jus), a. & n. Imbued with religion, pious, god-fearing, devout; of, belonging to, a monastic order; of, concerned with, religion; scrupulous, conscientious, (*with r. care, exactitude*, &c.); hence **reli·gious**LY[2] adv., **reli·gious**NESS n. (N.; as sing. with *a* &c., & as pl. in same form with *the, some, several*, &c.) person bound by monastic vows. [f. L *religiosus* (RELIGION, -OSE[1])]

reline. See RE- 9.

reli·nquish, v.t. Give up, abandon, cease from, resign, surrender, (habit, plan, hope, belief, right, possession); loose hold of (object held.) Hence **reli·nquish**MENT n. [f. OF *relinquir* f. L *re(linquere* leave), RE- 3, -ISH[2]]

re·liquary, n. Receptacle for relic(s). [f. F *reliquaire* (RELIC, -ARY[1])]

relĭ·quiae, n. pl. Remains; (Geol.) fossil remains of animals or plants; (Bot.) withered remains of leaves decaying on stem. [L (*reliquus* remaining, f. *relinquere* RELINQUISH, -IA[1])]

re·lish[1], n. Flavour, distinctive taste *of*; slight dash or tinge *of* some quality; appetizing flavour, attractive quality, (*meat has no r. when one is ill*; *horseplay loses its r. after childhood*); thing eaten with plainer food to add flavour; enjoyment of food or other things, zest, liking *for*, (*eat, read, appreciate jest*, &c., *with great r.*; *has no r. for poetry*). [earlier & OF *reles* aftertaste (*relesser* RELEASE[1]) w. assim. to -ISH[2]]

re·lish[2], v.t. & i. Serve as r. to, make piquant &c.; get pleasure out of, like, be pleased with, (*thought he could r. a lobster*; *does not r. the prospect*), whence **re·lish**ABLE a.; taste, savour, smack, suggest presence, *of*; affect the lit. or fig. taste *well, badly*, &c. [f. prec.]

relive, reload. See RE- 8.

relu·cent (-ōō-), a. (rare). Shining, bright. [f. L *re(lucēre* shine), RE- 6, -ENT]

relu·ct, v.i. Feel or show reluctance, make opposition, (*at, against*). So **relu·ct**ATE[3] (in same sense) v.i., **relucta·**TION n. [f. L *re(luctari* struggle), RE- 2]

relu·ctant, a. Struggling, offering resistance, hard to work or get or manage, (esp. poet.); unwilling, disinclined, *to* do or abs. (*am very r. to admit*; *gave me r. assistance*). Hence **relu·ct**ANCE n., **relu·ctant**LY[2] adv. [as prec., -ANT]

relu·me (-ōō-, -ū-), v.t. Rekindle (light or flame lit. or fig.); make (eyes &c.) bright again; light (sky &c.) up again. [RE- 9, & as ILLUME]

rely·, v.i. Put one's trust, depend with confidence, (*up*)*on* person or thing (*is relying upon a broken reed*; *I r. upon you to do it, its being done, today*; *you may r. upon it that he will be here*). [earlier senses *rally, adhere to, be vassal of*; f. OF *relier* bind together, f. L *re(ligare* bind), RE- 9]

remai·n[1], v.i. Be left over after abstraction or use of or dealing with the rest (*the few pleasures that r. to an old man*; *worse things r. to be told*; *nothing remains but to draw the moral*); abide, stay in same place or condition, continue to exist, be extant, be left behind, (*r. three weeks in Paris*; *let it r. as it is*; *as things have been they r.*; *the Parthenon remains to attest* or *as a proof of it*; *this visit will always r. in my memory*; *the luggage unfortunately remained on the platform*; *victory remained with the Thebans*); (with compl.) continue to be (*one thing remains certain*; *r. faithful* &c.; *I r. yours truly* &c., formula concluding letter). [f. OF *remaindre* f. L *re(manēre* stay), RE- 3]

remai·n[2], n. (Usu. pl.) what remains over, surviving members or parts or amount, (*the rr. of a nation, family, meal, stock, building, of* one's *conscience* or *strength*, &c.; also in pl. as sing., & in sing., as *here there is the rr., a r., of a temple*); (usu. pl.) relics or relic of obsolete custom or of antiquity; (pl.) works, esp. those not before or yet published, left by author (rarely in sing. of single work); (pl.) dead body, corpse. [OF (prec.)]

remai·nder, n., & v.t., (Law) residual interest in estate devised to another (cf. REVERSION) simultaneously with creation of estate (*r. man*, devisee of r.), right of succession to title or position on holder's decease, whence **remai·nder**SHIP n.; residue, remaining persons or things; (Arith.) number left after subtraction; (Bookselling) copies left unsold when demand has ceased & often offered at reduced price, (vb) treat or dispose of (edition) as r.; (attrib.) left over. [AF (REMAIN[1]*dre*, -ER[4])]

remake, see RE- 8; **reman**, RE- 8, 9.

rema·nd, v.t., & n. Send back *to*, reconsign, (now rare in gen. sense); send back (prisoner) into custody to allow of further inquiry; (n.) recommittal to custody. [f. L *re(mandare* commit), RE- 9]

rĕ·manent, a. Remaining, residual, (now rare exc. in *r. magnetism*, that left in iron after electric excitation). [f. L part. as foll., see -ENT]

re·manĕt, n. Remaining part, residue; postponed lawsuit or parliamentary bill. [L, = it remains (REMAIN[1])]

remargin. See RE- 8.

remar·k[1], v.t. & i. Take notice of, perceive, regard with attention, observe, (person, thing, fact, *that* &c.); say by way of comment; make comment (*up*)*on*. [f. F *re(marquer* MARK), RE- 6]

remar·k[2], n. Noticing, observing, (*worthy of r.*, remarkable), commenting (*is the theme of general r.*; *let it pass without r.*); a written or spoken comment, anything said, (*his rr. are often interesting*; *make a r.*, speak). [f. F *remarque* (prec.)]

remar·kable, a. Worth notice, exceptional, striking, conspicuous. Hence **remar·kable**NESS n., **remar·kab**LY[2] adv. [f. F *remarquable* (REMARK[1], -ABLE)]

remarque (F), n. Mark, usu. marginal sketch, indicating certain state of engraving plate.

remarry &c., **remast.** See RE- 8.

Rembrandte·sque (-sk), a. & n. (After) the style of Rembrandt, with marked effects of light & shade. [-ESQUE]

re·medy, n., & v.t. Cure for disease, healing medicine or treatment, means of removing or counteracting or relieving any evil (*for*), redress, legal or other reparation, whence or cogn. **remē·di**AL a., **reme·dial**LY[2] adv., (now poet. or rhet.) **remē·di**LESS (*or* re·-) a., **reme·diless**LY[2] adv. (Vb) cure medically (now rare); rectify, make good; so **remē·di**ABLE a. [vb f. L *remediare*, n. f. AF *remedie*, f. L *re(medium* f. *medēri* heal), RE- 1]

reme·mber, v.t. Retain in the memory, not forget, recall to mind, recollect, know by heart, (person, thing, fact, *that, to* do, *how to* do, *when, why*, &c., or abs.; *r. oneself*, bethink oneself of one's manners or intentions after a lapse; also refl. with *me, him*, &c., archaic, as *I r. me that, they remembered them of*), whence **reme·mber**ABLE a.; make present to, tip, (*remembered me in his will*; *r. the waiter*); mention in one's prayers; convey greetings from (person) *to* another (*r. me kindly to them*; *begs to be remembered to you*). [f. OF *remembrer* f. LL *re(memorari* f. L *memor* mindful), RE- 9]

reme·mbrance, n. Remembering or being remembered, memory, recollection, (*has escaped my r.*; *have in, call to, r.*; *put in r.*, remind; *have no r. of it*; *more than once within my r.*; *a pillar in r. of the exploit*);

keepsake, souvenir, memorial; (pl.) greetings conveyed through third person. [F (prec., -ANCE)]

reme·mbrancer, n. *King's, Queen's, R.*, officer collecting debts due to sovereign; *City R.*, representing Corporation of City of London before parliamentary committees &c.; reminder, memento, *of*. [AF (prec., -ER¹)]

remigrate &c. See RE- 9.

remi·nd, v.t. Put (person) in mind *of, to* do, *that, how*, &c., or abs. [RE- 8, MIND vb]

remi·nder, n. Thing that reminds or is meant to remind. [-ER¹]

remi·ndful, a. Acting as a reminder, reviving the memory, *of*. [-FUL]

remini·scence, n. Remembering, recovery of knowledge by mental effort, (*Platonic doctrine of r.*, that all knowledge is such recovery of things known to the soul in previous existences); remembered (& related) fact or incident, (pl.) collection in literary form of incidents that person remembers; point in thing reminding or suggestive *of* other thing (*there is a r. of the Greek type in her face*). Hence **reminisce·ntIAL** a. [f. LL *reminiscentia* f. L *re(minisci* cogn. w. MIND) remember, RE- 9, -ENCE]

remini·scent, a. Recalling past things, given to or concerned with retrospection, mindful or having memories *of*; reminding or suggestive *of*. Hence **remini·scentLY²** adv. [as prec., -ENT]

remint. See RE- 8.

remi·se¹ (-ēz), n., & v.i. (Archaic) coachhouse, carriage hired from livery-stable; (Fenc.) second thrust made for recovery from first (vb, make r.). [F, vbl n. f. *remettre* REMIT¹]

remi·se² (-īz), v.t. (legal). Surrender, make over, (right, property). [f. F *remis(e)* p.p. as prec.]

remi·ss, a. Careless of duty, lax, negligent; lacking force or energy. Hence **remi·ssLY²** adv., **remi·ssNESS** n. [f. L REMIT*tere*]

remi·ssible, a. That may be remitted. [f. L *remissibilis* (REMIT, -IBLE)]

remi·ssion (-shn), n. Forgiveness *of* sins &c., forgiveness of sins; remitting of debt, penalty, &c.; diminution of force, effect, degree, violence, &c.; act of remitting in other senses (rare). So **remi·ssIVE** a. [OF, f. L *remissionem* (foll., -ION)]

remi·t, v.t. & i. (-tt-). (Usu. of God) pardon (sins &c.); refrain from exacting or inflicting or executing (debt, punishment, sentence); abate (t. & i.), slacken, mitigate, partly or entirely cease from or cease, (*r.* one's *anger* or *efforts, the siege; pain, enthusiasm, begins to r.*); refer (matter for decision &c.) *to* some authority, send back (case) to lower court; send or put back (*in*)*to* previous state; postpone, defer, *to* or *till*; transmit (money &c.), get conveyed by post &c., whence **remi·tter¹** [-ER¹], **remittEE·**, nn. Hence **remi·ttAL(2)** n. [f. L *re(mittere miss-* send), RE- 5]

remi·ttance, n. Money sent to person; consignment of goods sent (rare); sending of money; *r.-man*, emigrant subsisting on rr. from home (esp. typical idler). [prec., -ANCE]

remi·ttent, a. & n. (Fever) that abates at intervals (cf. INTERMIT*tent*). [REMIT, -ENT]

remi·tter², n. (legal; for *r.*¹ see REMIT). Substitution, in favour of holder of two titles to estate, of the more valid for the other by which he entered on possession; remitting of case to other court; restoration to rights, rehabilitation, (rare). [-ER⁴]

re·mnant, n. *The* little or few that remain(s), small remaining quantity or piece or number of persons or things; surviving trace *of*; fragment, scrap, esp. piece of cloth &c. offered at reduced price when greater part has been used up. [short for obs. & OF *remenant, -manant*, (*remanoir* REMAIN¹, -ANT)]

remodel. See RE- 8.

remŏ·netize (*or* -mŭ-), v.t. Restore (metal &c.) to former position as legal tender. Hence **remonetizA·TION** a. [RE- 9]

remo·nstrance, n. (Hist.) formal statement of public grievances (*the Grand R.*, from House of Commons to Crown 1641); remonstrating, expostulation, *a* protest. [OF (foll., -ANCE)]

remo·nstrate, v.i. & t. Make protest, expostulate, (*against* course, *with* person, *on* or *upon* matter, or abs.); urge in remonstrance (*that* or parenth.). Hence or cogn. **remo·nstrANT** a. & n., **remo·nstrantLY²**, **remo·nstrātingLY²**, advv., **remo·nstratIVE** a., **remo·nstrātOR²** n. [f. med. L *re(monstrare* show), RE- 2, -ATE³]

remo·ntant, a. & n. (Rose) blooming more than once in year. [F (*remonter* REMOUNT², -ANT)]

re·mora, n. The sucking-fish, formerly supposed to stay course of ship to which it adhered; obstruction, impediment, (now rare). [L (RE- 2, *mora* delay), =impediment, sucking-fish]

remor·se, n. Bitter repentance for wrong committed, whence **remor·seFUL** a., **remor·sefulLY²** adv.; compunction, compassionate reluctance to inflict pain or be cruel, (chiefly in *without r.*), whence **remor·seLESS** a., **remor·selessLY²** adv., **remor·selessNESS** n. [OF *remors* f. LL *re(morsus -ūs* f. *mordēre mors-* bite), RE- 3]

remo·te, a. (-er, -est). Far apart; far away or off in place or time, not closely related, distant or widely different or by nature separate *from*, (*lies r. from the road; came from the remotest parts of the earth*;

memorials of r. ages; *a r. ancestor, descendant, kinsman*; *r. causes, effects*; *introduces considerations r. from the subject*); out-of-the-way, secluded, (*a r. village*; *lives r.*); (chiefly superl., of idea &c.) slight(est), faint(est), least, (*have not the remotest, have only a very r., conception of what he means*). Hence **remo·te**LY² adv., **re-mo·te**NESS n. [f. L *remotus* (REMOVE¹)]

remould, remount¹. See RE- 8.

remou·nt², v.t. & i. Go up, get on to, (hill, ladder, horse, &c.) again; go up again, get on horseback again, make fresh ascent; go back *to* specified date, period, source. [f. OF *re(monter* MOUNT), RE- 9]

remo·vable, a. & n. In vbl senses; esp., (of magistrate or official) subject to removal from office, holding office during pleasure of Crown or other authority; (n.) r. magistrate in Ireland. Hence **remov-**ABI·LITY n. [foll., -ABLE]

remo·ve¹ (-ōōv), v.t. & i. Take off or away from place occupied, convey to another place, change situation of, get rid of, dismiss, (*r.* one's *hat, the tea-things, all traces*; *r. mountains*, do miracle; *cardinal was removed by poison*; *r. magistrate from office*; *boy is removed from school*, taken away by parents &c.; *this will r. all apprehension, the last doubts*; *r. furniture*, for persons changing house, as special trade, whence **remo·**VER¹ n.), (pass., of course at dinner &c.) be succeeded *by* (*boiled haddock removed by hashed mutton*); change one's residence, go away *from*, (*am removing from London to Oxford*; *truth has removed from earth*); (p.p.) distant or remote *from* (*is not many degrees removed from the brute*), (of cousins) *once, twice*, &c., *removed*, with difference of one, two, &c., generations (*my first cousin once, twice, removed*, cousin's child or parent's cousin, cousin's grandchild or grandparent's cousin). Hence **remo·**VAL (2) n. (not of cousinship). [f. OF *removoir* f. L *re(movēre* MOVE), RE- 4]

remo·ve², n. Dish that succeeds another at table; promotion to higher form at school (*has not got his r.*); (in some schools) a certain form or division; (rare) change of residence, departure, removal; (rare) distance (*at a certain r. its shape seems to change*); stage in gradation, degree, (*is but one r., few rr., from*), esp. in consanguinity (cf. prec.). [f. prec.]

remū·nerate, v.t. Reward, pay for service rendered; serve as or provide recompense for (toil &c.) or to (person). Hence **remuner**A·TION n., **remu·ner**ATIVE a., **remu·nerative**LY² adv., **re-mu·nerative**NESS n. [f. L *re(munerari* f. *munus -eris* reward), RE- 1]

renai·ssance (or as F), n. Revival of art & letters under influence of classical models in 14th–16th cc., period of its progress, style of art & architecture developed by it, (often attrib., as *r. painters, architecture, church*); any similar revival. [F (*renaître* be born again) after *naissance* birth, cf. RENASCENCE]

rē·nal, a. Of the kidneys. [f. LL *renalis* (*ren* kidney, -AL)]

rename. See RE- 8.

rena·scence, n. Rebirth, renewal; =RENAISSANCE. [foll., -ENCE]

rena·scent, a. Springing up anew, being reborn. [f. L *re(nasci* be born), RE- 8, -ENT]

rencou·nter (ow-), **renco·ntre** (*-er*, or as F), n. (now rare). Encounter, battle, skirmish, duel; casual meeting. [f. F *rencontre* (*rencontrer*, see RE-, ENCOUNTER)]

rend, v.t. & i. (rent). Tear or wrench (*off, away, out of, from, asunder, apart*, &c., or abs.; archaic or rhet.; *a province rent from the empire*; *r.* one's *garments, hair*, in sign of grief &c.; *turn & r.* one, fig., abuse him unexpectedly); split or divide (t. & i.) in two or in pieces or usu. into factions (*r. laths*, make them by splitting wood; *Europe was rent in two by the question*; *shouts r. the air*, sound explosively; *heart is rent by contending emotions*; *the veil rends*). [OE *rendan* cf. OFris. *renda*]

re·nder, v.t., & n. Give in return (*r. thanks, good for evil*); give back (archaic), hand over, deliver, give *up*, surrender, (chiefly archaic; *r. to Caesar the things that are Caesar's*; *grave renders up its dead*; *fortress was rendered on terms*); pay (tribute &c.), show (obedience &c.), do (service &c.), (usu. *to* or with ind. obj.); produce for inspection, submit, present, send in, (account, reason, &c.; *will have to r. an account of*; *account rendered*, bill previously sent in & not yet paid, phr. used as substitute for repetition of items); reproduce, portray, give representation or performance or effect of, execute, translate, (*painter has hardly rendered the expression*; *the quartet, Iago, the dramatist's conception, were well rendered*; *how would you r.* solvitur ambulando*?*; *poetry can never be adequately rendered in another language*), whence **re·nder**ING¹(1, 2) n.; (with obj. & compl.) make, cause to be, convert into, (*age had rendered him peevish*; *the tone rendered it an insult*); melt (fat) down, extract by melting, clarify; cover (stone, brick) with first coat of plaster; *r.-set* v.t., plaster (wall &c.) with two coats, n. & a., (plastering) of two coats; (n., legal) return in money or kind or service made by tenant to superior. [f. OF *rendre* ult. f. L *reddere reddit-* (RE-, *dare* give)]

rendezvous (raw·ndĭvōō), n. (pl. same, pr. -ōōz), & v.i. (*-ouses, -oused, -ousing*, pr. -ōōz, -ōōd, -ōōing). Place appointed for assembling of troops or ships; place of common resort; meeting-place agreed on, meeting by agreement (*place of r.*); (vb) meet at r. [F, f. *rendez vous* (*rendre*, see prec.) betake yourselves]

rendi·tion, n. (now rare). Surrender of

place or person. [F (obs.), f. *rendre* RENDER, -ION]

re·negāde n. & v.i., **renegā·do** (archaic) n. Apostate, esp. from Christianity to Mohammedanism; deserter of party or principles, turncoat. (Vb) turn r.; so **renega·TION** n. [Sp. (-*o*), f. med. L *re(negatus* f. *negare* deny), RE- 9]

renew·, v.t. & i. Restore to original state, make (as good as) new, resuscitate, revivify, regenerate, (*nature dies & is renewed*; *r.* person's *life, sorrow, energy*; *r. the golden age*; *rose from her knees renewed by the Holy Spirit*; *renewed by baptism*); patch, fill up, reinforce, replace, (*coat renewed in places*; *r. the water in the bowl*; *r. garrison, tires,* &c.); get, begin, make, say, or give, anew, continue after intermission, (*r.* one's *youth, strength,* &c., grow young &c. again; *r. attack, correspondence, speech, game, efforts*; *r.* one's *vows, statements,* &c.; *r. lease, bill,* grant or be granted continuation of it), (abs.) r. lease or bill; (rare) become new again (*the clamour renewed*; *feel my youth renewing*). Hence **renew·ABLE** a., **renew·AL**(2) n. [RE-, NEW]

rē·niform, a. Kidney-shaped. [REINS, -FORM]

re·nnet[1], n. Curdled milk found in stomach of unweaned calf, or preparation of stomach-membrane or of kinds of plant, used in curdling milk for cheese &c. [f. *renne* obs. form of RUN[1]]

re·nnet[2], n. Kinds of dessert apple. [f. F *reinette*, prob. f. *reine* queen f. L REGINA, -ETTE]

renou·nce (-ow-), v.t. & i., & n. Consent formally to abandon, surrender, give up, (claim, right, possession); repudiate, refuse to recognize longer, decline association or disclaim relationship with, withdraw from, discontinue, forsake, (*r. treaty, principles,* person's *authority, all thought of, design, attempt, son* &c., *friend, friendship*; *r. the world,* abandon society or temporal affairs); (Law) refuse or resign right or position esp. as heir or trustee; (Cards) follow with card of another suit for want of right one (cf. REVOKE), (n.) playing of such card, opportunity of doing so (*has a r. in hearts*). Hence **renou·nceMENT** n. [f. F *renoncer* f. L *re(nuntiare* ANNOUNCE), RE- 5]

re·novate, v.t. Make new again, repair, restore to good condition or vigour. Hence **renova·TION, re·novatoR**[2], nn. [f. L *re(novare* f. *novus* new), RE- 9, -ATE[3]]

renow·n, n. Celebrity, fame, high distinction. (*man, town,* &c., *of r.* or *great* &c. *r.*, famous). [AF *renoun* = OF *renon* f. *renomer* make famous f. L *re(nominare* NOMINATE), RE- 8]

renow·ned, a. Famous, celebrated. [obs. *renown* celebrate f. OF *renomer* see prec.]

rent[1]. See REND.

rent[2], n. Tear in garment &c., opening in clouds &c. resembling tear; cleft, fissure, gorge. [f. obs. *rent* vb, var. of REND]

rent[3], n., & v.t. & i. Tenant's periodical payment to owner or landlord for use of land or house or room; payment for hire of machinery &c.; *r.-charge,* periodical charge on land &c. reserved by deed to one who is not the owner; *r.-free* a. & adv., with exemption from r.; *r.-roll,* register of person's lands &c. with rr. due from them, sum of one's income from r.; *r.-service,* (tenure by) personal service in lieu of or addition to r.; hence (of land &c., with *low, high,* &c.) **-re·ntED**[2] a. (Vb) take, occupy, use, at a r.; let or hire for r.; be let *at* specified r.; impose r. on (tenant; *rents his tenants low*); hence **re·ntABLE** a. [f. OF *rente* ult. f. L *reddita* fem. p.p. as RENDER]

re·ntal, n. Income from rents; amount paid or received as rent. [AF (prec., -AL)]

rente (F), n. Income, esp. that consisting of life-annuity or dividends.

rentier (F), n. Person living on rente, person not needing to earn his living.

renu·mber. See RE- 8.

renuncia·tion (-sĭā-), n. Renouncing, document expressing it; self-denial, giving up of things. So **renu·nciANT**(1) n. & a. (-shĭ-), **renu·nciATIVE** (-sha-), **renu·nciatoRY** (-shatrĭ), aa. [f. L *renunciatio* (RENOUNCE, -ATION)]

reo-. See RHEO-.

reoccupy &c., **reopen,** see RE- 9; **reorganize** &c., RE- 8.

rep[1], **repp, reps,** n. Textile fabric with corded surface used in upholstery. [f. F *reps* etym. dub.]

rep[2], n. (school slang). Verse &c. learnt by heart. [abbr. of *repetition*]

rep[3], n. (slang). Person of loose character. [perh. for REPROBATE[2]]

repaganize &c., **repaint.** See RE- 9.

repair·[1], v.i., & n. Resort, have recourse, go often or in numbers, *to*; (n., archaic) resort (*have r. to*), haunt, being visited by numbers (*a place of great, little, r.*). [f. OF *repaire(r)* f. LL *re(patriare* f. L *patria* native land), RE- 9]

repair·[2], v.t. Restore (building, machine, garment, tissue, strength, &c.) to good condition, renovate, mend, by replacing or refixing parts or compensating loss or exhaustion, whence **repair·ABLE** a.; remedy, set right again, make amends for, (loss, wrong, error). [f. OF *reparer* f. L *re(parare* make ready), RE- 9]

repair·[3], n. Restoring to sound condition (*health, bicycle, house, boots, need r.*; *shop is closed during rr.*; *rr. done while you wait*); good condition, relative condition, for working or using (*is in, out of, r.*;

must be kept in good, is in bad, r.). [f. prec.]

repa·nd, a. (bot., zool.). With undulating margin, wavy. Hence **repa·ndo-** comb. form. [f. L *re(pandus* bent), RE- 9]

repaper. See RE- 8.

re·parable, a. (Of loss &c.) that can be made good. [F, f. L *reparabilis* (REPAIR[2], -ABLE)]

repara·tion, n. Repairing or being repaired, repair, (pl.) repairs, (now usu. *repair, repairs*); making of amends, compensation (esp., pl., for war damages). So **re·par**ATIVE (*or* repă·-) a. [f. OF *reparacion* f. L *reparationem* (REPAIR[2], -ATION)]

repartee·, n., & v.i. Witty retort; (making of) witty retorts (*a great power, a storehouse, of r.*); (vb, now rare) make rr. [f. F *repartie* fem. p.p. of *re(partir* PART[2]) start fresh, RE- 8]

repartition, see RE- 8; **repass** &c., RE- 9.

repa·st, n. (Food supplied for or eaten at) meal (usu. *rich, plentiful, slight, delicate, luxurious,* &c., *r.*). [OF, f. *repaistre* f. LL *re(pascere past-* feed), RE- 8]

repă·triate, v.t. & i. Restore or return to native land. Hence **repatri**A·TION n. [f. LL *re(patriare* f. L *patria* fatherland), RE- 9]

repay·, v.t. & i. (-paid). Pay back (money); return, retaliate, (blow, visit, service, &c.); give in recompense *for*; make repayment to (person); make return for, requite, (action); make repayment. Hence **repay·**ABLE a., **repay·**MENT n. [f. OF *re(paier* PAY[2]), RE- 9]

repea·l, v.t., & n. Revoke, rescind, annul, (law &c.); hence **repea·l**ABLE a. (N.) abrogation, repealing; (Irish Pol.) cancelling of the Union demanded by O'Connell &c., whence **repea·l**ER[1] n. [f. OF *rapel(er)* (RE- 9, APPEAL[1])]

repea·t, v.t. & i., & n. Say or do over again, recite, rehearse, report, reproduce, give imitation of, (*r. action, statement, poem, conversation, attempt, pattern, signal,* &c.; *action was repeated several times*, whence **repea·ted**LY[2] adv.; *language will not bear repeating*, is too foul &c. to r.), (of watch &c., abs.) strike last quarter &c. over again when required (so *repeating watch* &c. or **repea·t**ER[1] n.), (of firearms) fire several shots without reloading (*repeating rifle* &c.); recur, appear again or repeatedly, (*the last three figures r.*; *food repeats*, is tasted intermittently for some time); (refl.) recur in same form, say or do same thing over again, (*history repeats itself*; *does nothing but r. himself*); hence **repea·t**ABLE a. (N.) repeating, esp. of item in programme in response to encore; (Mus.) passage intended to be repeated, mark indicating this; pattern repeated in wall-paper &c.; (Commerc.) fresh consignment similar to previous one, order given for this. [f. F *répéter* f. L *re(petere* seek), RE- 8]

repe·l, v.t. (-ll-). Drive back, repulse, ward off, refuse admission or acceptance or approach to, (*r. assailant, attack, temptation, weapon, blow, suggestion, plea, offer,* person's *advances*; *first attracts & then repels the magnet*); be repulsive or distasteful to, exert mental repulsion upon, whence **repe·l**LENT a., **repe·llent**LY[2] adv. [f. L *re(pellere puls-* drive), RE- 2]

rē·pent[1], a. (chiefly bot.). Creeping, esp. growing along or just under surface of ground. [f. L *repere* creep, -ENT]

repe·nt[2], v.t. & i. (Refl., with archaic refl. pron.) feel regret or penitence about something or *of* (archaic; *I now r. me*; *he repenteth him of the evil*); (impers.) affect with penitence or regret (archaic; *it repents me that I did it*); think with contrition *of*, think with contrition of, be regretful about or *of*, be contrite, wish one had not done, (*you shall r. this, of this*, or abs.; *have nothing to r. of*; *r. my kindness, setting off when I did*). So **repe·nt**ANCE n., **repe·nt**ANT a., **repe·ntant**LY[2] adv. [f. F *re(pentir* f. L *paenitēre* make sorry), RE- 3]

repeople. See RE- 9.

repercussion &c. See RE- 9.

re·pertoire (-twar), n. Stock of pieces &c. that company or performer knows or is prepared to give (*r. company* or *system*, relying on r. & not on long runs.) [F (*ré-*), f. L as foll.]

re·pertory, n. Place for finding something, store or collection, esp. of information, instances, facts, &c.; =prec. [f. L *repertorium* (*reperire -pert-* find f. RE-, OL *parire* =L *parere* produce, -ORY)]

reperuse &c. See RE- 8.

repete·nd, n. Recurring figures of decimal; recurring word or phrase, refrain. [f. L as REPEAT, -ND[1]]

repeti·tion, n. REPEATing or being repeated; piece set to be learnt by heart; copy, replica; ability of musical instrument to repeat note quickly. Hence **repeti·tion**AL, **repeti·tion**ARY[1], **repeti·tio**US, **repĕ·titi**VE, aa. (rare). [f. L *repetitio* (RE- 8, PETITION)]

repiece. See RE- 9.

repi·ne, v.i. Fret, be discontented, (*at, against,* or abs.). Hence **repi·ning**LY[2] adv. [RE- 6, PINE[2]]

repi·que (-ēk), n., & v.t. & i. Winning of 30 points on cards alone before beginning to play in piquet; (vb) score r. against (opponent), make r. [f. F *repic* (RE-, PIQUE[2])]

repla·ce, v.t. Put back in place; take place of, succeed, be substituted for, (pass.) be succeeded or have one's or its place filled *by*, be superseded; fill up place of (*with, by*), find or provide substitute for. Hence **repla·ce**ABLE a., **repla·ce**MENT n. [RE- 9, PLACE[2]]

replant &c. See RE- 8.

replĕ·nish, v.t. Fill up again (*with* or abs.); (p.p.) filled, fully stored, full, (*with* or abs.). Hence **reple·nish**MENT n. [f.

OF *re(plenir* ult. f. L *plenus* full), RE- 9, -ISH[2]]

reple·te, a. Filled, stuffed, fully imbued, well stocked, *with*; gorged, sated, (*with*). So **reple·tion** n. (esp. *full to -ion*). [f. L *re(plēre plet-* fill), RE- 6]

replĕ·vin, n. Restoration or recovery of distrained goods on security given for submission to trial & judgement; writ granting r.; action arising out of r. [AF, f. OF as foll.]

replĕ·vy, v.t. Recover by replevin. [f. OF *re(plevir* etym. dub.; see PLEDGE[1]), RE- 9]

re·plica, n. Duplicate made by original artist of his picture &c.; facsimile, exact copy. [It. (*replicare* REPLY)]

re·plicate[1] (-*at*), n. Tone one or more octaves above or below given tone. [as foll.]

re·plicate[2] (-*at*), a. (bot.). Folded back on itself. [as foll., -ATE[2]]

re·plicāte[3], v.t. (rare). Repeat; make replica of; fold back. [L *re(plicare* fold), RE- 9, -ATE[3]]

replica·tion, n. Folding back, fold, (rare); replying, rejoinder, answer, esp. reply to answer, (Law) plaintiff's reply to defendant's plea; echo; copy, copying. [OF, f. L *replicationem* (prec., -ATION)]

reply·, v.i. & t., & n. Make answer, respond, in word or action (*to*; abs., *that* &c., or parenth.; *rose to r. for the ladies*, represent them in returning thanks for toast; *the batteries replied to our fire*; *he replied that I must please myself*; *'Please yourself' he replied*); (n.) act of replying (*what he says in r.*), what is replied, response; *r. paid*, (of telegram) with cost of r. prepaid by sender. [f. OF *replier* f. L as REPLICATE[3]]

repoint, repolish. See RE- 9.

répondez s'il vous plaît (F), formula appended (usu. in abbr. *R.S.V.P.*) to invitation or other letter, = please answer.

repopulate. See RE- 9.

repor·t[1], v.t. & i. Bring back account of, state as ascertained fact, tell as news, narrate or describe or repeat esp. as eyewitness &c. (*to*), relate as spoken by another, make official or formal statement about, inform against (offence, offender) *to* authorities or abs., announce one*self* as returned or arrived, (*reports open water at pole, pole to be accessible, that he reached pole*; *it is reported*, commonly said; *reported all details of the scene to me*; *my actual words & those reported to you were quite different*; *reported speech*, oblique oration; *chairman of committee reports bill to House*, announces conclusion of committee's dealings with it between 2nd & 3rd reading; *r. progress*, state what has been done so far, *move to r. progress* in House of Commons, propose that debate be discontinued, often for obstructive purposes; *all variations are to be reported daily*; *shall r. you, your unpunctuality, to senior partner*); take down word for word or epitomize or write description of for publication (*r. law case, proceedings, meeting*; also abs., as *reports for the* Times); make, draw up, or send in r. usu. (*up*)*on*; give r. *of* conveying that one is *well* or *badly* impressed (*reports well of the prospects*; *is badly reported of*). Hence **repor·table** a., **repor·ter[1]** n. [f. OF *reporter* f. L *re(portare* bring), RE- 9]

repor·t[2], n. Common talk, rumour, (*mere r. is not enough to go upon*; *the r. goes*, it is said); way person or thing is spoken of, repute, (*things of good r.*; *faithful through good & evil r.*); account given or opinion formally expressed after investigation or consideration, description or epitome or reproduction of scene or speech or law case esp. for newspaper publication, (*r. stage* in House of Commons, treatment of bill when committee has reported, see prec.); sound of explosion (*went off with a loud r.*). [OF (*reporter* see prec.)]

repo·se[1] (-z), v.t. Place (trust &c.) *in*. Hence **repo·sal**(2) n. [f. L *re(ponere posit-* place), RE- 4, w. assim. to *depose*, foll., &c.]

repo·se[2] (-z), v.t. & i., & n. Rest (one*self* or abs.); lay (one's *head* &c.) to rest (often *on* pillow &c.); give rest to, refresh with rest; lie, be lying or laid, esp. in sleep or death (*in, on*, or abs.), be supported or based *on* (*the whole system reposes on fear*); (of memory &c.) dwell *on*. (N.) rest, cessation of activity or excitement, respite from toil, sleep, peaceful or quiescent state, stillness, tranquillity; restful effect, harmonious combination in art, composure or ease of manner, (esp. in *lacks r.*); hence **repo·seful** a., **repo·sefully[2]** adv. [f. F *repos(er* f. LL *re(pausare* PAUSE; RE- 5); meaning influenced by prec.]

repŏ·sitory (-z-), n. Receptacle; place where things are stored or may be found, museum, warehouse, store, shop, (*book, person, &c., is a r. of curious information*); burial-place; recipient *of* confidences or secrets. [f. L *repositorium* (REPOSE[1], -ORY)]

repossess &c. See RE- 9.

repost. See RIPOSTE.

repot. See RE- 8.

repoussé (repōō·sā), a. & n. (Ornamental metal work) hammered into relief from reverse side. [F, p.p. of *re(pousser* PUSH[1]), RE- 3]

repp. See REP[1].

repped, a. Having surface like rep. [-ED[2]]

reprehe·nd, v.t. Rebuke, blame, find fault with. So **reprehe·nsible** a., **reprehe·nsibly[2]** adv., **reprehe·nsion** n. [f. L *re(prehendere* seize), RE- 2]

represe·nt (-z-), v.t. Call up by description or portrayal or imagination, figure, place likeness of before mind or senses, serve or be meant as likeness of, (*can you r. infinity to yourself?*; *can only r. it to you by metaphors*; *picture represents murder of Abel*; *is represented in hunting costume*); try to bring (facts influencing conduct) home (*to*), state by way of expostulation or incentive, (*represented the rashness of it, that it could not succeed*); make out *to* be &c., allege *that*, describe or depict *as*, (*am not what you r. me to be* or *as*; *in the corner is the Pope represented as a beggar*; *represents that he has* or *himself to have seen service*); act (play &c.), play part of on stage; symbolize, act as embodiment of, stand for, correspond to, be specimen of, (*sovereign represents majesty of State*; *inch of rain represents 100 tons to acre*; *globe represents totality*; *camels are represented in the New World by llamas*; *Welsh football is represented in the team by Morgan*); fill place of, be substitute or deputy for, be entitled to speak for, be sent as member to House of Commons by, (*King was represented by the Duke of Norfolk*; *members representing urban constituencies*). Hence or cogn. **represe·nt**ABLE a., **representa·**TION n. (*proportional -ion*, electoral system so arranged that minorities are represented in proportion to their strength), **representa·tion**AL a. [f. L *re(praesentare* PRESENT[4]), RE- 8]

represe·ntative, a. & n. Serving as portrayal or symbol *of* (*a group r. of the theological virtues*); that presents or can present ideas to the mind (*imagination is a r. faculty*); typical of a class or classes, containing typical specimens of all or many classes, (*the truth of an allegory is r., not literal*; *call a meeting of r. men*; *a very r. selection, collection*); (of species in nat. hist. &c.) corresponding in a locality to others elsewhere; consisting of elected deputies or rr. (*r. chamber, house*, &c.), based on representation by such deputies (*r. government, institutions*); hence **represe·ntative**LY[2] adv., **represe·ntative**NESS n. (N.) sample, specimen, typical embodiment, analogue, *of*; person's agent, delegate, substitute, successor, or heir; deputy in r. chamber (*House of Rr.*, lower house of U.S. Congress). [f. med. L *repraesentativus* (REPRESENT, -ATIVE)]

repre·ss, v.t. Check, restrain, put down, keep under, quell, suppress, prevent from sounding or bursting out or rioting. So **repre·ss**ION (-shn) n. (esp., in Psychol., of natural promptings), **repre·ss**IVE a. [f. L *re(primere = premere* PRESS[2]), RE- 5]

reprie·ve, v.t., & n. Suspend or delay execution of (condemned person), (fig.) give respite to. (N.) reprieving or being reprieved; (warrant for) remission or commutation of capital sentence; respite. [n. f. vb, earlier *reprie, -pry*, in sense *remand*, first in p.p., prob. f. F *re(pris* p.p. of *prendre* f. L *prehendere* take), RE- 8; -V- unexplained]

re·primand, n., & v.t. Official(ly) rebuke (*for* fault). [f. F *réprimande(r)* f. *réprimer* REPRESS]

reprint. See RE- 8.

repri·sal (-zl), n. (Hist.) forcible seizure of foreign subjects' persons or property in retaliation (*letters of r.*, official warrant authorizing this); act of retaliation (usu. *make rr.* or *r.*). [f. F *reprisaille* as foll. + -AL(2)]

repri·se (-ĭz), n. (Law) rent-charge or other payment to be made yearly out of estate (*beyond, besides, above, rr.*, remaining after all rr. have been paid); (rare) resumption of action, one of the times devoted to something not done all at once. [F, fem. of *repris* see REPRIEVE]

reproa·ch (-ōtsh), v.t., & n. Upbraid, scold, (person, often *with* offence); rebuke (offence); (of look &c.) convey protest or censure to (*his eyes r. me*); hence **reproa·ching**LY[2] adv. (rare for *reproachfully*). (N.) thing that brings disgrace or discredit (*to*; *the state of the roads is a r. to civilization*), whence **reproa·ch**LESS a. (rare for *irreproachable*); opprobrium, disgraced or discredited state, (*live in r. & ignominy*; *the things that had brought r. upon him*; *has taken away my r.*); upbraiding, rebuke, censure, (*abstain from r.*; *heap rr. on*; *the mute r. in his eyes*; *term of r.*, word implying censure), whence **reproa·ch**FUL a., **reproa·chful**LY[2] adv., **reproa·chful**NESS n.; (pl.) Good-Friday chiefly R.-C. set of antiphons & responses representing rr. of Christ to people. [f. F *reproche(r)* perh. ult. f. L *reprobare* REPROVE]

re·probāte[1], v.t. Express or feel disapproval of, censure; (of God) cast off, exclude from salvation. Hence **reproba·**TION n. [f. L *re(probare* APPROVE), RE- 7, -ATE[3]]

re·probate[2] (-*a*t), a. & n. (Person) cast off by God, hardened in sin, of abandoned character, immoral. [as prec., -ATE[2]]

reproduce &c. See RE- 8.

reproo·f, n. Blame (*a word, glance, of r.*; *spoke in r. of idleness*); a rebuke or expression of blame. [f. OF *reprove* (*reprover* REPROVE)]

repro·ve (-ōōv), v.t. Rebuke, chide, (person, rarely sin &c.). Hence **repro·ving**LY[2] adv. [f. OF *reprover* f. L as REPROBATE[1]]

reprovision. See RE- 8.

reps. See REP[1].

re·ptant, a. (nat. hist.). Creeping. [f. L *reptare* frequent. of *repere* crawl, -ANT]

re·ptile, n. & a. Crawling animal; member of the *Reptilia* or class of animals including snakes, lizards, crocodiles, turtles, & tortoises, whence **repti·l**IAN a. & n., **reptili·**FEROUS, **repti·li**FORM, aa.; mean grovelling person. (Adj.) (of animals) creeping; mean & grovelling (*the r. press*, subservient semi-official newspapers esp. in pre-war Germany). [(n. f. *reptile* neut.) f. LL *reptilis* (*repere rept-* crawl, -IL)]

repu·blic, n. A State in which the government is carried on nominally & usu. in fact also by the people or its elected representatives, commonwealth, (fig.) society of persons or animals with equality between members (*the r. of letters*, literary men, literature). [f. L *respublĭca* (abl. *republica*) f. *res* concern, PUBLIC*us*]

repu·blican, a. & n. Of, constituted as, characterizing, republic(s); (person) advocating or supporting r. government; (member) of U.-S. political party favouring liberal interpretation of constitution, extension of central power, & protective tariff; (of birds) social, living in large communities. Hence **repu·blican**ISM(3) n., **repu·blican**IZE(3) v.t. [-AN]

republish &c. See RE- 8.

repū·diate, v.t. & i. Divorce (one's wife; esp. of the ancients or non-Christians); disown, disavow, reject, refuse dealings with, deny; refuse to recognize or obey (authority) or discharge (obligation, debt), (of State) r. public debt. Hence **repudi**A·TION, **repu·diat**OR², nn. [f. L *repudiare* (*repudium* divorce, f. RE-, *pudēre* be ashamed, -ATE³)]

repūg·n, v.i. & t. (rare). Offer opposition; strive *against*; strive against; affect disagreeably, be repugnant to. [f. L *re(pugnare* fight) oppose, RE- 2]

repu·gnance, n. Inconsistency, incompatibility, of ideas, statements, tempers, &c. (*of, between, to, with*); antipathy, dislike, aversion, (*to, against*). [f. L *repugnantia* (prec., -ANCE)]

repu·gnant, a. Contradictory (*to*), incompatible (*with*); (poet.) refractory, resisting; distasteful (*to*). [f. L as REPUGN + -ANT]

repū·llulate, v.i. Sprout afresh, shoot out again; (of diseases) start again, recur. Hence **repullul**A·TION n. [f. L *re(pullulare* PULLULATE), RE- 9, -ATE³]

repu·lse, v.t., & n. Drive back, (attack, attacking enemy) by force of arms, (fig.) foil in controversy; rebuff (friendly advances or maker of them), refuse (request, offer, or maker of it). (N.) repulsing or being repulsed, rebuff, (*inflict, meet with, suffer*, &c., *r.* or usu. *a r.*). [(n. f. L *repulsa* or *repulsus -ūs*) f. REPEL*lere*]

repu·lsion, n. Repulsing (rare); (Physics) tendency of bodies to repel each other or increase their mutual distance (opp. ATTRACTION; also fig.), *capillary r.*, tendency in some liquids (e.g. quicksilver in glass) to shrink from wall of capillary tubes so that upper surface is convex; dislike, aversion, repugnance. [f. LL *repulsio* (REPEL, -ION)]

repu·lsive, a. Offering resistance (poet.); (Physics) exercising repulsion; (archaic, of behaviour &c.) repellent, cold, unsympathetic; exciting aversion or loathing, loathsome, disgusting, whence **repu·lsive**LY² adv., **repu·lsive**NESS n. [REPULSE v., -IVE]

repurchase, repurify. See RE- 9.

re·pūtable, a. Of good repute, respectable. Hence **re·putab**LY² adv. [REPUTE n., -ABLE]

reputa·tion, n. What is generally said or believed about a person's or thing's character (*has not justified his r.*); state of being well reported of, credit, distinction, respectability, good fame, (*persons of r.*; *has a r. for integrity*); *the* credit or discredit *of* doing or *of* being (*has the r. of racking his tenants, of being* or *of the best shot in England*). [f. L *reputatio* (REPUTE, -ATION)]

repu·te, v.t., & n. (Rare in active) consider or reckon, (pass.) be generally considered or reported of, (with compl., *to* be, or *as*; *is reputed the best doctor* or *to be* or rarely *as the best*); (pass.) be generally *well, ill*, &c., thought or spoken *of*; (p.p.) passing as but probably not being (*his reputed father, clemency*, &c., *reputed pint* &c., bottle of beer &c. sold as pint &c. but not guaranteed as imperial pint &c.); hence **repu·ted**LY² adv. (N.) reputation. [f. L *re(putare* think), RE- 6]

reque·st, n., & v.t. Act of asking for something, petition made, thing asked for, (*came at his r.*; *shall make two rr.*; *you shall have your r.*; *make r. for*; *by r.*, in response to expressed wish); state of being sought after, demand, (*is now in great, came into, r.*). (Vb) seek permission *to* do; ask to be given or allowed or favoured with (*r. candid consideration, person's presence*, &c.); ask *that*; ask (person) *to* do. [f. OF *requeste(r)*, see RE- 6, QUEST]

requicken. See RE- 9.

re·quiem, n. Special mass for repose of souls of the dead; musical setting for r.; dirge. [initial L wd (=rest) of the mass]

requie·scăt, n. Wish for dead person's repose; *r., requiescant, in pace*, abbr. R.I.P., inscription = may he, they, rest in peace, used esp. on R.-C. tombs. [L, = may he rest]

require·, v.t. & i. Order (person), demand (*of* person), *to* do (*they r. me* or *of me to appear*); demand or ask in words (person's action, act *of* person, thing *at* person's *hands, that*, &c.) esp. as of right (*they r. my appearance, an oath of me, a gift at my hands, that I should appear*); lay down as imperative (*had done all that was required by the Act*); need, call for, depend for success &c. on, (*the emergency requires it, that it should be done*; *irony re-*

quires care in its use; land requires 10 lb. of seed to the acre; place would r. an army to take it; machine requires no attention; it required all his authority to keep them in hand); (rare) be necessary (*do not tie it more tightly than requires*). Hence **re-quire·**MENT n. [f. L *re(quirere -quisit- =quaerere* seek), RE- 6]

re·quisite (-ĭzĭt), a. & n. Required by circumstances, necessary to success &c., called for; hence **re·quisite**NESS n. (N.) requirement, thing needed for accomplishment of some purpose (*for*). [f. L p.p. as prec.]

requisi·tion (-z), n., & v.t. Requiring, demand made, esp. formal & usu. written demand that some duty should be performed; order given to town &c. to furnish certain military supplies; being called or put into service (*is under* or *in r.*, being used or applied; *put in, call into, r.*, have recourse to). (Vb) demand use or supply of for military purposes; demand such supplies &c. from (town &c.); press into service, call in for some purpose. [f. L *requisitio* (REQUIRE, -ION)]

requi·te, v.t. Make return for, reward or avenge, (service, wrong, injury, treatment; often *with*); make return to, repay with good or evil, (person; often *for* treatment received, *with* treatment given); give in return (*r. like for like*). Hence **requi·**TAL(2) n. [RE- 1, *quite* var. of QUIT²]

re-read. See RE- 8.

rēre·dos, n. Ornamental screen covering wall at back of altar. [earlier *areredos* (REAR¹, F *dos* back f. L *dorsum*)]

rēs (-z), n. (L). Thing (*r. judicata*, =CHOSE JUGÉE); property (*r. angusta domi*, poverty).

resaddle, resale &c. See RE- 9.

rescind (-sĭ-), v.t. Abrogate, annul, revoke, cancel. So **resci·**SSION (-zhn), n. [f. L *re(scindere sciss-* cut), RE- 5]

rē·script, n. Roman emperor's written reply to appeal for guidance esp. from magistrate on legal point; Pope's decretal epistle in reply to question, any papal decision; ruler's or government's or official edict or announcement; thing rewritten, rewriting; palimpsest. [f. L p.p. neut. of *re(scribere script-* write), RE- 1]

re·scue, v.t., & n. Deliver from or *from* attack, custody, danger, or harm; (Law) unlawfully liberate (person), forcibly recover (property); hence **re·scu**ER¹ n. (N.) rescuing or being rescued, succour, deliverance, illegal liberation, forcible recovery. [f. OF *rescoure* (L RE-, EX*cutere* =*quatere* shake)]

resear·ch (-ertsh), n., & v.i. Careful search or inquiry *after* or *for*; (usu. pl.) endeavour to discover facts by scientific study of a subject, course of critical investigation, (*his rr. have been fruitful; is engaged in r.*). (Vb) make rr.; hence **re-sear·ch**ER¹ n. [f. obs. F *recerche(r)*, now *rechercher*, see RE- 6, SEARCH]

reseat. See RE- 8.

rese·ct, v.t. (surg.). Pare down (bone, cartilage, &c.). So **rese·ct**ION n. [f. L *re(secare sect-* cut), RE- 5]

resē·da, n. Genus of plants including mignonette & Dyer's weed; (usu. *réséda* F) pale green colour as of mignonette. [L, perh. imperat. of *re(sedare* quiet) allay, RE- 5, used as first wd of charm in applying plant to tumours]

reseek, see RE- 8; **reseize** &c., **resell,** RE- 9.

rese·mble (-z-), v.t. Be like, have similarity to or feature(s) in common with or same appearance as, & so **rese·mbl**ANCE (*to, between, of*) n., **rese·mbl**ANT (*to*) a. (rare); (archaic) liken *to*. [f. OF *re(sembler* f. L *similare, simulare*, f. *similis* SIMILAR), RE- 1]

rese·nt (-z-), v.t. Show or feel indignation at or retain feelings about (insult or injury sustained). Hence **rese·nt**FUL [perh. through obs. *resent* resentment] a., **re-sentful**LY² adv., **rese·nt**MENT n. [f. F *ressentir* (RE- 1, L *sentire* feel)]

reserva·tion, n. In vbl senses; also or esp.: (Eccl.) right reserved to Pope of nomination to vacant benefice, power of absolution reserved to superior, practice of retaining for some purpose a portion of the Eucharistic elements (esp. the bread) after celebration; (Law) right or interest retained in estate being conveyed, clause reserving it; (U.S.) tract of land reserved esp. for exclusive occupation by native tribe; express or tacit limitation or exception made about something (*mental r.*, qualification tacitly added in making statement, oath, &c. [f. LL *reservatio* (foll., -ATION)]

reser·ve¹ (-z-), v.t. Postpone use or enjoyment or treatment of, hold over, keep back for later occasion, (*r. oneself for*, not put forth one's energies till); retain possession or control of esp. by legal or formal stipulation (*for* or *to* oneself or another; *reserved seats* at entertainment &c., that may be booked; *reserved list*, of naval officers removed from active service but liable to be called out), (pass.) be left by fate *for*, fall first or only *to*; set apart, destine, *for* some use or fate; (p.p. as adj.) reticent, slow to reveal emotions or opinions, uncommunicative, whence **reser·vĕd**LY² adv. [f. OF *reserver* f. L *re(servare* keep), RE- 3]

reser·ve², n. Something reserved for future use, extra stock or amount, (*banker's r.*, amount kept on hand to meet probable demands; *has a great r. of energy*; often attrib., as *his r. strength*); (Mil., sing. or pl.) troops withheld from action to reinforce or cover retreat, forces outside regular army & navy liable to be called out in emergencies, member of such forces (also

reser·VIST n.), (in games) extra player chosen in case substitute should be needed; being kept unused but available (*has it in r.*); place reserved for some special use; (at exhibitions) distinction conveying that exhibit will have prize if another is disqualified; limitation, exception, restriction, or qualification, attached to something (*I accept your statement without r.*, fully; *sale* or *auction without r.*, not subject to a fixed price's being reached; *r. price*, than which less will not be accepted; *we publish this with all r., all proper rr.*, without endorsing it); self-restraint, abstinence from exaggerated or ill-proportioned effects, in artistic or literary expression; reticence, avoidance of plain speaking, coolness of manner, lack of cordiality; intentional suppression of truth. [f. F *réserve* (*réserver*, OF *reserver* RESERVE[1])]

re·servoir (-vwar), n., & v.t. Receptacle constructed usu. of earthwork or masonry in which large quantity of water is stored; any natural or artificial receptacle esp. for or of fluid, place where fluid &c. collects, part of machine or organ of body holding fluid (*r. pen*, containing its own supply of ink), reserve supply or collection *of* something e.g. knowledge or facts, &c.; (vb) store in r. [f. F *réservoir* (LL *reservatorium*, cf. COUNTER[1], PARLOUR) f. *réserver* see prec., -ORY(2)]

rese·t[1], v.t. & i. (-tt-; archaic). Receive (stolen goods); receive stolen goods. So **rese·tt**ER[1] n. [f. OF *receter* f. L *receptare* frequent. of *recipere* RECEIVE]

reset[2], **resettle** &c., **reshape,** see RE- 8; **reship** &c., RE- 9; **reshuffle,** RE- 8.

resi·de (-z-), v.i. (Of persons) have one's home, dwell permanently, *at, in, abroad*, &c.; (of officials) be in residence; (of power, rights, &c.) rest or be vested *in* person &c.; (of qualities) be present or inherent *in*. [f. L *re*(*sidēre* = *sedēre* sit), RE- 3]

re·sidence, n. Residing (*have, take up*, one's *r.*, dwell, begin to dwell; *honoured the place with her r.*; *r. is required*, official &c. must live on the spot for certain periods or altogether; so *in r.*); place where one resides, abode *of*; house esp. of considerable pretension, mansion, (*desirable family r. for sale*). [f. F *résidence* f. L *residentia* (prec., -ENCE)]

re·sidency, n. Official residence of Governor-general's representative at Indian native court. [as prec., -ENCY]

re·sident, a. & n. Residing (*whether r. at home or abroad*; *the r. population*); (of birds &c.) non-migratory; bound to residence, having quarters on the spot, (*r. surgeon, tutor, political agent*); inherent, located, *in* (*a right r. in the nation*; *powers of sensation r. in the nerves*). (N.) permanent inhabitant of town or neighbourhood (opp. *visitor*); Indian Governor-general's political agent residing at native court, British government agent in other semi-dependent State, whence **re·sident**SHIP n. [f. L (RESIDE, -ENT)]

reside·ntial (-shl), a. Suitable for or occupied by private houses (*r. estate, street, quarter*); connected with residence (*the r. qualification for voters*). [RESIDENCE, -AL]

reside·ntiary (-sha-), n. & a. Ecclesiastic bound to residence; (adj.) bound to, requiring, of or for, official residence (usu. after n.; *Canon, Canonry, r.*; *at his r. house*). [f. med. L *residentiarius* (RESIDENCE, -ARY[1])]

resi·dual, a. & n. (Math.) resulting from subtraction (n., r. quantity); remaining, left over, left as residuum, (n., remainder, substance of the nature of a residuum); (of error in calculations) still unaccounted for or not eliminated. [RESIDUUM, -AL]

resi·duary, a. Of the residue of an estate (*r. bequest, clause, legatee, &c.*); of, being, a residuum, residual, still remaining, (*mere r. substances*; *the r. aberration*; *some r. odds & ends*). [RESIDUUM, -ARY]

re·sidue, n. Remainder, rest, what is left or remains over; what remains of estate after payment of charges, debts, & bequests; (Chem. &c.) residuum. [f. F *résidu* RESIDUUM]

resi·duum (-z-), n. (pl. *-dua*). What remains, esp. (Chem. &c.) substance left after combustion or evaporation, (in calculations) amount not accounted for or residual error; lowest stratum or dregs of population. [L, neut. of *residuus* remaining (RESIDE)]

resig·n[1] (-z-), v.t. & i. Relinquish, surrender, give up, hand over, (office, right, claim, property, charge, task, life, hope; often *to* person, *into* person's hands &c.; *r.* one*self to* another's *guidance, to sleep, rest, meditation*, &c.); reconcile one*self*, one's *mind*, &c. (*to* one's *fate* &c., *to doing*, or abs. = accept the inevitable without repining), whence **resig·n**ED[1] a., **resig·nĕd**LY[2] adv.; give up office, retire. [f. OF *resigner* f. L *re*(*signare* seal) unseal, cancel, RE- 7]

re-sign[2], v.t. & i. Sign again. [RE- 8]

resigna·tion (-zĭg-), n. In vbl senses (RESIGN[1]); esp.: resigning of an office, document conveying it (*give, send in*, one's *r.*); being resigned, uncomplaining endurance of sorrow or other evil. [f. F *résignation* (RESIGN[1], -ATION)]

resi·le (-z-), v.i. (Of elastic bodies) recoil, rebound, resume shape & size after stretching or compression; have or show elasticity or buoyancy or recuperative power. Hence **resi·li**ENCE, **resi·li**ENCY, nn., **resi·li**ENT a. [f. L *re*(*silire* = *salire* jump), RE- 9]

rĕ·sin (-z-), n., & v.t. Adhesive substance

insoluble in water (cf. GUM) secreted by most plants & exuding naturally or upon incision esp. from fir & pine; kinds of similar substance got by chemical process; (v.t.) rub or treat with r. Hence **resin**A·CEOUS, **resini·**FEROUS, **re·sini**FORM, **re·sin**OUS, aa., **re·sin**OID a. & n., **re·sin**ATE[1](3) n., **re·sini**FY v.t. & i., **re·si**NIFICA·TION n., **re·sino**- comb. form. [f. F *résine* f. L *resina* cogn. w. Gk *rētinē*]

resipi·scence, n. Recognition of error, return to good sense. So **resipi·sc**ENT a. [f. L (*-ntia*) f. *re(sipiscere* f. *sapere* see SAPIENT), RE- 9]

resi·st (-z-), v.t. & i., & n. Stop course of, successfully oppose, keep off or out, prevent from penetrating, repel, be proof against or unaffected or uninjured by, abstain from, (projectile, weapon, edge, frost, heat, moisture, attack, temptation, power, infection, influence, suggestion, &c.; *who can r. God's will?*; *cannot r. a joke*, must make it if it suggests itself, or must be amused by it), whence **resi·st**IBLE a., **resi·st**LESS a. (poet.), **resi·stless**LY[2] adv.; strive against, oppose, try to impede, refuse to comply with; offer resistance, make opposition, whence or cogn. **resi·st**ANT, **resi·st**ENT, **resi·st**IVE, aa., **resi·st**ER[1] n. (*passive r.*, person refusing on grounds of justice to pay education rate). (N.) composition applied to surfaces for protection from some agent employed on them, esp. to parts of calico that are not to take dye. [f. L *re(sistere* redupl. of *stare* stand), RE- 2]

resi·stance, n. (Power of) resisting (*passive r.*, refusal to comply; *something with greater r. for its weight than steel*); hindrance, impeding or stopping effect, exercised by material thing upon another (*overcome the r. of the air*; *r. of fluids varies with their specific gravity*; *line of r.*, direction in which it acts; *take line of least r.* fig., adopt easiest method or course); (Electr., Magnet., Heat) non-conductivity; (Electr.) part of apparatus used to offer definite r. to current. [f. F *résistance* (prec., -ANCE)]

resistibi·lity, n. Being resistible; power of offering resistance. [RESIST*ible*, -BILITY]

resole. See RE- 8.

re·soluble (-zolōō-, -lū-), a. That can be resolved, (usu.) analysable *into*, resolvable. [f. LL *resolubilis* (RESOLVE, & see SOLUBLE)]

re·solute (-zolōōt, -ūt), a. (Of person or his temper or action) determined, decided, bold, not vacillating, unshrinking, firm of purpose. Hence **re·solute**LY[2] adv. [f. L p.p., see RESOLVE]

resolu·tion (-lōō-, -lū-), n. Separation into components, decomposition, analysis, conversion *into* other form, (Med.) disappearance of inflammation without suppuration, (Pros.) substitution of two short syllables for one long, (Mus.) making of discord to pass into concord, (Mech.) replacing of single force by two or more jointly equivalent; solving *of* doubt, problem, question, &c.; formal expression of opinion by legislative body (cf. MOTION) or public meeting, form proposed for this; resolve, thing resolved on, (*good rr.*, intentions that one formulates mentally for virtuous conduct); determined temper or character, boldness & firmness of purpose. [f. L *resolutio* (RESOLVE, -ION)]

re·solutive, a. & n. Having dissolving power (chiefly med.; *r. cataplasm* &c.; n., r. application or drug); (Law) *r. condition*, whose fulfilment terminates contract &c. [prec., -IVE]

reso·lve (-z-), v.t. & i., & n. Dissolve (t. & i.; *into*), disintegrate, analyse, break up into parts, dissipate, convert or be converted *into*, reduce by mental analysis *into*, (*used vinegar to r. the rocks*; *blood first coagulates & then resolves*; *r. thing, thing is resolved* or *resolves itself* or *resolves, into its elements*; *telescope resolves nebula into stars*; *inflammation, tumour, is resolved* or *resolves*, passes away without suppuration; *House resolves itself into a committee*; *might r. Christianity into a system of morality*), (Mus.) convert (discord) or be converted into concord; solve, explain, clear up, settle, (*all doubts were resolved*; *r. me this* archaic, answer this question; *the problem of its origin has not yet been resolved*); decide upon, make up one's mind *upon* action or do*ing* or *to* do, form mentally or (of legislative body or public meeting) pass by vote the resolution *that*, (of circumstances &c.) bring (person) to resolution *to* do or *upon* action or do*ing*, (*he resolved upon* or rarely *resolved amendment*; *resolved that nothing should induce him, that he would do, upon doing*; *the House began by resolving that . . .*; *this discovery resolved us on going* or *to go*; p.p. used in minutes of meeting, = the following resolution was passed, namely *that*; p.p. as adj., resolute, whence **reso·lvĕd**LY[2] adv.); hence **reso·lv**ABLE a. (N.) resolution come to in the mind (*& she kept her r.*); (poet.) resolution, steadfastness, (*a mind, deeds, of high r.*). [f. L *re(solvere solut-* SOLVE), RE- 5]

reso·lvent, a. & n. (chiefly med. & chem.). (Drug, application, substance) effecting resolution of tumour &c. or division into component parts. [prec., -ENT]

re·sonant (-z-), a. (Of sound) echoing, resounding, continuing to sound, reinforced or prolonged by vibration or reflexion; (of bodies, rooms, &c.) tending to reinforce or prolong sounds esp. by vibration; (of places) resounding *with*. Hence or cogn. **re·son**ANCE n., **re·sonant**LY[2] adv. [f. L *re(sonare* sound), RE- 6, -ANT]

re·sonator, n. Instrument responding to single note & used for detecting it in combinations; appliance for giving resonance to sounds. [as prec., -OR[2]]

resor·b, v.t. Absorb again. Hence **re-sor·b**ENCE n., **resor·b**ENT a. [f. L *re(sorbēre sorpt-* ABSORB), RE- 9]

resor·cin (-z-), n. Compound got by action of potash on resin used chiefly as dye-stuff. [RESIN, ORCIN]

resor·ption, n. Resorbing or being resorbed. [RESORB, -ION]

resor·t¹ (-z-), v.i. Turn for aid *to* (*r. to force, experiment,* &c., or rarely concrete object or person); go in numbers or often *to* (*visitors resorted to him, to the shrine, by the hundred; watched the inn to which he was known to r.*). [f. OF *re(sortir* come out, etym. dub.), RE- 8]

resor·t², n. Thing to which recourse is had, what is turned to for aid, expedient, (*a carriage, repetition of the experiment, was the only r.*); recourse (*cannot be done without r. to compulsion; in the last r.*, when all else has failed, as final attempt); frequenting or being frequented (*encouraged the r. of scholars; a place of great r.*); place frequented usu. for specified purpose or quality (*health, holiday, r.; mountain, seaside, r.*). [OF (prec.)]

re-sor·t³, v.t. Sort again. [RE- 8]

resou·nd (-zow-), v.i. & t. (Of place) ring or echo (*with*); (of voice, instrument, sound, &c.) produce echoes, go on sounding, fill place with sound; (of fame, event, &c.) be much talked of, produce sensation, (often *through* Europe &c.); repeat loudly (usu. *the praises* &c. *of*); (of place) give back (sound). Hence **resou·nding-**LY² adv. [RE- 9, SOUND, after L as RESONANT]

resour·ce (-sōrs), n. (Usu. in pl.) means of supplying a want, stock that can be drawn on, (pl.) country's collective means for support & defence; (after French; now rare) possibility of aid (*lost without r.*); expedient, device, shift, (*flight was his only r.; am at the end of my rr.*); leisure occupation (*reading is a great r.; a man of no rr.*); skill in devising expedients, practical ingenuity, quick wit, (*is full of r.*). Hence **resour·ce**FUL, **resour·ce**LESS, aa., **resour·ceful**NESS, **resour·celess-**NESS, nn., **resour·ceful**LY² adv. [f. F *ressource* f. OF *re(s)sourdre* f. RE- 9, L *surgere* rise]

respe·ct¹, n. Reference, relation, (*to; the terms have r. to position alone; is true with r. to the French; with r. to possible routes, there are three; ablative, accusative, of r.* in Lat. Gram., those translatable by *with r.* or *as to*); heed or regard *to* or *of*, attention to, (*have not had* or *paid r. to anything but colour; did it quite without r. to the results; r. of persons,* partiality or favour shown esp. to the powerful); particular, detail, point, aspect, (*of; is admirable in r. of style; in all, many, some, rr.; in one, this, r.*); (archaic) consideration *that* (*is out of the question, in r. that it stultifies the whole plan*); deferential esteem felt or shown towards person or quality (*has won the r. of all; have the greatest r. for him; is held in r.*; SELF-*r.*); (pl., with *my* &c.) polite messages or attentions (*give him my, sends his, rr.; went to pay his rr. to*). [f. L *respectus -ūs* (*respicere* see foll.)]

respe·ct², v.t. Pay heed to (archaic; *r. persons,* discriminate unfairly between them under influence of wealth &c., whence **respe·ct**ER¹ n. *of persons*); relate to, be concerned with, (now rare exc. in part., as *legislation respecting property,* also used as prep., as *am at a loss respecting his whereabouts*); regard with deference; avoid degrading or insulting or injuring or interfering with or interrupting, treat with consideration, spare, (*r. oneself,* refrain from unworthy conduct or thoughts, have self-r.; *r. innocence* or *the innocent,* refrain from offending or corrupting or tempting; *respected my silence,* let me remain silent; *r. privileges, property, neutral territory,* &c.). [f. L *re(spicere spect-* = *specere* look at), RE- 6]

respectabi·lity, n. Being, those who are, *a* person who is, socially respectable. [foll., -BILITY]

respe·ctable, a. & n. Deserving respect (*did it from r. motives*); not inconsiderable in amount &c., of some merit or importance, fairly good or many or much, tolerable, passable, (*a r. hill, antiquity, painter, minority; r. talents*); of fair social standing, having the qualities necessary for such standing, not disreputable, honest & decent in conduct, (of pursuits, clothes, &c.) befitting r. persons; hence **respe·ctab**LY² adv. (N.) *a* r. person (usu. in pl.). [-ABLE]

respe·ctful, a. Showing deference (*r. behaviour; stood at a r. distance*). Hence **re-spe·ctful**LY² adv., **respec·tful**NESS n. [-FUL]

respe·ctive, a. Each's own, proper to each, individual, several, comparative, (*go to your, put them in their, r. places; were given places according to their r. rank* or *ranks; A & B contributed the r. sums of 4d. & 3d.; the election depends on the r. popularity of the candidates*). Hence **re-spe·ctive**LY² adv. [f. LL *respectivus* (RESPECT², -IVE)]

respell. See RE- 8.

re·spirable (*or* -īr·-), a. (Of air, gas, &c.) that can, fit to, be breathed. [f. LL *respirabilis* (RESPIRE, -ABLE)]

respira·tion, n. Breathing; single inspiration & expiration; plant's absorption of oxygen & emission of carbon dioxide. [f. L *respiratio* (RESPIRE, -ATION)]

re·spirātor, n. Apparatus of gauze &c. worn over mouth (& nose) to warm or filter inhaled air; (Mil.) kinds of chemical filtering-apparatus worn for defence against poison gas (*box r.*, the British pattern). [f. L as foll. + -OR²]

respire·, v.i. & t. Breathe, inhale & exhale, air, whence **re·spirā**TORY a.; breathe (air &c.); (rare) exhale (perfume, amiability, &c.); breathe again, take breath, recover hope or spirit, get rest or respite. [f. L *re(spirare* breathe), RE- 9]

re·spite, n., & v.t. Delay permitted in the discharge of an obligation or suffering of a penalty; interval of rest or relief. (Vb) grant r. to, reprieve, (condemned person); postpone execution or exaction of (sentence, obligation); give temporary relief from (pain, care) or to (sufferer); (Mil). withhold (pay), withhold pay from. [f. OF *respit* f. L RESPECT¹*us*]

resple·ndent, a. Brilliant, dazzlingly or gloriously bright. Hence or cogn. **re-sple·nd**ENCE, **resple·nd**ENCY, nn., **re-sple·ndent**LY² adv. [f. L *re(splendēre* glitter), RE- 6, -ENT]

respo·nd¹, v.i. Make answer (esp. of congregation making set answers to priest &c.); perform answering or corresponding action (*responded with a drop-kick, left-hander*, &c.); show sensitiveness *to* by behaviour or change (*does nor r. to kindness*; *nerve responds to stimulus, string to note*, &c.); (rare) correspond, be analogous, whence or cogn. **respo·nd**ENCE, **re-spo·nd**ENCY, nn. [f. L *re(spondēre spons-* pledge) answer, RE- 1]

respo·nd², n. (Eccl.) = RESPONSORY, also response to versicle; (Arch.) half-pillar or half-pier attached to wall to support arch. [OF (*respondre* answer, as prec.)]

respo·ndent, a. & n. Making answer; responsive *to*; in position of defendant. (N.) one who makes answer, defends thesis, &c.; defendant esp. in divorce case. [as RESPOND¹, -ENT]

respo·nse, n. Answer given in word or act, reply, retort, (*in r. to*; *made no r.*; *the rr. of the oracles*; *his r. was the proclamation of martial law*); feeling, movement, &c., elicited by stimulus or influence (*called forth no r. in his breast*); (Eccl.) = RESPONSORY, also any part of liturgy said or sung in answer to priest. [f. L *responsum* neut. p.p. (RESPOND¹)]

responsibi·lity, n. Being responsible (*declines all r. for it*; *will take the r. of doing it*; *did it on his own r.*, without authorization; *is not afraid of r.*, of having to act without detailed guidance); charge for which one is responsible (*a family is a great r.*; *asked to be relieved of his r.* or *rr.*). [foll., -BILITY]

respo·nsible, a. Liable to be called to account, answerable (*to* person, *for* thing, or abs.; *r. ruler, government*, not autocratic), morally accountable for actions, capable of rational conduct; of good credit or position or repute, respectable, apparently trustworthy; involving responsibility (*a r. office*). Hence **respo·nsib**LY² adv. [obs. F (L RESPOND¹*ēre*, -IBLE)]

respo·nsions, n. pl. First of three examinations for Oxford B.A. degree (also *smalls* colloq.; cf. *moderations, greats, final schools*). [f. L *responsio* (RESPOND¹, -ION)]

respo·nsive, a. Answering, by way of answer, (of liturgy &c.) using responses; responding readily to or *to* some influence, impressionable, sympathetic. Hence **re-spo·nsive**LY² adv., **respo·nsive**NESS n. [f. LL *responsivus* (RESPOND¹, -IVE)]

respo·nsory, n. Anthem said or sung by soloist & choir after lesson. [f. LL *responsoria* neut. pl. (RESPOND¹, -ORY)]

ressaldar·, n. Native captain in Indian cavalry regiment. [f. Hind. *risaladar* (*risalah* squadron f. Arab. *arsala* he sent, *dar* having)]

rest¹, v.i. & t. Be still, cease or abstain or be relieved from exertion or action or movement or employment, lie in sleep or death, be tranquil, be let alone, (*waves that never r.*; *r. upon* one's *oars*, temporarily cease rowing or any exertion; *never let your enemy r.*; *let us r. here*, cease walking &c.; *r. from* one's *labours*; *rests in the church-yard*, lies buried; *let her r. in peace*; *is too feverish to r.*; *could not r. under an imputation, till he got his wish*; *land was allowed to r.*, left fallow; *the matter cannot r. here*, must be further examined &c.), give relief or repose to (*stayed a day to r. myself*; *r. your men for an hour*; *says the goggles r. his eyes*; *must r. the ground*; *r.* or *God r. his soul*, may God give it repose), (p.p.) refreshed or reinvigorated by resting (*are you quite rested?*); lie, be spread out, be supported or based, depend, rely, (of eyes &c.) alight or be steadily directed, (*up*)*on* (*shadow, light, rests on his face*; *roof rests on four arches*; *their left rested on the river*; *hand resting on the table*; *science rests on phenomena*; *I r. upon your promise*; *his gaze rested on a strange object*), be propped *against*, repose trust *in* (*be content to r. in God*), place for support or foundation (*up*)*on* (*r.* one's *elbow, load, on the table*; *r.* one's *case on equity, unimpeachable evidence*); *resting-place*, provided or used for resting (*last r.-p.*, the grave). [OE *ræstan*, cf. G *rasten*, Du. *rusten*]

rest², n. Repose or sleep esp. in bed at night (*go, retire, to r.*; *take r.* or one's *r.*); abstinence or freedom from or absence of exertion or activity or movement or care or molestation, a period of such abstinence &c., (*day of r.*, Sunday; *a r. from work* &c.; *give person, horse, machine*, &c., *a r.*; *take a short r.*; *at r.*, still, not agitated or troubled, often of the dead; *set question*, person's *mind, at r.*, settle, relieve; *lay to r.*, bury); lodging-place or shelter provided for sailors, cabmen, or other class; prop or support or steadying-piece, e.g.

for gun in aiming, billiard-cue, cutting-tool in lathe, or foot on bicycle; (Mus.) appointed interval of silence or sign denoting it; pause in elocution, caesura in verse; *r.-balk,* ridge left unploughed between furrows; *r.-cure,* r. usu. of some weeks in bed as medical treatment; *r.-day,* day spent in r., (rare) Sunday; *r.-house,* dawk-bungalow. [OE *ræst,* cf. G *rast,* Du. *rust*]

rest[3], v.i. Remain over (archaic; *whatever rests of hope*); *r. with,* be left in the hands or charge of (*it rests with you to propose terms; the management of affairs rested with Wolsey*); remain in specified state (*the affair rests a mystery; r. assured, satisfied,* &c.; also archaic in epistolary forms, as *I r. your devoted friend*). [f. F *rester* f. L *re(stare* stand), RE- 3]

rest[4], n. *The* remaining part(s) or individuals *of, the* remainder of some quantity or number, *the* others, (*& the* or *all the r. of it,* & all else that might be mentioned; *for the r.,* as regards anything beyond what has been specially mentioned); (Banking) reserve fund; (Commerc.) stocktaking & balancing; (Tennis &c.) spell of continuous returns. [f. F *reste* (prec.)]

rest[5], n. (hist.). Check holding butt of medieval tilter's spear when couched for charging (*with, lay* or *set* one's, *lance in r.*). [for ARREST[1], & see REST[3]]

restamp, restart, restate &c. See RE- 8.

re·staurant (*-or-, or as F*), n. Place where meals or refreshments may be had. [F (*restaurer* RESTORE, -ANT)]

restaurateur (F), n. Restaurant-keeper.

re·stful, a. Favourable to repose, free from disturbing influences, soothing. Hence **re·stful**LY[2] adv., **re·stful**NESS n. [-FUL]

re·st-harrow, n. A tough-rooted shrub, cammock. [obs. *rest* v. as REST[5], HARROW[1]]

restiff. See RESTIVE.

re·stitute, v.t. & i. (rare). Make restitution (of). [f. L *re(stituere -tut- =statuere* set up), RE- 8]

restitu·tion, n. Restoring of or *of* thing to proper owner, reparation for injury, (esp. *make r.; r. of conjugal rights,* name of a matrimonial lawsuit); restoring of thing to its original state (esp. theol. *the r. of all things*); resumption of original shape or position by elasticity. [f. L *restitutio* (prec., -ION)]

re·stive, re·stiff (archaic), a. (Of horse) refusing to advance, stubbornly standing still or moving backwards or sideways, jibbing, refractory; (of person) unmanageable, rejecting control. Hence **re·stive**LY[2] adv., **re·stive**NESS n. [earlier sense *inert*; orig. form *-iff,* f. OF *restif* (REST[3], -IVE)]

re·stless, a. Finding or affording no rest, uneasy, agitated, never still, ever in motion, unpausing, fidgeting. Hence **re·stless**LY[2] adv., **re·stless**NESS n. [REST[2], -LESS]

restock. See RE- 8.

restora·tion, n. In senses of RESTORE; also or esp.: (period of) re-establishment of monarchy in 1660; model or drawing representing supposed original form of extinct animal, ruined building, &c. [earlier *restauration* f. L *restauratio* (RESTORE, -ION) w. assim. to *restore*]

restora·tionism, n. Doctrine that all men will ultimately be restored to happiness in future life. So **restora·tion**IST(2) n. [-ISM]

restŏ·rative, a. & n. Tending to restore health or strength; (n.) r. food, medicine, or agency. Hence **restor·ative**LY[2] adv. [f. OF *restauratif -ive* (foll., -IVE)]

restore·, v.t. Give back, make restitution of; (attempt to) bring back to original state by rebuilding, repairing, repainting, emending, &c. (*church, picture, text, has been restored, spoilt in restoring, restored out of all recognition,* &c.); make representation of supposed original state of (extinct animal, ruin, &c.); reinstate, bring back *to* dignity or right; bring back to or *to* health &c., cure (person); re-establish, renew, bring back into use; reinsert by conjecture (missing words in text, parts of extinct animal, &c.); replace, put back, bring *to* former place or condition. Hence **restor·**ABLE a., **restor·**ER[1] n. [f. OF *restorer* f. L *re(staurare* cf. Gk *stauros* stake), RE- 9]

restrai·n[1], v.t. Check or hold in *from,* keep in check or under control or within bounds, repress, keep down; confine, imprison. Hence **restrai·n**ABLE a., **restrai·nĕd**LY[2] adv. (esp., with self-restraint). [f. OF *restrai(g)n-* st. of *restraindre* f. L *re(stringere strict-* tie), RE- 2]

re-strai·n[2], v.t. Strain again. [RE- 8]

restrai·nt, n. Restraining or being restrained, stoppage, check, controlling agency or influence, confinement esp. in asylum, (*without r.,* freely, copiously; *is under r.,* esp. as lunatic); constraint or reserve of manner; self-control, avoidance of excess or exaggeration, austerity of literary expression; *r. of princes,* embargo. [f. OF *restrainte* (RESTRAIN[1])]

restri·ct, v.t. Confine, bound, limit, (*to, within; has a very restricted application; am restricted to advising; is restricted within narrow limits*). Hence or cogn. **restri·ct**ION n., **restri·ct**IVE a., **restri·cted**LY[2], **restri·ctive**LY[2], advv. [f. L, see RESTRAIN]

restuff. See RE- 8.

resu·lt (-z-), v.i., & n. Arise as actual or follow as logical consequence (*from* conditions, causes, premisses, &c., or abs.); have issue or end in specified manner esp. *in* failure &c. (*resulted badly, in a large profit*). (N.) consequence, issue, or outcome of something (*without r.*, in vain, fruitless), whence **resu·lt**FUL, **resu·lt**LESS, aa.; quantity, formula, &c., given by calculation. [n. f.vb, f. L *re*(*sultare* = *saltare* frequent. of *salire* jump), RE- 9]

resu·ltant, a. & n. Resulting, esp. as total outcome of more or less opposed forces; (n.) composite effect of two or more forces acting in different directions at same point (esp. in Mech., also transf.). [prec., -ANT]

resu·me (-z-), v.t. & i. Get or take again or back, recover, reoccupy, (*r.* one's *spirits, sway, liberty, seat*; *r. gift, grant, territory*); begin again (upon), go on (with) after interruption, begin to speak or work again, recommence t. & i., (*House resumed work* or *its labours*, or *resumed*; *r. thread of* one's *discourse*; *r. pipe*, go on smoking again; '*No, it is hopeless*' *he resumed*); make résumé of, recapitulate, summarize. [f. L *re*(*sumere sumpt-* take), RE- 8]

résumé (rĕ·zōōmā, *or as F*), n. Summary, epitome, abstract. [F, p.p. of *résumer* RESUME]

resummons. See RE- 8.

resu·mption (-z-), n. Resuming. So **resu·mpt**IVE a., **resu·mptive**LY[2] adv. [f. L *resumptio* (RESUME, -ION)]

resū·pinate (-at), a. (bot.). (Of leaf &c.) inverted, bottom up. Hence **resupin**A·TION n. [f. L *re*(*supinare* make SUPINE), RE- 9]

resur·ge, v.i. (rare exc. facet.). Experience resurrection, revive, rise or arise again. So (in ordinary use) **resur·g**ENT(1) n. & a., **resur·g**ENCE n. [f. L *re*(*surgere surrect-* rise f. SUR-[1], *regere* direct), RE- 9]

resurre·ct, v.t. (colloq.). Raise from the dead (rare); revive practice or memory of; take from grave, exhume. [back form. f. foll.]

resurre·ction (-z-), n. (Festival in memory of) rising of Christ from the grave; rising again of men at the last day; exhumation lit. or fig., resurrecting (*r. man*, BODY-snatcher), whence **resurre·ction**IST(1) n.; revival from disuse or inacti ity or decay, restoration to vogue or memory, (*r. pie*, made from remains of previous meals.) Hence **resurre·ction**AL a. [f. LL *resurrectio* (RESURGE, -ION)]

resurvey. See RE- 8.

resu·scitate (-sĭ-), v.t. & i. Revive, return or usu. restore to life, consciousness, vogue, vigour, or vividness. Hence or cogn. **resuscit**A·TION, **resu·scitat**OR[2](1, 2), nn., **resu·scit**ATIVE a. [f. L *re*(SUS*citare* CITE), RE- 9, -ATE[3]]

ret, rate, rait, v.t. & i. Soften (flax, hemp) by soaking or exposing to moisture; (of hay &c., in pass. or intr.) be spoilt by wet, rot. [cf. Du. *reten, roten*, Sw. *röta*; cogn. w. ROT[2]]

retā·ble, n. Shelf, or frame enclosing decorated panels, above back of altar. [f. F *rétable* (RE-, TABLE), cf. med. L *retrotabulum*]

rē·tail[1], n. Sale of goods in small quantities (esp. *by r.*, or attrib. as *r. trading, dealer*; also adv., esp. in conjunction w. *wholesale*, as *Do you buy wholesale or r.?*). [OF, = piece cut off f. *re*(*taillier* cut, see TAILOR), RE- 5]

retai·l[2], v.t. & i. Sell (goods) by r.; (of goods) be retailed (esp. *at* or *for* specified price); recount, relate details of. Hence **retai·l**ER[1] n. [prob. f. prec.]

retai·n, v.t. Keep in place, hold fixed, (*retaining wall*, supporting & confining mass of earth or water; *retaining force* mil., posted to keep part of enemy inactive &c.); secure services of (esp. barrister) by engagement & preliminary payment (*retaining fee*, retainer); keep possession of, not lose, continue to have; continue to practise or recognize, allow to remain or prevail, not abolish or discard or alter; succeed in remembering, not forget. Hence **retai·n**ABLE a. [f. OF *retenir* f. L *re*(*tinēre tent-* = *tenēre* hold), RE- 3]

retai·ner, n. 1. (Law) formal retention of something as one's own, authorization to retain thus; being retained to serve in some capacity; fee paid to barrister &c. for right to his services if required. 2. In vbl senses; esp. (hist.), dependant or follower of person of rank. [RETAIN + (sense 1) -ER[4], (sense 2) -ER[1]]

retake. See RE- 9.

retă·liate, v.t. & i. Repay (injury, insult, &c., rarely kindness &c.) in kind; retort (accusation) *upon* person; do as one is done by, esp. return evil, make reprisals, (Pol. Econ.) impose duties on imports from foreign State in return for its import duties. Hence **retali**A·TION n., **reta·li**ATIVE, **reta·liat**ORY, aa. [f. L *re*(*taliare* f. *talis* such), RE- 1]

retar·d, v.t. & i., & n. Make slow or late, delay progress or arrival or accomplishment or happening of; (esp. of physical phenomena, e.g. motion of tides, waves, or celestial bodies) happen, arrive, behind normal or calculated time; hence or cogn. **rētard**A·TION, **retar·d**MENT, nn., **retar·d**ATIVE, **retar·dat**ORY, aa. (N.) retardation (*r. of tide* or *high water*, interval between full moon & following high water). [f. F *retard*(*er*) f. L *re*(*tardare* f. *tardus* slow), RE- 3]

retaste. See RE- 8.

rētch, v.i., & n. Make motion of vomiting esp. ineffectually & involuntarily; (n.) such motion or sound of it. [OE *hrǣcan* spit (*hrāca* spittle, cf. ON *hraki*)]

retell. See RE- 8.

rete·ntion, n. RETAIN*ing*; esp. (Med.) failure to evacuate urine or other secretion. [OF, f. L *retentionem* (RETAIN, -ION)]

rete·ntive, a. (Of memory, or rarely of

person in that respect) tenacious, not forgetful; (of substances) *r. of* moisture &c., apt to retain it (also *r.* abs., retentive of moisture); (Surg., of ligature &c.) serving to keep something in place. Hence **rete·ntive**LY[2] adv., **rete·ntive**NESS n. [OF (*-if, -ive*), see RETAIN, -IVE]

retenue (F), n. Reserve, self-control.

rē·tiary (-sh*a*-), n. Net-making or geometrical spider. [f. L *retiarius* (gladiator) with net (*rete* net, -ARY[1])]

re·ticence, n. Reserve in speech, avoidance of saying all one knows or feels, abstinence from over-emphasis in art; holding back of some fact; disposition to silence, taciturnity. So **re·tic**ENT a. (*on, upon, about*), **re·ticent**LY[2] adv. [f. L *reticentia* f. *re*(*ticēre* = *tacēre* be silent), RE- 4]

rĕ·ticle, n. Network of fine threads or lines in object-glass of telescope to help accurate observation. [f. L RETICULUM]

reti·culate, v.t. & i. Divide or be divided in fact or appearance into a network, arrange or be arranged in small squares or with intersecting lines. So (see etym.) **reti·cul**ATE[2] (*-at*) a., **reti·culate**LY[2] adv., **reticul**A·TION n., **reti·culat**o- comb. form. [vb by back form. f. *reticulated* f. *reticulate* a. (RETICULUM, -ATE[2])]

rĕ·ticule, n. =RETICLE; lady's netted or other bag carried or worn to serve purpose of pocket; (Astron.) a Southern constellation. [f. F *réticule* f. L (foll.)]

retĭ·culum, n. (pl. *-la*). Ruminant's second stomach or honeycomb; netlike structure, reticulated membrane &c., whence **reti·cul**AR[1], **reti·cul**OSE[1], aa., **reti·culo**- comb. form. [L (*rete* net, -CULE)]

rē·tiform, n. Netlike, reticulated. [f. L *rete* net, -I-, -FORM]

rĕ·tina, n. (pl. *-as, -ae*). Layer at back of eyeball sensitive to light. Hence **re·tin**AL a., **retin**I·TIS n. [med. L, perh. f. L *rete* net]

re·tinue, n. Suite or train of persons in attendance upon some one. [f. OF *retenue* fem. p.p. of *retenir* RETAIN]

retire·, v.i. & t., & n. Withdraw (intr.), go away, retreat, seek seclusion or shelter, recede, go (as) to bed, (*r. from the world*, become recluse; *r. into oneself*, be uncommunicative or unsociable, whence **retir·**ING[2] a., **retir·ing**LY[2] adv., **retir·ing**NESS n.; *the ladies r.*, leave dining-room after dessert; *always retires before midnight*, often *to rest, to bed, for the night*, &c.; *general, army, was forced to r., retired in good order*, often *from* position, *to* place, *before* enemy, &c.; *background does not r. as it should*; *retiring-room*, for retiring to, esp. lavatory); (p.p., f. obs. trans. use) withdrawn from society or observation, secluded, (*lives retired*; *a retired life*; *in a retired valley*), whence **retire·d**NESS n.; cease *from* or give up office or profession or employment or candidature, (Cricket) voluntarily terminate one's innings, compel (officer, employee) to r., (*r. from the army, from business, on a pension*; *batsman retired hurt*; *was compulsorily retired as incompetent*; *retiring pension*, allowed to one who retires at normal time), (p.p., see -ED[1](2) for sense) that has retired (*a retired general, grocer*; *retired pay*, pension; *retired list*, of retired officers); (Mil.) order (troops) to r.; (Finance) withdraw (bill, note) from operation or currency. (N., mil.) signal to troops to r. (usu. *sound the r.*). [n. a use of imperat. of vb, f. F *re*(*tirer* draw f. Teut., cf. Goth. *tairan*, OHG *zeran*, TEAR v.), RE- 9]

retire·ment, n. In vbl senses; also: seclusion, privacy; secluded place. [F (prec., -MENT)]

retor·t[1], v.t. & i., & n. Requite (humiliation, insult, attack) in kind; turn (mischief &c.), fling (charge, sarcasm, jest), back (*on* or *upon* author or aggressor), make (argument) tell against or *against* its user; make, say by way of, repartee or counter-charge or counter-argument; (p.p.) recurved, twisted or bent backwards. (N.) incisive reply, repartee; turning of charge or argument against its author; piece of retaliation. [f. L *re*(*torquēre tort-* twist), RE- 9]

retor·t[2], n., & v.t. Vessel usu. of glass with long downward-bent neck used in distilling liquids; kinds of receptacle of various shapes & materials used in purifying mercury & making gas & steel; (vb) purify (mercury) by heating in r. [f. med. L *retorta* fem. p.p. as prec.]

retor·tion, n. Bending back (lit. & fig.); (Internat. law) retaliation by State upon subjects of another. [f. med. L *retortio* (RETORT[1], -ION)]

retouch. See RE- 8.

retra·ce, v.t. Trace back to source or beginning; look over again; recall the course of in memory; go back over (one's *steps* or *way*; often fig. of undoing actions). [f. F *retracer* (RE- 8, TRACE v.)]

retra·ct, v.t. & i. 1. Draw (esp. part of one's body) back or in, (of such part &c.) shrink back or in or be capable of being retracted, (*snail retracts its horns*; *cat's claws r.* or *can be retracted*; *surgeon retracts skin with instrument, organ is retracted by muscle, called* **retra·ct**OR[2] n.; *if the piston is suddenly retracted*); hence or cogn. **retra·ctable**[1] [-ABLE] & (in same sense) **retra·ct**ILE aa., **retractĭ·**LITY n., **retra·c**TIVE a., **retra·ction**[1] [-ION] n. 2. Withdraw, revoke, cancel, refuse to abide by, acknowledge falsity or error of, expressly abandon, (statement, promise, opinion), (abs.) r. opinion or statement; hence or cogn. **retra·ctable**[2] [-ABLE] a., **rētrac-**

TA·TION, **retra·ction**² [-ION], nn. [sense 1 f. L *re(trahere tract-* draw), RE- 4; sense 2 partly as 1, but chiefly f. L *re(tractare* draw frequent. of *trahere* draw), RE- 9, & L *re(tractare* pull about or handle), RE- 8, as in archaic *retractation* rehandling now only in title of Augustine's *Retractations*]

rē·tral, a. (nat. hist. &c.). Hinder, posterior, at the back. [RETRO-, -AL]

retransfer, retransform, retranslate &c., **retread.** See RE- 9.

retrea·t, v.i. & t., & n. Go back, retire, relinquish a position, (esp. of army &c.); (trans., chiefly in chess) move (piece) back from forward or threatened position; recede (*a retreating chin, forehead*). (N.) act of, (Mil.) signal for, retreating (*sound the* or *a r.* mil.; *beat a r.*, r., abandon undertaking; *make good* one's *r.*, get safely away; *intercept r. of*, cut off; *are in full r.*), (Mil.) bugle-call at sunset; withdrawing into privacy or security, (place of) seclusion, (Eccl.) temporary retirement for religious exercises, asylum for inebriates or lunatics or pensioners, lurking-place, place of shelter. [f. OF *retrait(er)* f. p.p. of *retraire* f. L as RETRACT (1)]

retre·nch, v.t. & i. Cut down, reduce amount of, (expenses, things causing outlay); cut off, deduct, (*retrenched a year from the established period*); make excisions in or of, shorten or remove, (literary work or passages in it); cut down expenses, introduce economies; (Fortif.) furnish with inner line of defence usu. consisting of trench & parapet. Hence **retre·nch**MENT n. [f. obs. F *retrencher* var. of *retrancher* (RE-, TRENCH)]

retrial. See RE- 8.

retribu·tion, n. Recompense for evil or rarely for good done, vengeance, requital. So **retri·but**IVE a., **retri·butive**LY² adv. [f. L *re(tributio* f. *tribuere -ut-* assign, -ION), RE- 1]

retrie·ve, v.t. & i., & n. (Of dogs, esp. of special breed) find & bring in (killed or wounded bird &c., or abs.), whence **retrie·**VER¹ n. Recover by investigation or effort of memory, restore to knowledge or recall to mind; regain possession of; rescue *from* bad state &c.; restore to flourishing state, revive, (esp. one's fortunes &c.); make good, repair, set right, (loss, disaster, error); hence **retrie·**VABLE a., **retrie·**VAL(2) n. (N.) possibility of recovery (*beyond, past, r.*). [f. OF *re(trover, trouver,* find, compose in verse, ult. f. L f. Gk *tropos* TROPE), RE- 9]

retrim. See RE- 8.

retro- (usu. rē- exc. in the commoner wds, esp. *rĕtrograde, rĕtrospect*), pref. f. L *retro* adv. & pref.: (1) chiefly in L derivatives (*retroact, retrograde*) or wds formed on L anal. of L elements (*retroflex, retroject*) with senses *backwards, back again, in return*; (2) chiefly in scientific esp. anat. wds with sense *behind* (*retrosternal* a. behind the breastbone), *hinder* (*retrochoir* part behind high altar).

rētrōă·ct, v.i. React; operate in backward direction; have retrospective effect. Hence **retroa·ct**IVE a., **retroa·ctive**LY² adv., **retroacti·**VITY, **retroa·ct**ION, nn. [f. L RETRO(*agere act-* act)]

rē·trocede¹, v.i. Move back, recede; (of gout) strike inward. So **retroce·d**ENCE n., **retroce·d**ENT a. [f. L RETRO(*cedere cess-* go)]

rētroce·de², v.t. Cede (territory) back again. [f. F *rétrocéder* (RETRO-, CEDE)]

retroce·ssion, n., **retroce·ssive,** a. In vbl senses (RETROCEDE¹, ²). [-ION, -IVE]

rē·trochoir (-kwīr), n. Part of cathedral or large church behind high altar. [f. med. L RETRO(*chorus* CHOIR)]

rē·troflected, -flex, -flexed, aa. (anat., path., bot., &c.). Turned backwards. So **retrofle·**XION (-ĕkshn) n. [f. L RETRO(*flectere flex-* bend)]

rĕtrograda·tion, n. (Astron.) apparent backward motion of planet in zodiac, motion of heavenly body from E. to W., backward movement of lunar nodes on ecliptic; =(the now usu.) RETROGRESSION. [f. L RETRO(*gradatio* f. *-gradare* f. *-gradus* -walking, -ATION)]

rĕ·trograde, a., n., & v.i. (Astr.) in or showing RETROGRADATION; directed backwards (*r. motion*), retreating; reverting esp. to inferior state, declining; inverse, reversed, (*in r. order*; *r. imitation* in music, with notes of passage repeated backwards); hence **re·trograde**LY² adv. (N., rare) degenerate person; backward tendency. (Vb): (Astr.) show RETROGRADATION; move backwards, recede, retire, decline, revert. [f. L *retrogradus, -gradare* (prec.)]

rē·trogre·ss, v.i. Go back, move backwards, deteriorate. Hence **retrogre·s**SIVE a., **retrogre·ssive**LY² adv. [f. L RETRO(*gradi gress-* walk)]

rĕtrogre·ssion, n. (Astr.) retrogradation; backward or reversed movement; return to less advanced state, reversal of development, decline, deterioration. [f. L (prec.) + -ION]

rē·troject, v.t. Cast back (chiefly as opp. *project* in lit. senses). [RETRO-, & as PROJECT¹]

retropu·lsion, n. (path.). Shifting of external disease to internal part. [RETRO-, L *pellere puls-* drive, -ION]

retror·se, a. (nat. hist.). Turned back, reverted. Hence **retror·se**LY² adv. [f. L *retrorsus* = RETRO(*versus* p.p. of *vertere* turn)]

rĕ·trospect, n. Regard (to be) had *to* precedent or authority or previous conditions; (rare) retrospective force, retroaction; backward view (rare), survey of past time or events (*is pleasant in the r.*, when looked back on; *a short r. is now necessary*). [f. L RETRO(*spicere spect-* = *specere* look) after PROSPECT n.]

rĕtrospe·ction, n. Action of looking back esp. into the past, indulgence or engagement in retrospect. [as prec., -ION]

rĕtrospe·ctive, a. Of, in, proceeding by, retrospection; (of statutes &c.) not restricted to the future, licensing or punishing &c. past actions, having application to the past, retroactive; (of view) lying to the rear. Hence **retrospe·ctive**LY[2] adv. [as prec., -IVE]

retrou·ssé (-ōō·sā), a. Turned up (of nose). [F]

rē·trovert, v.t. Turn backwards (esp. path. in p.p. of womb). So **retrover·**SION n. [f. LL RETRO(*vertere vers-* turn)]

retry &c. See RE- 8.

re·ttery, n. Flax-retting place. [RET, -ERY]

returf. See RE- 8.

retur·n[1], v.i. & t. Come or go back (*gone never to r.*; *r. home, the way* one *came*; p.p. somet. as in -ED[1](2), as *a returned emigrant, they are* or usu. *have returned*); revert (*shall r. to the subject*; *unto dust shalt thou r.*; *r. to* one's *old habits*; *property returns to original owner*); bring, convey, give, yield, put, send, or pay, back or in r. or requital (*fish must be returned to the water*; *r. borrowed book* or *sum*; *investments r. a profit*; *r. sword to scabbard*, or *r. swords* mil.; *r. ball*, strike &c. it back in tennis &c.; *r. like for like, the compliment, a blow, an answer*; *r. thanks*, express them esp. in grace at meals or in response to toast; *r.* person's *love, greeting*, &c., reciprocate it; *returned empties*, packing-cases &c. sent back; *r. clubs* &c. or *partner's lead* at cards, lead from same suit); say in reply, retort; state, mention, or describe, officially esp. in answer to writ or formal demand(*liabilities were returned at £5000*; *were all returned guilty, unfit for work*; *returning officer*, official conducting election & announcing name of person elected), (of constituency) elect as M.P. Hence **retur·n**ABLE a. [f. OF *re(turner* TURN), RE- 9]

retur·n[2], n. Coming back (*his r. was the signal for riots*; *r. of* POST[2]; *r. ticket* or *r.*, ticket for there-&-back journey, as *took a first-class r. to Leeds*; *r. passenger, voyage, cargo*, &c.; *many happy rr. of the day* or *rr.*, birthday or festival greeting; *have had a, no, r. of the symptoms*); (Archit.) part receding from line of front, e.g. side of house or of window-opening (*r. angle, side, wall*, &c.); (coming in of) proceeds or profit of undertaking (often pl.; *the rr. were large*; *brings an adequate r.*; *small profits & quick rr.*, motto of cheap shop &c. relying on large trade); giving, sending, putting, or paying, back, or thing so given &c., esp. sheriff's report on writ, (returning officer's announcement of) candidate's election as M.P., or formal report with statistics &c. compiled by order (*sheriff made a r. of* nulla bona; *secured his r. for Colchester*; *table littered with rr. & pamphlets*; *must ask for the r. of the book* or *loan*; *received a ticket in r. for his fare, neglect in r. for attention*; *fencer's r.*, i.e. riposte, *is slow*; fielder *has a good r.* in cricket, sends ball in fast & straight; *r. match* or *game*, or *r.*, between same sides as before); (pl.) kind of mild pipe-tobacco (orig. sense *refuse of tobacco*). Hence **retur·n**LESS a. [AF (prec.)]

retu·se, a. (bot., entom.). With broad end & central depression (of leaf or similar part). [f. L *re(tundere tus-* beat), RE- 9]

rēū·nion, n. Reuniting or being reunited, reunited state; social gathering, esp. of intimates or persons with common interests (often in F form *ré-*). [f.F *réunion* (RE-, UNION)]

reu·nionist, -ism, nn. Seeker, seeking, of reunion between R.-C. & Anglican Churches. [-IST, -ISM]

reunite, see RE- 9; **reurge, revaccinate** &c., RE- 8.

rĕvale·nta, n. Food prepared from lentil & barley flour. [orig. *erv-* (L *ervum lens* LENTIL)]

revalue &c. See RE- 8.

revanche (F), n. Return match (esp. as name of the revenge for the Franco-German war desired by France from 1870).

revea·l[1], v.t. (Esp. of God) make known by inspiration or supernatural means (*revealed religion*, opp. *natural*); disclose, divulge, betray, bewray; display, show, let appear (*r. itself*, come to sight or knowledge). Hence **revea·l**ABLE a. [f. L *re(velare* f. *velum* VEIL), RE- 7]

revea·l[2], n. Internal side surface of opening or recess, esp. of doorway or window-aperture. [f. obs. vb *revale* f. OF *re(valer* lower f. *à val* downwards f. L *ad vallem* to the valley), RE- 4]

revei·lle (-vĕlĭ, -vālye). Military waking-signal sounded in morning on bugle or drums. [f. F *réveillez* imperat. pl. of *réveiller* (RE-, *veiller* f. L *vigilare* watch, see VIGIL)]

rĕ·vel, v.i. & t. (-ll-), & n. Make merry, be riotously festive, feast, carouse, whence **re·vell**ER[1] n.; take keen delight *in*; throw *away* (money, time) in revelry. (N.) revelling, (occasion of indulgence in) merry-making, (often pl., as *the rr. began*; *r. rout*, party of revellers, f. obs. *r.-rout* revelry); hence **re·vel**RY(4, 5) n. [f. OF *revel(er)* riot f. L REBEL[2]*lare*]

revela·tion, n. Disclosing of knowledge, knowledge disclosed, to man by divine or supernatural agency (*The R.*, also pop. *Rr.* or *the Rr.*, abbr. *Rev.*, last book of N.T., Apocalypse), whence **revela·tion**AL a.; striking disclosure (*it was a r. to me*;

what a r.!); revealing *of* some fact. [f. L *revelatio* (REVEAL[1], -ATION)]

revela·tionist, n. *The R.*, author of Apocalypse; believer in divine revelation. [-IST]

revenant (F), n. One returned from the dead or from exile &c.

revendica·tion, n. (diplom.). Formal claiming back, or recovery by such claim, of lost territory &c. [F (RE-, VINDICATION)]

reve·nge[1] (-j), v.t. & i. Satisfy one*self*, (pass.) be satisfied, with retaliation (*for* offence, *on*, *upon*, *of*, offender); retaliate, requite, exact retribution for, (offence to oneself or another; *on*, *upon*, offender); avenge (person); take vengeance. [f. obs. F *re(venger* f. L *vindicare* VINDICATE), RE- 1]

reve·nge[2], n. Revenging, act done in revenging; desire to r., vindictive feeling, whence **reve·nge**FUL a., **reve·ngeful**LY[2] adv., **reve·ngeful**NESS n.; (Games) opportunity given for reversing former result by return game (*give* one his *r.*). [f. prec.]

re·venue (*in Parl. usage often* -vĕ·-), n. Income, esp. of large amount, from any source (pl., collective items of it, usu. w. possess. as *his rr.*); State's annual income from which public expenses are met (INLAND *r.*; *r. tax*, imposed solely to raise r., not to affect trade, opp. *protective*; *r. cutter*, *officer*, &c., employed to prevent smuggling), department of civil service collecting it. [OF, p.p. of *revenir* f. L *re(venire* come) return, RE- 9]

rever·berate, v.t. & i. Return, beat back, echo, reflect, (t. & i. of sound, light, heat; *reverberating furnace* or *kiln*, constructed to r. heat on substance dealt with, whence **rever·berat**ORY, *pr.* -*ra*-, a. & n.); (of emotion &c., rare) react *upon*; (of ball &c., rare) rebound. So **reverbera**·TION n., **rever·ber**ATIVE, **rever·ber**ANT (poet.), aa. [f. L RE- 9(*verberare* beat), -ATE[3]]

rever·berātor, n. Reflector, reflecting lamp. [-OR[2]]

revere·, v.t. Regard as sacred or exalted, hold in deep & usu. affectionate or religious respect, venerate. [f. L RE(*vereri* fear)]

re·verence, n., & v.t. Revering (see prec.; *hold in*, *regard with*, *r.*; *feel r. for*, *pay r. to*); capacity for it (*the rising generation lacks r.*), (archaic) gesture showing it, bow, curtsy, obeisance; so **revere·nt**IAL a., **revere·ntial**LY[2] adv.; being revered (*saving your r.* archaic, apology for use of coarse term; *your*, *his*, *r.* archaic or vulg. or facet., titles used to, of, clergyman); (vb) regard with r., venerate. [f. L *reverentia* (prec., -ENCE)]

re·verend, a. & n. Deserving reverence by age, character, or associations (of person, place, custom, &c.; esp. as title, abbr. *Rev.*, or otherwise, of clergyman; *Very R.*, of dean; *Right R.*, of bishop; *Most R.*, of archbishop; *the Right R. John Smith* or *the Right R. the bishop of* —; *Rev.* or *the Rev. John* or *J. Smith*, or vulg. *Rev.* or *the Rev. Smith*; *the r. gentleman*, the clergyman in question; as n., usu. pl., = clergyman &c., as *rr. & right rr.*, clergy & bishops); of the clergy (*r. utterances* &c.); (archaic) = foll. [f. L *reverendus* (REVERE, -ND[1])]

re·verent, a. Feeling or showing reverence. Hence **re·verent**LY[2] adv. [f. L *reverens* (REVERE, -ENT)]

rĕ·verie (-ĭ, -ē), n. (Fit of) musing, daydream(ing), (*was lost in r.* or *a r.*); (archaic) fantastic notion or theory, delusion; (Mus.) dreamy instrumental piece. [OF (*rever*, *resver*, now *rêver* dream etym. dub., -ERY); cf. RAVE[2]]

revers (revār·), n. (pl. the same). Turned-back edge of coat, bodice, &c. displaying lining. [F]

rever·se[1], a. Opposite or contrary (*to*, or abs.) in character or order, inverted, back or backward, upside down, (*in the r. direction to the time before*; *the r. side* &c. *of a coin, picture*, &c.; *r.* Q; *r. fire*, *battery*, &c., playing on enemy's rear or into works from rear; *r. flank*, opposite to pivot end in wheeling). Hence **rever·se**LY[2] adv. [f. L *re(vertere vers-* turn), RE- 9]

rever·se[2], v.t. & i. Turn (trans.) the other way round or up or inside-out, invert, transpose, convert to opposite character or effect, (*r. arms*, hold rifles butt upwards; *r. motion*, *policy*, *order*, &c.: *r. engine*, make it work backwards); revoke, annul, (decree, attainder, &c.); (Danc., esp. in waltz) begin to revolve in opposite direction. Hence **rever·s**AL(2) n., **rever·s**IBLE a., **reversi**BI·LITY n. [f. F *reverser* (RE-, L *versare* frequent. of *vertere* turn)]

rever·se[3], n. *The* contrary (*of*, or abs.; *with others the r. of this* or *the r. happens*; *on the r.* in motoring, with car moving backwards; often w. adj. as periphr. for its opposite, as *made remarks the r. of complimentary*); (device on) subordinate side of coin &c. (opp. OBVERSE); = VERSO; = *r.*[1] *side* (*take in r.*, subject to *r.*[1] *fire*); piece of misfortune, disaster, esp. defeat in battle (*the rr. of fortune*; *suffered a r.*). [OF (-*rs*, -*rse*) as REVERSE[1]]

rever·si (or -ē), n. Game on draught-board with counters coloured differently above & below. [F]

rever·sion, n. (Return to grantor or his heirs or passing to ultimate grantee or **rever·sion**ER[1] n. of, also right of ultimate succession to) estate granted till specified date or event, esp. death of original grantee (*in r.*, on such conditions); sum payable on person's death esp. by way of life-insurance; thing to which one has a right or expects to succeed when relinquished by another; return to a previous state, habit, &c., esp. (Biol.) to ancestral type. Hence **rever·sion**AL, **rever·sion**ARY[1], aa., **rever·sional**LY[2] adv. [OF, f. L *re(versionem* f. *vertere vers-* turn, -ION), RE- 9]

rever·t, v.i. & t., & n. Go back (rare); (of property, office, &c.) fall in by REVERSION, whence **rever·t**ER[4] n. (legal); return *to* former state &c. (cf. prec.; n. after *convert, pervert,* person who readopts his original faith), (abs.) fall back into wild state; recur *to* subject in talk or thought; turn (eyes, rarely steps) back. [f. OF *revertir* f. L as prec.]

rever·tible, a. (Of property) subject to reversion. [prec., -IBLE]

reve·t, v.t. (-tt-). Face (rampart, wall, &c.) with masonry &c. esp. in fortification. [f. F *revêtir* f. L *re(vestire* clothe f. VEST*is*), RE- 8]

reve·tment, n. Retaining-wall or facing (as prec.). [f. F *revêtement* (prec., -MENT)]

revictual. See RE- 8.

review[1] (-vū), n. Revision (esp. legal; *is not subject to r.*; *court of r.*, before which sentences &c. come for revision); display & formal inspection of troops, fleet, &c. (*r. order*, dress & arrangement usu. at rr., & transf. full fig; *pass in r.* fig. t. & i., examine or be examined); retrospect, survey of the past; critique of book &c.; periodical publication with articles on current events, new books, art, &c.; second view. [f. F *reveue* (now *-vue*) orig. fem. p.p. of *revoir* f. L *re(vidēre* see), RE- 9]

review[2], v.t. & i. View again; subject to esp. legal revision; survey, glance over, look back on; hold r. of (troops &c.); write r. of (book &c.), write rr., whence **review·**ER[1] n. Hence **review·**ABLE a., **review·**AL(2) n. [RE-, VIEW]

revi·le, v.t. & i. Call by ill names, abuse, rail at; talk abusively, rail. Hence **revi·l**ER[1], **revi·l**ING[1](1), nn., **revi·ling**LY[2] adv. [f. OF *reviler* (RE- 6, VILE)]

revi·se (-z), v.t., & n. Read or look over or re-examine or reconsider & amend faults in (literary matter, printers' proofs, law, constitution, &c.; *Revised Version*, abbr. R.V., revision made 1870–84 of Authorized or 1611 Version of Bible); hence or cogn. **revi·s**ABLE, **revi·s**ORY, aa., **revi·s**AL(2), **revi·s**ION (-zhn), nn., **revi·sion**AL a., **revi·s**ER[1] (esp. in pl. of authors of R.V.), (N.) revision, revising, (rare); revised form (rare); (Print.) proof-sheet embodying corrections made in earlier proof. [n. f. vb, f. F *re(viser* look at f. L *vidēre vis-* see), RE- 8]

revisit, see RE- 8; **revitalize,** RE- 9.

revi·val, n. Bringing or coming back into vogue (*r. of learning, letters*, &c., at Renaissance; *r. of architecture*, 19th-c. reversion to Gothic; *r. of book, play, word, custom*, &c.), (special effort with meetings &c. to promote) reawakening of religious fervour, whence **revi·val**ISM(3), **revi·val**IST(2), nn.; restoration to bodily or mental vigour or to life or consciousness. [foll., -AL(2)]

revi·ve, v.i. & t. Come or bring back to consciousness, life, existence, vigour, notice, activity, validity, or vogue; (Chem.) restore (metal, esp. mercury) to natural form. Hence **revi·v**ABLE a. [f. LL *re(vivere* live), RE- 8; trans. use prob. f. *is* &c. *revived* as -ED[1](2)]

revi·ver, n. In vbl senses; esp.: (slang) stimulating drink; preparation for restoring faded colour &c. [-ER[1]]

revi·vify̆, v.t. Restore to animation, activity, vigour, or life; (Chem.) = REVIVE. Hence **revivi**FICA·TION n. [f. LL *re(vivificare* VIVIFY), RE- 8]

revivi·scence, n., **revivi·scent,** a. Returning to life or vigour. [f. L RE- 8- (*viviscere* incept. of *vivere* live), -ENCE, -ENT]

revi·vor, n. (law). Proceeding for revival of suit after death of party &c. [REVIVE, -OR[2]]

revo·ke, v.t. & i., & n. Repeal, annul, withdraw, rescind, cancel, (decree, consent, promise, permission; also rarely abs., withdraw promise &c.), so **re·voc**ABLE, **re·vocăt**ORY, aa., **revoca·tion** n.; (Whist &c.) make r. (N.) card-player's failure to follow suit though he could; (rare) revocation (*beyond r.*). [f. L *re(vocare* call), RE- 9]

revō·lt, v.i. & t., & n. Cast off allegiance, make rising or rebellion, fall away *from* or rise *against* ruler, go over *to* rival power, (n., act of revolting or state of having revolted, rising, insurrection; so *in r.*; p.p. as -ED[1](2), as *his revolted subjects*); feel revulsion or disgust *at*, rise in repugnance *against*, turn in loathing *from*, (*common sense, nature*, one's *heart, revolts at* or *against* or *from it*; n., sense of loathing, rebellious or protesting mood); affect with strong disgust, nauseate, whence **revo·lt**ING[2] a., **revo·lting**LY[2] adv. [f. F *révolte(r)* f. RE- 2, L *volutare* frequent. of *volvere volut-* roll]

re·volute[1] (-ōōt, -ūt), a. (bot. &c.). With back-rolled edge. [f. L REVOLVE*re*]

revolu·te[2] (-ōōt), v.i. (slang). Engage in political revolution. [back formation f. foll.]

revolu·tion (-ōōshn, -ū-), n. Revolving, motion in orbit or circular course or round axis or centre, rotation, single completion of orbit or rotation, time it takes, cyclic recurrence; complete change, turning upside down, great reversal of conditions, fundamental reconstruction, esp. forcible substitution by subjects of new ruler or polity for the old (*the R.*, expulsion of Stuarts 1688; *French R.*, overthrow of monarchy 1789 &c.; *American R.*, overthrow of British rule 1775 &c.), whence **revolu·tion**IZE(1, 3) v.t.; **revolu·tion**ISM(3), **revolu·tion**IST(2), nn. [f. LL (*-tio*) as REVOLVE, -ION]

revolu·tionary, a. & n. (Instigator) of revolution; involving great & usu. violent changes; (rare) of rotation or revolving. [-ARY¹]

revo·lve, v.t. & i. Turn (t. & i.) round or round & round, rotate, go in circular orbit, roll (intr.) along, (*r. problem, fact, in the mind* &c. or abs., ponder over it; *mechanism for revolving the turn-table*; *Earth revolves both round* or *about sun & on its axis*; *seasons, years, r.*). [f. L *re(volvere volut-* roll), RE- 6]

revo·lver, n. Pistol with revolving mechanism enabling user to fire several shots without reloading (*policy of the big r.*, of threatening foreign States with retaliatory tariff). [-ER¹]

revue·, n. Loosely constructed play or series of scenes or spectacles presenting or satirizing current events. [F]

revu·lsion, n. Counter-irritation, treatment of one disordered organ &c. by acting upon another; (rare) drawing or being drawn away (*the r. of capital from other trades*); sudden violent change of feeling, sudden reaction in taste, fortune, trade, &c. [f. L *re(vulsio* f. *vellere vuls-* pull), RE- 9]

revu·lsive, a. & n. (chiefly med.). Of, producing, revulsion; (n.) counter-irritant application. [prec., -IVE]

rewar·d (-ord), n., & v.t. Return or recompense for service or mérit, requital for good or evil, retribution; sum offered for detection of criminal, restoration of lost property, &c.; hence **rewar·d**LESS a. (Vb) repay, requite, recompense, (service or doer of it, offender, offence). [f. ONF *reward(er)* = OF REGARD¹(*er*)]

rewin, see RE- 9; **reword, rewrite,** RE- 8.

Rex, n. (abbr. *R.*). Reigning king (in use as REGINA). [L]

Rey·nard (rĕ-, rā-), n. (Proper name for) the fox; a fox. [f. OF *Renart* name of fox in the *Roman de Renart*]

rha·bdomancy, n. Use of divining-rod, esp. for discovering subterranean water or ore. [f. LL f. Gk *rhabdomanteia* (*rhabdos* rod, -MANCY)]

Rhădama·nthus, n. Stern & incorruptible judge. Hence **Rhadama·nth**INE² a. [name of judge in Gk Hades]

Rhae·tian (-shn), a. & n. *R. Alps*, part of Alps about the Engadine; = RHAETO-ROMANIC a. & n. [L *Rhaetia*, -IAN]

Rhae·tic, a. & n. (Of) *the* set of strata intermediate between lias & trias prevailing in Rhaetian Alps. [f. L *Rhaeticus* (prec., -IC)]

Rhaeto-Romă·nic, -a·nce, aa. & nn. (Of, in) any of the Romance dialects of S.E. Switzerland & Tyrol, esp. Romansh & Ladin. [L *Rhaetus* Rhaetian, -O-]

rha·psode (-ōd), n. Ancient-Greek minstrel or reciter of epic poems. [f. Gk *rhapsō(i)dos* (*rhaptō* stitch, ODE)]

rha·psodize, v.t. & i. Recite (t. & i.) as rhapsode; talk or write rhapsodies (usu. *about, on,* &c.). So **rha·psod**IST(1) n. [foll., -IZE]

rha·psody, n. (Gk Ant.) epic poem, or part of it, of length for one recitation; enthusiastic extravagant high-flown utterance or composition, emotional irregular piece of music, whence **rhapsŏ·d**ICAL a., **rhapsŏ·dical**LY² adv. Hence **rhapsŏ·d**IC a. [f. L *rhapsodia* f. Gk *rhapsōidia* (RHAPSODE, -IA¹)]

rhă·tany, n. (Extract, used medicinally & in adulterating port, of root of) S.-Amer. shrub. [f. Port. *ratanhia* f. native *ratañá*]

rhe·a, n. S.-Amer. three-toed ostrich. [name of Gk goddess]

Rhē·mish, a. Of Rheims (*R. Bible, Testament, version, translation,* N.T. translated by Roman Catholics of English College at Rheims 1582). [obs. E *Rhemes*, -ISH]

Rhē·nish, a. & n. (archaic). Of the Rhine & districts on its banks (now usu. *Rhine* attrib.); (n.) R. wine (now usu. *Rhine wine* or *hock*). [f. OF *rinois* or MHG *rînisch* or MDu. *rijnsch* w. assim. to L *Rhenus* Rhine]

rheo-, reo-, comb. form in electr. terms of Gk *rheos* stream, = current-, as *rheo·*-METER, *rhe·*OSCOPE; *rhe·otome*, device for interrupting current; *rhe·ostat*, instrument regulating current to constant degree of force.

rhē·tor, n. Ancient Greek or Roman teacher or professor of rhetoric; (mere) orator (rare). L, f. Gk *rhētōr* (*eirō*, perf. *eirēka*, speak)]

rhĕ·toric, n. (Treatise on) the art of persuasive or impressive speaking or writing; language designed to persuade or impress (often w. implication of insincerity, exaggeration, &c.); persuasiveness of or *of* looks or acts. [f. L f. Gk *rhētorikē* (*tekhnē* art) of RHETOR (-IC)]

rhetŏ·rical, a. Expressed with a view to persuasive or impressive effect, artificial or extravagant in language, of the nature of rhetoric, (*r. question*, asked not for information but to produce effect, as *who cares?* for *nobody cares*); of the art of rhetoric; given to rhetoric, oratorical. Hence **rheto·rical**LY² adv. [f. L f. Gk *rhētorikos* (RHETOR, -IC) + -AL]

rhetori·cian, n. = RHETOR; rhetorical speaker or writer. [f. OF *rethoricien* (RHETORIC, -ICIAN)]

rheum (ro͞om), n. (archaic). Watery secretion or discharge of mucous membrane &c. such as tears, saliva, or mucus; catarrh; (pl.) rheumatic pains. [f. OF *reume* f. L f. Gk *rheuma -atos* stream (*rheō* flow, -M)]

rheumă·tic, a. & n. Of, suffering from, subject to, producing, or produced by, rheumatism (*r. fever*, non-infectious fever with inflammation & pain in joints; *r. walk* &c., impeded by r. stiffness); hence **rheuma·tic**ALLY adv., **rheuma·ticky**[2] a. (colloq.), **rheu·mato-** comb. form, **rheu·mat**OID a. (N.): (pl.) rheumatism (colloq.); r. patient. [f. L f. Gk *rheumatikos* (prec., -IC)]

rheu·matism, (vulg.) **-tiz,** n. Disease marked by inflammation & pain in joints (*acute r.*, rheumatic fever). [f. LL f. Gk *rheumatismos* (*rheumatizō* f. RHEUM*a*, -IZE, -ISM)]

rheu·my, a. (archaic). Consisting of, flowing with, rheum; (of air) damp, raw. [-Y[2]]

rhī·nal, a. (anat. &c.). Of nostril or nose. [RHINO-, -AL]

rhine[1], n. (S.-W. dial.). Large open ditch. [prob. f. OE *ryne* RUNE]

Rhine[2], n. German river (*R.-wine*, kinds esp. of white wine from R. vineyards, cf. RHENISH; *Rhinestone*, kind of rock-crystal, also paste gem imitating diamond).

rhi·no[1], n. (slang). Money (often *ready r.*). [?]

rhi·no[2], n. (slang). (Short for) rhinoceros.

rhīno-, comb. form of Gk *rhis rhinos* nostril, nose, as *-phary·ngeal*, of nose & pharynx; *-pla·stic*, *-plasty*, (of) plastic surgery of the nose; *rhi·no*SCOPE, *-scŏ·p*IC, *rhino·scop*Y[1].

rhīnŏ·ceros (-os), n. Large unwieldy African & S.-Asiatic quadruped with horn or two horns on nose & thick folded & plated skin. So **rhinocerŏ·t**IC a. [f. LL f. Gk RHINO(*kerōs* f. *keras* horn)]

rhīzo-, comb. form of Gk *rhiza* root chiefly in bot. terms as *-carp*, plant with perennial root but perishing stems.

rhī·zome, n. Prostrate rootlike stem emitting roots, rootstock. [f. Gk *rhizōma* (*rhizoomai* take root as prec., -M)]

rho, n. Greek letter (Ρ, ρ) = r. [Gk]

Rhodes scholar, n. Holder of any of 190 scholarships tenable at Oxford by members of British Dominions or United States. [Cecil *Rhodes*, founder]

Rhō·dian, a. & n. (Native) of Rhodes. [L *Rhodius* f. L f. Gk *Rhodos* Rhodes + -AN]

rhō·dium[1], n. (Also *r.-wood*) scented wood of Canary convolvulus, rosewood, (*oil of r.*, rosewood oil got from it). [mod. L, neut. adj. (sc. *lignum* wood) = roselike f. Gk *rhodon* rose]

rhō·dium[2], n. Hard white metal of platinum group (*r. pen*, steel pen tipped with it). Hence **rho·d**IC, **rho·d**OUS, aa. (chem.). [Gk *rhodon* rose, -IUM, from colour of solution of its salts]

rhōdo-, comb. form of Gk *rhodon* rose, as *-sper·mous* with red spores.

rhodode·ndron (-on), n. Kinds of large-flowered evergreen shrubs akin to azalea. [LL f. Gk (prec., *dendron* tree)]

rhomb (-b usu. mute exc. before vowel), n. Oblique equilateral parallelogram, diamond or lozenge, object or part with such outline; (Cryst.) rhombohedron. Hence **rho·mb**IC a., **rhombo-** comb. form. [f. L f. Gk *rhombos*]

rhombohē·dron, n. (chiefly cryst.; pl. *-ra, -rons*). (Crystal in shape of) solid bounded by six equal rhombs. Hence **rhombohe·dr**AL a. [RHOMBO- (prec.), Gk *hedra* base]

rho·mboid, a. & n. Of or near the shape of a rhomb (*r. muscle*, connecting scapula with vertebrae). (N.) quadrilateral of which only opposite sides & angles are equal; r. muscle. [f. LL f. Gk *rhomboeidēs* (RHOMB, -OID)]

rhomboi·dal, a. Having shape of a rhomboid (prec., n.); = prec. (adj.). Hence **rhomboi·dal**LY[2] adv. [prec., -AL]

rho·mbus, n. (pl. *-i, -uses*). = RHOMB; kinds of flat-fish including turbot & brill. [L (RHOMB)]

rhō·tacism n., **rho·tacize** v.i. (Speak with) excessive or peculiar pronunciation of r.; conversion of, convert, other sounds into r. [n. f. vb f. Gk *rhōtakizō* (RHO, -IZE)]

rhu·barb (rōō-), n. (Purgative made from) root of Chinese & Tibetan plant (usu. *Chinese, East Indian, Russia*, or *Turkey r.*, from channels of importation); (fleshy leaf-stalks of) kinds of garden plant, cooked in spring as substitute for fruit (sometimes *English, French, common*, or *garden r.*); (attrib., of colour) yellowish-brown like Chinese r. Hence **rhu·barb**Y[2] a. [f. OF *rubarbe* f. med. L *rhabarbarum* foreign rha or rhubarb (*rha* Gk, perh. f. *Rha* the Volga, BARBAROUS), w. assim. to L f. Gk *rhēon* rhubarb]

rhumb (-m), n. (naut.). (Also *r.-line*) line cutting all meridians at same angle, line followed by ship sailing on one course; angular distance between two successive points of compass, 11° 15′. [thr. F or Sp. f. L RHOMBUS]

rhyme[1], **rime,** n. Identity of sound between words or verse-lines extending from the end to the last fully accented vowel & not further (greet *&* deceit, shepherd *&* leopard, quality *&* frivolity, stationary *&* probationary, is it *&* visit, *give rr., but* seat *&* deceit, station *&* crustacean, visible *&* invisible, *do not*; *single* or *male* or *masculine, double* or *female* or FEMININE, *treble* or *triple, quadruple, r.*, according to number of syllables included; *imperfect r.*, as in *love* & *move*, *phase* & *race*; *without r. or reason*, quite unaccountable, -bly); verse marked by rr. (pl. or sing.), a poem with rr., the employment of r., (*should be written in r.*; *prefer blank verse to r.*; *am sending you some rr.*; NURSERY *r.*; *was reading an old r.*; *r. royal*, stanzas of seven ten-syllable lines with rr. as *ababbcc*, as in Chaucer's *Clerkes Tale* &c.); word providing a r. (*to* another; *can't find a r. to* teacups; *English is badly off for double rr.*). Hence **rhy·me**LESS a., **rhy·meless**NESS n. [*rhyme* assim. to RHYTHM of earlier & OF *rime* f. L f. Gk *rhuthmos* RHYTHM]

rhyme², **rime**, v.i. & t. Write rr., versify (intr.), whence **rhy·mer**¹, **rhy·me**STER, nn.; put or make (story &c.) into r. (*rhymed verse*, opp. *blank verse*); while (time) *away* in rhyming; (of words or lines) exhibit r., (of word) supply or act as r. *to* or *with*, (of person) treat (word) as rhyming *with*, select rr., (*rhymes carelessly*; *rhymes* law *with* four; *rhyming*¹-*dictionary*, of words arranged by terminations for versifiers' use), whence **rhy·m**IST(1) n. [f. OF *rimer* as prec.]

rhy̆·thm (-dhm, -thm), n. Metrical movement determined by various relations of long & short or accented & unaccented syllables, measured flow of words & phrases in verse or prose; (Mus.) systematic grouping of notes according to duration, structure resulting from this; (Art) harmonious correlation of parts; (Physics, Physiol., & gen.) movement with regular succession of strong & weak elements. Hence or cogn. **rhy·thmic**(AL) aa., **rhy·thmical**LY² adv., **rhy·thm**LESS a., **rhy·thm**IST(3) n. [f. L f. Gk *rhuthmos* cf. *rheō* flow]

rī·ant, a. Smiling, cheerful, (of face, eyes, &c., & esp. of landscape). [F (*rire* f. L *ridēre* laugh, -ANT)]

rib, n., & v.t. One of curved bones reaching from spine round upper part of body (*true, sternal, r.*, joined also to breastbone, opp. *false, floating, asternal, short, r.*; *poke* one *in the rr.*, to draw his attention facetiously; *smite under fifth r.* bibl., stab; *r.* or *rr. of beef* &c., as joint of meat; SPARE-*r.*); (joc. w. ref. to *Gen.* ii. 21) wife, woman; ridge or long raised piece often of thicker material across thinner surface serving to support as part of framework or strengthen or adorn, e.g. vein of leaf, shaft of feather, spur of mountain, vein of ore, ridge between furrows, wave-mark on sand, raised line in knitting, one of ship's curved timbers to which planks are nailed or corresponding ironwork, arch supporting vault, groin, raised moulding on groin or across ceiling &c., wooden or iron beam helping to carry bridge, hinged rod of umbrella-frame; *r.-grass, -wort*, Narrow-leaved Plantain; hence **(-)ribb**ED², **ri·b**LESS, aa. (Vb) provide with rr., act as rr. of, whence **ri·bb**ING¹(3, 6) n.; mark with ridges; plough with rr. between furrows, half-plough, rafter. [com.-Teut., cf. ON *riff*, G *rippe*, Du. *rib*]

ri·bald (-*a*-), n. & a. Irreverent jester, user of scurrilous, blasphemous, or indecent language; so **ri·bald**RY(4, 5) n. (Adj., of language or its user) scurrilous, obscene, irreverent. [earlier sense *low-born retainer, menial*, f. OF *ribaut, -auld*, etym. dub.]

ri·band n., **ri·banded** a. =RIBBON(*ed*). [f. F *riban* (now *ru-*), etym. dub.]

ri·bband (-*a*-), n. Wale, strip, scantling, or light spar, of wood, used esp. in shipbuilding to hold ribs in position, launching, & making of gun-platform or pontoon-bridge. [f. RIB, BAND¹, or var. of prec.]

ri·bbon, n. (Piece or length of) silk or satin or other fine material woven into narrow band esp. for adorning costume; r. of special colour &c. worn to indicate membership of knightly order, club, college, athletic team, &c. (BLUE¹ *r.*; *R. Society*, Irish R.-C. secret society formed in early 19th c. & associated with agrarian crime, whence **Ri·bbon**ISM n.); long narrow strip of anything, r.-like object or mark, (pl.) driving reins, (*hang in, torn to, rr.*, ragged strips; *handle, take, the rr.*, drive); *r.-fish*, long slender flat kinds; *r.-grass*, slender-leaved kind; *r.-man*, member of R. Society. Hence **(-)ribbon**ED² a. [var. of RIBAND]

rī·bēs (-z), n. (bot.). Currant or gooseberry plant. [med. L, = sorrel, f. Arab. *ribas*]

Ri·bston pi·ppin, n. Kind of dessert apple. [*R.* Park in Yorks.]

Ricar·dian, a. & n. (Adherent) of the political economist Ricardo (d. 1823), according to his views. [-IAN]

rice, n. (Pearl-white seeds, used as staple food in many Eastern countries, & in England in puddings, cakes, &c., or as table-vegetable, of) chiefly oriental plant grown in marshes; *r.-bird*, Java sparrow, also bobolink; *r.-milk*, boiled & thickened with r.; *r.-paper*, kind made from pith of a Formosan plant & used by Chinese artists for painting on (named after r. in error). [f. OF *ris* f. It. *riso* (L f. Gk *oruza* prob. f. Oriental source)]

rich (-tsh), a. (Of persons, societies, States, &c.) wealthy, having riches, (also as n. in *the r., r. & poor*); (of countries, periods, soil, &c.) abounding in or *in* natural resources or some valuable possession or production, fertile; valuable (*r. offerings, a r. harvest*); (of dress, furniture, buildings, banquets, &c.) splendid, costly, elaborate, (*with* lace, sculpture, &c.); (of food or diet) containing or involving large proportion of fat, oil, butter, eggs, sugar, spice, &c.; (of colours, sounds, smells) mellow, deep, full, not thin;

abundant, ample; (of incidents) highly amusing, full of entertainment or material for humour; *rich-*, richly (*r.-clad, -bound, -glittering*, &c.). Hence **ri·ch**EN[6] v.i. & t. (rare), **ri·ch**NESS n. [com.-Teut.; OE *rīce*, cf. Du. *rijk*, G *reich*, ON *rikr*; perh. early Teut. adoption of L *rex* king]

Ri·chard, pers. name. *R. Roe*, typical name for defendant in ejectment suit (cf. JOHN *Doe*); *Poor R.'s sayings*, maxims from almanacs issued by Benjamin Franklin with *Poor R.* as pseudonym; *R.'s himself again* (f. interpolation in Cibber's version of Shak. *R. III*), said by or of person recovered from despondency, fear, illness, &c.

ri·ches (-tshĭz), n. (usu. as pl.). Abundant means, wealth, valuable possessions, being rich. [f. obs. & OF *richesse* (*riche* RICH, -ESS[2])]

ri·chly, adv. In adj. senses; also (chiefly with *deserve*) fully, thoroughly, (*r. deserves a thrashing, to succeed*). [-LY[2]]

rick[1], n., & v.t. Stack of hay, corn, peas, &c., esp. one regularly built & thatched; *r.-barton*, =r.-yard; *r.-cloth*, canvas cover for unfinished r.; *r.-stand*, short wooden or stone pillars bearing joists to raise r. from ground; *r.-yard*, enclosure for rr.; (vb) form into rick(s). [OE *hrēac*, cf. Du. *rook*, Norw. *rauk*]

rick[2]. See WRICK.

ri·ckets, n. (as sing. or pl.; *-et* in comb. &c., as *ricket-producing, rickety*). Children's disease with softening of bones, esp. of spine, & bow-legs &c., rachitis. [etym. dub.; taken by writer (1645) of treatise on it for corrupt. of RACHITIS, which he introduced as its sci. name]

ri·ckety, a. Suffering from, of (the nature of), rickets; feeble, shaky, tottering, weak-jointed, fragile, insecure, (of persons or things, esp. furniture). Hence **ri·ckety**NESS n. [-Y[2]]

ricksha(w). See JINRICKSHA.

ri·cochet (-shā, -shĕt), n., & v.i. & t. (-t- or -tt-, *pr.* -shād *or* -shĕtĭd, -shāĭng *or* -shĕtĭng &c.). Skipping on water or ground of cannon-ball or bullet, hit made after it, (often attrib., as *r. fire, shot, battery*). (Vb): (of bullet &c.) skip once or more; (of gun, gunner, &c.) hit or aim at with r. shot(s). [vb f. n., F, etym. dub.]

ri·ctus, n. Expanse or gape of person's or animal's mouth, bird's beak, or flower with two-lipped corolla. [L (*ringi* open the mouth)]

rid, v.t. (past *ridded, rid*; p.p. *rid*, rarely *ridded*). Make (person, place) free, disencumber, *of* (usu. in p.p. with *be* or *get*; *glad to be, must get, r. of him*); (archaic) abolish, clear away, get r. of, (pest). Hence **ri·dd**ANCE n. (esp. *a good r.* as excl. of joy; person &c. *is a good r.*, better away). [earlier sense *clear* (land &c.); f. ON *rydhja*]

ri·d(d)el, n. (eccl.). Altar-curtain. [f. OF *ridel* (F *rideau*) curtain]

ridden. See RIDE.

ri·ddle[1], n., & v.i. & t. Question, statement, or description, designed or serving to test ingenuity of hearers in divining its answer or meaning or reference, conundrum, enigma; puzzling or mysterious fact, thing, or person. (Vb) speak in, propound, (part.) expressed in, rr., whence **ri·ddling**LY[2] adv.; solve (r.; often *r. me* as challenge). [OE *rǣdels* (READ, suf. *-els* as in BURIAL), cf. Du. *raadsel*, G *rätsel*]

ri·ddle[2], n., & v.t. Coarse sieve for corn, gravel, cinders, &c.; plate with pins used in straightening wire. (Vb) pass (corn &c.) through r., sift, (fig.) test (evidence, truth); fill (ship, person) with holes esp. of gunshot, (fig.) pelt with questions, refute (person, theory) with facts. [OE *hriddel*, earlier *hridder* (*hrid-* shake), cf. G *reiter*, L *cribrum*]

ride, v.i. & t. (*rode*, archaic *rid*; *ridden*, archaic *rid*), & n. Sit on & be carried by horse &c., go on horseback &c. or on bicycle &c. or in train or other public conveyance (cf. DRIVE[1]), sit or go or be *on* something as on horse esp. astride, sit on & manage horse, lie at anchor, float buoyantly, (of sun &c.) seem to float, (of things normally level or even) project or overlap, (*r. a-*COCK-HORSE, BODKIN, ROUGH-*shod, 50 miles, full speed, a race*; *r. to hounds*, hunt; *r. for a fall*, r. or fig. act recklessly; *r. 12 st.* &c., weigh that in riding-trim; *r. over*, in horse-racing as WALK *over*; *r.* one *down*, overtake him by riding, also put one's horse at him; *r.* one *off* at polo, edge him away; *r. off on* a side issue, use it to evade the main point; *r. & tie*, of two or more travellers sharing horse, one riding ahead & then leaving it tied to await the other; *riding on his father's shoulders, back, knee, foot*; *rides well, cannot r., learn to r., riding-lessons* or *-school*; *bird, ship, rides on the wind, waves*; *ship rode at anchor*; *r. out the storm* lit. & fig., come safely through it; *moon was riding high*; *bone rides* in fracture, one part overlaps other; *rope rides*, has one turn crossing over another), traverse on horseback &c., r. over or through, (*r. the country, desert*, &c.; *r. a ford*, pass through it on horseback); r. on, sit heavily on, oppress, haunt, dominate, tyrannize over, (*r. horse*; *r.* one's *horse at* fence or enemy, urge it forward; *r.* one's *horse*, & fig. hobby or method or jest, *to death*, kill or overdo it; *nightmare rides* sleeper: *r. the whirlwind*, direct it; *ship rides the waves*; *ridden by fears, prejudices*, &c.; *priest* &c. *-ridden*); give r. to, cause to r., (*r. child on* one's *back*; *r.* one *on rail*, carry him astride on it as torture); (of ground) be of specified character for riding on (*rides well, soft, hard*, &c.); hence **ri·d**ABLE a. (N.) journey in public conveyance, spell of riding on horse, bicycle, person's back, &c.; road esp. through wood for riding on; (Mil.) batch of mounted recruits. [com.-Teut.; OE *ridan*, cf. Du. *rijden*, G *reiten*]

ri·del. See RIDDEL.

ri·der, n. In vbl senses; also or esp.: (Naut., pl.) additional set of timbers or iron plates strengthening ship's frame, (sing.) overlying rope or rope-turn; (Curl.) stone that ousts another; additional clause amending or supplementing document, esp. parliamentary bill at third reading; corollary, naturally arising supplement; expression of opinion, recommendation &c., added to verdict; (Math.) problem testing student's mastery of principles on which its solution depends; piece in machine &c. that surmounts or bridges or works over others. Hence **ri·der**LESS a. [OE *ridere* (prec.)]

ridge, n., & v.t. & i. Line of junction in which two sloping surfaces meet (*the r. of a roof, the nose*, &c.); long narrow hill-top, mountain range, watershed; (Agric.) one of a set of raised strips separated by furrows; (Gard.) raised hot-bed for melons &c.; any narrow elevation across surface; *r.-piece*, beam along r. of roof; *r.-pole*, horizontal pole of long tent, also =*r.-piece*; *r.-tile*, used for roof-r.; *r.-tree*, =*r.-piece*; *ridgeway*, road along r.; hence **ri·dg**Y[2] a. (Vb) break up (land) into rr.; mark with rr.; plant (cucumbers &c.) in rr.; gather (t. & i. esp. of sea) into rr. [com.-Teut.; OE *hrycg*, cf. LG *rüg*, G *rücken*]

ri·dicule, n., & v.t. Ridiculous thing, ridiculousness, (archaic); holding or being held up as laughing-stock, derision, mockery; (vb) make fun of, subject to r., laugh at. [f. L *ridiculum* neut. of *ridiculus* laughable (*ridēre* laugh)]

ridi·culous, a. Deserving to be laughed at, absurd, unreasonable. Hence **ridi·culous**LY[2] adv., **ridi·culous**NESS n. [as prec. + -OUS, or f. L *ridiculosus*]

ri·ding[1], n. In vbl senses; also, road for riders, esp. green track through or beside wood; *r.-breeches*; *r.*-HABIT[1]; *r.-lamp, -light* (shown by ship r. at anchor. [-ING[1]]

ri·ding[2], n. Administrative division (*East, W.*, or *N., R.*) of Yorkshire; similar division of other U.-K. or colonial county. [for *thriding* (THIRD, -ING[3]) third part, with loss of *th-* owing to preceding -t(h) of *east* &c.]

rifacime·nto (-ahtsh-), n. (pl. *-ti* pr. -tē). Remodelled form of a literary work or the like. [It.]

rife, pred. a. Of common occurrence, met with in numbers or quantities, prevailing, current, numerous, (usu. *be*, also *grow, wax*, &c., *r.*); well provided *with* (*language is r. with maxims*). Hence **ri·fe**NESS n. [OE *rȳfe*, cf. MDu. *rijf*, ON *rífr*]

ri·ff-răff, n. *The* rabble, disreputable persons. [earlier *riff & raff* f. F *rif et raf*]

ri·fle[1], v.t. & i. 1. Search & rob. esp. of all that can be found in various pockets or storing-places; carry off as booty; 2. make spiral grooves in (gun or its barrel or bore) to produce rotatory motion in projectile (p.p. of projectile, with studs fitting such grooves); 3. shoot (t. & i.) with r. Hence **ri·fl**ING[1] n. [1 f. OF *rifler* graze, scratch; 2 (from 1635) ult. f. same source, cf. LG *rifeln*, G *riefeln*, Da. *rifle*, Sw. *reffla*; 3 f. foll.]

ri·fle[2], n. One of the grooves made in rifling a gun; (formerly *r.-gun*) musket or carbine with rifled barrel, (pl.) troops armed with rr.; *r.-bird*, dark-green Australian bird; *r. brigade*, certain regiments of British army; *r.-corps*, of volunteer riflemen; *r.(-)green* n. & a., (of) dark green as in rifleman's uniform; *r.*-GRENADE; *rifleman*, soldier armed with r., esp. member (*R-* when prefixed = Private) of r. brigade, also =*r. bird*; *r.-pit*, excavation as cover for riflemen firing at enemy; *r.-range*, distance r. carries, place for r.-practice; *r.-shot*, distance r. carries, *good* &c. r.-marksman, shot fired with r. [f. prec. 2]

rift, n., & v.t. Cleft, fissure, chasm, in earth or rock; rent, crack, split, in an object, opening in cloud &c. (*little r. within the lute*, often fig. of incipient madness or dissension); *r.-valley*, steep-sided formed by subsidence of earth's crust; hence **ri·ft**LESS, **ri·ft**Y[2], aa. (Vb, usu. in p.p.) rend apart, cleave. [f. Scand.; cf. Da. *rift* a cleft, ON *ripta* to break (a bargain &c.)]

rig[1], v.t. & i., & n. Provide (ship), (of ship) be provided, with necessary spars, ropes, &c., or **ri·gg**ING[1](3) n., prepare (t. & i.) for sea in this respect; fit (*out, up*, or rarely abs.) with or *with* clothes or other equipment; set *up* (structure) hastily or as makeshift or by utilizing odd materials; *rigging-loft*, gallery in dockyard for fitting rigging, (Theatr.) space over stage from which scenery is worked. (N.) way ship's masts, sails, &c., are arranged, whence **-rigg**ED[2] a.; (transf.) person's or thing's look as determined by clothes &c. (*r.-up, -out*, such accessories). [etym. dub.; cf. Norw. *rigga* bind up]

rig[2], n., & v.t. Trick, dodge, way of swindling; (Commerc.) = CORNER; (vb) manage or conduct fraudulently (*r. the market*, cause artificial rise or fall in prices). [?]

Ri·ga, n. A port of the Baltic (*R. deal, hemp*, &c.; *R. balsam*, essential oil distilled from kind of pine & used medicinally).

rĭge·scent, a. Growing rigid, rather stiff. So **rige·**SCENCE n. [f. L *rigescere* (*rigēre* be stiff, -ESCENT)]

ri·gger, n. In vbl senses (RIG[1, 2]); also: (Mech.) band-wheel; =OUTRIGGER; = THIMBLE-*r.*; *-r.*, ship rigged in specified way. [-ER[1]]

right (rīt), a., v.t. & i., n., & adv. (Archaic) straight (now only in *r. line, r.-lined*); (of angle) neither acute nor obtuse, of 90°, made by lines meeting not obliquely but perpendicularly, (*at r. angles*, turning or placed with such angle), whence **right-angl**ED[2] a.; involving r. angle(s), not oblique, (*r. sailing*, due N., S., E., or W.; *r.* ASCENSION; *r. cone, cylinder, prism*, &c., with ends or base perpendicular to axis); (of conduct &c.) just, morally good, required by equity or duty, proper, (*acted a r. part; it is only r. to tell you, that you should know*), whence **right-mind**ED[2] a., **right-mi·nded**NESS n.; correct, true, (*r. use of words; did not give a r. account of the matter; your opinions are r. enough*); *the* preferable or most suitable, *the* less wrong or not wrong, (*which is the r. way to —?; the r. man in the r. place; does not do it the r. way; the r. heir*; cf. *Mr, Miss, R.*, destined husband, wife; *took the r. way to offend us; a fault on the r. side; the r. side* of a fabric &c., that meant for show or use; so *r. side up; on the r. side of forty* &c., not yet 40 years old); in good or normal condition, sound, sane, satisfactory, well-advised, not mistaken, (*in* one's *r. mind*, not mad &c.; *is not r. in his head; are you r. now?*, comfortable, recovered, &c.; *all's r. with the world; is as r. as a trivet, as rain*, &c., quite; *set* or *put r.*, restore to order, health, &c., also correct mistaken ideas of, also justify one*self* usu. *with* person; *get r.*, bring or come into r. state; *r., r. you are*, forms of approval, or, & so also *all r., r. oh!* slang, of assent to order or proposal), whence **righ·t**EN[6] v.t. (rare); (archaic) rightful, real, veritable, properly so called, (*r.* WHALE; *r. cognac* &c.); (of position) having the relation to front & back that equinoctial sunrise has to north & south, on or towards that side of human body of which the hand is normally more used, on or towards that part of an object which is analogous to person's r. side or (with opposite sense) which is nearer to spectator's r. hand, (cf. LEFT[1]; *r. side, eye*, &c.; *r. wing* or *flank* of army &c.; *r. bank*, on r. side of one looking down stream; *r.* CENTRE[1]. *R. & left*: adv., to or on both sides, on all hands, as *the crowd divided, he was abused, r. & l.*; adj., with or of or to both hands or sides, as *a r.-&-l. shot*, with both barrels, *r.-&-l. screw*, with contrary threads at two ends; n., r.-&-l. shot, also pugilist's two blows in quick succession with different hands. *R. arm*, (fig.) one's most reliable helper. *R. hand*: hand of r. side; this as the better hand, as *put* one's *r. h. to the work*; this w. ref. to handshaking, as *give the r. h. of fellowship*; region or direction on this side of person, as *at, on, to*, one's *r. h.*; one's indispensable or chief assistant; *r.-h.*, placed on the r. h.; *r.-h. man*, soldier on one's r. h. in line, also assistant as above; *r.-h. screw*, with thread turning to r.; *r.-handed*, using r. h. more than left; *r.-handed blow* &c., struck with r. h.; *r.-handed tool* &c., made to suit r. h.; *r.-handed rotation* &c.; *r.-hander*, r.-handed blow or person. *R. turn*, into position at r. angles with original one; *r.-about turn* or *face*, r. turn prolonged to rear (see ABOUT[1] for mil. use); *r.-about*, = r.-a. turn, reversal of front, hurried retreat as in *send to the r.-a.*, send packing, also as v.t. & i. =reverse or make reverse front); hence **righ·t**NESS n. (Vb) restore to proper or straight or vertical position (*r. helm*, put it amidships; *boat rights herself; could not r. the boat, car*); *r.* one*self*, recover balance, (of ship) recover vertical position; make reparation for or to, avenge, (wrong, wronged person); vindicate, justify, rehabilitate; correct (mistakes &c.), correct mistakes in, set in order, (often refl., as *that is a fault that will r. itself*); hence **righ·t**ABLE a. (N.) what is just, fair treatment, (*r. & might, r. & wrong; do* one *r.*, treat or think of him fairly; *by r.* or now usu. *rr.*, if r. were done; *the r.*, the juster cause, as *God defend the r.; be in the r.*, have justice or truth on one's side); justification, fair claim, being entitled to privilege or immunity, thing one is entitled to, (*has a, the, no, r. to* thing, *to* do, *of* doing, *of search* &c.; *r. divine* or DIVINE *r.; claims in r. of his wife; reigns by r. of worth; belongs to him of* or *by r.; rr. & duties; woman's rr.*, of equality with men, whence **woman's-righ·t**ER[1] n.; *r. of way*, r. established by usage to pass over another's ground, also path subject to such r.; *Declaration* or *Bill of Rr.*, constitutional settlement of 1689; *assert* or *stand on* one's *rr.*, refuse to relinquish them; *peeress in her own r.*, not by marriage; *admiration is her r.*), whence **righ·t**LESS a.; (pl.) r. condition, true state, (*set* or *put to rr.*, arrange properly; *have not heard, do not know, the rr. of the case*); r.-hand part or region or direction (*is on your* or *the, to the, r.; to, from, r. & left; work round the enemy's r.*), (Pol.) reactionary or conservative members of foreign parliament &c., whence **righ·t**WARD a. & adv., **righ·t**WARDS adv., (rare). (Adv.) straight (*wind was r. behind us; go r. on; went r. at him; r. off, away*, chiefly U.S., immediately, without pause); all the way *to, round*, &c., completely *off, out*, &c., (*sank r. to the bottom; veranda r. round house; took gate r. off hinges; turned r. round*); exactly, quite, (*r. in the middle*); very, to the full, (*know r. well; banqueted r. royally; was r. glad to hear; r.* HONOURABLE, REVEREND; *r.-down*, thorough, -ly, as *is a r.-d. scoundrel, was r.-d. sorry*); justly, properly, correctly, aright, truly, satisfactorily, (*whether they act r. or wrong; does not hold his pen, do the sum, r.; serves* *him r.*, is no worse than he deserves; *nothing goes r. with me*; *if I remember r.*; *guessed r.*); to r. hand (*eyes r.!*, order to soldiers dressing; *looks neither r. nor left*). [com.-Teut.; OE *riht* a. & n., *rihtan* v., *rihte* adv., cf. Du. & G *recht* &c., also L *rectus* DIRECT²]

righ·teous (-tsh*u*s, -ty*u*s), a. Just, upright, virtuous, law-abiding, (of person, life, action). Hence **righ·teously**² adv., **righ·teousness** n. [OE *rihtwis* (prec. n. + WISE a., or prec. a. + WISE n.) w. assim. to *bounteous* &c.]

righ·tful, a. (Of actions &c.) equitable, fair; (of persons) legitimately entitled to position &c. (*the r. king, heir, owner*), (of office, property, &c.) that one is entitled to. Hence **righ·tfully**² adv., **righ·tfulness** n. [-FUL]

righ·tly, adv. Justly, fairly, properly, correctly, accurately, justifiably. [-LY²]

ri·gid, a. Not flexible, stiff, unyielding, (*a r. bar, stem, frame, airship*); inflexible, harsh, strict, precise, punctilious, (*r. justice, principles, Catholics, adherence to rules, economy*). Hence or cogn. **rigi·dity** n., **ri·gidly**² adv. [f. L *rigidus* (as RIGOR)]

ri·gmarole, n. Rambling or meaningless talk or tale; (attrib.) incoherent. [prob. f. obs. *ragman roll* = catalogue, etym. dub.]

ri·gor (-or), n. (path.). Sudden chill with shivering before fever &c.; *r. mortis*, stiffening of body after death. [L (*rigēre* be stiff, -OR¹)]

ri·gour (-*er*), n. Severity, strictness, harshness, (pl.) harsh measures; strict enforcement *of* rules &c. (*with the utmost r. of the law*); extremity or excess *of* weather, hardship, famine, &c., great distress; austerity of life, Puritanic strictness of observance or doctrine, so **ri·gorism**(3), **ri·gorist**(2), nn.; logical accuracy, exactitude. So **ri·gorous** a., **ri·gorously**² adv. [OF, f. L (prec.)]

ri·gsdag, n. Danish Parliament. [Da.]

Rig-ve·da (-vā-), n. The chief VEDA. [f. Skr. *ṛigveda* (*ṛic* praise)]

ri·ksdag, n. Swedish parliament. [Sw.]

rile, v.t. (slang). Raise anger in, irritate. [var. of obs. & U.S. *roil* make muddy, cf. obs. F *ruiler* mix mortar]

rilie·vo (rēlyā-), n. = RELIEF², RELIEVO. [It.]

rill, n., & v.i. Small stream, runnel, rivulet; hence **ri·llet**¹ n. (Vb) issue or flow as r. [cf. Du. *ril*, G *rille*]

rille, n. (astr.). Trench or narrow valley of moon's surface. [G (prec.)]

rille·tt(e)s, n. pl. Preparation of minced ham, chicken, fat, &c. [F (-*es*)]

rim¹, n., & v.t. Outer ring of wheel's framework, not including tire; frame of sieve; (poet.) circular object (*golden r.*, crown); (Naut.) surface *of* the water; raised edge or border, margin, verge, esp. of something more or less circular; *r.-brake*, acting on r. of wheel; hence **ri·mless**, **(-)rimmed**², aa. (Vb) furnish with r., serve as r. to, edge, border. [OE *rima*, cf. ON *rime* ridge]

rim², n. (archaic). *R.* (*of the belly*), peritoneum. [OE *rēoma*, cf. Du. *riem*, G *riemen*, strap]

rime¹, n., & v.t. = RHYME¹, ². [earlier *rime* (RHYME) was corrected c. 1560 to RHYTHM, which served for senses *rhythm* & *rhyme* till *rhyme* was established c. 1700 as different.; obs. *rime* was revived c. 1870 & is often used by writers on prosody & literature]

rime², n., & v.t., (chiefly poet.). Hoarfrost; hence **ri·my**² a. (Vb) cover with r. [OE & ON *hrim*, cf. Du. *rijm*]

ri·mer, n. = REAM²*er*. [dial. *rime* var. of REAM², -ER¹]

rī·mose, rī·mous, aa. (bot. &c.). Full of chinks or fissures. [f. L *rimosus* (*rima* chink, -OSE¹), -OUS]

rīnd, n., & v.t. Bark of tree or plant (vb, strip r. from); peel of fruit or vegetable; harder enclosing surface of cheese or other substance; skin of bacon &c.; external aspect, surface. Hence **-rinded**² a. [OE, cf. Du. *run*, G *rinde*]

ri·nderpest, n. Disease of ruminants esp. oxen, cattle-plague. [G (*rinder* pl. of *rind* ox)]

ring¹, n., & v.i. & t. Circlet usu. of precious metal & often set with gem(s) worn round finger as ornament or token (esp. of betrothal or marriage) or signet, or (usu. *nose, arm,* &c., *-r.*) hung to or encircling other part of body; circular appliance of any material & any (but esp., cf. *hoop*, no great) size; raised or sunk or otherwise distinguishable line or band round, rim of, cylindrical or circular object; circular fold, coil, bend, structure, part, or mark (*rr.* of tree, concentric bands of wood corresponding in number to tree's years; *has livid rr. round his eyes*; *puffing out rr. of smoke*; *rr.* in water, circular ripples expanding from centre of agitation); persons, trees, &c., disposed in a circle, such disposition, (Commerc. &c.) combination of traders or politicians acting together for control of market or policy; circular enclosure or space for circus-riding, prize-fighting (PRIZE-*r.*), betting at races (*the r.*, bookmakers), showing of cattle, &c.; circular or spiral course (*make rr. round*, go or do things incomparably quicker than); *r.-bark* v.t., cut r. in bark of (tree) to kill it or to check its growth & bring it into bearing; *r.-bolt*, bolt with r. attached for fastening rope to &c.; *r.-bone*, (horse-disease with) deposit of bony matter on pastern-bones; *r.-cartilage*, CRICOID; *r.-dove*, wood-pigeon; *r.-fence*, completely enclosing estate &c.; *r.-finger*, third esp. of left hand; *r.-goal*, game in which light hoop is thrown towards goal with sticks; *r.-hunt*, in which beasts are driven inwards by r. of fire;

ri·ngleader, (one of) chief instigator(s) in mutiny, riot, &c.; *r.-lock*, opened by right adjustment of several grooved rr.; *r.-man*, bookmaker; *r.-master*, manager of circus performance; *r.-neck*, r.-necked plover or duck; *r.-necked*, with band(s) of colour round neck; *r.-net*, kind of salmon net, also of lace; *r. ouzel*, kind of bird allied to blackbird; *r.-snake*, common European grass-snake (from coiling); *r.-stand*, for keeping finger-rr. on; *r.-straked* (bibl.), marked with rr. of colour round body; *r.-tail*, female of hen-harrier, also golden eagle till its third year, also r.-tailed opossum or phalanger; *r.-tailed*, with tail ringed in alternate colours, also (of phalanger) with tail curled at end; *r.-taw*, game with marbles in r.; *r.-wall*, as *r.-fence*; *ringworm*, skin-disease esp. of children in circular patches; hence **(-)ring**ED[2], **ri·ng**LESS, aa. (Vb): (of hawk &c.) rise in spirals; (of hunted fox) take circular course; encompass (usu. *round, about, in*; often in p.p.), hem in (game, cattle) by riding or beating in circle round them; put r. upon, put r. in nose of (pig, bull), (*r.-the-bull*, game with r. to be thrown or swung on to hook); =*r.-bark* above; cut (onions, apples) into rr. [com.-Teut.; OE *hring*, cf. ON *hringr*, Du. & G *ring*]

ring[2], v.i. & t. (*rang*, now rarely *rung*; *rung*), & n. Give forth clear resonant sound (as) of vibrating metal (*bell, trumpet, coin, sound, rings*, often *out*, &c.; *with a ringing laugh*; *a shot rang out*; *a ringing frost*, in which ground rings under foot; *r. true, false*, of coin tested by throwing on counter, & fig. of sentiments &c.), (of bell) *r. to* or *for* prayers, dinner, &c., convey summons by ringing; (of place) resound, re-echo, (*with* sound, *to* sound or its cause, *with* fame, &c. or its theme, with talk *of*; often *again*); (of utterance or other sound) *r. in* one's *ears, heart*, &c., linger in one's hearing, haunt the memory; (of ears) be filled with sensation as of bell-ringing (so *has a ringing in the ears*) or *with* sound; make (bell) r. (*r. the bell*, esp. as summons to servant; *r. up bell*, raise church bell over beam & r. it there; *ringing engine*, pile-driver worked by ropes like peal of bells), throw (coin) on counter to test it; r. bell as summons (*r. at door*, to get admittance &c.; *r. for* servant, coffee, one's boots, &c.; *did you r., sir?*); sound (peal, knell, BOB[4] *major, the* CHANGE[1]*s*) on bells (or with *bell* or *bells* as subj.; *r. the knell of*, announce or herald abolition &c. of); announce (hour &c.) by sound of bell(s); summon *up* &c. by ringing bell (*r. up* on telephone, get or seek communication with; *r. off*, terminate telephone interview; *r. curtain up* or *down* in theatre, direct it by bell to be raised or lowered); usher *in, out*, with bell-ringing. (N.) set *of* (church) bells; ringing sound, ringing tone in voice &c., resonance of coin or vessel; act of ringing bell, sound so produced, (*three rr. for the hall porter*; *give bell a r.*; *heard a loud r. at the door*). [OE *hringan*, cf. ON *hringja*, G *ringen*, perh. imit.]

ri·ngent (-j-), a. Gaping, grinning, (esp. bot. of wide labiate corolla). [as RICTUS, -ENT]

ri·nger (-nger), n. Quoit that falls round pin; fox that runs in ring when hunted; bell-r.; device for ringing bell. [RING[1], [2], -ER[1]]

ri·nglet (-ngl-), n. Small ring, fairy ring on grass, ring-shaped mark &c., (rare); curly lock of hair, curl, whence **ri·nglet**ED[2], **ri·nglet**Y[2], aa. [-LET]

rink, n., & v.i. Stretch of ice used for game of curling; sheet of natural or artificial ice, floor, for (roller-)skating. (Vb) skate on r. esp. with roller-skates, whence **ri·nk**ER[1] n. [earlier sense *jousting-ground*; from 14th c.; prob. f. OF *renc* RANK[1]]

rinse, v.t., & n. Wash out or *out* (vessel, mouth) by filling with water &c., shaking, & emptying; pour liquid over or wash lightly; put (clothes) through clean water to remove soap; clear (impurities) *out* or *away* by rinsing; wash (food) *down* with liquor; (n.) rinsing (*give it a r.*). [f. F *rincer*, OF *raincer* perh. = med. L *re(sincerare* f. *sincerus* pure), RE- 8]

ri·ot (-ot), n., & v.i. & t. Loose living, debauchery; loud revelry, a revel; unrestrained indulgence in or display or enjoyment of something (*a r. of emotion, colour, sound*); (Hunt.) following of any scent indiscriminately (*run r.*, orig. of hounds doing this, now usu. fig. of person or his tongue or fancy throwing off all restraint); disorder, tumult, disturbance of the peace, outbreak of lawlessness, on part of a crowd (*R. Act*, by which persons not dispersing after official reading of part of it incur guilt of felony; *read the R.A.*, lit., & joc. of parent &c. announcing that noise &c. is to cease); hence or cogn. **ri·otous** a., **ri·otous**LY[2] adv., **ri·otous**NESS, (rare) **ri·ot**RY(2), nn. (Vb) live wantonly, revel; throw *away* (time, money), wear *out* (life), in dissipation; make or engage in a political r. or offence against the R. Act, whence **ri·ot**ER[2](4) n. [f. OF *riote(r)*, cf. Pr. *riota*, It. *riotta*, etym. dub.]

rip[1], n. Worthless horse, screw; dissolute person, rake. [perh. var. of REP[3]]

rip[2], v.t. & i., & n. Cut or tear (thing) quickly or forcibly away from something (*r. out the lining*; *r. the boards off*); make long cut or tear in (n., such cut &c.), cut or tear vigorously apart (often *up*; *had his belly ripped up*); split (wood, rock), saw (wood) with the grain (*r.-saw*, used thus); strip (roof) of tiles or slates &

laths; make (fissure, passage) by ripping; open *up* (wound, quarrel, sorrow, the past) again; come violently asunder, split (intr.); rush along (of ship, & transf.; so *let her r.*, do not check speed or interfere), (part., slang, cf. *rattling*) fine, splendid, enjoyable, firstrate, (also as adv. with *good* &c., as *a ripping good time*), whence **ri·pping**LY[2] adv. [cf. Fris. *rippe*]

rip[3], n. Stretch of broken water in sea or river, overfall. [perh. f. prec.]

rīpār·ian, a. & n. Of, on, river-bank (esp. *r. proprietor, rights*); (n.) r. proprietor. [L *riparius* (*ripa* bank, -ARY[1]) + -AN]

ripe, a., & v.t. & i. Ready to be reaped, gathered, eaten, drunk, used, or dealt with, fully developed, mellow, mature, prepared or able *to* undergo something, in fit state *for*, (*r. corn, fruit, cheese, wine, seed*; *r. lips*, red & full like r. fruit; *r. beauty*, of grown woman; *r. scholar, scholarship, judgement, experience, understanding*; *die at a r. age*, old; *persons of riper years*, not immature; *opportunity r. to be seized*; *is r. to hear the truth*; *mood* or *person, plan, disease, r. for mischief, execution, treatment*; *soon r. soon rotten*, prov. depreciating precocity); hence **ri·pen**[6] v.t. & i., **ri·pely**[2] adv., **ri·peness** n. (Vb, chiefly poet.) =ripen. [OE *ripe*, cf. Du. *rijp*, G *reif*]

ripō·ste, n., & v.i. Quick return thrust in fencing, (transf.) counterstroke, retort; (vb) deliver r. [F, f. It. *risposta* RESPONSE]

ri·pper, n. In vbl senses; esp.: tool for ripping roof; rip-saw; (slang) ripping person or thing. [-ER[1]]

ri·pple[1], n., & v.t. Toothed implement used to clear away seeds from flax; (vb) treat with r. [cf. Du. *repel(en)*, G *riffel(n)*]

ri·pple[2], n., & v.i. & t. Ruffling of water's surface, small wave(s); wavy or crinkled appearance in hair, ribbons, &c.; gentle lively sound that rises & falls (esp. *a r. of conversation*); *r.-mark*, ridge, ridged surface, left on sand or mud or rock by water or wind; hence **ri·pplet**[1] n., **ri·pply**[2] a. (Vb) form, flow in, show, agitate or mark with, sound like, rr. [vb found earlier than n.; etym. dub.; cf. RIP[3] (found later), -LE(3)]

Ripuār·ian, a. Of the ancient Franks living on Rhine between Meuse & Moselle (esp. *R. law*, code observed by them). [f. med. L *Ripuarius* (perh. irreg. f. L *ripa* bank) + -AN]

Rip van Winkle, n. Person of utterly antiquated ideas or information. [hero of tale by W. Irving who slept 20 years]

rise[1] (-z), v.i. & t. (*rose* pr. -z, *risen* pr.-zn; p.p., see -ED[1](2), often with *is* &c.). Get up from lying or sitting or kneeling position, get out of bed, (of meeting &c.) cease to sit for business, recover standing or upright position, become erect, leave ground, come to life again or usu. *again* or *from the dead*, (*r. from table*, leave meal; *all rose to receive him*; *house*, i.e. theatre audience, *rises at* actress &c., in universal applause; *found he could not, was too weak to, r.*; *r., Sir Thomas* &c., formula in knighting; *r. betimes, at 5.0 a.m., with the lark*; *r. up early*; *Parliament will r. next week*; *fell never to r. again*; *the hair rose on his head*; *horse rises on its hind-legs*; *horse rises to a fence*, takes off for leap; *birds r. well today*); cease to be quiet, abandon submission, make revolt, (*if a wind should r.*; *r. in arms, rebellion, &c., against oppression, oppressor*; *town rose on its garrison*; *gorge, stomach, rises*, indignation or disgust is felt; *my whole soul rises against it*, finds it intolerable); come or go up, grow upwards, ascend, mount, soar, project or swell upwards, become higher, reach higher position or level or amount, increase, incline upwards, come to surface, become or be visible above or *above* surroundings, develop greater energy or intensity, be progressive, (*sun, star, morning, dawn, rises*; *the risen sun*; *rising cupboard*, kitchen lift; *the rising generation*, the young; *smoke rises straight up*; *tree rises 20 ft*, attains that height; *fabric rose like a dream*; *blisters r.*, form; *bread will not r.*, swell with yeast; *balloon rises*; *should r. above petty jealousies*, be superior to; *picture, idea, rises before the mind*; *river, tide, flood, level, rose 6 ft, is rising*; *the mercury, barometer* or *glass, is rising*; *spirits r.*, become more cheerful; *prices, demands, r.*; *the funds, sugar, r.*, increase in value or price; *a rising lawyer*; *a man likely to r.*; *r. in the world*, attain higher social position; *r. to greatness*; *rising ground*, sloping up; *in a rising series*; *rises in a gentle curve*; *the interest rises with each act*; *bubbles r.*; *fish rises*, comes to surface to feed; *drowning man rises three times*; *in the foreground rises a castle*; *does not r. above mediocrity*; *the wind is rising*; *her colour rose*, became brighter or deeper; *rising 5, 14*, getting on for that age); develop powers equal *to* (*does not r. to an occasion*; *rose to the emergency, requirements*, &c.); have origin, begin to be, flow, *from, in, at*, &c. (*river rises from a spring, in the Grampians*, &c.; *earth & heaven rose at His word*; *the difficulty rises from misapprehension*); (rare, usu. poet.) arise (*a feud, rumour, rose*); (causative in spec. senses) make or see r. (*did not r. a fish, a bird, all day*; *r. ship*, see it appear from top downwards in approaching it). [com.-Teut.; OE *risan* (usu. *arisan* ARISE), cf. Du. *rijzen*, G (of sun) *reisen*]

rise[2], n. Coming up *of* sun &c. (rare; *at r. of sun, day*; cf. *sunr.* &c.); ascent, upward slope, knoll, hill, (*came to a r. in the road*; *chapel stands on a r.*); social advancement, upward progress, increase in power, rank, value, price, amount, height, pitch, wages, &c., (*has had a r. in life*; *the r. & fall of statesmen*; *the r. of the tide is 30 ft*; *asks for a r.*, higher wages; *prices are on the r.*, increasing); movement of fish to surface (*not a sign of a r.*; fig., *get* or *take a r. out of* one, draw him into display of temper or other foible); vertical height of step, arch, incline, &c., (also **ri·ser**[1] f. prec.) vertical piece connecting two treads of staircase; origin, start, (*has, takes, its r. in, from*; *give r. to*, occasion, suggest). [f. prec.]

ri·sible (-z-), a. Inclined to laugh, so **risibi·lity** n.; of laughter (*r. nerves, faculties*, &c.); (rare) laughable, ludicrous. [f. LL *risibilis* (*ridēre ris-* laugh, -IBLE)]

ri·sing, n. In vbl senses; esp.: *r.*(*-again*), resurrection; insurrection, revolt; boil, pimple. [-ING[1]]

risk, n., & v.t. Hazard, chance of or *of* bad consequences, loss, &c., exposure to mischance, (*there is the r. of his catching cold*; *run rr., a r., the r.*, often *of*, expose oneself or be exposed to loss &c.; *take rr.* &c., expose oneself so; *at the r. of his life*; *at owner's* &c. *r.*, he to bear any contingent loss); *r.-money*, allowance to cashier to cover accidental deficits; hence **ri·sk·ful, ri·skless**, aa. (Vb) expose to chance of injury or loss; venture on, take the chances of, (*r. the jump, a battle, a sprained ankle*). [f. F *risque(r)* f. It. *risco* n., *riscare* v., etym. dub.]

ri·sky, a. Hazardous, full of risk; (also, & after, F *risqué*) involving suggestion of indecency, offending against propriety, (of story, dramatic situation, &c.). Hence **ri·skily**[2] adv., **ri·skiness** n. [-Y[2]]

risqué. See prec.

ri·ssole, n. Fried ball or cake of meat or fish mixed with bread-crumbs &c. [F, perh. ult. f. L *russeolus* reddish]

ritarda·ndo (rē-), mus. direction. Slower. [It.]

rite, n. (Form of procedure, action required or usual, in) a religious or solemn ceremony or observance (*the rr. of hospitality*; *the r. of confirmation*; *burial* or *funeral rr.*; *conjugal* or *nuptial rr.*, sexual intercourse between husband & wife; *the Latin, Anglican*, &c., *r.*, body of usages characteristic of a Church). Hence **ri·teless** a. [f. L *ritus -ūs*]

ri·tual, a. & n. Of, with, consisting in, involving, religious rites; hence **ri·tually**[2] adv. (N.) prescribed order of performing religious service; book containing this; performance of r. acts, whence (w. implication of excess) **ri·tualism**(3), **ri·tualist**(2), nn., **rituali·stic** a., **rituali·stically** adv., **ri·tualize**(2, 3) v.i. & t. [f. L *ritualis* (prec., -AL)]

rī·vage (-ĭj), n. (poet.). Coast, shore, bank. [F (OF *rive* f. L *ripa* bank, -AGE)]

rī·val, n., attrib. a., & v.t. & i. (-ll-). Person's competitor for some prize (esp. a woman's or man's love) or in some pursuit or quality (also of things; *without a r.*, unapproached for excellence &c.); hence **ri·valry**(2, 4), **ri·valship**, nn. (Adj.) that is a r. or are rr. (Vb) vie with, be comparable to, seem or claim to be as good &c. as; (rare) be in rivalry. [f. L *rivalis* (*rivus* stream, -AL) orig. = on same stream]

rive, v.t. & i. (*rived*; *riven*, rarely *rived*). Rend, cleave, wrench *away* or *off* or *from*, strike asunder, (archaic, poet.); (of artisan) split (wood, stone), make (laths) by splitting, whence **ri·ver**[1] [-ER[1](1)] n.; be split, gape under blow &c., (of wood &c.) admit of splitting. [f. ON *rífa* perh. cogn. w. G *reiben* rub]

rĭ·vel, v.i. & t. (-ll-; archaic). Wrinkle, crumple, shrivel. [prob. back formation f. *rivelled*, OE *rifelede* perh. f. **rifel* a fold +ED[2]]

riven. See RIVE.

rĭ·ver[2], n. (for *river*[1] see RIVE). Copious stream of water flowing in channel to sea or lake or marsh or another r. (*the r.* often prefixed to name, as *the r. Thames*); *the* boundary between life & death; copious flow or stream *of* (*a r. of lava*; *rr. of blood*, much bloodshed); (attrib., prefixed to many names of animals, plants, & things) living in, situated or used on, river(s); *r.*-BED[1](2); *r.-god*, mythological being dwelling in & personifying a r.; *r.-horse*, hippopotamus; *riverside*, ground along r.'s bank (often attrib., as *a r.-s. villa*). Hence **(-)rivered**[2], **ri·verless**, aa. [f. OF *rivere* f. pop. L **riparia* (L *ripa* bank, -ARY[1])]

ri·verain, a. & n. Of river or its neighbourhood; situated, dwelling, by river; (n.) person dwelling by river. [F (*rivière* as prec., -AN)]

ri·verine, a. Of, on, river or its banks, riparian. [-INE[1]]

rĭ·vet, n., & v.t. Nail or bolt for holding together metal plates &c., its headless end being beaten out after passing through two holes. (Vb) clinch (bolt); join or fasten with rr. (*together, down, to, into, on* adv. or prep., &c.); fix, make immovable, (*r. error* &c.); concentrate, direct intently, (eyes, attention, &c., *upon*); engross (attention), engross attention of; hence **ri·veter**[1](1, 2) n. [vb f. n., OF (*river* clinch, etym. dub.)]

ri·vière (-ĭār, *or as F*), n. Gem necklace, esp. of more than one string. [F, as RIVER[2]]

rĭ·vūlet, n. Small stream; kinds of moth. [perh. f. It. *rivoletto* (L *rivus* stream, -UL-, -ET[1])]

ri·x-dollar, n. (hist.). Silver coin & money of account (4/6–2/3) of 16th–19th cc. in some continental States. [f. Du. *rijcksdaler*, cf. G *reichstaler*, see (*bishop*)*ric*, DOLLAR]

roach[1] (rōtsh), n. Small freshwater fish allied to carp (*sound as a r.*, in firstrate health &c.); *r.-backed, -bellied* (convex in profile). [f. OF *roche* etym. dub.]
roach[2], n. (naut.). Upward curve in foot of square sail. [?]
road[1], n. (Usu. pl.; also *roadstead*) piece of water near shore in which ships can ride at anchor; line of communication between places for use of foot-passengers, riders, & vehicles (*on the r.*, travelling; *take the r.*, set out; *the r.*, the highway; *take to the r.* archaic, become highwayman; *rule of the r.*, custom regulating side to be taken by vehicles, riders, or ships, meeting or passing each other); way of getting *to* (*the r. to York, ruin, success*; *royal r. to*, way of attaining without trouble); one's way or route (*in the, my,* &c., *r.* colloq., obstructing some-one or something; so *get out of the, my,* &c., *r.*); *R. Board*, authority making & improving rr.; *r.-book*, describing rr. of country &c., itinerary; *r.-hog*, dangerous scorching motorist; *roadman* (repairing rr.); *r.-metal*, broken stone for r.-making; *r.-side*, border of r. (esp. attrib., as *r.-s. plants, inn*); *roadway*, r., central part of r. (opp. *side-path*), part of bridge or railway used for traffic; *roadworthy*, fit to be used on the r., (of person) fit to travel. Hence **(-)road**ED[2], **roa·d**LESS, aa. [OE *rád* (*rīdan* RIDE)]
road[2], v.t. (Of dog) follow up (game-bird, or abs.) by foot-scent. [?]
roa·dster, n. Ship at anchor in roadstead; horse, bicycle, &c., for use on the road; experienced traveller. [-STER]
roam, v.i. & t., & n. Ramble (v., & rarely n. as *a half-hour's r.*), wander; walk or travel unsystematically over or through or about (country, seas, &c.). [?]
roan[1], a. & n. (Of animal) with coat of which the prevailing colour is thickly interspersed with another, esp. bay or sorrel or chestnut mixed with white or grey (often with chief colour prefixed, as *black, blue, red, r.*); (n.) r. horse, cow. [OF, cf. Pr. *rouant*, It. & Sp. *roano*]
roan[2], n. Soft sheepskin leather used in bookbinding as substitute for morocco. [perh. f. *Rouen* in France]
roar, v.i. & t., & n. (Utter, send forth) loud deep hoarse sound (as) of lion, person or company in pain or rage or loud laughter, the sea, thunder, cannon, furnace, &c. (*the r. of the waves*; *rr. of laughter*; *lions roaring after their prey*; *roared with pain* or *laughter* or *for mercy*; *you need not r.*, talk so loud; *set table in a r.*, make company laugh loud); (of horse) make loud noise in breathing due to disease, whence **roar·**ER[1], **roar·**ING[1], nn.; (of place) be full of din, re-echo, (often *again*); say, sing, utter, (words, chorus, oath, &c., often *out*) in loud tone; make *deaf, hoarse,* &c., put *down*, by roaring; (part.) riotous, noisy, boisterous, brisk, (*a roaring night*, stormy, also spent in revelry; *a roaring blade* archaic, fast liver; *the roaring game*, curling; *roaring forties*, see FORTY; *in roaring health*; *drive a roaring trade*). [n. f. vb, OE *rárian*, cf. LG *raren*, G *rehren*, prob. imit.]
roast, v.t. & i. (p.p. in vb forms *-ed*, as adj. *roast*), & n. Cook (esp. meat) by exposure to open fire or (improp. for *bake*) in oven (*prefers r. beef, his meat roasted*); heat or calcine (ore) in furnace; heat (coffee-beans) as preparation for grinding; expose (victim for torture, one*self* or some part for warmth) to fire; ridicule, banter, chaff; undergo roasting; (part.) very hot; *roasting-jack*, appliance keeping meat in motion while roasting. (N.) r. meat or a dish of it (*rule the r.*, be master); operation of roasting. [n. partly f. OF *rost*, partly f. vb, f. OF *rostir* f. Teut. (OHG *rôsten* f. *rôst* gridiron)]
roa·ster, n. In vbl senses; esp.: kind of oven for roasting; ore-roasting furnace; coffee-roasting apparatus; pig, potato, &c., fit for roasting. [-ER[1]]
rob, v.t. Despoil (person &c.) of or *of* property by violence, feloniously plunder (person, place, often *of*), deprive *of* what is due, (*r.* PETER); (abs.) commit robbery. So **ro·bber** [-ER[1], -ER[2](4)], **ro·bb**ERY(2, 4), nn. [f. OF *rob*(*b*)*er* f. Teut. (REAVE)]
robe, n., & v.t. & i. Any long loose outer garment (rare, poet., metaph.); (trade name of) kind of lady's dress in one piece; outer garment of baby in long-clothes; (often pl.) long outer garment worn as indication of wearer's rank, office, profession, &c., gown, vestment, (*the long r.*, legal or clerical dress; *gentlemen of the r.*, lawyers); *r.-de-chambre* (F), dressing-gown, wrapper. (Vb) invest (person) in r., dress; assume one's rr. or vestments. [OF, conn. w. prec., orig. sense *booty*]
rŏ·bin, R-, n. (Also *r. redbreast*) small red-breasted bird; (with or without distinctive epithet) kinds of Amer., Colonial, & Indian bird; *r.-, r.'s-*, in plant names, as *R.-run-the-hedge* ground-ivy, *r.'s-eye* herb-Robert; *R. Goodfellow*, a sportive goblin; *R. Hood*, (type of) medieval forest outlaw; ROUND[1] *r.* [OF, fam. for *Robert*]
rō·borant, a. & n. (med.). Strengthening (drug). [L *roborare* (*robur -oris* strength), -ANT]
rō·bot, n. An apparently human automaton, an intelligent & obedient but impersonal machine; (transf.) machine-like person. [term in Capek's play *R.U.R.*; cf. Pol. *robotnik* workman]
rō·burite (-er-), n. A strong flameless explosive. [L *robur* strength, -ITE[1](2)]
robu·st, a. (-er, -est). Of strong health & physique, not slender or delicate or weakly, (of persons, animals, plants, body, health, &c.); (of exercise, discipline, &c.) tending to or requiring strength, invigorating, vigorous; (of intellect &c.)

sensible, straightforward, not given to nor confused by subtleties. Hence **robu·st**LY[2] adv., **robu·st**NESS n. [f. L *robustus* (*robur* strength)]

robu·stious, a. Boisterous, self-assertive, noisy. [earlier in common use = prec.; now chiefly w. ref. to *Hamlet* III. ii. 10]

roc, n. Gigantic bird of Eastern tales. [f. Arab. *rokh*]

rŏ·cambole, n. Kind of leek, Spanish garlic. [F, etym. dub.]

rŏ·chet (-tsh-), n. Surplice-like vestment used chiefly by bishops & abbots. [OF, f. Teut. (G *rock* coat)]

rock[1], n. Solid part of earth's crust underlying soil (*dug down to the living r.*; often *bed-r.*; *built, founded, on the r.*, lit., & fig., secure; *R. of ages*, Christ), mass of this projecting & forming a hill, cliff, &c., or standing up into or out of sea &c. from bottom (*the R.*, Gibraltar; *run upon the rr., see rr. ahead*, &c., of lit. or fig. shipwreck or danger of it; *on the rr.* slang, hard up; *r. of water* &c., ref. to *Numb.* xx. 11); stone as a substance (*a mass, needle of r.*); large detached stone, boulder; (Geol.) any particular igneous or stratified mineral constituent of earth's crust including sands, clays, &c.; kinds of hard sweetmeat (usu. *almond* &c. *r.*); (also *blue r.*) = *r.-pigeon*; *r.-bed*, base of r., rocky bottom; *r.-bird*, esp. puffin; *r.-bottom* (slang, of prices &c.), very lowest; *r.-cake*, bun with hard rough surface; *r.-cork*, variety of asbestos; *r.-crystal*, transparent colourless silica or quartz usu. in hexagonal prisms; *r.-dove*, r.-pigeon; *r.-drill*, r.-boring tool or machine; *r. English*, mixed language of Gibraltar; *r. fever*, kind of enteric prevalent at Gibraltar; *r.-fish*, kinds of goby, bass, wrasse, &c.; *r.-goat*, ibex; *r.-hewn*, cut out of the r.; *r.-leather*, as *r.-cork*; *rockling* [-LING[1]], kinds of fish esp. sea-loach; *r.-oil*, native naphtha; *r.-paper*, as *r.-cork*; *r.-pigeon*, kind of dove haunting rr. & supposed source of domestic pigeon; *r.-ribbed*, (of earth, coast, &c.) with ribs of r.; *r.-rose*, kinds of cistus with yellow, rose, or salmon flowers; *r.-salt*, found stratified in free state; *R. scorpion*, (nickname for) person born at Gibraltar; *r.-silk*, as *r.-cork*; *r.-sucker*, sea lamprey; *r.-tar*, petroleum; *r.-whistler*, Alpine marmot; *r.-wood*, as *r.-cork*; *r.-work* or **ro·ck**ERY(3) n., pile of rough stones with soil in interstices for growing ferns &c. on, also natural group or display of rr. Hence **ro·ck**LESS, **ro·ck**LIKE, aa., **ro·ck**LET n. [f. OF *roke, rocque, roche*, etym. dub.]

rock[2], n.(hist.). Distaff. [cf. Du. *rok(ken)*, G *rocken*, It. *rocca*]

rock[3], v.t. & i., & n. Move (t. & i.) gently to & fro (as) in cradle, set or keep (cradle &c.) or (of cradle &c.) be in such motion, (*r. him to sleep*; *ship rocking on, rocked by, the waves*; *sat rocking himself* or *rocking in his chair*; *rocked in security, hopes*, &c.); (Gold-min.) work (CRADLE), work cradle, shake in cradle; sway (t. & i.) from side to side, shake, oscillate, reel, (*earthquake rocks house, house rocks, a rocking gait*); *ro·cking-chair*, mounted on rockers, or with seat arranged to r.; *ro·cking-horse*, wooden horse on rockers for child; *rocking-stone*, poised boulder easily rocked; *rocking-turn* in skating, from any edge to same in opposite direction with body revolving away from convex of first curve (*counter-r.-t.* or *-rocker* or *counter*, same turn with body revolving away from concave); *r.-shaft*, that oscillates about axis without making complete revolutions; *r.-staff*, part of apparatus working smith's bellows; (n.) rocking motion, spell of rocking. [OE *roccian*; cf. Du. *rukken*, G *rücken*, tug]

ro·cker, n. In vbl senses; esp.: one of the curved bars on which cradle &c. rocks; gold-miner's cradle; skate with highly curved blade; (Skat.) *r., counter-r.*, = (*counter-*) ROCK[3]*ing-turn*. [ROCK[3], -ER[1]]

ro·cket[1], n. Kinds of plant of which some are used as salad & some grown for flowers (*Garden, Roman*, &c., *r.*; *R. gentle*; *Base r.*, wild mignonette; *Blue r.*, kinds of wolfsbane & larkspur, also bluebell). [f. F *roquette* f. It. *ruchetta* (*ruca* f. L *eruca*, -ETTE)]

ro·cket[2], n., & v.t. & i. Cylindrical paper or metal case that can be projected to height or distance by ignition of contents, used in firework displays, for signalling, to carry line to ship in distress, &c. (Vb) bombard with rr.; (of horse or its rider) bound upwards or dart like r.; (of pheasant &c.) fly straight upwards, fly fast & high, whence **ro·cket**ER[1] n. [f. F *roquet* or It. *rocchetta* (*rocca* ROCK[2], w. ref. to cylindrical shape), -ETTE]

ro·cky, a., & n. (pl.). Of rock, full of or abounding in rocks, (*the R. Mountains*, or as n. *the Rr.*, western N.-Amer. range); like rock in ruggedness, firmness, solidity, &c.; (rare) unsteady, tottering. Hence **ro·ck**ILY[2] adv., **ro·ck**INESS n. [ROCK[1, 3], -Y[2]]

rocō·co, a. & n. (Of furniture, architecture, &c.) with much conventional decoration, tastelessly florid, in the Louis-Quatorze or Louis-Quinze style, (n., the r. style); antiquated, out of date. [F, perh. f. *rocaille* pebble-work]

rod, n. Slender straight round stick growing as shoot on tree or cut from it or made from wood, switch, wand, (somet. as symbol of office &c., see esp. BLACK[1] *r.*; AARON'S-ROD; *divining, dowsing, -r.*, see DOWSING); such stick, or bundle of twigs, for use in caning or flogging (*the r.*, use of this; *spare the r. & spoil the child*; *make* &c. *a r. for* one's *own back*, prepare trouble for oneself; *kiss the r.*, take punishment meekly or gladly; *have a r.*

in pickle for, be ready to punish when time comes); =FISH[2]*ing-r.*; (also *rodman* & **ro·dster** n.) angler; (as measure) = PERCH[2]; slender metal bar, connecting bar, shaft, (*curtain, piston*, &c., *-r.*); (Physiol.) r.-shaped structure. Hence **ro·dless, ro·dlike**, aa., **ro·dlet** n. [OE *rodd*, cf. ON *rudda* club]

rode. See RIDE.

rō·dent, a. & n. (Animal) of the order *Rodentia* with strong incisor & no canine teeth, whence **rode·ntial** a.; gnawing (esp. in Path. of ulcers). [f. L *rodere ros-* gnaw]

rode·o (-dāō), n. A round-up of cattle on a western American range for branding &c., enclosure for this; exhibition of cowboys' skill. [Sp., f. *rodear* go round]

rŏdomonta·de, n., a., & v.i. Boastful, bragging, (saying or talk). (Vb) brag, talk big; hence **rodomonta·der**[1] n. [vb & adj. f. n., F (*Rodomont* f. It. *Rodomonte* character in *Orlando Furioso*, -ADE)]

roe[1] (rō), n. (collect. sing. somet. for pl.). Small kind of European & Asiatic deer; *roebuck*, male r.; *r.-deer*, r. [com.-Teut.; OE *rāha*, cf. Du. *ree*, G *reh*]

roe[2] (rō), n. Mass of eggs (also *hard r.*) in fish's ovarian membrane (*r.-corn*, one egg); *soft r.*, male fish's milt; *r.-stone*, oolite. Hence **(-)roed**[2] a. [cf. MDu., MLG, MHG, *roge*]

roga·tion, n. (Pl.) litany of the saints chanted on the three days before Ascension Day (*r. days*, these; *r. week, Sunday*, including, preceding, them,; *r. flower*, milk-wort), whence **roga·tional** a.; (Rom. Ant.) law proposed before the people by consul or tribune (*Licinian* &c. *rr.*, proposed by Licinius &c.). [f. L *rogatio* (*rogare* ask, -ATION)]

Rŏ·ger (-j-), male name (*the jolly R.*, pirates' black flag; *R.* or *Sir R. de Coverley*, a country-dance & tune).

rōgue (-g), n., & v.t. Idle vagrant (archaic); knave, rascal, swindler, (often playfully of mischievous child or waggish or arch-mannered person); inferior plant among seedlings (vb, weed out rr. from); (also *r. elephant, buffalo*, &c.) wild beast, esp. elephant, driven or living apart from the herd & of savage temper; shirking racehorse or hunter. Hence **ro·guery**(4) n., **ro·guish**[1] a., **ro·guishly**[2] adv., **ro·guishness** n. [16th-c. cant wd, etym. dub.]

roi, n. (F for) king (*r. fainéant*, ruler, chairman, &c., who is a mere figure-head like the Merovingian kings whose power was usurped by mayors of the palace; *le r. le veult, le r. s'avisera*, forms of giving, refusing, the royal assent to parliamentary bill, =the king wills it, will consider).

roi·nek, rooi-, n. New-comer, esp. British or European immigrant, in S. Africa; (in Boer war) British soldier. [S.-Afr.-Du. (*rooi-*), = red-neck]

roi·ster, v.i. Revel noisily, be uproarious, (esp. in part. as adj.). Hence **roi·sterer**[1], **roi·stering**[1], nn. [f. obs. *roister* roisterer f. F *rustre* var. of *ruste* f. L RUSTICUS]

Rō·land, name of nephew of Charlemagne celebrated in legend often with his comrade Oliver (*a R. for an Oliver*, effective retort).

role, *rôle*, n. Actor's part; one's function, what one is appointed or expected or has undertaken to do. [F (*rô-*, as foll.)]

rōll[1], n. Cylinder formed by turning flexible fabric such as paper or cloth over & over upon itself without folding (*rr. of carpet, printing-paper*, &c.; SWISS *r.*), (in Ionic capital) volute; document, esp. official record, in this form (*Master of the Rr.*, judge of Court of Appeal with charge of certain public records; *the Rr.*, buildings in which these were formerly kept now superseded by Public Record Office, also court of Master of the Rr.), register or catalogue (*in the r. of saints*; *a long r. of heroes*; *on the rr. of fame*; RENT[3]*-r*; *r. of honour*, esp. list of those who have died for their country in war), the official list of qualified solicitors (*strike off the rr.*, debar from practising for dishonesty &c.), a list of persons esp. soldiers or schoolboys used to detect absentees (*r.-call*, calling over of this); more or less (semi)-cylindrical straight or curved mass of anything however formed (*a r. of butter, soap, straw, tobacco, hair*; *has rr. of fat on him*; *r. of bread* or usu. *r.*, small loaf esp. for breakfast use), (Arch., also *r.-moulding*) moulding of convex section; turned-back edge of something, e.g. coat-collar; (Book-bind.) revolving patterned tool for marking cover; cylinder or roller. [f. OF *rolle* (now *rôle*) f. L *rotulus* collat. form of *rotula* (foll.)]

rōll[2], v.t. & i., & n. Move (t. & i.) or send or go in some direction by turning over & over on axis often with aid of gravitation (*r. barrel*; *barrel started rolling*; *ball, coin, rolled under the table, into a hole*; *river rolls down stones*; *rolling stone* GATHERS *no moss*; *planets r. on their courses*; *years r. on* or *by*, go smoothly; *r.* one *over*, send him rolling or sprawling), make revolve between two surfaces (*rolling a marble between his palms*), wrap usu. *up in* by rolling motion (*rolled himself up in the blankets*); (t. & i. of eyes) change direction (of) with rotatory motion (*his eyes r. strangely*; *rolled his eyes on us*); wallow, turn about in fluid or loose medium, (of horse &c.) lie on back & kick about, (*porpoise, swimmer, rolls in the water*; *rolling in money, luxury, ease*; *mule tried to r.*, as way of getting rid of rider or load); sway or rock (t. & i.), walk with swaying gait as of sailor, reel, (*rolled himself from side to side*; *ship rolls & pitches*; *he rolled up to her*); undulate, show undulating surface or motion, go or propel or carry with such motion, (*sea, river, rolls; river rolls its waters to sea; waves r. in; smoke rolls up; chimney rolls up smoke; the mist rolled away; a rolling expanse* or *plain*); (t. & i. of sound) utter or be uttered, sound, with vibratory or undulating or trilling effect (*r. out verses, song,* &c.; *thunder, drum, organ, voice, echo, rolls; r.* one's rs); (of wheeled vehicle) advance or convey usu. *along, by,* &c., (of person) be so conveyed, (*carriage rolled along, rolled them by; he rolled past in his carriage; rolling-stock,* railway company's wagons & trucks); flatten by passing roller over or by passing between rollers (*r. lawn, metal, paste for pies,* &c.; *rolled gold,* thin coating so applied; *rolling-pin,* roller for paste; *rolling-press,* copperplate-printer's press with revolving cylinder, also press with rollers for various purposes); turn (t. & i.) over & over upon itself into more or less cylindrical shape (usu. *up; the way to r. a great-coat; hedgehog rolls itself into a ball* or *rolls up*); form (t. & i.) in(to) cylindrical or spherical shape, or accumulate into mass, by rolling (*r. cigarettes, a huge snowball, snow* or *string into ball; the reckoning is rolling up,* increasing in amount; *saint & philosopher rolled into one*); *r.-top desk,* with flexible cover sliding in curved grooves; *r. up* (Mil.), drive flank of (enemy line) back & round so that line is shortened or surrounded; hence **ro·ll**ABLE a. (N.) rolling motion (*the r. of the sea, ship*); spell of rolling (*a r. on the grass*); rolling gait; quick continuous beating of drum; long peal of thunder or shout; rhythmic flow of words. [f. OF *roller* = It. *rotolare* (L *rotula* dim. of ROTA)]

rō·ller, n. In vbl senses; esp.: cylinder of wood, stone, metal, &c., & of various proportions used alone or as rotating part of machine for lessening friction, smoothing ground, pressing, stamping, crushing, spreading printer's ink, rolling up cloth on, &c.; (usu. *r. bandage*) long surgical bandage rolled up for convenience of applying; kind of tumbler-pigeon; long swelling wave; brilliant-plumaged bird allied to crows, also German breed of canary, [G, f. *rollen* to roll]; *r.* SKATE², *skating; r. towel,* endless, working on r. [-ER¹]

rŏ·lley. See RULLEY.

rŏ·llick, v.i., & n. Be jovial, indulge in high spirits, enjoy life boisterously, revel, (esp. in part. as adj.). (N.) exuberant gaiety; frolic, spree, escapade. [?]

rō·ly-pō·ly, n. & a. (Also *r. pudding*) pudding made of sheet of paste covered with jam &c., formed into roll, & boiled; (adj., usu. of child) podgy, plump. [prob. formed on ROLL²]

Rom, n. (pl. *Roma*). Male gipsy, (pl.) gipsies. [Romany wd]

Romā·ic, a. & n. (Of, in, &c.) the vernacular language of modern Greece. [f. Gk *Rōmaikos* Roman (used esp. of Eastern empire)]

Romā·ika, n. National dance of modern Greece. [mod. Gk (*-kē*), orig. fem. adj. (prec.)]

Rō·man¹, n. Citizen, soldier, native, or inhabitant, of ancient Rome, member of ancient-R. State, (*King, Emperor, of the Rr.,* sovereign head of Holy R. Empire); inhabitant of medieval or modern Rome; (pl.) Christians of ancient Rome (*Rr.,* or in full *Epistle to the Rr.,* N.-.T. book, abbr. *Rom.*); (Print.) ROMAN² type (abbr. in press-correcting, *rom.*); = ROMAN CATHOLIC. [f. L *Romanus* (ROME, -AN)]

Ro·man², a. Of ancient Rome or its territory, people, or (rarely; usu. *Latin*) language (*R. Empire,* that established by Augustus 27 B.C. & divided by Theodosius A.D. 395 into WESTERN or Latin & eastern or Greek empires, of which the eastern lasted till 1453, & the western, after lapsing in 476, was revived 800 by Charlemagne & continued to exist as the *Holy Roman Empire* till 1806; *R. law,* code developed by ancient Rr. & forming basis of many modern codes; *R. pottery, bricks, road,* &c., surviving from period of R. rule; *R. cement,* trade name for a hydraulic cement named after ancient-R. kind; *R. balance, beam,* or *steelyard,* ordinary steelyard; *R. simplicity, honesty, virtue, patriotism,* &c., as of Rr. of early Republic; *R. nose,* with high bridge, aquiline, whence, of person or horse, **Roman-nos**ED² a.; *R. letters* or *type,* of the plain upright type used in ordinary print, opp. *Gothic* or *black letter* & *italic; R. alphabet,* that used by Rr. & still with slight modifications in W. Europe; *R. numerals,* the letters I, V, &c. used in composing number-symbols, see below* for mod. use, & cf. ARABIC; *R. architecture,* COMPOSITE, & see ORDER¹; *R. history, historian,* &c., of ancient Rome); of papal Rome, esp. = ROMAN CATHOLIC, whence **Ro·man**ISH¹(2) a., **Ro·manize**R¹ n.; of medieval or modern Rome (*R. school,* painting school of Raphael; *R. fever,* malaria prevalent at Rome; *R.* SNAIL; *R. vitriol,* sulphate of copper; *R.* CANDLE). Hence **Ro·man**ISM(3, 4), **Ro·man**IST(2, 3), nn., **Romani·s**TIC a., **Ro·man**IZE(2, 3, 4) v.t. & i., **Romaniza**·TION n., **Romā·no**- comb. form. *Mod. use of R. numerals, differing in some respects from the ancient: The only symbols now used are I = 1, V = 5, X = 10, L = 50, C = 100, D = 500, M = 1000; the letters composing a number are ranged in order of value, & the number meant is found by addition, e.g. MDCLXVI = 1666; if a letter or set of letters is placed before a letter of higher value, it is to be subtracted from it before the addition is done, e.g. IIC = 98, MCM = 1900; IIII is usu. preferred to IV on clock-faces. [as prec.]

Roman Catholic, a. & n. (Member) of the Church of Rome. Hence **Roman-Catho·lically, Roman-Ca·tholicly**[2], advv., **Roman-Catho·licism**(3) n. [f. *c.* 1600, perh. orig. as non-controversial compromise between *Roman(ist)*, *Romish*, &c., & *Catholic*]

roma·nce, n. & a., & v.i. 1(*R*-): Vernacular language of old France mainly developed but distinguished from Latin, corresponding language of Spain, Provence, &c., (collect.) the languages descended from Latin (adj., of languages, thus descended). 2(*r*-): Medieval tale usu. in verse of some hero of chivalry (named as written in R.); prose or rarely verse tale with scene & incidents remote from every-day life, class of literature consisting of such tales; set of facts, episode, love affair, &c., suggesting such tales by its strangeness or moving nature; atmosphere characterizing such tales, mental tendency to be influenced by it, sympathetic imaginativeness, whence **roma·nceless** a.; (an) exaggeration, (a) picturesque falsehood, (vb, exaggerate, draw the long-bow); (Mus.) short piece of simple character. [f. OF *romanz* f. pop. L **romanice* (opp. *Latine* in Latin) adv. f. ROMANIC*us*]

roma·ncer, n. Medieval or other writer of romances; fantastic liar. [f. *romance* vb (prec.) partly in obs. sense]

Rŏ·manĕs, n. Gipsy language. [Gipsy (adv.)]

Rōmane·sque (-k), a. & n. =ROMANCE 1 (a. & n.); (Arch.) (in) style of building prevalent in Romanized Europe between the classical & Gothic periods. [-ESQUE]

Romă·nic, a. & n. Descended from Latin, Romance (a. & n.); descended from, inheriting civilization &c. of, the Romans, Romance-speaking. [f. L *Romanicus* (ROMAN[1], -IC)]

Romă·nity, n. (rare). Civilization & influence of Roman empire. [ROMAN[2], -ITY]

Roma·nsh, Rou-, Ru-, n. & a. (In) the RHAETO-ROMANIC tongue of N.-W. part of E. Switzerland; =*Rhaeto-Romanic.* [as ROMANCE]

roma·ntic, a. & n. Characterized by or suggestive of or given to romance, imaginative, remote from experience, visionary, (*a r. story, scene, adventure, girl*); (of music) subordinating form to theme, imaginative, passionate; (of projects &c.) fantastic, unpractical, quixotic, dreamy; (of literary or artistic method &c.) preferring grandeur or picturesqueness or passion or irregular beauty to finish & proportion, subordinating whole to parts or form to matter, (opp. CLASSIC, CLASSICAL), whence **roma·nticist**(2) n.; hence **roma·ntically** adv., **roma·nticism**(2, 3) n., **roma·nticize**(2, 3) v.i. & t. (N.): (pl.) r. ideas or talk; romanticist. [f. F *romantique* (*romant* tale, now *roman*, var. of *romanz* ROMANCE, -IC)]

Rŏ·many, n. & a. Gipsy (n. & a.); (pl., also collect. sing.) *the* gipsies, (pl.) gipsies; the gipsy language. [f. Gipsy *Romani* fem. & pl. of *Romano* adj. (ROM)]

romau·nt, n. (archaic). A romance or tale of chivalry &c. [f. OF *romant* see ROMANTIC]

Rome, n. City or ancient State of R. (*R. was not built in a day*, encouragement to fainthearted; *do in R. as R. does, as the Romans do*, adapt oneself to surroundings); Roman empire; Church of R., whence **Ro·meward** a. & adv., **Ro·mewards** adv., **Ro·mish**[1] a. (contempt.). [OF, f. L *Roma*]

romp, v.i. & n. (Of children &c.) play about together, chase each other, wrestle, &c.; (Racing slang) get *along, past*, &c., without effort, come *in* or *home* as easy winner. (N.) child or woman fond of romping, tom-boy; spell of romping, boisterous play, (often *game of rr.*); hence **ro·mpy**[2] a. [perh. n. f. vb, var. of RAMP[2]]

ro·mper, n. (Sing. or pl.) child's overall. [prec., -ER[1](2)]

ro·ndeau (-dō), n. Ten-line or thirteen-line poem with only two rhymes throughout & opening words used twice as refrain. [F, earlier RONDEL]

ro·ndel, n. (Special form of) RONDEAU. [F, *rond* ROUND[1], -LE(2)]

ro·ndo, n. Piece of music with leading theme to which return is made. [It., f. F RONDEAU]

ro·ndure, n. (poet.). Round outline or object. [f. F *rondeur* (ROUND[1], -OR[1])]

Rö·ntgenogram (rŭntyen-), n. Photograph taken by Röntgen rays. [foll., -O-, GRAM]

Röntgen rays. See RAY[1].

rōōd, n. The cross of Christ (archaic; often in oaths, as *by the R.*); crucifix, esp. one raised on middle of *r.-screen*, wooden or stone carved screen separating nave & choir; *r.-arch*, between nave & choir; *r.-beam*, cross-beam, usu. as head of r.-screen, supporting r.; *r.-cloth*, veiling r. in Lent; *r.-loft*, gallery on top of r.-screen; quarter of an acre (esp. as loose term for small piece of land; *not a r. remained to him*). [OE *rōd* cross, cf. OFris. *rōde*, cogn. w. ROD]

rōōf, n., & v.t. Upper covering of house or building usu. supported by its walls (*under* one's *roof*, in one's house, esp. w. ref. to hospitality; also fig., as *the r. of heaven*; *r. of the world*, high mountain range; *r. of the mouth*, palate; *under a r. of foliage*), top of covered vehicle esp. when used for outside passengers; *r.-tree*, ridge-pole of r.; hence **roo·fage**(1) n., **(-)roofed**[2], **roo·fless,** aa. (Vb) cover with r., be r. of, (often *in, over*); hence **roo·fing**[1](3)n. [OE *hrōf*, cf. OFris. *rhoof*, MDu. *roof*]

roo·fer, n. (colloq.). Letter of thanks for entertainment sent by departed visitor. [ROOF, -ER¹]

rŏŏk¹, n., & v.t. Black hoarse-voiced bird of crow tribe nesting in colonies; sharper, esp. at dice or cards, person who lives on inexperienced gamblers &c., (cf. PIGEON); *r. pie*, of young rr.; *r.-rifle*, of small bore for r.-shooting; hence **roo·klet**, **roo·kling¹**, nn., **rŏŏ·ky²** a. (Vb) win money from at cards &c. esp. by swindling; charge (customer) extortionately. [OE *hróc*, cf. Du. *roek*, G *ruch*; prob. imit.]

rŏŏk², n. (chess). =CASTLE¹. [f. OF *roc* ult. f. Pers. *rukh*]

roo·kery, n. (Clump of trees with) colony of rooks; colony of penguins &c. or seals; crowded cluster of mean houses or tenements. [-ERY]

rŏŏ·kie, n. (army slang). Recruit. [corrupt. of *recruit*]

rōōm, n., & v.i. Space that is or might be occupied by something, capaciousness or ability to accommodate contents, (*takes up too much r.*; *there is plenty of r.*; *no r. to turn in, to swing a* CAT¹; *would rather have his r. than his company*, wish him away; *we have no r. here for idlers*; *make r.*, vacate standing-ground &c. or post &c. for or *for* another, withdraw, retire, also clear a space *for* person or thing by removal of others; *R. for* archaic, ellipt. command to make way for some one; *in one's r.*, *in the r. of*, instead of, in succession to, as substitute for), whence **roo·my²** a., **roo·miness** n., **roo·mily²** adv.; opportunity, scope, *to* do or *for* (*r. to deny ourselves*; *no r. for dispute*; *leave r. for evasion*; *there is r. for improvement*, things are not as good as they should be); part of house enclosed by walls or partitions, floor, & ceiling, (pl.) set of these occupied by person or family, apartments or lodgings, (transf.) the company in a r. (*set the r. in a roar*), whence **roo·mful**(2) n., **-roomed²** a. (Vb, U.S.) have room(s), lodge, board, whence **roo·mer¹** n. [com.-Teut.; OE *rúm*, cf. G *raum*, Sw. & Da. *rum*]

roost¹, n., & v.i. & t. Bird's perching or resting place, esp. hen-house or part of it in which fowls sleep, (transf.) sleeping-accommodation, bed(room), (*go to r.*, retire for the night; *at r.*, perched, in bed; *curses come home to r.*, recoil upon curser). (Vb): (of birds or persons) settle for sleep, be perched or lodged for the night; provide with sleeping-place. [vb f. n., OE *hróst*, cf. MDu. *roest*]

roost², n. Tidal race about Orkneys & Shetlands. [f. ON *rost*]

roo·ster, n. Domestic cock (esp. U.S.). [-ER¹]

root¹, n. Part of plant normally below earth's surface & serving to attach it to earth & convey nourishment from soil to it, (pl.) such part divided into branches or fibres, corresponding organ of epiphyte, part attaching ivy to its support (also **roo·tlet** n.), permanent underground stock of plant, small plant with r. for transplanting, (plant, such as turnip or carrot, with) edible r., (*pull up by the rr.*, uproot lit. & fig.; *take, strike, r.*, begin to draw nourishment from soil, fig. get established; *lay axe to r. of* tree or institution, set about destroying it; *r. &* BRANCH¹); (bibl.) scion, offshoot, (*there shall be a r. of Jesse*); imbedded part of some bodily organ or structure, part of thing attaching it to greater or more fundamental whole, (*r. of tongue, tooth, nail*, &c.; *r. of a gem*, esp. of emerald, cloudy part by which it adhered to stone; *rr. of mountain*, its base); source or origin (*of*; *love of money is the r. of all evil*; *a r. of bitterness*; *r. fallacy, idea*, &c., the one from which the rest originated); basis, dependence, means of continuance or growth, (*has its r.* or *rr. in selfishness*; *has no r. in the nature of things*); bottom, essential substance or nature, (*get at the rr. of things*; *has the r. of the matter in him*, is essentially sound, w. ref. to *Job* xix. 28); (Math.) *r. of*, number or quantity that when multiplied by itself a usu. specified number of times gives (specified number &c.; *square* or *second r. of 4*, or ellipt. *r. of 4* or *r. 4*, symbol $\sqrt{4}$, *is 2*; $\sqrt{3}$ *is irrational*; *cube* or *third r. of 27*, symbol $\sqrt[3]{27}$, *is 3*); (Philol.) ultimate unanalysable element of language, basis (whether itself existing as a word or not) on which words are made by addition of prefixes or suffixes or by other modification, (symbol √, as *sopor is from* √SWEP); (Mus.) fundamental note of chord; *r.-stock*, = RHIZOME, also primary form whence offshoots have arisen. Hence **roo·tage**(1, 3) n., **roo·tless**, **roo·ty¹** (-Y²), aa. [OE f. ON *rót*; cogn. w. L *radix*, & w. WORT]

root², v.t. & i. (Cause to) take r., fix firmly to the spot, establish, (*some kinds r. freely*; *take care to r. them firmly*; *fear rooted him to the ground*; esp. in p.p., as *her affection was deeply rooted, rooted objections to, obedience rooted in fear*, whence **roo·tedly²** adv., **roo·tedness** n.); drag or dig *up* by the rr.; *r. out*, exterminate; uproot, tear away, *from* (poet.). [f. prec.]

root³, **rout** (rowt), v.i. & t. (Of swine &c.) turn up ground with snout, beak, &c., in search of food; turn *up* (ground) thus; (transf.) search *out*, hunt *up*, rummage (*among, in*). [earlier *wroot*, f. OE *wrótan* (*rót* ROOT¹)]

roo·tery, n. Pile of roots & stumps for growing garden plants on (cf. ROCK¹*ery*). [-ERY]

roo·tle, v.i. & t. =ROOT³. [-LE(3)]

roo·ty², n. (for *r.*¹ see ROOT¹). (Mil. slang) bread. [Anglo-Ind., f. Hind. *rōṭī*]

rope, n., & v.t. & i. (Piece of) stout cordage (prop. over 1 in. in circumf., cf. CABLE¹, CORD) made by twisting strands of hemp, flax, hide, or wire, into one (*the r.*, halter for hanging person, also = TIGHT-*r.*; *on the* HIGH *rr.*; *the rr.*, those enclosing prize-ring or other arena; *know, learn, put* one *up to, the rr.*, the conditions in some sphere of action; *give* one *r.*, *r. enough to hang* him*self, plenty of r.*, &c., not check him, trust to his bringing about his own discomfiture; *r. of sand*, delusive security; *r. of onions, ova, pearls*, these strung together; *on the r.* of mountaineers, roped together); viscid or gelatinous stringy formation in beer or other liquid; *r.-dancer, -cing*, performer, -ming, on tight-r.; *r.-drill*, in which a r. stretched by two men represents company &c.; *r.-ladder*, two long rr. connected by short cross-rr. as ladder; *ropemanship*, skill in r.-walking or r.-climbing; *r.-moulding*, cut spirally in imitation of r.-strands; *r.-quoit*, ring of r. used in quoits played on board ship; *r.'s-end*, short piece of r. used to flog (esp. sailor) with; *r.-walk*, long piece of ground used for twisting r.; *r.-walker, -king*, = r.-dancer, -cing; *r.-yard*, r.-making establishment; *r.-yarn*, (piece of the) material (esp. when unpicked) of which r.-strands consist, mere trifle; hence **ro·**PING[1](6) n., **ro·**PY[2] a., **ro·**PINESS n. (Vb) fasten or secure with r.; (Mountaineering) connect (party) with r., attach (person) to r., put on r.; use rr. in towing &c.; enclose, close *in*, (space) with r.; *r. in*, secure adherence of, decoy; (Racing) check (horse), check horse, (of athlete) not put forth full powers, in order to lose race; become ropy or viscid. [com.-Teut.; OE *rāp*, cf. Du. *reep*, G *reif*, Icel. & Norw. *reip*]

Roquefort (rŏ·kforr), n. Kind of French cheese of goats' & ewes' milk resembling Stilton. [*R.* in France]

rŏ·quelaure (-ke-), n. (hist.). Man's cloak reaching to knees (18th c.). [F (Duke of *R.*)]

rō·quet (-kĕ), v.t. & i. (*-eting, -eted*, pr. -ĭing, -ĭd), & n. Cause one's ball to strike, (of ball) strike, another ball at croquet; strike another ball thus; (n.) act or fact of roqueting. [arbitrary f. CROQUET[2] & orig. in same sense]

ror·qual, n. Whale with dorsal fin, finback. [F, f. Norw. *röyrkval* (*raud* red, *kval* whale)]

ror·ty, raugh·ty, a. (slang). Enjoyable (*had a r. time*); fond of amusement & excitement. [?]

rō·sace (-zās), n. Rose-window; rose-shaped ornament or design. [F (ROSE)]

rosā·ceous (-z-), a. Of the order *Rosaceae*, of which the rose is the type. So **ro-sa·cean** n. [f. L *rosaceus* (ROSE, -ACEOUS)]

rosă·niline (-z-), n. (Kinds of red dye obtained from) an organic base derived from aniline. [ROSE, ANILINE]

rosar·ian, n. Rose-fancier; (R.-C. Ch.) member of a Confraternity of the Rosary. [f. L *rosarium* ROSARY, -AN]

rosar·ium, n. Rose-garden. [L (foll.)]

rō·sary (-z-), n. Rose-garden, rose-bed; (R.-C. Ch.) form of prayer in which fifteen decades of Aves are repeated, each decade preceded by Paternoster & followed by Gloria, book containing this, string of 165 beads for keeping count in this (*lesser r.*, of 55). [f. L *rosarium* (ROSE, -ARIUM); R.-C. sense f. LL sense *chaplet*]

Ro·scian (-shĭ-), a. Like or worthy of Roscius, famous Roman actor of 1st c. B.C. [-AN]

rose[1] (-z), n., a., & v.t. (Prickly bush or shrub bearing) a beautiful & usu. fragrant flower usu. of red or yellow or white colour (BLUSH[2], BRIER[1], CABBAGE, DAMASK, MOSS[1], MUSK, TEA, &c., -*r.*; also in names of other flowering plants, as ROCK-*rose*, CHRISTMAS *r.*, *R. of Jericho*, the Resurrection plant with dried fronds unfolding under moisture, *R. of Sharon*, unidentified eastern flower, *R. of May*, white narcissus; ATTAR, OTTO, *of rr.*; *red as a r.*; *gather rr.* or *life's rr.*, seek pleasure; *path strewn with rr.*, life of delights; *bed of rr.*, pleasant easy post or condition, esp. in *is no b. of rr.*; so *is not all rr.*; *r. without a thorn*, impossible happiness, unalloyed delight; *the white r. of virginity, innocence*, &c.; *the r. of* with place-name, most beautiful girl or woman in; *Wars of the Rr.*, 15th-c. civil wars between Yorkists with white & Lancastrians with red r. as emblem; *under the r.*, = SUB *rosa*), whence **ro·**SERY(3) n.; representation of the flower in heraldry or decoration (esp. as national emblem of England, cf. THISTLE, SHAMROCK, LEEK OR DAFFODIL; *Golden r.*, ornament blessed by Pope on 4th Sunday in Lent & sent as compliment to some R.-C. sovereign, city, &c.), r.-shaped design; rosette worn on shoe or clerical hat; protuberance round base of animal's horn or some birds' eye; sprinkling-nozzle of watering-pot or hose, whence **(-)ros**ED[2] a.; =*r. diamond*; =*r. window*; light crimson colour, pink, (usu. pl.) rosy complexion (*has quite lost her, spoiled her natural, rr.*); *the r.*, erysipelas; *r.-apple*, tropical tree cultivated for foliage & fruit, its fruit; *r.-bay*, oleander, rhododendron, azalea, willow-herb; *rose-bud*, bud of r. (often attrib., as *r.-b. mouth*), pretty girl, (U.S.) débutante; *r.-bush*, r. plant; *r.-chafer*, green or copper-coloured beetle frequenting rr.; *r.-colour*, rosy red, pink, (fig.) pleasant state of things or outlook (*life is not all r.-c.*); *r.-coloured*, rosy, (fig.) optimistic, sanguine, cheerful, (*takes r.-c. views*; *see things through r.-c. spectacles*); *r.-cut*, cut as a *r. diamond*, hemispherical with curved part in triangular facets; *r.-drop*, skin-disease with red blotches; *r.-engine*, appendage to lathe for engraving curved patterns; *r.-gall*, excrescence on dog-r. &c. made by insect; *r.-*

leaf, leaf, usu. petal, of r. (*crumpled r.-l.*, slight vexation alloying general felicity); *r.-lipped*, with rosy lips; *r. nail*, with head shaped like r. diamond; *r. noble*, 15th–16th c. gold coin of varying value stamped with r.; *r.-pink*, pigment of chalk or whiting coloured with Brazil-wood decoction, also = *r.-colour(ed)* lit. & fig.; *r.-rash*, = ROSEOLA; *r.-red* a. & n., red as (of) a r.; *r.-root*, kinds of plant with root smelling like r. when dried or bruised; *r.-tree*; *r. vinegar*, infusion of rr. in vinegar for application in headache &c.; *r.-water*, perfume made from rr., (fig.) compliments, gentle handling, &c. (*r.-water surgery*; *revolutions are not made with r.-w.*); *r. window*, circular, usu. with spokelike mullions; *rosewood*, kinds of cabinet wood named from their fragrance; hence **ro·se**LESS, **ro·se**LIKE, aa. (Adj.) coloured like a pale red r., of warm pink. (Vb) make (face, snow-slope, &c.) rosy (esp. in p.p.). [OE *rose*, *róse*, f. L *rosa* prob. f. Gk *rhodea* rose-tree (*rhodon* rose)]

rose[2]. See RISE[1].

rō·seate (-zĭat), a. = ROSE-*coloured* (lit. & fig.). Hence **ro·seate**LY[2] adv. [f. L *roseus* (ROSE[1]) rosy + -ATE[2]]

rō·semary (-zm-), n. Evergreen fragrant shrub with leaves used in perfumery &c. & taken as emblem of remembrance. [earlier *rosmarine* f. L *ros marinus* (*ros* dew, MARINE) w. assim. to *rose*, *Mary* (prob. the Virgin)]

rō·seo-, comb. form in names of salts & alkalis of L *roseus* rose-coloured, as *-cobalt*.

rose·ola (-zē-), n. Rosy rash in measles &c.; German measles. Hence **rose·ol**AR[1], **rose·ol**OUS, aa. [mod. L (prec., *-ola* dim. termination)]

rose·tte (-z-), n. Rose-shaped ornament for dress or harness made of ribbons, leather strips, &c.; (Arch.) carved or moulded conventional rose on wall &c., also rose-window; (Biol.) rose-like cluster of organs, markings resembling rose; = ROSE *diamond*; roselike object or arrangement of parts. Hence **rose·tt**ED[2] a. [F (ROSE[1], -ETTE)]

Rōsicru·cian (-z-, -shn), n. & a. (Member) of a society devoted to occult lore & magic said to have been founded 1484 by Christian Rosenkreuz. Hence **Rosicru·cian**ISM(3) n. [f. L *rosa*, rose, *crux crucis* cross, + -AN, as latinization of *Rosenkreuzian*]

rŏ·sin (-z-), n., & v.t. = RESIN (esp. of solid residue after distillation of oil of turpentine from crude turpentine); hence **ro·sin**Y[2] a. (Vb) smear, seal up, rub (esp. bow or string of fiddle &c.), with r. [changed f. RESIN]

Rŏsina·ntĕ (-z-), **Roz-**, n. Worn-out horse, jade. [f. Sp. *Rocinante* (*rocin* jade, cf. obs. E *rouncy* riding-horse) Don Quixote's horse]

rosō·lio (-z-), n. A S.-Europ. sweet cordial. [It., f. L *ros* dew, *solis* of the sun, cordial being orig. made from plant sundew]

rō·ster, n. List or plan showing turns of duty for individuals or companies esp. of a military force. [f. Du. *rooster* list, orig. gridiron (*roosten* ROAST), w. ref. to parallel lines]

ro·stral, a. (Of column &c.) adorned with beaks actual or sculptured &c. of ancient war-galleys; (Zool. &c.) of, on, the rostrum. [f. LL *rostralis* (ROSTRUM, -AL)]

rostra·ted, a. (Of column &c.) = prec.; (Zool. &c.) having, ending in, a rostrum. [f. L *rostratus* (ROSTRUM, -ATE[2])]

ro·strum, n. (pl. *-ra*, *-rums*). (Sing., or pl. *-ra* of single specimen but usu. w. pl. constr.; pl. in pl. sense, *-ra* or *-rums*) platform for public speaking (orig. that in Roman forum adorned with beaks of captured galleys), pulpit, office &c. that enables one to gain the public ear; (Rom. Ant.) beak of war-galley (pl. usu. *-ra*); (Zool., Ent., Bot.) beak, stiff snout, beak-like part, whence **ro·str**ATE[2], **rostri·**FEROUS, **ro·stri**FORM, aa., **rostro-** comb. form. [L, = beak (*rodere* gnaw)]

rŏ·sulate (-z-), a. (bot.). (Of leaves) packed over each other like rose-petals. [LL *rosula* (ROSE[1], -ULE), -ATE[2], see -UL-]

rō·sy (-zĭ), a. Coloured like a red rose (esp. of complexion as indicating health, of blush, wine, sky, light, &c.), (fig.) = ROSE-*coloured*; (now rare) smelling like a rose, made of or covered or strewn with roses; *r. cross*, emblem of ROSICRUCIANS; *r.-fingered*, epithet of *dawn* &c. Hence **ro·si**LY[2] adv., **ro·si**NESS n. [-Y[2]]

rot[1], n. & int. Decay, putrefaction, rottenness, (esp. in timber, cf. DRY[1]-*r.*); virulent liver-disease of sheep (usu. *the r.*); (slang; also *tommy r.*) nonsense, absurd statement or argument or proposal (often as int. of incredulity or ridicule), foolish course, undesirable state of things, (*don't talk r.*; *it is perfect r. to trust him*; *what tommy r. that it is not open on Sundays!*); (Cricket, War, &c.) sudden series of unaccountable failures on one side (*a r. set in*). [prob. f. Scand. (Icel., Norw., *rot*), cogn. w. foll.]

rot[2], v.i. & t. Undergo natural decomposition, decay, putrefy, (*r. off*, drop from stem &c. through rottenness), (fig., of society, institutions, &c.) gradually perish from want of vigour or use, (of prisoner) pine away (*left to r. in gaol*); cause to r., make rotten, (slang) spoil or disconcert (*has rotted the whole plan*); (slang) chaff, banter, tease, (abs.) talk ironically (*he is only rotting*); *r.-gut* a. & n., (liquor) injurious to stomach. [com.-Teut.; OE *rotian*, cf. Fris. *rotsje*, Du. *rotten*, Icel. *rota*]

rō·ta, n. List of persons acting, or duties to be done, in rotation, roster; (R.-C. Ch.)

supreme ecclesiastical & secular court. [L, = wheel]

rō·tary, a. & n. Acting by rotation; (n.) r. machine; (*the*) *R.*, a U.-S. & British society with many branches for international service to humanity, orig. named from clubs entertaining in rotation, whence **Rotār·**IAN a. & n., (member) of R. [f. LL *rotarius* (prec., -ARY[1])]

ro·tate[1], a. (bot.). Wheel-shaped. [ROTA, -ATE[2]]

rota·te[2], v.i. & t. Move (t. & i.) round axis or centre, revolve; arrange (esp. crops) or take in rotation. Hence **rō·**TATIVE, **ro·tat**ORY, **rota·**TABLE, aa. [f. L ROTAre, -ATE[3]]

rota·tion, n. Rotating; recurrence, recurrent series or period, regular succession in office &c., (often *in, by, r.*; *r. of crops,* growing of different crops in regular order to avoid exhausting soil). Hence **rota·tion**AL a. [f. L *rotatio* (prec., -ATION)]

rota·tor, n. (Anat.) muscle that rotates a limb &c.; revolving apparatus or part. [L (ROTATE[2], -OR[2])]

rotch(e), n. The little auk. [earlier *rotge,* cf. Fris. *rotgies* brent-goose]

rote, n. Mere habituation, knowledge got by repetition, unintelligent memory, (only *by r.*, as *say, know, do, by r.*). [perh. OF, = ROUTE]

rō·tifer, n. Wheel-animalcule, member of class *Rotifera* with rotatory organs used in swimming. [L ROTA, -FEROUS]

rō·tograph, n. Print of MS. page &c. got by sensitized roll. [prec., -GRAPH]

rō·tor, n. Rotary part of machine; upright revolving cylinder on ship taking the place of mast & sails (*r. ship,* so propelled). [irreg. for ROTATOR]

ro·tten, a. Decomposed or decomposing, putrid, perishing of decay, falling to pieces or friable or easily breakable or tearable from age or use; (of sheep) affected with the rot; morally, socially, or politically corrupt, effete, (*r.* BOROUGH; *something is r. in the state of Denmark, Haml.* I. iv. 90, things are unsatisfactory); inefficient, worthless; (slang; of state of things, plan, &c.) disagreeable, regrettable, beastly, ill-advised; *r.-stone,* decomposed siliceous limestone used as polishing-powder. Hence **ro·tten**LY[2] adv., **ro·tten**NESS n. [f. ON *rotinn* cogn. w. ROT[2], RET]

Ro·tten Row (rō), n. (Now usu. *the Row*) track in Hyde Park, fashionable resort for riding. [perh. f. prec.]

ro·tter, n. (slang). Useless or inefficient or disliked person. [ROT[2], -ER[1]]

rotu·nd, a. Circular, round, (rare), whence **rotu·nd**ATE[2] a., **rotu·ndi-, rotu·ndo-,** comb. forms, (bot.); (of mouth) rounded in speaking &c., (of speech, literary style, &c.) as from r. mouth, sonorous, sounding, grandiloquent; (of persons) plump, podgy. Hence or cogn. **rotu·ndi**TY n., **rotu·nd**LY[2] adv. [f. L *rotundus* cogn. w. ROTA]

rotu·nda, n. Building of circular groundplan, esp. one with dome; circular hall or room. [earlier *rotonda,* It., fem. of *rotondo* = prec.]

roturier (F), n. Plebeian. [F (*roture* plebeian tenure, prob. f. L *ruptura* breaking, -IER)]

rou·ble (rōō-), n. The Russian monetary unit (before the great war a silver coin = 2/1½). [F, f. Russ. *ruble*]

roucou (rōōkōō·), n. (W.-Ind. tree yielding) orange dye. [F, f. Braz. *urucú*]

roué (rōō·ā), n. Debauchee, rake. [F, p.p. of *rouer* break on wheel, = one deserving this]

rouge[1] (rōōzh), a., n., & v.t. & i. Red (only in *R. Croix* pr. krwah, *R. Dragon,* two pursuivants of English college of Arms, & in *r.-royal marble,* reddish Belgian kind). (N.) fine red powder made from safflower & used for colouring cheeks & lips; plate-powder of oxide of iron; revolutionary politician; *r. et noir* (-ān-wah·r), card-game played on table with red & black marks on which money staked is laid (*r.*, the red in this). (Vb) colour, adorn oneself, with r. [F, f. L *rubeus* cogn. w. RED]

rouge[2] (rōōj), n. Scrummage, also touchdown counting as point to opponents, in Eton football. [?]

rough (rŭf), a., adv., n., & v.t. Of uneven or irregular surface, not smooth or level or polished, diversified or broken by prominences, hairy, shaggy, coarse in texture, rugged, (*r. skin, hands, paper, bark, road, cloth, country*; *book with r. edges,* in which edges of original sheets are left untrimmed; *r. leaf,* first true leaf of springing plant after the smooth leaves or cotyledons, *in the r. l.*, at this stage; *r. rice,* unhusked rice, paddy); not mild or quiet or gentle, unrestrained, violent, stormy, boisterous, disorderly, riotous, inconsiderate, harsh, unfeeling, drastic, severe, grating, astringent, (*r. manners, soldier, play*; *r. water, sea, weather, wind*; *r. words*; *r. element of the population, quarter of the town*; *r. usage, handling*; *r. remedies*; *r. barytone voice*; *r. claret*; *r. tongue,* habit of rudeness; *gave him a lick with the r. side of my tongue,* spoke severely to him; *r. passage,* crossing over r. sea; *r. work,* violence, also task requiring it, & see below; *have a r. time,* suffer r. handling or hardship; *horse has r. paces,* jolts rider; fact &c. *is r. luck,* or *r., on* person, worse luck than he deserves; *r.* MUSIC); deficient in finish or elaboration or delicacy, incomplete, rudimentary, entirely or partly unwrought, merely passable, inexact, approximate, preliminary, (*r. nursing, style, welcome, kindness, plenty, accommodation, sketch, drawing*; *r. work,* & see above; *r. state,* *attempt, makeshift, circle*; *r. stone*, not dressed; *r.* DIAMOND; *r. justice*; *r. translation, estimate*; *r. copy* of picture &c., reproducing only essentials; *r. draft*; *r.* COPY[1]; *r. coat*, first coat of plaster laid on; *r. coating*, r.-cast; *r. & ready*, not elaborate, just good enough, not over-particular, roughly efficient or effective); *r.-&-tumble*, (adj.) irregular, scrambling, disorderly, regardless of procedure-rules, (n.) haphazard fight, scuffle; *r.-cast*, (adj., of wall &c.) coated with mixture of lime & gravel, (of plan &c.) imperfectly elaborated, (n.) plaster of lime & gravel for walls, (v.t.) coat (wall) with r.-c., prepare (plan, essay, &c.) in outline; *r.-dry*, dry (clothes) without ironing &c.; *r.-footed*, with feathered feet (in names of birds); *r.-grind*, give preliminary grinding to (edged tool &c.); *r.-hew*, shape out roughly, give crude form to, (p.p., uncouth, unrefined); *r.-hound*, kind of dogfish; *r.-legged*, with hairy or feathered legs (of breeds of horse & bird); *r.-rider*, horsebreaker, man who can ride unbroken horses, (Mil.) irregular cavalryman; *roughshod*, (of horse) having shoes with the nail-heads projecting (*ride r.-s.*, domineer *over*); *r.*-SPOKEN; *r.-wrought*, with the earlier processes done; hence **rou·gh**EN[6] v.t. & i., **rou·gh**ISH[1](2) a., **rou·gh**LY[2] adv. (*roughly* SPEAK*ing*), **rou·gh**NESS n. (Adv.) in r. manner (*land should be ploughed r.*; *play r.*; chiefly in compds, of which some are given above). (N.) r. ground (esp. *over r. & smooth*), (Golf) *the* r. ground bordering, or between greens of, links; one of the spikes inserted in roughing horse; hard part of life, piece of hardship, (usu. *the r. & the smooth, the rr. & the smooths*); rowdy, hooligan, man or boy of lower classes ready for lawless violence; *the* unfinished or *the* natural state, *the* general way, (*shape it from the r.*; *have seen it only in the r.*; *is true in the r.*). (Vb) turn *up* (feathers, hair, &c.) by rubbing against the grain (*r.* one *up the wrong way*, irritate him); secure (horse or its shoes) against slipping by insertion of spikes or projecting nails in shoes; *r. it*, do without ordinary conveniences of life; break in (horse); shape or plan *out* roughly; sketch *in* roughly; tune *up* (piano) roughly; give first shaping to (gem, lens, &c.). [OE *rúh*, cf. Du. *ruig*, G *rauh*]

roulade (rōōlah·d), n. Quick succession of notes rhythmically equivalent to one. [F (*rouler* ROLL[2], -ADE)]

rouleau (rōōlō·), n. (pl. *-x* or *-s*, pr. -z). Cylindrical packet of gold coins; coil or roll. [F (*rôle* ROLL[1])]

roule·tte (rōō-), n. Gambling game on table with revolving centre; (Math.) curve generated by point on rolling curve; device for keeping hair in curl; revolving toothed wheel used in engraving, similar wheel for perforating postage stamps. [F, dim. of *rouelle* dim. of *roue* f. L *rota* wheel]

Rou·man, Roumā·nian, (rōō-), nn. & aa. (Native or language) of Roumania. [f. F *Roumain* f. native *Romîn* f. L ROMAN[1]-*us*; -IAN]

Rouma·nsh. See ROMANSH.

Roumē·liote, (rōō-), n. Native of Roumelia. [-OT[2]]

rou·ncival (row-), n. (Also *r. pea*) large variety of pea. [from 16th c.; perh. f. *Roncesvalles* place-name]

round[1] (row-), a. Spherical or circular or cylindrical or approaching these forms, presenting convex outline or surface, (*the r. world*; *r. shot*, spherical ball for smooth-bore cannon; *r. buckler, hole, mat*, of circular outline; *r. table*, with disk top; *the R. Table*, at which Arthur & his knights sat that none might have precedence; *r. table conference*, held at r. table for same purpose; *r. game*, proper for r. table, players being of any number & without sides or partners; *r. face*, as broad as long; *r. jacket*, cut level below, without skirts; *r. hand* or *text*, writing with bold curves; *r. tower, post, limbs*; *r. arch*, semicircular as in Romanesque, opp. *pointed*; *r. cheeks*, plump, not hollow; *r. shoulders*, so bent forward that back is convex, whence **round-shoulder**ED[2] a.; *r. vowel* in Phonet., pronounced with rounded lips); done with or involving circular motion (*r. dance*, waltz; *r. trip, voyage*, with return to starting-point; *r.* or *r.-arm* or *r.-hand bowling*, with arm swung horizontally, cf. *underhand, overhand*; *r. towel*, endless on roller; *r. robin*, written petition with signatures in circle to conceal order in which they were written); entire, continuous, all together, not broken or defective or scanty, sound, smooth, plain, genuine, candid, outspoken, (*r. dozen, score*, that & no less, so many together; *r. numbers*, tens, hundreds, &c., with neglect of minor denominations, whence = roughly correct; *a r. sum*, considerable; *a r. style*, flowing; *at a r. trot*, vigorous; *a r. voice*, not harsh; *r. unvarnished tale*, the plain truth; *be r. with* one, archaic, speak home-truths to him; *a r. oath*, unmistakable); *roundhead*, member of Parliament party in 17th-c. civil war (from custom of wearing hair close cut); *r.-house*, (Hist.) lock-up or place of detention, (Naut.) cabin or set of cabins on after part of quarterdeck chiefly in old sailing-ships); *r.-top*, platform about masthead, formerly circular. Hence **rou·nd**ISH[1](2) a., **rou·nd**NESS n. [f. OF *rund-, rond-* (F *rond*), f. L RO-TUND*us*]

round[2], n. R. object (*this earthly r.*, earth; *rr. of ladder*, rungs; *r. of beef*, thick disk from haunch as joint; *r. of toast*, disk &c. cut across loaf); (Sculpt.) solid form as opp. *relief*; circumference, bounds, extent, of (*in all the r. of Nature*); revolving motion, circular or circuitous or recurring course, circuit, cycle, series, (*the earth in its daily* or *yearly r.*; *the daily r.*, ordinary occupations of the day; *go for a good r.*, long walk out & home; *a r. of days, pleasures, visits*; *make, go*, one's *rr.*, take customary walk esp. of inspection; *make the r. of*, go r.; *news, story, goes the r.*, is passed on), (Mil., pl.) watch that goes r. inspecting sentries or circuit it makes, (Golf) playing of all holes in course once, (Mus.) kind of canon for three or more equal voices; allowance of something distributed or measured out, one of set or series, one bout or spell, one stage in competition, (*serve out a r. of spirit, 20 rr. of ball cartridge*; *never fired a single r.*; *r. after r. of cheers*; *a fight of ten rr.*; *threw up the sponge after the third r.*; *the winners in the first r. are paired for the second*); *roundsman*, tradesman's employee going r. for orders & with goods. [f. F *rond* (prec.) & prec.]

round[3], adv. & prep. With more or less circular motion, with return to starting-point after such motion, with rotation, with change to opposite position lit. or fig., (*sun goes, summer comes, r.*; *brings us r. to winter*; *sleep the clock r.*, for twelve or twenty-four hours; *all the year r.*; *6 in. r.*, in girth; *wheels go r.*; *he turned short r.*; *soon won him r.*); to or at or affecting all or many points of a circumference or area or members of a company &c., in every direction from a centre or within a radius, (*glasses r.*, for all present to drink; *tea was served r.*; *send r. the* HAT; *Home Rule all r.*, for each nationality; *an all-r. man*, one of varied talents; *show* one *r.*, take him to all points of interest; *room hung r. with portraits*; *spread destruction r.*; *all the neighbours for a mile r.*); by circuitous way (*will you jump or go r.?*; *go a long way r.*; *ask* one *r.*, out of his house into one's own; *order the carriage r.*, from coach-house to door); *all r., right r., r. & r.*, emphatic forms of *r.*; *r. about*, in a ring (about), all r. (adv. & prep.), on all sides (of), with change to opposite position, circuitously; *roundabout*, (n.) circuitous way, piece of circumlocution, merry-go-r. (*lose on the swings what you make on the roundabouts*, end where you began after ups & downs), (adj.) circuitous, circumlocutory, plump or stout. (Prep.) so as to encircle or enclose (*tour r. the world*; *has a wrapper r. her*); with successive visits to, at or to points on the circumference of, (*hawks them r. the cafés*; *station them r. the field*; *seated r. the table*); in various directions from or with regard to (*diffuses cheerfulness r. her*; *shells bursting r. me*); having as axis of revolution or central point (*turns r. its centre of gravity*; *argue r. & r. subject*, not come to close quarters with it; *write book r. a subject*); so as to double or pass in curved course, having thus passed, in the position that would result from thus passing, (*go, be, find* person, *r. the corner*; GET *r.*); *all r., right r., r. & r.*, emphatic forms of *r.* [f. ROUND[1, 2]]

round[4], v.t. & i. Invest with, assume, r. shape (*rounded eyes, mouth*; *her form is rounding*; *r. vowel*, pronounce it with rounded lips; *r. off* or *r. the angles*, make them less sharp; *r. dog's ears*, crop them); bring to complete or symmetrical or well-ordered state (often *off*; *r. off* or *r. a sentence, estate, career*); gather *up* (cattle, & transf.) by riding r., whence **rou·nd-up** n.; pass r., double, (cape &c.); turn (t. & i.) r. (rare, chiefly naut.; *rounded on his heel to look at me*; *r. boat off* &c., turn her to meet wave &c.; *ship rounds to*, comes to wind & heaves to); *r. on*, make unexpected retort to (friend &c.), (of informer) peach upon. [f. ROUND[1, 3]]

round[5] (row-), v.i. & t. (archaic). Whisper (t. & i.; chiefly w. double obj. as *rounded him in the ear that*, told him secretly that). [OE *rúnian* (*rún* RUNE)]

rou·ndel (row-), n. Small disk, esp. decorative medallion &c.; rondeau or rondel. [f. OF *rondel*, see ROUND[1], -LE(2)]

rou·ndĕlay (row-), n. Short simple song with refrain; bird's song. [f. F *rondelet* (RONDEL, -ET[1]) w. assim. to LAY[1]]

rou·nder, n. In vbl senses of ROUND[4]; also, (pl.) game with bat & ball between two sides with r. (or complete run of player through all the bases arranged in a round) as unit of scoring. [ROUND[4, 2], -ER[1]]

rou·ndly, adv. In thorough-going manner (*go r. to work*); bluntly, with plain speech, without qualification, severely, (*told him r. that he would not*; *r. asserts that it is true*; *was r. abused*); in circular way (*r. oval*; *swells out r.*). [-LY[2]]

roup[1] (ro͞op), v.t., & n., (Sc. & north.). Sell by auction; (n.) an auction. [n. f. vb (orig. sense *shout*), cf. Icel. *raupa* boast][1]

roup[2] (ro͞op), n. Kinds of poultry-disease (a) with swellings on rump, (b) with purulent catarrh. Hence **rou·py**[2] a. [(a) etym. dub., (b) perh. imit. of hoarse breathing]

rouse[1] (rowz), n. (archaic). Draught of liquor, bumper, toast, revel, drinking-bout, (*take* one's *r.*, carouse; *give a r.*, propose or drink toast). [prob. for CAROUSE, perh. f. wrong division of *drink carouse*]

rouse[2] (rowz), v.t. & i., & n. Startle (game) from lair or cover; wake or stir up or startle (person) from sleep or inactivity or confidence or carelessness (often *up, from, out of, to* action, *to* energy, *to* do, &c.; *r. oneself*, overcome one's indolence; *wants rousing*, is indolent; *a rousing cheer, song, sermon, lie*); provoke temper of, inflame with passion, (*is terrible when* *roused*); evoke (feelings); stir (liquid, esp. beer while brewing); (Naut.) haul vigorously *in, out, up*; cease to sleep, become active, (usu. *up*); (n., mil.) the reveille. [orig. as hunting term; etym. dub.]

rouse[3] (rowz), **roose** (-z), v.t. Sprinkle (herring &c.) with salt in curing. [earlier *arrouse* f. F *arrouser* f. L AD(*rorare* f. *ros roris* dew)]

rou·ser, n. In vbl senses of ROUSE[2]; esp.: implement for rousing beer; outrageous or rousing lie. [-ER[1]]

Rousseau·ism (rōōsō-), n. (Adherence to) views on religion, politics, education, &c., of Jean Jacques Rousseau, French author 1712–78. So **Rousseau**E·SQUE, **Rousseau·**IAN, **Rousseau·**ISH[1], **Rousseau·**AN, aa., **Rousseau·**IST(2), **Rousseau·**ITE(1), nn. & aa. [-ISM]

Roussillon (F), n. A red wine. [*R.*, old French province]

rout[1] (rowt), n., & v.t. Assemblage or company esp. of revellers or rioters, (Law) assemblage of three or more persons engaged in unlawful act; riot, tumult, disturbance, clamour, fuss; (archaic) large evening party or reception (*r.-seat*, light bench hired out for rr.); disorderly retreat of defeated army or troops (*put to r.*, utterly defeat); (vb) put to r. [f. OF ROUTE in senses obs. in F]

rout[2] (rowt), v.i. & t. =ROOT[3]; also, force or fetch *out* (*of bed* or from bed or house or hiding-place). [var. of ROOT[3]]

route (rōōt *& mil.* rowt), n., & v.t. Way taken in getting from starting-point to destination; (Mil.) marching orders (*get, give, the r.*), *column of r.*, formation of troops on the march, *r.-march*, training march of battalion &c.; *en r.* (F), on the way(*is, did it*, en r.). (Vb) plan r. of (goods &c., esp. by rail). [F (now=road), f. L *rupta* (*via* way) fem. p.p. of *rumpere* break, with other senses in OF, see ROUT[1]]

routine (rōōtē·n), n. Regular course of procedure, unvarying performance of certain acts, (attrib.) performed by rule (*r. duties* &c.). Hence **routi·n**ISM(3), **routi·n**IST(2), nn. [F (prec., -INE[4])]

rove[1], v.i. & t., & n. Wander without settled destination, roam, ramble (*roving sailor*, kinds of creeper), (of eyes) look in changing directions; wander over or through; (Angling) troll with live bait; (n.) act of roving (esp. *on the r.*). [orig. term in archery =shoot at casual mark with range not determined; etym. dub.]

rove[2], n., & v.t. Sliver of cotton, wool, &c., drawn out & slightly twisted. (Vb) form into rr.; hence **ro·ver**[1] [-ER[1]] n. [?]

rove[3], n. Small metal plate or ring for rivet to pass through & be clinched over. [f. ON *ró*]

rove[4]. See REEVE[3].

ro·ver[2] (for *r.*[1] see ROVE[2]), n. 1. (Archery) mark chosen at undetermined range, also mark for long-distance shooting, (usu. *shoot at rr.*); wanderer; (Croquet) ball that has passed all hoops but not pegged out, its owner. 2. Sea robber, pirate; senior boy scout. [1 f. ROVE[1], -ER[1]; 2 MDu. (*roven* rob cogn. w. REAVE, -ER[1])]

row[1] (rō), n. Number of persons or things in a more or less straight line (*in a r., rr.*, so arranged); r. of houses, street with this on one or each side (often in street names); *the R.*, ROTTEN ROW; line of seats in theatre &c. (*in the front, third*, &c., *r.*); r. of plants in garden (*a hard r. to hoe* U.S., difficult task). [OE *ráw*, cf. G *reihe*]

row[2] (rō), v.i. & t., & n. Propel boat, propel (boat), convey (passenger) in boat, with oars or sweeps (*r. over*, WALK over in boat-race; also with cogn. obj., as *r. a race, a few strokes, a fast stroke, 30 to the minute*); r. race with; *r. down*, overtake in rowing, esp. bumping, race; be oarsman of specified number in boat (*rows 5 in the Oxford crew*); (of boat) be fitted with (so many *oars*); *r.-boat*, rowing-boat; (n.) spell of rowing, boat-excursion. Hence **row·**ER[1] n. [OE *rówan*, cf. Du. *roeijen*, ON *róa*; cogn. w. L *remus*, Gk *eretmon*, oar]

row[3] (-ow), n., & v.t., (colloq.). Disturbance, commotion, noise, dispute, (*what's the r.?*, what is the matter?; *make, kick up, a r.*, raise noise, also make protest); shindy, free fight, (*town-&-*GOWN *r.*); being reprimanded (*shall get into a r.*). (Vb) reprimand, rate; hence **row·**ING[1](1) n. [from 1787; etym. dub.]

row·an (rō-, row-), n. (Sc. & north.). (Scarlet berry of) mountain ash (also *r.-tree*). [f. Scand. (Sw. *rön*, Icel. *reynir*)]

row-de-dow·, n. Din, uproar. [imit.]

row·dy (row-), n. & a. Rough & disorderly & noisy (person); so *r.-dowdy* a. Hence **row·di**NESS, **row·dy**ISM(2), nn., **row·dy**ISH[1](2) a. [U.S., etym. dub.; orig. sense *backwoodsman*]

row·el (row-), n., & v.t. (-ll-). Spiked revolving disk at end of spur (vb, urge with r.); circular piece of leather &c. with hole in centre inserted between horse's skin & flesh to discharge humours (vb, insert r. in). [f. OF *rouel* f. *roue* f. L *rota* wheel, -LE(2)]

row·lock (rŭ-), n. Pair of thole-pins or other contrivance on boat's gunwale serving as fulcrum for oar. [prob. assim. of earlier *oarlock*, OE *árloc* (OAR, LOCK[2]), to ROW[2]]

Ro·xburghe (-ŭru), n. Style of bookbinding with plain leather gilt-lettered backs, cloth or paper sides, & leaves with untrimmed edges & bottoms. [Duke of *R.* 1740–1804]

roy·al, a. & n. Of, from, suited to, worthy of, belonging to family of, in service or under patronage of, a king or queen (after its noun in some phrr., as *the blood r.*, r. family, RHYME[1] *r.*, PRINCESS *R.*, cf. *R.*

Princess used of any of r. family; *r. charter, warrant,* &c.; *the r. anger, hands,* &c., the sovereign's; *R.* ACADEMY; *R.* AIR[1] *Force*; *R. Artillery*; *r. blue,* a deep pure vivid shade; *r. burgh,* holding charter from Crown; *R. Courts of Justice,* building in Strand, London, in which superior courts of law & appeal are held; *R. Engineers,* engineer branch of army; *r. evil,* =KING[1]*'s evil*; *R. Exchange,* building in Cornhill, London, for dealings between merchants; *R. Field Artillery*; *R. Flying Corps,* army branch of R. Air Force; *R. Garrison Artillery*; *R.* HIGHNESS; *R.* HORSE[1] *Artillery*; *R.* HUMANE *Society*; *R. Institution,* founded 1799 for diffusion of scientific knowledge; *R. Irish Constabulary,* Imperial semi-military police in Ireland, disbanded 1921; *R. Marine Artillery, R. Marine Light Infantry,* two branches of *R. Marines,* soldiers serving on warships; *R. Military Academy,* at Woolwich for Engineer & Artillery cadets; *R. Military College,* at Sandhurst for infantry & cavalry cadets; *R. Naval Air Service,* naval branch of R. Air Force; *R. Naval Division,* military force raised in the great war from surplus sailors & marines; *R. Naval Reserve,* drawn from mercantile marine; *R. Naval Volunteer Reserve,* drawn from landsmen used to the sea; *R. Navy*; *r. oak,* in which Charles II hid after Worcester; *r.* ROAD *to*; *R.* SOCIETY; *r. standard,* square banner with r. arms); kingly, majestic, stately, splendid, first-rate, on great scale, of exceptional size &c., (*r. magnanimity*; *gave us r. entertainment*; *in r. spirits*; *had a r. time*; BATTLE[1] *r.*; *r. paper,* 24×19 in. for writing & 25×20 for printing; *r. octavo* &c., folded from this; *r. fern,* osmund; *r. stag,* with head of 12 or more points; *r. sail, mast,* above topgallant sail & mast; *r. arch,* degree in free-masonry); hence **roy·al**LY[2] adv. (N.) member of r. family (colloq.); r. stag; r. sail or mast; (pl.) first regiment of foot. [f. OF *roial* f. L *regalis* (*rex* king, -AL)]

roy·alist, n. Monarchist, supporter of monarchy as an institution or of the royal side in civil war &c. (also attrib.). So **roy·al**ISM(3) n., **royali·st**IC a. [-IST]

roy·alty, n. Office or dignity or power of king or queen, sovereignty; royal persons; member of royal family (usu. in pl.); (usu. in pl.) prerogative(s) or privilege(s) of the sovereign; royal right (now esp. over minerals) granted by sovereign to individual or corporation, lessee's payment to land-owner for privilege of working mine, sum paid to patentee for use of patent or to author &c. for each copy of his book &c. sold. [f. OF *roialté* (ROYAL, -TY)]

Roy·ston crow, n. Hooded or grey crow. [place-name]

rub[1], v.t. & i., & n. Subject to friction, slide one's hand or an object along over or up & down the surface of (*r.* one's *hands,* each with the other usu. in sign of keen satisfaction; *r. shoulders,* come into contact *with* other people; *r. noses* of some savages, greet each other; *r. the wrong way,* stroke against the grain, irritate or repel as by stroking cat upwards); polish, clean, abrade, chafe, make *dry, sore, bare,* &c., by rubbing; reproduce design of (sepulchral brass or stone) by rubbing paper laid on it with coloured chalk &c., whence **ru·bb**ING[1](2) n.; slide (hand, object) *against* or *on* or *over* something, (objects) together or *together,* with friction; bring (stain &c.) *out,* (nap &c., or fig. novelty, shyness, &c.) *off* or *away,* force (liniment &c., or fig. lesson, humiliating fact, &c.) *in* or *into,* reduce *to* powder &c., force *through* sieve, bring size or level of *down,* spread (ointment &c.) *over,* groom (horse, one*self*) *down,* freshen or brush (tarnished object, or fig. one's memory, Greek, &c.) *up,* mix (chocolate, pigment, &c.) *up* into paste, by rubbing lit. or fig.; come into or be in sliding contact, exercise friction, *against* or *on*; (of bowl) be retarded or diverted by unevenness of ground, (fig., of person, process, &c.) go *on, along, through,* with more or less restraint or difficulty; (of cloth, skin, &c.) get frayed or worn or sore or bare with friction; *r.-stone,* (piece of) stone used for sharpening, smoothing, &c. (N.) spell of rubbing (*give it a r., r.-up, r.-down,* &c.); (Bowls) inequality of ground impeding or diverting bowl, the being diverted &c. by this (prov., *those who play at bowls must look for rr.*), (transf.) impediment or difficulty (*there's the r.,* that is the point at which doubt or difficulty arises; *the rr. & worries of life*), (Golf) *r. of* or *on the green,* accidental interference with course or position of ball. [etym. dub.; cf. LG *rubben*]

rub[2]. See RUBBER[2].

rŭ·b-a-dub, n., & v.i. (Make) rolling sound of drum. [imit.]

ruba·to (-ah-), a. & n. (mus.). (*Tempo*) *r.,* time varied for expression. [It., = robbed]

ru·bber[1], n., & v.t. In vbl senses; also or esp.: masseur or masseuse; Turkish-bath attendant; implement used for, part of machine operating by, rubbing; caoutchouc or india-r. (often attrib.; vb, coat with r.); *rubberneck* (U.-S. slang), inquisitive person. [-ER[1]; last sense from use in rubbing out pencil-marks]

ru·bber[2], n. Three successive games between same sides or persons at whist, cribbage, backgammon, &c. (*have a r. of whist* &c. or *a r.*); *the r.* (also abbr. *the rub*), winning of two games in r., third game when each side has won one. [etym. dub.; as term in bowls from c. 1600; in early use often *a rubbers*]

ru·bbish, n. & int. Waste material, debris,

refuse, litter; worthless material or articles, trash, (*a good riddance of bad r.*, esp. at departure of person one dislikes), absurd ideas or suggestions, nonsense (often as excl. of contempt), whence **ru·bbish**Y[2] & colloq. in same sense **ru·bbishing,** aa. [ME *robows, robeux*, perh. AF pl. of foll.]

ru·bble, n. Waste fragments of stone, brick, &c., from old houses; pieces of undressed stone used, esp. as filling-in, for walls; (Geol.) loose angular stones &c. as covering of some rocks, also water-worn stones. Hence **ru·bbl**Y[2] a. [cf. Icel. *rubb(i)* refuse]

ru·befy, -ify, (ro͞o-), v.t. Make red; (Med., of counter-irritant) stimulate (skin &c.) to redness, so **rube**FA·CIENT a. &, see -ENT(2), n., **rube**FA·CTION n. [ult. f. L *rubefacere* (*rubēre* be red, -FY)]

ru·bicelle (ro͞o-), n. Orange-red precious stone, kind of spinel ruby. [F, prob. dim. of *rubis* or *rubace* RUBY]

Ru·bicon (ro͞o-), n. *The* boundary by passing which one becomes committed to an enterprise (usu. *pass* or *cross the R.*). [name of stream limiting Caesar's province & crossed by him before war with Pompey]

ru·bicund (ro͞o-), a. (Of face, complexion, or person in these respects) ruddy, high-coloured. Hence **rubicu·nd**ITY n. [f. L *rubicundus* (*rubēre* be red, -ND[1])]

rubi·dium (ro͞o-), n. Soft silvery metal grouped with caesium, lithium, potassium, & sodium. [L *rubidus* red (w. ref. to spectrum lines), -IUM]

rubi·ginous (ro͞o-), a. Rust-coloured. [L *rubigo -inis* rust, -OUS]

ru·bious, a. (poet.). Ruby-coloured. [-OUS]

ru·bric (ro͞o-), n. Heading of chapter, section, &c., also special passage or sentence, written or printed in red or in special lettering; direction for conduct of divine service (prop. in red) inserted in liturgical book, whence **rubric**AL a. **ru·brical**LY[2] adv., **rubri**·CIAN (-ĭshn), **ru·bric**ISM(3), **ru·bric**IST(2), nn.; (red-letter entry in) calendar of saints (now rare). [f. L *rubrica* (*ruber rubr-* red)]

ru·bricate, v.t. Mark with, print or write in, red; furnish with rubrics. Hence **rubric**A·TION, **ru·bricat**OR[2], nn. [L *rubricare*, -ATE[3]]

ru·by (ro͞o-), n. & a., & v.t. Rare precious stone (also *true* or *Oriental r.*) of colour varying from deep crimson or purple to pale rose (*balas, spinel, r.*, stones of less value resembling r.; *above rr.*, of inestimable value); (of) glowing purple-tinged red colour; red pimple on nose or face; red wine; (Pugil.) blood; a size of TYPE; *r. glass*, coloured with oxides of copper, iron, lead, tin, &c.; *r.-tail*, insect of deep metallic bluish-green with upper side of abdomen bright red (also *Gold wasp*); (vb) dye or tinge r.-colour. [f. OF *rubi(s)*, prob. ult. f. L *rubeus* red]

ruche (ro͞osh, *or as F*), n. Frill or quilling of gauze, lace, &c. Hence **ruch**ED[2] a. [F]

ruck[1], n. Main body of competitors left out of the running. [earlier senses *stack of fuel, heap, large quantity*; perh. cogn. w. RICK[1]]

ruck[2], **ru·ckle**[1], nn., & vv.i. & t. Crease, wrinkle, (as vb usu. *r. up*). [*ruck* vb f. n., f. ON *hrukka*; *ruckle* f. *ruck*, -LE(3)]

ru·ckle[2], v.i., & n. (Make) gurgling sound esp. in throat of dying person. [f. Scand. (Norw. dial. *rukla* vb)]

ru·cksack (ro͝o-), n. Bag slung by straps from both shoulders & resting on back for carrying walker's or climber's necessaries. [G]

ru·ction, n. (slang). Disturbance, tumult, row, (*there will be rr.*, things will not be allowed to proceed quietly). [from 1825; etym. dub.]

rudd, n. Fresh-water fish resembling roach, red-eye. [prob. f. obs. *rud* red colour; cogn. w. RED]

ru·dder, n. Broad flat wooden or metal piece hinged to vessel's stern-post for steering with, (fig.) guiding principle &c.; (Brewing) paddle for stirring malt in mash-tub; *r.-fish*, kinds that follow ships. Hence **ru·dder**LESS a. [OE *róther*, cf. Du. *roer*, G *ruder*, f. st. of ROW[2]]

ru·ddle, n., & v.t. Red ochre, esp. of kind used for marking sheep; (vb) mark or colour (as) with r. [as RUDD]

ru·ddock, n. Robin redbreast. [OE *ruddue* (RUDD, -OCK)]

ru·ddy, a., & v.t. & i. (Of face or its owner) freshly or healthily red, rosy, (*r. health, youth*, &c., marked by ruddiness); (of light, fire, sky, object lighted up, &c., also in animal names as *r. plover, squirrel*) reddish; (slang) bloody, damnable; hence **ru·ddi**LY[2] adv., **ru·ddi**NESS n. (Vb) make or grow r. [OE *rudig* (*rud* see RUDD, -Y[2])]

rude, a. Primitive, simple, unsophisticated, in natural state, rugged, unimproved, uncivilized, uneducated, roughly made or contrived or executed, coarse, artless, wanting subtlety or accuracy, (*r. times, men, simplicity, ignorance, chaos; r. produce, ore; r. scenery; r. plough, beginnings, methods; r. path, verses, drawing; r. fare, plenty; r. writer, style; r. observer, version, classification*); violent, not gentle, unrestrained, startling, sudden, abrupt, (*r. passions, blast, shock, awakening, reminder*); vigorous, hearty, (*r. health*); insolent, impertinent, offensive, (*r. remarks; say r. things; be r. to*, insult). Hence **ru·de**LY[2] adv., **ru·de**NESS n., **ru·d**ISH[1](2) a. [f. L *rudis*]

Ru·desheimer (ro͞odĕs-hī-), n. A white Rhine wine. [G (*Rü-*)]

ru·diment (ro͞o-), n. (Pl.) elements or first principles of or *of* knowledge or some subject; (pl.) imperfect beginning *of* something that will develop or might under other conditions have developed, (sing.) part or organ imperfectly developed as having no function (e. g. the breast in males). Hence **rudime·nt**AL (rare), **rudime·nt**ARY[1], aa. [f. L *rudīmentum* (RUDE, -MENT)]

rue[1], v.t., & n. Repent of, bitterly feel the consequences of, wish undone or unbefallen, (*you shall r. it*; *r. the day, hour*, &c., *when* —). (N., archaic) repentance, dejection at some occurrence, whence (in ordinary & esp. facet. use) **rue·**FUL a. (*Knight of the -ful countenance*, Don Quixote), **rue·ful**LY[2] adv., **rue·ful**NESS n.; compassion, ruth. [OE *hrēow(an)*, cf. Du. *rouw(en)*, G *reu(en)*]

rue[2], n. Perennial evergreen shrub with bitter strong-scented leaves formerly used in medicine. [F, f. L *ruta* f. Gk *rhutē*]

rue·-raddy, n. Belt or rope passed over shoulder to drag something with. [?]

rufe·scent (rōō-), a. (zool. &c.). Reddish. [L *rufescere* (*rufus* red, -ESCENT)]

ruff[1], n. Deep projecting frill of several folds of linen or muslin starched & separately goffered worn round neck esp. in 16th c., projecting or conspicuously coloured ring of feathers or hair round bird's or beast's neck, whence **(-)ruff**ED[2] a.; kind of domestic pigeon. [perh. shortened f. RUFFLE]

ruff[2], n. (fem. *reeve*). Bird of sandpiper kind of which male has r. & ear-tufts in breeding season. [perh. f. prec.; but the fem. apparently made from it by vowel change (cf. *fox vixen*) suggests that it is an older wd & separate]

ruff[3], n. Small freshwater fish of perch family with prickly scales. [perh. f. ROUGH]

ruff[4], n., & v.i. & t. Trump(ing) at whist; (also *cross* or *double r.*) state of game in which partners out of different suits give each other alternate chances of trumping. [perh. f. *ruff* obs. card-game f. OF *roffle, ronfle*, perh. corrupt. of *triomphe* TRIUMPH, cf. TRUMP]

ru·ffian, n. Brutal violent lawless turbulent person, desperado, bully, rough. Hence **ru·ffian**ISM(2) n., **ru·ffian**LY[1] a. [OF, cf. Pr. & Sp. *rufian*, It. *ruffiano*, etym. dub.]

ru·ffle, v.t. & i., & n. Disturb smoothness or tranquillity of (feathers, hair, water, temper or person in regard to it, brow; *bird ruffles up its feathers*, in anger or to keep off cold; *nothing ever ruffled him*); (of sea, hair, temper, &c.; rare) suffer ruffling, lose smoothness or calmness; swagger about, behave arrogantly or quarrelsomely, whence **ru·ffl**ER[1] n. (N.) perturbation, bustle, (rare; *without r. or excitement*), rippling effect on water; ornamental gathered or goffered frill of lace &c. worn at opening of garment esp. about wrist or breast or neck, RUFF[1] of bird &c., whence **ru·ffl**ED[2] a.; (now rare) a contention, dispute; (Mil.) vibrating drum-beat, [etym. dub.; cf. LG *ruffelen* crumple, goffer; senses *swagger, contention, drum-beat*, perh. independent]

ru·fous (rōō-), a. (chiefly nat.-hist.). Red-dish-brown. So **rufi-**, **rufo-**, comb. forms. [L *rufus*, -OUS]

rug, n. Large wrap or coverlet of thick woollen stuff; floor-mat of shaggy material or thick pile, esp. (often *hearth-r.*) laid down before fireplace. [perh. f. Scand. (Norw. dial. *rugga* coverlet, Sw. *rugg* ruffled hair)]

Rugbei·an (-bēan), n. & a. (Member) of Rugby School.

Ru·gby, n. *R. football* or *R.*, also **ru·gg**ER[1] n. slang, one of the two chief forms of football, distinguished from *Association* or *socker* esp. by players' being permitted to carry the ball & to hold opponent doing this; *R. Union*, of clubs using R. football rules. [*R.* school]

ru·gged (-gĭd), a. Of rough uneven surface (*r. bark*; *r. ground, country*, full of abrupt ups & downs, craggy, wooded, &c.; *r. features*, strongly marked, of irregular outline); unsoftened, unpolished, lacking gentleness or refinement, harsh in sound, austere, unbending, involving hardship, (*r. manners, grandeur, kindness, honesty, character, verse, times, life*). Hence **ru·gged**LY[2] adv., **ru·gged**NESS n. [prob. f. Scand., cogn. w. RUG, RAG[1], ROUGH]

rugo·se (rōō-), a. (chiefly nat. hist.). Wrinkled, corrugated. Hence or cogn. **rugo·se**LY[2] adv., **ru·g**ATE[2], **ru·g**OUS, aa., **rugo·**SITY n. [f. L *rugosus* (*ruga* wrinkle, -OSE[1])]

Rühmkorff coil, n. Kind of induction coil. [H. D. *Rühmkorff*, maker]

ru·in, n., & v.t. & i. Downfall or fallen or wrecked or impaired state, lit. (of building or structure; *the crash of r.*; *tumble, lie, lay, in r.*) or fig. (*the r. of my hopes*; *bring to r.*, complete loss of property or position; *dates her r. from his arrival*; RACK[1] *& r.*); (often pl.) what remains of building, town, structure, &c., or fig. of person, that has suffered r. (*the rr. of Rome*, remains of ancient Rome or of the Roman imperial system; *is but the r. of what he was*; *lies in rr.*; *is a r.*; *lives in an old r.*); what causes r., destroying agency, havoc, (*will be the r. of us*; BLUE[1] *r.*; *rapine & red r.*), so [f. obs. *ruinate* vb] **ruin**A·TION n. (Vb) reduce (place) to rr. (esp. in p.p.); bring to r. (*her extravagance ruined him*; so *r. oneself*; *r. girl*, seduce her; *r.* one's *new hat, prospects*); (poet.) fall headlong or with a crash. [f. F *ruine(r)* f. (vb thr. med. L *ruinare*) L *ruina* (*ruere* fall., -INE[4])]

ru·inous, a. In ruins, dilapidated; bringing ruin, disastrous, (*r. folly, expense*), whence **ru·inous**LY[2] adv. Hence **ru·inous**NESS n. [f. L *ruinosus* (prec., -OSE[1])]

rule, n., & v.t. & i. Principle to which action or procedure conforms or is bound or intended to conform, dominant custom, canon, test, standard, normal state of things, (*deduce rr. of action*; *the rr. of decorum, cricket*, &c.; *r. of the* ROAD[1]; *there was a r. that* —; *standing r.*, made by corporation to govern its procedure; *r. of thumb*, based on experience or practice, not theory, often *r.-of-t.* attrib.; *r. of three*, method of finding number that bears same ratio to one given as exists between two others given, also attrib., as *r.-o.-t. sum*; GOLDEN *r.*; *by r.*, in regulation manner, mechanically; WORK[2] *to r.*; *hard & fast r.*, rigid formula; EXCEPTION *proves r.*; *large families are the r. & not the exception*; *as a r.*, usually, more often than not); sway, government, dominion, (*bear r.*, hold sway; *under British r.*; *the r. of force*; *entrusted with the r. of half the tribe*); (Eccl.) code of discipline observed by religious order; (Law) order made by judge or court w. ref. to particular case only (*r.* NISI; *r. absolute*, making r. *nisi* no longer contingent); (Hist.) *the rr.*, limited area outside Fleet & King's-Bench prisons in which prisoners were allowed to live on certain terms; graduated often jointed straight measure used by carpenters &c. (often *foot-r.*, *2 ft r.*, &c.); (Print.) thin slip of metal for separating headings, columns, &c., also short (*en r.*) or long (*em r.*) dash in punctuation &c.; *r.-joint*, of kind usual in jointed carpenter's r.; hence **ru·le**LESS a. (Vb) exercise sway or decisive influence over, keep under control, curb, (person, conduct, one's passions; *ruling passion*, motive that habitually directs one's actions), (pass.) consent to follow advice, be guided *by*; be the ruler(s) or have the sovereign control of or *over*, bear r., (*r. the* ROAST; *rules over many millions*; *kings should r. by love*); (of prices, or goods &c. in regard to them or to quality &c.) have a specified general level, be for the most part, (*corn, prices, the market, ruled high* &c.; *crops r. good*; *ruling prices*, those current); give judicial or authoritative decision (usu. *that*; also *r.* person or thing *out of order*; *r. out*, exclude, pronounce irrelevant or ineligible), whence **ru·l**ING[1] (2) n.; make parallel lines across (paper), make (straight line), with ruler or mechanical help. [f. OF *riule(r)* f. L *regula, regulare*, see REGULAR]

ru·ler, n. Person or thing bearing (esp. sovereign) rule (often *of*), whence **ru·ler**SHIP n.; straight strip or cylinder usu. of wood used in ruling paper or lines. [-ER[1]]

ru·lley, rŏl-, n. Flat four-wheeled dray, lorry. [?]

rum[1], n. Spirit distilled from sugar-cane; *r.*-SHRUB[2]. [formerly *rumbullion, rumbustion, rumbo*, etym. dub.]

rum[2], ru·mmy, aa. (slang). Odd, strange, queer; *r. customer*, (esp.) person or animal that is dangerous to meddle with; *r. start* (slang), surprising occurrence. Hence **ru·m**LY[2], **ru·mmi**LY[2], advv., **ru·m**NESS, **ru·mmi**NESS, nn. [16th-c. cant, orig. =*fine, spirited*, perh. var. of ROM; -Y[2]]

Rumansh. See ROMANSH.

ru·mble, v.i. & t., & n. Make sound (as) of thunder, earthquake, heavy cart, air in the bowels, &c.; go *along, by*, &c., making or in vehicle making such sound; utter, say *out*, give *forth*, with such sound. (N.) rumbling sound; hind part of carriage arranged as extra seat or for luggage; *r.-tumble*, lumbering vehicle, rough motion. [ME *romblen*, cf. Du. *rommelen*, G *rummeln*, prob. imit.]

rumbu·stious, a. (colloq.). Boisterous, uproarious. [perh. var. of ROBUSTIOUS]

ru·men (rōō-), n. Ruminant's first STOMACH. [L, = throat]

ru·minant, n. & a. Animal that chews cud. (Adj.) belonging to the rr.; contemplative, given to or engaged in meditation. [foll., -ANT]

ru·minate, v.i. & t. Chew the cud; meditate, ponder, (i., rarely t.; often *over, about, of, on*), whence or cogn. **ru·mina**TIVE a., **ru·minative**LY[2] adv., **ru·minator**[2] n. So **rumina·**TION n. [f. L *ruminari* (RUMEN), -ATE[3]]

ru·mmage (-ĭj), v.t. & i., & n. Ransack (ship, house, pockets, records, book), make search in or *in*, make search; fish *out* or *up* from among other things; disarrange, throw *about*, in searching. (N.) things got by rummaging, miscellaneous accumulation; rummaging, search (esp. of ship by Customs officer); *r.-sale*, clearance sale of unclaimed articles at docks &c., sale of odds & ends contributed to raise money for charity bazaar. [n. in mod. senses f. vb; vb orig. f. n. in obs. sense *arranging of casks &c. in hold*, f. F *arrumage* (now *arri-*) f. *arrumer* etym. dub.]

ru·mmer, n. Large drinking-glass. [f. WFlem. *rummer* or Du. *romer* or G *römer* perh. = Roman glass]

rummy. See RUM[2].

ru·mour (rōō-), n., & v.t. General talk, report, or hearsay, of doubtful accuracy; *a* or *the* current but unverified statement or assertion (often *that, of*). (Vb, chiefly in pass.) report by way of r. (*it is rumoured that* —; *he is rumoured to* be &c.; *the rumoured disaster*). [OF, f. L *rumorem* nom. *-or*]

rump, n. Tail-end, posterior, buttocks, of beast or bird or rarely of person, whence (of tailless fowl) **ru·mp**LESS a.; small or contemptible remnant of a parliament or similar body, esp. (hist.) that of Long Parliament either after its restoration 1659 or from Pride's Purge 1648 to its first dissolution 1653; *rumpstea·k*, cut from ox's r. [prob. f. Scand. (Da. *rumpe*, Sw. & Norw. *rumpa*)]

ru·mple, v.t. Wrinkle, crease, tousle, disorder, (fabric, leaves, garment, hair, &c.). [cf. MDu. *rompelen*, MLG *rumpen*]

ru·mpus, n. (slang). Disturbance, brawl, row, uproar. [?]

ru·mpy, n. Manx tailless cat. [RUMP, -Y²]

rum-tum, n. Light sculling-boat on lower Thames. [?]

run¹, v.i. & t. (*ran, run*; p.p. rarely as -ED¹(2), as *a fresh-r. salmon*). (Of men) progress by advancing each foot alternately never having both on ground at once (cf. WALK¹; *running jump*, in which jumper runs to the take-off), (of animals) go at quicker than walking pace, amble, trot, canter, gallop, &c.; (start to) cross cricket pitch to score r.; flee, abscond, (chiefly now in *r. for it, cut & r.* slang; *running fight* naut., kept up by retreating ship or fleet with pursuer); go or travel hurriedly, precipitately, &c. (*r. to meet* one's *troubles*, anticipate them; *r.* RIOT; *r. to help* another; *r. over* or *down* or *up*, to place for flying visit; *he who runs may read*, said of easily intelligible exposition &c.); be allowed to grow or stray *wild*; compete in or *in* race (*r. second* &c., come in so), seek election &c. (*for* parliament, president, &c.); (of fish, ship, &c.) go straight & fast (*a running whale*; *salmon r.*, go up river from sea; *ship runs before the wind, into port, ashore, on the rocks*, FOUL *of* or *aboard* another); advance (as) by rolling or on wheels, spin round or along, revolve (as) on axle, go with sliding or smooth or continuous or easy motion, be in action, work freely, be current or operative, (*ball, carriage, wheel, spindle, sledge, time, runs*; *rope runs in pulley*; *his life runs smoothly*; *running knot*, that slips along rope & enlarges or diminishes running noose; *running hand*, writing in which pen &c. is not lifted after each letter; *how your tongue runs!*, how incessantly you talk!; *verse runs*, is smooth; *tune runs in head*, seems to be heard over & over again; *lease, contract, runs for seven* &c. *years*; *play ran 100 nights*, was kept on stage; *courage runs in the family*, is found in all members of it; *the works have ceased running*; *place where writs do not r.*, are not valid or respected); (of public conveyance by land or water) ply (*from, to, between*), (of fire, news, enthusiasm, &c.) spread rapidly from point to point (*news ran like wild-fire*; *a cheer ran down the line*; *running fire*, successive shots from different points); (of colour in fabric) spread from the dyed to the undyed parts; (of thought, eye, memory, &c.) pass in transitory or cursory way (*thoughts r. through* one's *head*; *eyes r. over object*; *running commentary*, touching on a point here & there; *r. back over the past*, survey it summarily); (of liquid, grain, sand, &c., also of vessel containing or object emitting &c., & fig.) flow, be wet, drip, flow with, (*till the blood ran*; *ran blood*; *fountains r. wine*; *is running with oil*; *tide runs strong*; *river runs clear, thick*; *feeling ran high*; one's *blood runs cold*, he is horrified; *the sands are running out*, time of grace &c. is nearly up; *running sore*, suppurating; *nose, eyes, r.*, drop mucus or tears; *r. at the nose*; *r. with sweat*; *r. dry*, cease to flow, be exhausted; *r. low, short*, become scanty; *candle runs*, gutters); extend, be continuous, have a certain course or order, progress, proceed, have a tendency or common characteristic or average price or level, (*fence runs round the house*; *running head-line, head*, or *title*, repeated or different heading of page; *whereof the memory of man runneth not to the contrary*, phr. applied to immemorial tradition or custom; *running account*, = *current* ACCOUNT²; *road runs at right angles to, along, the ridge*; *story, title, document, runs in these words*; *must not r. to extremes*; *runs to sentiment*; *our pears r. big this year*, are so for the most part; *prices r. high*; *oats r. 44 lb. to the bushel*), (in part., placed after pl. n.) following each other without interval, in succession, (*happened three days, hit the bull's-eye seven times, running*); (w. cogn. obj.) pursue, follow, traverse, cover, make way swiftly through or over, wander about in, perform, essay or be exposed or submit to, (course, way, race, a mile, r. at cricket; *things must r. their course*, be left to themselves; *r. a scent*, follow it up; *r. the streets*, be street arab; *r. errands, messages*, be a messenger; *the Derby was r. in a snow-storm*; *r. the* GAUNTLET²; *r.* RISKS; *runs a chance of being*, may be; *r. rapids*, shoot them; *r. croquet-hoop*, send ball clear through it; *r.* BLOCKADE¹); sew (fabric) slightly; chase, hunt, have running race with, (*r. fox five miles*; *r. to earth*, chase to its lair, & often fig. = discover after long search; *will r. you for £50 a side*; *r.* one *hard* or *close*, press him severely in race, competition, or comparative merit &c.); (in causative senses) make r. or go (*r. cattle* &c., turn out to graze; *r. brandy*, &c., smuggle it in by evading coast-guard &c.; *r. ship aground, to New York*; *r. boat down to the water*; *r. train through*; *r.* one's *head against*; *r. cart into wall*; *r. sword, pin, into*; *r.* one's *hand, eye, along, down, over*, something; *r. rope through eyelet*; *r. coach, steamer, business, person*, keep them going, manage them, conduct their operations; *r. the show* slang, dominate in an undertaking &c.; *r. horse*, send him in for race, so *r. candidate*; *r. metal into mould*; *r. the water off*; *r. parallel, simile*, &c., *too far*; *ran his fingers, comb, through his hair*; *r.* thing *fine*, leave very little margin of time or amount concerning it); *ru·nabout* a., roving, (n.) light motor-car; *ru·naway* n. & a., fugitive, bolting (horse), *r.-a. match* or *marriage*, after elopement, *r.-a. ring* or *knock*, given at door by practical joker who immediately makes off. With prepp.: *r. across*, fall in with; *r. after*, pursue with attentions, seek society of, give much time to (pursuit &c.); *r. against*, fall in with; *run at*, assail by charging or rushing; *r. in* (incur) *debt*; *r. into*, fall into (practice, absurdity, &c.), be continuous or coalesce with, have collision with, reach or attain (*some length, five editions*, &c.); *r. on*, be concerned with (*talk, mind, runs on* a subject); *r. over*, review, glance over, peruse, recapitulate, touch (notes of piano &c.) in quick succession, (of vehicle) pass over (prostrate person); *r. through*, examine cursorily, peruse, deal successively with, consume (estate &c.) by reckless or quick spending, pervade; *r. to*, reach (amount, number, &c.), have money or ability or (of money &c.) be enough for (some expense or undertaking), fall into (ruin), (of plants) tend to develop chiefly (seed), (of persons) indulge inclination towards (coarseness &c.); *r. upon*, (of thoughts &c.) be engrossed by, dwell on, (of person) encounter suddenly. With advv.: *r. about*, bustle, hurry from one person &c. to another, (esp. of children) play or wander without restraint; *r. away*, flee, abscond, elope, (of horse) bolt, (of horse or person) get clear away *from* competitors in race; *r. away with*, carry off (person, stolen property, &c.), accept (notion) hastily, (of expense &c.) consume (money &c.), (of horse &c.) bolt with (rider, carriage or its occupants); *r. down*, (of clock &c.) stop for want of winding, (of person or his health &c.) become enfeebled from overwork, poor feeding, &c. (also in p.p. as *is, feels, much r. d.*), knock down or collide with (person, ship, &c.), overtake (game, person) in pursuit, discover after search, disparage; *r. in*, (of combatant) rush to close quarters, (Rugby footb.) carry ball over opponents' goal-line & touch it down, pay short visit (*to* person or house), (colloq.) arrest & take to prison, (colloq.) secure election of (candidate); *r. off*, flee, flow away, digress suddenly, write or recite (poem, list, &c.) fluently, drain (liquid) off, decide (race) after tie or trial heats; *r. on*, be joined together (of written characters), continue in operation, elapse, speak volubly, talk incessantly, (Print.) begin (t. & i. of sentence &c.) in same line as what precedes; *r. out*, come to an end (of period, also of stock of something or its owner; *r. out of*, exhaust one's stock of), escape from containing vessel, advance from block to hit ball in cricket, pass or be paid out (of rope), jut out, come out of contest in specified position &c. or complete required score &c., complete (race), advance (gun &c.) so as to project, put down wicket of (batsman while running), exhaust one*self* by running; *r. over*, overflow (of vessel or contents), recapitulate, review, glance over; *r. through*, pierce with sword &c., draw line through (written words); *r. up*, grow quickly, rise in price, amount *to*, be RUNNER-up, accumulate (number, sum, debt) quickly, force (rival bidder) to bid higher, force up (price or commodity in that respect), erect (wall, house) to great height or in unsubstantial or hurried way, add up (column of figures). [ME *rinnen, rennen*, prob. f. ON *rinna*, cf. MDu. & G *rinnen*; OE has *rinnan* very rarely, & usu. the metathetic forms *irnan* intr. & *ærnan* trans.]

run², n. Act or spell of RUN¹ning (*have a r. for* one's *money*, get some enjoyment &c. out of expenditure or effort, orig. w. ref. to scratching of horse after bets; *had a good r.*, esp. in hunting or on ship, train, &c.; *on the r.*, fleeing, also bustling about; *at a r.*, running; *a r. on the Continent, to Paris*, &c., short excursion or visit); (Cricket) traversing of pitch by both batsmen without either's being put out, point scored thus or otherwise, notch; rhythmical motion, way things tend to move, direction, (*cannot get the r. of the metre*, or *of* some process or operation, see how it goes; *the r. of the market was against us*; *the r. of the hills is* N.W.); rapid fall (*come down with a r.*, of building &c., person, mercury in barometer &c., prices, &c.); (Mus.) roulade; continuous stretch or spell or course, long series or succession, general demand, (*a 500 ft r. of pipe*; *a long r. of power, office*; *a r. of luck*; *in the* LONG¹ *r.*; *a r. on the bank*, sudden demand from many customers for immediate payment; *r. on rubber, book*, &c., great demand for it; so *book* &c. *has a considerable r.*; *r. on the red* in rouge-et-noir, its coming many times running; *play has a r. of 50 nights, a long r.*, &c.); common, general, average, or ordinary type or class (*the common r. of men*, average men), class or line of goods, batch or drove of animals born or reared together, shoal of fish in motion; regular track of some animals, enclosure for fowls &c., range of pasture (usu. *sheep* &c. *-r.*); trough for water to run in; part of ship's bottom narrowing towards stern; licence to make free use of (*allowed him the r. of their books, house*; *the r. of* one's *teeth*, free board); *r.-in*, act of running in (see prec.) at football; *r.-off*, deciding race after dead heat; *r.-up*, race between greyhounds up to hare's first turn. [f. prec.]

rŭ·nagate, n. (archaic). Vagabond. [assim. of RENEGADE to *run* & obs. *agate* away]

ru·ncinate (-*a*t), a. (bot.). Saw-toothed, with lobes curved towards base. [L *runcina* plane (wrongly supposed to be saw), -ATE²]

ru·ndāle, n. Joint occupation of (esp. Irish) land, each holder having several strips not contiguous. [RUN¹, obs. *dale* north. var. of DOLE¹]

rune, n. Any letter of earliest Teutonic alphabet used esp. by Scandinavians & Anglo-Saxons, dating from as early as 2nd c. & formed by modifying Roman or Greek characters to suit carving; similar mark of mysterious or magic significance; (division of) Finnish poem; *r.-staff,* magic wand inscribed with rr., also runic calendar. [f. ON *rún,* cogn. w. OE *rún* whisper, secret counsel, whence ROUND⁵]

rung¹, n. Short stick attached at each end as rail, spoke, or cross-bar in chair &c. or esp. in ladder (often fig., as *the lowest, topmost, r. of Fortune's ladder*). Hence **rung**ED², **ru·ng**LESS, aa. [OE *hrung,* cf. Du. *rong,* G *runge*]

rung². See RING².

ru·nic, a. & n. Of, in, marked with, runes; (of poetry &c.) of the ancient-Scandinavian type; (of ornament) interlacing as on r. monuments & metal-work. (N.) r. inscription; kinds of moth; (Print.) ornamental type of thick face & condensed form. [-IC]

ru·nlet¹, n. (archaic). Cask of varying size for wine &c. [f. OF *rondelet* dim. of *rondelle* dim. of *ronde* (ROUND¹)]

ru·nlet², n. Small stream. [RUN², -LET]

ru·nnel, n. Brook, rill; gutter. [OE *rynel* f. RUN¹, -LE(1)]

ru·nner, n. In vbl senses; also or esp.: messenger, scout, collector, or agent for bank &c., tout; (Hist., esp. BOW-STREET *r.*) police-officer; the bird water-rail; =BLOCKADE¹-*r.*; revolving millstone; (Naut.) rope in single block with one end round tackle-block & other having hook; creeping stem that issues from main stem of strawberry &c. & takes root; kinds of twining bean, esp. SCARLET *r.*; ring &c. that slides on rod, strap, &c.; one of the long pieces of wood &c. on which sledge &c. slides, (blade of) FEN¹-*r.*; groove or rod for thing to slide along, roller for moving heavy article; *r.-up,* dog beaten only in final heat at coursing, competitor similarly beaten at golf &c. [-ER¹]

ru·nning, n. In vbl senses; esp.: (w. ref. to racing) *make, take up, the r.,* take the lead, set the pace, (lit., & fig. of talk &c.), *in, out of, the r.* (of competitor), with good, no, chance of winning; *r. powers,* right granted by railway to another to run trains over its line. [-ING¹]

ru·nrig, n. (Sc.). =RUNDALE. [RUN¹, Sc. & north. *rig* RIDGE]

runt, n. Ox or cow of small esp. Scotch-Highland or Welsh breed; large breed of domestic pigeon. [?]

rupee· (rōō-), n. Indian monetary unit & silver coin, 1s. 4*d.* (*pl. abbr.* Rs; Rx, tens of rr., in statistics &c.). [f. Hind. *rupiyah* f. Skr. *rupya* wrought silver]

ru·pture (-tsher), n., & v.t. & i. Breach of harmonious relations, disagreement & parting; (Path.) tumour formed by protrusion of part of an organ through breach in wall of containing cavity esp. in abdomen, hernia; breaking, breach. (Vb) burst, break, (cell, vessel, membrane); sever (connexion, marriage, &c.); affect with hernia; suffer r. [f. L *ruptura* (*rumpere rupt-* break, -URE)]

rur·al (-roor-), a. In, of, suggesting, the country (opp. URBAN), pastoral or agricultural, (*r.* DEAN¹; *in r. seclusion*; *r. policeman, constituency, sports,* &c.). Hence **rura·l**ITY n., **rur·al**IZE(2, 3) v.i. & t., **ruraliza·**TION n., **rur·al**LY² adv. [f. L *ruralis* (*rus ruris* country, -AL)]

ruridecā·nal (roor-; *also* -dĕ·ka-), a. Of rural DEAN¹ or deanery. [L *rus* (prec.), -I-]

ru·sa, n. Large E.-Ind. deer. [Malay]

ruse (rōōz, *or as F*), n. Stratagem, feint, trick. [OF (*ruser* drive back, retreat, cogn. w. RUSH²)]

rusé (F), a. (fem. *-ée*). Given to ruses, sly, cunning, (of person, procedure, look, &c.).

rush¹, n., & v.t. Marsh or water-side plant with naked slender tapering pith-filled stems (prop. leaves) formerly used for strewing floors & still for making chair-bottoms & plaiting baskets &c., a stem of this, (collect.) rr. as a material; thing of no value (*don't care, not worth, a r.*); *r.-bearing,* annual northern festival on occasion of carrying rr. & garlands to strew floor & decorate walls of church; *r. candle,* made by dipping pith of a r. in tallow; *ru·shlight,* r. candle (usu. fig. of feeble glimmer of intelligence, scanty information, &c.; *r. ring,* ring made of rush(es) formerly used in (esp. mock) weddings; hence **ru·sh**LIKE, **ru·sh**Y², aa. (Vb) supply (chair-bottom), strew (floor), with rr. [OE *risc* & rare *rysc,* cf. MDu. *risch,* also Du. & G *rusch*]

rush², v.t. & i., & n. Impel, drag, force, carry along, violently & rapidly (*rushed them into danger, round the sights*; *ball is rushed down the field*; *r. bill through,* get it hurriedly passed; *refuse to be rushed,* insist on doing things at one's own pace); (Mil.) take by sudden vehement assault; pass (obstacle, stream, fence, &c.) with a rapid dash; swarm upon & take possession of (goldfield, platform at meeting, &c.); charge (customer) exorbitant price (*they r. you shockingly, rushed us £1 a head*); run precipitately, violently, or with great speed, go or resort without proper consideration (*in*)*to,* (*r. into, out of, the room*; *r. at,* charge; *dark horse rushed past the favourite*; *r. into extremes*; *r. into print,* write to newspaper, publish book, &c.); flow, fall, spread (intr.), roll (intr.), impetuously or fast (*river rushes past*;

a rushing mighty wind; *avalanches r. down*; *blood rushed to his face*; *his past life rushed into his memory*). (N.) act of rushing, violent or tumultuous advance, spurt, charge, onslaught, (*the r. of the tide*; *carry the citadel with a r.*; *a r. of blood to the head*; *a great r. of business*); (Footb.) combined dash of several players with the ball; sudden migration of large numbers esp. to new goldfield; strong run *on* or *for* some commodity; *r.-hours* (at which traffic is busiest). [n. f. vb, AF *russher* f. OF *re(h)usser, ruser*, perh. f. L *re(fundere fus-* pour), RE- 9, cause to flow back]

rusk, n. Piece of bread pulled or cut from loaf & rebaked. [f. Sp. or Port. *rosca* twist, coil, roll of bread]

Ruski·nian, a. & n. After the manner or principles, follower, of John Ruskin writer on art & social subjects d. 1900. So **Ruskin**E·SE, **Ruskin**E·SQUE, aa. & nn., **Ru·skin**ISM(3) n. **Ru·skin**IZE(2, 3, 4) v.i. & t. [-IAN]

Russ, n. & a. A Russian; the Russian language; (adj.) Russian. Hence **Ru·ssi**FY v.t., **Russi**FICA·TION n., **Russo-** comb. form, **Ru·sso**PHIL n. & a., **Russo·phil**ISM(3) n., **Ru·sso**PHOBE n. & a., **Russo**PHO·BIA n. [f. Russ. *Rusi* Russian people or country]

Russell (cord), n. Ribbed fabric of cotton & wool used for scholastic gowns &c. [?]

ru·sset, n. & a. (Hist.) coarse home-spun reddish-brown or grey cloth worn by peasants; reddish brown; kind of rough-skinned r.-coloured apple. (Adj.) reddish-brown (also **ru·sset**Y[2] a.); (archaic) rustic, homely, simple. [f. OF *rousset* (*rous* red f. L *russus*, -ET[1])]

Russia (leather) (-sha), n. Durable bookbinding leather from skins impregnated with birch-bark oil. [*Russia*]

Ru·ssian (-shn), n. & a. Native, language, of Russia. (Adj.) of or from Russia (*R. boots*, loosely enclosing calf); of or in R.; hence **Ru·ssian**IZE(3) v.t. [f. med. L *Russianus* (prec., -AN)]

Ru·ssniak, n. & a. (Member, language) of the Little Russian or Ruthenian race in Galicia. [f. native *Rusnyak*]

rust, n., & v.i. & t. Yellowish-brown coating formed on iron or steel by oxidation esp. as effect of moisture & gradually corroding the metal, similar coating on other metals, (fig.) impaired state due to disuse or inactivity, inaction as deteriorating influence; (plant-disease with rust-coloured spots caused by) kinds of fungus, blight, brand; hence **ru·st**LESS a. (*-less steel*, esp. ferro-chromium alloys used for stainless cutlery &c.). (Vb) contract r., undergo oxidation or blight; (of bracken &c.) become r.-coloured; lose quality or efficiency by disuse or inactivity (*better wear out than r. out*, exhortation to maintain activity in old age &c.); affect with r., corrode. [OE *rūst*, cf. Du. *roest*, G *rost*; cogn. w. RED]

ru·stic, a. & n. (Now less usual for) rural; having the appearance or manners of country-people, characteristic of peasants, unsophisticated, unpolished, unrefined, uncouth, clownish; of rude or country workmanship (*r. seat, bridge, work*, of untrimmed branches or rough timber), (of lettering) irregularly formed, (Arch.) with rough-hewn or roughened surface or with chamfered joints (*r.-work*, such masonry); hence or cogn. **ru·stic**ALLY, **ru·stic**LY[2] (rare), advv., **rusti·c**ITY n. (N.) countryman, peasant. [f. L *rusticus* (*rus* the country)]

ru·sticate, v.i. & t. Retire to, sojourn in, the country, lead a rural life; send down temporarily from university as punishment; countrify; mark (masonry) with sunk joints or roughened surface. Hence **rustic**A·TION n. [f. L *rusticari* live in the country (prec.), -ATE[3]]

ru·stle (-sl), v.i. & t., & n. (Give forth) sound (as) of dry leaves blown, rain pattering, or silk garments in motion; go with r. (*along* &c.; *r. in silks*, be clad in silk); cause to r. by shaking &c. Hence **ru·stling**LY[2] adv. [n. f. vb, imit.; cf. Du. *ridselen*]

ru·sty[1], a. Rusted, affected with rust; of antiquated appearance; (of voice) croaking, creaking; stiff with age or disuse, antiquated, behind the times, impaired by neglect, in need of furbishing, (*his Greek is a little r.*); (of black clothes) discoloured by age; rust-coloured. Hence **ru·sti**LY[2] adv., **ru·sti**NESS n. [-Y[2]]

ru·sty[2], a. Rancid (esp. of bacon). [=obs. *resty* f. OF *resté* left over, stale]

rut[1], n., & v.t. Track sunk by passage of wheels; established mode of procedure, beaten track, groove; hence **ru·tt**Y[2] a. (Vb) mark with rr. (usu. in p.p.). [?]

rut[2], n., & v.i. Periodic sexual excitement of male deer (also of goat, ram, &c.), heat; (vb) be affected with r. Hence **ru·tt**ISH[1](1) a. [OF, also *ruit*, f. L *rugitus -ūs* (*rugire* roar)]

ruth (rōōth), n. (archaic). Pity, compassion. Hence (mod.) **ru·th**LESS a., **ru·thless**LY[2] adv., **ru·thless**NESS n. [RUE[1], -TH[1]]

-ry, suf., shortened form of -ERY (which see for numbered meanings), as in *chantry* (ME *chaunterie*), *jewry, bottomry, foundry, poultry, jewel(le)ry*; somet. also in direct formations, as *rivalry*.

rye (rī), n. (Grain of) a N.-Europ. cereal used for bread in northern Continental countries & for fodder in U.K. [OE *ryge*, cf. ON *rugr*, Da. *rug*; cogn. w. Du. *rogge*, G *roggen*]

rye·-grass, n. Kinds of fodder grass. [f. obs. *ray* etym. dub. w. assim. to prec.]

rye·peck (rī-), n. Ironshod pole for securing punt &c. [?]

ry·mer, n. One of the posts in weir or lock holding paddles. [?]
ry·ot, n. Indian peasant. [f. Hind. *raiyat* f. Arab. as RAYAH]

S

S (ĕs), letter (pl. *S*s, S's). (Also) S-shaped object (COLLAR[1] *of S, Ss, SS*, or *esses*) or curve (*river makes a great S*).

Abbreviations (1): S., *sacrosanctae*, **S.T.P.** (*theologiae professor*); saint (pl. SS.), as **S.** John, **SS.** Peter & Paul; salvation, **S.A.** (army); *senatus*, **S.P.Q.R.** (*populusque Romanus*); sergeant, **S.M.** (major); **S.**(ignor); simultaneous, **S.B.** (broadcast); small, **S.P.Q.R.** (profits & quick returns); social, **S.D.F.** (democratic federation); society, **S.J.** (of Jesus) **S.P.C.K.** (for promoting Christian knowledge), **S.P.E.** (for pure English), **S.P.G.** (for propagation of gospel), **S.P.R.** (for psychical research); **S.S.J.E.** (of St John Evangelist); Sodor, **S. & M.** (Man); soprano, **S.A.T.B.** (alto, tenor, bass); south, **S.**, **S.A.**(frica), **S.C.**(arolina), **S. Dak.**(ota), **S.E.**(ast), **S.W.**(est); southern, **S.R.**(ailway); steam, **S.S.** (ship). s., screw, **s.s.** (steamer); small, **s. caps** (capitals); *solidus, solidi*, **s. d.** (denarii, as 7*s.* 6*d.*); son; sub, **s.f.** (*finem*), **s.v.** (*voce*).

Abbreviations (2): **Salop.**, Shropshire; **Sam.**(uel; O.-T. book); **Sarum.**, bp of Salisbury; **Sask.**(atchewan); **sc.**(*ilicet*); **sc.**(*ulpsit, -ulpserunt*); **scil.**(*icet*); **Sec.**-(retary); **sen.**(ior); **seq(q).**, *sequentes, -tia*; **Sergt**, Sergeant; **sf.**(*orzando*); **Skr.**, Sanskrit; **Soc.**(iety); **Song of Sol.**-(omon); **SOS** (see in dict. place); **sq.**-(uare); **St**, saint; **st**, street; **st.**(one); **st.**-(umped); **Staffs.**, Staffordshire; **stg** (sterling); **sup.**(*ra*); **Supt**, superintendent; **sus.**(*pendatur*) **per col.**(*lum*); **syn.**(onym).

's, used for (1, archaic) *God's* in *'sblood* & other oaths; (2, colloq.) *is* in *he's, she's, it's, Smith's*, &c.; (3, colloq.) *has* as in (2), esp. before p.p. as *he's done it*; (4, colloq.) *us* in *let us*, as *let's go*.
Sab(a)e·an, a. & n. (Native) of ancient Yemen; (erron.) = SABIAN. [f. L f. Gk *Sabaios* (*Saba* f. Arab. *Saba'* people of Yemen) + -AN]
Sā·baism (-ba-), n. Star-worship. [f. Heb. *çaba* host, -ISM]
Să·bāoth, n. pl. *Lord of S.* in N.T. & *Te Deum*, Lord of Hosts. [f. Heb. pl. (prec.)]
sabbatar·ian, n. & a. Sabbath-keeping Jew; Christian who accepts (& inculcates) the obligation to observe Sunday strictly as sabbath; Christian individual or member of sect observing Saturday as sabbath, seventh-day baptist &c.; hence **sabbatar·ian**ISM(3) n. (Adj.) of s. tenets. [f. L *sabbatarius* (foll., -ARY[1]) + -AN, see -ARIAN]
sa·bbath, n. (Also *s. day*) seventh day of week as day of religious rest appointed for Israel (*s.-day's journey*, distance Israelite might travel on s., about ⅔ m., also transf. easy journey); (also *s. day*) Christian Sunday esp. as day of obligatory abstinence from work & play (chiefly in Presbyterian, nonconformist, & distinctively protestant use, or facet.; *keep, break, the s.*; *s.-breaker*), whence **sa·bbath**LESS a.; period of rest; (usu. *witches' s.*) annual midnight orgy of the devil, demons, sorcerers, & witches. [f. L *sabbatum*, Gk *-ton*, f. Heb. *shabbāth* (*shābath* to rest)]
sabbă·tic(al), aa. Of, appropriate to, the sabbath (*-al river*, one in Jewish legend flowing except on sabbath; *s. year*, seventh year in which Israelites were to cease tilling & release debtors & Israelite slaves). Hence **sabba·tical**LY[2] adv. [f. Gk *sabbatikos* (prec., -IC), -AL]
sa·bbatize, v.i. & t. Keep the, have a, sabbath; make (day) into, keep as, a sabbath. [f. L *sabbatizare* f. Gk *sabbatizō* (SABBATH, -IZE)]
Sabe·llian[1], a. & n. (Rom. hist.). (Member) of the group of tribes in ancient Italy including Sabines, Samnites, Campanians, &c. [f. L *Sabelli* SABINES + -IAN]
Sabe·llian[2], a. & n. (Holder) of the doctrine of Sabellius (3rd c.) that the three Divine persons are merely aspects of one. [-AN]
Sā·bian, a. & n. (Member) of a sect classed in Koran with Moslems, Jews, & Christians, as believers in the true God; (erron.) (adherent) of SABAISM. [f. Arab. *çabi'* (perh. f. Aram. vb = baptize) + -AN]
Să·bine, a. & n. (One) of the *S*s, ancient Italians of central Apennines. [f. L *Sabinus*]
să·ble[1], n. Small brown-furred arctic & subarctic carnivorous quadruped allied to martens; its skin or fur. [OF, = s.-fur, prob. f. Slav. (Pol. & Czech *sobol*, Hung., *czoboly*, the s.)]
să·ble[2], n. & a. Black as a heraldic colour; (poet., rhet.) the colour black; (poet. & rhet.; pl.) mourning garments, whence **sa·bl**ED[2] a.; (also *s. antelope*) large stout-horned antelope of which male is black. (Adj., poet. & rhet.) black, dusky, gloomy, dread, (of Negro, sky, sea, night, Fate, &c.; *his s. Majesty*, the devil); hence **sa·bl**Y[2] adv. [F (herald.), perh. f. prec.]
să·bot (-ō), n. Shoe hollowed out from one piece of wood worn by French lower classes; wooden-soled shoe; (Mil.) wooden disk riveted to spherical, metal cup strapped to conical, projectile; (Mech.) shoe or armature of pile, boring-rod, &c. Hence **sa·bot**ED[2] (-ōd) a. [F, cf. *savate* shoe, etym. dub.]
să·botage (-ij), n. Doing of damage to plant &c. by workmen on bad terms with

their employers (*the derailing of the train is attributed to s.*; *acts of s.*). [F]

să·bre (-*er*), n., & v.t. Cavalry sword with curved blade (*the s.*, military force or rule); (in pl.) cavalry unit (cf. *rifle*), cavalry soldier & horse, (*has 3000 ss.*); copper tool for skimming molten glass; *s.-bill*, *-wing*, kinds of bird; *s.-cut*, blow with s., wound made or scar left by it; *s.-toothed lion* or *tiger*, extinct mammal with long s.-shaped upper canines; (vb) cut down or wound with s. [F, earlier *sable* f. G *sabel* prob. of Oriental orig.]

să·bretache (-*er*tăsh), n. Cavalry officer's satchel on long straps from left of waist-belt. [F, f. G *säbeltasche* (prec., *tasche* pocket)]

sabreur (sahbrer·), n. Cavalryman with sabre, esp. (often *beau s.*) cavalry officer of dashing appearance. [F]

să·bulous, a. Sandy, of sand, (pedant.); (Med., of secretions esp. in urinary organs) granular. [f. L *sabulosus* (*sabulum* sand, -OSE[1])]

sabu·rra, n. (med.). Foul granular matter deposited in stomach. L, = sand, cf. prec.]

sac, n. Bag-like membrane-enclosed cavity in animal or vegetable organism; membranous envelope of hernia, cyst, tumour, &c.; (of dress) = SACK[1]. [f. L *saccus* SACK[1]]

sa·ccāte, a. (Bot.) dilated into bag; contained in sac. [f. med. L *saccatus* (prec., -ATE[2])]

sa·cchar- (-k-), stem, f. Gk *sakkharon* SUGAR, of many words chiefly in scientific use; *sa·cchar*ATE[1](3), salt of *sacchă·r*IC *acid*, a dibasic acid formed by nitric acid on dextrose, also a monobasic acid formed by bases on glucoses; *sacchari·*-FEROUS, sugar-bearing; *sa·cchari*FY, convert (starch) into sugar; *sacchari·*METER, instrument for testing sugars by polarized light; *sa·cchar*IN(*e*) n., intensely sweet substance got from coal-tar & used to sweeten food for the gouty, diabetic, &c.; *sa·cchar*INE[1] a., sugary, of or containing or like sugar; *sacchar*O-, sugar-&-; *sa·cchar*OID a. (geol.), granular like sugar, (n.) sugarlike substance; *saccharo·*METER, hydrometer used, esp. in brewing, to estimate amount of sugar in solution by specific gravity; *sa·cchar*OSE[2], any of the group of sugars distinguished from the glucose group.

sa·cciform (-ks-), a. Sac-shaped. [SAC, -FORM]

sa·ccule, n. Small sac or cyst. Hence (see -UL-) **sa·ccul**AR[1], **sa·ccul**ATE[2], **-ated**, aa., **saccul**A·TION n. [f. L *sacculus* (SAC, -ULE)]

să·cerdōcy, n. (rare). Sacerdotalism; priestly function. [f. L *sacerdotium* (*sacerdos -otis* priest lit. sacrifice-giver f. *sacer* holy, *dare* give)]

sa·cerdōtage, n. (joc.). Sacerdotalism; priest-ridden state. [as prec. w. ref. to *dotage*, cf. *anecdotage*]

să·cerdō·tal, a. Of priest(s) or priesthood, priestly; (of doctrines &c.) ascribing sacrificial functions & supernatural powers to ordained priests, claiming excessive authority for the priesthood. Hence **sacerdo·tal**LY[2] adv., **sacerdo·tal**ISM(3), **sacerdo·tal**IST(2), nn., **sacerdo·tal**IZE(3) v.t. [F, f. L *sacerdotalis* (as SACERDOCY, -AL)]

să·chem (-tsh-), n. Supreme chief of some Amer.-Ind. tribes; big-wig, eminent person. [Amer.-Ind.]

să·chet (-shā), n. Small perfumed bag; (packet of) dry perfume for laying among clothes &c. [F, dim. of *sac* f. L SACcus]

sack[1], n., & v.t. Large usu. oblong bag for storing & conveying goods usu. open at one end & made of coarse flax or hemp (*give* one, *get*, *the s.*, dismiss him, be dismissed, from service, cf. '*On luy a donné son sac*, hee hath his pasport given him' in Cotgrave), whence **sa·ck**ING[1](3) n.; s. with contents (usu. *of*; also **sa·ck**FUL n.); amount (of corn, coal, flour, wool, potatoes, &c.) usu. put in s. as unit of measure or weight (*at 12/- the s.*); (of dress; also as pseudo-F *sacque, sac*) kind of lady's loose gown (archaic), also pleated silk appendage attached to shoulders of dress & falling to ground & forming train, also man's or woman's loose-hanging coat not shaped to back; *sackcloth*, coarse fabric of flax or hemp, sacking, (fig.) mourning or penitential garb (esp. *in s.-c. & ashes* bibl.); *s.-race*, between competitors tied in ss. up to the neck. (Vb) put into sack(s); (colloq.) give the s. to, dismiss from service; (colloq.) defeat in match or fight. [OE *sacc* f. L f. Gk *sakkos* f. Heb. *saq*]

sack[2], v.t., & n. (Of victorious army or its commander) plunder, give over to plunder, (captured city &c.); (of burglars &c.) carry off contents of; (n.) sacking of captured place. [vb prob. f. n. f. F *sac* in phr. *mettre à sac* put to sack, f. It. *sacco* etym. dub. (perh. f. *saccare* put in SACK[1])]

sack[3], n. (hist.). Kinds of white wine formerly imported from Spain & the Canaries (*sherry*, *Canary*, &c., *s.*; *s. posset*, *whey*, &c., beverages containing it; *half-pennyworth of bread to intolerable deal of s.*, absurd excess of the unessential, w. ref. to *1 Henry IV*, II. iv. 592). [earlier *wyne seck*, f. F *vin sec* dry wine]

sa·ckbut, n. Obsolete bass trumpet with slide for altering pitch. [f. F *saquebute* sackbut from 15th c., prob. = ONF *saqueboute* hook for pulling man off horse (*saquier* pull, *boute* of doubtful sense); in *Dan.* iii *s.* is mistransl. of Aram. *sabbeka* (a stringed instrument) due to accidental likeness of the wds]

sa·ckless, a. (archaic, Sc. & north.). Innocent (*of*), harmless, feeble-minded. [OE *sacléas* (*sacu* litigation, -LESS)]

sacque. See SACK[1].

sā·cral, a. (Anat.) of the sacrum; (Anthropol.) of or for sacred rites. [SACRUM, -AL]

să·crament, n., & v.t. Religious ceremony or act regarded as outward & visible sign of inward & spiritual grace (applied by the Eastern, pre-Reformation Western, & R.-C. Churches to the seven rites of baptism, confirmation, the eucharist, penance, extreme unction, orders, & matrimony; restricted by most Protestants to baptism & the eucharist; *the s., the s. of the altar, the Blessed* or *Holy S.*, the eucharist, also the consecrated elements esp. the bread or Host; *take, receive, the s. to* do or *upon*, as confirmation of some promise or oath); thing of mysterious & sacred significance, sacred influence, symbol, &c.; oath or solemn engagement taken (vb, bind by oath, esp. in p.p.). [f. F *sacrement* f. L *sacramentum* military oath, legal caution-money, f. *sacrare* (*sacer sacr-* SACRED), -MENT, used in Christian L as transl. of Gk *mustērion* MYSTERY[1]]

sacrame·ntal, a. & n. Of (the nature of) a or the sacrament, whence **sacramenta·l**ITY n.; (of doctrine &c.) attaching great importance to the sacraments, whence **sacrame·ntal**ISM(3), **sacrame·ntal**IST(2) nn.; hence **sacrame·ntal**LY[2] adv. (N.) observance analogous to but not reckoned among the sacraments, e.g. use of holy water or sign of the cross. [f. LL *sacramentalis* (prec., -AL)]

sacramentār·ian, a. & n. (Hist.; also *sacramentary*) denying, denier of, the Real Presence (as holding that ' body & blood of Christ ' was used only in a sacramental, i.e. symbolic, sense); (mod.) holding or involving, holder of, high sacramental doctrine, whence **sacramentar·ian**ISM(3) n. [f. med. L SACRAMENT(*arius* -ARY[1]), see -ARIAN]

sacrār·ium, n. (pl. *-ia*). (Rom. Ant.) shrine, adytum, room of Penates in house; (also *sanctuary*) part of church within altar-rails; (R.-C.) piscina. [L (*sacer sacr-* holy, -ARIUM)]

să·cré (-ā), v.i. (-créd, -créing). (Of Frenchman) say *sacré*, swear. [f. F *sacré* interj. = foll.]

sā·cred, a. (rarely *-est*). Consecrated or held dear *to* a deity, dedicated or reserved or appropriated *to* some person or purpose; made holy by religious association, hallowed, (*s. book, writings*, embodying laws &c. of a religion; *s. history*, related in Bible; *s. number*, associated with religious symbolism, e.g. 7; *s. poetry, music*, on religious themes; *s. concert*, of s. music; as specific epithet of beasts &c. now or once s. to some god, as *s. ibis, monkey, beetle*); safeguarded or required by religion or reverence or tradition, indefeasible, inviolable, sacrosanct, (*His most S. Majesty the King*; *the s. right of insurrection*; *regards it as a s. duty*; *their property, persons, will be held s.*; *no place was s. from him, from outrage*). Hence **sa·cred**LY[2] adv., **sa·cred**NESS n. [p.p. of obs. *sacre* consecrate f. F *sacrer* f. L *sacrare* (*sacer sacr-* holy)]

să·crifice, n., & v.t. & i. Slaughter of animal or person, surrender of a possession, as offering to a deity, (fig.) act of prayer or thanksgiving or penitence as propitiation; what is thus slaughtered or surrendered or done, victim, offering; (Theol.) the Crucifixion, the Eucharist as either a propitiatory offering of the body & blood of Christ or an act of thanksgiving; giving up of thing for the sake of another that is higher or more urgent, thing thus given up, loss thus entailed, (*will gain nothing by the s. of your principles*; *at some s. of regularity*; *surplus stock for sale at a large s.*; *his health was the s. demanded of him*; *the great* or *last s.*, esp., death for one's country in war; SELF-*s.*); so **sacrifi·**CIAL (-ĭshl) a., **sacrifi·cial**LY[2] adv. (Vb) offer (as) s. (*to*); give up, treat as secondary or of inferior importance, devote, *to* (*has sacrificed herself, her whole life, her pleasures, to his interest*; *s. accuracy to vividness*); resign oneself to parting with. [vb f. n., F, f. L *sacrificium* (*sacrificus* as prec., -FIC)]

să·crilege (-ĭj), n. Robbery or profanation of sacred building, outrage on consecrated person or thing, violation of what is sacred. Hence **sacrilē·gi**OUS (-jus) a., **sacrile·gious**LY[2] adv., **sacrilē·gi**ST(1) n. (rare). [OF, f. L *sacrilegium* f. *sacrilegus* (SACRED, *legere* collect)]

sā·cring, n. (archaic). Consecration of elements in the mass; ordination & consecration of bishop, sovereign, &c.; *s.-bell*, rung at elevation of Host. [obs. *sacre* (SACRED), -ING[1]]

sā·crist, n. Official keeping sacred vessels &c. of religious house or church. [OF, (*-e*), f. L *sacrista* (SACRED, -IST)]

să·cristan, n. Sexton of parish church (archaic); = prec. [f. med. L SACRIST*anus* (-AN)]

să·cristy, n. Repository for vestments, vessels, &c., of a church. [F (*-ie*), f. med. L *sacristia* (SACRIST, -IA[1])]

să·crosanct, a. (Of person, place, law, &c.) secured by religious sanction against outrage, inviolable. Hence **sacrosa·nc**TITY n. [f. L *sacrosanctus* (*sacro* abl. of *sacrum* SACRED rite, SAINT a.)]

sā·crum, n. Composite triangular bone of anchylosed vertebrae forming back of pelvis. Hence **sa·cr**AL a., **sacro-** comb. form. [f. L *os sacrum* sacred bone (from sacrificial use)]

sad, a. Sorrowful, mournful, showing or causing sorrow, (*a sadder & a wiser man,* of one who has had distressing experience; *in s. earnest*, seriously); (contempt., usu. joc.) shocking, deplorably bad, incorrigible, (*is a s. slut, coward*, &c.; *s. dog*, rake, scapegrace; *writes s. stuff*); (of pastry, bread, &c.) heavy, doughy; (of colour) dull, neutral-tinted; *s.-iron*, solid flat-iron. Hence **sa·dd**EN[6] v.t. & i., **sa·d**LY[2] adv., **sa·d**NESS n., **sa·dd**ISH[1](2) a. [earlier senses *sated, weary, solid, serious*; com.-Teut.; OE *sæd* cf. Du. *zat*, G *satt*, cogn. w. L *sat(is)*, Gk *hadēn*, enough]

sa·ddle, n., & v.t. Rider's seat placed on back of horse &c. (usu. concave-shaped of leather with side-flaps & girths & stirrups) or forming part of bicycle &c. or of some agricultural machines (PACK[1], SIDE, -*s.*; *in the s.*, mounted, fig. in office or control; *put s. on right, wrong, horse*, blame right, wrong, person); part of shaft-horse's harness that bears shafts; s.-shaped thing, e.g. ridge between two summits, support for cable or wire on top of suspension-bridge pier or telegraph-pole, joint *of* mutton or venison consisting of the two loins; *saddleback*, (Arch.) tower roof with two opposite gables, saddlebacked hill, kinds of bird (esp. the Grey Crow) & fish, (adj.) saddlebacked; *saddlebacked*, with upper outline concave, (Arch.) having saddleback; *s.-bag*, one of pair of bags laid across horse behind s., kind of carpeting (in imitation of Eastern s.-bb. of camels) used in upholstering chairs &c.; *s.-boiler*, of concave form used in heating-apparatus; *s.-bow*, arched front of s. [BOW[1]]; *s.-cloth*, laid on horse's back under s.; *saddlefast*, firmly seated in s.; *s.-horse*, for riding; *s.-pin*, by which bicycle &c. s. fits into socket; *s.-tree*, frame of s., also N.-Amer. tulip-tree (with s.-shaped leaves); hence **sa·ddle**LESS a. (Vb) put s. on (horse &c.); burden (person) *with* task, responsibility, &c.; put (burden) *(up)on* (person). [com.-Teut.; OE *sadol(ian)*, cf. Du. *zadel(en)*, G *sattel(n)*; perh. cogn. w. SIT]

sa·ddler, n. Maker of or dealer in saddles & other equipment for horses; (Mil.) man in charge of cavalry regiment's saddlery. Hence **sa·ddl**ERY(1, 2, 3) n. [-ER[1]]

Sa·ddūcee, n. Member of a Jewish sect or party (cf. PHARISEE, ESSENE) of time of Christ that denied resurrection of the dead, existence of spirits, & obligation of the traditional law. Hence or cogn. **Sadduce·**AN a., **Sa·dducee**ISM(2) n. [f. LL f. Gk *Saddoukaios* f. Heb. *Çadduqi* prob. = descendant of *Zadok*]

sa·dism (sah-), n. Form of sexual perversion marked by love of cruelty. [f. F *sadisme* (Count de *Sade* 1740–1814, -ISM)]

safe[1], n. (Also *meat-s.*) ventilated cupboard for provisions; fire-proof & burglar-proof receptacle for valuables. [orig. *save*, f. SAVE[1]]

safe[2], a. (Pred., after *come, arrive, bring, keep*, &c.) uninjured (*parcel came s.*; *saw them s. home*; often *s. & sound*); secure, out of or not exposed to danger (*from*), (*now we are, can feel, s.*; *is s. from his enemies*). Affording security or not involving danger (*put it in a s. place*; *is it s. to leave him?*; *s. custody, convoy*, &c.; *err, error, on the s. side*, with margin of security against risks; *dog is not s. to touch*; *it is s. to say*, may be said without risk of exaggeration or falsehood), debarred from escaping or doing harm (*have got him s.*); cautious & unenterprising, consistently moderate, that can be reckoned on, unfailing, certain *to* do or be, sure to become, (*a s. critic, statesman*; *s. methods*; *a s.* CATCH[2], *winner*; *is a s. first*, sure to take a first class; *is s. to win, be there*); hence **sa·fe**NESS n. *S. conduct*, (document conveying) privilege granted by sovereign, commander, &c., of being protected from arrest or harm on particular occasion or in district; *s.-guard*, = *s. conduct*, (also & usu.) proviso or stipulation or quality or circumstance that tends to prevent some evil or protect, (v.t.) guard, protect, (esp. rights &c.) by precaution or stipulation (*-ing duties*, on imports, against competition held to be unfair); *s. keeping*, custody. Hence **sa·fe**LY[2] adv. [ME & F *sauf* f. L *salvus* uninjured cogn. w. Gk *holos* WHOLE]

sa·fety (-ftĭ), n. Being safe, freedom from danger or risks, (*there is s. in numbers* prov.; *is in s.*; *cannot do it with s.*; *play for s.*, avoid risks in game or fig.; *s. first!*, motto inculcating caution); safeness, being sure or likely to bring no danger, (*is the s. of the experiment certain?*; *factor* or *coefficient of s.* in engineering, ratio of material's strength to strain to be allowed for); (also *s.-bolt*) contrivance for locking gun-trigger, gun with this; (also *s.-bicycle*) bicycle of usual low-saddled modern form (opp. *ordinary*); *s.-fuse*, that can be ignited at safe distance; *s.-lamp*, miner's so protected as not to ignite fire-damp; *s.-match*, only igniting on prepared surface; *s.-pin*, with point that returns to head & is caught in a guard so that wearer may not be pricked nor pin come out; *s. razor*, kinds with guard to prevent cutting chin &c.; *s.-valve* in steam-boiler, opening automatically to relieve excessive pressure, (fig.) means of giving harmless vent to excitement &c. (*sit on the s.-v.*, follow policy of repression). [f. F *sauveté* f. med. L *salvitatem* (prec., -I-, -TY)]

sa·ffian, n. Leather of goatskin or sheepskin tanned with sumach & dyed in bright colours. [f. Russ. *safiyanu*]

sa·fflower (-owr), n. A thistle-like plant yielding red dye used esp. in rouge; its dried petals; the dye made from them. [f. Du. *saffloer* f. OF *saffleur* f. early It. *saffiore* etym. dub.]

sa·ffron, n., a., & v.t. Orange-coloured stigmas of the Autumnal Crocus used for colouring & flavouring confectionery & liquors (*Bastard S.*, the plant safflower); (a. & n.) s.-colour(ed), whence **sa·ffron**Y[2] a.; *s. cake*, cake flavoured with s., also tablet of pressed s.; (vb) colour with or like s. [f. F *safran* ult. f. Arab. *za'faran*]

să·franin, n. Colouring-matter of saffron; yellowish-red coal-tar colour. [prec., -IN]

sag, v.i. & t., & n. Sink or subside under weight or pressure; hang sideways, be lopsided, (*gate, bridge, sags*); have downward bulge or curve in middle (*ceiling, beam, stretched rope, ladder, sags*), (trans.) cause to curve thus; (Commerc.) decline in price; (of ship) drift from course (esp. *s. to leeward*); hence **sa·gg**Y[2] a. (N.) amount that rope &c. sags, distance from middle of its curve to straight line between supports; sinking, subsidence; decline in price; (Naut.) tendency to leeward. [cf. Du. *zakken* subside, Da. *sakke* lag; perh. cogn. w. SINK]

sa·ga (sah-), n. A medieval Icelandic or Norwegian prose narrative, esp. one embodying history of Icelandic family or Norwegian king, (transf.) story of heroic achievement or adventure. [ON, = narrative, cogn. w. SAW[2]]

sagā·cious (-sh*us*), a. Mentally penetrating, gifted with discernment, practically wise, acute-minded, shrewd; (of sayings, plans, &c.) showing sagacity; (of animals) exceptionally intelligent, seeming to reason or deliberate. Hence or cogn. **saga·cious**LY[2] adv., **sag**Ă·CITY n. [f. L *sagax* (*sagire* discern acutely), -ACIOUS]

să·gamore, n. = SACHEM (1st sense). [f. Amer.-Ind. *sagamo*]

sage[1], n. Aromatic herb with dull greyish-green leaves; its leaves used in cookery (*s. & onions*, stuffing used for goose, duck, pork, &c.); *s.-brush*, growth of alkaline plants characterizing some sterile districts of U.S. (*s.-cock, -grouse, -hare*, &c., found in this); *s. cheese*, flavoured & mottled by addition of s.-infusion to the curd; *s.-green*, colour of s.-leaves; *s. tea*, medicinal infusion of s.-leaves. Hence **sa·gy**[2] a. [ME & F *sauge* f. L *salvia*]

sage[2], a. & n. Wise, discreet, judicious, having the wisdom of experience, of or indicating profound wisdom, (often iron.); wise-looking, solemn-faced; hence **sa·ge**LY[2] adv., **sa·ge**NESS n. (N.) profoundly wise man (often iron.), esp. any of the ancients traditionally reputed wisest of their time (*the seven ss.*, 7 Greeks each credited with a notable saying); hence **sa·ge**SHIP n. [F, f. com.-Rom. *sabio* f. pop. L **sapius* (L *sapere* be SAPIENT)]

sa·ggar, n. Case of baked fireproof clay enclosing pottery while it is baked. [perh. contr. of *safeguard*]

Sagi·tta, n. A northern constellation, the Arrow. [L, = arrow]

Săgittār·ius, n. Constellation & ninth sign of zodiac, the Archer. [L (prec., -ARY[1])]

să·gittate(d), aa. (bot., zool.). Shaped like arrow-head. [SAGITTA, -ATE[2]]

sā·go, n. (Kinds of palm & cycad with pith yielding) kind of starch used as food in puddings &c. [f. Malay *sagu*]

saha·, int. (nav.). Goodbye.

Sahar·a, n. Great Libyan desert; arid tract (lit. & fig.). Hence **Sahar·**AN, **Sahar·**IAN, **Sahar·**IC, aa. [f. Arab. *çahra*]

Sah·ib, n. (Anglo-Ind.). Englishman or European in India as spoken of or to by natives (MEM-SAHIB); (appended to name of S.) Mr, as *Jones S.* [Hind., f. Arab. *çahib* friend]

said. See SAY[2].

sai·ga (*or* sī-), n. Antelope of steppes. [Russ.]

sail[1], n. Piece of canvas or other textile material extended on rigging to catch wind & propel vessel, (collect.) some or all of ship's ss. (CARRY, CROWD[2], *hoist, lower*, MAKE[1], SET[1], SHORTEN, STRIKE, *s.*; *take in s.* fig., moderate one's ambitions; *take* WIND[1] *out of ss.*; *full s.* adv., with all s. spread lit. & fig.; *under s.*, with ss. set); (collect.) ships (in giving number of ships in squadron or company; *a fleet of twenty s.*), ship (esp. in *s. ho!*, cry announcing that ship is in sight); wind-catching apparatus, now usu. set of boards, attached to arm of windmill; s.-fish's dorsal fin, tentacle of nautilus; (also *wind-s.*) funnel-shaped bag on ship's deck or above mine giving ventilation; *s.-arm*, arm of windmill; *s.-axle*, on which s.-arms revolve; *s.-cloth*, canvas for ss., also dress-material; *s.-fish*, kinds with large dorsal fin, esp. Basking shark. Hence **(-)sail**ED[2], **sai·l**LESS, aa. [com.-Teut.; OE *seg(e)l*, cf. Du. *zeil*, G *segel*]

sail[2], v.i. & t., & n. (Of vessel or person on board) travel on water by use of ss. (*sailing-ship, -vessel*, opp. *steamer*; *s. close to* or *near the wind*, nearly against it, also fig. come near transgressing a law or moral principle); (of vessel or person on board) travel on water by use of ss. or engine-power, start on voyage, (*we s. next week*; *list of sail*ING[1]*s from London*; *sailing orders*, instructions to captain for departure, destination, &c.); (of bird, cloud, moon, &c.) glide in air; (esp. of women) walk in stately manner; travel over or along, navigate, glide through, (*the sea, Spanish main, sky*, &c.); control navigation of (ship; *plain sail*ING[1], used pred. to describe task &c. that is not perplexing; *sailing-master*, officer navigating yacht), set (toy-boat) afloat; *s. into* (slang), inveigh against, scold, rate, attack. (N.) voyage or excursion in sailing-vessel (*go for a s.*); voyage of specified duration (*is ten days' s. from Plymouth*). [OE *siglan, segl(i)an*, (prec.)]

sai·ler, n. Ship of specified sailing-power (*fast, good, bad, s.*). [-ER[1]]

sai·lor, n. Seaman, mariner, esp. one below rank of officer (*good, bad, s.*, person not, very, liable to sea-sickness; *s. hat*, of straw with straight narrow brim & flat top worn by women, also with turned-up brim in imitation of sailor's worn by children; *s.-man*, (vulg. & joc. for) s.; *sailors' home*, institution for lodging ss. cheaply ashore; *s.'s knot*, way of tying neck-tie. Hence **sai·lor**ING[1](1) n., **sai·lor**LESS, **sai·lor**LY[1], aa. [var. of prec., see -ER[1], -OR[2]]

sain, v.t. (archaic). Make sign of the cross on, bless, protect by divine power or enchantment. [OE *segnian*, cf. G *segnen* bless, f. L *signare* mark (SIGN[1]*um*)]

sai·nfoin, n. Low-growing herb used as fodder. [F (*sain* SANE, *foin* hay f. L *faenum*)]

saint, a. (snt; *abbr.* St, S., *in pl.* Sts, SS.), n., & v.t. Holy, canonized or officially recognized by the Church as having won by exceptional holiness a high place in heaven & veneration on earth, (usu. as prefix to name of person or archangel as *St Paul, St Michael*, whence ellipt. names of churches as *St Peter's*, & of towns called after their churches often with loss of possessive sign as *St Andrews* & *St Albans*, & many Christian & family names taken either from patron s. or from local names as above; also in some names of churches not called after ss., as *St Saviour's, Sepulchre's, Faith, Cross*; *St —'s day*, Church festival in memory of particular s.; *St Andrew*, patron s. of Scotland (*St A.'s day*, 30th Nov.); *St Anthony's, Elmo's*, FIRE[1]; *St Bartholomew*: *St B.'s*, (used for) St B.'s Hospital in London, abbr. *Bart's*; *massacre of St B.*, of Huguenots in France on St B.'s day, 24 Aug., 1572. *St Bernard* (*the Great, Little, St B.*, Alpine passes); *St Bernard dog* or *St Bernard*, breed kept by monks of Hospice on Great St Bernard pass for rescue of travellers. *St Cecilia*, patron s. of music; *St Charles*, King Charles I as canonized martyr; *St David*, patron s. of Wales (*St D.'s day*, 1st Mar.); *St Denis*, patron s. of France. *St George*, patron s. of England (*St G.'s day*, 23rd Ap.); *St G.'s*, (used for) St G.'s Hospital in London; *St G.'s, Hanover Square*, London church at which many West-end weddings take place; *St G.'s cross*, the *Greek* CROSS[1]. *St Germain* (or *Faubourg St G.*), aristocratic quarter of Paris; *St Gotthard* (*the St G.*, the Alpine pass of St G. or the tunnelled railway used instead of it). *St Helē·na*, (used for) place of exile (w. ref. to Napoleon, 1815–21). *St James's* (or *the Court of St James's* or *St James*), the British court (esp. in distinction from foreign courts; w. ref. to St James's Palace in London); (also) fashionable district in London about St James's Palace. *St-John's-wort*, kinds of yellow-flowered wild & garden plant. *St Leger*, horse-race at Doncaster for three-year-olds, f. founder's name; *St Lubbock's day*, any of the BANK[3]-holidays instituted 1871 by Sir J. Lubbock's Act; *St Luke's* SUMMER. *St Mark's*, (used for) St M.'s church in Venice; *St Martin's-le-Grand*, (used for) the General Post Office; *St Martin's* SUMMER; *St Michael & St George*, order of knighthood; *St Michael*, kind of orange, f. one of the Azores so called; *St* MONDAY. *St Patrick*, patron s. of Ireland (*St P.'s Day*, Mar. 17th; *order of St P.*, Irish order of knighthood); *St Paul's*, cathedral of see of London; *St Peter's*, (used for) the church of St Peter in the Vatican in Rome; *St Peter's chair*, (used for) the office of Pope. *St Sophia*, (used for) the mosque of St S. in Constantinople; *St Stephen's*, (used for) Parliament (w. ref. to former use of St S.'s chapel, Westminster, for meetings of H. of C.); *St Swithun*, the day (15th July) whose rain or absence of rain presages the same for 40 days. *St Thomas's*, (used for) St Thomas's Hospital in London. *St* VALENTINE'*s day*; *St Vitus's* DANCE[2]. (N.) one of the blessed dead or other member of the company of heaven (*departed s.*, phr. used by or attributed to mourners, = deceased person); canonized person (see adj. sense; *patron s.*, selected as heavenly protector of person or place, esp. church, often named after him); (bibl., archaic, & with some mod. sects) one of God's chosen people, member of the Christian Church or speaker's branch of it; person of great real or affected holiness (*would provoke, try the patience of, a s.*; *young ss. old devils* or *sinners*, early piety is no good sign; LATTER-*day ss.*); *s.'s-day*, Church festival in memory of a s., often observed as holiday at schools &c.; hence **sai·nt**DOM, **sai·nt**HOOD, **sai·nts**HIP, **sai·nt**LING[1], nn., **sai·nt**LIKE, **sai·nt**LY[1], aa., **sai·ntli**NESS n. (Vb) canonize, admit to the calendar of ss.; call or regard as a s.; (p.p.) worthy to be so regarded, of saintly life, (of place &c.) sacred. [vb f. n. f. adj., OF, f. L *sanctus* p.p. of *sancire* consecrate]

Saint-Simo·nian, a. & n. (Advocate) of the socialism of the Comte de Saint-Simon (1760–1825) with State control of property & distribution of produce. So **Saint-Sī·mon**IST(2), **Saint-Sī·mon**ITE[1](1), **Saint-Sī·mon**ISM(3), **Saint-Simo·nian**ISM(3), nn. [-IAN]

saith. See SAY[2].

Sāi·tic, a. Of Sais, ancient capital of Lower Egypt (*S. dynasties*, 26th–30th of Egyptian kings). [f. L f. Gk *Saïtikos* (*Saïtēs* f. *Sais*, -ITE[1])]

sake, n. *For the s. of —, for —'s* or *my* &c. *s.*, out of consideration for, in the interest of, because of, owing to, in order to please or honour or get or keep, (common n. with sibilant ending does not take the extra syllable of the possessive before *s.*, but has usu. the apostrophe, as *for peace', conscience', goodness', s.*, cf. *for God's, the children's, Phyllis's, s.*; *for my own s. as well as yours*; *for both, all, our ss.* or rarely *s.*; *for his name's s.*, because he bears the name he does or in the interest of his reputation; *persecuted for opinion's s.*; *for any s.* in entreaties, for one reason if not for another; *for old s.'s s.*, in memory of old days). [OE *sacu* contention, charge, fault, sake, cf. Du. *zaak* lawsuit, cause, thing, G *sache* affair, also OE *sacan* to quarrel; cogn. w. SEEK]

să·kė (-ā), n. Japanese fermented liquor made from rice. [f. Jap. *sake*]

sā·ker, n. Large lanner falcon used in hawking, esp. the female larger than the male or **sa·ker**ET[1] n.; (Hist.) old form of cannon. [f. F *sacre* (in both senses) f. Sp., Port., *sacro* prob. f. Arab. *çaqr*]

sa·kia (sah-), n. Eastern water-wheel for irrigation. [Arab. *sāqiya* (*saqā* irrigate)]

sal (sahl), **saul**, n. Valuable Indian timber (tree). [Hind.]

salaa·m (-lahm), n., & v.i. & t. Oriental salutation 'Peace'; Indian obeisance with this, low bow of head & body with right palm on forehead; (vb) make s. (to). [f. Arab. *salam*]

sā·lable, a. Fit for sale, finding purchasers; *s. price*, that article will fetch. Hence **sala**BI·LITY n. [-ABLE]

salā·cious (-shus), a. Lustful, lecherous. Hence or cogn. **sala·cious**LY[2] adv., **sala·cious**NESS, **sal**Ă·CITY, nn. [f. L *salax* (*salire* leap), -ACIOUS]

să·lad (-ad), n. Cold dish of uncooked usu. sliced vegetables such as lettuce or endive seasoned with oil, vinegar, &c., & eaten with or including cold fish, meat, hard-boiled eggs, &c.; vegetable or herb suitable for eating raw; *s.-days*, inexperienced youth; *s.-dressing*, mixture of oil, vinegar, cream, &c., taken with s.; *s.-oil*, superior quality of olive-oil. [f. OF *salade* ult. f. L *sal* salt, -ADE(1)]

să·lamănder, n. Lizard-like animal supposed to live in fire; person who can endure great heat, fire-eating soldier &c.; spirit living in fire (cf. *sylph, gnome, nymph*); (Zool.) kinds of tailed amphibian, whence **salama·ndr**OID a. & n.; red-hot iron for firing gunpowder, hot iron plate for browning omelettes &c. Hence **salama·ndr**IAN, **salama·ndr**INE[1], aa. [F (*-dre*), f. L f. Gk *salamandra*]

sala·mĕ (-lah-), n. Italian sausage highly salted and flavoured often with garlic. [It.]

săl-ammō·niac, n. Ammonium chloride. [L *sal* salt, AMMONIAC]

să·langane (-ngg-), n. Swallow making edible nest. [F, f. *salamga* name in Luzon]

să·lary, n., & v.t. Fixed periodical payment made to person doing other than manual or mechanical work (cf. *wages*); (vb; chiefly in p.p.) pay s. to. [AF (*-ie*), =OF *salaire* f. L *salarium* orig. soldier's salt-money (*sal* salt, -ARY[1])]

sale, n. Exchange of a commodity for money or other valuable consideration, selling (*on, for, s.*, offered for purchase; *s. &*, or *or, return*, arrangement by which retailer takes quantity of goods with right of returning all that he fails to sell), amount sold (*the ss. were enormous*); public auction (*put up for s.*, offer at auction); rapid disposal at reduced prices of shop's stock at end of season; BILL[4] *of s.*; *s.-ring*, ring of buyers at auction; *salesman, -woman*, person engaged in selling goods in shop or as middleman between producer & retailer, whence **sa·lesman**SHIP n., skill in this art. [OE *sala* prob. f. ON *sala* cogn. w. SELL]

Sā·lem, n. Nonconformist chapel. [*Heb.* vii. 2]

să·lep, n. Nutritive meal from dried tubers of some orchidaceous plants. [F f. Turk., f. Arab. *tha'leb*]

sălera·tus, n. (U.S.). Impure bicarbonate of potash or sodium bicarbonate as ingredient in baking-powders. [f. mod. L *sal aeratus* AERATED salt]

Sā·lian[1], a. Of the Salii or priests of Mars. [L *Salii* pl. (*salire* leap), -AN]

Sā·lian[2], a. & n. (Member) of Frankish tribe near Zuyder Zee from which the Merovingians were descended. [LL *Salii* the tribe, -AN]

Să·lic, Sali·que (-ēk), aa. (Form *-ic*) =prec. adj. (*S. law*, Frankish law-book extant in Merovingian & Carolingian times); (*-ic, -ique*) *S. law*, law excluding females from dynastic succession, esp. as alleged fundamental law of French monarchy (based on a quotation, not referring to such succession, from the law-book above). [F (*-que*) f. *Salii* (prec.), -IC]

să·licin, n. Bitter crystalline principle got from willow-bark & used medicinally. So **sa·lic**YL n., **salicȳ·l**IC a. (*-ic acid*, used as antiseptic & for rheumatism), **sali·cyl**ATE[1](3) n., **sali·cyl**IZE(5) & in same sense **sali·cyl**ATE[3] vv.t., **sali·cyl**ISM(5) n., **sali·cyl**OUS (chem.) a. [F (*-ine*), f. L *salix -icis* willow, -IN]

sali·cional (-shon-), **să·licet**, nn. Organ stop of soft reedy tone as of willow pipe. [G, f. L *salix* (prec.) w. suff.]

sā·lient, a. & n. Leaping or dancing (pedant., facet.), (of water &c., poet.) jetting forth, (*s. point* archaic, initial stage or origin or first beginning, from old med. use = heart as it first shows in an embryo); (of angle, esp. in Fortif., opp. RE-ENTRANT) pointing outwards; jutting out, prominent, conspicuous, most noticeable, (*s. points, features, character-*

istics); (n.) a s. angle or part in fortification (*the S.*, that at Ypres in the great war). Hence **sa·li**ENCE, **sa·li**ENCY, nn., **sa·lient**LY[2] adv. [f. L *salire* leap, -ENT]

sali·ferous, a. (geol.). (Of strata) containing much salt. [L *sal* salt, -I-, -FEROUS]

să·līne (*or* salī·n), a. & n. (Of natural waters, springs, &c.) impregnated with salt or salts, whence **sălino·**METER n.; (of taste) salt; of chemical salts, of the nature of a salt; (of medicines) containing salt(s) of alkaline metals or magnesium; hence **salī·**NITY n., **salī·no-** comb. form, (*sa*-). (N.) salt lake, spring, marsh, &c.; salt-pan, salt-works; s. substance; s. purge; solution of salt & water. [prec., -INE[1]]

Salique. See SALIC.

salī·va, n. Colourless liquid given by mixed secretions of salivary & mucous glands discharged into mouth & assisting mastication, spittle. So **să·liv**ARY[1] a. [L]

să·livate, v.t. & i. Produce unusual secretion of saliva in (person) usu. with mercury; secrete or discharge saliva esp. in excess. So **saliv**A·TION n. [f. L SALIVA*re*, -ATE[3]]

salle (F), n. Hall, room, (of foreign countries; *s.-à-manger*, dining-room, coffee-room; *s.-d'attente*, waiting-room at station).

să·llenders, n. pl. Dry eruption inside hock of horse's hind-leg (cf. MALANDERS). [cf. F *solandre*; etym. dub.]

să·llow[1] (-ō), n. Willow-tree, esp. of low-growing or shrubby kinds, whence **sa·llow**Y[2] a.; a shoot, the wood, of this. [OE *sealh*, cf. OHG *salaha*, ON *selja*, also L *salix*, Gk *helikē*]

să·llow[2] (-ō), a., n., & v.t. & i. (Of human skin or complexion or person in these respects, rarely of foliage) of sickly yellow or pale brown; hence **sa·llow**ISH[1](2) a., **sa·llow**NESS n. (N.) s. hue. (Vb) make or grow s. [OE *salo*, cf. MDu. *salu* discoloured, OHG *salo* dark]

sa·lly[1], n., & v.i. Rush of besieged upon besiegers, sortie; a going forth, excursion; sudden start into activity, outburst; escapade (rare); witticism, piece of banter, lively remark esp. by way of attack upon person or thing or of diversion in argument; *s.-port*, opening in fortification for making ss. from. (Vb) make military s. (often *out*); go *forth* or *out* on a journey, for a walk, &c.; issue, come out, suddenly (rare). [vb f. n., f. F *saillie* (*saillir* issue, in OF also dance, f. L *salire* leap)]

sa·lly[2], n. First movement of bell when set for ringing (also *hand-stroke*, opp. *back-stroke*), bell's position when set; part of bell-rope prepared with inwoven wool for holding; *s.-hole*, through which bell-rope passes. [perh. f. prec. in obs. sense *swinging motion*]

Sa·lly[3], fam. for *Sarah* (AUNT *S.*; *S. Lunn*, sweet light tea-cake served hot, perh. f. name of girl hawking them at Bath c. 1800).

sălmagu·ndĭ, n. Dish of chopped meat, anchovies, eggs, onions, &c., & seasoning; general mixture, miscellaneous collection, of articles, subjects, qualities, &c. [f. F *salmigondis* etym. dub.]

să·lmi (-ē), n. Ragout esp. of game-birds. [F, prob. short for prec.]

săl·mon, n. (collect. sing. usual for pl.), & a. Large silver-scaled pink-fleshed anadromous fish much prized for food & sport; *s.-colour(ed)*, (of) the orange-pink colour of s.-flesh; *s.-ladder, -leap, -pass, -stair*, series of steps or other arrangement for allowing s. to pass dam & ascend stream; *s. steak*, fried slice of s.; *s. trout*, N.-Europ. fish resembling s.; hence **sa·lmon**OID a. & n. (Adj.) s.-coloured, orange-pink. [AF *samoun* f. L *salmonem* nom. *-o* prob. cogn. w. *salire* leap]

Sălomŏ·nic, Salomō·nian, aa. Of, as of, Solomon. [L *Salomon* Solomon, -IC, -IAN]

salon (F), n. Reception-room in continental, esp. French, great house; (reunion of notabilities in) reception-room of (esp. Parisian) lady of fashion; *the S.*, annual exhibition of living artists' pictures in Paris.

saloo·n, n. Hall or large room, esp. in hotel or place of public resort, fit for assemblies, exhibitions, &c.; large cabin for first-class or for all passengers on ship; (also *s.-car, -carriage*) luxurious railway carriage without compartments furnished as drawing-room &c. (also *sleeping, dining, -s.*); public room(s) or gallery for specified purpose (*billiard, dancing, shaving, shooting*, &c., *-s.*); (U.S.) drinking-bar; *s. deck*, reserved for s. passengers; *s.-keeper* (U.S.), of bar; *s. pistol, rifle*, adapted for short-range practice in shooting-s. [f. prec., f. It. *salone* (*sala* hall f. Teut. cf. G *saal*, -OON)]

saloo·p, n. =SALEP; hot drink of salep or sassafras formerly sold as substitute for coffee at London street-stalls. [var. of SALEP]

Salō·pian, a. & n. (Native) of Shropshire; (member) of Shrewsbury school. [*Salop* Shropshire f. AF *Sloppesberie* corrupt. of OE *Scrobbesbyrig* Shrewsbury, -IAN]

salpiglo·ssis, n. Herbaceous showy-flowered garden-plant allied to petunia. [irreg. f. Gk *salpigx* trumpet, *glōssa* tongue]

să·lsifȳ, n. British & Continental plant with long cylindrical fleshy roots eaten as vegetable, Purple Goat's-beard. [f. F *salsifis* cf. It. *sassefrica* etym. dub.]

salt (sawlt, sŏlt), n., a., & v.t. (Often *common s.*) substance that gives sea-water its characteristic taste got in crystalline forms from strata consisting of it or by evaporation of brine pumped from these or of sea-water & used for seasoning or preserving food & other purposes, sodium chloride, (BAY-SALT, SEA-*s.*, ROCK[1]-*s.*; *white s.*, refined for household use from the brownish rock-s.; *table s.*, powdered or easy to powder for the s.-cellar; *in s.*, sprinkled with s. or immersed in brine as preservative; *eat s. with*, be guest of; *eat* one's *s.*, be his guest or dependant; *is not, any one, worth his s.*, efficient, worth keeping; *drop pinch of s. on tail of*, capture, w. ref. to directions given children for catching bird; *take with a grain of s.*, regard as exaggerated, be incredulous about, believe only part of; *am not made of s.*, can go out in rain without fear of dissolving; *the s. of the earth*, people or classes for whose existence the world is better, moral élite, see *Matt.* v. 13); sting, piquancy, pungency, wit, (*no s. in such tears*; *talk full of s.*; ATTIC[1] *s.*); (Old Chem.) solid soluble non-inflammable sapid substance (obs. exc. in some compd names, as *s. of* LEMON[1], GLAUBER'S SALT, SMELL*ing ss.*, EPSOM *s.*); (Chem.) compound of basic & acid radicals, acid with whole or part of its hydrogen replaced by a metal; =*s.-cellar* (chiefly now in trade use; & hist. in *above, below*, &c., *the s.*, seated at table among the family & their equals, among the servants & dependants); (also *s.-marsh*, **sa·lt**ING[1] n.) marsh overflowed by sea, often used as pasture or for collecting water for s.-making; (pl.) exceptional rush of sea-water up river; experienced sailor (esp. *old s.*); *sa·lt-cat* [*cat* unexpl.], mass of s. mixed with gravel, urine, &c., to attract pigeons & keep them at home; *sa·lt-cellar* [assim. of obs. *saler* (f. OF *salier* salt-box f. L as SALARY) to *cellar*], vessel holding s. for table use; *s.-glaze*, glaze on stone-ware made by throwing s. into furnace; *s.-lick*, place where animals collect to lick earth impregnated with s.; *s.-mine*, yielding rock-s.; *s.-pan*, depression near sea, vessel, used for getting s. by evaporation; *s.-pit*, pit yielding s.; *s.-pond*, natural or artificial for evaporating sea-water; *s.-spoon*, usu. with short handle & roundish deep bowl for helping s.; *s.-well*, bored well yielding brine; *s.-works*, s. manufactory; *sa·ltwort*, kinds of maritime & s.-marsh plants; hence **sa·lt**LESS, **sa·lty**[2], aa., **sa·lti**NESS n. (Adj.) impregnated with, containing, tasting of, cured or preserved or seasoned with, s. (cf. FRESH); (of plants) growing in sea or s.-marshes; (of tears, grief, &c.) bitter, afflicting; (of wit &c.) pungent; (of stories, jests, &c.) indecent, spicy; (of bill, charge, &c.; slang) exorbitant; *s. horse* naut. slang, s. beef; *s.* JUNK[1]; *s. water*, sea water, tears; *s.-water*, of, living in, the sea; hence **sa·lt**ISH[1](2) a., **sa·lt**LY[2] adv., **sa·lt**NESS n. (Vb) cure or preserve with s. or brine (*s. down money* or *stock* slang, put it by); sprinkle (esp. snow to melt it in street) with s.; make s., season, (lit. & fig.); (p.p.; of horses or persons) proof against diseases incident to climate or special conditions by habituation, hardened; treat (esp. paper in Photog.) with solution of s. or mixture of ss.; (Commerc., slang) *s. an account* &c., put down extreme price for articles, *s. the books*, represent receipts as larger than they have been; (Mining, slang) *s. a mine*, introduce extraneous ore &c. to make it seem rich. [com.-Teut.; OE *sealt(an)*, cf. Du. *zout(en)*, G *salz(en)*; cogn. w. Gk *hals*, L *sal*]

săltare·llo, n. Italian & Spanish dance with sudden skips for one couple. [It. & (*-elo*) Sp.]

sălta·tion, n. Leaping, dancing, a jump; sudden transition or movement. So **sa·ltat**ORY, **saltator·**IAL, aa. [f. L *saltatio* (*saltare* frequent. of *salire salt-* leap, -ATION)]

sa·lter, n. Manufacturer of, dealer in, salt; =DRY[1]-*s.*; workman at salt-works; person who salts fish &c. [OE *sealtere* (SALT n. & v., -ER[1])]

sa·ltern, n. A salt-works; set of pools for natural evaporation of sea-water. [OE *sealtærn* (SALT, *ærn* hut)]

să·ltigrade, a. & n. (Spider) with legs adapted for jumping. [L *saltus -ūs* leap (*salire salt-*), *-gradus* -walking]

să·ltimba·nco, n. Mountebank, quack. [It.]

să·ltire, n. (herald.). Ordinary formed by bend & bend sinister crossing like a St Andrew's cross (*in s.*, *per s.*, so arranged). Hence **sa·ltire**WISE adv. [f. OF *sautoir* stile, saltire, f. L *saltatorium* (SALTATION, -ORY)]

saltpē·tre (*-ter*), n. Potassium nitrate, nitre, white crystalline salty substance used as constituent of gunpowder, in preserving meat, & medicinally (*Chili* or *cubic s.*, sodium nitrate); *s.-paper*, TOUCH-paper; *s. rot*, white efflorescence on new or damp walls. [earlier & OF *salpetre* f. med. L *salpetra* prob. for *sal petrae* salt of stone (i.e. found as incrustation) w. assim. to *salt*; *petrae* f. LL f. Gk *petra* rock]

să·ltus, n. (pl. *-ūs*). Sudden transition, breach of continuity. [L, = leap]

salu·brious (-ōō-, -ū-), a. Healthy (chiefly of climate, air, &c.; rarely of food, exercise, &c.). Hence or cogn. **salu·brious**LY[2] adv., **salu·bri**TY n. [L *salubris* (as SALUTARY), -OUS]

Salu·ki (-ōōgĭ), n. Breed of dog, Arabian gazelle-hound.

să·lūtary, a. Salubrious (now rare); producing good effects, beneficial. [f. L *salutaris* (*salus -utis* health, -AR[1]), -ARY[2]]

sălūta·tion, n. (Use of) words spoken or written to convey interest in another's health &c., pleasure at sight of or communication with him, or courteous recognition of his arrival or departure, (rarely, now usu. *salute*) gesture of similar import, (*the Angelic S.*, the Ave Maria). Hence or cogn. **saluta·tion**AL, **salu·tat**ORY (-ōō-, -ū-), aa. [OF (*-cion*, f. L *salutationem* (foll., -ATION)]

salu·te (-ōōt, -ūt), v.t. & i., & n. Make salutation to, greet; (rare) hail as (king &c.); perform s. to or *to*, perform s.; (archaic) kiss (person, cheek, hand) esp. at meeting or parting; accost or receive *with* a smile, oath, volley, &c.; become perceptible to (eye, ear, person arriving). (N.) gesture expressing respect, homage, or courteous recognition, to person esp. when arriving or departing, (Mil., Naut.) prescribed movement or position of body or weapons, or use of flag(s) or discharge of gun(s) in sign of respect, (*a s. of 7 guns was fired*; *the s.*, attitude taken by individual soldier, sailor, policeman, &c., in saluting; *take the s.* esp. of highest officer present, acknowledge it as meant for him by gesture), (Fenc.) formal performance of certain guards &c. by fencers before engaging; kiss given, prop. as greeting (archaic or facet.; often *a chaste s.*). [vb f. L *salutare* (*salus -utis* health); n. f. F *salut* partly f. L *salutem* nom. *-us* & partly f. com.-Rom. & L *salutare*]

saluti·ferous, a. (now rare). Promoting health. [f. L *salutifer* (prec., -FEROUS)]

să·lvage (-ĭj), n., & v.t. (Payment made or due for) saving of a ship or its cargo from loss by wreck or capture (also attrib., as *s. money*); rescue of property from fire &c.; property salvaged; (vb) make s. of, save from wreck, fire, &c. [OF (L *salvare* SAVE[1], -AGE)]

sa·lvarsan, n. Drug used esp. in syphilis. [proprietary name]

sălva·tion, n. Saving of the soul; deliverance from sin & its consequences & admission to heaven brought about by Christ (*find s.*, be converted, also joc. discover formula that will enable one to abandon one's principles &c.); preservation from loss, calamity, &c., thing that preserves from these (esp. *be the s. of*); *S. Army*, organization on military model for revival of religion among the masses, whence (& w. ref. to religious revivals in general) **salva·tion**ISM(3), **salva·tion**IST (2), nn. [OF (*-cion*), f. L *salvationem* (SAVE[1], -ATION)]

salve[1] (sahv), n., & v.t. Healing ointment for sores or wounds (now chiefly poet. & in *lip-s.*); mixture of tar & grease for smearing sheep; something that soothes wounded feelings or uneasy conscience or (archaic) glozes over discrepancy or palliates fault (usu. *for*). (Vb) anoint (wound &c.; archaic exc. in fig. use = *soothe* as below); smear (sheep); smooth over or make good (defect, disgrace, &c.; archaic); soothe (pride, self-love, conscience, &c.); account for, dispose of, harmonize, vindicate, (difficulty, doubt, discrepancy, person's honour); save (ship, cargo) from loss at sea or (property) from fire, whence **să·lv**ABLE a. [n. in 1st sense OE *sealf*, cf. Du. *zalf*, G *salbe*, cogn. w. Skr. *sarpis* clarified butter & perh. Gk *olpē* oil-flask, in 2nd sense f. vb; vb partly f. n., partly f. L *salvare* SAVE esp. as connected w. SALVO[1], & in last sense back formation f. SALVAGE]

***sa·lvē*[2]**, n. (Also *S. regina*) R.-C. antiphon beginning with *s.* recited after Divine Office from Trinity Sunday to Advent, music for it. [L (vb imperat. = hail)]

sa·lver, n. Tray usu. of gold, silver, brass, or electro-plate, on which servants hand refreshments, letters, cards, &c. [f. F *salve* tray for presenting certain things to king f. Sp. *salva* assaying of food (*salvo* SAFE[2]) + -ER[1]]

sa·lvo[1], n. (pl. *-oes*). Saving clause, reservation, (often *of*; *with an express s. of their rights*); tacit reservation, quibbling evasion, bad excuse; expedient for saving reputation or soothing pride or conscience. [f. L abl. of *salvus* SAFE[2] as used in *salvo jure* &c. without prejudice to the right &c.]

sa·lvo[2], n. (pl. *-oes*). Simultaneous discharge of cannon or other fire-arms esp. as salute, or in seafight; round or volley of applause. [earlier & It. *salva* salutation, perh. com.-Rom. f. L SALVE[2]]

sal volă·tilē, n. (Aromatic solution, taken for faintness &c., of) ammonium carbonate. [mod. L, = volatile salt]

să·lvor, n. Person, ship, making or assisting in salvage. [SALVE[1] vb, -OR[2]]

Sam, n. (slang). *Stand S.*, bear the expense esp. of drink; *upon my S.*, asseveration. [?]

Samă·ritan, n. & a. Native, language, of Samaria (*good S.*, genuinely charitable person, w. ref. to *Luke* x. 33 &c.); adherent of the S. religious system; (adj.) of Samaria or the Ss. (*the S. pentateuch*, recension used by Ss. of which MSS. are in S. or archaic-Hebrew characters). Hence **Sama·ritan**ISM(2, 3, 4) n. [f. LL *Samaritanus* f. Gk *Samareitēs* (*Samareia* Samaria) + -AN]

sa·mbo, n. (pl. *-os, -oes*). Half-breed esp. of Negro & Indian or European blood; (*S-*; nickname for) Negro. [1st sense f. Sp. *zambo* perh. = *zambo* bandy-legged; 2nd sense etym. dub.]

Sam Browne, n. Army officer's belt & straps. [f. Gen. Sir *S.* J. *Browne*]

sa·mbur, n. Indian elk. [f. Hind. *sa(m)-bar*]

same, a. Monotonous, uniform, unvarying, (*the life is perhaps a little s.*), whence **sa·me**NESS n.; (with *this, these, that, those*; often w. depreciatory intention) aforesaid, previously alluded to or thought of, (*what is the use of this s. patience?*); (vulg. or commerc.) = *the s.* (pron. & adv., as specified below). *The s.*, a., pron., & adv.: (Adj.) identical, not different, indifferent, unchanged, (also *the very s.*, *just the s.*, & in sing. *one & the s.*; *t. s. causes produce t. s. effects*; *the difference between a body in motion & t. s. body at rest*; *t. s. observations are true of the others also*; *all planets travel in t. s. direction*; *belong to one & t. s. class*; *say t. s. thing twice over*; *several of the very s. birds*; *bigotry is t. s. in every age*; *she was always t. s. to me*; *it is all, just, t. s. to me*, makes no difference; *much t. s.*, not appreciably different; *at t. s. time*, often introducing fact &c. in apparent conflict with what precedes but also true or to be remembered; *by t. s.* TOKEN); identical *with* (*words of t. s. nature with those he had first heard*; *expectation of pleasure is t. s. thing with desire*); (emphatic substitute—before full or elliptical relative clause with *that*, *where* &c., or esp. *as* which often replaces *that* under its influence—for) the, that, those, (*at t. s. time that I am endeavouring*; *to t. s. place where I had found it*; *on t. s. grounds that he would defend suicide*; *I have t. s. bible my mother gave me*; *Rhenish wine at t. s. price as French is sold at*; *sailors received t. s. pay as soldiers*; *Olympia, t. s. city as Pisa*; *gave t. s. answer as before*); (pron.) t. s. person (now rare exc. in *To*, *From*, *t. s.* as heading of letter or poem addressed to or coming from s. person as the preceding one), t. s. thing (*we must all say, do, t. s.*; *would do t. s. again*), the aforesaid thing or person (archaic, legal, commerc., & vulg.; somet. in commerc. & vulg. use with omission of *the*; *grace & power faithfully to fulfil t. s.*; *he that shall endure unto the end, t. s. shall be saved*; *& never met, found, t. s. again*; *to repairing sleeve of s. 1/3*); (adv.) in t. s. manner (*think t. s. of*, *feel t. s. to*, remain in t. s. mind regarding; *we take what pleasure we can get t. s.*, or vulg. *s.*, *as you do*; *all t. s.*, nevertheless, notwithstanding, even under different circumstances; *just t. s.*, in spite of changed conditions). [ON, cf. OHG & Goth. *sama*; cogn. w. Skr. *sama*, Gk *homos*]

să·mel, a. (Of brick, tile) imperfectly baked, soft, from being outmost in the baking. [perh. f. OE *sam-* half, cogn. w. SEMI-, *ǣlan* burn]

Sā·mian, a. & n. (Native) of Samos (*S. ware*, fine pottery found on Roman sites). [L f. Gk *Samios* (*Samos*), -AN]

să·mite, n. (archaic). Rich medieval dress-fabric of silk sometimes interwoven with gold. [f. (OF *samit* or) med. L *samitum* f. late Gk *hexamitum* (*hex* six, *mitos* thread) perh. = fabric in which weft-threads are caught only at every sixth warp-thread, cf. DIMITY]

sa·mlet, n. Young salmon. [SALMON, -LET]

Sa·mnite, n. & a. Member of an ancient-Italian people at war with republican Rome; (adj.) of the Ss. [f. L *Samnitęs* pl.]

Samo·an, a. & n. (Native, language) of Samoa. [-AN]

sămovar·, n. Russian tea-urn with interior heat-tube. [f. Russ. *samovaru* = self-boiler]

Să·moyĕd (-*o*-), n. Member of a race of Siberian Mongols (also attrib.); their language; white Arctic breed of dog. [f. Russ. *Samoyedu*]

Samoyĕ·dic, a. & n. Of the Samoyeds; (n.) their language. [-IC]

sa·mpăn, n. Any small boat of Chinese pattern. [f. Chin. *san-pan* (*san* three, *pan* board)]

sa·mphire, n. Cliff plant with aromatic saline fleshy leaves used in pickles. [earlier *sampere* f. F (*herbe de*) *St Pierre* St Peter('s herb)]

sa·mple, n., & v.t. Small separated part of something illustrating the qualities of the mass &c. it is taken from, specimen, pattern, (esp. as offered by dealer in commodities sold by weight or measure; also of immaterial things, as *if that is a fair s. of his proceedings*); *s.-card*, card with sample(s) of goods attached. (Vb) take or give ss., try the qualities, get a representative experience, of; hence **sa·mpler**[1] [-ER[1]] n. [f. obs. *essample* var. of EXAMPLE]

sa·mpler[2], n. Piece of embroidery worked by girl as specimen of proficiency & often preserved & displayed on wall &c.; young tree left standing when others are cut down. [f. OF *essemplaire* f. L *exemplaris* (EXAMPLE, -AR[1], -ER[2])]

Sa·mson, -pson, n. Person of great strength or resembling S. (*Judg.* xiii–xvi) in some respect; (Naut.) *S.'s-post*, strong pillar passing through hold or between decks, post in whale-boat to which harpoon rope is attached. Hence **sa·msonite**[1] (2) n., an explosive. [L, f. Gk (-*psŏn*) f. Heb. *Shimshon*]

să·murai (-ŏŏrī), n. (Jap.; pl. same). Military retainer of daimios, member of military caste, (hist.); army officer. [Jap.]

să·native, -tory, aa. Healing, of or tending to physical or moral health, curative. [-*ive* f. med. Lt *sanativus*, -*ory* mod., f. L *sanare* cure, -IVE, -ORY]

sanator·ium, n. (pl. -*ia*). Establishment for treatment of invalids esp. convalescents & consumptives; place with good climate &c. frequented by invalids. [as prec., -ORY(2)]

sănbeni·to (-nē-), n. (pl. -*ōs*). Penitential scapular-shaped yellow garment with red St Andrew's cross before & behind worn by confessed & penitent heretic under Spanish Inquisition; similar black garment painted with flames & devils worn by impenitent heretic at auto-da-fé. [Sp. (*samb*-), f. *San Benito* St Benedict (shaped like scapular introduced by him)]

sa·nctifȳ, v.t. Consecrate, set apart or observe as holy; purify or free from sin (p.p. often iron. = *sanctimonious*; *such sanctified airs*); impart sanctity to, make legitimate or binding by religious sanction, give colour of innocence to, justify, sanction (*the end sanctifies the means*); make productive of or conducive to holiness. So **sancti**FICA·TION n. [f. OF *saintifier* f. eccl. L *sanctificare* (L *sanctus* holy, -FY)]

sanctimō·nious, a. Making a show of sanctity or piety. Hence **sanctimo·niousLY**[2] adv., **sanctimo·nious**NESS n. [foll., -OUS]

sa·nctimony (-mo-), n. Sanctimoniousness. [OF (*-ie*), f. L *sanctimonia* sanctity (*sanctus* SAINT, -MONY)]

sa·nction, n., & v.t. Law, decree, (hist.; PRAGMATIC *s.*); penalty (also *vindicatory* or *punitive s.*) or reward (also *remuneratory s.*) for (dis)obedience attached to a law, clause containing this, (Eth.) consideration operating to enforce obedience to any rule of conduct; confirmation or ratification of law &c. by supreme authority, express authoritative permission, countenance or encouragement given to action &c. by custom &c.; hence **sa·nction**LESS a. (Vb) ratify, invest with authority, make binding; authorize; countenance (action &c.); attach penalty or reward to (law). [vb f. n., f. L *sanctio* (*sancire sanct-* make sacred, -ION)]

sa·nctitude, n. (now rare). Saintliness. [f. L *sanctitudo* (SAINT, -TUDE)]

sa·nctity, n. Holiness of life, saintliness, (ODOUR *of s.*); sacredness, being hallowed, right to reverence, inviolability, (pl.) sacred obligations, feelings, &c. (*the ss. of the home*). [f. OF *saincteté* f. L *sanctitatem* (SAINT, -TY)]

sa·nctuary, n. Place recognized as holy, church, temple, tabernacle, HOLY place, HOLY of holies, SACRARIUM, penetralia, inmost recess, (lit. & fig.); sacred place by retiring to which fugitive from law or debtor was secured by medieval Church law against arrest or violence, place in which similar immunity was established by custom or law, asylum or place of refuge (*London, the s. of political refugees*); (right of affording) such immunity (*violate* or *break s.*, arrest or use violence to person in a s.; *take, seek*, &c., *s.*, resort to a s.; *rights* &c. *of s.*); (Hunt. &c.) close time or place for beast, bird, or fish. [f. OF *sainctuarie* f. L *sanctuarium* (irreg. as SAINT, -ARY[1])]

sa·nctum (sanctor·um), n. Holy place (*s.*), HOLY of holies (*s.s.*), in Jewish temple (usu. transf. of inner retreat, esoteric doctrine, &c.); person's private room, study, den. [L, transl. of Heb.]

sa·nctus, n. The hymn 'Holy, holy, holy' closing the Eucharistic preface, music for this; *s. bell*, bell in turret at junction of nave & chancel, or hand-bell, rung at the s. [L, = holy]

sand, n., & v.t. Minute fragments resulting from wearing down of esp. silicious rocks & found covering parts of the seashore, riverbeds, deserts, &c., (also pl.) shoal or submarine bank of s., (usu. in pl.) grain of s., (pl.) expanse or tracts of s., (*numberless as the s.* or *ss.*; ROPE *of s.*; *built* &c. *on s.*, unstable; PLOUGH *the s.* or *ss.*; *the ss. are running out* &c., time of grace &c. is nearly at end, w. ref. to hourglass &c.; *children playing on the ss.*; *scour saucepan, adulterate sugar, dry ink* or *writing, with s.*); *s.-bag* n., filled with s. for use (a) in fortification for making temporary defences, (b) as ballast esp. for boat or balloon, (c) as ruffian's weapon inflicting heavy blow without leaving mark, (d) as support for engraving-plate, (e) to stop draught from window or door; *sa·ndbag* v.t., barricade or defend, provide (window, chink), with s.-bag(s), fell with blow from s.-bag; *s.-bank*, shoal in sea or river; *s.-bar*, s.-bank at mouth of harbour or river; *s.-bath*, vessel of heated s. as equable heater in chem. processes; *s.-bed*, stratum of s.; *s.-blast*, jet of s. impelled by compressed air or steam for giving rough surface to glass &c.; *s.-box*, castor for sprinkling s. over wet ink (hist.), mould of s. used in founding, box of s. on locomotive for sprinkling slippery rails, (Golf) receptacle for s. used in teeing; *s.-boy*, (prob.) boy hawking s. for sale (now only in *jolly as a s.-b.*); *s.-cloud*, driving s. in simoom; *s.-crack*, disease of horses' hoofs, crack in human foot from walking on hot s., crack in brick due to imperfect mixing; *s.-eel*, an eel-like fish; *s.-fly*, kind of midge, kind of fishing-fly; *s.-glass*, wasp-waisted reversible glass with two bulbs containing enough s. to take a definite time (*hour, minute*, &c., *-glass*) in passing from upper to lower bulb; *s.-hill*, dune; *s.-iron*, golf-club for lifting ball from s.; *s.-man*, (also *dustman*) power causing children's eyes to smart towards bed-time; *s.-martin*, kind nesting in side of s.-pit or sandy bank *s.-paper*, with s. stuck to it for polishing, (v.t.) polish with s.-p.; *s.-piper*, kinds of bird haunting open wet sandy places; *s.-pump*, for clearing drill-hole, caisson, &c., of wet s.; *s.-shoes*, usu. of canvas with rubber or hemp soles for use on ss.; *s.-spout*, pillar of s. raised by desert whirlwind; *sandstone*, rock of compressed s. (*old, new, red, s.-s.*, series of British rocks below, above, carboniferous); *s.-storm*, desert storm of wind with clouds of s. (Vb) sprinkle with s.; overlay with, bury under, s.; adulterate (sugar, wool, &c.) with s.; polish with s. [com.-Teut.; OE; cf. G *sand*, Du. *zand*]

să·ndal[1] (-dl), n., & v.t. (-ll-). Sole without uppers attached to foot by thongs passing over instep & round ankle (worn chiefly by ancient Greeks & Romans, by some Orientals, & as modern revival esp. by children); strap for fastening low shoe passing over instep or round ankle. (Vb) put ss. on (feet, person; esp. in p.p.); fasten or provide (shoe) with s. [f. L f. Gk *sandalion* cf. *sanbalon* etym. dub.]

să·ndal²(wood), n. Kinds of scented wood (*white, yellow, red, s.-w.*); *sandal-tree,* the Malabar white s.-w. tree. [f. med. L *sandalum,* cf. Arab. *çandal*]

să·ndarac, n. = REALGAR; (also *gum s.*) kind of resin used in preparing spirit varnish & pounce. [f. L f. Gk *sandarakē*]

sa·nd-blind, a. (archaic). Dim-sighted, purblind. [prob. for *samblind* cf. SAMEL]

sa·nderling, n. A small wading bird. [?]

sa·nders, saun-, n. = SANDALWOOD; RED *s.* [f. OF *sandre* var. of *sandle* SANDAL²]

Sa·ndhurst, n. (Used for) Royal Military College, S., for army cadets.

să·ndiver, n. Glass-gall, liquid saline matter given off in glass-making. [prob. f. F *suin de verre* exhalation (*suer* sweat) of glass]

sa·ndwich (-tsh), n., & v.t. Two slices of bread with meat or other relish between (*ham, egg, caviare, cucumber,* &c., *s.*; also fig., as *a s. of good & bad*); (usu. *s.-man, -boy,* &c.) man &c. walking street with two advertisement-boards hung one before & one behind; *s.-board,* one of such boards; *s.-boat* in bumping race, boat rowing last in higher & first in lower division on same day; (vb) insert (thing, statement, &c.) between two of another character. [perh. f. Earl of *S.* (said to have eaten slices of bread & toast while gaming for 24 hrs)]

sa·ndy¹, a. In n. senses; also, (of hair) yellowish-red, (of person) with such hair. Hence **sa·ndi**NESS n., **sa·ndy**ISH¹(2) a. [-Y²]

Sa·ndy², n. (Nickname for) Scotchman. [usual Sc. shortening of *Alexander*]

sane, a. Of sound mind, not mad; (of views &c.) moderate, sensible. Hence **sa·ne**LY² adv. [f. L *sanus* healthy]

sang. See SING.

sa·nga(r) (-ngg-), n. Stone breastwork used by Indian hill-tribes. [f. Hind. *sunga*]

sangaree· (-ngg-), n. Cold drink of wine diluted & spiced. [f. Sp. *sangria* (lit. bleeding) drink of lemon-water & red wine]

sang-de-bœuf (F), n. & a. (Of) a deep red colour found on old Chinese porcelain. [F, = ox's blood]

sang-froid (F), n. Composure, coolness, in danger or under agitating circumstances. [F, = cold blood]

sangrail, -real. See GRAIL².

sanguifica·tion (-gwĭ-), n. Formation of, conversion of food into, blood. [L *sanguis* blood, -FICATION]

sa·nguinary (-gwĭ-), a. Attended by, delighting in, bloodshed or slaughter, bloody, bloodthirsty, (of laws) inflicting death lightly; (euphem., substituted in reporting foul language, or used orig. as milder form, for) bloody. Hence **sa·nguinari**LY² adv., **sa·nguinari**NESS n. [f. L *sanguinarius* (*sanguis -inis* blood, -ARY¹)]

sa·nguine (-nggw-), a., n., & v.t. Blood-red (literary, & in Nat. Hist. = L *sanguineus,* as *S. ant, sponge, turtle*); of blood (rare; *s. rain*), sanguinary (rare; *s. slaughter*); (hist.) of the temperament in which the blood predominates over the other HUMOUR¹s, with ruddy complexion & courageous hopeful amorous disposition; (of complexion) bright, ruddy, florid; habitually hopeful, confident, expecting things to go well, whence (& rarely in other senses) **sa·nguine**LY² adv., **sa·nguine**NESS n. (N.) crayon coloured red with iron oxide; a drawing in red chalk. (Vb, poet.) stain with blood, stain red. [f. F *sanguin* f. L *sanguineus* (prec.)]

sangui·neous, a. Of blood (med.); blood-coloured (esp. bot.); full-blooded, plethoric. [f. L as prec., -OUS]

să·nhedrim (-nĭ-), n. Highest court of justice & supreme council in ancient Jerusalem, of 71 members. [f. late Heb. *sanhedrin* f. Gk *sunedrion* (SYN-, *hedra* seat)]

să·nicle, n. An umbelliferous plant. [OF, f. med. L *sanicula* prob. f. L *sanus* SANE]

să·nifȳ, v.t. Make healthy, improve sanitary state of, (place). [f. L *sanus* healthy, -I-, -FY]

să·nitary, a. Of the conditions that affect health esp. with regard to dirt & infection; free from or designed to obviate influences deleterious to health; *s. towel* (of kind used in menstruation). Hence **sanitar**AR·IAN (-ār-), n. & a., **sa·nitari**LY² adv., **sa·nitari**NESS, **sa·nitar**IST(2), nn. [f. F *sanitaire* (L as SANITY, -ARY¹)]

să·nitās, n. (Trade name of) an antiseptic & disinfectant preparation. [L, see SANITY]

sanita·tion, n. Improving of sanitary conditions. Hence **sanita·tion**IST(2) n., (by back formation) **sa·nitate** v.t. & i. [irreg. f. SANITARY, -ATION]

să·nity, n. Being sane, mental health; tendency to avoid extreme views. [f. F *sanité* f. L *sanitatem* (SANE, -TY)]

sa·njak, n. One of the administrative districts of a Turkish vilayet. [Turk.]

sank. See SINK¹.

sans, prep. Without (as E wd, pr. sănz, now chiefly w. ref. to Shaks. *A. Y. L.* II. vii. 166, *s. teeth, s. eyes, s. taste, s. everything.* As F wd, pr. as F, in phrr. & compounds: *s. cérémonie* adv., with rude or hurried or kindly neglect of usual formalities; *sansculo·tte,* pr. as F or E, lit. =

breechless, republican of Parisian lower classes in French Revolution, any ex-extreme republican or revolutionary, whence *sansculo·tterie* [-ERY(4, 5)] n., *sansculo·tt*IC a., *sansculo·tt*ISM n.; *s. doute* adv., doubtless; *s. façon* adv., outspokenly, unceremoniously; *s.-gêne* n., absence of constraint, familiarity, making oneself at home; *s. peur et s. reproche* a., of chivalrous character, cf. BAYARD; *s. phrase* adv., in a word, without qualification; *s.-souci* n., gay carelessness, unconcern.) [OF, ult. f. L *sine*]

sansĕ·rif, n. & a. (Form of type) without serifs. [prob. f. prec. +SERIF, but found earlier than *serif*]

Sa·nskrit, -scrit, n. & a. (Of, in) the ancient & sacred language of India, oldest known member of INDO-European family. Hence **Sanskri·t**IC a., **Sa·nskrit**IST(3) n. [f. Skr. *saṃskṛta* composed (*saṃ* together, cogn. w. SAME, *kṛ* make)]

Sa·nta Clau·s (-z), n. Personage who fills children's stockings with Christmas presents by night. [U.S., f. Du. *Sint Klaas* St Nicholas]

sa·nton, n. Mohammedan monk or hermit. [Sp. (*santo* SAINT)]

santŏ·nica, n. Kind of wormwood. [L (*Santones* Aquitanian tribe, -IC)]

sa·ntonin, n. Extract of santonica used as anthelmintic. [-IN]

Saorstat Eireann (sayor·stath ār·an), n. The Irish Free State. [Ir.]

sap[1], n., & v.t. Vital juice circulating in plants (also fig., as *the s. of youth, there is no s. in a written constitution*); (also *s.-wood*) soft outer layers of wood, alburnum; *s.-green* n. & a., pigment made from buckthorn berries, (of) colour of this; *s.-lath*, made of s.-wood; hence **sa·p**FUL, **sa·p**LESS, **sa·pp**Y[2], aa., **sa·ppi**NESS n. (Vb) drain or dry (wood) of s., (fig.) exhaust vigour of (*his energy, constitution, belief, had been sapped by*; cf. foll.); remove s.-wood from (log). [OE *sæp*, cf. Du. *sap*, G *saft*; perh. cogn. w. L *sapere* taste]

sap[2], n., & v.i. & t. Making of trenches to cover assailants' approach to besieged place, (fig.) insidious or slow undermining of belief, resolution, &c.; covered siege-trench; *s.-head*, front end of s.; *s.-roller*, large gabion covering s.-head. (Vb) dig s., approach (i. & t.) by s.; undermine, make insecure by removing foundations, (fig.) destroy insidiously (cf. prec.), (*walls, cliffs, sapped by the stream, tide*; *health sapped by the damp climate*; *science was sapping old beliefs*). [(vb f. F *saper*) f. F *sappe* or It. *zappa* spade, sap, etym. dub.]

sap[3], v.i., & n., (school slang). Be studious, work hard at books or lessons. (N.) studious or hard-working person; tiresome task, trouble, grind, (*it is such a, too much, s.*). [prob. fig. use of prec.]

să·pajou (-jōō), n. Small S.-Amer. monkey often kept as pet. [F, earlier *-iou*, said to be Cayenne wd]

să·pan-wood, -pp-, n. Wood yielding red or yellow dye from tropical Asia. [Malay *sapan*, cf. Tamil *shappangam*]

să·pid, a. Having (esp. agreeable) flavour, savoury, palatable, not insipid, (of talk, writing, &c.) not vapid or uninteresting. So **sapi·d**ITY n. [f. L *sapidus* (*sapere* taste, -ID[1])]

să·pient, a. Wise (now rare); would-be wise, of fancied sagacity, aping wisdom. Hence or cogn. **sa·pi**ENCE n., **sa·pient**LY[2] adv. [f. L *sapient-* part. st. of *sapere* be wise]

sapie·ntial, a. Of wisdom (esp. *the s. books*, Prov., Eccl., Ecclus., Cant., Wisd., &c.). [f. eccl. L *sapientialis* (L *sapientia* wisdom as prec., -AL)]

sa·pling, n. Young tree, (fig.) a youth, greyhound in first year (*s. stakes* in coursing). [SAP[1], -LING[1]]

săpodi·lla, n. Large evergreen trop.-Amer. tree with durable wood & edible fruit (*s. plum* or NASEBERRY). [f. Sp. *zapotilla* dim. of *zapote* f. Mex. *zapotl*]

săpona·ceous, a. Of, like, containing, soap, soapy (lit. &, in joc. use, fig.). [f. L *sapo -onis* soap, -ACEOUS]

sapŏ·nifȳ, v.t. & i. Turn (t. & i. of fat or oil) into soap by combination with alkali. Hence or cogn. **sapo·nifi**ABLE a., **saponifica·tion** n. [f. F *saponifier* (prec., -FY)]

să·por (-or), n. Quality perceptible by taste, e. g. sweetness; distinctive taste of substance; sensation of taste. [L (*sapere* taste, -OR[1])]

sa·pper, n. In vbl senses of SAP[1, 2, 3]; also, private of Royal Engineers (*Royal Ss. & Miners*, former title of R.E.). [-ER[1]]

sapperme·nt, a German oath. [corrupt. of G *sakrament* sacrament]

Sa·pphic (săf-), a. & n. Of Sappho (Lesbian lyric poetess 600 B.C.; *S. vice*, also **Sa·pph**ISM n., unnatural sexual relations between women; *S. verse, stanza*, in Gk metres invented by Sappho & imitated in L by Horace, esp. the four-line stanza with short fourth line roughly copied in E light verse as *Needy knife-grinder, whither do you wander?*); (n. pl.) verse in S. stanzas. [f. F *saphique* f. L f. Gk *Sapphikos* (*Sapphō*, -IC)]

sa·pphire (săf-), n. & a. A transparent blue precious stone, (Mineral.) any precious native crystalline alumina including s. & ruby; bright blue of s., azure; kinds of humming-bird; so **sa·pphir**INE[2] a. (Adj.) of s. blue. [f. OF *safir* f. L f. Gk *sappheiros* lapis lazuli]

săpr(o)-, comb. form of Gk *sapros* rotten in scient. terms: *saprae·mia*, septic poisoning, so *sapraemic* a., [Gk *haima* blood]; *-ge·nic*, causing or produced by putrefaction; *-phile* a. & n., (bacterium) inhabiting putrid matter; *-phyte*, vegetable organism living on decayed organic matter.

sar, n. A fish, the sea bream. [F, f. L *sargus*]

să·raband, n. Slow Spanish dance in triple time, piece of music for or in rhythm (with second note of measure lengthened) of this. [F (*-de*), f. Sp. *zarabanda* prob. of oriental orig.]

Să·racen, n. & a. (General name among later Greeks & Romans for) nomad of Syro-Arabian desert; Arab or Moslem of time of crusades; *S. corn*, buckwheat; *S.'s head*, as heraldic charge or inn-sign; hence (esp. of Moslem archit.) **Saracĕ·nic** a. (Adj.) = Saracenic. [f. LL f. late Greek *Sarakēnos* etym. dub.]

Săratō·ga (trunk), n. Lady's large travelling-trunk. [prob. f. *Saratoga* Springs, New York watering-place]

sar·casm, n. Bitter or wounding remark, taunt, esp. one ironically worded; language consisting of, faculty of uttering, use of, such remarks; so **sarcă·stic** a., **sarca·stically** adv. [f. LL f. late Gk *sarkasmos* (*sarkazō* gnash the teeth, tear flesh, see SARCO-, *-asm* corresp. to -ISM)]

sar·căst, n. (rare). Sarcastic person. [as prec., *-ast* cf. -IST]

sarce·lle, n. Kinds of small duck or teal. [f. OF *cercelle* f. L *querquedula*]

sarcenet. See SARSENET.

sarco-, comb. form of Gk *sarx sarkos* flesh: *-logy*, anatomy of fleshy parts of body; *-plasm*, interfibrillar substance of muscle.

sar·code, n. Animal protoplasm. [prec., -ODE]

sarco·ma, n. (pl. *-ata*). Tumour of embryonic connective tissue. [f. Gk *sarkōma* (*sarkoō* see SARCO- become fleshy, -M)]

sarcŏ·phagus, n. (pl. *-gi* pr. -gī, -jī). Stone coffin usu. adorned with sculpture or inscription. [L, f. Gk *sarkophagos* orig. = flesh-consuming (stone) as SARCO- + *-phagos* -eating]

sar·cous, a. Consisting of flesh or muscle. [SARCO-, -OUS]

sard, n. Yellow or orange cornelian. [F (*-e*), f. L *sarda*, L f. Gk *sardios* (*Sardis* in Lydia)]

Sardanapā·lian, a. As of, like, Sardanapalus king of Nineveh notorious for effeminate luxury. [-IAN]

sarde·lle, n. Fish like & treated like sardine. [f. It. *sardella* dim. of L *sarda* SARDINE[2]]

sar·dine[1], n. Precious stone in *Rev.* iv. 3. [prob. erron.; RV gives *sardius* (SARD)]

sardi·ne[2] (-ēn), n. Small fish of herring kind found off Sardinia & Brittany, or young pilchard of Cornish coast, cured & tinned in oil (*packed like ss.*, of crowded company). [F, f. It. f. L *sardina* (*sarda* f. Gk *sardē* cf. *Sardō* Sardinia)]

Sardi·nian, a. & n. (Inhabitant) of the island or of the kingdom (1720–1859, including also Piedmont &c.) of Sardinia. [-AN]

sardŏ·nic, a. Bitter, scornful, mocking, sneering, cynical, (of laugh, laughter, affected merriment, &c.). Hence **sardo·nically** adv. [f. F *sardonique* f. L f. Gk *sardonios* assim. of Homeric *sardanios* etym. dub. to *Sardonios* Sardinian, owing to belief that convulsive laughter ending in death resulted from eating a Sardinian plant, + -IC]

sar·donyx, n. Onyx with white layers alternating with sard. [L, f. Gk *sardonux* (SARDios, ONYX)]

sarga·sso, n. (pl. *-os*, *-oes*). (Also *gulf-weed*) kinds of seaweed with berry-like air-vessels found floating in island-like masses in the Gulf-stream & esp. in N.-Atlantic region called *S. sea*. [f. Port. *sargaço*]

sari·ssa, n. (Gk ant.; pl. *-ae*). Long lance of ancient Macedonians. [Gk]

sark, n. (Sc.). Shirt or chemise. Hence **sar·king**[1] n., boarding between rafters & roof. [OE *serc*, cf. ON *serkr*]

Sarma·tian (-āshn), a. & n. (Inhabitant) of ancient Sarmatia (Russia & Poland); (poet.) Pole, Polish. [-AN]

sar·mentose, -e·ntous, aa. (bot.). With long thin trailing shoots. [f. L *sarmentosus* (*sarmenta* pl. twigs, brushwood, f. *sarpere* prune, -MENT, -OSE[1], -OUS)]

sarsapari·lla, n. Kinds of tropical-American smilax esp. the Jamaica s. (so called as chief source of the medicinal s. for which Jamaica was emporium); dried roots, or extract of these used as tonic &c., of (esp. Jamaica) s. [f. Sp. *zarzaparrilla* (*zarza* bramble, perh. + dim. of *parra* vine)]

sar·sen, n. Sandstone boulder on chalk downs esp. in Wilts. [prob. f. SARACEN]

sar·senet, -ce-, (-sn-), n. Fine soft silk material now used chiefly for linings. [AF *sarzinett* (prob. f. *sarzin* SARACEN + -ET[1] after OF *drap sarrasinois* Saracen cloth)]

sartor·ial, a. Of tailor, tailoring, or men's clothes. [f. L *sartorius* (*sartor* tailor f. *sarcire* patch), -AL]

Sār·um, eccl. name of Salisbury (*S. use*, order of divine service used in diocese of Salisbury from 11th c. to Reformation). [med. L, prob. f. misread abbr. of L *Sarisburia* Salisbury, cf. *viz* for *videlicet*]

sash[1], n. Ornamental scarf worn by man usu. as part of uniform or insignia over one shoulder or round waist or by woman or child round waist. Hence **sashed**[1] [-ED[2]] a. [earlier sense *turban-band*, f. Arab. *shash* muslin]

sash[2], n. Frame usu. of wood holding pane(s) of glass & usu. made to slide up & down in grooves of window aperture, glazed sliding light of glass-house or garden-frame, (opp. CASEMENT); (rare) = casement; *s.-cord*, *-line*, strong kind attaching s.-weights to s.; *s.-pocket*, space on each side of window-frame in which s.-weights run; *s.-pulley*, for s.-cord to work over; *s.-tool*, kinds of glazier's & painter's brush; *s.-weight*, attached to each end of s. to balance it at any height; *s.-window*, with s. or usu. two ss. of which one or each can be slid over the other to make opening. Hence **sashed**[2] [-ED[2]], **sa·sh**LESS, aa. [corrupt. of CHASSIS prob. taken for pl.]

sa·shmaray, n. French lugger-rigged coasting vessel. [f. F *chasse-marée* = chase-tide]

să·sin, n. Indian antelope. [Nepalese]

sassā·by, n. Large S.-Afr. antelope. [native]

sa·ssafrăs, n. (Small N.-Amer. tree yielding) a bark used medicinally; infusion of this. [Sp. (*sasa-*), etym. dub.]

Sassā·nian, Sa·ssanid, nn. & aa. (Member, esp. a king) of family of Sa(s)san, rulers of Persian empire A.D. 211–651. [-IAN, -ID[3]]

Sa·ssenach (-ch), n. & a. (Sc. & Ir. for) English(man). [thr. Gael. & Ir. f. *Saxon*]

sat. See SIT.

Sā·tan, (archaic) **Să·tanăs**, n. The Devil, Lucifer. [L f. Gk, f. Heb. *ṣaṭan* enemy]

Sată·nic(al rare), a. Of, like, or befitting Satan, diabolical, hellish, (*his S. majesty*, Satan; *S. school*, orig. Byron, Shelley, &c., also any set of writers accused of defiant impiety &c.). Hence **Sata·nical**LY[2] adv. [-IC, -ICAL]

Sā·tanism, n. Deliberate wickedness, pursuit of evil for its own sake, diabolical disposition, so **Sa·tan**IZE(3) v.t.; characteristics of SATANIC school; (esp. French 19th-c.) professed worship of Satan. So **Sa·tan**IST(2) n. [-ISM]

Sātano·logy, n. (History or collection of) beliefs concerning the Devil. [-O-, -LOGY]

satar·a, n. Heavy broadcloth with horizontal rib. [*S.* in India]

sa·tchel (-tshl), n. Small bag usu. of leather & hung from shoulder with strap for carrying books &c. esp. to & from school. Hence **sa·tchell**ED[2] a. [f. OF *sachel* f. L *saccellus* (SACK[1], -EL)]

sate, v.t. Gratify (desire, person feeling it) to the full; cloy, surfeit, weary with over-abundance (*sated with*). Hence **sa·te**LESS a. (poet.). [earlier *sade*, OE *sadian* (SAD), assim. to L *sat(is)* enough]

satee·n, n. Cotton or woollen fabric with glossy surface. [f. SATIN after VELVETEEN]

să·tellite, n. Person's follower or henchman or hanger-on, member of great man's retinue, underling; planet revolving round another (often fig.), whence **satelli·t**IC a. [F, f. L *satellitem* nom. *-les* guard]

sati. See SUTTEE.

sā·tiate[1] (-shyat), a. Satiated. [L *satiare* (SATIS), -ATE[2]]

sā·tiāte[2] (-shĭ-), v.t. =SATE. So **sa·ti**ABLE (-sha-) a. (rare), **sati**A·TION (sāsĭ-, sāshĭ-) n. [as prec., -ATE[3]]

satī·ety, n. Glutted or satiated state, feeling of having had too much of something, cloyed dislike *of*, (*to s.*, to extent beyond what is desired); (rare) over-abundance. [f. F *satiété* f. L *satietatem* (*satis* enough, -TY)]

să·tin, n. & a., & v.t. Silk fabric with glossy surface on one side got by catching warp-threads only at intervals (*Denmark s.*, smooth worsted material used for ladies' slippers; *white s.*, the plant Honesty, also kind of moth; *s.* or *white s.* slang, gin; (adj. or attrib.) smooth as s.; *s. beauty, carpet*, kinds of moth; *s. cloth*, a woollen cloth woven like s.; *s. finish*, polish given to silver with metallic brush; *s.-flower*, Honesty, also Greater Stitchwort; *s. gypsum*, fibrous kind with pearly lustre; *s. paper*, fine glossy writing-paper; *s. pug, pygmy*, kinds of moth; *s. sheeting*, fabric of waste silk & cotton; *s.-spar*, fibrous carbonate of lime; *s.-stitch*, giving appearance of s. in embroidery & wool-work; *s.-stone*, s. gypsum; *s.-straw*, soft & flexible for hats; *s. white*, artificial sulphate of lime; *s.-wood*, choice timber of a tropical tree; hence **sa·tin**Y[2] a., **satin**E·TTE(2) & in same sense **sa·tin**ET[1] nn. (Vb) give glossy surface to (paper). [F, prob. ult. f. L *seta* silk, -INE[1]]

să·tire, n. (Rom. Ant.) poetic medley, esp. poem aimed at prevalent vices or follies; a composition in verse or prose holding up vice or folly to ridicule or lampooning individual(s), this branch of literature, (often *upon*); thing that brings ridicule upon something (*our lives are a s. upon our religion*); use of ridicule, irony, sarcasm, &c., in speech or writing for the ostensible purpose of exposing & discouraging vice or folly. [f. L *satira* in 1st sense above, var. of *satura* (*lanx satura* full dish)]

sati·ric, a. Of satires or satire, containing satire, writing satires, (*s. verse, poem, poet, writer, intent, stroke*). [F (*-ique*), f. LL *satiricus* (prec., -IC)]

sati·rical, a. = prec.; given to the use of satire in speech or writing or to cynical observation of others, sarcastic, humorously critical. Hence **sati·rical**LY[2] adv. [prec., -AL]

sa·tĭrist, n. Writer of satires; satirical person. [-IST]

sa·tĭrize, v.t. Assail with satire, write satire(s) upon, describe satirically. [f. F *satiriser* (SATIRE, -IZE)]

să·tis, Latin adv. & n. = enough, used in phrr. *jam s.* already enough, *s. sūper·quĕ* enough & too much.

satisfa·ction, n. Payment of debt, fulfilment of obligation, atonement (*for*), thing accepted by way of s., (Eccl.) performance of penance, (Theol.) atonement made by Christ for sins of men, (*make s.*;

in s. of; *enter s.* legal, place on record of court that payment ordered has been made; *Christ is the s. for our sins*); opportunity of fighting duel with person one complains of (*give, demand, s.*); satisfying or being satisfied in regard to desire or want or doubt, thing that satisfies desire or gratifies feeling, (*find s. in*; *give s.*; *to the s. of*; *heard it with great s.*; *their s. at* or *with the results*; *if you can prove it to my s.*; *the s. of not having to do it*; *it is a great s. that it need not be done*; *would be a s. to me*; *thinks only of present s.*). [F, f. L *satisfactionem* (SATISFY)]

satisfa·ctory, a. (Theol.) serving as atonement for sin; satisfying expectations or needs, leaving no room for complaint, causing satisfaction, adequate, (*s. proof, method, result, pupil, pair of boots, expedition, marriage, compromise*). Hence **satisfa·ctori**LY[2] adv., **satisfa·ctori**NESS n. [f. F *satisfactoire* f. med. L *satisfactorius* (SATISFY, -ORY)]

să·tisfy, v.t. & i. Pay (debt, rarely creditor), fulfil (obligation), comply with (demand), (of Christ) make atonement for sins of men; meet the expectations or desires of, come up to (notion, preconception, &c.), be accepted by (person, his taste, &c.) as adequate, content, (*s. the examiners* at univv., receive pass without honours); (pass.) be content or pleased (*with*), demand no more than or consider it enough *to* do, (*rest satisfied,* make or take no further demands or steps); (intr.) give satisfaction, leave nothing to be desired; dispose of (an appetite or want), rid (person) of an appetite or want, by sufficient supply; furnish with adequate proof, convince, (*of* fact, *that it is so*; *s.* one*self,* attain to practical certainty); adequately meet (objection, doubt, request, conditions). Hence **sa·tisfi**ABLE a., **sa·tisfy**ING[2] a., **sa·tisfying**LY[2] adv. [f. OF *satisfier* f. L SATIS*facere fact-* (-FY)]

să·trap, n. Holder of provincial governorship or **sa·trap**Y[1] n. in ancient-Persian empire, viceroy; modern subordinate ruler, colonial governor, &c. (esp. rhet. with implication of luxury or tyranny). [f. L f. Gk *satrapēs* f. OPers. *khsatra-pava* province-guardian]

Sa·tsūma, (ware), n. Cream-coloured Japanese pottery. [name of province]

să·tūrate (*or* -tsher-), v.t. Impregnate, soak thoroughly, imbue *with*; (Chem. &c.) charge (substance, air, vapour, metal) with or cause to combine with or absorb or hold the greatest amount possible of another substance, moisture, magnetism, electricity, &c., (p.p., of colour) free from admixture of white, full, rich. Hence or cogn. **sa·tur**ATE[2] (*-at*) a. (poet. exc. of colour), **sa·tur**ABLE a., **satur**A·TION n. [f. L *saturare* (*satur* full cogn. w. SATIS), -ATE[3]]

Să·turday (-dĭ), n. Seventh day of week (HOLY, HOSPITAL, *S.*; *S.-to-Monday,* = the now usu. WEEK-*end*). [OE *Sæternes)dæg* transl. of L *Saturni dies* day of SATURN]

Să·turn, n. (Rom. Ant.) Italic god of agriculture later identified with Greek Cronos father of Zeus, ruler of the world in a golden age of innocence and plenty; a planet, the furthest off of the 7 anciently known, with 8 moons & broad flat ring, credited in astrology with producing cold sluggish gloomy temperament in those born under its influence. [f. L *Saturnus* (*serere sat-* sow)]

saturnā·lia, n. pl. & (see below) sing. Ancient-Roman festival of Saturn in December observed as time of unrestrained merrymaking with temporary release of slaves, predecessor of modern Christmastide (*S-*); scene or time of wild revelry or tumult (*s-*, *S-*; often as sing. as *a s. of crime*). Hence **saturna·li**AN a. [L, neut. pl. of *Saturnalis* (prec., -AL)]

Satur·nian, a. & n. Of the god or the planet Saturn; *S. metre, verse,* metre used in early Latin poetry before introduction of Greek metres & generally taken to have been an iambic dimeter catalectic followed by three trochees (e.g. *dabunt malum Metelli Naevio poetae*). (N.) inhabitant of Saturn; (pl.) S. verse. [f. L SATURN*ius*, -AN]

satur·nic, a. (path.). Affected with lead-poisoning. So **Sa·turn**ISM(5) n. [SATURN in alch. sense *lead,* -IC]

sa·turnine, a. Of sluggish gloomy temperament, (of looks &c.) suggestive of or produced by such temperament, whence **sa·turnine**LY[2] adv.; of lead (*a s. poultice, red,* &c.); of, affected by, lead-poisoning (*s. patients, symptoms*). [SATURN (cf. prec.), -INE[1]]

să·tyr (*-er*), n. One of a class of Greek woodland deities in human form with horse's ears & tail (or, as represented by Romans, with goat's ears, tail, legs, & budding horns); lustful or beastly-minded man; (rare) orang-utan. [f. L f. Gk *saturos*]

satў·ric, a. Of satyrs (esp. *s. drama,* kind of Greek play with chorus of satyrs). [f. L f. Gk *saturikos* (prec., -IC)]

sauce, n., & v.t. Liquid preparation taken as relish with some article of food (*bread, egg, mint, parsley, tomato,* &c., *s.,* with these as prominent ingredient; *white s.,* of melted butter, flour, &c.; *hunger is the best s.*; *s. for the* GANDER; *serve with the same s.,* subject to same usage), (fig.) something that adds piquancy (*is tame without the s. of danger*); solution of salt & other ingredients used in some manufacturing processes; sauciness, impertinent speech, cheek, (*none of your s.!*); *s.-alone,* hedge-weed formerly used to flavour salads & ss.; *s.-boat,* vessel in which s. is served; *s.-box,* impudent person; *saucepan* (*-an*), metal vessel usu. cylindrical with long handle projecting from side for boiling things in cookery; hence **sau·ce**LESS a. (Vb) season with ss. or condiments (rare), (fig.) make piquant, add relish to; (vulg.) be impudent to, cheek, (person). [vb f. n., F, f. pop. L *salsa* fem. of *salsus* (*salere sals-* to salt f. *sal* salt)]

sau·cer, n. Shallow vessel for standing cup on to intercept spillings of tea &c. (*s. eye,* large & round as a s., whence **saucer-eye**ED[2] a.); vessel placed under flowerpot to prevent water from running away at once; any small shallow round vessel resembling tea-s. Hence **sau·cer**FUL(2) n., **sau·cer**LESS a. [earlier sense *condiment-dish,* f. OF *saussier* (SAUCE, -ARY[1])]

sau·cy, a. Impudent to superiors, cheeky; (slang) sprightly, smart, stylish. Hence **sau·ci**LY[2] adv., **sau·ci**NESS n. [earlier sense *savoury*; SAUCE, -Y[2]]

sauerkraut (sowr·krowt), n. German dish of pickled cabbage. [G]

saul. See SAL.

saunders. See SANDERS.

sau·nter, v.i., & n. Walk in leisurely way or without destination, stroll, (also fig., as *s. through life*); hence **sau·nter**ER[1] n., **sau·ntering**LY[2] adv. (N.) leisurely ramble or gait. [?]

saur·ian, a. & n. (One) of the *Sauria* or order of lizards including crocodiles, alligators, & extinct kinds such as ichthyosaurus & plesiosaurus. So **sauro-** comb. form, **saur·**OID a. & n. [Gk *sauros* lizard, -IAN]

saur·y, n. A long-billed sea-fish. [prob. f. mod. L f. Gk *sauros* lizard]

sausage (sŏ·sĭj), n. Pork or other meat minced, seasoned, & stuffed into long cylindrical cases prepared from entrails & divided when full into lengths of a few inches by twisting or tying, *a* length of this, (*Bologna s.,* large kind made of bacon, veal, pork-suet, &c., & sold ready for eating cold; (army slang) KITE balloon; *s.-filler, -grinder, -machine,* s.-making appliances; *s.-meat,* used as stuffing for turkeys &c. instead of being enclosed in skins; *s. roll,* s.-meat enclosed in pastry & cooked. [f. ONF *saussiche* f. LL *salsicia* (L *salsus* see SAUCE)]

sauté (sō·tā), a. (in fem. *-ée*; pl. *-és,* fem. *-ées*). Quickly fried in hot pan with little grease. [F]

Sauterne (sōtār·n), n. Kinds of sweet white French wine. [place-name]

sauve-qui-peut (sō·vkēper·), n. Precipitate flight in various directions. [F, f. phr. *sauve qui peut* let him find safety who can]

să·vage (-ĭj), a., n., & v.t. Uncultivated, wild, (archaic; *a s. scene*); uncivilized, in primitive state, (*s. tribes, life*); fierce, cruel, furious, (*s. persecution, persecutor, revenge, criticism, blow*); (colloq.) angry, out of temper; (Herald.; of human figure) naked; hence or cogn. **sa·vage**LY[2] adv., **sa·vage**NESS, **sa·vage**RY(2, 4), nn. (N.) member of s. tribe esp. of one living by hunting & fishing, whence **sa·vage**DOM n.; brutally cruel or barbarous person. (Vb; of horse) attack & bite or trample (person; *was savaged by his horse*). [earlier & OF *salvage* f. L *silvaticus* (*silva* a wood, -ATIC, cf. -AGE)]

sava·nna(h), n. Treeless plain, great tract of meadow-like land, esp. in tropical America. [f. Sp. *zavana* perh. of Carib orig.]

savant (F), n. Man of learning, esp. distinguished scientist. [part. of F *savoir* know, as SAPIENT]

sava·te (-aht), n. French boxing, in which feet & head are used as well as fists.

save[1], v.t. & i., & n. Rescue, preserve, deliver, from or *from* danger or misfortune or harm or discredit (*saved my life, me from drowning, the State*; *s. me* or *God s. me from my friends* &c., comment upon well-meant inopportune officiousness; *s. us!,* excl. of surprise; *s.* one's BACON, FACE[1]; *s. the situation,* find or provide way out of difficulty, avert disaster; *s. appearances,* put a good face on something), (Footb.) prevent opponents from scoring (n., such prevention, as *a clever s.*); bring about spiritual salvation of, preserve from damnation, (*who then can be saved?*; *the saving of souls*), (part.) redeeming (*by the saving grace of God*; *has the saving grace of humour*); keep for future use, husband, reserve, abstain from expending, lay by money, live economically, (*s.* one's *breath,* be silent; *a saving housekeeper*; *is saving his strength*; *has never saved,* put by money; *s. up,* try to accumulate money by economy; *you may s. your pains* or *trouble,* need not take, will take in vain), whence **sa·**VER[1](1) n., **sa·**VING[1](2) n. (usu. in pl.), **sa·ving**LY[2] adv.; relieve (person) from need of expending (money, trouble, &c.) or from exposure to (annoyance &c.), obviate need of, reduce requisite amount of, (*that will s. me £50*; *his secretary saved him much time* or *labour, many interviews*; *s. the follow-on* in cricket, get enough runs to prevent it; *stitch in time saves nine*; *soap saves rubbing*), whence **-sav**ER[1](2) n., **-sav**ING[2] a.; avoid losing, be in time for, succeed in catching, (*write hurriedly to s. the post*; *shall we s. the tide?,* get in or out while it serves); make reservation concerning, make reservation, (esp. *saving clause,* containing stipulation of exemption &c.; *saving your reverence,* apology for unseemly expression &c., cf. *s. the* MARK[1]), (part. as prep.) except, with the exception of, SAVE[2]; *s.-all,* pan with spike fcr urning up candle-ends; *savings-bank,* receiving small deposits from the poor & conducted solely in depositors' interests (*Post-office s.-b.,* with branches at local post offices). Hence **sa·**VABLE a. [f. OF *salver* f. L *salvare* (*salvus* safe)]

save[2], prep. & conj. Except, but, (with n. in obj. case, or with *that* clause; archaic, poet., or with formal or pretentious effect in ordinary writing, also pleonast. in *s. & except*; *forty stripes s. one*; *all s. him*, & see conj.; *I am well s. that I have a cold*). (Conj.; archaic) unless, but, (*thou seest no beauty s. thou make it*; *all the conspirators s. only he*; *happy s. for one want*). [f. SAFE[2] after F *sauf* & SALVO[1]]

să·veloy, n. Highly seasoned dried sausage. [earlier & OF *cervelat* f. It. *cervellata* (*cervello* brain f. L CEREBELLUM), named as orig. made of pig's brain]

să·vin, n. (Tree or shrub with) tops yielding a volatile oil used medicinally. [f. OF *savine* f. L *sabina* (*herba*) SABINE (herb)]

sā·viour, n. Deliverer, redeemer (*the, our, S.*, Christ), person who saves a State &c. from destruction &c. [f. OF *sauveour* (SAVE[1], -IOUR)]

săvoir faire· (-vwar), n. Quickness to see & do the right thing, address, tact. [F]

savoir vi·vre (-vwar-vē·vr), n. Good breeding, being at home in society. [F]

sā·vory, n. Herb of mint family used in cookery. [ult. f. L *satureia* prob. w. assim. in F to foll.]

sā·vour, n., & v.i. & t. Characteristic taste, flavour, relish, or (now rare) smell, power to affect the taste (lit. or fig.); quality suggestive, perceptible admixture, suspicion, smack, *of* (*a not unpleasing s. of preciosity*); hence **sa·vour**LESS a. (Vb) appreciate or perceive the lit. or fig. taste of (archaic); give flavour to (rare); smack, offer suggestion, suggest presence, *of* (*the offer savours of impertinence*). [f. OF *savour*(*er*) f. L *saporem* (*sapere* taste, -OR[1])]

sa·voury (-verĭ), a. & n. With appetizing taste or smell; (of places &c.; only w. neg.) free from bad smells; (of dishes &c.) of salt or piquant & not sweet flavour (*sweet or s. omelette*); hence **sa·vouri**LY[2] adv., **sa·vouri**NESS n. (N.) s. dish, esp. one served at beginning or end of dinner as stimulant or digestive. [f. OF *savouré* p.p. (SAVOUR)]

savoy·, n. Kind of cabbage with wrinkled leaves. [S. in France]

Savoy·ard, n. & a. (Native) of Savoy. [F (*Savoie* Savoy, -ARD)]

sa·vvy, corrupt. of Sp. *sabe* knows, in slang use = do you understand? (*no s.*, I do, he &c. does, not know or understand), also as n. = understanding, wits, savoir-faire.

saw[1], n., & v.t. & i. (p.p. *sawn*, rarely *sawed*). Implement usu. of steel worked by hand or mechanically & with variously shaped blade or edge having teeth of various forms cut in or attached to it for dividing wood, metal, stone, &c., by reciprocating or rotatory motion (*annular, crown, cylinder, s.*, cylinder with toothed edge for making circular hole; BAND[1], BOW[1], FRAME[2], FRET[1],-*s.*; CIRCULAR *s.*; *cross-cut, rip-, s.*, for cutting wood across, along, the grain; *hand-s.*, held with one hand; HACK[2]-*s.*; *jig-s.*, frame-s. worked mechanically in connexion with table holding the wood &c. (*j.-s. puzzle*, of pieces sawn with j.-s. to be put together); *pit-s.*, worked by two men one above & one in pit; *reciprocating s.*, worked mechanically with backward & forward strokes; *stone-s.*, toothless frame-s. cutting stone by friction with sand & water); (Zool. &c.) serrated organ or part; *s.-doctor*, machine for making teeth of s.; *sawdust*, wood fragments produced in sawing used in packing, pugging, stuffing, drying moisture, &c. (*let the s.-d. out of* fig., expose pretentiousness or unsubstantial character of, w. ref. to doll's stuffing); *s.-fish*, large kind with toothed snout used as weapon; *s.-fly*, kinds injurious to plants with serrated ovipositor; *s.-frame*, in which s.-blade is held taut; *s.-gate*, s.-frame; *s.-gin*, cotton-GIN[1] with s.-teeth; *s.-horse*, rack supporting wood for sawing; *s.-mill*, driven by water or steam for mechanical sawing; *s.-pit*, in which lower of two men working pit-s. stands; *s.-set*, tool for wrenching s.-teeth in alternate directions to give kerf wider than blade & let s. work freely; *s.-wort*, plant yielding yellow dye named from serrated leaves; *s.-wrack*, a serrated seaweed; *s.-wrest*, s.-set. (Vb) cut (wood &c.) with, make (boards &c.) with, use, s.; move (t. & i.) backward & forward, divide (the air &c.), with motion as of s. or person sawing; (quasi-pass.) admit of being sawn *easily, badly*, &c.; (Bookbind.) make incisions to receive binding-bands in (gathered sheets); *sawbones* slang, surgeon. [vb f. n., OE *saga*, cf. Du. *zaag*, G *säge*, cogn. w. L *secare* cut]

saw[2], n. Proverbial saying, old maxim, (usu. *old* or *wise s.*). [OE *sagu*, cogn. w. SAY[2]]

saw[3]. See SEE[1].

saw·der, n. *Soft s.*, compliments, flattering speeches, blarney. [= SOLDER]

Saw·ney, n. (Nickname for) Scotsman; simpleton. [prob. as SANDY[2]]

saw·yer, n. Man employed in sawing timber (TOP-*s.*); (U.S.) uprooted tree floating or stranded in river (named as sawing up & down); kinds of wood-boring larva. [-YER]

sax, zax, n. Slater's chopper, with point for making nail-holes. [OE *seax* knife (see SAXON), cf. Icel. *sax*]

sa·xatĭle, a. (nat. hist.). Living, growing, on or among rocks. [f. L *saxatilis* (*saxum* rock, -ATILE)]

saxe, n. Kind of photographic paper; a colour, = SAXON *blue*. [F, = Saxony (place of origin)]

sa·xhorn, n. Instrument of trumpet class. [A. *Sax,* inventor]

saxi·coline, -lous, aa. (nat. hist.). =SAXATILE. [L *-cola* inhabitant of (*colere* inhabit)]

sa·xifrāge (*or* -ĭj), n. Kinds of Alpine or rock plant with tufted foliage & panicles of white or yellow or red flowers. [OF, f. L *saxifraga* spleenwort (*saxum* stone, *frangere* break) prob. named as growing in rock-clefts]

Sa·xon, n. & a. Member, language (often *old S.*), of the Teutonic N.-German people by which England was conquered in 5th & 6th cc.; =ANGLO-SAXON, whence **Sa·xon**DOM n.; native of modern Saxony; Teutonic (opp. Latin or Romance) elements of English. (Adj.) of the Ss. (*S. architecture,* rude Romanesque preceding Norman in England); in S. (*S. words* in English, of Teutonic origin), whence **Sa·xon**ISM(2, 4), **Sa·xon**IST(2), nn.; *S. blue,* solution of indigo in sulphuric acid as dye; hence **Sa·xon**IZE(2, 3) v.i. & t. [F, f. L *Saxonem* f. WG (OE *Seaxan* pl., perh. f. *seax* knife)]

sa·xony, n. Fine kind of wool, cloth made from it. [f. *S.* in Germany]

sa·xophone, n. Powerful keyed brass reed instrument with large inverted bell. [as SAXHORN, Gk *phōnē* sound]

sa·xtūba, n. Large SAXHORN. [TUBA]

say[1], n. (now rare). Fine serge-like cloth. [f. F *saie* f. L *saga* pl. of *sagum* military cloak]

say[2], v.t. & i. (*said,* pr. sĕd; archaic 3rd sing. pres., *saith* pr. sĕth), & n. Utter, make (specified remark), recite, rehearse, in ordinary speaking voice (*s. the word,* give the order &c.; *s. no more,* cease speaking; *s. a good word for,* commend or excuse; *to be said or sung*; *s. no, yes,* refuse, grant, request, also deny, confirm or accept, statement; *s. out,* express fully or candidly; *s.* one *nay,* refuse him something; *has said his s.,* finished what he had to s.; *s. lesson,* repeat it to teacher; *s. grace, prayer*; *s. something,* s. grace, also make a speech; *that is to s.,* in other words, as *the whole family, t. i. t. s. four persons,* also =or at least, as *he never went, t. i. t. s. it is not recorded that he did,* also ellipt. *s.* in giving sum in words after figures, as *£500, s. five hundred pounds*; *he said 'You lie'*; *says* or *said he* &c., *said I, says I* colloq., forms inserted in repeating conversation; *saying & doing,* speech & action; *I s.,* excl. used to draw attention, open a conversation, or express surprise, as *I s., who was that?, I s., what a beauty!,* or in same sense *I say!* alone); state, promise, prophesy, (*he says all men* or *that all men are liars*; *you said you would*; DARE *s.*; *they s., it is said,* forms introducing rumour; *it says in the Bible,* the Bible says; *goes without saying,* is too obvious to need mention; *hear s.,* hear it reported; *so he says, he says so*; *you may well s. so,* your statement is fully justified); speak, talk, (rare; *s. away,* s. what you have to s.; *he said, & turned his back,* in narrative poetry &c.); put into words, express, (*that was well said*); adduce or allege in argument or excuse (*there is much to be said on both sides*; *have you nothing to s. for yourself?*); form & give opinion or decision as to or abs. (*there is no saying, it is hard to s., who it was*; *I cannot s.,* do not know *whether* &c. or abs.; *do s. which you will have*; *what s. you to a theatre?,* are you inclined for it?; *& so s. all of us,* & that is our opinion too); select as example, assume, take (specified number &c.) as near enough, (*let us s.,* or usu. ellipt. *s.*; *any country, let us s. Sweden, might do the same*; *well, s. it were true, what then?*; *a few of them, s. a dozen or so*). (N.): (opportunity of saying) what one has to s., share in decision, (*s. your s.*; *let him have his s.*; *had no s. in the matter*). [OE *secgan,* cf. ON *segja,* G *sagen*]

say·ing, n. In vbl senses; esp., sententious remark, maxim, adage, (*as the s. is,* form used in quoting proverb or phrase). [-ING[1]]

sbĭ·rro, n. (pl. *-ri* pr. -ē). Italian policeman. [It.]

scab, n., & v.i. Dry rough incrustation formed over sore in healing, cicatrice; mange, itch, or similar skin-disease; kinds of fungous plant-disease; mean dirty fellow (archaic), (Trade unionism) workman who refuses to join strike or union or takes striker's place, blackleg; *s.-wort,* elecampane; hence **scabb**ED[2], **sca·bb**Y[2], aa., **sca·bb**ILY[2] adv., **sca·bbi**NESS n. (Vb; of sore) form s., heal over. [f. ON (Da. *skab,* Sw. *skabb,* cf. OE *sceab, scæb,* (SHABBY)]

sca·bbard, n. Sheath of sword, bayonet, &c. (*fling, throw, away the s.,* commit oneself to fighting a matter out to the end); *s.-fish,* silvery-white sea-fish shaped like sword-s. [earlier *scawberk* cf. AF *escaubers* pl.; prob. ult. f. Teut. (SHELL, HAUBERK)]

scā·biēs, n. The itch. [L (*scabere* scratch)]

scā·bious, a. & n. Scabby, affected with mange, itch, &c.; (n.) kinds of wild & cultivated annual or perennial herb with blue, pink, or white, pincushion-shaped flowers. [(n. f. *scabiosa herba* named as specific against itch) f. L *scabiosus* (prec., -OSE[1])]

scā·brous, a. (Zool., Bot., &c.) with rough surface, scurfy; (Literature; of subject, situation, &c.) requiring tactful treatment, hard to handle with decency. Hence **sca·brous**NESS n. [f. L *scaber* rough, cf. prec., + -OUS]

scad, n. Kind of fish called also horse-mackerel. [?]

sca·ffold n. & v.t., **sca·ffolding** n. Elevated platform of timber usu. for execution of criminals (*-old*; *the s.*, death by executioner's hands) or rarely (*-old*, *-ing*) for display of something or accommodation of spectators; (usu. *-ing*) temporary structure of poles & planks providing workmen with platform(s) to stand on while building or repairing house &c., (*-ing*) materials for this; (Anat., Embryol.; *-old*, *-ing*) framework outlining parts to be formed on it later (*the s. of the skull*); *scaffolding-pole*, mastlike pole helping to support building-platform; (vb) attach scaffolding to (house). [f. OF *escadafault* (now *échafaud*) perh. f. EX- + It. *catafalco* CATAFALQUE]

scăg·lia, n. Reddish Italian limestone. [It.]

scaglio·la (-alyō-), n. Imitation stone of plaster mixed with glue & variously coloured or diversified. [It. (*-iuola*)]

scā·lable, a. In vbl senses of SCALE[1, 2, 3]. [-ABLE]

scală·riform, a. (bot., zool.). Ladder-shaped (of veins in insect's wings, or of alternating thick & thin strips in structure). [L *scalaria* staircase (neut. pl. of *scalaris* f. *scala* SCALE[3], -AR[1]), -FORM]

scă·lawag, -lla-, -lly-, n. Undersized or ill-fed animal; good-for-nothing person, scamp, scapegrace. [U.S., etym. dub.]

scald[1] (-aw-), v.t., & n. Injure or pain (skin, or person or animal or part in regard to it) with hot liquid or vapour (*was scalded to death by the steam*; *scalding tears*, of bitter grief); raise (milk) to near boiling-point (*scalded cream*, from milk scalded & allowed to stand), whence **sca·ld**ER[1](2) n.; cleanse (vessel; often *out*) by rinsing with boiling water; (n.) injury to skin by scalding (*for ss. & burns*). [f. ONF *escalder* f. L EX(*caldare* f. *calidus* hot)]

scald[2] (-aw-), **sk-**, n. Ancient-Scandinavian composer & reciter of poems in honour of great men. Hence **sca·ld**IC a. [ON *skáld* etym. dub.]

sca·ld-head (-aw-), n. Scalp-disease of children. [SCALL, -ED[2]]

scaldi·no (-ē-), n. (pl. *-ni* pr. -ē). Small earthenware brazier used in Italy for warming the hands &c. [It.]

scale[1], n., & v.t. & i. One of the thin horny overlapping plates protecting the skin of many fishes & reptiles; plate or thin outer piece with some resemblance to fish-s. in organic or other object, e.g. pod, husk, rudimentary leaf or feather, bract, metamorphosed hair of lepidoptera, bulb-layer, flake of skin, scab, lamina on surface of rusty iron; (without *a*) incrustation inside boiler &c., tartar on teeth; *s.-armour*, of metal ss. attached to leather &c.; *s.-board*, very thin for back of mirror, picture, &c.; *s.-borer*, machine for removing s. from boiler-tubes; *s.-fern*, ceterach; *s.-insect*, kinds that cling fast to plants & secrete a shield-like s. as covering; *s.-moss*, kinds of plant with s.-like leaves resembling moss; *s.-winged*, lepidopterous; *s.-work*, overlapping arrangement, imbrication; hence **(-)scal**ED, **sca·le**LESS, **sca·l**Y[2], aa., **sca·li**NESS n. (Vb) take away scale(s) from (*s. fish, almonds, peas, teeth, iron*); (of skin, metal, &c.) form, come off in, drop, ss.; (of ss.) come *off*. [f. OF *escale* f. OTeut. *skalā*; cogn. w. foll.]

scale[2], n., & v.t. Dish of simple balance (*throw sword into s.*, back claim with arms; *turn the s.* of motive or circumstance, be decisive); (Astr.) *the Ss.*, = LIBRA; (pl.) a simple balance (also *pair of ss.*) or weighing-instrument (*hold the ss. even*, be impartial judge). (Vb) weigh in ss. (rare); (of thing weighed) show (specified weight) in the ss. (*scales 10 st., 100 lb.*). [f. ON *skál* bowl f. OTeut. *skǣlā*; cogn. w. OE *scealu* shell & w. prec.]

scale[3], n., & v.t. & i. Series of degrees, ladderlike arrangement or classification, graded system, (*is high in the s. of creation* or *social, intellectual*, &c., *s.*; *sink in the s.*, fall to lower rank or level; *at the top, bottom, of the s.*; *sliding s.*, see SLIDE[1]); (Mus.) set of sounds belonging to a KEY[1] arranged in order of pitch (DIATONIC, CHROMATIC, MAJOR[2], MINOR, *s.*; *play, sing, run over* one's, *ss.*, as exercise for fingers or voice); (often *s. of notation*) basis of numerical system as shown in ratio between units in different places of number (the *ordinary* or *denary* or *decimal s.*, with successive places denoting units, tens, hundreds, &c.; *binary s.*, denoting units, twos, fours, &c.; *ternary s.*, denoting units, threes, nines, &c.; thus fourteen is written in binary s. 1110 i.e. nought + two + four + eight, in ternary s. 112 i.e. two + three + nine, in septenary s. 20 i.e. nought + two sevens, & in denary s. 14 i.e. four + ten); relative dimensions, ratio of reduction & enlargement in map &c., (*philanthropy, armies, on a vast s.*; *a building of small s. but fine proportions*; *large, small, -s. map*; *to s.*, with uniform reduction or enlargement; *the s. to be one to fifty thousand, an inch to the mile, 1/1000*, &c.); set of marks at measured distances on a line for use in measuring or making proportional reductions & enlargements, rule determining intervals between these, piece of metal &c. or apparatus on which they are marked (GUNTER'*s s.*). (Vb) climb (wall, steep place, or abs.) with ladder or by clambering; represent in dimensions proportional to the actual ones, reduce to common s., (*s. up, down*, make larger, smaller, in due proportion); (of quantities &c.) have common s., be commensurable; *scaling-ladder*, used in escalades. [f. L *scala* ladder (*scandere* climb)]

scale·ne, a. & n. Unequal-sided (*s. tri-*

angle, with no two sides equal; *s. cone, cylinder*, with axis inclined to base; *s. muscle*, any of several connecting spine & ribs); (n.) s. triangle or muscle. [f. LL f. Gk *skalēnos*]

scall (-awl), n. (archaic). Scaly eruption on skin (*dry s.*, the itch; *moist s.*, eczema). [f. ON *skalle* bare head]

scallawag. See SCALAWAG.

scă·llion, n. Kind of onion or shallot. [f. AF *scaloun* = OF *eschalogne* SHALLOT]

scă·llop, sco-, n., & v.t. Bivalve mollusc with shell divided into grooves & ridges radiating from middle of hinge & edged all round with small semicircular lobes; (also *s.-shell*) one valve of this (hist.) as pilgrim's badge, (mod.) as utensil in which oysters, shredded fish, mince, &c., are cooked & served, small shallow pan similarly used; (pl.) ornamental edging cut in material in imitation of s.-edge. (Vb) cook in s.; ornament (edge, material) with ss. or **sca·llop**ING[1](6) n. [f. OF *escalope* f. Teut. (Du. *schelp* cogn. w. SCALE[1], [2], SHELL)]

scallywag. See SCALAWAG.

scalp, n., & v.t. Top of head; skin with hair &c. of head excluding face, this or part of it cut as trophy from enemy's head by Red Indians (*take s.*; *out for ss.*, on the war-path, often fig. = in aggressive or pugnacious or savagely critical mood); bare rounded hill-top; whale's head without lower jaw; *s.-lock*, single lock on Red Indian's shaven head left as challenge to enemies; hence **sca·lp**LESS a. (Vb) take s. of; criticize savagely. [cf. MSw. *skalp*, ON *skálpr*, sheath, MDu. *schelpe* shell; cogn. w. SCALLOP, SCALE[1], SHELL]

sca·lpel, n. Surgeon's small light knife shaped for holding like pen. [f. L *scalpellum* (*scalprum* chisel, f. *scalpere* scrape, -EL)]

sca·lper, scau·per, n. Gouge used by engravers. [f. L *scalprum* (prec.)]

sca·lpriform, a. Chisel-shaped (of incisor teeth). [L *scalprum* see SCALPEL, -I-, -FORM]

sca·mmony, n. (Kind of Asiatic convolvulus yielding) a gum resin used as drastic purgative. [f. L f. Gk *skammōnia*]

scamp[1], n. Rascal, knave, (also in playful use as term of endearment). Hence **sca·mp**ISH[1] a. [prob. of same orig. as SCAMPER]

scamp[2], v.t. Do (work &c.) in perfunctory or inadequate way. [prob. var. of SCANT]

sca·mper, v.i., & n. Run impulsively like (or of) frightened animal or playing child; take s. *through*. (N.) hasty run; gallop on horseback for pleasure; rapid tour or course of reading (*through Normandy, Dickens*, &c.). [earlier sense *flee* (of army &c.), f. ONF (*s'*)*escamper* (EX-, L *campus* field) + -ER[5]]

scan, v.t. & i. Test metre of (line &c.) by examining number & quantity of feet & syllables, read over with emphasis on rhythm; be metrically correct (*line does not s.*), admit of rhythmic reading (*line will not s., scans smoothly, badly*); look intently at all parts successively of (face, horizon, &c.). [f. L *scandere* climb, perh. with loss of *-d* by confus. w. -ED[1]]

sca·ndal (-dl), n. (Thing that occasions) general feeling of outrage or indignation esp. as expressed in common talk, opprobrium, (*it is a s. that such things should be possible*; *a grave s. occurred*; *gave rise to s.*); malicious gossip, backbiting, whence **sca·ndal**MONGER n.; (Law) public affront, irrelevant abusive statement in court, (cf. LIBEL, SLANDER). So **sca·ndal**OUS a., **sca·ndalous**LY[2] adv., **sca·ndalous**NESS n. [ME *-dle*, f. ONF *escandle* f. eccl. L f. Gk *skandalon* snare, stumbling-block]

sca·ndalize[1], v.t. Offend moral feelings, sense of propriety, or ideas of etiquette, of, shock. [f. F *scandaliser* f. eccl. L f. Gk (*-izō*) as prec., see -IZE]

sca·ndalize[2], v.t. (naut.). Reduce area of (a sail). [corrupt. of obs. SCANT*elize*]

sca·ndalum magnā·tum, n. (hist.). Defamation of magnates. [med. L]

Scandinā·vian, a. & n. (Native, family of languages) of Scandinavia (Denmark, Norway, Sweden, & Iceland). [-AN]

sca·nsion, n. Metrical scanning, way verse scans. [f. L *scansionem* (*scandere scans-* climb, -ION)]

scansor·ial, a. Habitually climbing, adapted for climbing, (of birds, their feet, &c.). [L *scansorius* (prec., -ORY), -AL]

scant, a., & v.t. Barely sufficient, deficient, with scanty supply *of*, (archaic, poet., & in isolated phrr. as *with s. courtesy, s. of breath*); hence **sca·nt**LY[2] adv. (Vb; archaic) skimp, stint, provide grudgingly, (supply, material, person). [f. ON *skamt* short, whence also SCAMP[2]]

sca·ntling, n. Specimen, sample, (archaic); modicum, small amount, one's necessary supply *of*; small beam under 5 in. in breadth & depth; size to which stone or timber is to be cut; set of standard dimensions for parts of structure esp. in ship-building; trestle for cask. [f. OF *escantillon* etym. dub.]

sca·nty, a. Of small extent or amount, barely sufficient, (opp. *ample*). Hence **sca·nti**LY[2] adv., **sca·nti**NESS n. [-Y[2]]

scape[1], n., & v.t. (archaic). Escape (still in *hairbreadth ss.*). [for ESCAPE]

scape[2], n. (Bot.) radical stem bearing fructification & no leaves as in primrose; (Entom.) base of antenna; shaft of feather; spring, usu. with curve, of column from base. [f. L *scapus* cf. SCEPTRE]

sca·pegoat, n. (O.T.) goat allowed to escape when Jewish chief priest had laid sins of people upon it (*Lev.* xvi); person bearing blame due to others. [SCAPE[1]]

scā·pegrace, n. Harebrained person, esp. child, who constantly gets into trouble. [=one who gets no grace (SCAPE[1])]

scapement. =ESCAPEMENT.

scă·phoid (-f-), a. & n. (anat.). Boat-shaped (*s. bone*, one in tarsus & one in carpus); (n.) s. bone. [f. Gk *skaphoeidēs* (*skaphē, skaphos*, bowl, boat, -OID)]

scă·pūla, n. (pl. *-lae*). SHOULDER-blade. [LL, sing. of L *scapulae*]

scă·pular, a. & n. Of shoulder or shoulder-blade (*s. arch*, = *shoulder*-GIRDLE[1]; *s. feathers*, growing near insertion of wing). (N.) monastic short cloak covering shoulders; badge of admission to an ecclesiastical order, consisting of two strips of cloth hanging down breast & back & joined across shoulders (also *scapulary*); bandage for shoulder-blade; s. feather. [(n. in first sense f. F *scapulaire*) f. LL *scapularis* (prec., -AR[1])]

scapulo-, comb. form of SCAPULA, as *-hu·meral, -ra·dial, -u·lnar*, of scapula & humerus, & radius, & ulna. [-O-]

scar[1], n., & v.t. & i. Mark left after healing of wound or burn or sore, cicatrice, (also fig. of abiding effects of grief &c.); mark on plant left by fall of a leaf &c., hilum; hence **scar·**LESS a. (Vb) mark with s. or ss. (esp. in p.p.); heal (i. & t.) over, form s. [f. OF *escare* f. LL *eschara* scar f. Gk *eskhara* hearth, burn]

scar[2], **scaur,** n. Precipitous craggy part of mountain side. [f. ON *sker* isolated rock in sea, cogn. w. SHEAR[1]]

scă·rab, n. Sacred beetle of ancient Egypt; =foll.; ancient-Egyptian gem cut in form of beetle & engraved with symbols on flat side. [f. F *scarabée* f. L *scarabaeus*]

scarabae·id, n. Member of *Scarabaeidae*, family of beetles including prec., cockchafer, &c. [prec., -ID[3]]

scarabae·oid, a. & n. Like a scarab or a scarabaeid; (n.) counterfeit scarab. [-OID]

scă·ramouch (-owtsh), n. (archaic). Boastful poltroon, braggart. [F (*-e*), f. It. *Scaramuccia* stock character in Italian farce]

scārce, a. & adv. Insufficient for the demand or need, not plentiful, scanty, (usu. pred., & of food, money, or other necessaries of life), whence **scar·**CITY n. (*of*, or abs. = dearth of food); seldom met with, rare, hard to find, (*a s. book, moth*; *make oneself s.* colloq., retire, make off, keep out of the way), whence **scar·ce**NESS n.; (adv.; archaic, poet., rhet.) scarcely. [f. ONF *escars*, cf. It. *scarso* perh. f. LL *scarpsus* for L EX(*cerptus* = *carptus* f. *carpere* pluck) select]

scar·cely, adv. Hardly, barely, only just, (*is s. seventeen years old*; *had s. arrived when he was told that* —; *I s. know him*); surely not, not unless the unlikely happens or is true, (*you will s. maintain that*; *he can s. have said so*); (mild or apologetic substitute for) not (*I s. think so, know what to say*). [-LY[2]]

scār·cement, n. Set-back in a wall, ledge resulting from this. [SCARCE + -MENT]

scare, v.t., & n. Strike (esp. child, foolish person, or animal) with sudden terror, frighten (as) with a bugbear, (*scared face, expression*, &c., betraying terror; *s. away*, drive off by fright); keep (birds) away from sown land &c.; *scare·crow*, figure of man hung with old clothes & set up in field to keep birds away, bugbear, badly dressed or grotesque-looking or skinny person. (N.) unreasoning terror, esp. baseless general apprehension of war, invasion, &c., whence **scare·**MONGER n.; commercial panic. [ME *skerre*, f. ON *skirra* (*skiarr* timid)]

scarf[1], n. (pl. *-fs, -ves*). Long narrow strip of material worn for ornament or warmth round neck, over shoulders, or baldric-wise; man's neck-tie (*s.-pin, -ring*, usu. of gold or jewelled for holding ends of this together); *s.-loom*, for weaving narrow fabrics; *s.-skin*, outermost layer of skin constantly scaling off (esp. of that adhering to base of nails); *scarf-wise*, baldric-wise. Hence **scarf**ED[2] a. [prob. f. ONF *escarpe* f. Teut.; cogn. w. SCRIP[1]]

scarf[2], v.t., & n. Join ends of (pieces of timber, metal, or leather) by bevelling or notching so that they overlap without increase of thickness & then bolting, brazing, or sewing them together; flench (whale). (N.) joint made by scarfing timber or leather (also *s.-joint*) or metal (also *s.-weld*); notch, groove. [n. f. vb, perh. f. Sw. *skarfva* join (*skarf* seam)]

scăr·ificator, n. In vbl senses; esp., surgical instrument for scarifying, in which several lancet-points protrude at once from plane surface on touching of trigger. [SCARIFY, -OR[2]]

scăr·ifier, n. In vbl senses; esp.: =prec.; agricultural machine with prongs for stirring without turning soil; spiked road-breaking machine. [foll., -ER[1]]

scăr·ifȳ, v.t. (Surg.) make superficial incisions in, cut off skin from, (fig.) pain by severe criticism &c.; stir (soil) with scarifier. So **scari**FICA·TION n. [f. F *scarifier* f. L *scarificare* by assim. to *-ficare* -FY of *scarifare* f. Gk *skariphaomai* (*skariphos* style, cogn. w. L *scribere* write)]

scār·ious, a. (bot.). Thin, dry, & membranaceous (of bracts &c.). [f. F *scarieux* f. mod. L *scariosus* etym. dub.]

scarlati·na (-tē-), n. Scarlet fever. [It. (*-tt-*), f. *scarlatto* SCARLET]

scar·let, n. & a. (Of) brilliant red colour inclining to orange; s. cloth or clothes (*dressed in s.*); *s. admiral*, kind of butterfly; *s. fever*, infectious fever with s. rash, (joc.) tendency to fall in love with soldiers; *s.-grain*, scale-insect from which red dye is made in Russia & Turkey; *s. hat*, cardinal's, (allus.) cardinalate; *s. rash*, roseola; *s. runner*, s.-flowered trailing bean-plant; *s. woman, whore*, pagan

Rome, papal Rome, or the worldly spirit (acc. to interpretation put on *Rev.* xvii). [f. OF *escarlate* f. Pers. *saqalat* s. cloth (also *saqlatun*, whence ME *ciclatoun*)]

scă·roid (*or* skār-), a. & n. (Fish) of scarus genus, resembling scarus. [-OID]

scarp, n., & v.t. Inner wall or slope (cf. COUNTERSCARP) of ditch in fortification; any steep slope; (vb) make (slope) perpendicular or steep, provide (ditch) with steep s. & counters., (p.p. of, hillside &c.) steep, precipitous. [f. It. *scarpa*]

scār·us, n. Kinds of bright-hued fish with parrotlike beak (also *parrotfish*) of wrasse family. [L, f. Gk *skaros*]

scāthe (-dh), v.t., & n. Injure esp. by blasting or withering up (now rare exc. in part. used by exag. of severe speech, as *scathing sarcasm, ridicule, remarks*, whence **sca·thing**LY² adv.), (in neg. context) do the least harm to (*shall not be scathed*; esp. *unscathed*); (n.; rare, & usu. in neg. context) harm, injury, (*without, guard from, s.*), whence **sca·the**LESS a. (usu. pred.). [f. ON *skathe* n., *skatha* vb, cf. OE *sceathan*, G & Du. *schaden*; cogn. w. Gk *askēthēs* unharmed, in which *a-* = A-(7)]

scato·logy, n. Study of coprolites. [Gk *skōr skatos* dung, -LOGY]

scato·phagous, a. Feeding on dung. [prec., Gk *-phagos* -eating]

sca·tter, v.t. & i. Throw here & there (*s. seed*), strew (*s. gravel on road, road with gravel*), sprinkle; disperse (t. & i.), turn (t. & i.) in dispersed flight, rout, be routed; dissipate (cloud, hopes); diffuse (light); (of gun) send charge, send (charge), in spreading manner; (p.p.) not situated together, wide apart, sporadic, (*scattered hamlets, garrisons, instances*); *s.-brain*, heedless person; *s.-brained*, heedless, desultory. Hence **sca·ttering**LY² adv. [ME, etym. dub.]

scaup(-duck), n. Kinds of duck named from frequenting mussel-scaups or beds of mussels exposed at low tide. [var. of SCALP]

scau·per, var. of SCALPER.

scaur. See SCAR².

scă·venger, n., & v.i. Person employed to keep streets clean by carrying away refuse; animal feeding on carrion (esp. *s.-beetle, -crab*), writer &c. delighting in filthy subjects; hence **sca·venge** (by back formation) v.t. & i., **sca·veng**ERY (2, 5) n. (Vb) be, act as, s. [earlier *scavager* (cf. *messenger, passenger*) inspector of imports (AF *scawage* inspection f. ONF *escauwer* inspect f. Teut. cf. SHOW + -AGE, -ER¹)]

scā·zon, n. Greek & Latin iambic, ending with ⏑ – – ⏓ instead of ⏓ – ⏑ ⏓, used in short poems, choliamb; other metres of limping character. [f. Gk *skazōn* (*skazō* limp)]

scena (shā·nah), n. (mus.). Scene or portion of opera; elaborate dramatic solo usu. including recitative. [It.]

scenar·io (shānar-), n. (Table of) scene-distribution, appearances of characters, &c., in dramatic work, skeleton libretto. [It.]

scend. See SEND².

scene (sēn), n. Stage of theatre (archaic; still in fig. use *quit the s.*, esp. = die), place on which something is exhibited as on the stage (*this world is a s. of strife*); place in which events set forth in drama or tale are supposed to occur, locality of event, (*the s. is laid in India*; *the s. of the disaster was the North Sea*); portion of a play during which action is continuous or (esp. of French plays) in which no intermediate entries or exits occur, subdivision (or rarely the whole) of an act, (*in the third s. of Act II*; *Act II. s.* III. *l. 220*; *the famous duel s.*; CARPENTER-*s.*), (transf.) description with more or less abrupt beginning & end of an incident or part of person's life &c. (*ss. of clerical life, from a gold-field*, &c.), actual incident that might occasion such description (*distressing ss. occurred*), agitated colloquy esp. with display of temper (*now don't make a s.*); any of the pieces of painted canvas, woodwork, &c., used to help in representing s. of action on stage, or whole of these together (*behind the ss.*, among the stage machinery or the actors off the stage, usu. fig. = having information not accessible to the public; CARPENTER-*s.*; *ss. painted by* —; *set s.*, made up of many parts fitted together; DROP-SCENE), (transf.) landscape or view spread before spectator like s. in theatre (*a silvan, desolate, s.*; *a s. of destruction*; *change of s.*, variety of surroundings esp. secured by travel); *s.-dock*, space near stage where ss. are stored; *s.-painter, -ting*, of theatre ss.; *s.-shifter*, person helping to change ss. in theatre. [f. F *scène* f. L f. Gk *skēnē* tent, stage]

sce·nery, n. Accessories used in theatre to make stage resemble supposed scene of action; spectacles presented by natural features of a district (*the s. is imposing, tame*). [earlier *scenary* f. It. *scenario* f. L *scenarius* (prec., -ARY¹) of the stage, assim. to -ERY]

scē·nic, a. Of, on, the stage (*s. performances*); of the nature of a show, picturesque in grouping; (of picture &c.) telling a tale, crystallizing an incident; (of emotion &c.) dramatic, affected, put on. Hence **sce·ni**CALLY adv. [f. F *scénique* f. L f. Gk *skēnikos* (SCENE, -IC)]

sceno·graphy, n. Drawing or painting in perspective (esp. of representing building not in ground-plan or elevation, but as spectator sees it). So **sce·no**GRAPH(1), **sceno·**GRAPHER, nn., **sceno**GRA·PHIC a., **scenogra·phi**CALLY adv. [f. L f. Gk *skēnographia* (SCENE, -GRAPHY)]

scent (sĕ-), v.t. & i., & n. Discern by smell (*s. game* &c.), (fig.) begin to suspect presence or existence of (*s. treachery, a job*); *s. out,* discover by smelling about or search; make fragrant or rank (*rose, carrion, scents the air*), apply perfume to (handkerchief &c.; *scented dames, cigarettes*); exercise sense of smell, apply this to, (*goes scenting about; lifts its head & scents the air*). (N.) odour, esp. of agreeable kind, proceeding from or belonging to something (*the s. of hay*), whence **sce·nt**LESS a.; (Hunt.) trail perceptible to hounds' sense of smell left by animal (often fig.; *follow up, lose, recover,* &c., *the s.,* lit., & of investigation; *on the s.,* having clue; *put off the s.,* deceive by false indications; COLD[1], HOT[1], *s.*), paper strewn by paperchase hares (*false s.,* laid to deceive about course, also fig.); power of detecting or distinguishing smells or of discovering presence of something, flair, (*some dogs have practically no s.; keen-scented; has a wonderful s. for snobbery, young talent,* &c.); liquid perfume distilled from flowers &c.; *s.-bag,* pouch containing special odoriferous substance in some animals, also bag of aniseed &c. as substitute for fox in hunting; *s.-bottle,* for perfume; *s.-gland,* secreting musk, civet, &c.; *s.-organ,* s.-bag or s.-gland; hence **(-)sce·nt**ED[2] a. (*s. caper,* kind of tea; *s. fern,* kind smelling like citron). [n. f. vb, earlier *sent,* f. F *sentir* perceive, smell, f. L *sentire* perceive]

sce·psis (sk-, sĕ-), **sk-,** n. Philosophic doubt, sceptical philosophy. [f. Gk *skepsis* inquiry (*skeptomai* examine)]

sce·ptic (sk-, sĕ-), **sk-,** n. Ancient or modern holder of PYRRHONISM; person who doubts truth of the Christian or of all religious doctrines, agnostic, (pop.) atheist; person of sceptical habit of mind, or unconvinced of truth of particular fact or theory, or who takes cynical views. So **sce·ptic**ISM(3) n. [ult. f. Gk *skeptikos* (prec., -IC)]

sce·ptical (sk-, sĕ-), **sk-,** a. Inclined to suspense of judgement, given to questioning truth of facts & soundness of inferences, critical, incredulous; accepting PYRRHONISM, denying possibility of knowledge; holding, designed to support, inspired by, the ideas of SCEPTICS. Hence **sce·ptical**LY[2] adv. [-AL]

sceptre (sĕ·pter), n. Staff borne as symbol of personal sovereignty; royal or imperial authority. Hence **sce·ptr**ED[2] (-terd), **sce·ptre**LESS, aa. [OF, f. L f. Gk *skēptron* (*skēptō* prop)]

sche·dule (shĕ-; U.S. skĕ-), n., & v.t. Tabulated statement of details, inventory, list, &c., esp. as appendix or annexe to principal document; *s. time,* that stated in time-table; (vb) make s. of, include in s. [ME & OF *cedule* f. LL *scedula* (L *sceda* papyrus-strip, -ULE)]

scheik. =SHEIKH.

schē·ma (sk-), n. (pl. *-ta*). Synopsis, outline, diagram; (Log.) syllogistic figure; (Gram., Rhet.) figure of speech; (Kantian Philos.) general type, essential form, conception of what is common to all members of a class. So **schemă·tic** a., **schema·tic**ALLY adv. [med. L, f. Gk *skhēma -atos* shape (*ekhō, skh-,* hold, be)]

scheme (sk-), n., & v.i. & t. Systematic arrangement proposed or in operation (*s. of colour,* principle on which colours have been chosen & grouped in picture &c.), table of classification or of appointed times, outline, syllabus; plan for doing something; artful or underhand design. (Vb) make plans, plan esp. in secret or underhand way (*to* do, *for,* or abs.), intrigue, whence **sche·m**ER[1] n., **sche·m**ING[2] a.; plan to bring about. [f. L SCHEMA]

scherza·ndo (skārts-), mus. direction. In playful manner. [It.]

scherzo (skār·tsō), n. Light playful passage or movement usu. following slow one in sonata or symphony. [It., f. Teut. (G *scherz* jest)]

Schieda·m (skĭd-), n. Holland gin. [place]

schi·pperkĕ (sk-, sh-,), n. Kind of lapdog. [Du.]

schism (sĭ·zm), n. Division of a community into factions (rare in gen. sense), esp. separation of a Church into two Churches or secession of part of a Church owing to difference of opinion on doctrine or discipline; offence of causing or promoting such separation. [f. OF *scisme* f. eccl. L f. Gk *skhisma -atos* (*skhizō* split, -M)]

schismă·tic a. & n., **-ical** a. Tending or inclined to, guilty of, schism; hence **schisma·tical**LY[2] adv. (N.) holder of s. opinions, member of s. faction or seceded branch of a Church. [f. OF *scismatique* f. eccl. L f. Gk *skhismatikos* (prec., -IC), -AL]

schist (sh-), n. Kinds of foliated rock presenting layers of different minerals & splitting in thin irregular plates. Hence **schi·st**OSE[1] a. [f. F *schiste* f. L f. Gk *skhistos* split (SCHISM)]

schīza·nthus (sk-), n. Kinds of flowering annual with handsome white, violet, or crimson flowers & much-divided leaves. [Gk *skhizō* split, *anthos* flower]

schī·zomȳce·te, n. Any of the *Schizomycetae,* a class of minute often single-cell vegetable organisms between algae & fungi including bacilli, bacteria, microbes, &c. [Gk *skhizō* split, *mukēs -ētos* mushroom]

schme·lze (-tse), n. Kinds of coloured glass, or esp. Bohemian glass prepared to receive colour, for decorative use. [f. G *schmelz* enamel, cf SMELT[1], SMALT]

schnap(p)s, n. A spirit resembling Holland gin. [G]

schnŏ'rrer (shn-), n. Jewish beggar. [Yiddish, f. G dial. *schnurrer* beggar]

scho'lar (sk-), n. Schoolboy, schoolgirl, (archaic or vulg.); person's disciple (rhet.); person who learns (*proved an apt, dull, s.*; *at 90 he was still a s.*); learned person, person versed in literature esp. that of ancient Greece & Rome, (*a s. & a gentleman*, person of good education & breeding), whence **scho'lar**LY[1] a., **scho'lar**SHIP(3) n.; (Univv., Pub. Schh.) undergraduate or boy admitted to foundation usu. after competitive examination & receiving education gratis or for reduced fees (RHODES *s.*), whence **scho'lar**SHIP(1) n. [AF *escoler* (SCHOOL, -ER[1]) refash. on LL *scholaris* (-AR[1])]

schola'stic, a. & n. Of universities, schools, schooling, dons, or schoolmasters, educational, academic, pedantic, formal, (*a. s. education, post*; *s. attire, manners, precision, life*; *s. agent*, finding posts for teachers); (as) of the SCHOOL[1]men, dealing in logical subtleties, (*s. theology*, much concerned with precise definition of & deduction from dogma); hence or cogn. **schola'sti**CALLY adv., **schola'stici**SM (2, 3) n. (N.) SCHOOLman; modern theologian of s. tendencies; Jesuit between novitiate & priesthood. [f. L f. Gk *skholastikos* (*skholazō* be at leisure, see SCHOOL, -IC)]

schō'liast, n. Commentator, esp. ancient grammarian who wrote scholia on the classics. Hence **scholia'sti**C a. [f. LL f. Gk *skholiastēs* (*skholiazō* write scholia (foll.)]

schō'lium, n. (pl. *-ia*). Marginal note, explanatory comment, esp. one by ancient grammarian on passage in classical author. [f. med. L f. Gk *skholion* (*skholē* see foll.)]

school[1] (sk-), n., & v.t. Institution for educating children or giving instruction usu. of more elementary or more technical kind than that given at universities (BOARD[1], BOARDING, DAY, GRAMMAR, MIXED, NIGHT, NORMAL, PRIMARY, PRIVATE, PUBLIC, RAGGED, SECONDARY, SUNDAY, *s.*; *national s.*, one founded by the National Society started 1811 to promote education of the poor; *continuation s.*, at which those who have left esp. primary s. for an occupation can have further teaching in leisure time; *evening-s.*, = night-s.; *free s.*, open without fees; *high s.*, secondary s., or chief s. of a town &c.; *technical s.*, giving TECHNICAL education; *keep a s.*, manage private s.), buildings of such institution, any of its rooms used for teaching in (*the fifth-form, chemistry, s.*), its pupils (*the whole s. knows*), time during which teaching is done (*there will be no s. today*; *go to s.*, attend lesson); being educated in a s. (*go to, leave, s.*, begin, cease, this; *go to s. to* transf., imitate or learn from), (fig.) circumstances or occupation serving to discipline or instruct (*in the s. of adversity*; *learnt his generalship in a severe s.*; *the duel is a good s. of manners*); medieval lecture-room (*the ss.*, medieval universities & their professors & teaching & disputations; *the theology of the ss.*; *s. doctors*, schoolmen), any of the branches of study with separate examinations at university (*the history, mathematical, Greats, s.*), hall in which university examinations are held, (pl.) such examination (*in the ss.*, undergoing this; *in for his ss.*, of candidate); disciples or imitators or followers of philosopher, artist, &c., band or succession of persons devoted to some cause or principle or agreeing in typical characteristics, (*left no s. behind him*: *s. of Epicurus, Raphael, &c.*; *Bolognese, Venetian, Roman, British, &c., s.*, of painters; *lake, romantic, &c., s.*, of literature; *peripatetic, Hegelian, &c., s.*, of philosophy; *laissez-faire, blue-water, &c., s.*, of politics, strategy; *Tübingen s.*, of rationalistic theological criticism; *a gentleman of the old s.*, according to the older acceptation of the word); (Mus.) manual of (*—'s violin s., s. of counterpoint*); *s.-board*, local education authority responsible (1870–1902) for providing BOARD[1]*-ss.*; *s.-book*, for use in ss.; *schoolboy*, boy at s. (often attrib., as *s.-b. slang, mischief, spirits*); *s.-dame*, keeper of old-fashioned DAME-S.; *s.-days*, time of being at s. esp. as looked back upon; *s. divine*, scholastic theologian, so *s. divinity*; *s. fee(s)*, amount periodically paid by pupil's parent &c.; *schoo'lfellow*, member past or present of same s.; *schoo'lgirl* (as *s.-boy*); *schoo'lhouse*, building of esp. village s.; *school house*, headmaster's or central boarding-house at public s.; *s.-inspector*, reporting on efficiency of ss. provided at public expense; *s.-ma'am, -marm* colloq., U.-S. s.-mistress; *schoo'lman*, teacher in medieval European university, theologian dealing with religious doctrines by rules of Aristotelian logic; *schoo'lmaster*, head or assistant male teacher in s., pedagogue; *s.-mate*, contemporary at same s.; *s. miss*, inexperienced or bashful girl; *schoo'lmistress* (as *s.-master*); *s.pence*, money brought weekly by elementary-s. child as fee; *schoo'lroom*, used for lessons in s. or private house; *s.-ship*, training-ship; *s.-teacher*, master or mistress esp. in elementary s.; *s.-time*, lesson-time at s. or home, also = s.-days. (Vb) send to s., provide for education of, (rare), whence (in common use) **schoo'**LING[1] n.; discipline, bring under control, deliberately train or accustom *to*, induce to follow advice, (*must s. his temper*; *s. oneself to patience, to take an interest in*; *will not be schooled*). [OE *scōl* f. L *schola* school f. Gk *skholē* leisure, philosophy, lecture-place]

school[2] (sk-), n., & v.i. Shoal of or *of* fish; *s.-fish*, kinds that s., esp. the menhaden; (vb) form ss. [Du., cf. SHOAL[2]]

schoo·lable, a. Liable by age &c. to compulsory education. [-ABLE]

schoo·ner (sk-), n. Fore-&-aft-rigged vessel with two or more masts. [perh. f. an alleged Sc. & New-England *scun, scoon,* skim or skip; orig. (*c.* 1713) *scooner,* name given by first designer, now *sch-* by assim. to its derivative Du. *schooner*]

schorl (sh-), n. Black tourmaline. [f. G *schörl*]

schotti·sche (sh-, -ēsh), n. Kind of polka; music for it. [G (*-sch*), = *Scottish*]

sciă·graphy (sī-), **ski-,** n. Art of shading in drawing &c.; photography by Röntgen rays (usu. *sk-*); (Arch.; also & usu. *-graph*) vertical section showing interior of house &c.; (Astron.) finding of time by shadows as in sundial. So **sci·agram** n., Röntgen-ray picture, **sciagramma·tic** a., **-ically** adv., **sci·**AGRAPH(1, 2, 3) n. & v.t., **scia·**GRAPHER n., **scia**GRA·PHIC a., **sciagra·phi**CALLY adv. [f. Gk *skiagraphia* (*skia* shade, -GRAPHY)]

sciă·machy (sī-, -kĭ), **scio-,** n. Fighting with shadows, imaginary or futile combat. [f. Gk *skiamakhia* (prec., *-makhos* -fighting f. *makhomai* fight, -IA[1])]

sciă·tic (sī-), a. Of the hip (*s. nerve, artery,* &c.); of, affecting, the s. nerve; suffering from or liable to sciatica. Hence **scia·tic**ALLY adv. [f. F *sciatique* f. LL *sciaticus* f. L f. Gk *iskhiadikos* subject to sciatica (*iskhias -ados* loin-pain f. *iskhion* socket of thigh-bone)]

scia·tica, n. Neuralgia of hip & thigh, pain in sciatic nerve. [med. L, fem. of LL as prec.]

sci·ence (sī-), n. Knowledge (archaic), whence (in mod. use) **scie·nt**IAL a., **scie·ntial**LY[2] adv.; systematic & formulated knowledge (*moral, political, natural,* &c., *s.,* such knowledge in reference to these subjects), pursuit of this or principles regulating such pursuit (*man of s.*); (also *natural s.*) the physical or natural ss. collectively (*s. now shares the curriculum with literature, history, & mathematics*); (with *a* & pl.) branch of knowledge, organized body of the knowledge that has been accumulated on a subject, (*the s. of optics, ethics, philology*; *exact s.,* admitting of quantitative treatment; *pure s.,* one depending on deductions from self-evident truths, as mathematics, logic; *natural, physical, s.,* one dealing with material phenomena & based mainly on observation, experiment, & induction, as chemistry, biology, whence esp. **sci·en**TIST, **sci·ent**ISM, nn.; *the dismal s.,* political economy); expert's skill as opp. strength or natural ability, esp. in pugilism or other fighting. [F, f. L *scientia* (*scire* know, -ENCE)]

scie·nter, adv. (legal). Wittingly. [L (prec., -ENT, *-er* adv. term.)]

scienti·fic, a. (Of investigation &c.) according to rules laid down in science for testing soundness of conclusions, systematic, accurate; of, used or engaged in, esp. natural science (*s. instruments, books, terminology, men*); (of act or agent) assisted by expert knowledge (*a s. boxer, game*; *s. cruelty*). Hence **scienti·fi**CALLY adv. [f. LL *scientificus,* see SCIENCE, -FIC)]

sci·licet (sī-), adv. (abbr. *sc., scil.*). To wit, that is to say, namely, (introducing word to be supplied or explanation of ambiguous one). [L, = *scire licet* it is allowed to know]

sci·metar (sĭ-), n. Oriental curved sword usu. broadening towards point. [f. Rom. (It. *scimitarra,* F *cimeterre*) perh. f. Pers. *shamshir*]

scinti·lla (sĭ-), n. Spark, atom, (esp. *not a s. of evidence* &c.). [L]

sci·ntillate, v.i. Sparkle, twinkle, emit sparks. So **sci·ntill**ANT a., **scintill**A·TION n. [f. L *scintillare* (prec.), -ATE[3]]

sci·olist (sī-), n. Superficial pretender to knowledge, smatterer. Hence or cogn. **sci·ol**ISM(2) n., **scioli·st**IC a. [f. LL *sciolus* smatterer (*scire* know), -IST]

scio·lto (shŏ-), mus. direction. In free manner, according to taste; staccato. [It.]

sciomachy. See SCIAMACHY.

sci·on (sī-), n. Shoot of plant, esp. one cut for grafting or planting; descendant young member of (esp. noble) family. [F (earlier also *cion*), etym. dub.]

Sci·ōt(e) (sī-), a. & n. (Inhabitant) of Scio, the ancient Chios. [-OT[2]]

scir·e fă·ciăs (sīrī, -shĭ-), n. Writ to enforce or annul judgement, patent, &c. [L, = let (party) know]

scirocco. See SIROCCO.

sci·rrhus (sĭ-, skĭ-), n. Hard tumour as early stage of cancer. Hence or cogn. **sci·rrh**OID, **sci·rrh**OUS, aa., **scirrhŏ·**SITY n. [LL, f. Gk *skir(r)os* (*skiros* hard)]

sci·ssel (sĭ-), n. Waste clippings of metal or remainder of metal plate from which disks have been punched in coining. [f. F *cisaille* f. *ciseler* CHISEL, -AL(2)]

sci·ssile (sĭ-), a. Able to be cut. [f. L *scissilis* (*scindere sciss-* cut, -IL)]

scission (sĭ·shn), n. Cutting, being cut, division, split. [F, f. LL *scissionem* (prec., -ION)]

sci·ssor, v.t. Cut (*off, up, into,* &c.) with scissors; clip out or *out* (cutting from book &c.), whence **sci·ssor**ING[1](2) n. [f. foll.]

sci·ssors (sĭz-), n. pl. Instrument for cutting fabrics, paring nails, &c., made of two blades with handles for thumb & one finger or the fingers & so pivoted that their cutting edges work by leverage against each other (often *pair of s.*; *I want a pair of, some, s.*; *where are my s.?*; *buttonhole s.,* with gaps in blades near pivot so that cutting begins inside edge of cloth; *lamp, nail, -s.,* of special shapes for trimming wicks, nails; *s. & paste,* compiling of books out of cuttings from others); *scissor-bill*, the bird SKIMMER; *scissor-bird* or *-tail*, kinds of bird with long forked tail esp. fork-tailed fly-catcher; *scissor-tooth*, tooth in carnivora acting like s. against one in other jaw. Hence **sci·ssor**WISE adv. [ME *sisours* f. OF *cisoires* f. L *cisorium* (as CHISEL, -ORY)]

sciū̆r·ine (sĭ-), a. Of the squirrel tribe; squirrel-like. So **sciur·**OID a. [L f. Gk *skiouros* squirrel (*skia* shade, *oura* tail), -INE¹]

Sclav, Sclavonic, &c. See **Slav** &c.

sclē̆r·a, n. =SCLEROTIC n. (anat.). Hence **sclē̆rī·**TIS, **sclero·**TOMY, nn. [f. fem. of Gk *sklēros* hard]

sclē̆rī·asis, n. (path.). Hardening of tissue. [Gk (*sk*-), = induration of eyelid (foll., -ASIS)]

sclē̆r(o)-, comb. form of Gk *sklēros* hard: *sclere·nchyma*, hard tissue of coral, tissue forming hard parts of plants such as nutshell or seed-coat; *-der·m(at)ous*, with hard outer skin (of reptiles, fish, &c.); *-gen*, hard matter deposited on inner surface of plant-cells, e.g. that lining walnut shell; *-mē·ninx*, DURA MATER; *-ske·leton*, hard parts resulting from ossification of tendons as in turkey's leg &c.; *sclero·steous*, of the nature of sclero-skeleton.

sclē̆r·oid, a. (bot., zool.). Of hard texture. [f. Gk *sklēroeidēs* (prec., -OID)]

sclē̆ro·ma, sclē̆ro·sis, nn. (pl. *-mata, -sēs*). Morbid hardening of tissue; (Bot.; *-sis*) hardening of cell-wall by SCLEROgen. Hence **scler·os**ED² a. [Gk (*sk*-), see SCLERO-, -M, -OSIS]

sclē̆rŏ·tic, a. & n. Of, with, sclerosis; of the s. (N.) membrane coating eye round iris, white of eye; hence **scleroti·**TIS n. [SCLERO-, -OTIC]

sclē̆r·ous, a. (path., anat., bot.). Indurated, bony. [Gk *sklēros* hard, -OUS]

scobs, n. Sawdust, shavings, filings, dross. So **scō·bi**FORM a. (bot., of seeds). [L]

scoff, n., & v.i. Mocking words, taunt, gibe; object of ridicule, laughing-stock. (Vb) speak derisively esp. of religion or object of respect; aim ss. or mockery *at*; hence **sco·ff**ER¹ n., **sco·ffing**LY² adv. [vb f. n., ME *scof*, cf. ON *skop*]

scōld, v.i. & t., & n. Find fault noisily, rail; rate, rebuke, (chiefly of parent, employer, speaking to child, servant), whence **sco·ld**ING¹(1) n. (N.) railing or nagging woman. [vb f. n., f. ON *skáld* SCALD²]

scō·lex, n. (pl. *-ē·cēs*). Tape-worm in embryonic stage. [f. Gk *skōlēx* worm]

scŏlio·sis, n. Lateral curvature of spine. Hence **scolio·**TIC a. [Gk (*sk*-), f. *skolioō* make crooked (*skolios*), -OSIS]

scollop. See SCALLOP.

scŏlopa·ceous, scolŏ·pacine, scolŏ·pacoid, aa. Of, like, the snipes. [Gk *skolopax -akos* perh. = woodcock, -ACEOUS, -INE¹, -OID]

scolope·ndrine, a. Of, like, related to, centipede(s). [L f. Gk *skolopendra* millepede, -INE¹]

scolope·ndrium, n. Kinds of fern, hart's-tongue &c. [L, f. Gk *skolopendrion* (prec.)]

sco·mber, n. Mackerel or kinds of fish allied to it. Hence **sco·mbr**ID³(1) n., **sco·mbr**OID a. & n. [L, f. Gk *skombros*]

scon. See SCONE.

sconce¹, n. Flat candlestick with handle; bracket candlestick to hang on wall. [earlier sense, lantern; f. OF *esconse* dark lantern f. med. L *sconsa* f. L *absconsa* var. of ABSCONDita fem. p.p.]

sconce², n. (Old joc. term for) head, crown of head (*a crack on the s.*). [perh. a use of prec. or foll.]

sconce³, n. Small fort or earthwork, usu. covering a ford, pass, &c.; (archaic) shelter, screen; (north.) fixed slab seat by fireplace. [f. Du. *schans*, etym. dub.]

sconce⁴, v.t., & n. (At Oxford) inflict forfeit of beer &c. for offence against table etiquette upon (member of company or his offence; *Jones was, Latin quotations are, sconced*); (hist., of university officials &c.) fine for breach of discipline (*Vice-chancellor sconced all that were without their hoods*); (n.) the forfeit. [?]

scŏn(e), n. Soft cake of barley-meal or wheat-flour of size for single portion & usu. triangular cooked on griddle. [perh. f. MDu. *schoon*(*brot*) fine (bread)]

scoop, n., & v.t. Short-handled deep shovel for taking up & transferring such things as grain, sugar, coal, specie; large long-handled ladle-shaped dipping-vessel for liquids; gouge-like instrument e.g. for surgical use or for helping cheese; coal-scuttle; motion as of, act of, scooping (*with a, at one, s.*), (slang) large profit made quickly or by anticipating competitors; *s.-net*, formed for sweeping river-bottom, also hand-net for catching bait; *s.-wheel*, with buckets on circumference raising water for irrigation &c. (Vb) lift (usu. *up*), hollow (usu. *out*), (as) with s.; (slang) secure (large profit &c.) by sudden action or stroke of luck. [cf. Du. *schoep* bucket & *schop* shovel, G *schöpfen* draw (water); cogn. w. SHOVE]

scoo·per, n. In vbl senses; esp.: engraver's tool; kind of avocet. [-ER¹]

scoot, v.i. (slang). Run, dart, make off. Hence **scoo·t**ER¹(2) n., child's toy, a footboard with two tandem wheels on which one foot is set while the other propels & a long handle (*motor scooter*, similar machine propelled by motor). [earlier *scout* in naut. use; reimported as *scoot* f. U.S.]

scō·pa, scŏ·pula, nn. (entom.; pl.-*ae*). Small brushlike tuft of hairs esp. on bees' legs. Hence **sco·**PATE², **sco·pul**ATE², **sco·pi**FORM, **sco·puli**FORM, **scopi·**FEROUS, aa. [*scopa* sing. of L *scopae*, = twigs, broom, *-la* mod. sing. of L *scopulae* pl.]

scope, n. End aimed at, purpose, intention, (now rare); outlook, purview, sweep or reach or sphere of observation or action, tether, extent to which it is permissible or possible to range, opportunity, outlet, vent, (*mind, undertaking, of wide s.*; *is beyond my s.*; *gives no, ample, s. for expatiating, to ability*; *seeks s. for his energies*); (Naut.) length of cable out when ship rides at anchor. [earlier sense *target* (perh. thr. It. *scopo*) f. Gk *skopos* mark to shoot at, watcher, (*skeptomai* look at, cf. L *specere*)]

-scope, suf. repr. Gk *skopos* watcher (prec.). *Horoscope* is f. Gk *hōroskopos* (watcher of) a nativity. *Telescope* is f. Gk *tēleskopos* far-seeing. In wds of mod. formation the suf. usu. has the sense *instrument for observing or showing*, as *stetho-, gyro-, laryngo-*, and the hybrid *muto-*. Hence *-scŏ·pic*, adj. suf., pertaining to the -scope, somet. w. extended meaning also, as in TELESCOPIC, MICROSCOPIC; *-scopy*, n. suf., use of or examination by the -scope, as *laryngoscopy*.

scorbū·tic, a. & n. Of, like, (person) affected with, scurvy. Hence **scorbu·tic**ALLY adv. [f. F *scorbut* scurvy prob. f. MLG *schorbûk* (*schoren* break, *bûk* belly) + -IC]

scorch, v.t. & i., & n. Burn surface of with flame or heat-rays so as to discolour or injure or pain, affect with sensation of burning (*a wit that scorches*), whence **scor·ch**ING² a., **scor·ching**LY² adv.; become discoloured &c. with heat; (of motorist or cyclist; slang) go at utmost speed (n., spell of such driving or riding). [earlier *scorken* perh. f. ON *skorpna* be shrivelled]

scor·cher, n. In vbl senses; also, (slang) fine specimen of its kind. [-ER¹]

score, n., & v.t. & i. Notch cut or line cut or scratched or drawn (*rock covered with ss. or striations*; *the ss. of the whip showed on his back*; *made a s. in the tally*; *lightning had made ss. in the mountain side*), mark showing starting-point in race or standing-place in shooting-match (now rare; hence perh. *go off at s.*, start off vigorously esp. to discourse on pet subject), (Naut.) groove in block or dead-eye to hold strap; running account kept by ss. against customer's name esp. for drink in old inns, reckoning esp. for entertainment, (*pay* one's *s.*, settle reckoning; *death pays all ss.*; *pay off old ss.* fig., pay person out for past offence; so *quit ss. with*); number of points made by player or side in some games, register of items of this, (*make a good s.*; *what is the s. now?*; *s.-book, -card, -sheet*, prepared for entering esp. cricket-s. in; *keep s.*, register it as it is made); (Mus.) copy of a composition on set of staves braced & barred together (named from bar drawn through all staves; *full s.*, with separate staff for each part; *compressed, close, short, s.* in vocal music, with treble & alto on one staff, tenor & bass on another; *in s.*, with parts arranged below each other & corresponding); twenty, set of twenty, (for use of *s.*, *ss.*, see DOZEN; *three s. & ten*, phr. for normal length of human life; *ss. of people*, great numbers); category, head, (*rejected on the s. of absurdity*, as being absurd; *you may be easy on that s.*, so far as that matter is concerned); (slang) remark or act by which person scores off another (*given to making cheap ss.*), piece of good fortune (*what a s.!*). (Vb) mark with notches or incisions or lines, slash, furrow, make (line &c.) with something that marks, (*s. out words*, draw line through them; *s. under*, underline); mark *up* in inn-score, enter (item of debt *against* or *to* customer; often *up*), (fig.) mentally record (offence *against* or *to* offender), record (point in cricket &c. s.; abs., keep the s., whence **scor·**ER¹ n.); win & be credited with (*has scored a success, a century at cricket*), make points in game (*failed to s.*), secure an advantage or have good luck (*that is where he scores*; *we shall s. by it*); *s. off* slang, worst in argument or repartee, inflict some humiliation on; (Mus.) orchestrate, whence **scor·**ING¹(6) n., arrange *for* another instrument, write out in s. [OE *scoru* twenty f. ON *skor* twenty, notch; cogn. w. SHEAR; sense *twenty* perh. from twentieth notch's larger size]

scor·ia, n. (pl. *-ae*). Cellular lava or fragments of it. Hence **scori**A·CEOUS a. [L, f. Gk *skōria* refuse (*skōr* dung)]

scor·ify̆, v.t. Reduce to dross, assay (precious metal) by scorifying a portion of its ore fused with lead & borax. Hence **scori**FICA·TION, **scor·ifi**ER¹(2), nn. [prec., -FY]

scorn, n., & v.t. Disdain, contempt, derision, (*think s. of*, despise; LAUGH *to s.*), whence **scor·n**FUL a., **scor·nful**LY² adv., **scor·nful**NESS n.; object of contempt, (usu. *a s. to*, *the s. of*, persons &c.). (Vb) hold in contempt, consider beneath notice, abstain from or refuse *to* do as unworthy (*scorns lying, a lie, to lie*); hence **scor·n**ER¹ n. (archaic exc. w. *of*). [ME *skarn* n., *scarne* vb, f. OF *escarn*(*ir*) f. Teut., cf. Du. *scherne*(*n*) ridicule n. & v.]

Scor·pio, n. Zodiacal constellation & eighth sign of zodiac, the Scorpion. [L, also *scorpius* f. Gk *skorpios* scorpion, *skorpiōn* ballista]

scor·pioid, n. & a. (bot.). (Inflorescence) curled up at end like scorpion's tail & uncurling as flowers develop. [f. Gk *skorpioeidēs* (prec., -OID)]

scor·pion, n. Arachnid with lobster-like

claws & jointed tail that can be bent over to inflict poisoned sting on prey held in claws, falsely reputed to sting itself to death if encircled with fire & to contain a substance serving as antidote for its poison; (bibl.; prob.) whip armed with metal points (1 *Kings* xii. 11); =SCORPIO; kind of ballista; *s.-broom*, kind of genista; *s.-fish*, kind with spines on head & fins; *s.-plant*, Javan orchid with creamy white flower, also s.-broom; *s.-shell*, kind of shell-fish with long spines fringing outer lip of aperture; *s.-thorn*, s.-broom. [F, f. L *scorpionem* SCORPIO]

scorzonē·ra, n. Black salsify or Viper's-grass, a plant with parsnip-like root used as vegetable. [It., prob. f. *scorzone* adder 'because it doeth heale the bytinges of this beast']

scot[1], n. (hist.). Payment corresponding to modern tax, rate, or other assessed contribution (*pay s. & lot*, share pecuniary burdens of borough &c.); *s.-free* (in mod. use), not having to pay (rare), (usu.) unharmed, unpunished, safe, (esp. *go s.-f.*). [f. OF *escot* f. ON *skot* shot, contribution, cf. OE *sceot* whence SHOT[3]]

Scot[2], n. (Pl.) Gaelic tribe that migrated from Ireland to Scotland about 6th c. (often PICTS *& Ss.*); native of Scotland. [OE *Scottas* pl., f. LL *Scottus*]

Scotch[1], a. & n. Of Scotland or its inhabitants, in the dialect(s) of English spoken in Lowlands of Scotland, (the S. themselves usu. prefer the form *Scottish* also used by the English esp. in dignified style or context, or *Scots* rare in Engl. use exc. in compliment to S. hearers; *the S.*, S. people or nation; *S.* FIR, KALE, MIST; POUND *Scots*; *S. broth*, soup or liquid stew with pearl barley and vegetables; *S. catch* or *snap* in music, shortening of first of two tones played to same beat; *S. cap*, of shapes worn with Highland costume, Glengarry, Tam-o'-Shanter, &c.; *S. whisky*, kind with smoky flavour orig. made in Scotland; *S. pebble*, kinds of agate & jasper, cairngorm, &c.; *S. collops*, steak & onions; *S. woodcock*, eggs on anchovy toast; *S.-&-English*, prisoners' base); *Scotchman,-woman, Scotsman* (Sc.), *Scotswoman* (Sc.), natives of Scotland (*flying Scotchman*, a northern express train). (N.) the S. dialect of English (Sc. *Scots*; also *Lowland S.*; BROAD *S.*); S. whisky (*S. & soda*, glass of this with soda-water). [contr. of SCOTTISH]

scotch[2], v.t., & n., (archaic). Make incisions in, score, wound without killing, slightly disable, (esp. 'We have scotch'd the snake, not killed it', see *Macbeth* III. ii. 13); (n.) slash, mark on ground for HOP[2]-S. [?]

scotch[3], n., & v.t. Wedge or block placed before wheel &c. to prevent motion downhill; (vb) hold up (wheel, barrel) with s. [perh. var. of *scatch* stilt, see SKATE[2]]

sco·ter, n. Large sea-duck. [?]

scō·tia (-sha), n. Concave moulding esp. in base of column. [L f. Gk *skotia* darkness (SCOTO-) w. ref. to shadow produced]

Scō·tism, n. (hist.). Metaphysical doctrines of Duns Scotus (d. 1308). So **Sco·tist**(2) n. [L *Scotus* the Scot, -ISM]

Scotland Yard. (Used for) the London police, the headquarters of the detection of crime. [*Great, New, S. Y.*, successive headquarters of metropolitan police]

scŏto-, comb. form of Gk *skotos* darkness; *-dī·nia*, giddiness [Gk *dinē* whirl]; *-graph*, machine for writing in darkness.

scoto·ma, n. (path.; pl. *-ata*). Obscuration of part of the field of vision. [LL, f. Gk *skotōma* f. *skotoō* darken (prec., -M)]

Scots. See SCOTCH[1]. [ME *Scottis* SCOTTISH]

Sco·t(t)ĭcè (-ē), adv. In Scotch. [med. L (LL *Scot(t)icus* Scotch)]

Sco·tticism, -ŏti-, n. Scotch phrase, word, or idiom. [as prec., -ISM(4)]

Sco·tticize, -ŏti-, v.i. & t. Imitate the Scotch in idiom or habits; imbue with, model on, Scotch ways. [prec., -IZE]

Sco·ttish, a. See SCOTCH[1]. [SCOT[2], -ISH[1]]

scou·ndrel (-ow-), n. Unscrupulous person, villain, rogue, rascal. Hence **scou·ndrel**DOM, **scou·ndrel**ISM(3), nn., **scou·ndrel**LY[1] a. [?]

scour[1] (-owr), v.t., & n. Cleanse or brighten by friction (*s. metal*, with sand &c.; *s. clothes* &c., with soap or chemicals); (of water, or person with water) clear out (channel, harbour, pipe, &c.) by flushing or flowing through or over; (of drug, physician, &c.) purge (bowels) drastically (*s. worms*, purge them by placing in damp moss &c. to fit them for bait); clear (rust, stain, &c.) *away, off*, by rubbing &c. (also fig.); *scouring-rush*, kind of HORSE[1]-tail with silicious coating used for polishing wood &c.; hence **(-)scour**ER[1](1, 2) n. (N.) clearing action of swift current on channel &c. (*the s. of the tide*); diarrhoea in cattle; substance used for scouring fabrics. [prob. f. MLG *schûren* (G *scheuern*) f. OF *escurer* f. med. L *scurare* (L EX*curatus* taken good care of, see CURE[2])]

scour[2] (-owr), v.i. & t. Rove, range, go along hastily, esp. in search or pursuit; hasten over or along, search rapidly, (*s. the plain, coast, woods*). [perh. f. ON *skúr* a storm, & cogn. w. SHOWER]

scourge (skerj), n., & v.t. Whip for chastising persons (archaic); person or thing regarded as instrument or manifestation of divine or other vengeance or punishment (e.g. barbarian conqueror, pestilence, war; *the white s.*, consumption as an endemic disease). (Vb) use whip on (archaic); chastise, afflict, oppress, harass. [n. f. AF *escorge* f. p.p. (=thong) of LL EX(*coriare* f. *corium* hide); vb f. OF *escorgier* perh. f. the LL vb =flay]

scout[1] (-owt), n., & v.i. (Mil. &c.) man

sent out to get information about enemy or surroundings (*boy s.*, member of organization intended to develop character, resourcefulness, & public spirit); ship designed for reconnoitring; small fast single-seat aeroplane; (Oxf.) college servant (cf. GYP, SKIP²); (Crick.; archaic) fielder; act of seeking (esp. mil.) information (*on the s.*); kinds of bird, auk, guillemot, puffin; *s.-master*, officer directing ss. or boy ss. (Vb) act as s. (esp. *out scouting*). [vb f. n., f. OF *escoute* spy, eavesdropper, (*escouter* listen f. L as AUSCULTATION)]

scout² (-owt), v.t. Reject (proposal, notion) with scorn or ridicule. [cf. ON *skúta* a taunt, Sw. *skjuta* to shoot; prob. cogn. w. SHOOT]

scow, n. Kind of flat-bottomed boat (esp. U.S.). [f. Du. *schouw* ferry-boat]

scowl, v.i. & t., & n. Wear sullen look, look sour, frown ill-temperedly; *s. down*, master or overbear (person, opposition, &c.) with s.; hence **scow·ling**LY² adv. (N.) scowling aspect, angry frown. [cf. Da. *skule* look down]

scra·bble, v.i. Scrawl, scribble, (bibl.); scratch or grope about to find or collect something (usu. *about*). [f. Du. *schrabbelen* dim. of *schrabben* SCRAPE]

scrag, n., & v.t. Lean skinny person, animal, plant, &c.; bony part of animal's carcass as food, esp. neck of mutton or inferior part of it, (slang) person's neck; hence **scra·ggy**² a., **scra·ggi**LY² adv., **scra·ggi**NESS n. (Vb) put to death by hanging, garotte, wring neck of, (slang); (Footb.) tackle by the neck; (school slang) squeeze neck of with arm by way of torture. [prob. f. obs. (& Sc.) *crag* neck (cf. Du. *kraag*, G *kragen*) with acquired *s*-]

scra·mble, v.i. & t., & n. Make way as best one can over steep or rough ground by clambering, crawling, &c.; take part in physical or other struggle to secure as much as possible of something from competitors (usu. *for*; *s. for pennies*, of children &c. among whom coin is thrown; *s. for place, wealth, a living*); throw (coins &c.) to be scrambled for; cook (eggs) by breaking into pan with butter, milk, &c., stirring slightly, & heating; hence **scra·mbling**LY² adv. (N.) climb or walk over rough ground &c.; eager struggle or competition for or *for* something. [f. 16th c., etym. dub.]

scran, n. (slang). Food, eatables, broken victuals; *bad s. to —!* (Anglo-Ir.), bad luck to —. [?]

scra·nnel, a. (archaic). (Of sound) weak, reedy, feeble, (chiefly w. allus. to Milton, *Lycidas* 124). [cf. Norw. *skran* thin, lean, dry]

scrap¹, n., & v.t. Small detached piece of something, fragment, remnant, (pl.) odds & ends, useless remains, whence **scra·pp**Y² a., **scra·ppi**LY² adv., **scra·ppi**NESS n.; picture, paragraph, &c., cut from book or newspaper for keeping in a collection (*s.-book*, for pasting these into); *s. of paper*, negligible promise &c. (w. ref. to violation of Belgian neutrality 1914); (collect.) rubbish, waste material, clippings &c. of metal collected for reworking (also *s.-iron, -metal*), (*s.-heap*, collection of waste stuff, also fig.; *s.-h. policy*, practice of discarding promptly what is past its prime); (sing. or pl.) residuum of melted fat or of fish with the oil expressed (*s.-cake*, compressed fish s.). (Vb) consign to s.-heap, condemn (ships, supplies, &c.) as past use, discard. [f. ON *skrap* (SCRAPE)]

scrap², n., & v.i., (slang). Fight, scrimmage, esp. of unpremeditated kind (*had a bit of a s. with*); (vb) have s. [?]

scrape, v.t. & i., & n. Level surface of, clear of projections, abrade, smooth, polish, shave, or graze, by drawing sharp or angular edge breadthwise over or by causing to pass over such edge (*s. ship's bottom*, clear of barnacles &c.; *s.* one's *chin*, shave; *s.* one's *boots*, remove dirt from soles by drawing over scraper; *s.* one's *plate*, leave no food on; *ship scraped her side, paint, against the pier*; *s. away*, reduce by scraping; *s. down*, s. away, also s. all over, & see below); take (projection, stain, &c.) *off, out*, or *away*, by scraping (*s. off the paint*); excavate (hollow) by scraping (often *out*); draw along with scraping sound, produce such sound from, emit such sound, (*s.* one's *feet*, in restlessness or to drown speaker's voice, also *s.* abs., esp. = draw back foot in making clumsy formal bow; *s. down*, silence by scraping feet; *s. bow across fiddle-strings, s. fiddle*, also *s.* abs. = play fiddle &c.; *branches scraping against the window*); pass along something so as to graze or be grazed by it or just avoid doing so (*scraped against, along, the wall*; *s. through* adv. or prep., get through with a squeeze or narrow shave, often fig. of passing examination &c.); amass by scraping or with difficulty or by parsimony, contrive to gain, (usu. *up, together*; *must s. up enough for*; *s.-penny*, miser; *s. acquaintance with*, thrust one's acquaintance on), (abs.) practise economy (*work & s. as one may*); hence **scra·p**ING¹ (esp. 2), **scra·p**ER¹(1, 2), nn. (N.) Act or sound of scraping (*a s. of the pen*, writing of a, esp. important, word or two e.g. signature); scraping of foot in bowing; awkward predicament esp. resulting from escapade. [f. ON *skrapa*; cogn. w. OE *screpan* scratch]

scratch¹, v.t. & i., n., & a. Score surface of, make long narrow superficial wounds in, with nail, claw, or something more or less pointed (*threatened to s. my face*; *s. the surface of*, not penetrate far into; *s. a Russian, & you find a Tartar*; *stones* *scratched with rude letters or pictures; much scratched with thorns*), get (some part of one) scratched (*have scratched my hands badly*); form (letters, representation), excavate (hole), by scratching, scribble (*a few lines* &c.); scrape without marking esp. with nails to relieve itching (*s.* one's *head*, esp. as sign of perplexity; *s. my back & I will s. yours*, = CLAW[2] *me*), (abs.) s. oneself, s. ground &c. in search (*s. about for stray seeds, evidence*, &c.); scrape *together* or *up*; score (written words &c.) *out* or *through*, strike *off* with pencil &c., erase (horse's name in list of entries for race, competitor's name), withdraw (horse, candidate, or intr. for refl.) from competition; *s. along* slang, manage to live &c. (N.) mark or sound made by scratching (*a s. of the pen*, signature or written order easily given); spell of scratching oneself; slight wound (*got off with a s. or two*); line from which competitors in race start (*toe, come to* or *up to, the s.*, put in appearance at right time, not shirk, often transf.; *s.-race*, with all on equal terms, opp. handicap; *s. man* or *s.*, competitor in handicap receiving no start); (pl.) horse-disease with dry chaps above heel; (also *s.-wig*) wig covering part only of head; *s.-cat*, spiteful child or woman; *s.-work*, graffito decoration. (Adj.) collected by haphazard, scratched together, heterogeneous, (*a s. crew, collection, team*). [perh. mixture of ME *scratte* (cf. MSw. *kratta* scrape w. AF pref. *es-* EX-) with ME *cracche* (cf. MDu. *kratsen*)]

Scratch[2], n. *Old S.*, the devil. [f. obs. *scrat*, hermaphrodite = ON *skratta* goblin]

scra·tchy, a. (Of drawing &c.) done in scratches, careless or unskilful; (of pen) making sound of scratching or given to catching in paper; (of crew &c.) of scratch character, not well matched or working well together. Hence **scra·tchi**LY[2] adv., **scra·tchi**NESS n. [-Y[2]]

scrawl, v.i. & t., & n. Write (t. & i.) in hurried more or less illegible way; mark (paper &c.) *over, all over*, with bad writing or lines like writing; (n.) piece of bad writing, hurried note or letter. [earlier senses, sprawl, crawl; perh. = *crawl* w. acquired *s-*]

scray, n. Common tern, sea swallow. [cf. W *yscraen*]

scream, v.i. & t., & n. Utter piercing cry expressing terror, pain, or pretence of these, (of steam-engine &c.) whistle or hoot shrilly; laugh uncontrollably (usu. *s. with laughter*; *screa·m*ING[1] *farce, fun*, &c., causing spectators to s., intensely funny); utter, say, in screaming tone (usu. *out*; *screamed that she did not dare jump*; *s. out a curse, order*, &c.); hence **screa·ming**LY[2] adv. (N.) screaming cry or sound (*ss. of pain, laughter*); (slang) irresistibly comical affair; (without article) violent over-emphasis in style or sentiment, whence **screa·m**Y[2] a., **screa·mi**LY[2] adv., **screa·mi**NESS n. [ME *scræmen* etym. dub.]

screa·mer, n. In vbl senses; also or esp.: kinds of bird, e.g. the swift; (slang) tale &c. that raises screams of laughter, extraordinarily fine specimen of anything. [-ER[1]]

scree, n. (Mountain slope covered with) small stones that slide down when trodden on (often pl. in same sense). [f. ON *skritha* (*skritha* glide)]

screech, v.i. & t., & n. Scream (vb & n.) with, of, fright or pain or anger, or in harsh or uncanny tones (usu. contempt. or facet., & esp. w. ref. to disagreeable nature of sound); *s.-owl*, kinds that s. instead of hooting, esp. the BARN-owl. [imit.; earlier *scritch, scrike*, &c.]

screed, n. Long tiresome harangue (esp. list of grievances) or letter; one of the fillets of mortar or strips of wood by which a surface to be plastered is divided into compartments. [var. of SHRED]

screen, n., & v.t. Partition of wood or stone separating without completely cutting off one part of church or room from another, esp. that between nave & choir of cathedral &c. (ROOD-*s.*), decorated wall enclosing court &c., façade of church; movable piece of furniture designed to shelter from excess of heat, light, draught, &c., or from observation (*fire, window, folding*, &c., *-s.*); any object utilized as shelter esp. from observation, expression of face or measure adopted for concealment, protection afforded by these, (*prepared the attack behind a s. of trees*; *put on a s. of indifference*; *a cavalry s.*, cavalry thrown out to keep enemy's scouts from getting in touch with main body; *under s. of night*); board, often with wire-netting cover, on which notices are posted; sheet on which lantern or shadow pictures are thrown; body proof against electric or magnetic induction or having property of interrupting other such physical processes; large sieve or riddle esp. for sorting coal &c. into sizes. (Vb) afford shelter to, hide partly or completely, (*from*; often fig. of protecting another from deserved censure &c. by taking blame upon oneself or diverting it); show (object, scene) on lantern or cinema s.; riddle (coal &c.; *screened coal*, from which dust &c. has been removed; *screenings*, refuse separated by sifting). [cf. OF *escren* prob. f. OHG *skirm* (G *schirm*) shelter]

screeve v.i., **scree·ver** n., (slang). (Be) pavement artist. [ult. f. L *scribere* write]

screw[1], n., & v.t. & i. Cylinder with spiral ridge called the thread running round it outside (MALE or *exterior s.*) or inside (FEMALE or *interior s.*), metal male s. with slotted head & sharp point for fastening pieces of wood together with more security than nail (also *wood-, common, s.*)

or with blunt end to receive nut & bolt things together (also *s.-bolt*), wooden or metal male or female s. as part of appliance or machine acting as one of the MECHANICAL powers to exert pressure in various ways, (ARCHIMEDEAN *s.*; *endless* or *perpetual s.*, threaded revolving shaft engaging with & working cogwheel; *differential* or *Hunter's s.*, arrangement of ss. with threads of different pitch working inside each other giving great lifting-power; *left-handed s.*, advanced by turning leftwards contrary to usu. arrangement; *right-&-left s.*, cylinder with threads in opposite directions at the two ends; *interrupted s.*, with parts of thread cut away; *have, there is, a s. loose*, phrr. suggesting that something, esp. person's brain, is out of working order; *put the s. on*, exert pressure esp. in way of extortion or intimidation); (also *s.-propeller*) revolving shaft with spiral blades projecting from ship or airship at stern & propelling it by acting on s. principle upon water or air; (also *s. steamer*, abbr. *s.s.*) steamer propelled by s. or ss.; one turn of a s. (*give it another s.*); oblique curling motion or tendency as of billiard-ball struck sideways; small twisted-up paper *of* tobacco &c.; miser, stingy or extortionate person; (slang) amount of salary or wages; *s. coupling*, right-&-left female s. for joining ends of pipes or rods; *s.-cutter*, hand-tool for cutting ss.; *s.-driver*, tool like blunt chisel for turning ss. by the slot; *s.-eye*, s. with loop for passing cord &c. through instead of slotted head; *s. gear*, endless s. with cogwheel or pinion; *s.-hook*, hook to hang things on with s. at end of shank to fasten it in with; *s.-jack*, dentist's implement for regulating distance between crowded teeth, (also) carriage JACK[1] worked by s.; *s.-pile*, with s. at lower end, & sunk by rotation; *s.-pine*, plant with leaves arranged spirally & resembling those of pine-apple; *s.-plate*, metal plate for holding s.-cutting dies, also steel plate with threaded holes for making male ss.; *s.-pod*, kind of mesquit with spirally twisted pods; *s. press*, press worked by simple s. used esp. by printers & binders; *s.-tap*, tool for making female ss.; *s. valve*, stopcock opened & shut by s., valve moved by s.; *s.-wheel*, worked by endless s.; *s.-wrench*, for turning ss. with angular head or nuts, also wrench with jaws worked by s. (Vb) fasten, tighten, &c., by use of s. or ss. (*s. up door*, make fast, esp. as practical joke at university; *s. up* person, s. up his door; *boards are screwed down*; *his head is screwed on the right way*, he has sense); turn (s.), twist round like s., (w. ref. to twisting pegs of fiddle; usu. *up*) make tenser or more efficient (*s.* one's *courage to the sticking-place*, *s. up* one's *courage*, gather resolution; *he, the management, wants screwing up*); put the s. upon, press hard on, oppress; be miserly; squeeze, extort, (consent, money, &c.) *out of*; contort, distort, contract, (*s.* one's *face into wrinkles*; *s. up* one's *eyes*); (of s.) revolve (*s. stiffly, to the right*, &c.); (of rolling ball, also of person &c.) take curling course, swerve; hence **screw·**ABLE a. [f. OF *escro(u)e* etym. dub.; cf. SCROLL]

screw[2], n. Vicious, unsound, or worn-out horse. Hence **screw·**Y[2] a. [perh. f. prec.]

screwed, a. (slang). Drunk, drunken. [prob. f. SCREW[1], -ED[1]]

scriba·cious, a. (rare). Given to writing. [f. L *scribere* write, -ACIOUS]

scri·bble[1], v.t. & i., & n. Write (t. & i.) hurriedly or carelessly in regard either to handwriting or composition; be a journalist or author (w. implication, often mock-modest, of inferiority), write poetry &c., whence **scri·bbler**[1] [-ER[1]] n.; *scribbling-paper, -diary*, for casual jottings; hence **scri·bble**MENT n. (rare). (N.) careless handwriting or thing written in it, scrawl, hasty note, &c. [f. med. L *scribillare* dim. of L *scribere* write]

scri·bble[2], v.t. Card (wool, cotton) coarsely, pass through scribbling-machine or **scri·bbler**[2] [-ER[1]] n. [prob. f. LG, cf. Sw. *skrabbla*; cogn. w. SCRUB[2]]

scribe, n., & v.t. Person who writes or can write (rare; *am no great s.*, do not write well); (bibl.) ancient-Jewish maker & keeper of records &c., also Jewish theologian & jurist of type prevalent in time of Christ; hence **scri·b**AL a. (Also *s.-awl*) pointed instrument for marking lines on wood, bricks, &c., to guide saw &c., or writing words on barrel &c. (vb, mark with s.; *scribing-compass*, for scratching circles &c.; *scribing-iron*, **scrib**ER[1] n., = *s.* n.). [vb f. n., f. L *scriba* (*scribere* write)]

scrim, n. Lining-cloth in upholstery &c. [?]

scri·mmage, scrŭ-, (-ĭj), n. Tussle, confused struggle, row, brawl, skirmish, (usu. *scri-*); (Rugby footb.; usu. *scru-*; also abbr. *scrum*) tight mass of all the forwards with ball on ground in middle. [varr. of SKIRMISH]

scrimp, v.t. & i. Skimp. Hence **scri·mp**Y[2] a. [f. 18th c. only; cf. SHRIMP]

scri·mshank, v.i. (mil. slang). Shirk duty. Hence **scri·mshank**ER[1] n. [f. 1890; etym. dub.]

scri·mshaw, v.t. & i., & n. Adorn (shells, ivory, &c.), adorn shells &c., with carved or coloured designs (as sailors' amusement at sea); (n.) piece of such work. [perh. f. person's name]

scrī·nium, n. (Rom. ant.; pl. *-ia*). Cylindrical or other box for rolled MSS. [L, see SHRINE]

scrip[1], n. (archaic). Beggar's or traveller's or pilgrim's wallet, satchel. [prob. f. OF *escrepe*; cf. SCARF[1]]

scrip², n. Provisional certificate of money subscribed to bank or company entitling holder to formal certificate in due time & to dividends &c., (collect.) such certificates. [abbr., = (sub)scrip(tion receipt)]

script, n. (Law) original document (opp. *copy*); handwriting, written characters (opp. *print*); printed cursive characters, imitation of handwriting in type. [f. L *scriptum* thing written (*scribere script-* write)]

scriptor·ium, n. (pl. *-s, -ia*). Room set apart for writing esp. in monastery. [med. L (prec., -ORY)]

scri·ptural (-tshŏŏ-), a. Founded on, reconcilable with, laying stress on, appealing to, doctrines contained in the Bible, whence **scri·pturalISM**(3), **scri·pturalIST**(2), nn.; of, taken from, the Bible (rare; usu. now *scripture* attrib.). Hence **scri·pturalLY**² adv., **scri·pturalNESS** n. [foll., -AL]

scri·pture (-tsh*er*), n. The Bible with or without the Apocrypha (usu. without article; also *Holy S.* or *the Ss.*; *a doctrine not found in S.* or *the Ss.*); *a* or *the* quotation from the Bible; (attrib.) taken from or relating to the Bible (*a s. text, lesson*; cf. SCRIPTURAL); sacred book of non-Christian community; (archaic) inscription; *s.-reader*, person who reads Bible to the poor in their homes. [f. L *scriptura* (SCRIPT, -URE)]

scrĭ·vener, n. (hist.). Writer, drafter of documents, notary, broker, moneylender; (in mod. use) *s.'s palsy*, WRITER's cramp. [f. OF *escrivain* f. LL *scribanus* (SCRIBE, -AN) + -ER¹]

scrobi·culate (-*a*t), **-āted**, aa. (bot., zool.). Pitted, furrowed. [LL *scrobiculus* (*scrobis* ditch, -CULE), -ATE²]

scrŏ·fūla, n. Morbid constitutional condition with glandular swellings & tendency to consumption. Hence **scro·fulOUS** a., **scro·fulousLY**² adv., **scro·fulousNESS** n. [med. L sing. f. LL *scrofulae* scrofulous swelling, orig. dim. of *scrofa* a sow]

scrōll, n., & v.t. & i. Roll of parchment or paper, book or volume of the ancient roll form, (archaic) schedule or list; ornamental design esp. in architecture carved or drawn or otherwise made to imitate s. of parchment more or less exactly, volute of Ionic capital or of chair &c., head of fiddle, flourish in writing, ribbon bearing heraldic motto, &c.; any tracery of spiral or flowing lines; *s.-bone*, turbinated; *s. gear*, with s.-wheel; *s.-head*, volute at ship's bow; *s.-lathe*, for spiral work; *s.-saw*, fretsaw; *s.-wheel*, cogwheel in shape of disk with cogs in spiral lines on one side causing variation of pace according as outer or inner parts are in action; *s.-work*, ornament of spiral lines esp. as cut by s.-saw. (Vb) curl up (t. & i.; rare) like paper; adorn with ss. (chiefly in p.p.). [earlier *scrowl* dim. of ME *scrowe* f. OF *escro(u)e* (cf. SCREW¹) f. Teut.; cogn. w. SHRED]

scroop, n., & v.i. (Make) grating noise. [imit.]

scrō·tum, n. (pl. *-ta*). Bag containing testicles. Hence **scro·tAL** a., **scrotI·TIS**, **scro·toCELE**, nn. [L]

scrounge (-ownj), v.i. & t. (slang). Appropriate things, cadge; acquire thus. Hence **scrou·ngER**¹ n. [?]

scrub¹, n. (Ground covered with) brushwood or stunted forest growth; worn or short-bristled brush or moustache; stunted or insignificant person, animal, or plant; *s.-oak*, American dwarf kinds. Hence **scru·bbY**² a., **scru·bbiNESS** n. [var. of SHRUB¹]

scrub², v.t. & i., & n. Rub hard to clean or brighten esp. with soap & water applied with scrubbing-brush; (v.i.) use such brush (*would rather s. for my living*); eliminate, or extract for use, certain elements from (coal-gas); hence **scru·bbER**¹ (esp., apparatus for scrubbing gas), **scru·bbING**¹, nn. (N.) scrubbing or being scrubbed (*give it, he wants, a good s.*). [perh. f. MDu. *schrubben* imported as naut. term]

scru·bber, n. In vbl senses: also, apparatus for purifying coal-gas from ammonia & tar by spraying with water. [-ER¹(1, 2)]

scruff, n. Back *of the neck* as used to grasp & lift or drag animal or person by (*take by the s. of the neck*). [corrupt. of SCUFF²]

scrum(mage). See SCRIMMAGE.

scru·mptious (-shus), a. (slang). Delightful, delicious, first-rate. [arbitrary; cf. GOLUPTIOUS]

scrunch. = CRUNCH. [*s-* as in SCRAG &c.]

scru·ple (-ōō-), n., & v.i. & t. Weight-unit (in apothecaries' wt) of 20 grains; very small quantity (archaic); feeling of doubt or hesitation on grounds of morality or propriety about acting or approving of action, conscientious objection, (*make no s. to do*, do without such hesitation or with easy conscience; *have ss. about* doing; *man of no ss.*, unscrupulous; *did it without s.*). (Vb) feel or be influenced by ss. (rare); be deterred from or hindered in (do*ing* or n. of action; archaic; *would s. lying* or *a lie*) by ss.; hesitate owing to ss. *to* do (esp. w. neg.; *does not s. to say*). [vb f. n., f. F *scrupule* f. L *scrupulus* (*scrupus* sharp stone, -ULE)]

scru·pūlous, a. Careful to offend in nothing, conscientious even in small matters, not neglectful of details, punctilious, marked by extreme thoroughness, unfailing, (*s. persons*; *s. honesty, cleanliness, care, methods, respect, attention*, &c.); over-attentive to details, esp. to small points of conscience, whence **scrupulo·SITY** n. Hence **scru·pulousLY**² adv., **scru·pulousNESS** n. [f. F *scrupuleux* f. L *scrupulosus* (prec., -OSE¹)]

scruta·tor, n. Person given to scrutiny (chiefly as signature to newspaper letters &c.). [L (SCRUTINY, -OR[2])]

scrutin (F), n. *S. d'arrondissement, de liste*, contrasted methods by which voter votes for one or more representatives of small district only, or for large number representing wide area.

scrutineer·, n. Person examining ballot papers for irregularities. [SCRUTINY, -EER]

scru·tinize, v.t. Look closely at, examine in detail. Hence **scru·tinizing**LY[2] adv. [foll., -IZE]

scru·tiny (-ōō-), n. Critical gaze, close investigation, examination into details; official examination of votes cast in election to test their validity when closeness of contest or suspicion of irregularity makes it desirable (*demand a s.*). [f. LL *scrutinium* (*scrutari* search f. *scruta* broken pieces)]

scry, v.i. Use the crystal in CRYSTAL-*gazing*. Hence **scry·**ER[1] n. [=(DE)SCRY]

scud, v.i., & n. Run or fly straight & fast esp. with smooth or easy motion, skim along; (Naut.) run before the wind. (N.) spell of scudding; vapoury driving clouds. [f. 16th c., etym. dub.]

scū·do (*or* -ōō-), n. (pl. *-di* pr. -ē). Old Italian silver coin of about 4/-; Italian five-franc piece. [It., f. L *scutum* shield]

scuff[1], v.i. Walk with dragging feet, shuffle with the feet. [f. 18th c., etym. dub.]

scuff[2], n. Nape (now usu. *scruff*). [also *scuft, scruft*, etym. dub.]

scu·ffle, v.i., & n. (Engage in) confused struggle in which disputants chiefly push each other about, disorderly fight. [prob. of Scand. orig. & cogn. w. *shove, shuffle*]

scug, n. (sch. slang). Person lacking spirit, sociability, manner, sportsmanship, &c. [?]

scull, n., & v.t. & i. One of pair of small oars used by single rower each with one hand; oar resting in nick on boat's stern & worked with twisting strokes to propel like ship's screw; (vb) propel (boat), propel boat, with scull(s). [f. 14th c., etym. dub.]

scu·ller, n. User of scull(s); boat intended for sculling. [-ER[1]]

scu·llery, n. Back kitchen, room for washing-up dishes &c. [f. OF *escuelerie* f. L *scutella* (SCUTTLE[1]) + -ERY]

scu·llion, n. (archaic, poet., rhet.). Cook's boy, washer of dishes & pots. [perh. assim. to prec. of F *souillon* scullion, orig. dirty fellow (as SOIL[2])]

sculp, v.t. (Colloq. for) SCULPTURE. [f. L *sculpere*; now regarded as abbr.]

scu·lpin, n. Kinds of small American sea-fish with large spiny head. [perh. corrupt. of obs. *scorpene* f. L f. Gk *skorpaina* a fish]

scu·lpsit, sculpsē·runt, (abbr. *sc.* or *sculps.*), v. sing. & pl. 3rd pers. (So-&-so) carved or sculptured or engraved (this work; used with artist's signature). [L, see SCULPTURE]

scu·lptor, n. One who sculptures. Hence **scu·lptr**ESS[1] n. [L (foll., -OR[2])]

scu·lpture (-tsh*er*), n., & v.t. & i. Art of forming representations of objects in the round or in relief by chiselling stone, carving wood, modelling clay, casting metal, or similar processes; a work of s.; (Zool., Bot.) raised or sunk markings on shell &c.; hence **scu·lptur**AL, **sculptur**E·SQUE, aa., **scu·lptural**LY[2] adv. (Vb) represent in s.; adorn with s.; be a sculptor, do s.; (p.p., Zool. & Bot.) having s. [vb. f. n., f. L *sculptura* (*sculpere sculpt-*, perf. *sculpsi*, -URE)]

scum, n., & v.t. & i. Impurities that rise to surface of liquid esp. in boiling or fermentation, floating film; (fig.) worst part, refuse, offscouring, (*of*); hence **scu·mm**Y[2] a. (Vb) take s. from, skim; be or form a s. on; (of liquid) develop s. [Teut. (cf. G *schaum*, Da. *skum*) perh. thr. OF *escume*; see also SKIM]

scu·mble, v.t., & n. Soften (oil-painting) by covering with very thin coat of opaque colour; (n.) softening of tints produced. [prec., -LE(3)]

scu·ncheon (-tshn), n. Stones or arches across angles of square tower supporting alternate sides of octagonal spire. [f. OF *escoinson* (EX-, COIN[1])]

scu·pper[1], n. Hole in ship's side to carry off water from deck. [perh. f. SCOOP vb + -ER[1]]

scu·pper[2], v.t. (slang). Surprise & massacre, sink (ship, crew), do for. [perh. f. prec.]

scurf, n. Flakes on surface of skin cast off as fresh skin develops below, esp. those of head (also *dandruff*); any scaly matter on a surface. Hence **scur·f**Y[2] a., **scur·fi**NESS n. [OE, cogn. w. *sceorfan* scarify, cf. Sw. *scorv*]

scu·rrilous, (archaic) **scu·rril(e),** aa. Grossly or obscenely abusive (of person or language), given to or expressed with low buffoonery. Hence or cogn. **scu·rrilous**LY[2] adv., **scurri·l**ITY n. [f. obs. *scurril* f. L *scurrilis* (*scurra* buffoon), -OUS]

scu·rry, v.i., & n. Run hurriedly esp. with short quick steps, scamper, (*the scurrying mice*); (n.) act or sound of scurrying. [perh. shortened f. *hurry-scurry* redupl. of *hurry*]

scur·vy, a. & n. Paltry, low, mean, dishonourable, contemptible, (*a s. trick, fellow*); hence **scur·vi**LY[2] adv. (N.) diseased state of blood with swollen gums, livid spots, & prostration, attacking sailors & any who feed on salt meat & lack vegetables; *s.-grass* [corrupt. of *-cress*], plant of mustard family used against s.; hence **scur·vi**ED[2] a. [n. (expressing pitiful state) f. adj. orig. = scurfy (SCURF, -Y[2])]

scut, n. Short tail esp. of hare, rabbit, or deer. [etym. dub.; cf. Icel. *skott* fox's tail]
scū·tage (-ĭj), n. (hist.). Money paid by feudal landowner in lieu of personal service. [f. med. L *scutagium* (*scutum* shield, -AGE)]
scutch, v.t., & n. Dress (fibrous material, esp. retted flax) by beating; *s.-blade, scutching-sword,* **scu·tch**ER[1](2) n., implements for scutching flax. (N.) scutcher; coarse tow separated in scutching flax. [perh. f. OF *escousser* f. L EX(*cutere cuss-* =*quatere quass-* shake)]
scŭ·tcheon (-tshn), n. =ESCUTCHEON; pivoted cover of keyhole; plate for name or inscription. [short for ESCUTCHEON]
scute. See SCUTUM.
scute·llum, n. (nat. hist.; pl. *-lla*). Small shield, plate, or scale, in plants, insects, birds, &c., esp. one of the horny scales on birds' feet. Hence **scu·tell**ATE[2](d), **scute·ll**AR[1], aa., **scutell**A·TION n. [mod. L, dim. of SCUTUM]
scu·tter, v.i. Scurry. [var. of SCUTTLE[3]]
scu·ttle[1], n. (Usu. *coal-s.*) metal or other vessel in which small supply of coal esp. for single fireplace is brought & kept. [OE *scutel* dish f. L *scutella* salver, dim. of *scutra* tray]
scu·ttle[2], n., & v.t. Hole with lid in wall or roof of house or ships' deck, side, or hatchway-covering; *s.-butt, -cask,* water-butt usu. on deck with hole in top for dipping from; (vb) make hole(s) in (ship) esp. for purpose of sinking. [cf. F *escoutille,* Sp. *escotilla,* hatchway; perh. all f. Du. *schutten* to shut]
scu·ttle[3], v.i., & n. Hurry along, scurry, run away, make off, fly from danger or difficulty; (n.) hurried gait, precipitate flight or departure. [earlier also *scuddle,* f. SCUD, -LE(3)]
scu·tum, n. (pl. *-ta*). (Rom. Ant.) legionary's shield of oblong, oval, or semi-cylindrical shape; (Anat.) knee-pan; (Zool. &c.; also *scute*) shield-like plate or scale, piece of bony armour in crocodile, sturgeon, turtle, armadillo, &c., whence **scu·t**AL, **scu·t**ATE[2], aa. Hence **scu·ti**FORM a. [L, cogn. w. Gk *skutos* hide, SKY, SCUM, &c.]
Scy·lla (sĭ-), n. *S. & Charybdis,* six-headed monster living on a rock, & whirlpool, so placed on opposite sides of Straits of Messina that it was hard to steer clear of one without being caught by the other (see Homer, *Od.* xii).
scy·phus (sī-), n. (pl. *-phī*). (Gk Ant.) footless drinking-cup with two handles not higher than rim; (Bot.) cup-shaped part as in narcissus flower or in lichens, whence **scy·ph**OSE[1] a. Hence **scy·phi**FORM a. [L, f. Gk *skuphos*]
scythe (sīdh),n., & v.t. Mowing & reaping implement of long slightly curved blade swung over ground by usu. crooked pole about 5 ft. long with two short handles projecting at right angles from it; blade continuing axle of ancient war-chariot at each end, whence **scyth**ED[2] a.; (vb) cut with s. [OE *sithe,* cf. Du. *zeis,* ON *sigdhr*; cogn. w. L *secare* cut, SICKLE]
Scy·thian (sĭdh-, -th-), a. & n. (Inhabitant) of ancient Scythia, the region north of the Black Sea; =TURANIAN. [L f. Gk *Skuthia* (*Skuthēs* a S.), -AN]
'sdeath, int. (archaic) expressing anger, surprise, &c. [short for *God's death*]
se-, L pref. = apart, without.
sea, n. Expanse of salt water that covers most of earth's surface & encloses its continents & islands, the ocean, any part of this as opposed to dry land or fresh water, (*by s. & land*; *at the bottom of the s.*; *jumped into the s.*; *on the s.,* in ship &c., also situated on seashore; *go to s.,* become sailor; *follow the s.,* be sailor; *put to s.,* leave port or land; *arm of the s.,* deep gulf; *at s.,* away from & esp. out of sight of land, also fig. = perplexed, not knowing conditions &c. or what to do; *between* DEVIL[1] *& deep s.*; *as good* FISH[1] *in the s.*; *when the s. gives up its dead,* at the resurrection; also pl. in same sense, as *beyond, over, s.* or *ss.,* to or in countries separated by s.; *the high ss.,* the open s. outside the three-mile limit to which nearest country's jurisdiction extends; *mistress of the s.* or *ss.,* chief naval power at any time); particular tract of s. partly or sometimes wholly enclosed by land & usu. distinguished by special name (*the North, Mediterranean, Caspian, Dead, S.*; *inland s.,* entirely landlocked as the Caspian, also rarely of great freshwater lakes; *closed s.,* = MARE[1] *clausum*; *the seven ss.,* Arctic, Antarctic, N. & S. Pacific, N. & S. Atlantic, & Indian, Oceans; *the four ss.,* those enclosing Great Britain); local motion or state of the s., swell, great billow, (*a heavy s.,* with great waves; *ss. mountains high*; of boat &c. *ship a s.,* be flooded by a wave; *long s.,* with long regular waves; *short s.,* choppy & irregularly agitated; *s. like looking-glass* or *sheet of glass,* quite smooth; *half ss. over,* having drunk too much); vast quantity or expanse *of* (*a s. of troubles, care, flame, upturned faces*; also pl., as *ss. of blood,* ruthless bloodshed); (bibl.) *brazen* or *molten s.,* = LAVER[2]; (attrib. & in comb.) living or used in or on, of, near, like, the s. (often prefixed to name of animal, fruit, &c., to form name of marine thing with merely superficial resemblance to what it is named after, as *s. canary, cucumber, -fox, raven,* below); *s. acorn,* barnacle; *s. air,* air at seaside esp. as recommended for invalids &c.; *s.-anchor,* DRAG[2]-anchor; *s.* ANEMONE; *s.-angel,* ANGEL-fish; *s.-arrow,* flying squid; *s. asparagus,* kind of soft-shelled crab; *s.-barrow,* skate's egg-case; *s. bathing,* in s.; *s. bear,* polar bear, also

kind of fur-seal; *s.-bells*, seashore bindweed; *s.-belt*, sweet fucus, a seaweed with belt-like fronds; *sea·board*, seashore, coast region, line of coast; *s.-boat*, ship &c. of specified seagoing qualities (*is a good, bad*, &c., *s.-b.*); *s.-born*, born of the s. (poet., esp. of Aphrodite); *s.-borne*, conveyed by s. (*s.-b. commerce, goods*): *s.-bow*, rainbow effect in s.-spray; *sea·-breeze*, blowing landward from s. esp. during day in alternation with land-breeze at night; *s. breeze*, any breeze at s.; *s.-calf*, common seal; *s. canary*, white whale (from its whistling); *s. captain*, (poet., rhet.) great sailor or commander at sea, (in ord. use, chiefly where army-captain is to be excluded) past or present captain of ship in navy or merchant service; *s. change*, transformation (w. ref. to *Tempest* I. II. 400); *s. chestnut*, s.-urchin; *s.-cloth*, used in theatre to represent shore; *s. coal* archaic, coal (orig. of coal brought from Newcastle by sea, opp. charcoal &c.); *s. coast*; *s.-cock*, kinds of bird & fish, (also) valve by which s. water can be let into ship's interior; *s. colander*, brown seaweed with fronds perforated like colander; *s. cook*, naut. term of abuse; *s.-cow*, sirenian, also walrus; *s. crow*, kind of gull; *s. cucumber*, any holothurian, esp. *bêche-de-mer*; *s.-devil*, kinds of fish; *s.-dog*, kinds of seal, also dogfish, also old sailor (esp. of the Elizabethan sea-captains), & see *sea*-DOG[1]; *s. eagle*, kinds of fishing eagle, also osprey; *s.-ear*, ormer; *s. elephant*, large kind of seal with proboscis; *s.-fan*, kind of coral; *sea·faring* a. & n., traversing the s. esp. habitually (*s.-f. man*, sailor), so **sea·farER**[1] n. (rare); *s. fennel*, samphire; *s.-fight*, between war-ships; *s.-flower*, s. anemone; *s. fog*, caused by difference of land & s. temperature & extending only short way inland; *s.-fowl*; *s.-fox*, long-tailed shark; *s. front*, part of town facing s.; *s. furbelow*, kinds of brown seaweed; *s.-gauge*, ship's draught, also kind of sounding-instrument; *s. gherkin*, s. cucumber; *s. gilliflower*, s. pink; *s.-girt*, surrounded by sea (poet., rhet., of island &c.); *s.-god(dess)*; *sea·going*, (of ship) for crossing s. not coasting, (of person) seafaring; *s. grape*, shrub allied to firs, also gulf-weed, also (pl.) cuttle-fish eggs; *s.-green* a. & n., (of) bluish green as of s.; *s.-gull*; *s. hedgehog*, s.-urchin; *s.-hog*, porpoise, (slang) fast liner; *s.-horse*, creature harnessed to s. god's chariot having horse's head & fish's tail, also walrus, also hippocampus; *s. kale*, kind of colewort with young shoots used as table vegetable; *s. kidney*, kidney-shaped polypidom; *s.-king*, medieval Scandinavian pirate chief; *s. lace*, kind of seaweed with long cord-like fronds; *s. lawyer*, (naut. term of contempt for) captious person; *s.-legs*, ability to walk on deck of rolling ship (*has not yet got his s.-l.*); *s. lemon*, a yellow oval mollusc; *s. leopard*, kinds of spotted seal; *s. level*, level continuous with that of s. half-way between high & low water (also *mean s. l.*) as used in reckoning height of hills &c. & for barometric standard (*corrected to s. l.*); *s. lily*, crinoid; *s.-line*, horizon at s.; *s. lion*, kinds of large eared seal, esp. one with mane; *sea·man* (pl. *-men*), sailor, (Nav.) sailor below rank of officer (ABLE-*bodied s.-m.*; *ordinary s.-m.*, below rating of A.B.), person expert in practical management of ship, *good, bad, no*, &c., navigator, whence **sea·manLIKE**, **sea·manLY**[1], aa., **sea·manSHIP**(3) n.; *s.-mark*, beacon, lighthouse, &c., or elevated conspicuous object, used to direct course at s.; *s.-mat*, polyzoan forming flat matted coralline; *s. melon*, kind of holothurian; *s.-mew*, gull; *s. mile*, geographical MILE; *s. monster*, any huge, terrible, or strange s.-animal; *s. moss*, mosslike polyzoan or seaweed; *s.-mouse*, an iridescent s.-worm; *s. mud*, saline deposit of salt marshes &c. used as manure; *s. necklace*, string of whelk egg-cases; *s. needle*, garfish; *s. nettle*, jelly-fish; *s.-nymph*; *s. oak*, kind of seaweed; *s. ooze*, s. mud; *s. orange*, globose orange-coloured holothurian; *s.-orb*, globe-fish; *s. otter*, kind with very valuable fur; *s.-owl*, = LUMP[2]; *s.-ox*, walrus; *s.-pad*, starfish; *s. parrot*, puffin; *s. pass*, neutral ship's passport in time of war; *s.-pay*, for active service at s.; *s. peach, pear*, kinds of ascidium; *s.-pen*, feather-shaped polyp; *s. pie*, sailors' pie of salt meat &c., also a shore-bird, the oyster-catcher; *s.-piece*, picture of scene at s.; *seapi·et*, s. pie (bird); *s.-pig*, porpoise, also dugong; *s.-pike*, garfish, hake, & other fish; *s. pilot*, s. pie (bird); *s. pincushion*, skate's egg-case; *s. pink*, common coast-flower, thrift; *s.-plane*, aeroplane constructed for rising from & alighting on water; *s. poacher*, a small fish; *sea·port*, town with harbour; *s. pumpkin*, s. melon; *s.-purse*, skate's egg-case; *s. raven*, sculpin; *s. robin*, red gurnard; *s.-room*, clear space at s. allowing ship to turn &c.; *s. rover*, pirate or piratical ship; *s.-salt*, got by evaporating s.-water; *s.-scape*, s.-piece; *s. serpent*, kinds of snake living in sea, also (*the s.-s.*) enormous serpentine s. monster occasionally reported as seen but disbelieved in by naturalists; *seashore·*, land close to s., (Law) space between high & low water marks; *sea·sick*, vomiting or inclined to vomit from motion of ship &c., whence **sea·sickNESS** n.; *seasi·de*, places or some unspecified place close to s. as permanent or esp. as holiday residence (*do you like the s.-s.?*; *must go to the s.-s.*); *s.-sleeve*, cuttlefish; *s. snail*, small slimy fish, the unctuous sucker, also periwinkle or similar shellfish; *s. snipe*, the dunlin, also the snipe-fish; *s. squirt*, any ascidium; *s.*

strawberry, kind of polyp; *s. sunflower*, s. anemone; *s. swallow*, tern; *s.-tang(le)*, kinds of seaweed; *s.-toad*, the angler; *s.-urchin*, echinus; *s.-wall*, wall or embankment made to check encroachment of s.; *s.-ware*, seaweed collected for manure or other uses; *s.-water*; *s.-way*, ship's progress, also place where ship lies in rough water (*in a s.-w.*); *sea·weed*, any alga or other plant growing in s.; *s.-whip*, whip-shaped coral; *s. whipcord*, kind of seaweed; *s.-wife*, fish allied to wrasse; *sea·wind*, = *seabreeze*; *s.-wing*, a bi-valve mollusc; *sea·withwind*, s.-bells; *s.-wolf*, s. elephant, also kinds of fish, also viking or pirate; *sea·worthy*, (of ship) in fit state to put to s., strong & well rigged &c., whence **sea·worthi**NESS n. Hence **sea·**WARD a., adv., & n., **sea·**WARDS adv. [OE *sǽ*, cf. Du. *zee*, G *see*]

seal[1], n., & v.i. Kinds of carnivorous amphibious marine mammal with short limbs modified to serve chiefly for swimming but having fur or hair & beastlike face, feeding on fish & hunted for their oil & skin & the valuable fur of some species (*eared s.* or *otary*, kinds distinguished from *common s.* by having visible external ears, & including the larger kinds, as sea bear, sea lion, sea elephant, & the fur-ss.); *s.-fishery* or **sea·l**ERY n.; *s.-rookery*, seals' breeding-place; *sea·l(skin)*, skin of s., or usu. prepared fur of ss. as material for women's jackets &c., jacket of this; (vb) hunt ss. [OE *seolh*, cf. ON *selr*, Da. *sæl*]

seal[2], n., & v.t. Piece of wax, lead, or other such material, impressed with device & attached in some way to document usu. in addition to signature as guarantee of authenticity (*given under my hand & s.*, signed & sealed by me; *set* one's *s. to*, authorize or confirm) or to envelope or to any receptacle such as box or room or house to prevent its being opened without knowledge of owner &c. (*leaden s.*, stamped piece of lead holding ends of a wire used as fastening; *under s. of confession, confidence, silence*, &c., fig. of communications for which secrecy is stipulated or obligatory), impression stamped on or paper disk stuck to document as symbol equivalent to wax s.; (fig.) significant or prophetic mark (*has the s. of death in his face*); gem, piece of metal, &c., serving as stamp to produce s. on wax &c. or paper (*s.-ring*, finger-ring with s.; *the ss.*, those held during tenure of office by Lord Chancellor or Secretary of State; *Great S.*, s. in charge of Lord Chancellor or Lord Keeper used in sealing Parliament-writs, treaties, & important State papers; PRIVY *S.*; *Fisher's S.*, papal s. with St Peter fishing as device); act done, thing given, event regarded, as confirmation or guarantee *of* (*s. of love*, kiss, birth of child, &c.; *baptism & the Lord's Supper are ss. of God's covenant with us*); substance used to close aperture &c., esp. water standing in drain-trap to prevent ascent of foul air (*s.-pipe*, DIP[2]-pipe); *s.-wort*, SOLOMON'S *s.* (Vb) affix s. to, stamp or fasten with s., certify as correct with s. or stamp (*Sealed Book*, one of perfect copies of Book of Common Prayer certified by Great S. under Charles II), show genuineness of (devotion &c.) *with* one's life &c.; close securely or hermetically, stop up or *up*, (*my lips are sealed*, I must not speak; *sleep sealed his eyes*; *is a sealed book to me*, is something of which I have & can get no knowledge; *windows must be sealed up*, e.g. by pasting paper along all crevices; *s. up tin*, solder it so that air has no access; *s. pipe* &c., provide it with water-s. by means of trap &c.); set significant mark on, set apart, destine, decide irrevocably, (*death has sealed her for his own*; *is sealed to* or *for salvation, damnation*, &c.; *his fate is sealed*), (of Admiralty) officially adopt (design); confine securely (often *up*); fix (staple &c.) into wall &c. with cement &c.; *sealing-wax*, mixture of shellac & rosin with turpentine & pigment used for ss. [vb f. n., f. OF *seel* f. L *sigillum* see SIGILLATE]

sea·ler, n. In vbl senses of SEAL[1], [2]; esp., ship or man engaged in seal-hunting. [-ER[1]]

Sea·lyham, n. *S.* (*terrier*), a breed of terrier.

seam, n., & v.t. Line of junction between two edges esp. those of two pieces of cloth &c. turned back & sewn together or of boards fitted edge to edge, fissure left by gaping of parallel edges (*ship's ss. want caulking*); scar, cicatrice; line of separation between two strata; thin stratum of coal &c. between thicker strata; (Anat.) suture; *s.-lace*, seaming-lace; *s.-presser*, agricultural implement for flattening down furrow-ridges after the plough, also tailors' goose; hence **sea·m**LESS a. (Vb) unite with s. (rare); mark or score with s., fissure, or scar (chiefly in p.p.; *seamed with wounds, cracks*, &c.); (Knitting) make ridges in (stocking &c.); *seaming-lace*, galloon or other trimming sewn over ss. in upholstery &c. [OE *séam*, cf. Du. *zoom*, G *saum*; cogn. w. SEW]

sea·mstress (sĕm-), **semp-**, n. Sewing-woman. [OE *séamestre* (prec., -STER) + -ESS[1]]

sea·my, a. Showing seams (*s. side*, inside of garment &c. where turning-back of seams is visible, chiefly fig. of the less presentable or attractive aspect of life &c.). [-Y[2]]

Seanad Eireann (shă·nadh ār·an), n. Upper Chamber of the Irish Free State legislature. [Ir., = senate of Ireland]

se·ance (sā-), ***séance*** (F), n. Sitting of a society or deliberative body; meeting for exhibition or investigation of spiritualistic phenomena [F, f, L *sedēre* sit]

sear[1] a. & v.t., **sere** a. (Of leaves, flowers, &c., & fig. of age &c.) withered, dried up (*the s., the yellow leaf,* old age). (Vb) wither up, blast, (rare); scorch surface of esp. with hot iron, cauterize, brand; make callous (*a seared conscience*); *searing-iron,* for cauterizing. [vb f. adj., OE *séar,* cf. O Du. *sore* dry; cogn. w. Gk *auos* dry, & AUSTERE]

sear[2]. See SERE[1].

search (sertsh), v.t. & i., & n. Look or feel or go over (person or his face or pockets, receptacle, place, book) for what may be found or to find something of which presence is suspected, probe (lit. & fig.; *s. a wound, men's hearts*); (of shrapnel, gunners) penetrate all recesses of (trench &c.); (archaic) look for, seek out or (still current) *out*; make s. or investigation (*for* or abs.); (part., of examination &c.) thorough, leaving no loopholes, whence **sear·ching**LY[2] adv.; hence **sear·cher**[1](1, 2) n., **sear·ch**LESS a. (poet.). (N.) act of searching, investigation, quest, (*am in s. of,* trying to find; *the s. for* or *of*; *right of s.* in internat. law, belligerent's right to stop neutral vessel & s. it for contraband; *s.-light,* electric arc-light with concentrated beam that can be turned in any direction for use esp. on ships for discovering enemy or lighting-up channel; *s.-party,* persons going out to look for lost or concealed person or thing; *s.-warrant,* granted by justice of peace to enter premises of person suspected of concealing stolen property &c. [ME *serchen, cerchen,* f. OF *cerchier* (F *chercher*) f. LL *circare* go round (CIRCUS)]

sear·ching, n. In vbl senses; esp., *ss. of heart,* misgivings caused by guilt or otherwise. [-ING[1]]

sea·son (-zn), n., & v.t. & i. Proper time, favourable opportunity, time at which something is plentiful or in vogue or active, (*a word in s.,* advice given when it is likely to be taken or is needed; *in s. & out of s.,* at all times without selection; *oysters, venison, strawberries, are in s.,* to be had in good condition & without special difficulty; *the holiday s.,* any of the times when most people keep holiday, esp. Christmas, Easter, Whitsuntide, or August; *the London, Brighton, Parisian, s.,* when society is busy or visitors many there; *London in the s., the theatrical, publishing, cricket, s.*; *close, open, s.,* when hunting &c. of some animal is prohibited, permitted); period of indefinite or various length (*may endure for a s.*; *a s. of inaction*; *s.-ticket,* issued at reduced rates for any number of journeys taken, performances attended, &c., within a year, six months, or other period); one of the divisions of the year with distinguishable characteristics of temperature, rainfall, vegetation, &c. (*the four ss.,* spring, summer, autumn, winter, beginning astronomically each at an equinox or solstice but popularly having different dates in different countries; *the dry, rainy, s.,* two ss. recognized in the tropics instead of the four of temperate countries); hence **sea·son**AL, **sea·son**LESS, aa., **sea·sonal**LY[2] adv. (Vb) bring into efficient or sound condition by habituation, acclimatization, exposure, special preparation, use, or lapse of time, inure, mature, (*seasoned soldiers, timber, wine*); make palatable or piquant by introduction of salt, condiments, wit, jests, &c., give zest to, flavour, (*highly seasoned dishes*; *conversation seasoned with humour*), whence **sea·son**ER[1](2), **sea·son**ING[1](4), nn.; temper, moderate, (*let mercy s. justice*); become fit for use by being seasoned. [vb f. n., f. OF *seson,* f. L *sationem* (*serere sat-* sow, -ION) in LL sense *season*]

sea·sonable, a. Suitable to, of the kind usual at, the season (esp. *s. weather,* frost &c. in winter); opportune, meeting the needs of the occasion, (*s. aid, caution,* &c.; *the s. arrival of*). Hence **sea·sonable**NESS n., **sea·sonab**LY[2] adv. [prec., n., -ABLE]

seat, n., & v.t. Thing used, esp. one made, for sitting on, chair, throne, stool, bench, or other sitting-accommodation, (*the ss. are uncomfortable*), occupation of a s. (*took his s. on the throne, a rock*; *pray take a s.,* sit down), whence **sea·t**ING[1](6) n., **-seat**ER[1] n. (motor-car, aeroplane, &c., with ss. for specified number); part of chair &c. on which sitter's weight directly rests, part of machine that supports another part (*s. of valve,* surface &c. on which it slides or works); the buttocks, part of trousers &c. covering them; site or location, temporary or permanent scene, abiding-place, *of* (*the liver is the s. of disease*; *the disease has its s. in the liver*; *the s. of war is mountainous*; *an ancient s. of learning*); country mansion esp. with park or large grounds (*has a s. in Norfolk*; *the country ss. of England*); right to sitting-accommodation or to sit as member of board or esp. House of Commons (*have taken two ss. for* Macbeth; *has a s. on the Board*; *lost his* or *the s.,* failed to secure re-election to Parliament); manner of sitting horse, bicycle, &c. (*has a good, firm, graceful, s.*); hence **sea·t**LESS a. (Vb) make sit, place oneself in sitting posture, (p.p.) sitting, (*took up the child & seated him on the bookcase*; *s. candidate,* elect him to Parliament; *seated himself in state*; *found him seated on a reversed bucket*; *pray be seated,* sit down); fit or provide (church, room, &c.) with ss. (*is seated for 5000*); (of room &c.) have ss. for (number); mend s. of (chair, trousers); establish in position, fix in particular place, (*s. machinery,* put it on its supports; *the seated hills* poet.; *a deep-seated disease*; *the Turks seated themselves on the Bosphorus*). [vb f. n., f. ON *sæti*, cogn. w. SIT]

sebā·ceous (-shus), a. Of tallow or fat, fatty, *s. gland, follicle, duct*, secreting or conveying oily matter or *s. humour* to lubricate hair & skin). [L *sebaceus* (*sebum*, tallow), -OUS]

sebe·stan, -en, n. Plumlike fruit of the tree *Cordia Myxa*, used medicinally in the East & formerly in Europe. [Arab. *sabastān*]

sec, a. (Of wine) dry. [F]

sĕ·cant, a. & n. (math.). Cutting; (n.) s. line, esp. radius of circle produced through end of arc to meet tangent to other end, ratio of this to radius, *s. of angle*, ratio of greater to less of its containing lines as bounded by a perpendicular to either (abbr. *sec*; *sec 60° = 2*). [L *secare* cut, -ANT]

sécateur (sĕ·kater), n. Pair of pruning clippers. [F, irreg. f. L *secare* cut]

se·cco, n. Tempera-painting. [It.]

se·ccotine (-ēn), n., & v.t. A liquid substitute for glue; (v.t.) stick with s. (*on, together*, &c.). [proprietary name introduced 1894 by J. Stevenson]

sece·de, v.i. Withdraw formally from membership of some body, esp. a Church or federal or other State. Hence **sece·der**[1] n. [f. L SE(*cedere cess-* go)]

secer·nent, a. & n. (physiol.). That secretes or can secrete. (N.) secreting organ; drug that promotes secretion. [as SECRETE, -ENT]

sece·ssion, n. Act of seceding (*War of S.*, American civil war of 1861–5 caused by s. of eleven Southern States). Hence **sece·ssionism**(3), **sece·ssionist**(2), nn. [f. L *secessionem* (SECEDE, -ION)]

seclu·de, v.t. Keep (person, place, esp. one*self*) retired or away from company or resort (*s.* one*self from society*; *a secluded spot, life*, &c.). Hence **seclu·dedly**[2] adv. [f. L SE(*cludere -clus-* = *claudere* shut)]

seclu·sion (-zhn), n. Secluding or being secluded, retirement, privacy, avoidance of intercourse, whence **seclu·sionist**(2) n.; secluded place. [f. med.L *seclusionem* (prec., -ION)]

sĕ·cond, a., n., & v.t. Next after first (*the, a, s.*, often as n. with ellipse of n., esp. = s. day of month; often further defined, as *the s. man you meet, was the s. to come*; *in the s. place*, secondly; *s. to none*, surpassed by no other; *s.* CLASS; *s. cabin*, s.-class accommodation in passenger-ship; *come in, finish, s.*, be s. in race; *s. floor*, that two floors above ground-floor; *s. distance*, space in landscape between foreground & background); other besides one or the first, additional, supplementary, (*s. advent*, return of Christ esp. as preliminary to His expected personal reign on earth, whence **second-a·dventist** n.; *s. ballot*, electoral method by which, if the winner on the first ballot has not polled more than half the votes cast, a second is taken in which only he & the next candidate are eligible; *s. chamber*, upper House in bicameral parliament; *s. coming*, s. advent; *s.* DIVISION; *s. nature*, acquired tendency that has become instinctive, as *habit is s. n., self-sacrifice is now s. n. with him*; *s.* SELF; *s. teeth*, those of adults, cf. MILK[1]*-teeth*; *s. thoughts*, opinion or resolution formed on reconsideration; *s.* WIND[1]); of secondary kind, subordinate, derived, unoriginal, imitative, metaphorical, (*s. cause*, that is itself caused; *s.* CHILDHOOD, COUSIN; *s. Daniel, Solomon*, &c., person comparable to these; *s. fiddle*, taking s. part, esp. fig. in *play s. fiddle*, be of only secondary importance, often *to* other person; *at s. hand*, by hearsay, not actual observation &c.; *s.* INTENTION, SIGHT[1]); *s.-best*, of s. quality (*come off s.-b.*, get the worst of it); *s.-class*, of s. or of inferior position or quality (*s.-c. passenger, ticket*, using, entitling to use of, s.-c. railway-carriage &c.); *s.-hand*, (of clothes, books, furniture, &c.) bought after use by a previous owner, (of information &c.) taken on another's authority & not got by original observation or research; *s. lieutenant*, army OFFICER; *s.-pair back, front*, room on s. floor in back, front, of house (see PAIR[1]); *s.* PERSON (gram.); *s.-rate*, not of superior quality, (of ship, also as n.) rated in s. class. (N.) s. person &c. in race &c. (*a good s.*, close up); s. class in examination for honours, person who takes this; another person or thing besides the previously mentioned or principal, whether regarded as next, inferior, or equal; (Mus.) next tone to given one in diatonic series, interval between or combination of these two, second tone in scale, s. voice or instrument or part in harmony with the air; (pl.) goods of s. quality, esp. coarse flour or bread made from it; supporter chosen by principal in duel or pugilism to see fair play &c.; sixtieth part of a MINUTE of time or angular measurement (see etym.), (loosely) short time (*wait a s.*); *s. of* EXCHANGE[1]; *s.-hand*, extra hand in some watches & clocks recording ss.; *s.-mark*, mark (″) used with s.-figures in statements of angular measurement or time (*1° 6′ 40″*; *1 h. 35′ 15″*), or denoting linear inches. (Vb) supplement, support, back up, (*s. words with deeds*; *will you s. me if I ask him?*); (of member of debating body) give the necessary formal support to (motion &c. or its proposer) by rising with or without speech to show that mover is not isolated, whence **se·conder**[1] n.; (Mil.; usu. *seco·nd*) put (officer) into temporary retirement with a view to staff or other extra-regimental appointment. [F, f. L *secundus* (*sequi* follow); *s.* of time &c. f. F *seconde* f. med.L (*minuta*) *secunda* secondary minute, i.e. minute of a minute]

se·condary, a. & n. Next below, coming in place or time after, depending on or derived from, of less importance or originality than, what is primary, of the second rank &c., supplementary, of inferior rank or importance *to*, (*s.* COLOUR[1]; *s. education, school,* for those who have received elementary or primary instruction but not yet proceeded to university or occupation, esp. boys & girls of 13–19; *s. planet,* planet's satellite); (Geol.) = MESO*zoic*; hence **se·condari**LY[2] adv. (N.) deputy or delegate; minor cathedral dignitary; s. planet; feather growing on second joint of wing; insect's hind wing; s. strata. [f. L *secundarius* (prec., -ARY[1])]

seco·nde, n. Fencing-position. [F (SECOND)]

se·condly, adv. In the second place (in enumerations). [-LY[2]]

seco·ndo, n. Second performer or lower part in duet (cf. PRIMO[1]). [It. (as SECOND)]

se·crecy, n. Keeping of, ability to keep or habit of keeping, secrets (*he promised s.*; *can rely on his s.*; *the gift of s.*; *done with great s.*); tendency to concealment, secretiveness; unrevealed state, being kept secret, (*there can be no s. about it*; *in s.*, in secret). [earlier *secretee, -tie* (foll., -TY)]

sē·cret, a. & n. (To be) kept private, not (to be) made known or exposed to view, privy, (*s. treaty, understanding, errand, door, passage, sin, process, arrival, influence*; *the s. parts,* parts of body of which exposure is avoided esp. the genitals; *s.-service money,* applied by Government to securing information &c. without obligation to state details of expenditure), whence **se·cret**LY[2] adv.; given to or having faculty of secrecy, secretive, close, reticent, not leaky; (of place &c.) secluded, retired. (N.) thing (to be) kept s. (*keep a* or *the s.*, abstain from revealing it); thing known only to a limited number (*in the s.*, among the number of those allowed to know it; *open s.*, thing s. only to those who do not trouble to learn it); mystery, thing of which explanation is sought in vain, (*the ss. of nature*); true but not generally recognized method for attainment *of* (*the s. of health, success, happiness, salvation, is temperance, to try again,* &c.); secrecy (only in *in s.*, secretly); (R.-C. Ch.) celebrant's private prayer in Mass; (pl.) s. parts of body. [F, f. L *secretus* f. SE(*cernere cret-* sift) put apart]

sĕcretaire·, n. Escritoire. [F (*-cré-*), as foll.]

sĕ·cretary, n. Person employed by another to assist him in correspondence, literary work, getting information, & other confidential matters (often *private s.*; *unpaid s.*, esp. of person acting as s. to prominent politician for sake of experience); official appointed by society or company or corporation to conduct its correspondence, keep its records, & deal in the first instance with its business (*honorary s.*, abbr. *hon. sec.*, unpaid s. usu. of society not conducted for profit); minister in charge of a Government Office (*the S. of State for the Home Department, Foreign Affairs, War, the Colonies, India,* or *Home, Foreign, War, Colonial, Indian, S.*; *the S. for Scotland*; *under-s.*, one of two attached to each S. of State, one as permanent manager of the connected office, the other usu. as representative in other House of the S. of State; *permanent s.*, under-s. as above; *s. of legation* or *embassy,* ambassador's chief subordinate & deputy); secretaire, escritoire; (Print.) script type imitating engrossing-hand; *s.-bird,* African bird preying on snakes, with crest likened to pen stuck over writer's ear. Hence **secretār·**IAL a., **secretār·**IATE[1](1), **se·cretary**SHIP(1), nn. [earlier sense *confidant*; f. med.L *secretarius* (SECRET, -ARY[1])]

secre·te, v.t. Put (object, person, one*self*) into place of concealment; (Physiol.; of gland or organ or the person &c. of which it is part) produce by secretion, whence **secre·**TOR[2](2) n., **secre·**TORY a. [f. L SECRET*us*]

secre·tion, n. Act of concealing (*the s. of stolen goods*); (Physiol.) process by which special substances are separated from blood or sap for service in the organism or for rejection as excretions, any substance produced by such process, as saliva, urine, resin. [F (*sécré-*), f. L *secretionem* (SECRET, -ION)]

sē·cretive (*or* sĭkrē·-), a. Given to making secrets, intentionally uncommunicative, needlessly reserved. Hence **se·cretive**LY[2] adv., **-ive**NESS n., (*or* sĭkrē·-). [f. SECRET + -IVE]

sect, n. Body of persons agreed upon religious doctrines usu. different from those of an established or orthodox Church from which they have separated & usu. having distinctive common worship, nonconformist or other Church as described by opponents, party or faction in a religious body, religious denomination, so **sectār·**IAN a. & n., **sectar·ian**ISM(2, 3) n., **sectar·ian**IZE(3) v.t.; followers of a particular philosopher or philosophy or school of thought. [f. L *secta* faction, following, f. stem of *sequi secut-* follow, cf. *sectari* pursue]

se·ctary, n. (archaic). Member of a sect, esp. of the Independents, Presbyterians, &c., at time of the Civil War. [f. F *sectaire* f. med.L *sectarius* (prec., -ARY[1])]

se·ctile, a. Able to be cut (esp. of soft minerals such as talc). [F, f. L *sectilis* (*secare sect-* cut, -IL)]

se·ction, n., & v.t. Separation by cutting; part cut off from something, one of the parts into which something is divided arbitrarily or may naturally be considered as divided (e.g. length of cane-stem between two rings), one part of a structure such as boat or wooden house that is made in parts for transportation, one of the minor subdivisions of a book usu. indicated by the *s.-mark* (§; § 20), (Mil.) subdivision of the platoon, part of community having separate interests or characteristics (whence **se·ctionalISM** n., **se·ctionalIZE** v.t.), (*microscopic s.*, thin slice cut from something for examination with microscope; *subject falls into five ss.*; *last s. of the journey*; *conveyed to Tanganyika in ss.*; *ss. have been preferred to chapters*; *s.-commanders will be responsible*; *popular with all ss. & classes*); cutting of solid by plane (*conic ss.*, study of curves of intersection produced by allowing plane to cut cone at various angles), representation of internal structure of something supposed to be cut thus (*vertical, horizontal, longitudinal, oblique*, &c., *s.*, according to position chosen for plane); (Nat. Hist.) group, esp. subgenus; the s. mark (see above) used as mark of marginal reference or with or without number to indicate beginning of s.; hence **se·ctionAL** a., **se·ctionalLY**[2] adv. (Vb) arrange in, divide into, ss. [f. L *sectionem* (prec., -ION)]

se·ctor, n. Plane figure enclosed between two radii of circle, ellipse, &c., & the arc cut off by them (*s. of sphere* &c., solid generated by revolution of plane s. round one radius); (Mil.) any of the parts into which the space occupied by opposing armies is distributed according as each lies within the tactical purview of a headquarters at the focus or centre in rear; mathematical rule of two flat pieces working on rule-joint with lines representing sines, tangents, &c., radiating from centre of joint for use in making diagrams &c. Hence **se·ctorAL** a. [LL, =sector f. L =cutter (prec., -OR[2])]

sector·ial, a. & n. (Carnivore's tooth) acting with tooth in opposite jaw like scissors (of specialized molar or premolar). [prec., -IAL]

sĕ·cūlar, a. & n. Occurring once in or lasting for an age or a century (*s. games*, ancient-Roman festival held at long intervals; *s. hymn*, composed for this; *the s. bird*, phoenix); lasting or going on for ages or an indefinitely long time (opp. *periodical, cyclic*; *s. change*, going on slowly but persistently; *s. cooling* or *refrigeration*, that of the earth from fluid state; *s. acceleration*, slow increase in motion of heavenly body; *s. fame*, enduring; *the s. rivalry between France & England, Church & State*, &c.); concerned with the affairs of this world, worldly, not sacred, not monastic, not ecclesiastical, temporal, profane, lay, (*s. affairs, education, music*; *the s. clergy*, parish priests &c., opp. *regular*; *the s. arm* hist., civil jurisdiction to which criminal was transferred by ecclesiastical courts for severer punishment); sceptical of religious truth or opposed to religious education &c., whence **se·cularISM**(3)n., **se·cularIST**(2)n. & a., **se·cularIZE**(3) v.t., **se·cularizA·TION** n.; hence **seculă·RITY** n., **se·cularLY**[2] adv. (N.) s. priest. [(in senses lay, worldly, f. OF *seculer*) f. L *saecularis* (*saeculum* generation, age, perh. f. st. of *serere sat-* sow)]

secu·nd, a. (bot., zool.). Arranged on one side only (as flowers in lily-of-the-valley). Hence **secu·ndLY**[2] adv. [f. L as SECOND]

secu·ndo. See PRIMO[2].

secu·ndum, L prep. = according to: *s. artem*, artificially, also skilfully or scientifically; *s. naturam*, naturally, not artificially; *s. quid*, in some respect only, not absolutely or generally, with limitations.

secu·ndus. See PRIMUS[1].

secure·, a., & v.t. Untroubled by danger or apprehension (*a quiet s. existence*; *dwell s.*), (archaic) confident or unsuspecting (*a s. fool*, dupe &c.; *the s. hope of salvation*); safe against attack, impregnable; reliable, certain not to fail or give way, (*a s. foundation, fastening, foothold, grasp*); (usu. pred.) in safe keeping, firmly fastened, (*have got him s.*; *are you sure it is s.?*); having sure prospect *of*, safe *against* or *from*, (*s. of victory*; *s. against assault*; *s. from interruption*); hence **secure·LY**[2] adv. (Vb) fortify (town, harbour, &c., usu. *with* wall &c.); confine, enclose, fasten, or close, securely (*s. prisoner, valuables, buckle, window*; *s. vein* &c. in surgery, compress to prevent bleeding; *s. arms* mil., hold rifles with lock in armpit to guard from rain); guarantee, make safe against loss, (*loan secured on landed property* &c.; *how can I s. myself against the consequences?*; *to s. the labourer the* or *in the fruits of his labour*); succeed in getting, obtain, (esp. something coveted or competed for, as *have secured front places, a first-class cook, the prize, my ends*); hence **secur·ABLE** a. [vb f. a., f. L SE(*curus* f. *cura* care)]

secūr·iform, a. (esp. nat. hist.). Axe-shaped. [L *securis* axe (*secare* cut), -I-, -FORM]

secūr·ity, n. In adj. senses; also or esp.: over-confidence; thing that guards or guarantees (*pride should at least be a s. against meanness*; *in s. for*, as guarantee for), thing deposited or hypothecated as pledge for fulfilment of undertaking or payment of loan to be forfeited in case of failure, document as evidence of loan, certificate of stock, bond, exchequer bill, &c. [f. L *securitatem* (SECURE, -TY)]

seda·n(-chair), n. 17th & 18th c. vehicle seated for one & carried by two chairmen with poles; =LADY-*chair*. [?]

seda·te, a. (Of person or his manner, look, speech, or writing) tranquil, equable, composed, settled, not impulsive or lively. Hence **seda·te**LY[2] adv., **seda·te**NESS n. [L *sedare* settle (*sedēre* sit), -ATE[2]]

sĕ·dative, a. & n. (Drug, influence, &c.) tending to soothe. [f. F *sédatif* as prec. +-IVE]

sē dĕfende·ndo, adv. In self-defence (as plea in cases of homicide). [L]

sĕ·dentary (-dn-), a. & n. Sitting (*s. posture, statue*); (of person) inclined by nature or driven by occupation to, (of occupation) involving, (of life &c.) characterized by, much sitting, whence **se·dentar**ILY[2] adv., **se·dentari**NESS n.; (Zool. &c.) not migratory, free-swimming, &c., (of spider) lying in wait till prey is in web. (N.) s. person; s. spider. [f. F *sédentaire* f. L *sedentarius* (*sedēre* sit, -ENT, -ARY[1])]

sedĕr·unt, n. Sitting of ecclesiastical assembly or other body, or of a company over the wine or in talk (*had a long* s.). [L, = (the following persons) sat]

sedge, n. Kinds of grass-like plant with jointless stems growing in marshes or by waterside, bed of such plants; *s.-warbler, -wren*, kind of warbler frequenting s. Hence **se·dg**Y[2] a. [OE *secg*, cf. LG *segge*; cogn. w. SAW[1], SECTION, prob. w. ref. to swordlike blades]

sedi·lia, n. pl. (sing. *sedī·lĕ*, rare). Set of usu. three stone seats for priests in S. wall of chancel often canopied & otherwise decorated. [f. L *sedile* seat (*sedēre* sit)]

sĕ·diment, n. Matter that settles to bottom of liquid, lees, dregs. Hence **sedime·nt**ARY[1] a. [F (*sé*-), f. L *sedimentum* (prec., -MENT)]

sedi·tion (-shn), n. Agitation directed against the authority of a State's executive, conduct or speech tending to rebellion or breach of public order. So **sedi·tious** a., **sedi·tious**LY[2] adv., **sedi·tious**NESS n. [OF, f. L *seditionem* (*sed*- =SE-, *ire it*- go, -ION)]

sedu·ce, v.t. Lead astray, tempt into sin or crime, corrupt; persuade (woman) into surrender of chastity, debauch. Hence **sedu·c**IBLE a., **sedu·cing**LY[2] adv., **sedu·ce**MENT (rare), **sedu·c**ER[1], nn. [f. L SE(*ducere duct*- lead)]

sedu·ction, n. Seducing or being seduced; thing that tends to seduce, tempting or attractive quality *of* (often with merely playful or no imputation of blame), (*the ss. of a great capital, beauty, the country*, &c.), so **sedu·ct**IVE a., **sedu·ctive**LY[2] adv., **sedu·ctive**NESS n. [F (*sé*-), f. L *seductionem* (prec., -ION)]

sĕ·dūlous, a. Diligent, persevering, assiduous, (of action &c.) deliberately & consciously continued, painstaking, (*with s. care*; *s. flattery, attentions*; *play the s. ape*, acquire literary style by imitation). Hence or cogn. **se·dulous**LY[2] adv., **sedu·l**ITY, **se·dulous**NESS n. [L *sedulus*, -OUS]

see[1], v.i. & t. (saw, seen). Have or exercise the power of discerning objects with the eyes (*sees best at night*; *cannot s. till the ninth day*; *s. into millstone, through brick wall*, fig. of preternatural acuteness of intelligence; *seeing is believing*, one's own observation is the best evidence; *s.* DOUBLE[1] adv.; *s. red* slang, s. things as blood-coloured, be filled with homicidal fury; *seeing ye shall s. & shall not perceive*; *s. through* fig., not be deceived by, penetrate, detect nature of); descry, discern by sight, observe, look at or over, (*come where we cannot be seen*; *children should be seen & not heard*; *please s. whether it is there, where it is*; *s. the light*, be born or alive; *things seen*, not imaginary &c.; *s. visions*, be a seer &c.; *s. things*, have hallucinations &c.; *s. stars*, have dancing lights before eyes from blow on head; *was seen to fall* or *falling*; *saw him fall* or *falling*; *s. the back*, be quit *of* visitor, invader, &c.; *cannot see my way*; s. one's *way to* do or *to* doing, manage, contrive; *s. the sights, town*, &c., as SIGHT[1]-seer; *s. over* house &c., go round examining; *worth seeing*, notable; *s.p. 15* &c., look at, *vide*; *s. thing done*, supervise doing of it); learn from the newspaper (*I s. Roberts died yesterday*); discern mentally, attain to comprehension of, apprehend, excogitate, ascertain by search or inquiry or reflection, consider, (*cannot s. a* or *the joke, point*; *do you s. what I mean?*, also *s.?* ellipt. in same sense colloq.; *you s.* parenth., as you no doubt understand, also = I must explain; *I s.*, now that you have explained I understand; *as far as I can s.*, to the best of my understanding or belief; *must s. what can be done*; *do not s. the good, fun, advantage*, &c., *of doing*; *do not s. how to do it*; *you s. what it is to have faith*), (part. as prep. or conj.) considering or inasmuch as (*seeing that you do not know it yourself*; *seeing no other course is open to us*); experience, go through more or less observantly, have presented to one's attention, contemplate & abstain from interference with, (*shall never s. death*; *have seen five reigns*; *will never s. 50* &c. *again*, is over that age; *s. life*, gain experience of men & manners esp. by dissipation &c.; so perh. *well seen* archaic, accomplished *in*, as intr. p.p.; *have seen the day when*, in drawing attention to past state of affairs; *never saw such doings*; *has seen service*, is expert or worn; *has seen better*, or *its* &c. *best, days*, has declined; *you will not s. me shot like a dog?*; *s.* person or thing *blowed* or *damned*, before one will do what he asks or trouble about it; *s. thing through* or *out*, not abandon undertaking before it is completed); grant interview or be at home to, pay visit to, secure interview with, (*refused to s. me*; *can I s. you on business?*; *when will you come & s. us?*; *must s. the lawyer, doctor,* &c.; *can s. you for five minutes*); call up picture of, imagine, (*cannot s. myself submitting to it*); recognize as tolerable, consent willingly to, (*do not s. being made use of*); escort, conduct, stand by & countenance, (*may I s. you home?*; *mind you s. him off the premises*; *s. off* nav. slang, outdo, defeat; *saw him off by the Mauretania*; *will you s. me through the difficulty?*); take view of, have opinion, (*I s. life, things, it, differently now*; *s. good,* consider it right or expedient *to* do; *s.* EYE[1] *to eye*); make provision, take care, give attention, make sure, (*s. that it is done*; *s. you don't catch your foot*; *s. to* one's *business*; *will s. about it,* & see below; *s. after,* take care of; *s. to it that,* take care that); make examination, hold inquiry, (*must s. into it*); reflect, take time to consider, (esp. *let me s.,* appeal for time to think before making answer or giving particulars, or confession that coming statement may need reconsideration; *will s. about it,* form for declining to act at once, & see above); (Gambling &c.) accept or take on (challenge to bet or competition, person offering it); *s.-bright,* the plant clary (w. ref. to use as eye-salve founded on pop. etym. of *clary* as = clear-eye). Hence **se·**ER[1] n. [OE *séon,* cf. Du. *zien,* G *sehen*]

see[2], n. What is committed to (arch)-bishop, (archi-)episcopal unit, (usu. *the s. of Norwich, Canterbury, Rome,* &c.; *Holy S., S. of Rome,* the Papacy or Papal court; cf. BISHOPRIC, DIOCESE; *several new ss. were created*). [f. OF *se(d)* f. L *sedes* seat (*sedēre* sit)]

seed, n., & v.i. & t. Flowering plant's unit of reproduction or germ capable of developing into another such plant, (collect.) ss. in any quantity esp. as collected for sowing, (*its ss. are, s. is, black*; *is full of s.*; *drops its ss.* or *s. everywhere*; *to be kept for* or *as s.*; *go, run, to s.,* cease flowering as s. comes, fig. grow shabby &c.); male fecundating fluid, semen, milt; (bibl.) offspring, progeny, (*raise up s.,* beget children; *the s. of Abraham,* Hebrews); germ, prime cause, beginning, *of* (*ss. of strife, vice*; *sow the ss. of,* initiate); *s.-cake,* containing whole ss. esp. caraway as flavouring; *s.-coral,* in small s.-like pieces; *s.-corn,* reserved for s.; *s.-drill,* DRILL[2]; *s.-eater,* kind of bird; *s.-fish,* ready to spawn; *s.-leaf,* primary leaf or developed cotyledon; *s.-lobe,* cotyledon; *s.-oysters,* young ones for planting; *s.-pearl,* small; *s.-plot,* piece of nursery-ground, (fig.) hotbed *of* sedition &c.; *seedsman,* dealer in ss.; *s.-time,* sowing season; *s.-vessel,* pericarp; *s.-wool,* raw cotton before ss. have been removed from fibre; hence **see·d**LESS **a.** (Vb) go to s., produce or let fall s.; sprinkle (as) with s.; remove ss. from (fruit &c.); separate s. from straw of (flax), (Sport) sort stronger from weaker (competitors) to secure good later matches in tournament; *seeding-machine,* mechanical s.-sower; *seeding-plough,* with hopper depositing s. in furrow as made. [OE *sǽd,* cf. Du. *zaad,* G *saat*; cogn. w. SOW[1]]

see·der, n. Seed-drill; apparatus for seeding raisins &c.; spawning fish. [-ER[1]]

see·dling, n. Plant raised from seed & not from cutting &c.; young tender plant. [-LING[1]]

see·dy, a. Full of seed, going to seed; (of brandy) having flavour attributed to weeds among the vines; (colloq.) shabby-looking, in worn clothes, out of sorts, feeling ill, whence **see·di**LY[2] adv.; *s.-toe,* disease of horse's foot. Hence **see·di**NESS n. [-Y[2]]

seek, v.t. & i. (*sought,* pr. sawt). Make search or inquiry for, try or be anxious to find or get, ask (thing *of* person), aim at, pursue as object, endeavour *to* do, make for or resort to (place, person, for advice, health, &c.), (*what are you seeking?*; *seeks a situation as cook, wealth, scope for his energies,* &c.; *sought of him a sign*; *seeks my aid*; *seeks my life* or *to kill me*; *came seeking advice*; *sought his bed, a fortune-teller, the shore*; *s. dead!,* order to retriever to find killed game; *s. out,* single out for pursuit &c., esp. make special efforts to secure society of); search (place, receptacle) *through*; make search or inquiry *after* or *for* (*sought-after,* much in demand, generally desired or courted); (archaic) resort in numbers *to* (person, place): *is* &c. *to s.* or *much to s.,* is deficient, wanting, or not yet found (*politeness is much to s. among them*; *is to s. in intelligence, grammar*; *an efficient leader is yet to s.*). Hence **(-)seek**ER[1] n. [OE *sécan,* cf. Du. *zoeken,* G *suchen*; cogn. w. L *sagire* perceive, Gk *hēgeomai* consider]

seel, v.t. (archaic). Close (eye), close eyes of (hawk), by sewing up lids, (fig.) hoodwink. [f. OF *siller, c-,* (*cil* eyelid f. L as CILIA)]

seem, v.i. Have the air or appearance or sensation of being, appear or be apparently perceived or ascertained *to* do or have done, (*be what you s. to be* or *s.*; *the man who seemed the ringleader*; *seems to be tired, a hopeless absurdity*; *seems to be a good fellow, saint,* &c.; *I s. to be* or *s. deaf today, s. to see him still*; *do not s. to* slang, somehow do not, as *I do not s. to like him, fancy it*; *s. good to,* be adopted as best course by; *what seemeth him good* archaic, what he chooses; *seems to have died at 35*); appear to be true or the fact (with anticipatory *it* & following *that*-clause, or parenth. with *it* only, often with implication of anger or remonstrance; *it seems* *to me that it will rain, such talk is absurd, we had better make up our minds to it*; *so we are to get nothing, it seems*; *it seems you were lying*; also *it should* or *would s.* in same senses; *me seems, -seemeth, -seemed,* archaic, it seems, seemed to me); (part.) ostensible, apparent only, apparent but perhaps not real, apparent & perhaps real, (*the seeming & the real*; *a seeming friend*; *with seeming sincerity*; *seeming-virtuous* &c., usu. with suggestion of falsity), whence **see·mingLY**[2] adv. [ME *seme* f. ON (Icel. *sæma* conform to), cogn. w. SAME]

see·mly, a. & adv. Decent, decorous, becoming; hence **see·mliNESS** n. (Adv.; rare) decorously. [f. ON *sæmiligr* (*sæmr* becoming f. *samr* SAME, -LY[1])]

seen. See SEE[1].

seer, n. Prophet, person who sees visions, person of preternatural insight esp. as regards the future. [different. in sense & pronunc. of *se·er* (SEE[1], -ER[1])]

seer·sucker, n. Indian blue-&-white-striped linen. [f. Pers. *shīr o shakkar* lit. milk & sugar]

see·saw, a., adv., n., & v.i. With backward & forward motion as of a saw (*s. motion*; *go s.*, vacillate or alternate). (N.) game in which two persons sit one at each end of long board balanced on central support & move each other up & down alternately, board thus balanced. (Vb) play at s.; move up & down as in s.; vacillate in policy &c. [redupl. of SAW[1]]

seethe (-dh), v.t. & i. (*seethed*; archaic past *sod*; archaic p.p. SODDEN). Cook (t. & i.) by boiling (archaic; prov. *thou shalt not s. a kid in his mother's milk*); (fig.) boil, bubble over, be agitated, (*the seething waters*; *India was seething with discontent*; *madness, enthusiasm, seething in his brain*). [OE *séothan*, cf. Du. *zieden*, G *sieden*]

segar. (Incorrect for) CIGAR.

se·gment, n., & v.i. & t. Part cut off or separable or marked off as though separable from the other parts of something (e.g. one ring of a worm, one division of a limb or the skull, one wedge of orange-pulp); (Geom.) part cut off by line or plane from any figure (*s. of circle*, part enclosed between arc & chord; *s. of sphere*, part cut off by any plane not passing through centre), *s. of line*, part included between two points; *s.-gear, -rack, -wheel*, with cogs occupying arc of circle only; *s.-saw*, with teeth extending over s. of circle, also circular saw made up of segmental saw-plates, also saw for cutting into segmental shapes; *s.-shell*, having between explosive within & lead casing without a case of iron made in ss. to facilitate bursting; *s.-valve*, closed by slide turning radially across seat; hence **segme·ntAL, se·gmentARY**[1], aa., **segme·ntalLY**[2] adv. (Vb) divide (i. & t.) into ss., (of embryo) undergo cleavage or divide into parts; (Physiol.) reproduce by gemmation; hence **segmentA·TION** n. [f. L *segmentum* (*secare* cut, -MENT)]

sē·gregāte[1], v.t. & i. Put apart from the rest, isolate; (intr.; Crystallog.) separate from a mass & collect about centres or lines of fracture. Hence or cogn. **segregA·TION** n., **se·gregATIVE** a. [f. L SE(*gregare* f. *grex gregis* flock), -ATE[3]]

se·gregate[2] (-*at*), a. Set apart, separate, (archaic); (Zool.) simple or solitary, not compound; (Bot.) *s. polygamy*, inflorescence in which each floret within common calyx has its own perianth also. [prec., -ATE[2]]

Se·id (sā-, *or* sēd), n. Descendant of Mohammed through Fatima & Ali. [f. Arab. *sayyid* prince]

Sei·dlitz powder (sĕd-), n. Aperient medicine of two powders mixed separately with water & then poured together giving effervescence. [named as substitute for mineral water of *Seidlitz* in Bohemia]

seigneur (sānyer·), **seig·nior** (sē-), n. Feudal lord, lord of manor, whence **seignior·IAL** a.; *grand seigneur* (F), person of high rank or whose demeanour &c. correspond to popular ideal of great nobleman; *the Grand Seignior*, = GRAND *Signior*. [F (*-eur*), as SENIOR]

seig·niorage (sē-), n. Something claimed by sovereign or feudal superior as prerogative, esp. Crown's right to percentage on bullion brought to mint for coining. [OF (*-norage*), see prec., -AGE]

seig·niory, n. Lordship, sovereign authority; seignior's domain; municipal council of medieval Italian republic. [f. OF *seignorie* (SEIGNEUR, -Y[1])]

seine (sān, sēn), n., & v.t. & i. Fishing-net for encircling, with floats at top & weights at bottom edge, & usu. hauled ashore; *s.-gang*, set of men working s.; *s.-needle*, for netting ss.; *s.-roller*, cylinder over which s. is hauled. (Vb) fish, catch, with s., whence **sei·NER**[1] n. [OE *segne*, f. L f. Gk *sagēnē*]

seise, seisin. See **seiz-.**

sei·smic, sei·smal (rare), (sīz-), aa. Of earthquake(s). [Gk *seismos* earthquake (*seiō* shake), -IC]

sei·smo- (sīz-), comb. form = earthquake-: *-gram*, record given by *sei·smo*-GRAPH (2) or *seismo·*METER or *sei·smo*SCOPE, instruments showing force, place, &c., of earthquake; so *-graphy, -grapher, -gra·phic(al), -metry, me·tric(al), -sco·*PIC; *-logy, -logist, -lo·gical(ly)*. [prec., -O-]

seize (sēz), v.t. & i. (Law; also *seise*) put in possession *of* (chiefly in p.p. *seized* or *seised of*, having in legal possession, &, fig., aware or informed of; often *stand seized of*); take possession of (contraband goods, documents, &c.) by warrant or legal right, confiscate, impound, atttach, whence **sei·ZOR**[2] n. (legal), **sei·ZABLE** a.;

lay hold of forcibly or suddenly, snatch, grasp with hand or mind, comprehend quickly or clearly, (*s. fortress, sceptre,* person *by the neck* &c., person's *hand, opportunity* or *occasion, an idea, a distinction, the point, the essence of the matter*; *was seized by apoplexy, with remorse* or *panic*); lay hold eagerly *upon* (*s. upon a chance* or *pretext*); (Naut.) lash, fasten with several turns of cord, (*s.* one *up,* lash him to rigging for flogging; *s. ropes together*), whence **sei·z**ING¹(4) n. (usu. pl.). [f. OF *seisir, sai-*, give seizin, f. LL *sacire* take possession of perh. f. Teut. & cogn. w. SET¹)]

sei·zin, sei·sin (-z-), n. (legal). Possession of land by freehold; act of taking such possession; what is so held. [f. OF *seisine, sai-* (prec., -INE¹)]

sei·zure (-zh*er*), n. In vbl senses; esp., sudden attack of apoplexy &c., stroke. [f. F *saisir* SEIZE w. assim. to -URE cf. PLEASURE]

sē·jant, a. (herald.). Sitting with forelegs upright. [AF *seiant* (*seier* var. of OF *seoir* f. L *sedēre* sit, -ANT)]

sē·jugous (-jŏŏ-), a. (bot.). With six pairs of leaflets. [L *sejugis* team of six (*sex* six, *jugum* yoke), -OUS]

seju·nction, n. (archaic). Disjoining, separation. [f. L SE(*junctio* JUNCTION)]

sē·kŏs, n. (archaeol.). Sacred enclosure esp. of ancient temple, adytum. [Gk (*sē*-)]

selā·chian (-k-), n. & a. Any fish of shark or dogfish kind; of or like such fishes. So **sĕ·lach**OID a. & n. [Gk *selakhos* shark, -IAN]

sē·lah, Hebrew word of unknown meaning retained in Bible version of Psalms & supposed to be a musical direction.

sela·mlik (-ah-), n. Men's part of Mohammedan house. [Turk.]

se·ldom (-om), adv. (rarely *-er, -est*). Rarely, not often, (*s. or never*; *very s.*; *not s.*). [OE *seldan*, cf. Du. *zelden*, G *selten*; *-om* by assim. to adv. dat. ending as in *whilom*]

sele·ct, a., & v.t. Chosen for excellence, choice, picked, got by rejection or exclusion of what is inferior; (of society &c.) exclusive, cautious in admitting members; hence **sele·ct**NESS n. (Vb) pick out as best or most suitable; hence **sele·ct**IVE a., **sele·ctive**LY² adv., **sele·ct**OR² n. [vb f. adj., f. L SE(*ligere lect-* =*legere* pick)]

sele·ction, n. Selecting, choice; what is selected (*a fine s. of summer goods*; *what is your s. for the Derby?*; *the new headmaster is a good s.*); (Biol.) sorting out in various ways (*natural, sexual, physical, artificial, methodical, unconscious, s.*) of the types of animal or plant better fitted to survive or multiply regarded as a factor in evolution. [f. L *selectio* (prec., -ION)]

selenite, n. Crystallized or foliated sulphate of lime often in transparent thin plates (sĕ·-); (Chem.) salt of selenium (sĕ·-); (*S*-; sĭlē·-) inhabitant of moon. Hence **sĕleni·t**IC a. [f. Gk *selēnitēs* (*lithos*) moon(-stone) f. *Selēnē*, -ITE¹]

selē·nium, n. Non-metallic element grouped with sulphur & tellurium & with special uses due to difference in its electric resistance under light & darkness. Hence **selen**IC a., **sĕ·len**ATE¹(3) n., **sele·ni**OUS (chem.) a. [Gk *Selēnē* moon, -IUM; named w. ref. to TELLURIUM]

selēn(o)-, comb. form of Gk *selēnē* moon; *-ce·ntric*, as seen &c. from centre of moon; *sele·nodont*, (mammal) with crescent-ridges on crowns of teeth; -GRAPHY, study or mapping of the moon, so -GRAPH(1), *-grapher, -gra·phic*; -LOGY, *-logist*; *-trŏ·pic*, curving towards the moon (of plant-organs influenced in growth thus), so *-tropism, -trop*Y¹.

Seleu·cid, n. (pl. *-ids, -idae*). One of the dynasty founded by Seleucus that governed Syria c. 312–64 B.C. [-ID³]

self, n. (pl. *-ves*) & a. Person's or thing's own individuality or essence, person or thing as object of introspection or reflexive action, (*the study of the s.*; *the consciousness of s.*; one's *former, better,* &c., *s.*, oneself as one formerly was, one's nobler impulses &c.; one's *second s.*, intimate friend, right-hand man; chiefly *his, its,* &c., *own* or *very s.* as form of *himself* &c. when divided; *Caesar's, pity's,* &c., *s.*, rhet. for *Caesar himself, pity itself*); one's own interests or pleasure, concentration on these, (*cares for nothing but, refers everything to, s.*; *s. is a bad guide to happiness*); flower of uniform, or of the natural wild, colour; (commerc., vulg., joc.) =*myself, yourself, himself,* &c. (*cheque drawn to s.*; *a ticket admitting s. & friend*); *our noble ss.* (joc., as toast); (adj.) (of colour) uniform, the same throughout, (of flower) s.-coloured; HERSELF, HIMSELF, ITSELF, MYSELF, ONEs., OURSELF, THEMSELVES, YOURSELF. [OE, cf. Du. *zelf*, G *selbe*; etym. dub.; orig. appended, as adj. or in apposition, to pronoun & declined with it, *he self, his selfes,* dat. *him selfum,* acc. *hine selfne*; in ME also adj. = same, very]

self-, pref. (prec.) expr. direct or indirect reflexive action, automatic or independent action, or sameness; freely used as living pref.; the more established wds are given alphabetically with references to the numbered classes following:

1. Expressing direct reflexive action with part. of any vb that can have *self* for object, & hence with the p.p. in sense *by* oneself or *itself*, & with vbl nn. & adjj. & advv. in sense *of -self*; so from 'I accuse myself' come *s.-accusing, -accused,* aa., *-accuser, -accusation,* nn., *-accusatory* a., *-accusingly, -accusatorily,* advv.

2. By extension it is prefixed also to any word, whether participle or other vbl deriv. or not, to which *self* might be attached by a preposition; in a large class (2a) the sense is *without external agency or assistance*; so from 'acts by or of itself' come *s.-acting, s.-action, s.-activity*; from 'evident of itself' comes *s.-evident*; in other wds (2b) the relation expressed is various; so from 'conceited about one self' *s.-conceited* & *s.-conceit*, from 'be absorbed, confide, in oneself' *s.-absorbed, -absorption, -confidence*, from 'inflict on oneself' *s.-inflicted*, from 'be conscious, despair, of oneself' *s.-consciousness, -despair*, from 'depend on oneself' *s. dependence*, from 'righteous as seen by oneself' *s.-righteous*, from 'seek things for oneself' *s.-seeker, -seeking* a. & n., from 'suffice, use violence, to oneself' *s.-sufficing, -sufficient, s.-violence.*

3. To a few nn. & their derivv. in -ED[2] *self-* is prefixed with sense *uniform*, or *natural & not artificially produced.*

s.-abandonment, s.-abasement, s.-abhorrence, s.-abnegation, 1; *s.-absorbed, s.-absorption*, 2b; *s.-abuse* 1, onanism; *s.-accusation, s.-accusatory*, &c., 1; *s.-acting, s.-action, s.-activity*, 2a, automatic (action); *s.-adjusting, s.-adjustment*, 1, of machinery &c.; *s.-admiration, s.-aggrandizement, -appointed, -appreciation, -approval, -approbation*, 1; *s.*-ASSERT*ing, -assertive, -assertion*, &c., 1; *s.-assumed* 2b, of title &c. not conferred but taken esp. without right; *s.-begotten* 1, by exag. for *not begotten by another*; *s.-betrayal* 1; *s.-binder* 2a, reaping-machine with automatic arrangement for binding sheaves; *s.-blinded* 1; *s.-born* 1, as *s.-begotten*; *s.-centred(ness)* 2b, preoccupied with one's own personality or affairs; *s.-closing* 1; *s.-cocking* 1, of gun in which hammer is raised by trigger, not by hand; *s.-collected* 2b, having or showing presence of mind or composure; *s.-colour(ed)* 3, of flower or material in which colour is uniform throughout, or flower whose colour has not been changed by cultivation &c.; *s.-command* 1, power of controlling one's emotions; *s.-communion* 2b, meditation esp. upon one's own character or conduct; *s.-complacent, -complacency*, 2b, of person too easily pleased with himself; *s.-conceit(ed)* 2b; *s.-condemned, -condemnation*, 1; *s.-confidence, -confident(ly)*, 2b; *s.-congratulation, -conquest*, 1; *s.-conscious-(ness)* 2b, esp. of person embarrassed or made theatrical by inability to forget himself in society, also philos. &c. of man as having faculty of self-contemplation; *s.-consistent, -consistency*, 2b; *s.-constituted* 1, esp. of person who assumes function without right to it; *s.-consuming* 1; *s.-contained* 1, not communicative, also compact or complete in itself; *s.-contempt, -contemptuous(ly)*, 1; *s.-content* n., *-contented*, 2b; *s.-contradiction, contradictory, -control, -convicted*, 1; *s.-created, -creation*, 1, as *s.-begotten*; *s.-critical, -criticism, -culture, -deceiving, -deceiver, -deceit, -deception*, 1; *s.-defence* 1 (*in s.-d.*, not by way of aggression; *art of s.-d.*, boxing); *s.-delusion* 1; *s.*-DENY*ing* (*s.-d. ordinance*, resolution of Long Parliament 1645 depriving members of Parliament of civil & military office; also often used allusively), *-denial*, 1; *s.-dependent, -ence*, 2b; *s.-depreciation, -depreciative*, 1; *s.-despair* 2b; *s.-destroying, -destruction*, &c., 1; *s.-determining, -determination*, &c., 1, esp. w. ref. to free will as opp. fatalism &c., &, in recent Pol., of a nation's right to determine its own polity; *s.-development* 1; *s.-devotion* 1, devoting of oneself to person or cause; *s.-discipline, -disparagement, -display, -dispraise, -distrust-(ful), -educated, -education, -effacement*, 1; *s.-elective* 1, esp. = proceeding &c. by cooptation; *s.-esteem* 1; *s.-evident(ly)* 2a, without need of demonstration; *s.-examination* 1; *s.-executing* 1, not needing legislation &c. to enforce it; *s.-existent* 2a; *s.-explaining, -explanatory*, 1; *s.-faced* 3, (of stone) unhewn, undressed; *s.-feeding, -feeder*, 1, (furnace, machine, &c.) that renews its own fuel or material automatically; *s.-fertilizing, -fertilized*, 1, *-fertile, -fertility*, 2a, of plants fertilized by their own pollen, not from others; *s.-flattering, -flattery*, 1; *s.-forgetful(ness)* 1, unselfish(ness); *s.-generating* 1; *s.-glazed* 3, (of porcelain) covered with glaze of one tint; *s.-glorification* 1; *s.-governing* (esp. *the s.-g. colonies* opp. CROWN[1]*-colony*), *-government*, 1; *s.-gratulation* 1; *s.-heal* 1, kinds of plant named as enabling patient to do without doctor; *s.-help* 1, working for oneself without waiting for external aid; *s.-humiliation, -immolation*, 1; *s.-important, -importance*, 2b, in one's own eyes, & hence pompous &c.; *s.-imposed* 2b, of task &c.; *s.-impotent* 2a, opp. *s.-fertile*; *s.-improvement* 1; *s.-inductive, -induction*, 2a, (Electr.) (capable of) production of extra current in circuit by variation of current in that circuit; *s.-indulgent, -indulgence*, &c., 1, yielding to temptations of ease or pleasure; *s.-inflicted* 2b; *s.-interest(ed)* 2b, (actuated by or absorbed in) what one conceives to be for one's own interests; *s.-invited* 1, having had to ask for, having come without, an invitation; *s.-involved* 2b, wound up in oneself; *s.-justification, -kindled, -knowledge, -laudation*, 1; *s.-love* 1, selfishness, impulse towards s.-indulgence, vulnerable conceit, also rarely desire of s.-development &c.; *s.-luminous* 2a; *s.-made* 1, of person who has risen by his own exertions, often with implication of vulgarity &c.; *s.-mastery, -mortification*, 1; *s.-moving, -motion, -murder(er)*, 1; *s.-opinion, -opinioned, -opinionated*, 2b, of stubborn adherence to one's own opinions; *s.-partial(ity)* 2b; *s.-pity, -pleasing* a. & n., 1; *s.-poised* 2a; *s.-pollution* 1, s.-abuse; *s.-possessed, -possession,* 1, cool(ness), composed, composure, in agitating circumstances &c.; *s.-praise* 1 (*s.-p. is no recommendation*); *s.-preservation* 1, esp. the primary instinct impelling conscious beings to go on living & avoid injury; *s.-profit* 2b; *s.-propagating* 1; *s.-raker* 2a, reaping-machine with set of rakes automatically preparing corn for binding; *s.-realization* 1, development of one's faculties esp. as ethical first principle; *s.-recording* 2a, of scientific instrument &c.; *s.-regarding, -regard,* 1, opp. *altruism* &c. without the censure implied in *selfish* &c.; *s.-registering* 2a, as *s.-recording*; *s.-regulating* 1, of machinery; *s.-reliant, -ance,* 2b; *s.-renunciation* 1, unselfishness; *s.-repression, -reproach(ful),* 1; *s.-repugnant* 2b, inconsistent; *s.-respecting, -respect, -respectful,* 1, of person who has & acts up to a standard of worthy conduct; *s.-restrained, -restraint, -revealing* a., *-revelation,* 1; *s.-reverent, -reverence,* 1, rhet., poet., theol., &c., for *s.-respect* &c.; *s.-righteous(ness)* 2b; *s.-righting* a. 1, of boat; *s.-sacrificing* a., *-sacrifice,* 1, postponing private interest & desires to those of others; *selfsame* 3, emphatic form of *same*; *s.-satisfied, -satisfaction,* 2b, conceit(ed); *s.-scorn* 1; *s.-seeking* a. & n., *-seeker,* 2b; *s.-slaughter* 1; *s.-sown* 1, sprung from seed that has dropped without human agency; *s.-starter* 2a, electric appliance for starting motor-car without use of crank-handle; *s.-sterile, -sterility,* 2a, as *s.-impotent*; *s.-styled* 1, having taken the name without right &c., pretended, would-be; *s.-sufficing* 2b, requiring nothing from outside, independent; *s.-sufficient, -ency,* 2b, = *s. sufficing,* also & usu. sufficient in one's own opinion, presumptuous; *s.-suggestion* 2b, reflexive suggestion of the mesmeric or hypnotic kind; *s.-support(ing), -surrender, -sustaining, -sustained, -taught, -tormenting* &c., *-torture* &c., 1; *s.-violence* 2b, esp. suicide; *s.-will(ed)* 2b, as *s.-opinion* &c.; *s.-winding* 1, of clock with automatic winding apparatus; *s.-worship* 1.

se·lfhood, n. (rare). Personality, separate & conscious existence. [-HOOD]

se·lfish, a. Deficient in consideration for others, alive chiefly to personal profit or pleasure, actuated by self-interest, (of motives &c.) appealing to self-interest (*s. theory of morals,* that pursuit of pleasure of one kind or another is the ultimate spring of every action). Hence **se·lfish**LY[2] adv., **se·lfish**NESS n. [-ISH[1]]

se·lfless, a. Oblivious of self, incapable of selfishness. Hence **se·lfless**NESS n. [-LESS]

se·lfness, n. (rare). =SELFHOOD. [-NESS]

Selju·k (-ōōk), n. Member of 11th–13th-c. Mohammedan dynasties in central & Western Asia descended from the chieftain Seljuk. Hence **Selju·k**IAN a. & n.

sell, v.t. & i. (sōld), & n. Make over or dispose of in exchange for money (cf. BUY, BARTER; *s.* one's *life dearly* fig., kill or wound assailants before being killed; *selling-race, -handicap,* &c., in which winning horse must be sold to highest bidder; *s.* one *a pup* slang, swindle him); keep stock of for sale or be a dealer in (*do you s. candles?*; *bookselling* &c.); betray for money or other reward (*s.* one's *country* &c.); prostitute for money or other consideration, make a matter of corrupt bargaining, (*s. justice, oneself,* one's *honour* or *chastity*); (slang) disappoint by not keeping engagement &c., by failing in some way, or by trickery (*sold again!,* excl. used by or to disappointed person; n., such disappointment, as *what a s.!*); (of goods) find purchasers (*will never s.*; *selling like wildfire*); *s. off,* s. remainder of (goods), clear out stock, at reduced prices; *s. out,* leave army by selling commission (hist.), s. (all or some of one's shares in company, whole stock-in-trade, &c., or abs.); *s. up,* s. goods of (debtor) by distress or legal process. Hence **(-)sell**ER[1] n. [OE *sellan,* cf. ON *selja,* OHG *sellen* deliver up; cogn. w. SALE]

sellanders. See SALLENDERS.

se·ltzer(-water), n. Medicinal mineral water from *Selters* in Germany; artificial substitutes for this, soda-water.

se·ltzogene, n. =GAZOGENE. [f. F *selzogène* (prec., -GEN)]

se·lvage (-ĭj), **-edge,** n. Edge of cloth so woven that it cannot unravel, border of different material or finish along edge of cloth intended to be torn off or hidden, list; edge-plate of lock with opening for the bolt. Hence **se·lvag**ED[2] a. [f. MDu. *selfegge* (SELF, EDGE)]

selves. See SELF.

sema·ntics, n. pl. Semasiology. [f. Gk *sēmantikos* significant (*sēmainō* mean)]

sē·maphore, n., & v.i. & t. Signalling apparatus of post with oscillating arms, arrangement of lanterns, &c., for use (esp. now on railways) by day or night; military signalling by operator's two arms or two flags (vb, signal, send, by s.). Hence **semaphŏ·r**IC a., **semapho·r**ICALLY adv. [irreg. f. Gk *sēma -atos* sign, *pherō* bear]

sēmăsio·logy, n. Branch of philology concerned with meanings. So **semasiolo·gical** a., **-ly** adv. [f. Gk *sēmasia* meaning + -LOGY]

semă·tic, a. (nat. hist.). (Of colour or markings in animals) significant, serving to warn off enemies or attract attention. [prec., -IC]

se·mblable, a. (archaic). Having semblance of something, seeming. [OF (foll., -ABLE)]

se·mblance, n. What looks like, the outward appearance of, something (*put on a* *s. of anger*; *bears the s. of an angel & the heart of a devil*). [F (*sembler* f. L as SIMULATE, -ANCE)]

sĕ'mée, sĕ'mé, (-mĭ), a. (herald.). Covered with small bearings of indefinite number (e.g. stars, fleurs-de-lis) arranged over field. [F, p.p. of *semer* sow (SEMEN)]

semeiology, semeiotics. See **semio-.**

sē'men, n. Generative fluid of male animals. [L, genit. *-inis*, = seed (*serere* sow, -MEN)]

seme'ster, n. Half-year course or term in German & other universities. [G, f. L *semestris* six-monthly (*sex* six, *mensis* month)]

sĕmi-, pref. = L *semi-* half- [cf. Gk *hēmi-*, OE *sam-*, Skr. *sami*, perh. cogn. w. SAME], attached to any E wd as living pref. (cf. BI-, DI-², DEMI-, HEMI-); the more established or illustrative wds are given alphabetically w. reff. to the following numbered senses: 1. the half of (*-circle*); 2. on one of two sides (*-detached*), in one of two directions (*-infinite*), in some particular (*-vowel*); 3. little more or better than (*-barbarism*); 4. rather less than (*-official*) in low degree (*-civilized*), not quite deserving the description (*-smile*); 5. imperfect(ly) (*-bull, -double*); 6. occurring, published, &c., each half — or twice in a —(*-annual*; cf. BI- 1e): *s.-annual(ly)* 6; *s.-barbarian, -barbarism,* 3; *se'mibreve* 1, whole note or time occupied by it (see BREVE); *s.-bull* 5, issued by Pope after election & before coronation with one side of seal left blank; *s.-centennial* 6, occurring &c. every fifty years; *s.-chorus* 1, half or part of choir, passage given by it; *semicircle, -cir'cular* a., 1, (amounting to, arranged as or in, shaped like) half of a circle or of its circumference, set of objects ranged in or object forming a s.-c., instrument for measuring angles; *semico'lon* 4, punctuation-mark (;) now used as the chief stop (the colon being mostly reserved for special uses) of intermediate value between comma & full stop; *s.-cylinder, -cylindrical,* 1, (of, forming, &c.) half of a cylinder cut longitudinally; *s.-demi-semiquaver* 1; *s.-detached* 2, (of house) joined to another by party-wall on one side only; *s.-dome* 1, 4, half-dome formed by vertical section, part of structure more or less resembling dome; *s.-double* 5 (bot.), having outer stamens only converted to petals; *s.-final* 4, match or round preceding the final; *s.-fluid* a. & n. 4, viscous (fluid); *s.-fused* 5; *s.-infidel* 3; *s.-infinite* 2, limited in one direction & stretching to infinity in the other; *semilu'nar* 1, 4, halfmoon-shaped, crescent-shaped, (esp. in anat. names, as *s.-l. bone, cartilage, fold, fossa, lobe, valve*); *s.-monthly* 6; *s.-mute* a. & n. 3, (person) practically dumb owing to (esp. congenital) deafness; *s.-official(ly)* 4, esp. of communications made to newspapers by official with stipulation that they shall not be formally attributed to him; *s.-plume* 2, feather with firm stem but downy web; *s.-precious* 4, of stones; *se'miquaver* mus. 1, note with double-hooked shaft; *s.-smile* 4; *se'mitone* mus. 1, interval approximately equal to half a tone on the scale (CHROMATIC *s.-t.*; *diatonic s.-t.*, between 7th & 8th note of major scale); *s.-transparent* 4; *s.-tropical* 4, (as) of regions bordering on the tropics; *s.-tubular* 1, shaped like half a tube cut longitudinally; *s.-uncial* 5, betwen uncial & minuscule; *se'mivowel, -vo'cal* a., 2, sound, or letter representing it, intermediate between vowel & consonant (e.g. *y, w*), consonant that is not mute (e.g. *l, m, z*); *s.-weekly* 6.

sĕ'minal, a. Of seed or semen or reproduction, germinal, reproductive, propagative, (*s. fluid*, semen; *in the s. state*, rudimentary, still undeveloped; *s. principles*, pregnant with consequences). Hence **se'minal**LY² adv. [F (*sé-*), f. L *seminalis* (SEMEN, -AL)]

sĕ'minary, n. Place of education (formerly in pretentious use for *school*, cf. ACADEMY; now rare exc. either fig. as *a s. of vice* &c., or of R.-C. & esp. Jesuit schools, whence **se'minar**IST n.). [f. L *seminarium* seed-plot (SEMEN, -ARY¹)]

sĕmina'tion, n. (bot.). Process, plant's manner, of seeding. [f. L *seminatio* (*seminare* f. SEMEN, -ATION)]

sĕmini'ferous, a. Bearing seed; conveying semen. [SEMEN, -I-, -FEROUS]

sĕmio'logy, sĕmio'tics, -meio- (-mīŏ-), nn. Branch of pathology concerned with symptoms. [Gk *sēmeion* sign (*sēma* mark), *sēmeiōtikos* of signs, -LOGY, -ICS]

Sĕ'mite, n. & a. (Member) of any of the races supposed to be descended from Shem (*Gen.* x. 21 foll.) including esp. the Hebrews, Arameans, Phoenicians, Arabs, & Assyrians. So **Semĭ'tic** a. (also n. = S. languages), **Sĕ'mit**ISM(2, 4), **Se'mit**IST(3), nn., **Se'mit**IZE(3) v.t. [LL f. Gk *Sēm* Shem, -ITE¹]

sĕmoli'na (-lē-), **sĕ'mola,** n. Hard grains left after bolting of flour, used in puddings &c. [*-ina* f. It. *semolino* dim. of *semola* bran f. L *simila* fine flour]

sempiter'nal, a. (Rhet. for) eternal; everlasting, never to end, (rare). [OF (*-nel*) f. L *sempiternus* (*sempi-* for *semper* always, w. suf. as in *aeternus* eternal) + -AL]

se'mplice (-ētshā), mus. direction. Without embellishments or liberties. [It., = SIMPLE]

se'mpre (-ā), mus. direction. Throughout (with other direction, as *s. piano*). [It.]

sempstress. See SEAMSTRESS.

sen, n. Japanese copper coin, 1/100 of yen.

senār'ius, n. (pl. *-iī*). Latin verse of six feet, esp. iambic trimeter. [f. L (*versus*) *senarius* (*seni* six each, -ARY¹)]

sē·nary, a. On basis of six, by sixes, (*s.* SCALE³, cf. BINARY). [f. L as prec.]

sĕ·nate (-*at*), n. State-council of the ancient-Roman republic & empire dividing legislation with the popular assemblies, administration with the magistrates, & judicial power with the equites; council of ancient Athens & Sparta; upper or second chamber in some parliaments; (rhet.) any legislature or its proceedings or members (*the s., the pulpit, & the press*); governing body of Cambridge Univ. & other institutions; *S.-house* (esp. at Cambridge). [f. OF *senat* f. L *senatus* (*sen-* old, -ATE¹)]

se·nator, n. Member of senate. Hence or cogn. **senator·**IAL a., **senator·ial**LY² adv., **se·nator**SHIP n. [OF (-*our*), f. L *senatorem* nom. -*or* (prec., -OR²)]

senā·tus, n. The ancient-Roman senate (*s. populusque Romanus* the senate & people of Rome, abbr. S.P.Q.R., official name of ancient Rome as a State; *s.-consult(um)*, decree of the s.). [L, =SENATE]

send¹, v.t. & i. (sent). Bid go, secure conveyance of, to some destination (destination given by *to* or other prep. or by ind. obj. of person, or merely implied; *s. message* or *messenger to*; *sent me a book*; *will send an army*; *s. goods all over* or *round the world*; *s.* COALS *to Newcastle*; *s. word*, have message taken *that*, *to* do, &c.; *s. up* or *in* one's name, an exhibit, &c., enter oneself or it for competition); (of God, providence, &c.) grant, bestow, inflict, bring about, cause to be so-&-so, (*s. rain, a judgement, pestilence*; *God s. it may not be so!*; *s. him victorious!*); propel, cause to move, (*s. bullet*; *sent his temperature up, down*; *s. out* or *forth leaves, steam, odour*); dismiss, with or without force (with *off, away*, or compl. or adv. phr.; *sent him away, packing, flying, about his business, to the right-about*; *s. to* COVENTRY; *s. down*, rusticate or expel from university; *s. off letter, parcel*, &c., get it off one's own hands & started on its way; *s. off* person, witness his departure as sign of respect &c., so *s.-o.* n., also laudatory review of book &c.); drive *mad* or *crazy*; s. message or letter (*sent to warn me, depose him, to me to take care*; *s. for him*, telling him to come; *s. for the book*, ordering it as purchase). Hence **se·nd**ER¹ n. [OE *sendan*, cf. Du. *zenden*, G *senden*]

send², sc-, n., & v.i., (naut.; -ended). Impulse given by the down slope of a wave (usu. *s. of the sea*); (vb, of vessel) plunge or pitch owing to this (n., such plunge). [prob. =prec., with *sc-* by confusion with *descend*]

se·ndal, n. Medieval silken fabric used for rich dresses, pennons, &c. [Rom. (OF, Sp., Port., *cendal*) prob. ult. f. Gk *sindōn* fine linen]

sĕ·nega, -ka, n. (Drug, used in cough-mixtures, made from root of) American plant called also *S.-snake-root*. [f. name of *Seneca* Indians]

sene·scent, a. Growing old. Hence **sene·**SCENCE n. [f. L *senescere* (SENIOR, -ESCENT)]

sĕ·neschal (-shl), n. Steward or major-domo of medieval great house. [OF, f. Teut. (Goth. **sins* old, found in *sinista* oldest, cogn. w. L *senex*, *skalks* servant, cf. MARSHAL)]

se·ngreen (-n-g-), n. =HOUSE¹-*leek*. [OE *singréne* evergreen]

senhor·, senhor·a, senhori·ta (-rē-), (-ny-), used of or to Portuguese as SIGNOR.

sē·nile, a. Showing the feebleness &c. of, incident to, old age (*s. atrophy, apathy, garrulity, dementia*, &c.). Hence **seni·l**ITY n. [f. L *senilis* (foll., -IL)]

se·nior (-*er*), a. & n. More advanced in age or older in standing, superior in age or standing *to*, of higher or highest degree, (opp. JUNIOR; *the s. service*, Navy as opp. Army; *the s. members of the family, university*, &c.; *the s. partner*, head of firm; *s. optime*, see WRANGLER; *s. classic*, competitor placed highest in classical tripos when names were arranged according to merit; *s.* WRANGLER; *s. man* at university, opp. FRESH*man*; *is two years s. to me*), so **senio·r**ITY n.; (appended to name for distinction; abbr. *sen.*, *sr*; opp. JUNIOR) s. to another of same name (esp. with father's Christian name & surname when son has same, as *John Smith sen.*, or at school with surname when two or more boys have same, as *Smith sen.*). (N.) person of advanced age or comparatively long service &c.; one's elder or superior in length of service, membership, &c. (*is my s.*); s. wrangler, classic, or man. [L, =older, old(ish) man, compar. f. st. of *senex senis* old (man)]

sēnior·ēs prior·ēs, L sentence (=elders first) used in reminding the young of precedence due to seniority.

se·nna, n. (Dried leaflets, used as laxative, of) kinds of cassia. [f. Arab. *sanā*]

se·nnet, n. (hist.). Signal call on trumpet (in stage-directions of Shaksperian & other plays). [var. of SIGNET]

se·nnight (-īt), n. (archaic). Week (esp. *Tuesday* &c. *s.*). [for *seven-night*]

se·nnit, si·nnet, n. (naut.). Braided cordage made in flat or round or square form from 3–9 cords (*common* i. e. flat, *round, square, s.*). [?]

señor·, señor·a, sĕñori·ta (-rē), (-ny-), used of or to Spaniards as SIGNOR &c.

Senou·s(s)i (-ōō-), n. Religious & political Mohammedan fraternity in N. Africa named after founder (usu. *the S.* as sing. or pl.).

sensa·tion, n. Consciousness of perceiving or seeming to perceive some state or affection of one's body or its parts or senses or of one's mind or its emotions, contents of such consciousness, (*had a s.*

of giddiness, heat, pain, comfort, thirst, falling, sourness, deafness, pride, stupidity; pressing the eyeball in the dark will produce the s. of light or *of seeing light; in search of a new s.*), whence **sensa·tion**ARY[1] a. (rare); stirring of the emotions common to many people or of eager interest among them, display of intense common emotion or interest, literary or other use of material calculated to excite it, (*made a great s.*, was eagerly discussed or viewed; *s. among the audience*, shown by deep silence, applause, or other general manifestation; *a three-days s.*; *what is the latest s.?*; *the essence of melodrama is s.*; *deals largely in s.*). Hence **sensa·tion**AL a., **sensa·tional**LY[2] adv. [f. med. L *sensatio* (LL *sensatus* having sense f. *sensus* SENSE, -ATE[2], -ION)]

sensa·tionalism, n. (Philos.) theory that ideas are derived solely from sensation; pursuit of the sensational in literature, political agitation, &c. So **sensa·tional**IST(2) n. [-ISM]

sense, n., & v.t. Any of the special bodily faculties by which sensation is roused (*the five ss.*, sight, hearing, smell, taste, & touch; *sixth* or *muscular s.*, producing sensation of muscular effort; *has quick, keen, ss., a dull s. of smell*), (pl.) person's sanity or ordinary state of mind regarded as secured by possession of these (*have you taken leave of, are you out of, your ss.?*, are you mad?; *he will soon come, we must bring him, to his ss.*, out of mad folly; *frightened out of his ss.*, into loss of faculties; *in* one's *ss.*, sane); ability to perceive or feel or to be conscious of the presence or properties of things, sensitiveness of all or any of the ss., (*s.-perception*; *errors of s.*, mistakes in perception; *the pleasures of s.*, those depending on sensation; *has a plant s.?*); consciousness *of* (*a* or *the s. of pleasure, pain, gratification, having done well*, ones' *own importance, shame, responsibility*; *labouring under a s. of wrong*, feeling wronged); quick or accurate appreciation *of*, instinct regarding or insight into specified matter or habit of squaring conduct to such instinct, (*s. of locality, distance, the ridiculous, humour, duty, beauty, gratitude*; *a keen s. of honour*; *the religious, moral, aesthetic, s.*); practical wisdom, judgement, common sense, conformity to these, (*sound, good*, COMMON[1], *s.*; *a man of s.*, sagacious; *had not the s. to* do; *has plenty of s.*; *what is the s. of talking like that?*; *has more s. than to* do; *now you are talking s.*); meaning, way in which word &c. is to be understood, intelligibility or coherence or possession of a meaning, (*in what exact s. we shall rise again is doubtful*; *the s. of the word is clear*; *does not make s.*, is unintelligible; *in the strict, limited, literal, figurative, moral, metaphorical, legal*, PICKWICKIAN, *proper, full, s.*; *in a vague, in every, s.*; *in a s.*, provided the statement is taken in a particular way, under limitations, as *what you say is true i. a s.*; *make s. out of nonsense*); prevailing sentiment among a number of people (*take the s. of the meeting*, ascertain this by putting question &c.); *s.-body, -capsule, -cavity, -cell, -centre, -organ*, parts of animals concerned in producing sensation; hence **se·nse**LESS a. (esp. = foolish; *knock senseless*, stun), **se·nseless**LY[2] adv., **se·nseless**NESS n. (Vb) perceive by s., (esp.) be vaguely aware of. [f. F *sens* f. L *sensus -ūs* (*sentire sens-* feel)]

sensibi·lity, n. Capacity to feel (*skin lost its s.*); exceptional openness to emotional impressions (*sense & s.*), delicacy of feeling, susceptibility (*s. to kindness* &c.), over-sensitiveness, (pl.) susceptibility in various directions. [f. L *sensibilitatem* (foll., -TY)]

se·nsible (-*si*-), a. Perceptible by the senses (*s. phenomena, things*); great enough to be perceived, appreciable, (*a s. difference, increase*); (archaic) sensitive (*to*); aware, not unmindful, *of*, (*was s. of his peril, your kindness*); of good sense, reasonable, judicious, moderate, practical, (*a s. man, course, compromise*; *that is very s. of him*). Hence **se·nsib**LY[2] adv., **se·nsible**NESS n. [F, f. L *sensibilis* (SENSE, -BLE)]

se·nsitive, a. & n. Of the senses, sensory, (rare); having sensibility *to*, very open *to* or acutely affected by external impressions esp. those made by the moods or opinions of others in relation to oneself; (of instrument &c.) readily responding *to* or recording slight changes of condition (*s. market*, liable to quick changes of price); (Chem.) readily affected by or responsive *to* appropriate agent, (Photog.) *s. paper*, prepared to receive impressions from light, whence **se·nsit**IZE(3) v.t., **sensitiza·**TION, **se·nsitiz**ER[1](2), **sensito·**METER, nn.; *s. plant*, kind of mimosa whose leaves curve downwards & leaflets fold together at nightfall or when touched; hence **se·nsitive**LY[2] adv., **se·nsitive**NESS, **sensiti·**VITY (chem., photog., physiol., psychol.), nn. (N.; Hypnotism &c.) person s. to hypnotic &c. influences. [F (-*if, -ive*), f. med. L *sensitivus*, irreg. f. L *sentire sens-* feel, -IVE]

sensor·ium, n. (pl. -*ia*, -*s*). The seat of sensation, the brain, brain & spinal cord, or grey matter of these; (Biol.) whole sensoryapparatus including nerve-system &c. [LL (foll.)]

se·nsory, sensor·ial, aa. Of the sensorium or sensation or the senses. [SENSE, -ORY, -AL]

se·nsūal (*or* -shŏŏ-), a. Of sense or sensation, sensory, (rare); of or depending on the senses only & not the intellect or spirit, carnal, fleshly, (*s. pleasures*); given to the pursuit of s. pleasures or gratification of the appetites, self-indulgent in regard to food & sexual enjoyment, voluptuous, licentious; (Philos.) holding the doctrine of, according to, of, sensationalism. Hence or cogn. **se·nsual**IZE(3) v.t., **se·nsualiz**A·TION, **se·nsual**ISM(2, 3), **se·nsual**IST(1, 2), **sensua·l**ITY, nn., **se·nsual**LY² adv. [f. LL *sensualis* (SENSE, -AL)]

se·nsūous, a. Of, derived from, affecting, the senses (chiefly as substitute, free of implied censure, for prec.; cf. *non-moral* & *immoral*). Hence **se·nsuous**LY² adv., **se·nsuous**NESS n. [SENSE, -OUS]

sent. See SEND.

se·ntence, n., & v.t. (Archaic) one's opinion for or against some course or conclusion (*my s. is for war*); (archaic) pithy saying, briefly expressed thought, maxim, proverb, so (in common use) **sente·nti**OUS a., **sente·ntious**LY² adv., **sente·ntious**NESS n.; verdict (rare), (declaration of) punishment allotted to person condemned in criminal trial (also transf.); (Gram.) set of words complete in itself, containing subject & predicate (either, or part of either or both, somet. omitted by ellipsis), & conveying a statement, question, or command (e.g. *I go, will you go?, go* =go thou or you, *what?* =what did you say?, *hearts trumps*= hearts are trumps; *simple s.*, with single subject & predicate; *compound s.*, with more than one of either or both; *complex s.*, with subordinate clause or clauses), so **sente·nti**AL a. (rare); (loosely in Gram.; usu. *subordinate s.*) subordinate clause; small amount of speech, usu. that between two full stops often including several grammatical sentences (e.g. *I went & he came*). (Vb) state s. of (condemned criminal, or transf.), declare condemned *to*. [OF, f. L *sententia* (for *sentie-*) f. *sentire* be of opinion, -ENCE]

se·ntient (-shnt), a. Having the power of sense-perception. Hence **se·nti**ENCE n., **se·ntient**LY² adv. [L *sentire* feel, -ENT]

se·ntiment, n. A mental feeling, the sum of what one feels on some subject, a tendency or view based on or coloured with emotion, such feelings collectively as an influence, (*the s. of pity, patriotism*; *animated by noble ss.*; *my s. towards him is one of respect*; *s. unchecked by reason is a bad guide*; *these are*, often facet. *them's, my ss.*, that is what I think about it); (Art) moving quality resulting from artist's sympathetic insight into what is described or depicted; tendency to be swayed by feeling rather than by reason, emotional weakness, mawkish tenderness or the display of it, nursing of the emotions, whence **sentime·nt**AL a., **sentime·ntal**LY² adv., **sentimenta·l**ITY, **sentime·ntal**ISM, **sentime·ntal**IST, nn., **sentime·ntal**IZE(2, 3) v.i. & t.; (sense intended to be conveyed by) the expression of some desire or view esp. as formulated for a toast &c. (*the s. is good though the words are injudicious* &c.; *conclude* one's *speech with a s.*; *I call upon Mr Jones for a song or a s.*). [OE (*-tement*), f. med.L *sentimentum* (L *sentire* feel, -MENT)]

se·ntinel (-nl), n., & v.t. (-ll-). Soldier posted to keep guard (cf. foll.); (also *s. crab*) Indian-Ocean crab with long eye-stalks. (Vb) keep guard over or in (poet.); station ss. at or in (rare). [f. OF *sentinelle* f. It. *sentinella*, both fem. & perh. orig. = watchtower]

se·ntry, n. (Term in ordinary mil. use for) sentinel; *s.-board*, platform for s. outside ship's gangway; *s.-box*, wooden cabin large enough to hold s. standing; *s.-go*, duty of pacing up & down as s. [perh. f. *centrinel* 16th-c. var. of prec.]

se·nza (-tsa), It. prep. = without, in mus. directions as *s. tempo* not in strict time.

sĕ·pal, n. One of the divisions of the calyx, calyx-leaf, (cf. PETAL). [assim. of L *separ* separate to term. of *petal*]

sĕ·parate¹ (-at), a. & n. Physically disconnected, forming a unit that is or may be regarded as apart or by itself, distinct, individual, of individuals, (*from*, or abs.; *the s. members of the body*; *the s. volumes may be had singly*; *live in s. rooms*; *live s.*; *the two questions are essentially s.*; *one is quite s. from the other*; *s. & corporate* or *common ownership*; *s. estate*, married woman's property when not subject to husband's control; *s. maintenance*, husband's allowance to wife from whom he lives s. by consent, cf. *alimony*; hence **se·parate**LY² adv., **se·parate**NESS n., & (esp. w. ref. to political or ecclesiastical independence, opp. *unionism, -ist*) **se·parat**ISM(3) n., **se·parat**IST(2) n. & a. (N.) copy of single article &c. reprinted from proceedings of society, magazine, &c., for s. distribution. [f. L SE(*parare* arrange), -ATE²]

se·parāte², v.t. & i. Make s., sever, disunite, keep (trans.) from union or contact, part (t. & i.), secede *from*, go different ways, disperse (intr.); sort or divide (milk, grain, ore, fruit, light, &c.) into constituent parts or sizes, get (cream &c.) by such process for use or rejection, whence **se·parāt**OR²(2) n. Hence **se·par**ABLE, **se·par**ATIVE, **se·parat**ORY (rare), aa., **se·parab**LY² adv., **separab**I·LITY, **se·parable**NESS, nn. [as prec., -ATE³]

separa·tion, n. In vbl senses; esp. partial divorce, divorce from bed & board without dissolution of marriage tie (*judicial s.*, ordered by court); *s. allowance*, that made by soldier, with large Government augmentation, to his wife &c. [OF, f. L *separationem* (prec., -ION)]

separa·tum, n. (pl. *-ta*). =SEPARATE¹ n. [L neut. p.p.]

Sephar·di (-ē), n. (pl. *-im*). Spanish or Portuguese Jew. [f. Heb. *Sephārād* (see *Obad.* 20) Spain]

sē·pia, n. Black fluid of CUTTLE-fish; brown pigment prepared from this used in monochrome drawing & in water-colours (*warm s.*, mixture of this with some red), dark reddish-brown colour, (also *s.-drawing*) a drawing done in s. [L f. Gk (*sē-*), = cuttle or its ink]

sē·poy, n. Native Indian soldier disciplined by European methods, esp. one of those serving in British-Indian army (*s. mutiny*, = *Indian* MUTINY). [f. Hind. *sipahi* native soldier f. Pers. *sipahi* soldier (*sipah* army)]

seps, n. Kinds of skink, serpent lizard. [Gk (*sē-*), f. *sēpō* rot, w. ref. to effect of bite]

se·psis, n. (med.). Putrefaction, contamination from festering wound &c., blood-poisoning. [Gk (*sē-*), as prec.]

sept, n. Clan, esp. in Ireland. [f. OF *septe* var. of SECTE]

sept-, septem-, septi-, comb. forms of L *septem* seven: *se·ptan*, (of fever) recurring every 6th (inclus. 7th) day; *se·ptangle, -a·ngular*, heptagon(al); *septempar·tite*, divided into 7 parts; *septenār·ius*, verse (esp. Latin) of 7 feet esp. trochaic tetrameter catalectic; *septē·nary* a. & n., of or involving the number 7, on basis of 7, by sevens, septennial, set of 7; *se·ptenate* (bot.,) having 7 parts; *septe·nnate*, (arrangement made for) period of 7 years; *septe·nnial(ly)*, of, for, (recurring) every, 7 years; *septe·nnium* (pl. *-ia*), period of 7 years; *septe·t(te)*, (musical work for) 7 voices, singers, instruments, or players, in combination, (transf.) any set of 7; *se·ptfoil*, the plant tormentil, seven-lobed figure esp. as R.-.C. symbol of the 7 sacraments; *septilă·teral*, seven-sided; *septi·llion*, seventh power of a million, 1 with 42 ciphers; *septisy·llable*, word of 7 syllables; *se·ptūple* a. & n. & v.t. & i., sevenfold (amount), multiply by 7, increase sevenfold.

septa. See SEPTUM.

se·ptal, a. Of sept(s), septum, or septa. [-AL]

se·ptate, a. (bot., zool., anat.). Having septum or septa, partitioned. Hence **septa·tion** n. [SEPTUM, -ATE[2]]

Septe·mber, n. Ninth month of year. [OF (*-bre*), f. L *September* (SEPT-, cf. DECEMBER)]

Septe·mbrist, n. Participator in the massacres in Paris Sept. 2, 3, 1792. [F (*-e*), see -IST]

se·ptic, a. & n. (med.). Of or involving sepsis, not aseptic; *s. tank* (in which sewage is made innocuous by bacterial treatment); hence **se·ptically** adv., **septi·city** n. (N.) s. substance. [f. LL f. Gk *sēptikos* (*sēptos* f. *sēpō* rot, -IC)]

septicae·mia (-sēm-), n. (path.). Blood-poisoning. Hence **septicae·mic** a. [med. L, f. Gk *sēptikos* see prec., *haima* blood, & -IA[1]]

se·ptimal, a. Of the number 7. [f. L *septem* seven after *decimal*]

se·ptime (-ēm), n. Fencing-position. [f. L *septimus* seventh (*septem* seven)]

septimus. See PRIMUS[1].

septuagenār·ian, a. & n. (Person) between 69 & 80. [foll., -AN]

septuagē·nary, a. Of seventy. [f. L *septuagenarius* (*septuageni* seventy each f. *septuaginta* seventy, -ARY[1])]

Septuagĕ·sima, n. (Also *S. Sunday*) Sunday before Sexagesima. [L, = seventieth (day), prob. named loosely as before SEXAGESIMA]

se·ptuagint, n. Greek version of O.T. including the apocrypha said to have been made about 270 B.C. by seventy translators. [f. L *septuaginta* seventy]

se·ptum, n. (anat., bot., zool.; pl. *-ta*). Partition such as that between the nostrils or the chambers of a poppy-fruit, dissepiment. [L (also *sae-*), = fence (*saepire saept-* f. *saepes* hedge)]

sepu·lchral, a. Of sepulchre(s) or sepulture (*s. mound, pillar*, &c.; *s. customs*); suggestive of the tomb, funereal, gloomy, dismal, (*a s. look, voice*). Hence **sepu·lchrally**[2] adv. [f. L *sepulcralis* (foll., -AL)]

sĕ·pulchre (-ker), n., & v.t. Tomb esp. cut in rock or built of stone or brick, burial vault or cave, (*the Holy S.*, in which Christ was laid; *whited s.*, hypocrite, w. ref. to *Matt.* xxiii. 27); (vb) lay in s. [OF (*-cre*), f. L *sepulcrum* (*sepelire sepult-*, suf. *-crum* cf. *simulacrum*)]

se·pulture (-tsher), n. Burying, putting in the grave. [OF, f. L *sepultura* (prec., -URE)]

sequa·cious, a. (pedant.). Inclined to follow, lacking independence or originality, servile; (of reasoning or reasoner) not inconsequent, coherent. Hence **sequa·ciously**[2] adv., **sequă·city** n. [L *sequax* (*sequi* follow), -ACIOUS]

sē·quel, n. What follows after, continuation or resumption of a story or process or the like after a pause or provisional ending, (*in the s.*, as things developed afterwards); after effects, upshot; (rare) result of a chain of argument, logical inference, conclusion. [OF (*-lle*), as foll.]

sequē·la, n. (path.; usu. in pl. *-ae*). Morbid condition or symptom following upon some disease (*heart-disease is one of the* sequelae *of rheumatic fever*). [L (*sequi* follow)]

se·quence, n. Succession, coming after or next, set of things that belong next each other on some principle of order, series without gaps, (*shall follow the s. of events, give the facts in historical s.*; *calamities fall in rapid s.*; *a s. of clubs* &c. in cards, three or more next each other in value; *the s. spring, summer, autumn, winter*); mere succession without implication of causality (s. *is related to* consequence *as* post hoc *to* propter hoc; *is causality, is a law of nature, anything beyond invariable s.?*), so (& rarely in other senses) **se·quENT**, **seque·ntIAL** (-shl), aa., **seque·ntialLY**[2] adv., **sequentia·lITY** (-shĭ-) n.; (Mus.) succession of similar melodic phrases at different pitches; (Gram.) *s. of tenses*, accommodation of subordinate vb in tense or mood according to certain rules to tense or mood of principal verb (e.g. *I should think you* were *satisfied now*); (Eccl.) rhythmical or metrical phrase said or sung after the Alleluia that precedes the Gospel (also *prose*). [f.LL *sequentia* (prec., -ENCE)]

seque·ntēs, seque·ntia, (abbr. *seq.* or *seqq.*), L wds = (&) the following lines, (&) what follows, appended (with or without *et* and) to line or page numbers in references. [pl. part. of L *sequi* follow]

seque·ster, v.t. & i. Seclude, isolate, set apart, (*s. oneself from the world*; esp. in p.p.; as *a sequestered life, retreat, cottage*); (Law; also **seque·strATE**[3], *or* sē·-, v.t.) seize temporary possession of (debtor's estate &c.), remove (debatable property) from control of party to lawsuit, (intr.; of widow) renounce concern in husband's estate; (also *sequestrate*) confiscate, appropriate; hence or cogn. **sequestrA·TION**, **se·questratOR**[2], nn., **seque·strABLE** (*or* sē·-) a. [f. LL *sequestrare* commit for safe keeping (L *sequester* trustee, agent, cf. *secus* apart)]

seque·strum, n. (pl. *-ra*). Piece of dead bone detached from living bone but remaining in place. Hence **seque·strAL** a., **sēquestro·TOMY** n. [neut. of L *sequester* adj. standing apart]

sē·quin, n. (Hist.) Venetian gold coin of about 9/4; coinlike ornament of silver, jet, &c., sewn on to dresses &c. [F, f. It. *zecchino* (*zecca* mint f. Arab. *sikka* die)]

sequoi·a, n. Kinds of Californian coniferous tree of great height. [f. *Sequoiah*, a Cherokee pers. name]

séra·c (sĕ-), n. One of the castellated masses into which a glacier is divided at steep points by the crossing of crevasses (usu. in pl.). [Swiss F, orig. name of a cheese]

serag·lio (-ahlyō), n. Walled palace, esp. (hist.) that of Sultan with government offices &c. at Constantinople; harem. [f. It. *serraglio* enclosure (*serrare* lock, f. LL *serare* f. L *sera* bolt f. *serere* join, *-aglio* = L *-aculum*)]

serai· (-rī, -rā, -rah·ĭ), n. = CARAVANSERAL.

sera·ng, n. (Anglo-Ind.). Native head of a Lascar crew. [f. Pers. *sarhang* commander]

sĕ·raph, n. (pl. *-phim, -phs*). Celestial being; one of the highest ORDER[1] of ninefold celestial hierarchy gifted esp. with love & associated with light, ardour, & purity; (*Order of the Seraphim*, Swedish order of knighthood). Hence **seră·phIC** a. (*the S. Doctor*, St Bonaventura), **sera·phICALLY** adv. [earlier *-in* &c. as with CHERUB; f. Heb. *seraphim* pl., seraphs, perh. f. *sāraph* to burn]

sĕraphi·na (-ē-), **sĕ·raphine** (-ēn), n. Early form of harmonium. [prec., -INE[1]]

sĕraskier·, n. Turkish general commanding, commander-in-chief, or minister of war (*seraskier·at*, war office). [Turk. f. Pers. = head of army]

Serb n., **Ser·bia(n)** aa. & nn. (Native, language) of Serbia. Hence **Serbo-** comb.-form. [f. Serb. *Srb, Serb*]

Serbō·nian bog, n. Treacherous bog formerly existing between delta of Nile & isthmus of Suez, (fig.) situation from which escape is difficult. [Gk *Serbōnis*, -IAN]

sere[1], **sear,** n. Catch of gun-lock holding hammer at half or full cock. [f. OF *serre* lock (*serrer* f. LL *serare* see SERAGLIO)]

sere[2]. See SEAR[1].

serein (F), n. Fine rain falling in tropical climates from cloudless sky.

sĕrĕnā·de, n., & v.t. Evening song or instrumental piece sung or played by lover at his lady's window; = foll. (Vb) sing or play s. to; hence **serena·dER**[1] n. [OF, f. It. *serenata* (*sereno* open air f. L as SERENE); see -ADE]

sĕrĕna·ta (-nah-), n. (mus.). Cantata with pastoral subject for open-air performance; simple form of symphony. [It. (prec.)]

sere·ne, a. & n., & v.t. (Of sky, air, &c.) clear & calm, (of sea &c.) unruffled; placid, tranquil, unperturbed, (*a s. temper, look, life*); (slang) *all s.*, all right; *His, Her, Their, Your, S. Highness(es)*, *abbr.* H.S.H., T.S.H., titles used of or to certain continental princes; hence or cogn. **sere·neLY**[2] adv., **serĕ·nITY** n. (*your* &c. *Serenity*, Serene Highness). (N.) s. expanse of sky, sea, &c. (Vb; poet.) make (sky, brow, &c.) s. [f. L *serenus*]

serf, n. Villein, person whose service is attached to the soil & transferred with it (cf. SLAVE); oppressed person, drudge. Hence **ser·fAGE**, **ser·fDOM**, **ser·fHOOD**, nn. [OF, f. L *servus* slave]

serge, n. Kind of durable twilled worsted fabric used esp. for rough wear (*silk s.*, used for tailor's linings). [orig. a silk stuff; OF, f. L *serica* fem. of *sericus* silken (*Sericus* Chinese f. Gk *Sēres* pl. the Chinese, -IC)]

sergeant, -j-, (sar·jnt), n. (Hist.) lawyer of high rank (*-j-*); (Mil.; *-g-*; abbr. *Sergt*) non-commissioned officer above corporal, one of four to the company, employed to teach drill, command small detachments, &c. (*s. major* or *regimental s.m.*, R.S.M., warrant officer assisting adjutant of regiment or battalion; *company s. major*, C.S.M., highest warrant officer of company; *lance-s.*, corporal acting as s. with corporal's pay); police officer ranking between inspector & constable; *serjeant-at-arms*, title of certain court, parliamentary, & city officials with ceremonial duties; *common serjeant*, officer of City of London; ***s.-fish*** (*-g-*), sea-fish with lateral stripes suggesting chevron. Hence **ser·geant**SHIP n. [f. OF *sergent* f. L *servientem* nom. *-ens* servant (L *servire* SERVE, -ENT)]

serge·tte, n. Thin serge. [F (SERGE, -ETTE)]

sēr·ial, a. & n. Of, in, forming, a series, whence **seria·**LITY n.; (of story &c.) issued in instalments (*s. rights*, copyright in regard to story &c. so issued), whence **ser·ial**IST (1) n.; (of publication) periodical; hence **ser·ial**LY² adv. (N.) s. story; a s. publication, periodical, (rare). [SERIES, -AL]

ser·iate (*-at*), **-āted,** aa., **ser·iāte** v.t. (Arrange) in the form of a series, in orderly sequence. Hence **seri**A·TION n. [L SERIES, -ATE², ³]

sĕriā·tim (*or* sēr-), adv. Point by point, taking one subject &c. after another in regular order, (*consider, examine, discuss, take*, &c., *s.*). [med. L (prec., *-im* advl term.)]

Sēr·ic, a. (rhet. &c.). Chinese. [f. L as SERGE]

seri·ceous (-sh*u*s), a. (bot., zool.). Of silky or satiny surface, soft & shiny, covered with glossy down. [f. L *sericeus* silken (*sericum* silk, see SERGE), -OUS]

sĕ·ri(ci)culture, n. Silkworm-breeding, production of raw silk. Hence **seri(ci)-cu·ltur**AL a., **seri(ci)cu·ltur**IST(3) n. [F (*-ci-*), see prec., -I-, CULTURE]

sĕriē·ma, n. Sonorous-voiced Brazilian bird of heron size preying on serpents. [native]

sēr·iēs (-z), n. (pl. same). Number of things of which each is similar to the preceding or related to it as it to its predecessor, sequence, succession, order, row, set, (*a s. of kings, misfortunes*; *in s.*, in ordered succession; *s. of stamps, coins*, &c., of different denominations but issued at one time, in one reign, &c.; *the whole s. of reform acts*); (Bibliog.) set of successive issues of a periodical, of articles on one subject or by one writer, &c., esp. (*first, second*, &c., *s.*) when numbered differently from a preceding or following set, also set of independent books in common *format* or under common title or supervised by common editor-in-chief, (*Guesses at Truth, 2nd s.*; *the Men-of-Letters s.*); (Geol.) set of strata with common characteristic; (Chem.) set of elements with common properties or of compounds with common radical; (Math.) set of terms constituting a progression or having the several values determined by a common relation (*arithmetical, geometrical, s.*, one in ARITHMETICAL, GEOMETRICAL, progression); (Electr.) set of batteries &c. having positive electrode of each connected with negative of next; (Zool.) number of connected genera, families, &c. (used vaguely like GROUP). [L (*serere* join, cf. Gk *eirō* bind)]

sĕ·rif, (now rare) **ceriph,** n. Cross-line finishing off a stroke of a letter (esp. in SANSERIF; This has ss.: This is sanserif). [?]

sĕ·rin, n. Central-Europ. finch related to canary. [F, etym. dub.]

serine·tte, n. Instrument for training song-birds. [F (*seriner* teach to sing f. prec., -ETTE)]

seri·nga (-ngg*a*), n. Kinds of Brazilian rubber-tree. [Port., = (rubber for)—SYRINGE(S)]

sērio-co·mic, a. Combining the serious & the comic, jocular in intention but counterfeiting seriousness or vice versa. Hence **serio-co·mic**ALLY adv. [-O-]

sĕrio·so, mus. direction. With solemnity. [It.]

sēr·ious, a. Thoughtful, earnest, sober, sedate, responsible, not frivolous or reckless or given to trifling, (*has a s. look, air*; *a s. young person*; *s. politician*, who gives his best energies to politics; *s. thought*, real deliberation); important, demanding consideration, not to be trifled with, not slight, (*this is a s. matter, question, step*; *made a s. alteration*; *have a s. rival in her affections*; *s. illness, danger, wound, damage, accident, defeat*); sincere, not ironical or jesting, in earnest, (*are you s.?*, do you mean what you say?; *made a s. attempt*, not merely perfunctory; *& now to be s.*); concerned with religion or ethics, not worldly or secular, (*s. subjects* &c.); (now chiefly joc.) religious-minded, with thoughts concentrated on salvation. Hence **ser·ious**LY² adv. (esp. as preface to sentence implying that irony &c. is now to cease), **ser·ious**NESS n. [f. LL *seriosus* (L *serius* etym. dub., -OSE¹)]

sĕ·riph, n. = SERIF.

serjeant. See SERGEANT.

ser·mon, n., & v.t. Extempore or written discourse delivered from the pulpit by way of religious instruction or exhortation, similar discourse (often *lay s.*) on religious or moral subject delivered elsewhere or published, (*S. on the Mount*, discourse of Christ reported *Matt.* v–vii); moral reflection suggested by natural objects &c. (esp. *ss. in stones*); piece of admonition or reproof, lecture, (vb, administer such s. to). Hence **sermon**E·TTE, **ser·mon**ET¹, nn., **ser·mon**IZE(1, 2) v.t. & i., **ser·moniz**ER¹ n. [OF, f. L *sermonem* nom. *-o* speech]

sēro-, comb. form of SERUM: *-puru·lent*, of serum & pus; *-sangui·nolent*, & blood.

sĕ·rotine, n. Chestnut-coloured European bat. [F (*sé-*), f. L *serotinus* late (*serus* late)]

serŏ·tinous, a. (bot.). Appearing late in season. [prec., -OUS]

sēr·ous, a. Of or like serum, watery, whey-like. Hence **sērO·SITY** n. [f. F *séreux* f. L *serosus* (SERUM, -OUS)]

ser·pent, n. Scaly limbless reptile, snake esp. of the larger kinds, (preferred to SNAKE chiefly in rhet. use; *the, the old, S.*, the devil, w. ref. to *Gen.* iii, *Rev.* xx), (fig.) treacherous person esp. one who worms himself into favour for base ends; *the S.*, a northern constellation; wind-instrument now little used, a wooden tube with several bends giving powerful note; *Pharaoh's s.*, chemical toy of small cone that when ignited issues in long coiling serpentlike ash; *s.-charmer*, person who charms ss. esp. by music; *s.-eater*, SECRETARY-bird; *s.-grass*, Alpine bistort; *s. lizard*, seps; *s.'s-tongue*, ADDER'*s-tongue*. Hence **serpe·ntiFORM, ser·pentLIKE,** aa. [OF, f. L *serpentem* nom. *-ens*, orig. part. of *serpere* creep, cogn. w. Gk *herpō* creep, Skr. *sarpa* snake]

ser·pentine, a. & n., & v.i. Of or like a serpent lit. or fig., writhing, coiling, tortuous, sinuous, meandering, cunning, subtle, treacherous, (*s. windings*, of stream, road, &c., or of insinuation; *s. motion*; *s. wisdom*, profound, w. ref. to *Matt.* x. 16; *s. dance*, with sinuous movements enhanced by special drapery; *s. verse*, line beginning & ending with same word; *the S.*, ornamental water in Hyde Park). (N.) kinds of hydrous silicate of magnesium, soft rocks of dark green & other colours sometimes mottled or spotted like serpent's skin, taking high polish & used as decorative material; (Skating) wavy line produced by changes of edge. (Vb) move sinuously, meander. [f. OF *serpentin* a., *serpentine* n., f. L *serpentinus -a* (prec., -INE[1])]

serpi·ginous, a. (path.). Affected with herpes; (of skin-disease &c.) creeping from one part to another. [obs. & med. L, *serpigo -ginis* ringworm (L *serpere* creep), -OUS]

ser·pūla, n. (pl. *-ae*). Kinds of marine worm inhabiting beautifully coloured tortuous calcareous tubes often massed together. [LL, = small serpent (L *serpere* creep)]

se·rra, n. (anat., bot., zool.; pl. *-ae*). Serrated organ, structure, or edge. [L, = saw, perh. f. *secare* cut]

serradi·lla, n. Kind of clover grown as fodder. [Port., dim. of *serrado* SERRATE a.]

se·rrate a., **serra·te** v.t., (chiefly anat., bot., zool.). Notched like saw; (vb, usu. in p.p. as adj.) provide with saw-like edge. Hence **serrA·TION** n. [f. L SERRA*tus* (-ATE[2]), -ATE[3]]

se·rrefile (-refīl), n. (mil.; usu. in pl.). Person in (pl.) the line of supernumerary & non-commissioned officers in rear of squadron or troop. [F, f. *serrer* (see SERRIED) + *file* (see FILE[3])]

serri-, comb. form (-I-) of SERRA: *-corn*, (beetle) with serrate antennae; -FEROUS; -FORM; *-ro·strate*, (of bird) with serrated bill.

se·rried, a. (Of ranks of soldiers, rows of trees, &c.) shoulder to shoulder, without gaps, close. [angliciz. of F *serré* p.p. of *serrer* close f. LL *serare* see SERAGLIO]

se·rromōtor, n. Steam reversing-gear attached to marine engine. [SERRA (in sense *cog*), -O-, MOTOR]

se·rrulate (-rŏŏ-), **-ated,** aa. Finely serrate, with series of small notches. Hence **serrulA·TION** n. [L *serrula* (SERRA, -ULE), -ATE[2]]

sēr·um, n. Whey; thin transparent part of the blood; chyle, lymph, watery animal fluid. [L, cf. Gk *oros* whey, Skr. *sara(s)* flowing]

ser·val, n. Tawny black-spotted African tiger-cat. [F, f. Port.]

ser·vant, n. Person who has undertaken usu. in return for stipulated pay to carry out the orders of an individual or corporate employer, esp. one who lives in house of master or mistress receiving board & lodging & wages & performing domestic duties (*public ss.*, State officials; *railway company's ss.*, its employees; *civil s.*, member of the civil service; *outdoor s.*, groom, gardener, &c.; *indoor s.*, cook, butler, footman, housemaid, &c.; *domestic*, GENERAL, LIVERY, *s.*; *s.-girl, -maid*; *the s. question*, problem of getting & controlling ss.; *keeps three ss.*; *servants' hall*, room in which ss. of large household have meals &c.; *s. of ss.*, lowest of dependants, esp. as title assumed by Popes, transl. of *servus servorum Dei*; *a good s. but a bad master*, of things that should be treated as means & not ends); devoted follower, person willing to serve another, (*a s. of Jesus Christ*; *your humble s.* archaic, form of ironical courtesy; *your obedient s.*, epistolary form preceding signature now used only in letters of official type). [OF (SERVE, -ANT)]

serve, v.t. & i., & n. Be servant (to), do service (to), be useful (to), (*s. two masters*, be divided between two conflicting principles &c.; *s. the Lord* or *God*, be religious or virtuous; *s. the devil*, be wicked; *s. tables*, postpone spiritual to bodily needs, see *Acts* vii. 2; *s. at table*, act as waiter; *has served his generation*; *would do much to s. you*; *indiscretion sometimes serves us well*; *s. in army, navy*, &c., be employed in it; *has served in India*, been employed esp. as soldier); meet needs (of), avail (t. & i.), suffice (t. & i.), satisfy, perform function, be suitable, do what is required for, (*s. a purpose*; *s. the purpose of*, take place of, be used as; *to s. some private ends*; *serves the* or one's *turn* or *need*, does well enough; *it will s.*, do what is absolutely necessary; *that excuse will not s. you*; *it serves to show the folly of*; *1 lb. serves him for a week*; *nothing would s. him* or *s. but absolute submission*; *a sofa serving him*, or *serving, as* or *for a bed*; *as memory serves*, whenever one remembers; *as occasion serves*, when it is favourable; *the tide serves*, is suitable for getting out of harbour &c.; *curate serves two parishes*, does the work; *s. an office*, go through a tenure of it; *s.* one's *apprenticeship*, go through training; *s. a sentence*, undergo it for the full time; *s.* one's *time*, hold office for normal period, also s. a sentence; *s. time*, undergo imprisonment &c.; *s. gun, battery*, keep it firing; *s. mare* &c., cover, esp. of stallion &c. hired for purpose; *s. rope* &c. naut., bind with small cord to save fraying); dish *up*, set (food) on table, set out ready, distribute (trans. & abs.), supply (person *with*), make legal delivery of (writ &c.), set ball or set (ball) in play, (*fish served up nearly cold*; *asparagus served with butter*; *s. up dinner*; *dinner is served*, servant's announcement that it is ready; *s. ammunition, rations*, &c., *out* or *round*; *was serving a customer with stockings, serving in the shop*; *have them served with soup*; *s. with the same sauce* fig., retaliate upon; *s. person, the town*, &c., *with gas, water*; *s. with writ* &c., = s. writ &c. on; *s. warrant, writ, notice, process, attachment*, &c., usu. *on* person, deliver document to person concerned in legally formal manner; *tennis, racquet*, &c., *player serves a ball, serves well, badly*, &c., sends ball to opponent in first stroke of round); treat, treat to, pay (person) *out*, (*has served me shamefully*; *you may s. me as you will*; *served them a trick*, played it on them; *s.* or *serves him right!*, excl. of satisfaction at sight of offender getting his deserts; *shall manage to s. him out*, retaliate); *serving-man*, male servant; hence **(-)ser'ver**[1](1, 2) n. (N.; tennis &c.) first stroke of round, turn for delivering this (*whose s. is it?*). [f. OF *servir* f. L *servire* (*servus* slave)]

Ser'vian[1], var. of, & till 1914 more usual than, SERBIAN.

Ser'vian[2], a. (Rom. Ant.). Of Servius Tullius sixth king of Rome (*S. wall*, built by him & still existing in parts). [-AN]

ser'vice[1], n. Being servant, servant's status, master's or mistress's employ, (*girl* &c. *goes out to, goes into, tries, is in, s.*; *take s. with*, become servant to; *take into* one's *s.*, employ); department of royal or public employ or of work done to meet some general need, persons engaged in it, employment in it, (*the fighting*, or *the, ss.*, navy, army, & air force; *the public ss.*; *the* CIVIL, COVENANTED, *consular*, SECRET, *omnibus, railway*, &c., *s.*; *the preventive s.*, coastguards, customhouse, &c.; *is on s., in active s.*, actually engaged in such employ; *see s.*, have experience esp. as soldier or sailor), (attrib.) of the kind issued to the s. (*the s. rifle*); person's disposal or behalf (*at your* &c. *s.*, ready to obey orders or be used; *on his, her, Majesty's s.*, abbr. O.H.M.S., frank stamped on official letters &c.); what employee or subordinate is bound to, work done or doing of work on behalf of employer, benefit conferred on or exertion made on behalf of someone, expression of willingness to confer or make these, (*personal s.*, feudal obligation of homage &c.; *feudal, menial, willing*, YEOMAN'*s, s.*; *has a right to my s.*; *asks for my ss.*; *will you do me a s.?*; *exaggerates his own ss.*; *has seen s.*, been much used, shows signs of wear; *my s. to him*, form of respectful message); use, assistance, (*can I, will it, be of s. to you?*); liturgical form or office appointed for use on some occasion, (whole proceedings, usu. including one such s. or more, of) single meeting of congregation for worship, musical setting of all or several of the invariable parts of a liturgy adapted for such treatment, (*the communion, burial*, &c., *s.*; *special ss.*; *divine s.* usu. without *a*, meeting for worship; *holds four ss. every Sunday*; *are you going to s.* or *the s.?*; *—'s s.*, setting by particular composer; *full s.*, performed by choir without solos, also s. with music wherever possible; *plain s.*, read or monotoned; *s.-book*, book of offices of a Church, e.g. the Book of Common Prayer; CHURCH[1]*-service*); legal serving of or *of* writ &c. (*personal s.*, delivery with announcement of contents to person affected; *s. by publication, substitution*, publishing of writ &c. by posting up or insertion in newspaper or by handing to neighbour &c. recognized as sufficient under some conditions; ACCEPT *s.*); set of dishes, plates, &c., required for serving meal (*dinner, dessert, tea*, &c., *s.*); (Traffic) set of trains, steamers, omnibuses, &c., plying at stated times; (single act of) serving in tennis &c., serve, manner of serving, person's turn to serve, (*his s. is weak, terrific*; *whose s. is it?*; *s.-line*, marking limit short of which serve must fall); *s.-pipe*, conveying house's water from the main. [OF, f. L *servitium* (*servus* slave)]

ser'vice[2], n. (Usu. *s.-tree*) European tree rare in England with leaves like those of mountain-ash & small pear-shaped fruit (*s.-berry* or *s.*) eaten when over-ripe. [f. *serves* pl. of obs. *serve* f. L *sorbum* berry of the *sorbus* taken as sing. & assimilated to prec.]

ser'viceable (-*sa*-), a. Of use, useful, willing & able to render or capable of rendering service, (*a s. person, reminder, instrument*); durable, suited for rough use or ordinary wear rather than for ornament. Hence **ser·viceab**LY[2] adv., **ser·vice-able**NESS n. [f. OF *serviçable* (SERVICE[1], -ABLE)]

servie·tte, n. Table-napkin (chiefly used by & to waiters or servants). [F]

ser·vīle (*or* -ĭl), a. Of, being, a slave or slaves, slave-, (*s. war*, between revolted slaves & their owners; *s. class, labour*; *s. letter* fig., having no other function than to indicate pronunciation of another, as *e* in manageable, saleable); as of a slave, slavish, cringing, mean-spirited, menial, completely dependent, (*s. spirit, creature, submission, flattery, fear, imitation*), so **servĭ·l**ITY n. Hence **ser·vile**LY[2] adv. [f. L *servilis* (*servus* slave, -IL)]

ser·vitor, n. Attendant, henchman, servant, (archaic, poet.); (Oxf. Univ.; hist.) undergraduate assisted from college funds & performing menial duties in return, whence **ser·vitor**SHIP n. [OF f. LL (SERVE, -OR[2])]

ser·vitude, n. Slavery lit. or fig., subjection esp. involuntary to a master, bondage (PENAL *s.*); (Law) subjection of tenement to an easement. [F, f. LL *servitudo* (*servus* slave, -TUDE)]

Servo-, = Serbo- (see SERBIAN).

sĕ·same (-ĭ), n. Annual herbaceous tropical & subtropical plant with seeds used in various ways as food & yielding an oil used in salads & as laxative; its seeds; *open s.*, (w. ref. to Arabian-Nights tale) magical or mysterious means of commanding access to what is usu. inaccessible. [f. L f. Gk *sēsamē*]

se·samoid, a. & n. Shaped like a sesame-seed, nodular, (esp. of small independent bones developed in tendons passing over angular structure, as the knee-pan & the navicular bone); (n.) such bone. [f. L f. Gk *sēsamoeidēs* (prec., -OID)]

sĕ·selĭ, n. Genus of white-flowered umbelliferous perennial plants. [OF f. L f. Gk]

sesqui-, L pref. (perh. f. *semis-que* & a half), = one & a half (*sesquipedalis* a foot & a half long), proportioned as $1\frac{1}{2}:1$ or $3:2$ (*sesquialter*), proportioned as $n+1:n$ (*-tertius, -quartus*, &c., in ratios 4 : 3, 5 : 4, &c.). Hence in E (1) chem. wds for compounds in which there are three equivalents of the named element to two others, as *sesquioxide, -sulphide*; *-basic* (of salt), with three of base to two of acid; (2) math. wds expressing ratios as above, *-alteral* 3 : 2, *-tertial* 4 : 3, *-quartal, -quintal, -sextal, -septimal, -octaval, -nonal* 10 : 9; (3) mus. wds in *-a* corresponding to the above & expressing intervals (*-altera* interval having ratio 2 : 3, *-tertia* 3 : 4, &c.); (4) miscellaneous wds, as *-ocellus* entom., large spot with smaller one within it (also *sesquialter*); *-pedalian* (of word) $1\frac{1}{2}$ ft long, cumbrous & pedantic; *-plicate*, in ratio of cube to square; *-tone*, musical interval of $1\frac{1}{2}$ tone.

sess. See CESS.

se·ssĭle, a. (bot., zool.). (Of flower, leaf, eye, &c.) attached directly by the base without stalk or peduncle. [f. L *sessilis* (*sedēre sess-* sit, -IL)]

session (sĕ·shn), n. Being seated, sitting posture, (rare); being assembled esp. for transaction of deliberative or judicial business, single uninterrupted meeting for such purpose, period during which such meetings are held daily or at short or regular intervals, period (usu. one in a year) between meeting & prorogation of Parliament, (*in s.*, sitting or assembled for business, not keeping vacation; *had a long s.*, sat assembled a long time, *autumn s.*, incorrectly for *autumn sitting*, resumption of s. of Parliament sometimes required by pressure of business after long adjournment in summer without prorogation); (esp. Sc. & U.S.) university term; QUARTER-*ss.*; BREWSTER-SESSIONS; *petty ss.*, meeting of two or more justices of the peace for summary trying of certain offences; *Court of S.*, supreme civil court of Scotland; KIRK-*s.* Hence **se·ssion**AL a. (*s. order* Parl., valid only for, renewable each, session). [F, f. L *sessionem* (prec., -ION)]

se·sterce, sester·tius (-sh*us*; pl. *-iī*), nn. Ancient-Roman silver (& later bronze) coin & money of account = $\frac{1}{4}$ denarius or $2\frac{1}{2}$ asses (about 2*d.*). [f. L (*-ius*) orig. adj. with *numus* coin = $2\frac{1}{2}$ (**semistertius* half-third)]

sester·tium (-shm), n. (pl. *-ia*). Ancient-Roman money of account = 1000 sesterces. [orig. gen. pl. of prec. after *millia* thousands]

seste·t, n. = SEXTET; last six lines of sonnet. [f. It. *sestetto* (*sesto* f. L *sextus* sixth, -ET[1])]

sesti·na (-tē-), n. Form of rhymed or unrhymed poem with six stanzas of six lines & final triplet, each stanza having same words as the others ending its lines but in different order. [It. (prec., -INE[4])]

set[1], v.t. & i. (set). Put, lay, stand (trans.), (usu. with adv. or advl phr.; *s. load* or *passenger down, statue up, meat before* person, *flowers in water, one brick on another, his bow in heaven*; *s. foot*, tread *on*; *s.* thing *against* another, balance, reckon as counterpoise or compensation; *s. apart*, reserve, separate; *s. aside*, reserve, reject, disregard, annul; *s. by*, reserve, save for future use; *s. stone out*, lay it with edge projecting beyond one below; *s.* person *over* others or thing, put in authority); apply (thing) *to* (*s. pen to paper, bugle to* one's *lips, spurs to horse*; *s.* one's *hand, seal, to* document, sign, seal; *s.* one's *hand to* task, begin; *s. fire to*, kindle; *s. the axe to*, begin to cut down or destroy; *s.* one's *wits to* question, try to solve; *s.* one's *wits to* another's, argue with him; *s.* SHOULDER *to wheel*); station, place ready, place or turn in right or specified position or direction, dispose suitably for use or action or display, (*s. a* or naut. *the watch*, put sentinels &c. in place; *s. chairs*, for visitors &c.; *s. clock* or *watch*, put hands to right time; *s. alarum*, provide for its sounding at desired time; *s. hen*, cause to sit on eggs; *s. eggs*, place for hen to sit on; *s. seed, plant*, put in ground; QUICKS.; *s. butterfly* &c., arrange as specimen; *s. sail*, hoist, also = start on voyage; *s. trap*; *s. razor*, give even edge to after grinding; *s. saw*, give teeth alternate outward inclination; *s. table*, lay for meal; *s.* or *s. up type*, arrange it in words &c.; *s. up* MS., put it in type; *s. close, wide*, &c., print with small, large, spaces between words or letters; *s. out*, s. wide; *s.* one's CAP[1] *at*); join, attach, fasten, fix, determine, decide, appoint, settle, establish, (*s. leg, bone, joint*, put parts into right relative position after fracture or dislocation, also by extension *s. fracture* or *dislocation*; *s. eyes on*, catch sight of; *s. diamond* &c., insert in gold &c. as frame or foil; *s. stake in ground*; *close-s.*, inserted with little interval; *s.* one's *heart, mind, hopes*, &c., *on*, aspire confidently to, expect, be resolved to get; *s.* one's *life on a chance* &c. metaph. from gambling, risk it; *s. price on*, announce salable value of; *s.* person *against* another or a thing, fill with settled dislike for; *s. price on* one's *life* or *head*, offer specified reward for his killing; *s. store* or *much by*, & ellipt. *s. by*, estimate or value highly; *s.* one's *face* or one*self against*, stedfastly oppose or discountenance; *s.* one's *teeth*, clench them, esp. fig. = make up one's mind inflexibly; often in p.p., = unmoving, fixed, as *s. smile, eyes, look, purpose*; *of s. purpose*, intentionally, deliberately; *s. time*, prearranged; *s. scene*, built up of more or less solid material; *s. piece* in fireworks, built up on scaffolding; *s. forms of prayers* &c., not extempore; *s. speech*, composed beforehand; *s. fair* of weather, fine without sign of breaking; *s. on* or *upon*, determined to get, absorbed in; *batsman is s.*, has got his eye in); bring by placing, arranging, impelling, or other means, into specified state (*s. things right, to rights, in order, in motion*; *s.* one's *house in order*, often fig., introduce reforms; *s. question*, person's *heart, at rest*; *s. machine going, cask abroach*; *s.* person *on his feet* lit. & fig., *box on its end*; *s.* one *in the way*, direct him; *s.* one *on his way* archaic, go part way with him; *s.* one *right*, disabuse him of error, correct, often with implication of officiousness &c.; *s.* one *at ease*, relieve his anxieties or bashfulness; *s. at liberty, s. free*, release; *s.* persons *by the ears, at variance* or *loggerheads*, produce quarrel; *s. on fire*, kindle; *s. Thames on* FIRE[1]; *s. movement* &c. *on foot*, start it; *s. table, company*, &c., *laughing* or *on* or *in a roar*, stir laughter; *s. teeth on* EDGE[1]); *s. at defiance*, defy; *s. at naught*, mock, disregard; make sit down *to* task, order to apply energies *to* do*ing*, cause *to work*, apply oneself *to work*, (*s. him to dictation, wood-chopping, work at his Greek*; *shall s. to work now*, begin; *s.* one*self to* do, make up one's mind, resolve or undertake); exhibit or arrange as pattern or as material to be dealt with (often w. ind. obj.; *s., s.* person, *an example, task, problem*, &c., to be followed, done, solved, by him; *s. the fashion, the pace*, determine it by leading; *s. paper*, draw up questions to be answered by examinees; *s. the* TEMPERAMENT in piano-tuning, arrange intervals of one octave as standard for the rest); *s.* (*to music*), provide (song, words) with music usu. composed for the purpose; make insertions in (surface) *with* (*gold, field, sky, s. with gems, daisies, stars*; *shall s. top of wall with broken glass, this bed with geraniums*); turn (i., rarely t.) to solid or hard or rigid from liquid or soft or mobile state, curdle, solidify, harden, take shape, develop (usu. intr.) into definiteness or maturity, (*egg sets*, by cooking or incubation; HARD-*s.*; *blossom sets*, forms into fruit; *fruit sets*, develops out of blossom; *tree sets*, develops fruit; *plaster of Paris sets quickly*; *the jelly, junket, has* or *is s.*; *when his body, character, has s.*; THICKS.; *over-exercise sets a boy's muscles prematurely*; *face sets*, takes hard expression; *eyes s.*, become motionless in death, swoon, &c.); sink below horizon (*sun, moon, sets*; *the star of Rome, his star, has* or *is s.*, greatness is departed); (of tide, current, &c., & transf. of feelings, customs, &c.) have motion, gather force, sweep along, show or feel tendency, (*tide sets in, out*; *current sets strongly, eastwards*; *opinion is setting against it*; *his soul s. to grief*); (of sporting dog) take rigid attitude indicating presence of game; (of dancers) take position facing partners (often *s. to partners*); (of garment) adapt itself to figure, sit, *well, badly*, &c.; SHARP[1]-*s.* Special senses with advv. & prepp.: *s. about*, begin, take steps towards, (task, do*ing*); *s. back*, impede or reverse progress of; *s. down*, put in writing, attribute *to*, explain or describe to oneself *as*; *s. forth*, make known, declare, expound, adorn, begin journey or expedition; *s. forward*, assist progress of, begin going forward (archaic); *s. in*, arise, get vogue, become established, (*reaction, rain, s. in*; *it s. in to rain*); *s. off*, act as adornment or foil to, enhance, make more striking, start (person) laughing or talking on pet subject, begin journey; *s. on* adv., instigate, advance to the assault; *s. on* prep., urge (dog &c.) to attack (person &c.), attack; *s. out*, embellish, demonstrate, exhibit, declare, begin journey; *s. to* adv., begin doing something vigorously, esp. (usu. w. pl. subj.) fighting or arguing; *s. up*, develop figure of by physical training (esp. in p.p., as *a well s.-u. man*), start (institution, business, one's carriage, &c.), occasion (soreness &c.), establish (person) or provide with means of establishment or establish oneself in some capacity (*his father, £50, s. him up as a tobacconist* or *in the tobacco trade*; *shall s. up as a dentist*), provide adequately *in* or *with* some article (*am s. up with novels for the winter*), place (standard, notice, &c.) in view, begin uttering (protest, shriek, &c.) loudly, propound (theory), restore from ill-health or depression; *s. up for*, make pretensions to the character of (*sets up for a scholar, moralist*, &c.); *s. upon*, = *s. on* prep. [OE *settan* (*sittan* SIT), cf. Du. *zetten*, G *setzen*]

set[2], n. Number of things or persons that belong together as essentially similar or as complementary to each other, group, clique, collection, (*s. of studs, chairs, golf-clubs, fire-irons, lectures*; *s. of teeth*, natural or artificial; *a fine s. of men, players, officers*, &c.; *dinner s.*, dinner SERVICE[1]; *toilet s.*, vessels of wash-hand-stand; *the fast, best, racing, smart, literary, political*, &c., *s.*, sections of society consorting together; *s. of quadrilles* or *s.*, figures that make up a quadrille; *s. of dancers* or *s.*, number needed to make up square dance; *a, the first*, &c., *s.* in tennis &c., group of games counting as unit to side that wins more than half the games in it; *s. of exchange*, first &c. of EXCHANGE[1] collectively); slip or shoot for planting; young fruit just s.; setting *of* sun or day (poet.); way current or wind or opinion &c. sets, drift or tendency *of*, (*the s. of the current, public feeling*, &c.; *the s. of his mind is towards intolerance*); configuration, conformation, habitual posture, way head &c. is set on or carried, way dress &c. sits or flows, (usu. *of*; *the s. of the hills, his head, the drapery*), warp or bend or displacement caused by continued pressure or position (*has got a s. to the right*); (amount of) alternate deflection of saw-teeth; last coat of plaster on wall; timber frame supporting gallery &c. in coal-mine; amount of margin in type causing letters to be close or wide s.; number of eggs in nest, or number laid before bird sits, clutch; setter's pointing in presence of game (often *dead s., make dead s. at* transf., combine to attack esp. by argument or ridicule); badger's burrow; granite paving-block; kinds of wrench & punch; (Theatr.) s. scene; *s.-back*, reversal or arrest of progress, relapse; *s.-down*, rebuff, snub; *s.-off*, thing s. off against another, thing of which the amount or effect, may be deducted from that of another of opposite tendency, counterpoise, counter-claim, thing that embellishes, adornment *to* something, (Arch.) sloping or horizontal member connecting lower and thicker part of wall &c. with upper receding part; *s.-out*, commencement or start (esp. *at the first s.-o.*), things s. out, equipment, display of food or utensils or goods; *s.-to*, combat esp. with fists; *s.-up*, erectness or carriage of body. [in 1st sense prob. corrupt. of SECT; in others f. prec.]

sētā·ceous (-sh*u*s), a. Bristly, having bristles, shaped like a bristle. Hence **seta·ceous**LY[2] adv. [f. L *seta* bristle, -ACEOUS]

sēti·ferous, seti·gerous, seto·se, aa. Having bristles. [L *seta* bristle, *setiger, setosus*, bristly, -FEROUS, -GEROUS, -OSE[1]]

sē·ton, n. (surg.). Skein of cotton or the like passed below skin and left with ends protruding to maintain an artificial issue as counter-irritant &c. esp. in veterinary practice; *s.-needle*, for inserting s. [f. med. L *setonem* silk (L *seta* bristle)]

set square, n. Draughtsman's appliance consisting of a triangular plate of wood or metal with angles of 90°, 60°, 30°, or of 90°, 45°, 45°, for drawing lines at such angles. [p.p. of SET[1]]

sett, arbitrary var. of SET[2] in some of its more technical senses.

settee·[1], Long seat variously constructed to seat more than one person, esp. kind of double arm-chair or short sofa with ends alike for tête-à-tête. [perh. irreg. dim. f. SETTLE[1]; see -EE]

settee·[2], n. Mediterranean sharp-prowed lateen-sailed vessel with two or three masts. [f. It. *saettia* (*saetta* f. L SAGITTA)]

se·tter, n. In vbl senses; esp., breeds (*English, Irish, Gordon, s.*) of long-haired dog trained to stand rigid on scenting game; *s.-on*, instigator. [SET[1], -ER[1]; dog named from native habit of crouching on same occasion]

se·tterwort (-ert), n. A plant, Bear's-foot or Fetid Hellebore. [prob. f. MLG or MHG (*sitro-, sutten-*, &c., WORT)]

se·tting, n. In vbl senses; esp.: the music of a song &c.; the metal or other frame in which a gem is set, (transf.) surroundings of any object regarded as its framework or as accessories setting it off, environment, (Theatr.) way a play is put on the stage, scenery, properties, costumes, &c.; *s.-board*, on which entomological specimens are set; *s.-box*, in which s.-boards are kept like shelves or drawers; *s.-needle*, needle in wooden handle used in setting specimens; *s.-rule*, brass rule or steel plate with which type is kept temporarily in place as it is set up; *s.-stick*, used in setting type. [-ING[1]]

se·ttle[1], n. Bench with high back & arms & often with chest from seat to floor. [OE *setl*, cf. Du. *zetel*, G *sessel*; cogn. w. SIT, SET[1]]

se·ttle², v.t. & i. Establish or become established in more or less permanent abode or place or way of life (often *down*), (cause to) sit down or *down* to stay for some time, cease from wandering or motion or change or disturbance or turbidity (often *down*), bring to or attain fixity or composure or certainty or clarity or decision, determine, agree upon, decide, appoint, (*he settled detachments of Jews in Assyria*; *shall s. in London, Australia*; *s. feet in stirrups, plant's root well down in ground, invalid among pillows, oneself in chair*; *s. down to dinner, whist, reading, married life*; *settled down to defensive play, a series of skirmishes*; *marry & s. down*; *cannot s. to work, to anything*, of restless or excited or desultory person; *bird settles on tree*, alights; *stand beer to s.*, get clear; *let the excitement s. down*; *things will soon s. into shape*; *must get it settled up*, finally arranged; *s. coffee, soup, with white of egg*, clarify; *man, expression, of settled convictions, melancholy*; *settled order, state, habitation, government, weather*; *a liqueur to s.* one's *dinner*, facilitate digestion; *s. the day*, fix date; *s. quarrel, question, doubts, the pattern of, waverers*; *what have you settled on* or *settled?*; *s. the succession*, determine who shall succeed; *that settles the matter* or *question*, there is no more to be said; *s.* one's *affairs*, esp. before death by making will &c.); colonize, establish colonists in, s. as colonists in, (country); subside, sink to bottom of liquid or into lower position, (*the solid matter soon settles*; *soil, house, foundation, settles*, comes gradually to lower level by gravitation & giving way of what is below; *ship settles*, shows loss of buoyancy, tends to sink); deal effectually with, dispose or get rid of, do for, pay (bill), pay bill, (*s.* person, get rid of his importunity or obstruction by argument or conflict or killing; *let us s. up our accounts* or *s. up*, draw up & liquidate balance; *s.* person's HASH² or *business*; *settled*, written on paid bill in acknowledging payment; *will you s. for me?*, pay the bill; *s. with creditors*, pay their bills or such proportion as they will agree to accept; *settling-day*, esp. fortnightly account day at Stock Exchange); bestow legally for life *on* (*settled an annuity on him*; *settled all his property on his wife*; *settled estate*, held by tenant for life under specified conditions). [OE *setlan* (prec.), perh. with admixture of OE *sahtlian* reconcile (*saht* reconciliation)]

se·ttlement, n. In vbl senses; esp.: (Law) conveyance of, or creation of estate(s) in, property to make provision for one or more beneficiaries differing from what would result from simple conveyance or statutory inheritance (*marriage s.*, usu. made in favour of wife, her children, &c.; company of persons aiming at social reform who establish themselves in a poor district to live in intimate relations with the working class; newly settled tract of country, colony; subsidence of wall, house, &c.; *Act of S.*, statute of 1701 vesting crown in Sophia of Hanover & her heirs. [-MENT]

se·ttler, n. In vbl senses; esp.: one who settles in new colony, early colonist; (slang) decisive blow, argument, or event. [-ER¹]

se·twall, n. Kind of valerian formerly in medicinal use. [AF *zedewale*, as ZEDOARY]

sĕ·ven, a. & n. One more than six, 7, VII, (often agreeing with understood n., as *s. of the men, s. of them, s. o'clock* or *s.*; *one & s.*, 1/7; *s. & six*, 7/6; *twenty-s.* or *s.-&-twenty*, & so on to s.-&-ninety; *was s. last birthday*, years old; *one-&-sevenpenny* &c., costing 1/7 &c.; *the s.* SAGE²*s* or *wise men*; *the s. sleepers*, Christians who fell asleep in a cave while hiding from Decian persecution & woke 200 years later when Roman Empire was Christian; *the s.* VIRTUES, *deadly* SINS, WONDER¹*s of the world*; *s.-league boots*, giving wearer power of going 7 leagues at each stride; *seventy times s.*, large indefinite number, w. ref. to *Matt.* xviii. 22); *s.-gills*, kind of shark; hence **se·venFO·LD** a. & adv., **se·venTEE·N** a. & n. (*sweet s.*, age of girlish beauty), **seventee·NTH²** a. & n. (N.) the number 7, the symbol 7, set of 7 persons or things esp. 7-pipped card, (*twice s. is 14*; *make a large s.*; *by ss.*, in sets of 7; *at* SIXES *& ss.*). [Aryan: OE *seofon*, cf. Du. *zeven*, G *sieben*, L *septem*, Gk *hepta*, Skr. *saptá*]

se·venth, a. & n. Next after sixth (*the, a, s.*, often as n. with ellipse of n., esp. *the s.* = 7th day of month; *s. day*, Saturday in Quaker speech & with sects keeping Saturday instead of Sunday as sabbath (*s.-day*, sabbatarian; *S.-day Adventists*, a millenarian sect); *in the s.* HEAVEN, in the greatest happiness or satisfaction; *s. part*, one of 7 equal parts into which thing may be divided). (N.) = s. part; (Mus.) tone 7 diatonic degrees from given tone, this interval, harmonic combination between tone & its s. [-TH²]

se·venthly, adv. In the 7th place (in enumerations). [-LY²]

se·venty, a. & n. Seven times ten, 70, LXX, (*s.-one* &c., or *one-&-s.* &c.; *s.-first* &c.; *the s.*, the disciples of *Luke* x, also the sanhedrim, also the Septuagint translators); *s.-four* hist., war-ship with 74 guns; *s.-five*, French 75 mm. gun, = *soixante-quinze*; hence **se·ventiETH** a. & n. (N.) the number or symbol 70; *the ss.*, years between 69 & 80 in life or century. [-TY²]

sĕ·ver, v.t. & i. Separate, divide, part, disjoin, disunite, (t. & rarely i.; *s. husband & wife, friends* or *friendship, rope, neck, connexion*; *sea severs England &* or *from France*; *the rope severed under the strain*); cut or break off, take away, (part) from or *from* whole (*severed his head, his head from his body*; *s.* one*self from the Church*); (Law; of person in joint action) conduct case independently of the rest. Hence **se·ver**ABLE a., **se·ver**ANCE n. [f. OF *sevrer* f. L as SEPARATE]

sĕ·veral, a. & pron. Separate, diverse, distinct, individual, respective, (*all of us in our s. stations*; *each has his s. ideal*; *went their s. ways*; *indictment of three s. counts*; *the s. members of the Board*; *each s. ship sank her opponent*; *collective & s. responsibility*, of persons as a body & as individuals; *joint & s. bond* &c., signed by more than one person, of whom each is liable for whole sum; *s. estate*, not shared with others), whence **se·veral**LY[2] adv.; a few, more than two but not many, (*have called s. times*; *myself & s. others*). (Pron.) a moderate number, more than two but not many, of the previously mentioned or implied persons or things (*s. of you have seen him*; *went mushroom-hunting & found s.*). [AF, f. med. L *separale* separate thing (L *separ* SEPARATE, -AL)]

se·veralty, n. Individual or unshared tenure of estate &c. (usu. *in s.*). [-TY]

severe·, a. (-er, -est). Austere, strict, harsh, rigorous, unsparing, (*s. look, discipline, critic, master, sentence, inspection, self-control*; *s. upon*, hard on); violent, vehement, extreme, (*s. weather*, very cold or stormy; *a s. winter*; *s. attack of gout*); trying, making great demands on endurance, energy, skill, or other quality, (*s. test, pain, competition, requirements*); unadorned, stripped of all that is unessential, without redundance, restrained, terse, (*s. architecture, beauty, simplicity, style*); sarcastic or satirical (*s. remarks*; *you are pleased to be s.*). Hence or cogn. **severe·**LY[2] adv. (*leave* or *let -ly alone*, abstain from dealing with as mark of disapproval, also joc. avoid meddling with as too formidable or difficult); **sevĕ·ri**TY n. (w. pl. = severe treatment). [f. L *severus* etym. dub.]

sĕ·very, n. (archit.). Compartment of vaulted ceiling. [f. OF *civoire* f. L CIBORIUM]

Sèvres (sā·vr), n. Porcelain made at S.

sew (sō), v.t. & i. (p.p. *sewn, sewed*). Fasten (material, pieces) by passing thread again & again through holes made with threaded needle or with awl &c. (*s. cloth, calico, leather, pieces together, sheets of book*), whence **sew·**ING[1](5) n.; make by sewing (*s. seam, pleat, shirt, book, boot, buttonhole*); fasten *on* or *in*, attach, by sewing (*s. on a button*; *can you s. buttons?*; *s. in a patch, band, gusset, rib*, &c.); close *up* (hole, rent, wound, bag) by sewing; enclose, fasten *up*, by sewing receptacle (*s. up money in a bag*; *s. money into* one's *belt*); *s.* one *up* slang, utterly exhaust, (esp. in p.p.) intoxicate; use needle & thread or sewing-machine; *sewing-machine*, apparatus in which needle is worked mechanically by crank or treadle; *sewing-press*, apparatus for sewing books. Hence **sew·er**[1] [-ER[1]] n. [Aryan: OE *siwian*, OHG *siuwen*, L *suere*, Gk *kassuō* (CATA-), Skr. *siv*]

sew·age (-ĭj), n., & v.t. Matter conveyed in sewers; *s.-farm*, on which s. is used as manure, esp. one that utilizes & disposes of a town's s.; *s.-grass*, grown on sewaged land; (vb) manure with s. [prob. formed f. SEWER[3] by change of (supposed) -ER[1] to -AGE]

sew·er[2] (for *s.*[1] see SEW), n. (hist.). Person who set out table, placed guests, carried & tasted dishes, &c. [f. AF *asseour* f. OF *asseoir* to seat, set, f. L AS(*sidēre* = *sedēre* sit) sit beside]

sew·er[3], n., & v.t. Conduit or channel usu. covered over for carrying off the drainage & excrementitious matter of a town, public drain; *s.-gas*, foul air of ss.; *s. rat*, common brown or Norway rat; hence **sew·er**AGE(1) n. (Vb) drain, provide, with ss. [f. OF *seuwiere* sluice f. L *EX*aquaria* (*aqua* water, -ARY[1]); cf. EWER]

sew·in, -en, n. Kind of salmon trout. [?]

sewn. See SEW.

sex, n. Being male or female or hermaphrodite (*what is its s.?*; *s. does not matter*; *without distinction of age or s.*), whence **se·x**LESS a., **se·xless**NESS n.; males or females collectively (*all ranks & both ss.*; *the fair, gentle, softer, weaker, s.*, & facet. *the s.*, women; *the sterner s.*, men; *is the fairest of her s.*). [f. L *sexus* -ūs]

sex-, sexi-, comb. forms of L *sex* six, in derivatives of L compds & in mod. formations: *se·xangle*, hexagon; *sexangular(ly)*, hexagonal(ly); *sexcentē·nary* (or -sĕ·-) a. & n., of 600, 600-year, 600th anniversary; *sexdi·gitate*, six-fingered; *sexe·nnial(ly)*, lasting, (occurring) once in, six years; *sexfid* bot., cleft in 6; *sexfoil*, 6-lobed figure in architectural or other decoration, also 6-leaved plant; *sexi·llion*, 6th power of a million, 1 with 36 ciphers; *sexisylla·bic, -able*, (word) of 6 syllables; *sex(i)valent* chem., combining with 6 atoms of hydrogen, having 6 combining equivalents; *sexpar·tite*, divided in 6; *se·xtūple* a. & n. & v.t. & i., sixfold (amount), multiply by 6.

sexagenār·ian, a. & n. (Person) between 59 & 70. [L *sexagenarius* (foll.), -AN]

sexagē·nary, a. Of 60, going by sixties. [f. OF *sexagenaire* f. L *sexagenarius* (*sexageni* 60 each f. *sexaginta* 60, -ARY[1])]

Sexagĕ·sima, n. (Also *S. Sunday*) Sunday before Quinquagesima. [L, fem. adj. = 60th (day), prob. named loosely as preceding QUINQUAGESIMA]

sexagĕ·simal, a. & n. Sixtieth, of 60, proceeding by sixties, (*s. fractions*, or *ss.* n., with denominators proceeding in ratio of 60 as in the divisions of the circle & hour). Hence **sexage·simal**LY[2] adv. [f. LL *sexagesimalis* f. L *sexagesimus* 60th (*sexaginta* 60), -AL]

sext, sexte, n. (eccl.). The office of the 6th hour, recited at noon. [f. fem. *sexta* (*hora* hour) of L *sextus* sixth]

se·xtain, n. Stanza of 6 lines. [L *sextus* sixth, -AN; cf. QUATRAIN]

se·xtan, a. (Of fever &c.) recurring every fifth (by inclusive reckoning sixth) day. [as prec.]

se·xtant, n. Sixth part of circle (obs.); instrument including a graduated s. used in navigation & surveying for measuring angular distances. [f. L *sextans -ntis* sixth part (*sextus* sixth, -ANT, as if f. **sextare* divide by 6)]

sexte·t(te), n. (Musical work for) 6 voices, singers, instruments, or players, in combination; (transf.) any set of 6. [f. L *sextus* sixth, as QUARTETTE]

sexti·llion, n. =SEX*illion*. [F (prec., BILLION)]

se·xto, n. (pl. *-ōs*). Book formed by folding sheets in six. [f. L *sextus* sixth, as QUARTO]

sextodĕ·cimo, n. (*abbr.* 16mo, usu. read *sixteenmo*). Sheet of paper folded in 16 leaves; this way of folding (*in s.*); book made by folding thus. [orig. *in s.* L (IN^5, *sextus decimus* 16th)]

se·xton, n. Officer charged with care of church, its vessels, vestments, & churchyard, & often with duties of parish clerk & grave-digger; *s. beetle*, kinds that bury carrion to serve as nidus for eggs. [ME *sekesteyn* &c., corrupt. of SACRISTAN]

sextus. See PRIMUS^1.

se·xūal (*or* -kshōō-), a. Of sex, a sex, or the sexes (*s. organs*, genitals; *s. intercourse* or *commerce*, copulation; *s. affinity*, mutual attraction of two individuals of opposite sexes; *s.* SELECTION; *s. appetite, indulgence*, for, in, s. intercourse); (Bot.; of classification) based on the distinction of sexes in plants, whence **se·xual**IST(2) n. Hence **sexua·**LITY n., **se·xual**LY^2 adv. [f. LL *sexualis* (SEX, -AL)]

se·xualize, v.t. Attribute sex to. Hence **sexualiz**A·TION n. [-IZE]

sforza·ndo (-ts-) mus. direction. With sudden emphasis. [It.]

sfuma·to (-ōōmah-), a. (paint.). With indistinct outlines. [It., lit. smoked]

sha·bby, a. Scurvy, contemptible, paltry, dishonourable, (*played me a s. trick*); close-fisted, mean; worn, threadbare, dilapidated, seedy, in bad repair or condition; *s.-genteel*, retaining traces of better days, attempting to keep up appearances. Hence **sha·bbi**LY^2 adv., **sha·bbi**NESS n., **sha·bby**ISH^1(2) a. [OE *scæb, sceabb*, SCAB, + -Y^2]

shă·brack, n. Cavalry saddlecloth. [f. G *schabracke* of E.-Europ. orig.]

shack, n. (U.S., Can.). Rough hut. [?]

sha·ckle, n., & v.t. Metal loop or staple, bow of padlock, link closed by bolt for connecting chains &c., coupling link; long link joining pair of wrist or ankle rings, (pl.) fetters, impediments, or restraints (*the ss. of convention*); kind of insulator for telegraph wires; *s.-bolt*, for closing s., also bolt with s. at its end; *s.-joint*, in some fishes, formed by bony ring passing through hole in other bone; (vb) fetter, impede, trammel. [OE *sceacul* loose bond, etym. dub.]

shad, n. Kinds of anadromous deep-bodied fish, of which the American or White S. is much esteemed as food. [OE *sceadd*, cf. Ir. & Gael. *sgadan*, W *ysgadan*, herrings]

sha·ddock, n. (Fruit, sometimes weighing 15 lb., of) orig. Malayan & Polynesian tree of orange kind. [*S.*, introducer to W. Indies]

shade^1, n. Comparative darkness (& usu. coolness) caused by interception of light (& usu. heat) rays, (fig.) comparative obscurity (*throw into the s.*, outshine); (often pl.) place sheltered from sun, cool or sequestered retreat; (pl.) darkness *of* night or evening; darker part of picture (*without light & s.*, of paintings, also fig. of descriptions or characters, monotonous, uniformly glaring or sombre); a colour esp. with regard to its depth or as distinguished from one nearly like it, gradation of colour, material so coloured, (*in all ss. of purple*; *I want the same colour in a lighter s.*; *all the newest ss. in stock*; also fig., as *people of all ss. of opinion, delicate ss. of meaning*); slight difference, small amount, (*am a s. better today*); unsubstantial or unreal thing (*is the shadow of a s.*, delusive); soul after death (*spoke with the s. of Homer*; *went down to the ss.*, died, visited Hades; *S. of Priscian* &c.*!*, exclamation at blunder, crime, &c., that would have outraged person invoked); screen excluding or moderating light, heat, &c. (usu. in comb., as SUN, *candle, lamp, -s.*), eye-shield, glass cover for object. Hence **sha·de**LESS a. [Aryan; = SHADOW; OE *scead, sceadu*, cf. Du. *schaduw*, G *schatten*, Gk *skotos*]

shade^2, v.t. & i. Screen from excessive light (*shaded his eyes with his hand*; *trees s. the street*); cover, keep off, or moderate power of (luminous object, light) with or as intervening object; make dark or gloomy (*a sullen look shaded his face*); (Drawing) darken (parts of object represented) esp. with parallel pencil lines to give effects of light & shade or gradations of colour, whence **sha·d**ING^1(6) n.; (of colour or light, & fig. of opinion, practice, &c.) pass *off* by degrees into (or *into*) other colour or variety, make (colour &c.) pass thus *into* another; modify pitch of (organ-pipe). [f. prec.]

shadoo·f, n. Pole with bucket & counterpoise used esp. in Egypt for raising water. [f. Arab. *shādūf*]

shă·dow[1] (-ō), n. Shade (*sitting in the s.*; *the s. of death is on his face*; VALLEY *of the s. of death*; *the ss. of night*; *under the s. of misfortune*), dark part of picture, room, &c.; patch of shade, dark figure projected by body that intercepts light rays, this regarded as person's or thing's appendage (*may your s. never grow less!*, nor consequently you thin), (fig.) one's inseparable attendant or companion; reflected image; type, faint representation, adumbration, premonition (*coming events cast their ss. before*); slightest trace (*without a s. of doubt*); unsubstantial or unreal thing or counterfeit (*what ss. we are!*; *catch at ss.*; *having only the s. of freedom*), phantom, ghost, (*is but the s. of his former self*; *worn to a s.*; *a terrible s. with uplifted hand*); privacy, obscurity, (*content to live in the s.*); shelter, protection, (*under the s. of the Almighty*); (Yacht.) kind of light sail used in fair winds; *s.-stitch*, kind of ladder-work in lace-making. Hence **sha·dow**LESS, **sha·dow**Y[2], aa., **sha·dowi**NESS n. [OE *sceadu*, see SHADE[1]]

sha·dow[2], v.t. Overspread with s. (chiefly poet.); set *forth* dimly, in outline, allegorically, or prophetically; dog, secretly watch all movements of. [f. prec.]

shā·dy, a. Giving, situated in, shade; (of actions, conduct, &c.) shunning the light, disreputable, of dubious honesty; *on the s. side of forty* &c., more than. Hence **sha·di**LY[2] adv., **sha·di**NESS n. [-Y[2]]

shaft, n. (Slender pole of) lance or spear; long-bow arrow (often CLOTH-*yard s.*; also fig., as *ss. of satire, ridicule, envy*); ray *of* light, bolt or stroke *of* lightning; stem, stalk, column between base & capital, one of group of clustered columns, spire, part of chimney above roof, rib of feather, part more or less long & narrow & straight supporting or connecting part(s) of greater thickness &c.; (Mech.) large axle, revolving bar transferring force by belts or cogs, whence **sha·ft**ING[1] (3, 6) n.; handle of tool &c.; one of pair of bars between which horse of vehicle is harnessed (*s.-horse*, so placed, opp. LEADER in tandem); vertical or inclined excavation giving access to mine; tunnel of blast-furnace; (also *ventilating s.*) upward vent for smoke or bad air from tunnel, drain, &c. [OE *sceaft* spear-shaft, perh. orig. shaven rod (SHAVE, suf. *-t*), cf. Du. *schacht*, G *schaft*]

shag[1], n. Rough growth or mass of hair &c., whence **sha·gg**ED[2] a. (rare); (archaic) long-napped rough cloth; coarse kind of cut tobacco. [OE *sceacga*, cf. ON *skegg* beard (*skaga* jut out)]

shag[2], n. Crested cormorant. [prob. f. prec.]

sha·ggy, a. Hairy, rough-haired, (of hair) coarse, wildly abundant, unkempt, (of land &c.) overgrown with forest or rough vegetation, (of trees &c.) with rough branches or twigs, (Bot., Biol.) villous. Hence **sha·ggi**LY[2] adv., **sha·ggi**NESS n. [-Y[2]]

shagree·n, n. Kind of untanned leather with artificially granulated surface made from skin of horse, ass, camel, &c., & usu. dyed green; shark-skin rough with natural papillae used for rasping & polishing. [as CHAGRIN, which is differentiated in sense]

shah, n. King of Persia, padishah. [Pers., =ruler; cf. CHECK[1]]

shake[1], v.t. & i. (shŏŏk, shaken). Move (thing, person) violently or quickly up & down or to & fro with the hand(s) &c. (*like a terrier shaking a rat*; *deserves a good* **sha·king**[1](1) n.; *s. hands*, *s.* one *by the hand*, clasp right hands with or without shaking at meeting or parting, in reconciliation or congratulation, or over concluded bargain; *s. a carpet*); (make) tremble or rock or quiver or vibrate or wave, jolt, jar, brandish, (*s. the house*; *the earth shook*; *hand shakes*, is unsteady; *s.* one's *fist*, *stick*, &c., *in* person's *face* or *at*, threaten with fist &c.; *s. a* LEG; *s.* one's *head*, move it from side to side in refusal, denial, disapproval, or concern *over* or *at* or abs.; *s. with fear*, *cold*, &c., tremble violently; *s. in* one's *shoes*, tremble with apprehension); agitate, shock, disturb, (*was much shaken by*, *with*, *at*, *the news*; *s. him out of his lethargy*; *shook my composure*); weaken, impair, make less convincing or firm or stable or courageous, (*the firm's credit was shaken*; *shook the witness's evidence*; *his faith in Providence was greatly shaken*; *the ranks were shaken but not broken*); (of voice, musical note, singer, &c.) make tremulous sounds, change pitch or power with rapid alternations, trill, (*his voice shook with emotion*; *must learn to s.*); (imperat.; colloq., chiefly U.S.) s. hands; *s. down*, fetch or send down by shaking (fruit from tree; straw or blankets &c. on floor for bed, whence **sha·kedown** n.; grain &c. in vessel into least compass), (intr.) become compact, get comfortably settled or into harmony with associates or circumstances; *s. off*, get rid of (dust &c., & fig. undesirable companion or worry) by shaking (*s. o. the* DUST[1] *from* one's *feet*); *s. out*, empty (vessel, garment, &c.) of contents or dust, (contents) from vessel &c., spread or open (sail, flag, reef); *s. up*, mix (ingredients), restore (pillow &c.) to shape, by shaking, rouse from stagnant or lethargic or convention-ridden state. Hence **shā·k**ABLE a. [OE *scacan*, cf. ON & Sw. *skaka*]

shake[2], n. Shaking or being shaken (see prec.; *with a s. of the head*; *give it*, *had*, *a s.*; *all of a s.*, trembling; *the ss.*, ague), jolt, jerk, shock; trill, quick alternation of two notes with voice or on instrument; moment (*in two* &c. *ss. of a lamb's tail* &c.

or *ss.*, very quickly, in no time); crack in growing timber; (slang) *is no great ss.*, not very good or efficient; *s.-out* (St. Exch.), crisis in which weaker speculators are driven out of market; *s.-up*, shaking or being shaken up. [f. prec.]

sha·ker, n. In vbl senses; also (*S*-) member of religious sect founded in Manchester, & still existing in U.S., holding that Christ's second coming has taken place (named from religious dances), whence **Sha·ker**ESS[1], **Sha·ker**ISM(3), nn. [-ER[1]]

Shāk(e)spe(a)r·ian (-pēr-), a. (In the style) of Shakspere. So **Shak(e)spe(a)ri**A·NA n. pl. [-IAN]

shă·ko, n. Form of military hat, more or less cylindrical with peak & upright plume or tuft. [f. Hung. *csákó*]

sha·ky, a. Unsteady, apt to shake, trembling, unsound, infirm, unreliable, tottering, wavering, (*a s. hand, table, old man, house*; *s. credit, voters, courage*; *feel, look, s.*). Hence **sha·ki**LY[2] adv., **sha·ki**NESS n. [-Y[2]]

shale, n. Kinds of clayey stone splitting readily into thin plates & resembling slate but softer & less solid; *s.-oil*, kind of naphtha got from bituminous s. Hence **sha·l**Y[2] a. [prob. f. obs. *shale* shell f. OE *scealu*, cf. SCALE[2]]

shăll, v. aux. (pres. *I, he, we, you, they, s.*, *thou shalt*; past & condit. *I, he, we, you, they, should* pr. shŏŏd, *thou shouldst* pr. shŏŏdst, or *shoul·dest* pr. shŏŏ-; neg. forms *shall not* or *shan't* pr. -ah-, *should not* or *shouldn't*; no other parts used). *S.* & *should* are used (1) in first person (the others having *will, would*) to form a plain future or conditional statement or question (*we s. hear about it tomorrow*; *I should have been killed if I had let go*; *s. I hear from you soon?*); (2) in 2nd & 3rd persons (1st having *will, would*) to form a future or conditional statement expressing speaker's will or intention (*you s. not catch me again*; *he should not have gone if I could have prevented it*); (3) alternatively with *will, would*, in sentences of type 1 changed in reporting from 1st to other person (*he says* or *said, you say* or *said, that he, you, s.* or *should never manage it*; now more usu. *will, would*) or from other person to 1st (*he says I s.* or *will never manage it*, reporting *you will never*; *will* now rare); (4) in reporting sentences of type 2 that contained *s.* or *should* (*you promised I, he, should not catch you at it again*); (5) in 2nd-person questions corresponding to type 1, by attraction to expected answer (*shall you be going to church?*); (6) in any person to form statements or questions involving the notions of command & future or conditional duty, obligation, &c. (*thou shalt not steal*; *I, you, he, should really have been more careful*; *s. I, he, open the door?*; *why should I, you, he, obey?*); (7) in all persons to form conditional protasis or indefinite clause (*if, when, we s. be defeated* or *defeat s. overtake us*; *any one who should say*; *if you should happen to be there*; & with inversion *should I, you, he, be there, it would be talked about*); (8) alternatively with *may, might*, in all persons in final clauses (*to the end that I, you, he s.* or *should not be able*); (9) in some miscellaneous idioms (*it should seem*, it seems; *you shall find* archaic, be sure you will find; *it is surprising* &c. *that I, you, he, should be* or *have been so foolish*). [OE *sceal*, cf. Du. *zal*, G *soll*, cogn. w. G *schuld* debt, guilt]

shalloo·n, n. Light cloth for coat-linings & women's dresses. [f. *Chalons* in France]

shă·llop, n. Light open boat. [f. F *chaloupe* SLOOP]

shal(l)o·t, n. Plant of onion kind with cloves like, but of milder flavour than, those of garlic. [earlier *eschalot* f. F *eschalotte* dim. of *eschaloigne* f. L *ascalonia* orig. fem. adj. f. *Ascalon* in Palestine]

shă·llow (-ō), a. (-er, -est), n., & v.i. & t. Of little depth (lit. & fig.; *s. water, a s. stream, dish*; *a s. mind, argument, love, man*, superficial, trivial; so *s.-brained, -hearted, -pated*); hence **sha·llow**LY[2] adv., **sha·llow**NESS n.; (n.) s. place, shoal; (vb) become shallower, make s. [15th-c. *schalowe* etym. dub.; cf. SHOAL[1]]

shalt. See SHALL.

sham, v.t. & i., n., & a. Feign, simulate, (*s. illness, sleep, a faint, fear*; *is only shamming*); pretend to be (*shammed ill, dead, asleep*); hence **sha·mm**ER[1] n. (N.) imposture, pretence, humbug, (*this age of ss.*); person or thing pretending or pretended to be something that he or it is not; (also *sheet, pillow, -s.*) embroidered linen laid on bed in day for show. (Adj.) pretended, counterfeit, (*s. fight*, imitation battle for training troops; *s. plea* &c. in law, advanced only to gain time.) [17th-c. slang, etym. dub.]

Shā·manism, n. Religion of Siberian tribes involving belief in secondary gods & in power of shamans or priests to influence these. [f. G *schamane* of Mongol origin, -ISM]

sha·mble, v.i., & n. Walk or run in shuffling or awkward or decrepit way (*shambling gait*, of person who shambles); (n.) shambling gait. [prob. f. obs. *shamble* adj. straddling, wry, perh. f. *shamble* bench (see foll.) w. ref. to straddling trestles]

sha·mbles, n. pl. (often w. sing. constr.). Butchers' slaughter-house; scene of carnage (*the place became a s.*). [pl. of obs. *shamble* stool, OE *scamel* f. L *scamellum* dim. of *scamnum* bench]

shame[1], n. Feeling of humiliation excited by consciousness of guilt or shortcoming, of having made oneself or been made ridiculous, or of having offended against propriety, modesty, or decency, (*flushed with s.*; *begin with s. to take the lowest room*); restraint imposed by, desire to avoid, such humiliation (*for s.!*, appeal to person not to disregard or reproof for disregarding this; *cannot do it for very s.*; *is quite without* or *lost to s.*), whence **sha·me**LESS a., **sha·meless**LY[2] adv., **sha·meless**NESS n.; state of disgrace or ignominy or discredit (*s. on you!*; *put* one *to s.*, disgrace him esp. by exhibiting superior qualities &c.), person or thing that brings disgrace (*is a s. to his parents*; *would think s. to do it*; *is a sin & a s.*), whence **sha·me**FUL a., **sha·meful**LY[2] adv., **sha·meful**NESS n. [OE *sc(e)amu*, cf. Da. *skam*, G *scham*]

shame[2], v.i. & t. Be ashamed, refuse from s., *to* (archaic; usu. with negative, as *he shamed not to say*); bring s. on, be a s. to, make ashamed; put (superior) to the blush by outdoing (*a dog's fidelity shames us*); frighten by s. *into* or *out of* doing, conduct, &c. [OE *sc(e)amian* (prec.)]

sha·mefaced (-āst), a. Bashful, shy; (poet., of virtue, flowers, &c.) modest, retiring, inconspicuous. Hence **sha·me-facĕd**LY[2] adv., **sha·mefaced**NESS (-āsĭd-, -āst-) n. [f. obs. *shamefast*, OE *scamfæst* (SHAME[1], FAST[3]) by confusion w. *-fac*ED[2]]

sha·mmy, shă·moy, n. = CHAMOIS(2).

shampoo·, v.t., & n. Subject (body &c.) to kneading or massage after hot bath (orig. sense, now rare); lather, wash, & rub (head, hair); (n.) *a* shampooing of the head. [f. Hind. *chámpná* press, shampoo]

sha·mrock, n. Kinds of trefoil or clover serving as national emblem of Ireland (cf. rose, thistle, leek). [f. Ir. *seamróg* trefoil, dim. of *seamar* clover]

sha·ndrydăn, n. Light two-wheeled cart; old rickety vehicle. [?]

sha·ndygăff, n. Mixed drink of beer & ginger-beer. [?]

shanghai· (-hī), v.t. (naut. slang). Drug & ship as sailor while unconscious. [*S.* in China]

shank, n., & v.i. Leg (*Shanks's mare*, one's own legs as opp. riding &c.); leg from knee to ankle; shin-bone; upright part of bird's foot; footstalk of flower; leg of stocking; shaft of pillar &c., shaft of tool between head &c. & handle, stem of key, spoon, anchor, &c., straight part of fish-hook, narrow middle of boot-sole; hence **(-)shank**ED[2] a. (Vb) *s. off* (of flowers) fall off by decay of s. [OE *sc(e)anca*, cf. Du. *schonk* bone, G *schinken* ham]

sha·nny, n. Oblong olive-green European sea-fish, the smooth blenny. [?]

shan't. See SHALL.

shă·nty[1], n. Hut, cabin, mean dwelling. [f. Canad.-F *chantier* log hut f. F = workshop]

sha·nty[2], var. of CHANTY.

shape[1], v.t. & i. (p.p. *-ed*, archaic *-en*). Create, form, construct; model, mould, fashion, bring into desired or definite figure or form (p.p., having such figure, as *shaped like a pear*); adapt, make conform, *to*; plan, devise; direct, aim, (one's course &c.); frame mentally, imagine, call up image of; assume form, develop into s., give signs of future s. (*shapes well*, is promising). Hence **sha·p**ABLE a. [OE *scieppan*, cf. G *schaffen*, Du. *scheppen*, create, cogn. w. -SHIP & (*land*)*scape*]

shape[2], n. Configuration, form, total effect produced by thing's outlines, (*spherical in s.*; *has the s. of a boat*); appearance, guise, (*monster in human s.*); concrete presentment, embodiment, (*intention took s. in action*; *showed me politeness in the s. of an invitation*); kind, description, sort, (*made no overtures in any s. or form*); symmetrical or definite form, orderly arrangement, proper condition, (*get* one's *ideas into s.*; LICK *into s.*; *give s. to*), whence **sha·pe**LESS a., **sha·peless**LY[2] adv., **sha·peless**NESS n.; person considered as impressing the sight, & esp. as indistinctly seen or imagined, apparition, ghost, (*a s. loomed through the mist*; *a grim mysterious s. stalked towards me*); pattern for workman &c., mould for shaping hats &c.; jelly, blancmange, &c. shaped in mould; padding worn by actor. Hence **(-)shap**ED[2] a. [OE *gesceap* (Y-, prec.)]

sha·pely, a. Well formed or proportioned, of the right or a pleasing shape. Hence **sha·peli**NESS n. [-LY[1]]

sha·per, n. In vbl senses; esp., kinds of machine for turning, planing, stamping, moulding, &c. [-ER[1]]

shard, sherd, n. (archaic). Potsherd (still used by gardeners of fragment put over hole of flowerpot); beetle's wing-cover. [OE *sceard* (SHEAR[1], SHARE)]

share[1], n. Portion detached for individual from common amount (*must get a s. of the plunder*); part one is entitled to have or bound to contribute, equitable portion, (*that is your fair s.*; *took, bore, my* or *more* or *less than my s. of the burden*; *go ss.*, make equitable division with others; *s. & s. alike*, with equal division; LION'*s s.*); part one gets or contributes (*had a large s. in bringing it about, but no s. of the credit*); part-proprietorship of property held by joint owners (*has a s. in the bank, estate*, &c.), esp. one of the equal parts into which company's capital is divided entitling holder to proportion of profits (*holds 50 ss. in*; *an issue of 10,000 ss.*; *deferred ss.*, on which lower dividend or none is to be paid till fixed date or contingent event; *preference* or *preferred ss.*, on which fixed dividend is guaranteed before payment begins on *ordinary ss.*; *shareholder*, owner of ss.; *s.-list*, of current prices of ss. in various companies.) [OE *scearu* (*sceran* SHEAR[1])]

share², v.t. & i. Apportion (food, property, task, &c.) among others, give each a s. of; give away part of (*would s. his last crust*); get or have s. of, possess or use or endure jointly with others; have share(s), be sharer(s), (*will s. with you in the undertaking*; *we must s. alike*); *s. out*, distribute, whence *share·-out* n., provident club's distribution. Hence **shār·**ER¹ n. [f. prec.]

share³, n. Plough-share; blade of seeding-machine or cultivator; *s.-beam*, part of plough in which s. is fixed. [OE *scear* (*sceran* SHEAR¹)]

shark, n., & v.i. & t. Kinds of long-shaped lateral-gilled inferior-mouthed sea-fish many species of which are large & voracious (*Basking, Man-eating, White, Blue, Dusky, Bonnet-headed*, &c., *S.*); rapacious person, swindler, (LAND-s.); *s.-moth*, kinds of moth named from shape; *s.-oil*, got f. s.'s liver & used like cod-liver oil; *s.'s-mouth*, opening in awning for mast &c. (Vb) play the swindler, adventurer, &c. (*sharks for a living*), whence **shar·**KING² a.; gather *up* by dishonest or dishonourable means; swallow voraciously. [f. 16th c., etym. dub.]

sharp¹, a., n., & adv. With fine edge or point, not blunt; peaked, pointed, edged, (*s. gable, summit, ridge*); well-defined, clean-cut, (*s. outline, distinction, impression, features*; so *s.-cut*); abrupt, angular, (*s. turn, incline*); keen, pungent, acid, tart, shrill, piercing, biting, harsh, acrimonious, severe, intense, painful, (*s. flavour, wine, voice, cry, frost, air, words, tongue, temper, reproof, contest, attack of gout*); acute, sensitive, quick to see or hear or notice, keen-witted, vigilant, clever, (*s. eyes, ears, intelligence, attention*; *s.-sighted, -witted*, &c.; *keep a s. look-out*; *a s. remark, child*; *as s. as a needle*, very intelligent); quick to take advantage, bent on winning, artful, unscrupulous, dishonest, (*was too s. for me*, overreached me; *s. practice*, barely honest dealings); vigorous, speedy, not loitering, impetuous, (*take a s. walk*; *s.'s the word*, exhortation to be quick; *s. work*, said of matter quickly dispatched or fight &c. that takes all one's energy); (Phonet., of mutes) unvoiced, hard; (Mus., opp. FLAT) above true pitch (*piano is s.*; *B, D*, &c., *s.*, a semitone higher than B, D, &c.), (of key) having sharp(s) in signature; *sharp-shooter*, skilled shot posted where marksmanship is required; hence **shar·p**EN⁶ v.t. & i., **(-)sharpen**ER¹(1, 2) n., **shar·p**LY² adv., **shar·p**NESS n. (N.) sewing-needle of slender make; (Mus.) note raised a semitone above pitch, symbol indicating this raising, *ss. & FLAT²s*; s. consonant. (Adv.) punctually (*at six o'clock s.*); (Mus.) above true pitch (*is singing s.*); LOOK¹ *s.*; *s.-set*, hungry; *s.-shod*, calked. [OE *scearp*, cf. Du. *scherp*, G *scharf*]

sharp², v.t. & i. Sharpen, whet, (archaic or vulg.); raise pitch of (note) or mark as s.; play unfairly, swindle, at cards &c., whence **shar·p**ER¹ n. [f. prec.]

sha·tter, v.t. & i. Break (t. & i.) suddenly & violently in pieces; utterly derange, destroy, dissipate, (*shattered nerves, constitution, hopes*). [f. 14th c., etym. dub.]

shave¹, v.t. & i. (p.p. *-ed* &, chiefly as adj., *-en*). Remove (hair), free (chin &c.) of hair, relieve (person) of hair on chin &c., with razor (*has shaved off* or *shaved his beard*, now wears none; *a shaven chin*); (intr.) s. oneself (*he does not s. every day*); pare surface of (wood &c.) with spoke-shave, plane, &c., whence **sha·**VING¹(2) n.; pass close to without touching, skirt, miss narrowly, nearly graze; *s.-hook*, tool for scraping surface of metal before soldering; *shaving-brush*, for lathering chin &c. before shaving; *shaving-horse*, bench with clamp for holding wood to be shaved. [OE *sc(e)afan*, cf. Du. *schaven*, G *schaben*, perh. cogn. w. L *scabere* scratch, Gk *skaptō* dig]

shave², n. Having one's beard &c. shaved (*must have a s.*; *a penny s.*); close approach without contact, narrow miss or escape or failure, (*had a close s. of it*); knife-blade with handle at each end for shaving wood &c.; trick, deception, hoax. [(the tool f. OE *sceafa*) f. prec.]

sha·veling, n. (archaic). Shaven person, monk, friar, priest. [-LING¹]

sha·ver, n. In vbl senses; also (colloq.), lad, youngster, (usu. *young s.*). [-ER¹]

Shā·vian, a. (In the manner) of G. B. Shaw, dramatist. [-IAN]

shaw, n. (archaic & poet.). Thicket, wood. [OE *scaga*, cogn. w. SHAG¹]

shawl, n., & v.t. Rectangular garment, often square to be folded into triangle, chiefly worn by women as outer covering, for shoulders; *s.-dance*, in which dancer waves a s.; *s.-pattern*, variegated design like that of Oriental ss.; (vb) put s. on (person). [f. Pers. *shāl*]

shawm, n. Obsolete musical instrument with reed. [f. OF *chalemie* f. L f. Gk *kalamos* reed]

shay, n. (Archaic, facet., or vulg., for) CHAISE. [back form. f. *chaise* taken for pl.]

she, pron. (obj. HER¹, possess. HER², HER²s, pl. THEY &c.), n., & a. The female (or thing personified as female, e.g. ship or train) previously mentioned or implied or easily identified; (n.) female, woman, (*the not impossible s.*, woman one might love; *is the child a he or a s.?*; *had a litter of two shes & a he*, two bitches & a dog); (adj., usu. hyphened) female (*s. goat, -ass, -bear*, &c.; *s.-devil, -cat*, malignant or spiteful woman; *s.-oak*, kinds of Australian shrub, esp. BEEF*wood*; *s.-pine*, Australian conifer). [OE *séo* fem. of def. art., orig. demonstr. pron., *se*; cf. Du. *zij*, G *sie*, Gk *hē*]

she·a, n. W.-Afr. tree yielding a vegetable butter (*s.-butter*). [native]

shea·ding (-ĕd-), n. Administrative division (six) of I. of Man. [SHED[1], -ING[1]]

sheaf, n. (pl. *-ves*), & v.t. Bundle of things laid lengthwise together & usu. tied (*s. of papers, arrows*, &c.), esp. armful of corn-stalks tied after reaping (*s.-binder*, tool for tying these); (vb) make into ss., sheave. [OE *scéaf*, cf. Du. *schoof*, G *schaub*; cogn. w. SHOVE]

shear[1], v.t. & i. (past *-ed* & archaic *shore*; p.p. *shorn*, rarely *sheared*). Cut with sword &c. (poet.; t. & i.; *shore off his plume*; *shore through the bone*); clip, cut with scissors or ss., (trans.; *s. sheep*, clip its wool; also abs., *shall be shearing*, i.e. my sheep, *tomorrow*; *s. cloth*, remove or reduce nap by clipping), (fig.) fleece, strip bare, (*come home shorn*; *shorn of wool, glory*, &c.); (of structure, material, &c.) be distorted or broken by the strain called a s., (of pressure) distort or break thus; *shear-water*, kinds of low-flying sea-bird. Hence **shear·**ER[1] n. [OE *sceran*, cf. Du. & G *scheren*, Gk *keirō* shave; cogn. w. SHARD, SHARE, SCAR[2], &c.]

shear[2], n. (Pl.) clipping-instrument with two meeting blades pivoted as in scissors or connected by spring & passing close over each other edge to edge (*hand me the ss.*; *want a pair of ss.*; *shear* in comb. or attrib., as *shearbill*, the bird scissorbill or skimmer; *s.-grass*, kind with sharp-edged leaves; *s.-legs*, SHEER[4]s; *s. steel*, cf special quality fit for ss. & other cutting tools; *sheartail*, humming-bird with tail like ss.); (Mech.) kind of strain produced by pressure in structure of a substance, its successive layers being shifted laterally over each other. [OE *scéar* sing. (prec.)]

shear·ling, n. Sheep once shorn. [-LING[1]]

shea·t-fish, n. Largest European fresh-water fish. [f. G *scheidfisch* (*scheid* of doubtful etym. & meaning)]

sheath (-th), n. (pl. pr. -dhz). Close-fitting cover, esp. for blade of weapon or tool; (Bot., Zool., Anat.) investing membrane, tissue, skin, horny case, &c.; structure of loose stones for confining river within banks. Hence **shea·th**LESS a. [OE *scǽth*, cf. Du. *scheede*, G *scheide*; cogn. w. SHED[1]]

sheathe (-dh), v.t. Put into sheath (*s. the sword*, cease from war, & fig.); encase, protect with casing or **shea·th**ING[1](3) n. [f. prec.]

sheave[1], n. Grooved wheel in pulley &c. for rope to run on. [cf. G *scheibe* slice, disk, Icel. *skífa* slice n. & v.]

sheave[2], v.t. Gather (corn &c.) into sheaves, sheaf. [f. SHEAF]

sheaves. See SHEAF.

shebee·n, n. (Ir.). Pot-house, unlicensed house selling drink. [Ir.]

shed[1], v.t. (shed). Part with, let fall off, (*tree, stag, snake, crab, prime minister, sheds leaves, horns, skin, shell, colleagues*); drop (*s. tears*, weep; *s.* one's *blood for* one's *country*, be wounded or killed); cause (others' blood) to flow; disperse, diffuse, spread abroad, (*s. light on*, illuminate, esp. fig.; *s. love, radiance, perfume*, &c., *around* one). Hence **she·dd**ER[1] n. [OE *sc(e)ádan* part, cf. Du. & G *scheiden*, prob. cogn. w. Gk *skhizō*, L *scindere*]

shed[2], n. One-storeyed shelter for storing goods or vehicles or keeping cattle &c. or for use as workshop &c. & consisting of roof with some or all or no sides open. Hence **she·dd**ING[1](3) n. [var. of SHADE]

sheen, n. Splendour, radiance, brightness. Hence **shee·n**Y[2] a. (poet.). [f. obs. adj. *sheen* beautiful, OE *sciene*, cf. G *schön*; sense affected by confusion with unrelated *shine*]

sheep, n. (pl. the same). Kinds of wild or domesticated timid gregarious woolly sometimes horned ruminant mammal of which male is named *ram*, female *ewe*, & young *lamb* (*s. & goats*, the good & the bad, see *Matt.* xxv. 33; BLACK[1] *s.*; *cast s.'s eyes*, glance amorously *at*; *follow like s.*, said of persons with no initiative or independence; *as well be hanged for a s. as a* LAMB[1]; *s. that have no shepherd*, helpless crowd &c.; WOLF *in s.'s clothing*); bashful embarrassed person (so **shee·p**ISH[1] a., **shee·pish**LY[2] adv., **shee·pish**NESS n.); (usu. pl., now chiefly facet.) member(s) of minister's flock, parishioners &c.; = sheepskin leather; *s.-bot*, fly & larva injurious to s.; *s.-cote* (archaic), *-fold, -pen* (rare), enclosure for penning s.; *s.-dip*, preparation for cleansing s. of vermin or preserving their wool; *s.-dog*, collie, also breed of rough-coated short-tailed dog used by shepherds; *s.-farmer, -master*, breeder of s.; *s.-hook*, shepherd's crook; *s.-louse, -tick*, kinds of parasite on s.; *s.-pox*, s.-disease resembling smallpox; *s.-run*, extensive s.-walk, esp. in Australia; *s.'s-bit*, plant resembling scabious; *s.'s fescue*, a pasture grass; *sheepshank*, bight & hitches used to shorten rope's length temporarily; *s.'s-head* lit., also kind of sea-fish used for food; *s.-shearing*, (festival at) shearing of s.; *sheepskin*, garment or rug of s.'s skin with wool on, also leather of s.'s skin used in bookbinding &c., also parchment of it or deed or diploma engrossed on this; *s.-walk*, tract of land on which s. are pastured; *s.-wash*, lotion for killing vermin or preserving wool on s. [OE *scéap*, cf. Du. *schaap*, G *schaf*, etym. dub.]

sheer[1], a. & adv. Mere, simple, unassisted, undiluted, uncompounded, neither more nor less than, absolute, (*did it by s. force*; *is s. waste, nonsense, folly*; *a s. impossibility*); (of rock, fall, ascent, &c.) perpendicular, unrelieved by slope; (Commerc., of cambric &c.) diaphanous; (adv.) plumb, perpendicularly, outright, (*fell 3000 ft s.*;

torn s. out by the roots; *rises s. from the water*). [ME *schēre* = ON *skǽrr* bright (*skína* SHINE v.), cogn. w. OE *scīr* bright]

sheer², v.i. (Naut.) deviate from course; (also in gen. use) *s. off*, part company, depart, esp. from person one dislikes or fears or is offended by. [perh. f. Du. *scheren* SHEAR¹]

sheer³, n. Upward slope of ship's lines towards bow & stern; deviation of ship from course. [perh. f. SHEAR¹]

sheer⁴, n. (Pl.; also *s.-legs* or *shear-legs*) hoisting-apparatus of two poles attached at or near top and separated at bottom for masting ships or putting in engines &c., used in dockyards or on *s.-hulk*, dismasted ship used for the purpose. [var. of SHEAR²; named from resemblance to pair of shears]

sheet¹, n. Rectangular piece of linen used in pairs as inner bed-clothes (*between the ss.*, in bed), whence **shee·**TING¹(3) n.; broad more or less flat piece *of* some thin material (*a s. of iron, glass*, &c.); wide expanse *of* water, snow, ice, flame, colour, &c.; complete piece of paper of the size in which it was made (*book is in ss.*, printed but not bound; *s. of notepaper*, usu. folded once for writing on; *s. of quarto* &c., the four &c. leaves given by folding a s. twice &c.); newspaper (*a penny, scurrilous*, &c., *s.*); rope or chain at lower corner of sail for regulating its tension &c. (*flowing s.*, not close-hauled, eased for free wind; *a s., three ss., in the wind* slang, rather, very, drunk); *s.-anchor* [see etym.], carried outside waist of ship for use in emergencies, (fig.) last dependence or security; *s. copper, iron, metal*, &c., spread by rolling, hammering, &c., into thin ss.; *s. glass*, kind made first as hollow cylinder, which is cut open & flattened in furnace; *s.* LIGHTNING. [OE *scéte, scýte*, linen cloth, with mixture of sense of OE *scéat* corner, fold, all cogn. w. SHOOT; orig. sense *projection*; *s.-anchor*, earlier *shut(t(e)-, shot(e)-, shott-*, may be f. obs. *shot* spliced cables]

sheet², v.t. Furnish with ss.; cover with s. (*the sheeted dead*); form into ss. (*sheeted rain*); secure (sail) with s. (esp. *s. home*). [f. prec.]

sheik(h) (-ēk, -āk), n. Chief, head of Arabian or Mohammedan tribe, family, or village; (transf.) masterful husband or lover; *S. ul Islam*, grand mufti at Constantinople, chief authority on sacred law in Turkish empire. [Arab. *shaikh*, = elder, chief]

shekarry. See SHIKAREE.

shĕ·kel (-kl), n. Jewish weight & silver coin; (pl.) money, riches, pelf. [f. Heb. *sheqel* (*shāqal* weigh)]

Shekī·nah, -ch-, n. Visible glory of Jehovah resting over mercy-seat. [Heb. (*-k-*) f. *shākan* dwell]

she·ldrake, n. (fem. somet. *shelduck*). Kinds of bright-plumaged wild duck. [prob. f. dial. *sheld* piebald = MDu. *schillede*, DRAKE]

shelf, n. (pl. *-ves*). Projecting slab of stone or board let into or hung on wall to support things, one of the boards in cabinet, bookcase, &c., on which books &c. stand, (*on the s.*, put aside, done with, esp. of person past work); ledge, horizontal step-like projection in cliff face &c.; reef or sandbank under water. Hence **shelv**ED² a., **she·lf**FUL(2) n. [prob. f. LG *schelf*, cogn. w. OE *scylfe* of doubtful meaning & *scylf* crag]

shell¹, n. Hard outer case enclosing nuts, kinds of seed or fruit, eggs, some animals or parts of them, &c., husk, crust, pod, carapace, scale, conch, wing-case, pupa-case, (*come out of* one's *s.*, throw off reserve, become communicative); walls of unfinished or gutted house, ship, &c.; outline of plan &c.; inner coffin; light racing-boat; hollow metal or paper case to contain explosives for fireworks, cartridges, &c.; explosive projectile or bomb for use in cannon or mortar, whence **she·ll-**PROOF² a.; handguard of sword; (poet.) lyre; (at schools) intermediate form; outward show, mere semblance; (short for) s.-jacket; *s.-back* (naut., slang), old sailor; *s.-bark*, kinds of hickory; *s.-bit*, gouge-shaped boring-bit; *s. button*, made of two metal disks enclosed in cloth &c.; *s.-fish*, aquatic shelled mollusc (oyster &c.) or crustacean (crab, shrimp, &c.); *s.-gun*, cannon throwing ss. horizontally (cf. MORTAR¹); *s.-heap* or *-mound*, kitchen MIDDEN; *s.-jacket*, army officer's undress jacket reaching only to waist behind; *s.-marble*, kinds containing fossil ss.; *s.-shock*, disorganization of mental faculties, power of speech, &c., resulting from exposure to bombardment & other war strains; *s.-work*, ornamentation of ss. cemented on wood &c. Hence **(-)shell**ED², **she·ll-**LESS, **she·ll**Y², aa. [OE *scell*, cf. Du. *schel*; cogn. w. SCALE¹]

shell², v.t. & i. Take out of s., remove s. or pod from, (*s. peas*); provide, cover, or pave, with shell(s); bombard (town &c.), fire at (troops), with ss., whence **she·ll**ING¹(1) n.; (of metal &c.) come *off* in scales; *s. out* slang, pay up (t. & i.), hand over required sum. [f. prec.]

shella·c, n., & v.t. (-cking, -cked). LAC¹ melted into thin plates, used for making varnish; (vb) varnish with s. [SHELL¹, LAC¹]

she·lter¹, n. Thing serving as shield or barrier against attack, danger, heat, wind, &c.; screen or cabin built to keep off wind & rain (*cabman's s.*); place of safety or immunity; shielded condition (*find, take, s.*). Hence **she·lter**LESS a. [f. 16th c. only, etym. dub.; perh. f. *shield* vb + -URE]

she·lter², v.t. & i. Act or serve as s. to,

protect, conceal, harbour, defend *from* blame, screen, shield; *s.* one*self under, beneath, behind,* &c., use the protection afforded by; take s. *under, in, from*; *sheltered trades,* those not exposed to foreign competition, e.g. building & inland transport. [f. prec.]

she·lty[1], **-tie,** n. (Sc.). Shetland pony. [prob. f. ON *Hjalti* Shetland]

she·lty[2], n. (Sc.). Rude cabin or hut. [cf. Sc. *sheal(ing)* in same sense]

shelve[1], v.t. Put on shelf (books &c.), (fig.) abandon or defer consideration of (plan &c.), cease to employ (person); fit (cupboard &c.) with shelves, whence **she·lv**ING[1](3) n. [f. SHELF]

shelve[2], v.i. Slope gently. [cf. WFris. *skelf* oblique; unconnected w. *shelf*]

shelves. See SHELF.

Shema· (-ah), n. The *Hear, O Israel,* Jews' confession of faith. [the initial wd, Heb. = hear]

Shē·ōl, n. Hebrew Hades, place of the dead, the grave. [Heb.]

she·pherd (-perd), n., & v.t. Man who tends sheep at pasture, pastor (lit., & fig., esp. of minister in relation to his flock; *the good S.,* Christ); *s.'s-club, -joy, -knot, -purse, -rod,* &c., plants; *s.'s crook,* staff with hook at one end used by ss.; *s.'s pie,* minced meat baked under mashed potatoes; *s.'s plaid,* small black & white check pattern in cloth; hence **she·pherd**ESS[1] n. (Vb) tend (sheep, also fig.) as s., marshal or conduct or drive (crowd &c.) like sheep. [SHEEP, HERD[2]]

she·ppy, n. Sheep-cote. [f. SHEEP; perh. a pseudo-archaism]

Shĕ·raton, n. Severe 18th-c. style of furniture (often attrib. as *S. chairs*). [T. *S.* maker & designer]

sher·bet (-et), n. Eastern cooling drink of diluted fruit-juices (in pop. Engl. use, made effervescent). [Turk. & Pers., f. Arab. *shariba* to drink]

sherd. See SHARD.

sheri·f (-ēf), **-eef,** n. Descendant of Mohammed through Fatima, entitled to wear green turban or veil; chief magistrate of Mecca. [f. Arab. *sharīf* lofty]

shĕ·riff, n. Chief officer of crown in county or shire, charged with the keeping of the peace, administering justice under direction of the courts, executing writs by deputy, presiding over elections, &c. [OE *scīr-gerēfa* (SHIRE, REEVE)]

she·riffalty, she·riffdom, she·riffhood, she·riffship, nn. Shrievalty, office of sheriff. [*-alty* after *shrievalty*; -DOM, -HOOD, -SHIP]

she·rry, n. White wine of Xeres or of South Spain (*brown s.,* dark varieties); *s.-glass,* wineglass containing about four table-spoons; *s.* COBBLER. [earlier *sherris* f. *Xeres*]

She·tland, n. Group of islands NNE of Scotland (*S. lace,* openwork woollen trimming; *S. pony,* small hardy breed; *S. wool,* fine kind).

shew. See SHOW[1]; *shew·bread,* see SHOW[1].

Shi·ah, Shi·ite, (-ē-), nn. Member of the Mohammedan sect (cf. *Sunni,* see SUNNAH) that regards Ali as first imam or successor of Mohammed & rejects first three Sunni Caliphs. [Arab., = sect]

shi·bboleth, n. Test word or principle or behaviour or opinion, the use of or inability to use which betrays one's party, nationality, &c. (see *Judg.* xii. 6); old-fashioned & generally abandoned doctrine once held essential. [Heb.]

shield, n., & v.t. Variously shaped & sized detached piece of armour made of leather, wood, or metal, for wearing on left arm to receive thrust or stroke, esp. (cf. *buckler, target*) one of elongated form large enough to cover most of body (*the other side of the s.,* the aspect of a question &c. that is less obvious, or that is not the one lately presented); protective plate or screen in machinery &c.; person or thing that protects one; s.-like part in animal or plant; (Her.) drawing &c. of s. used for displaying person's coat of arms; *s.-fern,* common handsome fern with s.-shaped covers to fruit-dots; *s.-hand* archaic, left hand; hence **shie·ld**LESS a. (Vb) protect, screen, esp. from censure or punishment (often with implication of illegitimate concealment of facts). [OE *sceld,* cf. Du. & G *schild*]

shi·er, -est. See SHY[1].

shift[1], v.t. & i. Change or move (t. & i.) from one position to another, substitute one specimen of for another, undergo such substitution, change form or character, (*s.* one's *ground,* take up new position in argument &c.; *s.* one's *lodging*; *s. load into other hand*; *s. the scene, the scene shifts,* in theatre, novel, &c.; *s.* one's *shirt* &c. archaic, change it; *cargo shifted,* got shaken out of place; often *s. about*; *s. off* responsibility &c., get rid of, transfer to another; *wind shifts round to the E.*); use expedients, take whatever course is available, contrive to do something, manage or get along or make a livelihood, (*must s. as I can, for himself*); equivocate, practise evasion, (rare; *shifts & prevaricates*). [OE *sciftan,* divide, cf. Du. *schiften* divide, ON *skipta* divide, shift]

shift[2], n. Change of place or character, substitution of one thing for another, vicissitude, rotation, (rare; *the ss. & changes of life*; *s. of crops,* rotation); relay of workmen, time for which it works; new device, expedient, resource, whence **shi·ft**LESS a., **shi·ftless**LY[2] adv., **shi·ftless**NESS n.; dodge, trick, artifice, piece of evasion or equivocation, whence **shi·ft**Y[2] a. (*s. eyes,* deceitful), **shi·fti**LY[2] adv., **shi·fti**NESS n.; *make s.* or *a s.,* manage or contrive (*to* do, or abs.), get along somehow (*must make s. without it*); (archaic) chemise; arrangement by which joints of successive tiers in brickwork &c. do not coincide. [ME *schift* cogn. w. prec.; cf. ON *skipti* division, exchange, Sw. *skift* spell, relay]

Shiite. See SHIAH.

shikar·, n.(Anglo-Ind.). Hunting. [Hind.]

shikar·ee, -i, sheka·rry, n. (Anglo-Ind.). Hunter; native attendant of sportsman. [Hind. (*-i*), f. prec.]

shille·lagh (-āla), **-ālah, -elah, -aly,** n. Irish cudgel of blackthorn or oak. [*Shillelagh* in Ireland]

shi·lling, n. (abbr. *s.*, as 3*s.*). British silver coin & money of account = 1/20 of sovereign or twelve pence (*1/6*, a s. & sixpence; £1 1*s.* 1*d.*; *take King's* or *Queen's s.*, enlist as soldier, w. ref. to now obs. method of recruiting; *cut off* one's heir &c. *with a s.*, leave one's property to others; *shilling's*-WORTH[1]). [OE *scilling*, cf. Du. *schelling*, G *schilling*; perh. = thin slice (SKILL, -LING[1])]

shi·lly-shălly, n., & v.i. Inability to make up one's mind, indecision, vacillation; (vb) vacillate, be undecided, hesitate to act or choose one's course. [f. *shall I?* w. redupl.]

shily. See SHY[1].

shim, n., & v.t. Thin slip or wedge used in machinery &c. to make parts fit; (vb) fit or fill up thus. [?]

shi·mmer, v.i., & n. (Shine with) tremulous or faint diffused light. [OE *scymrian*, cf. G *schimmern*]

shi·mmy, n. (Colloq., nursery, &c., for) CHEMISE.

shin, n., & v.i. & t. Front of leg below knee (*s.-bone*, tibia; *s. of beef*, ox's shank); *s.-guard*, worn at football. (Vb) climb *up* (tree, wall, ladder, &c.; or with *up* adv.); kick ss. of, hack. [OE *scinu*, cf. Du. *scheen*, G *schiene*; perh. orig. = thin slice]

shi·ndy, n. Brawl, disturbance, row, noise, (often KICK[2] *up a s.*). [perh. f. Sc. *shinny* or *shinty* kind of hockey]

shine[1], v.i. & t. (*shone*, pr. -ŏn). Emit or reflect light, be bright, glow, (lit. & fig.; *face shone with soap* or *with gratitude* &c.); be brilliant, be a luminary, excel, in some respect or sphere (*does not s. in conversation, society*; *is a shining example*); (colloq.) make bright, polish, (boots, fireplace, brass, &c.). [OE *scīnan*, cf. Du. *schijnen*, G *scheinen*]

shine[2], n. Light, brightness, (chiefly colloq.; *rain or s.*, whatever the weather; *put a good s. on* boots &c.; *take the s. out of*, impair brilliance or newness of, also throw into the shade by surpassing); (slang) disturbance, shindy, sensation. [f. prec.]

shi·ner, n. (slang). A coin, esp. sovereign, (pl.) money. [SHINE[1], -ER[1]]

shi·ngle[1] (-nggl), n., & v.t. Rectangular slip of wood used like roof-tile on roofs, spires, &c.; (vb) roof with ss.; cut (hair of head) so that all ends are exposed like roof-ss., cut hair of (head, person) thus. [n. f. L *scindula*, earlier *scandula*]

shi·ngle[2] (-nggl), n. Small rounded pebbles lying on sea-shore. Hence **shi·ngly**[2] a. [earlier *ch-*, perh. imit., cf. *chink*]

shi·ngles (-ngg-), n. pl. Skin-disease forming inflamed band often round right half of body at waist. [f. med. L *cingulus* f. L *cingulum* girdle (*cingere* gird)]

Shi·nto, n. Japanese religion partly ousted by Buddhism. Hence **Shi·ntōISM, Shi·ntōIST,** nn. [f. Chin. *shin tao* way of the gods]

shi·ny, a. Glistening, polished, rubbed bright, (*s. hat, boots*, &c.; *s. coat, seams*, with nap worn off). Hence **shi·nINESS** n. [-Y[2]]

ship[1], n. (regarded as fem., w. pron. *she, her*). Vessel with bowsprit & three, four, or five square-rigged masts (cf. BARQUE, BRIG, SCHOONER, SLOOP); any sea-going vessel of considerable size (BATTLE[1]-*s.*, *s. of the* LINE[2], MERCHANT-*s.*, SAIL[2]*ing-s.*, WAR[1]-*s.*; *sister s.*, built on same plan as another; *s. of the desert*, camel; ABOUT[2] *s.*; PUMP-*s.*; *take s.*, embark; *on* BOARD[1] *s.*; *when my* &c. *s. comes home*, when I &c. make my &c. fortune); (slang) boat, esp. racing-boat; *on shipboard*, on board s.; *s. biscuit*, hard coarse kind made for keeping used on board s.; *s.-breaker*, contractor who breaks up old ss.; *s.-broker*, agent transacting s.'s business in port, dealer in ss., marine-insurance agent; *s.-builder, -building*; *s.-canal*, for conveying ss. inland; *s.*-CHANDLER(*y*); *s.-fever*, typhus; *s.-letter*, conveyed by other than mail-s.; *shipload*, quantity of something forming whole cargo; *shipmate*, person belonging to or sailing on same s. as another, esp. fellow sailor; *s.-money* hist., impost for providing ss. for navy, revival of which by Charles I was a cause of Great Rebellion; *shipowner*, person owning (shares in) ship(s); *s.-railway*, for transportation of ss. overland from water to water; *s.-rigged*, as s. in first sense; *s.'s articles*, terms on which seamen take service on her; *s.'s* COMPANY[1]; *s.'s* CORPORAL[3]; *shi·pshape* adv. or pred. a., in good order (& see BRISTOL); *s.'s husband*, s.-broker in first sense; *s.'s papers*, documents establishing ownership, nationality, nature of cargo, &c., of s.; *s.-way*, inclined structure on which s. is built & down which it slides to be launched; *s.-worm*, mollusc boring into s. timbers; *shi·pwreck* n., destruction of s. by storm, foundering, stranding, striking rock, &c., (fig.) ruin (*make shipwreck*, be ruined; *make* or *suffer shipwreck of* one's *hopes* &c.); *shi·pwreck* v.t. & i., inflict s.-w. lit. or fig. on (person, hopes, &c., rarely ship), suffer s.-w.; *s.-wright*, s.-builder; *s.-yard*, s.-building establishment. Hence **shi·pLESS** a. [OE *scip*, cf. Du. *schif*, G *schiff*]

ship[2], v.t. & i. Put, take, or send away (goods, passengers, sailors) on board s.; (Commerc.) deliver (goods) to forwarding agent for conveyance by land or water; fix (mast, rudder, &c.) in its place on s. (*s. oars*, take from rowlocks & lay inside boat); (of s. or boat) *s. a sea*, be flooded by wave; take s., embark, (of sailor) take service on s. [f. prec.]

-ship, suf. f. OE *-scipe* (cf. Du. *-schap*, G *-schaft*) f. Teut. root *skap* form, make, forming abstract nn. on adjj. as *hardship*, *worship* (*worth* adj.), & on nn. as *lordship*, *friendship*, *scholarship*, *apprenticeship*; in the latter use it is a living suf.; meaning, (1) being so-&-so, status, office, honour, (2) tenure of office, (3) skill in certain capacity. *Landscape* also contains the suf.

shi·pment, n. Putting of goods &c. on ship; amount shipped, consignment. [SHIP[2], -MENT]

shi·pper, n. Merchant &c. who sends or gets goods by ship. [-ER[1]]

shi·pping, n. In vbl senses; also: ships, esp. the ships of a country, port, &c.; *s.-agent*, person acting for ship or line of ships at a port &c.; *s.-articles*, agreement between captain & seamen as to wages &c.; *s.-bill*, manifest of goods shipped; *s.-master*, official in whose presence s.-articles are signed, paying off is done, &c.; *s.-office*, s.-agent's or s.-master's. [-ING[1]]

shīre (*as suf. pr.* -sher), n. County (chiefly now as suf. in names of certain counties & districts, as *Hampshire*, *Hallamshire*, with some of which it is omissible, as *Devonshire* or *Devon*, & in pl. *the ss.*, band of counties stretching NE from Hampshire & Devonshire ending in *-shire*, also loose term for the midland counties, & for the hunting district including Leics. & Rutland & Northants.); *s.-bred horse*, *s.-horse*, largest breed of draught horse raised esp. in Lincolnshire & Cambridgeshire; KNIGHT *of the s.* [OE *scīr* business, administration, province, etym. dub.; not connected w. *shear*, *share*]

shirk, v.t., & n. Avoid meanly, get out of, shrink selfishly from, (duty, responsibility, fighting, &c.; also abs.); hence **shir·k**ER[1] n. (N.) shirker. [f. obs. *shirk* n. sponger, sharper, perh. f. G *schurke*]

shir(r), n., & v.t., (U.S.). Elastic webbing; elastic thread woven into fabric; gathered trimming, gathering in costumery; (vb) gather (material) with parallel threads run through; hence **shir·r**ING[1] n. [?]

shirt, n. Man's sleeved under-garment worn under cloth clothes, extending from neck to thighs, usu. visible at collar & wrist-bands, & made of linen, cotton, flannel, or silk (NIGHT-*s.*; *stripped to the s.*, *in* one's *s.-sleeves*, without coat & waistcoat, coat; *near is my s., but nearer is my skin*, self is the first consideration; *keep* one's *s. on* slang, keep one's temper; *get* one's *s. off* slang, make him angry; *put* one's *s. on, upon*, slang, bet all one has upon; *give* one *a wet s.*, work him till he sweats); woman's blouse with stiff collar & cuffs; *s.-front*, breast of s., usu. stiffened & starched (*s.-f. wicket*, absolutely true & smooth cricket pitch), also dicky. Hence **-shirt**ED[2], **shir·t**LESS, aa., **shir·t**ING[1](3) n., **shir·t**Y[2] a. (slang), in a rage, annoyed. [OE *scyrte*, cf. ON *skyrta* shirt, G *schürze* apron, cogn. w. SHORT, SKIRT]

shit, v.i., & n., (vulg.). Evacuate bowels. (N.) ordure (& as term of abuse). [earlier *sc(h)-*, cf. ON *skita*, Du. *schijten*, G *scheissen*]

shĭ·ver[1], v.i., & n. (Experience or show) quick slight vibrating movement (such as is) caused by sensation of cold, tremble with cold; *shivering-fit*, as in ague; hence **shi·vering**LY[2] adv. (N.) momentary shivering movement (often pl., as *gives me the ss.*), whence **shi·ver**Y[2] a. [ME *chiveren*, etym. dub.]

shĭ·ver[2], n. (usu. pl.), & v.t. & i. (One of) the many small pieces into which thing is shattered by blow or fall; (vb) break (t. & i.) into ss. (*s. my timbers*, reputed naut. imprecation). [ME *scifre*, cf. obs. *shive* slice, & G *schiefer* slate]

shoal[1], a., n., & v.i. Shallow, not deep, (only lit., of water); (n.) shallow place, submerged sand-bank esp. one that shows at low water, (fig., usu. pl.) hidden danger(s) or impediment(s), whence **shoa·l**Y[2] a., **shoa·l**INESS n.; (vb) get shallower. [OE *sceald*]

shoal[2], n., & v.i. Multitude, crowd, great number, esp. of fish swimming in company (also SCHOOL[2]), (*ss. of people*; *gets letters in ss.*); (vb, of fish) form ss. [perh. f. OE *scolu* troop of soldiers, cf. OSax. *scola* multitude; but prob. a re-adoption f. Du. of SCHOOL[2]]

shock[1], n. Violent collision, concussion, or impact (*three ss. of earthquake were felt*; *clashed with a mighty s.*; *s. tactics*, use of cavalry to charge in masses; *s.-troops*, German special-service troops in the great war); sudden & disturbing physical or mental impression (*news came upon me with a s.*, *was a great s.*; *electric s.*, stimulation of nerves by passage of current through body), (Path.) state of prostration following overstimulation of nerves by sudden pain as of wound &c. or violent emotion (*died of s.*; *the s. is more dangerous than the loss of blood*); injury inflicted on credit, stability, &c., great disturbance of organization or system. [f. F *choc* (*choquer*, see foll.)]

shock[2], v.t. & i. Affect with indignation, disgust, or horror, appear improper or outrageous or scandalous to (*was shocked at, by, to hear*, &c.), whence **sho·ck**ING[2] a. & adv. (*shocking bad* &c. colloq.),

sho·ckingLY[2] adv., **sho·ckingNESS** n.; collide violently (poet.). [f. F *choquer* clash, etym. dub.]

shock[3], n., & v.t. Group of usu. twelve corn-sheaves stood up close together in field; (vb) arrange (corn) in ss. [cf. MDu. *schok* s., sixty, MHG *schoch* heap, sixty, MSw. *skokk* crowd]

shock[4], n. Unkempt or shaggy mass of hair; *s. head*, rough head of hair, whence **shock-headED**[2] a. [perh. f. obs. *shock-dog* or *shough* poodle, etym. dub.]

sho·cker, n. (colloq.). Very bad specimen of anything; sensational cheap novel (esp. *shilling s.*). [-ER[1]]

shod. See SHOE[2].

sho·ddy, n. & a. Fibre made from old cloth &c. shredded; inferior cloth made partly of such fibre; anything of worse quality than it claims or seems to have; (adj.) counterfeit, pretentious, trashy. [prob. f. OE *sceddan* SHED[1]]

shoe[1] (-ōō), n. Outer foot-covering, esp. not reaching above ankle (*that's another pair of ss.*, another matter; *dead men's ss.*, property or position as looked forward to by expectant successor; *be in* person's *ss.*, in his plight; *die in* one's *ss.*, by violence, esp. hanging; *where the s. pinches*, hardships of one's own lot; *put the s. on the right foot*, apportion blame &c. truly); metal rim nailed to hoof of horse &c.; thing like s. in shape or use, e.g. wheel-drag, socket, ferrule, mast-step; *ss. & stockings*, bird's-foot trefoil; *shoe·black*, boy or man who blacks ss. of passers-by; *s.-buckle*, for fastening s. over instep (now usu. worn only as ornament); *shoe·horn*, instrument of horn, metal, &c., for helping s. on to foot; *s.-lace*, *-string*, for lacing up s.; *s.-latchet* (bibl.), fastening of s.; *s.-leather*, leather for ss., ss. (*as good a man as ever trod s.-l.*, lived); *s.-lift*, =*shoehorn*; *s.-maker*, maker of boots & ss. Hence **shoe·LESS** a. [OE *scóh*, cf. Du. *schoen*, G *schuh*; perh. cogn. w. SHAED, SKY]

shoe[2], v.t. (*shod*; part. *shoeing*). Fit with shoe(s) (esp. with *horse* &c. as obj., or in p.p. as *neatly shod feet, pole shod with iron*). [f. prec.]

shō·gun (-ōōn), n. (hist.). Japanese hereditary commander-in-chief & virtual ruler for some centuries until the office was abolished 1868. Hence **shō·gunATE**[1] n. [Jap., = general]

shone. See SHINE[1].

shoo, int., & v.i. & t. (Utter) sound used to frighten birds away; drive *away* thus. [imit.]

shook[1]. See SHAKE[1].

shōōk[2], n., & v.t. Set of staves & headings for cask ready for putting together; (vb) pack in ss. [prob. p.p. of *shake*; *shaken cask* is used in same sense]

shōōt[1], v.i. & t. (shot). Come vigorously or swiftly *out, forth, along, up*, &c., or abs., sprout, dart, (*boat shot out from the creek*; *shooting* STAR[1]; *flash shoots across sky*; *s. ahead*, come quickly to front of competitors &c.; *buds are shooting*; *tree shoots*, puts forth buds; *fountain, flame, shoots up*; *prices shot up*, rose suddenly; *cricket-ball shoots*, darts along ground when it touches, instead of bouncing; *child is shooting up*, growing tall; *pain shoots through nerves* &c.; *corn, tooth, shoots*, inflicts intermittent pain); project abruptly *out* (*mountain-spur, cape, shoots out*); send out, discharge, propel, emit, violently or swiftly (*s. rubbish* &c., let it slide from cart or receptacle; *bow, gun, shoots arrow, shell*; *passengers were shot out of coach*; *sun shoots its rays*; *s. out* one's *lips* bibl., protrude in scorn; *s.* one's *linen*, display wristbands by shaking them down; *s. the cat* slang, vomit; *s. fishing-net*, extend it across river &c.; *s. bolt* of door, send it home; *tree shoots out branches*); discharge (bullet &c.) from gun &c., cause (bow, gun, &c.) to discharge missile, discharge gun &c., make use *well* &c. of gun &c., kill or wound (person, animal) with missile from gun &c., hunt game &c. habitually or on one occasion with gun, s. the game *over* estate &c., s. game on (estate &c.), (of gun &c.) go off, send missile *straight* &c., (*fool's* BOLT[1] *is soon shot*; *I'll be shot if —*, form of negative asseveration; *can army* or *sportsman, does gun, s. straight?*; *was shot for a spy*; *had his arm shot off*, torn off by cannon-ball &c.; *s. a match*, engage in shooting-match; *will s. the coverts tomorrow*; *neither rides nor shoots*; *was out shooting*; *have shot away all our ammunition*); (Assoc. Footb., v.i.) take a shot at goal; *s. up* (U.S. slang), terrorize (village, district) with punitive rifle-shooting, firing of houses, &c.; *s. the sun* naut., take its altitude with the sextant at noon; *s. the moon* slang, remove one's goods by night to avoid paying rent; be, have one's boat, swept swiftly under or down (bridge, rapid fall; *s. Niagara*, attempt desperate enterprise); (p.p., of coloured material) so woven &c. as to show different colours at different angles (*shot silk*; *crimson shot with maize-colour*); *shooting-box*, sportsman's lodge for use in shooting-season; *shooting-coat, -jacket, -boots*, of patterns useful in shooting game; *shooting-iron* slang, fire-arm; *shooting-range*, ground with butts for rifle practice. Hence **shoo·TABLE** a. [OE *scéotan*, cf. Du. *schieten*, G *schiessen*]

shoot[2], n. Young branch or sucker; rapid in stream; inclined plane down which water &c. may flow or things slide, chute; shooting party or expedition or practice or (=SHOOTING) land. [f. prec.]

shoo·ter, n. In vbl senses; esp.: ball that shoots at cricket; (in comb.) shooting-implement (PEA-*s.*; *six* &c. *-s.*, revolver firing six &c. shots). [-ER[1]]

shoo·ting, n. In vbl senses (for compounds see SHOOT[1]); esp.: right of s. over particular land; estate &c. rented to shoot over. [-ING[1]]

shop, n., & v.i. Building, room, &c., for retail sale of some commodity (*chemist's, butcher's, fruit-, s.*; *come to the wrong s.* transf., apply to wrong person &c.), or in which manufacture or repairing is done (*engineering-s.*; *fitting, pattern,* &c., *-s.*, departments of manufactory); (slang) institution, establishment, &c. (e.g. one's school, university, &c.; esp. of R.M.A., Woolwich; *the other s.*, rival institution); one's profession, trade, or business, things connected with it, or talk about it, (*shut up s.*, cease doing something; *talk s.*; *sink the s.*, refrain from talking s., also conceal one's occupation; SMELL *of the s.*), whence **sho·ppy**Y[2] a.; *all over the s.* (slang), in disorder, in every direction, wildly, (*have looked for it a. o. t. s.*; *my books are a. o. t. s.*; *hitting, steering,* &c., *a. o. t. s.*); *s.-bell,* on door to give notice of customer's entrance; *s.-boy, -girl,* assistants in s.; *shopkeeper,* owner of s. (*nation of shopkeepers,* the English); *s.-lifter,* pretended customer who steals goods in s.; *shopman,* shopkeeper or his assistant; *s.-steward,* person elected by his fellow workmen in a factory or branch of it as their spokesman on conditions of work &c.; *sho·pwalker,* attendant in large s. who directs customers; *s. window,* window of s. used for display of wares (*has everything in the s. w.* transf., is superficial); *s.-worn,* soiled or faded by being shown in s.; (vb) go to shop(s) to make purchases, whence **sho·pp**ING[1] n.; (slang) imprison, (of informer) cause (accomplice) to be imprisoned. [OE *sceoppa* booth, cf. G *schopf* porch, shed]

shore[1], n. Land that skirts sea or large body of water (*in s.*, on the water near or nearer to s.); (Law) land between ordinary high & low water marks. Hence **shore·**LESS a., **shore·**WARD a. & adv. [ME *schore,* cf. Du. *schoor* prob. cogn. w. SHEAR[1]]

shore[2], n., & v.t. Prop, beam set obliquely against ship, wall, tree, &c., as support; (vb) support, hold *up,* with shore(s). Hence **shor·**ING[1](3) n. [ME *schore,* cf. Du. *schoor,* ON *skortha*]

shore[3], **shorn.** See SHEAR[1].

short, a., adv., & n. Measuring little from end to end in space or time, soon traversed or finished, (*a s. way off*; *a s. time ago*; *s. story,* of the character of a novel but less length; *s.* CUT[1]; *s. circuit,* electric circuit made through a small resistance, esp. one acting as a shunt to one of greater resistance, form of this due to a fault that allows current's escape to earth; *s.-circuit* v.t., establish s. c. in, cut off current from thus; *s.* DIVISION; *s. drink* slang, cocktail &c. before dinner; *shorter* CATECHISM; *s. rib,* = *false* RIB; *s.* SHRIFT; *s.* WHIST[3]; *a s. sea,* s. broken waves; *make s. work of,* dispose of or destroy or consume quickly; *he, his joy* &c., *had but a s. life,* whence **shortliv**ED[2] a.; *s. temper,* self-control that is soon or easily lost, whence **short-temper**ED[2] a.; *s. waist* in dress, made high up, whence **short-waist**ED[2] a.; *s. wind,* easily exhausted breathing-power, inability to run long or fig. to talk or write at any length, whence **short-wind**ED[2] a., **short-wi·nded**NESS n.; *s. clothes* or *coats,* dress of child too old for long-clothes, whence **shor·t-coat** v.t.); of small stature, not tall, (usu. of human beings, or of upright things, as chimney, tower, tree); not far-reaching, acting near at hand, deficient, scanty, in want *of,* below the degree *of,* abruptly finished, (*s. sight,* not seeing clearly at distance or fig. into the future, whence **short-sighted**ED[2] a., **short-sigh·ted**LY[2] adv., **short-sigh·ted**NESS n.; *at s. range*; *take s. views,* consider the present only; *s. date,* early date for maturing of bill &c., whence **short-dat**ED[2] a.; *s. bill, paper,* &c., dated for early payment; *s.* LEG, SLIP, in cricket; *has a s. memory*; *are s. of hands,* have not enough workmen, whence **short-hand**ED[2] a.; *s. of breath,* panting, s.-winded; *s.* COMMONS; *s. weight,* less than it is represented to be; *a s. ten miles, mile, hour,* &c., less or seeming less than that; *cut s.,* bring to end before natural time; *come s.,* disappoint expectations &c., fail *of* one's duty or proper development, whence **shor·t-com**ING[1] n.; *fall s.,* be insufficient or inadequate; *run s.,* have or be too little, as *our tea ran s., we ran s. of tea*; *an escape nothing s. of marvellous*); concise, brief, curt, sullenly or snappishly reticent, (*the* LONG[1] *& the s. of it*; *in s.,* to use few words, without circumlocution, to give the conclusion briefly; *is called Bob for s.,* by way of s. name; *was very s. with me,* uncivil); (Phonet., Pros.; of vowel or syllable) (prop.) having the less of the two recognized durations, (pop.) unstressed, (also, of vowel) having the or an other sound than that called LONG[1] (e.g. those in *met, pull, but*); (of pastry, clay, &c.) friable, crumbling, not tenacious, (cf. COLD-SHORT); (St. Exch. &c.; of stocks, stockbroker, crops, &c.) sold, selling, &c., when the amount is not in hand in reliance on getting the deficit in time for delivery; *something s.,* a drink of strong liquor, esp. spirits; *shor·tbread, shor·tcake,* brittle dry cake made with flour & much butter & sugar; *shortha·nd,* methods of compendious writing used for taking verbatim reports of speeches &c., stenography; *shor·thorn,* name of s.-horned breed of cattle; hence **short**ISH[1] (2) a., **shor·t**NESS n. (Adv.) abruptly, before the natural or expected time, in s.

manner, (*took him up s.*, interrupted him; *stop s.*, suddenly cease, not go on to the end; *bring*, or *pull, up s.*, check or pause abruptly; *be taken s.*, have sudden motion of bowels; *s.-spoken*, given to brevity of speech; *sell s.*, when one has not the articles in hand, see the adj.); *s. of*, except, putting out of the question, (*s. of committing suicide he does his best to keep out of the way*). (N.) s. syllable (LONG[1]s *&* ss.) or vowel; mark indicating that vowel is s., as ă; (pl.) garment like trousers cut s. worn by athletes, boy scouts, boys, &c. [OE *sceort*, cf. OHG *scurz*, cogn. w. SKIRT, SHIRT]

shor·tage (-ĭj), n. (Amount of) deficiency (*there is no s., a s. of 100 tons*). [-AGE]

shor·ten, v.i. & t. Become or make actually or apparently shorter or short, curtail; reduce the amount of *sail* spread. [-EN[6]]

shor·tly, adv. Before long, a short time *before* or *after*; in few words, briefly; curtly. [-LY[2]]

shot[1], n. (pl. *-s*, also *shot* see below), & v.t. Single missile for cannon or gun, non-explosive projectile, (usu. with qualification or in comb., as *round, solid*, CHAIN-, GRAPE-, CASE[2]-, BUCK[1]-, *s.*; *chilled s.*, case-hardened for armour-piercing; *a s. in the* LOCKER); (pl. usu. *shot*) small lead pellets of which a quantity is used for single charge or cartridge esp. in sporting guns, such pellets collectively, (*s. does* or *do well for cleaning decanters*; *put three s.* or *ss. of different sizes on the gut*; *s. is made in various ways*; *about a dozen nº 10 s. were extracted from his leg*); discharge of cannon or gun (*several ss. were fired, heard*, &c.), attempt to hit with projectile or missile or fig. to make stroke in game or guess or do something (*at each s. he was nearer the bull's-eye*; *a beautiful s. from cover-point took off the bails*; *made a bad s.*, guessed wrong; *am going to have a good s. at winning*; *snap s.*, discharging of rifle &c. with momentary aim, cf. SNAP*shot*; *flying s.*, at bird on wing or moving object; PARTHIAN, *random, s.*; *-s.*, range, reach, distance to or at which thing will carry or act, as *bow, rifle, ear, -s.*); possessor of specified skill with rifle, gun pistol, &c. (*is a good, bad, crack* or *firstclass*, or *no, s.*); *s.-tower*, in which s. is made from molten lead poured through sieves at top & falling into water at bottom; hence **sho·t**PROOF[2] a. (Vb) load, weight, &c., with s. [OE *gesceot* (Y-, *scēotan* SHOOT[1]), cf. G *schoss*]

shot[2]. See SHOOT[1].

shot[3], n. Reckoning, (one's share of) tavern-bill, (usu. *pay* one's *s.*). [var. of SCOT[1]]

should. See SHALL.

shou·lder (-ōl-), n., & v.t. & i. Part of body at which arm or foreleg or wing is attached, either lateral projection below or behind neck, (also *s.-joint*) combination of end of upper arm with those of collarbone & blade-bone, (pl.) upper part of back, (pl.) body regarded as bearing burdens, (of slaughtered animal) foreleg with parts usu. kept with it in dismembering, (HEAD[1] *&* ss.; *dislocate* one's *s.*; *s. to s.*, with closed ranks or united effort; *has broad ss.*, is strong, can bear much weight or responsibility; *old head on young ss.*, youthful wisdom, wise young person; *put, set, s. to wheel*, make effort; *straight from the s.*, said of well delivered blow or telling invective; *s.-of-mutton sail*, triangular fore-&-aft sail hoisted abaft mast; COLD[1] s.; COLD[1]-s. v.t.; *lay the blame, burden*, &c., *on the right ss.*); part of mountain, bottle, tool, &c., projecting like human s.; (Mil.) position of soldier who has shouldered arms (see vb); *s.-belt*, baldric, bandolier, or other band passing over one s. & under opposite arm; *s.-blade*, either large flat bone of upper back, scapula; *s.-brace*, contrivance for flattening round back of child &c.; *s.-knot*, of ribbon or metal lace worn on s. by livery servant; *s.-pegged* of horse, stiff in ss.; *s.-strap*, band from s.-tip in soldier's uniform, keeping s.-belts in place & bearing name or number of regiment &c.; hence **(-)shoulder**ED[2] a. (Vb) push (t. & i.) with s., jostle, make way thus; take (burden lit. or fig.) on one's ss.; (Mil.) *s. arms*, hold rifle vertical supported by right hand at lock (cf. SLOPE v.). [OE *sculder*, cf. Du. *schouder*, G *schulter*, etym. dub.]

shout (-owt), v.i. & t., & n. Make loud articulate or inarticulate cry or vocal sound, speak loudly, (*shouted with laughter*; *s. for joy*; *s. at*, speak loudly to &c.; *all is over but the shouting*, contest is virtually decided); say loudly, call out, express in loud tones, (*s. approbation*; *shouted that the coast was clear*; *shouted to* or *for me to come*; '*Go back*' *he shouted*). (N.) Loud utterance or vocal sound from individual or company expressing joy, (dis)approval, defiance, &c., or calling attention (*my* &c. *s.* slang, turn to order drink &c. for the company). [f. 14th c., etym. dub.]

shove (-ŭv), v.t. & i., & n. Push (t. & i.) vigorously, move (t.) along by hard or rough pushing; make one's way *along, past, through*, &c., by pushing, jostle (person); *s.-halfpenny*, modern gambling form of shovelboard; (colloq.) put somewhere (*s. it in the drawer*); *s. off*, start from shore in boat. (N.) push (*give* one *a s. off*, help him to start); woody centre of flax-stem. [OE *scūfan*, cf. Du. *schuiven*, G *schieben*]

sho·vel (-ŭvl), n., & v.t. (-ll-). Scooping implement for shifting coal, earth, &c., often in form of spade with sides of blade turned up; *s. hat*, broad-brimmed as worn by Anglican dignitaries; *s.-head,* kinds of sturgeon & shark, also *s.-nose*; hence **sho·vel**FUL(2) n.; (vb) shift (coal &c.) with or as with s. (*s. food into* one's *mouth,* eat greedily). [OE *scofl,* cf. Du. *schoffel* hoe, G *schaufel*; cogn. w. prec.]

sho·velboard (-ŭvl-), n. Game played (now esp. on ship's deck) by impelling disks (formerly coins) with hand or mace over marked surface. [earlier *shove-board, -groat* (SHOVE)]

sho·veller, n. In vbl senses; also, the spoonbill duck. [-ER¹]

show¹, shew, (-ō), v.t. & i. (p.p. *-n,* rarely *-ed*). Let be seen, disclose, manifest, offer (thing, person thing, thing *to* person) for inspection, exhibit, produce, give (treatment, person treatment, treatment *to* person), reveal, (*clothes s. signs of wear*; *an aperture shows the inside*; *showed neither joy nor anger, that he was annoyed, how much he felt it,* &c.; *s.* oneself, be seen in public; *s. me, I was shown, a specimen*; *has nothing to s. for it,* no token of achievement &c.; *s. your tickets, please*; *got prizes for all the dogs he showed*; *s.* CAUSE¹; *s. favour, mercy, to*; *showed me kindness* or *unkindness*; *s. fight,* not yield tamely; *s.* one's COLOUR¹s; *s.* one's *hand* orig. in cards, let out one's designs; *s. the hoof* or *cloven hoof,* see CLEAVE¹; *s. white* FEATHER¹; *s.* CLEAN¹ *pair of heels*; *s. a leg,* get out of bed; *s.* thing *the fire,* slightly heat it); be visible or noticeable, come into sight, appear in public, have some appearance, (*the blood shows through her skin*; *stain will never s.*; *buds are just showing*; *her husband never shows at her at-homes* colloq.; *shows white, like a disk, from here*); demonstrate, prove, expound, point out, cause (person) to understand (thing), (*has shown the falsity of the tale, that* it *is false, how false* it *is,* it *to be false*; *s.* one *the way,* by words, pointing, or going with or before him, also encourage by doing thing first; *s.* person *how to write, what to do,* &c.; *s.* person *the* DOOR; *it only shows how little you know*; *on your own showing,* even according to your own admission or contention); conduct (*showed us round the house*; *s.* one *out* or *in,* esp. open door for his exit or entrance); *s. forth* archaic, exhibit, expound; *s. off* trans., display to advantage, intr., try to make impression by exhibiting one's wealth or skill; *s. up,* make or be conspicuous or clearly visible, expose (fraud, impostor); *shew-bread,* twelve loaves displayed in Jewish temple & renewed each sabbath; *show-case,* glazed case for exhibiting goods, curiosities, &c.; *show-room, -window,* in which wares are kept, hung up, for inspection; *s.-place,* that tourists &c. go to see. [OE *scéawian* see, make see, cf. Da. *schouwen,* G *schauen*; cogn. w. L *cavēre* be cautious, Gk *koeō* observe]

show², n. Showing (*voted by s. of hands*; DUMB¹ *s.*); spectacle, exhibition, pageant, display, collection of things shown esp. for money to entertain, (*flower, horse,* &c., *-s.*; *Lord Mayor's s.,* procession of symbolic cars &c.; *a fine s. of blossom*); outward appearance, semblance, impression produced, parade, ostentation, pomp, display, (*pierce beneath the ss. of things*; *there is a s. of reason in it*; *good enough in outward s.*; *did it for s.*; *is fond of s.*; *S. Sunday,* that before Commemoration at Oxford), whence **show·**Y² a., **show·i**LY² adv., **show·**INESS n.; (slang) concern, undertaking, organization, (RUN¹ or BOSS³ *the s.*; *give away the s.,* betray its inadequacy or pretentiousness); (slang) opportunity of acting, defending oneself, &c. (*had no s. at all*; *give him a fair s.*); (Obstetr.) discharge indicating approach of labour; *showman,* proprietor or manager of menagerie or other such s. [f. prec.]

shower (-owr), n., & v.t. & i. Brief fall of rain, or *of* hail, arrows, bullets, dust, stones, &c. (also fig., as *a s. of gifts, honours*; *letters come in ss.*); *s.-bath,* in which water descends from above through perforated plate; hence **shower·**Y²(-owrĭ) a., **shower·**INESS n. (Vb) discharge (water, missiles, &c.) in a s., bestow (gifts &c. usu. *upon*); descend or come in a s. [OE *scúr,* cf. Du. *schoer,* G *schauer*]

shram, v.t. (dial.; usu. in p.p.). Benumb with or *with* cold. [perh. cogn. w. OE *scrimman* shrivel]

shrank. See SHRINK.

shra·pnel, n. Bullets contained in shell timed to burst slightly short of objective & let them fly on in shower; part of bomb &c. so scored as to break & scatter. [inventor's name]

shred, n., & v.t. (*shredded,* archaic *shred*). Scrap, fragment, rag, strip, torn or broken piece, small remains, least amount, (*tore it to ss.*; *without a s. of clothing on him*; *not a s. of evidence, reputation,* &c.; *tear* an argument &c. *to ss.,* completely refute it); (vb) tear or cut into ss. [OE *scréade* n., *scréadian* vb, cf. G *schrot*; cogn. w. SHROUD, doublet of SCREED]

shrew, n. Scolding woman, whence **shrew·**ISH¹ a., **shrew·ish**LY² adv., **shrew·ish**NESS n.; (also *s.-mouse*) small mammal like long-snouted mouse feeding on insects. [OE *scréawa* s.-mouse]

shrewd, a. (Of pain, cold, &c.) sharp, biting, (literary, esp. *s. blow, knock, thrust, turn*); sagacious, sensible, discriminating, astute, judicious, (*can make a s. guess*; *a s. observer*; *s. face* &c., sagacious-looking). Hence **shrew·d**LY² adv., **shrew·d**NESS n. [ME *shrewed* (prec., -ED², cf. *dogged, crabbed*)]

shriek (-rēk), v.i. & t., & n. (Utter) shrill & usu. inarticulate cry of terror, pain,

&c., screech, scream; laugh uncontrollably (usu. *s. with laughter*); *s. out*, say in shrill agonized tones. [var. of SCREECH]

shrie·valty (-rē-), n. Sheriff's office or jurisdiction, tenure of this. [as SHERIFF w. F suf. as COMMONALTY]

shrift, n. (Archaic) confession to priest, confession & absolution, (now only in *short s.*, little time between condemnation & execution or punishment). [OE *scrift* (SHRIVE)]

shrike, n. Kinds of bird called also butcher-bird with strong hooked & toothed bill & habit of impaling its prey of small birds & insects on thorns. [prob. f. OE *sric* missel-thrush or perh. any shrill-voiced bird; cogn. w. SHRIEK]

shrill, a., & v.i. & t. Piercing & high-pitched in sound; (fig.) importunate, insisting on being heard esp. in complaint or accusation; hence **shri·lLY**[2] (-l-li) adv., **shri·llNESS** n. (Vb, poet. or rhet.): (of cry &c.) sound shrilly; (of person &c.) utter, send *out*, (song, complaint, &c.) shrilly. [f. 14th c.; cf. Sc. *skirl*, LG *schrell*]

shrimp, n., & v.i. Kinds of long-tailed ten-footed saltwater crustacean of which the common British species is about two inches long of translucent greenish-grey while alive & brown when cooked; diminutive person. (Vb) go catching ss.; hence **shri·mpER**[1] n. [f. 14th c.; cf. MHG *schrimpen* shrink up]

shrine, n., & v.t. Casket, esp. one holding sacred relics; tomb usu. sculptured or highly ornamented of saint &c.; altar or chapel of special associations; place hallowed by some memory; (vb) enshrine. [OE *scrin* f. L *scrinium* chest for writing-materials (*scribere* write)]

shrink, v.i. & t. (*shrank*; *shrunk* & rarely in vbl, commonly in adj., use *shrunken*), & n. Become of less dimensions, grow smaller, whence **shri·nkAGE**(3) n.; recoil, retire from observation, (*s. into* oneself, become reserved), flinch *from*, whence **shri·nkingLY**[2] adv.; be averse *from* do-*ing*; make smaller (esp. in pass.; *his face has a shrunken look*), make s. (flannel &c., in order that it may not do so later; *s. wheel-tire* &c. *on*, slip it on while expanded with heat & let it tighten as it cools), whence **shri·nkABLE** a.; (n.; rare) shrinking (*how much must we allow for the s.?*). [OE *scrincan*, cf. MDu. *schrinken*]

shrive, v.t. (archaic; *shrove*, *shriven*). Hear confession of, assign penance to, & absolve; (of penitent) submit oneself to priest for this purpose. [OE *scrifan* prob. f. L *scribere* write]

shri·vel, v.i. & t. (-ll-). Contract or wither (i. & t.) into wrinkled, folded, rolled-up, contorted, or dried-up state. [cf. Sw. dial. *skryvla*]

shroud (-owd), n., & v.t. Winding-sheet, garment for the dead, whence **shrou·dLESS** a.; concealing agency (*wrapped in a s. of mystery*); (pl.) set of ropes forming part of standing rigging & supporting mast or topmast. (Vb) clothe (corpse) for burial; cover & conceal or disguise. [OE *scrūd* garment, cogn. w. SHRED]

Shrove Tue·sday, n. Day before Ash Wednesday, on which & the preceding days or *Shrovetide* it was customary to be shriven. [*shrove* formed f. SHRIVE (cf. ABODE), = SHRIFT]

shrub[1], n. Woody plant of less size than tree & usu. divided into separate stems from near the ground. Hence **shru·bbY**[2] a., **shru·bbERY**(3) n. [OE *scrybb*, cf. Norw. *skrubba* dwarf cornel]

shrub[2], n. Cordial made of fruit-juice & spirit (usu. *rum-s.*). [f. Arab. *sharāb*; cogn. w. SHERBET, SYRUP]

shrug, v.t. & i., & n. Slightly & momentarily raise (shoulders), raise shoulders, to express indifference, helplessness, contempt, vexation, &c.; (n.) this motion (*of the shoulders*, or abs.). [f. 1400, etym. dub.]

shrunk(en). See SHRINK.

shuck, n., & v.t. Husk, pod; (vb) remove ss. of, shell. [?]

shu·dder, v.i., & n. (Experience) sudden shivering due to fear, horror, repugnance, or cold; feel strong repugnance &c. (*I s. to think what might happen*). Hence **shu·dderingLY**[2] adv. [ME *shodre*, cf. G *schaudern*]

shu·ffle, v.i. & t., & n. Move (t. & i.) with scraping or sliding or dragging or difficult motion (*shuffles along rheumatically*; *shuffles his* or *with his feet*; *s. cards*, slide them over one another so as to change their relative positions; so *s.* things of any sort, intermingle, confuse; *s. the cards* fig., change the parts, try new policy, &c.); slip (clothes, burden) *off* or *on* (*s. off responsibility upon others*; *shuffled on his clothes*); keep shifting one's position lit. or fig., fidget, vacillate, prevaricate, whence **shu·fflER**[1] n.; hence **shu·fflingLY**[2] adv. (N.) shuffling movement; shuffling of cards, general change of relative positions; piece of equivocation or sharp practice; quick scraping movement of feet in dancing (*double s.*, executed twice with one & then the other foot). [perh. f. LG *schüffeln*, cogn. w. SCUFFLE]

shun, v.t. Avoid, keep clear of, eschew. Hence **shu·nLESS** a. (poet.). [OE *scunian*, etym. dub.]

'shun !, abbr. of *attention!* as word of command.

shunt, v.t. & i., & n. Divert (train, electric current, &c.), (of train &c.) diverge, on to a side track, esp. to clear line for more important traffic, whence **shu·ntER**[1] n. (in vbl senses, &, slang, able organizer); postpone or stifle discussion of (subject), lay aside (project), leave (person) inactive. (N.) turning or being turned on to side track; (Electr.) conductor joining two points of circuit, over which more or less of current may be diverted. [perh. f. SHUN]

shut, v.t. & i. (shut). Move (door, sash, lid, lips, &c.) into position to stop an aperture (*s. the door upon,* refuse to consider, make impossible); s. door &c. of (room, window, box, eye, mouth, &c.; *s. your eyes*; *s.* one's *eyes* or by extension *ears to,* pretend not or refuse to see or hear); become or admit of being closed, swing or fall or contract into closed position, (*the door s. with a bang*; *lid shuts automatically*; *pimpernels s. in rainy weather*); keep (person, sound, &c.) *out* or *in* by shutting door &c., send (person) *into* or *out of* room &c. & fasten door &c. against him, bar (person) *out from* hope &c.; catch or pinch (finger, dress, &c.) by shutting something on it (*s. his finger into the door-hinge*); bring parts of together (*s. his teeth, a knife,* &c.); *s. down,* push or pull (window-sash &c.) down into closed position, (intr., of mill &c.) cease working; *s. in,* (of hills, houses, sea, &c.) encircle, prevent free prospect or egress from or access to; *s. off,* check flow of (water, gas, &c.) by shutting valve, separate *from* society &c.; *s. out,* exclude (landscape &c.) from view, prevent (possibility &c.); *s. to* adv., close (door &c., or intr. of door &c.) tight; *s. up,* close all doors & windows of or bolt & bar (house; *s. up shop,* cease business for the day or permanently), close (box &c.) securely or decisively or permanently, imprison (person), put (thing) away in box &c., desist (colloq.; esp. *s. up* imperat.), reduce to silence by rebuke or refutation. [OE *scyttan* cogn. w. SHOOT (f. shooting of bolt)]

shu·tter, n., & v.t. In vbl senses of prec.; esp.: one of a set of wooden panels or iron plates, hinged, sliding, folding, or detachable, placed inside or outside glass of window to keep out light or burglars (*put up the ss.,* cease business for the day or permanently); structure of jointed laths or metal slats on rollers serving same purposes; blind of swell-box in organ for regulating loudness; piece that opens & closes lens of photographic camera; hence **shu·tter**LESS a. (Vb) provide with ss., put up ss. of. [-ER[1]]

shu·ttle, n. Weaving-implement shaped like cigar with two pointed ends by which weft-thread is carried or shot across between threads of warp; carrier of lower thread in lock-stitch sewing-machine; *shuttlecock,* cork stuck with feathers & struck to & fro in BATTLEDORE *& s.* [*-cock* prob. f. flying motion]. [OE *scytel* bolt, cogn. w. SHOOT, SHUT, see -LE(1)]

shy[1], a. (*shyer, -est,* rarely *shi-*). (Of beasts, birds, fish, &c.) easily startled, timid, avoiding observation; bashful, coy, uneasy in company; avoiding company *of* person, chary *of doing,* (FIGHT[1] *s. of*); elusive, hard to find, catch, interpret, &c. Hence **shy·**LY[2] adv., **shy·**NESS n. [OE *scéoh*; cf. Du. *schuw*]

shy[2], v.i., & n. Start suddenly aside (*at* object or noise, or fig. *at* proposal &c.) in alarm (usu. of horse, or fig. of person). Hence **shy·**ER[1] n. [f. prec.]

shy[3], v.t. & i., & n., (colloq.). Fling, throw, (stone &c., or abs.); (n.) act of shying (*have a s. at,* try to hit with missile, jeer at, make an attempt to get). [?]

Shy·lock, n. Hard-hearted money-lender. [character in *Merchant of Venice*]

si (sē), n. (mus.). Seventh note of octave. [added perh. c. 1600 to names of hexachord; see GAMUT; perh. f. initials of *Sancte Johannes* in sapphics given under *gamut*]

sī·amang (*or* sē-), n. Kind of gibbon from Sumatra & Malay peninsula. [Malay]

Sīame·se, a., & n. (pl. *-ese*). (Native, language) of Siam; *S. twins,* two S. (d. 1874) joined by cartilaginous band from one's right to other's left side, (fig.) inseparable friends &c. [-ESE]

sib, a. (archaic & Sc.). Related, akin, (*to*). [OE *sib*(*b*), cf. MDu. *sib*(*be*), OHG *sippi*]

Sībē·rian, a. & n. (Inhabitant) of Siberia (*S. dog,* of breed much used for sledging). [-AN]

si·bilant, a. & n. Hissing, sounded with a hiss (esp. of letter or set of letters, as s, sh); hence **si·bil**ANCE, **si·bil**ANCY, nn. (N.) s. letter(s). [f. L *sibilare* hiss (*sibilus* a hissing), -ANT]

si·bilate, v.t. & i. Pronounce with hissing sound. Hence **sibil**A·TION n. [as prec., -ATE[2]]

si·byl, n. One of the women who in ancient times acted at various places (*Cumaean, Erythraean,* &c., *s.*) as mouthpiece of some god, & to whom many collections of oracles & prophecies were attributed, pagan prophetess; old fortune-teller, sorceress, or hag. [f. L f. Gk *Sibulla*]

siby·lline, a. Issuing from an ancient sibyl, oracular, mysteriously prophetic; *the s. books,* collection of oracles belonging to ancient-Roman State & often consulted by magistrates for guidance, (fig., with ref. to story of their acquisition) thing that one refuses & is afterwards glad to get on worse terms. [f. L *Sibyllinus* (prec., -INE[1])]

sic, Latin adv. = so, appended in brackets after a word or expression in a quoted passage as guarantee that it is quoted exactly, though its incorrectness or absurdity would suggest that it was not. Also in the phrr. *s. volo s. jubeo* (such is my will & command) used as **n.** = arbitrary order, *s. vos non vobis* (so ye not for yourselves) used w. ref. to work of which the credit &c. falls to another than the doer.

Sicā·nian, n. & a. Aboriginal inhabitant of Sicily (cf. *Sicel, Siceliot, Sicilian*); (adj.) of the Ss. [f. L *Sicanius* (L f. Gk *Sikanoi* pl.), -AN]

si·ccative, a. & n. (Substance &c.) of drying properties, esp. one mixed with oil-paint to dry it. [f. LL *siccativus* (DESICCATE, -ATIVE)]

sice[1], n. The six on dice. [f. OF *sis* SIX]

sice[2], syce, n. (Anglo-Ind.). Groom. [f. Hind. f. Arab. *sā'is*]

Si·cel, Si·kel, Sicū·lian, nn. & aa. Member of race that immigrated into Sicily perh. c. 11th c. B.C., native as opposed to Greek ancient Sicilian (cf. foll.); (adj.) of the Ss. [f. Gk *Sikeloi* pl., & L *Siculi* pl., -AN]

Sicē·liot, Sik-, n. & a. Ancient-Greek settler in Sicily; (adj.) of the Ss. [f. Gk *Sikeliōtēs* (*Sikelia* Sicily, -OT[2])]

Sici·lian, a. & n. Of Sicily or its inhabitants (*S. Vespers*, massacre of French residents by natives in 1282, with vesper bell as signal); (n.) native of Sicily. [f. L *Sicilia* Sicily + -AN]

sick[1], a. Ill, incapacitated by illness, feeling effects *of* some disease, (*a s. man*; *the S. Man*, Turkish Empire; *s. of a fever*; *the s.*, those who are ill; *be, feel, make, s.* in mod. use, vomit, be disposed or cause to vomit; *turn s.*, feel or make feel as if about to vomit); disordered, perturbed, suffering effects *of*, disgusted, pining *for*, (*am s. at heart*; *s. of love*, lovesick; *makes me s. to think of it*; *is awfully s. at being beaten*; *s. for a sight of home*); surfeited & tired *of* (*s. of flattery, rain, waiting*); (of ship) needing repair (esp. of specified kind, as *nail-s., paint-s.*); *s.*-BAY[3]; *s.-bed*, invalid's bed, invalid state; *s.-call*, military summons on bugle &c. for s. men to attend; *s.-flag*, yellow, indicating presence of disease at quarantine station or on ship; *s. headache*, due to biliousness; *s.-leave*, leave of absence granted for reason of health; *s.-list*, of the s. esp. in regiment, ship, &c. (*on the s.-l.*, laid up); *s.-room*, occupied by s. person, or kept ready for the s. Hence **si·ck**ISH[1](2) a. [OE *sēoc*, cf. Du. *ziek*, G *siech*]

sick[2], v.t. Set upon (usu. in imperat. *s. him!* &c. urging dog to worry rat &c.). [var. of SEEK]

si·cken, v.i. & t. Begin to be ill, show symptoms of illness (*child is sickening for something*); feel nausea or disgust *at, to see, &c.*; affect with inclination to vomit, loathing, or disgust (*a sickening sight*) or with weariness or despair *of* (*was sickened of trying to make peace*), whence **si·cken**ER[1](2) n., **si·ckening**LY[2] adv. [-EN[6]]

si·ckle, n. Reaping-hook, short-handled semicircular-bladed implement now chiefly used for lopping & trimming, formerly for cutting corn; *the* constellation Leo; *sicklebill*, kinds of bird with s.-shaped bill; *s.-feather*, one of long middle feathers of cock's tail; *s.-wort*, the plant Heal-all. [OE *sicol*, cf. Du. *sikkel*, G *sichel*, perh. f. L *secula* (*secare* cut)]

si·ckly, a., & v.t. Apt to be ill, chronically ailing, of weak health; suggesting sickness, as of sick person, languid, faint, pale, (*s. look, smile, complexion*); causing ill health, inducing or connected with nausea, (*s. climate, smell, taste*); mawkish, weakly sentimental; (v.t.) cover *over* or *o'er* with a s. hue (w. ref. to *Haml.* III. i. 85). Hence **si·ckli**NESS n. [-LY[1]]

si·ckness, n. Being ill, disease; a disease (FALL[1]*ing s.*; *sleeping s.*, fatal African disease, *morbus dormitivus*, marked by somnolence & nerve-paralysis, caused by certain trypanosomes introduced by kinds of tsetse; *sleepy s.*, a world-wide recently identified disease, epidemic encephalitis or *encephalitis lethargica*, not yet traced to a parasitic cause, but distinct from sleeping s., though lethargy is a mark of both); vomiting or inclination to vomit. [-NESS]

Siculian. See SICEL.

Si·culo-, comb. form of L *Siculi* Sicilians, as *-Arabian*, Arabian as modified in Sicily. [-O-]

side[1], n. One of the flat(tish) surfaces bounding an object (*cube has six ss.*), esp. a more or less vertical outer or inner surface (*s. of house, cave, mountain, &c.*; so perh. COUNTRY-*s.*); such surface as distinguished from top & bottom, or front & back, or ends (*four*, or *two*, *ss. of box*; *two ss. of house*); either surface of thing regarded as having only two (*two ss. of sheet of paper, board, &c.*; *sent him six ss. of argument*, pages of notepaper so filled; *the* INSIDE *&* OUTSIDE *of a bowl*; *right, wrong, s. of cloth* &c., surface meant, not meant, to be visible; BACK[1]*side*; SHADY, SEAMY, SILVER[1], *s.*); (Math.) bounding line of superficial figure (*opposite ss. of a parallelogram*); part of person or animal that is on his or its right or left, esp. that of it which extends from armpit to hip or from foreleg to hindleg (*s. of mutton, bacon*, &c., this part of carcass; BLIND[1] *s.*; *s. by s.*, standing close together, esp. for mutual support; *shake* one's *ss.*, laugh heartily; *s.-splitting*, causing violent laughter, amusing); part of object turned in same direction as observer's right or left & not directly towards or away from him, or turned in specified direction (*right, left, s.*; *debit, credit, s.*, in account book; *epistle, gospel, s.*, south, north, end of altar; DECANI, CANTORIS, *s.*; *the north, landward, s.*); part or region near margin and remote from centre or axis of thing, subordinate or less essential or more or less detached part, (*s. of room, road, table*, &c.), (attrib.) subordinate (*s. issue*, point that distracts attention; *s. line*, work &c. carried on apart from one's main work); region external but contiguous to, specified direction with relation to, person or thing (*on one s.*, aside; *look on all ss.*; *came from all ss.* or *every s.*; *standing at my s.*; *on the north s. of*); partial aspect of thing, aspect differing from or opposed to other aspects (*study all ss. of the question*; *has many ss. to his character*; *the s. of the moon visible to us*); (cause represented by, position in company with) one of two sets of opponents in war, politics, games, &c. (*the Lord is on my s.*; *there is much to be said, there are faults, on both ss.*; *take ss.*, decide to espouse one or other cause; *join the winning s.*; ON[1], OFF, *s.*; *Cambridge has a strong s.*, team for cricket, football, &c.); position nearer or farther than, right or left of, dividing line (*on this s. of*, or *on this s., the Alps*; *on this s. the grave*, in life; *on the right, wrong, s. of forty*, below, above, 40 years of age; *on the wrong s. of the door*, shut out; *on the wrong s. of the* BLANKET[1]); line of descent through father, or mother (*well descended on the mother's* or *maternal s.*; DISTAFF or *spindle*, SPEAR, *s.*); (Billiards) spinning motion given to ball by striking it on s.; (slang) assumption of superiority, swagger, (*puts on, has too much, s.*), whence **si·dy**[2] a. *S.-arms*, swords or bayonets; *si·deboard*, table or flat-topped chest at s. of dining-room for supporting and containing dishes, decanters, &c.; *si·de-bone*, (in carving fowls) either small forked bone under wing; *s.-car* = JAUNT*ing-car*, (also) car for passenger(s) attachable to s. of motor-cycle; *s.-chapel*, in aisle or at side of church; *s.-dish*, extra dish often of elaborate kind at dinner &c.; *s.-drum*, small double-headed drum in military band hung at drummer's s.; *si·delight*, light from s., (fig.) incidental illustration &c., (Naut.) red port or green starboard light on ship under way; *s.-note*, marginal note; *s.-saddle*, for rider, usu. woman, with both feet on same s. of horse; *s.-seat* in vehicle &c., in which occupant has back against s. of vehicle; *s.-show*, minor show attached to principal one; *s.-slip*, skid v. & n., (Aeron.) move (vb) or motion broadside on instead of forward, also shoot of tree & (fig.) illegitimate child, also (theatr.) division at s. of stage for working scenery; *si·desman*, deputy churchwarden; *s.-step*, step taken sideways, step for getting in & out of carriage &c.; *s.-stroke*, stroke towards or from a s., incidental action, kinds of swimming action opp. breast-stroke; *s.-track*, siding, (v.t.) turn into siding, shunt, postpone treatment or consideration of, (chiefly U.S.); *s.-view*, view obtained sideways, profile; *s.-walk*, path at s. of road for foot-passengers (chiefly U.S.); *s.-wind*, wind from a s., indirect agency or influence. Hence **-sid**ED[2] a., **-si·ded**LY[2] adv., **-si·ded**NESS n., **si·de**LESS a. [OE *side*, cf. Du. *zijde*, G *seite*, & prob. OE *sīd* spacious]

side[2], v.i. Take part, be on same s., *with* disputant &c. [f. prec.]

si·delong, adv. & a. Inclining to one side, oblique(ly), (*move s.*; *a s. glance*). [-LONG]

sīdēr·ĕal, a. Of the constellations or the fixed stars (*s. day*, time between successive meridional transits of star, esp. of first point in Aries, about 4′ shorter than solar day; *s. year*, time in which earth makes one complete revolution round sun, longer than tropical year by difference due to precession; *s. time*, measured by apparent diurnal motion of stars). [f. L *sidereus* (*sidus -eris* star), -AL]

sĭdero·graphy, n. A process of engraving on steel. [f. Gk *sidēros* iron, -GRAPHY]

si·deward(s), adv. & a. Lateral(ly), to or from a side, (*moved s.*; *s. motion*). [-WARD(S)]

si·deways, adv. & a. = prec. [-WAYS]

sī·ding, n. Short track by side of railway line & opening into it at one end or both for shunting purposes. [-ING[1]]

sī·dle, v.i. Walk obliquely, esp. in timid or cringing manner (often *along, up*). [back formation f. obs. *sideling* (now SIDELONG)]

Sīdō·nian, a. & n. (Inhabitant) of Sidon. [f. L f. Gk *Sidōnios* (*Sidōn*), -AN]

siege (sēj), n., & v.t. Operations of encamped attacking force to take or compel surrender of fortified place, period during which these last, besieging or being besieged, (often fig.; *push the s.*, continue it vigorously; *raise the s. of*, abandon attempt to take; *lay s. to*, begin besieging; *s. lasted 100 days*; *stood a long s.*, before or without surrendering); persistent attempt to force or persuade reluctant person to do something; *s.-basket*, gabion; *s.-gun*, used in ss., too heavy for field use; *s.-train*, artillery & other appliances for besieging; *s.-works*, trenches, shelters, &c., of besiegers; (vb; archaic) besiege. [OF, orig. = seat, ult. f. L *sedes*]

Siene·se, -nnese, (sēĕ-), a., & n. (pl. *-ese*). (Inhabitant) of Sienna (*S. school*, of 13th–14th-c. painters). [-ESE]

sie·nna, n. Ochrous earth used raw or burnt as pigment of brownish-yellow (*raw s.*) or reddish-brown (*burnt s.*) colour. [f. It. (*terra di*) *Siena* (earth of) Sienna]

siĕ·rra, n. Long jagged mountain-chain; Spanish mackerel. [Sp., f. L *serra* saw]

sie·sta, n. Mid-day nap or rest in hot countries. [Sp., f. L *sexta* (*hora*) sixth hour]

sieve (sĭv), n., & v.t. Utensil for separating finer from coarser particles by letting finer pass when shaken through holes too small for coarser, usu. a shallow wooden cylinder with cross wires or hairs stretched across bottom; coarsely plaited basket often used as measure; person who cannot keep secrets; (vb) put through, sift with, s. [OE *sife*, cf. Du. *zeef*, G *sieb*]

siffleur (F), n. (fem. *-euse*). Whistling artiste.

sift, v.t. & i. Separate into finer & coarser parts with sieve, separate (finer parts) *from* material or its coarser parts or *out*, sprinkle (sugar &c.) from perforated spoon &c.; closely examine details of (evidence, facts, &c.) with regard to credibility or authenticity or relevance, analyse character of; (of snow, light, &c.) fall as from sieve. Hence **(-)sift**ER[1](1, 2) n. [OE *siftan* (*sife* SIEVE)]

sigh (sī), v.i. & t., & n. Draw deep audible breath expressive of sadness, weariness, aspiration, relief from tension, cessation of effort, &c.; yearn *for* (person or thing desired or lost); utter or express with ss. (usu. *out*); (of wind &c.) make sound like sighing; hence **sigh·ing**LY[2] adv. (N.) act of, sound made in, sighing (*a s. of relief*). [ME *sihen* prob. f. OE *sican*]

sight[1] (sīt), n. Faculty of vision (*long, short* or *near, s.*, requiring objects to be unusually far, near, for clear definition; *short s.* fig., lack of discernment or foresight; *has good, bad, s.*; *know by s.*, be familiar with appearance only of; *loss of s.*, becoming blind; *second s.*, power of internal vision by which future or distant occurrences are presented), whence **-sight**ED[2] a., **-sigh·ted**LY[2] adv., **-sigh·ted**NESS n.; seeing or being seen, way of looking at or considering thing, (*catch, lose, s. of*, begin, cease, to see; *have lost s. of Jones*, no longer know his movements &c.; *get a s. of*, manage to see; *take a s.* (*of, at*) slang, cock a snook; *at, on, s.*, as soon as person or thing has been seen; *plays music at s.*, without preliminary study or practice of piece; *payable at s.*, of draft &c.; *at first s.*, prima facie; *the s. of her distress unmanned him*; *she found favour in his s.*; *do what is right in* one's *own s.*); range or unobstructed space within which person &c. can see or object be seen (*is in, out of, s.*, visible, not visible; HEAVE[1] *in s.*; *the millennium is in s.*, clearly near at hand; *put out of s.*, hide, ignore; *came in s. of the fort*, so as to see it or be seen from it; *out of s. out of mind*, we forget the absent; *out of my s.!*, rhetorical order to depart); thing seen, visible, or worth seeing, display, show, spectacle, (*a sad s. awaited us*; *a s. for sore eyes*, person or thing one is glad to see, esp. welcome visitor; *went to see the ss.*, noteworthy features of town &c., whence **sigh·tsē**ER[1], **sigh·tsee**ING[1], nn.; *the daffodils were a s. to see* or *a s.*; *his face is a perfect s.*, disfigured with wounds &c.; *make a s. of* oneself, dress in bizarre fashion &c.); (colloq.) great quantity (*will cost a s. of money*; *is a long s. better*); (kinds of device for assisting) precise aim with gun or observation with optical instrument (*forgot to put up the leaf of his back s.*, in rifle-shooting; *took a careful s. before firing*; *the ss. of, a s. with, quadrant* or *compass*); *sigh·tworthy*, worth seeing. [OE *gesihth* (Y-, SEE, -TH[1]), cf. G *sicht*]

sight[2], v.t. Get s. of, esp. by coming near (*s. land, game*); take observation of (star &c.) with instrument; provide (gun, quadrant, &c.) with ss.; adjust ss. of (*sighting shot*, experimental one to guide rifleman &c. in this); aim (gun &c.) with ss. [f. prec.]

sigh·tless, a. Blind; (poet.) invisible. [-LESS]

sigh·tly, a. Not unsightly. Hence **sigh·t**LINESS n. [-LY[1]]

si·gillate, a. (Of pottery) with impressed patterns; (Bot.) having seal-like marks. [f. LL *sigillatus* (*sigillum* seal dim. of SIGN*um*, -ATE[2])]

si·gma, n. Greek letter (Σ or C, ς or σ) corresponding to s. [Gk, perh. f. *sizō* hiss, -M]

si·gmate[1], a. Sigma-shaped; S-shaped. [-ATE[2]]

si·gmate[2], v.t. Add sigma or s to. Hence **sigm**A·TION n. [-ATE[3]]

sigmă·tic, a. Formed with sigma (esp. *s. aorist*). [SIGMA *-atos*, -IC]

si·gmoid, a. & n. (Chiefly anat.) curved like the uncial sigma (C), or (now usu.) like S; (n.) reversed or inverted curve. [-OID]

sign[1] (sīn), n. Mark traced on surface &c. (esp. *the s. of the cross*, made by Christian priests in blessing or laymen in reverence with finger on forehead or breast; *s. manual*, signature written with person's own hand); written mark conventionally used for word or phrase, symbol, thing used as representation of something, (*positive* or *plus s.*, +; *negative* or *minus s.*, —; *words are the ss. of ideas*; *a sacrament is an outward & visible s. of an inward & spiritual grace*); (thing serving as) presumptive evidence or indication or suggestion or symptom *of* or *that*, distinctive mark, token, guarantee, password, miracle evidencing supernatural power, portent, (*violence is a s. of weakness* or *that one is weak*; *shows all the ss. of decay*; *gave earth & water in s. of submission*; *by this s. ye shall know them*; *did ss. & wonders*; *s. & countersign*, secret sentences &c. by which confederates recognize each other; *ss. of the times*, things showing the tendency of affairs); (often *signboard*) fanciful device usu. painted on a board displayed formerly by traders of any sort & still by many taverns & some barbers &c. as advertisement of their business (*at the s. of the White Hart* &c. archaic, formerly used as address); natural or conventional motion or gesture used instead of words to convey information & esp. order or request (*gave him a s. to withdraw*; *deaf-&-dumb ss.*, those used in finger-talk; *make no s.*, seem unconscious, not protest, &c.); any of twelve divisions of ZODIAC named from constellations formerly situated in them; *s.-painter*, of sign-boards, shop-front inscriptions, &c.; *sig·npost*, at cross-roads &c. with names of places on each road. [f. F *signe* f. L *signum*]

sign², v.t. & i. Mark with s. (esp. *s. infant* &c. *with the s. of the cross* in baptism); acknowledge or guarantee (letter, deed, picture, book, article, petition, &c., or abs.) as one's own production or as having one's authority or consent by affixing or having affixed one's name or initials or recognized mark (*the will had never been signed*; *a signed masterpiece of Turner's*; *signed as usual with a dicky-bird*; *does not s. his contributions to the press*; *nothing shall induce me to s.*), whence **sig·n**ABLE a.; write (one's name) as signature; convey (right, property, &c.) *away* by signing deed &c.; take, acknowledge being taken, *on* for some employment to which employee binds himself by signature; communicate by gesture (*s. assent*), give order or make request by gesture *to* person *to* do (*signed to me to come*). [f. L *signare* (*signum*, see prec.)]

si·gnal¹, a. Remarkably good or bad, conspicuous, noteworthy, exemplary, condign, (*s. victory, defeat, reward, punishment, virtue, example*). Hence **si·gnal**LY² adv. [f. L *signum* SIGN¹, -AL)]

si·gnal², n., & v.t. & i. (-ll-). Preconcerted or intelligible sign conveying information or direction esp. to person(s) at a distance, message made up of such signs, (*the s. was to be the dropping of a handkerchief*; *ss. are made by day with flags & by night with lights*; *gave the s. for advance*; FOG¹-*s.*; *s. of distress*, appeal for help, esp. from ship made by firing guns; *storm-s.*, cone &c. hoisted at meteorological station; *code of ss.*, *s.-book*, body of ss. arranged for sending complicated messages esp. in naval & mil. use); immediate occasion *for* some general movement (*the earthquake was the s. for an outbreak of the primitive instincts*); *s.-box*, hut on railway with signalling-apparatus; *s.-man*, signaller. (Vb) make signal(s), make signal(s) to, transmit (order, information) by s., announce (event, *that*) by s., direct (person *to* do) by s.; hence **si·gnall**ER¹ n. [F, f. med. L *signale* (orig. neut. adj. as prec.)]

si·gnalize, v.t. Make noteworthy or remarkable, lend distinction or lustre to, (*his accession was signalized by an amnesty*). [SIGNAL¹, -IZE]

si·gnatory, a. & n. (Party, esp. State) that has signed an agreement esp. a treaty (*the ss.* or *s. powers to the treaty of Berlin*). [f. L *signatorius* of sealing (*signare* mark, -TORY)]

si·gnature (-tsher, -tūr), n. (Archaic) significant appearance or mark (*has the s. of passion, of early death, in his face*; *herb's yellow flowers are a s. indicating that it will cure jaundice*); person's name or initials or mark used in SIGN²ing; letter or figure placed by printer at foot of first page of each sheet of book as guide in making up for binding, such sheet after folding; (Mus.) signs placed at beginning of staff to indicate key & rhythm, consisting of clef, key-s. or sharps & flats, & rhythm-s. or numerals stating number & length of beats in measure. [F, f. med. L *signatura* (prec., -URE)]

si·gnet, n. Private seal for use instead of or with signature as authentication (*the s.*, royal seal formerly used for special purposes; WRITER *to the s.*); *s.-ring*, finger-ring with seal set in it. [OF (SIGN¹, -ET¹)]

signi·ficance, n. Being significant, expressiveness, (*there is no s. in his eyes*; *with a look of deep s.*); covert or real import, what is meant to be or may be inferred, (*those were the words, but what is their s.?*); importance, noteworthiness, (*what he thinks about it is of no s.*). [OF, f. L *significantia* (SIGNIFY, -ANCE)]

signi·ficant, a. Having a meaning (*-kin is a s. termination*); expressive, suggestive, with pregnant or secret sense, inviting attention esp. from part only of company; noteworthy, of considerable amount or effect or importance, not insignificant or negligible, (usu. in negative contexts, as *the only s. event was* —). Hence **signi·ficant**LY² adv. [as SIGNIFY, -ANT]

significa·tion, n. Act of signifying (rare); exact meaning or sense (usu. *of* something, esp. of a word or phrase). [OF, f. L *significationem* (SIGNIFY, -ATION)]

signi·ficātive, a. Offering signs or presumptive evidence *of*. [OF (*-if*, *-ive*), see foll., -ATIVE]

si·gnifȳ, v.t. & i. Be a sign or indication or presage of (*a long upper lip signifies obstinacy*; *a halo signifies rain*); mean, have as meaning, (*D.D. signifies doctor of divinity*); communicate, make known, (*he signified his reluctance, that he could not consent*); be of importance, matter, (esp. in negative contexts, as *it does not s.*). [f. F *signifier* f. L *significare* (SIGN¹, -FY)]

Signior. See GRAND.

Si·gnor, Signor·a, Signori·na (-ēna), (sēny-), nn. (pl. *-ri* pr. -rē, *-re* pr. -rā, *-ne* pr. -nā). Titles used of or to Italians corresponding to Sir & Mr, Madam & Mrs, young lady & Miss. [It.]

Sikh (sĭk, sēk), n. Member of Hindu community founded as monotheistic sect c. 1500 in Punjab & after achieving independence annexed 1849 to British India. [Hind., = disciple]

sī·lage (-ĭj), n., & v.t. =ENSILAGE; (vb) put into silo. [SILO, -AGE]

sī·lence, n., & v.t. Abstinence from speech or noise, being silent, taciturnity, non-betrayal of secret &c., fact of not mentioning a thing, (*the s. of Scripture on the subject*; *s. gives consent*; *keep, break, s.*, abstain from speaking, speak; *put to s.*, esp. refute in argument); absence of sound, stillness, (*in s.*, without speech or other sound); oblivion, state of not being mentioned, (*have passed into s.*); *S.!* (order to cease from speech or noise). (Vb) make silent by force, superior argument, &c. (*silenced the enemy's batteries, the best debaters in the House, the voice of conscience*). Hence **si·lencER**[1] n., kinds of device for rendering (comparatively) noiseless the escape of gas from gun, oil-engine, &c., by means of retarding spiral or plates. [vb f. n., OF, f. L *silentium* (*silēre* be silent)]

sī·lent, a. Not speaking, not uttering or making or accompanied by any sound, (*s. letter*, one written but not pronounced, e.g. *b* in *doubt*; *s. partner*, with no voice in management of business; *the s. system* in prisons, by which prisoners are never allowed to speak); taciturn, speaking little; saying nothing on some subject (*history is s. upon it*). Hence **si·lentLY**[2] adv. [f. L *silēre* be silent, -ENT]

Sīlē·nus, n. Rollicking drunken bloated old man. [L, f. Gk *Seilēnos* name of one of Bacchus's attendants]

silē·sia (-sha), n. Kinds of thin cloth used for blinds & dress-linings. [orig. made in Silesia]

silhouette (sĭlōōĕ·t), n., & v.t. Portrait of person in profile showing outline only, all inside the outline being usu. black on white ground or cut out in paper; appearance of person or object as seen against light so that outline only is distinguishable (*in s.*, so seen or placed); (vb) represent or (usu. pass.) exhibit in s. [named after French minister of finance 1759 w. ref. to his parsimony]

si·lica, n. Silicon dioxide, a hard white or colourless widely distributed mineral present in many precious & other stones & esp. in quartz & sand. Hence **sili·cIC**, **silici·FEROUS**, **sili·ciOUS** or **sili·CEOUS** (-shus), aa., **si·licATE**[1](3) n., **silici-**, **silico-**, comb. forms. [f. L *silex -icis* flint]

si·licated, a. Coated, mixed, combined, or impregnated, with silica. [prec., -ATE[3], -ED[1]]

sili·cif̄y, v.t. & i. Impregnate with silica, turn (t. & i.) into silica, petrify. Hence **sili·cIFICA·TION** n. [prec., -FY]

si·licon, n. A non-metallic element found only in combination. [as SILICA]

si·liqua (pl. *-ae*), **sili·que** (-ēk), n. Pod of plants of mustard family. Hence **si·liquOSE**[1], **si·liquOUS**, (-kw-), aa. [L]

silk, n. Fine soft thread produced in making cocoon by *silk-worm* or larva of kinds of moth feeding esp. on mulberry leaves (*spun s.*, see SPIN; *thrown s.*, ORGANZINE); similar thread spun by some spiders &c. or (*artificial s.*) drawn by various processes out of viscid matter; cloth woven of s. (*take s.*, become K.C. or Q.C. & exchange stuff for s. gown), (pl.) kinds, or garments made, of such cloth; *S-*, = K.C. or Q.C.; peculiar lustre seen in some sapphires & rubies; (attrib., now usu. preferred to *silken*) made of s. (*s. stockings* &c.; *make a s. purse out of a sow's ear*, get better results from a person than his qualities admit of); *s.-fowl*, breed with silky plumage; *s.-gland*, secreting the substance produced as s.; *s.-reel, -winder*, for unwinding s. from cocoon & winding it as thread. [OE *seolc* f. L *sericum* neut. adj. (L f. Gk *Sēres* prob. the Chinese, -IC)]

si·lken, a. Made of silk (archaic, poet.); clad in silk; soft, lustrous, as silk; (of manner &c.) suave, insinuating. [-EN[5]]

si·lky, a. Like silk in smoothness, softness, fineness, or lustre (*s. manner* &c., suave). Hence **si·lkiNESS** n. [-Y[2]]

sill, n. Shelf or slab of stone or wood at foot of door or esp. window. [OE *syll(e)*, cf. ON *syll*, *svill*, Da. *syld*, G *schwelle*]

si·llabub, n. Dish made of cream or milk mixed with wine &c. into soft curd & sometimes whipped or solidified with gelatine. [also *sillibouk* (& *merribowk*), perh. f. SILLY (& *merry*) + dial. *bouk* belly]

si·ller, n. (Sc.). Silver; money. [=SILVER]

Si·llery, n. Kinds of sparkling & still champagne. [place-name]

si·lly, a. & n. Innocent, simple, helpless, (archaic); foolish, weak-minded, imprudent, unwise, imbecile; (n., chiefly in childish talk) s. person (*don't be a s.*); *the s. season*, August & September as the season when newspapers start general discussions for lack of news; *s. point, short leg* (placed close up to batsman). Hence **si·lliLY**[2] adv., **si·lliNESS** n. [earlier sense *fortunate*; OE *sǣlig*, cf. Du. *zalig*, G *selig*, blessed]

sī·lo, n., & v.t. Pit or airtight structure in which green crops are pressed & kept for fodder, undergoing fermentation; (vb) make ensilage of. [Sp., f. L f. Gk *siros*]

silt, n., & v.t. & i. Sediment deposited by water in channel, harbour, &c.; (vb) choke or be choked with s. (usu. *up*; *the passage has or is silted up*). [cf. Du. *zult*, Da. *sylt*, salt marsh, G *sülze* brine; cogn. w. SALT]

Silūr·ian, a. & n. Of the Silures, a people of ancient Britain; (of) a series of rocks forming the lowest subdivision of the Palaeozoic & underlying the Devonian, named as first investigated in district of the Silures. [f. L *Silures*, -IAN]

si·lvan, sy-, a. Of the, having, woods; rural. [f. L *silvanus* (*silva* wood, -AN)]

si·lver[1], n. A white lustrous precious metal used chiefly with alloy of harder metals for coin, plate, & ornaments, & in chem. combinations for photography &c. (*German s.*, *nickel s.*, &c., white alloys used as substitutes for s. in table articles &c., or for coating with s.; *fulminating s.*, an explosive powder; OXIDIZED *s.*); s. coins (*have you any s. on you?*); s. vessels or implements or articles of furniture (*melted down all his s. in the king's service*); any of the salts of s. used in sensitizing photographic paper; (attrib.; usu. now preferred to **si·lvern** a. archaic see -EN[5]) made of s., second-best, (*the s. age*, see BRAZEN[1], also spec. the period of Latin literature that followed the Augustan; so *s. Latin*; *a s. cup*; *speech is s.* or *silvern, but silence is golden*, better be silent than speak), (as substitute for **si·lvery**[2] a., whence **si·lveri**NESS n.) resembling s. in whiteness, lustre, ringing sound, &c. (*s. hair*, white & lustrous; *has a s.* or *silvery tone*; *has a s. tongue*, is eloquent, whence **silver-tongu**ED[2] a.; *every cloud has a s. lining*, misfortune has its consolations); *s.-bath*, (tray for holding) solution of s. nitrate used for sensitizing; *s. fir*, kind with two s. lines on under side of leaves; *s.-fish*, kinds of fish, esp. a colourless variety of gold-fish, (also) silvery insect found in books & mouldy places; *s.* FOIL[1]; *s. fox*, variety of common fox with black grey-tipped fur; *s. gilt*, s. gilded over, also imitation gilding of yellow lacquer over s. leaf; *s.-grey*, lustrous grey; *s.* LEAF; *s. paper*, fine white tissue-paper, (loosely) tin foil; *s. plate*, vessels, spoons, &c., of s.; *s. point*, (process of sketching on prepared paper with) s.-pointed style (*a head in s. p.*); *s. print*, photographic positive on paper sensitized by a salt of s.; *s. sand*, fine kind used in gardening; *s. side*, best side of round of beef; *si·lversmith*, worker in s., manufacturer of s. articles; *s. solder*, solder for joining s.; *s. standard*, use of s. money alone as full legal tender; *s.-stick*, field-officer of Life-guards on palace duty; *s. streak, the* English channel; *s.-top*, a disease in grasses; *s.-weed*, yellow-flowered roadside plant with silvery lower leaf-surfaces. [OE *seolfor*, cf. Du. *zilver*, G *silber*, etym. dub.]

si·lver[2], v.t. & i. Coat or plate with s.; provide (mirror-glass) with backing of tin foil, mercury, &c.; (of moon or white light) give silvery appearance to; (with *hair* as obj. or subj.) turn (t. & i.) grey or white. [f. prec.]

sĭ·mian, a. & n. (Zool.) (of) one of the *Simiidae* or anthropoid apes; (Gen.) ape(-like), monkey(-like). So **si·mi**OID a. [f. L *simia* ape, -AN]

si·milar, a. & n. Like, alike, having mutual resemblance or resemblance *to*, of the same kind; (Geom.) shaped alike; hence or cogn. **similă·r**ITY n., **si·milar**LY[2] adv. (N.) thing resembling another, (pl.) s. things. [f. F *similaire* (L *similis* like, -AR[1])]

sĭ·milĕ, n. The introduction, esp. in poetry or poetical style, ostensibly for explanatory or illustrative purposes but often in fact for ornament only, of an object or scene or action with which the one in hand is professedly compared & usu. connected by a comparative conjunction such as *as* (*a style rich in s. & metaphor*); a comparison of this kind (*the s. of the dome of many-coloured glass*; cf. METAPHOR, ALLEGORY, PARABLE). [f. L neut. of *similis* like]

simĭ·litude, n. Likeness, guise, outward appearance, (*in, assume, the s. of*); simile, comparison, (*talks in ss.*); counterpart, facsimile, (rare; *is the very s. of*). [OF, f. L *similitudo* (prec., -TUDE)]

si·milize, v.i. & t. Use simile; illustrate by simile(s). [SIMILE, -IZE]

si·mmer, v.i. & t., & n. Be, keep (trans.), on the point of boiling, boil (t. & i.) very gently; (fig.) be in a state of suppressed anger, indignation, or laughter; (n.) simmering state (esp. *at a* or *on the s.*). [earlier *simper*, prob. imit.]

si·mnel-cake, n. Rich ornamental boiled cake made esp. at Easter, Christmas, and Mid Lent. [f. OF *simenel* f. L *simila* finest flour, cf. Gk *semidalis*]

sīmō·niac, n. Person guilty of simony. [f. OF *simoniaque* (SIMONY, -AC)]

simonī·acal, a. Guilty, of the nature, of simony. Hence **simoni·acal**LY[2] adv. [-AL]

Sī·mon Pure, n. The real or genuine person or article (usu. *the real S.P.*). [character in Centlivre's *Bold Stroke for a Wife*]

sĭ·mony, n. Buying or selling of ecclesiastical preferment. [OF *simonie* f. med. L *simonia* f. *Simon* (*Magnus*), see *Acts* viii. 18, -Y[1]]

sĭmoo·m, n. Hot dry suffocating dust-laden wind moving in straight narrow track and passing in a few minutes, chiefly in Arabian desert. [f. Arab. *semūm* (*samm* to poison)]

si·mper, v.i. & t., & n. Smile affectedly, smirk; express by or with simpering (*simpered consent*); hence **si·mpering**LY[2] adv., **si·mper**ER[1] n. (N.) affected smile. [cf. Da. & Norw. *semper*, G *zimp(f)er*, delicate, affected]

si·mple, a. & n. Not compound, consisting of one element, all of one kind, involving only one operation or power, not divided into parts, not analysable, (*s. sentence*, without subordinate clauses; *s.* INTEREST[1]; *a s. quantity*, expressible by single number; *induction by s. enumeration*, based merely on random examples without selection or tests; *s. addition*, of numbers of one denomination; *s. equation*, not involving the second or any higher power of unknown quantity, cf. QUADRATIC; *s. machine*, any of the MECHANICAL powers; *s. leaf*, of one blade; *s. pistil*, of one carpel; *s. eye* of insect, OCELLUS; *s. fracture*, breaking of bone only, cf. COMPOUND²; *s. idea*, that cannot be analysed into elements); not complicated or elaborate or adorned or involved or highly developed (*the style is s. and devoid of ornament*; *s. diet*; *the s. life*, practice of doing without servants & luxuries, attempt to return to more primitive conditions; *the greatest works of art are the simplest*; *in s. beauty*, unadorned; *a s. form of pump*; *s. forms of life*, creatures low in scale of evolution); absolute, unqualified, mere, neither more nor less than, just, (*to give an infant alcohol is s. murder* or *madness*; *his s. word is as good as an oath*; *pretends to be no more than a s. gentleman*; FEE *s.*); plain in appearance or manner, unaffected, unsophisticated, ingenuous, natural, artless, (*a s. person*; *s. attire*; *a s. heart* or *mind*, whence **simple-heart**ED², **simple-mind**ED², aa., **simple-mi·nded**NESS n.); foolish, ignorant, inexperienced, (*am not so s. as to suppose*); easily understood or done, presenting no difficulty, (*gave a s. explanation*; *the problem is very s.*; *can be cured by a s. device*); of low rank, humble, insignificant, trifling, (GENTLE *& s.*; *her s. efforts to please*); hence or cogn. **si·mple**NESS (rare), **simpli·**CITY, nn., **si·mp**LY² adv. (N.) a herb used medicinally, the medicine made from it; *be cut for the ss.*, undergo operation for cure of folly. [OF, f. L *simplic-* st. of *simplex* onefold (*sim-* one-, cf. *semel* once, *simul* at once, *singuli* one by one, + *-plic-*, cf. *plicare* to fold)]

si·mpleton, n. Foolish, gullible, or half-witted person. [fancy noun f. prec.]

simplĭ·citer, adv. Absolutely, universally, without limitation, not relatively or in certain respects only (cf. SECUNDUM *quid*). [L]

simplifȳ, v.t. Make simple, make easy to do or understand. So **simpli**FICA·TION n. [f. L *simplus* simple, -FY]

si·mplism, n. Affected simplicity. [-ISM]

simūlā·crum, n. (pl. *-cra*). Image of something; shadowy likeness, deceptive substitute, mere pretence. [L (SIMULATE)]

si·mūlant, a. Having the appearance *of* (esp. biol., as *stamens s. of petals*). [foll., -ANT]

si·mūlate, v.t. Feign, pretend to have or feel, put on, (*s. virtue, indignation*, &c.); pretend to be, act like, resemble, wear the guise of, mimic, (of word) take or have an altered form suggested by (word wrongly taken for its source), (*actor simulates king* &c.; *chameleon simulates its surroundings*; amuck, *for* amok, *simulates the English* muck). So **simul**A·TION n. [f. L *simulare* (*similis* like), -ATE³]

simultā·neous, a. Occurring or operating at the same time (*with*). Hence **simu·ltanē**·ITY, **simulta·neous**NESS, nn., **simulta·neous**LY² adv. [f. L *simul* together, -ANEOUS, perh. after L *momentaneous* f. *momentum*]

simur·g, n. Monstrous bird of Persian myth. [f. Pers. *sīmurgh*]

sin, n., & v.i. Transgression, *a* transgression, against divine law or principles of morality (ORIGINAL *s.*; *living in open s.*; *deadly* or *mortal s.*, such as kills the soul or is fatal to salvation; *the seven deadly ss.*, pride, covetousness, lust, anger, gluttony, envy, sloth; one's *besetting s.*, to which one is especially tempted; *for my ss.* joc., as a judgement for something or other; *the unpardonable s.*, that described *Matt.* xii. 31–2; *man of s.* archaic or joc., reprobate, also Antichrist; *like s.* adv. slang, vehemently); offence *against* good taste, propriety, &c.; *s.-offering*, sacrifice &c. in expiation of s.; hence **si·n**FUL, **si·n**LESS, aa., **si·nful**LY², **si·nless**LY², advv., **si·nful**NESS, **si·nless**NESS, nn. (Vb) commit s.; offend *against* (*more sinned against than sinning, King Lear* III. ii. 60, often of victim of seduction); *s.* one's *mercies*, be ungrateful for good luck; hence **si·nn**ER¹ n. (often joc., as *you young -er*; *as I am a -er*, form of asseveration). [vb f. n., OE *synn*, cf. Du. *zonde*, G *sünde*; perh. cogn. w. L *sons sontis* guilty]

Sīnaĭ·tic (-*na*-), a. Of Mount Sinai or the peninsula of Sinai. [f. mod. L *Sinaiticus*]

si·napism, n. Mustard plaster. [f. F *sinapisme* f. L f. Gk *sinapismos* (*sinapizō* cover with *sinapi* mustard)]

since, adv., prep., & conj. After specified or implied past time, throughout (usu. *ever s.*) or at some or any point in the period between such time & that which is present or being dealt with, (*has* or *had been healthy ever s.*; *then more flourishing than ever before or s.*; *has s. been cut down*; *have* or *had not seen him s.*); ago (*happened many years s.*; *how long s. is it?*; *saw him not long s.*). (Prep.) after (specified past time or event), through or in period between time present or being dealt with & (such time), (*has* or *had been going on, has happened, s. 1900* or *Christmas*; *have eaten nothing s. yesterday*; *s. seeing you I have* or *had heard* —). (Conj.) from the past time when, through or in the period between time present or being dealt with & that when (*what have you done s. we met?*; *nothing has happened, there had been a disturbance, s. we parted*); seeing that, inasmuch as, (*s. that is so, there is no more to be said*); (ellipt.) as being (*a more dangerous, s. unknown, foe*). [earlier *sithence* f. OE *siththan* after that (*sith* after, cf. G *seit, thon* instr. case of demonst. pron.) + -ES]

sincere·, a. Free from pretence or deceit, the same in reality as in seeming or profession, not assumed or put on, genuine, honest, frank. Hence or cogn. **sincĕ·**RITY n., **sincere·**LY[2] adv. (esp. in *yours s.* before signature of letter). [f. L *sincerus* etym. dub.]

si·ncipŭt, n. Head from forehead to top (cf. OCCIPUT). [L (*semi-* half, *caput* head)]

sine[1], n. (trigon.). (*S. of arc*) line drawn from one extremity of arc perpendicularly to radius at other extremity; (*s. of angle*) ratio of above line to radius (abbr. *sin*, as *sin A*, ratio of the perpendicular subtending the angle A to the hypotenuse; *versed s.*, abbr. *vers*, unity minus the cosine). [f. L *sinus* curve]

si·nĕ[2], L prep. Without (*s. dīē*, without date, of business indefinitely adjourned; *s. quā nŏn*, indispensable condition or qualification).

si·nĕcure, n. Office of profit or honour without duties attached, esp. benefice without cure of souls. Hence **si·necūr**ISM (3), **si·necur**IST(2), nn. [f. L *sine cura* without care]

si·new, n., & v.t. (Piece of) tough fibrous tissue uniting muscle to bone, tendon; (pl., loosely) muscles, bodily strength, wiriness, (fig.) what forms the strength of or sustains or holds together, framework, resources, (esp. *the ss. of war*, money); hence **si·new**LESS, **si·new**Y[2], aa., **si·newi**NESS n. (Vb, poet.) serve as ss. of, sustain, hold together. [OE *sinu*, cf. Du. *zenuw*, G *sehne*)]

sing, v.i. & t. (*sang* or, now rare, *sung*; *sung*). Utter words, utter (words), in tuneful succession, esp. in accordance with a set tune (*s.* one's *praises*, be always praising him), whence **si·ng**ABLE (-ng-) a.; produce vocal melody, utter (song, tune), (*birds were singing*; *s. another song* or *tune*, *s. small*, become more humble, be crestfallen); make inarticulate melodious or humming or buzzing or whistling sounds (*wind, kettle, bee, sings*), (of ears) be affected as with buzzing sound (also *have a singing in* one's *ears*); compose poetry, celebrate (hero, beauty, great event, &c.) in verse; usher (esp. old or new year) *out* or *in* with singing; put *to sleep*, *into good humour*, &c., with singing; *s. out* t. & i., call out loudly, shout; *singing-man* [-ING[2]], paid singer; *singing-master* [-ING[1]], teacher of singing; *singing-voice* [-ING[1]], voice as modulated in singing. Hence **si·ng**ER[1] (-ng-) n. [OE *singan*, cf. Du. *zingen*, G *singen*]

singe (-j), v.t. & i. (*singeing*), & n. Burn (t. & i.) superficially (*s.* person's *hair*, burn off tips as hairdressing operation; *s. pig, fowl*, burn off bristles, down, after killing or plucking; *s. King of Spain's beard*, harry his coasts; *your dress is singeing*; *his reputation is a little singed*; *s.* one's *feathers* or *wings*, take some harm esp. in venturesome attempt); (n.) superficial burn (rare). [OE *sengan* perh. related to prec. w. ref. to hissing sound made in burning; cf. Du. *zengen*, G *sengen*]

Singhalese. =CINGALESE.

si·ngle[1] (-nggl), a. & n. One only, not double or multiple, united, undivided, designed for or used or done by one person &c. or one set or pair, (*s.* COMBAT, ENTRY, FILE[3]; *s. flower*, that grows one on a stem, also that has not double corolla; *s. game*, with one player on each side; *s. wicket*, rudimentary form of cricket; *s. court* in lawn tennis, fives, &c., of size &c. for s. game; *s. bed, room*, for one person; *s. eye-glass*, for one eye, monocle; *a multitude inspired with a s. purpose*); solitary, lonely, unaided, (*a s. tree stands on the ridge*; *paid either by instalments or in a s. sum*; *s. life, state, man, woman*, unmarried; *s. blessedness* facet., unmarried state); (in negative contexts) not to speak of more (*did not see a s. one, a s. person*; *can a s. argument be advanced for it?*); free from duplicity, sincere, consistent, guileless, ingenuous, (*a s. eye*, devotion to one purpose, whence **single-eyed**[2] a.; *s. heart* or *mind*, simplicity of character, whence **single-heart**ED[2], **single-mind**ED[2], aa., **single-mi·nded**NESS n.); *s.-acting* of engine &c., with steam admitted only to one side of piston; *s.-breasted* of coat &c., with only one set of buttons & buttonholes, not overlapping & buttoning either way; *s.-cut* of file, with grooves cut in one direction only, not crossing; *s.-fire* of cartridge, not meant to be recharged after use; *s.-handed* a. & adv., (*done* &c.) without help from other persons (*by his s.-handed efforts*; *cannot be done s.-handed*), also with or for one hand (*the men played s.-handed against the women with both hands*; *two-handed* & *s.-handed swords*); *s.-loader*, breechloading rifle without magazine; *si·nglestick*, (fencing with) basket-hilted stick of about sword's length; hence **si·ngle**NESS n., **si·ng**LY[2] adv. (N.) s. game; hit for one in cricket; (short whist) game won by 5–4; (pl.) twisted s. threads of silk. [OF, f. LL *singulus* (L *singuli* one by one, cf. SIMPLE)]

si·ngle[2], v.t. Choose *out* as an example or as distinguishable or to serve some purpose. [f. prec.]

si·nglet (-ngg-), n. Garment worn below shirt, vest. [SINGLE,[1] -ET[1]; prob. orig. =unlined garment on anal. of DOUBLET]

si·ngleton, n. Whist-hand with a one-card suit (*s. lead*, playing of such card as lead). [f. SINGLE on anal. of *simpleton*]

si·ngsong, a. & n., & v.i. & t. In, recited with, monotonous rhythm. (N.) monotonous rhythm; monotonous cadence in speaking; impromptu vocal concert, meeting for amateur singing. (Vb) recite (verse &c.), speak, in s. manner. [SING, SONG]

si·ngūlar (-ngg-), a. & n. (Gram.) of the form used in speaking of a single person or thing, not dual or plural, (n., the s. NUMBER[1], a word in the s. number); single, individual, (esp. *all & s.*, all whether taken together or separately); unexampled, unique, (now rare); unusual, remarkable from rarity, much beyond the average in degree, extraordinary, surprising; eccentric, unconventional, strangely behaved. Hence **si·ngular**LY[2] adv. [f. F *singulier* f. L *singularis* (*singuli* one by one, -AR[1])]

singulă·rity, n. In adj. senses; esp., uncommonness, being remarkable, odd trait or peculiarity. [f. F *singularité* f. L *singularitatem* (prec., -TY)]

si·ngularize, v.t. Strip (word) of termination mistaken for that of plural (pease & Chinese *are singularized into* pea, Chinee). Hence **si·ngularīz**A·TION n. [-IZE]

Sinhalese. = CINGALESE.

si·nister, a. (Herald.) on left side of shield &c. (i.e. on right as seen by observer; BEND[1], BAR[1], *s.*; cf. DEXTER); (facet.) left; of evil omen; (usu. of person in regard to his appearance, or of his face or look) ill-looking, of malignant or villanous aspect; wicked, flagitious, (*a s. design*). Hence **si·nister**LY[2] adv. [f. OF *sinistre* f. L *sinistrum* nom. *-ter* left]

sini·stral, a. Of, on, the left (rare); (of spiral shells) with whorls going to left & not as usu. to right. Hence **sini·stral**LY[2] adv. [prec., -AL]

sini·stro-, comb. form of L *sinister* left, as *-ce·rebral* of the left hemisphere of the brain; *si·nistrorse*, with leftward motion or aspect (esp. in Bot. of climbing plants &c.).

sink[1], v.i. & t. (*sank* or now rarely *sunk*; *sunk* or in adj. use usu. *sunken*). Fall slowly downwards, decline, disappear below surface of liquid or below horizon, come gradually to lower level or pitch, droop, despond, subside, settle down, gradually expire or perish or cease, (*sun is sinking, sank*; *my heart, spirits, sank*; *ship sinks*, goes to the bottom; *her eyes sank*, were turned downwards; *his head, chin, sank on his shoulder, chest*; *voice sinks*, becomes lower-pitched, or quieter; *sick man, life, is sinking*, becoming weaker, dying; *prices s.*, become lower; *storm, river, sinks*, subsides; *ground sinks*, slopes down, also comes to lower level by subsidence; *darkness sank upon the scene*, descended; *s. into feebleness, degradation, the grave, a quicksand, a chair*; *s. in* one's *estimation*, lose credit with him; *his eyes, cheeks, have sunk in* or *sunk*, fallen inwards, become hollow; so *sunken cheeks, eyes*; *here goes, s. or swim*, said in running risks & taking chances); penetrate (intr.), make way, *in* or *into* (*bayonet sank in to the hilt*; *impression, lesson, sinks into the mind* or *memory*, becomes fixed; *dye sinks in*, is absorbed); cause or allow to s., send below surface of liquid or ground, lower level of, keep (trans.) in obscurity or background, conceal, put out of sight, make no reference to, excavate, make by excavating, engrave, (*would sooner s. the ship than surrender*; *s. shaft, well*, dig or bore it; *s.* one's *head on* one's *chest*, let it droop; *drought had sunk the streams*; *s.* one's *title, name, office*, &c., keep it temporarily secret, not obtrude it; *s. the* SHOP; *s. a fact*, keep it quiet; *s. oneself* or one's *own interests*, be altruistic; SINKING-*fund*; *s. a die*, engrave it; *s. money*, invest it in undertaking from which it cannot be readily withdrawn, also lose it by such investment; *sunk* FENCE[1]). Hence **si·nk**ABLE a. [OE *sincan*, cf. Du. *zinken*, G *sinken*]

sink[2], n. Place in which foul liquid collects (now usu. fig.; *the Chinese quarter is a s. of iniquity*); basin or box usu. of lead or porcelain with outflow pipe into which slops are thrown in kitchens &c.; pool or marsh in which river's water disappears by evaporation or percolation; opening in stage through which scenery is raised & lowered. [f. prec.]

si·nker, n. In vbl senses; esp.: weight used to sink fishing or sounding line; DIE[1]-*s.* [-ER[1]]

si·nking, n. In vbl senses; also: internal bodily sensation caused by hunger or apprehension; *s.-fund*, moneys set aside for the purpose of sinking or wiping out a State's or corporation's debt by degrees (*the s.-f.*, surplus of revenue over expenditure, devoted to payment of national debt; *raid the s.-f.*, use such surplus in any year for other purposes). [-ING[1]]

si·nnet. See SENNIT.

Sinn Fein (shĭn fān), n. A 20th-c. patriotic movement & party in Ireland aiming at national revival in language &c. as well as political independence. [Ir., = we ourselves]

sino·logue (-ōg, -ŏg), n. Person versed in sinology. [F (foll., -LOGUE)]

sino·logy, n. Knowledge of the Chinese language, history, customs, &c. Hence **sino·**LOGIST n. [f. Gk *Sinai* the Chinese, -O-, -LOGY]

si·nter, n. Siliceous or calcareous rock formed by deposit of springs. [G, cf. CINDER]

si·nuate (-*a*t), a. (esp. bot.). Wavy-edged, with distinct inward & outward bends along edge. Hence **si·nuate**LY[2] adv., **sinu**A·TION n. [f. L *sinuare* (SINUS) bend, -ATE[2]]

sinuŏ·sity, n. Being sinuous; a bend, esp. in a stream or road. [foll., -ITY]

si·nuous, a. With many curves, serpentine, tortuous, undulating. Hence **si·nuous**LY[2] adv. [f. L *sinuosus* (SINUS, -OUS)]

sī·nus, n. (pl. *-uses, -ūs*). (Anat., Zool.) cavity of bone or tissue, pouch-shaped hollow; (Path.) fistula; (Bot.) curve between lobes of leaf. [L, = bosom, recess]
-sion (-shn, -zhn), suf. forming nn. of action or condition (= -s- of L p.p. st. + -ION, & see -ATION), as *tension* (*tendere tens-*).
Sioux (sōō, sū), n. (pl. the same, pr. sōō, sū, sōōz, sūz), & a. Member of a N.-Amer.-Indian tribe; (adj.) of the S. [F, f. native name]
sip, v.t. & i., & n. Drink (t. & i.) in repeated tiny mouthfuls or by spoonfuls; (n.) small mouthful of liquid imbibed (*a s. of brandy*). [f. 14th c.; perh. dim. in form & sense of SUP]
si·pahee (sē-), n. = SEPOY.
sī·phon, n., & v.i. & t. Pipe or tube shaped like inverted V with unequal legs for conveying liquid over edge of vessel & delivering it at lower level by utilizing atmospheric pressure; (also *s.-bottle*) aerated-water bottle from which liquid is forced out by pressure of gas through s.-tube; (Zool.; also *siphuncle*) canal or conduit esp. in molluscs or shells, sucking-tube of some insects &c.; *s. barometer,* with tube bent at bottom like inverted s.; *s.-cup,* lubricating apparatus with oil led over edge of reservoir by capillary action through wick; *s. gauge,* glass s. attached to reservoir & containing mercury for indicating pressure &c. inside reservoir; hence **si·phon**AL, **sipho·nic**, aa. (Vb) conduct or flow (as) through s. (*water is siphoning from the vase on to the tablecloth*); hence **si·phon**AGE(3) n. [f. L f. Gk *siphōn* tube]
sī·phonet, n. One of two tubes through which aphides exude honeydew. [prec., -ET[1]]
sī·phuncle, n. See SIPHON. [f. L *siphunculus* (SIPHON, -UNCLE)]
si·ppet, n. Small piece of bread &c. soaked in liquid; one of the pieces of toast or fried bread served round mince &c. [perh. dim. of SOP, see -ET[1]]
sī quis, n. Notice posted in ordination-candidate's parish church serving similar purpose to banns. [L, = if anyone (know an impediment)]
sir, n. (also v.t., see below) used (1) as vocative in addressing a master or superior, the Speaker of the House of Commons either in his own person on points of order or as embodiment of the House in ordinary debate, any male whose name is or is to be understood to be unknown to speaker, or boy &c. who is to be rebuked (pl. *sirs,* for which *gentlemen* is usu. substituted); (2) as titular prefix to name of knight or baronet, always followed by Christian name, or its initial & surname, or the whole name (*Sir John Moore, Sir J. Moore,* or, in familiar use esp. as vocative, *Sir John*); (vb) address as *sir* (*don't s. me*). [shortened f. SIRE]
sir·car, n. (Anglo-Ind.). The Government of India; head of government or household; house-steward; native accountant. [f. Hind. f. Pers. *sarkār* (*sar* head, *kār* work)]
sir·dar, n. (In India &c.) person in command, leader; (in Egypt) commander-in-chief (since 1882 a British officer) of army. [f. Hind. f. Pers. *sardār* (prec., *-dār* holding)]
sire, n., & v.t. Father or male ancestor (poet.); male parent of beast, esp. stallion kept for breeding; (voc.) Your Majesty (in addressing king or sovereign prince); (v.t.) beget (esp. of stallions). [OF, f. L SENIOR]
sīr·en, n. (Gk Myth.; pl.) women, or half women & half birds, living on a rocky isle to which they lured unwary seafarers with enchanting music; sweet singer; dangerously fascinating woman, temptress, tempting pursuit &c.; (attrib.) irresistibly tempting, as of a s.; = SIRENIAN; instrument used in acoustic experiments & for making loud sound as warning &c. by revolution of perforated disk over jet of compressed air or steam. [f. OF *sereine* f. LL *Sirena* f. L f. Gk *seirēn* etym. dub.]
sīrē·nian, a. & n. (Member) of the *Sirenia,* an order of fish-like mammals resembling cetaceans, including manatee & dugong. [mod. L *Sirenia* (prec.), -AN]
sir·gang, n. Bright-green Asiatic bird, the green jackdaw. [E.-Ind.]
sirī·asis, n. Sunstroke; sun-bath as medical treatment. [L, f. Gk *seiriasis* (*seiriaō* be hot, -ASIS)]
Si·rius. See DOG[1]. [L, f. Gk *Seirios,* cf. prec.]
sir·kar. = SIRCAR.
sir·loin, n. Upper part of loin of beef, with meat both above & (*undercut* or *fillet*) below the bone. [corrupt. of *surloin* (1554) f. F *surlonge* (SUR-[2], LOIN)]
siro·cco, sci-, n. (Italian name for) Sahara wind or simoom when it reaches Italy, (also for) warm sultry rainy wind prevailing in winter. [It., f. Arab. *sharq* the East]
si·rrah (archaic), **sir(r)ee·** (U.S.), nn. voc. replacing *sir* in imperious or contemptuous use. [f. SIR]
sirup. See SYRUP.
sirvente (F), n. Medieval usu. satirical lay of special metrical form. [orig. sense *service-song* (i.e. not love-song), F, f. Pr. *sirventes* (L *servire* serve, -ENT, -ESE)]
si·sal-grass, -hemp, nn. Prepared fibre of American aloe used for cordage. [*Sisal* port of Yucatan]
si·skin, n. Olive-green songbird, kind of finch, often kept in cage. [f. G dial. *sisschen* prob. of Slav. orig., cf. Pol. *czyżik*]

si·ster, n. Daughter of same parents (also *s. german*) or (strictly *half-s.*) parent as another person (the latter usu. specified by *my* &c. or possessive case; *the Fatal Ss.* or *Ss. three* or *three Ss.*, the Fates; *S. Anne*, person watching on behalf of another for an arrival, w. ref. to *Bluebeard*); (prop. *s.-in-law*) one's husband's or wife's s. or brother's wife; close female friend, female fellow member of class or sect or human race; member of religious community of women (*s. of* CHARITY; *s. of mercy*, member of nursing sisterhood, esp. of R.-C. one founded in Dublin 1827; *little Ss. of the poor*, French R.-C. charitable sisterhood; LAY² s.); hospital nurse in authority over others; personified quality or thing regarded as female that closely resembles another (*prose, younger s. of verse*; *s. ships*, built on same design); *s.-hook*, double hook that opens to admit rope &c. & closes into a figure 8. Hence **si·ster**LESS, **si·ster**LY¹, aa., **si·sterli**NESS n. [Aryan; OE *swuster*, cf. Du. *zuster*, G *schwester*, L *soror*, Skr. *svasā*]

si·sterhŏŏd (-r-h-), n. Being a sister or sisters, relation between sisters; society of women bound by monastic vows or devoting themselves to religious or charitable work. [-HOOD]

Si·stine, a. Of one of the popes called *Sixtus* (*S. chapel*, in Vatican, with frescoes by Michelangelo; *S. Madonna*, picture by Raphael removed from church of San Sisto in Piacenza). [f. It. *Sistino* (*Sisto* Sixtus, -INE¹)]

si·strum, n. (pl. *-tra*). Jingling instrument or rattle used by ancient Egyptians esp. in rites of Isis. [L, f. Gk *seistron* (*seiō* shake)]

Sisyphē·an, a. As of Sisyphus, Greek condemned in Tartarus to push a stone up hill & begin again when it rolled down, everlastingly laborious. [f. L f. Gk *Sisupheios* (*Sisuphos*), -AN]

sit, v.i. & t. (sat). Take or be in position in which body is supported more or less upright by buttocks resting on ground or raised seat (*sits well*, has good seat in riding; *s. tight* colloq., remain firmly in one's place, not be shaken off or move away or yield to distractions), be engaged in some occupation in which this position is usual (*s. in judgement*, assume right of judging others, be censorious; *s. for* one's *portrait*, give painter interviews or sittings; *s. for fellowship* &c., undergo examination for it; *s. for borough* &c., represent it in Parliament; *Parliament, Courts, are sitting*, in session; *s. at home*, be inactive); (of birds & some animals) rest with legs bent & body close to ground or perch (*shoot bird, hare, sitting*, when not on wing or running), remain on nest to hatch eggs (*sitting hen*, engaged in hatching; *wants to s.*, is broody); (chiefly of inanimate things) be in more or less permanent position (*sits the wind there?*, is it in that quarter?, is that the state of affairs?; *food sits heavy on the stomach*, is not soon digested; *her dress, imperiousness*, &c., *sits well on her*, suits, fits; *sitting tenant*, one in present occupation; *his principles s. loosely on him*, do not bind him much); keep one's seat on (horse &c.; *he could not s. his mule*); *s. down*, take seat after standing (also refl. archaic, as *sat him, pray s. you, d.*), (Mil.) encamp *before* place to besiege it; *s. down under*, submit tamely to (insult &c.); *s. on* or *upon*, (of jury &c.) hold session concerning, *s. on his head* (as way of keeping fallen horse quiet), (slang) repress or rebuke or snub (*he wants sitting upon*); *s. out*, take no part in something, esp. in particular dance (also trans. as *sat out the next dance*), also s. outdoors, (trans.) outstay (other visitors) or stay till end of (performance); *s. under*, be one of congregation preached to by (minister); *s. up*, rise from lying to sitting posture, remain (*late, nursing*, &c.) out of bed, s. erect without lolling (*make* one *s. up* colloq., subject him to hard work, pain, surprise, &c.); *si·tfast*, horny sore on horse's back. [Aryan; OE *sittan*, cf. Du. *zitten*, G *sitzen*, L *sedēre*, Gk *hezomai*, Skr. *sad*]

site, n. Ground on which town or building stood, stands, or is to stand; *s.-value*, value of land fixed as the standard with which its later value was to be compared in estimating increment under the budget of 1909. [f. L *situs*]

sith, conj. (archaic, bibl.). Since. [see SINCE]

sīt(i)o-, comb. form of Gk *sitos, sition*, food, as *sit(i)o·logy* dietetics, *sit(i)opho·bia* morbid aversion to food.

si·tter, n. In vbl senses; esp.: person sitting for portrait; *good, bad, s.*, hen that sits well &c.; (slang, from *to shoot bird sitting*) easy shot, thing easily done. [-ER¹]

si·tting, n. In vbl senses; esp.: time during which one sits continuously (*wrote the whole poem at a s.*; *all-night s. of House of Commons*; *can you give me six ss.?*, for portrait); clutch of eggs; seat in church appropriated to a person; *s.-room*, space enough to accommodate seated persons, also a room used for sitting in (opp. *bedroom*). [-ING¹]

si·tuāted, si·tuate (*-at*; archaic), aa. In specified situation (*situated on the top of the hill*; *awkwardly situated*, in a difficulty). [f. LL *situatus* (L *situs* position, -ATE²)]

situa·tion, n. Place, with its surroundings, occupied by something (*house stands in a fine s.*; *unrivalled for s.*); set of circumstances, position in which one finds oneself, (*came out of a difficult s. with credit*); critical point or complication in drama (*curtain falls on a strong s.*); employee's, esp. domestic's, place or paid office (*cannot find a s.*). [F (prec., -ATION)]

sitz-bath. See BATH.

Si·va (sē-), n. Hindu god held supreme by his special votaries, & by others associated as principle of destruction with Brahma & Vishnu in a triad. Hence **Sivai·stic** [-IST, -IC] a., **Si·vaITE**[1](1) n. & a. [Hind., f. Skr. *çiva* propitious]

six, a. & n. One more than five, 6, vi, (often agreeing with understood noun, as *s. of the men, s. of them, s. o'clock* or *s.*; *s. to one,* long odds; *two & s.*, half-a-crown; *s. & eight(pence)*, common item in solicitors' bills; *s. & s.*, 6/6; *it is s. of one & half-a-dozen of the other*, difference is merely nominal; *twenty-s.* or *s.-&-twenty*, & so on to *s.-&-ninety*; *am not s. yet*, years old); *s.-footer*, person 6 ft in height, thing 6 ft long; *si·xpence*, (silver coin worth) 6*d*. (*have not got a sixpence*); *si·xpenny* a., costing or worth 6*d*. (*sixpenny bit*, or *sixpenny* as n., the coin sixpence; *seven-&-sixpenny* &c., costing 7/6 &c.); *s.-shooter*, s.-chambered revolver; hence **si·xFOLD** a. & adv. (N.) the number s. (*twice s. is twelve*; *at ss. & sevens*, in confusion); card or die-face of s. pips (*the s. of spades*; *double ss.*, die-throw of two ss.); (pl.) candles made s. to the lb. [Aryan; cf. Du. *zes*, G *sechs*, L *sex*, Gk *hex*, Skr. *shash*]

si·xain, n. Six-line stanza. [F (*six* f. L *sex*)]

si·xer, n. Hit for six in cricket. [-ER[1]]

sixte, n. One of the positions in fencing. [F, f. L *sextus* sixth]

sixtee·n, a. & n. One more than fifteen, 16, xvi; *sixteenmo* or *16mo*, = SEXTODECIMO; hence **sixtee·nTH**[2] a. & n.; (n.) the number s. (*twice s. is thirty-two*). [-TEEN]

sixth, a. & n. Next after fifth (*the, a, s.*, often as n. with ellipse of noun, esp. *the s.* = 6th day of month; *s.* FORM[1]); *s. part*, one of six equal parts into which thing, may be divided. (N.) = s. part; *the* s. form; (Mus.) tone six diatonic degrees above or below given tone, this interval, harmonic combination of tone & its s. [OE *sixta*, w. assim. to FOURTH, see -TH[2]]

si·xthly, adv. In the sixth place (in enumerations). [-LY[2]]

si·xty, a. & n. Six times ten, 60, lx, (*s.-one, -eight*, &c.; *s.-first, -fourth*, &c.); *s.-four-mo*, (size of) book or page given by folding sheet six times into 64 leaves (for L *in quarto et sexagesimo*); hence **si·xtiETH** a. & n. (N.) the number s.; *the ss.*, years between 59 & 70 in life or century. [OE *siextig* (-TY[2])]

si·zable, a. Of large size. [SIZE[1], -ABLE]

si·zar, n. Student at Cambridge or Trinity College, Dublin, paying reduced fees & formerly charged with certain menial offices. Hence **si·zarSHIP** n. [foll. = ration, -ER[1] (cf. *scholar*)]

size[1], n., & v.t. & i. (Hist.) standard of weight or measure for some article esp. of food or drink; (Camb. Univ.; also **si·zING**[1] n.) ration of food or drink from buttery; dimensions, magnitude, (*is of vast, diminutive, s.*, very large or small; *s. matters less than quality*; *are both of a*, i.e. the same, *s.*; *is the s. of*, i.e. as big as, *an egg*; *what s.*, i.e. how big, *is it?*; *that's about the s. of it* colloq., a true account of the matter), one of the usu. numbered classes into which things, esp. garments, otherwise similar are divided in respect of s. (*is made in several ss.*; *takes s. 7 in gloves*; *is quite a s., three ss., too big*; OUT *s.*); implement for sizing pearls; *s.-stick*, shoemaker's measure for taking length of foot; hence **-sizED**[2] a. (Vb): (Camb. Univ.) order s.; group or sort in ss. or according to s., whence **si·zER**[1](2) n.; *s. up*, estimate s. of, (colloq.) form judgement of (person &c.). [f. OF *sise* shortened f. *assise* ASSIZE]

size[2], n., & v.t. Gelatinous solution used in glazing paper & stiffening textiles & in many manufacturing processes; hence **si·zY**[2] a. (Vb) glaze or stiffen or treat with s. [perh. = prec.]

si·zzle, v.i. & n. (colloq.). Make sputtering sound as in frying; (n.) such noise. [imit.]

sja·mbok (zh-), n. Rhinoceros-hide whip. [S.-Afr. Du. f. Malay *chamboq* f. Pers. *chābuk* whip]

skald. See SCALD[2].

skat, n. A three-handed card-game popular in Germany. [G, f. It. *scarto* a discard]

skate[1], n. Kinds of ray-fish, esp. (*Blue, Grey, S.*) rhomboidal long-tailed kind. [f. ON *skata*]

skate[2], n., & v.i. & t. One of pair of implements, each with steel blade or set of rollers, attached beneath boots & enabling wearer to glide in curves over ice or (*roller-s.*) hard floor. (Vb) move, perform (specified figure), on ss. (*s. over thin ice*, talk on subject needing tactful treatment); *skating-rink*, piece of ice artificially made, or floor reserved, for skating; hence **ska·tER**[1] n. [earlier *schates* pl. f. Du. *schaatsen* pl. f. ONF *escache* stilt]

skean, skene, skain, n. Gaelic dagger used in Ireland & Scotland; *s.-dhu* (-dōō), dagger stuck in stocking as part of Highland costume. [f. Gael. *sgian* knife, *dubh* black]

skeda·ddle, v.i., & n., (colloq.). Run away, disperse in flight; (n.) hurried flight or dispersal. [U.S., etym. dub.]

skee. See SKI.

skein (-ān), n. Bundle of yarn or thread or silk made by coiling it many times, drawing it out to the coil's length, & folding it; flock of wild geese &c. in flight; (fig.) tangle, confusion. [f. OF *escaigne*, etym. dub.]

skĕ·leton, n. Hard internal or external framework of bones, cartilage, shell, woody fibre, &c., supporting or containing an animal or vegetable body, whence **ske·let**AL a., **ske·leto-** comb. form, **skeleto·**GRAPHY n., &c.; dried bones of human being or other animal fastened together in same relative positions as in life (*s. at the feast*, something that alloys pleasure, intrusive care; *s. in the cupboard, family s.*, discreditable or humiliating fact concealed from strangers), part of anything that remains after its life or usefulness is gone; framework or essential part of anything (*s. crew, regiment*, &c., permanent nucleus ready for filling up, cadre; *s. drill*, with companies &c. represented by two men separated by long rope; *s. key*, fitting many locks by having interior of bit hollowed; *s.* or *s.-face type*, with thin strokes); outline sketch, epitome, abstract; (by exag.) thin person. [Gk, orig. neut. of *skeletos* dried-up (*skello* parch)]

ske·letonize, v.t. Reduce to skeleton or abstract by destroying flesh, the tissue between veins of leaves, &c., or by omitting details. [-IZE]

skene. See SKEAN.

skep, n. Kinds, varying locally, of wooden or wicker basket; straw or wicker beehive. [f. ON *skeppa*, cf. Du. *schepel*]

skepsis, skeptic, &c. See **sce-.**

sketch, n., & v.t. & i. Preliminary, rough, slight, merely outlined, or unfinished drawing or painting often as experiment for, or memorandum for use in, regular picture; brief account without many details conveying general idea of something, rough draft, general outline; slight play often of musical kind or short descriptive article; musical composition of single movement; *s.-block, -book*, arrangements of drawing-paper leaves for doing series of ss. on; *s.-map*, with outlines but little detail; hence **ske·tch**Y[2] a., **ske·tch**ILY[2] adv., **ske·tch**INESS n. (Vb) make or give s. of; make ss. esp. of landscape (*went out sketching*); hence **ske·tch**ER[1] n. [f. Du. *skets* f. It. *schizzo*, perh. f. L f. Gk *skhedios* off-hand, extempore]

skew, a. & n. Oblique, slanting, sideways, distorted, (now chiefly in Arch., Mech., & Math.; *s. bridge*, with line of arch not at right angles to abutment; *s. chisel*, with oblique edge; *s. wheel*, bevel wheel with oblique teeth; *s. curve*, in three dimensions); (Math.) having symmetry distorted by reversal of some element on opposite sides; *skewbald*, (esp. of horse) with irregular patches of white & some colour (prop. not black, cf. *piebald*); *s.-eyed*, squinting. (N.) sloping top of buttress; coping of gable; stone built into bottom of gable to support coping. [f. obs. *skew* vb sidle, shy, f. ONF *eskiuer* = OF *eschever* ESCHEW]

skew·er, n., & v.t. Pin of wood or iron for holding meat compactly together while cooking; (joc.) sword &c.; (vb) fasten together, pierce, (as) with s. [f. 17th c.; also *skiver*; etym. dub.]

ski (shē, skē), n. (pl. *ski, skis*), & v.i. (*ski'd, skiing*). One of pair of wooden runners about 8 ft long & 4 in. broad fastened under feet for travelling over snow esp. in Scandinavia. [Norw., f. ON *skidh* billet, snow-shoe, cf. *skid*]

skiagraphy &c. See **scia-.**

skid, n., & v.t. & i. Piece of frame or timber serving as buffer, support, inclined plane, &c.; wooden or metal shoe preventing wheel from revolving used as drag (also *s.-pan*), other kinds of wheel-locking contrivance; slip or slide of wheel on muddy ground. (Vb) support or move or protect or check with s.; (of wheel or vehicle) slide forwards or backwards or sideways on slippery ground. [perh. cogn. w. ON *skidh* billet, cf. ME *shide* slip of wood, & SHEATH]

skier (shē·*er*), n. Person using SKI (cf. SKYER). [-ER[1]]

skiff, n. Light rowing or sculling boat. [f. F *esquif* prob. f. OHG *scif* SHIP]

ski·lful, a. Having or showing skill (*at, in*), practised, expert, adroit, ingenious. Hence **ski·lful**LY[2] adv. [foll., -FUL]

skill, n. Expertness, practised ability, facility in doing something, dexterity, tact. [f. ON *skil* discernment (*skilja* to separate), cf. Sw. *skäl* reason]

skilled, a. Having or showing skill, skilful, (rare exc. in phrr. *s. labour, workman*, &c., = trained, or followed by *in*). [-ED[2]]

ski·llet, n. Small metal pot with long handle & usu. legs used in cooking. [f. 15th c., etym. dub.]

ski·ll-less, a. (rare). Without skill, knowing nothing *of*. [-LESS]

skills, v.i. 3rd sing. impers. (archaic). *It s. not*, makes no difference, is of no use, (usu. *to* do). [f. ON *skilja* see SKILL]

ski·lly, n. Thin broth or soup or gruel usu. of oatmeal & water flavoured with meat often served out in prisons, work-houses, &c. [earlier *skillygalee, -golee*, etym. dub.]

skim, v.t. & i., & a. Take scum or cream or floating layer from surface of (liquid), take (cream &c.) from surface of liquid, (*s. the cream off* often fig., take best part of; *skimming-dish* slang, flat-bottomed racing yacht); keep touching lightly or nearly touching (surface) in passing over, (intr.) go thus *over* or *along* surface, glide along in air; read (t. & i.) superficially, look over cursorily, gather salient facts contained in; (adj.) *s. milk*, from which cream has been skimmed. [prob. f. OF *escumer* (*escume* SCUM)]

ski·mmer, n. In vbl senses; esp.: ladle &c. for skimming liquids; kinds of water-bird, esp. *Black S.*, with flat mandibles. [-ER[1]]

skimp, v.t. & i. Supply (person with or *in* food, money, &c.; material, expenses, &c.) meagrely, stint; be parsimonious. Hence **ski·mpy**² a., **ski·mpingly**² adv. [f. 19th c. only; cf. SCRIMP]

skin¹, n. Flexible continuous covering of human or other animal body (*with a whole s.*, unwounded; *save* one's *s.*, get off safe; *change* one's *s.*, undergo impossible change of character &c.; *would not be in his s.*, should not like to be he; *is only s. & bone*, very thin, & so **ski·nny**² a., **ski·nniness** n.; *escape with the s. of* one's *teeth*, narrowly; *thick, thin, s.*, imperviousness, sensitiveness, to affront or criticism; *fair, dark*, &c., *s.*, complexion; *near is my* SHIRT, *nearer my s.*), (Anat.) one layer of this (*true* or *inner s.*, derma; *outer s.*, epidermis); hide of flayed animal with or without the hair &c.; material prepared from ss. esp. of smaller animals (cf. *hide*); vessel for wine or water made of animal's whole s.; outer coating of plant, fruit, &c., rind; planking or plating of ship or boat inside or outside ribs; GOLD-*beaters' s.*; *s.-bound*, with s. tightly stretched over flesh; *s.-deep*, (of wound, also of emotion, impression, beauty, &c.) superficial, not deep or lasting; *s.-friction*, lateral resistance to way of ship &c. passing through water; *skinful* (*of wine* &c., or abs.), as much liquor as one can hold; *s.-game* (U.S. slang), swindle; *s.-grafting*, surgical substitution of s. cut from another part or person for damaged part. Hence **-skinned**², **ski·nless**, aa. [f. ON *skinn*, cogn. w. G *schinden* flay]

skin², v.t. & i. Cover (sore &c., usu. *over*) as with s., (of wound &c.) form or become covered with new s., cicatrize, (usu. *over*); strip of s., withdraw s. from, flay, (*keep your eyes skinned* slang, be watchful or cautious), (colloq.) strip oneself, strip (another), of tight garment such as jersey; *ski·nflint*, niggard, miser. [f. prec.]

skink, n. Kinds of small-limbed lizard. [f. L f. Gk *skigkos*]

ski·nner, n. In vbl senses; esp., (now chiefly in name of a city company) dealer in skins, furrier. [-ER¹]

skip¹, v.i. & t., & n. (Of lambs, kids, children, &c.) jump about, gambol, caper, frisk, move lightly from one foot on to the other; (of children, esp. girls) use skipping-rope; shift quickly from one subject or occupation to another, be desultory, (usu. *off, from*, &c.); (slang) make off, disappear; omit, make omissions, in dealing with a series or in reading (*do them all without skipping any* or *skipping*; *always s. the descriptions*; *skips as he reads*; *s. every tenth row*); *ski·pjack*, jumping toy made of bird's merrythought, also kinds of fish & butterfly & beetle named from their movements; *skipping-rope*, length of rope with two wooden handles used in girls' game of skipping; hence **ski·ppingly**² adv. (N.) skipping movement, esp. quick shift from one foot to other (HOP³, *s., & jump*). [f. Scand., cf. MSw. & Norw. *skopa* vb]

skip², n. College servant, scout, esp. at Dublin. [perh. f. obs. *skip-kennel* lackey (prec.)]

skip³, n. Captain or director of side at bowls & curling. [perh. for SKIPPER²]

skip⁴, n. Cage, bucket, &c., in which men or materials are lowered & raised in mines & quarries. [var. of SKEP]

ski·pper¹, n. In vbl senses; esp., (Zool.) =SKIP¹*jack*. [-ER¹]

ski·pper², n. Sea captain, esp. master of small trading vessel; *s.'s daughters*, (with pun on prec.) tall white-crested waves; (transf.) captain of side in games. [f. MDu. *schipper* (*schip* SHIP¹, -ER¹)]

ski·ppet, n. (hist.). Small cylindrical wooden box used to enclose and protect large seal attached by ribbon to deed. [?]

skirl, v.i., & n. (Make) sound characteristic of bagpipes. [Sc., prob. f. Scand.]

skir·mish, n., & v.i. Piece of irregular or unpremeditated fighting esp. between small or outlying parties, slight engagement; encounter of wit, argument, &c. (Vb) fight in small parties, loose order, or unpremeditated way; hence **skir·misher**¹ n. [n. f. vb, f. OF *eskermir* (-ISH²) fence, f. OHG *scirman* (*scirm*, whence G *schirm* shelter); cf. *scrimmage*]

ski·rret, n. Kind of water parsnip formerly much used as table vegetable. [prob. f. OF *eschervis* var. of *carvi* CARAWAY]

skirt, n., & v.t. & i. Part of coat or shirt that hangs below waist; woman's outer garment shaped like petticoat from waist downwards (*divided s.*, loose trousers resembling s.), whence **skir·ting**¹(3) n.; edge, border, extreme part, (often pl.; *on the ss. of London*, just inside or outside of it); *s. of beef* &c., the diaphragm & other membranes as cheap food-material; *s.-dance(r), -cing*, with full s. waved about giving graceful effects; hence **-skirted**², **skir·tless**, aa. (Vb) go along or round or past the edge of, be situated along; go *along* coast, wall, &c.; *skirting-board*, along bottom of room-wall. [f. ON *skyrta*; cogn w. SHORT, & doublet of SHIRT]

skit, n. Light piece of satire, burlesque, literary squib, (often *upon*). [f. obs. *skit* shoot, dart, jump, perh. f. Scand., cf. ON *skjóta* SHOOT]

ski·tter, v.i. (Of wild-fowl) go splashing along water in rising or settling; fish by drawing bait along surface. [as prec., -ER¹]

ski·ttish, a. (Of horses &c.) nervous, inclined to shy, excitable, playful, fidgety; (chiefly of women) capricious, coquettish, flirting, lively, given to amusement, gadding about, affecting youthfulness, wanton. Hence **ski'ttishly**[2] adv., **ski'ttishness** n. [as SKIT, -ISH[1]]

ski'ttle, n. *Ss.*, game played with nine pins (*ss.* or *s.-pins*) set up at end of *s.-alley* or *s.-ground* to be bowled down with *s.-ball* (*beer & ss.*, amusement, as *life is not all beer & ss.*); (slang, as int.) *ss.!*, rubbish, nonsense. [formerly also *kittle-pins*; etym. dub.]

skiv, n. (slang). Sovereign, £1. [?]

skive, v.t. Split or pare (hide, leather); grind away surface of (gem). [f. ON *skifa*]

skī'ver, n. Knife for skiving leather; thin leather got by skiving. [-ER[1]]

sku'a, n. Kinds of gull, esp. the *Great S.*, largest of gull kind, chiefly dark-coloured. [f. ON *skúfr*]

skulk, v.i. Lurk, keep oneself concealed esp. in cowardice or with evil intent, stay or sneak away in time of danger, shirk duty, avoid observation. Hence **sku'lker**[1] & (in same sense) **skulk** nn., **sku'lkingly**[2] adv. [f. Scand., cf. Da. *skulke*, Norw. *skulka*]

skull, n. Bony case of the brain, frame of the head, cranium, (*s. & cross-bones*, representation of bare s. with two thigh-bones crossed below it as emblem of death); *s.-cap*, close-fitting cap usu. of velvet worn indoors chiefly by old men, also kinds of plant with helmet-shaped flower. Hence **-skulled**[2] a. [f. 13th c., etym. dub.]

skunk, n. Black white-striped bushy-tailed American carnivorous animal about size of cat able to emit powerful stench from liquid secreted by anal glands as defence; its fur; stinking or contemptible fellow. [f. Amer.-Ind. *segongw*]

Sku'pshtina (-ōōp-), n. Serbian parliament. [Serb., = assembly]

sky, n., & v.t. (The vault of) heaven (*blue, clear, cloudy, overcast*, &c., *s.*; *if the s. fall we shall catch larks*, unlikely cataclysms are not worth providing against; *under the open s.*, out of doors; often pl., as *laud to the ss.*, highly; *was raised to the ss.*, taken up to heaven); climate, atmosphere, (*try what a warmer s., warmer ss., will do for you*); *s.-blue* a. & n., colour(ed) like clear sky; *s.-born* poet., of divine birth; *s.-clad* facet., naked; *s.-high* adv. & a., so as to reach, reaching, the s.; *sky'-lark* n., lark that flies spirally upwards singing, v.i. (with pun on LARK[1], [2], & perh. of naut. orig., w. ref. to clambering about rigging), frolic, play tricks or practical jokes, ballyrag, &c.; *sky'light*, window set in plane of roof or ceiling; *s.-line*, outline of hill &c. defined against s. (*is on the s.-l.*, seen outlined on s.); *s. pilot* slang, parson; *s.-rocket*, discharged upwards; *sky'sail*, light sail above royal in square-rigged ship; *sky'scape*, picture chiefly representing s.; *s.-scraper* facet., =*skysail*, also building of many storeys, tall chimney, &c.; *s.-writing*, legible smoke-trails made as advertising method by aeroplane; hence **sky'ey**[2], **sky'less**, aa., **sky'ward(s)** adv. & a. (Vb) hit (cricket-ball) high up; hang (picture) high on wall, treat picture of (artist) so. [earlier sense *cloud*; f. ON *ský* cloud, cf. OE *scéo*]

Skye (terrier), n. Small long-bodied short-legged long-haired slate or fawn coloured variety of Scotch terrier, named from Skye.

sky'er, n. High hit at cricket (cf. SKIER). [*sky* + -ER[1]]

slab[1], n., & v.t. Thin flat usu. square or rectangular piece of stone or other rigid material; (of timber) outer cut sawn from log; *s.-stone*, kinds of stone that split readily into ss. (Vb) remove ss. from (log, tree) to prepare it for sawing into planks; *slabbing-gang*, set of saws for doing this. [f. 13th c., etym. dub.]

slab[2], a. (archaic). Viscous, (of liquid) thick & sticky, (chiefly w. ref. to *Macbeth* IV. i. 32). [f. prov. E *slab* puddle, cf. Icel., Sw., & Norw., *slabb* mud]

slabber. =SLOBBER.

slack, a., adv., n., & v.t. & i. Sluggish, remiss, relaxed, languid, loose, inactive, negligent, (*s. water*, about turn of tide, esp. low tide; *s. in stays* naut., slow in going about; *a s. rope*, not taut; *keep a s. hand* or *rein*, ride, or fig. govern, carelessly; *s. trade, business, market*, with little doing; *s. weather*, inclining to indolence); *s. lime*, slaked lime; hence **sla'cken**[6] v.t. & i., **sla'ckly**[2] adv., **sla'ckness** n. (Adv., in comb. w. *dry, bake*, &c.) slowly, insufficiently, (*s.-dried hops*; *to s.-bake bread*). (N.) s. part of rope (*haul in the s.*); s. time in trade &c.; (pl.) trousers; [perh. f. G *schlacke* SLAG] coal-dust used chiefly for making briquettes &c. (Vb) slacken; make loose (rope; often *off, away*); (colloq.) take a rest, be indolent, whence **sla'cker**[1] n.; =SLAKE (lime); *s. off*, abate vigour; *s. up*, reduce speed of train &c. before stopping. [OE *sleac*, cogn. w. LAX; & cf. ON *slakr*]

slag, n., & v.i. Dross separated in fused state in reduction of ores, vitreous smelting-refuse, clinkers; volcanic scoria; *s.-wool*, = *mineral* WOOL; hence **sla'ggy**[2] a. (Vb) form s., cohere into s.-like mass. [f. MLG *slagge*, whence Sw. *slagg*, cf. G *schlacke*, cogn. w. prec.]

slain. See SLAY.

slake, v.t. Assuage, satisfy, (thirst, & rhet. revenge &c.), whence **sla'keless** a. (poet.); (also *slack*) combine (lime) chemically with water. [var. of SLACK]

slam, v.t. & i., & n. Shut (t. & i., of door &c.; often *to* adv.) with loud bang; put *down* (object) with similar sound; (slang) hit, beat, gain easy victory over. (N.)

sound (as) of slammed door; gaining of every trick in whist or euchre. [perh. f. Scand., cf. Norw. *slemba*, imit.]

sla·nder, n., & v.t. False report maliciously uttered to person's injury; uttering of such reports, calumny; (Law) false oral defamation (cf. LIBEL, SCANDAL); hence or cogn. **sla·nder**OUS a., **sla·nderous**LY[2] adv., **sla·nderous**NESS n. (Vb) utter s. about, defame falsely; hence **sla·nder**ER[1] n. [f. OF *esclandre* f. L SCANDAL*um*]

slang, n., & v.t. Words & phrases in common colloquial use, but generally considered in some or all of their senses to be outside of standard English; words & phrases either entirely peculiar to or used in special senses by some class or profession, cant, (*racing, thieves', artistic, schoolboy*, &c., *s.*); (vb) use abusive language to. [cant word, etym. dub.]

sla·ngy (-ngĭ), a. Of the character of, given to the use of, slang. Hence **sla·ngi**LY[2] adv., **sla·ngi**NESS n. [-Y[2]]

slant, v.i. & t., a., & n. Slope (i. & t.), diverge from a line, lie or go obliquely to a vertical or horizontal line; hence **sla·nting**LY[2] adv., (facet. on *perpendicular*) **slantingdi·cular** or **slantendi·cular** a. (Adj., chiefly poet.) sloping, inclined, oblique. (N.) slope, oblique position, (*on the* or *a s.*, aslant), whence **sla·nt**WISE adv.; (archaic) indirect censure, disparaging remark; (Naut.) *a s. of wind*, favourable breeze. [f. ON (Norw. *slent* n. side-slip, *slenta* vb)]

slap, v.t., n., & adv. Strike with palm of hand, smack; (part. as adj. & adv.) very fast, big, good, &c. (*a slapping pace, great girl, dinner*). (N.) such stroke (*s. in the face* lit., also fig. rebuff, insult). (Adv.) with the suddenness or effectiveness or true aim of a blow, suddenly, just, quite, full, (*ran s. into him*; *hit me s. in the eye*); *s.-bang*, violently, noisily, headlong; *sla·pda·sh* adv., vehemently, recklessly; *sla·pdash* a., impetuous, random, happy-go-lucky, n., such action or work, also =ROUGH*cast*, (v.t.) =ROUGH*cast*; *s.-up* a. vulg., quite up to date, in the latest fashion, with all modern appliances. [imit., cf. LG *slapp* sounding blow]

slash, v.i. & t., & n. Make sweeping or random cut(s) with sword, knife, whip, &c. (*slashing criticism*, with outspoken condemnation); make long narrow gashes in (*slashed sleeve* &c., with slits cut to show lining or puffing of other mater al); lash (person &c.) with whip, crack (whip); (Mil.) fell (trees) to form abatis; (n.) (wound or slit made by) slashing cut. [perh. f. OF *esclachier* break in pieces]

slat[1], n. Thin narrow piece of wood, esp. used in sets in Venetian blinds, lath. [f. OF *esclat* = *esclate*, see SLATE[1]]

slat[2], v.i. & t. (Of sails, cordage, &c.) flap against mast &c. with reports; strike noisily with or on a surface. [f. SLAT[1], or imit.]

slate[1], n., a., & v.t. Kinds of grey, green, or bluish-purple rock easily split into flat smooth plates; piece of such plate used as roofing-material; piece of it usu. framed in wood used, by school-children, small shop-keepers, &c., for writing on with *s.-pencil* or small rod of soft s. (*clean the s.*, rid oneself of or renounce obligations); *s.-black, -blue, -grey*, modifications of these tints such as occur in s.; *s.-club*, mutual benefit society with small weekly contributions; *s.-colour(ed)*, (of) dark bluish or greenish grey; hence **sla·t**Y[2] a. (Vb) cover with ss. esp. as roofing; hence **sla·t**ER[1] n. [f. OF *esclat(e)* (now *éclat*) f. *esclater* shiver in pieces, etym. dub.]

slate[2], v.t. (colloq.). Criticize severely (esp. author in reviews), scold, rate. Hence **sla·t**ING[1](1) n. [?]

sla·ttern, n. Sluttish woman. Hence **sla·ttern**LY[1] a., **sla·tternli**NESS n. [perh. for *slattering* (dial. *slatter* be wasteful)]

slaugh·ter, n., & v.t. Slaying, esp. of many persons or animals at once, carnage, massacre, (*s.* or *massacre of the* INNOCENTS); *s.-house*, shambles, place for killing cattle or sheep, place of carnage; hence **slaugh·ter**OUS a. (rhet.), **slaugh·terous**LY[2] adv. (Vb) kill (people) in ruthless manner or on great scale; butcher, kill for food; hence **slaugh·ter**ER[1] n. [f. ON *slátr* meat, cogn. w. SLAY]

Slav (-ahv), n. & a. One of a race spread over most of Eastern Europe and including Russians, Bulgarians, Illyrians, Poles, Silesians, Pomeranians, Bohemians, &c.; hence **Sla·**VOPHIL, **Sla·**VOPHOBE, nn. & aa., **Sla·**VISM(2, 3) n. (Adj.) of the Ss., Slavonic, Slavonian. [earlier *Sclave* f. med. L *Sclavus*, late Gk *Sklabos*, f. Slavonic]

slave, n., & v.i. Person who is the legal property of another or others and is bound to absolute obedience, human chattel (WHITE *s.*); helpless victim *to* or *of* some dominating influence (*is a s. to drink, the s. of his wife's caprices*, &c.; *the ss. of fashion*); drudge, person of no leisure; mean contemptible person; *s.-bangle* (of gold, glass, &c., worn by ladies above elbow); *s.-born* (in slavery, of s. parents); *s.-driver*, overseer of ss. at work, (transf.) hard taskmaster; *s.-grown*, (of commodities) produced by s.-labour; *s.-holder*, owner of ss.; *s.-hunter*, person who hunts esp. Negroes to sell them as ss.; *s.-ship*, employed in s.-trade; *s. States*, southern States of N. America in which slavery prevailed before civil war; *s.-trade*, procuring, transporting, & selling as ss., of human beings, esp. African Negroes; so *s.-trader*. (Vb) work like s., drudge. [f. OF *esclave* f. med. L *sclavus* Slav captive, see prec.]

slā·ver[1], n. Ship or person engaged in slave-trade. [-ER[1]]

slă·ver[2], v.i. & t., & n. Let spittle flow from mouth; let one's spittle fall upon (garment &c., or another's cheek in kissing). (N.) spittle running from mouth, (fig.) fulsome or servile flattery; hence **sla·very**[1] [-Y[2]] a. [f. Scand. (Icel. *slafur* n., *slafra* vb), cf. LG *slabbern*]

slā·very[2] (for *s.*[1] see prec.), n. Condition of a slave; slave-holding; exhausting labour, drudgery. [-ERY]

sla·vey, n. (slang). Maid-servant, esp. in lodgings or boarding-house. [-Y[3]]

Sla·vic (-ah-), a. & n. (Language) of the Slavs, Slavonic. [-IC]

sla·vish, a. As of, having the characteristics of, slaves, abject, servile, base, (*s. imitation,* without any attempt at development or originality). Hence **sla·vish**LY[2] adv., **sla·vish**NESS n. [-ISH[1]]

Slavō·nian, a. & n. (Language, member) of the Slav race; (inhabitant) of the Austrian district Slavonia. [f. med. L *S(c)lavonia* country of Slavs, -AN]

Slavŏ·nic, a. & n. (Language) of the Slavs. Hence **Slavŏ·nic**IZE(3) v.t. [as prec.,-IC]

slay, v.t. (*slew* pr. -ōō, *slain*). Kill (chiefly poet., rhet., or facet.; often abs., as *went forth slaying & spoiling*). Hence **(-)slay**ER[1] n. [OE *slēan*, cf. Du. *slaan*, G *schlagen*, strike]

slea·zy, a. (Of textiles, & rarely transf.) flimsy. [f. 17th c., etym. dub.]

sled, sledge[1], **sleigh** (-ā), nn., & vv.i. & t. Vehicle on runners instead of wheels for conveying loads or passengers esp. over snow drawn by horses or dogs or reindeer or pushed or pulled by hand, toboggan, (*sled* now little used in England except of structure on runners for dragging loads in agriculture; *sleigh* chiefly of runner-carriage for driving over snow; *sledge* in all senses); *sleigh-bell,* one of the tinkling bells often attached to harness of s.-horse &c.; (vv.) travel, go, convey, in s. [*sled* f. MDu. *slede* cogn. w. SLIDE; *sledge* f. MDu. *sleedse*; *sleigh* (-*gh* arbitrary) shortened f. *sled*, cf. Du. *slee* for *slede*]

sledge[2]**(-hammer),** n. Blacksmith's large heavy hammer (*s.-h.* often attrib. & fig., as *s.-h. blows, arguments, style*). [OE *slecg* (*slēan* smite, SLAY), cf. Du. *slegge*)]

sleek, a., & v.t. Smooth & soft & glossy (of hair, fur, skin, or animal or person with such hair &c.); hence **slee·k**LY[2] adv., **slee·k**NESS n.; (vb) make s. esp. by stroking or pressing down. [var. of SLICK, ME *slike*, cf. OE *slician* & Icel. *slíkja* make s.]

sleep[1], n. Bodily condition, normally recurring every night & lasting several hours, in which nervous system is inactive, eyes are closed, muscles relaxed, & consciousness nearly suspended, prolonged similar condition of hibernating animals, (BEAUTY *s.*; *in* one's *s.*, while asleep; *the s. of the just,* sound; *s. that knows not breaking,* death; *broken s.*, with disturbed intervals; *go to s.*, fall asleep; *fall on s.* archaic, go to s., fig. die); *a* period of or single indulgence in s. (*shall try to get a s.*); (fig.) rest, quiet, negligence, death, &c.; *s.-walker, -walking,* somnambulist, -ism. Hence **slee·p**LESS a., **slee·p-less**LY[2] adv., **slee·pless**NESS n. [OE *slǣp*, cf. Du. *slaap*, G *schlaf*, cogn. w. LG *slap*, G *schlaff*, loose]

sleep[2], v.i. & t. (slept). Be immersed in s., fall or be asleep, (*let sleeping dogs lie,* avoid stirring up trouble; *s. like a log* or *top,* soundly; *s. on, upon, over,* a question, leave it till tomorrow; *s. the clock* ROUND[3]); spend in or affect by sleeping (*s. the hours away*; *slept off his vexation, headache, debauch*); be inactive or dormant (*sword sleeps in the scabbard*; *top sleeps,* spins so steadily as to seem motionless; *sleeping partner,* not sharing management); lie in the grave; sojourn for the night *at, in,* &c.; provide sleeping accommodation for (*lodging-house sleeps 300 men*); *sleeping-bag,* for sleeping out-of-doors in; *sleeping-car(riage),* railway wagon provided with beds; *sleeping-draught,* opiate; *sleeping-*SICKNESS; *sleeping-suit,* pyjamas. [OE *slǣpan*, cf. Du. *slapen*, G *schlafen*, & see prec.]

slee·per, n. In vbl senses; also, wooden beam or piece of other material used as support for rails &c.; =SLEEP[2]*ing-car*. [-ER[1]]

slee·py, a. Drowsy, ready for sleep; habitually indolent, unobservant, &c.; without stir or bustle (*a s. little town*); (of fruit, esp. pears) insipid & dry with incipient decay; *slee·pyhead,* s. or inattentive person (esp. in voc.); *s.* SICKNESS. Hence **slee·pi**LY[2] adv., **slee·pi**NESS n. [-Y[2]]

sleet, n., & v.i. impers. Hail or snow falling mixed with rain; (vb) *it sleets* &c., s. falls. Hence **slee·ty**[2] a., **slee·ti**NESS n. [f. 14th c.; cf. G *schlosse* hailstone]

sleeve, n. Part of garment that covers arm (LAWN[1] *ss.*; LEG-*of-mutton s.*; *mandarin s.*, loose & open below elbow; *laugh in* one's *s.*, slyly, secretly; *have card, plan,* &c., *up* one's *s.*, in reserve, concealed but ready for use; *turn, roll, up* one's *ss.*, prepare to fight or work; *wear* one's HEART *upon* one's *s.*); tube enclosing rod or smaller tube; *s. coupling,* tube for connecting shafts or pipes; *s.-fish,* kind of cuttlefish, squid; *s.-link,* two buttons linked for fastening wristband; *s.-nut,* long nut with right-hand & left-hand screw-threads for drawing together pipes or shafts conversely threaded. Hence **(-)sleeve**D[2], **slee·ve**LESS, aa. [OE *sliefe*, *slȳf*, cf. MDu. *slove*, *sloof*, covering]

sleigh. See SLED.

sleight (-it), n. Dexterity, cunning, deceptive trick or device or movement, (archaic); *s.-of-hand,* juggling, legerdemain, prestidigitation, quickness of hand in fencing &c. [f. ON *slǽgdh* (*slǽgr* SLY, -TH[1])]

sle·nder, a. Of small girth or breadth, slim, not stout, (*s. stem, waist, pillar, girl, hand*); scanty, slight, meagre, inadequate, relatively small, (*s. hopes, means, store, income, acquaintance with subject, foundations for belief*). Hence **sle·nder**LY[2] adv., **sle·nder**NESS n. [f. 14th c., etym. dub.]

slept. See SLEEP[2].

sleu·th-hound (-lōō-, -lū-), n. Bloodhound (lit. & fig.); (also *sleuth*, esp. U.S.) detective. [*sleuth* var. of SLOT[2]]

slew[1], slue, (-ōō), v.t. & i., & n. Turn or swing forcibly or with effort out of the forward or ordinary position (often *round, to the left*, &c.); (n.) such change of position. [naut. wd, etym. dub.]

slew[2]. See SLAY.

slice, n., & v.t. & i. Thin broad piece or wedge cut off or out esp. from meat, bread, or cake; share, part taken or allotted, (*a s. of territory, of the profits*, &c.); kinds of implement with thin broad blade e.g. (also *fish-s.*) for helping fish, (also *s.-bar*) for clearing furnace-bars of clinker, or for lifting things out of frying-pan &c. (Vb) cut (often *up*) into ss., cut (piece) *off* adv. or prep., go through (air &c.) with cutting motion; make incorrect slicing motion with oar (also trans. *s. the water*) or golf-club (also trans. *s. the ball*). [vb f. n., f. OF *esclice* splinter (*esclicer* f. OHG *slizan*, G *schleissen*, cogn w. SLIT)]

slick, a. & adv. (colloq.). Dextrous, not marred by bungling, carried smoothly through; simple, absolute, unqualified, mere, (*did it out of s. perversity*); (adv.) directly, exactly, completely, (*came s. into the middle of them; hit him s. in the eye; bowled his middle stump s. out of the ground*). [var. of SLEEK]

slide[1], v.i. & t. (slid). Progress along smooth surface with continuous friction on same part of object progressing (cf. ROLL; *slid sitting down a grass slope; piston slides noiselessly up & down*), make move thus (*s. the drawer into its place*); glide over ice on both feet without skates with momentum got by running (*s. over delicate subject*, barely touch upon it); glide, go smoothly along; go without interference (*let things s.*, be negligent); go unconsciously or by imperceptible degrees (*slides into sin; s. from one note to another* in music); *sliding door*, drawn across aperture on s. instead of turning on hinges; *sliding keel*, CENTRE-board; *sliding, s.-, rule*, graduated, with sliding part for doing certain mathematical processes automatically; *sliding scale*, schedule for automatically varying one thing (esp. tax, wages, prices) in direct or inverse proportion to fluctuations of another; *sliding seat*, mounted on runners esp. in racing boats to lengthen rower's or sculler's stroke. Hence **sli·d**ER[1](1, 2) n., **sli·d**ABLE a. [OE *slidan*, cf. SLED]

slide[2], n. Track on ice made by persons' sliding; slope prepared with snow or ice for tobogganing; act of sliding; inclined plane down which goods &c. s. to lower level, shute; (also *s.-way*) part(s) of machine on or between which sliding part works; part of machine or instrument that slides, (also *s.-valve*) sliding piece that opens and closes aperture by sliding across it; thing slid into place, esp. glass holding object for microscope or magic-lantern picture. [f. prec.]

slight[1] (-īt), a. Slender, slim, frail-looking, (*saw a s. figure approaching; supported by a s. framework*); *a* or *some* inconsiderable (*has a s. cold; took a s. repast; have made a s. inquiry, some s. inquiries, into it*); not much or great or thorough, inadequate, scanty, *not* even *the* small*est*, (*after s. inquiry; did it with s. inconvenience to himself; there is not the slightest excuse for it; a conclusion based on very s. observation; a structure raised on s. foundations; paid him s. attention*). Hence **sligh·t**ISH[1](2) a., **sligh·t**LY[2] adv., **sligh·t**NESS n. [cf. ON *sléttr*, Du. *slecht*, G *schlecht* bad, *schlicht* smooth]

slight[2], v.t., & n. Treat or speak of (person, branch of study, &c.) as not worth attention, fail in courtesy or respect towards, markedly neglect; hence **sligh·t-ing**LY[2] adv. (N.) marked piece of neglect, omission of due respect &c., (*put a s. upon*, s.). [f. prec.]

sli·ly, var. of SLY*ly*.

slim, a. Of small girth or thickness, slenderly built, of slight shape; (f. S.-Afr. Du.) clever in stratagem, crafty, unscrupulous. Hence **sli·m**LY[2] adv., **sli·m**MISH[1](2) a., **sli·m**NESS n. [Du., = sly, bad, cf. G *schlimm* bad, cunning]

slime, n., & v.t. & i. Fine oozy mud or other substance of similar consistence, e.g. liquid bitumen or mucous exudation of fish &c.; *s.-gland* in molluscs &c. secreting s.; *s.-pit*, of liquid bitumen. (Vb) cover with s. (esp. of snake preparing prey for gorging); (slang) get *through, away, past, out of it*, &c., by physical or moral slipperiness. [OE *slim*, cf. Du. *slijm*, G *schleim*, also L *limus* mud]

sli·my, a. Of the consistence of slime; covered or smeared with or full of slime; slippery, hard to hold; cringingly dishonest; repulsively meek or flattering. Hence **sli·mi**LY[2] adv., **sli·mi**NESS n. [-Y[2]]

sling[1], v.t. & i. (slung), & n. Throw (rare; *s. ink* slang, be an author or journalist, write); hurl (stone &c.) from s., use s., whence **sli·ng**ER[1] (-ng-), n.; suspend with s., allow to swing suspended, arrange so as to be supported from above, hoist or transfer with s.; *s.-cart*, in which load is slung from axletree; *slung shot,* metal ball attached by thong &c. to wrist & used esp. by criminals as weapon. (N.) strap or string used with the hand to give impetus to small missile; kinds of apparatus used to support hanging weight, e.g. injured arm, rifle, ship's boat, goods being transferred; *s.-dog,* one of pair of hooks used to grapple goods for hoisting. [vb f. ON *slyngva,* cf. G *schlingen* entwine, twist; n. cogn., but prob. f. various Teut. nn.]

sling[2], n. (chiefly U.S.). Kind of toddy (esp. *gin-s.*). [?]

slink[1], v.i. (*slunk* or rarely *slank, slunk*). Go in secretive manner or with guilty or ashamed or sneaking air (usu. *off, away, by,* &c.). [OE *slincan* creep, cf. G *schlinken*]

slink[2], v.t. & i., & n. (Of animal) miscarry, produce (young, or abs.) prematurely. (N.) animal, esp. calf, so born; its flesh; *s.-butcher,* who deals in s. [perh. = prec., perh. var. of SLING[1]]

slip[1], v.i. & t. Slide unintentionally for short distance, lose footing or balance or place by unintended sliding, (*slipped in the mud* or *over the edge and fell*; *blanket slipped off bed*; *foot slips out of stirrup, ring off finger*); go with sliding motion (*as the door closes the catch slips into place*; *s. along* slang, go at great speed; *s. into* slang, pummel, belabour, eat heartily of); escape restraint or capture by being slippery or hard to hold or by not being grasped (*eel, opportunity, slipped through his fingers*; *let reins s. out of his hands*; *let s. the dogs of war* poet., begin war); make way unobserved or quietly or quickly (*how time slips away!*; *s. by, past*; *s. out of the room*; *s. off* or *away,* depart without leave-taking &c.; *just s. across to the baker's*; *errors will s. in*); make careless mistake (*slips now & then in his grammar*); let go from restraint of some kind (*s. greyhounds,* from leash; *s. anchor,* detach ship from it; *cow slips its calf,* produces it prematurely); pull (garment &c.) hastily *on, off*; insert stealthily or casually or with gliding motion (*slipped half a crown into the porter's hand, a white powder into her glass, the papers into his pocket, a marker between the pages*); escape from, give the s. to, (*dog slips his collar, prisoner his guard*; *the point had slipped my attention*). [ME, = escape, glide, prob. f. MLG *slippen*; & cf. OE *slipor* SLIPPERY]

slip[2], n. Act of slipping, blunder, accidental piece of misconduct, (*a s. on a piece of orange-peel may be fatal*; *there's many a s. 'twixt the cup & the lip,* nothing is certain till it has happened; *give* one *the s.,* escape from him; *s. of the tongue, pen,* thing said or written accidentally for something else; *a few ss. in youth are inevitable*); kinds of loose covering or garment, e.g. pillow-case, under bodice, petticoat, pinafore; leash for slipping dogs, device for suddenly loosing clip or attachment; artificial slope of stone as landing-stage; inclined plane on which ships are built or repaired; long narrow strip of thin wood, paper, &c., printer's proof on such paper; cutting taken from plant for grafting or planting, scion, (*a s. of a boy,* slim boy); one of the fielders (*short, long, s.*) stationed for balls glancing off bat to off side behind batsman, (sing. or pl.) this part of ground (*was caught in the ss.* or *at s.*); (without pl. or article) semifluid clay for coating or making pattern on earthenware; (Theatr.; pl.) part from which scenes are slipped on, part where actors stand before entering. [chiefly f. prec.; sense *clay* f. OE as in COWSLIP; senses *scion, strip,* prob. f. MDu. *slippe* strip]

slip-, comb. form of SLIP[1, 2]. *S.-carriage,* railway carriage on express for casting loose at station where rest of train does not stop; *s.-cover,* of calico &c. for furniture out of use; *s.-galley,* long narrow tray for holding composed type; *s.-hook,* with contrivance for loosing it readily at need; *s.-knot,* that can be undone by a pull, also knot that slips up & down string & tightens or loosens loop; *s.-rope,* with both ends on board so that casting loose either end frees ship from moorings; *sli·pshod,* having shoes down at heel, slovenly, (fig., of speech, writing, speaker, writer, method of work, &c.) negligent, careless, unsystematic, casual, loose in arrangement; *sli·pslop,* = slipshod (fig.), (as n.) slipshod writing &c., also (as redupl. of *slop*) washy stuff lit. or fig., weak drink, slops, sentimental talk or writing; *sli·pway,* shipbuilding or landing slip.

sli·pper, n., & v.t. Loose comfortable indoor shoe (HUNT[1]*-the-s.*; *bed-s.,* s.-shaped BED[1]-pan), whence **sli·pper**ED[2] a.; skid or shoe placed under wagon-wheel as drag; person who slips greyhounds in coursing-match; *s.-bath,* shaped like s., with covered end; *sli·pperwort,* calceolaria. (Vb) chastise (child &c.) with s.; hence **sli·pper**ING[1](1) n. [-ER[1]]

sli·ppery, a. (Of ground) hard to stand on, causing slips by its smoothness or muddiness, (fig., of subject) requiring tactful handling; (of object or person) hard to hold firmly owing to polish or sliminess or elusive motion, (fig.) unreliable, incalculable, shifty, unscrupulous. Hence **sli·pperi**LY[2] adv., **sli·pperi**NESS n. [f. OE *slipor* slippery (cf. SLIP[1]), -Y[2]]

sli·ppy, a. Slippery (vulg.); *look* or *be s.* slang, look sharp, make haste. [-Y[2]]

slit, v.t. & i. (slit), & n. Cut or (t. & i.) tear lengthwise, make long incision or rent in, cut into strips, (*threatened to s. his nose, tongue,* &c.; s. one's *weasand,* cut his throat; *s. hide into thongs, sheet of metal into strips* or *rods*; *if you strain it too hard it will s.*; *has s. my coat-sleeve from shoulder to wrist*); *slitting-rollers*, ribbed pair fitting into each other & slitting metal sheet by pressure. (N.) long incision; long narrow opening comparable to cut (*a s. is provided for the coin to drop through*; *the windows are mere ss.*; *the ss. on the neck are gill-openings*). [ME *slitten* (w. change of vowel) f. OE *slītan*, cf. Du. *slijten* wear out, G *schleissen* & *schlitzen* slit; cogn. w. SLICE]

sli·ther (-dh-), v.i. (colloq.). Slide unsteadily, go with irregular slipping motion. [var. of obs. *slidder*, OE *slidrian*, cf. SLIDE & OE *slidor* slippery]

sli·ver, n., & v.t. & i. Piece of wood torn from tree or timber, splinter, (vb, break t. & i. off as s., break t. & i. up into ss.); (in fishing; pr. slī-) side of small fish cut off as bait (vb, cut ss. from). [f. obs. *slive* vb f. OE *slīfan* split + -ER[1]]

slo·bber, v.i. & t., & n. Run at the mouth in infantile helplessness or maudlin emotion; wet (clothes, other person in kissing) with saliva; do (task) badly, botch, bungle. (N.) running saliva; maudlin talk, emotion, or kisses; hence **slo·bbery**[2] a., **slo·bberiness** n. [cf. Du. *slobberen* be messy]

sloe, n. (Small bluish-black plum, fruit of) BLACK[1]*thorn* (*s.-gin*, liqueur of ss. steeped in gin). [OE *slá*, cf. Du. *slee*]

sloe-worm. Var. of SLOW-WORM.

slog, v.i. & t., & n. Hit (i. & t.) hard & wildly esp. in boxing & at cricket; walk or work doggedly (usu. *on, away*); hence **slo·gger**[1] n. (N.) hard random hit. [?]

slō·gan, n. (Sc.). Highland war-cry; party cry, watchword, motto. [f. Gael. *sluaghghairm* (*sluagh* host, *gairm* outcry)]

sloid, sloyd, n. A system (orig. Finnish) of manual training, esp. by means of wood-carving, used in schools. [f. Sw. *slöjd* skill, cogn. w. SLEIGHT]

sloop, n. Small one-masted fore-&-aft-rigged vessel with mainsail & jib, & usu. gaff topsail & forestaysail; *s. of war*, cutter-rigged ship mounting guns; *s.-rigged*, rigged like s. [f. Du. *sloep* perh. f., perh. the source of, F *chaloupe* SHALLOP]

slop[1], n. (in pl. only), & v.i. & t. (Pl.) dirty water or liquid, waste contents of kitchen or bedroom vessels; (pl.) liquid food, as broth, gruel, &c., non-alcoholic drinks; *s.-basin*, for receiving dregs of cups at table; *s.-pail*, for removing bedroom ss. (Vb) spill (i. & t.), (allow to) flow over edge of vessel, (often *over, out*); make mess with ss. (or with ss. as subj.) upon (clothes, floor); *s. over* fig., gush, be maudlin. [earlier sense in sing. *puddle*; OE *-sloppe* liquid droppings, cf. *slyppe* in COWSLIP]

slop[2], n. (in pl. only). (Archaic) wide knickerbockers; ready-made clothing, clothes & bedding supplied to sailors in navy; *s.-room*, from which ss. are issued on man-of-war; *s.-seller, -shop*, of ready-made clothes. [f. ON *sloppr* gown (cf. OE *oferslop* upper garment)]

slop[3], n. (slang). Policeman. [=*ecilop* (*police* spelt backwards)]

slope, n., & v.i. & t. Inclined position or direction, the having of one end or side at higher level than the other, difference in level between two ends or sides of thing, the lying in a line neither parallel nor perpendicular to level ground or a line serving as standard, (*there is always a certain s. in a ship's deck*; *cut this side straight & the other with a s. to the right*; *the whole s. may amount to 2 ft*); piece of rising or falling ground, incline; position of soldier with rifle sloped (*come to the s.*); hence **slo·pewise** adv. (Vb) have or show s., lie or tend obliquely esp. to ground level, slant esp. up or down, whence **slo·pingly**[2] adv.; place or arrange or make in or at a s. (*s. arms*, place rifle at a s. over shoulder; *must s. the sides of the pit*); (slang) make off, go away, also saunter, walk about. [n. & v. 17th & 16th c. formations f. obs. or archaic adj. *slope*, which was perh. for *slopen* p.p. of *slip*, or perh. for ASLOPE]

slo·ppy, a. (Of road) wet with rain, full of puddles; (of floor, table, &c.) wet with slops, having water &c. spilt on it; (of work) unsystematic, not thorough; (of sentiment or talk) weakly emotional, maudlin. Hence **slo·ppily**[2] adv., **slo·ppiness** n. [SLOP[1], -Y[2]]

slosh &c. See SLUSH &c.

slot[1], n., & v.t. Groove, channel, slit, or long aperture, made in machine &c. to admit some other part, esp. slit for penny or other coin that sets working a *s.-machine* or automatic retailer of small wares; stage trapdoor; (vb) provide with slot(s). [f. OF *esclot* hollow of the breast, etym. dub.]

slot[2], n. Track of deer &c. esp. as shown by footprints. [f. AF & OF *esclot* hoof-print prob. f. ON *slódh* trail, cf. SLEUTH-HOUND]

slōth, n. Laziness, indolence, whence **slo·thful** a., **slo·thfully**[2] adv., **slo·thfulness** n.; kinds of S.-Amer. mammal with curved long-clawed feet living entirely in trees & capable only of very slow motion on ground; *s.-bear*, large-lipped black shaggy honey-eating bear of India & Ceylon; *s.-monkey*, kind of loris. [ME *slowthe* (SLOW, -TH[1])]

slouch (-owtsh), v.i. & t., & n. Droop, hang down negligently; go or stand or sit with loose ungainly attitude; bend one side of brim of (hat) downwards (opp. *cock*); hence **slou·chingly**[2] adv. (N.) slouching attitude or walk, stoop, downward bend of hat-brim (opp. *cock*);

(slang) incompetent or slovenly worker or operator or performance (esp. *is no s. at, this show* &c. *is no s.*); *s. hat,* with slouched brim. [cf. Icel. *slókr* slouching fellow, etym. dub.]

slough[1] (-ow), n. Quagmire, swamp, miry place, (*the S. of Despond,* state of hopeless floundering in sin). Hence **slough·y**[1] [-Y[2]] a. [OE *slóh,* etym. dub.]

slough[2] (-ŭf), n., & v.i. & t. Snake's cast skin, any part that an animal casts or moults; dead tissue that drops off from living flesh &c.; (fig.) habit &c. abandoned; hence **slou·ghy**[2] [-Y[2]] a. (Vb) drop off (t. & i.; often *off, away,* esp. in intr. sense) as s.; cast off s. [cf. LG *sluwe* husk]

Slova·k, n. & a. (Member) of a North-Hungarian Slav race. [Boh.]

slo·ven (-ŭ-), n. Personally untidy or dirty, careless & lazy, or unmethodical person. Hence **slo·ven**LY[1] a., **slo·venli**NESS n., **slo·ven**LY[2] adv. (archaic), **slo·v-en**RY n. [perh-f. Du. *slof* careless + *-ain* -AN]

Slove·ne, n., **Slovē·nian,** a. & n. (Member) of Slav race in Styria, Carinthia, &c.; (*-ian*) language of the Ss. [G, f. OSlav. (*slovo* word), whence also SLAV]

slow (-ō), a., adv., & v.i. & t. Not quick, deficient in speed, taking a long time to traverse a distance or do a thing, (*s. & steady wins the race*; *s. & sure,* haste is risky; *s. march,* of troops in funeral procession &c.; *s. music*), gradual (*s. growth, progress*), whence **slow·**LY[2] adv.; tardy, reluctant, lingering, (was not *s. to defend himself*), not hasty or easily moved (*is s. to anger*); (of clock &c., usu. pred.) behind correct time (*is 20′ s.*); dull-witted, stupid, (*is s. of speech, of wit,* whence **slow-witt**ED[2] a., &c.); deficient in interest or liveliness, dull, tedious, (*entertainment was voted s.*); *slow·coach,* person s. in action, dull of wit, or behind the times in opinions &c.; *s.-match,* s.-burning for igniting explosives; *s.-worm,* see foll.; hence **slow·**NESS n. (Adv., compar. *-er,* sup. *-est*) at s. pace, slowly, (being ousted by *slowly,* but still common when the adv. & not the vb gives the essential point, as *how s. he climbs!, please read* or *go s.* or *slower, watch goes s.,* cf. *I saw a man climb slowly up*; placed always after vb exc. in excl. with *how* or in comb. with part. as *s.-going, -moving*). (Vb) reduce one's speed, reduce speed of (train, ship, &c.), (usu. *down, up, off*). [OE *sláw,* cf. Du. *slee(uw),* Sw. *slö,* & perh. L *laevus* & Gk *laios* left]

slow-worm (-ō-), n. Small harmless reptile between snakes & lizards, blind-worm. [OE *slá-wyrm,* cf. MSw. *slā,* Norw. *slo,* slow-worm]

sloyd. See SLOID.

slub, n., & v.t. Wool slightly twisted as preparation for spinning; (vb) twist thus. [?]

slu·bber, v.t. & i. Do carelessly or bunglingly; slaver, slobber. [cf. Da. *slubbre,* G *schlubbern,* & SLOBBER]

sludge, n. Thick greasy mud; sewage. Hence **slu·dg**Y[2] a. [see SLUSH]

slue. See SLEW[1].

slug, n., & v.i. 1. Kinds of shell-less snail destructive to small plants; (vb) collect & destroy ss. in garden &c. 2. Bullet of irregular shape; roundish lump of metal; line of type in linotype printing. [sense 1 f. obs. n. = SLUGGARD; sense 2 either f. 1 w. ref. to shape, or as 1 w. ref. to weight, or f. obs. *slug* = SLOG]

slu·g-abed, n. (archaic). Person who lies late in bed. [as foll., ABED]

slu·ggard, n. Lazy sluggish person. [f. obs. *slug* be slothful f. Scand., + -ARD]

slu·ggish, a. Inert, inactive, torpid, indolent, slow-moving, (*a s. stream, circulation, temper, person*). Hence **slu·ggish**LY[2] adv., **slu·ggish**NESS n. [obs. *slug* SLUGGARD, -ISH[1]]

sluice (slo͞os), n., & v.t. & i. (Also *s.-gate, -valve*) sliding gate or other contrivance for changing level of a body of water by controlling flow into or out of it, floodgate; water above or below or issuing through floodgate; (also *s.-way*) artificial water-channel; *a* rinsing. (Vb) provide with sluice(s); flood with water from s.; rinse; pour or throw water freely upon; (of water) rush *out* &c. (as) from s. [f. OF *escluse* f. LL *exclusa* floodgate (orig. fem. p.p. see EXCLUDE)]

slum, n., & v.i. Dirty back street or court or alley in city. (Vb) go about the ss. to visit or examine condition of inhabitants; hence **slu·mm**ER[1] n. [cant wd, etym. dub.]

slu·mber, v.i. & t., & n. Sleep (distinguished in sense only by an implication of comfort or ease, which is not invariable, e.g. *fell into a troubled s.*; & in use by a rhet. or poet. tinge; the n. is often in pl., as *his ss. were interrupted by a knock*); *s. away,* waste (time) in s.; *s.-suit* (shop), pyjamas. Hence **slu·mb(e)r**OUS a., **slu·mb(e)rous**LY[2] adv., **slu·mber**ER[1] n. [earlier sense *doze*; n. f. vb, f. ME *slumen* (*slume* n. f. OE *slúma*) + -ER[5]; -b- as in NUMBER; cf. G *schlummern*]

slu·mmock, v.t. & i. (colloq.). Swallow greedily, wolf down; move or speak in awkward disorderly way. [cf. dial. *slammakin* sloven]

slump, n., & v.i., (slang). Sudden or rapid or great fall in prices or diminution of demand for commodity or interest taken in subject or undertaking; (vb) undergo s., fall in price, fall through, fail utterly. [earlier (17th-c.) sense *be bogged*; prob. imit., cf. PLUMP[2]]

slung. See SLING[1].

slunk. See SLINK[1].

slur, v.t. & i. (part. *slur·ring*), & n. Write

(t. & i.) or pronounce (t. & i.) indistinctly with letters or sounds running into one another; (Mus.) sing one syllable, sing (syllable), to more than one note, also sing or play legato, also mark s. over two or more notes in MS.; pass (fault, fact, &c.) lightly *over*, conceal or minimize; (archaic) put s. upon (person, character), make insinuations against. (N.) imputation, blame, stigma, (*he put a s. upon me*; *it is no s. upon his reputation that he should have* or *to say that*); piece of slurring in handwriting, pronunciation, or singing; curved mark used in music-writing to show that two or more notes are to be sung to one syllable or played or sung legato. [f. obs. *slur* thin mud, etym. dub.]

slush, n. Watery mud or thawing snow (cf. SLUDGE); (fig.) silly sentiment. Hence **slu·sh**Y[2] a. [f. 17th c., w. varr. *sludge* & *slutch*, also 19th c. *slosh*; etym. dub.]

slut, n. Slovenly woman, slattern; (joc.) girl. Hence **slu·tt**ERY(4) n., **slu·tt**ISH[1] a., **slu·ttish**LY[2] adv., **slu·ttish**NESS n. [perh. f. Scand., cf. Sw. dial. *slåta*, Norw. *slott* idler]

sly, a. (slyer, slyest). Cunning, wily, hypocritical; practising concealment (*s. dog*, person who keeps his peccadilloes or pleasures quiet), done &c. in secret (*on the s.*, privately, without publicity); knowing, arch, bantering, insinuating, ironical; *sly·boots*, s. person (in playful use, esp. to or of child or animal). Hence **sly·**LY[2] adv., **sly·**NESS n. [ME *sleigh* f. ON *slœgr*, perh. cogn. w. SLAY; cf. SLEIGHT]

slype, n. Passage from cathedral transept to chapter-house or deanery. [var. of SLIP[2]]

smack[1], n., & v.i. Flavour, taste that suggests presence of something; barely discernible amount *of* some food-material &c. or *of* a quality &c. present in dish or person's character, tinge, tincture, spice, dash, *of*, (*has a s. of ginger*, *of the cask*, *in it*, *of recklessness*, *of the old Adam*, *in him*). (Vb) have a slight curious or unexpected or secondary taste (rare); taste slightly *of*, suggest by taste or otherwise the presence or effects *of*, (*wine smacking of the cork*; *his manner smacked of superciliousness*). [vb f. n., OE *smæc*, cf. G *geschmack* n., *schmecken* vb]

smack[2], n., v.t. & i., & adv. Slight explosive report as of surface struck with palm, of lips parted suddenly, or of whip cracked; blow with palm, slap; hard hit at cricket; loud kiss (*gave her a hearty s.*). (Vb) slap (person's face &c.) with palm; part (t. & i. of lips) noisily in eager anticipation or enjoyment of food or other delight; crack (t. & i. of whip). (Adv., colloq.) with a s., in sudden direct violent way, outright, exactly, (*went s. through windows*, *into ditch*; *hit him s. on the nose*). [prob. imit., & unconnected w. prec.; cf. MDu. *smack* n., *smacken* vb]

smack[3], n. Sloop esp. for fishing; *sma·cks-man*, sailor on s. [f. MDu. *smacke*, etym. dub.]

sma·cker, n. (slang). Loud kiss; sounding blow; large or remarkable specimen of anything. [SMACK[2], -ER[1]]

small (-awl), a., n., & adv. Not large, of deficient or comparatively little size or strength or power or number, consisting of minute units (*s. rain*), (of agent) not doing thing on large scale, (usu. without emotional implications of LITTLE, e.g. not *a dear s. pony* or *a dirty s. scoundrel*; *s. farmer*, *shopkeeper*, on s. scale; *has a s. voice*; *s.* FRY[1]; *s.* HOURS; *s. & early*, party with few guests & not kept up late; *the still s. voice*, conscience; *coat is s.* or *too s. for me*; *s. craft*, boats; *came in s. numbers*; *this beer is very s.*, weak, watery); (as distinctive epithet) of the smaller kind (*s.-sword*, rapier or sword for thrusting only; *s. beer* archaic, of light kind); *think no s. beer of* oneself, be conceited; *chronicle s. beer*, talk of trifles as important; *look*, *feel*, *s.*, be humiliated; *s. change*, copper & silver coins, (transf.) trivial remarks; *s. gross*, ten dozen; *s.-arms*, fire-arms other than cannon; *s. letters*, not capitals; *s. capitals*, of less height than the fount's regular capitals; *s. pica*, size of TYPE; *s. hand*, ordinary writing, opp. *text-hand*; *s. debt*, not above largest amount recoverable in county court; *s.-clothes* archaic, knee-breeches; not much of (*& s. blame to him*, *& s. wonder*, comments on conduct &c. just described; *there was no s. excitement about it*; *has s. Latin*, knows little of it); unimportant, trifling, (*s. talk*, ordinary society conversation; *the s. worries of life*; *is great in s. matters*); socially undistinguished, poor, obscure, humble, (*great & s.*, all classes; *lives in a s. way*, unpretentiously; *have experimented with radium in a s. way*; *s. people love to talk of great*); morally mean, ungenerous, petty, paltry, (*his s. spiteful nature*; *only a s. man would think of that at such a time*; *I call it s. of him to remind me of it*), whence **small-mind**ED[2] a.; *sma·llpox*, highly contagious & fatal disease with fever & pustules; hence **sma·ll**ISH[1](2) a., **sma·ll**NESS n. (N.) *the* slenderest part *of* something, esp. *s. of the back*, hinder part of waist; (pl., at Oxford) responsions. (Adv.) SING *s.* [OE *smæl*, cf. Du., Da., & Sw. *smal*, G *schmal*, thin]

sma·llage (-awlĭj), n. Wild celery. [prec., F *ache* f. L *apium* parsley]

smalt (-awlt), n. Glass coloured blue with cobalt; pigment made by pulverizing this. [F, f. It. *smalto* f. Teut., cogn. w. SMELT[1]]

smart[1], v.i., & n. (Of person or part of him, or of wound lit. or fig. or the missile or insult &c. that has inflicted it) feel or give acute pain, rankle, (*my finger smarts*; *rushed off smarting with nettle-stings, under disappointment*, &c.; *with the gibe yet smarting in his brain*; *s. for*, be paid out for, suffer consequences of, esp. as threat *you shall s. for this*); (n.) bodily or mental sharp pain, stinging sensation; *s.-money*, paid or exacted as penalty or compensation; *smar·tweed*, the Water Pepper. [OE *smeortan*, cf. Du. *smarten*, G *schmerzen*; cogn. w. L *mordēre* bite, Gk *smerdaleos* terrible]

smart[2], a. Severe, sharp, vigorous, lively, brisk, (*gave him a s. rap over the knuckles*; *had a s. skirmish, walk, bout of toothache*; *went off at a s. pace*); clever, ingenious, showing quick wit or ingenuity, keen in bargaining, quick to take advantage, (*a s. talker, retort, saying, device, invention*; *a s. officer, servant, lad*, ready & intelligent; *s. dealing*, selfishly clever to verge of dishonesty); bright & fresh in appearance, spruce, in perfect order or repair, in gay or fashionable clothes, well groomed, showing bright colours or new paint, (*s. clothes, a s. garden*; *person, house, ship, looks quite s.*); conspicuous in society, leading the fashion, stylish, (*s. people*; *the s. set*). Hence **smar·t**EN[6] v.t. & i., **smar·t**LY[2] adv., **smar·t**NESS n. [OE *smeart*, cf. prec.]

smash, v.t. & i., n., & adv. Break (t. & i.) utterly to pieces (often *up*), shatter, bash *in* with crushing blow, (*a smashing blow*, of irresistible force); utterly rout & disorganize (enemy); hit (lawn-tennis ball) downwards over net with great force; (of business firm) break, go bankrupt, come to grief; (of vehicle &c.) crash *into* another or an obstacle; (slang) utter false coin. (N.) breaking to pieces; violent fall or collision or disaster (*go to s.*, be spoilt or disorganized or ruined); smashing stroke in lawn tennis (see vb); violent blow with fist &c.; bankruptcy, series of commercial failures; drink of spirit & water iced & flavoured (usu. *brandy-s.*); *s.-up*, complete s. (Adv., with vbs of motion) with a s. (*went s. into a goods train*). [prob. imit.]

sma·sher, n. In vbl senses; esp. (slang), convincing argument or smashing blow or heavy fall. [-ER[1]]

smatch, n. (now rare). = SMACK[1] n.

sma·ttering, n. Slight superficial knowledge of a language or subject. So **sma·tter**ER[1] n. [f. obs. *smatter* talk ignorantly, prate, earlier (14th c.) defile, etym. dub.]

smear, v.t. & i., & n. Daub with greasy or sticky substance or with something that stains, (of grease &c.) make marks on, make a s.; blot, obscure outline of, (writing, drawing). (N.) blotch made by smearing; hence **smear·**Y[2] a., **smear·i**NESS n. [OE *smerian* (*smeru* n., fat, cf. G *schmeer*); cogn. w. Gk *muron* ointment]

sme·ctite, n. Kind of whitish clay used for taking out grease from cloth &c. [f. Gk *smēktis* fuller's earth (*smaō* wipe), -ITE[1](2)]

smeech, smitch, n. (dial.). Smell of burning or smouldering. [OE *sméc, smíc*, cogn. w. *smoke*]

sme·gma, n. Sebaceous soaplike secretion in folds of the skin, esp. of the prepuce. Hence **smegmă·t**IC a. [f. Gk *smēgma -atos* soap (*smēkhō* = *smaō* see prec., -M)]

smell, n., & v.t. & i. (*smelt* or rarely *smelled*). Nasal sense by which odours are perceived (*s. is less acute in man than in most animals*; *has a fine sense of s.*; *is perceptible to s. as well as sight*); quality in substances that affects this sense, odour, (*has no, a sweet, pungent, disgusting, peculiar, close, s.*; *the s. of thyme, carrion*); bad odour, whence **sme·ll**Y[2] a. (colloq.); act of inhaling in order to ascertain s. (*take a s. at it*); hence **sme·ll**LESS a. (Vb) perceive s. of, detect presence of by s., (*am sure I s. gas*; *horses smelt the water a mile off*; *s. a rat* fig., suspect foul dealing &c.), whence **sme·ll**ABLE a.; inhale s. of, set one's sense of s. to work *at* (*smelt it* or *at it to see if it was high*; *came up & smelt at my calves*); (of dog) hunt *out* by s., (fig. of person) find *out* (secret, plotter, &c.) by investigation, (of dog or fig. of person) sniff or search *about*; perceive ss., have sense of s. (*can, do, fishes s.?*); emit s. usu. of kind specified by adj. or adv., suggest or recall the s. *of*, (*flowers that do not s.*; *smells sweet, nice, disgustingly, of garlic, of brandy*; *s. of the lamp*, seem to have been composed laboriously at night; *s. of the shop*, be over-technical; *s. of jobbery, nepotism*, &c., suggest these); stink, be rank; seem from the s. to be (*dish, milk, smells good, sour*); *smelling-bottle*, pocket phial of *smelling-salts*, ammonium carbonate mixed with scent to be sniffed as cure for faintness &c. [ME *smel(len)*, excl. E]

sme·ller, n. In vbl senses; also (slang): the nose; severe blow esp. on the nose. [-ER[1]]

smelt[1], v.t. Extract metal from (ore) by melting; extract (metal) from ore by melting. [cf. Da. *smelte*, G *schmelzen*, & the prob. connected MELT[2]]

smelt[2], n. Small fish allied to salmon & prized as food. [OE, cf. Du. *smelt*, G *schmelte*, sand-eel]

smelt[3]. See SMELL.

smew, n. Kind of fishing duck. [also *smee, smeath*, etym. dub.]

smī·lax, n. Genus of climbing shrubs some of which yield sarsaparilla; a Cape vine much used in decoration. [L f. Gk]

smile, v.i. & t., & n. Relax features often by parting lips into pleased or kind or gently amused or indulgently contemptuous or sceptical expression or forced imitation of these, look (*up*)*on* or *at* with such expression, (*s. sweetly, indulgently, cynically, bitterly*; *s. at the claims of*, ridicule or show indifference to them), whence **smi·ling**LY[2] adv.; express by smiling (*s. welcome, consent, appreciation*, &c.); give *a s.* of specified kind (*smiled an ironical, a curious, s.*); drive (person's vexation &c.) *away*, bring (person) *into* or *out of* a mood, by smiling; *come up smiling*, face fresh difficulty (w. ref. to boxer beginning new round); be or appear propitious, have bright aspect, seem to look propitiously (*up*)*on*, (*fortune, occasion, smiles on us*; *all nature looks smiling & gay*). (N.) act of smiling, smiling expression or aspect; hence **smi·le**LESS a. [cf. MHG *smielen*]

smirch, v.t., & n. Stain, soil, smear, spot, (lit., & fig. as *a smirched reputation*). [perh. f. OF *esmorcher* torture, brand]

smirk, v.i., & n. (Put on or wear) affected or silly smile, simper. [OE *smercian*, excl. E]

smite, v.t. & i. (*smote* & archaic *smit*, *smitten* & archaic *smit*), & n. Strike, hit, (chiefly archaic or joc.; *whosoever shall s. thee on thy right cheek*; *smote his hands together*; *smote the harpstrings*; *s. off his head*; *smote the first ball for four*; *an idea smote him*, suddenly came); inflict severe defeat on (*s. them hip & thigh*, utterly defeat them; *we hope to s. them*); chastise (*God shall s. thee*; *his conscience smote him*); (chiefly in p.p.) strike or seize or infect or possess *with* disease or desire or fascination (*city, person, smitten with plague, palsy*; *am smitten with her charms* or *her* or abs.; *smitten with a desire to*; come forcibly or abruptly (*up*)*on* (*wave smote upon the cliff*; *sun's rays smiting upon him*; *sound smites upon the ear*); hence **smi·**TER[1] n. (N.) blow, stroke, attempt, (colloq.). [OE *smitan*, cf. Du. *smijten*, G *schmeissen* (OHG *smîzan* to stroke, smear)]

smith, n. Worker in metal esp. one who forges iron, blacksmith, (the gen. sense chiefly in comb., as *gold, silver, tin, white, -s.*). [OE cf. Du. *smid*, G *schmied*]

smitheree·ns, smi·thers, (-dh-) nn. pl. Small fragments (*smash* &c. *to* or *into s.*). [19th c. only, etym. dub.; *-een* Ir. dim. ending]

smi·thery, n. Smith's work; (esp. in Admiralty dockyards) smithy. [-ERY]

Smi·thfield, n. (Used for) the London meat market. [*S.* in London]

smi·thy (-dhĭ), n. Blacksmith's workshop, forge. [f. ON *smidhja*, cf. obs. E *smithe* f. OE *smiththe*]

smitten. See SMITE.

smock, n., & v.t. Chemise (archaic); child's overall; *s.-frock*, field-labourer's outer linen garment of shirtlike shape & with upper part closely gathered; *s.-mill*, windmill of which the cap only & not the body revolves. (Vb) adorn with SMOCKING. [OE *smoc* (*smúgan* creep into), cf. OHG *smoccho*]

smo·cking, n. Honeycomb ornamentation on garment of which the basis is close gathers as on smock-frock. [-ING[1]]

smoke[1]**,** n. Volatile products of combustion, esp. visible vapour with carbon &c. in suspension emitted by burning substance (*a column, cloud, of s.*; *end in s.*, come to nothing; *no s. without* FIRE[1]; *from s. into smother*, from one evil to another or a worse; *like s.* slang, without check or difficulty, rapidly, easily); spell of tobacco-smoking (*must have a s.*); (slang) cigar; *s.-ball*, projectile filled with material emitting dense smoke used to conceal military operations &c., also ball used in trap-shooting & giving puff of s. when struck, also medical appliance for inhaling vapour from in asthma &c.; *s.-bell*, suspended over lamp &c. to protect ceiling; *s.-consumer*, apparatus for utilizing instead of releasing s. of furnace or fireplace, & so *s.-consuming* a.; *s.-dried*, cured in s.; *s.-jack*, machine for turning roasting-spit by use of current of hot air in chimney; *s.-plant, -tree*, ornamental shrub with feathery s.-like fruit-stalks; *s.-rocket*, contrivance for injecting s. into drain to discover leak; *s.-screen* (mil., nav.), s. diffused to hide operations; *s.-stack*, funnel & steam escape pipes of steamer; *s.-stone*, cairngorm. Hence **smo·ke**LESS a., **smo·keless**LY[2] adv., **smo·keless**NESS n. [OE *smoca*, cf. *sméocan* to smoke; cogn. w. Du. *smook*, G *schmauch*]

smoke[2]**,** v.i. & t. Emit s. or visible vapour, reek, steam, (*altars s.*; *his smoking blade, steeds*; *meat smoking on the board*; *lamp is smoking*, not burning clear), (of chimney or fire) discharge s. into room; colour or darken or obscure, spoil taste of in cooking, preserve or cure, suffocate, rid of insects &c., with s. (*lamp smokes ceiling*; *smoked wood*, fumed; *smoked glass*, darkened with s. for looking at sun &c.; *the porridge is smoked*; *smoked ham, haddock*, &c.; *s. insects, plants*, kill, cleanse, them by fumigation; *s. out wasps, wasps'-nest*, &c., destroy by injecting s.); inhale & exhale s. of (tobacco-pipe, cigar, cigarette, tobacco, opium, stramonium, cane, brown paper; *put that in your pipe & s. it*, reflect upon what has been said, esp. some admonition or rebuke), whence **smo·k**ABLE a.; s. tobacco (*smokes too much* or *like a chimney*; *will you s.?*), bring one*self* into specified state by smoking (*has smoked himself ill, sick, stupid, into tranquillity*); (schoolboy slang) blush; get inkling, become suspicious or aware, of, (archaic) quiz, make fun of, (person &c.); *smoking-cap, -jacket*, of ornamental kind worn while one smokes; *smoking-car*(*riage*) or *compartment,* reserved for smokers on railway-train; *smoking concert,* concert at which smoking is allowed; *smoking-mixture,* blend of tobaccos for smoking in pipe; *smoking-room,* in hotel or house kept for smoking in (*s.-r. talk* &c., esp. such as is suited for men only); *smoking-tobacco* (esp. for use in pipes). [OE *smocian* (prec.)]

smo·ker, n. In vbl senses; also or esp.: person who habitually smokes tobacco (*s.'s heart, throat,* ailments due to excessive smoking); smoking-carriage on train, smoking-concert. [-ER[1]]

smo·ky, a. Emitting, veiled or filled with, obscure (as) with, stained with or coloured like, smoke (*a s. fire, city, room, hue, ceiling*). Hence **smo·ki**LY[2] adv., **smo·ki**NESS n. [-Y[2]]

smōlt, n. Second-year salmon at stage between parr & grilse after development of silvery scales. [cf. OE *smolt* serene]

smōōth[1] (-dh), a. Of relatively even & polished surface, free from perceptible projections or lumps or indentations or roughness or (of liquid) undulations, not wrinkled or pitted or scored or hairy, that can be traversed without check, (*s. skin, surface, morocco, brow, chin*; *am now in s. water,* have passed obstacles or difficulties; *bring the paste to a s. consistence*; *had a s. passage,* across sea; *course of true love never did run s.*; *s. hair,* esp. flattened down on head); free from harshness of sound or taste (*s. verse,* with easy & correct rhythm; *s. claret, spirit,* &c.; *s. breathing* in Gk Gram., unaspirated sound of initial vowel, also symbol of this); equable, unruffled, polite, conciliatory, complimentary, flattering, (*s. temper, manners*; *s. face,* esp. hypocritically friendly, whence **smoothfac**ED[2] a.; *s. things,* esp. flattery or insincere encouragement, whence **smooth**SPOKEN, **smooth-tongu**ED[2], aa.); *s.-bore,* gun with unrifled barrel. Hence **smoo·th**LY[2] adv., **smoo·th**NESS n. [OE *smóđh* (rare, usu. *smēđhe*); excl. E]

smooth[2], v.t. & i., & n. Make s. (often *out, over, down, away*; *s. over* or *away differences, perplexities, difficulties,* &c., reduce or get rid of in fact or appearance); free from impediments or discomfort (*s. the way*; *will s. his declining years*); cloak *over* faults &c.; become s. (usu. *down*; *sea presently smoothed down*); (n.) smoothing touch or stroke (*gave his hair a s.*); *smoothing-iron,* implement usu. heated to s. linen &c.; *smoothing-plane,* small plane for finishing the planing of wood. [f. prec.]

smote. See SMITE.

smo·ther (-ŭdh-), n., & v.t. & i. Smouldering ashes &c. (archaic; *from the* SMOKE[1] *into the s.*); cloud of dust, spray, smoke, &c., or obscurity caused by it (rare). (Vb) suffocate, stifle, kill by stopping breath of or excluding air from, (*smothered mate* in chess, when king having no vacant space to move to is checked by knight); overwhelm *with* kisses, gifts, kindness, &c.; put out or keep down (fire) by heaping with ashes &c.; suppress, conceal or secure concealment of, keep from notice or publicity, burke, (often *up*; *s. a yawn*; *with smothered curses*; *the facts, the recommendations of the committee, were smothered up*); cover entirely *in* (*strawberries smothered in cream*); (rare) perish of suffocation, have difficulty in breathing. [vb f. n., ME *smorther* (OE *smorian* stifle, cf. Du. *smoren* stifle, stew, G *schmoren* stew, + agent-suf. *-ther*)]

smo·thery, a. Stifling. [-Y[2]]

smou·lder (-ō-), v.i., & n. Burn without flame, burn inwardly or in suppressed way or unseen; (of feelings &c.) exist, operate, be nursed, undetected or without conspicuous effects (*smouldering discontent, hatred, rebellion*); (n.) smouldering combustion (*the s. will soon be a flame*). [n. f. vb, ME *smolderen* (obs. *smolder* n. smoke), etym. dub.]

smudge[1], **smutch** (archaic), v.t. & i., & n. Smear or blot or blur lines of (writing, drawing); make dirt-mark or confused blot or smear on (face, paper, surface); (usu. *-tch*) defile, sully, stain with disgrace, impair purity of, (person's record, fame, &c.); (of ink, drawing, &c.) become blurred (*smudges easily*). (N.) dirt-mark lit. or (esp. *-tch*) fig., blotted line, blurred mark; hence **smu·dg**Y[2] a., **smu·dg**ILY[2] adv., **smu·dg**INESS n. [*-ge* older as vb (1430), *-tch* as n. (1530); etym. dub.]

smudge[2], n. Outdoor fire with dense smoke made to keep off insects &c. [?]

smug, a. & n. Of commonplace respectable narrow-minded self-satisfied comfortable unambitious unimaginative character or appearance; hence **smu·g**NESS n. (N., chiefly university slang) person ill-fitted for society or without athletic pursuits or interests. [?]

smu·ggle, v.t. Import or export (goods, or abs.) illegally, esp. without payment of customs duties (often *in, out, over*), whence **smu·ggl**ER[1], **smu·ggl**ING[1], nn.; convey secretly *in, out,* &c., or put *away* &c. into concealment. [f. LG *smuggeln*]

smut, n., & v.t. & i. (Spot or smudge made by) small flake of soot; *ditto, brother s.* (nursery &c.), tu quoque retort to criticism; obscene talk or words or stories; disease of corn by which parts of the ear change to black powder; *s.-ball,* kinds of fungus; *s.-mill,* machine for cleansing grain from s.; hence **smu·tt**Y[2] a., **smu·tt**ILY[2] adv., **smu·tt**INESS n. (Vb) mark with s. or ss.; infect (corn) with, (of corn) contract, s. [cf. Sw. *smuts* dirt, G *schmutz* dirt, the corn-disease]

smutch. See SMUDGE.

Smyrˑniot(e), a. & n. (Native or inhabitant) of Smyrna. [-OT[2]]

snack, n. Slight or casual or hurried meal; *go ss.*, go shares (*ss.!*, claim to share). [orig. sense *snap* n. & v. (of dog), cf. MDu. *snac* n., *snakken* vb, snap]

snaˑffle, n. Bridle consisting of *s.-bit*, or plain slender jointed bit without curb, & single rein; *ride* one *on the s.* (fig.), manage him gently. Hence **snaˑffl**ED[2] a. [cf. Du. *snavel*, G *schnabel*, mouth, beak]

snag, n., & v.t. Jagged projecting point, e.g. irregular or broken tooth, stump of branch remaining on tree, pointed root or stump poking out of ground, piece of rough timber or rock embedded in river or sea bottom & impeding navigation; hence **snagg**ED[2], **snaˑgg**Y[2], aa. (Vb) run (ship) on s.; clear (land, waterway, tree-trunk) of ss. [prob. f. Scand. (Norw. *snag* spike)]

snail, n., & v.t. & i. Kinds of slimy slow-creeping gasteropod mollusc, most of them with spiral shell & horns or retractile eye-stalks, some used as food esp. in France, whence **snaiˑl**ERY(3) n., & many destructive in gardens (*Roman s.*, the chief edible kind; *s.'s gallop, pace*, very slow locomotion); (also *s.-wheel*) notched wheel in clock resembling s. in outline determining number of strokes in striking the hours; (also *s.-clover, -trefoil*) kinds of leguminous plant including lucerne with spiral pods; *s.-fish*, with ventral sucker for clinging; *s.-slow*, slow as a s.; hence **snaiˑl**LIKE a. (Vb) rid (garden) of, hunt for, ss. [OE *snægl*, cf. OHG *snegil*, ON *snigill*]

snake, n. Serpent (commoner in ordinary speech, more loosely applied so as to include s.-like lizards &c., & specially used of the common British harmless kind; *s. in the grass*, hidden danger or secret enemy; *warm, cherish*, &c., *a s. in* one's *bosom*, meet with ingratitude or receive evil for good; SCOTCH[2] *the s.*; *see ss.*, have delirium tremens; *raise* or *wake ss.*, make disturbance, start violent quarrel; *Ss.!*, int. of anger); treacherous cold-hearted person; *s.-charmer, -ming*, see SERPENT; *s.-fence* (of horizontal tree-trunks only, laid zigzag with overlapping ends to support each other); *s. lizard*, kinds of lizard with rudimentary or no legs; *s.-locked*, with ss. instead of hair; *snaˑkeshead*, the fritillary plant; *s.-stone*, ammonite; *s.-weed*, bistort. [OE *snaca*, cf. MLG *snake*, ON *snákr*, Sw. *snok*]

snaˑky, a. Infested with snakes; snake-like in appearance or in such attributes as venom, guile, coldness, ingratitude; *s. hair* (of the Furies with snakes for hair). Hence **snaˑki**NESS n. [-Y[2]]

snap, v.t. & i., & n. Make sudden audible bite (*dog snapped viciously*; *s. at*, try to bite, also speak irritably to; *s. at bait, offer, chance*, &c., accept eagerly), (fig.) say ill-tempered or spiteful things (*s. out*, say irritably), whence **snaˑpp**ISH[1] a., **snaˑppish**LY[2] adv., **snaˑppish**NESS n.; bite *off* (*s. off* one's *nose*, esp. fig. interrupt him angrily or rudely); pick *up* (scraps, or fig. bargain &c.) hastily, whence **snaˑpp**ER[1]**-up** n.; take *up* (interlocutor) without letting him finish; break (t. & i.) with sharp crack (*s. the string, a stick*; *oar, wire, snaps*); produce report from, emit report or crack, (*s. pistol, whip*; *s.* one's *fingers*, make audible fillip esp. *at* person &c. in contempt; *pistol snaps*, either in going off or in missing fire), close (t. & i.) &c. with snapping sound (*s. the clasp*, one's *teeth together*; *the door snapped to*); take instantaneous photograph of (esp. unconscious or unwilling subject); *snapping turtle*, ferocious American freshwater kind. (N.) act or sound of snapping (also quasi-adv., as *s. went an oar*); spring-catch fastening bracelet &c.; kinds of small crisp cake; a card-game; (usu. *cold s.*) sudden spell of frost; crispness of style, fresh vigour or liveliness in action, go, dash, spring, whence **snaˑpp**Y[2] a.; =*snapshot* n. (see below); (Theatr.) short engagement as actor; (attrib., esp. of parliamentary or other deliberative proceedings) taken by surprise, brought on without notice, &c. (*a s. division, debate, crisis*, &c.); *s.-bolt, -lock*, going home automatically with spring on closing of door &c.; *snaˑpdragon*, kinds of plant with bag-shaped flower that can be made to gape, antirrhinum, also Christmas game of plucking raisins from dish of burning brandy; *s.-hook, -link*, with spring allowing entrance but barring escape of cord, link, &c.; *snap shot* n., shot taken with little or no delay in aiming; *snapˑshot*, instantaneous photograph taken with hand camera, (v.t., also *-shoot*) take such photograph of. [f. MLG *snappen* (*snavel* beak), cf. G *schnappen*]

snare, n., & v.t. Trap for catching birds or animals, esp. one made with cord; (Surg.) wire loop for catching & extracting polypi &c.; device for tempting enemy or dupe to expose himself to capture, defeat, failure, disgrace, loss, &c.; thing that acts as a temptation (*popularity is often a s.*); (pl.) twisted strings of gut or hide stretched across lower head of side-drum to produce rattling sound. (Vb) catch (bird &c.) in s., whence **-snar**ER[1] n.; get (person) into s. (less common, & with more of the lit. sense, than *ensnare*). [f. ON *snara*, cf. Du. *snaar* string]

snarl[1], v.i. & t., & n. (Of dog) make high-pitched quarrelsome growl; (of person) speak cynically, make ill-tempered complaints or criticisms; *s. out*, utter in snarling tone; express (discontent &c.) by snarling; hence **snarˑl**ER[1] n., **snarˑl-**

ingLY[2] adv. (N.) act or sound of snarling; hence **snar·ly**[2] a. [frequent. of earlier *snar*, cf. MHG & MLG *snarren* (G *schnarren*)]

snarl[2], v.t. & i., & n. (Archaic) entangle, become entangled, (*a snarled skein*, intricate business); adorn exterior of (narrow metal vase) with raised work made by indirect internal hammering with *snarling-iron*; (n., archaic) tangle. [frequent. of SNARE]

snatch, v.t. & i., & n. Seize quickly, eagerly, or unexpectedly, esp. with suddenly outstretched hand(s), rescue narrowly *from*, secure with difficulty, carry suddenly *away* or *from*, (*snatched his gun up, down*; *wind snatched my cap off*; *child snatches its food*; *s. kiss, opportunity*, &c.; *was snatched from the jaws of death*; *s. a half-hour's repose*; *s. victory out of defeat*; *snatched away, from us, by premature death*); shoot out hand(s) *at* to seize (also fig., as *s. at offer*, take it eagerly). (N.) act of snatching (*made a s. at it*); (usu. pl.) fragment(s) or short burst(s) *of* song or recitation or talk, short spell(s) of action (*only works by ss.*, fits & starts), whence **sna·tchy**[2] a., **sna·tchi**LY[2] adv. [ME *snacchen*, etym. dub.; perh. cogn. w. SNACK, SNECK]

sneak, v.i. & t., & n. Slink, go furtively, (often *in, out, past, round, about, off, away*, &c.), whence **snea·kers** n. pl. slang, silent shoes; (part.) furtive, not avowed, (*have a sneaking kindness for him*, an affection that one cannot justify by reason); (schoolboy slang) peach, tell tales; (slang) make off with, steal; hence **snea·king**LY[2] adv. (N.) mean cowardly underhand person; (schoolboy slang) informer, telltale; (Cricket) ball bowled along the ground; *s.-thief* (stealing from open doors or windows). [f. 16th c., etym. dub.]

sneck, n., & v.t. (chiefly Sc.). Latch. [ME (n.), perh. cogn. w. SNACK, SNATCH]

sneer, v.i. & t., & n. Smile derisively (often *at*); utter derisive words esp. of a covert or ironical kind (usu. *at*); put (person) *down, out of countenance*, &c., take *away* (person's reputation, happiness, &c.), by sneering; hence **sneer·**ER[1] n., **sneer·ing**LY[2] adv. (N.) sneering look or remark. [earlier sense *snort*; cf. NFris. *sneer* a taunt, *sneere* to scorn]

sneeze, v.i., & n. Make explosive sound in involuntarily expelling anything that irritates interior of nostrils (*not to be sneezed at*, passable, not contemptible); *s. into a basket* (euphem.), be guillotined; (n.) act or sound of sneezing. [ME *snesen*, var. of *fnesen* (due to misreading of *f* as *ſ* when *fnese* had been made unfamiliar by substitution of *neeze*) f. OE *ge-fnēsan* cf. Du. *fniezen*, Gk *pneō* breathe]

snick, v.t., & n. Cut small notch or make small incision in; (Cricket) slightly deflect course of (ball) with bat. (N.) slight notch or cut; (Cricket) snicking touch with bat. [?]

sni·cker, v.i., & n. Whinny, neigh; = SNIGGER. [imit.]

sni·ckersnee·, n. (facet.). Knife, esp. one usable as weapon. [perh. f. obs. *snick-or-snee* a fight with knives, earlier *stick or snee*, f. Du. *steken* thrust, *snijen* cut]

snide, a. & n. (slang). Counterfeit, bogus; (n.) s. jewelry or coin(s); *snidesman*, utterer of false coin. [cant word, etym. dub.]

Sni·der, n. (Also *S.-rifle*) early pattern of breechloading rifle. [inventor]

sniff, v.i. & t., & n. Draw up air audibly through nose to stop it from running or as expression of contempt (*s. at*, try the smell of, also show contempt for or discontent with, also, of dog, show disposition to bite person's *calves*); draw up or *up* (air, liquid, scent), draw up scent of (flower, brandy, meat, &c.), into nose; (n.) act or sound of sniffing, amount of air &c. sniffed up. [imit.; f. 14th c.]

sni·ffy, a. (colloq.). Disdainful, contemptuous; (of thing that should be odourless) slightly malodorous. [-Y[2]]

sni·fting-valve, n. Air-escape valve in steam-engine cylinder. [f. obs. *snift* = SNIFF]

sni·gger, v.i., & n. (Give) half-suppressed secretive laugh esp. of cynical kind or of amusement at obscenity or indecency. [imit., cf. SNICKER]

sni·ggle, v.i. Fish *for eels* by pushing bait into hole. [f. dial. *snig* eel, etym. dub.]

snip, v.t. & i., & n. Cut with scissors or shears esp. in small quick strokes (*s. cloth, a hole*; *s. off the ends*; *s. at*, make snipping strokes at), whence **sni·pp**ING[1](2) n. (N.) act of snipping; piece snipped off; (colloq.) tailor. [cf. Du. *snippen*]

snipe, n. (collect. sing. usu. for pl.), & v.i. & t. Kinds of gamebird with long straight bill & angular flight frequenting marshes (*common* or *whole, great* or *double* or *solitary, small* or *half* or *jack, s.*, British kinds); *s.-eel, -fish*, &c., kinds with long slender snout; hence **snī·py**[2] a. (Vb) go s.-shooting; (Mil.) fire shots from hiding esp. at night into enemy's camp, kill or hit thus, whence **sni·p**ER[1] n. [cf. Icel. *-snipa*, Da. *sneppe*, G *schnepfe*]

sni·ppet, n. Small piece cut off, snipping; (pl.) detached fragments of knowledge or information, odds & ends, whence **sni·ppet**Y[2] a., **sni·ppeti**NESS n. [-ET[1]]

snip-snap-snor·um, n. A round card-game. [f. LG *snipp-snapp-snorum*]

snĭ·vel, v.i. (-ll-), & n. Run at the nose; be lachrymose, affect contrition, show maudlin emotion; hence **sni·vell**ER[1] n., **sni·vell**ING[2] a. (N.) running mucus; whining & weeping; hypocritical talk, cant. [ME *snevelen* (OE *snofl* mucus)]

snob, n. Man of low birth or breeding or social position (archaic); (at universities & public schools; archaic) townsman; person with exaggerated respect for social position or wealth & a disposition to be ashamed of socially inferior connexions, behave with servility to social superiors, & judge of merit by externals, whence **sno·bb**ISH[1] a., **sno·bbish**LY[2] adv., **sno·bbish**NESS, **sno·bb**ERY(4, 5), **sno·b**LING[1](2), **snobo·**CRACY, nn. [earlier sense in dial. *cobbler's man*, etym dub.]

snōōd, n. (Sc. & literary) fillet worn by maidens in Scotland to confine hair, whence **snoo·d**ED[2] a.; any of the short lines attaching hooks to a main line in sea fishing. [OE *snód*, etym. dub.]

snōōk[1], n. Kinds of fish esp. the sea pike. [f. Du. *snoek*]

snōōk[2], n. (slang). Contemptuous gesture with thumb to nose & fingers spread out (*cock, cut, make, a s.* or *ss.*; *Ss.!*, int. of contempt). [?]

snōō·ker, n. Game on billiard-table combining pool & pyramids (*snookered*, having one's object-ball covered by another); (slang) newly joined cadet at Woolwich. [?]

snooze, v.i. & t., & n. (Take) short sleep esp. in day-time; pass time in lazy indifference; *s. time* &c. *away*, spend it indolently. [?]

snore, v.i. & t., & n. (Make) hoarse rattling or grunting noise in breathing esp. during sleep; pass time *away* in snoring; bring one*self awake, into a nightmare*, &c., by snoring. Hence **snor·**ER[1] n. [prob. imit.; cf. *snort*]

snort, v.i. & t., & n. (Make) explosive noise due to sudden forcing of breath through nose & usu. expressing anger or indignation or incredulity, or (of steam-engine &c.) noise resembling this; express (defiance &c.) by snorting (often *out*), throw *out* (words) with snorting. [prob. imit.; cf. *snore*]

snor·ter, n. In vbl senses; also (slang); boisterous gale; performance &c. conspicuous for vigour or violence. [-ER[1]]

snot, n. (not in decent use). Mucus of the nose (also of person as low term of abuse); *s.-rag*, handkerchief. [OE *gesnot*, cf. Du. & Da. *snot*; cogn. w. SNOUT]

sno·tty, a. & n. (not in decent use). Running or foul with snot (also as low abusive epithet); hence **sno·tti**LY[2] adv., **sno·tti**NESS n. (N., nav. slang) midshipman. [-Y[2]]

snout (-owt), n. Nose (& mouth) of animal or (contempt.) human being; pointed front of something, nozzle, (s. of glacier, of battleship's ram, &c.); *s.-beetle*, kinds with beaked head; *s.-ring*, inserted in pig's s. to prevent rooting. Hence **(-)snout**ED[2] a. [cf. Du. *snuit*, G *schnauze*; cogn. w. OE *snȳtan* blow the nose]

snow (-ō), n., & v.i. & t. Atmospheric vapour frozen into ice crystals & falling to earth in white flakes or spread on it as a white layer (*red s.*, s.-plant, see below), (pl.) falls or accumulations of s. (*where are the ss. of last year?*); substance &c. resembling s. esp. in whiteness (*her breast of s.*; *the ss. of seventy years*, white hair; *apple, chestnut*, &c., *s.*, kinds of pudding); *snow·ball* n., mass of s. pressed into hard ball esp. for use as missile, fund each subscriber to which finds *n* others, kinds of pudding e.g. apple enclosed in rice, (v.t. & i.) pelt or have pelting-match with snowballs; *snowball-tree*, guelder-rose; *s.-berry*, garden shrub with white berries; *s.-bird*, kinds of white or partly white finch, esp. the *s. bunting*; *s.-blind(ness)*, unable, inability, to see owing to exhaustion of retina by reflection of light endured in traversing s.-fields &c.; *s.-blink*, reflection in sky of snow or ice fields; *s.-boots*, over-boots of rubber & cloth; *s.-bound*, kept from going out or travelling by s.; *s.-cap*, white-crowned humming-bird; *s.-capped*, (of mountain) covered at top with s.; *s.-drift*, bank of s. heaped by wind; *snow·-drop*, early spring white-flowered plant; *s.-fall*, esp. amount of s. that falls on one occasion or in a year at any place as measured by *s.-gauge*; *s.-field*, esp. permanent wide expanse of snow in mountainous or polar regions; *s.-flake*, one of the small collections of crystals in which s. falls; *s.-goggles*, darkened spectacles worn by mountaineers &c. to prevent s.-blindness; *s.-goose*, arctic white goose with black-tipped wings, the wavy; *s.-grouse*, ptarmigan; *s.-ice*, opaque white ice formed from s.-slush; *s.-leopard*, ounce; *s.-line*, level above which s. lies permanently at any place; *s. man*, figure made of s. by children &c. & set up; *s.-on-the-mountain*, kinds of white-flowered garden plant; *s.-*, or usu. *snowy, owl*, the great white owl; *s.-plant* or *red s.*, microscopic alga growing in s. & colouring it red; *s.-plough*, contrivance drawn by horses or attached to front of locomotive for clearing track by pushing s. aside; *s.-shoes*, racket-heads or (also SKI) long narrow boards attached to feet & enabling wearer to traverse s. without sinking in; *s.-shovel*, large wooden shovel for s.; *s.-slip*, avalanche; *s.-storm*, heavy fall of s. esp. with wind; *s. under* (U.S.), cover (as) with s., overwhelm with numbers &c. (esp. in pass. of election candidate defeated by huge majority); *s.-white*, white as s.; hence **snow·**LESS, **snow·**Y[2], aa., **snow·i**LY[2] adv., **snow·i**NESS n. (Vb): (impers.) *it snows, will s.*, &c., s. falls &c.; sprinkle or scatter, come, like s.; *snowed up, in*, s.-bound, blocked up with s. [Aryan; OE *snāw*, cf. Du. *sneeuw*, G *schnee*, L *nix nivis*, Gk *nipha* accus.]

snub[1], v.t., & n. Rebuff, reprove, put down, humiliate, with sharp words or marked want of cordiality, whence **snu·bb**ING[1](1) n., **snu·bbing**LY[2] adv.; check way of (ship) esp. by rope wound round *snub(bing)-post* or bollard; (n.) snubbing, rebuff. [n. f. vb, f. ON *snubba* chide]

snub[2], a. & n. (Of nose) short & stumpy or turned up, whence **s.-nos**ED[2] a.; (n., rare) s. nose. [f. prec. vb in old sense *check growth of*]

snuff[1], v.i. & t., & n. =(the now more usu.) SNIFF vb; also, take s., whence **snu·ff**ER[1] n. (N.): =(the now more usu.) SNIFF n.; also: powdered tobacco taken by sniffing as stimulant or sedative (*take* thing *in s.* archaic, take offence at it; *up to s.* slang, not childishly ignorant or innocent), whence **snu·ff**Y[2] a., **snu·ffi**NESS n.; medicinal powder taken by sniffing; *s.-box*; *s.-colour(ed)*, (of) dark yellowish-brown; *s.-mill*, for grinding s., also s.-box; *s.-taker, -king*. [n. f. vb. f. MDu. *snuffen* clear the nose, cf. G *schnauben* snort; sense *tobacco* &c. prob. f. Du. *snuf* abbr. of *snuiftabak* snuffing-tobacco]

snuff[2], v.t. & i., & n. Trim s. from (candle or its wick) with fingers or scissors or esp. **snu·ffers** n. pl., kind of scissors with box to catch s. (*s. out* v.t., extinguish by trimming, also fig. as *I was nearly, his hopes were, snuffed out*; *s. out* v.i. slang, die; *can s. a candle with a pistol*, shoot off top of wick without putting flame out); *snuffer-tray*, holding snuffers. (N.) charred part of candle-wick, esp., in bad wick, black excrescence obscuring light; *s.-dish*, snuffer-tray. [n. f. vb, etym. dub.]

snu·ffle, v.i. & t., & n. Sniff (intr.), make sniffing sounds; speak nasally, whiningly, or like one with a cold, esp. as form of religious affectation ascribed to puritans & dissenters, whence **snu·ffl**ER[1] n.; *s. out*, utter with snuffling; hence **snu·ffling**LY[2] adv. (N.) sniff; snuffling sound, tone, or talk. [SNUFF[1], -LE(3)]

snug, a. Sheltered from weather & cold, well enclosed or packed in or fixed in place, comfortably situated, cosy, (*as s. as a bug in a rug*); (of income, dinner, &c.) good enough for modest requirements. Hence **snu·g**LY[2] adv., **snu·g**NESS n. [cf. ON *snoggr* smooth (of hair), Sw. *snygg* neat]

snu·ggery, n. Snug place, esp. person's private room or den; bar-parlour of inn. [-ERY]

snu·ggle, v.i. & t. Shift one's position or lie close *up to* for warmth; draw (child &c.) close *to* one, cuddle. [f. obs. *snug* vb (SNUG) + -LE(3)]

so, adv., conj., int., & pron. To the extent or in the manner set forth by preceding or following *as* clause or implied in context, thus, equally, similarly, analogously, (now used to express degree before *as*-clause only with negative, as *I am not so eager*, but *I am as eager, as you*; *as the tree falls, so must it lie*; *as bees love sweetness, so flies love rottenness*; rarely used twice correlatively, as *so many men so many minds*; *when he saw her so frightened*; *why are you panting so?*; *so & so only can it be done*; *stand just so*; *did not expect to live so long*; *did not get it by force & ought not to be so deprived of it*; often in sentence appended as explanation, as *I paid him double, I was so pleased*; *ever* or *never so bad* &c. in condit. clause, as bad &c. as possible; *so far*, up to this time or point or extent, as *so far it has not happened, so far you are right*; *so* or *in so far as* or archaic *so far forth as*, to whatever extent; *& so forth, & so on*, et cetera, & the like; *so long as*, with the proviso, on the condition, that; *so be it*, form of acceptance, resignation, &c.; *so long*, good-bye till we next meet; *so much for*, that is all that need be done or said about; *is only so much rubbish*, all rubbish; *at so much a week, a head*, &c., a definite but unspecified sum &c.; similarly *so much of one ingredient & so much of another*; *not so much as*, less than, not even; *is not so much discontented as unsatisfied*); to the degree or in the manner or with the intent or result set forth by following *that*-clause or *but*-clause or *as to* (*so high that you cannot reach it*; *so run that ye may obtain*; *warned him so that he might avoid the danger*; *all precautions have been taken, so that we expect to succeed*; *not so deaf but he can hear a cannon*; *was so fortunate as to escape*; *put it so as not to offend him*; *it so happens that he was not there*); to a degree that demands exclamatory emphasis (*so many worlds, so much to do!*; *I am so glad, tired!*; *she is so beautiful!*; *so kind of you!*; also colloq. or vulg. with *ever*, as *that is ever so much better, he is ever so angry!*); on condition that or *that*, on condition set forth in *as*-clause or implied, (*so that* or *so it is done, it matters not how*; *so may you find forgiveness as now you forgive me!*; *so help me God!*, form of asseveration); accordingly, consequently, therefore, as appears or results from preceding or implied statements or fact, (*he says he was not there, so he doubtless was not*; *so* or *and so I cannot come*; *so you are back again*; *so that's that*, colloq. winding up of statement or discussion; *so look to yourself*); (accompanying emphasis on some later word) moreover, also, as well, in actual fact, (*well, so I* did; *you said it was good, & so it* is; *yes, I denied it, but* or *& so did* you; '*your birthday? yes, so it* is'); (as substitute, often preceding vb, for obj. of *say, call, speak, tell, think, hope, suppose, do*, &c.) it, this, that, the same, this is what, (*so he said*; *so spake Achilles*, i.e. what precedes, *& Patroclus so*, i.e. what follows; also ellipt., as *So Satan, whom the archangel thus rebukes*; *do you think so?*; *& so say all of us*; *I suppose so*, form of agreement; *I told you so*, warned you in vain; *she is ill & he thinks himself so*; *so-called*, epithet questioning accuracy of description; *so to say* or *speak*, apology for exaggeration, metaphor, neologism, &c.; *you don't say so?*, formula of surprise); in that state or condition, actually the case, (*he, it, is better so*; *God said Let there be light, & it was so*; *must it be so?*; *but perhaps it is not, even if it were, so*; *though it was*, or *things were, ever* or *never so* vulg., however bad the state of things; also with omission of *it is* &c., as *how so?*, *why so?*, *if so, not so*; also ellipt. for *is that so?* chiefly in imit. of German, as 'He went off yesterday' 'So?'; *quite so, just so*, forms of agreement); (archaic) *and so*, after which I, they, &c., proceeded (*& so to dinner, a division*, &c.); (archaic) *so please you*, by your favour, if you please; (ellipt. after conditional clause; archaic) let it be so, very well, (*if you are content, so*); (as int., also *soh*) that will do, stay as you are, stand still, be quiet; (in comb. with relative words) -ever (also with *-ever* appended, as *whoso, whosoever*); *so-&-so*, particular person or thing not needing to be specified (*never mind what so-&-so says*; *tells me to do so-&-so*); *so so*, pred. adj. or adv., not more than passable, -bly; *or so*, or thereabouts (after expressions of quantity or numbers; *send me half-a-dozen or so*; *1lb. or so will do*). [OE *swá*, cf. Du. *zoo*, G *so*]

soak, v.t. & i., & n. (Of absorbent substance) take *up* or suck *in* (liquid); place or leave or lie in or *in* liquid for saturation, steep t. & i., make or be wet through, (of rain &c.) drench, whence **soa·k**ING[1](1) n.; (of moisture) make way *in(to)* or *through*, make its *way*, by saturation, whence **soa·k**AGE(3) n.; drink persistently, booze. (N.) soaking; drinking-bout; hard drinker. [OE *socian* (*súcan* SUCK)]

soa·ker, n. In vbl senses; esp.: hard drinker; drenching shower. [-ER[1]]

soap, n., & v.t. & i. Compound of fatty acid with soda or potash or (*insoluble ss.*) with an earth or metallic oxide, of which the soluble kinds yield when rubbed in water a lather used in washing (*soft s.*, made with potash & remaining liquid, also fig. flattery); *s.-berry, -nut, -plant, -pod, -root, -wort*, kinds of plant yielding substances serving purpose of s.; *s.-boiler, -ling*, manufacture(r) of s.; *s.-bubble*, iridescent globe of air enclosed in film of soapy water made by blowing through pipe dipped in s.-suds; *s.-earth, s.-stone*, steatite; *s.*-SUDS; *s.-works*, s. manufactory; hence **soa·p**LESS a. (Vb) apply s. to, scrub or rub with s.; use s. upon oneself. [OE *sápe*, cf. Du. *zeep*, G *seife*]

soa·py, a. Like, smeared or impregnated with, suggestive of, soap; (of person or his manners or talk) unctuous, flattering. Hence **soa·pi**LY[2] adv., **soa·pi**NESS n. [-Y[2]]

soar, v.i. Fly high (lit. & fig.), mount to or be at a great height above earth, hover or sail in the air without flapping of wings, (*soaring eagle, spire, thoughts, ambition, ideals*). Hence **soar·ing**LY[2] adv. [f. F *essorer* f. LL EX(*aurare* f. *aura* breeze)]

sōa·vĕ, sōavĕme·ntĕ, (-ah-), mus. direction. With tenderness. [It.]

sob, v.i. & t., & n. Draw breath in convulsive gasps usu. with weeping under mental distress or physical exhaustion; *s. out*, utter with ss.; hence **so·bbing**LY[2] adv. (N.) convulsive drawing of breath esp. in weeping; *s.-stuff* (U.S.), pathos, sentimental writing [prob. imit.]

sō·ber, a., & v.t. & i. Not drunk (*as s. as a judge*; *appeal from Philip drunk to Philip s.*, suggest that opinion &c. represents passing mood only); temperate in regard to drink (*is a s. man*); moderate, well-balanced, sane, tranquil, self-controlled, sedate, not vehement or passionate or excited or wayward or fanciful or exaggerated, (of colour) quiet & inconspicuous, (*in s. fact*, in fact as opp. fancy; *a s. estimate*; *s.-minded*; *s.-sides*, sedate person; *s.-suited* poet., clad in s. colours), whence **so·ber**LY[2] adv. (Vb) make or become s. or less wild, reckless, enthusiastic, visionary, &c. (often *down*). [f. OF *sobre* f. L *sobrius* perh. f. *so-, se-*, apart from, *ebrius* drunk, etym. dub.]

Sōbra·nje (-ahnyĕ), n. Bulgarian national assembly. [Bulg.]

sobri·ety, n. Being SOBER. [f. F *sobriété* f. L *sobrietatem* (SOBER, -TY)]

sō·briquet, sou- (sōō-) (-kā), n. Nickname, assumed name. [F, etym. dub.]

sŏ̄·c(c)age (-ĭj), n. Feudal tenure of land involving payment of rent or other service to superior. [AF, f. OE *sóc* jurisdiction (*sécan* SEEK) + -AGE]

soccer. (Anomalous spelling, cf. BACCY, of) SOCKER.

sō·ciable (-sh*a*-), a. & n. Fitted for companionship, ready & willing to converse, not averse to society, communicative, liking company; (of meeting &c.) marked by friendliness, not stiff or formal; hence **socia**BI·LITY n., **so·ciab**LY[2] adv. (N.) open carriage with facing side seats; tricycle for two riders side by side; S-shaped couch allowing two occupants to face each other. [F, f. L *sociabilis* (*sociare* f. *socius* fellow cogn. w. *sequi* follow, -ABLE)]

sō·cial (-shl), a. & n. Living in companies, gregarious, not fitted for or not practising solitary life, interdependent, cooperative, practising division of labour, existing only as member of compound organism, (*man is a s. animal*; *s. bees, wasps*, kinds having common nests &c.; *s. birds*, building near each other in communities; *s. plants*, kinds that grow thickly together & monopolize ground they grow on; *s. polyp* &c.); concerned with the mutual relations of men or classes of men (*s. problems, science, morality, students, philosophers*; *the s. contract* or rarely *compact*, agreement among men to exchange the individual freedom of the state of nature for legal restriction, assumed by 18th-c. thinkers as basis of political society; *s. democrat*, politician aiming at improving condition of lower classes by gradual advance towards socialism; *the s. evil*, prostitution); of or in or towards society (*s. intercourse, life, code, etiquette, pleasures, duties*; one's *s. superiors & inferiors*; *s. rank, position, distinctions*; *has s. tastes*; *a s. evening, gathering*); of or with allies (*the S. war* in Rom. Hist.). (N.) s. gathering, esp. one organized by club, congregation, &c. Hence or cogn. **socia·**LITY (-shĭ-) n., **so·cial**LY[2] adv. [f. L *socialis* (*socius* see prec., -AL)]

so·cialism, n. Principle that individual freedom should be completely subordinated to interests of community, with any deductions that may be correctly or incorrectly drawn from it, e.g. substitution of cooperative for competitive production, national ownership of land & capital, state distribution of produce, free education & feeding of children, & abolition of inheritance (*Christian s.*, attempt to apply Christian precepts in ordinary life resulting in some approximation to the aims of s.). Hence **so·cial**IST(2) n. & a., **sociali·st**IC a., **sociali·st**ICALLY adv. [-ISM]

so·cialize, v.t. Make social; arrange socialistically. Hence **socializ**A·TION n. [-IZE]

soci·ety, n. Social mode of life, the customs & organization of a civilized nation, (*the progress of s. is an evolution*; *pests of s.*, persons who prey on the community); any social community (*no s. can retain members who flout its principles*); the upper classes of a community whose movements & entertainments & other doings are more or less conspicuous, the socially distinguished, fashionable & well-to-do & well-connected people, (*was welcomed by s.*; *the customs of polite s.*; *s. does not approve*; *leaders of s.*; often attrib., as *s. lady, people, gossip, news, journal*; *s. verse*, of light topical witty kind); participation in hospitality, other people's houses or company, (*goes a great deal into, avoids, is at his best* or *embarrassed in, s.*); companionship, company, (*s. & solitude*; *always enjoy his s.*; *seek, avoid, the s. of*); association of persons united by a common aim or interest or principle (*S. of Friends*, quakers; *S. of Jesus*, abbr. *S.J.*, see JESUIT; FRIENDLY *s.*; *Royal S.*, founded 1662 for improving natural knowledge; *S. for the Propagation of the Gospel*, abbr. *S.P.G.*; DORCAS *s.*; *building, cooperative, s.*). [f. OF *societe* f. L *societatem* (*socius* see SOCIABLE, -TY)]

Socĭ·nian, a. & n. (Follower, following or according to doctrine) of the 16th-c. Italian theologians Laelius & Faustus Socinus, whose opinions resemble those of modern unitarians. Hence **Soci·nian**ISM(3) n. [-IAN]

sōcio·logy (-sĭ-, -shĭ-), n. Science of the development & nature & laws of human society. Hence **socio**LO·GICAL a., **sociolo·gical**LY[2] adv., (-sho-), **socio·**LOGIST n. [F (*-gie*), f. L *socius* see SOCIABLE, -LOGY]

sock[1], n. (shop pl. *sox*). Short stocking not reaching knee; removable inner sole put into shoe for warmth &c.; ancient comic actor's light shoe (also used allusively for comedy &c., cf. BUSKIN). [OE *socc* f. L *soccus* comic actor's shoe]

sock[2], v.t., n., & adv., (slang). Fling (ball, stone) *at*; hit (person) with hand-flung missile; (n.) blow inflicted by missile or fist (esp. *give him ss.!*); (adv.) with such blow, plump, right, (*hit him s. in the eye*). [?]

sock[3], n., & v.t. & i., (school slang). Sweets, pastry, &c., eaten at odd times, tuck, grub; (vb) treat to s., indulge in s., give (person thing). [?]

sockdŏ·loger, n. (slang). Decisive blow or argument. [U.S., perh. corrupt. of *doxology*]

so·cker, n. (slang). Association football, form of football in which (cf. RUGBY) ball may not be touched with hand. [*Association*, -ER[1]]

so·cket, n. Natural or artificial hollow for something to fit into or stand firm or revolve in (*eye-s.*; *s. of the hip*; *candle too large for s.*; BALL[1] *& s.*); *s.-joint*, =BALL[1]-*&-s. joint*; *s.-pipe*, with enlarged end to receive another. Hence **so·cket**ED[2] a. [f. OF *soket* dim. of *soc* ploughshare]

sŏ·cle, n. (archit.). Plain low rectangular block serving as support for pedestal, vase, statue, &c. [F. f. It. *zoccolo* f. L *socculus* (*soccus* SOCK[1], -ULE)]

Socră·tic, a. & n. Of, like, following, &c., Socrates (*S. method*, dialectic, procedure by question & answer; *S. irony*, pose of ignorance assumed in order to entice others into display of supposed knowledge); (n.) follower of Socrates. Hence **Socra·t**ICALLY adv. [f. L f. Gk *Sōkratikos* (*Sōkratēs*, -IC)]

sod[1], n., & v.t. Turf, upper layer of grass land including blades & roots & earth,

(*under the s.*, in the grave); piece of turf pared off; hence **so·ddy**² a. (Vb) cover (ground) with ss. (*sodding mallet, spade*, implements used); pelt with ss. [cf. Du. *zode*, LG *sode*]
sod². See SEETHE.
sod³, n. (vulg.). Sodomite. [abbr.]
sō·da, n. One of the compounds of sodium in common use, esp. sodium carbonate or bicarbonate; (also *s.-water*) water made effervescent by impregnation with carbonic acid under pressure & used alone or with spirit or wine or milk as a drink (orig. made with sodium carbonate; *some s.-water*; *some* or *a brandy & s.*; *s.-fountain*, vessel in which s.-water is stored under pressure to be drawn out). [med. L, etym. dub.]
sodă·lity, n. A confraternity or association esp. of religious character (chiefly in titles of R.-C. societies). [f. L *sodalitas* (*sodalis* comrade, -TY)]
so·dden, a., & v.t. & i. Saturated with liquid, soaked through; (of bread) doughy, heavy & moist; stupid or dull in fact or appearance with habitual drunkenness; hence **so·dden**NESS n. (Vb) become or make s. [orig. p.p. of SEETHE]
sō·dium, n. A silver-white metal existing chiefly in soda & other compounds, burning with bright yellow flame, and igniting in warm water. Hence **sō·d**IC a. [SODA, -IUM]
sŏ·domite, n. Person practising sodomy. [f. L f. Gk *Sodomitēs* inhabitant of Sodom, see -ITE¹(1)]
sŏ·domy, n. Copulation between male persons. [f. OF *sodomie* (L *Sodoma* Sodom, see *Gen.* xix. 4 foll., -IA¹)]
sōĕ·ver, suf. somet. separable usu. appended to relative pronouns, adverbs, or adjectives, but sometimes following them at an interval, to give indefinite meaning (*whosoever, howsoever*, &c.; *how great s. it may be*; *with what end s. he did it*). [SO, EVER]
sō·fa, n. Couch with raised ends & back on which several persons can sit or one lie; *s. bed(stead)*, piece of furniture serving as s. by day & bed by night. [f. Arab. *soffah* bench]
so·ffit, n. Lower surface of architrave, arch, balcony, &c. [f. F *soffite* f. It. *soffitta* ceiling, fem. p.p. = fixed under (L SUB², *figere* fix)]
sofi(sm). See SUFI(*sm*).
soft (saw-, sŏ-), a., n., adv., & int. Comparatively wanting in hardness, yielding to pressure, malleable, plastic, easily cut, (*s. as butter*; *s. stone, iron*; *s. coal*, bituminous, opp. *anthracite*; *s. corn*, moist thickening of skin between toes confused with CORN³; *s. tissues* of body, not bony or cartilaginous; *s. palate*, hinder part of palate; *s. wicket* at cricket, moist or sodden turf; *s. goods*, textiles; *s. money*, notes & bills; *s. solder*, kinds used for easily fusible metal, cf. *s.* SAWDER; *s.* SOAP; *s. tack* naut., bread, opp. *hard tack* or biscuit; *s. roe*, of male fish); of smooth surface or fine texture, not rough or coarse, (*s. skin, hair, raiment*); mellow, mild, balmy, not noticeably cold or hot, (*s. air*; *a s. winter*); rainy or moist or thawing (*s. weather*; *a s. day*); (of water) free from mineral salts & so good for washing or cooking; not astringent or sour or bitter (*s. claret* &c.); not crude or brilliant or dazzling (*s. colours, light, eyes*); not sharply defined (*s. outline*); not strident or loud, low-toned, (*a s. voice*; *s. music*; *s.* PEDAL¹; *s. whispers, murmurs*); (Phonet.) sibilant (*g is s. in* gin), voiced (*b, g, d, are s. mutes*), unaspirated (*s.* or *smooth* BREATHING¹); gentle, quiet, conciliatory, complimentary or amorous, (*s. rain*; *s. drink*, U.S. slang, non-alcoholic; *s. manners*; *a s. answer*, esp. a good-tempered one to abuse or accusation; *s.-spoken*, see SPEAK; *s. nothings*, amorous talk); sympathetic, compassionate, (*has a s. heart*, whence **softheart**ED² a., **soft-hear·t**EDNESS n.); tranquil (*s. slumbers*); (slang) easy (*has a s. job*; *s. thing*, light well-paid office &c.); flabby, weak, feeble, unstrung, effeminate, silly, (*the national character has gone s.*; *a s. luxurious people*; *s. muscles*; *s.-headed, s.-witted*, half idiotic); hence **so·ft**ISH¹ a., **so·ft**LY² adv., **so·ft**NESS n. (N.) silly weak person, also **so·ft**Y³ n. (Adv., commoner in compar. than in posit.) softly (*play s., softer*; *s.-whispering* &c.). (Int., archaic) wait a moment; hush!. [OE *sófte* (usu. adv.), *séfte* a., cf. G *sanft*, Du. *zacht*]
sŏ·fta, n. Moslem student of sacred law & theology. [Turk.]
so·ften (-fn), v.i. & t. Become or make SOFT or softer; *softening* (morbid degeneration) *of the brain*. Hence **so·ften**ER¹(1, 2) n. [-EN⁶]
so·ggy (-gĭ), a. Sodden, saturated, dank. Hence **so·ggi**NESS n. [f. dial. *sog* a swamp, etym. dub.]
soh. See SO.
soho·¹, int. used in quieting horse &c. [AF hunting-cry]
Soho·², n. District in London associated with foreign restaurants &c.
soi-disant (F), a. Self-styled, pretended.
soil¹, n. The ground, upper layer of earth in which plants grow consisting of disintegrated rock usu. with admixture of organic remains, mould, (*good, poor, clayey, alluvial, light, rich*, &c., *s.*; NIGHT-*s.*; one's *native s.*, ground of one's native land or place). Hence **-soil**ED² a. [AF, f. L *solium* seat confused w. *solum* ground]
soil², v.t. & i., & n. Make dirty, smear or stain with dirt, tarnish, defile, (*soiled linen*; *would not s. my hands with it* fig.), so **soi·l**URE n. (archaic); admit of being

soiled (*soils easily*). (N.) dirty mark, stain, smear, deflement; *s.-pipe*, discharge-pipe of water-closet; hence **soi·l**LESS a. [n. f. vb, OF *soillier* defile, perh. f. L *suculus* dim. of *sus* pig; doublet of SULLY]

soil³, v.t. Feed (cattle) on fresh-cut green fodder (orig. for purging). [perh. f. SOIL² in sense *dung* (cf. *soil-pipe*)]

soirée (swar·ā), n. Social evening, evening gathering esp. for music, conversation, the advancement of some society's objects, or the like. [F, = evening (-party) f. L *serus* late, *-ata* see -ADE(1)]

soixante-quinze (F), n. French 75 mm. gun, famous in the great war. [F, = 75]

so·journ (sŭ·jern, sŏ-), v.i., & n. (Make) temporary stay in or *in* place or *with* or *among* person(s). Hence **so·journ**ER¹ n. [f. OF *sojourner* (L SUB-, *diurnare* f. *diurnus* DIURNAL]

Sŏl¹, n. (joc.). The sun. [L]

sŏl², n. (mus.). Fifth note of octave. [1st syl. of L *solve*, see GAMUT]

sō·la, n. Pithy-stemmed tropical swamp plant (*s. topi*, Indian sun-helmet of the pith). [f. Hind. *sholā*]

sŏ·lace (-*as*), n., & v.t. Comfort (v. & n.) in distress or disappointment or tedium (*s. oneself with*, find compensation or relief in; *tobacco, the poor man's s.*; *found s. in religion*). [f. OF *solas* f. L *solacium* (*solari* CONSOLE¹)]

sō·lan(-goose), n. The gannet. [f. ON *súla*, perh. + *ond* duck]

solā·num, n. Large genus of plants including potato, nightshade, & many kinds (often spoken of as *s.*) cultivated as ornamental creepers or for flowers or foliage. [L, = nightshade]

sō·lar, a. Of, concerned with, determined by, the sun (*s.* DAY, *eclipse, spectrum, time,* YEAR; *s. flowers*, that remain open only for some hours in the day; *s. month*, an exact twelfth of the year; *s. myth*, tale explained as symbolizing s. phenomena; *s. plexus*, the complex of nerves at pit of stomach; *s. system*, the sun & the heavenly bodies whose motion is directly or indirectly determined by it). [f. L *solaris* (*sol* sun, -AR¹)]

so·larism, n. Belief in solar myths as chief source of mythology. So **so·lar**IST(2) n. [-ISM]

solār·ium, n. Place often enclosed in glass for enjoyment or esp. medical use of sun's rays. [L, = sun-dial, sunning-place (SOLAR, -ARY¹)]

so·larize, v.i. & t. (photog.). Spoil (i. & t.) by long exposure. Hence **solariz**A·TION n. [-IZE]

solā·tium (-shĭ-), n. (pl. *-tia*). Thing given as compensation or consolation. [L, = SOLACE]

sold. See SELL.

sŏldane·lla, n. Kinds of Alpine plant some of which (esp. the Blue moonwort) are grown in gardens. [It., etym. dub.]

sŏl·der, n., & v.t. Kinds of fusible alloy used to join edges of less fusible metals (*hard*, SOFT, *s.*, fusible at higher, lower, temperature & so serving for different metals), (fig.) cementing agency. (Vb) join with s.; *soldering-iron*, tool used hot for applying s. [vb f. n., f. OF *soudure* (*souder* f. L *solidare* f. SOLIDUS, -URE)]

sō·ldier (-jer), n., & v.i. Member of army (lit. & fig.; *ss. & sailors*; *go, enlist, for a s.*; *play at ss.*, of children, also of volunteers &c.; *tin, toy, ss.*; *s. of Christ*, active or proselytizing Christian; *the unknown S.*, see WARRIOR; *every* INCH¹ *a s.*; *old s.*, lit., also person of experience, also empty bottle, also cigar-end; *come the old s. over*, claim to dictate to in virtue of greater experience; *s. of fortune*, ready to take service under any State or person that will hire him; *red s.*, pig-disease; *s.'s wind* naut., fair wind for going & returning); private or N.C.O. in army (*both officers & ss.*; often *common s.*); military commander of specified ability (*a great, fine, poor, s.*; *no s.*), whence **so·ldier**SHIP(3) n.; hence **so·ldier**LIKE a., **so·ldier**LY¹,² a. & adv.; (Naut., slang) man, esp. sailor, who shirks work; (slang) red herring; (also *s. ant*) one of fighting section of ant or termite colony; (also *s. beetle*) kinds of reddish-coloured insect with carnivorous larvae; (also *s. crab*) kind of hermit crab; *s. orchis*, kind with helmet-shaped sepals. (Vb) serve as s. (chiefly in gerund, as *go, tired of, soldiering*); (Naut., slang) shirk work. [OF (*soude* pay f. SOLIDUS, -ARY¹)]

so·ldiery, n. *The* soldiers (of a State, in a district, &c.); *a* set of troops of specified character (*a wild, licentious,* &c., *s.*). [-ERY]

sŏ·ldo, n. (pl. *-di*, pr. -dē). Italian halfpenny. [It., f. SOLIDUS]

sole¹, n., & v.t. Lower surface of human or other plantigrade foot; part of shoe or boot below foot; bottom or foundation of various things, e.g. plough, carpenter's plane, wagon, golf-club head; *s.-channel*, groove in s. of boot &c. in which sewing is sunk; *s.-leather*, compressed for use in ss.; *s.-plate*, bed-plate of engine &c.; hence **-sol**ED² a. (Vb) provide (boot &c.) with s. [OF, f. med. L *sola* f. L *solea*]

sole², n. Kind of flat-fish much esteemed as food (LEMON² *s.*). [OF, f. L *solea* (prec.)]

sole³, a. One & only, exclusive, (*his s. reason is this*; *on my own s. responsibility*); (Law) unmarried (only in FEME SOLE); (archaic) alone, unaccompanied, (*went forth s.*; CORPORATION *s.*). Hence **so·le**LY² adv. [f. OF *sol* f. L *solus*]

sŏ·lĕcism, n. Offence against grammar or idiom, blunder in the manner of speaking or writing; piece of ill breeding or incorrect behaviour. So **so·lec**IST(1) n., **soleci·st**IC a. [f. L f. Gk *soloikismos* (*soloikizō* f. *soloikos* barbarous, said to be f. *Soloi* town in Cilicia noted for bad Attic, *-oikos* -dwelling, -IZE), -ISM]

sŏ·lemn (-m), a. Accompanied with ceremony, done &c. in due form, formally regular, (*s. feast-day, sacrifice, oath; the S. League & COVENANT; probate in s. form*); mysteriously impressive (*s. silence; a s. cathedral*); full of importance, weighty, (*a s. occasion, truth, warning*); grave, sober, deliberate, slow in movement or action, (*s. music, a s. promise, s. looks; a s. pace*); pompous, affecting gravity or importance, dull, (*put on a s. face; a s. fool*). Hence **so·lemn**LY[2] adv., **so·lemn**NESS n. (rare). [ME & OF *solempne* f. L *sollemnis*, etym. dub.]

sole·mnity (-mn-), n. Rite, celebration, festival, piece of ceremony; being solemn, solemn character or feeling or behaviour. [f. OF *solempnite* f. LL *sollemnitatem* (prec., -TY)]

sŏ·lemnize, v.t. Celebrate (festival &c.); duly perform (marriage ceremony); make solemn. Hence **solemnīz**A·TION n. [f. OF *solempniser* (SOLEMN, -IZE)]

sō·len, n. A bivalve, the Razor-shell. [L, f. Gk *sōlēn* tube, shell-fish]

solē·noid, n. Magnet made of wire coiled into cylinder & traversed by electric current. [f. F *solénoïde* (prec., -OID)]

sŏ·l-fa· (-ah), v.i. & t., & n. =SOLMIZATE, SOLMIZATION; TONIC *s.* [SOL[2], FA]

sŏlfĕ·ggio (-jō), n. (pl. *-gi*, pr. -jē). Solmization, sol-fa; sol-fa exercise for voice. [It., (prec. +suf. *-eggio*)]

sŏlferi·no (-rē-), n. A purplish-red colour made from rosaniline. [discovered in year of battle of *S.*, cf. MAGENTA]

soli·cit, v.t. & i. Invite, make appeals or requests to, importune, (*marvels s. his attention* or *senses; we s. you for your custom; was known to have solicited the judges*), (of prostitute) entice (man, or abs.) in public place; ask importunately or earnestly for (*s. favours, office, custom*). So **solicit**A·TION n. [f. OF *soliciter* f. L *sollicitare* (*sollicitus* anxious perh. f. *sollus* whole, *ciēre cit-* rouse)]

soli·citor, n. One who solicits (rare); member of the legal profession competent to advise clients & instruct & prepare causes for barristers but not to appear as advocate except in certain lower courts (cf. BARRISTER, LAWYER, ATTORNEY); *S. General*, Crown law officer below Attorney General, & like him appointed by the Government of the day & advising & representing it in legal matters. [f. OF *solliciteur* (prec., -OR[2])]

soli·citous, a. Eager *to* do; desirous *of*; anxious, troubled, (*about, concerning, for*, &c., or abs.). Hence **soli·citous**LY[2] adv. [f. L *sollicitus* see SOLICIT, -OUS]

soli·citude, n. Being solicitous, anxiety, concern. [OF, f. L *sollicitudo* (prec., -TUDE)]

sŏ·lid, a. & n. Of stable shape, not liquid or fluid, having some rigidity, (*s. food; water becomes s. at 32° F.*); of s. substance throughout, not hollow, without internal cavities or interstices, uninterrupted, whole, (*s. sphere* or *ball; s. tire*, without central tube; *s. square* mil., formation of equal depth & length; *s.-hoofed, -horned*, &c.; *s. printing*, without leads between lines; *a s. hour, day*, &c.); strongly constructed, not flimsy, (*s. house, pier, furniture; man of s. build*); homogeneous, alike all through, (*of s. silver* &c.; *s. colour*, covering the whole of an object, without pattern &c.; *a s. vote* &c., unanimous, undivided; *go* or *be s. for*, be united in favour of; *the s. South*, southern States of U.S. consistently voting for democratic party); well grounded, sound, reliable, real, genuine, not fancied or pretended or showy, (*s. arguments, sense, comfort; a s. man*, sensible but not brilliant, also of sound financial position; *have s. grounds for supposing; s. consideration*, thing that can fairly be regarded as an inducement in contracts &c.); of three dimensions (*s. foot* &c., cubic; *s. angle*, formed by three or more plane angles in different planes meeting at point; *s. number*, integer with three prime factors); concerned with ss. (*s. geometry; s. measure; s. problem* math., involving curves that are sections of ss. & requiring cubic equation); hence or cogn. **soli·di**FY v.t. & i., **solidi**FICA·TION n., **soli·difi**ABLE a., **soli·d**ITY n., **so·lid**LY[2] adv. (N.) body consisting of particles that maintain their relative positions against some degree of pressure; (Geom.) body or magnitude having three dimensions (cf. *point, line, surface; regular s.*, bounded by equal & regular planes equally inclined, see REGULAR). [f. OF *solide* f. L *solidus* cogn. w. Gk *holos*, Skr *sarva(s)*, whole]

solidă·rity, n. Holding together, mutual dependence, community of interests, feelings, & action. So **so·lidary** a. [f. F *solidarité* (*solidaire* f. *solide*=prec., -ARY[1], -TY)]

solidu·ngular, -ate, aa. Solid-hoofed, of horse family, equine. [f. L SOLID*us*, *ungula* hoof, -AR[1], -ATE[2]]

sŏ·lidus, n. (pl. *-dī*). (Hist.) gold coin introduced by Roman Emperor Constantine; (only in abbr. *s.*) shilling(s), as 7*s.* 6*d.*, £1 1*s.*; the shilling line (for ſ or long s) as in 7/6. [L, a noun use of SOLID*us*]

sōlifi·dian, a. & n. (Holder) of doctrine that faith by itself suffices for salvation. [L *solus* alone, *fides* faith, + -IAN]

soli·loquy, n. Talking without or regardless of the presence of hearers (*a s.*, piece of this esp. on part of character in play). Hence **soli·loqu**IZE(2) v.i., **soli·loqu**IST(1) n. [f. L *soliloquium* (*solus* alone, -I-, *loqui* speak)]

sŏ·lipĕd, a. & n. Solidungulate (animal). [L *solus* alone, *pes pedis* foot]

soli·psism, n. (metaphys.). View that the self is the only knowable, or the only existent, thing. So **soli·psIST** n. [f. L *solus* alone, *ipse* self, -ISM]

sŏlitaire·, n. Ear-ring, shirt-stud, &c., having a single gem; shirt-cuff fastening in one piece; game played by one person with marbles on special board; (now usu. *patience*) kinds of card-game for one player; kinds of W.-Ind. & Amer. thrush; (now rare) a recluse. [F, see foll.]

sŏ·litary, a. & n. Living alone, not gregarious, without companions, unfrequented, secluded, single, lonely, sole, (*s. ants, bees*, &c., kinds not living in communities; *a s. life, walk, valley, instance*; *s. confinement*, isolation in separate cell); hence **so·litariLY**[2] adv., **so·litariNESS** n. (N.) recluse, anchoret. [f. L *solitarius* (*solus* alone)]

sŏ·litude, n. Being solitary; lonely place. [OF, f. L *solitudo* (SOLE[3], -TUDE)]

so·lmizate, v.i., **solmiza·tion,** n. (Use) system of associating each note of scale with particular syllable (see GAMUT), such syllables representing either C, D, &c., of natural scale or first, second, &c., note of any scale. [*-ate* f. F *solmiser* (SOL[2], MI, -IZE)]

sō·lo, n. (pl. *-os*, *-i* pr. -ē). Song or musical piece or passage given by one person or instrument with strictly subordinate or no accompaniment (also attrib., as *a s. passage*; *s. organ*, partial organ with special or *s. stops* fit for use in ss.), whence **so·loIST**(1) n.; (Cards) kind of whist in which one player opposes three or undertakes other tasks, similar varieties of other games. [It., as SOLE[3]]

Sŏ·lomon, n. King of Israel reputed wisest of men (*is no S.*; SONG *of S.*), whence **Solomŏnic** a.; *S.'s seal*, kinds of flowering plant with some likeness to lily of the valley.

Sō·lon, n. Sage, wise legislator. [name of Athenian lawgiver]

so·lstice, n. Either time (*summer, winter*, *s.*, about 21st June, 22nd Dec.) at which sun is furthest from equator & appears to pause before returning; (also *solstitial point*) point in ecliptic reached by sun at s. So **solsti·tiAL** (-ĭshl) a. [OF, f. L *solstitium* (SOL[1], *sistere -stit-* make stand f. *stare* stand)]

sŏ·lūble, a. That can be dissolved in some fluid; that can be solved. Hence **solubi·LITY** n. [OF, f. L *solubilis* (SOLVE, -BLE)]

sō·lus, pred. a. (fem. *-la*). Alone, unaccompanied, (esp. in stage directions, as *enter king s.*; also joc., as *found myself s.*). [L]

solu·tion (-ōō-, -ū-), n. Separation, dissolution, abolition of union, (chiefly in *s. of continuity* surg., separation of tissues by fracture &c., & transf.); dissolving or being dissolved, esp. conversion of solid gas into liquid form by mixture with liquid called the solvent or menstrum (*chemical s.*, involving change in chem. properties of components; *mechanical s.*, without such change), state resulting from this (*held in s.* &c.; *his ideas are in s.*, in a state of flux, unsettled), liquid & solid or gas so mixed (*a s. of alum*; *strong, weak, s.*, with small, large, proportion of solvent); resolution, solving, answer, method for the solving, of a problem, puzzle, question, doubt, difficulty, &c. (*of, for, to*). [OF, f. L *solutionem* (foll., -ION)]

Solū·trian, a. (archaeol.). Of the palaeolithic period represented by remains found at the Solutré cave, Saône-et-Loire, France.

solve, v.t. Untie, loosen, unravel, dissolve, (knot, tangle, cohesion, &c.; archaic); find answer to (problem) or way out of (difficulty). Hence **so·lvABLE** a., **solvABI·LITY** n. [f. L *solvere solut-* (*se-* apart, *luere*, cf. Gk *luō*, loosen)]

so·lvent, a. & n. Having the power of dissolving or forming SOLUTION with something or fig. of weakening the hold of traditions or beliefs; having money enough to meet all pecuniary liabilities, whence **so·lvENCY** n. (N.) s. liquid or substance, menstruum, (see SOLUTION; *water is the commonest s.*; *alcohol is the s. of resinous substances*); dissolving or weakening agent (*science as a s. of religious belief*). [f. L SOLVE*re*, -ENT]

-som. See -SOME.

somă·tic, a. Of the body, corporeal, physical, (opp. *mental, spiritual, psychic*; *s. death*, of the body as a whole). [f. Gk *sōmatikos* (*sōma -atos* body, -IC)]

sō·mato-, comb. form (prec., -O-) = of body or the human body, as *-gĕ·nic*, originating in the body, -LOGY, science of living bodies physically considered, also physics, also human anatomy & physiology.

so·mbre (*-er*), a. Dark, gloomy, dismal, as *a s. sky, s. prospect, man of s. character*. Hence **so·mbreLY**[2] adv., **so·mbreNESS** n., **so·mbrOUS** (poet.) a. [F, etym. dub.; cf. Sp. *sombrio* sombre, *sombra* shade]

sombrer·o (-ārō), n. Broad-brimmed felt hat common in America. [Sp. (*sombra*, see prec.)]

some (sŭm, sum), a., pron., & adv. Particular but unknown or unspecified (person or thing), as *s. fool has locked the door, saw it in s. book* (*or other*), *ask s. experienced person, s.* (*people*) *say yes & s.* (or *others* or *other people*) *say no*; a certain quantity or number of (something), as *drink s. water, eat s. bread, bring s. pens, I have s. already, have s. more, s. of it is spoilt, s. of them were late,* *can we* or *can't we have s. milk?* (but *we cannot have any milk*), *if I find s.* (or *any*) *I will send them*; an appreciable or considerable quantity of, as *went s. miles out of our way, had s. trouble in arranging it, s. years ago, that is s. help*; such to a certain extent, as *that is s. guide, test, proof*; (emphat. in meiosis, U.S. & slang) such in the fullest sense, something like (a), as *this is s. war!, I call that s. poem*; (usu. stressed) not quite no, as *do have s. mercy on our nerves, has after all s. sense of decency*; approximately so many or much of (something), as *waited s. 20 minutes, scales s. 15 stone, we were s. 60 in all*; ALL *& s.*; (adv., slang) in s. degree, as *he seemed annoyed s.*; *so·mebody*, s. person, (w. pl. *-dies*) person of consequence; *so·mehow*, in s. unspecified or unexplained manner, for s. reason or other, as *he somehow dropped behind, somehow or other I never liked him*, (stressed) no matter how, as *must get it finished somehow*; *so·meone*, = *somebody* (not in pl.); *s. one*, any particular (one), as *choose s. one place as a centre, take s. one as a type*; *so·mething*, s. thing (esp. *or something* as vague substitute for noun, adj., vb, or adv.), as *have something to tell you*; *we hope to see something of* (occasionally meet) *them, has lost something or other, take a drop of something* (liquor), *he is* or *has something* (s. official, s. employment) *in the record office, can spare something out of so much, there is something* (truth, point) *in what you say, thinks himself something* (of s. consequence), *felt there was a little something wanting, something of preciosity in his style, am something of* (am in s. sense or degree) *a carpenter, it is something* (s. comfort) *to be safe home again, his temper is, his fads are, something awful, was made a bishop or something, has sprained his ankle or something* (s. other part), *is neurotic or something, lost his train or* (did) *something, turned the tap too soon or too hard or* (*too*) *something*, (adv., archaic exc. *something like*) in s. degree, as *was something impatient, something troubled, shaped something like a cigar*, (colloq., w. stress on *like*) *this is something like a* (is a large or good) *pudding, that's something like* (is capital)*!*; *s. time* adv., for s. time, as *have been waiting s. time*, at s. time, as *must see him about it s. time*; *so·metime* adv. & a. (archaic), former(ly), as *was sometime mayor of Barnstaple*, (*the*) *sometime sheriff*; *so·metimes* adv., at s. times, as *have sometimes thought, is sometimes hot & sometimes cold*; *so·meway*, in s. way; *so·mewhat*, (adv.) in s. degree, as *it is somewhat difficult, was somewhat puzzled, answered somewhat hastily*, (pron., archaic exc. when indisting. f. adv.) *found somewhat to detain him, loses somewhat* (perh. adv.) *in the telling, loses somewhat of its force*; *so·mewhen* (rare, affected), at s. time or other; *so·mewhere*, in, at, to, s. place, as *lives somewhere near us, sent him somewhere, Burton says somewhere in the Anatomy, will see him somewhere* (in hell &c.) *first*; *so·mewhither* (archaic), to s. place. [OE *sum*, cf. ON *sumr*, Da. *somme* pl.]

-some, -som, suf. forming adjj., OE *-sum*, repr. Du. *-zaam*, G *-sam*; joined to nn. w. sense 'adapted to, productive of', as *handsome, quarrelsome, gladsome* (f. obs. *glad* n.), to adjj., as *lithesome* (also *lissom*), *blithesome, fulsome*, & to trans. vbs w. sense 'apt to', as *tiresome, winsome, wearisome, gruesome* (f. *grue* in impers. trans. use *it grues me*). Written *-om* in *lissom, buxom*, &c.; in *two, three, four, -some* the suf. was orig. the pronoun OE *sum* some; *-som* in RANSOM is of dif. orig.

so·mersault, -set[1], (sŭ-), n., & v.i. Spring, bound, in which person turns heels over head (*double, treble, s.*, twice, thrice) in the air; *turn a s.*, make such spring; (v.i.) turn s. [f. OF *sombre saut* f. Pr. *sobresaut* f. L *supra* above + *saltus -ūs* leap (*salire*)]

so·merset[2] (sŭ-), n. Padded saddle esp. for one-legged rider. [f. Lord F. *S.*, who used one]

So·merset House (sŭ-), n. Building in London containing chief place of deposit of proved wills, & inland revenue offices, & often mentioned allusively in these connexions.

sō·mite, n. Segment of (esp. articulate or vertebrate) animal body, metamere. Hence **somi·tic** a. [f. Gk *sōma* body + -ITE[1](2)]

somna·mbūlism, n. Walking or performing other action during sleep; condition of brain inducing this; *artificial s.*, hypnotism. Hence or cogn. **somna·mbulANT** (rare), **somnambuli·stIC**, aa., **somna·mbulATE**[3] v.i. (rare), **somna·mbulIST** n. [f. L *somnus* sleep + *ambulare* walk]

somni- in comb. = L *somnus* sleep, as: *-ferous*, inducing sleep, narcotic; *-loquence, -loquism, -loquy*, habit of talking in sleep; *-loquous, -loquist*, (person) given to this; *-pathist*, hypnotic subject; *-pathy*, hypnotic sleep.

so·mnolent, a. Sleepy, drowsy; inducing drowsiness; (Path.) in state between sleeping & waking. Hence or cogn. **so·mnolENCE, -ENCY**, nn., **so·mnolentLY**[2] adv. [f. L *somnolentus, -nul-* (*somnus* sleep, see -LENT)]

so·mnolism, n. Hypnotic sleep. [f. prec. + -ISM]

son (sŭn), n. Male child of a parent (*s. & heir*, esp. eldest s.); *s.-in-law*, one's daughter's husband; *he is his father's s.* (like, worthy of, his father); *the S. of Man*, (N.T.) Christ, the Messiah, (O.T.)

descendant of Adam, esp. as form of address in *Ezekiel*; *the ss. of men*, mankind; *the S.* (*of God*), = GOD[1] *the S.*; *s. of a* GUN; *every* MOTHER[1]'*s s.*; descendant, as *ss. of Abraham*; (as form of address esp. of old man to young man, confessor to penitent, &c.) *my s.*; *s. of the soil*, recognizable native of a district, worker on the land, dweller in the country; native of a country, as *Britain's ss.*; person viewed as inheriting an occupation, quality, &c., as *s. of toil*, *s. of Mars* (soldier), *s.* (=*man*) *of* BELIAL, *ss. of light, darkness*, &c.; *Ss. of Liberty*, *of the* (*American*) *Revolution*, &c., American patriotic &c. organizations. Hence **so·n**LESS a., **so·n**SHIP n. [OE *sunu*, cf. Du. *zoon*, G *sohn*, ON *sunr*, *sonr*]

-son, suf., = -TION in some wds f. F, as *reason*, *season* (F *raison*, *saison*, L *rationem*, *sationem*), *treason* (OF *traison*, L *traditionem*), *benison* (OF *beneison*, L *benedictionem*), POISON, VENISON, ORISON, COMPARISON.

sō·nant, a. & n. (Sound, letter) capable of being sounded continuously, accompanied by vocal vibration, voiced, not surd, (e.g. *b, d, g, j, v, z*). Hence **so·n**ANCY n. [f. L *sonare* sound (*sonus*), see -ANT]

sona·ta (-nah-), n. Instrumental composition, esp. for piano, of three or four movements (one or more in s. form) in contrasted rhythms but related keys; *s. form*, mode of composition in which two themes are successively set forth, developed, & restated. [It. (as prec., see -ADE)]

sōnati·na (-tē-), n. Simplified form of sonata. [It. dim. of prec.]

song, n. Singing, vocal music, as *burst forth into s.*; musical cry of some birds (*s.-birds*); short poem set to music or meant to be sung; short poem in rhymed stanzas; poetry, verse, as *renowned in s.*; (Mus.) *s. form*, mode of composition usu. in three sections, the first & third being nearly the same & the second contrasted with the first; *bought, sold, it for a s.* or *an old s.* (mere trifle); *S. of* DEGREES or *ascents* (in O.T., Psalms 120–134); *S. of Ss.*, *S. of Solomon*, Canticles; *s.*-THRUSH; *s.-sparrow*, hedge-sparrow & other birds. Hence **so·ng**LESS a. [OE, Da., G, *sang*, cf. Du. *zang*; as SING]

so·ngster, n. Singer; song-bird; poet. Hence **so·ngstr**ESS[1] n. [-STER]

soni·ferous, a. Conveying or producing sound. [f. L *sonus* sound + -FEROUS]

so·nnet, n. Poem of 14 lines (usu. rhyming thus; *pig bat cat wig jig hat rat fig*; *lie red sob die bed rob* or *lie red die bed pie wed*; or otherwise e.g. as in Shakspere's ss.); (now rare) any short lyric. So **sonnet**EER· n., & v.i., (usu. contempt.) [F, f. It. *sonetto* (*suono* SOUND[2] n., -ET[1])]

so·nny (sŭ-), n. Familiar form of address to a boy. [f. SON + -Y[3]]

sonŏ·meter, n. Kinds of instrument for testing deaf person's hearing, measuring sounds, &c. [f. L *sonus* sound + -METER]

sōnore·scent, a. (Of hard rubber &c.) emitting sounds corresponding to pulsations of radiant heat or light. So **sonore·sc**ENCE n. [as SONOROUS + -ESCENT]

sōnori·fic, a. Producing (esp. other than vocal) sound. [as foll. + -FIC]

sonor·ous, a. Resonant; loud-sounding; (of speech, style, &c.) high sounding, imposing; *s. figures* (formed in layer of sand &c. by sound-vibration); *s. râle* (heard in some diseases). Hence or cogn. **sonor·**ITY, **sonor·ous**NESS, nn., **sonor·ous**LY[2] adv. [f. L *sonorus* (*sonor* sound f. *sonare* vb) + -OUS]

sōōn, adv. Not long after the present time or time in question or *after* specified time, in a short time, as *shall s. know the result*, *was s. convinced of his error*, *arrived s. after four*, *s. after the gate was closed*, *least said soonest mended*; *as* (or *so*, esp. after negative, or when causality or other close connexion is suggested) *s. as*, the moment that, not later than, as early as, as *came as* (or *so*) *s. as I heard of it*, *will get there as s. as they* (*do*), *did not arrive so* (or *as*) *s. as I expected*, *drops his fine theories so* (or *as*) *s. as they clash with his interests*, *so s. as* (*ever*) *there is any talk of paying he cools down*; (w. expressed or implied comparison) willingly, as *I would just as s. stay at home* (*as go*), *would sooner die than let him* (or *than that he should*) *find it out*, *which would you soonest do?*; early, as *what makes you come so s.?*, *you spoke too s.*; *we had no sooner sat down than* (the moment we sat down) *she burst into tears*, *no sooner said than done*, it was done the moment it was proposed &c.; *the sooner the better*; *you will repent it sooner or later* (some day, in the long run). [OE *sóna*, cf. OHG *sân*]

sōōt, n., & v.t. Black substance rising in fine flakes in the smoke of wood, coal, oil, &c., during combustion & sticking to sides of chimney &c., used as fertilizer; *s.-cancer*, *-wart*, disease of scrotum in sweeps. Hence **soo·ti**LY[2] adv., **soo·ti**NESS n., **soo·t**LESS, **soo·t**Y[2], aa. (Vb) cover with s. [OE & ON *sót*, cf. Da. *sod*]

sōō·terkin, n. (archaic). Dutch woman's false birth produced by sitting over stove; (fig.) abortive scheme. [?]

sōōth, n. (archaic). Truth, fact, esp. *in* (*good*) *s.*, really, truly. [OE *sóth* (for *santh*), cf. ON *sannr*, Sw. *sann*, Da. *sand*, true]

sōōthe (-dh), v.t. Calm (person, nerves, passions); soften, mitigate, (pain); flatter, humour, (person, his vanity). Hence **soo·th**ER[1] n. (in vbl senses, & esp. rubber teat for child to suck),

soo·thingLY[2] adv. [OE (*ge*)*sóthian* confirm, assent to (*ge-* Y- + *sóth* SOOTH)]

soo·thfast, a. (archaic). Truthful; true; loyal, steadfast. [OE *sóthfæst* (SOOTH, cf. STEADFAST)]

soo·thsayer, n. One who foretells the future, diviner. Hence **soo·thsay** v.i. [SOOTH + SAY + -ER[1]]

sop, n., & v.t. & i. Piece of bread &c. dipped in broth &c. (*s. in the pan*, fried bread); MILK[1]*sop*; something given (*to* formidable or troublesome animal, person, &c., esp. *to Cerberus*) to pacify, bribe; (v.t.) soak (bread &c. in broth &c.), take *up* (water &c.) by absorption in towel &c., wet thoroughly; (v.i.) be drenched, as *am sopping with rain, clothes are sopping* (vbl n. as adv.) *wet*, whence **so·ppy**[2] a. [OE *sopp* n., *soppian* vb, cf. ON *soppa* n.; cogn. w. *súpan* SUP]

sŏ·phism, n. False argument intended to deceive (cf. PARALOGISM). [ME & OF *sophisme* f. L f. Gk *sophisma* (as foll., see -M)]

sŏ·phist, n. Ancient-Greek paid teacher of philosophy & rhetoric; captious or fallacious reasoner, quibbler. Hence or cogn. **sophi·st**IC(AL) aa., **sophi·stical**LY[2] adv., **so·phist**RY(4, 5) n. [f. L f. Gk *sophistēs* (*sophizō* instruct f. *sophos* wise, -IST)]

sŏ·phister, n. (hist.). Student of varying seniority at some English & American universities. [f. OF *sophistre* var. as prec.]

sophi·sticate, v.t. & i. Involve (subject) in sophistry; mislead (person) thus; deprive (person, thing) of simplicity, make artificial; tamper with (text &c.) for purposes of argument &c.; use sophistry; adulterate (wine &c.). So **sophistic**A·TION n. [f. med. L *sophisticare* (*sophisticus* sophistic), see -ATE[3]]

sŏ·phomore, n. (U.S. univv.). Second-year student. [prob. f. *sophom* obs. var. of SOPHISM + -OR[2]]

Sō·phy, n. (hist.). Ruler of Persia in 16th & 17th cc. [f. Pers. *Çafī* surname of dynasty]

sŏpori·fic, a. & n. (Drug) tending to produce sleep. So **sopori·**FEROUS, **so·po**ROSE[1], **so·por**OUS, aa. [f. L *sopor* sleep + -I- + -FIC]

sopra·no (-rah-), n. (pl. *-nos, -ni* pr. -nē), (Music for) highest female or boy's voice, treble (often attrib.); (also **sopra·n**IST n.) singer with this. [It. (*sopra* above f. L *supra*)]

-sor, suf. forming agent-nn. on L p.p. st. in -s-, as *professor*; see -OR[2].

sor·a, n. Bird frequenting marshes of Carolina &c. in autumn & used as food. [native]

sorb, n. Service-tree; (also *s.-apple*) its fruit. Hence **sor·b**ATE[1](3) n., **sor·b**IC a., (chem.). [f. L *sorbus*]

sorbĕfā·cient (-shnt), a. & n. (med.). (Drug &c.) causing absorption. [f. L *sorbēre* suck in + -FACIENT]

sor·bet, n. Flavoured water-ice; = SHERBET. [F, as SHERBET]

Sorbo·nne (-ŏn), n. (Hist.) theological faculty in University of Paris having great influence in 16th & 17th cc.; the seat of the *Académie* of Paris & of the faculties of theology, science, & literature. [F, f. R. de *Sorbon*, founder about 1250]

sor·cerer, n. User of magic arts, wizard, enchanter (often fig.). So **sor·cer**ESS[1], **sor·**CERY(4, 5), nn. [earlier *sorcer* f. OF *sorcier* f. LL *sortiarius* caster of lots (*sors -rtis* lot, see -ARY[1]) + -ER[1]]

sordame·ntĕ, adv. (mus.). In a muffled manner. [It.]

sor·did, a. Mean, niggardly; ignoble, base; (Bot., Zool., of colours) impure, muddy, as *s. blue*; (archaic) dirty, squalid. Hence **sor·did**LY[2] adv., **sor·did**NESS n. [f. F *sordide* f. L *sordidus* (*sordēre* be dirty, *sordes* filth, see -ID[1])]

sor·dine (-ēn), n. (mus.). Mute for stringed instruments. [f. It. *sordina* f. L as SURD]

sore, a., n., & adv. (Of parts of body, person) morbidly tender, as *has a s. arm, is* FOOT[1]*sore*, (*clergyman's*) *s.* THROAT, *touched him on a s. place* (often fig.), *a sight for s. eyes* (welcome, pleasant), *like a bear with a s. head* (grumpy); irritated, aggrieved, touchy, as *is very s. about his defeat*; arousing painful feelings, irritating, esp. a *s. subject*; (archaic, poet.) distressing, grievous, severe, as *in s. distress, a s. struggle, affliction s. long time he bore*, whence **sore·**LY[2] adv. (N.) s. place on body e.g. where skin or flesh is bruised or inflamed; (fig.) s. subject, painful memory, esp. *re-open old ss.*; BED[1]*sore*; EYE[1]*sore*. (Adv.) grievously, severely, as *s. oppressed, bested, afflicted.* Hence **sore·**NESS n. [(n. & adv. f. adj.) OE *sár* painful, cf. Du. *zeer* sore, ON *sárr* sore, G *sehr* sorely, very]

sorel. See SORREL[2].

sor·ghum (-gum), n. Kinds of grass including millet & Chinese sugar-cane. [mod. L, f. It. *sorgo* etym. dub.]

sor·icine, a. Of, related to, the shrew-mouse. [f. L *soricinus* (*sorex -icis* shrew-mouse, -INE[1])]

sorī·tēs, n. Chain-syllogism (e.g. a cat is a quadruped, quadruped is an animal, animal is a substance; therefore a cat is a substance); form of sophism leading by gradual steps from truth to absurdity and based on the absence of precise, esp. numerical, limits to terms (e.g. a man with only 1 hair is bald, therefore man with 2, 3, 4, . . . 10,000, hairs is bald). So **sorī·**TICAL a. [L f. Gk *sōritēs* lit. heaper (*sōros* heap, see -ITE[1])

sorn, v.i. (Sc.). Obtrude oneself *on* (person) for bed & board. Hence **sor·n**ER[1] n. [f. obs. Ir. *sorthan* free quarters]

sorō·sis, n. (bot.). Fleshy compound fruit, e.g. pine-apple, mulberry. [as SORUS + -OSIS]

so·rra, adv. (Ir., slang). Not, never, (*s. a one, a bit*, &c., = the devil a). [=*sorrow*]

sŏrrel[1], n. Kinds of acid-leaved herb allied with dock. [f. OF *sorele* f. Teut. *sūr* SOUR]

sŏ·rrel[2], a. & n. (Of) reddish-brown colour; s. animal esp. horse; (also *sorel*) buck of third year. [f. OF *sorel* s. horse, dim. of *sor* s. (horse), etym. dub.]

sŏ·rrow, n., & v.i. Grief, sadness, caused by loss of good or occurrence of evil, whence **so·rrow**FUL a., **so·rrowful**LY[2] adv., **so·rrowful**NESS n.; occasion of this, misfortune, trouble, as *has had many ss., much s.*; *the Man of Ss.*, Christ; *s.-stricken* (with s.); lamentation, as *his s. was loud & long*; (v.i.) grieve, feel sorrow, (*at, over, for*, misfortune &c., *for*, i.e. on behalf of, person &c.), mourn (*after, for*, lost person or thing), whence **so·rrow**ER[1] n., **so·rrow**ING[2] a. [ME *sorwe*, OE & ON *sorg*, cf. Du. *zorg*, G *sorge*]

sŏ·rry, a. Feeling regret, regretful, as *will be s. for this some day, felt s. for him* (on his account), *s. for* one*self* (colloq. = depressed), *am s. for* (regret) *that, am so s.* (*that*) *you must go, am s. to hear it*, (as informal apology for trifling offence) *s.!*; wretched, paltry, shabby, of poor quality, as *a s. fellow, in a s. plight, in s. clothes, a s. excuse*, whence **so·rri**LY[2] adv., **so·rri**NESS n. [OE *sárig* (SORE, -Y[2]); not connected w. prec.]

sort[1], n. Group of things &c. with common attributes, class, kind, species, as *biscuits of several ss., a new s. of bicycle, people of every s. & kind*; *of ss.*, (in inventories &c.) unassorted, mixed; (in foll. uses = KIND[1]) *nothing of the s., coffee of a s., what s. of tree?, these s. of men, a s. of stockbroker* &c., *I s. of expected it*; *a s. of war* &c., *a war* &c. *of a s.* or colloq. *of ss.*, not fully deserving the name; (colloq.) *an awfully good s.* (of person), *that's your s.* (the way to do it); (archaic) manner, way, as *in seemly, courteous*, &c., *s.*, *after* or *in a s.* (= FASHION); *in some s.* (literary), to a certain extent; (Print.) any letter or piece in fount of type, as *copy is hard* (or *runs*) *on ss.* (requires many of some ss.); *out of ss.*, out of health, spirits, or temper, (Print.) short of ss. [f. OF *sorte* f. L *sortem* (nom. *sors*) lot, chance, state]

sort[2], v.t. & i. Separate into sorts (often *over, out*); select (things of one s.) from miscellaneous group, as *sorted out those of the largest size*; (archaic) correspond or agree *with* (*his actions s. ill, well, with his professions*). Hence **sor·t**ABLE a., **sor·t**ER[1] n. [f. prec.]

sor·tēs, n. pl. *S. Virgiliā·nae, Biblicae* or *Sacrae, Homericae*, divination by chance selection of passages from Virgil, the Bible, or Homer. [L, pl. as SORT[1]]

sor·tie (-tē), n. Sally esp. of beleaguered garrison. [F, f. *sortir* go out, etym. dub.]

sor·tilege (-ĭj), n. Divination by lots. [f. OF *sortilege* f. med. L *sortilegium* f. L *sortilegus* a. (as SORT[1] + *legere* choose, read)]

sorti·tion, n. Casting of lots. [f. L *sortitio* (*sortiri* cast lots)]

sor·us, n. (bot.; pl. *-rī*). Heap, cluster, esp. of spore-cases on back of fern-frond. [f. Gk *sōros* heap]

-sory, suf., a spec. form of -ORY in aa. or nn. f. L vbs that form p.p. in -s-, as *accessory* (*cedere cess-*), *promissory* (*mittere miss-*).

S O S (ĕsōĕs), wireless code-signal of extreme distress. [arbitrary]

so·-so, pred. a. & adv. Not very good. [so]

sostenu·to (-nōō-), adv. (mus.). In sustained or prolonged manner. [It.]

sot, n., & v.i. Confirmed drunkard, person stupefied by habitual drunkenness; (v.i.) tipple. Hence **so·tt**ISH[1] a., **so·ttish**LY[2] adv., **so·ttish**NESS n. [OF, = fool, etym. dub.; cf. Du. *zot*, med. L *sottus*]

So·theby's (sŭth*e*-), n. A sale-room in London for books, MSS., &c.

Sō·thic, a. Of the dog-star, esp. *S. year* (Egyptian, fixed by heliacal rising of dog-star), *S. cycle* (of 1460 S. or 1461 solar years). [f. Gk *Sōthis* f. Egypt. name of dog-star]

so·tto vo·ce (-tshā, -sĭ), adv. In an undertone, aside. [It., = beneath the voice]

sou (sōō), n. (pl. *-s* pr. -z). (Hist.) French coin of various values; (loosely) five-centime piece; (colloq.) *hasn't a s.* (a farthing, any money). [F]

soubrette (sōōbrĕ·t), n. Maid-servant or similar character (esp. w. implication of pertness, coquetry, intrigue, &c.) in comedy. [F]

sou·chong (sōōsh-), n. Kind of black tea made from youngest leaves. [F, f. Chin. *siao* small + *chung* sort]

Soudane·se (sōō-, -z), a. & n. (pl. same). (Inhabitant) of the Soudan, district of Africa south of Sahara. [-ESE]

souffle (sōō·fl), n. (med.). Low murmur heard in auscultation of various organs &c. [F, f. *souffler* blow f. L SUF(*flare* blow)]

soufflé (sōō·flā), a. & n. Made light & frothy, as *omelet s.*; such dish, usu. made with beaten whites of eggs. [F, p.p. as prec.]

sough (sŭf, sow, sōōch), n., & v.i. (Make) moaning, whistling, or rushing sound as of wind in trees &c. [OE *swógan* resound, prob. imit.]

sought. See SEEK.

soul (sōl), n. The immaterial part of man, as *immortality of the s., commend* one's *s. to God* (of person at point of death), *'pon my s.* (asseveration); moral & emotional part of man, as *his whole s. revolted from it,* CURE[1] *of ss., has a s. above sherry & bitters*; intellectual part of man, vital principle & mental powers of animals including man, as *keep* BODY[1] *& s. together, cannot call his s. his own* (is dominated by another); animating or essential part, person viewed as this, as *he was the (life &) s. of the enterprise, of the party*; person viewed as embodying moral or intellectual qualities, as *the greatest ss. of antiquity, left that to meaner ss.*; (often without *a*) emotional or intellectual energy e.g. as revealed in work of art, as *the fellow has no s., his pictures lack s.*; (of persons) personification or pattern *of (is the s. of honour,* is incapable of dishonourable conduct); departed spirit, as ALL *Souls' Day*; disembodied spirit; person, as *not a s. to speak to for miles round, ship went down with 200 ss.,* (expr. familiarity, patronage, pity, contempt, &c.) *my good s., there's a good s., the poor little s. had lost her way, a simple s.*; (in comb.) *s.-destroying, -stirring, -subduing,*&c. Hence **(-)soul**ED[2], **sou·l**LESS, aa., **sou·lless**LY[2] adv., **sou·llessness** n. [OE *saw(e)l, -ol, -ul,* cf. Du. *ziel,* G *seele*]

sou·lful, a. Having, expressing, appealing to, the (esp. higher) emotional or intellectual qualities. Hence **sou·lful**LY[2] adv., **sou·lful**NESS n. [-FUL]

sound[1] (sow-), a. & adv. Healthy, not diseased nor injured nor rotten, as *a s. body, s. mind, s. in life & limb, s. fruit, timbers, ship*; correct, logical, well-founded, judicious, as *s. doctrine, theologian, argument, views, policy, is he s. on free trade?*; (Commerc., of company &c.) solvent; thorough, unqualified, as *a s. sleep(er), flogging*; (adv.) s. (fast) *asleep, will sleep the sounder for it.* Hence **sou·nd**LY[2] adv., **sou·nd**NESS n. [ME, Da., Sw., *sund,* cf. OE & G *gesund,* Du. *gezond*]

sound[2] (sow-), n., & v.i. & t. The sensation produced through the ear, what is or may be heard; vibrations causing this sensation; *musical s.* (produced by continuous & regular vibrations, opp. to *noise*); any of a series of articulate utterances, as *vowel, consonant, ss.*; mere words (*s. & fury*); (fig.) mental impression produced by oral or other statement &c., as *will have a queer s., don't like the s. of it*; *s.-board,* = *sounding-board*; *s.-bow,* thick edge of bell against which tongue strikes; *s.-film,* cinema show with audible dialogue, songs, &c.; *s.- hole, -post,* hole in belly, small prop between belly & back, of some musical instruments; *s.*-PROOF[2]; *s.-shadow,* interception of s. by large object; *s.-wave* (of condensation & rarefaction, by which s. is propagated in elastic medium e.g. air). (Vb) give forth s., as *the trumpets s.*; (w. ref. to impression created, often fig.) *sounds to me like something cracking, sounds as if a tap were running, sounds as if he wanted to back out of it, will s. very strange to say you hadn't time, that* (excuse &c.) *sounds very hollow, that* (report, explanation) *sounds all right* (promising, plausible, &c.); (part.) having more s. than sense or truth, as *sounding rhetoric, promises,* imposing, as *sounding titles*; make (trumpet &c.) s.; utter, as *s. a note of alarm*; pronounce (*the h in hour is not sounded*); give notice of (*an alarm, the retreat,* &c.) with bell &c., cause to resound, make known, as *s. his praises far & wide*; test (railway-carriage wheel &c., lungs &c.) by noting s. produced by hammer, by auscultation; *sounding-board,* canopy over pulpit &c. serving to direct s. towards audience, thin plate of wood in musical instrument increasing s. Hence **sou·nd**LESS a. [(n.) AF *soun* f. OF *son* f. L *sonus,* for *-d* cf. LEND, ROUND[5], HIND[2]; (vb) f. OF *soner* f. L *sonare*]

sound[3] (sow-), v.t. & i., & n. Test the depth of (sea, channel, pond, &c., or abs.) & the quality of its bottom with *sounding-line* or *-apparatus* (often furnished with cup &c. for bringing up sample); find depth of water in (ship's hold) with *sounding-rod*; (Med.) examine (bladder &c.) with probe; (of fish, esp. whale) dive to the bottom; inquire esp. in cautious or reserved manner into the sentiments or inclination of (person *about, on, as to*); (n.) surgeon's probe. [(n. f. vb) f. F *sonder* (*sonde* SOUND[4])]

sound[4] (sow-), n. Narrow passage of water connecting two seas or sea with lake &c., strait; fish's air-bladder; cuttle-fish. [OE, ON, Da., Sw., G, *sund,* cogn. w. SWIM, = variously swimming, water, sea, strait, air-bladder, ferry]

sou·nder[1] (sow-), n. (Archaic) herd of wild swine; (pseudo-archaic) young wild boar. [f. OF *sundre* f. Teut., cf. OE *sunor,* OHG *swaner*]

sou·nder[2], n. In vbl senses of SOUND[2], esp.: telegraphic receiving instrument for reading message by sound. [-ER[1]]

sou·nder[3], n. In vbl senses of SOUND[3]; *flying s.,* sounding-apparatus that can be used without reducing ship's speed. [-ER[1]]

sou·nding, n. In vbl senses of SOUND[3], also: (pl.) place near enough to shore to admit of s., as *be in, come into, ss.* [-ING[1]]

soup (sōōp), n. Liquid food made of stock & other ingredients (*in the s.,* slang, in difficulties); *s.-kitchen,* public establishment for supplying s. gratis to the poor; *s.-ticket* (entitling holder to s. at s.-kitchen); *s. maigre* (-ger), thin s. chiefly of vegetables; *s.-plate,* deep kind for s.; PEA *s.* Hence **sou·py**[2] a. [f. F *soupe* (*souper* SUP)]

soupçon (F), n. Very small quantity, dash, (*of* flavouring, quality, &c.).
sour (sowr), a., & v.i. & t. Of acid taste, esp. as result of unripeness, as *s. apples, s.* GRAPES, or of fermentation, as *s. milk, bread*, (of smell) suggestive of fermentation; (of soil) dank; (of person or temper) harsh, peevish, morose; *s. dock*, common sorrel; (vb) make, become, sour (esp. fig.), as *soured by misfortune*. Hence **sour·**ISH[1] a., **sour·**LY[2] adv., **sour·**NESS n. [OE *sur*, cf. Du. *zuur*, G *saure*, ON *surr*]
source (sōrs), n. Spring, fountain-head, from which stream issues, as *the ss. of the Nile*; origin, place from which thing comes or is got, as *the s. of all our woes, reliable s. of information, drawn from all ss.* [f. OF *sourse*, fem. p.p. as n. of *sourdre* rise f. L *surgere*]
sourdine (soordē·n), n. Harmonium stop producing soft effect; =SORDINE. [F, cf. SORDINE]
sour·-sop, n. A W.-Ind. fruit & tree. [SOUR + SOP]
souse (sows), n., v.t. & i., & adv. Pickle made with salt; food in pickle, esp. head, feet, & ears, of swine; dip, plunge, drenching, in water; (vb) put in pickle, as *soused mackerel*, plunge (t. & i., *into* liquid), soak (thing *in* liquid), throw (liquid *over* thing); (adv.) with swift descent, headlong, as *came s. into our midst*. [vb f. n., OF *sous* pickle f. OHG *sulza* (*salzan* to SALT); adv. partly f. obs. *souse* swoop cogn. w. *source*]
soutache (sōō·tahsh), n. Ornamental braid for sewing on fabric in designs. [F, f. Hung. *szuszak* ringlet]
soutane (sōōtah·n), n. (R.-C. Ch.). Priest's cassock. [F]
souteneur (sōōtener·), n. Man cohabiting with & living on the earnings of a prostitute. [F, = protector]
south (sowth), adv., n., a., (abbr. *S.*), & v.i. (Towards, at, near) point of horizon directly opposite to north; point of compass opposite north; DUE[1] *s.*; *s.* BY[1] *east* or *west*; *s. of*, further s. than; *s.-east, s.-s.-west*, &c., advv., aa., & nn., POINT[1]s of the compass, corresponding regions, (with uses & derivatives corresp. to those of south, e.g. *s.-s.-easterly*); southern part of England, Scotland, Ireland, or Europe; the Southern STATE[1]s; *s.* (*wind*), wind from the south; *s.-east, s.-west*, (abbr. *S.E., S.W.*) London postal districts. (Adj.) situated or dwelling in, looking towards, the s.; *S. Downs* (of Hampshire & Sussex), *sou·thdown* a. & n., (sheep) of a breed originating on S. Downs esteemed for their flesh; *S. Kensington*, (used for) the museums of S. K. or the atmosphere of culture & art & instruction associated w. them; *S. Sea* (hist.), the Pacific; *S. Sea Bubble*, scheme for trading in Spanish America, which collapsed in 1720. (Vb) move towards s., (of moon &c.) cross the meridian of a place. Hence **sou·th**WARD a. & n., **sou·th**WARD(S) adv. [OE *súth*, cf. ON *suthr*]
southea·ster, sou·ther, nn. Wind from SE, from S. [-ER[1]]
sou·therly (sŭdh-), a. & adv. Towards the south; (of wind) blowing from the south. [f. SOUTH, as EASTERLY]
sou·thern (sŭdh-), a. & n. Of, in, the south; *S.* HEMISPHERE, CROSS[1], CONFEDERACY, STATES; looking south, as *a s. aspect*; (of wind, rare) = prec.; (n.) inhabitant of the south, esp. of the Southern States, whence **sou·thern**ER[1] n.; *sou·thernwood*, kind of wormwood with scented leaves. Hence **sou·thern**MOST a. [-ERN]
sou·thing (sowth-), n. In vbl senses, also (Naut.) difference of latitude made in sailing south. [-ING[1]]
sou·thron (sŭdh-), a. & n. (archaic Sc.). English, Englishman, (usu. contempt.). [var. of SOUTHERN]
southwe·ster, n. Wind from SW; (usu. *sou'w-*) waterproof hat with broad brim behind to protect neck. [-ER[1]]
souvenir (sōō·venēr), n. Thing given, kept, &c., to recall the past, memento (*of* occasion, place, &c.; also, in the war, as French children's request for keepsake to foreign soldiers). [F (n. f. vb), = remember, souvenir, f. L SUB(*venire* come) occur to the mind]
sovereign (sŏ·vrĭn), a. & n. Supreme, as *s. power, the s. good* (= SUMMUM BONUM); lofty, as *with s. contempt*; possessing s. power, as *s. States*, royal, as *our s.* LORD, whence **so·vereign**TY n.; very good, esp. *a s. remedy*; hence **so·vereign**LY[2] adv. (archaic). (N.) supreme ruler, esp. monarch; (colloq. abbr. *sov*) English gold coin worth £1; *half s.*, gold coin worth 10s. [(n. f. adj.) f. OF *soverain* f. LL SUPER(*anus* -AN); *-g-* by assoc. w. *reign*]
sōviĕ·t, n. Any of the councils elected by the workers & soldiers of a district in revolutionary Russia, or of a smaller number elected by these, or the all-Russian congress of delegates from these latter; *Union of S. Socialist Republics* (abbr. U.S.S.R.), the revolutionary government of Russia. [Russ.]
sow[1] (sō), v.t. (sowed, sown *or* sowed). Scatter (seed, or abs.) on or in the earth for purpose of growth; (fig.) *s.* (*the seeds of*) *dissension* &c., *must reap what you have sown, s. the wind* (see WHIRL); plant (field &c. *with* seed) by sowing; (fig.) cover thickly *with*. Hence **sow·**ER[1](1, 2), **sow·**ING[1], nn. [OE *sáwan*, cf. Du. *zaaien* G *säen*, ON *sá*]
sow[2] (sow), n. Adult female hog; *get the wrong s. by the ear*, fix on wrong person or thing, reach wrong conclusion; *as drunk as a s.* (completely); (also *s.-bug*) woodlouse; main trough through which molten iron runs into side-channels to form pigs, large block of iron that solidifies in this;

sow·back, low ridge of sand &c.; *sow·bread,* kind of cyclamen; *s.-thistle,* plant with small yellow flowers & milky juice. [OE *sugu,* cf. Du. *zog,* G *sau,* ON *sýr*]

soy, n. Kind of sauce made in Japan & China from the *s.-bean* or *-pea.* [f. Jap. *shoyu*]

spa (-ah, -aw), n. (Place where there is a) mineral spring. [*Spa,* place in Belgium]

space[1], n. Continuous extension viewed with or without reference to the existence of objects within it; interval between points or objects viewed as having one, two, or three dimensions, as *separated by a s. of 10 ft, clear a space* (area), *box occupies too much s., would take up too much s.* (on paper) *to go into detail*; (Print.) blank between words &c., type securing this; interval of time, as *in the s. of an hour, after a short s., let us rest a s.*; *s.-bar,* bar in typewriter for making s. between words; *space-time* (philos.), a fusion of the concepts of s. & time, regarded as a continuum in which the existent exists, & as the fourth dimension non-recognition of which confines the Euclidean or three-dimensional geometry to the range of practical experience & leaves it philosophically assailable beyond that range; *s.-writer, -writing* (in newspaper, paid according to area occupied). Hence **spa·ce**LESS a. [f. F *espace* f. L *spatium*]

space[2], v.t. & i. Set at intervals, put spaces between, (esp. words, letters, lines, in printing; make a space between words on typewriter &c., as *don't forget to s.,* whence **spa·c**ER[1](2) n.; *s. out* (print.) put more or wider spaces between. Hence **spa·c**ING[1](1) n. [f. prec.]

spā·cious (-shus), a. Enclosing a large space, roomy. Hence **spa·cious**LY[2] adv., **spa·cious**NESS n. [f. F *spacieux* f. L *spatiosus* (as SPACE[1], see -OUS)]

spade, n., & v.t. Tool for digging & cutting ground, turf, &c., with sharp-edged iron blade & wooden handle used with both hands; *call a s. a s.,* call things by their names, speak plainly or bluntly; tool of similar shape for various purposes, e.g. for removing blubber from whale; *s. bayonet* (with broad blade, used as both s. & weapon); *s. husbandry* (with deep s.-digging instead of subsoil-ploughing); (playing-card with) black figure(s) shaped like heart with small handle, (pl.) suit of these cards; *s. guinea* (of George III, with shield shaped like s. on cards); *s.-work,* (fig.) hard work with attention to details (*continual s.-w. is necessary on the Insurance question*); (v.t.) dig over (ground), cut blubber from (whale), with s. Hence **spa·de**FUL n. [OE *spadu* perh. f. LG (Da., Sw., Norw., *spade*), cogn. w. L f. Gk *spathē* broad blade; in card sense f. Gk thr. Sp. *espada* sword]

spa·dger, n. (slang). Corrupt. of SPARROW.

spadi·lle (-ĭl), n. Ace of spades in ombre & quadrille. [F, f. Sp. *espadilla* dim. as SPADE[1]]

spā dix, n. (bot.; pl. *-dī·cēs*). Spike of flowers closely arranged round fleshy axis & usu. enclosed in a spathe. Hence or cogn. **spadĭ·c**EOUS, **spa·dic**OSE[1], aa. [L f. Gk, = palm-branch]

spā·do, n. (law). Person incapable of procreation. [L, f. Gk *spadōn* eunuch]

spaghe·ttĭ (-gĕ-), n. Kind of macaroni. [It.]

spahi, -ee (spah·hē), n. Member of 14th-c. Turkish irregular cavalry; member of native Algerian cavalry in French service. [f. Turk. f. Hind. *sipahi* SEPOY]

spake. See SPEAK.

spall (-awl), v.t. & i., & n. Splinter, chip; (Mining) prepare (ore) for sorting by breaking it up. Hence **spa·ld**ER[1] n. [n. f. 15th c., etym. dub.; cf. G *spellen* to split]

spă·lpeen, n. (Ir.). Mean fellow, rascal.

span[1], v.t. & i. (Of bridge, arch, &c., fig. of memory &c.) stretch from side to side of, extend across, (river &c., fig. period &c.), (of builder &c.) bridge (river &c.); measure, cover, the extent of (thing) with one's grasp &c.; (Naut.) confine (booms &c.) with ropes; move in distinct stretches like span-worm. [f. OE *span* n., see foll.]

span[2], n. Full extent from end to end, as *s. of a bridge, of an arch, our brief s.* (*of life*), *the whole s. of Roman history*; each part of a bridge &c. between piers or supports; greenhouse or similar structure with s. roof; maximum distance between tips of thumb & little finger, esp. as a measure = 9 in.; short distance, as *our life is but a s.*; (Naut.) rope fastened by both ends to take a purchase in the loop, double rope connected with thimbles; (Colon., U.S.) pair of horses or mules, yoke of oxen; *s.-dogs,* pair of iron bars with claws for grappling timber; *s. roof* (with two inclined sides, opp. to pent-roof or lean-to); *s.-worm,* larva of geometer. [senses *measure, extent,* f. OE *span* (of the hand); naut. & colon. senses f. Du. *span* (*spannen* fasten)]

spa·ndrel, n. Space between either shoulder of arch & surrounding rectangular moulding or framework, or between shoulders of adjoining arches & moulding above; *s. wall* (built on curve of arch, filling in s.). [?]

spa·ngle (-nggl), n., & v.t. Small piece of glittering material esp. one of many as ornament of dress &c.; any small sparkling object; (also *oak-s.*) spongy excrescence on oak-leaves, oak-apple; (v.t). cover with spangles (esp. in p.p.). Hence **spa·ngl**Y[2] a. [f. earlier *spang* f. MDu. *spange* metal clasp + -LE]

Spă·niard (-yerd), n. Native of Spain. [f. OF *Espaignart* (*Espaigne* Spain, -ARD)]

spă·niel (-yel), n. Kinds of dog with long silky coat, drooping ears, & docile & affectionate disposition, some used by sportsmen & some kept as pets (*King Charles's s.*, small black-&-tan kind); (fig.) fawning or cringing person. [ME, f. OF *espaigneul* f. Sp. *español* Spanish f. *España* Spain f. L *Hispania*]

Spă·nish, a. & n. Of Spain or the Spaniards or their language; *S.* (=*Invincible*) ARMADA; *S. black, brown, red, white,* pigments; *S.* CHESTNUT; *S. fly,* bright green insect dried & used for raising blisters, as aphrodisiac, &c.; *S. fowl,* breed of domestic fowl with glossy greenish-black plumage; *S. grass,* esparto; *S. main* (hist.), NE coast of S. America between Orinoco river & Panama, & adjoining part of Caribbean sea; *S. windlass,* use of stick as lever for tightening cord or bandage; *War of the S. succession* (between France & Bavaria on one side & England, Prussia, & United Provinces, on the other, on death of Charles II of Spain without issue, 1701-14); (n.) S. language. [ME *Spainisc* (*Spain,* see -ISH¹)]

spank, v.t. & i., & n. Slap on buttocks with open hand or slipper &c., whence **spa·nking¹** [-ING¹] n.; urge forward esp. by slapping or whipping; (of horse &c.) move briskly esp. at a step between trot & gallop; (n.) slap, blow with open hand &c., on buttocks. [imit.]

spa·nker, n. In vbl senses; also or esp.: fast-going horse; (colloq.) person or thing of notable size or quality, stunner, whopper; (Naut.) fore-&-aft sail set on after side of mizzenmast. [-ER¹]

spa·nking² (for s.¹ see SPANK), a. & adv. In vbl senses; also: (colloq.) striking, notable, excellent, as *had a s. time, a s.* (strong) *breeze,* (adv.) *a s. fine woman.* [-ING², cf. *whacking, thumping, whopping*]

spa·nless, a. (poet.). Beyond measure. [-LESS]

spa·nner, n. In vbl senses; also: instrument for turning nut on screw &c.; cross-brace of bridge &c.; connecting-rod in parallel motion of engine; =SPAN²-*worm.* [-ER¹; mech. sense f. G *spanner*]

spar¹, n., & v.t. Stout pole esp. such as is used for mast, yard, &c., of ship; *s.-buoy* (made of a s. with one end moored so that other stands up); *s.-deck,* upper deck extending from bow to stern, including quarterdeck and forecastle; (v.t.) furnish with s., help (ship) over shallow bar with ss. [ME *sparre,* cf. Du. *spar,* G *sparren,* ON *sparri*]

spar², n. Kinds of crystalline mineral, easily cleavable & non-lustrous, as *calcareous s.,* calcite, *Derbyshire* (=FLUOR) *s., Iceland s.,* transparent calcite much used for optical purposes. [f. MLG *spar,* cogn. w. OE *spæren* gypsum]

spar³, v.i., & n. Make motions of attack & defence with closed fists, use the hands (as) in boxing, (often *at* opponent); (fig.) bandy words, as *they are always sparring* (*at each other*); (of cocks) fight esp. with protected spurs; (n.) sparring motion, boxing-match, cock-fight. [orig. = (of cock) strike out with spurs; etym. dub.]

spă·rable, n. Headless nail for soles & heels of boots. [corrupt. of *sparrow-bill*]

spare¹, a. & n. Scanty, frugal, as *s. diet,* lean, thin, as *man of s. frame,* whence **spare·**LY² adv., **spare·**NESS n.; *spareri·b,* upper part of row of ribs of pork with small amount of meat adhering; that can be spared, not required for ordinary use, as *how to use your s. time, have no s. cash;* reserved for emergency or extraordinary use, as *always take a s. cap, s. room* (bedroom for visitor); (n.) s. part for substitution in machine. [OE *spær,* cf. ON *sparr,* Da. *spar*(*som*), Sw. *spar*(*sam*)]

spare², v.t. & i. Be frugal or grudging of, as *s. the rod & spoil the child, must not s. expense,* whence **spar·ing**LY² adv., **spar·ing**NESS n.; dispense with, do without, as *cannot s. him just now, s. me a penny, could have spared the explanation;* (archaic) forbear (*to* do); abstain from inflicting (with double object), as *s. me these protestations;* abstain from killing, hurting, wounding, &c., as *s.* (do not kill) *me, s. my life, s. his feelings,* (loosely) *s.* (do not provoke) *his blushes;* be frugal. [OE *sparian,* cf. prec., & Du. & G *sparen*]

spar·ger, n. Sprinkling-apparatus, esp. in brewing. [f. rare vb *sparge* f. L *spargere,* -ER¹]

spark¹, n. Fiery particle thrown off from burning substance, or still visibly alight in ashes, or struck out by impact from flint &c. (*as the ss. fly upward,* with the certainty of a law of nature); small bright object or point e.g. in gem; (fig.) brilliant emanation of wit &c., esp. *strike ss. out of* person, provoke him to lively or original conversation; (usu. neg. or quasi-neg.) particle of fire or (fig.) of a quality &c., as *not a s. of life remained, if you had a s. of generosity in you;* (Electr.) luminous effect of sudden disruptive discharge, electric s. serving to fire explosive mixture in oil-engine of motor &c., as *advance, retard, the s.* (in the cycle of operation in the engine); *Ss.,* (nickname for) wireless operator; *fairy ss.,* phosphorescent light from decayed vegetable matter &c.; *s.-arrester,* device for preventing (injury from) SPARK²ing in electrical apparatus, netting &c. to catch ss. on steam-engine. Hence **spar·k**LESS a., **spar·k**LET n., small s., carbonic-acid charge for use in some gazogenes. [OE *spearca,* cf. MDu. *sparke,* & ON *spraka,* Da. *sprage,* crackle; perh. f. crackle of burning wood &c.]

spark², v.i. Emit sparks of fire or electricity; *sparking-plug,* device for firing explosive mixture in motor-engine; (Electr.) produce sparks at point where continuity of circuit is interrupted. [prob. f. prec.]

spark[3], n., & v.i. Gay fellow; gallant; (v.i.) play the gallant. Hence **spar·kish**[1] a. [(vb f. n., prob. fig. use of SPARK[1]]

spar·kle, v.i., & n. Emit sparks, (of gems &c. & fig. of wit &c.) glitter, glisten, scintillate, whence **spar·kler**[1] n., **spar·klingly**[2] adv.; *sparkling wines* (giving out carbonic-acid gas in small bubbles, cf. STILL); (n.) sparkling, gleam, spark. [ME *sparkle* n., *-klen* vb, f. SPARK[1], [2] + -LE(1,3)]

spă·rrow (-ō), n. Kinds of small plain-coloured bird, esp. *house s.*, European kind noted for attachment to human dwellings, prolificness, and pugnacity; *s.-bill*, = SPARABLE; *s.-grass* (vulg.), asparagus; *s.-hawk*, kinds of small hawk preying on ss. &c. [OE *spearwa*, cf. ON *sporr*, Da. *spurv*]

spar·ry, a. Of, like, rich in, SPAR[2]. [-Y[2]]

sparse, a. (Of population &c.) thinly scattered, not dense; (Bot., Zool.) placed, occurring, at distant or irregular intervals. Hence **spar·sely**[2] adv., **spar·seness** n. [f. L *spargere spars-* scatter]

Spar·tacist, a. & n. (Member) of the Spartacus group of extremists in the German revolution. [*Spartacus*, leader in anc.-Roman servile war, -IST]

Spar·tan, a. & n. (Native) of Sparta (esp. w. allusion to supposed characteristics of Ss., as *S. endurance, simplicity*). [f. L *Spartanus* (*Sparta* f. Gk *Spartē*, see -AN)]

spa·sm (-zm), n. Excessive muscular contraction (CLONIC, TONIC, *s.*); sudden convulsive movement, wrench, or strain, as *a s. of coughing*, (fig. *ss. of grief* &c.; *functional s.*, nervous disorders caused by occupation, e.g. writer's cramp. Hence **spasmo·logy** n. [f. L f. Gk *spasmos* (*spaō* draw)]

spasmŏ·dic, a. Of, caused by, subject to, spasm(s), as *a s. jerk, s. asthma*; occurring, done, by fits & starts, as *s. efforts*. Hence **spasmo·dically** adv. [f. Gk *spasmōdēs* (as SPASM, see -OID) + -IC]

spă·stic, a. (med.). = prec. [f. L f. Gk *spastikos* drawing (*spaō* draw, see -IC)]

spat[1], n., & v.i. & t. Spawn of shell-fish esp. oyster; (v.i., of oyster &c.) spawn; (v.t.) shed (spawn). [prob. cogn. w. SPIT[2]]

spat[2], n. (usu. pl.). Short gaiter covering instep & reaching little above ankle. [for SPATTER*dash*]

spat[3]. See SPIT[2].

spa·tchcock, n., & v.t. Fowl killed & cooked in a hurry; (v.t., colloq.) insert (words) hastily in telegram &c. [usu. expl. as *dispatch-cock*, but perh. f. confus. w. SPITCHCOCK]

spate, n. River-flood, esp. *river is in s.* [orig. Sc., etym. dub.]

spāthe (-dh), n. (bot.). Large bract or pair of bracts enveloping spadix or flower-cluster. Hence **spa·those**[1], **spa·thous**, (-th-), aa. [f. L f. Gk *spathē* broad blade &c.]

spă·thic, a. Of SPAR[2], like spar esp. in cleavage. So **spă·thiform** a. [G *spath* spar + -IC]

spā·tial (-shl), n. Of space, as *s. relations, extent*. Hence **spatiă·lity** (-shĭ-) n., **spa·tially**[2] adv. [f. L as SPACE + -AL]

spa·tter, v.t. & i., & n. Scatter (liquid, mud, &c.) here & there in small drops; splash (person *with* mud, slander, &c.) thus; (of liquid) fall here & there in drops; (n.) spattering, splash (*of* mud &c.), quick succession of light sounds, pattering; *spa·tterdashes*, cloth or other leggings to protect stockings &c. from mud &c. [cf. Du. *spatten* burst, spout, -ER[5]]

spă·tūla, n. Broad-bladed instrument for working pigments &c.; surgeon's instrument for pressing tongue down or to one side. [L, dim. as SPATHE]

spă·tule, n. (zool.). Broad racket-shaped formation or part, esp. end of bird's tail-feather. Hence **spa·tular**[1], **spa·tulate**[2], **spa·tuliform**, aa. [OF, f. L as prec.]

spă·vin, n. Disease of horse's hock-joint; *blood, bog, s.*, distension of the joint by effusion of lymph within it; *bone s.*, deposit of bony substance uniting the bones. Hence **spa·vined**[2] a. [f. OF *espavain, esparvain*, etym. dub.]

spawn, v.t. & i., & n. (Of fish, frog, mollusc, crustacean, contempt. of human being or other animal) produce (eggs, or abs.), generate; (of eggs or young of fish &c.) be produced, issue; (n.) eggs of fish &c., (contempt.) human or other offspring (*s. of the devil, of Cobden*, scoundrels, free-traders), white fibrous matter from which fungi are produced, mycelium, as *mushroom s.* [(n. f. vb) f. OF *espandre* EXPAND]

spay, v.t. Castrate, remove ovaries of, (female animal). [f. AF *espeier* (OF *espee* sword)]

speak, v.i. & t. (*spoke*, archaic *spake*; *spoken*). Use articulate utterance in ordinary (not singing-) voice, as *child is learning to s., wish you would s. distinctly*; (p.p., as stage direction) to be said, not sung (also as n., such part); hold conversation (*with, to*, person, *of, about*, thing), as *have heard him s. of it, will s. to him about it*; *portrait speaks* (is lifelike), so *speaking likeness*; make oral address, deliver speech, before assembly, magistrate, tribunal, &c.; utter (words); make known (one's opinion, *the truth*, &c.) thus, esp. *s.* one's *mind* (bluntly &c.); use (specified language) in speaking, as *cannot s. French*, whence **Fre·nch** &c. **-speaker**[1] n., **-speaking**[2] a.; *strictly, roughly, generally, speaking* (quasi-adv.), in the strict, rough, &c., sense of the word(s), as *am not strictly speaking a member of the staff*;

legally &c. *speaking*, from the legal &c. point of view; (as an apology for loose or strong or figurative expression) *so to s.*, if I may use such an expression; hail & hold communication with (ship); (archaic, of conduct, circumstance, &c.) show (person) to be (so-&-so), as *his conduct speaks him generous*, be evidence of, as *this speaks a little mind*; (of fact &c.) *s. volumes*, be very significant; *s. volumes* &c. *for*, *s. well for*, be abundant evidence of, place in favourable light, as *speaks volumes for his forbearance*; (of dog) bark esp. when ordered; (fig., of mus. instrument &c.) sound; make mention in writing *of*, *s. by the* or *like a* BOOK¹; *s.* (person) *fair*, use polite language to; *s. for*, act as spokesman of, state the sentiments of; *s. of*, mention; *nothing to s. of*, nothing worth mentioning, practically nothing; *s. out* (also *up*), s. freely, s. one's whole opinion; *s. to*, address (person &c.), s. in confirmation of or in reference to, as *I can s. to his having been there, will s. to that point later*; *s. up* (also *out*), s. loud(er); *s. without book*, give facts &c. from memory; *fair, smooth, ill, well*, &c., *-spoken* [as if *-speech*ED²], (given to) using such language; *s.-easy* (U.-S. slang) illicit liquor shop [OE *sp(r)ecan*, cf. Du. *spreken*, G *sprechen*]

spea·ker, n. One who speaks esp. in public; (*S*-) presiding officer in H. of Commons charged with preservation of order &c. & having casting vote in case of equal division, similar officer in U.S. House of Representatives &c., whence **Spea·ker**SHIP n. [-ER¹]

spea·kies, n. pl. (slang). Acted plays as opp. MOVIES. [f. *speak* on anal. of MOVIES]

spea·king, n. In vbl senses: *s. acquaintance*, person one knows well enough to exchange conversation with him, this degree of familiarity; *not on s. terms*, not, esp. no longer, having s. acquaintance *with* (usu. implying estrangement); *s.-trumpet*, instrument for conveying voice to a distance; *s.-tube*, tube for conveying voice from one room or building to another. [-ING¹]

spear (spēr), n., & v.t. & i. Hunter's or foot-soldier's thrusting or hurling weapon consisting of stout staff with point usu. of steel (cf. LANCE, PIKE); (poet.) = *spearman*; sharp-pointed & barbed instrument for stabbing fish &c.; *spear·man*, person esp. soldier who uses s.; *spear·mint*, common garden mint; *s. side*, male branch of family (cf. DISTAFF); (v.t.) pierce, strike, with s.; (v.i.) shoot into a long stem. [(vb f. n.) OE *spere*, cf. Du. & G *speer*]

spec, n. (colloq.). Speculation, speculative enterprise, as *it turned out a good s., did it on s.* [abbr. of SPECULATION]

spĕ·cial (-shl), a. & n. Of a particular kind, peculiar, not general, (cf. ESPECIAL), as *lacks the s. qualities required, word used in a s. sense, what is your s. work?, its s. charm did not appeal to him, s. anatomy* (of particular organs of human body), *s.* JURY, *s. hospital* (for particular class of diseases); for a particular purpose, as *appointed s. agents, received s. instructions*; (*also especial*) exceptional in amount, degree, intensity, &c., as *took s. trouble, find no s. excellence in his work*; *s. case*, written statement of facts submitted by litigants to court, (also) exceptional or peculiar case; *s. constable* (sworn in to assist in maintaining public peace in case of riot &c.); *s. correspondent* (appointed by newspaper to report on s. facts); *s. edition* (including later news than ordinary edition of newspaper); *s. licence* (enabling priests to marry parties without publication of banns or at time or place other than those usually necessary); *s. logic*, rules for thinking concerning s. class of objects; *s. pleader*, member of Inns of Court whose business it is to give verbal or written opinions on matters submitted to him & to deal with various proceedings out of usual course; *s. pleading*, (Law) allegation of s. or new matter as opp. to denial of allegations of other side, (pop.) specious but unfair argument, statement of case designed to favour speaker's point of view rather than to discover the truth; *s. train*, extra train for s. purpose; *s.* VERDICT. (N.) s. constable, train, examination, edition of newspaper (esp. EXTRA-*s.*), &c. Hence **spe·cial**LY² adv. [f. OF (*e*)*special* f. L *specialis* (*species*, see -AL)]

spĕ·cialist, n. One who devotes himself to particular branch of a profession, science, &c. Hence or cogn. **spe·cial**ISM n., **speciali·st**IC a. [-IST]

spĕciă·lity (-shĭ-), n. Special feature or characteristic; (also *specialty*) special pursuit, product, operation, &c., thing to which a person gives special attention, as *jam(-making) is our s.* [f. OF (*e*)*specialité* f. LL *specialitatem* (as SPECIAL, see -TY)]

spĕ·cialize, v.t. & i. Make specific or individual; modify, limit, (idea, statement); (Biol.) adapt, set apart, (organ &c.) for particular purpose, differentiate; be differentiated, become individual in character; be(come) a specialist. Hence **specializa·**TION n. [f. F *spécialiser* (SPECIAL, -IZE)]

spĕ·cialty (-shl-), n. (Law) instrument under seal, sealed contract; = SPECIALITY (2nd sense). [f. OF *specialté* SPECIALITY]

spē·cie (-shĭē, -shē), n. (no pl.). Coin as opp. to paper money, as *s. payments, paid in s., shortness of s.* [f. L abl. of foll. in phr. *in specie*]

spē·cies (-shĭēz, -shēz), n. (Nat. Hist.) group subordinate in classification to *genus* (cf. CLASS) & having members that differ only in minor details; *the* or *our s.*, mankind; (Logic) group subordinate to GENUS & containing individuals agreeing in some common attribute(s) & called by a common name; kind, sort, as *has a s. of cunning, a s. of dogcart*; (Law) form, shape, given to materials. [L, = appearance, kind, beauty, f. *specere* look]

speci·fic, a. & n. Definite, distinctly formulated, as *a s. statement, has no s. aim*; of a species, as *the s. name* of plant &c.; *s. difference* (what differentiates a species); possessing, concerned with, the properties that characterize a species, as *the s. forms of animals, draws a s. distinction between them*; relating to particular subject; peculiar, as *has a s. style, a style s. to that school of painters*; *s. cause* (producing a particular form of disease); *s. centre*, place or period at which differentiation from a common stock takes place; *s.* GRAVITY, HEAT[1]; *s. medicine*, having distinct effect in curing a certain disease; (n.) s. medicine or remedy. Hence **speci·fi**CALLY adv., **specifi·ci**TY, **speci·fic**NESS, nn. [f. med. L *specificus* (as SPECIES, see -FIC)]

spĕcifica·tion, n. Specifying; specified detail, esp. (pl.) detailed description of construction, workmanship, materials, &c., of work undertaken by architect, engineer, &c.; description by applicant for patent of the construction & use of his invention; (Law) working up of materials into a new product not held to be the property of the owner of the materials. [f. med. L *specificationem* (foll., -FICATION)]

spĕ·cifȳ, v.t. Name expressly, mention definitely, (items, details, ingredients, &c.; often abs.); include in (e.g. architect's) specifications, as *a slate-course was not specified*. Hence **spe·cifi**ABLE a. [f. OF *specifier* f. med. L *specificare* (as SPECIFIC, see -FY)]

spĕ·cimen, n. Individual or part taken as example of a class or whole, esp. individual animal or plant or piece of a mineral &c. used for scientific examination, as *ss. of copper ore, zoological ss., fine s. of the Swallow-tail, of mosaic work, a s. of his skill, generosity*, *s. page* (of book, printed in prospectus to show size, type, &c.), (colloq. contempt.) *what a s.* (person)*!*. [L, = characteristic mark (*specere* look, -MEN)]

spēcio·logy (-shĭ-), n. Science of (origin &c. of) species. Hence **speciolo·gi**CAL a. [-LOGY]

spē·cious (-sh*us*), a. Of good appearance, plausible, fair or right on the surface, as *s. argument, tale, pretence, person, appearance*. Hence or cogn. **specio·**SITY, **spe·cious**NESS, nn., **spe·cious**LY[2] adv. [f. L *speciosus* beautiful (SPECIES, see -OUS)]

speck[1], n., & v.t. Small spot, dot, stain; particle (*of* dirt &c.); spot of rottenness in fruit; (v.t.) mark with ss. (esp. in p.p.). Hence **spe·ck**LESS a. [OE *specca*, cf. SPECKLE]

speck[2], n. (U.S. & S. Afr.). Fat meat, bacon, pork; fat of seals, whales, &c., blubber. [f. Du. *spek* or G *speck*, cf. OE *spic* bacon]

spe·ckle, n. Small spot or stain; (v.t.) mark with ss. or patches (esp. in p.p.). [SPECK[1] + -LE; cf. Du. *spikkel*]

specktioneer·, -si-, (-shon-), n. (whaling). Chief harpooner. [f. Du. *speksnijer* (SPECK[2], *snijden* cut, -ER[1])]

specs, n. pl. (colloq.). Pair of spectacles. [abbr.]

spe·ctacle, n. Public show, whence **spectă·cul**AR[1] a., **specta·cular**LY[2] adv.; object of sight, esp. of public attention, as *a charming s., drunken woman is a deplorable s., sure to make a s.* (= EXHIBITION) *of himself*; (*pair of*) ss. or colloq. *specs*, pair of lenses to correct or assist defective sight, set in frame without spring (cf. EYE[1]*-glass*) constructed to rest on nose & ears, (fig.) *sees everything through rose-coloured* &c. *ss.*, takes cheerful &c. views, (Crick.) *pair of ss.*, two DUCK[1]s. [OF, f. L *spectaculum* show (*spectare* see, frequent. of *specere* look)]

spe·ctacled, a. Wearing spectacles; (of animals) marked in a way that suggests spectacles, esp. *s. bear*, the S.-Amer. bear. [-ED[2]]

specta·tor, n. One who looks on esp. at a show, game, &c., as *the ss. were moved to tears, was a mere s., an unconcerned s.*, (as title of paper) *The S.* Hence **specta·tr**ESS[1] n. [L (*spectare*, see SPECTACLE & -OR[2])]

spe·ctral, a. Ghostlike, of ghosts; of spectra or the spectrum, as *s. colours, analysis*. Hence **spe·ctral**LY[2] adv. [SPECTRUM, -AL]

spe·ctre (-*er*), n. Ghost; haunting presentiment (*of* ruin, war, madness, &c.); *s. of the Brocken*, huge shadowy image of the observer projected on mists about mountain-top, first observed on the Brocken; (in names of animals compared to s. from thinness of body &c.) *s.-bat, -crab, -insect, -lemur, -shrimp*. [F, f. SPECTRUM]

spectro- in comb. = SPECTRUM, as: *-graph*, apparatus for photographing or otherwise reproducing the spectrum, *-gram*, representation obtained by this, so *-gra·phic* a., *-graphy* n.; *-logy*, science of spectral analysis, so *-lo·gical(ly)* a. & adv.; *-meter*, instrument for measuring deviation of light-rays in passing through prism; *-phone*, modification of spectroscope in which succession of sounds takes the place of observation of eye.

spe·ctroscope, n. Instrument for forming & analysing the spectra of rays, consisting usu. of collimating tube, prism or diffraction grating, small telescope, & measuring apparatus. Hence **spectro-**

scŏ·pic(AL) aa., **spectrosco·pical**LY[2] adv., **spectro·scop**IST (*or* spĕ·-), **spectro·scop**Y[1] (*or* spĕ·-), nn. [F (SPECTRO- + -SCOPE)]

spe·ctrum, n. (pl. *-ra*). (Also *ocular s.*) image of something seen continuing when the eyes are closed or turned away; image formed by rays of light or other radiant energy in which the parts are arranged in a progressive series according to their refrangibility; *diffraction, prismatic, s.* (produced by means of diffraction grating, by means of prism); *solar s.* (formed from rays of sun); *s.* (or *spectral*) *analysis,* chemical analysis by means of spectroscope. [L, = appearance, image, f. *specere* look]

spĕ·cular, a. Of (the nature of) a speculum, esp. reflecting, as *s. surface.* [f. L *specularis* (SPECULUM, see -AR[1])]

spĕ·culate, v.i. Pursue an inquiry, meditate, form theory or conjectural opinion, (*on, upon, about,* subject, the nature, cause, &c., of a thing, or abs.); make investment, engage in commercial operation, that involves risk of loss, as *has been speculating in stocks, in rubber,* (esp. w. implication of rashness) *is believed to s. a good deal.* Hence or cogn. **spe·cula**TIVE a., **spe·culative**LY[2] adv., **spe·culative**NESS, **spe·culat**OR[2], nn. [f. L *speculari* spy out, observe, (*specula* watch-tower, as SPECULUM), see -ATE[3]]

specula·tion, n. Meditation on, inquiry into, theory about, a subject, as *much given to s., sorry to disturb your ss.*; speculative investment or enterprise, practice of speculating, in business, as *ruined by* (*a single unlucky*) *s., bought it as a s.* (or *on* SPEC, rarely *on s.*); game in which cards are bought & sold. [f. L *speculationem* (as prec., see -ATION)]

spĕ·culum, n. (pl. *-la*). (Surg.) instrument for dilating cavities of human body for inspection; mirror, usu. of polished metal e.g. *s.-metal* (alloy of copper & tin), esp. in reflecting telescope; (Ornith.) specially coloured area on wing of some birds, also = OCELLUS. [L, = mirror (*specere* look)]

sped. See SPEED.

speech (-tsh), n. Faculty of speaking; thing said, remark, as *after this unlucky s. he remained silent*; public address, as *after-dinner,* MAIDEN, *s., s. for the defence, a set s.* (studied, prepared), *make* (deliver) *a s.*: *King's* or *Queen's s., s. from the throne,* brief statement of foreign & domestic affairs & of the chief measures to be considered by Parliament, prepared by ministry & read by sovereign in person or by commission at opening of Parliament; language of a nation; sounding-quality of organ-pipe &c.: FIGURE[1] *of s.*; PART[1]*s of s.*; *s.-reading,* deaf-mute's interpretation of s. by watching speaker's lips; *s.-day,* annual day for delivering prizes in schools usu. marked by recitations &c. [OE *spǣc,* earlier *sprǣc,* as SPEAK]

spee·chifȳ, v.i. (contempt.). Make speeches, hold forth in public. Hence **speechi**FICA·TION, **spee·chifi**ER[1], nn. [-FY]

spee·chless, a. Dumb; temporarily deprived of speech by emotion &c., as *s. with rage*; (slang) dead drunk. Hence **spee·chless**LY[2] adv., **spee·chless**NESS n. [OE *spǣcléas,* see -LESS]

speed, n., & v.t. & i. (*sped,* exc. as below). Rapidity of movement, as *with all s., more haste less s., at full s.*; rate of progress or motion, as *attains a high s., depends on the s. required, three-s. engine, tricycle,* &c. (with adaptable gear for going at different ss.); (archaic) success, prosperity, as *send me good s.* (cf. GOD[1]*-s.*); *s.-cone,* contrivance for adjusting ratio of s. between parallel shafts by means of belt; *spee·dwell,* kinds of herb with creeping or ascending stems & bright-blue flowers. (Vb) go fast, as *sped down the street* (now chiefly literary); (archaic) send fast, send on the way, as *s. an arrow from the bow, s. the parting guest*; (archaic) be or make prosperous, succeed, give success to, as *how have you sped?, God s. you!.* (Past & p.p. *speeded*): regulate s. of (engine &c.), cause to go at fixed s.; *s. up,* cause to work at greater s. (*the train service wants speeding up*). [(vb f. OE *spēdan*) OE *spēd* (*spōwan* prosper), cf. Du. *spoed,* OHG *spuot, spôt,* success]

spee·der, n. Kinds of device for regulating or increasing speed of machinery. [-ER[1]]

speedo·meter, n. Appliance indicating the speed at which motor-car &c. is moving. [SPEED, -O-, -METER]

spee·dy, a. Rapid; expeditious, prompt, coming without delay, as *s. answer, vengeance.* Hence **spee·di**LY[2] adv., **spee·di**NESS n. [-Y[2]]

speiss (-is), n. Compound of arsenic, iron, &c., found in smelting some lead ores. [f. G *speise* food, amalgam, f. pop. L *spesa* EXPENSE]

spēlae·an, a. Of, dwelling in, caves. [f. L f. Gk *spēlaion* cave (*speos* cave) + -AN]

spelicans. See SPILLIKIN.

spell[1], n. Words used as charm, incantation or its effect (*under a s.,* mastered by or as by a s.); attraction, fascination, exercised by person, pursuit, quality, &c.; *spe·llbinder* (U.S.), political speaker who can hold audiences s.-bound; *spellbound,* bound (as) by a s. [OE *spel(l)* saying, story, cf. ON *spjall*; cogn. w. foll.]

spell[2], v.t. (*spelt* or *spelled* pr. -lt). Write or name the letters that form (a word), as *how do you s. ' analyse '?, must not be spelt with a z, can't s. his own name,* (abs.) *wish you would learn to s.* (*correctly*); *s. out* or *over,* make out (words, writing) laboriously letter by letter; *s. backward*, repeat or write the letters of (word) in reverse order, (fig.) misinterpret, pervert meaning of; (of letters) make up, form, (word), as *what does* c a t *s.?*, (fig., of circumstances, scheme, &c.) have as necessary result, involve, as *these changes s. ruin to the farmer*. [f. OF *espeler* f. Teut. (OE *spellian* tell f. prec.)]

spell³, n., & v.t. Turn of work, as *did a s. of carpentering*; short period, as *wait (for) a s.*; (v.t., rare) relieve, take the place of, (person) in work &c. [OE *spelian* vb, *gespelia* & *spala* nn., = substitute]

spe·ller, n. In vbl senses of SPELL²; also =SPELLING-*book*. [-ER¹]

spe·lling, n. In vbl senses, as *his s. is weak, not sure of the s. of 'aneurysm', another s. of the same word*; *s.-bee*, competition in s. usu. with prizes; *s.-book* (for teaching s.). [-ING¹]

spelt¹, n. Kind of wheat giving very fine flour, German wheat. [OE, f. LL *spelta*]

spelt². See SPELL².

spe·lter, n. (now commerc.). Zinc. [cf. OF *espeautre*, Du. & G *spiauter*, & PEWTER]

spence, -se, n. (archaic). Buttery, larder. [OF, short for *despense* (see DISPENSE)]

spe·ncer¹, n. (hist.). Man's, woman's, short over-jacket. [f. Earl *S.*, d. 1834]

spe·ncer², n. (naut.). =TRY*sail*. [?]

Spe·ncerism, n. Doctrine of Herbert Spencer (d. 1903) referring the ordered universe to the necessary laws of mechanics, synthetic philosophy. So **Spencēr·**IAN a., **Spencer·ian**ISM n. [-ISM]

spend, v.t. & i. (spent). Pay out (money) for a purchase &c. (also abs., as *s. profusely*); use, use up, consume, as *our ammunition was all spent, shall s. no more breath, trouble, &c., on him, how do you s. your time?, spent a pleasant day*; exhaust, wear out, as *his anger will soon s. itself, storm is spent, spent cannon-ball* (with little impulse left); (Naut.) lose (mast); be consumed, as *candles s. fast in draught*; emit spawn; *spent herring* &c. (that has deposited its spawn); *spe·ndthrift*, extravagant person, prodigal, (often attrib.). Hence **spe·nd**ABLE a., **spe·nd**ER¹ n. [OE *spendan* f. L EX(*pendere* weigh) spend]

Spe·nlow & Jor·kins, n. Plan of attributing one's (S.'s) hard dealings to a supposed hard partner (J.) kept in background. [persons in Dickens's *David Copperfield*]

spense. See SPENCE.

Spensēr·ian, a. Of the poet Edmund Spenser (d. 1599), esp. *S. stanza*, that used in the *Faerie Queen*; (n. pl.) S. stanzas. [-IAN]

spent. See SPEND.

sperm¹, n. Male generative fluid. [f. L f. Gk *sperma -matos* seed (*speirō* sow, see -M)]

sperm², n. (Also *s.-whale*) cachalot, whale yielding spermaceti; =foll. [abbr.]

spermacē·ti, n. White brittle fatty substance contained in solution in heads of sperm-whale &c., used for candles & ointments. [med. L, =SPERM¹+*ceti* of whale f. Gk *kētos* (s. being regarded as whale-spawn)]

sper·mary, n. Male germ-gland, testicle or equivalent organ. [SPERM¹+-ARY¹]

spermă·tic, a. Of SPERM¹ or the spermary. [f. OF *spermatique* f. L f. Gk *spermatikos* (as SPERM¹, see -IC)]

sper·mato- in comb. = SPERM¹, as: *-blast*, germ of a spermatozoon; *-ge·nesis*, development of spermatozoa, so *-genous* a., *-geny* n.; *-logist, -logy*, student, study, of sperm, so *-lo·gical* a.; *-phore*, capsule containing spermatozoa; *-rrhoe·a* (-rēa), involuntary seminal discharge; *-zō·on* (pl. *-zōa*), male fertilizing element contained in semen of animals, similar element in lower plants, so *-zo·al, -zo·an*, aa.

spermo- in comb. = Gk *sperma* seed, semen, as: *-blast* =SPERMATO*blast*; *-logy*, =SPERMATO*logy*, (Bot.) study of seeds, so *-lo·gical* a., *-logist* n.

spew, spue, v.t. & i. Vomit (t. & i.); (of gun) droop at muzzle from too quick firing. [OE *spēowan, spīwan*, cf. ON *spýja*, G *speien*, L *spuere*, Gk *ptuō*]

sphă·celate, v.t. Affect, be affected, with gangrene or necrosis. Hence **sphacel**A·TION n. [f. Gk *sphakelos* gangrene + -ATE³]

sphaer(o)- in comb. = Gk *sphaira* ball, in many scientific esp. nat. hist. terms.

spha·gnum, n. (bot.; pl. *-na*). Kinds of moss growing in bogs and peat, and used as packing &c. [mod. L, f. Gk *sphagnos* a moss]

sphēn(o)- in comb. = Gk *sphēn* wedge, chiefly in sense 'of the sphenoid bone'; also: *-gram*, cuneiform character, so *-gra·phic* a.

sphē·noid, a. & n. (anat.). Wedge-shaped, esp. *s. (bone)*, compound bone at base of skull. Hence **sphenoi·d**AL a., **sphenoi·do-** comb. form. [f. Gk *sphenoeidēs* (*sphēn* wedge, -OID)]

sphere (-ēr), n., & v.t. Solid figure generated by revolution of semicircle about its diameter, or every part of whose surface is equidistant from a point within called the centre; ball, globe; (poet.) the heavens, the sky; any heavenly body; globe representing the earth or the apparent heavens; each of the revolving globe-shaped shells in which the heavenly bodies were formerly supposed to be set, esp. *music, harmony, of the ss.* (produced by movements of the ss.); one's field of action, influence, or existence, one's natural surroundings, one's place in society, as *has done much within his peculiar s., earnest young lady in search of a s., great mistake to take him out of his s.*, *moves in quite another s.*, State's *s.* (claimed or recognized area) *of influence in Africa*; *celestial s.*, surface on which heavenly bodies appear to lie; *doctrine of the s.*, spherical geometry & trigonometry; *great, small, circle of s.*, section made by plane passing, not passing, through its centre; *oblique, right, parallel, s.*, sphere of apparent heavens at a place where there is oblique angle, right angle, no angle, between equator & horizon. (V.t.) enclose (as) in s., make s.-shaped, (poet.) exalt to the (celestial) s. Hence **spher·Y**[2] a. (poet.). [(vb f. n.) f. OF *espere* f. L f. Gk *sphaira* ball, globe]

sphĕ·ric, a. & n. (Poet.) of the heavens, celestial, exalted; (rare) = foll.; (n. pl.) geometry & trigonometry of the sphere. [f. LL f. Gk *sphairikos* (as prec., see -IC)]

sphe·rical, a. Shaped like a sphere, globular, whence or cogn. **sphe·ricalLY**[2] adv., **spheri·CITY** n.; of spheres, as *s. geometry*; *s. lune, triangle, polygon* (bounded by arcs of great circles of sphere). [-AL]

sphēr·ograph, n. Stereographic projection of the earth on disk, with meridians & parallels of latitude marked in single degrees. [SPHERE + -O- + -GRAPH]

sphēr·oid, n. Sphere-like but not perfectly spherical body; solid generated by revolution of ellipse about its major (*prolate* or *oblong s.*) or minor (*oblate s.*) axis, as *the earth is an oblate s.* Hence **spheroi·dalLY**[2] adv., **spheroi·d(IC)AL** aa., **spheroidi·CITY** n. [f. L f. Gk *sphairoeidēs* (as SPHERE, see -OID)]

sphero·meter, n. Instrument for finding radius of sphere & for exact measurement of thickness of small bodies. [f. F *sphéromètre*, see SPHERE, -METER]

sphĕ·rule, n. Small sphere. Hence **sphe·rulAR**[1], **sphe·rulATE**[2](2) (entom.), aa. [f. L *sphaerula* (as SPHERE, see -ULE)]

sphe·rulite, n. Vitreous globule as constituent of some rocks. Hence **spheruli·tIC** a., **sphe·rulitIZE**(3), v.t. [f. prec. + -ITE[1]]

sphi·ncter, n. Muscle surrounding & serving to close an opening or tube. Hence **sphi·ncterAL**, **sphinctēr·IAL**, **sphinctē·RIC**, aa. [L, f. Gk *sphigktēr* (*sphiggō* shut tight)]

sphinx, n. (Gk Myth., *S*-) winged monster of Thebes with woman's head & lion's body who proposed a riddle to the Thebans, killed all who could not guess it, & on Oedipus's solving it threw herself from the rock on which she sat & died; (Egypt. Ant.) figure with lion's body & man's or animal's head; enigmatic person; hawk-moth; kind of baboon. [L, f. Gk *sphigx*, perh. f. *sphiggō* strangle]

sphragi·stics (-j-), n. pl. (often treated as sing.). Study of engraved seals. [f. Gk *sphragistikos* (*sphragizō* seal vb f. *sphragis* n.)]

sphy̆gmo- in comb. = foll., as: *-graph*, instrument for showing character of pulse in series of curves, *-gram*, record so produced, so *-gra·phic* a., *-graphy* n.; *-logy*, study of the pulse; *-phone, -scope*, instrument for making audible, visible, the action of the pulse.

sphy·gmus, n. (physiol.). Pulse, pulsation. [mod. L, f. Gk *sphugmos* f. *sphuzō* throb]

spi·ca, n. (Bot.) spike, whence **spi·CATE**[2], **-ated**, aa.; (Surg.) spiral bandage with reversed turns. [L, = spike, ear of grain]

spice, n., & v.t. Aromatic or pungent vegetable substance used to flavour food, e.g. cloves, pepper, mace; ss. collectively, as *dealer in s.*. *sugar & s. & all that's nice*, so **spi·CERY**(1) n.; (fig.) smack, dash, flavour, (*of* malice &c. *in* person's character, writings, &c.); *spi·cebush*, aromatic American shrub of laurel family; (v.t.) flavour with s. [(vb f. n.) f. OF *espice* spice f. L SPECIES]

spick, a. *S. & span*, smart & new, brand-new. [earlier *s.-&-span-new*, redupl. of ME *span new* f. ON *spán-nýr* = chip-new]

spĭ·cule, n. Small sharp-pointed body; (Zool.) small hard body esp. in framework of sponge; (Bot.) small or secondary spike. Hence **spi·culAR**[1], **spi·culATE**[2] (2), aa. [f. L *spiculum* dim. of SPICA]

spi·cy, a. Of, flavoured or fragrant with, spice; (fig.) piquant, pungent, improper (*s. story*), showy, smart. Hence **spi·ciLY**[2] adv., **spi·ciNESS** n. [-Y[2]]

spī·der, n. Eight-legged animal of the order *Araneida*, many species of which spin webs esp. for capture of insects as food (*s. & fly* fig., ensnarer & ensnared); kinds of arachnid like s.; thing compared to s. esp. as having prominent legs, e.g. kind of three-legged gridiron; sulky with very large light wheels; *s.-catcher*, kinds of bird; *s.-crab*, crab with long thin legs; *s.-line*, thread of s.'s web substituted for wire in scales &c. for minute work; *s.-monkey*, kind with long limbs & long prehensile tail; *s.-wasp*, wasp that stores its nest with ss. for its young. Hence **spi·derLIKE** a., **spi·deryY**[2] a. (esp., of writing, legs, spokes, &c.) very thin. [ME *spithre* (SPIN[1] + *-ther* agent suf.)]

spiegeleisen (spē·gelīzn), n. Kind of cast iron containing manganese, much used in Bessemer process. [G (*spiegel* mirror f. L *speculum* + *eisen* iron)]

spi·f(f)licate, v.t. (slang). Trounce, do for. Hence **spif(f)licA·TION** n. [?]

spĭ·got, n. Small peg or plug esp. one for insertion into gimlet-hole in cask; plain end of pipe fitting into socket of next one. [f. OPr. *espiga* ear of corn f. L SPICA]

spike, n., & v.t. Sharp point; pointed piece of metal e.g. one of a set forming top of iron fence &c. or worn in bottom of shoe to prevent slipping; large stout nail esp. as used for railways; (Bot.) flower-cluster of many sessile flowers arranged closely on long common axis; separate sprig of any plant in which flowers form s.-like cluster; [f. F *spic*] kind of lavender; *s. oil* (got from lavender); *s. plank*, bridge before mizzenmast of vessel meant for arctic service; (v.t.) fasten with ss., furnish with ss., fix on or pierce with s., plug up vent of (cannon) with s. Hence **spi·ke**LET n. (bot.), **spi·ke**WISE adv., **spi·k**Y[2] a. [(vb f. n.) ME, cf. Sw. & Norw. *spik*, Du. *spijker*, nail; partly also f. L *spica* ear of corn]

spī·kenard (-kn-), n. (Ancient costly aromatic ointment made chiefly from) perennial herb allied to valerian; kinds of fragrant oil. [f. LL SPICA *nardi* (of NARD)]

spile, n., & v.t. Wooden peg, spigot; large timber for driving into ground, pile; (v.t.) make s.-hole in (cask). [(vb f. n.) cf. Du. *spijl* spile, bar, G *speil* skewer; in sense *pile* perh. corrupt. of PILE[1]]

spi·ling, n. Set of piles; (Naut.) edge-curve of plank in vessel's hull. [f. prec. +-ING[1]; naut. sense, earlier *spoiling*, etym. dub.]

spill[1], v.t. & i. (*spilt* or *spilled*), & n. Allow (liquid, substance in small particles) to fall or run out from vessel, as *spilt the salt, no use crying over spilt milk*, (of liquid &c.) fall or run out; *s. blood*, be guilty of bloodshed, *s. the blood of*, kill; *s. money* (slang), lose it in betting &c.; (Naut.) empty (belly of sail) of wind; throw from saddle or vehicle, as *horse spilt him, was spilt from a dog-cart*; (n.) such throwing, as *had a nasty s.*; *spi·llway*, passage for surplus water from dam. [OE *spillan* destroy, cf. ON *spilla*, Du. *spillen*, G (*ver*)*spillen*, also OE *spildan* (the orig. form)]

spill[2], n. Thin strip of wood, spiral tube &c. of paper for lighting candles &c. [ME, perh. cogn. w. SPILE]

spi·ller, n. Seine put into a larger one to take out fish when the larger cannot be hauled ashore. [?]

spi·llikin, n. Splinter of wood, bone, &c., used in some games; (pl., also *spělicans*) game played with ss. [f. SPILL[2], see -KIN)]

spilt. See SPILL[1].

spilth, n. (archaic). What is spilt; excess, surplus. [-TH[1]]

spin[1], v.t. & i. (*spun* or *span, spun*). Draw out & twist (wool, cotton, or abs.) into threads; make (yarn) thus; (of spider, silkworm, &c.) make (web, gossamer, cocoon, or abs.) by extrusion of fine viscous thread; form (cup &c.) in lathe or similar machine; (fig.) produce, compose, (narrative, literary article, &c.; often *out* i. e. at great length), esp. *s. a yarn* (orig. naut.), tell a story; *s. out*, spend, consume, (time, one's life, &c., *by* discussion &c., *in* occupation &c.), prolong (discussion &c.); cause (top &c.) to whirl round, (of top) whirl round, turn (person, thing) quickly round, (of person &c.) turn thus, e.g. as result of blow, as *sent him spinning*; fish in (stream, pool) with swivel or spoon-bait; (slang) reject (candidate) after examination; (p.p., slang) tired out, done; *spun glass* (spun when heated into filaments that remain pliant when cold); *spun gold, silver*, gold, silver, thread prepared for weaving; *spun silk*, cheap material of short-fibred & waste silk often mixed with cotton; *spun yarn* (naut.), line formed of rope-yarns twisted together. [OE *spinnan*, cf. Du. & G *spinnen*, ON *spinna*, cogn. w. SPAN]

spin[2], n. Spinning motion, whirl; secondary revolving motion esp. as developed in rifle bullet, or in billiard or tennis ball struck aslant; brisk or short run or spell of driving, rowing, bicycling, &c., as *went for a s.* [f. prec.]

spi·nach, -age, (-ĭj), n. Garden vegetable with thick succulent leaves used when boiled as food; other plants similarly used. Hence **spin**A·CEOUS a. [f. OF *espinache, -age*, perh. f. Arab. *isfināj* f. Pers. *isfānāj*, but usu. assoc. w. L *spina* thorn]

spī·nal, a. Of the spine, as *s. curvature, complaint*; *s. column*, spine; *s. cord*, cylindrical structure within s. canal, a part of the central nervous system. [f. LL *spinalis* (SPINE, -AL)]

spi·ndle, n., & v.i. Pin in spinning-wheel used for twisting & winding the thread; small bar serving same purposes in hand-spinning; pin bearing bobbin of spinning-machine; pin, axis, that revolves or on which a thing revolves; *live* (revolving) *s., dead* (non-revolving) *s.*; slender thing or person; varying measure of length for yarn; *s.-shanked*, with long thin legs, *s.-shanks*, person with such legs; *s.-shaped*, of circular cross-section & tapering towards each end; *s.-tree*, shrub or small tree with hard wood used for ss.; hence **spi·nd**LY[2] a., slender, attenuated; (v.i.) have, grow into, long slender form. [(vb f. n.) OE *spinl*, as SPIN[1]+phonetic *-d-*+ -LE(1)]

spi·ndrift, n. Spray blown along surface of sea; *s. clouds*, light feathery clouds. [var. of *spoon-drift* or *spoom-drift*, etym. dub.]

spine, n. The series of the vertebrae, backbone; *railway s.*, concussion of s. due to railway accident; (Bot.) stiff sharp woody process due to degeneracy or modification of some organ; sharp ridge or projection; *spi·neback*, kinds of fish with ss. in or in front of dorsal fins. Hence **spine**D[2], **spi·no**SE[1], **spi·no**US, aa., **spino**·SITY n. [f. OF *espine* thorn f. L *spina* thorn, backbone]

spi·nel, n. Kinds of mineral of various colours occurring in regular crystals; *s. ruby*, valuable red variety. [f. OF (*e*)*spinelle*, etym. dub.]

spi·neless, a. Having no spine, invertebrate; (fig.) limp, weak, having no backbone; (of fish) having no fin-spines. [-LESS]

spinĕ·t (*or* spĭ·-), n. (hist.). Musical instrument like small harpsichord. [f. ME *espinette* prob. f. G. *Spinetti,* inventor]

spīni- in comb. = L *spina* thorn, backbone, as: *-cĕ·rebrate,* having brain & spinal cord; *-ferous,* having or producing spines; -FORM.

spi·nnaker, n. Large jib-shaped sail carried on mainmast of racing-yacht running before wind. [f. *Sphinx,* name of yacht using it]

spi·nner, n. In vbl senses, esp.: thread-spinning machine; person who shapes vessels &c. in lathe; (also **spi·nner**ET[1] n.) spinning-organ in spider, silkworm, &c. [-ER[1]]

spi·nney, n. Small wood, thicket. [f. OF *espinaye* (*espine,* see SPINE)]

spi·nning, n. In vbl senses; *s.-house* (chiefly hist.), house of correction for prostitutes; *s.-jenny,* mechanism for s. more than one strand at a time; *s.-machine,* (esp.) machine that spins fibres continuously; *s.-wheel* (hist.), household implement for s. yarn or thread, with fly-wheel driven by crank or treadle. [-ING[1]]

Spĭ·nozism (*or* -nō·z-), n. Doctrine of B. de Spinoza, a Spanish Jew (d. 1677), that there is one sole & infinite substance of which extension & mind are attributes & individual beings are changing forms. So **Spi·noz**IST n., **Spinozi·st**IC a. [-ISM]

spi·nster, n. Unmarried (esp. elderly in pop. use) woman. Hence **spi·nster**HOOD n. [ME, orig. = woman who spins (SPIN[1], see -STER)]

spinthă·riscope, n. Instrument showing by sparks the emission of rays from radium. [f. Gk *spintharis* spark + -SCOPE]

spi·nule, n. (bot., zool.). Small spine. Hence **spinuli·**FEROUS, **spi·nul**OSE[1], **spi·nul**OUS, aa. [f. L *spinula* (as SPINE, see -ULE)]

spi·ny, a. Full of spines, prickly, esp. in names of animals, as *s. crab, lobster, rat*; (fig.) perplexing, troublesome, thorny. Hence **spi·ni**NESS n. [-Y[2]]

spīr·acle, n. (zool.). Kinds of breathing-hole in animals, e.g. blow-hole of cetaceans. Hence **spiră·cul**AR[1], **spira·cul**ATE[2](2), aa. [f. L *spiraculum* (also used in E) f. *spirare* breathe]

spīrae·a, n. Kinds of rosaceous plant with small white or pink flowers. [L, f. Gk *speiraia* meadowsweet (*speira* coil)]

spīr·al, a., n., & v.t. (-ll-). Coiled; winding continually about & constantly receding from a centre, whether remaining in same plane like watch-spring or rising in a cone; winding continually & advancing as if along cylinder, like thread of screw; *s. balance* (measuring weight by torsion of s. spring); *s. wheel* (with teeth cut at angle to axis); (n.) plane or other s. curve, s. spring, s. formation in shell &c.; (v.t.) make s. Hence **spira·l**ITY n., **spir·al**LY[2] adv. [f. med. L *spiralis* (as SPIRE[2], see -AL)]

spīr·ant, a. & n. (Consonant) uttered with perceptible expulsion of breath & in producing which the organs are near together but not wholly closed, continuable (consonant) (cf. EXPLOSIVE), e.g. *f, v, th, dh,* & sometimes *w, y,* & others. [f. L *spirare* breathe, see -ANT]

spire[1], n., & v.i. & t. Tapering structure in form of tall cone or pyramid rising above tower; continuation of tree trunk above point where branching begins; any tapering body, e.g. stalk of grass; (v.i.) shoot up; (v.t.) furnish with s. Hence **spīr·**Y[2] a. [OE *spir,* cf. Du. & G *spier*]

spire[2], n. Spiral, coil; single twist of this. Hence **spīr·**Y[2] a. [F, f. L f. Gk *speira* coil]

spi·rit[1], n. Intelligent or immaterial part of man, soul; *in* (*the*) *s.,* inwardly, as *groaned in s., was vexed in s., shall be with you in* (*the*) *s.*; person viewed as possessing this, esp. w. reference to particular mental or moral qualities, as *one of the most ardent ss. of his time, a meeting of choice ss., a master-s.,* person of commanding intellect &c.; rational or intelligent being not connected with material body, disembodied soul, incorporeal being, elf, fairy, as *God is a s., the Holy S.* (third person of the Trinity), *has seen a s., ss. must have been at work,* ASTRAL *ss.,* FAMILIAR *s., peace to his departed s.*; person's mental or moral nature or qualities, as *a man of an unbending s., the poor in s.,* the meek; courage, self-assertion, vivacity, energy, dash, as *if you had the s. of a mouse, do show a little s., went at it with s., infused s. into his men, people of s.*; person viewed as supplying this (= *soul,* but usu. w. adj.), as *was the animating s. of the rebellion*; mental or moral condition or attitude, mood, as *took it in a wrong s., depends on the s. in which it is done, did it in a s. of mischief, objections made in a captious s.*; real meaning opp. to verbal expression, as *must consider the s. of the law, not the letter, have followed out the s. of his instructions*; animating principle or influence, mental or moral tendency, as *cannot resist the s. of the age* or *times*; (formerly) immaterial principle governing vital phenomena, whence (mod.) ANIMAL *ss., high* or *great ss.,* cheerfulness & buoyancy, *poor* or *low ss.,* depression; (usu. pl.) strong distilled liquor esp. alcohol, e.g. brandy, whisky, gin, rum, as *glass of ss. & water,* ARDENT *ss., touches no s. but gin*; solution (*of* volatile principle) in alcohol, tincture; *s.* or *ss. of wine,* alcohol; METHYLATED *s.*; *s. blue,* aniline blue soluble in alcohol; *s. duck,* kinds of duck diving rapidly at flash of gun &c.; *s.-lamp* (burning alcohol instead of oil); *s.-level*, glass tube partly filled with s. for testing horizontality; *s.-rapper*, person professing to hold intercourse with departed ss. by means of their raps on table &c., so *s.-rapping*; *s.-room* (naut.), paymaster's store-room, formerly used for ss. [f. L *spiritus* breath, spirit, f. *spirare* breathe]

spi·rit[2], v.t. Convey (usu. *away, off*, &c.) rapidly and secretly (as) by agency of spirits; cheer (person, usu. *up*). [f. prec.]

spi·rited, a. Full of spirit, animated, lively, brisk, courageous, as *a s.·translation, attack, reply*; having specified spirit, as *high, mean, proud, jealous, -s.*; having specified spirits, as *low-s.* Hence **(-)spi·rited**LY[2] adv., **-spi·rited**NESS a. [-ED[2]]

spi·ritless, a. Wanting in courage, vigour, or vivacity. Hence **spi·ritless**LY[2] adv. [-LESS]

spĭrĭtō·so, adv. (mus.). With spirit. [It.]

spi·ritual, a. Of spirit as opp. to matter; of the soul esp. as acted on by God, as *s. life*; of, proceeding from, God, holy, divine, inspired, as *s. songs, the s. law*; *the s. man*, inner nature of man, (also, esp. in N.T.) regenerate man (opp. to *natural, carnal*); concerned with sacred or religious things, as *our s. interests, s.* (ecclesiastical) *courts, s. corporations, lords s.*, bishops & archbishops in H. of Lords; having the higher qualities of the mind. Hence **spi·ritual**LY[2] adv., **spi·ritual**NESS n. [f. OF *spirituel* f. L *spiritualis* (as SPIRIT, see -AL)]

spi·ritualism, n. Belief that departed spirits communicate with & show themselves to men, esp. (also *modern s.*) at seances by means of spirit-rapping, -handwriting, &c., so **spi·rit**ISM, **spi·rit**IST, nn.; (Philos.) doctrine that spirit exists as distinct from matter or that spirit is the only reality (cf. MATERIALISM). Hence or cogn. **spi·ritual**IST n., **spiritu-ali·stic** a. [-ISM]

spiritua·lity, n. Spiritual quality; (usu. pl.) what belongs or is due to the Church or to an ecclesiastic as such, as *the ss. of his office, s. of benefices*, tithes of land &c. [f. OF *spiritualité* f. LL *spiritualitatem* (as SPIRITUAL, see -TY)]

spi·ritualize, v.t. Make spiritual, elevate, (character, person, thoughts); (rare) infuse life into, animate; attach spiritual as opp. to literal meaning to. Hence **spiritualiz**A·TION n. [f. F *spiritualiser* (as SPIRITUAL, see -IZE)]

spiritue·l(le), a. (Chiefly of women) marked by refinement, grace, or delicacy, of mind. [F, as SPIRITUAL]

spi·rituous, a. Containing much alcohol, distilled not fermented, as *s. liquors* (also used loosely of beer &c.). Hence **spi·rituous**NESS n. [f. OF *spiritueux* f. L as SPIRIT, -OUS]

spīr·itus, n. (Gk gram.). *S. asper, lēnis*, =*rough, smooth*, BREATHING[1]. [L]

spī·rivalve, a. Having spiral shell; (of shell) spiral. [f. L *spira* SPIRE[2]+*valva* door]

spir·keting, n. Inside planking between top of waterways & lower sills of ports. [f. obs. *spirket, spur-*, etym. dub.]

spīro-[1] in comb. = Gk *speira* coil.

spīro-[2] in comb. (irreg.) = L *spiro* breathe in sense 'breath', as: *-graph*, instrument for marking breathing movement; *-meter, -scope*, instrument for measuring lung capacity, so *-me·tric* a., *-metry* n.; *-phore*, instrument for inducing respiration in cases of suspended animation.

spirt, spurt, v.i. & t., & n. Gush out in a jet or stream; cause (liquid &c.) to do this; (n.) sudden gushing out, jet. [?]

spit[1], n., & v.t. Slender bar on which meat that is to be roasted is made to rotate before fire; small point of land running into sea; (v.t.) thrust a s. through (meat &c.), (fig.) pierce, transfix, with sword &c. [(vb f. n.) OE *spitu*, cf. Du. *spit*, G *spiess*]

spit[2], v.i. & t. (*spat* or archaic *spit*), & n. Eject saliva (*s. & polish*, furbishing work of soldier or sailor); eject (saliva, blood; food &c. *out*) from mouth; (fig.) utter (oaths, threats, &c.) vehemently (*s. it out* slang, exhortation to speak or sing louder); (of cat &c., fig. of person) make noise as of spitting as sign of anger or hostility; (of rain) fall lightly, (of fire, candle, pen) send out sparks, stray ink, &c.; *s. at* or *upon*, (fig.) treat with ignominy; *spi·tfire*, person of fiery temper, (also *spi·tdevil*) toy cone of wet gunpowder spitting when ignited. Hence **spi·tt**ER[1] n. (N.) spitting (esp. of cat), spawn of some insects; (rare) spittle; *the (very) s. of* (exact counterpart of, likeness of, as *he is t. v. s. o. his father*). [(n. f. vb) OE *spittan*, also *spǣtan* (whence past & p.p. *spat*); prob. cogn. w. ON *spýta*, Da. *spytte*, Sw. *spotta*, and w. SPOUT]

spit[3], n. Spade-depth (*dig it two ss.* or *s. deep*). [Du., cf. OE *spittan* dig]

spi·tchcock, n., & v.t. Eel split & broiled; (v.t.) prepare thus (eel, fish, bird). [f. 16th c., etym. dub.]

spite, n., & v.t. Ill will, malice, as *did it from pure s.* or *in* or *out of s.*; grudge, as *has a s. against me*; (*in*) *s. of*, notwithstanding; (v.t.) thwart, mortify, annoy, as *does it to s. me, cut off* one's *nose to s.* one's *face*, injure oneself by vindictive or resentful conduct. Hence **spi·te**FUL a., **spi·teful**LY[2] adv., **spi·teful**NESS n. [(vb f. n.) short for DESPITE]

spi·ttle, n. Saliva esp. as ejected from mouth. [OE *spātl* (*spǣtan* SPIT[2])]

spittoo·n, n. Vessel to spit into, usu. round metal or earthenware vessel with funnel-shaped top. [irreg. f. SPIT[2]+-OON]

spitz, n. (Also *s.-dog*) small kind of dog with pointed muzzle, Pomeranian. [G *spitz(hund)* f. *spitz* pointed, *hund* dog]

spla·nchnic (-ngk-), a. Of the entrails, intestinal. So **splanchno-** comb. form, **splanchno·**LOGY, **splanchno·**TOMY, nn. [f. Gk *splagkhnikos* (*splagkhna* entrails, see -IC)]

splăsh, v.t. & i., & n. Bespatter (person &c. *with* water, mud, &c.); dash, spatter, (liquid *about, on* or *over* person &c.); (of liquid) fly about in drops or scattered portions; (of person) cause liquid to do this, make one's *way*, move *across, along,* &c., thus; step, fall, plunge, &c., *into* (water &c.) so as to s. it; decorate with scattered ornamentation. (N.) splashing; quantity of liquid splashed; resulting noise, as *we heard a s.*; spot of dirt &c. splashed on to things; patch of colour esp. on animal's skin; *make a s.*, (fig.) attract much attention, create sensation; complexion powder usu. of rice-flour; *s.-board*, guard in front of wheeled vehicle to keep mud off occupants. Hence **spla·sh**Y[2] a. [=PLASH with emphat. *s-* (=OF *es-* f. L EX-)]

spla·sher, n. In vbl senses; also: kinds of guard placed over wheels of locomotive &c. to keep off mud &c.; screen behind wash-stand to protect wall. [-ER[1]]

spla·tter, v.i. & t. Make continuous splashing sound; speak (a language, or abs.) unintelligibly; *s.-dash*, noise, clamour; *s.-dashes*, =SPATTER*dashes*. [prob. var. of SPATTER]

splay, v.t. & i., n., & a. Construct (aperture) with divergent sides (*splayed loophole, window, doorway*, with opening wider at one side of wall), (of aperture or its sides) be so shaped or set; dislocate (esp. horse's shoulder); (n.) surface making oblique angle with another, e.g. splayed side of window, embrasure; (adj.) wide & flat, turned outward; *s.-foot* n. & a., (having) broad flat foot turned outward; *s. mouth*, wide mouth, mouth stretched wide in grimace. [(n. & adj. f. vb) ME *splayen*, short for DISPLAY]

spleen, n. Organ producing certain modifications in the blood of most vertebrates, situated in mammals at left of stomach; lowness of spirits, ill temper, spite, as *a fit of s., vented his s.*, whence **splee·n**FUL, **splee·**NISH[1], **splee·**NY[2], aa., **splee·nful**LY[2], **splee·nish**LY[2], advv.; *splee·nwort*, kinds of fern formerly used for s. disorders. Hence **splee·n**LESS a. [f. L f. Gk *splēn*]

splen- in comb. = Gk *splēn* spleen, as: *-a·lgia*, pain in (region of) spleen, so *-a·lgic* a.; *-e·ctomy*, excision of spleen; *-ī·tis*, inflammation of spleen; so *-ĭ·tic* a.; *-ŏ·logy*, study of spleen, so *-olo·gical* a.; *-ŏ·tomy* incision into, dissection of, spleen.

sple·ndent, a. (mineral., entom.). Having bright metallic lustre. [f. L *splendēre* shine, see -ENT]

sple·ndid, a. Magnificent, gorgeous, sumptuous, glorious, brilliant, as *a s. palace, gift, achievement, victory*; (of person) affecting splendour (*in* surroundings &c.); (colloq.) excellent, capital, as *here is a s. chance of escape*. Hence **sple·ndid**LY[2] adv. [f. L *splendidus* (as prec., see -ID[1])]

splendi·ferous, a. (colloq.). Splendid. [irreg. f. foll. + -FEROUS]

sple·ndour, n. Great or dazzling brightness; magnificence, grandeur; (Herald.) *sun in s.* (with rays & human face). [OF, f. L *splendorem* (as SPLENDENT, see -OR[1])]

splenĕ·tic, a. & n. Ill-tempered, peevish, whence **splene·t**ICALLY adv.; of the spleen; (n.) medicine for, sufferer from, disease of the spleen. [f. LL *spleneticus* (as SPLEEN, see -ETIC)]

splē·nial, a. (anat.). Acting like a splint; of the splenius. [-AL]

splĕ·nic, a. Of, in, the spleen, as *s. fever*, anthrax. So **splē·n**OID a. [f. L f. Gk *splēnikos* (as SPLEEN, see -IC)]

splē·nius, n. (pl. *-iī*). (Either section of) muscle on back & sides of neck serving to draw back the head. [f. Gk *splēnion* bandage]

splēniza·tion, n. Conversion of lung into substance resembling spleen. [-IZE, -ATION]

splice, v.t., & n. Join ends of (ropes) by interweaving strands; join (pieces of timber &c.) in overlapping position; (colloq.) join in marriage, as *when did he* or *they get spliced?*; *s. the* MAIN[3] *brace*; (n.) junction of two ropes or pieces of wood &c. by splicing; EYE[1]*-s.* [(n. f. vb) f. MDu. *splissen* perh. cogn. w. SPLIT]

spline, n., & v.t. Rectangular key fitting into grooves in hub & shaft of wheel & allowing longitudinal play; slat; flexible wood or rubber strip used in drawing large curves esp. in railway work; (v.t.) fit with s. [?]

splint, n., & v.t. Strip of rigid or flexible material for holding broken bone when set or for basketwork &c.; (Anat., also *s.-bone*) either of two small bones in horse's foreleg lying behind & in close contact with cannon-bone, (in man) fibula; tumour on, callus due to disease of, s.-bone of horse; *s.-coal*, cannel coal of slaty structure; (v.t.) confine (broken limb &c.) with ss. [(vb f. n.) f. MDu. or MLG *splinte* metal plate or pin]

spli·nter, v.t. & i., & n. Split (t. & i.) into long thin pieces, shiver; (n.) sharp-edged or thin piece broken off from wood, stone, &c.; *s.-bar*, cross-bar in vehicle supporting springs or to which traces are attached; *s.-bone*, fibula; *s.-proof* (against ss. of bursting shells). [(n. f. vb) MDu., cf. prec.]

spli·ntery, a. Of splinters; splinter-like; apt to splinter. [-Y[2]]

split[1], v.t. & i. (split). Break forcibly, be broken, into parts esp. with the grain or plane of cleavage; divide into parts, thicknesses, &c., as *s. it into three layers, the job, sum,* &c., *was s.* (usu. *up*) *among 6 of us, s.* one's *vote,* vote for each of opposed candidates, *s. the difference,* take mean quantity &c. between two proposed; *s. hairs,* draw over-subtle distinctions, so HAIR-*splitting*; divide (t. & i.) into disagreeing or hostile parties (*on* question &c.); *s.* (one's *sides* or intr.), be convulsed with laughter, so *side-splitting* a. & n., *side-splitter* (person or joke); *head is splitting* (feels acute pain), *a splitting* (acute) *headache*; *s. on* (slang), betray the secrets of (accomplice &c.); *s. cloth* (surg.), bandage with several tails esp. for head & face; *s. gear, wheel* (made in halves for removal from shaft); *s. infinitive* (with adverb &c. inserted between *to* and verb, e.g. *seems to partly correspond*); *s. moss,* kinds of which capsules split at maturity; *s. peas(e)* (dried & s. in half for cooking); *s.* PIN[1]; *s. ring* (usu. of steel on the pattern of those used for bunches of keys); *s. shot, stroke,* stroke at croquet driving two touching balls in different directions. Hence **(-)splitt**ER[1](1, 2) n. [f. MDu. *splitten,* cf. Du. *splitten* & *splijten,* G *spleissen*]

split[2], n. Splitting; fissure, rent, crack; separation into parties, schism, rupture; split osier &c. for parts of basket-work; each of the strips of steel, cane, &c., of reed in loom; single thickness of split hide; (in faro) turning up of two cards of equal value so that stakes are divided; half bottle of aerated water, half glass of liquor; (pl.) acrobat's trick of sitting on ground with legs spread out laterally, as *do ss.* [f. prec.]

splotch, splodge, nn. Daub, smear. Hence **splo·tch**Y[2] a. [*-tch* f. 17th, *-dge* 19th, c.; etym. dub.]

splurge, n., & v.i. (Make) noisy display or effort. [U.S. wd, prob. imit.]

splu·tter, v.i. & t., & n. =SPUTTER. Hence **splu·tter**ER[1] n. [for *-l-* cf. *sp(l)atter*]

Spode, n. A fine pottery. [J. *S.,* maker, d. 1827]

spo·ffish, a. (slang). Bustling, fussy. [?]

spoil[1], n. (Usu. pl. or collect. sing.) plunder taken from enemy in war, (fig.) profit, advantage, accruing from success in contest &c., emoluments of public office &c.; *ss. system* (U.S.), practice of giving public offices to adherents of successful party, whence *spoi·lsman,* advocate of, one who seeks to profit by, this; a draw in the game of *s.-five,* in which each player has five cards. [f. OF *espoille* f. L *spolium* skin stripped off animal, (usu. pl.) spoil]

spoil[2], v.t. & i. (*spoilt* or *spoiled*). (Archaic, literary; never *-lt*) plunder, deprive (person *of* thing), by force or stealth, as *s. the Egyptians* (persons regarded as one's natural enemies &c.; *Exod.* xii. 36); impair the qualities of, or person's enjoyment of, as *was quite spoilt by the rain, will s. all the fun, always s. a joke in the telling, the news spoilt his dinner, s.* one's *beauty for him* (with black eye &c.); injure character of (person &c.) by indulgence, as *spare the rod & s. the child, are determined to s. me, is the spoilt child of fortune*; (slang) maim or kill or do for (person); (of fruit, fish, &c., fig. of joke &c.) decay, go bad, as *will not s. with keeping, dog is spoiling* (ripe, eager) *for a fight*; *s.-sport,* one who spoils sport. Hence **spoi·l**ER[1] n. [f. OF *espoillier* f. L *spoliare* strip, plunder (as prec.)]

spoi·lage (-ĭj), n. Paper spoilt in printing. [-AGE]

spoke[1], n., & v.t. Each of the bars running from hub to rim of wheel, whence **spo·ke**WISE adv.; rung of ladder; each radial handle of steering-wheel of vessel; bar used to prevent wheel from turning esp. in going down hill, as (fig.) *put a s. in* person's *wheel,* thwart his purposes; *s.-bone,* radius of fore-arm; *s.-shave,* plane-bit between two handles, used for ss. & other esp. curved work where ordinary plane is not available; (v.t.) furnish with ss., check (wheel) with s.; *spoking-machine* (for giving uniform inclination to ss. of wheel). [(vb f. n.) OE *spáca,* cf. Du. *speek,* G *speiche*]

spoke[2], **spoken, -spoken.** See SPEAK.

spo·kesman (-ks-), n. One who speaks for others, representative. [irreg. f. SPOKE[2] + -ES + MAN]

spŏ·lia opi·ma, n. (Rom. Ant.) arms stripped from hostile general by Roman commander in single combat; (fig.) supreme achievement or distinction. [L, =rich spoils]

spōlia·tion, n. Plunder, pillage, esp. of neutral vessels by belligerent, (fig.) extortion; (Eccl.) taking of fruits of benefice under pretended title, *writ of s.* (for recovery of these); (Law) destruction, mutilation, alteration, of document to prevent its being used as evidence. Hence or cogn. **spo·liat**OR[2] n., **spo·lia**TORY a. [F, f. L *spoliationem* (as SPOIL[2], see -ATION)]

spondā·ic, a. Of spondees; (of hexameter) having spondee as fifth foot. [f. F *spondaique* ult. f. Gk *spondeiakos* (as foll., see -AC)]

spo·ndee, n. Metrical foot – –. [f. L f. Gk *spondeios* (*pous* foot) used in making treaty (*spondai* n. pl. f. *spendō* make libation)]

spo·ndўl(e), n. Joint of backbone, vertebra. Hence **spo·ndyl**(o)- comb. form. [F (*-le*), f. L f. Gk *spondulos* (prop. *spho-*)]

sponge[1] (-ŭnj), n. Aquatic animal of low order with pores in the body-wall, whence **spongo·**LOGIST, **spongo·**LOGY, (spŏ-), nn.;

skeleton of a s. or colony of ss. (whence **spo·ngi**FORM a.), esp. elastic kind chiefly from the Levant used as absorbent in bathing, cleansing surfaces, &c.; *throw up the s.*, (of boxer or his attendant) throw into the air as token of defeat the s. used between rounds, (fig.) abandon contest, own oneself beaten; *pass the s. over*, agree to forget (offence &c.); thing of s.-like absorbency or consistence, e.g. piece of leavened dough, s.-cake, absorbent pad used in surgery, kind of mop for cleaning bore of cannon, iron or other metal in finely-divided condition; (fig.) parasite, person who contrives to live at another's expense; *s.-*BATH, *s.-cake*, light cake of s.-like consistence; *s. cucumber, -gourd, vegetable s.*, kind of gourd used in Turkish baths as rubber or towel; *s. tent*, compressed s. for keeping wound &c. open; *s.-tree*, spiny tropical shrub of bean family with globose heads of fragrant yellow flowers. [OE, f. L f. Gk *spoggia* var. of *sp(h)oggos*, cf. FUNGUS]

sponge², v.t. & i., & n. Wipe, cleanse, with sponge; sluice water over (parts of body &c., or abs., often *down, over*) with sponge; wipe out, efface, (writing, fig. memory of thing &c., usu. *out*) with sponge; absorb, take *up*, (water &c.) with sponge; gather sponges; procure by sycophantic arts; *s. on*, live as the parasite of, be meanly dependent on (person *for* thing); (n.) sponging, bath with sponge, as *had a s. down*. Hence **spo·nger**¹(1, 2) n. [(n. f. vb) f. LL *spongiare* (as prec.)]

spo·nging, n. In vbl senses; *s.-house* (hist., in archaic sense *squeezing*), bailiff's house for temporary lodging of arrested debtor. [-ING¹]

spongiopī·line, n. Substitute for poultice made of sponge & fibre backed with rubber. [as SPONGE¹ + Gk *pilos* felt + -INE⁴]

spo·ngy, a. Like sponge; porous, compressible, elastic, absorbent, as sponge; (of metal) finely divided & loosely coherent. Hence **spo·ngi**NESS n. [-Y²]

spo·nsion, n. Being surety for another; (Internat. Law) engagement made on behalf of State by agent not specially authorized. [f. L *sponsio* (*spondēre spons-* promise, see -ION)]

spo·nson, n. Projection from side of warship to enable gun to be trained forward & aft; triangular platform before & abaft paddle-box. [?]

spo·nsor, n. Godfather or godmother; person who makes himself responsible for another. Hence **sponsor·**IAL a., **spo·nsor**SHIP n. [L (*spondēre spons-* promise, see -OR²)]

spontā·neous, a. Acting, done, occurring, without external cause; voluntary, without external incitement, as *made a s. offer of his services*; (of sudden movements &c.) involuntary, not due to conscious volition; growing naturally without cultivation; (Biol., of structural changes in plants, muscular activity in esp. young animals) instinctive, automatic, prompted by no motive; (of bodily movements, literary style, &c.) gracefully natural & unconstrained; *s. combustion*, ignition of mineral or vegetable substance (e.g. heap of rags soaked with oil, mass of wet coal) from heat engendered by rapid oxidation; *s. generation*, production of living from non-living matter as inferred from appearance of life (due in fact to bacteria &c.) in some infusions; *s. suggestion* (from association of ideas without conscious volition). Hence or cogn. **spontanē·**ITY, **sponta·neous**NESS, nn., **sponta·neous**LY² adv. [f. L *spontaneus* (*sponte* of one's own accord, see -ANEOUS)]

spontōō·n, n. (hist.). Kind of halberd used by some British infantry officers. [f. F *sponton* f. It. *spontone* f. *puntone*, *punto*, point]

spōōf, v.t., & n., (slang). Swindle, humbug, hoax. Hence **spoo·fer**¹ n. [arbitrary]

spōōk, n. Ghost. Hence **spoo·kish**¹, **spoo·ky**², aa. [Du., cf. G *spuk*]

spōōl, n., & v.t. Reel for winding yarn, photographic film, &c., on; revolving shaft of angler's reel; (vb) wind on s. [f. MDu. *spoele*, cf. Sw. *spole*, G *spule*]

spōōn¹, n., & v.t. & i. Utensil consisting of round or usu. oval bowl & a handle for conveying esp. liquid food to mouth, usu. of silver or plated metal for table use (*tea, dessert, table, -s.*, of small, medium, large, size, esp. as recognized measure for medicine; APOSTLE *s.*, EGG¹, *salt, mustard, -s.*; *marrow-s.*, for getting marrow from bones) & of wood or iron for cooking &c.; BORN *with silver s. in mouth*; *long s. & the devil* (see SUP); *wooden s.* (hist.), (wooden s. given to) last man in Cambridge mathematical tripos; EGG¹*-&-s. race*; s.-shaped thing, esp. (oar with) broad curved blade, kinds of golf-club with striking-surface hollowed out; *s.(-bait)*, bright revolving s.-shaped piece of metal used as lure in fishing; *spoo·n-beak, -bill*, kinds of bird; *s.-drift*, see SPINDRIFT; *s.-fed*, (fig., of industries &c.) artificially encouraged by bounties or import duties; *s.-meat*, liquid food, food for infants (also fig.); *s.-net*, angler's landing-net. (Vb) take (liquid &c., usu. *up, out*) with s.; fish with s.-bait; (Croquet) make pushing stroke; (Crick.) strike (ball) feebly, send *up* (ball, a catch) thus, with bat. Hence **(-)spoo·nful** n. [(vb f. n.) OE *spón*, cf. Du. *spaan*, G *span*]

spoon², n., & v.i. Simpleton; silly or demonstratively fond lover; *be ss. on*, be sillily in love with; (vb) behave amorously, behave thus towards (girl &c.). [f. prec.]

Spōō·ner(ism), n. Accidental transposition of initial letters &c. of two or more words (e.g. *has just received a blushing crow, for real enjoyment give me a well-boiled icycle*). [f. Rev. W. A. *Spooner*, esteemed for ss., + -ISM]

spoo·ny, a. & n. Soft, silly; sentimental, amorous, sweet (*up*)*on*; (n.) mild simpleton. Hence **spoo·ni**LY[2] adv., **spoo·ni**NESS n. [prob. f. SPOON[2], -Y[2]]

spoor, n., & v.t. & i. Track, scent, of animal; (vb) follow by s. Hence **spoor·**ER[1] n. [Du, perh. cogn. w. SPUR, cf. OE & ON *spor*, G *spur*]

sporă·dic, a. Occurring only here & there, separate, scattered. Hence **spora·dic**AL a. (rare), **spora·dical**LY[2] adv., **spora·dical**NESS n. [f. med. L f. Gk *sporadikos* (*sporas -ados* scattered, cf. *speirō* sow, see -IC)]

sporă·ngium (-j-), n. (bot.). Case in which spores are produced. [f. Gk *spora* SPORE + *aggeion* vessel]

spore, n. (Bot., in cryptogamous plants) single cell that becomes free & capable of individual development; (Biol.) minute organic body that develops into new individual; (fig.) seed, germ, of anything. [f. Gk *spora* sowing, seed, f. *speirō* sow]

sporo- in comb. = prec., as: *-ge·nesis*, spore-formation; *-genous*, producing spores.

spo·rran, n. Pouch, usu. covered with fur &c., worn by Highlander in front of kilt. [f. Gael. *sporan*]

sport, n., & v.i. & t. Amusement, diversion, fun; *in s.*, jestingly; *make s. of*, turn into ridicule, make fun of; *be the s.* (plaything, butt) *of Fortune* &c.; pastime, game; outdoor pastime, e.g. hunting, fishing, racing; *have good s.*, esp. make good bag or basket when shooting &c.; *athletic ss.*, running, jumping, putting weight, &c., meeting of athletes to compete in these, as *school ss.*, *inter-university ss.* (*ss. coat, jacket*, kinds worn for golf &c.); animal, plant, deviating suddenly or strikingly from normal type; (slang) good fellow, sportsman; *sportsman, -woman*, person fond of ss. esp. hunting, shooting, or fishing, (fig.) person who regards life as a game in which opponents must be allowed fair play, person ready to play a bold game, whence *spor·tsmanship* n.; *spor·tsmanlike*, befitting, worthy of, a sportsman. (Vb) divert oneself, take part in pastime; (part.) interested in s., as *a sporting man*, sportsmanlike, as *sporting conduct, sporting offer*, whence **spor·ting**LY[2] adv.; (Bot., Zool.) become or produce a s.; wear, exhibit, produce, esp. ostentatiously, as *sported a gold tie-pin*; *s.* one's OAK. [short for DISPORT]

spor·tive, a. Playful. Hence **spor·tive**LY[2] adv., **spor·tive**NESS n. [-IVE]

spŏ·rule, n. Spore; small spore. Hence **spo·rul**AR[1] a. [-ULE]

spot[1], n. Particular place, definite locality, as *dropped it on this precise s.*, *the s. where William III landed*; *a tender s.*, (fig.) subject on which one is touchy; small part of the surface of a thing distinguished by colour, texture, &c., usu. round or less elongated than a streak or stripe, small mark or stain, pimple, as *a blue tie with pink ss.*, SUN-*s.*, *can the leopard change his ss.?*; (fig.) moral blemish, stain, as *without a s. on his reputation*; kinds of fish & domestic pigeon; (slang) act of spotting winner &c., horse &c. so spotted; (Billiards) small round black patch near each end of table equidistant from sides, *s.-stroke*, pocketing red ball when placed on s. remote from balk, *s.-barred game* (in which successive s.-strokes are not allowed), *s.* (*-ball*), white ball distinguished from the other by black s.; *on the s.*, without delay or change of place, then & there, (of person) wide awake, equal to the situation, in good form at game &c.; (Commerc.) *s. cash, cotton, wheat, prices* (to be paid or delivered immediately on sale), *ss.*, commodities sold for s. cash. Hence **spo·t**LESS, **spo·tt**Y[2], aa., **spo·tless**LY[2] adv., **spo·tless**NESS, **spo·tti**NESS, nn. [ME, cf. MDu. *spotte, spot*]

spot[2], v.t. Mark, stain, soil, with spots (lit., & fig. of character &c.); (of material &c.) be (liable to be) marked with spots; (colloq.) single out beforehand (winner of race &c., horse &c. as winner *for* event); (colloq.) detect, recognize nationality &c. of, as *spotted him at once as an American, can always s. a dun*; (p.p.) marked with ss., esp. in names of animals; *spotted dog* (slang), = PLUM-*duff*; *spotted fever*, cerebro-spinal meningitis. Hence **spo·tted**NESS n. [f. prec.]

spouse (-owz), n. Husband or wife. [f. OF *sp*(*o*)*us* masc., *spuse* fem., f. L p.p. of *spondēre* promise]

spout (-owt), v.t. & i., & n. Discharge, issue, forcibly in a jet, as *blood spouts from wound, wounds s. blood, whale spouts water*; utter (verses &c., or abs.) in declamatory manner, speechify; (slang) pawn. (N.) projecting tube through which liquid &c. is poured from tea-pot, kettle, gutter of roof, &c.; sloping trough down which thing may be shot into receptacle, esp. shoot in pawnbroker's shop, as *his watch is up the s.* (in pawn); jet, column, of liquid or grain &c.; WATER[1]-*s.*; (also *s.-hole*) spiracle of whale. Hence **spou·t**ER[1] n., **spou·t**LESS a. [ME *spouten* vb, *spoute* n., cf. Du. *spuiten*; cogn. w. SPIT[2]]

sprag, n. Billet of wood or similar device for checking wheel of car &c. [?]

sprain, v.t., & n. Wrench (ankle, wrist,

&c.) violently so as to cause pain & swelling but not dislocation; (n.) such wrench, resulting inflammation & swelling. [f. 17th c., etym. dub.]

sprai̇nts, n. pl. Otter's dung. [f. OF *espraintes* lit. out-pressings f. OF *espreindre* f. L EX(*primere* = *premere* press)]

sprang. See SPRING[1].

sprat, n., & v.i. Small European herring-like fish much used as food; other kinds of fish, e.g. sand-eel, young herring; *throw a s. to catch a herring* or *mackerel* or *whale*, risk a little to gain much; (joc.) thin child; *s.-day*, Nov. 9, on which s. season begins in England; (v.i.) fish for ss., whence **spra·tt**ER[1], **spra·tt**ING[1], nn. [(vb f. n.) OE *sprot*, cf. G *sprott*, Du. *sprot*]

sprawl, v.i. & t., & n. Spread oneself, spread (one's limbs), out in careless or ungainly way; (of writing, plant, &c.) be of irregular or straggling form; open out (troops) irregularly; (n.) sprawling movement or attitude. [OE *spreawlian*, cf. NFris. *spraweli*]

spray[1], n. Branch of tree with branchlets or flowers, esp. slender or graceful one, sprig of flowers or leaves; ornament in similar form, as *a s. of diamonds* &c.; *s.-drain*, drain in field &c. made by filling trench with branches. Hence **spray·ey**[1] a. [cf. CLAYEY]. [ME, etym. dub.]

spray[2], n., & v.t. Water or other liquid flying in small drops from force of wind, dashing of waves, or action of atomizer &c.; medical or other liquid preparation to be applied in this form with atomizer &c.; (v.t.) throw (liquid, or abs.) in form of s., sprinkle (object) thus; *s.-board* (on boat's gunwale to keep off s.). Hence **spray·**ER[1](1, 2) n., **spray·ey**[2] a. [cf. MDu *spraeyen*, MHG *spreien*, to sprinkle]

spread[1] (-ĕd), v.t. & i. (spread). Extend the surface of, cause to cover larger surface, by unrolling, unfolding, smearing, flattening out, &c., (fig.) display thus to eye or mind, as *peacock spreads its tail*, *s. oneself* (slang, = talk bumptiously), *s. a banner*, *s. out a rug on the grass*, *s. butter on bread*, *map lay s. out on the table*, *the view s. out before us*, whence **sprea·d**ER[1](2) n.; show extended or extensive surface, as *river here spreads out to a width of half a mile*, *on every side s. a vast desert*, *spreading yews*; diffuse, be diffused, as *his name s. fear in every quarter*, *rumour s. from mouth to mouth*, *has s. a malicious report*; cover surface of, as *slices of bread s. with jam*, *a table s. with every luxury*, *meadow s. with daisies*; *s. eagle*, figure of eagle with legs & wings extended as seen on coins &c., skating movement on both inside edges at once one forward & the other back, (colloq.) fowl split open down the back & broiled, (Naut.) person lashed in rigging with arms and legs s. out as punishment, (adj., *s.-e.*) bombastic, esp. noisily patriotic, whence *s.-ea·gleism* n.; *s.-over* (*system*), elasticity in accommodating restricted work-hours to special needs. [OE *sprǣdan*, cf. Du. *spreiden*, G *spreiten*]

spread[2], n. Spreading; capability of expanding, as *inferior to the eagle in s. of wings*; breadth, compass, as *arches of equal s.*; diffusion (*of* education &c.); (colloq.) feast, meal, as *had no end of a s.*; (U.S., commerc.) difference between cost of manufacture & selling price. [f. prec.]

spree, n., & v.i. Lively frolic, bout of drinking &c., as *is on the* (having a) *s.*; (v.i.) have a s. [19th-c. slang, etym. dub.]

sprent, a. (archaic). Sprinkled, overspread, (*with* drops, particles, &c.). [p.p. of obs. *spreng* f. OE *sprengan* make SPRING[1]]

sprig, n., & v.t. Small branch, shoot; ornament of s. form; small headless nail; (usu. contempt.) youth, young man, as *who is this s.?*, *a s. of the nobility*; (v.t.) ornament with ss., as *sprigged muslin*; *spri·gtail*, kinds of duck & grouse with pointed tail. Hence **spri·gg**Y[2] a. [sense *nail* f. 14th, *shoot* f. 15th, c.; prob. two wds; etym. dub.]

sprigh·tly, a. Vivacious, lively, gay. Hence **sprigh·tli**NESS n. [f. SPRITE + -LY[1]]

spring[1], v.i. & t. (sprang, sprung). Leap, jump, move rapidly or suddenly, (often *up*, *down*, *out*, *over*, *through*, *away*, *back*, &c.), as *sprang* (*up*) *from his seat*, *sprang through the gap*, *at his throat*, *to their assistance*, *blood sprang to her cheeks*; move rapidly as from constrained position or by action of a spring, as *branch sprang back*, *door sprang to*; come into being (usu. *s. up*), arise (often *from* source), appear, as *a breeze sprang up*, *the piers from which the arches s.*, *is sprung from* or *of a royal stock*, *the buds are springing*, *the belief has sprung up*, *his actions s. from a false conviction*, (to person arriving suddenly or unexpectedly or whose presence is only now realized) *where do* or *did you s. from?*; (of wood) warp; (t. & i. of wood) split, crack, as *bat is* or *has sprung*, *have sprung my racket*; (p.p., colloq.) tipsy; rouse (game) from earth or covert; cause to act suddenly by means of a spring, produce or develop suddenly or unexpectedly, as *s. a trap*, *has sprung a new theory*, *loves to s. surprises on us*; cause (mine) to burst; (Naut., of ship) *s. a butt*, loosen end of plank by labouring in heavy sea, *s. a leak*, develop leak from starting of timbers, *s. the* or *her luff*, yield to helm & sail nearer to wind. [OE *springan*, cf. Du. & G *springen*, ON *springa* burst]

spring[2], n. Leap, as *took a s.*, *rose with a*

s.; season in which vegetation begins, season preceding summer (esp. from about March 21 to June 22); place where water or oil wells up from earth, basin so formed, as *hot, mineral, ss.*; backward movement from constrained position, recoil, e.g. of bow; elasticity, as *his muscles have no s. in them*; elastic contrivance usu. of bent or coiled metal used esp. as motive power in clockwork &c. or for preventing jar as in carriage, as *bow s.* (bow-shaped), CEE *s., air* or *pneumatic s.* (working by compression of air), HAIR-*s.*, MAIN[2]*s.*; (fig.) motive actuating person &c., source, origin, as *the ss. of human action, the custom had its s. in another country*; upward curve of beam &c. from horizontal line; starting of plank; springing of leak; DAY-*s.*; *s. balance* (measuring weight by tension of s.); *s.-beam*, beam stretching across wide space without intermediate support, elastic bar used as s. in tilt-hammer &c.; *s. bed, mattress*, mattress formed of spiral ss. in wooden frame; *s.-board*, elastic board giving impetus in leaping, diving, &c.; *s.-carriage, -cart* (mounted on ss.); *s. gun* (contrived to go off when trespasser or animal stumbles on it); *s.-halt*, convulsive movement of horse's hind leg in walking; *s. tide*, high tide occurring shortly after new & full moon in each month; *spri·ngtide, spri·ngtime*, season of s.; *s. water* (from s., opp. to river or rain water). Hence **spri·ng**LESS, **spri·ng**LIKE, aa., **spri·ng**LET n. [OE, f. prec.]

spri·ngal(d), n. (archaic). Youngster. [f. 15th c., etym. dub.]

spri·ngbok, n. S.-Afr. gazelle with habit of springing in play or when alarmed; (pl., nickname for) S. Africans, S.-African football team &c. [S.-Afr. Du.]

springe (-j), n. Noose, snare, for small game. [ME (SPRING[1])]

spri·nger (-ng*er*), n. In vbl senses; also or esp.: (Archit.) part of arch where curve begins, lowest stone of this part, bottom stone of coping of gable, rib of groined roof or vault; kind of spaniel used to spring game; grampus; springbok. [-ER[1]]

spri·ngy (-ngĭ), a. (Of movement or substance) elastic. Hence **spri·ngi**NESS n. [-Y[2]]

spri·nkle, v.t. & i., & n. Scatter (liquid, ashes, crumbs, &c.) in small drops or particles, whence **spri·nkl**ER[1](2) n.; subject (ground, object) to sprinkling (*with* liquid &c.); (of liquid &c.) fall thus on; (n.) light shower (*of* rain &c.), so **spri·nkl**ING[1](2) n. (esp., fig., *a* few here & there *of*). [(n. f. vb) earlier *sprenkle*, cf. Du. *sprenkelen*, G *sprenkeln*]

sprint, v.i. & t., & n. Run short distance, run (specified distance), at full speed; (n.) such run. Hence **spri·nt**ER[1] n. [cf. ON *spretta*]

sprit, n. Small spar reaching diagonally from mast to upper outer corner of sail; *spri·tsail* (-sāl, -sl), sail extended by s., (formerly) sail extended by yard set under bowsprit. [OE *spréot* pole, cogn. w. SPROUT]

sprite, n. Elf, fairy, goblin. [ME, as SPIRIT]

spro·cket, n. Each of several teeth on wheel engaging with links of chain; *s.-wheel*, such wheel, e.g. for engaging bicycle chain. [?]

sprout (-owt), v.i. & t., & n. Begin to grow, shoot forth, put forth shoots; spring up, grow to a height; produce by sprouting, as *has sprouted horns, a moustache*; (n.) shoot of plant; BRUSSELS *ss.* [(n. f. vb) OE *sprútan*, cf. Du. *spruiten*, G *spriessen*]

spruce[1], a., & v.t. Neat in dress & appearance, trim, smart; (v.t.) smarten (one*self* &c., usu. *up*). Hence **spru·ce**LY[2] adv., **spru·ce**NESS n. [prob. as foll., w. ref. to Prussian leather]

spruce[2], n. (Also *s. fir*) kinds of fir; *s.-beer* (made from leaves and small branches of s., useful as antiscorbutic). [f. AF *Pruce* (F *Prusse*) Prussia, cf. med. L *Sprucia*, used attrib. = Prussian]

sprue[1], n. Passage through which metal is poured into mould; metal filling s. [?]

sprue[2], n. Tropical disease (also *psilosis*) with ulcerated mucous membrane of mouth & chronic enteritis. [f. Du. *spruw* THRUSH[2]]

sprung. See SPRING[1].

spry, a. (spryer, -est). Active, lively. [dial. & U.S., etym. dub.]

spud, n., & v.t. Kinds of small spade for cutting roots of weeds &c.; short thick thing, whence **spu·dd**Y[2] a.; (colloq.) potato; (v.t.) remove (weeds, often *up, out*) with s. [f. 15th c., etym. dub.]

spu·ddle, v.i. (dial.). Dig lightly, dig about, (of amateur gardeners &c.). [orig. alteration of *puddle*; now assoc. w. prec.]

spue. See SPEW.

spume, n., & v.i. Froth, foam. Hence **spume·**SCENCE, **spu·mi**NESS, nn., **spume·**SCENT, **spu·m**OUS, **spu·m**Y[2], aa. [f. L *spuma*]

spun. See SPIN[1].

spunge. (Archaic for) SPONGE.

spunk, n. Courage, mettle, spirit; anger. Hence **spu·nk**Y[2] a. [orig. = spark, tinder; obs. *funk* (cf. G *funke*), & *punk*, spark are perh. the same word]

spur, n., & v.t. & i. Pricking instrument with point or (also *rowel-s.*) rowel worn on horseman's heel (*put* or *set ss. to*, = s. vb; *need the s.*, be sluggish, also of persons); *win* one's *ss.*, (hist.) gain knighthood, (fig.) gain distinction, make a name; (fig.) stimulus, incentive; *on the s. of the moment*, impromptu, on a momentary impulse; s.-shaped thing, e.g. hard projection on cock's leg, steel point fastened to this in cockfight, projecting mountain (range), climbing-iron, wall crossing part of rampart and joining it to interior work, slender hollow projection from some part of flower; *s. royal*, coin of James I bearing s.-like sun with rays; *s.-wheel*, cog-wheel with radial teeth; *spur·wort*, plant with whorls of leaves like rowel of s.; (v.t.) prick (horse) with ss. (*s. a willing horse* fig., be needlessly importunate), incite (person *on to* effort, *to* do, &c.), furnish (person, boots, gamecock, esp. in p.p.) with ss.; (v.t.) ride hard (*on*, *forward*, &c.). Hence **spur·**LESS a. [(vb f. n.) OE *spura*, *spora*, cf. Du. *spoor*, G *sporn*; perh. cogn. w. SPOOR]

spurge, n. Kinds of plant with acrid milky juice. [f. OF *espurge* (*espurger* purge, as EXPURGATE)]

spūr·ious, a. Not genuine, not being what it pretends to be, not proceeding from the pretended source, as *s. coin*, (*reading in*) *MS.*, *affection*; (Zool.) resembling an organ &c. but not having its function, having the function of organ &c. but morphologically different, as *s. eyes*, *legs*. Hence **spur·ious**LY[2] adv., **spur·ious**NESS n. [f. L *spurius* + -OUS]

spur·ling-line, n. (naut.). Line from steering-wheel to telltale in cabin for showing position of helm. [?]

spurn, v.t. & i., & n. Repel, thrust back, with foot; (also archaic *s. at*) reject with disdain, treat with contempt, (offer, advances, person, &c.); (n.) spurning, contemptuous rejection. [OE *spurnan*, cf. ON *spyrna*, *sperna*; cogn. w. SPUR]

spur·rier (*or* spŭ·-), n. Spur-maker. [-IER]

spŭ·rry, -rey, n. Kinds of herb of pink family, esp. *corn-s.*, a weed in cornfield &c. [f. Du. *spurrie*, cf. med. L *spergula*]

spurt[1], v.i., & n. (Make) short sudden violent effort esp. in racing. [var. of SPIRT, etym. dub.]

spurt[2]. See SPIRT.

spu·tter, v.t. & i., & n. Emit with spitting sound; speak, utter, (words, threats, a language, &c.) rapidly or incoherently; speak in hurried or vehement fashion (often *at* person &c.); (n.) such speech. Hence **spu·tter**ER[1] n., **spu·ttering**LY[2] adv. [imit., cf. Du. *sputteren*]

spū·tum, n. (pl. *-ta*). Saliva, spittle; expectorated matter esp. as characteristic of disease. [L, neut. p.p. of *spuere* spit]

spy, n., & v.t. & i. Person who goes, esp. in disguise, into enemy's camp or territory to inspect works, watch movements, &c., & report the result; person who keeps (esp. secret) watch on movements of others, as *refuse to be a s. on his conduct*; (v.t.) discern, make out, esp. by careful observation, as *spied a horseman approaching*, *is quick at spying his neighbours' faults*, *s. out*, explore secretly, discover by this means; (v.i.) play the s., keep close & secret watch (*upon* person, movements, &c., *into* secret &c.); *spyglass*, small telescope; *s.-hole*, peep-hole. [ME *spie* n., *spien* vb, f. OF *espie* n., *espier* vb ESPY]

squab (-ŏb), a., adv., & n. Short & fat, squat, whence **squa·bb**Y[2] a.; (adv.) with heavy fall, as *come down s. on the floor*; (n.) short fat person, young esp. unfledged pigeon, stuffed cushion, ottoman; *s.-chick*, unfledged bird; *s. pie*, pigeon-pie, pie of mutton, onions, & apples. [cf. Sw. dial. *sqvabb* loose flesh, *sqvabba* fat woman, &c.]

squa·bble (-ŏbl), v.i. & t., & n. Engage in petty or noisy quarrel (*with* person *about* thing); (Print.) disarrange (composed type); (n.) petty or noisy quarrel. Hence **squa·bbl**ER[1] n. [prob. imit., cf. Sw. dial. *skvabbel* n. dispute]

squă·cco, n. Small crested heron of S. Europe, Africa, & Asia. [f. It. *sguacco*]

squad (-ŏd), n. (Mil.) small number of men assembled for drill &c. (*s. drill*, elementary); *awkward s.* (of recruits not yet competent to take place in regimental line, also fig.); small party of persons. [f. F *escouade* var. of *esquadre* f. It. *squadra* SQUARE]

squa·dron (-ŏd-), n., & v.t. Principal division of cavalry regiment, consisting of two troops & containing 120 to 200 men; any orderly body of persons; detachment of war-ships employed on particular service, as *flying s.* (equipped for rapid cruising); *s.-commander* (see AIR[1] *Force*); (v.t.) form (men) into ss. [f. It. *squadrone* (prec., -OON)]

squail, n. (Pl.) game with small wooden disks (*ss.*) on round table or board (*s.-board*). [?]

squai·ler, n. Stick with leaded knob for striking or throwing at squirrels &c. [f. dial. *squail* strike with s. + -ER[1]]

squa·lid (-ŏl-), a. Dirty, mean, poor, in appearance. Hence or cogn. **squali·d**ITY, **squa·lid**NESS, **squa·l**OR[1], nn., **squa·lid**LY[2] adv. [f. L *squalidus* (*squalēre* be stiff or dirty, -ID[1])]

squall (-awl), v.i. & t., & n. Cry out, scream, violently as in fear or pain; utter in screaming or discordant voice. Hence **squa·ll**ER[1] n. (N.) sudden & violent gust or successive gusts of wind, esp. with rain or snow or sleet (*arched s.*, s. occurring near equator with sudden collection of black clouds in form of arch & usu. violent thunderstorm; *black s.*, with dark cloud; *white s.*, arising in fair weather without formation of clouds), whence **squa·ll**Y[2] a.; *look out for ss.*, (fig.) be on one's guard against danger or trouble; [f. the vb] discordant cry, scream. [imit]

squā·loid, a. Like a shark. [f. L *squalus*, kind of sea-fish, (mod.L) genus of sharks, +-OID]

squā·ma, n. (bot., zool.; pl. *-ae*). Scale, scale-like feather or part of bone. Hence or cogn. **squami-**, **squamo-**, comb. forms, **squa·mose**[1], **squa·mous**, aa., **squa·mule** n. [L]

squa·nder (-ŏn-), v.t. Spend (money, time, &c.) wastefully; dissipate (fortune &c.) thus. Hence **squa·nderer**[1] n., **squa·nderingly**[2] adv., **squandermania** n. (Government & other extravagance prevalent after the war). [f. 16th c., etym. dub.]

square (-ār), n., a., adv., & v.t. & i. Equilateral rectangle; object (approximately) of this shape; quadrilateral area planted with trees &c. or ornamentally laid out & surrounded with buildings esp. dwelling-houses, as *Trafalgar S.*, *Russell S.*, *lives in the next s.*; block of buildings bounded by four streets; L-shaped or (*T-s.*) T-shaped instrument for obtaining or testing right angles; *out of s.*, not at right angles; standard, pattern, (usu. fig., & archaic exc. *on the s.*, fairly, honestly, as *can be trusted to act on the s.*, *by the s.*, exactly); product of a number multiplied by itself, as *the s. of 9 is 81, of x^2 is x^4, 9 is a perfect s.* (has rational root); body of infantry drawn up in rectangular form, *hollow s.*, so drawn up with space in middle for baggage &c., or with files facing inwards to receive orders from officers in central space; (also *word-s.*) set of words (to be guessed from description &) arranged in a s. so as to read alike across & downwards (e.g. *cab ace bed*); MAGIC *s.*; 100 s. ft as measure of flooring &c. (Adj.) of s. shape; *s. foot, inch,* &c., (area equal to that of) s. whose side is a foot, inch, &c.; *s. measure* (expressed in s. feet &c.); *a table 4 ft s. has an area of 16 s. ft*; rectangular, as *table with s. corners*; at right angles *to*; *s. number*, s. of an integer, e.g. 1, 4, 9, 16, &c.; *s. root* of a given number, number of which it is the s., as *the s. root of 9 is 3, of x^6 is x^3, of 2 is irrational*; *s. dance, game* (in which four couples, players, face inwards from four sides); having the breadth more nearly equal to the length or height than is usual, as *a man of s. frame*; angular, not round, as *s. peg in round* HOLE[1]; *has a s. jaw*; properly arranged, in good order, as *must tidy up & get things s.*; thorough, uncompromising, as *was met with a s. refusal, made a s. meal*; fair, honest, as *his play is not always quite s.*, *a s. deal*, fair bargain; on a proper footing, even, quits, as *am now s. with all the world, get s. with* (pay, compound with) *our creditors*; *s.-built*, of comparatively broad shape; *square·head* (U.S.), Scandinavian in U.S. or Canada (cf. DAGO); *s. leg* (crick.), fielder at some distance to batsman's left & nearly opposite wicket, his place, as *was put at s. leg*; *s.-rigged*, with principal sails extended by horizontal yards slung to mast by the middle, opp. to *fore-&-aft rigged*; *square sail*, four-cornered sail extended on yard slung to mast by middle esp. on fore-&-aft rigged vessel; *s.-shouldered*, with broad & not sloping shoulders, esp. opp. to *round-shouldered*; *s.-toed*, (having boots) with s. toes, (fig.) formal, prim; *s.-toes*, s.-toed person. Hence **square·ly**[2] adv., **square·ness** n., **squar·ish**[1] a. (Adv.) squarely, as *sat s. on his seat, hit him s. on the jaw, do you think he plays s.* (fair)?, FAIR[2] *& s.* (Vb) make s.; make rectangular, give rectangular edges to (timber); multiply (number) by itself, as *3 squared is 9, x squared is written x^2*; adjust, make or be suitable *to* or consistent *with*, reconcile, as *decline to s. my conduct to* or *with his interests, his practice does not s.* or *he does not s. his practice with his principles*; settle, pay, (bill &c.), esp. *s. accounts with* (fig. have revenge on), (abs. in some senses) *s. up*; (colloq.) pay, esp. bribe, as *can you s. the porter?*, *has been squared to hold his tongue*; secure acquiescence &c. of (person) thus; assume attitude of boxer, move *up to* (person) thus; *s. the circle*, construct s. equal in area to given circle, express area of circle exactly in s. measure, (fig.) perform demonstrable impossibility; (Naut.) lay (yards) at right angles with keel making them at same time horizontal, get (dead-eyes) horizontal, get (ratlines) horizontal & parallel to one another. [f. OF *esquarre* n. (cf. It. *squadra*), *esquarré* a., *esquarrer* vb, f. pop. L *EX(*quadra* n., *-are* vb, square; cf. QUADRI-)]

squa·rrose, -ous, (-ŏr-), aa. (bot., zool.). Rough with scale-like processes. [f. alleged LL *squarrosus* prob. mistake for *squamosus* (as SQUAMA, see -OSE[1], -OUS)]

squar·son, n. (facet.). Squire & parson in one. [portmanteau wd]

squash[1] (-ŏ-), v.t. & i., & n. Crush, squeeze flat or into pulp; pack tight, crowd; (fig.) silence (person) with crushing retort; squeeze one's way (*into* &c.). (N.) squashed thing or mass, whence **squa·shiness** n., **squa·shy**[2] a.; crowd; (sound of) fall of soft body; (also *s. rackets*) game played with rackets & soft ball in fives-court; LEMON[1] *s.*; *s. hat* (of soft felt &c.). [f. OF *esquasser* f. pop. L *EX(*quassare* see QUASH)]

squash[2] (ŏ-), n. Kinds of gourd. [f. Amer.-Ind. *askutasquash*]

squat (-ŏt), v.i. & t., a., & n. Sit on ground &c. with knees drawn up & heels close to or touching hams, crouch with hams resting on backs of heels; put (oneself, person) into this position; (of animals) crouch close to ground; (colloq.) sit (*down, on,* &c.). (Adj.) in squatting posture; (of person &c.) short & thick, dumpy. (N.) squatting posture; s. person. [(adj. & n. f. vb) f. OF *esquatir* flatten (*es-* EX- + *quatir* f. L *coactus*, see COGENT)]

squa·tter, n. In vbl senses; also: (Austral.) person who gets right of pasturage from government on easy terms, also, any stock-owner; person who settles on new esp. public land without title. [f. prec. + -ER¹)]

squaw, n. Amer.-Indian woman or wife; *s.-man,* white married to s. [f. native *squa*]

squawk, v.i., & n. (Chiefly of birds) utter harsh cry of pain or fear; (n.) such cry. [imit.]

squeak, v.i. & t., & n. Utter short shrill cry as of mouse or unoiled hinge; utter (words) shrilly; (slang) turn informer, peach. (N.) short shrill sound, whence **squea·ki**LY² adv., **squea·k**Y² a.; (*narrow*) *s.*, narrow escape, success barely attained; BUBBLE¹-*and-s.* [imit., cf. Sw. *sqväka* croak]

squea·ker, n. In vbl senses; also, young bird esp. pigeon. [-ER¹]

squeal, v.i. & t., & n. Utter shrill cry as of child from pain, fear, anger, joy, &c.; utter (words) thus; (slang) protest excitedly e.g. against taxation; (slang) turn informer; *make* one *s.* (slang), blackmail him; (n.) shrill cry of child, pig, &c. [imit.]

squea·ler, n. In vbl senses; also, young bird esp. pigeon. [-ER¹]

squea·mish, a. Easily nauseated; fastidious, overnice, overscrupulous in questions of propriety, honesty, &c. Hence **squea·mish**LY² adv., **squea·mish**NESS n. [earlier *squeamous* f. AF *escoymous* etym. dub., altered to -ISH¹]

squee·gee (*or* -ē·), **squi·lgee,** nn., & vv.t. Rubber-edged implement for sweeping wet deck or road; small similar instrument or roller used in photography; (v.t.) treat with s. [*squee-* f. *squil-* etym. dub. (also *squillage*), altered on SQUEEZE]

squeeze, v.t. & i., & n. Exert pressure upon (sponge, lemon, &c.) esp. in order to extract moisture, compress with hand or between two bodies, as *s.* person's *hand* (as sign of sympathy, affection, &c.), *squeezed orange* fig., person, thing, from whom or which no more is to be had, *was squeezed to death in the crowd*; thrust (one*self,* person, thing, *into* vehicle, room, &c., *out of,* &c.) forcibly; make one's way by squeezing (*into* &c.); harass by exactions, extort money &c. from; constrain, bring pressure to bear on, as *could s. the government to any extent*; get (money &c. *out of* person &c.) by extortion, entreaty, &c.; produce with effort (*a tear* &c.); take impression of (coin &c.) esp. with sheets of damp paper. (N.) application of pressure, as *gave him a s.* (*of the hand*); crowd, crush, as *we all got in, but it was a* (*tight*) *s.*; impression of coin &c., esp. as above. Hence **squeeza**BI·LITY n., **squee·z**ABLE a. [cf. obs. *quease, squize, squiss,* & OE *cwésan*]

squee·zer, n. In vbl senses; also or esp.: machine for expressing air-bubbles &c. from puddled iron; (pl.) playing-cards with value shown at top right-hand corner so that they need not be opened out. [-ER¹]

squelch, v.t. & i., & n., (colloq.). Stamp on, crush flat, put an end to; disconcert, silence; make sucking sound as of hoof drawn out of thick mud; (n.) act or sound of squelching. [imit.]

squib, n., & v.t. & i. Firework thrown by hand & exploding like rocket or burning with hissing sound; tube of gunpowder used to fire a charge; short satirical composition, lampoon; (vb) write, attack with, lampoons. [f. 16th c., etym. dub.]

squid, n., & v.i. Kind of cuttle-fish used as bait; kinds of artificial bait; (v.i.) fish with s. [?]

squi·ffer, n. (slang). Concertina. [?]

squi·ffy, a. Slightly drunk. [?]

squilgee. See SQUEEGEE.

squill, n. Plant of lily family; its bulb, used as diuretic, purgative, &c.; (also *s.-fish*) a crustacean. [f. L *squilla* f. Gk *skilla*]

squinch, n. Straight or arched structure across interior angle of square tower as support for side of octagon. [var. of obs. *scunch* abbr. of SCUNCHEON]

squint, v.i. & t., n., & a. Have the eyes turned in different directions, have strabismus; look obliquely (*at* &c.); close (eyes) quickly, hold (eyes) half-shut. Hence **squi·nt**ER¹ n. (N.) affection of eyes in which their axes are differently directed, as *has a fearful s.*; stealthy or sidelong glance; (colloq.) glance, look, as *let's have a s. at it*; leaning, inclination, (*to, towards,* policy &c.); oblique opening through wall of church esp. affording view of altar from transept. (Adj.) squinting, looking different ways; *s.-eyed,* (fig.) malignant. [f. obs. adv. *squint* obliquely, abbr. ASQUINT]

squire, n., & v.t. Country gentleman, esp. *the* chief landed proprietor in a district; woman's escort or gallant; *s. of dames,* man who is attentive to or frequents company of women; (Hist.) attendant on knight; (v.t., of man) attend upon, escort, (woman). Hence **squire·**HOOD, **squire·**LET, **squire·**LING¹, **squire·**SHIP, nn., **squire·**LY¹ a. [as ESQUIRE]

squire·archy (-kĭ), n. Government by, influence of, landed proprietors esp. before Reform Bill of 1832; the class of landed proprietors, so **squire·arch** n.

Hence **squire·archAL, squirear·chICAL,** aa. [f. prec. + Gk *-arkhia* rule f. *arkhō*]
squiree·n, n. Small landed proprietor esp. in Ireland. [f. SQUIRE + *-een* dim. suf.]
squirm, v.i., & n. Wriggle, writhe; (fig.) show, feel, embarrassment or discomfiture; (n.) wriggling movement, (Naut.) twist in rope. [imit.]
squi·rrel, n. Kinds of rodent quadruped of active arboreal habits with bushy tail & pointed ears; *barking s.*, prairie-dog; *s.-fish*, kinds of fish covered with sharp spines; *s.-hawk*, large hawk preying on ss.; *s.-monkey*, marmoset & other small monkeys; *s.-tail*, kinds of grass allied to barley. [f. OF *escureul* f. med. L *scurellus* irreg. dim. of L f. Gk *skiouros* (pop. explained as f. *skia* shadow + *oura* tail)]
squirt, v.t. & i., & n. Eject (liquid, powder) in a jet as from syringe; (of liquid &c.) be discharged thus. (N.) syringe; jet *of* water &c.; (also *s.-gun*) kind of toy syringe; (colloq.) insignificant self-assertive fellow. [(n. f. vb) cf. LG *swirtjen*]
St. For St Andrew &c. see SAINT.
stab, v.t. & i., & n. Pierce, wound, with (usu. short) pointed weapon e.g. knife or dagger; aim blow with such weapon (*at*); (fig.) inflict sharp pain on (person, his feelings, conscience, &c.), aim blow *at* (reputation, person, &c.); *s.* (vb & n.) *in the back*, slander; roughen (brick wall) with pick before plastering; (n.) blow, thrust, with knife &c., wound thus made, blow or pain inflicted on person's feelings. Hence **sta·bbER**[1] n. [n. f. 15th, vb f. 16th, c.; etym. dub.]
Stā·băt Mā·ter (*or* stah-, mah-), n. (Musical setting for) Latin hymn on agony of the Virgin Mary at the crucifixion. [L, = the mother was standing, first wds of the hymn]
stā·ble[1], a. Firmly fixed or established, not easily to be moved or changed or destroyed, as *doubt whether the structure is s.*; firm, resolute, not wavering nor fickle, as *the only s. politician of his day*; *s.* EQUILIBRIUM. Hence or cogn. **stabi·lITY, stăbilizA·TION, sta·bleNESS,** nn., **stă·bilIZE**(3) v.t., **sta·bilizER**[1] n. (esp. = aircraft's fixed horizontal tailplane), **stā·bLY**[2] adv. [f. OF *estable* f. L *stabilis* (*stare* stand, see -BLE)]
stā·ble[2], n., & v.t. & i. Building set apart & adapted for lodging & feeding horses or (less usu.) cattle; race-horses of particular s.; AUGEAN *ss.*; *s.-boy, -man* (-mn), (employed in s.); *s.-call*, cavalry signal for grooming & watering horses; *s.-companion*, horse of same stable, (colloq.) member of same school, club, &c.; (v.t.) put, keep, horse in s., as *where can we s. our horses?*; (v.i., of horse &c., fig. of person) be stabled, as *must s. where they can.* [f. OF *estable* f. L *stabulum* (*stare* stand)]
sta·bling, n. In vbl senses of prec., esp. accommodation for horses &c. [-ING[1]]
stă·blish, v.t. (archaic). Fix firmly, establish, set up. [as ESTABLISH]
stacca·to (-kah-), a. & adv. (To be played) in abrupt sharply detached manner, cf. LEGATO; *s. mark*, dot above or below s. note. [It.]
stack, n., & v.t. Circular or rectangular pile of grain in sheaf or of hay, straw, &c., usu. with sloping thatched top; *s.-funnel*, pyramidal frame ventilating centre of s.; *s.-stand* (on which s. is built for dryness & exclusion of vermin); (as measure of wood) pile of 108 cub. ft; pile, heap, of anything; (colloq.) large quantity, as *have ss., a whole s., of work to get through first*; pyramidal group of rifles, pile; number of chimneys standing together; (also *smoke-s.*) chimney, funnel, of locomotive or steamer; high detached rock esp. off coast of Scotland & Orkneys; (v.t.) pile in s., *s.* (= PILE[3]) *arms.* [(vb f. n.) f. ON *stakkr* haystack, cf. Sw. *stack* stack]
sta·ctē, n. A sweet spice used by ancient Jews in making incense. [f. L f. Gk *staktē* oil trickling from myrrh &c. (*stazō* drip)]
stactŏ·meter, n. Tube for measuring a liquid in drops. [f. Gk *staktos* vbl adj. f. *stazō* drip + -METER]
stā·dium, n. (pl. *-ia*). (Gk Ant.) measure of length, about 202 yds, course for foot-race; modern athletic ground; (Med.) stage, period, of disease. [L, f. Gk *stadion* (*sta-* stand)]
sta·d(t)hōlder (stahd-, staht-, stă-), n. (hist.). Viceroy or governor of province or town in Netherlands; chief magistrate of United Provinces. Hence **sta·d(t)-holderSHIP** n. [altered f. Du. *stadhouder* deputy (*stad* STEAD + *houder* HOLDER)]
staff[1], n. (pl. now *staffs* exc. Mus. *staves*). Stick, pole, for use in walking or climbing or as weapon (now chiefly fig.), as *bread is the s.* (support) *of life, you are the s. of his old age*, QUARTER[1]-*s.*; this as sign of office or authority, as *pastoral s.* (borne by or before bishop &c.); shaft, pole, as support or handle, as FLAG[4]*s.*; stick used in surveying &c., esp. JACOB'S *s.*; kinds of instrument for taking altitude at sea, as *back, cross, fore, -s.*; surgeon's steel instrument for guiding knife into bladder; (Mil.) body of officers assisting officer in high command & concerned with army or regiment as a whole, as *regimental s., general s.* (at main headquarters of army, acting as personal s. of commander-in-chief), *s. officer, -sergeant*, (serving on s.), *s. college* (in which officers are prepared for s. as opp. to regimental duties); body of persons carrying on work under manager &c., as *editorial s. of newspaper, diplomatic s.*, whence **(-)staffED**[2] a.; (Mus.) set of five parallel lines on any one or between any

two of which a note is placed to indicate its pitch, *s. notation* (by means of s., esp. opp. to TONIC *sol-fa*). [OE *stæf*, cf. Du. *staf*, G *stab*, ON *stafr*]

staff², n. Mixture of plaster-of-Paris, cement, &c., as building-material. [?]

stag, n. Male of red deer or of other large kinds of deer; bull castrated when (nearly) full-grown; (St. Exch.) person who applies for allotments in new concerns with a view to selling at once at a profit; (slang) irregular dealer in stocks; *s.-beetle* (with branched mandibles like s.'s antlers); *s.-evil*, lockjaw in horses; *s.-horn*, kinds of club-moss & coral; *sta·ghound*, large kinds of hound hunting deer by sight or scent. [cf. ON *steggr*, *-gi*, he-bird]

stage¹, n. Raised floor or platform, e.g. scaffold for workmen's use in building, *hanging s.* (suspended on ropes for painters' use), *landing-s.* (at quay &c. for landing from vessel), surface on which object is placed for inspection through microscope; platform on which plays, &c. are exhibited; (fig.) the drama, dramatic art or literature, actor's profession, as *went on the s.*, became actor, *the French s.*; (fig.) scene of action, as *quitted the s. of politics, the s. of his operations, a larger s. opened to him*; point or period in development &c., as *reached a critical s., at this s. an interruption occurred, passed through a long s. of inactivity, is in the hoyden s., larval s.*; regular stopping-place in route, distance between two of these, as *travelled by easy stages, got down at the next s.*; *s.-coach*, coach running regularly by ss. between two places, *s.-coachman*, driver of this; *s.-craft*, skill or experience in writing or staging plays; *s. direction*, written or printed instruction in play as to movement, position, tone, &c., of actor; *s. door*, actors' & workmen's entrance at back of s.; *s. effect*, effect produced in acting or on the s., artificial or theatrical effect produced in real life; *s. fever*, inordinate desire to go on the s.; *s. fright*, nervousness on facing audience esp. for first time; *s. manager*, person superintending production of play, managing rehearsals, &c.; *s. right*, exclusive right to perform particular play; *s.-struck*, struck with s. fever; *s. whisper*, aside, whisper meant to be heard by others than the person addressed. [f. OF *estage* f. L **staticum* (*stare* stand)]

stage², v.t. & i. Put (play) on stage; (of play) lend itself to representation, as *does not s. well*. [f. prec.]

stā·ger, n. *Old s.*, experienced person, old hand. [STAGE¹ + -ER¹]

sta·ggard, -t, n. Stag four years old. [-ARD]

sta·gger (-g-), v.i. & t., & n. Walk or stand unsteadily, totter; hesitate, waver in purpose; cause to totter, as *received a staggering blow*; cause to hesitate or waver, as *the question staggered him, his resolution*; arrange in zigzag order, esp. set (spokes of wheel) leaning alternately to right & left. Hence **sta·ggering**LY² adv. (N.) tottering movement; (Mech.) overhanging or slantwise or zigzag arrangement of like parts in a structure &c.; (pl., also *blind ss.*) kinds of disease of brain & spinal cord esp. in horses & cattle; (pl.) giddiness. [(n. f.vb) earlier *stacker* f. ON *stakra* frequent. of *staka* push]

sta·ggerer, n. In vbl senses, esp. disconcerting argument, objection, event, &c. [-ER¹]

sta·ging, n. Putting play on stage; driving or running stage-coaches; scaffolding. [-ING¹]

Stă·girite (-j-), n. *The S.*, Aristotle. [f. L f. Gk *Stageiritēs* native of *Stageira* (-ITE¹)]

sta·gnate, v.i. (Of liquid) be(come) motionless, have no current, cease to flow; (of life, action, mind, business, person) be(come) dull or sluggish. Hence or cogn. **sta·gn**ANCY, **stagn**A·TION, nn., **sta·gn**ANT a., **sta·gnant**LY² adv. [f. L *stagnare* (*stagnum* pool), -ATE³]

stagnĭ·colous, a. Living in swamps or stagnant water. [f. L *stagnum* pool + *colere* inhabit + -OUS]

sta·gy (-jĭ), a. Theatrical in manner, style, appearance, &c. Hence **sta·gi**NESS n. [f. STAGE¹ + -Y²]

staid, a. Of steady & sober character; sedate. Hence **stai·d**LY² adv., **stai·d**NESS n. [= *stayed* p.p. of STAY]

stain, v.t. & i., & n. Discolour, make foul, soil, as *cigarettes s. the fingers, wine will s. the cloth, warranted not to s. clothes*; (fig.) sully, blemish, (reputation, name, person; p.p. often in comb., as *guilt, sin, -stained*); colour (wood, glass, &c.) by process other than painting or covering the surface; impregnate (substance) for microscopic examination with colouring matter that acts more powerfully on some parts than on others; print colours on (wall-paper). Hence **stai·n**ABLE a., **stai·n**ER¹ n. (N.) discoloration, spot or mark caused esp. by contact with foreign matter, as *cloth is covered with tea-ss.*; staining-material; (fig.) blot, blemish, as *without a s. on his character*. Hence **stai·n**LESS a. (usu. of reputation, also of kind of cutler's steel), **stai·nless**LY² adv. [(n. f. vb) also obs. *distain* f. OF *desteindre* f. DIS- + L *tingere* dye]

stair, n. Each of a set of (now usu. indoor) steps, as *the top s. but one*; (now usu. pl.) set of these, as *passed him on the ss., down a winding s.*; *flight, pair, of ss.*, set of ss. in continuous straight line or from one landing to another; *below ss.*, in the basement of house esp. as part belonging to servants, as *was coolly* *discussed below ss.* (by the servants); *down, up, ss.,* on, to, the lower, upper, floor(s) of house; BACK[1]*s.*; *stair·case,* (part of building containing) flight of ss., *corkscrew s.-c.* (winding round central pillar); *s.-rod* (for securing s.-carpet in angle between two steps. [OE *stǣger*, cf. Du. *steiger*, cogn. w. OE *stīgan*, OHG *stīgan*, ON *stīga*, & Gk *steikhō*, go up, go]

stake, n., & v.t. Stick sharpened at one end & driven into ground as support, boundary mark, &c.; post to which person is bound to be burnt alive, (fig.) death by burning, as *was condemned to, suffered at, the s.*; tinsmith's small anvil fixed on bench by pointed prop; money &c. wagered on an event, esp. deposited with third party (*sta·keholder*) by each of those who make a wager, (pl.) money to be contended for esp. in horse-race, (pl.) such race, as *maiden, trial, ss.*; *have a s. in the country,* be materially concerned in its welfare, e.g. as landowner; (fig.) principle &c. contended for, as *consider the immensity of the s.*; *at s.*, at issue, in question, risked, as *life itself is at s.*; *s.-boat* (anchored to mark course for boat-race &c.); *s.-net,* fishing-net hung on ss. (Vb) fasten, secure, support, with s. or ss.; mark *off, out* (area) with ss.; wager, risk, (money &c. *on* event &c.). [(vb f. n.) OE *staca*, cf. MDu. *stake*; cogn. w. STICK]

stala·ctite (*or* stă·-), Deposit of carbonate of lime, usu. in form like large icicle, hanging from roof of cave &c. & formed by trickling of water. Hence **stala·c·tic**, **stala·ctiform**, **stălacti·tic**, aa. [f. mod. L *stalactītēs* (Gk *stalaktos* vbl adj. f. *stalassō* drip, see -ITE[1])]

stala·gmite (*or* stă·-), n. Deposit as prec. on floor of cave &c. often uniting with stalactite. Hence **stălagmi·tic** a., **stalagmi·tically** adv. [f. mod. L *stalagmītēs* (Gk *stalagmos* dripping, as prec.)]

stale[1], a., n., & v.t. & i. Not fresh, insipid, musty, or otherwise the worse for age; *s. bread* (musty; also, not of the day's baking, as *s. bread is best for toast*); (fig.) lacking novelty, trite, as *s. joke, news, devices*; (of athlete) overtrained; *stalema·te* (Chess), draw resulting from player's having no move available, his king not being in check, (v.t.) reduce (player) to this position, (fig.) bring to a standstill. Hence **sta·lely**[2] adv., **sta·leness** n. (N.) urine of horses & cattle. (Vb) make s. or common; (of horse &c.) make water. [n. f. vb, prob. f. OF *estaler* make water, cf. It. *stallare*, Du. & MHG *stallen*, Sw. *stalla*, Da. *stallen*; adj. perh. also f. vb (cf. Flem. *stel* adj., used of beer & urine), or f. Teut. *sta-* stand; *stale(mate)* perh. f. OF *estaler* f. OE as STALL vb]

stale[2], n. (archaic). Decoy bird; dupe, laughing-stock. [prob. f. AF *estale* of Teut. orig. cf. OE *stæl(hrān* reindeer) decoy reindeer f. *stellan* to place]

stalk[1] (-awk), v.i. & t., & n. Stride, walk in stately or imposing manner (often *along* &c.); steal up to game under cover; pursue (game) stealthily; *stalking-horse,* horse behind which hunter conceals himself, (fig.) pretext. (N.) stalking of game, imposing gait. Hence **(-)stalker**[1] n. [OE *stealcian* walk warily, cogn. w. STEAL]

stalk[2] (-awk), n. (Bot.) stem, main axis, of plant, (loosely) any support of an organ; s.-like support of organ &c. in animals; stem of wine-glass &c.; (Archit.) ornament like s. of plant; tall chimney of factory &c.; *s.-eyed,* (of crab &c.) having the eyes mounted on ss. Hence **(-)stalked**[2], **stal·kless** aa., **stal·klet** n. [ME *stalke* perh. dim. f. OE *stalu* side or rung of ladder]

stall[1] (-awl), n., & v.t. & i. (Single compartment for one animal in) stable, cowhouse; FINGER-*s.*; booth in market &c., compartment in a building, for sale of goods, table in this on which goods are exposed, as *picked it up in* or *on a book-s.*; fixed seat in choir or chancel of church more or less enclosed at back & sides & often canopied, esp. one appropriated to clergyman, as *canon's, dean's, s.,* (fig.) office, dignity, of canon &c., as *how long has he had his s.?*; each of a set of seats in theatre usu. between pit & stage; working-compartment in coal-mine; *s.-feed,* fatten (cattle) in s., so *s.-fed* a. (Vb) place, keep, (cattle &c.) in s. esp. for fattening, as *a stalled ox*; furnish (stable &c.) with ss.; (of horse or cart) stick fast as in mud or snow, (of motor-engine) stop working, (of aeroplane or airman) become unstable by loss of pace. [(vb f. n.) OE *steal(l)*, cf. Du. *stal*, G *stall*, ON *stallr*; cogn. w. STABLE]

stall[2] (-awl), n. Pickpocket's confederate who diverts attention during theft & assists thief's escape &c. [var. of STALE[2]]

sta·llage (-ĭj), n. Space for, rent for, right to erect, stall(s) in market &c. [AF *estalage* (*estal* STALL[1], -AGE)]

stă·llion, n. Uncastrated male horse, esp. one kept for breeding. [f. OF *estalon* (OHG *stal* STALL[1], see -OON), so called because kept in stall]

stalwart (staw·lwert), a. & n. Strongly built, sturdy; courageous, resolute, determined, as *s. supporters*; (n., Pol.) strong party man. Hence **sta·lwartly**[2] adv., **sta·lwartness** n. [earlier *stalworth*, OE *stǣl-wyrthe*, prob. for *statholwyrthe* (*stathol* foundation + *wyrthe* WORTH]

stā·men, n. Male organ of flowering plants, organ containing pollen. Hence **(-)stamened**[2], **stami·neal**, **stami·neous**, **stamini·ferous**, aa. [L, gen. *-minis*, = warp in upright loom, thread]

stă·mina, n. Staying-power, power of

endurance. [L pl. of prec. now usu. as sing.]

stă·minal, a. Of stamens or stamina. [-AL]

stă·minate (-*at*), a. Having stamens but no pistils; having stamens. [-ATE²(2)]

sta·mmer, v.i. & t., & n. Speak (habitually, or on occasion from embarrassment &c.) with halting articulation esp. with rapid repetitions of same syllable, whence **sta·mmer**ER¹ n., **sta·mmering**LY² adv.; utter (words) thus, as *stammered out an excuse*; (n.) stammering speech, tendency to s. [OE *stamerian*, cf. Du. *stameren*, G *stammeln*]

stamp, v.t. & i., & n. Impress pattern, name, mark, upon (metal, butter, paper, &c.) with die or similar instrument of metal, wood, rubber, &c.; affix postage or other s. to (envelope, document); crush, pulverize, (ores &c.); bring down one's foot, bring down (foot), heavily on ground; *s. out*, put an end to, crush, destroy, (rebellion &c.); assign a character to, characterize, as *this alone stamps the story* (*as*) *a slander*; impress *on* the memory. Hence **(-)sta·mp**ER¹(1, 2) n. (N.) instrument for stamping pattern or mark; mark made by this; impression of official mark required to be made for revenue purposes on deeds, bills of exchange, &c., as evidence of payment of tax; piece of paper impressed with official mark as evidence of payment of tax or fee & meant to be affixed to letter, postcard, receipted account, &c.; mark impressed on, label &c. affixed to, commodity as evidence of quality &c. (fig.) characteristic mark, impress, as *bears the s. of genius*; character, kind, as *avoid men of that* or *his s*; block that crushes ore in s.-mill; heavy downward blow with foot; *s. act*, act concerned with s.-duty, esp. that imposing duty on American colonies in 1765 & repealed in 1766; *s.-collector* (of postage-ss. as curiosities); *s.-duty* (imposed on certain kinds of legal instrument); *s.-machine* (for beating rags &c. into pulp for paper); *s.-mill* (for crushing ore &c.); *s.-office* (for issue of government ss. & receipt of s.-duty &c.). [ME *stampen*, cf. Du. *stampen*, G *stampfen*; or f. OF *estamper* f. Teut.]

stampe·de, n., & v.i. & t. Sudden fright & scattering of a number of horses or cattle; sudden flight or hurried movement of soldiers due to panic; (U.S. Polit.) unconcerted movement of many persons by common impulse; (vb) (cause to) take part in s. [f. Sp. *estampida* crash]

stance, n. (golf, cricket). Position taken for stroke. [OF, f. It. STANZA]

stanch¹, staunch, (-ah-, -aw-), v.t. Check the flow of (esp. blood); check the flow from (esp. wound). [f. OF *estanchier*, cf. It. *stancare* to weary, perh. f. L as STAGNATE]

stanch² &c. See STAUNCH &c.

sta·nchion (-shn), n., & v.t. Post, pillar, upright support; upright bar, pair of bars, for confining cattle in stall; (v.t.) supply with s., fasten (cattle) to s. [(vb f. n.) f. OF *estanchon* dim. of OF *estance* prop f. pop. L as STANZA]

stand¹, v.i. & t. (stŏŏd). Have or take or maintain upright position, be set upright, as *tell him to s. up*, *s. at* EASE¹, *s.* EASY, *s. in* person's LIGHT¹, *in the* BREACH¹, *stood there till I was tired*, *was too weak to s.*, *chair will not s. on two legs*, *hair stands on end* (with terror); be of specified height, as *stands six foot three*; be situated, be, as *on each side s. two pillars*, *a stranger stood in the doorway*, *the cups s. on the top shelf*, *here once stood a huge oak*; assume stationary position, as *s. still*, *was commanded to s.*, *s.* (*& deliver*) *!*, highwayman's order; maintain position, avoid falling or moving or being moved, as *don't s. there arguing*, *house will s. another century*, *whether we s. or fall*, *has stood through worse storms*, *s. on* one's *own* BOTTOM¹, *s. fast*, *s. firm*, *all standing* (naut. & transf.), without time to lower sails or prepare; *it stands to reason*, it is logically demonstrable (*that*), (pop.) I shall lose my temper if you deny (*that*); hold good, remain valid or unaltered, as *the former conditions may s.*, *the passage must s.*, *the same remark stands good*; be, find oneself, in specified situation, rank, &c., as *stands convicted of treachery*, *in need of help*, *in an awkward position*, *under heavy obligations*, *I s. corrected* (accept correction); *thermometer stood at 90°*, *corn stands higher* (is dearer) *than ever*, *the matter stands thus*, *stands first on the list*, *alone among his contemporaries*, *in the same relation to both parties*, *stands well* (is on good terms or in good odour) *with the authorities*, *how do we s. in the matter of* (have we enough or suitable) *horses?*, *I s. prepared to dispute it*, *s. in awe of*, *have often stood his friend*, *s. at* BAY⁴; move to & remain in specified position, as *s. back*, *clear*, *aside*, *aloof*, *away*; (Naut.) hold specified course, as *s. in for the shore*; (of dog) point, set; place, set, in upright or specified position, as *s. the jug on the table*, *s. it against the wall*, *shall s. you in the corner* (as punishment); endure without succumbing or complaining, as *nerves could not s. the strain*, *how does he s. pain?*, *could never s. the fellow*, *shall s. no nonsense*, *can't s. these French matches*, *s. fire* (receive fire of enemy without giving way), *failed to s. the test*; *s.* one's *ground*, maintain one's position (lit., & fig. of argument &c.); undergo (trial), be faced with (CHANCE¹); provide at one's expense, as *stood him a drink*, *stood a bottle to the company*, *who is going to s. treat?*; *s. by* (prep.), uphold, support, side with, (person), adhere to, abide by, (terms, promise), (Naut.) take or s. ready to take hold of (anchor &c.); *s. by* (adv.), stand near, be a bystander, stand & look on, as *will not s. by & see him ill-treated,* (orig. naut.) stand ready, be on the alert; *s.-by,* thing, person, that one can depend upon; *s. down,* retire from witness-box or similar position; *s. for,* represent, signify, imply, as *P.O. stands for postal order, tariff reform stands for a great deal more than that,* be candidate for (office), be candidate for representation of (constituency) in Parliament, espouse the cause of (free trade &c.); s. (person) *in* (sum), cost, as *coat stood me in £4, wife stands him in £50 yearly for motor tires*; s. (person) *in good* STEAD; *s. in with,* be in league with; *s. off,* move away, keep one's distance; *s. off & on* (naut.), sail alternately away from & towards shore so as to keep a point in sight; *s. on* (prep.), insist on, observe scrupulously, esp. *s. on ceremony*; *s. on* (adv., naut.), continue on same course; *s. out,* hold out, persist in opposition (*against*) or endurance, be prominent or conspicuous; *s. over,* be postponed; *s. to* (prep.), abide by (promise &c.), stick to, not desert, (one's *post, guns,* esp. fig., *duty,* &c.), *s. to it,* maintain stoutly (*that*), *s. to sea* (naut.), sail out to sea; *s. to* (adv., archaic), fall to, set to work; *s. to win, lose,* have one's bets or other dispositions so made that one is sure to win or lose something or a specified amount (*whoever loses, I s. to win*; *how much do you s. to lose?*; *if Ladas is scratched I s. to win £5000*); *s. up,* rise to one's feet from sitting or other position, maintain erect position; *s. up for,* side with, maintain, support, (person, cause); *s. upon,* = *s. on*; *s. up to,* meet, face, (opponent) courageously; *s. up with,* take one's place with (partner) for dance, dance with; *s.-o·ffish* a., distant, reserved, not affable, whence *s.-offishly* adv., *s.-offishness* n.; *s.-up* a., (of collar) upright, high, opp. to *turn-down,* (of fight) thorough, fair & square. [OE *standan, ston-,* cf. Goth. *standan,* ON *standa*; cogn. w. L *stare,* Gk *histēmi* (st. *sta-*)]

stand[2], n. Cessation from motion or progress, stoppage, as *came, was brought, to a s.*; *be at a s.* (archaic), be unable to proceed, be in perplexity; stationary condition assumed for purpose of resistance, esp. *make a s.* (*against* enemy, *for, against,* principle &c.); position taken up, as *took his s. near the door, I take my s.* (base argument &c., rely) *on the precise wording of the act*; table, set of shelves, rack, &c., on or in which things may be placed, as *music, hat, umbrella, -s.*; INK*s.*; WASH-(*hand-*)*s.*; stall in market &c., as *fruit-s.*; standing-place for vehicles &c., as CAB[1]-S.; raised structure for persons to sit or stand on, as BAND[1]*s.*, GRAND *s.*; standing growth (*of* clover &c.); *s. of arms,* complete set for one man; *s. of colours,* regiment's flags; *s.-pipe,* vertical pipe for various purposes; *sta·ndpoint,* point of view; *s.-rest,* high stool with sloping top for supporting person standing at easel &c.; *sta·ndstill,* stoppage, inability to proceed, as *am brought to a s.-s.* [f. prec.]

sta·ndard, n. Distinctive flag, esp. flag of cavalry regiment (opp. to *colours* of infantry), as *the* (*English*) *royal s.* (square banner with national arms), (fig.) rallying principle (*raise the s. of revolt, free trade*); weight or measure to which others conform or by which the accuracy of others is judged (often attrib., as *s. pound, yard,* &c.); thing serving as basis of comparison; degree of excellence &c. required for particular purpose, as *does not come up to the s., must set a low s.*. thing recognized as model for imitation &c., esp. attrib., as *the s. work on the subject, s. novels* (those of admitted merit); average quality, as *work was of a low s.*; *monetary s.,* proportion of weight of fine metal & alloy in gold or silver coin (*gold, silver, s.*) or in both (*double s.*); *multiple, tabular, s.,* s. of value obtained by averaging prices of a number of products; upright support (often attrib., as *s. lamp,* set on tall usu. telescopic pillar); upright water or gas pipe; tree, shrub, that stands alone without support; shrub grafted on upright stem & trained in tree form; *s.-bearer,* soldier who bears s., (fig.) prominent leader in a cause; *s. bread* (wheaten, of mixed flours). [ME, f. OF *estandard & estendard* (f. L as EXTEND + -ARD); partly also f. STAND[1]]

sta·ndardize, v.t. Make to conform to standard; (Chem.) obtain by analysis specific value of (solution &c.) for purposes of comparison. Hence **standardiz**A·TION n. [-IZE]

sta·nding[1], n. In vbl senses; esp.: estimation in which one is held, repute, position, as *men of high s., is of no s.*; duration, as *a dispute of long s.*; *s.-room,* space to stand in. [-ING[1]]

sta·nding[2], a. In vbl senses, esp.: established, as *a s. rule, has become a s.* (stock) *jest*; permanent, not made, raised, &c., for the occasion, as *s. army, s. orders* (esp. those respecting manner in which business shall be conducted in Parliament), *s. rigging* (fixed stays); *s. corn* (not cut); *s. jump* (performed without preliminary run); s. (stagnant) *water.* [-ING[2]]

sta·ndish, n. (archaic). Ink-stand. [STAND + DISH]

sta·ndpatter, n. (U.S.). Politician who is for strict adherence to party platform, esp. on tariffs. [f. *stand pat* in poker, = = abide by hand dealt to one]

stă·nhope (-nop), n. Light open carriage of 2 or 4 wheels; (also *S. press*) iron printing press invented by Lord S.; *S. lens* (with convex surfaces of different curves). [name of inventors]

stă·niel, n. Kestrel. [OE *stángella* (*stán* stone + *gellan* YELL)]

stank. See STINK v.

sta·nnary, n. & a. Tin-miNE; tin-mining district; *s. court* (for regulation of tin-mines in Cornwall & Devon). [f. med. L *stannaria* n. (LL *stannum*, *stag-*, tin, see -ARY[1])]

sta·nnic, a. (chem.). Of tin esp. in its higher valence, as *s. acid.* So **sta·nnATE**[1](3) n., **stanni·**FEROUS, **sta·nn**OUS, aa. [f. LL *stannum* tin + -IC]

sta·nza, n. Group of (usu. four or more) rhymed lines, as *Spenserian s.*; group of four lines in some Greek & Latin metres, esp. *Alcaic, Sapphic, s.* Hence **(-)stanza'd, -za**ED[2], **stanzā·**IC, aa. [It., = chamber, stanza, f. pop. L **stantia* abode (*stare* stand, see -ANCE)]

stā·ple[1], n., & v.t. Hoop-shaped bar or piece of wire with pointed ends for driving into post &c. to take point of hook, hasp, &c.; box-shaped part into which lock of door &c. shuts; metal tube holding the reeds of oboe & similar instruments; bent wire used in wire-stitching; (v.t.) furnish, fasten, with s.; *stapling - machine,* bookbinder's wire - stitching machine. [(vb f. n.) OE *stapul,* cf. Du. *stapel* chair-leg, Da. *stabel* stake, G *staffel* rung, step, *stapel* stake; prob. cogn. w. STEP]

stā·ple[2], n., a., & v.t. Important or principal article of commerce, as *the ss. of that country, of British industry*; raw material; (fig.) chief element or material, as *formed the s. of conversation*; fibre of cotton, wool, &c., viewed as determining its quality, as *cotton of fine, short, s.*; (adj.) *s.* (principal) *commodities* &c.; (v.t.) sort, classify, (wool &c.) according to fibre, whence **sta·pl**ER[1] n. [(vb & adj. f. n.) = market, f. OF *estaple* f. MLG *stapel,* = prec.]

star[1], n. Celestial body appearing as luminous point; (also *fixed s.*) such body so far from earth as to appear motionless except for diurnal revolution of the heavens; *double, multiple, s.,* group of two, of three to six, fixed ss. appearing to naked eye as one, *binary s.,* two ss. revolving round one another; EVENING, MORNING, *s.*; *day·star* (poet.), morning star, sun; LODEs.; *north, polar,* (= POLE[2]-) *s.*; *shooting s.,* small meteor appearing like s. moving rapidly and disappearing; thing suggesting s. by its shape, esp. figure or object with radiating points e.g. as decoration of an order; *ss. & stripes,* U.S. national flag; asterisk; white spot on forehead of horse &c.; (Pool) additional life bought by player whose lives are lost; principal actor in a company (*the s. system,* of relying on a s. or two to make up for weak company); brilliant or prominent person, as *literary s., bright particular s.* (object of one's devotion); heavenly body considered as influencing person's fortunes &c., as *born under an unlucky s., his s. was in the ascendant, you may thank your ss. you were not there, the ss. were against it* (cf. ILL-*starred*); *S.-chamber* [perh. diff. wd], court of civil & criminal jurisdiction primarily concerned with offences affecting crown interests, noted for summary & arbitrary procedure, & abolished 1640; *s.-drift,* common proper motion of a number of fixed ss. in same region; *star-finch,* redstart; *star·fish,* echinoderm with five or more radiating arms; *s.-gazer* (facet.), astronomer; *star·light,* light of ss., as *walked home by s.-l.,* (adj., also *star·lit*) lighted by the ss., as a *s.-l. night*; *s. of Bethlehem,* plant of lily family with s.-like white flowers striped with green on outside; *S. of India,* order of knighthood instituted 1861 to commemorate assumption of direct government of India; *s. shell,* kind designed to burst in air & light up enemy's position; *s.-spangled,* spangled with ss. (esp. of U.S. flag); *s.-stone,* kind of sapphire. Hence **star·**LET n., **star·**LESS, **star·**LIKE, **star·ry**[2], aa. [OE *steorra,* cf. Du. *ster,* G *stern,* ON *stjarna,* & L *stella,* Gk *astēr*]

star[2], v.t. & i. Set, adorn, (as) with stars (esp. in p.p.); affix asterisk to (name in list &c.); appear as star actor; (Pool) buy additional life. [f. prec.]

star·board (-*erd*), n., & v.t. Right side of vessel looking forward (cf. PORT[5], LARBOARD; often attrib.); (v.t.) turn, put, (helm) to s. [(vb f. n.) OE *stéorbord* (*stéor* rudder, see STEER[1], + *bord* BOARD), early Teut. ships being steered with a paddle over the right side]

starch (-tsh), a., n., & v.t. (Now rare) precise, prim, whence **star·ch**LY[2] adv., **star·ch**NESS n. (N.) white odourless tasteless powder procured chiefly from corn & potatoes but found in all plants except fungi & valuable in digestion; preparation of this with usu. boiling water for stiffening linen &c. before ironing; (fig.) stiffness of manner, formality. Hence **star·chi**NESS n., **star·chy**[2] a., (lit. & fig.). (V.t.) stiffen with s. (often fig. esp. in p.p., whence **star·chĕd**LY[2] adv., **star·ched**NESS n.); CLEAR[1]-*s.* Hence **(-)starch**ER[1] n. [adj. f. n. f. vb, ME *sterche* stiffen f. STARK]

stare, v.i. & t., & n. Look fixedly with eyes wide open (*at, upon,* &c., or abs.) from surprise, admiration, bewilderment, stupidity, horror, impertinent curiosity, &c.; (chiefly in part.) be unpleasantly prominent or striking, as *a staring waistcoat, tie was of a staring red,* (adv.) *stark staring mad*; reduce (person) to specified condition by staring, as *stared* *him out of countenance, into silence, dumb*; *s. down,* outstare; *s.* (person) *in the face,* be evident or imminent, as *the facts s. us in the face, ruin stared him in the face.* Hence **star·ing**LY[2] adv. (N.) staring gaze. [(n. f. vb) OE *starian,* cf. Du. *staren,* ON *stara*]

stark, a. & adv. Stiff, rigid, as *s. & stiff, lies s. in death*; (poet.) strong; (poet.) stubborn, resolute; downright, sheer, as *s. madness*; (adv.) quite, wholly, (chiefly in *s. mad, naked*). [OE *stearc* strong, stiff, cf. Du. *sterk,* G *stark,* ON *sterkr*; *s. naked* was orig. *start* (=tail) *-naked* (OE *steort* tail, cf. REDstart & Du. *staart,* G *sterz,* ON *stertr*)]

star·ling[1], n. Bird of blackish-brown plumage with light speckles & metallic purple & green reflections, of great imitative powers & easily tamed. [OE *stærlinc* (*stær* starling, cf. G *staar,* Da. *stær,* L *sturnus*) + -LING[1]]

star·ling[2], n. Protective piling round pier of bridge [f. 17th c., perh. corrupt. of obs. *staddling,* OE *statholung* (*statholian* establish f. *stathol* foundation, -ING[1])]

start[1], v.i. & t. Make sudden movement from pain, surprise, &c., as *started in his seat, started at the sound of my voice*; change position abruptly as from shock or sudden impulse, as *s. aside, from* one's *chair*; (of timbers &c.) spring from proper position, give way; set out, begin journey, as *we s. at six*; make a beginning (*on* journey, enterprise, book, cigar, &c.); begin (*work, doing,* colloq. or vulg. *to* do); *s. in* (colloq.), begin (*to* do); *s. out* (colloq.), take steps as intending (*to* do); *s. up,* rise suddenly e.g. from seat, arise, come into existence or action, occur to the mind, as *many difficulties, rivals, have started up*; rouse (game) from lair &c.; originate, set going, (enterprise, newspaper, business, clock after winding, objections, quarrel, &c.); cause to begin doing (*this started me coughing*); cause or enable (person) to commence business &c.; give signal to (persons) to s. in race; cause or experience the starting of (timbers, tooth, &c.); (Naut.) pour out (liquor) from cask; *to s. with,* in the first place, as *you have no right to be here, to s. with,* at the beginning, as *had 6 members to s. with.* [ME *sterte,* perh. f. OE *styrtan,* cogn. w. Du. *storten,* Da. *styrte,* G *stürzen,* hurl &c.]

start[2], n. Sudden movement of surprise, pain, &c.; (pl.) intermittent or spasmodic efforts or movements, esp. (*works*) *by fits & ss.*; beginning of journey or action or race, as *shall make an early s. for town, is difficult work at the s., the s. is fixed for 3 p.m.*; starting-place of race; advantage conceded in race, as *will give you 60 yards s., 15 seconds s.*; advantageous position gained in business &c., as *got a good s. in life, got the s. of* (gained advantage over) *his rivals*; *a rum s.* colloq., surprising occurrence. [ME *stert,* as prec.]

star·ter, n. In vbl senses, esp.: one who gives signal to start in race; horse, competitor, starting in race, as *list of probable ss.*; (slang, w. ref. to aperient effect) dried fig. [-ER[1]]

star·ting, n. In vbl senses; *s.-gate,* removable barrier for securing fair start in horse-races; *s.-post* (from which competitors start in race); *s. prices* in horse-races, final odds at start. [-ING[1]]

star·tle, v.t. Cause (person &c.) to start with surprise or sudden alarm, give shock to, take by surprise, whence (of person, news, &c.) **star·tl**ER[1] n.; (part.) surprising, alarming, as *startling news, discovery, development,* whence **star·tling**LY[2] adv. [ME *startlen, ster-,* f. START[1], see -LE(3)]

starve, v.i. & t. Die of hunger; suffer from lack of food; suffer extreme poverty; (colloq.) feel hungry, as *am simply starving*; (now rare) perish with, suffer from, cold; (fig.) suffer mental or spiritual want, feel strong craving *for* (sympathy, amusement, knowledge, &c.); cause to perish with hunger; deprive of, keep scantily supplied with, food (lit. & fig.); compel (garrison &c. *into* surrender &c.) thus; cause to perish, affect severely, with cold. Hence **starv**A·TION n. [OE *steorfan* die, cf. Du. *sterven,* G *sterben,* die]

star·veling (-vl-), n. & a. Starving or ill-fed person or animal; (adj.) starving. [-LING[1]]

stā·sis, n. (path.). Stoppage of circulation of any of the fluids of the body. [Gk, = standing]

state[1], n. & a. Condition in which a thing is, mode of existence as determined by circumstances, as *s. of life* (one's rank & occupation), *a precarious s. of health, found him in the same s., in a s. of deep depression, things were in an untidy s., in a bad s. of repair, what a* (dirty, untidy) *s. you are in!,* (colloq.) *he was in quite a s.* (quite excited or anxious) *about it*; (often *S*-) organized political community with government recognized by the people, commonwealth, nation; such community forming part of federal republic, esp. *the United Ss.* (*of America*); (pl.) legislative body in Jersey & Guernsey; civil government, as *Church & S.*; rank, dignity, as *in a style befitting his s.*; pomp, as *arrived in great s., keep s.,* maintain one's dignity, be difficult of access, *in s.* (with all due ceremony); (archaic) throne (also *chair of s.*), dais, canopy over throne; (of dead person) *lie in s.* be placed on view in public place; *free, slave, S.* (U.S.), S. in which slavery did not, did, exist; *Southern Ss.* (in southern part of U.S.); *Ss. of the Church,*

Papal Ss., former temporal dominions of Pope chiefly in central Italy; *Ss. General*, legislative bodies of (1) the Netherlands (2) France before 1879; *sta·tecraft*, art of conducting affairs of S. (Adj.) of, for, concerned with, the S., as *s. criminal*, political offender, *s. documents, service, s. prisoner*, person under arrest for felony, also political prisoner, *s. trial*, prosecution by S. esp. for political offence; *S. rights* (U.S.), rights & powers not delegated to United States but reserved to individual Ss.; *S. socialism, socialist*, policy, advocate, of S. control of manufactures, railways, &c. for the benefit of the masses; reserved for, done on, occasions of ceremony, as *s. apartments, carriage, s. call* (colloq.), formal visit; *s.-room*, room so reserved, also, private sleeping-apartment on steamer. [(adj. f. n.) f. OF *estat* f. STATUS]

state², v.t. Express, esp. fully or clearly, in speech or writing, as *have stated my opinion, must s. full particulars, this condition was expressly stated, no precise time was stated, did not s. why, states that arrangements are complete*; fix, specify, (date &c.), as *at stated intervals*, whence **sta·ted**LY² adv.; (Alg.) express the conditions of (problem, relation, &c.) in symbols. Hence **sta·t**ABLE a. [f. prec.]

sta·tely, a. (Of manner, language, person, literary style, rhythm, building, proportions, &c.) dignified, imposing, grand. Hence **sta·teli**NESS n. [as STATE¹, see -LY¹]

sta·tement, n. Stating, expression in words, as *requires clearer s.*; thing stated, as *the s. is unfounded*; formal account of facts, e.g. of liabilities & assets, as, *the Bank issues monthly ss.* [-MENT]

stā·ter, n. Ancient Greek coin of various values, esp. gold coin worth 20 drachmae. [L, f. Gk *statēr* (*sta-* stand, *histēmi* weigh)]

sta·tesman, n. Person taking prominent part, person skilled, in management of State affairs; sagacious far-sighted practical politician; (North.) small working landowner; *the Elder Ss.*, the Japanese ss. who mainly directed the evolution of Japan between the re-establishment of the Mikado (1868) & the end of the 19th c. Hence **sta·tesman**LIKE, **sta·tesman**LY¹, aa., **sta·tesman**SHIP(3) n. [=*state's man*]

stă·tic(al), a. Concerned with bodies at rest or forces in equilibrium, whence **sta·t**ICS n. pl. (or as sing.); acting as weight but not moving, as *s. pressure*; *s. electricity* (at rest); *static ataxia*, inability to stand without falling or swaying. Hence **sta·tical**LY² adv. [f. Gk *statikos* (*sta-* stand, see -IC & -AL)]

stā·tion, n., & v.t. Standing, being still, (opp. *motion*; now rare; *a s. like the herald Mercury*); place, building, &c., in which person or thing stands or is placed esp. habitually or for definite purpose, as *was assigned a s. in the valley, returned to their several ss., took up a convenient s., coastguard s.* (occupied by coastguardsmen), POLICE *s., life-boat s.* (where life-boat is kept), *naval s.*, place affording shelter or harbour for ships with dockyard &c., (pl. Nav.) posts assigned to members of ship's complement in readiness for battle; subordinate depot or office serving local needs; stopping-place on railway with buildings for accommodation of passengers & goods or (*goods-s.*) of goods only; position in life, (high) rank, status, employment, as *occupied a humble s., men of (exalted) s., the duties of his s.*; (Surv.) point from which measurements are made, standard distance usu. 100 or 66 ft; military post esp. in India, officers or society residing there; (Austral.) sheep-run or its building; (Eccl.) fast on Wed. & Frid. (hist.), (also *s. of the cross*) each of series of 14 images or pictures representing Christ's passion before which devotions are performed in some churches; church esp. in Rome to which pilgrims &c. go for devotions; (Bot., Zool.) nature of the habitat of plant or animal in respect of climate, soil, &c.; *s.-bill* (naut.), list of appointed posts of ship's company; *s.-calendar*, board showing successively the starting-time of trains at each platform; *s.-house*, police-station; *s.-master*, official in charge of railway-s.; *s.-pointer*, three-armed protractor for locating place on chart from certain data; (v.t.) assign s. to, place (person, one*self*) in s. [(vb f. n.) F, f. *stationem* (*stare* stand, -ATION)]

sta·tionary, a. & n. Remaining in one place, not moving, as *balloon was now s.*; not meant to be moved, not portable, as *s. engine, troops*; (of planet) having no apparent motion in longitude; not changing in magnitude, number, quality, efficiency, &c., as *s. temperature, population, intelligence*; *s. air* (remaining in lungs during ordinary respiration); *s. diseases*, local diseases due to atmospheric conditions & disappearing after a period; (n.) s. person, esp. (pl.) s. troops. Hence **sta·tionari**NESS n. [f. L *stationarius* (as prec., see -ARY¹)]

sta·tioner, n. One who sells writing-materials &c.; *Stationers' Hall* (of Stationers' Company in London, at which book is *entered*, i.e. registered, for purposes of copyright). Hence **sta·tion**ERY (1) n. [earlier = bookseller (as prec. in med. L sense *shopkeeper* as opp. pedlar)]

stā·tist, n. Dealer in statistics. [earlier = politician, f. STATE¹ + -IST]

stati·stics, n. pl. Numerical facts systematically collected, as *ss. of population, crime*; (treated as sing.) science of collecting, classifying, & using ss. So **stati·st**IC(AL) aa., **stati·stical**LY² adv., **stătisti·**CIAN, **statisto·**LOGY, nn. [prec. + -ICS]

stă·toscope, n. Aneroid barometer for

showing minute variations of pressure. [f. Gk *statos* fixed (*sta-* stand) + -SCOPE]

sta·tuary, a. & n. Of or for statues, as *s. art, s. marble* (fine-grained white); (n.) sculptor, (art of making) statues. [f. L *statuarius* (as foll., see -ARY[1])]

stă·tue, n. Sculptured or cast or moulded figure of person or animal (esp. one not much below life size, opp. to **statue·tte** n.); EQUESTRIAN *s.* Hence **sta·tued**[2] a. [OF, f. L *statua* (*stare* stand)]

statue·sque (-k), a. Like, having the dignity or beauty of, a statue. Hence **statue·squely**[2] adv., **statue·squeness** n. [-ESQUE]

stă·ture (-yer), n. Height of (esp. human) body, as *increased in s., of mean s.* Hence **(-)statured**[2] a. [OF, f. L *statura* standing posture (*stare stat-* stand, see -URE)]

stā·tus, n. (pl. prob. not used). Social position, rank, relation to others, relative importance, (*his s. is a matter of doubt, their s. is wholly different, his s. among novelists*); (Law) person's relation to others as fixed by law; position of affairs, esp. *s. (in) quo,* unchanged position (cf. IN[5] *statu quo*) or (also *s. q. ante*) the previous position. [L, gen. *-ūs,* = standing (*stare* stand)]

sta·tutable, a. = STATUTORY. Hence **sta·tutably**[2] adv. [-ABLE]

stă·tute, n. A written law of a legislative body, e.g. Act of Parliament; *s. law,* a s., (collect.) the ss. (opp. to COMMON[1] *law*); ordinance of corporation, founder, &c., intended to be permanent, as *University ss.*; (bibl.) divine law, as *kept thy ss.*; *declaratory s.* (fixing interpretation of existing law); *private s.* (affecting individuals, opp. to *general, public, s.*); *s.-book,* book(s) containing the s. law; *s.-roll,* engrossed s., s.-book; *ss. at large* (in full as originally enacted). [f. F *statut* f. LL *statutum* neut. p.p. as n. of L *statuere* establish (*stare* stand)]

sta·tutory, a. Enacted, required, imposed, by statute, as *s. provisions, minimum.* [-ORY]

staunch (-aw-, -ah-), **stanch,** a. Trustworthy, loyal, as *s. friend, supporter*; (of ship, joint, &c.) watertight, airtight. Hence **stau·nchly**[2] adv., **stau·nchness** n. [earlier also = water-tight, f. OF *estanche* fem. adj. as STANCH[1]]

staur·oscope, n. Instrument for examining effects of polarized light on crystals. [f. Gk *stauros* cross + -SCOPE]

stave[1], n. Each of the curved pieces of wood forming sides of cask &c.; each of the boards forming curb of well or hollow cylinder; rung of ladder; stanza, verse; (Mus.) = STAFF; *s.-rhyme,* alliteration esp. in old Teut. poetry. [var. of STAFF, due to pl. *staves*]

stave[2], v.t. (*staved* or *stove*). Break a hole in (cask, boat; often *in* adv.); (usu. *s. in*) crush or bash (hat, box) out of shape; furnish, fit, (cask, &c.) with staves; *s. off,* avert, ward off, defer, (ruin, exposure, &c.); make (metal &c.) firm by compression. [f. prec.]

sta·vesacre (-vzāker), n. Kind of larkspur whose seeds are used as poison for vermin. [f. L *staphisagria* (Gk *staphis* dried grapes + *agria* wild)]

stay[1], v.t. & i., & n. (Now chiefly literary) check, stop, (progress, inroads of disease &c.); *s.* one's *stomach,* appease hunger esp. temporarily; postpone (judgement, decision); support, prop (often *up*) as or with buttress &c.; remain, as *s. here till I return, will not stay where it is put* (also, U.S., *will not s. put*), *has come to s.* (colloq.), must be regarded as permanent; (w. adv.) *s. away, on, out,* &c.; (colloq.) wait long enough to partake of (*can you s. supper?*); dwell temporarily (*at* hotel &c., *in* town &c., *with* person); pause in movement, action, speech (esp. in imperat.), &c. as *get him to s. a minute, s.!—you forget one thing*; show endurance esp. in race, as *does not seem able to s.,* whence **stay·er**[1] n.; *s.-at-home* a. & n., (person) remaining habitually at home. (N.) remaining, esp. dwelling, in a place, duration of this, as *made a long s. in London, your s. has been very short*; suspension of judicial proceedings (esp. *s. of execution,* i.e. of carrying out judgement given); (chiefly literary) check, restraint, (*will endure no s., a s. upon his activity*); endurance, staying-power; prop, support, (*you have been the s. of my old age*); (pl.) corset, whence **stay·less** a.; *s.-bar, -rod,* support in building or machinery; *s.-lace, -maker* (of corsets). [n. f. vb, prob. f. OF *ester* f. L *stare* stand; sense *support* v. & n. perh. f. OF *estaye(r),* f. Teut. as foll., in transferred uses].

stay[2], n., & v.t., (naut.). Rope supporting mast or spar; *ship is (hove) in ss.* (going about from one tack to another); *miss ss.,* fail in endeavour to tack; *stay·sail* (-sāl, *naut.* -sl), any sail extended on s.; (v.t.) support (mast &c.) by ss., put (ship) on other tack. [vb f. n., OE *stæg,* cf. G, Du., & ON *stag,* cogn. w. STEEL]

stead (-ĕd), n. (now chiefly literary). *Stand* (person) *in good s.,* be advantageous or serviceable to; *in* person's *s.,* instead of him, as his substitute. [OE & Du. *stede* place, cogn. w. Du. *stad,* G *stadt,* town, & w. STAND; seen in *bedstead, homestead*]

stea·dfast (-ĕd-), a. Constant, firm, unwavering. Hence **stea·dfastly**[2] adv., **stea·dfastness** n. [OE *stedefæst* (prec., FAST[3])]

stea·ding (stĕd-), n. Farmstead. [-ING[1]]

stea·dy (-ĕdĭ), a., n., & v.t. & i. Firmly fixed or supported or standing or balanced, not tottering, as *not s. on his legs, must level table's legs to make it s., s. as a rock, has not acquired a s. seat on bicycle*; done, moving, acting, happening, in uniform & regular manner, as *went off at a s. pace, had a s. wind behind us, requires a s. light, observe a s. increase in the numbers*; (as command or warning) *s. !*, be s., abstain from erratic or boisterous behaviour, premature action, hasty inference, &c., (Naut., also *keep her s.*) keep direction of ship's head unchanged; constant in mind or conduct, not changeable, as *s. in his principles, allegiance*; of industrious & temperate habits; (n.) kinds of support for hand or tool. Hence **stea·di**LY² adv., **stea·di**NESS n. (Vb) make, become, s., as *s. the boat, boat steadied, adversity will s. him, he will soon s. (down)*. [STEAD + -Y²]

steak (stāk), n. Slice of beef, pork, venison, or fish, cut for broiling &c., as *beefs.*, RUMP-, PORTER²-*house, s., fillet s.* (from undercut of sirloin); *Hamburg s.*, cake of chopped & seasoned beef cooked in covered frying-pan. [f. ON *steik* (*steikja* roast on spit)]

steal, v.t. & i. (stole, stolen), & n. Take away (thing, or abs.) secretly for one's own use without right or leave, take feloniously, as *who steals my purse steals trash, stolen fruit*; obtain surreptitiously or by surprise, as *stole a kiss, a stolen interview*; (also *s. away*) win, get possession of, (esp. person's *heart*) by insidious arts, attractions, &c.; *s. a march on*, get the start of, anticipate; (intr.) move (*in, out, away, up, by*, &c.) secretly or silently, as *stole out of the room, mist stole over the valley*; (n.) successful long stroke in golf. Hence **(-)steal**ER¹ n. [OE *stelan*, cf. Du. *stelen*, G *stehlen*]

stealth (-ĕl-), n. Secrecy, secret procedure, esp. *by s.*, surreptitiously. Hence **stea·lthi**LY² adv., **stea·lthi**NESS n., **stea·lth**Y² a. [-TH¹]

steam¹ (-ēm), n. Vapour of water, esp. the gas into which water is changed by boiling, largely used as motive power owing to its elasticity; *saturated s.* (in contact with, & at same temperature as, boiling water); *superheated s.* (having higher temperature at given pressure, & greater volume for a given weight, than saturated s.); *wet, dry, s.* (containing, not containing, mechanically suspended particles of water); visible particles of water resulting from condensation of s.; any vaporous exhalation; (colloq.) energy, as *get up s.*, summon energy for special effort, so *put on, let off, work off, s.*; *stea·mboat*, vessel propelled by s.; *s.-boiler*, vessel in which water is boiled to generate s. esp. for working engine; *s.-box, -chest* (through which s. passes from boiler to cylinder); *s. brake, crane, gun, hammer, plough, whistle, winch*, &c. (worked by s.); *s.-coal* (used in heating s.-boilers); *s.-colour* (fixed on printed cloth by action of s.); *s.-cylinder* (in which piston of s.-engine moves); *s.-engine*, locomotive or stationary engine in which the motive power depends on elasticity & expansion or rapid condensation of s.; *s.-gas*, superheated s.; *s.-gauge* (attached to boiler to show pressure of s.); *s.-heat*, heat required to produce s. from water at freezing-point, also, heat given out by s. from radiators &c.; *s.-jacket*, casing round cylinder &c. with space between to be filled by s. for heating the cylinder &c.; *s. navvy*, excavating machine; *s.-port*, each of two oblong passages from s.-chest into cylinder, any passage for s.; *s.-power*, force of s. applied to machinery &c.; *stea·mship* (propelled by s.); *s.-tight*, capable of resisting passage of s.; *s. tug*, steamer for towing ships &c. Hence **stea·mi**NESS n., **stea·m**Y² a. [OE *stéam*, cf. Du. *stoom*, etym. dub.]

steam², v.t. & i. Cook (food) by s.; treat with steam, soften (timber) for bending by steam; give out steam or vapour, as *a sirloin steamed on the table, water steaming hot*; rise in vapour; move by agency of steam, as *we, the vessel, steamed down the river*; (colloq.) work vigorously, make great progress, esp. *s. ahead, away*. [OE *stēman* (prec.)]

stea·mer, n. In vbl senses; also or esp.: vessel propelled by steam; fire-engine worked by steam; vessel in which things are steamed, esp. cooked by steam; *boiler is a bad s.* (generator of steam). [-ER¹]

stē·arin, n. Chief ingredient of suet & tallow; (pop.) stearic acid separated from s. by steam & used for candles. Hence **ste·ar**ATE¹(3) n., **steă·r**IC a. [f. Gk *stear* fat + -IN]

ste·arinery, n. Manufacture of stearin (products). [-ERY]

stē·atite, n. Kind of talc, soapstone. Hence **steati·t**IC a. [f. L *steatites* (f. Gk as foll., -ITE¹)]

stēat(o)- in comb. = Gk *stear -atos* fat.

steed, n. (poet., rhet., or facet.). Horse, esp. war-horse. Hence **stee·d**LESS a. [OE *stēda* (*stod* STUD²)]

steel, n., & v.t. Kinds of malleable alloy of iron & carbon largely used as material for tools, weapons, &c., & capable of being tempered to many different degrees of hardness (often attrib., as *s. pen*), whence **stee·li**FY v.t.; BESSEMER *s.*; *cold s.*, sword &c. as opp. to firearm; *a grip, muscles, a heart, of s.* (very tight, strong, hard); rod of s., usu. tapering & roughened, for sharpening knives; strip of s. for stiffening corset or expanding skirt; (poet., rhet., not in pl.) sword (*a foe worthy of* one's *s.*); *s. cap*, simple form of helmet; *s.-clad*, clad in armour; *s. engraving*, engraving on, impression taken from, s. plate; *stee·lwork*, s. articles, s. for these; (v.t.) harden (*oneself*, one's *heart*, &c., *to* do, *to* action, *against* compassion &c.). [OE *stȳle* & *stǣli*, cf. Du. *staal*, G *stahl*, ON *stál*, cogn. w. STAY²]

stee·ly, a. Of, hard as, steel; inflexibly severe, as *s. glance, composure.* Hence **stee·li**NESS n. [-Y²]

stee·lyard, n. Kind of balance with short arm to take the thing weighed & long graduated arm along which a weight is moved till it balances this. [prob. f. STEEL & YARD¹, but usu. taken as for *s. beam,* i.e. balance of Hanseatic 'Steelyard' (MLG *stâlhof* = sample-house mistranslated) in London]

stee·nbok (stā-, stē-), n. Kinds of small African antelope. [Du., lit. stone buck]

stee·ning, n. Stone lining of well. [f. dial. *steen* pave (OE *stǽnan* to STONE) + -ING¹]

stee·nkirk, n. (hist.). Cravat, other articles of dress &c., named in allusion to Battle of *Steenkerke* in Belgium 1692.

steep¹, a. & n. Having decided slope, sheer, as *s. hills*; (colloq., of demand, price, &c.) exorbitant, unreasonable, as *seems a bit s. that we should have both the trouble & the expense,* (of story &c.) exaggerated, incredible; (n.) s. slope, precipice. Hence **stee·p**EN⁶ v.i. & t., **stee·p**LY² adv., **stee·p**NESS n., **stee·p**Y² (poet.) a. [OE *stéap,* cf. OFris. *stâp,* cogn. w. STOOP]

steep², v.t., & n. Soak in liquid; bathe with liquid; *s. in* (fig.), impregnate with, pervade with, as *steeped in Greek & Latin, misery, slumber*; (n.) process of steeping (esp. *in s.*), liquid in which thing is steeped. [ME *stepen,* cf. Sw. *stöpa*; perh. cogn. w. STOUP]

stee·per, n. Vessel in which things are steeped. [-ER¹]

stee·ple, n. Lofty structure, esp. tower surmounted with spire, rising above roof of church; *stee·plechase,* horse-race (perh. orig. with s. as goal) across tract of country with ditches, hedges, &c., to jump, (also) cross-country foot-race, *s.-chaser,* rider in s.-c., horse trained for s.-c., *s.-chasing,* the sport of riding in s.-cc.; *s.-crowned hat* (with tall pointed crown); *s.-jack,* man who climbs ss. &c. to do repairs &c.; *s.-top,* polar whale with spout-holes ending in cone. Hence **stee·pl**ED² a., **stee·ple**WISE adv. [OE *stépel* & *stýpel* (as STEEP¹)]

steer¹, v.t. & i. Guide (vessel) by rudder or helm, guide vessel in specified direction, (*steering-wheel,* vertical wheel with handles along rim for controlling rudder); guide (motor, aircraft, &c.) by handle &c.); (chiefly colloq. or poet.) direct (one's course), direct one's course, in specified direction, as *steered his flight heavenwards, we steered (our course) for the railway station, s. clear of* (avoid) *the local meteorologist*; *steer·sman,* one who steers vessel, *steer·smanship,* skill in steering. Hence **steer·**ABLE a., **steer·**ER¹(1, 2) n. [OE *stieran, stéoran* (*stéor* rudder, cf. Du. *stuur,* G *steuer,* ON *stýri,* cogn. w. ON *staurr,* Gk *stauros,* stake)]

steer², n. Young male of ox kind, esp. castrated bullock raised for beef. [OE *stéor,* cf. Du. & G *stier* bull, ON *thjórr*]

steer·age (-ĭj), n. (Now rare) steering; (Naut.) effect of helm on ship, as *ship went with easy s.*; part of ship allotted to *s. passengers* (travelling at cheapest rate), variously placed; (in man-of-war) part of berth-deck just forward of ward-room, quarters of junior officers, clerks, &c.; *s.-way,* amount of headway required by vessel to enable her to be controlled by helm. [-AGE]

steeve¹, v.i. & t., & n., (naut.). (Of bowsprit) make angle with horizon; cause (bowsprit) to do this; (n.) such angle. [perh. f. OF *estive* ploughtail f. L *stiva*]

steeve², n., & v.t., (naut.). Long spar used in stowing cargo; (v.t.) stow with this. [(n. f. vb) f. OF *estiver* cram f. L *stipare*]

Stei·nberger (stī-, -*ger*), n. White wine grown on Rhine near Wiesbaden.

stei·nbock (stīn-), n. A wild goat, the Alpine ibex. [G, = stone buck]

stē·lē, n. (Gk archaeol.; pl. *-ae*). Upright slab or pillar usu. with inscription & sculpture, esp. as gravestone. [Gk]

ste·llar, a. Of stars. So **stelli·**FEROUS, **ste·lli**FORM, aa. [f. LL *stellaris* (*stella* star, see -AR¹)]

ste·llāte(d), aa. Arranged like a star, radiating, esp. (Bot.) *s. leaves* (surrounding stem in a whorl). Hence **ste·llate**LY² adv. [f. L *stellare* set with stars (*stella* star), see -ATE²]

ste·llenbosch (-sh), v.t. (mil. slang). Supersede without formal disgrace by appointing to unimportant command. [f. *S.* in S. Africa, military base so utilized]

ste·llular, a. Shaped like, set with, small stars. So **ste·llul**ATE² a. [f. LL *stellula* dim. of *stella* star + -AR¹]

stem¹, n., & v.t. Main body or stalk (usu. rising into light & air but sometimes subterranean) of tree, shrub, or plant; slender stalk supporting fruit, flower, or leaf, & attaching it to main stalk or branch or twig; s.-shaped part, e.g. slender part of wine-glass between body & foot, vertical line rising or falling from head of note in music, various winding-parts of watch (*s.-winder,* watch wound by turning head on end of s., not by key), tubular part of tobacco-pipe; part of noun, verb, &c. (derived from & sometimes identified with a root) to which case-endings &c. are added, part that appears or would originally appear unchanged throughout the case of a noun, persons of a tense, &c.; line of ancestry, branch of family, as *descended from an ancient, a collateral, s.*; carved timber or metal piece to which ship's sides are joined at fore end, piece joined to & forming upright continuation of keel at fore end, as *from s. to stern,* from end to end; *false s.,* sharp-edged piece in front of s. serving as cutwater; (v.t.) remove s. of (esp. tobacco, whence **ste·mm**ER[1](1) n.). Hence **ste·m**LESS, **(-)stemm**ED[2], aa., **ste·m**LET n. [(vb f. n.) OE *stefn, stemn,* stem (of tree, ship, family), cf. Du. *stam* trunk, *steven* prow, ON *stafn, stamn,* stem of ship, Da. *stamme,* G *stamm,* trunk]

stem[2], v.t. Check, dam up, (stream &c., lit. & fig.); make headway against (tide, current, &c., lit. & fig.). [sense *check* f. ON *stemma,* cf. Da. *stemme,* G *stemmen,* cogn. w. STAMMER; 2nd sense f. prec.]

ste·mma, n. (pl. *-ta*). Family tree, pedigree; lineal descent; (Zool.) simple eye, facet of compound eye. [L, f. Gk *stemma* wreath (*stephō* wreathe, see -M)]

ste·mple, n. Each of several cross-bars in shaft of mine serving as supports or steps. [cf. G *stempel*]

stench, n. Offensive smell; *s.-trap* (in sewer &c., to prevent upward passage of gas). [OE *stenc* (any) smell, cf. Du. & G *stank,* cogn. w. STINK]

ste·ncil, n., & v.t. (-ll-). (Also *s.-plate*) thin plate of metal &c. in which pattern (interrupted when necessary by a thin bar of the material left to prevent piece from falling out) is cut out; decoration, lettering, &c., produced by s.; (v.t.) produce (pattern) on surface, ornament (surface) with pattern, by brushing paint &c. over s.-plate laid on the surface. Hence **ste·ncil**LER[1] n. [perh. f. OF *estenceler* sparkle, cover with stars, f. *estencele,* see TINSEL]

steno- in comb. = Gk *stenos* narrow, chiefly in scientific wds.

stenŏ·chromy, n. Art of printing in several colours at one impression. [f. STENO- + Gk *khrōma* colour + -Y[1]]

stĕ·nograph, n. Character used, piece of writing, in shorthand; kinds of machine for writing in shorthand. Hence **steno·graph**ER[1], **steno·graph**IST, **stenograph**Y[1], nn., **stenogră·phic** a., **stenogra·ph**ICALLY adv. [STENO- + -GRAPH]

Ste·ntor, n. Person with powerful voice. Hence **stentor·**IAN a. [L f. Gk *Stentōr,* herald in Trojan war]

step[1], v.i. & t. Shift & set down foot or alternate feet (*s. out, short,* take long, short, ss.; *s. through a dance,* perform its ss.; *s. high,* lift feet high esp. of trotting horse, so HIGH-*ste·pper*); go short distance or progress in some direction by stepping (*s. back, forward, across the road, into the boat*; *s. this way,* polite formula for *come here*; *s. in, out,* enter, leave, room or house; *s. in* fig., intervene to help or hinder; *s. up, down*; *s. aside,* lit., & fig. = make digression); perform (dance; also *s. it,* dance), measure (distance), by stepping; (Naut., prob. f. n.) set up (mast) in s.; *stepping-stone,* raised usu. as one of set in stream or muddy place to enable passengers to cross dry-shod, (fig.) means to an end. [OE *steppan* plant foot, go, cf. Du. *stappen,* G *stapfen*]

step[2], n. Complete movement of one leg in walking or running or dancing, distance gained by it, mark left by foot on ground, sound made by setting foot down, manner of stepping as seen or heard, simultaneous stepping with corresponding legs by two or more persons or animals, (fig.) measure taken esp. as one of a series in some course of action, (*took a s. back* or *forward*; *s. by s.,* gradually, cautiously, by degrees; *that is a long s. towards success*; *it is but a s. to my house, from life to death,* exag. for short distance or quick transition; *do not move a s.*; *turn* one's *ss.,* go in a specified direction; *found his ss.* or usu. *footss. in the soil*; *in his* &c. *ss.,* following his &c. example; *do you hear a, know her, s.?*; *walks with a rapid s.*; *one-s., two-s.,* dance names; *in, out of, s.,* stepping, not stepping, in time with others or with drum-beat &c.; *keep, break, s.,* keep in, get out of, s.; *keep s. with* person, *to* band &c.; FALSE *s.*; *must take ss. in the matter, to prevent it,* &c.; *a rash, ill-advised, prudent,* &c., *s.*); surface provided or utilized for placing foot on in ascending or descending, e.g. tread or riser & tread of staircase, block of stone or other platform before door or altar &c., rung of ladder, notch cut for foot in ice-climbing, attached piece of vehicle for stepping up or down by, (pl., also *s.-ladder* or *pair* or *set of ss.*) kind of short ladder with flat ss. & prop used without being leant against wall &c., (fig.) one of the degrees in some scale of precedence or advancement, advance from one of these to another, (*staircase of 50 ss.*; *stone, oak, ss.*; *door, altar, -s.*; *on the top s. of the ladder*; *run down the ss.*; *cutting ss. with his ice-axe*; *when did you get your s.?,* promotion esp. in army; *give him a s. in the peerage*); (Naut.) socket or platform supporting mast, (Carpent.) piece of timber with another fixed upright in it, (Mech.) lower socket or bearing for shaft; *s.-dance,* in which the ss. are peculiar or difficult or of more importance than the figure, usu. danced as display by one performer. Hence **stepp**ED[2] a., **ste·p**WISE adv. [OE *stæpe* (prec.)]

step-, pref., = holding nominal relationship analogous to that specified owing to death of one and remarriage of the other of a married pair; *ste·pchild, son, daughter,* one's wife's or husband's child by previous marriage; *ste·pfather, mother, -parent,* one's parent's later husband or wife; *ste·pmother* or archaic *dame,* harsh or neglectful mother lit. or fig., whence **ste·pmother**LY[1] a.; *step-brother, -sister,* child of previous marriage of one's s.-

parent. [OE *stéop* orphaned, cf. Du. & G *stief-*, OHG *stiufan* deprive of parents or children; applied first to child & later extended to parent &c.]

stĕphanō·tis, n. Climbing hothouse plant with fragrant waxy flowers. [Gk fem. adj. = fit for a wreath (*stephanos*)]

steppe, n. Level plain devoid of forest esp. in Russia & Siberia. [f. Russ. *stepi*]

-ster, suf. forming agent nn.; OE *-estre*, cf. Du. & Fris. *-ster*. In OE the suf. was orig. confined to the fem., but this restriction appears in mod. E only in *spinster*. Exx.: *brewster, huckster* (which however seems to have existed before the obs. vb *huck*), *gamester, punster*, & perh. *holster, bolster*. In *seamstress* -ESS[1] is added to *-ster*; *-ster* in *lobster* is of different orig., but perh. assimilated.

stercora·ceous, ster·coral, aa. Of ordure or faeces. [L *stercus -oris* dung, -ACEOUS, -AL]

stĕreo, n. (colloq.; pl. *-os*). Stereotype (often attrib., as *s. plate*). [shortening]

stĕreo-, comb. form of Gk *stereos* solid, stiff: *-bate*, solid platform on which a building is erected; *-che·mistry*, branch dealing with composition of matter as affected by relations of atoms in space; *-chrōmy*, painting with pigments fixed by WATER[1]-glass; *-graphy*, art of delineating solid form on plane, so -GRAM, -GRAPH(1), -GRA·PHIC, *-gra·ph*ICALLY; *-meter*, instrument for measuring solid capacity, also instrument for determining specific gravity of liquids, porous bodies, &c.; so -METRY, *-me·tr*IC(AL), *-me·trical*LY[2]; *-scope*, instrument combining two views of object taken at slightly different angles into single image with effect of solidity, so *-scŏ·p*IC(ALLY), *-scop*Y[1].

ste·reotype, n., & v.t. Printing-plate cast from a papier-mâché or other mould of a piece of printing composed in movable type; making, use, of such plates; *s.-block*, on which s. is mounted for use; hence **ste·reotyp**IST(1), **ste·reotyp**Y[1], **stereotypo·**GRAPHY, nn. (Vb) make ss. of; print by use of ss.; (fig.) make unchangeable, impart monotonous regularity to, fix in all details, formalize; hence **ste·reotyp**ER[1] n. [f. F *stéréotype* a. & n. (prec., TYPE)]

stĕ·rile, a. Unfruitful, unproductive, barren, not producing crop or fruit or young or complete seed or result (*s. land, cow, plant, year, effort, discussion*); free from living germs esp. bacilli or bacteria or microbes (usu. *sterilized*); (of style) jejune, bald. Hence or cogn. **ste·ril**IZE(3) v.t., **steriliz**A·TION, **ste·riliz**ER[1](2), **steri·l**ITY, nn. [f. L *sterilis*, cogn. w. Skr. *starī*, Gk *steira*, barren cow]

ster·let, n. Kind of small sturgeon. [f. Russ. *sterlyadi*]

ster·ling, a. (Of coins & precious metals) genuine, of standard value or purity, (abbr. *stg*; with coins, chiefly appended to sum expressed in sovereigns without odd money, as *£20 stg*; *is of s. gold, silver*); (transf.) of solid worth, not showy, that is what it seems to be, (*is a s. fellow*; *s. sense, qualities, character*; *the s. nature of*). [orig. as n., = the English silver penny, money of that quality, genuine English money; etym. dub.; the traditional derivation f. *Easterling* is unlikely, requiring loss of the stressed syllable; perh. = little star, w. ref. to star found on some early Norman pennies; see -LING[1] (2)]

stern[1], a. Severe, grim, rigid, strict, enforcing discipline or submission, not compassionate or indulgent or yielding, (*s. countenance, ruler, treatment, rebuke, virtue, father, tutor*; *sterner* SEX). Hence **ster·n**LY[2] adv., **ster·n**NESS n. [OE *styrne*; perh. cogn. w. STEREO-, STARE]

stern[2], n. Hind part of ship or boat (opp. *bow, stem*; *from stem to s.*, throughout ship; *s. chase*, pursuit of ship by another straight behind it; *s. foremost*, moving backwards; *s. on*, with s. presented; BY[1] *the s.*); buttocks, rump; tail esp. of foxhound; *s.*-CHASE[1](*r*); *s.-fast*, rope or chain securing s. to quay &c.; *s.-post*, central upright timber or iron of s. usu. bearing rudder; *s. sheets*, space in boat aft of rowers' thwarts often with seats for passengers [perh. f. SHEET in naut. sense *rope*]; *s.-way*, backward motion or impetus of ship; *s.-whee·ler*, steamer propelled by one large paddle-wheel at s. Hence **-stern**ED[2], **ster·n**MOST, aa., **ster·n**WARD a. & adv., **ster·n**WARDS adv. [f. ON *stjórn* steering cogn. w. STEER[1]]

stern(o)-, comb. form of foll. esp. in names of muscles &c. connecting sternum with other part; *sterna·lgia*, chest-pain, esp. angina pectoris; *sternoclavi·cular*, of sternum & clavicle; *-fa·cial*; *-thyr·oid*; *-tra·cheal*.

ster·num, n. (pl. *-na*). Bone running from neck to stomach & having ribs articulated with it, the breastbone. Hence **ster·n**AL a. [mod. L, f. Gk *sternon* chest]

sternūta·tion, n. Sneezing, sneeze. [f. L *sternutatio* (*sternutare* frequent. of *sternuere* sneeze cf. Gk *ptarnumai*, -ATION)]

sternu·tative a., **sternu·tatory** a. & n. (Substance, e.g. snuff) causing to sneeze. [L *sternutare* (prec.), -IVE, -ORY]

ster·torous, a. (Of breathing or breather, esp. in apoplexy &c.) making snore-like sounds. Hence **ster·torous**LY[2] adv., **ster·torous**NESS n. [L *stertere* snore, -OR[1], -OUS]

stet, proof-correcting direction & v.t. Let it (i.e. the original form) stand (in margin to cancel a correction); (vb) write *s.* against, cancel correction of. [L, 3 sing. subj. of *stare* stand]

stĕ·thoscope, n., & v.t. Instrument used in auscultation esp. of the heart; (vb) examine with s. Hence **stetho·scop**IST, **stetho·scop**Y[1], nn., **stethoscŏ·pic** a., **stethosco·pic**ALLY adv. [F (*sté-*), f. Gk *stēthos* breast, -SCOPE]

ste·tson, n. Slouch hat worn by Anzac soldiers. [maker's name]

stē·vĕdore, n. Man employed in loading & unloading ships. [f. Sp. *estivador* (*estivar* f. L *stipare* pack tight, -TOR)]

stew[1], n. (archaic). Brothel (usu. *the ss.*). [earlier sense (cf. BAGNIO) *bath room* or *house,* f. OF *estuve* f. med. L *stup(h)a* etym. dub.; prob. cogn. w. E STOVE, G *stube* room]

stew[2], v.t. & i., & n. Cook (t. & i.) by long simmering in closed vessel with little liquid (*let* person, thing, *s. in his* &c. *own juice* or *grease,* abstain from helping &c.; *stew*ING[1] *pears* &c., fit for eating stewed, not raw; *the tea is stewed,* is bitter or strong with too long soaking), (fig.) be oppressed by close or moist warm atmosphere,(slang) = SWOT; *s.-pan, -pot,* shallow saucepan, covered crock, used for stewing. (N.) dish made by stewing (*Irish s.,* of mutton, potato, & onion); (fig., colloq.) *in a s.,* agitated with perplexity, anxiety, or anger. [n. f. vb, f. prec. in sense *hot bath*]

stew[3], n. Fishpond, tank for keeping fish alive in; artificial oyster-bed. [f. OF *estui* (*estuier* shut up)]

stew·ard (-*erd*), n. Person entrusted with management of another's property, esp. paid manager of great house or estate; purveyor of provisions &c. for a college, club, guild, ship, &c.; passengers' attendant & waiter on ship; any of the officials managing a race-meeting, ball, show, &c.; *Lord High S. of England,* official managing coronation or presiding at trial of a peer; *Lord S. of the Household,* high court officer. Hence **stew·ard**ESS[1], **stew·ard**SHIP, nn. [OE *stigweard* (*stig* house &c. cogn. w. STY[1], WARD[1])]

sthĕ·nic, a. (path.). (Of disease &c.) with morbid increase of vital action esp. of heart & arteries. [Gk *sthenos* strength, -IC]

sti·chomy̆th, stichomy̆·thia, (-k-), n. Dialogue in alternate lines of verse as employed in Greek plays. [f. Gk *stikhomuthia* (*stikhos* line, MYTH)]

stick, v.t. & i. (stuck), & n. Thrust point of *in(to)* or *through* (*s. the spurs in*; *s. bayonet, pin, into* or *through*); insert pointed thing(s) into, stab, (*s. pigs,* of butcher, also of mounted sportsman spearing wild pig; *will pull out a knife & s. you*; *tipsy-cake stuck over* or *stuck with almonds*; *cushion stuck full of pins*); fix *(up)on* pointed thing, be fixed (as) by point *in(to)* or *on (to),* (colloq.) put in specified position, (*heads were stuck on spikes of gateway*; *arrows s. in target*; *work with needle, body with dagger left, sticking in it*; *s. feather, rose, in cap, buttonhole*; *s. pen behind* one's *ear*; *s. up a target,* erect it; *s. your cap on*; *s. them in your pocket*; *s. a few commas in*; *just s. it on the table, down anywhere*); (with *out, up*) protrude, (cause to) project, be or make erect, (*s.* one's *head out of window*; *his hair sticks straight up*; *s.-up collar,* not turned down; *s. out* one's *chest*; *how his stomach sticks out!*; *stuck-up,* conceited, insolently exclusive, prob. f. carriage of head; *s. up to,* not humble oneself before, offer resistance to; *s. up for,* maintain cause or character of esp. absent person); fix or become or remain fixed (as) by adhesion of surfaces, (cause to) adhere or cleave, (*s. postage-stamp on*; *this envelope will not s.*; *if you throw* MUD *enough, some of it will s.,* innocence is not proof against scandal; *limpet sticks to rock*; *s. to the point,* not digress; *s. to business,* avoid distractions; *the name stuck to him* or *stuck,* was not forgotten; *friend that sticketh closer than a brother*; *can you s. on a horse?,* escape being thrown; *some of the money stuck in* or *to his fingers,* was appropriated or embezzled by him; *friends should s. together*; *s. to friend, resolve, promise, word,* &c, abide by, remain faithful to; *s. bills,* post placards on wall &c.; *s. to it,* persist, not cease trying; *s. in photographs,* paste them in book &c.; *sticks like a bur,* is not to be got rid of; *are you going to s. in* or *indoors all day?,* remain at home; so perh. *s. out for higher price, better terms,* &c., refuse to take lower); *s. it out* or *s. it* (slang), endure the conditions (*could not s. it any longer*); *s. it on* (slang), make high charges, exaggerate in narration; lose or deprive of power of motion through friction, jamming, suction, difficulty, or other impediment (*s. in the mud* lit., & fig. be unprogressive; *s.-in-the-mud* a., slow, unprogressive, n. person of such kind; also slang *Mrs* &c. *S.-i.-t.-m.,* Mrs &c. So-&-so; *sticks in my throat,* I cannot swallow it lit. or fig.; *sticks in* one's *gizzard,* cannot be digested fig.; *s. fast,* be hopelessly bogged &c.; *is stuck on a sandbank*; *got up to the fourth form, through some ten lines, & there stuck*; *s. at nothing,* allow nothing, esp. no scruples, to deter one; *stuck up* slang, completely at a loss; *that will s. him up,* puzzle him; *s. up bank, mail-coach,* &c. slang, terrorize officials, passengers, &c., in order to rob); provide (plant) with s. as support or to climb up; set (type) in COMPOSING-*s.,* whence **sti·ck**FUL(2) n.; *sticking-place, -point,* at which screw becomes jammed (usu. fig. w. ref. to *Macbeth* I. vii. 60); *sticking-plaster,* adhesive plaster for wounds &c.; *s.-jaw* (slang), pudding &c. hard to masticate. (N.) shoot of tree cut to convenient length for use as walking-cane or bludgeon, staff, wand, rod, piece of wood whether as part of something or separate more or less resembling these in shape & size, (*cut a s. from the hedge*; *cannot walk without a s.*; *gathering ss. to make a fire*, twigs; *any s. to beat a dog*, hatred makes unscrupulous; GOLD, SWORD, SINGLE[1], BROOM, FIDDLE, DRUM[1], *umbrella, rocket, -s.*; *riding on broomstick*, witch's way of transporting herself through air; *house was pulled down & not a s. left standing*; *a few ss. of furniture*, chairs &c. of simple kind; *wants the s.*, should be caned; *as* CROSS[3] *as*, DEVIL[1] *on, two ss.*; *in a cleft s.*, see CLEAVE[1]; CUT[2] one's *s.*), (Naut., joc.) mast or spar, (Mus.) conductor's baton, (fig.) person of no vigour or intelligence or social qualities; slender more or less cylindrical piece *of* sugar-candy, sealing-wax, shaving-soap, &c.; (short, with aid of context, for) fiddle-s., drum-s., composing-s., &c.; *s.-insect*, = WALK*ing-s. insect*. [vb a mixture of ME *stikien* (OE *stician*) & ME *steken*; cogn. w. Gk *stizō* prick, L *instigare* INSTIGATE, Skr. *tigmá* sharp; n., OE *sticca* (*stician*), orig. = peg]

sti·cker, n. In vbl senses; also or esp.: *pig-s.*, long-bladed sharp-pointed knife; BILL[4]*-s.*; batsman who scores slowly & is hard to get out; person who stays too long on visit; (Organ-build.) wooden rod transmitting motion between ends of two reciprocating levers. [-ER[1]]

sti·ckleback, n. Small fish with sharp spines on back. [OE *sticel* a prickle, sting, f. *stician* STICK, -LE(1), BACK[1]]

sti·ckler, n. *S. for*, person who insists on or pertinaciously supports or advocates (*is a great, am no, s. for authority, precision*, &c.). [f. obs. *stickle* be umpire, prob. f. ME *stightlen* arrange f. OE *stihtan* make, found, cf. MDu. *stichten*, G *stiften*; -ER[1]]

sti·cky, a. Tending to stick to what is touched, glutinous, viscous. Hence **sti·cki**LY[2] adv., **sti·cki**NESS n. [-Y[2]]

stiff, a. & n. Rigid, not flexible, unbending, unyielding, uncompromising, obstinate, (*s. shirt-front*; *lies s. in death*; *has a s. leg*, incapable of bending at knee; *s.-necked*, stubborn; *keep a s. upper lip*, show firmness of character; *s. ship*, heeling little under sail, not crank; *s. market*, with prices remaining firm; *met the charge with a s. denial*); lacking ease or grace or graciousness or spontaneity, constrained, reserved, haughty, formal, (*s. manners*; *a s. reception, bow*, &c.; *s. movement, attitude*, &c.; *writes in a s. style*); not working freely, sticking, offering resistance, (*a. s hinge, piston*, &c.; *s. un*, veteran athlete &c.; *s. neck*, rheumatic affection in which patient cannot turn head without pain), (of muscle, limb, &c., or person in regard to them) aching when used as result of previous exertion; hard to cope with, calling for strength or capacity of some kind, trying, (*s. examination, climb, slope, breeze*; *a s. price*, high; *a s. glass of grog*, strong; *a s. subject*, requiring application to master it); (of moist clay, batter, &c.) thick & viscous, not fluid, in or approaching plastic state; *s.-bit*, horse's bit made of unjointed bar with rings at ends; hence **sti·ff**LY[2] adv., **sti·ff**NESS n., **sti·ff**ISH[1](2) a., **sti·ff**EN[6] v.t. & i., **sti·ffen**ER[1] (2), **sti·ffen**ING[1](1, 4), nn. (N., slang) negotiable paper; (slang) corpse. [OE *stif*, cf. Du. *stijf*, G *steif*; cogn. w. L *stipes* stem, *stipare* pack]

stī·fle[1], v.t. & i. =SMOTHER vb. Hence (preferred to corresp. wds f. *smother*) **sti·fl**ING[1] a., **sti·fling**LY[2] adv. [earlier *stuf(f)le*, perh. f. OF *estouffer*, -LE(3)]

stī·fle[2], n. (Also *s.-joint*) joint of horse's hind leg between hip & hock; disease of s.-joint or s.-bone, whence **sti·fl**ED[2] a.; *s.-bone*, bone of s.-joint, horse's knee-pan; *s.-shoe*, kind with which stifled horse is shod on sound leg to make it use & so strengthen the weak one. [?]

sti·gma, n. (pl. *-s*, & *-ata* as specified below). Mark branded on slave, criminal, &c. (archaic); imputation attaching to person's reputation; stain on one's good name; (Path.) definite characteristic of some disease; (Anat., Zool.) spot, pore, small natural mark on skin &c., small red spot on person's skin (pl. *-ata*) that bleeds periodically or under mental stimulus, (Bot.) part of style or ovary-surface that receives pollen in impregnation, so **stigmă·**TIC, **sti·gmat**OSE[1], aa.; (Eccl.; pl. *-ata*; usu. in pl.) mark(s) corresponding to those left by the nails & spear at the Crucifixion developed by St Francis of Assisi & others (whence **sti·gmat**IST n.) & attributed to divine favour. [L f. Gk, genit. *-atos* (*stizō* prick, brand, -M)]

sti·gmatize, v.t. Use opprobrious terms of, describe opprobriously *as*, (*shall not s. him as he deserves*; *s. him, it, as a coward, cowardice*); produce stigmata on (person) by hypnotic suggestion &c. Hence **stigmatiz**A·TION n. [f. med. L f. Gk *stigmatizō* (prec., -IZE)]

stile[1], n. Steps or some provision other than gate enabling passengers to get over or through fence or wall but excluding cattle &c. (*help lame* DOG[1] *over s.*). [OE *stigel* f. *stigan* climb, cf. G *steigen*, -LE(1)]

stile[2], n. Vertical piece (cf. RAIL[1]) in frame of panelled door, wainscot, &c. [?]

stile·tto, n. (pl. *-os, -oes*), & v.t. Small dagger (vb, stab with s.); pointed implement for making eyelets &c. [It., dim. of *stilo* f. L *stilus* STYLE[1], -ET[1]]

still[1], a., n., v.t. & i., & adv. Without or almost without motion or sound or both (*stand, sit, lie, keep, s.*, motionless; *a s. lake*, unruffled; *s.* WATER[1]*s run deep*; *s. as the grave*; *a s. evening*; *how s. everything is!*; *in s. meditation*; *s. small voice*, that of conscience, w. ref. to 1 *Kings* xix. 12; *all sounds are s.*, hushed; *s. life* in painting, representation of inanimate things such as fruit & furniture; *s. hock* &c., not sparkling; *s. birth*, delivery of dead child, so *s.-born*); *s.-bugle*, naval call requiring crew to remain motionless till next call; *s.-fish* v.i., fish from anchored boat; hence **sti·lly**[1] (-l-lĭ) [-LY[2]] adv. (rare), **sti·ll**NESS n. (N.) deep silence (*in the s. of night*). (Vb) quiet, calm, appease, assuage, silence; (rare) grow calm (*when the tempest stills*). (Adv.) constantly, habitually, (archaic); then or now or for the future as before, even to this or that past or present or future time; nevertheless, for all that, on the other hand, all the same; (with comparat.) even, yet. [OE *stille* adj. & adv., *stillan* vb, cf. Du. *stil(len)*, G *still(en)*]

still[2], n., & v.t. Distilling-apparatus, esp. for making spirituous liquors, consisting essentially of a boiler & a condensing chamber, the vapour from the former passing into a spiral tube or worm surrounded by cold water or other refrigerating matter that fills the latter & issuing in drops as it condenses; *s.-room*, room for distilling, housekeeper's storeroom in large house. (Vb) distil (poet.); make (spirit) in s. [vb in 2nd sense f. n.; n. f. vb in first sense, partly short for DISTIL, partly f. L *stillare* drip]

sti·llage (-ĭj), n. Bench, frame, &c., for keeping articles off floor while draining, waiting to be packed, &c. [prob. f. Du. *stellagie* (*stellen* to place, -AGE)]

sti·lling, sti·llion, n. Support for cask. [perh. f. Du. *stelling* scaffold (as prec., -ING[1])]

sti·lly[2] (for *s.*[1] see STILL[1]), a. (poet.). Still, quiet. [STILL[1], -LY[1]]

stilt, n. Pole with rest for foot used generally in pairs with upper part of pole bound to leg or held with hand & raising user from ground (*on ss.* lit., & fig. = bombastic, stilted); (also *s.-bird* or *-plover* or *-walker*) long-legged bird resembling plover in having three-toed feet; *s.-petrel, -sandpiper*, long-legged kinds. [cf. Sw. *stylta*, Du. *stelt*, G *stelze*]

sti·lted, a. (As) on stilts; (of literary style &c.) pompous, bombastic, whence **sti·lted**LY[2] adv., **sti·lted**NESS n.; (of arch) with pieces of upright masonry between imposts & feet of the true arch. [-ED[2]]

Sti·lton, n. Superior kind of cheese named from S. in Huntingdonshire.

sti·mulant, a. & n. Stimulating (rare in gen. sense); (Med.) producing rapid transient increase of vital energy in organism or some part of it (n., s. agent or substance, as warmth, electricity, joy, &c., or exciting drug or article of food esp. alcoholic drink; *never takes ss.*, usu. = drinks no alcohol). [f. L as foll., -ANT]

sti·mulate, v.t. Apply stimulus to, act as stimulus upon, animate, spur on, excite to (more vigorous) action. Hence or cogn. **sti·mulat**ING[2], **sti·mul**ATIVE, aa., **stimu**LA·TION, **sti·mulat**OR[2], nn. [L *stimulare* (foll.), -ATE[3]]

sti·mŭlus, n. (pl. *-lī*). Thing that rouses to activity or energy (*so lethargic that no s. affects him*), rousing effect (*under the s. of hunger*); (Physiol.) thing that evokes functional reaction in tissues; (Bot.) sting, whence **sti·mul**OSE[1] a.; (Eccl.) point at end of crozier, pastoral staff, &c. [L, = goad]

sti·my, n., & v.t., (golf). Lie of balls on green such that player has other's ball between his & hole; (vb; usu. in p.p.) hinder by s. [also *stymy*; etym. dub.; cf. Sc. *styme* glimmer, glance]

sting, v.t. & i. (stung), & n. Wound with s. (*a bee, nettle, stung him, his finger*); affect with acute physical or mental pain (*pepper stings one's tongue*; *the cane, his bat-handle, the blow, his conscience, the imputation, stung him*; *stung by reproaches, with envy* or *desire*; *a stinging insult*), whence **sti·nging**LY[2] adv.; (of part of one's body) feel acute pain or communicate it to sensorium (*my hand, tooth, stings*); be able to s., have a s. (*some bees do not s.*; *stinging-nettle*, opp. DEAD-*nettle*). (N.) sharp-pointed weapon often tubular & connected with poison-gland in some insects & other animals (in tail as with bee, in head as with gnat, in claws as with centipede; also of snake's poison-fang) & plants (projecting as hair from surface as in nettle); infliction of wound with s., wound so made, pain caused by it, wounding quality or effect, rankling or acute pain of body or mind, keenness or vigour, (*was hurt by a s.*; *face covered with ss.*; *the s. of hunger, ss. of remorse*; *a jest with a s. in it*; *this air, bowling, has no s. in it*, is relaxing, feeble); *s.-bull* or *-fish*, kind of weever; *s.-nettle*, stinging-nettle; *s.-ray*, kinds of fish with flexible tail having sharp serrated projecting spine used as weapon; *s.-winkle*, beaked shell-fish that bores holes in other shell-fish; hence **sti·ng**LESS a. [OE *stingan*, cf. Da. *stinge*, Sw. & ON *stinga*]

sti·ngaree (-ngg-), n. = STING-*ray*. [corrupt.]

sti·nger (-ng-), n. In vbl senses; esp., smart painful blow. [-ER[1]]

sti·ngo (-nggō), n. (archaic). Strong beer. [STING, w. ref. to pungency, with fancy ending]

sti·ngy (-jĭ), a. Meanly parsimonious, niggardly. Hence **sti·ngi**LY[2] adv., **sti·ngi**NESS n. [spec. sense & pronunc. of obs. *stingy* (-ngĭ) nipping (of wind &c.) f. STING, -Y[2]]

stink, v.i. & t. (*stank* or *stunk, stunk*), & n. (Have or emit) strong offensive smell (*s. in* NOSTRILS *of*; *s.* one *out*, drive him from room &c. by s.), whence **sti·nking**LY[2] adv.; (slang) *s. of money*, be notoriously rich; (slang) perceive s. of (*can s. it a mile off*); (n. pl., slang) chemistry, natural science, as subject of study; (part., slang) objectionable in any way, that one dislikes; (part., as distinctive epithet of animals or plants) having recognizable & usu. disagreeable smell (*stinking camomile*; *stinking cedar* or *yew*, savin & allied trees; *stinking crane's-bill, hellebore, horehound, nightshade,* &c.; *stinking-weed* or *-wood*, kind of cassia; *stinking badger*, teledu); *s.-alive*, the fish bib (from rapid putrefaction after death); *s.-ball*, vessel containing explosives &c. generating noxious vapours used formerly in naval warfare & still by Eastern pirates; *s.-horn*, kinds of ill-smelling fungus; *s.-pot*, any receptacle containing something that stinks, also =*s.-ball*, also as abusive term for person or thing; *s.-stone*, kind of limestone giving off fetid smell when quarried; *s.-trap*, appliance to prevent escape of effluvia from drains when opened. [OE *stincan*, cf. Du. & G *stinken*; cogn. w. STENCH]

sti·nkard, n. Stinking person or animal, esp. the teledu. [-ARD]

sti·nker, n. Stinkard, stinkpot; kinds of large petrel. [-ER[1]]

stint, v.t., & n. Cease do*ing* or *to* do (archaic); keep on short allowance (*s.* one*self* or person or animal *in* food &c.); supply or give in niggardly amount or grudgingly (*s. food, money, service,* &c.); hence **sti·nting**LY[2] adv. (N.) limitation of supply or effort (usu. *without, no, s. laboured without s.*, without sparing effort), whence **sti·nt**LESS a.; fixed or allotted amount of or *of* work (*do* one's *daily s.*); kinds of small sandpiper, esp. dunlin. [OE *styntan* (*stunt* short of wit, dull, cf. ON *stuttr* short)]

stī·pate, a. (bot.). Crowded, close-set. [L *stipare* pack, -ATE[2]]

stipe, stī·pēs, n. (bot., zool.). Stalk or stem (in Bot. esp. support of carpel, stalk of frond, stem of fungus). Hence **sti·pi(ti)**FORM, **sti·pit**ATE[2], aa. [*stipe* F, f. L *stipes -itis* stem]

stī·pel, n. (bot.). Secondary stipule at base of leaflets of compound leaf. Hence **sti·pell**ATE[2] a. [f. F *stipelle* (prec., -EL)]

stī·pend, n. Fixed periodical money allowance for work done, salary, esp. clergyman's official income. [f. OF *stipende* f. L *stipendium* (for *stipip-*) f. *stipem* alms &c. in small coin, *pendĕre* pay]

stipe·ndiary, a. & n. (Person) receiving stipend, paid, not serving gratuitously; *s.* (*magistrate*), paid police magistrate in large towns appointed by Home Secretary. [f. L *stipendiarius* (prec., -ARY[1])]

stipes. See STIPE.

sti·pple, v.t. & i., & n. Engrave (plate, thing portrayed), paint or draw, in dots, not lines; use this method; hence **sti·ppl**ER[1](1, 2), **sti·ppl**ING[1], nn. (N.) dotted work; *s.-graver*, engraver's stippling-tool. [f. Du. *stippelen* (*stippen* to prick, f. *stip* point)]

stī·pūlate[1], v.i. & t. *S. for*, mention or insist upon as essential part of agreement; demand as part of bargain or agreement *that*; (p.p.) laid down as part of the terms of an agreement (*is not of the stipulated quality*). So **stipula·tion**[1] [-ATION], **sti·pulat**OR[2], nn. [L *stipulari* (OL *stipulus* firm, cogn. w. STIPES) bargain, -ATE[3]]

stī·pule, n. Small leaf-life appendage to leaf usu. at base of leaf-stem. Hence **stipul**A·CEOUS, **sti·pul**AR[1], **sti·pul**ARY[1], **sti·pulate**[2] [-ATE[2]], **sti·puli**FORM, aa., **stipula·tion**[2] [-ATION], n. [F (STIPE, -ULE)]

stir, v.t. & i., & n. Set, keep, or (begin to) be, in motion (*not a breath stirs the lake, leaves*; *sit without stirring a foot* &c. or *stirring*; *if you s., I shoot*; *never stirred abroad* or *out of the house*, went out; *is not stirring yet*, is still in bed; *s. the fire*, use poker; *s. your stumps* colloq., make haste, walk &c. faster; *s. tea, porridge, soup*, &c., move spoon &c. round & round in to mix ingredients, keep from burning in pot, &c.; *there is no news stirring*, going about; *lead stirring life*, be busy; *s. up*, mix well by stirring; *s. up the mud, sediment*, &c., make it rise from bottom of liquid by stirring); rouse (*up*), excite, animate, inspirit, (*s. up strife, mutiny, discontent, curiosity*; person *wants stirring up*, is indolent or torpid; *s.* one's *blood*, excite him to enthusiasm, desire, &c.; *s.* one's *wrath, bile*, &c., enrage, disgust, &c.; *stirring events, times, music*, &c., exciting, stimulating; *a stirring speech, picture, tale*), whence **stir·ring**LY[2] adv.; *s.-about*, (n.) porridge, (adj.) bustling; hence **stir·r**ER[1](1, 2) n. (N.) commotion, bustle, disturbance, excitement, sensation, (*full of s. & movement*; *person, event, makes a great s.*, is much discussed &c.); slightest movement (*not a s.*), whence **stir·**LESS a.; act of stirring (*give the fire a s.*). [OE *styrian*, cf. Norw. *styrja*; perh. cogn. w. Du. *storen*, G *stören*, disturb, & w. STORM]

stir·piculture, n. Breeding of special stocks or strains. [foll., -I-, CULTURE]

stirps, n. (Law) progenitor of family; (Zool.) classificatory group. [L, =stock]

sti·rrup, n. Rider's foot-rest usu. consisting of iron loop with flattened base hung by a strap or *s.-leather* from *s.-bar*, iron attachment let into saddle; s. & s.-leather as a whole; (Naut.) rope with eye giving hold in reefing; *s.-bone*, small bone, s.-shaped in man, in mammal's ear; *s.-cup*, of wine &c. presented to person mounted for departure; *s.-iron*, s. without s.-leather; *s.-piece* in carpentry &c., hanging support. [OE *stirāp* (*stigan* climb, cf. STILE, ROPE)]

stitch, n., & v.t. & i. Acute internal pain in the side such as often results from running &c. soon after eating; single pass of needle in sewing (*a s. in time* SAVE[1]*s nine*), result of it or of single complete movement in knitting, crochet, embroidery, &c. (*if one s. gives the rest will*; *what long ss.!*; *has not a dry s. on him*, is wet through; *drop a s.* in knitting, let loop fall off needle-end spoiling the continuity; *put a s.* or *ss. in* in surgery, sew up wound with gut, silk, wire, &c.), method followed in making ss. or kind of work produced (*am learning a new s.*; LOCK[3], *buttonhole*, HERRING-*bone*, &c., *-s.*, CROSS-STITCH); *s.-wheel*, harness-maker's notched wheel for pricking leather in places where ss. are to go; *sti·tchwort*, kinds of chickweed, esp. one with erect stem & white star flowers (named as cure for s. in side); (vb) sew (t. & i.; *s. up*, usu. mend by sewing; *stitching-horse*, harness-maker's clamp for holding work). [vb f. n., OE *stice* pricking (*stician* pierce), cf. G *stich*, *sticken* vb]

sti·thy (-dhĭ), n. (archaic & poet.). Smith's shop, forge. [f. ON *stethi* (Teut. *sta-* stand)]

stī·ver, n. Even the smallest coin (usu. *don't care, has not, a s.*). [f. Du. *stuiver* small obsolete coin]

sto·a, n. (pl. *-ae*). Portico in ancient-Greek architecture (*the s.*, the PORCH, see STOIC). [Gk]

stoat[1], n. The ermine, esp. in its summer coat (also as general name for ermine & allied kinds, weasel, ferret, &c.). [f. 15th c., etym. dub.]

stoat[2], v.t. Sew up (tear, cloth edges) with invisible stitches. [?]

stock, n., & v.t. & i. Stump, butt, main trunk, plant into which graft is inserted, body-piece serving as base or holder or handle for working parts of implement or machine, (source of) family or breed, raw material of manufacture, store ready for drawing on, equipment for trade or pursuit, (*they nest in the ss. of trees*, archaic use; *ss. & stones*, inanimate things, lethargic persons; *laughing, gazing*, &c., *-s.*, butt for ridicule &c.; *must be grafted on a sound s.*; *s. of rifle, plane, plough*, main part, usu. of wood, into which barrel, blade, share, &c., are fastened; *s. of bit*, brace; *s. of anvil*, base it rests on; *s. of anchor*, cross-bar; *lock, s., & barrel* fig., completely, root & branch; *comes of a good, Puritan, treacherous*, &c., *s.*, family of distinct character; *polyp* &c. *-s.* in Zool., aggregate organism; *paper* &c. *s.*, rags &c. from which paper &c. is made; *soup-s.* or usu. *s.*, liquor made by stewing bones &c. as basis for any sort of soup; *has a great s. of information, hardware*; ROLL[2]*ing s.*; *take over a farm with the s.*, its animals, also *live s.*, & implements, also *dead s.*; *s.-in-trade*, all requisites for a trade, also fig. as *the politician's s.-in-t. of a dozen catch-words*; *renew* one's *s.*; *lay in a s. of*; *have in s.*, have ready without need of procuring specially; *take s.*, review one's s. for accurate knowledge of what one has in s.; so *s.-taking* n.; *take s. of* fig., observe with a view to estimating character &c. of; *s. argument, comparison, remark, joke*, &c., one that requires no fresh thought but is always at hand & perpetually repeated whether by individual or by people in general); kinds (*common* or *ten-weeks, Virginia*, &c., *s.*) of fragrant-flowered usu. hoary-leaved garden plant (orig. *s.-gilliflower*, named as having stronger stem than clove-gilliflower or pink); (pl., hist.) timber frame with holes for feet & sometimes hands in which petty offenders were confined in sitting position; (pl.) timbers on which ship rests while building (*on the ss.*, in construction or preparation, often transf.); stiff wide band of leather or other material formerly worn round neck, now displaced in general use by collar & tie, but surviving in some military uniforms & sometimes revived in modified forms by fashion; (Finance) money lent to a government & involving payment of fixed interest to lenders or whomsoever their rights have passed to by purchase &c. (*buy, hold, s.*, the right to receive such interest on some amount of s.; *the ss.*, State's funded debts as a whole; *has money, £50,000, in the ss.*; *take s. in* fig., concern oneself with), capital of corporation or company contributed by individuals for prosecution of some undertaking & divided into (esp. £100) shares entitling holders to proportion of profits (also JOINT[2]*-s.*; *bank, railway*, &c., *s.*; PREFERENCE or *preferred s.*; *s. certificate*; WATER[2] *s.*); *s.-account, -book*, showing amount of goods laid in & amount disposed of; *s.-breeder*, raiser of live s.; *s.-broker, -king*, (person engaged in) buying & selling for clients on commission of ss. held by s.-jobbers; *s.-car*, cattle-truck; *stoc·kdove*, European wild pigeon smaller & darker than rockdove [perh. from breeding in ss. of trees]; *s. exchange*, place where ss. & shares are publicly bought & sold, esp. *the S. E.*, (building in London occupied by) association of dealers in ss. conducting business according to fixed rules (*is on the S. E.*, a member of this association); *s.-farm(er)*, that breeds live s.; *stoc·kfish*, cod & similar fish split & dried in sun without salt; *s.-gang*, gang of saws in frame cutting log into boards at one passage; *s.-jobber, -bing, -bery*, (person engaged in) speculating in ss. with view of profiting by fluctuations in price, cf. *s.-broker*; *s.-list*, daily or periodical s.-exchange publication giving current prices of ss. &c.; *s.-man* (Austral.), man in charge of live s.; *s.-market*, s. exchange or transactions on it; *s.-owl*, the great eagle owl; *s.-pot*, for making or keeping soup-s.; *s.-rider* (Austral.), herdsman on unfenced station; *s.-still*, motionless; *s.-whip*, with short handle & long lash for herding cattle; *s.-yard*, enclosure with pens &c. for sorting or temporary keeping of cattle; hence **sto·ck**LESS a. (esp. of gun, anchor, &c.). (Vb) fit (gun &c.) with s.; (Hist.) confine in the ss.; provide (shop, farm, &c.) with goods or live s. or requisites (*a well-stocked larder, library*, &c.); keep (goods) in s. (*we do not s. the out sizes*); fill or cover (land) with permanent growth esp. of pasture-grass; (of plant) =TILLER³. [OE *stocc*, cf. Du. *stok*, G *stock*]

stockā·de, n., & v.t. (Fortify with) breastwork or enclosure of upright stakes. [f. F *estacade* f. Sp. *estacada* f. *estaca* f. Teut., see STAKE, -ADE(1), w. assim. to prec.]

sto·ckinet, n. Elastic knitted material used esp. for underclothing. [foll., -ET¹; or corrupt. of older *stocking-net*]

sto·cking, n. Tight covering usu. knitted or woven of wool or cotton or silk for foot & leg up to or slightly above knee (usu. in pl., esp. *pair of ss.*; *is* or *stands six feet in his ss.* or *s.-feet*, when measured without his boots; *elastic s.*, surgical appliance of elastic webbing like s. or part of it worn for varicose veins, strained muscles, &c.; *white* &c. *s.* in horse &c., lower part of leg differently coloured from rest); *s.-frame, -loom, -machine*, knitting-machine. Hence **sto·cking**LESS a. [STOCK, -ING³; formerly also *stock(s)* short for *nether-stock(s)* opp. *upper-stock(s)* = knee-breeches, *stock* having sense *docked part* (of the original hose or single garment for abdomen & legs)]

sto·cky, stu·ggy (colloq.), a. Thickset, short & strongly built, (of person; also in Bot. & Zool.). Hence **sto·cki**LY², **stug-**, adv., **sto·cki**NESS, **stug-**, n. [-Y²]

stodge, n., & v.i., (school slang). Food esp. of heavy kind; full meal, feast; greedy eater; (vb) eat greedily. [perh. imit.]

sto·dgy (-ŏjĭ), a. (Of food) heavy, filling, indigestible; (of receptacle) packed, bulging; (of book, style, &c.) over-full of facts or details, wanting in lightness or interest. Hence **sto·dgi**NESS n. [-Y²]

stoep (-ōōp), n. (S.-Afr.). Terraced veranda in front of house. [Du., cogn. w. STEP]

sto·ic, n. Philosopher of the school founded at Athens *c.* 308 B.C. by Zeno making virtue the highest good, concentrating attention on ethics, & inculcating control of the passions & indifference to pleasure & pain (*S-*; often attrib., as *S. philosopher, doctrines, indifference*); (*s-*) person of great self-control or fortitude or austerity, whence **sto·ic**AL a. **sto·ical**LY² adv. Hence **Sto·ic**ISM(2, 3), **s-**, n. [f. L f. Gk *stōikos* (*stoa*, porch, w. ref. to Zeno's teaching in *Stoa Poecile* Painted Porch at Athens, -IC)]

stoke, v.t. & i. Feed & tend (furnace). feed furnace of (engine &c.), act as stoker; (fig.; colloq.) take food esp. in hurried way; *s.-hole*, compartment in which steamer's fires are worked. [back form. f. foll.]

sto·ker, n. Man who tends furnace esp. that of steamer or steam-engine (*mechanical s.*, automatic feeder for furnace). [Du. (*stoken* stoke)]

stole¹, n. (Rom. Ant.; also L *stola* pl. *-ae*) outer dress of ancient-Roman matron; ecclesiastical vestment, a strip of silk or other material hanging from back of neck over shoulders & down to knees (worn by deacon over left shoulder only), woman's wrap similarly worn; *groom of the s.* [orig. *stoole*, i.e. king's close-stool], first LORD of the Bed-chamber. Hence **(-)stol**ED² a. [f. L f. Gk *stolē* robe (*stellō* array)]

stole². =STOLON.

stole³, stolen. See STEAL.

stŏ·lid, a. Phlegmatic, unemotional, lacking animation, not easily agitated, hard to stir, obstinate, apparently stupid. Hence or cogn. **stoli·di**TY n., **sto·lid**LY² adv. [f. L *stolidus*]

stō·lon, stole⁴, n. Reclined or prostrate branch that strikes root & develops new plant; underground shoot of mosses developing leaves; (Zool.) rootlike creeping growth. Hence **sto·lon**ATE², **stoloni·**FEROUS, aa. [f. L *stolo -onis*]

sto·mach (-ŭmak), n., & v.t. Internal cavity in which chief part of digestion is carried on, being in man a pear-shaped enlargement of the alimentary canal extending from end of gullet to beginning of gut (*coat of the s.*, its mucous inmost lining; *coats of the s.*, the peritoneum or serous coat, the muscular, submucous, & mucous layers); (in some animals, esp. ruminants), one of several digestive cavities either of similar character or differing in action or function (*ruminant's ss.*, first s. or paunch or rumen, second s. or honeycomb or reticulum, third s. or psalterium or omasum, fourth or true s. or reed or abomasum; *muscular s.*, acting by grinding or squeezing, as the gizzard; *glandular s.*, acting esp. by gastric juices); (loosely) belly, abdomen, lower front of body, (*pit of the s.*, depression below bottom of breastbone, the wind or mark; *what a s. he has got!*, corporation); appetite for or *for* food (STAY¹ one's *s.*); taste or readiness or sufficient spirit *for* (or archaic *to*) controversy, conflict, danger, or an undertaking (*had no s. for the fight*), *proud* or *high s.*, haughtiness; *s.-ache*, pain in belly, esp. in bowels; *s. cough*, caused by irritation of s. or small intestine; *s.-pump*, kind of syringe for emptying s. or forcing liquid into it; *s.-staggers*, apoplexy in horses due to paralysis of s.; *s.-tooth*, lower canine milk-tooth in infants, cutting of which often disorders s.; *s.-tube*, for introducing through gullet into s. to wash it out or empty it by siphon action; hence **sto·machAL**, **sto·machLESS**, aa., **sto·machFUL** (2) n. (Vb) eat with relish or toleration, find sufficiently palatable to swallow or keep down, (fig.) pocket or put up with (affront &c.), (usu. w. neg., as *cannot s. it*). [ME *stomak* f. F *estomac* f. L f. Gk *stomakhos* gullet, dim of *stoma* mouth]

sto·macher, (-tsher), n. (hist.). Front-piece of 15th–17th-c. female dress covering breast & pit of stomach, ending downwards in point often lapping over skirt, & often set with gems or richly embroidered. [f. AF or OF *estomachier* (prec.), whence the pronunc.]

stomă·chic (-k-), a. & n. Of the stomach; aiding s. action, promoting digestion or appetite (n., s. draught or drug, bitters &c.). [f. L f. Gk *stomakhikos* (STOMACH, -IC)]

stŏmato-, comb. form of Gk *stoma -atos* mouth, as *-ga·stric*, of mouth & stomach.

stone, n., a., & v.t. Piece of rock of any shape usu. detached from earth's crust & of no great size, esp. a pebble, a cobble, or a single piece used or usable in building or roadmaking or as missile (STOCKS *& ss.*; *built of great ss.*; *as hard as a s.*; ROLL[3]*ing s.*; ROCK[3]*ing s.*; SERMONS *in ss.*; *ss. will cry out*, wrong is great enough to move inanimate things; *give a s. for bread*, offer a mockery of help; *mark with a white s.*, record as a joyful day, w. ref. to ancient-Roman use of chalk; *meteoric s.*, meteorite; *leave no s. unturned*, try every possible means, often *to* do; *break ss.*, get living by preparing road metal, as phr. for being reduced to extremities; *cast, throw, ss.* or *a s. at*, lit., & = make aspersions on character &c. of; *those who live in glass houses should not throw ss.*, aspersion provokes retort; *shower of ss.*, thrown, or rolling down hill &c.; *kill two* BIRDS *with one s.*; *s.'s cast* or *throw*, distance s. can be thrown); (usu. *precious s.*) a gem (*no s. in it worth less than £100*; *Bristol s.*, Bristol DIAMOND; CAIRNGORM *s.*); ss. or rock as a substance or material (often with defining pref., as SAND, LIME[1], *-s.*; *Bath, Caen, Portland, s.*, kinds of building s.; *built of s.*; *s. buildings* &c.; *s. jar* &c., of s.-ware; *s.* JUG[1]; HOLYSTONE; *artificial s.*, kinds of concrete; *Cornish s.*, kaolin; *has a heart of s.*, is hard-hearted; *harden into s.*, petrify lit. or fig.; *the s. age*, stage of civilization at which implements & weapons were of s., not metal; PHILOSOPHERS' *s.*); piece of s. of definite & designed shape (often with purpose specified by word in comb., or easily supplied from context; GRIND, GRAVE[1], HEARTH, MILL[1], WHET, *-s.*; *Moabite, Rosetta, s.*, stelae with historically important inscriptions); thing resembling s. in hardness or pebble in shape, e.g. calculus (as single concretion or as the malady), hard case of kernel in drupe or s.-fruit, seed of grape, testicle, pellet of hail, (GALL[1]*-s.*; *underwent an operation for s.* or *the s.*, *remove the ss. from plums, grapes*, &c.; *hail-storm with ss. as big as marbles*); weight of 14 lb. or of other amounts varying with the commodity (*rides 12st.*, weighs that in the saddle; *s. of meat* or *fish* 8 lb., *s. of cheese* 16 lb., &c.); *s.-axe*, with two obtuse edges for hewing s.; *s.-blind* (quite); *s.-blue*, compound of indigo with starch or whiting; *s.-boiling*, primitive method of boiling by putting heated ss. into water; *s.-borer*, kinds of mollusc; *s.-break*, saxifrage; *s.-buck*, steenbok; *s.-butter*, kind of alum; *s.-cast*, = *stone's cast* above; *stone-*CHAT[2]; *s.-coal*, anthracite; *s.-cold* (quite); *sto·necrop*, kinds of low creeping plant growing esp. on walls & rocks; *s.-curlew*, thick-knee or thick-kneed plover; *s.-dead, -deaf*, (quite); *s.-eater*, = *s.-borer*; *s.-fence* (U.S. slang), whisky & cider, or similar mixed drink; *s.-fern*, ceterach; *s.-fly*, insect with aquatic larvae found under ss., used as bait for trout; *s.-fruit*, with seeds enclosed in hard shell surrounded by pulp, drupe, e.g. plum, peach, cherry; *s.-gall*, round mass of clay in variegated sandstone; *s.-horse* archaic, stallion; *s. man*, cairn; *s.-mason*, dresser of or builder in s.; *s.-parsley*, a hedge plant; *s.-pine*, S.-Ital. kind with branches at top spreading like umbrella; *s.-pit*, quarry; *s. pitch*, inspissated pitch; *s.-plover*, large kind called also *thick-knee* & *s.-curlew*; *s.-race* (of runners who must pick up ss. laid at intervals); *s.-rag*, kind of lichen; *s.-rue*, kind of fern; *s.-saw*, untoothed iron blade stretched in saw-frame for cutting s. with aid of sand; *s.-weed*, gromwell; *s.-snipe*, large N.-Amer. kind; *stonewa·ll* v.i. & t., obstruct by *s.-walling*; *s.-wa·lling*, (Cricket) excessively cautious batting, (Politics, esp. Austral.) parliamentary obstruction; *s.-ware*, pottery made from very silicious clay or from composition of clay & flint; *s.-work*, masonry; *sto·newort*, kinds of plant, esp. s.-parsley; hence **(-)stonED**[2], **sto·neLESS**, aa. (Vb) pelt with ss. (*s. to death*); free (fruit) from ss.; face, pave, &c., with s. [OE *stán*, cf. Du. *steen*, G *stein*]

sto·ny, a. & adv. Full of, covered with, having many, stones; hard, rigid, fixed, as stone (*a s. stare*, refusing response or recognition; *s. heart*, obdurate or unfeeling heart, also hard core or interior, whence **stony-heartED**[2] a.); hence **sto·nILY**[2] adv., **sto·niNESS** n. (Adv.) utterly (only in *s.* BROKE[2]). [-Y[2]]

stood. See STAND.

stoo͝k, n., & v.t., (chiefly Sc. & north). =SHOCK[3]. [ME *stouk*, cf. MLG *stûke*]

stool, n., & v.i. Backless seat for one, often consisting of wooden slab on three legs (*office s.*, high s. used by clerks &c.; MUSIC, CAMP[1], *-s.*; *three-legged s.*; *folding s.*, made to fold up; *s. of repentance*, orig. that on which fornicators &c. were set to receive rebuke in churches in Scotland, & now transf.; *fall between two ss.*, fail from vacillation between two courses &c.); low bench for kneeling on; =FOOT-*s.*; (Archit.) window-sill; (place for) evacuation of bowels, faeces evacuated, (*go to s.*; CLOSE[1], NIGHT[1],-*s.*); root or stump of plant from which shoots spring; piece of wood to which decoy-bird is attached; *s.-ball*, old game resembling cricket still played in Sussex esp. by girls; *s.-pigeon*, pigeon used, person acting, as decoy. (Vb) throw up shoots from root; go to s., evacuate bowels. [OE *stōl*, cf. Du. *stoel*, G *stuhl*; cogn. w. STAND]

stoop[1], v.i. & t., & n. Bring one's head nearer the ground by bending down from standing position, (fig.) deign or condescend *to* do, descend or lower oneself *to* some conduct (*s. to conquer*, gain power or one's end by preliminary self-abasement); carry one's head & shoulders bowed forward, whence **stoo·ping**LY[2] adv.; (of hawk &c., & transf.; archaic, poet.) swoop, pounce; incline (head, neck, shoulders, back) forward & down; tilt (cask) forward. (N.) stooping carriage of body; (archaic) swoop of hawk &c. [OE *stūpian*, cf. MDu. *stûpen*, ON *stúpa*; cogn. w. STEEP[1, 2]]

stoop[2], n. =STOUP.

stoop[3], n. (U.S., Can.). Uncovered platform in front of house (cf. STOEP). [f. Du. STOEP]

stop[1], v.t. & i. Stuff up or *up*, prevent or forbid passage through, make impervious or impassable, close, bar, stifle, stanch, (*s. a leak, hole*, &c.; *stopped pipe* in organ, with upper end plugged, giving note an octave lower; *s.* one's *ears*, put fingers in to avoid hearing, also fig. refuse to listen; *s. a tooth*, fill cavity in it with **sto·pp**ING[1] n. of gold, amalgam, cement, &c.; *s. a wound*, stanch its bleeding; *s.* one's *mouth* fig., induce him by bribery or other means to keep silence about something; *s. a gap*, serve to meet a temporary need; *s. the way*, be or act as obstruction, prevent progress); put an end to (motion &c.), completely check progress or motion or operation of, effectively hinder or prevent, (*s. progress* &c.; *s. horse* &c., esp. when running away; *s. ball*, esp. of batsman or field in cricket; *s. thief!*, cry of pursuer; *s. blow*, parry it in boxing; *s. blow with* one's *head* &c. facet., receive it, esp. *s. a bullet*, be shot; *thick walls s. sound*, render it inaudible; *s.* one's *breath*, kill him by smothering or otherwise; *s. clock, factory*, &c., make it cease working; *s.* person's *doing*, person *from* doing; *shall s. that nonsense*, not allow it to go on); cut off, suspend, decline customary giving of or permission for, (*shall s. your wages, holidays, meetings*; *the cost must be stopped out of his salary*; *s. payment of a cheque*, direct one's banker not to cash; *s. payment*, declare oneself unable to meet obligations, break financially; *why has our gas, water, been stopped?*); change pitch of (stringed or other musical instrument, string of instrument) by pressing string, closing hole, &c.; cease, come to an end, cease from *doing*, discontinue (one's action), cease from motion or speaking or action, make a halt or pause, (*noise, annuity, stops*; *do not s.*, go on, continue; *s. dead* or *short*, cease abruptly; *shall s. playing, subscribing, my visits, my endeavours*; *do s. grumbling, your complaints, that noise*; *he stopped in the middle of a sentence*; *my watch has stopped*; *train does not s. at, before, Exeter*; *he never stops to think*); (colloq.) remain, stay, sojourn, (*shall s. in bed, at home*; *s. up*, not go to bed; *shall you s. for the sermon?*; *have been stopping in Cornwall with friends*); provide with ss., punctuate, (*a badly spelt & stopped letter*); (Naut.) make fast, stopper, (cable &c.); (Etching) *s. out*, cover (parts that are to be protected from action of acid) with defensive coating (*stopping-brush*, for doing this); (Photog.) *s. down*, obscure part of (lens) with diaphragm; (Founding) *s. off*, fill in (part of mould not to be used) with sand. Hence **sto·pp**AGE(3) n. [OE *(for)stoppian* f. pop. L *stuppare* (*stup(p)a* cf. Gk *stuppē* tow)]

stop[2], n. Stopping or being stopped, pause, check, (*put a s. to*; *make, come to, bring to, a s.*; *is at a s.*, not proceeding or unable to proceed; *train runs from London to Crewe without a s.*); punctuation-mark, esp. comma, semi-colon, colon, or period (*full s.*, period; *come to a full s.* transf., cease completely); (Mus.) change of pitch effected by stopping (see prec.), also fret or key or lever in instrument to assist stopping, (in organ) set of pipes having special tone, also knob &c. by which these are put in or out of action, (fig.) manner of speech adopted to produce particular effect (*can put on* or *pull out the pathetic, blustering, virtuous*, &c., *s. at will*); batten, peg, or the like, meant to s. motion of something at fixed point; (Opt., Photog.) diaphragm; (Phonet.) mute consonant sound made by closure of organs concerned (as k, t, p); (Naut.) small line used as lashing, also projection of lower mast-head supporting trestle-trees. Hence **sto·p**LESS a. [f. prec.]

stop-, comb. form of STOP[1, 2]: *sto·pcock*,

tap; *s.-collar,* ring checking motion of shaft; *s.-cylinder,* kind of printing-press; *s.-drill,* with shoulder limiting depth of penetration; *sto·pgap,* temporary substitute; *s.-knob,* knob actuating organ-stop; *s.-motion,* arrangement for automatic stopping of machine when out of order; *s.-order,* order to stockbroker to buy or sell on stock's reaching specified price; *s.-plate,* limiting play of axle on bearings; *s.-press,* (news) inserted in paper after printing has begun; *s. -valve,* closing pipe against passage of liquid; *s.-watch,* with mechanism for starting & stopping it at will, used in timing races &c.

sto·pper, n., & v.t. In vbl senses; esp.: plug for closing bottle &c. usu. of same material as the vessel (*put a s. on* something, bring about cessation of it); *tobacco-s.,* implement for pressing down tobacco in pipe-bowl; (Naut.) rope, clamp, double claw, &c., for checking & holding rope cable or chain cable; *s. bolt,* ring-bolt in deck to which ss. are secured; *s.-knot,* finishing of end of s.-rope made by interlacing its strands; (vb) close or secure with s. [-ER¹]

sto·pple, n., & v.t. Stopper of bottle or other vessel; (vb) close with s. [STOP¹, -LE(1)]

stor·age, n. Storing of goods, method of doing this (*cold s.,* in refrigerators &c.); space available for it; cost of warehousing. [STORE + -AGE]

stor·ax, n. (Tree yielding) a resinous vanilla-scented balsam formerly much used in medicine & perfumery; *liquid s.,* a balsam got from the Oriental sweet-gum tree. [L, f. Gk *sturax*]

store, n., & v.t. Abundance, provision, stock of something ready to be drawn upon, (sing. with or, archaic exc. of intangible things, without *a,* & pl.; *has s., good s., a s.,* or *ss., of wine, wit, anecdote, wisdom*; *in s.,* laid up in readiness, about to come, destined, as *I have, tomorrow has, a surprise in s. for you*); place where things are kept for sale, (chiefly U.S.) ordinary shop (*s. clothes* &c., esp. = ready-made; *book* &c.-*s.*), (Brit.) large commercial establishment selling goods of many different kinds usu. for cash & at low prices (*the ss.,* these opp. ordinary shops, as *I get most things at the ss.*; COOPERATIVE *s.* or *ss.*; *Army & Navy,* &c., *ss.,* selling only to members, who must have specified qualification); (pl.) articles of particular kind or for special purpose accumulated for use, supply of things needed, (*military, naval,* &c., *ss.*; *marine ss.,* old ship materials); (attrib.) kept for future use (*s. cattle* &c., not yet being fattened); *set s. by,* reckon precious or important, esp. *set no great s. by*; *store·house,* place where things are stored up, granary &c., esp. fig. (*person, book, is a s.-h. of information* &c., cf. MINE¹); *s.-keeper,* shopkeeper (U.S.); *s.-room,* in which household requisites are kept; *s.-ship,* carrying ss. for fleet, garrison, &c. (Vb) stock or furnish with or *with* something (usu. with knowledge or the like; *s. your mind with facts*; *a well-stored memory*); lay up or *up* for future use (*harvest has been stored,* got in; *s. up a saying in* one's *heart*); deposit (furniture &c.) in a warehouse for temporary keeping; (of receptacle) hold, keep, contain, have storage-accommodation for (*a single cell can s. 2,000,000 foot-pounds of energy*); hence **stor·**ABLE a. [vb f. n., f. OF *estor* f. *estorer* build f. L IN(*staurare* cf. RESTORE) renew]

stor·ey (pl. *-eys*), **stor·y,** n. Any of the parts into which a house is divided horizontally, the whole of the rooms &c. having a continuous floor, (*fell from a third-s. window*; *a house of five ss.*; *upper s.* or *ss.* fig., the brain, as *is a little wrong in the u. s.*); *s.-post,* upright supporting a beam on which rests a floor or wall. Hence **(-)storey**ED², **-ied,** a. [f. 13th-c. Anglo-L *hystoria, istoria,* perh. orig. meaning tier of STORIED windows or sculpture, & = STORY¹; spelling *-ey* is for different. f. STORY¹]

stor·iated, a. (Of title-pages &c.) with elaborate decorative designs. [for HISTORIATED]

stor·ied, a. Celebrated in legend, associated with legends or stories or history; adorned with legendary or historical representations. [STORY¹, -ED²]

stork, n. Tall stately wading bird allied to heron, the best-known species pure white except for black wing-tips & reddish bill & feet, sometimes half domesticated & nesting on buildings, & credited with peculiar affection both to its young & its parents (*King S.,* oppressively active ruler, cf. *King* LOG¹); *s.'s-bill,* kinds of plant. [OE *storc,* cf. Du. *stork,* G *storch*]

storm, n., & v.i. & t. Violent disturbance of the atmosphere with thunder, strong wind, or heavy rain or snow or hail, a tempest, (*cyclonic s.*; *thunder, rain, snow, wind, -s.*; *s. in a teacup,* great excitement over small matter); violent disturbance of the established order in human affairs, tumult, agitation, war, invasion, dispute, &c. (*s. & stress,* period of fermenting ideas & unrest in person's or nation's life, f. G *Sturm und Drang,* name of a play characteristic of the literary movement in Germany 1770–82); vehement shower *of* missiles or outbreak of hisses, applause, indignation, &c.; direct assault by infantry on fortified place, capture *of* place by such assault, (*take by storm,* of such capture, & transf. of captivating audience or person rapidly); *s.-beaten,* battered by lit. or fig. ss.; *s.-belt,* tract in which ss. are frequent; *s.-bird*, stormy petrel; *s.-bound*, prevented from leaving port or continuing voyage by ss.; *s.-card*, chart assisting navigator of ship in s. to conjecture position of s.-centre & so to direct course; *s.-centre*, point to which wind blows spirally inward in cyclonic storm, (fig.) subject &c. upon which agitation or disturbance is concentrated; *s.-cloud*, heavy rain-cloud, state of affairs that threatens disturbances; *s.-cock*, kinds of bird, esp. missel-thrush, fieldfare, or green woodpecker; *s.-cone*, tarred-canvas cone hoisted as warning of high wind, upright for north & inverted for south; *s.-door*, additional outer door for protection in bad weather or winter; *s.-drum*, cylinder added to s.-cone for expected s. of great violence; *s.-finch*, stormy petrel; *s.-glass*, sealed tube containing a solution of which the clarity is affected by temperature formerly regarded as efficient weather-glass; *s.-petrel*, stormy petrel; *s.-sail*, of smaller size & stouter canvas than the corresponding one used in ordinary weather; *s.-signal*, s.-cone, s.-drum, or other device for warning of an approaching s.; *s.-tossed*, lit. & fig.; *s.-wind*; *s.-window*, as *s.-door*; *s.-zone*, s.-belt; hence **stor·m**LESS, **stor·m**PROOF[2], aa. (Vb.): (of wind, rain, &c.) rage, be violent; talk violently, rage, bluster, fume, scold (intr.), (often *at* object of displeasure); take by s. (*storming-party*, detachment told off to begin assault; so **stor·m**ER[1] n.). [vb f. n., OE, also Du., Sw., & Da., cf. G *sturm*; cogn. w. STIR]

stor·my, a. Of marked violence, raging, vehement, boisterous, (*s. wind, sea, waves, passions, temper, abuse*); infested or troubled with lit. or fig. storms (*a s. coast, sea, night, debate, life*); associated with or threatening storms (*s. petrel*; *a s. sunset*). Hence **stor·mi**LY[2] adv., **stor·mi**NESS n. [-Y[2]]

stor·t(h)ing (-tĭ-), n. Norwegian Parliament. [Norw. (*-ti-*), f. *stor* great, *t(h)ing* assembly]

stor·y[1], n. History (archaic; *versed in classic s.*); past course of person's or institution's life (*his s. is an eventful one*; *in our rough island-s.*); account given of an incident (*they all tell the same s.*; *according to his own s.*, suggestion of doubt as to his veracity; *to make a long s. short*, formula excusing omission of details; *it is quite another s. now*, we now hear a different account, esp. = things have changed; *the s. goes*, it is said); piece of narrative, tale of any length told or printed in prose or verse of actual or fictitious events, legend, myth, anecdote, novel, romance, (*tell me a s.*; *but is the s. true?*; *short s.*, relating usu. a single incident & published as article in magazine or as one of a collection; *good, funny, s.*, amusing anecdote often embodying witticism or ludicrous situation; *but that is another s.*, formula for breaking off & tantalizing reader with allusion); main facts or plot of novel or epic or play (*reads only for the s.*; *the s. is the least part of the book*); facts or experiences that deserve narration (*that face must have a s. belonging to it*); (Nursery) lie, fib, liar (*oh you s.!*); *s.-book*, containing s. or ss.; *s.-teller*, Eastern making a living by telling ss. to audience, writer of ss., retailer of anecdotes in society, (Nursery) liar. [AF *estorie* f. OF *estoire* f. L as HISTORY]

story[2]. See STOREY.

stoup (-ōōp), n. (archaic). Flagon, beaker, drinking-vessel; holy-water basin. [f. ON *staup*, cf. Du. *stoop*, OE *stéap*]

stout (-owt), a. & n. Brave, doughty, resolute, vigorous, sturdy, stubborn, staunch, strongly built, (*s. fellow* archaic, good at fighting &c.; *a. s. heart*, courage, whence **stoutheart**ED[2] a., **stout-hear·t-ed**LY[2] adv., **stout-hear·ted**NESS n.; *made a s. resistance*; *a s. opponent*; *a s. stick, ship*, &c.); corpulent, bulky, tending to fatness; hence **stou·t**ISH[1](2) a., **stou·t**LY[2] adv., **stou·t**NESS n. (N.) strongest kind of porter. [f. OF *estout* f. Teut. (Du. *stout*, G *stolz*, proud), perh. f. L *stultus* stupid]

stove[1], n., & v.t. Kinds of closed apparatus in which heat is produced by consumption of wood, coal, charcoal, oil, gas, or other fuel, for use in warming rooms, cooking, &c.; (Gardening) hothouse with artificial heat (vb, force, raise, in s.); *s.-pipe*, conducting smoke & gases from s. to chimney (*s.-pipe hat* U.S., tall silk hat). [earlier sense *heated room, bath*; prob. f. MDu. *stove*, cf. OE *stofa* hot-air bath, G *stube* room, & STEW[1]]

stove[2]. See STAVE[2].

stow (-ō), v.t. Pack (goods &c.) in right or convenient places without waste of room (*s.* thing *away*, place it where it will not cause obstruction); fill (receptacle) with articles compactly arranged; (slang, usu. in imperat.) abstain from, cease to indulge in, (*s. larks, that nonsense*, &c.); *stow·away*, person getting free passage by going aboard ship & hiding till she is at sea (*s.a.* as v.i., do this); *s.-wood*, billets used for chocking casks in ship's hold. Hence **stow·**AGE(1, 3, 4) n. [ME, f. OE *stów* a place, cogn. w. STAND]

strabi·smus (-z-), n. Squinting, squint, (*cross-eyed s.*, with eye or eyes turning inward; *wall-eyed s.*, outward). Hence **strabi·sm**IC, **strabi·sm**AL, aa. [mod. L, f. Gk *strabismos* (*strabos* squinting, -ISM)]

strabŏ·tomy, n. Operation of cutting eyeball muscle to cure squint. [prec., -TOMY]

stra·ddle, v.i. & t., & n. Take or be in attitude with legs wide apart; stand or sit across (thing) thus (*cannot s. his horse*; *stood straddling the ditch*); part (one's legs) widely; (Nav.) drop shots short of & beyond (target, enemy) esp. to find range; (fig.) vacillate between two policies &c., sit on the fence. (N.) act of straddling lit. or fig.; (St. Exch.) contract giving holder the right of either calling for or delivering stock at fixed price. [STRIDE, -LE(3)]

Strădivar·ius (*or* -ār-), (colloq.) **Strad,** n. Violin or other stringed instrument made by S. of Cremona (d. 1737).

strafe (-ahf), v.t., & n., (slang). Bombard, worry with sniping &c., reprimand or abuse or thrash; (n.) piece of strafing (*the morning s.*, German gunfire at dawn). [joc. adaptation of G 1914 catchword *Gott s.* (God chastise) *England*]

stra·ggle, v.i. Stray from the main body, fail to remain compact, get dispersed, proceed in scattered irregular order, be sporadic, occur here & there, (*crowd straggled along*; *plant straggles*, grows long & weedy; *straggling village, houses*, &c.). Hence **stra·ggler**[1] n., **stra·gglingly**[2] adv., **stra·ggly**[2] a. [perh. f. ME *straken* roam cogn. w. STRETCH, -LE(3)]

straight (-āt), a., n., & adv. Without curve or bend, extending uniformly in same direction, (*s. line* in Geom., lying evenly between any two of its points; *s. arch*, shaped like inverted V, without curves; *a s. back*, not bowed; *a s. knee*, not bent; *s. legs*, not bandy or knock-kneed; *s. hair*, not curly); (of aim, look, blow, course) going direct to the mark; upright, honest, candid, (*s. dealings, speaking*; *is perfectly s. in all his dealings*; *s. thinking*, logical, not swayed by emotion); in proper order or place, level, symmetrical, (*are the pictures s.?*; *put things s.*, get rid of disorder; *accounts are s.*, made up in due form; *a s. race, fight*, &c., in which competitors do their best to win); direct from source (*s. tip*, hint esp. as to likely winner of race or prospects of investment got from good authority); *the s. ticket* U.S., the party programme without modification; *straightfor·ward*, honest, open, frank, (of task &c.) presenting no complications; so *straightfor·wardly* adv., *straightfor·wardness* n.; *straigh·tway* archaic, at once, immediately; hence **straigh·ten**[6] v.t. & i., **straigh·tness** n. (N.) s. condition (*is out of the s.*, crooked); straight part of something, esp. concluding stretch of racecourse (*they were even as they reached the s.*); sequence of cards in poker. (Adv.) in a s. line, direct, without deviation or circumlocution, (*go s.*; *hit s. from the shoulder*, in boxing; *ride s.*, taking fences &c. instead of going round; *comes s. from Paris*; *is making s. for a precipice*; *told it him s. out*); in right direction, with good aim, (*shoot s.*); correctly (*does not see s.*); (archaic) at once (also in *s. away* slang, immediately; *s. off*, without hesitation, deliberation, &c., as *cannot tell you s. o.*); *s.-cut*, (tobacco) cut lengthwise into long silky fibres. [ME *stregt*, p.p. of *streccan* STRETCH]

strain[1], v.t. & i. Stretch tightly, make taut, exercise to greatest possible or beyond legitimate extent, press to extremes, wrest or distort from true intention or meaning, (*s. parchment across the aperture*; *s. rope to breaking-point*; *s. every nerve*, do one's utmost; *s.* one's *ears, eyes, voice*, &c., listen &c. to best of one's power, & see below; *s.* one's *authority, powers, rights*, &c., or *the law* &c., apply them beyond their province or in violation of their true intention; *s. a point*, go further than one is entitled or can be expected to, esp. in the way of concession, to effect a purpose; *a strained interpretation* or *sense*, got by pressing some rule of grammar &c. too far; *straining-beam, -piece*, horizontal beam used as strut between tops of queen-posts); hug (person) *to* oneself or one's breast &c.; (p.p.) produced under compulsion or by effort, artificial, forced, constrained, not spontaneous, (*the quality of mercy is not strained*, mercy should be spontaneous; *strained manner, laugh, cordiality*, &c.); overtask, injure or try or imperil by over-use or making of excessive demands, (*take care not to s. your eyes, voice*, &c.; *for fear of straining his followers' loyalty*; *has strained a muscle, his leg, his heart*, &c.; *ship is strained*, has had parts wrenched out of rigid state; *strained relations*, over-sensitiveness between parties who have tried each other's forbearance too far); make intense effort, strive intensely *after*, tug *at*, hold out with difficulty under or *under* pressure, (*the straining horses, masts*; *plants straining upwards to the light*; *dogs, horses, rowers, s. at the leash, collar, oar*; *porter straining under his load*; *strains too much after epigram, effect*, &c.); clear (liquid) of solid matter by passing through sieve or other **strai·ner**[1](2) n., filter (solids) *out* from liquid, (of liquid) percolate; *s. at*, be over-scrupulous about (ref. to *Matt.* xxiii. 24, prop. *s. out*, see R.V., in prec. sense). Hence **strai·nable** a. [ME *streinen* f. OF *estreindre estreign-* f. L *stringere strict-*]

strain[2], n. Pull, stretching force, tension, demand upon or force that tries cohesion or strength or stability or resources, exertion required to meet such demand or to do something difficult, injury or change of structure resulting from such exertion or force, (*the s. on the rope was tremendous*; *was a great s. on my resources, attention, credulity*; *the s. of modern life*; *is suffering from s.* or *over-s.*; *all his senses were on the s.*, exerted to the utmost; *is* *epigrammatic without s.*, appearance of undue effort; *has a s. in his leg*); (Physics, Mech.) condition of a body subjected to stress, molecular displacement; (poet. & rhet., usu. in pl.) burst or snatch or spell of music or poetry (*martial, inspiriting, pathetic*, &c., *ss.*, music or poetry of such character; *the ss. of the harp, of the Elizabethan poets*, &c.); tone or key or pitch adopted in talking or writing, tendency of discourse, (*he went on in another s.*; *& much more in the same s.*); moral tendency forming part of a character (*there is a s. of weakness, ferocity, mysticism, in him*); breed of animals, human stock or family, (*comes of a good s.*). [first sense from prec.; last f. OE *stréon* gain, product, progeny; others of mixed orig.]

strait, a. & n. Narrow, limited, confined or confining, (archaic exc. in *s. gate* w. ref. to *Matt.* vii. 14, *s. jacket* or usu. *waistcoat*, strong garment put on maniacs to confine arms, which are either in sleeves so long that the ends can be tied or strapped within body of jacket, & in *s.-laced* now fig. only, severely virtuous, morally scrupulous, puritanic); strict (archaic exc. in *straitest sect of* w. ref. to *Acts* xxvi. 5); hence **strai·t**LY[2] adv. (archaic), **strai·t**NESS n. (archaic), **strai·t**EN[6] v.t. (*straitened circumstances*, poverty; *is straitened for*, ill supplied with). (N.) narrow passage of water connecting two seas or large bodies of water (usu. in pl. when used of particular s. with name, as *the Ss. of Messina, Dover*; *Ss. Settlements*, Crown colony on Ss. of Malacca & Singapore; *the Ss.*, formerly of Gibraltar, now usu. of Malacca); (usu. pl.) difficult position, need, distress, (esp. *in ss.*). [ME *streit* f. OF *estreit* f. L p.p. as STRAIN[1]]

strake, n. Continuous line of planking or plates from stem to stern of ship (GARBOARD *s.*). [var. of STREAK]

strami·neous, a. (archaic). Of, light or worthless as, coloured like, straw. [L *stramineus* (*stramen -inis* straw f. *sternere strat-* strew, -MEN), -OUS]

stramō·nium, n. (Drug, much used in asthma, from seeds or leaves of) kind of datura. [mod. L, etym. dub.]

strand[1], n., & v.t. & i. Margin of sea, lake, or river (rhet., poet.). (Vb) run (t. & i. of ship) aground; (p.p.) in difficulties, unable to get along esp. for want of funds or other resources, left behind while others advance. [com.-Teut.; OE, Du., G, Sw., & Da., *strand*; etym. dub.]

strand[2], n., & v.t. One of the strings or wires by twisting which a rope is made; (fig.) element or strain in any composite whole; (vb) break a s. in (rope). [cf. OF *estran* rope]

strānge (-j), a. Foreign, alien, not one's own, not familiar or well known (*to*), novel, queer, peculiar, eccentric, singular, surprising, unaccountable, unexpected, (*in a s. land*; *worship s. gods*; *cannot play on a s. ground, with a s. racket*; *the place, work, handwriting, is s. to me*; *it is a s. thing, story*; *how s. that you should not have heard!*; *wears the strangest clothes*; *is very s. in his manner*, seems mad &c.; *truth is stranger than fiction*; *repeating the question with s. persistency*; *feel s.*, not in one's usual condition, esp. dizzy &c.; *it feels s.*, is a novel sensation), whence **stra·nge**LY[2] adv.; fresh or unaccustomed *to*, unacquainted, bewildered, (*am s. to the work*; *am quite s. here*, do not know my way about or the people &c.; *feel s.*, not at home, out of one's element &c.). Hence **stra·nge**NESS n. [f. OF *estrange* f. L EXTRA*neus*]

stra·nger, n. Foreigner, person in a country or town or company that he does not belong to, person unknown to or *to* one (in U.S. as rustic voc. = *sir* &c.), person entirely unaccustomed *to* some feeling or practice or experience, (*am a s. here*, do not know my way about &c.; *spy* or *see ss.* in House of Commons, demand expulsion of all but members or officials; *make a, no, s. of*, treat distantly, cordially; *you are quite a s.*, seldom show yourself here; *is no, a, s. to me*, I know, do not know, him; *is a, no, s. to fear, court-intrigues*, has had no, much, experience of; *the little s.*, newborn child). [f. OF *estrangier*, see prec., -ER[2](2)]

stra·ngle (-nggl), v.t. Throttle, kill by squeezing windpipe; (of collar &c.) squeeze (neck); (fig.) suppress (movement, impulse, &c.); *stra·nglehold*, deadly grip (usu. fig. in Pol. or commerce). [f. OF *estrangler* f. L *strangulare* f. Gk *straggalaō* (*straggalē* halter f. *straggos* twisted)]

stra·ngles, n. pl. (usu. treated as sing.). Infectious catarrh in horse, ass, &c. [f. prec.]

stra·ngūlate (-ngg-), v.t. Strangle (rare); (Path., Surg.) prevent circulation through (vein, intestine, &c.) by compression. Hence **strangul**A·TION n. [f. L as STRANGLE, -ATE[3]]

stra·ngūry (-ngg-), n. Disease in which urine is passed painfully & in drops; disease produced in plants by bandaging. So **strangūr·i**OUS a. [f. L f. Gk *straggouria* (*stragx -ggos* drop, *ouron* urine)]

strap, n., & v.t. Strip of leather; strip of leather or other flexible material with buckle or other fastening for holding things together or other purpose (SHOULDER-*s.*; *rug, umbrella*, &c., *-s.*, pair of ss. with holder joining them for making bundle); strip of metal used to secure or connect, leaf of hinge, &c.; (Bot.) tongue-shaped part in ligulate floret; *the s.*, chastisement with a s.; *s.-hanger*, bus or train passenger who has to stand & hold on by s. for want of sitting space; *s.-laid*, (of rope) made by laying ropes side by side & joining them into a flat band; *s.-oil*, beating given with s.; *s.-work*, ornamentation imitating plaited ss.; *s.-wort*, kind of white-flowered knotgrass. (Vb) secure with s. (often *up*, *down*, &c.; *strapped trousers*, held down by s. passing below instep for riding &c.); strop, whet, (razor, knife); (Surg.) close (wound), bind (part), up or *up* with adhesive plaster or **stra·p-**PING[1](4) n.; flog with s.; (part. as adj., cf. *thumping*, *whacking*, *whopping*) big, lusty, tall, (*a strapping girl*, *fellow*), whence **stra·pp**ER[1] n. [OE *strop* prob. f. L *struppus*, cf. Gk *strophos* band (*strephō* twist)]

strappā·do, n., & v.t. Torture inflicted, punish, by securing person's hands or other part in ropes, raising him, & letting him fall till brought up by taut rope. [f. F *strapade* f. It. *strappata* (*strappare* pull); for *-o* see -ADO(2)]

strata. See STRATUM.

stră·tagem, n. (An) artifice, trick(ery), device(s) for deceiving enemy, (*devised a s.*; *must be effected by s.*). [f.F *stratagème* f. L f. Gk *stratēgēma* (*stratēgeō* be STRATEGUS, -M)]

stratē·gic, a. Of, dictated by, serving the ends of, strategy (*s. skill*, *considerations*, *movement*, *position*). Hence **strate·gic**AL a. (now rare), **strate·gical**LY[2] adv., **strate·gi**CS n. [f. Gk *stratēgikos* (foll., -IC)]

stratē·gus, n. (Gk ant.; pl. *-gi* pr. -gī *or* -jī). Military commander, esp. one of annually appointed board of ten at Athens. [L, f. Gk *stratēgos* (*stratos* army, *agō* lead)]

stră·tegy, n. Generalship, the art of war, (lit. & fig.); management of an army or armies in a campaign, art of so moving or disposing troops or ships as to impose upon the enemy the place & time & conditions for fighting preferred by oneself, (cf. TACTICS). Hence **stra·teg**IST(3) n. [f. F *stratégie* f. Gk *stratēgia* (prec., -IA[1])]

străth, n. (Sc.). Broad mountain valley; *strathspey·* (-ā), Scotch dance resembling reel but slower (named f. *Strathspey* valley of the Spey). [f. Gael. *srath*, cf. W *ystrad*]

strati·culate (-at), a. (geol.). Arranged in thin layers. [STRATUM, -I-, -CULE, -ATE[2]]

stră·tify̆, v.t. Arrange in strata(esp. p.p.). Hence **strati**FICA·TION n. [f. F *stratifier* (STRATUM, -I-, -FY)]

strāto-, comb. form of STRATUS, as *-ci·rrus*, *-cu·mulus*.

strato·cracy, n. Military government, domination of soldiers. [Gk *stratos* army, -CRACY]

strā·tum, n. (pl. *-ta*). (Geol.) layer, or set of successive layers, of any deposited substance; (transf.) social grade (*the various ss. of society*). Hence **stra·t**AL, **stra·ti**FORM, aa., **strati·**GRAPHY(2) (-at-) n., **străti**GRA·PHIC a., **stratigra·phi**CALLY adv. [L, = spread thing, coverlet, neut. p.p. of *sternere* strew]

strā·tus, n. (pl. *-tī*). Continuous horizontal sheet of cloud. [assim. of prec. to termination of *cumulus* & other CLOUDS]

straw, n., & v.t. Dry cut stalks of kinds of grain as material for bedding, thatching, packing, hats, &c. (*made of*, *thatched* &c. *with*, *s.*; *a load of s.*; *s. mattress*, *hat*, *rope*, &c.; *in the s.* archaic, in child-bed; *man of s.*, stuffed effigy, imaginary person set up as opponent &c., person without substantial means); s. hat; single stalk or piece of s., insignificant trifle, (*with a s. in his mouth*; *lemonade sucked through ss.*; *draw ss.*, draw lots with ss. of different lengths; *make bricks without s.*, of persons set to work without adequate means, see *Exod.* v. 7; *catch at a s.*, resort to utterly inadequate expedient like drowning man; *the last s.*, slight addition that makes something no longer tolerable as with camel's load; *a s. shows which way the wind blows*, slight hint may suggest much; *is not worth*, *don't care*, *a s.*); *s.-board*, coarse cardboard made of s.; *s.-colour(ed)*, (of) pale yellow; *s.-stem*, wineglass with stem not made separately & attached but drawn out of bowl; *s.-worm*, caddis; hence **straw·**Y[2] a. (Vb, archaic) strew. [OE *strēaw*, cf. Du. *stroo*, G *stroh*; cogn. w. STREW (of which the vb is perh. a var,) & L *sternere strat-* strew]

straw·berry (-erĭ), n. (Kind of perennial plant throwing out runners & producing) pulpy red fruit having surface studded with yellow seeds (*crushed s.*, kind of dull crimson; *the s. leaves*, ducal rank, w. ref. to ornamentation of duke's coronet); *s.-mark*, soft reddish birthmark; *s. pear*, (fruit of) W.-Ind. cactaceous plant; *s. roan*, red ROAN[1]; *s.-tree*, evergreen arbutus bearing s.-like fruit. [OE *strēawberige* (prec., w. ref. to runners, BERRY)]

stray, v.i. (p.p. as -ED[1], 2), n., & a. Wander, go aimlessly, deviate from the right way or from virtue, lose one's way, get separated from flock or companions or proper place. (N.) strayed domestic animal; WAIFS *&* *ss.*; property of deceased person escheating to crown in default of heirs; (Wireless, usu. in pl.) = ATMOSPHERICS. (Adj.) strayed; scattered, sporadic, occurring or met with now & then or casually or unexpectedly, (*a few stray instances*; *a stray customer or two came in*; *hit by a s. bullet*). [(n. & a. f. AF *estrai*, *stray*) f. OF *estraier* prob. ult. f. L as EXTRAVAGANT]

streak, n., & v.t. Long narrow irregular line or band or layer-edge, esp. one distinguished by colour, visible on a surface (*black with red ss.*; *a s. of light above the horizon*; *bacon with ss. of fat & lean*; *s. of lightning*, flash; *like a s. of lightning*, or *a s.*, swiftly; *the silver s.*, English Channel; *has a s. of humour, superstition*, &c., *in him*, strain or element); hence **strea·ky**² a., **strea·kily**² adv., **strea·kiness** n. (Vb, usu. in p.p.) mark with streak(s). [OE *strica* stroke, line, cf. G *strich*, Du. *streek*; cogn. w. STRIKE]

stream, n., & v.i. & t. Body of water running in bed, river, or brook, (*on the banks of a s.*; *up, down, s.*, moving or situated upwards, downwards, on river), whence **strea·mless** a., **strea·mlet** n.; flow of any liquid, onward moving fluid mass or crowd, (sing. or pl.) large quantity of or *of* something that flows or moves along, (*saw a s. of lava*; *came out, went by, in a s.* or *ss.*; *a s., ss., of blood, tears, people*); current, direction of flow, (GULF-s.; *with, against, the s.*; *go with the s.*, do as others do; *the s. of tendency, thought, is the other way*); *s.-anchor*, intermediate between bower & kedge esp. for use in warping; *s.-line*, natural course of water or air currents (*s.-l. shape* in aircraft, that calculated to cause least resistance); hence **strea·my**² a. (rare). (Vb) flow or move as a s.; run with liquid (*streaming eyes, windows, umbrella*); (of banner, loose hair, &c.) float or wave in the wind; emit s. of (blood &c.). [OE *strēam*, cf. Du. *stroom*, G *strom*; cogn. w. Skr. *sru*, Gk *rheō*, flow]

strea·mer, n. Pennon, ribbon attached at one end & floating or waving at the other; column of light shooting up in aurora. [-ER¹]

street, n. Town or village road that has houses on one side or both, this with the houses, (*go down, across, the s.*; *main, side, broad*, &c., *s.*; *live in the s.*, be constantly outside one's house; *lives in a fashionable s.*; MAN¹ *in the s.*; *not in the same s. with* colloq., utterly inferior to in ability &c.; *window looks on the s.*; *in the s.*, said of St.-Exch. business done after closing hours; *on the ss.*, living by prostitution; KEY¹ *of the s.*; GRUB-STREET; LOMBARD, QUEER, *-s.*; *s.* ARAB; *s. cries*, of hawkers; *s. orderly*, scavenger); *s.-door*, opening on s.; *s.-sweeper*, esp. machine with revolving brush for cleaning ss.; *stree·twalker*, common prostitute. Hence **(-)streeted**² a., **stree·tward** adv. & a. [OE *strǣt* f. LL *strata* (*via*) paved (way) f. *sternere strat-* lay]

stre·ngth, n. Being STRONG, degree in which person or thing is strong, (*the s.* of *a man, rope, beam, fortress, current, argument, fleet*; *the s. of wine, acid, tea, evidence*; *s. of body, mind, will, memory, judgement*; *his s. is in endurance*; *has the s. of a horse*, is as strong; *has not the s. to lift a cup, walk upstairs*; *that is beyond human, too much for my, s.*; MEASURE² one's *s. with*; *on the s. of*, encouraged by or relying on or arguing from, as *I did it on the s. of your promise*); what makes strong (*God is our s.*; *his s. is patience*); proportion of whole number present (*were there in great, full, s.*); (Mil.) *on the s.*, on the muster-roll (*was taken, is, on the s.*). Hence **stre·ngthless** a. [OE *strengthu* (*strang* STRONG, -TH¹)]

stre·ngthen, v.t. & i. Make or become stronger; *s.* one's *hands* fig., encourage him to vigorous action. [-EN¹]

strĕ·nuous, a. Energetic, unrelaxing, ardently persistent. Hence **stre·nuously**² adv., **stre·nuousness** n. [L *strenuus*, cf. Gk *strēnēs* strong, + -OUS]

Strĕ·phon, n. Fond lover (*S. & Chloe*, pair of lovers). [character in Sidney's *Arcadia*]

strĕpito·so, mus. direction. Boisterously, with impetuosity. [It.]

streptoco·ccus, n. (pl. *-cī*). Bacterial organism of chaplet form. [Gk *streptos* torque (*strephō* turn), *kokkos* a grain]

stress, n., & v.t. Constraining or impelling force *of* (*under, driven by, s. of weather, poverty*, &c.); effort, demand upon energy, (STORM *& s.*; *subjected to great s.*; *times of slackness & times of s.*); emphasis (*lay s. on*, convey that one attaches importance to); accentuation, emphasis laid on syllable or word, *a* or *the* accent, (*s. & quantity are different metrical principles*; *the s. is on the first syllable, on the word 'permissive'*); (Mech.) force exerted between contiguous bodies or parts of a body; hence **stre·ssless** a. (Vb) lay the s. on, accent, emphasize; subject to mechanical s. [vb in present sense f. n., which is partly aphetic for DISTRESS¹ & partly f. the vb f. OF *estrecier* f. pop. L **strictiare* see DISTRESS²]

stretch, v.t. & i., & n. Make taut, tighten, straighten, place somewhere in tight-drawn or outspread state, (*the rope must be stretched tight*; *s. a wire across the road*; *with a canopy stretched over them*; *s. trousers*, remove creases &c. by pulling out in frame; *s. oneself* or *s.* abs., tighten muscles after sleeping &c. by extending limbs &c. in various directions; *s.* one's *legs*, straighten them by walking as relief from sitting &c.; *s.* one *on the ground*, knock him sprawling; (p.p.) lying *at full length, on the lawn*, &c.; *s. out hand, foot*, &c., extend it by straightening arm or leg; *s. out* abs., reach out hand, also begin to lengthen stride); strain, exert to utmost or beyond legitimate extent, make the most of, do violence to, exaggerate, (*s. a point, a principle*, one's *powers*, one's *credit*, = *strain*; *s. the truth* or *s.* abs., exaggerate, lie); have specified length or extension, be continuous between points or to or from a point, (*stretches from end to end*, *across the sky, to infinity*; *road stretches away, memory stretches down, from* or *to* place or period); draw, be drawn or admit of being drawn, out into greater length or extension or size (*gloves, boots, want stretching*; *it stretches like elastic*); (slang) hang (person). (N.) stretching or being stretched (*with a s. & a yawn*, whence **stre·tchy**² a., **stre·tchiness** n.; *by a s. of authority, language*, &c.; *with every faculty on the s.*); continuous expanse or tract or spell (*a s. of road, open country*, &c.; *works ten hours at a s.*), (Naut.) distance covered on one tack. [OE *streccan*, cf. Du. *strekken*, G *strecken*; perh. cogn. w. STARK]

stre·tcher, n. In vbl senses; esp.: brick or stone laid with side in face of wall (cf. HEADER); board in boat against which rower presses feet; appliance, often of canvas stretched on oblong frame, for carrying disabled person on; (slang) exaggeration, lie; *s.-bond*, method of building in which all bricks are ss. but joints of contiguous courses do not coincide. [-ER¹]

strew, v.t. (p.p. *-n, -ed*). Scatter (sand, flowers, small objects) over a surface; (partly) cover (surface, object) with small objects scattered. [OE *streawian* (STRAW), cf. G *streuen*; prob. cogn. w. L *sternere strat-*]

stri·a, n. (anat., zool., bot., geol.; pl. *-ae*). Linear mark on surface, slight ridge or furrow or score. Hence **stri·ate**² a., **stria·te**³ v.t., **stri·ately**² adv., **stria·tion**, **stri·ature** (-tsher), nn. [L]

stricken. See STRIKE.

stri·ckle, n. Rod used in STRIKE-*measure*. [OE *stricel* (STRIKE)]

strict, a. Precisely limited or defined, accurate, tense, without irregularity or exception or deviation, requiring implicit obedience or exact performance, not lax, (*in the s. sense*; *keep s. watch*; *s. time* in music; *lives in s. seclusion*; *was told me in s. confidence*; *gave s. orders*; *a s. code of laws* or *customs*; *s. morals*, admitting no laxity; *s. parents, schoolmaster, discipline*). Hence **stri·ctly**² adv. (*-ly speaking*, if one is to use words in their s. sense), **stri·ctness** n. [f. L *stringere strict-* tighten]

stri·cture (-tsher), n. (Usu. in pl.) piece of censure, critical remark, (usu. *on* or *upon*); (Path.) morbid contraction of some canal or duct in the body, whence **stri·ctured**² a. [f. L *strictura* contraction (*stringere*, see prec. & STRIGIL, -URE)]

stride, v.i. & t. (past *strode*, rare p.p. *stridden* or *strid*), & n. Walk with long steps; pass over (ditch &c.) with one step; bestride, straddle (trans.). (N.) single step esp. in respect of length, gait as determined by length of s., (*walks with vigorous ss.* or *a vigorous s.*; *take* obstacle *in* one's *s.*, clear it without changing step to jump, fig. find no serious impediment in it); distance between feet parted either laterally or as in walking. [OE *stridan*, cf. Du. *strijden*, G *streiten*, contend]

stri·dent, a. Loud & harsh in sound. Hence **stri·dently**² adv. [L *stridere* creak, -ENT]

stri·dulate, v.i. (entom.). Make shrill jarring sound by rubbing together hard parts of body (of cicadas, grasshoppers, &c.). So **stri·dulant** a., **stridula·tion**, **stri·dulator**²(1, 2), nn. [L *stridulus* creaking (prec.), -ATE³]

strife, n. Contention, state of conflict, struggle between opposed persons or things. [f. OF *estrif*, cf. *estriver* STRIVE]

stri·gil (-j-), n. Skin-scraper used by ancients at bath. [f. L *strigilis* (*stringere* graze), cf. Gk *stleggis, streggis*]

stri·gose, stri·gous, aa. (bot.). With short stiff hairs or scales. [L *striga* swath, -OSE¹, -OUS]

strike, v.t. & i. (*struck, struck* & as specified below *stricken*), & n. Hit, hit upon or (*up*)*on*, deliver blow(s) or stroke(s), (*struck me in the mouth, with his fist*; *s. ball out of court* &c., send it with blow; *s. weapon up* or *down* or *aside*, divert it by blow; *s.* one's *foot against a stone*, one's *hand on the table*; *s. while* IRON¹ *is hot*; *striking-force*, esp. military corps ready to deliver blow at short notice; *within striking-distance*, near enough to s.; *s. a blow*, or *s., for freedom*; *hammer strikes on* or *strikes bell*; *ship strikes rock* or *on rock* or *strikes*, runs on it; *s. hands* archaic, touch or clasp them in sign of agreement made; *was struck by a stone, lightning*; *a stricken heart*, afflicted by strokes of grief; *stricken with fever, pestilence, paralysis*, &c.; *a stricken field*, pitched battle or scene of it; *stricken in years*, enfeebled by age; *s. out*, hit from the shoulder, also use arms & legs in swimming or feet in skating; *s. upon an idea, plan*, &c., have it luckily occur to one; *s.* OIL¹; *light strikes upon* object, illuminates it; *s. at*, aim blow at; *s. at the root of*, threaten destruction to; *s. back*, return blow; *s. home*, get blow well in; *s. all of a heap* colloq., dumbfound; *s. fish* or *s.* abs., jerk tackle in order to secure hook in mouth; *s. the track*, come upon it); produce or record or bring into specified state by stroke(s) or striking (*s. coin*, make it by stamping; *s. bargain*, make it as by striking hands; *s. sparks, fire, light, out of flint*; *s. a match*, ignite by striking against something; *s. a light*, produce by striking match; *match will not s.*, give light when struck; *clock strikes the hour, five*, &c.; *the hour has struck*, clock has struck it, & fig. the critical moment has come or gone; *s.* one *blind, deaf*, &c., blind, deafen, &c.,

him at one stroke; *s. me dead!*, vulg., form of asseveration; *s. down*, fell with blow lit. or fig.; *s. his head off*, behead; *s. out plan* &c., forge or devise; *s. out a line for oneself*, be original; *s. item* or *name out* or *off*, *s. word through*, expunge with pen-stroke; *s. up an acquaintance*, start it rapidly or casually; band or person *strikes up a tune* or *strikes up*, starts playing or singing as by stroke of drum; printer *strikes off 1000 copies*, makes as by stamping); arrest attention of, occur to mind of, produce mental impression on, impress *as*, (*what struck me was the generosity of the offer*; *it strikes me he* or *that he may have misunderstood*; *an idea suddenly struck me*; *how does it s. you?*, what do you think about it?; *it strikes me as ridiculous, absolutely perfect*), (part.) sure to be noticed, arresting, impressive, whence **stri·king**LY[2] adv., **stri·king**NESS n.; lower or take down (flag, sail, tent), signify surrender by striking flag, surrender, (*s.* one's *flag*, surrender ship or fortress to enemy, also resign a naval command; *s. tents*, break up camp; *town, ship, strikes*, surrenders); cease (work), cease work, (of workmen) refuse to go on working unless employer accedes to some demand (cf. LOCK[3] *out*; *s. for higher pay, against long hours*, &c.); (cause to) penetrate (*struck a knife, terror, into his heart*; *cold strikes through his clothes, into his marrow, the wind strikes cold*; *plant strikes its roots into the soil*; *strikes root*, or *strikes* abs.; *oysters s.*, attach themselves to bed; *rays s. through fog*; *struck with terror, panic, dizziness*, &c., suddenly filled with); direct one's course somewhere, take specified direction, diverge *to*, start *into*, (*then s. to the right*; *s. into* or *out of a track, subject*, &c.; *s. in*, intervene in talk, often *with* suggestion &c.; *gout strikes in*, attacks interior instead of extremities; *s. into a gallop*, begin galloping); level (grain &c. or the measure) in *s. measure* (see n.), ascertain (balance) by deducting credit or debit from the other, arrive at (average) by equalizing all items, compose (jury) by allowing both sides to reject same number; suddenly & dramatically assume (attitude); *s.-a-light*, apparatus for getting light from flint; hence **stri·ker**[1] (1, 2) n. (N.) concerted refusal to work by employees till some grievance is remedied (*on s.*, acting on such refusal; *s.-breakers*, workmen brought in to replace strikers; *s. pay*, allowance for subsistence made by trade union to workmen who have struck; *general s.*, by workmen of all or most trades with a view to securing some common object by paralysing business; *sympathetic s.*, by unaggrieved trade to give moral support to one on s.); =STRICKLE (*s. measure*, when grain &c. is measured by passing a rod across top of heaped vessel to secure that it shall be full & no more). [OE *strīcan* go, cf. Du. *strijken*, G *streichen*, smooth, stroke, cogn. w. L *stringere* graze]

string, n., & v.t. & i. (strung). Twine or fine cord, piece of this or of leather, ribbon, webbing, or other material, used for tying up, lacing, drawing or holding together, actuating puppet, &c., (*want some s. & brown paper*; APRON, *bonnet*, BOW[1], *kite*, &c., *-s*; *two ss. to* one's BOW[1]; *first, second, s.*, person or thing that one's chief, alternative, reliance is set on, w. ref. to prec. phr.; *pull the ss.*, be the real actuator of what another does; HEART-*ss.*); tough piece connecting two halves of pod in beans &c.; stretched piece of catgut, cord, or wire, yielding musical tone(s) in piano, harp, violin, & other instruments (*harp-, fiddle-, bass, soprano*, &c., *s.*; *touch the ss.*, play; *harp on one s.*, dwell on single subject; *touch a s.* fig., excite particular feeling in person's heart; *the ss.*, the stringed instruments in a band or part contributed by them to the effect, cf. *the* WIND[1]), whence **(-)string**ED[2] a.; set of or usu. *of* objects strung together or persons or things of one kind coming one after another (*a s. of beads, pearls*; *filed past in a long s.*; *a s. of porters, carriages, instances, lies*); (Billiards) scoring-board with buttons sliding on wires, the score, stroke made in stringing for lead; *s. alphabet*, code for the blind in which special knots on s. represent letters; *s. band*, of stringed instruments only; *s.-bark*, STRINGY-bark; *s.-board*, supporting timber in which ends of staircase steps are set; *s.-course*, raised horizontal band or course running round or along building; *s.-halt*, = SPRING[2]-*halt*; *s.-piece*, long timber supporting & connecting the parts of a framework; hence **stri·ng**LESS a. (Vb) supply with string(s), tie with s.; secure (bow) in state ready for use by bending it & slipping loop of s. into notch, (fig., chiefly in p.p.) tighten *up* or make ready or sensitive or excited (senses, nerves, resolution, or person in regard to them; *was strung up to do the deed*; *high-strung* or *highly strung nerves* or *person*, neurotic, susceptible, oversensitive); thread (beads &c.) on a s. strip ss. from (beans); *s. up* colloq., kill by hanging; (of glue &c.) become stringy; (Billiards) make the preliminary strokes that decide which player shall begin. [OE *streng*, cf. Du. *streng*, G *strang*; cogn. w. STRANGLE, STRICT]

stringe·ndo (-j-), mus. direction. With increased speed & loudness. [It.]

stri·ngent (-j-), a. (Of rules, stipulations, &c.) strict, precise, requiring exact performance, leaving no loophole or discretion; (of money-market &c.) tight, hampered by scarcity, unaccommodating, hard to operate in. Hence **stri·ng**ENCY n., **stri·ngent**LY[2] adv. [L *stringere* draw tight, -ENT]

stri·nger (-ng-), n. In vbl senses; also, STRING-board. [-ER[1]]

stri·ngy (-ngĭ), a. Fibrous, like string, (*s.-bark*, kinds of gum-tree); (of liquid) viscous, ropy. Hence **stri·ngi**NESS n. [-Y[2]]

strip[1], v.t. & i. Denude, lay bare, deprive *of* covering or appurtenance or property, (*s.* one *to the skin*, leave him no clothes; *stripped*, naked; *stripped of fine names, it is a swindle*; *s. house, ship, tree*, remove furniture, rigging, bark & branches; *s. cow*, milk to last drop; *s. tobacco*, remove stems from; *s. screw*, tear thread from it); pull or tear (covering lit. or fig., appurtenance, property) off or *off* from or *from* something; put off one's clothes, undress; (of screw) lose thread, (of projectile) issue from rifled gun without spin; *s.-leaf*, tobacco with stems removed. Hence **stri·pp**ER[1](1, 2) n. [OE *strýpan*, cf. Du. *stroopen*, G *streifen*]

strip[2], n. Long narrow piece (*a s. of card, paper, cloth, garden, territory, board*). [prob. f. MLG *strippe* strap]

stripe, n. Long narrow band usu. of uniform breadth on a surface from which it differs in colour or texture (*black with a red s.*; STAR[1]*s & ss.*; *ss. on soldier's trousers*; *sergeant's, corporal's, ss.*, chevron; *get, lose*, one's *ss.*, be promoted, degraded; *zebra's ss.*), whence **(-)strip**ED[2], **stri·p**Y[2], aa., **stri·pi**NESS n.; (archaic) blow with scourge (usu. in pl.), (pl.) flogging. [prob. f. MDu. *strīpe*, cf. G *streifen*, ON *strip* striped fabric, also STRIP[1]; sense *blow* perh. as STRIP[2]]

stri·pling, n. Lad, young man whose figure has not yet filled out. [prob. f. STRIP[1], -LING[1]]

strive, v.i. (strove, strĭven). Struggle, endeavour, try hard, make efforts, contend, vie, (*to* do, *for* or *after* desired end, *with* or *against* opponent or temptation or difficulty; *s. together*, or *with each other*, quarrel, dispute pre-eminence &c.). [f. OF *estriver* (from, or whence, *estrif* strife), prob. f. Teut. (Du. *straven*, G *streben*)]

strō·bile, n. Cone of pine &c. [f. L f. Gk *strobilos* (*strephō* twist)]

strode. See STRIDE.

stroke[1], n., & v.t. & i. Blow, shock given by blow, (*to receive 20 ss. of the birch*; *with one s. of his sword*; *killed by a s. of lightning* or *lightning-s.*; *finishing s.*, coup de grâce, final & fatal blow; *s. of paralysis* or *apoplexy*, or *s.*, sudden disabling attack; SUN-*s.*); single effort put forth, one complete performance of a recurrent action or movement, time or way in which such movements are done, (*has not done a s. of work*; *s. of wing, oar*, &c., whole of motion till starting-position is regained; *s. of piston*, whole motion in either direction; *golfer does hole in five ss.*, successive single dealings with ball; *row a fast, slow, long*, &c., *s.*; *vary the s.*; *second boat is gaining at every s.* or *s. by s.*); method of striking in games &c., specially successful or skilful effort, (*invented a new s. in cricket*; *s. of genius*, original idea; *s. of wit, diplomacy*, &c.; *s. of business*, profitable transaction; *a clever s.*; MASTER[1]-*s.*); *s. of luck*, unforeseen opportune occurrence; mark made by movement in one direction of pen or pencil or paint-brush, detail contributing to general effect in description, (*up, down, -s.*, part of letter so written; HAIR-*s.*; *thick, thin, horizontal*, &c., *s.*; *dash off picture with a few ss.*; *could do it with a s. of the pen* by exag., by writing signature; *finishing ss.*, finishing touches; *description is full of ss. from the life*); sound made by striking clock (*it is on the s. of nine*, nine is about to strike; *was there on the s.*, punctually); (also, now rarely, *s. oar*) oarsman rowing nearest stern & setting time of s. (*row, pull, s.*, act as s.); (vb) act as s. to (boat, crew). [ME *strōk, strāk*, (STRIKE)]

stroke[2], v.t., & n. Pass the hand gently, & usu. repeatedly in same direction, along surface of (*s.* one or one's *hair the wrong way*, irritate him; *s.* one *down*, mollify his anger &c.); hence **stro·king**LY[2] adv. (N.) act or spell of stroking. [OE *strácian*, cf. Du. *streeken*, G *streichen*; cogn. w. STRIKE]

strōll, v.i. & t., & n. Saunter, go for short leisurely walk, (n., such walk; *take, go for, a s.*); go from place to place giving performances &c., traverse *the country* thus, (*strolling players*; *a strolling company*). Hence **stro·ll**ER[1] n. [f. 17th-c., etym. dub.]

stro·ma, n. (biol.; pl. *-ata*). Framework of an organ or cell, usu. of connective tissue. Hence **stromă·t**IC a. [L f. Gk (-ō-), =coverlet (*strōnnumi* spread, -M)]

strong, a. (*comp. & sup. pr.* -ngg-). Having power of resistance, not easily broken or torn or worn or injured or captured, tough, healthy, firm, solid, (*s. china, stick, cloth*; *a s. constitution*, not liable to, able to overcome, disease; *s. nerves*, proof against fright, irritation, &c.; *s. fortress, town*, &c.; *s.-box, -room*, proof against burglars &c. for keeping valuables in; *s. conviction, faith, character*; *the s.*, those who have good health; *are you quite s. again?*, restored to health; *a s. foundation*; *a s. market*, steadily high or rising prices; *s. meat* bibl., solid food, fig. doctrine or measures acceptable only to vigorous or instructed minds); capable of exerting great force or doing much, muscular, powerful by size or numbers or resources or quality or ability, convincing, striking, powerfully affecting the senses, (*s. to do, suffer*, *labour, save,* &c.; *is s. enough to*; *s. in judgement, Greek, numbers, health,* well equipped in these respects; *s. eyes, memory,* &c.; *a s. man,* muscular; *by the s. arm* or *hand,* by force; *is as s. as a horse,* can do or stand much work; *the s.,* those who have might on their side; *s. army, fleet,* &c., numerous & well equipped; *a s. detachment,* numerous; *a company 200 s.,* numbering 200; *how many s. are you?,* what are your numbers?; *a s. combination,* set capable of doing much when united; *a s. candidate,* formidable, likely to win; *s. drink, waters,* alcoholic liquors; *s. tea, toddy,* made with large proportion of the flavouring element; *s. situation,* conjuncture in play or story calculated to move audience deeply; *s. voice,* loud or penetrating; *s. mind,* capable of sound reasoning; *s.-minded,* having such mind, also & usu. in spec. sense of woman, claiming mental & legal equality with men; *s. evidence, argument, case*; *s. light, shadow, colour, flavour*; *s. cheese, onion,* pungent; *s. butter, bacon,* rancid; *s. breath,* ill-smelling); energetic, effective, vigorous, decided, (*a s. wind, tide, attraction*; *have a s. hold upon* or *over,* be able to influence; *a s. literary style,* vivid & terse; *has a s. inclination to*; *s. language,* forcible expressions esp. of abusive or blasphemous kind; *give s. support to,* support with all one's power; *a s. partisan, Tory, advocate*; *s. man,* administrator who acts without hesitation, masterful person; *s. measures,* drastic action; *is s. against compromise,* will have nothing to do with it; *going strong* slang, continuing race or other occupation vigorously, also in good health or trim; *come* or *go it s.* slang, go to great lengths in something); (Gram., of vbs) forming inflections by vowel-change within stem rather than by addition of suffix (e.g. *swim swam, give gave, break broke,* cf. *float floated*); *stro·nghold,* fort, fastness, citadel, place where some cause or sentiment still prevails (*Liverpool is a s.-h. of protestantism*). Hence **stro·ng**ISH[1](2) a., **stro·ng**LY[2] adv. [OE *strang,* cf. ON *strangr,* Du. *streng,* G *streng* strict; cogn. w. L *stringere* STRAIN]

stro·ntia (-sh*a*) n., **stro·ntian** (-shn) n. & a. An oxide of strontium of which the nitrate is used in fireworks to colour flame red; (adj.) of strontia or strontium. [*-a* f. foll.; *-an* (n.) f. *Strontian* in Argyle, (adj.) f. foll. + -AN]

stro·ntium (-shm), n. A dark-yellow metal. [*Strontian* (prec.), -IUM]

strop, n., & v.t. Strip of leather on which razor is sharpened, implement or machine serving same purpose; collar of leather or spliced rope or iron used in slinging pulley &c.; (vb) sharpen on or with s. [as STRAP]

strŏ·phĕ, n. (Lines recited during) turn made in dancing by ancient-Greek chorus (*s., antistrophe, epode,* three sections of a choral ode or of one division of it, s. & antis. exactly corresponding in metre. So **stro·phi**C a. [Gk (*-ē*), orig. = turning (*strephō* turn)]

strove. See STRIVE.

strow (-ō), v.t. (p.p. *strown* or *-ed*). (Archaic for) STREW.

struck. See STRIKE.

stru·cture (-tsh*er*), n. Manner in which a building or organism or other complete whole is constructed, supporting framework or whole of the essential parts of something, make, construction, (*the s. of a house, machine, animal, organ, poem, sentence*; *a sentence of loose, a rock of columnar, s.*; *its s. is ingenious*; *ornament should emphasize & not disguise the lines of s.*), whence **stru·ctur**AL, **stru·cture**LESS, **(-)stru·ctur**ED[2], aa., **stru·ctural**LY[2] adv.; thing constructed, complex whole, a building, (*a fine marble s.*; *a lumbering s. drawn by six horses*). [f. L *structura* (*struere struct-* build, -URE)]

stru·ggle, v.i., & n. Throw one's limbs about in violent effort to get free or escape grasp (*child struggled & kicked*); make violent or determined efforts under difficulties, strive hard *to* do, contend *with* or *against* opponent or obstacle or difficulty, (*struggled to express himself, control his feelings*; *struggling with his infirmity, against superior numbers* or *the forces of nature*); make one's way with difficulty *through, up, along, in,* &c. (*light struggled in through dirty panes*), (part.) experiencing difficulty in making a living or getting recognition (*a struggling artist* &c.); hence **stru·ggling**LY[2] adv., **stru·ggl**ER[1] n. (N.) spell of struggling, confused wrestle or jostling, mêlée, hard contest, effort under difficulties; *the s. for existence,* the competition between organisms esp. as an element in natural selection. [ME *strogelen,* cf. Norw. *stru* refractory]

stru·ldbrug, n. One of those cursed with immortality in *Gulliver's Travels.* [arbitrary]

strum, v.i. & t., & n. Touch notes or twang strings of piano or other stringed instrument (esp. unskilfully); s. on (piano, guitar, &c.); (n.) sound made by strumming (*the s. of a guitar*). [imit., cf. THRUM]

stru·ma (-ōō-), n. (pl. *-ae*). Scrofula; goitre; (Bot.) cushion-like dilatation of an organ. So **stru·mo**SE[1], **stru·mo**US, aa. [L, = scrofulous tumour]

stru·mpet, n. Prostitute. [f. 14th c., etym. dub.]

strung. See STRING.

strut[1], v.i., & n. (Walk with) pompous or affected gait. Hence **stru·tting**LY[2] adv. [OE *strūtian* project, cf. foll.]

strut[2], n., & v.t. Piece of wood or iron

inserted in a framework & intended to bear weight or pressure in the direction of its length, brace, esp. one set obliquely from rafter to king-post or queen-post; (vb) brace with strut(s). [cf. ON *strútr* conical cap, Norw. *strut* spout, Sw. *strut* paper cornet]

stru·thious (-ōōth-), a. Of or like an ostrich, of the ostrich tribe. [L *struthio* f. Gk *strouthiōn* ostrich (*strouthos* sparrow), -OUS]

strў·chnia, strў·chnĭn(e), (-k-), nn. Vegetable alkaloid got from plants of genus *Strychnos*, highly poisonous & used in minute doses as nerve-stimulant. Hence **stry·chnic** a., **stry·chn(in)ism**(5) nn. [L *strychnos* f. Gk (*s*)*trukhnos* kind of nightshade, -INE[5]]

Stu·art, n. *The Ss.*, sovereigns James I–James II, Mary, & Anne.

stub, n., & v.t. Stump of tree, tooth, &c., left projecting; remnant *of* pencil, cigar, dog's tail, or similar object; *s.-iron*, used for gun-barrels & made of old horse-shoe or other nails; *s.-mortise*, *-tenon*, going only part of the way through; hence **stu·bby**[2] a. (Vb) grub up (s.) by the roots; clear (land) of ss.; *s.* one's *toe*, hurt it by striking against something. [OE *stybb*, cf. Du. *stobbe*, ON *stubbr*, Gk *stupos*]

stu·bble, n. Stumps of grain left sticking up after harvest, cropped hair or beard. Hence **stu·bbly**[2] a. [f. OF *estuble* f. LL *stupula* f. L *stipula* (*stipes* stock, -ULE)]

stu·bborn (*-ern*), a. Obstinate, unyielding, obdurate, inflexible, refractory, intractable, (*facts are s. things*, will not adapt themselves to theory). Hence **stu·bbornly**[2] adv., **stu·bbornness** n. [ME *stoburn*, *stiborn*, perh. f. OE *stybb* STUB w. unexplained suf.]

stu·cco, n. (pl. *-oes*), & v.t. Kinds of plaster or cement used for coating wall surfaces or moulding into architectural decorations; (vb) coat with s. [It., f. OHG *stukki* a crust (whence G *stück* piece)]

stuck(-up). See STICK.

stud[1], n., & v.t. Large-headed nail, boss, or knob, projecting from a surface esp. for ornament; rivet, cross-piece in each link of chain-cable; two-headed button for use with two button-holes esp. in shirt-front (*collar-s.*, long kind going through four holes); post to which laths are nailed, whence **stu·dding**[1] n., woodwork of lath-&-plaster wall. (Vb) set with ss. by way of strengthening or usu. of decorating, (p.p.) thickly set or strewed *with* (*door, lawn, sea, sky, studded with nails, trees, islands, stars*); be scattered over or about (surface). [OE *studu* post, cf. ON *stoth*, Sw. *stöd*, G *stütze* prop]

stud[2], n. Number of horses kept for some purpose as breeding, racing, hunting, coaching; *s.-book*, containing pedigrees of horses; *s. farm*, place where horses are bred; *s.-horse*, stallion. [OE *stód*, cf. ON *stóth*, G *gestüt*; cogn. w. STAND]

studding-sail (stŭ·nsl), n. Sail set on small extra yard & boom beyond leech of square sail in light winds. [etym. dub.]

stū·dent, n. Person studying in order to qualify himself for some occupation or devoting himself to some branch of learning or under instruction at university or other place of higher education or technical training (*medical, theological, historical, s.*; *s. interpreter*, civil servant qualified or qualifying for consular service in China, Persia, &c., by study of the language required; *a s. of archaeology, law, botany, manners*; *numbers its ss. by the thousand*); person of studious habits; (at some colleges) recipient of stipend from foundation, fellow or scholar, whence **stu·dentship** n. [L *studēre* (*studium* STUDY[1]), -ENT]

stū·dio, n. Working-room of painter, sculptor, photographer, &c., often with skylights or windows specially designed to secure suitable light. [It., f. L as STUDY[1]]

stū·dious, a. Given to study, occupied with reading; taking care *to* do, anxiously desirous *of doing*; studied, deliberate, intended, zealous, anxious, painstaking, (*with s. care, attention, politeness*). Hence **stu·diously**[2] adv., **stu·diousness** n. [f. L *studiosus* (foll., -OSE[1])]

stŭ·dy[1], n. Thing to be secured by pains or attention (*it shall be my s. to please, to write correctly*; *your comfort was my s.*; *make a s. of*, try to secure); (now usu. *brown s.*) fit of musing, reverie, (*there he stood for an hour in a s.*; *is in a brown s.*, too intent on his thoughts to observe what is passing); devotion of time & thought to acquiring information esp. from books (often pl.), pursuit of some branch of knowledge, (*gives his hours to s.*; *make a s. of*, investigate carefully; *my ss. have convinced me that*; *the s. of mathematics, morals*; *continue your ss.*, go on with your lessons); thing that is or deserves to be investigated (*the proper s. of mankind is man*; *his face was a s.*); (Paint. &c.) sketch made for practice in technique or as preliminary experiment for picture or part of it (*his ss. are exquisite, but his finished work disappointing*; *a s. of a head*); (Mus.) composition designed to test or develop player's skill; (Theatr.) *good, slow*, &c., learner of parts (UNDERSTUDY); room used for literary occupation, transaction of business, &c. (*you will find him in his, the, s.*). [AF & OF *estudie* f. L *studium* zeal, study]

stu·dy[2], v.t. & i. Make a s. of, take pains to investigate or acquire knowledge of (subject) or to assure (result sought), scrutinize or earnestly contemplate (visible object), (*s. law, French, philosophy*; *s. book*, read it attentively; *s.* one's *part*, try to learn it by heart; *s. up*, get up for examination &c.; *s. out*, succeed in finding out by hard thinking; *studies others' convenience, his own interests*; *s.* person's *face* or *character, a map, the stars*); apply oneself to s. esp. reading (*s. for the bar*, read law); (archaic) meditate, muse; be on the watch, try constantly to manage, *to* do (*studies to avoid disagreeable topics*); (p.p.) deliberate, intentional, affected, (*a studied insult*; *with studied politeness, rudeness, unconcern, abandon*), whence **stu·died**LY[2] adv. [f. OF *estudier* f. med. L *studiare* f. L as prec.]

stuff, n., & v.t. & i. Material that thing is made of or that is or may be used for some purpose (*the s. that dreams, heroes, are made of*; *has good s. in him*, sterling qualities; *some s. they call petrol*; *this punch, book, is good, sorry, s.*; *household s.* archaic, furniture &c.; *bread, food, -ss.*, things made into bread, used as food; *green, garden, s.*, vegetables; *doctors' s.*, physic; *inch s.*, boards 1 in. thick; *thick s.*, planking over 4 in. thick; *the s.* colloq., available supply of something e.g. timber, shells); any woollen fabric (opp. silk, cotton, linen; *s. gown*, worn by barrister who has not taken SILK); valueless matter, refuse, trash, nonsense (n. & int.), (*Take that s. away. Smith a liar? s. & nonsense!. What s. he writes!*); (slang) HOT *s., the s. to give 'em* (way to proceed &c.). (Vb) pack, cram, stop *up*, fill, distend, (*s.* one's *ears with wool, cushion with down*; *stuffed birds, beasts*, skin with interior removed & replaced by enough material to restore original shape; *stuffed fowl, turkey, haddock, veal*, with minced seasoning inserted before cooking; *s. child, goose*, &c., make it eat largely; *a head stuffed with romance, facts, folly*), whence **stu·ff**ING[1](4) n. (*stuffing-box*, chamber in machinery through which rod can work without allowing passage of air &c., all vacant space being filled with stuffing); ram or press into receptacle (*stuffed his necessaries into a small bag, his fingers into his ears, the food into his mouth*); gull with lies, hoax; gorge oneself, eat greedily; hence **(-)stuff**ER[1] n. [vb f. n., OF *estoffe*, cf. Pr., Sp., & Port. *estofa* cloth, It. *stoffa* woven piece, etym. dub.; G & Sw. *stoff*, Da. *stof*, are f. the OF]

stu·ffy, a. (Of valley, room, &c., or atmosphere in it) lacking fresh air or ventilation, close, hard to breathe in, fusty; (U.S.) angry, sulky. Hence **stu·ffi**NESS n. [-Y[2]]

stuggy &c. See **stock-.**

stu·ltify̆, v.t. (Of act, statement, agent, speaker) reduce (previous act &c.) to absurdity, exhibit (act &c. or one*self*) in ridiculous light, make (act &c.) of no effect, neutralize (one*self*) as agent, by later inconsistent act &c. Hence **stulti**FICA·TION n. [f. LL *stultificare* (L *stultus* foolish, -I-, -FY)]

stum, n., & v.t. Unfermented grape-juice, must; (vb) prevent from fermenting, secure (wine) against further fermentation in cask, by introduction of antiseptic. [f. Du. *stom* n., *stommen* vb (*stom* a. quiet, cf. G *stumm*)]

stu·mble, v.i. & t., & n. Lurch forward, have partial fall, from catching or striking foot or making false step (*s. along*, go with frequent ss.); make blunder(s) in doing something (*stumbles in his speech*; *s. through a recitation*); be offended, feel scruples, *at*; come accidentally (*up*)*on* or *across*; (archaic) give pause to, excite scruples in; *stu·mbling-block*, obstacle, circumstance that causes difficulty or hesitation or scruples; hence **stu·mbling**LY[2] adv. (N.) act of stumbling. [f. 14th c.; cf. Norw. *stumla*, & STAMMER]

stū·mer, n. (slang). Worthless cheque, counterfeit coin or note. [?]

stump, n., & v.i. & t. Projecting remnant of cut or fallen tree, corresponding remnant of broken branch or tooth or amputated limb, useless end of cigar or pencil, worn-down brush or other implement, stub; (pl., facet.) legs (usu. STIR one's *ss.*); s. of tree used by orator to address meeting from (*on the s.*, colloq., engaged in political speech-making or agitation; *s. oratory*, of kind suitable for such speeches); (Cricket) one of the three uprights of a wicket (OFF, *middle*, LEG, *s.*); cylinder of rolled paper or other material with conical ends for softening pencil-marks & other uses in drawing. (Vb) walk stiffly & noisily as on wooden legs; (of question &c.; colloq.) pose, be too hard for, (*am stumped*, at a loss, at my wits' end), whence **stu·mp**ER[1](2) n.; (Cricket) put (batsman who is not in his ground) out by disturbing wicket while holding ball, whence **stu·mp**ER[1](1) n. (slang, =wicket-keeper); make s. speeches, traverse (district) doing this; use s. on (drawing, line, &c.); *s. up* slang, pay over the money required, produce (sum). [cf. Du. *stomp*, G *stumpf*; perh. cogn. w. STAMP, STUB]

stu·mpy, a. Thickset, stocky, of small height or length in proportion to girth, (*a s. man, book, tail, pencil*). Hence **stu·mpi**LY[2] adv., **stu·mpi**NESS n. [-Y[2]]

stun, v.t. (Of sound) deafen temporarily, bewilder; (of blow lit. or fig.) knock senseless, reduce to insensibility or stupor, benumb, overwhelm; (part. as adj., slang) ravishingly good in some respect, splendid, delightful, ripping, whence **stu·nning**LY[2] adv., & so **stu·nn**ER[1] n. [prob. f. OF *estoner* ASTONISH]

Stu·ndism, Stu·ndist, (-ōō-), nn. Doctrines, adherent, of a religious body in Russia, orig. of peasants, rejecting ceremonies of Orthodox Church & basing itself on the Bible as translated 1861 into modern Russian. [G *stunde* hour, lesson (the movement originating with German colonists), -ISM, -IST]

stung. See STING.

stunk. See STINK.

stu·nsail, stuns'l, n. = STUDDING-SAIL.

stunt[1], v.t. Check growth or development of, dwarf, cramp, (esp. in p.p.). [f. OE *stunt* a. dull, cf. ON *stuttr* short]

stunt[2], n. (slang). Special effort, feat, show performance, display of concentrated energy, advertising device. [etym. dub.; first in U.S. college athletics]

stūpe[1] (*or* -ōōp), n., & v.t. Flannel &c. wrung out of hot water & applied as fomentation; pledget of soft material used as surgical dressing; (vb) apply s. to, foment. [f. L *stup(p)a* tow]

stupe[2], n. (slang). Fool. [for STUPID]

stū·pefȳ, v.t. Make stupid or torpid, deprive of sensibility, (*stupefied with drink, narcotics, grief,* &c.). Hence or cogn. **stupe**FA·CIENT a. & n. (med.), **stupe**FA·CTION, **stu·pefi**ER[1](1, 2), nn., **stu·pefact**IVE a. [f. F *stupéfier* f. L *stupefacere* (*stupēre* be torpid, -FY)]

stūpe·ndous, a. Amazing, prodigious, astounding, esp. by size or degree (*a s. structure, error, achievement; s. folly*). Hence **stupe·ndous**LY[2] adv., **stupe·ndous**NESS n. [L *stupendus* (*stupēre* be amazed at, -ND[1]), -OUS]

stū·peous, a. (entom.). With long loose scales like tow. [L *stup(p)eus* (*stupa* tow), -OUS]

stū·pid, a. & n. In a state of stupor or lethargy; dull by nature, slow-witted, lacking in sensibility, obtuse, crass, characteristic of persons of this nature, (*a s. person, joke, idea, book, fright; what a s. place to put it in!*), whence **stupi·di**TY n.; uninteresting, dull, (*a s. place, visit, time*). Hence **stu·pid**LY[2] adv. [f. L *stupidus* (as STUPENDOUS, -ID[1])]

stū·por, n. Dazed state, torpidity, whence **stu·por**OUS a. (med.); helpless amazement. [L (as STUPENDOUS, -OR[1])]

stūpo·se, a. (bot., zool.). With tow-like tufts of long hair. [as STUPEOUS, -OSE[1]]

stur·dy[1], a. Robust, hardy, vigorous, lusty, strongly built, (*s. child, opponent, legs, frame, resistance, courage; s. beggar* archaic, able-bodied but not working). Hence **stur·di**LY[2] adv., **stur·di**NESS n. [earlier sense *reckless*; f. OF *estourdi* amazed, etym. dub.]

stur·dy[2], n. Vertigo in sheep caused by tapeworm in brain. Hence **stur·di**ED[2] a. [f. OF *estourdie* giddiness (prec.)]

stur·geon (-jn), n. Kinds of large anadromous fish resembling shark in general shape, having mailed body & head, yielding caviare & isinglass, & esteemed as food. [f. OF *esturgeon* f. med. L *sturionem* nom. *-o* f. OHG *sturjo*, cf. OE *styrga*; perh. cogn. w. STIR]

Sturm und Drang. See STORM *& stress.*

stu·tter, v.i. & t., & n. Keep repeating parts, esp. initial consonants, of words in effort to articulate; utter in this way (often *out*); hence **stu·tter**ER[1] n., **stu·ttering**LY[2] adv. (N.) act or habit of stuttering. [obs. *stut* in same sense (cf. G *stossen* strike) + -ER[5]; cf. Du. *stotteren*, G *stottern*]

sty[1], n. (pl. *-ies*), & v.t. & i. (*Pig*)*sty*, enclosure for keeping pig(s) in, (fig.) mean or dirty hovel or room, place of debauchery; (vb) lodge (t. & i.) in s. [OE (& ON) *sti*]

sty[2], **stye,** n. Inflamed swelling on edge of eyelid (usu. *a s. in* one's *eye*). [prob. f. obs. *styany* (= *styan eye* f. OE *stigend* sty, lit. riser, f. *stigan* rise + *eye*) shortened as though = sty on eye]

Stȳ·gian, a. (As) of the Styx or of Hades, murky, gloomy. [L f. Gk *Stugios* (STYX), -AN]

style[1], n., & v.t. Ancient writing-implement, a small rod with pointed end for scratching letters on wax-covered tablets & blunt end for obliterating (whence **sty·li**FORM a.), (poet.) pen or pencil, (transf.) thing of s.-like shape as etching-needle or styloid process in Anat.; manner of writing, speaking, or doing, esp. as opposed to the matter to be expressed or thing done (*the s. is better than the matter; written in a florid, cumbrous, lucid, delightful, s.; different ss. of rowing; slashed about him in fine s.; good, bad, s.,* = *good, bad,* FORM[1]); collective characteristics of the writing or diction or artistic expression or way of presenting things or decorative methods proper to a person or school or period or subject, manner exhibiting these characteristics, (*in the s. of Shakspere, Raphael, Wagner; the epic, lyric, dramatic, s.; lapidary* or *monumental s.*, fit or resembling that fit for inscriptions on stone; *pre-Raphaelite, impressionist, s.*, in painting; *baroque, Louis XIV, rococo, renaissance, s.*, in architecture or furniture or dress; GOTHIC, *classical,* ROMANESQUE, *s.*, in architecture; *Norman, early English, decorated, perpendicular, ss.*, kinds of esp. ecclesiastical architecture prevailing successively in England 1066–1189, 1189–1272, 1272–1377, 1350–1600, & marked respectively by round arches & heavy pillars, pointed arches & lancet windows & simple tracery, flowing tracery & elaborate ornament, slender pillars & vast windows divided by vertical & horizontal lines; *Tudor, Jacobean, Queen Anne, ss.*, kinds of esp. domestic architecture); descriptive formula, designation of person or thing, full title, (*is entitled to the s. of* Right honourable, King, Esquire; *did not recognize him under his* *new s.*; *my s. is plain* John Smith; *regret that I am not acquainted with your proper s.*; *old*, *new*, *s.*, abbr. *O.S.*, *N.S.*, appended to dates, = so called when reckoned by the Julian, GREGORIAN, CALENDAR[1]); noticeably superior quality or manner esp. in regard to breeding or fashion, distinction, (*there is no s. about her*, she looks commonplace; *let us do the thing in s. if we do it at all*), whence **sty·**LISH[1] a., **sty·lish**LY[2] adv., **sty·lish**NESS n.; kind, sort, esp. with regard to appearance (*what s. of house, servant, do you require?*; *a gentleman of the old s.*); make, shape, pattern, (*this s. 2/6*; *in all sizes & ss.*); (vb) use specified designation of (*is styled king, folly*). [ME *stile* f. OF *stile, style*, f. L *stilus* incorrectly spelt *stylus* by late writers w. assim. to Gk (foll.)]

style[2], n. Gnomon of sun-dial; (Bot.) narrowed extension of ovary supporting stigma. [f. Gk *stulos* pillar]

style[3], n. (Incorrect spelling for) STILE.

stў·let, n. Slender pointed instrument, stiletto; (Surg.) stiffening wire of catheter, probe. [F, f. It. STILETTO]

sty·list, n. Person with or aiming at good literary style. [-IST]

styli·stic, a. Of literary style. Hence **styli·sti**CALLY adv. [-IC]

sty·lite, n. Medieval ascetic living on top of a pillar. [f. late Gk *stulitēs* (STYLE[2], -ITE[1])]

sty·lo, n. (colloq. abbr.; pl. *-os*). Stylograph.

stylo-, comb. form of *styloid* in names of muscles = of the styloid process & —, as *-hy·oid*, *-maxi·llary*. [f. L as STYLE[1], -O-]

sty·lobate, n. Continuous basement supporting a row or rows of columns. [f. L f. Gk *stulobatēs* (STYLE[2], *bainō* stand)]

sty·lograph, n. Kind of pen containing reservoir of ink & marking with point instead of split nib. Hence **stylogra·phi**C a., **stylogra·phi**CALLY adv. [STYLE[1], -O-, -GRAPH]

sty·loid, a. & n. *S.* (*process*), spine projecting from base of temporal bone. [STYLE[1], -OID]

sty·mie, n., & v.t. (Var. of) STIMY.

sty·ptic, a. & n. (Substance) that checks bleeding. [f. LL f. Gk *stuptikos* (*stuphō* contract)]

stўr·ax, n. Kinds of tree & shrub, some of which yield valuable gums. [L, f. Gk *sturax*]

Stў·rian, a. & n. (Native) of Styria.

Styx, n. (Gk. myth.). River encompassing Hades (*cross the S.*, die; *black* &c. *as S.*). [L, f. Gk *Stux -ugos*]

Suabian. See SWABIAN.

sū·able, a. That can be sued. Hence **sua**BI·LITY n. [-ABLE]

suasion (swā·zhn), n. Persuasion as opposed to force (esp. *moral s.*). [f. L *suasionem* nom. *-o* (*suadēre suas-* urge, cogn. w. foll., -ION)]

suave (swāv), a. Bland, soothing, mollifying, polite, (*s. person, speech, manners, wine, medicine*). Hence or cogn. **sua·ve**LY[2] adv., **suă·vi**TY n. [F, f. L *suavis* cogn. w. SWEET]

sua·viter (swā-). *S. in mō·do, for·titer in re*, gently but firmly, with iron hand in velvet glove. [L, = suavely in manner, strongly in matter]

sub[1], n. (colloq.). Subaltern; subscription; substitute. [abbr.]

sub[2], L prep., = under, in some L phrr.: *s. fi·nem* (abbr. *s.f.*), towards the end (of the chapter &c. referred to); *s. ju·dicĕ* (-jōō-), under judicial consideration (*newspaper comment on cases s.j. is prohibited*), not yet decided, still debatable (*the matter is still s.j.*; cf. RES *judicata*); *s. rō·sa* (-zā *or* -za), (of communications, consultations, &c.) in confidence, under express or implied pledge of secrecy [lit. under the rose, as emblem of secrecy]; *s. sĭle·ntio* (-tĭō, -shĭō), in hushed-up manner, privately; *s. vo·cĕ*, abbr. *s.v.*, (in references to dictionaries &c.) under the word in question, under the word —.

sub-, pref. f. L *sub* prep. & *sub-* pref. = under.

1. Many words are from L compounds, in which *sub-* (or often by assim. &c. *suc-*, *suf-*, *sug-*, *sum-*, *sup-*, *sur-*, *sus-*) expresses clearly or obscurely the ideas of lower position (*subjacent, subordinate, subscribe, subsist, substance*), motion to this (*subject, subjugate, subjunctive, submerge, submit, subside, succumb, suppose, suppress*) or from this (*subtract, succinct, suspect, suspend, suspire*), covertness or secrecy or tacitness (*subaudition, suborn, summon, surreptitious*), inclusion (*subsume*), closeness (*subjoin, subjunctive, sublime, subsequent, suburb, succeed*), inferiority (*subaltern, subserve, succentor*), support (*subsidy, subvention, succour, suffer, suffice, sustain*), addition (*suffix, supplement*), or substitution (*substitute, supplant, surrogate*).

2. *Sub-*, without the above changes into *suc-* &c., is also used as a living pref. with more definite senses:

a. On anal. of L *subterraneus* underground (*sub terra* below the earth) adjj. are formed from *sub*, the abl. of any L noun, & an adj. ending, esp. as anat. terms with sense *situated under the* — (*substernal* f. L *sub sterno* below the breastbone); in others *sub-* has the secondary sense *below in degree* (*subnormal* below normal), & in some having this sense, as in b below, *sub-* is prefixed directly to a derived E adj. (*subhuman* less than human, as from *sub homine*).

b. On anal. of L *subacidus* slightly acid,

For words in *sub-* not given see SUB-.

adjj. & rarely nn. are formed by prefixing *sub-* to E adjj. & nn. whether of L orig. or not, the pref. having an effect equivalent to rather (*subacid*), more or less (*subaquatic*), roughly (*subcylindrical*), incipient (*subdelirium*), not quite (*subconscious*), approaching the specified character (*suberect*), on the borders of (*subalpine*).

c. On anal. of med. L *subprior* under-prior, *sub-* is prefixed to nn. & vv. with sense *under-*, *subordinate(ly)*, *secondary -ily*, *further*, (*subprefect, subheading, subspecies, subdivide, sublet*).

d. On anal. of *substruction* f. L *substructio*, *sub-* is rarely prefixed to E nn. with sense *underlying* (*subsoil, subway*).

e. With multiplicative adjj. (*double, triple, quadruple, quintuple, sextuple, septuple, octuple, decuple*) *sub-* inverts the sense; so, *double, triple*, expressing the ratios 2:1, 3:1, *subdouble, subtriple*, =1:2, 1:3.

The following list contains, with letters of reference & further explanation when necessary, the words in *sub-* whether compounded in L or in E that fall under 2; the L wd needed to give the meaning of wds marked *a* will be found by reference to the simple adj. that is left when *sub-* is removed, or to wd added in brackets:— *subabdo·minal*, a; *-a·cid, -aci·dity*, b, (lit., & fig. of words &c.); *suba·gent, -a·gency*, c; *-a·lpine*, b; *-ā·nal*, a; *-ande·an*, b (of Andes mountains); *-a·pennine*, b; *-aposto·lic*, b, of period after that of apostles; *-aqua·tic*, b, of more or less aquatic habits or kind, also a, underwater; *-ā·queous*, a; *-ar·ctic*, b; *-a·stral*, a, terrestrial; *-aur·al*, a; *-a·xillary*, a; *su·b-branch, -breed*, nn., c; *-cau·dal*, a; *-ce·ntral*, a, b; *-ce·rebral*, a (esp. of reflex action in which the spinal cord is concerned, but not the brain); *su·bclass*, c; *-cla·vate*, b; *-clā·vian, -clavi·cular*, a (CLAVICLE); *su·b-commi·ssion(er), -commi·ttee*, c; *-co·ncave, -co·nical, -co·nscious(ly, -ness)*, b; *-co·ntinent* n., b, region whose size & importance would justify the name *continent* if it were not part of one, e.g. India, S. Africa; *su·b-co·ntract* n., *-contra·ct* v.i., *-contra·ctor* n., c; *-co·ntrary* a. & n. pl., *-contrari·ety* n., b, contrary in some degree only (esp. in logic, as '*some men are mortal*' *&* '*some men are not mortal*' *are sub-contraries, whereas* '*all men are mortal*' *&* '*no man is mortal*' *are contraries*); *-co·nvex*, b; *-cor·date*, b; *-cor·neous*, b, rather horny, also a, placed under horn, nail, &c.; *-cor·tical, -co·stal, -cra·nial*, a; *-cry·stalline*, b; *-cuta·neous(ly), -cuti·cular*, a; *-cyli·ndrical*, b; *su·bdea·con, -dea·conship, -dean, -dea·nery, -deca·nal*, c; *-de·cuple*, e; *-deli·rium*, b, incipient or mild or intermittent; *-dermal*, a (DERM); *-dia·conate*, c; *-divi·de* v.t. & i. [f. L *subdividere*], *-division*, c; *-do·minant* n. mus., a, tone below dominant, fourth; *-dor·sal*, a; *-dou·ble, -du·plicate*, e; *-e·dit, -e·ditor*, c; *-epider·mal*, a (EPIDERMIS); *-e·qual*, b (esp. of quantities in a group such that no one is as large as the sum of the rest); *-equila·teral*, b; *-ere·ct*, b; *su·bfa·mily*, c (in zool. classif.); *-fe·brile*, b; *su·bflavour*, d; *su·b-form*, c; *su·bfusc*, b, dusky, dull-coloured [f. L *suffuscus* see FUSCOUS]; *-gela·tinous*, b; *su·b-gēnus, -gene·ric*, c; *-gla·cial*, a; *-glo·bular, -grallator·ial*, b; *su·b-group, -head* (in classif.), *-heading*, c; *-hepa·tic*, a, b; *-himalay·an*, b; *-hu·man*, a; *-hu·meral*, a (HUMERUS); *-infeuda·tion, -inspe·ctor*, c; *-inte·stinal*, a (INTESTINE[1]); *su·bjoint*, c, one of subdivisions of regular joint in leg &c. of insect &c.; *su·bkingdom*, c, main division of animal or vegetable kingdom; *-la·nceolate*, b; *su·blease* n. & v.t., *-lessee·, -le·ssor, -let* v.t., *su·b-librar·ian, su·b-lieute·nant*, c; *-li·minal*, a (LIMEN; of sensations so faint that subject is not conscious of them); *-li·ngual*, a; *-li·ttoral*, b; *-lu·nar* (poet.), *-lu·nary*, a, of this world, earthly, (*s. affairs* &c.); *-ma·mmary*, a (MAMMA[2]); *-mar·ine*, a (*s. plant, cable, volcano*, &c.; *s. boat*, or *s.* as noun, that can be submerged esp. for torpedo work with store of compressed air for crew); *su·bmaster*, c, second master in some schools; *-maxi·llary*, a (MAXILLA); *-me·mbranous*, b; *-me·ntal*, a (MENTAL[2]); *-meta·llic*, b; *-mo·ntane*, a; *-mu·cous*, b; *-mu·ltiple* a. & n., e; *-narco·tic*, b; *-na·sal, -na·tural* (opp. *supernatural*), *-nor·mal, -occi·pital* (OCCIPUT), *-ocea·nic*, a; *-oce·llate*, b (OCELLUS); *-o·ctuple*, e; *-o·cular, -oesopha·geal* (OESOPHAGUS), *-or·bital* (ORBIT), a; *su·border, -or·dinal*, c (in bot. & zool. classif.); *-o·val*, b; *-pari·etal, -phary·ngeal* (PHARYNX), *-phre·nic*, a; *-pi·lose*, b; *-pleur·al*, a; *-po·lar*, b, of nearly polar character or situation, also a, directly below pole of heavens (astron.); *-pre·fect(ure), -pri·or*, c; *-pyra·midal, -quadra·ngular, -qua·drate*, b; *-qua·druple, -qui·ntuple*, e; *-ra·mose*, b; *su·breader*, c (in Inns of Court); *-recta·ngular*, b; *su·brector*, c, rector's deputy; *su·bregion*, c, division of faunal region; *su·brent* v.t., c; *-re·tinal*, a (RETINA); *-rhomboi·dal*, b; *-sa·cral*, a (SACRUM); *-satu·rated, -satura·tion*, b; *-sca·pular*, a; *su·bsection*, c; *-se·nsible*, a, below the reach of the senses; *-se·ptuple*, e; *-ser·ous, -se·ssile*, b; *-se·xtuple*, e; *su·bsoil*, d; *su·bspecies, -speci·fic* a., c; *-sphe·rical, -spi·nous* (SPINE), b; *su·bstation*, c; *-ster·nal*, a (STERNUM); *substra·tum* (pl. *-ta* rare), d, what underlies something, lower layer, foundation, basis, (often fig., as *it has a s. of truth*); *-stru·ction* or *-stru·cture, -stru·ctural*, d; *-te·mperate*, b (of climate &c.); *su·btenant, -tenancy*, c; *-ter·minal*, b, nearly at the end; *-terra·nean*, a, underground (lit. & fig.), so *-terra·neously*; *-thora·cic*, a (THORAX); *su·btitle*, c; *su·b-*

tonic n. (mus.), a, note next below tonic; *-transpar·ent*, *-tria·ngular*, b; *su·btribe*, a (zool. & bot. classif.); *-tri·ple*, *-tri·plicate*, e; *-tro·pical*, b (of climate, fauna, flora, &c.); *-u·ngulate*, b, hoofed, but with several digits; *-ur·sine*, b; *su·bvariety*, c (in classif.); *-ver·tebral*, a; *-ver·tical*, *-vi·treous*, b; *su·bway*, d, covered usu. underground way.

subahdar· (sōō-), n. (Anglo-Ind.). Chief native officer of company of sepoys. [Hind. (*subah* province, *dār* master)]

sŭ·baltern, a. & n. Of inferior rank, (Log., of propositions) particular, not universal; (n., mil.) junior officer below rank of captain. [f. LL SUB(*alternus* ALTERNATE[1])]

***subau·dī*,** v. imperat. Supply (specified word or words) by way of subaudition. [L]

sŭbaudi·tion, n. Mental supplying of omitted word(s), understanding of what is not expressed, reading between the lines. [f. L *subauditio* f. SUB(*audire* hear)]

subdu·ce, subdu·ct, vv.t. (rare). Withdraw, deduct, subtract. So **subdu·ction** n. [f. L SUB(*ducere -duct-* draw)]

subdue·, v.t. Conquer, subjugate, overcome, vanquish, master, tame, bring into subjection, discipline, (*s. enemies, nature, rough land*, one's *passions*; *subdued by kindness*); soften, make gentle, tone down, mitigate, (esp. in p.p., as *subdued colour, light, tone, effect, mood, manners, satisfaction*, whence **subdue·dness** n.). Hence **subdu·able** a., **subdu·al**(2) n. [ME *sodewe* f. OF *soduire* repr. in form L SUBDUCE*re*, but in sense L SEDUCE*re*, while the E vb has the sense of L SUB[2](*dere* put) conquer]

sūbĕr·eous, sūbĕ·ric, sū·berose, aa. Corky, of or like cork. [(*-ous* f. LL *subereus* + -OUS) f. L *suber* cork, -IC, -OSE[1]]

subja·cent, a. Underlying, situated below. [f. L SUB(*jacēre* lie), -ENT]

su·bject[1], a. & adv. (Archaic, poet.) subjacent (*survey the s. plains*); under government, not independent, owing obedience *to*, (*a s. province, tribe*; *is held s.*, in subjection; *has long been s. to France*; *States s. to foreign rule*; *we are all s. to the laws of nature, the law of the land*); liable or exposed or prone *to* (thing; *persons s. to gout*; *is very s. to damage, envy*, &c.); *s.* (a. & adv.) *to*, conditional(ly) upon, on the assumption of, without precluding, (*treaty is s. to ratification*, not valid unless ratified; *the arrangement is made*, or *is, s. to your approval*; *s. to your consent, I propose to try again*; *s. to correction, these are the facts*). [ME & OF *suget*, f. L p.p. of SUB(*jicĕre -ject-* = *jacĕre* throw)]

su·bject[2], n. Person s. to political rule, any member of a State except the Sovereign, any member of a s. State, (*rulers & ss.*; *the ss. of the Sultan*; *the loyalty of My ss.*; *the liberty of the s.*, such immunities as are secured to ss. under constitutional rule; fig., as *the ss. of King Shakspere*); (Log., Gram.) that member of a proposition about which something is predicated, the noun or noun-equivalent with which the verb of a sentence is made to agree in number &c., (*s. & predicate are the essential parts of a sentence*; *every verb has a s. expressed or understood, not every verb has an object*); (Metaphys.) thinking & feeling entity, the mind, the ego, the conscious self, as opp. all that is external to the mind (*s. & object*, the ego & the non-ego, self & not-self, the consciousness & what it is or may be conscious of), the substance or substratum of anything as opp. its attributes; theme of or *of* discussion or description or representation, matter (to be) treated of or dealt with, (*never talks on serious ss.*; *proposed a s. for the debate*; *on the s. of*, concerning, about; *a tabooed, ticklish, interesting, dull, s.*; *what is the s. of the poem, story, picture?*; *constantly wanders from the s.*; *pastoral, genre, marine, historical*, &c., *s.* in painting; *s. of piece of music*, base-melody, leading phrase, motif; *s. for dissection*, or *s.*, dead body; *was made the s. of an experiment*; *could write if I could think of a s.*; *change the s.*, talk of something else, esp. as way out of embarrassment); circumstance that gives occasion *for* specified feeling or action (*is a s. for ridicule, pity, rejoicing, congratulation*); person of specified usu. undesirable bodily or mental tendencies (*a sensitive, bilious, plethoric, hysterical, ill-conditioned*, &c., *s.*); *s.-heading*, in index collecting references to a s.; *s.-matter*, matter treated of in book &c.; *s.-object*, object of sense or thought as it is conceived of (opp. *object-object*, as it is in fact). Hence **su·bjectless** a. [f. L masc. & neut. p.p. (prec.)]

subje·ct[3], v.t. Subdue (nation &c. usu. *to* one's sway &c.); expose, make liable, treat, *to* (*rudeness subjects one to retorts in kind*; *must be subjected to great heat*; *shall s. it to criticism*). So **subje·ction** n. [f. OF *subjecter* f. L as SUBJECT[1]]

subje·ctive, a. & n. (Philos.) belonging to, of, due to, the consciousness or thinking or perceiving subject or ego as opp. real or external things, (pop.) imaginary; (of art & artists) giving prominence to or depending on personal idiosyncrasy or individual point of view, not producing the effect of literal & impartial transcription of external realities, whence **subje·ctiveness, subjecti·vity,** nn.; (Gram.) of the subject (*s. case*, or *s.* as n., the nominative; *s. genitive*, as in 'by the act *of God*', cf. OBJECTIVE). Hence **subje·c-**

tiveLY[2] adv. [f. LL *subjectivus* (SUBJECT[2], -IVE)]
subje·ctivism, n. Doctrine that knowledge is merely subjective & that there is no external or objective test of truth. So **subje·ctivIST**(2) n. & a. [prec., -ISM, -IST]
subjoi·n, v.t. Add at the end, append, (illustration, anecdote, &c.). [f. OF *subjoindre* f. L SUB(*jungere junct-* join)]
su·bjugate, v.t. Subdue, vanquish, bring under bondage or into subjection. Hence or cogn. **su·bjugABLE** a., **subjugA·TION, su·bjugatOR**[2], nn. [f. L *subjugare* bring under the yoke (SUB[2], *jugum* yoke), -ATE[3]]
subju·nctive, a. & n. *S. mood* or *s.*, a verbal MOOD[2], obsolescent in English, named as being used in the classical languages chiefly in subordinate or subjoined clauses (cf. CONJUNCTIVE; the two names denote the same forms & are sometimes used indifferently; sometimes *s.* is restricted to the subordinate uses while *conjunctive* either includes all uses or is restricted to principal-clause verbs, as in apodosis of conditional sentence). Hence **subju·nctiveLY**[2] adv. [f. L *subjunctivus* (SUBJOIN, -IVE)]
sublapsā·rian, a. & n. =INFRALAPSARIAN. [SUB- 2a]
su·blimāte[1], v.t. Convert from solid state to vapour by heat & allow to solidify again; (fig.) refine, purify, idealize. Hence **sublimA·TION** n. [as foll., -ATE[3]]
su·blimate[2], (-*at*), a. & n. Sublimated (substance); CORROSIVE *s.*; *blue s.*, pigment made from mercury, flowers of sulphur, & sal ammoniac. [f. L *sublimare* SUBLIME[2], -ATE[2]]
subli·me[1], a. Of the most exalted kind, so distinguished by elevation or size or nobility or grandeur or other impressive quality as to inspire awe or wonder, aloof from & raised far above the ordinary, (*s. mountain, scenery, tempest, ambition, virtue, heroism, self-sacrifice, love, thought, beauty, genius, poet,* &c.; *s. indifference, impudence,* &c., as of one too exalted to fear consequences; *the S.* PORTE; *the s.*, all that is s., sublimity), whence or cogn. **subli·meLY**[2] adv., **subli·mITY** n.; (Anat.) lying near the surface, not deep-sunk. [F, f. L *sublimis*, perh. f. SUB[2], *limen* lintel, = reaching up to the lintel]
subli·me[2], v.t. & i. Sublimate (lit.), whence **subli·mER**[1](2) n.; undergo sublimation; purify or elevate, become pure, as by sublimation; make sublime. [f. OF *sublimer* f. L *sublimare* in med. L sense *sublimate* (prec.)]
submer·ge, v.t. & i. Place below water, flood with water, inundate, (also fig.; *the submerged tenth,* the part of the population that is plunged in debt or permanently in distress); (of submarine or its crew or commander) dive, go below surface. Hence or cogn. **submer·gENCE, submer·sION,** nn. [f. L SUB(*mergere mers-* dip)]
submer·se, v.t., & a. (rare). Submerge (rare ex. in p.p. used in Bot. of parts of plants growing under water); (adj., rare, bot.) submersed. Hence (in common use) **submer·sIBLE** a. [f. L p.p. (prec.)]
submi·ssion (-shn), n. Submitting or being submitted (*shall be satisfied with nothing short of complete s.*; *demands the s. of the signature to an expert*); (in legal use) theory &c. submitted by counsel to judge or jury (*my s. is that,* I submit that); humility, meekness, resignation, acceptance of authority, obedient conduct or spirit, so **submi·ssIVE** a., **submi·ssiveLY**[2] adv., **submi·ssiveNESS** n. [f. L *submissionem* (foll., -ION)]
submi·t, v.t. & i. (-tt-). Surrender one*self* for control &c. *to* (*wives s. yourselves unto your own husbands*); present for consideration or decision (*should like to s. it to your inspection*; *s. a case to the court*); urge or represent deferentially *that* (*I s. that a material fact has been passed over*; also parenth., as *that, I s., is a false inference*); give way, make submission, yield, cease or abstain from resistance, (*will never s., s. to indignity, s. to being parted from you*; *had to s. to defeat, God's will*). [f. L SUB(*mittere miss-* send)]
subor·dinate[1] (-*at*), a. & n. Of inferior importance or rank, secondary, subservient, (*to*; *s. clause,* sentence made by addition of a conjunction or by position to serve as a noun or adj. or adv. in another sentence); hence **subor·dinateLY**[2] adv. (N.) person working under another (*leaves everything to, never trusts, ss.* or *his ss.*). [f. med. L SUB(*ordinatus* f. L *ordinare* ORDAIN)]
subor·dināte[2], v.t. Make s., treat or regard as of minor importance, bring or put into subservient relation, (*to*). Hence **subordinA·TION** n., **subor·dinATIVE** a. [as prec., -ATE[3]]
subordina·tionism, n. (theol.). Doctrine that second & third persons of Trinity are inferior to the Father as regards (orthodox view) order only or (Arian view) essence. [-ISM]
subor·n, v.t. Induce by bribery or otherwise to commit perjury or other unlawful act. Hence or cogn. **subornA·TION, subor·nER**[1], nn. [f. L SUB*ornare* equip or incite secretly]
subpoe·na (-pēn*a*), n., & v.t. (-*aed* pr. -*ad*, -*a'd*). Writ commanding person's attendance in court of justice; (vb) serve s. on. [orig. two words, L, = under penalty, the first in the writ]
subre·ption, n. Obtaining of something by surprise or misrepresentation. [f. L *subreptio* purloining f. SUB(*ripere -rept-* =*rapere* snatch)]
subscri·be, v.t. & i. Write (one's name or rarely other inscription) at foot of docu-

ment &c. (*the subscribed names carry weight*; *some one has subscribed a motto*); write one's name at foot of, sign, (document, picture, &c.); express one's adhesion *to* an opinion or resolution (*cannot s. to that*); enter one's name in a list of contributors, make or promise a contribution, contribute (specified sum), to or *to* a common fund or *for* a common object, raise or guarantee raising of by subscribing thus, (*s. to a charity, for a testimonial, £10*; *s. for a book*, engage before it is published to take copy or copies; *s. to a newspaper*, engage to take it for specified time; *the sum needed was subscribed several times over*). Hence or cogn. **subscri·ber**[1] (*the -er*, the under-signed), **subscri·ption**, nn. [f. L SUB(*scribere script-* write)]

su·bscript, a. (Gk gram.). Written below (only in *iota s.*, small iota written below ā, ē, & ō). [f. L p.p. (prec.)]

subse·llium, n. (pl. *-ia*). =MISERICORD (last sense). [L (SUB[2], *sella* seat)]

su·bsequent, a. That follow(s) or followed the event &c. indicated in the context, of later time or date than something, posterior in time *to*. Hence **su·bsequence** n., **su·bsequently**[2] adv. [f. L SUB[2](*sequi* follow), -ENT]

subser·ve, v.t. Serve as means in promoting (purpose, end, &c.). [f. L SUB[2](*servire* SERVE)]

subser·vient, a. Useful as means, having merely instrumental relation, (*to*); cringing, obsequious. Hence **subser·vience, subser·viency,** nn., **subser·viently**[2] adv. [f. L as prec., -ENT]

subsi·de, v.i. (Of water, esp. flood) sink in level, run off, disappear; (of ground) cave in, sink; (of building, ship, &c.) settle down lower in ground or water; (of suspended matter) fall to bottom, be precipitated; (of person, usu. joc.) sink into sitting or kneeling or lying posture (*subsided into an armchair*); cease from activity or agitation, become tranquil, abate, (*storm, tumult, apprehension, excitement, subsides*). Hence **su·bsidence** (*or* subsī·-) n. [f. L SUB[2](*sīdere* settle cogn. w. *sedēre* sit)]

subsi·diary, a. & n. Serving to assist or supplement, auxiliary, supplementary, whence **subsi·diarily**[2] adv.; (of troops) subsidized, hired by another nation; (n., usu. in pl.) s. thing or person, accessory. [f. L *subsidiarius* (SUBSIDY, -ARY[1])]

su·bsidize, v.t. Pay subsidy to. [foll., -IZE]

su·bsidy, n. (Hist.) parliamentary grant of money to the sovereign for State needs, tax levied on particular occasion; money grant from one State to another in return for military or naval aid or other equivalent; money contributed by State to expenses of commercial undertaking, charitable institution, &c., held to be of public utility. [f. L *subsidium* reserve troops f. SUB[2](*sīdere* = *sedēre* sit)]

subsi·st, v.i. & t. Exist, continue to exist, remain in being; keep oneself alive, support life, be kept in life, find sustenance, (*on vegetables, charity*, &c., *by begging* &c.); provide sustenance for (*undertook to clothe, arm, & s. 1000 men*). [f. F *subsister* f. L SUB[2](*sistere* set, stand, causal f. *stare* stand)]

subsi·stence, n. Subsisting; means of supporting life, livelihood, what one lives on or by. [f. LL *subsistentia* substance (prec., -ENCE)]

su·bstance, n. (Metaphys.) the substratum that the cognizable properties or qualities or attributes or accidents of things are conceived as inhering in or affecting, the essential nature underlying phenomena, (*s. & accidents in metaphysics correspond to subject & predicate in logic*; *a s. is a being subsisting in itself & subject to accidents*; *being of one s. with the Father*); essence or most important part of anything, pith, purport, real meaning, (*I agree with you in s.*, generally, apart from details; *can give you the s. of his remarks*; *the s. of religion*); material as opposed to form (*the s. is good, but the style repellent*); reality, solidity, solid worth, actual possessions, (*sacrifice the s. for the shadow*; *there is no s. in him*; *an argument of little s.*; *a man of s.*, with property, cf. *man of* STRAW; *waste* one's *s.*, be spendthrift); particular kind of matter (*a heavy, porous, yellow, transparent, s.*; *the small number of ss. that make up the world*). [OF, f. L *substantia* (SUB[2], *stare* stand, -ANCE)]

substa·ntial (-shl), a. Having substance, actually existing, not illusory, (*the ghost proved s. after all*); of real importance or value, of considerable amount, (opp. *nominal, verbal*; *a s. argument, point*; *made a s. contribution, s. progress, s. concessions*); of solid material or structure, not flimsy, stout, (*a s. house*; *a man of s. build*); possessed of property, well-to-do, commercially sound, (*a s. yeoman*; *deal only with s. firms*); deserving the name in essentials, virtual, practical, (*s. truth, agreement, success, performance of contract*). Hence or cogn. **substantia·lity** n., **substa·ntially**[2] adv. [f. LL *substantialis* (prec., -AL)]

substa·ntialism, n. (philos.). Doctrine that behind phenomena there are substantial realities. So **substa·ntialist**(2), n. [-ISM]

substa·ntialize, v.t. & i. Invest with or acquire substance or actual existence. [-IZE]

substa·ntiate (-shĭ-), v.t. Prove the truth

of, give good grounds for, (charge, statement, claim). Hence **substantia·tion** (-sĭ-, -shĭ-) n. [SUBSTANCE, -ATE[3]]

su·bstantive, a. & n. Expressing existence (*the s. verb*, the vb *be*); having a separate & independent existence, not merely inferential or implicit or subservient or parasitic, (*s. enactment, motion*, &c., made in due form as such; *noun s.*, old name for the noun in the now usual sense distinguishing it from the *noun adjective* now called *adjective* simply); hence **su·bstantively**[2] adv. (esp. in gram., = *substantivally*). (N.) noun s., noun in the now usual sense excluding adjectives; so **substanti·val** a., **substanti·vally**[2] adv. [OF (*-if, -ive*), f. LL *substantivus* self-existent (SUBSTANCE, -IVE)]

su·bstitute, n., & v.t. Person or thing performing some function instead of another. (Vb) make (person or thing) fill a place or discharge a function for or *for* another, (vulg.) replace (person or thing) *by* or *with* another; put in exchange (*for*); so **substitu·tion** n., **substitu·tional, substitu·tionary**[1], **su·bstitutive,** aa., **substitu·tionally**[2] adv. [f. L SUB(*stituere -ut-* = *statuere* see STATUTE)]

subsu·me, v.t. Include (instance &c.) under a rule or class. Hence **subsu·mption** n. [SUB-, L *sumere sumpt-* take]

subte·nd, v.t. (geom.). (Of chord, side of triangle) be opposite to (arc, angle). [f. L SUB(*tendere tens-* stretch)]

subte·nse, n. Line subtending arc or angle. [f. L p.p. (prec.)]

subter-, pref. = under, less than, esp. in wds formed as opposites to compounds of SUPER-, as *-position, -human, -natural.* [L (SUB[2], *-ter* as in INTER[2])]

su·bterfuge, n. Attempt to escape censure or defeat in argument by evading the issue, statement &c. resorted to for such purpose, use of such statements &c. [f. L *subterfugium* f. SUBTER(*fugere* flee)]

sŭb·til(e), a. (Archaic for) SUBTLE. Hence or cogn. **sub·tilize**(2, 3) v.t. & i., **subtiliza·tion** n., **sub·tilty** n. (archaic). [f. F *subtil* f. L *subtilis* perh. orig. = finewoven (SUB[2], *tela* web)]

subtle (sŭ·tl), (archaic) **sub·til(e),** a. Tenuous or rarefied (archaic), pervasive owing to tenuity, (*the s. air, a s. vapour*; *of s. texture, a s. perfume*); evasive, mysterious, hard to grasp or trace, (*s. magic, charm, power, art*; *a s. distinction*); making fine distinctions, having delicate perception, acute, (*s. senses, perception, insight*; *a s. observer, philosopher, intellect, mind*); ingenious, elaborate, clever, (*a s. device, fancy, workman, explanation, policy*; *s. fingers*); crafty, cunning, (*now the serpent was more s. than any beast*; *a s. enemy*). Hence **sub·tly**[2] adv. [ME & OF *sotil* f. L as prec.]

sub·tlety, n. In adj. senses; also, a fine distinction, a piece of hair-splitting. [f. OF *soutilté* f. L *subtilitatem* (SUBTIL, -TY)]

subtra·ct, v.t. Deduct (part, quantity, number) from or *from* whole or greater quantity or number, esp. in arithmetic or algebra. Hence or cogn. **subtra·ction** n., **subtra·ctive** a. [f. L SUB(*trahere tract-* draw)]

su·btrahend, n. What is to be subtracted in a subtraction sum. [L as prec., -ND[1]]

sū·bŭlate (-at), **su·buliform,** aa. (bot., zool.). Awl-shaped. [L *subula* awl (*suere* sew), -ATE[2], -I-, -FORM]

su·burb, n. Outlying district of city (*the ss.*, all or one of such districts, as *a house in the ss.*, also the environs). So **subur·ban** a. [f. OF *suburbe* f. L SUB(*urbium* f. *urbs urbis* city)]

subve·ntion, n. Grant of money in aid, subsidy. [OF, f. LL *subventionem* f. SUB(*venire, vent-* come) assist, -ION]

subver·t, v.t. Overturn, upset, effect destruction or overthrow of, (religion, monarchy, the constitution, principles, morality). Hence or cogn. **subver·sion** n., **subver·sive** a. [f. L SUB(*vertere vers-* turn)]

suc-, = SUB- in L compounds of *sub* with words in c- & their derivatives.

succa·des, n. pl. (commerc.). Candied fruits in syrup. [f. OF *succade, chucade*, etym. dub.]

succedā·nĕum (-ks-), n. (pl. *-ea*). Substitute, thing or rarely person that one falls back on in default of another. So **succeda·neous** a. [neut. of L *succedaneus* (foll., -ANEOUS)]

succee·d (-ks-), v.t. & i. Take the place previously filled by, follow (t. & i.) in order, come next (to), ensue, be subsequent (to), come by inheritance or in due order to or *to* office or title or property, (*day succeeds day* or *to day*; *agitation succeeded calm* or *succeeded*; *succeeding ages will reverence his memory*; *Elizabeth succeeded Mary, succeeded to the throne, succeeded*); have success (*in doing* &c.), be successful, prosper, accomplish one's purpose, (of plan &c.) be brought to successful issue. [f. F *succéder* f. L SUC(*cedere cess-* go)]

succe·ntor (-ks-), n. Leading bass in choir; precentor's deputy. [LL, f. L SUC(*cinere -cent-* = *canere* sing), -OR[2]]

succès d'estime (F), n. Passably cordial reception given to performance or work from respect rather than appreciation.

succe·ss, n. Issue of undertaking (rare; *with good or bad s.*); favourable issue, accomplishment of end aimed at, attainment of wealth or fame or position, (*have inquired for it without s.*; *military ss.*; *spoilt by s.*; *nothing succeeds like s.*, one s. leads to others), whence **succe·ssful** a., **succe·ssfully**[2] adv.; thing or person that turns out well (*the experiment is a s.*; *was a great s. as a bishop*). [f. L *successus -ūs* (SUCCEED)]

succe·ssion (-shn), n. A following in order (esp. *in s.*; *three great victories in s.*, **running**, without intervening defeat); series of things in s. (*a s. of disasters*, several running); (right of) succeeding to the throne or any office or inheritance, set or order of persons having such right, (*laws regulating the s.*; *claimed, was excluded from, the s.*; *in s. to*, as successor of; *the s. must not be broken*; *is second in the s.*; *was left to him & his s.*, heirs; *apostolic s.*, uninterrupted transmission of spiritual authority through bishops from the apostles downwards; *law of s.*, regulating inheritance esp. in cases of intestate decease; *s. duties*, taxes on property passing by s.); *the S. States*, those resulting from dismemberment of Austria-Hungary; (Biol.) order of descent in development of species. Hence **succe·ssion**AL a. [f. L *successionem* (SUCCEED, -ION)]

succe·ssive, a. Following one after another, in uninterrupted succession, running, consecutive. Hence **succe·ssive**LY[2] adv. [f. med. L *successivus* (SUCCEED, -IVE)]

succe·ssor, n. Person or thing that succeeds to another (*to*, *of*; cf. PREDECESSOR). [OF f. L (SUCCEED, -OR[2])]

succi·nct (-ks-), a. Terse, concise, briefly expressed. Hence **succi·nct**LY[2] adv., **succi·nct**NESS n. [f. L *succinctus* f. SUC(*cingere cinct-* gird) tuck up]

su·ccory, n. = CHICORY. [corrupt. of *cicoree* = CHICORY]

su·ccotash, n. (U.S.). Dish of green maize & beans (& salt pork) boiled together. [f. Amer.-Ind. *msiquatash*]

su·ccour (-ker), v.t., & n. Come to the assistance of, give aid to, (person in danger or difficulty). (N.) aid given at time of need; (pl., archaic) reinforcements, troops coming to the rescue; hence **su·ccour**LESS a. [vb f. OF *sucurre* f. L SUC(*currere curs-* run); n. f. OF *socors* f. med. L *succursus -ūs* (*succurrere*)]

su·ccūba, -bus, n. (pl. *-bae, -bī*). Female demon having sexual intercourse with sleeping men. [LL (*-ba*) & med. L (*-bus*) f. SUC(*cumbere* lie)]

su·ccūlent, a. Juicy (of lit. or fig. food); (Bot.) thick & fleshy, having such leaves or stems. Hence **su·ccul**ENCE n., **su·ccu·lent**LY[2] adv. [f. L *succulentus* (*succus* juice, -LENT)]

succu·mb (-m), v.i. Be overcome, have to cease from resistance or competition or other effort, be forced to give way *to*, die owing *to*, die, (*s. to* one's *enemies, superior numbers, grief, temptation*). [f. OF *succomber* f. L SUC(*cumbere* lie)]

succur·sal, a. (Of chapel of ease) subsidiary. [f. F (*église*) *succursale* subsidiary (church) f. med. L as SUCCOUR, -AL]

such (-tsh), a. (placed not between *a* & its n. but before or after them), & pron. Of the same kind or degree *as* (*s. people, people s., as these*; *s. beauty as yours*; *experiences s. as this are rare*; *s. grapes as you never saw*; *s. as* also = of the or a kind that, as *s. a scarlet as makes the eyes ache*); so great, so natured in some respect, *as to* do or *that* (*is s. as to make one despair*; *had s. a fright that she hardly survived it*); of the kind or degree already described or implied or intelligible from the context or circumstances (*never had s. sport*; *there are no s. doings now*; *s. things make one despair*; *s. are the privileges of fatherhood*; *don't be in s. a hurry*; *how could you leave him at s. a time?*; *saw just s. another yesterday*; *long may he continue s.!*; often colloq. preceding adj. & n. with the effect of *so* modifying the adj., as *s. horrid language*, language so horrid, *was it s. a long time ago?*, *don't want s. a big one* or *s. big ones*; also rarely used twice as relative & correl., as *s. master s. servant*, the servant is s. as the master is); (in legal or formal style) the aforesaid, of the aforesaid kind (*whoever shall make s. return falsely*); so great !, of a kind that demands exclamatory description, (*we have had s. sport!*, *s. an enjoyable evening!*); of a kind or degree sufficient to account for the preceding or following statement (*he cannot come too often, he gives s. pleasure*; *there was s. a draught, it is no wonder he caught cold*); (also *s.-&-s.*) particular, of particular kind, but not needing to be specified (*s. an one*, *s. a one*, archaic, *s.-&-s. a person*, some one, so-&-so; *s.-&-s. results will follow from s.-&-s. causes*); *su·chlike*, of s. kind (now chiefly vulg.; & see below). (Pron.) *s. as*, those who (chiefly archaic or poet. or rhet.; *s. as sit in darkness*); that, the action &c. referred to, (*I may have offended, but s. was not my intention*); *as s.*, as being what has been named (*in country places a stranger is welcome as s.*); *all s.*, persons of s. character (*so perish all s.!*); (also *suchlike*; chiefly vulg.) things of s. kind (*do not hold with theatres & balls & s.* or *s.-l.*); (vulg. or commerc.) the aforesaid thing(s), it, they or them, (*those who leave parcels in the train cannot expect to recover s.*). [OE *swylc* (*swá* so, -LY[1]); cf. Du. *zulk*, G *solch* f. OHG *solih*]

suck, v.t. & i., & n. Draw (milk, liquid) into mouth by making vacuum with muscles of lips &c., (fig.) imbibe or gain (knowledge, advantage, &c.; also *s. in knowledge, s. advantage out of*); draw milk or liquid or sustenance or advantage from (*s. ary*, exhaust of contents thus; *s. the breast of*; *the mother whom he sucked*; *sucked orange*, thing in which there is no goodness left; *s.* one's *brains*, extract his ideas for one's own use); roll the tongue about, squeeze in the mouth, (*s. sweets*, one's *teeth*, &c.); (of absorbent substance) *s. in* or *up*, absorb; (of whirlpool &c.) *s.*

in, engulf; s. the breast or udder (part., not yet weaned, as *sucking child, sucking-pig*, also fig. unpractised, budding, as *sucking barrister, saint*), s. something, use sucking action, make sucking sound, (*sat sucking at his pipe*; *pump* &c. *sucks*, makes gurgling or drawing sound; *sucking-disk*, sucker); *s. up* (schoolboy slang), play toady (*to*; *s.-up* n., a toady). (N.) opportunity of sucking the breast (*give s.*, of mother or nurse or animal suckling child &c.); drawing action of whirlpool &c.; spell of sucking with lips or in mouth (*take a s. at it*); small draught of or *of* liquor; (schoolboy slang, pl.) sweets; (schoolboy slang) disappointment, fiasco, (*what a s.!*, *ss.!*, intt. expr. amusement at another's failure after confidence). [OE *súcan*, cf. L *sugere suct-*, G *saugen*, Du. *zuigen*]

su·cker, n., & v.t. & i. Person or thing that sucks, esp. sucking-pig or new-born whale; kinds of fish that suck in food or have mouth suggesting suction or adhere by sucking-disk; piston of suction-pump; pipe through which liquid is drawn by suction; (also *sucking-disk*) flat or concave surface (as organ in some animals, also *acetabulum*, or artificial of rubber &c. in machinery or appliances) that adheres by suction & atmospheric pressure to what it is placed against; (Bot.) shoot springing from subterranean part of stem, from part of root remote from main stem, from axil, or abnormally from bole or branch (v.t., remove ss. from; v.i., produce ss.). [-ER[1]]

su·ckle, v.t. Give suck to. [perh. back form. f. foll.]

su·ckling, n. Unweaned child or animal (*babes & ss.*, the utterly inexperienced). [SUCK vb, -LING[1]]

sū·crose, n. Cane-sugar or any of the sugars of the same composition & properties. [F *sucre* SUGAR, -OSE[2]]

su·ction, n. Sucking; production of partial vacuum by removal of air &c. for purpose of enabling external atmospheric pressure to force in liquid or produce adhesion of surfaces; *s.-chamber, -pipe*, in s.-pump; *s.-fan*, for withdrawing chaff &c. from grain by s.; *s.-plate*, holding set of artificial upper teeth & adhering to palate by s.; *s.-pump*, drawing water through pipe into chamber exhausted by piston. [L *sugere suct-* SUCK, -ION]

suctor·ial, a. (zool.). Adapted for or capable of sucking, having sucker for feeding or adhering. [mod. L *suctorius* (prec., -ORY), -AL]

Sudane·se (sōō-). =SOUDANESE.

sūdār·ium, n. (pl. *-ia*). Kerchief of St Veronica miraculously stamped with face of Christ; any miraculous portrait of Christ; napkin about Christ's head (*John* xx. 7). [L, = handkerchief (*sudor* sweat, -ARY[1])]

sudator·ium, n. (pl. *-ia*). Hot-air bath. [L neut. as foll.]

su·datory, a. & n. Promoting perspiration. (N.) s. drug; =prec. [f. L *sudatorius* (*sudare* SWEAT, -ORY)]

sudd, n. Floating plants, trees, &c., impeding navigation of White Nile. [Arab., =barrier]

su·dden (-dn), a. & n. Occurring or come upon or made or done unexpectedly or without warning, abrupt, abnormally rapid, hurried, (*s. death, need, fear*; *a s. resolve, departure, change, turn of the wrist, bend in the road*; *is very s. in his movements*); hence **su·dden**LY[2] adv., **su·dden**NESS n. (N.) *of* or *on a*, rarely *on the, s.*, suddenly. [f. OF *soudain* f. L *subitaneus* (*subitus* sudden f. SUB*ire -it-* come up, -ANEOUS)]

sūdori·ferous, a. Sweat-producing (of glands). [f. LL *sudorifer* (*sudor* sweat, -FEROUS)]

sudori·fic, a. & n. (Drug) causing sweat. [L *sudor* sweat, -I-, -FIC]

Su·dra (sōō-), n. Lowest of four great Hindu castes. [Skr.]

suds, n. pl. Froth of soap & water (usu. *soap-s.*). [perh. f. MDu. *sudse* marsh]

sue, v.t. & i. Prosecute (person) in law-court; entreat (person), make entreaty or application *to* person or law-court, (*for* redress or a favour, esp. woman's hand in marriage); *s. out*, make petition in law-court for & obtain (writ, pardon, &c.). [f. AF *suir* f. OF *sivre* (now *suivre*) follow f. pop. L **sequere* for L *sequi*]

suède (swād), n. Undressed kid as used for gloves & slippers (usu. attrib.). [f. F (*gants de*) *Suède* (gloves of) Sweden]

su·et, n. Hard fat of kidneys & loins of oxen, sheep, &c. Hence **su·et**Y[2] a. [OF *seu* f. L *sebum* tallow, -ET[1]]

suf-, =SUB- in L compds with wds in f- & their derivatives.

su·ffer, v.t. & i. Undergo, experience, be subjected to, (pain, loss, grief, defeat, change, punishment, wrong, &c.); undergo pain or grief or damage or disablement (*suffers acutely*; *suffering mortals*; *was suffering from neuralgia*; *your reputation will s.*; *the engine suffered severely*; *trade is suffering from the war*), whence **su·ffer**ER[1], **su·ffer**ING[1](1), nn. (often pl.); (of condemned man) be executed (*was to s. the next morning*); permit *to* do, allow to go on, put up with, tolerate, (*s. them to come*; *should not s. it for a moment*; *how can you s. him* or *his insolence?*, whence, chiefly w. neg., **su·ffer**ABLE a.). [f. OF *soffrir* f. L SUF(*ferre* bear)]

su·fferance, n. (Archaic) submissiveness; tacit consent, permission or toleration implied by abstinence from objection, (esp. *on s.*, in virtue of such toleration). [f. OF *suffrance* f. LL *sufferentia* (SUFFER, -ENCE)]

su·ffete, n. One of two chief magistrates

of ancient Carthage. [f. L *sufes -etis* f. Punic]

suffi·ce, v.i. & t. Be enough (*to* do, *for* person or purpose, or abs.), be adequate, (*your word will s.*; *that suffices to prove it*; *s. it to say that,* I will content myself with saying that); satisfy, meet the needs of, (*half-a-dozen sufficed him*). Hence **suffi·cing**LY[2] adv. [ME *suffisen* f. OF *suffire* (part. *-fisant*) f. L SUF(*ficere*= *facere* make)]

suffi·ciency, n. (Archaic) being sufficient, ability, efficiency; adequate resources, a competence, a sufficient amount of or *of* something. [f. L *sufficientia* (foll., -ENCY)]

suffi·cient (-ishnt), a. & n. Sufficing, adequate esp. in amount or number to the need, enough, (*is s. to feed a hundred men*; *had not s. courage for it*; *has impudence s. for anything*; *have you s. provisions?*), whence **suffi·cient**LY[2] adv.; (archaic) competent, of adequate ability or resources; SELF-*s.*; (n.) enough, a s. quantity, (chiefly vulg. for *enough*; *have you had s.?*). [f. L part. (SUFFICE, -ENT)]

suffi·x[1], v.t. Append (letter, syllable) in word-formation. [f. L SUF(*figere fix*- fasten)]

su·ffix[2], n. Suffixed letter or syllable (cf. *prefix, affix*). [f. L p.p. (prec.)]

su·ffocate, v.t. & i. Choke or kill by stopping respiration (of person, superincumbent mass, fumes, &c.); produce choking sensation in, impede breath or utterance of, (*suffocated by* or *with grief, excitement,* &c.); feel suffocated, gasp for breath. Hence or cogn. **su·ffocating**LY[2] adv., **suffoca·tion** n. [f. L *suffocare* (SUB[2], *fauces* throat)]

su·ffragan, a. & n. *S. bishop* or *s.*, bishop consecrated to assist bishop of see by managing part of diocese, also any bishop in relation to his archbishop or metropolitan (*s. see* &c., of s. bishop). Hence **su·ffragan**SHIP n. [OF, f. med. L *suffraganeus* assistant (bishop) f. L *suffragari* support with vote (foll.)]

su·ffrage (-ij), n. Vote, approval or consent expressed by voting, (*the electors gave their ss. for free trade*; also transf., as *the biplane has my s.*, I think it preferable); the right of voting in political elections (*the s.*, or *manhood, woman, universal,* &c., *s.*; *manhood s.*, extended to all adult males without property tests &c.; *woman s.*, extended to women as well as men; *universal s.*, extended to all adults); (Eccl.) short petition of congregation, esp. one said in response to priest, (archaic) an intercessory prayer. [F, f. L *suffragium*]

suffrage·tte, n. (Facet. name for) woman who agitated for woman suffrage. [incorrect use of -ETTE]

su·ffragist, n. One who attaches importance to (esp. some extension of) the suffrage (*woman-s.* &c.). [-IST]

suffu·se (-z), v.t. (Of colour or moisture) well up from within & colour or moisten (*a blush, tears, suffused her cheeks, eyes*; often in p.p., as *skies suffused with amethyst*). So **suffu·sion** n. [f. L SUF(*fundere fus-* pour)]

su·fi (sōō-), **sō·fi,** n. Mohammedan pantheistic mystic. Hence **su·fic, so-,** a., **su·fism**(3), **so-,** n. [f. Arab. *çūfī* man of wool (*çūf* wool)]

sug-, = SUB- in L compds w. wds in g- & their derivatives.

su·gar (shŏŏ-), n., & v.t. & i. Kinds of sweet crystalline substance prepared from various plants esp. the s.-cane & beet for use in cookery, confectionery, brewing, &c. (*cane, beet, maple,* &c., *s.*, named from plant of origin; *brown, white, powdered,* LUMP[1], CASTOR[2], LOAF[1], *s.*); sweet words, flattery, anything serving purpose of s. put round pill in reconciling person to what is unpalatable; (Chem.) kinds of soluble sweet-tasting fermentable carbohydrate divided according to their composition into glucoses & saccharoses; *s.-basin,* holding s. for table use; *s.-bean,* kinds of pulse & kidney-bean; *s.-beet,* kinds from which s. is extracted; *s.-bird,* kinds that suck flowers; *s. candy,* candy; *s.-cane,* a grass with jointed stems 18–20 ft high from which s. is made; *s.-gum,* Australian gum-tree with sweet foliage; *s.-house,* establishment in which raw s. is made; *s.*-LOAF[1]; *s.-maple,* tree from sap of which s. is made; *s.-mill,* for crushing s.-cane & expressing s.; *s.-mite,* kind infesting unrefined s.; *s.-orchard,* of s.-maples; *su·garplum,* sweetmeat, esp. small ball of boiled *s.*; *s.-refiner(y),* (establishment of) manufacturer who refines raw s.; *s.-tongs,* small tongs for taking up lump-s. at table; hence **su·gar**Y[2], **su·gar**LESS, aa., **su·gar**INESS n. (Vb) sweeten with s. lit. or fig.; (slang) work lazily, not do one's full share of work, not put forth all one's strength, whence **su·gar**ER[1] n. [f. OF *zuchre* f. Arab. *sukkar*; cf. Pers. *shakar*, Skr. *çarkara* gravel, candy, & Gk *sakkharon*]

sugge·st (*suj*-), v.t. Cause (idea) to present itself, call up the idea of by mention or association, (*thing suggests itself,* comes into the mind); propose (theory, plan, often expressed in *that*-clause) for acceptance or rejection, set up the hypothesis *that,* (*suggested a retreat, that they should retreat*; *I s. that,* formula of examining counsel in imputing motives &c. = *I put it to you,* as *I s. that you had a secret understanding with them*). [f. L SUG(*gerere gest-* bring)]

sugge·stible, a. That may be suggested; open to hypnotic suggestion. Hence **suggestibi·lity** n. [-IBLE]

sugge·stio fă·lsī (-tiō), n. Positive misrepresentation not involving direct lie but going beyond concealment of the truth (cf. SUPPRESSIO VERI). [L]

sugge·stion (-stshn), n. Suggesting (*full of s.*, suggesting many ideas, stimulating reflection); theory or plan suggested; suggesting of prurient ideas; insinuation of a belief or impulse into the mind of a hypnotic subject, such belief or impulse. So **sugge·stIVE** a. (*of*), **sugge·stiveLY**² adv., **sugge·stiveNESS** n. [OF *suggestioun*, f. L SUGGEST*ionem* (-ION)]

su·ī, genit. of L *suus* his, her, its, or their, own: *s. gĕ·neris* pred. a., not classifiable with others, unique; *s. juris* pred. a., of full age & capacity, independent.

su·icide, n. 1. Person who intentionally kills himself; (Law) s. of years of discretion & sane mind. 2. Intentional self-slaughter (in law, as in 1; esp. *commit s.*, kill oneself); action destructive to one's own interests or continuance in some capacity (*commit political s.*, ruin one's prospects as a politician; *race-s.*, failure of a people to maintain its numbers); hence **suici·dAL** a., **suici·dalLY**² adv. [formed on false anal. of *fratricide* &c. f. L *sui* genit. of *se* self, -CIDE(1, 2)]

su·illine, a. Of the hog family. [L *suillus* of pigs (*sus* pig), -INE¹]

suit (sūt), n., & v.t. & i. Suing, petition, seeking of woman's hand in marriage, (*make s.*, urge a humble request; *with lowly s.*; *has a s. to the king*; *press, push*, &c., one's *s.*; *prosper in* one's *s.*); legal prosecution of a claim, action in law-court, (also *law-s.*, *s. at law*; *criminal, civil*, &c., *s.*); any of the four sets (hearts, diamonds, spades, clubs) into which pack of cards is divided (*follow s.*, play from s. that was led, fig. conform to another's movements), player's holding in it (*long, short, s.* in whist, of more than three, less than four, cards); set of man's clothes esp. when of same cloth, consisting usu. of coat, waistcoat, & trousers or knickerbockers or breeches (often *s. of clothes*; *dress s.*, for evening dress; *s. of dittos*; *s.-case*, kind of small portmanteau), whence **sui·TING**¹(3) n.; (in recent use, usu. *2, 3, 4, -piece s.*) woman's costume; set *of* sails, set *of* armour, for simultaneous use. (Vb) accommodate, adapt, make fitting or appropriate, *to* (*s. the action to the word*, carry out promise or threat at once; *s.* one's *style to* one's *audience*), (p.p.) appropriate *to*, well adapted or having the right qualities *for*, (*democracy is not suited to* or *for Negroes*; *is not suited to be* or *for an engineer*); satisfy, meet the demands or requirements or interests of, (*does not s. all tastes*; *it suits me* or, prob. w. ref. to betting, *my book to put up with him*; *s. yourself*, do as you choose, also find something that satisfies you, esp. as servant's formula in giving warning), (of food, climate, &c.) improve or be consistent with the health of, agree with, (*cold, asparagus, does not s. me*); comport with or *with*, go well with appearance or character of, become, (*red does not s. with* or *s. her complexion*; *the part suits him admirably*; *mercy suits a king*); be convenient (*that date will s.*). [vb f. n., f. OF *suitte* following f. med. L *secuta* (L *sequi secut-* follow)]

sui·table, a. Suited *to* or *for*, well fitted for the purpose, appropriate to the occasion. Hence **suitaBI·LITY**, **sui·tableNESS**, nn., **sui·tabLY**² adv. [prec., -ABLE]

suite (swēt), n. Retinue, set of persons in attendance; set of things belonging together, esp. *s. of rooms* or *furniture*, (Mus.) series of dance tunes. [F, as SUIT]

sui·tor, n. Party to law-suit; petitioner; wooer, man who asks for woman's hand in marriage. [AF *seutor* f. LL *secutor* (L *sequi* follow, -OR²)]

suivez (swē·vā), mus. direction instructing accompanist to suit his time &c. to soloist's performance. [F]

Su·key (sŏŏ-), n. (colloq.). *S.* or *black S.*, kettle. [*Susan*]

su·lcate, a. (bot., anat.). Grooved, fluted, channelled. [L *sulcus* furrow, -ATE²]

sulk, n., & v.i. Sulky fit (usu. pl., esp. *in the ss.*); (vb) be sulky. [f. 18th c. only; etym. dub.]

su·lky, a. & n. Sullen, morose, silent or inactive or unsociable from resentment or ill-temper; hence **su·lkiLY**² adv., **su·lkiNESS** n. (N.) light two-wheeled one-horse vehicle for single person. [-Y²]

su·llage, n. Filth, refuse, sewage. [prob. f. F as SOIL² + -AGE]

Su·llan, a. (Rom. hist.). Of, enacted by, L. Cornelius Sulla. [-AN]

su·llen (-en), a. & n. Passively resentful, unforgiving, gloomy-tempered, unsociable, not responding to friendliness or encouragement or urging, stubbornly ill humoured, morose, of dismal aspect; hence **su·llenLY**² adv., **su·llenNESS** n. (N., pl.) *the ss.*, s. frame of mind, ill temper, depression. [ME *soleyn* lonely (L *solus* SOLE³, -AN)]

su·lly, v.t. Soil, tarnish, (chiefly poet.); diminish the purity or splendour of (reputation, character, victory, &c.), disgrace. [prob. f. F *souiller* SOIL²]

sulph(o)-, comb. forms of SULPHUR: *sulphă·mic*, derived from an amic acid of sulphuric acid, so *su·lphamATE*¹(3); *su·lphate*, salt of sulphuric acid (*s. of copper*, blue vitriol; *s. of iron*, green vitriol; *s. of magnesium*, Epsom salts; *s. of sodium*, Glauber's salts; *s. of zinc*, white vitriol); *su·lphide*, compound of sulphur with element or radical; *su·lphite*, salt of sulphurous acid; *sulphocya·nic*, containing sulphur & cyanogen; *sulph(o)indigŏ·tic*, of sulphuric acid & indigo; *su·lphonal*, a hypnotic & anaesthetic drug; *sulphovi·nic*, of sulphuric acid & alcohol.

su·lphur, n., a., & v.t. Pale-yellow non-metallic element occurring in crystalline & amorphous modifications, burning with blue flame & stifling smell, & used in making gunpowder, matches, vulcanite, & sulphuric acid, & in medical treatment of skin-diseases (*flowers, milk, of s.*, yellow, white, powders got by treating s. in certain ways; *roll, stick, -s.*, s. refined & cast in moulds, brimstone); kinds of yellow butterfly; material of which hell-fire & lightning were held to consist; *s.-ore*, iron pyrites; *s.-spring*, of water impregnated with s. or its compounds; *s.-wort*, yellow-flowered herb formerly used in medicine; hence **su·lphur**Y² a. (Adj.) of pale slightly greenish yellow. (Vb) apply s. to, fumigate with s. [f. OF *soufre* f. L *sulfur, -phur*]

su·lphūrate, v.t. Impregnate or fumigate or treat with sulphur, esp. in bleaching. Hence **sulphur**A·TION, **sul·phura**TOR²(2), nn. [f. LL SULPHUR(*atus* -ATE²), -ATE³]

sulphūr·eous, a. Of, like, suggesting, sulphur; (Bot.) sulphur-coloured. [L *sulphureus* (SULPHUR), -OUS]

sulphūre·tted, a. Having sulphur in combination (chiefly in *s. hydrogen*, a transparent colourless fetid gas). [obs. *sulphuret* (SULPHUR, -ET¹) sulphide, -ED²]

sulphūr·ic, a. (chem.). Containing sulphur in its higher combining proportion (cf. SULPHUROUS; *s. acid*, oil of vitriol, a dense oily colourless highly acid & corrosive fluid much used in the arts; *s. ether*, =ETHER in chem. sense). [f. F *sulfurique* see SULPHUR, -IC (chem.)]

su·lphurize (-er-, -ūr-), v.t. =SULPHURATE. Hence **sulphuriz**A·TION n. [-IZE]

su·lphurous (-er-, -ūr-), a. =SULPHUREOUS; (Chem.) containing sulphur in its lower combining proportion (cf. SULPHURIC; *s. acid*). [f. L SULPHUR(*osus* -OSE¹)]

su·ltan, n. Moslem sovereign (*the S.* hist., s. of Turkey), whence **su·ltan**ATE¹ n.; kinds of gorgeously coloured bird of rail family; variety of white domestic fowl from Turkey; *sweet, yellow, s.*, kinds of garden flower. [F f. Arab.]

sulta·na (-tah-), n. Sultan's mother, wife, or daughter; mistress of king &c.; sultan-bird; kind of seedless raisin grown at Smyrna & used in puddings & cakes. [It., f. *sultano* (prec.)]

su·ltaness, n. =prec. (first sense). [-ESS¹]

su·ltry, a. (Of atmosphere or weather) hot & close or oppressive. Hence **su·ltri**LY² adv., **su·ltri**NESS n. [f. obs. *sulter* vb prob. = SWELTER, -Y²]

sum, n., & v.t. & i. Total amount resulting from addition of items, brief expression that includes but does not specify details, substance, summary, (also *s. total*; *the s. of all my wishes is happiness*; *the s. of two & three is five*; *s., remainder, product, quotient*, results of addition, subtraction, multiplication, division; *the s. or s. & substance of his objections is this*; *in s.*, briefly & comprehensively put); particular amount of money (*what s. would you give for it?*; *for the s. of 15/-*; *a good, round, considerable, s.*; LUMP¹ *s.*); (working out of) an arithmetical problem (*good at ss.*; *did a rapid s. in his head*). (Vb) collect into or express or include as one total or whole (often *up*), gather *up* (evidence, points of argument &c., already treated in detail) into brief review; *s. up* (intr.), make recapitulation of evidence or argument (esp. of judge after both sides have been heard; so *summing-up* n.). [f. OF *somme(r)* f. L *summa* n. orig. fem. of *summus* highest (SUPER-), *summare* vb]

sū·mac(h) (-k; also shōō·măk), n. (Dried & ground leaves, used in tanning & dyeing, of) kinds of shrub. [F (*-ac*) f. Arab. *summāq*]

Sūmēr·ian, a. & n. (archaeol.). Of the non-Semitic element in the civilization of Babylonia; (n.) the S. language, a S. person. [f. *Sumer*, a district of Babylonia]

su·mmarize, v.t. Make or be a summary of, sum up. So **su·mmar**IST(1) n. [foll., -IZE]

su·mmary, a. & n. Compendious, brief, dispensing with needless details or formalities, done with dispatch, (*a s. account*; *s. methods, jurisdiction*, &c.); hence **su·mmari**LY² adv. (N.) brief account, abridgement, epitome. [n. f. L *summarium*, adj. f. med. L *summarius*, (SUMMA, -ARY¹)]

summa·tion, n. Addition, finding of total or sum. [f. L SUM*mare*, -ATION]

su·mmer¹, n., & v.i. & t. Second or hot season of the year, May–July (Astr., 21 June–21 Sep.), (INDIAN, *St* MARTIN's, *s.*; *St Luke's s.*, period of fine weather expected about 18th October); (usu. in pl. with number &c.) year of life or age (*a child of ten ss.*); (attrib.) characteristic of or fit for s. (*s.-house*, light building in garden &c. for sitting in; *s. lightning*, distant sheet lightning; *s. school*, long vacation meeting for lectures &c., esp. at university; *s.-time* or *su·mmertime*, the weather or season of s.; *s. time*, that indicated by clocks advanced in s. to facilitate use of daylight); hence **sum·mer**LY¹, **su·mmer**Y², **su·mmer**LESS, aa. (Vb) pass the s. usu. *at* or *in* place; pasture (cattle) *at* or *in*. [OE *sumor*, cf. Du. *zomer*, G *sommer*, Skr. *samā* half year]

su·mmer², **summer-tree,** nn. Horizontal bearing beam, esp. one supporting joists or rafters. [see BREASTSUMMER]

summersault, -set. =SOMERSAULT.

su·mmit, n. Highest point, top, apex, highest degree, (*the icy ss. of the Alps*; *at the s. of power*; *the s. of my ambition is*). Hence **su·mmit**LESS a. [f. OF *somet, sommette*, (*som* top f. L *summum* neut. of SUM*mus*, -ET¹)]

su·mmon, v.t. Demand the presence of, call upon to appear, esp. as defendant or witness in lawcourt, cite, convoke, invite; call upon (town &c.) to surrender; *s. up*, gather *courage, spirit*, &c., usu. *to* do or *for* undertaking. [f. OF *somondre* f. L SUB(*monēre* warn)]

su·mmons, n. (pl. *-ses*), & v.t. Authoritative call or urgent invitation to attend on some occasion or do something; citation to appear before judge or magistrate (vb, serve with s.). [f. OF *somonse* f. a pop. L fem. p.p. (*summonsa*) f. L as prec.]

su·mmum bŏ·num, n. The chief good, esp. as the end or ultimate determining principle in an ethical system. [L]

sump, n. Pit or well for the reception of (esp. superfluous) water, oil, or other liquid in mines, machines, &c.; cesspool. [earlier sense, now dial., marsh; f. MLG *sump* marsh; cf. SWAMP]

su·mpter, n. (Archaic) pack-horse or its driver; *s.-horse, -mule, -pony,* pack-animals. [f. OF *sommetier* pack-horse driver f. LL **sagmatarius* (=*sagmarius* see BREASTSUMMER) f. Gk *sagma -atos* pack-saddle (*sattō* pack, -M)]

su·mption (-shn), n. Major premiss of syllogism. [f. L *sumptio* f. *sumere sumpt-* take=SUB-, *emere* take, buy, -ION]

su·mptuary, a. Regulating expenditure (*s. law, edict,* &c., limiting private expenditure in the interest of the State). [f. L *sumptuarius* (*sumptus -ūs* cost as prec.)]

su·mptuous, a. Rich & costly, suggesting lavish expenditure. Hence **su·mptuous**LY[2] adv., **su·mptuous**NESS n. [f. OF *somptueux* f. L *sumptuosus* (prec., -OSE[1])]

sun, n., & v.t. & i. The heavenly body that the earth travels round & receives warmth & light from, such light or warmth or both, (*s. rises, sets,* is brought by earth's revolution above, below, the horizon; *his, its,* &c., *s. is set,* time of prosperity or existence is over; *rise with the s.*, get up early; *Order of the Rising S.*, Japanese order; *hail* or *adore the rising s.*, curry favour with new or coming power; *empire* &c. *on which the s. never sets,* world-wide; *let not the s. go down upon your wrath,* limit it to one day; *the midnight s.*, seen in arctic & antarctic regions; *nothing new under the s.*, in the world; *mock s.*, parhelion; *S. of righteousness,* Christ; *see the s.*, be alive; *make* HAY *while the s. shines*; *hold a candle to the s.*, prov. of superfluous action; *take,* or slang *shoot, the s.* naut., ascertain its altitude in order to fix latitude; *with, against, the s.*, CLOCK[1]-wise, counterclockwise, whence **su·n**WISE adv.; *s.'s eyelashes, s.'s backstays* naut., *s. drawing water,* phenomenon given by rays piercing aperture in cloud & illuminating suspended particles in parallel lines; *s. & planet,* system of gearing in which cogged wheel on reciprocating rod both rotates on its axis & travels round the wheel that it engages & communicates motion to; *exclude, let in, the s.*; *in the s.*, exposed to s.'s rays; *a place in the s.*, fig., favourable situation or conditions; *take the s.*, expose oneself to s.-light); any fixed star with satellite(s); (poet.) day or year; (also *s. burner*) set of gas-jets, electric lights, &c., massed as one great light in ceiling; *s.-bath,* exposure of naked body to s.; *su·nbeam,* ray of s.; *s.-bird,* kinds of small bright-plumaged Old-World birds with resemblance to humming-birds; *s.-blind,* window-shade; *s.-bonnet,* of linen &c. with projection & pendent back to shade face & neck; *s.-bow,* prismatic bow given by s.-light on spray &c.; *su·nburn,* tanning of face &c. by exposure to s., so *su·nburnt* or *-burned* a.; *s.-dance,* of N.-Amer. Indians in honour of s.; *su·ndew,* kinds of small bog-plant with hairs secreting drops of moisture; *s.*-DIAL; *s.*-DOG[1]; *su·ndown,* sunset; *su·ndowner,* Australian tramp who times his arrival for the evening; *s.-dried,* dried by s. & not by artificial heat; *su·nfish,* large fish of almost spherical shape; *su·nflower,* kinds of tall garden-plant with showy golden-rayed flowers; *s.-glow,* whitish or faintly coloured corona of light sometimes seen round s.; *s.-god,* the s. worshipped as a deity; *s.-hat, -helmet,* adapted by material or shape to keep s. off; *su·nlight*; *su·nlit*; *s.-myth,* SOLAR myth; *s.-picture,* photograph; *su·nrise,* (moment of) s.'s rising; *su·nset,* (moment of) s.'s setting, western sky with colours characterizing s.-s. (attrib., resembling these), (fig.) declining period of life; *su·nshade,* parasol, also awning of shop-window; *su·nshine,* light of sun (*s.-s. recorder,* instrument recording duration of s.-s.), surface illuminated by it, fair weather, (fig.) cheerfulness or bright influence, so *su·nshiny* a.; *s.-snake,* ornament found in early N.-Europ. art shaped like S with small circle at centre; *s.-spot,* one of the dark patches, changing in shape & size & lasting for varying periods, sometimes observed on s.'s surface; *s.-star,* red starfish with many rays; *s.-stone,* kinds of quartz (esp. cat's-eye) & feldspar; *su·nstroke,* acute prostration from excessive heat of weather; *s.-worship(per)*; hence **su·n**LESS a., **su·n-less**NESS n., **su·n**LIKE, **su·n**PROOF[2], aa., **su·n**WARD a. & adv., **su·n**WARDS adv. (Vb) expose to the s. (*s. oneself,* bask in s.-light); s. oneself. [OE *sunne,* cf. Du. *zon,* G *sonne,* ON *sunna*; cogn. w. L *sol,* Goth. *sauil,* ON *sól*]

su·ndae (-dĭ), n. (U.S.). Portion of ice-cream mixed with crushed fruit, nuts, &c. [?]

Su·nday, n. First day of week, Lord's day, observed as day of rest & worship (HOSPITAL, LOW[1], PALM[1], ROGATION, SHOW[2], *S.*; *month of Ss.*, long period; *S. letter,* dominical letter; *S. best* usu. facet., best clothes kept for S. use; *S.-school*, for religious instruction on Ss.). [OE *sunnan dæg* day of the sun]

su·nder, v.t. & i. Separate (t. & rarely i.), sever, keep (trans.) apart. Hence **su·nder**ANCE n. (rare). [OE *sundrian* (*sundor* asunder) cf. ON *sundra*, G *sondern*]

su·ndry, a. & n. Divers, several, (chiefly archaic & joc.; *all & s.*, each & all, everyone collectively & individually). (N., pl.) oddments, accessories or items not needing special mention. [OE *syndrig* (*sundor* see prec., -Y[2])]

sung. See SING.

sunk(en). See SINK[1].

sunn(-hemp), n. E.-Ind. hemplike fibre. [f. Hind. *san* f. Skr. *sana*]

Su·nna(h), n. Traditionary portion of Mohammedan law based on Mohammed's words or acts, but not written by him, accepted as authoritative by the orthodox (**Su·nn**ITE[1] or **Su·nni** pr. -ē, nn.) & rejected by the Shiites. [Arab. (*-a*), = tradition]

su·nny, a. Bright with or as sunlight; of the sun (rare); exposed to, warm with, the sun (*the s. side*, side of house &c. that gets sun, also fig. the more cheerful aspect of circumstances &c.); cheery, bright in disposition, diffusing cheerfulness. Hence **su·nni**LY[2] adv., **su·nni**NESS n. [-Y[2]]

sup, v.t. & i., & n. Take (soup, tea, &c.) by sips or spoonfuls (*he must have a long spoon that sups with the devil*, parleying with doubtful characters is risky); take supper (*on, off*, specified food); (of food or host) provide supper for. (N.) mouthful of liquid (esp. *neither bit* or *bite nor s.*). [OE *súpan*, cf. Du. *zuipen*, ON *súpa*, OHG *sûfan*; partly also f. OF *souper* see SUPPER]

sup-, = SUB- in L compds w. wds in p- & their derivatives.

sū·per, n. & a. (colloq., shop). Supernumerary actor, (fig.) extra or unwanted or unimportant person &c.; (Commerc.) superfine cloth or manufacture. (Adj.) superfine; (of measure) superficial, in square (not linear or solid) measure (*120 s. ft*, or *120 ft s.*). [abbr. *supernumerary, superfine, superficial*]

sūper-, pref. f. L *super* prep., *super-* pref-, over, beyond [compar. form f. SUB[2], cf. Gk *huper*, Skr. *upari*]. 1. In adjj. (& their derivv.) formed on anal. of L *supernumerarius* f. L phr. consisting of *super* & n. governed by it; *super numerum* = beyond the number, *supernumerary* = being beyond the number. The distinguishable varieties of meaning are:

a. situated directly over, as *-columnar* above columns, *-humeral* over the shoulder;

b. not in or under but above, as *-aqueous, -terrene, -celestial*, above water, earth, sky;

c. exceeding, going beyond, more than, transcending, too exalted for contact or connexion with, as *-normal* beyond the norm, *-natural* beyond what nature will account for, *-sensible* out of reach of sense, *-ethical* above the sphere of ethics.

2. In vbs & adjj. & their derivv. adapted from or made on anal. of L wds to which *super-* was prefixed with advl sense. Varieties of meaning are:

a. on the top of something, as *-impose, -scribe, -stratum*;

b. observation from above, as *-intend, -stition, -vise*;

c. besides, in addition, as *-add, -erogation, -fetation*;

d. to a degree beyond the usual or the right, as *-eminent, -saturate, -subtle*;

3. In nn. & their derivv. on anal. of L *superficies* (*facies* face) in which *super-* is prefixed w. adj. force;

a. upper or outer, as *-canopy, -cilious, -hive*;

b. of higher kind, in higher than the ordinary sense, esp. in names of classificatory divisions, as *-class* group including more than one class;

c. in the second degree, as *-parasite* the parasite of a parasite, *-tuberation* the forming of tubers on tubers.

4. In math. wds expressing ratio on anal. of L *supertertius* exceeding by $\frac{1}{3}$, *-bipartient* or *-bitertial* = exceeding by $\frac{2}{3}$ or in the ratio 5:3, *-biquintal* in ratio 7:5, *-tripartient* or *-triquartal* = in ratio 7:4, *-quadripartient* or *-quadriquintal* = in ratio 9:5, *-sesquialteral* in ratio 5:2, *-sesquitertial* in ratio 7:3.

superabou·nd v.i., **-abu·ndance** n., **-abu·ndant** a., **-abu·ndantly** adv., 2d; **supera·dd** v.t., **-addi·tion** n., 2c; **su·peraltar** n., 3a, slab of stone consecrated & placed on unconsecrated altar; **supera·nal** a., 1a (ANUS); **superange·lic** a., 1c; **supera·nnuate** v.t., 1c (L *annus* year), declare too old for work or use or continuance, dismiss or discard as too old, send into retirement with pension, (p.p.) past work or use, so **superannua·tion** n.; **supera·queous** a., 1b; **superbĭpar·tient, superbiqui·ntal, superbiter·tial,** aa., 4; **superca·lendered** a., 2d; **superca·nopy** n., 3a; **su·percargo** n., 1, person in merchant-ship managing sales &c. of cargo [f. Sp. *sobrecargo*]; **supercele·stial** a., 1b, also 1c = *superangelic*; **su·percharger** n., 2d, pump used in motorcars & aeroplanes to force an extra quantity of explosive mixture into cylinders of engine & so increase its efficiency; **superci·liary** a., 3a [L *supercilium* eyebrow f. *cilium* eyelid cf. Gk *kula* parts below eye], of the brows, over the eye; **superci·lious** a., **superci·liously** adv., **superci·liousness** n., 3a [f. LL *superciliosus* w. ref. to raised eyebrows, see prec.], contemptuous, showing haughty indifference, assuming superiority; **superci·vilized** a., 2d; **su·perclass** n., 3b; **supercolu·mnar** a., 1a; **supercolumnia·tion** n., 1a, placing of one architectural order over another; **superdrea·dnought** n., 1c, battleship more powerful than the Dreadnought type; **super-eleva·tion** n., 3b, amount by which outer rail at a curve is higher than inner; **supere·minent** a., 2d; **supereroga·tion** n., 2c [f. L *supererogare* pay out beyond what is expected], doing of more than duty requires (esp. *works of s.* in Theol., such as form a reserve fund of merit that can be drawn on in favour of sinners), so **superero·gatory** a.; **supere·thical** a., 1c; **supere·xcellent** a., **-e·xcellence, excita·tion,** nn., 2d; **su·perfamily** n. (biol.) 3b; **superfa·tted** a., 2d (of soap); **superfecunda·tion, superfeta·tion,** nn., 2c, second conception occurring during gestation; **superfi·cial** (-ĭshl) a., **superficia·lity** (-shĭ-) n., **superfi·cially** adv., 3a (foll.), of or on the surface only, not going deep, without depth, (*s. colour, resemblance, knowledge, wound, accomplishments*; *a s. person*, with no reserve of knowledge or feeling behind what he shows), (of measure) square (see SUPER a.); **superfi·cies** (-shĭēz) n. (pl. the same), 3a [L, f. *facies* face], a surface; **su·perfine** a., 2d, (commerc.) of extra quality, (gen.) affecting great refinement (so **superfi·neness** n.); **superflu·ity** n., 2d (foll.), superfluous amount (*give of* one's *s.*), thing not needed; **super·fluous** a., **super·fluously** adv., **super·fluousness** n., 2d (L *superfluus* f. *fluere* flow), more than enough, redundant, needless; **superhea·t** v.t., 2d, (esp.) heat (steam) to temperature higher than that of boiling water, so **superhea·TER**[1](2) n.; **su·perhive** n., 3a, removable upper compartment of hive; **superhu·man** a., **superhu·manly** adv., 1c; **superhu·meral** n., 1a (L HUMERUS), Jewish ephod, also amice[1], also archiepiscopal pallium; **superimpo·se** v.t., 2a, lay on or *on* something else; **superimpregna·tion** n., 2c, superfecundation; **superincu·mbent** a., 2a, lying on something (*the s. mass* &c.); **superindu·ce** v.t., 2c, develop or bring in as an addition; **superinstitu·tion** n., 2c, institution of person into benefice already occupied; **superinte·nd** v.t. & i., 2b (L INTEND*ere* attend to), have the management (of), arrange & inspect working (of), so **superinte·ndence** n., **superinte·ndent** n., person who superintends; **superja·cent** a., 2a (L *jacēre* lie), superincumbent; **super·lative** a. & n., 2d [f. LL *super(lativus* f. *ferre lat-* carry)], of the highest degree (*s. wisdom, beauty,* &c.; *s. degree* in Gram., the forms of the adjective & adverb by which the highest or a very high degree of a quality is expressed, as *bravest, most absurdly*), so **super·latively** adv., **super·lativeness** n., (n.) the s. degree or form (*not used in the s.*; *what is the s. of shy?*), a word in the s. (*his talk is all ss.*, he exaggerates); **superlu·nar(y)** a., 1b, (esp.) not of this world; **su·perman** n., 3b, OVERMAN; **superme·dial** a., 1a; **supermo·lecule** n., 3b, compound molecule, combination of molecules acting as physical unit; **supermu·ndane** a., 1c, superior to earthly things; **supernă·culum** adv. & n., 1 [mod. L *naculum* fingernail f. G *nagel*], *drink s.*, to the bottom (w. ref. to pouring of the last drop on thumbnail), (n.) choice wine worthy of being so drunk; **supernā·tant** a., 2a (NATATION), floating on surface; **superna·tural** a., **superna·turally** adv., **superna·turalness** n., 1c, due to or manifesting some agency above the forces of nature, outside the ordinary operation of cause & effect, so **superna·turalism, superna·turalist,** belief, believer, in the s., **superna·turalize**, elevate into the s. region; **supernor·mal** a., 1c; **supernu·merary** a. & n., 1c, (person or thing) in excess of the normal number, esp. extra person engaged for odd jobs; **supernutri·tion** n., 2d; **su·peroctave** n., 3c, organ-stop two octaves above principal; **su·perorder** n., **superor·dinal** a., 3b (in classif.); **superor·dinary** a., 1c; **superorga·nic** a., 1c (of psychical things considered apart from the organisms in which they are manifested), also, 3b, social, organic in a higher metaphorical sense; **superoxygena·tion** n., 2d; **superpa·rasite** n., **superparasi·tic** a., 3c; **superpho·sphate** n., 2d, phosphate with greatest possible proportion of phosphoric acid; **superphy·sical** a., 1c; **superpo·se** v.t., **superposi·tion** n., 2a, lay (thing) on or (*up*)*on* another; **superquadripar·tient, superquadriqui·ntal,** aa., 4; **supersa·cral** a., 1a (SACRUM); **supersa·turate** v.t., **supersatura·tion** n., 2d; **su·perscribe** v.t., 2a [f. LL *super(scribere script-* write)], write (inscription) at top of or outside something, write inscription over or on (thing), so **su·perscript** a., written above the line, superior, **superscri·ption** n., superscribed word(s); **superse·de** v.t. [f. OF *superseder* desist f. L *super(sedēre sess-* sit) desist from], set aside, cease to employ, adopt or appoint another person or thing in place of, (of person or thing appointed or adopted) take the place of, oust, supplant; **superse·nsible** a., 1c; **superse·nsitive** a., 2d; **superse·nsual, superse·nsuous,** aa., 1c, supersensible; **supersesquia·lteral, supersesquiter·tial,** aa., 4; **superse·ssion,** superseding or being superseded; **superso·lar** a., 1b; **su·persolid** n., 3b, a solid of more than three dimensions; **superspi·ritual** a., **superspiritua·lity** n., 2d; **supersti·tion** n., 2b [OF, f. L *super(stitionem* f. *stare stat-* stand) perh. orig. = standing over in awe], credulity regarding the supernatural, irrational fear of the unknown or mysterious, misdirected reverence, a religion or practice or particular opinion based on such tendencies, so **supersti·tious** a., **supersti·tiously** adv., **supersti·tiousness** n.; **superstra·tum, superstru·ction** or **su·perstructure** nn., **superstruc·tural** a., 2a; **supersubsta·ntial** a., 1c; **supersub·tle** a., **supersub·tlety** n., 2d; **su·pertax** n., 3b, tax on incomes above a certain amount levied in addition to ordinary income tax; **supertellū·ric** a., 1b (L *tellus -uris* the earth); **superte·mporal** a., 1a, above the temples of the head, also 1c, transcending time; **superte·rrene, superterre·strial,** aa., 1b; **su·pertonic** n., 1c, tone in musical scale next above tonic; **supertrīpar·tient, supertrīquar·tal,** aa., 4; **supertūbera·tion** n., 3c; **supervacā·neous** a., 2d [f. L *super(vacaneus* f. *vacare* be empty)], superfluous, unnecessary; **superve·ne** v.i., 2a [f. L *super(venire vent-* come)], occur as an interruption to or change from some condition or process, so **superve·ntion** n.; **supervi·se** (-z) v.t., 2b (L *vidēre vis-* see), direct or watch with authority the work or proceedings or progress of, oversee, so **supervi·sion** n.

su·perable, a. Not insuperable. [f. L *superabilis* f. *superare* overcome (*super* over, see prec.), -ABLE]

super·b (sōō-, sū-), a. Of the most impressive or splendid or exalted kind, grand, (*s. beauty, courage, impudence; a s. view, display, collection, specimen, voice, binding*). Hence **super·bLY**[2] adv. [f. L *superbus* proud]

supēr·ior (sōō-, sū-), a. & n. Upper, in higher position, of higher rank, (*s. officer, rank, court; s.* LIMIT[1]; *s. genus*, higher in the classificatory series & so more comprehensive; *s. wings*, folding over others; *s. figures* or *letters*, written or printed above the line; *s. limb* of sun &c., upper edge; *ovary, calyx, is s.*, grows from the top of or above the other); better or greater in some respect, related as the better or greater *to*, (*by s. wisdom, cunning, &c.; is s. in speed to any other machine; s. numbers*, esp. more men or their presence, as *was overcome by s. n.*); of quality or qualities above the average, having or showing consciousness of such qualities, (*made of s. leather; my cook is a very s. woman; s. persons*, the better educated &c., also & usu. iron., prigs; *he remarked with a s. air*); above giving attention or yielding or making concessions *to* (*s. to bribery, temptation, revenge, fortune; rise s. to*, be unaffected by); hence or cogn. **supērio·rITY** (*or* -pĕ-) n., **supēr·iorLY**[2] adv. (chiefly in describing position in Bot., Anat., &c.). (N.) one's better, person s. to one, in rank or *in* some respect (*is deferential to his ss.; you are my s. in ability & I yours in application; has no s. in courage*); head of monastery &c. (often *Father, Mother, Lady, S.*), whence **supēr·iorESS**[1] n. (rare). [OF, f. L *superiorem* nom. *-or*, comp. of *superus* high (*super* above, see SUPER-)]

sūper·nal, a. (poet., rhet.). Heavenly, divine, of the sky, lofty. [OF, f. L SUPER*nus*, -AL]

***supersē·dĕās*,** n. Writ staying proceedings. [L 2 sing. pres. subj. as SUPER*sede*]

sū·pinate, v.t. Turn (hand) palm upward (cf. PRONATE). Hence or cogn. **supinA·TION** n., **su·pinatOR**[2](2) n. (as name of two muscles). [L *supinare* (foll.), -ATE[3]]

sū·pine[1] (*or* -ī·n), a. Lying face upward (cf. PRONE); disinclined for exertion, indolent, lethargic. Hence **supi·neLY**[2] adv., **supi·neNESS** n. [f. L *supinus* (st. of SUPER-,-INE[1])]

su·pine[2], n. (L gram.). Verbal noun with accusative in *-um* & ablative in *-u* formed from p.p. st of L vbs & used in special constructions. [f. L (*verbum*) *supinum* (prec., sense doubtful)]

su·pper, n. A meal taken at the end of a day, the last meal of the day when dinner is not the last. Hence **su·pperLESS** a. [f. OF *soper* (now *souper*) f. *soper* take supper, etym. dub.]

suppla·nt, v.t. Oust & take the place of esp. by underhand means. Hence **suppla·ntER**[1] n. [f. OF *supplanter* f. L SUP(*plantare* f. *planta* sole) trip up]

su·pple, a., & v.t. & i. Easily bent, pliant, flexible; given to compliance, avoiding overt resistance, wanting in sturdiness of character, artfully submissive, fawning; *s.-jack*, (walking-cane of) kinds of strong twining shrub; hence **su·ppleNESS** n., **su·ppLY**[2] adv. (Vb) make or grow, s. (*s. horse*, train him to obey slightest touch of rein). [f. OF *souple* f. L SUP(*plex -plicis* f. *plicare* fold) submissive]

su·pplement[1] (-lĭment), n. Thing added to supply deficiencies, esp. fuller treatment of special subject issued with newspaper &c.; (Math.) the angle that added to another will make the sum two right angles. Hence **suppleme·ntAL, suppleme·ntARY**[1], aa. [f. L SUP(*plementum* f. *plēre* fill, -MENT)]

su·pplemĕnt[2], v.t. Make addition(s) to. Hence **supplementA·TION** n. [f. prec.]

For words in *super-* not given, see SUPER-.

su·ppliant, a. & n. Supplicating, expressive of supplication; hence **su·ppliant**LY[2] adv. (N.) humble petitioner. [F (*supplier* f. L as foll., -ANT)]

su·pplicate, v.t. & i. Make humble petition to or *to* person or for or *for* thing. Hence or cogn. **su·pplicating**LY[2] adv., **supplic**A·TION n., **su·pplicat**ORY a. [f. L *supplicare* (*supplex* SUPPLE), -ATE[3]]

supply·, v.t., & n. Furnish, provide, (thing needed, or person, receptacle, &c., with or *with* thing needed), whence **suppli**·ER[1] n.; make up for, meet, serve to obviate, (deficiency, need, loss); fill (place, vacancy, pulpit) as substitute. (N.) providing of what is needed (*Committee of S.*, House of Commons discussing details of estimates for public service; *s. department*, charged with supplying some need, esp. stores & provisions for army &c.); stock, store, amount of something provided or at hand or get-at-able, (*s. & demand* in Pol. Econ., chief factors regulating price of commodities; *an inexhaustible s. of fish, coal,* &c.; *water &c.-s.*), (pl.) collected necessaries for army &c.; (pl.) grant of money by Parliament for cost of government, money allowance to person (*his father cut off the ss.*). [n. f. vb, f. OF *supploier* f. L SUP(*plēre* fill)]

suppor·t, v.t., & n. Carry (part of) weight of, hold up, keep from falling or sinking, (*foundation, buttress, supports house, wall*; *supported by a life-belt*; *had to be supported home*); enable to last out, keep from failing, give strength to, encourage, (*what supported him* or *his strength was a glass of brandy, a good conscience, hope, your approval*; *too little food to s. life*); endure, tolerate, (*supports fatigue well*; *I can s. life, such insolence, no longer*), whence **suppor·t**ABLE a., **suppor·tab**LY[2] adv.; supply with necessaries, provide for, (*s. a family*); lend assistance or countenance to, back up, second, further, (*s. a cause, policy, leader, candidate*; *s. actor* or other performer, take secondary part to him; *s. resolution* &c., speak in favour of it; *s. lecturer* &c., appear on his platform; *s. institution*, subscribe to its funds); bear out, tend to substantiate, bring facts to confirm, (statement, charge, theory, &c.); keep up or represent (part, character) adequately. (N.) supporting or being supported (*give s. to*; *requires s.*; *gets no s.*; *troops stationed in s.*, as reserve; *s. trench*, the second of three lines, between fire-trench & reserve trench; *speak in s. of*, advocate); person or thing that supports (*shelf must have another s.*; *he is the chief s. of the cause*); hence **suppor·t**LESS a. [f. F *supporter* f. L SUP(*portare* carry)]

suppor·ter, n. In vbl senses; esp., (Herald.) representation of living creature holding up or standing (usu. as one of pair) beside an escutcheon. [-ER[1]]

suppo·se (-z), v.t. Assume as a hypothesis (*let us s. a second flood*; *well, s. it was so*; in part. or imperat. with conjunctional force = *if*, as *supposing white were black you would be right, s. your father saw you what would he say?*; also in imperat. as formula of proposal, as *s. we went for a walk, s. we try another*); (of theory, result, &c.) require as a condition (*that supposes mechanism without flaws*; *design in creation supposes a creator*); take for granted, presume, assume in default of knowledge, be inclined to think, accept as probable, (*I s. we shall be back in an hour*; *you cannot s., it is not to be supposed, that*; *I s. he won't* or *I don't s. he will come*; *what do you s. he meant?*; *I s. so*, form of hesitating assent; also abs. in parenth., as *you will not be there, I s.*); (p.p.) believed to exist, believed to have specified character, (*the supposed music of the spheres*; *his supposed brother, generosity*), whence **suppo·sed**LY[2] adv. Hence or cogn. **suppo·**SABLE a., **supposi·**TION n. [see below], **supposi·tion**AL a., **supposi·tional**LY[2] adv., **supposi·**TIOUS(2) a., hypothetical, assumed. [f. F SUP(*poser* POSE[1]); *supposition* &c. f. L SUP(*positionem* f. L *ponere posit-* place, -ION), cf. DEPOSITION]

suppŏsiti·tious (-shus), a. Substituted for the real, spurious, (*s. child, writings*). Hence **suppositi·tious**LY[2] adv., **suppositi·tious**NESS n. [f. L *suppositicius* f. SUP(*ponere posit-* place) substitute, -ITIOUS[1]]

suppŏ·sitory, n. (med.). Cone or cylinder of medicinal substance introduced into rectum or vagina or uterus & left to dissolve. [f. LL *suppositorium* (prec., -ORY)]

suppre·ss, v.t. Put down, quell, put an end to activity or existence of, (rebellion, sedition, agitators, conscience, piracy, monasteries, &c.); restrain, keep in, not give vent to, withhold or withdraw from publication, keep secret, not reveal, (groan, yawn, feelings, name, book, evidence, facts). So **suppre·**SSIBLE a., **suppre·**SSION (-shn), **suppre·**SSOR[2], nn. [f. L SUP(*primere press-* = *premere* press)]

suppre·ssio vēr·i, n. Suppression of truth, misrepresentation by concealment of facts that ought to be made known. [L]

su·ppūrate, v.i. Form pus, fester. So **suppur**A·TION n., **su·ppur**ATIVE a. [L SUP(*purare* f. PUS), -ATE[3]]

sūpra-, pref. f. L *supra* adv. & prep. above, freely used in forming anat. terms indifferently with SUPER- 1a as *-clavi·cular* above the clavicle, *-or·bital* above the eye-sockets, *-re·nal* above the kidney, or with SUPER- 3a as *-maxi·llary* a. & n. (of) the upper jaw; also in other wds w. sense *over, beyond, before, after*, often in contrast with compds of INFRA-, SUB-, as *-mu·ndane* above or superior to the world, *-lapsār·ian(ism)* a. & nn., (holding, holder of) doctrine that God's decrees of election & reprobation were not due to the Fall but preceded it & his prescience of it (cf. INFRALAPSARIAN); *-pro·test*, acceptance or payment of bill by third person after protest for non-acceptance or non-payment.

suprĕ·macy, n. Being supreme, highest authority, (*Act, oath, of s.*, securing ecclesiastical s. to the Crown & excluding the authority of the Pope). [foll., -ACY(2)]

supre·me (sōō-, sū-), a. & n. Highest in authority or rank (*the S. Being* or *the S.* as n., God; *S. Council of the Allies*, small body, also *the Big Four, Five*, settling by conference the Allied common policy 1919–1921, each Great Power having a representative; *S. Court of* JUDICATURE; *s. end* or *good*, SUMMUM BONUM; *s. Pontiff*, the Pope); greatest possible, uttermost, extreme, last & greatest or most important, (*s. wisdom, courage*, &c.; *the s. test of fidelity*; *a* or *the s. hour, moment*, &c.). Hence **supre·me**LY[2] adv. [f. L *supremus* superl. of *superus* see SUPRA-]

sur-[1], =SUB- in some L compds w. wds in r- & their derivatives, as *surge, surreptitious.*

sur-[2], =SUPER- in many wds taken into E f. OF, as *surcharge, surface, surloin, surprise, surrender*, also sometimes for *super-, supra-*, in anat. wds as *surrenal* SUPRArenal.

sura(h[1]***)*** (soor·*a*), n. Chapter of Koran. [Arab.]

sū̆r·ah[2], n. Kind of soft twilled usu. one-coloured silk. [perh. f. *Surat* in India]

sū̆r·al, a. Of the calf of the leg (*s. artery* &c.). [L *sura* calf, -AL]

sura·t (sōō-), n. Kind of cotton grown, kind of cotton cloth made, in the Bombay Presidency. [place-name]

surcea·se, n., & v.i., (archaic). Cessation; (vb) cease. [AF *sursise* delay, orig. fem. p.p. of OF *surseoir* f. L as SUPER*sede*, w. assim. to *cease*]

surchar·ge, n., & v.t. Excessive or additional load or burden or amount of money charged; supply of force, electricity, &c., in excess of what is required; additional charge made by assessors as penalty for false returns of taxable property; mark printed on postage-stamp changing its value; amount in official account not passed by auditor & having to be refunded by person responsible; showing of omission in account for which credit should have been given. (Vb) overload, fill or saturate to excess; (of assessor, auditor) exact s. from, exact (sum) as s., fine (person sum) as s.; show omission of credit in (account). [f. OF *surcharge(r)*, see SUR-[2]]

sur·cingle, n., & v.t. Band round horse's body rarely as saddlegirth, usu. to keep blanket &c. in place; girdle of cassock; (vb) gird (horse), fasten (blanket &c.), with s. [f. OF SUR[2](*cengle* girth f. L *cingula* f. *cingere* gird)]

sur·coat, n. (hist.). Loose robe worn over armour; 15th–16th-c. woman's jacket. [OF SUR[2](*cote* COAT)]

sur·culose, -lous, aa. (bot.). Producing suckers. [f. L *surculosus* (*surculus* sucker, -OSE[1]), -OUS]

surd, a. & n. (Math.) irrational (a. & n.); (Phonet.) (consonant, consonantal sound) uttered with the breath & not the voice (as p, f, s, cf. *sonant* or *vocal* of b, v, z). [f. L *surdus* deaf, noiseless; math. sense by mistransl. into L of Gk *alogos* (1) irrational, (2) speechless]

sure (shoor), a. & adv. Having or seeming to have adequate reason for belief, convinced *of* or (*that*), having certain prospect or confident anticipation or satisfactory knowledge *of*, free from doubts *of*, (*are you s.?*; *you may be s. of his honesty, he is* or *that he is honest*; *he feels* or *is s. of success*; *I did not feel s. of my company, could not feel s. about it*; *if one could be s. of living to 70*; *I'm sure I didn't mean to hurt you*, form of asseveration; *well, I'm s.!*, excl. of surprise); safe, reliable, trusty, unfailing, (*sent it by a s. hand*; *put it in a s. place*; *a s. shot*, marksman who never misses; *a s. draw*, covert certain to yield fox, remark &c. certain to draw person; *s. card*, scheme &c. certain to succeed; SLOW *& s.*; *there is only one s. way*; *s.-footed*, never stumbling or making false step lit. or fig.); to be relied on, certain, *to* do (*is s. to turn out well*; *would be s. to dislike him*); undoubtedly true or truthful (*one thing is s.*; *to be s.*, formula of concession = to avoid over-statement, as *t. b. s. she is not perfect, is pretty*, also as excl. of surprise, as *so it is, t. b. s.!. well, to be s.!*; *make s.*, ascertain absolutely that something is as supposed, take measures to secure that something is as desired; *make s. of*, establish the truth or ensure the happening of; also *make s. of* or *that*, have confident but often false anticipation of or that); hence **sure·**NESS n. (Adv.): (archaic) I admit, you will admit, (*'tis pleasant, s., to see one's name in print*); *as* certainly *as* (*as s. as eggs is eggs, as s. as a gun*, colloq. forms of asseveration); *s. enough*, in fact as well as in prospect (*I said it would be, & s. e. it is*), with practical certainty (*he will come s. e.*). [f. OF *sur* f. L *securus* SECURE]

sure·ly, adv. With certainty or safety (*he knows full s. that*; *will diminish slowly but s.*; *mule plants its feet s.*); if strong belief or experience or probability or right is to count for anything (*it s. cannot have been he*; *s. I have met you before*; *there is no truth in it, s.*; *s. you will not desert me*); (in answers, archaic) certainly, undoubtedly, (' *Should you be willing to try?* ' '*S.*'). [-LY²]

sure·ty, n. (Archaic) certainty (esp. *of a s.,* certainly); thing pledged as security for payment or performance (now rare); person who makes himself responsible for another's appearance in court or payment of sum or performance of engagement (*stand s.,* become so responsible, go bail, *for* another; *find s.* or *ss.,* said of person primarily liable), whence **sure·tyship** n. [f. OF *seurte* f. L *securitatem* (SURE, -TY)]

surf, n. Foam & commotion of sea breaking on shore or reefs; *s.-bird,* coast-bird related to sand-piper; *s.-boat,* of buoyant build for use in s.; *s.-man,* skilled in managing s.-boats; *s.-riding* (on boards, as a sport). Hence **sur·fy²** a. [earlier *suffe,* etym. dub.]

sur·face (-ĭs), n., & v.t. The outside of a body, (any of) the limits that terminate a solid, outward aspect of material or immaterial thing, what is apprehended of something upon a casual view or consideration, (*has a smooth, uneven, s.*; *presents a large s. to view*; *its upper s. is as cold as ice*; *looks only at the s. of men & things*; *his politeness is only of* or *on the s.*; *one never gets below the s. with him*), (attrib.) of the s. only (*s. plausibility, impressions,* &c.); (Geom.) that which has length & breadth but no thickness (*plane s.,* that contains the whole of the straight line connecting any two points in it; *curved s.,* that may be so cut by a plane through any point in it that the line of section shall be a curve; *developable s.,* that may be unfolded into a plane without doubling or separation of parts, e.g. s. of cone or cylinder); *s.-colour,* used in *s.-printing,* printing from raised s. as with ordinary type or woodcuts & not from incised lines; *s.-man,* keeping permanent way of railway in order; *s.-tension,* tension of a liquid causing it to act as an elastic enveloping membrane seen in drop or bubble; *s.-water,* that collects on & runs off from s. of ground &c.; hence *-surfaced²* a. (Vb) put special s. on (paper &c.). [F (SUR-², FACE)]

sur·feit (-fĭt), n., & v.t. & i. Excess esp. in eating or drinking, oppression or satiety resulting. (Vb) overfeed (t. & i.), (cause to) take too much of something, cloy, satiate *with.* [vb f. n., f. OF *sorfait* orig. p.p. of *sorfaire* (SUR-², L *facere fact-do*)]

surge, v.i., & n. Move up & down or to & fro (as) in waves (of sea, crowd, standing corn, emotion, &c.); (Naut., of rope or chain on windlass) slip back with a jerk; (of wheel) revolve without advancing on rail or road; (n.) waves, a wave, surging motion. [n. f. vb, f. OF *sourdre sourge-* f. L *surgere* rise contraction of SUR¹(*rigere* = *regere* direct)]

sur·geon (-jn), n. Medical man treating injuries & deformities & diseases by manual operation (*house-s.,* on staff of hospital), person skilled in surgery; medical practitioner having a diploma qualifying him to practice surgery (*s. dentist,* dentist thus qualified); (formerly, opp. *physician*) general practitioner dispensing drugs & attending out-patients & not confining himself to consultation; medical officer in navy or army or military hospital; *s.-fish,* kind named from lancet-shaped spines on each side of tail. [AF *surgien* f. OF *cirurgien* (*cirurgie* f. L f. Gk *kheirourgia* handiwork, surgery, f. *kheir* hand, -O-, *ergō* work)]

sur·gery, n. Manual treatment of injuries or disorders of the body, operative therapeutics, surgical work, (*antiseptic, clinical, plastic,* &c., *s.*; *conservative s.,* avoiding amputations &c.); surgeon's consulting-room & dispensary. [f. OF *cirurgerie* (*cirurgie* see prec., -ERY)]

sur·gical, a. Of surgeons or surgery (*s. skill, operations, instruments*; *s. fever,* caused by s. operation through sepsis). Hence **sur·gically²** adv. [as SURGEON, -ICAL]

sū̆r·icate (-at), n. S.-Afr. animal resembling polecat & ferret. [native]

surloin, obs. form of SIRLOIN.

sur·ly, a. Uncivil, given to making rude answers, showing unfriendly temper, churlish. Hence **sur·lily²** adv., **sur·liness** n. [earlier *sirly* (SIR, -LY¹) = masterful]

sur·master, n. Second master or vice-master in St Paul's School. [SUR-²]

surmi·se (-z), n., & v.t. & i. Conjecture, suspicion of the existence or guess at the nature of something. (Vb) infer doubtfully, suspect the existence of; make a guess, try to divine something. [vb f. n., OF, orig. fem. p.p. of SUR²(*mettre* put f. L *mittere miss-* send) lay to person's charge]

surmou·nt, v.t. Cap, be on the top of, (usu. in pass.; *peaks surmounted with snow*); overcome, get over, (difficulty, obstacle), whence **surmou·ntable** a. [f. OF SUR²(*monter* MOUNT²)]

surmu·llet, n. The red mullet. [f. OF *surmulet* perh. f. *sor* SORREL², MULLET]

sur·name, n., & v.t. Additional name of descriptive or allusive kind attached to a person & sometimes becoming hereditary; the name common to all members of a family (cf. CHRISTIAN *name*). (Vb) give s. to; give (person s.); (p.p.) called by way of additional name, having as family name. [SUR-², NAME, after F SUR²(*nom* f. L *nomen* see NOMINAL)]

surpa·ss, v.t. Outdo, excel. Hence **surpa·ssing²** a., **surpa·ssingly²** adv. [f. F SUR²(*passer* PASS¹)]

sur·plice, n. Loose full-sleeved white-linen vestment descending to hips or knees or ankles & worn usu. over cassock by clergy & choristers at divine service; *s. choir*, wearing ss.; *s.-fee*, paid to clergy for marriages, funerals, &c. Hence **sur·plic**ED[2] a. [f. OF SUR[2]*plis* f. med. L SUPER(*pelliceum* f. L *pellicius* see PELISSE)]

sur·plus, n. What remains over, what is not required for the purpose in hand, esp. excess of public revenue over expenditure for the financial year, (opp. *deficit*; often attrib., as *s. population*). So **sur·plus**AGE(1) n. [OF, f. med. L SUPER(PLUS)]

surpri·se (-z), n., & v.t. Catching of person(s) unprepared (*the fort was taken, the truth must be elicited, by s.*; *determined to attempt a s.*; *a s. visit*, without notice); emotion excited by the unexpected, astonishment, (*full of s.*; *his s. was visible*; *to my great s.*, much against my expectations; *s. packet*, with unexpected contents, e.g. packet of sweets with coin, also often fig.); event &c. that excites s. (*was a great s. to me*; *I have a s. for you*, piece of unexpected news, unexpected gift, &c.; *what a s.!*). (Vb) capture (place, person) by s., attack at unawares, come upon (person) off his guard (*surprised him in the act*); affect with s., astonish, turn out contrary to expectations of, be a s. to, (*should you be surprised to learn —?*; *I am surprised at you*, shocked, scandalized; *more surprised than frightened*), whence **surpri·s**ING[2] a., **surpri·sing**LY[2], **surpri·sĕd**LY[2], advv.; hurry (person) by s. *into* conduct or act or doing (*surprised me into rudeness, consent, dropping the reins*); hence **surpri·s**AL(2) n. [OF, orig. fem. p.p. of SUR[2](*prendre* f. L *prehendere* take)]

sŭrrebu·t (-tt-), **sŭrrejoi·n,** vv.i. (Of plaintiff) reply, make **surrebu·tt**ER[4], **surrejoi·nd**ER[4], nn., to defendant's rebutter, rejoinder (order of pleadings at common law: Plaintiff's *declaration*, Defendant's *plea*, P.'s *replication*, D.'s *rejoinder*, P.'s *surrejoinder*, D.'s rebutter, P.'s *surrebutter*). [SUR-[2]]

surre·nder, v.t. & i., & n. Hand over, give into another's power or control, relinquish possession of, esp. upon compulsion or demand (*s. fortress, army, ship, freedom, hopes, chastity, privilege, office*, &c.; *s. insurance policy*, abandon claim in return for repayment of part of premiums); give one*self* over *to* habit, emotion, influence, &c.; (of fortress, ship, or force, or its commander) accept enemy's demand for submission; give oneself up, cease from resistance, submit, (*s. to* one's *bail*, appear in court after being admitted to bail). (N.) surrendering or being surrendered (*s. value*, amount payable to surrenderer of insurance policy). [f. OF SUR[2](*rendre* RENDER)]

sŭrrepti·tious (-ĭshus), a. Underhand, kept secret, done by stealth, clandestine. Hence **surrepti·tious**LY[2] adv. [L *surrepticius* f. SUR[1](*ripere -rept-* =*rapere* snatch), -ITIOUS[1]]

sŭ·rrogate (-*a*t), n. Deputy, esp. of bishop or his chancellor. Hence **su·rrogate**SHIP n. [L SUR[1](*rogare* ask) elect as substitute, -ATE[2]]

surrou·nd (-ow-), v.t., & n. Come or be all round, invest, enclose, encompass, encircle, environ, (*the surrounding country*, the neighbouring district; *surrounded with* or *by*); (n.) floor-covering between walls & carpet. [earlier sense *overflow*; f. OF SUR[2](*onder* f. L *undare* see ABOUND); present sense by confus. w. *round*]

surrou·ndings, n. pl. Sum total or general effect of all that is in the neighbourhood of a person or thing (*picturesque healthy, degraded, cultured, s.*). [-ING[1]]

sur·tax, n., & v.t. (Impose) additional tax (on). [f. F SUR[2](*taxe, -taxer*, TAX)]

sur·tout (-tōō), n. (now rare). Overcoat, esp. of frock-coat shape. [F, f. *sur tout* over all]

survei·llance (-vāl*a*ns, -lyans), n. Supervision, close observation, invigilation, (esp. *under s.*, not trusted to work or go about unwatched). [F, f. SUR[2](*veiller* f. L as VIGILANT)]

survey·[1] (-vā), v.t. Let the eyes pass over, take general view of, form general idea of the arrangement & chief features of; examine condition of (building &c.); collect by measurement &c. all facts needed for determining the boundaries, size, position, shape, contour, ownership, value, &c., of (country, coast, district, estate, &c.), whence **survey·**ING[1](1) n. [AF SUR[2](*veier* f. OF *veeir* f. L *vidēre* see)]

sur·vey[2], n. General view, casting of eyes or mind over something; inspection of the condition, amount, &c., of something, account given of result of this; department carrying on, operations constituting, piece of, surveying of land &c. (see prec.), map or plan setting forth results of such s. (ORDNANCE *s.*). [f. prec.]

survey·or, n. Official inspector *of* (*s. of weights & measures* &c.), whence **survey·or**SHIP n.; person professionally engaged in SURVEY[1]ing. [AF *surveour* (SURVEY[1], -OR[2])]

survī·val, n. Surviving (*s. of the fittest*, process or result of *natural* SELECTION); person or thing that has remained as a relic of an earlier time. [foll., -AL(2)]

survi·ve, v.t. & i. Outlive, be still alive or in existence after the passing away of, come alive through or continue to exist in spite of, (*s.* one's *children, contemporaries*, &c.; *s.* one's *usefulness*; *s. all perils*); continue to live or exist, be still alive or existent. Hence **survi·vor**[2] n., **survi·vor**SHIP n. (esp. right of joint tenant to whole estate on other's death). [f. F *survivre* f. LL SUPER(*vivere* live)]

sus-, = SUB- in L compds w. wds in c-

(also suc-, cf. *succeed, susceptible*), in p- (also sup-, cf. *suppose, suspend*), & in t-, & their derivatives. [for *subs* var. of *sub*; cf. ABS-]

susce·ptible (-sĕ-), a. (Pred.) admitting *of* (*passage is s. of another interpretation*; *facts not s. of proof*), open or liable or accessible or sensitive *to* (*very s. to pain, injury, kindness, female charms*); impressionable, sensitive, readily touched with emotion, touchy. Hence or cogn. **susceptibi·lity** n. (often in pl. = sensitive points of person's nature), **susce·ptibly**² adv. [f. med. L *susceptibilis* f. L sus(*cipere -cept-* = *capere* take), -IBLE]

susce·ptive, a. Concerned with the receiving of emotional impressions (cf. prec. & *receptive*; *the s. faculties, nature*). [f. med. L *susceptivus* as prec., -IVE]

su·sī (sōō-), n. E.-Ind. cotton fabric with stripes of different-coloured silk. [Hind.]

suspe·ct¹, v.t. Have an impression of the existence or presence of (*danger, a plot, foul play, collusion, a causal relation*); half believe *to be* (*I s. him to be my brother, a liar, dying*); be inclined to think that or *that* (*I s. you once thought otherwise*; also parenth., as *you, I s., don't care*); incline to mentally accuse *of* or inculpate, doubt the innocence of, distrust, (*I s. him of lying, of deep designs*; *a suspected criminal*, person suspected of being one; *suspected persons*; *the ignorant s. everybody*); hold to be uncertain, mistrust, doubt the genuineness or truth of, (*s. the authenticity of, the evidence*). Hence **suspe·ctable** a. (rare). [f. L *suspect-* (foll.)]

suspe·ct², pred. a. & n. Of suspected character, subject to suspicion, not unimpeachable, (*the statement of an interested party is naturally s.*); (n.) suspected person (*political ss. are kept under surveillance*). [F, f. L *suspicere suspect-* (SUB-, *specere* look)]

suspe·nd, v.t. Hang up, (p.p., of solid particles or body in fluid medium) sustained somewhere between top & bottom (*a balloon suspended in mid-air*; *suspended particles of dust*), so **suspe·nsible** a., **suspensibi·lity** n.; keep in undecided or inoperative state for a time, defer, temporarily annul, adjourn, debar temporarily from office or function or privilege or membership, (*s. judgement*, one's *indignation, the rules, the Habeas-Corpus Act, proceedings, a clergyman*; *s. payment*, fail to meet financial engagements, admit insolvency; *suspended animation*, state of insensibility without death). [f. L sus(*pendĕre pens-* hang)]

suspe·nder, n. In vbl senses; esp., (pl.) pair of braces (chiefly shop), pair of (sets of) attachments to which tops of socks or stockings are hung. [-ER¹]

suspe·nse, n. State of usu. anxious uncertainty or expectation or waiting for information (*keep* one *in s.*, delay acquainting him with what he is eager to know); (Law) suspension, temporary cessation of right &c.; *s. account* in bookkeeping (in which items are temporarily entered till proper place is determined). [OF, f. p.p. of L SUSPENDere]

suspe·nsion, n. In vbl senses (SUSPEND); esp. *s.-bridge*, in which roadway is hung across stream &c., usu. on wire cables passing over towers & anchored, without support from below. So **suspe·nsive** a. (*-ive veto*, operating only for a time, not definitive), **suspe·nsory** a., **suspe·nsively**² adv. [f. LL *suspensionem* (SUSPEND, -ION)]

sus. per coll., n. The entry recording that a person was hanged (often facet. = hanged, hanging). [abbr. of L *suspendatur per collum* let him be hanged by the neck]

suspi·cion (-ishn), n., & v.t. Feeling of one who suspects, suspecting or being suspected (*above s.*, too obviously good &c. to be suspected), partial or unconfirmed belief esp. that something is wrong or some one guilty; soupçon *of*; hence **suspi·cionless** a. (Vb, U.S. slang) have s. that or *that*. [AF *suspecioun* (OF *souspeçon*) f. med. L *suspectionem* f. L *suspicere* SUSPECT, -ION]

suspi·cious, a. Prone to, feeling, indicating, suggesting or justifying, suspicion (*the ignorant are s.*; *he became s.*; *with a s. glance*; *under s. circumstances*). Hence **suspi·ciously**² adv., **suspi·ciousness** n. [OF, f. L *suspiciosus* (prec., -OSE¹)]

suspire·, v.i. (poet.). Sigh. So **suspira·tion** n. [f. L *suspirare* (SUB-, *spirare* breathe)]

sustai·n, v.t. Bear weight of, hold up, keep from falling or sinking (cf. *support*); enable to last out, keep from failing, give strength to, encourage, (exx. as in SUPPORT; *sustaining food*, that keeps up the strength); endure without giving way, stand, bear up against, (*sustained the shock of the enemy's cavalry*; *will not s. comparison with*); undergo, experience, suffer, (*s. a defeat, severe contusion, loss*, &c.); (of court or other authority) allow validity of, give decision in favour of, uphold, (*s. the objection, the applicant in his claim*, &c.); bear out, tend to substantiate or corroborate, confirm, (statement, charge, theory, &c.); keep up or represent (part, character) adequately; keep (sound, effort, &c.) going continuously (*a sustained note, effort*). Hence **sustai·nable** a., **sustai·nment** n. (rare). [f. OF *sustenir* f. L sus(*tinēre tent-* = *tenēre* hold)]

su·stenance, n. Nourishing (now rare; *given for the s. of our bodies*); nourishing quality, subsistence, food lit. or fig., (*there is no s. in it*; *how shall we get s.?*; *lived a week without s. of any kind*). [OF (*sos-*), f. *sostenir* SUSTAIN, -ANCE]

sustenta·tion, n. Support of life (rare; *s. fund*, collected to support indigent clergy). [OF, f. L *sustentationem* (*sustentare* frequent. of *sustinēre* SUSTAIN, -ION)]

sūsurra·tion n., **susu·rrous** a., (rare). Whispering, rustling. [L *susurrare*, *susurrus* a., (*susurrus* a whisper), -ATION, -OUS]

su·tler, n. Camp-follower selling provisions &c. [f. Du. *soeteler* (*soetelen* befoul, cf. G *sudeln* to sully)]

Su·tra (sōō-), n. Set of aphorisms in Sanskrit literature. [Skr., orig. = string, cogn. w. SEW]

suttee·, sati· (-ē), n. Hindu widow who immolates herself on her husband's funeral pyre; custom requiring such immolation, also **suttee·**ISM(2) n. [Skr. (*sa*-), = virtuous wife]

sū·ture (-tsh*er*), n., & v.t. Seamlike articulation of two bones at their edges, esp. one of those in the skull, similar junction of parts in Bot., Entom., &c.; (Surg.) uniting of edges of wound by stitching, thread or wire used for this, (vb, unite thus). Hence **su·tur**AL a., **su·tural**LY[2] adv., **sutur**A·TION n., **su·tur**ED[2] a. [F, f. L *sutura* (*suere sut-* sew, -URE)]

sū·zerain, n. Feudal lord, lord paramount, sovereign or State having nominal sovereignty or right of general control over semi-independent or internally autonomous State. So **su·zerain**TY n. [F, f. *sus* above f. L *su(r)sum* upward (SUB-, VERSUS) on anal. of *souverain* SOVEREIGN]

***svelte*,** a. Lightly built, lissom, supple, (chiefly of human, esp. female, figure). [F, f. EX(*vellitus* pop. L p.p. of L *vellere* pull)]

swab (-ŏb), v.t., & n. (Clean with water &) mop or other arrangement of absorbent material on handle for cleaning (*s. down* or *s. the deck* &c.); absorbent pad used in surgery; *s. up*, take up (moisture) with s.; (Naut. slang) officer's epaulet; (Naut. slang) clumsy fellow, also **swa·bb**ER[1] n. [back form. f. *swabber* f. Du. *zwabber* ship-drudge, cf. MLG *swabben* to splash in mud]

Swā·bian, Sua-, a. & n. (Inhabitant) of Swabia (*S. emperors*, Hohenstaufens, 1138–1254). [*Suabia* (mod. L f. G *Schwaben*), -AN]

swa·ddle (-ŏdl), v.t. Swathe in bandages or many or thick wraps or garments (*swaddling-bands, -clothes*, in which infants are wrapped, also fig. influences that restrain freedom of action or thought). [SWATHE, -LE]

Swade·shi (-dā-), n. Movement in India for boycotting British goods as means of bringing political pressure to bear. [Bengali, = own country]

swăg, n. (slang). Booty carried off by burglars &c., (transf.) gains made by political or other jobbery; (Austral.) tramp's, miner's, or bush-traveller's bundle. [f. obs. *swag* vb hang swaying (of bundle, fat belly, &c.), prob. f. Scand., & cogn. w. SWAY]

swage, n., & v.t. Kinds of die or form for shaping wrought iron &c. by hammering or pressure; *s.-block*, with variety of perforations, grooves, &c., for this purpose; (vb) shape with s. [vb f. n., f. OF *souage* etym. dub.]

swăgger (-g-), v.i. & t., & n. & a. Walk like a superior among inferiors, show self-confidence or self-satisfaction by gait, go *about, in, out*, &c., with such walk; behave in domineering or defiant way; talk boastfully (*about* prep.) or in hectoring manner; bluff (person) *into, out of*, &c.; hence **swa·gger**ER[1] n., **swa·ggering**LY[2] adv. (N.) swaggering gait or manner or talk; dashing or confident air or way of doing something, freedom from tameness or hesitancy, smartness; *s.-cane*, carried by soldiers when walking out. (Adj.) smart, fashionable, (*s. clothes, society*, &c.). [obs. SWAG vb, -ER[5]]

swain, n. Young rustic; bucolic lover; (facet.) lover, suitor. [f. ON *sveinn* lad, cf. OE *swān* swineherd]

swa·llet (-ŏl-), n. (dial.). Underground stream; hole into which a stream flows, SWALLOW[1]-hole. [prob. f. foll.]

swa·llow[1] (-ŏlō), v.t. & i., & n. Cause or allow (food &c.) to pass down one's throat (*s. a* CAMEL, make no difficulty about something incredible or impossible or outrageous); engulf, absorb, exhaust, draw in, make away with, (usu. *up*; *the earth swallowed them up*; *the expenses more than s. up the earnings*; *death is swallowed up in victory*); accept (statement) with ready credulity (*will s. anything you tell him*); put up with, pocket, stomach, (affront); recant (one's words); perform muscular operation of swallowing something. Hence **swa·llow**ABLE a. (N.) gullet; act of swallowing; amount swallowed at once; (also *s.-hole*) funnel-shaped cavity in limestone. [ME *swolowen* f. OE *swelgan*, cf. Du. *zwelgen*, G *schwelgen* gorge]

swa·llow[2] (-ŏlō), n. Kinds of usu. migratory, long-winged, swift-flying, wide-gaped, weak-legged, fork-tailed, insectivorous bird associated with summer (*one s. does not make a summer*, warning against hasty inference); *s. dive* (with arms outspread till close to water); *s.-fish*, kind of gurnard; *s.-hawk, -plover, -shrike*, &c., fork-tailed kinds of hawk &c.; *s.-tail*, deeply forked tail, kinds of butterfly & humming-bird having this, points of burgee, (sing. or pl.) s.-tailed coat; *s.-tailed*, with deeply forked tail (of butterflies, birds, &c.; *s.-t. coat*, kind with tapering tails formerly worn in ordinary costume & still in evening dress); *s.-wort*, milk-weed, also celandine. [OE *swalewe*, cf. Du. *zwaluw*, G *schwalbe*]

swam. See SWIM.

swamp (-ŏ-), n., & v.t. Piece of wet spongy ground, bog, marsh, (attrib., in many names of plants & animals found in ss.); hence **swa·mpY**[2] a. (Vb) entangle in s. (usu. in p.p.); (of water) overwhelm, flood, soak, (boat or its crew or contents, house, provisions, &c.); make helpless with excessive supply of something (*am swamped with letters, applications, work*); (of greater quantity or numbers) swallow up, make invisible &c., prevent from being noticed or taking effect. [f. 17th c. in Virginia; prob. cogn. w. SUMP; cf. OHG & MLG *swamp*, OE & Goth. *swamm*, sponge or fungus, & Gk *somphos* spongy]

swan (-ŏn), n. Kinds of large water-bird with long flexible neck, webbed feet, and in most species snow-white plumage, formerly supposed to sing melodiously at point of death (*white, black-necked, black, mute* or *tame* or *common, hooper* or *hooping, trumpeter*, &c., *s.*; *black s.*, name given before discovery of black species to extreme rarity; *all his geese are ss.*, see GOOSE), (fig., w. ref. to sweetness of dying song) poet (esp. *S. of Avon*, Shakspere); the constellation Cygnus; *s.-flower*, kind of orchid; *s.-goose*, long-necked China goose; *s.-herd*, royal officer having charge of s.-marks; *s.-mark*, cut in skin of beak to show ownership; *s.-neck*, curved end of discharge-pipe; *s.'s-down*, down of s. used in trimmings & esp. in powder-puffs, also kind of thick cotton cloth with soft nap on one side; *s.-shot*, of large size; *s.-skin*, kind of fine twilled flannel; *s.-song*, of dying s., also person's last production &c.; *s.-upping*, annual taking up & marking of Thames ss. Hence **swa·nLIKE** a., **swa·nnERY**(3) n. [OE, cf. Du. *zwaan*, G *schwan*; perh. cogn. w. Skr. *swan*, L *sonare*, sound]

swănk, n., & v.i., (slang). Show(ing) off, swagger, bounce, bluff. [dial. wd (=strut), etym. dub.]

swap. See SWOP.

Swara·j (-ahj), n. Home-rule or self-government as the watchword of Indian Nationalists. Hence **swara·jIST** n. & a. [f. Skr. *svaraj* self-ruling; cf. L *suus* one's own, & see RAJ]

sward (-ord), n. Expanse covered with short grass, lawnlike ground; turf, whence **swar·dED**[2] a. [OE *sweard* skin, cf. Du. *zwoord* bacon-rind, G *schwarte* bark, rind]

sware. See SWEAR.

swarm[1] (-orm), n., & v.i. Large number of insects, birds, small animals, sharpshooters, horsemen, &c., moving about in a cluster or irregular body esp. round prey or enemy (*ss.*, great numbers *of* children, stars, people, bills, &c.); cluster of honey-bees emigrating from hive with queen bee to establish new home; *s.-cell, -spore*, zoospore. (Vb) move in a s. (*s. round*, about, over, &c., prepp.), (of bees) cluster for emigration; congregate in numbers, be very numerous; (of places) be overrun, be crowded, abound, *with* (*road, hills, house, swarming with beggars, rebels, fleas*). [OE *swearm*, cf. Du. *zwerm*, G *schwarm*, perh. cogn. w. Skr. *svára* to sound, L *susurrus* whisper]

swarm[2] (-orm), v.i. & t. Climb rope or tree or pole (always *up*), climb (rope &c., or *up* rope &c.), by clipping with knees & hands. [?]

swart (-ort), a. (archaic). Dark-hued, swarthy. [OE *sweart*, cf. Du. *zwart*, G *schwarz*]

swar·thy (-ordhĭ), a. Dark-complexioned. Hence **swar·thiLY**[2] adv., **swar·thiNESS** n. [obs. *swarth* var. of prec., -Y[2]]

swash (-ŏ-), v.t. & i., & n. (Archaic) strike violently (*swa·shbuckler*, bully, bravo; *swashing blow*, hard); (of water &c.) wash about, make sound of washing or rising & falling (n., such motion or sound; *s.-plate*, inclined disk revolving on axle & communicating up-&-down motion to bar whose end rests on it). [imit.]

swă·stika, n. Fylfot. [Skr., lit. =fortunate (*sú* well, *asti* being)]

swat (-ŏt), v.t. Slap, crush (fly &c.). [U.S.]

swath (-aw-), n. Ridge of grass, corn, &c., lying after being cut, or space left clear after one passage of mower &c. [OE *swæth, swathu*, track, cf. Du. *zwad*, G *schwad*; cogn. w. LG *swade* scythe]

swāthe (-dh), v.t., & n. Bind with bandages, enclose in wraps or cloths or warm or many garments; (n., rare) a bandage or fold. [OE *swathian* vb, *swath*(*um* dat. pl.) n.; cf. SWADDLE]

sway, v.i. & t., & n. Lean unsteadily to one side or in different directions by turns, have unsteady swinging motion, oscillate irregularly, waver, vacillate; give swaying motion to, govern the motion of, wield, control direction of, have influence over, govern, rule over, (*wind sways trees*; *s. sceptre, cricket-bat, sword*; *his speech swayed votes*; *is too much swayed by the needs of the moment*; *sways a fifth of mankind*); (p.p., of horse, also *sway-backed*) with back abnormally hollowed. (N.) swaying motion or position; rule, government. [f. LG *swâjen* be blown to & fro, cf. Sw. *svaja*, G *schweien*, Du. *zwaaien*]

swear (swār), v.t. & i. (*swore* or archaic *sware, sworn*), & n. State something on oath, take oath (*to*, that or *that*), promise (conduct, *to* do) on oath, take (oath), (colloq.) say emphatically that, (*will you s., s. it, s. to it, s. you* or *that you were not there, on the Testament?*; *s. eternal fidelity*; *had sworn*, or *sworn a solemn oath, to return*; *I s. it is too bad of him*; *s. to* or *by*, appeal to as witness & guarantee of oath: *s. by* colloq., profess or have great belief in, regularly resort to or recommend; *s. off drink* &c., take oath to abstain); use profane oaths to express anger or as expletives (often *at*); cause to take oath, administer oath to, (*s. witness* &c.; *s.* person *to secrecy*; *sworn brothers* or *friends*, close intimates; *sworn enemies*, open & irreconcilable; *sworn broker*, admitted to profession with oath against fraud &c.; *s. in*, induct into office by administering oath), (p.p., of evidence &c.) given on oath; make sworn affirmation of (offence) *against* (*s. treason against*; *s. the peace against*, make oath that one is in danger of bodily harm from); hence **swear·**ER[1] n. (N.) spell of profane swearing (*relieved his feelings by a hearty s.*); (colloq., also *s.-word*) a profane oath. [OE *swerian*, cf. Du. *zweren*, G *schwören*]

sweat (-ĕt), n., & v.i. & t. Moisture exuded from the skin, perspiration, (*running, dripping, wet, with s.*; *in* or *by the s. of* one's *brow*, by dint of toil; *bloody s.*, exudation of blood mixed with s.); sweating state, spell of sweating, piece of exercise that induces s., (*in a*, colloq. *all of a, s.*; *nightly ss.*; *a cold s.*, as in death, swoon, terror, &c.; *a s. will do him good*); (colloq.) state of anxiety (*in a s.*); (chiefly colloq.) drudgery, toil, effort, a laborious task or undertaking, (*cannot stand the s. of it*; *says it is a horrid s.*; *will not take the s.*); drops exuding from or condensing on any surface; *s.-band*, leather or flannel lining of hat or cap; *s.-cloth*, esp. thin blanket under horse's saddle or collar; *s.-duct*, by which s. exudes from *s.-gland*, secreting s. below skin; *s.-shop*, in which sweated workers are employed; hence **swea·t**LESS, **swea·t**Y[2], aa., **swea·ti**LY[2] adv., **swea·ti**NESS n. (Vb) exude s., perspire; (fig.) be in state of terror or suffering or repentance (*he shall s. for it*, repent it); emit (blood, gum, &c.) like s.; (of wall &c.) exhibit surface moisture; toil, drudge; make (horse, athlete, &c.) s. by exercise; employ (labour, workers) at starvation wages for long hours, exploit to the utmost by utilizing competition, (*sweated clothes* &c., made by sweated workers), (of workers) work on such terms; subject (hides, tobacco) to fermentation in manufacturing; deprive (coins) of part of metal by shaking in bag; remove s. from (horse) by scraping; fasten (metal part) *on* or *in* by partial fusion; *sweating-bath*, for producing s.; *sweating-iron*, for scraping s. from horse; *sweating-room*, in Turkish bath; *sweating-sickness*, epidemic fever prevalent in 15th & 16th cc. [vb f. n., OE *swāt*, cf. Du. *zweet*, G *schweiss*; cogn. w. Skr. *svédas*, Gk *hidrōs*, L *sudor*]

swea·ter, n. In vbl senses; esp.: sweating employer; thick woollen jersey worn during or after exercise to reduce weight or prevent chills. [-ER[1]]

swede, n. Native of Sweden (*S-*); Swedish turnip. [MLG, MDu.]

Swēdenbor·gian, a. & n. (Adherent) of the Swedish philosophical & religious mystic Emanuel Swedenborg (1688–1772) or his doctrines or New Church. Hence **Swedenbor·gian**ISM(3) n. [-IAN]

Swē·dish, a. & n. (Language) of Sweden or its inhabitants. [SWEDE, -ISH[1]]

swee·ny, n. (U.S.) Atrophy of muscle, esp. of shoulder, in horse. [prob. f. dial. G *schweine* atrophy]

sweep, v.i. & t. (swept), & n. Glide swiftly, speed along with impetuous unchecked motion, go majestically, extend (intr.) in continuous curve or line or slope, (*eagle sweeps past*; *wind sweeps along*; *cavalry sweeps down on the enemy*; *she swept out of the room*; *his glance sweeps from right to left*; *with a sweeping stroke*; *coast sweeps northward*; *plain sweeps away to the sea*); (part.) of wide range, regardless of limitations or exceptions, (*sweeping remark, generalization*, &c.), whence **swee·ping**LY[2] adv., **swee·ping**NESS n.; impart sweeping motion to, carry *along* or *down* or *away* or *off* in impetuous course, clear *off* or *away* or *out of* existence &c. or *from*, (*swept his hand across*; *river sweeps away bridge*, *sweeps logs down with it*; *was swept away by an avalanche*; *the plague swept off thousands*; *s. away slavery, feudalism*, abolish swiftly; *he swept his audience along with him*, won enthusiastic support; *s. all obstacles from* one's *path*); traverse or range swiftly, pass lightly across or along, pass eyes or hand quickly along or over, scan, scour, graze, (*s. the seas*, traverse in all directions, & see below; *wind sweeps the hillside*; *s. the strings, lute*, &c., of hand or its owner; *s. the horizon*, of eyes or their owner; *s. river-bottom* &c., drag it to find something; *dress sweeps the ground*); (of artillery &c.) include in line of fire, cover, enfilade, rake, (*battery sweeps the approaches, glacis, street*); clear everything from, clear of dust or soot or litter with broom (often *up*), gather *up* or collect (as) with broom, push *away* &c. (as) with broom, (*s. the seas*, drive all enemies from them, & see above; *s. floor, carpet, chimney*; *s. up the room*; *s. away the snow*; *swept & garnished*, generally renovated, w. ref. to *Luke* xi. 25; *s. the board*, win all the money on gaming-table, & transf. win all possible prizes &c.; *s. a constituency* &c., receive nearly all votes, have large majority; *sweeps everything into his net*, seizes all that comes; *s. up litter* &c., whence **swee·p**ING[1](2) n. usu. in pl.); propel (barge &c.) with ss.; *s.-net*, long fishing-net, also entomologist's net; *s.-seine*, large seine; *swee·pstake(s)*, form of gambling on horse-races &c. in which the sum composed of participators' stakes goes to the drawer(s) of winning or placed horse(s) &c.; hence **(-)sweep-er**[1](1, 2) n. (N.) sweeping motion or extension, curve in road &c., piece of curving road &c., (*with a s. of his arm, eyes, scythe*; *a s. of mountain country*; *river makes a great s. to the left*; *house is approached by a fine s.* or *carriage s.*); range or compass of something that has sweeping motion (*within, beyond, the s. of the scythe, net, telescope, eye, human intelligence*); act of sweeping (as) with broom (*give it a thorough s.* or *s.-up* or *s.-out*; *make a clean s.*, have complete riddance *of* old furniture, officials, &c.); long oar worked by standing rower(s) on barge, becalmed sailing-ship, &c. (*had to get out the ss.*); long pole mounted as lever for raising bucket from well; man who sweeps chimneys (often *chimney-s.*); (colloq.) = *sweepstake.* [ME *swepen*, derivative vb f. OE *swápan* SWOOP; cf. ON *sveipa*, G *schweifen*, E SWIPE]

sweet, a. & n. Tasting like sugar or honey (*s. apples* &c.; *s. stuff*, sweetmeats; *likes her tea s.*, with much sugar; *a s. tooth*, a liking for s. things; *s. wine*, opp. DRY[1]; *tastes s.*, has s. taste); smelling like roses or perfumes, fragrant, (*smells s.*; so **sweet-scented**[2] a.; *air is s. with thyme*; *s. violet*, of scented kind, opp. *dog-violet*; *s. breath*); melodious or harmonious in sound (*has a s. voice*; *sounds s.*; *s. song, singer*, &c.); fresh & sound, not salt or salted or sour or bitter or rancid or high or stinking, (*s. water*, fit for drinking, neither salt nor bitter nor putrid; *is the meat, milk, butter, still s.?*; *keep the room clean & s.*); highly agreeable or attractive or gratifying, inspiring affection, dear, beloved, amiable, gentle, easy, (colloq.) pretty or charming or delightful, (*'tis s. to hear one's own praises*; *s. toil*, that one loves; *s. love, dalliance, idleness, sleep*; *what a s. blouse, moustache, collie!*; *s. temper*, amiability, whence **sweet-tempered**[2] a.; *a s. nature, face*, &c.; *a s. girl*, lovable, affectionate; *s. one* voc., darling; *a s. one* slang, painful blow with fist &c.; *s. going*, travelling over well-laid road or in smooth-going carriage); *at* one's *own s. will*, just as or when one pleases, arbitrarily, at random; *s.* (*up*)*on* (colloq.), (inclined to be) in love with, very fond of; *swee·tbread*, pancreas (*belly s.-b.*) or thymus-gland (*throat* or *neck s.-b.*) esp. of calf as food; *sweet* BRIER[1]; *s.* GALE[1]; *swee·theart*, either of pair of lovers, (vb) be engaged in love-making (esp. *go sweethearting*); *s.-john*, kinds of pink or of narrow-leaved s.-william; *swee·tmeat*, shaped morsel of confectionery usu. consisting chiefly of sugar or chocolate, a fruit preserved in sugar, bonbon, sugarplum, goody; *s. oil*, (esp.) olive oil; *s. pea*, garden annual with showy s.-scented flowers; *s.* POTATO; *s.-root*, liquorice; *s. rush*, kind of sedge with thick creeping aromatic rootstock used in medicine & confectionery; *s.-sop*, (s.-pulped fruit of) an evergreen shrub of tropical America; *s.* SULTAN; *s.-water*, kind of white hothouse grape; *s.-wi·lliam*, a garden-plant, kind of pink with close-clustered flowers often particoloured in zones; *s. willow*, s. gale; hence **swee·ten**[6] v.t. & i., **swee·tening**[1](4) n., **swee·tish**[1](2) a., **swee·tly**[2] adv., **swee·tness** n. (N.) s. part (*the s. & the bitter* or *ss. & bitters of life*); a sweetmeat, bonbon, (also **swee·ty**[3] n.); (usu. pl.) s. dish(es) such as puddings, tarts, creams, jellies, forming a course at table; (usu. pl.) fragrance (*flowers diffusing their ss. on the air*); (pl.) delights, gratifications, pleasures, (*the ss. of office, domestication, flattery, success*); (chiefly in voc.) darling. [Aryan; OE *swéte*, cf. Du. *zoet*, G *süss*, Skr. *svādús*, Gk *hēdus*, L *suavis* pleasant, *suadēre* persuade]

swee·ting, n. Kind of sweet apple; (archaic) darling. [-ING[3]]

swell, v.i. & t. (p.p. *swōllen*, rarely *swelled*), & n. & a. (Cause to) grow bigger or louder, dilate, expand, rise or raise *up* from surrounding surface, bulge *out*, increase in volume or force or intensity, (*river swollen with melted snow*; *the injured wrist began to s. up* or *s.*, whence **swe·lling**[1](2) n.; *the swelling sails*; *toad swelling himself to size of ox*; *swelling oratory*, of inflated kind; *sound swells on the breeze*; *murmur swelled into a roar*; *ground swells into an eminence*; *heart swells*, feels like bursting with emotion; *s. with pride, indignation*, &c., be or seem hardly able to contain it; *s. like a turkey-cock*, put on blustering air; *wind swells the sails*; *the swelling tide*; *expenditure swollen by extravagance*; *swollen estimates*, inordinately high; *a thousand voices s. the sound*; *items s. the total*; *s. note* in music, sing or play it with alternate crescendo & diminuendo; *emotion swells & subsides*; *swelled head* slang, conceit). (N.) act or condition of swelling (*the s. of the hymn floated past*; *the s. of the ground*); heaving of sea with waves that do not break after storm; part of any more or less cylindrical object that swells out (*the s. of the fore-arm*); (Mus.) crescendo followed by diminuendo, mechanism in organ for swelling or subduing tones at will by opening or closing apertures in box containing pipes &c.; (colloq.) person of distinction or ability, member of good society, person of dashing or fashionable appearance, (*is a s. in politics, at cricket*, &c.; *what a s. you are!*, how finely dressed; *has been* *asked to dinner by some ss.*), whence **swe·ll**DOM n.; *s.-blind*, one of the slats of *s.-box*, in organ (see above); *s.-fish*, kinds that can inflate themselves into nearly globular form; *s.-keyboard*, of s.-organ; *s. mob(smen)*, (class of) pickpockets dressed like gentlemen; *s.-organ*, partial ORGAN with pipes enclosed in s.-box; *s.-pedal*, controlling slats of s.-box; *s.-rule* in printing, dash swelling into diamond in middle & tapering towards ends. (Adj., colloq.) of distinction (*a s. pianist*; *s. parties, society*, &c.); smart, finely dressed, (*s. clothes*; *looks very s.*); hence **swe·ll**ISH[1](2) a. [OE *swellan*, cf. Du. *zwellen*, G *schwellen*]

swe·lter, v.i., & n. Be faint or moist or languid or oppressive with heat (of atmosphere &c., or of things or persons suffering from it; *under a sweltering sky*; *city sweltered in the plain*; *the sweltering horses*); (n.) sweltering atmosphere or conditions (*in the s. of the Indian night*). [OE *sweltan* die, cf. ON *svelta*, Goth. *swiltan*, OHG *swelzan* be consumed by fire or love, -ER[1]]

swept. See SWEEP.

swerve, v.i. & t., & n. Diverge from regular line of motion, go off in changed direction, dodge, (*never swerves an inch from his duty*; *bird, ball, swerves in the air*; *horse, three-quarters* at football, *swerved suddenly*); cause (ball) to s. in the air. (N.) divergence from course, swerving motion; hence **swer·ve**LESS a. [OE *sweorfan* rub, file, cf. Du. *zwerven* swerve, OFris. *swerva* creep, ON *sverfa* file]

swift, a., adv. (*-er, -est*), & n. Fleet, rapid, quick, soon coming or passing, not long delayed, (now chiefly poet. & rhet.; *s. runner, movement, feet, retribution, anger, laughter, response, riddance*; so **swift-foot**ED[2], **swift-wing**ED[2], aa.); prompt, quick *to* do, (*has a s. wit*; *s. to anger*; *be s. to hear, slow to speak*; so **swift-hand**ED[2] a.); hence **swi·ft**LY[2] adv., **swi·ft**NESS n. (Adv.) swiftly (*he answered s.*; *they that run swiftest*; esp. in comb., as *s.-coming, -passing*). (N.) kinds of very long-winged & s.-flying insectivorous bird with resemblances to swallows, whence **swi·ft**LET n. (small kind); kinds of small lizard; the common newt; breed of pigeons; kinds of moth; revolving frame for winding yarn &c. from. [OE (*swifan* move quickly, cf. ON *svifa*, cogn. w. SWEEP)]

swig, v.t. & i., & n., (slang). Take draughts (of); (n.) (act of taking) a draught of liquor. [vb f. n. (16th c.) in obs. sense *liquor*, etym. dub.]

swill, v.t. & i., & n. Rinse, pour water over or through, flush, (often *out*); drink (t. & i.) greedily. (N.) rinsing (*give it a s.* or *s. out*); bout of drinking (rare); inferior liquor; hog-wash, slops. [OE *swilian* wash, etym. dub.]

swim, v.i. & t. (swăm, swum), & n. Float on or at surface of liquid (SINK[1] *or s.*; *vegetables swimming in butter*; *with bubbles swimming on it*); progress at or below surface of water by working legs, arms, tail, webbed feet, fins, flippers, wings, body, &c., traverse or accomplish (stream, distance, &c.) thus, compete in (race) thus, compete with thus, cause (horse, dog, &c.) to progress thus, (fig.) go with gliding motion, (*s. on* one's *chest, back, side*, methods of human swimming; *s. across, out, back, the channel, a mile, a race, person a hundred yards*, one's *horse across*; *cannot s. a stroke*; *s. with the tide* or *stream*, act with the majority; *s. to the bottom* or *like a stone* or *tailor's goose* facet., sink; *she swam into the room*; *moon swims in sky*), whence **swi·mm**ER[1] n.; appear to undulate or reel or whirl, have dizzy effect or sensation, (*everything swam before his eyes*; *my head swims*; *has a swimming in the head*); be flooded or overflow with or *with* or *in* moisture (*eyes, deck, swimming with tears, water*; *swimming eyes*; *floor swimming in blood*); *swimming-bath*, large enough to s. in; *swimming-bell*, bell-shaped swimming organ of jelly-fish &c.; *swimming-belt*, to keep learner afloat; *swimming-bladder*, fish's sound; *swimming-stone*, kind of spongy quartz. (N.) spell of swimming; swimming-bladder (rare); deep pool frequented by fish in river; (fig.) main current of affairs (esp. *in the s.*, engaged in or acquainted with what is going on). [OE *swimman*, cf. Du. *zwemmen*, G *schwimmen*]

swi·mmeret, n. Swimming-foot in crustaceans. [*swimmer*, -ET[1]]

swi·mmingly, adv. With easy & unobstructed progress (esp. *go on s.*). [-LY[2]]

swi·ndle, v.t. & i., & n. Cheat (person, *money out of* person, person *out of* money &c., or abs.); so **swi·ndl**ER[1] n., **swi·nd-ling**LY[2] adv. (N.) fraudulent scheme, imposition, piece of swindling, person or thing represented as what it is not. [back formation f. *swindler* f. G *schwindler* visionary projector, swindler, (*schwindeln* be dizzy, f. OHG *suindan* waste away)]

swine, n. (pl. the same). Kinds of ungulate non-ruminant omnivorous mammal, pig (which name has displaced it exc. in poet., rhet., zool., agricult., & U.-S. use), whence **swi·n**ERY[3] n.; person of greedy or bestial habits; *s.-bread*, the truffle, also = SOW[2]*-bread*; *s.-fever*, s.-plague; *s.-herd*, tender of s.; *s.-plague*, infectious lung-disease of s.; *s.-pox*, form of chicken-pox; *s.'s-snout*, dandelion. Hence **swi·n**ISH[1] a., **swi·nish**LY[2] adv., **swi·n-ish**NESS n., (chiefly of persons & their habits). [OE *swin* (sing. & pl.), cf. Du. *zwijn*, G *schwein*; perh. orig. an adj. form, cf. L *suinus* of pigs (*sus* sow, -INE[1])]

swing, v.i. & t. (*swung* or rarely *swang, swung*), & n. Move (t. & i.) with to-&-fro or curving motion of object having fixed point(s) or side but otherwise free, sway (t. & i.) or so hang (t. & i.) as to be free to sway like a pendulum or door or branch or tree or hammock or anchored ship, oscillate, revolve, rock, wheel, (*he shall s. for it*, be hanged; *door swung to*, closed; *boat, boom, swings round, across*; *ship swings at anchor*; *s. child* &c., work the s. in which he sits; *sat on table swinging his legs*; *s.* one's *arms, a bell, Indian clubs, bat, basket*; *s. a hammock*, suspend it by ends; *no room to s. a* CAT[1]; *officer swings his company, company swings, into line*, brings, comes, by wheeling); (part., of gait, melody, &c.) vigorously rhythmical (*at a long swinging trot*; *a swinging chorus*); go with swinging gait (*he swung out of the room*; *s. along, past, by*, &c.), whence **swi·nging**LY[2] adv.; *s. the lead* (nav. & mil. slang), malinger or scrimshank. (N.) act of swinging, oscillation, swinging movement, (*work is in full s.*, active; *the s. of the pendulum* fig., tendency to alternation, esp. tendency of electorate to put parties in power alternately); swinging gait or rhythm (*goes with a s.*); normal duration of activity (*let it have its s.*, have free course till it rests of itself like pendulum); seat slung by ropes or chains for swinging in (*ss. &* ROUND[3]-*abouts*), spell of swinging in this; compass to which thing swings (*has a s. of 3 ft*); *s.-boat*, boat-shaped carriage hung from frame for swinging in; *s. bridge*, that can be swung aside as a whole or in sections to let ships &c. pass; *s. plough*, without wheels. [OE *swingan*, cf. Sw. *svinga*, G *schwingen*]

swinge (-j), v.t. (swingeing). Strike hard, beat, (archaic exc. in *a swingeing blow* &c.); (part.) huge (*swingeing majority, lie, damages*; cf. *thumping, whopping*, &c.) [OE *swengan*, causal of prec.]

swi·ngle (-nggl), n., & v.t. Wooden instrument for beating flax & removing woody parts from it; swinging part of flail; *swi·ngletree*, crossbar pivoted in middle to ends of which traces are fastened in cart, plough, &c. (Vb) clean (flax) with s.; *swingling-tow*, coarse part of flax. [f. MDu. *swinghel*, as SWING, -LE(1)]

swink, v.i., & n., (archaic). Toil. [OE (*-nc, -ncan*), cogn. w. SWING]

swipe, v.i. & t., & n. Hit at or hit cricket-ball &c., hit (cricket-ball &c.), hard & recklessly, slog; hence **swi·per**[1] n. (N.) reckless hard hit or attempt to hit at cricket &c., slog. [var. of SWEEP]

swipes, n. pl. Washy or turbid or otherwise inferior beer. [f. prec. in obs. sense *drink off*]

swirl, v.i. & t., & n. Eddy, carry (object) or be carried with eddying motion; (n.) eddying motion of water, air, &c., commotion made by fish &c. rushing through water. [cf. Norw. *swirla* frequent. of *sverra* hum, whirl, & G *schwirren*]

swish, v.t. & i., & n. Flog with birch; audibly cut the air with (cane &c.), cut (flower &c.) *off* thus; make such audible cut *with* cane &c., (make, move with) sound as of cane or lash or swift bird cutting the air or of scythe cutting grass; a stroke of a birch or cane or lash. [imit.]

Swiss, a., & n. (pl. the same). (Native) of Switzerland (*S. French, German*, dialects of French & German spoken in Switzerland; *S. guards*, S. mercenaries formerly employed in France &c. & still at the Vatican; *S. roll*, kind of jam sandwich rolled up & baked). [f. F *Suisse* f. MHG *Swiz*]

switch, n., & v.t. & i. Flexible shoot cut from tree, tapering rod resembling this; tress of dead hair tied at one end used in hairdressing; kinds of mechanism for making & breaking connexion between corresponding parts of a system by which railway trains are diverted from one line to another, electric circuits completed or interrupted, &c.; *s.-back*, zigzag railway for ascending or descending steep slopes, also railway (chiefly used for amusement at fairs &c.) in which train's ascents are effected solely by momentum acquired in previous descents; *s.-bar*, part of railway or electric s.; *s.-board*, arrangement for varying the connexion between a number of electric circuits; *s.-lever*, handle & lever operating a s.; *s.-man*, in charge of railway ss.; *s.-signal*, flag or lantern or semaphore board indicating position of railway s. (Vb) whip with s.; swing (thing) round quickly, snatch suddenly, whisk, (*cow switches her tail*; *I switched my head round*; *he switched it out of my hand*); transfer (train, current) with s., (fig.) direct (thoughts, talk) to another subject; turn (electric light, current) *off* or *on*; put (user of telephone) *on* to or cut (him) *off* from another (*s. off* intr., cut off connexion). [cf. LG *zwukse* n., *zwuksen* vb to bend or swish]

Swi·tzer, n. (archaic). A Swiss. [MHG (G *Schweizer*, Du. *Zwitser*) f. *Switz* Switzerland, -ER[1]]

swi·vel (-vl), n., & v.i. & t. (-ll-). Ring & pivot serving as connexion between two parts of something & enabling one of them to revolve without the other (*s. chain, bookrest, gun, -hook, -joint, rowlock*, &c., provided with s.); *s.-eye(d)*, (with) squinting eye; (vb) turn (t. & i.) on s. [OE *swifan* see SWIFT, -LE(1)]

swob(ber), var. of SWAB(*ber*).

swollen, swoln (archaic), p.p. of SWELL.

swoon, v.i., & n. (Have) fainting-fit (*swooned for joy, with pain*, &c.); (of music &c.) die languidly away, whence **swoo·ning**LY² adv. [n. f. vb, ME *swoune* perh. back form. f. *swogning* n. f. *iswogen* p.p. = OE *geswógen* fainted (*swógan* to choke) + -ING¹]

swoop, v.i. & t., & n. Come down or *down* with the rush of a bird of prey, make sudden attack from a distance, (often *upon* prey, place, &c.); (colloq.) snatch, *up*, snatch, the whole of, at one s. (N.) sudden attack or downward plunge as of bird of prey; snatching action carrying off many things at once; *at one fell s.* (in describing completeness & extent & suddenness of catastrophe &c., see *Macb.* IV. iii. 219). [n. f. vb, OE *swápan* rush, cf. ON *sveipa*, G *schweifen* ramble; cogn. w. SWEEP, SWIPE]

swop, swap (-ŏp), v.t. & i., & n., (slang). Exchange (v.t. & i., & n.) by way of barter (*never s. horses while crossing the stream*, leave changes till crisis is past; *swopped my knife for bread*; *will you s. places* &c.?, or abs.; *shall we try a s.?*). [f. 14th c. in obs. sense *hit*, prob. imit.]

sword (sord), n. Offensive weapon consisting of long variously shaped blade for cutting or thrusting or both & hilt with hand-guard (BROADS.; *cavalry s.*, sabre; *court, dress, s.*, worn with court dress; *double-edged, two-handed,* &c., *s.*; *duelling, small-, s.*, kind with straight edgeless blade of triangular section used for thrusting only; SCUTCH*ing-s.*; *s. of State*, borne before sovereign on State occasions; *the s. of the spirit*, the word of God; *cross* or *measure ss.*, have fight or controversy or open rivalry, often *with*; *draw, sheathe, the s.*, begin, cease from, war; *throw* one's *s. into the scale*, back claim &c. with arms; *put to the s.*, kill, esp. of victors or captors; *fire & s.*, rapine, destruction spread by invading army; *the s. of justice*, judicial authority; *the s.*, war, the arbitrament of war, military power, sovereign power); (army slang) bayonet; *s.-arm*, right; *s.-bayonet*, kind with short s.-blade & hilt; *s.-bearer*, person carrying sovereign's or other great person's s. on some occasions; *s.-belt*, to which scabbard is attached; *s.-bill*, long-billed humming-bird; *s.-cane*, hollow walking-stick enclosing s.-blade; *s.-cut*, wound given with s.-edge, scar left by it; *s.-dance*, in which ss. are brandished, or women pass under men's crossed ss., or performer treads about ss. laid on ground; *s.-fish*, large Atlantic & Mediterranean kind with upper jaw elongated into sharp weapon capable of piercing other fish or ship's timbers; *s.-flag*, esp. yellow iris; *s.-flighted* of birds, having flight-feathers of separate colour & looking when closed like s. worn at side; *s.-grass*, gladiolus, kinds of sedge with s.-like leaves; *s.-guard*, part of s.-hilt that protects hand; *s.-hand*, right; *s.-knot*, ribbon or tassel attached to s.-hilt orig. for securing it to wrist; *s.-law*, military domination; *s.-lily*, gladiolus; *s.-play*, fencing, (fig.) repartee, cut-&-thrust argument; *swor·dsman*, person of (usu. specified) skill with s., whence **swo·rdsman**SHIP(3) n.; *s.-stick*, s.-cane. Hence **(-)sword**ED², **swo·rd**LESS, **swor·d**LIKE, **swor·d**PROOF², aa. [OE *sweord*, cf. Du. *zwaard*, G *schwert*, etym. dub.]

swore, sworn. See SWEAR.

swot, v.i. & t., & n., (school slang). Work hard esp. at books, sap; *s.* (subject) *up*, study it hurriedly. (N.) hard study; (thing that demands) effort, a sweat, (*it is too much s.*; *what a s.!*); person who works hard esp. at learning, a sap. [var. of SWEAT]

swum, swung. See SWIM, SWING.

sȳ-, = SYN- in Gk compds with wds in s- followed by consonant or in z- & their derivv.

Sȳ·barite, n. & a. Inhabitant of ancient-Greek colony of Sybaris in Italy noted for luxury; luxurious & effeminate (person). Hence **sybari·tic** a., **sy·barit**ISM(2) n., **sybari·tic**ALLY adv. [f. L (*-ta*) f. Gk *Subaritēs* (*Subaris*, -ITE¹)]

sȳ·bil, n. (Erron. for) SIBYL.

sȳ·camine, n. (bibl.). The black mulberry tree. [f. L f. Gk *sukaminos* mulberry-tree f. Heb. *shiqmah* sycamore]

sȳ·camore, n. (Also *s. fig* or *Egyptian* or *oriental s.*) kind of fig.-tree growing in Syria & Egypt; (also *s. maple*) large timber-tree allied to maple & plane. [f. OF *sicamore* f. L f. Gk *sukomoros* (*sukon* fig, *moron* mulberry)]

syce. See SICE².

sȳcee· (silver), n. Ingots of pure silver bearing banker's or assayer's seal & used in China for payments by weight. [f. Chin. *sí sz'* fine silk (as capable of being drawn out fine)]

sȳchnocar·pous (-k-), a. (bot.). Bearing fruit several times before dying, perennial. [Gk *sukhnos* numerous, *karpos* fruit, -OUS]

sȳcō·nium, n. (bot.; pl. *-ia*). Fleshy hollow receptacle developing into multiple fruit as in fig. [mod. L (Gk *sukon* fig)]

sȳ·cophant, n. Flatterer, toady, parasitic person. So **sy·coph**ANCY n., **sycopha·n**TIC a. [f. L (*-ta*) f. Gk *sukophantēs* informer, perh. f. *sukon* fig, *phainō* show (informing against export of figs or plunder of sacred fig-trees)]

sȳco·sis, n. Skin-disease of bearded part of face or scalp also called *barber's itch*. [f. Gk *sukōsis* figlike ulcer (*sukon* fig, -OSIS)]

sȳ·enite, n. Grey crystalline rock of feldspar & hornblende with or without quartz. Hence **syeni·tic** a. [F (*syé-*), f. L *Syenites* (*lapis* stone) of Syene in Egypt, see -ITE¹]

syl-, =SYN- in Gk compds w. words in l- & their derivatives.

sy·llabary, n. List of characters representing syllables & serving the purpose, in some languages or stages, of an alphabet. [L *syllaba* SYLLABLE, -ARY[1]]

sylla̋·bic, a. Of syllable(s) (often in comb., as *mono, di, tri, quadri, -s.*, having 1, 2, 3, 4, syllables); (of symbols) representing a whole syllable; articulated in syllables. Hence **sylla·bICALLY** adv. [f. Gk *sullabikos* (SYLLABLE, -IC)]

syllă·bicate, sylla·bifȳ, sy·llabize, vv.t. Divide into or articulate by syllables. Hence **syllăbicA·TION, syllabiFICA·TION**, nn. [Gk *sullabē* see foll., -IC, -ATE[3], -FY, -IZE]

sy·llable, n., & v.t. Unit of pronunciation forming a word or part of a word & containing one vowel sound & often consonant(s) preceding or following or preceding & following this; (transf.) so much as a word, the least amount of speech, (*not a s.!*, do not speak); hence **(-)syllablED**[2] a. (Vb) pronounce by ss., articulate distinctly; (poet.) utter (name, word). [f. OF *sillabe* f. L f. Gk *sullabē* (SYL-, *lambanō* take); for *-le* cf. PRINCIPLE, PARTICIPLE]

syllabub, var. of SILLABUB.

sy·llabus, n. (pl. *-bī*). Abstract giving heads or main subjects of a lecture, course of teaching, &c., conspectus or programme of hours of work &c.; (R.-C. Ch.) summary of points decided by an ecclesiastical decree, esp. catalogue of eighty heretical doctrines or practices or institutions condemned by Pius IX in 1864. [mod. L based on a prob. nonexistent Gk *sullabos*]

syllĕ·psis, n. (gram.; pl. *-psēs*). Application of a word to two others in different senses (e.g. *in a flood of tears & a sedan-chair*) or to two of which it grammatically suits one only (e.g. *neither you nor he knows*). So **syllĕ·ptIC** a., **sylle·ptICALLY** adv. [LL, f. Gk *sullēpsis* (*sullambanō* see SYLLABLE) comprehension]

sy·llogism, n. Form of reasoning in which from two given or assumed propositions called the premis(s)es & having a common or middle term a third is deduced called the conclusion from which the middle term is absent (FIGURE[1], MOOD[2], *of s.*; *false s.*, one whose conclusion does not necessarily follow from its premisses because it fails to fulfil the rules of logic regarding the nature & mutual relations of the major & minor & middle terms necessary if the inference is to be sound); (transf.) deductive reasoning as opp. induction. So **syllogi·stIC** a., **syllogi·stICALLY** adv. [f. OF *silogime* f. L f. Gk *sullogismos* f. *sullogizomai* (SYL-, *logizomai* to reason f. *logos* reason), -ISM]

sy·llogize, v.i. & t. Use syllogisms; throw (facts, argument) into syllogistic form. [f. med. L *syllogizare* f. Gk *sullogizomai* (prec.)]

sȳlph, n. Elemental spirit of the air (cf. *nymph, gnome, salamander*, of water, earth, fire) in Paracelsus's system, whence **sy·lphLIKE** a.; (transf.) slender girl; kinds of long-tailed humming-bird. [f. mod. L *sylphes* or G *sylphen* (pl.), prob. invented by Paracelsus]

sylvan. See SILVAN.

sȳm-, =SYN- in Gk compds with words in b-, m-, p-, as: *-bion(t)*, organism living in symbiosis [Gk *biōn -ountos* part. of *bioō* f. *bios* life]; *-bio·sis*, permanent union between organisms each of which depends for its existence on the other as the fungus & alga composing lichen [f. Gk as *symbion*, -OSIS], whence *-bio·tIC* a., *bio·tICALLY* adv.; *-pa·lmograph*, apparatus exhibiting sound-curves usu. by double pendulum with style attached [Gk *palmos* vibration f. *pallō* brandish]; *-pe·lmous*, (of bird) having tendons of toe-flexors united at a point [Gk *pelma* sole]; *-pe·talous*, having petals united; *-phy·llous*, with leaves united [Gk *phullon* leaf]; *-phȳsis*, growing together, (place or line of) union between two corresponding bones or other parts, coalescence, [Gk *phuō* grow], whence *symphy·seAL* a.; *-pĭĕso·meter*, instrument for measuring force of current of water, also barometer in which atmospheric pressure is balanced partly by column of liquid & partly by elastic pressure of confined gas [Gk *piesis* pressure f. *piezō* press]; *-pō·dium*, stem whose successive sections are strictly branches each springing from the preceding, as in the vine [Gk *pous podos* foot], so *sympo·diAL* a., *sympo·dialLY*[2] adv.

sy·mbol (-bl), n., & v.t. (-ll-). Thing regarded by general consent as naturally typifying or representing or recalling something by possession of analogous qualities or by association in fact or thought (*white, the lion, the thunderbolt, the cross, are ss. of purity, courage, Zeus, Christianity*; *values the handle to his name only as a s.*); mark or character taken as the conventional sign of some object or idea or process, e.g. the astronomical signs for the planets, the letters standing for chemical elements, letters of the alphabet, the mathematical signs for addition & infinity, the asterisk; hence or cogn. **symbŏ·lIC(AL)** aa., **symbo·lic-alLY**[2] adv., **symbo·lICS** n., **sy·mbolISM**(3), **sy·mbolIST**(3), nn. (esp. denoting certain recent schools of painters & of French poets), **sy·mbolIZE** v.t. (see vb), **symbolizA·TION, symb(ol)o·LOGY, symb(ol)o·LATRY**, nn. (Vb, rare, also & usu. *symbolize*): be the s. of; represent by means of s., speak of under a s.; (*-ize* only) treat (story &c.) as symbolic & not literal, import symbolism into. [f. F *symbole* f. LL f. Gk *sumbolos, -on*, token, watchword, f. *sumballō* (SYM-, *ballō* throw) agree]

symme·trian, symmetri·cian, sy·mmetrist, nn. (rare). Person insisting on symmetry. [-AN, -ICIAN, -IST]

sy·mmetry, n. (Beauty resulting from) right proportion between the parts of the body or any whole, balance, congruity, harmony, keeping; such structure as allows of an object's being divided by a point or line or plane or radiating lines or planes into two or more parts exactly similar in size & shape & in position relatively to the dividing point &c., repetition of exactly similar parts facing each other or a centre, whence (in art) **symmetroPHO·BIA** n.; approximation to such structure, possession by a whole of corresponding parts correspondingly placed, (Bot.) possession by flower of sepals & petals & stamens & pistils in (multiples of) the same number. Hence or cogn. **symmĕ·triC(AL)** aa., **symme·tricalLY**[2] adv., **sy·mmetrIZE**(3) v.t., **summetriZA·TION** n. [f. LL f. Gk *summetria* f. SYM(*metros* f. *metron* measure) commensurate, symmetric]

sympathĕ·tic, a. & n. Of, full of, exhibiting, expressing, due to, effecting, sympathy (*s. heart, person, conduct, words*; *s. landscape* &c., that touches the feelings by association &c.; *s. pain* &c., caused by pain or injury to some one else or in another part of the body; *s. sound, resonance, string,* sounding by vibration communicated through the air or other medium from vibrating object; *s. nerve,* any, esp. either of two extending the length of the vertebral column, of a system of nerves uniting viscera & blood-vessels in common nervous action; *s. ink,* writing done with which is invisible till brought out by warmth or other agency); (as Gallicism, & in critics' slang) capable of evoking sympathy, appealing *to* reader &c.; hence **sympathe·tICALLY** adv. (N.) s. nerve or system; person peculiarly sensitive to hypnotic or similar influence. [f. late Gk *sumpathētikos* (SYMPATHY, PATHETIC)]

sy·mpathize, v.i. Feel or express sympathy, share feeling or opinion *with* person &c., agree *with* sentiment. Hence **sy·mpathizER**[1] n. [f. F *sympathiser* (foll., -IZE)]

sy·mpathy, n. Being simultaneously affected with the same feeling, tendency to share or state of sharing another person's or thing's emotion or sensation or condition (*with*), mental participation in another's trouble (*with*), compassion (*for*), agreement in opinion or desire. [f. LL f. Gk *sumpatheia* f. SYM(*pathēs* f. *pathos* feeling) sympathetic]

sy·mphony, n. (Archaic) harmony, consonance of sounds, whence **symphō·niOUS** a. (rare); (Mus.) elaborate orchestral composition of several contrasted but closely related movements, (also) instrumental prelude, interlude, or close, to the accompaniment of a song. Hence **symphŏ·nIC** a. [f. OF *simphonie* f. L f. Gk *sumphōnia* f. SYM(*phōnos* f. *phōne* sound) harmonious]

sympŏ·siarch (-k), n. President of symposium, toast-master, feast-master. [f. Gk *sumposiarkhos* (foll., *-arkhos* -ruler f. *arkhō* rule)]

sympŏ·sium (-z-), n. (pl. *-ia*). Ancient-Greek after-dinner drinking-party with music, dancers, or conversation; any drinking-party; philosophical or other friendly discussion; set of contributions on one subject from various authors & points of view in magazine &c. Hence **sympo·siAL** a. [f. L f. Gk *sumposion* f. SYM(*pinō* drink, cf. *posis* drinking) drink together]

sy·mptom, n. Perceptible change in the body or its functions indicating disease (*subjective, objective, ss.,* directly perceptible only to patient, to others); sign or token of the existence of something. Hence or cogn. **symptomă·tIC** a., **symptoma·tICALLY** adv., **symptomato·LOGY** n. [f. F *symptome* f. L f. Gk *sumptōma -atos* chance, symptom, f. SYM(*piptō* fall, -M)]

sўn-, pref. (appearing also as SYL-, SYM-, *syr-* before r-, *sys-*, before s- not followed by consonant, & SY-; the Gk change of *sun- to sug-* before gutturals is disregarded in mod. derivatives) repr. Gk *sun* prep. & pref., with, together or alike, in wds derived directly f. Gk wds (*syncope*) or made f. Gk (*syngnathous*) or very rarely f. non-Gk (*synovial*) elements:—*syn(a)er·esis* (-nēr-), contraction of two vowels or syllables into one [Gk *haireō* take]; *-allagmă·tic,* (of treaty or contract) imposing reciprocal obligations [Gk *allassō* exchange]; *-al(o)e·pha* (-lē-), elision or obscuration of final before initial vowel [Gk *aleiphō* smear]; *-a·ntherous,* with stamens coalescent by the anthers; *-a·nthous,* with flowers & leaves appearing simultaneously [Gk *anthos* flower]; *-aphe(i)·a* (-ēa), continuity between lines or sections of lines in verse, allowing the ordinary rules of elision & quantity to operate with the final syllable [Gk *haptō* join]; *-arthro·sis* (pl. *-osēs*), immovable articulation, as in sutures of skull & socketing of teeth; *-carp,* aggregate or multiple fruit, e.g. blackberry, fig, so *-car·pous* a. [Gk *karpos* fruit]; *-chondro·sis,* (nearly) immovable articulation of bones by layer of cartilage, as in spinal vertebrae; *-cla·stic,* concave, or convex, all over (opp. *anticlastic,* partly concave & partly convex) [Gk *klaō* break]; *-cli·nal,* (of strata) dipping towards a common line or point (opp. *anticlinal,* dipping away);

-cotylē·donous, with cotyledons united; *-cretism*, attempt to sink differences & effect union between sects or philosophic schools, so *-crē·tic*, *-cretist*, *-creti·stic*, *-cretize* v.t. & i. [Gk *sugkrētizō* etym. dub., combine against common enemy]; *-cў·tium* (pl. *-ia*), mass of protoplasm with several nuclei but forming one cell [-CYTE]; *-da·ctyl(ous)* aa., with digits united as in webbed feet &c., so *-da·ctylism*; *-desmo·sis*, articulation by ligaments, so *-desmŏ·tic*, *-desmo·logy*, *-desmo·graphy* [Gk *desmos* bond f. *deō* bind]; *-dĕ·tic*, of, using, conjunctions [ASYNDETON]; *sy·ndrome* (-mĭ), concurrence of, set of concurrent, symptoms in disease; *-e·cdoche* (-kĭ), extended acceptation by which when a part is named the whole it belongs to is understood, as in *50 sail* (for *ships*) [Gk *ek* out, *dekhomai* accept]; *sў·nesis*, violation of grammatical rule due to influence exerted by the sense (as *neither of them* are *right*) [Gk *sunesis* understanding (*hiēmi* send)]; *-gĕ·nesis*, formation of embryo partly from the male & partly from the female element; *-gnathous*, (of fish) with jaws united into tubular snout; *-izē·sis* (pl. *-esēs*), pronunciation of two vowels not making a diphthong as one syllable [Gk *hizō* to seat]; *synoe·cious* (-nē-), having male & female organs in one inflorescence or receptacle, as in composite flowers & mosses [Gk *oikos* house]; *-osteo·logy*, science of the joints of the body; *-ost(e)o·sis*, anchylosis, so *-ostŏ·tic* a.; *-ō·via*, albuminous fluid secreted by membranes in interior of joints & in other places needing lubrication, so *syno·vial* a. [invented by Paracelsus from unknown elements]; *-tony*, the tuning or accommodation to each other of wireless-telegraphy apparatuses, so *-to·nic* a., *-tonize* v.t. [TONE].

sy·nagogue (-ŏg), n. Jewish congregation with organized religious observances & instruction, its place of meeting. Hence **synagŏ·gICAL** (-g-, -j-) a. [f. LL f. Gk *sunagōgē* (prec., *agōgē* bringing f. *agō* bring)]

sy·nchronize, v.i. & t. Occur at the same time, be simultaneous or **sy·nchronOUS** a. (whence **sy·nchronousLY**[2] adv.), (*with*); ascertain or set forth the correspondence in date of (events); cause (clocks) to show, (of clocks) show, a standard or uniform time. Hence or cogn. **sy·nchronISM**(1) or rarely **sy·nchronY**[1], **synchronizA·TION**, nn. [f. Gk *sugkhronizō* (SYN-, *khronos* time, -IZE)]

sy·ncopate, v.t. Shorten (word) by dropping interior letter(s) or syllable(s), as in *symbology* for *symbolology*, *Gloster* for *Gloucester*; (Mus.) invert rhythm of (note, tone) by beginning on unaccented & sustaining into accented beat. Hence **syncopA·TION** n. [L *syncopare* swoon (foll.), -ATE[3]]

sy·ncopĕ, n. (Gram.) syncopated spelling or pronunciation; (Med.) fainting, loss of consciousness from fall of blood-pressure, whence **syncŏ·p(t)IC** a.; (Mus.) syncopation, also such combination of voice-parts that two or more notes in one coincide with one in another. [f. Gk *sugkopē* (SYN-, *koptō* strike)]

sy·ndic, n. Official of kinds differing in different countries & times, (Camb. Univ.) member of special committee of senate. [F, f. LL f. Gk *sun(dikos* f. *dikē* justice) advocate]

sy·ndicalism, n. A movement among industrial workers having as its object the transfer of the means of production & distribution from their present owners to unions of workers, the method generally favoured for the accomplishment of this being the general strike. [f. F *syndicalisme* (*syndicat* trade union, SYNDICATE, -ISM]

sy·ndicate, n. (-*a*t), & v.t. (-āt). Body of syndics (esp. at Camb.); combination of commercial firms &c. associated to forward some common interest (vb, esp. in p.p., form into s., whence **syndicA·TION** n.). [vb f. n., f. F *syndicat* (prec., -ATE[1])]

syne, Sc. for *since* (*auld lang s.*, the days of long ago, esp. as title & refrain of song sung at parting &c.).

sў·nod, n. Ecclesiastical council (*oecumenical* or *general*, *national*, *provincial*, *diocesan*, *s.*, attended by bishop(s) & delegated clergy of all nations, a nation, a province, a diocese); (Presb.) ecclesiastical court above presbyteries & subject to General Assembly; any meeting for debate; (Astron.) conjunction of planets or stars. So **sy·nodAL**, **synŏ·dIC(AL)**, aa., **syno·dICALLY** adv. [f. LL f. Gk *sunodos* (SYN-, *hodos* way) meeting]

sy·nonym, n. Word identical & coextensive in sense & usage with another of the same language (as *caecitis*, cf. *typhlitis*); word denoting the same thing(s) as another but suitable to different context (as *leap*, *slay*, cf. *jump*, *kill*) or containing different suggestion (as *blind-worm*, cf. *slow-worm*); word equivalent to another in some only of either's senses (as *ship*, cf. *vessel*). Hence or cogn. **synony·mITY** n., **synŏ·nymOUS** a. (*with*), **syno·nymousLY**[2] adv. [f. LL f. Gk *sunōnumos* of like sense (SYN-, *onuma -atos* name)]

synonў·mic, a. Of or using synonyms. [prec., -IC]

syno·nymy, n. Synonymity; collocation of synonyms for emphasis (as *in any shape or form*); system or collection of, treatise on, synonyms. [f. LL f. Gk *sunōnumia* (SYNONYM, -Y[1])]

syno·psis, n. (pl. *-psēs*). Summary, conspectus. [f. LL f. Gk SYN(*opsis* seeing f. *op-* see)]

syno·ptic, a. & n. Affording a conspectus or general survey (*s. gospels*, those of

Matthew, Mark, & Luke); of the s. gospels; hence **syno·ptic**AL a., **syno·ptical**LY[2] adv. (N., also **syno·pt**IST) writer of a s. gospel. [f. Gk *sunoptikos* (prec., -IC)]

synta·ctic, a. & n. Of, according to, syntax; hence **synta·ct**ICALLY adv. (N., pl.) branch of mathematics relating to the number of ways of putting things together under conditions. [f. Gk *suntaktikos* (foll.)]

sy·ntax, n. Sentence-construction, the grammatical arrangement of words in speech or writing, set of rules governing this. [F (*-xe*), f. LL f. Gk *suntaxis* (SYN-, *tassō* order) marshalling, syntax]

sy·nthesis, n. (pl. *-thesēs*). Combination, composition, putting together, (opp. *analysis*); building up of separate elements esp. of conceptions or propositions or facts, into a connected whole, esp. a theory or system; (Chem.) artificial production of compounds (called ' synthetic rubber, indigo ', &c.) from their constituents as opp. extraction from plants &c.; (Gram.) making of compound & derivative words, preference of composition & inflexion to use of prepositions &c.; (Surg.) joining of divided parts. Hence or cogn. **synthĕ·t**IC(AL) aa., **synthe·t**ICALLY adv., **sy·nthes**IZE(1), **-tize,** vv.t., **sy·nthet**IST(1), **-sist,** nn. [L, f. Gk *sunthesis* (SYN-, *tithēmi* put); the irreg. *-thesize* more used than the correct *-thetize*]

sȳ·pher, v.t. Join (planks) with overlapping edges into flush surface; *s.-joint*, thus made. [var. of CIPHER in obs. sense]

sȳ·philis, n. Pox, an infectious venereal disease affecting first some local part (*primary s.*), secondly the skin & mucous membrane (*secondary s.*), & thirdly the bones & muscles & brain (*tertiary s.*). Hence **syphili·t**IC, **sy·phil**OUS, **sy·phil**OID, aa., **sy·phil**IZE(5) v.t., **syphilo·**LOGY n. [F, f. *Syphilus*, (character in) 16th-c. Latin poem on the subject]

syphon, syren, erron. for **si-.**

Sȳ·riac, n. & a. (In) the language of ancient Syria, western Aramaic. Hence **Sy·riac**ISM(4) n. [f. L f. Gk *Suriakos* (*Suria* Syria f. *Suros* a Syrian, -AC)]

Sy·rian, a. & n. (Native) of Syria. [*Syria*, -AN]

sȳri·nga (-ngg*a*), n. The mock orange, a shrub with strong-scented white usu. clustered flowers. [SYRINX (w. ref. to use of stems cleared of pith as pipe-sticks),-A]

sy·ringe (-j), n., & v.t. Cylindrical tube with nozzle & piston into which liquid is first drawn by suction & then ejected in fine stream used in surgery, gardening, &c., squirt, (*hypodermic s.*, needle-pointed for hypodermic injections); hence **syringe**FUL(2) n. (Vb) sluice or spray (ears, plants, &c.) with s. [f. med. L *siringa* f. Gk as foll.]

sȳ·rinx, n. (pl. *-es, -ngēs*). Pan-pipe; (Archaeol.) narrow rock-cut gallery in Egyptian tombs; (Anat.) Eustachian tube from throat to drum of ear supplying latter with air, whence **syringi·**TIS n.; lower larynx or song-organ of birds, whence **syri·nge**AL a.; (Surg.) fistula, whence **syringo·**TOMY n. [L, f. Gk *surigx* pipe]

Sȳro-, comb. form f. Gk *Suros* Syrian, as *-ara·bian, -phoeni·cian.* [-O-]

syr·tis, n. (pl. *-tēs*). Quicksand. [L, f. Gk *surtis* (*surō* draw)]

sȳ·rup, si-, n. Water (nearly) saturated with sugar, this combined with flavouring as beverage or with drug(s) as medicine; condensed sugarcane-juice, part of this remaining uncrystallized at various stages of refining, molasses, treacle, (*golden s.*, trade name for pale kind). Hence **sy·rup**Y[2] a. [f. OF *sirop* f. Arab. *sharāb* beverage, cf. SHERBET]

syssarco·sis, n. Connexion between bones by intervening muscle. [f. Gk *sussarkōsis* (SYN-, *sarkoō* f. *sarx sarkos* flesh, -OSIS)]

syssī·tia, n. pl. (Gk ant.). Public messes of Spartans & some other Dorians at which citizens were required to feed with a view to the promotion of patriotism, military efficiency, discipline, & simplicity. [Gk (*su-*) pl. of *sussition* (SYN-, *sitos* food)]

systa·ltic, a. Contracting & dilating by turns, having systole & diastole, pulsatory. [f. LL f. Gk *sustaltikos* (SY-, *stellō* place, -IC)]

sy·stem, n. Complex whole, set of connected things or parts, organized body of material or immaterial things, (*s. of pulleys*, several arranged to work together; *s. of philosophy*, set of coordinated doctrines; *mountain s.*, range or connected ranges; *river, railway, s.*, river, railway, with its tributaries or branches, also rivers, railways, of a country, continent, &c.; *solar s.*, sun & planets; *nervous, muscular,* &c., *s.*, the nerves, muscles, of a person's or animal's body; *digestive* &c. *s.*, all bodily parts subserving digestion &c.; *the s.*, the body as a functional whole, as *the poison has passed into the* or *his s.*; *Ptolemaic* &c. *s.*, set of hypotheses or principles composing Ptolemy's &c. theory; *Devonian* &c. *s.*, set of strata &c. so named); method, organization, considered principles of procedure, (principle of) classification, (*s. of government*; *what s. do you go on?*; *lacks, works with, s.*; *Linnaean, natural,* &c., *s.*, classifications with different criteria), whence **sy·stem**LESS a.; (Mus.) braced staffs of score. [f. LL f. Gk *sustēma -atos* (SY-, *histēmi* set, -M)]

systemă·tic, a. Methodical, according to a plan, not casual or sporadic or unintentional, (*s. worker, liar, insolence, nomenclature*). Hence or cogn. **systema·t**ICALLY

adv., **sy·stematize**(3) v.t., **sy·stematism** (1), **sy·stematist**(1), **sy·stematizer**[1], **systematiza·tion**, nn. [f. LL f. late Gk *sustēmatikos* (prec., -IC)]
systĕ·mic, a. (physiol.). Of the bodily system as a whole, not confined to a particular part. Hence **syste·mically** adv. [-IC]
sy·stolĕ, n. (physiol.). Contraction of heart &c. alternate with DIASTOLE. Hence **systŏ·lic** a. [f. Gk *sustolē* (*sustellō*, see SYSTALTIC)]
sy·style, a. With columns set comparatively close together. [f. L f. Gk SY(*stulos* STYLE[2])]
sy·stȳlous, a. (bot.). With styles united. [as prec., -OUS]
sȳ·zygy, n. (astron.). Conjunction or opposition. [f. LL f. Gk *suzugia* f. *suzeugnumi* (SY-, *zeugnumi* f. *zugon* yoke)]

T

T, t, (tē), letter (pl. *Ts*, T's). T-shaped thing, esp. attrib., as *T-bandage, -bar, -bolt, -joint, -pipe*, -SQUARE; *suits me, hit it off*, &c., *to a T*, exactly, to a nicety; *cross the T's*, (fig.) be minutely accurate, also, emphasize a point.

Abbreviations (1): T., tank, **T.C.**(orps); territorial, **T.F.**(orce); Thames, **T.R.C.** (rowing club); their, **T.R.H., T.S.H.**, (Royal, Serene, Highnesses); torpedo, **T.B., T.B.D.**, (boat, destroyer); trade, **T.U.C.** (union congress); Trinity, **T.C.D.** (College, Dublin); turn, **T.O.** (over). t., taken, **t. & o.** (offered).

Abbreviations (2): TEMP.; **Tenn.**(essee); **Tex.**(as); **Thess.**(alonians), **Tim.**(othy), **Tit.**(us), N.-T. books; **Thos**, Thomas; **TNT**, trinitrotoluene; **Toc H** (see in dict. place); **trs.**, transpose; **Truron.**, bp of Truro.

ta (tah), sentence & n. (nursery, colloq.). Thank you, as *ta muchly, must say ta*. [?]
taal (tahl), n. *The t.*, Cape Dutch patois. [Du., = language, cogn. w. TALE]
tab, n. Small flap, strip, tag, or tongue, as part of or appendage to garment &c., e.g. metallic binding at end of boot-lace, (also *ear-t.*) flap at side of cap to protect ear; (Mil.) mark on collar distinguishing staff-officer. [?]
tă·bard, n. (Hist.) coarse outer garment worn by the poor, knight's garment worn over armour; herald's coat blazoned with arms of sovereign. [OF, etym. dub.]
tă·baret, n. Upholstery fabric of alternate satin & watered-silk stripes. [mod. trade wd, perh. f. TABBY]
tăbasheer·, -shir (-ēr), n. Kind of opal found in joints of bamboo & used in E.-Ind. medicine. [Hind. & Arab. (-*ir*)]
ta·bby, n., & v.t. Watered fabric esp. silk (often attrib.); (also *t. cat*) brindled or mottled or streaked cat, esp. of grey or brownish colour with dark stripes; cat, esp. female; gossiping woman esp. old maid; (also *t. moth*) kinds of moth; kind of concrete; (vb) give wavy appearance to (fabric). [(vb f. n.) f. F *tabis* f. Arab. *'attābiy* a quarter of Bagdad; some senses perh. f. *Tabitha*]
tăbĕfa·ction, n. Emaciation due to disease. [f. LL *tabefacere* (*tabēre* f. TABES, see -FACTION)]
tă·berdar, n. Scholar of Queen's College, Oxford. [= *tabarder* (TABARD + -ER[1]), from former dress]
tă·bernăcle, n., & v.t. & i. (Bibl.) fixed or movable habitation usu. of slight construction, (fig.) human body; *Feast of Tt.*, Jewish autumn festival commemorating the dwelling of the Jews in wilderness; (Jewish Hist.) tent used as sanctuary before final settlement of Jews in Palestine; (often contempt.) place of public worship; receptacle for pyx or eucharistic elements; (Archit.) canopied stall, niche, or pinnacle, *t.-work*, series, tracery characteristic, of such tt., whence **ta·bernacled**[2] a.; socket or double post for hinged mast that requires lowering to pass under bridges; (vb, fig.) provide with shelter, dwell temporarily. So **tabernă·cular**[2] a. [(vb f. n.) F, f. L *tabernaculum* tent (*taberna* hut, see -CULE)]
tā·bēs (-z), n. (med.). Emaciation; *dorsal t.*, wasting disease of spinal cord, locomotor ataxia. [L]
tabĕ·tic, a. & n. Of, affected with, (esp. dorsal) tabes; (n.) t. patient. So **tabe·scence, tă·bitude**, nn., **tabe·scent, tă·bic, tă·bid**[1], aa., **ta·bidly**[2] adv. [irreg. f. prec. + -*t*- + -IC]
tă·binet, n. Watered fabric of silk & wool. [as TABARET]
tă·blature (-tsher), n. (archaic). Mental picture; graphic description. [F (as see foll., -URE)]
tā·ble, n., & v.t. Article of furniture consisting of flat top of wood or marble &c. & one or more usu. vertical supports esp. one on which meals are laid out, articles of use or ornament kept, work done, or games played; *breakfast, luncheon, dinner, tea, supper, -t.*, t. used for such meals or on which such meal is laid out (*at t.*, while taking meal at t., as *refused to talk politics at t.*; *under the t.*, esp. drunk after dinner); each half of folding backgammon-t.; *billiard-t.* (for billiards, with slate top covered with green cloth); LORD'S, ROUND[1], KNEE[1]-*hole*, DRESSING-, TOILET-, *t.*; part of machine-tool on which work is put to be operated on; slab of wood, stone, &c.; matter written on this, esp. *the two tt.* or *the tt. of the law* or *covenant* or *testimony*, ten commandments, *the twelve tables*, laws promulgated in Rome 451–0 B.C., principal source of Roman jurisprudence; level area, plateau; (Archit.) flat usu. rectangular surface, horizontal moulding esp. cornice; flat surface of

gem, cut gem with two flat faces; (Palmistry) palm, esp. part indicating character or fortune; each of two bony layers of skull; company seated at (dinner- &c.) t., as *kept the t. amused*; (quantity & quality of) food provided at t., as *keeps a good t., expenses of his t.*; list of facts, numbers, &c., systematically arranged esp. in columns, matter contained in this, as *mathematical tt.* (of logarithms, trigonometrical ratios, &c.), *tt. of weights & measures, knows his multiplication t. up to 12 times 12, t. of* (i.e. *prohibited*) DEGREES, *t. of* CONTENT[1]*s*; *lay, lie, on the t.*, postpone (measure, report, &c., in Parliament &c.), be postponed, indefinitely; *turn the tt.* (*on* person or abs.), reverse relations (between), esp. pass from inferior to superior position [f. backgammon sense of *tt.*]; *t.-beer*, ordinary beer used at t.; *t.-book*, ornamental usu. illustrated book kept on t.; *t.-clamp* (for fastening thing to t.); *t.-cloth* (of white linen &c. for use at meals, of coloured material for use at other times); *t.-cut*, (of gem) cut with flat top; *t.-flap*, hinged end of t.-top, lowered when not in use; *t.-knife*, steel knife for use at t.; *t.-land*, extensive elevated region with level surface, plateau; *t.-leaf*, piece that may be inserted in top of t. to increase its length, also, t.-flap; *t.-lifting, -moving, -rapping, -tipping, -turning*, lifting &c. of t. apparently without physical force, as spiritualistic phenomenon; *t.-linen*, t.-cloths, napkins, &c.; *t.-money*, allowance to higher officers in army & navy for official hospitality, charge to members of club for use of dining-room; *t.*-SPOON; *t.-talk*, miscellaneous talk at t. (often as title of book); *t.-tomb*, flat-topped chest-like tomb in Roman catacombs; *t.-ware* (for use at t.); *t.-water*, mineral water bottled for use at t. Hence **ta·ble**FUL n. (Vb) lay (measure &c., as above) on the t.; set (timbers) together with alternate grooves & projections in each to prevent shifting; strengthen (sail) with wide hems. Hence **ta·bl**ING[1](1, 2) n. [(vb partly f. OF *tabler*) F, f. L *tabula* board, tablet, &c.]

tă·bleau (-lō), n. (pl. *-eaux* pr. -ōz). Picturesque presentation, esp. (also *t. vivant*, F, lit. living picture) silent & motionless group of persons &c. arranged to represent a scene; dramatic or effective situation suddenly brought about; (as int., after description of incident) picture the scene!; *t. curtains* (theatr.), pair of curtains to draw across & meet in the middle of the stage in place of the usual drop-curtain. [F, = picture, dim. of prec.]

table d'hôte (tahbldō·t), n. Common table for guests at hotel; *t. dinner* &c. (served in hotel &c. at fixed hour & price). [F, = host's table]

tă·blet, n. Thin sheet of ivory, wood, &c., for writing on, esp. each of a set fastened together; (usu. pl.) such set; small slab esp. with or for inscription, as *votive t.*; small flat piece of prepared substance, esp. (also **ta·bl**OID n., proprietary name) fixed weight or measure of a drug brought by pressure or addition of gum into convenient shape; (also *table·tte*) projecting horizontal coping of wall. [f. OF *tablete* (TABLE, -ETTE)]

tablier· (-ā), n. Woman's small apron or apron-like part of dress. [F]

tabōō·, n., a., & v.t. (Among Polynesians &c.) system, act, of setting apart person or thing as accursed or sacred; ban, prohibition; (adj.) under a ban, prohibited, consecrated; (vb) put (thing, practice, &c.) under t., exclude or prohibit by authority or social influence, as *the subject was tabooed.* [(vb f. n.) f. Polynes. *tapu* a. & n.]

tā·bor, n. (hist.). Small drum, esp. one used to accompany pipe. [f. OF *tabour* perh. f. Arab., cf. TAMBOUR]

tă·bouret (-berĭt), n. Small seat usu. without arms or back, stool; embroidery-frame. [OF, = stool, dim. as prec.]

tă·būla, n. (pl. *-ae*). (Anat.) hard flat surface of bone &c.; *t. rasa*, erased tablet, fig. human mind at birth viewed as having no innate ideas. [L, = board, table, pl. tablets]

tă·bular, a. Of, arranged in, computed &c. by means of, tables, as *a t. statement, t. values, results, computations, arranged in t. form, t. difference* (between successive logarithms &c. in mathematical tables); broad & flat like a table, as *t. surface*; (formed) in thin plates, as *t. structure.* Hence **ta·bular**LY[2] adv. [f. L *tabularis* (prec., see -AR[1])]

tă·bulate, v.t., & a. Arrange (figures, facts) in tabular form, whence **tabul**A·TION, **ta·bulat**OR[2], nn.; give flat surface to; (adj.) having flat surface, composed of thin plate. [f. TABULA + -ATE[2, 3]]

tă·camahăc, n. Gum resin from some S.-Amer. & other trees; the balsam poplar. [Sp. (*-ca*), f. Aztec *tecomahiyac*]

tă·c-au-tă·c (-ō-), n. (fencing). Parry combined with riposte; rapid succession of attacks & parries. [F, imit.]

tă·cē, v.i. imperat. Be silent (*t. is Latin for a candle*, veiled injunction = MUM[1]). [L]

tă·cĕt, mus. direction indicating silence of voice or instrument. [L, = is silent]

tach (tătsh), n. (bibl.). A clasp, link. [see TACK]

tachŏ·meter (-k-), n. Instrument for measuring velocity. So **tacho·**METRY n. [f. Gk *takhos* speed + -METER]

tăchycar·dia (-kĭ-), n. (path.). Abnormally rapid heart-action as a disease. [f. Gk as foll., & see CARDIAC]

tachy̆·graphy (-k-), n. Stenography, esp. that of ancient Greeks & Romans. Hence

tachy·grapher[1] n., **tachygră·phic(al)** aa. [f. Gk *takhus* swift + -GRAPHY]
tă·chylyte, n. A vitreous form of basalt. Hence **tachylў·tic** a. [as prec. + *-lutos* f. *luō* loose, from ready fusion under blowpipe]
tachy·meter, n. Surveyor's instrument for rapid location of points. [as prec. + -METER]
tă·cit, a. Understood, implied, existing, without being stated, as *t. consent, agreement, understanding*; abstaining from speech or action (*t. spectator*). Hence **ta·citly**[2] adv. [f. L *tacitus* silent (*tacēre* be silent)]
ta·citurn, a. Reserved in speech, not given to much speaking. So **tacitur·nity** n. [f. L *taciturnus* as prec.]
tack, n., & v.t. & i. Small sharp flat-headed nail of iron, copper, &c., for securing carpet &c. (*tin-t.*, iron t. coated with tin; BRASS *tt.*); (pl.) long stitches as temporary fastening in needlework; (Naut.) rope for securing corner of some sails, corner to which this is fastened, direction in which vessel moves as determined by position of sails (*port, starboard, t.*, with wind on port, starboard, side), temporary change of direction in sailing to take advantage of side wind &c., esp. each of several alternate movements to port & starboard (*t. & t.*, by successive tt.); (fig.) course of action or policy, as *must change our t., am on the right* or *wrong t., try another t.*; = foll. (parl. sense); sticky condition of varnish &c., whence **ta·ckiness** n., **ta·cky**[2] a.; [prob. diff. wd] food, fare, esp. HARD *t.*, *soft t.*, bread, good fare; *t.-driver*, machine that automatically places & drives tt.; *t.-hammer*, light hammer for driving tt., usu. with claw for extracting tt. (Vb) fasten (carpet &c., often *down*) with tt., stitch (pieces or parts of cloth &c.) lightly together, (fig.) annex, append, (thing *to* or *on to* another, esp. as in foll.); change ship's course (often *about*) by shifting tt. & sails (cf. WEAR[3]), (fig.) change one's conduct, policy, &c. Hence **ta·cker**[1](1, 2) n. [(vb f. n.) doublet of TACH (*Exod.* xxvi. 6) f. OF *tache* clasp, nail, cf. ATTACH, & G *zacken* prong, Du. *tak* twig]
ta·cking, n. In vbl senses, esp.: (Law) priority of a third or subsequent mortgage &c. to a second of which notice was not given; (Parl.) appending of an extraneous clause to a money bill to secure its passing H. of Lords, which cannot amend money bills. [-ING[1]]
ta·ckle, n., & v.t. & i. Mechanism esp. of ropes, pulley-blocks, hooks, &c., for lifting weights, managing sails or spars, &c. (*naut. pr.* tā·kl); windlass with its ropes & hooks; requisites for a task or sport, as *fishing-t.*; grasping or holding esp. of opponent in football; *t.-block*, pulley over which rope runs; *t.-fall*, rope connecting blocks of a t. (Vb) grapple with, grasp with endeavour to hold or manage or overcome, (opponent, awkward thing or business, problem); (Footb.) seize & stop (player running with ball); secure by means of t.; *t. to* (colloq.), fall to work vigorously, set to. Hence **ta·ckling**[1](1, 3, 6) n. [(vb f. n.) ME & LG *takel* f. MLG *taken* lay hold of, cogn. w. TAKE]
tact, n. Intuitive perception of what is fitting esp. of the right thing to do or say, adroitness in dealing with persons or circumstances, whence **ta·ctful, ta·ctless,** aa., **ta·ctfully**[2] adv., **ta·ctlessness** n.; (Mus.) stroke in beating time. [f. L *tactus -ūs* (sense of) touch (*tangere tact-* touch)]
ta·ctical, a. Of tactics; adroitly planning or planned. Hence **ta·ctically**[2] adv. [f. Gk *taktikos* (foll.) + -AL]
ta·ctics, n. (As sing. or pl.) art of disposing military or naval forces esp. (cf. STRATEGY, LOGISTICS) in actual contact with enemy; (pl.) procedure calculated to gain some end, skilful device(s), as *cannot approve these t.* Hence **tacti·cian** n. [f. Gk *taktika* neut. pl. (*tassō* arrange, see -IC)]
ta·ctile, a. Of, perceived by, connected with, the sense of touch, as *t. impression, organ*, so **ta·ctual** a., **ta·ctually**[2] adv.; tangible; (Paint.) producing or having to do with the effect of solidity (*t. values* &c.). Hence **tacti·lity** n. [f. L *tactilis* (*tangere tact-* touch, see -ILE)]
ta·dpole, n. Larva of batrachian e.g. frog from time it leaves egg till loss of gills & tail; *t.-fish*, European fish with large flat head. [ME *tadpolle* (TOAD + POLL[1], f. size of head)]
tae·dium vī·tae, n. (path.). Weariness of life with tendency to suicide. [L]
tael (tāl), n. Chinese ounce (= $1\frac{1}{3}$ oz avoirdupois) esp. of silver as monetary unit. [Port., f. Malay *tahil* weight]
tae·nia, n. (pl. *-ae*). (Archit.) fillet on top of Doric epistyle; (Anat.) ribbon-like part esp. of brain; roller bandage; tapeworm; (Gk & Rom. Ant.) fillet, head-band. Hence **tae·nioid** a. [L, f. Gk *tainia*]
tă·ffeta, n. Kinds of silk or linen fabric esp. thin glossy silk of plain texture. [f. F *taffetas* f. Pers. *tāftah* (*tāftan* twist)]
tă·ffrail, ta·fferel, n. Rail round stern of vessel; (*-erel*) upper part of stern. [f. Du. *tafereel* dim. of *tafel* f. L as TABLE, assim. to RAIL[1]]
Tă·ffy[1], n. (colloq.). Welshman. [W pronunc. of *Davy* = *David*]
taffy[2]. See TOFFEE.
tă·fia, n. (W. Ind.). Kind of rum distilled from molasses &c. [native]
tag, n., & v.t. Metal point at end of lace; loop at back of boot used in pulling it on; address label, esp. one for tying on; loose or ragged end of anything; ragged

lock of wool on sheep; appendage; (Theatr.) closing speech addressed to audience; trite quotation, stock phrase, refrain of song; (tip of) animal's tail; [perh. diff. wd] children's game in which one chases the rest (*cross-*, *long*, &c., *t.*, forms of this); *t.-rag*, = RAG[1]*t.*; *t.-sore*, pustular disease of sheep; *ta·gtail*, kind of worm, sycophant. (Vb) furnish (lace &c., literary composition) with a t.; join (thing, esp. piece of writing, *to* or *on to* another, things *together*), find rhymes for (verses), string (rhymes) together; shear away tt. from (sheep); (colloq.) follow closely or persistently; touch (person pursued) in game of t. [(vb f. n.) f. 14th c., etym. dub.]

tā·getēs (-j-), n. Kinds of plant of aster family with showy yellow or orange flowers. [f. L *Tages*, Etruscan divinity]

ta·gger, n. In vbl senses; also or esp.: pursuer (also called *it*) in game of tag; (pl.) thin sheet iron, whether coated with tin or (*black tt.*) not. [-ER[1]]

tail[1], n., & v.t. & i. Hindmost part of animal esp. when prolonged beyond rest of body, as *dog* WAG[1]*s his t.*, *tail* WAG[1]*s dog*, *dog has his t. between his legs* (as sign of alarm or dejection; often fig. of person), *turn t.*, turn one's back, run away, *twist the* LION'*s t.*, *drop pinch of* SALT *on t. of*, PASHA *of three* &c. *tt.*; thing like or suggesting t. in shape or position, hind or lower or subordinate or inferior part, slender part or prolongation, as *t.* (luminous train) *of comet*, *t.* (outer corner) *of the eye*, *t.* (*end*) *of procession* &c., *t.* (weaker members) *of the XI* (or other sports team), *t. margin* (at foot of page), *followed by a t.* (long train) *of attendants*, *at the t.* (back) *of a cart*, *t.* (string & paper appendage at lower end) *of a kite*, *cow's-t.*, frayed end of rope &c., *t.* (=STEM[1]) *of musical note*, *t.* (part below line) *of a* g &c., *t.* (exposed end) *of slate* or *tile* in roof, *t.* (unexposed end) *of brick* or *stone* in wall, *t.* (slender backward prolongation) *of butterfly's wing*, *t.* (comparative calm at end) *of a gale*, *t.* (calm stretch following rough water) *of a stream*, *t. of the trenches* (fortif.), part first made by advancing party, *make* HEAD[1] *or t. of*, PIGTAIL; (pl.) =*t.-coat*, as *boys go into tt. at sixteen*; (tossing) *t.* or usu. *tt.*, reverse of coin turned upwards (see HEAD); *t.-bay*, part of canal lock between t.-gate & lower pond; *t.-board*, hinged or removable back of cart; *t.-braid* (for protecting hem of skirt); *t. coat*, man's morning or evening coat with long skirt divided at back into tt. & cut away in front; *t.-gate*, lower gate of canal lock; *t.-light* (carried at back of train, car, cycle, &c.); *t.-piece*, decoration in blank space at end of chapter &c., triangular piece of wood to which lower ends of strings are fastened in some musical instruments; *t.-pipe*, suction-pipe of pump, (v.t.) fasten something to t. of (dog, fig. person); *t.-race*, part of mill-race below water-wheel. Hence **(-)tail**ED[2], **tai·l**LESS, aa. (Vb) furnish with t.; (colloq.) remove the ends of (fruit); join (thing *on to* another); *t. after*, follow closely; *t. away* or *off*, (of persons, dogs, &c.) fall behind or away in scattered line; *t. in*, fasten (timber) by one end into wall &c.; *t. to the tide*, *t. up and down stream*, (of anchored vessel) swing up & down with tide. [(vb f. n.) OE *tæg(e)l*, cf. ON *tagl*, Sw. *tagel*, dial. G *zagel*]

tail[2], n. & a. (law). Limited ownership (*in t.*, on those terms); estate limited to a person & heirs of his body; (adj.) so limited, esp. *estate t.*, FEE-*t.* [f. OF *taille* notch, cut, tax, f. *taillier* cut f. LL *taliare* (L *talea* slip of wood)]

tai·ling, n. In vbl senses of TAIL[1]; also or esp.: unexposed end of brick or stone or beam in wall; (pl.) refuse or inferior part of grain, ore, &c.; blur or other fault in calico-printing. [-ING[1]]

tai·lor, n., & v.i. & t. Maker of (esp. men's) garments esp. to order (*the t. makes the man*; *nine tt. go to a man*; *ride like a t.*, badly); *t.-bird*, kinds of small bird sewing leaves together to form nest; *t.-made*, (esp. of woman's dress) made by t. usu. w. little ornament & w. special attention to exact fit; *tailor's chair* (without legs), for sitting cross-legged as t. at work; *tailor's cramp* (in fingers & thumbs); *tailor's twist*, kind of strong silk thread; (slang) kill (bird) badly. Hence **tai·lor**ESS[1] n. (Vb) be, work as, a t., whence **tai·lor**ING[1] n.; make clothes for (chiefly in p.p., as *well-tailored*). [f. OF *taillour* f. LL *taliatorem* (*taliare* TAIL[2], -OR[2])]

tain, n. Thin tin plate; tin foil for backing mirror. [F, = *étain* tin]

taint, n., & v.t. & i. Spot, trace, of decay or corruption or disease (lit. & fig.), corrupt condition, infection, as *there was a t. of insanity in the family*, *the moral t. had spread among all classes*, *without t. of commercialism*; (vb) introduce corruption or disease into, infect, be infected, as *tainted meat*, *taints all it touches*, *meat will t. readily in hot weather*, *his mind was tainted*; *tainted goods* (in trade-unionism), goods that members of a union must not handle because non-union labour has been employed on them or for similar reasons. Hence **tai·nt**LESS a., **tai·ntless**-LY[2] adv. [f. F *teint* n. & p.p. of *teindre* TINGE; partly also aphetic f. ATTAINT]

Tai·-pi·ng, Tae-, (tī-), n. One of those who took part in a rebellion in China (1850–64). [f. Chin. *t'ai p'ing* great peace]

taj (tahj), n. Tall cap of Mohammedan dervish. [Pers. f. Arab.]

take[1], v.t. & i. (to͝ok, taken). Lay hold of with the hand(s) or other part of the body or with any instrument (lit. & fig.), grasp, seize, capture, catch by pursuit or surprise, captivate, win, gain, as *t. it between your finger & thumb, took him by the throat, t. it up with the tongs, t. the* BULL¹ *by the horns, deuce t. it !, t.* BIT¹ *between teeth, t. a fortress, t. by* STORM, *took 113 prisoners, was taken prisoner* or *captive, took his bishop* (at chess), *t. the odd trick* (at cards), *takes* (gains, receives in payment) *£40 a week, took* (gained) *little by this move, took first prize, t. the* CAKE or *biscuit* (slang), *rabbit taken in trap, took* (surprised, caught) *him in the act* or *at a disadvantage, was taken ill* or colloq. *bad, taken aback, what takes* (captivates) *my fancy, was much taken* (charmed) *with* or *by her manners, novel did not t.* (become popular), *vaccine did not t.* (operate); assume possession of, procure e.g. by purchase, acquire, avail oneself of, use, use up, consume, require as instrument, material, agent, &c., as *takes whatever he can lay his hand on, wish you would not t. my bicycle, t.* (assume or enjoy as one's right) *precedence, took his degree, t.* ORDER¹s, *t.* SILK, *shall t. a holiday,* (cooking direction) *t. 1 oz of curry-powder, do you t.* (buy regularly, subscribe to) *Punch ?, am not taking any* (slang), decline offer, *took* (engaged) *seats in advance, must t. lessons, lodgings, a cab, will t.* (buy) *2 lb., t. legal, medical, &c., advice,* consult lawyer &c. (& see below), *t.* (as instance) *the French Revolution, has taken a partner, a wife,* (archaic) *took to* (as) *wife Jane Smith, t. a* BACK¹ *seat, took his seat on the railing, must t. the liberty of differing from you, must t. leave to differ, took a mean advantage, do not t. advantage* (avail yourself unfairly) *of his youth, t. the opportunity, will t.* (drink) *a cup of tea, takes too much alcohol, these things t. time, t. your time,* do not hurry, *it takes a lot of doing* (is hard to do), *takes a poet to translate Virgil, transitive verbs t. an object*; cause to come with one, carry with one, conduct, convey, remove, dispossess person &c. of, as *t. the letters to the post, the dog for a walk, the children to the pantomime, the corkscrew from the shelf, takes his readers with him* (engrosses their attention), *t. him through* (make him read) *a book of Livy,* took him *into partnership, takes all the fun out of it, t. to* TASK, *t. in hand,* undertake, start doing or dealing with, undertake the control or reform of (*the boy wants taking i. h.*), (see also special uses w. advv. & prepp.): catch, be infected with, (cold, fever, &c.); conceive, experience, indulge, give play to, exert, as *t. offence, umbrage, t. a fancy to, takes a pride in his work, a pleasure in contradicting, t. pity on him, t. no notice, t. heed, pains, trouble*; ascertain (person's measure, height, temperature, address, &c.) by inquiry, measurement, &c.; apprehend, grasp mentally, infer, conclude, understand, interpret, as *I t. your meaning* or (archaic) *you, I t. this to be ironical, I t. it that we are to wait here, t.* person *at his* WORD¹, *how would you t.* (translate, interpret) *this passage ?, t. it for granted,* assume it, *do you t. me for* (think me) *a fool ?*; treat or regard in specified manner, adopt specified attitude towards, as *t. things coolly, t. it easy, should t. it kindly of you* (be obliged) *if you would answer my letter, must not t. it ill of him* (resent his conduct), *t. to* HEART, *t. as read,* dispense with the actual reading of (minutes &c.); accept, put up with, submit to, adopt, choose, receive, derive, as *t. the offer, t. what you can get, the bet was taken, taken & offered* (abbr. *t. & o.*, phr. used in recording betting odds), *I took him* (his bet), *must t. us as you find us, will take no nonsense, will not t. this treatment, took it like a lamb, will not t. a hint, t. advice,* act on it (& see above), *you may t. it from me* or *t. my word for it,* I, a well-informed person, assure you, *t. sides,* join one of two parties, *t.* (hold, adopt) *a different view, takes its name from the inventor*; perform, execute, make, undertake, negotiate, deal with, as *took work for a friend, t. notes, t. a photograph, took a sudden leap, horse will not t. fence, t. a walk, t.* (be examined in) *the mathematical tripos, t.* (conduct) *the evening service, t. a glance round you, took a deep breath, t. an oath*; photograph, come out *well* &c. when photographed, as *t. him in cap & gown, does not t. well*; *t. account of,* include in one's reckoning, not overlook; *t. aim,* direct weapon or missile (*at* object); *t. care,* be careful, be on one's guard, not neglect or fail, be cautious in arranging or deciding, as *t. care !, t. care to leave plenty of room, t. care not to wake the baby, t. care how you speak* or *what you say to him*; *t. care of,* be careful of, be in charge of; *t.* one's *chance,* accept risk (*of*); *t. earth,* (of fox &c., fig. of person) escape into hole; *t.* EFFECT¹, EXCEPTION, HEART (*of grace*), HOLD², LEAVE¹ (*of*); *t.* one's *life in* one's *hand,* risk it; *t.* person's esp. God's *name in vain,* use it lightly or profanely; *t.* PART¹; *t. place,* happen; *t.* STOCK (*of, in*); *t. the* WALL, *t.* WIND¹. Spec. uses w. prepp., advv., & adv. phrr.: *T. after,* resemble (person, esp. parent or relation) in character, feature, &c. *T. back* colloq., retract (words). *T. down*: write down, as *t. down his name & address, took down the sermon in shorthand*; humble, esp. *t.* person *down a* PEG¹ *or two*; swallow (food &c.) esp. with difficulty or reluctance; remove (building, structure) by taking it to pieces. *T. from,* diminish, lessen, weaken, as *such faults do not t. from his credit as a historian. T. in*: admit, receive, (lodgers, guest, &c.); *t.* (lady) *in* (often *to dinner*), conduct from drawing-room to dining-room & sit beside; receive (washing, sewing, typewriting, &c.) to be done at home; include, comprise; reduce (garment &c.) to smaller compass, furl (sail); understand, digest mentally; believe (false statement); deceive; cheat; t. (newspaper &c.) by subscription; *t.-in* n., a fraud, deception, piece of humbug. *T. into*: *t. into* one's *confidence*, confide in; *t. into* one's *head*, conceive, get hold of, (idea), imagine, adopt the belief, (*that, it . . . that*), resolve (*to* do). *T. off*: remove (clothes, hat, &c.) from the body (*t. o.* one's *hat to* fig., applaud as admirable); remove, conduct away, as *took him off to the station, took himself off*, went off; deduct (part of price); drink off; ridicule by imitation, mimic; jump, spring, (*from, at*, place); *t.-off* n., caricature, spot from which one jumps, (Croquet) stroke causing one's own ball to go forward while touching but scarcely moving another. *T. on*: undertake (work, responsibility); *t.* person *on at golf* &c., play with him; (colloq.) show violent emotion, make a fuss. *T. out*: cause to come out, bring or convey out, as *t. him out for a walk, books must not be taken out of the library*; remove (stain &c.); *t. the nonsense* &c. *out of* person, cure him of it; accept payment of (debt &c.) or compensation for (injury &c.) *in*, as *took it out in cigars & drinks*; *t. it out of*, have revenge on, get satisfaction from, exhaust the strength of; procure, get issued, (patent, summons, &c.). *T. over*, succeed to management or ownership of (business &c.). *T. to*: begin, fall into the habit of, begin to busy oneself with, as *took to humming a tune, t. to bad habits, literature*; conceive a liking for (person &c.). *T. up*: lift up; absorb, occupy, engage, as *sponges t. up water, takes up all my time, my attention*; *train stops to t. up* (admit) *passengers*; t. into custody; adopt as protégé; interrupt or correct (speaker); enter upon (profession, subject); pursue (matter, inquiry) further; secure, fasten, (dropped stitch, artery, &c.); furnish the amount of (loan &c.); *t. up with*, consort with; *t. up the* CUDGELS, GAUNTLET[1], GLOVE; *t.-up* n. (mech.), kinds of device for tightening band &c. in machine, drawing up slack of thread, removing material that has been operated on, &c. *T.* (*it*) *upon* or *on* one *to*, venture, presume, to. [late OE *tacan* f. ON *taka*, cf. Sw. *taga*, Da. *tage*, cogn. w. TACKLE]

take[2], n. Amount (*of* fish, game, &c.) taken or caught; (Print.) amount of copy set up at one time; takings, esp. money received at theatre for seats. [f. prec.]

ta·ker, n. In vbl senses, esp. one who takes a bet, as *no tt., a few tt. at 5 to 4.* [-ER[1]]

ta·kin (tah-), n. Tibetan horned ruminant. [native]

ta·king[1], n. In vbl senses, esp.: (pl.) money taken in business, receipts; (archaic) state of agitation, as *was in a great t.* [-ING[1]]

ta·king[2], a. Attractive, captivating; catching, infectious. Hence **ta·king**LY[2] adv., **ta·king**NESS n. [ING[2]]

tă·lapoin, n. Buddhist monk in Ceylon, Siam, &c.; kind of monkey. [f. Port. *talapão*, of E.-Ind. orig.]

talār·ia, n. pl. Winged boots or sandals as attribute of Mercury, Iris, & others. [L]

ta·lbotype (tawl-), n. Photographic process invented by W. H. Fox Talbot in 1840, the basis of that now used. [TYPE]

talc, n., & v.t. A magnesium silicate usu. found in flat smooth often transparent plates & used as lubricator &c.; (pop., commerc.) mica esp. as glazing-material. Hence **ta·l(c)k**Y[2], **ta·lc**OID, **ta·lc**OSE[1], **tă·lc**OUS, aa. (Vb) treat with t. [F, f. Arab. *ṭalq*]

ta·lcite, n. A massive variety of talc. [-ITE[1]]

tale, n. True or usu. fictitious narrative esp. one imaginatively treated, story, as *tell him a t., a true t. of the Crusades, old wives' tt., marvellous legendary tt., t. of a tub*, idle fiction, *prefer to tell my own t.* (give my own account of the matter), *thing tells its own t.* (is significant, requires no comment, explains itself); malicious report whether true or false, as *all sorts of tt. will get about, if all tt. be true* (esp. as preface to scandal), *tell tt.* (*out of school*), report esp. with malicious intention what is meant to be secret, *ta·lebearer*, person who does this, so *ta·lebearing* a. & n.; *ta·leteller*, one who tells tt. (in either sense); (archaic, rhet., poet.) number, total, as *the t. is complete, shepherd tells his t.* (of sheep). [OE *talu* narrative, cf. Du. TAAL, ON *tala* talk, tale, number, G. *zahl* number, cogn. w. TELL]

tă·lent, n. Special aptitude, faculty, gift, (*for* music &c., *for doing*; see *Matt.* xxv. 14–30), high mental ability, whence **ta·lent**ED[2], **ta·lent**LESS, aa.; persons of t., as *all the t. of the country, looking out for local t.*; (Sport. slang) *the t.*, those who take odds &c. relying on their own judgement & knowledge, opp. to bookmakers; ancient weight & money of account among Greeks, Romans, Assyrians, &c., of varying value, as *Attic t.* (about £243. 15*s.*); *t.-money*, bonus to professional cricketer &c. for especially good performance. [f. L *talentum* f. Gk *talanton* balance, t. (weight, money), cogn. w. *talas* adj. enduring, *tla-* endure, sustain]

tā·lēs (-z), n. (law). Writ for summoning jurors, list of persons who may be so summoned, to supply deficiency; *pray a* t., plead for completion of jury thus; *ta·lēsman* (*or* -lz-), person so summoned. [L *t.* (*de circumstantibus*) such (of the bystanders), first wds of writ]

Tăliaco·tian (-ōshn), a. *T. operation*, formation of new nose by means of flap taken from arm or forehead but severed only after union has taken place. [f. *Tagliacozzi*, Italian surgeon d. 1599 + -AN]

tă·lion, n. (Also L *lex talionis*) the law of retaliation inflicting punishment of same kind & degree as injury (see *Lev.* xxiv. 20). Hence **taliŏ·**NIC a. [F, f. L *talio -onis* (*talis* such)]

tă·lipĕd, a. & n. Club-footed; (Zool., of sloth &c.) having feet twisted into unusual position; (n.) t. person or animal. [as foll.]

tă·lipēs (-z), n. Club-foot(edness); taliped formation. [mod. L (TALUS, *pes pedis* foot)]

tă·lipot, -ut, n. A fan-leafed palm. [f. Hind. *tālpāt* f. Skr. *tālapattra* (*tala* palm + *patra* leaf)]

tă·lisman, n. Charm, amulet, thing capable of working wonders; (Astrol.) magical figure cut or engraved & capable of benefiting its possessor. Hence **talismă·**NIC a. [f. Arab. *ṭilsam* f. late Gk *telesma* rite (Gk *telĕō* pay f. *telos* end, initiation, -M)]

talk (tawk), v.i. & t., & n. Converse, communicate ideas, by spoken words, as *was talking with* or *to a friend, what are you talking about?, t.* BIG, TALL, *people will t.* (scandal), *now you're talking* (slang = I welcome that offer &c.); have the power of speech, as *child is learning to t., parrots can t.*; use this to excess, as *is always talking*; express, utter, discuss, in words, as *you are talking nonsense, t. treason, philosophy,* SHOP; use (language), as *t. French, talks nothing but English*; bring into specified condition &c. by talking, as *talked himself hoarse, t.* person *round,* persuade him, *talked him out of his resolution, into his grave, would t. a horse's hind leg off,* is talkative; *t. about,* discuss, as *do not want to be talked about* (made subject of gossip); *t. at,* address to one of a company remarks covertly hostile to & meant to be heard by (another); *t. away,* consume (time) in talking; *t. back,* reply defiantly; *t. down,* silence (person) by superior loudness or persistency; *t. of,* discuss, mention, as *talking* (while we are on the subject) *of muffins, what time do you have tea?,* express some intention of (do*ing*); *t. out* (bill, motion, in Parl.), get rid of it by prolonging discussion till time of adjournment; *t. over,* discuss at some length, win over by talking; *t. round,* discuss (subject) at length without reaching conclusion; *t. through* one's *hat* slang, exaggerate or bluff or make wild statements; *t. to,* speak to, (colloq.) reprove, give a piece of one's mind to, so *gave him a talking-to*; *t. up,* discuss (subject) in order to rouse interest in it. Hence **tal·**KER[1] n. (N.) conversation, as *let us have a t.,* SMALL *t., it will end in t.* (nothing will be done); theme of gossip, as *they, their quarrels, are the t. of the town* [(n. f. vb) ME *talken* (OE *tal-* as in TALE + frequent. -k)]

tal·kative, a. Fond of talking. Hence **tal·kative**NESS n. [-ATIVE]

tal·kee-tal·kee, n. Incessant chatter; broken English of Negroes &c. [TALK]

ta·lkies, n. pl. (slang). = SOUND[2]*-films.* [f. TALK, after MOVIES]

tal·king, a. In vbl senses, esp.: having the power of speech, as *t. parrot*; expressive, as *t. eyes.* [-ING[2]]

tall (tawl), a. & adv. (Of person) of more than average height; (of tree, steeple, mast, &c.) higher than the average or than surrounding objects; of specified height, as *he is six feet t.* (now usu. *high*), *how t. is it?*; *ta·llboy,* bedroom chest of drawers 5 ft or more high sometimes in lower & upper sections or mounted on legs or on dressing-table, kind of chimney-pot; (slang) extravagant, boastful, excessive, as *a t. story, t. talk, a t. order* (exorbitant or unreasonable demand), (adv.) *talk t.,* boast. Hence **ta·ll**NESS n. [prob. f. OE *getæl* quick, prompt, cf. OHG *gizal* quick]

tă·ll(i)age, n. (hist.). Form of taxation abolished in 14th c. [ME & OF *taillage* (*tailler* cut, see TAIL[2] & -AGE)]

tă·llith, n. Scarf worn by Jews esp. at prayer. [Heb.]

tă·llow (-ō), n., & v.t. Substance got by melting the harder & less fusible kinds of (esp. animal) fat, used for making candles & soap, greasing machinery, &c.; *vegetable t.,* kinds of vegetable fat similarly used; *t.-chandler,* maker, vendor, of t. candles, so **ta·llow**ER[1] n.; *t.-drop,* style of cutting precious stones with dome on one or both sides; *t.-face,* pale person; *t.-tree,* kinds of tree yielding vegetable t. Hence **ta·llow**ISH[1], **ta·llow**Y[2], aa. (Vb) grease with t.; fatten (sheep). [(vb f. n.) ME *talgh,* cf. G, Da., Sw., *talg*]

tă·lly, n., & v.t. & i. Piece of wood scored across with notches for the items of an account & then split into halves of which each party kept one; account so kept, score, reckoning; mark made to register a fixed number of objects delivered or received, such number used as unit, as *buy goods by the t.* (dozen, hundred, &c.); (in counting goods aloud as delivered) *16, 18, t.* (20), *96, 98, t.* (100); ticket, label of wood or metal or paper with name &c. attached to thing for identification, as *horticultural tt.,* plant labels; corresponding thing, counterpart, duplicate, (*of*); *ta·llyman,* one who keeps a t. or t.-shop, one who sells goods by sample; *t.-sheet,* paper on which t. is kept; *t.-shop,* conducted on t. system; *t. system, trade* (of sales on short credit with account kept by t.). (Vb) record, reckon, by t.; (Naut.) haul (sheet) taut; agree, correspond, (*with*), as *goods do not t. with invoice.* Hence **ta·lli**ER[1] n. [(vb f. n.) AF *tallie* f. L *talea,* see TAIL[2]]

tă·lly-ho·, int., n., & v.t. & i. Huntsman's cry to hounds; (vb) utter, urge (hounds) with, this. [f. F *taïaut*]

ta·lma, n. Woman's or man's long cape or cloak in first half of 19th c. [F. J. *T.*, French tragedian]

tă·lmi-gold, n. Brass thinly coated with gold. [G, etym. dub.]

Tă·lmud, n. Body of Jewish law & legend comprising the Mishnah (precepts of the elders codified *c.* 200 A.D.) & the Gemara (commentary on the Mishnah in recensions at Jerusalem *c.* 400 & at Babylon *c.* 500), (also, in limited sense) the Babylonian Gemara. Hence **Talmŭ·d**IC(AL) aa. [late Heb., = instruction (*lāmad* teach)]

Ta·lmudist, n. Compiler, adherent, or (now usu.) student, of the Talmud. Hence **Talmudi·st**IC a. [-IST]

tă·lon, n. Claw esp. of bird of prey; cards left after deal; shoulder of bolt against which key presses in shooting it; ogee moulding; heel of sword-blade. Hence **(-)talon**ED[2] a. [OF, =heel, f. LL *talo -onis* ankle f. L *talus* heel]

talu·k (-ōōk), **-ook**, n. District in India subject to revenue collection by native officer; tract of proprietary land in India; *talu·kdar*, such officer, proprietor of t. [Hind. (*-uk*)]

tā·lus, n. (pl. *-lī*). (Anat.) ankle(-bone); form of club-foot; slope of wall that tapers to the top or rests against bank; (Geol.) sloping mass of fragments at foot of cliff. [L, = ankle, heel (in sense *slope*, thr. OF *talu*)]

tama·ndūa, ta·manoir (-war), nn. Kinds of ant-eater. [(*-ua*) Braz., (*-oir*) F corrupt.]

tă·marack, n. Kinds of Amer. tree, esp. =HACKMATACK. [Amer.-Ind.]

tă·marin, n. Kinds of S.-Amer. marmoset. [native]

tă·marind, n. (Tropical tree with) fruit whose pulp is used in making cooling drinks &c.; *t.-fish*, preparation of fish with t. pulp. [ult. f. Arab. *tamr* ripe date +*Hind* India]

tă·marisk, n. Kind of plant, esp. *common* or *French t.*, evergreen shrub with feathery branches & white or pink flowers suitable for planting near sea. [f. LL *tamariscus*, etym. dub.]

tama·sha (-mah-), n. (Anglo-Ind.). A show or entertainment or function. [Arab.]

ta·mbour, n., & v.t. Drum, esp. bass drum; circular frame on which silk &c. is stretched to be embroidered, stuff so embroidered; (Archit.) cylindrical stone in shaft of column, circular part of various structures, ceiled lobby with folding doors in church porch &c. to obviate draught; kinds of fish making drumming noise or like drum in shape; (Fortif.) palisaded defence for road, gate, &c.; (vb) decorate, embroider, (stuff or abs., on t. [(vb f. n.) F, f. Arab. *ṭanbūr* lute, drum]

ta·mbourin, n. Long narrow drum used in Provence; (music for) dance accompanied by this. [F, dim. of prec.]

tambouri·ne (-ēn), n. Small drum made of wooden or metal hoop with parchment stretched over one end & loose jingling metal disks; (music for) Provençal dance orig. executed to tabor & pipe; kind of African pigeon. [prob. f. prec.]

tame, v.t., & a. Make gentle & tractable, domesticate, break in, (wild beast, bird, &c.); subdue, curb, reduce to submission, humble, (person, spirit, courage, ardour, &c.). Hence **tama**BI·LITY, **ta·mable**NESS, **(-)tame**R[1], nn., **ta·m**ABLE, **ta·me**LESS (poet.), aa. (Adj.) made tractable, domesticated, not wild, (*t. cat* fig., person tolerated as useful hanger-on); (colloq., of land or plant) cultivated, produced by cultivation; submissive, spiritless, inert, feeble, flat, insipid, as *the tamest of slaves, t. acquiescence, scenery, description.* Hence **ta·me**LY[2] adv., **ta·me**NESS n. [OE *temian* vb, *tam* a., cf. Du. *tam*, G *zahm*, cogn. w. L *domare*, Gk *damaō*]

Tă·mil, n. Language, member, of a race inhabiting S. India & Ceylon. Hence **Tamĭ·l**IAN a. [native]

Ta·mmany, n. Central organization of democratic party in *T. Hall*, New York (often implying political corruption). Hence **Ta·mmany**ISM n.

tam-o'-sha·nter, ta·mmy, n. Round woollen or cloth cap fitting closely round brows but large & full above. [f. Burns's *T. o' S.*]

tamp, v.t. Pack (blast-hole) full of clay &c. to get full force of explosion, whence **ta·mp**ING[1](3) n.; ram down (road material &c.). [perh. back form. f. *tamping* corrupt. of TAMPION]

ta·mpan, n. Venomous S.-Afr. tick. [native]

ta·mper, v.i. *T. with*: meddle with; make unauthorized changes in (will, MS., &c.); exert secret or corrupt influence upon, bribe. Hence **ta·mper**ER[1] n. [var. of TEMPER]

ta·mpion, n. Wooden stopper for muzzle of gun; plug e.g. for top of organ-pipe. [f. F as foll.]

ta·mpon, n., & v.t. Plug used to stop haemorrhage; pad for the hair; (vb) plug (wound &c.) with t. [(vb f. n.) F, var. of *tapon* (*tape* bung, -OON)]

tampona·de, n. Use of tampon for wound &c. So **ta·mpon**AGE, **ta·mpon**MENT, nn. [-ADE]

tamtam. See TOMTOM.

tan[1], v.t. & i., n., & a. Convert (raw hide) into leather by soaking in liquid containing tannic acid or by use of mineral salts &c., whence **ta·nn**ABLE a., **ta·nn**AGE(3),

ta·nner[1] [-ER[1](1)], **ta·nnERY**(2, 3), nn.; make, become, brown by exposure to sun; treat (imitation marble, fish-nets, &c.) with hardening process; (slang) beat, thrash. Hence **ta·nnING**[1](1) n. (N.) bark of oak or other tree bruised & used for tanning hides; colour of this, yellowish-brown; the bronze of sunburnt skin; *the t.* (slang), the circus; (also *spent t.*) t. from which tannic acid has been extracted, used for covering roads &c.; *t.-balls* (of spent t., used for fuel); *t.-liquor, -ooze, -pickle*, liquid used in tanning; *t.-yard*, tannery. (Adj.) of t. colour; BLACK[1] *& t.* [(vb f. n.) F, prob. f. Celt., cf. Bret. *tann* oak]

tan[2]. See TANGENT.

ta·na (tah-), ***tă·nna***, n. Military post, police-station, in India; *tan(n)adar*, chief officer of this. [f. Hind. *thāna*]

tă·nager (-j-), n. Kinds of Amer. birds of finch family & mostly of brilliant plumage. Hence **ta·nagrINE**[1], **ta·nagrOID**, aa. [f. Braz. *tangara*]

tă·ndem, adv., n., & a. (Of horses in harness) one behind another; *drive t.* (with horses so harnessed); (n.) (carriage with) horses t., bicycle or tricycle with seats for two or more one behind another; (adj., of bicycle) so arranged. [L, = at length (of time), orig. facet. use in E]

tă·ndstickor, n. Swedish wooden lucifer match. [f. Sw. *tandsticka* match, pl. *-or* (*tända* kindle + *sticka* splinter)]

tang[1], n., & v.t. Point, projection, esp. part of chisel &c., that goes into handle (vb, furnish with t.); strong taste or flavour, characteristic property, whence **ta·ngY**[2] (-ngĭ) a. [ME, f. ON *tange* point]

tang[2], n. Kinds of sea-weed. [cf. Norw. & Da. *tang*, Icel. *thāng*]

tang[3], v.t. & i., & n. Ring, twang, sound loudly, (t. & i.); induce (bees) to settle by striking pieces of metal together; (n.) twang. [imit.]

ta·ngent (-j-), a. & n. Meeting a line or surface at a point but not (when produced if necessary) intersecting it. (N.) straight line t. to a curve at any point; *fly, go, off at a t.*, diverge impetuously from matter in hand or from normal line of thought or conduct; (Trig., abbr. *tan*) *t. of an angle*, ratio of the perpendicular subtending it in any right-angled triangle to the base; *t.-balance* (showing weight by position of beam as shown on graduated arc). Hence **ta·ngENCY** n., **tange·ntIAL** a., **tange·ntIALLY**[2] adv. [f. L *tangere* touch, see -ENT]

Tangeri·ne (-ēn), a. & n. (Native) of Tangiers; *T.* (*orange*), small flattened kind. [f. *Tanger* Tangiers, see -INE[1]]

ta·nghin (-nggĭn), n. Madagascar tree the fruit of which has poisonous kernel formerly used in ordeals. [F, f. native *tangena*]

ta·ngible, a. Perceptible by touch; definite, clearly intelligible, not elusive or visionary, as *t. advantages, scheme, distinction*; (Law) corporeal. Hence or cogn. **tangibI·LITY**, **ta·ngibleNESS**, nn., **ta·ngibLY**[2] adv. [f. L *tangibilis* (*tangere* touch, see -BLE)]

ta·ngle[1], v.t. & i., & n. Intertwine (threads, hair, &c.), become involved, in confused mass; entrap, entangle; complicate, as *a tangled affair*; *ta·nglefoot* (U.S. slang), whisky or intoxicants. (N.) confused mass of intertwined threads &c.; confused state, as *skein, business, is in a t.*; device used in dredging for delicate forms of marine life. Hence **ta·ngleSOME**, **ta·nglY**[2], aa. [n. f. vb, ME, var. of *tagle* entangle, prob. of Scand. orig.]

ta·ngle[2], n. = TANG[2].

ta·ngo (-nggō), n. A S.-Amer. dance recently introduced into Europe. [?]

ta·ngram, n. Chinese puzzle square cut into seven pieces to be combined into various figures. [?]

tă·nist, n. (hist.). Successor apparent to Celtic chief, usu. most vigorous adult of his kin. [f. Ir. *tánaiste* heir]

ta·nistry, n. Celtic mode of tenure according to which a lord's successor was chosen from his family by election (abolished in Ireland under James I). [-RY]

tank, n. Large metal or wooden vessel for liquid, gas, &c.; part of locomotive tender containing water for boiler; (E.-Ind.) storage-pond, reservoir for water; (Mil.) steel box travelling by motor power, containing crew & guns, & serving as peripatetic fort in battle (*male, female, t.*, more, less, powerful types); *t. drama* (Theatr. slang), sensational drama in which water is used for representing rescue from drowning &c.; *t. engine*, railway engine carrying fuel & water receptacles on its own frame, not in tender. [f. Port. *tanque* f. LL as STANCH[1]; or perh. of Ind. orig.]

ta·nkage (-ĭj), n. (Charge for) storage in tanks; cubic content of tank(s); kind of fertilizer got from refuse fats &c. [-AGE]

ta·nkard, n. Large drinking-vessel usu. of silver or pewter & often with cover; contents of, amount held by, this, as *a t. of ale*; COOL[1] *t.*; *t. turnip*, kinds with oblong root usu. rising high above ground. [cf. Du. *tanckaert*, F *tanquart*, etym. dub.]

ta·nker, n. Ship with tank for carrying mineral oil in bulk. [-ER[1]]

ta·nner[2] (for *t.*[1] see TAN[1]), n. (slang). A sixpence. [?]

ta·nnic, a. Of tan; *t. acid* (also **ta·nnIN** n.), astringent substance got chiefly from bark &c. of oak & other trees & used in preparing leather & writing-ink & in medicine. So **ta·nnATE**[1](3) n. (chem.), **tanni·FEROUS** a. [-IC]

ta·nsy (-zĭ), n. Herb with yellow flowers & finely-toothed bitter aromatic leaves used in medicine & cookery. [f. OF *tanesie* f. med. L f. Gk *athanasia* immortality (*a-* not + *thanatos* death)]

ta·ntalize, v.t. Torment, tease, (person &c.) with hopes that seem continually on point of fulfilment or with object almost within his grasp or with imperfect information &c. Hence **tantaliz**A·TION n., **ta·ntalizing**LY[2] adv. [f. TANTALUS + -IZE]

ta·ntalum, n. A rare metal used for incandescent filament in electric lamps. [f. foll. w. ref. to its non-absorbent quality + -UM]

Ta·ntalus, n. (Gk Myth.) son of Zeus condemned in Tartarus to stand up to chin in water that receded whenever he stooped to drink; kinds of ibis; spirit-stand in which decanters are locked up but visible; *T.-cup,* toy cup containing figure of man illustrating principle of siphon. [L, f. Gk *Tantalos*]

ta·ntamount, a. Equivalent, as *his message was t. to a flat refusal.* [orig. as vb, f. AF *tant amunter* AMOUNT to so much (*tant* f. L *tantus* so great)]

tantar·a, n. Succession of notes on trumpet or horn. [imit.]

tanti·vy, n., a., adv., & v.i., (archaic). Hunting cry; swift movement, gallop, rush; (adj.) swift; (adv.) swiftly; (vb) hurry, rush. [perh. imit. of hoof-strokes]

ta·ntra, n. Each of a class of recent Sanskrit religious works dealing chiefly with magic. Hence **ta·ntr**ISM(3), **ta·ntr**IST(2), nn. [Skr., = loom, groundwork, doctrine]

ta·ntrum, n. Display of temper or petulance, as *is in, went into, her tt.* [f. 18th c., etym. dub.]

Ta·oism (tahō-, tow-), n. Religious doctrine of Lao-tsze, Chinese philosopher (c. 500 B.C.). [f. Chin. *tao* way + -ISM]

tap[1]**,** n., & v.t. Cock through which liquid is drawn from cask or flows from pipe; plug used to close opening in cask; liquor of a particular brewing &c. w. ref. to quality, as *an excellent t., you know the t.*; = *t.-room,* as *found him in the t.*; instrument for cutting threads of internal screws; *on t.,* (of cask) furnished with t., (of liquor) in such cask, ready to be drawn; *t.-borer,* auger for boring tapering hole in cask; *t.-room* (in which liquor is sold & drunk); *t.-root,* chief descending root of plant. (Vb) furnish (cask) with cock; pierce (cask &c.) to let out liquid, let out thus; (Surg.) give vent to (fluid accumulated in body), operate thus on (person); draw sap from (tree) by cutting into it; penetrate to, get into communication with, establish trade &c. in, (district &c.); apply to, solicit, (person *for*); broach (subject); divert part of current from (telegraph wires &c.) to intercept message; make internal screw-thread in. [(vb OE *tæppan* f. n.) OE *tæppa,* cf. Du. *tap,* ON *tappi,* G *zapfen*]

tap[2]**,** v.t. & i., & n. Strike lightly, as *t. the door with your knuckles, pavement with your stick, tapped his forehead knowingly*; cause (thing) to strike lightly *against* &c., as *tapped his stick against the window*; strike gentle blow, rap, (*at* door &c.); apply leather to (heel of shoe). (N.) light blow, rap; sound of this, as *heard a t. at the door*; (pl.) men's dinner-call in barracks, (U.S.) signal on drum or trumpet for lights to be put out in soldiers' quarters. [(n. f. vb) imit., perh. thr. F *tap(p)er*]

ta·pa (tah-), n. Bark of a tree used in Pacific islands for clothes, mats, &c. [native]

tape, n., & v.t. Narrow cotton or linen strip used for tying up parcels & in dressmaking &c. (RED *t.*); such strip stretched across racing-track between winning-posts, as *breast the t.,* win race; narrow band of strong fabric rotating on pulleys &c. in machinery; continuous strip of paper in receiving instrument of recording telegraph; = *t.-measure, tapeworm*; (slang) spirituous liquor; *t.-line, -measure,* strip of t. or thin flexible metal marked for use as measure, & often coiled up in cylindrical case; *ta·peworm,* kinds of t.-like many-jointed worm infesting alimentary canal of man & most vertebrates. Hence **ta·pe**LESS a. (Vb) furnish, tie up, with t.; join sections of (book) with bands of t. [(vb f. n.) OE *tæppe*]

tā·per, n., a., & v.i. & t. Slender candle, wick coated with wax &c.; (adj., now chiefly poet. or rhet.) growing gradually smaller towards one end like cone or pyramid, as *t. fingers,* whence **ta·per**NESS n., **ta·per**WISE adv.; (vb, often *t. off*) make or become t., (cause to) grow gradually less, as *the upper part tapers* or *is tapered off to a point,* whence **ta·pering**LY[2] adv. [(vb f. adj. f. n., w. ref. to shape) OE]

tă·pestry, n. Textile fabric in which woof is supplied with spindle instead of shuttle, with design formed by stitches across warp, used for covering walls, furniture, &c.; *Bayeux t.,* ancient roll of t. representing scenes in life of William I preserved at Bayeux; *Russian t.,* stout linen or hemp stuff used for blinds &c. Hence **(-)tapestri**ED[2] a. [f. F *tapisserie* (*tapisser* furnish with t., f. TAPIS, see -ERY)]

tăpiō·ca, n. Starchy substance n hard white grains got by heating cassava & used for puddings &c. [Port., f. Braz. *tipioca* juice of cassava (*tipi* dregs + *ok* pluck, squeeze)]

tā·pir, n. Hoofed swine-like mammal with short proboscis, allied to rhinoceros. Hence **ta·pir**OID a. & n. [f. Braz. *tapira*]

tapis· (-pē, *also* tă·pĭs), n. (Of subject) *be, come, on the t.* (under consideration or discussion). [OF, = tapestry, carpet, f. LL f. Gk *tapētion* dim. of *tapēs -ētos*; phrr. f. use of tapestry for table-cloths]

tapō·tement (-tm-), n. (med.). Percussion as part of massage treatment.

ta·ppet, n. Arm, collar, cam, &c., used in machinery to impart intermittent motion; *t. loom* (in which hammers are worked by tt.). [perh. f. TAP[2] + -ET[1]]

tap rate, n. (financ.). Current rate for Treasury additional paper. [= T.A.P.]

ta·pster, n. Person employed at a bar to draw & serve liquor. [OE *tæppestre*, orig. fem. (TAP[1], -STER)]

tapu. See TABOO.

tar[1], n., & v.t. Dark viscid liquid got by dry distillation of wood, coal, &c., & used as preservative of timber & iron, antiseptic, &c.; *a touch of the t.-brush*, admixture of Negro blood as shown by colour of skin; *t.-board*, stout millboard of tarred rope &c.; *t. macadam* (also abbr. as trade mark *tar·mac*), road-materials of stone or slag with t.; *t.-water*, cold infusion of t. used as medicine, also, tarry ammoniacal water obtained in gas-manufacture. (Vb) cover with t.; *t. & feather*, smear with tar & then cover with feathers as punishment; *tarred with the same brush* or *stick*, having the same faults. [(vb f. n.) OE *teoru*, cf. Du. *teer*, ON *tjara*, Da. *tjære*, cogn. w. TREE]

tar[2], n. (Also *Jack t.*) sailor. [abbr. of TARPAULIN]

tăradi·ddle, tarra-, n. (colloq.). Fib, lie. [?]

tar·a(-fern), n. Edible fern of New Zealand &c. [Tasmanian]

tărantă·ss, n. Springless four-wheeled Russian vehicle. [f. Russ. *tarantasu*]

tărante·lla, -elle (-ĕl), n. (Music for) rapid whirling Ital. dance for one couple, once held a cure for tarantism. [F (*-le*) f. It. (*-la*), as foll.]

tă·rantism, n. Dancing mania, esp. that originating in S. Italy among those who (thought they) had been bitten by the tarantula. [f. It. *Taranto* f. L *Tarentum*, S.-Ital. town, -ISM]

tara·ntūla, n. Large spider of S. Europe whose bite was formerly held to cause tarantism; other kinds of spider. Hence **tara·ntul**AR[1] a. [f. It. *tarantola*, as prec.]

tărată·ntara (*or* -tar·*a*), n. Sound of trumpet or bugle. [imit., cf. TANTARA]

tara·xacum, n. Kinds of plant of aster family including dandelion; drug prepared from this. [prob. of Arab. or Pers. orig.]

tarbōō·sh, n. Cap like fez. [f. Arab. *ṭarbūsh*]

tardame·ntĕ, adv. (mus.). Slowly. [It.]

Tardenoi·sean, a. (archaeol.). Of the mesolithic period represented by remains at Tardenois, Aisne, France. [-EAN]

tar·digrade, a. & n. (zool.). Slow-moving (animal). [f. L *tardigradus* (*tardus* slow + *gradi* walk)]

tar·do, a. & adv. (mus.). Slow(ly). [It.]

tar·dy, a. Slow-moving, slow, sluggish; late, coming or done late, as *t. retribution, amends, reform*; (of person &c.) reluctant, hanging back. Hence **tar·di**LY[2] adv., **tar·di**NESS n. [f. F *tardif* f. L *tardus* slow, see -IVE]

tare[1], n. Kinds of vetch, esp. common vetch (in *Matt.* xiii. 25, 36, perh. = darnel). [ME, etym. dub.]

tare[2], n., & v.t. Allowance made for weight of box &c. in which goods are packed, as *real, customary, average, t.*; weight of motor vehicle without fuel &c.; *t. & tret*, arithmetical rule for computing t. &c.; (Chem.) weight of vessel in which substance is weighed; (vb) ascertain weight of (box &c.). [F, f. Arab. *ṭarḥah* what is rejected (*ṭaraḥa* reject)]

targe. See foll.

tar·get (-g-), n. Circular stuffed pad with concentric circles painted on surface as mark in archery; similar usu. rectangular mark for rifles or pistols; (fig.) person, thing, serving as mark *for* (scorn &c.); circular railway signal e.g. at a switch; neck & breast of lamb as joint; (also *targe* archaic) shield, buckler, esp. small round one, whence **tar·get**ED[2] a.; *t.-card* (coloured like t., for keeping archer's score); *t. ship*, old ship used as t. [f. OF *targuete* dim. of *targue* (also *targe*) f. ON *targa*, cf. OHG *zarga* frame, border]

Tar·gum, n. Each of various ancient Aramaic or Chaldee paraphrases of the Hebrew scriptures. Hence **Targū·mic, Targumi·stic**, aa., **Tar·gum**IST(3) n. [Chald., = interpretation (*targēm* interpret)]

tă·riff, n., & v.t. List of duties or customs to be paid on imports or exports; such duties collectively; law imposing these; duty on particular class of goods; *preferential t.*, reduced duties on imports from favoured country; *retaliatory t.*, import duties levied by a nation to balance foreign duties imposed on its exports; *t. reform*, removal of inequalities &c. in t. (esp. as name given by opponents of free trade in U.K. to their policy); list of charges, as *railway, telegraph, refreshment-room, t.* (Vb) make t. of duties on (goods); put a valuation on. [(vb f. n.) f. It. *tariffa* arithmetic, ratebook, f. Arab. *ta'rīf* notification (*'arafa* notify)]

tar·latan, n. Thin kind of muslin. [f. F *tarlatane* earlier *tarn-*, etym. dub.]

tarn[1], n. Small mountain lake. [f. ON *tjörn*, cf. Sw. dial. *t(j)ärn*]

tarn[2]. See TERN[1].

tar·nal, tarna·tion, aa. & advv. (U.S. slang). Confounded(ly). [(*-ation* on *damnation*) corrupt. of ETERNAL]

tar·nish, v.t. & i., & n. Lessen or destroy the lustre of, lose lustre, as *has been tarnished by damp, will t. if exposed, does not easily t.*, (fig.) *a tarnished reputation*; (n.) loss of lustre, blemish, stain, (Mineral.) film of colour formed on exposed surface of mineral. Hence **tar·nish**ABLE a. [(n. f. vb) f. F *ternir* (*terne* dark), see -ISH[2]]

tar·o, n. Kinds of tropical plant of arum family with root used as food esp. in Pacific islands. [native]

tă·roc, -ot (-ō), n. Game played with, each card of, a pack of 78 cards. [f. F *tarot* f. It. *tarocchi*, etym. dub.]

tar·păn, n. Wild horse of Tartary. [native]

tarpau·lin, n. Waterproof cloth esp. of tarred canvas; sheet of this as covering; sailor's tarred or oiled hat; (colloq.) sailor. [f. TAR + *palling* covering f. *pall* vb cover f. PALL[1]]

Tarpei·an (-pēan), a. *T. rock*, cliff from which ancient Roman criminals were hurled. [f. L *Tarpeius* of Tarpeia (who was buried at foot of T. rock) + -AN]

tar·pon, n. Large game-fish common on south coast of U.S. [?]

tărradiddle. See **tara-.**

tă·rragon, n. Plant allied to wormwood & used in salads & in making *t. vinegar*. [f. Arab. *ṭarkhōn* perh. f. Gk as DRAGON]

Tarrago·na, n. Spanish wine like port. [*T.* in Spain]

tă·rras, n. See TRASS.

tă·rrock, n. Young kittiwake; common tern; guillemot. [?]

tar·ry[1], a. Of, like, smeared with, tar. [-Y[2]]

tă·rry[2], v.i. & t. (now literary). Remain, stay, lodge, (*at, in*, &c.); wait (often *for*) delay to come or appear, be late; wait for. [f. 14th c., etym. dub.]

tar·sia, n. Kind of mosaic woodwork. [It.]

tar·sier, n. Small large-eyed nocturnal lemur. [F (foll., from structure of foot)]

tar·sus, n. (pl. -ī). Collection of bones between lower leg & metatarsus, ankle; shank of bird's leg; (Entom.) terminal segment of limb; plate of connective tissue in eyelid. Hence **tar·**SAL a., **tarsi-, tarso-,** comb. forms. [mod. L, f. Gk *tarsos* flat of the foot]

tart[1], a. Sharp-tasted, acid; cutting, biting, as *a t. rejoinder*. Hence **tar·t**LY[2] adv., **tar·t**NESS n. [OE *teart*, perh. cogn. w. TEAR[1]]

tart[2], n. Pie containing fruit, as *apple, cherry, -t.*; *jam t.*, piece of pastry with jam on top; (slang) girl, woman, esp. of immoral character. So **tar·t**LET n. [f. OF *tarte* perh. var. of *to(u)rte* f. L *torquēre tort-* twist]

tar·tan[1], n. & a. Woollen fabric with stripes of various colours crossing at right angles esp. as worn by Scottish Highlanders; (other fabric) so striped, as *silk t., t. velvet*; Scotch plaid with distinctive pattern of a clan; Highlander; Highland troops. [f. 16th c., etym. dub.]

tar·tan[2], n. Kind of single-masted vessel used in Mediterranean. [f. F *tartane* f. It. *tartana*]

tar·tar[1], n. Pink or red deposit from completely fermented wine, forming hard crust on side of cask, whence **tartă·r**IC, **tar·tar**OUS, aa. (chem.), **tartariz**A·TION n., **tar·tar**IZE(5) v.t.; CREAM[1] *of t.*; incrustation of saliva, calcium phosphate, &c., forming on the teeth; *t. emetic*, double tartrate of potassium & antimony used as emetic, purgative, &c. [f. F *tartre* perh. f. Arab.]

Tar·tar[2], Ta·tar (tah-), a. & n. (Native) of Tartary, (member) of a group of peoples including Turks, Cossacks, &c., so **Tartār·**IAN a.; (*Tar-*) intractable or savage person (*catch a T.*, meet with person who is more than a match for one). [cf. Pers. *Tātār*, perh. the native form, whence *Tar-*, the usu. spelling, by assoc. w. foll.]

Tar·tarus, n. (Gk myth.). Abyss below Hades where Titans were confined; place of punishment in Hades. So **Tartār·**EAN a. [L, f. Gk *Tartaros*]

tar·trate, n. Salt of tartaric acid. [f. TARTAR[1] + -ATE[1]]

Tartu·f(f)e (-ōōf, *or as F*), n. Religious hypocrite. Hence **Tartu·f(f)**ISM n. [character in Molière's *T.*]

tasi·meter, n. Electrical apparatus for measuring changes in temperature, moisture, &c. Hence **tasime·tr**IC a. [f. Gk *tasis* stretching (*teinō* stretch) + -METER]

task, n., & v.t. Piece of work imposed; lesson to be learnt at school, as *has done his t.*; a work voluntarily undertaken, as *an arduous t., undertook the t. of classification*; *take* person *to t.*, accuse him of fault, rebuke him *for* (*doing*); *ta·skmaster, -mistress*, one who imposes t. (Vb) assign t. to; exact labour from, put strain upon, tax, (*powers, intellect*, &c.). [(vb f. n.) f. ONF *tasque* (OF *tasche*) TAX]

tass, n. (Sc.) Small draught (*of* brandy &c.). [f. OF *tasse* cup prob. f. Arab. *ṭass* basin]

ta·ssel, n., & v.t. (-ll-). Tuft of loosely hanging threads or cords as ornament for cushion, cap, &c.; t.-like head of some plants, esp. staminate inflorescence at top of stalk of Indian corn; ribbon sewn into book to be used as bookmark; = TORSEL; (vb) furnish with t., remove tt. of (Indian corn) to strengthen plant. [(vb f. n.) OF, perh. f. L *taxillus* small die]

tāste[1], v.t. & i. Learn flavour of (food &c., or abs.) by taking it into the mouth, as *t. this cheese, he tastes teas* (professionally) *for Smith & Co.*; eat small portion of or archaic *of* (esp. after negative), as *must just t. a snack, has not tasted food for 3 days*; perceive the flavour of, as *can t. nothing when you have a cold, fancy I t. garlic*; (archaic) relish, enjoy, as *cannot t. a joke against himself*; experience, have experience *of*, as *shall not t.* (*of*) *death, has never tasted* (*of*) *success*; (of food &c.,

or fig.) have a flavour *of*, smack *of*, as *tastes of mint, his writings t. of the schools.* Hence **ta·st**ABLE **a.** [f. OF *taster* handle, taste, ult. f. L *taxare* TAX]

tāste[2], **n.** Sensation excited in certain organs of mouth by contact of some soluble things, flavour, as *cannot endure the t. of onions, white of egg has no t.*; sense by which this is perceived; (rare) act of tasting; small portion (*of* food &c.) taken as sample (*give him a t. of the whip*, enough to show how it feels); liking, predilection, *for*, as *has no t. for sweet things, a t. for drawing, scenery, argument, is not to my t.* (liking), *tt. differ, there is no accounting for tt., add pepper* &c. *to t.* (to the amount desired); faculty of discerning & enjoying beauty or other excellence esp. in art & literature, as *is a man of t., true, false, t.*; disposition or execution of work of art, choice of language, conduct, &c., dictated by or seen in the light of this faculty, as *composed in admirable t., the remark was in bad t.* [ME, f. OF *tast* as prec.]

ta·steful, a. (Of person, work of art, &c.) having, showing, done in, good taste. Hence **ta·stefu**lLY[2] adv., **ta·steful**NESS n. [-FUL]

ta·steless, a. Having no flavour; insipid; lacking the physical sense of taste; lacking artistic taste; (of language, conduct, &c.) not in good taste. Hence **ta·steless**LY[2] adv., **ta·steless**NESS n. [-LESS]

ta·ster, n. In vbl senses, esp.: person employed to judge of teas, wines, &c., by taste; (fig.) publisher's reader; (hist.) person employed to taste food before it was touched by his employer; small cup used by wine-t.; instrument for extracting small cylindrical sample from a cheese. [-ER[1]]

ta·sty, a. (colloq.). Savoury, of pleasant flavour; (now vulg.; of dress, decoration, &c.) in good taste. Hence **ta·sti**LY[2] adv. [-Y[2]]

tat, v.i. & t. Do tatting; make by tatting. [prob. back formation f. TATTING]

tata (tah·tah·), int. Good-bye.

Tatar. See TARTAR[2].

Tate Gallery, n. London public gallery with permanent exhibition of pictures by British painters. [Sir H. *Tate*, donor]

ta·tter, n. Rag, torn piece, of cloth, paper, &c. (usu. in pl.); *tatterdemālion* [etym. dub.], ragged fellow. Hence **ta·tter**ED[2], **ta·tter**Y[2], aa. [cf. ON *tötrar* rags]

Ta·ttersall's, n. (Used for) headquarters of horse-dealing & betting rendezvous (*knows his T. better than his Greek Testament*). [R. *Tattersall*, founder of firm]

ta·tting, n. Kind of knotted work used for trimmings &c. [?]

ta·ttle, v.i. & t., & n. Prattle, chatter, gossip, whence **ta·ttling**LY[2] adv.; utter (words) idly; (n.) trivial talk. [(n. f. vb) perh. f. MFlem. *tatelen*, cf. MLG *tateren*]

ta·ttler, n. Prattler, gossip, (archaic *Tatler*, periodical of Steele & Addison); sandpiper. [f. prec. + -ER[1]]

tăttōō·[1], n., & v.i. Beat of drum, or bugle-call, at 10 p.m. recalling soldiers to quarters, elaboration of this with music & marching as entertainment; *beat the devil's t.*, drum idly with fingers &c.; (v.i.) rap quickly & repeatedly, beat the devil's t. [(vb f. n.) f. Du. *taptoe* tattoo, lit. (put the) tap to]

tăttōō·[2], v.t., & n. Mark (skin &c.) with indelible patterns by inserting pigments in punctures; (n.) such mark. [(n. f. vb) f. Tahitian *tatau* n.]

ta·tty, n. (Anglo-Ind.). Matting of cuscus-grass hung & kept wet to cool & perfume the air. [f. Hind. *ṭaṭṭi* wicker frame]

tau (taw), n. Greek letter (T, τ) = t; kinds of fish &c. marked with or suggesting this; (attrib.) T. shaped, as *T- cross.* [Gk]

taube (towbe), n. Type of German aeroplane. [G, = dove]

tau·chnitz (towk-), n. (Used for) any volume in the Library of British & American authors published by Tauchnitz of Leipzig, much used by travellers on the Continent.

taught. See TEACH.

taunt[1], v.t., & n. Reproach, upbraid, (person &c. *with* conduct &c.) contemptuously, whence **tau·nting**LY[2] adv.; (n.) contemptuous reproach, object of this, as *endured the tt. of, became a t. to, his neighbours.* [f. OF *tanter, tenter*, provoke, TEMPT; or f. F phr. *tant pour tant* so much for so much, tit for tat, f. L *tantum* so much]

taunt[2], a. (naut.). (Of mast) tall. [f. *ataunt* adv. naut. fully rigged f. F *autant* as much]

taur·ine, a. Bull-like, bovine, so **taur·i**FORM a.; of the zodiacal sign Taurus. [f. L *taurinus* (*taurus* bull, see -INE[1])]

taurŏ·machy (-kĭ), n. Bull-fight(ing). [f. Gk *tauromakhia* (*tauros* bull + *makhē* fight)]

Taur·us, n. A constellation; second sign of zodiac. [L, = bull]

taut (tawt), a. (naut.). (Of rope) tight, not slack; (of vessel &c.) in good order or condition. Hence **tau·t**EN[6] v.t. & i., **tau·t**LY[2] adv., **tau·t**NESS n. [ME *togt*, perh. = TIGHT w. assim. to p.p. of TOW]

tauto- in comb. = Gk *tauto, to auto*, the same, as: *-baryd* [f. Gk *barus* heavy], curve on which the pressure of a body moving under gravity is everywhere the same; *-chrone* [f. Gk *khronos* time], curve on which body sliding from state of rest under given force will reach lowest point in same time from whatever point it starts, so *-chronism* n., *-chronous* a.; *-phony*, repetition of same sound.

tauto·logy, n. Saying of the same thing twice over in different words (e.g. *arrived one after the other in succession*). Hence **tautolo·gic(al)** aa., **tautolo·gically**² adv., **tauto·logist**(1) n., **tauto·logize**(2) v.i. [f. LL f. Gk TAUTO(*logia* -LOGY)]

tă·vern, n. Public house for supply of food & drink. [f. OF *taverne* f. L *taberna* hut, tavern]

taw¹, v.t. Make (hide) into leather without use of tannin, esp. by soaking in solution of alum & salt. Hence **taw·er**¹, **taw·ery**(3), nn. [OE *tawian* prepare, cf. Du. *touwen* curry, MHG *zouwan* make, prepare]

taw², n. Game at marbles; limit line in playing marbles; a marble. [f. 18th c., etym. dub.]

taw·dry, a. & n. Showy but worthless, gaudy, having too much or ill-judged ornament, whence **taw·drily**² adv., **taw·driness** n.; (n.) cheap or excessive or tasteless finery. [f. *St Audry's* fair held in Isle of Ely (*Audry* corrupt. of *Etheldrida*, who founded Ely Cathedral)]

taw·ny, a. Brownish-yellow, tan-coloured. Hence **taw·niness** n. [f. OF *tané* TAN¹ned]

taws(e), n. sing. or pl. (Sc.). Slit thong for chastising children. [prob. related to TAW¹; a sing. *taw* is much later]

tax¹, v.t. Impose tax on (subjects, citizens, &c., commodity, land, &c.), so **taxa·tion** n.; (N.T.) register (person) for purpose of imposing tribute; make demands upon, demand exertion from, (person's resources, powers, ingenuity, &c.); *cannot t. my memory*, cannot undertake to recollect the facts wanted; (Law) examine & (dis)allow items of (costs &c.); *taxed* (also *tax-*) *cart*, two-wheeled cart usu. for agricultural or trade purposes on which only reduced duty (& later none) was charged; charge (person *with* fault, *with* doing); *taxing-master*, law-court official who taxes costs. Hence **taxabi·lity, ta·xableness,** nn., **ta·xable** a., **ta·xably**² adv. [f. OF *taxer* f. L *taxare* censure, charge, compute, cf. TASK, TASTE¹]

tax², n. Contribution levied on persons, property, or business, for support of government, as DIRECT², INDIRECT, *capitation*, INCOME, *poll-*, *t.*; *single t.*, proposed sole t., on value of land irrespective of improvements; strain, heavy demand, (*up*)*on* (person, his energies &c.); *t.-cart*, see prec.; *t.-collector*, official who collects tt.; *t.-farmer*, one who buys from government the right to collect certain tt.; *t.-free*, exempt from tt.; *t.-gatherer*, = *t.-collector*; *ta·xpayer*. Hence **ta·xless** a. [f. prec.]

ta·xi, n., & v.i. & t. Motor-cab plying for hire & fitted with taximeter (also *t.-cab*), other motor-car of similar pattern; *ta·xi-man*, driver of t.; (vb) go or convey in t.; (aeron.) go along ground or water before or after flying. [abbr. TAXIMETER]

ta·xidermy, n. Art of preparing & mounting skins of animals in lifelike manner. Hence **taxider·mal, taxider·mic,** aa., **ta·xidermist**(3) n. [f. TAXIS + DERM]

taxi·meter, n. Automatic device fitted to cab & indicating fare due at any moment. [f. F *taximètre* (*taxe* tariff, TAX², -METER)]

ta·xin, n. Resinous substance from yew leaves. [f. L *taxus* yew + -IN]

ta·xis, n. (Surg.) manual pressure applied to restore parts to their place; (Gk Ant.) various divisions of troops; (Zool.) classification; (Gram., Rhet.) arrangement. [Gk, f. *tassō* arrange]

taxo·nomy, n. (nat. hist.). (Principles of) classification. Hence or cogn. **taxo·logy, taxo·nomist**(3), nn., **taxonŏ·mic(al)** aa., **taxono·mically**² adv. [f. F *taxonomie* (TAXIS + Gk-*nomos* f. *nemō* manage)]

tazza (tah·tsa), n. Saucer-shaped cup esp. one mounted on a foot. [It.]

tchick, n., & v.i. (Make) sound produced by pressing tongue against roof of mouth & quickly withdrawing it, esp. as used in urging horse. [imit.]

tea, n., & v.i. & t. (Also *t.-plant*) shrub or small tree of camellia family grown in China, India, &c.; leaves of this dried & prepared for use (*black, green, t.*, prepared by different processes; *bohea, congou, souchong, pekoe*, &c., *t.*, kinds of black, *hyson, gunpowder*, &c., *t.*, kinds of green; *tile t.*, in BRICK form); infusion or decoction of t.-leaves as beverage; infusion &c. of leaves of other plants or of other substance, as BEEF, CAMOMILE, *t.*; light afternoon meal with t., esp. *five-o'-clock t.*; (also *high t.*, *meat t.*) solid evening meal with t.; *t.-caddy*; *t.-cake*, kinds of cake eaten toasted or otherwise at t.; *t.-chest*, light lead-lined wooden box in which t. is exported; *t.-cloth* (for t.-table or -tray, also drying-cloth for cups &c.); *t.-cup*, cup in which tea is drunk (*storm in a t.-c.*, commotion in circumscribed circle or about trivial matter), (as measure, also *tea·cupful*) gill; *t.-fight* (colloq.), t.-party; *t.-garden* (in which t. is served to the public); *t.-gown*, woman's loose gown worn at t. &c.; *t.-house* (in which t. &c. is served in China & Japan); *t.-kettle* (used in making t.); *t.-leaf*, leaf of t. esp. (pl.) after infusion or soaking, used in sweeping floors; *t.-party* (at which t. is served); *t.-pot*, vessel in which t. is made; *t.-rose*, kinds with scent compared to that of t.; *t.-service, -set*, t.-pot, cups, &c., used in serving t.; *t.*-SPOON; *t.-table* (often attrib., as *t.-t. conversation*); *t.-things*, = *t.-set*; *t.-tray* (on which t.-set is used or carried); *t.-urn*, for boiling or holding water for t. (Vb) take t., as *we t. at 4*; give t. to (person). [(vb f. n.) earlier also *tay, tee*, f. Chin. dial. *t'e*, f. Chin. *ch'a*]

teach (tētsh), v.t. (taught *pron.* tawt). Enable or cause (person &c. *to* do) by instruction & training, as *t. him to swim, dog was taught to beg, misfortune has taught him to be thankful for small mercies, this* (punishment) *will t. you to speak the truth,* (colloq.) *I will t. him* (not) *to meddle in my affairs*; give lessons at school or elsewhere in or on (subject, game, instrument, &c., *to* person, or w. double object), as *taught him Greek, teaches Greek for a living, teaches the violin, t. me bridge, was never taught music, music was never taught to a more unwilling pupil, it is time the boy was taught something*; give instruction to, educate, (abs.) be a teacher; explain, show, state by way of instruction, (fact &c., *how, that,* &c., *to* person or w. double obj.), as *taught that we must forgive our enemies, I was taught that two sides of a triangle were greater than the third, was taught otherwise, was never taught this, who taught you that?*. Hence **tea·cher**[1], **tea·cher**SHIP, nn. [OE *tǽcan*, cogn. w. TOKEN]

tea·chable, a. Apt to learn, docile; (of subject &c.) that can be taught. Hence **teacha**BI·LITY, **tea·chable**NESS, nn. [-ABLE]

tea·ching, n. In vbl senses, esp. what is taught, doctrines, as *the tt. of the Church.* [-ING[1]]

Teague (tēg), n. (contempt.). Irishman. [f. *Tadhg*, common Irish name]

teak (tēk), n. (E.-Ind. tree with) heavy durable timber that does not warp or shrink or corrode iron, much used in shipbuilding. [f. Port. *teca* f. Malayalam *tēkka*]

teal (tēl), n. (pl. same). Kinds of small freshwater duck. [ME *tele*, cf. Du. *taling, te-*, etym. dub.]

team (tēm), n., & v.t. Two or more beasts of burden harnessed together, whence **tea·m**WISE adv.; set of players on one side in some games e.g. football; set of persons working together; *t.-work*, combined effort, organized cooperation. (Vb) harness (horses &c.) in t.; give out (work) to contractor who employs t. of workmen, whence **tea·m**ING[1] n. [OE *téam* family, set, cf. Du. *toom*, ON *taumr*, rein, G *zaum* bridle, cogn. w. L *ducere* lead]

tea·mster, n. Driver of a team. [-STER]

tea·poy (tēp-), n. Small three or four legged table esp. for tea. [f. Hind. *tīn* three + Pers. *pāē* foot; sense & spelling influenced by TEA]

tear[1] (tār), v.t. & i. (tore, torn), & n. Pull apart, rend, lacerate, as *tore up the letter, has torn his coat, t. it in half, in two, in pieces, torn to pieces by a tiger*; (fig.) *country was torn by factions, heart torn by conflicting emotions*; make (hole, rent) thus; pull violently (lit. & fig.), as *tore down the notice, t. out a page, t. off the cover, tree torn up by the roots, was torn* (forcibly parted) *from her parents, babe torn from the breast, could not t. myself* (make up my mind to go) *away*; pull violently *at*, as *tore at the cover of the parcel*; *t.* one's *hair*, pull it in anger or perplexity or despair; lend itself to tearing, as *tears easily, will not t.*; run or walk hurriedly or impetuously, as *tore down the hill, was simply tearing*; *tear·away* a., impetuous; (n.) rent in cloth &c. [(n. f. vb) OE *teran*, cf. Goth. *gatairan* break, G *zehren* consume, Gk *derō* flay]

tear[2] (tēr), n. (Also *t.-drop*) drop of saline liquid ordinarily serving to moisten & wash the eye but falling from it as result of grief or other emotion or of coughing or laughter, as *the tt. fell down her cheeks, wept tt. bitter of remorse, laughed till the tt. came, tt. were her only argument, a t.-stained face, found her in tt.* (weeping); t.-like thing, e.g. drop of fluid, solid drop of resin &c.; *tt. of strong wine*, drops forming on inside of partly-filled glass of port &c.; CROCODILE *tt.*; *t.*-(= LACHRYMATORY) *shell.* [OE *téar*, cf. ON *tár*, Da. *taar*, cogn. w. L *lacrima*, Gk *dakru(on)*]

tear·ful, a. Shedding tears, so **tear·**LESS a.; (of event, news, &c.) mournful, sad. Hence **tear·ful**LY[2] adv., **tear·ful**NESS n. [-FUL]

tear·ing, a. In vbl senses (TEAR[1]), also; violent, overwhelming (*t. pace, rage*). [-ING[2]]

tease (tēz), v.t., & n. Assail playfully or maliciously, vex, with jests, questions, or petty annoyances, whence **tea·sing**LY[2] adv.; importune (person *for* thing, *to* do); pick into separate fibres, comb, card, (wool, flax, &c.); dress (cloth &c.) with teasels. (N.) person given to teasing. [OE *tǽsan* pluck, pull, cf. Du. *teezen*]

tea·sel (-z-), **-zel, -zle,** n., & v.t. Kinds of plant with large prickly heads used in dressing cloth; such head; machine substituted for tt.; (vb) dress (cloth) with tt., whence **tea·sel**ER[1], **-zler,** n. [OE *tǽs(e)l* (as prec. + -LE)]

tea·ser, n. In vbl senses, esp.: teasing person; (colloq.) difficult question or problem or task, thing hard to deal with. [-ER[1]]

teat (tēt), n. Mammary nipple through which milk passes, pap of woman, dug of beast. Hence **(-)teat**ED[2], **tea·t**LIKE, aa. [f. OF *tete* prob. f. Teut. (OE *tit*, MDu. *titte*)]

tec, n. (slang). Detective. [abbr.]

te·chnic (-k-), a. & n. (Adj., rare) = foll.; (n.) = TECHNIQUE, (usu. pl.) doctrine of arts in general, (pl.) technical terms, details, methods, &c. Hence **te·chnic**IST n. [f. L f. Gk *tekhnikos* (*tekhnē* art, see -IC)]

te·chnical, a. Of or in a particular art, science, handicraft, &c., as *t. terms, skill, difficulty*; of, for, in, the mechanical arts, as *t. education, school.* Hence **te·chnical**LY[2] adv., **te·chnical**NESS n. [-AL]

technica·lity, n. Technicalness, technical expression, distinction, &c., as *legal tt.* [-ITY]

techni·que (-ēk), n. Mode of artistic execution in music, painting, &c.; mechanical skill in art. [F, as TECHNIC]

techno·logy, n. Science of the industrial arts; ethnological study of development of arts. Hence **technolo·gICAL** a., **techno·logIST** n. [f. Gk *tekhnologia* (*tekhnē* art, -LOGY)]

techy. See TETCHY.

tecto·logy, n. Structural morphology, i.e. that which treats an organism as composed of organic individuals. Hence **tectolo·gICAL** a. [irreg. f. Gk *tektōn* carpenter + -LOGY]

tectŏ·nic, a. & n. Of building or construction; (Geol.) due to a change in structural conditions caused by deformation; (n. pl.) whole art of producing useful and beautiful buildings, furniture, vessels, &c. [f. LL f. Gk *tektonikos* (*tektōn -onos* carpenter, see -IC)]

tector·ial, a. Forming a covering, esp. *t. membrane* (of ear). [f. L *tectorius* (as foll., see -ORY) + -AL]

tectrī·cēs, n. pl. (ornith.). Covering feathers of wings & tail. [f. L *tegere tect-* cover, -TRIX]

ted, v.t. Turn over and spread out (grass, hay) to dry. Hence **te·ddER**[1](1, 2) n. [f. Icel. *tedhja* spread manure (*tadh*)]

Te·ddy bear, n. Child's toy bear (named after *Theodore* Roosevelt).

Tē Dē·um, n. (Music for) hymn beginning *T.D. laudamus, We praise thee, O God,* sung at morning service, or on special occasions as thanksgiving; *sing T.D.*, (fig.) exult, triumph. [L]

tē·dious, a. Wearisome, irksome, tiresome. Hence **te·diousLY**[2] adv., **te·diousNESS** n. [f. LL *taediosus* (as foll., see -OUS)]

tē·dium, n. Tediousness. [f. L *taedium* (*taedet* it wearies)]

tee[1], n. Letter T; T-shaped thing esp. pipe.

tee[2], n., & v.t. & i. Mark aimed at in quoits, bowls, curling; (Golf) small pile of sand on which ball is placed at beginning of play for each hole, small appliance of rubber &c. for same purpose; (v.t.) place (ball) on t.; (v.i.) *t. off*, start from t., (fig.) start, begin. [?]

tee[3], n. Umbrella-shaped usu. gilded ornament crowning tope or pagoda. [f. Burm. *h'ti* umbrella]

teem[1], v.t. & i. (Archaic) bear (offspring); be prolific, be stocked to overflowing *with*, as *forests t. with snakes, book teems with blunders*; be abundant, as *fish t. in these waters.* [OE *týman* (TEAM)]

teem[2], v.t. (dial., tech.). Empty, discharge, pour out, (vessel, cart, coal, molten metal, &c.). Hence **tee·mER**[1] n. [f. ON *tœma* (*tómr* adj. empty)]

teen, n. (archaic). Grief; trouble; harm. [OE *téona* injury, cf. ON *tjón*]

-teen, suf. of numbers from 13 to 19 implying addition of ten (stress: four·teen, se·venteen, &c., in counting; elsewhere four·tee·n, se·ventee·n, &c., esp. when confusion w. forty, seventy, is to be avoided). [OE *téne, týne*, pl. of TEN]

teens, n. pl. Years of one's age from 13 to 19, esp. *in* one's *t.* [f. prec.]

teeny. See TINY.

teeth. See TOOTH.

teethe (-dh), v.i. Grow or cut teeth. Hence **tee·thING**[1] n. [f. prec.]

teetō·tal, a. Of, advocating, total abstinence from intoxicants, as *t. meeting, pledge*, whence **teeto·talISM** n.; (colloq.) total, entire, whence **teeto·talLY**[2] adv. [redupl. of *total*; from about 1833]

teeto·taller, n. Total abstainer. [-ER[1]]

teetō·tum, n. Children's four-sided top with sides lettered to determine gain or loss of the spinner; any top spun with the fingers (*like a t.*, spinning). [f. T (the letter on one side) + L *totum* the whole (stakes), for which it stood]

teg, n. Sheep in its second year. [f. 16th c., etym. dub.]

tĕ·gular, a. Of or like tiles. Hence or cogn. **te·gularLY**[2] adv., **te·gulated** [-ATE[2]] a. [f. L *tegula* tile (*tegere* cover) + -AR[1]]

tĕ·gument, n. Natural covering of (part of) animal body. Hence **tegume·ntAL**, **tegume·ntARY**[1], aa. [f. L *tegumentum* (*tegere* cover, see -MENT)]

tēhee·, n., & v.i. Restrained or contemptuous laugh; (v.i.) laugh thus, titter. [imit.]

Tē·ian, Tē·an, a. Of (the poet Anacreon born at) Teos. [f. L *Teius* (L f. Gk *Teōs*) + -AN]

teind (tēnd), n. (Sc.). Tithe. [ME *tende*, = TEN*th*]

tei·noscope (tī-), n. Instrument consisting of two prisms combined to correct chromatic aberration & increase or decrease dimensions of objects. [f. Gk *teinō* stretch, -SCOPE]

teknŏ·nymy, n. (anthrop.). Practice of naming parent from child. So **tekno·nymOUS** a. [f. Gk *teknon* child + *-ōnumos* -named + -Y[1]]

tĕlaesthē·sia, n. (psych.). Direct perception of distant occurrences or objects not effected by the recognized senses. Hence **telaesthe·tIC** a. [mod. L, f. TELE-, Gk *aisthēsis* perception, & -IA[1]]

tĕ·lamon, n. (archit.). Male figure as bear ing pillar (cf. CARYATID). [L, f. Gk *Telamōn* mythol. person]

telau·tograph, n. Telegraph that reproduces writing &c. So **telau·toGRAM** (5) n. [f. TELE- + AUTO- + -GRAPH]

tĕlĕ- in comb. = Gk *tēle-* far, esp. in names of instruments producing or recording results &c. at a distance, as: *-baro·meter*;

-meter, instrument for determining distances in surveying, artillery practice, &c., whence *-me·tric* a., *-metry* n.; *-ther-mo·meter.*

tĕ·ledu (-ōō), n. Stinking badger of Java and Sumatra. [native]

tele·gony, n. (biol.). Influence of previous sire seen in subsequent sire's progeny by same mother. Hence **telego·nic** a. [f. TELE- + Gk *-gonia* begetting]

te·legram, n. Telegraphic message. [-GRAM]

te·legraph[1], n. Apparatus for transmitting messages or signals to a distance esp. by electricity; semaphore; (in titles of newspapers) *Daily T.* &c.; *t.* (*-board*), board on which numbers of horses running in race, cricket scores, &c., are put up so as to be visible at distance; *t.-key*, device for making and breaking electric circuit of t.; *t.-line, -pole* or *-post, -wire* (used in forming telegraphic connexion); *t.-plant*, E.-Ind. plant whose leaves have spontaneous jerking motion. [f. F *télégraphe* (TELE-, -GRAPH)]

te·legraph[2], v.t. & i. Send (message *to* person, or abs.) by telegraph, as *t. the news to your father, t. me the result, t. to him to come, that we cannot come*; make signals (*to* person *to* do, *that*, &c.). [as prec.]

telĕ·grapher (*or* tĕ·-), n. Person skilled or employed in telegraphy. So **tele·graphist** n. [-ER[1]]

telegraphe·se, n. & a. (In) the elliptical style usual in telegrams. [-ESE]

telegra·phic, a. Of telegraphs or telegrams; of t. brevity, economically worded, with unessential words omitted; *t. address*, abbreviated or other registered address for use in telegrams. Hence **telegra·phically** adv. [-IC]

tele·graphy, n. Art of constructing, practice of communicating by, telegraph; *wireless t.*, transmission of signals through space by means of electric waves. [-Y[1]]

telekīne·sis, n. (psych.). Movement at a distance from the motive cause or agent without material connexion. [mod. L, f. TELE- + Gk *kinēsis* motion (*kineō* move)]

tĕ·lemark, n. Expert swing turn in skiing used to change direction or to stop short. [f. *T.*, district in Norway]

telemecha·nics, n. pl. Art of transmitting power by radio, & so controlling machinery from a distance. [TELE-]

teleo·logy, n. Doctrine of final causes, view that developments are due to the purpose or design that is served by them. So **teleolo·gic(al)** aa., **teleolo·gically**[2] adv., **teleo·logism, teleo·logist,** nn. [f. Gk *telos -eos* end + -LOGY]

tĕleosaur·us, n. Genus of fossil crocodiles. [f. Gk *teleos* complete + *sauros* lizard]

telĕ·pathy, n. Action of one mind on another at a distance through emotional influence without communication through senses. Hence **telepa·thic** a., **telepa·thically** adv., **tele·pathist**(2) n., **tele·pathize**(1, 2) v.t. & i. [TELE- + -PATHY]

te·lephone, n., & v.t. & i. Apparatus for transmitting sound esp. speech to a distance by wire or cord, esp. by means of electricity; *the t.*, system of communication by a network of tt. (*on the t.*, having an instrument connected with this, also by use of or while using the t.); (vb) send (message &c.), speak, (*to* person) by t. Hence **telephŏ·nic** a., **telepho·nically** adv., **tele·phonist**(3), **tele·phony**[1] n. [(vb f. n.) f. TELE- + Gk *phōnē* sound]

telephoto·graphy, n. Photographing of distant objects by means of a combination of telescope & ordinary photographic lens. So **telephotogra·phic** a. [TELE-]

te·lergy, n. (psych.). Force conceived as operating on the brain in telepathy. [TELE- + (*en*)*ergy*]

te·lescope, n., & v.t. & i. Instrument for making distant objects appear nearer & larger, whence **tele·scopist**(3), **tele·scopy**[1], nn.; (v.t.) press, drive, (sections of tube, colliding trains, &c.) together so that one slides into another like sections of small t.; (v.i.) close, be driven, be capable of closing, thus. [(vb f. n.) f. It. *telescopio* (TELE-, -SCOPE)]

telescŏ·pic, a. Of, made with, a telescope, as *t. observations*; visible only through telescope, as *t. stars*; consisting of sections that telescope, as *t. chimney* (of steamer), so **telescŏ·piform** a. Hence **telesco·pically** adv. [-IC]

te·leseme, n. System of electrical signalling including annunciator, used in hotels &c. [f. TELE- + Gk *sēma* sign]

televi·sion, n. The seeing, by aid of Hertzian waves or otherwise, of what is existing or happening at a place veiled by obstacles or distance from the observer's eyes. [TELE-]

tell, v.t. & i. (tōld). Relate in spoken or written words, as *t. me a tale, a story*; make known, divulge, state, express in words, as *t. me what you want, t. me all about it, will t. you a secret, t. it not in Gath* (let this news not reach and gladden the enemy, usu. joc. w. ref. to 2 *Sam.* i. 20), *t. that to the* (HORSE[1]-)*marines, told him my candid opinion, t. me your name, t.* TALES (*out of school*), *cannot t. you how glad I was, t.* FORTUNES; utter, as *you told me a lie, a* STORY[1], *are you telling the truth?*; give information or description, as *told me of* or *about his difficulties, he told of foreign lands, that tells a tale* (is significant, reveals something); decide, determine, as *how do you t. which button to press?, you never can t.* (appearances & probabilities are deceptive); distinguish, as *cannot t. them apart, him from his brother*; (childish) *don't t. on* (inform against) *me*; assure, as *I can t. you, it is* *not so easy*; produce marked effect, as *every blow tells, strain begins to t. on him*, whence **te·lling**[2] a., **te·llingly**[2] adv.; count (votes esp. in H. of Commons, one's BEAD[1]*s*; *we were 15 men all told*; *t. a hundred*; *tells over his gold every night*); *t. off*, count off, detach, for duty, as *6 of us were, I was, told off to get fuel*, (slang) t. (person) home truths, recite misdoings of. Hence **te·llable** a. [OE *tellan* (TALE), cf. Du. *tellen*, G *zählen*]

te·ller, n. In vbl senses, esp.: any of four persons appointed (two for each side) to count votes in H. of Commons; person appointed to receive or pay out money in bank &c. Hence **te·llership** n. [-ER[1]]

te·lltale, n. One who tells about another's private affairs, tattler; (fig.) thing, circumstance, that reveals person's thoughts, conduct, &c., esp. attrib., as *t. blushes, face, the t. clay on his shoes*; kinds of mechanical device for recording person's attendance at specified time &c., giving warning that cistern is full, &c.; (Naut.) index near wheel to show position of tiller, (also *t. compass*) compass hung usu. in captain's cabin for checking ship's course.

tellur·ian, a. (Inhabitant) of the earth. So **tellur·al** a. [as foll. + -IAN]

tellūr·ion, n. Instrument for illustrating succession of day & night & changes of seasons. [f. L *tellus -uris* earth]

tellur·ium, n. (chem.). A rare brittle silver-coloured element resembling sulphur. Hence **te·llurate**[1](3), **te·lluret, te·lluride,** nn., **te·lluretted**[1], **tellur·ic, te·llurous,** aa. [as prec. + -IUM]

tĕ·lotype, n. Printing electric telegraph; telegram so printed. [TELE-, -O-, TYPE]

te·lpher, a. Serving to transport (esp. goods) by electric locomotion, as *t. line*. Hence **te·lpherage**(1, 2) n. [for TELE-(PHORE)]

te·lson, n. Last joint in abdomen of Crustacea. [Gk, = limit]

tĕ·menos, n. (Gk ant.; pl. *-nē*). Sacred enclosure, temple precinct. [Gk (*temnō* cut)]

tĕmerār·ious, a. (literary). Reckless, rash. [f. L *temerarius* (*temere* rashly) + -OUS]

temĕ·rity, n. Rashness. [f. L *temeritas* (*temere* at random, rashly, see -TY)]

temp., abbr. (now usu. as playful pedantry) of L *tempore* in the time of, as *temp. Henry I.*

Tempē·an, (*or* tĕ·-), a. Of or like Tempe, beautiful vale in Thessaly celebrated by Gk & L poets. [-AN]

te·mper[1], v.t. & i. Prepare (clay &c.) by moistening, mixing, & kneading; bring (metal, esp. steel), (of metal) come, to proper hardness & elasticity by successive heating & cooling; modify, mitigate, (*justice* &c.) by blending *with* (*mercy* &c.); moderate, restrain, tone down; (Mus.) tune, modulate, (piano, organ) in particular TEMPERAMENT. Hence **te·mperable, te·mperative,** aa., **te·mperer**[1] n. [OE *temprian* f. L *temperare* (perh. f. *tempus -oris* time, due season)]

te·mper[2], n. Mixture, esp. suitable combination of ingredients (*of* mortar &c.); resulting condition or consistence; condition of metal as to hardness & elasticity; habitual or temporary disposition of mind, as *was of a saturnine, frigid, fiery, placid, t., persons of congenial t., found him in a good t.* (not irritable or angry), *in a bad t.* (peevish, angry); irritation, anger, as *fit of t., what a t. he is in!, naughty t.!*; *show t.*, be petulant; *lose* one's *t.*, become angry; *keep, control*, one's *t.*, not lose it; *out of t.*, angry. Hence **-tempered**[2] a., **-te·mperedly**[2] adv. [f. prec.]

te·mpera, n. = DISTEMPER[3]. [It.]

te·mperament, n. Individual character of one's physical organization permanently affecting the manner of acting, feeling, & thinking, as *a nervous t., the artistic t.*; *sanguine, lymphatic* or *phlegmatic, choleric* or *bilious, melancholic* or *atrabilious, t.* (formerly attributed to predominance of blood, lymph, yellow bile, black bile); (Mus.) adjustment of tones of piano &c. so as to fit the scale for all keys, esp. *equal* or *even t.*, in which the 12 semitones are at equal intervals. Hence **temperame·ntal** a. (in n. senses, & esp., of persons, liable to peculiar moods). [f. L *temperamentum* (as TEMPER[1], see -MENT)]

te·mperance, n. Moderation, self-restraint, in speech, conduct, &c., esp. in eating & drinking; moderation in use of, total abstinence from, alcoholic liquors as beverages; *t. hotel* (not supplying alcoholic drinks); *t. movement, society, league* (for restriction or abolition of use of alcoholic drinks). [AF (*-aunce*), f. L *temperantia* (as TEMPER[1], see -ANCE)]

te·mperate (*-at*), a. Moderate; self-restrained; abstemious; of mild temperature, as *north, south, t. zone* (between tropic of Cancer & arctic circle, Capricorn & antarctic). Hence **te·mperately**[2] adv., **te·mperateness** n. [f. L TEMPER[1]*atus*]

te·mperature (-tsh*er*, -tūr), n. Degree or intensity of sensible heat of a body or of the atmosphere esp. as shown by thermometer, as *high, low, t.*; (Med.) internal heat of the body (*normal t.* in man, 98°·4; *take* one's *t.*, ascertain his variation from this in illness &c.); *absolute* ZERO *of t.*; *t. curve* (showing variations of t.). [f. L *temperatura* (as TEMPER[1], see -URE)]

te·mpest, n. Violent storm of wind often with rain, snow, &c.; (fig.) violent tumult or agitation. [f. OF *tempeste* f. L *tem-*

pestatem time, weather, storm (*tempus* time, see -TY)]

tempe·stūous, a. (Of weather, time, &c., and fig. of person or mood) stormy, violent. Hence **tempe·stuous**LY[2] adv., **tempe·stuous**NESS n. [f. LL *tempestuosus* (prec., -OUS; for *-u-* cf. VOLUPTUOUS)]

te·mplar, n. (*T-*) member of religious military order (*Knights Tt.*) for protection of pilgrims to Holy Land, suppressed in 1312; lawyer, law student, with chambers in the Temple; *Free, Good, Tt.*, secret temperance societies. [f. OF *templier* =med. L *templarius* (TEMPLE[1], -ARY[1])]

template. See TEMPLET.

te·mple[1], n. Edifice dedicated to service of (esp. ancient Greek, Roman, Egyptian) god; any of three successive religious edifices of the Jews in Jerusalem; place of Christian public worship, esp. Protestant church in France; (fig.) place in which God resides (1 *Cor.* vi. 19); *Inner, Middle, T.*, two INNS *of Court* on site of *the T.* (establishment of Knights Templars) in London; *T. Bar*, gateway (removed 1879) that marked the westward limit of the City Corporation's jurisdiction, at junction of Fleet Street & Strand in London. [f. L *templum* cogn. w. Gk TEMENOS]

te·mple[2], n. Flat part of either side of head between forehead & ear. [OF, f. L *tempora* the tt. (sing. *tempus*)]

te·mple[3], n. Device in loom for keeping cloth stretched. [F, = foll.]

te·mplet, -āte, n. Pattern, gauge, usu. thin board or metal plate, used as guide in cutting or drilling metal, stone, wood, &c.; timber or plate used to distribute weight in wall or under beam &c.; wedge for building-block under ship's keel; =prec. [perh. f. L *templum* rafter + -ET[1]]

te·mpo, n. (mus.). Time, rapidity of movement; characteristic style of movement, as *t. di menuetto*. [It.]

te·mporal, a. & n. Of this life, secular, esp. opp. to *spiritual*, as *t. affairs, interests*, whence **te·mporal**LY[2] adv., **te·mporal**NESS n.; *t. lords*, peers of realm, cf. SPIRITUAL; *t. power*, of ecclesiastic esp. Pope in t. matters; of or in or denoting time (*t. & spatial*, of time & space; *t. conjunctions*, when &c.), (Gk Gram.) *t. augment* (made by lengthening initial vowel); of the temple(s) of the head, as *t. artery, bone*; (n.) t. bone. [F, f. L *temporalis* (*tempus -oris*, see TEMPER[1], TEMPLE[2], + -AL)]

tempora·lity, n. A secular possession, esp. properties & revenues of religious corporation or ecclesiastic (usu. pl.); (Law) temporariness. [f. LL *temporalitatem* (as prec., see -TY)]

te·mporalty, n. The laity; =prec. (1st sense). [f. OF *temporalité* as prec.]

te·mporary, a. Lasting, meant, only for a time, as *t. buildings, relief, possession, office*. Hence **te·mporari**LY[2] adv., **te·mporari**NESS n. [f. L *temporarius* (*tempus -oris* time, see -ARY[1])]

te·mporize, v.i. Pursue indecisive or time-serving policy; avoid committing oneself, act so as to gain time; comply temporarily with requirements of occasion. Hence **temporiza·**TION, **te·mporizer**[1], nn., **te·mporizing**LY[2] adv. [f. F *temporiser* f. L *tempus -oris* time + -IZE]

te·mporo- in comb. =L *tempora* temples of head, as *-fa·cial*, of temporal & facial regions.

tempt, v.t. (Archaic, bibl.) test, try the resolution of, as *God did t. Abraham*; entice, incite, (*to* do, *to* action esp. evil one); *I am tempted* (strongly disposed) *to question this*; allure, attract, whence **te·mpting**LY[2] adv.; (archaic, bibl.) provoke, defy, as *shalt not t. the Lord*. Hence or cogn. **tempta**BI·LITY n., **te·mpt**ABLE a. [f. OF *tenter, tempt-*, f. L *temtare, tempt-*, handle, test, try]

tempta·tion, n. Tempting or being tempted (*the T.*, see *Matt.* iv); thing that attracts, attractive course. [f. OF *temptacioun* f. L *temptationem* (prec., -ATION)]

te·mpter, n. One who tempts; *the T.*, the devil. So **te·mpt**RESS[1] n. [ME *temptour* f. L *temptatorem* (as prec., see -OR[2])]

ten, a. & n. One more than nine, 10, X; (as round number) *t. times as easy, t. to one he forgets it*; HART *of t.*; UPPER *t.*; *ten*PENNY *nail*; *t.-pou·nder* (hist.), person having vote in parliamentary election by occupation of property of rental value of £10. Hence **te·n**FOLD a. & adv., **ten**TH[2] a. & n., **te·nth**LY[2] adv. [OE *tien* cf. Du. *tien*, G *zehn*, & L *decem*, Gk *deka*]

tĕ·nable, a. That can be maintained or defended against attack, as *a t. position, fortress, theory*; (of office &c.) that can be held *for* specified time, *by* person, &c. Hence **tena**BI·LITY, **te·nable**NESS, nn. [F (*tenir* hold f. L *tenēre*, see -ABLE)]

tĕ·nace (-ĭs), n. (whist). (Holding of) two cards, one next above, the other next below, the opponents' highest of the suit (*major, minor, t.*, variations of this variously defined). [f. Sp. *tenaza* lit. pincers]

tenā·cious (-shus), a. Holding fast; keeping firm hold (*of* property, rights, principles, &c.); (of memory) retentive; adhesive, sticky; strongly cohesive. Hence or cogn. **tena·cious**LY[2] adv., **tena·cious**NESS, **tenă·**CITY, nn. [f. L *tenax* (*tenēre* hold, see -ACIOUS)]

tenă·cūlum, n. (pl. *-la*). Surgeon's sharp hook for picking up arteries &c. [L, = holding instrument (*tenēre* hold)]

tenai·l, -aille, (-āl), n. (fortif.). Outwork in main ditch in front of curtain between two bastions. [F (*-le*), f. prec.]

tĕ·nant, n., & v.t. One who occupies land or tenement under a landlord; (Law) person holding real property by private ownership, also defendant in real action; occupant (*of* any place); *t. farmer* (cultivating farm he does not own); *t. right*, right of t. to continue tenancy, as long as he pays rent & acts properly, without injurious increase of rent, & to receive compensation from landlord if turned off; (v.t.) occupy as t. (esp. in p.p.). Hence or cogn. **te·nancy** n., **te·nantless** a. [F, f. L *tenēre* hold, see -ANT]

te·nantable, a. Fit to be occupied by a tenant. [-ABLE]

te·nantry, n. Tenants. [-RY]

tench, n. A European freshwater fish of carp family. [f. OF *tenche* f. LL *tinca*]

tend[1], v.i. Be moving, be directed, hold a course, lit. & fig., as *tends in our direction, downwards, this way, towards the coast, to the same conclusion*; be apt or inclined, serve, conduce, (*to* action, quality, &c., *to* do). [f. OF *tendre* stretch f. L *tendere tens-* or *tent-*]

tend[2], v.t. & i. Take care of, look after, (flocks, invalid, machine); wait *upon*; (Naut.) watch (ship at anchor) so as to keep turns out of her cable. So **te·ndance** n. (archaic). [shortened f. ATTEND]

te·ndency, n. Bent, leaning, inclination, (*towards, to*, thing, *to* do). [f. med. L *tendentia* (as TEND[1], see -ANCE)]

tende·ntious, a. (Of writing &c.) having an underlying purpose, calculated to advance a cause. [f. G *tendenziös* (TENDENCY, -OUS)]

te·nder[1], n. In vbl senses of TEND[2]; also: vessel attending larger one to supply her with stores, convey orders, &c.; carriage attached to locomotive & carrying fuel, water, &c.; small water reservoir fixed to mop &c. [-ER[1]]

te·nder[2], v.t. & i., & n. Offer, present, give in, (one's *services, resignation*, &c.); offer (money &c.) as payment; make a t. (*for* supply of thing or execution of work). (N.) offer, esp. offer in writing to execute work or supply goods at fixed price, as *are open to receive tt. for*; *plea of t.* (that defendant has always been ready to satisfy plaintiff's claim & now brings the sum into court); *legal t.*, currency that cannot be refused in payment of debt, as *silver is not l. t. above 40s.* [(n. f. vb) as TEND[1]]

te·nder[3], a. (-est). Soft, not tough or hard, as *t. steak*; easily touched or wounded, susceptible to pain or grief, as *a t. heart, conscience, place* (in body); delicate, fragile, (lit., & fig. of reputation &c.; *of t. age*, immature, young); loving, affectionate, fond, as *t. parents, wrote t. verses*; solicitous, considerate, (*of* one's honour, good name, &c.); afraid *of* (*doing* wrong thing); requiring careful handling ticklish, as *a t. subject*; *t.-eyed*, having gentle eyes, weak-eyed; *te·nderfoot* (colon. & U.S. slang), new-comer in bush &c., novice; *t.-hearted*, having t. heart, so *t.-hear·tedly* adv., *t.-hear·tedness* n.; (U.S.) *te·nderloin*, undercut of sirloin, (*T-*) amusements district of New York & other cities. Hence **te·nderly**[2] adv., **te·nderness** n. [f. OF *tendre* f. L *tener*]

te·ndon, n. Strong band or cord of tissue forming termination or connexion of fleshy part of muscle; *Achilles t.* (L *tendo Achillis*), t. connecting heel (where alone Achilles was vulnerable) with calf. So **te·ndinous** a. [f. med. L *tendo -inis* f. Gk *tenōn* w. assim. to *tendere* stretch]

te·ndril, n. Slender leafless plant-organ attaching itself to another body for support. Hence **te·ndrilled**[2] a. [cf. F *tendrillon* dim. of *tendron* bud (as TENDER[3])]

tĕ·nebrae, n. pl. (R.-C. Ch.). Matins & lauds for last three days of Holy Week, at which candles are successively extinguished. [L, = darkness]

tenebri·fic, a. Making darkness, as *t. stars* (believed to cause night). [f. prec., see -FIC]

tĕ·nebrous, a. (archaic). Dark, gloomy. [f. OF *tenebrus* f. L *tenebrosus* (TENEBRAE, -OUS)]

tĕ·nĕment, n. Piece of land held by an owner; (Law) any kind of permanent property, e.g. lands, rents, peerage, held of a superior, so **teneme·ntary**[1] a.; dwelling-house; set of apartments used by one family (*t.-house*, containing tt.). Hence **teneme·ntal** a. [OF, f. med. L *tenementum* (*tenēre* hold, see -MENT)]

tĕ·net, n. Principle, dogma, doctrine, of a person or school. [L, = he holds; formerly also *tenent*, = they hold]

te·nner, n. (colloq.). Ten-pound note. [-ER[1]]

te·nnis, n. Game for 2, 3, or 4 persons played by striking ball with rackets over net stretched across walled court; = LAWN *t.*; *t. arm, elbow*, affection of arm caused by t.; *t.-ball, -court* (for t.). [15th c. *tenetz*, prob. of F orig., perh. = *tenez* hold, take this, play (as foll.)]

tĕ·non, n., & v.t. End of piece of wood fitted for insertion into corresponding cavity (esp. MORTISE) in another piece; *t.-saw* (small, with strong brass or steel back, for fine work); (v.t.) cut into a t., join by means of t., whence **te·noner**[1] (1, 2) n. [F, f. *tenir* hold f. L *tenēre*]

tĕ·nor, n. Settled or prevailing course or direction, esp. fig. *of* one's *life, way*, &c.; general purport, drift, (*of* speech, writing, &c.); (Law) true intent, (also) exact copy; (Mus.) (music for, singer with) highest ordinary adult male voice, between barytone & alto (often attrib., as *t. voice*); instrument, esp. viola, playing part between bass & alto; *t. bell* (largest of peal or set). So **te·norist**(3) n. (mus.). [f. OF *tenour* f. L *tenorem* holding on, (med. L) chief melody (formerly assigned to adult male voice), f. *tenēre* hold, see -OR[1]]

teno·tomy, n. Tendon-cutting, esp. as remedy for club-foot. [irreg. f. Gk *tenōn, -ontos* tendon (*teinō* stretch) + -TOMY]

tense[1], n. (gram.). Form taken by verb to indicate the time (also continuance or completeness) of the action &c., as *present future, past, (im)perfect, pluperfect, aorist, t., primary, historic, tt.*; set of such forms for the various persons; SEQUENCE *of tt.* Hence **te·nse**LESS a. [f. OF *tens* f. L *tempus* time]

tense[2], a. (Of cord, membrane, nerve, fig. of mind, emotion), stretched tight, strained to stiffness. Hence **te·nse**LY[2] adv., **te·nse**NESS, **te·ns**ITY, nn. [f. L as TEND[1]]

te·nsile, a. Of tension, as *t. force*; capable of being drawn out or stretched, whence or cogn. **tensi**BI·LITY, **tensi·l**ITY, nn., **te·nsi**BLE a. [as prec., see -IL]

te·nsion, n., & v.t. Stretching, being stretched; tenseness; mental strain or excitement; strained (political, social, &c.) state; (Mech.) stress by which bar, cord, &c. is pulled when it is part of a system in equilibrium or motion; expansive force of gas or vapour; (v.t., only in p.p.) subject to t. Hence **te·nsion**AL a. [f. LL *tensio* (as TEND[1], see -ION)]

te·nson, -zon, n. Contest in verse between troubadours; subdivision of poem composed for this. [F (*-son*), = It. *tenzone*, as prec.]

te·nsor, n. (anat.). Muscle that tightens or stretches a part. [as TEND[1], see -OR[2]]

tent[1], n., & v.i. & t. Portable shelter of canvas, cloth, &c., supported by pole(s) & stretched by cords secured to *t.-pegs* driven into ground; *bell t.*, circular t. with one pole in middle; (Photog., also *dark t.*) portable dark room for outdoor use; *t.-bed* (with a t.-like canopy); *t.-fly*, piece of canvas stretched over ridge pole of tent leaving open space but keeping off sun & rain; *t.-pegging*, cavalry exercise in which rider tries at full gallop to carry off on point of lance t.-peg fixed in ground; *t.-stitch*, series of parallel diagonal stitches suggesting t.; (v.t.) cover (as) with t.; (v.i.) encamp in t. [ME & OF *tente* f. L *tenta* neut. pl. p.p. as TEND[1]]

tent[2], n., & v.t. Piece, bunch, roll, of linen &c. inserted into wound or natural opening to keep it open; (v.t.) keep open thus. [f. F *tente(r)* as TEMPT; earlier sense *probe*]

tent[3], n. Deep red wine chiefly from Spain, used esp. as sacramental wine. [f. Sp. *tinto* deep-coloured f. L as TINGE]

te·ntacle, n. Feeler, long slender flexible process or appendage of animal, used for exploration, prehension, or locomotion; (Bot.) sensitive hair or filament. Hence **te·ntacl**ED[2], **tentă·cul**AR[1], **tenta·cu-l**ATE[2], **-ated, tenta·culi**FORM, **tentacu-li**GEROUS, aa. [f. L as TEMPT + *-culum* seen in *spectaculum* &c.]

te·ntative, a. & n. Done by way of trial, experimental; (n.) experimental proposal or theory. Hence **te·ntative**LY[2] adv. [f. med. L *tentativus* (as TEMPT, see -IVE)]

te·nter[1], n. Person in charge of something, esp. of machinery in factory. [f. obs. & Sc. *tent* var. of TEND[2] + -ER[1]]

te·nter[2], n. Machine for stretching cloth to set or dry; *t.(-hook)*, each of the hooks that hold the cloth; *be on t.-hooks* or (archaic) *on the tt.* (in state of suspense or mental torment). [earlier also *tenture*, prob. f. L *tentura* (TEND[1], -URE); cf. BORDER]

tĕ·nŭis, n. (pl. *-es* pr. -ēz). Hard or surd mute (k, p, t), cf. MEDIA. [L, = thin]

tenŭ·ity, n. Slenderness; (of air, fluid) rarity, thinness; (of style) simplicity, absence of grandeur. [f. L *tenuitatem* (as prec., see -TY)]

tĕ·nuous, a. (rare). Thin, slender, small; (of distinctions &c.) subtle, over-refined. [f. L TENUIS + -OUS]

tĕ·nure (-*yer*), n. Kind of right or title by which (esp. real) property is held, as ALLODIAL, FEUDAL, *t.*, *military t.* (involving military service); (period of) holding, possession, enjoyment, as *during his t. of office, holds life on a precarious t.*; (Hist.) *t.-horn, -sword* (produced on certain occasions as evidence of t. of estates). [OF (*tenir* hold f. L *tenēre*, see -URE)]

tenu·to (-ōō-), a. (mus.). Sustained, given its full time value (cf. STACCATO). [It., = held]

tēoca·llĭ, n. Temple of Mex. & other Amer. aborigines, usu. on truncated pyramid. [Mex. (*teotl* god + *calli* house); also *teopan*]

tĕ·pefȳ, v.t. & i. Make, become, tepid. Hence **tepe**FA·CTION n. [f. L *tepefacere* (as TEPID, see -FY)]

te·phrite, n. Kinds of modern volcanic rock. [f. Gk *tephra* ashes, -ITE[1]]

tĕpid, a. Slightly warm, lukewarm (lit. & fig.). Hence or cogn. **tepi·**DITY, **te·pid**NESS, nn., **te·pid**LY[2] adv. [f. L *tepidus* (*tepēre* be lukewarm, see -ID[1])]

tepidār·ium, n. (Rom. ant.; pl. *-aria*). Intermediate room of moderate temperature in Roman baths; boiler for heating hot bath. [L (as prec., see -ARIUM)]

ter, adv. Three times (esp. mus.). [L]

-ter. See -THER.

tĕ·raph, n. (bibl.; only in pl. *-im*, used as sing. or collective sing.). Small image(s) as domestic oracle of ancient Hebrews. [Heb.]

tĕrato- in comb. = Gk *teras -atos* monster, as: *-gĕ·nic* a., *-geny* n., (of) production of monstrosities; *-lite*, kind of clay in Saxony formerly held to have curative properties; *-logy*, dealing in the marvellous, (Biol.) study of animal or vegetable monstrosities, so *-lo·gical* a., *-logist* n.

terce. See TIERCE.

ter·cel, a. Male falcon. [OF, f. pop. L *tertiolus* dim. of *tertius* third (hawk's third egg being held to produce small male)]

terce·ntenary (*or* -tē·n-), **-te·nnial,** aa. & nn. Of 300 years; (n.) 300th anniversary. [TER]

ter·cet, n. (Mus.; Pros., also *tiercet*) = TRIPLET. [f. It. *terzetto* (*terzo* third f. L *tertius*)]

tĕ·rebene, n. A hydrocarbon prepared by treating oil of turpentine with sulphuric acid, used as disinfectant &c. [f. foll. + -ENE]

tĕ·rebinth, n. Turpentine-tree, yielding Chian turpentine; *oil of t.*, oil of turpentine. [f. OF *therebinthe* f. L f. Gk *terebinthos*]

terebi·nthine, a. Of the terebinth; of turpentine, so **terĕ·bic** a. [f. L f. Gk *terebinthinos* (as prec., see -INE[2])]

tĕ·rebra, a. (pl. *-ae*). Boring ovipositor of some insects. Hence **te·rebrate**[2](2) a. [L, = borer]

terē·do, n. Ship-worm, mollusc that bores ships &c. [L, f. Gk *terēdōn* (*teirō* rub)]

ter·gal, a. Of the back, dorsal. [f. L *tergum* back + -AL]

tergĕ·minate (-*at*), a. (bot.). (Of leaf) having at base a pair of leaflets & forking with a pair on each branch. [f. L TER(*geminus* born together) + -ATE[2]]

ter·giversāte (-j-, -g-), v.i. Turn one's back on oneself, turn one's coat, apostatize, change one's party or principles; make conflicting statements. So **tergiversa·tion, ter·giversator**[2], nn. [f. L *tergiversari* turn one's back (*tergum* back + *vers-* f. *vertere* turn), see -ATE[3]]

term[1], n. (Somewhat archaic) boundary, limit, esp. of time, as *set a t. to his encroachments, awaited the t. of his existence,* whence **ter·mless** a. (poet., rhet.); limited period, as *for a t. of 5 years, his t. of office expired*; (Univv., School, Law) period during which instruction is given or court holds sessions, as *Michaelmas, Hilary, Easter, Trinity, t.* (w. ref. to administration of justice, now *sittings*), *will end it next t., during t.* (*-time*), EAT one's *tt.*; appointed day, esp. QUARTER[1]-day; (Law, also *t. of* or *for years*) estate or interest in land to be enjoyed for fixed period; (Math.) antecedent or consequent of ratio, part of expression joined to the rest by + or — (e.g. $3ax^2 - b + cz$ has three tt.); (Logic) word(s) that may be subject or predicate of a proposition, as MAJOR[2], MINOR, MIDDLE[1], *t.*; word used to express a definite conception esp. in particular branch of study &c., as *technical, scientific, law, t., in tt. of* (in the language peculiar to), CONTRADICTION *in tt., set* (definite) *tt.*; (pl.) language employed, mode of expression, as *in the most flattering tt.*; (pl.) conditions, as *cannot accept his tt., do it on your own tt.*, esp. charge, price, as *his tt. are 2 guineas a lesson,* INCLUSIVE *tt.*; *come to tt.*, yield, give way, (also *make tt.*) conclude agreement (*with*); *bring* person *to tt.*, cause him to accept conditions; (pl.) relation, footing, as *am on good, bad, familiar, tt. with him, are not on speaking tt.* [f F *terme* f. L TERMINUS]

term[2], v.t. Denominate, call, as *the music termed plain-song, I forget how* or *what he terms it, this he termed sheer robbery.* [f. prec.]

ter·magant, n. & a. (Hist., *T*-) imaginary Mohammedan deity of turbulent character, often appearing in morality plays; brawling woman, shrew, scold; (adj.) boisterous, turbulent, shrewish, whence **ter·magancy** n., **termagantly**[2] adv. [f. OF *tervagant* f. It. *trivigante, -vag-*, perh. = wandering under three names (Selene, Artemis, Persephone), f. L *tri-* thrice + *vagari* wander, -ANT]

ter·minable, a. That may be terminated; coming to an end after certain time, as *t. annuity*. Hence **ter·minableness** n. [f. obs. *termine* TERMINATE, see -ABLE]

ter·minal, a. & n. Of, forming, a limit or terminus, as *t. station*; (Math.) *t. value,* most concise form of an expression; (Bot.) borne at end of stem &c.; (Zool. &c.) ending a series, as *t. joints*; of, done &c., each term, as *t. accounts, subscription*; *t.* (TERMINUS) *figure*; (n.) terminating thing, extremity, esp. connecting-screw at each end of voltaic battery. Henc. **terminally**[2] adv. [f. L *terminalis* (TERMINUS, see -AL)]

ter·minate[1], v.t. & i. Bound, limit; bring, come, to an end; (of word) end *in* (such letters or syllable). Hence or cogn. **ter·minative, ter·minatory,** aa., **ter·minatively**[2] adv. [f. L *terminare* (TERMINUS), see -ATE[3]]

ter·minate[2], (-*at*), a. Coming to an end, bounded, as *a t. decimal.* [as prec., see -ATE[2]]

termina·tion, n. (In vbl senses, see TERMINATE[1], & esp.) word's final syllable or letter or group of letters esp. as an element in inflexion or derivation; *put a t. to, bring to a t.*, make an end of. Hence **termina·tional** a. (gram.). [f. L *terminationem* (TERMINATE[1], -ATION)]

ter·minator, n. Person, thing, that terminates; dividing line between light & dark part of heavenly body. [LL (as prec., -OR[2])]

ter·miner. See OYER.

ter·minism, n. Doctrine that every one has limited term for repentance; = NOMINALISM. So **ter·minist** n. [f. TERMINUS + -ISM]

termino·logy, n. Science of proper use of terms; terms used in an art &c. Hence **terminolo·gical** a. (*-al inexactitude* facet., lie), **terminolo·gically**[2] adv. [f. TERMINUS + -LOGY]

ter·minus, n. (pl. *-uses, -ī*). (Now rare) final point, goal; station at end of main or branch railway; (Rom. Ant., *T-*) god of boundaries; figure of human bust ending in square pillar; *t. ad quem, a quo,* terminating, starting, -point (of argument, policy, period, &c.). [L, cf. Gk *terma* limit]

termitar·ium, ter·mitary, nn. Nest of, cage for, termites. [f. foll. + -ARIUM, -ARY[1]]

ter·mite, n. White ANT. [f. LL *termes -itis* wood-worm f. *terere* rub]

ter·mly, a. & adv. (rare). (Occurring, paid, &c.) by the term, terminal(ly). [-LY[1]]

ter·mor, n. (law). One who holds lands &c. for a term of years, or for life. [AF *termer* (TERM, see -OR[2] s.f.]

tern[1], tarn, n. Kinds of sea-bird like gull but usu. smaller & with longer bill. [cf. Da. *terne,* Swed. *tärna,* ON *therna*]

tern[2], n. & a. Set of three, esp. three lottery numbers that when drawn together win large prize; such prize; (adj.) = TERNATE. [f. F *terne* f. L *ternas*]

ter·nary, a. Composed of three, so **ter·nAL** a.; (Math.) having three variables. [f. LL *ternarius* (L *terni* three each, see -ARY[1])]

ter·nāte (*or -at*), a. Arranged in threes, esp. (Bot., of leaves) having three leaflets, whorled in threes. Hence **ter·nateLY[2]** adv. [-ATE[2]]

terne, n. (Usu. *t.-plate*) inferior tin plate alloyed with much lead. [prob. f. F *terne* dull, see TARNISH]

Ter·psichorē·an (-k-), **t-,** a. Of Terpsichore, the Muse of dancing, as *the T. art.* [f. Gk *Terpsikhorē* + -AN]

te·rra, n. Earth (in various L & It. phrr.); *t. cārio·sa,* tripoli, rotten-stone; *terrae fi·lius,* son of the soil, humbly-born person; *t. firma,* dry land; *t. inco·gnita,* unknown region; *t. Japŏ·nica,* gambier [orig. thought to be earth from Japan]; *t. nera* (nār·a), pigment used by ancient artists [It., = black earth]; *t. verde,* green earth used as pigment [It.]. [L]

te·rrace (-as), n., & v.t. Raised level space, natural or artificial; (Geol.) raised beach; row of housing along top or face of slope (also as fancy name of street &c.); (v.t.) form into, furnish with, t. [F (prec., -ACEOUS)]

terrac·otta n. Hard pottery used as ornamental building-material & in statuary (often attrib.); statue, figurine, of this; (a. & n.) its brownish-red colour. [It., = baked earth]

tĕrrai·n, n. A tract of land as regarded by the physical geographer or the tactician. [F, as TERRENE]

terramare· (-ahr, -ār), n. Kinds of earthy deposit containing bones, phosphates, &c., & useful as fertilizer; S.-Europ. prehistoric deposit like kitchen MIDDEN. [F, f. dial. It. TERRA(*mara* = *marna* marl)]

terra·neous, a. (bot.). Growing on land. [f. TERRA, see -ANEOUS]

te·rrapin, n. Kinds of freshwater tortoise, esp. *salt-marsh t.* (also *diamond-back*), kind valued as food. [prob. of Amer.-Ind. orig.]

terrā·queous, a. (Of the earth) comprising both land & water. [TERRA, AQUA, -EOUS]

terre·ne, a. Of earth, earthy; terrestrial. [f. L *terrenus* (TERRA)]

terreplein (tār·plān), n. (fortif.). Surface of rampart behind parapet, where guns are mounted; base above, on, or below, the ground level, on which a battery is placed in field-works. [F (*terre* earth f. TERRA + *plein* f. L *plenus* full); orig. sense *earth-pack, talus*]

terre·strial, a. & n. Of the earth, esp. opp. to *celestial,* as *the t. seasons, the t. globe,* the earth, *a t. globe* (representing earth), *t.* MAGNETISM; of this world, worldly, as *t. aims, interests*; of land opp. to water; (Zool.) living on the ground, opp. to *aquatic, arboreal, aerial*; (n.) inhabitant of earth. Hence **terre·strialLY[2]** adv. [f. L *terrestris* (TERRA) + -AL]

te·rret, -it, n. Each of loops or rings on harness-pad for driving-reins to pass through. [f. OF *toret* dim. of TOUR]

te·rrible, a. Exciting or fit to excite terror, awful, dreadful, formidable; (colloq.) excessive, as *a t. bore*; ENFANT TERRIBLE. Hence **te·rribleNESS** n., **te·rribLY[2]** adv. (esp., slang, very). [F, f. L *terribilis* (*terrēre* frighten, see -BLE)]

terri·colous, a. Living on or in the earth, esp. of the *Terricolae,* group of annelids including earthworm. [f. L *terricola* (TERRA + *colere* inhabit) + -OUS]

te·rrier[1], n. Kinds of active & hardy dog with digging propensity; *black-&-tan,* BULL[1], FOX[1], *t.,* short-haired kinds; *Irish, Scotch, Skye, Yorkshire, t.,* rough-haired kinds; *Maltese, toy, t.,* small toy kinds; (colloq.) member of territorial army. [F, f. L as foll.]

te·rrier[2], n. Book recording site, boundaries, &c., of land of private persons or corporations; (Hist.) collection of acknowledgements of vassals or tenants of a lordship. [OF = rent-roll, = med. L *terrarius* (*liber* book) of lands]

terri·fic, a. Causing terror, terrible. Hence **terri·fICALLY** adv. [f. L *terrificus* (*terrēre* frighten, see -FIC)]

te·rrify, v.t. Fill with terror, frighten. [f. L *terrificare* (as prec., see -FY)]

terri·genous, a. Produced by the earth, as *t. deposits*; *t. metals,* metallic bases of earths, e.g. aluminium. [f. L *terrigenus* born of earth (TERRA + *-genus* = -born f. *gigno*) + -OUS]

terri·ne (-ēn), n. Earthenware vessel containing and sold with some table delicacy. [F, fem. of OF *terrin* earthen (L TERRA, -INE[1])]

territor·ial, a. & n. Of territory, as *t. possessions, acquisitions*; limited to a district, as *the right was strictly t.*; (*T*-) of (any of) the U.S. Territories; (Eccl.) *t. system* (in which civil rule claims supremacy as a natural right, whence **territor·ial**ISM n.); *t. army*, force organized for home defence to replace the older bodies of militia, yeomanry, and volunteers; (n.) member of t. army. Hence **territor·ial**LY[2] adv. [f. LL *territorialis* (as TERRITORY, see -AL)]

territor·ialize, v.t. Extend by addition of, reduce to state of, territory. [-IZE]

te·rritory, n. Extent of land under jurisdiction of sovereign, State, city, &c.; large tract of land; (U.S., *T*-) organized division of the country not yet admitted to full rights of a State. [f. L *territorium*, etym. dub.]

te·rror, n. Extreme fear; *t.-stricken, -struck* (with t.); person, thing, that causes this, as *a t. to evildoers*, (colloq.) *here comes this t.* (troublesome child) *again*; *king of tt.*, death (*Job* xviii. 14); *Reign of T., the T.*, period of French Revolution, 1793–4 (& of similar periods marked by sanguinary excesses of revolutionaries, also *Red T.*, or reactionaries, also *White T.*). [f. F *terreur* f. L *terrorem* (*terrēre* frighten, see -OR[1])]

te·rrorist, n. One who favours or uses terror-inspiring methods of governing or of coercing government or community, esp. (1) Jacobin under Reign of Terror, (2) Russian revolutionary. Hence or cogn. **te·rror**ISM(2, 3), **terroriz**A·TION, nn., **terrori·st**IC a., **te·rror**IZE(1) v.t. [F (-*e*), prec., -IST]

te·rry, n. A pile fabric with the loops uncut. [perh. f. F *tirer* draw f. LL *tirare* etym. dub.]

terse, a. (Of speech, style, writer) free from cumbrousness and superfluity, smooth and concise. Hence **ter·se**LY[2] adv., **ter·se**NESS n. [f. L *tergere ters-* wipe, polish]

ter·tian (-shn), a. & n. (Fever, disease) whose paroxysms occur every other day, as *t. ague.* [f. fem. of L *tertianus* (*tertius* third, see -AN)]

ter·tiary (-sha-), a. & n. Of the third order, rank, formation, &c.; (n.) *the T.*, third geological period, (Ornith.) flight-feather of third row, so **ter·ti**AL a. & n., (*T*-) member of 3rd order of monastic body. [f. L *tertiarius* (prec., -ARY[1])]

tertio (-shĭō). See PRIMO[2].

ter·tium quid (-shĭ-), n. A third something, esp. between mind and matter or between opposite things. [L]

ter·tius (-shus), a. (In schools) *Jones* &c. *t.* (third of the name); *t. gau·dens* (L, = glad third), third party expecting to profit by two others' quarrel. [L]

ter·za ri·ma (tārtsa-rē-), n. (pl. *-ze -me*, pr. -ā). Arrangement of (hen)decasyllabic triplets rhyming thus (bat pig cat fig box wig ox &c.) as in Dante's *Commedia*; such triplets. [It.]

terze·tto (tārts-), n. (mus.). Vocal trio. [It.]

te·ssellated, a. Formed of tesserae, as *t. pavement*; (Bot., Zool.) regularly checkered. So **te·ssell**AR[1] a., **tessell**A·TION n. [f. L *tessellatus* (*tessella* dim. of foll., see -ATE[2])]

te·ssera, n. (pl. *-ae*). Small hard non-square block used in mosaic, whence **te·sser**AL a.; (Rom. Ant.) small square of bone &c. used as token, ticket, &c. [L, f. Gk *tessares* four]

tessitur·a (-oora), n. (mus.). Range within which most tones of a voice-part fall. [It., = TEXTURE]

test[1], n. Critical examination or trial of person's or thing's qualities, as *has stood* (undergone) *the successive tt. of poverty and riches, must put it to the t.*; *a t. case* (serving to show the principle involved); means of so examining, standard for comparison or trial, circumstances suitable for this, as *success is not a fair t.*; ground of admission or rejection, as *is excluded by our t.*; (Chem.) reagent, substance employed to reveal presence of an ingredient in a compound, as *galls are a t. of* or *for iron*; movable hearth in reverberation furnace used in separating silver from lead; *T. Act* (of 1672, requiring all persons before holding office to *take the t.*, i.e. the oaths of supremacy and allegiance or equivalent t.; repealed in 1828); *t.-match*, one of the matches in a cricket tour &c. that are to count towards the total result; *t.-glass, -mixer, -paper, -tube*, (for tt. or other chem. purposes). [OF, f. L *testum* earthen pot, esp. (med. L) one for trying metals in]

test[2], v.t. Put to the test, make trial of, (person, thing, quality); try severely, tax, (one's powers of endurance &c.); refine (metal); (Chem.) examine by means of reagent. Hence **te·st**ABLE a., **te·ster**[1] (-ER[1](1, 2)] n. [f. prec.]

test[3], n. Shell, hard covering, of some animals. [f. L *testa* tile, jug, shell, &c., cogn. w. *testum* TEST[1]]

testā·ceous (-shus), a. Of shells or shell-fish, so **testa**·CEAN a. & n., **testaceo·**LOGY n.; with a hard continuous shell; (Bot., Zool.) of red brick colour. [f. L *testaceus* (TEST[3], -ACEOUS)]

te·stacy, n. Being testate. [-ACY]

te·stament, n. = WILL[2] (last sense), as MILITARY *t.*, so **testame·ntari**LY[2] adv., **testame·nt**ARY[1] a.; (bibl.) covenant, dispensation; *Old, New, T.*, the portion of the Bible dealing with the Mosaic, Christian, dispensation; (*T*-) copy of the N.T. [f. L *testamentum* will (TESTATE, -MENT); bibl. sense f. LL mistransl. of Gk *diathēkē* covenant, will]

testā·mur, n. (univv.). Certificate that

one has passed examination. [L, = we testify]

te·stāte (*or -at*), a. & n. (Person) who has made a will (and died leaving it in force). So **testa·tor**², **testa·trix**, nn. [f. L *testari* testify, make will, (*testis* witness), see -ATE²]

te·ster² (for *t.*¹ see TEST²), n. Canopy, esp. over FOUR-poster. [f. OF *testiere* (*teste* head, as TEST³)]

te·ster³, n. Shilling of Henry VIII; (archaic, facet.) sixpence. [var. of earlier and OF *teston* (as TEST³, see -OON)]

te·sticle, n. Each of two glands in male that secrete spermatozoa &c. Hence **testi·cular**¹ a. [f. L *testiculus* dim. of *testis* a t.]

testi·culate (*-at*), a. Having, shaped like, testicles; (Bot.) having a pair of organs so shaped. [f. LL *testiculatus* (prec., -ATE²)]

te·stify̆, v.i. & t. (Of person or thing) bear witness (*to* fact, state, assertion, *against* person &c., archaic *of* or *concerning* matter); (Law) give evidence; affirm, declare, (one's *regret* &c., *that*, *how*, &c.); (of things) be evidence of, evince. [f. L *testificari* (*testis* witness, see -FY)]

testimō·nial, n. Certificate of character, conduct, or qualifications; gift, money, presented to person, esp. in public, as mark of esteem, in acknowledgement of services, &c. [OF (adj.), f. LL *testimonialis* (TESTIMONY, -AL)]

testimo·nialize, v.t. Present (person) with testimonial. [-IZE]

te·stimony, n. Evidence, demonstration, as *called him in t.*, *produce t.* (*to*, *of*), *we have his t. for that*; (Law) oral or written statement under oath or affirmation; declarations, statements, as *must rely on the t. of history*, *of historians*; (archaic) solemn protest, as *for a t. against them*; (bibl.) the decalogue, esp. *the tables of the t.*, (sing. or pl.) the Scriptures. [f. L *testimonium* (*testis* witness, see -MONY)]

testudinār·ious, a. Mottled with red, yellow, and black, like tortoise-shell. [f. TESTUDO, see -ARIOUS]

testu·dinate, a. Arched like carapace of tortoise. [f. LL *testudinatus* (TESTUDO, see -ATE²)]

testudi·neous, a. Like carapace of tortoise. [f. L *testudineus* (foll., -EOUS)]

testū·do, n. (Rom. Ant.) screen formed by body of troops in close array with overlapping shields; similar screen used by miners where ground is likely to cave in; genus of tortoises, whence **testu·dinal** a. [L, gen. *-dinis*, = tortoise-shell (TEST³)]

te·sty, a. Irritable, touchy. Hence **te·stily**² adv., **te·stiness** n. [f. AF *testif*; OF has *testu* heady (TEST³)]

tetā·nic, a. & n. Of, such as occurs in, tetanus, as *t. spasm*; (n.) remedy acting on the muscles through the nerves, e.g. strychnia. [f. L f. Gk *tetanikos* (as foll., see -IC)]

tĕ·tanus, n. Disease marked by spasm of many or all muscles of voluntary motion, e.g. lockjaw; *artificial t.* (induced by strychnia &c.). Hence or cogn. **tetaniza·tion** n., **te·tanize**(3) v.t., **te·tanoid** a. [L, f. Gk *tetanos*, redupl. f. st. of *teinō* stretch]

te·tchy, **te·chy** (-tsh-), a. Peevish, irritable. Hence **te·(t)chily**² adv., **te·(t)chiness** n. [f. 16th c., etym. dub.]

tête-à-tête (tā·tahtā·t), adv., a., & n. Together in private; (adj.) private, confidential; (n.) private interview or conversation usu. between two, sofa for two. [F, lit. head-to-head]

tĕ·ther (-dh-), n., & v.t. Rope, chain, halter, by which grazing animal is confined; (fig.) scope, extent of one's knowledge, authority, &c. (*was beyond*, *at the end of*, *his t.*); (vb) tie (esp. grazing animal) with t. [vb f. n., prob. f. ON *tjódhr* (Sw. *tjuder*)]

tĕ·tra- in comb. = Gk *tetra-* comb. form of *tettares* four, as: *-chord*, scale series of half-octave (esp. in ancient mus.), so *-chor·dal* a.; *-cy·clic* bot., of four circles or whorls; *-da·ctyl* a. & n., *-ylous* a., four-toed (animal); *-gon*, figure of four angles, so *-gonal* a.; *-gram*, word of four letters, quadrilateral figure; *-gra·mmaton*, *Jehovah* or other sacred word written in four letters; *-gynous*, of four pistils; *hē·dron*, four-sided solid, esp. triangular pyramid, so *he·dral* a.; *-logy*, group of four dramatic or operatic works, esp. (Gk Ant.) three tragedies & satyric drama; *-meral*, *-merous*, having four parts; *-meter*, verse of four measures (cf. DIMETER); *-morph* (Christian art), union of attributes of four evangelists in one winged figure; *-pe·talous*, *-phy·llous*, of four petals, leaves; *-pod* a. & n., *-podous* a., (butterfly) with only four perfect legs; *-pody*, group, verse, of four feet; *-stich* (-k), group of four lines of verse; *-style* a. & n., (building) with four pillars esp. forming portico in front or supporting ceiling; *-sy·llable*, word of four syllables, so *-syllă·bic* a.

te·trad, n. The number four; set of four; atom, element, with combining-power of four atoms of hydrogen. [f. Gk *tetras -ados* (as prec., see -AD)]

tetra·ndrous, a. (bot.). Having four stamens. [f. TETRA- + Gk *anēr andros* male + -OUS]

tē·trarch (-k), n. (In Rom. empire) governor of fourth part of a country or province, subordinate ruler, whence or cogn. **te·trarchate**(1), **te·trarchy**¹, nn., **tetrar·chical** a.; commander of subdivision of ancient Greek phalanx. [f. LL *tetrarcha* f. Gk *tetrarkhēs* (TETRA- + *-arkhēs* f. *arkhō* rule)]

te·tter, n. Kinds of skin-disease; *te·tter-*

wort, larger celandine (supposed to cure these). [OE *teter*, cf. OHG *zitaroh*, G dial. *zittcroch*]

Teu·crian, a. & n. Ancient Trojan. [f. L *Teucri* + -AN]

Teuto-, comb. form (irreg.) of foll., as *Teuto*MA·NIA(C), *Teu·to*PHIL(E), -PHOBE, -PHO·BIA.

Teu·ton, n. Member of any of the Teutonic nations or (Hist.) of the tribe of *Tt.* first mentioned in 4th c. B.C. & dwelling perh. near mouth of Elbe. [f. L *Teutoni, -nes*; of Teut. orig., cf. DUTCH]

Teutŏ·nic, a. & n. Of the Teutons; of the Germanic peoples (including, in widest sense, Scandinavians & Anglo-Saxons as well as German races); *T. languages*, High & Low GERMAN[2] & Scandinavian; (n.) languages of the Teutons collectively. Hence **Teuto·nic**ISM(4), **Teu·ton**ISM(2, 4), **Teu·toniz**A·TION, nn., **Teu·ton**IZE(3) v.t. [f. L *Teutonicus* (prec., -IC)]

text, n. Original words of author esp. opp. to paraphrase of or commentary on them, as *there is nothing about this in the t., the t. is hopelessly corrupt* (altered by copyists); passage of Scripture quoted as authority or esp. chosen as subject of sermon &c.; subject, theme; *stick to one's t.*, not digress; main body of book opp. to notes, pictures, &c.; (also *t.-hand*) large kind of handwriting; CHURCH[1], GERMAN[2], *t.*; *t.-book*, manual of instruction, standard book in a branch of study. [f. F *texte* f. L *textus -ūs* (in med. L = Gospel) f. L *texere text-* weave]

te·xtĭle, a. & n. Of weaving, as *the t. art*; woven, suitable for weaving, as *t. fabrics, materials*; (n.) t. material. [f. L *textilis* (as prec., see -ILE)]

te·xtual, a. Of, in, the text, as *t. criticism, errors*. Hence **te·xtual**LY[2] adv. [ME & AF *textuel* (as TEXT, see -AL)]

te·xtualist, n. One who adheres strictly to the letter of the text, so **te·xtual**ISM n.; ready quoter of scriptural texts. [-IST]

te·xture (-tsher), n. Arrangement of threads &c. in textile fabric, as *loose t.*; arrangement of constituent parts, structure, (*of* skin, rock, literary work, &c.); representation of surface of objects in works of art; (Biol.) tissue, structure of this. Hence **te·xtur**AL a. [f. L *textura* (as TEXT, see -URE)]

te·xtureless, a. Without discernible texture, amorphous. [-LESS]

-th[1], suf. forming nn., = -NESS; usu. f. adjj. (*truth, wealth*), often with vowel change (*filth foul, breadth broad*); corrupted to *-t* in *drought, height*; also f. vv. (*tilth, ruth, growth*), meaning result or process, & (by assim. to *ruth* &c.) f. nn., as *faith* (OF *feid*). [of var. orig.]

-th[2], **-eth** after *-ty*, suf. forming ordinal numbers (adjj., & nn. expr. fractions), as *fourth, tenth, thirtieth, hundredth, millionth*; in *fifth, sixth*, &c., assim. f. earlier *-t*; in *eighth*, united w. end of stem. [OE *-tha*(-dh) in *fourth* (later numbers by assim.) f. OTeut. *-thon*, cf. Gk *-tos*, L *-tus*]

thă·lamus, n. (pl. -ī). (Gk Ant.) inner room, women's apartment; (Anat.) place where nerve emerges from brain, esp. *optic t.*; (Bot.) receptacle of flower. [L, f. Gk *thalamos*]

tha·ler (tah-), n. German silver coin. [G, see DOLLAR]

Thali·a, n. Muse of comedy & pastoral poetry. Hence **Thali·**AN a. [L, f. Gk *Thaleia* (*thallō* bloom)]

tha·llium, n. Rare soft white metallic element used in alloys & glass-making. Hence **tha·ll**IC, **tha·ll**OUS, aa. [f. foll. (from green line given in spectrum) + -IUM]

tha·llus, n. Plant-body without root, stem, or leaves. Hence **tha·ll**OID a. [L, f. Gk *thallos* young shoot (*thallō* bloom)]

than (dhan, -ăn), conj. (& quasi-prep.) introducing second member of comparison, as *you are taller t. he (is)*, (colloq.) *taller t. him, I know you better t. he (does)*, *better t.* (I know) *him, it is better to use hot water t. cold, do anything rather t. let him get off, would do anything rather t. that he should get off, a man t. whom no one is better able to judge*. [OE, = THEN, than; *A is better than B* orig. = *A is better, then B*]

thā·nage (-ĭj), n. Rank of, land granted to, -thane. [-AGE]

thănat(o)- in comb. = Gk *thanatos* death, as *thanatophĭ·dia* n. pl., poisonous snakes.

tha·natoid, a. Death-like, apparently dead; deadly. [as prec. + -OID]

thane, n. (In early Eng. Hist.) member of a rank between ordinary freemen and hereditary nobles. Hence **tha·ne**DOM, **tha·ne**HOOD, **tha·ne**SHIP, nn. [OE *theg(e)n* soldier, servant, thane, cf. OSax. *thegan*, ON *thegn*, cogn. w. Gk *teknon* child]

thank[1], v.t. Express gratitude to (person *for* thing); *t. you*, I t. you (polite formula acknowledging gift, service, offer accepted or refused); (as contempt. refusal) *t. you for nothing*; (anticipatory) *t. you (for that ball)!*, please throw it here; (as polite formula, now usu. iron. implying reproach) *I will t. you to shut the door, wipe your boots, leave my affairs alone*; *he may t. himself, has only himself to t., for that*, it is his own fault. [OE *thancian, tho-*, (foll.), cf. Du. & G *danken*]

thank[2], n. (now only in pl.). (Expression of) gratitude, as *give tt. to Heaven, expressed his heartfelt tt., she bowed her tt., small* (iron. *much*) *tt. I got for it*; *t.-offering* (bibl.), Jewish offering made as act of thanksgiving; (as formula) *tt.*, thank you; *tt. to* (as the result of) *my foresight, your obstinacy*. Hence **tha·nk**WORTHY a. (archaic.). [OE *thanc, thonc*, cf. Du. & G *dank*, cogn. w. THINK]

tha·nkful, n. Grateful; (of words or act)

expressive of thanks. Hence **tha·nk-fulLY**[2] adv., **tha·nkfulNESS** n. [-FUL]

tha·nkless, a. Not feeling or expressing gratitude; *a. t. task* (not likely to win thanks, unprofitable). Hence **tha·nk-lessLY**[2] adv., **tha·nklessNESS** n. [-LESS]

tha·nksgiving, n. Expression of gratitude esp. to God; form of words for this, as *General T.* (in Book of Common Prayer); *T. day* (set apart in U.S. for t. to God, usu. last Thursday of November); (bibl.) offering made as t.

thar (tar), n. Goat antelope of Nepal. [native].

that[1], a., pron., & adv. 1. Demonstr. adj. & pron. (pr. dhăt; pl. *those* pr. dhōz). The (person, thing), the person or thing, pointed to or drawn attention to or observed by the speaker at the time, or already named or understood or in question or familiar, as *observe t. dog in the next field, who is t. (woman) in the garden?, what was t. noise?, what noise is t.?, don't roll your eyes like t.* (as you are doing) or *in t. imbecile fashion, I knew all t. before, talked about responsibilities & all t.* (similar commonplaces), *t.* (your action, the action you tell me of) *is not fair, that's right!* (formula of approval, also vulg. = yes), (colloq.; also *there's*) *that's* (you, in view of present or future compliance &c., are) *a dear!, I use t.*(or *the*) *term in a special sense, much to the disgust of t.* (or *the*) *monarch, was cured from t. hour, things were easier in those days, so that's that* (formula closing narrative or discussion), *come out of t.* (slang form ordering person &c. to clear out), *wouldn't give t.* (a finger-snap) *for it*, AT *t.*; (with feeling) *I will not see t. boy put upon, why will you bring t. woman here?, when you have done thumping t. piano, shall not easily forget t. day*; (coupled or contrasted with *this*, & applied esp. to the farther, less immediate or obvious, &c., of two) *this poker is much heavier than t. (one), went to this doctor & t.* or *to this & t. doctor* (various doctors), *this, t., & the other* (various things), *put this & t.* (various facts &c.) *together*; (as pron. replacing *the* w. noun, w. sense completed by rel. pron. expressed or, in obj. case & archaic in subj., omitted) *those who drink water think water, those may try it who choose, had t. in his eye which forbade further trifling, all those (that) I saw, all those* (usu. *the*) *specimens that I saw, those* (usu. *the*) *few (books) that I had, a different pattern to that (which) I was used to*; (or by adj. or equivalent) *those unfit for use, those below the standard, a tunic like that described above, those* (usu. *the*) *persons most injured by the tax, like most of those issuing from German workshops, cost of oil is less than t. of gas*; (foll. by *that* conj.) such, such a, as *has t. confidence in his theory that he would put it into practice tomorrow, was wounded to t. degree that he resigned.* 2. Adv. (pr. dhăt). To such a degree, so, as (colloq.) *will go t. far, have done t. much,* (vulg.) *I was t. angry I could have struck him.* 3. Rel. pron. (pl. same; pr. dhat; used, exc. archaic, rhet., poet., only to introduce defining-clause essential or rhet. viewed as essential to identification; now largely replaced by WHO & to some extent by WHICH, esp. after antecedent *that*; in obj. case, & in archaic use in subj., *that* is often omitted; prep. governing *that* is always placed after it & usu. at end of clause). Exx.: *the book (t.* or *which) I sent you, the box (t.* or *which) you put them in, the man (t.* or usu. *whom) you stopped, the people (t.) you got it from* or *from whom you got it, the meanest flower t.* (rarely *which*) *blows, the best t.* (not *which*) *you can do, no one (t.*; not *whom) I ever heard of could see any difference.* [OE *thæt* that, THE, cf. Du. *dat*, G *das*; for *those* see THIS]

that[2] (dhat, *occas.* -ăt), conj. introducing subordinate clauses: (of statement or hypothesis) *they say (t.) he is better, there is no doubt (t.) he meant it, it is suggested t. the mistake was intentional, it is hoped t. all will go well, it is monstrous t. he should expect further help, to think (t.) he should use me so!*; (of purpose) *he lives t. he may eat, he withdrew (in order) t. the dispute might cease*; (of result) *am so sleepy (t.) I cannot keep my eyes open, his language was such t. we declined further dealings with him, what have I done t. he should cut me?, where is he, t. you come without him?*; (of reason or cause) *it is rather t. he has not the time, not t.* (I do not say this because) *I have any objection*; (of wish) *(O) t. that were all!, (O) t. I knew the truth!*; (archaic or literary) *in t.*, since, in so far as; *now t.*, since now, as *you ought to write now t. you know the address.* [OE, neut. as prec.]

thatch, n., & v.t. Roof-covering of straw, reeds, or (in tropical countries) coconut & other leaves; (v.t.) cover (roof, house, or abs.) with t. [(vb f. OE *theccan* f.) OE *thæc*, cf. Du. *dak*, G *dach*, cogn. w. Gk *tegos, stegē*, roof, L *toga* robe, *tegere* cover, &c.]

thau·matrope, n. Disk &c. on which are depicted images that appear to go through various movements when disk revolves. [irreg. f. Gk *thauma* wonder + *-tropos* -turning]

thau·maturge, n. Worker of miracles, wonder-worker. Hence or cogn. **thau-matur·GIC(AL)** aa., **thau·maturGIST, thau·maturGY**[1] nn. [f. med. L f. Gk *thaumatourgos* a. (*thauma -matos* wonder + -o- + *-ergos* -working)]

thaw, v.i. & t., & n. (Of ice, snow, frozen thing) pass to liquid state, melt, dissolve; (of weather, *it*) become so warm as to melt ice &c., rise above 32° Fahr.; (fig.) be freed from coldness or stiffness, unbend, become genial; cause to t. (lit. & fig.); (n.) thawing, warmth of weather that thaws, as *a t. has set in.* Hence **thaw·**LESS, **thaw·**Y[2], aa. [(n. f. vb) OE *thawian*, cf. Du. *dooien*, OHG *douwen*]

the (*bef. vowel* dhĭ, *bef. consonant* dhe, *emphat.* dhē), a. & adv. 1. Adj. applied esp. to person(s) or thing(s) already mentioned or under discussion, or from the nature of the case actually or potentially existent, or unique (as class or individual), or familiar, or otherwise sufficiently identified, as *tried to soothe t. child, gave t. fellow a shilling, shall let t. matter drop, how is t. game* or *score?*, *what is t. time?*, *depends on t. weather, t. Devil, sun, moon, stars, Thames, inflammation of t. lungs, pulled t. trigger, what was t. result?*, *you will be t. loser, revised by t. author, find their way to t. sea, went to t. baths, theatre, rink, t. King, t. Home Secretary, t. McGregor* &c. (chief of clan), *story does not lose in t. telling*; to sing. n. as repr. species, class, &c., as *t. lion, domestic cat, philosopher, cucumber, gavotte, general reader, man in the street, new woman,* (rhet., esp. bibl.) *t. oppressor, locust*; to some nn. used in restricted sense, esp. fig. repr. a pursuit &c., as *t. gloves, ribbons, table, stage, theatre, platform, hustings, bottle, pulpit, fancy*; to names of diseases &c. (now partly archaic), as *t. smallpox, measles, toothache, gout, fidgets, blues* (depression), *hump,* (vulg.) *t.* (habit of) *drink*; to nn. expr. a unit, as *4d. t.* (or *a* or *per*) *pound, yard,* &c., *£6 t. coat & skirt, allow 8 minutes* (to) *t. mile, 16 oz to t. pound*; with sense completed by rel. clause or adj. or equivalent, as *t. book* (*that*) *you borrowed, t. best* (*that*) *I can do for you, has not t. nerve for motoring, wonder you have t. impudence* (*to ask it* expr. or understood), (exclam.) *t. impudence of t. fellow!*, *t. cup on t. top shelf, t. one with a broken handle, t. bottom of a well, t. best way, t. only way, t. way out, t. upper classes, t. better man of the two*; w. adjj. used abs., as *none but t. brave* (brave men) *deserve t. fair, t. beautiful* (beauty), *t. sublime*; w. adjj. rhet. viewed as part of definition, as *t. virtuous & talented Duchess of X., details of t. shocking disaster, t. enraged animal*; (dhē; italics) applied to the person or thing best known or best entitled to the name, as *no relation to* the *Browning,* the *tobacco is* (advertiser's). 2. Adv. (a) rel., only in comb. w. (b). In whatever degree. (b) In that degree, by that amount, on that account. Exx.: *t. more he gets, t. more he wants*; *I play t. worse, t. more I practise*; *am not* (or *none*) *t. more inclined to help him because he is poor, on that account, for what you tell me*; *none t. better for seeing you*; *that makes it all t. worse* (in the full degree to be expected from what you say &c.); (tautologically) *so much t. worse for him*, t. worse, so much worse, for him. [f. OE masc. *the* (earlier *se*), fem. *thēo* (earlier *sēo*), neut. *thæt*; cf. Du. *de*, G *der, die, das*, L *iste, -ta, -tud*, Gk *ho, hē, to*, Skr. *tat.* 2. OE *thȳ́, thé*, instrumental case]

thĕa·ndric, a. Of the union, by joint agency, of divine & human nature in Christ. [f. eccl. Gk *theandrikos* (*theos* god, *anēr andros* man, -IC)]

thēanthrŏ·pic(al), aa. Both divine & human; tending to embody deity in human form. [f. eccl. Gk *theanthrōpos* god-man f. *theos* god + *anthrōpos* man + -IC]

thē·archy (-kĭ-), n. Government by god(s); class, order, of gods, as *the Olympian t.* [f. eccl. Gk *thearkhia* rule of god (Gk *theos* god + *-arkhia* f. *arkhō* rule)]

thē·atre, n. Building for dramatic spectacles, play-house; *patent t.* (established by letters patent, not licensed by Lord Chamberlain); room, hall, for lectures &c. with seats in tiers (*operating-t.*, for surgical demonstrations); dramatic literature or art; scene, field, of operation, as *the t. of war*; *t.-goer, -going,* frequenter, -ing, of tt. [(perh. thr. OF) f. L f. Gk *theatron* (*theaomai* behold f. *thea* spectacle)]

theă·trical, a. & n. (Of manner, speech, gesture, person) calculated for effect, showy, affected; of or suited to the theatre, of acting or actors, so **thea·tric** a. (rare); (n. pl.) t. performances, esp. *private* (amateur) *tt.* Hence **thea·trical**ISM(2, 4), **theatrica·**LITY, nn., **thea·trical**IZE(3) v.t., **thea·trical**LY[2] adv. [f. LL f. Gk *theatrikos* (as prec., see -IC) + -AL]

Thēbā·id (*or* thē·-), n. Territory around Thebes (in Egypt); (also L *-is*) poem on (siege of) Thebes (in Greece), esp. that of Statius. [f. L f. Gk *Thēbaïs -idos* (*Thēbai* Thebes)]

Thē·ban, a. & n. (Inhabitant) of Thebes. [-AN]

thee. See THOU.

theft, n. Stealing; larceny. [OE *thēoft* (*thēof* THIEF + -TH[1])]

thē·ic, n. One who drinks tea to excess. So **the·ism**[1] [-ISM(5)] n. [mod. L *thea* tea, -IC]

thē·ine, n. = CAFFEINE. [as prec. + -INE[1]]

their (dhār̆), possessive case of, & adj. corresponding to, THEY, with absolute form *theirs* (for uses cf. HER[2]). [f. ON *theira* gen. pl. of *sá* = OE *se* THE]

thē·ism[2] (for *t.*[1] see THEIC), n. Belief in existence of a God supernaturally revealed to man (cf. DEISM) & sustaining a personal relation to his creatures. So **the·**IST n., **thei·**STIC(AL) aa. [f. Gk *theos* god + -ISM]

them. See THEY.

themă·tic, a. (Mus.) of themes, as *t. treatment, t. catalogue* (giving opening themes as well as names &c.); (Gram.) of belonging to, a theme, as *t. vowel, form.* Hence **thema·tically** adv. [f. Gk *thematikos* (as foll., -IC)]

theme, n. Subject on which one speaks, writes, or thinks; school composition, essay, on given subject; (Gram.) stem of noun or verb. part to which inflexions are added; (Mus.) melodic subject usu. developed with variations; (Hist.) any of 29 provinces in Byzantine empire. [f. L f. Gk *thema -matos* (*tithēmi* set, place, see -M)]

Thĕ·mis, n. (Gk Myth.) goddess of law & justice; these personified. [L f. Gk *Themis* law]

themse·lves (dhem-), pron. Emphat. & reflex. form corresp. to THEY (for use, cf. HIMSELF). [THEM + pl. of SELF]

then (dhĕn), adv., conj., a., & n. (Adv.) at that time, as *was t. too much occupied, t. comes the trouble, the t. existing ordinances*; next, afterwards, after that, as *it must t. soak for two hours, & t. the operation is complete*; *now & then,* at one time & another, from time to time. (Conj.) in that case, therefore, it follows that, (often *well, t.*), as *t. you should have said so, t. it is no use your going,* (*but*) *t.* (if what you say is true) *why did you take it?*; (of grudging or impatient concession) if you must have it so, as *take it t., between you & I ... 'me', t.*; (resumptively, not as first word) accordingly, as *the new Governor, t., came prepared*; NOW *t.* (Adj.) existing &c. at that time, as *the t. Duke, secretary.* (N.) that time, as *before, till, by, from, t., every now & t.,* from time to time. [OE *thænne, tha-, tho-*, cogn. w. THAT[1], THE, cf. Du. *dan*, G *dann*]

thē·nar, n. (anat.). Palm of hand, sole of foot; (also attrib. *t. prominence, eminence*) ball of thumb. [Gk *thenar*]

thence (dh-), adv. (Archaic) from that place, from there; (somewhat archaic) from that source, for that reason, as *a discrepancy t. results, it t. appears*; *thencefor·th, thencefor·ward,* advv. & nn., from (or *from*) that time forward. [ME *thenne* (OE *thanon, tho-*, f. root of *this, that, then*) + -ES]

theo- in comb. = Gk *theos* god, as: *-cracy,* government or State governed by God directly or through a sacerdotal class &c., *the T.,* Jewish commonwealth from Moses to the monarchy; *-crat* ruler in, subject under, theocracy, so *-cra·tic* a.; *-cratist,* believer in direct intervention & authority of God through revelation in government of society; *-crasy* [f. Gk *krasis* mixture], union of soul with God through contemplation (among Neoplatonists, Buddhists, &c.); *-dicy,* vindication of divine providence in view of existence of evil; *-gony,* (poem dealing with) genealogy of the gods, so *-go·nic* a., *-gonist* n.; *-machy* (-kĭ), strife against or among the gods; *-ma·nia,* insane belief that one is God, also, religious insanity, so *-ma·niac* n.; *-phany,* appearance of God to man, so *-phă·nic* a.; *-phila·nthropist,* member of a society formed in Paris in 1796 with object of replacing Christianity by a form of deism, also, one who professes to unite love to God with love to man, so *-philanthro·pic* a., *-phila·nthropist, -phila·nthropy,* nn.; *-pneusty,* divine inspiration, so *-pneu·stic* a.; *-techny,* supernatural machinery, so *-te·chnic* a.

theŏ·dolite, n. Surveying-instrument for measuring horizontal and vertical angles by means of telescope. Hence **theodoli·tic** a. [orig. *-delite*; etym. dub.; perh. irreg. f. Gk *theaomai* observe, *dēlos* plain]

Theodō·sian, a. Of the emperor Theodosius (I, II, or III), esp. *T. code* (published under Theodosius II, d. 450). [-AN]

theolō·gian, n. Person skilled in, professor of, theology. [F (*-ien*), as foll. + -AN]

theo·logy, n. Science of (esp. Christian) religion: *natural t.* (dealing with knowledge of God as gained from his works by light of nature & reason); *positive, revealed, t.* (based on revelation); *dogmatic t.* (dealing with authoritative teaching of the Scriptures & the Church); *speculative t.* (giving scope to human speculation, not confined to revelation); *systematic t.,* methodical arrangement of the truths of religion in their natural connexion. Hence or cogn. **theolo·gical** a., **theolo·gically**[2] adv., **theo·logize**(1, 2) v.t. & i. [ME & OF *theologie* f. L f. Gk THEO(*logia* -LOGY)]

thĕor·bo, n. Two-necked musical instrument of lute class much used in 17th c. [f. F *téorbe* f. It. *tiorba* etym. dub.]

thē·orĕm, n. (Math.) proposition to be proved by chain of reasoning, a truth to be established by means of accepted truths, (cf. PROBLEM); algebraical or other rule, esp. one expressed by symbols or formulae, as *binomial t.,* formula for raising binomial to any power without multiplication; a speculative truth. Hence **theoremă·tic(al)** aa., **theorĕ·matist**(3) n. [f. LL f. Gk *theōrēma* (*theōreō,* see THEORY & -M)]

theorĕ·tic, a. & n. = foll.; (n. pl.) speculative parts of a science &c., so **theoreti·cian** n. [f. LL f. Gk *theōrētikos* (as THEORY, see -ETIC)]

theore·tical, a. Concerned with knowledge but not with its practical application, speculative; based on mere theory, not dealing with facts as presented by experience. Hence **theore·tically**[2] adv. [-AL]

theŏ·ric, a. (Gk ant.). Of, for, public

spectacles, esp. *t. fund* (for providing free seats at theatre for poor citizens &c.). [f. Gk *theōrikos* (as THEORY, see -IC)]

thē·ory, n. Supposition explaining something, esp. one based on principles independent of the phenomena &c. to be explained, opp. to HYPOTHESIS, as *atomic t., t. of gravitation, evolution*; speculative view, as *one of my pet tt.* (often implying fancifulness); the sphere of speculative thought, as *this is all very well in t., but how will it work in practice?*; exposition of the principles of a science &c., as *the t. of music*; (Math.) collection of results designed to illustrate principles of a subject, as *t. of chances, equations.* Hence **the·or**IST(3), **theoriz**A·TION, nn., **the·or**IZE(2) v.i. [f. LL f. Gk *theōria* f. *theōreō* behold, contemplate (*theōros* spectator f. *thea* spectacle)]

theo·sophy, n. Any of various ancient & modern philosophies professing to attain to a knowledge of God by spiritual ecstasy, direct intuition, or special individual relations. Hence or cogn. **the·o-soph, theo·soph**ER[1], **theo·soph**IST(2), nn., **theoso·ph**IC(AL), **theosophi·st**ICAL, aa., **theo·soph**IZE(2) v.i. [f. med.L f. late Gk *theosophia* f. THEO(*sophos* wise)]

-ther, -ter, suf. in pronominal & other wds w. idea of distinction or comparison (*other, either, whether*; NETHER, FURTHER; *hither* &c.; AFTER); *neuter, alter* vb, have the cogn. L suf. [cf. Gk *-teros*, L *-ter*, G *-der*]

therapeu·tic, a. & n. Curative; of the healing art; (n. pl.) branch of medicine concerned with treatment of disease & action of remedial agents in disease or health. Hence **therapeu·tic**AL a., **therapeu·tical**LY[2] adv., **therapeu·t**IST(3) n. [f. Gk *therapeutikos* (*therapeuō* wait on, cure, f. *theraps* servant, see -IC)]

there (dhār, dher *as below*), adv., n., & int. In or at that place, as *put it down t., what is that dog doing t.?, Are you t.?* (opening of telephone interview), *lived t. some years, have been t. before* (slang), know all about it, *all t.* (slang), in one's senses, sane, *t. it is—on the sofa,* (calling attention) *you t.!*; at that point in argument, progress of affairs, situation, &c., as *t. I agree with you, t. is* (or *comes in*) *the difficulty, you had* (the advantage of) *him t., t. it* (the trouble) *is, you see*; HERE *& t., neither* HERE *nor t.*; to that place, as *go t. every day, got t. in two minutes, get t.* (slang), succeed; *t. or thereabouts,* (transf.) about that amount, time, &c. (*'was it two years ago?' 'T.o.t.'*; *will come to £100, t.o.t.*); (merely expletive or introductory, usu. dher; preceding, or in interrog. or neg. or quasi-neg. sentence following, verb that normally precedes its subject, esp. *be*; in poet. or exclam. use subject may stand first) *t. was a cart close by, t. was nothing t., t. was plenty to eat, what is t. for supper?, not a sound was t. to indicate their presence, seldom has t. been more fuss, t. fell a deep silence, a knight t. was, a nice mess t. is* or *seems to be!*; *t.'s* (=THAT[1]'s) *a dear* &c. (N.) that place, as *was brought from t., lives somewhere near t., tide comes up to t., passed by t.* Int. expr. confirmation, triumph, dismay, &c., as *t.! what did I tell you?*, or used to soothe child &c., as *t., t., never mind. Thereabout(s)*, near that place, as *ought to be somewhere thereabouts*, near that number, quantity, &c., as *two gallons or thereabouts*; *therea·fter* (archaic), after that, according to that rule &c.; *there·ane·nt* (Sc.), about that matter; *therea·t* (archaic), at that place, on that account, after that; *thereby·* (or dhār·bī), by that means, as result of that (*& t.-b. hangs a tale*, in which connexion there is something to be told, see *As You Like It*, II. vii. 28); *therefor·* (archaic), for that object or purpose; *there·fore*, for that reason, accordingly, consequently; *there-fro·m* (archaic), from that or it; *therei·n* (archaic), in that place, in that respect; *thereina·fter, -before·*, later, earlier, in same document &c.; *therei·nto* (archaic), into that place; *thereo·f* (archaic), of that or it; *thereo·n* (archaic), on that or it (of motion & position); *thereou·t* (archaic), out of that, from that source; *therethrough·* (archaic), through that; *thereto·* (archaic), to that or it, in addition, to boot; *thereu·nto* (archaic), to that or it; *thereupo·n*, in consequence of that, soon or immediately after that, (archaic) upon that (of motion or position); *there-wi·th* (archaic), with that, thereupon; *therewitha·l*, in addition, besides. [OE *thǣr, thér*, cf. Du. *daar*, G *da*; f. stem of THAT[1]]

thēr·iăc, n. (Also *theriaca Andromachi, Venice treacle*) antidote to bites of poisonous animals compounded of many drugs. [f. LL f. Gk *thēriakē* antidote, fem. adj. as n. (*thērion* dim. of *thēr* wild beast, see -AC)]

thērianthro·pic, a. Of, worshipping, beings represented under form of man & beast. So **theria·nthrop**ISM(3) n. [f. Gk *thērion* beast + *anthrōpos* man + -IC]

therm, n. Amount of heat required to raise one gram of water at maximum density one degree centigrade; unit of coal-gas supplied (now reckoned by heat-producing capacity instead of by volume). [f. Gk *thermē* heat]

ther·mae, n. pl. (Gk & Rom. ant.). Hot springs or (esp. public) baths. [L, f. Gk *thermai* pl. as prec.]

ther·mal, a. Of heat, as *t. unit* (for measuring heat); *t. equator*, line along which greatest heat occurs on earth's surface; *t. springs*, hot springs; of thermae. Hence **ther·mal**LY[2] adv. [as THERM + -AL]

therma·ntidote, n. Apparatus for cooling the air, used in India. [as THERM + ANTIDOTE]

ther·mic, a. Of heat, as *t. rays, conditions.* [as THERM + -IC]

Thermidor·ian, n. Any of those who effected or favoured Robespierre's overthrow on Thermidor 9th, 1794. [f. F *thermidorien* (*thermidor*, republican month July-August, as THERM + Gk *dōron* gift), see -IAN]

thermi·on, n. An ION emitted by an incandescent substance. Hence **thermio·**NIC a. (*-ic valve* or *vacuum tube*, appliance giving copious flow of electrons used for many purposes & esp. in amplifying wireless waves in broadcast). [THERMO- + ION]

thermo- in comb. = Gk *thermos* warm, *thermē* heat, as: *-baro·meter*, apparatus for measuring atmospheric pressure by boiling-point of water, also, siphon barometer that can be used as thermometer; *-dynă·mics*, science of the relations between heat & mechanical work; *-electri·city*, electricity produced by difference of temperature, so *-ele·ctric* a.; *-electro·meter*, instrument for determining heating-power of electric current; *-ge·nesis*, production of heat esp. in human body, so *-genĕ·tic*, *-gĕ·nic*, aa.; *-gram*, record made by *-graph* (self-registering thermometer); *-mo·tive*, of motion produced by heat; *-mo·tor*, engine worked by means of heat, esp. by hot air; *-pile*, thermo-electric battery esp. arranged for measuring small quantities of radiant heat; *-scope*, instrument for detecting differences of temperature without measuring, so *-scŏ·pic(al)* aa.; *-stat*, automatic instrument for regulating temperature, so *-stă·tic* a.; *-sta·tics*, theory of the equilibrium of heat; *-te·nsile*, relating to tensile force as affected by temperature; *-type*, impression of section of wood &c. made by wetting the object with dilute acid, printing, & developing the impression by heat.

thermo·meter, n. Instrument for measuring temperature, usu. glass tube with small bore containing mercury or alcohol, & variously graduated (*Fahrenheit, Réaumur, Centigrade, t.*, with freezing-point at 32°, 0°, 0°, boiling-point of water at 212°, 80°, 100°); *clinical t.* (small, with range of 25° or less, for taking temperature of the body); MAXIMUM, MINIMUM, *t.* Hence **thermome·**TRIC(AL) aa., **thermome·trical**LY[2] adv., **thermo·**METRY n. [THERMO- + -METER]

ther·mos, n. *T. flask* or *t.*, kind of VACUUM flask. [proprietary name]

thēr·oid, a. (Esp. of idiot) having beast-like propensities. [f. Gk *thēr* wild beast + -OID]

thērо·logy, n. Science of mammals, mammalogy. So **thero·log**IST n. [as prec. + -LOGY]

thēsau·rus, n. Lexicon, cyclopaedia. [L, f. Gk *thēsauros* treasure (*tithēmi* place)]

these. See THIS.

thē·sis (*or* thĕ- *as below*), n. (pl. *thesēs*). Proposition to be maintained; dissertation, esp. one by candidate for degree; school or college exercise; (*also* thĕ-) unaccented syllable in English scansion (cf. ARSIS). [Gk (-ĕ-), = thing laid down, (Pros.) thesis or ARSIS, f. *tithēmi* place]

The·spian, a. Of Thespis, semi-legendary Greek dramatic poet of 6th c. B.C.; *the T. art*, the drama. [f. Gk *Thespis* + -AN]

thē·ta, n. Greek letter (Θ, θ) = th. [Gk]

thē·urgy, n. Supernatural agency esp. in human affairs; art of securing this; magical science of Neoplatonists; production of effects by supernatural agency opp. natural magic. Hence or cogn. **theur·**GIC(AL) aa., **the·urg**IST(3) n. [f. L f. Gk *theourgia* miracle f. *theourgos* (*theos* god + *-ergos* -working)]

thews, n. pl. Sinews, muscles; (fig.) mental or moral vigour. Hence **thew**ED[2], **thew·**LESS, **thew·**Y[2], aa. [OE *thēaw* habit, (pl.) manners]

they (dhā), pron. (obj. *them*, poss. THEIR). Pl. of HE, SHE, IT; *t.* (the persons) *who*; *t.* (people in general) *say*. [ME *thei* f. ON *thei-r* pl. of *sá* = OE *se* THE]

thick, a., n., & adv. Of great or specified depth between opposite surfaces, as *bread is (cut) too t., spread the butter t., a board two inches t., how t. was it?*; (of line &c.) broad, not fine, (of script, type, &c.) consisting of t. lines; arranged closely, crowded together, as *t. hair, forest, crowd grew thicker*; numerous, as *fell t. as peas*; abounding, packed, *with*, as *trees t. with leaves, air t. with snow*; of firm consistence, as *t. paste, soup*; turbid, muddy, cloudy, not clear, as *t. puddles, weather is still t.*; stupid, dull; (of voice) muffled, indistinct; (colloq.) intimate, esp. *t. as thieves*; *lay it on t.*, (slang) be profuse esp. in compliments; *a bit t., rather t., a little too t.*, &c. (slang), going beyond what is reasonable, too much of a good thing; *thi·ckhead*, blockhead; *t.-headed*, stupid; *thickset*, set or growing close together, heavily or solidly built, (n.) kind of stout fustian, (also *t.-s. hedge*) close-grown hedge; *t.-skinned*, (fig.) not sensitive to reproach, insult, &c., stolid; *t.-skulled, -witted*, stupid; *thick'un* (slang), sovereign (coin). (N.) the t. part of anything, esp. fig. *in the t. of it* (of fight &c.); (colloq.) stupid person; *through t. & thin*, under all conditions, resolutely, so *t.-&-thin* a., as *t.-&-thin supporters*. (Adv.) thickly, as *snow was falling t., blows came fast & t., heart beats t.* Hence **thi·ck**ISH[1] a., **thi·ck**LY[2] adv. [OE *thicce*, cf. Du. *dik*, G *dick*]

thi·cken, v.t. & i. Make or become thick; make (gravy &c.) of stiffer consistence, whence **thi·cken**ING[1](3) n.; *plot thickens* (becomes more intricate). [-EN[6]]

thi·cket, n. Number of shrubs, trees, &c., growing close together. [OE *thiccet* (as THICK)]

thi·ckness, n. Being thick; dimension other than length & breadth; piece of material of known t., as *three tt. of card-board will suffice.* [-NESS]

thief (-ēf), n. (pl. *-ves*). One who steals esp. secretly & without violence, whence **thie·**VERY(4), **thie·vish**NESS, nn., **thie·v**ISH[1] a., **thie·vish**LY[2] adv.; projection in wick of candle causing it to gutter; *thieves'* LATIN. [OE *théof*, cf. Du. *dief*, G *dieb*]

thieve, v.i. & t. Be a thief, practise stealing; steal (thing). [OE *théofian* (as prec.)]

thigh (thī), n. Part of human leg between hip & knee, corresponding part in other animals; *smite* HIP[1] *and t.*; *t.-bone*, single bone of t., femur. Hence **(-)thigh**ED[2] a. [OE *théo(h)*, cf. Du. *dij*, OHG *dioh*]

thill, n. Shaft of cart or carriage; (also **thi·ll**ER[1] n.) *t.-horse* (put between tt.). [f. 14th c., etym. dub.]

thi·mble, n. Metal cap (sometimes open at end) worn to protect finger & push needle in sewing; (Mech.) short metal tube, as *t. joint, coupling*; metal ring concave on outside & fitting in rope to prevent chafing; *thi·mbleful*, small quantity (of brandy &c.) to drink; *t.-pie*, rapping on head with t., as punishment; *thi·mblerig* n. & v.i., (play) sleight-of-hand trick with three t.-shaped cups & pea, bystanders betting which cup covers pea, *thi·mblerigger*, one who plays this, sharper. [OE *thȳmel*, as THUMB + -LE(1)]

thin[1], a. Having opposite surfaces close together, of small diameter, slender, as *t. wire, string, board, sheet*; not dense, as *t. air*; not full or closely packed, as *t. house* (theatre); of slight consistency, as *t. gruel*; lacking in important ingredient, as *t. beer, blood, voice, humour, eloquence*; (fig.) shallow, transparent, flimsy, as *t. disguise, excuse,* (colloq.) *that's too t.*; lean, not plump; (of lines) narrow, fine, of script, type, &c.) consisting of t. lines; (slang) uncomfortable, distasteful, (esp. *have a t. time*); *through* THICK *and t.*; *t.-skinned*, (fig.) sensitive; *t. captain*, kind of small dry plain biscuit. Hence **thi·n**LY[2] adv., **thi·n**NESS n., **thi·nn**ISH[1] a. [OE *thynne*, cf. Du. *dun*, G *dünn*, & L *tenuis*, Skr. *tanús*]

thin[2], v.t. & i. Make or become thin, reduce in bulk or numbers, as *his hair is thinning, nation had thinned under* (or *been thinned by*) *proscription*; remove some young fruit from (vine, tree) to improve growth of rest (also *t. out seedlings* &c.). [OE *thynnian*, as prec.]

thine. See THY.

thing, n. Whatever is or may be an object of thought (including or opp. to *person*), as: (of animate objects, esp. persons, expr. contempt, pity, affection, &c.) *poor t., spiteful t., a dear old t., dumb tt.,* (slang) OLD *t., & tt.* (colloq. = *& the like, etc,*); (of inanimate material object) *take those tt. off the table, platinum is a costly t., got my tt.* (clothes) *wet, pack up your tt.* (personal belongings); (of act, fact, idea, course, task, affair, circumstance) *a foolish t. to do,* SOFT *t.,* PUT[1]*-up t., strange t. that you cannot hold your tongue, that is not the same t., the only t. now is to take a cab, the t.* (to aim at) *is to improve the pace, tt. begin to look brighter, has made a mess of tt., takes tt. too seriously*; (of specimen or type of work &c.) *the latest t. in hats, a sweet t. in coal-scuttles, a little t. of mine I should like to read to you*; *not the* (conventionally proper) *t.*; *am not feeling at all the t.* (well); (Law) *tt. personal, real,* personal, real, property; (pl., with adj. following, often joc.) all that is so describable (*tt. Japanese, political, feminine, scholastic,* &c.); *make a good t. of,* make good profit by; *do the handsome t. by,* treat handsomely; *know a t. or two,* be experienced or shrewd. [OE, =thing, cause, sake, office, council, cf. Du. & G *ding*, ON *thing*]

thi·ngamy, thi·ngumajig, thi·ngumbob, thi·ngummy, nn. Person, thing, whose name one forgets or treats as known, what's-his-name, what-d'you-call-it. [prec.]

think, v.t. & i. (thought, *pron.* thawt). Consider, be of opinion, as *we t.* (*that*) *he will come, we do not t. it probable, I t. it a shame, it is not thought fair, is thought to be a fraud, I don't t.* (slang addition to ironical statement, as *you are a pattern of tact, I d. t.*); intend, expect, as *thinks to deceive us*; form conception of, as *cannot t. the infinite,* (colloq.) *I can't t. how you do it*; recognize presence or existence of, as *the child thought no harm*; reduce to specified condition &c. by thinking, as *cannot t. away a toothache, will t. himself silly*; exercise the mind otherwise than by passive reception of another's ideas, as *let me t.* (appeal for time before answering &c.), *t. twice before doing* (avoid hasty action), *t. in German* &c.; have half formed intention, as *I t. I'll try*; *t. about*, consider, esp. consider the practicability of (scheme, *doing*); *t. aloud*, utter one's thoughts in the order of their occurrence; *t. of,* consider, imagine, propose to oneself, entertain the idea of, hit upon, as *have many things to t. of, to t. of* (one can hardly imagine) *his not guessing it!, must be thinking of going, couldn't t. of such a thing, t. of a word beginning with B, would have telephoned if I had thought of it*; *t. better of,* decide on second thoughts to abandon (intention), (also) have higher opinion of (person, esp. *than to believe* &c.); *t. little* or *nothing of,* consider insignificant or contemptible, as *t. nothing* *of 30 miles a day, I t. nothing of your friend Jones*; *t. much, well, highly, meanly, of*, esteem thus, *t. no small* BEER *of*; *t. out*, consider carefully, devise (plan &c.); *t. over* (adv. or prep.), reflect upon, as *t. over what I have said, will t. it over*; *t. fit* or *good*, choose (*to* do esp. arbitrary or foolish thing). Hence **thi·nk**ABLE, **thi·nk**ING[2] (*all -ing men*, all who accept my view), aa., **thi·nk**ER[1] n. [OE *thenc(e)an*, past *thóhte*, cf. ON *thekkja*, G *denken*; cogn. w. THANK[2]]

third, a. & n. Next after second, whence **thir·d**LY[2] adv.; *t.* ESTATE, *t. of* EXCHANGE[1]; *t.-class, -rate*, (loosely) inferior, poor; (Crick.) *t. man*, (place of) fielder diagonally behind point away from wicket; *t. party* or *person* (see PERSON for gram. sense), another besides the two principals, bystander &c., (*t.-party risks* in insurance, damage to another than the insured, which the underwriter contracts to meet); one of three equal divisions of a whole; sixtieth of a second of time or angular measurement; (Mus.) (interval between a tone and) next tone but one, consonance of a tone & its t.; (pl.) t. part of husband's personal property, going to widow in certain cases. [OE *thridda* (THREE)]

thirst, n., & v.t. Suffering caused by want of drink, desire for drink (*have a t.* colloq., want a drink); (fig.) ardent desire, craving, (*of, for, after*, glory, person's blood, &c.); (v.i.) feel t. (now chiefly fig. *for, after*). Hence **thi·rst**LESS a. [OE *thyrstan* vb, *thurst* n., cf. Du. *dorst*, G *durst*, ON *thorsti*, cogn. w. L *torrēre* parch]

thir·sty, a. Feeling thirst (*be t.*, current E for *thirst* vb); fond of drink; (of country or season) dry, parched; (colloq.) causing thirst, as *this is t. work*. Hence **thir·sti**LY[2] adv. [OE *thurstig* (prec., -Y[1])]

thirtee·n, a. & n. One more than twelve, 13, xiii; *the t. superstition* (that t. as the number of persons at table, or of one's room &c., brings ill luck). Hence **thirtee·n**TH[2] a. & n. [OE *thréoténe, -týne* (as THREE, see -TEEN)]

thir·ty, a. & n. Three times ten, 30, xxx; *t.-one* &c., *t.-first* &c.; *T.-nine Articles* (subscribed to by person taking orders in Ch. of Eng.); *t.-two-mo*, 32*mo*, book with 32 leaves to the sheet. Hence **thir·ti**ETH, **thir·tyfold** (see -FOLD), aa. & nn. [OE *thritig, thrittig* (*thri* THREE, see -TY[2])]

this (dh-), a. & pron. (pl. *these* pron. dhēz). The (person, thing), the person or thing, close at hand or touched or pointed to or drawn attention to or observed by the speaker at the time, or already named or understood or in question or familiar (seldom idiomatically interchangeable with THAT[1], but often only equally applicable to the facts, the implication of greater nearness, familiarity, &c., being purely idiomatic), as *observe t. dog on the hearthrug, who are these people in the next room?, what is all t. noise?, fold it like t., I knew all t. before, t.* (your action, the action I am speaking of) *is not fair, t. term is liable to much abuse, things are easier in these days*; *t. and* THAT[1]; *t. much*, t. amount (esp. = what I am about to state, as *I know t. m., that the thing is absurd*); *t.*, THAT[1], *and the other*; (of time) *t. day*, today, *shall be* or *have been busy all t. week, ought to be ready by t.* (time), *before t.* (time), *have been asking for it these* (or *this*) *three weeks* (just past). [OE masc. *thes*, fem. *théos*, neut. *this*, prob. f. root of *thæt* (see THE); OE pl. *dǽs* gave *these*, *dás* gave *those* (now used as pl. of THAT[1])]

thi·sness, n. Quality of being this, = HAECCEITY. [-NESS]

thi·stle (-sl), n. Kinds of prickly composite plant with globular or cylindrical heads with purple, yellow, or white flowers, Scottish national emblem (cf. ROSE); *Order of the T.*, a Scottish order of knighthood. Hence **thi·stl**Y[2] a. [OE *thistel*, cf. Du. & G *distel*, ON *thistill*]

thither (dhĭ·dh*er*), adv. (archaic). To that place, there (of motion). Hence **thi·ther**WARD(S) adv. [OE *thider, thy-*, f. root of THE, cf. *hither*]

tho'. See THOUGH.

thole[1], v.t. (archaic). Undergo, endure, suffer, (pain, grief, &c., or abs.); permit, admit of. [OE *tholian*, cf. ON *thola*, Da. *taale*, G *geduld* patience, cogn. w. Gk **tlaō* suffer, L *tolerare*]

thole[2], n. (Also *t.-pin*) pin in gunwale of boat as fulcrum for oar; each of two such pins between which oar plays. [OE *thol*, cf. Du. *dol*, ON *thollr* tree, peg]

Tho·mism (tō-), n. Theological doctrine of Thomas Aquinas (d. 1274), who maintained predestination & efficacious grace, and denied the immaculate conception. So **Tho·m**IST n., **Thomi·st**IC(AL) aa. [-ISM]

thong, n., & v.t. Narrow strip of leather used as halter, reins, lash of whip, &c.; (v.t.) provide with t., strike with t. [OE *thwang*, cf. ON *thvengr*, cogn. w. TWINGE]

Thor, n. Scandinavian god of thunder, war, & agriculture; *T.'s hammer*, flint axe (-hammer). [f. ON *Thorr*]

thor·ax, n. (Anat., Zool.) part of trunk between neck and abdomen or tail, whence **thoră·c**IC a., **thoră·c**I(CO)-, **thoră·c**O-, comb. forms; (Gk Ant.) breastplate, cuirass. [L, f. Gk *thōrax -akos*]

thor·ite, n. A black compact mineral found in Norway. [THOR + -ITE[1]]

thorn, n. Prickle, spiny process on plant, esp. abortive branch; kinds of thorny shrub or tree, as *hawt., whitet., blackt.*; *a t. in* one's *flesh* or *side*, constant source of annoyance; *be, sit, on tt.*, be continuously uneasy esp. in expectation of being detected &c. at any moment; name of the obs. E letter þ (th); *thor·nback*, ray with spines on back and tail, British spider crab; *thor·nbill, thor·ntail*, kinds of humming-bird. Hence **thor·n**LESS, **thor·n**Y[2] (often fig. of affair, = hard to handle), aa. [OE & ON, cf. Du. *doorn*, G *dorn*]

thorough (thŭ·ru), a., n., prep., & adv. Complete, unqualified, not superficial, out-&-out, as *his work is seldom t., has caught a t. chill, wants a t. change, a t. scoundrel*; (n., hist.) uncompromising policy of Strafford & Laud under Charles I; (prep. & adv., archaic) through; *t.-bāss*, bass part accompanied by shorthand marks esp. numerals to indicate the general harmony, such system of marks, (loosely) harmonic composition; *t.-brace*, strap between C-springs of vehicle; *t.-bred* a. & n., (animal, esp. horse) of pure breed, high-spirited, mettlesome, (also fig. of persons); *tho·roughfare*, road, street, esp. one through which much traffic passes, *no thoroughfare*, (as notice at end of obstructed or private road) no passage; *t.-going*, uncompromising, out-&-out; *t.-paced*, (lit., of horse) trained to all paces, (fig.) complete, unqualified, as *a t.-p. rascal*; *t.-pin*, swelling in hollow of horse's hock. Hence **tho·rough**LY[2] adv., **tho·rough**NESS n. [= THROUGH]

thorp(e), n. Village, hamlet, (esp. in place-names). [OE & ON (*-p*), cf. Du. *dorp*, G *dorf*]

those. See THAT[1].

thou (dhow), pron. (object. *thee*, pl. YE, YOU), & v.t. & i. Sing. pron. of 2nd pers., now archaic or poet. exc. in addressing God and (usu. *thee* as subject. with 3rd pers. vb) as used by Quakers; (v.t.) address (person) as *t.*; (v.i.) use *t.* instead of *you*. [OE & ON *thú*, cf. Da. & G *du*, L *tu*, Gk *su, tu*]

though (dhō), **tho'**, conj. (Also *although*) notwithstanding the fact that, as *he finished first t. he began last, t. it was late we decided to set out*; (also *alt.*) on the supposition that, as *it is better to ask him* (*even*) *t. he* (*should*) *refuse* or *refuses*; *what t.* (what does it matter if) *the way is* (archaic *be*) *long?, as t.*, as if, as *it is as t. a man should ask alms of a beggar, he acts as t. he were mad, it looks as t. he meant* (vulg. *means*) *business*; (introducing what is virtually an independent sentence) and yet, as *I have no doubt he will understand—t. you never know*; (abs.) however, as *I wish you had told me, t.* [ME *thogh*, cf. ON *thó*, Du. & G *doch*]

thought[1] (thawt), n. Process, power, of thinking; faculty of reason; sober reflection (*in t.*, meditating); consideration, as *take t.* (consider matters), *after serious t., acts without t.*; idea, conception, chain of reasoning, &c., produced by thinking, as *an essay full of striking tt., a happy t.*, well-timed or apposite idea or suggestion; half-formed intention, as *had* (*some*) *tt. of resigning, had no t. of offending him*; (usu. pl.) what one thinks, one's opinion, as *will tell you my tt. of the matter*; subject of one's t., as *his one t. is how to get away, a* PENNY *for your tt.*; *you are much in my tt.*, I often think of you; *a t.*, a little, somewhat, as *cut it a t. shorter, seems to me a t. arrogant*; *quick as t.*, very quick; FREE[1] *t.*; *second tt.*, further consideration, as *second tt. are best, on second tt. I will take a cab*; *t.-reader, -reading*, reader, reading, of person's tt. by telepathy; *t.-transference*, telepathy; *t.-wave*, undulation of the supposed medium of t.-transference. Hence **(-)thought**ED[2] a. [OE (*ge*)*thoht* (THINK)]

thought[2]. See THINK.

though·tful, a. Engaged in or given to meditation; (of book, writer, remark, &c.) giving signs of original thought; (of persons or conduct) considerate, not haphazard or unfeeling. Hence **though·tful**LY[2] adv., **though·tful**NESS n. [-FUL]

though·tless, a. Careless of consequences or of others' feelings; due to want of thought. Hence **though·tless**LY[2] adv., **though·tless**NESS n. [-LESS]

thou·sand (-owz-), a. & n. Ten hundred, 1000, M (for uses cf. HUNDRED); (loosely) many, as *a t. times easier, one in a t.* (esp. rare or excellent one); (*a*) *t. & one*, myriad, numberless (*the t. & o. small worries of life*; *made a t. & o. excuses*); *a t. thanks, pardons, apologies*, &c. (forms of polite exaggeration); UPPER *ten t.* Hence **thou·sand**FOLD a. & adv., **(-)thou·sand**TH[2] a. & n. [OE *thúsend*, cf. Du. *duizend*, G *tausend*, ON *thúsund*, etym. dub.]

thrall (-awl), n., a., & v.t. Slave (*of, to*, person or thing, lit. & fig.); bondage, esp. *in t.*; (adj., archaic) enslaved (*to*); (v.t.) enslave. Hence **thra·l**DOM n. [OE *thræl*, f. ON *thrǽll*, cf. Da. *træl*]

thrash, -esh, v.t. (Usu. *-esh*) beat out or separate grain from (corn &c.) on *threshing-floor* or in *threshing-machine*, (fig.) *t. out*, arrive at, obtain, (the truth, rhyme, &c.) by repeated trial; (of paddle-wheel, branch, &c.) act like flail, deliver repeated blows, (of ship) keep striking the waves, make way against wind or tide (usu. *-ash*, as *t. to windward*); (*-ash*) beat esp. with stick or whip, conquer, surpass, whence **thra·sh**ING[1] n. [OE *therscan*, cf. ON *threskja*, Du. *dorschen*, G *dreschen*]

thra·sher, thre-, n. Kind of shark; (usu. *thre-*) person, machine, that threshes; (*thra-*) one who thrashes. [-ER[1]]

thrasŏ·nical, a. Bragging. Hence **thraso·nical**LY[2] adv. [f. L *Thraso -onis*, character in Terence, f. Gk *thrasus* bold, + -ICAL]

thread[1] (-ĕd), n. Spun-out filament of cotton, flax, silk, wool, &c., yarn, (*has* *not a dry t. on him,* is wet through); thin cord of twisted yarns; *gold t.* (of silk &c. with gold wire wound round it); LISLE THREAD; *t. & THRUM*[1]; t.-shaped thing, long slender body, e.g. spiral part of screw; thin seam or vein of ore; (fig.) *the t.* (course) *of life*; *hang by a t.*, (of person's life &c.) be in a precarious state, (of momentous issue &c.) be determinable either way by something still in doubt; *lost the t.* (chain, connexion) *of his argument*; *resume* or *take up the t. of*, proceed with after interruption; *gather up the tt.*, bring the divisions of subject &c. into relation after separate treatment; *threa·dbare*, (of cloth) worn so that nap is lost and t. visible, wearing such clothes, (fig.) well-worn, hackneyed, whence *threa·dbareness* n.; *t. lace* (made of t.); *t.-mark*, mark made in bank-note paper with highly-coloured silk fibres to prevent counterfeiting; *t.-needle*, children's game (OLD *lady of Threadneedle St*); *t.-paper*, (strip of) soft thin paper used for rolling up t.; *threa·dworm*, kinds of t.-like worm, esp. one infesting rectum of children. Hence **threa·di**NESS n., **threa·dy**[2] a. [OE *thrǣd* (as THROW), cf. Du. *draad*, G *draht*]

thread[2], v.t. Pass thread through eye of (needle); string (beads &c.) on thread, make (chain &c.) thus; pick one's way through (maze, streets, crowded place, &c.), make one's *way* thus; streak (hair &c.) as with threads. [ME *threden*, as prec.]

threat (-ĕt), n. Declaration of intention to punish or hurt; (Law) such menace of bodily hurt or injury to reputation or property as may restrain person's freedom of action; indication of coming evil (*there is a t. of rain*). [OE *thrēat* crowd, calamity, threat, cf. *thrēotan*, past *thrēat*, afflict, urge, & Du. *verdrieten* vex, cogn. w. L *trudere* push]

threa·ten (-ĕtn), v.t. & i. Use threats towards (person &c., or abs.; *with* the evil threatened), as *threatened me with death, am threatened with a visit*; give warning of the infliction of (injury &c., or abs.), announce one's intention (*to* do), as punishment or in revenge &c., as *threatens every kind of torment, t. to resign*, (fig.) *clouds t.* (*an interruption* or *to interrupt us*), *the practice threatens to become general*. Hence **threa·tening**LY[2] adv. [OE *thrēatnian* (THREAT)]

three, a. & n. One more than two, 3, iii; (Skat.) any of four turns in which direction & edge are both changed; *t. times t.*, t. cheers thrice repeated; *the t. F's*, free sale, fixity of tenure, fair rent, (demands of Irish Land League); *the t. R's*, reading, writing, arithmetic; RULE *of t.*; *t.-bottle man*, old-fashioned hard drinker; *t.-colour process* (of reproducing natural colours by combining photographs in red, blue, & yellow); *t.-cornered*, triangular, (of contest &c.) between three parties each for himself; *t.-de·cker*, war-vessel with t. gun-decks, t.-storeyed pulpit; *t.-handed*, with t. hands, played by t. persons, as *t.-h. euchre*; *t. halfpence*, $1\frac{1}{2}$*d.*; *T. in One*, the Trinity; *t.-legged race*, of couples each having a right & left leg tied together; *t.-ma·ster*, vessel esp. schooner with t. masts; *t.-pair*, (of room) up t. pair of stairs (usu. *t.-p. back* or *front*); *three·pence* (-ĕp-, -ĭp-, -ēp-), sum of t. pence; *three·-penny* (*bit*) (same pron.), coin worth t. pence; (*the*) *t.-per-cents*, (government) bonds bearing that interest; *t.-ply*, of t. strands, webs, or thicknesses, (as n.) t.-p. wood made by gluing together 3 layers with grain in different directions; *t.-quarter(s)*, (a.) of t. fourths of normal size or numbers, (of portrait) going down to hips, showing t. fourths of face, (n.) any of 3 or 4 players behind HALF-backs; *threescore·*, (age of) sixty (*t.-s. & ten*, age of 70 as normal limit of life). Hence **three·**FOLD a. & adv. [OE *thrēo*, *thri*, cf. Du. *drie*, G *drei*, L *tres*, Gk *treis*]

three·some, n. & a. (chiefly Sc.). Set of three persons; game &c. for three; (adj.) of three. [-SOME]

thremmatŏ·logy, n. Science of breeding animals & plants. [f. Gk *thremma -matos* nursling (*trephō* nourish, -M), -O-, -LOGY]

thrē·node, -ody, nn. (Song of) lamentation esp. on person's death. Hence or cogn. **threne·tic**, **threne·tic**AL, **threnō·di**AL, **threnŏ·dic**, aa., **thre·nod**IST(3) n. [f. L f. Gk *thrēnōidia* (*thrēnos* wailing + *ōidē* ODE]

thresh &c. See THRASH &c.

thre·shold (-sh-hō-, -shō-), n. Plank or stone at bottom of door in dwelling-house, church, &c.; (loosely, esp. fig.) entrance, as *at the t. of a discussion, on the t. of a revolution, of a new century*. [OE *therscold* (*therscan* THRASH + -LE)]

threw. See THROW.

thrice, adv. (archaic or literary). Three times (now chiefly in comb. = highly, as *t.-blessed, -favoured*). [ME *thries* (THREE, -ES)]

thrid, v.t. (archaic). = THREAD.

thrĭ·dace, n. Inspissated juice of lettuce, used as sedative. [f. Gk *thridax -akos* lettuce]

thrift, n. Frugality, economical management, whence **thri·ft**LESS a., **thri·ftless**LY[2] adv., **thri·ftless**NESS n.; kinds of plant, esp. sea-pink. [ME & ON (as THRIVE, see -TH[1])]

thri·fty, a. Frugal, economical; thriving, prosperous. Hence **thri·fti**LY[2] adv. [-Y[2]]

thrill, v.t. & i., & n. Penetrate (person &c.) with wave of emotion or sensation, as *his voice thrilled the listeners*; be thus penetrated or agitated (*with* horror &c.); (of emotion &c.) pass *through*, *over*, *along*, as *fear thrilled through my veins*; quiver, throb, (as) with emotion; (n.) wave of emotion or sensation, as *a t. of joy*, throb, pulsation, (Med.) kinds of tremor or resonance observed in auscultation, (slang) sensational story. Hence **thri·ll**ER[1](2) n. (esp. sensational play or tale), **thri·lling**LY[2] adv., **thri·lling**NESS n. [(n. f. vb) OE *thyrlian* (*thýrel* a. & n. bored, hole, f. *thurh* THROUGH)]

thrips, n. Kinds of insect, esp. (improp.) some injurious to vines &c. [L f. Gk, = woodworm]

thrīve, v.i. (*thrōve* rarely *thrived*, *thrĭven* rarely *thrived*). Prosper, flourish; grow rich; (of animal or plant) grow vigorously. Hence **thri·ving**LY[2] adv., **thri·ving**NESS n. [ME *thriven*, past *thraf*, *-of*, f. ON *thrífa* grasp, cf. Da. *trives*, Sw. *trifvas*, thrive]

thro', thro. See THROUGH.

throat, n., & v.t. Front of neck between chin & collar-bone, jugular region, (*cut one's t.*, esp. with intent to kill him; *take by the t.*, try to throttle); gullet; windpipe, as *words stuck in my t.*; t.-shaped thing, e.g. narrow part of river between rocks, (also in many naut. wds); *sore t.*, inflammation of lining membrane of gullet &c., *clergyman's sore t.*, form of this affecting those who speak much in public, often of nervous origin; *cut* one's *own t.*, *one another's tt.*, adopt suicidal, mutually destructive, policy; *lie in* one's *t.*, lie grossly; *give* person *the lie in his t.*, accuse him of lying grossly; *thrust* thing *down* one's *t.*, force it on his attention; (v.t.) channel, groove. Hence **-throat**ED[2] a. [OE *throte*, cf. OHG *drozza*, G *drossel*, perh. cogn. w. Du. *strot* throat & ON *throti* swelling]

throa·ty, a. Guttural, uttered in the throat; having prominent or capacious throat. Hence **throa·ti**NESS n. [-Y[2]]

throb, v.i., & n. (Of heart, bosom, temples, &c.) palpitate, pulsate esp. with more than usual force or rapidity; (fig.) quiver, vibrate, (as) with emotion; (n.) palpitation, pulsation, as *heart-tt.*, *tt. of pleasure*. Hence **thro·bbing**LY[2] adv. [ME *throbben*; excl. E; perh. imit.]

throe, n., & v.i. (Usu. pl.) violent pang(s), esp. of childbirth lit. & fig., anguish; (v.i.) be in agony. [ME *throwe* n., etym. dub.]

Throgmor·ton Street. (Used for) the London Stock Exchange or its members or operations.

thrombō·sis, n. Coagulation of blood in blood-vessel or organ. Hence **thrombŏ·**TIC a. [Gk *thrombōsis* curdling (*thrombos* lump, see -OSIS)]

throne, n., & v.t. Chair of state for sovereign, bishop, &c., usu. decorated & raised on dais; sovereign power, as *came to the t.*, *lost his t.*; (pl.) third ORDER[1] of angels; (v.t.) enthrone (lit. & fig.). Hence **thro·ne**LESS a. [f. OF *trone* f. L f. Gk *thronos* seat, chair]

throng, n., & v.i. & t. Crowd of people; multitude esp. in small space (*of* people or things); (v.i.) come, go, press, (*round* &c.) in multitudes; (v.t.) fill (street &c.) with a crowd or as crowd does, (archaic) press hard upon (person). [(vb f. n.) OE (*ge*)*thrang* f. *thringan* vb crowd, cf. Du. & G *drang*]

thro·stle (-sl), n. Song-thrush; (also *t.-frame*) machine for spinning wool, cotton, &c. [OE, cf. MHG *drostel*; cogn. w. L *turdus* thrush]

thro·ttle, n., & v.t. Throat, gullet, windpipe; (also *t.-valve*) valve controlling flow of steam &c. in engine. (V.t.) choke, strangle; control (steam &c., engine) with t.-valve. [vb (f. 1400) perh. f. THROAT + -LE(3); n. (f. 1550) perh. f. north. *thropple* throat, etym. dub.]

through, thro', thro, (-ōō), prep., adv., & a. From end to end or side to side of, between the sides or walls or parts of, as *marched t. the town*, *arrow went t. his arm*, *see t. a telescope*, *look t. the window*, *pass t. the doorway*, *swam t. the waves*, *pushes his fingers t. his hair*; (fig.) *went t. many trials*, *got t. his examinations*, *saw t. his hypocrisy*, *wait t. ten long years*, *flashed t. his mind*; by reason of, by agency, means, or fault of, as *it all came about t. his not knowing the way*, *concealed it t. shame*, *it was all t. you that we were late.* (Adv.) from side to side, from end to end, from beginning to end, as *let us stroll t.*, *would not let us t.* (gate &c.), *ice gave & I went t.*, *read it carefully t.*, *read it t. & t.* (t. again & again), *looked him t. & t.* (observed searchingly), *lasted all t.* (all the time); (colloq.) *are you t.* (*with that job*)?, have you finished (it)?; CARRY, *drop* or FALL[1], PULL[1], *t.*; GO[1] *t. with.* (Adj.) going, concerned with going, t., as *a t. bolt*, *t.-stone*, = BOND[1]-*stone*, esp. (of railway or steamboat travelling) going all the way without change of line &c., going over different companies' lines with same ticket, as *t. carriage*, *train*, *passenger*, *ticket* (for t. passenger), *fares*. [OE *thurh* prep. & adv., cf. Du. *door*, G *durch*, cogn. w. Goth. *thairh* through & *thairkô* hole]

through·ly, adv. (archaic). Thoroughly. [f. THROUGH + -LY[2]]

throughou·t, adv. & prep. Right through, in every part, in all respects, as *timber was rotten t.*, *followed a sound policy t.*; (prep.) right through, from end to end of, as *t. the length & breadth of the land*, *t. the 18th century.* [OUT]

throw[1] (-ō), v.t. & i. (*threw* pr. -ōō, *thrown* pr. -ōn). Release (ball, object) after imparting motion, propel through space, send forth or dismiss esp. with some violence, fling or hurl or cast (lit. & fig.), as *must not t. stones* (lit., & fig. = cast imputations), *threw the ball over his* *head, learnt to t. a fly* (in fishing), *mortars t. shell, hose throws water, house thrown down by earthquake, ship was thrown upon the coast, thrown from his horse, was thrown into a dilemma* or *upon his own resources, t.* COLD[1] *water on, t. a* SOP *to, t. light on the matter,* help to explain it, *t. down the* GLOVE, *t.* DUST[1] *in* person's *eyes, t.* one*self,* one's *daughter, at the head of* (openly seek as husband), *t.* (as FLING) *in* one's *teeth, t. good money after bad* (lose more in trying to recoup a loss), (w. ind. obj.) *t. me a rope, t.* one *a kiss* (wave hand to him after kissing it); (Cricket, of bowler) deliver ball with sudden straightening of elbow (*was no-balled for throwing*); (of wrestler, horse) bring (antagonist, rider) to the ground; put (clothes &c.) carelessly or hastily *on, off, over* one's *shoulders* &c., (of snake) cast (skin); (of animals, e.g. rabbits, pigeons) bring forth (young); make (specified cast) with dice, as *threw deuce-ace*; twist (silk &c.) into threads; shape (round pottery) on potter's wheel; turn, direct, move esp. quickly (esp. part of body), as *threw his eyes to the ground, a glance backwards, his arms up, his head back, t. a chest* (slang, = stand erect with chest expanded). *T. away,* (fig.) part with needlessly or recklessly, lose by neglect, as *threw away all his advantages, an excellent offer*; (p.p.) wasted, as *the advice was thrown away upon him. T. back,* revert to ancestral character. *T.* one*self down,* lie down. *T. in*: (also *t. into the bargain*) add (thing) to a bargain without extra charge; interpose (word, remark) by way of parenthesis or casually; *t. in* one's *lot with,* decide to share the fortunes of. *T.* one*self into,* engage vigorously in. *T. off*: discard (acquaintance &c.); contrive to get rid of (illness, troublesome companion); abandon (disguise); produce, deliver, (poem, epigram) in offhand manner; (of hounds or hunt, & transf.) begin hunting, make a start, begin speaking, playing, &c.; (& see above). *T.* one*self on, upon,* place one's reliance on (*the mercy of the court* &c.). *T. open*: open suddenly or wide; make accessible (*to* all comers &c.); *t. open the door to,* make possible. *T. out*: cast out; build (wing of house, pier, projecting or prominent thing); suggest, insinuate; reject (bill in Parliament); distract (person speaking, thinking, or acting) from the matter in hand so that he blunders or stops; (Cricket, of fielder) put out (batsman) by throwing at wicket. *T. over,* desert, abandon. *T. overboard,* see OVER-(2). *T. up*: lift up (window-sash); resign (office); vomit (t. & i.); *t.* one's *eyes up* (as sign of horror or outraged propriety); *t. up the* SPONGE. Hence **(-)thrower**[1] n. [OE *thrāwan,* past *thrēow,* twist, hurl, cf. G *drehen,* Du. *draaien,* twist, whirl]

throw[2] (-ō), n. Throwing, cast; cast of dice; cast of fishing-line; distance a missile is or may be thrown, as *record t. with the hammer, a stone's t.,* (loosely) slight distance; fall in wrestling; (Crick.) bowler's illegitimately delivered ball; (Geol., Mining) fault, leap, in strata; machine, device, giving rapid rotary motion; *t.-off,* start in hunt or race; *t.-stick,* club, stick, meant to be whirled from the hand, e.g. boomerang. [f. prec.]

throw'ster, n. One who throws silk. [-STER]

thrum[1], n., & v.t. Fringe of threads remaining on loom when web has been cut off; single thread of this; any loose thread or tuft; *thread & t.,* all alike, good & bad; (v.t.) make of, cover with, tt. Hence **thru'mmy**[2] a. [OE, cf. ON *thromr* edge, Du. *dreum,* G *trumm,* end, thrum]

thrum[2], v.i. & t., & n. Play monotonously or unskilfully on or *on* (stringed instrument); drum, tap, idly on or *on* (table &c.); (n.) such playing, resulting sound. [imit.]

thrush[1], n. Family or genus of birds, esp. European *song-t.,* throstle. [OE *thrȳsce*]

thrush[2], n. Disease, esp. of children, marked by pearl-coloured fungous vesicles in mouth & throat; disease affecting frog of horse's foot. [f. 17th c., etym. dub.; cf. Da. *troske*]

thrust, v.t. & i. (thrust), & n. Push with sudden impulse or with force (lit. & fig.), as *t. his fist into my face, t. the letter into his pocket, t. a pin into the cushion, I t. out my hand, t. him forth* (out of room &c.), *was t. from his rights*; *t.* oneself or one's *nose in,* obtrude, interfere; pierce (person &c.) *through*; make sudden push *at* (person &c. *with* dagger &c.); force oneself *through, past,* &c.; make one's *way* thus; hence **thru'ster**[1] n. (esp., foxhunter who endangers others or the hounds in securing a forward place). (N.) sudden or forcible push, (Mil.) strong attempt to penetrate enemy's line or territory; attack with point of weapon; remark aimed at a person (*a shrewd,* HOME[1], *t.*; *he parried the t.*); stress between two bodies esp. parts of structure, e.g. arch, rafters, crushing of coal-mine pillars by weight of roof; *t.-hoe* (worked by t., not pull). [(n. f. vb) ME *thrusten* f. ON *thrȳsta,* perh. cogn. w. L *trudere*]

thud, v.i., & n. (Make, fall with) low dull sound as of blow on soft thing. [prob. imit.; but cf. OE *thyddan* strike, thrust]

thug, n. Member of a religious organization of assassins in India suppressed about 1825; cut-throat, ruffian. [f. Hind. *ṭhag, -ug*]

thu'ggee (-gē), n. The practice of the thugs. So **thu'ggery, thu'ggism,** nn. [f. Hind. *ṭhagi* as prec.]

Thū·lē, n. Name given by Pytheas of Massilia to some (is)land north of Gt Britain; *ultima* (=farthest) *T.*, any far-away unknown region.

thumb (-m), n., & v.t. Short thick finger set apart from & opposite to the others on human hand; digit of other animals corresponding to this in position; *tt. up!* (slang excl. of satisfaction); RULE *of t.*; *his* FINGERS *are all tt.*; *under* person's *t.* (influence, domination); *t.-blue*, washing indigo in small lumps; *t.-latch* (raised by pressing end of lever with t.); *t.-mark* (made by t. esp. on leaf of book); *t.-nail sketch*, portrait of t.-n. size, hasty word-picture; *t.-nut* (shaped for t. to turn); *t.-print*, impression of t. esp. as used for identification; *t.-screw*, instrument of torture for squeezing tt.; *t.-stall*, sheath, pad, &c., to protect t.; (v.t.) wear, soil, (pages &c.) with t., handle (piano keys &c.) or play (music) awkwardly. Hence **thu·mb**LESS a. [OE *thúma*, cf. Du. *duim*, G *daumen*, L *tumēre* to swell]

thu·mmim. See URIM.

thump, v.t. & i., & n. Beat heavily esp. with fist; deliver heavy blows *at*, *on*, &c.; *t. the* or *a cushion* (of vehement preacher emphasizing his words with blows on pulpit cushion); (n.) heavy blow, bang. [imit.]

thu·mper, n. In vbl senses, also: (colloq.) large, striking, or impressive person or thing, esp. lie, so **thu·mping**[2] a. [-ER[1]]

thu·nder, n., & v.i. & t. Loud noise following flash of lightning & due to discharge of electricity through the air; thunderbolt, as *Jove's tt.*; (fig.) loud noise, as *tt. of applause*, *blood-&-t.*, (of novel &c.) sensational; (pl.) authoritative censure or threats (*the tt. of* The Times, *the Church*); (v.i.) give forth t., usu. *it thunders*, make loud noise, as *voice thundered in my ears*, utter violent threats &c. *against* &c.; (v.t.) emit (threats &c.) in loud or impressive manner; *t.-&-lightning*, =OXFORD *mixture*; *thu·nderbolt*, flash of lightning with crash of t., imaginary bolt or shaft viewed as substance of lightning, kinds of stone or fossil supposed to be such bolt, formidable threat &c.; *t.-clap*, crash of t. (esp. fig. or in simile of sudden terrible event or news; *the t.-c. of Napoleon's escape*; *the news came on me like a t.-c.*); *t.-cloud* (producing t.); *t.-storm* (with t.); *t.-struck*, struck by lightning, amazed. Hence **thu·nder**LESS, **thu·nder**OUS, **thu·nder**Y[2], aa., **thu·nderous**LY[2] adv. [(vb, OE *thunrian*) OE *thunor*, cf. Du. *donder*, G *donner*, ON *thórr* (cf. THOR), cogn. w. L *tonare* thunder, Gk *stenō* groan]

thu·nderer, n. In vbl senses, esp. *the T.*, Jupiter, (facet.) *Times* newspaper. [-ER[1]]

thu·ndering, a. & adv. In vbl senses, also or esp.: (colloq.) unusual(ly), remarkable, -bly, decided(ly), as *a t. nuisance, was t. glad to get back, a t. great fish*; *the T. legion*, Roman legion containing Christian soldiers whose prayers were held to have procured a thunderstorm that terrified the enemy. Hence **thu·ndering**LY[2] adv. [-ING[2, 1]]

thūri- in comb.=L *thus thuris* frankincense, as: *-fer*, acolyte who carries censer; *-ferous*, producing frankincense; *-fica·tion*, burning of incense.

thūr·ible, n. Censer. [f. L *thuribulum* (*thus*, see prec., f. Gk *thuos* f. *thuō* sacrifice)]

Thur·sday (-zdĭ), n. Fifth day of week; HOLY, MAUNDY, *T.* [OE *thúres dæg* THOR'S DAY f. ON *thórs-dagr*, on L *dies Jovis* Jupiter's day]

thus (dh-), adv. In this way, in the way (to be) indicated, whence **thu·s**NESS n. (facet.); accordingly, as a result or inference; to this extent, so, as *t. far*, *t. much.* [OE, cf. Du. *dus*, prob. cogn. w. THAT[1]]

thwack, v.t. & n. =WHACK. [imit.]

thwaite, n. Piece of wild land made arable (now in place-names, as *Est.*, *Stonet.*). [f. ON *thveit* paddock, cogn. w. OE *thwitan* cut, WHITTLE]

thwart, adv., prep., & a., (archaic), v.t., & n. Across, athwart; (Naut.) *t.-hawse*, across the hawse, *t.-ship* a., *-ships* adv., (lying) across ship; (adj.) lying across, transverse; (v.t.) frustrate, cross, (wish, purpose), whence **thwar·ting**LY[2] adv.; (n.) oarsman's bench placed across boat. [ME (adv.), f. ON *thvert*, cf. OHG *twer*, G *quer*, Du. *dwars*; cogn. w. L *torquēre* twist]

thy, thine, (dh-), pron. & a. Possessive case of, & adj. corresp. to, THOU (now archaic &c. as THOU; before vowel usu. *thine*), also (*thine*) in abs. use, as *it was thy fault, lift thine eyes, the fault is thine, do what thou wilt with thine own.* [OE *thin*, cf. ON *thinn*, G *dein*; *thy* by oss of *-n*]

thȳ·lacine, n. Zebra wolf, a Tasmanian carnivorous marsupial. [F, f. Gk *thulakos* pouch, -INE[1]]

thyme (tīm), n. Kinds of plant, esp. *common garden t.*, shrub with pungent aromatic leaves used in cookery, *shepherd's* or *wild t.*, kind with mildly aromatic leaves. Hence **thy·mol** (th-) n. (a powerful antiseptic), **thy·my**[2] a. [f. F *thym* f. L f. Gk *thumos* (*thuō* sacrifice)]

thȳr·oid, a. & n. (anat., zool.). Shield-shaped, as *t. cartilage*, large cartilage of larynx projection of which in man forms Adam's apple; connected with the t. cartilage, as *t. artery*; *t. body* or *gland*, large ductless organ of no known function situated on larynx & trachea, the seat of goitre (*t. gland* or *t.*, drug prepared in various forms from the t. gland of animals & used in cretinism & other diseases); having shield-shaped markings, as *t. woodpecker*. Hence **thyro-** comb. form (anat.). [irreg. f. Gk *thureoeidēs* (Galen) f. *thureos* shield f. *thura* door, see -OID]

thyr·sus, n. (Gk ant.; pl. -ī). Staff tipped with ornament like pine-cone, an attribute of Bacchus. [L, f. Gk *thursos*]

thyself, pron. Reflexive & emphat. form corresp. to *thou, thee*. [THY + SELF]

ti (tē), n. Kinds of tree with edible roots. [Polynesian name]

tiar·a, n. Ancient Persian turban worn erect by king, depressed by others; Pope's diadem pointed at top & surrounded by three crowns, (fig.) the papal office; ornamental coronet. Hence **tiar·a'd** [-ED[2]] a. [L f. Gk, prob. of Pers. orig.]

ti·bia, n. (anat.; pl. -*ae*). The shin-bone; fourth joint of leg in insects; drumstick of fowl. So **ti·bi**AL a., **ti·bio-** comb. form. [L (tī-), = shin-bone, flute]

tic, n. Habitual spasmodic contraction of muscles esp. of face; (in full *t. douloureux* pr. dŏlorōō· *or as F*, lit. painful t.) severe form of facial neuralgia with convulsive twitchings. [F, etym. dub.]

tice, n. = YORKER. [f. obs. *tice* ENTICE]

tick[1], v.i. & t., & n. (Make) slight recurring click, esp. that of watch or clock (*to* or *on the t.*, with exact punctuality); *t.-tack*, pulsating sound esp. of the heart (see also TRICK-TRACK); *t.-t.*, (nursery for) watch; small mark set against items in list &c. in checking; (v.t.) mark (item, usu. *off*) with t.; (of clock &c.) *t. away* (the time &c.); (of tape-machine) *t. out* (news &c.). [ME *tek* light touch, cf. Du. *tik(ken)* n. & vb, touch, pat; in sense 'click' perh. imit.]

tick[2], n. Kinds of parasitic insect infesting various animals, as *dog, sheep, cattle, -t.* [OE *ticia* (once, perh. erron. for *tica*), ME *teke*, cf. MDu. *teke*, G *zecke*]

tick[3], n. Cover, case, of bedding; (also **ti·ck**ING[1] n.) stout usu. striped linen or cotton material used for this. [earlier *teke* f. L f. Gk *thēkē* case (*tithēmi* place)]

tick[4], n., & v.i., (colloq.). Credit, as *buy goods on t.*; (v.i.) give credit. [abbr. of TICKET]

ti·cker, n. In vbl senses of TICK[1], esp. (colloq.) watch, telegraphic tape, (facet.) the heart. [-ER[1]]

ti·cket, n., & v.t. Written or printed piece of card or paper entitling holder to admission to place of entertainment &c., conveyance by train &c., or other right, as *concert, theatre, bath, lottery, railway, excursion*, SEASON, THROUGH, RETURN, *t.*; (Mil. slang) discharge (*get* one's *t.*); label attached to thing & giving price or other particulars; notice, usu. of card, set up in window &c. of house to let &c.; *the t.* (colloq.), the proper thing, as *not quite the t.*; (U.S. Polit.) list of candidates put forward by a party, (fig.) principles of a party, as *the democratic t.*; *t. of leave* (allowing liberty with certain restrictions to prisoner or convict who has served part of his time), *t.-of-leave man*, holder of such t.; *t.-day* (St. Exch.), day before settling-day, when names of actual purchasers are handed to stockbrokers; *t.-night*, performance at theatre proceeds of which are divided among several persons in proportion to number of tt. disposed of by each; *t.-porter*, licensed porter identified by badge; *t.-punch* (for punching tt.); (v.t.) put t. on (article for sale &c.). [f. OF *e(s)tiquet(te)* ticket, bill, f. OLG *stekan* to STICK]

ti·ckle, v.t. & i., & n. Apply light touches to (person, part of his body, or abs.) so as to excite the nerves & usu. produce laughter & in extreme case convulsion, as *t. him with a feather, t. the soles of her feet, don't t.*; feel this sensation, as *my foot tickles*; excite agreeably, amuse, divert, (person, his sense of humour, vanity, &c.), as *I was hugely tickled at the idea, this will t. his palate*; catch (trout &c.) with the hand; (n.) act, sensation, of tickling. [ME *tikelle*, perh. by metath. f. ON *kitla*, cf. KITTLE]

ti·ckler, n. In vbl senses, also; puzzling or delicate question or matter; feather used by revellers to tickle faces. [-ER[1]]

ti·cklish, a. Easily tickled, sensitive to tickling; (of question or thing to be dealt with) difficult, critical, delicate, requiring careful handling. Hence **ti·cklish**LY[2] adv., **ti·cklish**NESS n. [-ISH[1]]

ticpolo·nga (-ngga), n. Venomous serpent of India & Ceylon. [f. Cingalese *titpolongā* spot-viper]

ti·dal, a. Of tide(s); *t. air* (passing in & out of lungs at each respiration); *t. basin, dock, harbour* (subject to rise & fall of tide); *t. friction* (of t. wave, retarding diurnal rotation of earth); *t. river* (affected by tide to some distance from mouth); *t. wave*, wave following sun & moon from east to west & causing tides, (improp.) any extraordinary ocean wave e. g. one attributed to earthquake, (fig.) widespread manifestation of feeling &c. Hence **ti·dal**LY[2] adv. [-AL]

tidbit. See TITBIT.

ti·ddl(e-d)y-winks, n. Game in which counters are flicked into tray &c. on centre of table. [?]

tide[1], n. Time, season, (now chiefly in *even-t., Whitsunt., Christmast., yule-t.*, &c., otherwise archaic); period of time, as *work double tt.* (night & day); periodical rise (*flood-t.*) & fall (*ebb-t.*) of sea due to attraction of moon & sun, whence **tido·**LOGY n.; *high, low, t.*, completion of flood, ebb. -t.; *spring, neap, -t.*, maximum, minimum, t. when solar & lunar tt. act together, act 90° apart; LAG[1]*ging*, PRIMING[2], *of the tt.*; *meteorological* *t.* (due to regular alternations of wind &c.); (fig.) trend of opinion or fortune or events (*go with the t., the t. turns*); *t.-gate* (opened to admit water or let vessels pass during rising tide, closed to keep water in during ebb); *t.-gauge* (showing extremes or present level of t.); *t.-lock* (between tidal harbour & basin behind it); *t.-rip(s)*, rough water caused by opposing tt.; *tide-waiter*, customs officer who boards ship on arrival to enforce customs regulations; *t.-way*, channel where t. runs, ebb or flow in such channel. Hence **ti·de**LESS a. [OE *tīd* time, cf. Du. *tijd*, G *zeit*, ON *tīth*]

tide[2], v.i. & t. Drift with tide, esp. work in or out of harbour with help of tide; get *over* (difficulty &c.), as *t. over this business, t. it over.* [(in obs. sense happen, betide) OE *tīdan*; mod. senses direct f. prec.]

tī·dings, n. pl. (now chiefly literary; treated as sing. or pl.). (Piece of) news, as *the t. come(s) too late.* [OE *tīdung* (as prec.), ME *tīdinde* f. ON *tīthindi* f. corresp. ON vb]

tī·dy, a., n., & v.t. (Of dress, room, person, habits) neatly arranged, neat, orderly; (colloq.) pretty large, considerable, as *left a t. sum behind him, a t. day's work*; (colloq.) fairly well in health, as *am feeling pretty t.*; (n.) detachable usu. ornamental cover for chair-back &c., receptacle for odds & ends (*street t.*, bin for paper &c.); (v.t.) make (room, table, &c., one*self*, or abs.; often *up*) neat, put in good order. Hence **ti·di**LY[2] adv., **ti·di**NESS n. [ME, =seasonable, tidy, (TIDE[1] + -Y[2])]

tie[1], v.t. & i. (tying). Attach, fasten, with cord or the like, as *t. the dog to the railings*, RIDE *& t., t. his legs together, t. up a parcel*; secure (shoe, bonnet) by tightening & knotting its strings; arrange (string, ribbon, tie, &c.) to form knot, bow, &c., as *t. your tie, t. it in a bow*; form (knot, bow) thus; *t.* (dress fish-hook to look like) *a fly*; bind (rafters &c.) by crosspiece &c.; restrict, bind, (person &c. *to, down to*, conditions, occupation, &c.); *tied to* woman's APRON-*strings*; *t.* person's *tongue*, secure, compel, his silence; *t. up*, restrict, esp. annex conditions to (bequest &c.) to prevent its being sold or diverted from its purpose; *tied house*, public-house bound to deal exclusively with one firm; (Mus.) unite (notes) by tie; make same score as (person) in game &c., be equal in score *with.* [OE *tīgan*, as foll.]

tie[2], n. Cord, chain, &c., used for fastening; =NECK[1]-*t.*; (fig.) thing that unites persons, bond, obligation, as *tt. of blood, friendship*; rod, beam, holding parts of a structure together, (U.S.) rail sleeper; *t.-beam*, horizontal beam connecting rafters; (Mus.) curve set above notes that are to be played &c. continuously; equality of score among competitors in game, *play, shoot*, &c., *off a t.*, play further game &c. to decide between such competitors; match between any pair of several competing players or teams, as *cup-tt.* (in competition for cup); *t.-up*, obstructed situation, standstill, esp. (U.S.) strike of railway men &c.; *t.-wig* (tied behind with ribbon). [OE *teáh* rope f. *téo(ha)n* pull, cf. ON *taug* tie, string]

tier (tēr), n., & v.t. Row, rank, esp. one of several placed one above another as in theatre; *tt. of cable*, circles it forms when coiled; (v.t.) pile (often *up*) in tt. [(vb f. n.) f. OF *tire* sequence (*tirer* to draw)]

tierce (tērs), n. One third of a pipe as old wine-measure, cask containing certain quantity (varying with the goods) esp. of provisions; (Mus.) =THIRD; sequence of three cards; (Fencing) third position for guard, parry, or thrust (*t. & quart*, fencing); (Eccl., also *terce*) office of third hour. [ME, f. F *tiers*, fem. *-rce*, third, f. L TER*tius*]

tiercel. See TERCEL.

tiercet. See TERCET.

tiers état (tyārzētah), n. =*third* ESTATE. [F]

tiff, n., & v.t. & i. Draught of liquor; fit of peevishness, slight quarrel; (v.t.) sip, drink; (v.i.) be in a pet, (Anglo-Ind.) lunch. [different wds, etym. dub.; last sense f. TIFFIN]

ti·ffany, n. Kind of gauze muslin. [orig. dress for Twelfth Night, f. OF *tiphanie* f. LL THEO*phania* manifestation of God, EPIPHANY]

ti·ffin, n., & v.i. (Anglo-Ind.). (Take) light meal esp. of curried dishes & fruit, lunch. [TIFF vb + -ING[1]; orig. in sense 'drinking']

tige (tēzh), n. (Archit.) shaft of column; (Bot.) stem, stalk. [F, f. L TIBIA]

tī·ger (-g-), n. Large Asiatic striped feline quadruped, esp. *Bengal t.*; *American t.*, jaguar; *red t.*, cougar; *work* &c. *like a t.* (with fierce energy); dissolute swaggerer or bully, whence **ti·ger**ISM(2) n.; groom accompanying master in light vehicle; (U.S. slang) yell supplementary to three cheers, final burst; *t.-beetle*, predaceous kinds with spotted or striped wing-covers; *t.-cat*, any moderate-sized feline beast resembling the t., e.g. ocelot, serval, margay; *t.('s)-eye*, a gem of brilliant lustre; *t.-lily*, garden kind with flowers of dull orange spotted with black or purple; *t.-moth*, kinds with richly-streaked hairy wings suggesting t.'s skin; *t.-wood* (imported from Brit. Guiana for cabinet-making). So **tī·gr**ESS[1] n. [ME & OF *tigre* f. L f. Gk *tigris* of oriental orig.]

tī·g(e)rish, a. Like, cruel as, a tiger. [-ISH[1]]

tight (tīt), a., n., & adv. Closely & firmly put together, as *t. ship*; impermeable, impervious, esp. (in comb.) to specified thing, as *air, gas, water, wind, -t.*; closely held, drawn, fastened, fitting, &c., as *t. knots, cork is too t., corn caused by a* (too) *t. shoe*; neat, trim, compact, as *a t. lass, t. little island*; tense, stretched so as to leave no slack, as *t. rope* (*t.-r.*, one on which rope-dancers &c. perform); (colloq.) drunk; *money is t.* (not easily obtainable), *a t. money-market* (in which money is t.); produced by, requiring, great exertion or pressure, as *a t. squeeze, am in a t. place* (usu. fig., difficult situation); *t.-fisted*, stingy; (n. pl.) close-fitting garments as used by acrobat &c.; (adv.) tightly, as *squeeze it, hold it, t.* Hence **tigh·ten**[6] v.t. & i. (*-en* one's *belt* joc., go without food), **tigh·tener**[1] (1, 2), **tigh·tness**, nn., **tigh·tly**[2] adv. [earlier *thight* f. ON *théttr*, cf. G *dicht*]

tike, ty-, n. Cur; low fellow; *Yorkshire t.*, Yorkshireman. [ME, f. ON *tik* bitch]

til (tēl), n. The TILDE in Port. use (over vowel, repr. lost nasal n).

ti·lbury, n. (hist.). Kind of gig. [maker]

ti·ldě, n. Mark put over Spanish *n* when it is pronounced ny (so *señor*). [Sp., var. of *titulo* TITLE]

tile, n., & v.t. Thin slab of baked clay for roof, pavement, drain, &c.; similar slab glazed & often decorated for hearth, fireplace, wall, &c.; *have a t. loose* (slang), be rather mad; *Dutch t.* (painted usu. in blue & with scriptural subjects); PANTILE; *plain t.*, flat roofing-t. usu. about $10\frac{1}{2} \times 6\frac{1}{2}$ in.; (colloq.) silk hat; *t.* TEA; *ti·lestone*, kinds of flagstone serving when split for *tt.*; (v.t.) cover (roof &c. or abs.) with tt., (Freemasonry) guard (lodge, meeting) against intrusion by placing tiler at door, whence (gen.) bind (person) to secrecy; *t. in*, enclose in tt. Hence **ti·ling**[1](1, 2, 6) n. [(vb f. n.; in Freem. sense f. foll.) OE *tigele* f. L *tegula* f. *tegere* cover]

ti·ler, n. One who makes or lays tiles, whence **ti·lery**(3) n.; (Freemasonry, also archaic *tyler*) doorkeeper of lodge. [-ER[1]]

till[1], v.t. Cultivate (soil). Hence **ti·llable** a., **ti·llage**(3) n. [OE *tilian, teolian*, strive for, till, f. *til* useful, cogn. w. foll., cf. Du. *telen* breed, till, G *zielen* aim at]

till[2], prep. & conj. Up to, as late as, (specified day, hour, season), as *wait t. evening, four o'clock, then, Monday, next week*; up to the time of (event expected to happen sooner or later), as *was true t. death, waited t. the end, t. his return, arrival, departure* (but not *t. his accident*); (conj.) up to the time when, as *ring t. you get an answer, walk on t. you come to the gate.* [f. ON *til* to, orig. a noun = OE *till* fixed point, cf. G *ziel*]

till[3], n. Money-drawer in shop counter. [f. 15th c., etym. dub.]

till[4], n. Stiff clay with boulders, sand, &c., boulder-clay. Hence **ti·lly**[2] a. [?]

ti·ller[1], n. One who tills. [-ER[1]]

ti·ller[2], n. Lever fitted to head of rudder for steering; *t.-chain, -rope* (connecting t. with wheel). [f. OF *telier* crossbow-stock, orig. weaver's beam, f. L *tela* web, -ARY[1]]

ti·ller[3], n., & v.i. Shoot of plant springing from bottom of original stalk; sapling; sucker; (v.i.) put forth tt. [OE *telgor*, cf. Du. *telg*, MHG *zelch*]

tilt[1], v.i. & t., & n. (Cause to) assume sloping position, heel over, as *table is apt to t. over, don't t. the table, cask wants tilting* (to facilitate emptying); (Geol., t. & i. of strata) turn *up* at steep angle; make a charge with lance (often *at* opponent, esp. fig.); *t. at the ring* (suspended for horseman to carry off on point of lance); hammer (steel &c.) with t. (N.) tilting, sloping position; charging with spear against antagonist or mark (*t.-yard*, place used for this); device of crossed sticks &c. for showing when fish has taken hook; *full t.*, at full speed, with full force, esp. *come, run, full t. against*; *t.(-hammer)*, heavy pivoted hammer used in forging. Hence **ti·lter**[1](1, 2) n. [(n. f. vb) ME *tilten* f. OE *tealt* unsteady, cf. Norw. *tylten* unsteady, Sw. *tulta* waddle]

tilt[2], n., & v.t. Covering of canvas &c. esp. for cart; (v.t.) furnish with t. [OE *teld*, cf. MDu. *telde*, G *zelt*, ON *tjald*]

tilth, n. Tillage, cultivation; depth of soil affected by this. [OE (TILL[1] + -TH[1])]

ti·mbal, -ul, ty-, n. Kettledrum. [f. F *timbale*, earlier *attabale* f. Arab. *al ṭabl* the drum]

timbale (F), n. Drum-shaped raised pie in crust of paste or macaroni.

ti·mber, n. Wood prepared for building, carpentry, &c.; trees suitable for this; woods; piece of wood, beam, esp. (Naut.) any of the curved pieces forming ribs of vessel, whence (invoking destruction) *shiver my tt.*; (Hunting) fences & gates; *t.-cart* (high-wheeled, with tackle for lifting t.); *t.-head*, top end of t. rising above deck & used for belaying ropes &c.; *t.-toe(s)* colloq., person with wooden leg; *t.-yard* (lit., &, in cricket slang, batsman's wicket). Hence **(-)ti·mbered**[2] a., **ti·mbering**[1](2, 3) n. [OE, cf. Du. dial. *timmer*, G *zimmer* room, timber, ON *timbr*, cog. w. Gk *demō* build, L *domus* house]

timbre (tă·mber, or as F), n. Characteristic quality of sounds produced by each particular voice or instrument, depending on the form of the vibrations. [F, = timbre, clock-bell, drum, f. TYMPANUM]

ti·mbrel, n. Tambourine. [dim. of ME *timbre* f. prec.]

time[1], n. Duration, continued existence; progress of this viewed as affecting persons or things, as *t. will show who is right, has stood the test of t.*, (personified) *assaults of* (*old, Father*) *T.*; more or less definite portion of this associated with particular events or circumstances, historical or other period, as *the tt. of the Stuarts, the* *t. of the Black Death, for the t.* BEing, *prehistoric tt., those godless tt., the good old tt., things have changed since those tt., the scientists of the t.*; allotted or available portion of t., the t. at one's disposal, as *it will last our t.* (lives), *have no t. for such frivolities, had no t. to discuss it, spend, lose, waste, t., will take all your t.* (colloq. =tax your powers), *give me t. & I will pay,* (colloq.) *got there t.* (soon) *enough to see him, gain t.,* procure it esp. by temporizing measures; moment or definite portion of t. destined or suitable for a purpose &c., as *there is a t. for everything, will fix a t. for seeing him, now is the t. to press your point, now is your t.* (opportunity), *I must bide my t., it is* (HIGH) *t. to go, t. for lunch, lunch-t., it is t. I was going* (for me to go), *in the* NICK[1] *of t., t.* (for boxing-round &c.) *is up,* (umpire's call) *t.!, is serving his t.* (as apprentice &c.), *is doing t.* (in prison), *is far on in her t.* (of gestation), *is near her t.* (of childbirth), *my t.* (death) *is drawing near*; (often pl.) conditions of life, prevailing circumstances, of a period, as *hard, bad, good, tt.* (esp. hard &c. to get a living in), *had a good t.,* enjoyed myself, *those were* (fine) *tt!, what a t.* (trouble) *you will have getting him home!*; occasion, as *the first t. I saw him, wait till next t., did it seven tt. running, have told you a dozen tt., tt. out of number, t. & again, many a t., t. after t., for the last t. of asking, three, four,* &c. *tt.* (but *twice,* not *two tt.*) *9 is 27* &c., *is three tt. the size of mine, ten tt. easier* or *as easy*; *past, present, future, t.,* the portions into which all t. may at any moment be accurately or loosely divided (esp., Gram., with reference to tenses); (amount of) t. as reckoned by conventional standards, as *the t. allowed was four years, months, minutes, did a mile in record t., astronomical* (mean solar) *t., apparent* (SOLAR) *t.,* SIDEREAL *t.,* esp. stated in hours & minutes of the day, as *the t. fixed was 4.30, what is the t.?, is that the correct* (GREENWICH) *t.?, at this t. of day* (fig., at this late stage in history, in the negotiations, &c.); (Mus.) (a) duration of a note as indicated by semibreve, minim, &c., (b) style of movement depending on number & accentuation of beats in a bar, as *binary, ternary, t.* (with two, three, beats in bar), COMMON[1] *t.,* (c) rate of execution, =*tempo*; *against t.,* with utmost speed, as *working, riding, against t.*; *ahead of,* (*born*) *before,* one's *t.* or *tt.,* having notions too enlightened to be appreciated or put into practice; *all the t.,* during the whole of the time referred to (*they were laughing a. t. t.*), (U.S.) at all times (*is a business man a. t. t.*); *at the same t.,* simultaneously, notwithstanding, all the same; *at tt.,* now & then; *at one t.,* during a known but unspecified past period (*a. o. t. we met frequently*); *beat t.,* indicate, follow t., of music with stick, hand, &c.; *civil t.* (expressed by CIVIL year &c.); CLOSE[1] *t.*; *from t. to t.,* occasionally; *in t.,* not late, early enough (*to* do, *for* thing), eventually, sooner or later, in accordance with, following, the t. of music &c.; *in no t.,* rapidly, in the twinkling of an eye; *keep t.,* walk, dance, sing, &c., in t., (of clock &c.) *keep good, bad, t.,* record t. (in)-accurately; *mean t.* (regulated by average); *one, two,* &c., *at a t.,* each, each two &c., separately; *out of t.,* unseasonable, -bly, (of singing &c.) not in t.; *t. immemorial* or *out of mind,* (for, from) a longer time than any one can remember or trace; *the t. of day,* hour by clock, (colloq.) *pass the t. of day,* exchange greeting &c. (*with* person), (slang) *so that's the t. of day* (the state of affairs, your little game, &c.)!; *the t. of* one's *life* (slang), a period of exceptional enjoyment or pleasant or unpleasant excitement (*have the t. of* one's, *give* one *the t. of* his, *life*); *what t.* (poet.), while, when; *the Tt.,* the newspaper so named, esp. (*shall write to the Tt.*) as used by correspondents for ventilating grievances &c.; *t.-ball* (dropped from top of staff at observatory to indicate fixed moment of mean time, usu. 1 P.M.); *t.-bargain,* contract for sale of stock &c. at future t. (often a form of gambling); *t.-book, -card, -sheet* (for recording workmen's hours of work); *t.-fuse* (calculated to burn for given t.); *t.-honoured,* venerable by antiquity; *ti·mekeeper,* one who records t. esp. of workmen, *watch* &c. *is good, bad, t.-k.* (keeps good, bad, t.); *ti·mepiece,* t.-measuring instrument esp. portable but stationary clock; *t.-server,* one who, esp. for selfish ends, adapts himself to opinions of the tt. or of persons in power, so *t.-serving* a. & n.; *t.-table,* scheme of school work &c., table showing tt. of trains; *t.-work* (paid for by time, not PIECE-*w.*). [OE *tima,* cf. ON *timi,* Da. *time,* cogn. w. TIDE]

time[2], v.t. & i. Choose the time for, do at chosen time, as *must t. your blows, remark was ill, well, timed*; ascertain the time taken by (race, runner, &c.), whence **ti·mer**[1](1, 2), **ti·ming**[1], nn.; keep time, harmonize, *with.* [f. prec.]

ti·meless, a. (rare). Unending; untimely. [-LESS]

ti·mely, a. Seasonable, opportune. Hence **ti·meliness** n. [-LY[1]]

tĭ·mĕo Dă·naōs et do·na ferentēs, phr. inculcating or expressing distrust of a conciliatory enemy. [L, = I fear (the combination) Greeks & gift-bringers]

timeous. See TIMOUS.

ti·mid, a. Easily alarmed; shy. Hence or cogn. **timi·dity, ti·midness,** nn., **ti·midly**[2] adv. [f. L *timidus* (*timēre* fear, -ID[1])]

tīmo·cracy, n. Form of government in which there is a property qualification for office. So **timocră·tic** a. [f. OF *tymo-*

cracie f. med. L f. Gk *timokratia* (*timē* honour, worth, value, see -CRACY)]

ti·morous, a. Timid, easily alarmed. Hence **ti·morous**LY[2] adv., **ti·morous**NESS n. [f. L *timor* fear f. *timēre*, -OUS]

ti·mothy(-grass), n. A fodder-grass. [*T.* Hanson, who introduced it in N. America]

ti·mous, a. (chiefly Sc.). Timely. Hence **ti·mous**LY[2] adv. [f. TIME[1] + -OUS]

tin, n., & v.t. White highly malleable metal taking high polish, little affected by atmosphere, & much used for cooking-utensils &c. esp. in form of *t. plate* (sheet iron coated with t.); vessel &c. of t., esp. for preserving meat, fruit, &c., as *sardine-t.*; (attrib.) made of t. or of iron covered with t.; (slang) money; *cry of t.*, crackling sound it makes if bent; *salt of t.*, *t.-liquor*, solutions of t. used as mordants by dyers &c.; *t. fish* (naut. slang), torpedo; *t. foil*, foil of t. or t.-like alloy, used as wrapper for soap, tobacco, &c. (v.t.) cover or coat with this; *t. god*, object of mistaken veneration; *t. hat* (army slang), modern soldier's steel cap; *t. Lizzie*, nickname for Ford motor-car; *t.-plate* v.t., coat w. t.; *ti·nman, t.- smith*, worker in t. plate, so **ti·nner**[1] n.; *ti·nstone*, principal ore of t.; *ti·nware*, vessels &c. of t. or t. plate; *t. whistle*, = *penny* WHISTLE. Hence **ti·nny**[2] a.; (v.t.) cover, coat, with t.; pack (meat, fruit, &c.) in tt. for preservation. [OE, ON, Du., Da., cf. G *zinn*; not conn. w. L *stannum, stag-*, whence F *étain*]

ti·namou (-ōō), n. S.-Amer. quail-like game-bird. [F, of S.-Amer. orig.]

ti·ncal, -kal, (-ngkl), n. Unrefined borax. [f. Malay *tingkal* f. Skr. *ṭankaṇa*]

tinctor·ial, n. Of colour or dyeing, producing colour. [f. L *tinctorius* (TINGE, -ORY) + -AL]

ti·ncture (-tsher), n., & v.t. Alcoholic solution of some (usu. vegetable) principle used in medicine, as *t. of quinine*; slight flavour, spice, smack, (*of* thing, fig. *of* moral quality &c.); tinge (*of* colour); (v.t.) colour slightly, tinge, flavour, (fig.) affect slightly (*with* quality). [(vb f. n.) f. L *tinctura* dyeing (as TINGE, see -URE)]

ti·nder, n. Dry substance readily taking fire from spark, esp. charred linen &c. used in *t.-box* (containing t., flint, & steel, for kindling fire); *German t.*, = AMADOU. Hence **ti·ndery**[2] a. [OE *tyndre* (*-tendan* kindle, cf. Da. *tænde*, Sw. *tända*]

tine, n. Point, prong, e.g. of antler, harrow, or fork. Hence **(-)tined**[2] a. [OE *tind*, cf. ON *tindr*, Sw. *tinne*]

ting, n., & v.i. (Make) tinkling sound as of bell. [imit.]

tinge, v.t., & n. Colour slightly (*with* red &c.); (fig.) modify by mixture (*with* envy &c.); (n.) tint, slight colouring, flavour (lit. & fig.). [f. L *tingere tinct-* dye, stain]

ti·ngle, v.i. & t., & n. (Feel) prickling or stinging sensation; cause this, as *the reply tingled in his ears*; (rare) make (ear &c.) t. [var. of TINKLE]

ti·nker, n., & v.t. & i. Mender (esp. itinerant) of kettles, pans, &c. (*don't care a t.'s damn*, at all); rough-&-ready worker, botcher; patching, botching, as *had an hour's t. at it*; kinds of fish, bird, & seal; (v.t.) repair (metal-work), patch (anything, lit. & fig., often *up*) roughly; work in amateurish or clumsy fashion *at* (thing) in the way of repair or alteration. Hence **ti·nker**LY[1] a. [(vb f. n.) f. 13th c., etym. dub.]

ti·nkle, v.i. & t., & n. (Make) succession of clinking sounds; make (bell &c.) t.; (obs.) tingle. [(n. f. vb) f. obs. *tink* to chink + -LE(3)]

ti·nkler, n. In vbl senses, esp.: (slang) small bell. [-ER[1]]

tinnī·tus, n. (med.). Ringing in the ears. [L, f. *tinnire -it-*, imit., cf. TING]

ti·nsel, n., a., & v.t. (-ll-). Kinds of glittering metallic substance made in thin sheets & used in strips, threads, &c., to give sparkling effect; dress-fabric &c. adorned with t.; (fig.) superficial brilliancy or splendour; (adj.) showy, gaudy, cheaply splendid; (v.t.) adorn with t. (lit. & fig.). [(a. & vb f. n.) f. MF *estincelle, ét-*, spark (for loss of *é-* cf. *ticket*) f. L *scintilla* perh. corrupted to *stincilla*]

tint, n., & v.t. A variety of a colour, esp. one made by diluting with white; (rare) tendency towards, admixture of, a different colour, as *red of* or *with a blue t.*; *autumn tt.* (of dying leaves); (Engrav.) set of parallel lines cut with *t.-tool* to give uniform shading; *t.-block*, block bearing design to be printed in faint colour as background, *ruled, crossed, t.*, surface of this with parallel, crossing, lines; (v.t.) apply t. to, colour. Hence **ti·nt**LESS a. [f. It. *tinta* (as TINGE); earlier also *tinct* f. L]

ti·nter, n. Person who tints; instrument for tinting; magic-lantern slide of plain coloured glass. [-ER[1]]

ti·ntinnābula·tion, n. Tinkling of bells. [f. foll. + -ATION]

tintinnă·būlum, n. (pl. *-la*). Bell, esp. small tinkling one, whence **tintinna·bu**LAR(Y)[1], **tintinna·bul**OUS, aa.; rattle made of small bells or metal plates. [L, = bell, f. *tintinnare* redupl. form as TINNITUS]

tinto·meter, n. Instrument for determining tints. [-METER]

ti·nty, a. Discordantly tinted. [-Y[2]]

ti·ny, tee·ny (nursery), a. Very small, as *a t. little boy, little t. boy*. [earlier *tine, tyne*, used as n. & adj., a bit, little, etym. dub.]

-tion, suf. of nn. of action or condition (= *-t-* of L p.p. stem + -ION, cf. -ATION), as *attention*.

tip[1], n., & v.t. Extremity, end, esp. of small or tapering thing, as *the tt. of the fingers, walk on the tt. of your toes, t. of a* *cigar, bird measures 15 in. from t.* (of one wing) *to t.* (of other), *had it on the t. of my tongue*, was just going to say it; kinds of brush used in gilding; small piece or part attached to end of thing, e.g. ferrule; *ti·pstaff* (hist.; pl. *-staves*), (metal-tipped staff as badge of) sheriff's officer; *t.-tilted*, (of nose) turned up at t.; *ti·ptoe*, (adv., also *on tiptoe*) on the tt. of the toes, (v.i.) walk t.; *tipto·p*, (n.) highest point of excellence, (a. & adv.) first-rate; (v.t.) furnish with t. [ME, Du., Da.]

tip², v.t. & i., & n. (Cause to) lean or slant, tilt, topple, (*over, up*, &c.) esp. with slight effort; strike or touch lightly (*t. & run*, form of cricket in which batsman must run if bat touches ball); overturn, cause to overbalance, (person *into* pond &c.); discharge (contents of jug &c. *out, into*, &c.) thus; (slang) throw lightly, hand, give, communicate, in informal manner, as *t.* (throw) *us a copper, t. us your fin*, shake hands, *t. us a song, a yarn, might have tipped me the wink* (given me warning wink); (Sport. slang) give secret information about horse &c. to; make usu. small present of money to, as *must t. the porter, tipped me* (now rarely *with*) *half-a-crown*. (N.) small money present; secret information about horse-racing, money-market, &c., as *will give you the straight* (correct) *t.*; good dodge or recipe for doing something; *miss* one's *t.*, fail in one's object; slight push; light stroke esp. in base-ball; place where refuse is tipped; *t.-car, -cart* (pivoted for tipping); *t.-cat*, (game with) short piece of wood tapering at ends & struck with stick; *t.-up seat*, of the kind used in theatres &c. to allow of free passing. Hence **ti·ppER**¹ (1, 2) n. [of doubtful & prob. various orig.]

Tipperār·y, n. Song specially associated with the B.E.F. of 1914. [*It's a long way to T.*, first wds]

ti·ppet, n. Cape, muffler, of fur &c. covering shoulders & coming down to some distance in front, worn by women & as part of official costume by judges, clergy, &c. [f. 1300; prob. f. TIP¹ + -ET¹]

ti·pple, v.i. & t., & n. Drink strong drink habitually; drink (liquor) slowly & repeatedly; (n.) strong drink. Hence **ti·pplER**¹ n. [cf. Norw. *tipla* frequent. of *tippa* drip from tip]

ti·pster, n. One who gives tips about races &c. [-STER]

ti·psy, a. Intoxicated; proceeding from, showing, intoxication, as *a t. lurch*; *t.-cake*, sponge-cake soaked in wine & served with custard. Hence **ti·psiFY** v.t., **ti·psiLY**² adv., **ti·psiNESS** n. [prob. f. TIP², = inclined to lean, unsteady; for *-sy* cf. *tricksy*]

tirā·de, n. Long vehement speech esp. of censure; long passage of declamation &c.; (Mus.) diatonic run filling interval between notes. [F, = long speech, f. It. *tirata* drawing, pulling, f. It. & LL *tirare* draw, see -ADE]

tirailleur· (*-alēr or as F*), n. Sharp-shooter, skirmisher.

tire¹, v.t. & i. Make or grow weary; *am tired*, have had enough *of*, am sick *of*, (thing, do*ing*), am exhausted *with*. Hence **tire·dNESS** n., also (rhet., poet.) **tire·less**¹ [-LESS] a., **tire·lessLY**² adv. [OE *tiorian, té-*; excl. E]

tire², **tyre**, n., & v.t. Band of metal, rubber, &c., placed round rim of wheel to strengthen it or prevent jar; PNEUMATIC *t.*; (v.t.) place t. on (wheel). Hence **(-)tirED**², **tire·less**² [-LESS], aa. [prob. = foll.]

tire³, n., & v.t., (archaic). Head-dress; attire; (v.t.) adorn, attire, as *she tired her head*; *tire·woman* (archaic), woman employed to dress another. [for ATTIRE]

tire·some, a. Tending to tire, fatiguing; tedious; annoying, as *how t.!—I have left my watch behind*. Hence **tire·someLY**² adv., **tire·someNESS** n. [TIRE¹ + -SOME]

tīr·o, tyro, n. Beginner, novice. [L (*ti-*), = newly levied soldier]

tirocī·nium, n. Apprenticeship, first rudiments of an art. [L, = first service of soldier (prec.)]

'tis (-z), contraction of *it is*.

tīsa·ne (-zăn), n. = PTISAN. [F]

ti·ssue (-sū, -shū, -shōō), n. Any fine woven fabric; (Biol.) substance of an organ, fabric formed of cells & cell-products, as *adipose, connective, muscular, nervous, t.*; (fig.) interwoven series, set, collection, (*of* lies, crimes, &c.); *t.(-paper)*, thin soft unsized paper for wrapping or protecting delicate articles, engraving in book, &c. Hence **(-)tissuED**² a. [f. F *tissu* woven (thing) f. **tistre* weave (mod. F *tisser*) f. L *texere*]

tit¹, n. Kinds of small bird, including *ti·tlark* & *ti·tmouse* (both also called *ti·tling*); (archaic) small or poor horse, child, girl. [prob. imit. of littleness; cf. Icel. *tittr* pin, titmouse]

tit², n. *T. for tat*, blow for blow, retaliation. [perh., = earlier *tip for tap*]

Ti·tan, n. (Gk Myth.) each of a gigantic race, the children of Uranus & Ge, (also) the sun-god, brother of Helios; *the weary T.*, British or other large empire (w. ref. to ATLAS); person of superhuman size, strength, intellect, &c., whence **Ti·tanESS**¹ n.; = foll. So **TitanE·SQUE, tită·nIC**, aa. [L f. Gk]

titā·nium, n. A dark-grey metallic element. Hence **ti·tanATE**¹(3) n. [prec. + -IUM]

ti·tbi·t, n. Delicate bit, choice morsel. [earlier *tidbit* f. dial. *tid* delicate, wanton]

tithe (-dh), n., & v.t. Tax of one-tenth, esp. one payable in kind; (often pl.) tenth part of annual proceeds of land (*predial tt.*) & personal industry (*personal tt.*) taken for support of clergy & church;

mixed tt. (from) pigs, sheep, &c., fed on the land); *t. commissioners* (arranging commutation of tt. &c.); *t.-pig,* tenth pig set apart for t.; (rhet.) tenth part, esp. *not a t. of*; (v.t.) subject to tt. Hence **ti·th**ABLE a. [(vb OE *téothian*) OE *téotha* (as TEN, see -TH[2])]

ti·thing, n. Taking tithe; (Hist.) ten householders living near together & bound over as sureties for each other's peaceable behaviour. [OE *téothung* (*téothian,* prec., -ING[1])]

ti·tillate, v.t. Tickle; excite pleasantly. So **titill**A·TION n. [f. L *titillare,* see -ATE[2]]

ti·tivate, titti-, v.t. & i. (colloq.). Adorn, smarten, (one*self* &c.); adorn onself. [earlier *tid-*, perh. f. *tidy* after *cultivate*]

ti·tle (-tl), n. Distinguishing appellation placed at head of chapter, poem, &c.; contents of t.-page of book, short essential part of these used in reference (e.g. *Adam Smith's Wealth of Nations*); formula at head of legal document, statute, &c.; division of statute &c.; personal appellation, hereditary or not, denoting or implying office (e.g. *king, queen, judge, mayor, rector, captain*) or nobility (e.g. *duke, marquis, earl, viscount, baron,* any of which exc. *duke* may be COURTESY t. of son &c. of duke &c.) or distinction or merit (e.g. *baronet, knight*) or (usu. *degree*) qualification (e.g. *D.D., M.A.*), or used in addressing or referring to person (e.g. *Lord, Lady, Sir, Mrs, Miss, Doctor, Professor,* prefixed to name; *your* or *her* or *his Majesty, Grace,* &c.); (Law) right to ownership of property with or without possession, the facts constituting this, (also *t.-deed*) legal instrument as evidence of right; just or recognized claim (*to*), service, merit, &c., that constitutes this; fineness of gold as expressed in carats; fixed sphere of work & source of income as condition to ordination; (district attached to) parish church in Rome; *t.-page,* page at beginning of book giving particulars of subject, authorship, publication, &c.; *t.-role,* part in a play that gives it its name (e.g. *Othello*). Hence **ti·tle**LESS a. [OF, f. L *titulus*]

ti·tled, a. Having title of nobility. [-ED[2]]

ti·tling[1], n. See TIT[1]. [f. ON *titlingr* (as TIT[1], see -LING[1])]

ti·tling[2], n. Impressing of title in goldleaf &c. on back of book. [-ING[1]]

ti·tmouse, n. (pl. *-mice*). = TIT[1]. [ME *titmōse* (TIT[1] + OE *máse* t., cf. Du. *mees,* G *meise*]

ti·trate, v.t. Determine quantity of given constituent in (compound) by observing quantity of a standard solution necessary to convert this constituent into another form. So **titr**A·TION n. [f. F *titre* TITLE + -ATE[2]]

ti·tter, v.i., & n. Laugh, giggle, in restrained manner; (n.) such laugh. Hence **ti·tter**ER[1] n. [imit.]

ti·ttle, n. Particle, whit, esp. *not one jot or t.* [ME, = stroke over word or letter, f. L as TITLE, cf. TILDE]

ti·ttlebat, n. Stickleback. [corrupt.]

ti·ttle-tattle, n., & v.i. Gossip. [redupl. f. *tattle*]

ti·ttup, v.i., & n. Go *along* &c., move, conduct oneself, in lively or frisky fashion; (naut. &c. slang) toss for drinks; (n.) spring, prance. Hence **ti·ttup(p)**Y[2] a. [perh. imit. of hoof-beat]

titūba·tion, n. (med.). Fidgetiness esp. as caused by nervous irritation. [f. L *titubatio* (*titubare* totter, see -ATION)]

ti·tūlar, a. & n. Held by virtue of a title, as *t. possessions*; existing, that is such, only in name, as *t. sovereign(ty)*; *t. bishop,* (R.-C. Ch.) bishop bearing name of a former Christian see esp. in Mohammedan countries; *t.* (*saint*), patron saint of church; (n.) holder of office &c. esp. benefice without corresponding functions or obligations. Hence **ti·tular**LY[2] adv. [f. L as TITLE + -AR[1]]

ti·tyre-tū, n. Member of gang of London street-ruffians in time of Charles II. [*Tityre, tu,* first wds of first eclogue of Virgil]

ti·zzy, n. (slang). Sixpence. [?]

tmē·sis, n. (gram.). Separation of the parts of a word by intervening word(s) (e.g. *to us ward,* L *cere-* comminuit *-brum*). [Gk *tmēsis* cutting f. *temnō* cut]

TNT, n. = TRI*nitrotoluene, -ol.*

to[1] (before consonant te, before vowel tŏŏ, emphat. or at end of clause tōō), prep. In the direction of (place, person, thing, condition, quality, &c.; with or without the implication of intention or of arrival), as *was walking over to Bath, on his way to the station, fled to Rome, throw it to me, got to the house by four, to bed with you!, fluttered to the pavement, was committed to the flames, house looks to the south, held it to the light, to arms!, hand to hand, told him to his face, was carried to destruction, letter has come to hand, fell to work, fell to musing, tends* or *has a tendency to indolence, slow to anger, appointed to a post, born to a great fortune, all to no purpose, to his shame be it said*; as far as, not short of, as *true to the end, cut him to the heart, a Home-ruler to the core, fought to the last gasp, hit it to the boundary, correct to a hair's-breadth, suits him to a T, acted his part to perfection, might run to £5, drank himself to death, might argue to all eternity, & so on to the end of the chapter*; (of comparison, ratio, adaptation, reference, &c.) *this is nothing to what it might be, 3 is to 4 as 6 is to 8, ten to one he will find it out, two to one is not fair play, not up to the mark, equal to the occasion, made to order, drawn to scale, not to the point, true to life, will speak to that question later, sang to his guitar, cannot do it to his liking, corresponding, compared, inferior,* &c., *to*; (archaic) for, by way of, as *took her to wife, has a duke to his father-in-law*; (introducing indirect object of vb, recipient, possessor, &c., or person or thing affected by the action, quality, &c.; alternative constrr. as shown) *lend it* or *them,* or *this* &c., or *your knife* &c., *to John* or *to him* (also *lend John* or *him this* &c. or *your knife* or rarely *it* or *them, lend it* or rarely *them him* or rarely *John,* but not *lend this* &c., or *your knife him,* or *John,* nor *lend to him* or *John it* or *them,* nor in ordinary prose *lend to him* or *John this* &c. or *your knife*), *write to me, explain it to me, apply to the secretary, seems to me absurd, to my mind* or *thinking, revolting to sane minds, pleasant to the taste, impervious to weather, obedient to command, unkind to him, has been a good father to them, what's that to you?, drink to me only with thine eyes, here's to you* (your health), *broken in to the saddle, accustomed to it, next door to us, ready to his hand, has not a shilling to his name, takes no wine to his dinner* (archaic), *there is a moral to it, there is no end to it*; *would to God* (I wish it were or had been God's will) *that*; (as sign of infinitive, expressing purpose, consequence, &c., limiting the meaning of adj., or merely forming verbal n.; omitted after *can, do, may, must, shall, will,* & as shown, cf. also DARE, NEED, GO) *he proposes to stay, declines to go, wants to know, began to sing* (or *began singing*), *fail to understand, does it to annoy, the matter is difficult to explain, it is useless to rebel* (rebellion is useless), *allow me to remind* (but *let me remind*) *you, was seen to fall* (but *I saw him fall*), *was heard to complain* (but *I heard him complain*), *floor was felt to tremble* (but *felt the floor tremble*), *was never known* or *found to fail, have sometimes known* or *found it* (*to*) *fail, make him repeat it, he was made* (usu. *to*) *repeat it, help me* (*to*) *lift this, please* (*to* usu. omitted) *shut the door, was pleased* (thought fit) *to be angry, I prefer to go* (but *had rather go, had as lief go*), *had my work to do, had to do my work* (but *will not have you talk such nonsense*), *was about to protest,* (archaic) *he is much to seek* (deficient) *in that respect,* (archaic) *what went ye out for to see?, to* WIT[1]; (as substitute for infinitive) *meant to call but forgot to, had no time to, you promised to.* [OE *tó* prep. & sign of gerund as distinct from infinitive, cf. Du. *toe,* G *zu*]

to[2] (tōō), adv. To the normal or required position or condition, esp. to a standstill, as BRING, COME, FALL, GO, HEAVE, LIE[3], *to*; *the door is to* (just not shut); *to & FRO.* [f. prec.]

toad, n. Reptile like frog but with clumsy & usu. warty body & not aquatic except when breeding; detestable or disgusting person; *t. in a* (or *the*) *hole,* beef baked in batter; *t.-eater,* sycophant, obsequious parasite, so *t.-eating* a. & n.; *t.-flax,* perennial plant with spurred yellow flowers marked with orange spot; *t.-spit,* = CUCKOO-*spit*; *toa·dstone,* stone, sometimes precious, supposed to resemble or to have been formed in body of t., formerly used as amulet &c., [f. G *todtes gestein* dead rock] kind of volcanic rock; *toa·dstool,* kinds of umbrella-shaped fungus. Hence **toa·dish**[1] a. [OE *tádige,* etym. dub.]

toa·dy, n., & v.t. = TOAD-*eater*; (v.t.) fawn servilely upon (person, or abs.) Hence **toad·yish**[1] a., **toa·dyism** n. [19th c. wd, perh. shortened f. TOAD-*eater*]

toast, n., & v.t. & i. (Slice of) bread browned on each side esp. at open fire (*anchovies* &c. *on t.,* so served at table; *have* one *on t.* slang, have him at one's mercy; *as warm as a t.,* glowing with warmth); (archaic) *a t.,* piece of t. in cup of wine; person esp. woman whose health is drunk, thing, sentiment, similarly named in drinking, as *was a great t. in her day*; *t.-list, t.-master,* (person who announces) tt. at public dinner; *t.-rack* (for holding slices of t. at table); *t.-water* (in which t. has stood, used as cooling drink; also *t. & water*). (Vb) brown, cook, (bread, muffin, cheese, bacon, or intr. of these) before fire; warm (one's feet &c.) thus; drink to the health or in honour of. Hence **toa·ster**[1](1, 2) n. ([vb f. n.) ME *tost* f. OF *toster* vb f. L *tostus* p.p. of *torrēre* parch; drinking sense of anecd. orig.]

toa·sting, n. In vbl senses; *t.-fork,* long fork for t. bread &c., (facet., also *t.-iron*) sword. [-ING[1]]

toba·cco, n. (pl. *-os*). (Also *t.-plant*) plant of Amer. origin with narcotic leaves used for smoking, chewing, or snuff; its leaves esp. as prepared for smoking &c. (abbr. *baccy*); *t.-cutter,* instrument for shredding t.; *t. heart,* disorder of heart caused by excessive use of t.; *t.*-PIPE[1]; *t.-pouch* (for carrying about small quantity of t.); *t.-stopper,* instrument for pressing down t. in pipe. [f. Sp. *tabaco,* of native orig.]

toba·cconist, n. Dealer in tobacco. [irreg. f. prec. + -IST; *-n-* perh. after *Platonist* &c.]

Tō·bin('s tube), n. Kind of room ventilator. [inventor]

tobo·ggan, n., & v.i. Long narrow sled used for going down-hill esp. over snow or ice; *t.-shoot, -slide,* slide for tt., usu. divided into different courses to prevent collision; (v.i.) go in t. Hence **tobo·gganer**[1], **tobo·gganing**[1], nn. [of Amer.-Ind. orig.]

tō·by, n. Jug or mug usu. in form of old man with three-cornered hat (also *T. Fillpot*); *t. collar,* broad turned-down goffered collar like Punch's dog T.'s. [pers. name]

tocca·ta (-kah-), n. (mus.). Composition for piano, organ, &c., orig. intended to exercise the touch. [It., f. *toccare* TOUCH, see -ADE]

toccate·lla, -ti·na (-ēna), nn. Short or simple toccata. [It., dimm. of prec.]

Toc H, n. Society with many branches carrying on comradeship from the great war. [signallers' letter T, + H, for *Talbot House* started at Ypres in memory of Gilbert Talbot]

Tochar·ian (-kār-), a. & n. (Of, in) a lately discovered extinct Aryan language. [f. *Tochari* a Scythian tribe (in Strabo)]

tō·co, -ko, n. (slang). Punishment; pain. [perh. f. Gk *tokos* interest, as schoolboy jest]

to·csin, n. (Bell rung as) alarm-signal (now chiefly fig.). [f. OF *toquassen* f. Pr. *tocasenh* (*tocar* TOUCH + *senh* signal-bell f. L as SIGN)]

tod¹, n. (archaic). Bush; mass of foliage; weight for wool, usu. 28 lb. [f. 15th c.; cf. ON *toddi* piece, Du. *tod*(*de*) rag, G *zotte* tuft]

tod², n. (dial.). Fox. [f. 12th c., etym. dub.]

today·, to-day·, adv. & n. (On) this present day, as *saw* or *shall see him t.*, *t. is his birthday*. [OE *tó dæge* on (this) day (*tó* TO¹ + dat. of DAY); so *tonight*, *tomorrow*]

to·ddle, v.i. & t., & n. Walk with short tottering steps, as child learning to walk; make (one's *way*), perform (distance), thus; take casual or leisurely walk (*round*, *to*, &c.); (n.) toddling walk, (colloq.) toddling child. Hence **to·ddl**ER¹ n. [f. 17th c., etym. dub.]

to·ddy, n. Sap of some kinds of palm, from which when fermented arrack is obtained; sweetened drink of spirits & hot water. [f. Hind. *tāṛī* (*tār* palm f. Skr. *tâla* palmyra)]

to-do·, n. = ADO. [TO¹ + DO]

tō·dy, n. W.-Ind. bird related to kingfisher. [f. F *todier* f. L *todus*, a small bird]

toe (tō), n., & v.t. & i. Digit of foot; part of stocking, shoe, boot, that covers the tt.; fore part of hoof; piece of iron under front of horseshoe to prevent slipping; projection from foot of buttress &c. to give stability; end of head of golf-club; (Mech.) lower end of vertical shaft resting in a step, arm on valve-lifting rod of steam-engine; *ball* (callous fleshy pad on under side) *of t.*; *great, little, t.*, largest, smallest, t. of human foot; *tread on* person's *tt.*, offend his feelings or prejudices; *the light fantastic t.*, (joc.) dancing; (slang) *turn up* one's *tt.*, die; *from top to t.*, from head to foot, completely; *heel-&-toe* WALK¹*ing*; *t.-cap*, outer covering of t. in boot or shoe; *t.-drop*, inability to raise toes, from paralysed muscles; *t.-nail*, nail of human t., metal nail driven obliquely through end of board &c. (Vb) furnish with t., mend t. of, (stocking, shoe); (school slang) kick (person &c.); touch (*the line, mark, scratch*) with t. before starting in race (*t. the line* fig., conform esp. under pressure to the requirements of one's party); (Golf) strike (ball) with part of club too near t.; *t. in, out*, turn tt. in, out, in walking. Hence (-)**to**ED, **toe·**LESS, aa. [OE & ON *tá*, cf. G *zehe*]

to·-fall, n. (archaic, poet.). Close, decline, (*of* day &c.). [TO² + FALL]

toff, n. (slang). Distinguished person, swell. [perh. corrupt. of TUFT]

to·ffee (-ĭ), **-fy**, n. Kinds of sweetmeat made of sugar, butter, &c., as *almond t.* [earlier, & still Sc. & U.S., *taffy*, etym. dub.]

toft, n. (law). Homestead; land once occupied by this; *to·ftman* (hist.), occupier of t. [OE, f. ON *topt*]

tog, n., & v.t., (slang). (Usu. pl.) garment(s); (Naut.) *long tt.*, shore-clothes; (v.t.) dress (person, one*self*, often *out*). Hence **to·gg**ERY(5) n. [perh. f. foll.]

tō·ga, n. Ancient Roman's loose flowing outer garment, esp. w. allusion to Roman citizenship, to civil career, or (also *t. virī·lis*, manly t.) to its assumption as sign of manhood (at age of 14). Hence **to·ga'd, to·ga**ED² (-*a*d), a. [L, cogn. w. *tegere* cover]

togĕ·ther (-dh-), adv. In company or conjunction, as *walking t.*, *lived t.*; simultaneously, as *both t. exclaimed*; *compared t.* (one with another); into conjunction, so as to unite, as *sew them t.*, *tied t.*, GET, HANG¹, *t.*, *put* TWO *& two t.*; *t. with*, as well as, & also, as *sent a host of foot-soldiers t. with some cavalry*. [OE *tógædere* (*tó* TO¹ + *gædre* together, cf. GATHER)]

to·gger, n. (Oxf. slang for) TORPID n.

to·ggle, n. (Naut.) pin put through eye of rope &c. to keep it in place &c.; pair of rods or plates hinged together by *t.-joint* (knee-joint) so as to transmit pressure at right angles; *t.-iron*, harpoon with movable blade instead of fixed barbs; *t.-press* (acting by means of t.-joints). [perh. cogn. w. TUG & TANGLE¹]

toil¹, v.i., & n. Work long or laboriously (*at, on, through*, task); move painfully or laboriously (*up* hill &c., *along*); labour, drudgery; *t.-worn* (by t.). Hence **toi·l**ER¹, **toi·lsome**NESS, nn., **toi·l**FUL, **toi·l**LESS, **toi·l**SOME, aa., **toi·lful**LY², **toi·lsome**LY², advv. [(n. f. vb) prob. f. OF *toillier* mix, pester, prob. f. L *tudiculare*, stir up f. *tudicula* olive-bruising machine (*tudes* mallet f. *tundere* beat, -CULE)]

toil², n. (now only in pl.). Net, snare, (lit. & fig.), as *taken in the tt.* [f. OF *toile* cloth, (pl.) toils, f. L *tela* web f. *texere* weave]

toile (twahl), n. *T. cirée* (sērā·), fine kinds of oil-cloth; *t. colbert* (-ār), canvas for embroidery; *t. d'Alsace* (-ahs), *de Vichy* (vēshē·), linen materials for woman's summer dress. [F, see prec.]

toi·let (toi-), **toilette** (twahlĕ·t), n. Process of dressing, arranging the hair, &c., as *make* one's *t.*; (style of) dress, costume, as *an elaborate t.*, *a t. of white satin*; (also *t.-table*) dressing-table usu. with looking-glass; *t.-cover*, cover for this; *t.-paper* (for water-closet); *t.-set* (of utensils for t.); *t. soap* (for use in t.); *t. vinegar* (aromatic kind for mixing with washing-water); (Med.) cleansing of a part after operation. [F (*-te*), orig. = cloth, clothes-bag, dim. of prec.]

toiline·t(te), n. Cloth of mixed wool, cotton, & silk. [irreg. f. TOILE]

toison d'or (F), n. =*Golden* FLEECE.

Tokay· (-ā), n. Rich aromatic wine made at T. in Hungary; kind of grape.

tō·ken, n. Sign, symbol, evidence, (*of* affection &c.; often *in t. of*); memorial of friendship, keepsake; ring, coin, &c., serving as proof of authenticity; (bibl.) preconcerted signal (*Mark* xiv. 44); (Hist.) piece of metal like & used instead of coin, but worth much less than nominal value & issued by tradesmen, bank, &c., without sanction of government; (archaic or facet.) *by* (*this, the same*) *t.*, *more by t.*, in corroboration of what I say; *t. money*, coins of higher nominal than intrinsic value but exchangeable for full-standard money at the higher rate; *t. vote*, Parliamentary vote of money in which the amount stated *pro formâ* is not meant to be binding. Hence **to·ken**LESS a. [OE *tác(e)n*, cf. Du. *teeken*, G *zeichen*, ON *teikn*, cogn. w. TEACH]

To·kenhouse Yard, n. Auction mart of landed property (often allusively w. ref. to price of land, forced sale of estates, &c.). [*T.Y.* in London]

to·ko. See TOCO.

tō·la, n. Unit of weight in Indian empire, =180 grains troy. [Hind., f. Skr. *tulā*]

Tolē·do, n. Fine sword(-blade) made at T. in Spain.

to·lerable, a. Endurable; fairly good, not bad, as *am in t. health*, *had a t. passage*. Hence **to·lerable**NESS n., **to·lerab**LY[2] adv. [F (*-lé-*), f. L *tolerabilis* (as foll., see -BLE)]

tŏ·lerate, v.t. Endure, permit, (practice, action, person's do*ing*); forbear to judge harshly or rigorously (person, religious sect, opinion); endure society of or intercourse with; sustain, endure, (suffering &c.), esp. (Med.) sustain use of (drug &c.) without harm. Hence or cogn. **to·ler**ANCE, **to·lerat**OR[2], nn., **to·ler**ANT a., **to·lerant**LY[2] adv. [f. F *tolérer* f. L *tolerare*, -ATE[3]]

tolera·tion, n. Tolerating; forbearance; recognition of right of private judgement in religious matters, liberty to uphold one's religious opinions & forms of worship or to enjoy all social privileges &c. without regard to religious differences, whence **tolera·tion**IST(2) n.; *Act of T.* (conditionally freeing Dissenters from some restrictions on the exercise of their forms of worship, 1689). [F (*-lé-*), f. L *tolerationem* (as prec., see -ATION)]

tōll[1], n., & v.i. Tax, duty, paid for use of market, public road, &c., or for service rendered; (Law) *t. thorough* (taken by town for use of highway, bridge, &c.). *t. traverse* (for passing over private land); grain retained by miller as compensation for grinding (still, fig., in *take t.* = abstract a portion *of*); *t.-bar*, *-gate*, bar or usu. gate across road to prevent passage of person, vehicle, &c., without paying t.; *tol(l)-booth* (archaic, Sc.), town gaol [orig. temporary structure for collection of market tt. & detention of those who did not pay & others]; *toll-house* (occupied by collector at t.-gate); (v.i.) take, pay, t. [OE (also *toln*), cf. Du. *tol*, G *zoll*, ON *tollr*, perh. f. L f. Gk *telōnion* t.-house (*telos* tax)]

tōll[2], v.t. & i., & n. Cause (bell, or abs.) to ring with slow uniform strokes; (of bell or clock) give out (stroke, knell, hour of day), give out measured sounds, ring on account of (person, his death, &c.); (n.) tolling, stroke, of bell. [ME *tollen* draw, entice, etym. dub.]

tō·llable, a. (Of person or goods) subject to toll. [TOLL[1] + -ABLE]

tol-lo·l(lish), a. (slang). In fair state, so-so, middling. [f. *tol(erable)* w. redupl.]

To·ltec, n. One of a race traditionally held to have ruled in Mexico before the Aztecs. Hence **To·ltec**AN a. [Mex.]

tolū· (*or* tō·-), n. Balsam got from a S.-Amer. tree & used in perfumery & medicine. Hence **tolu·**IC a., **tŏ·lu**ENE & **tŏ·lu**OL nn., benzylic hydride. [name of place]

tom, n. (*T-*) abbr. of *Thomas*; *T., Dick, & Harry*, persons taken at random, ordinary commonplace people; male animal, esp. *t.(-cat)*; *long t.*, (naut.) long gun esp. one carried amidships on swivel-carriage; *Old T.*, strong kind of gin; *T. & Jerry* (U.S.), rum & water beaten up with eggs &c.; *to·mboy*, romping girl, hoyden; *to·mfoo·l*, fool, trifler, (v.i.) play the fool, act in trifling manner (*tomfoo·lery*, foolish trifling, foolish knick-knacks &c.); *T. Fool* (type of witlessness, esp. in proverb *there's more knows T. Fool than T. Fool knows* =notoriety is not honour); *tomno·ddy*, blockhead, fool; *T. Thumb*, a legendary dwarf, any diminutive person, dwarf variety of various plants; *T. Tiddler's ground*, children's game, place where money can be had for the picking up; *to·mti·t*, kinds of small bird, esp. titmouse.

tŏ·mahawk (-h-), n., & v.t. War-axe of N.-Amer. Indian, with head of horn, stone, or steel; *bury the t.* or HATCHET; (vb) strike, kill, with t., criticize savagely in review. [of native orig.]

tomă·ll(e)y, n. Soft greenish substance (called the liver) in lobster, used as sauce. [Carib]

toma·n (-ahn), n. Persian gold coin worth about 7/2. [Pers.]

toma·to (-mah-), n. (pl. *-oes*). (Plant with) red or yellow pulpy edible fruit; *currant t.* (with small fruit about size of currant); *tree-t.*, kind that grows erect & sustains fruit without support. [f. Sp. *tomate* f. Mex. *tomatl*; formerly called *love-apple*]

tomb (tōōm), n., & v.t. Hole (made) in earth or rock to receive dead (esp. human) body, grave; subterranean or other vault for the dead; sepulchral monument; (fig.) *the t.*, death; *to·mbstone*, monumental stone placed over grave; (v.t.) enclose as or in or as in t. Hence **tom·b**LESS a. [f. OF *tumbe* f. LL *tumba* f. Gk *tumbos* sepulchral mound]

tŏ·mbac, -k, n. Kinds of copper-&-zinc alloy, used under various names as material for cheap jewelry. [F (-c), f. Malay *tambâga* copper]

to·mbola, n. (In France & southern U.S.) kind of lottery with fancy articles for prizes. [It., prob. f. *tombolare* TUMBLE]

tome, n. Volume, esp. large heavy one. [F, f. L f. Gk *tomos* section f. *temnō* cut]

tome·ntum, n. (Bot.) kind of pubescence composed of matted woolly hairs; (Anat.) flocculent inner surface of pia mater. Hence **tōmento·se**[1], **tome·nto**US, aa. [L, = padding of wool &c.]

to·mmy, n. (*T-*) familiar form of TOM; *T. Atkins*, the British soldier, whence *T.* or *t.* (slang), private in army; (Mech.) kinds of wrench or turnscrew, (also *t.-bar*) short bar for working box-spanners; bread, provisions, esp. as given to workman in lieu of wages; this system of payment, truck system (now illegal); *t.-shop*, (formerly) in which t. was enforced, (now) shop in works where provisions may be bought, any baker's shop; food carried by workmen; *t.* ROT[1]; *soft t.* (naut.), soft or fresh bread (cf. HARD *tack*). [-Y[3]]

tomo·rrow, to-morrow, adv. & n. (On) the day after today, as *will write t.*, (prov.) *t. never comes*; (attrib.) *t. morning, afternoon*, &c. (used as nn. & advv.; *t. week*, eight days hence). [TO[1]+MORROW, cf. TODAY]

to·mpion, var. of TAMPION.

to·mtŏm, n., & v.i. Native Indian drum; gong; (v.i.) beat t. [f. Hind. *tamtam*, imit.]

-tomy, suf. = Gk *-tomia* -cutting (*temnō* cut), chiefly in names of surgical operations (*anatomy, phlebotomy, tracheotomy*).

ton[1] (tŭn), n. Measure of weight, 2240 or (U.S., also *short t.*) 2000 lb. avoirdupois; *metric t.*, 1000 kilograms; measure of capacity (often varying) for timber (40 ft), stone (16 cub. ft), salt (42 bushels), lime (40 bushels), coke (28 bushels), wheat (20 bushels), wine (see TUN), &c.; unit of internal capacity (100 cub. ft) or carrying capacity (40 cub. ft) of ship; (colloq.) large number or amount, as *bag weighs (half) a t.* (several pounds, ounces, &c.), *tt. of people, have asked him tt. of times.* [var. of TUN]

ton[2] (F), n. Prevailing mode, fashion, as *in the t.*, BON TON.

tō·nal, a. Of tone or tones; of tonality. Hence **to·nal**LY[2] adv. [f. med. L *tonalis* (TONE, -AL)]

tona·lity, n. (Mus.) character, quality, of tone, also, system of tones, key; colour scheme of picture. [-ITY]

to·-name, n. (chiefly Sc.). Name added esp. to person's Christian name & surname for distinction. [OE *tó-nama* (TO[1], NAME)]

tondi·no (-dē-), n. Tondo with bowl-like centre; (Archit.) = ASTRAGAL. [It., dim. of foll.]

to·ndo, n. Easel painting, or relief, of circular form. [It., = round (plate), f. L *rotundus* round]

tone[1], n. Sound, esp. w. ref. to pitch, quality, & strength; *heart tt.*, sounds of heart heard in auscultation; musical sound (FUNDAMENTAL, HARMONIC, *t.*); modulation of voice to express emotion, sentiment, &c., as *impatient, lively, imploring, despondent, bantering, suspicious, t.*; (Gram.) stress on one syllable of word; (Mus.) ancient esp. Gregorian psalm-tune, (also *whole t.*) any of the larger intervals in diatonic scale, opp. to *semitone*; (Med.) proper condition of the bodily organs, state of health in which animal functions are duly performed, as *has lost, recovered, t.*; prevailing character of morals, sentiments, &c., as *the t. of the nation must be raised, gave a flippant t. to the debate*; general effect of colour or of light & shade in picture; tint, shade of colour; degree of luminosity of colour; (Photog.) colour of finished positive picture. Hence **to·ne**LESS a., **to·neless**NESS n. [f. F *ton* f. L f. Gk *tonos* thing stretched, tone, f. root of *teinō* stretch]

tone[2], v.t. & i. Give tone or quality (of sound or colour) to (*toned paper*, esp. of pale amber tint); (Mus.) tune (instrument); (Photog.) give (picture), (of picture) receive, altered colour in finishing by means of chemical solution; harmonize (usu. intr.), as *does not t. with the wallpaper*; *t. down*, soften colouring of (picture), render (statement, expression, &c.) less pronounced or confident, (intr.) become softer, less pronounced, &c.; *t. up*, give, receive, higher tone or character or greater vigour. [f. prec.]

to·nga (-ngga), n. Light two-wheeled vehicle used in India. [f. Hind. *tāngā*]

tongs, n. pl. (Also *pair of t.*) kinds of instrument for grasping & holding usu. with two limbs pivoted together near either end or connected by spring piece, as *fire-t.* (for grasping coal &c.), *asparagus, sugar, blacksmith's, wire,* LAZY, *-t.*; HAMMER[1] *& t.*; *would not touch* (repulsive person or thing) *with a pair of t.* (still less without). [OE *tang(e)* sing., cf. Du. & Da. *tang*, G *zange*, cogn. w. Gk *daknō* bite]

tongue[1] (tŭng), n. Fleshy muscular organ in the mouth, serving purposes of taste, mastication, swallowing, & (in man) of speech (*put out* one's *t.*, as grimace, or for doctor's inspection; *on the tt. of men*, much talked of; *furred* or *dirty t.*, symptom of illness); this as article of food, as *ox-, sheep's, reindeer's, t., smoked, rolled, t.*; faculty of, tendency in, speech, as *has a ready* or *fluent t., sharp, caustic, dangerous, long* (talkative), *t.*; *put, speak with,* one's *t. in* one's *cheek*, speak ironically, humour one's hearer; *keep a civil t. in* one's *head*, avoid rudeness; language of a nation &c., as *the German t.*, one's *mother t., gift of tt.*, power of speaking in unknown tt. esp. as miraculously conferred on early Christians, *confusion of tt.* (*Gen.* xi. 1–9); thing like t. in shape (esp. tapering) or function, e.g. long low promontory, strip of leather closing gap in front of shoe, clapper of bell, pin of buckle, projecting edge of MATCH[1]-board, slip connecting two grooved boards &c., index of scale or balance, vibrating slip in reed of some musical instruments, jet of flame, pointed rail in railway-switch; *have lost, find,* one's *t.*, be too bashful, recover power of speech; *give* or *throw t.*, (of hounds) bark esp. on finding scent; *hold* one's *t.*, be silent; *on the* TIP[1] *of* one's *t.*; *wag* one's *t.*, talk indiscreetly or volubly; *t.-bit* (with plate preventing horse from getting t. over mouthpiece); *t.-bone*, = HYOID; *t.-tie*, impediment in speech due to shortness of fraenum of t., *t.-tied*, having this, (fig.) debarred from speaking out. Hence **(-)tongue**ED[2], **to·ngue**LESS, aa., **to·ngue**LET n. [OE *tunge*, cf. ON & Sw. *tunga*, Du. *tong*, G *zunge*, cogn. w. L *lingua*, OL *dingua*]

tongue[2], v.t. & i. Produce staccato &c. effects with (flute &c.) by use of tongue, use tongue thus; *t. & groove*, furnish (MATCH[1]-board &c.) with tongue & groove. [f. prec.]

tŏ·nic, a. & n. (Of medicine, medical treatment, &c., fig. of success, misfortune, punishment) serving to invigorate, bracing; (Mus.) of tones, esp. of the key-note; *t. accent*, stress on syllable; *t. spasm*, continuous muscular contraction (cf. CLONIC); *t. sol-fa* (-fah), system of musical (esp. (vocal) notation in which all diatonic scales are written alike (i.e. *doh*, key-note, *ray, me, fah, sol, lah, te*, usu. written *d, r*, &c., with vowel-change for accidentals, e.g. *de, re, ma*), time-value being shown by vertical lines & colons, *t.-sol-fa·ist*, advocate of, expert in, this; (n.) t. medicine &c. (lit. & fig.), (Mus.) key-note. Hence **to·n**ICALLY adv. [f. Gk *tonikos* (as TONE[1], see -IC)]

toni·city, n. Tone; being tonic; healthy elasticity of muscles &c. [-ITY]

tonigh·t, to-night, adv. & n. (On) the present night, (on) the night of today. [TO[1] + NIGHT, cf. TODAY]

tŏ·nish, tonn-, a. (now rare). In the TON[2], modish, stylish. Hence **to·n(n)ish**NESS n. [-ISH[1]]

tō·nite, n. A powerful gun-cotton explosive. [f. L *tonare* thunder + -ITE[1]]

tonk, v.t. (slang). Hit (bowling, person) hard, defeat easily in contest. [?]

To·nka bean, t-, n. Fragrant seed of a tree found in Guiana &c., used in perfumery &c. [native *tonka*, the bean]

tonnage (tŭ·nĭj), n. Internal cubic capacity, or freight-carrying capacity, of ship in TON[1]s; total freightage esp. of a country's merchant marine; duty on vessels formerly reckoned on t., now on registered size; charge per ton on cargo or freight; *t. & poundage* (hist.), customs duties on the tun of wine & the pound's-worth of merchandise imported or exported, granted as subsidies (orig. for the defence of the realm) at intervals in the 14th–18th cc. & levied unconstitutionally by Charles I without consent of Parliament; *t.-deck* (upper of two, second of three or more). [TON[1], -AGE]

tonneau (tŏ·nō, *or as F*), n. Part of some motor-cars that contains the back seats. [F, lit. cask, tun]

-to·nner, n. Vessel of so many tons, as *two-thousand-t.* [-ER[1]]

tonŏ·meter, n. Tuning-fork or other instrument for measuring pitch of tones. [as TONE[1] + -METER]

to·nsil (-sl), n. Either of two oral organs on each side of the fauces. Hence **to·nsil**AR[1] a., **tonsilli·tis** n. [f. L *tonsillae* pl.]

tonsor·ial, a. (facet.). Of a barber or his work. [f. L *tonsorius* (*tondēre tons-* shave, see -OR[2]) + -AL]

to·nsure (-sher), n., & v.t. Rite of shaving the crown (R.-C. Ch.) or whole head (Gk Ch.) of person entering priesthood or monastic order; bare part of monk's or priest's head; (fig.) admission to holy orders; (v.t.) shave head of, give t. to. [f. L *tonsura* (as prec., see -URE)]

tonti·ne (-ēn), n. Annuity shared by subscribers to loan, the shares increasing as subscribers die till last survivor gets all; *t. policy of insurance* (in which associated policy-holders agree to receive no dividend, return-premium, &c., till end of fixed period called *t. period*). [f. It. *tontina* (Lorenzo *Tonti*, originator of tt. about 1653)]

tōō, adv. & a. In a higher degree than is admissible for a specified or understood purpose, standard, &c. (not used to qualify vb, cf. VERY), as *t. ripe for cooking, t. good to be true, allows t. long an interval, t. long intervals, t. large for me, my taste,* *my purpose, is t. fond of comfort, t.* MANY *for*; *t. much* (*of a good thing*), intolerable (*this is really t. m.* or *t. m. o. a g. t.*); (in affected or gushing use) *is quite t., is t. t.*, (*delightful* &c., often omitted); also, as well, as *take the others t., mean to do it t.* (as well as threaten); moreover, as *achieved, t., at small cost*; (adj.) *t.-t.*, gushing. [=TO[1]]

took. See TAKE.

tōōl[1], n. Mechanical implement, as *carpenter's, joiner's, gardener's, engraver's, mason's, tt.*; (usu. *machine-t.*) machine used in making machinery, e.g. lathe; (fig.) thing used in an occupation or pursuit, as *literary tt., the tt. of* one's *trade*; person used as mere instrument by another, cat's-paw; separate figure in tooling of book; *broad t.*, = TOOLER; EDGE[1]-, *edged, t.*; *t.-holder*, device for holding t. in lathe, handle for use with different tt.; *t.-post, -rest*, holder or support for cutting-t. in lathe. [OE *tól*, cf. ON *tól* pl., OE *tawian* prepare, Goth. *taujan* make, cause]

tool[2], v.t. & i. Dress (stone) with chisel; ornament (edges of book-cover) with tooling; work with t.; (slang) drive (coach &c.), (intr.) drive, ride, (often *along* &c.) esp. in casual or leisurely manner. [f. prec.]

too·ler, n. In vbl senses, esp.: stonemason's broad chisel for tooling. [-ER[1]]

too·ling, n. Stone-dressing in parallel lines; ornamentation of edges of book-cover with designs impressed by heated tools (*blind t.*, without gilding). [-ING][1]

tōōn, n. E.-Ind. tree with close-grained red wood much used for furniture &c. [f. Hind. *tun*]

tōōt, v.t. & i., & n. Sound, esp. produce harsh or dismal sound with, (horn, cornet, whistle, &c.); sound horn &c. thus; (of horn &c.) give out such sound; (of grouse) call; (n.) sound of horn, trumpet, &c. [imit., cf. G *tuten*, Du. *tuyten*]

tōōth, n. (pl. *teeth*), & v.t. & i. Each of several hard dense structures growing in jaws of vertebrates & used for mastication; CANINE, EYE[1]-, INCISOR, MILK[1]-, MOLAR[1], WISDOM, *t.*; *false, artificial, t.* (made by dentist); t.-shaped projection or thing, e.g. cog, point, &c., of gear-wheel, saw, comb, rake; SWEET *t.*; *cast* thing *in* person's *tt.*, reproach him with it; *in the tt. of*, in spite of (opposition &c.), in opposition to (directions &c.), in the face of (the wind &c.); *armed to the tt.* (completely, elaborately); *cut* one's *eye-tt.*, gain worldly wisdom; *escape by the skin of* one's *tt.* (narrowly); *fight, struggle, t. & nail* (with utmost effort); *from the tt. outwards* (archaic), insincerely, not from the heart; LIE[2] *in* one's *tt.*; *set* one's *tt. on* EDGE[1]; *show* one's *tt.*, take threatening tone; *take the* BIT[1] *between* one's *tt.*; *too·thache*, ache in t.; *t.-billed*, (of bird) having t.-like process(es) on cutting edges of bill; *t.-brush* (for cleaning tt.); *t.-comb* (with fine close-set tt.); *t. ornament*, = DOG[1]-*t.*; *t.-paste, -powder* (for cleaning or preserving tt.); *too·thpick*, small sharp instrument of quill, wood, gold, &c., for removing matter lodged between tt. (Vb) furnish with tt.; (of cog-wheels) interlock. Hence **(-)tooth**ED[2], **too·th**LESS, aa., **too·th**LET n. [OE *tóth*, cf. Du. *tand*, G *zahn*, L *dens -ntis*, Gk *odous -ontos*, f. root *ed-* EAT]

too·thful, n. Small draught of spirit &c., thimbleful. [-FUL]

too·thing, n. In vbl senses, esp.: projecting bricks or stones left at end of wall to provide for continuation; *t.-plane* (with serrated edge for roughening surface). [-ING[1]]

too·thsome, a. Pleasant to eat. Hence **too·thsome**LY[2] adv., **too·thsome**NESS n. [-SOME]

too·tle, v.i. Toot gently or repeatedly esp. on flute. [-LE(3)]

tōō·tsy(-wōōtsy), n. (nursery). Foot. [?]

top[1], n. & a. Summit, highest part, as *t. of a hill, hill-t., at the t. of the tree* (fig., of highest rank in profession &c.); *come to the t.*, win distinction; *on t.*, above; *on the t. of*, in addition to; leaves &c. of plants grown for the root, as *turnip-tt.*; surface (of ground), upper surface (of table &c.); upper part of shoe; cover of carriage; lid of saucepan &c.; head (of page in book); upper edges of book, as *gilt t.*; (person occupying) highest rank, foremost place, as *came out* (*at the*) *t. of the school, the t.* (upper end, head) *of the table*; utmost degree, height, as *realized the t. of my ambition, called at the t. of his voice, ran at the t. of his speed*; crown of the head, as *from t. to toe*; *the t. of the morning* (*to you*), Irish morning greeting; (Naut.) platform round head of lower mast serving to extend topmast shrouds, as *maint., foret., mizzent.*; (pl.) metal buttons plated &c. only on face; bunch of hair, fibres, &c., esp. as measure $=1\frac{1}{2}$ lb.; (adj.) highest in position or degree, as *the t. rail, at t. speed, t. dog* (slang, =victor, master, opp. *under dog*), whence **to·p**MOST a.; *t.-boot* (also *t.*), boot with high t. usu. of different material or colour & made to look as if turned down; *t.-coat*, overcoat; *t.-dress*, apply manure on the t. of (earth) instead of ploughing it in, *t.-dressing*, this process, manure so applied; *topga·llant* (tŏpg-, tog-), mast, sail, yard, rigging, immediately above topmast & topsail; *t. hamper*, light upper sails & rigging; *t. hat*, tall silk hat; *t.-heavy*, overweighted at t. so as to be in danger of falling (often fig. of scheme &c.); *t.-hole* slang, first-rate; *to·pknot*, knot, bow of ribbon &c., tuft, crest, worn or growing on head; *t.-lantern, -light*, light displayed from mizzentop of flagship; *to·pman*, t.-sawyer (lit.), (Naut., also *to·psman*) man doing duty in a t.; *to·pmast* (next above lower mast); *to·psail* (-sl), square sail next above lowest; *topsaw·yer*, sawyer in upper position in saw-pit, (fig.) person in superior or high position; *topsides*, sides of ship above water-line. [OE, Du., Da., cf. ON *toppr*, G *zopf* tuft, tree-top]

top², v.t. Provide with top or cap; (Naut.) raise one end of (yard &c.) above the other; remove top of (plant) to improve growth &c.; reach the top of (hill &c.); be higher than; be superior to, surpass, as *tops all I ever saw*, whence **to·pping²** a., **to·ppingly²** adv.; *t.* one's *part*, act or discharge it to perfection; (Golf) hit (ball) at t. instead of true; *t. off* or *up*, put an end or a finishing touch to (thing, or abs.); be of (specified height), as *he tops 6 ft.* [f. prec.]

top³, n. Kinds of wooden or metal toy, usu. conical, spherical, or pear-shaped, rotating on sharp point at bottom when set in motion by hand, spring, or string; HUMMING, PEG, WHIP¹*ping* or *whip*, *-t.*, SLEEP² *like a t.* (sound); *t.-shell*, kinds of shell-fish with t.-shaped shell. [cf. MHG *topf*, MLG *doppe*]

tō·paz, n. A transparent or translucent mineral, a silicate of aluminium, yellow, white, green, blue, or colourless; *false t.*, kind of yellow quartz; kind of humming-bird. [f. OF *topaze* f. L f. Gk *topazos*, *-zion*, etym. dub., cf. Skr. *tapas* fire, *tap* shine]

topă·zolite, n. Yellow or green kind of garnet. [prec. + -O- + -LITE]

tope¹, v.i. Drink alcoholic liquors to excess esp. habitually. Hence **to·per¹** n. [perh. f. F *tôper* cover stake in dicing, whence (*je*) *tôpe!* int. agreed!, done!, (in drinking) I pledge you]

tope², n. (Anglo-Ind.). Mango or other grove. [f. Tamil *tōppu*]

tope³, n. Buddhist monument, usu. dome or tower. [f. Hind. *tōp* f. Skr. *stūpa* mound]

tope⁴, n. Small species of shark, dogfish. [?]

tŏph, tō·phus, nn. Gouty deposit of calcareous matter round teeth & at surface of joints. Hence **topha·ceous** a. [L (*-us*), = sandstone, tufa]

Tō·phet, n. Place in Valley of Hinnom near Jerusalem used for idolatrous worship & later for depositing refuse, for consumption of which fires were kept burning; hell. [f. Heb. *topheth* etym. dub.]

topi, -ee. See SOLA.

tō·pia, n. Ancient-Roman style of mural decoration with heterogeneous landscape scenes. [L, = landscape gardening or painting, f. Gk *topos* place]

tō·piary, a. *The t. art* (of clipping shrubs &c. into ornamental shapes). Hence **topiār·ian** a., **to·piarist** n. [f. L *topiarius* landscape gardener (as prec., see -ARY¹)]

tŏ·pic, n. Theme for discussion, subject of conversation or discourse; (Logic, Rhet.) class of considerations from which arguments can be drawn. [f. L f. Gk (*ta*) *topika* topics, as title of a treatise of Aristotle (*topos* place, see -IC)]

to·pical, a. Of topics; dealing with esp. current or local topics, as *t. allusion*, *song*; local, esp. (Med.) affecting a part of the body. Hence **to·pically²** adv. [-AL]

topŏ·graphy, n. Detailed description, representation on map &c., of natural & artificial features of a town, district, &c.; such features; (Anat.) mapping of surface of body with reference to the parts beneath. Hence **topo·grapher¹** n., **topogră·phic(al)** aa., **topogra·phically²** adv. [f. LL f. Gk *topographia* (*topos* place, see -GRAPHY)]

topŏ·nymy, n. Study of the place-names of a region. [f. Gk *topos* place, *onuma* name, -Y¹]

to·pper, n. In vbl senses, also: (colloq.) = TOP¹ *hat*; (commerc.) fine fruit &c. put at top of stock for show. [f. TOP² + -ER¹]

to·pple, v.i. & t. (Cause to) totter & fall (often *over*, *down*). [f. TOP¹ + -LE(3)]

topsytur·vy, adv., a., n., & v.t. Upside down; (in) utter confusion; (v.t.) turn t. Hence (facet.) **topsytur·vydom**, **topsyturvifica·tion**, nn., **topsytur·vify** v.t. [f. 16th c., etym. dub.; prob. containing TOP¹ + obs. *terve* overturn cogn. w. OE *tearflian* turn, roll over]

tōque (-k), n. (Hist.) small kinds of man's & woman's hat; small bonnet; kinds of monkey with cap-like arrangement of hair. [F, cf. It. *tocca*, Sp. *toca*]

tor, n. Hill, rocky peak, esp. on Dartmoor. [OE, cf. W *twr* heap]

-tor, suf. forming agent nn. on L p.p. stems in *-t-* (*doctor*, *narrator*); see -OR².

tor·ah, n. Revealed will of God, esp. Mosaic law; Pentateuch. [Heb. *torāh* instruction]

torch, n. Piece of resinous wood or twisted flax &c. soaked in tallow &c. for carrying lighted (*t. of Hymen*, passion of love); other appliance for this purpose, e. g. oil-lamp on pole; *electric t.*, stick-shaped portable electric lamp; *t.-fishing* (also **tor·ching¹** n.) mode of catching fish by t.-light; *t.-race*, ancient-Greek festival performance of runners handing lighted tt. to others in relays; *hand on the t.*, keep knowledge &c. alive (w. ref. to t.-race). [f. F *torche* perh. ult. f. L *torquēre tort-* twist]

tor·chon (-shn, *or as* F), n. attrib. *T. paper*, paper with rough surface used esp. for water-colours; *t. board* (covered with t. paper); *t. mat*, MAT³ of t. paper; *t. lace*, peasants' bobbin lace with geometrical designs. [F, = dishcloth (*torcher* wipe)]

tore¹. See TEAR¹.

tore[2], = TORUS (first sense).

tŏrēador·, n. Spanish (usu. mounted) bullfighter. [Sp. (*torear* engage in bullfight f. *toro* bull f. L *taurus*, see -OR[2])]

toreu·tic (-rōō-), a. & n. (N. pl., art) of chasing, carving, & embossing, esp. metal, [f. Gk *toreutikos* (*toreuō* bore, chase, see -IC)]

tor·goch (-ch), n. Red-bellied char. [W (*tor* belly + *coch* red)]

tor·ment[1], n. Severe bodily or mental suffering, as *was in t., suffered tt.*; source of this, as (colloq.) *the child is a positive t.* [OF, f. L *tormentum* engine for hurling stones, rack, torment, (*torquēre* twist, see -MENT)]

torme·nt[2], v.t. Subject to torment, as *tormented with neuralgia, suspense, inquiries.* Hence **torme·nting**LY[2] adv. [f. OF *tormenter* (prec.)]

tor·mentil, n. Low herb with bright yellow flowers & highly astringent rootstock used in medicine. [f. med. L *tormentilla* f. TORMENT[1]; sense-connexion unknown]

tormen·tor, n. Person, thing, that torments, whence **torme·ntr**ESS[1] n.; long fork used on ship for taking meat from coppers; kind of harrow on wheels. [-OR[2]]

tor·mina, n. Griping pains in bowels, colic. [L (*torquēre* twist)]

torn. See TEAR[1].

tornā·do, n. (pl. *-oes*). Violent storm of small extent, esp. in W. Africa at beginning & end of rainy season & in U.S. from April to July, having usually a rotary motion, & often accompanied by funnel-shaped cloud; (fig.) outburst or volley *of* cheers, hisses, missiles, &c. Hence **tornă·d**IC a. [perh. assim. of Sp. *tronada* thunderstorm (*tronar* to thunder) to Sp. *tornar* to turn]

tor·ous, toro·se, aa. (Bot.) cylindrical with bulges at intervals; (Zool.) knobby. [f. L *torosus* (TORUS, see -OSE[1], -OUS)]

torpē·do, n. (pl. *-oes*), & v.t. Electric ray, a fish with electric apparatus for numbing or killing its prey &c.; kinds of explosive mine or petard; cigar-shaped self-propelling submarine missile that can be aimed at a ship &c. & explodes on touching it (*aerial t.*, discharged from aircraft); *t.-boat*, small fast steamer for carrying or discharging tt.; *t.(-boat)-catcher, t. gunboat*, large vessel intended to catch t.-boat; (*t.-boat*) *destroyer*, small fast boat used to catch t.-boat or carry tt.; *t.-net* (hung round ship to intercept tt. or t.-boat); *t.-tube* (from which tt. are discharged); (vb) destroy, attack, with t., (fig.) paralyse, make (policy, institution, &c.) ineffective. [(vb f. n.) L, = t. fish (*torpēre* be numb)]

tor·pid, a. & n. (Of hibernating animal) dormant; numb; sluggish, dull, apathetic; (n. pl.) Lent boat-races at Oxford between second crews of colleges, (sing.) boat rowing in these. Hence or cogn. **torpi·d**ITY, **tor·pid**NESS, **tor·por**[1], nn., **tor·pid**LY[2] adv., **tor·pi**FY v.t., **torpori·**FIC a. [f. L *torpidus* (prec., -ID[1])]

Torps, n. (nav. slang). Ship's torpedo officer. [abbr.]

tor·quāte(d), aa. (zool.). With ring of peculiar colour or texture of hair or plumage about the neck. [f. L *torquatus* (foll., -ATE[2])]

torque (-k), **torc**, n. Necklace of twisted metal, esp. of Gauls; (Mech., *-que*) twisting-MOMENT. [f. L *torques* necklace, as TORT]

tŏ·rrefȳ, v.t. Parch with heat, roast, dry, (metallic ores, drugs). So **torre**FA·CTION n. [f. F *torréfier* f. L *torrefacere* (*torrēre* parch, see -FY)]

tŏ·rrent, n. Rushing stream of water &c.; (pl.) great downpour *of rain* (also *rain falls in tt.*); (fig.) violent flow (*of* abuse, grief, questions). Hence **torre·nt**IAL (-shl) a., **torre·ntial**LY[2] adv. [F, f. L *torrentem* lit. boiling stream (*torrēre* parch, see -ENT)]

Torrice·llian, a. *T. experiment* (with mercury in tube, leading to principle on which barometer is made); *T. tube* (used for this). [E. *Torricelli* d. 1647 + -AN]

tŏ·rrid, a. (Of land &c.) parched by sun, very hot; *t. zone*, part of earth's surface between tropics. Hence **torri·d**ITY, **to·rrid**NESS, nn. [f. L *torridus* (*torrēre* parch, see -ID[1])]

tor·sel, n. Twisted ornament e. g. scroll; block of wood in brick wall for joist &c. to rest on. [prob. var. of TASSEL]

tor·sion (-shn), n. Twisting; (Bot.) state of being spirally twisted, so **tor·s**IVE a.; (Med.) twisting of cut end of artery after operation &c. to check haemorrhage; *t. balance* (for measuring minute forces by means of fine twisted wire). Hence **tor·sion**AL, **tor·sion**LESS, aa., **tor·sional**LY[2] adv. [F, f. LL *tortionem, -si-* (as TORT, see -ION)]

torsk, n. Fish of cod family. [Sw. & Da.]

tor·so, n. Trunk of statue apart from head & limbs; (fig.) unfinished or mutilated work. [It., = stalk, stump, torso, f. THYRSUS]

tort, n. (law). Private or civil wrong. [F, = wrong, harm, f. L *torquēre tort-* twist]

tortico·llis, n. (path.). Rheumatic affection of muscles of neck, stiff neck. [f. L as prec. + *collum* neck]

tor·tile, a. Twisted, curved; (Bot.) coiled. Hence **torti·l**ITY n. [f. L *tortilis* (TORT, -ILE)]

torti·lla (-ēlya), n. Flat maize cake, Mexican substitute for bread. [Sp.]

tor·tious (-shus), a. (law). Constituting a tort, wrongful. Hence **tor·tious**LY[2] adv. [AF *torcious* (TORSION, -OUS), assoc. in sense w. *tort*]

tor·toise (-t*u*s, -toiz), n. Land (& freshwater) varieties of turtle, reptile encased in two scaly or leathery shields forming a box; ALLIGATOR *t.*; (Rom. Ant.) = TESTUDO; *hare & t.*, ability beaten by persistence; *t.-shell*, mottled & clouded outer shell or scale of some sea turtles used for combs &c., *t.-shell cat, butterfly* (with black & yellow markings suggesting t.-shell). [ME *tortuce, tortu* (thr. OF *tortue*), f. LL *tortuca* (perh. as TORT, w. ref. to t.'s crooked feet)]

tor·tūous, a. Full of twists or turns, so **tortuo·SE**[1] a. (bot.); (fig., of policy &c.) devious, circuitous, crooked, not straightforward. Hence or cogn. **tortuŏ·SITY, tor·tuousNESS,** nn., **tor·tuousLY**[2] adv. [AF, f. L *tortuosus* (*tortus -ūs* twist, foll., -OUS)]

tor·ture (-tsh*er*), n., & v.t. Infliction of severe bodily pain e.g. as punishment or means of persuasion, as *was put to the t.*, *instruments of t.* (rack, thumbscrew, &c.); severe physical or mental pain. (V.t.) subject to t., as *tortured with neuralgia, tight boots, anxiety*; (fig.) force out of natural position or state, pervert meaning of (words, passage). Hence **tor·turABLE, tor·turOUS,** aa., **tor·turER**[1] n., **tor·turingLY**[2] adv. [(vb. f. n.) F, f. L *tortura* twisting (*torquēre tort-* twist, see -URE)]

tŏ·rula, n. (pl. *-ae*). Kinds of yeast-like fungus; chain of spherical bacteria, whence **to·ruliFORM** a.; (Bot.) small torus. [mod. L dim. of TORUS]

tor·us, n. (pl. *-rī*). Large moulding of semicircular profile esp. as lowest member of base of column; (Bot.) receptacle of flower, modified end of stem; (Anat.) smooth ridge as of muscle. [L, = protuberance, bed]

tor·y, n. & a. (Member) of the party that opposed the exclusion of the Duke of York (James II), inclined to the Stuarts after 1689, accepted George III and the established order in Church & State, opposed Reform Bill of 1832, & has been succeeded by Conservative party (cf. WHIG); *T. Democrat*, Conservative who inclines to some democratic principles. Hence **tor·yISM** n. [orig. = Irish robber, f. Ir. *tóraidhe* pursuer (*tóir* pursue)]

-tory, suf., most freq. form of -ORY, in wds f. L vbs w. p.p. stem in *-t-* (*amatory, factory*).

tosh, n. (slang). Rubbish, twaddle; (Cricket, lawn tennis, &c.) easy bowling or service. [?]

tŏ·sher, n. (slang). Unattached student (see UNATTACHED). [corrupt.]

tŏss, v.t. & i. (*tossed* or poet. *tost*), & n. Throw up (ball &c.) with the hand esp. with palm upward, (of bull &c.) throw (person &c.) up with the horns; throw (thing *to* person, *away, aside*, &c.) lightly or carelessly; throw (coin) into air to decide choice &c. by way it falls, settle question or dispute with (person *for* thing) thus, as *will t. you for* (or *who has*) *the armchair*; (Lawn tennis) strike (ball, or abs.) high into air; *toss* (person) *in blanket*, jerk him upwards out of it by pulling suddenly on all corners; throw back one's *head* esp. in contempt or impatience; *t. a pancake*, jerk it up so that it returns upside down to pan; throw (thing, one*self*) about from side to side, throw oneself about thus in bed &c., roll about restlessly, (of sea, ship, branch, &c.) roll or swing with fitful to-&-fro motion; separate heavy from light parts of (tin ore) by agitation in vessel; *t. oars* (of boat's crew bringing oars to upright position blades upward as salute); *t. off*, drink off at a draught, dispatch (work) rapidly or without apparent effort; *t. up*, toss coin as above, prepare (food) hastily; *toss-pot* (archaic), toper. (N.) tossing of coin, head, &c. as *win the t.*, have its decision in one's favour; *a contemptuous t. of the head*; *full t.* (slang), full pitch at cricket; *t.-up*, tossing up of coin, doubtful question, as *is quite a t.-up whether he comes or not*; PITCH[2]-*&-t.*; throw from horse-back &c. (*take a t.*, be thrown). [(n. f. vb) f. 16th c., etym. dub.]

tot[1], n. Small child, esp. *a tiny t.*; (colloq.) dram of liquor. [f. 18th c., etym. dub.]

tot[2], n., & v.t. & i., (colloq.). Set of figures to be added; (vb) add usu. *up*, (of items) mount *up* (*t. up to*, amount to). [abbr. of foll. or of L *totum* the whole]

tō·tal, a., n., & v.t. (-ll-). Complete, comprising the whole, as *the t. number of persons, t. population, sum t., t. tonnage*; absolute, unqualified, as *was in t. ignorance of it*; *resulted in t. loss of his fortune, t.* ABSTINENCE, *abstainer, t. eclipse* (in which whole surface is obscured); (n.) t. number or amount; (v.t.) find the t. of (things, set of figures), amount in number to, as *the visitors totalled 131*. Hence **totă·lITY** n. (esp., time for which an eclipse is t.), **to·talLY**[2] adv. [(n. & vb f. adj.) F, f. LL *totalis* (*tōtus* entire, see -AL)]

to·talize, v.t. & i. Collect into a total, find the total of; use totalizer in betting. Hence **totalizA·TION** n. [-IZE]

to·talizer, n. Device showing number & amount of bets staked on race with a view to dividing the total among betters on winner. So **to·talizatOR**[2] n. [-ER[1]]

tote[1], n. (slang). = prec. [abbr.]

tote[2], v.t. (U.S.). Convey, transport, (supplies, timber, &c.). [f. 1676; etym. dub.]

tō·tĕm, n. Natural object esp. animal assumed among N.-Amer. Indians as emblem of clan or individual on ground of relationship; image of this; *t.-post* (on which tt. are carved or hung); *t. stage*, stage of mental development in which tt. are taken as clan-names & objects of worship. Hence **totĕ·mic, totemi·stic,** aa., **to·temism**(3), **to·temist**(2), nn. [of native orig.]

t'o·ther, to·ther, (tŭ-), a. & pron. The other; *tell t. from which* (joc. variant of *tell one from the other*). [earlier *the tother* f. wrong division of ME *thet* (THAT) *other*; now understood as = *the other* & usu. used without *the*]

tō·tidĕm ver·bīs, adv. In so many words, in these very words, as *he said, t.v., that he would write in either case.* [L]

tō·tiēs quō·tiēs (*or* tō·shiēs kwō·shiēs), adv. On each occasion, every time, as *offer was refused t.q.* [L, = as often as]

tō·to cae·lo (sē-), adv. *Differ* t.c. (by an immense distance). [L, = by the whole heaven]

to·tter, v.i. Stand or walk unsteadily (esp. of child learning to walk); (part., of steps) unsteady; (of tower &c., fig. of State, system, &c.) be shaken, be on the point of falling. Hence **to·tterer**[1] n., **to·tteringly**[2] adv., **to·ttery**[2] a. [f. 1200, etym. dub.; cf. Norw. dial. *totra* quiver, Du. *touteren* swing]

toucan (tōōkah·n, tōō·kn), n. Kinds of tropical American bird with immense beak. [f. Braz. *tucana*]

touch[1] (tŭtsh), v.t. & i. Be separated at one or more points by no intervening space or object from (thing &c.), be in or come into contact with, bring part of body esp. hand into contact with, establish this relation towards (thing *with* one's *hand, stick,* &c.), cause (two things) to come into contact, (of two things) be in contact, as *two rocks t.* (*each other*) *at the bases, you are touching wet paint, t. pitch,* have to do with shady transaction or person, *he touched me on the shoulder, t. the table with your stick, wouldn't t. him* (unpleasant person) *with a barge-pole, just touched them together & they cracked, I never touched him* (hostilely), *can just t. bottom* (of water with toes), *t.* BOTTOM[1], *touched his hat* (as salutation), *was touched by the king* (to cure KING[1]'s evil), *t. wood* (to propitiate Nemesis after boasting &c.), *t. the spot* (find out, or do, exactly what is requisite); (Geom.) be a tangent to (circle &c.); apply slight force to, as *he touched* (rang) *the bell*; strike (keys, strings, of musical instrument), strike keys or strings of; delineate, mark lightly, put *in,* (features &c.) with brush, pencil, &c.; reach, as *can just t. the ceiling,* (fig.) approach in excellence &c., as *no one can t. him in light comedy, in the spot-barred game, for purity of style*; affect with tender feeling, soften, as *it touched me to the heart, was visibly touched by her appeal*; rouse painful or angry feeling in, as *touched him home, touched him to the quick,* = *touched him on a raw* or *tender place* (also lit.); treat of (subject) lightly or in passing; concern, as *the question touches you nearly*; (chiefly neg.) have to do with, as *refuses to t.* (risk capital in) *breweries, dare not t.* (drink) *beer*; injure slightly, as *flowers are a little touched with the east wind*; (p.p.) slightly crazy; affect slightly, modify, as *morality touched with emotion*; (neg.) produce slightest effect on, cope with, as *brass polish won't t. these candlesticks, couldn't t. the algebra paper*; (slang) *t.* one *for,* get (sum) out of him (*touched me for £5*; cf. TAP[1]); *t. at* (naut.), call at (port &c.); *t. down* (football), t. ball on ground behind own goal to prevent opponent's doing so; *t. on* or *upon,* treat (subject) briefly; *t. off,* make (sketch) hastily, make hasty sketch of, (also) discharge (cannon), break off telephone interview; *t. up,* correct, give finishing touches to (picture, writing, &c.), strike (horse) with whip, jog (memory); *tou·chwood*[1] (see also foll.), children's game in which touching wood gives immunity from pursuit. Hence **tou·chable** a. [ME, f. OF *tochier,* cf. Pr., Sp., & Port. *tocar,* It. *toccare*]

touch[2], n. Act or fact or touching, contact, as *gave him a t., felt a t. on my arm, royal t.* (for KING[1]'s evil), *at a t.* (if touched, however lightly); sense by which contact is perceived, whence **tou·chless** a.; light stroke with pencil, brush, &c., in drawing &c., as *added a few tt., finishing tt.,* (often fig. of writing, management of business, &c.); small amount, slight tinge or trace, as *wants a t. of salt, an occasional t. of irony, felt a t. of rheumatism*; performer's manner of touching keys or strings of musical instrument, manner or degree in which keys &c. respond to this, manner or style of workmanship in carving &c. or in writing, as *has a light* or *firm t. on piano, piano is wanting in t., writer has light t.* (produces required effect simply, without laboured emphasis, &c.); *the Nelson t.,* Nelson's unique handling of a situation; mental correspondence, sympathy, communication, esp. *keep in t.,* remain in sympathy or not cease from correspondence or personal intercourse (*with*); magnetization of steel bar by repeated contact with magnet; (archaic) touchstone, test, as *put it to the t.*; *near t.,* close shave, narrow escape; (Med.) exploration of organs &c. by sense of t.; (Footb.) part of field outside the side limits (*t.-lines*) & between goal-lines produced, *t.-in-goal,* each of the four outside corners enclosed by t.-lines & goal-lines, *t.-down,* touching down (as in prec.); *t.-&-go,* (adj.) of uncertain event, risky, placed in risky circumstances, as *it was t.-&-go whether we got past, a t.-&-go business, we were t.-&-go all the time,* (n.) such situation; *t.-body, -corpuscle* (concerned in sense of t.); *t.-hole,* small hole in cannon by which it is fired; *t.-last,* children's game;

t.-needle, needle of gold alloy of known composition used as standard in testing other alloys on touchstone; *t. of nature*, natural trait, (pop.) exhibition of feeling with which others sympathize (f. misinterpretation of Shaksp. *T. & C.* III. iii. 175); *t.-paper* (steeped in nitre, for firing gunpowder &c.); *tou·chstone*, fine-grained dark schist or jasper used for testing alloys of gold &c., (fig.) standard, criterion; *tou·chwood*[2] (see also prec.), soft substance into which wood is changed by some fungi, used as tinder. [f. prec.]

tou·cher, n. In vbl senses, also: (slang) *near t.*, close shave, *as near as a t.*, very nearly, almost exactly. [-ER[1]]

tou·ching, a. & prep. Affecting, pathetic, as *a t. incident, shows the most t. confidence in us*, whence **tou·ching**LY[2] adv., **tou·ching**NESS n.; (prep. archaic or literary, also *as t.*) concerning, about. [-ING[2]]

tou·chy, a. Apt to take offence, over-sensitive. Hence **tou·chi**LY[2] adv., **tou·chi**NESS n. [perh. corrupt. of TETCHY]

tough (tŭf), a. Flexible but not brittle, hard to break or cut, as *a beefsteak as t. as leather, requires the toughest steel*; (of clay &c.) stiff, tenacious; able to endure hardship, hardy; unyielding, stubborn; difficult, as *found it a t. job*; (colloq., of luck &c.) hard, severe, unpleasant; (U.S. slang) ruffianly, turbulent & criminal, (n.) street ruffian. Hence **tou·gh**EN[6] v.t. & i., **tou·gh**ISH[1] a., **tou·gh**LY[2] adv., **tou·gh**NESS n. [OE *tóh*, cf. Du. *taai*, G *zäh(e)*]

toupee· (tōō-), n. Artificial patch of hair worn to cover bald spot. [f. F *toupet* dim. of *toupe* tuft (as TOP[1])]

toupet (tōō·pā), n. Front of false hair. [F, see prec.]

tour (toor), n., & v.i. & t. Journey through a country from place to place; *the grand t.* (hist.), journey through France, Italy, &c., as finishing touch to education; rambling excursion, short journey, walk, as *a t. of observation through the town*; (Mil.) spell of duty on service, time to be spent at a station; *t. de force*, feat of strength or skill; (vb) make t. (*through, about*, &c.), make a t. of, travel through, (country &c.). [F, =turn, round, tour, f. *tourner* TURN]

tourbi·llion (toor-), n. Kind of firework spinning in air so as to look like scroll or spiral column of fire. [f. F *tourbillon* whirlwind]

tour·ist, n. Person who makes a tour, as *place is overrun with tt.*; *t. ticket*, railway &c. ticket issued to t. on special terms, esp. return ticket available for extended period. [f. F *touriste* (TOUR, see -IST)]

tour·malin(e) (toor-), n. Mineral of various colours possessing powerful electric properties & used as gem; *t. granite* (containing t.). [F, f. Cingalese *tòramalli*]

tour·nament (toor-, ter-), n. (Hist.) pageant in which two parties of mounted & armed men contended with blunted weapons; any contest of skill between a number of competitors, as *chess, lawn-tennis, t.* [f. OF *torneiement* (*torneier* TOURNEY, see -MENT)]

tour·nay (toor-), n. Printed worsted upholstering-material. [f. *Tournay*, in Belgium]

tour·ney (ter-, toor-), n., & v.i. (Take part in) tournament (hist.). [f. OF *torneier* vb, *tornei* n., f. *tourner* TURN]

tour·niquĕt (toor-, -k-), n. Instrument for stopping flow of blood through artery by compression effected with screw. [F, f. *tourner* TURN]

tournure (toornūr· *or as F*), n. Curve, contour; pad &c. worn by women to give rounded outline to hips, back drapery of dress. [F (as TURN, see -URE)]

tousle (tow·zl), v.t. Pull about, handle roughly, make (esp. hair) untidy. [f. *touse* (now dial. or obs. cf. *Towzer* as dog's name), ME *tusen*, cf. G *zausen*, + -LE(3)]

tous-les-mois (tōōlămwah·), n. Food starch got from tubers of species of canna. [F, lit. = every month, prob. corrupt. of S.-Amer. *toloman*]

tou·sy (-zĭ), a. Rough, shaggy, dishevelled. [f. *touse* (TOUSLE) + -Y[2]]

tout (towt), v.i., & n. Solicit custom, pester possible customers with applications (*for* orders); spy out movements & condition of horses in training; (n.) instance of, (also **tou·ter**[1] n. rare) person employed in, touting. [ME *toten* peep, pry, OE *tótian* project, peep out, cf. ON *túta* peak, Sw. *tut* point, Da. *tud* spout]

tout court (tōō koor), adv. (Of name &c.) without addition or explanation. [F, lit. =quite short]

tout ensemble (F), n. See ENSEMBLE.

tow[1] (tō), v.t., & n. (Of vessel, horse on bank, &c.) pull (boat, barge, &c.) along in water by rope or chain; pull (person, thing) along behind one; drag (net) over surface of water, drag net over (water), to collect specimens; (n.) towing, being towed, esp. *take, have, in t.*, (fig.) assume direction of, take possession of, (person); *tow(ing)-line, -rope* (used in towing); *tow(ing)-net* (for dragging water); *tow(ing)-path* (along river or canal for use in towing). Hence **tow·**AGE(3, 4) n. [OE *togian*, cf. ON *toga* pull, OHG *zogôn* draw, cogn. w. G *ziehen* draw & w. L *ducere* lead, draw]

tow[2] (tō), n. Coarse & broken part of flax or hemp. Hence **tow·**Y[2] a. [f. 14th c., etym. dub.; cf. ON *tó* tuft of wool for spinning]

toward[1] (tō·*erd*), a. (archaic). Docile, apt. Hence **tow·ard**LY[1] a., **tow·ard**NESS n., (archaic). [as foll.]

towards, toward[2], (tōrdz, tō·*erdz*, twordz, towor·dz), prep. (-*s* now more usu. in prose & colloq.). In the direction of, as *looks t. the sea, set out t. town, I look t. you* (in drinking health); as regards, in relation to, as *felt some animosity t. him, his attitude t. Home Rule*; (archaic esp. bibl.) *to usward*, t. us; for, for the purpose of, as *saved something t. his education*; near, as *t. noon, t. the end of our journey*; (archaic, as adv.) *feast is toward* (coming). [OE *tóweard* a. future (TO, -WARD), see -ES]

tow·el, n., & v.t. & i. (-ll-). Cloth for drying oneself after bath &c.; *roller t.*, endless t. on revolving bar; *t.-horse*, frame for hanging tt. on; (old slang) *lead t.*, bullet, *oaken t.*, cudgel; (v.t.) wipe (one*self* &c.) with t., (slang) thrash; (v.i.) wipe oneself with t. Hence **tow·elling**[1](1, 3) n. [f. OF *toaille* f. OHG *dwahila* (G dial. *zwehle*) f. *twahan* wash, cf. OE *thwéan*]

tow·er, n., & v.i. Tall usu. equilateral (esp. square) or circular structure, often forming part of church or other large building; (fig.) place of defence, protector (*t. of strength*, champion, comforter, &c.); MARTELLO *t.*; *water-t.*, pipe used to secure high head of water at fires, also, t. supporting tank for distribution of water at high pressure; *the T. (of London)*, assemblage of buildings now used as arsenal & repository of objects of public interest, orig. a fortress & palace & later used as State prison; (v.i.) reach high (*above* surroundings, often fig. of eminent person, as *towers above his contemporaries*), (of eagle &c.) soar or be poised aloft, (of wounded bird) shoot straight up, (part.) high, lofty, (fig.) *a towering* (violent) *rage, passion*. Hence **tow·ered**[2], **tow·ery**[2], aa. [(vb f. n.) f. OF *tur* f. L *turris*]

town, n. (Hist.) collection of houses enclosed by wall or hedge; considerable collection of dwellings &c. (larger than *village*; often opp. to *country*), esp. one not created a CITY; the people of a t., as *the whole t. knows of it, is the talk of the t.* (talked about by everyone in the t.); (without *the*) London or the chief city or town in speaker's neighbourhood, as *went up to t.* (London) *from York, is not in t., is out of t.*; *man about t.*, fashionable idler esp. in London; PAINT[2] *the t. red*; COUNTY *t.*; *t. & GOWN*; *t. clerk*, official who makes & keeps t. records; *t. council(lor)*, (member of) governing body in municipality; *t.* CRIER; *t. hall*, building for transaction of official business of t., often also used for public entertainment &c.; *t. house*, one's t. (as opp. to *country*) residence; *tow·nsfolk*, inhabitants of a particular t. or of tt.; *tow·nsman*, inhabitant of a town, fellow citizen; *tow·nspeople*, the people of a t.; *t. talk*, the talk of the t. Hence **tow·nless**, **tow·nward**, aa., **tow·nlet** n., **tow·nward(s)** adv. [OE *tūn*, cf. Du. *tuin*, ON *tūn*, G *zaun* hedge]

townee·, n. (univ. slang). Inhabitant of university town who is not a member of the university. [-EE]

tow·nship, n. (Hist.) community inhabiting a manor, parish, &c., manor or parish as a territorial division, small town or village forming part of a large parish, or being one of the parishes into which a larger one had been divided; (U.S. & Can.) division of county with some corporate powers, district six miles square; (Austral.) site laid out for town. [OE *túnscipe*, see TOWN, -SHIP]

to·xic, a. Of poison, as *t. symptoms*; poisonous; *t. anaemia, epilepsy*, &c. (caused by poison). Hence **to·xically**, **toxicolo·gically**[2], advv., **to·xicant** a. & n., **toxicolo·gical** a., **toxico·logist**, **toxico·logy**, **toxicoma·nia**, **toxico·sis**, **toxipho·bia**, nn. [f. L f. Gk *toxikon* poison, orig. for dipping arrows in, neut. of *toxikos* (*toxa* bow & arrows, -IC)]

to·xin, n. A poison, esp. one secreted by a microbe & causing some particular disease. [prec., -IN]

toxŏ·philite, n. & a. (Student, lover) of archery. Hence **toxophili·tic** a. [f. Gk *toxon* bow + -PHIL + -ITE[1]]

toy, n., & v.i. Plaything esp. for child; knick-knack, thing meant rather for amusement than for serious use, as *the spinthariscope is a pretty t.*; occupation followed in trifling or unpractical manner, hobby, as *she makes a t.* (amuses herself with needless elaboration) *of housekeeping*; *t.-box* (for keeping one's tt. in); *t. dog, spaniel, terrier*, small kinds kept as pets or curiosities; *toy·shop*; *t. soldier* (of lead &c., or of an army that has no fighting to do); (v.i.) trifle, amuse oneself, *t. with*, deal with, handle, in trifling or fondling or careless manner, as *toyed with a plate of strawberries*, whence **toy·ingly**[2] adv. [(vb f. n.) etym. dub.; once in 1303, =amorous play; common f. 1530, cf. Du. *tuig* tool, stuff, trash, (*speeltuig* toy). & G *zeug* (*spielzeug* toy)]

Toy·nbee Hall, n. Institution in Whitechapel founded in 1885 by members of Oxf. & Camb. Univv. as a SETTLEMENT in memory of A. Toynbee, social reformer.

tra-, pref. alternating with TRANS- before consonants in some wds of L orig.

trābea·tion, n. Use of beams (not arches or vaulting) in construction. So **tra·beate(d)** [-ATE[2](2)] aa. [f. L *trabs* beam + -ATION]

trabĕ·cula, n. (pl. *-ae*). (Anat.) supporting band or bar of connective tissue &c.; (Bot.) beam-like projection or process. Hence **trabe·cular**[1], **trabe·culate(d)** [-ATE[2](2)], aa. [L, dim. of *trabs* beam]

traca·sseries (-rē), n. pl. Petty worries & entanglements & quarrels. [F]

trace[1], v.t., & n. Delineate, mark out, sketch, write esp. laboriously, as *traced (out) a plan of the district, traced the words* *with a shaking hand,* (fig.) *the policy traced* (*out*) *by him was never followed*; (also *t. over*) copy (drawing &c.) by following & marking its lines on superimposed sheet (esp. of *tracing-paper* made transparent with oil of turpentine &c.) through which they are visible or on sheet placed below with carbon paper between; follow the track or path of (person, animal, footsteps, &c., *along, through, to,* &c.); ascertain position & dimensions &c. of (ancient road, wall, &c.) by its remains; observe or find vestiges or signs of, as *his resentment can be clearly traced in many passages, cannot t.* (often = do not think I received) *any letter of that date*; *t. back,* go back over the course of, as *have traced his genealogy back to* (*the time of*) *William I, the report has been traced back to you*; pursue one's way along (path &c.). Hence **tracea**BI·LITY, **tra·ceable**NESS nn., **tra·ce**ABLE a., **tra·ceab**LY[2] adv., **tra·c**ER[1](1, 2) n. (esp. mil., projectile whose course is made visible to gunner by smoke or flame). (N.) track left by person or animal walking or running, footprints or other visible signs of course pursued (usu. pl.); visible or other sign of what has existed or happened, as *of these buildings no t. remains, sorrow has left its tt. on her face, tt. of Italian influence abound in his earlier works*; (loosely) small quantity, as *contains tt. of soda.* Hence **tra·ce**LESS a., **tra·celess**LY[2] adv. [f. F *trace(r)* vb & n. ult. f. L *trahere tract-* draw]

trace[2], n. Each of the two side straps or chains by which horse draws vehicle; *in the tt.*, in harness (lit. & fig.); *kick over the tt.*, (fig., of person) become insubordinate; *t.-horse* (that draws in tt. or by single t., esp. one hitched on to help up hill &c.). [ME *trays* f. OF *trais,* orig. pl. of TRAIT]

trā·cery, n. Stone ornamental open-work esp. in head of Gothic window; decorative pattern or natural outline (e.g. in insect's wing) suggesting this. Hence **tra·ceri**ED[2] a. [f. TRACE[1] + -ERY]

trachē·a (-k-; *or* trā·k-), n. (pl. *-ae*). Principal air-passage of body from larynx to bronchial tubes; each of the passages by which air is conveyed from the exterior in insects, arachnids, &c.; (Bot.) duct, vessel. Hence **trā·che**AL, **tra·che**AN, **tra·che**ATE[2](2), aa., **tra·cheo**- comb. form, **tra·cheo**CELE, **tra·cheŏ·**TOMY, **tra·che**I·TIS, nn. [med. L f. Gk *trakheia* (*artēria*), lit. rough artery, f. *trakhus* rough]

trachē·lo- (-k-) in comb. = Gk *trakhēlos* neck.

trachō·ma (-k-), n. Disease of eye marked by granular excrescences on inner surface of lids. Hence **trachŏ·mat**OUS a. [f. Gk *trakhōma* roughness (*trakhus* rough, see -M)]

trăchy- (-k-) in comb. = Gk *trakhus* rough, as *-phō·nia* hoarseness.

tră·chyte (-kīt), n. Light-coloured volcanic rock rough to the touch. Hence **trachy̆·t**IC a. [F, f. Gk *trakhutēs* roughness (*trakhus* rough) on wds in -ITE, cf. BARYTES]

track, n., & v.t. & i. Continuous line, series of marks, left by person, animal, or thing, in passing along, (pl.) such marks, esp. footprints, as *watched the broad t. of departing ship, followed his t. through the snow, am on his t.* (in pursuit of him, fig. in possession of clue to his conduct, designs, &c.), *presently came on some more of his tt., keep t. of* (follow the course or development of); course taken, as *followed in his t., indicated the t. in which we were to go, t. of a comet*; path. esp. one beaten by use, (fig.) course of life or routine, as *a rough t. runs round the hill-side, covered with sheep-tt., afraid to leave the beaten t.* (of ordinary life; also lit.); prepared racing-path, esp. *cinder-t.* (for runners); continuous line of railway, as *single, double, t.*, one pair, two pairs, of rails; (Mech.) band of the CATERPILLAR kind enabling tractor &c. to do without roads, whence (of vehicle) **tra·ck**ED[2] a.; *in* one's *tt.* (slang), where one stands, there & then; *make tt.* (slang), go or run away, make off; *make tt. for* (slang), go in pursuit of, go after; *off the t.*, off the scent, (fig.) away from the subject; *t.-clearer,* kinds of device attached to locomotive, mowing-machine, &c., for clearing t. in front or behind. Hence **tra·ck**LESS a., **tra·ckless**LY[2] adv., **tra·ckless**NESS n. (V.t.) follow the t. of (animal, person, *to* lair &c.); *t. down,* reach, capture, by tracking; trace, make *out,* (course, development, &c.) by vestiges; tow (boat) by rope &c. from bank; (v.i., of wheels) so run that the hinder is exactly in the first's t. Hence **tra·ck**ER[1] n. (in vbl senses, & esp. wooden connecting-rod in organ mechanism). [f. OF *trac* perh. f. MDu, *treck* (*trecken* draw); vb f. n., but in sense *tow* direct f. Du.]

tra·ckage (-ĭj), n. Towage; railway-tracks collectively, amount of these. [-AGE]

tract[1], n. Region, area, of indefinite (usu. large) extent, as *a t. of sand, pathless tt.*; (Anat.) area of organ or system, as *olfactory, optic, respiratory, t.*; (archaic) period (*of* time &c.). [f. L *tractus -ūs,* vbl n. f. *trahere tract-* draw]

tract[2], n. Short treatise or discourse esp. on religious subject; (R.-C. Ch. &c.) a form of anthem; *Tt. for the Times, Oxford Tt.*, see TRACTARIANISM. [abbr. of TRACTATE]

tra·ctable, a. (Of persons, rarely of materials &c.) easily handled, manageable, pliant, docile. Hence **tractab**I·LITY **tra·ctable**NESS, nn., **tra·ctab**LY[2] adv.

[f. L *tractabilis* (*tractare* handle, freq. of *trahere tract-* draw, -BLE)]

Tractār·ian, a. & n. (Adherent, promoter) of Tractarianism. [TRACT[2] + -ARIAN]

Tractar·ianism, n. (Also *Oxford movement*) High-Church reaction towards Roman-Catholicism & against rationalism & formalism, voiced by Newman, Pusey, Keble, Froude, &c., in 90 tracts (*Tracts for the Times*) published at Oxford 1833–41. [-ISM]

tra·ctāte, n. Treatise. [f. L *tractatus -ūs* (*tractare*, see TRACTABLE)]

tra·ction, n. Drawing of a body along a surface, as *electric, steam, t.*; *line of t.*, that in which the force of t. acts, *angle of t.* (between line of t. & plane in which body is drawn); contraction e.g. of muscle, as *t. aneurysm* (produced by t.); *t.-engine*, movable steam-engine for dragging heavy load on ordinary road, or gang of ploughs &c.; *t.-wheel*, driving-wheel of locomotive &c. Hence or cogn. **tra·ctionAL, tra·ctIVE,** aa. [f. med. L *tractionem* f. L *trahere tract-* draw, see -ION]

tra·ctor, n. Traction-engine; stationary or locomotive motor engine for hauling; aeroplane with engine in front (opp. *pusher*). [LL, = puller (*trahere* see prec., -OR[2])]

trade, n., & v.i. & t. Business, esp. mechanical or mercantile employment opp. to *profession*, carried on as means of livelihood or profit; JACK[1] *of all tt.*; *two of a t. never agree*; *trick of the t.*, device for attracting custom, gaining advantage of rival, &c.; *the t.*, (colloq.) the licensed victuallers, (naut. slang) submarine branch of navy; exchange of commodities for money or other commodities, commerce, as *foreign t.*, exportation & importation of goods from & to home country or exchange of commodities of different countries, *domestic* or *home t.* (carried on within a country); *is good, bad, for t.*, induces, discourages, buying; *carrying-t.*, transportation of goods from one country to another by water; the persons engaged in a t., as *the t. will never submit to it, is unpopular with the book t.*; *Board of T.*, committee of Privy Council supervising commerce & industry, BALANCE[1] *of t.*; FREE[1] *t.*; FAIR[2] *t.*; = *t.-wind*; *t. hall* (for meetings of traders &c.); *t. mark*, device or word or words legally registered (or, formerly, established by use) as distinguishing a manufacturer's or trader's goods; *t. name*, that by which a thing is called in the t., also, name given by manufacturer to proprietary article; *t. price* (charged by manufacturer &c. to dealer for goods that are to be sold again); *tra·desman*, person engaged in t., esp. shopkeeper; *tra·despeople*, tradesmen & their families; *t. union*, organized association of workmen of a t. formed for protection & promotion of common interests, *t.-u·nionism*, this system of association, *t.-u·nionist*, advocate of this, member of t. union; *t.-wind*, wind blowing continually towards thermal equator within parallels 30° N. & 30° S. in Atlantic & Pacific & deflected westwardly by rotation of earth, (pl.) the t.-wind & the (30°–60°) ANTI-TRADE. (Vb) buy & sell, engage in t. (*in* commodity, *with* person); have a transaction (*with* person *for* thing); carry merchandise (*to* place); exchange in commerce, barter, (goods); make a t. of one's political influence, make corrupt bargains in politics, (esp. in part.); *t. on*, take (esp. unscrupulous) advantage of (person's good-nature, one's knowledge of a secret, &c.). [(vb f. n.) ME f. MLG, orig. = path (as TREAD)]

tra·der, n. Person engaged, vessel regularly employed, in trade. [-ER[1]]

tradi·tion, n. Opinion or belief or custom handed down, handing down of these, from ancestors to posterity; (Theol.) doctrine &c. supposed to have divine authority but not committed to writing, esp. (1) laws held by Pharisees to have been delivered by God to Moses, (2) oral teaching of Christ not recorded in writing by immediate disciples, (3) words & deeds of Mohammed not in Koran; artistic or literary principle(s) based on accumulated experience or continuous usage, as *stage t., the tt. of the Dutch School*; (Law) formal delivery. Hence or cogn. **tradi·tionAL, tradi·tionARY[1],** aa., **tradi·tionalLY[2]** adv. [f. OF *tradicion* f. L *traditionem* surrender, delivery, tradition, f. TRA(*dere dit-* = *dare* give), -ION]

tradi·tionalism, n. (Excessive) respect for tradition esp. in religion; philosophical system referring all religious knowledge to divine revelation & tradition. So **tradi·tion(al)IST** nn., **traditionali·stIC** a. [-ISM]

trā·ditor, n. (pl. *-ors, -or·ēs*). Early Christian who to save his life surrendered copies of Scripture or Church property to persecutors. [L (*tradere*, see TRADITION, -OR[2])]

tradu·ce, v.t. Calumniate, misrepresent. Hence **tradu·cER[1], tradu·ceMENT,** nn., **tradu·cIBLE** a. [f. L TRA(*ducere duct-* lead) bring over, display, disgrace, propagate]

tradu·cian(ist), nn. One who believes that soul as well as body is propagated (cf. CREATIONISM, 1st sense). So **tradu·cianISM** n. [f. LL *traducianus* f. L *tradux -ucis* layer of vine (as prec.), see -AN]

Trafa·lgar Square, n. London square often made use of for popular demonstrations, with plinth of Nelson column as platform.

tra·ffic, v.i. & t. (-ck-), & n. Trade (*in* commodity lit. & fig.), carry on commerce; barter (esp. fig.). Hence **tra·ffick-**

ER[1] n. (N.) trade (*in* commodity lit. & fig.), as *the t. in raw hides, unscrupulous t. in lucrative appointments*; transportation of goods, coming & going of persons or goods by road, rail, steamship route, &c., number or amount of persons or goods conveyed, as *there is little t. on these roads, the t.-returns* (periodical statements of t.) *on all railways show marked decrease, apply to the superintendent of t.* (on railway). Hence **tra·ffic**LESS a. [(n. f. vb) f. F *trafiquer* f. It. *trafficare* perh. = TRANS.- + -*ficare* -FY in sense *transact*]

tră·gacanth, n. White or reddish gum from certain herbs, used in pharmacy, calico-printing, &c. [f. F *tragacante* f. L f. Gk *tragakantha,* name of shrub (*tragos* goat + *akantha* thorn)]

tragē·dian, n. Writer of tragedies; (w. fem. *tragedienne,* pr. -ĕn) actor in tragedy. [f. OF *tragediane* fem. -*enne,* or f. foll. + -AN]

tră·gĕdy (-j-), n. Drama in prose or verse of elevated theme & diction & with unhappy ending (*t. queen,* tragic actress); (*T*-) t. personified; sad event, calamity, serious accident or crime. [ME & OF *tragedie* f. L (-*oed*-) f. Gk *tragōidia* f. *tragōidos* lit. goat-singer (*tragos* goat + -*ōidos* singer f. *aeidō* sing), hist. doubtful]

tră·gic(al), aa. (-*ic*) of, in the style of, tragedy, as *t. drama, the t. stage, in a t. voice, t. actor, t. irony,* use in Gk tragedy of words having an inner esp. prophetic meaning for audience unsuspected by speaker; sad, calamitous, distressing, as *a t. tale, event, scene.* Hence **tra·gical**LY[2] adv., **tra·gical**NESS n. [f. L f. Gk *tragikos* (*tragos* see prec., -IC, -AL)]

tragico·medy, n. Drama of mixed tragic & comic elements. So **tragico·mic** a., **tragico·mi**CALLY adv. [f. F *tragicomédie* f. L *tragicocomoedia* (as prec., see COMEDY)]

tră·gopăn, n. Horned pheasant. [L f. Gk, name of fabulous bird (*tragos* goat, *Pan,* Gk god)]

trail, n., & v.t. & i. Part drawn behind or in the wake of a thing, long (real or apparent) appendage, as *engine left a t. of smoke behind it, the t. of a meteor*; lower end of gun-carriage; track left by thing that has moved or been drawn over surface, as *slimy t. of a slug*; track, scent, followed in hunting, as *got on, off, the t.*; beaten path esp. through wild region; *at the t.* (mil.), with arms trailed (see vb); *t.-net,* drag-net. (Vb) draw along behind one esp. on the ground, as *was trailing a toy cart, trailed her dress through the mud, trailing clouds of glory*; (Mil.) *t. arms,* let rifles hang balanced in one hand (*right, left, t.*) parallel to ground; tread down (grass &c.) so as to make path; be drawn along behind, as *skirt trails on the ground*; drag (one's limbs) along, walk wearily, lag, straggle; hang loosely; (of plant) grow to some length over ground, wall, &c.; *trailing-wheel,* either hind wheel of carriage. [cf. ONF *traille* & Du. *treil* tow-line, ONF *trailler* & Du. *treilen* to tow; prob. f. L *tragula* drag-net, sledge, f. *trahere* draw]

trai·ler, n. In vbl senses; also or esp.: trailing plant; wheeled chair drawn behind bicycle or tricycle, tram-car &c. drawn behind another. [-ER[1]]

train, v.t. & i., & n. Bring (person, child, animal) to desired state or standard of efficiency &c. by instruction & practice, as *t. up a child in the way he should go, was trained for the ministry, a trained nurse, soldier, trained faculties, did not escape his trained eye*; teach & accustom (person, animal, *to* do, *to* action), as *dog is trained to jump through hoop, trained to all out-door exercises, to obey* or *obedience*; bring (horse, athlete, one*self*), come, to physical efficiency by exercise & diet, as *is training for the boat-race, trains horses, is only half-trained, is over, under, -trained, t. down* (to lower weight), *t. fine* (into exact condition required; t. & i.), *always trains on vegetarian diet*; cause (plant) to grow in required shape (often *up, over,* wall &c.); point, aim, (cannon *upon* object &c.); (archaic) entice, lure, (*away, from* post &c.); (now rare) draw along (esp. heavy thing); (colloq.) go by t., perform (journey) thus, as *shall t. from York to Leeds, t. the rest of the way, we trained it all the way*; *t. off,* (of shot) go off obliquely. Hence **trai·n**ABLE a. **train**EE· n. (N.) thing drawn along behind or forming hinder part, esp. elongated part of woman's skirt trailing on ground or of official robe, long or conspicuous tail of bird; body of followers, retinue, as *formed part of his t., a t. of admirers*; succession or series of persons or things, as *long train of sight-seers, of camels, by an unlucky t. of events, suggested a whole t. of ideas, painful t. of thought, in the t. of* (as a sequel of; *war with pestilence in its t.*); series of railway carriages drawn by same engine(s), as *missed my t., put on a special t.,* EXPRESS[1], *fast, slow,* UP, DOWN[5], THROUGH, CORRIDOR, PARLIAMENTARY, *t., train de* LUXE (F); line of combustible material to lead fire to mine &c.; (archaic) ordered arrangement, condition, as *matters were in a fine t.*; series of connected wheels or parts in machinery; *t.-band* (hist.), each division of London citizen soldiery esp. in Stuart period; *t.-bearer,* person employed to hold up t. of robe; *t.-mile,* mile run by a t., as unit of work in railway accounts. Hence **trai·n**LESS a. [(n. f. F *traîne* & *train*) f. *traîner* vb trail, draw, f. L *trahere* draw]

trai·ner, n. In vbl senses, esp. one who trains horses, athletes, &c., for races &c. [-ER[1]]

trai·ning, n. In vbl senses; *be in* (process of) *t., go into t.,* (for race &c.); *t.-bit,* gag-bit for vicious horse; *t.-college, -school* (for t. teachers); *t.-ship* (on which boys are taught seamanship &c.). [-ING[1]]

trai·n-oil, n. Oil got from blubber of whale (esp. of the right whale). [earlier also *trane, train,* f. MDu. *traen* tear, t., cf. G *träne* tear, exudation from vine]

trait (-ā, U.S. -āt), n. Distinguishing feature in character physiognomy, habit, or protrayal; stroke, touch, (*of* humour &c.). [f. F *trait* n. & p.p. of *traire* draw f. L *trahere tract-* draw]

trai·tor, n. One who violates his allegiance or acts disloyally (*to* country, king, cause, religion, principles, him*self*, &c.). Hence or cogn. **trai·tor**OUS a., **trai·tor-ous**LY[2] adv., **trai·torous**NESS, **trai·tr**ESS[1], nn. [OF, f. L *traditorem* (*tradere,* see TRADITION & -OR[2])]

traje·ctory, n. Path described by projectile moving under given forces; (Geom.) curve or surface cutting system of curves or surfaces at constant angle. [f. L TRA(*jicĕre ject-* = *jacĕre* throw), see -ORY]

tram[1]**,** n., & v.i. & t. (Also *t.-car*) passenger car running on rails laid in public road; such rail; (also *tra·mway, t.-line*) line consisting of such rails; four-wheeled car used in coal-mines; *t.-road* (hist.), road with wooden, stone, or metal wheel-tracks; (v.t.) convey in t., perform (journey) in t.; (v.i.) go in t. [= LG *traam* balk, beam, barrowshaft; in E prob. first = shaft of car]

tram[2]**,** n. Kind of double silk thread used for some velvets & silks. [f. F *trame* f. L *trama* weft]

tra·mmel, n., & v.t. (-ll-). Kinds of net for fish, esp. (also *t.-net*) triple drag-net; shackle, esp. one used in teaching horse to amble; hook in fireplace for kettles &c.; instrument for drawing ellipses &c.; beam-compass; (usu. pl.) impediment(s) to free movement or action (chiefly fig.), as *tt. of etiquette, official routine*; (v.t.) confine, hamper, with tt. (usu. fig.); (p.p., of horse) with white marks on fore & hind feet of same or (*cross-trammelled*) different sides. [(vb f. n.) f. OF *tramail* f. med. L *tramacula* perh. f. *tri-* triple + *macula* MAIL[1]]

tramonta·na (-ah-, -ah-), n. (In Mediterranean) north wind; cold blighting wind in the Archipelago. [It., see foll.]

tramo·ntane, a. & n. (Situated, living) on other side of the Alps; (fig., from It. point of view) foreign, barbarous; (n.) t. person, also = prec. [f. It. *tramontano* f. L TRANS(*montanus* f. *mons -ntis* mountain) beyond the mountains]

tramp, v.i. & t., & n. Walk heavily, as *heard him tramping about overhead*; walk, go on foot, perform (journey), traverse (country), on foot (usu. w. implication of reluctance, weariness, &c.), as *have tramped up & down all day looking for you, decline to t. ten miles in this heat, have tramped the whole country in my time, missed the train & had to t. it*; be a t. (N.) sound of person(s) walking or marching or of horse's steps; journey on foot, walk; iron plate protecting sole of boot from wear & tear of spade in digging; person who tramps the roads in search of work or as vagrant, this mode of life (esp. *on the t.*); freight-vessel running on no regular line; *t.-pick,* lever for turning up hard soil. [ME & G *trampen,* cf. Da. *trampe,* Sw. *trampa*]

tra·mple, v.t. & i., & n. Tread under foot, crush thus, as *trampled to death by elephants*; *t. on,* tread heavily on, (fig.) treat roughly or with contempt, show no consideration for, (person, feelings, &c.); (n.) sound, act, of trampling. Hence **tra·mpl**ER[1] n. [-LE(3)]

tran-, pref. = TRANS- before *s.*

trance, n., & v.t. State suggesting that the soul has passed out of the body; ecstasy, rapture, extreme exaltation; (Path.) state of insensibility to external surroundings with partial suspension of vital functions, catalepsy, also, hypnotic state; (v.t., poet.) = ENTRANCE[2]. [(vb f. n.) f. OF *transe* f. *transir* fall into trance f. L TRANS(*ire* go) go over]

tra·nquil (-kw-), a. Calm, serene, unruffled, not agitated, as *preserved a t. mind, t. scene, t. surface of pond.* Hence or cogn. **tranqui·ll**ITY, **tranquilliz**A·TION, **tra·nquilliz**ER[1], nn., **tra·nquill**IZE(3) v.t., **tra·nquillizing**LY[2], **tra·nquil**LY[2], advv. [f. L *tranquillus*]

trans-, pref. (before s usu. *tran-*, before other consonants sometimes *tra-* in wds of L orig.), = L *trans-* across, beyond, on or to the other side, through, into a different state or place, (*transmit, transcend, transfer, transfix, transform, translate*); as living pref. chiefly in sense 'on other side of', as *-Appalachian, -Caucasian, -frontier* (esp. of Indian empire), *-Gangĕtic* (of the Ganges).

transa·ct (-z-), v.t. & i. Perform, carry through, (business); carry on business (*with* person). So **transa·ct**OR[1] n. [f. L TRANS(*igere act-* = *agere* ACT)]

transa·ction, n. Management of business, as *left the t. of the matter to him*; piece of esp. commercial business done, as *the tt. of a firm, the t. will not bear looking into, mixed up in shady tt.*; (pl.) reports of discussions, papers read &c., at meetings of some learned societies, as *Philosophical Tt.* (esp. of Royal Society of London); (Law) adjustment of dispute by mutual concessions, any act affecting legal rights. [f. L *transactionem* (as prec., see -ION)]

transa·lpine (-z-), a. & n. (Person living) beyond the Alps (usu. from Ital. point of view). [f. L TRANS(*alpinus* ALPINE)]

transatla·ntic (-z-), a. Beyond the Atlantic, American; crossing the Atlantic, as *t. line, steamer.* [TRANS-]

transce·nd (-sĕ-), v.t. & i. Be beyond the range or domain or grasp of (human experience, reason, description, belief, &c.); (t. & i.) excel, surpass. [f. L TRAN(*scendere* =*scandere* climb)]

transce·ndent, a. & n. Excelling, surpassing, as *t. merit, genius*; (Scholastic Philos.) higher than, not included under any of, the ten categories; (Kantian Philos.) not realizable in experience; (esp. of God) existing apart from, not subject to limitations of, the material universe; (n., philos.) t. thing. Hence or cogn. **transce·nd**ENCE, -ENCY, nn., **transce·ndent**LY² adv. [as prec., see -ANT, -ENT]

transcende·ntal, a. & n. =prec. (second sense); (Kantian Philos.) of a priori character, presupposed in & necessary to experience, as *t. cognition*, a priori knowledge, *t. object*, real (unknown & unknowable) object, *t. unity* (brought about by cognition); explaining matter & objective things as products of the subjective mind (esp. in Schelling's philosophy); (pop.) abstruse, vague, obscure, visionary; (Math., of functions) not capable of being produced by the algebraical operations of addition, multiplication, & involution, or the inverse operations, *t. curve* (represented by t. function). Hence **transcende·ntal**LY² adv. [f. med. L *transcendentalis* (prec., -AL)]

transcende·ntalism, n. Transcendental philosophy, esp. that of Schelling & his followers e. g. Emerson. So **transcende·ntal**IST n., **transcende·ntal**IZE(3) v.t. [-ISM]

transcontine·ntal, a. Extending across a continent, as *t. railway.* [TRANS-]

transcri·be, v.t. Copy out in writing. Hence or cogn. **transcri·b**ER¹, **transcri·pt**ION, nn., **transcri·ption**AL, **transcri·pt**IVE, aa. [f. L TRAN(*scribere script-* write)]

tra·nscript, n. Written copy. [as prec.]

transcu·rrent, a. (nat. hist.). Set or running crosswise. [f. L TRANS(*currere* run), -ENT]

transe·ction, n. Cross-section. [TRAN-]

tra·nsept, n. Transverse part of cruciform church, either arm (*north, south, t.*) of this. Hence **transe·pt**AL a. [f. TRAN- +SEPTUM]

transfer·¹, v.t. (-rr-). Convey, remove, hand over, (thing &c. *from* person or place *to* another); make over possession of (property, ticket &c. conferring rights, *to* person); convey (drawing &c.) from one surface to another esp. to lithographic stone by means of transfer-paper; remove (picture) from one surface to another esp. from wood or wall to canvas. Hence **transfera**BI·LITY, **transfer**EE·, **tra·nsfer**ENCE, **tra·nsfer**OR², **transfer·r**ER¹, nn., **tra·nsfer**ABLE a. (*the -ble vote,* electoral method for securing that elected candidate shall represent a majority, each voter signifying on his ballot-paper to which candidate his vote shall be transferred if no candidate has an absolute majority of first preferences), **transfere·nt**IAL, a. [f. L TRANS(*ferre lat-* bear)]

tra·nsfer², n. Transferring; conveyance of property or right, document effecting this; design &c. (to be) conveyed from one surface to another; small toy coloured picture or design transferable from paper on which it is sold to other surface; soldier exchanged from one regiment &c. to another; *t.-book,* register of tt. of property, shares, &c.; *t.-days* at Bank of England, days for t. of consols &c. free of charge (all but Sat. & Sun.); *t.-ink* (for making designs on lithographic stone or t.-paper); *t.-paper* (specially coated to receive impression of t.-ink & transfer it to stone). [f. prec.]

transfigūra·tion, n. Change of form or appearance, esp. that of Christ (*Mat.* xvii. 1–9); (*T-*) festival of Christ's t., Aug. 6. [f. L *transfigurationem* (as foll., see -ATION)]

transfi·gure (-*ger*), v.t. Change in form or aspect esp. so as to elevate or idealize. [f. OF *transfigurer* f. L TRANS(*figurare* FIGURE)]

transfi·x, v.t. Pierce with lance &c.; (of horror &c.) root (person) to the spot, paralyse faculties of. [f. L TRANS(*figere fix-* fix)]

transfi·xion (-kshn), n. Piercing through; (Surg.) amputation by piercing transversely & cutting outwards. [-ION]

transfor·m, v.t. Make (esp. considerable) change in the form, outward appearance, character, disposition, &c., of, as *caterpillar is transformed into butterfly, 10 years in India have transformed him* (in character or physique), *a beard may t. a man beyond recognition.* Hence **transfor·m**ABLE, **transfor·mat**IVE, aa. [f. L *trans*(*formare* FORM²), TRANS-]

transforma·tion, n. Transforming, being transformed, as *has undergone a great t.*; metamorphosis esp. of insects; change from solid to liquid or from liquid to gaseous state or vice versa; (Math.) change from one figure or expression to another equal in quantity; change in blood during passage through capillaries of vascular system; morbid change of tissue into form proper to some different part; *t.-scene,* elaborate spectacular scene in which chief pantomime characters are supposed to change into chief actors of the harlequinade that follows; (shop) woman's artificial head of hair. [f. LL *transformationem* (as prec., see -ATION)]

transfor·mer, n. In vbl senses, esp. (also **tra·nsformatOR²** n.) device for producing by means of an electric current another of different quantity & potential. [-ER¹]

transfor·mism, n. Fact, doctrine, of the development of one species from another; theory of development of complex animals from free organisms united into a colony & changed into organs of a complex whole. So **transfor·MIST** n., **transformi·stic** a. [F (*-me*), as TRANSFORM, -ISM]

transfu·se (-z), v.t. Cause (fluid, fig. quality &c.) to pass from one vessel &c. to another; (Med.) transfer (blood) from veins of person or animal to those of another person, inject (liquid) into blood-vessel to replace lost fluid, whence **transfu·sionIST**(2, 3) n. Hence or cogn. **transfu·SION** (-zhn) n., **transfu·SIVE** (-s-) a. [f. L TRANS(*fundere fus-* pour)]

transgre·ss (-z-, -s-), v.t. Violate, infringe, (commandment, law; often abs.). So **transgre·SSION, transgre·ssOR²**, nn. [f. F *transgresser* f. L TRANS(*gredi gress-* =*gradi* walk)]

tranship. See TRANS-SHIP.

tra·nsient (-z-), a. Not permanent, as *the t. affairs of this life*; of short duration, momentary, hasty, as *a t. gleam of hope, snatched a t. glance*; (Mus.) *t. chord, note* (unessential, serving only to connect). Hence **transiENCE, -ENCY**, nn., **tra·nsientLY²** adv. [f. L TRANS(*ire* go), see -ENT]

transi·lient, a. Extending across from one point of support to another. [f. L TRAN(*silire* = *salire* leap), see -ENT]

transillumina·tion (-z-), n. (med.). Throwing of strong light through organ &c. for purpose of diagnosis. [TRANS-]

transīr·ĕ (-z-), n. Custom-house permit for removal of goods. [L TRANS(*ire* go) go across]

tra·nsit (-z-), n., & v.t. Going, conveying, being conveyed, across or over or through, as *allowed 2 days for the t. of the lake, improved methods of t. by rail, goods delayed in t., loses quality in (the) t.*; passage, route, as *the overland t.*; =*t.-circle, -compass, -instrument*; apparent passage of heavenly body across meridian of place; passage of heavenly body (esp. of Venus as determining solar parallax, or of Mercury) across sun's disk &c.; ***t.-circle, -instrument***, instruments for observing t. of heavenly body across meridian; ***t.-compass***, surveyor's instrument for measuring horizontal angle; ***t.-duty*** (paid on goods passing through a country); (v.t.) cross the disk of (sun &c.). [(vb f. n.) f. L *transitus -ūs* f. TRANS(*ire it-* go)]

transi·tion (-z-), n. Passage, change, from one place or state or act or set of circumstances to another, as *came by an abrupt t. into hilly country, made a hurried t. to indifferent topics, is subject to frequent tt. from high spirits to depression*; (Mus.) change from key to key or from major to relative minor; (Art) change from one style to another, esp. (Archit.) from Norman to Early-English, as (attrib.) *t. stage, period*; *t. tumour* (tending, on recurrence after removal, to become malignant). Hence **transi·tionAL, transi·tionARY¹**, aa., **transi·tionalLY²** adv. [f. L TRANSIT*ionem* (-ION)]

tra·nsitive, a. & n. (gram.). (Verb) taking a direct object expressed or understood (e.g. *pick* in; *pick peas, pick till you are tired*; opp. to *intransitive* as in *picked at the hole to make it bigger*). Hence **tra·nsitiveLY²** adv., **tra·nsitiveNESS** n. [f. LL *transitivus* (as TRANSIT, see -IVE)]

tra·nsitory, a. Not permanent, lasting only a short time; *t. action* (law), one that can be brought in any country irrespective of where the transaction &c. occurred. Hence **tra·nsitoriLY²** adv., **tra·nsitoriNESS** n. [f. OF *transitoire* f. L *transitorius* (TRANSIT, -ORY)]

translate (-s-, -z-), v.t. Express the sense of (word, sentence, book) in or *into* another language, *has translated Homer (into English, from the Greek), his own novels into French*, (fig.) *kindly t.* (say what you mean in plain words); (quasi-pass., of language, style, &c.) lend itself *well* &c. to translation; convey, introduce, (idea, principle) *from* one art &c. *into* another; infer or declare the significance of, interpret, (signs, movements, conduct, hint, &c.), as *this I translated as a protest, translated his gestures to the bystanders*; remove (bishop) to another see; (bibl.) convey to heaven without death; (archaic) transform; (Teleg.) retransmit (message); (slang) make (esp. boots, shoes) of old material; (Mech.) cause (body) to move so that all its parts follow same direction, impart motion without rotation to. Hence or cogn. **transla·TABLE, transla·tionAL** (mech.), aa., **transla·TION, transla·TOR²**(1, 2), nn. [f. OF *translater* (as TRANSFER¹)]

transli·terate (-z-), v.t. Represent (word, or abs.) in the more or less corresponding characters of a different language. Hence **transliterA·TION, transli·teratOR²**, nn. [f. TRANS- + L *litera* letter + -ATE³]

translu·cent (-nz-), a. Transmitting light but not transparent; (loosely) transparent. Hence **translu·CENCE, -ENCY**, nn., **translu·CID¹** (rare) a. [f. L TRANS(*lucēre* shine), -ENT]

transmari·ne (-z-, -ēn), a. Situated beyond the sea. [f. L TRANS(*marinus* MARINE)]

tra·nsmigrate (*or* -mī·g-), v.i. (Of soul) pass into, become incarnate in, a different body; migrate. So **tra·nsmigr**ANT a. & n. (esp., alien passing through one country on way to another), **tra·nsmigrat**OR[2] n., **tra·nsmigrat**ORY a. [f. L TRANS(*migrare* MIGRATE)]

transmigra·tion, n. =METEMPSYCHOSIS, whence **transmigra·tion**ISM(3) n.; migration. [f. LL *transmigrationem* (as prec., see -ATION)]

transmi·t (-z-), v.t. (-tt-). Pass on, hand on, transfer, communicate, as *will t. the parcel, shall t. daily dispatches, will t. the title, the disease, the faculty, to his descendants, his writings have transmitted the principle to posterity*; suffer to pass through, be a medium for, serve to communicate, (heat, light, sound, electricity, emotion, news). Hence or cogn. **transmissi**BI·LITY, **transmi·ss**ION, **transmi·tt**AL, **transmi·tt**ER[1](1, 2), nn., **transmi·ss**IBLE, **transmi·ss**IVE, **transmi·tt**ABLE, aa. [f. L TRANS(*mittere miss-* send)]

transmŏ·grifȳ (-z-), v.t. (facet.). Transform esp. in magical or surprising manner. Hence **transmogri**FICA·TION n. [prob. thr. the n. as corrupt. of *transmigration* (of souls)]

transmuta·tion, n. Transmuting; change into another form, nature, or substance; (Alchem.) change of baser metals into gold &c.; (Geom.) change of figure or body into another of same area or content; (Biol.) change of one species into another, whence **transmuta·tion**IST(2) n.; *t. glaze,* iridescent porcelain glaze. [OF (as foll., see -ATION)]

transmu·te (-z-), v.t. Change the form, nature, or substance, of. Hence or cogn. **transmuta**BI·LITY, **transmu·t**ER[1], nn., **transmu·t**ABLE, **transmu·tat**IVE, aa., **transmu·tab**LY[2] adv. [f. L TRANS(*mutare* change)]

transnor·mal (-nz-), a. Beyond, exceeding, what is normal. [TRANS-]

transoceă·nic (-nz-), a. Situated beyond the ocean; crossing, concerned with crossing, the ocean, as *t. flight* of birds. [TRANS-]

tra·nsom, n. Horizontal (cf. MULLION) bar of wood or stone across window or top of door; *t. window* (divided by t. or placed above t. of door); each of several beams fixed across stern-post of ship; beam across saw-pit; strengthening cross-bar. Hence **tra·nsom**ED[2] a. [f. L TRANS(*trum,* agent-suf.)]

transpā·dane, a. Situated beyond (usu. =north of) the Po. [f. L TRANS(*padanus* f. *Padus* Po, see -AN)]

transpār·ency, n. Being transparent, so **transpār·**ENCE n.; picture, inscription, &c., painted on canvas or muslin & shown up by light behind, wooden framework supporting such picture; (Photog.) positive picture on glass hung in window as ornament or used as lantern slide; porcelain relief whose parts vary in thickness & t.; *his* &c. *T.* (burlesque title = G *Durchlaucht,* cf. SERENITY). [f. med. L *transparentia* (as foll., see -ENCY)]

transpār·ent, a. Transmitting rays of light without diffusion so that bodies behind can be distinctly seen; (fig., of disguise, pretext, &c.) easily seen through, (of motive, quality, &c.) easily seen through attempted disguise; bright, clear, (fig.) free from affectation or disguise, frank; *t. colours,* (in painting) such as when laid lightly on do not hide underlying colours & forms, (in stained glass) appearing only by transmission of light. Hence **transpar·ent**LY[2] adv., **transpar·ent**NESS n. [f. med. L *transparēre* appear, TRANS-, see -ENT]

transpier·ce, v.t. Pierce through. [f. F TRANS(*percer* PIERCE)]

transpire·, v.t. & i. Emit through excretory organs of skin or lungs, send off in vapour; be emitted thus, pass off as in insensible perspiration; (of gas or liquid) move through capillary tube under pressure; (Bot., of plant or leaf) exhale watery vapour; (fig., of secret &c.) ooze out, come to be known; (vulg.) happen. Hence or cogn. **transpīr·**ABLE, **transpīr·at**ORY, aa., **transpir**A·TION (-er-) n. [f. TRAN- + L *spirare* breathe]

transpla·nt, v.t. Plant in another place; remove & establish, esp. cause to live, in another place; (Surg.) transfer (living tissue) & implant in another part of body or in another person's body. Hence or cogn. **transpla·nt**ABLE a., **transplant**A·TION n. [f. L TRANS(*plantare* PLANT)]

transpla·nter, n. In vbl senses, esp.: hand-tool for lifting plants, machine for removing trees, with ball of earth about roots. [-ER[1]]

transpo·ntine, a. Of the part of London on Surrey side of Thames; cheaply melodramatic, like the plays formerly popular in t. theatres. [f. TRANS- + L *pons -ntis* bridge + -INE[1]]

transpor·t[1], v.t. Convey (person, goods, troops, baggage, &c.) from one place to another, whence **transpor·t**ER[1] n.; convey (criminal) to penal colony; carry away by strong emotion (chiefly in pass. as *transported with joy, anger, fear*), whence **transpor·ting**LY[2] adv. [f. L TRANS(*portare* carry)]

tra·nsport[2], n. Conveyance, transportation, from place to place (*T. Workers,* a trade union); (also *t. ship, vessel*) vessel employed to carry soldiers, stores, &c., to destination; transported convict; vehement emotion, as *in a t. of rage, was in tt.* (usu. of joy). [f. prec.]

transpor·table, a. That may be transported, whence **transporta**BI·LITY n.; (of offender or offence) punishable by transportation. [-ABLE]

transporta·tion, n. Conveying, being

conveyed, from place to place; removal to penal colony. [-ATION]

transpo·se (-z), v.t. Cause (two or more things) to change places; (Alg.) transfer (term) with changed sign to other side of equation; change the natural or the existing order or position of (words, a word) in sentence; (Mus.) write, play, in different key, as *transposed from G to B*; *transposing instrument* (producing tunes different in pitch from the written notes), *transposing piano* (on which transposition may be effected mechanically). Hence **transpo·SAL, transpo·SER**[1], nn. [f. F TRANS(*poser*, see COMPOSE)]

transposi·tion (-zĭ-) n. Transposing, being transposed. Hence or cogn. **transposi·tionAL, transpŏ·sitIVE**, aa. [F, f. med. L *transpositionem* f. TRANS(*ponere posit-* place), see -ION]

trans-shi·p (-z-), v.t. Transfer from one ship or conveyance to another. Hence **trans-shi·PMENT** n. [TRANS-]

transubsta·ntiate (-shĭ-), v.t. Change from one substance into another (esp. as foll.). [f. med. L TRAN(*substantiare*, as SUBSTANCE), see -ATE[3]]

transubstantia·tion, n. Change from one substance into another, esp. (Theol.) conversion of whole substance of eucharistic bread & wine into body & blood respectively of Christ (cf. CONSUBSTANTIATION). [f. med. L *transubstantiationem* (as prec., see -ATION)]

transu·de, v.i. (Of fluid) pass through pores or interstices of membrane &c. Hence **transudA·TION** n., **transu·datORY** a. [TRAN-, L *sudare* sweat]

transver·sal (-nz-), a. & n. (Of line) cutting a system of lines; (n.) t. line, (Anat., usu. L *tranversā·lis* pl. *-ēs, transver·sus* pl. *-ī*) muscle, structure, lying across certain parts. Hence **transversa·LITY** n., **transver·salLY**[2] adv. [f. med. L *transversalis* (foll., -AL)]

transver·se (-z-; *also* trā·-), a. & n. Situated, arranged, acting, in cross-wise direction, as *t. artery, ligament, magnet* (whose poles are at sides not ends), *section, strain*; (n.) t. muscle. Hence **transver·seLY**[2] adv., **transver·so-** comb. form. [f. L TRANS(*vertere vers-* turn)]

tra·nter, n. (dial.). Carrier; hawker. [f. med. L *travetarius*, etym. dub.]

trap[1], n., & v.t. & i. Pitfall or enclosure or mechanical structure for catching animals, affording entrance but not exit & often baited & having door or lid actuated by spring; FLY[1], RAT[1], *-t.*; (fig.) trick for betraying person into speech or act, as *is always setting tt. for me, walked straight into the t., is this* (question &c.) *a t.?*; contrivance for suddenly releasing bird, or throwing ball &c. into air, to be shot at; shoe-shaped wooden device with pivoted bar that sends ball from its heel into air on being struck at other end with bat, *t.-ball*, game played with this; U-shaped or other section of pipe so arranged as to prevent return flow of gas by means of liquid replaced whenever t. is used; kinds of wheeled vehicle, e.g. dog-cart; (slang) policeman; =*t.-door*; *t.-cellar*, space under stage of theatre; *tra·pdoor*, door in floor or roof (*t.-door spider*, kind that makes hinged t.-door at top of nest), (fig.) L-shaped tear in cloth &c. (Vb) catch (animal, fig. person) in t.; furnish (stage) with tt. for a play; set tt. in (wood, hedge, &c.); arrest (gas) in t.; supply (drain &c.) with t.; (of steam) be impeded in pipe &c. [OE *treppe, træppe*, cf. MDu. *trappe*, med. L *trappa*, OF *trape*; relation between Teut. & Rom. wds, & w. G *treppe*, Sw. *trappa*, stair, doubtful]

trap[2], n. Dark-coloured eruptive rock of columnar structure; (pl.) portable step-ladder. [f. Sw. *trapp* (*trappa* stair, see prec.)]

trap[3], v.t., & n. Furnish with trappings; (n. pl.) personal belongings, baggage, as *pack up your tt.* [f. F *drap(er)* cloth(e)]

trapan. See TREPAN[2].

trapes (-āps), n., & v.i. Slattern; (v.i., esp. of women) tramp or trudge wearily or in draggletailed way, go about on errands. [vb earlier also *trape*; perh. cogn. w. Du. *trappen* tread]

trapē·ze, n. Cross-bar(s) suspended by cords used as swing for gymnastic exercises; =foll., whence **trape·ziFORM** a. [f. F *trapèze*, = foll.]

trapē·zium, n. Four-sided plane figure of which no two (also, only two; cf. foll.) sides are parallel. [mod. L, f. Gk *trapezion* (*trapeza* table)]

tră·pezoid, a. & n. (Four-sided plane figure) of which only two (or no two; cf. prec.) sides are parallel. Hence **trapezoi·dAL** a. [f. late Gk *trapezoeidēs* (prec., -OID)]

tra·ppēan, a. Of the nature of the rock TRAP[2]. So **tra·ppOID, tra·ppOSE**[1], aa. [-EAN]

tra·pper, n. One whose business is to trap animals esp. for furs; one who tends air-doors in mines. [f. TRAP[1] + -ER[1]]

tra·ppings, n. pl. Harness of horse esp. when ornamental; (fig.) ornamental accessories (*of* office &c.). [f. TRAP[3] + -ING[1]]

Tra·ppist, n. Member of a Cistercian order founded 1140 at Soligny-la-Trappe & noted for silence & other austerities. [-IST]

tra·ppistine, n. Liqueur made at Trappist abbey of Grace-Dieu in France; (*T-*) nun of an order affiliated with Trappists. [-INE[1]]

tra·ppy, a. (colloq.). Tricky, treacherous, (chiefly of things). Hence **tra·ppiNESS** n. [f. TRAP[1] + -Y[2]]

trash, n., & v.t. Worthless or waste stuff, rubbish, refuse; loppings of trees &c.,

(W. Ind.) stripped leaves of sugarcane used as fuel; thing, e. g. literary production, of bad workmanship or material; nonsensical talk; *cane-t.*, refuse of crushed sugarcanes & dried leaves & tops, used as fuel; *t.-house* (on sugar-plantation, for storing bagasse & cane-t.); *t.-ice*, broken ice mixed with water (v.t.) strip (sugarcanes) of outer leaves. Hence **tra·sh**ERY(1), **tra·shi**NESS, nn., **tra·shi**LY[2] adv., **tra·sh**Y[2] a. [(n.) cf. Icel. *tros* rubbish, leaves & twigs as fuel]

trass, ta·rras, n. A volcanic earth formerly imported as cement-material. [Du. *terras, tras,* f. Rom. (L *terra* earth, -ACEOUS)]

trattori·a (-ēa), n. Italian eating-house. [It.]

trau·ma, n. Morbid condition of body produced by wound or external violence. So **trau·mat**ISM n. [f. Gk *trauma -matos* wound]

traumă·tic, a. & n. Of, (medicine) for, wounds. [f. LL f. Gk *traumatikos* (as prec., see -IC)]

tră·vail, n., & v.i., (archaic). (Suffer) pangs of childbirth; (make) painful or laborious effort. [(vb f. OF *travailler*) OF, = toil, prob. f. LL *trepalium* instrument of torture (L *tres* three, *palus* stake)]

tră·vel, v.i. & t. (-ll-), & n. Make a journey esp. one of some length to distant countries, as *ordered to t. for his health, spent his life in travelling*; act as COMMERCIAL traveller (*for* firm, *in* commodity); (of machine or part) move (*along* bar &c., *in* groove &c.); pass esp. in deliberate or systematic manner from point to point, as *his eye travelled over the scene, mind travels over the events of the day*; (of deer &c.) move onwards in feeding; move, proceed, in specified manner or at specified rate, perform (distance), as *horse travels slowly, light travels faster than sound, travels thousands of miles per second, train travelled 1,000 miles a day*; journey through, as *travelled France from end to end*; cause (herds &c.) to t.; (p.p.) experienced in travelling, as *is a travelled man*; *t. out of the record*, wander from subject; *travelling-cap, -dress,* &c. (of form convenient for travelling). (N.) travelling esp. in foreign countries, as *is much improved by t., has returned from his tt., is going to publish* (account of) *his tt., cannot read books of t.* or *tt.*; range, rate, mode, of motion of a part in machinery, as *has extended, improved, the t. of the valves*; (of person, clothes, &c.) *t.-soiled, -stained, -worn,* &c. (as result of t.). [differentiated f. prec.]

tra·veller (-vl-), n. In vbl senses, esp.: kinds of moving mechanism (esp. overhead crane on rails); = COMMERCIAL *t.*; *bona fide t.*, one entitled to call for refreshment on Sunday at public house by having walked 3 miles; *tip* person *the t.*, impose on him, tell him lies; *t.'s tale*, presumable lie; *t.'s-joy*, a climbing plant. [-ER[1]]

tră·velogue (-ŏg), n. Illustrated lecture-narrative of expedition &c. [irreg. f. *travel* + -LOGUE]

tră·verse, a., n., & v.t. & i. (Archaic in gen. use) = TRANSVERSE; (Herald.) crossing shield from side to side; *t. sailing* (on zigzag track). (N.) thing, esp. part of structure, that crosses another; (Fortif.) earthwork in form of parapet protecting covered way &c., double or quadruple right-angle in trench (˥, ˥˩˥) to prevent enfilading; gallery from side to side of church &c.; (Geom.) transversal line; (Naut.) zigzag line taken by ship owing to contrary winds or currents (*work, solve, a t.*, compute direct distance so covered); sideways movement of part in machine; sideways motion across face of precipice from one practicable line of ascent or descent to another, place where this is necessary; (Law) denial esp. of allegation of matter of fact; (archaic) thwarting circumstance; turning of gun to required direction; *t.-table*, nautical table used in solving tt., platform for shifting engine &c., from one line of rails to another. (Vb) travel or lie across, as *must t. a vast extent of country, district traversed by canals, wall traversed by beam*; make a t. in climbing; (fig.) consider, discuss, the whole extent of (subject); turn (gun); plane (wood) across grain; deny esp. (Law) in pleading; thwart, frustrate, oppose, (plan, opinion); (of needle of compass &c.) turn (as) on pivot; (of horse) walk crosswise; *traversing pulley* (running over rope &c. that supports it). [(vb f. F *traverser*, n. partly thr. adj.) f. F *travers -rse*, f. L as TRANSVERSE]

tra·verser, n. In vbl senses, esp. railway traverse-table. [-ER[1]]

tră·vertin(e), n. Porous light-yellow rock, a calcareous deposit from springs, hardening on exposure and used in Italy for building. [f. It. *travertino* f. L *tiburtinus* (*lapis* stone) of Tibur (Tivoli), see -INE[1]]

tră·vesty, v.t., & n. Make (subject &c.) ridiculous (intentionally or not) by treatment of it; (of person or thing, e.g. literary work) be a ridiculous imitation of (another); (n.) such treatment, such imitation, (*of*). [(vb & n. f. obs. adj.) f. F *travesti* p.p. of *travestir* disguise, change the clothes of, f. It. TRA(*vestire* clothe f. L *vestire* f. *vestis* clothing)]

trawl, v.t. & i.. & n. Drag (t.-net), catch fish in t.-net. Hence **traw·l**ING[1] n. (N.): (also *t.-net*) large bag-net with wide mouth held open by beam (*beam-t.*) or otherwise, meant to be dragged along the bottom by boat; (U.S.; also *t.-line*) long sea-fishing line buoyed & supporting short lines with baited hooks; *t.-anchor* (for anchoring t.-line); *t.-boat* (for setting t.-line or drawing t.-net). [f. 16th c., etym. dub.]

traw·ler, n. Person who trawls; trawl-boat. [-ER¹]

tray, n. Flat shallow vessel usu. of wood or metal for placing or carrying esp. small articles on, as *tea-t.*, *pen-t.*, *developing-t.* (in photography); shallow lidless box forming a compartment in trunk. Hence **tray·**FUL n. [OE *trig*, cogn. w. TREE]

trea·cherous (-ĕtsh-), a. Violating allegiance, betraying trust, perfidious; not to be relied on, deceptive, as *t. memory*, *t. ice* (apt to give). Hence or cogn. **trea·cherous**LY² adv., **trea·cherous**NESS, **trea·cher**Y¹, nn. [f. OF *trechereus* (*trecheur* a cheat f. *trechier* deceive perh. cogn. w. TRICK, -OUS)]

trea·cle (-ēkl), n. Syrup got in refining sugar; (loosely) = MOLASSES; kinds of saccharine fluid, e. g. sap of birch. Hence **trea·cl**Y² a. [earlier = THERIAC; f. OF *triacle* f. L as THERIAC]

tread (-ĕd), v.i. & t. (*trod*, archaic *trode*; *trodden*), & n. Set down one's foot, walk, step, (of foot) be set down, as *do not t. on the grass*, *trod on a snake*, *t. lightly*, (fig.) deal cautiously with delicate subject, *where no foot may t.*, *where angels fear to t.*, *t. in* person's (*foot*)*steps*, (fig.) follow his example, *t. on* person's *corns* or *toes*, (fig.) offend him, *t. on the heels of*, (lit., & fig. of event &c.) come closely or immediately after, *t.* or *seem to t. on air* (of person transported with joy), *t. on* or *as on eggs* (of person in situation requiring much tact), *t.* (set one's foot lit. or fig. as sign of supremacy) *on the neck of* person, *t.* AWRY; walk upon, press or crush with the feet, as *treads a perilous path*, *trod the room from end to end*, *t. grapes* (in making wine), *wine*; perform, execute, in walking &c., as *trod a dozen hurried paces*, *t. a measure* (in dancing); (of cock) copulate with (hen, or abs.); *t. down*, press down with feet, trample on, destroy, as *t. down the earth round the roots*, *t. down Satan under our feet*; *t. in*, press in or into earth &c. with feet; *t. out*, stamp out (fire, fig. insurrection &c.), press out (wine, grain) with feet; *t. the stage* or *boards*, be an actor, appear on stage; *t. under foot*, (fig.) destroy, treat contemptuously; *t. water*, maintain upright position in deep water. (N.) manner, sound, of walking, as *recognized his heavy t.*, *approached with cautious t.*; (of male bird) copulation; (also *t.-board*) top surface of step or stair, each step of treadmill; piece of metal or rubber placed on step to lessen wear or sound; part of wheel that touches ground or rails, part of rail that wheels touch; part of stilt on which foot rests; part of boot-sole that rests on ground; distance between pedals of bicycle; cicatricule of egg (formerly supposed to appear only in fecundated eggs); *trea·dmill*, appliance for producing motion by the stepping of man or horse &c. on movable steps on revolving cylinder, esp. kind used in prisons as punishment, (fig.) monotonous routine; *t.-wheel*, treadmill or similar appliance. [(n. f. vb) OE *tredan*, cf. Du. *treden*, G *treten*, ON *trotha*]

trea·dle (-ĕdl), n., & v.i. Lever moved by foot & imparting motion to machine, e.g. lathe, sewing-machine, bicycle, reed-organ; *t.-machine*, *-press*, printing-press worked by t.; (v.i.) work t. Hence **trea·dl**ER¹ n. [(vb f. n.) OE *tredel* step (as prec.)]

trea·son (-ēzn), n. (Also *high t.*) violation by subject of allegiance to sovereign or to chief authority of State (e. g. compassing or intending sovereign's death, levying war against him, adhering to his enemies, killing his wife or heir, violating his wife or eldest unmarried daughter or heir's wife, killing chancellor or treasurer or justice, abetting marriage of sovereign under 18 years of age without written consent of regent & parliament); breach of faith, disloyalty, (*to* cause, friend, &c.); *constructive t.* (held in law as equivalent to t. though not intended or realized as such); MISPRISION¹ *of t.*; *t.-felony*, attempt to depose sovereign or levy war in order to compel change of measures, intimidate parliament, or stir up foreign invasion. Hence **trea·son**OUS a. [f. OF *traïson*, as TRADITION]

trea·sonable, a. Involving the crime, guilty, of treason. Hence **trea·sonable**NESS n., **trea·sonab**LY² adv. [-ABLE]

trea·sure (-ĕzh*er*), n., & v.t. Precious metals or gems, hoard of these, accumulated wealth, as *buried t.*, *had amassed great t.* or *tt.*, *a voyage in quest of t.*, (not now in colloq. use); thing valued for rarity, workmanship, associations, &c., as *art tt.*, *absorbed in his latest t.* (book, picture, &c.); (colloq.) beloved person esp. child, as (voc.) *my t.*; (colloq.) highly efficient or satisfactory person e. g. servant, as *the girl is a perfect t.* (Vb) store (usu. *up*) as valuable; receive, regard, as valuable, store (usu. *up*) in memory, (person's words, looks, &c.); *t.-city* (bibl.), city for stores & magazines; *t.-house*, place where tt. (esp. fig.) are kept; *t. trove* [see TROVER], gold &c. found hidden in earth & of unknown ownership. [f. OF *tresor* f. L f. Gk *thēsauros*]

trea·surer, n. Person in charge of funds of society, company, club, &c.; officer authorized to receive & disburse public revenues; *Lord High Treasurer* (hist.), crown officer with duties now discharged by Lords of the Treasury; *T. of the Household*, official ranking next to Lord Steward. Hence **trea·surer**SHIP n. [f. OF *tresor*(*i*)*er* f. LL *thesaurarius* (as prec., see -ARY¹, -IER)]

trea·sury (-zh*er*ĭ), n. Place, building, where treasure is stored, (fig.) book, person, &c., viewed as repository of information &c.; place where public revenues are kept; department managing public revenue of a country, officers of this; *T. Board, Lords* (*Commissioners*) *of the T.*, board in charge of British public revenue, viz. *First Lord of the T.*, usu. prime minister, Chancellor of the Exchequer, & 3 junior lords; *T. bench*, front bench on right hand of Speaker in H. of Commons, occupied by First Lord of T. (if a commoner), Chancellor of Exchequer, & other members of ministry; *t. bill*, bill of exchange issued by the T. to raise money for temporary needs & sold to highest bidder; *t. note*, = CURRENCY *note*, (U.S.) note issued by T. & receivable for government dues; *T. warrant* (issued by T. for sums disbursed by Exchequer). [f. OF *tresorie* (as TREASURE, see -Y[1])]

treat (-ēt), v.t. & i., & n. Act towards, behave to, as *how did they t. you?, treated me abominably, kindly, as if I were a child, better t. it as a joke*; deal with (person, thing) with view to result, apply process to, subject to chemical agent &c., as *treated him for smallpox, how would you t. a sprained ankle?, must next be treated with sulphuric acid*; manipulate, present, express, (subject) in literature or art; give (person) food or entertainment at one's expense, as *I will t. you all, think you might t. me to an ice, a theatre,* (of candidate for election) give food &c. or cause these to be given to (electors) in order to influence election, whence **trea·t**ING[1] n.; negotiate terms (*with* person); *t. of*, handle, discuss, (subject). (N.) thing that gives great pleasure, as *pantomime is a great t. to him, what a t. it is not to have to get up early*; entertainment designed to do this, as *school-t.*, picnic &c. for (esp. Sunday-) school children; *stand t.*, bear expense of entertainment. Hence **trea·t**ABLE a., **trea·t**ER[1] n. [(n. f. vb) f. OF *traitier* f. L *tractare* handle frequent. of *trahere tract-* draw]

trea·tise (-ĭz), n. Literary composition dealing more or less systematically with definite subject. [AF *tretiz* (*traitier* as prec.)]

trea·tment, n. (Mode of) dealing with or behaving towards a person or thing, as *received strange t. from him, must vary the t., is now ready for t. with an acid.* [as TREAT, see -MENT]

trea·ty, n. Formally concluded & ratified agreement between nations; agreement between persons (*to* do &c.); *be in t.* (negotiating) *with* (person *for* purchase &c.); *t. port*, one that a country is bound by t. to keep open to foreign trade. [f. F *traité* p.p. of *traiter* (OF *-ier*) TREAT]

trĕ·ble, a. & n., & v.t. & i. Threefold, triple, whence **tre·b**LY[2] adv.; multiplied by three, three times (amount &c., as *the enemy had t. our numbers*); (esp. of boy's voice or boy) = SOPRANO; (n., whist) game won by 5 to 0 counting three points; (vb) multiply, be multiplied, by three, as *has trebled its value, its value has trebled.* [(vb & n. f. adj.) OF, f. L *triplus* TRIPLE; mus. sense from early contrapuntal music in which t. was third part]

trĕ·būchet (-sh-), **trĕ·bucket**, n. (Hist.) military engine for throwing stones &c.; tilting balance for weighing light articles; kind of trap for small birds &c. [OF, f. *trebucher* tumble, f. TRANS- + OF *buc* trunk of body f. WG *bûh* belly (G *bauch*)]

trece·nto (trātsh-), n. The 14th century in Italian art & literature. So **trece·n**TIST(2, 3) n. [It., = three (for thirteen) hundred]

trechŏ·meter (-k-), n. = HODOMETER. [f. F *trechomètre* (Gk *trekhō* run, -METER)]

tree, n., & v.t. Perennial plant with single woody self-supporting stem or trunk usu. unbranched (cf. SHRUB[1]) for some distance above ground; piece or framework of wood for various purposes, e. g. AXLE, BOOT[1], ROOF, SADDLE, SWINGLE, *-t.*, CROSS-TREES; (archaic) gibbet, cross used for (esp. Christ's) crucifixion; CHRISTMAS *t.*; (Math.) diagram of branching lines; *family* or GENEALOGICAL *t.*; *up a t.*, (fig.) cornered, non-plussed; *at the top of the t.*, at the top of one's profession; *t. agate* (with t.-like markings); *t. calf*, calf binding for book stained with t.-like design; *t.-creeper*, kinds of small bird; *t.-fern*, kinds of fern attaining size of t.; *t.-gorse*, = BARNACLE[2](1); *t.-milk*, juice of a shrub used in Ceylon instead of milk; *tree-nail*, pin of hard wood for securing planks &c.; *t. of knowledge of good & evil* (*Gen.* iii); *t. of liberty* (dedicated to liberty & set up in public place); *t. of life* (*Gen.* ii. 9). Hence **tree·**LESS a., **tree·less**NESS n. (Vb) force (animal, fig. person) to take refuge in t.; stretch (boot) on boot-t. [(vb f. n.) OE *trēo* tree, timber, cf. ON *tré*, Da. *træ*, Sw. *trä*]

trĕ·foil, n. & a. Kinds of leguminous plant with leaves of three leaflets & flowers of various colours, clover; kinds of plant with similar leaves; three-lobed ornamentation in tracery &c.; (thing) arranged in three lobes, whence **tre·foil**ED[2] a. [f. OF *trifoil, trefeul*, f. L TRI(*folium* leaf)]

treha·la (-ah-), n. Manna of starch, sugar, & gum, excreted in cocoon form by an insect in Turkey & Persia. [f. native *tīqālah*]

trek, v.i., & n., (S.-Afr.). (Of ox) draw vehicle, pull load; travel by ox-wagon; migrate; (slang) clear out or depart; (n.) such journey, each stage of journey, organized migration. Hence **tre·kk**ER[1] n. [f. Du. *trekken* vb, *trek* n.]

tre·llis, n., & v.t. (Also *t.-work*) lattice,

grating, of light wooden cross-bars nailed together where they cross, similar structure of wire or metal; summer-house, screen, &c., made of t.-work; (vb) furnish, support (vine &c.), with t. [(vb f. n) f. OF *treliz* f. L TRI(*licem*, nom. *-ix*, f. *licium* warp-thread) three-ply]

tre·mble, v.i., & n. Shake involuntarily from fear, agitation, physical weakness, &c., as *he trembled with anger, voice trembled with excitement, hands t. from over-smoking* &c.; (fig.) be in state of extreme agitation, fear, suspense, &c., as *I t. to think what has become of him, t. at the thought, no cause to t. before his judge, hear & t.* (be duly impressed)*!*, *I t.* (am alarmed) *for his safety, in trembling uncertainty*; move in quivering manner, as *leaves t. in the breeze, trembling* POPLAR, (fig.) *his fate, life,* &c., *trembles in the balance* (has reached a critical point, is in extreme danger). Hence or cogn. **tre·mble**MENT n. (poet. rare), **tre·mbling**LY² adv., **tre·mbl**Y² a. (N.) trembling, quiver, as *there was a t. in her voice,* (colloq.) *was all of a t.* (trembling all over); (pl.) kinds of (esp. cattle-) disease, with trembling. [(n. f. vb f. F *trembler* f. med. L *tremulare* as TREMULOUS]

tre·mbler, n. In vbl senses; also or esp.: automatic vibrator for making & breaking electric circuit; electric bell. [-ER¹]

trĕ·mellose, a. (bot.). Jelly-like, shaking like jelly. [f. mod. L *Tremella*, genus of jelly-like fungi, + -OSE¹]

treme·ndous, a. Awful, fearful, overpowering, (colloq.) considerable, as *a t. explosion, revolution, makes a t. difference, a t.* (huge) *blue-bottle*. Hence **treme·ndous**LY² adv., **treme·ndous**NESS n. [f. L *tremendus* (*tremere* tremble, see -ND¹) + -OUS]

tremola·ndo, adv. (mus.). Tremulously. [It.]

trĕ·molant, -mulant, n. Device in organ for producing tremolo effect. [(*-ol-* f. It. *tremolante*) f. med. L as TREMBLE, see -ANT]

trĕ·molo, n. (mus.). Intentionally tremulous effect in vocal or instrumental music; = prec. [It., as TREMULOUS]

trĕ·mor, n. (Of leaf, part of body, voice, person) shaking, quivering; thrill (of fear, exultation, &c.); *intention t.* (in part of body when it moves to do something); *metallic t.*, trembling palsy of metal-workers. Hence **tre·mor**LESS a. [ME & OF, f. L *tremorem* (*tremere* tremble, see -OR¹)]

trĕ·mulous, a. Trembling, quivering, as *t. leaves, voice, hand*; *t. line* (drawn by t. hand); timid, vacillating. Hence **tre·mulous**LY² adv., **tre·mulous**NESS n. [f. L *tremulus* (*tremere* tremble, shake) + -OUS]

trench (-tsh), v.t. & i., & n. Dig ditch in (ground); turn over the earth of (field &c.) by digging succession of contiguous ditches; cut groove in (wood &c.); proceed, make one's way, (*down, along,* &c.) by trenching; encroach (*up*)*on* (person's rights, privacy, &c.); verge or border closely (*up*)*on* (heresy, vulgarity, &c.). Hence **tre·nch**ER¹ [-ER¹] n. (N.) deep furrow or ditch; (Mil.) ditch often 7 ft deep with earth thrown up to form parapet, as *open* (begin digging) *the tt., mount* (guard in) *the tt.*; *t.-cart*, hand-cart on low wheels for use in tt.; *t. coat*, soldier's mackintosh; *t. foot*, affection of feet or legs with sloughing &c. caused by much standing in water; *t. mortar*, light simple kind throwing heavy charge of high explosive short distance for use in tt. [f. OF *trenchier* cut prob. ult. f. L *truncare* TRUNCATE]

tre·nchant, a. Sharp, keen, as *t. sword, blade*, (now rare in lit. sense); (fig., of style, language, policy, &c.) penetrating, incisive, decisive, vigorous. Hence **tre·nch**ANCY n., **tre·nchant**LY² adv. [OF, part. as prec.]

tre·ncher² (for *t.*¹ see TRENCH), n. Wooden platter now chiefly used for cutting bread on at table; (archaic) the pleasures of the table, eating, (chiefly attrib. or in comb., as *t. companions, t.-valiant, good, poor,* &c., *tre·ncherman*, great, small, &c., eater); *t. cap*, square college cap; *t.-fed*, (of hounds) kept by separate members of the hunt, not all together in hunt kennels. [f. OF *trencheoir* (as TRENCH)]

trend, v.i., & n. Have specified general direction, bend or turn away in specified direction, as *coast trends* (*towards the*) *south*; (fig.) be chiefly directed, have general tendency, (*towards* &c.); (n.) general direction & tendency (esp. fig. *of* events, opinion, &c.). [(n. f. vb) OE *trendan* cf. Da. & Sw. *trind* a. round]

tre·ntal, n. Set of 30 successive daily masses for the dead. [f. med. L *trentale* f. L *triginta* thirty + -AL]

trente-et-quarante (F), n. = ROUGE¹*-et-noir*. [lit. = 30 & 40]

trepa·n¹, n., & v.t. (-nn-). Surgeon's cylindrical saw for removing part of bone of skull to relieve brain; borer for sinking shafts; (v.t.) perforate (skull) with t. So **trepan**A·TION, **trepa·nn**ING¹ n. [f. F *trépan*(*er*) n. & vb f. med. L *trepanum* f. Gk *trupanon* (*trupaō* bore f. *trupa* hole)]

trepa·n², v.t. (-nn-). Trap, ensnare, beguile, (*into, from,* place &c., *into doing*). [f. obs. *trapan* a decoy; perh. connected w. *trap*]

trepa·ng, n. Edible sea-slug used in China for soup. [f. Malay *tripang*]

trephi·ne (-ēn, -īn), n., & v.t. Improved form of trepan with guiding centre-pin; (vb) operate on (skull, eyeball, person) with this. [(vb f. n.) assim. of TREPAN¹ to L *tres fines* three ends w. ref. to its shape]

trepida·tion, n. Alarm, flurry; trembling of limbs e.g. in paralysis; (hist.) oscillation of ecliptic formerly assumed to account for precession of equinoxes &c. [f. L *trepidationem* (*trepidare* be agitated, tremble, f. *trepidus* flurried, see -ATION)]

tre·spass (-*as*), v.i., & n. Make unlawful or unwarrantable intrusion (*on*, *upon*, land, rights, &c., or abs.; *t. on* one's *preserves*, fig., meddle in a matter that he has made his own); make unwarrantable claim *on* (chiefly in polite formulas, as *shall t. on your hospitality*); offend (*against* person, law, principle, rights; now literary), as *forgive them that t. against us*. Hence **tre·spass**ER[1] n. (N.) transgression of law or right; (Law) any transgression that is not (misprision of) treason or felony; trespassing (see vb, 1st sense) on another's land with damage; (also *action of t.*) common-law action for recovery of damages for t.; *t.-offering*, sacrifice atoning for t. against Mosaic law. [(n. f. OF *trespas*) f. OF *trespasser* pass over, trespass (*tres-* TRANS- + *passer* PASS)]

tre·ss, n., & v.t. Portion, lock, plait, of hair of human esp. woman's or girl's head; (pl.) hair of esp. woman's or girl's head. Hence **(-)tress**ED[2], **tre·ss**Y[2], aa. (Vb) arrange (hair) in tt. (chiefly in p.p.). [(vb f. F *tresser*) f. F *tresse*, cf. med. L *trecia* perh. f. Gk *trikha* threefold (TRI-)]

tre·stle (-sl), n. Supporting structure for table or flat form or carpenter's work &c., consisting of bar supported by two divergent pairs of legs or of two frames fixed at an angle or hinged; (also *t.-work*) open braced framework of wood or metal for supporting bridge &c.; (Naut., also *t.-tree*) each of a pair of horizontal pieces on lower mast supporting topmast &c. [f. OF *trestel* ult. f. dim. of L *transtrum* TRANSOM]

tret, n. Allowance of extra weight formerly made to purchasers of some goods for waste in transportation. [perh. f. OF *traite* transportation &c. (as TRAIT)]

trevet. See TRIVET.

trews, n. pl. Highlander's tartan trousers. [Ir. *trius* f. *trouse* see TROUSERS]

trey (-ā), n. Card, die, with three spots. [f. OF *treis* three f. L *tres*]

tri- (-ī- before vowel, & before consonant exc. as shown), pref. = L & Gk *tri-* three-, having or composed of three, triple, as: *-ade·lphous*, with stamens in 3 sets; *-a·ndrous*, with 3 stamens; *-a·psidal*, with 3 apses; *-bā·sic*, with 3 hydrogen atoms replaceable by base or basic radical; *-brā·chial* (-k-), three-armed implement &c., esp. a flint implement; *-ca·psular* (bot., zool.), with 3 capsules (to each flower); *-car·pous*, bearing 3 fruits or carpels; *-centenary*, = TERCENTENARY; *-chord* (-k-) a. & n., three-stringed (instrument esp. lute), (of piano) with 3 strings to each note; *-chroma·tic*, three-coloured (*t.-c. photography*, THREE-*colour process*), (of the eye) having the normal three colour sensations, i. e. red, green, & purple, so *-chrō·matism* n.; *-corn*, having 3 horns, (n.) three-cornered hat, (pop., also *-corne*) French gendarme's two-cornered hat; *-cor·poral*, *-cor·porate* (-*at*), (herald.) having 3 bodies & one head; *-cotylē·donous*, with 3 cotyledons; *-crŏ·tic*, (of pulse) with 3 beats; *-cu·spid*, with 3 cusps or points, as *t. valve* of heart, *t. murmur* (heard when this is deranged); *-da·ctyl(ous)*, with 3 fingers or toes; *-de·ntate*, with 3 teeth or prongs; *-di·gitate*, = *-dactyl*; *-dime·nsional*, of 3 dimensions; *-fā·cial* a. & n., (of) the trigeminus; *-flor·al*, *-flor·ous*, bearing 3 flowers; *-fō·liate*, *-fō·liolate*, (of compound leaf) with 3 leaflets, (of plants) having such leaves; *-fo·liated*, (Bot.) = prec., (Archit.) trefoiled; *-form(ed)*, formed of 3 parts, having 3 forms or bodies; *-fur·cate* (-*at*) a., divided into three forks, (v.t. & i., -āt) divide thus; *-gĕ·minal* a. & n., triple, (of) the trigeminus; *-gĕ·minus*, cranial nerve with the 3 functions of motion, common sensation, & taste; *-glot*, written in 3 languages; *-goneu·tic* (entom.), having 3 broods in a year; *-gram*, *-graph*, group of 3 letters representing one sound; *-gynous* (trĭ·j-), having 3 pistils; *-hĕ·dral*, with 3 surfaces; *-ju·gate*, *-ju·gous*, (bot.), having, arranged in, 3 pairs; *-labe*, three-pronged surgical instrument for removing calculi &c.; *-lā·biate*, three-lipped; *-lă·minar*, of 3 layers; *-lă·teral* a. & n. (adv. *-lly*), of 3 sides, (of dealings) to which there are 3 parties, (n.) triangle, t. district &c.; *-le·mma*, choice between 3 things; *-lĭ·near*, of 3 lines; *-li·ngual*, of, expressed in, 3 languages; *-lĭ·teral*, of 3 letters, (of Semitic languages) having (most of) their roots in 3 consonants, so *-li·teralism*, *-litera·lity*, nn.; *-lith*, monument of 3 stones, esp. two upright & one across their tops, so *-lĭ·thic* a.; *-lō·bate*, three-lobed; *-lobite*, member of palaeozoic group of animals with body in 3 main divisions, so *-lobĭ·tic* a.; *-lŏ·cular*, with 3 cells or compartments; *-me·nsual*, *-me·str(i)al*, occurring every 3 months; *-merous*, of 3 members or joints (also *3-merous*); *-mor·phism*, *-mor·phous*, (biol., bot., crystallog.), existence, existing, in 3 distinct forms; *-ner·vate*, three-nerved; *-nō·dal* (anat., bot.), having 3 joints; *-no·mial* a. & n., (technical name, algebraical expression) consisting of 3 terms; *-no·mialism*, use of 3 terms in naming objects in natural history; *-oe·cious* (-ēs-), having male, female, & hermaphrodite flowers each on different plants; *-o·xide*, oxide containing 3 oxygen atoms; *-pe·nnate*, = *-pi·nnate*; *-pĕ·talous*, having 3 petals; *-phthong* (-ĭ-), 3 vowels forming one sound; *-phtho·ngal* (-nggl), so formed;

-phy'llous, three-leaved; *-pi'nnate*, having 3 series of leaflets; *-rā'dial*, *-rā'diate(d)*, radiating in 3 directions; *-ser'ial*, *-ser'iate*, (anat., bot.) disposed in 3 rows; *-sper'mous*, containing 3 seeds; *-spor'ous*, *-spor'ic*, having 3 spores; *-stichous* (trĭs-tik-) (bot.), arranged in 3 vertical rows; *-stigma'tic*, *-sty'lous*, (bot.), having 3 stigmas, styles; *-su'lcate*, (bot.) three-grooved, (zool.) divided into 3 digits or hoofs; *-ter'nate* (bot.) thrice ternate, having 27 leaflets; *-tone*, (mus.) interval of 3 tones; *-valent* (trī-) (chem.), having combining power of 3.

trī'able, a. That may be tried. [-ABLE]

triacontahē'dral, a. Having 30 sides or surfaces. [f. Gk *triakonta* 30 + *hedra* seat, -AL]

trī'ad, n. Group of three; (Chem.) element, radical, with combining power of three; (Mus.) chord of three tones, common chord; Welsh form of literary composition depending on arrangement in groups of three. Hence **triă'dic** a. [f. L f. Gk *trias -ados* (*treis* three, see -AD)]

trī'age (-ĭj), n. Refuse of coffee-beans. [F, = sifting (as TRY, see -AGE)]

trī'al, n. Process or mode of testing the qualities of a thing, experimental treatment, test, as *made t. of his strength*, *was found on t. to be incompetent*, *shall subject* or *put it to further t.*, *will make the t.* (try the experiment), *has been making tt.* or (attrib.) *t. ascents with an aeroplane*; *t. of the* PYX; *bicycle is hired*, *clerk employed*, *on t.* (to be retained only if efficient), *will give you a t.* (employ you on t.); =*t.* HEAT[1]; trying thing or experience or person, esp. hardship, trouble, as *old age has many tt.*, *fear you will find the boy*, *the piano next door*, *a great t.*; judicial examination & determination of issues between parties by judge with or without jury or by referee &c., as *was on his t.* or *stood* or *underwent t. for murder*, *granted a new t.* (on ground of error or injustice in former t.); *t. balance* (of ledger in double-entry book-keeping), comparison of Dr & Cr totals, inequality of which reveals certain errors in posting; *t. eights*, two experimental crews tried against each other with a view to selection of crew for boat-race; *t. trip*, new vessel's trip to test sailing qualities &c., (fig.) experiment. [AF (TRY, -AL)]

trī'angle (-nggl), n. Figure (esp. plane) bounded by three (esp. straight) lines, as *equilateral*, *isosceles*, *scalene*, *right-angled*, *t.*, *spherical t.* (formed on surface of sphere by intersection of three great circles; any three points not in one straight line together with the imaginary lines joining them; implement &c. of this shape, e.g. right-angled t. as drawing-implement, (Naut.) device of three spars for raising weights, (Mus.) rod of polished steel in form of t. open at one angle sounded by striking with steel rod, (hist.) frame of three halberds joined at top to which soldier was bound for flogging; *the* ETERNAL *t.*; *tt. of the neck* (regions into which it is divided for surgical purposes); (*T-*) a northern constellation; *solution of a t.*, finding of the remaining angles & sides when some are given; *t. of forces*, t. whose sides represent in magnitude & direction three forces in equilibrium, fact that such forces can always be represented by a t. [f. L *triangulum* f. TRI(*angulus* ANGLE) a.]

tria'ngular, a. Of the shape of a triangle, three-cornered, so **tria'nguloid** a.; *t. treaty*, *duel*, &c. (between three parties); *t. compasses* (with three legs); *t. numbers*, sums of the series 1, 2, 3, &c., taken to any number of terms, e.g. 1, 6, 28, 55 (w. ref. to mode of disposing such number of points in form of equilateral triangle); *t. pyramid* (with t. base). Hence **triangula'rity** n., **tria'ngularly**[2] adv. [f. LL *triangularis* (as prec., see -AR[1])]

tria'ngulate[1], v.t. Make triangular; divide (area &c.) into triangles for surveying purposes; determine (height, distance, &c.) thus. Hence **triangula'tion** n. [f. TRIANGLE + -ATE[3]]

tria'ngulate[2] (-at), a. (zool.). Marked with triangles. Hence **tria'ngulately**[2] adv. [f. med. L *triangulatus* (prec., -ATE[2])]

trī'as, n. (geol.). Division of rocks underlying the jurassic. Hence **tria'ssic** a. [as TRIAD, f. threefold subdivision in Germany]

triă'tic stay, n. (naut.). Stay connecting fore & main mastheads in fore-&-aft-rigged ships. [?]

trĭ'badism, n. Unnatural vice between women. [f. L f. Gk *tribas -ados* lewd woman (*tribō* rub) + -ISM]

trī'balism, n. Tribal organization. [-ISM]

tribe, n. Group of barbarous clans under recognized chiefs; (Rom. Hist.) each of the political divisions (orig. three, probably representing clans, ultimately 35) of the Romans; any similar division whether of natural or political origin, e.g. *the twelve tt.* of the Israelites (*the ten tt.*, these without Judah & Benjamin; *the lost tt.*, the ten tt. after deportation by Shalmaneser); (Zool., Bot.) group of plants or animals usu. ranking between genus & order; (usu. contempt.) set, number, of persons esp. of one profession &c., as *the whole t. of parasites*, *actors*, *the scribbling t.*; *tri'besman*, member of a t. or of one's own t. Hence **trī'bal** a., **trī'bally**[2] adv. [f. L *tribus*, etym. dub.]

trĭ'blet, trĭ'bolet, n. Mandrel used in making tubes, rings, &c. [f. F *triboulet* etym. dub.]

trībo'meter, n. Sled-like apparatus for measuring friction. [f. F *tribomètre* f. Gk *tribos* rubbing + -METER]

trī'brăch (-k), n. Metrical foot ⏑⏑⏑.

Hence **tribra·ch**IC a. [f. L f. Gk TRI(*brakhus* short)]

tribula·tion, n. Severe suffering or trial. [OF (*-cion*), f. LL *tribulationem* (*tribulare* press, oppress, f. *tribulum* sledge for threshing, f. *terere trit-* rub, see -ATION)]

tribu·nal, n. Judgement-seat, seat or bench for judge(s) or magistrate(s); court of justice (rhet., & often fig., as *before the t. of public opinion*); (in the great war) local board hearing claims for exemption from military service. [L (as TRIBUNE[1], see -AL)]

trĭ·bune[1], n. (Rom. Hist.) each of (orig. two, ultimately ten) officers chosen by the people to protect their liberties against senate & consuls, also, kinds of military, fiscal, & other officers; (esp. as title of newspaper) champion of the people. Hence or cogn. **tri·bun**ATE[1](1), **tri·bune**SHIP, nn., **tri·bun**ARY[1], **tribuni·ci**AL, **-tial** (-shl), **tribuni·**CIAN (-shn), aa. [f. L *tribunus* (as TRIBE)]

trĭ·bune[2], n. Raised floor for magistrate's chair in apse of Roman basilica; bishop's throne, apse containing this, in basilica; platform, pulpit, esp. that used by speakers in French Chamber of Deputies. [F, f. med. L *tribuna* (prec.)]

trĭ·butary, a. & n. Paying, subject to, tribute, as *t. States*; contributory, auxiliary; (of river) serving to swell a larger river; (n.) t. State, person, stream. Hence **tri·butari**LY[2] adv., **tri·butari**NESS n. [f. L *tributarius* (as foll., see -ARY[1])]

trĭ·bute, n. Money or equivalent paid periodically by one prince or State to another in acknowledgement of submission or as price of peace or protection, or by virtue of treaty; state of being subject to tribute, as *was laid under t.*; (fig.) contribution, esp. thing done, said, given, &c., as mark of respect &c., as *the t. of a tear, will not withhold my t. of praise, the tt.* (gifts, compliments, attentions) *of her admirers, floral tt.* (flowers to actress, at funeral, &c.); (Mining) proportion of ore, its equivalent, paid to miner for his work, *t.-work* (so paid). [f. L *tributum* (*tribuere -ut-* give)]

trice[1], v.t. (naut.) Haul up (usu. *up*); haul up & secure in place (usu. *up*); tie up (usu *up*). [f. MDu. *trîsen* hoist, etym. dub.]

trice[2], n. *In a t.*, in a moment. [prob. f. prec., but cf. Sp. *en un tris* in a trice (*tris* clink of breaking glass)]

trī·ceps, a. & n. (Of muscle) three-headed; (n.) t. muscle, esp. large muscle of back of arm. [L (TRI- + *caput -itis* head)]

trĭ·chi. See TRICHINOPOLI.

trichī·asis (-k-), n. Urinary disease in which hair-like filaments appear in urine; disease of breasts in child-bearing women; inversion of eyelashes; disease marked by matted state of hair. [LL, f. Gk *trikhiasis* (as foll., see -ASIS)]

trĭ·china (-k-), n. (pl. *-ae*). Hair-like worm parasitic in body of man, swine, rat, &c., usu. introduced into human body by use of imperfectly cooked pork, & causing often fatal disease. Hence **trichinī·**ASIS, **trichiniz**A·TION, **trichino·**SIS, nn., **tri·chin**IZE(3) v.t., **tri·chinos**ED[2], **trichino·**TIC, **trĭ·chin**OUS, aa. [f. Gk *trikhinos* of hair (TRICHO-, -INE[2])]

trichinŏ·poli, trĭ·chĭ, (-tsh-), n. Kind of Indian cheroot. [*Trichinopoli* in India]

trĭcho- (-k-) in comb. (before vowel *trich-*) = Gk *thrix trikhos* hair, as: *-gen* n., *-genous* a., (preparation) promoting growth of hair; *-logy*, study of the hair; *-pa·thic* a., *-pathy* n., (treatment) of diseases of hair.

trī·chome (-k-), n. Hair, scale, or other outgrowth from epidermis of plant. [f. Gk *trikhōma* (*trikhoō* furnish with hair, see prec. & -M)]

trichō·sis, n. Any disease of hair. [as TRICHO- + -OSIS]

tricho·tomy (-k-), n. Division into three, esp. of human nature into body, soul, & spirit. Hence **tricho·tom**OUS a. [f. Gk *trikha* threefold (*treis* three) + -TOMY]

trick, n., & v.t. & i. Fraudulent device or stratagem, as *I suspect some t., t. of the* TRADE, *shall not serve me that t. twice*; feat of skill or dexterity, knack, precise mode of doing or dealing with a thing, as *conjurer's tt., do the t.* (slang, = accomplish one's purpose), *my dog knows no tt., I know a t. worth two of that* (better expedient), *shall soon get* or *learn the t. of it* (best way of doing or handling it), (attrib.) *t. cyclist* &c.; peculiar or characteristic practice, habit, mannerism, as *has a t. of repeating himself, these are private-school tt., style is disfigured by tt., must cure himself of the t. of archaism*; mischievous or foolish or discreditable act, practical joke, prank, as *is always playing mad tt., a dirty* or *shabby* or *dog's t. to play on any one*; (Cards) the cards played in a round, as *take up the t.*, such round, point gained as result of this, as *won, lost, saved, the t., the* ODD *t.*; (Naut.) man's turn at helm, usu. two hours; *t.-line*, cord used in making changes in pantomime; *t. scene* (made without dropping curtain); *t. wig* (of which hair can be made to stand on end); (Vb) deceive by t., cheat, (person, often *out of* thing, *into doing*, &c.); (of thing) foil, baffle, disappoint the calculations of, take by surprise; play tt.; (usu. *t. out* or *up*) dress, decorate, deck. Hence **tri·ck**ER[1], **tri·ck**ERY(4, 5), **tri·ck**STER, nn., **tri·ck**ISH (now rare, = TRICKY) a. [vb f. n., f. OF *trique* = *triche* (*trechier* see TREACHEROUS)]

tri·ckle, v.i. & t., & n. (Of liquid) flow in

drops or in small stream, as *tears trickled down her cheeks, water trickles through crevice,* (fig.) *the information trickled* (came gradually) *out*; cause (liquid) to do this, pour out in drops; (n.) trickling stream. Hence **tri·ckl**ET[1] n., **tri·ckl**Y[2] a. [ME *triklen*, etym. dub.]

tri·cksy, a. Playful, frolicsome; quaint. [perh. f. *tricks* pl. + -Y[2], but cf. *tipsy, cocksy, Betsy*]

tri·ck-track, ti·ck-tack, n. Complicated form of backgammon. [f. F *trictrac*, prob. imit. of sound]

tri·cky, a. Crafty, prone to deceit; skilful at evasion, resourceful, adroit; (of task &c.) requiring adroitness, full of pitfalls, ticklish. Hence **tri·cki**LY[2] adv., **tri·cki**NESS n. [TRICK + -Y[2]]

tricli·nium, n. (Rom. Ant.; pl. *-ia*). Dining-table with couches along three sides, room containing this. [L, f. Gk TRI(*klinion* f. *klinē* couch)]

trī·colour, -or, a. & n. (Also **trī·colour**ED[2] a.) of three colours; (n.) flag of three colours in about equal proportions, esp. French national standard of red, white, & blue, adopted during Revolution. [f. F TRI(*colore* f. L as COLOUR)]

tricot (trē·co), n. Hand-knitted woollen fabric, imitation of this; kind of ribbed cloth; *t.-stitch*, kind of crochet stitch. [F, = knitting]

trī·cȳcle, n., & v.i. & t. (Ride on) three-wheeled cycle; TANDEM, SOCIABLE, (*t.*). Hence **tri·cycl**IST(1) n. [(vb f. n.) F (TRI-)]

trī·dent, n. Three-pronged implement e. g. fish-spear; such spear or sceptre as attribute of Posidon or Neptune. [f. L TRI(*dens -ntis* tooth)]

Trīde·ntine, a. & n. Of the Council of Trent (1545–63) esp. as basis of Roman Catholic doctrine & practice, as *T. theology*; (n.) Roman Catholic. [f. med. L *Tridentum* Trent + -INE[1]]

trī·duo, -uum, n. (R.-C. Ch.). Three days' service of prayer in preparation for saint's day or for obtaining saint's intercession. [(*-o* It.) f. L TRI(*duum* f. *dies* day) space of three days]

trie·nnial, a. & n. Lasting, happening or done every, three years, as *t. plants, parliaments, T. Act* (requiring t. parliaments, repealed 1716); (n.) t. plant, mass performed daily for three years for soul of dead person, every third anniversary of event. Hence **trie·nnial**LY[2] adv. [f. L TRI(*ennium* f. *annus* year) space of three years + -AL]

trī·er, n. In senses of TRY, esp. (also *trior*) person appointed to decide whether challenge to juror is well founded. [-ER[1]]

trī·erarch (-k), n. (Gk ant.). Commander of trireme; wealthy person compelled to build & equip trireme at his own expense. Hence **trī·erarch**AL a. [f. L f. Gk *triērarkhos* f. *triērēs* trireme + *arkhō* rule]

trī·erarchy, n. Office, duty, of trierarch; (Athenian formation of fleet at expense of) the trierarchs. [f. Gk *triērarkhia* (prec., -Y[1])]

trī·fid, a. (bot., zool.). Partly or wholly divided into three, three-cleft. [f. L TRI(*fidus* f. root of *findere* cleave)]

trī·fle, n., & v.i. & t. Thing, fact, circumstance, of slight value or importance, as *wastes time on tt., the merest t. puts him out,* (iron.) *shall probably break our necks, but that is a t.*; small amount esp. of money, as *spare a t. for the porter,* (adv.) *seems a t.* (rather) *angry*; confection of whipped cream or white of eggs, with pastry &c. soaked in wine, fruit, almonds, &c.; common pewter; *t.-ring*, kinds of puzzle-ring. (Vb) talk or act frivolously; *t. with*, treat (person, thing, matter) with flippancy or derision, refuse to take seriously, (also) occupy oneself carelessly with, toy with, (novel, cigarette, &c.); throw or fool *away* (time, energies, money, &c., *on* object); (part.) *a trifling error, correction, circumstance,* &c. (unimportant). Hence **trī·fl**ER[1] n., **trī·fling**LY[2] adv. [(vb f. n.) ME & OF *trufle* mockery, var. of *truffe* jest, etym. dub.]

trīfor·ium, n. (pl. *-ia*). Gallery, usu. in form of arcade, above arches of nave & choir (& transepts) of church. [med. (Anglo-)L, etym. dub.; prob. not f. TRI- + L *fores* door, being applied f. 12th to 18th cc. only to Canterbury, where the openings are not triple]

trig[1], a., v.t., & n. Trim, spruce, smart; (vb) smarten, deck, (often *up, out*); check, stop, (wheel) with skid, stone, &c.; prop *up*; (n.) obstacle &c. used. [cf. ON *tryggja* vb (*tryggr* firm)]

trig[2], school abbr. of *trigonometry*.

tri·gamous, a. Thrice married or having three wives or husbands at once, whence or cogn. **tri·gam**IST, **tri·gam**Y[1], nn.; (Bot.) having male, female, & hermaphrodite flowers in same head (cf. TRI-*oecious*). [f. LL f. Gk TRI(*gamos* -married) + -OUS]

tri·gger, n. Device for releasing spring or catch & so setting mechanism in action, esp. projecting tongue in firearm that liberates hammer of lock; HAIR *t.* Hence **(-)trigger**ED[2] a. [earlier *tricker* f. Du. *trekker* (*trekken* pull, cf. TREK)]

trī·glyph, n. Each of the grooved tablets alternating with metopes in Doric frieze. Hence **trī·glyph**AL, **triglȳ·ph**IC(AL), aa. [f. L f. Gk TRI(*gluphos* f. *gluphō* carve)]

trī·gon, n. (Astrol.) each of four groups (*watery, earthly, airy, fiery, t.*) of three signs of zodiac; triangular instrument used in dialling; = TRINE; (Gk Ant.) game at ball for three persons, (also *trigō·non*) triangular lyre or harp; (Math.) triangle, whence **trigŏ·n**IC a. [f. L f. Gk TRI(*gōnon* f. *gōnia* angle) triangle]

trī·gonal, a. (Math.) triangular; (Bot., Zool.) triangular in cross-section, as *t.*

stem, antennae. Hence or cogn. **tri·gonal**LY[2] adv., **tri·gon**OUS a. [-AL]

trigonŏ·meter, n. Instrument for solution of plane right-angled triangles by inspection. [TRIGON + -O- + -METER]

trigonŏ·metry, n. Branch of mathematics dealing primarily with relations of sides & angles of a triangle, much used in astronomy, surveying, & navigation. Hence **trigonome·tr**IC(AL) aa., **trigonome·trical**LY[2] adv. [TRIGON + -O- + -METRY]

trike, n. & vb (colloq.). = TRICYCLE. [abbr.]

tri·lby, n. *T.* (*hat*), soft felt kind (colloq.); (pl., slang) feet. [f. G. du Maurier's novel so named]

trill, v.i. & t., & n. (Of person or thing) give forth sound with tremulous vibration, as *trilling laughter*; sing (t. & i.) in quavering manner, esp.(Mus.) with shake. (N.) quavering sound, esp. (Mus.) quick alternation of two notes a (semi)tone apart, shake; consonant pronounced with trilling sound, e.g. *r*. [(n. f. vb) f. It. *trillare* imit.]

tri·lling, n. Compound crystal of three individuals; each of three children born at a birth. [f. L *tres* three + -LING[1]]

tri·llion, n. & a. A million million million; (U.S., after F) a million million. Hence **tri·llion**TH[2] a. & n. [f. TRI- on MILLION, cf. BILLION]

tri·logy, n. (Gk Ant.) set of three tragedies to be performed in immediate succession; set of three literary compositions, speeches, &c., each complete in itself but with common theme. [f. Gk TRI(*logia* -LOGY)]

trim, a., v.t. & i., & n. In good order, well arranged or equipped, neat, spruce, whence **tri·m**LY[2] adv., **tri·m**NESS n. (Vb) set in good order, make neat or tidy, remove irregular or superfluous or unsightly parts from, (lamp or strictly its wick, hedge, beard, &c.); remove (such parts, often *off, away*) by clipping, pruning, planing, &c.; make (person, *oneself*, often *up*) neat in dress & appearance; ornament (dress &c. *with* ribbon, lace, &c.); (of school of fish) *t.* (move along close to) *the shore*; (Naut.) adjust balance of (ship, boat) by distribution of cargo or passengers &c., arrange (yards, sails) to suit wind, as *t.* BY[1] *the head, stern*; hold middle course in politics or opinion, attach oneself to neither of contesting parties, be a time-server; (colloq.) rebuke sharply, thrash, worst in bargain &c.; (colloq.) *t.* person's *jacket*, flog him. (N.) state, degree, of adjustment or readiness or fitness, as *found everything in perfect t., am in no t.* (state of dress, health, &c.) *for rough work, in fighting t.*, (of ship, & fig.) ready for battle; good order (esp. Naut.), as *in, out of, t.*; (Naut.) *t.* (relative position) *of the masts.* [(n. f. vb, OE *trymian* make firm, set in order) f. OE *trum* strong, cf. LG *trim*]

tri·meter, n. & a. (Verse) consisting of three measures (see DIMETER), esp. *iambic t.*, six-foot iambic line usual in ancient Greek dramatic dialogue. Hence **trĭme·tr**IC(AL) aa. [f. L f. Gk TRI(*metros* f. *metron* measure)]

tri·mmer, n. In vbl senses, esp.: one who trims articles of dress, as *coat, hat, -t.*; person who stands neutral, time-server, (orig. of party following Marquis of Halifax 1680–90); kinds of instrument for clipping &c.; piece of timber framed across opening (e.g. for hearth) to carry ends of the truncated joists. [-ER[1]]

tri·mming, n. In vbl senses, esp.: ornamentation of lace &c. on dress &c.; (pl., colloq.) *leg of mutton* &c. *& tt.* (accessories). [-ING[1]]

trine, a. & n. Threefold, triple, made up of three parts, whence **tri·n**AL, **tri·n**ARY[1], aa.; *t. aspersion* or *immersion*, thrice sprinkling in baptism; (Astrol.) of a t., in t. (N.): (Astrol.) aspect of two planets 120° apart, *in t.*, so related (*to*). [f. F *trin trine* f. L *trinus* threefold (*tres* three)]

tri·ngle (-nggl), n. Curtain-rod: supporting rod for canopy of bedstead; (Archit.) small square moulding or ornament; (Gunn.) bar on traversing-platform to check recoil. [F, etym. dub.]

trinitrotŏ·luene, -uol, n. A high explosive (also abbr. *trotyl* & TNT) much used in the great war. [f. TRI-, NITRO-, TOLU, -ENE, -OL]

tri·nity, n. Being three; group of three; *the T.*, union of three persons (Father, Son, Holy Spirit) in one Godhead, doctrine of this, whence **Trinit**AR·IAN(ISM) nn.; symbolical representation of the T. in art; triple pipe-cleaner; *t. ring*, kinds of ancient bronze ring with three bosses &c. found in Ireland; *T. Sunday*, next after Whitsunday; *T. Brethren*, members of *T. House*, association concerned with licensing of pilots, erection of lighthouses, &c.; *T.* TERM. [f. OF *trinite* f. LL *trinitatem* (as TRINE, see -TY)]

tri·nket, n. Trifling ornament, jewel &c. worn on the person; small fancy article. Hence **tri·nket**RY(1, 5) n. [f. 16th c., etym. dub.; cf. obs. *trenket* (TRENCH) small knife, & *trick*]

tri·o (-ēō, -īō), n. (Mus.) composition for three vocal or instrumental parts, set of three performers, second division of minuet, march, &c., orig. performed by t. of instruments; set of three persons &c.; three aces, kings, queens, or knaves, in piquet. [F f. It., f. L *tres* three]

tri·ole (trē-), n. (mus.). = TRIPLET. [dim. of prec.]

For other words in *tri-* see TRI-.

tri·olet (trē-), n. Poem of 8 (usu. 8-syllabled) lines with rhymes as shown, first line recurring as fourth & seventh & second as eighth (cat dog bat cat fat hog cat dog). [F (-LET)]

trī·onal, n. A hypnotic & anaesthetic drug. [TRI- (as containing 3 ethyl groups) + ending of *sulphonal*]

Trīō·nēs, n. pl. = CHARLES'S WAIN. [L, = plough-oxen]

trior. See TRIER.

trip, v.i. & t., & n. Walk or dance with quick light tread, (fig., of rhythm &c.), run lightly, whence **tri·pping**LY[2] adv.; (archaic) take journey or excursion, whence (in mod. use) **tri·pper**[1] n.; make false step, stumble, (often *over* obstacle); make mistake, commit inconsistency or inaccuracy or moral delinquency, as *caught him tripping in his dates, all apt to t.*; (of person or obstacle) cause (person) to stumble by entangling or suddenly arresting his feet (often *up*); detect (person) in blunder (often *up*); (Naut.) loose (anchor) from bottom by means of cable, turn (yard &c.) from horizontal to vertical position; release (part of machine) suddenly by withdrawing catch &c. (N.) journey, voyage, excursion, as *round t.* (to a place & back), *cheap tt. to the Riviera*; nimble step; stumble (lit. & fig.); tripping or being tripped up; the fish caught during a voyage; *t.-hammer*, kind of TILT[1]-hammer. [(n. f. vb) f. OF *treper, trip(p)er*, f. Teut., cf MDu. *trippen*, G *treppe* step]

trīpar·tite (or trĭ·p-), a. Divided into 3 parts; (Bot., of leaf) divided into 3 segments almost to the base; *t. indenture* (with 3 corresponding parts or copies); made, existing, between 3 parties, as *t. treaty*. Hence **tri·partite**LY[2] adv., **tri·parti·tion** n. [f. L TRI(*partitus* p.p. of *partiri* divide f. *pars -rtis* part)]

tripe, n. Principal part of stomach of ox &c. as food, as *will stand anything but t.* (archaic *a t.*); (now vulg., usu. pl.) entrails, belly; (slang) inferior stuff, nonsense, easy bowling &c.; *t.-de-roche* (trē·p-derō·sh) [F, lit. rock-t.], bitter nutritive vegetable substance obtained from some lichens & used at a pinch by hunters &c. as food; *tri·peman*, man who prepares & hawks t. Hence **tri·pery**(3) n. [OF, cf. Sp. & Port. *tripa*, etym. dub.]

tri·plane, n. Aeroplane with three planes. [TRI-, PLANE[3]]

tri·ple, a., & v.t. & i. Threefold, of three parts (often in comb., as *t.-headed, -nerved*); *T. Alliance*, (1) between England, Sweden, & Netherlands, in 1668 against Louis XIV, (2) between France, Great Britain, & Netherlands, in 1717 chiefly against Spain, (3) between Germany, Austria, & Italy, in 1882–3 against Russia & France, (4) of three trade unions combined for political action (railwaymen, miners, & transport workers), dissolved 1921; *t. crown*, pope's tiara; *T.* ENTENTE; (Mus.) *t. time* (of 3 or 9 beats in bar). (Vb) increase (t. & i.) threefold; be three times as great or many as; alter (engine) to t. expansion. [(vb f. adj.) F, f. L TRI*plus* f. Gk *triplous*]

trĭ·plet, n. Set of three things; 3 verses rhyming together; (Mus.) 3 notes performed in the time of two; (colloq.) each of 3 children born at a birth; (Naut.) 3 links of chain between cable & anchor-ring. [f. prec. + -ET[1]]

tri·plex, n. (mus.). Triple time; composition in three parts. [L TRI(*plex -plicis* f. *plicare* fold) threefold]

tri·plicate[1] (-*at*), a. & n. Threefold, esp. of which three copies are made, as *t. certificate*; *t. ratio* of two numbers, ratio of their cubes; (n.) each of a set of 3 copies or corresponding parts, state of being t., as *document drawn up in t.* [f. L *triplicare* (TRIPLEX), -ATE[2]]

tri·plicāte[2], v.t. Treble, make triplicate. So **triplica·tion**, **tri·plicature**, nn. [-ATE[3]]

trĭ·plice (-tshā), n. = TRIPLE *alliance* (3). [It., = triple]

tripli·city, n. State of being triple. [f. LL *triplicitatem* (TRIPLEX, -ITY)]

trī·pod, n. Stool, table, utensil, resting on three feet or legs, whence **tri·pod**AL a.; three-legged stand for supporting camera &c.; (Gk Ant.) bronze altar at Delphi on which priestess sat to utter oracles, imitation of this esp. as prize in Pythian games &c. [f. L *tripus* f. Gk TRI(*pous podos* foot)]

tri·polĭ, n. = ROTTEN-*stone*. [f. *T.* in Africa]

trī·pŏs, n. (Camb. univ.). (List of successful candidates in) honours examination. [as TRIPOD, w. ref. to stool on which B.A. sat to deliver satirical speech at commencement]

tri·ptych (-ĭk), n. Picture or carving on three panels side by side, set of three associated pictures so placed; set of three writing-tablets hinged or tied together. [f. Gk TRI(*ptukhon* f. *ptussō* fold) three-layered, neut. adj. as n.]

trīpū·diate, v.i. (pedant.). Dance for joy; dance in triumph or contempt *upon*. [f. L *tripudiare* (*tripudium* a dance, perh. f. TRI-, *pes pedis* foot), -ATE[3]]

trīquē·tra, n. (pl. *-ae*). Symmetrical ornament of three interlaced arcs. [L, fem. of TRI(*quetrus* unexpl.) three-cornered]

trīque·trous, a. Three-cornered, esp. (Bot., of stem) having 3 acute angles. Hence **trique·trous**LY[2] adv. [f. L as prec. + -OUS]

trī·ēme, n. Ancient esp. Greek warship with three banks of oars. [f. L TRI(*remis* f. *remus* oar)]

Trisă·gion (-g-), n. Hymn in Greek & oriental liturgies with triple invocation of

God as holy. [f. Gk *trisagios* (*tris* thrice +*hagios* holy)]

trise·ct, v.t. Divide (line, angle, &c.) into three esp. equal parts. Hence **trise·ct**ION n. [f. TRI- + L *secare sect-* cut]

tri·smus (-z-), n. (path.). Lockjaw. [f. Gk *trismos* creaking (*trizō* squeak)]

tri·stful, a. (archaic). Sad. [obs. *trist* f. OF *triste* f. L *tristis* sad + -FUL]

trisy·llable, n. Word of three syllables. **trisyllă·b**IC a., **trisylla·b**ICALLY adv. [n. f. TRI- + SYLLABLE; adj. f. L f. Gk TRI(*sullabos*, see SYLLABLE) adj.]

tritagō·nist (*or* -ă·go-), n. Third actor in Greek play (cf. DEUTERAGONIST). [f. Gk *tritagōnistēs* (*tritos* third + *agonistēs* actor, see AGONISTIC)]

trite, a. (Of expression, sentiment, quotation, &c.) commonplace, hackneyed, worn out. Hence **tri·te**LY[2] adv., **tri·te**NESS n. [f. L *terere trit-* rub]

trī·thēism, n. Doctrine that there are (esp. that Father, Son, & Holy Spirit are) 3 Gods. So **tri·the**IST n., **trithei·st**IC(AL) aa. [TRI-]

Trī·ton, n. (Gk Myth.) son of Posidon & Amphitrite, each of a race of minor sea-gods usu. represented as men with fishes' tails & sometimes with forefeet of horse & carrying shell-trumpet; *T. among the* MINNOWS; kinds of gastropod & salamander. [L, f. Gk *Tritōn*]

tri·tūrate, v.t. Grind to fine powder; grind with molar teeth, masticate thoroughly. Hence or cogn. **tri·tur**ABLE a., **tritur**A·TION, **tri·turat**OR[2](1, 2), nn. [f. LL *triturare* f. L *tritura* rubbing, as TRITE, see -URE & -ATE[3]]

tri·umph, n., & v.i. (Rom. Ant.) procession & ceremony in honour of victory & victorious general; state of being victorious or successful, signal success, great achievement, thing that constitutes this, as *returned home in t., has achieved great tt., the tt. of science, hat is a t. of ugliness*; joy at success, manifestation of this, exultation, as *great was his t. on hearing* &c., *could detect no t. in his eye.* (Vb): (Rom. Ant.) enjoy a t.; gain victory, be successful, prevail, (*over* enemy, opposition, &c.); exult (*over* fallen enemy &c., or abs.), whence **tri·umphing**LY[2] adv. [(vb f. OF *triumpher*) f. OF *triumphe* f. L *triumphus* cf. Gk *thriambos* hymn to Bacchus]

triu·mphal, a. Of, used in, celebrating, a triumph, as *t. car, progress, hymn, t. crown* (Roman general's laurel wreath); *t. arch* (built to commemorate victory &c.). [f. F *triomphal* f. L *triumphalis* (as prec., see -AL)]

triu·mphant, a. Victorious, successful; (of person, speech, voice, &c.) exulting. Hence **triu·mphant**LY[2] adv. [f. F *triomphant* (as TRIUMPH vb, see -ANT)]

trīu·mvir, n. (pl. *-rī, -rs*). (Rom. Ant.) each of three men united in office; (Rom. Hist.) each member of first or second triumvirate. Hence **triu·mvir**AL a. [L (*trium*, gen. of *tres* three, + *vir* man)]

triu·mvirate (-*at*), n. Office of a triumvir; set of triumviri; (Rom. Hist.) *first t.*, (coalition 60 B.C. between) Pompey, Julius Caesar, & Crassus, *second t.*, (that in 43 B.C between) Mark Antony, Octavian, & Lepidus; party, set, of three. [f. L *triumviratus* (prec., see -ATE[1])]

trī·une, a. Three in one, as *t. Godhead.* Hence **triu·n**ITY n. [f. TRI- + L *unus* one]

trī·vet, n. Iron tripod for holding cooking-vessels by the fire; iron bracket designed to hook on to bars of grate for similar purposes; *right* (orig. = steady) *as a t.*, (colloq.) all right (adj. & adv.), in good health or position or circumstances; *t. table* (with three feet). [earlier also *tre-*; f. L TRI(*pes pedis* foot) three-footed]

trī·vial, a. Of small value or importance, trifling, as *t. matters, a t. loss* (of something t.), *raised t. objections*; (of person) trifling, shallow, lacking ability or moral qualities; commonplace, humdrum, as *the t. round* (of daily life &c.); (Bot., Zool., of name) popular, not scientific, also, specific opp. to *generic.* Hence or cogn. **tri·vial**ISM(2, 4), **trivia·l**ITY, **tri·vial**NESS, nn., **tri·vial**IZE(3) v.t., **tri·vial**LY[2] adv. [f. L *trivialis* commonplace f. TRI(*vium* f. *via* road) cross-road, see -AL]

trī·vium, n. (hist.). (In medieval schools) the first three liberal arts, grammar, rhetoric, & logic. [see prec.]

-trix, suf. forming fem. agent nn. corresp. to masc. nn. in -TOR, f. L *-trix -tricis*, chiefly in legal terms (*executrix, administratrix*).

troat, v.i., & n. (Make) cry of rutting buck. [imit.]

trō·car, n. (med.). Instrument used in dropsy &c. for withdrawing fluid from body. [F (*trois* three + *carre* side f. L *quadra* square)]

trochā·ic (-k-), a. & n. (Composed) of trochees, as *t.* DIMETER, TETRA*meter*; (n. pl.) t. verse. [f. L f. Gk *trokhaïkos* (as TROCHEE, see -IC)]

tro·chal (-kl), a. (zool.). Wheel-shaped. [f. Gk *trokhos* wheel (*trekhō* run) + -AL]

trocha·nter (-k-), n. (anat., zool.). Each of several bony processes on upper part of thighbone; second joint of insect's leg. [F, f. Gk *trokhantēr* ball of hip-bone (*trekhō* run)]

trōche (-k, -sh, -tsh, -kē), n. Small medicinal circular cake or lozenge. [back form. f. obs. *trochisk* (taken as *trochies* pl.) f. F *trochisque* f. L f. Gk *trokhiskos* dim. of *trokhos* wheel]

trō·chee (-k-), n. Metrical foot – ⏑. [f. L f. Gk *trokhaios* (*pous*) running foot (*trekhō* run)]

For other words in *tri-* see TRI-.

trŏ·chil(us) (-k-), n. Kinds of small bird esp. (1) humming-bird, (2) bird mentioned by ancient writers as picking crocodile's teeth. [f. L f. Gk *trokhilos* (*trekhō* run)]
trŏ·chlĕa (-k-), n. (anat.; pl. *-ae*). Pulley-like part or arrangement. Hence **tro·ch·lear**[1] (anat., bot.), **tro·chleate**[2] (bot.), aa. [f. L *trochlea* pulley, cf. Gk *trokhilia*]
trŏ·choid (-k-), a. & n. (Anat.) rotating on its own axis; (of curve) generated by a point in the plane of one curve that rolls on another; (Conch.) top-shaped; (n.) t. joint, t. curve, kinds of gasteropod. Hence **trochoi·dal** a. [f. Gk *trokhoeidēs* wheel-like (TROCHAL, -OID)]
trocho·meter (-k-), n. =HODOMETER. [as TROCHAL + -METER]
trod(den). See TREAD.
trŏ·glodyte, n. Cave-dweller, esp. of prehistoric W. Europe (often attrib.); (fig.) hermit; kinds of wren & anthropoid ape. Hence or cogn. **troglodȳ·tic(al)** aa., **tro·glodȳtism**(2) n. [f. L (*-ta*) f. Gk *trōglodutēs* (*trōglē* cave + *duō* enter)]
troi·ka, n. (Vehicle with) team of three horses abreast. [Russ.]
trois-temps. See WALTZ.
Trō·jan, a. & n. (Inhabitant) of Troy; *T. War* (between Greeks under Agamemnon & Trojans under Priam); (fig.) person who works or fights or endures courageously, esp. *like a T.* [f. L *Trojanus* f. *Troja* Troy f. L f. Gk *Trōs* Trojan, see -AN]
trōll[1], v.t. & i., & n. Sing (parts of song) in succession; sing (song, or intr.) in casual or careless fashion; fish for, fish in (water), fish, with rod & line & dead bait or with spoon-bait (*trolling-spoon*) drawn along behind boat; (archaic) cause (bottle) to circulate at table &c. (N.) song sung in successive parts, catch; reel of fishing-rod; trolling-spoon. [(n. f. vb) earlier sense *roll*, f. OF *troller*, perh. f. G *trollen* roll, troll]
trōll[2], n. Supernatural being, giant or (later) friendly but mischievous dwarf, in Scandinavian mythology. [ON & Sw., cf. Da. *trold*]
trŏ·lley, -ly, n. Kind of truck that can be tilted; costermonger's cart pushed by hand or drawn by donkey; low truck worked by hand-lever along the rails for conveying railwaymen to work; pulley used for conveying current in electric street-railway (*t.-pole*, with t. at upper end for this purpose); (also *t.-lace*) lace of which the pattern is outlined with thick thread. [prob. f. TROLL[1]]
trŏ·llop, n. Slatternly woman; prostitute. Hence **tro·llopish**[1], **tro·llopy**[2], aa. [perh. f. TROLL[1]]
tro·mba, n. (mus.). Trumpet. [It.]
tro·mbone, n. Large musical instrument of trumpet family with sliding tube or with valves. Hence **tro·mbōnist**(3) n. [It. (as prec., see -OON)]
tro·mmel, n. (mining). Revolving cylindrical sieve for cleaning ore. [G, = drum]
tromŏ·meter, n. Instrument for measuring very slight earthquake shocks. [f. Gk *tromos* trembling (*tremō* tremble) + -METER]
trompe, n. Apparatus for producing blast in furnace. [F, = TRUMP[1]]
trōōp, n., & v.i. & t. Assembled company, assemblage of persons or animals, as *a t. of school-children, of antelopes, surrounded by tt. of friends*; (pl.) soldiers, as *lost a third of his tt.*, HOUSEHOLD *tt.*; cavalry unit consisting of usu. 60 troopers with two lieutenants & captain (cf. COMPANY), command of this (*get* one's *t.*, be promoted captain); particular call of drum as signal for marching; company of performers, troupe; *t.-horse*, cavalry horse; *t.-ship*, transport. (Vb) assemble, flock together, (often *up*, *together*, &c.); move along in a t. (*along*, *in*, *out*, &c.); (w. pl. subject) walk hurriedly *off*, *away*; form (regiment) into tt.; *trooping the colour(s)*, ceremony at public mounting of garrison guards. [(vb f. n.) f. F *troupe*, OF *trope*, f. LL *troppus* flock, etym. dub.]
troo·per, n. Horse-soldier, private soldier in cavalry; *swear like a t.* (much); cavalry horse; troop-ship. [-ER[1]]
tropae·olum, n. Indian cress, kinds of trailing plant with spurred yellow or scarlet flowers including NASTURTIUM (2nd sense). [mod. L f. Gk *tropaion* TROPHY, w. ref. to likeness of flower & leaf to helmet & shield]
trope, n. Figurative (e. g. metaphorical, ironical) use of a word. [F, f. L f. Gk *tropos* turn, way, trope, (*trepō* turn)]
trŏ·phic, a. Concerned with nutrition, as *t. nerves.* [f. Gk *trophikos* (*trophē* nourishment f. *trephō* nourish + -IC)]
trŏpho- in comb. = Gk *trophē* food, as *-neurō·sis*, defective nutrition due to nervous derangement.
trŏ·phy, n. (Gk Ant.) arms &c. of vanquished enemy set up on field of battle or elsewhere to commemorate victory; Roman memorial of victory in imitation of this but usu. permanent; anything, e.g. captured standard, kept as memorial of victory (lit. & fig.); prize; memento; ornamental group of symbolic or typical objects arranged on wall &c. Hence **(-)trophied**[2] a. [f. F *trophée* f. L f. Gk *tropaion* (*tropē* rout f. *trepō* turn)]
trŏ·pic, n. & a. Parallel of latitude 23° 27′ north (*t. of Cancer*) or south (*t. of Capricorn*) of the equator; *the tt.*, region between these; each of the two corresponding circles on celestial sphere where sun appears to turn after reaching greatest declination; *t.-bird*, kinds of bird like tern seen usu. in the tt.; (adj.) = foll. exc. last sense. [f. L f. Gk *tropikos* (*kuklos*) tropic (circle) f. *tropē* turning, solstice, (*trepō* turn), see -IC]

tro·pical, a. Of, peculiar to, suggestive of, the tropics, as *t. plants, diseases, heat, abscess* (of liver, induced by residence in hot climate), *t. year* (between two successive passages of sun through same equinox); (fig.) fervid, passionate; [f. TROPE] figurative. Hence **tro·pical**LY[2] adv. [-AL]

tropicopŏ·litan, a. & n. (Animal, plant) confined & common to the tropics. [f. TROPIC on *cosmopolitan*]

tropŏ·logy, n. Figurative use of words; figurative interpretation esp. of the Scriptures, so **trō·**PIST(2) n. Hence **tropolo·gi**CAL a., **tropolo·gical**LY[2] adv. [f. LL *tropologia* (TROPE, -LOGY)]

tro·ppo, adv. (mus.). Too, as *andante* &c. *ma non t.* (but not too much so). [It.]

trot, v.i. & t., & n. (Of horses &c.) proceed at steady pace faster than walk lifting each diagonal pair of legs alternately with brief intervals during which body is unsupported; cause (horse &c.) to do this; (of person) run at moderate pace esp. with short strides (often *along* &c.); perform (distance) by trotting; bring (person, horse, &c.) to specified condition by trotting, as *trotted him off his legs, to death*; *t. out,* cause (horse) to trot to show his paces, (fig.) produce, introduce, (person, thing, superior information, subject) to excite admiration. (N.) action, exercise, of trotting, as *proceeded at a t., went for a t.*; (fig.) brisk steady movement or occupation, as *kept him on the t.* (busy); toddling child. [f. OF *trot(er)*, cf. Pr., Sp., Port., *trotar*, It. *trottare*]

trōth, n. (archaic). Truth, esp. (*in*) *t.*, truly, upon my word; *plight* one's *t.*, pledge one's word esp. in betrothal. [OE *tréowth* TRUTH]

tro·tter, n. In vbl senses; also or esp.: horse of special breed noted for trotting; (pl.) animal's feet used as food, as *pigs', sheep's, tt.*; (facet.) human foot. [TROT, -ER[1]]

trottoir· (-twahr), n. Side pavement. [F]

trō·tyl, n. (chem.). Trinitrotoluol. [(*trini*)-*trot*(*oluol*) + -YL]

trou·badour (-ōō-, -oor), n. Lyric poet of a class originating in Provence (cf. TROUVÈRE) in 11th c. [F, f. Pr. *trobador* f. *trobar* = F *trouver* find f. LL **tropare* make poetry (as TROPE) or f. L *turbare* (cf. CONTRIVE), see -OR[2]]

trou·ble (trŭ-), v.t. & i., & n. Agitate, disturb, be disturbed or worried, as *troubled waters, don't let it t. you, don't t. about it, has been troubled about* or *with money matters, a troubled countenance*; afflict, as *am troubled with neuralgia, how long has it been troubling you?*; subject, be subjected, to inconvenience or exertion (chiefly in polite formulas), as *may I t. you to shut the door?, to mind your own business?, will t. you for* (to pass) *the mustard, sorry to t. you, don't t.* (*to explain* &c., or abs.), *why should I t.* (*myself*) *to explain?, I will t.* (I defy) *you to translate this, will t. you for* (invite your comment on) *his last exploit.* (N.) vexation, affliction, as *has been through much t., till this great t. came upon them, life is full of small tt.*; disease, as *liver, digestive, tt.*; inconvenience, unpleasant exertion, source of this, as *did it to spare you t., shall not put you to any t. in the matter, fear the child is a great t. to you, will never take the t. to write, is incapable of taking t., an omelette is no t.* (*to make*), *French beans are a great t. to prepare,* (as polite formula) *no t.* (*at all*); *ask* or *look for t.* (slang), meddle, be rash, &c.; *be in, get into, t.*, incur censure, punishment, &c.; (Mining) small fault. [f. OF *trouble(r), tourbler,* ult. f. L *turba* crowd]

trou·blesome, a. (Of person or thing) causing trouble, vexatious. Hence **trou·blesome**LY[2] adv., **trou·blesome**NESS n. [-SOME]

trou·blous, a. (archaic). Full of troubles, agitated, disturbed, as *t. times.* [f. OF *troubleus* (TROUBLE, -OUS)]

trough (-ŏf, -awf), n. Long narrow open wooden or other receptacle for holding water or food for sheep &c., kneading dough, washing ore, &c.; wooden or other channel for conveying liquid; *t. of the sea,* hollow between two waves; (also *t.-battery*) voltaic battery formed of t. divided into cells; *t. of barometric depression,* line of greatest depression in area of moving barometric pressure. [OE, Du., ON, G, *trog,* cogn. w. TREE]

trounce (-ow-), v.t. Beat severely, castigate, (lit. & fig.). Hence **trou·ncing**[1] n. [cf. OF *troncer* cut back (as TRUNK)]

troupe (-ōōp), n. Company of actors, acrobats, &c. [F, see TROOP]

trous-de-loup (trōō de loo·), n. pl. Small conical pits with stake in centre of each as defence against cavalry. [F, lit. wolf-holes]

trou·ser (-owz-), n. (Pl., also *pair of tt.*) two-legged outer garment reaching from waist to ankles; (vulg.) pair of tt., as *here, again, is a smart & dressy t.*; *t.-button* (of certain sizes & materials); *t.* or *tt. pocket* (esp. as holding one's money, or hands when idle); *t.-stretcher,* apparatus for stretching tt. to preserve shape; early 19th-c. woman's long frilled drawers reaching to ankles. Hence **trou·ser**ED[2] a., **trou·ser**ING[1](3) n. [pl. form (cf. *tweezers*) of obs. *trouse* sing. (cf. TREWS) f. Ir. *triubhas* a Celtic garment of close breeches, somet. w. stockings attached]

trousseau (trōōsō·, trōō·sō), n. Bride's outfit of clothes &c. [F, lit. bundle, OF *troussel* dim. as TRUSS]

trout (-owt), n. (pl. usu. same), & v.i. Kinds of freshwater fish esteemed as food & game; *t.-coloured,* (of white horse) speckled with black, bay, or sorrel; (vb) fish for t. Hence **trou·t**LET, **trou·t**LING[1], nn., **trou·ty**[2] a. [OE *truht* f. L *tructa* f. Gk *trōktēs* lit. gnawer (*trōgō* gnaw), a sea-fish]

trouvaille (F), n. Lucky find, windfall.

trouvère (trōōvār·), n. Epic poet of a class originating in N. France (cf. TROUBADOUR) in 11th c. [F (as TROUBADOUR)]

trove. See TREASURE.

trō·ver, n. (law). Acquisition of personal property; common-law action to recover value of personal property wrongfully taken or detained. [OF, F *trouver* (TROUBADOUR, -ER[4])]

trow (-ō, -ow), v.t. (archaic). Think, believe; (added to question) *what ails him, (I) t.* (I wonder)?. [OE *trúwian* (*trúwa* faith), *tréowian* (*tréowe* faith)]

trow·el, n., & v.t. (-ll-). Mason's or bricklayer's flat-bladed tool for spreading mortar &c.; *lay it on with a t.*, (fig.) flatter grossly; gardener's scoop for lifting plants &c.; (vb) apply (plaster &c.), dress (wall &c.), with t. [(vb f. n.) f. F *truelle* f. LL *truella* dim. of L *trua* ladle, cf. *trulla* spoon]

troy, n. (Also *t. weight*) system of weights used for gold & silver (cf. AVOIRDUPOIS), as *weighs 3 lb. 5 oz t., t. pound contains 12 oz, 5760 grains.* [prob. f. *Troyes*, town in France]

tru·ant, n., a., & v.i. One who absents himself from place of work, esp. child who stays away from school without leave; *play t.*, stay away thus; *t.-school*, industrial school for t. children; (adj., of person, conduct, character, thoughts, &c.) shirking, idle, loitering, wandering; (vb) play t. Hence **tru·**ANCY n., **tru·ant**LY[2] adv. [(vb f. n.) ME & OF, prob. f. Celt. (W *truan*, Gael. *truaghan*, wretched)]

truce, n. (Agreement for) temporary cessation of hostilities (FLAG[4] *of t.*); respite from pain &c., rest from work &c. (*a t. to* —, archaic, demand that — shall cease); *t. of God* (hist.), suspension of private feuds esp. during certain church festivals &c. Hence **tru·ce**LESS a. [ME *trewes*, pl. of OE *tréow* compact, faith, see TRUE]

truck[1], v.i. & t., & n. Make an exchange, trade, bargain, (*with* person *for* thing); exchange (thing *for* another); hawk (wares) about. (N.) exchange, barter, traffic, (*have no t. with*, avoid dealing with); small wares; (colloq.) rubbish, (fig.) nonsense, as *shall stand no t.*; (also *t. system, tommy*) practice of paying workmen in goods instead of money or in money on the understanding that they will buy provisions &c. of their employers, *T. Acts* (of 1831 & 1870, providing for suppression of or inquiry into t. system), *t. shop* (conducted on t. system). [f. F *troque*(*r*) etym. dub.]

truck[2], n., & v.t. Strong usu. four or six wheeled vehicle for heavy goods; open railway wagon; porter's two, three, or four, wheeled barrow for luggage at railway station &c.; set of wheels in framework for supporting whole or part of railway-carriage &c.; (Naut.) wooden disk at top of mast with holes for halyards; (now rare) small tireless wheel; *t.-bolster*, crossbeam on car-t. supporting one end; (vb) convey on t. Hence **tru·ck**AGE(3, 4) n. [f. L f. Gk *trokhos* wheel (*trekhō* run)]

tru·ckle, v.i., & n. Submit obsequiously, cringe, (*to*), whence **tru·ckl**ER[1] n.; (n. usu. *t.-bed*) low bed on wheels that may be wheeled under another, esp. as formerly used by servants &c. [(vb, earlier = sleep in t.-bed, f. n.) f. TRŎCHLEA]

trŭ·cŭlent (*or* trōō-), a. Of or showing bellicose aggressive merciless temper. Hence or cogn. **tru·cul**ENCE, -ENCY, nn., **tru·culent**LY[2] adv. [f. L *truculentus* (*trux trucis* fierce, see -LENT)]

trudge, v.i. & t., & n. Walk esp. laboriously, perform (distance) thus; (n.) such walk. [f. 16th c., etym. dub.]

tru·dgen, n. *T.* (*stroke*), swimming with alternate right & left over-arm strokes & ordinary leg action. [J. *T.*, person]

true, a., adv., & v.t. In accordance with fact or reality, not false or erroneous, as *his story is t., that is only too t., is it t. that he refused?, his words have come t.* (been realized in fact), (as formula of concession), *t., it would cost more*; in accordance with reason or correct principles or received standard, rightly so called, genuine, not spurious or hybrid or counterfeit or merely apparent, having all the attributes implied in the name, as *could not form a t. judgement, frog is not a t. reptile, is a t. benefactor, the t. heir, t. ribs* (complete, articulating with breast-bone, not floating), *t.* HORIZON; accurately conforming *to* (type &c.); (of voice) in perfect tune; loyal, constant, adhering faithfully, (*to* one's word, friend, one*self*, &c.; often *t. as steel*); (of wheel, post, beam, &c.) in correct position, balanced or upright or level; (archaic) not given to lying, veracious; (archaic) honest, as *t. men*; *t. bill*, bill of indictment endorsed by grand jury as being sustained by evidence; *t.-blue* a. & n., (person) of uncompromising principles or loyalty; *t.-born*, of genuine birth, truly such by birth, as *a t.-b. Englishman*; *t.-bred*, of genuine or good breed; *t.-hearted*(*ness*); *t.-love*, person truly loved or loving, sweetheart, plant with four leaves arranged like *t.-love*(*r's*) *knot* (kind of double knot with interlacing bows on each side); *true·penny* (archaic), honest fellow; (adv.) truly (rare exc. w. certain vbs, as *tell me, aim, breed, t.*); (v.t.) bring (tool, wheel, frame, &c.) into exact position or form required. Hence **true·**NESS n. (rare). [OE *tréowe* (*tréow*, see TRUCE), cf. Du. *getrouw*, G *treu*, ON *tryggr*]

trŭ·ffle (*or* trōō-), n. Subterranean fungus used for seasoning dishes. Hence

tru·ffLED[2] a. [f. OF *trufle* prob. f. L *tubera* pl. of *tuber*]

trug, n. Wooden milk-pan; shallow garden basket made of wood strips. [perh. var. of TROUGH]

tru·ism, n. A self-evident or indisputable truth; proposition that states nothing not already implied in one of its terms (e. g. *I don't like my tea too hot* = *I don't like it hotter than I like it*); hackneyed truth, platitude. [f. TRUE + -ISM]

trŭll, n. (archaic). Prostitute. [cf. G *trulle,* Swiss *trolle*]

tru·ly, adv. Sincerely, genuinely, as *am t. grateful, a t. alarming state of affairs, a t. courageous act,* (as purely neutral formula for closing letter) *yours* (*very*) *t. W. Jones,* (hence, facet.) *won't do for yours t.* (me); (usu. parenthet., & now chiefly literary or archaic) really, indeed, as *t., I should be puzzled to say*; faithfully, loyally, as *has served him t.*; accurately, truthfully, as *it has been t. stated, is not t. represented.* [OE *tréowlīce* (as TRUE, see -LY[2])]

trumeau (F), n. (archit., pl. *-eaux*). Piece of wall, pillar, between two openings, e. g. pillar dividing large doorway.

trump[1], n. (archaic, poet.). Trumpet, its sound, as *last t., t. of doom.* [f. F *trompe,* etym. dub.]

trump[2], n., & v.t. & i. Each card of a suit temporarily ranking above others, as *a call for tt.* (conventional signal to partner to lead tt.); *t. card,* card turned up to determine which suit shall be tt., any card of this suit, (fig.) valuable resource; (colloq.) person of admirable courage, resource, generosity, &c., excellent fellow; *put* person *to his tt.,* (fig.) reduce him to his last resources; *turn up tt.* (colloq.), turn out better than was expected, (also) have a stroke of luck; (vb) defeat (card) with a t., play a t. (also fig.); *t. up,* fabricate, forge, (story, excuses, &c.). [f. F *triomphe* TRIUMPH, a game of cards]

tru·mpery, n. & a. Worthless finery; rubbish; nonsense; (adj.) showy but worthless, delusive, shallow, as *t. furniture, arguments.* [f. F *tromperie* (*tromper* deceive, etym. dub., -ERY)]

tru·mpet, n., & v.t. & i. Kinds of musical wind-instrument esp. of brass with long often bent or coiled tube & bell-shaped mouth, the sounds being modified by player's lips or by slides, valves, &c.; trumpeter, esp. (hist.) one sent as envoy; reed-stop in organ; EAR, SPEAKING, *-t.*; t.-shaped thing e.g. kind of funnel; sound (as) of t.; *feast of tt.,* Jewish festival celebrating beginning of year; FLOURISH[2] *of tt.*; BLOW[1] one's *own t.*; *t.-call,* call by sound of t., (fig.) urgent summons to action; *t.-conch, -shell, sea-t.,* kinds of gasteropod with turreted shell; *t.-flower, -leaf,* kinds of plant with t.-shaped flowers, leaves; *t. major,* head trumpeter of cavalry regiment. (Vb) proclaim (as) by sound of t. (usu. fig., = celebrate), blow t., (of elephant &c.) make loud sound as of t. [(vb f. n.) F *trompette* dim. as TRUMP[1]]

tru·mpeter, n. One who sounds a trumpet, esp. cavalry soldier giving signals with trumpet (*be* one's *own t.,* = BLOW one's *own trumpet*); kind of domestic pigeon with peculiar coo, other birds making trumpet-like sound, esp. (also *t. swan*) a large N.-Amer. swan. [-ER[1]]

tru·ncal, a. Of the trunk of a body or tree. [f. L as TRUNK + -AL]

trŭncāte, v.t., & a. Cut the top or end from (tree, body, cone, pyramid, fig. quoted passage &c.); (Crystallog.) replace (edge) by plane; (adj.) truncated, (Bot., Zool., of leaf, feather, &c.) ending abruptly as if cut off at tip, whence **tru·ncateLY**[2] adv. So **truncA·TION, tru·ncatURE** (zool.), nn. [f. L *truncare* (TRUNK), -ATE[2], [3]]

tru·ncheon (-shn), n. Short club or cudgel e. g. that carried by policeman; baton, staff of authority, esp. (Herald.) that of Earl Marhsal. [f. OF *tronchon* dim. as TRUNK]

tru·ndle, n., & v.t. & i. Small broad wheel, e. g. castor; small wheel with cylindrical teeth; low-wheeled truck; (also *t.-bed*) = TRUCKLE-*bed*; head of lower drum of double capstan. (Vb) roll (t. & i., of hoop, truck, &c., often *along, down,* &c.); (slang) bowl at cricket; hence **tru·ndlER**[1] n. (esp., slang, bowler). [(vb f. n.) var. of OE (& MHG & MLG) *trendel* circle, cogn. w. TREND]

trunk, n., & v.t. Main body of tree opp. to branches & roots; human or animal's body without head & limbs & tail; main part of any structure; (also *t.-line*) main line of railway or canal, telephone main line (esp. of lines from town to town); box with hinged lid, often covered with leather, for carrying clothes &c. on journey; kinds of shaft, conduit, or trough, usu. rectangular & of wood, for ventilation, separation of ores, &c.; open cylinder used instead of piston-rod in some marine & other engines (*t.-engines*); proboscis esp. of elephant; (pl., also *t. hose*) 16th–17th-c. breeches from waist to middle of thigh; *t.-call,* telephone call on t.-line with special charges according to distance; *t. drawers* (shop), drawers reaching only to knees; *t.-nail,* nail with large ornamental head for t., coffin, &c.; *t.-road,* main road. Hence **tru·nkFUL** n., **tru·nkLESS** a. (Vb) separate (ore) by use of t. [(vb f. n.) f. OF *tronc* f. L *truncus* a. & n., maimed, trunk]

tru·nnion, n. Supporting cylindrical projection on each side of cannon or mortar; hollow gudgeon supporting cylinder in steam-engine & giving passage to steam. Hence **tru·nnionED**[2] a. [f. F *trognon* core, stump, etym. dub.]

truss, v.t., & n. Support (roof, bridge, &c.) with t. (see below); fasten (wings of fowl &c.), fasten wings &c. of (fowl &c.), before cooking, tie arms of (person) to his sides; (archaic) fasten, tighten, (garment, usu. *up*), hang (criminal, usu. *up*), (of hawk &c.) seize (bird). (N.) supporting structure or framework of roof, bridge, &c., e. g. pair of rafters with tie-beam, king-post, & struts (*t.-bridge* &c., so strengthened); bundle of old (56 lb.) or new (60 lb.) hay or (36 lb.) straw; compact terminal flower-cluster; large corbel supporting monument &c.; (Naut.) heavy iron fitting securing lower yards to mast; (Surg.) padded belt or encircling spring used in rupture. [f. F *trousse*(*r*) perh. f. L *tors-* p.p. st. of *torquēre* twist]

trust, n., & v.t. & i. Firm belief in the honesty, veracity, justice, strength, &c., of a person or thing, as *our t. is in God, I repose considerable t. in him, put no t. in him*; confident expectation (*that*); person, thing, confided in, as *he is our sole t.*; reliance on truth of statement &c. without examination, as *takes everything on t.*; commercial credit, as *supplied with goods on t.*; responsibility arising from confidence reposed in one, as *am in a position of t.*; (Law) confidence reposed in person by making him nominal owner of property to be used for another's benefit, right of the latter to benefit by such property, property so held, legal relation between holder & property so held, as *have accepted a t., the property is merely a t., is held in t.*, (attrib.) *t.-money*; thing, person, committed to one's care, resulting obligation, as *would not desert his t., have fulfilled my t.*; (Commerc.) organized association of several companies for purpose of defeating competition &c., the shareholders in each transferring all or most of the stock to central committee & losing their voting power while remaining entitled to profits; *t.-deed*, deed by debtor conveying property to trustee for payment of his debts, deed conveying property to creditor to sell & pay himself & restore the residue, any instrument of conveyance that creates a t. (Vb) place t. in, believe in, rely on the character or behaviour of, as *have never trusted him, if we may t. this account, do not t. him with* (let him use) *your typewriter, cat cannot be trusted with* (will steal) *milk, would t. him with untold gold*, whence **tru·sting**LY[2] adv.; consign (thing *to* person &c.), place or leave (thing *with* person &c., *in* place &c.), without misgiving; allow credit to (customer *for* goods); entertain an earnest or (rarely) confident hope, as *I t. he is not hurt*(?), *I t. to hear better news*; place reliance *in*; *t. to*, place (esp. undue) reliance on, as *we must t. to meeting someone who knows, does not do to t. to memory for these things.* [ME *trost* n., *trusten* vb, f. ON *traust* n. (*traustr* strong), *treysta* vb (cf. G *trösten* to comfort)]

trustee·, n. Person who holds property in trust for another (*the Public T.*, State official charged, since 1908, with executing wills & trusts when invited); (pop.) each of a body of men, often elective, managing affairs of college &c. Hence **trustee·**SHIP n. [-EE]

tru·stful, a. Full of trust, confiding. Hence **tru·stful**LY[2] adv., **tru·stful**NESS n. [-FUL]

tru·stworthy, a. Worthy of trust, reliable. Hence **tru·stworthi**NESS n.

tru·sty, a. & n. (Chiefly archaic) trustworthy, as *t. steed, sword, servant*, whence **tru·sti**LY[2] adv., **tru·sti**NESS n.; (n.) well-behaved & privileged convict. [-Y[2]]

truth (trōōth; pl. -dhz), n. Quality, state, of being true or accurate or honest or sincere or loyal or accurately shaped or adjusted, as *the t. of the rumour is doubted, there is t. in what he says, may depend on his t., wheel is out of t.*; what is true, as *have told you the* (*whole*) *t., the t. is that I forgot, am a lover of t.* (or *T.* personified), *fundamental tt., home tt.* (unpalatable facts about oneself), GOD[1]'*s t.*, GOSPEL *t.*; *in t.* (literary), *of a t.* (archaic), truly, really; *to tell the t., t. to tell*, formulas introducing confession. [OE *trēowth* (as TRUE, see -TH[1])]

tru·thful, a. Habitually speaking truth, veracious; (of tale &c.) true. Hence **tru·thful**LY[2] adv., **tru·thful**NESS n. [-FUL]

tru·thless, a. (Of statement) false; (of person) faithless, not adhering to promise &c. Hence **tru·thless**NESS n. [-LESS]

try, v.t. & i., & n. Test (quality), test the qualities of (person, thing), by experiment, subject (person &c.) to suffering or hard treatment (as if) for this purpose (whence **try·**ING[2] a., **try·ing**LY[2] adv.), as *t.* (*the effect of*) *soap & water, t.* (buy) *our ginger ale, did you ever t. quinine* (as cure) *for it?*, (*strength of*) *rope must be tried before it is used, each machine is tried before it leaves the shops, t. your hand* (skill) *at, this will t. his courage, patience has been sorely tried, should not t. your eyes with that small print*; make experiment in order to find out, as *t. how far you can throw, let us t. which takes longest, whether it will break*; *t.* CONCLUSIONS, *a* FALL[2]; investigate (case, issue) judicially, subject (person) to trial (*for* murder &c., also *for* his *life*); settle (question, disputed point) by examination or experiment; attempt to achieve or perform, as *tried a jump & fell, better t. something easier*; attempt, endeavour, (*to* do or abs.; colloq. often & do, seldom after neg. or quasi-neg. & never after past tense), as *do t. to* (or *&*) *attend, must t. to* (or *&*) *get it finished tonight, if at first you don't succeed t., t., t. again, no use trying to persuade him, don't t. to* (rarely *&*) *palliate it, have often tried to mend it*; (also *t. up*) dress (roughly-planed board) with *trying-plane* to give fine surface; (also *t. out*) purify (metal, fat, oil) by melting or boiling; *t. back*, = HARK (intr.) *back*, lit. & fig.; *t. for*, aim at (a calmer tone &c.), apply or compete for (appointment &c.); *t. on*, put (clothes &c.) on to test fit, begin (*it*, one's *games, tricks*, &c., often *with* person) experimentally to see how much will be tolerated, as *no use trying it on with mē*; *t. out*, put to the test, test thoroughly; *try·sail*, small fore-&-aft sail set with gaff in heavy weather on mainmast or foremast or supplementary mast instead of mainsail or foresail [f. obs. naut. sense of vb, = lie to]; *try(ing)-square*, carpenter's square usu. with one wooden & one metal limb; *try-works*, apparatus for trying blubber. (N.): (colloq.) attempt, as *have* (make) *a t. at it, for it, to catch it*; (Rugby footb.) right to carry ball in front of goal & t. to kick goal. [n. f. vb f. OF *trier* etym. dub.]

trȳ·panosōme, n. Kinds of blood-parasite some of which cause sleeping-sickness & other diseases. [f. Gk *trupanon* auger, *sōma* body]

trȳst, n., & v.t., (archaic). Appointed meeting, appointment, as *keep, break, t.*; (vb) engage to meet (person), appoint (time, place) for meeting. [f. OF *trist(r)e* station to watch in hunting, prob. of Scand. orig. cogn. w. TRUST]

tsar &c. See CZAR &c.

tsĕ·tse (-ĭ), n. S.-Afr. fly whose bite is often fatal to horses, cattle, dogs, &c. [S.-Afr.]

tub, n., & v.t. & i. Open wooden usu. round vessel of staves held together by hoops used for washing (*wash-t.*) or holding butter, liquids, &c. (*let every t. stand on its own bottom*, everyone look to himself); varying measure of capacity for butter, corn, tea, &c.; sponge-bath, bath taken in this, as *jumped into his t., seldom has a t., a cold t. would do him good*; (Mining) kinds of bucket or box for conveying ore, coal, &c.; clumsy slow boat (contempt.); boat used for practice rowing, as *t.-pair, -eight*, &c. (for so many oarsmen); *t.-thumper*, ranting preacher, so *t.-thumping* a. & n.; *t.-wheel*, bowl-shaped water-wheel, rotating drum for washing skins &c. in. Hence **tu·b**FUL n. (Vb) bathe (t. & i.) in t.; plant in t.; row in t., coach (oarsman, -men) in t.-pair; (Mining) line (shaft) with wood or iron casing. Hence **tu·bb**ING[1](1, 2) n. [(vb f. n.), cf. MDu. *tobbe, tubbe*]

tū·ba, n. Large low-pitched kind of trumpet; an organ reed-stop. [L, = trumpet]

tu·bby, a. Tub-shaped, fat & round, corpulent, so **tu·bb**ISH[1] a.; (of musical instrument) sounding dull, lacking resonance. [-Y[1]]

tube, n., & v.t. Long hollow cylinder esp. for conveying or holding liquids &c.; cylinder of thin flexible metal with screw cap for holding paint &c. (*t. colours*, kept in tt.); main body of wind instrument; (Anat.) hollow t.-shaped organ, esp. one conveying air, as *bronchial t.*, whence **tu·b**AL, **tu·b**AR[1], aa.; each of several tubular electric railways in London; *Crookes's t.*, vacuum t. for showing certain phenomena connected with gases; *pneumatic t.* (for pneumatic dispatch); TEST[1]-*t.*; *t.-flower*, ornamental E.-Ind. shrub of vervain family; *t.-shell*, kinds of bivalve forming shelly t.; *t.-well*, iron pipe with sharp point & perforations at bottom for getting water from underground; (vb) furnish with, enclose in, t. or tt. Hence **tu·b**ING[1](2) n. [(vb f. n.) F, f. L *tubus*]

tū·ber, n. Short thick part of an underground stem covered with modified buds, e. g. potato, artichoke, whence **tuberi·**FEROUS, **tu·beri**FORM, aa.; kinds of underground fungus, truffle; (Anat.) swelling part, prominence. [L, = bump, tumour]

tū·bercle, n. Small rounded projection esp. of bone; small granular tumour or nodule formed within the substance of an organ tending to degeneration & (in lungs &c.) to production of pulmonary consumption &c.; (Bot.) wart-like excrescence, small tuber. Hence **tu·bercl**ED[2], **tuber·cul**AR[1], **tuber·culate(d)** [-ATE[2] (2)], **tuber·cul**OID, **tuber·cul**OSE[1], **tuber·cul**OUS, aa. [F, f. L TUBER*culum* (-CULE)]

tubercula·tion, n. Formation, set, system, of tubercles. [-ATION]

tuber·cul(ar)ize, vv.t. Infect with tuberculosis. Hence **tuberculiz**A·TION **n.** [-IZE]

tuber·culō·sis, n. Disease affecting most tissues of the body marked by tubercles & the presence of a characteristic bacillus; *pulmonary t.*, consumption. Hence **tuber·culos**ED[2] a. [-OSIS]

tū·berose, a. & (*pop. pron.* tū·brōz) **n.** Covered with tubers, knobby; of the nature of a tuber; bearing tubers. Hence or cogn. **tuberŏ·**SITY, **tu·berous**NESS, nn., **tu·ber**OUS a. (N.) garden & greenhouse bulb with creamy-white fragrant flowers. [(n. f. L fem. adj.) f. L *tuberosus* (TUBER, see -OSE[1])]

tūbi- in comb. = L *tubus* tube, as: *-corn* a. & n., (ruminant) with hollow horns; -FORM; *-li·ngual*, with tubular tongue.

tu·bular, a. Tube-shaped; having, consisting of, contained in, tube(s), as *t. boiler* (in which heat or water to be heated passes through many tubes), *t. bridge*, rectangular tube through which railway &c. passes; (of sound in breathing) like sound of air passing through tube. So **tu·bul**OSE[1], **tu·bul**OUS, aa. [f. foll. + -AR[1]]

tu·bule, n. Small tube. Hence **tu·buli**-comb. form. [f. L *tubulus* dim. as TUBE]

tuck[1], v.t. & i., & n. Gather (material) into flat folds for stitching; draw or thrust or roll the parts of (cloth &c. *up, in*) close together, as *t. in the loose ends, tucked up his shirt-sleeves* (so as to leave arms bare); draw together into small compass, as *tucked his legs under him like a tailor, bird tucks his head under his wing*; cover (person, one*self*) snugly & compactly *up* or *in*, as *tucked himself up in bed*; stow away (thing *in* corner &c., *away*, &c.); (of spare material &c.) be disposed of by tucking away; empty (seine) by means of small one; (slang) hang (criminal) *up*; *t. in* (slang), eat heartily (*at* food, or abs.). (N.) flat fold, often one of several parallel folds, in fabric fixed in place by stitches as ornament or to dispose of spare stuff, as *make a t. in sleeves* (when too long); (Naut.) part of vessel's hull where after planks meet; (slang) eatables esp. pastry & sweets, *t.-in, -out*, full meal, *t.-shop* (where t. is sold); *t.-net, -seine*, small net for taking fish from larger one. [(n. f. vb) ME *tukken*, cf. LG *tukken, to-*, G *zucken*, & TOUCH]

tuck[2], n. (archaic). Blast, flourish, of trumpet; (Sc.) *t.* (beat) *of drum*. [f. Picard *toquer* var. of F *toucher* TOUCH]

tu·cker, n. In vbl senses; also or esp.: piece of lace, linen, &c., covering neck & shoulders of woman in 17th & 18th c. (*best* BIB[2] *& t.*); part of sewing-machine used in making tucks; (slang) food. [TUCK[1] + -ER[1]]

tu·cket, n. (archaic). Flourish on trumpet. [cf. TUCK[2], & It. *toccata* prelude (*toccare* TOUCH, cf. -ADE)]

tu·cum (tōō-), n. Brazilian palm with fibre used for cordage &c. [Braz.]

-tude, suf. forming abstract nn. f. L adjj. & p.pp., usu. ending in *-ti-* (*desuetude, consuetude*, for *-suetitude*); in wds direct f. L (*altitude*), thr. F (*aptitude, attitude*), or on L anal. (*correctitude*). [F, f. L *-tudinem*, nom. *-tudo*]

Tū·dor, a. Of the (period of the) *Tt.*, English sovereigns from Henry VII to Elizabeth, as *T.* (late perpendicular) *style* in architecture, *T. rose*, five-lobed flower, *T. flower*, trefoil ornament, used in T. style. [Owen *T.* of Wales, grandfather of Henry VII]

Tue·sday (tūz-), n. Third day of week; SHROVE *T.* [OE *Tīwes dæg* (*Tīwes* genit. of *Tīw* god of war, cogn. w. L *deus* god, Gk *Zeus* Jupiter + *dæg* DAY]

tū·fa, n. Rock of rough or cellular texture of volcanic or other origin. Hence **tufA·CEOUS** a. [It., as foll.]

tuff, n. Kinds of volcanic fragmentary rock; *t.-cone* (of ashes &c. round volcanic opening). [f. F *tuf* f. It. *tufo, tufa*, f. L *tophus* soft sandy stone]

tuft, n., & v.t. & i. Bunch, collection, of threads, grass, feathers, &c., held or growing together at the base, whence **tu·ftY**[2] a.; (Anat.) bunch of small blood-vessels; imperial (beard); titled undergraduate [from t. formerly worn on cap]; *t.-hunter, -hunting*, one who seeks, practice of seeking, society of titled persons. (Vb) furnish with t. or tt.; make depressions at regular intervals in (mattress &c.) by passing thread through; grow in tt. [(vb f. n.) f. F *touffe* prob. of Teut. orig., cf. G *zopf*]

tug, v.t. & i., & n. Pull with great effort or violently; make vigorous pull *at*; tow (vessel) by means of steam t., (of steam t.) tow (vessel); (fig.) drag (subject &c. *in* &c.) forcibly. (N.) tugging, violent pull, as *gave a t. at the bell*; violent or painful effort, esp. fig., as *felt a great t. at parting, parting was a t., had a great t. to persuade him*; (Eton slang) colleger; (also *tu·gboat*) small powerful steam-vessel for towing others; loop from saddle supporting shaft or (in double harness) trace, *t.-spring*, spring-frame to which this is fastened to lessen jerk in starting &c.; (Mining) iron hoop to which a tackle is fixed; *t. of war*, contest in which each of two groups of persons holding same rope tries to pull the other across line marked between them, supreme contest. [(n. f. vb) ME *toggen*, cogn. w. OE *tēon* draw, & TAUT, TIGHT, TIE, TOW[1], TOUGH]

tū·ism, n. Doctrine that all thought is addressed to a second person, esp. to one's future self as this. [f. L *tu* thou + -ISM]

tūi·tion (-shn), n. Teaching, esp. as a thing to be paid for; fee for this. Hence **tui·tionAL, tui·tionARY**[1], aa. [OF, f. L *tuitionem* (*tuēri tuit-* watch, guard, see -ION)]

tu·la-work (tōō-), n. = NIELLO. [*Tula*, in Russia]

tŭ·lchan, -in, (-ch-), n. (Sc.). Calf-skin stuffed with straw or spread on mound beside cow to make her give milk; *t. bishops*, titular bishops in whose names revenues of Scotch sees were drawn by lay barons after Reformation. [Gael., = mound]

tū·lip, n. Kinds of plant with brilliant bell-shaped flowers of various colours; bell-shaped outward swell of muzzle of gun; *t.-root*, disease of oats causing base of stem to swell; *t.-tree*, N.-Amer. tree with flowers like large greenish-yellow tt., marked with orange inside. [thr. F *tulippe* or It. *tulipa(no)* f. Turk. *tulbant* f. Pers. *dulband* TURBAN]

tulipomā·nia, n. Craze for tulips, esp. that in Holland about 1634. Hence **tulipoMA·NIAC** n. [prec. + -O- + -MANIA]

tulle (tōōl, *or as F*), n. Fine silk net used for veils & dresses. [*T.*, city in France]

tŭ·lwar, n. Sabre used by some N.-Indian tribes. [Hind. *talwār*]

tum, tu·mtum, n. Sound of banjo or similar instrument. [imit.]

tu·mble, v.i. & t., & n. Fall (*down, over, off, from,* &c.) suddenly or violently; (of waves, sick person, &c.) roll, toss, up & down or from side to side; move, walk, run, in headlong or blundering fashion (*came tumbling along, tumbled up the stairs, tumbled into* or *out of bed*); perform acrobatic feats; pull about, disorder, rumple, (clothes, hair, &c.); overturn, fling headlong, throw or push (*down, out, in,* &c.) roughly or carelessly; bring down (bird, hare, &c.) by shooting; polish (castings &c.) in tumbling-box; *t. in,* fit (piece of timber) into another, (Naut., also *t. home,* of ship's sides) incline inwards above extreme breadth, (slang) go to bed; *t. to* (slang), understand, grasp, (idea &c.). (N.) fall, as *had a slight, nasty,* &c., *t.*; somersault or other acrobatic feat; untidy or confused state, as *things were all in a t.*; *t.-bug,* kinds of dung-beetle; *tu·mbledown,* dilapidated. [(n. f. vb) f. OE *tumbian* + -LE(3), cf. Du. *tuimelen,* G *taumeln, tummeln,* stagger]

tu·mbler, n. In vbl senses; also or esp.: one who turns somersaults &c., acrobat; kind of pigeon that turns somersaults during flight; toy figure of sitting mandarin &c. contrived to rock when touched; flat-bottomed stemless drinking-glass (formerly with rounded bottom so as not to stand upright), whence **tu·mbler**FUL n.; part of the mechanism of a lock or gunlock. [-ER[1]]

tu·mbling, n. In vbl senses; *t.-barrel, -box, -wheel,* revolving box or barrel containing emery-powder &c. in which castings &c. are cleaned by friction against each other or the walls of the box; *t.-bob,* weighted lever reacting when lifted to a certain point. [-ING[1]]

tu·mbly, a. (rare). = TUMBLE*down.* [TUMBLE, -Y[2]]

tu·mbrel, -il, n. (Mil.) two-wheeled covered cart for carrying tools, ammunition, &c.; dung-cart; (Hist.) instrument of punishment perh. the same as CUCKING-STOOL. [f. OF *tumb(e)rel* (*tomber* fall, of Teut. orig., cf. TUMBLE)]

tū·mĕfȳ, v.t. & i. (Cause to) swell, inflate; be inflated, (lit. & fig.). So **tume**FA·CIENT a. (path.), **tume**FA·CTION n. (path.). [f. F *tuméfier* ult. f. L *tumefacere* (*tumēre* swell, see -FY)]

tū·mid, a. (Of parts of body &c.) swollen, inflated, so **tume·**SCENCE n., **tume**·SCENT a.; (fig., of style &c.) inflated, bombastic. Hence or cogn. **tumi·**DITY, **tu·mid**NESS, nn., **tu·mid**LY[2] adv. [f. L *tumidus* (*tumēre* swell, -ID[1])]

tu·mmy, n. (nursery). = STOMACH. [-Y[3]]

tū·mour, n. Local swelling esp. from morbid growth; *malignant t.* (tending to recur after removal & cause death, opp. to *benign t.*). [f. L *tumorem* (*tumēre* swell, -OR[1])]

tŭ·mtŭm[1], n. W.-Ind. dish of boiled plantains beaten soft in a mortar; (Anglo-Ind.) light vehicle, dog-cart. [?]

tumtum[2]. See TUM.

tū·mult, n. Commotion of a multitude esp. with confused cries &c.; noisy uprising of mob &c.; uproar; confused & excited state of mind, as *the t. within him had subsided.* Hence or cogn. **tumu·ltu**ARY[1] (esp. undisciplined, riotous), **tumu·ltu**OUS (esp. vehement, uproarious), aa., **tumu·ltuous**LY[2] adv. **tumu·ltuous**NESS n. [f. L *tumultus* (as foll.)]

tū·mūlus, n. (pl. *-lī*). Sepulchral mound often enclosing masonry. Hence or cogn. **tu·mul**AR(Y)[1] aa. [L (*tumēre* swell)]

tun, n., & v.t. Large cask for wine, beer, &c., esp. formerly as measure of capacity (252 wine gallons); brewer's fermenting-vat; *tu·ndish,* kind of funnel esp. in brewing; (v.t.) store (liquor) in t. [(vb f. n.) OE *tunne,* cf. Du. *ton,* G *tonne,* ON *tunna*]

tund, v.t. (Winch. Coll. slang). Thrash with stick. [f. L *tundere* beat]

tu·ndra (too-), n. Mossy & often marshy plain in N. Russia. [Lappish]

tune, n., & v.t. & i. Melody with or without harmony, air, as *psalm, hymn, -t.*; correct intonation in singing or playing, due adjustment of instrument for this, as *piano is out of t., sings out of t., must learn to sing in t.*; agreement, concord, harmonious relation, as *in, out of, t. with* one's *surroundings* or *company*; suitable mood (*for* purpose &c.); *change* one's *t., sing another t.,* assume a different style of language or manner, e.g. change from insolent to respectful tone; *to the t.* (serious or exorbitant amount) *of £5* &c. (Vb) put (violin, piano, &c.) in t., whence **tu·n**ER[1](1, 2) n.; (fig.) adjust, adapt, (thing *to* standard, purpose, circumstances, &c.); be in harmony (*with,* lit. & fig.); (poet.) produce (music), as *lark tunes his song*; express, celebrate, in music; *t. in,* set wireless instrument to right wave-length; *t. up,* (of orchestra) bring instruments to common pitch, begin to play or sing, (facet., of child) begin to cry. Hence **tu·n**ABLE a., **tu·nable**NESS n., **tu·nab**LY[2] adv. [(vb f. n.) 14th-c. var. of TONE]

tu·neful, a. Melodious, musical. Hence **tu·neful**LY[2] adv., **tu·neful**NESS n. [-FUL]

tu·neless, a. Not in tune; unmelodious; (of mus. instrument) not played, silent. [-LESS]

tu·ngsten, n. A steel-grey heavy metallic element. Hence **tu·ngst**ATE[1](3), n., **tu·ngst**IC, **tu·ngst**OUS, aa. (chem.). [Sw. (*tung* heavy + *sten* stone)]

tū·nic, n. Ancient Greek or Roman short-sleeved body-garment reaching about to knees; woman's loose blouse or coat gathered or belted at waist; close-fitting short coat of soldier's or policeman's dress. (Zool.) leathery envelope of ascidia &c., (Anat.) membrane enclosing an organ, (Bot.) any of the layers of a bulb, integument of a part, whence **tu·nic**ATE[2] a. (zool., anat., bot.), & n. (zool.); (Eccl.) = foll. [f. OF *tunique* f. L *tunica*]

tu·nicle, n. Fine or delicate tunic (esp. bot., zool.); (Eccl., esp. R.-C. Ch.) short vestment of deacon at eucharist &c., (pl.) this & dalmatic worn by bishop. [f. L *tunicula* dim. as prec.]

tu·ning, n. In vbl senses; *t.-crook,* hook for varying pitch in cornet &c.; *t.-fork,* two-pronged steel fork designed to give particular note (esp. middle C) when struck; *t.-hammer,* hammer-shaped wrench for altering tension of strings in piano &c. by turning the pegs (*t.-pegs, -pins*) to which they are attached. [-ING[1]]

tunnage. See TONNAGE.

tu·nnel, n., & v.t. & i. (-ll-). Artificial subterranean passage through hill &c. or under river &c.; subterranean passage dug by burrowing animal; (Mining) adit or level open at one end; main flue of chimney; *t.-borer,* kinds of machine for making tt.; *t.-net,* fishing-net wide at mouth & narrow at other end. (Vb) make a t. through (hill &c.); furnish with t.; make one's way (*through, into,* &c.), make one's *way,* by tunnelling. [(vb f. n.) f. OF *tonnel* dim. of *tonne* TUN]

tu·nny, n. Large oceanic scombroid fish used as food. [f. F *thon* f. L f. Gk *thunnos*]

tū·ny, a. (Of music) having marked or catchy tunes. Hence **tu·ni**NESS n. [TUNE, -Y[2]]

tup, n., & v.t. Male sheep, ram; striking-face of steam hammer &c.; (vb) copulate with (ewe). [ME *tope, tupe,* etym. dub.]

tūque (-k), n. Kind of Canadian cap. [Canad. F form of TOQUE]

tū quō·quĕ, n. The retort *So are* (or *did* &c.) *you.* [L, = you too]

Tūrā·nian, a. Of the Asiatic languages that are neither Semitic nor Indo-European, esp. of the Ural-Altaic group of languages. [f. Pers. *Turān* region beyond Oxus, + -IAN]

tur·ban, n. Oriental man's head-dress of scarf wound round cap; modification of this, esp. early-19th-c. European woman's head-dress; modern woman's or child's hat with narrow or no brim; spire of univalve shell; *t.-shell,* kinds of gasteropod or shell; *t.-stone,* Mohammedan pillar tombstone with t. carved on top; *t.-top,* kind of mushroom. Hence **tur·ban**ED[2] a. [f. Turk. *tulbant* f. Pers. *dulband*]

tur·bary, n. Right of digging turf on another's ground; place where turf or peat is dug. [f. OF *torberie* (*tourbe* TURF f. Teut., -ERY)]

tur·bid, a. (Of liquid or colour) muddy, thick, not clear; (fig.) confused, disordered. Hence **turbi·d**ITY, **tur·bid**NESS, nn., **tur·bid**LY[2] adv. [f. L *turbidus* disturbed (*turbare* disturb f. *turba* crowd, tumult, see -ID[1])]

tur·binate (-*at*), a. Shaped like a top or inverted cone, so **tur·bini**FORM, **tur·bin**OID, aa.; (Anat., esp. of some nasal bones) of scroll-like formation; whirling like a top. So **tur·bin**AL a., **turbin**A·TION n. [f. L *turbinatus* (as foll. see -ATE[2])]

tur·bīne, n. Kinds of water-wheel driven by impact or reaction or both of a flowing stream of water; *air t.,* wheel of similar form driven by wind or by air from tube, *steam t.* (driven by steam jets); *t. boat* &c. (driven by tt.). [F, f. L *turbo -inis* wheel, top, whirlwind, (med. L) turbot]

tur·bit, n. Kind of domestic pigeon with flat head & short beak. [perh. f. L as prec., w. ref. to shape]

tur·bot, n. Large kind of flat-fish esteemed as food. [f. OF *tourbout,* as prec.]

tur·būlent, a. Disturbed, in commotion; tumultuous; insubordinate, riotous. Hence or cogn. **tur·bul**ENCE n., **tur·bulent**LY[2] adv. [f. L *turbulentus* (*turba* tumult, see -LENT)]

Tur·co (ter-, *or as F*), n. Algerian tirailleur in French service. [F]

Turco-, Turko-, in comb. Of the Turks. So **Tur·co**PHIL, **Turco·phil**ISM, **Tur·co**PHOBE, nn. [f. med. L as TURK, -O-]

turd, n. (not in polite lang.). Ball or lump of excrement. [OE *tord,* cf. MDu. *torde*].

tur·dīne, a. Thrush-like. So **tur·di**FORM, **tur·d**OID, aa. [f. L *turdus* thrush + -INE[1]]

tūree·n, n. Deep covered dish for holding soup &c. at table. [earlier *terreen* f. F TERRINE]

turf, n., & v.t. Surface earth filled with matted roots of grass &c.; piece of this cut from the ground, sod; (in Ireland) peat; *the t.,* the race-course, occupation or profession of horse-racing, esp. *on the t.,* so occupied; *t.-bound,* covered with close t.; *t. drain* (covered with t.); *tur·fman,* person interested in horse-racing, so **tur·f**ITE[1] n.; (v.t.) cover (ground) with t. Hence **tur·fi**NESS n., **tur·f**Y[2] a. [OE & Du., cf. ON & Sw. *torf,* Da. *törv*]

tur·gid, a. Morbidly swollen or inflated or enlarged, whence **turge·**SCIBLE a.; (fig., of language) pompous, bombastic, inflated. Hence or cogn. **turge·**SCENCE, **turgi·d**ITY, nn., **turg**E·SCENT a., **tur·gid**LY[2] adv. [f. L *turgidus* (*turgēre* swell, see -ID[1])]

tūr·ion, n. (bot.). Young scaly shoot rising from ground as in asparagus, hops, &c. Hence **turioni·**FEROUS a. [f. L *turio -onis* shoot]

Turk, n. Ottoman, Osmanli; member of the race from whom the Ottomans are derived; ferocious, wild, or unmanageable person (now chiefly facet. of children); Mohammedan; Turkish horse;

T.'s-cap, kinds of lily & other plants; *T.'s-head,* head on post for sword displays, turbanlike ornamental knot, kinds of round brush or broom, kind of baking-pan for cakes. Hence **Tur·kism** n. [cf. F *Turc,* med. L *Turcus,* Pers. & Arab. *Turk*]

tur·key, T-, n. Large (esp. domestic) gallinaceous bird native of America related to pheasant, esteemed as food & associated with Christmas festivities; (*T-*) country of the Turks; *t. buzzard, vulture,* an American vulture; *T. carpet* (made entirely of wool, & of velvety appearance); *t.-cock,* male of t. (*red as a t.-c.,* of person flushed with anger &c.), (fig.) pompous or self-important person; *T. corn,* maize; *T. leather,* kind treated with oil before the hair side is removed; *t.-poult,* young of t.; *T. red,* a pigment or colour, cotton cloth dyed with this; *T. stone,* kind of oil-stone for sharpening knives &c.; *t. trot,* a modern dance. [cf. F *Turquie* Turkey (prec., -IA[1]), whence the bird was held to come (as prec.)]

Tur·kish, a. & n. (Language) of Turkey or the Turks; *T. bath,* hot-air bath followed by soaping, washing, rubbing, kneading, &c., (also pl.) building used for this; *T.*(=TURKEY) *carpet*; *T. delight,* a sweetmeat in gelatinous slabs coated with powdered sugar; *T. music* (produced with instruments of percussion); *T. pound* (usu. written *£T,* as *£T50*), coin worth about 18/2; *T. towel* (rough with long nap usu. of uncut loops). [-ISH[1]]

Tur·koman, Tur·kman, Tur·co-, n. (pl. -ns.). Member of any of various Turkish hordes in Turkestan, Afghanistan, Persia, & Russia; *T. carpet,* rich-coloured kind with soft long nap. [f. Pers. *Turkumān* (TURK, *mān-dan* resemble)]

tur·malin(e). See TOURMALIN.

tur·meric, n. E.-Ind. plant of ginger family: powdered root of this as dye-stuff, stimulant, & condiment esp. in curry-powder; *t.-paper* (saturated with t. & used as test for alkalis). [f. F *terre-mérite* perh. corrupt. of Arab. as CURCUMA]

tur·moil, n., & v.t. Agitation, trouble; (vb, archaic, chiefly in p.p.) agitate, trouble. [f. 16th c., etym. dub.]

tur·mut, var. of *turnip* used by writers as characteristic of rustic speech.

turn[1], v.t. & i. Move (t. & i.) on or as on axis, give rotary motion to, receive such motion, as *crank turns wheel, wheel turns, t. the key in the lock, t. the tap, tap will not t., he turned on his heel(s), t.* person *round* one's FINGER, *everything turns* (depends) *on his answer*; execute (somersault &c.) with rotary motion; change from one side to another, invert, reverse, (fig.) revolve mentally, as *turns everything upside down* or *inside out* (into state of confusion), *whole world has turned topsy-turvy, umbrella turns inside out, turned the body with its face upwards, turned* (inverted) *comma, turned period* (˙), *t.* TURTLE, *t. the* TABLES *on, t. over pages of book* (to read on other side), *t. over new* LEAF, *not t. a* HAIR, *dress must be turned* (the soiled outside becoming the inside), *t.* one's COAT, *t. an honest* PENNY, *have turned the matter over & over in my mind*; give new direction to, take new direction, adapt, be adapted, as *t. your face this way, river turns to the right, turned his flight northwards, scarcely know where* or *which way to t.* (fig. what course to follow, where to seek help), *turned to God in her trouble, t.* one's BACK[1] *on,* t. *a* DEAF *ear to, t. the edge of* (knife &c., fig. remark &c.), blunt, *t. your attention to this, have often turned my thoughts, thoughts have often turned, to the subject, can t. his hand to* (learn to do) *any thing, turns even his errors to account* (profits by them), *all turns* (tends) *to his profit, tide turns* (at ebb or flow); move to other side of, go round, flank, as *t. the* CORNER, *t. the scale,* cause it to sink, fig. decide question in suspense, *t.* (*the flank* or *position of*) *an army,* pass round so as to attack it from flank or rear, *t.* person's *flank,* outwit him, defeat him in argument &c.; *be turned* (have passed the age) (*of*) *40* &c.; cause to go, send, put, as *was turned adrift in the world, t. it out into a basin, never turned* (*away*) *a beggar from his door, will t.* (resist or divert) *a bullet*; change (t. & i.) in nature, form, condition, &c., change for the worse, (cause to) become, as *turned water into wine, has been turned into a joint stock company, fear he will t. crusty, has turned traitor, Mohammedan, botanist, joy is* or *has turned to bitterness, t.* (translate) *it into French, how would you t. this passage?, milk will t.* (*sour*), *thunder will t. milk* (*sour*), *turned pale at the thought, very thought turns me pale, sight of raw meat turns* (nauseates) *my stomach, stomach turns at the sight, success has turned his head* (intoxicated him), *head has turned with success, head turns* (with giddiness), *overwork has turned his brain*; shape (object) in lathe, (of material) lend itself (*easily, well,* &c.) to treatment in lathe; give (esp. elegant) form to, as *can t. a compliment, could t. a Latin verse in my day, well-turned phrase, exquisitely-turned wrist.* Spec. uses with advv. & prepp.: *T. about,* t. so as to face in new direction. *T. against,* become hostile to. *T. down*: fold down; place (playing card) face downwards; reduce flame of (gas, lamp, &c.) by turning tap &c., (slang) reject (proposal, its maker, &c.). *T. in*; fold inwards; incline inwards, as *his toes t. in*; (colloq.) go to bed. *T. off*: check passage of (water, gas, &c.) by means of tap &c., achieve, produce, (epigram, piece of work); dismiss (servant &c.) from employment; (slang) hang (criminal), marry (couple). *T. on* (adv.): give free passage to (water &c.) by turning tap; (colloq.) give free scope to, as *t. on the waterworks*, begin to cry. *T. on* (prep.): depend upon; face hostilely, become hostile to. *T. out*: expel; cause to point or incline outwards, as *t. out your toes*; produce (manufactured goods &c.); t. inside out, bring to view, as *made him t. out his pockets*; assemble for duty &c., as *15 men turned out*; get out of bed; (Mil.) *t. out the guard*, call them from guard-room; be found, prove to be the case, as *this turns out to be true, he turned out a humbug, it turns out that he was never there, we shall see how things t. out*. *T. over*: cause to fall over, upset; transfer the conduct of (thing *to* person); do business to the amount of, as *turns over £500 a week*. *T. round*: face about; adopt new opinions or policy. *T. to* (prep.), apply oneself to, set about, (work, do*ing*). *T. to* (adv.), begin work. *T. up*: (Cards) expose (trump card); disinter, as *plough turns up skulls*; make one's appearance, as *turned up an hour late, unexpectedly*; (of event, opportunity, &c.) happen, present itself; (colloq.) cause to vomit, as *the sight turned me up*. *T. upon*, = *t. on*. *T.-bench*, watchmaker's portable lathe; *t.-buckle*, device for connecting parts of metal rod; *t.-cap*, revolving chimney-top; *tur·ncoat*, one who turns his COAT; *tur·ncock*, person employed to t. on water for mains &c.; *t.-down*, (of collar) doubled down; *tur·nkey*, person in charge of prison keys; *t.-out*, turning-out esp. for duty, strike of employees, assembly of persons to see spectacle &c., equipage, quantity of goods manufactured &c. in given time; *tur·nover*, upsetting of carriage &c., semicircular pie or tart, amount of money turned over in business, newspaper article running on to second page; *tur·npike*, (hist.) defensive frame of pikes, gate set across road to stop carts &c. till toll is paid, such road; *t.-screw*, screw-driver; *tur·nside*, giddiness in dogs; *tur·nsole*, kinds of plant supposed to t. with the sun; *tur·nspit*, long-bodied short-legged dog formerly used to t. spit; *tur·nstile*, post at entrance of building esp. where admission fee is charged with four horizontal arms that move round as person passes through; *tur·nstone*, bird allied to plover; *t.-table*, circular revolving platform for reversing locomotives &c.; *t.-up* (colloq.), commotion. [OE *tyrnan, turnian*, f. L *tornare* turn in lathe (*tornus* = Gk *tornos*)]

turn[2], n. Rotary motion, changed or change of direction or position or tendency, deflection, deflected part, bend, as *a single t. of the handle, a t. of Fortune's wheel* (change of luck), *with a neat t. of the wrist, took a sudden t. to the left, complaint took a favourable t., milk is on the t.* (just turning sour), *tide is on the t.* (turning), *gave a new t. to the argument, path is full of tt. & twists, walked along a t. of the river*, (Mil. as wds of command) *right, left, about, t.!*, any of the THREES (*t. A, B, C, D*) in figure-skating; character, tendency, disposition, formation, as *was of a humorous t., do not like the t. of the sentence, the t. of an ankle*; *have a fine, pretty*, &c., *t. of speed* &c., be able to go very fast &c. on occasion; short walk, stroll, drive, ride, or performance, as *take a t. in the garden, on a bicycle, took a t. of work, short tt.* (songs, recitations, &c., in music-hall &c.); opportunity, occasion, privilege, obligation, coming successively to each of several persons &c., as *it is your t. to watch, it was now my t. to be angry, must not speak out of* (before or after) *your t., will hear you all in t.* (succession), *we dug by tt.* (in rotation of individuals or groups), *take tt.*, work &c. alternately, *work t. & t. about* (alternately), *went hot & cold by tt.*; *did not serve my t.* (purpose); *did me a good, an ill, t.* (service, disservice; *one good t. deserves another*); (Mus.) kinds of grace consisting of principal tone with those above & below it; (pl.) menses; each round in coil of rope &c.; (Print.) inverted type as temporary substitute for missing letter, letter turned wrong side up; (colloq.) nervous shock, as *gave me quite a t.*; *meat is done to a t.* (enough & not too much). [f. prec.]

tur·ner, n. In vbl senses; also or esp.: one who works with lathe, so **tur·**NERY (1, 2, 3) n.; kind of tumbler-pigeon. [-ER[1]]

tur·ning, n. In vbl senses, esp.: use of lathe; place where road meets another, such road, as *stop at the next t., take the second t. to the left*; *t.-point*, point in place, time, development, &c., at which decisive change occurs, as *has reached the t.-point, this may be the t.-point of his life*. [-ING[1]]

tur·nip, n. Biennial plant of mustard family; its fleshy globular root used as vegetable & for feeding cattle &c.; *t.-top*, growing top of t. used as vegetable. Hence **tur·nip**Y[2] a. (esp. tasting of tt.). [OE has *næp* f. L *napus*; *tur-* perh. = *turn* or F TOUR, w. ref. to shape]

tur·pentine, n., & v.t. Oleo-resin secreted by several coniferous trees & (*Chian t.*) by terebinth, used in mixing paints & varnishes & in medicine; (also pop. *turps*) oil or spirit of t.; *t.-tree*, terebinth. Hence **turpenti·**NIC a. (Vb.) apply t. to. [f. OF *ter(e)bentine* f. L f. Gk *terebinthinos* (as TEREBINTH, see -INE[2])]

tur·peth, n. Cathartic root of an E.-Ind. plant. [f. OF *turbith* f. Arab. & Pers. *turbid*]

tur·pitude, n. Baseness, depravity. [F, f. L *turpitudinem* (*turpis* base, see -TUDE)]

tur·quoise (-koiz, -kw-), n. Opaque sky-blue or greenish-blue precious stone; *t. green*, pale colour between green & blue. [F, fem. of *turquois* Turkish (*Turc* TURK)]
tu·rret, n. Small tower connected with main building whether rising from ground or projecting from wall or corbels; (Mil.) low flat usu. revolving tower for gun & gunners in ship or fort; (Hist.) square many-storeyed building on wheels used in attacking fortified place; *t. gun* (for use in revolving t.); *t.-ship* (with guns in tt.). Hence **tu·rret**ED[2] a. [f. F *tourette* dim. of *tour* TOWER]
turri·culate(d), aa. (conch.). (Of shell) having a long spire. [f. L *turricula* (*turris* tower, see -CULE, -ATE[2])]
tur·tle[1], n. (Now usu. *t.-dove*) kinds of dove, esp. a common wild kind noted for soft cooing & affection for mate & young. [OE f. L *turtur*, imit.]
tur·tle[2], n., & v.i. Marine reptile encased as tortoise & with flippers used in swimming, esp. (also *green t.*) kind much used for soup; MOCK[2] *t.*; *turn t.* (naut. slang), capsize; *t.-shell*, tortoise-shell, esp. dark kind used for inlaying, (also *t.-cowry*) large handsome kind of cowry; (v.i.) hunt for tt., whence **tur·tl**ER[1], **tur·tl**ING[1], nn. [=*tortu(e)* TORTOISE, assim. to prec.]
Tu·scan, a. & n. (Language, inhabitant) of Tuscany; *T.* ORDER[1]; *T. straw*, fine yellow wheat-straw used for hats &c. [f. LL *Tuscanus* (L *Tuscus*, see -AN)]
tush[1], int., n., & v.i. (archaic). Pshaw.
tush[2], n. Long pointed tooth, esp. canine tooth of horse. [var. of TUSK]
tu·shery, n. (literary). Use of archaisms such as TUSH[1]. [-ERY; word made by R. L. Stevenson]
tusk, n., & v.t. Long pointed tooth, esp. protruding from closed mouth as in elephant, walrus, &c.; t.-like tooth or part in harrow, lock, &c. Hence **(-)tusk**ED[2], **tu·sky**[2], aa. (Vb) gore, thrust, tear up, with t. or tt. [(vb f. n.) OE *tusc*, *tux*, cf. OFris. *tusk*]
tu·sker, n. Elephant with developed tusks. [-ER[1]]
tu·sser, -ur, -ore, n. Oak-feeding silk-worm yielding strong but coarse silk; (also *t.-silk*) silk of this & some other silkworms. [f. Hind. *tasar* f. Skr. *tasara* shuttle]
tu·ssive, a. (med.). Of a cough. [f. L *tussis* cough, see -IVE]
tu·ssle, n., & v.i. Struggle, scuffle, (*with* person, *for* thing). [as TOUSLE]
tu·ssock, n. Clump, hillock, of grass &c.; tuft, lock, of hair &c.; (also *t.-moth*) kinds of moth with tufted larvae; *t.-grass*, tall elegant grass on boggy ground in Patagonia &c. Hence **tu·ssock**Y[2] a. [f. 16th c., etym. dub.]
tussore. See TUSSER.
tut[1], **tut-tu·t**, int., n., & v.i. Int. expr. impatience, contempt, or rebuke; (n.) this exclamation; (vb) exclaim *t.* [instinctive]
tut[2], n., & v.i., (mining). Job; *t.-work*, piece-work (cf. TRIBUTE); (vb) work by the job. [?]
tutā·nia, n. Kind of Britannia metal. [*Tutin*, inventor]
tū·tĕlage (-ĭj), n. Guardianship; (period of) being under this. [f. L *tutela* (*tuēri tuit-* or *tut-* watch) + -AGE]
tū·tĕlar(y), aa. Serving as a guardian, protective; of a guardian, as *t. authority*. [f. LL *tutelarius* (as prec., see -ARY[1])]
tū·tĕnăg, n. Zinc imported from China & E. Indies; white alloy like German silver. [f. Marathi *tuttinăg* perh. f. Skr. *tuttha* blue vitriol + *nāga* tin]
tū·tor, n., & v.t. & i. Private teacher, esp. one having general charge of person's education; (Eng. Univv.) college official, usu. a fellow, directing studies of undergraduates assigned him; (Law) guardian of a minor. Hence or cogn. **tu·tor**AGE(2), **tu·tor**ESS[1], **tu·tor**SHIP, nn., **tutor·**IAL a., **tutor·ial**LY[2] adv. (Vb) act as t. to, instruct; exercise restraint over (*oneself*, one's passions, another); make one's living as t. [f. OF *tutour* f. L *tutorem* (*tuēri tut-* watch, see -OR[2])]
tu·tsan, n. St.-John's-wort, plant once held to heal wounds &c. [earlier *totsane* f. L *totus* whole, *sanus* sound, prob. thr. F]
tutti (tŏŏ·tē), mus. direction, & n. All (voices, instruments) together; (n.) music for these. [It.]
tutti-frutti (tŏŏ·tē frŏŏtē), n. Confection, ice-cream, of mixed fruits. [It., = all fruits]
tu·tty, n. Impure zinc oxide used as polishing-powder. [f. OF *tutie* f. Arab. *tūtiyā*]
tū·um. See MEUM.
tu-whi·t (tŏŏ-) n., **tu-whoo·** (tŏŏ-) n., & v.i. (Make) cry of owl. [imit.]
tŭxē·do, n. (U.S.). Dinner-jacket. [place-name]
tuyère (twēyār·, tōōyār·, twēr), **twȳ·er**, n. Pipe through which air is forced into furnace &c. [F (*tu-*), =nozzle]
twa·ddell (twŏ-), n. Kind of hydrometer for liquids heavier than water. [inventor's name]
twa·ddle (twŏ-), v.i., & n. (Indulge in) senseless, feeble, or prosy talk. Hence **twa·ddl**ER[1] n., **twa·ddl**Y[2] a. [orig. *-ttle*, var. of TATTLE]
twain, a. & n. (archaic). Two; two persons or things; *cut* &c. *in t.* (in two). [see TWO]
twang, v.i. & t., & n. (Cause to) make ringing metallic sound as of string of musical instrument or bow when plucked, (contempt.) play on or *on* (fiddle &c.) thus, as *the fiddles twanged, twanged (on) his fiddle, twanged his bow*, whence **twa·ngl**E(3) v.i. & t.; speak, utter, with nasal sound; (n.) sound of tense string when plucked, nasal tone. [imit.]

twa·nkay, n. Kind of green tea. [f. Chin. *Tun-ki*, name of a stream]
'twas (-*oz*), contraction of *it was.*
tway·blade, n. Kinds of orchid with green or purple flowers & single pair of leaves. [*tway* var. of TWAIN + BLADE]
tweak, v.t., & n. Pinch & twist sharply, pull with sharp jerk, twitch; (n.) twitch, sharp pull, pinch; (slang) dodge, device, wrinkle. Hence **twea·ker**[1] n. (slang), boy's catapult. [f. 17th c., cf. TWITCH]
tweed, n. Twilled woollen or wool-&-cotton fabric with unfinished surface & usu. two colours combined in the yarn, used esp. for men's clothes & largely made in S. Scotland. [anecdot. explained as corrupt. of *twill* (Sc. *tweel*) encouraged by assoc. with *Tweed*]
twee·dle, n. Sound as of fiddle; *tweedle-du·m & tweedledee·*, things differing only or chiefly in name. [prob. imit.]
'tween, adv. & prep. Between, esp. *'t-decks*, (space) between decks. [abbr.]
twee·ny, n. (colloq.). Servant assisting two others e. g. cook & housemaid; small cigar. [prec. + -Y[3]]
tweet, n. & v.i. Chirp (of bird). [imit.]
twee·zer, n., & v.t. (Pl., also *pair of tt.*) minute pair of tongs for taking up small objects, plucking out hairs, &c.; (vb) extract (hair, thorn, &c.) with tt. [(vb f. n.) f. obs. *tweese, pair of tweeses*, case, esp. folding case, for small instruments, f. F ETUI]
twelfth, a. & n. Next in order after eleventh (*the t.*, of August, as beginning of grouse-shooting); *T.-day* (after Christmas, festival of Epiphany); *T.-night*, eve of this, celebrated with various festivities &c.; *T.-cake*, prepared for T.-night; (n.) each of 12 equal parts. Hence **twe·lfth-ly**[2] adv. [OE *twelfta* (foll., -TH[2])]
twelve, a. & n. One more than eleven, 12, xii; *the T.* (apostles); *T.* TABLES; *in tt.* (duodecimo); *long, square, tt.*, duodecimo pages of sheet variously folded; *twe·lve-*FOLD **a.** & **adv.**; *twe·lvemo, 12mo*, = DUODECIMO; *twe·lvemonth*, year, as *has been there a t.-m.*, (adv.) *this day t.-m.*, a year hence or ago; *twe·lvepence* (archaic exc. shop), a shilling; *twe·lvepenny*, shilling (adj.). [OE *twelf*, lit. two over (as TWO + -*lif* cogn. w. LEAVE[2])]
twe·nty, a. & n. Twice ten, 20, xx; *have told him t.* (several) *times*; *t.-one, -two,* &c., or *one, two,* &c., *& t.*; *twe·ntymo, twentyfour·mo*, (*20mo, 24mo*), leaf of sheet folded into 20, 24, equal parts, book made up of such leaves. Hence **twe·ntieth** a. & n., **twe·ntyfold** a. & adv. [OE *twentig* (*twēgen* TWO, see -TY[2])]
'twere, contr. of *it were.*
twi- in comb. = two, double, in TWILIGHT & in some archaic or pseudo-archaic forms, as: *-bill*, double-bladed battle-axe, kind of mattock; *-blade*, = TWAYBLADE; *-fold* **a.** & **adv.**, two-fold; *-folded*; *-forked*; *-formed.*

twice, adv. Two times (esp. of multiplication), on two occasions, as *t. 3 is 6, told him t.*; doubly, in double degree or quantity, as *t. as strong, has t. the strength, is t. the man he was* (t. as strong &c.); (colloq.) *did it in t.* (two attempts or instalments). [ME *twies*, written *-ce* to show pronunc. (-s *not* -z), OE *twiges* (as TWO, see -ES)]
twi·cer, n. Compositor who is also pressman. [f. prec. + -ER[1]]
twi·ddle, v.t. & i., & n. Twirl idly, esp. *t.* one's *thumbs* (for lack of occupation); trifle *with* (object); *twiddling-line*, string attached to compass-gimbal & pulled to make compass-card play freely; (n.) slight twirl. [perh. dim. of *twirl* or *twist*]
twig[1], n. Small shoot or branch of tree or plant; (Anat.) small branch of artery &c.; (Electr.) small distributing conductor; divining-rod, esp. *work the t.*; *hop the t.* (colloq.), die. Hence **(-)twigged**[2], **twi·gless, twi·ggy**[2], aa. [OE, cf. Du. *twijg*, G *zweig*, cogn. w. TWO]
twig[2], v.t. (colloq.). Understand, catch the meaning of, (person, words, plan, *that* &c., or abs.); perceive, observe. [f. 18th c., etym. dub.]
twi·light, n., & v.t. (-lighted). Light from sky when sun is below horizon in morning or (usu.) evening; faint light; (fig.) state of imperfect knowledge, understanding, &c.; *t. arc(h)* or *curve* (bounding the brightest region of t. where atmosphere receives solar rays direct); *t. of the gods* (Norse myth.), conflict in which gods & giants destroyed each other; *t. sleep*, name of a modern method of making childbirth painless; (vb) illuminate faintly. [ME (TWI- + LIGHT[1])]
twill, n., & v.t. Textile fabric in which weft-threads pass alternately over one warp-thread & under (not one as in plain weaving but) two or more, thus producing diagonal lines; (vb) weave (material) thus (esp. in p.p.). [OE TWILI, cogn. w. OHG *zwilih*, two-threaded, after L BI(*lix* f. *licium* thread)]
'twill, contr. of *it will.*
twin, a., n., & v.t. & i. Forming, being one of, a closely related pair esp. of children born at a birth, as *t. children, brother(s), sister(s), the T. Brothers* or *Brethren*, Castor & Pollux; (Bot.) growing in pairs; consisting of two closely connected & similar parts; *t. boat, steamer* (with two hulls supporting one deck & having paddle-wheel between them); *twi·nflower*, slender creeping evergreen bearing a pair of fragrant flowers; *t.-screw*, steamer with two propellers on separate shafts having opposite twists. (N.) each of a closely related pair esp. of children born at a birth; exact counterpart of person or thing; compound crystal one part of which is in a reversed

position with reference to the other; *The Tt.*, Gemini; SIAMESE *tt.* Hence **twi·**NLING[1], **twi·**NSHIP, nn. (Vb) join intimately together, couple, pair, (*with*; t. & i.); *twinning-machine*, *-saw* (for cutting out teeth of combs, these being cut in pairs). [(vb & n. f. adj.) OE *twinn* double, cf. ON *tvinnr*, cogn. w. TWO]

twine, n., & v.t. & i. String of two or more strands of hemp, manilla, &c., twisted together; coil, twist, as *snaky tt.*; interlacing, tangle. (Vb) form (thread) by twisting strands together, whence **twi·**NER[1](2) n.; form (garland &c.) of interwoven material, garland (brow &c.) *with*; interweave; coil, wind, (thing *about*, *round*, another); (of plant, snake) coil itself or *itself* (*round*). Hence **twi·ning-**LY[2] adv. [(vb ME *twinen* cogn. w.) n. OE *twin*, cf. Du. *twijn*, ON *tvinni*, G *zwirn*, cogn. w. TWO]

twinge (-j-), v.t. (rare), & n. (Affect with) sharp darting pain, as *conscience twinged him*, *a t. of tooth-ache*, *rheumatism*, *conscience*, *remorse*. [(n. f. vb) OE *twengan*, etym. dub.]

twi·nkle, v.i. & t., & n. (Of light, star, &c.) shine with quick gleams, sparkle; (of eyelids, feet in dancing, &c.) move rapidly up & down or to & fro; blink, wink, (one's eyes, or intr. of person or eye); (of eyes) sparkle (*at* jest &c.); emit (light) in quick gleams. Hence **twi·nk-**LER[1] n. (N.) twitching of eyelid, blink, wink; sparkle, gleam, of the eyes, as *a humorous*, *mischievous*, *t.*; short rapid movement e. g. of feet in dancing; quick tremulous light, glimmer. [(n. f. vb) OE *twinclian*; cf. obs. *twinken* & G *zwinken* to wink]

twi·nkling, n. In vbl senses, esp. *in a t.*, *in the t. of an eye*, *in the t. of a* BED[1]*post*, in a moment, very quickly. [-ING[1]]

twirl, v.t. & i., & n. Revolve (t. & i.) rapidly, spin, whirl, (often *round*); turn (one's *thumbs* &c.) round & round in purposeless way, twiddle; (n.) rapid or idle circular motion, flourish or curl made with pen &c. [(n. f. vb), f. 16th c., etym. dub.]

twist, n., & v.t. & i. Thread, rope, &c., made by winding two or more strands &c. about one another; kinds of strong silk thread & of cotton yarn; roll of bread, tobacco, &c. in form of t.; paper packet with screwed up ends; act of twisting, condition of being twisted, as *give it a t.*, *has a curious t.*, *full of turns & tt.*; manner or degree in which thing is twisted, e. g. inclination of rifle-grooves, whirling motion given to ball in cricket &c. to make it take special curve; peculiar tendency of mind, character, &c.; (Physics) twisting strain, (angle showing) amount of torsion of rod &c., forward motion combined with rotation about an axis; kinds of mixed drink, as *gin t.*; (colloq.) appetite, as *had a tremendous t.*; *Damascus t.*, process of twisting Damascus iron to form gun-barrel; *t. of the wrist*, fig. dexterity, knack. (Vb) wind (strands &c.) one about another; form (rope &c.) thus; interweave (thing *with* or *in with* another); give spiral form to (rod, column, &c.) as by rotating the ends in opposite directions; receive, grow in, spiral form; cause (ball, esp. in billiards) to rotate while following curved path; twine (flowers &c. *into* garland &c.), make (garland &c.) thus; make one's way, make one's *way*, (*through* crowd &c., *along*, &c.) in winding manner; wrench out of natural shape, distort, as *limbs twisted on the rack*, *features twisted with pain*, (fig.) *wants to t. my words into an admission of error*; *t.* one's *arm*, force his hand or wrist round as torture; *t. off*, break off (piece) by twisting; *t. up*, t. (paper &c.) into spiral form. Hence **twi·st**ABLE a. [(vb ME *twisten* cogn. w.) n. OE *twist* (in *mæst-twist* mast-rope), f. root of TWO]

twi·ster, n. In vbl senses; also or esp.: twisting ball in cricket or billiards; girder; inner part of thigh as proper place to rest upon on horseback. [-ER[1]]

twit, v.t. Reproach, upbraid, taunt, (person *with* fault &c.). Hence **twi·tting-**LY[2] adv. [OE *ætwitan* (*æt* at + *witan* blame)]

twitch[1], v.t. & i., & n. Pull (thing *off* &c.) with light jerk; pull at, jerk at, (person's sleeve &c.) esp. to call attention; (of features, muscles, limbs) move or contract spasmodically; (n.) sudden involuntary contraction or movement, sudden pull or jerk; veterinary appliance for stilling horse during operation. [(n. f. vb) ME *twicchen*, cf. G *zwicken*, OE *twiccian*]

twitch[2], n. = QUITCH. [dial. var.]

twite, n. Kind of linnet. [perh. imit. of cry]

twi·tter, v.i. & t. & n., (Of bird) utter succession of light tremulous sounds, chirp; utter, express, thus; (n.) such series of sounds, (colloq., also **twitter-**A·TION n.) excited state. [(n. f. vb) ME *twiteren*, cf. G *zwitschern*]

'twixt, prep. = BETWIXT. [abbr.]

two (tōō), a. & n. One more than one, 2, ii; *one or t.*, a few (also lit.); *cut*, *divide*, &c., *in t.* (into t. parts); *t. can play at that game*, threat of retaliation; *put t. & t. together*, make inference from data; *in t. twos*, in a very short time; *t.-cleft* (bot.), divided nearly to the middle in t. parts; *t.-edged*, (of sword &c.) having an edge on each side, (fig., of argument, compliment, &c.) cutting both ways, ambiguous; *two·fold* a. & adv., double, doubly; *t.-handed*, having t. hands, (of sword) requiring to be used with both hands, (of saw, game, &c.) to be worked, played, &c., by t. persons; *t.-handled, -legged, -tipped, -masted, -petalled, -toothed,* &c., (having t. handles &c.); *t.-line* a. (print.), having a depth double that of the size specified, as *t.-line pica*; *twopence* (tŭ·pns), sum of, silver coin (now only as maundy money) worth, t. pence (*t.-p. coloured,* cheap &, as opp. *penny plain,* gaudy); *twopenny* (tŭ·penĭ), (adj.) worth or costing twopence, cheap, worthless, (n.) kind of beer, (slang) *tuck in your t.-p.* (head, at leap-frog); *t.-ply,* of t. strands, layers, or thicknesses, as *t.-ply rope, carpet*; *t.-speed,* adapted for t. rates of speed, as *t.-speed gear, bicycle*; *t.-sided,* having t. sides, aspects, &c.; *t.-step,* kind of round dance in march or polka time; *t.-tongued,* double-tongued, deceitful; *t.-way,* (Plumbing, of cock) permitting fluid to flow in either of t. channels, (Math.) having double mode of variation. Hence **two·**NESS n. [OE *twēgen* masc., *twā* fem., *twā* or *tu* neut., cf. Du. *twee,* G *zwei,* ON *tve'r,* L *duo,* Gk *duo*]

two·some, a. & n. (Sc.). (Game, dance, &c.) for two persons. [-SOME]

'twould, contr. of *it would.*

twy- pref., var. of TWI-.

twyer. See TUYÈRE.

-ty¹, -ity, -ety, suff. in abstract nn., repr. F *-té* f. L *-tatem* (nom. *-tas*). L adj. or n. stems in *-i-* took *-tas* without change, as *felicitas, docilitas, civitas*; adj. stems in *-o-* changed *-o-* to *-i-* or when preceded by *-i-* to *-e-*, as *aequitas, benignitas, pietas* (*pius*), *varietas* (*varius*), *satietas* (as if f. *satius*); consonantal stems (nn. or rarely adjj.) sometimes added *-i-*, as *auctoritas* but *paupertas*; nn. f. comparatives, as *priority, seniority, majority, superiority,* date only f. med. L; in *plenitas, bonitas,* F dropped *-i-*, & this type was followed in E *plenty, bounty, fealty, loyalty, penalty,* &c.

-ty², suf. = tens, as *twenty, thirty, ninety,* (two, three, &c. tens); OE *-tig,* cogn. w. *ten* & Goth. *tigjus,* Gk *dekas* (*deka* ten), decade.

Ty̆·burn, n. (hist.). Place of execution in London; *T. ticket* (hist.), exemption from parish offices &c. granted to one who prosecuted a felon to conviction; *T. tippet,* halter; *T. tree,* gallows. Hence **Ty̆bur·nia** n., fashionable London district north of Hyde Park.

Ty̆chŏ·nic (-k-), a. Of the Danish astronomer Tycho Brahe (d. 1601) or his system. [-IC]

ty̆cōō·n, n. Title applied by foreigners to shogun of Japan 1854–68. Hence **tycoo·**NATE¹(1) n. [f. Jap. *taikun* great prince]

tying. See TIE¹.

tyke. See TIKE.

tyler. See TILER.

ty̆·lopod, a. & n. (Animal) with padded not hoofed digits, e. g. camel. Hence **tylŏ·pod**OUS a. [f. Gk *tulos* knob + *pous podos* foot]

ty̆lo·sis, n. (Path.) inflammation of eyelids with hardening of the margins; (Bot.) kind of growth formed in the cavity of a duct. So **tylo·**TIC a. [f. Gk *tuloō* make knotty (*tulos* knob), see -OSIS]

ty̆·lote, n. (zool.). Cylindrical sponge-spicule knobbed at ends. [as prec.]

tymp, n. Crown of opening in front of hearth in blast-furnace; short horizontal roof-timber in mine. [abbr. of foll.]

ty·mpan, n. Stretched sheet of membrane or thin material; frame for equalizing pressure in some printing-presses; (Anat., Archit.) = TYMPANUM. [OF, f. TYMPANUM]

tympă·nic, a. Like, acting like, a drum-head; (Anat.) of the tympanum; *t. membrane,* drum-membrane of ear; *t.* (*bone*), bone of ear supporting this. [-IC]

tympanī·tēs, n. Swelling of abdomen caused by air in intestine &c. Hence **tympanĭ·**TIC a. [LL f. Gk *tumpanitēs* of drum (TYMPANUM, -ITE¹)]

tympanī·tis, n. Inflammation of living membrane of tympanum. [-ITIS]

ty·mpanum, n. (Anat.) middle ear, (also *tympanic membrane*) ear-drum; modified end of trachea in ducks &c.; (Archit.) triangular space forming field of pediment, similar space over door between lintel & arch, door-panel; drum-wheel for raising water from stream; kind of tread-mill. [L, f. Gk *tumpanon* drum]

Ty̆·nwald (-nwŏld), n. Isle of Man legislature. [f. ON *thing-vollr* place of assembly (*thing* assembly + *vollr* field)]

type¹, n. Person, thing, event, serving as illustration, symbol, prophetic similitude, or characteristic specimen, of another thing or of a class, as *water may serve as a t. of instability, paschal lamb is a t. of Christ, these things are a t.* (have a prophetic significance), *the treatment he received is but a t. of what patriots must expect, person is an admirable t. of modern athleticism* or *of the modern athlete*; class of things &c. having common characteristics, as *her beauty was of* or *belonged to another t., dislike men of that t.*; (Biol. &c.) plan of structure, as *deviates from the t.,* main division of animal or vegetable kingdom characterized by this, as *the vertebrate t.,* organism having the essential characteristics of its group (so *t. genus,* genus giving its name to & having the characteristics of a higher group, e. g. a family), whence **ty·**PAL a.; (Chem.) compound whose structure illustrates that of many others, esp. hydrochloric acid, water, ammonia, & marsh-gas; (Fine Arts) object, conception, work of art, serving as model for subsequent artists; device on either side of medal or coin; (Print.) piece of metal or wood having on its upper surface a letter or character for use in printing, (collect.

sing.) set or supply or (with pl.) kind of these, as *wooden tt. are* or *t. is now used only for posters, ran short of t., short of certain tt., was printed in various tt.* (kinds or sizes of t.), *printed in large t., a large-t. Bible, brilliant, diamond, pearl, ruby, nonpareil, emerald, minion, brevier, bourgeois, long primer, small pica, pica, English, great primer, canon, t.* (principal sizes in ascending order), BLACK[1]*-letter*, CHURCH[1]*-text*, CLARENDON, GERMAN[2]*-text*, GOTHIC, ITALIC, ROMAN[2], RUNIC, SCRIPT, *t.*, FOUNT[2] *of t.*; *t.-bar*, line of tt. in solid bar as cast in some t.-setting machines; *t.-high*, (of woodcut &c.) of proper height to print with t.; *t.-metal*, alloy used for printing-tt.; *t.-setter*, compositor, (also) composing machine; *t.- setting*, setting of tt. in proper order for printing, *t.-s. machine* (for simplifying this process, sometimes including the making of tt. as they are needed); *t.-wheel*, wheel bearing letters in relief as used in some t.-writers & telegraphs; *t.-write*, print (copy &c., or abs.) with t.-writer; *t.-writer*, machine for producing printed characters on paper as substitute for handwriting, (also) typist. [F, f. L f. Gk *tupos* blow, impress, model, f. *tuptō* strike]

type[2], v.t. Be a type of; type-write. [prec.]

tȳphlī·tis, n. Inflammation of caecum & vermiform appendix. Hence **typhlī·**TIC a. [f. Gk *tuphlos* blind, w. ref. to CAECUM, + -ITIS]

ty·phoid, a. & n. Like typhus; *t. (fever)*, infectious fever with eruption of red points on chest & abdomen & severe intestinal irritation, enteric; *t. bacillus*, germ held to cause t.; *t. condition* (of depressed vitality, occurring in many acute diseases); *t. pneumonia* (combined with t.). Hence **typhoi·d**AL a. [f. TYPHUS + -OID]

typhomā·nia, n. Muttering delirium characteristic of typhus. [Gk (*tuphō-*) f. *tuphos* TYPHUS, -MANIA]

tȳphōō·n, n. Violent hurricane in the China seas occurring esp. from July to October. Hence **typhŏ·n**IC a. [partly f. Arab. *tūfān* perh. f. Gk *tuphōn* whirlwind, partly f. Chin. *tai fung* big wind]

tȳ·phus, n. Fever marked by eruption of purple spots, great prostration, & usu. delirium; *malignant, simple, t.*, severe, mild, for ı of t. Hence **ty·ph**OUS a. [mod. L f. Gk *tuphos* smoke, stupor]

tȳ·pic, a. *T. fever*, one that is regular in its attacks or follows particular type. [f. F *typique*, f. L f. Gk *tupikos* (as TYPE[1], see -IC)]

tȳ·pical, a. Serving as a type or characteristic example, representative, symbolical, emblematic, (*of*), as *a t. genus, plant, Scotchman, is t. of the genus, was t. of* (foreshadowed) *Christ's second coming*; characteristic of, serving to distinguish, a type, as *t. markings, structure, phraseology.* Hence **ty·pical**LY[2] adv., **ty·pical**NESS n. [f med. L *typicalis* (prec., -AL)]

tȳ·pifȳ, v.t. Represent by a type, foreshadow; be a type of, embody the characteristics of. Hence **typi**FICA·TION, **ty·pifi**ER[1], nn. [as TYPE[1] + -FY]

ty·pist, n. User of typewriter. [f. TYPE[1] + -IST]

ty·po, n. (colloq.). =TYPOGRAPHER. [abbr.]

typo- in comb. (bef. vowel *typ-*) = TYPE, as: *-graph*, machine for making & setting type; *-lite*, stone impressed with figure of animal &c., fossil; *-logy*, doctrine, interpretation, of (esp. biblical) types, so *-lo·gical* a.; *-onym* (biol.), name based on a type, so *-ŏ·nymal, -onȳ·mic*, aa.

typŏ·graphy, n. Art of printing, whence **typo·graph**ER[1] n.; character, appearance, of printed matter, as *faults of t., the t. was admirable.* Hence **typogra·ph**IC(AL) aa., **typogra·phical**LY[2] adv. [F (*-ie*), = TYPE + -O- + -GRAPHY]

tȳra·nnic(al), a. (*-ic* rare). Acting like, characteristic of, a tyrant; arbitrary, imperious, despotic. Hence or cogn. **tyra·nnical**LY[2], **tȳ·rannous**LY[2], advv., **tyra·nnical**NESS n., **tȳ·rann**OUS a. [*-ic* f. F *tyrannique* f. L f. Gk *turannikos* (TYRANT, -IC) + -AL]

tȳra·nnicide, n. Killer, killing, of a tyrant. Hence **tyrannici·d**AL a. [F, f. L *tyrannicida, -cidium* (as TYRANT, see -CIDE)]

tȳ·rannize, v.i. & t. Play the tyrant, rule despotically or cruelly (*over* person &c.); (now rare) rule (person &c.) despotically. [f. F *tyranniser* (TYRANT, see -IZE)]

tȳ·ranny, n. Despotic or cruel exercise of power; instance of this, tyrannical act or behaviour; rule of (Greek) tyrant, period of this. [f. OF *tyrannie* f. med. L (*-ia*) f. Gk *turannia, -is*, as foll.]

tȳr·ant, n. Oppressive or cruel ruler; (Gk Hist.) absolute ruler owing his office to usurpation, *Thirty Tt.*, oligarchs ruling Athens 404–3 B.C.; *t.-bird, t. fly-catcher*, kinds of Amer. passerine bird. [OF, f. L f. Gk *turannos*, w. assim. to -ANT]

tyre[1], n. (Anglo-Ind.) Curdled milk & cream. [Tamil *tayir*]

tyre[2]. See TIRE[2].

tyro. See TIRO.

Tȳrole·se (-z), a. & n. (pl. same). (Native) of the Tyrol. [-ESE]

Tȳrōlie·nne (-ĕn), n. Dance of Tyrolese peasants, song suitable for this. [F]

tȳroto·xicon, n. A ptomaine produced in milk or cheese. [f. Gk *turos* cheese + *toxikon* poison]

Tȳ·rrhene, Tyrrhē·nian, aa. Etruscan. [f. L f. Gk *Turrhēnos* + -IAN]

tzar &c. See CZAR &c.

tzetze. See TSETSE.

Tziga·ne (-ahn), a. & n. Of the Hungarian Gipsies or their music; (n.) Hungarian Gipsy. [F, f. Magyar *czigány*]

U

U, u, (ū), letter (pl. *Us*, U's). *U-boat*, German submarine [G *untersee*, underwater]. *U-bolt, -tube*, &c. (shaped like U); U.P. (slang pronunc. of *up* adv., esp. *it's all U.P.*).

Abbreviations (1): U., union, **U.D.C.** (of democratic control), **U.S.S.R.** (of socialist soviet republics); united, **U.K.** (kingdom), **U.K.A.** (-kingdom alliance), **U.P.** (presbyterian), **U.S.** (States, i.e. of America), **U.S.A.** (States of America, States Army), **U.S.N.** (States Navy); Utah, **U.T.** (Territory). u., under, **u.p.** (proof); upper, **u.c.** (case).

Abbreviations (2): **ult.**(*imo*); **Univ.**-(ersity); **Ut.**(ah).

ūbi·ety, n. Being in definite place, local relation, whereness. [f. L *ubi* where, see -TY]

ubiquitar·ian, a. & n. (theol.). Of, believer in, the omnipresence of Christ's body. Hence **ubiquitar·ian**ISM n. [foll., -ARIAN]

ūbi·quity, n. Omnipresence; being everywhere or in an indefinite number of places at same time; *u. of the king* (law), his official presence in courts in the person of his judges. Hence **ubi·quit**OUS a., **ubi·quitous**LY² adv., **ubi·quitous**NESS n. [L *ubique* everywhere f. *ubi* where, -ITY]

ūbi sū·pra, adv. In the place (in book &c.) above mentioned. [L, lit. where above]

ū·dal, n. Kind of freehold right based on uninterrupted possession prevailing in N. Europe before feudal system & still in Orkney & Shetland (often attrib., as *u. tenure*); *u·dalman*, holder of property by u., so **u·dall**ER¹ n. [f. ON *óthal*, cf. OHG *uodil* inherited property]

u·dder, n. Mammary glands of cattle &c. esp. when large & having more than one teat. Hence **(-)udder**ED², **u·dder**LESS, aa. [OE *úder*, cf. Du. *uijer*, G *euter*, cogn. w. L *uber*, Gk *outhar*]

ūdŏ·meter, n. Rain-gauge. Hence **udome·tr**IC a. [f. F *udomètre* f. L *udus* damp + -O- + -METER]

ugh (ŏŏh &c.), int. expr. disgust or horror.

ŭ·gly, a. & n. Unpleasing or repulsive to sight, as *an u. beast of a bulldog, must not make u. faces, the ugliest house I have seen, has an u. scar on the forehead*; morally repulsive, vile, discreditable, unpleasant, unpleasantly suggestive, threatening, unpromising, as *u. vices, his conduct has an u. look, u. rumours are about, an u.* (awkward) *job, an u. customer*, formidable person, *cloud has an u. look, have had u. weather, an u. gash*; *u. duckling*, person who turns out the genius &c. of the family after being thought the dullard &c. (w. ref. to cygnet in brood of ducks in an Andersen tale). Hence **u·gli**FY v.t., **u·gli**LY² adv., **u·gli**NESS n. (N.) shade worn as appendage to bonnet about middle of 19th c. [f. ON *uggligr* fearful (*uggr* fear + *-ligr* -LY¹)]

U·grian, U·gric, (ŏŏ-), aa. Finnic. [f. name of a tribe + -IAN, -IC]

uh·lan (ŏŏ-, ū-), n. Cavalryman armed with lance in some European armies. [G, f. Pol. *ulan* f. Turk. *oghlān* son, child]

ūka·se (-ās), n. Edict of Russian government. [f. Russ. *ukaz'* ordinance, edict]

ukulele (ŏŏkŏŏlā·lĕ), n. Four-stringed Hawaiian guitar. [native]

-ul- in comb. = -ULE, forming derivative adjj. &c. with or without dim. sense & often preferred to direct formations from parent noun (*glandular, globulin, nodulose*).

u·lcer, n. Open sore on external or internal surface of body with secretion of pus &c.; (fig.) moral blemish, corrupting influence, &c. Hence or cogn. **u·lcer**ED², **u·lcer**OUS, aa., **u·lcerous**LY² adv., **u·lcerous**NESS n. [f. L *ulcus -eris* sore, cf. Gk *helkos* wound, sore]

u·lcerate, v.i. & t. Form, convert or be converted into, affect with, an ulcer (lit. & fig.). Hence or cogn. **u·lcer**ABLE, **u·lcer**ATIVE, aa., **ulcer**A·TION n. [f. L *ulcerare* (prec.), -ATE³]

-ule, suf. of dimm. f. L wds in *-ulus, -ula, -ulum*, as *globule* (L *globulus* f. *globus*), *granule, pustule*, & in mod. wds on L anal. *anguillule*; also *-le*, as *angle*. In *pendule, -ule* has diff. orig.

U·lĕma (ŏŏ-), n. Moslem doctors of sacred law & theology esp. in Turk. empire. [f. Arab. *'ulema* pl. of *'alim* learned f. *'alama* know]

-ulent, suf. of adjj. f. L, repr. L *-ulentus*, the normal form of *-lentus* -LENT, as in *fraudulent, turbulent, truculent*. Hence n. suf. *-ulence*.

ūli·ginose, a. (bot.). Growing in muddy places. [f. L *uliginosus* (*uligo -ginis* moisture, see -OSE¹)]

u·llage (-ĭj), n. (commerc.). What a cask &c. wants of being full. [AF *ulliage*, OF *ouillage* (*ouiller* fill up, -AGE)]

u·lmin, n. (chem.). Black gummy substance found on elm & other trees & in vegetable mould &c. Hence **u·lm**IC, **u·lm**OUS, aa. (chem.). [f. L *ulmus* elm + -IN]

u·lna, n. (pl. *-ae*). Inner of two bones of forearm (cf. RADIUS). Hence **u·ln**AR¹ a., **u·lno-** comb. form. [L, = elbow, cf. Gk *ōlenē*, & ELL]

ūlo·trichan a. & n., **-ous** a., (-k-). Woolly-haired, esp.: (member) of the woolly-haired division of mankind. [f. Gk *oulos* woolly + *thrix trikhos* hair + -AN, -OUS]

u·lster, n. Long loose overcoat often with belt orig. of Ulster frieze, whence **u·lster**ED² a.; *U. custom*, form of tenant right in U.

ulter·ior, a. Situated beyond; more remote, not immediate, in the future, in the background, beyond what is seen or avowed, (*u. views, object, plans*). Hence **ulter·ior**LY[2] adv. [L, compar. of adj. seen in ULTRA-]

u·ltima, a. Last, most remote, (in phrr.: *u. ratio*, final argument esp. force, *u. ratio rē·gum*, last argument of kings, resort to arms, *u.* THULE). [L, fem. of *ultimus*, superl. as prec.]

u·ltimate (-*at*), a. Last, final, beyond which no other exists or is possible, as *u. result, analysis*; fundamental, primary, as *u. basis, u. principles, truths, u. cause* (beyond which no other can be found), *the u. facts of nature* (beyond reach of analysis). Hence **u·ltimate**LY[2] adv., **u·ltimate**NESS n. [f. LL *ultimare* come to an end (*ultimus*, as prec.), see -ATE[3]]

ultimā·tum, n. (pl. *-tums, -ta*). Final proposal or statement of terms, rejection of which by opposite party may lead to rupture, declaration of war, &c.; ultimate conclusion; fundamental principle. [neut. p.p. as prec.]

u·ltimo, adj. (usu. abbr. *ult.*). In the month preceding that now current (cf. PROXIMO, INSTANT[1]), *as your letters of the 28th ult. & 3rd inst.* [L, = in last (*mense* month), see ULTIMA]

ultimoge·niture, n. System in which youngest son (cf. PRIMOGENITURE) takes inheritance, = BOROUGH-ENGLISH. [f L *ultimus* (see ULTIMA) on PRIMOGENITURE]

u·ltra, a. & n. Favouring, advocate of, extreme views or measures. [orig. as abbr. of F *ultra-royaliste*]

ultra-, pref. = L *ultra* beyond, on the other side of, esp. as living pref. to adjj. & their derivatives w. sense ' excessively, beyond what is usual or natural or reasonable ', as: *-classical -conservatism, -conservative*; *-cosmopolitan*; *-critical*; *-fashionable*; *-partisan*; *-Protestant(ism)*; *-religious*.

u·ltraist, n. Holder of extreme opinions in politics, religion, &c. So **u·ltra**ISM n. [-IST]

u·ltramari·ne (-ēn), a. & n. Situated beyond the sea. (N.) blue pigment got from lapis lazuli; *artificial u.* (made by mixing clay, carbonate of soda, sulphur, & resin), *u. ashes*, residuum of lapis lazuli after extraction of u., used by old masters for neutral flesh tints &c. [f. med. L ULTRA(*marinus* MARINE); n. sense from fact that lapis lazuli was brought from beyond sea]

ultramo·ntane, a. & n. Situated south of the Alps; Italian; favourable to the absolute authority of the Pope in matters of faith & discipline, whence **ultramo·ntan**ISM, **ultramo·ntan**IST, nn.; (n.) one who resides south of the Alps, person holding u. views. [f. med. L ULTRA(*montanus* f. L *mons -ntis* mountain + -ANE); earlier in senses ' north of Alps ', ' unfavourable to Pope ', &c., cf. TRAMONTANE, CIS*montane*]

ultramu·ndane, a. Beyond the world or the solar system; of another life. [f. LL ULTRA(*mundanus* MUNDANE)]

u·ltra-vi·olet, a. (Of invisible rays of the spectrum) beyond the violet rays. [ULTRA-]

u·ltra vīr·ēs, adv. or pred. a. Beyond one's power or authority. [L]

ultrōmoti·vity, n. Power of spontaneous movement. [f. L *ultro* of one's own accord + MOTIVITY]

ū·lūlate, v.i. Howl; hoot. So **u·lul**ANT a., **ulul**A·TION n. [f. L *ululare*, see -ATE[3]]

-um. See -IUM.

u·mbel, n. (bot.). Flower-cluster in which stalks nearly equal in length spring from common centre & form a flat or convex or concave surface as in parsley. Hence **u·mbell**AL, **u·mbell**AR[1], **u·mbell**ATE[2](2), **umbelli·**FEROUS, **umbe·lli**FORM, aa., **u·mbell**ET[1], **umbe·ll**ULE, nn. [f. L *umbella* sunshade dim. of UMBRA]

u·mber, n., a., & v.t. Natural pigment like ochre but darker & browner (*raw u.*, this in natural state, of dark yellow colour, *burnt u.*, redder & deeper in colour), whence **u·mber**Y[2] a.; grayling; *u.-bird* (also *umbre·tte*), Afr. bird allied to stork & heron; (adj.) of u. colour, dark, dusky; (v.t.) colour with u. [(vb & adj. f. n.) f. OF *ombre* (or *terre d'ombre*) f. L *umbra* shade, or f. fem. of L *Umber* Umbrian]

umbĭ·lical (*or* -ī·kl), a. Of, situated near, the umbilicus, as *u. cord*, rope-like structure passing from foetus to placenta; central; connected through the female line, as *an u. ancestor*. [f. med. L *umbilicalis* (UMBILICUS, -AL)]

umbi·licate (-*at*), a. Shaped like a navel, whence **umbilic**A·TION n.; having an umbilicus. [f. L *umbilicatus* (UMBILICUS, -ATE[2])]

umbili·cular, a. Of the navel; *u. contemplation*, sitting with gaze fixed on one's navel (practised by Indian mystics as means of attaining great sanctity). [-UL-, -AR[1]]

umbilī·cus, n. Navel, whence **umbilĭ·**FEROUS, **u·mbili**FORM, aa.; (Bot., Zool., Conch.) navel-like formation; (Geom.) point in a surface through which all lines of curvature pass; (Rom. Ant.) boss at each end of stick on which MS. was rolled. [L, cogn. w. Gk *omphalos*, & NAVEL]

u·mbo, n. (pl. *-os, -ō·nēs*). Boss of shield, esp. in centre; (Bot., Zool., &c.) boss, knob, protuberance. Hence **u·mbon**AL, **u·mbon**ATE[2], **umbŏ·n**IC, aa. [L, gen. *-onis*]

u·mbra, n. (pl. *-ae*). (Astr.) total shadow (cf. PENUMBRA) cast by the earth or moon in an eclipse; dark central part of sun-spot (cf. PENUMBRA); (Rom. Ant.) uninvited guest brought by a guest. Hence **u·mbrAL** a. [L, =shade]

u·mbrage (-ĭj), n. Sense of slight or injury, offence, as *give, take, u.*; (chiefly poet.) shade, what gives shade, so **umbrā·geOUS** a. [f. F *ombrage* f. L *umbraticum* (UMBRA, see -AGE)]

umbre·lla, n. Light circular canopy of silk or other material attached to radiating folding frame sliding on stick carried in the hand as protection against rain or (now usu. *sunshade, parasol*) sun; (fig.) formula or compromise enabling politicians &c. of divergent views to coalesce (*under the Unionist, anti-communist,* &c., *u.*); gelatinous disk of jelly-fish &c. by contraction & expansion of which it swims; (also *u.-shell*) gasteropod with u.-like shell; *u.-bird*, kinds of S.-Amer. bird with radiating crest; *u.-stand* (for holding closed uu., usu. with pan at bottom to catch drippings); *u.-tree*, small kind of magnolia with leaves in u.-like whorl at end of branch, (colloq.) tree so grafted or trained that its branches droop in u. form. Hence **umbre·lla'd** [-ED²] a. [f. It. *ombrella*, dim. of *ombra* shade f. UMBRA]

umbrette. See UMBER.

U·mbrian, a. Of (ancient or modern) Umbria; *U. school*, school of painting to which Raphael & Perugino belonged; (n.) language, inhabitant, of ancient Umbria. [-AN]

umbri·ferous, a. Affording shade. [f. L *umbrifer* (UMBRA, see -FEROUS]

umiak (ōō·myăk), n. Eskimo boat worked by women. [Esk.]

umlaut (ōō·mlowt, ŏŏ·m-), n., & v.t. (In Germanic languages) vowel change due to *i* or *u* (now usu. lost or altered) in following syllable (e. g. German *mann männer, fuss füsse*, English *man men*); (vb) modify (form, sound) by the u. [G (*um-* around + *laut* sound)]

u·mpire, n., & v.i. & t. (Law) third person called in to decide between arbitrators who disagree; person chosen to decide question; person chosen to enforce rules & settle disputes in cricket or other game. Hence **u·mpirAGE**(3), **u·mpireSHIP**, nn. (Vb) act as u. (*for* persons, *in* game &c.), act as u. in (game). [(vb f. n.) ME *nompere* f. OF *nomper* peerless, not equal, in sense *third man, odd man*, (*non* not + *per* PEER¹); for loss of *n-* cf. ADDER]

ŭ·mpteen, a. (slang). Several, many, a lot of. [facet. form. on -TEEN]

'un, pron. (colloq.). One, as *that's a good 'un, he's a tough 'un, stiff-'uns' race.*

un-¹, pref. of vbs w. neg. sense & usu. denoting action contrary to or annulling that of the simple vb. The pref. being unlimited in use, only a selection of the existing vbs & derivative wds is here given. Adjj. in *-able, -ed,* & *-ing*, are identical in form with wds in UN-², with or without material difference in meaning; *undoable, unstrappable,* may mean 'that can be undone, unstrapped', or 'that cannot be done, strapped'; *unbracing* may mean 'that unbraces' or 'that does not brace'; an *unbending* person is one fond of or averse to relaxation; an *un²coiled* rope must be coiled before it can be *un¹coiled*; an *unbridlED¹* horse may (*un-¹*) or may not (UN-²) have been previously bridled, in either case he is now *un²bridlED²*. As a rule, the UN-² forms of such adjj. are current, the others not. The stress in the foll. wds is not marked, being the same as in the simple vb or n. or, where that is monosyllabic, falling on the second syllable (*undecei·ve, unsay·*); but p.pp. or adjj. in *-ed*, whether in *un-¹* or UN-², tend in attrib. use to take stress on *un-* (cf. -ED²), as *an u·nmasked villain, an u·nmuzzled hound, villain was unma·sked, dog was unmu·zzled.*

(1) Wds formed upon a simple verb & with contrary sense (rarely w. intensified negative sense, as *unloose*). The distinction between some of these & the vbs in the following groups, which appear to be formed rather on a noun, is necessarily arbitrary, the assumed simple vb (identical in form with the noun, from which it is usu. derived) being often rare or non-existent in the required senses of 'furnish with', 'place in', &c. Exx.: *unanchor* v.t. & i.; *unattire* v.t. & i.; *unbalance* v.t.; *unbank* v.t., cause (fire) to burn briskly by removing ashes from top; *unbar* v.t., remove bar from (gate &c.), unlock, open, (often fig.); *unbear* v.t., take off or relax bearing-rein of (horse); *unbend* v.t. & i., change from bent position, straighten, relax (mind &c.) from strain or exertion, rid oneself of constraint, be affable, whence *unbending¹* a., (Naut.) unfasten (sails) from yards & stays, cast (cable) loose, untie (rope); *unbeseem* v.t. be unbecoming to; *unbias* v.t., free from bias; *unbind* v.t., release from bonds or binding; *unblindfold* v.t.; *unblock* v.i. (whist), play high card to avoid interrupting partner's long suit; *unbolt* v.t., release (door &c.) by drawing back bolt; *unbonnet* v.i. & t., take off cap &c. e. g. in salutation, remove the bonnet of: *unbosom* v.i. & t., disclose one's secret feelings, disclose (thoughts &c.); *unbrace* v.t., remove the braces of, free from tension, relax (nerves &c.); *unbraid* v.t., separate the strands of; *unbreech* v.t., free the breech of (cannon) from fastenings &c.; *unbridle* v.t., remove bridle from (horse, fig. person, tongue, &c.); *unbuckle* v.t., release the buckle of (strap, shoe, &c.); *unburden* v.t., relieve of burden, relieve (one*self*,

conscience, &c.) by confession &c. *to* person; *unbutton* v.t., open (coat &c.) by withdrawing buttons from buttonholes; *unchain* v.t.; *unchristianize* v.t.; *unclasp* v.t., loosen the clasp of; *unclench, -inch,* v.t. & i.; *unclog* v.t.; *unclose* v.t. & i., open; *unclothe* v.t.; *uncock* v.t., let down hammer of (gun) softly so as not to explode charge; *uncoil,* v.t. & i.; *uncord* v.t.; *uncork* v.t., draw cork from (bottle), (colloq.) give vent or expression to (feelings &c.); *uncouple* v.t., release (dogs, railway-cars, &c.) from couples or couplings; *uncover* v.t. & i., remove covering from, lay bare, disclose, take off one's hat or cap, (Mil., of front line) expose (the line behind) by wheeling to right or left; *uncreate*[1] v.t., annihilate; *uncross* v.t., remove (legs, arms, knives, &c.) from crossed position; *uncurb* v.t.; *uncurl* v.t.; *undeceive* v.t., free from deception, whence *undeceived*[1] a.; *undeify* v.t.; *undo* v.t., annul (*cannot u. the past, our past actions*), untie or unfasten or unloose (coat, button, parcel), unfasten the buttons or garments or stays of (person), ruin the prospects or reputation or morals of, whence *undoer, undoing,* nn., *undone*[1] a.; *undomesticate* v.t.; *undrape* v.t.; *undress*[1] v.t. & i., take off the clothes of, take off one's clothes, whence *undressed*[1] a.; *unegoize* v.t.; *unentangle* v.t.; *unequalize* v.t.; *unfasten* v.t., whence *unfastened*[1] a.; *unfetter* v.t., whence *unfettered*[1] a.; *unfeudalize* v.t.; *unfile* v.t., remove (paper) from file; *unfit* v.t., make unsuitable (*for*); *unfix* v.t., whence *unfixed*[1] a.; *unfold*[1] v.t. & i., open the folds of, spread out, (fig.) reveal (thoughts, designs), become opened out, develop; *unform* v.t.; *unfurl* v.t. & i., spread out (sail), become spread out; *ungear* v.t., strip of gear, throw out of gear; *ungild* v.t.; *ungird* v.t.; *unglaze* v.t.; *unha·llow* v.t., profane, desecrate; *unhand* v.t., take one's hands off, release from one's grasp; *unhang* v.t., remove from hanging position, strip (wall &c.) of hangings; *unharness* v.t.; *unhasp* v.t., loose from hasp; *unhinge* v.t., take (door) off its hinges, disorder (mind &c.), whence *unhinged* a.; *unhitch* v.t.; *unhook* v.t., remove from hook, open (dress &c.) by detaching its hooks; *unhoop* v.t., *unhouse* v.t., deprive of shelter, drive from house; *unhumanize* v.t.; *unjoin* v.t.; *unjoint* v.t., separate joints of (fishing-rod &c.); *unkink* v.t. & i.; *unknit* v.t.; *unknot* v.t.; *unlace* v.t., loose or open by undoing lace(s) of (boot, stays, &c.); *unlade* v.t.; *unlash* v.t. (naut.); *unlatch* v.t., release latch of (door); *unlay* v.t. (naut.), untwist; *unlearn* v.t., expel from one's memory, forget the knowledge of, rid oneself of (esp. false or misleading information, habit, &c.); *unline* v.t., remove lining of; *unlink* v.t.; *unload* v.t., remove load from (ship, cart, &c., or abs.), remove (load) from ship &c., withdraw charge from (gun &c.); *unlock* v.t., release lock of (door, box, &c., fig. mind &c.), (fig.) disclose (secret &c.); *unlodge* v.t., dislodge; *unloose* v.t., loose; *unmake* v.t., destroy, annul; *unmask* v.t. & i., remove the mask from, expose (villain, villainy), take off one's mask, reveal one's true character &c.; *unmew* v.t. (poet., rhet.), release; *unmoor* v.t., loose the moorings of (vessel &c. or fig., also abs.), weigh one of two or more anchors of (vessel); *unmortise* v.t.; *unmould* v.t., change the form of; *unmuffle* v.t. & i., remove muffler from (face, bell, &c.), remove muffler &c. from one's face; *unmuzzle* v.t., (esp., fig.) relieve of obligation to remain silent; *unnaturalize* v.t., make unnatural; *unnerve* v.t., deprive of nerve or strength or resolution, whence *unnerved* a.; *unpack* v.t., open & remove contents of (package, box, &c., or abs.), take out (contents) from package &c.; *unpeg* v.t., remove the peg(s) from or of, open thus; *unpeople* v.t., depopulate; *unpick* v.t., undo (stitches, garment &c.) by picking, open with pick; *unpin* v.t., unfasten by removing pins; *unplait* v.t.; *unplug* v.t.; *unpreach* v.t., recant in preaching; *unravel* v.t., separate (threads &c.), separate the threads of (material), disentangle (lit. & fig.); *unreel* v.t. & i., unwind, become unwound, from reel; *unreeve* v.t. (naut.); *unrein* v.t., give the rein to (often fig.); *unriddle* v.t., solve or explain (riddle, mystery); *unrig* v.t. (naut.); *unrip* v.t., rip open or apart; *unrivet* v.t.; *unroll* v.t. & i., open (roll of cloth &c.), (of roll) be opened, display, be displayed; *unromanize* v.t.; *unroot* v.t., pull up by root; *unsa·ddle* v.t. (often abs.); *unsay* v.t., retract (statement), whence *unsaid*[1] a.; *unscrew* v.t., unfasten by removing screws, loosen (screw); *unseal* v.t., break the seal of, open, (letter &c.); *unseam* v.t., rip open (garment &c.) at seam; *unseat* v.t., remove from seat, throw from seat on horseback, depose (M.P. &c.) from seat, whence *unseated*[1] a.; *unset* v.t., remove (gem) from its setting; *unsettle* v.t., disturb orderly arrangement of, discompose, disincline to routine &c. (*holidays u. me*), derange (intellect), whence *unsettled*[1] a.; *unshackle* v.t.; *unsheathe* v.t.; *unship* v.t., unload (cargo), disembark (passenger), (Naut.) remove (oar, tiller, &c.) from place where it is fixed or fitted, whence *unshipped*[1] a.; *unsling* v.t. (esp. naut.); *unspeak* v.t., retract; *unsteel* v.t., soften, relax, (resolution, person); *unstick* v.t., separate (thing stuck to another); *unstitch* v.t., undo stitches of; *unstock* v.t., deprive of stock, remove (gun-barrel) from stock; *unstop* v.t., free from obstruction, remove stopper from; *unstrap* v.t., remove or undo the strap(s) of; *unstring* v.t., remove the strings of, loosen strings of (harp &c.), take (beads &c.) off string, weaken (nerves), weaken nerves of (person &c.), whence *unstrung* a.; *unswaddle* v.t.; *unswathe* v.t.; *unswear* v.t., recant by oath; *untack* v.t., disjoin, separate, (thing tacked to another); *untangle* v.t.; *unteach* v.t.; *untemper* v.t., take away the temper of (metal &c.); *untether* v.t.; *unthink* v.t., retract in thought; *unthread* v.t., take thread out of (needle), find one's way out of (maze); *untie* v.t., undo (knot &c.), undo the cords &c. of (bundle, package, &c.), liberate from bonds, whence *untied*[1] a.; *untruss* v.t.; *untuck* v.t.; *untune* v.t., put out of tune (lit. & fig.); *untwine* v.t. & i.; *untwist* v.t. & i.; *unveil* v.t. & i., remove veil from, remove one's veil, remove concealing drapery from (statue &c.) with ceremonies; *unvote* v.t., retract by vote (what has been voted); *unwarp* v.t., restore from warped state; *unweave* v.t., take to pieces (textile fabric), separate (woven threads); *unwill* v.t., will the reverse of (what one has willed); *unwind* v.t. & i., draw out at length (what is wound), become thus drawn out, whence *unwound*[1] a.; *unwork* v.t., undo, destroy, (fabric &c.); *unwrap* v.t.; *unwrinkle* v.t.; *unyoke* v.t. & i., release (as) from yoke, (fig.) cease work.

(2) Vbs formed on n. or vb—see (1)—& having sense 'deprive of', 'separate from'. A simple vb sometimes exists in same sense, e. g. *(un)bone, (un)husk, (un)shell.* Exx.: *unapparel* v.t.; *unarm* v.t., deprive of arms or armour, whence *unarmed*[1] a.; *unballast* v.t.; *unbelt* v.t.; *unbone* v.t.; *unboot* v.t. & i.; *unbowel* v.t.; *uncap* v.t.; *uncloak* v.t.; *uncowl* v.t., uncover (face) by removing cowl, unmonk; *uncrown* v.t., deprive (esp. fig. king &c.) of crown; *unedge* v.t., destroy edge of, blunt; *unface* v.t., expose; *unfeather* v.t.; *unfence* v.t.; *unflesh* v.t.; *unflower* v.t.; *unframe* v.t.; *unfrock* v.t., deprive of frock or (fig.) of ecclesiastical rank; *ungirdle* v.t.; *unglove* v.t. & i., deprive of, take off one's, gloves; *ungown* v.t.; *ungum* v.t.; *unhair* v.t.; *unhat* v.t.; *unhelm* v.t.; *unhusk* v.t.; *unlead* v.t. (print.), remove leads from (types); *unlimber* v.t. & abs.; *unman* v.t., deprive (esp. ship) of men, see also (4); *unmantle* v.t.; *unnail* v.t., take nails out of, unfasten (box &c.) thus; *unplume* v.t.; *unprop* v.t.; *unring* v.t.; *unrobe* v.t. & i., undress; *unroof* v.t.; *unrumple* v.t.; *unscale* v.t., remove scales of; *unself* v.t., rid of self, unegoize; *unsex* v.t., deprive (usu. woman) of the qualities of the sex; *unshell* v.t.; *unshoe* v.t., take shoe(s) off (horse &c.); *unshot* v.t., remove shot from (gun); *unshutter* v.t.; *unsinew* v.t.; *unsister* v.t.; *unsolder* v.t.; *unspar* v.t.; *unstarch* v.t., free from starch or (fig.) stiffness or reserve; *unstopper* v.t.; *untile* v.t.; *untin* v.t.; *untooth* v.t.; *unturf* v.t.

(3) Vbs similarly formed with sense 'release from', 'take out of', 'displace from'. Exx.: *unbag* v.t.; *unbed* v.t.; *unbitt* v.t. (naut.); *unbox* v.t.; *uncage* v.t.; *uncart* v.t.; *uncase* v.t.; *unchurch* v.t., excommunicate; *uncloister* v.t.; *uncoop* v.t.; *undock* v.t.; *unearth* v.t., drive (fox &c.) from an earth, dig up, (fig.) bring to light; *unfold*[2] v.t., release (sheep) from fold; *unhive* v.t.; *unhorse* v.t., throw from horse, (of horse) throw (rider), cause to dismount; *unleash* v.t.; *unnest* v.t.; *unpen* v.t.; *unperch* v.t.; *unroost* v.t.; *unsnare* v.t.; *unspell* v.t., release from spell; *unsphere* v.t.; *unstep* v.t. (naut.); *untent* v.t.; *unthrone* v.t.; *untomb* v.t.

(4) Occasional vbs formed chiefly f. nouns with sense 'cause to be no longer', 'degrade from the position of'. Exx.: *unbishop* v.t.; *unduke* v.t.; *unking* v.t.; *unlord* v.t.; *unman* v.t., deprive of manly qualities, break the courage of, dishearten, emasculate, see also (2); *unmonk* v.t.; *unpope* v.t.; *unprelate* v.t.; *unpriest* v.t.; *unprince* v.t.; *unqueen* v.t.; *unsquire* v.t.; *unvicar* v.t. [OE, cf. Du. *ont-*, G *ent-*, Goth. *and-* (as in ANSWER[1])]

un-[2], pref. giving negative sense to adjj. with their derivative nn. & advv., & to a miscellaneous group of nn. chiefly of independent formation.

(1) Of the many adjj. formed with *un-*, esp. of those in *-able, -ed, -ing,* for which cf. UN-[1], only a selection is here given. The sense of *un-* is either simply 'not' (as in most adjj. in *-able, -ed, -ing,* & in some others, as *unofficial*) or more commonly 'the reverse of', with implication of praise, blame, &c. Between *un-* & IN-[2] a differentiation has been suggested according to which *inartistic* means 'contrary to rules of art', 'such as an artist would condemn', & *unartistic* means 'not concerned with rules of art'; & pairs of words may be found that bear out the distinction, esp. where one of the pair has long been restricted to the proposed sense & the other has been manufactured or revived to supply its deficiencies (*immoral, unmoral*). But the purely neutral sense thus ascribed to *un-* is not that found in many of the most familiar adjj. (*unbeautiful, unfair, ungraceful, ungracious, unkind, unjust, ungenerous, untrue, unscrupulous, unmanly, unscholarly, unladylike, unchristian*), including some of the exact type of *unartistic* (*unscientific, unphilosophical*): when we say that a thing is *untrue*, we do not mean that it does not matter for our purpose whether it is true or not, but that it is culpably inconsistent with truth. Apart from the adjj. in *-able, -ed, -ing,* both *un-* & *in-* more commonly have this implication of

blame &c., the purely neutral sense being often given by NON-(5). IN-[2] is preferred to *un-* with certain terminations of L orig., e. g. *-ate*, *-ite*, *-ant*, *-ent*, *-ble* (exc. *-able*, now a living E suf.), is for the most part archaic with *-ed*[1, 2] (*indigested* &c., but cf. *inexperienced*), and is not used with *-ing*, *-ful*, *-like*, *-ly*, &c. Derivatives in *-ly*, *-ness*, *-ity*, &c., are briefly recorded. stress follows that of the simple adj.; but for adjj. in *-ed* see UN-[1]. Exx.: *unabashed*; *unabated*; *unabbreviated*; *unabetted*; *unabiding*; *unable*, not able (*to* do); *unabridged*; *unabsorbable*; *unabsorbed*; *unabsorbent*; *unaccented*; *unaccentuated*; *unacceptable*; *unaccommodating*; *unaccompanied*, not accompanied, (Mus.) without accompaniment; *unaccomplished*, not accomplished or achieved, lacking accomplishments; *unaccordant*; *unaccountable* (*-bility*, *-bleness*, *-bly*), that cannot be explained, strange, not responsible; *unaccoutred*; *unaccredited*; *unaccused*; *unaccustomed*, not accustomed (*to*), not usual (*his u. silence*); *unachievable*; *unachieved*; *unacknowledged*; *unacquainted*; *unacquirable*; *unacquired*; *unacted*; *unadaptable*; *unadapted*; *unaddicted*; *unaddressed*; *unadjudged*; *unadjusted*; *unadministered*; *unadmired*; *unadmonished*; *unadorned*; *unadulterated*; *unadventurous*; *unadvisable* (*-bility*); *unadvised* (*-ĕdly*), indiscreet, rash, without advice; *unaffable*; *unaffected* (*-ly*, *-ness*), free from affectation, genuine, sincere, not affected (*by*); *unaffiliated*; *unafflicted*; *unaggressive*; *unaided*; *unalarmed*; *unalleviated*; *unallotted*; *unallowable*; *unalloyed*; *unalterable* (*-bility*, *-bleness*, *-bly*); *unaltered*; *unamazed*; *unambiguous* (*-ly*, *-ness*); *unambitious* (*-ly*, *-ness*); *unamenable*; *unamendable*; *un-American*, not American, foreign to American customs or ideas; *unamiable* (*-bility*, *-bleness*, *-bly*); *unamusing*; *unanalysable*; *unanalysed*; *unanimated*; *unannounced*; *unanswerable* (*-bility*, *-bleness*, *-bly*), that cannot be answered or refuted; *unanswered*; *unanticipated*; *unapocryphal*; *unapostolic*, contrary to apostolic usage, not having apostolic authority; *unappalled*; *unapparelled*; *unapparent*; *unappeasable*; *unappeased*; *unappetizing* (*-ly*); *unapplied*; *unappreciated*; *unappreciative*; *unapprehended*; *unapprehensive*; *unapprised*; *unapproachable* (*-bility*, *-bleness*, *-bly*); *unappropriated* (*u. blessing* facet., old maid); *unapproving* (*-ly*); *unapproved*; *unapt* (*-ly*, *-ness*); *unarmed*[2]; *unarmoured*; *unarranged*; *unarrayed*; *unarrested*; *unartificial* (*-ly*), not artificial, natural; *unartistic*; *unascertainable*; *unascertained*; *unashamed*; *unasked*; *unaspirated*; *unaspiring* (*-ly*); *unassailable*, not assailable, (of statement &c.) against which nothing can be said; *unassayed*; *unassignable*; *unassimilated*; *unassisted*; *unassuming*, making little of one's merits or status; *unattached*, not attached, (Law) not seized for debt, (Mil.) not assigned to regiment or company, (Univv., of student) belonging to no college; *unattainable* (*-ness*); *unattempted*; *unattended*; *unattested*; *unattractive* (*-ly*, *-ness*); *unaugmented*; *unauthentic* (*-ity*); *unauthenticated*; *unauthorized*; *unavailable*; *unavailing* (*-ly*), ineffectual; *unavenged*; *unavoidable* (*-bly*); *unavowed*; *unaware*, not aware (*of*, *that*, &c.); *unawares* [-ES] adv. & n., unexpectedly, by surprise, unintentionally, as *was taken u. by his question*, *must have dropped it u.*, (n.) *at u.*, unexpectedly; *unbacked*, not supported, having no backers (esp. in betting), (of horse) unbroken, not taught to bear rider; *unbalanced*, (esp., of the mind) disordered, violently impulsive; *unbaptized*; *unbearable* (*-bly*); *unbeaten*, not beaten, not surpassed (*u. record* &c.); *unbeautiful*, ugly; *unbecoming* (*-ly*, *-ness*), indecorous (*an u. speech*), not befitting (person, *to* or *for* person), not suited to the wearer (*an u. hat*); *unbefitting*; *unbefriended*; *unbegotten*; *unbeknown*, *-knownst* [-ES], colloq., not known, esp. *u. to* quasi-adv., without the knowledge of, as *did it u. to him*; *unbelievable*; *unbelieving* (*-ly*), not believing esp. in divine revelation; *unbeloved* (-vd); *unbending*[2] (*-ly*, *-ness*), not bending, inflexible, firm, austere; *unbeneficed*; *unbeseeming* (*-ly*); *unbesought*; *unbespoken*; *unbias(s)ed*; *unbiblical*, not in or authorized by the Bible; *unbidden*, not commanded, not invited; *unbigoted*; *unbleached*; *unblemished*; *unblest*; *unblooded*, (of horse &c.) not thoroughbred; *unblushing* (*-ly*, *-ness*); *unbookish*; *unborn*; *unbounded* (*-ly*, *-ness*), not bounded (*by*, or abs.), infinite; *unbred*; *unbribable*; *unbridled*, not bridled, esp. fig. as *u. insolence*, *tongue*; *unbroken* (*-ly*, *-ness*), not broken, not subdued, not interrupted (*u. slumber*, *peace*), not surpassed (in *u. record*), not broken in (*u. horse*); *unbrotherly*; *unburdened*; *unburied*; *unbusinesslike*; *uncalled*, not called, esp. *u. for*, impertinently obtruded, as *the remark was u. for*, *his u.-for remark*; *uncandid* (*-ly*); *uncanny* (*-iness*), weird, mysterious, not canny; *uncanonical* (*-ly*, *-ness*); *uncanonized*; *uncared-for*, disregarded, neglected; *uncarpeted*; *uncastrated*; *uncatalogued*; *uncaused*, not caused, not created, self-existent; *uncauterized*; *unceasing* (*-ly*); *unceremonious* (*-ly*, *-ness*), informal, familiar, abrupt in manner, wanting in courtesy; *uncertain* (*-ly*, *-ty*), not certainly knowing or known (*am u. which he means*, *u. of his meaning*, *is of u. age*, *the result is u.*), not to be depended on (*is u. in his aim*), changeable (*u. temper*, *weather*); *uncertificated*; *unchallenged*; *unchancy* (chiefly Sc.), unlucky, unseasonable; *unchangeable* (*-bly*,

-*ness*); *uncharitable* (-*bly*, -*ness*), censorious, severe in judgement; *unchartered*; *unchary*; *unchaste* (-*ly*, -*tity*); *unchastened*; *unchivalrous*; *unchristian* (-*ly*, -*ness*), not Christian, contrary to the Christian character; *uncircumcised*, (fig.) heathen, unregenerate; *uncircumstantial*, not going into details; *uncivil* (-*ly*), ill-mannered, rude; *uncivilized*; *unclad*; *unclaimed*; *unclean* (-*ness*), not clean, foul, unchaste, ceremonially impure (in Jewish law); *unclerical*; *unclothed*; *unclouded* (esp. of happiness &c., cf. *cloudless*); *u·nco*, a., n., & adv. (Sc.), strange, unusual, (n.) stranger, (adv.) remarkably, very, [dial. var. of *uncouth*]; *uncoined*; *uncoloured*, not coloured, (fig.) not exaggerated or heightened in description (*u. account* &c.); *uncombed*; *uncome-at-able* (-kumăt-) colloq., not accessible or attainable; *uncomely* (-*iness*); *uncomfortable* (-*bly*); *uncommercial*, not commercial, contrary to commercial principles; *uncommitted*; *uncommon* (-*ly*, -*ness*) a. & colloq. adv., not common, unusual, remarkable, (adv.) remarkably (*an u. fine girl*); *uncommunicative* (-*ly*, -*ness*), reserved, taciturn; *uncompanionable*; *uncomplaining* (-*ly*, -*ness*); *uncomplaisant* (-*ly*); *uncomplicated*; *uncomplimentary*; *uncompounded*; *uncompromising* (-*ly*), not admitting of compromise, decided, inflexible, unyielding; *unconcerned* (-*ĕdly*), not concerned (*in*, *with*), easy in mind, free from anxiety or agitation; *uncondemned*; *uncondensed*; *unconditional* (-*ity*, -*ness*, -*ly*), not subject to conditions, absolute, (*u. surrender*, *refusal*); *unconfirmed* (esp. of rumour &c.); *unconformable* (-*bly*, -*ness*); *uncongenial* (-*ly*); *unconnected*; *unconquerable* (-*bly*); *unconquered*; *unconscientious* (-*ly*, -*ness*); *unconscionable* (-*bly*, -*ness*), wholly unreasonable, not guided or restrained by conscience, (Law) *u. bargain*, contract too grossly unfair to be enforced, [prob. f. *conscion*, formed as sing. of *conscience* taken as pl.]; *unconscious* (-*ly*, -*ness*), not conscious, as *was u. of any change, lay u. for some hours, u.* CEREBRATION, *the u.* (as n.; see PSYCHO-*analysis*); *unconsecrated*; *unconsidered*, disregarded; *unconstitutional* (-*ity*, -*ly*), (of measures, acts, &c.) opposed to a country's constitution; *unconstrained* (-*ĕdly*); *unconsumed*; *uncontainable*; *uncontaminated*; *uncontemplated*, not expected; *uncontracted*; *uncontradicted*; *uncontrollable* (-*bly*, -*ness*); *uncontrolled* (-*ĕdly*); *uncontroversial* (-*ly*); *uncontroverted*; *unconventional* (-*ity*, -*ly*), not bound by convention or custom, free in character or action or treatment; *unconversable*; *unconversant*; *unconverted*; *unconvinced*; *uncooked*; *uncorroborated*; *uncorroded*; *uncorrupted*; *uncountenanced*; *uncoupled*; *uncourtly*; *uncovenanted*, not promised by or based on a covenant (*u. mercies* of God), not enjoying a covenant (*u. civil service* in India); *uncovered*; *uncoveted*; *uncreated*, not yet created, (also archaic *uncreate*²) existing without being created; *uncritical* (-*ly*), disinclined or incompetent to criticize, not according to principles of criticism; *uncrossed*, not crossed (*u. cheque* &c.), not thwarted; *uncrowned* (*u. king*, not yet crowned, also, having power but not name of king); *unculled*; *uncultivable*; *uncultivated*; *uncultured*; *uncurbed*; *uncurtailed*; *uncushioned*; *uncustomed*, not liable to duty, having paid no duty; *uncut*, not cut, esp. (of book) with full untrimmed margins; *undamaged*; *undated*, not dated; *undaunted* (-*ly*, -*ness*), not daunted, fearless; *undebated*; *undebauched*; *undeceived*²; *undecided* (-*ly*), not settled (*point is still u.*), irresolute (*he stood u.*); *undecipherable*; *undefended*, (esp., of suit) in which no defence is put in; *undefiled*; *undefined*; *undelivered*; *undemonstrated*; *undemonstrative*, not given to showing strong feelings, reserved; *undeniable* (-*bly*), that cannot be denied or disputed, decidedly good; *undenominational* (*u. education*); *undenounced*; *undependable*; *undeplored*; *undeposed*; *undepraved*; *undepreciated*; *undepressed*; *undescried*; *undeserved* (-*ĕdly*); *undeserving*; *undesignated*; *undesigned* (-*ĕdly*), not designed, esp. not intended; *undesirable* (-*bility*, -*bleness*, -*bly*) a. & n., not desirable, unpleasant, inconvenient, (n.) u. person; *undesired*, not desired or solicited; *undesirous*; *undetachable*; *undetected*; *undetermined*, not settled, irresolute; *undeterred*; *undeveloped*; *undeviating* (-*ly*); *undevout* (-*ly*); *undifferentiated*; *undiffused*; *undigested* (esp. fig., of ill arranged facts &c.); *undignified*, lacking or inconsistent with dignity; *undiluted*; *undiminished*; *undimmed*; *undiplomatic*; *undirected*; *undiscerned*; *undiscerning* (-*ly*); *undischarged*; *undisciplined*; *undisclosed*; *undiscomfited*; *undisconcerted*; *undiscoverable* (-*bly*); *undiscovered*; *undiscriminating* (-*ly*); *undiscussed*; *undisguised* (-*ĕdly*), not veiled, open, (*u. reluctance* &c.); *undismayed*; *undispelled*; *undispersed*; *undisplayed*; *undisputed*; *undissected*; *undissembled*; *undissolved*; *undistinguishable* (-*bly*, -*ness*); *undistinguished*; *undistracted*; *undistressed*; *undistributed* (*u. middle*, fallacy resulting from failure to DISTRIBUTE middle term); *undisturbed* (-*ĕdly*); *undiversified*; *undiverted*; *undivided*; *undivorced*; *undivulged*; *undomesticated*; *undone*², not done; *undoubted*; *undoubtedly* adv., without doubt (implying certainty on speaker's part, cf. DOUBTLESS); *undoubting* (-*ly*); *undraped*; *undreamed-of*, -*mt-of*; *undressed*²; *undrilled*; *undrinkable*; *undue* (-*duly*), excessive, disproportionate, (*spoke with u. warmth*), improper (*u. influence*, by which person, e. g. testator, is induced to do what he would not of his own free will), (of bill &c.) not yet due; *undurable* (*-bly*); *undutiful* (*ly, -ness*); *undying* (*-ly*), immortal (*u. fame* &c.); *unearned*, not earned (*u. increment*, increased value of land due to external causes e. g. increased population, not to owner's labour or outlay); *unearthly* (*-iness*), not earthly, supernatural, ghostly, weird, (*u. cry, pallor*); *uneasy* (*-ily, -iness*), disturbed or uncomfortable in body or mind (*you seem u., passed an u. night*), disturbing (*had an u. suspicion*); *uneatable*; *uneaten*; *unecclesiastical*; *uneclipsed*; *uneconomic*, (esp., of rent) too low to repay owner & builder; *uneconomical*; *unedified*; *unedifying*, (esp.) tending to suggest evil or offend moral delicacy; *unedited*; *uneducated*; *uneffaced*; *uneffected*; *unelated*; *unelected*; *unelucidated*; *unemancipated*; *unembarrassed*; *unemotional* (*-ly*); *unemphatic* (*-ally*); *unemployable* a. & n., (person) unfitted by character, by age, or otherwise, for paid employment; *unemployed*, not used, lacking employment, out of work & wages (*u. capital, energies, the u.*); *unempowered*; *unenclosed*; *unencumbered* (*u. estate*, having no liabilities on it); *unendangered*; *unending* (*-ly, -ness*), having no end; *unendorsed*; *unendowed*; *unendurable* (*-bly*); *unenforced*; *unenfranchised*; *unengaged*; *un-English*, not (characteristic of the) English; *unenjoyable*; *unenlightened*; *unenrolled*; *unenslaved*; *unenterprising* (*-ly, -ness*); *unentertaining* (*-ly, -ness*); *unenthusiastic*; *unenumerated*; *unenviable* (*-bly*); *unenvied*; *unequable*; *unequal* (*-ly*), not equal (*to*), of varying quality; *unequalled*; *unequipped*; *unequivocal* (*-ly, -ness*), not ambiguous, plain, unmistakable; *unerased*; *unerring* (*-ly, -ness*), not erring or failing or missing the mark (*u. judgement, wisdom, aim*); *unescapable*; *unespied*; *unessayed*; *unessential* a. & n., not essential, not of the first importance, (n.) u. part or thing; *unestablished*; *unestimated*; *unestranged*; *unevangelical*; *unevaporated*; *uneven* (*-ly, -ness*), not level or smooth, not uniform or equable (*makes u. progress, has an u. temper*), (of number, rare) odd; *uneventful* (*-ly*); *unexamined*; *unexampled*, without precedent; *unexcelled*; *unexceptionable* (*-bly, -ness*), with which no fault can be found; *unexcised*, not subject to excise; *unexclusive* (*-ly*); *unexecuted*; *unexemplified*; *unexercised*; *unexhausted*; *unexpensive*; *unexpected* (*-ly, -ness*); *unexpiated*; *unexpired*, (of lease &c.) still running; *unexplained*; *unexplored*; *unexposed*; *unexpounded*; *unexpressed*; *unexpurgated*; *unextended*, not extended, occupying no space, dimensionless; *unfadable*, that cannot fade; *unfading* (*-ly, -ness*); *unfailing* (*-ly, -ness*), not failing, not running short (*u. supply*), not disappointing one's expectations &c. (*u. resource, supporter*, &c.); *unfair* (*-ly, -ness*), not equitable or honest or impartial (*an u. advantage, got by u. means, u. play*); *unfaithful* (*-ly, -ness*); *unfaltering* (*-ly*); *unfamiliar* (*-ity, -ly*); *unfashionable* (*-bly, -ness*); *unfashioned*, not brought into shape; *unfastened*[2]; *unfathered*, (poet.) fatherless, (fig.) not acknowledged by its author (*u. theory* &c.); *unfatherly*; *unfathomable* (*-bly*); *unfathomed*; *unfavourable* (*-bly, -ness*); *unfeasible*; *unfed*; *unfeed*, not FEED[3]; *unfeeling* (*-ly, -ness*), lacking sensibility, harsh, cruel; *unfeigned* (*-ĕdly*); *unfelt*, not FELT[2]; *unfeminine*; *unfermented*; *unfertilized*; *unfettered*[2]; *unfigured*, not marked with figures (*u. muslin, vase*); *unfilial* (*-ly*); *unfilled*; *unfiltered*; *unfinished*; *unfit* (*-ly, -ness*), not fit (*to* do, *for* purpose, *for a doctor* &c., to be one); *unfitted*, not fit, not fitted, not furnished with fittings; *unfitting* (*-ly*); *unfixed*[2]; *unflagging*; *unflattering* (*-ly*); *unflavoured*; *unfledged*, not yet fledged or (fig., of person &c.) developed; *unfleshed*; *unflinching* (*-ly*); *unfordable*; *unforeseen*; *unforgettable*; *unforgivable*; *unforgiven*; *unforgiving* (*-ly, -ness*); *unforgotten*; *unformed*, not formed, shapeless; *unformulated*; *unfortified*; *unfortunate* (*-ly*) a. & n., the reverse of fortunate, unlucky, unhappy, (n.) u. person; *unfounded*, without foundation (*u. rumour, hopes*), not yet founded; *unfrequented*; *unfriended*, lacking friends; *unfriendly* (*-iness*); *unfruitful* (*-ly, -ness*); *unfulfilled*; *unfunded*, (of debt) floating not funded; *unfurnished*, not supplied (*with*), without furniture; *unfused* (FUSE[1, 2]); *ungallant* (*-ly*), not gallant to women; *ungalvanized*; *ungarbled*; *ungarnered*; *ungarnished*, not decorated; *ungauged*; *ungenerous* (*-ly*); *ungenial*; *ungenteel* (*-ly*); *ungentle* (*-ness, -tly*), harsh, rude, ill-bred; *ungentlemanly* (*-iness*), unworthy of a gentleman, rude, ill-bred; *unglazed*; *unglutted*; *ungodly* (*-ily, -iness*); *ungovernable* (*-bly*), unruly, licentious, wild, violent, (*u. passions*); *ungraceful* (*-ly, -ness*); *ungracious* (*-ly, -ness*), not kindly or courteous (*u. reply, reception*); *ungraduated*; *ungrammatical* (*-ly*), contrary to rules of grammar; *ungrateful* (*-ly*); *ungrounded*, (of statement &c.) unfounded; *ungrudging* (*-ly*); *unguarded* (*-ly*), not guarded, incautious, thoughtless (*an u. expression, admission*); *unhackneyed*; *unhallowed*; *unhampered*; *unhandsome* (*-ly, -ness*), (of appearance, conduct, &c.) not handsome; *unhandy* (*-ily, -iness*), awkward to handle, inconvenient, (of person) clumsy; *unhanged*, (esp.) who has escaped hanging (*the greatest scoundrel u.*); *unhappy* (*-ily, -iness*), not happy, unlucky, wretched; *unharmed*; *unhatched* (HATCH[2, 3]); *unhealthful* (*-ly, -ness*); *unhealthy* (*-ily, -iness*), (esp., mil. slang, of places) dangerous, exposed to fire; *unheard*, not heard (*u. of*, unprecedented);

unheeded; *unheedful* (*-ly*); *unheeding*; *unhelpful* (*-ly*); *unhemmed*; *unheralded*; *unheroic*; *unhesitating*(*-ly*); *unhewn* (lit., &, fig., rough, incondite); *unhidden*; *unhistoric*(*al*), (esp.) merely legendary; *unholy* (*-ily*, *-iness*), not holy, impious, wicked; *unhonoured*; *unhuman*, not human; *unhung*; *unhurt*; *unidea'd*, having no ideas; *unideal*, not ideal, prosaic, ordinary, dull, inferior; *unidentified*; *unilluminated*; *unillustrated*; *unimaginable*; *unimaginative* (*-ly*, *-ness*); *unimpaired*; *unimpassioned*; *unimpeachable* (*-bility*, *-bleness*, *-bly*), giving no opening to censure, beyond reproach or question; *unimpeded*; *unimportant* (*-ance*); *unimposing*; *unimpressionable*; *unimpressive* (*-ly*, *-ness*); *unimproved*, (esp. of land) not improved; *unimpugned*; *unindexed*; *unindicated*; *uninflammable*; *uninflated*; *uninflicted*; *uninfluenced*; *uninfluential*; *uninformed*, (esp.) ignorant; *uninhabitable*; *uninhabited*; *uninitiated*; *uninjured*; *uninspired*, (esp., of oratory &c.) commonplace; *uninstigated*; *uninstructed*; *uninstructive*; *uninsulated*; *uninsured*; *unintelligent* (*-ly*); *unintelligible* (*-bility*, *-bly*); *unintentional* (*-ly*); *uninteresting* (*-ly*, *-ness*); *unintermittent* (*-ly*); *unintermitting* (*-ly*); *uninterpretable*; *uninterred*; *uninterrupted* (*-ly*); *uninventive* (*-ly*); *uninvestigated*; *uninvited*; *uninviting* (*-ly*), unattractive, repellent; *uninvoked*; *uninvolved*; *unirrigated*; *unisolated*; *unissued*; *unjaundiced*; *unjust* (*-ly*), contrary to justice, not just; *unjustifiable* (*-bly*, *-ness*); *unkind* (*-ly*, *-ness*), not kind, harsh, cruel; *unkingly*; *unkneaded*; *unknightly* (*-iness*); *unknowable* (*-bility*, *-bleness*, *-bly*); *unknowing* (*-ly*), not knowing, unconscious, (*of*, or abs.); *unknown* a., n., & adv., not known (*he*, *his purpose*, *what he wanted*, *that district*, *was u. to me*, *a youth to fame u.*, *of u. ingredients*, x *&* y *denote u. quantities* in equation &c., *the U.* WARRIOR), (n. or abs. adj.) *we all dread the u.*, *equation of two uu.*, (adv.) *u. to*, without the knowledge of (*did it u. to me*); *unlabelled*; *unlaboured*, (of style &c.) easy, spontaneous; *unladylike*; *unlamented*; *unlawful* (*-ly*, *-ness*); *unlearnèd*, not LEARNED; *unlearnt*, *-ned* (*pr.* -nd), not learnt; *unleavened* (lit. & fig.); *unlettered*, illiterate; *unlicensed*; *unlicked*, not licked into shape, unmannerly; *unlike* (*-ness*) a. & prep., not like (*is u. both his parents*, *the two are u.*, *portrait is utterly u.*, *u. signs*, + & —, *plays quite u. anyone I have heard before*); *unlikely* (*-ihood*, *-iness*), improbable, unpromising, (*u. tale*, *errand*); *unlimited* (*-ly*, *-ness*), boundless, unrestricted, very great or numerous (*has u. scope*, *possibilities*, *his powers are u.*, *u. expanse of sea*, *drinks u. coffee*); *unlined*, (esp.) with no lining, (of face &c.) not wrinkled; *unliquidated*; *unlit*; *unlocated*; *unlooked-for*, not expected; *unlopped*; *unlovable*; *unloved*; *unlovely* (*-iness*), not amiable or attractive; *unloverlike*; *unloving*; *unlucky* (*-ily*), not lucky or fortunate or successful, hapless, wretched, unsuccessful, bringing bad luck, ill-timed, ill-contrived, (*u. toss* of coin, *always u. at cards*, *u. fellow*, *asked in an u. hour*, *single magpie is u.*, *his u. efforts to please*, *an u. expedient*); *unmade*; *unmaidenly*; *unmailable*, that must not or cannot be sent by post; *unmaimed*; *unmaintainable*; *unmalleable* (*-bility*); *unmanageable* (*-bly*, *-ness*), not (easily) to be managed or manipulated or controlled (*u. child*, *material*, *situation*); *unmanful* (*-ly*); *unmanlike*, not like a man, esp. womanish or childish; *unmanly* (*-iness*); *unmannerly* (*-iness*), rude, ill-bred; *unmarked*, not marked, not noticed; *unmarketable*; *unmarriageable* (*-ness*); *unmarried*; *unmartial*, unwarlike; *unmasculine*, not masculine or manly; *unmasticable*; *unmatchable*; *unmatched*; *unmated*; *unmaterial*, not consisting of matter; *unmatured*; *unmeaning*, (*-ly*, *-ness*), without meaning, senseless; *unmeant*, not intended; *unmeasured*, not measured, (poet.) immeasurable; *unmechanical*; *unmeet* (*-ly*, *-ness*) archaic, not fit (*to* do, *for* purpose); *unmelodious* (*-ly*, *-ness*); *unmelted*; *unmendable*; *unmentionable* (*-ness*) a. & n., that it is improper to mention, (n. pl., facet.) trousers; *unmerchantable*; *unmerciful* (*-ly*, *-ness*); *unmerited*; *unmethodical*; *unmetrical* (*-ly*), not metrical, violating requirements of metre; *unmilitary*; *unmindful* (*-ly*, *-ness*); *unminted*; *unmirthful* (*-ly*); *unmistakable* (*-bly*), that cannot be mistaken or doubted, clear; *unmitigated*, unqualified, absolute, (*u. blackguard*, *lie*); *unmixed*; *unmodern*; *unmodified*; *unmodulated*; *unmolested*; *unmoral* (*-ity*), non-moral; *unmortgaged*; *unmotherly*; *unmounted*, not mounted (*u. police*, *picture*, *jewel*); *unmourned*; *unmoved*, not moved, not changed in purpose, not affected by emotion; *unmown*; *unmurmuring* (*-ly*), not complaining; *unmusical* (*-ity*, *-ly*), not pleasing to the ear, unskilled in or indifferent to music; *unmutilated*; *unnamable*, (esp., of vices) too horrible to be named; *unnamed*; *unnational*; *unnatural* (*-ly*, *-ness*), contrary or doing violence to nature, monstrous, (*u. crimes*, *vices*), lacking natural feelings (*u. parent*, *child*), artificial, forced, affected; *unnaturalized*, not naturalized; *unnavigable*; *unnecessary* (*-ily*) a. & n., not necessary, more than is necessary (*with u. care*), (n., usu. pl.) u. thing(s); *unneedful* (*-ly*); *unnegotiable*; *unneighbourly* (*-iness*); *unnoticed*; *unnourished*; *unnumbered*, not marked with number, not counted, countless; *unobjectionable* (*-bly*); *unobliging*; *unobliterated*; *unobscured*; *unobservant*; *unobserved*; *unobstructed*; *unobtainable*; *unobtrusive* (*-ly*, *-ness*); *unoccupied*; *un-*

offending, harmless, innocent; *unoffered*; *unofficial*, (esp., of news) not officially confirmed; *unofficinal*; *unopened*; *unopposed*; *unordained*; *unorganized*; *unoriginal*, not possessing originality, derived; *unornamental*, not ornamental, unsightly; *unornamented*; *unorthodox*; *unostentatious* (*-ly, -ness*); *unowned*; *unpacified*; *unpaged*, with pages not numbered; *unpaid*, (of sum, bill, debt, or person) not paid (*the great u.*, u. magistrates or justices); *unpaired*; *unpalatable* (*-bly*); *unparalleled*, having no parallel or equal; *unpardonable* (*-bly, -ness*); *unpared*; *unparental*, unworthy of a parent; *unparliamentary* (*-ily, -iness*), contrary to parliamentary usage (*u. language*, oaths, abuse); *unpatented*; *unpatriotic* (*-ally*); *unpatronized*; *unpaved*; *unpawned*; *unpeaceful*; *unpedantic*; *unpedigreed*; *unpeeled*; *unpensioned*; *unperceived*; *unperforated*; *unperformed*; *unperjured*; *unpersuadable*; *unpersuaded*; *unpersuasive*; *unperturbed*; *unperused*; *unperverted*; *unphilosophical* (*-ly, -ness*), not according to philosophical principles, wanting in philosophy; *unpicked*, not selected, (of flowers) not plucked; *unpicturesque*; *unpiloted*; *unpitied*; *unpitying* (*-ly*); *unplaced*, not placed esp. in race or list; *unplagued*; *unplaned*; *unplanned*; *unplanted*; *unplastered*; *unplastic*; *unplated*; *unplausible* (*-bly*); *unplayable* (esp. of ball or serve in games); *unpleasant* (*-ly*), not pleasant, disagreeable; *unpleasantness* n., in adj. senses, also, misunderstanding, quarrel, *the late u.* (U.S. facet.), the civil war; *unpleasing* (*-ly*); *unpliable* (*-bly*); *unpliant* (*-ly*); *unploughed*; *unplucked*; *unplumbed*; *unpoetical* (*-ly, -ness*); *unpointed*, having no point, not punctuated, without vowel points (in Hebrew &c.), (of masonry) not pointed; *unpolished*; *unpolitical*, not concerned with politics; *unpolled*, not polled (*u. elector, vote*); *unpolluted*; *unpopular* (*-ity, -ly*), not popular, esp. not liked by the public; *unportioned*, portionless; *unpossessed*, not possessed, not possessed *of*; *unposted*, uninformed, (of letter) not posted; *unpractical* (*-ity, -ly*), (of person, plan, method, &c.) not practical; *unpractised*, not experienced or skilled, not put into practice; *unpraised*; *unprecedented*, for which there is no precedent, unparalleled; *unprefaced*; *unprejudiced*, (esp.) impartial; *unprelatical*; *unpremeditated* (*-ly*), not previously thought over, not deliberately planned, unintentional; *unpreoccupied*; *unprepared* (*-ness*), not prepared (*found everything u., was u. for this objection, delivered an u. speech*); *unprepossessing*; *unprescribed*; *unpresentable*, not presentable, not fit to be presented to company, not fit to be seen; *unpresuming*; *unpresumptuous*; *unpretending* (*-ly*), *unpretentious* (*-ly, -ness*), **aa.**, not given to display, making little show; *unpreventable*; *unpriced*, with the price(s) not fixed or marked or stated (*u. goods, catalogue*); *unpriestly*; *unprimed*; *unprincely*; *unprincipled*, lacking or not dictated by good moral principles (*u. person, conduct*); *unprintable*, (esp.) too blasphemous, indecent, &c., to appear in print; *unprinted*; *unprivileged*; *unprized*, not valued; *unprobed*; *unproclaimed*; *unprocurable*; *unproductive* (*-ly, -ness*); *unprofaned*; *unprofessional* (*-ly*), not pertaining to one's profession, not belonging to a profession, contrary to professional etiquette &c., (*knows nothing of u. matters, ask any u. man, u. conduct*); *unprofitable* (*-bly, -ness*; *u. servants*, persons content to do no more than their duty); *unprogressive* (*-ness*), not progressive, conservative; *unprohibited*; *unprolific*; *unpromising*; *unprompted*, spontaneous; *unpromulgated*; *unpronounceable*; *unpropagated*; *unprophetic*; *unpropitious* (*-ly, -ness*); *unproportional*, not proportional; *unproposed*; *unprosperous* (*-ly, -ness*); *unprotected*; *unprotested*; *unprovable*; *unproved, -en*; *unprovided*, not supplied (*with* money &c.), not prepared; *unprovoked*, (of person or act) without provocation; *unpruned*; *unpublished*, not made public, (of MS. &c.) not published; *unpunctual* (*-ity, -ly*); *unpunctuated*; *unpunishable*; *unpunished*; *unpurified*; *unquailing* (*-ly*); *unqualified* (*-ly*), not competent, not legally or officially qualified, not modified, (*am u. to serve, an u. practitioner, gave his u. assent*); *unquarried*; *unquelled*; *unquenchable* (*-bly*); *unquenched*; *unquestionable* (*-bly, -ness*), that cannot be questioned or doubted; *unquestioned*, not disputed or doubted, not interrogated; *unquestioning* (*-ly*), asking no questions (*u. obedience* &c., yielded without questions asked); *unquiet*, restless, agitated, (*u. spirit, times*); *unquilted*; *unquotable* (as *unprintable*); *unquoted*; *unransomed*; *unrazored*, unshaven; *unreachable*; *unread*, (of book &c.) not read, (of person) not well-read; *unreadable* (*-ness*); *unready*, not ready, not prompt in action; *unreal* (*-ity, -ly*), illusive, sham, visionary; *unrealizable*; *unrealized*; *unreaped*; *unreasonable* (*-bly, -ness*), not reasonable, exceeding the bounds of reason (*u. demands, conduct*, &c.), not guided by or listening to reason; *unreasoned*, not rationally thought out; *unreasoning* (*-ly*), not using or guided by reason; *unrebuked*; *unrecallable*; *unrecalled*; *unreceipted*; *unreceived*; *unreciprocated*; *unreckoned*; *unreclaimed*; *unrecognizable* (*-bly*); *unrecognized*; *unrecompensed*; *unreconciled*; *unrecorded*; *unrectified*; *unredeemed*, not redeemed, (of promise) not fulfilled, (of bills &c.) not recalled by payment, not taken out of pawn, (of faults &c.) not mitigated or relieved (*by* merits &c. or abs.); *unredressed*; *unrefined*, not refined (*u. sugar, manners*); *unreflecting* (*-ly*); *unreformable*; *unreformed*; *unrefuted*; *unregal*; *unregarded*; *unregenerate*; *unregistered*; *unregretted*; *unregulated*; *unrehearsed* (esp. of results that surprise their authors); *unrelated*; *unrelaxed*; *unrelenting* (*-ly, -ness*); *unreliable* (*-bility, -bleness, -bly*); *unrelieved*, (esp.) lacking the relief given by contrast or variation; *unreligious*, not concerned with religion; *unremembered*; *unremitting* (*-ly*), not abating, incessant, (*u. care, exertions*); *unremunerative*, not profitable; *unrenewed*; *unrenounced*; *unrepealed*; *unrepentant* (*-ance*); *unrepining* (*-ly*); *unreplenished*; *unreported*; *unrepresentative*; *unrepresented*; *unreproachful*; *unreproved*; *unrequited*, not requited or returned (*u. affection*); *unrescinded*; *unresented*; *unresenting* (*-ly*); *unreserved* (*-ědly, -ness*), without reservation (*u. compliance* &c.), open, frank, (*an u. nature*), not reserved (*u. seats*); *unresisted*; *unresisting* (*-ly*); *unresolved*, not having formed a decision, not solved or cleared up (*u. doubts, problem*), not separated into constituent parts; *unrespected*; *unresponsive* (*-ness*); *unrestful* (*-ly, -ness*); *unresting* (*-ly*); *unrestored*; *unrestrainable* (*-bly*); *unrestrained* (*-ědly, -ness*); *unrestricted* (*-ly*); *unretarded*; *unretentive*; *unrevenged*; *unreversed*; *unrevised*; *unrevoked*; *unrewarded*; *unrhetorical*; *unrhymed*; *unrhythmical*, without (satisfactory) rhythm; *unridable*; *unridden*; *unrighted*; *unrighteous* (*-ly, -ness*), not upright or honest or just, evil, wicked; *unripe* (*-ness*), not ripe (lit. & fig.); *unrisen*; *unrivalled*, having no equal, peerless; *unromantic* (*-ally*); *unroofed*; *unroyal* (*-ly*), unlike or unworthy of a king; *unruffled*; *unruled*, not governed, not ruled with lines; *unru·ly* (*-iness*), lawless, refractory, [f. rare *ruly* (RULE, -Y ²)]; *unsafe* (*-ly, -ness*), dangerous; *unsaid* ²; *unsaintly*; *unsalable* (*-bility, -bleness*); *unsalaried*; *unsalted*; *unsanctified*; *unsanctioned*; *unsanitary*, unhealthy; *unsated*; *unsatisfactory* (*-ily, -iness*); *unsatisfied*; *unsatisfying* (*-ly*); *unsaved*, not saved (esp. in religious sense); *unsavoury* (*-ily, -iness*), uninviting, disgusting, (*an u. dish, smell, theme*); *unsayable*; *unscalable*, that cannot be climbed; *unscannable*, that cannot be scanned (*u. verses*); *unscared*; *unscarred*; *unscathed*, without injury suffered; *unscented*; *unscheduled*; *unscholarly*; *unschooled*; *unscientific* (*-ally*), (esp.) transgressing scientific principles; *unscoured*; *unscourged*; *unscreened* (esp. of coal); *unscriptural* (*-ly*), not in accordance with Scripture; *unscrupulous* (*-ly, -ness*), having no scruples, shameless, unprincipled; *unsculptured*, not covered with sculpture, (Zool.) smooth; *unsealed*; *unsearchable*, beyond the reach of search; *unsearched*; *unseasonable* (*-bly, -ness*); *unseasoned*; *unseated* ², not provided or furnished with seat(s); *unseaworthy* (*-iness*); *unseconded*; *unsectarian* (*-ism*), free from sectarian limitations; *unsecured*; *unseduced*; *unseductive*; *unseeing*, blind, unobservant; *unseemly* (*-iness*) a. & (archaic) adv.; *unseen* a. & n., not seen (*the u.*, the world of spirits), *u.* (*translation*), translation of unprepared passages as school exercise; *unseizable*; *unselect*, promiscuous, mixed; *unselected*; *unselfish* (*-ly, -ness*), regardful of others' interests rather than of one's own; *unsensational* (*-ly*); *unsent*; *unsentenced*; *unsentimental*; *unseparated*; *unserviceable* (*-bly, -ness*); *unset*, not set (*sun, gem, trap, broken leg, is u.*); *unsettled* ², not settled, liable to change, open to further discussion, not paid, having no fixed abode, (of lands) not occupied by permanent inhabitants, (*his mind is still u., u. weather, the point, the bill, is u.*); *unsevered*; *unshackled*; *unshaded*; *unshadowed*; *unshaken*, not shaken esp. in resolution; *unshapely*; *unshared*; *unshaven*; *unshed*; *unsheltered*; *unshipped* ²; *unshocked*; *unshod*; *unshorn*, not shorn or shaven; *unshown*; *unshrinkable*, that will not shrink (*u. flannel*); *unshrinking* (*-ly*), unhesitating, fearless, firm; *unshrunk*; *unshut*; *unshuttered*; *unsifted*; *unsighted*, not sighted, not furnished with sights, (*ship is still u., u. gun*); *unsightly* (*-iness*), repulsive to the sight, ugly; *unsigned*; *unsinged*; *unsisterly* (*-iness*); *unsized*, not stiffened with size; *unskilful* (*-ly, -ness*); *unskilled*, not possessing or requiring skill or special training (*u. labour*, simple forms of manual labour); *unslaked*; *unsleeping*, *unslumbering*, (fig.) watchful; *unsmoked*; *unsociable* (*-bility, -bleness, -bly*); *unsocial*; *unsoiled*; *unsolaced*; *unsold*; *unsoldierly*; *unsolicited* (esp. *u. testimonials*); *unsolicitous*; *unsolid* (*-ity*); *unsolvable*; *unsolved*; *unsophistical*; *unsophisticated* (*-ness*), artless, innocent, simple, not adulterated, not artificial; *unsoothed*; *unsorted*; *unsought*; *unsound* (*-ness*), not sound, diseased, morbid, rotten, ill-founded, erroneous, fallacious, unreliable, (*u. lungs, fruit, doctrine, policy, argument*; *of u. mind*, insane); *unsounded*, unfathomed; *unsoured*; *unsown*; *unsparing* (*-ly, -ness*), profuse, lavish, (*u. praise, u. of* or *in praise, u. in his efforts*), merciless; *unspeakable* (*-bly, -ness*), that words cannot express, good, bad, &c., beyond description (*u. joys, an u. bore*); *unspecified*; *unspeculative*; *unspent*; *unspilt*; *unspiritual* (*-ity, -ly*); *unspliced*; *unspoiled, -lt*; *unspoken*; *unspontaneous*, forced, artificial; *unsportsmanlike* (colloq. also *unsporting*); *unspotted*, not spotted or (fig.) contaminated; *unsquared*; *unstable*; *unstaid*; *unstained*, not stained (esp. fig.); *unstamped*, without stamp (*u. deed, letter*); *unstarched*; *unstartled*; *unstated*; *unstatesmanlike*; *unstatutable*(*-bly*), not warranted by statute;

unsteadfast (*-ly, -ness*); *unsteady* (*-ily, -iness*), not steady or firm, shaking, reeling, changeable, fluctuating, of irregular habits, (*an u. hand, walked with u. steps, ladder is u., was u. in his adherence, u. winds, is notoriously u.*, dissipated); *unstigmatized*; *unstimulated*; *unstinted*; *unstirred*; *unstocked*, not stocked (*with*, or abs.); *unstopped*; *unstored*; *unstrained*, not forced, not subjected to strain, not put through a strainer; *unstratified*; *unstressed*, not pronounced with stress; *unstudied*, easy, natural, spontaneous, (*u. ease, eloquence*); *unstuffed*; *unstung*; *unsubdued*; *unsubjugated*; *unsubmissive* (*-ly, -ness*); *unsubscribed*; *unsubstantial* (*-ity, -ly*), having little or no solidity or reality (*u. air, visions, forms, an u. building*); *unsubstantiated*, not confirmed or established (*u. rumours*); *unsuccessful* (*-ly*); *unsugared*; *unsuggestive*; *unsuitable* (*-bility, -bly*); *unsuited*, unfit (*for* purpose), not adapted (*to*); *unsullied*; *unsummed*; *unsummoned*; *unsung*, not sung or (poet.) sung of; *unsunned*, not lighted by sun; *unsupple*; *unsupplied*; *unsupportable* (*-bly, -ness*); *unsupported*; *unsuppressed*; *unsure*; *unsurgical*; *unsurmised*; *unsurmounted*; *unsurpassable* (*-bly*); *unsurpassed*; *unsurrendered*; *unsurveyed*; *unsusceptible*; *unsuspected* (*-ly*); *unsuspicious* (*-ly, -ness*); *unsustainable*; *unsustained*; *unswallowed*; *unswayed*, not controlled or influenced; *unsweetened*; *unswept*; *unswerving* (*-ly*); *unsworn*, not sworn (*u. oath, witness*); *unsymbolical*; *unsymmetrical* (*-ly*), failing in or not characterized by symmetry; *unsympathetic* (*-ally*); *unsympathizing* (*-ly*); *unsystematic* (*-ally*); *untainted*; *untalented*; *untamable* (*-ness*); *untamed*; *untanned*; *untarnishable*; *untarnished*; *untasked*; *untasted*; *untaught*, (of person &c. or subject &c.) not taught, ignorant; *untaxed*; *unteachable* (*-ness*); *untearable*; *untechnical*; *untempered*, not tempered (*u. mortar, steel, severity*); *untempted*; *untenable* (*-bility, -bleness*); *untenantable*, not fit to be occupied; *untenanted*; *untended*; *untendered*, not offered; *unterrified*; *untested*; *untethered*; *unthanked*; *unthankful* (*-ly, -ness*); *unthatched*; *unthinkable*, that cannot be conceived in thought, (colloq.) unlikely; *unthinking* (*-ly*), thoughtless; *unthought*, not thought, esp. *u.-of*; *unthoughtful* (*-ness*); *unthrashed*; *unthreadable*; *unthreaded*; *unthreshed*; *unthrifty*; *unthwarted*; *untidy* (*-ily, -iness*); *untied*²; *untiled*; *untillable*; *untilled*; *untimbered*; *untimely* (*-iness*) a. & adv.; *untimous* (Sc.); *untinctured*; *untinged*; *untired*; *untiring* (*-ly*); *untithed*, not subject to tithes; *untitled*; *untold*, not told, not counted, beyond count (*u. gold*); *untormented*; *untorn*; *untortured*; *untouched*; *untoward* (archaic), perverse, refractory, awkward, unlucky, (*an u. generation, accident*); *untraceable*; *untraced*; *untracked*, not followed by means of or marked with tracks; *untragic*, not tragic or suited to tragedy; *untrained*, not trained or practised or instructed, not prepared by exercise, diet, &c., for race &c.; *untrammelled*; *untransferable*, that cannot or must not be transferred; *untranslatable* (*-bility, -bleness, -bly*); *untransmutable*; *untransportable*; *untravelled*, that has not travelled; *untried*, (esp.) inexperienced; *untraversable*; *untrimmed*; *untrodden*; *untroubled*, not troubled, calm; *untrue* (*-uly*), not true, contrary to the fact, false, not faithful or loyal (*to* person, principle, &c.), deviating from correct standard; *untrussed* (*u. fowl* &c.); *untrustworthy* (*-iness*); *untruthful* (*-ly, -ness*); *untuned*; *untuneful* (*-ly*); *unturned*, not turned (*leave no* STONE *u.*); *untutored*, not taught or schooled; *unurged*; *unused*; *unusual* (*-ity* rare, *-ness, -ly*), not usual, remarkable; *unutilized*; *unutterable* (*-bly*), above or beyond description (*u. torment, joy*, &c., *an u. fool*); *unuttered*; *unvaccinated*; *unvalued*, not esteemed or prized, not estimated or priced; *unvanquished*; *unvaried*; *unvarnished*, not varnished or embellished (*u. surface, the u. truth*); *unvarying* (*-ly*); *unvenerable*; *unvenerated*; *unvenomous*; *unventilated*; *unveracious*; *unverifiable*; *unverified*; *unversed*, not versed or skilled (*in*); *unvexed*; *unvictualled*; *unvindicated*; *unviolated*; *unvisited*; *unvitiated*; *unvoiced*, not spoken or uttered, (Phonet.) not voiced; *unvouched*, not vouched (usu. *-for*); *unwak(en)ed*; *unwanted*; *unwarlike*; *unwarmed*; *unwarned*; *unwarped*; *unwarrantable* (*-bly, -ness*), indefensible, unjustifiable, improper; *unwarranted*, unauthorized, not guaranteed; *unwary* (*-ily, -iness*); *unwashed*, not washed (*the great u.*, the rabble); *unwatched*; *unwatchful* (*-ness*); *unwatered*, not watered or diluted or supplied with water (*u. milk, horse, capital*); *unwavering* (*-ly*); *unweaned*; *unwearable*; *unwearied*; *unweary*; *unwearying* (*-ly*), not growing weary, persistent, (*u. efforts* &c.); *unwedded*; *unweeded*; *unweighed*; *unwelcome*; *unwelcomed*; *unwell*, not in good health, indisposed, menstruating; *unwept* (rhet., poet.), not wept for; *unwetted*; *unwhipped*; *unwhitened*; *unwhitewashed*; *unwholesome* (*-ly, -ness*); *unwifely*; *unwilling* (*-ly, -ness*), not willing or inclined (*to* do, *for* thing, *for* thing *to* be done, *that*, or abs.); *unwinged*; *unwinking*, not winking, vigilant; *unwise* (*-ly*), foolish, imprudent; *unwished*, not wished (usu. *-for*); *unwithdrawn*; *unwithering*; *unwithered*; *unwitnessed*; *unwitting* (*-ly*), not consciously or intentionally [see WIT¹]; *unwomanly*; *unwon*; *unwonted*; *unwooded*; *unwooed*; *unworkable*; *unworkmanlike*; *unworldly* (*-iness*), not worldly, spiritual, (*u.-minded*, &c.); *unworn*, that has not been worn or impaired by wear; *unworshipped*; *unworthy* (*-ily*, *-iness*), not worthy or befitting the character (*of*), discreditable, unseemly; *unwound*²; *unwounded*; *unwoven*; *unwreaked*; *unwrinkled*; *unwritable*; *unwritten*, not written (*u. law*, resting originally on custom or judicial decision, not on written statutes &c.); *unwrought*; *unwrung*, not wrung (WITHERS *u.*); *unyielding* (*-ly*, *-ness*), firm, obstinate; *unyoked*; *unyouthful*; *unzealous*.

(2) Nouns are occasionally formed either directly on a simple noun (*unbelief*, *unfriend*, *unrepair*) or by back formation or otherwise on corresp. adj. Exx.: *unbelie·f*, incredulity, disbelief esp. in divine revelation or in a particular religion, so *unbelie·ver*; *uncha·stity*; *uncircumci·sion*, not being circumcised, (N.T.) *the u.*, the Gentiles; *unconcer·n*, freedom from anxiety, indifference, apathy; *unconstrai·nt*, freedom from constraint; *undre·ss*², ordinary dress opp. to full dress or uniform, loose negligent dress, (often fig. & attrib.); *unea·se* (archaic), uneasiness, distress, discomfort; *unemploy·ment*, lack of employment, state of things in which many workers cannot find work or wages; *unfai·th* (rare), want of faith; *unfrie·nd* (archaic), enemy; *unpre·judice*, freedom from prejudice; *unrea·son*, lack of reason, nonsense, folly (ABBOT *of U.*); *unrepair·*, dilapidation, want of repair; *unreser·ve*, absence of reserve, frankness; *unre·st*, lack of rest, disturbed or agitated condition of person or nation (*the u. in Turkey*; *unrestrai·nt*; *unrigh·t* (archaic), wrong, injustice; *unsucce·ss*, want of success, failure; *unsuspi·cion* (rare); *unsy·mmetry*, absence or violation of symmetry; *u·nthrift* (archaic), prodigal(ity); *untru·th*, being untrue, falsehood, lie, (*the manifest u. of this statement*, *told me an u.*); *unwi·sdom*, lack of wisdom, folly, imprudence. [OE & G, cf. Du. *on-*, cogn. w. L IN-² & *ne*, Gk *a(n)-*, *nē-*]

unanchor. See UN-¹(1).

ūnă·nimous, a. All of one mind, agreeing in opinion, as *we were*, *the meeting was*, *u.* (*for reform*, *as to the policy to be pursued*, *in protesting*, &c.); (of opinion, vote, &c.) formed, held, given, with one accord. Hence or cogn. **unani·**MITY, **una·nimous**NESS, nn., **una·nimously**LY² adv. [f. L *unanimus*, *-mis*, (*unus* one + *animus* mind) + -OUS]

unapparel, unarm, unarmed¹, see UN-¹(2); **unattire,** UN-¹(1); **unbag,** UN-¹(3); **unbalance,** UN-¹(1); **unballast,** UN-¹(2); **unbank, unbar, unbear,** UN-¹(1); **unbed,** UN-¹(3); **unbeknown(st),** UN-²(1); **unbelief, unbeliever,** UN-²(2); **unbelt,** UN-¹(2); **unbend, unbending**¹, UN-¹(1).

unberu·fen (ŏŏnbĭrōō-), a. Unsummoned (in E use as deprecating Nemesis after boastful remark &c.). [G]

unbeseem, unbias, unbind, see UN-¹(1); **unbishop,** UN-¹(4); **unbitt,** UN-¹(3); **unblindfold, unblock, unbolt,** UN-¹(1); **unbone,** UN-¹(2); **unbonnet,** UN-¹(1); **unboot,** UN-¹(2); **unbosom,** UN-¹(1); **unbowel,** UN-¹(2); **unbox,** UN-¹(3); **unbrace, unbraid, unbreach, unbridle, unbuckle, unburden, unbutton,** UN-¹(1); **uncage,** UN-¹(3); **uncanny,** UN-²(1); **uncap,** UN-¹(2); **uncart, uncase,** UN-¹(3).

uncate. See UNCINATE.

unchain, see UN-¹(1); **unchastity,** UN-²(2); **unchristianize,** UN-¹(1); **unchurch,** UN-¹(3).

u·ncia, n. (Rom. ant.; pl. *-ae*). Twelfth part, esp. (as coin or amount) of the as; ounce; inch. [L]

u·ncial (-shl), a. & n. Of, written in, a kind of majuscule writing found in MSS. of 4th to 8th c. with characters partly resembling modern capitals; (n.) u. letter or MS. [f. L *uncialis* (prec., see -AL), in sense *inch-high*, *large*]

u·ncinate, a. (Also *uncate*) hooked, crooked. So **unci·**FEROUS, **u·nci**FORM, **u·ncin**AL, aa. [f. L *uncinatus* (*uncinus* hook f. L *uncus* hook, see -ATE²)]

uncircumcision, see UN-²(2); **unclasp,** UN-¹(1).

uncle, n. Father's or mother's brother; aunt's husband; (U.S., as familiar mode of address) *U. Tom's Cabin* &c., *U. Sam*, government or typical citizen of U.S.; (slang) pawnbroker; (colloq., often w. name added, as voc. or not) elderly friendly person, e.g. B.B.C. announcer; *talk to* (person) *like a Dutch u.* (with kindly severity). Hence **u·ncle**SHIP n. [AF, f. L *avunculus* maternal uncle (*avus* grandfather, see foll.)]

-uncle, suf. in nn. of L orig. or on L anal., repr. L *-unculus*, *-la*, a special form of *-culus* -CULE prob. due to use of *-culus* w. stems in *-on-*, as *sermunculus* (*sermon-*), *carbunculus* (*carbon-*), *oratiuncula*, &c., and its extension to other stems (*avunculus*, st. *avo-*, *furunculus*, st. *fur-*). E has also *-uncule* (*homuncule*), & L *-culus* is sometimes kept (*ranunculus*).

unclench, -inch, see UN-¹(1); **uncloak,** UN-¹(2); **unclog,** UN-¹(1); **uncloister,** UN-¹(3); **unclose, unclothe,** UN-¹(1); **unco,** UN-²(1); **uncock, uncoil,** UN-¹(1); **unconcern,** UN-²(2); **unconscionable,** UN-²(1); **unconstraint,** UN-²(2); **uncoop,** UN-¹(3); **uncord, -cork, -couple,** UN-²(2).

uncou·th (-ōōth), a. (Obs. or archaic) not known of, unfamiliar, unusual; (of places; now literary) unfrequented, desolate, wild, (of life) uncivilized, comfortless; (of persons, looks, conduct, &c.) strange, awkward, clumsy, uncultured, (of language) harsh, rugged, pedantic. Hence **uncou·th**LY² adv., **uncou·th**NESS n. [OE *uncúth* unknown (UN-² + *cúth* p.p. of *cunnan* know, CAN²)]

For adjj. in *un-* not given see UN-²(1).

uncover, see UN-¹(1); **uncowl,** UN-¹(2); **uncreate, uncross,** UN-¹(1); **uncrown,** UN-¹(2).

u·nction, n. Anointing with oil or unguent for medical purposes or as religious rite or ceremonial (EXTREME *u.*); thing used in anointing, unguent, (fig.) soothing or flattering words or thought or circumstance (see FLATTER); fervent or sympathetic quality in words or tone caused by or causing deep religious or other emotion; simulation of this, affected enthusiasm, gush; excessive suavity; keen or lingering enjoyment in narration, gusto, (*told the story with much u.*). [f. L *unctionem* (*ungere unct-* anoint, see -ION)]

u·nctuous, a. Full of (esp. simulated) unction; greasy, esp. (of minerals) having a soapy feel when touched. Hence **u·nctuous**LY² adv., **u·nctuous**NESS n. [f. med. L *unctuosus* f. L *unctus -ūs* anointing (as prec.), see -OUS]

uncurb, uncurl, see UN-¹(1).

u·ndé (-ā), **u·ndee,** a. (herald.). Wavy. [f. F *ondé* (L *unda* wave, -ATE²)]

undeceive, undeceived¹, undeify, see UN-¹(1).

u·nder, prep., adv., & a. In or to a position lower than, below, as *it lay, fell, u. the table, assembled u.* (at the foot of) *the castle wall, struck him u. the left eye, nothing new u. the sun* (anywhere), *u.* FOOT¹, *u.* HATCH¹*es*, *u.* one's NOSE, *u.* (in & covered by) *water*, *u.* one's WING; within, on the inside of, (surface &c.), as *inserted a knife-blade under the bark, was seen to blush u. his dusky skin, with a good meal u. his belt* (in his stomach), *u. the* LEE *of*; inferior to, less than, as *no one u. a bishop, incomes u. £160, cannot be done u.* (at less cost than) *£5, total falls u. what was expected, speak u.* one's *breath* (in a whisper); in the position or act of supporting or sustaining, subjected to, undergoing, liable to, on condition of, subject to, governed or controlled or bound by, in accordance with, in the form of, in the time of, as *sank u. the load* (lit. & fig.), *u. a* CLOUD, *groaning u. tyranny, is now u. repair, u. examination, a few acres u.* (planted with) *corn, u.* FIRE¹, *u.* (propelled by) *sail, u.* WAY, *u.* ARM²*s, forbidden u. pain of death, a criminal u. sentence of* (condemned to) *death, have sat u.* (attended sermons of) *famous preachers, country prospered u. him* or *his rule, might succeed u. other conditions, is u. a delusion, was u. the impression, u. the circumstances, u. the rose,* = SUB²*rosa, u.* FAVOUR¹, *u.* (attested by) one's *hand & seal, was u. a vow, known u. an assumed name, appears u. various forms, u. pretence of ignorance, lived u. the Stuarts.* (Adv.) in or to a lower place or subordinate condition, as BRING, KEEP¹, KNOCK¹, KNUCKLE, GO¹, *u., a cloth should be spread u.* (usu. *underneath, beneath*). (Adj.) lower (now largely merged in foll.), as *the u. jaw, u. layers, u. servants*; *u. dog* (slang), dog, person, who has the worst of an encounter. Hence **u·nder**MOST a. [com.-Teut.: OE *under* (adv. & prep.), cf. Du. *onder*, G *unter*, ON *undir*, cogn. w. L *infra* below]

under-, pref. = prec. prep. or adv. or adj.

1. As prep. governing the noun to which it is prefixed, w. sense 'below', *under-* forms a few advv. & adjj., as: *underfoo·t* adv., under one's feet; UNDERGROUND; UNDERHAND; *u·nderproof* a., with less alcohol than proof spirit.

2. *Under-* is prefixed to vbs & their derivatives w. adv. or prep. force in sense 'beneath', 'lower than', 'below', as: *underbi·d* v.t., make lower bid than (person); *undercu·t*¹ v.t., cut away material of (design &c. in carving) so as to make it stand out in relief, (Golf) hit (ball) so that it rises high & does not roll far on alighting, (commerc.) offer lower terms than (competitor); *underdrai·n*¹ v.t., drain (ground) by forming channels beneath it; *underlay·* v.t. & i., lay something under (thing), esp. (Print.) lay paper under (types) to raise them, (Mining, intr.) incline from the vertical; *u·nderlay* n., paper laid under types, (Mining) = inclined lode or shaft; *underle·t* v.t., let below true value, sublet; *underli·ne*¹ v.t., draw line under (word) to secure emphasis or to indicate italics; *underme·ntioned* a.; *underpi·n* v.t., place support of masonry &c. under (wall, overhanging bank, &c.); *underplay·* v.i. (whist), play low card while retaining high one of same suit; *u·nderplay* n., underplaying; *underpro·p* v.t., put prop under; *underquo·te* v.t., quote lower prices than (person), quote lower prices than others for (goods &c.); *underru·n* v.t. & i., run or pass under; *underscore·* v.t., = *underline*¹; *underse·ll* v.t., sell cheaper than (person); *u·nderseller* n.; *underse·t*¹ v.t., support (masonry &c.) by prop; *u·ndershot* a., (of wheel) worked by water passing under it, = UNDERHUNG; *undersig·ned* a., *I, we, the u.*, (whose signatures appear below); *undertru·mp* v.t., play lower trump than (person, trump played).

3. *Under-* in sense 'insufficiently', 'incompletely', is prefixed to vbs (used in p.p.) & to some adjj., w. their derivatives. Adjj. & p.pp. tend in attrib. use (cf. UN-¹, -ED²) to take stress on first syllable (*beef was underdo·ne, hate u·nderdone beef*; *an u·nder-exposed* or *u·nder-expo·sed negative*). Exx.: *undera·ct* v.t., act (a part, or abs.) inadequately; *underbre·d* a., ill-bred, vulgar; *underchar·ge* v.t., charge too little

for (thing) or to (person), put insufficient charge into (gun &c.); *u·ndercharge* n., insufficient charge; *under-deve·lop* v.t. (photog.); *underdo·* v.t., cook insufficiently, esp. in p.p. *underdone*; *underdo·se* v.t.; *under-draw·* v.t., depict inadequately; *underdre·ss* v.t. & i., dress too plainly or too lightly; *undere·stimāte* v.t., form too low an estimate of; *undere·stimate* (-at), *-ation*, nn.; *under-expo·se* v.t., *under-exposure* n., (photog.); *underfee·d* v.t. & i.; *under-fire·d* a., (of pottery) not baked enough; *undergrow·n* a.; *underma·n* v.t., furnish (ship &c.) with too few men; *underma·sted* a.; *underpay·* v.t., pay (workmen &c.) inadequately; *under-produ·ction* n., production less than is usual or required; *underra·te* v.t., underestimate; *under-re·ckon* v.t.; *under-ri·pe* a.; *undersi·zed* a., of less than the usual size, dwarfish; *understa·te* v.t.; *understa·tement* n.; *understo·ck* v.t., supply (farm, shop, &c.) with insufficient stock; *underti·med* a., = *under-exposed*; *undervalua·tion* n.; *underval·ue* v.t.

4. *Under-* in adj. relation with noun replaces or is interchangeable with *under* a., in senses ' situated beneath ', ' subordinate '. In the less-established compounds the hyphen is usu. retained & the stress variously placed on either component or both. Exx.: *under-agent* n.; *u·nderbrush* n., = *undergrowth*; *u·nderclay* n., clay bed under coal; *under-clerk(ship)* nn.; *u·nderclothes, u·nderclothing*, nn., clothes worn under others esp. next to skin; *underdrain*[2] n., drain placed underground; *u·nderflow* n., current flowing beneath surface; *u·ndergarment* n., garment worn under others; *u·ndergrowth* n., shrubs or small trees growing under larger ones; *under-king* n., inferior or subordinate king; *under-lease* n., lease granted by lessee for shorter term than his own; *u·nderline*[2] n., advance announcement of production of subsequent play at foot of play-bill; *u·nderlinen* n., linen or (loosely) other undergarments; *u·nderplot* n., subordinate plot in play or novel; *u·nder-se·cretary(ship)* nn. (esp. of permanent chief of department under Secretary of State); *under-servant* n.; *u·nderset*[2] n. (naut.), undercurrent in contrary direction to that of wind or surface water; *under-sheriff* n., sheriff's deputy; *undershirt* n.; *u·ndershrub* n., plant like shrub but smaller; *u·nderskirt* n.; *u·ndersleeve* n., sleeve, esp. detached one, worn under another; *u·ndersoil* n.; *u·nderstrapper* n., inferior agent, underling; *under-stratum* n.; *under-tenant* n., tenant's tenant; *under-tenancy* n.; *u·ndertint* n., subdued tint; *u·ndertone* n., subdued tone esp. in speaking, thin or subdued colour; *u·ndertow* n., backward flow of wave breaking on beach, = *underset*; *u·nderwear* n., (clothes meant for) wearing underneath; *u·nderwing* n., kinds of moth with conspicuous markings &c. on u. wings; *u·nderwood* n., = *undergrowth*; *u·nderworld* n., antipodes, infernal regions, lowest social stratum.

underact, see UNDER- 3; **under-agent,** UNDER- 4; **underbid,** UNDER- 2; **underbred,** UNDER- 3; **underbrush,** UNDER- 4; **undercharge,** UNDER- 3; **under-clay, underclothes, underclothing,** UNDER- 4.

u·ndercroft, n. Crypt. [UNDER, ME *croft* f. L *crupta* CRYPT]

u·ndercurrent, n. Current below the surface; (fig.) unperceived influence or feeling of different or contrary tendency; (Mining) large shallow box beside main hydraulic sluice serving to aid in saving gold. [UNDER- 4]

undercut[1]**.** See UNDER- 2.

u·ndercut[2]**,** n. Under side of sirloin; upward blow in boxing. [UNDER- 4]

under-develop, underdo, underdose, see UNDER- 3; **underdrain**[1] v.t., UNDER- 2, **underdrain**[2] n., UNDER- 4; **underdraw, underdress, underestimate, underestimation, under-expose, under-exposure, underfeed, under-fired,** UNDER- 3; **underflow,** UNDER- 4; **underfoot,** UNDER- 1; **undergarment,** UNDER- 4.

undergo·, v.t. Be subjected to, suffer, endure esp. with firmness, as *has undergone many trials, underwent a rapid change, an operation.* [OE UNDER(*gán* GO)]

undergra·duate, n. Member of university who has not taken his first degree (often attrib.). Hence **undergra·duateship** n. [UNDER- 4]

undergrou·nd, adv., a., & n. Beneath surface of earth; (adj., in attrib. use ŭ·n-, & n.) situated u., as *the u. (railway).* [UNDER- 1]

undergrown, see UNDER- 3; **undergrowth,** UNDER- 4.

underha·nd, adv. & a. (*in attrib. use* ŭ·n-). Clandestine(ly), secret(ly), not aboveboard; (Crick., of bowling) (performed) with hand underneath both elbow & ball, as *bowls u., u. bowling.* [UNDER- 1, 4]

underhu·ng (*attrib.* ŭ·n-), a. (Of lower jaw) projecting beyond upper jaw; having u. jaw. [UNDER- 2]

under-king, see UNDER- 4; **underlay** v.t. & i., & n., UNDER- 2; **under-lease,** UNDER- 4; **underlet,** UNDER- 2.

underlie·, v.t. Lie, be situated, under (stratum &c. or abs.); (fig., of principle &c.) be the basis of (doctrine, law, conduct, &c., or abs. esp. in part.). [UNDER-2]

underline[1] v.t., see UNDER- 2; **underline**[2]**, underlinen,** UNDER- 4.

u·nderling, n. Subordinate (usu. contempt.). [ME (-LING[1])]

underman, undermasted, see UNDER- 3; **undermentioned,** UNDER- 2.

undermi·ne, v.t. Make mine or excavation under, wear away base or foundation of, as *rivers u. their banks, u. the walls*; injure (person, reputation, influence, &c.) by secret means; injure, wear out, (health &c.) insidiously or imperceptibly. Hence **undermi·ner**[1] n. [UNDER- 2]

underneath, adv., prep., a., & n. At or to a lower place (than), below (not in fig. senses); lower (surface, part). [OE *underneodhan* (UNDER, cf. BENEATH)]

underpay, see UNDER- 3; **underpin, underplay** v.i., & n., UNDER- 2; **underplot,** UNDER- 4; **under-production,** UNDER- 3; **underproof,** UNDER- 1; **underprop, underquote,** UNDER- 2; **underrate, underreckon, under-ripe,** UNDER- 3; **underrun, underscore,** UNDER- 2; **under-secretary(ship),** UNDER- 4; **undersell(er),** UNDER- 2; **under-servant,** UNDER- 4; **underset**[1] v.t., UNDER- 2; **underset**[2] n., **under-sheriff, under-shirt,** UNDER- 4; **undershot,** UNDER- 2; **undershrub,** UNDER- 4; **undersigned,** UNDER- 2; **undersized,** UNDER- 3; **underskirt, undersleeve, undersoil,** UNDER- 4.

understa·nd, v.t. & i. (p.p. archaic *-standed*). Comprehend, perceive the meaning of, (words, person, or language &c.), as *does not u. what you say, do you u. me?, French?, tongue not understanded of the people,* foreign language; grasp mentally, perceive the significance or explanation or cause or nature of, know how to deal with, as *do not u. why he came, what the noise is about, the point of his remark, quite u. your difficulty, cannot u. him, his conduct, his wanting to go, thoroughly understands children, could never u. mathematics,* (abs.) *you don't u.* (the situation &c.); infer esp. from information received, take as implied, take for granted, as *I u. that doors open at 7.30, that they are almost destitute, him to be* or *that he is a distant relation, I quite understood that expenses were to be paid, no one could u. that from my words, what did you u. him to say* (u. from his words)?, (expr. uncertainty or surprise or indignation) *do I u.* (*you to say*) *that* or *am I to u. that you refuse?,* (introducing warning or threat) *now u. me, he gave me* or *I was given to u.* (I thought he said or meant) *that it was done*; supply (word) mentally, as *the verb may be either expressed or understood.* [OE UNDER(*standan* STAND)]

understa·nding[1], a. Having insight. [-ING[2]]

understa·nding[2], n. In vbl senses, esp.: intelligence, as *has an excellent u., men without u.*; power of apprehension, power of abstract thought, (often opp. to *reason*); agreement, harmony, union of sentiments, convention, thing agreed upon, as *must come to an u. with him disturbed the* (*good*) *u. between them, had a secret u. with other firms, consented only on this u., on the distinct u. that*; (pl., slang) feet, legs, shoes, &c. [-ING[1]]

understate(ment), understock, see UNDER- 3; **understrapper, under-stratum,** UNDER- 4.

u·nderstudy, n., & v.t. One who studies theatrical part in order to play it at short notice in absence of the usual actor; (vb) study (part) thus. [UNDER- 4]

underta·ke, v.t. & i. Bind oneself to perform, make oneself responsible for, engage in, enter upon, (work, enterprise, responsibility); accept an obligation, promise, (*to* do); (archaic) engage with (person) in combat, argument, &c.; guarantee, affirm, as *I will u. that he has not heard a word, that you shall* or *will be no loser by it*; (archaic) be guarantee *for* (person fact); (colloq.) manage funerals. [ME UNDER(*taken* TAKE)]

u·ndertaker, n. In vbl senses, esp.: one who manages funerals; (Hist.) influential person who undertook to procure particular legislation esp. to procure supplies from Commons if king would grant some concession. [-ER[1]]

underta·king, n. In vbl senses, esp.: work &c. undertaken, enterprise, as *a serious u.*; management of funerals (ŭ·n-). [-ING[1]]

under-tenant, under-tenancy, see UNDER- 4; **under-timed,** UNDER- 3; **undertint, undertone, undertow,** UNDER- 4; **undertrump,** UNDER- 2; **undervaluation, undervalue,** UNDER- 3; **underwear, underwing, underwood, underworld,** UNDER- 4.

underwri·te, v.t. & i. Execute & deliver (policy of insurance esp. on marine property), practise marine insurance, whence **u·nderwriter**[1] n.; engage to buy all stock in (company &c.) not bought by the public; write below, as *the underwritten names.* [UNDER- 2]

u·ndies, n. pl. (slang). Underclothing. [abbr., -Y[3]]

undi·ne (-ēn), n. Female water-sprite who by marrying a mortal & bearing a child might receive a soul. Hence **undi·nal** a. [f. L *unda* wave + -INE[1]]

undo, see UN-[1](1); **undock,** UN-[1](3); **undoer, undoing, undomesticate, undone**[1], UN-[1](1).

u·ndose, a. (entom.). Wavy, undulating. [f. L *undosus* (*unda* wave, see -OSE[1])]

undrape, undress[1] v.t. & i., see -UN[1](1); **undress**[2] n., UN-[2](2); **undressed**[1], UN-[1](1); **unduke,** UN-[1](4).

u·ndŭlāte[1], v.i. Have wavy motion or look. Hence **u·ndulant** a. (esp. *-ant fever,* Malta fever), **u·ndulatingly**[2] adv. [as foll., -ATE[3]]

u·ndulate[2] (-at), a. Wavy, going alternately up & down or in & out, as *leaves with u. margins.* Hence **un·dulately**[2] adv. [f. L *undulatus* (*unda* wave, see -UL-, -ATE[2])]

undula·tion, n. Wavy motion or form, gentle rise & fall, each wave of this; set of wavy lines; (Path.) sensation of undulating movement in the heart. [as prec. + -ATION]

u·ndulatory, a. Undulating, wavy; of, due to, undulation; *u. theory of light* (that light is propagated through the ether by wave-motion imparted to the ether by molecular vibrations of the radiant body), so **undula·tion**IST(2), n. [-ORY]

unearth, see UN-[1](3); **unease,** UN-[2](2); **unedge,** UN-[1](2); **unegoize,** UN-[1](1); **unemployment,** UN-[2](2); **unentangle, unequalize,** UN-[1](1); **unface,** UN-[1](2); **unfaith,** UN-[2](2); **unfasten, unfastened**[1], UN-[1](1); **unfeather, unfence,** UN-[1](2); **unfetter, unfettered**[1], **unfeudalize, unfile, unfit, unfix, unfixed**[1], UN-[1](1); **unflesh, unflower,** UN-[1](2); **unfold**[1], UN-[1](1); **unfold**[2], UN-[1](3); **unform,** UN-[1](1); **unframe,** UN-[1](2); **unfriend,** UN-[2](2); **unfrock,** UN-[1](2); **unfurl,** UN-[1](1).

ungai·nly, a. & adv. (Of persons or animals or their movements) ill-made, awkward-looking, clumsy; (adv.) in u. manner. Hence **ungai·nli**NESS n. [UN-[2] + obs. *gain* a. f. ON *gegn* straight + -LY[1]]

ungear, ungild, ungird, see UN-[1](1); **ungirdle,** UN-[1](2); **unglaze,** UN-[1](1); **unglove, ungown,** UN-[1](2).

u·ngual (-gw-), a. Of, like, bearing, a nail or hoof or claw. So **ungui·cul**AR[1], **ungui·cul**ATE[2], [-CULE, usu. without dim. force], **ungui·**FEROUS, **u·ngui**FORM, aa. [f. L *unguis* claw, nail, + -AL]

u·nguent (-gw-), n. Any soft substance used as ointment or for lubrication. So **u·nguent**ARY[1] a. [f. L *unguentum* (*unguere* anoint)]

u·ngŭla, n. (pl. *-ae*). Hoof, claw, talon, whence **u·ngul**ATE[2](2) a. & n. (zool.); hooked instrument for extracting dead foetus; cone, cylinder, with top cut off by plane oblique to base. Hence **u·ngul**AR[1] a. [L, dim. as UNGUAL]

ungum, unhair, see UN-[1](2); **unhallow, unhand, unhang, unharness, unhasp,** UN-[1](1); **unhat, unhelm,** UN-[1](2); **unhinge(d), unhitch,** UN-[1](1); **unhive,** UN-[1](3); **unhook, unhoop,** UN-[1](1); **unhorse,** UN-[1](3); **unhouse, unhumanize,** UN-[1](1); **unhusk,** UN-[1](2).

ūni- in comb. = L *unus* one, as: *-arti·culate,* single-jointed; *-a·x(i)al,* having a single axis, whence *-a·xially* adv.; *-ca·meral,* of only one chamber (*u. legislature*); *-ca·psular,* of one capsule; *-ce·llular,* one-celled; *-co·lour(ed),* of one colour; *-cor·nous,* one-horned; *-co·state,* single-ribbed; *-cu·spid* a. & n., (tooth) of one cusp; *-cycle* (ū·-), single-wheeled velocipede; *-flor·ous,* bearing one flower; *-fo·liate,* having one leaf; *-la·teral,* one-sided (*u. leaves,* leaning to one side of stem, *u. contract,* binding one party only), whence *-la·terally* adv.; *-li·teral,* consisting of one letter; *-lo·cular, -lo·culate,* (bot., zool.), single-chambered; *-parous* (unĭ·-), producing one at a birth, (Bot.) having one axis or branch; *-par·tite,* not divided; *-ped* (ū·-), single-footed; *-per·sonal,* (of Deity) existing only in one person, (of verb) used only in one person; *-plā·nar,* lying in one plane; *-po·lar,* (Biol., of cell &c.) having only one pole, (Electr.) showing only one kind of polarity, whence *-pola·rity* n.; *-ra·diate(d),* having only one arm or process; *-ser·ial,* set in one row; *-se·xual,* of one sex, not hermaphrodite, having stamens or pistil but not both, whence *-sexua·lity* n., *-se·xually* adv.; *-su·lcate,* (bot., zool.), single-grooved; *-valent* (ūnĭ·-) (chem.), having a combining power of one, whence *-valence, -valency,* nn.; *-valve* (ū·-) a. & n., (mollusc) of one valve; *-vocal* (ūnĭ·-) a. & n., (word) of only one proper meaning, (Mus.) having a unisonous sound, whence *-vocally* adv.; *-voca·tion,* agreement of name & meaning.

U·niat, -āte, (ū-), n. Member of any community of Oriental Christians that acknowledges Pope's supremacy but retains own liturgy &c. [f. Russ. *uniyat* f. L *unus* one]

u·nicorn, n. Fabulous animal with horse's body & single straight horn (in *Deut.* xxxiii. 17 mistransl. of Heb. *re'em,* a two-horned animal); heraldic representation of this, with goat's beard & lion's tail; (also *u.-fish, -whale, sea-u.*) narwhal; kind of single-horned beetle; caterpillar with horn-like prominence on back (*u. moth,* of this); pair of horses with third horse in front, turn-out with these; (also *u.-shell*) kinds of gasteropod with spine on lip of shell. [f. L UNI(*cornis* f. *cornu* horn)]

u·niform, a., n., & v.t. Not changing in form or character, the same, unvarying, as *present a u. appearance, of u. size & shape, keeps a u. temperature, behaved with u. moderation, u. acceleration* (not varying with time); (of tax, law, &c.) not varying with time or place; conforming to same standard or rule; (n.) u. dress worn by members of same body, e.g. by soldiers, sailors, policemen; (vb) make u., clothe in u. Hence **u·niform**LY[2] adv. [(n. & vb f. adj.) f. F *uniforme* f. L UNI(*formis* -FORM)]

unifor·mity, n. Being uniform, sameness, consistency; *Act of U.* (for securing u. in public worship, esp. that of 1662); *doctrine of u.* (that u. has prevailed in physical causes & effects in all ages, opp. to CATASTROPHISM), whence **uniformit**AR·IAN(ISM) nn. [f. L *uniformitas* (as prec., see -TY)]

For other words in *uni-* see UNI-.

u·nifȳ, v.t. Reduce (things or abs.) to unity or uniformity. Hence or cogn. **uni**FICA·TION, **u·nifi**ER[1], nn. [f. med. L UNI(*ficare* -FY)]

Unigĕ·nitus (ū-, -j-), n. (hist.). Bull of Clement XI against Jansenism in 1713. [mod. L, = only-begotten, its first wd]

unintelligible. See UN-[2](1).

ū·nion, n. Uniting, being united, coalition, junction, as *effected a u., the u. of the parts was imperfect, u. by first or second* INTENTION, *the U.* (of England & Scotland in 1706, also, of Great Britain & Ireland); matrimony, marriage; concord, agreement, as *lived together in perfect u.*; a whole resulting from combination of parts or members, esp. (1) *the* U.S., (2) *the* United Kingdom, TRADE *u.*; POSTAL *u.*; two or more parishes consolidated for administration of poor-laws, (in full *u. workhouse*) workhouse erected by such u.; association of independent (esp. Congregational or Baptist) churches for purposes of co-operation; part of flag with device emblematic of u. normally occupying upper corner next staff (*ensign hoisted u. down*, with u. below as signal of distress); *U. Jack* or *flag*, national ensign of United Kingdom formed by u. of crosses of St George, St Andrew, & St Patrick; kinds of joint or coupling for pipes &c.; shallow vat in which beer is left to clear; fabric of mixed materials, e.g. cotton with linen or silk or jute; *u. suit* (U.S.), combinations (garment). [F, f. LL *unio* unity (*unus* one, see -ION)]

ū·nionist, n. Member of a trade union, advocate of trade unions; person opposed to rupture of legislative union between Great Britain & Ireland, opponent of home rule in Ireland, as LIBERAL *u.*, (attrib.) *u. party, principles*; (U.S. Hist.) one who during the civil war opposed secession. So **u·nion**ISM n., **unioni·st**IC a. [-IST]

ūni·que (-ēk), a. & n. Unmatched, unequalled, having no like or equal or parallel, as *his position was u., this vase is so far as is known u.*, (vulg.) *the most u.* (remarkable) *man I ever met*; (n.) u. thing. Hence **uni·que**LY[2] adv., **uni·que**NESS n. [F, f. L *unicus* (*unus* one)]

u·nison (-zn, -sn), a. & n. (Mus.) coinciding in pitch, whence or cogn. **uni·son**AL, **uni·son**ANT, **uni·son**OUS, aa., **uni·son**ANCE n.; *u. string* (tuned in u. with another string & meant to be sounded with it). (N.) unity of pitch in sounds or notes, (Mus.) this regarded as an interval; interval of an octave; state of sounding at same pitch, esp. *in u.*; =*u. string*; concord, agreement, as *acted in perfect u.* [f. LL UNI(*sonus* sound)]

ū·nit, n. Individual thing or person or group regarded for purposes of calculation &c. as single & complete, each of the individuals or groups into which a complex whole may be analysed, as *take the family as the u. of society*; quantity chosen as a standard in terms of which other quantities may be expressed, as *abstract u.*, the number one (1), *C.G.S. system of uu.* (in which centimetre, gramme, second, are the uu. of length, mass, & time), *electrical, magnetic, thermal, u.* [shortened f. UNITY]

unitār·ian, n. & a. (*U*-) one who, member of a Christian body that, maintains against the doctrine of the Trinity that God is one person, whence **Unitar·ian**ISM n., **Unitar·ian**IZE v.t.; advocate of unity or centralization e.g. in politics. (Adj.) of the Uu., as *U. Church*; =foll. [-ARIAN]

u·nitary, a. Of a unit or units, as *u. method*, a rule in arithmetic used for same purpose as rule of three; marked by uni(formi)ty. [-ARY[1]]

ūni·te, v.t. & i. Join (t. & i.) together, make or become one, combine, consolidate, amalgamate, as *u. the parts with cement, give the parts time to u., the two nations gradually* (*became*) *united, oil will not u. with water, United* STATE[1]*s, United* KINGDOM, *United Irishmen*, Irish society formed in 1791 for purposes of parliamentary reform &c., *United Provinces*, Holland, Zealand, & 5 other provinces united in 1579 & forming basis of republic of Netherlands, *United Brethren*, the MORAVIAN sect; agree, combine, co-operate, (*in* sentiment, conduct, *doing*). Hence **uni·ted**LY[2] adv., **u·nĭt**IVE a. [f. L *unire -it-* (*unus* one)]

u·nitism, n. =MONISM. [-ISM]

u·nitize, v.t. Reduce to, treat as, a unit. [-IZE]

ū·nity, n. Oneness, being one or single or individual, being formed of parts that constitute a whole, due interconnexion & coherence of parts, as *disturbs the u. of the idea, pictures lack u., national u.*; thing showing such u., thing that forms a complex whole, as *a person regarded as a u.*; (Math.) the number one, factor that leaves unchanged the quantity on which it operates; *the dramatic uu., uu. of time, place, & action*, limitation of supposed time of drama to that occupied in acting it or to a single day, use of same scene throughout, & abstention from all that is irrelevant to development of single plot; harmony, concord, between persons &c., as *dwell together in u., at u. with*; (Law) joint tenancy of different tenants, joint possession by one person of different rights. [f. L *unitatem* (*unus* one, see -TY)]

univer·sal, a. & n. Of or belonging to or done &c. by all persons or things in the world or in the class concerned, applicable to all cases, *the terror was u., met* *with u. applause, has the u. sanction of philosophers, the rule does not pretend to be u., u. agent* (empowered to do all that can be delegated), *u.* PROVIDER, *u. compass* (with legs that may be extended for large circles), *u. coupling* or *joint* (transmitting power by a shaft at any selected angle), *u. legatee* (to whom the whole of a property is bequeathed), *u. proposition* (in which predicate is affirmed or denied of the entire subject). Hence or cogn. **universa·lity, universaliza·tion**, nn., **univer·salize**(3) v.t., **univer·sally**[2] adv. (N.): (Logic) u. proposition; (Philos.) general notion or idea, thing that by its nature may be predicated of many. [f. OF *universel* f. L *universalis* (as UNIVERSE, see -AL)]

univer·salist, U-, n. One who holds, esp. member of an organized body of Christians who hold, that all mankind will eventually be saved. Hence or cogn. **univer·salism** n., **universali·stic** a. [-IST]

u·niverse, n. All existing things; the whole creation (& the Creator); all mankind; (Logic) all the objects under consideration. [f. F *univers* f. L *universum* neut. of UNI(*versus* p.p. of *vertere* turn) combined into one, whole]

univer·sity, n. Educational institution designed for instruction or examination or both of students in all or many of the more important branches of learning, conferring degrees in various faculties, & often embodying colleges & similar institutions; members of this collectively; team, crew, &c., representing a u., as *the u. had four wickets to fall*; *U.* EXTENSION; *U. Test Act* (abolishing subscription to Thirty-nine Articles &c. as requisite to taking of degree, 1871). [f. OF *université* f. L *universitas* whole, universe, corporation, (as prec., see -TY), understood also w. ref. to number of subjects taught]

universo·logy, n. Science of all created things; science of all that is of human interest. Hence **universolo·gical** a., **universo·logist** n. [f. UNIVERSE + -O- + -LOGY]

unjoin, unjoint, see UN-[1](1).

unke·mpt, a. Uncombed, dishevelled; untidy, of neglected appearance; (of language) careless, rough, incondite. [UN-[2] + ME *kempt* p.p. of *kemben* comb, OE *cemban*]

unking, see UN-[1](4); **unkink, unknit, unknot, unlace, unlade, unlash, unlatch, unlay,** UN-[1](1); **unlead,** UN-[1](2); **unlearn,** UN-[1](1); **unleash,** UN-[1](3).

unle·ss, conj. If not, except when, as *shall* (*not*) *go u. I hear from him, u. absolutely compelled, always walked u. I had a bicycle*; *u. & until* (verbose for *until* in condit. use cf. *if & when*). [earlier *onless* (ON + LESS); *u. I hear* = on less provocation than my hearing, short of my hearing, cf. F *à moins que* or *de*]

unlimber, see UN-[1](2); **unline, unlink, unload, unlock, unlodge, unloose,** UN-[1](1); **unlord,** UN-[1](4); **unmake,** UN-[1](1); **unman,** UN-[1](2, 4); **unmantle,** UN-[1](2); **unmask, unmew,** UN-[1](1); **unmonk,** UN-[1](4); **unmoor, unmortise, unmould, unmuffle, unmuzzle,** UN-[1](1); **unnail,** UN-[1](2); **unnaturalize, unnerve(d),** UN-[1](1); **unnest,** UN-[1](3); **unpack, unpeg,** UN-[1](1); **unpen,** UN-[1](3); **unpeople,** UN-[1](1); **unperch,** UN-[1](3); **unpick, unpin, unplait, unplug,** UN-[1](1); **unplume,** UN-[1](2); **unpope,** UN-[1](4); **unpreach,** UN-[1](1); **unprejudice,** UN-[2](2); **unprelate, unpriest, unprince,** UN-[1](4); **unprop,** UN-[1](2); **unqueen,** UN-[1](4); **unravel,** UN-[1](1); **unreason,** UN-[2](2); **unreel, unreeve, unrein,** UN-[1](1); **unrepair, unreserve, unrest, unrestraint,** UN-[2](2); **unriddle, unrig,** UN-[1](1); **unright,** UN-[2](2); **unring,** UN-[1](2); **unrip, unrivet,** UN-[1](1); **unrobe,** UN-[1](2); **unroll, unromanize,** UN-[1](1); **unroof,** UN-[1](2); **unroost,** UN-[1](3); **unroot,** UN-[1](1); **unrumple,** UN-[1](2); **unsaddle, unsaid**[1], **unsay,** UN-[1](1); **unscale,** UN-[1](2); **unscrew, unseal, unseam, unseat, unseated**[1], UN-[1](1); **unself,** UN-[1](2); **unset, unsettle, unsettled**[1], UN-[1](1); **unsex,** UN-[1](2); **unshackle, unsheathe,** UN-[1](1); **unshell,** UN-[1](2); **unship, unshipped**[1], UN-[1](1); **unshoe, unshot, unshutter, unsinew, unsister,** UN-[1](2); **unsling,** UN-[1](1); **unsnare,** UN-[1](3); **unsolder, unspar,** UN-[1](2); **unspeak,** UN-[1](1); **unspell, unsphere,** UN-[1](3); **unsquire,** UN-[1](4); **unstarch,** UN-[1](2); **unsteel,** UN-[1](1); **unstep,** UN-[1](3); **unstick, unstitch, unstock, unstop,** UN-[1](1); **unstopper,** UN-[1](2); **unstrap, unstring, unstrung,** UN-[1](1); **unsuccess, unsuspicion,** UN-[2](2); **unswaddle, unswathe, unswear,** UN-[1](1); **unsymmetry,** UN-[2](2); **untack, untangle, unteach, untemper,** UN-[1](1); **untent,** UN-[1](3); **untether, unthink, unthread,** UN-[1](1); **unthrift,** UN-[2](2); **unthrone,** UN-[1](3); **untie, untied**[1], UN-[1](1).

unti·l, prep. & conj. = TILL[2] (preferred when its clause or phrase stands first, as *U. you told me I had no idea of it*, & somet. in leisurely or dignified or pompous style, as *unless & u.*). [ME *untill* f. ON *und* as far as + TILL[2]]

untile, untin, see UN-[1](2).

u·nto, prep. (archaic). = TO[1] (in all uses except as sign of infinitive). [as UNTIL, w. TO[1] substituted for TILL[2]]

untomb, see UN-[1](3); **untooth,** UN-[1](2); **untruss,** UN-[1](1); **untruth,** UN-[2](2); **untuck, untune,** UN-[1](1); **unturf,** UN-[1](2); **untwine, untwist, unveil,** UN[1]-(1); **unvicar,** UN-[1](4); **unvote, unwarp, unweave,** UN-[1](1).

unwie·ldy, a. Slow or clumsy of movement, difficult to use or manage, owing to size or weight or shape. Hence **unwie·ldi**LY[2] adv., **unwie·ldi**NESS n. [UN-[2] +obs. *wieldy* (obs. *wield* n. control, cf. WIELD v., + -Y[2]) vigorous]

unwill, unwind, see UN-[1](1); **unwisdom,** UN-[2](2); **unwitting(ly),** UN-[2](1); **unwound**[1], **unwork, unwrap, unwrinkle, unyoke,** UN-[1](1).

up, adv., prep., a., & n. To or in a high(er) place, position, degree, amount, value, &c., to or in a capital or university or place further north or otherwise conventionally regarded as high(er), as *bird flew up to the eaves, high up in the air, what is he doing up there?, horse might have won with a better jockey up* (in saddle), *lives four floors up, a few feet further up, flames mount up, total mounts up, tide is coming up, water came up to his chin, a hundred up* (on scoring-board, scored in game), *it is u. to* (incumbent on) *us to foot the bill, sums up to £5, lives up to* (spends all) *his income, up to the* MARK[1], *u. against* (confronted with) *a hard job, am not up to* (fit for) *travelling, custom is traced up* (back) *to the Stuarts, up to* DATE[2], *lift up your head, as far up* (north) *as Aberdeen, Oxford men just going up, stayed up* (at Oxford &c.) *for the vacation, ran up to town* (London) *for the day, was had up* (before magistrate) *on a charge of drunkenness, sailed up* (towards source) *as far as the river was navigable, corn is up* (at high price), *is high up in the school, went up three places in class, ran up a bill, have looked for it up & down* (in every direction); to the place in question or in which the speaker &c. is, as *child came up & asked me the time, went straight up to the door, sure to* TURN[1] *up late*; to or in erect or vertical position (lit. & fig.) esp. as favourable to activity, out of bed or lying or sitting or kneeling posture, in(to) condition of efficiency or activity, as *sprang up from his seat, stand up,* (with *get, stand,* &c. understood) *up !, up with you,* get up, *up with it,* put it up, *up* (opp. *down with*) *the Bolsheviks !, was* (already) *up early this morning, was* (still) *up late last night, must be up & doing, Home Secretary is up* (has risen to speak, is speaking), *Parliament is up* (no longer sitting, prorogued), *stir up sedition,* GET *up, screw up your courage, wind up watch, put the helm up* (so place it as to force ship away from wind), *beer is not up* (is flat), *nation is up in arms* (armed & ready to fight lit. & fig., often *against*), *whole of the west was up* (in rebellion &c.), *his blood is up* (anger or spirit roused), *is well up* (instructed) *in mathematics, what is up* (going on)*?, what tricks have you been up to* (playing)*?, up to* SNUFF[1], *do not feel up* (equal) *to work, this cigar is not up to much* (is poor); (expr. complete or effectual result &c.) *eat, drink, burn, dry, tear, up, speak up* (loudly), *hunt up,* find by hunting, *follow up, praise up, save up,* accumulate by saving, *pack,* PUT[1], *bind, store, lock, chain, tie, fasten, fix, nail, seal, up* (securely), *time is up* (exhausted), GIVE[1] *up, hurry up,* MAKE[1] *up, cheer up, clear up, it is all up* (& slang *U.P.*) *with him,* his case is hopeless; HARD-*up*. (Prep.) to a higher point of, on or along in ascending direction, as *climbed up the ladder, up the hill, smoke goes up chimney, sailed up* (towards source of) *the river, walked up* (towards higher or more central part of, or simply along) *the street, up hill & down dale,* up & down in every direction, taking the country as it comes; at or in a higher part of, as *lives further up the road, somewhere up the river, saw him sitting half-a-mile up the hill, up a* TREE, *up the* POLE[1], *up the* SPOUT. (Adj.) moving, sloping, going, towards a higher point or to the capital, as *up stroke, line* (of railway), *train.* (N.) *ups & downs,* rises & falls, undulating ground, alternately good & bad fortune. [OE *up(p)* adv., cf. Du. *op,* G *auf*]

up-, pref. = prec. 1. Adv. pref. to vbs (esp. in p.p.) & vbl nn., chiefly archaic, poet., or rhet., exc. a few given separately (UPBRAID &c.), as: *upbear·* v.t., hold up, sustain aloft, esp. in p.p. *upborne*; *upbi·nd* v.t.; *upbla·ze* v.i.; *u·pbringing* n. (mod.), bringing up, education; *upca·st* v.t.; *u·pcast* n., casting up, upward throw, (Mining) shaft through which air passes out of mine; *u·pgrowth* n., growing up, development, what grows up; *uphea·p* v.t.; *uphea·val* n. (mod.), heaving up, esp. (Geol.) of part of earth's crust, (fig.) vast social or other change; *uphea·ve* v.t. & i.; *u·pkeep* n. (mod.), (cost, means, of) maintenance; *upli·ft* v.t.; *u·plift* n. (esp. U.S.), elevating influence, edifying effect, moral inspiration; *uprai·se* v.t.; *uprear·* v.t.; *upri·se* v.i.; *upri·sing* n., rising esp. from bed, rebellion, riot; *uproo·t* v.t. (mod.), tear up by roots (lit. & fig.); *upstanding,* well set up, erect, (of wages) fixed, not variable; *u·ptake* n., lifting, (Sc.) understanding, apprehension, as *quick in the u.*; *u·pthrow* n., throwing upward, esp. (Geol., Mining) upward displacement of rock on one side of fault; *u·pthrust* n. geol., = *upheaval*; *uptur·n* v.t., turn up (ground in ploughing &c.). 2. Pref. with prep. force forming advv. & adjj. f. nn., as: *u·p-country* a., toward the interior, inland, as *u.-c. districts* (cf. *up country* adv.); *uphi·ll* adv., with upward slope along hill or slope in upward direction, as *road runs u.,*

For other words in *up-* see UP.

riding u.; *u·phill* a., sloping upwards, (fig.) arduous, difficult, laborious, as *u. work*; *upstair·s* adv., *u·pstair(s)*, a., on, to, an upper storey; *up-strea·m* adv., *u·p-stream* a., (moving, done) against the current. 3. W. adj. force, as: *u·pland* a. & n. (sing. or pl.), (of) the higher or inland parts of a country; *u·pstroke*, upward line made in writing.

upa·nishad (ōōpah-, ōōpă-), n. Each of a series of Sanskrit philosophical treatises forming a division of the Vedas. [Skr.]

ū·pas, n. (Also *u.-tree, antiar*) Javanese tree yielding milky sap used as arrow-poison & held fatal to whatever came beneath its branches, (fig.) pernicious influence, practice, &c.; poisonous sap of this & other trees. [Malay, = poison]

upbra·id, v.t. Chide, reproach (person &c. *with, for*, fault &c., or abs.). Hence **upbrai·dING**[1] n., **upbrai·dingLY**[2] adv. [OE UP(*bregdan* BRAID[2]); orig. = bring up or adduce (a fault)]

up-end, v.t. & i. (dial.). Set on end; sit, stand, or rise, up. [UP adv.]

upho·ld, v.t. Hold up, keep erect, support; give support or countenance to (person, practice, &c.); maintain, confirm, (decision, verdict). Hence **up-ho·ldER**[1] n. [UP-]

uphō·lster, v.t. Furnish (room &c.) with hangings, carpets, furniture, &c.; provide (chair &c.) with textile covering, padding, springs, &c., cover (chair &c. *with, in*, tapestry &c.). [back formation f. foll.]

uphō·lsterer, n. One whose trade it is to upholster; *u.-bee*, kind that furnishes its cell with cut leaves &c. So **upho·ls-tERY**(1, 2) n. [earlier *uphold(st)er* repairer (UPHOLD, -STER) or dealer, + -ER[1]]

ū·phroe (-ō), n. (naut.). Long wooden block with holes through which cords are rove for adjusting an awning. [f. Du. *juffrouw* young lady, (naut.) ornamental pulley &c., (*jong* young + *vrouw* woman)]

upo·n, prep. = ON (*on* & *upon* are perhaps always idiomatically interchangeable; *on* is perhaps the commoner word esp. in colloq. use; *upon* is perhaps preferred when the prep. follows its object, as *had no evidence to go upon, nothing to depend upon, not enough to live upon*, but cf. *which table did you leave it on?*; other idiomatic preferences are perhaps rightly shown in *upon my word, on the whole, tier upon tier of seats, fell upon him unawares, had him on toast, came at once on receiving your message, take it on trust, will go on the chance, went on the spree, thrown upon his own resources, stretched upon the rack*). [formerly also as adv.; ME (UP + ON)]

u·pper, a. & n. Higher in place, situated above, as *u. lip, u. storey* (of house, also fig. = brain, as *something wrong in his u. storey*), *u.* (right-hand side of) *keyboard, u.* CASE[2], *have* or *get the u. hand* (mastery), *u. works* naut., parts of ship above water when she is balanced for voyage; higher in rank, dignity, &c., as *the u. servants, the U. House*, House of Lords, *the u. ten* (*thousand*), the aristocracy, *the U. Bench* (hist.), Court of King's Bench during exile of Charles II; (n.) u. part of boot or shoe, as *be on* one's *uu.* (poor, in difficulties), (pl.) cloth gaiters. [ME (UP + -ER[3])]

u·ppermost, a. & adv. Highest in place or rank, so **u·pMOST** a.; (adv.) on or to the top, as *said whatever came u.* (first suggested itself). [prec. + -MOST]

u·ppish, a. Self-assertive, pert. Hence **u·ppishLY**[2] adv., **u·ppishNESS** n. [f. UP + -ISH[1]]

u·pright (*in pred. use also* ŭprī·t), a., adv., & n. Erect, vertical, as *an u. post, posture*, PIANO[2], (pred. a. or adv.) *stood u., set it u.*; righteous, strictly honourable or honest, whence **u·prightLY**[2] adv., **u·prightNESS** n.; (n.) post or rod fixed u. esp. as support to some structure. [OE UP(*riht* RIGHT)]

u·proar, n. Tumult, violent disturbance, clamour. Hence **uproar·IOUS** a. (often of laughter, high spirits, &c.), **uproar·i-ousLY**[2] adv., **uproar·iousNESS** n. [f. Du. *oproer* (*op* up + *roer* a stir, cf. G *ruhr*)]

upse·t[1], v.t. & i., & n. Overturn, be overturned, as *carriage* (*was*) *u.*; disturb the composure or temper or digestion of, as *the news quite u. him, ate something that u. him*; shorten & thicken (metal, esp. tire) by hammering or pressure; (n.) upsetting, being upset. [UP-]

u·pset[2], a. *U. price*, lowest selling price of property in auction &c., reserve price. [UP-]

u·pshot, n. Final issue, conclusion; general effect, the long & short, (*of* a matter). [-UP]

u·pside-dow·n, adv. & a. With the upper part under, inverted, in total disorder, as *everything was* (*turned*) *u., an u. arrangement*. [altered f. ME *up so down*, lit. up as if down; cf. TOPSY-TURVY]

upsi·des, adv. (dial.). *Get u. with*, turn the tables on, avenge oneself upon. [UP, SIDE, -ES]

ūpsi·lon, n. Greek letter (Υ, υ) = u. [Gk (*psilos* bare)]

u·pstart, n. Person who has risen suddenly from humble position (often attrib.); person who assumes arrogant tone. [UP-]

u·pward a., **u·pward(s)** adv. Directed, moving, towards a higher place (lit. & fig.), as *an u. glance, prices show an u. tendency*, whence **u·pwardLY**[2] adv. (Adv.) in u. direction, as *look, move, u., followed the stream u.* (towards source); *children of 6 years old & upwards* (more); *found upwards of* (more than) *40 specimens*. [-WARD(S)]

ūrae·mia, n. (path.). Morbid condition of blood due to retention of urinary matter normally eliminated by kidneys. Hence **urae·mic** a. [f. Gk *ouron* urine + *haima* blood]

ūrae·us, n. Serpent as head-dress of Egyptian divinities & kings. [mod. L f. Gk *ouraios* repr. the anc.-Egypt. wd for cobra]

Ur·al-Altā·ic (ūr-), a. Of (the people of) the Ural & Altaic mountain ranges; (Philol.) of a family of Finnic, Mongolian, & other agglutinative languages of N. Europe & Asia.

uranian. See VENUS.

ūrā·nium, n. Heavy white metallic element found in pitch-blende &c. Hence **urā·nic, ur·anous,** aa. [f. URANUS + -IUM]

ūrano- in comb. = Gk *ouranos* heaven, as: *-graphy*, descriptive astronomy, so *-gra·phic(al)* aa., *-graphist* n.; *-logy*, astronomy; *-metry*, measurement of stellar distances, map showing positions and magnitudes of stars.

Ur·anus (ūr-), n. (Gk Myth.) son of Ge (Earth) & father of Cronus (Saturn), the Titans, &c.; planet discovered by Herschel in 1781, outermost of solar system except Neptune. [L, f. Gk *ouranos*, heaven, Uranus]

ur·ban, a. Of, living or situated in, a city or town, as *u. districts, population, u. sanitary district* (subject to u. sanitary authorities). [f. L *urbanus* of the city, refined, polished (*urbs urbis* city, see -AN)]

urba·ne, a. Courteous, suave, elegant or refined in manner. Hence **urba·nely**[2] adv. [as prec.]

urbă·nity, n. Courtesy, polished manners; (archaic) polished wit or humour. [f. L *urbanitas* (as prec., see -TY)]

ur·ceolate (-*at*), a. (bot.). Pitcher-shaped, with large body & small mouth. [f. L *urceolus* dim. of *urceus* pitcher + -ATE[2]]

ur·chin, n. Roguish or mischievous boy; boy, youngster; (usu. *sea-u.*) = ECHINUS; (archaic) hedgehog, goblin. [f. ONF *herichon* f. L *ericius* hedgehog]

Urdu (oor·dōō), n. Hindustani. [Hind., lit. = camp (language), as originating between Mohammedan conquerors & their subjects]

-ure, suf. forming nn., repr. F *-ure*, L *-ura*, added to p.p. stems of vbs (*apertura, captura, censura, dictatura*), rarely to others (*figura*). Wds in *-atura* lost *-t-* in F (*armatura* F *armure*, *tornatura* F *tournure*, *capellatura* F *chevelure*), & *-ure*, thus appearing to be added to pres. st., became living suf. in F forming nn. on vbs in *-er* not always of L orig. (*procédure, monture, brochure*), many of which are adopted in E. *Seizure, pleasure, failure, leisure, tenure*, are F infinitives in *-ir* assim. to wds in *-ure*; see also TREASURE, MANURE. Senses in E: (1) vbl action, (2) its result, (3) collective body of agents, as *legislature*, (4) term of (official) agency, as (rarely) *judicature*.

ūr·ea, n. (chem.). Soluble colourless crystalline compound contained esp. in urine of mammals. [f. Gk *ouron* urine]

-uret, suf. (chem.) of nn. & their derivatives indicating combination, now for the most part replaced by -IDE. [mod. L *-uretum* first applied to F wds in *-ure*]

ūrē·ter, n. Duct by which urine passes from kidney to bladder &c. Hence **ureteri·tis** n. [f. Gk *ourētēr* (*oureō* make water)]

urē·thra, n. Duct by which urine is discharged from bladder. Hence **ure·thral** a., **urethri·tis, ure·throcele, urethro·tomy,** nn. [LL, f. Gk *ourēthra* (as prec.)]

urĕ·tic, a. & n. = DIURETIC.

urge, v.t., & n. Drive forcibly, impel, hasten, cause to proceed with effort, as *urged his horse forward, urged him on, we urged our flight northwards*; entreat or exhort earnestly or persistently, as *u. him to action, to take steps*; advocate (measure &c.) pressingly; ply (person &c.) hard with argument or entreaty; dwell persistently or emphatically upon, as *in vain you u. his youth, urged the difficulty of getting supplies, argument was urged in vain*; (n., literary) impulsion, yearning. [f. L *urgēre* press, drive]

ur·gency, n. Being urgent; (Parl.) formal declaration, by vote of three to one in house of not less than 300, that matter is urgent & shall take precedence of all others. [f. foll., see -ENCY]

ur·gent, a. Pressing, calling for immediate action or attention, as *am in u. need, the matter is u., an u. demand*; importunate, earnest & persistent in demand, as *was u. with me for* (or *to disclose*) *further particulars.* Hence **ur·gently**[2] adv. [F (as URGE, see -ENT)]

ūr·ic, a. Of urine; *u. acid* (found in small quantities in healthy urine of man & quadrupeds, chief constituent in that of birds & reptiles). [f. F *urique* (URINE, -IC)]

ūr·im, n. *U. & thummim*, objects of unknown nature connected with breastplate of high priest (*Exod.* xxviii. 30). [Heb. *urim* pl. of *ur* light, *tummim* pl. of *tom* perfection]

ur·inal, n. Fixed vessel or receptacle for use of persons requiring to pass urine; public or private place containing such receptacles; vessel used by invalid for passing water in bed; glass vessel for containing urine for inspection. [OF f. L (URINE, -AL)]

ur·inary, a. & n. Of urine, as *u. organs, diseases*; (n.) reservoir for u. as manure. [-ARY[1]]

ur·inate, v.i. Pass urine. Hence **urina·tion** n. [f. med. L *urinare* (as foll.), see -ATE[3]]

ūr·ine, n. Pale-yellow fluid secreted from the blood by the kidneys, stored in bladder, & discharged through urethra.

So **ur·inous** a. [OF, f. L *urina*, cogn. w. Gk *ouron*, see -INE[4]]

urino- in comb. = prec., as: *-logy*, study of the urine; *-meter*, instrument showing specific gravity of urine, so *-me·tric* a., *-metry* n.; *-scopy*, inspection of urine, so *-sco·pic* a.

urn, n., & v.t. Vase with foot & usu. with rounded body, esp. as anciently used for storing the ashes of the dead or as vessel or measure; (fig.) anything in which dead body or its remains are preserved, e. g. grave; vase-shaped vessel with tap in which tea, coffee, &c., is kept hot, e.g. by means of spirit-lamp; *u.-flower*, kinds of bulbous plant with u.-shaped flower. Hence **ur·nFUL** n. (Vb) enclose in u. [(vb f. n.) f. L *urna* (*urere* burn)]

ūro-[1] in comb. = URINO-, as *-logy* &c.

ūro-[2] in comb. = Gk *oura* tail, in anat. terms.

Ur·sa, n. *U. Major*, *Minor*, Great, Little, BEAR[1]. [L, = she-bear]

ur·sine, a. Of, like, a bear, so **ur·siFORM** a.; (Entom.) thickly clothed with bristles. [f. L *ursinus* (*ursus* bear, see -INE[1])]

Ur·suline, a. & n. (Nun) of an order founded in 1537 for nursing the sick & teaching girls. [f. St *Ursula* + -INE[1]]

ur·ticate, v.t. Sting like a nettle; whip (paralytic limb &c.) with nettles to restore feeling. So **urticA·TION** n. [f. med. L *urticare* (L *urtica* nettle) see -ATE[3]]

urubu (ōō·rōōbōō), n. American black vulture. [Brazilian]

ūr·us, n. Kind of wild bull described by Caesar, = AUROCHS. [L, = Gk *ouros*]

us (ŭs, *us*), pl. obj. of I[2] (abbr. 's; somet., poet. & archaic, = ourselves, as *let's get us from the walls*), [OE *ūs*, cf. Du. *ons*, G *uns*, L *nos*, Gk *hēmas*, Skr. *asmān*]

usage (ū·zĭj), n. Manner of using or treating, treatment, as *met with harsh u.*, *damaged by rough u.*; habitual or customary practice esp. as creating a right or obligation or standard, as *sanctified by u.*, *an ancient u.*, *contrary to the u. of the best writers*; (Law) habitual but not necessarily immemorial practice. [ME & OF, f. med. L *usaticum* (as USE[1], see -AGE)]

u·sance (-z-), n. (commerc.). Time allowed for payment of foreign bills of exchange, as *the u. on Indian bills is 4 months*, *bill drawn at half* or *double u.* [OF (as USE[2], see -ANCE)]

use[1] (ūs), n. Using, employment, application to a purpose, as *should recommend the u. of a file*, *taught him the u. of the globes*, *put it to a good u.*, *is meant for u. not ornament*, *is in daily u.*, *becomes easier with u.*, *worn & polished with u.*, *made u. of* (employed) *a quibble*, *pray make u. of my telephone*; right or power of using, as *stipulated for the u. of the piano*, *lost the u. of his left arm*; availability, utility, purpose for which thing can be used, as *a blunt knife is of u. for this work*, *a foot-rule will be found of* (*great*) *u.*, *it is* (*of*) *no u. talking* or *to talk*, *what is the u. of talking?*, *talking is no u.*, *find a u. for banana-skins*, *I have no u. for it*; custom, wont, familiarity, as *long u. has reconciled me to it*, *in such matters u. is everything*, *according to his u. in emergencies*, *u. & wont*; ritual & liturgy of a church, diocese, &c., as *Sarum*, *Anglican*, *Roman*, u.; (Law) benefit or profit of lands & tenements in the possession of another who holds them solely for the beneficiary. [f. OF *us* f. L *usus -ūs* (as foll.); (in legal sense) AF *oes* f. L *opus* employment, need]

use[2] (ūz), v.t. & i. Employ for a purpose, handle as instrument, consume as material, exercise, put into operation, avail oneself of, as *seldom u. a knife*, *should u. oil for frying*, *we seem to u. a great deal of butter*, *never u. a dictionary*, *learn to u. your hands*, *u. your wits*, *must u. the services of an agent*, *shall u. every means*, *must u. your opportunities*, *u. your discretion*, *should at least u. some moderation*, *may I u. your name* (quote you as authority, reference, &c.)?, *do not fail to u.* (in argument, pleading, &c.) *this damaging fact*, *has used my absence to poison everyone against me*; treat in specified manner, as *has used me like a dog*, *how did he u. you?*, *used me ill*, *ill-used me*; (now only in past, usu. pron. ūst, esp. when followed immediately by *to*) be accustomed, have as one's constant or frequent practice, as *I used to take the bus*, *does not come as often as he used* (*to*), *bell used always to ring at one*, *what used he to say?*, *used not* (colloq. *didn't u.*) *to answer*; (now only in p.p., pron. as last sense) accustomed, as *am not used to this sort of thing*, *to being called a liar*, *have become used to a vegetarian diet*; *u. up*, consume the whole of (material &c.), find a use for (remaining material &c.), exhaust, wear out e. g. with overwork. Hence **u·sABLE** a., **u·ser**[1] [-ER[1]] n. [f. OF *user* f. LL *usare* frequent. of L *uti us-* use]

u·seful (-s-), a. Of use, serviceable, producing or able to produce good result, as *u. arts*, *ratchet-brace will be found u.*, *gave me some u. hints*, *must make himself generally u.* (perform miscellaneous services); (slang) highly creditable or efficient, as *a pretty u. performance*, *is pretty u. at Greek iambics*. Hence **u·sefulLY**[2] adv., **u·sefulNESS** n. [-FUL]

u·seless, a. Serving no useful purpose, unavailing, as *a mass of u. erudition*, *contents were rendered u. by damp*, *protest is u.*; (slang) out of health or spirits, unfit for anything, as *am feeling u.* Hence **u·selessLY**[2] adv., **u·selessNESS** n. [-LESS]

u·ser[2] (-z-; for *u.*[1] see USE[2]), n. (law). Continued use or enjoyment of a right &c.; *right of u.*, (1) right to use, (2) presumptive right arising from u. [OF (as USE², see -ER⁴)]

u·sher, n., & v.t. Officer or servant acting as doorkeeper of a court &c., showing persons to seats in public hall &c., or walking before person of rank, as (*gentleman u. of the*) BLACK¹*rod*; (now contempt.) under-teacher, assistant schoolmaster. Hence **u·sher**SHIP n. (Vb) act as u. to, precede (person) as u., announce, show *in* &c., as *was at length ushered (in)to his presence, star ushers in the dawn.* [(vb f. n.) AF *usser*, f. OF *(h)uissier* f. L *ostiarius* doorkeeper (*ostium* door, see -ARY¹)]

u·squebaugh (-kwĭbaw), n. Whisky; Irish cordial made of brandy &c. [f. Ir. *uisge beatha* water of life (*uisge* water, WHISKY¹, +*beatha* life)]

ustula·tion, n. Drying of moist substance to prepare it for pulverizing; burning of wine. [f. L *ustulare* scorch f. *urere ust-* burn, -ATION]

usual (ū·zhōōal), a. Such as commonly occurs, customary, habitual, as *asked the u. questions, with his u. disregard of convention, the courtesy u. with him, it is u. to tip the waiter, came earlier than* (was) *u., have forgotten something as* (is) *u.* or (vulg. facet.) *as per u.* Hence **u·sual**LY² adv., **u·sual**NESS n. [f. OF *usuel* f. L *usualis* (as USE¹, see -AL)]

usūca·ption (-ūz-), n. (civil law). Acquisition of the title or right to property by uninterrupted & undisputed possession for prescribed term. [also *-cāpion*, f. L *usucapio -onis* f. *usucapere* acquire by prescription (*usu* by USE¹ +*capere capt-* take)]

u·sūfruct (ūz-), n., & v.t. Right of enjoying the use & advantages of another's property short of destruction or waste of its substance; (vb) hold in u. [(vb f. n.) f. L *ususfructus* use & enjoyment (*usus* USE¹ +*fructus* FRUIT)]

usufru·ctuary, a. & n. Of, one who has, usufruct. [f. LL *usufructuarius* (prec., -ARY¹)]

u·surer (ūzher-), n. One who lends money at exorbitant interest. [AF, f. med. L *usurarius* (as USURY, see -ER²)]

usur·p (-ūz-), v.t. & i. Seize, assume, (throne, office, power, property, &c.) wrongfully; (rare) encroach (*up*)*on*. Hence or cogn. **usurp**A·TION, **usur·p**ER¹, nn., **usur·ping**LY² adv. [f. OF *usurper* f. L *usurpare* use, u., etym. dub.]

usury (ū·zhĕrĭ), n. Practice of lending money at exorbitant interest esp. at higher interest than is allowed by law, whence **ūsūri**OUS (-z-, -zh-) a., **usur·i-ous**LY² adv., **usur·ious**NESS n.; such interest; (now usu. fig.) interest, as *the service was repaid with u.* [f. med. L *usuria*, L *usura* (USE¹, -URE)]

ut¹ (ŏŏt), n. Key-note of a scale (now usu. DO³). [see GAMUT]

ŭt², adv. *Ut supra, infra*, as shown or stated above, below. [L]

ūte·nsil, n. Instrument, implement, esp. one in domestic use, as *kitchen, cooking-, uu.* [f. OF *utensile* f. L *utensilis* usable]

ū·terine, a. Of the uterus; born of same mother but not same father (*his u. brother*). [f. LL *uterinus* (foll., -INE¹)]

ū·terus, n. (pl. -ī). The womb. Hence **uteri·**TIS n. [L]

utilitār·ian, a. & n. Of, consisting in, utility; (holder) of utilitarianism. [-ARIAN]

utilitar·ianism, n. Doctrine that actions are right because they are useful; doctrine that greatest happiness of greatest number should be sole end of public action. [-ISM]

ūti·lity, n. Usefulness, profitableness; useful thing; =prec.; (Theatr., also *u.-man*) actor of the smallest parts in plays. [f. F *utilité* f. L *utilitatem* (*utilis* useful f. *uti* use, see -TY)]

ū·tilize, v.t. Make use of, turn to account, use. Hence **u·tiliz**ABLE a., **utiliz**A·TION n. [f. F *utiliser* (*utile* f. L *utilis*, see prec.)]

ū·tī possidē·tis, n. Principle that leaves belligerents in possession of what they have acquired. [L, = as you possess]

u·tmost, a. & n. Furthest, extreme, as *the u. limits*; that is such in the highest degree, as *showed the u. reluctance*; (n.) one's *u.*, all one can do. [OE *útemest*, double superl. of *út* OUT, cf. AFTERMOST]

Utō·pia (ū-), n. (Book published by Sir T. More in 1516 describing) imaginary island with perfect social & political system; ideally perfect place or state of things. [=nowhere, f. Gk *ou* not +*topos* place]

Uto·pian, u-, a. & n. (Inhabitant) of Utopia; (characteristic of an) ardent but unpractical reformer &c., whence **uto·-pian**ISM n. [-AN]

U·trecht (ū-), n. *U. velvet*, kind of mohair plush. [*U.* in Holland]

ū·tricle, n. Cell of animal or plant; small bag or cavity in the body, esp. one in the inner ear. Hence **utri·cul**AR¹ a. [f. L *utriculus* dim. of *uter* leather bag]

u·tter¹, a. Complete, total, unqualified, as *u. misery, saw the u. absurdity of it, an u. denial*; *u. barrister* (junior, addressing court from outside bar within which K.C. pleads). Hence **u·tter**LY² adv., **u·tter**MOST a., **u·tter**NESS n. [OE *úttera*, compar. adj. f. *út* OUT]

u·tter², v.t. Emit audibly (cry, groan, sigh, &c.); express in spoken or written wds (one's sentiments, a lie, the truth, &c.); put (notes, base coin, &c.) into circulation. [f. OUT, cf. Du. *uiteren* (*uit* out), G *äussern* (*aus* out)]

u·tterance¹, n. Uttering, expressing in words, as *gave u. to his rage*; power of speech, as *defective u.*; spoken words, as *his pulpit uu.* [-ANCE]

u·tterance², n. (literary). *Fight* &c. *to the u.* (bitter end). [f. OF *outrance* (*outrer* surpass, as ULTRA-)]

ū·vūla, n. (pl. *-ae*). Pendent fleshy part of soft palate; similar processes in bladder & cerebellum. Hence **u·vulAR**^{1} a. [med. L dim. of L *uva* bunch of grapes]

ŭxor·ious, a. Excessively fond of one's wife. Hence **uxor·iousLY**^{2} adv., **uxor·iousNESS** n. [f. L *uxorius* (*uxor* wife) + -OUS]

U·zbeg, n. Member of a Turkish race in central Asia. [native]

V

V, v, (vē), letter (pl. *Vs*, V's, Vees). V-shaped thing, e.g. joint; (Roman numeral) 5, as IV 4, VI 6, viii 8, viiii (now usu. ix) 9, xv 15, lv 55.

Abbreviations (1): **V.**, venereal, **V.D.** (disease); vice-, **V.C.** (chancellor); Victoria, **V.A.** (& Albert, Order of), **V.C.** (cross); Victorian, **V.O.** (order); voluntary, **V.A.D.** (aid detachment); volunteer, **V.D.** (decoration). **v.**, *varia*, **v.l.** (*lectio*); verse; *versus*; very, **v.f.**, **v.g.**, (fair, good); *vide*.

Abbreviations (2): **Va**, Virginia; **Ven.**-(erable, of Archdeacon); **verb.**(*um*) **sap.**-(*ienti*); **Vic.**(toria); **Vis.**(count); **viz**, videlicet; **vol.**(ume); **Vt**, Vermont; **Vulg.**(ate); **vulg.**(arly); **vv.**, verses.

va (vah), mus. direction. Go on, as *va rallentando*. [It.]

va·cancy, n. Being vacant or empty or unoccupied; emptiness of mind, idleness, listlessness; unoccupied post, as *has a v. on his staff, in his warehouse, must fill the v.* [f. LL *vacantia* (as foll., see -ANCY)]

vā·cant, a. Empty, not filled or occupied, as *house is still v., a v. smoking-compartment, have no v. space, will amuse your v. hours, applied for a v. post in the Treasury*; not mentally active, not rationally occupied, empty-headed, thoughtless, listless, stupid, as *his mind seems completely v., received the news with a v. stare, given up to v. frivolities*, whence **va·cantLY**^{2} adv. [OF (as foll., see -ANT)]

vaca·te, v.t. Go away from so as to leave empty or unoccupied, give up occupation or possession of, (military position, place, house, throne, office); annul (law, contract, &c.). [f. L *vacare* be empty (cf. VACUOUS), see -ATE^3]

vaca·tion, n. Vacating (*of* house, post, &c.); holiday, fixed period of cessation from work, esp. in law-courts & universities, as *Christmas, Easter, Whitsun, long* or *summer, v.* [OF, f. L *vacationem* (as prec., see -ATION)]

va·ccinate, v.t. Inoculate with vaccine to procure immunity from smallpox or with modified virus of any disease in order to produce it in mild form & so prevent serious attack. Hence **vaccinA·TION**, **vaccina·tionIST**(2), **va·ccinatOR**^{2} (1, 2), nn. [f. foll. + -ATE^3]

va·ccine, a. & n. Of cows or cowpox or vaccination; (n.) virus of cowpox as used in vaccination (*bovine, humanized, v.*, got direct from cow, got from human subject), modified virus of any disease similarly used, whence **va·ccinAL**, **vacci·NIC**, aa.; *v.-farm* (where v. is cultivated by inoculation of heifers); *v.-point*, pointed instrument used in inoculation. [f. L *vaccinus* a. (*vacca* cow, see -INE^1)]

vacci·nia, n. (med.). Cowpox, esp. inoculated. [mod. L, f. prec.]

vă·cillate, v.i. Move from side to side, oscillate, waver; fluctuate in opinion or resolution. Hence or cogn. **va·cillatingLY**^{2} adv., **vacillA·TION** n. [f. L *vacillare*, see -ATE^3]

va·cuole, n. (biol.). Minute cavity in organ &c. containing air, fluid, &c. Hence **va·cuolAR**^{1}, **va·cuolATE**^{2}(2), aa. [F, dim. of VACUUM]

vă·cūous, a. Empty, void; unintelligent, expressionless, vacant, as *a v. stare, remark*. Hence or cogn. **vacu·ITY**, **va·cuousNESS**, nn. [f. L *vacuus* + -OUS]

va·cuum, n. (pl. *-ums, -a*). Space entirely devoid of matter, as *nature abhors a v.*; space, vessel, from which air has been almost exhausted by air-pump &c. (*Guerickian, Torricellian, v.*, produced by air-pump, by mercury-pump as in mercurial barometer); (loosely) partial diminution of pressure below normal atmospheric pressure; *v. brake*, continuous train-brake in which pressure is caused by exhaustion of air from bellows pulling brake-rod; *v. cleaner*, apparatus for removing dust &c. by suction; *v. flask*, with two walls separated by v. jacket so that liquid in inner receptacle retains its temperature; *v.-gauge* (for testing pressure consequent on production of v.); *v.-tube*, sealed glass tube with almost perfect v. for observing passage of electric charge (see also THERMION). [L, neut. as prec. used as n.]

vā·dē-mē·cum, n. Handbook or other thing carried constantly about the person (often in title of book). [L, = go with me]

***vae vi·ctis*,** (vē), int. Woe to the vanquished (expressing victor's intention of exacting full fruits of victory). [L]

vă·gabond, a., n., & v.i. Having no fixed habitation, wandering; driven, drifting, to & fro; (of spider) not sedentary. (N.) wanderer, vagrant, esp. idle & worthless one; (colloq.) scamp, rascal. (Vb, now colloq.) wander about, play the v. Hence **va·gabondAGE**(2, 3), **va·gabondISM**(2), nn., **va·gabondISH**^{1} a., **va·gabondIZE**(2) v.i. [f. L *vagabundus* (*vagari* wander)]

vagār·y, n. Whimsical or extravagant notion; caprice; freak. [ult. f. L *vagari* wander]

vagi·na (-j-), n. Sheath, sheath-like covering, esp. (Anat.) sexual passage in female from uterus to external orifice, whence **văgini·**TIS, **vagino·**TOMY, nn.; (Bot.) sheath formed round stem by base of leaf. Hence **vă·gin**AL, **va·ginate(d)** [-ATE[2](2)], aa. [L]

vā·grant, a. & n. Wandering, roving, strolling, itinerant, as *a v. musician, indulging in v. speculations*; (n.) wanderer, idle rover, vagabond, (Law) idle & disorderly person of any of three grades liable to various terms of imprisonment. Hence **va·gr**ANCY n., **va·grant**LY[2] adv. [earlier *vagarant*, perh. f. AF *wakerant, walcrant*, of Teut. orig.; altered on L *vagari* wander]

vāgue (-g), a. Indistinct, not clearly expressed or identified, of uncertain or ill-defined meaning or character, as *returned only a v. answer, has some v. idea of going to Canada, have not the vaguest notion of his reasons, yields to v. terrors, heard a v. rumour to that effect.* Hence **va·gue**LY[2] adv., **va·gue**NESS n. [f. L *vagus* wandering]

vail[1], v.t. & i. (archaic, poet.). Lower or doff (one's plumes, pride, crown, &c.) esp. in token of submission; yield, give place, uncover as sign of respect &c. [f. F *avaler* see AVALANCHE]

vail[2], n. (archaic; usu. pl.). Gratuity, tip; present given for corrupt purpose. [=AVAIL]

vain, a. Unsubstantial, empty, trivial, as *v. boasts, v. triumphs, distinctions*; useless, unavailing, followed by no good result, as *in the v. hope of dissuading him, all resistance was v., to resist is v., it is vain to resist*; conceited, having too high an opinion *of* one's beauty, ability, &c.; *in v.*, to no purpose, as *we protested in v., it was in v. that we protested*; TAKE[1] person's *name in v.*; *vainglor·y*, boastfulness, excessive vanity, whence *vainglor·ious* a., *vainglor·iously* adv., *vainglor·iousness* n. Hence **vai·n**LY[2] adv., **vai·n**NESS n. (rare). [OF, f. L *vanus* empty, vain]

vair, n. (herald.). A fur represented by small shield-shaped figures alternately azure & argent. [F, f. L as VARIOUS]

vakee·l, -il (-ēl), n. (E.-Ind.). Ambassador, commissioner, residing at a court; native attorney or deputy. [Hind. (-*īl*)]

vă·lance, vă·lence[1], n. Kind of damask used for furniture; short curtain round frame or canopy of bedstead. Hence **va·lanc**ED[2] a. [perh. f. AF *valer* descend f. OF *avaler* see AVALANCHE]

vale[1], n. Valley (now chiefly poet. or in names as *White Horse V.*); small trough or channel carrying off water from pump &c. [f. OF *val* f. L *vallis*]

vā·lē[2], int. & n. Farewell. [L, imperat. of *valēre* be well, be strong]

vălĕdi·ction, n. (Words used in) bidding farewell. So **valedi·ct**ORY a. [f. L VALE(*dicere dict-* say) bid farewell, see -ION]

vā·lence[2] (for *v.*[1] see VALANCE), n. (chem.). Combining or replacing power of an atom as compared with standard hydrogen atom, as *hydrogen, carbon, has a v. of one, four.* [f. LL *valentia* strength (as VALE[2], see -ENCE)]

Valencie·nnes (-ĕnz, *or* vălensĕnz), n. Rich kind of lace; kind of pyrotechnic composition. [*V.*, in France]

va·lency, n. (chem.). Unit of combining capacity, as *carbon has 4 vv.*; =VALENCE. [-ENCY]

vă·lentine, n. *St V.'s day*, day on which St V. was beheaded & on which birds were supposed to pair, Feb. 14; sweetheart chosen on this; amatory or satirical letter or picture sent to person of opposite sex on St V.'s day. [f. L *Valentinus*, proper name]

valēr·ian, n. Kinds of plant, esp. *common v.*, herb with small pink or white flowers & strong odour esteemed by cats & rats; root of this used as mild stimulant &c., whence **vă·ler**ATE[1](3) n., **valĕ·**RIC a., (chem.). [f. OF *valeriane*, etym. dub.]

vă·let (-ĭt, -ā), n., & v.t. (-*eted*, pron. -ĭtĭd, -ād). (Also *v. de chambre*, pron. as F) manservant who attends on man's person; *v. de place* (de plahs), courier esp. in France; iron-pointed stick used in training horses; (vb) act as v. to [(vb f. n.) OF, var. of VARLET]

vălĕtūdinār·ian, a. & n. Of infirm health; seeking to recover health; unduly solicitous about health; (n.) v. person. Hence or cogn. **valetudinar·ian**ISM n., **valetu·din**ARY[1] a. & n. [f. L *valetudinarius* (*valetudo -dinis* health f. *valēre*, be well, see -TUDE & -ARY[1])]

Valha·lla, n. (Norse Myth.) palace in which souls of slain heroes feasted; building used as final resting-place of the illustrious dead, esp. Temple of Fame near Ratisbon. [f. ON *valhöll*, hall of the slain (*valr* slain + *höll* HALL)]

vă·liant, a. (Of person or conduct) brave, courageous. Hence **va·liant**LY[2] adv. [f. OF *vaillant* part. of *valoir* be worth f. L *valēre* be strong]

vă·lid, a. (Of reason, objection, argument, &c.) sound, defensible, well-grounded; (Law) sound & sufficient, executed with proper formalities, as *v. contract, the marriage was held to be v.* Hence or cogn. **vali·d**ITY n., **va·lid**LY[2] adv. [f. F *valide* f. L *validus* strong (as prec., see -ID[1])]

va·lidate, v.t. Make valid, ratify, confirm. So **valida·**TION n. [f. med. L *validare* (as prec.), see -ATE[3]]

vali·se (-ēs), n. Kind of small portmanteau; (Mil.) soldier's knapsack. [F, cf. med. L *valisia*, etym. dub.]

va·lkyr (-ēr), **valkȳ·ria, -iĕ,** n. (Norse myth.; pl. -*kyrs*, -*kyries*). Each of Odin's handmaidens who selected those destined to be slain in battle. Hence **valkȳ·**RIAN a. [f. ON *valkyrja* lit. chooser of slain (*valr* slain + *-kyrja* chooser cogn. w. *kjósa* CHOOSE)]

vallĕ·cŭla, n. (anat., bot.; pl. *-ae*). Groove, furrow. Hence **valle·cul**AR[1], **valle·cul**ATE[2], aa. [LL, dim. of L *vallis* vale]

va·lley, n. (pl. *-eys*). Low area more or less enclosed by hills & usu. with stream flowing through it; any depression compared to this; *v. of the shadow of death*, (period of) extreme affliction (*Ps.* xxiii. 4); (Archit.) internal angle formed by intersecting planes of roof. [f. OF *valee* (as VALE[1], cf. -ADE)]

vallō·nia, n. Acorn-cups of the *v. oak*, used in tanning, dyeing, & making ink. [f. It. *vallonia* ult. f. Gk *balanos* acorn]

va·llum, n. (Rom. Ant.) rampart; (Anat.) eyebrow. [L]

vă·lour, n. (now chiefly poet., rhet., or facet.). Personal courage esp. as shown in fighting, prowess. So **va·lor**OUS a., **va·lorous**LY[2] adv. [OF, f. LL *valorem* worth, courage (*valēre* be strong, see -OR[1])]

valse (vahls), n. Waltz. [F, f. G as WALTZ]

va·luable, a. & n. Of great value or price or worth, as *v. property, land, furniture, information, assistance*; capable of valuation, as *a service not v. in money*; (n., usu. pl.) v. thing(s), esp. small article(s) of personal property, as *sent all her vv. to the bank*. [f. VALUE + -ABLE]

valua·tion, n. Estimation (esp. by professional valuer) of a thing's worth, worth so estimated, price set on a thing, as *v. of land, disposed of at a low v., sets too high a v. on his abilities.* [OF, as foll. vb + -ATION]

vă·lue, n., & v.t. Worth, desirability, utility, qualities on which these depend, as *now learnt the v. of fresh water, a friend, quinine, accuracy, regular exercise*; worth as estimated, valuation, as *sets a high v. on his time*; *commercial, economic, exchange(able) v., v. in exchange*, purchasing power, power of a commodity to purchase others, amount of (pop.) money or (Pol. Econ.) other commodities for which thing can be exchanged in open market; FACE[1], SURRENDER, *v.*; *surplus v.*, surplus production of labour after subsistence of labourer & family; the equivalent of a thing, what represents or is represented by or may be substituted for a thing, as *v. received* (see BILL[4] *of exchange*), *got good v. for* (something well worth) *his money, paid him the v. of his lost property, the precise v.* (meaning) *of a word, acute accent has not always the same v., give the note* (in music) *its full time-v.* (the full time indicated by it); (Paint.) relation of one part of picture to others in respect of light & shade, as *out of v.*, too light or dark; amount, quantity, denoted by algebraical term or expression; (Biol.) rank in classification. (Vb) estimate the v. of, appraise (professionally, whence **va·lu**ER[1] n., or otherwise), as *should v. the whole at £2000*; have high or specified opinion of, attach importance to, prize, esteem, appreciate, pride one*self on*, as *v. sincerity (beyond all things), a valued friend, values himself on his conversational powers, do not v. that a brass farthing.* [(vb f. n.) OF, fem. p.p. of *valoir* be worth f. L *valēre* be strong]

va·lueless, n. Worthless. Hence **va·lue·less**NESS n. [-LESS]

valve, n. Kinds of automatic or other device for controlling passage of liquid or gas or the like through pipe &c., as *clack, rotary, screw, sliding, throttle, v., key v.* (of organ, flute, &c.), SAFETY-*v.*, THERMIONIC *v.*; (Anat., Zool.) membranous part of organ &c. allowing flow of blood &c. in one direction & not in another, as *vv. of the heart, veins, pulmonary vv.*, whence **valvul**I·TIS [-UL-] n.; (Conch.), each of two or more separable pieces of which shell consists, whole shell in one piece; (Bot.) each of the segments into which a capsule dehisces, each half of an anther after its opening; (now rare) leaf of folding door; *v. set*, wireless receiver with thermionic (v)v. (opp. *crystal set*). Hence or cogn. **va·lv**AL (bot.), **va·lv**AR[1], **va·lv**ATE[2] (anat., bot.), **(-)valv**ED[2], **valv**ELESS, **valvi·**FEROUS, **va·lvi**FORM, **va·lvul**AR[1] [-UL-], aa., **va·lv**ELET, **va·lv**ULE (anat., bot.), nn. [F, f. L *valva* leaf of folding door]

va·mbrāce, n. (hist.). Armour for forearm. [AF *vant-bras* (*avant* before, see ADVANCE[1], + *bras* arm f. L *brachium*)]

vamo·se, v.i. & t. (U.S. slang). Begone, decamp; decamp from (place). [f. Sp. *vamos* let us go]

vamp[1], n., & v.i. & t. Upper front part of boot or shoe; patch designed to make old thing look new; improvised accompaniment. (Vb) put new v. to (boot, shoe); repair, furbish usu. *up*; make *up* (literary article &c.) out of odds & ends; improvise accompaniment to, improvise accompaniments. Hence **va·mp**ER[1] n. [(vb f. n.) ME *vaumpe* f. MF *avant-pied* (*avant* before, see ADVANCE[1], + *pied* foot f. L *pedem* nom. *pes*)]

vamp[2], n., & v.t. & i., (U.S. slang). Adventuress, woman who exploits men; flirt; (vb) allure, exploit; flirt. [abbr. of foll.]

va·mpire, n. Ghost (usu. of wizard, heretic, criminal, &c.) that leaves grave at night & sucks blood of sleeping persons; person who preys on others; (U.S.) = prec. n.; (in full *v. bat*) kinds of bat, some of which suck blood of horses, cattle, & sleeping persons; (Theatr.) small spring trap of two flaps used for sudden (dis)-appearances of one person. Hence **vampi·**RIC a. [F, f. Magyar *vampir* perh. of Turk. orig.]

va·mpirism, n. Belief in existence of vampires; blood-sucking (lit. & fig.). [-ISM]

va·mplate, n. (hist.). Iron plate protecting hand when lance was couched. [f. AF *vant-* (as VAMBRACE) + PLATE]

van[1], n., & v.t. (Archaic) winnowing-machine; (archaic, poet.) wing; (vb) test quality of (ore) by washing on shovel or by machine, whence **va·nner**[1](1, 2) n., (n.) such test. [var. of FAN[1]]

van[2], n. Foremost division of army on the march or of fleet when sailing; front of army in line of battle; (fig.) leaders of a movement &c., as *in the v. of civilization*; *v.-bird*, migrant bird in advance, (fig.) harbinger, precursor; *va·nguard*, detachment of army marching in front to guard against surprise (also fig.). [abbr. of *vanguard*, f. OF *avant-warde, -garde* (*avant* before, see ADVANCE[1], WARD, GUARD)]

van[3], n., & v.t. Large usu. covered vehicle for conveying furniture or other goods; railway carriage for luggage (*luggage v.*) or for use of guard (*guard's v.*); (vb) convey in v. [abbr. of CARAVAN, cf. *bus, wig*]

vanā·dium, n. Rare white metallic element some salts of which yield intense permanent black colour. Hence **vă·nad**ATE[1](3) n., **vanā·d**IC, **va·nad**OUS, aa., (chem.). [f. ON *Vanadis* goddess in Scand. myth., + -IUM]

Va·ndal, a. & n. (Member) of a Germanic race that ravaged Gaul, Spain, N. Africa, & Rome, destroying many books & works of art; (fig., also *v-*) wilful or ignorant destroyer of works of art &c., whence **Va·ndal**ISM(2), v-, n. Hence **Vandă·l**IC, v-, a. [f. L *Vandalus* of Teut. orig.]

vandy·ke, n., a., & v.t. (*V-*; prop. *Van Dyck*) Flemish painter d. 1641, picture by him; each of a series of large points forming a border to lace, cloth, &c., (also *V. cape, collar*) cape, collar, with vv.; (adj., usu. *V-*) in the style of dress, esp. with pointed borders, common in V.'s portraits; (vb) cut (cloth &c.) in vv.

vane, n. Weathercock; similar device exposed to current of water &c. as in water-meter; (also *dog-v.*) cone or other device used on shipboard as weathercock; blade of windmill, screw propeller, &c.; sight of surveying instruments, sight of quadrant &c. Hence **van**ED[2], **va·ne**LESS, aa. [OE *fana* small flag, cf. Da *fane*, G *fahne*]

vang, n. (naut.). Each of two guy-ropes running from end of gaff to deck. [var. of FANG[1]]

va·ngee (-jē), n. Contrivance for working ship's pumps by barrel & crank-brakes. [?]

vani·lla, n. Kinds of tall orchid with fragrant flowers; (also *v.-bean*) fruit of this; extract obtained from v.-bean & used for flavouring ices, chocolate, &c. Hence **vani·ll**ATE[1](3) n., **vani·ll**IC a., (chem.). [f. Sp. *vainilla* pod dim. of *vaina* sheath, pod, f. VAGINA]

vani·llism, n. Eruptive itching skin-disease common among workers in vanilla. [-ISM(5)]

vă·nish, v.i., & n. Disappear suddenly; disappear gradually, fade away; pass away; cease to exist; (Math.) become zero (*vanishing fraction*, one that becomes zero for a particular value of the variable it contains); (Perspect.) *vanishing-point*, point in which all parallel lines in same plane tend to meet, *vanishing-line*, that which represents the line at infinity in which given plane cuts all parallel planes. (N., phonet.) slight sound with which a principal sound ends (e.g. o͝o, ĭ, at end of ō, ā). [aphetic f. OF as EVANISH]

vă·nity, n. Futility, unsubstantiality, unreality, emptiness, unsubstantial or unreal thing, as *the v. of worldly wealth, of political distinction, of human achievements, these things are v.* or *vv., all is v., pomps & v. of this wicked world, V. Fair*, the world (allegorized in *Pilgrim's Progress*) as a scene of v.; empty pride, conceit, based on personal attainments or attractions or qualities (*v. bag, case*, carried on the person & containing small mirror, powder-puff, &c.); ostentatious display; (O.T.) heathen deity, as *the vv. of the Gentiles*. [f. OF *vanite*, f. L *vanitatem* (as VAIN, see -TY)]

va·nquish, v.t. Conquer, overcome, (lit. & fig.; now chiefly rhet.). Hence **va·nquish**ABLE a., **va·nquisher**[1] n. [f. OF *veincre* (past *veinquis*, see -ISH[2]) f. L *vincere*]

va·ntage, n. = ADVANTAGE (now chiefly in tennis use & in *v.-ground*, COIGN *of v.*). [AF var.]

vă·pid, a. Insipid, flat, as *v. beer, conversation, moralizings*. Hence **vapi·d**ITY, **va·pid**NESS, nn., **va·pid**LY[2] adv. [f. L *vapidus*]

va·porize, v.t. & i. Convert, be converted, into vapour. Hence or cogn. **vapora**BI·LITY, **vaporiza·**TION, **va·porize**R[1](2), nn., **va·por(iz)**ABLE aa. [-IZE]

vā·pour, n., & v.i. Moisture in the air e.g. mist, (loosely) light cloudy substance e.g. smoke, (Physics) gaseous form of a normally liquid or solid substance (cf. GAS), whence **vapori·**FEROUS, **vapori·**FIC, **va·pori**FORM, aa., **vapori·**METER n.; (Med.) kinds of remedial agent to be inhaled, as *v. of iodine*; unsubstantial thing, vain imagination; (archaic) empty boasting; (pl., archaic) depression, spleen, hypochondria, whence **va·pour**ISH[1] a., **va·pourish**NESS n.; *v. bath* (also **va·por**AR·IUM n.), bath in v. or steam, apparatus or apartment for this; *v.-burner*, apparatus for vaporizing a hydrocarbon for lighting or heating purposes *v.-engine* (driven by steam or other elastic fluid). Hence or cogn. **va·porose**[1], **va·porous**, **va·poury**[2], aa., **vaporŏ·sity**, **va·porousness**, nn., **va·porously**[2] adv. (Vb) emit v.; utter idle boasts or empty talk, whence **va·pourer**[1] n. [(n.) AF, f. L *vaporem* nom. *-or*; (vb) f. L *vaporare* steam, reek]

văpula·tion, n. (facet.). Flogging. So **va·pulatory** a. [f. L *vapulare* be flogged + -ATION]

vaquer·o (-kārō), n. Mex. or U.-S. herdsman. [Sp., f. med. L *vaccarius* (*vacca* cow, -ARY[1])]

Vară·ngian (-j-), n. Norse rover, esp. of those who ravaged Baltic coasts about 9th c.; *V. guard*, body-guard of Byzantine emperors formed partly of Vv. [f. med. L *Varangus* f. ON *Væringi* lit. confederate (*várar* oaths)]

vă·rec, n. Impure sodium carbonate made in Brittany. [f. F *varech* prob. as WRECK]

var·iable, a. & n. That can be varied or adapted, as *rod of v. length, the pressure is v., a word of v. construction, v. gear* (designed to give varying speeds, e. g. slow advance & quick return); apt to vary, not constant, fickle, unsteady, as *v. wind, mood, temper, fortune*; (Math., of quantity) indeterminate, able to assume different numerical values; (Bot., Zool., of species) including individuals or groups that depart from the type; (Biol., of organism) tending to change in structure or function. Hence **variabi·lity**, **var·iableness**, nn., **var·iably**[2] adv. (N.) v. thing esp. quantity; (Naut.) shifting wind, (pl.) region between NE & SE trade-winds. [OF, f. L *variabilis* (VARY, -BLE)]

vā·ria le·ctio, n. Variant reading. [L]

var·iance, n. Disagreement, difference of opinion, dispute, lack of harmony, as *on that point we are at v.* (*among ourselves*), *at v. with the authorities, have had a slight v. with him, this theory is at v. with all that is known on the subject*; (Law) discrepancy between pleadings & proof or between writ & declaration. [OF, f. L *variantia* difference (as foll., see -ANCE)]

var·iant, a. & n. Differing in form or in details from the one named or considered, differing thus among themselves, as *a v. reading in some MSS., 40 v. types of pigeon*; variable, changing; (n.) v. form, spelling, type, reading, &c., as valet *is a v. of* varlet, *difficult to choose between these vv.* [OF (as VARY, see -ANT)]

varia·tion, n. Varying, departure from a former or normal condition or action or amount or from a standard or type, extent of this, as *is not liable to v., repeated vv. of temperature, is subject to a v. of several degrees, estimates the v. in value at 20 per cent*; (Gram.) inflexion; (Astron.) deviation of heavenly body from mean orbit or motion (*periodic, secular, v.*, compensated in short, in very long, period); (of magnetic needle) = DECLINATION (*v.-chart*, with lines drawn through places that have same v.); (Biol.) structural or functional deviation from type; (Alg.) (theory of) relation between quantities that VARY as each other, also, = PERMUTATION; thing that varies from a type, as *the scazon is a v. of* or *on the ordinary iambic trimeter*, esp. (Mus.) tune or theme repeated in a changed or elaborated form. Hence **varia·tional** a. [OF, f. L *variationem* (VARY, -ATION)]

va·ricated, a. (conch.). Having varices. So **varica·tion** n. [f. VARIX, see -ATE[2](2)]

vărice·lla, n. = CHICKEN-*pox*. Hence **varice·llar**[1], **varice·lloid**, aa. [mod. L, irreg. dim. of VARIOLA]

vă·ricocele, n. Tumour composed of varicose veins of spermatic cord. [as VARIX + -CELE]

vă·ricose, a. Of, affected with, designed for cure of, varix, as *v. ulcer, vein, bandage*, whence **va·ricosed**[1] a., **varicŏ·sity** n.; = VARICATED. [f. L *varicosus* (VARIX, see -OSE[1])]

vār·iĕgate, v.t. Diversify in colour, mark with irregular patches of different colours (chiefly in p.p., esp. Bot. of leaves partly pale from suppression of chlorophyll or of plants with such leaves, as *variegated geranium*). Hence **variega·tion** n. [f. L *variegare* (as VARIOUS + *agere* drive, make, cause), see -ATE[3]]

varī·ety, n. Being various, diversity, absence of monotony or uniformity, many-sidedness, as *was struck by the v. of his attainments, of his conversation, of the scene, London has for me the charm of v., cannot live without v.*; collection of different things, as *turned over a v. of silks, for a v. of reasons, v. entertainment* or *show* (consisting of dances, songs, acrobatic feats, &c.), *v. theatre* (for v. shows &c.); (specimen, member, of a) class of things differing in some common qualities from the rest of a larger class to which they belong; (Biol.) individual or group usually fertile with any other member of the species to which it belongs but differing from the type in some qualities capable of perpetuation, subspecies, as *climatic v.* (produced by climatic influences), *geographical v.* (confined to given area), whence **vari·etal** a., **vari·etally**[2] adv. [f. L *varietatem* (as VARIOUS, see -TY)]

var·iform, a. Having various forms. [-FORM]

varī·ola (va-), n. Smallpox. Hence **vari·olar**[1], **variŏ·lic**, **vari·olous**, aa. [med. L, as VARIOUS]

vārĭola·tion, n. Inoculation with smallpox virus. [f. prec. + -ATION]

vār·iole, n. (zool., bot.). Shallow pit like smallpox mark. Hence **var·iolate(d)** [-ATE[2]] a. [f. med. L VARIOLA]

vār·iolite, n. Rock with concretionary

structure causing on surface an appearance like smallpox pustules. Hence **varioli·tic** a. [as prec. + -ITE[1]]

vār·ioloid, a. & n. Like smallpox; (n.) mild form of smallpox esp. as modified by previous inoculation. [as prec. + -OID]

varior·um, a. With notes of various commentators, as *a v.* (*edition of*) *Horace.* [L, gen. pl. as VARIOUS]

vār·ious, a. Different, diverse, as *the modes of procedure were v., types so v. as to defy classification*; separate, several, more than one, as *came across v. people, for v. reasons*; (vulg., abs. or quasi-pron.) several, as *among the letters are v. anent motor-driving, this is denied by v., v. have assured me.* Hence **var·iously**[2] adv., **var·iousness** n. (rare). [f. L *varius* + -OUS]

vār·ix, n. (pl. *vă·ricēs*). (Path.) permanent abnormal dilatation of vein or other vessel, vein &c. thus dilated; (Conch.) each of the ridges across the whorls of a univalve shell. [L]

var·let, n. (Hist.) medieval page preparing to be a squire; (archaic, esp. facet.) menial, low fellow, rascal. [OF, earlier *vaslet*, prob. dim. as VASSAL]

var·mint, n. (vulg., facet.). Mischievous or discreditable person or animal; (Hunt. slang) *the* fox. [corrupt. of VERMIN]

var·nish, n., & v.t. Kinds of resinous solution applied to wood, metal, &c., to give hard shiny transparent surface; glaze on pottery &c.; artificial or natural glossiness; superficial polish of manner; favourable appearance given to misconduct &c., palliation, whitewash; *v.-tree*, kinds from which v. is obtained. (Vb) apply v. to (wood, picture, &c., fig. character, person, action, account, or abs.); *varnishing-day*, day before exhibition of pictures on which exhibitors may retouch or v. their pictures already hung. [(vb f. F *vernir*, see -ISH[2], earlier *vernisser*) f. OF *vernis* etym. dub.]

var·sal, a. (colloq., now rare). = UNIVERSAL. [corrupt.]

var·sity, n. (colloq.). University (often attrib., as *the v. boat*). [corrupt.]

varsovie·nne (-vyĕn), n. (Music for) dance imitating mazurka. [F, = (dance) of Warsaw (*Varsovie*)]

vār·us[1], n. (In full *talipes v.*) a deformity in which the foot is bent inwards; knock-kneed person. [L, = bent, knock-kneed]

vār·us[2], n. = ACNE. [L]

vār·y, v.t. & i. Change, make different, modify, diversify, as *can v. the* (direction, amount, &c., of) *pressure at will, seldom varies the routine, varies the treatment according to circumstances, never varies his style, style is not sufficiently varied, a varied scene*; (Mus.) make VARIATIONS of (theme); suffer change, be(come) different in degree or quality, be of different kinds, as *he, his mood, varies from day to day, climate varies, tried with varying success, varies from the type, opinions v. on this point*; *v.* (*directly*) *as, v. inversely as,* increase, decrease, in proportion or correspondingly to the increase of, as *attraction of bodies varies* (*directly*) *as their masses & inversely as the square of their distances, A varies as* (symbol ∝) *B, A varies as B & C jointly* (as their product). [f. L *variare* (as VARIOUS)]

văs, n. (anat.; pl. *vā·sa*). Vessel, duct, as *v. dēferens*, excretory duct of testis. Hence **vā·sal** a. [L, = vessel]

va·scular, a. Of, made up of, containing, vessels or ducts for conveying blood, sap, &c., as *v. functions, tissue, v.* (circulatory) *system, v. plants.* Hence **vascula·rity, vascularization,** nn., **va·scularize**(3) v.t., **va·scularly**[2] adv. [f. VASCULUM + -AR[1]]

va·sculose, n. & a. Chief substance of vessels of plants; (adj.) = prec. [foll., -OSE[2, 1]]

vă·sculum, n. (pl. *-la*). Botanist's (usu. tin) collecting-case; (Anat.) small vessel, penis. [L, dim. of VAS]

vase (vahz; *archaic* vawz, *archaic & U.S.* vās, -z), n. Vessel of baked clay or other material used for various purposes but primarily ornamental, as *flower-v.*; large usu. sculptured vessel of marble &c. used to decorate gate-post &c.; *coal-v.* (vulg. or shop), kinds of coal-scuttle in ornamental outer case; body of Corinthian or Composite capital; *v.-painting*, decoration of vv. with pigments esp. among ancient Greeks, instance of this. Hence **va·seful** n. [F, f. L VAS]

vă·sĕline, n. Unctuous substance got from petroleum & used in ointments &c. [proprietary term introduced by R. A. Chesebrough 1872; irreg. f. G *wasser* water + Gk *elaion* oil + -INE[5]]

vă̄si-, vă̄so-, in comb. = VAS, as: *va·siform, vas*-like, tubular; *vasoconstri·ctor, -dila·tor, -mo·tor,* aa. & nn. (nerve, drug) causing constriction, dilatation, either, of blood-vessels; *vasose·nsory*, supplying sensation to vessels.

va·ssal, n. (Hist.) holder of land by feudal tenure (*great, rear, v.*, holding directly from king, holding from great v.); (rhet.) slave, humble dependant. [OF, f. med. L *vassallus, vassus*, cf. Breton *goaz*, servant, W & Corn. *gwas*, OIr. *foss*]

va·ssalage (-ĭj), n. (Hist.) condition, obligations, service, of a vassal; servitude, dependence; fief; (rare; also **va·ssalry** n.) vassals collectively. [f. OF *vasselage* (prec., see -AGE)]

vast, a. & n. Immense, huge, very great, as *a v. expanse of water, v. plains, shook his v. frame, a v. multitude, scheme*; (colloq.) *gave him v. satisfaction, makes a v. difference.* Hence **va·stly**[2] adv. (esp. colloq.), **va·stness** n. (N., poet., rhet.) v. space, as *the v. of ocean, of heaven.* [f. F *vaste* f. L *vastus* empty, waste, huge]

vat, n., & v.t. Large tub, cistern, or other vessel, esp. for holding liquids or holding something in liquid in process of manufacture, as *fermenting, tan, -v.*, whence **va·t**FUL n.; (vb) place, treat, in v. [earlier *fat*; OE *fæt*, cf. Du. *vat*, G *fass*, ON *fat*, cogn. w. MDu. *vatten*, G *fassen*, seize, contain]

Vă·tican, n. Palace & official residence of Pope on V. hill in Rome; (fig.) papal government; *V. Council*, oecumenical council held 1869–70 & proclaiming infallibility of Pope when speaking ex cathedra, whence **Va·tican**ISM(3), **Va·tican**IST(2), nn. [f. L *Vaticanus* V. hill]

vati·cinate, v.t. Prophesy (often abs.). So **vaticin**A·TION, **vati·cinat**OR[2], nn. [f. L *vaticinari* (*vates* prophet + *canere* sing), -ATE[3]]

vaudeville (vō·dvĭl), n. Slight dramatic sketch interspersed with songs & dances; variety entertainment; French popular e. g. topical song with refrain; (Hist.) convivial song esp. any of those composed by O. Basselin, poet born at Vau de Vire in Normandy, d. 1418. Hence **vau·devill**IST(3) n. [F, f. *Vau* or *Val de Vire* Valley of the Vire]

Vaudois[1] (vōdwah·), a. & n. (pl. same). (Inhabitants, dialect) of Vaud in Switzerland. [F (*Vaud* + -*ois* -ESE)]

Vaudois[2] (vōdwah·), a. & n. (pl. same). (Member) of the Waldenses. [F, as WALDENSES]

vaudoo. See VOODOO.

vault[1], n., & v.t. (Archit.) arched roof, continuous arch, set or series of arches whose joints radiate from central point or line; v.-like covering, as *the v. of heaven*; arched apartment; arched or other cellar or subterranean chamber as place of storage (*wine-v.* &c.), of interment beneath church or in cemetery (*family v.*), &c.; (Anat.) arched roof of a cavity. (Vb) make in form of, furnish with, v. or vv. (esp. in p.p.). Hence **vau·lt**ING[1](6) n. [(vb f. n.) ME *voute*, f. OF *voute, volte*, vault, turn, fem. adj. as n. f. L *volutus* p.p. of *volvere* roll]

vault[2], v.i. & t., & n. Leap, spring, esp. while resting on the hand(s) or with help of pole, as *v. over the gate, from the saddle, upon a horse*; spring over (gate &c.) thus; *vaulting-horse*, wooden horse for practice in vaulting. Hence **vau·lt**ER[1] n. (N.) leap so performed. [(n. f. vb) f. OF *volter* leap, w. assim. to prec.]

vaunt, v.i. & t., & n. Boast, brag; boast of; (n.) boast. Hence or cogn. **vau·nt**ER[1] n., **vau·nting**LY[2] adv. [f. F *vanter* f. pop. L *vanitare* (as VANITY)]

va·vasory, n. (hist.). Tenure, lands, of a vavasour. [-Y[1]]

vă·vasour (-or, -*er*, -oor), (n. hist.). Vassal holding of a great lord & having other vassals under him. [f. OF *vavassour* f. med. L *vassus vassorum* VASSAL of vassals]

've, colloq. abbr. of *have* appended to *I, we, you,* & *they* (*I've* &c.).

veal, n. Flesh of calf as food, as *v. cutlet*; *v.-skin*, skin disease with smooth white tubercles usu. on face & neck. Hence **vea·l**Y[2] a. [f. OF *veël* f. L *vitellus* dim. of *vitulus* calf]

ve·ctor, n. (In quaternions &c.) line conceived to have fixed length & direction but no fixed position, quantity determining position of one point in space relative to another (*v. quantity*, one that may be represented by a v.); RADIUS *v.* Hence **vector·**IAL a. [L, = carrier (*vehere vect-* convey, see -OR[2])]

Ve·da (vā-), n. (Also in pl.) ancient Hindu scriptures written in old form of Sanskrit (*Rig, Sama, Yajur, Atharva, -V.*, four collections of hymns &c. composing the V.). Hence **Ve·d**IC a. [Skr., lit. knowledge]

Veda·nta, n. Hindu philosophy founded on the Veda. Hence **Veda·nt**IC a., **Veda·nt**IST(3) n. [Skr. (*vēda* + *anta* end)]

vede·tte (-ĕt), vi-, n. Mounted sentinel placed in advance of an outpost. [F (*ve-*), f. It. *vedetta* prob. f. *vedere* see f. L *vidēre*]

veer, v.i. & t. Change direction esp. (of wind, cf. BACK[2]) sunwise; (fig.) change one's mind, turn *round* in opinion or conduct or language; (Naut.) slacken, let out, as *v. away, out, the cable*; = WEAR[3]; *v. & haul*, tighten & slacken (rope &c.) alternately, (of wind) change alternately, (fig.) vacillate in opinion &c. Hence **veer·ing**LY[2] adv. [partly f. F *virer* to turn, etym. dub.; partly f. MDu. *vieren* let out]

ve·ga (vā-), n. Low moist tract in Spain or Cuba; Cuban tobacco-field. [Sp., etym. dub.]

vĕ·getable, a. & n. Of (the nature of), derived from, concerned with, comprising, plants, as *v. colic* (caused by use of unripe fruit), IVORY, *jelly* (=PECTIN), KINGDOM, MARROW, *naphtha, oyster* (= SALSIFY), *physiology*, SPONGE[1]. Hence **vegeta**BI·LITY n. (N.) plant, esp. herbaceous plant used for culinary purposes or for feeding cattle, e. g. cabbage, potato, turnip, bean, (often attrib., as *v. diet, soup*). [f. L *vegetabilis* animating (as VEGETATE, see -BLE)]

ve·getal, a. & n. Of (the nature of) plants, so **ve·geto-** comb. form; common to animals & plants, as *the v. functions* (of growth, circulation, generation, &c.); (n.) plant, vegetable. Hence **vegeta·l**ITY n. [f. L *vegetare* VEGETATE + -AL]

vegetar·ian, n. One who uses or advocates a diet of vegetable food (usu. with addition of milk, eggs, &c.) to the exclusion of meat (often attrib., as *v. food, diet, principles, craze*). Hence **vegetar·ian**ISM n. [-ARIAN]

vĕ·getate, v.i. Grow as plants do, fulfil vegetable functions; (fig.) live an idle or monotonous life. So **ve·getat**IVE a., **ve·getative**LY[2] adv., **ve·getative**NESS n. [f. L *vegetare* enliven (*vegetus* lively f. *vegēre* move, quicken), see -ATE[3]]

vegeta·tion, n. Vegetating (lit. & fig.); plants collectively, plant life, as *luxuriant v., no sign of v. for miles round*; (Path.) excrescence of surface of body. [f. med. L *vegetationem* (as prec., see -ATION)]

vē·hement (vēe-), a. Showing or caused by strong feeling, impetuous, ardent, passionate, as *a v. desire, protest, man of v. character*; acting with great force, violent, as *a v. wind, onset*. Hence or cogn. **ve·he**MENCE n., **ve·hement**LY[2] adv. [OF, f. L *ve(he)mentem*, nom. *-ns*, perh. f. *ve-* apart from +*mens -ntis* mind]

ve·hicle (vēĭ-), n. Carriage, conveyance, of any kind used on land; liquid &c. used as a medium for pigments, drugs, &c.; thing, person, used as a medium for thought or feeling or action, as *used the pulpit, the press, as a v. for his political opinions, will not be used as the v. of your resentment*. So **vehi·cul**AR[1] (-h-) a. [f. L *vehiculum* (*vehere* carry, see -CULE)]

vehmgericht (fā·mgericht), n. German system of irregular tribunals prevailing esp. in Westphalia in 14th & 15th cc. & trying the more serious crimes in secret night sessions; such tribunal. Hence **veh·mic** a. [G, also *f-*, f. *feme* punishment, tribunal, +*gericht* judgement, law]

veil (vāl), n., & v.t. Piece of usu. more or less transparent material attached to woman's bonnet or hat or otherwise forming part of head-dress, esp. one serving to conceal the face or as protection against sun, dust, &c., as *raised, dropped, her v.* (so as to uncover, cover, face), *took the v.*, became nun; curtain (*the v. of the temple*; *beyond the v.*, in the unknown state of after death); (fig.) disguise, pretext, as *under the v. of religion*; *draw a v. over*, avoid discussing or calling attention to; scarf on pastoral staff; (Bot., Zool.) = VELUM; slight huskiness of voice, natural or due to a cold &c. Hence **vei·l**ING[1](3) n., **vei·l**LESS a. (Vb) cover (one's face, oneself, or abs. in same sense) with v.; (fig.) conceal, disguise, mask, as *veiled resentment*. [vb v. n., AF *veile* (OF *voile*) f. L *vela* pl. of VELUM]

veilleuse (F), n. Shaded night-lamp esp. as subject for decorative art.

vein (vān), n., & v.t. Each of the membranous tubes that convey blood to the heart (cf. ARTERY; *pulmonary vv.*, returning oxygenated blood from lungs to left side, *systemic vv.*, returning venous blood from all parts to right side); (pop.) any blood-vessel; (Entom., Bot.) rib of insect's wing or of leaf; (Geol., Mining) fissure in rock filled with deposited matter (*vei·nstone*, = GANGUE); streak, stripe, of different colour in wood, marble, &c.; distinctive character or tendency, cast of mind or disposition, mood, as *was of an imaginative v., said in a humorous v., other remarks in the same v., am in the v. for high play, am not in (the) v. just now*. Hence **vei·n**LESS, **vei·n**LIKE, **vei·n**Y[2], aa., **vei·n**LET n. (Vb) fill or cover (as) with v. or vv. (esp. in p.p.). Hence **vei·n**AGE(1), **vei·n**ING[1](6), nn. [(vb f. n.) f. OF *veine* f. L *vena*]

velā·men (pl. *-mina*), ***vĕlame·ntum*** (pl. *-ta*), nn. Enveloping membrane esp. of brain. [L, = covering (*velare* f. VELUM, -MEN, -MENT)]

vē·lar, a. Of a veil or velum, as *v. gutturals*, sounds produced by aid of soft palate (e. g. gw, kw). [f. L *velaris* (VELUM, see -AR[1])]

veldt (-lt), n. S.-Afr. tract of land with little or no forest, grass country. [Du. (now *veld*), = FIELD]

vĕlita·tion, n. (archaic). Slight skirmish, controversy. [f. L *velitatio* (*velitari* skirmish, as foll., see -ATION)]

vē·lite, n. (Rom. ant.). Light-armed soldier. [f. L *veles -itis*]

vellē·ity, n. (archaic). Low degree of volition not prompting to action. [f. med. L *velleitas* (*velle* vb wish, see -TY)]

ve·llicate, v.t. & i. Twitch. Hence or cogn. **vellica·**TION n., **ve·llicat**IVE a. [f. L *vellicare* (*vellere* pluck), see -ATE[3]]

ve·llum, n. Fine parchment orig. from skin of calf; manuscript written on this; *v. paper* (imitating v.). Hence **ve·llum**Y[2] a. [f. OF *velin* (VEAL, -INE[1])]

veloce (vĕlō·tshā), adv. (mus.). With great rapidity. [It.]

velŏ·cipede (-ēd), n. Kinds of light vehicle impelled by rider (now chiefly hist. of obs. types e. g. hobby, also as general term = CYCLE). Hence **velo·cipede**IST(3) n. [f. F *vélocipède* f. L *velox -ocis* swift+*pes pedis* foot]

velŏ·city, n. Quickness, rate, of motion usu. of inanimate things, as *uniform, variable, v., a v. of 3 feet per second, initial v.*, v. of a body at starting, esp. (also *muzzle v.*) of projectile issuing from firearm. Hence **vĕloci·**METER n. [f. F *vélocité* f. L *velocitatem* (*velox -ocis* swift, see -TY)]

velours· (-oor), n. Kinds of plush used for hats &c. [F (OF *-our, -ous*), as VELVET]

vĕlouti·ne (-ēn), n. Kinds of corded fabric & of toilet-powder. [F]

vē·lum, n. (anat., bot., zool.; pl. *-la*). Kinds of membrane or membranous covering, esp. the soft palate. [L, = sail, veil, f. *vehere* carry]

vĕ·lure, n., & v.t. Velvet or similar fabric; velvet or other pad for smoothing silk hat; (vb) smooth with v. [(vb f. n.) f. OF as VELOURS]

velū·tinous, a. (bot., entom.). Velvety. [f. L as VELVET + -INE[1] + -OUS]

ve·lveret, n. Bad kind of velvet. [irreg. dim. of foll.]

ve·lvet, n. & a. Closely woven fabric wholly (also *silk v.*) or partly (*cotton v.*) of silk with thick short pile on one side (*terry v.*, with pile uncut); furry skin covering a growing antler; *v. pile*, fabric with pile like that of v.; (adj.) of, soft as, v. (often in names of animals & plants, as *v. ant, osier*); *v. glove*, outward gentleness cloaking inflexibility (*with an iron hand in a v. g.*); *v. paw*, of cat, fig. of cruelty &c. veiled under suave manner; *v. tread*, soft. Hence **ve·lveted**[2], **ve·lvety**[2], aa. [f. med. L *velluetum* ult. f. L *villus* shaggy hair]

velvetee·n, n. Cotton fabric with pile like velvet; kind of velvet made of silk & cotton. [prec. + *-een* -INE[4]]

ve·lveting, n. Velvet goods collectively; pile, nap, of velvet. [-ING[1]]

vē·nal, a. (Of person) that may be bought, ready to sell influence or services or to sacrifice principles from sordid motive; (of conduct &c.) characteristic of v. person. Hence or cogn. **vena·lity** n., **ve·nally**[2] adv. [f. L *venalis* (*venus, -um*, sale, see -AL)]

vena·tion, n. Arrangement of veins on leaf, insect's wing, &c. Hence **vena·tional** a. [as VEIN + -ATION]

vend, v.t. Sell (now chiefly legal, whence or cogn. **vendee·**, **ve·ndor**[2], nn.); offer (small wares) for sale, so **(-)ve·nder**[1] n. Hence or cogn. **vendibi·lity** n., **ve·ndible** a., **ve·ndibly**[2] adv. [f. L *vendere* = *venumdare* (*venum* sale, *dare* give)]

ve·ndace, n. Small & delicate fish found in some British & Continental lakes. [f. OF *vendese* dace, etym. dub.]

Vendē·an, a. & n. (Native) of Vendée, department of W. France; (member) of V. royalist party in 1793–5. [f. F *Vendéen* (*Vendée*, see -AN)]

vende·tta, n. Blood-feud in which family of injured or murdered man seeks vengeance on offender or his family; this practice as prevalent in Corsica &c. [It., f. L *vindicta*, see VINDICTIVE]

veneer·, v.t., & n. Cover (wood, furniture, &c.) with thin coating of finer wood; cover (pottery &c.) with thin coat of finer substance; (fig.) disguise (character &c.) under superficial polish of manner &c.; (n.) thin outer coating, veneering (lit. & fig.); *v.-moth*, kinds whose colouring suggests v. [f. G *furniren* f. F as FURNISH]

ve·nerable, a. Entitled to veneration on account of character, age, associations, &c., as *v. priest, relics, beard, ruins, river* (also in Ch. of Eng. as title of archdeacons, abbr. *Ven.*; in R.-C. Ch. as title of one who has attained first of three degrees of sanctity but is not canonized). Hence **venerabi·lity**, **ve·nerableness**, nn., **ve·nerably**[2] adv. [OF, f. L *venerabilis* (as foll., see -ABLE)]

vĕ·nerate, v.t. Consider worthy of & regard with deep respect or warm approbation; revere. So **ve·nerator**[2] n. [f. L *venerari*, -ATE[3]]

venera·tion, n. Profound respect, reverence; (Phrenol., often facet.) faculty of feeling reverence, as *organ, bump, of v.* [f. L *venerationem* (as prec., see -ATION)]

venēr·ĕal, a. Of sexual intercourse, as *v. desire*; *v. disease*, communicated by sexual intercourse; *v. remedies* (for v. disease). [f. L *Venereus* of VENUS + -AL]

vĕ·nery[1], n. (archaic). Hunting. [f. OF *venerie* (*vener* hunt f. L *venari*, see -ERY)]

vĕ·nery[2], n. (archaic). Sexual indulgence. [VENUS, -Y[1]]

vĕ·nĕsect v.t. & i., **venese·ction** n. = PHLEBOTOMIZE, PHLEBOTOMY. [vb f. n., f. L *venae sectio* cutting of vein]

Venē·tian (-shn), a. & n. Of Venice; *V. blind*, window blind of slats of wood that may be turned so as to admit or exclude light; *V. carpet* (of worsted, usu. with striped pattern); *V.* (= FRENCH) *chalk*; *V. glass*, glassware made at or near Venice, (also *Venice glass*) cup of this said to be destroyed by contact with poison; *V. lace*, kind of point lace; *V. mast*, spirally painted pole for use in street decorations; *V.* (solid artificial) *pearl*; *V. window* (with three separate openings). (N.) native of Venice; (usu. *v-*) V. blind, whence **vene·tianed**[2] a., (pl.) kind of tape for holding slats of this. [f. med. L *Venetianus* f. L *Venetia* country of the *Veneti*, -AN]

ve·ngeance (-jns), n. Punishment inflicted, retribution exacted, for wrong to oneself or to person &c. whose cause one espouses, as *will exact ample v.*, *took a bloody v. on the murderer* or *for the murder of his children, you lay yourself open to his v.*; *with a v.*, in a higher degree than was expected or desired, in the fullest sense of the word(s), & no mistake, as *this is punctuality with a v.* [F (*venger* avenge f. L as VINDICATE, see -ANCE)]

ve·ngeful, a. Disposed to revenge, vindictive. Hence **ve·ngefully**[2] adv., **ve·ngefulness** n. [f. obs. *venge* vb (as prec.) + -FUL]

vē·nial, a. (Of sin or fault) pardonable, excusable, not very wrong, (Theol.) not mortal. Hence **venia·lity**, **ve·nialness**, nn., **ve·nially**[2] adv. [OF, f. L *venialis* (*venia* pardon, see -AL)]

Vĕ·nice, n. (attrib.). *V.* (= VENETIAN) *glass*; *V. treacle*, = THERIAC.

venīr·e (fă·ciăs) (-sh-), n. (law). Writ directing sheriff to summon jury. [L, = make come]

vĕ·nison (-nzn), n. Deer's flesh as food. [f. OF *veneisun* f. L *venationem* hunting (*venari* hunt, see -ATION, -SON)]

Venī·tĕ, n. (Musical setting of) *Ps.* xcv. [L, = Come ye, first word of psalm]

vĕ·nom, n. Poisonous fluid secreted by serpents, scorpions, &c., & introduced into system of victim by bite or sting; (fig.) malignity, virulence, of feeling or language or conduct. Hence or cogn. **ve·nom**ED[2], **ve·nom**OUS, aa., **ve·nomous**LY[2] adv., **ve·nomous**NESS n. [ME & OF *venim* f. L *venenum* poison]

venŏ·sity, n. Excess of venous blood in organ &c.; deficient aeration of venous blood in lungs with afflux of venous blood into arteries. [as foll., see -OSITY]

vē·nous, -ose, aa. (anat., zool., bot.). Of, full of, contained in, veins, as *v.* (opp. to arterial) *blood, v. congestion,* accumulation of v. blood in organ &c. Hence **ve·nous**LY[2] adv. [f. L *venosus* (as VEIN, see -OSE[1], -OUS)]

vent, n., & v.t. Hole or opening allowing passage out of or into confined space, e.g. touch-hole of gun, hole in top of barrel to admit air while liquid is being drawn out, finger-hole in musical instrument (also **ve·nt**AGE n.), flue of chimney, loophole in embattled wall; =*v.-faucet*; anus esp. of animals below mammals; (fig.) outlet, free passage, free play, as *gave v. to his indignation, impatience found a v.*; venting of otter &c. (see vb); *v.-faucet,* hollow gimlet for making v. in cask &c.; *v.-hole,* v.; *v.-peg,* peg for stopping v. of barrel, also =*v.-faucet*; *v.-plug,* plug for v. of gun, also = *v.-peg* (1st sense). Hence **ve·nt**LESS a. (Vb) make v. in (gun, cask, &c.); give v. to, as *vented his disgust in an epigram, with a snort, on the office-boy*; (of otter or beaver) come to surface for breath. [n. partly f. F *vent* f. L *ventus* wind, partly f. F *évent* (*éventer* f. EX- + *vent* wind); vb chiefly f. n.]

ve·nter, n. (Anat.) belly, also, protuberant or concave part of muscle or bone; (Law) womb, mother, as *a son by, the son of, another v.* [L, = belly, womb, (in legal sense thr. AF *ventre*)]

ve·ntiduct, n. (archit.). Air-passage, esp. subterranean one. [f. L *ventus* wind + DUCT]

ve·ntil, n. Valve in musical instrument; shutter for regulating air in organ. [G, f. med. L *ventile* sluice f. L *ventus* wind]

ve·ntilate, v.t. Cause air to circulate freely in (room &c.); purify by air, oxygenate, (blood); submit (question, subject, grievance, &c.) to public consideration & discussion. Hence or cogn. **ventila·**TION, **ve·ntilat**OR[2](2, 1; esp., appliance for ventilating room), nn., **ve·ntilat**IVE a. [f. L *ventilare* blow, winnow (*ventus* wind) see -ATE[3]]

ve·ntral, a. & n. (zool., bot.). Of the venter; on the belly (opp. DORSAL); *v. (fin),* either of the abdominal fins. Hence **ve·ntral**LY[2] adv. [F, f. L *ventralis* (VENTER, see -AL)]

ventre à terre (F), adv. At full speed (lit. with belly to ground).

ve·ntricle, n. (anat.). Any cavity of the body, hollow part or organ, as *vv. of the brain, right, left, v.* (*of the heart*). Hence **ventri·cul**AR[1], **ventri·cul**OUS, aa. [f. F *ventricule* f. L *ventriculus* dim. of VENTER]

ve·ntricose, -ous, aa. Having a protruding belly; (Bot.) distended, inflated. [f. VENTER + -IC + -OSE[1], -OUS]

ventri·loquism, n. Act, art, of speaking, or uttering sounds in such a manner that the voice appears to come from some other source than the speaker. So **ventrilocu·**TION, **ventri·loqu**IST(1), **ventri·loqu**Y[1], nn., **ventrilō·qui**AL, **ventriloqui·st**IC, **ventri·loqu**OUS, aa., **ventri·loqu**IZE(2) v.i. [f. L *ventriloquus* ventriloquist (VENTER + *loqui locut-* speak)]

ventro- in comb. = VENTER, as *-dor·sal,* extending from belly to back.

ve·nture (-tsh*er*), n., & v.t. & i. Undertaking of a risk, risky undertaking, as *declined the v., ready for any v.*; commercial speculation, as *one lucky v. made his fortune, failed in all his vv.*; (archaic) thing at stake, property risked; *at a v.,* at random. (Vb) dare, not be afraid, make bold, as *did not v. to stop him, I v. to differ from you*; dare to make or advance or put forward, hazard, as *would not v. an opinion, a guess, a step*; expose to risk, stake, as *men who v. their lives for the cause, will v. five shillings on it*; (abs.) undertake risk; *v.* (*up*)*on,* dare to engage in or grapple with or make, as *shall v. on a mild protest, will you v. on a slice of cucumber?.* Hence **ve·nture**SOME a., **ve·nturesome**LY[2] adv., **ve·nturesome**NESS n. [aphetic f. ADVENTURE]

vĕ·nue, n. (law). Country within which jury must be gathered & cause tried (orig. neighbourhood of crime &c.), as *change the v.* (to avoid riot, prejudiced jury, &c.); statement in indictment &c. indicating this; (pop.) rendezvous. [OF, = coming, f. *venir* come f. L *venire*]

Vē·nus, n. (Rom. Myth.) goddess of love; a PLANET[1]; sexual love, amorous influences or desires, (*uranian, pandemian, V.,* spiritual, sensual, sex love); a beautiful woman; *Mount of V.* (palmistry), base of thumb; *V.'s basin, bath,* common teazel; *V.'s comb,* annual of parsley family with comb-like fruit; *V.'s fly-trap,* herb with leaves that close on insects &c.; *V.'s slipper.* = LADY'*s-slipper.* [L, gen. *-eris*]

verā·cious, a. Speaking, disposed to speak, the truth; (of statement &c.) true, not (meant to be) false. Hence or cogn. **vera·cious**LY[2] adv., **ver**Ă·CITY n. [f. L *verax* (*verus* true, see -ACIOUS)]

verā·nda(h) (-dŭ), n. Open portico or gallery along side of house with roof supported on pillars. [f. Port. *varanda*]

vĕ·ratrīne, n. Poisonous compound from hellebore used esp. as local irritant in neuralgia & rheumatism. So **ve·ratr**ATE[1](3) n., **vera·tr**IC a., **ve·ratr**IZE (5) v.t. [F (*vé-*), f. L *veratrum* hellebore + -INE[5]]

verb, n. (gram.). Part of speech that predicates, word whose function is predication (e. g. italicized words in Time *flies*, Salt *is* good, You *surprise* me); *copulative* or *substantive v.*, be; AUXILIARY, DEPONENT, IMPERSONAL, (IN)TRANSITIVE, NEUTER, REFLEXIVE, *v.* [f. L *verbum* WORD, verb]

ver·bal, a. & n. Of, concerned with, words, as *v. distinctions, subtleties, critic(ism), accuracy*, INSPIRATION; (loosely) oral, not written, as *a v. communication, contract, v. evidence*; (of translation) literal, word for word; *v. note* (diplomacy), unsigned memorandum on matter that is not urgent but must not be overlooked; (Gram.) of (the nature of) a verb, as *v. inflexions, used in all the v. senses* (of the verb), *v. noun*, noun derived from verb & partly sharing its constructions (e.g. E nouns in -ING[1]); (n.) v. noun. Hence **ver·bal**LY[2] adv. [f. L *verbalis* (as prec., see -AL)]

ver·balism, n. Minute attention to words, verbal criticism. [-ISM]

ver·balist, n. Person concerned with words only, verbal critic. [-IST]

ver·balize, v.t. & i. Make (noun &c.) into a verb, so **ver·bi**FY v.t.; be verbose. Hence **verbaliz**A·TION n. [-IZE]

verbā·tim, adv. & a. Word for word, as *copied it v., a v. reprint.* [med. L (adv.), as VERB, cf. LITERATIM]

verbē·na, n. Kinds of plant of vervain family, as *lemon(-scented) v.* [L, = sacred bough of olive &c., VERVAIN]

ver·biage (-ĭj), n. Needless accumulation of words, verbosity. [F (as VERB, see -AGE)]

ver·bicide, n. (facet.). Word-butcher(y). [as VERB + -CIDE]

verbō·se, a. Using, containing, more words than are wanted, prolix. Hence **verbo·se**LY[2] adv., **verbo·se**NESS, **verbŏ·**SITY, nn. [f. L *verbosus* (as VERB, see -OSE[1])]

ver·bum (sat) săpiĕ·nti, sent. (abbr. *verb. sap.*). A word is enough to the wise. [L]

ver·dant, a. (Of grass &c.) green, fresh-coloured; (of field &c.) covered with v. grass &c.; (of person) unsophisticated, raw, green. Hence **ver·**DANCY n., **ver·dant**LY[2] adv. [perh. f. *verdure* + -ANT]

verd-anti·que (-ēk), n. Ornamental usu. green building-stone formed chiefly of serpentine; green incrustation on ancient bronze. [OF (*verd* green f. L *viridis* + ANTIQUE)]

ver·derer, -or, n. (hist.). Judicial officer of royal forests. [AF *verder* (*verd* f. L *viridis* green) + -ER[1], -OR[2]]

ver·dict, n. Decision of jury on issue of fact in civil or criminal cause, as *brought in a v. of not guilty, a v. for the plaintiff, open v.* (reporting commission of crime but not specifying criminal), *partial v.* (finding person guilty of part of the charge), *privy* or *sealed v.* (written v. delivered to clerk of court when court has adjourned during deliberation of jury), *special v.* (stating facts as proved but leaving court to draw conclusion from them); decision, judgement, as *the v. of the public was in its favour, does not dispute your v.* [ME & AF *verdit* f. L *vere dictum* thing truly said (*vere* truly + DICTUM)]

ver·digris, n. Green crystallized substance formed on copper by action of acetic acid & used in medicine & as pigment &c.; green rust on copper. [ME *verdegrese, verte grece*, f. AF *vert de Grece* green of Greece (as VERDURE + *Greece* f. L *Graecia*)]

ver·diter, n. *Blue, green, v.*, pigments got from copper nitrate. [f. OF *verd de terre* green of earth (as foll. + *terre* f. L *terra* earth)]

ver·dure (-dyer), n. Greenness of vegetation, green vegetation, whence **ver·dur**ED[2], **ver·dure**LESS, **ver·dur**OUS, aa.; (fig.) freshness; French tapestry with prominent foliage. [F (OF *verd* green, f. L *viridis*, see -URE)]

verein (ferī·n), n. Association of persons or parties, organized body. [G]

verge[1], n. Extreme edge, brink, border, (usu. fig.), as *drew near to the very v. of the stream, on the v. of 70, destruction, betraying his secret*; grass edging of flower-bed &c.; wand, rod, carried before bishop, dean, &c., as emblem of office; kinds of shaft or spindle in various mechanisms; (Archit.) shaft of column, edge of tiles projecting over gable, *v.-board*, = BARGE-*board*; (Hist.) area of jurisdiction of Marshalsea. [OF, f. L *virga* twig, rod]

verge[2], v.i. Incline downwards or in specified direction (*the now verging sun; v. towards old age, to a close*); *v. on*, border on, approach closely, as *path verges on the edge of a precipice, a solemnity verging on the tragic.* [f. L *vergere* bend, incline; sense influenced by prec.]

vergee· (-jē), n. Channel-Island measure of area, four-ninths of acre. [f. F *vergée* measured (VERGE[1])]

ver·gency, n. (optics). Reciprocal of focal distance of lens as measure of divergence or convergence of rays. [VERGE[2], -ENCY]

ver·ger, n. Official in a church who shows persons to their seats &c.; officer who bears staff before bishop, vice-chancellor of university, &c. Hence **ver·ger**SHIP n. [prob. as VERGE[1], cf. med. L *virgarius* rod-bearer]

veri·dical, a. Truthful (usu. iron.); (Psych., Spirit.; of visions &c.) coinciding with realities. Hence or cogn. **veri·dical**LY[2] adv., **veri·dic**OUS a. [f. L *veridicus* (*verus* true + *dicere* say) + -AL]

vĕ·rifȳ, v.t. Establish the truth of, examine for this purpose, as *must v. the statement, his figures, am now verifying the items*; (of event, action, &c.) bear out, make good, fulfil, (prediction, promise); (Law) append affidavit to (pleadings), support (statement) by proofs. Hence or cogn. **verifiabi·lity, verifica·tion, ve·rifier**[1], nn., **ve·rifiable** a. [f. OF *verifier* f. med. L *verificare* (*verus* true, see -FY)]

vĕ·rily, adv. (archaic). Really, truly, in very truth. [f. VERY + -LY[2]]

vĕrisimi·litude, n. Air of being true, semblance of actuality, (*the v. of the tale*; *v. is not proof*); *a* thing that seems true. So **verisi·milar**[1] a. [f. L *verisimilitudo* f. *verisimilis* probable (*veri* gen. of *verus* true + *similis* like), see -TUDE]

vĕ·ritable, a. Real, rightly so called, as *a v. boon.* Hence **ve·ritably**[2] adv. [OF (as VERITY, see -ABLE)]

vĕ·ritās, n. (Also *bureau véritas*) French ship register like Lloyd's. [F (*vé-*), f. L as foll.]

vĕ·rity, n. Truth (*of* statement &c.); true statement; really existent thing, as *these things, alas! are vv.*; *of a v.* (archaic), in truth, really. [f. OF *verite* f. L *veritatem* (*verus* true, see -TY)]

ver·juice, n. Acid liquor got from crab-apples, sour grapes, &c., & used in cooking. Hence **ver·juiced**[2] a. [f. OF *verjus* (*verd*, see VERDURE, + *jus* JUICE)]

ver·meil (-mĭl), n. Silver gilt; varnish used to give lustre to gilding; orange-red garnet; (poet.) vermilion. [OF, see VERMILION]

vermi- in comb. = L *vermis* worm, as: *-cide*, drug that kills worms, so *-cidal* a.; *-form*, worm-shaped (*v.* APPENDIX), structurally allied to worms; *-fuge*, drug that expels intestinal worms, so *-fugal* a.; *-grade*, moving like worm, wriggling along; *-vorous* feeding on worms.

ver·mian, a. Of worms, worm-like. So **vermeŏ·logist, vermeo·logy,** nn. [f. L *vermis* worm + -AN]

vermice·llĭ, n. Paste of same materials as macaroni made in slender threads. [It., pl. of *vermicello* dim. f. L *vermis* worm]

vermĭ·cular, a. Like a worm in form or movements, as *v.* (= VERMI*form*) *appendix*; of worm-eaten appearance; marked with close wavy lines. [f. med. L *vermicularis* (L *vermiculus* dim. of *vermis* worm, see -AR[1])]

vermi·culate, a. = prec. (rare, usu. fig.). [f. L *vermiculari* be full of worms (prec.), -ATE[2, 3]]

vermicula·tion, n. Being eaten or infested by or converted into worms; vermicular marking; worm-eaten state. [f. L *vermiculatio* (prec., -ATION)]

vermĭ·lion, n., a., & v.t. Cinnabar; brilliant red pigment made by grinding this or artificially; (of) this colour; (vb) colour (as) with v. [(vb f. n.) f. OF *vermillon* vermilion, kermes insect (*vermeil* vermilion f. L *vermiculus* dim. of *vermis* worm, see -OON)]

ver·min, n. (usu. treated as pl.). Mammals & birds injurious to game, crops, &c., e. g. foxes, weasels, rats, mice, moles, owls, &c.; noxious insects, e. g. fleas, bugs, lice; parasitic worms or insects; (fig.) vile persons, as *the v. that infest racecourses.* So **ver·minous** a., **ver·minously**[2] adv. [ME & OF *vermine* ult. f. L *vermis* worm]

ver·minate, v.i. Breed vermin, become infested with parasites. So **vermina·tion** n. [f. L *verminare* (*vermis* worm), see -ATE[3]]

ver·m(o)uth (-o͞oth), n. Liqueur flavoured with wormwood. [f. F *vermout* f. G *wermuth* wormwood]

vernă·cular, a. & n. (Of language, idiom, word) of one's native country, native, indigenous, not of foreign origin or of learned formation; (of disease) = ENDEMIC; (n.) the language or dialect of the country, as *Latin gave place to the v.* Hence **verna·cularism**(4), **vernacula·rity, vernacularization,** nn., **verna·cularize**(3) v.t., **verna·cularly**[2] adv. [f. L *vernaculus* native (*verna* home-born slave, see -CULE) + -AR[1]]

ver·nal, a. Of, appearing or occurring or done in, spring, as *v. breezes, flowers,* EQUINOX, *migration, v.* (malarial) *fever, v. grass*, sweet-scented grass grown among hay. Hence **ver·nally**[2] adv. [f. L *vernalis* (*vernus* f. *ver* spring, see -AL)]

verna·tion, n. (bot.). Arrangement of leaves (cf. AESTIVATION) within leaf-bud. [f. L *vernare* bloom (*ver* spring, see -ATION)]

ver·nier, n. Small movable scale for obtaining fractional parts of the subdivisions on fixed scale of theodolite &c. [F, f. P. *V.*, inventor, d. 1637]

vĕ·ronal, n. An opiate. [?]

Vĕrone·se (-ēz), a., & n. (pl. the same). (Inhabitant) of Verona. [-ESE]

verŏ·nica, n. Kinds of herb or shrub with blue, purple, pink, or white flowers; cloth with representation of Christ's face, esp. one miraculously so impressed after being used by St V. to wipe sweat from Christ's face. [*V.*, woman's name]

ve·rricule, n. (entom.). Thick tuft of upright hairs. Hence **verri·culate**[2] a. [f. L *verriculum* net (*verrere* sweep)]

verru·ca, n. (path., zool., bot.). Wart, wart-like elevation. Hence or cogn. **verru·ciform, ve·rrucose**[1], **ve·rrucous, verru·culose**[1] [-UL-], aa. [L]

ver·sant, n. Extent of land sloping in one direction, general slope of land. [F, f. L *versare* frequent. of *vertere vers-* turn]

ver·satĭle, a. Turning readily from one subject or occupation to another, capable of dealing with many subjects, as *v. author, genius, disposition, mind*; capable of being moved or turned as on hinge, as *v. spindle*; (Bot., Zool.) moving freely about or up & down on a support, as *v. anther, head, antennae*; changeable, inconstant. Hence or cogn. **ver·satilely**[2] adv., **versatĭ·lity,** n. [F, f. L *versatilis* (as prec., see -ATILE)]

verse, n., & v.t. & i. Metrical line containing definite number of feet, as *quoted some vv. of the Iliad, had a good v. here & there,* CAP² *vv.*; group of definite number of vv., stanza; metrical composition in general, particular type of this, as *wrote pages of v., expressed in indifferent v., what is not prose is v., a prize for Latin v.,* BLANK¹, SOCIETY, *elegiac, iambic, trochaic,* &c., *v.*; each of the short divisions of chapter in Bible (CHAPTER *& v.*); short sentence as part of liturgy; solo part of anthem &c.; *v.-monger(ing),* maker, making, of bad vv. Hence **ver·se**LET n. (Vb) express in v., make vv. [(vb f. n.) OE *fers* f. L *versus -ūs* turning, line, row, verse, f. *vertere vers-* turn]

versed, a. Experienced, skilled, proficient, (*in* subject, occupation, &c.); reversed (now only in *v.* SINE). [adaptation of L *versatus* p.p. of *versari* be engaged in, see VERSANT; trig. sense f. L *versus* p.p. as prec.]

ver·set, n. (mus.). Short prelude or interlude for organ. [OF, dim. of *vers* VERSE]

ver·sicle, n. Short verse, esp. of each series of short verses in liturgy said or sung alternately by minister & people. [f. L *versiculus* (as VERSE, see -CULE)]

ver·sicolour(ed), aa. Variegated; changing from one colour to another in different lights. [f. L *versicolor* (*vertere vers-* turn + *color* COLOUR)]

versi·cular, a. *V. division* (into verses). [as VERSICLE (see -UL-) + -AR¹]

ver·sify̆, v.t. & i. Turn (prose) into verse; express in verse; make verses. Hence or cogn. **versi**FICA·TION, **ver·sifi**ER¹, nn. [f. OF *versifier* f. L *versificare* (as VERSE, see -FY)]

ver·sion, n. Book &c. translated into another language, as *Authorized, Revised, V.* (of the Bible, made 1604–11, 1870–84; abbr. *A.V., R.V.*); piece of translation, esp. into foreign language, as school exercise; account of a matter from particular person's point of view, as *now let me have your own v. of the affair*; turning of child improperly placed for delivery so that head or feet may be first presented. Hence **ver·sion**AL a. [F, f. L *versionem* (L *vertere vers-* turn, see -ION)]

vers libre (F), n. Versification or verses in which different metres are mingled, or prosodical restrictions disregarded, or variable rhythm substituted for definite metre. **versli·brist** (vārlē-) n., writer of v.

ver·so, n. (pl. *-os*). Any left-hand page of book (cf. RECTO); reverse of coin. [L, abl. p.p. as VERSE]

verst, n. Russian measure of length, 3,500 feet. [f. Russ. *verstá*]

ver·sus, prep. (abbr. *v.*). Against, as (Law) *Jones* v. *Smith,* (Cricket &c.) *Surrey* v. *Kent.* [L, = towards, against]

vert¹, n. (Law, hist.) all that bears green leaves in forest, right to cut this; (Herald.) the tincture green. [OF, f. L *viridis* green]

vert², n., & v.i., (colloq.). Convert or pervert; (vb) leave one Church for another. [coined as neutral form]

ver·tebra, n. (pl. *-ae*). Each segment of backbone (*false v.,* fixed, as os sacrum & coccyx in man, *true v.,* movable; neither expression now used in human anat.). Hence **ver·tebr**AL a., **ver·tebral**LY² adv., **vertebro-** comb. form. [L (*vertere* turn)]

ver·tebrate (-*at*), a. & n. (Animal) having a spinal column or a notochord, esp. (member) of the division *Vertebrata,* including mammals, birds, reptiles, amphibians, & fishes. Hence **ver·tebrāted** [-ATE²] a. [f. L *vertebratus* jointed (as prec., see -ATE²)]

vertebra·tion, n. Formation of, division into, vertebrae or similar segments. [-ATION]

ver·tex, n. (pl. usu. *-icēs*). Highest point, top, apex; (Anat.) crown of head; (Geom.) each angular point of triangle, polygon, &c., *v. of an angle,* meeting-point of lines that form it. [L, gen. *-icis,* = whirlpool, head, vertex, (*vertere* turn)]

ver·tical, a. Of, at, the vertex or highest point; at the zenith; perpendicular to plane of horizon; (Anat.) of the crown of the head; *v. angles,* each pair of opposite angles made by two intersecting lines; *v.* (= AZIMUTH-) *circle*; *v. fins* (dorsal, anal, & caudal); *v. plane,* plane perpendicular to the horizon. Hence **vertica·**LITY n., **ver·tical**LY² adv. (N.) v. line, plane, or circle; *out of the v.,* not v. [F (prec., see -AL)]

ver·ticil, n. (bot., zool.). Whorl, set of parts radiating from axis. Hence **verti·cillate(d)** [-ATE²] aa., **verti·cillate**LY² adv. [f. L *verticillus* whorl of spindle, dim. of VERTEX]

ver·tigo (*or* -tī·-), n. Giddiness, dizziness, as *subjective, objective, v.* (in which patient feels as if he, as if surrounding objects, were turning round), *essential v.* (without apparent cause). Hence **verti·gin**OUS a., **verti·ginous**LY² adv., **verti·ginous**NESS n. [L, gen. *-ginis,* = whirling, dizziness, (*vertere* turn)]

vertu. See VIRTU.

Verulā·mian (-rōō-), a. Of Francis Bacon, Baron Verulam, Viscount St Albans, d. 1626; of St Albans. [*Verulam,* ancient city near site of St Albans, + -IAN]

ver·vain, n. Kinds of weedy plant with small blue, white, or purple flowers, formerly believed to have various virtues & used as amulet &c. [f. OF *verveine* f. L VERBENA]

verve (vārv), n. Enthusiasm, energy, vigour, in artistic or literary work. [F, etym. dub.]

ver·vet, n. A small S.-Afr. monkey often employed by organ-grinders. [F, etym. dub.]

vĕ·ry[1], a. & adv. Real, true, genuine, that is such in the truest or fullest sense, as *v. God of v. God, has shown himself a v. knave, the veriest simpleton knows that, must consent from v. shame,* (somewhat archaic exc. in foll. uses); (with *the, this, that,* or possessive adj., emphasizing identity, coincidence, significance, or extreme degree) *this is the v. spot I found it on, speaking in this v. room, the v. fact of his presence is enough, you are the v. man I am looking for, a needle is the v. thing (for our purpose), come here this v. minute, grieves me to the v. heart, the v. stones cry out, his v. servants bully him, drank it to the v. dregs*; (with *a*) *a v. little more will do, give me only a v. little*; (adv., perh. orig. adj., with superl. adj. often abs., or with *my* &c. *own*) in the fullest sense, as *drank it to the v. last drop, the v. last thing I expected, did the v. best I could, did my v. utmost, may keep it for your v. own*; (adv.: used with advv. & the positive of non-verbal adjj.; with partt. established as independent adjj., as *a v. dazzling effect, effect was v. dazzling, a v. trying time*; with p.pp. in attrib. use applied to what is not the real object of the vbl action, as *wore a v. pained, pleased, puzzled, troubled, vexed, annoyed, surprised,* &c., *expression,* but not *his expression was v. pained* &c.; & colloq. with the same p.pp. in pred. use applied to the true object & fulfilling purely vbl function, as *I was v. pleased, surprised, annoyed,* &c.; not otherwise used with vbs) in a high degree, as *that is v. easily done, v. often fails, v. easy, not v. much use, find v. few instances, gives v. little trouble,* but not *v. better* &c.; *v. well,* formula of consent or approval. [(adv. f. adj.) ME & OF *verai* ult. f. L *verus* true]

Vĕ·ry[2], n. attrib. *V. light* (projected from *V. pistol* for temporarily illuminating part of battle-field &c.). [S. W. *V.*, inventor]

vesī·ca, n. (anat., bot.). Bladder, cyst, sac, esp. (whence **vĕ·sico**CELE, **vĕsico·**TOMY, nn.) urinary bladder; *v.* (*piscis* or *piscium* = fish's or fishes'), the pointed oval (()) used as an aureole in medieval sculpture & painting. Hence **vĕ·sic**AL a., **vesico**- comb. form. [L]

vĕ·sicate, v.t. Raise blisters on. Hence **ve·sic**ANT(2), **ve·sicat**ORY, aa. & nn., **vesica·**TION n. [f. prec. + -ATE[3]]

vĕ·sicle, n. (anat., bot., geol.). Small bladder, cell, bubble, or hollow structure. Hence **vesi·cul**AR[1], **vesi·cul**ATE[2], **vesiculi·**FEROUS, **vesi·culi**FORM, **vesi·cul**OSE[1], **vesi·cul**OUS, aa., **vesicula·**TION n., **vesiculo**- comb. form. [f. L *vesicula* dim. of VESICA]

ve·sper, n. (*V-*) Venus as evening-star, (poet.) evening; (pl.) sixth of the seven canonical hours of the breviary, EVEN[1]-song; *v.* (*-bell*), bell that calls to vv.; *Sicilian Vv.*, massacre of French residents in Sicily in 1282, begun at stroke of v.-bell. [L, cf. HESPERUS]

ve·spertine, a. Of, done in, the evening; (Bot., of flowers) opening, (Zool.) flying, in the evening; (Astron.) descending towards horizon at sunset. [f. L *vespertinus* (VESPER)]

ve·spiary, n. Nest of wasps. [irreg. f. L *vespa* wasp, after *apiary*]

ve·spine, a. Of wasps. So **ve·spi**FORM a. [f. L *vespa* wasp + -INE[1]]

ve·ssel, n. Hollow receptacle esp. for liquid, e. g. cask, cup, pot, bottle, dish; ship, boat, esp. large one; (Anat.) duct, canal, holding or conveying blood or other fluid, esp. *blood-v.*; (Bot.) chain of cells that have lost intervening partitions, duct; (bibl. or allus. esp. facet.) person viewed as recipient or exponent, as *chosen v.* (*Acts* ix. 15), *weaker v.*, woman (1 *Pet.* iii. 7), *vv. of wrath* (*Rom.* ix. 22). Hence **ve·ssel**FUL n. [AF, f. OF *vaissel* f. L *vascellum* dim. of VAS]

vest[1], n. (Shop) waistcoat; (also *underv.*) knitted or woven undergarment; piece, usu. V-shaped, on front of body of woman's gown; (archaic) clothing, dress. Hence **ve·st**ING[1](3) n. [f. F f. It. *veste* f. L *vestis* garment, cogn. w. Gk *esthēs* dress]

vest[2], v.t. & i. Furnish (person *with* authority, powers, property, &c.); *v.* (property, power) *in* (person), confer formally on him an immediate fixed right of present or future possession of it (*vested rights, estate,* &c., possession of which is determinately fixed in a person & is subject to no contingency); (of property, right, &c.) *v. in* (person), come to him; (poet.) clothe. [f. OF *vestir* f. L *vestire -it-* clothe (as prec.)]

ve·sta, n. (Rom. Myth., *V-*) goddess of the hearth; (Astron., *V-*) an asteroid; (*wax*) *v.*, wax match to be ignited by friction (*fusee v.*, kind for use in strong wind). [L, cf. Gk *Hestia*]

ve·stal, a. & n. Of the goddess Vesta or the v. virgins; *v.* (*virgin*), virgin consecrated to Vesta, vowed to chastity, & charged with care of sacred fire perpetually burning on her altar, hence, woman of spotless chastity, esp. one who devotes her life to religion, nun. [f. L *Vestalis* a. & n. (as prec., see -AL)]

ve·stibule, n. Ante-chamber, hall, lobby, next to outer door of house & from which doors open into various rooms; porch of church &c.; (U.S.) *v.* (= CORRIDOR) *train*; (Anat.) chamber or channel communicating with others, esp. *v. of the ear,* central cavity of labyrinth of internal ear. Hence **vesti·bul**AR[1], **vesti·bul**ATE[2] (anat.), **ve·stibul**ED[2], aa. [f. L *vestibulum,* etym. dub.]

ve·stige, n. Foot-print (now only fig.), track, trace, evidence, sign, as *vv. of an* *earlier civilization, found no vv. of his presence*; (loosely, w. neg.) atom, particle, as *without a v. of clothing, has not a v. of evidence for this assertion*; (Biol.) part, organ, now degenerate & of little or no utility but ancestrally well developed. Hence **vesti·gi**AL (esp. biol.), **vesti·gi**ARY[1], aa. [F, f. L *vestigium* footstep, etym. dub.]

ve·stiture (-tsh*er*), n. (zool.). Hair, scales, &c., covering a surface. [f. med. L *vestitura* f. L as VEST[2], -URE]

ve·stment, n. Garment, esp. official or state robe; any of the official garments of clergy, choristers, &c., worn during divine service, esp. chasuble; altar-cloth. [f. OF *vestement* f. L *vestimentum* (as VEST[2], see -MENT)]

ve·stry, n. Room, building, attached to church & in which vestments are kept & put on; chapel attached to non-liturgical church & used for prayer-meetings &c.; (also *common, general, ordinary, v.*) ratepayers of a parish, (also *select v.*) representatives of these, assembled for dispatch of parochial business; (room used for) meeting of either of these bodies; *v.-clerk*, officer chosen by v. to keep parish accounts &c.; *ve·stryman*, member of a v. Hence **ve·str**AL a. [f. OF *vestiarie* f. L *vestiarium* wardrobe (as VEST[1], see -ARIUM)]

ve·strydom, n. (Corrupt, inefficient) government by vestry. [-DOM]

ve·sture (-tsh*er*), n., & v.t., (poet., rhet.). Garments, dress, clothes; covering; (vb) clothe. [OF, as VESTITURE]

ve·sturer, n. Church official in charge of vestments; sub-treasurer of cathedral or church. [f. prec. + -ER[1]]

Vesū·vian, v-, a. & n. Of Vesuvius; volcanic. (N., *v*-) kind of fusee match; (also **vesu·vian**ITE[1] n.) brown or green mineral first found on Vesuvius. [f. L *Vesuvius* + -AN]

vet, n., & v.t., (colloq.). = VETERINARY; (vb) examine or treat (beast, & transf.). [abbr.]

vetch, n. Kinds of plant of bean family largely used, wild or cultivated, for forage, esp. *common v.*, tare. Hence **ve·tch**Y[2] a. [f. ONF *veche* f. L *vicia*]

ve·tchling, n. Plant allied to vetch. [-LING[1]]

vĕ·teran, a. & n. (Person) who has grown old in or had long experience of (esp. military) service or occupation, as *Wellington's vv., a v. golfer*; of a v., composed of vv., as *v. service, troops.* Hence **ve·teran**IZE(3) v.t. [f. L *veteranus* a. & n. (*vetus -eris* old, see -AN)]

vĕ·terinary, a. & n. Of, for, (the treatment of) diseases & injuries of domestic animals, as *v. surgeon, science, college*; (n., abbr. *vet*; also **veterinār·i**AN n.) v. surgeon. [f. L *veterinarius* f. *veterinae* cattle]

vē·to, n. (pl. *-oes*), & v.t. Constitutional right of sovereign, president, governor, upper house of legislature, &c., to reject a legislative enactment (*suspensory v.*, suspending but not necessarily preventing completion of measure), whence **ve·to**IST(2) n.; (official message conveying) such rejection; prohibition, as *interposed his v., put a* or *his v. on the proposal*; (vb) exercise v. against (bill &c.), forbid authoritatively. [L, = I forbid, w. ref. to its use by tribune of the people in nullifying measures]

vettur·a (-oora), n. (pl. *-re* pron. -rā). Italian four-wheeled carriage. [It.]

vex, v.t. Anger by slight or petty annoyance, irritate, as *this would v. a saint, how vexing!*, whence **ve·xĕd**LY[2], **ve·xing**LY[2], advv.; (archaic) grieve, afflict; (poet., rhet.) put (sea &c.) into state of commotion; *a vexed* (much discussed) *question.* [f. OF *vexer* f. L *vexare*]

vexa·tion, n. Vexing, being vexed; harassing by means of malicious or trivial litigation; state of irritation or distress, as *conceive my v., in v. of spirit*; annoying or distressing thing, as *subjected to many vv.* Hence **vexa·tio**US a., **vexa·tious**LY[2] adv., **vexa·tious**NESS n. [f. L *vexationem* (as VEX, see -ATION)]

vexi·llum, n. (pl. *-a*). (Rom. Ant.) military standard esp. of maniple, body of troops under this; (Bot., also **ve·xil** n.) large upper petal of papilionaceous flower; web of a feather, whence **ve·xil**LATE[2] a.; (Eccl.) flag on or wound round bishop's staff, processional banner or cross. Hence or cogn. **ve·xill**AR(Y)[1] aa. [L (*vehere vect-* carry)]

vī·a, n. & prep. *V. La·ctēa*, Milky Way; *v. mē·dia*, mean between extremes (esp. of Anglican church as placed between Romanism & extreme Protestantism); (prep., also *viâ*) by way of, through, as *from Exeter to York* v. *London* (also facet. of connected subjects &c.). [L, = way, road]

vī·able, a. (Of foetus or new-born child) capable of maintaining life; (of plant, animal, &c.) able to live in particular climate &c. So **viabi·lity** n. [F (*vie* life f. L *vita*, see -ABLE)]

vī·aduct, n. Long bridge-like structure, esp. series of arches, for carrying road or railway over valley or dip in ground; such road or railway. [f. L *via* way after AQUEDUCT]

vī·al, n. Small (usu. cylindrical glass) vessel for holding liquid medicines &c.; LEYDEN *v.* (= *jar*); *pour out vv. of wrath*, take vengeance (*Rev.* xv. 7), (colloq.) give vent to anger. Hence **via·l**FUL n. [as PHIAL]

viă·meter, n. = HODOMETER. [L *via* way + -METER]

vī·and, n. (usu. in pl.). Article(s) of food, victual(s). [AF *viande*, = meat, food, f. L *vivenda* things to live on (neut. pl.

gerund. of *vivere* live, taken as fem. sing.)]

viă·ticum, n. (Rom. Ant.) supplies or sum of money allowed to officer for journey on State service; eucharist as given to dying person; portable altar. [L (*via* way, see -ATIC)]

vībră·cūlum, n. (pl. *-a*). Filamentous appendage of some polyzoa serving to bring food within reach by lashing movements. Hence **vibra·cul**AR[1] a. [f. L as foll.]

vībra·te, v.i. & t. Move to & fro like pendulum, oscillate; (of sound) throb (on ear, in memory, &c.); (Physics) move unceasingly to & fro, esp. rapidly; thrill, quiver, (*with* passion &c.); cause to oscillate; (of pendulum) measure (seconds &c.) by vibrating. Hence **vi·brat**IVE, **vi·brat**ORY, aa. [f. L *vibrare* shake, swing, see -ATE[3]]

vi·bratīle, a. Capable of vibrating. Hence **vibratĭ·l**ITY n. [-ILE]

vibra·tion, n. Vibrating, oscillation; (Physics) rapid motion to & fro esp. of the parts of a fluid or an elastic solid whose equilibrium has been disturbed (*amplitude of v.*, maximum departure of vibrating body from position of rest; *forced, free, v.*, whose period is, is not, modified by an outside force). Hence **vibra·tion**AL a., **vibra·ti**UNCLE n. dim. [f. L *vibrationem* (as VIBRATE, see -ATION)]

vibra·to (vēbrah-), n. Pulsating effect in singing produced by variation of emphasis on some tone. [It.]

vibra·tor, n. Person, thing, that vibrates, esp. (Electr., Teleg.) kinds of vibrating reed, (Mus.) reed in reed-organ, (Print. inking-roller with vibrating & rotary movements, (Med.) electric or other instrument used in massage. [-OR[2]]

vībri·ssae, n. pl. Stiff coarse hair about mouth of most mammals & in nostrils of man; bristle-like feathers about mouth of some birds. [L (as VIBRATE)]

vī·broscope, n. Instrument for observing vibrations. [-SCOPE]

vibur·num, n. Kinds of shrub of honeysuckle family. [L]

vĭ·car, n. Priest of a parish the tithes of which belong to chapter or religious house or layman (cf. RECTOR); *v. of Bray*, systematic turncoat, w. ref. to 17th-c. song; *clerk, lay, secular, v.*, cathedral officer singing some parts of service; *v. choral*, clerical or lay assistant in some (esp. musical) parts of cathedral service; *v. general*, (Ch. of Eng.) official assisting (arch)bishop in ecclesiastical causes &c. (usu. his chancellor), (R.-C. Ch.) bishop's assistant in matters of jurisdiction &c.; (R.-C. Ch.) *cardinal v.*, Pope's delegate acting as bishop of diocese of Rome, *v. apostolic*, missionary or titular bishop (whence **vĭcăr·i**ATE[1](1) n.), *v. forane*, dignitary appointed by bishop to exercise limited local jurisdiction, *V. of* (*Jesus*) *Christ*, Pope. Hence **vi·car**SHIP n. [f. OF *vicaire* f. L *vicarius* deputed, deputy, (as VICE-, see -ARY[1])]

vĭ·carage (-ĭj), n. Benefice, residence, of vicar. [-AGE]

vĭcār·ial, a. Of, serving as, a vicar. [-AL]

vĭcār·ious, a. Deputed, delegated, as *v. authority*; acting, done, for another, as *v. work, suffering, v. sacrifice* (of Christ in place of sinner). Hence **vicar·ious**LY[2] adv., **vicar·ious**NESS n. [f. L as VICAR*ius* + -OUS]

vice[1], n. Evil esp. grossly immoral habit or conduct, (particular form of) depravity, serious fault, as *has the v. of gluttony, drunkenness is not among his vv., v. is duly punished & virtue rewarded in fifth act, has no redeeming v.* (to relieve overpowering rectitude); defect, blemish, (*of* character, literary style, &c.); fault, bad trick, in horse &c., as *has no vv., is free from v., has one v.*; (now rare) morbid state of physical system, as *inherited vv. of constitution*; (*V-*) buffoon in a MORALITY. [OF, f. L *vitium*]

vice[2], n., & v.t. Instrument with two jaws between which thing may be gripped usu. by operation of screw so as to leave the hands free for working upon it, as *bench v.* (attached to carpenter's or machinist's bench), *instantaneous-grip v.*, *grips like a v.*; (vb) secure (material to be worked upon, or fig.) in v. [(vb f. n.) ME, = screw, winding-stair, f. OF *vis* f. L *vitis* vine]

vice[3] (vīs), n. (colloq.). = VICE-*president* &c.

vī·cĕ[4], prep. In the place of, as *gazetted as captain v. Captain Jones promoted.* [L, abl. of **vix vicis* change]

vice- (vīs), pref. (= prec.) forming nn. w. sense 'person acting or qualified to act in place of or next in rank to', w. their derivv., as: *-a·dmiral*, ADMIRAL of third grade; *-a·dmiralty*, office of v.-admiral (*v.-admiralty courts*, tribunals with admiralty jurisdiction in British colonial possessions); *-a·gent*; *-chair·man(ship)*; *-cha·mberlain* (esp. deputy of lord chamberlain); *-cha·ncellor*, (Univv.) deputy chancellor discharging most administrative duties, (Law, formerly) judge in chancery division of High Court of Justice, (R.-C. Ch.) cardinal at head of the branch of chancery in charge of bulls &c.; *-cha·ncellorship*; *-co·nsul(ship)*; *-dea·n*, subdean; *-go·vernor*; *-ki·ng*, = VICEROY; *-pre·sident(ship)*, *-pre·sidency*; *pri·ncipal*; *-quee·n* rare, woman acting as viceroy, viceroy's wife; *-re·gent*; *-reine* (rān), viceroy's wife; *-she·riff*; *-trea·surer-(ship)*; *-war·den.*

vicegĕ·rent (*also* -ēr-), a. & n. (Person) exercising delegated power, deputy, as *regard the Pope as God's v.* Hence **vicege·renc**Y n. [f. med. L *vicegerentem* nom. *-ens* (prec. + L *gerere* carry on, see -ENT)]

vice·nnial, a. Lasting, happening every, twenty years. [f. L *vicennium* period of 20 years (*viginti* 20 + *annus* year) + -AL]

vi·ceroy, n. Ruler exercising royal authority in colony, province, &c., as *V. of India.* Hence **vicerē·gAL, viceroy·AL,** aa., **viceroy·alTY, vi·ceroySHIP,** nn. [OF (VICE- + *roy* king f. L *regem* nom. *rex*)]

vi·cĕ ver·sa (-*a*), adv. or ellipt. sent. (The same is true, on the corresponding supposition, &c.) with the order of terms changed, the other way round, as *the man blames his wife & v. v.* (she him), *cat stole the dog's dinner & v. v.* (he hers), *calls black white & v. v.* (white black). [L, (VICE[4], *versa* abl. fem. p.p. of *vertere* turn)]

Vichy (water) (vē·shē), n. A mineral water. [*Vichy* in France]

vi·cinage (-ĭj), n. Neighbourhood, surrounding district; relation of neighbours. [refash. f. OF *voisinage* (*voisin* neighbouring f. L *vicinus* f. *vicus* village, quarter, + -AGE)]

vici·nity, n. Surrounding district; nearness in place (*to*); close relationship (*to*). [f. L *vicinitatem* (as prec., see -TY)]

vi·cious (-shus), a. Of the nature of vice, morally evil or injurious, as *v. tendencies, courses, life*; addicted to vice, as *v. companions*; (of horse &c.) having vices; (of language, reasoning, &c.) incorrect, faulty, unsound, corrupt, as *a v. style, a notoriously v. manuscript, v.* CIRCLE[1]; *v. union* (surg.), faulty joining of fractured ends of bone, resulting deformity; bad-tempered, spiteful, as *v. dog, mood, remarks.* Hence **vi·ciousLY**[2] adv., **vi·ciousNESS** n. [OF, f. L *vitiosus* (as VICE[1], see -OUS)]

vici·ssitude, n. Change of circumstances esp. of fortune, as *a life marked by vv.*; (archaic, poet.) regular change, alternation. Hence **vicissitu·dinOUS** a. [f. L *vicissitudo -dinis* (*vicissim* by turns, as VICE[4], see -TUDE)]

vi·ctim, n. Living being sacrificed to a deity or in performance of religious rite; person, thing, injured or destroyed in pursuit of an object, in gratification of a passion &c., or as result of event or circumstance, as *the vv. of his relentless ambition, fell a v. to his own avarice, the vv. of disease, of a railway accident*; prey, dupe, as *held the v. in his talons, the numerous vv. of the confidence trick.* [f. L *victima*]

vi·ctimize, v.t. Make (person &c.) the victim of a swindle &c. or of one's ambition, loquacity, &c.; (Trade-Un.) make (ringleader &c.) suffer by dismissal or other exceptional treatment. Hence **victimizA·TION** n. [-IZE]

vi·ctor, n. (rhet.). Conqueror in battle or contest (also attrib., as *v. troops, sword*). Hence **vi·ctrESS**[1] n. [L (*vincere vict-* conquer, -OR[2])]

victor·ia, n. Low light four-wheeled carriage with seat for two & raised driver's seat & with falling top; kinds of gigantic water-lily; kinds of domestic pigeon; *V. cross* (abbr. *V.C.*, *pron.* vē sē), decoration for conspicuous act of bravery founded by Queen V. in 1856. [L, = victory (as prec.)]

Victor·ian, a. & n. Of, (person esp. author) living in, the reign of Queen Victoria (1837–1901); = EARLY-*V.*; *V. order* (founded by Queen Victoria in 1896 & conferred usu. for great service rendered to sovereign). [-AN]

victori·ne (-ēn), n. Woman's fur tippet with long narrow ends. [f. 1849; perh. named f. Queen Victoria]

victor·ious, a. Conquering, triumphant; marked by victory (*v. day* &c.). Hence **victor·iousLY**[2] adv., **victor·iousNESS** n. [f. OF *victorieux* f. L *victoriosus* (VICTORIA, -OUS)]

vi·ctory, n. Defeat of enemy in battle or opponent in contest, as *battle ended in a decisive v., fought hard for v., hero of many vv.*, (fig.) *gained a* or *the v. over his passions, Cadmean* or PYRRHIC[2] *v.*, MORAL *v.*; (*V*-), (statue of) goddess of v. (*winged* &c. *V.*). [f. OF *victorie* f. L VICTORIA]

vic·tual (-tl), n., & v.t. & i. (Usu. pl.) food, provisions; (vb) supply with vv., obtain stores, eat vv. Hence **vic·tualLESS** a. [(vb f. n.) ME & OF *vitaille* f. LL *victualia* neut. pl. (taken as fem. sing.) of *victualis* of nourishment (L *victus -ūs* food f. *vivere* live, see -AL)]

victualler (vi·tler), n. One who furnishes victuals, esp. *licensed v.*, public-house-keeper licensed to sell spirits &c.; ship employed to carry stores for other ships. [f. OF *victuailleur* (prec., -OR[2])]

vic·tualling, n. In vbl senses; ***v.-bill***, custom-house warrant for shipment of bonded stores; *v.-note* (nav.), order authorizing ship's steward to victual a seaman; *v.-office* (for supplying provisions to navy); *v.-yard* (adjoining dockyard, for naval stores). [-ING[1]]

vicu·gna, -uña (-kōōnya), n. S.-Amer. mammal allied to camel & hunted for its flesh & wool; *v. wool* (commerc.), mixture of wool & cotton, also wool of the v. [Sp. f. Peruv.]

vi·dē (*or* -ĭ), vb imperat. (abbr. *v.*). (In formal or facet. reference to passage in book &c.) see, as *v. supra, infra,* see above, below, QUOD[2] *v., v. the press passim.* [L, imperat. of *vidēre*]

vidē·licĕt, adv. (abbr. *viz*, pron. nā·mlĭ). That is to say, in other words, namely, (usu. following words that promise or more or less clearly require explanation &c. as: *under the following conditions, viz that* &c.; *a permanent board of three, viz,* &c.; opp. to *i.e.*, which introduces rather optional explanation). [L (*vidēre licet* one may see)]

vidette. See VEDETTE.

vi·dimus, n. (pl. -*uses*). Inspection of accounts &c.; abstract of document &c. [L, = we have seen (*vidēre*)]

vie, v.i. (vying). Strive for superiority, carry on rivalry, (*with* another *in* quality, *in doing*). [ME (*en*)*vien* f. OF *envier* INVITE]

Viĕnnese (-ēz), a. & n. (pl. same). (Inhabitant) of Vienna. [-ESE]

vī ĕt ar·mĭs, adv. (law). With force & arms, with violence. [L]

view (vū), n., & v.t. Inspection by eye, survey, (*of* surroundings &c.); (Law) inspection by jury of place, property, &c., concerned in a case, or of dead body; power of seeing, range of vision, as *stood in full v. of* (visible to) *the crowd, came in v. of* (where one could be seen from or see) *the castle, passed from our v.* (sight); what is seen, scene, prospect, as *a superb v.*; picture &c. representing this; mental survey, as *take a general v. of the subject*; manner of considering a subject, opinion, mental attitude, as *takes a different v., his v. is that we are the aggressors, takes a favourable v. of her conduct, holds extreme vv.* (in politics &c.); intention, design, as *will this meet your vv.?, cannot fall in with your vv., cat has vv. upon the larder*; *in v. of*, having regard to, considering, as *in v. of recent developments we do not think this step advisable*, (vulg.) = *with a v. to* (1), (see also above); *on v.*, open to inspection; *with a v. to*, (1; also *with the v. of*; vulg. *with a v. of*) for the purpose of, as a step towards, as *with a v. to extending* (vulg. *extend*) *our trade, with a v. to further hostilities*, (2) in the hope or on the chance of getting, with an eye to, as *said this with a v. to the vacant secretaryship*, (3, vulg.) = *in v. of*; *to the v.*, openly, in public; BIRD'*s-eye v.*; *dissolving vv.* (see DISSOLVE); *have in v.*, have as one's object, also, bear (circumstance) in mind in forming judgement &c.; POINT[1] *of v.*; *private v.* (of picture exhibition, open only to exhibitors' friends, critics, &c.); *v.-finder*, part of camera showing limits of picture; *v. halloo·*, huntsman's shout on seeing fox break cover. (Vb) survey with the eyes; survey mentally, form mental impression or judgement of, as *subject may be viewed in different ways, does not v. the matter in the right light, he* or *the proposal is viewed unfavourably by the authorities*. Hence **view·**ABLE a. [(vb f. n.) AF, f. OF *veue* fem. p.p. as n. f. *voir* see f. L *vidēre*]

view·less, a. (poet., rhet.). Invisible. [-LESS]

view·y, a. (colloq.). Given to odd or fanciful views, faddy. Hence **view·**INESS n. [-Y[2]]

vĭ·gil, n. Keeping awake during the time usually given to sleep, watchfulness, as *keep v.*; (usu. pl.) nocturnal devotions; eve of a festival, esp. eve that is a fast. [f. OF *vigile* f. L *vigilia* (*vigil* awake)]

vĭ·gilance, n. Watchfulness, caution, circumspection, so **vĭ·gil**ANT a., **vĭ·gilant**LY[2] adv.; (Med.) insomnia; *v. committee*, self-organized body for maintenance of order &c. in imperfectly organized community. [F, f. L *vigilantia* (*vigilare* watch, as prec,. -ANCE)]

vignette (vēnyĕ·t), n., & v.t. (Archit.) ornament of leaves & tendrils; flourishes round capital letter in MS.; engraved illustration, esp. on title-page of book, not enclosed in definite border; photograph or portrait showing only head & shoulders with background gradually shaded off; (fig.) character sketch; (vb) make portrait of (person) in v. style, shade off (portrait) thus, whence **vigne·tt**ER[2](2), **vigne·tt**IST n. [F, dim. as VINE]

vigorō·so, adv. (mus.). With vigour. [It.]

vĭ·gour (-*er*), n. Active physical strength or energy; flourishing physical condition; healthy growth, vitality, vital force; mental strength or activity as shown in thought or speech or literary style, forcibleness, trenchancy, animation. Hence or cogn. **vĭ·gor**OUS, **vĭ·gour**LESS, aa., **vĭ·gorous**LY[2] adv., **vĭ·gorous**NESS n. [AF, f. L *vigorem* (*vigēre* be lively, see -OR[1])]

vī·king, n. Northern sea robber of 8th to 10th c. Hence **vī·king**ISM(2) n. [f. ON *víkingr*, perh. f. OE *wícing* (*wíc* camp, -ING[3])]

vila·yet (-lah-), n. Province of Turkish empire. [Turk., f. Arab. *welāyet* district]

vile, a. Worthless; morally base, depraved, shameful, abject, as *the v. trade of an informer, sycophant's v. practices, the vilest of mankind*; (colloq.) abominably bad, as *a v. pen, v. pastry*. Hence **vi·le**LY[2] adv., **vi·le**NESS n. [OF (*vil vile*), f. L *vilis*]

vĭ·lify, v.t. Defame, traduce, speak ill of; (rare) degrade, debase. Hence **vili**FICA·TION, **vĭ·lifi**ER[1], nn. [f. LL *vilificare* (prec., -FY)]

vĭ·lipend, v.t. (literary). Treat contemptuously, disparage. [f. L *vilipendere* (as VILE + *pendere* weigh)]

vi·lla, n. Country residence; detached suburban house. Hence **vi·lla**DOM n., suburban society. [L, = farm-house, cf. *vicus* village]

vi·llage (-ĭj), n. Assemblage of houses &c. larger than hamlet & smaller than town. [ME & OF f. L *villaticus* of a VILLA (see -AGE)]

vi·llager, n. Inhabitant of a village (usu. implying rusticity). [-ER[1]]

vi·llain (-*an*), n. & a. Person guilty or capable of great wickedness, scoundrel, as *has played the v., plays the vv. in melodramas*, (colloq., playful) *you little* &c. *v.* (rascal); (archaic) rustic, boor; (Hist., also *villein* a. & n.) feudal serf, tenant holding by menial services, so **vi·lla(i)n**AGE, **-e(i)nage**, n.; (adj.) of, done by, a v., as *v. services*. [ME & OF *vilein* f.

pop. L **villanus* farm-servant (as VILLA, see -AN)]
vi·llainous, a. Worthy of a villain, vile, wicked, so **vi·llainy**[2] n.; (colloq.) abominably bad, as *a v. scrawl, style, hotel.* Hence **vi·llainously**[2] adv., **vi·llainousness** n. [-OUS]
villane·lle (-ĕl), n. Form of (esp. French) poem of 19 lines on two rhymes. [F, f. It. *villanella*]
villeggiatur·a (-ĕjahtoora), n. Stay, retirement, in the country. [It.]
villein. See VILLAIN.
Ville Lumière (F), n. (Sobriquet of) Paris. [F, = town (that is) light or enlightenment]
vi·llus, n. (pl. -ī). (Anat.) each of the short hairlike processes on some membranes esp. on mucous membrane of intestine; (Bot., pl.) long soft hair covering fruit, flower, &c. Hence or cogn. **vi·lliform, vi·lloid, vi·llose**[1], **vi·llous,** aa., **villo·sity** n. [L, = shaggy hair]
vim, n. (colloq.). Vigour. [L, acc. of VIS]
vi·minal, a. (bot.). Of, producing, twigs or shoots. So **vimi·neous** a. [f. L *viminalis* (*vimen -minis* osier)]
vinā·ceous (-shus), a. Of wine or grapes; wine-red. [f. L *vinaceus* (*vinum* wine, -ACEOUS)]
vinaigre·tte (-nĭgrĕt), n. Bottle for holding aromatic vinegar &c., smelling-bottle. [F, dim. of *vinaigre* VINEGAR]
vi·ncible, a. (rare). Not invincible. [f. L *vincibilis* (*vincere* conquer, see -BLE)]
vi·ncŭlum, n. (pl. *-la*). (Alg.) line drawn over several terms to show that they have a common relation to what follows or precedes (e. g. $\overline{a+b}\times c = ac+bc$, but $a+b\times c = a+bc$; $a-\overline{b+c} = a-b-c$); (Print.) = BRACE[1]; (Anat.) = FRAENUM. [L, = bond (*vincire* bind)]
vi·ndicate, v.t. Maintain the cause of (person, religion, &c.) successfully; establish the existence or merits or justice of (one's veracity, courage, conduct, character, assertion). Hence or cogn. **vindicability, vi·ndication, vi·ndicator**[2], **vi·ndicatress**[1], nn., **vi·ndicable, vi·ndicative,** aa. [f. L *vindicare* (VIM + *dicare* assert, proclaim) lay claim to, see -ATE[3]]
vi·ndicatory, a. Tending to vindicate; (of laws) punitive. [-ORY]
vindi·ctive, a. Revengeful, given to revenge; *v.* (or *exemplary*) *damages* (awarded as punishment to defendant). Hence **vindi·ctively**[2] adv., **vindi·ctiveness** n. [f. L *vindicta* vengeance (VINDICATE) + -IVE]
vine, n. Climbing woody-stemmed plant whose fruit is the grape (*under* one's *v. & fig*[1]*-tree*); any plant with slender stem that trails or climbs, as *hop, melon, -v.*; *v.-borer,* kinds of insect destroying v.; *v.-disease,* due to PHYLLOXERA &c. Hence **vī·ny**[2] a. [f. OF *vigne* f. L *vinea* vineyard (*vinum* wine)]
vi·nĕgar, n., & v.t. Acid liquid got from wine, cider, &c., by acetous fermentation & used as condiment or for pickling (fig., often attrib., as type of sourness, as *a v. countenance*); *aromatic v.* (holding camphor &c. in solution); *toilet v.,* aromatic v. used for mixing with washing-water &c.; MOTHER[3] *of v.*; *V. Bible,* 1717 ed. with *parable of the vinegar* (for vineyard) above *Luke* xx; *v.-EEL*; *v.-plant,* microscopic fungus producing fermentation. Hence **vi·negarish**[1], **vi·negary**[2], aa. (Vb) apply v. to, make sour like v. (lit. & fig.). [f. OF *vinaigre* (*vin* wine f. L *vinum* + *aigre,* see EAGER)]
vī·nery (-erĭ), n. Vine greenhouse. [-ERY]
vi·neyard (-nyerd), n. Plantation of grape-vines. [VINE + YARD]
vingt-(et)-un (F), n. Card game in which the object is to reach the number of 21 pips without exceeding it. [F, = 21]
vini- in comb. = L *vinum* wine, as: *-culture,* cultivation of vines, so *-culturist*; *-ferous,* (of district) wine-producing; *-facteur* (-er), apparatus for making wine; *-ficator,* apparatus for collecting alcoholic vapours in wine-making.
vīno·meter, n. Apparatus for measuring alcohol in wine. [f. L *vinum* wine + -METER]
vin ordinaire (F), n. Cheap (usu. red) wine as drunk in France mixed with water.
vī·nous, a. Of, like, due to, wine, as *v. flavour, fermentation, eloquence.* So **vino·sity** n. [f. L *vinosus* (*vinum* wine, see -OUS)]
vint[1], v.t. Make (wine). [f. VINTAGE]
vint[2], n. A Russian card-game. [Russ., = screw]
vi·ntage (-ĭj), n. Season of gathering grapes; (wine made from) season's produce of grapes; *v. wines* (of well-known vv.); (poet., rhet.) wine. [f. OF *vendange* f. L *vindemia*; altered on *vintner*]
vi·ntager, n. Grape-gatherer. [prec., -ER[1]]
vi·ntner, n. Wine-merchant. Hence **vi·ntnery**(2) n. [earlier *vinter* f. OF *vinetier* f. L *vinum* wine, *vinetum* vineyard, see -ARY[1]]
vi·ol, n. Medieval (usu. 6-)stringed musical instrument, predecessor of violin &c. (*treble, tenor, bass, v.*); *bass v.* (mod.), = VIOLONCELLO; *v. class of instruments* (played with bow & capable, from having no frets, of continuous gradation). [f. OF *viele, viole,* etym. dub., cf. LL *vitula,* & FIDDLE]
viō·la[1], n. Kind of large violin, alto or tenor violin; (hist.) = prec. (*v. da braccio, da gamba,* tenor v. held in arm, bass v. held between legs). [It., as prec.]
vi·ola[2], n. Kinds of plant including pansy, esp. of single colour, & violet. [L, = violet]
violā·ceous (-shus), a. Of violet colour;

of violet family. [f. L *violaceus* (prec., -ACEOUS)]

vi·olate, v.t. Transgress, infringe, act against the dictates or requirements of (oath, treaty, law, terms, conscience); treat profanely or with disrespect (sanctuary &c.); break in upon, disturb, (person's privacy &c.); commit rape upon, ravish. So **vi·ol**ABLE a., **viola·**TION, **vi·olat**OR[2], nn. [f. L *violare* (VIS), see -ATE[3]]

vi·olence, n. Quality of being violent; violent conduct or treatment, outrage, injury, as *was compelled to use v., did v. to* (outraged, acted contrary to) *his feelings, our principles*; (Law) unlawful exercise of physical force, intimidation by exhibition of this. [OF, f. L *violentia* (as foll., see -ENCE)]

vi·olent, a. Marked by great physical force, as *a v. storm, came into v. collision, v. blows*; *v. death* (resulting from external force or from poison, cf. NATURAL); marked by unlawful exercise of force, as *laid v. hands on him*; intense, vehement, passionate, furious, impetuous, as *v. pain, sickness, abuse, controversy, discrepancy, revulsion, contrast, dislike, shock, apt to form v. attachments, is of* or *was in a v. temper*; *v. presumption* (law), one resting on almost conclusive evidence. Hence **vi·olent**LY[2] adv. [OF, f. L *violentus* (VIS, -LENT)]

vi·olet, n. & a. Kinds of plant chiefly of genus VIOLA, with blue, purple, white, or other flowers, as *common blue v., sweet v., dog-v.*; (of) the colour seen at end of spectrum opposite red, produced by slight admixture of red with blue, so **viole·s**CENT a.; kinds of v. butterfly; *v.-powder*, toilet powder scented with orris or other perfume; *v.-wood*, myall & other kinds. [f. OF *violette* (flower) & *violet* (colour), dimm. of *viole* f. L VIOLA[2]]

violi·n[1], n. Modern 4-stringed instrument of viol class held in left arm & played with bow; (also **violi·n**IST n.) player on v., as *first, second, v.* (in orchestra); *keyed v.*, instrument like piano but with strings vibrated by small bows. [f. It. *violino* dim. of VIOLA[1]]

vi·olin[2], **-ine,** n. Emetic substance contained in sweet violet. [f. F *violine* (VIOLA[2] + -IN)]

vi·olist, n. Performer on viol(a). [-IST]

violonce·llo (vē-, -tshĕ-), n. (usu. abbr. *'cello*). Bass violin, 4-stringed instrument held between player's knees. Hence **violonce·ll**IST(3) n. [It., dim. of *violone* large viol (VIOLA[1], see -OON)]

vi·per, n. Kinds of venomous snake esp. *common v.*, adder, the only poisonous snake in Gt Britain; (fig.) malignant or treacherous person. Hence or cogn. **vi·per**IFORM, **vi·per**INE[1], **vi·per**ISH[1](fig.), **vi·per**OID, **vi·per**OUS (fig.), aa. [f. OF *vipere* f. L *vipera*, perh. as VIVIPAROUS]

virā·go, n. Turbulent woman, termagant; (archaic) woman of masculine strength or spirit. [L, = female warrior (*vir* man)]

vi·rĕlay, n. Kinds of (esp. old French) poem with two rhymes to a stanza variously arranged. [f. OF *virelai, -li*]

vire·scence, n. Greenness; (Bot.) abnormal greenness in petals &c. normally of some bright colour. So **vire·s**CENT a. [f. L *virescere* become green (*virēre* be green, see -ESCENT, -ENCE)]

vir·gate[1], a. (nat. hist.). Slim, straight, & erect. [f. L *virgatus* rod-like (*virga* rod, -ATE[2])]

vir·gate[2], n. (hist.). A varying measure of land. [f. L *virga* rod + -ATE[1], cf. VERGEE]

Virgi·lian, a. Of, in the style of, the Roman poet Virgil (d. 19 B.C.). [f. L *Virgilianus* (*Virgilius* Virgil, -AN)]

vir·gin, n. & a. Woman who has had no carnal knowledge of man, maid, whence or cogn. **vir·gin**HOOD, **virgi·n**ITY, nn.; member of any order of women under a vow to remain vv.; *the* (*Blessed*) *V.*(*Mary*) (abbr. *B.V.M.*), mother of Christ; picture, statue, of the B.V.M.; female insect producing eggs without impregnation; (Astr., *V-*) = VIRGO; *v.'s bower*, = TRAVELLER'S *joy*. (Adj.) that is a v.; of, befitting, a v., as *v. modesty*; undefiled, spotless; not yet used or tried, as *v. soil, v. clay* (not fired); (of insect) producing eggs without impregnation; *v. comb* (that has been used only once for honey & never for brood); *v. honey* (taken from v. comb, also, drained from comb without heat or pressure); *v. queen*, unfertilized queen bee, (*V.Q.*) Queen Elizabeth. [f. OF *virgine* f. L *virginem*, nom. *-go*, etym. dub.]

vir·ginal, a. & n. (Archaic) that is or befits or belongs to a virgin, whence **vir·ginal**LY[2] adv.; (n., hist.; also *vv., pair of vv.*) square legless spinet used in 16th–17th cc. [(adj.) OF, f. L *virginalis* (as prec., see -AL); origin of n. use unknown]

Virgi·nia, n. One of the U.S.; tobacco from V.; *V. creeper*, a woody vine cultivated for ornament. Hence **Virgi·ni**AN a. & n. [f. VIRGIN (Queen) + -IA[1]]

virgĭ·nibus pŭeri·squĕ, L. phr. (Addressed, suited) to girls & boys (i.e. respecting innocence).

Vir·go, n. Sixth zodiacal sign; a constellation; *v. intacta* (law), virgin with hymen intact. [L, = virgin]

viride·scent, a. Greenish, tending to become green. Hence **viride·s**CENCE n. [f. LL *viridescere* (*viridis* green, see -ESCENT)]

viri·dity, n. Greenness, esp. of oysters &c. after feeding on certain vegetable organisms. [f. L *viriditas* (*viridis* green, see -TY)]

vi·rĭle (*also* vīr-), a. Of man as opp. to woman or child; of, having, procreative power; (of mind, character, literary style,

&c.) having masculine vigour or strength. So **viri'lity** n. [OF (*-il, -ile*), f. L *virilis* (*vir* man, see -ILE)]

virile'scent, a. (Of female animal) assuming in advanced age some male characteristics. So **virile'scence** n. [f. L as prec., -ESCENT]

vi'rose, a. Poisonous, full of virus, so **vir'ous** a.; (Bot.) having fetid smell. [f. L *virosus* (VIRUS, see -OSE[1])]

virtu' (-ōō), n. Love of fine arts; *articles of v.* (interesting from workmanship, antiquity, rarity, &c.). [f. It. *virtù* VIRTUE, virtu]

vir'tūal, a. That is such for practical purposes though not in name or according to strict definition, as *is the v. manager of the business, take this as a v. promise, constitutes a v. exculpation*; *v. focus* (optics), point at which the lines of a pencil of rays would meet if produced; *v. velocity* or *displacement*, infinitesimal displacement of the point of application of a force measured in the direction of that force. Hence **virtua'lity** n., **vir'tually**[2] adv. [f. med. L *virtualis* (irreg. as foll., see -AL)]

vir'tue (-ū), n. Moral excellence, uprightness, goodness, as *v. is its own reward, make a v. of necessity,* feign alacrity or sense of duty while acting under compulsion; particular moral excellence, as *patience is a v., she has every v., the (s ven) cardinal vv.* (*natural vv.*, justice, prudence, temperance, fortitude, *theological vv.*, faith, hope, charity); chastity esp. of women, as *a woman of v.*; good quality, as *has the v. of being adjustable, of resisting temperature*; inherent power, efficacy, as *no v. in such drugs*; (pl.) seventh ORDER[1] of angels; *by* or *in v. of,* on the strength of, on the ground of, as *claims it in v. of his long service, is entitled to it by v. of his prerogative.* Hence **vir'tueless** a. [f. F *vertu* f. L *virtutem* nom. *-tus* (*vir*, see VIRILE)]

virtuō'so, n. (pl. *-i*, pron. -ē). Person with special knowledge of or taste for works of art or virtu; person skilled in the mechanical part of a fine art. Hence **virtuŏ'sity, virtuo'soship,** nn. [It. (as VIRTU, see -OSE[1])]

vir'tuous, a. Possessing, showing, moral rectitude; chaste. Hence **vir'tuously**[2] adv., **vir'tuousness** n. [f. OF *vertuous* f. LL *virtuosus* for *-tutosus* (as VIRTUE, see -OUS)]

vi'rulent (-ū-, -ŏŏ-), a. Poisonous; caused by or containing virus, as *v. ulcer*, so [irreg.] **viruli'ferous** a. (med.); malignant, bitter, as *v. animosity, tone, abuse.* Hence or cogn. **vi'rulence** n., **vi'rulently**[2] adv. [f. L *virulentus* (foll., see -LENT)]

vir'us, n. Morbid poison, poison of contagious disease, as *smallpox v.*; (fig.) moral poison; (fig.) malignity, acrimony. [L, = poison]

vīs, n. (mech.). *V.* INERTIAE; *v. mor'tūa*, force that does no work, dead force; *v. vī'va*, living force (= mass × square of velocity) of moving body. [L, = force]

visa. See VISÉ (etym.).

vi'sage (-zĭj), n. (now chiefly literary). Face, countenance. Hence **-visaged**[2] a. [OF, f. L *visus* look (*vidēre vis-* see), see -AGE]

visard. See VISOR.

vis-à-vis (vē'zahvē'), adv. & n. In a position facing one another; opposite *to.* (N.) person facing another esp. in some dances; kinds of carriage & couch in or on which persons sit facing each other. [F, = face to face (*vis* face f. L as VISAGE)]

viscă'cha, viz- (-tsha), n. S.-Amer. burrowing rodent with valuable fur. [of native orig.]

vi'scera, n. pl. The interior organs in the great cavities of the body (e. g. brain, heart, liver), esp. in the abdomen (e. g. the intestines). Hence **vi'sceral** a., **visceri-, viscero-,** comb. forms. [L, pl. of *viscus -eris*]

vi'scerate, v. t. Disembowel. [prec., -ATE[2]]

vi'scid, a. Sticky; semifluid. So **visci'dity** n. [f. LL *viscidus* (*viscum* mistletoe, birdlime, & see -ID[1])]

vi'scin, n. Sticky substance got from mistletoe & used in birdlime. [F, f. *viscum*, prec., -IN]

vi'scose, n. Cellulose dissolved to the viscous state in which it can be drawn into yarn for use as artificial silk; (attrib.) made from v., as *v. silk.* [f. obs. *viscose* a. f. L as VISCOUS]

viscŏ'sity, n. Stickiness; (Physics, of fluids, semifluids, & gases) internal friction, power of resisting a change in the arrangement of the molecules, whence **visco'meter, visco'metry, viscosi'meter,** nn. [f. OF *viscosite* (as VISCOUS, see -TY)]

vis'count, n. Noble ranking between earl & baron (esp. as courtesy title of earl's eldest son). Hence or cogn. **vis'countcy, vis'countess**[1], **vis'countship** or **vis'county**[4], nn. [f. OF *visconte* (VICE- + *counte* COUNT[3])]

vi'scous, a. Sticky; (Physics) having viscosity. Hence **vi'scousness** n. [f. L *viscosus* (as VISCID, see -OUS)]

visé (vē'zā), n., & v.t. (*viséd* or *-é'd*). Indorsement on passport &c. showing that it has been found correct; (vb) mark with v. [p.p. of F *viser* inspect f. L *vidēre vis-* see; F has *visa* n.]

vi'sible (-z-), a. That can be seen by the eye; that can be perceived or ascertained, apparent, open, as *has no v. means of support, spoke with v. impatience*; prepared to receive callers (*is she v.?*); *the v. church*, whole body of professed believers; *v. horizon*, the line that bounds sight; *v. speech*, system of alphabetical characters designed to represent all possible articulate utterances. Hence or cogn. **visibi·lity** (in adj. senses, & esp., meteorol., naut., conditions of light & atmosphere as regards distinguishing of objects by sight), **vi·sible**NESS, nn., **vi·sib**LY[2] adv. [OF, f. LL *visibilis* (*vidēre vis-* see, see -BLE)]

vi·sion (-zhn), n., & v.t. Act or faculty of seeing, sight, as *beyond our v., has impaired his v., the field of v.*, all that comes into view when the eyes are turned in some direction, *reflected, refracted, v.* (as affected by reflected, refracted, rays of light); thing seen in dream or trance; supernatural or prophetic apparition, phantom; thing seen in the imagination, as *romantic vv. of youth, had vv. of roast beef & plum pudding*; (vb) see, present, (as) in a v. [(vb f. n.) OF, f. L *visionem* (*vidēre vis-* see, see -ION)]

vi·sionary, a. & n. Given to seeing visions or to indulging in fanciful theories; existing only in a vision or in the imagination, imaginary, fanciful, unpractical; (n., also **vi·sion**IST n.) v. person. Hence or cogn. **vi·sion**AL a., **vi·sional**LY[2] adv., **vi·sionari**NESS n. [-ARY[1]]

vi·sit (-z-), v.t., & n. Go, come, to see (person, place, &c., or abs.) as act of friendship or ceremony, on business, or from curiosity, as *have never visited us, had no time to v. the Tower, hope to v. Rome*; go, come, to see for purpose of official inspection or supervision or correction; (of disease, calamity, &c.) come upon, attack; (bibl.) punish (person, sin), avenge (his *sins* &c.) *upon* person, comfort, bless, (person *with* salvation &c.). (N.) call on a person or at a place, temporary residence with person or at place, as *was on a v. to some friends, paid him a long v., during his second v. to the East*; formal or official call for purpose of inspection &c., as DOMICILIARY *v., right of v.* (see VISITATION). Hence **vi·sit**ABLE a. [(n. f. F *visite*) f. OF *visiter* f. L *visitare* frequent. of *visere* f. *vidēre vis-* see]

vi·sitant, a. & n. (Adj., poet.) visiting. (N.) migratory bird; (poet., rhet.) visitor; (*V-*) member of an order of nuns concerned with education of young girls. [f. L as prec., -ANT]

visita·tion, n. Official visit of inspection or the like esp. bishop's examination of the churches of his diocese; boarding of vessel belonging to another State to learn her character & purpose (*right of v.* or *visit*, right to do this, not including right of search); divine dispensation of punishment or reward, notable experience compared to this; (Eccl.) festival in honour of visit of B.V.M. to Elizabeth (*Luke* i. 39); (Zool.) unusual & large migration of animals; *Nuns of the V.*, = VISITANTS; *V. of the Sick*, office of Anglican Church. [OF, f. LL *visitationem* (as VISIT, see -ATION)]

vi·siting, n. Paying visits, making calls; *have a v. acquaintance with, be on v. terms with*, know well enough to v.; *v.-book* (for names of persons to be called upon); *v.-card*, small card with one's name, address, &c., left in making call &c. [-ING[1]]

vi·sitor, n. One who visits a person or place; (in colleges &c.) official with the right or duty of occasionally inspecting & reporting, whence or cogn. **visit(at)or·ial** aa.; *visitors' book*, book in hotel, boarding-house, &c., in which vv. write remarks. [f. OF *visiteur* (as VISIT, see -OR[2])]

vi·sor (z-), **-zor, vi·sard** (-z-), **-zard,** n. (Hist.) movable part of helmet covering face; projecting front part of cap; (Hist.) mask. Hence **vi·sor**ED[2], **vi·sor**LESS, aa. [ME & AF *viser* (F *vis* face, see VIS-À-VIS)]

vi·sta, n. Long narrow view as between rows of trees; long succession of remembered or anticipated events &c., mental prospect or retrospect, as *opened up new vv.* or *a new v. to his ambition, searched the dim v. of his childhood*. Hence **vi·sta'd** [-ED[2]] a. [It., = sight, n. & fem. p.p. of *vedere* see f. L *vidēre*]

vi·sual (-zhyŏŏ- *or* -zū-), a. Of, concerned with, used in, seeing, as *v. nerve, organ, v. angle* (formed at the eye by rays from the extremities of an object viewed), *v. field* (of VISION), *v. rays*, lines of light supposed to come from object to eye, *v. point*, point in the horizontal line in which the v. rays unite. Hence **visua·li**TY n., **vi·sual**LY[2] adv. [OF, f. LL *visualis* (*visus -ūs* sight f. *vidēre* see, see -AL)]

vi·sualize, v.t. Make visible to the eye, give outward & visible form to, (mental image, idea, &c.); call up distinct mental picture of (thing imagined or formerly seen, or abs.). Hence **visualiza·tion** n. [-IZE]

vi·ta glass, n. Kind of glass by which ultra-violet or actinic rays are not excluded as by ordinary glass, but allowed their vitalizing & curative effect. [proprietary name, f. L *vita* life]

vi·tal, a. & n. Of, concerned with or essential to, organic life, as *v. energies, functions, v. power* (to sustain life), *wounded in a v. part*; essential to existence or to the matter in hand, as *a v. question, question of v. importance, secrecy is v. to the success of the scheme*; affecting life, fatal to life or to success &c., as *a v. wound, error*; *v. centre* (med.), part in which wound appears to be instantly fatal, esp. respiratory nerve-centre in medulla oblongata; *v. force* or *principle* (assumed to account for organic life); *v. statistics* (of birth, marriage, death, &c.). Hence **vi·tal**LY[2] adv. (N. pl.) v. parts, e. g. lungs, heart, brain. [OF, f. L *vitalis* (*vita* life, cogn. w. *vivere* live & Gk *bios* life, see -AL)]

vi·talism, n. (biol.). Doctrine that life

originates in a vital principle distinct from chemical & other physical forces. So **vi·talIST** n., **vitali·stIC** a. [-ISM]

vita·lity, n. Vital power, ability to sustain life; (fig., of institution, language, &c.) ability to endure & to perform its functions. [f. L *vitalis* (as VITAL, see -TY)]

vi·talize, v.t. Endow with life. [-IZE]

vi·tamin, n. Any of a number of accessory food factors of which the chemical nature is still doubtful, but which are present in known foods & preventive of known ailments or necessary to known bodily functions; *v. A, B, C, D, E,* the vv. hitherto traced to & productive of particular sources & effects. [f. L *vita* life + *amine* = *am(monia)* + -INE⁵]

vi·taphone, n. SOUND²-film with gramophone dialogue. [prec., (GRAMO)PHONE]

vite·llin, n. (chem.). Chief proteid constituent of yolk of egg. [f. foll. + -IN]

vite·llus, n. (pl. *-i*). Yolk of egg, protoplasmic contents of ovum. Hence **vi·tel-lARY**¹, **vite·llINE**¹, aa., **vitelli-**, **vitello-**, comb. forms. [L, = yolk]

viti- in comb. = L *vitis* vine, as: *-cide,* insect &c. destructive to vines; *-colous,* living on vines; *-culture,* grape-growing, so *-cu·ltural* a., *-cu·ltur(al)ist* nn.

vi·tiate (-shĭ-), v.t. Impair the quality of, corrupt, debase, contaminate, as *constitution vitiated by excess, vitiated air, blood, mind, judgement*; make invalid or ineffectual, as *a word may v. a contract.* So **vitiA·TION**, **vi·tiatOR**², nn. [f. L *vitiare* (as VICE¹), see -ATE³]

vi·trĕous, a. Of (the nature of) glass; like glass in hardness, brittleness, transparency, structure, &c.; *v. body* or *humour,* transparent jelly-like tissue filling ball of eye; *v.* ELECTRICITY. Hence or cogn. **vitreo·SITY**, **vi·treousNESS**, **vitre·sCENCE**, nn., **vitre·SCENT**, **vi·triFORM**(1), aa. [f. L *vitreus* (*vitrum* glass) + -OUS]

vi·trifȳ, v.t. & i. Convert, be converted, into glass or glass-like substance. Hence or cogn. **vitriFA·CTION**, **vitrifiaBI·LITY**, **vitriFICA·TION**, nn., **vi·trifiABLE** a. [f. F *vitrifier* (as prec., see -FY)]

vi·triol, n. Sulphuric acid or any of its salts; (fig.) caustic speech, criticism, &c.; *black v.,* impure copper sulphate; *blue* or *copper v.,* copper sulphate; *oil of v.,* concentrated sulphuric acid; *v.-throwing,* throwing v. in person's face as act of vengeance &c. Hence **vitriŏ·lIC**, **vi·triolINE**¹, aa. [ME & OF, f. med. L *vitriolum,* dim. of L *vitrum* glass]

vi·triolize, v.t. Convert into a sulphate, so **vi·triolATE**³ v.t., **vitriolA·TION** n.; poison, burn, with vitriol. Hence **vi·triolizABLE** a., **vitrioliza·TION** n. [-IZE]

Vitru·vian, a. Of Vitruvius, Roman architect of the Augustan age; *V. scroll,* scroll pattern in frieze decorations &c. [-AN]

vi·tta, n. (pl. *-ae*). (Rom. Ant.) fillet, garland, as decoration of priest, victim, statue, &c.; lappet of mitre; (Bot.) oil-tube in fruit of some plants; (Zool.) strips of colour. So **vi·ttATE**² a. [L]

vitū·perate, v.t. Revile, abuse. Hence or cogn. **vituperA·TION**, **vitu·peratOR**², nn., **vitu·perativE** a., **vitu·perativeLY**² adv. [f. L *vituperare* (*vitu-* cogn. w. *vitium* VICE¹ + *parare* prepare), see -ATE³]

viva¹ (vē·vah), int. & n. (The cry) long live —. [It., 3rd pers. imperat. of *vivere* live, cf. VIVAT]

viva². See VIVA VOCE.

vivace (vēvah·tshā), adv. (mus.). In a lively manner. [It.]

vivā·cious, a. Lively, sprightly, animated, whence or cogn. **viva·ciousLY**² adv., **vivă·CITY** n.; (Bot.) tenacious of life, surviving winter, perennial. [f. L *vivax* (*vivere* live, -ACIOUS)]

vivandière (F), n. Woman attached to continental esp. French regiment & selling provisions & liquor.

vivār·ium, n. (pl. *-ia*). Place artificially prepared for keeping animals in their natural state, zoological garden or the like. [L (*vivus,* see VIVIFY & -ARIUM)]

vī·văt, int. & n. (The cry) long live, as *v. rex, regina,* long live the king, queen. [L, 3rd sing. subj. of *vivere* live]

vi·va vō·cĕ, adv., a., & n. Oral(ly); (n., colloq., also *viva*) oral examination. [L, = with the living voice]

vive (vēv), int. Long live, as *v. le roi* (the king), QUI VIVE. [F, 3rd sing. imperat. of *vivre* live f. L *vivere*]

vi·vers, n. pl. (Sc.). Food, victuals. [f. OF *vivres* (*vivre* live f. L *vivere*)]

vives, n. An ear disease esp. of young horses at grass. [f. F *avives* f. Sp. *avivas* f. Arab. *addhībah* (*al* the + *dhībah* she-wolf)]

vi·vid, a. (Of light or colour) bright, intense, glaring, as *v. flash of lightning, of a v. green*; (of mental faculty or impression) clear, vigorous, strongly marked, as *has a v. imagination, gave a v. description, have a v. recollection of the scene.* Hence **vi·vidLY**² adv., **vi·vidNESS** n. [f. L *vividus* (*vivere* live, see -ID¹)]

vi·vifȳ, v.t. Give life to, enliven, animate, (chiefly fig.). [f. F *vivifier* f. L *vivificare* (*vivus* living f. *vivere* live, see -FY)]

vivi·parous, a. (Zool.) bringing forth young alive, not hatching by means of egg, (cf. OVI*parous*); (Bot.) producing bulbs or seeds that germinate while still attached to parent plant. Hence **vivipă·RITY**, **vivi·parousNESS**, nn., **vivi·parousLY**² adv. [f. LL *viviparus* (*vivus,* see prec., + *parere* bring forth) + -OUS]

vi·visect, v.t. Dissect (animal, or abs.) while living. [f. foll.]

vivise·ction, n. Dissection of or (loosely) inoculation &c. tried upon living animals. Hence **vivise·ctionAL** a., **vivise·ctionIST**(2, 3), **vi·visectOR**², nn. [F, f. L *vivus,* see VIVIFY, + SECTION]

vi·vo (vē-), adv. (mus.). =VIVACE. [It.]

vi·xen, n. She-fox; quarrelsome woman, termagant. Hence **vi·xen**ISH[1], **vi·xen**LY[1], aa. [OE **fyxen*, fem. of FOX, cf. G *füchsin*]

viz. See VIDELICET.

vizard. See VISOR.

vizcacha. See VISCACHA.

vizi(e)r· (-zēr), n. High official, esp. State minister, in Mohammedan countries; *grand v.*, prime minister in Turkish empire & other countries. Hence **vizi(e)r·**ATE[1](1), **vizi(e)r·**SHIP, nn., **vizi(e)r·**IAL a. [f. Turk. *vezīr* f. Arab. *wazīr* counsellor, orig. porter (*wazara* bear burden)]

Vlach (-ahk, -ăk), a. & n. Member of a S.-E. European Latin-speaking people, Walachian or Roumanian. [Slav., ult. f. OHG *Walh* foreigner, Celt, Italian, Latin]

vō·cable, n. Word, esp. w. ref. to form rather than meaning. [F, f. L *vocabulum* (*vocare* call, cogn. w. *vox vocis* voice)]

vocă·bulary, n. (List, arranged alphabetically with definitions, of) the (principal) words used in a language or usu. in a particular book or branch of science &c., or by a particular author, as *a Livy with notes & v., a word not found in the Chaucerian v., the ever-increasing scientific v., his v.* (range of language) *is limited.* [f. med. L *vocabularius* (as prec., -ARY[1])]

vō·cal, a. & n. Of, concerned with, uttered by, the voice, as *a v. communication, v. auscultation* (of the sounds of the voice as heard through walls of chest), *v. cords*, folds of lining membrane of larynx about the opening of the glottis, *v. music* (written for or produced by the voice with or without accompaniment), *v. thrill* or *fremitus*, vibration of wall of chest in audible speech; (poet., of trees, water, &c.) endowed (as) with a voice; (Phonet.) voiced, sonant, (also) of vowel character. Hence or cogn. **vocă·l**ITY n., **vo·cal**LY[2] adv. (N.) vowel, whence **voca·l**IC a.; (R.-C. Ch.) person entitled to vote in certain elections. [f. L *vocalis* (as VOICE, see -AL)]

vo·calism, n. Use of voice in speaking or singing; vowel sound. [-ISM]

vo·calist, n. Singer (opp. to *instrumentalist*). [-IST]

vo·calize, v.t. & i. Form (sound), utter (word), with the voice, esp. make sonant, as f *is vocalized into* v; write (Hebrew &c.) with vowel points; (facet.) speak, sing, hum, shout, &c. So **vocaliz**A·TION n. [-IZE]

voca·tion, n. Divine call to, sense of fitness for, a career or occupation, as *felt no v.* (*for the ministry*), *has never had the sense of v., little or no v. to literature*; employment, trade, profession, as *mechanical vv., all vv. are overcrowded, mistook his* (chose the wrong) *v.* Hence **voca·tion**AL a., **voca·tional**LY[2] adv. [f. L *vocationem* (*vocare*, see VOCABLE & -ATION)]

vŏ·cative, a. & n. (gram.). (Case) employed in addressing person or thing. [f. L *vocativus* (*vocare*, see VOCABLE & -ATIVE)]

vōcĭ·ferate, v.t. Utter (words &c. or abs.) noisily, shout, bawl. Hence or cogn. **voci·fer**ANCE (rare), **vocifer**A·TION, **voci·ferat**OR[2], nn., **voci·fer**ANT(1) a. & n. [f. L *vociferari* (as VOICE + *ferre* bear)]

voci·ferous, a. (Of person, speech, &c.) noisy, clamorous. Hence **voci·ferous**LY[2] adv., **voci·ferous**NESS n. [f. prec. + -OUS]

vŏ·dka, n. Kind of fiery brandy distilled from rye &c. & drunk in Russia. [Russ.]

voe, n. (Shetland). Small bay, creek. [f. ON *vágr*]

vogue (vōg), n., & v.i. (Now chiefly literary) *the* prevailing fashion, as *the v. of large hats, large hats are the v.*; popular use or reception, as *has had a great v.*; *in v.*, in fashion, generally current; (vb) *v. la galère* (-ār), here goes (lit. let the galley set forth). [F, orig. = course, f. *voguer* f. It. *vogare* row in galley]

voice, n., & v.t. Sound uttered by the mouth, esp. human utterance in speaking, shouting, singing, &c., as *heard a v., did not recognize his v., cried out in a loud v., has lost her* (esp. singing-) *v., is not in v.* (proper vocal condition for singing or speaking), CHEST, HEAD[1], *-v., the v. of the cuckoo, veiled v.* (due to malformation &c.), (fig.) *sea, storm, lifts up its v.*, whence **-voice**D[2] a.; use of the v., utterance esp. in spoken or (fig.) written words, opinion so expressed, right to express opinion, as *gave v. to his indignation in a pamphlet, dog gave v. to his joy, took it* (natural phenomenon, calamity, popular outcry, &c.) *for the v.* (expression of the will, resentment, &c.) *of God, I count on your v.* (spoken or written support), *I have no v. in the matter, refused with one v.* (unanimously), (archaic, rhet.) *my v. is for peace*; (Phonet.) sound uttered with resonance of vocal chords, not with mere breath; (Gram.) set of forms of a verb showing relation of the subject to the action, as ACTIVE, PASSIVE, MIDDLE[1], *v.* (Vb) give utterance to, express, as *was chosen to v. their grievance, believe I am voicing the general sentiment when I say*; (Mus.) regulate tones of, tune, (organ &c.); (Phonet.) utter with v., make sonant, (esp. in p.p.). [(vb f. n.) f. OF *vois* f. L *vocem*, nom. *vox*]

voi·ceful, a. (poet.). Sonorous. [-FUL]

voi·celess, a. Speechless, dumb, mute; (Phonet.) not voiced. Hence **voi·celess**NESS n. [-LESS]

void, a., n., & v.t. Empty, vacant, as *a v. space, interval*; (of office) vacant, as *bishopric fell v.*; (esp. Law, of deed, promise, contract, &c.) invalid, not binding, as *null & v.*; (poet., rhet.) ineffectual, useless; *v. of*, lacking, free from, as *a proposal wholly v. of sense, his style is v. of affectation.* Hence **voi·d**LY[2] adv., **voi·d-**

NESS n. (N.) empty space, as *vanished into the v.*, (fig.) *the aching v. of his heart, cannot fill the v. made by death.* (Vb) render invalid; emit (excrement &c.); (archaic) quit, evacuate. Hence **voi·d**ABLE a. [(vb f. OF *voider*) f. OF *void(e)* perh. ult. f. L *vacuus* empty]

voi·dance, n. Ejection from benefice; vacancy in benefice; voiding. [OF (prec., -ANCE)]

voi·ded, a. In vbl senses, also (Herald., of bearing) having the central area cut away so as to show the field. [-ED[1]]

voiturette (F), n. Type of light motor vehicle.

vō·lant, a. (Zool.) flying, able to fly; (Herald.) represented as flying; (poet.) nimble, rapid. [F, f. L *volare* fly, see -ANT]

Volapü·k (-ōōk), n. Artificial international language invented about 1879 by J. M. Schleyer. Hence **Volapü·k**IST(2, 3) n. [Volapük (*vol* world + *-a-* + *pük* speech]

vō·lar, a. (anat.). Of the palm or sole. [f. L *vola* palm, sole, + -AR[1]]

vŏ·latile, a. Evaporating rapidly, as *v. salts, v.* (= ESSENTIAL) *oil*; (fig.) lively, gay, changeable, as *v. wit, writer, disposition.* Hence or cogn. **vo·latile**NESS, **volati·l**ITY nn. [OF (*-il, -ile*), f. L *volatilis* (*volare -at-* fly, -ILE)]

volă·tilize, v.t. & i. (Cause to) evaporate. Hence or cogn. **vola·tiliz**ABLE a., **volătiliz**A·TION n. [-IZE]

vol-au-vent (F), n. Kind of rich raised pie.

volcă·nic, a. Of, like, produced by, a volcano; *v. bomb,* mass of lava usually rounded & sometimes hollow; *v. glass,* obsidian. Hence **volca·n**ICALLY adv., **volcani·c**ITY n. [-IC]

volcā·no, n. (pl. *-oes*). Mountain, hill, having opening(s) in earth's crust through which lava, cinders, water, gases, &c., are expelled continuously or at intervals (*active, dormant, extinct, v.*; *submarine v.*, originating beneath sea & rising above surface by accumulation); *v.-ship,* ship loaded with combustibles for explosion on contact with another. Hence **vo·lcan**ISM(2), **vo·lcan**IST(3), **volcano·**LOGY, nn., **volcanolo·g**ICAL a. [It., f. L as VULCAN]

vole[1], n., & v.i. (In some card-games) winning of all the tricks in a deal; (vb) win all the tricks. [(vb f. n.) F, f. *voler* fly f. L *volare*]

vole[2], n. Kinds of mouse-like rodent; *water-v.*, large kind. [orig. *v.-mouse* field-mouse, cf. Icel. *vǒllr*, Norw. *voll*, Sw. *vall*, field]

vŏ·let (-ā), n. Panel, wing, of triptych. [F, = shutter, as VOLE[1]]

vŏ·litant, a. (zool.). = VOLANT. [f. L *volitare* frequent. of *volare* fly, see -ANT]

voli·tion (-shn), n. Exercise of the will; power of willing. Hence **vo·lition**AL, **voli·tion**ARY[1], **voli·tion**LESS, **vŏ·lit**IVE, aa., **voli·tional**LY[2] adv. [F, f. med. L *volitionem* (*velle* wish, pres. *volo,* see -ITION)]

vŏ·lkslied (f-, -lēt), n. Folk-song. [G]

vŏlksraad (f-, -raht), n. (hist.). Legislative assembly of Orange Free State. [S.-Afr. Du.]

vo·lley, n., & v.t. & i. Simultaneous discharge of missiles, missiles so discharged; (fig.) noisy emission (*of* oaths &c.) in quick succession; (Tennis, Lawn tennis) return of ball in play before it touches ground; (Crick.) sending of ball full to head of wicket; *half-v.*, (Lawn tennis) return of ball as soon as it touches ground, (Crick.) sending of ball so that after touching ground it flies towards head of wicket, (v.t.) return, send, (ball, or abs.) thus; *v.-gun,* machine gun discharging v. (Vb) discharge (missiles, abuse, &c., or abs.) in v.; (Tennis, Crick.) return, send, (ball, or abs.) in v.; (of missiles) fly in a v.; (of guns &c.) sound together. [(vb f. n.) f. F *volée* flight (as VOLE[1], cf. -ADE)]

vŏ·l-plane, n., & v.i. (Of aeroplane or its pilot) descent, descend, by gliding without use of engine. [f. F *vol plané* (*vol* flight, *planer* hover)]

vŏ·lt[1], v.i., & n. Make a volte; (n., var. of) VOLTE. [VOLTE]

vŏ·lt[2], n. Unit of electromotive force, the force that would carry one ampere of current against one ohm resistance. [as VOLTAIC]

vo·lta, n. (mus.; pl. *-te* pron. -tā). *Una v., due* &c. *vv.*, once, twice &c.; *prima* &c. *v.*, first &c. time. [It.]

volta- in comb. = VOLTAIC, as: *-ele·ctric,* of voltaic electricity; *-electro·meter, -meter,* instruments for measuring current, so *-me·tric* n.

vo·ltage (-ĭj), n. Electromotive force expressed in volts. [-AGE]

voltā·ic, a. Of electricity produced by chemical action, galvanic, as *v. battery, induction,* PILE[2]. Hence **vo·lta**ISM(2) n. [f. A. *Volta,* Italian physicist d. 1827, + -IC]

Voltair·(ian)ism, nn. Principles of Voltaire, scepticism. [-IAN, -ISM]

volte, n. (Fenc.) quick movement to escape thrust; circular tread of horse. [F, f. It. *volta* turn]

volte-face (-tfahs), n. Turning round, esp. (fig.) complete change of front in argument, politics, &c. [F]

vŏ·lūble, a. (Of speech or speaker) fluent, glib, whence or cogn. **volub**I·LITY, **vo·luble**NESS, nn., **vo·lub**LY[2] adv.; (archaic) revolving, rotating; (Bot., also **volu·bil**ATE[2], **vo·lubile,** aa.) twisting round a support, twining. [F, f. L *volubilis* (*volvere* roll, see -BLE)]

vŏ·lume, n. Set of (usu. printed) sheets of paper bound together & forming part or the whole of a work or comprising several works, (abbr. *vol.*), as *is now issued in 3 vv., an odd v. of* Punch, *library of 12000 vv.*, SPEAK *vv.* (*for*); (Hist.) scroll of papyrus &c., ancient form of book; (usu. pl.) wreath, coil, rounded mass, of smoke &c.; solid content, bulk, whence **volu·min**AL a.; (Mus.) fullness of tone. Hence **-volum**ED² a. [OF, f. L *volumen -minis* roll (*volvere*, see prec.)]

voluměno·meter, n. Instrument for measuring volume of a solid body by quantity of liquid &c. displaced. Hence **volumeno·**METRY n. [irreg. f. L as prec. + -O- + -METER]

volu·meter, n. Kinds of instrument for measuring volume of gas. Hence **volume·tric**(AL) aa., **volume·trical**LY² adv. [irreg. f. VOLUME + -METER]

volu·minous, a. Having coils or convolutions (of snakes, the brain, &c.; now rare); consisting of many volumes, as *a v. work*; (of writer) producing many books; of great volume, bulky, (of drapery &c.) loose or ample. Hence **volumino·**SITY, **volu·minous**NESS, nn., **volu·minous**LY² adv. [f. LL *voluminosus* (as VOLUME, see -OUS)]

vŏ·luntary, a. & n. Done, acting, able to act, of one's own free will, not constrained, purposed, intentional, as *a v. gift, there was no v. mis-statement, was a v. agent in the matter, v.* (opp. to *compulsory*) *service, army, v. confession* (of criminal, not prompted by promise or threat); brought about, produced, &c., by v. action, as *v. school* (supported by v. contributions), *v. waste* (of property by tenant's deliberate act or order); (of limb, muscle, movement) controlled by the will; (Law) *v. conveyance* (made without valuable consideration), *v. grantee* (in v. conveyance), *v. partition* (by mutual agreement, not by judgement of court). Hence **vo·luntari**LY² adv., **vo·luntari**NESS n. (N.) organ solo played before, during, or after service; one who holds that the Church or the schools should be independent of the State & supported by v. contributions, whence **vo·luntary**ISM (3) n., reliance on voluntary subscriptions & not on State aid for the maintenance of education; reliance on voluntary enlisting & not on compulsion for raising naval & military forces, **vo·luntary**IST(2) n.; (in competitions) special performance left to performer's choice. [f. F *volontaire* f. L *voluntarius* (*voluntas* free will f. *velle* will, part. st. *volent-*, **-unt-*, -ARY¹)]

volunteer·, n., & v.t. & i. Spontaneous undertaker of task &c.; person who voluntarily enters military or other service, esp. member of any of the corps of voluntary soldiers formerly organized in U.K. & provided with instructors, arms, &c., by government (often attrib., as *v. corps, manœuvres*); (vb) undertake, offer, (one's services, remark, explanation, &c., *to* do) voluntarily, make voluntary offer of one's services (*for* campaign, purpose), be a v. [(vb f. n.) as prec., w. assim. to -EER]

volu·ptuary, a. & n. Concerned with, (person) given up to, luxury & sensual gratifications. [f. L *volupt(u)arius* (as foll., see -ARY¹)]

volu·ptuous, a. Of, tending to, occupied with, sensuous or sensual gratification, as *v. life, liver, music, beauty*. Hence **volu·ptuous**LY² adv., **volu·ptuous**NESS n. [f. L *voluptuosus* (*voluptas -atis* pleasure, see -OUS; *-u-* as if f. vbl n. in *-us*; cf. *sensuous*, & VIRTUOUS)]

volū·te, n. & a. Spiral scroll characteristic of Ionic, Corinthian, & Composite capitals, whence **volu·t**ED² a.; kinds of (chiefly tropical) gasteropod often with beautiful shell, whence **vŏ·lut**OID a. & n.; (adj., bot.) rolled up. [F, f. L *voluta* (*volvere volut-* roll)]

volu·tion, n. Spiral turn; whorl(s) of spiral shell; (Anat.) convolution. [as prec., -ION]

vŏ·mit, v.t. & i., & n. Eject from stomach through mouth; puke, spew; (fig., of volcano, chimney, &c.) eject violently, belch forth. (N.) matter vomited from stomach; emetic; *black v.*, (black substance vomited in) yellow fever; *v.-nut*, = NUX VOMICA. [(n. f. L *vomitus -ūs*) f. L *vomere -it-*]

vo·mitory, a. & n. Emetic (a. & n.), so **vo·miti**VE a.; (n., Rom. ant.) each of a series of passages for entrance & exit in (amphi)theatre. [f. L *vomitorius* a., *-um* n., (as prec., see -ORY)]

vomitūrī·tion (-shn), n. Ineffectual attempt to vomit, retching; repeated vomiting. [VOMIT + L *-ur-*, desiderative, + -ITION]

vōō·dōō, n., & v.t. Use of, belief in, witchcraft & the like prevalent among W.-Ind. & U.-S. creoles & Negroes; (also *v. doctor, v. priest*) person skilled in this. Hence **voo·doo**ISM, **voo·doo**IST(2, 3), nn. (Vb) affect by v., bewitch. [(vb f. n.) Afr. *vodu*]

-vora. See -VOROUS.

vorā·cious, a. Greedy in eating, ravenous, (lit. & fig.), as *party of v. trippers, a v. appetite for scandal, a v. whirlpool*. Hence or cogn. **vora·cious**LY² adv., **vora·cious**NESS, **vorā·**CITY, nn. [f. L *vorax* (*vorare* swallow, see -ACIOUS)]

-vore. See foll.

-vorous, suf. f. L *-vorus* (*vorare* swallow) + -OUS, forming adjj. w. sense 'feeding on', as *carnivorous, graminivorous*; also *-vora*, in L neut. pl. names of animals classified by their food, as *herbivora*; also F & E *-vore* forming name of individual of such class, as *carnivore*.

vor·tex, n. (pl. *-ĭcēs, -exes*). Mass of whirling fluid, esp. whirlpool; (Physics) portion of fluid whose particles have rotatory motion; any whirling motion or mass, esp. (fig.) system, pursuit, &c., viewed as swallowing up or engrossing those who approach it, as *the v. of society*, *v.* (spiral arrangement of fibres at apex) *of the heart*; *v.-ring*, v. whose axis is a closed curve, e. g. smoke-ring puffed from smoker's lips or pipe; *v. theory* (that atoms are v.-rings in a frictionless ether). Hence **vor·tic**AL, **vor·tic**OSE[1], **vorti·cu**-LAR[1] [-UL-], aa., **vor·tical**LY[2] adv. [L, var. of VERTEX]

vor·ticel, n. Bell-shaped animalcule found in stagnant water &c. [dim. f. prec.]

vor·ticist, n. (Metaphys.) person regarding the universe, with Descartes, as a plenum in which motion propagates itself in circles; (Art) painter of recent school using vortices as the CUBIST uses cubes &c. So **vor·tic**ISM n. [f. *vortic-* st. of L VORTEX + -IST]

vorti·ginous, a. Whirling, vortical. [f. L VERTIGO, *vor-*, + -OUS]

vō·tary, n. Person vowed to the service *of* (God &c.); ardent follower, devoted adherent or advocate, (*of* system, pursuit, &c.). Hence **vo·tar**ESS[1] n. [f. L as foll. + -ARY[1]]

vote, n., & v.i. & t. Formal expression of will or opinion in regard to election of officer &c., sanctioning law, passing resolution, &c., signified by ballot, show of hands, voice, or otherwise, as *shall give my v. to* or *for the Unionist candidate*, *passed without a dissentient v.*, CAST[1] *v.*, SPLIT[1] one's *v.*, CASTING-VOTE, TRANSFERABLE *v.*; opinion expressed, money granted, by majority of vv., as *ministry received a v. of confidence*, *the army v.*; *the* collective vv. given or to be given by a party &c., as *will lose the Labour, Unionist, v.*, *the floating v.* (of persons not attached to a party; *the* right to v., as *shall women have the v.?*; ticket &c. used for recording v. Hence **vo·te**LESS a. (Vb) give a v. (*for*, *against*, person or measure); enact, resolve, (*that*), grant (sum), by majority of vv.; (colloq.) pronounce, declare, by general consent, as *was voted a failure*; (colloq.) propose (*that*); *v. down*, defeat (measure) by vv.; *v. in*, elect by vv. Hence **vo·t**ABLE a., **vo·t**ER[1] n. [(n. f. neut. p.p. as noun = wish) f. L *vovēre vot-* vow]

vo·ting, n. In vbl senses; *v.-paper* (used in v. by ballot in election of M.P. &c.); CUMULATIVE *v.* [-ING[1]]

vo·tive, a. Offered, consecrated, in fulfilment of a vow, as *v. offering*, *tablet*, *picture*. [f. L f. *votivus* (as VOTE, see -IVE)]

vouch (vowtsh), v.t. & i. Confirm, uphold, (statement) by evidence or assertion; answer *for*, be surety *for*, as *will v. for the truth of this*, *for him* or *his honesty*, *can v. for it that no step was taken*. [f. OF *vocher* f. L *vocare* call]

vou·cher, n. In vbl senses, esp. document, receipt, &c., establishing the payment of money or the truth of accounts. [AF (prec., -ER[4])]

vouchsa·fe, v.t. Condescend to grant, as *vouchsafed me no answer*, *v. me a visit*; condescend (*to* do). [VOUCH + SAFE, = guarantee securely]

voussoir (vōō·swar), n. Each of the wedge-shaped stones forming an arch. [f. OF *vossoir*, ult. f. L *volvere* roll]

vow, n., & v.t. Solemn promise or engagement esp. in the form of an oath to God, as *baptismal vv.* (given at baptism by baptized person or by sponsors), *monastic v.* (by which monk binds himself to poverty, celibacy, & obedience), *lovers' vv.* (promises of fidelity), *am under* (have taken) *a v. to drink no wine*; action, conduct, &c., promised by v., as *is this your v.?*. (Vb) promise solemnly (thing, conduct), as *vowed a temple to Apollo*, *v. obedience*, *vengeance against the oppressor*; (archaic) utter, make, *a v.*; declare solemnly (*that*); (archaic) declare, as *I v. you are most obliging*. [f. OF *vou*, *veu*, f. L as VOTE]

vow·el, n. Each of the more open sounds uttered in speaking, sound capable of forming a syllable, (opp. to, but not sharply divided from, *consonant*); letter representing this, e. g. a, e, i, o, u; *neutral v.* (heard in second syllable of *cousin*, *reason*, *haddock*); *v. gradation*, = ABLAUT; *v. mutation*, = UMLAUT; *v. point*, each of a set of marks indicating vv. in Hebrew & other Oriental languages. Hence **(-)vow-ell**ED[2], **vo·wel**LESS, **vow·ell**Y[2], aa. [f. OF *vouel* f. L *vocalis* (*littera*) VOCAL (letter)]

vow·elize, v.t. Insert the vowels in (Hebrew &c., shorthand). [-IZE]

vox, n. *V. bar·bara* (anat., bot., &c.), hybrid or incorrectly-formed word; *v. et praetĕ·rĕa nĭ·hil*, a voice & nothing more (i.e., esp., an empty word); *v. huma·na*, organ-stop with tones supposed to resemble human voice; *v. pŏ·pūlī*, the people's voice (i.e. public opinion, the general verdict, popular belief, or rumour). [see VOICE]

voy·age (-ĭj), n., & v.i. & t. Journey, esp. long one, by sea or water; *broken v.*, unsuccessful whaling &c. v.; (vb) travel, traverse, by water. Hence **voy·age**ABLE a., **voy·ag**ER[1] n. [(vb f. F *voyager*) f. OF *voiage* f. L VIATICUM]

vraisemblance (F), n. Appearance of truth, plausible appearance, verisimilitude.

vril, n. A natural wonder-working force assumed in Lytton's *The Coming Race* to have been discovered. [arbitrary]

Vu·lcan, n. (Rom. Myth.) god of fire & metal-working; *V. powder*, an explosive. [f. L *Volcanus*, *Vu-*]

vulcanic &c. See **vol-**.

Vu·lcanist, n. (geol.). Holder of PLUTONIC theory. [f. F *vulcaniste* (VULCAN, -IST)]

vu·lcanite, n. See foll. [-ITE[1]]

vu·lcanize, v.t. Treat (rubber) with sulphur at high temperature to increase elasticity & strength & yield hard (vulcanite) or soft flexible rubber. Hence **vu·lcaniz**ABLE a., **vulcaniz**A·TION, **vu·lcaniz**ER[1](1, 2), nn. [-IZE]

vu·lgar, a. Of, characteristic of, the common people, plebeian, coarse, low, as *v. expressions, mind, tastes, finery, an air of v. prosperity, the v.* HERD[1], (abs.) *the v.*, the common people; in common use, generally prevalent, as *v. errors, superstitions, the v.* (national, esp. formerly as opp. to Latin) *tongue, v.* FRACTION, *the v.* (Christian) *era.* Hence or cogn. **vu·lgar**ISM(4, 2), **vulgă·r**ITY, nn., **vu·lgar**LY[2] adv. [f. L *vulgaris*, *vo-*, (*vulgus*, *vo-*, common people, see -AR[1])]

vulgār·ian, n. Vulgar (esp. rich) person. [-IAN]

vu·lgarize, v.t. Make (person, manners, &c.) vulgar, infect with vulgarity; spoil (scene, sentiment, &c.) by making too common or frequented or well known. Hence **vulgariz**A·TION n. [VULGAR + -IZE (3)]

Vu·lgate (-*a*t), n. Latin version of the Bible prepared by Jerome late in the 4th c. [f. L *vulgata* (*editio* edition), fem. p.p. of *vulgare* make public (*vulgus*, see VULGAR)]

vu·lgus, n. (school slang). Greek or Latin verse-exercise in some schools. [corrupt. of 16th-c. *vulgars* = vulgar-tongue (i.e. English) passages for rendering into Latin]

vu·lnerable, a. That may be wounded (lit. & fig.), susceptible of injury, not proof against weapon, criticism, &c. Hence **vulnera**BI·LITY, **vu·lnerable**NESS, nn. [f. LL *vulnerabilis* (*vulnerare* wound f. *vulnus -eris* wound, see -BLE)]

vu·lnerary, a. & n. (Drug, unguent, &c.) useful or used for healing wounds. [f. L *vulnerarius* (*vulnus*, see prec. & -ARY[1])]

vu·lpine, a. Of (the nature of) a fox, so **vu·lpi**CIDE(1, 2) n.; crafty, cunning. [f. L *vulpinus* (*vulpes* fox, see -INE[1])]

vu·lture (-tsh*er*), n. Kinds of large bird of prey with head & neck more or less bare of feathers feeding chiefly on carrion; (fig.) rapacious person; *v. raven*, kinds of thick-billed African raven. Hence or cogn. **vu·ltur**INE[1], **vu·ltur**ISH[1], **vu·ltur**OUS, aa. [f. L *vultur*]

vu·lva, n. (anat.). Opening, orifice, esp. of female genitals. Hence **vu·lv**AR[1], **vu·lv**ATE[2], **vu·lvi**FORM, aa., **vulvi·**TIS n., **vulvo-** comb. form. [L]

vying. See VIE.

W

W (dŭ·blyōō), letter (pl. *W*s, W's).

Abbreviations(1); W.,war, **W.O.**(office); waste, **W.P.B.** (paper basket); weather, **W.P.** (permitting); west, **W.**, **W.C.** (central), **W.I.** (Indies); wireless, **W.T.** (telegraphy); women's, **W.A.A.C.** (army auxiliary corps), **W.R.A.F.**, **W.R.N.S.**, (royal air force, naval service), **W.S.P.U.** (social & political union); workers', **W.E.A.** (educational association); writer, **W.S.** (to the signet). **w.**, water, **w.c.**(loset); wrong, **w.f.**(ount).

Abbreviations (2): **War.**(wickshire); **Wash.**(ington); **Wigorn.**, bishop of Worcester; **Wilts.**(hire); **Winton.**, bishop of Winchester; **Wisc.**(onsin); **Wisd.**(om of Solomon); **Wm**, William; **Worcs.**, Worcestershire; **Wyo.**(ming).

wabble. See WOBBLE.

wa·cke (-k*e*), n. Kind of greyish-green or brownish clay resulting from decomposition of volcanic rock. [G, f. MHG *wacke* large stone]

wad (wŏd), n., & v.t. Small lump of soft material used to keep things apart or in place or to stuff up opening, esp. disk of felt &c. keeping powder or shot compact in gun; (U.S., slang) roll of notes, money. (Vb) press (cotton &c.) into w. or wadding; line (garment, coverlet), protect (person, walls, &c.), with wadding (also fig., as *well wadded with conceit*); stop up (aperture, gun-barrel), keep (powder &c.) in place, with w.; ram (w.) home. [cf. Sw. *vadd* wadding, G *watte*]

wa·dding (wŏ-), n. Spongy material usu. of cotton or wool used to stuff garments, quilts, &c., or to pack fragile articles in, cotton wool; material from which gun-wads are made. [-ING[1]]

wa·ddle (wŏ-), v.i., & n. Walk with the rocking motion natural to fat short-legged person or to bird with short legs set far apart as duck or goose; hence **wa·ddling**LY[2] adv. (N.) waddling gait. [WADE + -LE(3)]

wa·ddy (wŏ-), n. Australian war-club. [native]

wade, v.i. & t., & n. Walk through water or other impeding medium as snow, mud, sand (also fig., as *w. through slaughter* or *blood*, make one's way by massacre &c.; *w. through book*, read it in spite of dullness &c.); ford (stream) on foot, whence **wā·d**ABLE a.; *wading bird*, long-legged water-bird that wades (opp. short-legged web-footed swimmers); (n.) spell of wading. [OE *wadan* wade, trudge, cf. Du. *waden*, G *waten*; cogn. w. L *vadere* go, *vadum* ford]

wa·der, n. In vbl senses; esp.: wading bird (see prec.); (pl.) high waterproof boots worn in fishing. [-ER[1]]

wa·di, -y, (wah-), n. Rocky watercourse dry except in rainy season (chiefly of Eastern countries). [Arab. *wādī*]

wā·fer, n., & v.t. Kind of very thin sweet honeycomb-faced biscuit now chiefly eaten with ices (*thin as a w.*, whence **wa·fer**Y[2] a.); thin disk of unleavened bread used in Eucharist; small disk of dried paste formerly used for fastening letters, holding papers together, &c.; disk of red paper stuck on law papers instead of seal; (vb) attach or seal with w. [f. ONF *waufre* (cf. GOFER, GOFFER) f. MLG *wâfel* (cf. foll.), perh. cogn. w. G *wabe* honeycomb]

wa·ffle (wŏ-), n. Small batter cake baked in *w.-iron*, special utensil. [f. Du. *wafel* WAFER]

waft (wah-, wă-), v.t., & n. Convey (as) through air or over water, sweep smoothly & lightly along. (N.) single sweep of bird's wing; whiff of odour; fugitive sensation *of* peace, joy, &c.; (Naut., also *weft*) distress signal, e.g. ensign rolled or knotted or garment flown in rigging. [back form. f. obs. *wafter* convoying-ship prob. f. Du. *wachter* a guard (*wachten* to wait, watch)]

wag[1], v.t. & i., & n. Shake (t. & i., of thing attached by one end, as tail) to & fro, oscillate, (*dog wags his tail*, in sign of pleasure; *tail was wagging*; *tail wags dog*, least important member of society or section of party has control; *w.* one's *finger at*, in reproof &c.; *w.* one's *head*, in derision or amusement; *beards, chins, jaws, tongues, are wagging*, talk going on); (archaic, of the world, times, &c.) go along with varied fortune or characteristics (*how wags the world?*); *wa·gtail*, kinds of small bird (*pied, yellow*, &c., *w.*) with long tail in constant motion; (n.) single wagging motion (*with a w. of his tail, head*, &c.). [ME *waggen* f. root of OE *wagian* rock]

wăg[2], n. Facetious person, one given to jesting or practical jokes; (slang) truant (esp. *play w.* or *the w.*). Hence **wa·gg**ERY (4) n., **wa·gg**ISH[1] a., **wa·ggish**LY[2] adv., **wa·ggish**NESS n. [prob. for obs. *wag-halter* gallows-bird (prec. vb)]

wage[1], n. Amount paid periodically, esp. by the day or week or month, for time during which workman or servant is at employer's disposal (usu. pl. exc. in certain phrr.; *gets good ww.*; *brings his ww. home*; *at a w.* or *ww. of £1 a week*; *living w.*, ww. that allow earner to live without fear of starvation; *a fair day's work for a fair day's w.*); requital (usu. pl.; *the ww. of sin is death*); *wage(s)-fund* in Pol. Econ., part of community's capital devoted to paying ww. & salaries (*the w.-f. theory*, that wages can rise only if either capital increases or population diminishes). [OF, = *guage* GAGE[1]]

wage[2], v.t. Carry on (war, conflict). [earlier sense *declare* (*war*) f. ONF *wagier* (prec.)]

wā·ger, n., & v.t. = BET n. & v.t. (but not now in familiar use); (Hist.) *w. of battle*, ancient form of trial by personal combat between parties or champions, *w. of law*, COMPURGATION. [f. OF *wageure* (as prec., -URE)]

wă·ggle, v.i. & t., & n. = WAG[1] (but in more familiar use). Hence **wa·ggl**Y[2] a., unsteady. [-LE(3)]

wă·g(g)on, n. Four-wheeled vehicle for drawing heavy loads, often with removable semicylindrical tilt or cover, usu. drawn by two or more horses (*hitch* one's *w. to a star*, utilize powers higher than one's own); open railway truck; *w.-boiler, -ceiling, -roof, -vault*, shaped like w.-tilt. [f. Du. *wagen*, cf. OE *wægn* WAIN]

wa·g(g)oner, n. Driver of wagon; *the W.*, constellation Auriga. [-ER[1]]

wag(g)one·tte, n. Four-wheeled open pleasure vehicle (or with removable cover) for one or more horses & with facing side seats. [-ETTE]

wagon-lit (F), n. Sleeping-car on continental railway.

Waha·bi, -ee, (-hah-), n. One of a sect of Mohammedan puritans following the letter of the Koran. [Abd-el-*Wahhab*, founder c. 1700]

waif, n. Ownerless object or animal, thing cast up by or drifting in sea or brought by unknown agency; homeless & helpless person, esp. unowned or abandoned child; *ww. & strays*, odds & ends, unowned or neglected children. [AF, prob. of Scand. orig., cf. ON *veif* thing flapping about; n. corresp. to WAIVE]

wail, v.i. & t., & n. (Lament, i. & t., with) prolonged plaintive inarticulate usu. high-pitched cry; (fig.) lament(ation) in words (often *over*); (of wind &c.) sound (v. & n.) like person wailing. Hence **wai·l**FUL a. (poet.), **wai·ling**LY[2] adv. [cf. ON *væla* (*væ* int., see WOE)]

wain, n. Wagon (chiefly poet. or agricultural); *Charles's, Arthur's*, or *the W.*, CHARLES'S WAIN. [f. OE *wægn*, cf. Du. & G *wagen*; cogn. w. L *vehere* carry, Skr. *vahana* vehicle, Gk *okhos* car, & WEIGH]

wai·nscot, n., & v.t. Wooden panelling or boarding on room-wall; (vb) line with w., whence **wai·nscot**ING[1](3) n. [earlier sense *kind of oakwood*, f. MLG *wagenschot* perh. f. *wagen* waggon; for *schot* boarding cf. CAMPSHOT]

waist, n. Part of human body below ribs & above hips (*large, small, w.*, of such circumference; *long, short, w.*, of such vertical extent); contraction marking this in normal figure (*has no w.*, of stout person), analogous contraction in middle of long object, e.g. fiddle or hour-glass; part of ship between forecastle & quarter-deck; part of garment encircling w., band round w. from which petticoats &c. may be suspended; (U.S.) bodice; *w.-band, -belt*, worn round w.; *w.-cloth*, = LOINCLOTH; *wai·stcoat* (*also pr.* wĕ·skut), garment reaching down to w. with front showing when coat is open & usu. without sleeves (*sleeved w.-c.*, with sleeves for extra warmth or for use without coat by workmen); *w.-deep* or *-high* aa. & advv., up to w. Hence **-waist**ED[2] a. [ME *wast* (WAX[2]), cf. Goth. *wahstus* growth]

wait[1], v.i. & t. Abstain from action or departure till some expected event occurs, pause, tarry, stay, kick one's heels, be expectant or on the watch, (often *for, till*; *w. a minute*; *shall not w. here any longer*; *kept me waiting* or *made me w.*; *have a month to w. yet*; *w. till I come, for high water* or *a fine day*; *everything comes to those who w.*; *always has to be waited for*, is unpunctual); await, bide, (*is waiting his opportunity*; *you must w. my convenience*; *am only waiting the signal*); act as waiter, as servant shifting plates &c. at table, (*are you accustomed to waiting?*; often *at table*), or as attendant (LORD[1], GROOM, *in waiting*); defer (meal) till some one arrives (*don't w. dinner for me*); *wait-a-bit*, kinds of S.-Afr. shrub with hooked thorns; *w. (up)on*, watch (archaic), await convenience of, serve as attendant esp. at table, pay visit to (person regarded as superior), escort (archaic), (in race) purposely keep close behind (competitor), follow as result; *waiting-room*, provided for persons to w. in esp. at railway-station or house of consultant. [f. OF *guaitier* (now *guetter*) f. OHG *wahtên* to watch (*wahta* n. watch) cogn. w. WAKE[1]]

wait[2], n. 1. (Pl.) band(s) of persons singing carols &c. from house to house at Christmas. 2. Act or time of waiting (*had a long w. for the train*); watching for enemy, ambush, (*lie in* or *lay w.* usu. *for*). [sense 1 f. OF *waite* sentinel f. OF as prec.; sense 2 f. prec.]

wai·ter, n. In vbl senses; also or esp.: man who takes & executes orders, shifts plates, &c., at hotel or restaurant tables, whence **wai·tr**ESS[1] n.; tray, salver; DUMB[1]-*w.*; TIDE-*w.* [-ER[1]]

waive, v.t. Forbear to insist on or use, tacitly or implicitly relinquish or forgo, (right, claim, opportunity, legitimate plea, &c.). Hence **wai·**VER[4] n. (legal). [AF *weyver* f. OF *gaiver* make into a WAIF]

wake[1], v.i. & t. (past *woke, waked*; p.p. *waked, woken, woke*). Cease to sleep, rouse from sleep, (often *up*; also fig. as *spring wakes all nature, nature wakes*); be awake (archaic exc. in part. or gerund, as *in his waking hours, waking or sleeping*; *waking dream*, day-dream, reverie; cease or rouse from sloth, torpidity, inactivity, or inattention (usu. *up*; *w. up there!*; *wants something to w. him up*; *the insult waked his dull spirit*), rise or raise from the dead; (chiefly Ir.) hold w. over; disturb (silence, place) with noise, make re-echo; *w.-robin*, wild arum or lords-&-ladies. [mixture of OE **wacan wócarise*, be born, & *wacian* wake, watch, cf. Du. *waken*, G *wachen*; cogn. w. VIGIL, VEGETABLE]

wake[2], n. (Hist.) anniversary of dedication of church kept by watching all night, merry-making or fair in connexion with this; (Ir.) watch by corpse before burial, lamentations & merrymaking in connexion with it. [perh. f. ON *vaka* vigil, cogn. w. prec.]

wake[3], n. Strip of smooth water left behind moving ship (*in the w. of*, behind, following, after the example of). [f. ON *vaka* opening in ice, cogn. w. Gk *hugros*, L *humidus*, wet]

wa·keful, a. Unable to sleep, (of person's night &c.) passed with little or no sleep; vigilant. Hence **wa·keful**LY[2] adv., **wa·keful**NESS n. [WAKE[1], -FUL]

wā·ken, v.t. & i. Cause to be, become, awake (usu. = *wake up*, but conveying less of abruptness). [OE *wæcnan* (**wacan* WAKE[1])]

Wa·lach, Wall-, (wŏl-), n. = VLACH. Hence **Wal(l)ā·chian** (-kĭ-) a. (of the Ww. or of Walachia, a principality now forming part of Roumania) & n. (= *W.*, also the language of the Ww.). [see VLACH]

Walde·nsēs (wŏ-), n. pl. Puritan sect in valleys of Piedmont, Dauphiné, & Provence, started c. 1170 & much persecuted in 16th & 17th cc. Hence **Walde·ns**IAN a. & n. [Peter *Waldo* of Lyons, founder]

wale, weal, n., & v.t. Ridge raised on flesh by stroke of rod or whip; *wale-knot* or *wall-knot*, made at end of rope by intertwining strands to prevent unravelling or act as stopper; (vb) raise w. on. [OE *walu* stripe, ridge, cf. OFris. *walu*, ON *völr*, rod; also GUNWALE, CHANNEL[2]]

Wā·ler, n. Horse imported for Indian army from New South Wales. [N.S. *Wales*, -ER[1]]

Wales, n. Principality inhabited by the Welsh (*Prince of W.*, title usu. conferred on heir-apparent of Great Britain). [OE *Wealas* pl. of *wealh* see WELSH[1]]

Walhalla. See VALHALLA.

walk[1] (wawk), v.i. & t. (Of men) progress by advancing each foot alternately never having both off ground at once (*heel-&-toe walking*, in which both heel & toe are used, as required in walking-races; *w. backwards, sideways*, go in those directions with analogous motions; *w. over course* or *w. over*, have WALK[2] over; *w. away from*, easily out-distance), go with the gait usual except when speed is desired (*walking* DICTIONARY), (of animals) go with slowest gait corresponding to human w.; travel or go on foot (*w. into shop, up to person, down hill*, &c.; *please w. in*, invitation to enter; *w. up*, showman's invitation to circus &c.; *w. out with* esp. of servants &c., have as sweetheart; *w. about*, stroll; *walks two hours, ten miles, a day*; *ghost walks*, shows itself; *w. into* slang, thrash, abuse, eat heartily of; *w. off*, depart, esp. abruptly; *w. off* or *away with*, carry off, steal); (archaic) live with or in specified principle or manner, conduct oneself, (*w. in love, humbly, honestly, after the flesh, by faith, with God*,

&c.); perambulate, tread floor or surface of, (*Him that walked the waves*; *w. the streeets*, in gen. sense, also be prostitute; *w. the hospitals*, be medical student; *w. the boards*, be actor; *w. the* PLANK[1]; *w. the chalk*, prove sobriety to police &c. by walking straight between chalked lines), whence **wal·kABLE** a.; cause to w. with one, have walking-race with, (*w. horse*, when riding or driving or leading it; *policeman walked the man off*; *Smith will w. Jones for £100 a side*; *you have walked me off my legs*, tired out); (of farmer &c.) take charge of (hound puppy); *walk*ING[1] *chair*, = GO[1]*-cart*; *walk*ING[2] *delegate*, trade-union official who visits sick members, interviews employers, &c.; *walk*ING[1]*-dress*, for outdoor wear; *walk*ING[2]*-fern*, N.-Amer. kind with slender-tipped fronds that bow down to ground & take root; *walk*ING[2] *gentleman, lady*, actor, actress, of part requiring good presence but no skill; *walk*ING[2]*-leaf*, insect imitating leaf; *walk*ING[1]*-papers* or *-ticket* slang, dismissal; *walk*ING[1]*-stick*, carried in walking; *walk*ING[1]*-tour*, pleasure journey on foot. [OE *wealcan* roll, rove, cf. Du. *walken* press hats, Icel. *volka* roll, G *walken* full cloth]

walk[2], n. Walking gait, person's action in walking, (see prec.; *go at, never gets beyond, a w.*; *know him a mile off by his w.*); excursion on foot, stroll, constitutional, (*go for, take, a w.*; *across the hills from X to Z is a good w.*; *w. over*, race in which from absence or inferiority of competitors winner can go at a w. if he chooses, easy victory); person's favourite walking ground, round of hawker &c., place or track intended or suitable for strollers or foot-passengers, promenade, colonnade, footpath, (ROPE-*w.*; SHEEP-*w.*; *w. of life*, calling, profession, occupation). [f.prec.]

wal·ker[1], n. In vbl senses; esp.: SHOP-*w.*; STREET-*w.*; (class-name for) bird such as common fowl that neither flies nor swims, also bird that does not hop but walks on alternate feet. [-ER[1]]

Wal·ker[2] (waw-), int. (slang) expressing incredulity & suspicion of being hoaxed (also *Hookey W.*). [?]

Walkyrie. See VALKYR.

wall (wawl), n., & v.t. Continuous & usu. vertical & solid structure of stones,bricks, concrete, timber, &c., narrow in proportion to length & height serving to enclose (partly) or protect or divide off town, house, room, field, &c., surface of inner side(s) of room, (*party* or *partition w.*, separating two rooms, houses, fields, &c.; *w. of partition* fig., line of division, gulf; *blank w.*, without door or gate or window, also without decoration; *run* one's *head against a w.*, attempt impossibilities; *see through brick w.*, have miraculous insight; *ww. have ears*, eavesdroppers are or may be about; *with* one's *back to the w.*, brought to bay, fighting alone against odds; RETAIN*ing w.*); something resembling w. in appearance or effect (*mountain w.*, line of steep hills; *w. of armed men, fire, bayonets*, protection or obstacle consisting of these; *cell-w., ww. of the chest* &c., enclosing tissue or framework in Bot. or Anat.; *hanging, foot-, w.*, in mining, upper, lower, rock enclosing lode); (position next) w. as opp. kennel side of street footpath (*give one the w.*, allow him cleaner part in passing; *take the w. of*, refuse this courtesy to); side as opp. centre of road (*the weakest goes to the w.*, is pushed aside, gets the worst in competition); *w.-creeper*, kinds of bird; *w.-cress*, kinds of plant growing in stony places; *w.-fern*, common polypody; *wa·ll-flower*, fragrant spring garden-plant with usu. orange or brown clustered flowers, (colloq.) woman sitting out dances for lack of partners; *w.-fruit*, of trees fastened against w. for protection & warmth; *w. game*, an Eton form of football; *w.-painting*, on w. usu. of room, esp. fresco; *w.-paper*, for pasting over room-ww., usu. with decorative printed patterns; *w.-pepper*, kind of stone-crop; *w.-plate*, timber laid in or on wall to distribute pressure of girder &c.; *w.-rue*, small fern growing on ww. & cliffs; *w.-washer*, plate used with tie-rod in supporting shaky w.; hence **wa·ll-**LESS a. (Vb) provide or protect with w. (esp. in p.p., as *walled towns*); block *up* aperture &c. with w. [OE *weal* f. L *vallum* rampart, palisade]

wa·lla(h) (wŏ-), n. (Anglo-Ind.). Person or thing employed about or concerned with something, -man, (*competition-w.*, Indian civilian appointed by competitive examination; *punkah-w.*, servant who works punkah; *canal-w.*, ship built for voyage by Suez canal). [f. Hind. *-wālā* suf. = -ER[1](3)]

wa·llaby (wŏ-), n. Kinds of smaller kangaroo; *on the w.* (*track*), on tramp. unemployed. [Austral.]

Wallach. See WALACH.

wallaroo· (wŏ-), n. Kinds of larger kangaroo. [Austral.]

wa·llet (wŏ-), n. (Archaic) bag for carrying personal necessaries, food, &c., on journey, esp. pilgrim's or beggar's scrip; small leather case holding repairing tools for bicycle &c., fishing-kit, papers, or other small articles; flat case for holding paper money unfolded. [etym. dub.; perh. by metathesis for WATTLE]

wall-eye (waw·lī), n. (Affection of) eye with opaque white or pale iris showing diseased condition; (loosely) eye showing abnormal amount of white owing to squint &c., or large & glaring as in some fishes. [back formation . foll.]

wa·ll-eyed, a. Having wall-eye. [f. ON *vagl-eygr* (*vagl* unexp.., *auga* eye)]

wall-knot. See WALE.

Walloo·n, n. & a. Member, language (a French dialect), of people scattered in Belgium & neighbouring parts of France; (adj.) of the Ww. or in their language. [f. OF *Wallon* f. Teut. *walh*, cf. VLACH, WELSH]

wa·llop (wŏ-), v.t. (slang). Thrash, beat, hide; (part.) big, strapping, thumping. Hence **wa·llop**ING[1](1) n. [earlier senses *gallop, boil, bubble, flounder*; f. ONF as GALLOP]

wa·llow (wŏ-), v.i., & n. Roll about in mud, sand, water, &c. (*w. in money*, be very rich); take swinish or gross delight *in* sensuality &c.; (n.) place to which buffaloes &c. resort to w. [OE *wealwian* roll, cogn. w. L *volvere*]

Wa·llsend, (wawlz-), n. Kind of superior house coal orig. from W. on Tyne.

Wall Street, n. (Used for) the American money-market. [street in N.Y.]

wa·lnut (waw-), n. (Kinds of tree yielding) delicate-flavoured nut in pair of similar boat-shaped shells (*over the ww. & the wine*, at dessert); timber of w.-tree used in cabinet-making & for gunstocks. [f. OE *wealh* foreign, Gaulish (cf. WELSH[1]), NUT]

Walpur·gis-night (vahlpoorg-), n. Eve of 1st May, when witches meet at the Brocken or elsewhere & hold revels with the devil. [*Walpurgis*, female saint of 8th c.; connexion unknown]

wa·lrus (waw-, wŏ-), n. Kinds of large amphibious arctic long-tusked mammal related to seal, morse, sea-horse. [Du., prob. w. metath. f. Scand. (ON *hrosshvalr* kind of whale, *rosmhvalr* walrus)]

waltz (wawls), n., & v.i. Dance in which partners progress gyrating round each other in embrace (*trois-temps w.*, in ordinary time, *deux-temps w.*, faster); piece of w.-music. (Vb) dance w.; dance *in, out, round*, &c., in joy &c.; hence **wa·ltz**ER[1] n. [f. G *walzer* (*walzen* revolve]

wampee· (wŏ-), n. (Tree yielding) grape-like fruit grown in China & E. Indies. [Chin. (*hwang* yellow, *pī* skin)]

wa·mpum (wŏ-), n. Beads made from shells & strung for money or decoration by N.-Amer. Indians. [f. N.-Amer. Ind. *wampumpeag* (*wompi* white, *-ampi* string]

wan (wŏ-), a. Pale, colourless, bloodless, looking worn or exhausted, (chiefly of persons or their complexion or look, or of sky or light); (archaic, of night, water, &c.) dark, black. Hence **wa·n**LY[2] adv., **wa·n**NESS n. [OE *wann, wonn*, dark, black, etym. dub.]

wand (wŏ-), n. Slender rod for carrying in hand or setting in ground as temporary mark (chiefly now of conjurer's or music conductor's baton, or of staff symbolizing some officials' authority). [f. ON *vöndr*, perh. cogn. w. WIND[3] w. ref. to suppleness]

wa·nder (wŏ-), v.i. & t. Rove, stroll, go from country to country or from place to place without settled route or destination, (*Wandering Jew*, supposed to be still living from when Christ said 'Thou shalt w. on the earth till I return' as punishment for an insult, also person who never settles down, also kinds of climbing plant; *wandering cell, abscess, kidney*, &c., moving about, normally or abnormally attached to place in body; *wandering sailor*, kinds of climbing plant), whence **wa·nder**ER[1] n.; stray, diverge from the right way lit. or fig., get lost, depart from home; talk or think irrelevantly or disconnectedly or incoherently, stray from subject in hand, be inattentive or delirious, (*his wits are wandering*; *wanders in his talk*); traverse desultorily (*you may w. the world*, or usu. *the world through, & not find such another*). Hence **wa·nder**ING[1] (1) n. (usu. pl.), **wa·ndering**LY[2] adv. [OE *wandrian* (WEND, -ER[5]), cf. G & LG *wandern*]

wanderjahre (vah·nderyare), n. pl. (Time spent in travel by artisan, student, &c., as a mode of) apprenticeship. [G]

wanderoo· (wŏ-), n. Kind of Ceylon monkey. [Cingalese *wanderu*]

wane, v.i., & n. Decrease in size or splendour like moon after the full, lose power or vigour or importance or repute, decline; (n.) process of waning (esp. *is on the w.*, declining). [OE *wanian* (*wan* deficient), cf. ON *vana* diminish (*vanr*, see WANT[1]), & WANTON]

wă·ngle, v.t. (slang). Secure (favour, desired result) by plausibility or management or other dubious means; show in the desired light, cook, fake, (report &c.). [etym. dub.; first recorded (1888) as printers' slang]

wa·nion (wŏ-), n. *With a w.* (*to*), imprecation (archaic). [var. of *waniand* part. of WANE (waning moon = unlucky hour)]

want[1] (wah-, wŏ-), n. Lack, absence, deficiency, *of* (*ship rotting for w. of paint*; *shows great w. of thought, care, sense, judgement*); need *of*, need of sustenance, poverty, (*is in w. of money, a servant, &c.*; *living in the direst w.*; *w. is a severe but efficient teacher*); desire for thing as necessary to life or happiness or success or completion (whence **wa·nt**LESS a.), thing so desired, (*a man of few ww.*; *superfluities soon become ww.*; *is, supplies, a felt w.*; *can supply your ww.*). [f. ON *vant* neut. of *vanr* lacking, cf. OE *wan* (WANE)]

want[2], v.i. & t. Be without or deficiently supplied with, fall short *of*, fall short by (specified amount) *of* specified limit, (part.) lacking *in* quality or unequal *to* requirements or absent or deficient, (*wants, is wanting in, judgement*; *fortunately wants the power to do it*; *what was wanting, what we unfortunately wanted, was the will*; *wants something*, or *wants, of* *perfection*; *be found wanting*, or *wanting to the occasion*, one's *duty*, &c.; *head of statue is wanting*; *statue wants the head*; *infinitive wanting*, verb has none; *wants half a minute of the hour, an inch of the regulation measurement*); be in w. (*for*; *let him w. for nothing*; *must not be allowed to w.*); require (thing, *-ing*, *to be -ed*, *to* do; *boy wants the whip, whipping, to be whipped, to feel the whip*; *it wants careful handling*); desire, wish for possession or presence of, (*to* do, thing, person; *don't w. to go*; *I w. some sugar, it done, you to try*; *call me if I am wanted*; *is wanted by the police*, of suspected criminal &c.; *tell Jones I w. him*, send him to me). [f. ON *vanta* (prec.)]

wa·nting, prep. Without, minus, less, (*w. common honesty, nothing can be done*; *made a century w. one run*). [-ING[2]; use of part. either abs., cf. NOTWITHSTANDING, or in ordinary agreement]

wa·nton (wŏ-), a., n., & v.i. Sportive, gambolling, playful, irresponsible, capricious, (*w. child, kid, wind, mood*); luxuriant, unrestrained, wild, (*w. growth, ringlets, profusion*); licentious, unchaste, lewd, (*a w. woman*; *w. thoughts*); motiveless, serving no purpose, random, arbitrary, (*w. mischief, destruction*); hence **wa·nton**LY[2] adv., **wa·nton**NESS n. (N.) unchaste woman or rarely man; (rare) playful child. (Vb) sport, gambol, move capriciously; (rare) act lasciviously. [ME *wantoun*, *-towen* (*wan*, see WANE, used as pref. with sense *un-* as in obs. *wanhope* despair, OE *togen*, p.p. of *téon* draw, educate, cf. G *gezogen*)]

wap. See WHOP.

wa·pentake (wŏ-), n. (Old name in Anglian districts for) hundred or division of shire. [OE *wǽpengetæc* f. ON *vápnatak* (*vápn* weapon, *tac* taking f. *taka* TAKE) w. ref. to brandishing of weapons as form of voting]

wa·piti (wŏ-), n. N.-Amer. stag resembling red deer but larger. [f. Amer.-Ind. *wapitik* white deer]

war[1] (wor), n. Quarrel usu. between nations conducted by force, state of open hostility & suspension of ordinary international law prevalent during such quarrel, military or naval attack or series of attacks, (fig.) hostility or contention between persons, (*civil w.*, between parts of one nation for supremacy; *private w.*, feud between persons or families carried on in defiance of laws of murder &c., or armed attack made by members of one State without government sanction upon another; *holy w.*, waged in support of some religious cause; *make* or *wage w.*, begin or carry on hostile operations; *declare w.*, announce that hostilities may be expected, often *upon* another nation, also fig. *upon* institution, party, custom, &c.; so *declaration of w.*; *drift into w.*; *be at w.*, engaged in hostilities *with* enemy or abs., also fig.; *roll back tide of w.*, repel invasion; *go to the ww.* archaic, serve as soldier; *carry the w. into the enemy's country*, (fig.) make counter accusations &c., not confine oneself to defence; *has been in the ww.*, usu. fig. of person who has been mauled physically or otherwise; *on a w. footing*, of army, fleet, &c., with full establishment; *w. to the knife*, struggle to the bitter end usu. between persons; *Secretary of State for W.*, also *Secretary for W.*, *W. Secretary*, parliamentary head of W. Office; *art of w.*, strategy & tactics; *trade of w.*, soldier's profession; *sinews of w.*, money for waging w. or for effecting any object; TUG, CONTRABAND, COUNCIL, HONOUR[1]*s*, *of w.*; MAN[1]*-of-w.*; *laws of w.*, those recognized by civilized nations as limiting belligerents' action; *rights of w.*, those similarly permitting to belligerents certain acts illegitimate in peace; *the dogs of w.* poet., havoc attending w.; *ww. & rumours of ww.*, prevalence of the appeal to force among nations; *w. of the elements*, storms & catastrophes in nature; *all's* FAIR[2] *in love & w.*; *the w. to end w.*, that of 1914–18); *w. baby*, illegitimate child attributable to w. conditions, (joc.) naval cadet employed as naval officer in the great w.; *w.-cry*, phrase or name formerly shouted in charging or rallying to attack, party catchword, savages' battle-shout; *w.-cloud*, position of international affairs that threatens w.; *w.-dance*, indulged in by savages before w.; *w.-god*, one worshipped as giving victory in w., esp. the Greek Ares or Roman Mars; *w.-head*, explosive head of torpedo, removed in peace practice; *w.-horse*, charger (archaic & poet. exc. in phr. *like an old w.-h.* of person excited by memories of abandoned pursuit or controversy); *w.-lord* (rhet.), great captain (esp. of William II of Germany, & of Chinese civil-war generals); *W. Office*, State department in charge of army; *w.-paint*, put on body by savages before battle, (fig.) ceremonial costume, full fig; *w.-path*, (route of) warlike expedition of Amer. Indians (*be, go, on the w.-p.* fig., be engaged in, enter upon, any conflict, have taken, take, up the cudgels); *w.-plane*, military aeroplane; *w.-ship*, for use in w.; *w.-song*, sung by savages before battle, also any song on martial theme; *w.-whoop*, yell esp. of Amer. Indians in charging; *w.-worn*, experienced in or damaged or exhausted by w. [f. OF *werre* (now *guerre*) f. OHG *werra* confusion (*werran* embroil, cf. G *verwirren* confuse); cogn. w. WORSE]

war[2], v.i. & t. Make w. (archaic); bring or beat *down* by w.; (part.) rival, competing, inconsistent, (*warring creeds, principles*). [f. prec.]

war·ble[1] (wor-), v.i. & t., & n. Sing (i. &

t.) in gentle continuous trilling manner (esp. of birds, also of person or sound); speak, utter, in manner suggestive of bird's song; relate in verse. (N.) warbled song &c.; warbling voice (*spoke in a w.*). [f. OF *werble(r)* f. OHG *werbel* a rattle &c. (cf. MHG *wirbel* whirlpool, & WHIRL)]

war·ble[2] (wor-), n. Hard lump on horse's back from galling of saddle; (tumour produced by) larva of gadfly. [cf. MSw. *varbulde* boil (*var* pus, *bulde* tumour)]

war·bler, n. In vbl senses; esp., many kinds of small bird including nightingale, blackcap, robin, redstart, & hedge-sparrow, some not remarkable for song. [-ER[1]]

ward[1] (wor-), n. Act of guarding or defending place &c. (now only in *keep watch & w.*); guard or parry in fencing (archaic); confinement, custody, guardian's control, (archaic; *is under w.*; *put him in w.*; *to whom the child is in w.*); minor under care of guardian or Court of Chancery; administrative division of city; separate room or division in prison (*condemned* &c. *w.*) or hospital (*isolation* &c. *w.*) or workhouse (*casual* &c. *w.*); (pl.) notches & projections in key & lock designed to prevent opening by wrong key; *w.-mote*, meeting of city w. [OE *mót* meeting]; *w.-room*, on man-of-war for commissioned officers below commanding officer. [OE *weard* watching, cf. OHG *warta*; a doublet of GUARD]

ward[2], v.t. Have in keeping, protect, (chiefly now of God); parry (blow, often *off*), keep *off* danger, poverty, &c. [OE *weardian* (prec.)]

-ward(s), suf. repr. OE *weard* f. OE *weorthan* become, turn to, past *wearth*; cf. L *versus* towards, f. the cogn. *vertere* turn. In OE compds of *-weard* were orig. adjj., the adj. used sometimes becoming obs. & being redeveloped in later E f. the adv., as in *forward*. *-ward* formed advv. & prepp. by addition of -ES. In older E *-ward* could in some cases be separated f. its component, as in *to usward*. Mod. E retains many adjj. & advv. in *-ward* as *backward, forward, northward, homeward*, advv. in *-wards* as *backwards, inwards*, & the prep. *towards* (less usu. *-ward*); as living suffixes, *-ward, -wards*, form extempore adjj. & advv., often more or less facet., as *bankwards, bedward, Perthwards*.

war·den[1] (wor-), n. Watchman, sentinel, (archaic); guardian, president, governor, *of* (in obs. or existent titles, as *W. of the Marches, Merton College* &c., *the Cinque Ports*), whence **war·den**SHIP n. [f. OF *wardein* as GUARDIAN]

war·den[2] (wor-), n. Kind of cooking pear. [perh. f. AF *warder* to guard, = keeping pear]

war·der, n. Sentinel (archaic); jailor, whence **war·dr**ESS[1] n.; (Hist.) staff of authority carried by king or commander & sometimes used to give signals. [AF *wardour* (WARD[2], -OR[2])]

War·dour Street (wor-), n. A London street noted for antique furniture &c. (*W.-s. English*, affectedly archaic).

war·drobe (wor-), n. Place where clothes are kept, esp. large cabinet or movable cupboard with pegs, shelves, &c.; person's stock of clothes. [f. OF *warderobe* (as GUARD[2], ROBE)]

war·dship, n. Tutelage, guardian's care, (*under w.*; *has the w. of*). [WARD[1], -SHIP]

ware[1] (wār), n. Things manufactured for sale, esp. pottery of any kind (otherwise usu. in comb., as HARD*w.*, *tinw.*); (pl.) articles that person &c. has for sale (usu. *his* &c. *ww.*); (with distinctive epithet) kind of manufactured material esp. pottery, named from inventor, place of manufacture, or some characteristic (*Wedgwood, Delft* or *Delf, black*, &c., *w.*, kinds of pottery; *Tunbridge w.*, inlaid wood); *ware·house* (-s) n., building in which goods are stored, bonded, or displayed for sale, repository, wholesale or large retail store; *ware·house* (-z) v.t., store (esp. furniture or bonded goods) temporarily in repository; *ware·houseman*, owner of repository. [OE *waru*, cf. Du. *waar*, G *waare*, prob. cogn. w. GUARD]

ware[2] (wār), pred. a. (poet.). Aware. [OE *wær* heedful, cf. ON *varr*]

ware[3] (wor. wār), v.t. (Imperat.) look out for, be cautious about, (*w. hounds, wire, traps!*; esp. in hunting-field); (colloq., usu. imperat.) decline to have anything to do with, bar, avoid, fight shy of. [OE *warian* take heed (prec.)]

war·fare, n. State of war, campaigning, being engaged in war, (*after long w.*; *his w. is over*). [orig. sense *military expedition* (FARE[2])]

war·like, a. Martial, fond of or skilful in war; military, of or for war, (*w. preparations*); bellicose, threatening war. [-LIKE]

war·lock (wor-), n. (archaic). Sorcerer, wizard. [OE *wǽrloga* deceiver (*wǽr* truth, cogn. w. L *verus* true, *loga* liar f. *léogan* LIE[2])]

warm[1] (wor-), a. Hottish, of or at rather high temperature, (*hot, w., tepid, cool, cold*; *w. water, weather, countries*; *w. blood*, that of mammals & birds ranging from 98° to 112°, also fig. passionate or amorous or emotional disposition, whence **warm-blood**ED[2] a.; *w. with* slang, spirits & hot water with sugar), (of persons &c.) with temperature of skin raised by exercise or excitement or external heat; (of clothes &c.) serving to keep one warm; (of friendly relations or actions or agents) enthusiastic, hearty, zealous, (*a w. partisan, friend, welcome*, RECEPTION; *w. thanks*); animated, heated, exciting or excited, in or resulting from sanguine or offended or indignant or unreserved mood, (*when w. with wine*; *the dispute* or *disputants grew w.*; *w. work,* keen or dangerous conflict); (of position &c.) difficult or dangerous to maintain or meet (*a w. corner,* hot part of battle &c.; so *w.* RECEPTION; *make it* or *things w. for* one, create strong feeling against him); (of feelings &c.) sympathetic, emotional, affectionate, susceptible, (*has a w. heart,* whence **warm-heart**ED[2] a., **warm-hear·ted**LY[2] adv., **warm-hear·ted**NESS n.; *a w. temperament,* susceptible esp. to amorous impressions; *w. descriptions* &c., intended to appeal to amorous feelings, indelicate); (of colour) suggestive of warmth, esp. containing rich reds or yellows; (of scent in hunting) fresh & strong, indicating recent passage of quarry, (of seeker in children's hiding games) near the object sought, on verge of finding; (of person) comfortably off, rich; (of official &c.) no longer strange, comfortably established, *in* office. Hence **war·m**LY[2] adv., **warm**TH[1] n. [OE *wearm,* cf. Du. & G *warm*; perh. cogn. w. L *formus,* Gk *thermos,* Skr. *gharmá* heat]

warm[2], v.t. & i., & n. Make w., excite, (*fire warms room, person,* &c.; *wine to w. the heart*; *w. oneself at fire* &c.; *w.* person or his *jacket,* thrash him, whence **war·m**ING[1] n. slang); w. oneself at fire &c.; become w. or animated or sympathetic (often *up*; *room is warming up*; *he warmed up* or *warmed as he got into his subject*; *my heart warms to him*); *warming-pan,* flat closed long-handled usu. brass vessel holding live coals formerly used for warming inside of bed before it was occupied, (fig.) person holding office temporarily to keep it for another not yet of age &c.; hence **-warm**ER[1](2) n. (N.) act of warming oneself or something (*must have, give it, another w. first*). [OE *wirman, wearmian,* (prec.)]

warn (worn), v.t. Give notice to, put on guard, caution, admonish, (person *of* danger or consequences or future or unknown present circumstance, *against* person or thing or doing, *that* something impends or must be reckoned with, *that* he is or has neglected to do something, *to* do, or abs.). Hence **war·ning**LY[2] adv. [OE *w(e)arnian,* cf. G *warnen*; cogn. w. WARY, WARE[2]]

war·ning, n. In vbl senses (*take w.,* have one's caution excited, mentally register danger &c., act on a w.); also or esp.: thing that serves to warn (*palpitation is a w. of heart trouble*; *let this be a w. to you*); *give* (master, servant) *w.,* announce that employment is to terminate in specified (e. g. *a month's*) time. [-ING[1]]

warp[1] (worp), v.t. & i. Make or become crooked or perverted, change from straight or right or natural state, bias, (*sun had warped the boards*; *seasoned timber does not w.*; *hardship warped his disposition*; *judgement warped by self-interest*); (Naut.) haul (ship) in some direction by rope attached to fixed point, progress thus; fertilize by inundating with w. [OE *weorpan* throw, cf. ON *verpa,* Du. *werpen,* G *werfen*]

warp[2] (worp), n. Threads stretched lengthwise in loom to be crossed by woof; rope used in towing or warping; crooked state produced in timber &c. by uneven shrinking or expansion, (fig.) perversion or perverse inclination in mind; sediment or alluvial deposit, esp. that left by turbid water kept standing on poor land. [OE *wearp,* cf. ON *varp* cast of net, G *varf* warp; cogn. w. prec.]

wa·rrant[1] (wŏ-), n. Thing that bears person out in or authorizes action (*have no w. for what you do*; *his promise* or *order, our strength, is our w.*; *I will be your w.*; *with the w. of a good conscience*); voucher, written authorization to receive money (*dividend,* TREASURY, *w.*), carry out arrest or distress (*a w. is out against him*), represent principal in lawsuit (*w. of attorney*), &c.; certificate from War Office or Admiralty (cf. COMMISSION) held by *w.-officer* (between commissioned officers & N.C.O.s, as gunner, boatswain, sergeant major). [f. OF *warant* f. Teut. (G *gewähren* certify), -ANT]

wa·rrant[2], v.t. Serve as w. for, justify, (*nothing can w. such insolence*), whence **wa·rrant**ABLE a.; = (the now more usual) GUARANTEE v., esp. in sense *answer for genuineness* &c. *of* (goods; *warranted pure* &c., to be so), & in *I* or *I'll w.* (*you*) usu. parenthet. = no doubt, whence **wa·rrant**ER[1], **wa·rrant**OR[2], **warrant**EE· (one to whom warranty is given), nn. [f. OF *warantir* (prec.)]

wa·rranty, n. Authority or justification (usu. *for* doing or saying or supposing); (Law) express or implied undertaking on vendor's part that thing sold is vendor's & is fit for use or fulfils specified conditions. [f. OF *warantie* fem. p.p. of *warantir* WARRANT[2]]

wa·rren (wŏ-), n. Piece of ground in which rabbits are preserved or abound (*like rabbits in a w.,* of thick population). [f. OF *warenne* (*warir* keep, cogn. w. WARE[3])]

wa·rrior (wŏ·rier), n. Distinguished or veteran soldier (rhet., poet.); member of any of the fighting services (*the Unknown W.,* or *Soldier,* unidentified body of one killed in the great war selected for public burial as symbolizing his country's sacrifice); (attrib., of nation &c.) martial; (of savages) fighting man; *w. ant,* of kinds that make slaves of other species. [f. OF *guerreiur* (*guerreier* make WAR)]

wart (wor-), n. Small hardish excrescence on skin caused by abnormal growth of papillae (*paint* one *with his ww.,* without concealment of blemishes), similar lump on stem &c. of plant; *w.-grass, -weed, -wort,* kind of spurge with juice used to cure ww.; *w.-hog*, kinds of African large-headed swine with warty lumps on face. Hence **war·ty**[2] a. [OE *wearte*, cf. Du. *wrat*, G *warze*]

wār·y, a. Given to caution, habitually on the look out, circumspect; cautious *of doing*; showing, done with, caution. Hence **war·ily**[2] adv., **war·iness** n. [as WARE[2] + -Y[2]]

was. See BE.

wash[1] (wŏ-), v.t. & i. Cleanse with liquid (*w.* one's *face* &c., one*self*, or any object; *w.* thing *out*, clean its inside; *w.* one's *dirty* LINEN; *w.* one's *hands* fig., decline responsibility usu. *of*), (fig.) purify (*w. me throughly from mine iniquity*); take (stain, dirt, &c.) *out* or *off* or *away* by washing; *w. up* (plates &c., or usu. abs.), clean table utensils after use; (abs.) w. oneself or esp. one's (face &) hands (*must w. before dinner*), w. clothes (*washes for a living*); (of coloured material or dye) bear washing without loss of colour (*won't w.* fig. of argument &c., stand examination), whence **wa·shing**[2] a.; *washed out*, (fig.) enfeebled, limp, demoralized, esp. as effect of dissipation; moisten (*roses washed with dew*), (of river, sea, &c.) touch(coast, bank, country) with its waters; (of moving liquid) carry along in specified direction (chiefly in pass.; *a wave washed him overboard*; *was washed up by the sea*; *beef washed down with ale*), denude (*sea-washed cliffs*), scoop out (*water had washed a channel*), go splashing or sweeping *over*, *along*, *out*, *in*, or *into*; sift (ore) by action of water; brush thin coating of watery colour over (paper in water-colour or sepia painting, wall), coat (inferior metal) thinly with gold &c. Hence **wa·shable** a. [OE *wascan*, cf. Du. *wasschen*, G *waschen*; cogn. w. WATER]

wash[2], n. Washing or being washed (*give it a good w.*; *must get a w.*; *the w.*, treatment at laundry, as *send the linen to the w.*), quantity of clothes just (to be, being) washed; visible or audible motion of agitated water, esp. waves caused by passage of vessel; soil swept off by water, alluvium; kitchen water & scraps given to pigs; thin or weak or inferior liquid food (*this soup, tea, claret, is mere w.*), (fig.) twaddle, wishwash; liquid for spreading over surface to cleanse or heal or colour, lotion, cosmetic; thin coating of water-colour, wall-colouring, or metal. [f. prec.]

wash-, comb. form of WASH[1, 2], often = & used as substitute for *wash*ING[1]: *w.-basin*; *w.-board*, of ribbed wood for use in scrubbing clothes at wash, also board attached to gunwale, port, &c., to prevent water from washing in, also board skirting bottom of room-wall; *w.-boiler*, clothes-washing cauldron; *w.-bottle*, apparatus for purifying gases &c. by passage through liquid; *w.-bowl*; *w.-cloth*, piece of linen &c. used in washing dishes &c.; *w.-day*, on which clothes are washed; *w.-hand-basin*; *w.-hand-stand*, piece of furniture with toilet utensils; *w.-house*, laundry; *w.-leather*, chamois or similar leather; *w.-out* (army slang), complete failure esp. to hit target, fiasco; *w.-pot* (archaic exc. of pot with melted tin for final dipping of tinplate); *w.-stand*, = *w.-hand-stand*; *w.-tub*, esp. for clothes.

wa·sher, n. In vbl senses; also, flat ring or perforated piece of leather, rubber, metal, &c., used to give tightness to joint, nut, fastening, &c.; *wa·sherwoman*, laundress. [-ER[1]]

wa·shing, n. In vbl senses (& see WASH-); esp., linen &c. sent to the wash; *w.-stand*, = WASH-*stand*. [-ING[1]]

Washingtō·nia (wŏ-), n. Californian palm-tree named after George Washington. [-IA[1]]

wa·shy, a. (Of liquid food &c.) too watery, weak, thin, insipid; (of colour) faded-looking, thin; (of style, sentiment, &c.) diffuse, feeble, lacking vigour or compression. Hence **wa·shily**[2] adv., **wa·shiness** n. [-Y[2]]

wasp (wŏ-), n. Kinds of hymenopterous social or solitary insect of which the common kind has black & yellow transverse stripes, very slender waist, taste for fruit & sweets, & powerfully venomous sting (*has a waist like a w.'s*, whence **wasp-waisted**[2] a.); *w.-bee*, *-beetle*, *-fly*, kinds having some resemblance to w. [OE *wæps*, cf. G *wespe*; for metath. cf. ASK, HASP; cogn. w. WEAVE, w. ref. to nests, & w. L *vespa*]

wa·spish, a. Irritable, petulant, ill-tempered, sharp in retort. Hence **wa·spishly**[2] adv., **wa·spishness** n. [-ISH[1]]

wassail (wŏ·sl, wă·sl), n., & v.i., (archaic). Festive occasion, drinking-bout; kind of liquor drunk on such occasion; *w.-bowl*, *-cup*, *-horn*, &c.; (vb) make merry, hold festivities. [f. OE *wes* be thou (cf. *was* see BE), *hāl* WHOLE, form of salutation]

wast. See BE.

wā·stage (-ĭj), n. Amount wasted or that runs to waste, loss by waste. [-AGE]

wāste[1], a. (Of district &c.) desolate, desert, uninhabited, uncultivated, as result of natural barrenness &c. or of ravages or catastrophe (*lay w.*, ravage; *lie w.*, be uncultivated; *w. land*, not occupied for any purpose), (fig.) monotonous or presenting no features of interest (*the w. periods of history*), superfluous, refuse, no longer serving a purpose, left over after use, (*w. products*, useless by-products of manufacture; *w. energy*, *steam*, &c.; *w. paper*, esp. books or documents that fail or are valueless). [f. OF *wast* f. L VASTUS]

waste[2], v.t. & i. Lay WASTE[1]; (Law) bring (estate) into bad condition by damage or neglect; expend to no purpose or for inadequate result, use extravagantly, squander, (*w. money, time, food*, &c., or abs. as *w. not, want not*; *w. breath* or *words*, talk uselessly); wear (t. & i.) gradually away, wither, (archaic, of time) pass t. & i., (*his resources were wasted, were rapidly wasting*; *day wastes*, draws to a close; *sorcerer wasted his arm*; *a wasting disease*; *is wasting away for lack of food*); run to w. (*that water is wasting*). [f. OF *waster* (now *gâter*) f. L *vastare* (prec.)]

waste[3], n. Desert, w. region, dreary scene, (*a w. of waters*, unbroken expanse of sea); being used up, diminution by wear & tear, (*the w. of tissue is continuous*; *w. & repair balance each other*); w. material or food, useless remains, refuse, scraps, shreds; act of wasting, throwing away or extravagant or ineffectual use *of* time, money, food, &c., (*wilful w. makes woeful want*; *it is w. of time to argue further*; *run to w.* of liquid or fig. of affection &c., be wasted); (Law) injury to estate caused by act or neglect esp. of life-tenant. [as WASTE[1]]

waste-, comb. form of WASTE[1, 2, 3]: *w.-basket*, for w. odds & ends esp. of paper; *w.-book* in book-keeping, book in which rough preliminary entries of transactions are made; **wa·ste**FUL a., extravagant, given to or exhibiting waste, whence **wa·stefu**lLY[2] adv., **wa·steful**NESS n., **wa·ste**LESS a.; *w.-pa·per-basket*, receptacle for used papers &c.; *w.-pipe*, for carrying off used or superfluous water.

wa·ster, n. In vbl senses; also, article spoilt or flawed in manufacture; (slang) person whose existence is regrettable. [-ER[1]]

wā·strel, n. Thing spoilt in making; stray child, street arab, waif, good-for-nothing fellow; wasteful person. [f. WASTE[2] + -REL]

watch[1] (wŏ-), n. Wakefulness at night (now rare; *in the ww. of the night*, while one lies awake; *pass as a w. in the night*, be soon forgotten); alert state, being on the look-out, vigilance, constant observation, attention to what may come, (*keep w., a w., good* or *a good w.*; *w. & ward*, orig. guard by night & day, now emphatic reduplication of *w.*; *on the w.*, waiting usu. *for* expected or desired or feared occurrence), whence **wa·tch**FUL a., **wa·tchful**LY[2] adv., **wa·tchful**NESS n.; (Hist.) man or body of men charged with patrolling streets at night, guard (BLACK[1] *w.*, orig. an armed company); (Hist.) one of three or of four parts into which night was anciently divided (*first* &c. or *evening* &c. *w.*); four-hour spell of duty on board ship (DOG-*w.*, 2-hr), one of the halves (*starboard* & *port w.* from position of men's bunks) into which ship's crew is divided to take alternate duty; small timepiece worked by coiled spring for carrying on person (STOP-*w.*); *w.-case*, outer metal case enclosing w.-works; *w.-chain*, metal w.-guard; *w.-dog*, employed to give alarm of burglars &c.; *w.-fire*, at night in camps &c.; *w.-glass*, disk covering face of w.; *w.-guard*, chain or string for securing w. on person; *w.-key*, instrument for winding up w.-works; *w.-maker*; *wa·tchman*, (formerly, & still poet.) sentinel or member of street patrol, (now) man employed to look after empty building &c. at night; *w.-night*, last night of year as celebrated esp. by methodists with religious services; *w. oil*, fine thin kind for lubricating w.-works &c.; *w.-pocket*, in garment esp. waistcoat, or separate for attachment to bed &c., holding w.; *w.-spring*, kind used in w.-works, also mainspring of w.; *w.-stand*, small pillar &c. for hanging w. on; *w.-tower*, post of observation usu. fortified; *wa·tchword*, (formerly) military password, (now) phrase expressing briefly the principles of a party &c, (e. g. *Peace, retrenchment, & reform*). [OE *wæcce* (*wæccan*, see foll.)]

watch[2], v.i. & t. Remain awake for a purpose (now rare; *watched all night by his side*; *w. & pray*); be on the w., keep w., be vigilant, look out *for* opportunity &c., exercise protecting care *over*; keep eyes fixed on, keep under observation, follow observantly, (*had him watched by detectives*; *if you don't w. it* colloq., take care or precautions; *watched pot never boils*, strained expectation makes time seem long); look out for, bide, await, (opportunity; *w.* one's *time*, wait for right moment). Hence **wa·tch**ER[1] n. [OE *wæccan* doublet of *wacian* WAKE[1]]

wa·ter[1] (waw-), n. Colourless transparent tasteless scentless compound of oxygen & hydrogen in liquid state convertible by heat into steam & by cold into ice, kinds of liquid consisting chiefly of this seen in sea, lake, stream, spring, rain, tears, sweat, saliva, urine, serum, &c., body of w. as sea or lake or river, (*hot* & *cold, salt* & *fresh* or *sweet, smooth* or *still* & *rough* or *troubled*, HARD or SOFT, *aerated, saline, chalybeate, thermal*, BLUE[1], HOLY, MINERAL, &c., *w.*; *strong ww.* archaic, distilled spirits; *table ww.*, esp. mineral ww. bottled for use at meals; *red w.*, bloody urine; *in smooth w.*, going easily, past one's troubles; *on the w.*, in boat or ship; *by w.*, using ships, barges, &c., for travel or transport; *in deep w.* or *ww.*, floundering, in great difficulties, in affliction; *still ww. run deep*, quiet manner may cover depths of emotion, knowledge, or cunning; FISH[2] *in troubled ww.*; *cup of cold w.*, symbol of charitable intent; *get into, be in, hot w.*, bring or have brought trouble or rebuke on oneself by indiscretion &c.; *throw cold w. on* scheme &c., discourage or poohpooh it; *written in w.* of name, achievements, &c., transient; *keep* one's *head above w.*, chiefly fig., avoid financial ruin; *the ww.* rhet., the sea, as *cross the ww.*; *cast* one's *bread upon the ww.*, do good without looking for gratitude or immediate or definite return; *drink the ww.*, attend spa for health; *brings the w. to* one's *mouth*, makes it w.; FISH[1] *out of w.*; BETWEEN *wind & w.*; *pour* OIL[1] *on the ww.*; *spend money, shed blood, like w.*, lavishly or recklessly; *go through* FIRE[1] *& w.*; *fire & w.*, archaic, symbol of necessaries of life not to be supplied to outlaw; HOLD[1] *w.*; *make, pass, w.*, void urine; *tread w.*, maintain position in deep w. by action of marking time; *w. on the brain, knee*, &c., morbid accumulation of serum; *w. bewitched*, very weak tea &c. or spirit-&-w.; *w. of life*, spiritual enlightenment; *ww. of forgetfulness*, Lethe, oblivion, death); state of tide (*high, low, w.*; *in low w.* fig., in depressed condition, esp. badly off for money; *high, low, -w. mark*, highest, lowest point reached by tidal water, also fig. of best & worst results of fluctuating process); solution of specified substance in w. (*lavender, rose*, &c., *-w.*, scents; *soda, lithia, dill*, &c., *-w.*, beverages or medicines); transparency & brilliance of gem esp. diamond (*of the first w.*, of finest quality, often also transf. as *a genius, blunder, of the first w.*); (Finance) amount of nominal capital added by watering; *water-* (in compounds of which those especially that distinguish varieties of plants & animals are too numerous to be given separately), haunting, growing in, used or employed on, &c., the w., of, for, worked or effected by, made with, containing, using, yielding, &c., w. *W.-anchor*, = DRAG[2]-anchor; *w.-bailiff*, customhouse officer at port; *w.-bed*, rubber mattress filled with w. for invalid to avoid bed-sores; *w.-bellows*, blower made by suspension in w. of inverted valved vessel by raising & lowering of which air is drawn in & expelled; *w.-bird*; *w.-biscuit*; *w.-blister*, containing colourless serum, not blood; *w.-boatman*, kind of aquatic bug; *w.-borne*, (of goods) conveyed by w.; *w.-bottle*, esp. of glass for wash-hand-stand or dining table, also of metal &c. for soldier's kit; *w.-brash*, form of indigestion with copious saliva or w.-vomiting; *w.*-BREAKER[2]; *w.-butt*; *w.-carriage*, conveyance of goods by w.; *W.-carrier*, Aquarius; *w.-cart*, esp. with w. for sale or for watering roads; *w.-chute*, slope of boards slippery with running water for tobogganing down; *w.-closet*, privy with arrangement for flushing pan with w.; *w.-colour*, pigment mixed with w. & not oil, picture painted with such colours, (pl. or sing.) art of painting such pictures, whence **wa·ter-colour**IST(3) n.; *w.* COMPRESS[2]; *wa·tercourse*, brook, stream; *w.-cracker*, kind of biscuit; *wa·tercress*, creeping w.-plant eaten as salad; *w.-cure*, hydropathy; *w.-drinker*, (esp.) abstainer from alcohol; *wa·terfall*, stream falling over precipice or down steep hillside; *w.-finder*, dowser (DOWSING); *wa·terfowl* (usu. collect. as pl.), birds haunting w., esp. as objects of sport; *w.-gas*, got by decomposing water & used after treatment with carbon as illuminant; *w.-gate*, flood-gate, also gate giving access to river &c.; *w.-gauge*, glass tube &c. indicating height of w. inside reservoir, boiler, &c.; *w.-glass*, tube with glass bottom enabling objects under w. to be observed, also solution of flint sprayed over w.-colour painting on dry plaster to fix it, or used for preserving eggs; *w.-gruel*; *w.-hammer*, percussion made by w. in pipe when tap is turned off, or by w. in steam-pipe when live steam is admitted; *w.-hen*, = moorhen; *w.-ice*, flavoured & frozen w. & sugar; *w.-inch*, quantity discharged in 24 hrs through 1 in. pipe under least pressure; *w.-jacket*, case filled with w. & enclosing part of machine that is to be kept cool; *w.-joint*, proof against leakage; *w.-junket*, sandpiper; *w.-laid* of rope, = CABLE[1]*-laid*; *w.-lens*, magnifying lens made of glass-bottomed brass cell filled with w.; *w.-level*, surface of w. in reservoir &c., also plane below which ground is saturated with w., also levelling-instrument made of glass tube to be held horizontal with two upturned graduated open ends in which the contained w. must be at same height; *w.-lily*, kinds of plant with broad leaves & white or blue or yellow or red flowers floating on surface of w.; *w.-line*, along which surface of w. touches ship's side (when loaded, *load-w.-l.*, when empty, *light w.-l.*), also one of the semi-transparent parallel lines formed in some papers in manufacture; *wa·terlogged*, (of wood) so saturated, (of vessel) so filled, with w. as barely to float; *w.-main*, main pipe in w.-supplying system; *wa·terman*, boatman plying for hire, also oarsman *good, bad*, &c., at keeping boat truly balanced &c., whence **wa·terman**SHIP(3) n.; *wa·termark*, n. faint design seen in some paper when held against light indicating maker, size, &c., v.t., impress such mark on in making; *w.-meadow*, kept fertile by being flooded; *w.-melon*, one of two divisions of melon (the other being *musk-melon*) with ellipse shape, smooth skin, & watery juice; *w.-meter*; *w.-mill*, worked by w.-wheel; *w.-monkey*, jar with long narrow neck for w. used in hot countries; *w.-motor*, w.-wheel, turbine, small motor using w. under pressure; *w.-nymph*, naiad; *w.* OUZEL; *w.-pillar*, upright with revolving head for feeding steam-engines &c.; *w.-pipe*; *w.-plane*, plane passing through ship's w.-line, (also) = SEA*-plane*; *w.-plate*, with double bottom to hold hot w. for keeping food warm; *w.-platter*, kind of w.-lily with upturned edges to leaves; *Water Poet* (the),

John Taylor (d. 1653); *w. polo*, hand-ball game with goals played by swimmers; *w.-power*, mechanical force got from weight or motion of w., fall in stream capable of being utilized as force; *wa·terproof* a., impervious to w., w.-p. garment or material, v.t., make w.-p. with rubber &c., whence **wa·terproof**ER[1] n.; *w.-ram*, hydraulic ram; *w.-rat*, = *w. vole*; *w.-rate*, charge made for use of public w.-supply; *w.-sail*, below lower studding-sail close over w.; *w.-seal*, body of w. used in bent pipe or about mouth of pipe to prevent passage or escape of gas; *wa·tershed*, line of separation between ww. flowing to different rivers or basins or seas [cogn. w. SHED[1]]; *w.-shoot*, pipe or trough throwing off w. from house &c.; *watersi·de*, margin of sea, lake, or river; *w.-skin*, skin bag for carrying w.; *w.-soldier*, aquatic plant with flowers above surface; *w. souchet* or *souchy*, fish boiled & served in its own liquor; *wa·terspout*, phenomenon in which whirling cloud forms a funnel-shaped pendant, which descends towards sea & draws up corresponding volume of whirling water, the whole forming a pillar uniting sea & cloud; *w.-sprite*; *w.-supply*, providing & storing of w., amount of w. stored, for use of town, house, &c.; *w.-table*, string-course arranged to throw w. off building; *w.-tiger*, larva of certain w.-beetles; *wa·tertight*, (of joint, boots, cask, compartment in ship, &c.) tightly enough fastened or fitted to prevent ingress or egress of w. (*w.-t. compartments* fig., keeping of subjects &c. entirely separate); *w.-tower*, supporting elevated tank to secure pressure for distributing w.-supply; *w.-tube boiler*, in which w. circulates in tubes exposed to flames & hot gases; *w.-vole*, large vole haunting w.; *w.-way*, navigable channel, also thick planks at outer edge of deck along which channel is hollowed for w. to run off by; *w.-wheel*, kinds of wheel (*overshot, undershot, breast*, & *turbine, wheel*) worked by w. & working machinery; *w. - witch*, = *w.- finder*, also kinds of bird; *w.-withe*, W.-Ind. vine so full of sap that branch broken off yields draught of w.; *wa·terworks*, establishment for managing w.-supply, also ornamental fountain (*turn on the w.-w.* slang, shed tears). Hence **wa·ter**LESS a. [Aryan; OE *wæter*, cf. Du. *water*, G *wasser*, Gk *hudōr*, L *unda* wave, Skr. *udán*; cogn. w. WET]

wa·ter[2], v.t. & i. Sprinkle (road, plants, &c.), adulterate (milk, beer, &c.), with w.; give drink of w. to (horse, &c.), (of animals) go to pool &c. to drink; (of ship, engine, &c., or persons in charge) take in supply of w.; (of smarting eyes, or of mouth when food is seen or food or pleasure eagerly anticipated) secrete or run with w. (*makes* one's *mouth w.*, excites desire or envy); (chiefly in p.p., as *watered silk*) produce irregular wavy damask-like markings on (material) by moistening & pressing in manufacture; (Finance) increase (company's debt or nominal capital) by issue of new shares without corresponding addition to assets; *w. down*, make (details of story &c.) less vivid or horrifying; *watering-cart*, with perforated pipe or other device for watering road; *watering-place*, pool &c. at which animals w., also spa, also seaside place frequented at certain seasons by holiday-makers & invalids; *watering-pot*, with perforated nozzle for watering plants. [OE *wæterian* f. *wæter*, see prec.]

wa·terbury, n. Kinds of cheap American watch. [*W.* in U.S.]

wa·tery, a. Containing too much water, over-moist, sodden, (esp. of cooked vegetables or fish); (of eyes or lips) suffused or running with water; (of liquids) too thin, actually or apparently diluted, resembling water, (fig., of expression, talk, style, &c.) vapid, insipid, uninteresting, feeble, (of colour) pale, washed out; indicative of rain (*a w. moon, sky*). Hence **wa·teri**NESS n. [-Y[2]]

watt (wŏt), n. Unit of electric power, rate of working in circuit when electromotive force is one volt & intensity of current one ampere. Hence **wa·tt**METER n. [J. *W.* engineer d. 1819]

Watteau (wŏ·tō, *or as F*), n. French painter d. 1721 (*W. back*, arrangement of woman's dress-back with broad pleat falling from neck to ground without girdle; *W. bodice*, with square opening at neck & short ruffled sleeves).

wa·ttle[1] (wŏ-), n., & v.t. Interlaced rods & twigs as material of fences, walls, or roofs (*w. & daub*, plastered with mud or clay); (sing. or pl.) rods & twigs for such use; kinds of Australian acacia supplying such twigs, having bark used in tanning, & bearing golden flowers adopted as national emblem; (dial.) a wicker hurdle. (Vb) construct of w.; interlace (twigs &c.); enclose or fill up with w.-work. [OE *watul* etym. dub., cf. *wætla* a bandage]

wa·ttle[2] (wŏ-), n. Fleshy appendage on head or throat of turkey & other birds; BARB[1] of fish. Hence **wa·ttl**ED[2] a. [perh. f. prec. through the doubtful sense wicker-basket; perh. = obs. *wartle* dim. of WART]

waul, v.i. Squall, cry like cat. [imit.]

wave[1], v.i. & t. Vibrate or be stirred with sinuous or sweeping motions like those of flag or tree or field of corn in wind, flutter, undulate; impart waving motion to (*w. sword*, brandish it as encouragement to followers &c.; *w.* one's *hand* often *to* person, in greeting or as signal); w. hand or thing held in it usu. *to* person, give direction thus *to* person *to* do, send (person) *away* thus, summon (person) *nearer* thus, direct (person) thus *to* do, express *farewell* &c. thus; *w. aside*, dismiss as intrusive or irrelevant; give undulating surface or course or appearance to (hair of head, lines in drawing, &c.), make wavy, (of hair, line, &c.) have such appearance, be wavy. [OE *wafian* undulate, cf. MHG *waben*]

wave[2], n. Ridge of water between two depressions or (also *breaker*) long body of water curling into arched form & breaking on shore (*the ww.* or *w.* poet. & rhet., the sea, water; *attack in ww.*, mil., in successive lines advancing like sea-ww.); disturbance of the particles of a fluid medium e. g. water, air, ether, into a ridge-&-trough oscillation by which motion is propagated & heat, light, sound, electricity, &c., conveyed in some direction without corresponding advance or without any advance of the particles in the same direction, single curve in the course of such motion; temporary heightening of some influence or condition or feeling (*a w. of enthusiasm, prosperity, depression*; *heat, cold, -w.*, rise or fall of temperature travelling over large area;) undulating line or outline or surface, waviness; gesture of waving; *w.-length*, distance in any undulation from one crest to the next, varying greatly with different kinds of ray &c., stated for long waves (e. g. of Hertzian rays) in (kilo)-metres & for short waves (e. g. of X-rays) in Ångström units, & especially familiar as allocated in wireless. Hence **wa·ve**LESS a., **wa·ve**LET n. [f. prec.]

wā·ver, v.i. Oscillate unsteadily, flicker, quiver, (rare; chiefly of flame); (of troops) falter, become unsteady, begin to give way; be irresolute or undecided between different courses or opinions, be shaken in resolution or belief. Hence **wa·ver**ER[1] n., **wa·vering**LY[2] adv. [WAVE[1], -ER[5]]

wa·vy[1], a. Undulating, (of line or surface) consisting of or showing alternate contrary curves, (*w. hair*). Hence **wa·vi**LY[2] adv., **wa·vi**NESS n. [-Y[2]]

wā·vy[2], **-ey**, n. The snow-goose. [f. Amer.-Ind. *wawa*]

wawl. =WAUL.

wăx[1], n., & v.t. Sticky plastic yellowish substance secreted by bees as material of honeycomb cells, beeswax, white translucent scentless tasteless material got from this by bleaching & purifying & used for candles, in modelling, & for other purposes, (*mould* one *like w.*, form his character on desired lines or induce him to act just as desired); substance resembling w. in some respect, as the secretion of some other insects esp. *Chinese w.*, *ear-w.* or cerumen, *mineral w.* esp. ozocerite, bee-bread, *vegetable w.* or exudation of certain plants, SEAL[2]*ing-w.*, COBBLERS'*-w.*; (attrib., now usu. preferred to *waxen*) made of w.; *wa·xbill*, kinds of small bird with translucent bill; *w. candle*; *w.-chandler*, maker or seller of w. candles; *w.-cloth*, floor-cloth; *w. doll*, with face &c. of w., also person esp. woman with pretty but unexpressive face; *w.-insect*, kinds that secrete w., esp. that collected as Chinese w. from which superior candles are made; *w.-light*, taper or candle of w.; *w.-myrtle*, candleberry; *w.-painting*, encaustic; *w.-palm*, S.-Amer. palm with stem coated in mixture of resin & w.; *w.-paper*, waterproofed with layer of w.; *w.-pink*, garden-plant portulaca; *w.-pocket*, one of bee's w.-exuding apertures; *w.-pod*, = BUTTER-*bean*; *w.-tree*, kinds exuding w. or encrusted with it by insects; *wa·xwing*, kinds of bird with small horny tips like red sealing-w. to some feathers; *wa·xwork*, modelling-work, objects modelled, in w., esp. dummies of persons with face & hands of coloured w. clothed to look like life & be exhibited; (vb) smear, polish, encrust, treat surface of, with w. [com.-Teut.: OE *weax*, cf. Du. *was*, G *wachs*]

wăx[2], v.i. (Of moon between new & full) have progressively larger part of surface illuminated (cf. *wane*; *w. & wane* also transf. of influence &c., undergo alternations of increase & decrease), (archaic & poet.) grow or increase; (with adj. compl.) pass into specified condition or esp. mood or tone (*w. fat, old, merry, facetious, indignant, pathetic, angry*). [Aryan; OE *weaxan*, cf. Du. *wassen*, G *waschen*, Gk *auxanō*, L *augēre*, Skr. *vaksh*]

wăx[3], n. (slang). Fit of anger (*is in, got into, put him in, a w.*). [?]

wa·xen, a. Made of wax (being ousted by attrib. use of *wax*); presenting surface as of wax (esp. of complexion, used with less of depreciation than *waxy*); impressible as wax, plastic. [-EN[5]]

wa·xy, a. Resembling wax in some way, esp. easily moulded or presenting smooth pale translucent surface; (of tissue) having degenerated into consistency resembling wax (so *w. liver* &c.); (slang) angry, quick-tempered. Hence **wa·xi**LY[2] adv., **wa·xi**NESS n. [WAX[1, 3], -Y[2]]

way, n. Road or track lit. or fig. provided for passing along (HIGH*w.*; OVER *the w.*; *permanent w.*, complete piece of regular railroad track; *six-foot w.*, space left between each pair of rails & the next on railway; *covered w.*, roofed or in Fortif. screened passage; *Appian, Latin*, &c., *W.*, great Roman roads in Italy; MILKY *w.*; *the w. of the Cross*, series of paintings in church &c., to receive successive attention in certain services, illustrating Christ's progress to Calvary; *go the w. of all the earth, of all flesh, of nature*, die; *pave the w. for*, take steps that will facilitate or prepare people's minds to accept some change), (pl.) structure of timber &c. on which new ship is slid down at launch; best route or route taken or contemplated between two places or to place, method or plan for attaining object, person's desired or chosen course of action, (*ask the* or one's *w.*; *furthest w. about is nearest w. home*, short cuts are delusive; *find* one's or *the w.*, reach destination; *lose* one's or *the w.*, go astray; *parting of the ww.* usu. fig., time for momentous decision; *take* one's *w.*, go in some direction, usu. *to* or *towards*; *go* one's *w.* or *ww.*, depart; *came by w. of London*, viâ; *lead the w.*, act as guide or leader, show by example how thing can be done; *put* oneself *out of the w.*, inconvenience oneself to serve another; *is nothing out of the w.*, not uncommon or remarkable; *an out-of-the-w. corner*, remote, inaccessible; *go out of the* or one's *w. to be rude*, show wanton rudeness; *right & wrong ww. of doing a thing*; *that is the w. to do it*; *don't like the w. she smiles*; *where there 's a will there 's a way*; *you will never manage it that w.*; *will find or make a w.*; *will do it one w. or another*; *ww. & means*, methods esp. of providing money as in parliamentary *Committee of Ww. & Means*; *go, take*, one's *own w.*, act independently esp. against others' advice; *have* one's *own* or one's *w.*, get what one wants, see one's orders carried out or desires gratified); travelling-distance, length of road &c. (to be) traversed, (*India is a long w. off*; *went a little, a good, a long, some, w. with* or *to meet him*; ONCE *in a way*; *is still a long w. off perfection*); unimpeded opportunity of advance, room free of obstacles, ground over which advance is desired or would naturally take place, (GIVE[1], MAKE[1], *w.*; LION *in the w.*; *stand, be, in the w. of*, *in* one's *w.*, or *in the w.*, be obstacle to, be obstacle; *get out of, in, the w.*, cease, begin, to be impediment; *get* thing *out of the w.*, dispose of, get rid of, settle; *put* person *out of the w.*, confine or secretly kill him; *clear the w.*, remove obstacles, stand aside; RIGHT *of w.*; *put* one *in the w. of a good bargain, of* doing, give him opportunity); being engaged, time spent, in locomotion lit. or fig. (*with songs to cheer the w.*; *met him on the w. out* or *home*; *is on the w.*, travelling or approaching; *by the w.*, during journey, fig. incidentally, often used by speaker to introduce more or less irrelevant remark); specified direction (usu. in adv. phrr. without prep.; *which w. is he looking, going?*; *look the other w.*, avoid meeting person's eye, cut him; appended colloq. to names of places, as *lives somewhere London w.*); custom, manner of behaving, personal peculiarity, (*the good old ww.*, old fashions; *stand in the ancient ww.*, avoid what is new-fangled; *the w. of the world*, conduct no worse than is justified by custom; *it is not my w. to desert people in misfortune*; *has a little w. of leaving his bills unpaid*; *it is only his w.*, piece of rudeness &c. from him has no special significance); scope, sphere, range, line of occupation, branch of business, (*hunting is not, does not lie* or *come* or *fall, in my w.*; *is in the grocery w.*, a grocer; *want a few things in the stationery w.*); advance in some direction, impetus, progress, (*make* one's *w. home, into a shop*, &c.; *make* one's or one's *own w.*, prosper; *make the best of* one's *w.*, go as fast as one can; *make w.*, advance lit. or fig.; *gather, lose, w.*, gain or lose speed; *give w.* of oarsmen, row hard; *ship has w. on, is under w.*, moves through water); respect (*not a bad fellow in some ww.*; *is satisfactory in one* or *a w.*; *in a w.*, to a limited extent, not altogether; *no w. inferior*, not at all); ordinary course (*did it in the w. of business*); condition, assumption, hypothesis, state, train, degree, (*things are in a bad w.*; *have it* BOTH *ww.*; *each w., both ww.*, in backing horse &c., to win, to be placed; *any w.*, in either or any case or event; *we are all in the same w., live in a* SMALL *w., is an author, builds ships, in a small w.*, on small scale; *be in a w.* or *a great w.*, colloq., be agitated; *be in the family w.*, with child); *by w. of*, as substitute for or form of, with intention of, (*carries a stick by w. of weapon*; *did it by w. of apology, of discovering the truth*; *is by w. of making an effort*, represents himself to himself or others to be doing so). *W.-bill*, list of passengers or parcels on conveyance; *w.-board*, thin layer separating thicker strata; *way·farer, -faring*, traveller, travelling, esp. on foot; *way·faring-tree*, white-flowered shrub common along roadsides; *waylay·* v.t., lie in wait for, wait about for to rob or interview; *w.-leave*, right of way rented by mine-owners &c.; *w.-shaft* in steam-engine, rocking shaft for working slide-valve from eccentric; *waysi·de*, side of road (esp. attrib., as *w.-s. flowers, inn*); *w.-worn*, tired with travel. [com.-Teut.: OE, also Du. & G, *weg*, cogn. w. WAIN, L *vehere* carry, Skr. *vah* carry]

-ways, suf. forming advv. usu. of position or direction, & often used indifferently with -WISE; *lengthways, sideways, always*, &c. [prec., -ES]

way·ward, a. Childishly self-willed or perverse, capricious, unaccountable, freakish. Hence **way·ward**LY[2] adv., **way·ward**NESS n. [for *away*WARD, cf. *froward*]

way·zgoose, n. Printing-house's annual festivity. [earlier *waygoose* (1683; *wayz-* 1731), etym. dub.]

we, pl. subj. of I[2] (used, besides the ordinary pron. use, by royal person in proclamations &c. instead of *I*, by writer in unsigned article of newspaper &c., & as collective name for speaker & all others of the class that context shows him to be representing for the moment). [com.-Teut.: OE *wē*, cf. Du. *wij*, G *wir*, Skr. *vay-am*]

weak, a. Wanting in strength or power or number, fragile, easily broken or bent or defeated (*w. barrier, rope,* &c.; *w.* AS *a cat, water*; *a w. eleven,* of poor players; *offer but a w. resistance*; *w. vessel* usu. fig., unreliable person; *a w. crew,* short-handed; *w. hand,* deficient in high cards; *the weaker sex,* women; *weakest goes to* WALL; *w. knees* usu. fig., inability to stand firm, want of resolution, whence **weak-kneed**² a.; *w. ending* in blank verse, unaccented or proclitic word such as *if* at end); wanting in vigour, not acting strongly, sickly, feeble, (*w. constitution,* want of power to resist disease &c.; *w. stomach,* easily upset; *w. eyes, sight,* easily tired or not seeing well, whence **weak-eyed**², **weak-sighted**², aa.; *w. heart,* acting feebly; *w. mind, head,* below average in intelligence, verging on idiocy, whence **weak-minded**², **weak-headed**², aa.; so *w. intellect*; *w. imagination*; *w. voice,* easily tired or not reaching far; *w. demand* for goods or stocks, slack; so *the market was w.*); wanting in resolution or power of resisting temptation, easily led, (*w. character, man*; person's *w. side* or *point,* at which he is open to temptation), (of action) indicating want of resolution in agent (*a w. surrender, compliance*); unconvincing, logically deficient, (*w. logic, evidence*; *a w. argument*); (of mixed liquid or solution) watery, thin, (*w. tea, brandy-&-water, brine*); (of style &c.) not nervous or well-knit, diffuse, slipshod; (Gram.) inflected by consonantal additions to, not vowel change in, stem (in English esp. of verbs making past & p.p. by addition of *-ed*). Hence **wea·ken**⁶ v.t. & i., **wea·kish**¹(2) a., **wea·kly**¹ (-LY²) adv. [f. ON *veik-r* weak, cogn. w. OE *wác* pliant]

wea·kling, n. Feeble person &c. [-LING¹]

wea·kly², a. Sickly, not robust, ailing. [-LY¹]

wea·kness, n. In adj. senses; also or esp.: weak point or defect; inability to resist a particular temptation; foolish liking or inclination *for.* [-NESS]

weal¹, n. Welfare, prosperity, good fortune, (chiefly now in *w. & woe, w. or woe,* in COMMONWEAL, & in *for the public* or *general w.*). [OE *wela* wealth, cogn. w. WELL³]

weal². See WALE.

weald (wē-), n. District including parts of Kent, Surrey, Hants., & Sussex, with geologically interesting characteristics; *w.-clay,* beds of clay, sandstone, limestone, & iron-stone, forming top of w. strata, with abundant fossil remains. [OE, = forest, cogn. w. WOLD]

wea·lden, a. & n. Of the weald, resembling the weald geologically; (n.) series of lower-cretaceous fresh-water strata above oolite & below chalk best exemplified in the weald. [-EN⁵]

wealth (wĕ-), n. Welfare, prosperity, (archaic; *in health & w. long to live*); riches, large possessions, opulence, being rich; the rich; abundance, *a* profusion or great quantity or display, *of* (*a w. of illustration, wit, fruit*; *w. of words is not eloquence*). Hence **wea·lthy**² a., **wea·lthily**² adv., **wea·lthiness** n. [WEAL¹ + -TH¹, cf. Du. *weelde* luxury]

wean¹, v.t. Teach (sucking child or animal) to feed otherwise than from the breast (often *from* mother or breast); disengage or cure *from* or rarely *of* habit, specified company, &c., by enforced abstinence or counter-attractions. [OE *wenian* accustom, cf. Du. *wennen,* G *gewöhnen,* accustom; cogn. w. WONT]

wean², n. (Sc.). Child. [= *wee ane* little one]

wea·nling, n. New-weaned child &c. [-LING¹]

weapon (wĕ·pn), n. Material thing designed or used or usable as an instrument for inflicting bodily harm, e. g. cannon, rifle, sword, spear, stick, hammer, poker, horn, claw; action or procedure or means used to get the better in a conflict (*irony is a double-edged w.*; *use the w. of a general strike*; *tears, the woman's w.*). Hence **wea·ponless** a. [com.-Teut.: OE *wǽpen* cf. Du. *wapen,* G *waffe*]

wear¹ (wãr), v.t. & i. (wore, worn). Be dressed habitually in, have on, carry or exhibit on one's person or some part of it, (*wears green, serge, knickerbockers,* &c., as usual colour &c.; *is wearing diamonds,* on this occasion; *worn clothes,* that have been put on at least once; *w. the crown, sword, gown, willow, breeches,* be a monarch or martyr, soldier, lawyer, desolate lover, husband-ruling wife; *w.* one's *hair long, short,* &c.; *w. a face of joy, sour look,* &c.; *w.* HEART *on sleeve*; *w.* person or principle *in* one's *heart,* be devoted to; *w.* one's *years well,* remain young-looking), whence **wear·er**¹ n.; injure surface of, partly consume or obliterate, damage, attenuate, or alter, by rubbing or use, suffer such injury or consumption or change, come or bring into specified state by use, rub (t. & i.) *off* or *out* or *away* or *down,* (*step worn with pilgrims' knees*; *worn clothes,* the worse for wear; *inscription has been worn,* or *has worn, away*; *w. the freshness, the nap, off*; *impression soon wears off*; *clothes w. to one's shape,* fit better with use; *w.* one's *trousers, trousers have worn, into holes* or *bagginess*; *seams w. white, ragged, threadbare*; *is worn to a shadow with care*; *stick wears down to a stump*; *a worn* or *well-worn joke,* stale; *w. out,* use or be used till usable no longer); exhaust, tire or be tired *out,* put *down* by persistence, (*worn with travel*; *a wearing occupation, companion,* &c.; *w. out* one's *welcome,* go too often or stay too long as visitor &c.; *his patience wore,* or *was worn, out at last*; *succeeded in wearing down opposition*); endure continued use *well, badly,* &c., remain specified time in working order or presentable state, last long, (*won't w.*, of inferior material, transitory impression, &c.; *wears for years*; person *wears well*, retains youthful strength or esp. look); (of time) go slowly or tediously *on*, pass (t. & i. of time) gradually *away*, (*winter, time, day, wears on* or *away*; *w. away* or *out* one's *life* or *time* or *youth in trifles*; *w. through the day*, get through it somehow); make (hole, groove, channel) by attrition (usu. of incidental or undesigned action, cf. BORE; often of water); *wearing-apparel*, clothes; *wearing-iron* or *-plate*, piece of metal attached to protect surface exposed to friction. Hence **wear·**ABLE a. [Aryan: OE *werian*, cf. ON *verja*, Goth. *wasjan*; cogn. w. L *vestis*, Gk *esthēs*, clothes, Skr. *vas* to dress]

wear², n. Wearing or being worn on person, use as clothes, (*the best materials for Sunday, working, spring, seaside*, &c., *w.*; *serges are now in general w.*, fashionable; *the coat I have in w.*, am regularly wearing); thing to w., fashionable or suitable apparel, (in phrr. on type of *motley's the only w.*; also in *foot* &c. *-w.* chiefly in trade use as collective for things worn on feet &c.); damage sustained as result of ordinary use (esp. *w. & tear*; *will stand any amount of w.*; *is the worse for w.*, damaged by use); capacity for resisting w. & tear (*there is a great deal of, no, w. in it*). [f. prec.]

wear³ (wār), v.t. & i. (naut.; past & p.p. *wore*). Bring (ship), (of ship) come, about by putting up of helm (cf. *tack*). [etym. dub.; perh. corrupt. of VEER by confusion w. WEAR¹]

wear⁴ (wēr). = WEIR.

weary (wēr·ĭ), a., & v.t. & i. Tired, with energy abated, dispirited; sick or impatient *of*; tiring, tedious, irksome; hence **wear·**ILY² adv., **wear·**INESS n. (Vb) make w. (esp. of or with importunity or monotony), whence **wear·isome** a., **wear·isome**LY² adv., **wear·isome**NESS n.; grow w. (esp. *of* importunity or importunate person), whence **wear·**ILESS a.; (chiefly Sc.) long *to* do or *for*. [OE *wérig*, cf. OHG *wuarag* drunk; cogn. w. OE *wórian* go astray; not f. WEAR¹]

wea·sand (wēz-), n. (archaic). Wind-pipe (*slit* one's *w.*, cut his throat). [OE *wásend*, cf. OHG *weisunt*, etym. dub.]

weasel (wē·zl), n. Small nimble reddish-brown white-bellied slender-bodied carnivorous quadruped allied to stoat & ferret (*catch a w. asleep*, deceive wide-awake person); *w.-faced*, with thin sharp features. [OE *wesle*, cf. Du. *wezel*, G *wiesel*]

wea·ther¹ (wĕdh-), n. & a. Atmospheric conditions prevailing at a place & time, combination produced by heat or cold, clearness or cloudiness, dryness or moisture, wind or calm, high or low pressure, & electrical state, of local air & sky, (*April w.*, showers alternating with sunshine, fig. smiles & tears; FAIR², FOUL¹, DIRTY, FINE, SOFT, *w.*; *King's* or *Queen's w.*, fine on ceremonial occasion; *favourable, seasonable, good, bad*, &c., *w.*; *under stress of w.*, owing to storms &c.; CLERK *of the w.*; *make good* or *bad w.* naut., meet with; *make heavy w. of* fig., find trying; *under the w.* slang, in adversity); *w.-beaten*, seasoned by or bearing the marks of exposure to storms; *w.-board*, (n.) sloping board attached at bottom of door to keep out rain, (vb) supply with *w.-boarding, -boards*, horizontal boards of which each overlaps the next below to throw off rain as protective casing to wall &c.; *w.-bound*, unable to proceed owing to bad w.; *w.-box*, w.-indicator with figures of man & woman, one issuing to foreshow rain, the other fine w.; *w.-bureau*, meteorological office; *w.-chart*, diagram showing details of w. over wide area; *wea·thercock*, revolving pointer often in shape of cock mounted in high place esp. on church spire to show whence wind blows, (fig.) inconstant person; *w.-contact* or *-cross*, leakage from one telegraph wire to another due to wet w.; *w.-forecast*, prophecy of the day's w. posted at w.-bureau or printed in newspaper; *w.-glass*, barometer; *w.-map*, = *w.-chart*; *w.-moulding*, dripstone; *w.-*PROOF²; *w.-prophet*, person who foretells w.; *w.-service*, organization for meteorological observations; *w.-stain*, discolouration of wall &c. by exposure; so *w.-stained*; *w.-station*, post of observation in connexion with w.-service; *w.-strip*, piece of material used to make door or window proof against rain or wind; *w.-tiles*, arranged to overlap like w.-boarding; *w.-vane*, =*weathercock*; *w.-wise*, able to forecast w.; *w.-worn*, marked by storms &c. (Adj., naut.) windward (*on the w. quarter, beam, bow*, &c.; *have the w. gage* or GAUGE¹ *of*; *keep* one's *w. eye open* fig., be on the look-out); hence **wea·ther**MOST a. [com.-Teut.: OE *weder*, cf. Du. *weder*, G *wetter*; cogn. w. WIND¹, & w. Skr. *va*, Gk *aēmi*, blow]

wea·ther², v.t. & i. Expose to atmospheric changes; (usu. in pass.) discolour or partly disintegrate (rock, stones) by exposure to air (esp. in Geol.); be discoloured or worn thus; (of ship or its crew) get to windward of (cape &c.); come safely through (storm lit. or fig.); make (boards, tiles) overlap downwards, whence **wea·ther**ING² n. [f. prec.]

wea·therly, a. (naut.). (Of ship) making little lee-way, capable of keeping close to wind. Hence **wea·therli**NESS n. [-LY¹]

weave, v.t. & i. (*wove, woven* &, chiefly in some trade phrr., *wove*), & n. Form (thread &c.) into fabric, (fabric) out of thread &c., by interlacing, make fabric thus, work at loom; work up (facts &c.),

introduce (details), *into* a story or connected whole, fashion (tale, poem, &c.); contrive (plot); *wove(n) paper,* with uniform unlined surface given by making in frame of crossed wire-gauze; (n.) style of weaving. [com.-Teut.: OE *wefan,* cf. Du. *weven,* G *weben*; cogn. w. Gk *huphē* web]

wea·ver, n. In vbl senses; esp.: artisan who lives by weaving (*w.'s knot,* kind used esp. for joining cords of different size); (also *w.-bird*) kinds of bird remarkable for elaborate or dextrously made textile nests. [-ER[1]]

weazen. See WIZENED.

web, n. Woven fabric, amount woven in one piece, (also fig. as *a w. of lies*); cobweb (with help of context only; often *spider's w.*), similar product of any spinning creature, gossamer, &c.; membrane filling spaces between toes esp. of swimming bird or bat; connective tissue; vane of feather; large roll of paper used esp. in newspaper-printing; thin flat part connecting more solid parts in machinery &c., e. g. part of railway-carriage wheel between nave & rim; *w.-eye,* disease of eye with film or excrescence, whence **we·b-ey**ED[2] a.; *w.-fingers, -toes,* abnormally or normally connected with w., whence **web-finger**ED[2], **we·b-to**ED[2], aa.; *w.-foot,* with w.-toes, whence **web-foot**ED[2] a.; *w.-wheel,* with plate or w. instead of spokes, or with rim, spokes, & centre, in one piece as in watch-wheels; *w.-worm,* kinds of gregarious larvae spinning large ww. to sleep or to feed on enclosed foliage in. Hence **webb**ED[2] a. [OE *webb* (*wefan* WEAVE), cf. Du. *web,* G *gewebe*]

we·bbing, n. Strong narrow fabric such as is used for horse-girths, gymnastic belts, &c.; stronger edging of more delicate fabric. [-ING[1]]

wed, v.t. & i. (*wedded, wedded* or rarely & not in adj. use *wed*). (Of party, priest, or parent &c.) MARRY[1] (t. & i., rhet. exc. in p.p. *wedded* in adj. use, as *a wedded pair*; *wedded life, bliss,* &c., in matrimony); unite (qualities often separated; *w. efficiency to economy*); (p.p.) devoted *to* opinions, pursuits, &c., so as to be unable to abandon them. [OE *weddian* to pledge (*wed* a pledge, cogn. w. L *vas vadis*), cf. Du. *wedden,* G *wetten,* wager, & WAGE, WAGER, GAGE[1]]

we·dding, n. Marriage ceremony (& festivities); *silver, golden, diamond, w.,* 25th, 50th, 60th or 75th, anniversary of w.; *penny w.,* with money contributions from guests; *w. breakfast,* entertainment usual between w. ceremony & departure for honeymoon; *w.-cake,* distributed to w.-guests & sent in portions to absent friends; *w.-cards,* with names of pair sent to friends as announcement of w.; *w.-day,* day or anniversary of w.; *w.-favour,* white rosette or knot of ribbons worn in honour of w.; *w. garment,* qualification for participating in something (ref. to *Mat.* xii. 11); *w.-ring,* that put on bride's finger at w.-ceremony & usu. worn constantly as distinctive mark of married woman. [-ING[1]]

wedge, n., & v.t. Piece of wood or metal of which one end is an acute-angled edge formed by two converging planes used to split wood or rock or widen opening or exert force in various ways, one of the MECHANICAL powers (or a special application of the INCLINE[1]d plane), (*thin end of the w.,* change, measure, action, &c., that will lead to further changes or developments & is therefore of more importance than it seems); anything resembling a w. in being chiefly outlined by two radial planes or lines converging at acute angle (*a w. of cake* &c.; *the seats are disposed in ww.*; *drew up his men in a w.*); *w.-shaped,* like solid w., also V-shaped; *w.-tailed,* of birds having middle tail-feathers longest; hence **we·dge**WISE adv. (Vb) split with w. (rare); fasten by use of w.; thrust or pack (usu. *in*) tightly between other things or persons; push *off* or *away* like a w. [com.-Teut.: OE *wecg,* cf. Du. *wegge,* G *wecke* kind of loaf]

We·dgwood, n. Kind of semi-vitrified pottery. [J. *W.*, inventor d. 1795]

we·dlock, n. The married state (*born in lawful w.,* legitimately, of married parents). [OE *wedlác* (*wed* pledge, *lác* action) marriage vow]

Wed·nesday (wĕnz-), n. Fourth day of week (ASH[2] *W.*). [OE *wódnes dæg* day of Woden or Odin, transl. of LL *dies Mercurii*]

wee, a. Little, very small, (chiefly in nursery or Sc. use); *W. Frees,* nickname for part of Free Church of Scotland that refused inclusion in the United Free Church in 1900. [f. ME *wei, wee, we,* bit, usu. in phr. *a little we,* f. OE *wǽg* weight, balance, cf. WEY]

weed, n., & v.t. & i. Wild herb springing where it is not wanted (*ill ww. grow apace,* gibe at tall or fast-growing child); cigar (colloq.); *the* (*Indian, soothing,* &c.) *w.,* tobacco; lanky & weakly horse or person; *w.-grown,* weedy or overgrown with ww.; hence **wee·d**LESS, **wee·d**Y[2], aa., **wee·di**NESS n. (Vb) clear (ground) of ww. (also fig.), cut off or uproot ww., whence **wee·d**ER[1](1, 2) n.; sort *out* (inferior parts or members of a quantity or company) for riddance, rid (quantity or company) of inferior members &c. [vb (cf. Du. *wieden*) f. n., OE *wéod,* cf. OSax. *wiod,* etym. dub.]

weeds, n. pl. Mourning worn by widow (usu. *widow's w.*). [earlier sense in sing. *garment,* ME *wēde* f. OE *wǽd, wǽde,* cf. ON *vádh*]

week, n. Period of seven days reckoned

from midnight on Saturday – Sunday (*what day of the w. is it?*, is it Sunday. Monday, Tuesday, Wednesday, Thursday, Friday, or Saturday?; HOLY, PASSION, EASTER, *w.*; *w. of Sundays* or *ww.*, seven ww.; *feast of ww.*, Jewish PENTECOST; *middle of next w.*, see KNOCK[1]); period of seven days reckoned from any point (*can you come to us for a w.?*; *today w.*, 7 days hence; *tomorrow*, *yesterday*, *Friday*, &c., *w.*, day later, earlier, than such future, past, day by a w.; *have not seen you for ww.*; *did it ww. ago*); the six days between Sundays; *w.-day*, any day other than Sunday; *w.-end*, Sunday & parts of Saturday & Monday as time for holiday or visit, (v.i.) make w.-end visit &c., whence **week-end**ER[1] n. [com.-Teut.: OE *wice*, *wucu*, cf. Du. *week*, OHG *wehha*; also ON *vikja* to turn, G *wechsel* change]

wee·kly, a., adv., & n. (Occurring, issuing, done, &c.) once a week, every week; of or for or lasting a week; (n.) w. newspaper. [-LY[1, 2]]

ween, v.t. (poet.). Be of opinion (usu. *I w.* abs. & parenthet. also with *that* expressed or omitted), expect *to* get &c. [com.-Teut.: OE *wénan*, cf. Du. *wanen*, G *wähnen*, fancy]

weep, v.i. & t. (wept). Shed tears (*for* person; *for* pain, rage, joy, &c.); shed tears for, lament over, bewail; send forth or be covered with drops, come or send forth in drops, exude, sweat, drip, (*weeping eczema*, with exudation; *weeping pipe*, designed to drip at intervals); *Weeping Cross* (hist.), wayside cross for penitents to pray at (*come home by W. C.*, be made to repent one's conduct &c.); (of tree) have drooping branches (chiefly in part. as distinctive epithet of variety, *weeping birch*, *willow*, &c.); *w. out*, utter with tears; *w. oneself out*, w. one's fill; *w. away*, consume (time) in weeping. [com.-Teut.: OE *wépan* cry aloud (*wóp* outcry), cf. OHG *wuofan*, Goth. *wōpjan*]

wee·per, n. In vbl senses; also or esp.: hired mourner at funeral; crape hat-sash worn by men at funerals; widow's black crape veil; (pl.) widow's white cuffs. [-ER[1]]

wee·ver, n. Kinds of fish (*Dragon* & *Lesser W.*) with sharp dorsal spines inflicting wound that often festers. [f. OF *wivre* WIVERN, weever]

wee·vil (-vl), n. Kinds of beetle with head extended into a proboscis feeding on grain, nuts, fruit, & leaves; any insect damaging stored grain similarly to corn-w. Hence (of grain) **wee·vill**ED[2], **wee·vily**[2], aa. [OE *wifel*, cf. MDu. *wevel*, OHG *wibil*; perh. cogn. w. WEAVE]

weft[1], n. Cross-threads woven into warp to make web; (loosely) web. [OE *wefta*, cf. ON *vipta*, & WEAVE]

weft[2], var. of WAFT n. (naut.).

weigh (wā), v.t. & i., & n. Find weight of with scales or other machine, whence **weigh**·AGE(4) n., balance in hands (as if) to guess weight of, (*w. sugar*, *luggage*; *meditatively weighed his stick in his hand*; *w. out*, take definite weight of, take specified weight from larger quantity, distribute in definite quantities, by aid of scales, as *w. out butter*, *portions* or *3 lb. of butter*), ascertain one's own weight (*when did you w. last?*; *w. out*, *in*, of jockey before & after race, & transf. *w. in*, enter an appearance; *w. in with* argument &c., produce it triumphantly); estimate relative value or importance of, compare *with* or *against* or abs., consider with a view to choice or rejection or preference, (*w. consequences*, *pros & cons*, *oath* or *argument with* or *against* another; *w.* one's *words*, select such as express neither more nor less than one means; *w. the claims*, *merits*, &c., *of rival candidates*); be equal to or balance (specified weight) in the scales, (fig.) have specified importance, exercise pressure or influence, have weight or importance, be heavy or burdensome, (*weighs a ton*, *6 oz*, *little*, *nothing*, *light*, *heavy*, *heavily*; *w. heavy* &c., or abs., *upon*, be burdensome or depressing to; *the point that weighs with me*); bring *down* by weight lit. or fig., (of counterweight) force *up*, (*fruit weighs down branch*; *one good argument weighs down six bad ones*; *weighed down with cares*; *bucket is weighed up by mass of iron at end of lever*); raise from below water (*w. anchor*, start for voyage; *w. ship* rare, refloat it when sunk); *w.-beam*, portable steelyard suspended in frame; *w.-bridge*, weighing-machine with plate on to which horse & cart can be driven to be weighed; *w.-house*, building in which goods can be weighed officially; *w.-lock*, canal lock with provision for weighing barges; *weighing-machine*, usu. for great weights or of more complicated mechanism than simple balance. (N.) process or occasion of weighing; *under w.*, corruption of *under* WAY. [Aryan: OE *wegan* carry, cf. Du. *wegen* weigh, G *bewegen* move, *wägen* weigh, Skr. *vah* carry, L *vehere* carry]

weight[1] (wāt), n. Force with which body tends to centre of attraction (*the ww. of the planets*); (of terrestrial things) degree of downward tendency in body produced as resultant of earth's gravitation & centrifugal force (*the w. of a body varies with latitude & altitude, its mass does not*); relative mass or quantity of matter contained, downward force, heaviness, regarded as a property of bodies (*superior both in size & in w.*; *he is twice your w.*; DEAD *w.*; *w. of metal*, total amount that can be thrown by ship's guns at one discharge); body's mass numerically expressed in some recognized scale (*what is your w.?*; *reached the w. of 12 st.*), scale or notation for expressing ww. (TROY, AVOIRDUPOIS, *w.*); heavy body (*keep papers down with a w.*; *clock is worked by ww.*; *must not lift ww.*); piece of metal &c. of known mass used in scales for weighing articles (*where is the ounce w.?*); load to be supported (*the pillars have a great w. to bear*), heavy burden *of* care, responsibility, &c.; importance, convincing effect, influence, preponderance, (*considerations of no w.*; *men of w.*; *has great w. with me*; *the w. of evidence is against him*). Hence **weigh·t**LESS a. [OE *gewiht* (prec.)]

weight², v.t. Attach a w. to, hold down with a w. or ww.; impede or burden with load lit. or fig.; treat (fabric) with minerals &c. to make it seem stouter. [f. prec.]

weigh·ty, a. Weighing much, heavy; momentous, important; well-weighed, evidencing thought, deserving of consideration; influential, authoritative. Hence **weigh·ti**LY² adv., **weigh·ti**NESS n. [-Y²]

weir, wear, (wēr), n. Dam across river to raise level of water above it; enclosure of stakes &c. set in stream as trap for fish. [OE *wer* (*werian* defend), cf. G *wehr* defence]

weird¹ (wērd), n. Fate, destiny, (chiefly Sc.; DREE one's *w.*). [OE *wyrd* (*weorthan* be, happen, see WORTH²)]

weird², a. Connected with fate (*the w. sisters*, the fates, witches); supernatural, uncanny, unearthly; (colloq.) queer, odd, old-fashioned, strange, incomprehensible. Hence **weir·d**LY² adv., **weir·d**NESS n. [f. prec. used attrib. in *w. sisters*]

Wei·smannism (vīs-), n. A theory of heredity, in which transmission of acquired characters is denied. [August *Weismann*, German biologist, + -ISM]

Welch¹, a. Var. of WELSH¹ in names of some regiments (but *-sh Guards*).

welch²**(er)**. See WELSH².

we·lcome, int., n., v.t., & a. Hail, know that your coming gives pleasure (often with adv. addition, as *W. home, to Edinburgh!*). (N.) saying *w.* to person, kind or glad reception or entertainment of person or acceptance of offer, gift, &c., (*bid* one *w.*, assure him he is w.; WEAR¹ *out* or *outstay* one's *w.*; *give warm w.*, show great joy at arrival, also make vigorous resistance). (Vb) say *w.* to, greet on arrival, receive (guest, arrival, news, opportunity, event) with pleasure or signs of it. (Adj.) gladly received (*a w. guest, interruption, gift, rest, denial, sight*, &c.; *w. as snow in harvest*, unwelcome; *make* one *w.*, let him feel so); (pred. only) ungrudgingly permitted *to* do or given right *to* thing, absolved of thanking or recompensing, (*you are w. to take what steps you please*; *any one is w. to my share, to any service I can do*; *you are w.*, or ellipt. *w.*, no thanks required); hence **we·lcome**NESS n. [orig. f. OE *wilcuma* (*willa* pleasure, *cuma* comer) person who comes to please another, changed in sense by confusion with WELL³, COME, cf. ON *velkominn* a. welcome]

weld¹, n. Dyer's-weed, plant formerly used to dye yellow. [prob. cogn. w. WOLD]

weld², v.t. & i., & n. Unite (pieces of metal, esp. iron) into homogeneous mass by hammering or pressure (usu. when iron is softened by heat but not melted), make by welding, (of iron &c.) admit of being welded *easily* &c.; (fig.) bring (recruits, parts, arguments, &c.) into homogenous whole (usu. *into*); hence **we·ld**ABLE a., **weld**ABI·LITY n.; (n.) welded junction. [var. of WELL² in orig. sense *boil*]

we·lfare, n. Satisfactory state, health & prosperity, well-being, (usu. *of* person, society, &c., or with *my* &c.); *w.-work*, efforts to make life worth living for workmen &c. [WELL³, FARE²]

welk, v.i. (archaic). Fade, wither. [ME (cf. Du. & G) *welken* (OHG *welk* flaccid)]

we·lkin, n. (poet.). Sky. [OE *wolcnu* clouds, cf. G *wolke* cloud]

well¹, n. Spring or fountain, (fig.) source, (poet. or archaic; *w. of English undefiled*, Chaucer); shaft sunk in ground & lined with stone or other protection for obtaining subterranean water, oil, &c. (ARTESIAN *w.*); enclosed space more or less resembling w.-shaft, space in middle of house from floor to roof containing stairs (also *w. staircase*) or lift or surrounded by stairs (also *w.-hole*) or open for light & ventilation, railed space for counsel &c. in court, receptacle for ink in inkstand, &c.; *w.-deck*, space on main deck enclosed by bulwarks & higher decks; *w.-dish*, with hollow for gravy to collect in; *w.-head*, source, fountain-head; *w.-room*, where spa water is dispensed; *w.-sinker*, person whose occupation is sinking ww.; *w.-spring*, = *w.-head*. [OE *wella* cogn. w. *weallan* well up, boil, cf. G *welle* wave]

well², v.i. Spring (as) from fountain (often *up, out, forth*). [OE *wellan* causative of *weallan* (prec.)]

well³, adv. (better, best), pred. a. (better, best), attrib. a. (no comp.), & n. In good manner or style, satisfactorily, rightly, (*the work is w. done*; *that is w. said*; *a w. situated house*; *w. begun is half done*; *w. done!, run!*, &c., cry of commendation; *w. met!*, greeting to person one has been wanting to see; *come off w.*, have good luck, distinguish oneself; *wish I was w. out of it*, without disaster &c.; *you did w., it was w. done of you, to come*); thoroughly, with care or completeness, sufficiently, to a considerable distance or extent, with margin enough to justify description, quite, (*look w. to yourself*; *judge w. & truly*; *smack him, polish it, w.*; *is w. up in the list, w. on in life, w. advanced* or *stricken in years, w. past forty, w. among the leaders of thought*; *as w.*, in addition, to an equal extent, not less truly, as *but he is a Christian as w., he gave me clothes as w. as food*); heartily, kindly, laudatorily, approvingly, on good terms, (*love, like*, person *w.*; *treat* person *w.*; *think* or *speak w. of*; *it speaks w. for his discipline that he never punishes*, serves as commendation; *stand w. with* one, be in his good graces); probably, not incredibly, easily, with reason, wisely, advisably, (*it may w. be that* —; *can, cannot, w. manage it*; *you may w. ask, say, that*; *we might w. make the experiment*; *as w.*, with equal reason, preferably, without worse consequences, as *you might as w. throw your money into the sea as lend it to him, as w. be hanged for a sheep as a lamb, we may as w. begin at once*; *that is just as w.*, need not be regretted; *you might as w.*, nursery formula of request). (Pred. a., often indistinguishable from adv.) in good health (*is she w. or ill?*; *will soon be better*; *is best in the winter*; *quite w., thank you*; *am perfectly w.*); in satisfactory state or position, satisfactory, advisable, (*am very w. where I am*; *all's w.*; *it is all very w.*, ironical expression of discontent, or rejection of comfort, arguments, &c.; *it is w. with him*; *it would have been, were, w. for him if*; *it would be w. to inquire*; *w. enough*, tolerably good or good-looking; *as w.*, not unadvisable, as *it may be as w. to explain*; *w. & good*, formula of dispassionate acceptance of decision, as *if you choose to take my advice, w. & g.*; VERY *w.*). (Attrib. adj., rare) in good health (*a w. man should not be dawdling in bed*; *the w. are impatient of the sick*). (N.) good things (*I wish him w.*); what is satisfactory (*let w. alone*, do not meddle needlessly). [com.-Teut.: OE *wel*, cf. Du. *wel*, G *wohl*, cogn. w. WILL, w. sense *agreeably to wish*]

well[4], int. expressing great astonishment (*w., who would have thought it?*; *well!*: *w. to be sure!*), relief (*w., here we are at last*), concession (*w., come if you like*; *w., perhaps you are right*; *w. then, say no more about it*), resumption of talk (*w., who was it?*; *w., he says he must see you*), qualified recognition of point (*w., but what about Jones?*), expectation (*w. then?*), resignation (*w., it can't be helped*), &c. [ellipt. uses of prec. adv.]

well-. 1. In a few words *well-* or *well* is an inseparable pref.: *w.-being*, welfare; *w.-doer, -doing*, virtuous person, conduct; *w.-nigh* rhet., almost; *w.-wisher*, person who wishes well to one. 2. *Well* may precede any participle or word in -ED[2]; when the combination is used attrib. with n. following, it is usu. hyphened (*he is a w.-known person*); this is done in the pred. use also when the combination ends in -ING[2] or -ED[2], but not usu. when it ends in -ED[1] (*the stroke was w. timed*, cf. *a w.-timed stroke*) unless it has acquired a sense or use other or more restricted than that of the separate elements (*my watch is w. regulated*; *I do not think his action was well-advised*, cf. *he is not w. advised by his friends*); a list of the commoner combinations follows with special senses or contexts noted; *w.-advised*, prudent, wise, (chiefly of action taken); *w. aimed*; *w.-appointed*, having all necessary equipment (esp. of expedition, fleet, &c.); *w. armed*; *w. attested*; *w. authenticated*; *w.-balanced*, sane, sensible, (esp. of mind); *w.-behaved*; *w. beloved*; *w.-born*, of noble or distinguished family; *w.-bred*, having good breeding or manners, (of horse &c.) of good or pure stock; *w. chosen*, esp. of words or phrases; *w.-conditioned*, not querulous; *w.-conducted*, characterized by good conduct; *w.-connected*, connected by blood &c. with good families; *w. contented*; *w. contested*; *w. defined*; *w.-dined*, having had a good dinner; *w. directed*, esp. of blow or shot; *w.-disposed*, having good disposition or kindly feeling *to(wards)*; *w. done* of meat, cooked through; *w. dressed*; *w. drilled*; *w. earned*; *w. educated*; *w.-favoured*, good-looking; *w. fed*; *w. fought*; *w.-found* = *w.-appointed*; *w. founded*, having foundation in fact (of suspicion or other belief or sentiment); *w. furnished*; *w.-graced*, possessed of attractive qualities; *w. grounded* = *w. founded*, also w. trained in rudiments; *w.-informed*, having w.-stored mind or access to best information; *w.-intentioned*, aiming or aimed (usu. unsuccessfully) at good results; *w.-judged*, showing good judgement or tact or good aim (of action taken); *w.-knit*, compact, not loose-made or sprawling, (esp. of person or his frame); *w. known*; *w.-liking*, with w.-fed prosperous look (usu. *fat & w.-l.*); *w.-looking*, of attractive appearance; *w. loved*; *w. made*, (esp.) of symmetrical bodily make; *w.-mannered*, with good manners; *w. marked*, distinct, easy to detect; *w.-meaning*, = *w.-intentioned* (of person or attempt); *w. meant*, = *w.-intentioned* (of attempt); *w. oiled* (fig., of expression), complimentary; *w. ordered*, arranged in orderly manner; *w. paid*; *w. painted*; *w. pleased*; *w.-pleasing*; *w.-proportioned*; *w.-read*, having read much [cf. -ED[1](2)], with mind w. stored by reading; *w. regulated*, under proper control, not undisciplined; *w. remembered*; *w.-reputed*, of good repute; *w.-rounded*, complete & symmetrical; *w.-seeming*, apparently satisfactory or good; *w.-seen* archaic, accomplished *in*; *w. set*, compact, firmly knit, (esp., also *w. set up*, of bodily frame); *w. sifted* (esp. of facts or evidence); *w. spent* (esp. of time or effort); *w.-spoken*, refined in speech; *w.-timbered*; *w. timed*, opportune; *w. trained*; *w.-tried*, often tested with good result; *w.-trod-(den)*, frequented; *w. tuned*; *w. turned*, happily expressed (of compliment,phrase, verse); *w.-worn*, (esp.) trite, stale. 3. *W. off*, = fortunately situated (*does not know when he is w. o.*), sufficiently rich, is two words when used pred., but hyphened when attrib. (*w.-off people*); *w.-to-do*, = sufficiently rich, is hyphened when attrib. & usu. when pred. also.

welladay·, -away·, int. of grief (archaic or facet.). [OE *wálá wá* woe, lo ! woe]

Wellingtō·nia, n. Kinds of sequoia. [named after Duke of Wellington, -IA[1]]

We·llingtons, n. pl. Boots coming up or nearly up to knees. [as prec.]

Welsh[1] (& see WELCH[1]), a. & n. (Language, *the* people) of Wales (*W. mutton*, from small W. mountain sheep; *W. rabbit* or by pop. etym. *rarebit*, dish of toasted cheese); *We·lshman, -woman*, native of Wales. [OE *wælisc* foreign (*wealh* foreigner, Celt, -ISH[1])]

welsh[2], **welch**, v.t. & i. Decamp without paying (winner of bet on horse-race, or abs.). Hence **we·lsh**ER[1], **-ch-**, n. [f. 1857; etym. dub.]

welt[1], n., & v.t. Strip of leather sewn round edge of boot or shoe uppers to serve as attachment to sole; wale. (Vb) provide with w.; raise wales on, beat, flog. [ME *welte, walt*, etym. dub.]

welt[2] (v-), n. (German for) world (*w.-politik*, foreign policy on the grand scale; *w.-schmerz*, vague yearning & discontent with regard to the constitution of things). [G]

we·lter[1], v.i., & n. Roll, wallow, be washed about, be soaked or steeped or dabbled *in* blood &c.; (n.) general confusion, disorderly mixture or aimless conflict *of* creeds, policies, vices, &c. [f. MDu. *welteren* roll, cf. Icel. *velta*, G *wälzen*; cogn. w. WALTZ, WALLOW]

we·lter[2], n. Heavy rider (now rare); (attrib.) *w. race, cup, stakes, handicap*, &c., horse-races for heavy-weight riders (also ellipt. *w.* = w.-race); *w.-weight*, heavy-weight rider, also weight carried apart from weight for age as test, (Boxing) see BOX[5]*ing weights*; (colloq.) heavy blow, big person or thing. [prob. (orig. in last sense) f. WELT[1] flog + -ER[1], = big one, cf. WHACKER]

wen[1], n. More or less permanent tumour of benign character on scalp or other part of body; goitre; (fig.) abnormally large or congested city (*the great w.*, London). [OE *wenn*, cf. Du. *wen*, etym. dub.]

wen[2], n. The old English letter ƿ (w). [OE, var. of *wynn* joy (see WINSOME) used as beginning with the letter, cf. THORN]

wench (-tsh), n., & v.i. Girl or young woman, lass, (esp. of rustics or servants, or with playful depreciation, & colloq.; *a strapping, buxom*, &c., *w.*); (archaic) strumpet; (vb) whore, whence **we·nch**ER[1] n. (archaic). [ME *wenche(l)* f. OE *wencel* infant (*wancol* weak, tottering, cf. G *wanken* totter)]

wend[1], v.t. & i. Direct one's *way*; (archaic) go. [com.-Teut.: OE *wendan* turn t. & i., cf. Du. & G *wenden*; the past was formerly *went* (now used to supply past of GO[1])]

Wend[2], n. One of a Slavonic race formerly spread over N. Germany, & now inhabiting E. Saxony. Hence **We·nd**IC, **We·nd**ISH, aa. [f. G *Wende*, etym. dub.]

We·nsleydale, n. Kind of cheese. [*W.* in Yorks.]

went. See GO[1], WEND[1] etym.

we·ntletrap, n. Shell-fish with spiral shell of many whorls. [f. Du. *wenteltrap* orig. = winding stairs]

wept. See WEEP.

were. See BE.

were·wolf, wer·w-, n. (mythol.; pl. *-ves*). Human being turned into wolf. [OE *were-wulf* (*wer* man, cf. L *vir*, WOLF)]

wert. See BE.

Wer·therism (vārter-), n. Morbid sentimentality as of Werther in Goethe's *Sorrows of Werther*. [-ISM(3)]

Wesleyan (wĕzlē·-, *&, esp. among Ww.*, wĕ·slĭ-), a. & n. (Member) of the denomination founded by John Wesley (d. 1791). Hence **Wesley·an**ISM(3) (*or* wĕ·s-) n. [-AN; the normal form would be *Wesleian* (see -EAN), whence the doubtful pronunc.]

west, adv., n., & a., (abbr. W.). Towards or in the region in front of observer on equator at equinox who faces setting sun (*w.* BY[1] *north* or *south*; *w. of*, further w. than; DUE[1] *w.*; *lies* &c. *east & w.*, lengthwise along line between east & w.; *go, gone, w.* slang, die, dead); *w.-north-w.*, *w.-south-w.*, advv., nn., & aa., (regions) midway between w. & north-w., south-w. (with uses & derivatives corresponding to those of *west*, as *w.-north-westerly*, *w.-north-western*, *w.-north-westwardly*; see WESTERLY &c.); hence **we·st**WARD adv., n., & a., **we·st**WARDS adv. & n. (N.) cardinal point lying W.; western part of England, Scotland, Ireland, or Europe, part of U.S. beyond earlier settled States or w. of Mississippi; = OCCIDENT (*Empire of the W.*, WESTERN *Empire*); western part of any country; w. wind. (Adj.) situated, dwelling, in or more towards the w.; *w. longitude*; *w. central*, abbr. W.C., London postal district; *w. country*, part of England w. of line from Southampton to mouth of Severn; *W.* INDIES, whence *W.-Indian* a.; *W. End*, richer & more fashionable district in w. of London); (of wind) coming from the w.; *w.-country*, of or from or characteristic of the w. country; *w.-countryman* (or *-woman*), native of it; *W.-end*, in or characteristic of W. End. [com.-Teut.: OE, Du., G, &c.; prob. cogn. w. Gk *hesperos*, L *vesper*, evening]

we·stering, a. & part. Tending towards the west (usu. of sun). [f. obs. *wester* vb (prec. in vbl use, -ER[5])]

we·sterly, a. & adv. =foll. (rare); (of direction) towards the west; (of wind) blowing from the west or thereabouts. [f. WEST as EASTERLY]

we·stern, a. & n. Living or situated in, coming from, the west (*W. Empire*, one of two parts, with Rome as capital, cf. *Eastern Empire* with Constantinople, into which Theodosius divided Roman Empire 395; *W.* or *Latin Church*, part of Christian church that continued to acknowledge the popes at the Greek schism, see GREEK); =OCCIDENT*al*; (of wind) westerly (rare); hence **we·sterner**[1](4) n. (esp., in the great war, advocate of concentration on the French theatre as opp. Salonica, Gallipoli, Mesopotamia, &c.), **we·sternmost** a.; (n.) westerner. [-ERN]

we·sting, n. Westward progress or deviation esp. in sailing (cf. NORTHING). [-ING[1]]

We·stminster, n. City forming part of London (*W. Abbey* fig., glorious death such as would entitle one to place among celebrities there buried); (the Houses of) Parliament, the political arena; member of W. School.

wet, a., v.t., & n. Soaked, covered, dabbled, moistened, or supplied, with or *with* water or other liquid (*w. sponge, land, road, table, eyes, cheeks, clothes, feet*; *am w. to the skin*, with clothes soaked through); (U.S.) not prohibiting or opposing use of alcohol; *w.* BLANKET[1]; *w. bargain*, closed with drink; *w.* BOB[5]; *w. bulb*, see DRY[1]-*bulb thermometer*; *w. dock*, in which ship can float; *w. pack*, wrapping of body in w. cloths enclosed in dry blankets &c.; *w. plate* in photog., sensitized collodion plate exposed while w.); rainy (*w. day, weather*); *w.-nurse* n., woman employed to suckle another's child, v.t., act as w.-n. to (child); hence **we·tness** n., **we·ttish**[1](2) a. (Vb) make w. (*w. bargain*, close it with drink; *w.* one's *whistle*, drink); hence **we·tting**[1](1) n. (N.) moisture, liquid that wets something, rainy weather; (slang) a drink; (U.S.) opponent of prohibition. [OE *wǣt*, cf. ON *vátr*; cogn. w. WATER]

we·ther (-dh-), n. Castrated ram. [com.-Teut.: OE *wedher*, cf. Du. *weer*, G *widder*; prob. cogn. w. L *vitulus* calf]

wey (wā), n. Unit of weight varying from 2 cwt to 3 cwt with different kinds of goods. [OE *wǣge* weight (*wegan* WEIGH)]

wh-. In a few of the words beginning thus the w. is, as indicated in the pronunc. brackets, not sounded; in all others the h is silent in ordinary modern usage, but the correct sound, = hw, is retained by the Scotch, Irish, Welsh, & northern English, & by purists in pronunciation, as well as for the nonce in unfamiliar wds or such as might be confused with commoner wds having no -h- (*whet, whey*).

whack, v.t., & n. Strike heavily with stick &c., thwack, whence **wha·cking**[1](1) n.; (slang) go shares in, distribute. (N.) heavy blow esp. with stick; (slang) share (*have had my w. of pleasure*). [imit.]

wha·cker, n. (slang). Thing or person big of its kind. [-ER[1]; cf. *thumper, whopper*, &c.]

wha·cking, a. (slang). Big of its kind. [-ING[2]; see prec.]

whale, n., & v.i. Kinds of large fish-like marine mammal some of which are hunted for their oil, spermaceti, whalebone, ambergris, &c. (*right, arctic, Greenland*, or *bowhead w.*, kind yielding best whalebone; SPERM[2], *humpback, bottlenosed*, &c., *w.*; *bull, cow, w.*, adult male, female, w.; *very like a w.*, ironical assent to absurd statement, see *Hamlet* III. ii. 399); *w.-boat*, (double-bowed like those) used in whaling; *wha·lebone*, elastic horny substance growing in thin parallel plates in upper jaw of certain ww., & used in many kinds of manufacture; *w.-calf*, young w.; *w.-fin*, commerc. name for whalebone; *w.-head*, African bird allied to herons & storks; *w.-line*, superior rope 2 in. round used in whaling; *wha·leman*, seaman engaged in whaling; *w.-oil*, train oil or sperm oil got from ww. (Vb) be engaged in w.-fishing; *whaling-gun*, for firing harpoon &c. at ww.; *whaling-master*, captain of a whaler. [OE *hwæl*, cf. OHG *wal* (G *walfisch*)]

wha·ler, n. Whaling ship or man. [-ER[1]]

whang, v.t. & i., & n., (colloq.). Strike heavily & loudly, whack; (of drum &c.) sound (as) under blow; (n.) whanging sound or blow. [imit.]

wharf (worf), n. (pl. *-fs, -ves*), & v.t. Wooden or stone platform beside which ship may be moored for (un)loading &c.; hence **whar·fage**(1, 4) n. (Vb) moor (ship) at, store (goods) on, w. [OE *hwearf*, cf. Du. & G *werf*]

whar·finger (-j-), n. Wharf-owner. [for *wharfager* (WHARF*age*, -ER[1]) cf. *messenger*]

what (-ŏt), a. & pron. interrog., exclam., & rel. 1. Adj.: (*a*) interrog., asking for selection from indefinite number (cf. *which* from definite number; *w. books have you read?*; *don't know w. plan he will try*) or for specification of amount or number or kind (*w. money, men, abilities, has he?*; *w. news?*; *w. matter?*, w. does it matter?; *w. good, use, is it?*, w. purpose will it serve?; *w. manner of man is he?*; *I know w. difficulties there are*, cf. *c*): (*b*) exclam., = how great or strange or otherwise remarkable for good or ill (*w. a fool you are!*; *w. impudence!*; *w. an idea!*; *w. genius he has!*) or, before adj. & n.,

=how (*w. partial judges we are!*): (c) rel., =the — that, any — that, as much *or* many — as, (*dispose of w. difficulties there are*, cf. *a*; *lend me w. money* or *men you can*; *will give you w. help is possible*; *w. time* archaic, when, while). 2. Pron.: (*a*) interrog., = w. thing(s)?, with many modifications given by context, & often in ellipt. uses for sentence, some of which are here illustrated (*w. will people say?*, is it respectable to do it?; *What?*, i.e. did you say; *w. ho!*, excl. of greeting or hailing; *w. is he?*, i.e. in respect of occupation; *w., do you really mean it?*, i.e. I must have heard wrongly; *w. if we were to try?*, i.e. would result; *w. for?*, for w. reason or purpose?; *w. though we are poor?*, i.e. does it matter; *w. next?*, no absurdity can outdo this; *w. of* or *about —?*, i.e. w. news?, or how can you dispose of this point?; *well, w. of it?*, formula admitting fact but not inference &c. from it; *w. is he the better for it?*, in w. way or to w. extent; *w. is your name?*; *w. not* usu. without interrog. mark, many other things of the same kind, anything; *w.-not*, piece of furniture with shelves for knick-knacks; *w. like is he?*, provincial for *w. is he like?* or *what sort of man is he?*; *w.-d'ye-call-him, her, it, 'em, what's-his* (or *-her, -its*)-*name*, substitutes for name that has slipped memory; =*eh* after question or suggestion, a modern & prob. ephemeral use, as *Have you heard the latest, w.?*, *Come along, w.*; *I wonder w. you are*; *don't know w. he said*; *w. followed is doubtful*, cf. *c*; *cannot guess w. he was attempting*, cf. *c*; *I know w.*, have a new idea; *I'll tell you w.*, i.e. the truth or right course is; *know w.'s w.*, i.e. a good thing &c. from a bad &c.); (*b*) exclam., = w. thing(s)!, how much!, &c. (*w. he has suffered!*); (*c*) rel., = that or those which, the thing(s) that, anything that, a thing that, (*w. followed was unpleasant*, cf. *a*; *did w. he was attempting*, cf. *a*; *w. I have said I have said*; *w. I know not is not knowledge*; *give me w. you can*; *w. is called* the general reader; *come w. will* or *may*, in spite of any results &c.; *tell me what you remember of it*; *but, w. even you must condemn, he was lying*; *will do w. I can for you*; *use no arguments but w. you believe in yourself*; so also various more or less incorrect colloq. uses of *but w.* for *but*, as *not a day comes but w. makes a change, not a man but w. likes her, not a day but w. it rains, I never see him but w. I think, I don't know but w. I will*, NOT *but w.*; *w. with — w. with —*, between various causes &c., as *w. with drink & w. with fright, he did not know much about the facts*). [neut. of WHO]

whate·ver, whate'er (poet.; -ār), a. & pron. indef. rel. used (1)=prec. in rel. uses with addition of or emphasis on indefinite sense (*w. I have is yours*; *w. measures are considered best*; *do w. you like*); (2) in indef. concessive clauses where *what* is not possible, = though any(thing), as *w. results follow, w. happens, w. friends we may offend, we shall have done our duty*; (3) ellipt. for *w. it, he,* &c., *may be*, = *at all* after noun in negative context (never *whate'er*), as *there is no doubt w., is there any chance w.?, no one w. would accept, cannot see any one w.*; (4) vulg. for *what* EVER. [WHAT + EVER]

Wha·tman, n. (attrib.). *W.* (*paper*), brand of paper used for drawing, water-colours, engraving, & photography. [maker's name]

wha·tso (archaic), **whatsoĕ·ver** (emphatic), **whatsoe'er·** (poet.; -sōār), aa. & pronn. = WHATEVER 1, 2), & *whatsoever* = also WHATEVER (3). [SO]

whaup, n. Curlew (chiefly Sc.). [imit. of cry]

wheal, mis-spelling of **wale, weal.**

wheat, n. (Highly nutritious seeds of) kinds of corn-plant bearing dense four-sided spike of grain (esp. *winter* or *unbearded w.*, *summer* or *bearded w.*, & *German w.* or *spelt*); *w.-grass*, couch-grass. Hence **whea·tEN**[5] a. [OE *hwǣte*, cf. Du. *weit*, G *weizen*; cogn. w. WHITE]

whea·tear (-ēr), n. Small bird, the stone-chat or whitetail. [earlier *wheatears* (WHITE, ARSE)]

whee·dle, v.t. Coax *into* doing or *into* good temper &c., persuade by flattery or endearments, cajole, humour for one's own ends; get (thing) by wheedling *out of* person; cheat (person) *out of* thing by wheedling. Hence **whee·dlER**[1] n., **whee·dlING**[2] a., **whee·dlingLY**[2] adv. [perh. for *weadle* f. OE *wǣdlian* beg (*wǣdl* poverty)]

wheel[1], n. Circular frame or disk arranged to revolve on axis & used to facilitate motion of vehicle or for various mechanical purposes, machine &c. of which a w. is an essential part, object resembling a w., (BALANCE, CATHERINE, COG[1], FLY[3], MILL[1], OVERSHOT, PADDLE, POTTER'*s*, RATCHET, SPINN*ing*, STEER*ing*, SUN-*&-planet*, UNDERSHOT, -*w.*; *eccentric w.*, turning on axis not at its centre; *fifth w.*, apparatus enabling front wheels &c. of four-wheeled conveyance to be slewed, also see FIFTH *w.*; *ww. within ww.*, intricate machinery, indirect or secret agencies; *the ww. of life*, the vital processes &c.; *w. of life*, scientific toy converting series of pictures of successive attitudes into semblance of continuous motion; *Fortune's w.*, w. with which Fortune is depicted as symbol of ups & downs, also fig. vicissitudes; *break on the w.*, maim & kill on medieval instrument of torture that revolved with victim bound on it; BREAK[1] *butterfly on* *w.*; *a* FLY[1] *on the w.*; *put* SPOKE *in* one's *w.*, one's SHOULDER *to the w.*; *w. & axle*, utilization of leverage given by difference in circumference between w. & its axle, called one of the MECHANICAL *powers*; *go on ww.*, smoothly), Fortune's w. (*we may be rich at the next turn of the w.*), steering-w. (*don't speak to the man at the w.*); motion as of w., circular motion, motion of line as on pivoted end esp. as military evolution, (*street arab turning ww. in the gutter*; *the ww. & somersaults of the gulls*; *right, left*, &c., *w.*, words of command to company &c. in line to swing round on right, left, flank as pivot); *wheel*BARROW[2]; *w. chair*, invalid's on ww.; *w.-horse*, wheeler; *w.-house*, steersman's shelter; *w.-lock*, (gun with) antiquated lock having steel wheel to rub against flint &c.; *whee·lman*, cyclist; *w.-seat*, part of axle fitting into hub; *w.-tread*, part of carriage &c. w. that touches ground; *w. window*, circular with spokelike tracery; *w.-wright*, maker of ww. Hence **(-)wheel**ED[2], **whee·l**LESS, aa. [Aryan: OE *hwéol*, cf. Da. *hjul*, Du. *wiel*; cogn. w. Gk *kuklos* circle, wheel, & *polos* axis, L *colus* distaff]

wheel[2], v.t. & i. Swing (t. & i. of line of men &c.) round in line on one flank as pivot, (loosely) change direction lit. or fig., face another way, (often *round*); push or pull (wheeled thing esp. wheelbarrow or Bath chair or its load or occupant, or furniture on castors) in some direction; go in circles or curves; ride on bicycle. [f. prec.]

whee·ler, n. In vbl senses; also: pole or shaft horse in four-in-hand, tandem, &c. (cf. LEADER); FOUR-*wheeler*; wheelwright. [WHEEL[1, 2], -ER[1]]

wheeze, v.i. & t., & n. Breathe with audible friction; *w. out*, utter with wheezing. (N.) sound of wheezing, whence **whee·**ZY[2] a., **whee·**ZILY[2] adv., **whee·zi**NESS n.; (Theatr. slang) joke, anecdote, &c., interpolated by actor during performance. [prob. f. ON *hvæsa* to hiss]

whelk[1], n. Kinds of marine spiral-shelled mollusc, some used as food. [ME *wilk*, OE *wioloc* etym. dub., with *wh-* by assim. to foll.]

whelk[2], n. Pimple. Hence **whelk**ED[2] a. [OE *hwylca* (*hwelian* suppurate)]

whelm, v.t. (poet., rhet.). Engulf, submerge, overwhelm. [prob. f. obs. *whelve* f. OE *hwylfan* overturn, cogn. w. G *wölben* arch over, Gk *kolpos* bosom]

whelp, n., & v.i. & t. Young dog, pup; young lion, tiger, bear, wolf, &c., cub; disagreeable or ill-bred child or youth. (Vb) produce pups or cubs or (contempt.) child, give birth to (esp. contempt. of human mother); originate (evil scheme &c.). [OE *hwelp*, cf. Du. *welp*, G *welf*, etym. dub.]

when, adv. interrog. & rel., pron., & n. 1. Adv.: (a) interrog.: at what time?, on what occasion?, how soon?, how long ago?, (*w. did, shall, you see him?*; *don't know w. it was*; *say w.* ellipt., i. e. process is to begin or stop; in rhet. questions equivalent to neg. statement, as *w. shall we see his like again?*, *w. did I suggest such a thing?*); (b) rel.: (with *time* &c. as antecedent) at which (*the time w. such things could happen is gone*; *there are occasions, conjunctures*, &c., *w.*); at the or any time that, on the or any occasion that, at whatever time, as soon as, (*he exclaimed w. he saw me*; *w. Greek meets Greek*; *w. it rains he stays at home*; *shall have it w. you ask politely*; also ellipt. like WHILE[2], as *he looked in w. passing*, *w. found make a note of*; also introducing exclamatory clause with ellipse of apodosis, as *w. I think what I have done for that man!*); although, considering that, (*walks w. he might ride*; *how could you, w. you knew it might kill him?*; *how convince him w. he will not listen?*); after or upon which, but just then, & then, (*the conflict began, w. it soon appeared which was stronger*; *we were just coming to the point w. the bell interrupted us*). 2. Pron.: what (interrog.) or which (rel.) time (*till w. can you stay?*; *from w. does it date?*; *since w. things have been better*). 3. N.: time, date, occasion, (*told me the w. & the how of it*). [OE *hwanne*, *hwenne*, f. stem of WHO, cf. G *wann* when, *wenn* if, MDu. *wan, wen*]

whence, adv. interrog. & rel., pron., & n. From what place or source? (being ousted by *where — from* in lit. sense & *how, why*, &c., in fig.; *w. comes it that*, how is it that; *no one knows w. she comes*); (with *place* &c. as antecedent) from which (*the source w. these evils spring*; now usu. *from which*); to or rarely at or from the place from which (*return w. you came*; *abides w. he sent me*; *comes w. he came*; now usu. *where — from, from where — from*); *whenceso·ever*, from whatever place or source. (Pron.): what (interrog.) or which (rel.) starting-place (*from w. is he?*; *the source from w. it springs*). (N.) source (*we know neither our w. nor our whither*). [ME *whennes* (*whenne*, OE *hwanon* whence f. stem of WHO, + -ES)]

whene·ver, whene·er· (poet., -ār), **whenso·ever** (emphatic), adv. rel. indef. (cf. *when* EVER). At whatever time, on whatever occasion, as soon as, every time that. [SO, EVER]

where (-ār), adv. interrog. & rel., pron., & n. 1. Adv.: (a) interrog.: in or to what place or position lit. or fig., in what direction, at what part, in what respect, (*w. is Heaven?*; *w. did you read that?*, in what book; *w. are you going?*, now usu. preferred to *whither*; *showed me w. they were*; *w. does it touch our interests?*; *w. are you looking?*; *w. shall we be if prices fall now?*, how situated; *don't know w. to have him*, said of person of elusive character; often in rhet. questions = neg. statements, as *w. is the sense of it?*, *w. is the use of trying?*); (b) rel. (see also WHERE-); (with *place* &c. as antecedent) in which (*places w. they sing*; also with ellipse of noun, as *w. he is weakest is in his facts*); in or to the or any place, in the direction or part or respect, in which (*w. your treasure is*; *go w. you like*; *is, send him, w. he will be taken care of*; *w. the ancients knew nothing we know a little*; *that's w. it is* colloq., that is the real reason for it or point of it). 2. Pron.: what (interrog.) or which (rel.) place (*w. do you come from, are you going to?*; vulg. in rel. use, as *the place w. he comes from*). 3. N.: place, scene of something, (*the ww. & whens are important*; cf. *anyw., now., everyw.*). [OE *hwár*, cf. Du. *waar*, G *war(um)*; cogn. w. WHO, WHEN]

where-. 1. *Where* is written in one word with appended prep. as substitute for the prep. preceding or following *what* interrog. pron. or *which* rel. pron. (*whereby shall we know him?*; *the signs whereby he shall be known*; *whereby I saw that he was angry*), cf. corresp. compounds of *there*; the use is becoming rare exc. either in formal or poet. or in facet. or uneducated writing or in special uses as noted: **whereabout**(& see 2); **whereat; whereby; wherefore** (for what reason?, why?, on what account, on which account: also as n. pl. = reasons, as *the whys & wherefores*); **wherefrom; wherein** (also **whereinsoever**); **whereinto; whereof; whereon; whereout; wherethrough; whereto; whereunder; whereunto; whereupon** (still common introducing new sentence in narrative); **wherewith(al;** the longer form common as n. = money &c. needed for a purpose; *has not the wherewithal to do it*, or *the wherewithal*). 2. *Where* in its proper local use is qualified in sense by additions: **whereabouts** adv. interrog., where within considerable limits or vaguely (*whereabouts is he?*; *don't know even whereabouts to look*), n., person's or thing's locality roughly defined; **whereas** conj., taking into consideration or having as premiss the fact that (esp. in legal preambles), in contrast or comparison with the fact that, but in contrast with what has been said; **wherever, where'er** (poet.), **wheresoever** (emphat.), advv. rel. indef., in or to whatever place &c. (cf. *where* EVER).

whe·rry, n. Light shallow rowing-boat usu. for carrying passengers. [?]

whet, v.t., & n. Sharpen by rubbing on or with stone &c.; stimulate (appetite, stomach, desire); *whe·tstone*, shaped stone for tool-sharpening, thing that sharpens the wits. (N.) sharpening; small quantity taken to create or creating appetite for more; dram. [OE *hwettan* (*hwæt* bold), cf. Du. *wetten*, G *wetzen*]

whĕ·ther[1] (-dh-), a. & pron. interrog. & rel. (archaic). Which of the two. [OE *hwæther* (WHO,- THER), cf. ON *hvárr*, MHG *weder*]

whe·ther[2], conj. (1) introducing indirect questions of which the direct form would be answerable with *yes* or *no* (*don't know w. he will be here*); such questions involve an alternative, which may be unexpressed as above, expressed precisely (*w. he is here or w. he is in London*, or more usu. ellipt. *or in London*), or expressed comprehensively by the negative (*w. he is here or w. he is not here*, or more usu. ellipt. *or not*); i.e., the alternative if expressed has always *or*, after which *w.* is usu. repeated if subj. & vb are expressed; *w.*-clauses may be appended directly to many adjj. & nn. as well as to vbs (*doubtful, uncertain, anxious*, &c., *w.*; *the question* &c. *w.*), though *as to* is often needlessly inserted; DOUBT[2] *w.*; *w. or* NO[2]; formerly also with direct questions (*w. shall we live or die?*). (2) used with following *or* or *or whether* (according as second alternative has its subj. & vb expressed, as in 1) to introduce the protasis having alternatives corresponding to a single conditional apodosis (*w. we stay or w. we go, w. we go to him or he comes to us, w. we go or not, the result will be bad*); *w. or* NO[2]; formerly also when each alternative had apodosis (*w. we live, we live unto the Lord, & w. we die, we die* &c.). [f. prec.]

whew (hwū), int. expressing (usu. joc.) consternation.

whey (-ā), n. Part of milk that remains liquid when the rest forms curds; *w.-faced* archaic, pale esp. with fear. [OE *hwæg*, cf. Du. *wei*]

which, a. & pron. interrog. & rel. 1. Adj.: (a) interrog., asking for selection from alternatives conceived as limited in number or known (cf. WHAT; *w. way shall we go?*; *say w. chapter you prefer*): (b) rel., =&, now, although, since, &c., this *or* these, now rare exc. with n. serving to sum up details of a compound or vague antecedent (*a smile & a sixpence, w. equipment is within most people's reach, will suffice*; *w. things are an allegory*; *the w.*, archaic for *w.*). 2. Pron.: (a) interrog. = w. person(s), w. thing(s), (*w. of you am I to thank for this?*; *say w. you would like best*; *w. is w.?*, w. of two &c. given persons &c. corresponds to one of given descriptions &c., & w. to another?); (b) rel. (cf. THAT), used to convert what would in the simplest grammar be an independent sentence into a subord. clause by being substituted for a noun expressed in it after being expressed or implied in the sentence to which it is to be subordinated, =w. person or persons (archaic), w. thing(s) as modified by context, (*Our*

Father, w. art in heaven; *the river w.*, or better *that, flows through London*; *the meeting, w. was held in the Park, was a failure*; *he said he saw me there, w. was a lie*; occasionally in clause preceding antecedent, as *moreover, w. you will hardly credit, he was not there himself*; *the w.*, archaic for *w.*; in the possessive case *whose* is sometimes for convenience preferred to the usual *of which*, as *the only place whose supply of baths is adequate*). [OE *hwilc* (WHO, -LIKE), cf. Du. *welk*, G *welch*]

whiche·ver, whichsoe·ver (emphat.), aa. & pronn. rel. indef. used correspondingly to WHATEVER, WHATSOEVER, but with the restricted area of choice that distinguishes WHICH from WHAT (cf. *which* EVER). [SO, EVER]

whi·dah-bird, n. Small W.-Afr. bird, male of which has tail-feathers of enormous length. [orig. WIDOW-*bird*, altered f. assoc. w. *Whidah* in Dahomey]

whiff[1], n., & v.i. & t. Puff of air, smoke, odour, &c. (*w. of grape-shot*, a few discharges; *want a w. of fresh air*); (Commerc.) small cigar; light uncovered outrigged sculling-boat. (Vb) blow or puff (t. & i.) lightly. [imit.]

whiff[2], n. Kind of flatfish. [?]

whiff[3], v.i. Fish with line towing bait near surface. [?]

whiffle, v.i. & t., & n. (Of wind) blow lightly, shift about, drive (ship) in varying directions; (of flame, leaves, & fig. of thought &c.) flicker, flutter, wander; make the sound of a light wind in breathing &c.; (n.) slight movement of air. [f. WHIFF[1] + -LE(3)]

whig, n. & a. (Member) of the political party that, after the Revolution of 1688, aimed at subordinating the power of the crown to that of Parliament & the upper classes, passed the Reform Bill, & has been succeeded by the Liberals (opp. TORY; still applied to those liberals, & their opinions, who oppose further progress in the direction of democracy; DISH[2] *the ww.*). Hence **whi·gg**ERY(4), **whi·gg**ISM(3), nn., **whi·gg**ISH[1] a., **whi·ggish**LY[2] adv., **whi·ggish**NESS n. [earlier of Scotch covenanters, short for *whiggamor* nickname (perh. f. Sc. *whig* jog, drive, + MARE[2]) of western Scots who came to Leith for corn]

while[1], n., & v.t. Space of time, time occupied by or given to some action &c., (*have been waiting all this w.*; *go away for a w.*; *in a little w.*, soon; MEAN[2]*w.*; *once in a w.*, occasionally, at long intervals; *have not seen him for a long w.*, *this long w. past*; *happened a long w. ago*; *that is enough for one w.*, for some time; *worth w.* or *my* &c. *w.*, repaying the time spent in doing it &c.; *looked in her eyes the while* or *whilst*, during some other process; *the w.* or *whilst* poet., during the time that). (Vb) pass (time, hour, &c.) *away* in leisurely manner. [Aryan: OE *hwil*, cf. Sw. *hvila* rest, G *weile*; cogn. w. L *quies* QUIET]

while[2], **whiles** (archaic), conj. During the time that, for as long as, at the same time as, *please write while I dictate*; *Jones got 98 w. his partner was making 15*; *w. there is life there is hope*; also with ellipse of pronominal subject & *am, is, was*, &c., as *w. reading I fell asleep*, *we are safe w. in his care*, *he retained the consciousness of it w. asleep*); in contrast more or less marked with the fact that simultaneously, although, whereas, (chiefly journalistic) &, (*Nero fiddling w. Rome burns*; *w. I have no money to spend, you have nothing to spend money on*; *w. I admit his good points I can see his bad*; also erron. *w. admitting* &c., cf. the correct ellipses above; *Jones lost an arm, Brown a leg, w. Robinson had both amputated*). [f. a case of prec.; for *whiles* see -ES & cf. WHILST]

whi·lom, adv. & a. Once, formerly, (archaic); (adj.) quondam (*his w. friend*). [OE *hwilum* instr. pl. (WHILE[1])]

whilst, conj. & n. = WHILE[2]; (n.) *the w.*, = *the* WHILE[1]. [WHILE[1], -ES]

whim, n. Sudden fancy, caprice, crotchet; kind of windlass for raising ore from mine; *whi·mwham* archaic [redupl. of *w.*], plaything, toy, w. [perh. of Scand. orig., cf. ON *hvima* wander with the eyes]

whi·mbrel, n. Kind of curlew. [*whim*, imit. of its cry, -REL]

whi·mper, v.i. & t., & n. Make feeble querulous or frightened sounds, cry & whine softly; utter whimperingly; hence **whi·mper**ER[1] n., **whi·mpering**LY[2] adv. (N.) sound of whimpering. [imit.]

whi·msical, a. Capricious; odd-looking, fantastic. Hence **whimsică·l**ITY n., **whi·msical**LY[2] adv. [foll., -ICAL]

whi·msy (-zĭ), n. Crotchet, whim. [see WHIM]

whin[1], n. Gorse, furze, (used in pl. also); *w.-chat*, kind of small bird. [cf. Norw. *hvine*, Sw. *hven*, kinds of grass]

whin[2], **whi·nsill, whin·stone,** nn. Kinds of basaltic rock or hard sandstone. [?]

whine, v.i. & t., & n. (Make) long-drawn complaining cry (as) of dog; (utter) querulous talk; utter whiningly (often *out*). Hence **whi·n**ER[1] n., **whi·ning**LY[2] adv. [OE *hwinan*, cf. ON *hvina* whiz]

whi·nger (-ng-), n. Short sword, dirk, or long knife. [also *whinyard*; etym. dub.]

whi·nny, v.i., & n. Neigh gently or joyfully; (n.) whinnying sound. [imit., cf. WHINE]

whip[1], v.t. & i. Move (t. & i.) with sudden motion, snatch, dart, (always with adv. or prep.; *w. behind the cupboard*; *whipped away to France*; *whipped up her toy terrier*; *w. out sword, knife*; *w. off* one's *coat*); bind (cord, stick) with close covering of twine, sew (seam) with overhand stitches; flog, lash, (horse, boy, &c.; *w.*

in, off, together, of managing hounds with w., & transf. followers esp. in Parliament; *w. stream,* fish it with whipping motion; *w. horses on,* urge with w.; *w.* fault *out of* person; *w. eggs,* beat into froth), (slang) excel, defeat, (*w. creation,* beat all); hoist (coal &c.) with rope passed through pulley; *whipping-boy* hist., boy educated with & chastised for young prince; *whipping-post,* to which persons were tied to be whipped; *whipping-top,* kept spinning by blows of lash. Hence **whi·pp**ING[1](1, 4) n. [cf. Du. *wippen* skip, hasten, Sw. *vippa* to wag, G *wippen* move up & down; perh. cogn. w. L *vibrare* VIBRATE]

whip[2], **n.** Instrument for urging on or punishing with lash attached to short or long stick; *good, poor,* &c., coachman (esp. of four-in-hand or tandem driver); (also *whipper-in*) hunt official subordinate to huntsman charged with management of hounds, (transf.) official appointed to maintain discipline among, secure attendance of, & give necessary information to, members of his party in House of Parliament, also written notice (variously underscored with number of lines representing degrees of urgency, cf. FIVE-*line w.*) requesting attendance on particular occasion; (also *w.-&-derry*) rope-&-pulley hoisting apparatus; *whi·p-cord,* tightly twisted cord such as is used for making w.-lashes (*his veins stood out like w.-c.*); *w.-fish,* kind with dorsal fin produced into filament like w.-lash; *w.-gin,* tackle-block with hoisting rope; *w. hand,* hand that holds w. (esp. in *have the w. h. of,* be in position to control); *w.-ray,* ray-fish with long slender tail; *w.-saw,* narrow saw-blade with ends held by frame; *w.-snake,* slender kinds. [partly f. prec., partly f. cogn. LG nn.]

whi·pper, n. In vbl senses; esp.: *w.-in,* (now usu. shortened to) WHIP[2]; *w.-snapper,* small child, young & insignificant but presuming or intrusive person [perh. for *whipsnapper,* implying noise & unimportance; but cf. WHIPSTER]. [-ER[1]]

whi·ppet, n. Cross-bred dog of modified greyhound type used for racing; (Mil.) fast light tank. [f. 1610 in sense small dog; cf. obs. vb & n. = frisk]

whi·ppoorwill, n. American bird allied to goatsucker. [imit. of cry]

whi·pster, n. Small child; trifling frivolous person such as should still be subject to the whip. [-STER]

whir(r), v.i. (part. *whir·ring*), & n. (Make) continuous buzzing or softly clicking sound as of bird's wings quickly flapped or cogwheels in rapid action. [f. Da. *hvirre* whirl, or imit.]

whirl, v.t. & i., & n. Swing (t. & i.) round & round, revolve (t. & i.) rapidly (*whirling* DERVISH); send (missile &c.), (of moving body) travel, swiftly in orbit or curve; convey or go rapidly *away* &c. in wheeled conveyance; (of brain, senses, &c.) be giddy, seem to spin round, (of thoughts &c.) follow each other in bewildering succession; (n.) whirling movement (*my thoughts are in a w.*); *whir·lpool,* circular eddy in sea &c.; *whir·lwind,* mass of air whirling rapidly round & round in cylindrical or funnel shape (*sow wind & reap whirlwind,* suffer worse results of bad action). [f. ON *hvirfla,* cf. G *wirbeln*; cogn. w. OE *hweorfan* turn]

whir·ligig (-g-), **n.** Kinds of spinning toy, (fig.) revolving motion (*w. of time,* changes of fortune); merry-go-round; kinds of water beetle that circle about on surface. [prec., GIG[1]]

whisht. See WHIST[1].

whisk, n., & v.t. & i. Bunch of grass, hair, &c., to flap dust off, flies away, &c., with; instrument for beating up eggs or cream; quick movement (as) of w. or of animal's tail. (Vb) flap (dust, fly, &c.) *away* or *off*; beat up (eggs &c.); take *away* or *off* with sudden motion (*waiter whisked my plate off*); convey or go lightly & quickly esp. out of sight (*was whisked across channel in aeroplane*; *mouse whisks into its hole*); brandish lightly or flip or wave about (*went whisking a cane, her tail*). [earlier *wisk,* prob. of Scand. orig.; cf. Da. *viske* wipe, G *wischen* wipe, ON *visk* & OHG *wisc* wisp, LG *wisk* quick movement]

whi·sker, n. Hair of man's cheek (cf. *moustache, beard*; usu. in pl.); bristle growing from upper lip of cat &c., set of such bristles on one side. Hence **(-)whisker**ED[2] a. [prec., -ER[1]]

whi·sky[1], **n.** Spirit distilled from malted barley, other grains, or sugar &c.; *whiskified* facet., affected by w.-drinking; *w.-liver,* liver-complaint from alcoholic poisoning. [f. Gael. *uisge(-beatha)* water (of life), cf. USQUEBAUGH]

whi·sky[2], **n.** Kind of light gig or chaise. [f. WHISK, w. ref. to lightness of motion]

whi·sper, v.i. & t., & n. Speak without vibration of vocal cords; talk with intention of being audible only close at hand or to confidant; inform or bid (person) thus *that* or *to* do; converse privately, indulge in slander or plotting; put secretly in circulation (tale, *that*; esp. *it is whispered that*); (of leaves, stream, &c.) rustle; *whispering-gallery,* gallery, cave, &c., in which some acoustic peculiarity causes least sound made at a particular point to be audible at another far off; hence **whi·sper**ER[1], **whi·sper**ING[1](1), nn., **whi·spering**LY[2] adv. (N.) whispering speech (*always talks in a w.* or *ww.*); whispered remark; rumour of unknown origin, mysterious hint; rustling sound. [ONorthumb. *hwisprian,* cf. G *wispern*]

whist[1], **whisht,** int. enjoining silence (now rare exc. in representations of Irish talk, *-sht*). [cf. HIST, HUSH]
whist[2], a. (archaic). Silent. [f. prec.]
whist[3], n. Card game of mingled skill & chance for four or exceptionally three or two persons (*long, short, w.*, with ten, five, points to game; DUMMY, *double* DUMMY, BRIDGE[2], *w.*; RUBBER[2] *of w.*; *w. drive*, PROGRESSIVE w. party. [earlier *whisk* (perh. w. ref. to whisking off of cards from table), afterwards changed w. ref. to the silence usual in the game]
whi·stle (-sl), v.i. & t., & n. Make with the lips or with instrument for the purpose, or (of birds &c.) with the voice, or (of missile, wind, &c.) by rapid motion, the shrill sound of breath forced through small orifice formed with lips (*boy, bird, steam-engine* or its driver, *wind, bullet, whistles*; *w. for a wind*, of becalmed sailors, whence *may w. for it*, vainly wish; *let* one *go w.*, disregard his wishes; *whistling*, in names of kinds of bird & animal, as *Whistling eagle, marmot*); act as informer, peach; summon or give signal to (dog, attendant) by whistling (*w. down the wind* metaph. f. hawking, let go, abandon); give (tune &c.) by whistling. (N.) whistling sound or note; instrument for producing such sound (*penny w.*, tin pipe with six holes giving notes; *steam w.*, sounded by jet of steam; *pay for* one's *w.* of anecdotic orig., pay high for some caprice); throat (WET one's *w.*). [OE *hwistle* n., *hwistlian* make hissing sound, cf. ON *hvísla* whisper; imit.]
whi·stler, n. In vbl senses; esp.: kind of marmot; kinds of bird. [-ER[1]]
whit[1], n. Particle, least possible amount, (usu. in *no w.*, *not* or *never a w.*, not at all). [OE *wiht* WIGHT, whit]
Whit[2], **Whi·tsun,** aa. *Whit Sunday*, seventh Sunday after Easter, commemorating day of Pentecost; *Whit Monday, Tuesday*, those following, *Whit week*, that containing, Whit Sunday; *Whi·tsuntide*, Whit Sunday & following days; *Whitsun week*, Whit week. [OE *Hwita Sunnandæg*, lit. White Sunday; *Whitsun* short for *Whitsunday's*; *Whit Sunday = white Sunday*, so called because christenings, & therefore white robes, were common on it]
white[1], a., & v.t. Resembling a surface reflecting sunlight without absorbing any of the visible rays, of the colour of fresh snow or common salt or the common swan's plumage, having some approach to such colour, pale (*w. as a sheet*), less dark than other things of the same kind (*bleed w.*, fig., drain of wealth &c., w. ref. to hanging of calf to whiten veal), characterized by presence of some w., (*white-* in many -ED[2] compounds used esp. in naming animals &c., as *w.-backed, -beaked, -bearded, -bellied, -breasted, -crested, -crowned, -eyed, -faced, -footed, -fronted, -headed, -necked, -rumped, -tailed, -throated, -winged*); (of water, air, light) transparent, colourless; (fig.) innocent, unstained, of harmless kind; of w. men (see *w. man* below; *w. culture, civilization*, &c.); (Pol.) of royalist or counter-revolutionary or reactionary tendency (opp. RED, & cf. TERROR); *w. alloy*, any of the cheap imitations of silver; *whi·tebait*, small fish prob. the fry of several kinds eaten fried in quantities when about 2 in. long; *whi·tebeam*, small tree with silvery underleaf; *w. bear*, polar bear; *Whi·teboy*, member of 18th-c. illegal agrarian association in Ireland wearing w. frocks at nightly meetings & outrages; *w.-caps*, breakers out at sea; *w. corpuscle*, = LEUCO*cyte*; *w.* CROW[1], CURRANT, ELEPHANT; *w.* ENSIGN, flown by ships of British navy, cf. RED *ensign*; *w.* FEATHER[1]; *w.-fish* commerc., other than salmon, also of whiting & haddock in particular; *w.* FLAG[4], FRIAR, FROST; *w. gloves* (presented to assize judge who finds no criminal cases to try); *w.* GROUSE[1]; *w.-gum*, eruption on infant's neck & arms; *w. hands* lit., as sign of exemption from labour, fig. innocency or integrity; so *w.-handed*; *w. heart-cherry*, pale heart-shaped kind; *w.* HEAT[1] (lit., & fig. of passion &c.; so *w.-hot*); *w. horses*, waves with w. crests at sea; *W. House*, official residence of U.S. president; *w.* LEAD[1], LIE[1]; *w. light*, colourless, e.g. ordinary daylight, also fig. of unprejudiced judgement; *w.-lipped*, esp. with fear; *w.-livered*, cowardly; *w.* MAGIC; *w. man*, member of one of the paler races chiefly inhabiting or having inhabited Europe, & characterized by a certain type of civilization (cf. *black, brown, red, yellow, man*; *the w. m.'s burden*, task of leading the world forward), (colloq.) person of honourable character, good breeding, &c.; *w. meat*, poultry, veal, rabbits, pork; *w. metal*, = *w. alloy*; *w. mixture*, a hospital aperient; *w.-paper*, report issued by Government to give information; *w.* SCOURGE; *w. sheet*, penitent's garb (usu. *stand in a w. s.*, confess sin &c.); *w. slave*, girl entrapped (& exported) for purpose of prostitution (*the w.-s. traffic, w. slavery*); *whi·tesmith*, worker in tin, also polisher or galvanizer of iron; *w. squall*, sudden tropical storm at sea announced only by line of w. water approaching; *whi·tethorn*, hawthorn (cf. BLACK[1]*thorn*); *w.-throat*, kinds of small songbird; *W. Tsar*, (Asiatic phr. for) Tsar of Russia; *whi·tewash* n., solution of quicklime or of whiting & size for brushing over walls, ceilings, &c., to give clean appearance, also fig. means employed to clear person or his memory of imputations, (colloq.) glass of sherry after other wine, (v.t.) cover with whitewash, attempt to clear reputation of, (pass., of insolvent) get fresh start by

passage through bankruptcy court; *w. wine*, of amber or golden colour (opp. *red*); *w. witch* (using power for beneficent purposes only); hence **whi·te**LY² adv. (rare), **whi·ten**⁶ v.t. & i., **whi·te**NESS n., **whi·tish**¹(2) a. (Vb; archaic) make w. [OE *hwit*, cf. Du. *wit*, G *weiss*, Skr. *çvitrá*- whitish]

white², n. W. or nearly w. colour; kinds of w. pigment (*Chinese* &c. *w.*); w. clothes or material (*dressed in w.*); albuminous part round yolk *of* egg; visible part round iris *of* eye; =*w. man* (MEAN³ *w.*); kinds of butterfly; (Med.; pl.) LEUCO*rrhoea*. [f. prec.]

Whi·techapel, n., & v.i. *W. cart*, light two-wheeled spring-cart used by shopkeepers for sending goods round; (Whist) lead from one-card suit with a view to subsequent trumping. [*Whitechapel* in London]

Whi·tehall, n. (Used for) departmental government, the Government offices. [street in London]

whi·tening (-tn-), n. =WHITING¹. [*whiten* (WHITE¹), -ING¹]

whi·ther (-idh-), adv. interrog. & rel. (chiefly archaic), & n. To what place or point? (now usu. *where?*, *where — to?*, *how far?*, &c., but cf. *I see w. your question tends*), whence **whi·ther**WARD adv.; (rel., with antecedent *place* &c.) to which (now usu. *to which*, *where*), (without antecedent) to the or (also *w.-soever*) any place to which (now usu. *where*); =& thither; (n.) destination (*our whence & our w.*; *no w.* archaic, to no place). [OE *hwider* (WHICH, -THER)]

whi·ting¹, n. Chalk prepared by drying, grinding, &c., for use in whitewashing, plate-cleaning, &c. [WHITE¹ vb, -ING¹(4)]

whi·ting², n. Kind of sea-fish much used as food; *w.-pout*, fish with some resemblance to w. & an inflatable membrane over part of head. [WHITE¹ a., -ING³]

whi·tleather, n. White leather dressed with alum instead of being tanned. [WHITE¹]

whi·tlow, n. Inflammatory tumour on finger esp. about the nail. [earliest form *whitflawe*, perh. = white flaw, with *whit* = white as in WHIT² & prec.]

Whitsun. See WHIT².

whi·ttle¹, n. (archaic). Long knife, esp. such as is used by butchers. [ME *thwitel* f. OE *thwitan* pare, -LE(1)]

whi·ttle², v.t. & i. Trim, carve, slice off pieces from, (wood) with knife; shape, thin down, cut repeatedly *at*, piece of wood with knife; reduce amount or effect of by repeated subtraction (usu. *down*, *away*). [f. prec.]

whi·ty, a. Inclining to white (usu. in comb. with other colour-name, esp. *w.-brown*). [-Y²]

whiz, whizz, v.i., & n. (Make) sound given by friction of body moving at great speed through air; *w.-bang* (army slang), shell from a small-calibre high-velocity German gun. [imit.]

who (hōō), pron. pers. interrog. & rel. (obj. *whom* pr. hōōm; poss. WHOSE pr. hōōz). 1. Interrog.: What person(s)?, which person(s)?, what sort of person(s) in regard to position or authority?, (*w. said so?*; *whom* or colloq. *w. do you mean?*; *told him w. they were*, *whom* or colloq. *w. to look out for*; *whose son is he?*; *w. would have thought it?*, no one would; *w. are the Joneses? I should like to know*; *w. am I that I should object?*; *know who 's who*, who or what each person is; *a who 's who*, list with description of notables). 2. Rel.: (Person or persons) that (*the man whom you saw*; *those for whose benefit it was done*; *any one w. chooses can apply*; *there is no one w. we can believe is competent*, often incorrectly *whom*); (archaic) the or any person(s) that (*who breaks pays*; *whom the gods love die young*; *as w. should say*, like a person w. said, as though one said); &, but, though, since, if, &c., he, him, they, &c. (*sent it to Jones, w. passed it on to Smith*; *is flirting with Dick, whom she detests*). [Aryan: OE *hwá*, with neut. *hwæt*, gen. *hwæs*, dat. *hwám*, instr. *hwi*; cf. Du. *wie* who, *wat* what, *wiens* whose, *wien* whom, G *wer* who, *was* what, *wessen* whose, *wen* & *wem* whom, L *quis*, Skr. *ka*; the rel. senses are later than the interrog.]

whoa. See WO.

whoĕ·ver, who·so (archaic), **whosoe·ver** (emphat.), **whoe'er·** & **whosoe'er·** (poet.; -âr), (hōō-), pronn. pers. indef. rel. (cases as with WHO; *whomsoever* or the incorrect *w.* is usu. substituted without special emphasis for *whomever*, & *whosesoever* somet. for *whose-ever*), used (1) as mod. equivalent of archaic *who* in indef. rel. sense (*w. comes will be welcome*; *stopped whomsoever* or *w.* or *whomever he saw*; *return it to whose-ever* or *whosesoever address is on it*); (2) in indef. concessive clauses = though any one (*w. else objects, I do not*; *whose-ever it is, I mean to have it*; *whomsoever* or *w.* or *whomever I quote, you retain your opinion*); (3) vulg. for *who* EVER. [WHO, SO, EVER]

whole (hōl), a. & n. (Archaic) in good health, well, (*they that be w. need not a physician*); in sound condition, uninjured, not broken, intact, (*hope you will come back w.*; *got off with a w. skin*; *there is not a plate left w.*; *has swallowed a raisin w.*); integral, consisting of one or more units, without fractions, (*w. numbers*, integers); undiminished, without subtraction, (*bread made of w. meal*, not deprived by bolting of some constituents); (with *a* in sing.) not less than (*spent w. years of misery*; *went up a w. tone*; *lasted three w. days*; *w. regiments were cut down*; *talked a w. lot of nonsense*); (with *the, his*, &c.) all that there is of (*the w. truth, world, duty of man*; *do thing with* one's *w. heart*, heartily, with concentrated effort &c., without doubts &c., whence **whole-heartED**² a., **whole-hear·tedLY**² adv., **whole-hear·tedNESS** n.; *the w. priesthood, city*, &c., all members or inhabitants of it; COMMITTEE *of the w. House*; *go the w.* HOG¹, whence **whole-ho·ggER**¹ n., esp. thorough-going protectionist); *w.-coloured*, all of one colour; *w.-hoofed*, with undivided hoofs; *w.-length*, (portrait) representing person from head to foot; *who·lesale* n. (chiefly attrib.), selling of articles in large quantities to be retailed by others (*a w.-s. dealer*; *sells by w.-s.*; *w.-s. prices*), adj. & adv., on the w.-s. plan, (transf.) on large scale, (*our business is w.-s. only*; *sells w.-s.*; *a w.-s. slaughter took place*; *sends out begging letters w.-s.*); hence **who·leNESS** n. (N.) thing complete in itself; all that there is of something (often *of*; *the golden rule contains the w. of morality*; *on* or *upon the w.*, taking into consideration everything that bears on the question, after weighing pros & cons &c.); organic unity, complete system, total made up of parts, (*nature is a w.*; *the w. & the parts*). [OE *hál* HALE¹, cf. G *heil*, Du. *heel*; cogn. w. HEAL, HOLY]

who·lesome, a. Promoting physical or moral health, salubrious, salutary, not morbid, (*w. food, air, exercise, advice, neglect, excitement*). Hence **who·lesomeLY**² adv., **who·lesomeNESS** n. [prec., -SOME]

whō·lly (-l-lĭ), adv. Entirely, without abatement, (*I am w. yours*); exclusively, without admixture, (*a w. bad example*). [WHOLE, -LY²]

whom. See WHO.

whoop (h-). Var. of HOOP².

whop, v.t. (slang). Thrash, (fig.) defeat, overcome, whence **who·ppING**¹(1) n.; (part.) very large of its kind (esp. *a whopping lie*), whence **who·pPER**¹ n. [also *w(h)ap, wop*; etym. dub.]

whore (hōr), n., & v.i. (not in decent use). Prostitute, strumpet, (*the* SCARLET *W.*); *w.-master, -monger*, fornicator; hence **whore·DOM** n. (Vb, of man) practise fornication; (fig., archaic, esp. *go a-whoring after strange gods* &c.) practise idolatry or iniquity. [late OE *hóre* prob. f. ON *hóra* adulteress, cf. Du. *hoer*, G *hure*; cogn. w. L *carus* dear]

whorl, n. Ring of leaves or other organs round stem &c. of plant; one turn of a spiral; disk on spindle steadying its motion. Hence **whorlED**² a. [ME *wharwyl, whorwhil*, cf. OE *hweorfan* turn, -LE(1); or perh. var. of WHIRL]

whor·tleberry (wer-), n. = BILBERRY. [also *whortle, whort, hurtleberry, hurtle, hurt*, perh. f. F *heurte* a roundel azure in heraldry]

whose. Possessive case of WHO, used also as case of WHICH 2b; *whose-ever, whosesoever*, see WHOEVER.

whoso, whosoever. See WHOEVER.

why¹, adv. interrog. & rel., & n. (pl. *whys*). On what ground?, for what reason?, with what purpose?, (*w. did you do it?*; *cannot think w. you came*; often ellipt., as *You are late*; *why?*, esp. in *w. so?*, demand for grounds of statement or view); on account of which (*the reasons w. he did it are obscure*). (N.) reason, explanation, (*cannot go into the whys & wherefores now*). [OE *hwí* instr. of WHO, WHAT]

why², int. expr. surprised discovery or recognition (*w., it is surely Jones!*; *w., what a bruise you have got!*; *w., of course, that was it*), protest at simplicity of question &c. ('*What is twice two?*' *w., four. W., a child could answer that*), pause for reflection ('*Is it true?*' '*W., yes, I think so*'), objection (*w., what is the harm?*), introduction of apodosis (*if silver will not do, w., we must try gold*), &c. [ellipt. uses of prec. interrog.]

wick¹, n. (Piece of) fibrous or spongy material by which lamp or candle flame is kept supplied with melted grease or oil; (Surg.) gauze strip inserted in wound to drain it. [OE *wéoce, wéoc*, cf. MDu. *wiecke*, Da. *væge*]

wick², n. Town, hamlet, district, (rare exc. in place-names as *Hampton W.* or other compounds as *bailiwick*). [OE *wic* f. L *vicus*]

wi·cked, a. Sinful, iniquitous, vicious, given to or involving immorality, (*w. bible*, edition of 1632 with *not* omitted in seventh commandment), offending intentionally against the right; spiteful, ill-tempered, intending or intended to give pain, playfully mischievous, roguish. Hence **wi·ckedLY**² adv., **wi·ckedNESS** n. [ME, f. obs. *wick* of same sense (perh. adj. use of OE *wicca* wizard) + -ED¹ as in WRETCHED]

wi·cker, n. Plaited twigs or osiers as material of baskets, chairs, mats, protective covers, &c. (usu. attrib., as *w. chair*), whence **wi·ckerED**² a.; *w.-work*, (things made of) w. [earlier sense *pliant twig*, f. Scand. (MSw. *viker* osier cf. Sw. *vika* to bend, OE *wican* give way); cogn. w. WEAK]

wi·cket, n. Small door or gate, esp. one beside or in the compass of a larger one for use when the latter is not open (also *w.-door, -gate*); turnstile entrance; aperture in door or wall usu. closed with sliding panel; door closing only lower half of doorway; (Cricket) one set of three stumps & two bails (*keep w.*, be *w.-keeper* or fieldsman stationed close behind batsman's w.; *keep* one's *w. up*, succeed in not being put out), also the ww. as defended by one batsman (*5 ww. down*, five men out; *match won by 2 ww.*, with three of winning side still not out), also *good* &c. state of the pitch (*play began on a perfect w.*). [ME & AF *wiket*, mod. F *guichet*, f. uncertain Teut. source; cricket w. orig. resembled gate, being 2 ft wide by 1 ft]

wide, a., adv., & n. Measuring much or more than other things of same kind across or from side to side, broad, not narrow, (*w. door, road, river, brim, margin, cloth, interval*; *w. margin* fig., a good deal more allowed than is likely to be needed); (appended to measurement) in width (*a strip 3 ft w.*); extending far, embracing much, of great extent, (*has a w. range*; *w. fame*, known to many; *the w. world*, all the world great as it is; *a w. domain*, large; *is of w. distribution*, occurs in many places; *a w. generalization*, covering many particulars; *there is a w. difference between*; also adv., as *the principle ranges w.*, & esp. in *far & w.*), whence **wi·de**LY[2] adv.; not tight or close or restricted, loose, free, liberal, unprejudiced, general, (*w. knickerbockers*; *w. culture*, not specialized; *takes w. views*; *hazard a w. guess*, one allowing margin for errors of detail; *give w. berth to*, not go too near, keep clear of, avoid); open to full extent (*staring with w. eyes*; also adv. or pred. a., as *yawned w., open your mouth w., window is w. open, person is w. awake*); at considerable distance from a point or mark, not within reasonable distance *of*, (*w. ball* in cricket, also *w.* n., ball judged by umpire to pass wicket beyond batsman's reach & counting one to his side; *gave an answer quite w. of the mark* or *purpose*; also adv. or pred. a., as *is bowling, shooting, w., arrow fell w. of target*); *w. awake* a. colloq., wary, knowing; *w.-awake* n., soft w.-brimmed felt hat; *w.-spread*, widely disseminated (esp. of beliefs or impressions). Hence **wi·d**EN[6] v.t. & i., **wi·d**ISH[1](2) a. [com.-Teut.: OE *wid*, cf. Du. *wijd*, G *weit* far]

wi·dgeon (-jn), n. Kinds of wild duck. [perh. ult. f. L *vipio* kind of crane; cf. PIGEON, & F *vigeon, vingeon*, which however are not recorded as early as E *w.*]

wi·dow (-ō), n., & v.t. Woman who has lost her husband by death & not married again (GRASS *w.*; *w.'s* WEEDS; *w.'s cruse*, supply that looks small, but proves inexhaustible, see 1 *Kings* xvii. 10–16; *w.'s mite*, see *Mark* xii. 42; also attrib., as *w. lady, woman*); *w.-bird*, black-plumaged African bird of genus *Vidua* (L = w.); hence **wi·dow**HOOD n. (Vb) kill husband or mate of, deprive of husband or wife or mate, make into w. or widower, (usu. in p.p.; *the widowed father, mother*, &c.), (poet.) bereave *of* friend &c. [Aryan: OE *widewe*, cf. Du. *weduwe*, G *wittwe*; cogn. w. L *viduus* bereft, Gk *ēitheos* bachelor, Skr. *vidhavā*]

wi·dower, n. Man who has lost his wife by death & not married again. [prec., -ER[1]]

width, n. Distance or measurement from side to side; comprehensiveness or liberality *of* mind, views, &c.; piece of material of certain w. (*shall want three ww. of it*). [WIDE, -TH[1]]

wield, v.t. Control, sway, hold & use, manage with the hands or otherwise, (*w. power, the sceptre, a kingdom* &c. chiefly poet., *weapon* lit. or fig.). [OE *wieldan, wealdan* rule, cf. ON *valda*, G *walten*); perh. cogn. w. L *valēre* be strong]

wife, n. (pl. *-ves*). Woman, esp. one who is old & rustic or uneducated (now rare exc. in *old wives' tale*, foolish or superstitious tradition, & in comb. as FISH[1]*w.*, HOUSEWIFE, MIDWIFE); married woman esp. in relation to her husband (usu. *my* &c. *w., the w. of*, or with epithet as *will make a good w.*; *wedded, lawful, w.*, emphatic phrr. in contrast w. *mistress, concubine*, &c.; *all the* WORLD *& his w.*; *have, take, to w.*, = as w.). Hence **wi·fe**HOOD, **wi·fie**, [-Y[3]], nn., **wi·fe**LESS, **wi·fe**LIKE, **wi·fe**LY[1], aa. [OE *wif*, cf. Du. *wijf*, G *weib*, all neut. nn., etym. dub.]

wig[1], n. Artificial head of hair formerly much worn as ornament, & still to conceal baldness or disguise appearance or as part of official dress esp. of judge or lawyer or of servant's livery (*there will be ww. on the green*, a free fight). Hence **(-)wigg**ED[2], **wi·g**LESS, aa. [short for PERIWIG]

wig[2], v.t. Rebuke sharply, rate, (chiefly in the vbl n.). Hence **wi·gg**ING[1](1) n. [perh. w. ref. to bewigged superior reprimanding]

wi·gan, n. Stiff canvas-like material used for stiffening. [*Wigan* in Lancashire]

wight (wīt), n. (archaic or facet.). Person, being, (esp. *luckless, wretched*, &c., *w.*). [OE *wiht* creature, person, thing, cf. Du. *wicht* child, G *wicht* creature; doublet of WHIT[1]]

wi·gwăm (*or* -ŏm), n. N.-Amer. Indian's tent or hut of skins or mats or bark. [native]

wild, a., adv., & n. Not domesticated or cultivated (chiefly of animals & plants, & esp. of species allied to others that are not w.; in the commoner combinations *w.* & the n. are hyphened, or treated as one wd with accent on *w.*; *w. beast, plant*; *w. man*, savage; *w. ass*; *w.-boar*; *w.-duck*; *wi·ldfowl*; *w. vine*; *wi·ldcat* lit., also fig. as a. or attrib. of finance or commercial speculations, reckless, unsound; *wild-goose* lit., also in *w.-g. chase*, absurdly impossible enterprise; *w. horse*, also in *be drawn by w. horses*, form of torture & death; *w. hyacinth*, bluebell; *w.* OATS; *w. scenery* &c., of conspicuously desolate appearance; *woodnotes w.*, spontaneous &

artless poetry); (of horses, game-birds, &c.) shy, given to shying, easily startled, hard to get near; unrestrained, wayward, disorderly, irregular, out of control, unconventional, (*a w. fellow*; *settled down after a w. youth*; *w. work*, lawless doings; *hair hanging in w. locks*; *living in w. times*; *room is in w. disorder*; *run w.*, grow unchecked or untrained); tempestuous, violent, (*a w. wind, night*, &c.); intensely eager, excited, frantic, passionate, distracted, mad, (*is w. with excitement, to try it*; *the w. men*, extremists of a party &c.; *w. about* person or subject, enthusiastically devoted to; *w. delight, excitement, enthusiasm, grief, rage*; *w. looks, appearance*, &c., indicating distraction; *drive w.*, madden); haphazard, rash, ill-considered, ill-aimed, disturbed by excitement, (*a w. guess, shot, blow, venture*; *w. opinions, bowling*; also as adv., as *shoot, talk, w.*); *wi·ldfire*, = *Greek* FIRE[1] (*report spreads like w.-f.*, very fast); hence **wi·ld**ISH[1](2) a., **wi·ld**LY[2] adv., **wi·ld**NESS n. (N.) desert, w. tract. [com.-Teut.: OE *wilde*, cf. Du. & G *wild*; prob. cogn. w. WILL w. orig. sense *wilful*]

wildebeest (wē·ldebāst), n. The gnu. [S.-Afr. Du. (prec., BEAST)]

wi·lder, v.t. (poet.). Bewilder. [prob. shortened f. *wildern* see foll.]

wi·lderness, n. Desert, uncultivated & uninhabited tract, (*voice in the w.* &c., unregarded advocate of some reform, w. ref. to *Matt.* iii. 3 &c.; *wandering* &c. *in the w.*, of political party out of office, w. ref. to *Numb.* xiv. 33 &c.); part of garden left wild; unlimited number or quantity *of*. [prob. f. obs. *wildern* savage, f. OE *wild-déor* wild beast + -EN[5], + -NESS]

wi·lding, n. Plant sown by natural agency, esp. wild crab-apple, or fruit of such plant (also attrib.). [-ING[3]]

wile, n., & v.t. Trick, cunning procedure, artifice, (usu. in pl.). (Vb) lure, entice, *away, into*, &c. (also incorrectly for WHILE[1] vb). [ME *wil*, perh. f. Scand. (ON *vél* craft)]

wi·lful, a. For which compulsion or ignorance or accident cannot be pleaded as excuse, intentional, deliberate, due to perversity or self-will, (*w. murder, waste, ignorance, disobedience*); obstinate, self-willed, headstrong, refractory. Hence **wi·lful**LY[2] adv., **wi·lful**NESS n. [WILL, -FUL]

Wilhelmstrasse (vĭ·lhĕlmshtrahse), n. (Used for) the German Foreign Office. [Berlin street]

will[1], v.t. & aux. (pres. *I, he, we, you, they, w.* or *'ll, thou wilt* or *'lt*; past & condit. *I, he, we, you, they, would* pr. wo͝od or *'d, thou wouldst* pr. wo͝odst or *wouldest* or *'dst*; neg. forms *will not* or *wōn't, would not* or *wouldn't*, or *'d not*; no other forms or parts used). 1. (used irrespective of person with more or less of orig. sense of volition): Desire (thing; archaic; *what wilt thou?*; *what would they?*); want or desire or choose to (*the haven where I would be*; *come when you w.*); wish that, rarely *that* (usu. in condit. with optative effect; *I* often omitted; *it shall be as you w.*; *said it should be as we would*; *would* or *I would I were a bird!*; *would it were otherwise!*; *would God I had died!*, i.e. if only God had wished, or perh. ellipt. for *I would to God*; *I would to heaven I was dead*; *would-be*, prefixed as adj. or adv. to wd describing character that person vainly aspires to or that thing is meant to have, as *a would-be gentleman, smart saying*); consent or be prevailed on to (*w.* or *would not go any further*; *wound would not heal*; *would you pass the salt?*; *would not do it for £100*); refuse to be prevailed on not to (*boys w. be boys*; *accidents w. happen*; *you w. have your way*; *he w., would, get in my light*); be accustomed or observed from time to time to (*w. sit there for hours*; *now & then a blackbird would call*; *w. succeed once in ten times*); be likely to turn out to (*this w. be Waterloo, I suppose*; *I don't know who it would be*). 2. As tense & mood auxiliaries *w.* & *would* are used (a) in 2nd & 3rd person (1st having *shall, should*) to form a plain future or conditional statement or question (*you w. hear soon enough*; *they would have been killed if they had let go*; *w.* or *would you, they, be able to hear at such a distance?*, but cf. SHALL 5); (b) in 1st person (others having *shall, should*) to form a future or conditional statement expressing speaker's will or intention (*I will not be caught again*; *we would have come if you had given us longer notice*); (c) alternatively with *shall, should*, in sentences of type *a* changed in reporting to 1st from other person (*you say I w., said I would, never manage it*, reporting 'You w. never'; now more usu. *shall, should*) or from first to other person (*he said he would never manage it*, reporting 'I shall never'); (d) in reporting 1st pers. sentences of type *b* (*you promised you would not be caught again*). [Aryan: OE *willan*, cf. Du. *willen*, G *wollen*; cogn. w. L *velle* wish, & Skr. *vr̥* choose, also w. WELL[2]]

will[2], n. Faculty by which person decides or conceives himself as deciding upon & initiating action (*mind consists of the understanding & the w.*; *freedom of the w.*, *free will*, power of determining one's choice of action independently of causation); (also *w.-power*) control exercised by deliberate purpose over impulse, self-control, (*has a strong, weak*, &c., *w.*); deliberate or fixed intention (*the w. to live in a patient is the surgeon's best ally*; *the w. to power* &c., Germanisms for determination to win power &c.; *did it against my w., of my own free w.*; *where there 's a w. there 's a way*; *my poverty but not my* *w. consents*); energy of intention, power of effecting one's intentions or dominating other persons, (*do thing with a w.*, energetically; *has a w. that overbears all opposition*); contents of the w., what is desired or ordained by person, (*thy w. be done*; *what is your w.?*, what do you wish done?; *have* one's *w.*, get thing desired; *worked his wicked w. upon them*); arbitrary discretion (esp. *at w.*, whenever one pleases; *tenant at w.*, who can be turned out without notice; *w.-worship* archaic, religion constructed to suit oneself); disposition towards others, wishing of good or ill, (*good, ill, w.*, usu. as compd wds); directions written in legal form for disposition to be made of person's property & minor children after his death (often *last w. & testament*; *nuncupative w.*, see NUNCUPATE; *make* one's *w.*). Hence **-will**ED[2], **wi·ll**-LESS, aa. [OE *willa* (prec.)]

will[3], v.t. Have as contents of one's w., intend unconditionally, (*God wills, willeth, willed, that man should be happy*; *can we w. what we are told to w.?*; *he who wills success is half way to it*), (abs.) exercise w.-power (*has no power to w.*; *willing & wishing are not the same*); instigate or impel or compel by exercise of w.-power (*you can w. yourself into contentment*; *mesmerist wills patient to think himself well*; *willed the genie into his presence*); bequeath by w. (*shall will my money to a hospital*). [OE *willian*, f. prec.]

wi·llet, n. N.-Amer. snipe. [imit. of cry]

wi·lling, a. Not reluctant, cheerfully ready, (*to* do, or abs.; *do not spur a w. horse*); of, given &c. by, w. person (*w. hands, help*, &c.). Hence **wi·lling**LY[2] adv., **wi·lling**NESS n. [WILL[1], -ING[2]]

will-o'-the-wisp, n. = IGNIS FATUUS, JACK[1]*-o'-lantern*; also, person of uncertain whereabouts or appearances. [abbr. of *William*; *wisp* = handful of (lighted) tow &c.

wi·llow[1] (-ō), n. Kinds of tree & shrub with pliant branches growing usu. near water in temperate climates, many of which yield osiers & some timber used for cricket bats & other purposes (*wear the w.*, mourn loss or absence of one's beloved, formerly indicated by garland of w. leaves; *w.-pattern*, conventional design of Chinese type done in blue on white china &c. introduced in England 1780); cricket-bat (*handle the w.*, bat); *w.-herb*, kinds of plant, the commonest with leaves like w. & pale purple flowers. [OE *welig*, cf. Du. *wilg*]

wi·llow[2], v.t. & n., **wi·lly**, n. Clean (fibrous material) by beating, picking, &c., with machinery; (n., also *w., willowing, -machine*) machine for willowing. [OE *wilige* n. (prec.)]

wi·llowy, a. Abounding in willows; lithe & slender. [-Y[2]]

willynilly. See NILL.

wilt[1]. See WILL[1].

wilt[2], v.t. & i. Wither (t. & i. of plant, leaf, flower), (make) droop. [perh. var. of WELK]

Wi·lton, n. (Also *W. carpet*) kind of Brussels carpet with loops cut open into thick pile made at town of W.

wi·ly, a. Full of wiles, crafty, cunning. Hence **wi·li**LY[2] adv., **wi·li**NESS n. [WILE, -Y[2]]

Wi·mbledon, n. (Used for) the lawn-tennis tournaments with championship matches &c. held at W.

wi·mple, n., & v.t. & i. Covering of linen &c. worn by nuns & formerly by other women arranged in folds about head, cheeks, chin, & neck, (vb) put w upon, veil, arrange in folds; winding, twist, turn, ripple, (vb) fall in folds, (of stream) twist about, meander, ripple. [OE *wimpel*, cf. Du. & G *wimpel* streamer]

win, v.t. & i. (*won* pr. wŭn), & n. Secure as result of fighting or competition or (often *of* person) betting & gaming or of effort (*w. victory, fortress, prize, honour, fame, fortune*, one's BLUE[2], *wife*; *w.* one's *spurs*, be knighted, fig. get recognition as expert at something; *won £5 of him at cards*, whence **wi·nnings** n. pl., see -ING[1](2); *w.* one's *way*, progress by struggle &c., *w.* one's *bread*, earn livelihood, chiefly now in BREAD*-winner*; *w. fore* &c., get it from mine); be victorious in (*w. battle, game, bet, race*; *w. the field*, be victorious in battle or fig.; *w. the* TOSS), (abs.) w. race, contest, money, &c. (*w. by a* HEAD[1], *in a* CANTER, HAND[1]*s down, by two* &c. *lengths, easily*, &c.; *winn*ING[1]*-post*, marking end of race; *the winning horse, side*, &c.; *w. at cards*; *let those laugh who w.*), (part.) determining victory (*the winning hit, stroke, card*, &c.); make one's way to (*w. the shore, summit*, &c.); make one's way, or (with compl.) become by successful effort, (*w. home*; *w. through the day, through all difficulties*; *w. free, clear*, &c.); persuade, induce *to* do, gain *over*, (*you have won me*; *won him to consent*; *soon won his audience over*); exercise increasing attraction *upon* (*a theory that wins upon one by degrees*), (part. as adj.) charming, attractive, (*a winning smile, winning manners, personality*, &c.), whence **wi·nning**LY[2] adv.; *winning* HAZARD[1]; hence **(-)winn**ER[1] n. (N.) a success or victory in a game (*has had three ww. & no defeats*). [com.-Teut.: OE *winnan* fight, toil, cf. Du. *winnen*, G *gewinnen*]

wince, v.i., & n. Show bodily or mental pain or distress by slight start or loss of composure, flinch, (often *under pain, the knife, at allusion*, &c.); (n.) act of wincing. [cf. OF *guencir* f. Teut., cf. WINK]

wi·ncey, n. Strong material of wool & cotton or wool used for skirts &c. Hence **wincey**E·TTE(2) n. [perh. corrupt. of LINSEY-WOOLSEY]

winch (-tsh), n. Crank of wheel or axle; hoisting-machine, windlass. [OE *wince*, cogn. w. WINK]

Wi·nchester, n. *W. rifle* or *W.*, type of repeating rifle used esp. by big-game hunters. [*W.* in U.S.]

wind[1] (*rhet. &, esp. in rhyme, poet.* wī-), n. Air in more or less rapid natural motion, breeze or gale or blast, (*north* &c. *w.*, coming from N. &c.; *fair, contrary, w.*, helping, hindering, ship's course; *hot, cold, whistling, variable*, &c., *ww.*; *constant w.*, that always blows in same direction at same place; *periodical w.*, recurring at known periods; *w. rises*, begins to blow or gets stronger; *sound, scent, is carried by, comes on, the w.*; CAPFUL, SLANT, *of w.*; ILL *w.*; *before, down, the w.*, helped by its force; WHISTLE *down the w.*; BETWEEN *w. & water*; *sail, be, close to* or *near the w.*, as nearly against it as is consistent with using its force, fig. venture very near indecency or dishonesty; *in the w.'s eye, in the teeth of the w.*, directly against it; *on a w.*, naut., sailing against a w. on either bow; *off the w.*, naut., sailing with the w. on either quarter; *fling* or *cast* prudence &c. *to the ww.*, abandon, neglect, take no thought of; PUT[1] *the w. up* one; *get the w. up* slang, be frightened; *go like the w.*, swiftly; *there is something in the w.*, there are signs that some step is being secretly prepared; *find out how the w. blows* or *lies*, what developments are likely or what is the state of public opinion; *take the w. out of* one's *sails*, frustrate him by anticipating his arguments, using his material, &c.; *sow w. & reap* WHIRL*w.*; *raise the w.* fig., obtain money needed); windward position or *weather*-GAUGE[1] (*take* or *get the w. of*); (pl.) *the four* cardinal points (*came from the four ww.*, from all directions; *scatter to t. f. ww. of heaven*); mere empty words, unmeaning rhetoric; artificially produced air-current, air stored for use or used as current, (collect.) part of band consisting of w.-instruments, (*organ stops when the w. is exhausted*; *was knocked down by the w. of the blow*; *the strings were drowned by the w., the wood w.*, i.e. flutes &c., *by the brass*); smell conveyed on w., indication of thing's whereabouts or existence, commencing publicity, (*get w. of*, smell out, begin to suspect, hear rumour of; *take* or *get w.*, be rumoured); gas generated in bowels &c. by indigestion, flatulence, (*break w.*, release it by anus; *baby* &c. *is troubled with w.*); breath as needed in exertion, power of fetching breath without difficulty while running or making similar continuous effort, spot below centre of chest blow on which temporarily paralyses breathing, (*have lost, let me recover* or *get, my w.*; *has a good, bad, w.*; *broken w.*, see BROKEN-*winded*; *second w.*, recovery of w. in course of exercise after initial breathlessness; *have* one's *w. taken*, be paralysed by blow in the w.; *hit him in the w.*). *Wi·ndbag*, wordy orator; *w.-bound*, unable to sail for contrary ww.; *w.-chest*, box for compressed air in organ; *w.-colic*, pain caused by flatulence; *w.-cutter*, upper lip of mouth of flue-pipe in organ; *w.-egg*, unfertilized egg incapable of producing chicken; *wi·ndfall*, fruit blown down, fig. unexpected good fortune, esp. legacy; *w.-fanner*, = *windhover*; *w.-flower* poet., the plant anemone; *w.-gall*, soft tumour on horse's fetlock-joint; *w.-gauge*, anemometer, also instrument showing amount of w. in organ, also apparatus attached to sights enabling allowance to be made for w. in shooting; *wi·ndhŏver*, kestrel; *w.-instrument*, musical instrument in which sound is produced by current of air, as organ, flute; *w.-jammer* (slang), merchant sailing-ship; *wi·ndmill*, mill worked by action of w. on sails (*fight windmills*, tilt at imaginary foe or grievance, w. ref. to Don Quixote); *wi·ndpipe*, breathing-tube, trachea; *w.-row*, line of raked hay, corn-sheaves, peats, &c., made to allow of drying by w.; *w.-sail*, canvas funnel conveying air to lower parts of ship; *w.-screen* (of glass in front of motorcar driver); *w.-spout*, waterspout, tornado, or whirlwind; *w.-stick* (slang), propeller of aeroplane; *w.-sucker, -sucking*, (horse with) the vice of noisily drawing in & swallowing breath; *w.-swept*, exposed; *w.*-TIGHT; *wi·ndward* a. & n., (region) lying in the direction from which the w. blows, exposed to the w., (*look to w.-w.*; *the w.-w. side*; *get to w.-w. of*, avoid smell of, also get weather GAUGE[1] of or fig. advantage over). Hence **wi·nd**LESS a. [Aryan: OE, also Du. & G; cogn. w. L *ventus*, Skr. *vâta*, & see WEATHER[1]]

wind[2], v.t. Sound (horn, bugle, blast, call) by blowing (wī-; *winded* or by confusion w. foll. *wound*); detect presence of by scent (wĭ-; *winded*; *hounds, deer, w. the fox, stalkers*; *winded his tobacco half a mile off*); breathe, make breathe quick & deep by exercise, exhaust w. of, renew w. of by rest, (wĭ-; *winded*; *give horse a gallop to w. him*; *am quite winded by the climb*; *rested to w. the horses*). [f. prec.]

wind[3], v.i. & t. (*wound* pr. wow-), & n. Go in circular, spiral, curved, or crooked course, meander, (*path, river, winds*; *herd winds o'er the lea*; *creeper winds round pole*; *winding staircase*, spiral); make one's or its *way* &c. circuitously, insinuate one*self into*, (*brook winds its way*; *wound himself* or *his way into my affections*); coil (t. & i.), wrap closely (t. & i.), surround with coil, embrace, (*w. cotton on reel, wool into ball*, &c.; also with *off* adv. or prep. = unwind; *w.* person *round* one's *fingers*, exercise complete domination over; *wound the blanket round him, her* *arms round the child, the child in her arms*; *wind*ING[1]*-sheet*, in which corpse is wound; *w. pegtop*, coil string round it; *serpent winds itself* or *winds round victim*); hoist or draw by use of windlass &c. (*w. ship out of harbour, ore up from mine*); =*w. up* (clock &c.); *w. ship*, reverse positions of bow & stern; *w. up*, coil the whole of (*w. up piece of string*), tighten coiling or coiled spring or fig. tension or intensity or efficiency of (*w. up strings of fiddle*; *w. up clock* &c.; *is winding himself up for an effort* or *to do it*; *the administration needs winding up*, is slack; *person is wound up to fury*; *expectation was wound up to a high pitch*), bring to a conclusion, conclude t. & i., (*wound up his speech*, or *wound up, by declaring*; *shot his wife & child & wound up by stabbing himself*; *w. up company*, arrange its affairs & dissolve it; *company winds up*, ceases business, goes into liquidation, whence **wi·ndING[1]-up** n.); hence **wi·ndER**[1](1, 2) n., **wi·ndingLY**[2] adv. (N.) bend or turn in course; single turn in winding clock, string, &c.; *w.-up*, conclusion, finish. [OE *windan*, cf. Du. & G *winden*; cogn. w. WANDer, WEND[1]]

wi·ndage (-ĭj), n. Difference between projectile's & gun-bore's diameter allowing escape of gas; (allowance for) influence of wind in deflecting missile. [-AGE]

wi·ndlass, n., & v.t. Machine for hauling or hoisting on wheel-&-axle principle; (vb) hoist or haul with w. [prob. corrupt. of AF *windas* f. ON *vindáss* (*vinda* WIND[3], *áss* beam)]

wi·ndlestraw, n. Old stalk of kinds of grass. [OE *windelstrēaw* grass for plaiting (WIND[3], STRAW)]

wi·ndow (-ō), n. Opening in wall or roof of building, ship, carriage, &c., usu. filled with glass in fixed or sliding or hinged frames to admit light & sometimes air to room &c. (*look out of w.* or *the w.*; *have all* one's *goods in the w.*, be superficial; *blank, blind, false, w.*, mouldings or recess as for w. without aperture; BOW WINDOW; BAY[3], CASEMENT, DORMER, FRENCH, LATTICE, ORIEL, SASH[2], *w.*); *w.-box*, slide for weights in sash-w., also box on w.-sill in which flowers are grown; *w.-dressing*, art of arranging goods attractively in shop-w., often fig. of adroit presentation of statistics &c.; *w. envelope* (with transparent part allowing address inside to show). Hence **(-)windowED**[2] a., **wi·ndowLESS** a. [f. ON *vindauga* (WIND[1], EYE[1])]

Wi·ndsor (-nzer), n. Town in Berks. (*House of W.*, style of British Royal Family assumed 1917; *W. chair*, all of wood with curved support for back (& arms); *brown W. soap*, brown scented kind; *W. uniform*, blue coat with red collar & cuffs worn at Windsor by the royal family, & by others having royal grant.)

wi·ndy, a. Wind-swept (*w. hill-top, plain, situation*); in which wind is high (*w. night, weather, crossing*); wordy, verbose, empty, (*w. eloquence, logic, speaker*); generating or characterized by flatulence; (archaic) windward (*on the w. side of the law*, safely out of its reach); (slang) frightened. Hence **wi·ndiLY**[2] adv., **wi·ndiNESS** n. [-Y[2]]

wine, n. (Kinds of) fermented grape-juice (*is a sound w.*; DRY[1] or *sweet*, STILL[1] or *sparkling*, WHITE[1] or *red, w.*; *green w.*, in first year; *port w.*, port; COMET *w.*; *Adam's w.*, water; *good w. needs no* BUSH[1]; *new w. in old bottles*, new principle too powerful to be restrained by ancient forms; *take w. with*, pledge & be pledged by at table; SPIRIT *of w.*; TEAR[2]*s of strong w.*; *over the* WALNUTS *& the w.*; *w. whey*, beverage of w. & curdled milk; *in w.*, exhilarated or drunk with w.); (at universities) party for w.-drinking after dinner (*ww. have gone out of fashion*); fermented drink resembling w. made from specified fruit &c. (*cowslip, currant, gooseberry, orange, palm, w.*); (Med.) solution of drug in w. (*quinine w.*; *w. of opium*); *wi·nebag*, wineskin, or winebibber; *wi·nebibber*, tippler, drunkard; so *wi·nebibbing* a. & n.; *wi·nebottle*, glass bottle for w., also wineskin; *wi·nebowl*, lit., also drinking habits &c.; *w.-carriage*, wheeled utensil for circulating w.-bottle at table; *w.-cooler*, vessel in which w.-bottles are cooled with ice; *wi·necup*, as *winebowl*; *wi·nefat* archaic, winepress; *wi·neglass*, any glass for drinking w. from, esp. of size used for sherry, often as measure (also *wi·neglassful*) of medicine to be taken, =four tablespoons; *w.*-MARC; *w.-palm*, kind from which w. is made; *wi·nepress*, in which grapes are squeezed; *wi·neskin*, whole skin of goat &c. sewn up & used to hold w.; *w.-stone*, tartaric deposit in w.-casks; *w.-vault*, cellar in which w. is kept, also bar &c. where it is retailed. Hence **wi·neLESS, wi·nY**[2], aa. [OE *win* f. L *vinum*, cf. G *wein*, Du. *wijn*, Gk *oinos* wine, *oinē* vine]

wing, n., & v.t. & i. One of the limbs or organs by which the flight of a bird, bat, insect, angel, &c., is effected, part in non-flying bird or insect corresponding to w., supporting part of flying-machine, (*clip* one's *ww.*, limit his movements or ambitions or expenditure; *come on the ww. of the wind*, swiftly; *lend, add, ww. to*, accelerate; *take under* one's *w.*, treat as protégé; *his ww. are sprouting* &c., his virtues are too great for a being below the degree of an angel; *money takes to itself ww.*, disappears); (facet., esp. of wounding) arm; more or less separate projecting part of something, esp. of building or battle array (*the north w. was added in the 17th century*; *cavalry were massed on left w.*; *ww.* in theatre, sides of stage, pieces of side scenery); winged flight, wings, (*on the w.*, flying, travelling, in motion; *take w.*, start flying); *w.-beat*, one complete set of motions with w. in flying; *w.-case*, horny cover, a modified fore-w., protecting some insects' flying w.; *w.-commander*, officer of AIR[1]*-force*; *w.-covert*, one of small feathers covering insertion of bird's flying feathers; *w.-footed* poet., swift; *w.-sheath*, = *w.-case*; *w.-spread*, measurement across ww. when extended; *w.-stroke*, = *w.-beat*; hence **-wing**ED[2], **wi·ng**LESS, aa., **wi·ng**LET n. (Vb) equip with ww., enable to fly or mount, send in flight, lend speed to, (*w. arrow with eagle's feathers* or *at the mark*; *vengeance winged the shaft*; *winged words*, going like arrows to mark, significant; *ambition wings his spirit*; *fear winged his steps*; *winged horse*, Pegasus, poetry; *winged god*, Mercury; *winged Victory*, statue of goddess of victory with ww.); travel, traverse, on ww. (*bird wings its way*, *wings to its mate*, *wings the air*); wound (bird) in w., (person) in arm. [ON *vængr*, cf. Da. *vinge*]

wink, v.i. & t., & n. Close & open eyes, blink, close & open (eyes or eye), (of eye) close & open, (*like winking* slang, very quickly or vigorously); momentarily close one eye to awaken attention of or convey private intimation to person (usu. *at* person); (of light, star, &c.) twinkle, shine intermittently; *w. at*, shut one's eyes to, purposely avoid seeing, affect not to notice, connive at, (abuse, transgression, &c.). (N.) act of winking, esp. as signal &c. (*nod is as good as w. to blind horse*; *tip* one *the w.* slang, give him signal or intimation; *could not get a w. of sleep*; *did not sleep a w. all night*; *forty ww.*, nap). [OE *wincian* move sideways, cf. MDu. & G *winken* beckon; cogn. w. WINCE]

wi·nkle, n. Edible sea snail, periwinkle. [abbr. PERIWINKLE[2], cf. WIG[1]]

winnow (-ō), v.t. Fan (grain) free of chaff &c., fan (chaff &c.) *away* or *out* or *from*; sift, separate, clear of refuse or inferior specimens or falsehood, clear (refuse &c.) *out* or *away*, examine, sort, weed out; (poet.) fan (air with wings), flap (wings), stir (hair &c.). Hence **wi·nnow**ER[1](1, 2) n. [OE *windwian* (WIND[1])]

wi·nsome, a. (Of person or his appearance, manner, smile, &c.) charming, winning, attractive, engaging, bright. Hence **wi·nsome**LY[2] adv., **wi·nsome**NESS n. [OE *wynsum* (*wynn* joy, cogn. w. WIN, -SOME)]

wi·nter, n., & v.i. & t. Season between autumn & spring, three or four coldest months of year (in northern latitudes Nov. or Dec. to Jan. or Feb., or, Astron., from Dec. solstice to March equinox; *hard, mild, w.*, with, without, much frost), (attrib.) occurring, used, &c., in or lasting for the w. (*w. apple, cough, solstice*, &c.; *w. sleep*, hibernation; *w. quarters*, esp. to which troops retire for w.; *w. garden*, glass-covered space with plants &c. used as lounge); (Rhet., Poet.) year of life (*a man of 50 ww.*, 50 years old); *w.-green*, a genus of plants green through w.; *w.-lodge* bot., bud or bulb protecting plant's embryo through w.; *w.-tide* poet., w.; hence **wi·nter**LESS, **wi·nter**LY[2], aa. (Vb) spend the w. *at, in*, &c.; keep or feed (plants, cattle) during w. [OE, Du., & G; perh. cogn. w. WET, WATER]

wi·ntry, a. Having the temperature, storminess, or aspect appropriate to winter, cold, windy, cheerless, (*w.weather, day, sun, scene*); (of smile, greeting, &c.) lacking warmth or interest or vivacity. Hence **wi·ntri**NESS n. [-Y[2]]

wipe, v.t. & i., & n. Clean or dry surface of by rubbing with cloth, paper, hand, &c. (*w. table, dish, face, hands*, &c.; *w.* one's *eyes*, dry tears, cease weeping; *w.* one's *eye* slang, steal march on him, get advantage by anticipating him; *w. out bath* or other hollow utensil); get rid of, clear *away* or *off*, take *up*, wash *out*, by wiping (*w. away* or *w. your tears*; *w. up slops*; *w. out stain*, or fig. *disgrace, insult*, &c., esp. by vengeance); *w. out*, utterly destroy, annihilate, (*their very name, the whole army, was wiped out*); *w. the floor with* slang, inflict humiliating defeat or correction on (person); (slang) take or aim sweeping blow or stroke *at* (*wiped at me with his sword*). (N.) act of wiping (*give this plate a w.*); (slang) sweeping blow (*fetched* or *took a w. at him*; *fetched him a w.*); (slang) handkerchief. [OE *wipian*; cogn. w. WHIP]

wire, n., & v.t. & i. (Piece of) metal drawn out into form of thread or slender round or square or tapelike flexible rod (*platinum, silver, copper*, &c., *w.*; BARB[1]*ed*, LIVE[1], *w.*; *telegraph* &c. *ww.*; *private w.*, telegraph w. reserved for person's exclusive use; *was sent for, sent congratulations, by w.*, by telegraph; *pull the ww.*, control puppets by ww. or usu., fig., manage political party or movement by secret influence); telegraphic message (*sent me a w.*); *w.-cloth, w. gauze, netting*, fabrics woven or twisted of w.; *w.-cutter*, tool for cutting w.; *w.-dancer*, person performing on stretched w.; *wire·draw*, draw (metal) out into w., (fig.) refine or apply or press (argument, point, &c.) with idle or excessive subtlety (esp. in p.p.); *w.-edge*, false edge that turns back when blade is over-sharpened; *w. entanglement*, arrangement of barbed or other w. set up to prevent rapid attack of enemy; *w.-gun*, cannon made by coiling flat w. round tube; *w.-haired*, with stiff or wiry hair (esp. of dogs); *w.-heel*, disease of horse's foot; *wire·puller*, politician &c. who pulls the ww.; *w. rope*, made by twisting ww. together as strands; *w.-worm*, kinds of destructive larva; *w.-wove* of paper, = wove (WEAVE). (Vb) provide, fasten, &c., with wire(s); string (beads) on w.; snare (bird) with w.; telegraph (*w. me the result*; *wired to him*; *was wired for*); (slang) *w. in*, operate vigorously, put all one's force into some continuous effort. [OE *wir*, cf. ON *virr*, L *viēre* to plait; cogn. w. WITHE]

wire·less, a., n., & v.i. & t. Without wire(s), esp. in *w.* TELEGRAPHY; (n.) w. telegraphy or telegram; (vb) send w., send (message) or inform (person) by w. [-LESS]

wīr·y, a. Made of wire (poet.); tough & flexible as wire, (of persons) sinewy, untiring, whence **wir·ILY**[2] adv., **wir·INESS** n. [-Y[2]]

wis, v.i. pres. 1st sing. (pseudo-archaic). *I* know well (parenth.). [supposed pres. of *wist* (WIT[1]), obs. *ywis* certainly, cf. G *gewiss*, being read as *I wis*]

wi·sdom (-z-), n. Being wise, (possession of) experience & knowledge together with the power of applying them critically or practically, sagacity, prudence, common sense; wise sayings (*pour forth w.*; *W. of Solomon*, abbr. *Wisd.*, *W. of Jesus the Son of Sirach* or *Ecclesiasticus*, books of Apocrypha); *w.-tooth*, molar usu. cut after 20 years of age (*cut* one's *w.-teeth*, gain discretion). [OE *wisdóm* (WISE[1], -DOM)]

wise[1] (-z), a. (Of persons) having, (of action, course, speech, opinion, &c.) dictated by or in harmony with or showing, experience & knowledge judicially applied, sagacious, prudent, sensible, discreet; having knowledge (*w. after the event*, of person who has failed to foresee; *came away none the wiser* or *as w. as he went*, knowing no more than before; *where ignorance is bliss 'tis folly to be w.*); (archaic) having occult power or knowledge of mysterious things (*w. man*, wizard; *w. woman*, witch, fortune-teller, also midwife); suggestive of wisdom, oracular, (*with a w. shake of the head*; *w. saw*, proverbial saying). Hence **wi·seLY**[2] adv. [Aryan: OE *wis*, cf. Du. *wijs*, G *weis*; & see WIT[1]]

wise[2] (-z), n. Way, manner, guise, (*in solemn* &c. *w.* archaic; esp. *in some, no, any, w., on this w.*). [OE *wise* (*wisian* show way, orig. make wise, see prec.), cf. Du. *wijze*, G *weise*]

-wise, suf. = prec., forming advv. of manner as in *clockwise* with motion in direction of clock hands, *crosswise* with cross arrangement, *lengthwise* with length arranged in given direction, with regard to length, *nowise* in no way, not at all.

wī·seacre (-zāker), n. Sententious dullard. [corrupt of MDu. *wijsseggher*, itself corrupt. (as if =wise sayer) of MHG *wīzago* (= OE *witiga*) seer, cogn. w. WIT[1]]

wish, v.t. & i., & n. Have as a desire or aspiration (*that*-clause with *that* usu. omitted, or obj. & compl.; *w. I had never been born, were* or *was a bird, may live to see it*; *w. you would be quiet*; *it is to be wished that*, is desirable that; *I w. it may not prove*, fear it will; *could not w. it better*; *w. oneself dead, home, at home*, &c.; *w.* person *happy, away*; *w.* one *at the devil* or *further*, w. he were away); want with the kind of desire that tends to affect result (*to* do, person or thing *to* do, person or thing *-ed*, or rarely with simple obj. esp. pronoun; *I w. to go, you to do it, it finished* or *to be finished*; *what do you w.?*; *they say they w. peace, an interview*); be *well* or *ill* inclined to or *to* (*wishes me well, well to all men, wishes nobody ill*), whence **-wishER**[1] n.; say one hopes for (joy, luck, pleasant journey, sorrow, &c.) in person's favour or against him (ind. obj. or *to*; *I w. you joy, w. success to each & all*); *w.* person *joy of*, (iron.) hope he will enjoy; express desire *for* (*has nothing left to w. for*; *would not w. for anything better*); *wishing-bone*, merrythought (longer part of it when broken between two persons entitling holder to magic fulfilment of any w.); *wishing-cap*, magic cap securing to wearer fulfilment of any w. (N.): (expression of) desire or aspiration, request, implied command, (*w. is father to thought*, we believe thing because we w. it true; *if ww. were horses beggars might ride*; *has a great w. to go to sea*, whence **wi·shFUL** a. *to* do; *good ww.*, hopes felt or expressed for another's happiness &c.; *cannot grant your w.*; *he disregarded* or *disobeyed my ww.*); thing desired (*have got my w.*). [n. f. vb, OE *wȳscan*, cf. Du. *wenschen*, G *wünschen*; cogn. w. WINSOME, WEEN]

wi·sh-wash, n. Washy drink or talk. [redupl. of WASH[2]]

wi·shy-washy (-wŏ-), a. Thin, sloppy, (of soup, tea, talk, &c.). [redupl. of WASHY]

wisp, n. Small bundle or twist of straw &c. [f. 14th c., etym. dub.]

wist. See WIT[1].

Wistār·ia, n. Kinds of pale-purple-flowered leguminous tree. [C. *Wistar*, American anatomist, -IA[1]]

wi·stful, a. Affected with or betraying vague yearnings or unsatisfied desire to understand (of persons or usu. of eyes, look, voice, mood, &c.). Hence **wi·stfulLY**[2] adv., **wi·stfulNESS** n. [perh. assim. of obs. *wistly* adv. intently (cf. WHIST[1, 2]) to WISH*ful*, w. corresp. change of sense]

wit[1], v.t. & i. (archaic; pres. *I, he, wot, thou wottest*; past *wist*; inf. *wit*; part. *witting*; other parts not used). Know (*God wot*, knows; *I wot*, know well; *to w.*, that is to say, namely; *witting*, not unconscious or unintentional, whence **wi·ttingLY**[2] adv.). [Aryan: OE *witan*, cf. Du. *weten*, G *wissen*; cogn. w. L *vidēre* see, Gk *eidon* I saw, *oida* know, Skr. *veda* knowledge]

wit[2], n. (Sing. or pl.) intelligence, understanding, (*has not the w., the ww., w. enough, to see*; *remedy is past the w. of man to devise*; *out of* one's *ww.*, mad, distracted; *has his ww. about him*, is observant or of lively intelligence; *has quick, slow, &c., ww., a nimble w.*, whence **-witted**[2] a.; *at* one's *w.'s end*, utterly at a loss; *live by* one's *ww.*, by ingenious hand-to-mouth shifts; *the five ww.* archaic, the senses or the mind), whence **wi·tless** a., **wi·tlessly**[2] adv., **wi·tlessness** n.; (power of giving sudden intellectual pleasure by) unexpected combining or contrasting of previously unconnected ideas or expressions (*possessed of both w. &* HUMOUR; *pages sparkling with w.*), whence **wi·tty**[2] a., **wi·ttily**[2] adv., **wi·ttiness** n. [OE, = understanding (*witan* WIT[1])]

wit[3], n. Wise man (archaic); witty person (see prec.), person who talks wittily, whence **wi·tling**[1](2) n. [uses of prec.; 1st sense f. 15th, 2nd f. 17th, c.]

witch, n., & v.t. Woman or (now rarely) man practising sorcery (*white w.*, using powers for beneficent purposes only; *witches'* SABBATH), (fig.) fascinating or bewitching woman; ugly old woman, hag; *wi·tchcraft*, sorcery, use of magic; *w.-doctor*, = MEDICINE[1]*-man*; *w.-meal*, pollen of CLUB[1]*-moss*. (Vb) bewitch (*the witching time of night, Macb.* II. i. 51, time when ww. are active, midnight), esp. fig., fascinate, charm, whence **wi·tchery**(4, 5) n., **wi·tching**[2] a., **wi·tchingly**[2] adv. [OE *wicca* masc., *wicce* fem. (*wiccian* practise sorcery, etym. dub.); the mod. vb prob. aphetic f. *bewitch*]

witch-. See WYCH-.

wi·tenagĕmō·t (-g-), n. (hist.). Anglo-Saxon national council or parliament. [OE *witena* gen. pl. of *wita* wise man, *gemót* meeting]

with (-dh, -th), prep. In antagonism to, against, (*fight, quarrel, struggle, dispute, argue, compete, vie, w.*); in or into company of or relation to, among, beside, (*come, go, walk, eat, live, spend the day, mix* t. & i., *meet, w.*; *king is expected w.* or *together w. queen & court*; *numbered w. the transgressors*; *compare w.*; *have nothing to do w.*; *deal w.*; *w. God*, dead & in heaven; *have w. you* archaic, I accept your offer or challenge; so *done w. you*); agreeably or in harmonious relations to (*I feel, think, sympathize, w. you*; also with neg. wds in opp. sense, as *I disagree w. you*; *he that is not w. me is against me*; *vote with the Liberals*; *blue does not go with green*; *one w.*, part of same whole as); having, carrying, possessed of, characterized by, (*vase w. handles, man w. sinister expression*; *walking w. a gun*; *went out w. no hat on*; *w. child* or *young*, pregnant); in the care or charge or possession of (*have no money w. me*; *leave child, parcel, w. nurse, porter*; *it rests w. you to decide*; *the deal, decanter, next move, is w. you*); by use of as instrument or means (*cut it w. a knife*; *have no pen to write w.*; *walks w. a crutch*; *damn w. faint praise*); by addition or supply or acquisition or possession of as material (*fill it, overflowing, w. water*; *laden w. baggage*; *blessed w. beauty*; *adorn w. frescoes*); in same way or direction or degree or at the same time as (*changes w. the seasons*; *varies directly* or *inversely, increases, w.*; *rise w. the sun*; *w. that*, thereupon, simultaneously; *begin w.*, take as starting-point); because or by operation of, owing to, (*trembles w. fear*; *is down w. fever*; *stiff, silent, w. cold, shame*); displaying or so as to display, under favourable or unfavourable circumstances of, (*heard it with calmness*; *fought w. courage*; *won w. ease, difficulty, a good deal to spare*; *shot well w. a good, wretched, light*); in regard to, concerning, in the sphere of, in the mind or view of, (*be patient w. him*; *bear, do,* or *put up, w.*, tolerate, be indulgent to; *my dealings w. the natives*; *what do you want w. me?*; *away, down, up, to the devil, &c., w. him*, take or send or put him, he may go, away &c.; *can do anything, nothing, w. him*, influence or utilize him in any, no, direction; *w. God all things are possible*; *is it well w. thee?*; *it is holiday time w. us*; *the first object w. him is*; *has great influence w. the House*); so as to be separated from (*part, break, dispense, w.*); despite, notwithstanding, the presence of (*w. all his learning, he is the simplest of men*; *w. many admirable qualities, the best of intentions, he failed completely*). [OE, shortened f. *wither* against, cf. G *wider* against, ON *vidh*, Da. *ved*, Sw. *vid*; the senses of obs. *mid* with have passed to it]

witha·l (-awl), adv. & prep. (archaic). With it, in addition, moreover, as well, at the same time; (prep., always after its expressed or omitted obj.) with (*have nothing to, what shall he, fill his belly w.*). [prec., ALL]

withdraw·, v.t. & i. Pull aside or back (*w. curtain*, one's *hand*); take away, remove, (boy from school, coins from circulation, horse from race, troops from position, favour &c. from person); retract (offer, statement, promise; *cries of 'w.'*, demands that speaker shall unsay something as unparliamentary &c.); retire from presence or place, go aside or apart; *withdrawing-room* archaic, DRAWING-ROOM. Hence **withdraw·al**(2) n. [*with* in obs. sense *towards* (oneself, & so away from others), DRAW[1]]

wi·the (-dhĭ, *or* widh), **wi·thy** (-dhĭ), n. (pl. *-thes* pr. -dhĭz, or *-ths*). Tough flexible branch esp. of willow or osier used for binding bundles &c. [OE *withthe, withig,* cf. MDu. *wisse*, G *weide*, willow; cogn. w. Gk *itea* willow, L *vimen* twig, *vitis* vine]

wi·ther (-dh-), v.t. & i. Make or become dry & shrivelled (often *up*), deprive of or lose vigour or vitality or freshness or importance (often *away*), decline, languish, decay, (*has a withered arm*; *flowers & beauty w.*; *age cannot w. her*; *the individual withers*, ceases to be important); blight with scorn &c. (*w. one with a look* usu. joc.), whence **wi·ther**ING[2] a., **wi·ther·ing**LY[2] adv. [ME *widren* expose to WEATHER[1]]

wi·thers (-dh-), n. pl. Ridge between horse's shoulder-blades (*my w. are unwrung*, imputation &c. does not touch me). [named as the part that resists or takes strain of collar f. OE *wither* against, see WITH]

withhō·ld, v.t. (-held). Refrain from putting in action, refuse to grant, (*w.* one's *hand* archaic for *hold*, not take action; *w.* one's *consent, support, the light of* one's *countenance*, &c.). [WITH as in WITHDRAW, HOLD]

withi·n, adv., n., & prep. Inside, to or at or on the inside, indoors, internally, (chiefly archaic; *clean w. & without*; *go w.*, into house or room; *stay w.*, not go out of doors; *is Mr Jones w.?*, at home; *beauty without & foulness w.*; *make me pure w.*, in spirit; *Bishopsgate w.*, inside the walls). (N.) the inside (*as seen from w.*). (Prep.) to or on or in the inside of, enclosed by, (*w. doors*, in or into house; *safe w. the walls*; WHEEL[1]*s w. wheels*); not beyond, not too far for, not transgressing, so as not to pass or exceed, subject to, (*live, keep, w.* one's *income*; *w. the meaning of the Act* &c., covered by it; *immorality w. the law*, not illegal; *keep it w. bounds*; *a task well w. his powers*; *running w. himself*, without putting forth whole power; *is true w. limits*); not too far for, near enough to affect or be affected by, not farther off than (*of* with sense *from*, or abs.), (*is w. reach, sight, call*, near enough to reach or be reached &c.; often *of*, as *w. sight of port*; *is w. three miles of a station*; *was w. an ace of destruction*); in a time no longer than, before expiration or since beginning of, (*of* with sense *from*, or abs.; *shall have it w. an hour*; *w. a year of his death, w. a year, all was changed*; *have seen him w. these three days*). [OE *withinnan* on the inside (WITH, *innan* adv. in)]

withou·t, adv., n., prep., & conj. Outside, to or at or on the outside, out-of-doors, externally, (chiefly archaic; *white within & w.*; *stands disconsolate w.*, outside the house &c.; *listening to the wind w.*). (N.) the outside, external sources, (*as seen from w.*; *the suggestion came from w.*). (Prep.) outside of (*met us w. the gates*; *negotiations within & w. the House*; *is w. the pale of civilization*; *things w. us*, all that is not ourselves); not having, not with, with no, devoid of, lacking, in want of, free from, with freedom from, not feeling or showing, in or with absence of, less, (*came w. a hat*; *a rose w. a thorn*; *an w. friends* or *money*; *did it w. difficulty* or *being discovered*; *act w. hesitation*; *cannot live w. her, go away w. thanking you*; *is absolutely w. fear, anxiety*; *cannot make* OMELETTE *w. breaking eggs*; *w. health happiness is impossible*; *do, go, w.*, dispense with, also ellipt. dispense with something implied; COLD *w.*; *w. doubt*, admittedly, certainly; *w.* FAIL[1], PREJUDICE, RESERVE[2]; *w. end*, infinite, eternal; *goes w. saying*, is too well known or obvious to need mention). (Conj.; archaic or vulg.) unless. [OE *withūtan* (WITH, *ūtan* adv. out)]

withsta·nd, v.t. & i. (-stood). Resist, oppose, (person, force, hardship, wear, &c.); make opposition (poet.). [OE *withstandan* (WITH, STAND)]

withy. See WITHE.

wi·tness, n., & v.t. & i. Testimony, evidence, (*bear w. to* or *of*, state one's belief in, state facts tending to establish), thing stated by way of evidence (*my w. is not true*; archaic), confirmation (*stands there in w. of the event*; *call to w.*, appeal to for confirmation); thing or person whose existence, position, state, &c., serves as testimony *to* or proof *of* (*is a living w. to my clemency*); (also EYE-*w.*) spectator *of* incident, bystander, person present at event; person giving sworn testimony in lawcourt or for legal purpose (*w.* often used for *the w.*); person attesting genuineness of signature to document by adding his signature; *w.-box*, enclosure in lawcourt reserved for ww. (Vb) state in evidence (noun, *that*, &c.; archaic); give evidence (*against, for*), serve as evidence (usu. *against, for, to*; *w.* or *as w. my poverty*, of which let my poverty be the proof); be a or the w. (archaic; *w. Heaven!*, I call Heaven to w.); indicate, serve as evidence of, (*a deathly pallor witnessed his agitation*); see, be spectator of; sign (document) as w. [OE *witnes* (WIT[2], -NESS)]

wi·tticism, n. Witty remark, jest, (usu. in disparaging sense). [coined by Dryden f. WIT[1]*ty*, after *criticism*]

wittingly. See WIT[1].

wi·ttol, n. (archaic). Man who winks at wife's infidelity, acquiescent cuckold. [ME *wetewold*, prob. formed by substitution of WIT[1] for first syllable of *cokewold* CUCKOLD]

wive, v.t. & i. (now rare). Provide with, take, wife. [OE *wifian* (WIFE)]

wī·vern, wyf-, n. (herald.). Winged two-legged dragon with barbed tail. [f. OF *wyvre, wivre*, f. L VIPERA; for -n, cf. BITTERN]

wives. See WIFE.

wi·zard, n. Magician, sorcerer, male witch; person who effects seeming impossibilities; conjurer; *the W. of the North,* Sir Walter Scott; *the Welsh W.*, Mr Lloyd George. Hence **wi·zard**RY(4, 5) n. [ME *wisard* (WISE[1], -ARD)]

wi·zened, wi·zen, wea·zen, a. Of shrivelled or dried-up appearance (chiefly of person or his face or look). [f. OE *wisnian* become dry, cf. ON *visna* wither (*visinn* withered)]

wizier. See VIZIR.

wo, who·a, int. Stop (chiefly to horses); GEE-*wo*; *wo-back,* int. used in backing horses.

woad, n., & v.t. (Plant yielding) kind of blue dye; (vb) dye with w. [OE *wád,* cf. Du. *weede,* G *waid*]

wo·bble, wa·bble (wŏ-), v.i., & n. (Of top or revolving body) revolve with changing inclinations, rock; (of person, missile, &c.) go unsteadily, vibrate from side to side, swerve, stagger; (fig.) vacillate, waver, act inconsistently, be inconstant, whence **wo·bbl**ER[1] n.; (of voice or sound) quaver, pulsate; (n.) rocking movement, change of direction or policy, swerve, piece of vacillation. [*wa-*, now rare, is the earlier form; cf. MHG *wabelen* move restlessly, ON *vafla* waver, cogn. w. WAVE[1]]

woe, n. (chiefly poet. or facet.). Affliction, bitter grief, distress, (*weal & w.*, prosperity & adversity; *w. is me,* alas; *w. be to,* a curse upon; *w.* WORTH[2] *the day*), (pl.) calamities, troubles; *woe·begone* (-awn, -ŏn), dismal-looking [p.p. of OE *begán* (BY, GO) surround]. Hence **woe·**FUL a., **woe·ful**LY[2] adv., (often facet., as *woeful ignorance, woefully disappointed*). [Aryan: OE *wá* int., orig. cry of pain, cf. Du. *wee,* G *weh,* intt. & nn., L *vae* int.]

wōld, n. Piece of open uncultivated country, down or moor land. [com.-Teut: OE *weald, wald,* forest, cf. G *wald,* Du. *woud*; cf. WEALD]

wolf (wŏŏ-), n. (pl. *-ves*), & v.t. Erect-eared straight-tailed harsh-furred tawny-grey wild gregarious carnivorous quadruped allied to dog preying on sheep &c. or combining in packs to hunt larger animals (*cry w. too often,* raise false alarms till genuine ones are disregarded; *have, hold, w. by the ears,* be in situation where one can neither retreat, advance, nor stop; *keep w. from door,* avert starvation; *w. in sheep's clothing,* hypocrite); rapacious or greedy person, whence **wo·lf**ISH[1] a., **wo·lfish**LY[2] adv., **wo·lfish**NESS n.; (Mus.) discord in certain chords of keyboard instrument due to system of tuning or temperament; *w.-cub,* young w., junior boy scout; *w.-dog,* kinds of dog kept to guard sheep from ww., also dog-&-w. hybrid; *w.-fish,* large voracious kind; *w.-hound,* Russian breed of dog, (also) Alsatian breed popular in U.K.; *w.'s-bane,* monk's-hood, aconite; *w.'s-claws, -foot,* club-moss; *w.'s-fist,* puff-ball [OE *fist* fart]; *wo·lfskin,* (mat, cloak, &c., made of) w.'s skin; *w.'s-milk,* kind of spurge; *w. spider,* tarantula, also kinds that chase instead of netting prey; *w.-tooth,* supernumerary pre-molar in horse. (Vb) devour or swallow greedily (often *down*). [Aryan; OE *wulf,* cf. Du. & G *wolf,* Gk *lukos,* L *lupus,* Skr. *vṛkas*]

wo·lfram (wŏŏ-), n. Ore yielding tungsten, native tungstate of iron & manganese; (now rare) tungsten. [G, perh. f. WOLF + *ra(h)m* cream, or MHG *râm* dirt, soot]

wo·lverene, -ine (-ēn), n. American carnivorous mammal called also GLUTTON & *carcajou.* [irreg. dim. of WOLF, perh. after MHG *wölfelin*]

wolves. See WOLF.

wo·man (wŏŏ-), n. (pl. *wo·men* pr. wĭ-), & v.t. Adult human female (*every w. is to him a lady*; *w.'s* or *women's rights,* position of legal equality with men demanded for women; *there's a w. in it,* way of accounting for man's inexplicable conduct; *w. with a past,* with some scandal attaching to her past life; *w. of the world,* experienced in society, not raw & innocent; *play the w.*, weep or show fear; *make an honest w. of,* marry after seducing; *tied to w.'s apron-strings,* controlled like child by her; *single w.*, spinster; *the* SCARLET *w.*; WISE[1] *w.*); (without article) the average or typical w., the female sex, any w., (*how does w. differ from man?*; *man born of w.*, mortal man; *is an excellent thing in w.*; *w.'s wit,* instinctive insight or resource; *w.'s* REASON[1]; *O W.*, in apostrophes); queen's or great lady's female attendant, lady in waiting, (archaic; *sent one of her ww. to ask*); man with feminine characteristics (*is a w. in tenderness*; *the old ww. in the cabinet*; *all the old ww. of both sexes*); *the* feminine emotions (*all the w. in her rose in rebellion*; *stirred the w. in him*; *has much of the w. in his composition*); (attrib.) female (*w. doctor, friend, counsellor, councillor*; *w. suffrage,* extension or possession of political suffrage to or by ww.); (as suf.; chiefly in terms correl. to compounds in *-man*) w. concerned or dealing or skilful with (*countryw., shopw., horsew., churchw., chairw., ferryw., applew., needlew.*, &c.; also by close comb. with adj., as *gentlew.*); *w.-hater,* misogynist; *womankind,* ww. (one's *w.-k.* or *ww.-k.*, the ww. of one's family); *wo·menfolk,* ww., one's womankind; hence **wo·man**HOOD n. (= female maturity, womanly instincts, w.-kind), **wo·man**LESS, **wo·man**LIKE, aa. (Vb) make behave like a w., cause to weep &c.; address as 'w.', 'my good w.', &c., speak of as 'w.' (not 'lady'). [OE *wifman* (WIFE, MAN) i.e. woman person]

wo·manish, a. (Of man or his feelings, conduct, looks, &c.) like women or their ways &c. (usu. contempt.), effeminate. Hence **wo·manishly**[2] adv., **wo·manishness** n. [-ISH[1]]

wo·manize, v.t. & i. Make womanish; (of men) be licentious, frequent prostitutes. [-IZE]

wo·manly, a. (Of woman or her feelings, conduct, &c.) having or showing the qualities befitting a woman, not masculine or girlish, (*a truly w. woman*; *w. modesty, compassion, tact,* &c.). Hence **wo·manliness** n. [-LY[1]]

wo·mb (wōōm), n. Organ in woman & other female mammals in which child or young is conceived & nourished till birth, uterus, (*falling of the w.*, PROLAPSUS; *fruit of the w.*, children; also fig., as *in the w. of time,* of future events &c.). [com.-Teut: OE *wamb*, womb, belly, cf. Du. *wam*, G *wamme*]

wŏ·mbat, n. Australian marsupial mammal about size of badger. [f. native *womback, -at*]

women. See WOMAN.

won. See WIN.

wo·nder[1] (wŭ-), n. Miracle, prodigy, strange or remarkable thing or specimen or performance or event, (*signs & ww.*, miracles; *work ww.*, do miracles, succeed remarkably; whence **wo·nder-worker**[1] n.; *the child is a w.*, marvellously precocious &c.; *did ww.*, had remarkable success; *seven ww. of the world,* sights, of which one was the pyramids, so called in antiquity; *a nine-days' w.*, event of passing interest; *for a w.*, esp. by way of welcome exception, as *you are punctual for a w.*; *what w., it is no w., no w., that,* naturally, inevitably, of course, one cannot be surprised or might have guessed that, *that* usu. omitted; so *he refused, & no w.*; *is a w. of delicate workmanship*); emotion excited by what surpasses expectation or experience or seems inexplicable, surprise mingled with admiration or curiosity or bewilderment, (*were filled with w.*; *looked at him in silent* or *openmouthed w.*); *w.-land,* fairyland, a country of surprising fertility &c.; *w.-struck, -stricken,* filled or dumb with w. [OE *wundor* portent, cf. Du. *wonder*, G *wunder*, etym. dub.]

wo·nder[2], v.i. & t. Be filled with w., feel surprise, (usu. *at*, rarely *to* see &c., or abs. *shall never cease to w. at it*; *can you w. at it?*; *I w. at you* to child &c., am shocked by your conduct; *wondered to hear your voice*; *the kind of person that never wonders*), whence **wo·nderingly**[2] adv., **wo·nderment** n.; be surprised to find *that* (*that* usu. omitted: *I w. he didn't kill you*); be curious, desire, to know (*w. why pain exists, who invented gas-lamps, what the time is, how to proceed,* &c.). [OE *wundrian* (prec.)]

wo·nderful, a. Marvellous, surprising, exceeding what was expected, remarkable, admirable. Hence **wo·nderfully**[2] adv. [-FUL]

wo·ndrous, a. & adv. (poet., rhet.). Wonderful; hence **wo·ndrously**[2] adv., **wo·ndrousness** n. (Adv., qualifying adjj. only) wonderfully (*w. kind* &c.). [corrupt. on -OUS of obs. *wonders* (genit. of *wonder* n. used as adj. & adv.) wondrous(ly)]

wont[1] (wō-, wŭ-), pred. a. Accustomed *to* do (usu. after *is, was, are,* &c.; *as he was w. to say*). [OE *gewunod* p.p. of *gewunian* (*wunian* dwell, cf. G *wohnen*), ME *woned* p.p. of *wonen*]

wont[2] (wō-, wŭ-), v. aux. (poet.; pres. ind., *wont, wontest, wonts* or *wont*, pl. *wont*; past ind., *wont, wontest, wont,* pl. *wont*, or *wonted* for *wont*). Be accustomed (usu. *to* do). [prop. past, = *woned*, of ME *wonen* see prec.]

wont[3] (wō-, wŭ-), n. What is customary in general or habitual to a person (*use & w.*, established custom; *according to his w.*; *it is my w. to*). [perh. a use of the p.p., see WONT[1]]

won't. See WILL[1].

wo·nted (wō-, wŭ-), attrib. a. Habitual to person, (rarely) usual, (*heard me with his w. courtesy*; *met with the w. obstacles*). [f. *wont=woned* p.p. see WONT[1] w. erron. addition of -ED[1]]

woo, v.t. Ask in marriage, pay amorous court to, ask the love of, whence **woo·er**[1] n.; pursue, seek to win, (fame, fortune, &c.); (abs.) go courting, conduct oneself as wooer; coax, importune, try to persuade, (person usu. *to* do or *to* compliance &c.). Hence **woo·ingly**[2] adv. [ME *wowen*, cf. OE *dwógian*, etym. dub.]

woo·but, ou·bit (ōō-), n. =WOOLLY-*bear*. [ME *wolbode* (WOOL, perh. + OE *budda* beetle)]

wōōd, n. Growing trees occupying considerable tract of ground, forest, (also pl. in same sense, as *came upon a clearing in the ww.*; *cannot see w. for trees,* details impede general view; *don't halloo till you are out of the w.*, assume too soon that difficulties are over), whence **(-)wooded**[2] a.; fibrous substance between pith & bark of tree, whether growing or cut for timber or fuel; *the* cask or unbottled storage of wine &c. (*in, from, the w.*); (Mus.; also *w.-wind*) *the* wooden wind-instruments of a band &c.; *w.-agate,* showing grain of w.; *w. anemone,* the wild flowering ANEMONE; *woo·dbine* or *-bind,* wild honeysuckle, (also) cheap cigarette much used in the great war; *w.-block,* die usu. of boxwood from which woodcuts are taken; *woo·dcock,* kinds of game bird related to snipe; *w.-craft,* knowledge of forest conditions esp. as applied in hunting &c.; *woo·dcut,* (print, usu. as illustration in book or newspaper, taken from) engraving made on w.; *w.-cutter,* man who cuts w., engraver of woodcuts; *w.-engraver,* maker of woodcuts, kinds of boring insect; *w.-fibre*, fibre got from w. esp. as material for paper; *w.-gas*, carburetted hydrogen got from w.; *w. ibis*, kind of N.-Amer. stork; *woo'dland*, wooded country, woods, (often attrib., as *w.-l. scenery*; *the w.-l. choir*, birds); *w. leopard*, kind of moth; *w.-louse*, kinds of small wingless many-legged insect; *woo'dman*, forester, w.-cutter; *w.-notes*, spontaneous poetry; *w.-nymph*, dryad, kinds of humming-bird & moth; *w.-opal*, silicified w.; *w. paper*, made of w.-pulp; *w. pavement*, wooden blocks used as paving of road; *woo'dpecker*, kinds of bird that cling to tree-stems & tap them to discover insects; *w.-pie*, great spotted woodpecker; *w.-pigeon*, ringdove; *w.-pulp*, w.-fibre reduced to pulp as material for paper; *woo'druff*, kinds of plant, *sweet w.-r.* grown esp. for fragrance of leaves when dried or crushed; *woo'dsman*, dweller in or frequenter of ww.; *w. sorrel*, kinds of acid-juiced plant; *w. spirit*, crude methyl alcohol got from w.; *w.-tar*, got from w.; *w.-warbler*, kinds of bird; *w.-wasp*, kinds that hang nest in tree or burrow in rotten w.; *w.-wool*, fine pine shavings used as surgical dressing or for packing; *woo'dwork*, things made of w., esp. the wooden part of a house &c. Hence **woo'dless** a. [OE *wudu*, cf. ON *vithr*, OHG *witu*, also Gael. *fiodh*, W *gwŷdd*]

Woo'dbury-type, n. (Picture produced by) process transferring photograph from gelatine to soft metal. [inventor]

woo'dchuck, n. Kind of N.-Amer. marmot. [corrupt. of Amer.-Ind. *wejack*]

woo'den, a. Made of wood (*w. head*, stupidity, whence **wooden-headed**[2] a., **wooden-hea'dedness** n.; *w. horse*, by use of which Troy was taken; *w.* SPOON; *w. walls*, warships); stiff, clumsy, without animation, inexpressive, (*w. motions, manners, stare, face*, &c.), whence **woo'denly**[2] adv., **woo'denness** n. [-EN[5]]

woo'dy, a. (Of region) abounding in woods, well-wooded; of the nature, consisting, of wood (*the w. parts of a plant*; *w. stem, tissue*); (rare) found in woods (*w.* NIGHTSHADE). Hence **woo'diness** n. [-Y[2]]

woof, n. = WEFT. [ME *oof* f. OE *ōwef* (A-1, *wef* = WEB) = that which is woven on (to the warp); cf. ABB]

wool, n. Kind of hair distinguished by fineness & wavy structure & scaly surface forming fleece of sheep, goat, alpaca, &c., & occurring mixed with ordinary hair in coat of some other animals (*carding* or *short*, *combing* or *long*, *w.*, less, more, than 4 in. long & prepared by different processes for spinning; *dyed in the w.*, before spinning or weaving; *much cry & little w.*, disappointing result, fiasco; *go for w. & come home shorn*, have tables turned on one), whence **-wooled**[2] a.; woollen yarn, worsted, (*spent an hour matching ww.*; *Berlin w.*, fine dyed w. for knitting &c.); woollen garments or cloth (*safest to wear w.*); soft short under-fur or down; Negro's hair, (facet.) any person's hair (*lose one's w.* slang, show anger); kinds of w.-like substance (COTTON[1] *w.*; *mineral w.*, made from molten slag subjected to strong blast & used for packing walls &c.); *w.-ball*, esp. lump of concreted w. sometimes formed in stomach of sheep &c.; *w.-carding*, *-combing*, processes by which short, long, w. is prepared for spinning; *w.-dyed*, dyed in the w., see above; *w.-fat*, *-oil*, lanolin; *w.-fell*, skin of sheep &c. with fleece still on; *w.-gathering*, absent-minded(ness), inattentive (mood); *w.-hall*, w.-merchants' exchange or market; *w.-pack*, (formerly) 240-lb. bale of w., also fleecy cloud; *woo'lsack*, w.-stuffed cushion on which Lord Chancellor sits in House of Lords (*reach* &c. *the w.-s.*, become Lord Chancellor; *take seat on the w.-s.*, open proceedings in House of Lords); *w.-work*, embroidery with Berlin ww. imitating tapestry. [Aryan: OE *wull*, cf. Du. *wol*, G *wolle*; cogn. w. Skr. *ūrṇā*, Gk *lēnos*, L *lana* & *vellus* fleece]

woo'llen, a. & n. Made of wool. (N.) w. fabric, as blanket, flannel, cloth; *w.-draper*, retailer of ww.; hence **woollenette**(2) n. [-EN[5]]

woo'lly, a. & n. Bearing or naturally covered with wool or wool-like hair (*the w. flock*; *w. bear*, kinds of hairy caterpillar; *a w. puppy, head*); resembling or suggesting wool (*w. hair, clouds*; *w. voice*, husky), (Paint.) lacking in definition or luminosity or incisiveness (w. *texture, style*, &c.); (Bot.) downy, pubescent; (n.) woollen garment, esp. sweater. Hence **woo'lliness** n. [-Y[2]]

Woo'lwich (-lij), n. (Used for) W. Arsenal with magazines for naval & military stores; (used for) the Royal Military Academy, W., for cadets of Royal Engineers & Artillery; *W. infant* (name given to a 19th-c. pattern of exceptionally heavy gun). [*W.* in Kent]

woora'li, woorar'a. = CURARE.

wootz, n. Special kind of steel made in India & imported into Europe & America for edge-tools. [perh. misprint for *wook* repr. Canarese *ukku* steel]

wop[1]. See WHOP.

Wop[2], n. (U.-S. slang). Mid-European (e.g. Hungarian, Thracian) in U.S. (cf. DAGO, SQUARE*head*). [?]

word[1] (werd), n. Any sound or combination of sounds (or its written or printed symbol) recognized as a PART[1] of speech, conveying an idea or alternative ideas, & capable of serving as a member of, the whole of, or a substitute for, a sentence (*coin, play upon, torture, ww.*; *is not the w. for it*, not an adequate description; *have no ww. to express my gratitude* &c.;

takes ww. for things; ww. are the wise man's counters & the fool's money; in a or *one w.*, briefly, to sum up; *translate* or *repeat w. for w.*, literally or verbatim); speech (*honest in w. & deed; bold in w. only; by w. of mouth*, orally); thing said, saying, remark, conversation, (usu. in pl.; *take* one *at* his *w.*, act on assumption that he means what he says; *fair* or *good ww.*, complimentary, conciliatory, flattering, &c.; *high, hard, warm, hot, sharp*, &c., *ww.*, angry talk; *big ww.*, boasting, bluff; *burning ww.*, enthusiastic, inspiring, excited, &c.; *wild & whirling ww.*, not well weighed; *hard ww. break no bones, fine ww. butter no parsnips, ww. are but wind*, depreciations of talk as compared with action; so *ww. or things, ww. & deeds*; HOUSEHOLD *w.*; *have ww. with*, quarrel with; *they had ww.*, quarrelled; *have a w. with*, converse briefly with; so *a w. with you* as demand for interview; *suit the action to the w.*, do at once what one has threatened &c.; *on* or *with the w.*, as soon as something has been said; *a w. & a blow*, impetuous person's procedure; *proceed from ww. to blows*; *waste ww.*, talk vainly; *a w. in, out of, season*, well, ill, timed advice or interference; *have the last w.*, not let opponent in altercation speak last; *the last w.* on a subject, pronouncement including latest views & likely to be definitive; *a truer w. was never spoken*; *have a w. to say*, something worth hearing; *man of few ww.*, taciturn; *hasn't a w. to throw at a dog*, is unsociably or superciliously taciturn; *say a good w. for*, commend, defend; *give* person one's *good w.*, recommend him for post &c.; *eat* one's *ww.*, retract, apologize under compulsion; *w. of command*, w. or phrase giving direction esp. to soldiers being drilled; *a w. to the wise*, transl. of VERBUM SAPIENTI; *God's W.*, the scriptures; so *the W. of God*, & see below); news, intelligence, a message, (*send w. of*; *send w.*; *w. came that* or *of*); one's promise, assurance, or responsible statement (*give* person, *give, pledge, pass*, one's *w.*, make promise or rarely statement; *keep, break*, one's *w.*; *I give you my w. for it*, promise it shall be or state that it is so; so ellipt. *my w. upon it*; *upon my w.*, on my honour, also as excl. at something that shocks; *w. of honour*, promise or statement made upon one's HONOUR[1]; *a man of his w.*, a promise-keeper; *be as good as* one's *w.*, fulfil or exceed what one has promised; *his w. is as good as his bond*, may be relied on); command, order, password, motto, (*his w. is law*; *give the w. to* do or *for*; *act promptly at the w.*; *must give the w. before you can pass*; *sharp 's the w.*, exhortation to hurry); *the W.* (*of God*), Christ as mediator or manifestation of God to man; *w.-blind, -deaf*, incapacitated by kinds of brain trouble from attaching meaning to ww. seen or heard; *w.-book*, vocabulary; *w.-painter, -ting*, graphic or picturesque writer, writing; *w.-perfect*, knowing part, piece, &c., by heart; *w.-picture*, piece of w.-painting; *w.-play*, verbal fencing, also play on ww., pun, &c.; *w.-splitter, -ting*, (maker of) oversubtle verbal distinctions; *w.-square*, set of words so chosen that when they are written under each other the letters read downward in columns give same words, e.g. *rat, ado, too*. Hence **wor·d**LESS a. [cf. Du. *woord*, G *wort*; cogn. w. L VERB*um*, Gk *eirō* speak]

word[2], v.t. Put into ww., phrase, select ww. to express. Hence **wor·d**ING[1] n. [f. prec.]

wor·dy, a. Verbose, given to or expressed in many words, diffuse; in, consisting of, words (*w. warfare*). Hence **wor·di**LY[2] adv., **wor·di**NESS n. [-Y[2]]

wore. See WEAR[1, 2].

work[1] (werk), n. Expenditure of energy, striving, application of effort to some purpose, (*set to w.*, begin or make begin operations; *has got to, is at, w. at last*; *all w. & no play*; *never does a stroke of w.*; *never liked, will do no, w.*), (Physics) exertion of force in overcoming resistance or producing molecular change (*convert heat into w.*; *unit of w.*, lifting of 1 lb. for 1 ft; *internal w.*, exerted on molecules of a body); task (to be) undertaken, materials (to be) used in task, (*the w. of converting the heathen*; *have* one's *w. cut out for* one, no light task, as much as one can do; *all in the day's w.*, normal; *bring your w. downstairs*, i.e. sewing-materials, lesson-books, &c.); thing done, achievement, thing made, book or piece of literary or musical composition, literary or other product *of*, specimen *of*, (Theol., usu. in pl.) meritorious act as opposed to faith or grace, (*mighty ww.*, miracles; *a good day's w.*, much accomplished; *the ww. of God*, nature; *honest man the noblest w. of God*; *the ww. of Cicero*, his writings; *a learned, historical, w.*, book; *a w. of art*, fine picture, building, poem, &c.; *is the w. of the devil*; *ww. of mercy*, charitable actions; *covenant of ww.*, O.-T. dispensation; *ww. of* SUPER*erogation*); doings or experiences of specified kind (*sharp, bloody, wild, w.*; *thirsty, dry, w.*; *make short w. of*, quickly accomplish or get rid of or overcome); employment, esp. the opportunity of earning money by labour, laborious occupation, (*is out of, is in regular, wants, is looking for, w.*; *many hands make light w.*; *do you want the w. or the wages?*; *rich men's luxury makes w. for the poor*); (usu. in pl., & in comb. or with adj.) piece of fortification, structure for defence, (*the ww. are impregnable*; *advanced, detached, defensive, ww.* or *w.*; *outworks, earthworks*); (pl.) operations in building &c. (*public ww.*, such operations done by or for the State; *Board of Ww. & Public*

Buildings; CLERK *of the ww.*); (pl.) acting or operative part of machine (usu. *of*; *the ww. of a watch* &c.; *something must be wrong with the ww.*); (pl., often with sing. constr., usu. in comb. with attrib. n.) manufactory (*the owner of an iron, a glass, -ww.*; *the ww. will be closed from 1st Oct.*); (articles having) ornamentation of kind specified by adj. or by usu. hyphened attrib. n., things or parts made of material or with tools &c. so specified, (*covered with elaborate w.*; *rustic, embossed, beaten, frosted*, &c., *w.*; *woodw., ironw., stonew.*; *fancy, needle, stucco, relief, poker, -w.*); (Naut.) UPPER *ww.*; *wor'kaday*, fit for or used or seen on workdays, ordinary, practical, (now chiefly in *this workaday world*); *w.-bag, -basket, -box*, holding materials & implements for w., esp. for sewing; *wor'kday*, day other than Sunday or festival; *wor'khouse*, public institution for reception of paupers in parish or union of parishes; *wor'kman*, operative, man hired to do manual labour, person *good, bad, skilled*, &c., at his job (*an ill workman quarrels with his tools*); *wor'kmanlike*, characteristic of a good workman; *wor'kmanship*, person's relative skill in doing task, relative finish or execution seen in manufactured article or w. of art, one's making (*we are God's* or *of God's workmanship*); *w.-people*, workmen or workwomen; *w.-room*, in which work is done; *wor'kshop*, room or building in which manufacture is carried on; *w.-table*, with drawers for sewing-materials &c.; *wor'kwoman*, female operative. Hence **wor'kless** a. [Aryan: OE *weorc*, cf. Du. & G *werk*, Gk *ergon*]

work², v.t. & i. (*worked*; also *wrought* pr. rawt archaic exc. as specified below). Engage or be engaged in bodily or mental w., carry on operations, make efforts, be a craftsman *in* some material, (*men must w.*; *w. away* or *on*, continue to w.; *w. double* TIDES; *w. to rule*, make efficiency impossible by keeping every rule in & out of season, as substitute for open strike; *is working at Greek, history, social reform*; *works, worked* or *wrought, in brass, leather, oils, distemper*; person is *hard to w. with*, impracticable; *is working for, against, the cause*); (of machine, plan, &c.) operate, act, do its appointed work, (of person) put or keep (machine &c.) in operation, keep (person, horse, machine, &c.) going or at w., exact toil from, (*charm, drug, pump, scheme, works* or *will not w.*; *w. ship, typewriter*; *works his men* &c. *too hard, to death*); (of wheel &c.) run, revolve, go through regular motions, (*strap, handle, wheel, works on a wheel, pivot, axle*; *w. freely, stiffly*, &c.); carry on, manage, control, (*w. mine, scheme*; *works the coach from London to Brighton*, has charge of it; *my partner works the Liverpool district*; *is worked by wires, electricity*, &c.); have influence or effect, exercise influence on, (often *wrought*; *now let it w.*, leave it to produce its effect; *w. upon* person or his *mind* &c.; *all these things have worked together for good*; *the appeal wrought powerfully upon him*; *w. the* ORACLE); bring about, effect, accomplish, produce as result, (often *wrought*; *w. wonders, cures, mischief, a change*; *w.* one's *will*, accomplish one's purpose often *upon* person or thing; *will w. it if I can* slang, bring it about); be in motion, be agitated, cause agitation, ferment lit. & fig., (*face, features, worked violently*; *waves w. to & fro*; *thoughts, conscience, working within him*; *yeast began to w.*; *to be wroth with one we love doth w. like madness in the brain*); make way or make (way &c.) or cause to make way slowly or with difficulty or by shifting motions (usu. with adv. or prep.), gradually become (loose, free, tight, &c.) by motion, (*stockings, shirt, w. down, up*; *needle worked out eventually from her arm*; *ferrule has worked off, loose*; *w. your knife through the card, your point in*; *grub works its way into* or *out of*; *wind has worked round*; *ship is working eastwards*; *some influences w. upwards, some downwards, in society*; *angler works up stream*); knead, hammer, fashion, into shape or desired consistence (*w. dough, clay*, &c.; *butter should be thoroughly worked*; *wrought iron*, forged or rolled, not cast); artificially & gradually excite *into* (*worked his audience, himself, into enthusiasm, a rage*); do, make by, needlework or the like (*reads to them while they w.*; *w. pattern, intials*, &c., on linen &c.; *is working a shawl*); solve (sum) by mathematical processes; purchase (one's *passage*) with labour instead of money; *w. in*, find place for (illustration, subject, &c.), admit of being introduced; *w. off*, get rid of, get over, find customers &c. for, (*works off his bad temper on his servants*; *has worked off his debauch*; *w. off 3000 copies*; *works off old jokes on us*); *w. out*, find (amount &c.) or solve (sum) by calculation, (of amount &c.) be calculated *at* (*works out at £6 10s.*), (of sum) give definite result (*will not w. out*), exhaust with w. (*person, mine*, &c., *is quite worked out*), accomplish or attain with difficulty (*w. out* one's *salvation*), provide for or plan all details of (*has worked out a scheme of invasion*); *w. up*, bring gradually to efficient state, elaborate in description (often *wrought*), advance gradually *to* (climax), excite (persons, expectations, &c.) by degrees (often *wrought*; *his wrought-up nerves*; *is in a highly wrought-up state*, nervous, hysterical), mingle (materials) into whole, acquire familiarity with (subject) by study. [OE *wircan, wyrcan, wercan*, past *worhte* (prec.)]

wor'kable, a. That can be worked, that

will work, that is worth working, practicable, feasible. Hence **workabi·lity**, **wo·rkableness**, nn., **wor·kably**[2] adv. [-ABLE]

wor·ker, n. In vbl senses; esp., (also *w. bee, ant,* &c.) undeveloped female of various social insects. [-ER[1]]

wor·king[1], n. In vbl senses; also or esp.: way thing works or result of its working (*the ww. of his face, conscience, fancy*); mine, quarry, &c., or part of it in which work is being or has been done (*was found in a disused w.*); *w. day,* = WORK[1]*-day,* also hours of the twenty-four devoted to work; *w. capital, expenses,* those required by or devoted to actual carrying on of business; *w. drawing, plan* (serving as guide for building or construction); *w.-out,* calculation of results, elaboration of details. [-ING[1]]

wor·king[2], a. In vbl senses; esp., engaged in manual labour (*w. man*; *the w. class*). [-ING[2]]

world (wer-), n. Time or state or scene of existence (*the* or *this w.*, mortal life; *the other* or *next w., the w. to come,* life after death; *the lower w.*, hell, Earth; *Prince of this w.*, the devil; *we bring nothing into the w.*, at birth; *bring child into the w.*, beget or bear it; *make the best of both ww.*, reconcile secular & spiritual interests; *the end of the w.*, cessation of all mortal life by destruction of universe or otherwise; *w. without end,* for ever); secular interests & occupations (*the w., the flesh, & the devil,* kinds of temptation; *forsake the w.*); the universe, all creation, everything, (*the creation of the w.*; *the best of all possible ww.*; *in the w.*, at all, that exists, &c., as *who, how, what, in the w. was it?*, *nothing in the w.*; *for all the w. like,* precisely like; *carry the w. before* one, have rapid & complete success); everything that exists outside oneself (*the external w.*, all phenomena; *the w. of dreams,* things as they seem in dreams; *would not do it for the, to gain the whole, w.*; *she is all the w. to me*; *would give the w. to know*); the earth, heavenly body supposed to resemble it, its countries & their inhabitants, all people, the earth as known or in some respect limited, (*go round the w.*; *to the w.'s end,* to furthest attainable distance; *a universe of ww.*; *are there other ww. than ours?*; *federation of the w.*, combination of all peoples in one State; *citizen of the w.*, cosmopolitan; *all the w.'s a stage*; *make a noise in the w.*, be widely talked of; *all the w. knows,* it is generally known; *makes the whole w. kin*; *the wise old w.*, general experience & custom; *w. politics, movement, tendency,* affecting or seen among many peoples; *the Old W.*, Europe, Asia, & Africa, part known by ancients to exist; *the New W.*, America; *the Roman* &c. *w.*, as much of the w. as concerned Rome &c.; *the Anglo-Saxon, English-speaking,* &c., *w.*); human affairs, their course & conditions, active life, (*so wags the w.*; *how goes the w. with you?*; *know, see, the w.*, have, acquire, experience; *man of the w.*, experienced practical tolerant person; *begin the w.*, start one's career; *all's right with the w.*, expression of optimism; *take the w. as it is, as* one *finds it,* be adaptable; *let the w. slide,* not try to influence events, also disregard convention & public opinion); average or respectable or fashionable society or people or their customs or opinions (*the great w.*, fashionable society; *all the w. & his wife,* all with pretensions to fashion; *what will the w. say?*, dare we defy opinion?; *live out of the w.*, avoid society); all that concerns or all who belong to specified department or class, sphere, domain, (*the literary, scientific, sporting, animal, ancient, w.*; *the w. of letters, art, sport*); a vast or infinite number or amount or extent (*a w. of meaning, banknotes, trouble, faults*; *a w. of waters,* expanse of sea; *a w. too wide* &c., by far); *to the w.* (slang), utterly (*tired, drunk,* &c., *t. t. w.*, perh. by misapplication of *dead t. t. w.*); *w. language,* that was or will be or is meant to be universal, also spoken in more than one part of w.; *w.-old,* (usu. by exag.) old as creation; *w.-power,* powerful state whose policy &c. may affect the w. at large; *w.-weary,* tired of existence; *w.-wide,* spread over the w., known or found everywhere. [com.-Teut.: OE *weoruld* (*wer* man, ELD; lit. sense 'age of man'), cf. Du. *wereld,* G *welt*]

wor·ldling, n. Worldly person. [-LING[1]]

wor·ldly, a. Temporal, earthly, (*w. goods,* property); exclusively or preponderantly concerned with or devoted to the affairs of this life, esp. to pursuit of wealth or pleasure (*w. wisdom,* esp. prudence in advancing one's own interests; *w. people, life,* &c.); *w.-minded,* intent on w. things, whence **worldly-mi·ndedness** n.; *w.-wise,* having w. wisdom. Hence **wor·ldliness** n. [-LY[1]]

worm[1] (werm), n. Kinds of invertebrate limbless or apparently limbless creeping animal, esp. such as are segmented in rings or are parasitic in the intestines or tissues (also in compd names of larvae, insects, lizards, &c., with some resemblance to ww., as *silk, glow, slow, -w.*; *dog, child, has ww.*, internal parasites; *food for ww.*, of person when dead; *a w. will turn,* the meekest will resist or retaliate if pushed too far; *the w. of conscience,* gnawing pain of remorse; so *where their w. dieth not*; *am a w. today,* out of sorts & spiritless, w. ref. to *Ps.* xxii. 6); insignificant or contemptible person; spiral part of screw, spiral cartridge-extractor, spiral pipe of still in which vapour is cooled & condensed; ligament under dog's tongue; *w.-cast,* tubular mass of earth voided by earth-w.; *w.-eaten*, gnawn by ww., full of w.-holes, (fig.) antiquated; *w.-fishing*, with w. for bait; *w.-gear*, arrangement of toothed wheel worked by revolving spiral; *w.-hole*, left in wood, fruit, &c., by passage of w.; *w.-holed*, w.-eaten (lit.); *w.-seed*, (Levantine plant bearing) seed used to expel intestinal ww.; *w.-wheel*, wheel of w.-gear. Hence **wor·my**[2] a., **wor·miness** n. [OE *wyrm*, cf. Du. *worm*, G *wurm*; cogn. w. L *vermis*, Gk *(h)romos*]

worm[2], v.t. & i. Insinuate one*self into* (*favour*, person's *confidence*, &c.); convey one*self*, progress, make one's *way*, with crawling motion (*wormed himself* or *his way* or *wormed through the bushes*); draw (secret &c.) by crafty persistence *out* (*of* person); cut w. of (dog); rid (garden-bed &c.) of ww. [f. prec.]

wor·mul (wor-), n. (dial.). = WARBLE[2]. [perh. assim. to *worm*]

wor·mwood (wer-), n. Kinds of perennial herb with bitter, tonic, & stimulating qualities used in preparation of vermouth & absinth & in medicine; bitter mortification or its cause. [OE *wermod*, cf. OHG *wer(i)muota*, etym. dub., w. assim. to *worm*, *wood*]

worn. See WEAR[1].

wo·rrit (wŭ-), v.t. & i., & n. = foll. (vulg.).

wo·rry (wŭ-), v.t. & i., & n. (Of dogs) bite (rat, sheep, dog) repeatedly, shake or pull about with the teeth (*w. problem* &c. *out*, assail it again & again till it is solved; *w. the sword* in fencing, try to fluster opponent by small movements in quick succession); tease, harass, importune, be continuously or intermittently troublesome to, allow no rest or peace of mind to (*w.* one*self*, take needless trouble; *is much worried*, full of uneasiness; *wears a worried look*, looks anxious or troubled); give way to anxiety, let the mind dwell on troubles, fret; *w. along*, manage to advance in spite of obstacles; hence **wo·rri·ment** n., **wo·rryingly**[2] adv. (N.) hound's worrying of quarry; (usu. in pl.) care(s), thing(s) worrying person; cares, worried state, over-anxiety; hence **wo·rriless** a. [OE *wyrgan*, cf. Du. *worgen*, G *würgen*, strangle]

worse (wers), a. & adv. comp., & n. More BAD OR BADLY; (as pred. a.) in or into less good health (*is w. today, is getting w.*), in less good condition or circumstances (*is none the w. for it*). (N.) w. thing(s) (*have w. to tell*; *but w. followed, remains*); *the w.*, defeat in contest (*have, put to, the w.*, be defeated, defeat), w. condition (*a change for t. w.*). Hence **wor·sen**[6] v.t. & i. [OE *wyrs* adv., *wyrsa* adj., cf. OSax. *wirs*, *wirsa*, Goth. *wairs*, *wairsiza*, the last retaining the compar. suf. & corresponding to E obs. or vulg. *worser*; perh. cogn. w. G *wirren* twist]

wor·ship (wer-), n., & v.t. & i. (Archaic) worthiness, merit, recognition given or due to these, honour & respect, (*men of w.*, worthies; *win, have, w.*, reach, enjoy, high repute; so still in *your, his, W.*, used to or of certain magistrates, or to show respect for person of higher station or ironical pretence of this), whence **wor·shipful** a., **wor·shipfully**[2] adv., **wor·shipfulness** n.; reverent homage or service paid to God (*public w., the hours of w., forms of w.*, &c., church services; *place of w.*, church), adoration or devotion comparable to this felt or shown towards person or principle (*an object of w.*; *regarding her with w. in his eyes*; *the w. of rank, wealth, intellect, athletics*). (Vb) adore as divine, pay religious homage to; idolize, regard with adoration, (*worships the ground she treads on*); attend public w. (*where does he w.?*), whence **wor·shipper**[1] n.; be full of adoration. [OE *weordhscipe* (WORTH[1], -SHIP)]

worst (wer-), a. & adv. sup., n., & v.t. Most BAD, BADLY. (N.) w. part, feature, state, possible assumption, event, possible issue, or action (*the w. of the storm is over*; *the w. of it is that —*; *saw him at his w.*; *when things are at the* or *their w.*; *at w., at the w., our lives are safe*; *get the w. of it*, be worsted; *have, put to, the w.*, be defeated, defeat; *the w. has happened*; *be prepared for the w.*; *if the w. comes to the w.*, if the w. happens; *do your, let him* &c. *do his* &c., *w.*, expression of defiance). (Vb) get the better of, defeat, outdo, best. [OE *wyrst* adv., *wyrsta* adj. (WORSE, -EST); the vb (recorded from 17th c. only) f. the adj.]

wor·sted (wŏŏs-), n. Woollen yarn (often attrib., as *w. sock*). [*Worste(a)d* in Norfolk]

wort (wert), n. 1. Plant, herb, (rare exc. in comb., as *spleen, stitch, -w.*). 2. Infusion of malt before it is fermented into beer. [sense 1 f. OE *wyrt*, cf. G *wurz*, cogn. w. ROOT; sense 2 f. OE *wyrt*, cf. G *würze* spice, brewer's wort]

worth[1] (werth), pred. a. (governing noun like trans. part.) & n. Of value equivalent to (*is w. much, little, nothing, about 2/6*; *is little w.* poet., w. little; BIRD *in the hand is w. two in bush*; *what is the house w.?*; *the rarer it is the more it is w.*); deserving, worthy of, bringing compensation for, (*w.* one's *salt*, earning one's keep by good service; *w. doing, hearing, notice, the trouble*, WHILE[1], *an effort, troubling* one*self about*, &c.; *w. it* colloq., w. while; *to reign is w. ambition*; *game not w.* CANDLE; *I give you, you must take, this for what it is w.*, I do not guarantee its truth, wisdom, &c.); possessed of, having property amounting to, (*is, died, w. a million*; *spent all he was w. on it*; *for all* one *is w.* slang, with one's utmost efforts, without reserve); *w.-while* (in recent use as attrib. adj.), that is w. while (*a w.-w.*

experiment). (N.) what a person or thing is w., value, merit, high merit or excellence, (*of great, little, no, w.*; *persons of w.*; *true w. often goes unrecognized*), whence **wor·th**LESS a., **wor·thless**LY[2] adv., **wor·thless**NESS n.; coin's equivalent *of* commodity (*give me a shilling's, half a crown's, w. of stamps*; also in comb. as *pennyw., two-pennyw.* or *-pennorth, three-ha'porth* &c.). [OE *weorth* a. & n., cf. Du. *waard* a., G *werth* a. & n.]

worth[2] (werth), v.t. 3rd sing. subjunct. (archaic). Befall (only in *woe w. the day* =cursed be). [f. OE *weordhan* become, cf. G *werden*]

worthy (wer·dhĭ), a. & n. Estimable, having some moral worth, of a fair degree of merit, respectable, (*a w. man*; *has lived a w. life*; often with patronizing effect, cf. HONEST, as *I asked the w. rustic whether*); deserving *of* or deserving of or deserving *to* be or do (*is w. of* or rarely *w. remembrance* or *being remembered*; *is w. to be remembered, take the lead*; also in comb. as *praise, blame, -w.*); corresponding to the worth *of* or of, adequate, appropriate, of sufficient worth or merit, (*in words w. of* or *w. the occasion*; *is not w. of* or *w. my sword, steel*; *has found a w. adversary, received a w. reward*); hence **wor·thi**LY[2] adv., **wor·thi**NESS n. (N.) w. person, person of some distinction in his country, time, &c., (esp. in pl., as *the Ww. of England*; *an Elizabethan* &c. *w.*). [WORTH[1] n. + -Y[2]]

wot. See WIT[1].

would. See WILL[1].

woul·d-be, a. & adv. prefixed to n. or adj. expressing a quality aspired to or intended (*w. gentleman, facetious*). [WILL[1], BE]

wound[1] (wōō-), n., & v.t. Injury done by cut or stab or blow or tear to animal or vegetable tissues including & usu. going beyond the cutting or piercing or breaking or tearing of the skin or bark or other integument, (fig.) injury done to person's reputation &c. or pain inflicted on his feelings, (poet.) pangs of love, (*receive, inflict, make, heal, a w.*; *incised, punctured, contused, lacerated, w.*; *open, incurable, festering, mortal, w.*); *w.-wort*, kinds of plant supposed to have healing properties; hence **wou·nd**LESS a. (Vb) inflict w. on (often fig., esp. *wounded vanity, feelings*; *willing to w.*, spiteful). [com.-Teut.: OE *wund*, cf. Du. *wond*, G *wunde*; vb (OE *wundian*) f. n.]

wound[2]. See WIND[2, 3].

woura·li. See CURARE.

wove(n). See WEAVE.

wr-. In all words beginning thus w is silent.

wrack, n. Sea-weed cast up & used for manure &c.; wreckage; =RACK[1]. [OE *wræc* (*wrecan* WREAK) vengeance, damage, w. senses added f. MDu. *wrak* WRECK]

wraith, n. Person's double or apparition seen shortly before or after his death. [orig. Sc., etym. dub.]

wrangle (ra·nggl), v.i., & n. Brawl, (engage in) loud or vulgar or confused argument or altercation or quarrel. [cogn. w. WRING, -LE(3)]

wra·ngler, n. In vbl senses; also, (Camb. Univ.) person placed in first class of mathematical tripos (person in 2nd, 3rd, class being called *senior, junior, o·ptĭmē*; *senior w.*, first in first class when it was arranged in order of merit), whence **wra·ngler**SHIP n. [-ER[1]; spec. sense f. obs. sense of vb *dispute publicly on a thesis*]

wrap, v.t. & i., & n. Enfold, enclose or pack or conceal in folded or soft encircling material, (often *up*; *w. it in paper, cotton-wool*; *w.up parcel*; *mountain, affair, is wrapped in mist, mystery*; *wraps up his meaning in tortuous sentences, allegory*), (p.p. with *up*) engrossed or included (*mother, country's prosperity, is wrapped up in her child, its shipping*); *w. up*, put on ww. (*mind you w. up well if you go out*); arrange or draw (pliant covering) *round* or *about* person or thing (*wrapped her shawl closer about her*), whence **wra·p-p**ING[1](3) n.; overlap (intr.; *the edges should, do not, w.*); (n., usu. in pl.) shawl(s), rug(s), cloak(s), neckerchief(s), &c., as addition to ordinary clothes. [etym. dub.; cf. obs. *wlappen* in same sense, & LAP[2]]

wra·ppage (-ĭj), n. Wrapping(s). [-AGE]

wra·pper, n. In vbl senses; esp.: (garment resembling) dressing-gown; paper enclosing newspaper or similar packet for posting; detachable paper cover of book; outer tobacco-leaf of superior quality enclosing cigar. [-ER[1]]

wrapt. =RAPT.

wrăsse, n. Kinds of thick-lipped strong-toothed bright-coloured rock-haunting sea-fish. [f. Cornish *wrach, wrath*, cf. W *gwrach*]

wrath (raw-), n. Anger, indignation, (poet., rhet., or joc.; *vessels, children, of w.*, persons destined to divine chastisement; *slow to w.*, not irascible). Hence **wra·th**FUL a., **wra·thful**LY[2] adv. [OE *wrǣdhdhu* (WROTH)]

wreak, v.t. Avenge (wrong, wronged person; archaic); give play or satisfaction to, put in operation, (*vengeance, rage*, &c., usu. *upon* enemy &c.; rarely *desire* &c., as *w.* one's *thoughts upon expression*, find adequate words). [com.-Teut.: OE *wrecan* avenge, cf. Du. *wreken*, G *rächen*; orig. sense *drive*, cogn. w. WRACK, WRECK, L *urgēre* URGE, Gk *eirgō* hem in]

wreath (rēth), n. (*pl. pr.* -dhz). Flowers

For pronunciation of words in *wr-* see WR-.

or leaves strung or woven or wound together into ring for wearing on head or for decorating statue, building, coffin, &c., carved imitation of such w.; similar ring of soft twisted material such as silk; curl *of* smoke, circular or curved band *of* cloud, (poet.) circle *of* dancers or spectators. [OE *wridha* fillet cogn. w. WRITHE]

wreathe (-dh), v.t. & i. Encircle as or with or as with a wreath (*face wreathed in smiles*); form (flowers, silk, &c.) into wreath; wind one's *arms* &c. or (of snake &c.) *itself round* person &c.; make (garland); (of smoke &c.) move in shape of wreaths. [f. prec. & partly f. WRITHE]

wreck, n., & v.t. & i. Ruin, destruction, disablement, esp. of ship (*save ship*, one's *fortunes, from w.*; *gale caused many ww*; *the w. of the Hesperus, of his life*); ship that has suffered w., greatly damaged or disabled building or person, disorganized remains or sorry remnant *of*, (*shores are strewn with ww.*; *person, building, is a w.*; *is but a* or *the w. of his former self*); goods &c. cast up by the sea (*w. of the sea belongs to the Crown*); *w.-master*, officer appointed to take charge of goods &c. cast up from wrecked ship. (Vb) cause w. of (ship, train, hopes, undertaking, person or his fortunes), (p.p.) involved in shipwreck (*wrecked sailors, goods*); suffer w. (rare; *this is the obstacle your hopes will w. on*). [vb f. n., AF *wrec* f. ON (Norw., Icel., *rek*) f. st. of *wrekan* to drive, see WREAK]

wre·ckage (-ĭj), n. Wrecked material, remnants, fragments. [-AGE]

wre·cker, n. In vbl senses; also: man who tries from shore to bring about shipwreck with a view to profiting by wreckage or who steals such wreckage; person employed in recovering wrecked ship or its contents. [-ER[1]]

wren, n. Kinds of very small cock-tailed short-winged European songbird (often *Jenny W.*); *Wrens*, (punning name for) members of the W.R.N.S. [OE *wrenna*, cf. Icel. *rindill*]

wrench, n., & v.t. Violent twist or oblique pull or tearing off, (fig.) pain caused by parting, (*gave a w. to his ankle, at the door-handle*; *leaving home was a great w.*); implement made to grip & turn nuts, bolts, &c.; (vb) twist or pull violently round or sideways, injure or pull *off* or *away* by twisting, (*wrenched the door open, his horse's head round, his ankle, fowl's head off, opponent's sword from him*); pervert, wrest, (facts &c.). [n. f. vb, OE *wrencan* twist, practise guile, cf. OHG *renchan*]

wrest, v.t., & n. Twist, deflect, distort, pervert, (*wrests the law to suit himself*; *w. the facts, sense* or *words of a passage*, &c.); force or wrench away from person's grasp (*wrested his sword from him*); (n.) key for tuning harp &c.; *w.-block*, part of piano holding *w.-pins*, to which strings are attached. [OE *wrǽstan*, cf. Icel. *reista*, Da. *vriste*; cogn. w. WRITHE, WRIST]

wrestle (rĕ·sl), v.i. & t., & n. Grapple with & try to throw adversary esp. in sporting contest under code of rules (*with*, or abs); have wrestling-match with; contend, grapple, do one's utmost to deal, *with* evil, temptation, duty, task, problem, &c.; *w. with God* or *in prayer*, pray fervently; hence **wre·stl**ER[1], **wre·stl**ING[1], nn. (N.) wrestling-match; hard struggle. [prec., -LE(3)]

wretch, n. Very unfortunate or miserable person; despicable person, person without conscience or shame (often as term of playful abuse). [OE *wrecca* outcast (*wrecan* WREAK)]

wre·tched, a. Miserable, unhappy, afflicted; inferior, of bad quality or no merit, contemptible, unsatisfactory, causing discontent or discomfort or nuisance, confounded, (*w. weather, health, horse, inn, accommodation, poetry, poet*, &c.); (with nn. of condemnation) great, severe, excessive, (*w. insufficiency, stupidity*, &c.). Hence **wre·tched**LY[2] adv., **wre·tched**NESS n. [prec. + -ED[1], cf. WICKED]

wrick, rick, v.t., & n. Slightly sprain or strain (neck, back, joint); (n.) sprain or strain (*have a w. in my neck*; *gave my back a w.*). [cf. Du. *wrikken* stir to & fro (also ME *wricken* obs.)]

wri·ggle, v.i. & t., & n. (Of worm &c.) move body with short twistings, (of animals or persons) make wormlike motions, (fig.) be slippery, practise evasion; make way *along, through, out, in*, &c., by wriggling (often fig., as *w. out of a difficulty*); move one*self*, one's *body, tail, hand*, &c., with wriggling motion; make one's *way* by wriggling; (n.) wriggling movement. [f. LG *wriggeln* frequent. of *wriggen*, whence E dial. *wrig* to twist]

wright (rīt), n. Workman, maker, (now rare exc. in comb. as *ship, wheel, play, -w.*, or with help of context as *the wheel must go to the w. for repair*). [OE *wyrhta* (*wurh-* var. stem of WORK[2])]

wring, v.t. (wrung), & n. Squeeze, squeeze & twist, twist forcibly, break by twisting, pervert sense of, torture, (*w.* person's *hand*, press it with emotion; *w.* one's *hands*, squeeze them together in sign of great distress; *w. out* or *w. clothes*, press water from them by twisting; *wringing wet*, or colloq. *wringing*, so wet as to need wringing; *w. neck of*, kill *chicken* &c.; *has wrung the words from their true meaning*; *soul was wrung with agony*); extract by squeezing, get *out* by pressure or importunity, extort, (*w. water, groan, consent, money, from* or *out of* or *out*); hence **(-)wring**ER[1](2) n. (N.) squeeze (*gave my hand, give those clothes, a w.*). [OE *wringan*, cf. Du. *wringen*, G *ringen*]

wri·nkle[1], n., & v.t. & i. Furrow-like

crease or depression or ridge in the skin (esp. of the kind produced by age) or other flexible surface; hence **wri·nkly**[2] a. (Vb) produce ww. in (often *up*; *he wrinkled his forehead*; *wrinkled with age*); assume ww., show wrinkled appearance. [prob. backform. f. OE *gewrinclod* sinuous, etym. dub.]

wri·nkle[2], n. Piece of serviceable information not generally known, tip, dodge, (*is full of ww.*; *gave me, put me up to, a w. or two*). [perh. a use of prec.; so with pun in Swift]

wrist, n. Joint connecting hand with forearm; (effect got in fencing, ball-games, sleight-of-hand, &c., by) working of the hand from the w. alone (*his wonderful w.*; *that was all w.*); (Mech., also *w.-pin*) stud projecting from crank &c. as attachment for connecting-rod; *wri·stband* (-zb-), band usu. of folded & starched linen forming or concealing end of shirt-sleeve, cuff; *w.-drop*, paralysis of fore-arm muscles from lead-poisoning. [OE, cogn. w. WRITHE; orig. *hand-wrist* = hand-turner; cf. ON *rist* instep, G *rist* instep, wrist]

wri·stlet, n. Band or ring worn on wrist to strengthen or guard it or as ornament, bracelet, handcuff, &c. (*w. watch*, attached to w.). [-LET]

writ[1], n. *Holy, sacred, w.*, the bible; form of written command in name of sovereign, State, court, &c., issued to official or other person & directing him to act or abstain from acting in some way (*w. of attachment, habeas corpus, subpoena*, &c.; *serve w. on* one, deliver it to him; *w. runs* in district &c., is theoretically valid or is actually respected). [OE (*ge*)*writ* a writing (WRITE)]

writ[2]. See foll.

write, v.i. & t. (*wrote*, archaic *writ*; *written*, archaic *writ*). Trace symbols representing word(s) esp. with pen or pencil on paper or parchment, trace (such symbols), trace the symbols that represent or constitute (word, special script, &c.), (fig.) stamp marks indicating (quality or conditions) *on* or *in* or *over* person's face &c., (*w. well, legibly, disgracefully*, &c.; *w. in ink, in pencil*; *writes a good, niggling*, &c., *hand*, produces good &c. writing; *cannot read* or *w.*; *can w. his alphabet, the Greek letters, Greek*; *write your letters separate*; *w.* one's *name*; *has honesty written in his face*; *a paper written all over*, covered with writing; *a notice is written up on the wall*; *what I have written I have written*, of refusal to correct, see *John* xix. 22; *w. thing down*, record or take note of it in writing; *w. off*, w. & dispatch letter; *w. out*, w. the whole of, w. in full; *w. out fair*, make fair copy of; *name is written in book of life*, included in the list of the saved; *written in* or *on water*, unrecorded; *writ large*, aggravated, esp. w. ref. to intended remedy that reproduces former evils in greater degree); fill, draw up or fill in, with writing (*has written three sheets*; *w. cheque, certificate, application*, &c.; *w. up the books, reports*, &c., make entries bringing them up to date); compose for written or printed reproduction or publication, put into literary form & set down in writing, be engaged temporarily or permanently in such composition, compose books &c. *well* &c., (*is writing a book, article, his life, poetry, a novel, report, letter*, &c.; *w. off*, compose with facility; *writes cleverly, like an angel*; *writes a little, in* or *for the papers, for a living*, &c.); w. & send letter (*to* person or abs., also commerc. or vulg. without *to*; *writes home once a week*; *have written to him*; *we wrote you last week*; *will write off*, or *w., for a fresh supply*); send or convey (person or *to* person news, *that, how*, &c.) by letter (*w. me all the news, the result, how you got home*; *wrote to his mother that he was bullied*); state in writing or print (*Herodotus writes, it is written, that*); describe, put *down*, in writing as (*writes himself esquire*; *w. me down an ass*); *w. down*, disparage in writing, (also) reduce nominal value of (stock); *w. off*, cancel, recognize in writing the non-existence or annulment of, (bad debts, sums absorbed by depreciation, &c.); *w. out* refl., exhaust by writing (*has written himself out*, has no ideas &c. left); *w. up*, praise in writing, also elaborate account of (incident &c.). [OE *writan*, cf. ON *rita* score, write, G *reissen* tear; orig. sense *score, cut*]

wri·ter, n. In vbl senses; esp.: clerk in certain offices, whence **wri·ter**SHIP n.; author; manual teaching how to write specified language (*French* &c. *w.*); *w. to the signet*, abbr. *W.S.*, Scotch solicitor; *w.'s cramp* or *palsy*, muscular affection incapacitating for writing. [-ER[1]]

writhe (rīdh), v.i. & t., & n. Twist or roll oneself about (as) in acute pain, squirm; twist (one's *body* &c.) about; shrink mentally, be stung or bitterly annoyed, (*under, at*, insult &c.; *with* shame &c.); (n.) act of writhing. [OE *wrīdhan*, cf. ON *ridha*, OHG *rīdan*]

wri·ting, n. In vbl senses; also: written document; piece of literary work done, book, article, &c., (*the ww. of Plato*); *put thing in w.*, write it down; *w.-case*, holding w.-materials; *w.-desk*, desk; *w.-ink*, opp. *printing-ink*; *the w. on the wall*, ominously significant event &c. (see *Dan.* v); *w.-paper*, paper for w. on, esp. cut to size usual for letters; *w.-table*, KNEE[1]-hole or other table kept for w. at. [-ING[1]]

written. See WRITE.

wrong, a. (more, most), n., adv. (no comp.), & v.t. Out of order, in(to) bad condition, (*something is w. with him; my liver is* or *has gone* or *has got w.; what's w. with —?* colloq., surely no substitute is wanted); contrary to law or morality, wicked, (*knows the right from the w.; lying is w.*); other than the right or the more or most desirable (*always does the w. thing; took the w. way; the w. answer, move; in the w. box*, awkwardly placed, in a difficulty, at a disadvantage; *is w. side out*, inside out; *has hold of the w. end of the stick*, has inverted a theory, position, &c.; *on the w. side of 40* &c., older than; *w. side of the* BLANKET; *w. fount*, abbr. *w.f.*, notice to compositor that letter or wd is not of right FOUNT²); mistaken, in error, (*a w. opinion, guess, decision, hypothesis; I think you are, can prove you, w.*); *w.-headed*, perverse & obstinate; hence **wro·ng**LY² adv. (N.) what is morally w., w. action, (*the difference between right & w.; can two ww. make a right?; do w.*, sin, offend, transgress, whence **wro·ngdo**ER¹, **wro·ngdo**ING¹, nn.; *king can do no w.*, maxim expressing principle of ministerial responsibility in constitutional monarchy); injustice, unjust action or treatment, (*do w. to; suffer w.; has done me a great w.; you do me w.*, malign me; *complains of her ww.*); position of or responsibility for having caused quarrel, made the mistake, been the offender, &c. (*you were, they are both, in the w.; put* one *in the w.*, show or make it appear that he was the offender); hence (of actions) **wro·ng**FUL a., **wro·ngful**LY² adv., **wro·ngful**NESS n. (Adv., usu. placed last) amiss, in w. direction, with incorrect result, (*aim, guess, answer, do sum, sort things, w.; you told, led, me w.; go w.*, take w. path, esp. fig. of woman failing in chastity). (Vb) treat unjustly, do w. to, (*his deeply wronged wife*); mistakenly attribute bad motives &c. to (*I assure you you w. me*). [OE *wrang* n. f. ON (Icel. *rangr* awry, Da. *vrang* wrong a.); cogn. w. WRING; the adj. use not in OE]

wrote. See WRITE.

wroth (rō-, rŏ-), pred. a. (rhet., poet., or joc.). Angry. [OE *wrāth* (WRITHE) = perverted in temper, cf. Du. *wreed* cruel, OHG *reid* twisted]

wrought. See WORK².

wrung. See WRING.

wry, a. (*-ier, -iest*, or *-yer, -yest*). Distorted, turned to one side, skew, (*w. face, mouth*, grimace expressing disgust; *has a w. nose*); *wry·bill*, kind of plover; *wry·mouth*, kinds of fish; *w.-mouthed*, ironically flattering &c.; *wry·neck*, bird allied to woodpeckers able to turn head over shoulder. Hence **wry·**NESS a. [f. OE *wrigian* tend, incline, swerve, cf. WRIGGLE]

wy·andotte (-ŏt), n. American breed of fowl. [name of Amer.-Ind. tribe]

wȳch-, wich-, witch-, (-tsh), preff. in names of trees, as *w.-alder, -elm, -hazel*, f. OE *wice, wic*; orig. sense pliant, cogn. w. WEEK, WEAK.

wye, n. Letter Y; thing so shaped.

Wy·kehamist (wĭka-), a. & n. (Past or present member) of Winchester college. [William of *Wykeham*, founder, -IST]

wȳnd, n. (Sc.). Alley in Scotch town. [perh. var. of WIND³ n.]

wyvern. See WIVERN.

X

X (ĕks), letter (pl. *X*s, X's). (As Rom. numeral) 10, as IX 9, xv 15, lx 60, XC 90, MX 1010, DXL 540; (Alg.; *x*) first unknown quantity (cf. A, Y), (transf.) incalculable or mysterious factor or influence (*X*-RAY¹*s*); *XX* or *double-x*, *XXX* or *triple*-X, (*ale*), ales of certain strength (from brewers' marks on casks).

Abbr.: (x) = EX (i.e. not including right to) in **x-cp.**(coupon), **x-d.**(ividend), **x-i.**(interest), **x-n.**(ew shares); **Xmas,** Christmas, **Xt(ian),** Christ(ian), (prop. = Gk letter khi, ch, see CHIASMUS).

Xanthi·ppĕ (z-, -tĭ-, *or* -thĭ-), n. Shrewish wife. [*X.*, wife of Socrates]

xanth(o)- (z-), comb. form of Gk *xanthos* yellow: *xa·nthate*, a salt of xanthic acid; *xa·nthĕin(e)*, soluble part of yellow colouring-matter in flowers; *xa·nthic*, yellowish (*x. acid*, ethyl-disulpho-carbonic acid with yellow salts; *x. flowers*, typically yellow & never passing into blue but only into red or white, opp. *cyanic flowers* with blue as typical & red or white as alternative colours); *xa·nthin*, insoluble part of yellow colouring-matter in flowers, also colouring-matter of madder, also a substance related to uric acid occurring in blood, urine, liver, &c.; *xantho·chroi̅* n. pl. (ethnol.), blonds or fair whites (cf. MELANOCHROI), so *-chro·ic, -chroous*, aa.; *xanthomĕ·lanous* (ethnol.), with black hair & yellow or brown or olive skin; *xa·nthophyll*, yellow colouring-matter of autumn leaves (cf. *chlorophyll*); *xa·nthous* (ethnol.), yellow or Mongoloid.

xe·bec (zē-), n. Small three-masted Mediterranean vessel with some square & some lateen sails. [f. F *chebec* etym. dub., cf. OSp. *xabeque*, It. *sciabecco*, Turk. *sunbekī*]

xĕnēlă·sia (z-, gz-), n. (Gk hist.). Spartan system of excluding & expelling aliens. [Gk (-nē-), f. *xenos* stranger, *elaunō* drive]

xĕn(o)- (z-, gz-), comb. forms of Gk *xenos* strange(r): *xe·nial*, of hospitality or relations between host & guest: *xeno·gamy* bot., cross-fertilization.

xĕ·non (z-), n. (chem.). Heavy inert gaseous element discovered 1898. [Gk, neut. of *xenos* strange]

xēr(o)- (z-), comb. forms of Gk *xēros* dry: *xera·nsis* [Gk, f. *xērainō* dry up], desiccation, drying up; *xera·nthemum*, kinds of annual with everlasting composite flowers; *xero·philous* bot., adapted to hot & dry climate.

xi (ksī), n. Greek letter (Ξ, ξ) = x. [Gk]

xiph(i, -o)- (z-), comb. forms of Gk *xiphos* sword; *xi·phoid*, sword-shaped (*x. appendage, cartilage,* or *process,* or *x.* as n., lower end of sternum); *xiphister·num,* xiphoid appendage.

xo·anon (gz-, z-), n. (Gk ant.; pl. *-ana*). Primitive usu. wooden image of deity supposed to have fallen from heaven. [Gk (*xuō* scrape)]

xȳ·lem (z-), n. (bot.). Woody tissue (opp. PHLOEM). [foll., & as *phloem*]

xȳl(o)- (gz-, z-), comb. forms of Gk *xulon* wood: *xyloba·lsamum,* (decoction of) dried twigs of balm-of-Gilead tree; *xy·locarp,* (tree with) hard woody fruit, so *-car·pous* a.; *xy·lograph,* a (esp 15th-c.) wood-engraving, also a decorative pattern got by mechanical reproduction of wood-grain, so *-o·graphy, -o·grapher, -gra·phic*; *xy·lonite* = CELLULOID n.; *xylo·phagous,* (of insects) feeding on wood [-PHAGOUS]; *xy·lophone,* musical instrument of wooden bars graduated in length & vibrating when struck or rubbed.

xy·ster (z-), n. (surg.). Instrument for scraping bones. [f. Gk *xustēr* (*xuō* scrape)]

xy·stus (gz-, z-), n. (pl. *-tī*). Covered portico used by athletes for exercise in classical antiquity; garden walk or terrace. [L, f. Gk *xustos* orig. = polished (prec.)]

Y

Y (wī), letter, (pl. *Ys*, Y's). (Alg.; *y*) second unknown quantity (cf. X, B); Y-shaped arrangement of lines, piping, roads, &c., forked clamp or support, (often attrib., as *Y-branch, -cartilage, -joint, -ligament*; *Y-cross,* Y-shaped cross esp. on chasubles suggesting figure of crucified Christ; *Y-level,* surveying-level mounted on Ys; *Y-moth,* kind called also *gamma* with mark like Y or gamma on wings; *Y-track,* Y of railway-line with two branches running into main track enabling engine to reverse direction by running down one branch into stem & returning up the other.

Abbr. (1): (Y.) young, **Y.M.C.A., Y.W.C.A.,** (men's, women's, Christian association).

Abbr. (2): **yd,** yard; **y^e** (pr. as *the*) the (*y* a survival in corrupt form of obs. þ, symbol for th; still used as archaism); **Yorks.**(hire); **y^t** (pr. as *that*) that (conj.; as *y^e* above).

ȳ-, pref. common in ME & still found in a few archaic forms (*yclad* clad, YCLEPT, *ywis* surely), repr. OE, Du., & G *ge-* as pref. of p.pp., collective nn., & other wds; the same element is seen under different forms in ALIKE, AMONG, AWARE, EITHER, ENOUGH, HANDIWORK.

-y¹, suf. of abstract nn. & of adjj., repr. original L *-ius -ia -ium,* added directly to stem as *remedium* remedy, *furia* fury, or to another suf. as in wds in *-orius, -arius*; also repr. L *-iă* f. Gk *-iā*. The suf. being unaccented in L, *-i-* was in normal F absorbed into the accented syllable, as in *gloire, péremptoire, victoire, précaire,* or disappeared, as in *remède*; but learned formations also occur in *-ie* & are common in mod. F, as in *furie, centurie*; & L or mod. L wds, whether thr. F or not, have in E the corresponding *-y,* as *victory, glory, remedy, primary, peremptory*; but many adjj. add a new suf. as -OUS, -AL, (*meritorious, monitorial*).

-y², suf. forming adjj. f. nn., repr. OE *-ig*; used freely as a living suf., w. senses *full of, composed of, having the character of,* as *bony, thorny, milky, slangy*; also appended with sense of -ISH¹(2) to adj. of colour when it is to be used as comb. form (*whity-brown, pinky-white,* &c.); also forming adjj. chiefly poet. f. other adjj. without change of sense (*paly, steepy, lanky, stilly*). Mute -e is dropped before -y (*icy, stony*); a single final consonant of monosyllables, if preceded by a single vowel, is doubled (*knobby, finny,* but *beery, downy*); in wds of more than one syl. treatment varies, as *scoundrelly, fidgety*; in *clayey, skyey,* -e- is inserted to divide the *ys*. In *tardy* -y is of different origin.

-y³, suf. w. dim. sense added to monosyllabic personal names (*Johnny, Jenny, Annie*) or animal names (*piggy, doggie*) or other nouns (*lassie, cooky*) & somet. forming nn. f. monosyl. adjj. (*darky* nigger, *fatty*), with implication of affection or familiarity; the *-y* form somet. supplants the parent. n. in ordinary use (*baby*); for *-y,* after Sc., *-ie* is common; for treatment of final consonants & mute -e see prec.; a modern development is the colloq. substitution of -y for all except the first syllable of polysyllabic nn. & adjj. (*hanky, nighty, comfy,* for handkerchief, nightdress, comfortable).

-y⁴, suf. in nn. repr. F p.p. termm. *-é, -ée,* & ult. L *-atus, -ata, -atum,* cf. -ADE(1, 3), -ADO. So *deputy* (F *député,* = *-atus*), *army* (F *armée,* = *-ata*), *assembly* (OF *asembleé,* = *-ata*), *delivery* (AF *delivrée,* = *-ata*), *ditty* (OF *dité* f. L *dictatum*), *treaty* (F *traité* f. L *tractatum*); other wds are formed by anal., as *expiry, entreaty.*

yacht (yŏt), n., & v.i. Light sailing-vessel kept, & usu. specially built & rigged, for racing; vessel propelled by sails, steam, electricity, or motive power other than oars, & used for private pleasure excursions, cruising, travel, &c.; *y.-club,* esp. for y.-racing; *yach·tsman,* person who yachts. (Vb) race or cruise in y.; hence **yach·TING¹** n. [f. Du. *jacht, jagt,* cf. *jagen* to hunt; named f. its speed]

ya·ffle, ya·ffil, n. The green woodpecker. [imit. of laughing cry]
yā·ger (-g-), n. Member of certain German military corps esp. of riflemen. [f. G *jäger* orig. = hunter (*jagen* hunt)]
yah, int. of derision.
yahoo· (ya-), n. Brute in human shape (*Gulliver's Travels*); coarse person of bestial passions & habits. [made by Swift]
Yahveh· (-vā), n. **Yah·vist** n., **Yahvi·stic** a. =JEHOVAH, JEHOVIST(*ic*).
yak, n. Long-haired humped grunting wild or domesticated ox of Tibet; *y. lace*, heavy kind made from y.'s hair. [f. Tibetan *gyak*]
Yale lock, n. Cylinder lock for doors &c. invented by L. *Y.* (d. 1868).
yam, n. (Edible tuber of) kinds of tropical climbing plant. [f. Port. *inhame*, etym. dub.]
Ya·ma (yah-), n. Hindu god of departed spirits & judge of the dead. [Skr.]
ya·men, -un, (yah-), n. Chinese mandarin's official residence (*the Tsung li y.*, Chinese Foreign Office). [Chin. (*ya* general's marquee, *mun* gate)]
yank[1], v.t. & i., & n., (U.S. & slang). Pull (lever &c., or abs.) with a jerk; (n.) sudden hard pull. [?]
Yank[2], n. slang. Yankee. [abbr.]
Ya·nkee, n. Inhabitant of New England; Federal soldier or inhabitant of northern States in American civil war; (in Eng. & Europ. use) inhabitant of U.S., American; (attrib.) of or as of the Yy. (*Y. notions*, American appliances &c.); *Y. Doodle*, American tune & song regarded as a national air; *ya·nkeefied*, of acquired Y. character [-FY]. Hence **Ya·nkee**DOM, **Ya·nkee**ISM(2, 4), nn. [prob. f. Du. *Janke* dim. of *Jan* John used derisively; or perh. orig. pl. f. *Yengees* Indian corrupt. of *English*]
yap, v.i., & n. Bark shrilly or fussily; (n.) shrill or fussy bark. [imit.]
yapp, n. Kind of book-binding with limp leather cover projecting considerably. [inventor's name]
yar·borough, n. Whist or bridge hand with no card above a 9. [f. an Earl of *Y.* who betted against its occurrence]
yard[1], n. The unit of long measure, =3 ft, 36 in., or 1/1760 mile (abbr. *yd*; *100 yy.*, esp. flat-race distance; *square, cubic, y.*); y.-length *of* material (*5 yy., a y. & a half, of cloth*); cylindrical spar tapering to each end slung horizontally (*square y.*) or slantwise (*lateen y.*) across mast to support sail (*lower, topsail, topgallant, royal, y.*, according to sail supported; *man the yy.*, place men, stand, along yy. as form of salute); (archaic) penis; *y.-arm*, either end of sail-y.; *y. measure*, rod, tape, &c., a y. long & usu. divided into feet, inches, & quarters or fifths; *y.-stick, -wand*, rigid y.-measure. [OE *gyrd* stick, cf. Du. *garde*, G *gerte*, L *hasta* spear]
yard[2], n., & v.t. Piece of enclosed ground, especially one surrounded by or attached to building(s) or used for some manufacturing or other purpose often specified by combination with another word (CHURCH[1], COURT[1], DOCK[4], FARM[1], KALE, RICK[1], TIMBER, *-y.*, VINEYARD; *brick-y.*, where bricks are made; *cab-y.*, where cabs are kept; *railway-y.*, space near station where rolling-stock is kept, trains made up, &c.; *stock-y.*, where cattle are penned; *tan-y.*, tanning-ground); *y.-man, -master*, man working in, manager of, railway-y. (Vb) put (cattle) into stock-y., so **yar·d**AGE(4) n. [doublet of GARDEN; OE *geard*, cf. Du. *gaard*, G *garten*, L *hortus*, Gk *khortos*]
yarn, n., & v.i. Any spun thread esp. of kinds prepared for weaving, knitting, or rope-making (*y.-beam* or *roll*, on which warp-threads are wound for weaving); (colloq., esp. naut.) story, traveller's tale, anecdote, rambling discourse, (*spin a y., yy.*, tell yy.; vb, spin yy.). [OE *gearn*, cf. Du. *garen*, G *garn*; cogn. w. Gk *khordē* CORD]
ya·rrow (-ō), n. Common perennial herb with pungent smell & astringent taste, milfoil. [OE *gærwe*, cf. Du. *gerw*, G *garbe*]
ya·shmak, n. Veil worn by Moslem women in public. [Arab.]
yă·taghan (-găn), n. Mohammedan sword without guard or cross-piece. [Turk.]
yaw, v.i., & n., (naut.). (Of ship) fail to hold straight course, fall off, go unsteadily; (n.) deviation of ship from course. [cf. ON *jaga* swing]
yawl[1], v.i., & n., (rare). Howl, yell. [ME *youlen*, imit.]
yawl[2], n. Kinds of small boat, esp. ship's jolly-boat with four or six oars; two-masted fore-&-aft sailing-boat with after mast much smaller than main mast. [f. Du. *jol*, cf. Da. *jolle*; *jollyboat* is perh. of same orig.]
yawn, v.i. & t., & n. (Of chasm &c.) gape, be wide open, (*a yawning gulf, rent*, &c.; *hell yawns for him*), (of person or animal) open the mouth wide as effect of drowsiness, boredom, &c. (n., act of yawning); utter or say with a y. (*yawned goodnight*; *'What is the use?' he yawned*). Hence **yaw·ning**LY[2] adv. [OE *geonian, ginian*, cf. ON *gina*, MDu. *gênen*]
yaws, n. pl. Framboesia. [?]
ўcle·pt, a. (archaic, facet.). Called (so-&-so). [Y-, obs. *clepe* call, OE *clipian*, -ED[1]]
ye (yē *or* yĭ *acc. to emphasis*), 2nd pers. pron. pl. (cf. THOU, YOU) now only poet., archaic, religious, or facet. or colloq., & almost exclusively (after confusion in 15th–18th cc.) as subjective case (*blessed are ye when men shall hate you*; *ye zephyrs gay*; *ye gods!*, int.; *ye gods & little fishes!* facet.; *go it, ye cripples!*, facet. encouragement; also written or spoken for

you in some familiar phrr., as *How d'ye do?*, *What d'ye think?*, *Thank ye, I tell ye*). [Aryan; OE *gé*, *ge*, cf. Du. *gij*, G *ihr*, Goth. *jus*, Gk *humeis*, Skr. *yūyám*]

yea (yā), particle & n. (archaic; pl. *yeas*). Yes (*let your communication be y., y., nay, nay*, yes & no without oaths; *yy. & nays* archaic, ayes & noes, affirmative & negative votes; *y. &*, & moreover); indeed, nay, (*ready, y. eager*). [OE *géa*, cf. Du. & G *ja*]

yean, v.t. & i. Bring forth (lamb, kid), bring forth lamb or kid. [perh. = Y- + OE *éanian*, perh. cogn. w. EWE]

yea·nling, n. Young lamb or kid. [-LING[1]]

year, n. Time occupied by the earth in one revolution round the sun (also *astronomical, equinoctial, natural, solar, tropical, y.*; 365d. 5h. 48′ 46″ in length) or (*astral* or *sidereal y.*, longer by 20′ 23″) by the sun in recovering its previous apparent relation to the fixed stars or (*Platonic* or *Great* or *Perfect y.*, estimated by ancient astronomers at about 26000 yrs) by the celestial bodies in recovering their relative positions at the Creation; period of days (esp. *common y.* of 365 or *leap-y.* or *bissextile y.* of 366 reckoned from 1st Jan.) used by community for dating or other purposes commencing on a certain day & corresponding more or less exactly in length to the astronomical y. (also *legal, civil, calendar, y.*; *lunar y.*, of 12 lunar months; LUNI-SOLAR *y.*; NEW[1], OLD, *y.*; *Gregorian, Julian, y.*, as fixed by GREGORIAN, JULIAN, calendars; SABBATICAL *y.*; *y. of* GRACE, *of our* LORD; *in the y. 1929*; *in the y. 1*, lit., & = very long ago; *from y. to y., y. by y.*, as yy. go by, each y.; *y. in y. out*, right through the y., continuously); period of the same length as a civil y. commencing at any day (*Christian, Church, ecclesiastical, y.*, round of sacred seasons reckoned from & to Advent; *the fiscal y.*, reckoned from 1st April for taxing purposes; *the school y.*, y.'s school terms usu. reckoned from beginning of autumn term; *a y. & a day*, period specified in some legal matters; *was away for two yy.*; *it is yy. since we met*); (pl.) age, time of life, (*young for his yy.*, bearing age lightly; *in yy.*, old); *y.-book*, annual publication bringing information on some subject up to date; *year·long*, lasting a y. [OE *gé(a)r*, cf. Du. *jaar*, G *jahr*, ON *ár*; cogn. w. Gk *hōros, hōra*, season]

year·ling, n. & a. Animal more than one & less than two years old; (Racing) colt a year old dating from 1st Jan. of year of foaling; (adj.) a year old, having existed or been so-&-so for a year, (*y. heifer, bride*). [-LING[1]]

year·ly, a. & adv. (Occurring &c.) once a year or every year or by or for the year, annual(ly). [-LY[1, 2]]

yearn (yern), v.i. & (impers., archaic) t. Be filled with longing or compassion or tenderness (*for* or *after* rest, home, affection, &c.; *to* do; *towards* or *to* person &c.), whence **year·ning**[1] n., **year·ning**[2] a., **year·ningly**[2] adv.; *it yearns me* archaic, I y. or am troubled. [OE *giernan*, cf. ON *girna*, G *begehren*, desire; cogn. w. Gk *khairō* rejoice, L *hortari* exhort]

yeast, n. Yellowish frothy viscous substance consisting of fungous cells developed by germination in contact with saccharine liquids & producing alcoholic fermentation, used in brewing beer, making wine, distilling spirit, & raising bread &c.; *y.-powder*, substitute for y. used in bread-making. [OE *gist*, cf. Du. *gist*, G *gischt*; cogn. w. Gk *zeō* boil]

yea·sty (*or* yĕs-), a. Frothy like yeast (*y. waves* &c.); in a ferment, working like yeast, (*a y. conscience, turmoil, imaginings*); wordy, superficial, (*a y. fellow*; *y. talk, professions*). Hence **yea·stiness** n. [-Y[2]]

yelk. See YOLK.

yell, v.i. & t., & n. (Make, utter with) shrill cry of pain or anger or fright, high-pitched shout, or uncontrollable burst of laughter (*yelled with pain, fury, delight, laughter*; *y. out an oath, orders*; *yelled curses, my name, a refusal, defiance*; *with yy. of horror* &c.); (U.S. Univv.) organized cry used by students e.g. in encouraging their representatives in athletic contests. [OE *gellan*, cf. Du. *gillen*, G *gellen*]

ye·llow (-ō), a. (-er, -est) & n., & v.t. & i. Of the colour between green & orange in the spectrum, coloured like buttercup or primrose or lemon or sulphur or gold, (with many names of plants, animals, &c., as *y. rattle, wagtail, ochre, jaundice*; often also in comb. with parts of body &c., as *y.-bill, -head, -legs, -root, -rump, -seed, -shanks, -tail, -throat, -top, -wood*, forming animal & plant names; *y. boy*, slang, gold coin; *y. cartilage*, elastic kind forming artery-walls &c.; *y. fever*, or *Jack*, tropical fever with jaundice & black vomit; *y. jacket*, state garment in China for royal persons & subjects selected for high honour; *the* SERE *& y. leaf*; *y. men, races*, &c., Chinese, Japanese, Mongols, &c.; *y. metal*, brass of 60 parts copper & 40 parts zinc; *the y. peril*, the danger that the y. races may overwhelm the white or overrun the world; *the y. press*, sensational newspapers esp. of chauvinistic tendencies, orig. of U.S. newspapers urging war with Spain 1898; *y. spot*, point of acutest vision in retina); (fig., of looks, mood, feelings, &c.) jealous, envious, suspicious; *ye·llowback*, cheap novel in y. paper boards common in mid-19th c., also French novel in y. paper cover; *y.-gum*, infants' black jaundice; *y.-(h)ammer*, bunting with y. head & neck & breast [*hammer* prob. not a corruption, but of separate orig.]; hence **ye·llowish**[1] (2), **ye·llowy**[2]**-**, aa., **ye·llowly**[2] adv. (rare), **ye·llowness** n. (N.) y. colour; kinds of y. pigment; kinds of moth & butterfly; *the yy.* (archaic), jaundice, also jealousy, (U.S.) a peach-disease. (Vb) turn y. (*paper yellowed with age*; *the yellowing leaves*). [OE *geolu*, cf. Du. *geel*, G *gelb*, L *helvus*; cogn. w. GALL[1]]

yelp, v.i., & n. (Utter) cry (as) of dog in pain or in eager anticipation. [OE *gilpan* boast, cf. LG *galpen* croak]

yen, n. (pl. *yen*). Japanese monetary unit =about 2/1½. [Jap., f. Chin. *yüan* round, dollar]

yeo·man (yō-), n. (pl. *-men*). (Hist.) person qualified by possessing free land of 40/- annual value to serve on juries, vote for knight of shire, &c.; small landowner, farmer, person of middle class engaged in agriculture; member of the yeomanry force; *y.('s) service*, help in need; *y. of the guard*, BEEFeater. Hence **yeo·manly**[1] a. [ME *yoman*, *yeman*, prob. = YOUNG + MAN]

yeo·manry, n. Yeomen; volunteer cavalry force raised from farmers &c. [-RY]

-yer, suf. seen in *lawyer*, *sawyer*, *bowyer*, arising f. the use in ME of the suf. *-ien* in place of *-en* in causal vbs & vbs formed on nn. Thus OE *lufu* n. love gave *lufian* vb & in ME *lovien*, whence *lovier* n. as var. of *lover*. *Lawyer*, *sawyer*, *bowyer*, are formed on this anal. direct f. the nn. *law* &c.

yercum. See MUDAR. [Tamil]

yes, particle equivalent to affirmative sentence, & n. (pl. *yĕses*). The answer to your question is affirmative, it is as you say or as I have said, your request or command will be complied with, the statement made or course intended is correct or satisfactory, (*y. &*, *y. or*, forms for substituting stronger phr., as *I could endure, y., & enjoy it, he would beat me, y., or you either*; *y.?*, indeed?, is that so?); (in answer to summons or address) I am here, I hear or am attending to you, (*y.?*, what more have you to say?). (N.) the word or answer *y.* (*say y.*, consent; *confine yourself to y. & no* or *yy. & noes*). [OE *gése*, *gise*, prob. = *géa* yea + *sī* 3 s. pres. subj. of *bēon* BE]

yester- in comb. (1) in *ye·sterday* n. & adv., (on) the day before today (*he arrived y.*; *is but of y.*, of recent origin; *the day before yesterday*, n. & adv.; often attrib. as *yesterday morning*); (2) chiefly poet. with sense *of yesterday*, in compds serving as nn. & advv. for which ordinary usage prefers *yesterday* — or *last* —; so *-morn(ing)* (usu. *yesterday morning*), *-eve*, *-even(ing)*, (Sc.) *yestreen*, (usu. *yesterday evening*), *-night* (usu. *last night*); (3) poet. w. sense *last past* in *-year* n. & adv. (usu. *last year*). [OE *geostra* usu. in *geostran dæg* yesterday, cf. Du. *gisteren*, G *gestern*; cogn. w. L *hesternus*, Gk *khthes*, Skr. *hyás*; for *-ter* see -THER]

yet, adv. & conj. As late as now or then, with continuance to this or to that time, still, (*there is y. time*; *is he y. alive?*; *there is life in the old dog y.*; *much y. remains to be done*; *there is one y. missing*; *his hands were y. red with blood*; *his y. unfinished task*; *I seem to see him y.*; *while it was y. morning*); (w. neg. context) so soon as now or then, by this or by that time, so far, in the immediate future, (*it is not time y.*; *is he dead y.?*; *they have not y. heard*; *I have never y. lied*; *the largest y. found*; *haven't you learnt y. that fire burns?*; *need you go y.?*; *it will not happen just y.*; *these things are not y.*); again, in addition, (*y. once more* or *y. once*; *another & y. another*; *y. again*; *more & y. more*), (with *nor*) either (*won't listen to me nor y. to her*); before the matter is done with, before all is over, in the time that still remains (*he will win, I will be even with you, y.*); (w. compar.) even (*a y. more difficult, easier, task*); nevertheless, *and* in spite of that, *but* for all that, (*though they curse, y. bless thou*; *&, having nothing, y. hath all*; *it is strange, & y. it is true*; *strange & y. true*; *the logic seems sound, but y. it does not convince me*); *as y.*, up to now or then (esp. w. suggestion that the statement would not be true of later time; *it has worked well as y.*; *a conscience as y. clear*). (Conj.) but at the same time, & y., (*y. what is the use of it all?*; *faint y. pursuing*; *a rough y. ready helper*). [OE *giet*, cf. OFris. *ieta*]

yew, n. (Wood of) kinds of slow-growing dark-leaved evergreen tree (also *y.-tree*) often planted in graveyards & used formerly for making bows & still in cabinet-making. [OE *īw*, cf. G *eibe*]

Y·g(g)drasil, n. (Scand. myth.). Tree whose roots & branches bind together heaven & earth & hell. [ON *yg(g)drasill* perh. f. *Yggr* name of Odin + *drasill* horse]

Yi·ddish, a. & n. (In) a form of old German (with words borrowed from many modern languages) spoken by Jews in or from Slavonic countries. [f. G *jüdisch* Jewish]

yield, v.t. & i., & n. Produce or give or bring as fruit or result (*earth yields her increase*; *land yields good crops*; *investment yields 50%*; *tax yields a handsome revenue, little*; *sin yields bitter fruit*), (abs., of land &c.) repay cultivation &c. *well*, *poorly*, &c., (n.) amount yielded or produced, output, return; give up, deliver over, surrender (trans.), resign (trans.), comply with demand for, concede, (*y. fortress* &c.; *y. oneself prisoner*; *y. possession*, one's *pride of place*; *y. precedence to*; *y. the palm*, be surpassed; *y. submission*, *consent*, submit, consent; *y. up the ghost*, die; *y. the point*, concede it in argument);

surrender (intr.), make submission *to*, give consent or change one's course in deference *to*, comply with demand (whence **yie·ldING**[2] a., **yie·ldingLY**[2] adv.), be inferior or confess inferiority *to*, (*town yielded without awaiting assault*; *y. to superior force, persuasion*; *courage never to submit or y.*; *I y. to none in appreciation of his merits*). [OE *gieldan* pay, cf. Du. *gelden*, G *gelten* be worth]

-yl, suf. (chem.) used to form wds denoting a RADICAL. [f. Gk *hulē* material, substance]

yō·del, v.t. & i. (-dell-, -del-, -dl-), & n. Sing (t. & i.), make melodious inarticulate sounds, warble, with changes between falsetto & ordinary notes in the manner of Swiss & Tyrolese mountaineers; (n.) yodelling cry, match of yodelling. [f. G dial. *jodeln*]

yō·ga, n. Hindu system of philosophic meditation & asceticism designed to effect the reunion of the devotee's soul with the universal spirit. [Hind. f. Skr., =union]

yogh (yŏch), n. The middle-English letter ȝ used for certain values of g & y. [prob. f. ME *ȝoc* yoke, as beginning with the sound]

yo·gi (-gĭ), n. Devotee of yoga. Hence **yo·gISM**(3) n. [Hind. (prec.)]

yo·-heave-ho·, yoho·, intt. used by sailors in heaving together.

yoicks int. & n., **yoick** v.i. & t. Foxhunter's halloo; (vb) cry yoicks, urge (hounds) *on* &c. with it. [?]

yoke, n., & v.t. & i. Wooden cross-piece fastened over necks of two oxen &c. & attached to the plough or waggon that they are to (help to) draw, (Rom. Hist.) uplifted y. or arch of three spears symbolizing it under which defeated enemy was made to march (*send, pass* intr., *under the y.*), (fig.) sway or dominion or servitude (*submitted to his y.*; *the heavy y. of opinion*; *had never endured the y.*), (fig.) bond of union esp. the marriage tie; pair *of* oxen &c. (*y. of land* archaic, as much as one y. of oxen can plough in day); piece of timber shaped to fit person's shoulders & support pail &c. at each end; separately made shoulder-piece of shirt or coat or blouse, or waist-piece of skirt, from which the rest is suspended; cross-bar on which bell swings; cross-bar of rudder to whose ends ropes are fastened; coupling-piece of two pipes discharging into one; kinds of coupling or controlling piece in machinery; *y.-bone*, cheek-bone connecting bones of head & face; *yo·kefellow, yo·kemate*, partner in marriage, work, &c.; *y.-lines, -ropes*, with which rudder-y. is worked. (Vb) put y. upon; couple or unite (esp. pair) in marriage or otherwise, link (one *to* another); (intr.) match or work together (*together, with*, or abs.; *do not y. well*). [Aryan; OE *geoc*, Du. *juk*, G *joch*, L *jugum* (cf. *jungere* join), Gk *zugon*, Skr. *yugá-m*]

yō·kel, n. Rustic, country bumpkin. [f. 19th c., etym. dub.]

yolk (yōk), (now rare) **yelk**, n. Yellow part of egg; sebaceous secretion from skin of sheep, wool-oil; *y.-bag, -sac*, membrane enclosing y. of egg. Hence **(-)yolkED**[2], **yol·kY**[2], aa. [OE *geolca* (YELLOW)]

yon, a., adv., & pron. Yonder (a. & adv.; archaic or poet. or provincial); (pron.; archaic &c.) yonder person or thing. [OE *geon*, cf. G *jener*, ON *enn*]

yo·nder, a. & adv. (Situated) over there, in the direction towards which I am looking or pointing, within or conceived as within view but distant. [ME (prec., -THER)]

yore, n. Old times (now only in *of y.*, formerly, in or of old days). [OE *geára* long ago, etym. dub.]

York[1], n. *Y. & Lancaster*, rival royal houses & parties in the Wars of the Roses (*Y. - & - Lancaster rose*, parti-coloured kind); *House of Y.*, kings Edw. IV–Rich. III; *Y. stone*, kind used in building.

york[2], v.t. Bowl with yorker. [back form.]

yor·ker, n. Ball so bowled as to pitch immediately in front of batsman's block (also *tice*). [prob. f. *York*, as introduced in Yorkshire, -ER[1]]

Yor·kist, a. & n. (Adherent) of family descended from Edmund Duke of York son of Edward III, or of the White-rose party fighting for it in Wars of the Roses. [-IST]

Yor·kshire, n. County (*Y. flannel*, undyed; *Y. grit*, stone used in polishing marble; *Y. pudding*, batter baked under & eaten with meat esp. beef; *Y. stone*, kind used in building; *Y. terrier*, small shaggy toy kind).

you (ū *or* yŏŏ *acc. to emphasis*), 2nd pers. pron. sing. (w. pl. vb) & pl. (archaic &c. subj. pl. YE; archaic &c. sing. THOU, *thee*; possess. YOUR, YOURS). The person(s) or thing(s) addressed (*y. are mad, an angel, all fools*; *who sent y.?*; *I choose y. three*; *the rest of y. can stay here*; *y. & I* or *me*; *are y. there?*, opening of telephone conversation; *you're another* vulg., retort to one who calls names; somet. expressed w. imperat., as *don't y. go away, begin y.* or *y. begin*; as voc. w. n. in apposition =exclamatory statement, as *y. fool!*, *y. darling!*, somet. w. *y.* appended also, as *y. idiot y.!*; as voc. calling attention, as *y. there, what is your name?*); (archaic for) yourself (*get y. gone*, begone; *y. should find y. a wife*; *sit y. down*); (in general statements) one, any one, all concerned, every one, a person, (*y. never can tell*; *what are y. to do with a child like this?*; *it is bad at first, but y. soon get used to it*; *there's a shot for y.!*). [OE *éow* acc. & dat. of YE, supplanting *ye* f. more frequent use of obj. case, & *thou* & *thee* (cf. similar substitutes in F, G, It.) as more courteous form]

young (yŭ-), a. (*-er, -est*, pr. -ngg-), & n. (only in collect. sing.). Not far advanced in life or growth or development, of recent birth or origin or formation, not yet old, still vigorous, immature, youthful, inexperienced, (*a y. child, man, animal, plant, nation, institution*; *a y. family*, of y. children; *a y. person*, servants' phr. for unknown y. woman of lower classes; *the y. person*, those whose innocence must be shielded from the indecent in talk & literature; *y. people*, esp. the marriageable; *my* &c. *y. man* or *woman*, sweetheart; *the night, year, century, is yet y.*, still near its beginning; OLD *head on y. shoulders*; *y. &* OLD; *you y. rascal* &c., usu. in playful address to child; *a y. man in a hurry*, esp. ardent reformer; *y. for his* YEARS; *men are now y. at fifty*; *an old man but a y. convert*; *y.* BLOOD[1]; *younger son*, esp. member of noble family poor owing to primogeniture; *y. things*, often indulgently &c. of persons; *is y. in crime*, unpractised; *y. Jones*, esp. Jones the son; *y. 'un*, youngster, often as voc.; *in my y. days*, while I was y.; *y. love, ambition*, &c., felt in or characteristic of youth; *the younger* before or after name of person to be distinguished from another, as *the younger Pitt, Teniers the younger*; so *the y.* PRETENDER; *y. England, Ireland, Italy, Turks*, &c., esp. as names of political parties claiming to speak for the rising generation; *Y. Turks*, esp. the party that in 1908 forced the Sultan to restore the constitution; *youngers* somet. as n. pl. opp. *elders*, as *is kind to his youngers*). Hence **you·ngish**[1](2) a., **you·ngling**[1] n. (poet.). (N.) offspring esp. of animals before or soon after birth (*with y.*, pregnant; *cares for, deserts, its y.*). [Aryan; OE *geong*, Du. *jong*, G *jung*, W *ieuanc*, L *juvenis*, Skr. *yúvan*-]

you·ngster, n. Child, esp. active or lively boy. [-STER]

you·nker (yŭ-), n. Youngster (archaic or colloq.); =JUNKER. [f. MDu. *jonckher* (*jonc* young, *hêre* lord)]

your (ūr, yōr, yer, *acc. to emphasis*), attrib. a. Of, belonging to, spoken of by, done to or by, you (*y. danger, hat, expectations*; *so this is y. immaculate saint!*; *y. dismissal of him, by him*; *y. father & mine*; *y. & my father, fathers*; cf. foll.); (colloq. & chiefly archaic, now usu. w. depreciatory implication) much talked of, well known, familiar, (*no one so fallible as y. expert in handwriting*; *y. facetious bore is the worst of all*). [OE *éower* genit. pl. of YE]

yours (ūrz, yōrz), pron. & pred. a. The one(s) belonging to or of you (*my father & y.*; *y. & my father*, erron. for *your &*; *my father is not y.*; *I like y. better*; *y. is the only way*; *am no child of y.*; *that cough of y.*; *some friends of y.*; *you & y.*, you & your family, property, &c.; *y. is to hand*, your letter has come; so *y. of the 11th* &c.); (adj.) belonging to you, at your service, (*it is y. if you will accept it*; *ever y., y. truly*, FAITHFULLY, OBEDIENT*ly*, &c., epistolary formulae preceding signature; *y. truly* facet., I, as *but y. t. was not taking any*, I refused &c.). [prec., -ES, see OURS]

yourse·lf, pron. (pl. *-ves*). (Emphat.) you in person, in particular, in your normal state, & not another or others, or alone (usu. in apposition w. *you* except in commands, & either next after it or later, rarely substituted for it; *please see to it y.* or *yy.*; *you y. said so* or *you said so y.*; *y. have said it* archaic, poet., &c.,; *by y.*, alone, as *why are you sitting by y.?*, also unaided, as *you cannot do it by yy.*; *it is y. I want, not your money*; *how's y.?* slang, how are you?, esp. after answering similar inquiry; *you are not quite y. tonight*, are out of humour &c.); (refl.) the person(s) previously described as *you*, or to whom a command is addressed (*have you hurt y.?*; *you seemed pleased with yy.*; *ask y. whether it is not true*). [YOUR, SELF]

youth (ū-), n. (*pl. pr.* ūdhz). Being young, adolescence, (the vigour or enthusiasm or weakness or inexperience or other characteristic of) the period between childhood & full manhood or womanhood, (*has all the appearance of extreme y.*; *in my hot, raw, vigorous*, &c. *y.*; *from y. onwards*; *y.'s a stuff will not endure*; *the secret of perpetual, of keeping one's, y.*; *the y. of the world*, early times), whence **you·thful** a., **you·thfully**[2] adv., **you·thfulness** n.; young man (*as a y. of 20*; *promising, lanky*, &c., *yy.*); young men & women (*the y. of the country*; *loves to be surrounded by y.*; *our y. are infected with commerciality*). [OE *geoguth* (YOUNG, -TH[2])]

yowl, var. of YAWL[1].

ytter·bium, y·ttrium, nn. (chem.). Two rare metals. Hence **ytter·bic, y·ttric, y·ttrious**, aa., **yttro-** comb. form. [*Ytterby* in Sweden, -IUM]

yu·cca, n. Kinds of American white-flowered liliaceous plant. [Carib]

yule, n. The Christmas festival (also *y.-tide*; *y.-log*, burnt on Christmas Eve). [OE *géol*, cf. ON *jól*, etym. dub.]

Z

Z (zĕd), letter (pl. *Zs, Z's, zeds*), (Alg.) third unknown quantity (cf. C, X).

Abbr.: **Zech.**(ariah), **Zeph.**(aniah), O.T. books.

za·ffre (*-er*), **za·ffer**, n. Impure oxide of cobalt used in making cobalt-blue & as blue pigment in enamelling & porcelain-painting. [f. F *zafre*, etym. dub.]

Za·mbo, var. of SAMBO (in first sense).

za·ny, n. (Hist.) attendant clown awkwardly mimicking chief clown in shows, merry andrew; (mod.) person given to buffoonery, foolish jester, half-witted person. [f. F *zani* f. It. *zanni* abbr. of *Giovanni* John]

Zanzibar·i (-arĭ), n. & a. (Native) of Zanzibar.

za·ptieh (-ā), n. Turkish policeman. [f. Turk. *ḍabtiyeh* f. Arab. *ḍabt* administration]

Zarathustr-. See **Zoroastr-.**

zari·ba (-ē-), **-ē·ba,** n. Hedged or palisaded enclosure for protection of camp or village in the Soudan &c. [f. Arab. *zarība* pen]

zax, var. of SAX.

zeal, n. Earnestness or fervour in advancing a cause or rendering service, hearty & persistent endeavour. So **zea·lous** (zĕl-) a., **zea·lously**[2] adv. [ME *zele* f. L f. Gk *zēlos*]

zea·lot (zĕl-), n. Uncompromising or extreme partisan, fanatic, (*Z*-, one of a Jewish sect resisting the Romans A.D. 6–70). Hence **zea·lotry**(4) n. [f. eccl. L f. Gk *zēlōtēs* (prec., -OT[2])]

zebec(k), var. of XEBEC.

zē·bra, n. Kinds of striped quadruped (true or mountain z., Burchell's z., quagga) allied to ass or horse; (attrib., & in comb. w. names of animals &c.) striped like z. (*z. markings, z. caterpillar, z. woodpecker, z.-wood,* &c.). Hence **ze·brine**[1] a. [Congolese]

zē·bū, n. The E.-Ind. humped ox. [F (*zé*-)]

zed, n. Letter Z. [f. F *zède* f. L f. Gk *zēta*]

zĕ·doary (-ōa-), n. Kinds (*long, round, z.*) of aromatic gingerlike substance made from rootstock of E.-Ind. plants & used in medicine, perfumery, & dyeing. [f. med. L *zedoarium* f. Arab. *zedwār*]

zei·tgeist (tsītgī-), n. Spirit of the times, drift of thought & feeling in a period. [G]

Zelā·nian, a. (zoogeog.). Of New Zealand. [mod. L (*Nova*) *Zelania* (New) Zealand, -AN]

zelo·so, mus. direction. With fervour. [It.]

zemi·ndar, n. (Anglo-Ind.). (Hist.) district governor & revenue-farmer under Mogul empire; (mod.) Bengali landed proprietor paying land-tax to British government. [Hind., f. Pers. *zamīndār* (*zamīn* earth, *dār* holder)]

ze·mstvo, n. Local elective assembly regulating affairs of district in Russia. [Russ., f. *zemlya* land]

zena·na (-ah-), n. Part of house in which women of high-caste families are secluded in India (*z. mission,* of women visiting zz. to spread medical & other reform among inmates); *z.* (*cloth*), a light fabric for women's dresses. [Hind., f. Pers. *zanāna* (*zan* woman, cf. Gk *gunē*, & QUEAN)]

Zend, n. Ancient language of the Iranian family, allied to Sanskrit, named from the Zend-Avesta (Avesta or text & Zend or commentary) or Zoroastrian scriptures.

zĕ·nith, n. Point of heavens directly above observer (opp. NADIR); (transf.) highest point, time or place of greatest power or prosperity or happiness, (*is at his, its, the, z.*); *z.-distance,* arc intercepted between any body & z., complement of body's altitude. Hence **ze·nithal** a. [f. OF *cenit* f. Arab. *samt* (*ar-rās*) way (of the head)]

zĕ·phyr, n. The west wind personified (*Z*-); balmy breeze, light wind; athlete's thin gauzy jersey for running, rowing, boxing, &c. in; kinds of dress-material. [f. L f. Gk *zephuros* west wind]

Ze·ppelin, n. (colloq. *Zepp*). Large dirigible airship of type built for military use in Germany. [Count *Z.*, inventor]

zēr·o, n. Figure 0, cipher; no quantity or number, nil; starting-point in scales from which positive & negative quantity is reckoned (*z.* in thermometers, freezing-point of water or other point selected to reckon from; *absolute z.* in temperature, point at which the particles whose motion constitutes heat would be at rest, estimated at —273·7° C.), (Mil.) point of time from which the start of each movement in a timed programme is at a specified interval; lowest point, bottom of scale, nullity, nadir. [It., contr. of *zefiro* f. Arab. as CIPHER]

zest, n. Piquancy, stimulating flavour, (esp. fig.; *adds a z. to*); keen enjoyment or interest, relish, gusto, (*entered into it with z.*). [earlier sense *shred of lemon-peel*; OF, = skin of walnut kernel, etym. dub.]

zē·ta, n. Greek letter (Z, ζ) = z. [Gk (*zē*-)]

zētĕ·tic, a. (rare). Proceeding by inquiry. [f. Gk *zētētikos* (*zēteō* seek, -IC)]

zeu·gma, n. (gram.). Figure of speech in which a verb or adjective does duty with two nouns to one of which it is strictly applicable while the word appropriate to the other is not used (e. g. *kill the boys &* sc. destroy *the luggage, with weeping eyes &* sc. grieving *hearts*; cf. SYLLEPSIS). Hence **zeugmă·tic** a. [Gk (genit. *-atos*), f. *zeugnumi* yoke, -M]

Zeus, n. (Gk ant.). King of the Olympian gods. [Gk]

zi·bet, n. The Asiatic or Indian civet. [f. med. L *zibethum* as CIVET]

zi·gzag, a., n., adv., & v.i. (-gg-). With abrupt alternate right & left turns, with alternating salient & re-entrant angles, with motion as of tacking ship, (*a z. line, course, road, fence, trench, flash of lightning*); (n.) z. line or (esp. for mounting steep hill) road or (in sieges) set of trenches; (adv.) with z. course; (vb) go z. [F, etym. dub., cf. G *zickzack*]

zinc, n., & v.t. A white metal much used in the arts esp. as component of brass &

German silver, as roofing material, as coating for sheet iron (cf. GALVANIZE), in electric batteries, & in relief-printing blocks (*flowers of z.* or *z. oxide*, powder used as white pigment & in kinds of ointment & cement); hence (spelt, before -i-, with -c- or -k- or -ck-) **zi·ncic, zinci·**FEROUS, **zi·ncoid**, aa., **zi·nci**FY v.t., **zinci**FICA·TION n., **zi·nco**US (esp. of negative pole of voltaic battery), **zi·nky**[2], aa., **zinco-** comb. form. (Vb; *-k-* or *-ck-*), coat with z. [f. G *zink* etym. dub.]

zinco, n. (pl. *-os*), & v. =ZINCOGRAPH. [abbr.]

zi·ncode, n. Positive pole of voltaic cell (cf. PLATINODE). [ZINC, & as PLATINODE]

zi·ncograph, n., & v.i. & t. Zinc plate with design etched in relief on it for printing from, picture taken from it; (vb) etch (t. & i.) on zinc, reproduce (design) thus. So **zinco·**GRAPHY, **zinco·**GRAPHER, nn., **zinco**GRA·PHIC a. [ZINCO-, -GRAPH]

zi·ncotype, n. =prec. n. [as prec., TYPE]

Zi·ngaro (-ngg-), n. (pl. *-ri*). Gipsy. [It.]

zi·nnia, n. Kinds of composite plant with showy rayed flowers of deep red & other colours. [J. G. *Zinn* German botanist, -IA[1]]

Zi·on, n. (Holy hill of) ancient Jerusalem; the Hebrew theocracy; the Christian Church; the Heavenly Jerusalem or kingdom of heaven, whence **Zi·on**WARDS adv.; (name for) nonconformist chapel. [f. eccl. L *Sion* f. Heb. *Tsiyōn* orig. hill]

Zi·onist, n. Advocate of colonizing of Palestine by modern Jews. So **Zi·on**ISM (3) n. [-IST]

zir·con, n. A silicate of zirconium of which some varieties (HYACINTH, JARGON[2]) are cut into gems. [f. F *zircone* f. Arab. *zarqūn*]

zircō·nium, n. A metal found chiefly in zircon. Hence **zircŏ·nic** a. (*-ic acid*), **zir·con**ATE[1](3) n. [-IUM]

zi·ther(n), n. Simple stringed instrument with flat sounding-board played on table &c. Hence **zi·ther**IST(1) n. [G (as CITHER)]

zlo·ty, n. Polish coin (10*d.*).

Zo·ar, n. Place of refuge, sanctuary. [*Gen.* xix]

zō·diac, n. A belt of the heavens limited by lines about 8° from the ecliptic on each side, including all apparent positions of the sun & planets as known to the ancients, & divided into 12 equal parts called *signs of the z.* (Aries, Taurus, Gemini, Cancer, Leo, Virgo, Libra, Scorpio, Sagittarius, Capricornus, Aquarius, Pisces) each formerly containing the similarly named *zodiacal constellation* but now by precession of equinoxes coinciding with the constellation that bears the name of the preceding sign (e. g. the constellations Pisces, Aries, are now in the signs Aries, Taurus); (transf., now rare) complete course, circuit, or compass. [f. OF *zodiaque* f. late Gk *zōdiakos* f. *zō(i)dion* dim. of *zō(i)on* animal (*zōos* living cf. *zaō* live), -AC]

zodī·acal, a. Of, in, the zodiac (*z. light*, luminous tract of sky shaped like tall triangle sometimes seen in east before sunrise or in west after sunset esp. in tropics). [-AL]

zo·etrope, n. WHEEL[1] of life. [irreg. f. Gk *zōē* life, *tropos* turn]

Zo·har, n. A cabalistic textbook prob. of 14th c. called Bible of the Mystics. [Heb., =brightness]

zo·ic, a. Of animals; (Geol., of rocks &c.) containing fossils, with traces of animal or plant life. [f. Gk *zōikos* (*zōon* see ZODIAC, -IC)]

Zō·laism, n. Absence of reserve, detailed realism, in describing the gross or immoral. So **zo·la**IST(2) n., **zola**E·SQUE, **zolai·**STIC aa. [*Zola*, French novelist b. 1840, -ISM]

zollverein (tsō·lferīn), n. Union of States having a common customs-tariff against outsiders & usu. free trade with each other. [G]

zone, n., & v.t. Belt or girdle worn round the body (chiefly archaic & poet.; *maiden* or *virgin z.*, symbol of virginity; *loose the maiden z. of*, deprive of virginity); encircling band or stripe distinguishable in colour or texture or character from the rest of the object encircled; (Geog.) any of five divisions of the earth bounded by circles parallel to the equator (*frigid zz.*, N. of arctic, S. of antarctic, circle; *torrid z.*, between the tropics; *North, South, temperate z.*, between frigid & torrid zz.); area enclosed between two exact or approximate concentric circles; part of surface of sphere enclosed between two parallel planes, or of cone or cylinder between such planes cutting it perpendicularly to axis; any well-defined tract of more or less belt-like form; hence **zo·nal**, **zo·nary**[1], **zo·nul**AR[1] [-UL-], **zo·nate**[2] (bot., zool.), aa., **zo·nal**LY[2] adv. (Vb) encircle as or with z. [f. L f. Gk *zōnē* girdle (*zōnnumi* gird)]

Zōō, n. (colloq.). Zoological garden, esp. that in London. [abbr.]

zōō-, comb. form of Gk *zōos* living, *zōon* an animal (see ZODIAC), = of animals, of animal life, (somet. as opp. vegetables & minerals, somet. excluding man also or especially); *-che·mistry*, of constituents of animal bodies; *-dyna·mics*, animal physiology; *-gamy*, sexual reproduction; *-geny*, formation of animal organs; *-geo·graphy*, zoology dealing with local distribution of animals, so *-geo·grapher*, *-geogra·phic(al)*; *-gony*, = *zoogeny*; *-graft*, zooplastic graft; *-graphy*, descriptive zoology, so *-grapher*, *-gra·phic(al)*, *-graphist*; *-latry*, religious worship of animals; *-lite*, fossil animal, fossilized animal substance; *zoo·logy*, natural history of animals, science of their structure, physiology, classification, habits, & distribution, so *-lo·gical* (*-al garden*, public garden or park with collection of animals kept for exhibition), *-lo·gically*, *-logist*; *-ma·gnetism*, animal magnetism; *-mancy*, divination from appearances or behaviour of animals; *-mecha·nics*, = *zoodynamics*; *-mor·phic*, dealing with or represented under animal forms, having gods of beast-like form (cf. *anthropomorphic*), so *-mor·phism*; *-phy·sics*, study of physical structure of animals; *-phyte*, kinds of plant-like animal, esp. holothurians, starfishes, jelly-fishes, sea anemones, & sponges, so *-phȳtic*, *-phȳto·logy*, *-phytolo·gical*, *-phyto·logist*; *-pla·stic*, (of surgery) transferring live tissue from some animal to man; *-psycho·logy*, psychology of animals other than man; *-sperm*, spermatozoon, also zoospore; *-spore*, spore capable of motion, so *-spo·ric*; *-taxy*, classification of animals; *-thēism*, beast-worship, so *-thei·stic*; *-tomy*, dissection or anatomy of animals other than man.

zo·oid, a. & n. Of incompletely animal nature. (N.) organic body or cell resembling but not being animal or plant; more or less independent organism given by gemmation or fission; member of compound organism. [prec., -OID]

zoom, v.i. (aeron. slang). Force aeroplane to mount at high speed & steep angle. [?]

zŏ·ril, n. Carnivorous quadruped of Africa & Asia Minor allied to skunk & weasel. [f. F *zorille* f. Sp. *zorrilla* (*zorra* fox)]

Zŏroă·strian, Zarathu·str- (-thōō-), nn. & aa. (Follower) of Zoroaster, Zarathustra, or Zerduscht, (adherent) of the religious system taught by him & his followers in the Zend-Avesta based on the conflict between Ormuzd god of light & good & Ahriman god of darkness & evil, the religion of the magi & ancient Persia still held by Parsees & somet. called *fire-worship*. Hence **Zoroa·strian**ISM(3), **Zarathu·str(ian)ism**, nn. [f. L f. Gk *Zoroastrēs* f. Zend *Zarathustra*, -IAN]

zouave (zōō·ahv), n. Member of French light-infantry corps orig. formed of Algerians & retaining Oriental uniform; woman's short jacket like that of z. uniform. [name of tribe]

zounds (zow-), int. (archaic) of indignation. [=(*God*)'s *wounds* (i.e. Christ's on the cross)]

zucche·tta, -etto, (tsŏŏk-), n. R.-C. ecclesiastic's skull-cap, black for priest, purple for bishop, red for cardinal, & white for Pope. [It. (*-a*), dim. of *zucca* gourd]

Zulu (zōō·lōō), n. Member, language, of a S.-Afr. Kafir tribe.

zwieback (tswē·bahk), n. Kind of biscuit rusk or sweet cake toasted in slices. [G]

Zwi·ngiian (tswingg-), a. & n. (Follower) of the Swiss religious reformer Zwingli (1484–1531). [-IAN]

zȳ·gal, a. H-shaped (esp. of brain-fissures). [as foll., -AL]

zȳg(o)-, comb. forms of Gk *zugon* yoke: *zygapŏ·physis*, one of the processes on a vertebra serving as articulation with another; *zygoda·ctyl* a. & n., *-ylous* a., (bird) with toes disposed in pairs, two toes pointing forward & two backward; *zygomor·phous*, (of flower) divisible into similar halves only in one plane; *zy·gospore*, spore formed by conjugation of two similar gametes.

zȳgo·ma, n. (pl. *-ata*). Bony arch of cheek, yoke-bone. Hence **zygomă·**TIC a. [f. Gk *zugōma*, *-atos* yoke(bone) f. *zugoō* to yoke (prec.), -M]

zȳgo·sis, n. (biol.). =CONJUGATION. [f. Gk *zugōsis* joining (prec.)]

zȳ·gote, n. Product of the fusion of two gametes, e. g. zygospore. [f. Gk *zugoō* yoke (*zugon*)]

zȳmo·sis, n. Fermentation; zymotic disease in general or any form of it. [f. Gk *zumōsis* (*zumoō* ferment f. *zumē* leaven f. *zeō* boil)]

zymŏ·tic, a. Of fermentation (*z. diseases*, epidemic, endemic, contagious, or sporadic diseases regarded as caused by multiplication of germs introduced from without). [f. Gk *zumōtikos* (prec., -OTIC)]